O'CONNOR'S FEDERAL INTELLECTUAL PROPERTY CODES PLUS

EDITORS
PAUL W. FULBRIGHT
(COPYRIGHT & TRADE SECRETS)
ANNA RAIMER
(TRADEMARK)
COLLIN A. ROSE
(PATENT PROSECUTION)
CHRIS RYAN
(PATENT LITIGATION)
STEPHEN STOUT
(PATENT LITIGATION)

O'CONNOR'S
HOUSTON, TEXAS

THOMSON REUTERS®

O'CONNOR'S ANNOTATED CODES SERIES

Suggested cite form: *O'Connor's Federal Intellectual Property Codes Plus* (2018-19)

O'CONNOR'S®

Mailing address:
P.O. Box 3348
Houston, TX 77253-3348

Shipping address:
9364 Wallisville Rd., Ste. 150
Houston, TX 77013

Phone: (713) 335-8200
(800) OCONNOR (626-6667)
Fax: (713) 335-8201

www.oconnors.com

Print date: April 27, 2018
Printed in the United States of America

ISBN 978-1-53920-662-0

WHAT'S NEW

Copyright royalties. The Copyright Royalty Board promulgated new rule 37 C.F.R. §350.5 to create the eCRB, an electronic filing system that will be used to manage filings and cases with the Board. • 37 C.F.R. Part 360 was revised to account for the new eCRB system.

Generic drugs. 21 U.S.C. §355 was amended to require the FDA to prioritize review of, and act within eight months of submission on, generic drug applications for drugs for which there is a shortage or for which there are not more than three approved products and no blocking patents or exclusivities. The FDA must provide review status updates to applicants with pending generic drug applications. First-approved applicants for a competitive generic therapy are granted a 180-day marketing exclusivity period. There may be only one such period for a drug.

Medical imaging devices. 21 U.S.C. §355 was amended to allow the FDA to approve or classify a medical imaging device intended to be used with an approved contrast agent if differences from the approved use of the contrast agent do not adversely affect the safety and effectiveness of the contrast agent.

Pediatric drugs. 21 U.S.C. §355a was amended to expand the FDA to cover brand-name drug provisions that allow generic drugs to be approved and marketed without labeling for pediatric indications when the pediatric indications are protected by patent or marketing exclusivity.

Prescription drugs. 21 U.S.C. §355 was amended to extend through 2022 (1) marketing exclusivity for certain chemical variants of approved drugs and (2) support to defray the costs of developing drugs, devices, and medical food for rare conditions.

CURRENCY

The statutes in this book are current through P.L. 115-129. The regulations in 37 C.F.R. are current through April 4, 2018. The annotations are current for federal appellate opinions issued through February 28, 2018.

CONVENTIONS

In this book, the 2017 and 2018 changes to statutes and regulations are marked with Ⓐ or Ⓔ depending on whether the section was amended or enacted. Statutory language that takes effect in 2017 or 2018 is underlined or **bold** (depending on whether there are overlapping amendments), and deleted language is shown in ~~strikethrough~~ text. Italicized editor's notes under the code section headings explain the effect of AIA changes (e.g., effective dates, savings clauses).

Because of the AIA's staggered effective dates, several Patent Act sections have been printed twice. When the subject matter or terminology of the sections has changed dramatically, the identically numbered sections are marked with a bracketed letter (e.g., [A*] or [B*]) to help distinguish them in the context of the Patent Act and in the index.

To help you quickly determine which annotations may no longer be valid after the entire AIA is in effect, time-bomb symbols (💣) have been added next to Patent Act section headings and annotation headings.

Where Congress did not include a heading for a subsection, we supplied one ourselves. To make the statutes easier to read, we sometimes broke subsections included in the same paragraph into separate paragraphs. To conserve space, we made liberal use of abbreviations in the annotations. A list of these abbreviations is on the inside front cover of this book.

OUR ANNOTATIONS

Generally, our annotations are arranged according to three hierarchies. The first hierarchy is court rank. Annotations from higher-level courts precede annotations from lower-level courts. For example, a U.S. Supreme Court case precedes a circuit-court case, which in turn precedes a district-court case. The second hierarchy is reverse chronological order. This hierarchy is used to order annotations that come from the same court rank. For example, a circuit-court case from 2005 precedes a circuit-court case from 2003, which precedes a circuit-court case from 1999. The third hierarchy is reporter volume number. This hierarchy is used to order annotations from opinions issued in the same year. For example, if there are three annotations from 2005 that are published in three different reporter volumes, the annotations will appear in the following order: 420 F.3d, 419 F.3d, and 417 F.3d.

Because of our hierarchy system, annotations from precedential or frequently cited opinions may not always appear first. Whenever possible, we have tried to improve this situation by categorizing annotations. For example, because the case law for the patent-infringement statute, 35 U.S.C. §271, is voluminous, we have created categories for common issues that arise under §271, such as "*Claim Construction—Generally*," "*Claim Construction—§112, ¶6 Issues*," "*Doctrine of Equivalents—Generally*," and "*Willful Infringement*," as well as categories for the individual subsections of §271.

ABOUT THE EDITORS

PAUL W. FULBRIGHT

Paul W. Fulbright was admitted to the State Bar of Texas in 1992 and became a registered patent attorney in 1994. He received his Bachelor of Science in Chemical Engineering from Texas A&M University in 1984, his Master of Business Administration from Baylor University in 1986, his Doctorate of Jurisprudence from the University of Houston Law Center in 1992, his Master of Science in Telecommunications from Southern Methodist University in 2009, and his Master of Laws from the Southern Methodist University Dedman School of Law in 2016.

Mr. Fulbright is an Assistant Professor of Business Law at the Marilyn Davies College of Business at the University of Houston – Downtown. He teaches courses in business law, commercial law, and business ethics, and he focuses his research and service efforts in the areas of business law; high-tech/intellectual property/technology/innovation/licensing law; privacy/security law; compliance; entrepreneurship; negotiation; and ethics.

Mr. Fulbright is also the principal of the Law Office of Paul W. Fulbright, PLLC, a law firm he opened in Richardson, Texas, in 2003. Before that, he was Of Counsel at Strasburger & Price LLP of Dallas, Texas (2000-2003), Senior Intellectual Property Law Counsel at Nortel Networks Corporation in Richardson, Texas (1997-2000), Associate Attorney at Gardere & Wynne LLP in Dallas, Texas (1995-1997) and at Pravel, Gambrell, Hewitt, Kimball, & Krieger PC in Houston, Texas (1992-1995), and Computer Systems Analyst/Power Technology Engineer at E.I. du Pont de Nemours & Company (1986-1989). He has also served as Senior Intellectual Property Law Counsel at Nokia, Inc. in Irving, Texas (2007-2012), and as Senior Director/Head of Patents and Intellectual Property (Enterprise Segment) at Cisco Systems, Inc. in Richardson, Texas (2012-2016).

Mr. Fulbright is extremely active in community affairs. He has served as both an officer and a board member of the State Bar of Texas Intellectual Property (IP) Law Section. He lectures regularly at continuing legal education programs sponsored by the State Bar of Texas.

He has also served multiple times as debate moderator at the Richardson (East) Candidates Forum, a debate among the candidates for Richardson City Council and the Board of Trustees for the Richardson Independent School District. Mr. Fulbright was also the author and host of the "Ethics Roundtable," a program devoted to educating professionals about real-world techniques for analyzing and resolving ethical dilemmas. Finally, Mr. Fulbright has served as a director and officer of the Richardson East Rotary Club, one of the more than 31,000 nondenominational Rotary Clubs around the world dedicated to community and international service, the ethical advancement of the professions, and the global eradication of polio.

Mr. Fulbright thanks the entire staff at O'Connor's for their wonderful efforts on this project. This has been, and continues to be, a magnificent team effort.

ANNA RAIMER

Anna Raimer is a partner at Jones Day, where she focuses her practice on protecting and enforcing intellectual property rights. She works with clients to design and implement worldwide trademark protection programs, strengthen their intellectual property portfolios, and resolve domestic and international trademark disputes.

Anna has significant experience managing international brands for clients. She advises clients regarding the development and protection of intellectual property assets in a wide range of industries, including consumer products, food and beverage, personal care, industrial products, pharmaceuticals, apparel, entertainment, software, nonprofit, financial services, real estate, automotive, and energy. Anna oversees all aspects of trademark clearance, prosecution, and maintenance, as well as advising on trademark and copyright issues in license agreements and other corporate transactions.

Anna assists clients in policing, enforcing, and defending their intellectual property rights worldwide. She represents clients in enforcement actions in courts throughout the U.S. in cases involving trademark and trade dress infringement, copyright infringement, false advertising, unfair competition, and misappropriation of trade secrets. Anna routinely handles opposition and cancellation actions before the Trademark Trial and Appeal Board of the Patent and Trademark Office. She also counsels clients on the use and enforcement of trademarks on the Internet and in social media, and she represents clients in domain name disputes.

Anna is chair of the Trademark Transactions Committee of the Intellectual Property Section of the American Bar Association and a member of the International Trademark Association's Publications Committee. She also serves on the Board of Directors for the Association of Women Attorneys in Houston.

COLLIN A. ROSE

Collin grew up in Houston and earned a Bachelor of Science at Purdue University. Following Purdue, Collin returned to Houston and earned a Doctor of Jurisprudence from the University of Houston.

Collin joined Chamberlain Hrdlicka in 2011, and his practice includes providing full-service intellectual-property legal advice. Collin advises clients on all aspects of intellectual-property transactions on an international level. Collin helps clients develop and manage international intellectual-property portfolios. Collin also advises in adversarial legal proceedings and provides legal opinions regarding potential exposure to third-party patents. Collin also assists clients with patent reviews before the Patent Trial & Appeal Board of the U.S. Patent and Trademark Office.

Collin is admitted to the State Bar of Texas, the Southern District of Texas, the Eastern District of Texas, the Federal Circuit, and the United States Patent and Trademark Office. Collin is a member of the PTAB Bar Association and also served as a board member of the Houston Intellectual Property Lawyers Association. Collin is proud to be a native Houstonian and is grateful for the support of his wife, Lexie, and their two children, Parker and Ella.

CHRIS RYAN

Chris Ryan joined the Intellectual Property Section of Baker Botts in Austin, Texas, as a partner in 2015. Previously, Mr. Ryan practiced at Vinson & Elkins in 2002 and was admitted as a partner in 2011. Mr. Ryan has served clients as both plaintiff and defense counsel in patent-litigation and trial matters involving electrical, computer, semiconductor, and software-related technologies. His practice also includes counseling relating to patent, copyright, and trade-secret licensing. Mr. Ryan was formerly a management consultant with McKinsey & Company, where he advised technology clients in matters of business strategy and clients in other industry sectors in matters of technology strategy.

Mr. Ryan graduated with honors from the University of Texas School of Law in 2002. He received his undergraduate degree in Physics at Rice University in 1988, and after serving in the U.S. Peace Corps in Niger, where he taught physics and chemistry in a national lycée, he completed his masters in Electrical and Computer Engineering, also at Rice, in 1992.

Mr. Ryan is a member of the American Intellectual Property Law Association, the Austin Intellectual Property Law Association, and the College of the State Bar of Texas. He has been listed as a Texas Rising Star in Intellectual Property for 2010, 2011, and 2012 in *Texas Monthly*. In addition to being a member of the Texas State Bar, Mr. Ryan is admitted to practice before the Court of Appeals for the Federal Circuit and Fifth Circuit, and before the Western, Northern, Eastern, and Southern Districts of Texas. Mr. Ryan is also admitted to practice before the U.S. Patent and Trademark Office.

STEPHEN STOUT

Stephen Stout is a partner at Vinson & Elkins LLP where he focuses on technology-based litigation and counseling for clients. He has represented clients across the country in a wide variety of fields, ranging from biotechnology and pharmaceuticals to digital media and computer architecture. He is also an active member of the bar and has co-authored amicus briefs to the U.S. Supreme Court in several significant patent and veterans cases on behalf of the American Bar Association and the Federal Circuit Bar Association. Mr. Stout also routinely gives talks about intellectual property to classes at the University of Texas. For all of this work, Mr. Stout has been recognized as a Texas Rising Star each year since 2011.

Mr. Stout graduated with honors from the University of Texas School of Law in 2007. He has a B.S. from Texas A&M University in botany, an M.S. from Louisiana State University in plant health, and a Ph.D. from the University of Texas in plant biology. At the University of Texas, his Ph.D. research used molecular biology, bioinformatics, and electrophysiology approaches to study plant responses to gravity.

Mr. Stout is a member of the American Intellectual Property Law Association and the Austin Intellectual Property Law Association. He is admitted to practice in the Eastern District of Texas and the Western District of Wisconsin and is licensed to practice before the U.S. Patent and Trademark Office.

YOUR SUGGESTIONS

We welcome your comments. If you think we should have included (or excluded) something, or if you see anything that needs to be corrected, please let us know. Send your comments to the mailing address or fax number shown on the copyright page, or by e-mail to Carlos Goenaga, Managing Editor, at juan.goenaga@thomsonreuters.com.

CAVEAT

This book provides citations to important opinions that interpret the Lanham Act, Copyright Act, Patent Act, and Uniform Trade Secrets Act. You may disagree with the choice of cases for the various codes and rules in this book. You should therefore use this book only as a research guide. Read the codes, the rules, and the cases yourself and make your own evaluation of them.

EDITORIAL & PRODUCTION STAFF

As always, the staff of O'Connor's worked hard to prepare this publication, both in its substance and in its layout. The people who worked on this edition of ***O'Connor's Federal Intellectual Property Codes Plus*** are listed below.

MANAGING LEGAL EDITOR
Carlos Goenaga, J.D.

LEGAL EDITORS
Jamie Milne, J.D.
Sarah Arocha Ostriyznick, J.D.
Kristen K. Sheils, J.D.

LEGAL EDITORIAL ASSISTANTS
Eun-Jeong Choi, J.D.
Kalina Dalal, J.D.
Erin Gage, J.D.
Victoria R. Guzman, J.D.
Patrick M. Miller, J.D.
Colin K. Morrison, J.D.
Vardan Ramazyan, J.D.

PRODUCTION MANAGER
Donna E. Vass

PRODUCTION EDITOR
Annabelle M. Wilde

PRODUCTION STAFF
Sara Rhodes Bean
Evan Gabriel Bernard
Nicole E. Hammond
Clare Jensen
Rachel Kelly
Emily J. Viehman

PROOFREADERS
Sara Rhodes Bean
Evan Gabriel Bernard
Rachel Kelly
Kathryn A. Ritcheske, J.D.
Emily J. Viehman
Annabelle M. Wilde

HOUSTON, TEXAS

A BRIEF PRIMER ON THE LEAHY-SMITH AMERICA INVENTS ACT OF 2011

By Meredith J. Fitzpatrick and Rebecca J. Cantor[1]

On September 16, 2011, President Obama signed into law the *Leahy-Smith America Invents Act of 2011*, Pub. L. No. 112-29 ("AIA"). The AIA heralds a significant shift in many areas of substantive patent law and procedure in the United States Patent and Trademark Office ("USPTO"). This primer provides a high-level summary of the most significant changes to U.S. patent law including: (1) the shift from the 1952 Patent Act's "first-to-invent" system to the AIA's "first-inventor-to-file" system ("FITF"); (2) three new mechanisms for third-party challenges to a patent in the USPTO—preissuance submission, post-grant review, and inter partes review; and (3) selected litigation-related provisions.

I. The Shift Toward a First-Inventor-to-File System

Among the most significant and highly publicized changes of the AIA is a move from the U.S.'s previous "first-to-invent" system to the new FITF system, which brings us more in line with patent laws in foreign jurisdictions. The previous first-to-invent system allowed an applicant to patent an invention upon proving he invented it before anyone else. In contrast, the AIA rewards the first person who discloses the invention publicly or files a patent application, regardless of who invented the invention first.

The Shift Toward a First-Inventor-to-File System Substantially Changes 35 U.S.C. §102

The AIA fundamentally and radically alters 35 U.S.C §102 in order to achieve the shift from the first-to-invent system to the FITF system. The previous version of 35 U.S.C. §102(a) barred an applicant from receiving a patent when "the invention was known or used by others in this country, or patented or described in a printed publication in this or a foreign country *before the invention thereof* by the applicant for patent."[2] In contrast, the AIA bars patenting of any invention that was "patented, described in a printed publication, or in public use, on sale, or otherwise available to the public *before the effective filing date* of the claimed invention."[3] Further, the 1952 Patent Act section 102(b) provides a grace period that allows applicants to wait to file an application up to one year after the patenting or description of the invention in a printed publication or the public use or sale of the invention. The AIA greatly narrows this grace period by only allowing applicants to wait to file an application within one year of disclosure of the invention if the disclosure came from the inventor or someone who obtained the information from the inventor.[4] By greatly narrowing the one-year grace period between the public disclosure of the invention and the effective filing date of a U.S. patent application, as is available under the 1952 Patent Act section 102(b), the AIA places a critical emphasis on the filing of U.S. patent applications as early as possible, and before the disclosure of any invalidating prior art by others.

The AIA eliminates section 102(c), which barred an inventor from receiving a patent on an invention he previously abandoned. The abandonment provision of the previous section 102(c) provided an impetus to inventors to quickly and diligently disclose their inventions to the public. The FITF system provides that same motivation by awarding patent rights to the first inventor who files for a patent—thus obviating a need for a separate motivation to disclose more quickly under the previous section 102(c).

The AIA incorporates the previous section 102(d) into AIA section 102(a). Three things must occur for a patent to be invalid under the 1952 Patent Act section 102(d): (1) the applicant must file an application on the invention in another country; (2) more than 12 months later, the applicant must file for a patent on the same invention in this country; and (3) the foreign patent must issue before the applicant filed the U.S. patent application.[5] Under the AIA section 102(a), the first-filed foreign patent application becomes prior art to the later-filed U.S. patent application

1. Meredith J. Fitzpatrick and Rebecca J. Cantor are patent litigation and counseling attorneys in Vinson & Elkins' Austin and New York offices, respectively.
2. 35 U.S.C. §102(a) (emphasis added).
3. AIA §102(a)(1) (emphasis added).
4. The AIA grace period also applies if the disclosure in question postdates an earlier disclosure made by the inventor or someone who obtained the information from the inventor.
5. *Bayer AG v. Schein Pharms.*, 301 F.3d 1306, 1312 (Fed.Cir.2002).

once the foreign patent application becomes publicly available, the application is deemed published under section 122(b), or the first-filed patent is granted.

The shift to the FITF system negates the need for the 1952 Patent Act section 102(e). Under section 102(e) of the 1952 Patent Act, a patent that issues from an application published under section 122(b) by the USPTO or published as an international application[6] by another filed in the United States *before the invention* by the applicant for patent constitutes prior art. In other words, if inventor A filed a patent application, and then inventor B filed a patent application disclosing the same invention before inventor A's application published, inventor A's application constitutes prior art to inventor B's application under the 1952 Patent Act section 102(e), unless inventor B can show it invented before inventor A filed its application. The AIA section 102(b) bars patenting of an invention if it was described in a patent issued under section 151 or in an application for patent published or deemed published under section 122(b) in which the patent or application, as the case may be, names another inventor and was effectively filed *before the effective filing date* of the claimed invention. Thus, the AIA section 102(b) bars the same prior art as the 1952 Patent Act section 102(e), except that under the AIA, the second inventor to file cannot "swear behind" the first-filed reference by showing an earlier date of invention.

The AIA disposes of section 102(f), which barred applicants from patenting others' inventions. The FITF system does not bar this activity outright but provides derivation proceedings in which, upon a challenge from a third party, an applicant must prove he actually conceived of the invention. However, only other applicants to a patent can institute derivation proceedings, and they must do so within one year of first publication of a patent claiming an invention already claimed in an earlier-filed application. If an application goes unchallenged throughout this period, the AIA provides no bar to patenting of others' inventions.

Further, the AIA removes section 102(g), which bars an applicant from receiving a patent where, before the applicant conceived of his invention, a third party in the U.S. conceived of the same invention and diligently reduced it to practice before the applicant.[7] Section 102(g) defenses to invalidity during litigation often result in high costs associated with location of the prior art, third-party depositions, and expert testimony. Thus, removal of this sub-section will tend to lower litigation costs. Moreover, the FITF negates the need to quibble over which inventor conceived of and reduced their invention to practice first.

The First-Inventor-to-File System Expands the Scope of Prior Art

The AIA significantly expands the scope of what constitutes prior art. Previously, a prior publication anywhere in the world constituted prior art, but prior public knowledge, use, or sale constituted prior art only if it took place in the U.S. Under the AIA, as with printed publications, prior public use or sale anywhere in the world constitutes prior art. In addition, while public use or sale previously constituted prior art only when it occurred more than one year before the filing date, the same activities constitute prior art under the AIA up until the effective filing date. Further, the AIA does not distinguish between prior art activities of others and those of the inventor, as the 1952 Patent Act does. Under the AIA, all prior art based upon public activity occurring before the effective filing date, whether by the inventor or another, is lumped together in section 102(a)(1).

In addition, the AIA redrafted 35 U.S.C. §103 to expand the scope of prior art that can be considered in determining whether a patent is invalid for obviousness. Under the 1952 Patent Act, a claimed invention cannot be patented if it is proven to be obvious to a person of ordinary skill in the art at or before the time of *invention*. In other words, a patentee can "swear behind" a section 103 prior art reference that was available before the filing date of the patent by proving he conceived of the invention before the prior art reference was available and diligently worked to reduce the invention to practice. Under the AIA, the claimed invention must be nonobvious up until the *effective fil-*

---

6. An international application filed under the treaty defined in section 351(a) shall have the effects of an application filed in the United States only if the international application designated the United States and was published under Article 21(2) of such treaty in the English language. 35 U.S.C. §102(e).
7. 35 U.S.C. §102(g) will continue to apply to each claim of an application for patent and any patent issued thereon if such application or patent contains or contained at any time: (A) a claim to an invention having an effective filing date before March 16, 2013; or (B) a specific reference under 35 U.S.C. §§120, 121, or 365(c) to any patent or application that contains or contained at any time such a claim.

ing date. In other words, patentees can no longer swear behind section 103 prior art references. If a prior art reference is available before the effective filing date of a patent, it has potential to invalidate a patent, even if the date of invention predates the availability of the prior art reference.

The First-Inventor-to-File System Provides an Ambiguous Grace Period

The AIA provides a one-year grace period during which disclosures do not constitute prior art if the subject matter disclosed comes directly or indirectly from the inventor. While it appears clear that patents, published patent applications, and printed publications fall within the definition of "disclosures," a question remains as to whether public use, sale, or acts that make the invention "otherwise available to the public" similarly constitute disclosures falling within the one-year grace period.[8] The legislative history provides some argument that *all* activities are "disclosures" and hence within the scope of the grace period. Further clarification on this issue will likely be required by the courts.

The AIA Provides a Floating Transition Date to First-Inventor-to-File System

The changes toward the FITF system, particularly the redefinition of what constitutes prior art, are governed by a "floating" transition date. Instead of a firm transition date that makes the AIA applicable to any new application filed after a date certain, the new FITF system comes into effect for patent applications and patents issued on those applications that have ever contained: (1) a claim to a claimed invention where the filing date of the earliest application for which the claimed invention is entitled under sections 119, 365(a), 365(b), 120, 121, or 365(c) falls on or after March 16, 2013; or (2) a specific reference under sections 120, 121, or 365(c) to any patent or application that ever contained such a claim. Thus, applications filed on or after March 16, 2013, that claim priority back to patents filed before that date are governed by the old first-to-invent system rather than the FITF system, unless the application also claims priority to a patent filed on or after March 16, 2013. If the applicant makes a priority claim to a patent or application filed on or after March 16, 2013, then the FITF system governs, even if that priority claim is later canceled.

Derivation Proceedings Replace Interference Proceedings

In order to move toward a FITF system, the AIA provides mechanisms to ensure that the first person to file is the true inventor. The new law replaces interference proceedings with derivation proceedings in which the newly formed Patent Trial and Appeal Board (which replaces the Board of Patent Appeals and Interferences) will determine if an inventor named in an earlier-filed application derived the claimed invention from the inventor in a later-filed application.

Interference proceedings will remain available for certain legacy patents and applications. But under the new derivation proceedings, an applicant may file a petition for a derivation proceeding within one year of the first publication of a claim[9] to an invention that is the same or substantially the same as the earlier application's claim to invention. The applicant must do so within that year or permanently lose the opportunity to do so. The effective date of the derivation provision is March 16, 2013.

II. Mechanisms for Third-Party Challenge

The AIA creates three new mechanisms for a third party to challenge a patent in front of the USPTO—preissuance submission, post-grant review, and inter partes review.[10]

Preissuance Submission by Third Party

The AIA allows third parties to submit for consideration and inclusion in the record of any patent application any patent, published patent application, or other printed publication of relevance to the pending application. See 35

8. The AIA provides no definition of the term "disclosure."
9. The AIA does not define "publication" in this subsection.
10. The AIA does not substantively change the ex parte reexamination procedure.

U.S.C. §122(e). These documents must be submitted before the earlier of these events: (i) a notice of allowance is mailed; or (ii) the later of (a) six months after the application is published or (b) the USPTO issues a first rejection under 35 U.S.C. §132. In addition to submitting the references, the third party must also set forth a "concise description" of the asserted relevance of each submitted document. Preissuance submissions are available on September 16, 2012, one year after the enactment of the AIA.

Post-Grant Review

A post-grant review will allow a third party to challenge a patent on any ground that could be raised under 35 U.S.C. §§282(b)(2) or (3) (i.e., a third party will be able to argue invalidity on any ground it would be able to raise in a lawsuit). See 35 U.S.C. §§321-329. The third party will be required to file a petition for post-grant review within nine months of the patent grant or a patent reissue issuance.

A petition requesting a post-grant review will need to include, with particularity, each claim challenged and the grounds on which the challenge is based. This must be accompanied by evidence supporting the grounds, including copies of the prior art relied upon and affidavits or declarations supporting evidence and opinions. The third party will be allowed to rely on expert opinions. The patent owner will have the right to file a preliminary response to this petition within an amount of time that will be set by the USPTO.

A third party will be unable to file a petition if it has instituted an action challenging the validity of the claims (i.e., a declaratory judgment action). Moreover, if a petitioner institutes an action challenging the validity of the claims after filing a petition, the lawsuit will be stayed until: (i) the patent owner moves to lift the stay; (ii) the patent owner files a suit or counterclaim alleging infringement of the patent; or (iii) the petitioner moves to dismiss the lawsuit.

Once the petition has been filed, the Director of the USPTO will determine whether it is sufficient to institute a post-grant review. The Director is to institute a post-grant review if he determines that the information presented, if not rebutted, will more likely than not demonstrate that at least one of the claims is invalid. Alternatively, the Director may institute a post-grant review if the petition "raises a novel or unsettled legal question that is important to other patents or patent applications." The AIA gives no guidance on what might constitute such a "novel or unsettled" legal question.

If a post-grant review is instituted, it will be an adversarial proceeding conducted in front of the new Patent Trial and Appeal Board ("PTAB") under regulations to be promulgated by the USPTO. These regulations will govern, among other things, procedures for submission of supplemental information after the petition is filed, standards and procedures for discovery, providing protective orders, and requiring that a final determination be issued no later than one year after the Director institutes a post-grant review. During the course of the post-grant review, the patentee will be entitled to amend its claims once. These amendments may not enlarge the scope of the claims. Both parties will have a right to a hearing in front of the PTAB. In order to prevail, the petitioner will be required to show that the claims are invalid under a preponderance-of-the-evidence standard (a lower burden than the clear-and-convincing burden required to prove invalidity in court). Once the evidence is submitted, the PTAB will issue a final written decision with respect to the patentability of the claims being challenged. Any party to the post-grant review may appeal the PTAB's decision to the Court of Appeals for the Federal Circuit.

If the post-grant review results in a final written decision from the PTAB, the petitioner may not request or maintain any proceeding before the USPTO on any ground that the petitioner raised or reasonably could have raised during the post-grant review. The petitioner is further estopped from asserting invalidity in a civil action or in the International Trade Commission based on any ground that the petitioner raised or could have raised in the post-grant review.

While the AIA provides that the provisions regarding post-grant review will become effective one year after the AIA is enacted, it also provides that post-grant review will only be available for patents issued under the FITF system. Because the FITF system did not become effective until March 16, 2013, it will be several years before patent applications filed after that date will issue and can be challenged in a post-grant review.

Inter Partes Review

In the AIA, inter partes review replaces inter partes reexamination. An inter partes review can be considered a limited version of a post-grant review. See 35 U.S.C. §§311[B*]-319[B*]. In an inter partes review, the petitioner may only allege that claims are invalid under 35 U.S.C. §102 or 103. A petitioner may request an inter partes review at any time after the time to institute a post-grant review has expired (i.e., nine months after issuance), or, if the patent has been subject to a post-grant review, after the post-grant review is terminated.

Similar to a post-grant review, a third party will be unable to file a petition for an inter partes review if it has instituted a lawsuit challenging the validity of the claims. If a petitioner institutes a lawsuit challenging the validity of the claims after filing a petition, the lawsuit will be stayed until: (i) the patent owner moves to lift the stay; (ii) the patent owner files a suit or counterclaim alleging infringement of the patent; or (iii) the petitioner moves to dismiss the lawsuit. Additionally, an inter partes review may not be instituted if the petition is filed more than one year after the patent owner serves the petitioner with a complaint alleging patent infringement.

The requirements for a petition requesting an inter partes review will be similar to the petition required for a post-grant review. The patent owner will have the right to file a preliminary response to this petition within an amount of time that will be set by the USPTO. The Director will institute an inter partes review if the petitioner has shown a reasonable likelihood that it will prevail with respect to at least one of the claims challenged in the petition. This reasonable-likelihood standard also replaces the substantial-new-question-of-patentability standard for inter partes reexaminations as of the date of enactment of the AIA.

Similar to a post-grant review, an inter partes review is an adversarial proceeding conducted in front of the PTAB under regulations promulgated by the USPTO. These regulations are expected to be similar to the regulations the Director will implement for post-grant reviews. During the course of the inter partes review, the patentee will be entitled to amend its claims one time, but the amendments may not enlarge the scope of the claims. Both parties will have a right to a hearing in front of the PTAB. In order to prevail, the petitioner will be required to show that the claims are invalid under a preponderance-of-the-evidence standard (a lower burden than is required in federal district court). Once the evidence is submitted, the PTAB will issue a final written decision with respect to the patentability of the claims being challenged. Any party to the inter partes review may appeal the PTAB's decision to the Court of Appeals for the Federal Circuit.

If the inter partes review results in a final written decision from the PTAB, the petitioner will be estopped from asserting invalidity in a civil or International Trade Commission action based on any ground that the petitioner raised or reasonably could have raised in the inter partes review. Similar to the post-grant review, inter partes review will provide a viable, if limited, forum for a third party to challenge the patentability of claims. Inter partes review is available beginning on September 16, 2012, one year after AIA enactment, and is available for all patents, regardless of application or issue date.

III. Litigation-Related Provisions

Several provisions of the AIA will impact future patent litigation.

Inventor's Oath or Declaration

The AIA amends 35 U.S.C. §115 to allow a patent applicant to file a substitute statement instead of an inventor's oath or declaration in limited circumstances. Among these circumstances is where the inventor is required to assign his invention to the patent applicant but has refused to do so. The AIA further provides that if a patent grants with such a substitute statement, the patent will grant to the real party in interest, not to the inventor. This provision took effect on September 16, 2012, one year after enactment of the AIA.

The AIA Expands the Scope of the Prior-Commercial-Use Defense

Previously, it was a defense to an action for patent infringement if the defendant, acting in good faith, had actually reduced the subject matter to practice at least one year before the effective filing date of the patent and commercially used the subject matter before the effective filing date of such patent. This provision only applied to accusations of infringement of business-method patents. The new law expands this defense by broadly applying it to claims for infringement of any type of patentable subject matter. However, the new statute limits the scope of the defense to acts of commercial use that occurred at least one year before either the effective filing date or the date of disclosure, and does not apply to inventions that, at the time of the commercialization, were owned or subject to an obligation of assignment to either a university or an organization whose primary purpose is to promote the commercialization of university technology.

Although the movement toward a FITF system encourages early disclosures of technological information as a means to limit the scope of potential prior art, the changes to the prior-commercial-use statute discourage disclosure. Under both the 1952 Patent Act and the AIA, this defense allows people to practice business-method patents without the threat of patent litigation, even if their commercial use did not disclose to the public how the invention worked—what practitioners call a "non-self-disclosing use." The AIA expands the right to make non-self-disclosing uses by allowing people to make commercial uses of all types of inventions, not just business methods. Thus, the AIA provides a more expansive safe harbor for commercial uses that do not disclose the subject matter of the invention to the public. In other words, under the AIA, if a company chose to employ a non-self-disclosing process in secret, and then a third party independently invented the same subject matter at a much later date, the company would have a defense to the later inventor's patent infringement claims. This new approach will cause investors and inventors to reconsider whether they should choose to patent their inventions or develop them in secret and maintain trade secret protections. Patent practitioners anticipate this modification of the law to potentially cause fewer patent filings and mandatory disclosures accompanying them, and maybe even cause a shift toward development of more non-self-disclosing technologies.

Supplemental Examinations

Under the AIA, a patent owner may request a supplemental examination of a patent to consider, reconsider, or correct information believed to be relevant to the patent. If the USPTO concludes that the patent owner has raised a substantial new question of patentability, the patent will enter ex parte reexamination in accordance with 35 U.S.C. §30.

A patent owner may be able to prevent allegations that a patent is unenforceable for inequitable conduct through supplemental examination. After the reexamination is concluded, a patent generally may not be held unenforceable based on any of information that the USPTO considers during the supplemental examination. In effect, this gives a patent owner a way to cure prior inequitable conduct. There are some exceptions, however, to this general rule. First, this rule does not apply if, before the request for supplemental examination is made, a party pleads inequitable conduct with particularity in a civil action. Second, this rule does not apply in patent enforcement actions in federal court or the ITC unless the supplemental examination is concluded before the court proceeding is filed.

Supplemental examination also brings some risks for patent owners. If, during the course of a supplemental examination, the USPTO becomes aware that the patent owner committed material fraud on the USPTO, it is authorized to cancel any claims found to be invalid and to refer the matter to the U.S. Attorney General.

Tax Strategies Deemed Within the Art

The AIA provides that any strategy for reducing, avoiding, or deferring tax liability, whether known or unknown, is considered to be unpatentable in light of the prior art. This applies to federal, state, local, or foreign taxes. This provision does not, however, include a method, apparatus, technology, computer program, or system that is used solely for preparing tax returns or that is for financial management (to the extent that the financial management portion is severable from the tax strategy). This provision took effect September 16, 2011, and applies to all patents (including those issued before September 16, 2011) and patent applications.

Best Mode

Under the AIA, failure to satisfy the best-mode requirement of 35 U.S.C. §112 is no longer a basis for invalidity under 35 U.S.C. §282. This means that a litigant may not argue failure to satisfy the best-mode requirement as a basis for invalidity in a civil action. Additionally, because post-grant review is tied to 35 U.S.C. §282, a petition for post-grant review may not be based on the failure to satisfy the best-mode requirement. While the USPTO may still reject patent applications for failure to satisfy the best-mode requirement, third parties have no way to challenge issued patents for failure to satisfy the requirement. This provision took effect on September 16, 2011, and applies to proceedings commenced on or after that date.

Marking

The AIA eliminates the ability of third parties to bring qui tam actions alleging failure to comply with the marking statutes by providing that only the U.S. government may sue for false marking. A third party may only bring a suit for false marking if it can show that it has sustained a "competitive injury." The AIA does not give any guidance on what constitutes a "competitive injury."

The AIA also provides that a patentee may satisfy the marking requirement by including the word "patent" or "pat." on a product along with the URL of a website that associates the product with the patent number. In addition, it is no longer a violation of 35 U.S.C. §292 to mark a product with an expired patent. These amendments became effective the day the AIA was enacted and apply retroactively to all pending court cases alleging violations of 35 U.S.C. §292.

Post-Grant Review Proceedings for Covered Business-Method Patents

The AIA creates a transitional program during which petitioners may initiate a post-grant review proceeding for covered business-method patents to address growing concerns regarding the increasingly high volume of business-method patents of questionable validity issued in the recent post-*Bilski* years. The AIA defines "Covered Business Method Patent" to mean a patent that claims a method or corresponding apparatus for performing data processing or other operations used in the practice, administration, or management of a financial product or service, except that the term does not include patents for technological inventions. The proposed program functions in generally the same manner as other post-grant review proceedings, except that petitioners may not take advantage of this approach until sued for patent infringement, and the AIA narrows the scope of prior art applicable to the post-grant review proceedings.[11]

The AIA Alters Misjoinder Rules and Nonpracticing Entity Tactics

One provision of the AIA strips courts of their power to join multiple defendants in a single lawsuit simply based upon the fact that the defendants are all alleged to infringe the same patent. Under the new law, joinder of multiple defendants is still possible, but only if the right to relief against all parties arises out of the same transaction, occurrence, or series of transactions or occurrences relating to the acts of infringement and is based on common questions of fact. This misjoinder provision applies to all cases filed on or after September 16, 2011—the date President Obama signed the AIA. Patentees across the nation reacted to this situation by filing 54 new patent cases, accusing over 800 corporate entities of patent infringement on September 15. These filings represent an all-time high for single-day filings, and the average complaint accused over 16 entities of patent infringement. Although patentees may continue to file suits against several defendants, it appears many practitioners in the industry believe the AIA will make maintaining this type of joinder an uphill battle in the future.

The shift to the FITF system significantly reshapes several fundamental aspects of the Patent Act, including the scope of prior art, the inventors' grace period, and mechanisms to ensure that the first person to file is the true inventor. Additionally, the new mechanisms for challenging issued patents in the USPTO provide a new option for those wishing to challenge the validity of a patent. For challengers, these mechanisms will have the benefit of a lower burden of proof. However, there is a potential drawback to these mechanisms because prior art used in a USPTO challenge potentially cannot be used in a later court proceeding.

---

11. Petitioners may only use prior art that is described by AIA section 102(a) or prior art that discloses the invention more than one year before the date of the application for patent in the United States and would be described by the AIA section 102(a) if the disclosure had been made by another before the invention thereof by the applicant for patent.

SCHEDULE OF ENACTMENT

The AIA will bring about many changes over the next couple of years, and many of the provisions become effective on different days. The summary below provides a high-level overview of when the changes come into effect. For a chart detailing the different effective dates, see "America Invents Act Amendments Chart," p. 474.

Immediately Upon Signing of the Act – September 16, 2011

- Changes to requirements for standing to bring false-marking cases and marking requirements is effective immediately and applicable to pending proceedings.
- Limitations on joinder of defendants in infringement actions is effective immediately and applicable to all actions commenced on or after September 16, 2011.
- Best-mode violations no longer a basis for invalidating a patent in actions commenced on or after September 16, 2011.
- Changes to prior-commercial-use defense.
- Change of inter partes reexamination standard.
- Appeal of Board decisions in ex parte reexamination to Federal Circuit only.

10 Days from Signing of the Act – September 26, 2011

- A 15% surcharge will be added to all patent-related fees, including patent maintenance fees.
- USPTO will set fees for priority examination of important technologies.

60 Days from Signing of the Act – November 15, 2011

- USPTO will impose a $400 surcharge on certain original application for patent that are not filed electronically.

12 Months from Signing of the Act – September 16, 2012

- Changes to inventor's oath or declaration come into effect.
- The new rules on inter partes review become effective and apply to the institution and conduct of inter partes review commenced after enactment as to all patents, whether issued before, on, or after enactment.
- The new post-grant review process becomes effective.
- The new supplemental examination procedures become effective.
- Preissuance submissions become effective.
- The public may add prior art or written statements submitted by the patent owner in a proceeding either in federal court or in the USPTO to the file of an issued patent along with a statement of the pertinence and application of the prior art or written statements, for use in reexamination or post-grant review proceedings.

18 Months from Signing of the Act – March 16, 2013

- The FITF provisions take effect, but only apply to applications that have ever contained: (1) a claim to a claimed invention where the filing date of the earliest application for which the claimed invention is entitled under sections 119, 365(a), 365(b), 120, 121, or 365(c) falls on or after March 16, 2013; or (2) a specific reference under sections 120, 121, or 365(c) to any patent or application that ever contained such a claim.

TITLE 15. COMMERCE & TRADE

TABLE OF CONTENTS

TITLE 15. COMMERCE & TRADE

CHAPTER 22. TRADEMARKS

SUBCHAPTER I. THE PRINCIPAL REGISTER

§1051. APPLICATION FOR REGISTRATION; VERIFICATION

[LANHAM ACT §1]

(a) Application for use of trademark—

(1) The owner of a trademark used in commerce may request registration of its trademark on the principal register hereby established by paying the prescribed fee and filing in the Patent and Trademark Office an application and a verified statement, in such form as may be prescribed by the Director, and such number of specimens or facsimiles of the mark as used as may be required by the Director.

(2) The application shall include specification of the applicant's domicile and citizenship, the date of the applicant's first use of the mark, the date of the applicant's first use of the mark in commerce, the goods in connection with which the mark is used, and a drawing of the mark.

(3) The statement shall be verified by the applicant and specify that—

(A) the person making the verification believes that he or she, or the juristic person in whose behalf he or she makes the verification, to be the owner of the mark sought to be registered;

(B) to the best of the verifier's knowledge and belief, the facts recited in the application are accurate;

(C) the mark is in use in commerce; and

(D) to the best of the verifier's knowledge and belief, no other person has the right to use such mark in commerce either in the identical form thereof or in such near resemblance thereto as to be likely, when used on or in connection with the goods of such other person, to cause confusion, or to cause mistake, or to deceive, except that, in the case of every application claiming concurrent use, the applicant shall—

(i) state exceptions to the claim of exclusive use; and

(ii) shall specify, to the extent of the verifier's knowledge—

(I) any concurrent use by others;

(II) the goods on or in connection with which and the areas in which each concurrent use exists;

(III) the periods of each use; and

(IV) the goods and area for which the applicant desires registration.

(4) The applicant shall comply with such rules or regulations as may be prescribed by the Director. The Director shall promulgate rules prescribing the requirements for the application and for obtaining a filing date herein.

(b) Application for bona fide intention to use trademark—

(1) A person who has a bona fide intention, under circumstances showing the good faith of such person, to use a trademark in commerce may request registration of its trademark on the principal register hereby established by paying the prescribed fee and filing in the Patent and Trademark Office an application and a verified statement, in such form as may be prescribed by the Director.

(2) The application shall include specification of the applicant's domicile and citizenship, the goods in connection with which the applicant has a bona fide intention to use the mark, and a drawing of the mark.

(3) The statement shall be verified by the applicant and specify—

(A) that the person making the verification believes that he or she, or the juristic person in whose behalf he or she makes the verification, to be entitled to use the mark in commerce;

(B) the applicant's bona fide intention to use the mark in commerce;

(C) that, to the best of the verifier's knowledge and belief, the facts recited in the application are accurate; and

(D) that, to the best of the verifier's knowledge and belief, no other person has the right to use such mark in commerce either in the identical form thereof or in such near resemblance thereto as to be likely, when used on or in connection with the goods of such other person, to cause confusion, or to cause mistake, or to deceive.

Except for applications filed pursuant to section 1126 of title 15, no mark shall be registered until the applicant has met the requirements of subsections (c) and (d) of this section.

(4) The applicant shall comply with such rules or regulations as may be prescribed by the Director. The

Director shall promulgate rules prescribing the requirements for the application and for obtaining a filing date herein.

(c) Amendment of application under subsection (b) to conform to requirements of subsection (a).—At any time during examination of an application filed under subsection (b) of this section, an applicant who has made use of the mark in commerce may claim the benefits of such use for purposes of this chapter, by amending his or her application to bring it into conformity with the requirements of subsection (a) of this section.

(d) Verified statement that trademark is used in commerce—

(1) Within six months after the date on which the notice of allowance with respect to a mark is issued under section 1063(b)(2) of title 15 to an applicant under subsection (b) of this section, the applicant shall file in the Patent and Trademark Office, together with such number of specimens or facsimiles of the mark as used in commerce as may be required by the Director and payment of the prescribed fee, a verified statement that the mark is in use in commerce and specifying the date of the applicant's first use of the mark in commerce and those goods or services specified in the notice of allowance on or in connection with which the mark is used in commerce. Subject to examination and acceptance of the statement of use, the mark shall be registered in the Patent and Trademark Office, a certificate of registration shall be issued for those goods or services recited in the statement of use for which the mark is entitled to registration, and notice of registration shall be published in the Official Gazette of the Patent and Trademark Office. Such examination may include an examination of the factors set forth in subsections (a) through (e) of section 1052 of title 15. The notice of registration shall specify the goods or services for which the mark is registered.

(2) The Director shall extend, for one additional 6-month period, the time for filing the statement of use under paragraph (1), upon written request of the applicant before the expiration of the 6-month period provided in paragraph (1). In addition to an extension under the preceding sentence, the Director may, upon a showing of good cause by the applicant, further extend the time for filing the statement of use under paragraph (1) for periods aggregating not more than 24 months, pursuant to written request of the applicant made before the expiration of the last extension granted under this paragraph. Any request for an extension under this paragraph shall be accompanied by a verified statement that the applicant has a continued bona fide intention to use the mark in commerce and specifying those goods or services identified in the notice of allowance on or in connection with which the applicant has a continued bona fide intention to use the mark in commerce. Any request for an extension under this paragraph shall be accompanied by payment of the prescribed fee. The Director shall issue regulations setting forth guidelines for determining what constitutes good cause for purposes of this paragraph.

(3) The Director shall notify any applicant who files a statement of use of the acceptance or refusal thereof and, if the statement of use is refused, the reasons for the refusal. An applicant may amend the statement of use.

(4) The failure to timely file a verified statement of use under paragraph (1) or an extension request under paragraph (2) shall result in abandonment of the application, unless it can be shown to the satisfaction of the Director that the delay in responding was unintentional, in which case the time for filing may be extended, but for a period not to exceed the period specified in paragraphs (1) and (2) for filing a statement of use.

(e) Designation of resident for service of process and notices.—If the applicant is not domiciled in the United States the applicant may designate, by a document filed in the United States Patent and Trademark Office, the name and address of a person resident in the United States on whom may be served notices or process in proceedings affecting the mark. Such notices or process may be served upon the person so designated by leaving with that person or mailing to that person a copy thereof at the address specified in the last designation so filed. If the person so designated cannot be found at the address given in the last designation, or if the registrant does not designate by a document filed in the United States Patent and Trademark Office the name and address of a person resident in the United States on whom may be served notices or process in proceedings affecting the mark, such notices or process may be served on the Director.

History of 15 U.S.C. §1051: July 5, 1946, ch. 540, §1, 60 Stat. 427; Oct. 9, 1962, P.L. 87-772, §1, 76 Stat. 769; Jan. 2, 1975, P.L. 93-596, §1, 88 Stat. 1949; Nov. 16, 1988, P.L. 100-667, §103, 102 Stat. 3935; Oct. 30, 1998, P.L. 105-330, §§103, 201(a)(1), 112 Stat. 3064, 3069; Nov. 29, 1999, P.L. 106-113, §1000(a)(9), 113 Stat. 1536; Nov. 2, 2002, P.L. 107-273, §13207(b)(1), (2), 116 Stat. 1906.

Treatise Cross-References

McCarthy on Trademark & Unfair Competition

Ch. 4, *Explaining Terms of Art in Trademark & Unfair Competition Law*, §4:12
Ch. 16, *Acquisition & Priority of Trademark Rights*, §16:41
Ch. 17, *Loss of Trademark Rights*, §17:21
Ch. 19, *Federal Registration of Marks*, §§19:1; 19:1.25; 19:2; 19:12-19:14; 19:17-19:19; 19:22; 19:25; 19:26; 19:31; 19:34; 19:45.25; 19:46; 19:53; 19:109; 19:113; 19:125; 19:129
Ch. 20, *Inter Partes Trademark Proceedings in the Patent & Trademark Office*, §§20:13; 20:45
Ch. 21, *Appeal from Decisions on Trademark Registration*, §21:10
Ch. 26, *The Territorial Extent of Trademark Rights*, §§26:38; 26:39
Ch. 29, *International Aspects of Trademark Law*, §§29:14-29:16
Ch. 31, *Defenses to Infringement of Trademarks*, §31:76
Ch. 32, *Procedure in Trademark Infringement & Unfair Competition Litigation*, §32:18

ANNOTATIONS

Generally

Humanoids Grp. v. Rogan, 375 F.3d 301, 304-05 (4th Cir.2004). "[T]he PTO promulgated regulations providing that in order to receive a filing date, an application must contain: '(1) The name of the applicant; (2) A name and address for the correspondence; (3) A clear drawing of the mark; (4) A listing of goods or services; and (5) The filing fee....' When the PTO receives an application, it labels the application with a receipt date and then reviews the application for compliance with these 'minimum requirements for receipt of a filing date.' If the PTO determines that an application contains the required elements, the PTO assigns the application a filing date as of the date of receipt and enters the mark into its Trademark Electronic Search System, which the public may access through the PTO's website."

Harrods Ltd. v. Sixty Internet Domain Names, 302 F.3d 214, 229 (4th Cir.2002). "While it is the use of a mark, not its registration, that confers trademark protection, registration does confer certain benefits on the owner; for example, it serves as prima facie evidence of the mark's validity."

CAE, Inc. v. Clean Air Eng'g, 267 F.3d 660, 673 (7th Cir.2001). "In order to be registered, a mark must be capable of distinguishing the applicant's goods or services from those of others and must have been used in interstate commerce. To obtain registration, the applicant must present certain facts in a verified written application to the [PTO] and must pay a statutory filing fee."

Zazú Designs v. L'Oreal, S.A., 979 F.2d 499, 503 (7th Cir.1992). "Under the common law, one must win the race to the marketplace to establish the exclusive right to a mark. Registration modifies this system slightly, allowing slight sales plus notice in the register to substitute for substantial sales without notice."

Chien Ming Huang v. Tzu Wei Chen Food Co., 849 F.2d 1458, 1460 (Fed.Cir.1988). "No authority has been cited for excusing noncompliance with 15 U.S.C. §1051 [Lanham Act §1]. Neither the [TTAB] nor the courts can waive this statutory requirement."

Common-Law Protection

Quiksilver, Inc. v. Kymsta Corp., 466 F.3d 749, 757-58 (9th Cir.2006). "A product mark like 'ROXY,' even if always displayed with a house mark like 'QUIKSILVER,' may acquire independent trademark significance. [¶] In determining whether a mark has independent trademark significance, we consider whether the mark owner has engaged in 'a constant pattern or effort ... to use [product mark] in a manner separate and distinct from [house mark].' '[C]onsumer awareness of the product mark apart from the fame of the associated house mark,' the 'strength of the public reputation of the product mark,' and the 'nature and context of promotion' are also 'reliable test[s] of the independence of the product mark from its parent house mark.'"

Lucent Info. Mgmt. v. Lucent Tech., 186 F.3d 311, 316-17 (3d Cir.1999). "A party asserting trademark ownership in a trading area must show clear entitlement to protection of its trademark in a particular market. In other words, that party must introduce evidence to show its trademark has achieved market penetration that is significant enough to pose the real likelihood of confusion among the consumers in that area. [The] four-factor test to determine whether the market penetration of a trademark in an area is sufficient to warrant protection [is]: (1) the volume of sales of the trademarked product; (2) the growth trends (both positive and negative) in the area; (3) the number of persons actually purchasing the product in relation to the potential number of customers; and (4) the amount of product advertising in the area." (Internal quotes omitted.)

§1051(a)—Generally

American Express Co. v. Goetz, 515 F.3d 156, 161-62 (2d Cir.2008). "[T]he analogous use doctrine, where it applies, eases the technical requirements for trademarks and services marks in favor of a competing claimant who asserts priority on the basis of earlier analogous use of the mark. [¶] At the very least analogous use must be use that is 'open and notorious.' In other words, analogous use must be 'of such a nature and extent' that the mark has become 'popularized in the public mind' so that the relevant segment of the public identifies the marked goods with the mark's adopter. [¶] The doctrine, however, has not been stretched so far as to obviate the requirement that [mark proponent] show eventual actual use."

Sovereign Order of Saint John, Inc. v. Grady, 119 F.3d 1236, 1241 (6th Cir.1997). "[A] valid trademark registration requires only that the registrant 'believe' himself to be the owner of the mark."

In re Compagnie Generale Maritime, 993 F.2d 841, 843 n.3 (Fed.Cir.1993). 15 U.S.C. §1051, Lanham Act §1, "merely enumerates prerequisites for registration. It begins by saying that the owner of a mark 'may *register* his trade-mark' and then lists how he must do so. The list includes, among others, filing an application specifying various things, including use, paying fees, and following [PTO] rules. But nowhere does [§1051] refer to the jurisdiction of the [TTAB]. Nowhere does it suggest that for want of any specification required for registration, the PTO may not examine the application. Rather, the clear inference is that for lack of such specifications or proof, the mark will not be *registered*."

§1051(a)—Owner

Lyons v. American Coll. of Vet. Sports Med. & Rehab., 859 F.3d 1023, 1028 (Fed.Cir.2017). "A framework has developed in situations ... where there has been a departure from or change of membership in a group, and both the departing member and the remnant group claim ownership of the mark. [¶] For ownership disputes arising out of changes of membership in musical groups, [treatise] frames the inquiry as whether the mark 'identif[ies] the group regardless of its members.' To answer that question, [treatise] proposed a two-part analysis: first, one determines whether the mark is 'personal to the individual members or not'; and second, if it is not, then it must be determined 'for what quality or characteristic the group is known and who controls that quality.' The [TTAB] rephrased [treatise's] two-step inquiry in its findings to mean that 'the consuming public did not associate' the mark with the departing member, and the group, rather than any individual member, 'controlled the quality or characteristic of the band.' Thus, the [TTAB] determined that the band owned the mark, the departing member's application for registration was void *ab initio*, and the resulting registration was invalid."

Covertech Fabricating, Inc. v. TVM Bldg. Prods., 855 F.3d 163, 170 (3d Cir.2017). "In assessing the rightful ownership of the ... mark, the District Court relied on the 'first use test,' which determines initial ownership by asking which party was the first to use an unregistered trademark in commerce. [W]e conclude ... the first use test was not the correct test given the unique context of the manufacturer-distributor relationship.... *At 171-72:* [W]here initial ownership between a manufacturer and its exclusive distributor is at issue and no contract exists, the manufacturer is the presumptive trademark owner unless the distributor rebuts that presumption using a multi-factor balancing test designed to examine the distribution agreement in effect between the parties. The six factors that should be considered are: (1) '[w]hich party invented or created the mark'; (2) '[w]hich party first affixed the mark to goods sold'; (3) '[w]hich party's name appeared on packaging and promotional materials in conjunction with the mark'; (4) '[w]hich party exercised control over the nature and quality of goods on which the mark appeared'; (5) '[t]o which party did customers look as standing behind the goods, *e.g.*, which party received complaints for defects and made appropriate replacement or refund'; and (6) '[w]hich party paid for advertising and promotion of the trademarked product.' [¶] Our adoption of this test is also consistent with our sister Circuits, which, when asked to determine ownership in this context, have endorsed some version of the [treatise] test.... While some courts have distilled [treatise's] six factors to four, ... and others have varied the language, ... all have cited either to ... treatise itself or to cases that do so, applying the [treatise] test with only minor variations across the federal courts." *See also* ***TMT N. Am., Inc. v. Magic Touch GmbH***, 124 F.3d 876, 884 n.4 (7th Cir.1997); ***Sengoku Works Ltd. v. RMC Int'l***, 96 F.3d 1217, 1220 (9th Cir.1996).

Southern Cal. Darts Ass'n v. Zaffina, 762 F.3d 921, 930 (9th Cir.2014). "We hold that unincorporated associations ... have the capacity to own trademarks."

U.S. Ozone Co. v. U.S. Ozone Co. of Am., 62 F.2d 881, 885 (7th Cir.1932). "Any person, partnership, corporation, or unincorporated association capable of holding title to personalty may acquire the right to a trade-mark. The owner may be the manufacturer of the article to which the trade-mark is applied or the seller of goods of a particular manufacture or quality to which the distinguishing mark is applied."

§1051(a)—Specimen

In re Sones, 590 F.3d 1282, 1288 (Fed.Cir.2009). "[A] picture is not a mandatory requirement for a website-based specimen of use, and ... the test for an acceptable website-based specimen, just as any other specimen, is simply that it must in some way evince that the mark is 'associated' with the goods and serves as an indicator of source."

§1051(a)—Tacking

Hana Fin., Inc. v. Hana Bank, ___ U.S. ___, 135 S.Ct. 907, 909 (2015). "Rights in a trademark are determined by the date of the mark's first use in commerce. The party who first uses a mark in commerce is said to have priority over other users. Recognizing that trademark users ought to be permitted to make certain modifications to their marks over time without losing priority, lower courts have provided that, in limited circumstances, a party may clothe a new mark with the priority position of an older mark. This doctrine is called 'tacking,' and lower courts have found tacking to be available when the original and revised marks are 'legal equivalents' in that they create the same, continuing commercial impression. The question presented here is whether a judge or a jury should determine whether tacking is available in a given case. Because the tacking inquiry operates from the perspective of an ordinary purchaser or consumer, we hold that a jury should make this determination. *At U.S. ___, S.Ct. 911:* This is certainly not to say that a judge may never determine whether two marks may be tacked. If the facts warrant it, a judge may decide a tacking question on a motion for summary judgment or for judgment as a matter of law. And if the parties have opted to try their case before a judge, the judge may of course decide a tacking question in his or her factfinding capacity."

Quiksilver, Inc. v. Kymsta Corp., 466 F.3d 749, 758-59 (9th Cir.2006). "Under the tacking doctrine, a mark owner essentially seeks to tack his first use date in the earlier mark onto the subsequent mark. Tacking permits a mark owner to claim priority in a mark based on the first use date of a similar, but technically distinct, mark—but only in the exceptionally narrow instance where the previously used mark is the legal equivalent of the mark in question or indistinguishable therefrom such that consumers consider both as the same mark. The standard for tacking ... is exceedingly strict: The marks must create the same, continuing commercial impression, and the later mark should not materially differ from or alter the character of the mark attempted to be tacked. The later mark must be indistinguishable from the original mark at the time that the later mark is introduced. *At 759 n.10:* In deciding whether tacking applies, courts often compare the earlier mark with the subsequent mark to determine whether the two marks create the same, continuing commercial impression. The similarities or dissimilarities between two marks constitute evidence of whether consumers view them as indistinguishable." (Internal quotes omitted.)

§1051(a)—Use in Commerce

For more annotations on this topic, see 15 U.S.C. §1114, *§1114(1)—Commerce*, p. 64, 15 U.S.C. §1127, *Commerce*, p. 170, and *Use in Commerce*, p. 172.

George & Co. v. Imagination Entm't Ltd., 575 F.3d 383, 400 (4th Cir.2009). "In general, the party claiming ownership of a mark must be the first to use the mark in the sale of goods. The party claiming ownership must also use the mark as a trademark, that is, the mark must be used to identify the source of the goods to potential customers. Thus, so long as a person is the first to use a particular mark to identify his goods in a given market, and so long as that owner continues to make use of the mark, he is 'entitled to prevent others from using the mark to describe their own goods' in that market. [¶] However, if the owner of a mark ceases to use the mark without an intent to resume use in the reasonably foreseeable future, the mark is said to have been 'abandoned.' Once abandoned, a mark returns to the public domain and may, in principle, be appropriated for use by others in the marketplace, ... in accordance with the basic rules of trademark priority...."

International Mobile Machs. v. International Tel. & Tel., 800 F.2d 1118, 1120 (Fed.Cir.1986). "An initial commercial transaction is sufficient to support the validity of a registration so long as the initial transaction is not a sham transaction and is followed by a continuing effort or intent to engage in commercial use." *See also* ***Standard Pressed Steel Co. v. Midwest Chrome Process Co.***, 418 F.Supp. 485, 494 (N.D.Ill. 1976).

Standard Brands Inc. v. Schrage, 220 U.S.P.Q. 337, 339 (N.D.Ga.1982). "To be registrable under the Lanham Act a trademark must be used in interstate commerce. A single instance of interstate use is sufficient to obtain a registration of a trademark if the accompanying circumstances indicate that the applicant intends to continue that use. In applying for registration, [Ds] apparently satisfied the interstate commerce requirement by averring that they had shipped [trademarked product] from their only store in [home state], to customers residing in at least four other states."

Golden Door, Inc. v. Odisho, 437 F.Supp. 956, 962 (N.D.Cal.1977), *aff'd*, 646 F.2d 347 (9th Cir.1980). "Although the services are rendered locally, [P] has conducted extensive nationwide advertising and promotion with the purpose and effect of drawing clientele from many parts of the country. These facts suffice to qualify [P's] trade and service marks as being used in commerce."

§1051(b)

Kelly Servs. v. Creative Harbor, LLC, 846 F.3d 857, 864-65 (6th Cir.2017). "[T]he TTAB has provided several specific examples of objective circumstances which, if proven, may cast doubt on the bona fide nature of the intent or even disprove it entirely. For example, the applicant may have filed numerous intent-to-use applications to register the same mark for many more new products than are contemplated, numerous intent-to-use applications for a variety of desirable trademarks intended to be used on a single new product, numerous intent-to-use applications to register marks consisting of or incorporating descriptive terms relating to a contemplated new product, numerous intent-to-use applications to replace applications which have lapsed because no timely declaration of use has been filed, an excessive number of intent-to-use applications to register marks which ultimately were not actually used, an excessive number of intent-to-use applications in relation to the number of products the applicant is likely to introduce under the applied-for marks during the pendency of the applications, or applications unreasonably lacking in specificity in describing the proposed goods. Other circumstances may also indicate the absence of genuine bona fide intent to actually use the mark. [¶] Further, one prominent practitioner has recently compiled a list of affirmative activities that have been deemed indicative of the *presence* of a bona fide intent to use, including: conducting a trademark availability search; performing preparatory graphic design work or labeling on sales material for a product; using a mark in test marketing; testimony regarding informal, unwritten business plans or market research; obtaining necessary regulatory permits; obtaining a correlative domain name for the mark or setting up a website; making contacts with individuals who might help develop a business; correspondence mentioning the planned use of the mark; attempts to find licensees, including ones outside of the U.S.; and obtaining commercial space in which to perform the services. *At 875:* [W]e hold that when a §1(b) [intent-to-use] applicant lacks *bona fide* intent as to some, but not all, of the goods and services listed in her application, the application should not be voided in its entirety absent fraud or other egregious conduct. Rather, the court should determine as to which goods and services the applicant lacked *bona fide* intent, and excise the overbroad portions of the application." (Internal quotes omitted.)

M.Z. Berger & Co. v. Swatch AG, 787 F.3d 1368, 1375 (Fed.Cir.2015). "There is no statutory definition of the term 'bona fide,' but the language is clear on its face that an applicant's intent must be 'under circumstances showing the good faith of such person.' The reference to 'circumstances showing the good faith' strongly suggests that the applicant's intent must be demonstrable and more than a mere subjective belief. *At 1376:* [W]e hold that whether an applicant had a 'bona fide intent' to use the mark in commerce at the time of the application requires objective evidence of intent. Although the evidentiary bar is not high, the circumstances must indicate that the applicant's intent to use the mark was firm and not merely intent to reserve a right in the mark. The Board may make such determinations on a case-by-case basis considering the totality of the circumstances."

Aktieselskabet AF21. Nov. 2001 v. Fame Jeans Inc., 525 F.3d 8, 18 (D.C.Cir.2008). "While an intent-to-use application does not, by itself, confer any rights enforceable against others, it does give an applicant the right to engage in the statutorily prescribed application procedure. [P] may only contest [D's] application within the confines of that scheme. A trademark opposition must be based on 'a *statutory* ground'—such as a legal defect or deficiency in the application—'which negates the appellant's right to the subject registration.' [Lanham Act] §7(c) [15 U.S.C. §1057(c)] is a potential source of rights for a trademark registrant, not a requirement for or a source of defects in an application. [P] mistakes §7(c) for the true ground for its opposition, which is [Lanham Act] §2(d) [15 U.S.C. §1052(d)]. *At 21:* The TTAB has held [Lanham Act] §1(b) [15 U.S.C. §1051(b)] to require both actual intent to use a mark in commerce and evidence, contemporary with the application, that objectively demonstrate[s] such an intent.... The phrases 'bona fide' and 'good faith' ordinarily refer to a person's actual, subjective state of mind. Certainly a person will fail to have a 'bona fide' intent to use a trademark if his actual intent is otherwise. In addition, 'bona fide' means not fraudulent or feigned, ... and in some circumstances, showing a 'bona fide' intent will actually require proving certain objective facts.... Congress made clear that a 'bona fide intent to use' also involves an objective standard by specifying there must be 'circumstances showing ... good faith.'"

Humanoids Grp. v. Rogan, 375 F.3d 301, 307-08 (4th Cir.2004). "[T]he Lanham Act permits only '[a] person who has a bona fide intention ... to use a trademark in commerce [to] request registration of its trademark.' But nothing in the statute indicates that such an 'intent requirement' gives rise to an affirmative duty on the part of the PTO. No provision of the Lanham Act specifies how the PTO must process an application setting forth multiple marks, some of which the applicant does not intend to register. Certainly no statutory provision precludes the approach adopted by the PTO of generally rejecting applications that present multiple marks. If anything, such an 'intent requirement' would seem to place the onus on the applicant ... to submit a drawing of the mark that it intends to trademark, and only that mark."

Imperial Tobacco Ltd. v. Philip Morris, Inc., 899 F.2d 1575, 1578 n.3 (Fed.Cir.1990). For the intent-to-use applications made under 15 U.S.C. §1051(b), Lanham Act §1(b), "actual use of the mark in commerce is a prerequisite to the *issuance of a registration*. The same declaration of intent-to-use must now be made in connection with [15 U.S.C. §1126(e), Lanham Act §44(e),] applications, but such registration may issue without actual use."

Menashe v. V Secret Catalogue, Inc., 409 F.Supp.2d 412, 420 (S.D.N.Y.2006). "[Ps] concede that [intent-to-use] applicants have no Lanham Act rights to bring an offensive action in federal court—i.e., to charge another party with infringement—but argue that they may defend against claims of infringement by another party. [Ps] contend that by bringing a declaratory judgment action for non-infringement, they are acting defensively." Held: The court agrees and bases its holding on ***WarnerVision Entm't Inc. v. Empire, Inc.***, 101 F.3d 259 (2d Cir.1996). However, the court ultimately holds that Ps cannot prove noninfringement.

Lucent Info. Mgmt. v. Lucent Tech., 986 F.Supp. 253, 258 (D.Del.1997), *aff'd*, 186 F.3d 311 (3d Cir.1999). "The Lanham Act offers two ways to register a mark: (1) where the mark was already 'used in commerce'; and (2) where the party 'intends to use' the mark. The 'intends to use' statute requires the party to subsequently file a verified statement that the mark was actually 'used in commerce.' Thus, either way, registration of a trademark requires that the mark be 'used.'"

Fila Sport, S.p.A. v. Diadora, Inc., 21 U.S.P.Q.2d 1063, 1068 (N.D.Ill.1991). "The mere filing of an intent-to-use application under 15 U.S.C. §1051(b) [Lanham Act §1(b)] does not confer jurisdiction on the federal courts. Rather, [P] must allege that it has a valid federal trademark registration or allege the actual use of the marks in commerce."

§1051(d)

Eastman Kodak Co. v. Bell & Howell Document Mgmt. Prods., 994 F.2d 1569, 1572 (Fed.Cir.1993). The legislative history of the Trademark Law Revision Act of 1988 "emphasized that '[15 U.S.C. §1051(d)(1), Lanham Act §1(d)(1),] permits the [PTO] to raise issues of registrability that might not be evident until the applicant makes available specimens showing the mark as used and/or clarifying the nature of the goods or services involved.' Thus, the statute and legislative history provide for the situation where ... the question of mere descriptiveness cannot be answered until after use has begun. *At 1574:* [Section 1051] provides for the same substantive requirements to be met for intent-to-use and use-based applications. *At 1575 n.8:* [T]he applicant ... verifies at the time of application that he or she believes that the mark is registrable. ... It is not unreasonable for the PTO to assume that each application is bona fide until proven otherwise."

§1052. TRADEMARKS REGISTRABLE ON PRINCIPAL REGISTER; CONCURRENT REGISTRATION

[LANHAM ACT §2]

No trademark by which the goods of the applicant may be distinguished from the goods of others shall be refused registration on the principal register on account of its nature unless it—

(a) Consists of or comprises immoral, deceptive, or scandalous matter; or matter which may disparage or falsely suggest a connection with persons, living or dead, institutions, beliefs, or national symbols, or bring them into contempt, or disrepute; or a geographical indication which, when used on or in connection with wines or spirits, identifies a place other than the origin of the goods and is first used on or in connection with wines or spirits by the applicant on or after one year after the date on which the WTO Agreement (as defined in section 3501(9) of title 19) enters into force with respect to the United States.

(b) Consists of or comprises the flag or coat of arms or other insignia of the United States, or of any State or municipality, or of any foreign nation, or any simulation thereof.

(c) Consists of or comprises a name, portrait, or signature identifying a particular living individual except by his written consent, or the name, signature, or portrait of a deceased President of the United States during the life of his widow, if any, except by the written consent of the widow.

(d) Consists of or comprises a mark which so resembles a mark registered in the Patent and Trademark Office, or a mark or trade name previously used in the United States by another and not abandoned, as to be likely, when used on or in connection with the goods of the applicant, to cause confusion, or to cause mistake, or to deceive: *Provided*, That if the Director determines that confusion, mistake, or deception is not likely to result from the continued use by more than one person of the same or similar marks under conditions and limitations as to the mode or place of use of the marks or the goods on or in connection with which such marks are used, concurrent registrations may be issued to such persons when they have become entitled to use such marks as a result of their concurrent lawful use in commerce prior to (1) the earliest of the filing dates of the applications pending or of any registration issued under this chapter; (2) July 5, 1947, in the case of registrations previously issued under the Act of March 3, 1881, or February 20, 1905, and continuing in full force and effect on that date; or (3) July 5, 1947, in the case of applications filed under the Act of February 20, 1905, and registered after July 5, 1947. Use prior to the filing date of any pending application or a registration shall not be required when the owner of such application or registration consents to the grant of a concurrent registration to the applicant. Concurrent registrations may also be issued by the Director when a court of competent jurisdiction has finally determined that more than one person is entitled to use the same or similar marks in commerce. In issuing concurrent registrations, the Director shall prescribe conditions and limitations as to the mode or place of use of the mark or the goods on or in connection with which such mark is registered to the respective persons.

(e) Consists of a mark which (1) when used on or in connection with the goods of the applicant is merely descriptive or deceptively misdescriptive of them, (2) when used on or in connection with the goods of the applicant is primarily geographically descriptive of them, except as indications of regional origin may be registrable under section 1054 of title 15, (3) when used on or in connection with the goods of the applicant is primarily geographically deceptively misdescriptive of them, (4) is primarily merely a surname, or (5) comprises any matter that, as a whole, is functional.

(f) Except as expressly excluded in subsections (a), (b), (c), (d), (e)(3), and (e)(5) of this section, nothing in this chapter shall prevent the registration of a mark used by the applicant which has become distinctive of the applicant's goods in commerce. The Director may accept as prima facie evidence that the mark has become distinctive, as used on or in connection with the applicant's goods in commerce, proof of substantially exclusive and continuous use thereof as a mark by the applicant in commerce for the five years before the date on which the claim of distinctiveness is made. Nothing in this section shall prevent the registration of a mark which, when used on or in connection with the goods of the applicant, is primarily geographically deceptively misdescriptive of them, and which became distinctive of the applicant's goods in commerce before December 8, 1993.

A mark which would be likely to cause dilution by blurring or dilution by tarnishment under section 1125(c) of title 15, may be refused registration only pursuant to a proceeding brought under section 1063 of title 15. A registration for a mark which would be likely to cause dilution by blurring or dilution by tarnishment under section 1125(c) of title 15, may be canceled pursuant to a proceeding brought under either section 1064 or section 1092 of title 15.

History of 15 U.S.C. §1052: July 5, 1946, ch. 540, §2, 60 Stat. 428; Oct. 9, 1962, P.L. 87-772, §2, 76 Stat. 769; Jan. 2, 1975, P.L. 93-596, §1, 88 Stat. 1949; Nov. 16, 1988, P.L. 100-667, §104, 102 Stat. 3037; Dec. 8, 1993, P.L. 103-182,

§333(a), 107 Stat. 2114; Dec. 8, 1994, P.L. 103-465, §522, 108 Stat. 4982; Oct. 30, 1998, P.L. 105-330, §201(a)(2), (12), 112 Stat. 3069, 3070; Aug. 5, 1999, P.L. 106-43, §2(a), 113 Stat. 218; Nov. 29, 1999, P.L. 106-113, §1000(a)(9), 113 Stat. 1536; Oct. 6, 2006, P.L. 109-312, §3(a), 120 Stat. 1732.

See also 15 U.S.C. §70b; 37 C.F.R. §§6.1, 6.2; NAFTA art. 1708; Paris Convention arts. 6-10; TRIPs pt. II, §§2, 3.

Treatise Cross-References

McCarthy on Trademark & Unfair Competition

Ch. 7, *Trademark & Trade Dress Formats*, §§7:17.50; 7:21; 7:76; 7:94
Ch. 8, *Trade Dress*, §8:12
Ch. 10, *Literary, Artistic & Entertainment Rights*, §§10:3; 10:6.10
Ch. 11, *The Spectrum of Distinctiveness of Marks*, §§11:26; 11:43; 11:51; 11:51.50; 11:53; 11:55; 11:58; 11:59; 11:83
Ch. 12, *Generic Terms*, §§12:20; 12:56-12:58; 12:64
Ch. 13, *Personal Names as Marks*, §§13:25; 13:28; 13:30; 13:33; 13:35; 13:37-13:39
Ch. 14, *Geographic Term Marks*, §§14:26; 14:29; 14:31; 14:33; 14:34; 14:37-14:40
Ch. 15, *Secondary Meaning*, §§15:10; 15:32; 15:33; 15:34; 15:54; 15:59; 15:60; 15:62-15:68; 15:70; 15:76; 15:79-15:81
Ch. 16, *Acquisition & Priority of Trademark Rights*, §16:14
Ch. 19, *Federal Registration of Marks*, §§19:2; 19:6; 19:10; 19:11; 19:24; 19:31; 19:31.10; 19:37; 19:40; 19:41; 19:50; 19:56; 19:57; 19:64; 19:66; 19:67; 19:72; 19:75-19:78; 19:82; 19:92.50; 19:95; 19:101; 19:103; 19:118
Ch. 20, *Inter Partes Trademark Proceedings in the Patent & Trademark Office*, §§20:7; 20:11; 20:13-20:20; 20:27; 20:36; 20:38; 20:45; 20:46; 20:50.50; 20:52; 20:53; 20:54; 20:59; 20:67; 20:77; 20:80-20:82; 20:84; 20:87; 20:88; 20:96; 20:132
Ch. 21, *Appeal from Decisions on Trademark Registration*, §21:6
Ch. 22, *State Protection & Registration of Marks*, §22:5
Ch. 23, *Likelihood of Confusion: The Test of Trademark Infringement*, §§23:1; 23:64; 23:77-23:85; 23:88
Ch. 24, *Infringement by Use of Mark on Noncompetitive Goods or Services*, §§24:48; 24:63; 24:64; 24:94
Ch. 25, *Types of Trademark Infringement*, §25:67.50
Ch. 29, *International Aspects of Trademark Law*, §§29:4; 29:13; 29:23; 29:24
Ch. 31, *Defenses to Infringement of Trademarks*, §§31:69; 31:83
Ch. 32, *Procedure in Trademark Infringement & Unfair Competition Litigation*, §§32:146; 32:147; 32:197

ANNOTATIONS

Generally

Wal-Mart Stores v. Samara Bros., 529 U.S. 205, 211 (2000). "Nothing in [15 U.S.C. §1052, Lanham Act §2,] demands the conclusion that *every* category of mark necessarily includes some marks 'by which the goods of the applicant may be distinguished from the goods of others' *without* secondary meaning—that in every category some marks are inherently distinctive. *At 212:* It seems to us that [product] design, like color, is not inherently distinctive. The attribution of inherent distinctiveness to certain categories of word marks and product packaging derives from the fact that the very purpose of attaching a particular word to a product, or encasing it in a distinctive packaging, is most often to identify the source of the product."

Two Pesos, Inc. v. Taco Cabana, Inc., 505 U.S. 763, 768 (1992). "Marks are often classified in categories of generally increasing distinctiveness; ... they may be (1) generic; (2) descriptive; (3) suggestive; (4) arbitrary; or (5) fanciful. ... The latter three categories of marks, because their intrinsic nature serves to identify a particular source of a product, are deemed inherently distinctive, and are entitled to protection. In contrast, generic marks—those that 'refer to the genus of which the particular product is a species'—are not registrable as trademarks. *At 769:* Marks which are merely descriptive of a product are not inherently distinctive. When used to describe a product, they do not inherently identify a particular source, and hence cannot be protected. However, descriptive marks may acquire the distinctiveness which will allow them to be protected under the [Lanham] Act. ... This acquired distinctiveness is generally called 'secondary meaning.' [¶] The general rule regarding distinctiveness is clear: An identifying mark is distinctive and capable of being protected if it *either* (1) is inherently distinctive *or* (2) has acquired distinctiveness through secondary meaning." *See also* ***San Francisco Arts & Athletics, Inc. v. U.S. Olympic Cmte.***, 483 U.S. 522, 534 (1987). *But see* ***Amazing Spaces, Inc. v. Metro Mini Storage***, p. 11 (forsaking an analysis of symbols and designs with distinctiveness categories in favor of ***Seabrook Foods*** test).

Nola Spice Designs, L.L.C. v. Haydel Enters., 783 F.3d 527, 537-38 (5th Cir.2015). "To assess the distinctiveness of a word mark, our circuit ... divide[s] marks into five categories: (1) generic, (2) descriptive, (3) suggestive, (4) arbitrary, and (5) fanciful. While suggestive, arbitrary, and fanciful marks are inherently distinctive, generic marks cannot be distinctive, and descriptive marks are distinctive only if they have acquired 'secondary meaning.' In categorizing a term, we must examine the context in which the term is used. We consider how the term is used with other words, the products or services to which it is applied, and the *audience* to which the relevant product or service is directed. The question is, 'What do the buyers understand by the word for whose use the parties are contending?' Although summary judgment is rarely appropriate on the factual question of categorization, ... we may affirm a grant of summary judgment where the record compels the conclusion that the movant is entitled to judgment as a matter of law. [¶] A *generic* term is the name of a particular genus or class of which an individual article or service is but a member. The test for genericness is whether the public perceives the term primarily as the designation of the article. *At 539:* A *descriptive* term identifies a characteristic or quality of an article or service, such as its color, odor, function, dimensions, or ingredients. Examples of descriptive marks would include Alo with reference to products containing gel of the aloe vera plant and Vision Center in reference to a business offering optical goods and services. *At 540:* Arbitrary marks bear no relationship to the products or services to which they are applied. [A] mark's categorization ... depends on the context in which it appears and on the nature of the products sold. *At 543:* Because [P] has demonstrated that [D's] marks are descriptive, rebutting the presumption of inherent distinctiveness arising from [D's] registrations, [D] bears the burden of establishing secondary meaning at trial. *At 544:* The burden of demonstrating secondary meaning is substantial and requires a high degree of proof. ... Although secondary meaning is a question of fact, summary judgment may be upheld if the record compels the conclusion that the movant is entitled to judgment as a matter of law." (Internal quotes omitted.)

Fortres Grand Corp. v. Warner Bros. Entm't Inc., 763 F.3d 696, 705 (7th Cir.2014). "Trademark law protects the source-denoting function of words used in conjunction with goods and services in the marketplace, not the words themselves."

In re Chippendales USA, Inc., 622 F.3d 1346, 1354 (Fed.Cir.2010). "We agree with the PTO's argument ... that the proper time for measuring inherent distinctiveness is at the time of registration. [¶] Judging inherent distinctiveness at the time of first use would be fundamentally unfair. As we have noted, '[t]rademark rights are not static.' The test for inherent distinctiveness depends on whether the mark, or a variation thereof, has been in common use in general or in the particular field. A term or device that was once inherently distinctive may lose its distinguishing characteristics over time."

Amazing Spaces, Inc. v. Metro Mini Storage, 608 F.3d 225, 243-44 (5th Cir.2010). "We do not go so far as to hold that the ***Abercrombie*** test [for distinctiveness] is eclipsed every time a mark other than a word is at issue. Instead, we hold that the ***Abercrombie*** test fails to illuminate the fundamental inquiry in this case: whether the [mark's] intrinsic nature serves to identify [P] and its storage services. [¶] In contrast to the ***Abercrombie*** test, the ***Seabrook Foods*** test, articulated by the U.S. [C.C.P.A.], applies expressly to marks consisting of symbols and designs: In determining whether a design is arbitrary or distinctive this court has looked to (1) whether it was a 'common' basic shape or design, (2) whether it was unique or unusual in a particular field, (3) whether it was a mere refinement of a commonly-adopted and well-known form of ornamentation for a particular class of goods viewed by the public as a dress or ornamentation for the goods, or (4) whether it was capable of creating a commercial impression distinct from the accompanying words. The first three of the ***Seabrook Foods*** questions are merely different ways to ask whether the design, shape or combination of elements is so unique, unusual or unexpected in this market that one can assume without proof that it will automatically be perceived by customers as an indicator of origin—a trademark. As is true of the ***Abercrombie*** test, the ***Seabrook Foods*** test seeks an answer to the question whether a mark's intrinsic nature serves to identify a particular source. *At 247-48:* Secondary meaning occurs when, in the minds of the public, the primary significance of a mark is to identify the source of the product rather than the product itself. Secondary meaning is used generally to indicate that a mark or dress has come through use to be uniquely associated with a specific source. To establish secondary meaning, a manufacturer must show that, in the minds of the public, the primary significance of a product feature or term is to identify the source of the product rather than the product itself. The inquiry is one of the public's mental association between the mark and the alleged mark holder. Because the primary element of secondary meaning is a mental association in buyers' minds between the alleged mark and a single source of the product, the determination whether a mark or dress has acquired secondary meaning is primarily an empirical inquiry. [¶] In the context of trade dress, we have articulated seven factors to consider in determining whether secondary meaning has been shown: (1) length and manner of use of the mark or trade dress, (2) volume of sales, (3) amount and manner of advertising, (4) nature of use of the mark or trade dress in newspapers and magazines, (5) consumer-survey evidence, (6) direct consumer testimony, and (7) the defendant's intent in copying the trade dress. In considering this evidence, the focus is on how it demonstrates that the meaning of the mark or trade dress has been altered in the minds of consumers. We have consistently expressed a preference for an objective survey of the public's perception of the mark at issue." (Internal quotes omitted.) *But see* ***Tumblebus Inc. v. Cranmer***, 399 F.3d 754, 761 n.9 (6th Cir.2005) (applying ***Abercrombie*** seven-factor test for secondary meaning); ***Two Pesos, Inc. v. Taco Cabana, Inc.***, p. 10 (using distinctiveness categories).

Xtreme Lashes, LLC v. Xtended Beauty, Inc., 576 F.3d 221, 232 (5th Cir.2009). "Descriptiveness is construed broadly. Indicia include: (1) the mark's dictionary definition corresponds with its meaning and context; (2) upon hearing the mark, one need not use 'imagination, thought and perception to reach a conclusion as to the nature of goods'; (3) 'competitors would be likely to need the terms used in the trademark in describing their products'; and (4) others have used the term in marketing a similar service or product. We examine the context in which a term appears, and the audience to which it is directed, when determining eligibility for protection. We also look at a multi-word mark as a unitary whole in its given arrangement, and do not parse apart the constituent terms."

E.T. Browne Drug Co. v. Cococare Prods., 538 F.3d 185, 191 (3d Cir.2008). The Lanham Act "provides no protection for generic terms because a first-user of a term 'cannot deprive competing manufacturers of the product of the right to call an article by its name.' In contrast, the Lanham Act protects descriptive terms if they have acquired secondary meaning associating the term with the claimant. Finally, trademark law protects suggestive and arbitrary or fanciful terms without any showing of secondary meaning. *At 192:* 'The jurisprudence of genericness revolves around the primary significance test, which inquires whether the primary significance of a term in the minds of the consuming public is the product or the producer.' We ask 'whether consumers think the term represents the generic name of the product [or service] or a mark indicating merely one source of that product [or service].' If the term refers to the product (i.e., the genus), the term is generic. If, on the other hand, it refers to one source or producer of that product, the term is not generic (i.e., it is descriptive, suggestive, or arbitrary or fanciful). To give an example, 'Cola' is generic because it refers to a product, whereas 'Pepsi Cola' is not generic because it refers to the producer." *See also* ***A.J. Canfield Co. v. Honickman***, 808 F.2d 291, 305-06 (3d Cir.1986).

American Express Co. v. Goetz, 515 F.3d 156, 159-60 (2d Cir.2008). "[T]he same mark that performs [the] source-identifying role in one set of hands may constitute the creative work itself in another. Such distinction often is appropriate when an advertising agency licenses a slogan to a client for the client's use in marketing a product. In this scenario, the slogan is part of the advertising agency's creative work, but it may become a source identifier when used by the client. [¶] The [TTAB] has long recognized, in such situations, that the slogans cannot be registered as marks by the advertising agency, even if they would be subject to registration by the end users of the marks. The reason is plain: the slogan does not identify and distinguish the services of the advertising agency, but rather *is* the creative work itself."

Last Best Beef, LLC v. Dudas, 506 F.3d 333, 339-40 (4th Cir.2007). Held: Congress may pass a law to prevent particular phrase from being registered as trademark.

Synergistic Int'l v. Korman, 470 F.3d 162, 171-72 (4th Cir.2006). "We have recognized that the line between a descriptive mark and a suggestive mark is thinly drawn, and we have defined the distinction as follows: A word or figure is descriptive if it identifies a characteristic or quality of an article or service, and a suggestive term is one which suggests rather than describes, some characteristic of the goods to which it is applied and requires the consumer to exercise his imagination to reach a conclusion as to the nature of these goods. [G]enerally speaking, if the mark imparts information directly, it is descriptive. If it stands for an idea which requires some operation of the imagination to connect it with the goods, it is suggestive. The distinction between a descriptive mark and a suggestive mark is important, of course, because a mark's classification determines the level of protection it is entitled to receive. When a registered trademark contains a disclaimed word (here, the words 'GLASS' in [P's] GLASS DOCTOR® mark and 'WINDSHIELD' in [D's] THE WINDSHIELD DOCTOR mark), a reviewing court must look mainly at the use of the dominant word ('DOCTOR' for both marks) in making its assessment of whether a mark is suggestive or descriptive. [¶] If the

PTO believes a mark to be descriptive, the registrant must establish some secondary meaning before it grants registration. If the PTO did not require proof of secondary meaning, it has presumptively determined the mark to be suggestive. This presumption, however, can be rebutted by a party defending against an infringement claim. *At 173:* [A] suggestive mark is entitled to protection against the same or a confusing mark on the same product, or related products, and even on those which may be considered by some to be unrelated but which the public is likely to assume emanate from the trademark owner. As a result, the PTO's registration of a suggestive mark should be broadly construed, and the appropriate reading is not limited to the text of the mark's registered purpose." (Internal quotes omitted.) *See also* ***Lahoti v. Vericheck, Inc.***, 586 F.3d 1190, 1197-98 (9th Cir.2009).

Attrezzi, LLC v. Maytag Corp., 436 F.3d 32, 38 (1st Cir.2006). "Under the 'doctrine of foreign equivalents,' a foreign word is ordinarily translated into English to determine whether it is suggestive or descriptive."

Star Indus. v. Bacardi & Co., 412 F.3d 373, 382 (2d Cir.2005). "A design used in conjunction with other marks is separately protectable in its own right if it creates a separate and distinct impression from the impression created by the other marks. This will be true if either the mark is itself inherently distinctive ... or if the consuming public has come to associate the separate mark in itself with the particular product, vesting it with its own distinct secondary meaning.... *At 383:* Unshaded linear representations of common shapes or letters are referred to as 'basic.' They are not protectable as inherently distinctive, because to protect them as trademarks would be to deprive competitors of fundamental communicative devices essential to the dissemination of information to consumers. However, stylized letters or shapes are not 'basic,' and are protectable when original within the relevant market."

Tumblebus Inc. v. Cranmer, 399 F.3d 754, 761 n.5 (6th Cir.2005). "A suggestive mark suggests rather than describes an ingredient or characteristic of the goods and requires the observer or listener to use imagination and perception to determine the nature of the goods. *At 761 n.6:* An arbitrary mark has a significance recognized in everyday life, but the thing it normally signifies is unrelated to the product or service to which the mark is attached, such as CAMEL cigarettes or APPLE computers. *At 761 n.7:* A fanciful mark is a combination of letters or other symbols signifying nothing other than the product or service to which the mark has been assigned, such as EXXON or KODAK. *At 761 n.8:* A merely descriptive mark, as opposed to a common descriptive generic one, is often said to identify a characteristic of the thing. It is very similar to an adjective." (Internal quotes omitted.)

In re Oppedahl & Larson L.L.P., 373 F.3d 1171, 1174 (Fed.Cir.2004). "If a proposed mark includes a [top-level domain (TLD) indicator] such as '.com,' '.biz,' [or] '.info,' the examining attorney should present evidence that the term is a TLD, and, if available, evidence of the significance of the TLD as an abbreviation (*e.g.*, '.edu' signifies an educational institution, '.biz' signifies a business). Because TLDs generally serve no source-indicating function, their addition to an otherwise unregistrable mark typically cannot render it registrable. [¶] The law requires that a mark be 'considered in its entirety.' *At 1176:* The [TTAB] must, of course, determine the commercial impression of a mark in the proper context of the goods or services associated with that mark. ... TLD marks may obtain registration upon a showing of distinctiveness." *But see* ***Booking.com B.V. v. Matal***, below.

In re Boston Beer Co., 198 F.3d 1370, 1373 (Fed. Cir.1999). Applicant "does not dispute that 'The Best Beer in America' is a generally laudatory phrase. ... As in this case, a phrase or slogan can be so highly laudatory and descriptive as to be incapable of acquiring distinctiveness as a trademark."

Booking.com B.V. v. Matal, No. 1:16-cv-425 (E.D. Va.2017) (memo op.; 8-9-17). "[P] argues that '.com' should be read as a top-level domain (TLD), in the same family as '.net,' '.org,' and '.edu.' A TLD can be contrasted with a second-level domain (SLD), which is the next level of organization in the domain name hierarchy. For example, in 'booking.com,' 'booking' is the SLD and '.com' is the TLD. According to [P], the combination of 'booking' and '.com' signals a domain name, which is a unique identifier capable of indicating the source of a product or service. [Ds] argue that '.com' is merely a term that denotes services offered via the Internet, and point to Federal Circuit cases holding that a TLD has no source identifying significance. [¶] [T]his Court declines to rely on the Federal Circuit's precedents regarding TLDs and will treat this question as an issue of first impression. [T]he Court concludes that, when combined with an SLD, a TLD generally has source identifying significance and the combination of a generic SLD and a TLD is generally a descriptive mark that is protectable upon a showing of acquired distinctiveness." *But see* ***In re Oppedahl & Larson L.L.P.***, above.

§1052(a)

Matal v. Tam, ___ U.S. ___, 137 S.Ct. 1744, 1751 (2017). "We ... hold that [§1052(a)'s prohibition of trademarks that disparage, bring into contempt, or disrepute any persons, living or dead] violates the Free Speech Clause of the First Amendment. It offends a bedrock First Amendment principle.... *At U.S. ___, S.Ct. 1760:* Trademarks are private, not government, speech." *See also* ***In re Brunetti***, 877 F.3d 1330, 1335 (Fed.Cir.2017) (bar on registering immoral or scandalous marks is unconstitutional restriction of free speech).

In re Shinnecock Smoke Shop, 571 F.3d 1171, 1173 (Fed.Cir.2009). "[T]he Shinnecock Indian Nation is an 'institution' and thus falls within §1052(a)'s protection."

In re California Innovations, Inc., 329 F.3d 1334, 1336-37 (Fed.Cir.2003). "Although not expressly addressing geographical marks, [15 U.S.C. §1052(a), Lanham Act §2(a),] has traditionally been used to reject geographic marks that materially deceive the public. ... To deny a geographic mark protection under §1052(a), the PTO must establish that (1) the mark misrepresents or misdescribes the goods, (2) the public would likely believe the misrepresentation, and (3) the misrepresentation would materially affect the public's decision to purchase the goods. This test's central point of analysis is materiality because that finding shows that the misdescription deceived the consumer."

§1052(b)

In re City of Houston, 731 F.3d 1326, 1328 (Fed.Cir. 2013). This case "raise[s] a question of first impression—under the provisions of the Lanham Act, may a local government entity obtain a federal trademark registration for the entity's official insignia[?] We use the term 'official insignia' as a short-hand reference to the various types of insignia listed in the relevant provision of the Lanham Act; the specific piece of insignia for which registration is sought ... is the government entity's official seal. [¶] We conclude that the Board correctly interpreted [Lanham Act] §2(b) [15 U.S.C. §1052(b)] as prohibiting [city and district] from registering their seals, and therefore *affirm* both of the Board's final decisions."

In re Advance Indus. Sec., Inc., 194 U.S.P.Q. 344, 346 (T.T.A.B.1977). "Whether or not a simulation exists ... must necessarily be [a question] of first impression ... without a careful analysis and side-by-side comparison...."

§1052(c)

Gilbert/Robinson, Inc. v. Carrie Bev.-Mo., Inc., 989 F.2d 985, 990 (8th Cir.1993), *overruled on other grounds*, ***Lexmark Int'l v. Static Control Components, Inc.***, ___ U.S. ___, 134 S.Ct. 1377 (2014). 15 U.S.C. §1052(c), Lanham Act §2(c), "exists to protect the privacy and property interests of persons whom the public will associate with a mark. [¶] The Lanham Act's dominant interest in preventing consumer confusion argues strongly against rendering a registered mark unenforceable based upon a third party's long-expired §1052(c) rights."

Reed v. Bakers Eng'g & Equip. Co., 100 U.S.P.Q. 196, 199 (PO Ex.Ch.1954). Laches, "acquiescence, and estoppel have nothing to do with [Lanham Act] §2(c) [15 U.S.C. §1052(c)], which contains an absolute requirement for registration. [¶] The statute requires the written consent of a particular individual in certain cases and if this written consent does not exist in those cases in which it is required there can not be any registration. ... Consent to register must be distinguished from consent to use. There may very well be consent to use without any consent to register. And neither is consent to register sufficient under the statute unless it is a written consent as specified in the statute. [¶] [T]he statute uses the words 'a name' and not the words 'the name.' Hence 'name' in §2(c) is not restricted to the full name of an individual but refers to any name regardless of whether it is a full name, or a surname or given name, or even a nickname, which identifies a particular living individual, although in the case of the use of the surname only it is possible that the name may lose all significance of identifying a particular individual."

§1052(d)—Generally

Jean Patou, Inc. v. Theon, Inc., 9 F.3d 971, 975 (Fed.Cir.1993). Classification "is wholly irrelevant to the issue of registrability under [15 U.S.C. §1052(d), Lanham Act §2(d)], which makes no reference to classification."

§1052(d)—Concurrent Registration

Kentucky Fried Chicken Corp. v. Diversified Packaging Corp., 549 F.2d 368, 387 (5th Cir.1977). "Concurrent ownership of marks in separate geographical territories is clearly permissible."

J&D Home Imprv., Inc. v. Basement Doctor, Inc., 247 F.Supp.2d 575, 578 (D.Del.2003), *aff'd*, 90 Fed.Appx. 616 (3d Cir.2004). 15 U.S.C. §1052(d), Lanham Act §2(d), "does not provide original jurisdiction. ... Section 1052(d) does not create a 'civil action.' Section 1052(d) provides the court with the alternative remedy of concurrent registration when the court 'has finally determined that one or more person[s] is entitled to use the same or similar marks in commerce.' Thus, a party cannot seek to have a court determine concurrent use rights as an offensive response to cancellation proceedings initiated in the [PTO]."

§1052(d)—Likelihood of Confusion

For more annotations on this topic, see 15 U.S.C. §1114, *§1114(1)—Likelihood of Confusion—Generally*, p. 68, and 15 U.S.C. §1125, *§1125(a)(1)(A)—Likelihood of Confusion—Generally*, p. 137.

B&B Hardware, Inc. v. Hargis Indus., ___ U.S. ___, 135 S.Ct. 1293, 1306-07 (2015). "[T]he same likelihood-of-confusion standard applies to both registration and infringement. [¶] [I]t does not matter that registration and infringement are governed by different statutory provisions. ... Neither does it matter that the TTAB and the Eighth Circuit use different factors to assess likelihood of confusion. For one thing, the factors are not fundamentally different, and '[m]inor variations in the application of what is in essence the same legal standard do not defeat preclusion.' More important, if federal law provides a single standard, parties cannot escape preclusion simply by litigating anew in tribunals that apply that one standard differently."

Progressive Distrib. Servs. v. UPS, Inc., 856 F.3d 416, 426 (6th Cir.2017). "This Court has already held that a trademark examining attorney's opinion is not entitled to a procedural presumption or a reasonable inference drawn in its favor in circumstances when the USPTO fails to consider the same evidence that is subsequently placed in front of the district court. Similarly, the Ninth Circuit has held that a preliminary determination by a low-level USPTO administrator should not be accorded much weight, especially where the USPTO officer did not have access to the same type of information that informs a likelihood of confusion analysis. Finally, the Third Circuit has more recently endorsed the Ninth Circuit's decision, noting that while an 'initial [US]PTO determination ... may be considered, it need not be given weight when the [US]PTO attorney did not review all the evidence available to the District Court.'"

Midwestern Pet Foods, Inc. v. Societe des Produits Nestle S.A., 685 F.3d 1046, 1052 (Fed.Cir.2012). "[E]vidence of post-application fame, although not relevant to the issue of dilution of the opposer's mark, ... is relevant to the issue of likelihood of confusion. And while a party asserting dilution in an opposition proceeding must establish that its mark had become famous prior to the filing date of an intent-to-use application, ... no such restriction applies to the use of evidence of the strength of a mark for purposes of showing likelihood of confusion."

In re Viterra Inc., 671 F.3d 1358, 1362-63 (Fed.Cir. 2012). "The relevant [likelihood-of-confusion] factor requires examination of 'the similarity or dissimilarity of the marks in their entireties as to appearance, sound, connotation and commercial impression.' As is apparent from the plain language of this factor, marks must be viewed 'in their entireties,' and it is improper to dissect a mark when engaging in this analysis, including when a mark contains both words and a design. Although the court may place more weight on a dominant portion of a mark, for example if another feature of the mark is descriptive or generic standing alone, the ultimate conclusion nonetheless must rest on consideration of the marks in total. [¶] In the case of a composite mark containing both words and a design, 'the verbal portion of the mark is the one most likely to indicate the origin of the goods to which it is affixed.' Despite those statements, we also have cautioned that there is no general rule that the letter portion of the mark will form the dominant portion of the mark. Marks, therefore, must be considered on a case-by-case basis. Finally, where, as here, the goods at issue are identical, 'the degree of similarity necessary to support a conclusion of likely confusion declines.'"

Coach Servs. v. Triumph Learning LLC, 668 F.3d 1356, 1366-67 (Fed.Cir.2012). "The fame of the registered mark plays a 'dominant' role in the [likelihood-of-confusion] analysis, as famous marks 'enjoy a wide latitude of legal protection.' A famous mark is one that has 'extensive public recognition and renown.' [¶] Fame for purposes of likelihood of confusion is a matter of degree that 'varies along a spectrum from very strong to very weak.' Relevant factors include sales, advertising, length of use of the mark, market share, brand awareness, licensing activities, and variety of goods bearing the mark. The party asserting that its mark is famous has the burden to prove it. [¶] It is well-established that fame is insufficient, standing alone, to establish likelihood of confusion. Although fame cannot overwhelm the other [likelihood-of-confusion] factors, we are mindful that it 'deserves its full measure of weight in assessing likelihood of confusion.' *At 1369:* With respect to the [likelihood-of-confusion] factor assessing the similarity of the goods, [t]his factor requires a comparison between the goods or services described in the application and those described in the registration. [¶] When analyzing the similarity of the goods, 'it is not necessary that the products of the parties be similar or even competitive to support a finding of likelihood of confusion.' Instead, likelihood of confusion can be found 'if the respective products are related in some manner and/or if the circumstances surrounding their marketing are such that they could give rise to the mistaken belief that they emanate from the same source.' When trademarks would appear on substantially identical goods, 'the degree of similarity necessary to support a conclusion of likely confusion declines.' *At 1370:* [W]e consider the similarity or dissimilarity of the trade channels in which the parties' goods are sold and the purchasers to whom the parties' goods are marketed. The Board correctly recognized that, because [applicant's] description of goods is not limited to sales to educational professionals, the goods are presumed to travel in all normal channels and to all prospective purchasers for the relevant goods."

In re Mighty Leaf Tea, 601 F.3d 1342, 1346 (Fed. Cir.2010). "As applied to trademark registration, reasonable doubt as to the likelihood of confusion is resolved against the newcomer, 'for the newcomer has the opportunity of avoiding confusion, and is charged with the obligation to do so.'"

In re Chatam Int'l, 380 F.3d 1340, 1342 (Fed.Cir. 2004). "Likelihood of confusion under the Lanham Act is a legal determination based upon factual underpinnings."

American Legion v. Matthew, 144 F.3d 498, 499 (7th Cir.1998). "Section 1052(d) says that a trademark may not be registered if it so resembles another 'mark or trade name' that confusion is likely to ensue. Most of the time 'trademark' and 'trade name' operate as synonyms, but even when they are distinct the statutory definition of infringement remains. [P's] failure to prove confusion is fatal under §1052(d) whether 'Legionnaire' is a 'name' or a 'mark.'"

In re E.I. DuPont DeNemours & Co., 476 F.2d 1357, 1361 (C.C.P.A.1973). "In testing for likelihood of confusion under [15 U.S.C. §1052(d), Lanham Act §2(d),] the following, when of record, must be considered: (1) The similarity or dissimilarity of the marks in their entireties as to appearance, sound, connotation and commercial impression. (2) The similarity or dissimilarity of and nature of the goods or services as described in an application or registration or in connection with which a prior mark is in use. (3) The similarity or dissimilarity of established, likely-to-continue trade channels. (4) The conditions under which and buyers to whom sales are made, i.e. 'impulse' vs. careful, sophisticated purchasing. (5) The fame of the prior mark (sales, advertising, length of use). (6) The number and nature of similar marks in use on similar goods. (7) The nature and extent of any actual confusion. (8) The length of time during and conditions under which there has been concurrent use without evidence of actual confusion. (9) The variety of goods on which a mark is or is not used (house mark, 'family' mark, product mark). (10) The market interface between applicant and the owner of a prior mark: (a) a mere 'consent' to register or use. (b) agreement provisions designed to preclude confusion, i.e. limitations on continued use of the marks by each party. (c) assignment of mark, application, registration and good will of the related business. (d) laches and estoppel attributable to owner of prior mark and indicative of lack of confusion. (11) The extent to which applicant has a right to exclude others from use of its mark on its goods. (12) The extent of potential confusion, i.e., whether *de minimis* or substantial. (13) Any other established fact probative of the effect of use." *See also* ***M2 Software, Inc. v. M2 Comms.***, 450 F.3d 1378, 1381-82 (Fed.Cir.2006).

§1052(d)—Use

Aktieselskabet AF21. Nov. 2001 v. Fame Jeans Inc., 525 F.3d 8, 18 (D.C.Cir.2008). "[U]nder [Lanham Act] §2(d) [15 U.S.C. §1052(d)], an intent-to-use applicant prevails over any opposer who began using a similar mark after the intent-to-use filing date. Covering applications of all types, including [Lanham Act]

§1(b) [15 U.S.C. §1051(b)] applications, §2(d) simply says a mark is invalid if there is a likelihood of confusion with a mark 'previously used.' 'Previously used' must mean used before some date, and for a pending §1(b) application, there is only one date that could apply: the filing date. *At 20:* [P] need not 'meet the technical statutory requirements to register [a mark] to have a basis for objection to another's registration.' Section 2(d) requires only 'use[] in the U.S.,' and adoption of the mark by use analogous to strict trademark use will therefore suffice. An opposer may rely on myriad forms of activity besides sales themselves, including, among others, regular business contacts, after-sales services, advertising of various forms, and marketing. Even marketing of a trademarked product before the product is ready for sale has the potential to defeat a rival's registration. Still, desultory marketing such as sending out occasional press releases is not enough. Analogous use must be 'of such a nature and extent as to create public identification of the target term with the opposer's product.' *At 21-22:* A bona fide intent is a statutory requirement of a valid trademark application under §1(b), and the lack of such intent is therefore a ground on which [P] may oppose [D's] application. [¶] Thus, an opposer may defeat a trademark application for lack of bona fide intent by proving the applicant did not actually intend to use the mark in commerce or by proving the circumstances at the time of filing did not demonstrate that intent. To state a claim on the latter ground, an opposer only has to notify the applicant of the general 'circumstances, occurrences, and events' causing the flaw in the application. Although the complaint need not go into detail, it must at least notify the applicant of how the general circumstances fail to show intent." *See also* ***Herbko Int'l v. Kappa Books, Inc.***, 308 F.3d 1156, 1162 (Fed.Cir.2002).

First Niagara Ins. Brokers, Inc. v. First Niagara Fin. Grp., 476 F.3d 867, 870-71 (Fed.Cir.2007). The TTAB "based its [decision to dismiss foreign opposer's opposition to mark] on the assumption that an 'opposer's claim of prior use can succeed only if it has proved use of its marks in connection with services rendered in commerce lawfully regulated by Congress, as required under [Lanham Act] §45 ..., 15 U.S.C. §1127.' Such an assumption was unwarranted, however, in light of the plain language of the statute, which merely requires the prior mark to have been 'used in the U.S. by another.' ... Thus, a foreign opposer can present its opposition on the merits by showing only *use* of its mark in the U.S."

CreAgri, Inc. v. USANA Health Sci., Inc., 474 F.3d 626, 628 (9th Cir.2007). "[I]n order to acquire priority, a 'use in commerce' means a lawful use—here, a use compliant with federal labeling requirements. *At 634:* [T]he district court correctly cancelled [mark] from the supplemental register. A mark is only eligible for supplemental registration if it was in 'lawful use in commerce' prior to the date on which the holder applied for such registration." *See also* ***United Phosphorus Ltd. v. Midland Fumigant, Inc.***, 205 F.3d 1219, 1225 (10th Cir.2000).

Allard Enters. v. Advanced Programming Res., 249 F.3d 564, 572 (6th Cir.2001). "Typically, under [Lanham Act] §2(d) ..., 15 U.S.C. §1052(d), it is the senior user who has the right to a federal registration, subject only to the prior common law rights of a junior user who has used the mark prior to the senior user's application for federal registration."

Bright Beginnings, Inc. v. Care Comms., 30 U.S.P.Q.2d 1712, 1714 (C.D.Cal.1994), *aff'd*, 78 F.3d 592 (9th Cir.1996) (table case). In "order for a junior user to be a 'lawful user,' he must have adopted the mark in good faith in an area remote to the senior user."

CDS Inc. v. I.C.E.D. Mgmt., 80 U.S.P.Q.2d 1572, 1583-84 (T.T.A.B.2006). Held: Internet use does not automatically create confusion between two very similar marks used in separate geographic territories because P had displayed a disclaimer on its webpage specifying that it was doing business under "The Copy Club" mark only in the seven contested states. Because the disclaimer and P's "desire to eliminate overlapping territory" that existed in the past between the two companies were "helpful in avoiding confusion," the TTAB did not believe that "the creation of the Internet has rendered the concurrent use provision of the Trademark Act moot."

§1052(e)

Wal-Mart Stores v. Samara Bros., 529 U.S. 205, 213 (2000). When "it is not reasonable to assume consumer predisposition to take an affixed word or packaging as indication of source—where, for example, the affixed word is descriptive of the product ('Tasty' bread) or of a geographic origin ('Georgia' peaches)—inherent distinctiveness will not be found. That is why [15 U.S.C. §1052(e)(1), Lanham Act §2(e)(1),] generally excludes, from those word marks that can be registered as inherently distinctive, words that are 'merely descriptive' of the goods or 'primarily geographically descriptive of them[ ]'.... In the case of product design, as in the case of color, we think consumer predisposition to equate the feature with the source does not exist."

In re Reed Elsevier Props., Inc., 482 F.3d 1376, 1378 (Fed.Cir.2007). "The PTO bears the burden of proving a mark generic. In so doing, any competent source suffices to show the relevant public's understanding of a contested term, including purchaser testimony, consumer surveys, dictionary definitions, trade journals, newspapers, and other publications."

§1052(e)(1)

In re Cordua Rests., Inc., 823 F.3d 594, 599 (Fed. Cir.2016). "The critical issue in genericness cases is whether members of the relevant public primarily use or understand the term sought to be protected to refer to the genus of goods or services in question. [A] two-step test is applied to determine whether a given term is generic. First, what is the genus of goods or services at issue? Second, is the term sought to be registered or retained on the register understood by the relevant public primarily to refer to that genus of goods or services? Evidence of the public's understanding of the mark may be obtained from any competent source, such as consumer surveys, dictionaries, newspapers and other publications. *At 603:* While each trademark must always be evaluated individually, pluralization commonly does not alter the meaning of a mark. [¶] [A] term can be generic for a genus of goods or services if the relevant public—here, the restaurant-going public—understands the term to refer to a key aspect of that genus—e.g., a key good that characterizes a particular genus of retail services. A generic name of goods may also be a generic name of the service of selling or designing those goods. We have held that the test is not only whether the relevant public would itself *use* the term to describe the genus, but also whether the relevant public would *understand* the term to be generic." (Internal quotes omitted.)

DuoProSS Meditech Corp. v. Inviro Med. Devices, Ltd., 695 F.3d 1247, 1251-52 (Fed.Cir.2012). "A mark is merely descriptive if it consists merely of words descriptive of the qualities, ingredients or characteristics of the goods or services related to the mark. One articulation of that rule ... is that a mark is merely descriptive if it conveys information regarding a function, or purpose, or use of the goods. The line between a mark that is merely descriptive and may not be registered absent secondary meaning, and one that is suggestive and may be registered, is that a suggestive mark requires imagination, thought and perception to reach a conclusion as to the nature of the goods, while a merely descriptive mark forthwith conveys an immediate idea of the ingredients, qualities or characteristics of the goods. [¶] The determination of whether a mark is merely descriptive is a question of fact. As the party challenging the registrations' validity, [opposer] bears the burden of proving that the mark is merely descriptive by a preponderance of the evidence. *At 1255:* To determine whether a composite mark ... is merely descriptive, the Board was required to examine the meaning of each component individually, and then determine whether the mark as a whole is merely descriptive." (Internal quotes omitted.)

Lahoti v. VeriCheck, Inc., 636 F.3d 501, 506 (9th Cir.2011). "If consumer response requires any sort of multistage reasoning process to identify the characteristic of the product which the mark suggests, then the mark should not be regarded as 'merely descriptive.' Here, for example, consumers must separate 'veri' from 'check' and reason that 'veri' is short for 'verification services.' In addition, similar marks have been found to be suggestive. *At 507:* [W]hile a statutory presumption of distinctiveness only applies when the same mark has been registered, courts may also defer to the PTO's registration of highly similar marks." (Internal quotes omitted.)

In re Bayer A.G., 488 F.3d 960, 963-64 (Fed.Cir. 2007). "Descriptiveness of a mark is not considered in the abstract. Rather, it is considered in relation to the particular goods for which registration is sought, the context in which it is being used, and the possible significance that the term would have to the average purchaser of the goods because of the manner of its use or intended use. The examining attorney has the burden to establish that a mark is merely descriptive. [¶] The determination that a mark is merely descriptive is a factual finding, and this court reviews the [TTAB's] fact finding for substantial evidence. Substantial evidence 'means such relevant evidence as a reasonable mind might accept as adequate to support a conclusion.' [¶] Evidence that a term is merely descriptive to the relevant purchasing public 'may be obtained from any competent source, such as dictionaries, newspapers, or surveys.' *At 966:* Internet evidence is generally admissible and may be considered for purposes of evaluating a trademark. Definitions available from an online resource that are readily available and as such capable of being verified are useful to determine consumer perception. *At 967:* Search engine results—which provide little context to discern how a term is actually used on the webpage that can be accessed through the search result link—may be insufficient to determine the nature of the use of a term or the relevance of the search results to registration considerations. Web-based information that includes greater context for the use of a term, such as a complete webpage that is accessible as a link within the search engine results, will have greater probative value in determining how a term will be perceived. *At 969:* Information originating on foreign websites or in foreign news publications that are accessible to the U.S. public may be relevant to discern U.S. consumer impression of a proposed mark. The probative value, if any, of foreign information sources must be evaluated on a case-by-case basis." *See also* ***In re Stereotaxis, Inc.***, 429 F.3d 1039, 1042-43 (Fed.Cir.2005) (term was descriptive of medical equipment).

Nartron Corp. v. STMicroelectronics, Inc., 305 F.3d 397, 404 n.7 (6th Cir.2002). "A 'merely descriptive' mark, as opposed to a 'common descriptive' one, is often said to identify a characteristic of the thing. It is very similar to an adjective."

Bellsouth Corp. v. Datanational Corp., 60 F.3d 1565, 1569 (Fed.Cir.1995). "A generic term falls within [the §1052(e)(1)] prohibition because '[t]he generic name of a thing is in fact the ultimate in descriptiveness.' *At 1571:* The term 'use' plainly means use as a trademark. Thus the statute by its terms is applicable where there is more than one lawful user of the same or similar mark."

In re Berman Bros. Harlem Furniture Inc., 26 U.S.P.Q.2d 1514, 1515 (T.T.A.B.1993). "The test applied in the determination for whether or not a term is deceptively descriptive ... is twofold. First, it must be determined whether the proposed mark misdescribes a characteristic, quality, function, composition or use of the goods or services. If so, we reach the second part of the test, which is whether the misdescription is deceptive, or, in other words, whether prospective purchasers are likely to believe that the misdescription actually describes the goods or services."

§1052(e)(2)

In re Newbridge Cutlery Co., 776 F.3d 854, 859 (Fed.Cir.2015). "[R]efusal to register extends under both [§1052](e)(2) and (e)(3) only to those marks for which the geographical meaning is perceived by the relevant public as the *primary* meaning and that the geographical significance of the mark is to be assessed as it is used *on or in connection with the goods. At 860:* [T]his court has set out specific requirements for determining whether a mark is primarily geographically descriptive or primarily geographically deceptively misdescriptive. As the statute uses the phrase 'primarily geographically' in both the descriptive and deceptively misdescriptive subsections, this court's decisions relating to one subsection inform the meaning of the other and make clear that to refuse registration under either subsection the Trademark Examiner must show that: (1) the mark sought to be registered is the name of a place known generally to the public, ... and (2) the public would make a goods/place association, i.e., believe that the goods for which the mark is sought to be registered originate in that place. *At 861:* To refuse registration of a mark as being primarily geographically descriptive, the PTO must also show that (3) the source of the goods is the geographic region named in the mark. In applying prongs (1) and (2) of this test, our precedent establishes that the relevant public is the purchasing public in the U.S. of these types of goods. [W]e are not concerned with the public in other countries. [¶] Regarding the first prong of the test, that the population of the location is sizable and/or that members of the consuming public have ties to the location ... is evidence that a location is generally known. By contrast, that the geographic meaning of a location is minor, obscure or remote indicates that the location is not generally known. Of course, there are many probative factors to the question of whether a location is generally known, and these are just a few examples. [¶] In establishing the goods/place association required by the second prong of the test, we have explained that the PTO only needs to show a *reasonable predicate* for its conclusion that the public would be *likely* to make the particular goods/place association on which it relies. It need not show an 'actual' association in consumers' minds. A goods/place association can be shown even where the location is not 'well-known' or 'noted' for the relevant goods. If the Trademark Examiner establishes such a *prima facie* case, an applicant may[ ] rebut this showing with evidence that the public would not actually believe the goods derive from the geographic location identified by the mark. [¶] The PTO has long held that where: (1) a location is generally known; (2) the term's geographic significance is its primary significance; and (3) the goods do, in fact, originate from the named location, a goods/place association can be presumed. This presumption may well be proper, but, as this case can be decided on other grounds, we do not address its propriety and leave it for another day. *At 863:* [W]e do not foreclose the PTO from using gazetteer entries or internet websites to identify whether a location is generally known. ... Gazetteer entries and internet websites are valuable for the information they provide. But the mere entry in a gazetteer or the fact that a location is described on the internet does not necessarily evidence that a place is known generally to the relevant public." (Internal quotes omitted.) *See also* ***World Carpets, Inc. v. Dick Littrell's New World Carpets***, 438 F.2d 482, 486 (5th Cir.1971).

Barcelona.com, Inc. v. Excelentisimo Ayuntamiento, 330 F.3d 617, 629 (4th Cir.2003). "[A] geographic designation can obtain trademark protection if that designation acquires secondary meaning. On the record in this case, ... there was no evidence that the public ... associates 'Barcelona' with anything other than the City itself. ... Therefore, under U.S. trademark law, 'Barcelona' should have been treated as a purely descriptive geographical term entitled to no trademark protection."

§1052(e)(3)

In re Miracle Tuesday, LLC, 695 F.3d 1339, 1343-44 (Fed.Cir.2012). "A mark is primarily geographically deceptively misdescriptive, and thus barred from registration, if: (1) the primary significance of the mark is a generally known geographic location; (2) the consuming public is likely to believe the place identified by the mark indicates the origin of the goods bearing the mark, when in fact the goods do not come from that place; and (3) the misrepresentation was a material factor in the consumer's decision to purchase the goods. [¶] Whether a mark is primarily geographically deceptively misdescriptive is a question of fact. We review the Board's factual findings for substantial evidence. [¶] [W]e turn directly to the second element.... This element involves two questions: (1) whether there is an association between the goods and the place identified (a goods/place association); and (2) whether the applicant's goods in fact come from that place. [¶] As to the first inquiry, the examiner has the initial burden of submitting evidence to establish a goods/place association and the burden then shifts to the applicant to rebut this showing with evidence that the public would not actually believe the goods derive from the geographic location identified by the mark. This court has explained that the PTO is not required to establish an *actual* goods/place association. Instead, the PTO need only establish a *reasonable predicate* for its conclusion that the public would be *likely* to make the particular goods/place association on which it relies. [¶] Where ... a case involves goods rather than services, we have held that the goods-place association often requires little more than a showing that the consumer identifies the place as a known source of the product. Therefore, to establish a goods/place association, the case law permits an inference that the consumer associates the product with the geographic location in the mark because that place is known for producing the product. [¶] The second inquiry under this element asks whether the goods will in fact originate from the named place. It is undisputed that goods may be deemed to originate in a geographic location if they are manufactured there. Origin can be predicated on factors other than manufacture, however, where the circumstances justify such a connection. [I]n appropriate circumstances, the place of design can be enough. Similarly, if the goods contain a main component or ingredient from the place identified in the mark, that connection can be sufficient to find that the goods originate from that place. And, a product might be found to originate from a place where the applicant has its headquarters or research and development facilities, even when the manufacturing facilities, are elsewhere. *At 1346-47:* The third and final element of a [Lanham Act] §2(e)(3) [15 U.S.C. §1052(e)(3)] refusal focuses on materiality and asks whether a substantial portion of the relevant consumers is likely to be deceived by the mark's misrepresentation of a goods/place association. In ***Spirits International***, we held that, to establish a prima facie case of materiality there must be some indication that a substantial portion of the relevant consumers would be materially influenced in the decision to purchase the product or service by the geographic meaning of the mark. We have also held that the PTO may raise an inference in favor of materiality with evidence that the place is famous as a source of the goods at issue. [¶] [W]e [have] recognized that: (1) the standard under §2(e)(3) is more difficult to satisfy for service marks than for marks on goods; and (2) geographic marks in connection with services are less likely to mislead the public than geographic marks on goods. Given these differences, we drew a distinction between the evidence necessary to give rise to an inference of materiality for goods and that necessary to give rise to that same inference for services. Although for *goods*, evidence that a place is famous as a source of those goods is sufficient to raise an inference of materiality, when dealing with *service* marks, we held that there must be a heightened association between the services and geographic location." (Internal quotes omitted.)

In re Spirits Int'l, 563 F.3d 1347, 1351-52 (Fed.Cir. 2009). "One aspect of the doctrine of foreign equivalents generally requires considering the meaning of a mark in a non-English language to the speakers of that language. [U]nder the doctrine of foreign equivalents, foreign words from common languages are translated into English. ... However, the doctrine of foreign equivalents is not an absolute rule, for it does not mean that words from dead or obscure languages are to be literally translated into English for descriptive purposes. [¶] [T]he doctrine of foreign equivalents applies only in those situations where the ordinary American consumer would stop and translate the mark into English.... The ordinary American purchaser is not limited to only those consumers unfamiliar with non-English languages; rather, the term includes all American purchasers, including those proficient in a non-English language who would ordinarily be expected to translate words into English. [¶] [T]here are situations in which the doctrine does not require translation even with respect to foreign language speakers. The ordinary American consumer would not translate VEUVE CLICQUOT because its literal translation would be irrelevant to even those ordinary American consumers who speak French. ... Additionally, some marks would not be translated because of the particular context in which they occur. There may be many non-English marks that will not be translated in context but instead accepted at face value by the ordinary American consumer, including those familiar with the literal meaning of the mark in the non-English language. *At 1353:* [An earlier case] did not address the question of whether the materiality test of subsection (e)(3) embodies a requirement that a significant portion of the relevant consumers be deceived. We hold that subsection (e)(3) does incorporate such a requirement, and that the appropriate inquiry for materiality purposes is whether a substantial portion of the relevant consumers is likely to be deceived, not whether any absolute number or particular segment of the relevant consumers (such as foreign language speakers) is likely to be deceived. *At 1356:* That [substantial portion] is often the entire U.S. population interested in purchasing the product or service. [I]n some cases, the use of a non-English language mark can be evidence that the product in question is targeted at the community of those who understand that language. In such cases, the relevant consuming public will be composed of those who are members of that targeted community, and, as a result, people who speak the non-English language could comprise a substantial portion of the relevant consumers." (Internal quotes omitted.)

In re California Innovations, Inc., 329 F.3d 1334, 1339 (Fed.Cir.2003). Section 1052 "no longer treats [primarily] geographically deceptively misdescriptive marks differently from geographically deceptive marks. Like geographically deceptive marks, the analysis for primarily geographically deceptively misdescriptive marks under §1052(e)(3) focuses on deception of, or fraud on, the consumer. The classifications under the new §1052 clarify that these two deceptive categories both receive permanent rejection. Accordingly, the test for rejecting a deceptively misdescriptive mark is no longer simple lack of distinctiveness, but the higher showing of deceptiveness."

§1052(e)(4)

Earnhardt v. Kerry Earnhardt, Inc., 864 F.3d 1374, 1377-78 (Fed.Cir.2017). "A mark is primarily merely a surname if the surname 'is the primary significance of the mark as a whole to the purchasing public.' Because EARNHARDT COLLECTION is a combination of two terms, the PTO must consider the mark 'in its entirety' rather than merely 'consider[ing] the mark as two separate parts.' Thus, to evaluate whether the commercial impression of a mark that combines a surname with a second term is still primarily merely the surname, the PTO must determine whether the primary significance of the mark as a whole in connection with the recited goods and services is that of the surname. A key element in such an inquiry is determining the relative distinctiveness of the second term in the mark."

Peaceable Planet, Inc. v. Ty, Inc., 362 F.3d 986, 990 (7th Cir.2004). "The personal-name 'rule[ ]' ... is a common law rather than statutory doctrine. All that the Lanham Act says about personal names is that a mark that is 'primarily merely a surname' is not registrable in the absence of secondary meaning. There is no reference to first names. ... The extension of the rule to first names is a judicial innovation and so needn't be pressed further than its rationale, as might have to be done if the rule were codified in inflexible statutory language. Notice too the limitation implicit in the statutory term 'primarily.'"

Lane Capital Mgmt. v. Lane Capital Mgmt., 192 F.3d 337, 345 (2d Cir.1999). "Whether a mark is primarily merely a surname is a question of fact."

Avery Dennison Corp. v. Sumpton, 189 F.3d 868, 877 (9th Cir.1999), *overruled on other grounds, **Moseley v. V Secret Catalogue, Inc.***, 537 U.S. 418 (2003). "A long-standing principle of trademark law is the right of a person to use his or her own name in connection with a business. This principle was incorporated into the Lanham Act, which states that a mark that is 'primarily merely a surname' is not protectable unless it acquires secondary meaning."

Time, Inc. v. Petersen Publ'g, 173 F.3d 113, 117 (2d Cir.1999). "Secondary meaning attaches when 'the name and the business have become synonymous in the mind of the public, submerging the primary meaning of the term in favor of its meaning as a word identifying that business.'" *See also **In re Etablissements Darty et Fils***, 759 F.2d 15, 17 (Fed.Cir.1985).

Taylor Wine Co. v. Bully Hill Vineyards, Inc., 569 F.2d 731, 734 (2d Cir.1978). "The conflict between a first comer who has given a secondary meaning (as well as trademark registration) to a family name, and a later comer who wishes to use his own true family name as a trademark in the same industry has been one of the more interesting issues in the law of trademark infringement. The problem is made more difficult when the second comer has his own background of experience in the particular industry, and is not simply a newcomer."

§1052(e)(5)

TrafFix Devices, Inc. v. Marketing Displays, Inc., 532 U.S. 23, 32-33 (2001). "[A] functional feature is one the 'exclusive use of [which] would put competitors at a significant non-reputation-related disadvantage.' The Court of Appeals in the instant case seemed to interpret this language to mean that the necessary test for functionality is 'whether the particular product configuration is a competitive necessity.' ... This was incorrect as a comprehensive definition. [A] feature is also functional when it is essential to the use or purpose of the device or when it affects the cost or quality of the device."

McAirlaids, Inc. v. Kimberly-Clark Corp., 756 F.3d 307, 310 (4th Cir.2014). "[W]hen a company wants to protect a functional feature of a product design, it must turn to patent law rather than trademark law. [P]roof of a design element's functionality is a complete defense in a trademark-infringement action. Although the functionality doctrine originated in the common law, it has now been incorporated into the Lanham Act, which prohibits registration of trade dress that is 'as a whole ... functional.' *At 313:* When assessing a design element's functionality, courts often look at (1) the existence of utility patents, (2) advertising focusing on the utilitarian advantages of a design, (3) the availability of 'functionally equivalent designs,' and (4) the effect of the design on manufacturing."

ERBE Elektromedizin GmbH v. Canady Tech., 629 F.3d 1278, 1288 (Fed.Cir.2010). "Some factors courts use to determine functionality include whether the design yields a utilitarian advantage, alternative designs are available in order to avoid hindering competition, and the design achieves economies in manufacture or use."

Dippin' Dots, Inc. v. Frosty Bites Distrib., 369 F.3d 1197, 1202-03 (11th Cir.2004). "The functionality doctrine prevents trademark law, which seeks to promote competition by protecting a firm's reputation, from instead inhibiting legitimate competition by allowing a producer to control a useful product feature. Functional features are by definition those likely to be shared by different producers of the same product and therefore are unlikely to identify a particular producer. [T]hese features cannot be appropriated; otherwise, competitors would be prevented from duplicating the new product even to the extent permitted by the branches of the law of intellectual property that protect innovation rather than designations of source." (Internal quotes omitted.)

Tie Tech, Inc. v. Kinedyne Corp., 296 F.3d 778, 785 (9th Cir.2002). "Although the Lanham Act prohibits registration of a mark that 'comprises any matter that, as a whole, is functional,' ... not all aspects of functionality are precluded from protection. De jure, or legal, functionality must be distinguished from de facto functionality which still may support trademark protection."

Valu Eng'g v. Rexnord Corp., 278 F.3d 1268, 1278 (Fed.Cir.2002). If the TTAB "identifies *any* competitively significant single use in the recited identification of goods [in the registration application] for which the mark as a whole is functional, the Board should deny registration."

§1052(f)

Qualitex Co. v. Jacobson Prods. Co., 514 U.S. 159, 160-61 (1995). "The question in this case is whether the Trademark Act ... permits the registration of a trademark that consists, purely and simply, of a color. We conclude that, sometimes, a color will meet ordinary legal trademark requirements. And, when it does so, no special legal rule prevents color alone from serving as a trademark. *At 163:* We cannot find in the basic objectives of trademark law any obvious theoretical objection to the use of color alone as a trademark, where that color has attained 'secondary meaning' and therefore identifies and distinguishes a particular brand (and thus indicates its 'source')." *See also* ***Christian Louboutin S.A. v. Yves Saint Laurent Am. Holding, Inc.***, 696 F.3d 206, 225-26 (2d Cir.2012) (color used by fashion designer acquired secondary meaning because used consistently and prominently); ***ERBE Elektromedizin GmbH v. Canady Tech.***, 629 F.3d 1278, 1288 (Fed.Cir.2010) (color not registrable if it performs utilitarian function or has specific competitive advantage); ***Louisiana State Univ. v. Smack Apparel Co.***, 550 F.3d 465, 475 (5th Cir.2008) (school-color scheme protected as trademark because it acquired secondary meaning and is nonfunctional).

Department of Parks & Recreation for the State of Cal. v. Bazaar del Mundo Inc., 448 F.3d 1118, 1128 (9th Cir.2006). "To determine whether a descriptive mark has acquired secondary meaning, we consider: (1) whether actual purchasers of the product bearing the claimed trademark associate the trademark with the producer, (2) the degree and manner of advertising under the claimed trademark, (3) the length and manner of use of the claimed trademark, and (4) whether use of the claimed trademark has been exclusive." (Internal quotes omitted.) *See also* ***In re Dial-A-Mattress Oper. Corp.***, 240 F.3d 1341, 1347 (Fed.Cir.2001).

In re Slokevage, 441 F.3d 957, 959-60 (Fed.Cir. 2006). "[T]he determination whether trade dress is product design is a factual finding because it is akin to determining whether a trademark is inherently distinctive or whether a mark is descriptive, which are questions of fact. Inherent distinctiveness or descriptiveness involves consumer perception and whether consumers are predisposed towards equating a symbol with a source. Such issues are determined based on testimony, surveys, and other evidence as questions of fact. Determining whether trade dress is product design or product packaging involves a similar inquiry. We therefore will defer to the [TTAB's] finding on product design, affirming the Board if its decision is supported by substantial evidence. In addition, the inquiry into whether a mark is unitary is a factual determination. *At 961:* The Lanham Act provides protection not only for words and symbols, but also for 'trade dress,' a category of trademarks that has been described as involving the 'total image of a product,' including 'features such as size, shape, color or color combinations, texture, graphics, or even particular sales techniques.' The Supreme Court has recently observed that trade dress is a category that originally included only the packaging of a product, but has been expanded by courts to encompass the design of a product. In order for an applicant to gain protection for trade dress, the trade dress must be distinctive, either inherently or by acquiring distinctiveness. Trade dress is inherently distinctive when its 'intrinsic nature serves to identify a particular source of a product,' and, in contrast, acquires distinctiveness when the public comes to associate the product with its source. [¶] [T]he Court established a bright-line rule—product design cannot be inherently distinctive, and always requires proof of acquired distinctiveness to be protected. The Court did not recite the factors that distinguish between product packaging and product design trade dress, but stated that in 'close cases' courts should classify the trade dress as product design. *At 962:* [P]roduct design can consist of design features incorporated into a product. [¶] [U]nlike a trademark whose 'predominant function' remains source identification, product design often serves other functions, such as rendering the 'product itself more useful or more appealing.' [I]n such cases when the purchase implicates a utilitarian or aesthetic purpose, rather than a source-identifying function, it is appropriate to require proof of acquired distinctiveness." Held: Holes and flaps as part of the overall configuration of trousers and shorts are product design and are not registrable absent a showing of acquired distinctiveness.

In re Steelbuilding.com, 415 F.3d 1293, 1297 (Fed. Cir.2005). "Only in rare instances will the addition of a [top-level domain (TLD)] indicator to a descriptive term operate to create a distinctive mark. In those rare instances, a term that is not distinctive by itself may acquire some additional meaning from the addition of a TLD, such as '.com,' '.net,' etc. In those unusual circumstances, the addition of the TLD can show Internet-related distinctiveness, intimating some 'Internet feature' of the item. Because the evaluation of a mark proposed for registration requires consideration of the mark as a whole, the distinctiveness derived from a connection to the Internet, as indicated by the TLD indicator, is a part of the calculus for registration. *At 1299:* In this unusual case, the addition of the TLD indicator ['.COM' to 'STEELBUILDING'] expanded the meaning of the mark to include goods and services beyond the mere sale of steel buildings. Specifically, the TLD expanded the mark to include internet services that include 'building' or designing steel structures on the web site and then calculating an appropriate price before ordering the unique structure." Held: The "STEELBUILDING.COM" mark was merely descriptive and did not acquire a secondary meaning.

In re Wada, 194 F.3d 1297, 1301 (Fed.Cir.1999). Generic "terms are unregistrable because registration would preclude others from using terms that truthfully describe their products. Disclaimer of generic terms in composite marks allows marks containing generic terms to be registered as a whole while preventing any exclusive rights in the generic terms themselves."

In re Gyulay, 820 F.2d 1216, 1217 (Fed.Cir.1987). "A mark that is 'merely descriptive,' as the term is used in trademark law, is not registrable under [Lanham Act] §2(e) [15 U.S.C. §1052(e)], but may be registrable under [Lanham Act] §2(f), 15 U.S.C. §1052(f), if secondary meaning is shown. A suggestive mark, one that 'suggests, rather than describes,' is protectible without evidence of secondary meaning. Whether a given mark is suggestive or merely descriptive depends on whether the mark 'immediately conveys ... knowledge of the ingredients, qualities, or characteristics of the goods ... with which it is used,' or whether 'imagination, thought, or perception is required to reach a conclusion on the nature of the goods.'"

Ride the Ducks, L.L.C. v. Duck Boat Tours, Inc., 75 U.S.P.Q.2d 1269, 1275 (E.D.Pa.2005), *aff'd*, 138 Fed.Appx. 431 (3d Cir.2005). "[P's] service mark is ... 'a quacking noise made by tour guides and tour participants by use of duck call devices' throughout their tours. [P's] mark is not yet [incontestable] under [Lanham Act] §15 [15 U.S.C. §1065] as the registration is less than five years old. As such, the Court must endeavor to categorize the mark as arbitrary, fanciful, suggestive, or descriptive. *At 1276:* While [Ps] have presented circumstantial evidence from which the Court could find that the public, to some extent, associates the physical quacker itself with the [tour-service] experience, [Ps] have presented no evidence that a person apprehending a quacking noise on [city streets] would reflexively think of the services provided by [P]."

BigStar Entm't, Inc. v. Next Big Star, Inc., 105 F.Supp.2d 185, 196 (S.D.N.Y.2000). "While [Lanham Act] §2(f) ... (*see* 15 U.S.C. §1052(f)) permits registration of merely descriptive terms, the corresponding protection it accords demands, as a precondition, proof that the mark has acquired secondary meaning in its market. This test refers to demonstrable evidence that the mark, by means of sufficient marketing, sales, usage and passage of time, has established distinctiveness in commerce, measured by the extent to which it has become identified in the public mind with the particular source of the goods."

In re America Online, Inc., 77 U.S.P.Q.2d 1618, 1623 (T.T.A.B.2006). The mark "INSTANT MESSENGER" was not generic because "the mere fact that a record includes evidence of both proper trademark use and generic use does not necessarily create a mixed record that would overcome an examining attorney's evidence of genericness. [T]he evidence of generic use is offset by applicant's evidence that shows not only a significant amount of proper trademark use but also trademark recognition by customers, publishers, and third parties. *At 1625:* [Applicant also met its burden of showing that its mark had acquired distinctiveness because its] advertising had reached a significant percentage of people in the U.S. and it has provided some affidavits from customers who recognize its term as a mark for applicant's services."

§1053. SERVICE MARKS REGISTRABLE

[LANHAM ACT §3]

Subject to the provisions relating to the registration of trademarks, so far as they are applicable, service marks shall be registrable, in the same manner and with the same effect as are trademarks, and when registered they shall be entitled to the protection provided in this chapter in the case of trademarks. Applications and procedure under this section shall conform as nearly as practicable to those prescribed for the registration of trademarks.

History of 15 U.S.C. §1053: July 5, 1946, ch. 540, §3, 60 Stat. 429; Nov. 16, 1988, P.L. 100-667, §105, 102 Stat. 3938; Aug. 5, 1999, P.L. 106-43, §6(b), 113 Stat. 220.

Treatise Cross-References

McCarthy on Trademark & Unfair Competition

Ch. 19, *Federal Registration of Marks*, §19:80
Ch. 21, *Appeal from Decisions on Trademark Registration*, §21:6
Ch. 23, *Likelihood of Confusion: The Test of Trademark Infringement*, §23:76

ANNOTATIONS

American Express Co. v. Goetz, 515 F.3d 156, 161 (2d Cir.2008). "Unlike trademarks, service marks usually cannot be 'affixed' or displayed in close connection with the services, so advertisements and solicitations are often used as evidence of use. However, it cannot be said that a service mark is actually used if it is displayed in an advertisement for services that are non-existent or will only hypothetically be available at some point in the future."

Mid-State Aftermarket Body Parts, Inc. v. MQVP, Inc., 466 F.3d 630, 634 (8th Cir.2006). "'The Lanham Trademark Act affords the trademark holder the right to control the quality of the goods manufactured and sold under its trademark.' Service mark owners are entitled to the same protection, so [D] may control the services sold under its service mark."

Martahus v. Video Duplication Servs., 3 F.3d 417, 421 (Fed.Cir.1993). "Registration is barred ... if a service mark consists of or comprises a mark which so resembles a mark or trade name previously used in the U.S. by another, and not abandoned, as to be likely, when used in connection with the services of the applicant, to cause confusion, to cause mistake, or to deceive."

Lloyd's Food Prods. v. Eli's, Inc., 987 F.2d 766, 768 (Fed.Cir.1993). "A service mark is different from a mark for goods, especially in the manner it is used in commerce. The legally significant use giving rise to rights in a mark for goods is derived from the placing of the mark in some manner on the goods either directly or on their containers or packaging. A service mark, on the other hand, entails use in conjunction with the offering and providing of a service. This makes all the more important the use of the mark in 'sales' or 'advertising' materials of different description."

Larry Harmon Pictures Corp. v. Williams Rest. Corp., 929 F.2d 662, 664 (Fed.Cir.1991). Service "marks must be 'used in commerce' before they may be registered."

In re Kopy Kat, Inc., 498 F.2d 1379, 1380 (C.C.P.A. 1974). Registration "shall not be granted of a mark 'which ... when applied to the goods of the applicant is merely descriptive ... of them.' These words were written, of course, with respect to trademarks[,] but in view of [15 U.S.C. §1053, Lanham Act §3], which states that service marks are registrable subject to the provisions relating to the registration of trademarks, the word 'goods' must be read as comprehending services."

§1054. COLLECTIVE MARKS & CERTIFICATION MARKS REGISTRABLE

[LANHAM ACT §4]

Subject to the provisions relating to the registration of trademarks, so far as they are applicable, collective and certification marks, including indications of regional origin, shall be registrable under this chapter, in the same manner and with the same effect as are trademarks, by persons, and nations, States, municipalities, and the like, exercising legitimate control over the use of the marks sought to be registered, even though not possessing an industrial or commercial establishment, and when registered they shall be entitled to the protection provided in this chapter in the case of trademarks, except in the case of certification marks when used so as to represent falsely that the owner or a user thereof makes or sells the goods or performs the services on or in connection with which such mark is used. Applications and procedure under this section shall conform as nearly as practicable to those prescribed for the registration of trademarks.

History of 15 U.S.C. §1054: July 5, 1946, ch. 540, §4, 60 Stat. 429; Nov. 16, 1988, P.L. 100-667, §106, 102 Stat. 3938; Aug. 5, 1999, P.L. 106-43, §6(b), 113 Stat. 220.

See also 37 C.F.R. §§6.3, 6.4.

Treatise Cross-References

McCarthy on Trademark & Unfair Competition

Ch. 19, *Federal Registration of Marks*, §§19:90; 19:100
Ch. 20, *Inter Partes Trademark Proceedings in the Patent & Trademark Office*, §20:59
Ch. 21, *Appeal from Decisions on Trademark Registration*, §21:6
Ch. 32, *Procedure in Trademark Infringement & Unfair Competition Litigation*, §32:147

ANNOTATIONS

State of Idaho Potato Comm'n v. G&T Terminal Packaging, Inc., 425 F.3d 708, 715 (9th Cir.2005). "A certification mark ... is a mark used by someone other than its owner to signify that a product or service has a certain characteristic. The certification mark owner is required to license the mark to anyone who meets the certification criteria." *See also* ***Levy v. Kosher Overseers Ass'n***, 104 F.3d 38, 39 (2d Cir.1997).

Sebastian Int'l v. Longs Drug Stores, 53 F.3d 1073, 1075 (9th Cir.1995). "The language of the Lanham Act [expressly provides] that a collective mark shall have the same effect and provide the same protection as a trademark, effectively making the 'first sale' rule equally applicable to both."

Community of Roquefort v. William Faehndrich, Inc., 303 F.2d 494, 497 (2d Cir.1962). "A geographical name does not require a secondary meaning in order to qualify for registration as a certification mark. It is true that [15 U.S.C.] §1054 [Lanham Act §4] provides that certification marks are 'subject to the provisions relating to the registration of trademarks, so far as they are applicable....' But [15 U.S.C. §1052(e)(2), Lanham Act §2(e)(2)], which prohibits registration of names primarily geographically descriptive, specifically excepts 'indications of regional origin' registrable under §1054. Therefore, a geographical name may be registered as a certification mark even though it is primarily geographically descriptive. This distinction ... has significance. A trade-mark gives a producer exclusive rights; but a certification mark, owned by a municipality ... must be made available without discrimination 'to certify the goods ... of *any* person who maintains the standards or conditions which such mark certifies.'"

Schroeder v. Lotito, 577 F.Supp. 708, 716 (D.R.I. 1983), *aff'd*, 747 F.2d 801 (1st Cir.1984). When "the safeguarding of a valid collective mark against infringement by a third party is sought, it is wonted practice for the owner organization to bring suit on behalf of its members."

§1055. USE BY RELATED COMPANIES AFFECTING VALIDITY & REGISTRATION

[LANHAM ACT §5]

Where a registered mark or a mark sought to be registered is or may be used legitimately by related companies, such use shall inure to the benefit of the registrant or applicant for registration, and such use shall not affect the validity of such mark or of its registration, provided such mark is not used in such manner as to deceive the public. If first use of a mark by a person is controlled by the registrant or applicant for registration of the mark with respect to the nature and quality of the goods or services, such first use shall inure to the benefit of the registrant or applicant, as the case may be.

History of 15 U.S.C. §1055: July 5, 1946, ch. 540, §5, 60 Stat. 429; Nov. 16, 1988, P.L. 100-667, §107, 102 Stat. 3938.

Treatise Cross-References

McCarthy on Trademark & Unfair Competition

Ch. 3, *The Functions of Trademarks*, §3:11
Ch. 18, *Assignment & Licensing of Trademarks*, §§18:45.50; 18:46; 18:48; 18:49; 18:51-18:53
Ch. 19, *Federal Registration of Marks*, §19:53
Ch. 21, *Appeal from Decisions on Trademark Registration*, §21:6
Ch. 32, *Procedure in Trademark Infringement & Unfair Competition Litigation*, §32:18

ANNOTATIONS

Estate of Coll-Monge v. Inner Peace Movement, 524 F.3d 1341, 1347 (D.C.Cir.2008). "Ordinarily, a party establishes ownership of a mark by being the first to use the mark in commerce. Alternatively, the Lanham Act permits an applicant to establish ownership under the 'related companies' doctrine by showing that it controlled the first user of the mark. Under the doctrine of 'related companies,' the first use of a mark by a person controlled by the registrant or applicant for registration of the mark shall inure to the benefit of the controlling entity. *At 1348:* [15 U.S.C. §1055, Lanham Act §5,] does not expressly require formal corporate control, as the district court suggested. Instead, the statute requires control over only the use of a mark with respect to the nature and quality of the goods or services, ... which may include not only corporate control but also licensing agreements and other types of oversight." (Internal quotes omitted.)

Department of Parks & Recreation for the State of Cal. v. Bazaar del Mundo Inc., 448 F.3d 1118, 1125 (9th Cir.2006). "Registration under the Lanham Act has no effect on the registrant's rights under the common law, which requires a mark to have been used in commerce before a protectible ownership interest in the mark arises. 'To acquire ownership of a trademark it is not enough to have invented the mark first or even to have registered it first; the party claiming ownership must have been the first to actually use the mark in the sale of goods or services.'"

§1056. DISCLAIMER OF UNREGISTRABLE MATTER

[LANHAM ACT §6]

(a) Compulsory and voluntary disclaimers.—The Director may require the applicant to disclaim an unregistrable component of a mark otherwise registrable. An applicant may voluntarily disclaim a component of a mark sought to be registered.

(b) Prejudice of rights.—No disclaimer, including those made under section 1057(e) of title 15, shall prejudice or affect the applicant's or registrant's rights then existing or thereafter arising in the disclaimed matter, or his right of registration on another application if the disclaimed matter be or shall have become distinctive of his goods or services.

History of 15 U.S.C. §1056: July 5, 1946, ch. 540, §6, 60 Stat. 429; Oct. 9, 1962, P.L. 87-772, §3, 76 Stat. 769; Nov. 16, 1988, P.L. 100-667, §108, 102 Stat. 3938; Nov. 29, 1999, P.L. 106-113, §1000(a)(9), 113 Stat. 1536.

Treatise Cross-References

McCarthy on Trademark & Unfair Competition

Ch. 11, *The Spectrum of Distinctiveness of Marks*, §§11:26; 11:52
Ch. 19, *Federal Registration of Marks*, §§19:62; 19:67
Ch. 21, *Appeal from Decisions on Trademark Registration*, §21:6

ANNOTATIONS

Boston Duck Tours, LP v. Super Duck Tours, LLC, 531 F.3d 1, 22 (1st Cir.2008). "Although the PTO Examining Attorney is obligated to consider whether a disclaimer is appropriate for each application reviewed, the decision remains a discretionary choice rather than a conclusive legal determination. Therefore, a decision by the PTO to either require a disclaimer or not is merely a single piece of evidence in the court's overall genericism analysis."

In re Slokevage, 441 F.3d 957, 962 (Fed.Cir.2006). "The disclaimer requirement 'provides the benefits of the Lanham Act to applicants for composite marks with unregistrable components' and, at the same time, 'prevents an applicant from claiming exclusive rights to disclaimed portions apart from composite marks.' If a mark is unitary, meaning that it has no 'unregistrable components' and is an 'inseparable whole,' it is exempted from the disclaimer requirement because 'it does not fit within the language of 15 U.S.C. §1056(a) [Lanham Act §6(a)].' A unitary mark creates a 'single and distinct commercial impression.'"

In re Stereotaxis, Inc., 429 F.3d 1039, 1041 (Fed. Cir.2005). "The Director of the [PTO] 'may require the applicant to disclaim an unregistrable component of a mark otherwise registrable.' A mark or component is unregistrable if, 'when used on or in connection with the goods of the applicant,' it is 'merely descriptive ... of them.'"

First Interstate Bancorp v. Stenquist, 16 U.S.P.Q.2d 1704, 1706 (N.D.Cal.1990). "[I]t is well established that where a trademark owner engages in naked licensing, without any control over the quality of goods produced by the licensee, such a practice is inherently deceptive and constitutes abandonment of any rights to the trademark by the licensor."

§1057. CERTIFICATES OF REGISTRATION

[LANHAM ACT §7]

(a) Issuance and form.—Certificates of registration of marks registered upon the principal register shall be issued in the name of the United States of America, under the seal of the United States Patent and Trademark Office, and shall be signed by the Director or have his signature placed thereon, and a record thereof shall be kept in the United States Patent and Trademark Office. The registration shall reproduce the mark, and state that the mark is registered on the principal register under this chapter, the date of the first use of the mark, the date of the first use of the mark in commerce, the particular goods or services for which it is registered, the number and date of the registration, the term thereof, the date on which the application for registration was received in the United States Patent and Trademark Office, and any conditions and limitations that may be imposed in the registration.

(b) Certificate as prima facie evidence.—A certificate of registration of a mark upon the principal register provided by this chapter shall be prima facie evidence of the validity of the registered mark and of the registration of the mark, of the owner's ownership of the mark, and of the owner's exclusive right to use the registered mark in commerce on or in connection with the goods or services specified in the certificate, subject to any conditions or limitations stated in the certificate.

(c) Application to register mark considered constructive use.—Contingent on the registration of a mark on the principal register provided by this chapter, the filing of the application to register such mark shall constitute constructive use of the mark, conferring a right of priority, nationwide in effect, on or in connection with the goods or services specified in the registration against any other person except for a person whose mark has not been abandoned and who, prior to such filing—

(1) has used the mark;

(2) has filed an application to register the mark which is pending or has resulted in registration of the mark; or

(3) has filed a foreign application to register the mark on the basis of which he or she has acquired a right of priority, and timely files an application under section 1126(d) of title 15 to register the mark which is pending or has resulted in registration of the mark.

(d) Issuance to assignee.—A certificate of registration of a mark may be issued to the assignee of the applicant, but the assignment must first be recorded in the United States Patent and Trademark Office. In case of change of ownership the Director shall, at the request of the owner and upon a proper showing and the payment of the prescribed fee, issue to such assignee a new certificate of registration of the said mark in the name of such assignee, and for the unexpired part of the original period.

(e) Surrender, cancellation, or amendment by owner.—Upon application of the owner the Director may permit any registration to be surrendered for cancellation, and upon cancellation appropriate entry shall be made in the records of the United States Patent and Trademark Office. Upon application of the owner and payment of the prescribed fee, the Director for good cause may permit any registration to be amended or to be disclaimed in part: *Provided*, That the amendment or disclaimer does not alter materially the character of the mark. Appropriate entry shall be made in the records of the United States Patent and Trademark Office and upon the certificate of registration.

(f) Copies of United States Patent and Trademark Office records as evidence.—Copies of any records, books, papers, or drawings belonging to the United States Patent and Trademark Office relating to marks, and copies of registrations, when authenticated by the seal of the United States Patent and Trademark Office and certified by the Director, or in his name by an employee of the Office duly designated by the Director, shall be evidence in all cases wherein the originals would be evidence; and any person making application therefor and paying the prescribed fee shall have such copies.

(g) Correction of United States Patent and Trademark Office mistake.—Whenever a material mistake in a registration, incurred through the fault of the United States Patent and Trademark Office, is clearly disclosed by the records of the Office a certificate stating the fact and nature of such mistake shall be issued without charge and recorded and a printed copy thereof shall be attached to each printed copy of the registration and such corrected registration shall thereafter have the same effect as if the same had been originally issued in such corrected form, or in the discretion of the Director a new certificate of registration may be issued without charge. All certificates of correction heretofore issued in accordance with the rules of the United States Patent and Trademark Office and the registrations to which they are attached shall have the same force and effect as if such certificates and their issue had been specifically authorized by statute.

(h) Correction of applicant's mistake.—Whenever a mistake has been made in a registration and a showing has been made that such mistake occurred in good faith through the fault of the applicant, the Director is authorized to issue a certificate of correction or, in his discretion, a new certificate upon the payment of the prescribed fee: *Provided*, That the correction does not involve such changes in the registration as to require republication of the mark.

History of 15 U.S.C. §1057: July 5, 1946, ch. 540, §7, 60 Stat. 430; Aug. 17, 1950, ch. 733, 64 Stat. 459; Oct. 9, 1962, P.L. 87-772, §4, 76 Stat. 769; Jan. 2, 1975, P.L. 93-596, §1, 88 Stat. 1949; Nov. 16, 1988, P.L. 100-667, §109, 102 Stat. 3938; Oct. 30, 1998, P.L. 105-330, §201(a)(3), 112 Stat. 3070; Nov. 29, 1999, P.L. 106-113, §1000(a)(9), 113 Stat. 1536; Mar. 17, 2010, P.L. 111-146, §3(a), 124 Stat. 66.

Treatise Cross-References

McCarthy on Trademark & Unfair Competition

Ch. 11, *The Spectrum of Distinctiveness of Marks*, §11:43
Ch. 16, *Acquisition & Priority of Trademark Rights*, §§16:15-16:17; 16:18.50; 16:19
Ch. 19, *Federal Registration of Marks*, §§19:26; 19:29-19:31.10; 19:36; 19:49; 19:62; 19:133; 19:138; 19:142.75
Ch. 20, *Inter Partes Trademark Proceedings in the Patent & Trademark Office*, §§20:27; 20:28; 20:45; 20:71
Ch. 24, *Infringement by Use of Mark on Noncompetitive Goods or Services*, §24:65
Ch. 26, *The Territorial Extent of Trademark Rights*, §§26:31; 26:37; 26:38; 26:40; 26:44; 26:45; 26:53; 26:54

Ch. 29, *International Aspects of Trademark Law*, §29:21

Ch. 32, *Procedure in Trademark Infringement & Unfair Competition Litigation*, §§32:134-32:136

ANNOTATIONS

§1057(b)

In re Cordua Rests., Inc., 823 F.3d 594, 600 (Fed. Cir.2016). "The presumption of validity of ... §1057(b) does not carry over from registration of the older mark to a new application for registration of another mark that happens to be similar (or even nearly identical). The PTO is required to examine all trademark applications for compliance with each and every eligibility requirement, including non-genericness, even if the PTO earlier mistakenly registered a similar or identical mark suffering the same defect. *At 602:* We agree with [petitioner] that 'a proper genericness inquiry focuses on the description of services set forth in the certificate of registration.' 'The authority is legion that the question of registrability of an applicant's mark must be decided on the basis of the identification of goods set forth in the application regardless of what the record may reveal as to the particular nature of an applicant's goods, the particular channels of trade or the class of purchasers to which sales of the goods are directed.'"

Nola Spice Designs, L.L.C. v. Haydel Enters., 783 F.3d 527, 537 (5th Cir.2015). "The registration of [D's] marks with the PTO is prima facie evidence that the marks are inherently distinctive. However, [P] may rebut this presumption by demonstrating that the marks are not inherently distinctive. The analysis that our circuit follows to determine whether a mark is inherently distinctive differs for word marks and design marks. Therefore, we analyze separately the distinctiveness of [D's] word mark ... and the distinctiveness of its design mark...." *See also* ***Nola Spice Designs, L.L.C. v. Haydel Enters.***, p. 10 (word marks); ***Amazing Spaces, Inc. v. Metro Mini Storage***, p. 11 (design marks).

Amazing Spaces, Inc. v. Metro Mini Storage, 608 F.3d 225, 239 (5th Cir.2010). "[D's] introduction of evidence that the [mark] is not distinctive has reduced the presumption of validity to evidence that the PTO is of the opinion that the [mark] is sufficiently distinctive to be legally protectable as a mark. *At 240:* [A] mark is inherently distinctive if its intrinsic nature serves to identify a particular source. Inherent distinctiveness is attributable to a mark when the mark almost *automatically* tells a customer that it refers to a brand and immediately signals a brand or a product source." (Internal quotes omitted.)

Lahoti v. Vericheck, Inc., 586 F.3d 1190, 1199 (9th Cir.2009). "Although the statutory presumption of distinctiveness [under 15 U.S.C. §1115(a), Lanham Act §33(a),] applies only when the mark holder's own mark has been registered, courts may also defer to the PTO's registration of highly similar marks. In particular, we agree with the Fourth Circuit that nearly identical marks used for similar products may be viewed in a common light when the PTO has found one of them to be suggestive. *At 1200:* However, it should be noted that in some cases a series of prior registrations is evidence of the *descriptiveness* of a mark. [¶] The PTO Appeal Board has cautioned that a third party registration is not 'determinative' of distinctiveness if circumstances have materially changed since the third-party registration or if the registration is distinguishable because it combines one part of the disputed mark in that case with non-descriptive terms."

Emergency One, Inc. v. American Fire Eagle Engine Co., 332 F.3d 264, 269 (4th Cir.2003). Registration "of a trademark under the Lanham Act 'creates a presumption that the registrant is entitled to use the registered mark throughout the nation.' By contrast, a user claiming ownership of a mark under common-law principles does not enjoy the benefit of the presumptions conferred by registration and must 'establish his right to exclusive use'; in effect, registration 'shift[s] the burden of proof from the plaintiff ... to the defendant, who must introduce sufficient evidence to rebut the presumption of plaintiff's right to such [exclusive] use.'" *See also* ***Applied Info. Sci. Corp. v. eBay, Inc.***, 511 F.3d 966, 970 (9th Cir.2007).

U.S. Search, LLC v. US Search.com Inc., 300 F.3d 517, 524 (4th Cir.2002). With "the certificate of registration, 'the registrant obtains prima facie evidence that its mark is not generic in the eyes of the relevant public, and that its mark is not merely descriptive, but at a minimum is descriptive *and* has obtained secondary meaning.' We have held that a district court should not freely substitute its opinion for that of the PTO because a decision to register a mark, without requiring evidence of secondary meaning, is 'powerful evidence that the registered mark is suggestive and not merely descriptive.'"

Aromatique, Inc. v. Gold Seal, Inc., 28 F.3d 863, 869 (8th Cir.1994). "Registered marks ... are presumed to be distinctive and nonfunctional. [T]here is a split in the circuits over whether a party asserting a mark must prove the mark is nonfunctional or whether instead the party seeking to invalidate a mark must prove that it is functional. [W]e have settled the question in this circuit by requiring a party asserting a mark to prove that it is nonfunctional. But in all of those cases the plaintiffs were asserting unregistered marks. [P], as the owner of the registered marks at issue here, is entitled to the presumption that the marks are valid."

Martahus v. Video Duplication Servs., 3 F.3d 417, 421 (Fed.Cir.1993). Since "service mark registrations are presumed valid, one seeking cancellation of such a registration must rebut this presumption by a preponderance of the evidence as in any other cancellation proceeding." *See also* ***Cerveceria Centroamericana, S.A. v. Cerveceria India, Inc.***, 892 F.2d 1021, 1023-24 (Fed.Cir.1989).

DeCosta v. Viacom Int'l, 981 F.2d 602, 606 (1st Cir. 1992). 15 U.S.C. §1057(b), Lanham Act §7(b), "nowhere says that registration makes it easier for a registrant ... to prove that a relevant buying public may confuse some other person's mark with his own. [¶] Nor are we aware of any reason why registration here should significantly affect the proof about confusion. ... The fact of registration, at most, relates to ... the plaintiff's mark's strength."

WSM, Inc. v. Hilton, 724 F.2d 1320, 1326 (8th Cir. 1984). "The statutory presumption [in 15 U.S.C. §1057(b), Lanham Act §7(b),] may be overcome by establishing the generic nature of the mark."

Curtice-Burns, Inc. v. Northwest Sanitation Prods., 530 F.2d 1396, 1399 (C.C.P.A.1976). 15 U.S.C. §1057(b), Lanham Act §7(b), "does not accord 'prima facie effect' to every statement in a certificate of registration; as to ownership, it accords prima facie effect only to the statement of ownership of the mark for which the certificate is issued."

Harod v. Sage Prods., 188 F.Supp.2d 1369, 1375 (S.D.Ga.2002). "[I]f a junior user appropriates the mark in the same geographic area in which the registrant uses the mark, the registrant may be entitled to relief, provided that he has superior ownership rights."

Lucent Info. Mgmt. v. Lucent Tech., 986 F.Supp. 253, 258 (D.Del.1997), *aff'd*, 186 F.3d 311 (3d Cir.1999). Trademark "ownership is not solely established by registration. Trademark ownership is categorized and documented by the registration procedures, but is 'acquired by adoption and use' according to common law traditions. [¶] Determining the amount of activity that constitutes 'adoption and use' involves an inquiry into the facts of each case."

Trustees of Columbia Univ. v. Columbia/HCA Healthcare Corp., 964 F.Supp. 733, 742 (S.D.N.Y. 1997). "Although [P] has obtained federal service mark protection for [its] name ... for educational services, 'the presumption of an exclusive right to use a registered mark extends only to the goods and services noted in a registration certificate.'"

§1057(c)

Allard Enters. v. Advanced Programming Res., 146 F.3d 350, 360-61 (6th Cir.1998). "[Ds] claim only common law trademark rights, while [P] obtained federal registration of its mark. [T]he owner of a federally registered mark may claim constructive use of that mark as of the date of filing of the application for registration. Under this statutory scheme, [Ds'] rights to [their] mark extend only as far as the area where [their] continuous prior use of that mark preempted [P's] constructive use of its mark."

WarnerVision Entm't Inc. v. Empire, Inc., 101 F.3d 259, 260 (2d Cir.1996). "If, but only if, the mark completes the registration process and is registered, the [intent-to-use] applicant is granted a constructive use date retroactive to the [intent-to-use] filing date. This retroactive dating of constructive use permits a more orderly development of the mark without the risk that priority will be lost."

Sengoku Works Ltd. v. RMC Int'l, 96 F.3d 1217, 1219-20 (9th Cir.1996). The "registrant is granted a presumption of ownership, dating to the filing date of the application for federal registration, and the challenger must overcome this presumption by a preponderance of the evidence. However, the non-registrant can rebut this presumption by showing that the registrant had not established valid ownership rights in the mark at the time of registration—in other words, if the non-registrant can show that he used the mark in commerce first, then the registration may be invalidated."

Citicasters Licenses, Inc. v. Cumulus Media, Inc., 189 F.Supp.2d 1372, 1380 (S.D.Ga.2002), *aff'd*, 45 Fed.Appx. 879 (11th Cir.2002) (table case). Registration "gives a trademark holder nationwide rights in the mark. Nevertheless, the holder does not automatically receive the right to enjoin every infringer from using similar marks."

§1058. DURATION, AFFIDAVITS & FEES

[LANHAM ACT §8]

(a) Time periods for required affidavits.—Each registration shall remain in force for 10 years, except that the registration of any mark shall be canceled by the Director unless the owner of the registration files in the United States Patent and Trademark Office affidavits that meet the requirements of subsection (b), within the following time periods:

(1) Within the 1-year period immediately preceding the expiration of 6 years following the date of registration under this Act or the date of the publication under section 1062(c) of title 15.

(2) Within the 1-year period immediately preceding the expiration of 10 years following the date of registration, and each successive 10-year period following the date of registration.

(3) The owner may file the affidavit required under this section within the 6-month grace period immediately following the expiration of the periods established in paragraphs (1) and (2), together with the fee described in subsection (b) and the additional grace period surcharge prescribed by the Director.

(b) Requirements for affidavit.—The affidavit referred to in subsection (a) shall—

(1)(A) state that the mark is in use in commerce;

(B) set forth the goods and services recited in the registration on or in connection with which the mark is in use in commerce;

(C) be accompanied by such number of specimens or facsimiles showing current use of the mark in commerce as may be required by the Director; and

(D) be accompanied by the fee prescribed by the Director; or

(2)(A) set forth the goods and services recited in the registration on or in connection with which the mark is not in use in commerce;

(B) include a showing that any nonuse is due to special circumstances which excuse such nonuse and is not due to any intention to abandon the mark; and

(C) be accompanied by the fee prescribed by the Director.

(c) Deficient affidavit.—If any submission filed within the period set forth in subsection (a) is deficient, including that the affidavit was not filed in the name of the owner of the registration, the deficiency may be corrected after the statutory time period, within the time prescribed after notification of the deficiency. Such submission shall be accompanied by the additional deficiency surcharge prescribed by the Director.

(d) Notice of requirement.—Special notice of the requirement for such affidavit shall be attached to each certificate of registration and notice of publication under section 1062(c) of title 15.

(e) Notification of acceptance or refusal.—The Director shall notify any owner who files any affidavit required by this section of the Director's acceptance or refusal thereof and, in the case of a refusal, the reasons therefor.

(f) Designation of resident for service of process and notices.—If the owner is not domiciled in the United States, the owner may designate, by a document filed in the United States Patent and Trademark Office, the name and address of a person resident in the United States on whom may be served notices or process in proceedings affecting the mark. Such notices or process may be served upon the person so designated by leaving with that person or mailing to that person a copy thereof at the address specified in the last designation so filed. If the person so designated cannot be found at the last designated address, or if the owner does not designate by a document filed in the United States Patent and Trademark Office the name and address of a person resident in the United States on whom may be served notices or process in proceedings affecting the mark, such notices or process may be served on the Director.

History of 15 U.S.C. §1058: July 5, 1946, ch. 540, §8, 60 Stat. 431; Jan. 2, 1975, P.L. 93-596, §1, 88 Stat. 1949; Aug. 27, 1982, P.L. 97-247, §8, 96 Stat. 320; Nov. 16, 1988, P.L. 100-667, §110, 102 Stat. 3939; Oct. 30, 1998, P.L. 105-330, §105, 112 Stat. 3066; Nov. 29, 1999, P.L. 106-113, §1000(a)(9), 113 Stat. 1536; Nov. 2, 2002, P.L. 107-273, §13207(b)(3), 116 Stat. 1906; Mar. 17, 2010, P.L. 111-146, §3(d)(1), 124 Stat. 67.

Treatise Cross-References

McCarthy on Trademark & Unfair Competition

Ch. 5, *Historical Basis of Trademarks & Legislative History*, §5:10
Ch. 19, *Federal Registration of Marks*, §§19:133-19:140; 19:142.25; 19:142.75
Ch. 20, *Inter Partes Trademark Proceedings in the Patent & Trademark Office*, §20:58
Ch. 21, *Appeal from Decisions on Trademark Registration*, §21:10
Ch. 29, *International Aspects of Trademark Law*, §29:14
Ch. 31, *Defenses to Infringement of Trademarks*, §§31:79-31:81

§1059. RENEWAL OF REGISTRATION [LANHAM ACT §9]

(a) Period of renewal; time for renewal.—Subject to the provisions of section 1058 of title 15, each registration may be renewed for periods of 10 years at the end of each successive 10-year period following the date of registration upon payment of the prescribed fee and the filing of a written application, in such form as may be prescribed by the Director. Such application may be made at any time within 1 year before the end of each successive 10-year period for which the registration was issued or renewed, or it may be made within a grace period of 6 months after the end of each successive 10-year period, upon payment of a fee and surcharge prescribed therefor. If any application filed under this section is deficient, the deficiency may be corrected within the time prescribed after notification of the deficiency, upon payment of a surcharge prescribed therefor.

(b) Notification of refusal of renewal.—If the Director refuses to renew the registration, the Director shall notify the registrant of the Commissioner's[1] refusal and the reasons therefor.

(c) Designation of resident for service of process and notices.—If the registrant is not domiciled in the United States the registrant may designate, by a document filed in the United States Patent and Trademark Office, the name and address of a person resident in the United States on whom may be served notices or process in proceedings affecting the mark. Such notices or process may be served upon the person so designated by leaving with that person or mailing to that person a copy thereof at the address specified in the last designation so filed. If the person so designated cannot be found at the address given in the last designation, or if the registrant does not designate by a document filed in the United States Patent and Trademark Office the name and address of a person resident in the United States on whom may be served notices or process in proceedings affecting the mark, such notices or process may be served on the Director.

1. **Editor's note:** Probably should be "Director's."

History of 15 U.S.C. §1059: July 5, 1946, ch. 540, §9, 60 Stat. 431; Oct. 9, 1962, P.L. 87-772, §5, 76 Stat. 770; Nov. 16, 1988, P.L. 100-667, §111, 102 Stat. 3939; Oct. 30, 1998, P.L. 105-330, §106, 112 Stat. 3067; Nov. 29, 1999, P.L. 106-113, §1000(a)(9), 113 Stat. 1536; Nov. 2, 2002, P.L. 107-273, §13207(b)(4), 116 Stat. 1907.

Treatise Cross-References

McCarthy on Trademark & Unfair Competition

Ch. 5, *Historical Basis of Trademarks & Legislative History*, §5:10
Ch. 19, *Federal Registration of Marks*, §§19:133; 19:134; 19:142.25; 19:142.75
Ch. 20, *Inter Partes Trademark Proceedings in the Patent & Trademark Office*, §20:58
Ch. 32, *Procedure in Trademark Infringement & Unfair Competition Litigation*, §32:152

§1060. ASSIGNMENT [LANHAM ACT §10]

(a)(1) A registered mark or a mark for which an application to register has been filed shall be assignable with the good will of the business in which the mark is used, or with that part of the good will of the business connected with the use of and symbolized by the mark. Notwithstanding the preceding sentence, no application to register a mark under section 1051(b) of title 15 shall be assignable prior to the filing of an amendment under section 1051(c) of title 15 to bring the application into conformity with section 1051(a) of title 15 or the filing of the verified statement of use under section 1051(d) of title 15, except for an assignment to a successor to the business of the applicant, or portion thereof, to which the mark pertains, if that business is ongoing and existing.

(2) In any assignment authorized by this section, it shall not be necessary to include the good will of the business connected with the use of and symbolized by any other mark used in the business or by the name or style under which the business is conducted.

(3) Assignments shall be by instruments in writing duly executed. Acknowledgment shall be prima facie evidence of the execution of an assignment, and when the prescribed information reporting the assignment is recorded in the United States Patent and Trademark Office, the record shall be prima facie evidence of execution.

(4) An assignment shall be void against any subsequent purchaser for valuable consideration without notice, unless the prescribed information reporting the assignment is recorded in the United States Patent and Trademark Office within 3 months after the date of the assignment or prior to the subsequent purchase.

(5) The United States Patent and Trademark Office shall maintain a record of information on assignments, in such form as may be prescribed by the Director.

(b) An assignee not domiciled in the United States may designate by a document filed in the United States Patent and Trademark Office the name and address of a person resident in the United States on whom may be served notices or process in proceedings affecting the mark. Such notices or process may be served upon the person so designated by leaving with that person or mailing to that person a copy thereof at the address specified in the last designation so filed. If the person so designated cannot be found at the address given in the last designation, or if the assignee does not designate by a document filed in the United States Patent and Trademark Office the name and address of a person resident in the United States on whom may be served notices or process in proceedings affecting the mark, such notices or process may be served upon the Director.

History of 15 U.S.C. §1060: July 5, 1946, ch. 540, §10, 60 Stat. 431; Oct. 9, 1962, P.L. 87-772, §6, 76 Stat. 770; Jan. 2, 1975, P.L. 93-596, §1, 88 Stat. 1949; Nov. 16, 1988, P.L. 100-667, §112, 102 Stat. 3937; Oct. 30, 1998, P.L. 105-330, §107, 112 Stat. 3068; Aug. 5, 1999, P.L. 106-43, §6(a), 113 Stat. 220; Nov. 29, 1999, P.L. 106-113, §1000(a)(9), 113 Stat. 1536; Nov. 2, 2002, P.L. 107-273, §13207(b)(5), 116 Stat. 1907.

See also 10 U.S.C. §2260; 11 U.S.C. §365; 15 U.S.C. §3501; 26 U.S.C. §1253.

Treatise Cross-References

McCarthy on Trademark & Unfair Competition

Ch. 18, *Assignment & Licensing of Trademarks*, §§18:2; 18:7; 18:10; 18:11; 18:13; 18:21; 18:43

ANNOTATIONS

Generally

Brennan's Inc. v. Dickie Brennan & Co., 376 F.3d 356, 364 (5th Cir.2004). "A license gives one party the right to use another party's mark (i.e., to engage in otherwise infringing activity), generally in exchange for a royalty or other payment. [A] consent-to-use agreement [i]s not an attempt to transfer or license the use of a trademark ... but fixes and defines the existing trademark of each [so] that confusion and infringement may be prevented. Courts ordinarily will not find a licensing relationship when an authorization of trademark use is structured in such a way as to avoid misleading or confusing consumers as to the origin and/or nature of the respective parties' goods. [¶] With regard to licenses, the prevailing view is that one who exceeds the scope of the license is potentially liable not just for breach of the license agreement but also for trademark infringement." (Internal quotes omitted.)

Defiance Button Mach. Co. v. C&C Metal Prods., 759 F.2d 1053, 1059 (2d Cir.1985). A mark "ceases to be enforceable against others when it loses its significance as an indication of the origin of goods sold by and associated with the mark owner, such as when the owner makes the mark the subject of an unrestricted license or sale to others, or the owner assigns the mark without the goodwill associated with it. Under such circumstances the mark is held to have been abandoned for the reason that there 'are no rights in a trademark apart from the business with which the mark has been associated' and the '[u]se of the mark by the assignee in connection with a different goodwill and different product would result in a fraud on the purchasing public who reasonably assume that the mark signifies the same thing, whether used by one person or another.'"

EH Yacht, LLC v. Egg Harbor, LLC, 84 F.Supp.2d 556, 567-68 (D.N.J.2000). "It is well established that the law makes no distinction between voluntary and involuntary sales of trademarks, and that a trademark can be sold by a legal representative of the business when insolvent. Where the trademark involved is not a personal one and the transfer is made by operation of law through bankruptcy or a general assignment for the benefit of creditors, most courts have held that a trustee in bankruptcy has the power to sell the goodwill of a company and its symbolic trademarks with other assets of the bankrupt. If the goodwill and marks have been validly assigned, albeit by operation of law via bankruptcy, the mark and good will then may be sold by the trustee in bankruptcy, and the buyer has superior rights to the marks than does the bankrupt."

N.C.P. Mktg. Grp. v. Blanks, 337 B.R. 230, 236 (Bankr.D.Nev.2005), *aff'd*, 279 Fed.Appx. 561 (9th Cir.2008). "Because the owner of the trademark has an interest in the party to whom the trademark is assigned so that it can maintain the good will, quality, and value of its products and thereby its trademark, trademark rights are personal to the assignee and not freely assignable to a third party. *At 237:* Because we find that under applicable trademark law, trademarks are personal and non-assignable without the consent of the licensor, [trademark owner's] trademark would be unassumable as part of the bankruptcy estate of [D] without [trademark owner's] consent."

Goodwill

Berni v. International Gourmet Rests., Inc., 838 F.2d 642, 646 (2d Cir.1988). "[T]he transfer of a trademark or trade name without the attendant goodwill of the business which it represents is, in general, an invalid, 'in gross' transfer of rights." *See also* ***Sugar Busters LLC v. Brennan***, 177 F.3d 258, 262 (5th Cir.1999); ***In re Cult Awareness Network, Inc.***, 151 F.3d 605, 608 n.1 (7th Cir.1998).

In re Roman Cleanser Co., 802 F.2d 207, 208 (6th Cir.1986). "The issue here is whether a security interest in a trademark constitutes an impermissible 'assignment in gross' under the [Lanham] Act if the security interest fails to cover machinery and equipment needed to produce the trademarked goods. We hold that it does not.... *At 209:* We are of the opinion that the 'goodwill' spoken of in the statute does not mean machinery, and that the transfer of formulas and customer lists, both classic elements of goodwill, along with the trademarks satisfies the statutory requirement." *See also* ***Greenlon, Inc. v. Greenlawn, Inc.***, 542 F.Supp. 890, 895 (S.D.Ohio 1982).

Pilates, Inc. v. Current Concepts, Inc., 120 F.Supp.2d 286, 310 (S.D.N.Y.2000). "Good will is 'the value attributable to a going concern apart from its physical [assets]—the intangible worth of buyer momentum emanating from the reputation and integrity earned by the company. A trademark or service mark is merely the symbol by which the public recognizes that reputation and hence has no independent significance apart from the owner's good will.'"

In Writing

TMT N. Am., Inc. v. Magic Touch GmbH, 124 F.3d 876, 884 (7th Cir.1997). "Assignments of trademark rights do not have to be in writing, but an 'implied agreement to transfer' [such as in a distributorship agreement] requires conduct manifesting agreement, not just conduct that might be characterized as being shady or otherwise inequitable. Indeed, one prominent trademark commentator suggests that without documentary evidence, an assignment 'may be proven by the clear and uncontradicted oral testimony of a person in a position to have actual knowledge.'" *But see* ***UBU/Elements, Inc. v. Elements Pers. Care, Inc.***, No. 16-2559 (E.D.Pa.2016) (memo op.; 8-19-16) (footnote 1; holding ***TMT*** was wrongly decided based on misreading of trademark treatise's discussion of common-law trademarks).

Initial Ownership

Premier Dental Prods. v. Darby Dental Sup. Co., 794 F.2d 850, 856 (3d Cir.1986). "[W]hile the identity of the party exercising day-to-day control over the quality of a product is often relevant to trademark analysis, it is not essential that one perform this function to own a trademark. As we have earlier observed, one need not manufacture a product to possess goodwill in it. In particular, it has been consistently held that if an exclusive distributor is known as the exclusive domestic source and as the one who stands behind the product in this country, it may own and enforce the trademark." *See also* ***E.&J. Gallo Winery v. Gallo Cattle Co.***, 967 F.2d 1280, 1289 (9th Cir.1992).

Jurisdiction

Federal Treasury Enter. Sojuzplodoimport v. Spirits Int'l, 623 F.3d 61, 69 (2d Cir.2010). "[W]e ... consider whether [P] brought a proper challenge, in the proper forum, to [the] assignment. [Ds] essentially contend that [P] can only bring a state-law claim to challenge that assignment, and that, consequently, [P] has no federal claim. We reject that contention. We accept the premise that state law (or possibly Russian law) may govern the validity of the assignment.... However, we note that ownership of the relevant trademark is one of the 'necessary elements ... of trademark infringement under the Lanham Act.' Accordingly, federal courts may, applying the relevant law, adjudicate the ownership of a trademark as part of an infringement claim."

Licensor's Supervision

Miller v. Glenn Miller Prods., 454 F.3d 975, 992 (9th Cir.2006). "[W]hen the owner of a trademark licenses the mark to others, he retains a 'duty to exercise control and supervision over the licensee's use of the mark.' However, a provision recognizing the licensor's supervision and control is not an essential element of a trademark license. A license agreement need not contain an express quality control provision because trademark law, rather than the contract itself, confers on the licensor the right and obligation to exercise quality control. *At 993:* [A] trademark licensee ... may not sublicense without express permission from the original licensor."

Department of Parks & Recreation for the State of Cal. v. Bazaar del Mundo Inc., 448 F.3d 1118, 1131 (9th Cir.2006). Petitioner "posits that the quality-control provisions set forth in the Concession Agreement demonstrate the existence of an implied license because well-established trademark law imposes a duty upon the licensor to retain sufficient control over the mark to prevent public deception. 'The purpose of a trademark ... is to identify a good or service to the consumer, and identity implies consistency and a correlative duty to make sure that the good or service really is of consistent quality, i.e., really is the same good or service.' Without such control, 'the risk that the public will be unwittingly deceived will be increased [and] the only effective way to protect the public ... is to place on the licensor the affirmative duty of policing in a reasonable manner the activities of his licensees.' Because naked and uncontrolled licensing is 'inherently deceptive,' [petitioner] must have exercised a high degree of control and supervision over [respondent's] provision of restaurant services under the marks to even assert this basis for proving an implied licensing arrangement. *At 1132:* Here, however, [petitioner] points to no evidence revealing any effort to monitor or sample the quality of [respondent's] food and service. Nor is there any evidence that [petitioner] justifiably relied on [respondent's] reputation or had established a close working relationship with it to make a formal quality-control agreement unnecessary." *See also* ***Dawn Donut Co. v. Hart's Food Stores***, 267 F.2d 358, 367 (2d Cir.1959).

Prima Facie Evidence

Federal Treasury Enter. Sojuzplodoimport v. Spirits Int'l, 623 F.3d 61, 68 (2d Cir.2010). "Prima facie evidence of execution is not the same as conclusive evidence of the validity of an assignment. As the PTO has stated, '[t]he mere act of recording [an assignment] document is a ministerial act,' and '[t]he Assignment Branch [of PTO] does not examine the substance of the transaction'; rather, it records any assignment 'that appears on its face to be an assignment.' 'Since the act of recording a document is not a determination of the document's validity,' the existence of a recorded assignment 'does not preclude a party from ... establishing its ownership of the mark in a proper forum, *such as a federal court*.' If the mere fact that the registrant satisfied the requirements for incontestability could preclude [P's] claim, then incontestability would transform recording—a ministerial act—into a mechanism for conclusively defeating allegations (which must be credited on a motion to dismiss) challenging the legality of the assignment."

§1061. EXECUTION OF ACKNOWLEDGMENTS & VERIFICATIONS

[LANHAM ACT §11]

Acknowledgments and verifications required under this chapter may be made before any person within the United States authorized by law to administer oaths, or, when made in a foreign country, before any diplomatic or consular officer of the United States or before any official authorized to administer oaths in the foreign country concerned whose authority is proved by a certificate of a diplomatic or consular officer of the United States, or apostille of an official designated by a foreign country which, by treaty or convention, accords like effect to apostilles of designated officials in the United States, and shall be valid if they comply with the laws of the state or country where made.

History of 15 U.S.C. §1061: July 5, 1946, ch. 540, §11, 60 Stat. 432; Aug. 27, 1982, P.L. 97-247, §14(c), 96 Stat. 321.

§1062. PUBLICATION

[LANHAM ACT §12]

(a) Examination and publication.—Upon the filing of an application for registration and payment of the prescribed fee, the Director shall refer the application to the examiner in charge of the registration of marks, who shall cause an examination to be made and, if on such examination it shall appear that the applicant is entitled to registration, or would be entitled to registration upon the acceptance of the statement of use required by section 1051(d) of title 15, the Director shall cause the mark to be published in the Official Gazette of the Patent and Trademark Office: *Provided*, That in the case of an applicant claiming concurrent use, or in the case of an application to be placed in an interference as provided for in section 1066 of title 15, the mark if otherwise registrable, may be published subject to the determination of the rights of the parties to such proceedings.

(b) Refusal of registration; amendment of application; abandonment.—If the applicant is found not entitled to registration, the examiner shall advise the applicant thereof and of the reasons therefor. The applicant shall have a period of six months in which to reply or amend his application, which shall then be reexamined. This procedure may be repeated until (1) the examiner finally refuses registration of the mark or (2) the applicant fails for a period of six months to reply or amend or appeal, whereupon the application shall be deemed to have been abandoned, unless it can be shown to the satisfaction of the Director that the delay in responding was unintentional, whereupon such time may be extended.

(c) Republication of marks registered under prior acts.—A registrant of a mark registered under the provisions of the Act of March 3, 1881, or the Act of February 20, 1905, may, at any time prior to the expiration of the registration thereof, upon the payment of the prescribed fee file with the Director an affidavit setting forth those goods stated in the registration on which said mark is in use in commerce and that the registrant claims the benefits of this chapter for said mark. The Director shall publish notice thereof with a reproduction of said mark in the Official Gazette, and notify the registrant of such publication and of the requirement for the affidavit of use or nonuse as provided for in subsection (b) of section 1058 of this title. Marks published under this subsection shall not be subject to the provisions of section 1063 of this title.

History of 15 U.S.C. §1062: July 5, 1946, ch. 540, §12, 60 Stat. 432; Oct. 9, 1962, P.L. 87-772, §7, 76 Stat. 770; Jan. 2, 1975, P.L. 93-596, §1, 88 Stat. 1949; Nov. 16, 1988, P.L. 100-667, §113, 102 Stat. 3940; Oct. 30, 1998, P.L. 105-330, §104, 112 Stat. 3066; Nov. 29, 1999, P.L. 106-113, §1000(a)(9), 113 Stat. 1536.

Treatise Cross-References

McCarthy on Trademark & Unfair Competition

Ch. 19, *Federal Registration of Marks*, §19:125
Ch. 26, *The Territorial Extent of Trademark Rights*, §26:43

ANNOTATIONS

Genesee Brewing Co. v. Stroh Brewing Co., 124 F.3d 137, 148 n.11 (2d Cir.1997). "[A] trademark examiner may not send a mark to publication unless all unprotectable matter has been disclaimed."

Rolley, Inc. v. Younghusband, 204 F.2d 209, 211 (9th Cir.1953). "Upon registration the presumption as to date of first use by the registrant has been held to extend back to the filing date...."

Boyle v. U.S., 51 U.S.P.Q.2d 1585, 1589 (Fed.Cl. 1999), *aff'd*, 200 F.3d 1369 (Fed.Cir.2000). "The PTO's role in approving a registration is limited to reviewing the appropriateness of the service mark under specified standards and to determining whether there are similar pre-existing marks that could be confused with the proposed mark."

§1063. OPPOSITION TO REGISTRATION [LANHAM ACT §13]

(a) Any person who believes that he would be damaged by the registration of a mark upon the principal register, including the registration of any mark which would be likely to cause dilution by blurring or dilution by tarnishment under section 1125(c) of title 15, may, upon payment of the prescribed fee, file an opposition in the Patent and Trademark Office, stating the grounds therefor, within thirty days after the publication under subsection (a) of section 1062 of title 15 of the mark sought to be registered. Upon written request prior to the expiration of the thirty-day period, the time for filing opposition shall be extended for an additional thirty days, and further extensions of time for filing opposition may be granted by the Director for good cause when requested prior to the expiration of an extension. The Director shall notify the applicant of each extension of the time for filing opposition. An opposition may be amended under such conditions as may be prescribed by the Director.

(b) Unless registration is successfully opposed—

(1) a mark entitled to registration on the principal register based on an application filed under section 1051(a) of title 15 or pursuant to section 1126 of title 15 shall be registered in the Patent and Trademark Office, a certificate of registration shall be issued, and notice of the registration shall be published in the Official Gazette of the Patent and Trademark Office; or

(2) a notice of allowance shall be issued to the applicant if the applicant applied for registration under section 1051(b) of title 15.

History of 15 U.S.C. §1063: July 5, 1946, ch. 540, §13, 60 Stat. 433; Oct. 9, 1962, P.L. 87-772, §8, 76 Stat. 771; Jan. 2, 1975, P.L. 93-596, §1, 88 Stat. 1949; Jan. 2, 1975, P.L. 93-600, §1, 88 Stat. 1955; Aug. 27, 1982, P.L. 97-247, §9(a), 96 Stat. 320; Nov. 16, 1988, P.L. 100-667, §114, 102 Stat. 3940; Aug. 5, 1999, P.L. 106-43, §2(b), 113 Stat. 218; Nov. 29, 1999, P.L. 106-113, §1000(a)(9), 113 Stat. 1536; Oct. 6, 2006, P.L. 109-312, §3(b), 120 Stat. 1732.

See also 37 C.F.R. §§2.101-2.107, 2.116-2.136.

Treatise Cross-References

McCarthy on Trademark & Unfair Competition

Ch. 20, *Inter Partes Trademark Proceedings in the Patent & Trademark Office*, §§20:7; 20:13; 20:38

ANNOTATIONS

Generally

Mayer/Berkshire Corp. v. Berkshire Fashions, Inc., 424 F.3d 1229, 1234 (Fed.Cir.2005). Opponent to registration "presented evidence of changed circumstances in the five-year period after the district court's judgment [that registrants' mark did not infringe opponent's mark] that may be relevant to the issue of likelihood of confusion in the opposition proceeding, again rendering preclusion improper. [¶] Caution is warranted in the application of preclusion [by res judicata or collateral estoppel] by the PTO, for the purposes of administrative trademark procedures include protecting both the consuming public and the purveyors. Thus the party objecting to a registration may raise grounds not only of commercial injury to itself, but of confusion or deception or mistake to the consumer."

Enterprise Rent-A-Car Co. v. Advantage Rent-A-Car, Inc., 330 F.3d 1333, 1334-35 (Fed.Cir.2003). "[T]he owner of a famous mark cannot oppose registration based on dilution where its mark did not achieve fame prior to the applicant's prior use in a limited geographic area, and ... a trademark holder cannot oppose registration based on claims of dilution under state law. *At 1343:* Section 1063 does not provide for concurrent use registrations, an omission that must be seen as a deliberate choice made by Congress. It is not the province of this court or of the [TTAB] to read a new provision into the [Federal Trademark Dilution Act] to the effect that the [TTAB] may grant concurrent use registrations to avoid trademark dilution."

Eastman Kodak Co. v. Bell & Howell Document Mgmt. Prods., 994 F.2d 1569, 1575 (Fed.Cir.1993). "[T]he legislative history clearly shows that Congress considered the problem of placing the opposition proceeding of intent-to-use marks before actual use had occurred, but still *chose to* position the proceedings at that point in time for policy reasons. [T]he statute makes clear that the opposition proceedings occur before the statement of use is filed by the applicant...."

Money Store v. Harriscorp Fin., Inc., 689 F.2d 666, 671 (7th Cir.1982). "Nowhere does the Lanham Act specifically mandate a preapplication search by one who seeks federal registration of a mark. [¶] Placing the burden of investigation on a junior user makes a senior user's early opposition to registration unnecessary. The senior user can even challenge the junior user's registration *after* five years because a fraudulently obtained mark is not protected by the incontestability provision."

Intent to Use

M.Z. Berger & Co. v. Swatch AG, 787 F.3d 1368, 1375 (Fed.Cir.2015). "[W]e ... address the issue of whether lack of a bona fide intent is proper statutory grounds on which to challenge a trademark application. The PTO has long held that lack of such intent is a proper basis on which an opposer can challenge an applicant's registration. We agree. An opposer is 'entitled to rely on any statutory ground which negates appellant's right to the subject registration[.]' Because a bona fide intent to use the mark in commerce is a statutory requirement of a valid intent-to-use trademark application under [Lanham Act] §1(b) [15 U.S.C. §1051(b)], the lack of such intent is a basis on which an opposer may challenge an applicant's mark. We note that the one other circuit court to address this issue has likewise so held." *See also* ***Aktieselskabet AF21. Nov. 2001 v. Fame Jeans Inc.***, 525 F.3d 8, 21 (D.C.Cir.2008).

Standing

Coach Servs. v. Triumph Learning LLC, 668 F.3d 1356, 1376 (Fed.Cir.2012). "Standing is a question of law that this court reviews *de novo*."

Ritchie v. Simpson, 170 F.3d 1092, 1096-97 (Fed. Cir.1999). "In no case has this court ever held that one must have a specific commercial interest, not shared by the general public, in order to have standing as an opposer. Nor have we ever held that being a member of a group with many members is itself disqualifying. The crux of the matter is not how many others share one's belief that one will be damaged by the registration, but whether that belief is reasonable and reflects a real interest in the issue."

In re Mavety Media Grp., 33 F.3d 1367, 1374 (Fed. Cir.1994). The TTAB "has held that under ... §1063(a), any person who *believes* that he would be damaged by registration of a mark upon the principal register, thus including interested members of the composite of the general public, has standing to challenge registration in an opposition proceeding. Indeed, such a procedure establishes a meaningful opportunity for response by the applicant with evidence that a substantial composite of the general public would not consider the mark at issue scandalous in the context of contemporary attitudes and the relevant marketplace."

Otto Roth & Co. v. Universal Foods Corp., 640 F.2d 1317, 1319 (C.C.P.A.1981). 15 U.S.C. §1063, Lanham Act §13, "does not require that actual damage be proved before an opposition is sustained, 'nor does it provide that anyone who shows that he will be damaged by the registration will necessarily succeed in preventing registration.'" *See also* ***American Novawood Corp. v. U.S. Plywood-Champion Papers, Inc.***, 426 F.2d 823, 827-28 (C.C.P.A.1970).

Universal Oil Prods. v. Rexall Drug & Chem. Co., 463 F.2d 1122, 1124 (C.C.P.A.1972). "As the parent corporation of a wholly owned subsidiary, [opposer to registration] can reasonably believe that damage to the subsidiary will naturally lead to financial injury to itself. ... We conclude that [opposer to registration] has a real interest in this proceeding and therefore standing to institute and maintain it."

Use

First Niagara Ins. Brokers, Inc. v. First Niagara Fin. Grp., 476 F.3d 867, 870-71 (Fed.Cir.2007). "In the proceedings below, the [TTAB] based its [decision to dismiss foreign opposer's opposition to mark] on the assumption that an 'opposer's claim of prior use can succeed only if it has proved use of its marks in connection with services rendered in commerce lawfully regulated by Congress, as required under [Lanham Act] §45 ..., 15 U.S.C. §1127.' Such an assumption was unwarranted, however, in light of the plain language of the statute, which merely requires the prior mark to have been 'used in the U.S. by another.' ... Thus, a foreign opposer can present its opposition on the merits by showing only *use* of its mark in the U.S."

CreAgri, Inc. v. USANA Health Sci., Inc., 474 F.3d 626, 628 (9th Cir.2007). "[I]n order to acquire priority, a 'use in commerce' means a lawful use—here, a use compliant with federal labeling requirements. *At 634:* [T]he district court correctly cancelled [mark] from the supplemental register. A mark is only eligible for supplemental registration if it was in 'lawful use in commerce' prior to the date on which the holder applied for such registration." *See also* ***United Phosphorus Ltd. v. Midland Fumigant, Inc.***, 205 F.3d 1219, 1225 (10th Cir.2000).

Bourns, Inc. v. International Resistance Co., 341 F.2d 146, 147 (C.C.P.A.1965). "It is not necessary ... for an opposer [to registration] to aver and prove use of the mark in interstate commerce."

Truescents LLC v. Ride Skin Care, LLC, 81 U.S.P.Q.2d 1334, 1337-38 (T.T.A.B.2006). Held: Ownership of five marks that use "Genuine" did not create a family of marks because the goods were never advertised or marketed as a group and purchasers would not recognize "Genuine" as a surname for registration opposer's line of skin care products. Registration opposer's use did not qualify as family use under the test in ***Land-O-Nod Co. v. Paulison***, 220 U.S.P.Q. 61 (T.T.A.B.1983). The test is whether the marks are used and promoted together "in such a manner as to create public recognition coupled with an association of common origin predicated on the 'family,'" and the claimed "family" must be distinctive.

§1064. CANCELLATION OF REGISTRATION

[LANHAM ACT §14]

A petition to cancel a registration of a mark, stating the grounds relied upon, may, upon payment of the prescribed fee, be filed as follows by any person who believes that he is or will be damaged, including as a result of a likelihood of dilution by blurring or dilution by tarnishment under section 1125(c) of title 15, by the registration of a mark on the principal register established by this chapter, or under the Act of March 3, 1881, or the Act of February 20, 1905:

(1) Within five years from the date of the registration of the mark under this chapter.

(2) Within five years from the date of publication under section 1062(c) of title 15 of a mark registered under the Act of March 3, 1881, or the Act of February 20, 1905.

(3) At any time if the registered mark becomes the generic name for the goods or services, or a portion thereof, for which it is registered, or is functional, or has been abandoned, or its registration was obtained fraudulently or contrary to the provisions of section 1054 of title 15 or of subsection (a), (b), or (c) of section 1052 of title 15 for a registration under this chapter, or contrary to similar prohibitory provisions of such prior Acts for a registration under such Acts, or if the registered mark is being used by, or with the permission of, the registrant so as to misrepresent the source of the goods or services on or in connection with which the mark is used. If the registered mark becomes the generic name for less than all of the goods or services for which it is registered, a petition to cancel the registration for only those goods or services may be filed. A registered mark shall not be deemed to be the generic name of goods or services solely because such mark is also used as a name of or to identify a unique product or service. The primary significance of the registered mark to the relevant public rather than purchaser motivation shall be the test for determining whether the registered mark has become the generic name of goods or services on or in connection with which it has been used.

(4) At any time if the mark is registered under the Act of March 3, 1881, or the Act of February 20, 1905, and has not been published under the provisions of section 1062(c) of title 15.

(5) At any time in the case of a certification mark on the ground that the registrant (A) does not control, or is not able legitimately to exercise control over, the use of such mark, or (B) engages in the production or marketing of any goods or services to which the certification mark is applied, or (C) permits the use of the certification mark for purposes other than to certify, or

(D) discriminately refuses to certify or to continue to certify the goods or services of any person who maintains the standards or conditions which such mark certifies:

Provided, That the Federal Trade Commission may apply to cancel on the grounds specified in paragraphs (3) and (5) of this section any mark registered on the principal register established by this chapter, and the prescribed fee shall not be required.

Nothing in paragraph (5) shall be deemed to prohibit the registrant from using its certification mark in advertising or promoting recognition of the certification program or of the goods or services meeting the certification standards of the registrant. Such uses of the certification mark shall not be grounds for cancellation under paragraph (5), so long as the registrant does not itself produce, manufacture, or sell any of the certified goods or services to which its identical certification mark is applied.

History of 15 U.S.C. §1064: July 5, 1946, ch. 540, §14, 60 Stat. 433; Oct. 9, 1962, P.L. 87-772, §9, 76 Stat. 771; Aug. 27, 1982, P.L. 97-247, §9(b), 96 Stat. 320; Nov. 8, 1984, P.L. 98-620, §102, 98 Stat. 3335; Nov. 16, 1988, P.L. 100-667, §115, 102 Stat. 3940; Oct. 30, 1998, P.L. 105-330, §§201(a)(4), 301, 112 Stat. 3070; Aug. 5, 1999, P.L. 106-43, §2(c), 113 Stat. 218; Oct. 6, 2006, P.L. 109-312, §3(c), 120 Stat. 1732.

See also 37 C.F.R. §§2.111-2.136.

Treatise Cross-References

McCarthy on Trademark & Unfair Competition

Ch. 5, *Historical Basis of Trademarks & Legislative History*, §§5:8; 5:10
Ch. 12, *Generic Terms*, §§12:7; 12:21; 12:41; 12:56; 12:57; 12:60; 12:64
Ch. 18, *Assignment & Licensing of Trademarks*, §18:48
Ch. 19, *Federal Registration of Marks*, §§19:90; 19:92
Ch. 20, *Inter Partes Trademark Proceedings in the Patent & Trademark Office*, §§20:52; 20:60; 20:61; 20:62; 20:63; 20:67
Ch. 30, *Remedies for Trademark Infringement & Unfair Competition*, §§30:109; 30:110; 30:112
Ch. 31, *Defenses to Infringement of Trademarks*, §§31:59; 31:80; 31:89; 31:147

ANNOTATIONS

Generally

Patsy's Italian Rest., Inc. v. Banas, 658 F.3d 254, 266 (2d Cir.2011). "Local rights owned by another have been consistently viewed as sufficient to prevent a party from obtaining registration of a federal mark. [¶] Because registration of a federal mark confers upon the owner of the mark a presumption that the owner has the exclusive right to use the mark nationwide, … it is proper to consider the rights of users nationwide when determining whether a party is entitled to registration of their mark. [¶] In these circumstances, the principles applicable to the initial registrability of a mark should also be applied to a claim seeking the cancellation of a registration that has not yet become incontestable pursuant to [15 U.S.C.] §1065 [Lanham Act §15]."

Nasalok Coating Corp. v. Nylok Corp., 522 F.3d 1320, 1328 (Fed.Cir.2008). An earlier default judgment on infringement against P precluded a trademark cancellation action at the PTO because "challenges to the validity of a trademark registration should not be treated as compulsory counterclaims to trademark infringement actions. *At 1329:* [A]llowing [P] to proceed on its cancellation petition would undoubtedly impair [D's] rights as established in the infringement action, in particular its rights under the injunction, and would constitute a collateral attack on the district court's judgment."

Liberto v. D.F. Stauffer Biscuit Co., 441 F.3d 318, 325 (5th Cir.2006). "The district court held … that since [D] could have relied upon its incontestability defense in the 1996 [trademark-infringement] litigation but, instead, chose to settle, it is precluded from contesting the merits or raising any affirmative defenses in this action involving the same trademark infringement cause of action. [D] contends that trademark infringement has never been adjudicated, that the district court erred in ruling for [P], and that judgment should be rendered in its favor. We conclude that the district court should not have applied the doctrines of *res judicata* and judicial and licensee estoppel. *At 328:* The Final Judgment ordered by the district court neither clearly expresses nor is predicated upon the conclusion that [D] infringes [P's] mark. The Final Judgment in the 1996 litigation did not resolve the dispute." *See also* **Santos v. Hecht**, 82 U.S.P.Q.2d 1542, 1543 (E.D.N.Y.2006).

Papercutter, Inc. v. Fay's Drug Co., 900 F.2d 558, 563 (2d Cir.1990). "[D] may petition for cancellation of [P's] registration under [Lanham Act] §14 …, 15 U.S.C. §1064, 'either in a separate and independent action or as a counterclaim in an infringement suit,' by rebutting the presumption of a plaintiff's right to exclusive use of a registered mark by a preponderance of the evidence." *See also* ***On-Line Careline, Inc. v. America Online, Inc.***, 229 F.3d 1080, 1087 (Fed.Cir.2000).

Marcon, Ltd. v. Helena Rubenstein, Inc., 694 F.2d 953, 957 n.3 (4th Cir.1982). Prior "use is not a ground for cancellation…."

Likelihood of Confusion

Wallpaper Mfrs. v. Crown Wallcovering Corp., 680 F.2d 755, 763 (C.C.P.A.1982). Likelihood "of confusion of source ceases to be a ground for cancellation once a mark has been registered for five years. Thus, even one with an 'equal' right in a trademark based on priority may not attack the registration of another after five years on the grounds of likelihood of confusion of source."

Standing

Herbko Int'l v. Kappa Books, Inc., 308 F.3d 1156, 1161 (Fed.Cir.2002). "To obtain cancellation of the registration, the petitioning party must show both standing and valid grounds for cancellation. Standing requires only that the petitioner have a 'real interest' in the cancellation proceeding. In most settings, a direct commercial interest satisfies the 'real interest' test. Except when dealing with incontestable marks, any reason that would have precluded registration in the first instance suffices as a valid ground for cancellation."

International Nutrition Co. v. Horphag Research, Ltd., 220 F.3d 1325, 1329 (Fed.Cir.2000). "One situation in which parties have frequently been held to be in privity is when they hold successive interests in the same property. Thus, a judgment with respect to a particular property interest may be binding on a third party based on a transfer of the property in issue to the third party after judgment. *At 1330:* Because the cancellation proceeding does not derive from or involve an adjudication of [P's] rights in the French trademark ..., the transfer of the rights in that trademark [to P] did not render [P] in privity with [transferor of French trademark, P in prior U.S. trademark litigation,] for purposes of the opposition and cancellation proceedings [for U.S. trademark] at issue in this case."

Young v. AGB Corp., 152 F.3d 1377, 1379-80 (Fed. Cir.1998). Lanham Act §14, 15 U.S.C. §1064, "has been interpreted as requiring a cancellation petitioner 'to show (1) that it possesses standing to challenge the continued presence on the register of the subject registration and (2) that there is a valid ground why the registrant is not entitled under law to maintain the registration.' The standing requirement is based on the statutory requirement that a cancellation petitioner must believe that 'he is or will be damaged by the registration' and cases defining the scope of this language. The 'valid ground' that must be alleged and ultimately proved by a cancellation petitioner must be a '*statutory* ground which negates the appellant's right to the subject registration.' Although cancellation is most often premised on the grounds listed in [Lanham Act] §2 [15 U.S.C. §1052], other grounds which negate entitlement to maintain a registration also exist in the Lanham Act."

Star-Kist Foods, Inc. v. P.J. Rhodes & Co., 735 F.2d 346, 348 (9th Cir.1984). "[D's] argument that in order to have standing under §1064 [P] must prove that it would be damaged misapprehends the law. Proof of actual damage is only relevant, not requisite, to establishing standing."

§1064(1)

Park'N Fly, Inc. v. Dollar Park & Fly, Inc., 469 U.S. 189, 197 (1985). "Without regard to its incontestable status, a mark that has been registered five years is protected from cancellation except on the grounds stated in [15 U.S.C. §1064(3) and (5), Lanham Act §14(3) and (5)]. Pursuant to §14, a mark may be canceled on the grounds that it is merely descriptive only if the petition to cancel is filed within five years of the date of registration." *See also* ***Wilhelm Pudenz, GmbH v. Littlefuse, Inc.***, 177 F.3d 1204, 1211-12 (11th Cir. 1999).

Cold War Museum, Inc. v. Cold War Air Museum, Inc., 586 F.3d 1352, 1356-57 (Fed.Cir.2009). "A mark registered on the Principal Register is presumed to be valid [under 15 U.S.C. §1057(b), Lanham Act §7(b)]. Due to this presumption of validity, the burden of persuasion in a cancellation proceeding rests on the party seeking to cancel the registration. A party seeking to cancel a registration must overcome the registration's presumption of validity by a preponderance of the evidence. [¶] [T]he presumption of validity that attaches to a [15 U.S.C. §1052(f), Lanham Act §2(f),] registration includes a presumption that the registered mark has acquired distinctiveness. To rebut this presumption, a party seeking to cancel a [§1052(f)] registration must produce sufficient evidence for the [TTAB] to conclude, in view of the entire record in the cancellation proceeding, that the party has rebutted the mark's presumption of acquired distinctiveness by a preponderance of the evidence. *At 1358:* The burden of producing additional evidence or argument in defense of registration only shifts to the registrant if and when the party seeking cancellation establishes a prima facie showing of invalidity. The Board must then decide whether the party seeking cancellation has satisfied its ultimate burden of persuasion, based on all the evidence made of record during prosecution and any additional evidence introduced in the cancellation proceeding."

Jean Alexander Cosmetics, Inc. v. L'Oreal USA, Inc., 458 F.3d 244, 250-51 (3d Cir.2006). "[T]he case could have been resolved without the [TTAB's] determination that there was no likelihood of confusion between [P's and D's marks]. We must determine whether a finding that is an alternate, but independently sufficient, basis for a judgment should be deemed necessary to a decision for purposes of collateral estoppel. *At 255:* [W]e will follow the traditional view that independently sufficient alternative findings should be given preclusive effect."

§1064(3)—Abandoned

For more annotations on this topic, see 15 U.S.C. §1115, *§1115(b)(2)*, p. 83, and 15 U.S.C. §1127, *Abandoned*, p. 169.

Community of Christ Copyright Corp. v. Devon Park Restoration Branch of Jesus Christ's Ch., 634 F.3d 1005, 1010 (8th Cir.2011). "A registered mark is deemed abandoned 'when its use has been discontinued with intent not to resume such use' or when an owner causes the mark to 'lose its significance as a mark.' [D] has the burden of proving abandonment by clear and convincing evidence."

Doeblers' Pa. Hybrids, Inc. v. Doebler, 442 F.3d 812, 822 (3d Cir.2006). "A party arguing for abandonment has a high burden of proof: ... 'abandonment, being in the nature of a forfeiture, must be strictly proved.' *At 823-24:* Use of a trademark need not always be made directly by the trademark owner and is often made 'with the permission' of the owner via a licensing agreement. Indeed, sometimes the *only* use of a mark is through a licensee. [¶] A trademark license is typically written and contains express terms giving the licensor power to engage in quality control to ensure that the licensee does not engage in mere 'naked' use of the mark. Naked licensing is an '[u]ncontrolled licensing of a mark whereby the licensee can place the mark on any quality or type of goods or services,' raising 'a grave danger that the public will be deceived by such a usage.' [¶] Failure to provide quality control may constitute naked licensing, leading to abandonment of the mark. 'When the trademark owner fails to exercise reasonable control over the use of the mark by a licensee, the presence of the mark on the licensee's goods or services misrepresents their connection with the trademark owner since the mark no longer identifies goods and services that are under the control of the owner of the mark.' This may result in the trademark ceasing to function as a symbol of quality and controlled source, leading to an involuntary loss of trademark rights. [¶] To the extent that [P] may rely on a naked licensing theory, its burden is high. 'Because naked licensing if established is treated as an abandonment of the trademark, which triggers the loss of trademark rights against the world, anyone attempting to show such abandonment via naked licensing faces a stringent burden of proof.' [¶] Although it appears that there is no express written license agreement between the parties, a trademark license can also be implied. [¶] [T]he nature of the parties' relationship and conduct may evidence sufficient quality control. The Tenth Circuit has noted that a licensor may justifiably rely on its licensee for quality control where there is a 'special relationship' between the parties." *See also* ***Hokto Kinoko Co. v. Concord Farms, Inc.***, 738 F.3d 1085, 1098 (9th Cir. 2013); ***Mini Maid Servs. v. Maid Brigade Sys.***, 967 F.2d 1516, 1519 (11th Cir.1992).

Money Store v. Harriscorp Fin., Inc., 689 F.2d 666, 675 (7th Cir.1982). "An abandoned trademark is not capable of assignment because such a mark is subject to cancellation by the [PTO] or by the courts and is therefore invalid."

Board of Governors of Univ. of N.C. v. Helpingstine, 714 F.Supp. 167, 171 (M.D.N.C.1989). "[T]o establish abandonment it is imperative that [Ds] show both an intent to abandon as well as the loss of all indication as to the source of the mark's origin."

§1064(3)—Contrary to Provisions of §1054

F.R. Lepage Bakery, Inc. v. Roush Bakery Prods. Co., 851 F.2d 351, 354 (Fed.Cir.1988), *modified on other grounds*, 863 F.2d 43 (Fed.Cir.1988). "A basic principle pertaining to cancellation of registrations is that they were *obtained* contrary to the statute. The same principle logically applies (though the statute is silent on the point) if ownership is transferred to one who has no right, or would have had no right to obtain the registration. In this connection, [15 U.S.C. §1064(3), Lanham Act §14(3),] expressly provides for cancellation at any time if the registration was 'obtained fraudulently or *contrary to the provisions of* [*15 U.S.C.*] *§1054* [*Lanham Act §4*],' that being the section which provides for the registration of collective marks."

§1064(3)—Fraudulently Obtained

Hokto Kinoko Co. v. Concord Farms, Inc., 738 F.3d 1085, 1097 (9th Cir.2013). "To succeed on a claim for cancellation based on fraud, [D] must adduce evidence of (1) a false representation regarding a material fact; (2) the registrant's knowledge or belief that the representation is false; (3) the registrant's intent to induce reliance upon the misrepresentation; (4) actual, reasonable reliance on the misrepresentation; and (5) damages proximately caused by that reliance. A false representation in the original trademark application or an affidavit accompanying a renewal application may be grounds for cancellation if all five requirements are met. [D], however, bears a heavy burden of demonstrating that a trademark should be cancelled. Although a material false representation regarding an applicant's bona fide intent to use a trademark for a particular purpose may satisfy the test's first requirement, material falsity 'is only one aspect of the fraud claim.'" *See also* ***Patsy's Italian Rest., Inc. v. Banas***, 658 F.3d 254, 270-71 (2d Cir.2011).

In re Bose Corp., 580 F.3d 1240, 1243 (Fed.Cir. 2009). "Fraud in procuring a trademark registration or renewal occurs when an applicant knowingly makes false, material representations of fact in connection with his application. A party seeking cancellation of a trademark registration for fraudulent procurement bears a heavy burden of proof. [¶] [T]here is a material legal distinction between a 'false' representation and a 'fraudulent' one, the latter involving an intent to deceive, whereas the former may be occasioned by a misunderstanding, an inadvertence, a mere negligent omission, or the like. In other words, deception must be willful to constitute fraud. [¶] Several of our sister circuits have also required proof of intent to deceive before cancelling a trademark registration. *At 1245:* [W]e hold that a trademark is obtained fraudulently under the Lanham Act only if the applicant or registrant knowingly makes a false, material representation with the intent to deceive the PTO. [¶] Subjective intent to deceive, however difficult it may be to prove, is an indispensable element in the analysis. Of course, because direct evidence of deceptive intent is rarely available, such intent can be inferred from indirect and circumstantial evidence. But such evidence must still be clear and convincing, and inferences drawn from lesser evidence cannot satisfy the deceptive intent requirement. When drawing an inference of intent, the involved conduct, viewed in light of all the evidence must indicate sufficient culpability to require a finding of intent to deceive." (Internal quotes omitted.) *See also* ***Covertech Fabricating, Inc. v. TVM Bldg. Prods.***, 855 F.3d 163, 174-75 (3d Cir.2017); ***MPC Franchise, LLC v. Tarntino***, 826 F.3d 653, 658-59 (2d Cir.2016); ***Angel Flight v. Angel Flight Am., Inc.***, 522 F.3d 1200, 1209 (11th Cir.2008); ***Far Out Productions, Inc. v. Oskar***, 247 F.3d 986, 996 (9th Cir.2001); ***Aromatique, Inc. v. Gold Seal, Inc.***, 28 F.3d 863, 877-78 (8th Cir.1994); ***Meineke Disc. Muffler v. Jaynes***, 999 F.2d 120, 126 (5th Cir.1993); ***San Juan Prods. v. San Juan Pools***, 849 F.2d 468, 473 (10th Cir.1988); ***Money Store v. Harriscorp Fin., Inc.***, 689 F.2d 666, 670 (7th Cir.1982).

Angel Flight v. Angel Flight Am., Inc., 522 F.3d 1200, 1210 (11th Cir.2008). "'A misstatement of the date of first use in the application is not fatal to the securing of a valid registration as long as there has been valid use of the mark prior to the filing date.'" *See also* ***Opticians Ass'n v. Independent Opticians***, 920 F.2d 187, 194 (3d Cir.1990).

Marshak v. Treadwell, 240 F.3d 184, 193 (3d Cir. 2001). There "is no time limit on the assertion of fraudulent procurement as a defense to an infringement claim brought by the holder of a mark that has become incontestable." *But see* ***Pro-Football, Inc. v. Harjo***, 415 F.3d 44, 48 (D.C.Cir.2005) (laches is defense to cancellation based on fraud).

Daesang Corp. v. Rhee Bros., No. AMD 03-551 (D. Md.2005) (memo op.; 5-13-05). "It is well established that an applicant for a registration of a trademark has a duty of candor in his communications with the PTO. Consequently, there is no presumption of validity attached to a PTO registration where pertinent information is not presented to the PTO. Fraud arises, therefore, not only where the applicant makes false statements … but also where the applicant fails to make full disclosure of all material facts…."

Le Cordon Bleu, S.A. v. BPC Publ'g, 451 F.Supp. 63, 72 n.14 (S.D.N.Y.1978). "[W]hen an applicant fraudulently represents continued use under 15 U.S.C. §1058 [Lanham Act §8] and thereby secures his mark for 20 years, the mark has been obtained fraudulently within the meaning of 15 U.S.C. [§1064(3), Lanham Act §14(3)]."

§1064(3)—Genericness

Elliott v. Google, Inc., 860 F.3d 1151, 1155-56 (9th Cir.2017). "Over time, the holder of a valid trademark may become a victim of 'genericide.' Genericide occurs when the public appropriates a trademark and uses it as a generic name for particular types of goods or services irrespective of its source. For example, ASPIRIN, CELLOPHANE, and ESCALATOR were once protectable as arbitrary or fanciful marks because they were primarily understood as identifying the source of certain goods. But the public appropriated those marks and now primarily understands aspirin, cellophane, and escalator as generic names for those same goods. [¶] The question in any case alleging genericide is whether a trademark has taken the fateful step along the path to genericness. The mere fact that the public sometimes uses a trademark as the name for a unique product does not immediately render the mark generic. Instead, a trademark only becomes generic when the primary significance of the registered mark to the relevant public is as the name for a particular type of good or service irrespective of its source. [¶] We have often described this as a 'who-are-you/what-are-you' test. If the relevant public primarily understands a mark as describing 'who' a particular good or service is, or where it comes from, then the mark is still valid. But if the relevant public primarily understands a mark as describing 'what' the particular good or service is, then the mark has become generic. In sum, we ask whether the primary significance of the term in the minds of the consuming public is now the product and not the producer. *At 1157:* [W]e take this opportunity to clarify that a claim of genericide or genericness must be made with regard to a particular type of good or service. *At 1158:* Congress has instructed us that a speaker might use a trademark as a noun and still use the term in a source-identifying trademark sense. [¶] [T]he district court correctly rejected [P's] theory that verb use automatically constitutes generic use. Moreover, the district court aptly coined the terms 'discriminate verb' and 'indiscriminate verb' in order to evaluate [P's] proffered examples of verb use and determine whether they were also examples of generic use. Although novel, these terms properly frame the relevant inquiry as whether a speaker has a particular source in mind. We have already acknowledged that a customer might use the noun 'coke' in an indiscriminate sense, with no particular cola beverage in mind; or in a discriminate sense, with a Coca-Cola beverage in mind. In the same way, we now recognize that an internet user might use the verb 'google' in an indiscriminate sense, with no particular search engine in mind; or in a discriminate sense, with the Google search engine in mind. *At 1159:* A party applying for cancellation of a registered trademark bears the burden of proving genericide by a preponderance of the evidence. Moreover, the holder of a registered trademark benefits from a presumption of validity and has met its initial burden of demonstrating the lack of a genuine issue of material fact regarding genericide. Therefore, in light of the relevant inquiry under the primary significance test, [P] was required to identify sufficient evidence to support a jury finding that the primary significance of the word 'google' to the relevant public is as a name for internet search engines generally and not as a mark identifying the Google search engine in particular. *At 1160-61:* We next consider [P's] examples of alleged generic use by the media and by consumers. Documented examples of generic use might support a claim of genericide if they reveal a prevailing public consensus regarding the primary significance of a registered trademark. However, if the parties offer competing examples of both generic and trademark use, this source of evidence is typically insufficient to prove genericide. *At 1162:* Finally, we consider [P's] claim that there is no efficient alternative for the word 'google' as a name for the act of searching the internet regardless of the search engine used. Once again, a claim of genericide must relate to a particular type of good or service. In order to show that there is no efficient alternative for the word 'google' as a generic term, [P] must show that there is no way to describe 'internet search engines' without calling them 'googles.' Because not a single competitor calls its search engine 'a google,' and because members of the consuming public recognize and refer to different 'internet search engines,' [P] has not shown that there is no available substitute for the word 'google' as a generic term." (Internal quotes omitted.)

Princeton Vanguard, LLC v. Frito-Lay N. Am., Inc., 786 F.3d 960, 965 (Fed.Cir.2015). "We have said that determining a mark's genericness requires 'a two-step inquiry: First, what is the genus of goods or services at issue? Second, is the term sought to be registered or retained on the register understood by the relevant public primarily to refer to that genus of goods or services?' Evidence of the public's understanding of the mark may be obtained from 'any competent source, such as consumer surveys, dictionaries, newspapers and other publications.' In an opposition or cancellation proceeding, the opposer or petitioner bears the burden of proving genericness by a preponderance of the evidence."

Colt Defense LLC v. Bushmaster Firearms, Inc., 486 F.3d 701, 709 (1st Cir.2007). "The test for genericness is the 'primary significance of the mark to the *relevant* public.' Sometimes, the relevant public will not be the potential purchasing public as a whole but rather 'a relatively small group of highly trained and knowledgeable customers.'" *See also* ***Nartron Corp. v. STMicroelectronics, Inc.***, 305 F.3d 397, 406 (6th Cir.2002).

Creative Gifts, Inc. v. UFO, 235 F.3d 540, 544 (10th Cir.2000). "When the relevant public ceases to identify a trademark with a particular source of a product or service but instead identifies the mark with a class of products or services regardless of source, that mark has become generic and is lost as an enforceable trademark. For that purpose determinations of genericness are resolved under the statutory 'primary significance' test, and the 'relevant public' are the actual or potential purchasers of the particular goods or services in the marketplace."

Otokoyama Co. v. Wine of Japan Imp., Inc., 175 F.3d 266, 270 (2d Cir.1999). "[N]o trader may acquire the exclusive right to the use of a term by which the covered goods or services are designated in the language. Such a term is 'generic.' Generic terms are not eligible for protection as trademarks; everyone may use them to refer to the goods they designate. This rule protects the interest of the consuming public in understanding the nature of goods offered for sale, as well as a fair marketplace among competitors by insuring that every provider may refer to his goods as what they are. [¶] The same rule applies when the word designates the product in a language other than English. This extension rests on the assumption that there are (or someday will) be customers in the U.S. who speak that foreign language. *At 271:* Because of the diversity of the population of the U.S., coupled with temporary visitors, all of whom are part of the U.S. marketplace, commerce in the U.S. utilizes innumerable foreign languages. No merchant may obtain the exclusive right over a trademark designation if that exclusivity would prevent competitors from designating a product as what it is in the foreign language their customers know best. Courts and the USPTO apply this policy, known as the doctrine of 'foreign equivalents' ... to make generic foreign words ineligible for private ownership as trademarks."

Genesee Brewing Co. v. Stroh Brewing Co., 124 F.3d 137, 144 (2d Cir.1997). "The primary significance test is the law of the land.... Under this test, a plaintiff seeking to establish a valid trademark must show that the primary significance of the term in the minds of the consuming public is not the product but the producer. To satisfy this requirement, a trademark need not only and exclusively indicate the producer (the 'source'), but may, instead, serve a dual function—that of identifying a product while at the same time indicating its source. A mark is not generic merely because it has *some* significance to the public as an indication of the nature or class of an article. In order to become generic the *principal* significance of the word must be its indication of the nature or class of an article, rather than an indication of its origin." (Internal quotes omitted.)

Loglan Inst. v. Logical Language Grp., 962 F.2d 1038, 1040-41 (Fed.Cir.1992). If Loglan, a name for a logic-based language, "is used generically to designate a language, the term cannot properly be registered as a trademark for 'dictionaries and grammars' any more than English can be registered for a dictionary. ... Because a language is not 'goods' or 'services' under the [Lanham] Act, a name originated for a new language is inherently not registrable for the language. By the same token, a generic name of a language alone cannot function as a trademark to indicate origin of a dictionary describing that language."

Magic Wand, Inc. v. RDB, Inc., 940 F.2d 638, 640 (Fed.Cir.1991). "[A] proper genericness inquiry focuses on the description of services set forth in the certificate of registration."

Walker v. Klein, 47 U.S.P.Q.2d 1649, 1653 (S.D.Cal. 1998). "Generally, genericness can be demonstrated by several types of evidence including: (a) generic use of the terms by competitors which has not been challenged by the mark holder; (b) use by the mark holder of the term in a generic sense; (c) dictionary definitions; (d) generic usage in trade journals; (e) testimony of persons in the trade; and, (f) consumer surveys."

§1064(3)—Laches

Pro-Football, Inc. v. Harjo, 415 F.3d 44, 48 (D.C. Cir.2005). Section 1064(3) "does not bar the equitable defense of laches in response to §1064(3) cancellation petitions. [¶] [L]aches runs only from the time a party has reached his majority. *At 50:* In assessing prejudice [to D for P's delay in bringing cancellation suit], the district court should address both trial and economic prejudice. As to trial prejudice, the court should consider the extent to which [P's] post-majority delay resulted in a 'loss of evidence or witnesses supporting [D's] position.' As to economic prejudice, we express no view as to how such prejudice should be measured where ... what is at stake is not the trademark owner's right to use the marks but rather the owner's right to Lanham Act protections that turn on registration. We encourage the district court to take briefing on whether economic prejudice should be measured based on the owner's investment in the marks during the relevant years, on whether the owner would have taken a different course of action—e.g., abandoned the marks—had the petitioner acted more diligently in seeking cancellation, or on some other measure." *See also* ***Pro-Football, Inc. v. Harjo***, 57 U.S.P.Q.2d 1140, 1145 (D.D.C. 2000).

§1064(5)—Certification Marks

Midwest Plastic Fabricators, Inc. v. Underwriters Labs., 906 F.2d 1568, 1571 (Fed.Cir.1990). "[I]f a certification mark's owner also allowed the mark to be used as a trademark, there would be a basis for cancellation of the registration."

§1065. INCONTESTABILITY OF RIGHT TO USE MARK UNDER CERTAIN CONDITIONS

[LANHAM ACT §15]

Except on a ground for which application to cancel may be filed at any time under section 1064(3), (5) of title 15, and except to the extent, if any, to which the use of a mark registered on the principal register infringes a valid right acquired under the law of any State or Territory by use of a mark or trade name continuing from a date prior to the date of registration under this chapter of such registered mark, the right of the owner to use such registered mark in commerce for the goods or services on or in connection with which such registered mark has been in continuous use for five consecutive years subsequent to the date of such registration and is still in use in commerce, shall be incontestable: *Provided*, That—

(1) there has been no final decision adverse to the owner's claim of ownership of such mark for such goods or services, or to the owner's right to register the same or to keep the same on the register; and

(2) there is no proceeding involving said rights pending in the United States Patent and Trademark Office or in a court and not finally disposed of; and

(3) an affidavit is filed with the Director within one year after the expiration of any such five-year period setting forth those goods or services stated in the registration on or in connection with which such mark has been in continuous use for such five consecutive years and is still in use in commerce, and other matters specified in paragraphs (1) and (2) of this section; and

(4) no incontestable right shall be acquired in a mark which is the generic name for the goods or services or a portion thereof, for which it is registered.

Subject to the conditions above specified in this section, the incontestable right with reference to a mark registered under this chapter shall apply to a mark registered under the Act of March 3, 1881, or the Act of February 20, 1905, upon the filing of the required affidavit with the Director within one year after the expiration of any period of five consecutive years after the date of publication of a mark under the provisions of section 1062(c) of title 15.

The Director shall notify any registrant who files the above-prescribed affidavit of the filing thereof.

History of 15 U.S.C. §1065: July 5, 1946, ch. 540, §15, 60 Stat. 433; Oct. 9, 1962, P.L. 87-772, §10, 76 Stat. 771; Jan. 2, 1975, P.L. 93-596, §1, 88 Stat. 1949; Aug. 27, 1982, P.L. 97-247, §10, 96 Stat. 320; Nov. 16, 1988, P.L. 100-667, §116, 102 Stat. 3941; Nov. 29, 1999, P.L. 106-113, §1000(a)(9), 113 Stat. 1536; Mar. 17, 2010, P.L. 111-146, §3(b), 124 Stat. 67.

Treatise Cross-References

McCarthy on Trademark & Unfair Competition

Ch. 11, *The Spectrum of Distinctiveness of Marks*, §11:44
Ch. 12, *Generic Terms*, §§12:21; 12:56; 12:57; 12:60
Ch. 16, *Acquisition & Priority of Trademark Rights*, §16:18.50
Ch. 19, *Federal Registration of Marks*, §19:36
Ch. 20, *Inter Partes Trademark Proceedings in the Patent & Trademark Office*, §20:58
Ch. 26, *The Territorial Extent of Trademark Rights*, §§26:31; 26:44; 26:49; 26:53-26:56
Ch. 31, *Defenses to Infringement of Trademarks*, §§31:79-31:81
Ch. 32, *Procedure in Trademark Infringement & Unfair Competition Litigation*, §§32:140-32:142; 32:145; 32:147; 32:149; 32:152

ANNOTATIONS

Generally

Park'N Fly, Inc. v. Dollar Park & Fly, Inc., 469 U.S. 189, 205 (1985). "We conclude that the holder of a registered mark may rely on incontestability to enjoin infringement and that such an action may not be defended on the grounds that the mark is merely descriptive."

Specialized Seating, Inc. v. Greenwich Indus., 616 F.3d 722, 724 (7th Cir.2010). "The principal effect of incontestable status is to relieve the trademark proprietor of any need to show 'secondary meaning'—in other words, whether consumers associate a mark with a particular producer is not relevant when the mark is incontestable. … Because [a] mark is incontestable … the absence of confusion does not matter. Still, nine defenses [under 15 U.S.C. §1115(b)] are available to a person charged with infringing an incontestable mark."

Synergistic Int'l v. Korman, 470 F.3d 162, 170 (4th Cir.2006). "[T]he parties have stipulated that [P's] mark is protectible because it is incontestable. This stipulation of 'incontestability provides a strong presumption in favor of the mark's predictability and validity,' but it does not, in and of itself, establish the statutory requirement of likelihood of confusion."

KP Permanent Make-Up, Inc. v. Lasting Impression I, Inc., 408 F.3d 596, 606 (9th Cir.2005). "A descriptive mark that has become incontestable is conclusively presumed to have acquired secondary meaning. This means that a defendant in a trademark infringement action cannot assert that an incontestable mark is invalid because it is descriptive and lacks secondary meaning. [¶] [A] registered mark may be infringed even if the exact mark is not being imitated and, thus, the challenger of an incontestable mark cannot assert that the most salient feature of the mark is descriptive and lacks secondary meaning. When the holder of an incontestable mark is complaining that the most salient feature of its mark is being imitated and a likelihood of confusion may result, the holder of the mark does not have to show that the salient feature, apart from the mark, has acquired secondary meaning. Rather, the conclusive presumption that the mark has acquired secondary meaning extends to the most salient feature of the mark." *See also* ***Texas Pig Stands, Inc. v. Hard Rock Cafe Int'l***, 951 F.2d 684, 689 n.5 (5th Cir.1992). *But see* ***Igloo Prods. Corp. v. Brantex, Inc.***, 202 F.3d 814, 817 (5th Cir.2000) (prima facie presumption of secondary meaning applies to whole mark, not individual portion of mark).

Packman v. Chicago Tribune Co., 267 F.3d 628, 638 (7th Cir.2001). "Once a mark is registered, the [Lanham] Act affords a plaintiff one of two presumptions: (1) that her registered trademark is not merely descriptive or generic; or (2) that if descriptive, the mark is accorded secondary meaning."

Daddy's Junky Music Stores v. Big Daddy's Family Music Ctr., 109 F.3d 275, 282 (6th Cir.1997). "[F]or the purposes of assessing strength of a mark during an infringement action, incontestable status serves to confer upon a mark the strength accorded to a descriptive mark with secondary meaning. Accordingly, incontestable status benefits those marks which otherwise would lack inherent strength, i.e., generic marks or descriptive marks without secondary meaning."

Shakespeare Co. v. Silstar Corp., 9 F.3d 1091, 1098 (4th Cir.1993). "[A] court exercising its power under [15 U.S.C. §1119, Lanham Act §37,] is bound by the presumptions which accompany incontestability under [15 U.S.C. §1065, Lanham Act §15]."

Country Mut. Ins. v. American Farm Bur. Fed'n, 876 F.2d 599, 601 (7th Cir.1989). "Registration makes it hard for new firms to use marks that represent related goods, and an 'incontestable' registration, as its name suggests, puts the mark beyond challenge on the ground that it is 'descriptive.' Unless the PTO grants the application, however, the consequences of registration (as opposed to use) do not come to pass, and no damages are 'sustained in consequence thereof.' Firms might incur expenses to oppose the application, but as a rule legal fees are not 'damages' in American law."

Prudential Ins. v. Gibraltar Fin. Corp., 694 F.2d 1150, 1153 (9th Cir.1982). Incontestability "helps protect the registrant's mark from cancellation but is of no offensive use. Incontestability does not preclude a defense of laches."

Wrist-Rocket Mfg. v. Saunders Archery Co., 516 F.2d 846, 850 (8th Cir.1975). "An incontestable registration does not confer upon the registrant rights not possessed at common law. It is not a sword. To prevail in the infringement action, [registrant] had to establish his exclusive right to use the trademark independent of the registration." *See also* ***Tillamook Cty. Creamery Ass'n v. Tillamook Cheese & Dairy Ass'n***, 345 F.2d 158, 163 (9th Cir.1965).

Adverse Decisions

Skippy, Inc. v. CPC Int'l, 674 F.2d 209, 216 (4th Cir. 1982). "Unlike other statements required by [15 U.S.C. §1065, Lanham Act §15], the requirement that party state there be no adverse decisions has no express time limitation. Absent a specified limitation, we see no reason to impose one."

Attacking Incontestability

Progressive Distrib. Servs. v. UPS, Inc., 856 F.3d 416, 428 n.4 (6th Cir.2017). "An incontestable mark is one that has not been successfully challenged within five years of registration. *At 428-29:* The doctrine of incontestability and its evidentiary value is outlined in both 15 U.S.C. §§1065 and 1115(b) [Lanham Act §§15 and 33(b)]. And while there is no dispute that incontestable status serves as conclusive evidence of the registrant's exclusive right to use the mark, ... such use remains subject to proof of infringement as defined in [15 U.S.C.] §1114 [Lanham Act §32]. This Circuit has clearly noted that even where a trademark is incontestable: The significance of its presumed strength will depend upon its recognition among members of the public. Treating a valid, incontestable mark as an exceptionally strong mark for the purpose of determining whether confusion is likely to occur, without examining whether the mark is distinctive and well-known in the general population, would shift the focus away from the key question of whether relevant consumers are likely to believe that the products or services offered by the parties are affiliated in some way. Although a trademark may be strong and worthy of full protection because it is valid and incontestable ... does not necessarily mean that its strength is particularly relevant to the ultimate issue of whether confusion is likely to occur. [¶] To the extent that [P] wishes to rely solely upon the incontestable status of the mark, that by itself, is not sufficient when [D] has come forward with evidence of descriptiveness, third-party use, and a lack of commercial strength. Undoubtedly, [P's] claim of incontestability is entitled to a presumption of strength. However, a party may rebut the presumption of strength and show that a mark is not distinctive by presenting evidence of extensive third party use of similar marks. Third-party use weakens a mark because the mark is not an identifier for a single source. The presumption is that the third parties have muddled the mark's source. [¶] [T]here does not appear to be a specific number of third-party uses that are sufficient; rather, context matters." (Internal quotes omitted.)

Borinquen Biscuit Corp. v. M.V. Trading Corp., 443 F.3d 112, 117 (1st Cir.2006). "The effect of [the] presumption [of inherent distinctiveness] varies depending on whether the registered mark has attained incontestable status. If the registered mark has become incontestable through the owner's compliance with the applicable statutory formalities, the presumption is conclusive. If, however, the registered mark remains contestable, the putative infringer may defend a suit on the ground that the mark does not merit protection because it is not inherently distinctive (i.e., not suggestive, arbitrary, or fanciful) but, rather, is merely descriptive of the product. It follows, then, that under the Lanham Act, the effect of registration for a contestable mark is 'to shift the burden of proof from the plaintiff ... to the defendant, who must introduce sufficient evidence to rebut the presumption of the plaintiff's right to [exclusive] use' through proof that the mark is merely descriptive. *At 118:* When ... a mark is registered but contestable, a putative infringer must offer significantly probative evidence to show that the mark is merely descriptive. Then—and only then—does the burden of proof shift back, so that the party seeking protection must take an alternative route and assume the devoir of persuasion on the issue of whether its mark has acquired secondary meaning. Simply *alleging* descriptiveness is insufficient to compel the holder of a registered mark to go forward with proof of secondary meaning; the putative infringer must *prove* descriptiveness by a preponderance of the evidence before the mix of issues changes and the burden of persuasion on the new issue (secondary meaning) reverts to the trademark holder. If the putative infringer does not cross that threshold, the presumption holds and distinctiveness is presumed." *See also* ***Pebble Beach Co. v. Tour 18 I Ltd.***, 155 F.3d 526, 533 n.4 (5th Cir.1998), *overruled on other grounds*, ***TrafFix Devices, Inc. v. Marketing Displays, Inc.***, 532 U.S. 23 (2001).

Wilhelm Pudenz, GmbH v. Littlefuse, Inc., 177 F.3d 1204, 1206 (11th Cir.1999). Registered "trademarks that have become incontestable ... may still be declared invalid if they are found to protect the functional features of a product.... *At 1212:* The functionality doctrine is an important judicially created concept that was not abrogated by the enactment of the incontestability provisions of the Lanham Act."

Continuous Use

Elvis Presley Enters. v. Capece, 141 F.3d 188, 205 n.9 (5th Cir.1998). "[T]he nonuse of the mark during the period while no nightclub [that used the mark] was open may also break the period of continuous use required to establish the mark as incontestable...."

Brittingham v. Jenkins, 914 F.2d 447, 454 (4th Cir. 1990). "[T]he five-year continuous use provision of ... §1065 applies solely to the use of a mark in connection with the sale of goods and services, and not in relation to other business activities."

Casual Corner Assocs. v. Casual Stores, 493 F.2d 709, 712 (9th Cir.1974). 15 U.S.C. §1065, Lanham Act §15, "places upon a person claiming a prior state right the burden of showing that his has been a continuing use. To equate *continuing* with *a failure to abandon* would shift the burden from the state-right claimant to the owner of a valid and incontestable trademark. *At 713:* [R]egardless of whether §1065 controls [15 U.S.C. §1115, Lanham Act §33], [D] is precluded from claiming any rights arising out of the exception to §1065 because of its failure to demonstrate a use of the mark continuing from a date prior to the federal trademark registration and publication. Thus, it may raise only those defenses specifically enumerated in §1115."

Genericness

Yellow Cab Co. v. Yellow Cab, Inc., 419 F.3d 925, 928 (9th Cir.2005). "[A] registered mark may become generic and subject to cancellation. 'Generic terms are not registrable, and a registered mark may be canceled at any time on the grounds that it has become generic.' Competitors may use a term that was once distinctive if it has become generic over time. The crucial date for the determination of genericness is the date on which the alleged infringer entered the market with the disputed mark or term. *At 929:* 'To determine whether a term has become generic, we look to whether consumers understand the word to refer only to a particular producer's goods or whether the consumer understands the word to refer to the goods themselves.' If buyers understand the term as being identified with 'a particular producer's goods or services, it is not generic.' 'But if the word is identified with all such goods or services, regardless of their suppliers, it is generic.' [¶] We have often determined whether a mark is generic using the 'who-are-you/what-are-you' test: 'A mark answers the buyer's questions 'Who are you?' 'Where do you come from?' 'Who vouches for you?' But the generic name of the product answers the question 'What are you?'"

Soweco, Inc. v. Shell Oil Co., 617 F.2d 1178, 1191 n.34 (5th Cir.1980). "Although the Seventh Circuit held in [***Union Carbide Corp. v. Ever-Ready Inc.***, 531 F.2d 366 (7th Cir.1976),] that the incontestability of the mark there in question created a conclusive presumption of secondary meaning it noted ... that, '[i]f a mark is the common descriptive name of an item, it does not qualify for registration under [15 U.S.C. §1052(f), Lanham Act §2(f)]. If a mark becomes the common descriptive name of an item, it may be cancelled at any time and incontestability would be of no effect even if [15 U.S.C. §1065(4), Lanham Act §15(4),] had not been enacted.' Thus ... where the mark has become a common descriptive name, the presumption of secondary meaning stemming from the mark's incontestable status under ... §1065 does not apply. This is because the mark, being a common descriptive term, is not entitled to incontestable status under ... §1065(4), and thus not entitled to any presumption to which such status would normally entail. [P's] burden of proving secondary meaning is not satisfied by virtue of its mark being 'incontestable.'" *See also* ***Beer Nuts, Inc. v. Clover Club Foods Co.***, 805 F.2d 920, 924 (10th Cir.1986).

Senior User vs. Junior User

Watec Co. v. Liu, 403 F.3d 645, 653 (9th Cir.2005). "[A] litigant claiming §1065 senior rights in a mark must show: (1) that his or her 'use of the mark began before its registration and publication'; and (2) 'that there has been continuing use since that time.'"

Allard Enters. v. Advanced Programming Res., 249 F.3d 564, 572 (6th Cir.2001). "In the case in which a junior user applies for registration, ... the extent of the senior user/non-registrant's territory is frozen as of the date of actual registration to the junior user. [¶] The territorial rights of a holder of a federally registered trademark are always subject to any superior common law rights acquired by another party through actual use prior to the registrant's constructive use." *See also* ***Dorpan, S.L. v. Hotel Meliá, Inc.***, 728 F.3d 55, 62-63 (1st Cir.2013).

815 Tonawanda St. Corp. v. Fay's Drug Co., 842 F.2d 643, 646 (2d Cir.1988). "'[T]he plain meaning of [the second §1065 exception] is that if a party has acquired common-law trademark rights continuing since before the publication of the federal registration, then to that extent the registration will not be incontestable.'"

Dial-A-Mattress Oper. Corp. v. Mattress Madness, Inc., 841 F.Supp. 1339, 1353-54 (E.D.N.Y.1994). "An incontestable registration does not confer an unimpeachable right to exclusive use of the mark. Where the registrant is in fact the junior user of the mark, the senior user retains a right to use the mark in the geographic area wherein that user accrued common law rights superior to the registrant prior to the date of registration. In order to succeed in this defense, the claimed senior user must demonstrate (1) present rights in the mark, (2) acquired prior to the date of registration, (3) continual use of the mark since that date, and (4) use prior to the registrant on the goods or services that are in issue." *See also* ***Marshak v. Treadwell***, 240 F.3d 184, 198 n.10 (3d Cir.2001).

§1066. INTERFERENCE; DECLARATION BY DIRECTOR

[LANHAM ACT §16]

Upon petition showing extraordinary circumstances, the Director may declare that an interference exists when application is made for the registration of a mark which so resembles a mark previously registered by another, or for the registration of which another has previously made application, as to be likely when used on or in connection with the goods or services of the applicant to cause confusion or mistake or to deceive. No interference shall be declared between an application and the registration of a mark the right to the use of which has become incontestable.

History of 15 U.S.C. §1066: July 5, 1946, ch. 540, §16, 60 Stat. 434; Oct. 9, 1962, P.L. 87-772, §11, 76 Stat. 771; Aug. 27, 1982, P.L. 97-247, §11, 96 Stat. 321; Nov. 16, 1988, P.L. 100-667, §117, 102 Stat. 3941; Nov. 29, 1999, P.L. 106-113, §1000(a)(9), 113 Stat. 1536.

§1067. INTERFERENCE, OPPOSITION, & PROCEEDINGS FOR CONCURRENT USE REGISTRATION OR FOR CANCELLATION; NOTICE; TRADEMARK TRIAL & APPEAL BOARD

[LANHAM ACT §17]

(a) In every case of interference, opposition to registration, application to register as a lawful concurrent user, or application to cancel the registration of a mark, the Director shall give notice to all parties and shall direct a Trademark Trial and Appeal Board to determine and decide the respective rights of registration.

(b) The Trademark Trial and Appeal Board shall include the Director, Deputy Director of the United States Patent and Trademark Office, the Commissioner for Patents, the Commissioner for Trademarks, and administrative trademark judges who are appointed by the Secretary of Commerce, in consultation with the Director.

(c) Authority of the Secretary.—The Secretary of Commerce may, in his or her discretion, deem the appointment of an administrative trademark judge who, before August 12, 2008, held office pursuant to an appointment by the Director to take effect on the date on which the Director initially appointed the administrative trademark judge.

(d) Defense to challenge of appointment.—It shall be a defense to a challenge to the appointment of an administrative trademark judge on the basis of the judge's having been originally appointed by the Director that the administrative trademark judge so appointed was acting as a de facto officer.

History of 15 U.S.C. §1067: July 5, 1946, ch. 540, §17, 60 Stat. 434; Aug. 8, 1958, P.L. 85-609, §1(a), 72 Stat. 540; Jan. 2, 1975, P.L. 93-596, §1, 88 Stat. 1949; Oct. 15, 1980, P.L. 96-455, §1, 94 Stat. 2024; Nov. 29, 1999, P.L. 106-113, §1000(a)(9), 113 Stat. 1536; Nov. 2, 2002, P.L. 107-273, §13203(a)(1), 116 Stat. 1902; Aug. 12, 2008, P.L. 110-313, §1(b), 122 Stat. 3014.

ANNOTATIONS

Rosenruist-Gestao E Servicos LDA v. Virgin Enters., 511 F.3d 437, 443-44 (4th Cir.2007). "Procedure in *inter partes* matters diverges from that in district court at the trial stage, in that the taking of testimony does not occur in the presence of the TTAB. Instead, testimony is taken by deposition during set testimony periods, and the TTAB resolves all factual issues based on the written record submitted by the parties. [¶] *Inter partes* proceedings before the TTAB are governed by the Rules of Practice in Trademark Cases adopted by the PTO and set forth in [37 C.F.R.] Part 2.... The PTO's rules were 'adapted from the [FRCPs], with modifications appropriate to the administrative process.' Under the PTO's rules, the [FRCPs] generally apply to all phases of *inter partes* proceedings, including discovery and the taking of depositions. [¶] As an administrative tribunal of limited jurisdiction, the TTAB is empowered only to decide whether a given trademark is registrable. Although the TTAB has the authority to impose limited sanctions upon *parties* that fail to cooperate during discovery, the TTAB lacks the authority to compel witnesses through the subpoena power to appear for testimony in *inter partes* proceedings. [¶] Accordingly, Congress granted district courts subpoena authority under 35 [U.S.C.] §24 to command the appearance of witnesses in administrative proceedings before the PTO."

Rhoades v. Avon Prods., 504 F.3d 1151, 1165 (9th Cir.2007). "[W]e hold that the district court abused its discretion in declining to hear [P's] action. We agree with the Second Circuit that some situations might justify deferring a declaratory judgment case when related TTAB proceedings are pending; specifically, where the 'district court action involves only the issue of whether a mark is entitled to registration,' it might make more sense to resolve the registration claims at the TTAB first. On the other hand, if, as here, a potential infringement claim 'requires the district court to resolve much or all of [the registration issues], it would waste everyone's time not to settle the registration issue now[, in district court].' The deciding factor should be efficiency; the district court should exercise jurisdiction 'if this course is more efficient; otherwise, not.'"

EZ Loader Boat Trailers, Inc. v. Cox Trailers, Inc., 746 F.2d 375, 377-78 (7th Cir.1984). "The [TTAB] is limited by statute to determining whether to grant or deny registration of a trademark; it may not decide whether the use of a certain trademark violates the Lanham Act or grant an injunction against an infringing use. [T]he limited remedial powers of the [TTAB] are not in and of themselves an argument against the application of collateral estoppel. Courts have long held that where an agency acts in a judicial capacity and resolves disputes properly before it, the agency's findings may be given preclusive effect as long as the procedures utilized by the agency do not prevent the party against whom estoppel will be applied from having a fair opportunity to present its case. There is no question that the TTAB was acting in a judicial capacity. An opposition proceeding *is* an adversary proceeding. Both parties to this appeal were represented by attorneys before the Board; both presented evidence and submitted briefs."

§1068. ACTION OF DIRECTOR IN INTERFERENCE, OPPOSITION, & PROCEEDINGS FOR CONCURRENT USE REGISTRATION OR FOR CANCELLATION

[LANHAM ACT §18]

In such proceedings the Director may refuse to register the opposed mark, may cancel the registration, in whole or in part, may modify the application or registration by limiting the goods or services specified therein, may otherwise restrict or rectify with respect to the register the registration of a registered mark, may refuse to register any or all of several interfering marks, or may register the mark or marks for the person or persons entitled thereto, as the rights of the parties under this chapter may be established in the proceedings: *Provided*, That in the case of the registration of any mark based on concurrent use, the Director shall determine and fix the conditions and limitations provided for in section 1052(d) of title 15. However, no final judgment shall be entered in favor of an applicant under section 1051(b) of title 15 before the mark is registered, if such applicant cannot prevail without establishing constructive use pursuant to section 1057(c) of title 15.

History of 15 U.S.C. §1068: July 5, 1946, ch. 540, §18, 60 Stat. 434; Nov. 16, 1988, P.L. 100-667, §118, 102 Stat. 3941; Nov. 29, 1999, P.L. 106-113, §1000(a)(9), 113 Stat. 1536.

Treatise Cross-References

McCarthy on Trademark & Unfair Competition

Ch. 20, *Inter Partes Trademark Proceedings in the Patent & Trademark Office*, §§20:26; 20:27; 20:44; 20:45

§1069. APPLICATION OF EQUITABLE PRINCIPLES IN INTER PARTES PROCEEDINGS

[LANHAM ACT §19]

In all inter partes proceedings equitable principles of laches, estoppel, and acquiescence, where applicable may be considered and applied.

History of 15 U.S.C. §1069: July 5, 1946, ch. 540, §19, 60 Stat. 434; Jan. 2, 1975, P.L. 93-596, §1, 88 Stat. 1949; Nov. 16, 1988, P.L. 100-667, §119, 102 Stat. 3941.

§1070. APPEALS TO TRADEMARK TRIAL & APPEAL BOARD FROM DECISIONS OF EXAMINERS

[LANHAM ACT §20]

An appeal may be taken to the Trademark Trial and Appeal Board from any final decision of the examiner in charge of the registration of marks upon the payment of the prescribed fee.

History of 15 U.S.C. §1070: July 5, 1946, ch. 540, §20, 60 Stat. 435; Aug. 8, 1958, P.L. 85-609, §1(b), 72 Stat. 540.

§1071. APPEAL TO COURTS

[LANHAM ACT §21]

(a) Persons entitled to appeal; United States Court of Appeals for the Federal Circuit; waiver of civil action; election of civil action by adverse party; procedure—

(1) An applicant for registration of a mark, party to an interference proceeding, party to an opposition proceeding, party to an application to register as a lawful concurrent user, party to a cancellation proceeding, a registrant who has filed an affidavit as provided in section 1058 or section 1141k of title 15, or an applicant for renewal, who is dissatisfied with the decision of the Director or Trademark Trial and Appeal Board, may appeal to the United States Court of Appeals for the Federal Circuit thereby waiving his right to proceed under subsection (b) of this section: *Provided*, That such appeal shall be dismissed if any adverse party to the proceeding, other than the Director, shall, within twenty days after the appellant has filed notice of appeal according to paragraph (2) of this section, files notice with the Director that he elects to have all further proceedings conducted as provided in subsection (b) of this section. Thereupon the appellant shall have thirty days thereafter within which to file a civil action under subsection (b) of this section, in default of which the decision appealed from shall govern the further proceedings in the case.

(2) When an appeal is taken to the United States Court of Appeals for the Federal Circuit, the appellant shall file in the United States Patent and Trademark Office a written notice of appeal directed to the Director, within such time after the date of the decision from which the appeal is taken as the Director prescribes, but in no case less than 60 days after that date.

(3) The Director shall transmit to the United States Court of Appeals for the Federal Circuit a certified list of the documents comprising the record in the United States Patent and Trademark Office. The court may request that the Director forward the original or certified copies of such documents during pendency of the appeal. In an ex parte case, the Director shall submit to that court a brief explaining the grounds for the decision of the United States Patent and Trademark Office, addressing all the issues involved in the appeal. The court shall, before hearing an appeal, give notice of the time and place of the hearing to the Director and the parties in the appeal.

(4) The United States Court of Appeals for the Federal Circuit shall review the decision from which the appeal is taken on the record before the United States Patent and Trademark Office. Upon its determination the court shall issue its mandate and opinion to the Director, which shall be entered of record in the United States Patent and Trademark Office and shall govern the further proceedings in the case. However, no final judgment shall be entered in favor of an applicant under section 1051(b) of title 15 before the mark is registered, if such applicant cannot prevail without establishing constructive use pursuant to section 1057(c) of title 15.

(b) Civil action; persons entitled to; jurisdiction of court; status of Director; procedure—

(1) Whenever a person authorized by subsection (a) of this section to appeal to the United States Court of Appeals for the Federal Circuit is dissatisfied with the decision of the Director or Trademark Trial and Appeal Board, said person may, unless appeal has been taken to said United States Court of Appeals for the Federal Circuit, have remedy by a civil action if commenced within such time after such decision, not less than sixty days, as the Director appoints or as provided in subsection (a) of this section. The court may adjudge that an applicant is entitled to a registration upon the application involved, that a registration involved should be canceled, or such other matter as the issues in the proceeding require, as the facts in the case may appear. Such adjudication shall authorize the Director to take any necessary action, upon compliance with the requirements of law. However, no final judgment shall be entered in favor of an applicant under section 1051(b) of title 15 before the mark is registered, if such applicant cannot prevail without establishing constructive use pursuant to section 1057(c) of title 15.

(2) The Director shall not be made a party to an inter partes proceeding under this subsection, but he shall be notified of the filing of the complaint by the clerk of the court in which it is filed and shall have the right to intervene in the action.

(3) In any case where there is no adverse party, a copy of the complaint shall be served on the Director, and, unless the court finds the expenses to be unreasonable, all the expenses of the proceeding shall be paid by the party bringing the case, whether the final decision is in favor of such party or not. In suits brought hereunder, the record in the United States Patent and Trademark Office shall be admitted on motion of any party, upon such terms and conditions as to costs, expenses, and the further cross-examination of the witnesses as the court imposes, without prejudice to the right of any party to take further testimony. The testimony and exhibits of the record in the United States Patent and Trademark Office, when admitted, shall have the same effect as if originally taken and produced in the suit.

(4) Where there is an adverse party, such suit may be instituted against the party in interest as shown by the records of the United States Patent and Trademark Office at the time of the decision complained of, but any party in interest may become a party to the action. If there are adverse parties residing in a plurality of districts not embraced within the same State, or an adverse party residing in a foreign country, the United States District Court for the Eastern District of Virginia shall have jurisdiction and may issue summons against the adverse parties directed to the marshal of any district in which any adverse party resides. Summons against adverse parties residing in foreign countries may be served by publication or otherwise as the court directs.

History of 15 U.S.C. §1071: July 5, 1946, ch. 540, §21, 60 Stat. 435; July 19, 1952, ch. 950, §2, 66 Stat. 814; Aug. 8, 1958, P.L. 85-609, §1(c), 72 Stat. 540; Oct. 9, 1962, P.L. 87-772, §12, 76 Stat. 771; Jan. 2, 1975, P.L. 93-596, §1, 88 Stat. 1949; Jan. 2, 1975, P.L. 93-600, §2, 88 Stat. 1955; Apr. 2, 1982, P.L. 97-164, §162(1), 96 Stat. 49; Nov. 8, 1984, P.L. 98-620, §414(b), 98 Stat. 3363; Nov. 16, 1988, P.L. 100-667, §120, 102 Stat. 3942; Nov. 29, 1999, P.L. 106-113, §1000(a)(9), 113 Stat. 1536; Mar. 17, 2010, P.L. 111-146, §3(c), 124 Stat. 67; Sept. 16, 2011, P.L. 112-29, §9(a), 125 Stat. 316.

See also 28 U.S.C. §§1295, 1338; 48 U.S.C. §1405q.

Treatise Cross-References

McCarthy on Trademark & Unfair Competition

Ch. 21, *Appeal from Decisions on Trademark Registration*, §21:10

ANNOTATIONS

Generally

B&B Hardware, Inc. v. Hargis Indus., ___ U.S. ___, 135 S.Ct. 1293, 1299 (2015). "The question ... is whether the District Court ... should have applied issue preclusion to the TTAB's decision that SEALTITE is confusingly similar to SEALTIGHT. [W]e hold that a court should give preclusive effect to TTAB decisions if the ordinary elements of issue preclusion are met. *At U.S. ___, S.Ct. 1301:* After the TTAB decides whether to register the mark, a party can seek review in the U.S. Court of Appeals for the Federal Circuit, or it can file a new action in district court. In district court, the parties can conduct additional discovery and the judge resolves registration *de novo*. *At U.S. ___, S.Ct. 1303:* Although the idea of issue preclusion is straightforward, it can be challenging to implement. The Court, therefore, regularly turns to the Restatement (Second) of Judgments for a statement of the ordinary elements of issue preclusion. The Restatement explains that subject to certain well-known exceptions, the general rule is that '[w]hen an issue of fact or law is actually litigated and determined by a valid and final judgment, and the determination is essential to the judgment, the determination is conclusive in a subsequent action between the parties, whether on the same or a different claim.' [¶] Both this Court's cases and the Restatement make clear that issue preclusion is not limited to those situations in which the same issue is before two *courts*. Rather, where a single issue is before a court and an administrative agency, preclusion also often applies. *At U.S. ___, S.Ct. 1305:* [O]ne can seek judicial review of a TTAB registration decision in a *de novo* district court action, and some courts have concluded from this that Congress does not want unreviewed TTAB decisions to ground issue preclusion. But that conclusion does not follow. Ordinary preclusion law teaches that if a party to a court proceeding does not challenge an adverse decision, that decision can have preclusive effect in other cases, even if it would have been reviewed *de novo*. *At U.S. ___, S.Ct. 1306:* [I]ssue preclusion applies where 'the issues in the two cases are indeed identical and the other rules of collateral estoppel are carefully observed.' *At U.S. ___, S.Ct. 1307:* [It] does [not] matter that the TTAB and the Eighth Circuit use different factors to assess likelihood of confusion. For one thing, the factors are not fundamentally different, and '[m]inor variations in the application of what is in essence the same legal standard do not defeat preclusion.' More important, if federal law provides a single standard, parties cannot escape preclusion simply by litigating anew in tribunals that apply that one standard differently. [¶] The real question, therefore, is whether likelihood of confusion for purposes of registration is the same standard as likelihood of confusion for purposes of infringement. We conclude it is...."

Aktieselskabet AF21. Nov. 2001 v. Fame Jeans Inc., 525 F.3d 8, 13 (D.C.Cir.2008). "For a person challenging a TTAB decision, a civil action in district court is an alternative to review by the Court of Appeals for the Federal Circuit. [¶] The proceedings differ in important ways, with Federal Circuit review taking the form of an appeal and the district court alternative being an ordinary civil action. In a Federal Circuit appeal, the PTO transmits its record to the court, which 'shall review the decision from which the appeal is taken on the record.' In an *ex parte* case, the PTO must also explain the grounds for its decision, 'addressing all the issues involved in the appeal.' By contrast, in a [Lanham Act] §21(b) [15 U.S.C. §1071(b)] action, the PTO does not automatically transmit its record to the court; rather, any party may, on its own motion, enter the record into evidence. Once entered, '[t]he testimony and exhibits' of the PTO record 'have the same effect as if originally taken and produced in the suit.' The district court then decides *de novo* whether the application at issue should proceed to registration, or the registration involved should be canceled, or 'such other matter as the issues in the proceeding require, as the facts in the case may appear.'" *See also* ***CAE, Inc. v. Clean Air Eng'g***, 267 F.3d 660, 673 (7th Cir.2001).

Alltrade, Inc. v. Uniweld Prods., 946 F.2d 622, 625 (9th Cir.1991). "The ambiguity [of which party may appeal] begins with the language of [15 U.S.C. §1071, Lanham Act §21,] granting a right of appeal to parties '*dissatisfied* with the *decision*' of the [TTAB]. While 'dissatisfaction' hints at a broad construction of the statute—insofar as both parties might have cause for discontent—'decision' considerably narrows the scope—for a decision generally supports one party or the other. Courts that have construed this and analogous provisions typically have held that a party benefiting from a ruling, yet disagreeing with specific findings, cannot appeal."

Wagner Shokai, Inc. v. Kabushiki Kaisha Wako, 699 F.2d 1390, 1391 (Fed.Cir.1983). "The term 'decision' when used in [15 U.S.C. §1071, Lanham Act §21,] means a dispositive decision in which a right has been adjudicated. A denial of a motion to dismiss is not dispositive." (Internal quotes omitted.)

WNS, Inc. v. Deck the Walls, Inc., 4 U.S.P.Q.2d 1377, 1378 n.2 (N.D.Ill.1986). If "no mark is registered, the court has no power to determine the right to registration."

§1071(a)

In re Viterra Inc., 671 F.3d 1358, 1361 (Fed.Cir. 2012). "We review the [TTAB's] legal conclusions *de novo* and its factual findings for substantial evidence. The [TTAB's] determination of likelihood of confusion is a legal determination, ... as is its interpretations of the Lanham Act and the legal tests it applies in measuring registrability. The ultimate question of likelihood of confusion, however, is based upon factual underpinnings that we review for substantial evidence. For example, the question of similarity between two marks and the relatedness of goods are factual determinations. Within the broader question of the similarity of the marks, determinations as to the appearance, sound, connotation and commercial impression of the marks are also factual in nature. We will not disturb such factual findings if they are supported by substantial evidence in the record. [¶] Substantial evidence is more than a mere scintilla and is such relevant evidence as a reasonable mind would accept as adequate to support a conclusion. Accordingly, where two different conclusions may be warranted based on the evidence of record, the [TTAB's] decision to favor one conclusion over the other is the type of decision that must be sustained by this court as supported by substantial evidence." (Internal quotes omitted.)

§1071(b)

Shammas v. Focarino, 784 F.3d 219, 221 (4th Cir. 2015). "If [a dissatisfied trademark applicant] elects to proceed in a district court and no adverse party opposed his application before the [PTO], the applicant must name the Director of the PTO as a defendant and pay '*all the expenses* of the proceeding,' *whether he succeeds in the action or not*, unless the expenses are unreasonable. [¶] On appeal, [applicant] argues that the district court erred in 'shifting' the PTO's attorneys fees to him, contrary to the 'American Rule' under which each party bears his own attorneys fees, because the governing statute does not expressly provide for the shifting of attorneys fees. [¶] We reject this argument and affirm, concluding that the imposition of all expenses on a plaintiff in an ex parte proceeding, *regardless of whether he wins or loses*, does not constitute fee-shifting that implicates the American Rule but rather an unconditional compensatory charge imposed on a dissatisfied applicant who elects to engage the PTO in a district court proceeding. And we conclude that this compensatory charge encompasses the PTO's salary expenses for the attorneys and paralegals who represent the Director." *But see* ***NanKwest, Inc. v. Lee***, 162 F.Supp.3d 540, 545-46 (E.D.Va.2016) (explaining that Supreme Court's decision in ***Baker Botts L.L.P. v. ASARCO LLC***, ___ U.S. ___, 135 S.Ct. 2158 (2015), a bankruptcy case, is based on reasoning contrary to ***Shammas***).

Swatch AG v. Beehive Wholesale, LLC, 739 F.3d 150, 155 (4th Cir.2014). 15 U.S.C. §1071(b), Lanham Act §21(b), "permits a party in a trademark suit to initiate a civil action in the place of an appeal of the TTAB's determination to the Federal Circuit. [¶] In a §1071(b) action, the district court reviews the record de novo and acts as the finder of fact. The district court has authority independent of the PTO to grant or cancel registrations and to decide any related matters such as infringement and unfair competition claims. The district court must admit the PTO record if a party so moves, and if admitted, the record 'shall have the same effect as if originally taken and produced in the suit.' Whether or not the record is admitted, the parties have an unrestricted right to submit further evidence as long as it is admissible under the [FREs] and [FRCPs].

At 156: [W]here new evidence is submitted, de novo review of the entire record is required because the district court 'cannot meaningfully defer to the PTO's factual findings if the PTO considered a different set of facts.'" *See also* ***Kellogg Co. v. Toucan Golf, Inc.***, 337 F.3d 616, 623 (6th Cir.2003).

Board of Regents v. Phoenix Int'l Software, Inc., 653 F.3d 448, 451-52 (7th Cir.2011). "We ... hold that the Supreme Court's decision in ***Lapides v. Board of Regents*** ..., 535 U.S. 613 ... (2002), requires us to find that [state] waived its sovereign immunity when it filed suit in the federal district court seeking to overturn the decision of the TTAB. To maximize its chances of reversing the agency's decision, the state availed itself of the advantages of a fresh lawsuit, choosing that path over a number of others available. It would be anomalous if, after invoking federal jurisdiction, the state could declare that the federal court has no authority to consider related aspects of the case. [D's] counterclaims are compulsory in nature and thus lie well within the scope of [state's] waiver of immunity. [¶] We have mentioned that trademark law provides two avenues for review of TTAB decisions. The road not taken by [state] was a direct appeal to the Federal Circuit, which would have been restricted to the record developed before the TTAB and would have focused on whether substantial evidence supported the agency's decision. The option [state] chose was a new action in the district court. One advantage of this path for the state was the ability to expand the record by offering new evidence to fend off [D's] cancellation claim. A challenge to the TTAB's decision in a district court is 'both an appeal and a new action, which allows the parties to request additional relief and to submit new evidence.' In such an action, the district court wears two hats: '[it] is an appellate reviewer of facts found by the TTAB and is also a fact-finder based on new evidence introduced to the court.'"

Aktieselskabet AF21. Nov. 2001 v. Fame Jeans Inc., 525 F.3d 8, 12 (D.C.Cir.2008). "Although a district court owes a certain degree of deference to the TTAB's findings of fact, both parties may introduce new evidence in a [Lanham Act] §21(b) [15 U.S.C. §1071(b)] action. The question before us is whether a party may also introduce new issues not brought before the TTAB. We join several of our fellow circuits in allowing new issues in §21(b) actions."

CAE, Inc. v. Clean Air Eng'g, 267 F.3d 660, 674 (7th Cir.2001). In an appeal under 15 U.S.C. §1071(b), Lanham Act §21(b), "the district court sits in a dual capacity. It is an appellate reviewer of facts found by the [TTAB] and is also a fact-finder based on new evidence introduced to the court. Although the district court's review of the TTAB's decision is considered de novo when the parties present new evidence and assert additional claims, the district court also must afford deference to the fact findings of the TTAB. *At 676:* [F]indings of fact by the TTAB properly are reviewed under the substantial evidence standard set forth in [Administrative Procedure Act] §706(2)(E)...."

Material Sup. Int'l v. Sunmatch Indus., 146 F.3d 983, 990 (D.C.Cir.1998). "There is no reason ... for the district court to defer to the [TTAB and use the thorough-conviction standard of review] when that body grants summary judgment; the district court is just as able as the TTAB to determine an issue of law."

Goya Foods, Inc. v. Tropicana Prods., 846 F.2d 848, 851 (2d Cir.1988). "The narrow issue presented is whether the pendency of the registration proceeding before the [TTAB] was an appropriate basis for the denial of [P's] motion to amend its complaint seeking primarily a declaration of non-infringement. *At 854:* In relying on the pendency of TTAB registration proceedings as a basis for denying leave to amend, the District Judge applied an incorrect legal standard and thereby exceeded his discretion."

Formica Corp. v. Lefkowitz, 590 F.2d 915, 918 (C.C.P.A.1979). The Federal Trade Commission (FTC) says a petition of mandamus to the TTAB "is the equivalent of an appeal from a decision of the TTAB and should be governed by [Lanham Act] §21 ..., 15 U.S.C. §1071, the statutory provision for appeals from TTAB decisions. [I]f a dissatisfied party appeals to this court, an opponent may elect 'to have all further proceedings conducted as provided in §21(b),' by civil action in an appropriate district court." Held: The FTC is incorrect. A petition for mandamus is not an appeal because there has been no final decision. Therefore, the FTC may not elect under §1071(b) to have P's petition for mandamus reviewed by a district court.

Johnny Blastoff, Inc. v. Los Angeles Rams Football Co., 48 U.S.P.Q.2d 1385, 1393 (W.D.Wis.1998), *aff'd*, 188 F.3d 427 (7th Cir.1999). A rejection by the federal court of the other party's application as relief "is not available under ... §1071, which authorizes federal courts to hear appeals of final PTO rulings on trademark applications, and the Court of Appeals for the Seventh Circuit has held that the appeal provisions of §1071 provide the sole grounds for federal court 'jurisdiction over registration proceedings.'"

Scotch Whisky Ass'n v. Majestic Distilling Co., 681 F.Supp. 1297, 1301 (N.D.Ill.1988). "Courts have construed [15 U.S.C. §1071(b)(4), Lanham Act §21(b)(4),] to apply only where there are multiple defendants or a single defendant residing in a foreign country. Courts have also held that 'as §1071 is silent as regards a single adverse party [residing in the U.S.], it follows that the general law controlling on those subjects [of jurisdiction and venue] must apply.'"

§1072. REGISTRATION AS CONSTRUCTIVE NOTICE OF CLAIM OF OWNERSHIP

[LANHAM ACT §22]

Registration of a mark on the principal register provided by this chapter or under the Act of March 3, 1881, or the Act of February 20, 1905, shall be constructive notice of the registrant's claim of ownership thereof.

History of 15 U.S.C. §1072: July 5, 1946, ch. 540, §22, 60 Stat. 435.

Treatise Cross-References

McCarthy on Trademark & Unfair Competition

Ch. 16, *Acquisition & Priority of Trademark Rights*, §16:18.50
Ch. 19, *Federal Registration of Marks*, §§19:36; 19:145
Ch. 26, *The Territorial Extent of Trademark Rights*, §§26:32; 26:33; 26:38; 26:45; 26:54
Ch. 31, *Defenses to Infringement of Trademarks*, §31:40

ANNOTATIONS

Park'N Fly, Inc. v. Dollar Park & Fly, Inc., 469 U.S. 189, 199-200 (1985). 15 U.S.C. §1072, Lanham Act §22, "provides for constructive notice of registration and modifies the common-law rule that allowed acquisition of concurrent rights by users in distinct geographic areas if the subsequent user adopted the mark without knowledge of prior use."

In re International Flavors & Fragrances Inc., 183 F.3d 1361, 1367 (Fed.Cir.1999). "Registration serves as constructive notice to the public of the registrant's ownership of the mark and thus prevents another user of the mark from claiming innocent misappropriation as a trademark infringement defense." *See also* ***Veryfine Prods. v. Colon Bros.***, 799 F.Supp. 240, 250 (D.P.R.1992).

Circuit City Stores v. Carmax, Inc., 165 F.3d 1047, 1056 (6th Cir.1999). Once "there is [a] finding of infringement, ... the District Court [is] not required to find that [P] was about to enter [Ds'] market in order to grant injunctive relief. The law of this Circuit holds that no particular finding of likelihood of entry or irreparable harm is necessary for injunctive relief in trademark or unfair competition cases."

Beauty Time, Inc. v. Vu Skin Sys., 118 F.3d 140, 149 (3d Cir.1997). "It does not appear that the constructive notice provision of [15 U.S.C. §1072, Lanham Act §22,] applies to the submission of affidavits under [15 U.S.C. §1058, Lanham Act §8,] to register the trademark or under [15 U.S.C. §1065, Lanham Act §15,] to establish incontestability. The briefs of the parties and our own exhaustive search reveal no case law establishing that the act of confirming the trademark's continued use in commerce satisfies the constructive notice provision of §1072. Additionally, the language of §1072, which speaks to '[r]egistration of the trademark on the principal register' as constructive notice does not apply to the submission of affidavits five years later pursuant to [§§1058 and 1065]."

Champions Golf Club, Inc. v. Champions Golf Club, Inc., 78 F.3d 1111, 1123 (6th Cir.1996). "After registration, there can be no new 'innocent' users, and even an innocent prior user cannot expand the area of its use, because Lanham Act registration puts all would-be users of the mark (or a confusingly similar mark) on constructive notice of the mark."

In re Beatrice Foods Co., 429 F.2d 466, 472 (C.C.P.A.1970). "A federal registration gives certain procedural rights, such as the right to invoke jurisdiction of the federal courts, and the right to rely on certain evidentiary presumptions, but more importantly, the constructive notice provision of [15 U.S.C. §1072, Lanham Act §22,] takes away from future users of the mark registered the defense of innocent appropriation."

Dawn Donut Co. v. Hart's Food Stores, 267 F.2d 358, 362 (2d Cir.1959). 15 U.S.C. §1072, Lanham Act §22, "provides that registration of a trademark on the principal register is constructive notice of the registrant's claim of ownership. Thus, by eliminating the defense of good faith and lack of knowledge, §1072 affords nationwide protection to registered marks, regardless of the areas in which the registrant actually uses the mark."

General Bus. Servs. v. Rouse, 495 F.Supp. 526, 540 (E.D.Pa.1980). "Although 15 U.S.C. §1072 [Lanham Act §22] states that registration of a mark is constructive notice, this time designation is aimed at taking away from future users of the mark the defense of innocent appropriation. It is not provided for the purpose of supporting the defense of laches."

SUBCHAPTER II. THE SUPPLEMENTAL REGISTER

§1091. SUPPLEMENTAL REGISTER [LANHAM ACT §23]

(a) Marks registerable.—In addition to the principal register, the Director shall keep a continuation of the register provided in paragraph (b) of section 1 of the Act of March 19, 1920, entitled "An Act to give effect to certain provisions of the convention for the protection of trademarks and commercial names, made and signed in the city of Buenos Aires, in the Argentine Republic, August 20, 1910, and for other purposes," to be called the supplemental register. All marks capable of distinguishing applicant's goods or services and not registrable on the principal register provided in this chapter, except those declared to be unregistrable under subsections (a), (b), (c), (d), and (e)(3) of section 1052 of title 15, which are in lawful use in commerce by the owner thereof, on or in connection with any goods or services may be registered on the supplemental register upon the payment of the prescribed fee and compliance with the provisions of subsections (a) and (e) of section 1051 of title 15 so far as they are applicable. Nothing in this section shall prevent the registration on the supplemental register of a mark, capable of distinguishing the applicant's goods or services and not registrable on the principal register under this chapter, that is declared to be unregistrable under section 1052(e)(3) of title 15, if such mark has been in lawful use in commerce by the owner thereof, on or in connection with any goods or services, since before December 8, 1993.

(b) Application and proceedings for registration.—Upon the filing of an application for registration on the supplemental register and payment of the prescribed fee the Director shall refer the application to the examiner in charge of the registration of marks, who shall cause an examination to be made and if on such examination it shall appear that the applicant is entitled to registration, the registration shall be granted. If the applicant is found not entitled to registration the provisions of subsection (b) of section 1062 of title 15 shall apply.

(c) Nature of mark.—For the purposes of registration on the supplemental register, a mark may consist of any trademark, symbol, label, package, configuration of goods, name, word, slogan, phrase, surname, geographical name, numeral, device, any matter that as a whole is not functional, or any combination of any of the foregoing, but such mark must be capable of distinguishing the applicant's goods or services.

History of 15 U.S.C. §1091: July 5, 1946, ch. 540, §23, 60 Stat. 435; Oct. 9, 1962, P.L. 87-772, §13, 76 Stat. 773; Nov. 16, 1988, P.L. 100-667, §121, 102 Stat. 3942; Dec. 8, 1993, P.L. 103-182, §333(b), 107 Stat. 2114; Oct. 30, 1998, P.L. 105-330, §201(a)(5), 112 Stat. 3070; Nov. 29, 1999, P.L. 106-113, §1000(a)(9), 113 Stat. 1536; Nov. 2, 2002, P.L. 107-273, §13207(b)(6), 116 Stat. 1908.

See also NAFTA art. 1712.

Treatise Cross-References

McCarthy on Trademark & Unfair Competition

Ch. 7, *Trademark & Trade Dress Formats*, §§7:76; 7:95
Ch. 19, *Federal Registration of Marks*, §§19:33-19:35; 19:38-19:40; 19:42
Ch. 20, *Inter Partes Trademark Proceedings in the Patent & Trademark Office*, §20:80
Ch. 21, *Appeal from Decisions on Trademark Registration*, §21:6
Ch. 23, *Likelihood of Confusion: The Test of Trademark Infringement*, §23:77

ANNOTATIONS

In re Bush Bros., 884 F.2d 569, 570 (Fed.Cir.1989). "The test [of registrability on the Supplemental Register] is not whether the mark is already distinctive of the applicant's goods, but whether it is capable of becoming so. Thus a mark that is ineligible for registration on the Principal Register because it is 'merely descriptive' of the goods or services may be registered on the Supplemental Register."

Books on Tape, Inc. v. Booktape Corp., 836 F.2d 519, 520 (Fed.Cir.1987). "The statute does not require the anomalous result that a junior user is entitled to keep its Supplemental Registration for a descriptive term in which it has not established secondary meaning (as evidenced by registration on the Supplemental Register) because a *prior* user cannot show secondary meaning in that term either."

California Cooler, Inc. v. Loretto Winery, Ltd., 774 F.2d 1451, 1454 (9th Cir.1985). "Registration on the principal register shows that the Commissioner has determined that the mark is distinctive. Registration on the supplemental register means that the Commissioner has determined that the mark is 'capable of distinguishing.'"

Clairol Inc. v. Gillette Co., 389 F.2d 264, 267 (2d Cir.1968). "Registration of a mark on the Supplemental Register does nothing to enlarge the substantive rights of the registrant. *At 269 n.9:* [M]ost marks registered on the supplemental register will not, *prima facie*, receive protection as valid trademarks, for their very presence on that register indicates a preliminary determination that they are not distinctive of the applicants' goods. But a mark registered on the supplemental register is not necessarily different in this respect from one registered on the principal register, for while registration on the principal register confers certain advantages, it does not, taken alone, mean that the mark will be protected."

Novartis Consumer Health, Inc. v. McNeil-PPC, Inc., 53 U.S.P.Q.2d 1406, 1410 (D.N.J.1999). "A bona fide intent to use the mark in commerce does not satisfy the 'use in commerce' requirement for registration on the Supplemental Register. Although 15 U.S.C. §1095 [Lanham Act §27] provides that 'registration of a mark on the supplemental register shall not constitute an admission that the mark has not acquired distinctiveness,' there is nothing in the Lanham Act 'to preclude Supplemental Registration from being deemed an admission against interest that the term is not inherently distinctive.' The 'very presence [of a mark] on the Supplemental Register indicates a preliminary determination that the mark is not distinctive of the applicant's goods.'"

§1092. PUBLICATION; NOT SUBJECT TO OPPOSITION; CANCELLATION

[LANHAM ACT §24]

Marks for the supplemental register shall not be published for or be subject to opposition, but shall be published on registration in the Official Gazette of the Patent and Trademark Office.

Whenever any person believes that such person is or will be damaged by the registration of a mark on the supplemental register—

(1) for which the effective filing date is after the date on which such person's mark became famous and which would be likely to cause dilution by blurring or dilution by tarnishment under section 1125(c) of title 15; or

(2) on grounds other than dilution by blurring or dilution by tarnishment, such person may at any time, upon payment of the prescribed fee and the filing of a petition stating the ground therefor, apply to the Director to cancel such registration.

The Director shall refer such application to the Trademark Trial and Appeal Board which shall give notice thereof to the registrant. If it is found after a hearing before the Board that the registrant is not entitled to registration, or that the mark has been abandoned, the registration shall be canceled by the Director. However, no final judgment shall be entered in favor of an applicant under section 1051(b) of title 15 before the mark is registered, if such applicant cannot prevail without establishing constructive use pursuant to section 1057(c) of title 15.

History of 15 U.S.C. §1092: July 5, 1946, ch. 540, §24, 60 Stat. 436; Aug. 8, 1958, P.L. 85-609, §1(d), 72 Stat. 540; Oct. 9, 1962, P.L. 87-772, §14, 76 Stat. 773; Jan. 2, 1975, P.L. 93-596, §1, 88 Stat. 1949; Nov. 16, 1988, P.L. 100-667, §122, 102 Stat. 3943; Aug. 5, 1999, P.L. 106-43, §2(d), 113 Stat. 218; Nov. 29, 1999, P.L. 106-113, §1000(a)(9), 113 Stat. 1536; Oct. 6, 2006, P.L. 109-312, §3(d), 120 Stat. 1732.

Treatise Cross-References

McCarthy on Trademark & Unfair Competition

Ch. 19, *Federal Registration of Marks*, §19:41
Ch. 20, *Inter Partes Trademark Proceedings in the Patent & Trademark Office*, §20:80
Ch. 24, *Infringement by Use of Mark on Noncompetitive Goods or Services*, §24:100

§1093. REGISTRATION CERTIFICATES FOR MARKS ON PRINCIPAL & SUPPLEMENTAL REGISTERS TO BE DIFFERENT

[LANHAM ACT §25]

The certificates of registration for marks registered on the supplemental register shall be conspicuously different from certificates issued for marks registered on the principal register.

History of 15 U.S.C. §1093: July 5, 1946, ch. 540, §25, 60 Stat. 436.

§1094. PROVISIONS OF CHAPTER APPLICABLE TO REGISTRATIONS ON SUPPLEMENTAL REGISTER

[LANHAM ACT §26]

The provisions of this chapter shall govern so far as applicable applications for registration and registrations on the supplemental register as well as those on the principal register, but applications for and registrations on the supplemental register shall not be subject to or receive the advantages of sections 1051(b), 1052(e), (f), 1057(b), (c), 1062(a), 1063 to 1068, inclusive, 1072, 1115, and 1124 of title 15.

History of 15 U.S.C. §1094: July 5, 1946, ch. 540, §26, 60 Stat. 436; Nov. 16, 1988, P.L. 100-667, §123, 102 Stat. 3943; Oct. 30, 1998, P.L. 105-330, §201(a)(6), 112 Stat. 3070.

Treatise Cross-References

McCarthy on Trademark & Unfair Competition

Ch. 19, *Federal Registration of Marks*, §19:36

ANNOTATIONS

ERBE Elektromedizin GmbH v. Canady Tech., 629 F.3d 1278, 1288 (Fed.Cir.2010). "Federal registration on the Principal Register provides a presumption of the mark's validity [under 15 U.S.C. §1057(b), Lanham Act §7(b)]. Registration of a mark on the Supplemental Register, however, does not. [P] bears the burden of proving that it owns a valid mark [in its trademark-infringement suit]."

§1095. REGISTRATION ON PRINCIPAL REGISTER NOT PRECLUDED

[LANHAM ACT §27]

Registration of a mark on the supplemental register, or under the Act of March 19, 1920, shall not preclude registration by the registrant on the principal register established by this chapter. Registration of a mark on the supplemental register shall not constitute an admission that the mark has not acquired distinctiveness.

History of 15 U.S.C. §1095: July 5, 1946, ch. 540, §27, 60 Stat. 436; Nov. 16, 1988, P.L. 100-667, §124, 102 Stat. 3943.

Treatise Cross-References

McCarthy on Trademark & Unfair Competition

Ch. 19, *Federal Registration of Marks*, §§19:35; 19:43

§1096. REGISTRATION ON SUPPLEMENTAL REGISTER NOT USED TO STOP IMPORTATIONS

[LANHAM ACT §28]

Registration on the supplemental register or under the Act of March 19, 1920, shall not be filed in the Department of the Treasury or be used to stop importations.

History of 15 U.S.C. §1096: July 5, 1946, ch. 540, §28, 60 Stat. 436.

SUBCHAPTER III. GENERAL PROVISIONS

§1111. NOTICE OF REGISTRATION; DISPLAY WITH MARK; RECOVERY OF PROFITS & DAMAGES IN INFRINGEMENT SUIT

[LANHAM ACT §29]

Notwithstanding the provisions of section 1072 of title 15, a registrant of a mark registered in the Patent and Trademark Office, may give notice that his mark is registered by displaying with the mark the words "Registered in U.S. Patent and Trademark Office" or "Reg. U.S. Pat. & Tm. Off." or the letter R enclosed within a circle, thus ®; and in any suit for infringement under this chapter by such a registrant failing to give such notice of registration, no profits and no damages shall be recovered under the provisions of this chapter unless the defendant had actual notice of the registration.

History of 15 U.S.C. §1111: July 5, 1946, ch. 540, §29, 60 Stat. 436; Oct. 9, 1962, P.L. 87-772, §15, 76 Stat. 773; Jan. 2, 1975, P.L. 93-596, §§1, 2, 88 Stat. 1949; Nov. 16, 1988, P.L. 100-667, §125, 102 Stat. 1343.

Treatise Cross-References

McCarthy on Trademark & Unfair Competition

Ch. 19, *Federal Registration of Marks*, §§19:144-19:146; 19:147
Ch. 25, *Types of Trademark Infringement*, §25:15
Ch. 30, *Remedies for Trademark Infringement & Unfair Competition*, §§30:88; 30:94

ANNOTATIONS

U.S. v. Kim, 51 F.3d 92, 94 (7th Cir.1995). 15 U.S.C. §1111, Lanham Act §29, "does not create a defense; it is a limitation on remedies. ... Omission of [registered] symbol and lack of knowledge combined do not foreclose equitable remedies (including the confiscation of [D's] stocks of products) and therefore cannot be called a 'defense' under the Lanham Act."

Schroeder v. Lotito, 747 F.2d 801, 802 (1st Cir. 1984). "The limitations of [15 U.S.C. §1111, Lanham Act §29,] are incorporated by reference into 15 U.S.C. §1117 [Lanham Act §35], which authorizes recovery for profits, damages, costs, and attorney's fees. ... Section 1111, by its language, places a notice requirement only upon the recovery of profits and damages. Furthermore, the legislative history of the attorney's fees provision indicated that it was considered to be essentially an equitable remedy. We see no intent by Congress to limit this equitable remedy by requiring the statutory notice of §1111. The only requirement Congress placed upon the award of attorney's fees was that the case be 'exceptional.'"

§1112. CLASSIFICATION OF GOODS & SERVICES; REGISTRATION IN PLURALITY OF CLASSES

[LANHAM ACT §30]

The Director may establish a classification of goods and services, for convenience of Patent and Trademark Office administration, but not to limit or extend the applicant's or registrant's rights. The applicant may apply to register a mark for any or all of the goods or services on or in connection with which he or she is using or has a bona fide intention to use the mark in commerce: *Provided*, That if the Director by regulation permits the filing of an application for the registration of a mark for goods or services which fall within a plurality of classes, a fee equaling the sum of the fees for filing an application in each class shall be paid, and the Director may issue a single certificate of registration for such mark.

History of 15 U.S.C. §1112: July 5, 1946, ch. 540, §30, 60 Stat. 436; Oct. 9, 1962, P.L. 87-772, §16, 76 Stat. 773; Jan. 2, 1975, P.L. 93-596, §1, 88 Stat. 1949; Nov. 16, 1988, P.L. 100-667, §126, 102 Stat. 3943; Nov. 29, 1999, P.L. 106-113, §1000(a)(9), 113 Stat. 1536.

See also 37 C.F.R. §§6.1, 6.2.

Treatise Cross-References

McCarthy on Trademark & Unfair Competition

Ch. 19, *Federal Registration of Marks*, §19:56

§1113. FEES

[LANHAM ACT §31]

(a) Applications; services; materials.—The Director shall establish fees for the filing and processing of an application for the registration of a trademark or other mark and for all other services performed by and materials furnished by the Patent and Trademark Office related to trademarks and other marks. Fees established under this subsection may be adjusted by the Director once each year to reflect, in the aggregate, any fluctuations during the preceding 12 months in the Consumer Price Index, as determined by the Secretary of Labor. Changes of less than 1 percent may be ignored. No fee established under this section shall take effect until at least 30 days after notice of the fee has been published in the Federal Register and in the Official Gazette of the Patent and Trademark Office.

(b) Waiver; Indian products.—The Director may waive the payment of any fee for any service or material related to trademarks or other marks in connection with an occasional request made by a department or agency of the Government, or any officer thereof. The Indian Arts and Crafts Board will not be charged any fee to register Government trademarks of genuineness and quality for Indian products or for products of particular Indian tribes and groups.

History of 15 U.S.C. §1113: July 5, 1946, ch. 540, §31, 60 Stat. 437; Aug. 8, 1958, P.L. 85-609, §1(e), 72 Stat. 540; July 24, 1965, P.L. 89-83, §3, 79 Stat. 260; Jan. 2, 1975, P.L. 93-596, §1, 88 Stat. 1949; Dec. 12, 1980, P.L. 96-517, §5, 94 Stat. 3018; Aug. 27, 1982, P.L. 97-247, §3(f), 96 Stat. 319; Sept. 8, 1982, P.L. 97-256, §103, 96 Stat. 256; Dec. 10, 1991, P.L. 102-204, §5(f)(1), 105 Stat. 1640; Oct. 30, 1998, P.L. 105-330, §201(a)(7), 112 Stat. 3070; Nov. 29, 1999, P.L. 106-113, §1000(a)(9), 113 Stat. 1536.

§1114. REMEDIES; INFRINGEMENT; INNOCENT INFRINGEMENT BY PRINTERS & PUBLISHERS

[LANHAM ACT §32]

(1) Any person who shall, without the consent of the registrant—

(a) use in commerce any reproduction, counterfeit, copy, or colorable imitation of a registered mark in connection with the sale, offering for sale, distribution, or advertising of any goods or services on or in connection with which such use is likely to cause confusion, or to cause mistake, or to deceive; or

(b) reproduce, counterfeit, copy, or colorably imitate a registered mark and apply such reproduction, counterfeit, copy, or colorable imitation to labels, signs, prints, packages, wrappers, receptacles or advertisements intended to be used in commerce upon or in connection with the sale, offering for sale, distribution, or advertising of goods or services on or in connection with which such use is likely to cause confusion, or to cause mistake, or to deceive,

shall be liable in a civil action by the registrant for the remedies hereinafter provided. Under subsection (b) hereof, the registrant shall not be entitled to recover profits or damages unless the acts have been committed with knowledge that such imitation is intended to be used to cause confusion, or to cause mistake, or to deceive.

As used in this paragraph, the term "any person" includes the United States, all agencies and instrumentalities thereof, and all individuals, firms, corporations, or other persons acting for the United States and with the authorization and consent of the United States, and any State, any instrumentality of a State, and any officer or employee of a State or instrumentality of a State acting in his or her official capacity. The United States, all agencies and instrumentalities thereof, and all individuals, firms, corporations, other persons acting for the United States and with the authorization and consent of the United States, and any State, and any such instrumentality, officer, or employee, shall be subject to the provisions of this chapter in the same manner and to the same extent as any nongovernmental entity.

(2) Notwithstanding any other provision of this chapter, the remedies given to the owner of a right infringed under this chapter or to a person bringing an action under section 1125(a) or (d) of title 15 shall be limited as follows:

(A) Where an infringer or violator is engaged solely in the business of printing the mark or violating matter for others and establishes that he or she was an innocent infringer or innocent violator, the owner of the right infringed or person bringing the action under section 1125(a) of title 15 shall be entitled as against such infringer or violator only to an injunction against future printing.

(B) Where the infringement or violation complained of is contained in or is part of paid advertising matter in a newspaper, magazine, or other similar periodical or in an electronic communication as defined in section 2510(12) of title 18, the remedies of the owner of the right infringed or person bringing the action under section 1125(a) of title 15 as against the publisher or distributor of such newspaper, magazine, or other similar periodical or electronic communication shall be limited to an injunction against the presentation of such advertising matter in future issues of such newspapers, magazines, or other similar periodicals or in future transmissions of such electronic communications. The limitations of this subparagraph shall apply only to innocent infringers and innocent violators.

(C) Injunctive relief shall not be available to the owner of the right infringed or person bringing the action under section 1125(a) of title 15 with respect to an issue of a newspaper, magazine, or other similar periodical or an electronic communication containing infringing matter or violating matter where restraining the dissemination of such infringing matter or violating matter in any particular issue of such periodical or in an electronic communication would delay the delivery of such issue or transmission of such electronic communication after the regular time for such delivery or transmission, and such delay would be due to the method by which publication and distribution of such periodical or transmission of such electronic communication is customarily conducted in accordance with sound business practice, and not due to any method or device adopted to evade this section or to prevent or delay the issuance of an injunction or restraining order with respect to such infringing matter or violating matter.

(D)(i)(I) A domain name registrar, a domain name registry, or other domain name registration authority that takes any action described under clause (ii) affecting a domain name shall not be liable for monetary relief or, except as provided in subclause (II), for injunctive relief, to any person for such action, regardless of whether the domain name is finally determined to infringe or dilute the mark.

(II) A domain name registrar, domain name registry, or other domain name registration authority described in subclause (I) may be subject to injunctive relief only if such registrar, registry, or other registration authority has—

(aa) not expeditiously deposited with a court, in which an action has been filed regarding the disposition of the domain name, documents sufficient for the court to establish the court's control and authority regarding the disposition of the registration and use of the domain name;

(bb) transferred, suspended, or otherwise modified the domain name during the pendency of the action, except upon order of the court; or

(cc) willfully failed to comply with any such court order.

(ii) An action referred to under clause (i)(I) is any action of refusing to register, removing from registration, transferring, temporarily disabling, or permanently canceling a domain name—

(I) in compliance with a court order under section 1125(d) of title 15; or

(II) in the implementation of a reasonable policy by such registrar, registry, or authority prohibiting the registration of a domain name that is identical to, confusingly similar to, or dilutive of another's mark.

(iii) A domain name registrar, a domain name registry, or other domain name registration authority shall not be liable for damages under this section for the registration or maintenance of a domain name for another absent a showing of bad faith intent to profit from such registration or maintenance of the domain name.

(iv) If a registrar, registry, or other registration authority takes an action described under clause (ii) based on a knowing and material misrepresentation by any other person that a domain name is identical to, confusingly similar to, or dilutive of a mark, the person making the knowing and material misrepresentation shall be liable for any damages, including costs and attorney's fees, incurred by the domain name registrant as a result of such action. The court may also grant injunctive relief to the domain name registrant, including the reactivation of the domain name or the transfer of the domain name to the domain name registrant.

(v) A domain name registrant whose domain name has been suspended, disabled, or transferred under a policy described under clause (ii)(II) may, upon notice to the mark owner, file a civil action to establish that the registration or use of the domain name by such registrant is not unlawful under this chapter. The court may grant injunctive relief to the domain name registrant, including the reactivation of the domain name or transfer of the domain name to the domain name registrant.

(E) As used in this paragraph—

(i) the term "violator" means a person who violates section 1125(a) of title 15; and

(ii) the term "violating matter" means matter that is the subject of a violation under section 1125(a) of title 15.

(3)(A) Any person who engages in the conduct described in paragraph (11) of section 110 of title 17 and who complies with the requirements set forth in that paragraph is not liable on account of such conduct for a violation of any right under this chapter. This subparagraph does not preclude liability, nor shall it be construed to restrict the defenses or limitations on rights granted under this chapter, of a person for conduct not described in paragraph (11) of section 110 of title 17, even if that person also engages in conduct described in paragraph (11) of section 110 of such title.

(B) A manufacturer, licensee, or licensor of technology that enables the making of limited portions of audio or video content of a motion picture imperceptible as described in subparagraph (A) is not liable on account of such manufacture or license for a violation of any right under this chapter, if such manufacturer, licensee, or licensor ensures that the technology provides a clear and conspicuous notice at the beginning of each performance that the performance of the motion picture is altered from the performance intended by the director or copyright holder of the motion picture. The limitations on liability in subparagraph (A) and this subparagraph shall not apply to a manufacturer, licensee, or licensor of technology that fails to comply with this paragraph.

(C) The requirement under subparagraph (B) to provide notice shall apply only with respect to technology manufactured after the end of the 180-day period beginning on April 27, 2005.

(D) Any failure by a manufacturer, licensee, or licensor of technology to qualify for the exemption under subparagraphs (A) and (B) shall not be construed to create an inference that any such party that engages in conduct described in paragraph (11) of section 110 of title 17 is liable for trademark infringement by reason of such conduct.

History of 15 U.S.C. §1114: July 5, 1946, ch. 540, §32, 60 Stat. 437; Oct. 9, 1962, P.L. 87-772, §17, 76 Stat. 773; Nov. 16, 1988, P.L. 100-667, §127, 102 Stat. 3943; Oct. 27, 1992, P.L. 102-542, §3(a), 106 Stat. 3567; Oct. 30, 1998, P.L. 105-330, §201(a)(8), 112 Stat. 3070; Aug. 5, 1999, P.L. 106-43, §4(a), 113 Stat. 219; Nov. 29, 1999, P.L. 106-113, §1000(a)(9), 113 Stat. 1536; Apr. 27, 2005, P.L. 109-9, §202(b), 119 Stat. 223.

See also 18 U.S.C. §2320; 19 U.S.C. §1526.

Treatise Cross-References

McCarthy on Trademark & Unfair Competition

Ch. 9, *Corporation & Organization Trade Names*, §9:6
Ch. 18, *Assignment & Licensing of Trademarks*, §18:63
Ch. 19, *Federal Registration of Marks*, §19:144
Ch. 23, *Likelihood of Confusion: The Test of Trademark Infringement*, §§23:1; 23:10; 23:11.50; 23:76
Ch. 24, *Infringement by Use of Mark on Noncompetitive Goods or Services*, §§24:63; 24:101
Ch. 25, *Types of Trademark Infringement*, §§25:26; 25:28; 25:29
Ch. 27, *Lanham Act §43(a) & False Advertising*, §27:20
Ch. 29, *International Aspects of Trademark Law*, §§29:48; 29:51.75
Ch. 30, *Remedies for Trademark Infringement & Unfair Competition*, §§30:10; 30:37; 30:88; 30:94
Ch. 32, *Procedure in Trademark Infringement & Unfair Competition Litigation*, §§32:3; 32:12; 32:18

ANNOTATIONS

Generally

B&B Hardware, Inc. v. Hargis Indus., ___ U.S. ___, 135 S.Ct. 1293, 1299 (2015). "This case concerns the application of issue preclusion in the context of trademark law. [¶] Both a registration proceeding and a suit for trademark infringement ... can occur at the same time. ... In both registration proceedings and infringement litigation, the tribunal asks whether a likelihood of confusion exists between the mark sought to be protected ... and the other mark.... [¶] The question before this Court is whether the District Court in this case should have applied issue preclusion to the TTAB's decision that [respondent's mark] is confusingly similar to [petitioner's mark]. [W]e hold that a court should give preclusive effect to TTAB decisions if the ordinary elements of issue preclusion are met. *At U.S. ___, S.Ct. 1306-07:* [F]or a great many registration decisions issue preclusion obviously will not apply because the ordinary elements will not be met. [¶] [I]t does not matter that registration and infringement are governed by different statutory provisions. Often a single standard is placed in different statutes; that does not foreclose issue preclusion. Neither does it matter that the TTAB and the Eighth Circuit use different factors to assess likelihood of confusion. For one thing, the factors are not fundamentally different, and '[m]inor variations in the application of what is in essence the same legal standard do not defeat preclusion.' More important, if federal law provides a single standard, parties cannot escape preclusion simply by litigating anew in tribunals that apply that one standard differently. A contrary rule would encourage the very evils that issue preclusion helps to prevent. [¶] The real question, therefore, is whether likelihood of confusion for purposes of registration is the same standard as likelihood of confusion for purposes of infringement. We conclude it is…."

Ariel Invs. v. Ariel Capital Advisors LLC, 881 F.3d 520, 521 (7th Cir.2018). "The Lanham Act does not authorize nationwide service of process. A plaintiff therefore must secure personal jurisdiction under state law."

Savannah Coll. of Art & Design, Inc. v. Sportswear, Inc., 872 F.3d 1256, 1262 (11th Cir.2017). "The question for us is whether [P] has enforceable service mark rights that extend—beyond the services listed in its federal registrations—to goods in order to satisfy the first prong of an infringement analysis: the validity and scope of a contested mark. *At 1264:* [T]he holder of a federally-registered service mark need not register that mark for goods—or provide evidence of prior use of that mark on goods—in order to establish the unrestricted validity and scope of the service mark, or to protect against another's allegedly infringing use of that mark on goods." *But see* ***Murphy v. Provident Mut. Life Ins.***, 923 F.2d 923, 926 (2d Cir.1990) (service marks do not by their nature extend to goods or products).

Fortune Dynamic, Inc. v. Victoria's Secret Stores Brand Mgmt., 618 F.3d 1025, 1031 (9th Cir. 2010). "'[B]ecause of the intensely factual nature of trademark disputes, summary judgment is generally disfavored in the trademark arena.'"

Zino Davidoff SA v. CVS Corp., 571 F.3d 238, 243 (2d Cir.2009). "[T]he district court correctly found that [P] was likely to succeed on the merits in its contention that [D's] sales of its products with the UPC removed constituted trademark infringement. We recognize that, as a general rule, the Lanham Act does not impose liability for 'the sale of genuine goods bearing a true mark even though the sale is not authorized by the mark owner' because such a sale does not inherently cause confusion or dilution. However, we have held that goods are not genuine if they do not conform to the trademark holder's quality control standards, … or if they differ materially from the product authorized by the trademark holder for sale…. [¶] Where the alleged infringer has interfered with the trademark holder's ability to control quality, the trademark holder's claim is not defeated because of failure to show that the goods sold were defective. That is because the interference with the trademark holder's legitimate steps to control quality unreasonably subjects the trademark holder to the risk of injury to the reputation of its mark."

Beltronics USA, Inc. v. Midwest Inventory Distrib., 562 F.3d 1067, 1072-73 (10th Cir.2009). "We hold, as other federal circuit courts have held, that the unauthorized resale of a materially different trademarked product can constitute trademark infringement. [¶] We emphasize that not all differences are material. … A guiding principle in evaluating whether a difference between two products bearing the same trademark is material is whether the difference 'confuses consumers and impinges on the … trademark holder's goodwill.' For this reason, the materiality analysis must be undertaken 'on a case-by-case basis[ ]' … and must include 'an examination of the products and markets at issue.' Although no mechanical process exists for determining the threshold for materiality, … a difference is material if 'consumers [would] consider [it] relevant to a decision about whether to purchase a product.' Because many factors influence such considerations, the threshold 'must be kept low to include even subtle differences between products.' We review de novo the question of whether differences between trademarked goods and goods sold by an alleged infringer are material. [¶] [T]he district court did not commit an error of law in concluding that material differences may include the warranties and services associated with [P's products]. *At 1074:* So long as resellers of materially different products take the necessary steps to adequately alleviate this confusion and prevent injury to the trademark's goodwill—by, for example, sufficiently disclosing that the product differs from the originally sold product—those differences will be unlikely to trigger the liability [D] envisions." *See also* ***Brilliance Au-***

dio, Inc. v. Haights Cross Comms., 474 F.3d 365, 370 (6th Cir.2007) (same as annotation); ***Davidoff & CIE, S.A. v. PLD Int'l***, 263 F.3d 1297, 1302 (11th Cir.2001) (same as annotation); ***Iberia Foods Corp. v. Romeo***, 150 F.3d 298, 302-03 (3d Cir.1998) (gray-market goods); ***Martin's Herend Imps., Inc. v. Diamond & Gem Trading USA, Co.***, 112 F.3d 1296, 1301-02 (5th Cir. 1997) (same as annotation); ***Societe Des Produits Nestle, S.A. v. Casa Helvetia, Inc.***, 982 F.2d 633, 638-39 (1st Cir.1992) (same as annotation); ***Original Appalachian Artworks, Inc. v. Granada Elecs., Inc.***, 816 F.2d 68, 73 (2d Cir.1987) (same as annotation).

Mid-State Aftermarket Body Parts, Inc. v. MQVP, Inc., 466 F.3d 630, 633 (8th Cir.2006). "'While the distinction between a trademark and a service mark may be relevant for registration purposes, it is not particularly relevant for the purposes of the likelihood of confusion analysis.'"

Rock & Roll Hall of Fame & Museum v. Gentile Prod., 134 F.3d 749, 753 (6th Cir.1998). "[W]hether alleging infringement of a registered trademark, pursuant to 15 U.S.C. §1114(1) [Lanham Act §32(1)], or infringement of an unregistered trademark, pursuant to 15 U.S.C. §1125(a)(1) [Lanham Act §43(a)(1)], it is clear that a plaintiff must show that it has actually used the designation at issue *as a trademark*, and that the defendant has also used the same or a similar designation *as a trademark*."

Chanel, Inc. v. Italian Activewear, Inc., 931 F.2d 1472, 1476 (11th Cir.1991). "[A] showing of intent or bad faith is unnecessary to establish a violation of [15 U.S.C. §1114(1)(a), Lanham Act §32(1)(a)], or to seek remedies pursuant to [15 U.S.C. §1117(a), Lanham Act §35(a)]."

Exxon Corp. v. Humble Expl. Co., 695 F.2d 96, 103 (5th Cir.1983). "While [15 U.S.C. §1125, Lanham Act §43,] has a broader reach than [15 U.S.C. §1114, Lanham Act §32], and claims under it can be maintained by plaintiffs who are not owners of a trademark, when a claim is based on alleged ownership of a mark, the two sections must be applied in a parallel manner." *See also* ***Gucci, Inc. v. Action Activewear, Inc.***, 759 F.Supp. 1060, 1062-63 (S.D.N.Y.1991).

Quabaug Rubber Co. v. Fabiano Shoe Co., 567 F.2d 154, 159 (1st Cir.1977). "There appear to be no cases where a nonexclusive licensee has been permitted to maintain a trademark infringement suit in the absence of the 'registrant.'"

B&B Hardware, Inc. v. Hargis Indus., No. 4:06CV01654 BSM (E.D.Ark.2016) (order; 5-16-16). "[D] argues that 'registrant,' 'registered mark,' and 'registered on the principal register' all require [P] to maintain its registration for the duration of the suit, rather than simply possess it when [D] allegedly infringed. [¶] The statute does not direct what must occur, and this is an issue of first impression in the Eighth Circuit. [¶] '[R]egistrant' and 'registered mark' do not refer to a claimant's present condition, but only the situation at the time of infringement. ... Viewing the record in [P's] favor, it had a registered mark at the time of the infringement, and assuming there is a likelihood of confusion between the marks, [P] has a valid infringement claim."

Abercrombie & Fitch v. Fashion Shops, Inc., 363 F.Supp.2d 952, 962 (S.D.Ohio 2005). An "easy 'line' to draw [between a legal and an infringing situation] is ... demarcating any merchandise manufactured without [P's] approval or rejected by [P] and sold without a 'Sell-Off Compliance Agreement.' Under the first sale doctrine, this merchandise was not 'authorized to be made, in the first instance.'"

§1114(1)—Cause of Action

E.T. Browne Drug Co. v. Cococare Prods., 538 F.3d 185, 191 (3d Cir.2008). "To establish trademark infringement in violation of ... Lanham Act [§32], 15 U.S.C. §1114, a plaintiff must prove that (1) the mark is valid and legally protectable, (2) it owns the mark, and (3) the defendant's use of the mark is likely to create confusion concerning the origin of goods or services."

Applied Info. Sci. Corp. v. eBay, Inc., 511 F.3d 966, 969-70 (9th Cir.2007). "To prevail on its trademark infringement claim, [P] must show that: (1) it has a valid, protectable trademark, and (2) that [D's] use of the mark is likely to cause confusion. 'The threshold issue in any action for trademark infringement is whether the words used by a manufacturer in connection with his product are entitled to protection.' There are three ways in which [P] could have established it had a protectable interest: (1) it has a federally registered mark in goods or services; (2) its mark is descriptive but has acquired a secondary meaning in the market; or (3) it has a suggestive mark, which is inherently distinctive and protectable. [B]y demonstrating that it held a federal registration, [P] made a prima facie showing that it held a valid, protectable interest in the use of the [registered] mark in connection with the goods listed in its registration. [¶] A registered trademark holder's protectable interest is limited to those goods or services described in its registration. *At 971:* [T]he scope of validity and the scope of relief for infringement are not coextensive. Although the *validity* of a registered mark extends only to the listed goods or services, an owner's *remedies* against confusion with its valid mark are not so circumscribed. ... Thus a trademark owner may seek redress if another's use of the mark on different goods or services is likely to cause confusion with the owner's use of the mark in connection with its registered goods: [O]n the issue of validity, the recitation of goods and services in the registration limits the scope of presumptions of validity, but on the separate issue of infringement, the registered mark is infringed when used by another with any goods or services which creates a likelihood of confusion." *See also* ***Amazing Spaces, Inc. v. Metro Mini Storage***, 608 F.3d 225, 235-36 (5th Cir.2010); ***Virgin Enters. v. Nawab***, 335 F.3d 141, 146 (2d Cir.2003).

Lamparello v. Falwell, 420 F.3d 309, 313 (4th Cir. 2005). "Both infringement and false designation of origin have five elements. To prevail under either cause of action, the trademark holder must prove: (1) that it possesses a mark; (2) that the opposing party used the mark; (3) that the opposing party's use of the mark occurred 'in commerce'; (4) that the opposing party used the mark in connection with the sale, offering for sale, distribution, or advertising of goods or services; and (5) that the opposing party used the mark in a manner likely to confuse consumers." (Internal quotes omitted.) *See also* ***North Am. Med. Corp. v. Axiom Worldwide, Inc.***, 522 F.3d 1211, 1218 (11th Cir.2008); ***DeCosta v. Viacom Int'l***, 981 F.2d 602, 605 (1st Cir.1992).

§1114(1)—Commerce

For more annotations on this topic, see 15 U.S.C. §1051, *§1051(a)—Use in Commerce*, p. 6, 15 U.S.C. §1127, *Commerce*, p. 170, and *Use in Commerce*, p. 172.

Steele v. Bulova Watch Co., 344 U.S. 280, 281 (1952). "The issue is whether a U.S. District Court has jurisdiction to award relief to an American corporation against acts of trade-mark infringement and unfair competition consummated in a foreign country by a citizen and resident of the U.S." Held: The court has jurisdiction.

La Quinta Worldwide LLC v. Q.R.T.M., S.A. de C.V., 762 F.3d 867, 872 (9th Cir.2014). "[D] argues that we lack subject-matter jurisdiction because its expressions of intent to open a hotel are not sufficient to show a 'use in commerce' under the Lanham Act. The 'use in commerce' requirement that [D] relies on is found in §§32 and 43(a) of the Lanham Act [15 U.S.C. §§1114 and 1125(a)], which both lay out claims for infringement. We hold that the 'use in commerce' element of Lanham Act §§32 and 43(a) claims is not a jurisdictional requirement, and we have subject-matter jurisdiction under 15 U.S.C. §1121(a) [Lanham Act §39(a)]."

North Am. Med. Corp. v. Axiom Worldwide, Inc., 522 F.3d 1211, 1218-19 (11th Cir.2008). "[D] briefly argues that placing a competitor's trademarks within meta tags, which consumers never view, does not constitute a 'use' as required to find trademark infringement under the Lanham Act. However, we readily conclude that the facts of the instant case do involve a 'use' as contemplated in the Lanham Act—that is, a use in connection with the sale or advertisement of goods. ... Under the plain meaning of the language of [15 U.S.C. §1114(1)(a), Lanham Act §32(1)(a)], such use constitutes a use in commerce in connection with the advertising of any goods." *But see* ***1-800 Contacts, Inc. v. WhenU.Com, Inc.***, this page.

Lorillard Tobacco Co. v. Amouri's Grand Foods, Inc., 453 F.3d 377, 381 (6th Cir.2006). "We ... find ... no reason to restrict liability to those who actually create, manufacture or package the infringing items. Contrary to [D's] position, while a showing of 'likelihood of confusion' does require that consumers mistakenly believe that the infringing goods were 'sponsored or otherwise approved' by the plaintiff, there is no further requirement that those goods must have been produced by the defendant. Indeed, all the statutes demand is that the defendant have 'used' the goods 'in commerce' ([15 U.S.C.] §§1114(1)(a) and 1125(a) [Lanham Act §§32(1)(a) and 43(a)]), and we can think of no clearer 'use' of goods 'in commerce' than offering them for sale. In sum, as the Seventh Circuit has put it concisely, '[s]ellers bear strict liability for violations of the Lanham Act'...."

1-800 Contacts, Inc. v. WhenU.Com, Inc., 414 F.3d 400, 403 (2d Cir.2005). "We hold that, as a matter of law, [D] does not 'use' [P's] trademarks within the meaning of the Lanham Act ... when it (1) includes [P's] website address, which is almost identical to [P's] trademark, in an unpublished directory of terms that trigger delivery of [D's] contextually relevant advertising to [computer users]; or (2) causes separate, branded pop-up ads to appear on a [computer user's] computer screen either above, below, or along the bottom edge of [P's] website window." *But see* ***North Am. Med. Corp. v. Axiom Worldwide, Inc.***, p. 64.

Bosley Med. Inst. v. Kremer, 403 F.3d 672, 676 (9th Cir.2005). "While the meaning of the term 'commercial use in commerce' is not entirely clear, we have interpreted the language to be roughly analogous to the 'in connection with' sale of goods and services requirement of the infringement statute. *At 677:* [P] argues that it has met the commercial use requirement in three ways. First, it argues that a mark used in an otherwise noncommercial website or as a domain name for an otherwise noncommercial website is nonetheless used in connection with goods and services where a user can click on a link available on that website to reach a commercial site. *At 678:* [D's] website contains no commercial links, but rather contains links to a discussion group, which in turn contains advertising. This roundabout path to the advertising of others is too attenuated to render [D's] site commercial. [¶] [P's] second argument ... is that [D] created his website to enable an extortion scheme in an attempt to profit from registering [website]. [¶] [T]here is no evidence that [D] was trying to sell the domain name itself. [¶] [P's] third ... argument ... is that [D's] use of [P's] trademark was ... 'in connection with goods and services' because [D] prevented users from obtaining [P's] goods and services. *At 679:* [T]he ... inquiry is whether [D] offers *competing* services to the public. [D] is not [P's] competitor; he is their critic. His use of [P's] mark is not in connection with a sale of goods or services—it is in connection with the expression of his opinion *about* [P's] goods and services." *But see* ***People for the Ethical Treatment of Animals v. Doughney***, 263 F.3d 359, 365-66 (4th Cir.2001) (commercial-use requirement met because D's website had links to commercial websites).

Coca-Cola Co. v. Stewart, 621 F.2d 287, 290 (8th Cir.1980). "The word 'commerce' means all commerce which may lawfully be regulated by Congress."

Saint Louis Univ. v. Meyer, 625 F.Supp.2d 827, 830 (E.D.Mo.2008). "[T]here is no evidence that [D-professor] used [P-university's unregistered] marks in public. [D] told the newspaper's editor-in-chief ... that he had 'reserved the name' of the paper for the students' use, should they want it[, by forming a nonprofit corporation]. However, '[a] company's internal utilization of a trademark in a way that does not communicate it to the public is analogous to an individual's private thoughts about a trademark. Such conduct simply does not violate the Lanham Act, which is concerned with the use of trademarks in connection with the sale of goods or services in a manner likely to lead to consumer confusion as to the source of such goods or services.'"

800-JR Cigar, Inc. v. GoTo.com, Inc., 437 F.Supp.2d 273, 285 (D.N.J.2006). "[T]he pop-up advertising context, where the use of trademarks in internal computer coding is neither communicated to the public nor for sale to the highest bidder, [is different from D's use of P's marks]. [¶] Here, [D] makes trademark use of [P's] marks in three ways. First, by accepting bids from those competitors of [P] desiring to pay for prominence in search results, [D] trades on the value of the marks. Second, by ranking its paid advertisers before any 'natural' listings in a search results list, [D] has injected itself into the marketplace, acting as a conduit to steer potential customers away from [P] to [P's] competitors. Finally, through the Search Term Suggestion Tool, [D] identifies those of [P's] marks which are effective search terms and markets them to [P's] competitors." Held: D used P's marks in commerce.

Bertolli, Inc. v. Filippo Bertolli Fine Foods Ltd., 662 F.Supp. 203, 205 (S.D.N.Y.1987). 15 U.S.C. §1114(1), Lanham Act §32(1), "does not require that the allegedly infringing merchandise be available to the consuming public. That statute provides that a registered mark is infringed whenever any person merely uses in commerce any imitation of the mark. To meet the definition of 'use in commerce' it is sufficient that the goods be transported in commerce."

Council of Better Bus. Bur. v. Better Bus. Bur., Inc., 200 U.S.P.Q. 282, 288 (S.D.Fla.1978), *abrogated on other grounds*, ***Royal Palm Props., LLC v. Premier Estate Props., Inc.***, No. 10-80232-CV (S.D.Fla.2010) (no pub.; 4-15-10). "[T]he law is clear that it is sufficient to establish jurisdiction under the Lanham Act if the alleged infringing use has a substantial effect on [P's] interstate use of the Mark, even if the infringing use is strictly local or intrastate in character. The judicial interpretation given by this circuit is that in commerce is intended to refer to the impact that the infringement has upon the interstate use of the trademark and not to mean that an infringer is immune from interference with an interstate trademark so long as he keeps his infringement within the confines of a state." (Internal quotes omitted.)

§1114(1)—Contributory Infringement

Coach, Inc. v. Goodfellow, 717 F.3d 498, 499-500 (6th Cir.2013). "This case presents a question the Sixth Circuit has not directly addressed: Can a flea market operator be held contributorially liable for trademark infringement by vendors? [Ps] brought suit under the Lanham Act, alleging a … flea market operator is liable for sales of counterfeit products at his flea market. The district court granted [Ps'] motion for summary judgment on liability, entered judgment on the jury's damages verdict of $5,040,000, and awarded attorney's fees and costs to [Ps] in the amount of $186,666.61. [D] argues on appeal that the Lanham Act does not provide for contributory liability for trademark infringement by third persons and that this is not an 'exceptional case' warranting attorney's fees. Because we find the district court neither erred as a matter of law nor abused its discretion, we affirm." *See also* ***Fonovisa, Inc. v. Cherry Auction, Inc.***, 76 F.3d 259, 264-65 (9th Cir. 1996); ***Hard Rock Cafe Licensing Corp. v. Concession Servs.***, 955 F.2d 1143, 1149 (7th Cir.1992).

Tiffany (NJ) Inc. v. eBay Inc., 600 F.3d 93, 103-04 (2d Cir.2010). "Contributory trademark infringement is a judicially created doctrine that derives from the common law of torts. The Supreme Court most recently dealt with the subject in ***Inwood Labs. v. Ives Labs.***, 456 U.S. 844 … (1982). … According to the Court, 'if a manufacturer or distributor intentionally induces another to infringe a trademark, or if it continues to supply its product to one whom it knows or has reason to know is engaging in trademark infringement, the manufacturer or distributor is contributorially responsible for any harm done as a result of the deceit.' *At 106:* [W]hen applying ***Inwood*** to service providers, there are two ways in which a defendant may become contributorially liable for the infringing conduct of another: first, if the service provider 'intentionally induces another to infringe a trademark,' and second, if the service provider 'continues to supply its [service] to one whom it knows or has reason to know is engaging in trademark infringement.' *At 107:* For contributory trademark infringement liability to lie, a service provider must have more than a general knowledge or reason to know that its service is being used to sell counterfeit goods. Some contemporary knowledge of which particular listings are infringing or will infringe in the future is necessary." *See also* ***1-800 Contacts, Inc. v. Lens.com, Inc.***, 722 F.3d 1229, 1253 (10th Cir. 2013); ***Rosetta Stone Ltd. v. Google, Inc.***, 676 F.3d 144, 163 (4th Cir.2012).

Optimum Techs. v. Henkel Consumer Adhesives, Inc., 496 F.3d 1231, 1245 (11th Cir.2007). "[A]lthough there is no separate statutory provision for contributory trademark infringement, and although both actions stem from the general prohibitory language of 15 U.S.C. §1114(1) [Lanham Act §32(1)], the case law suggests that a contributory infringement claim requires, at a minimum, both an allegation of a direct infringement by a third party, and an allegation of an intentional or knowing contribution to that infringement by the defendant."

Perfect 10, Inc. v. Visa Int'l Serv., 494 F.3d 788, 807 (9th Cir.2007). "To be liable for contributory trademark infringement, a defendant must have (1) 'intentionally induced' the primary infringer to infringe, or (2) continued to supply an infringing product to an infringer with knowledge that the infringer is mislabeling the particular product supplied. When the alleged direct infringer supplies a service rather than a product, under the second prong of this test, the court must 'consider the extent of control exercised by the defendant over the third party's means of infringement.' For liability to attach, there must be '[d]irect control and monitoring of the instrumentality used by a third party to infringe the plaintiff's mark.'"

§1114(1)—Vicarious Infringement

Rosetta Stone Ltd. v. Google, Inc., 676 F.3d 144, 165 (4th Cir.2012). "[L]iability for vicarious trademark infringement requires 'a finding that the defendant and the infringer have an apparent or actual partnership, have authority to bind one another in transactions with third parties or exercise joint ownership or control over the infringing product.'" *See also* ***Grubbs v. Sheakley Grp.***, 807 F.3d 785, 793 (6th Cir.2015); ***Kelly-Brown v. Winfrey***, 717 F.3d 295, 314 (2d Cir.2013); ***Perfect 10, Inc. v. Visa Int'l Serv.***, 494 F.3d 788, 807 (9th Cir.2007).

§1114(1)—Counterfeit

General Elec. Co. v. Speicher, 877 F.2d 531, 534 (7th Cir.1989). "The literal sense [of the term 'counterfeiting'] might be the correct one if [15 U.S.C. §1114(1)(a), Lanham Act §32(1)(a),] were aimed just at 'counterfeiting.' But as the words 'reproduction,' 'copy,' and 'colorable imitation' suggest more clearly than 'counterfeiting,' the aim is broader: to prohibit the use of your trademark on someone else's product without your authorization. The usual violator of this prohibition copies, reproduces, imitates—or if you will 'counterfeits'—the trademark. He doesn't *have* the genuine trademark; if he did he wouldn't be an infringer—ordinarily. Sometimes, however, he has the genuine trademark but is an infringer for using it. The most common cases involve distributors. A distributor licensed to sell a trademarked product may decide to sell another product in the trademarked containers in which he received the trademarked product from his supplier. Or the distributor's trademark license may have expired, and rather than ceasing to use the trademark or returning the trademarked items to his supplier or otherwise complying with the terms of the license, the ex-licensee may continue to use the trademark."

Abercrombie & Fitch v. Fashion Shops, Inc., 363 F.Supp.2d 952, 957-58 (S.D.Ohio 2005). "To establish liability for trademark counterfeiting under [15 U.S.C.] §1114 [Lanham Act §32], a plaintiff must allege that: (1) the defendant infringed a registered trademark in violation of §1114; and (2) the defendant intentionally used the mark knowing it was a counterfeit, as the term counterfeit is defined in 15 U.S.C. §1116 [Lanham Act §34]. Therefore, a claim for trademark counterfeiting involves a higher burden of proof because a plaintiff must show both trademark infringement and the intentional use of a counterfeit mark."

U.S. v. 10,510 Packaged Computer Towers, 152 F.Supp.2d 1189, 1193 (N.D.Cal.2001). "Federal courts have held that the inquiry into whether a mark is 'counterfeit' must be conducted 'from the standpoint of an average purchaser.'"

§1114(1)—Damages

Visible Sys. v. Unisys Corp., 551 F.3d 65, 77 (1st Cir.2008). "There is no dispute that [P] was entitled to and received a jury trial for [P's] claim of its own damages for infringement, though the request was joined with a request for equitable relief. [¶] [P] argues that it was also entitled under both the [Lanham] Act and the Seventh Amendment to a jury trial.... *At 78:* [I]t seems clear that the Lanham Act itself does not create a right to a jury trial whenever the remedy of an accounting of defendant's profits is sought. *At 79:* Here, the court ruled that the issue of an accounting is for the court, not a jury. The trial judge also ruled that the evidence to support the remedy of an accounting was insufficient to reach the jury, stating that if the jury made such an award, the court would be forced 'to throw it out.' If the evidence was insufficient to justify an accounting (as we hold), then the question of whether there is a Seventh Amendment jury trial right to an accounting becomes academic and can be avoided."

Audi AG v. D'Amato, 469 F.3d 534, 542 (6th Cir. 2006). "[W]e use the same test to decide whether there has been trademark infringement, unfair competition, or false designation of origin: the likelihood of confusion between the two marks. [D] argues that the district court's finding of a likelihood of confusion should be reversed because [P] did not offer evidence demonstrating *actual* confusion. However, although proof that the buying public was actually deceived is necessary in order to recover *statutory damages* under the Lanham Act, only a 'likelihood of confusion' must be shown in order to obtain *equitable relief....*" *But see* ***Masters v. UHS of Del., Inc.***, 631 F.3d 464, 472 (8th Cir.2011) (proof of actual confusion is not necessary to recover monetary relief, e.g., profits).

Gracie v. Gracie, 217 F.3d 1060, 1068 (9th Cir. 2000). 15 U.S.C. §1114, Lanham Act §32, "requires only a *likelihood* of confusion combined with *willful infringement....* While *actual* confusion may be relevant as evidence of the *likelihood* of confusion (which *is* required for an award of profits under §1114), under our precedents a showing of actual confusion is not necessary to obtain a recovery of profits."

§1114(1)—Declaratory Judgment

Surefoot LC v. Sure Foot Corp., 531 F.3d 1236, 1242 (10th Cir.2008). "In light of ***MedImmune***'s [***MedImmune, Inc. v. Genentech, Inc.***, 549 U.S. 118 (2007),] direction, it seems to us clear that the [reasonable-apprehension-of-suit] test for declaratory judgment jurisdiction ... is no longer good law. *At 1248:* Instead, once the court is satisfied that [U.S. Const.] art. 3's jurisdictional requirements are met, it must then consider a number of factors ... to determine whether the suit warrants the district court's attention. These factors include: (1) whether a declaratory action would settle the controversy; (2) whether it would serve a useful purpose in clarifying the legal relations at issue; (3) whether the declaratory remedy is being used merely for the purpose of procedural fencing or to provide an arena for a race to *res judicata*; (4) whether use of a declaratory action would increase friction between our federal and state courts and improperly encroach upon state jurisdiction; and (5) whether there is an alternative remedy which is better or more effective." (Internal quotes omitted.)

§1114(1)—Disclaimer

Rosenfeld v. W.B. Saunders, 728 F.Supp. 236, 243 (S.D.N.Y.1990), *aff'd*, 923 F.2d 845 (2d Cir.1990) (table case). "The Second Circuit has repeatedly recognized that an effective disclaimer can significantly reduce the potential for consumer confusion caused by an infringing product if it clearly designates the source of the product. To successfully employ the use of a disclaimer, the infringing party has an affirmative duty to 'come forward with evidence sufficient to demonstrate that any proposed materials would significantly reduce the likelihood of consumer confusion.' Where the likelihood of confusion is substantial, the disclaimer must be prominent and disclose the competitive relationship between the two companies in a nonambiguous manner. Alternatively, where the likelihood of confusion is minimal to moderate, the court has broader discretion to uphold the adequacy of the disclaimer. Thus, courts must examine the effectiveness of disclaimers on a case by case basis 'by considering the circumstances of the relevant business and its consumers.'"

§1114(1)—Likelihood of Confusion—Generally

For more annotations on this topic, see 15 U.S.C. §1052, *§1052(d)—Likelihood of Confusion*, p. 15, and 15 U.S.C. §1125, *§1125(a)(1)(A)—Likelihood of Confusion—Generally*, p. 137.

AutoZone, Inc. v. Strick, 543 F.3d 923, 929 (7th Cir. 2008). "Whether consumers are likely to be confused about the origin of a defendant's products or services is ultimately a question of fact. That question of fact may be resolved on summary judgment only 'if the evidence is so one-sided that there can be no doubt about how the question should be answered.'" *See also* ***Sally Beauty Co. v. Beautyco, Inc.***, 304 F.3d 964, 972 (10th Cir.2002).

Perfumebay.com Inc. v. eBay Inc., 506 F.3d 1165, 1173 (9th Cir.2007). "In the internet context, 'the three most important ... factors in evaluating a likelihood of confusion are (1) the similarity of the marks, (2) the relatedness of the goods and services, and (3) the parties' simultaneous use of the Web as a marketing channel.' 'When this controlling troika or internet trinity suggests confusion is likely, the other factors must weigh strongly against a likelihood of confusion to avoid the finding of infringement.'" *See also* ***National Bus. Forms & Printing, Inc. v. Ford Motor Co.***, 671 F.3d 526, 532 (5th Cir.2012) (eight factors).

Leelanau Wine Cellars, Ltd. v. Black & Red, Inc., 502 F.3d 504, 515 (6th Cir.2007). "'The touchstone of liability under [15 U.S.C.] §1114 [Lanham Act §32] is whether the defendant's use of the disputed mark is likely to cause confusion among consumers regarding the origin of the goods offered by the parties.' The Sixth Circuit utilizes an eight-factor test in ascertaining whether a likelihood of confusion exists: (1) strength of the senior mark; (2) relatedness of the goods or services; (3) similarity of the marks; (4) evidence of actual confusion; (5) marketing channels used; (6) likely degree of purchaser care; (7) the intent of defendant in selecting the mark; and (8) likelihood of expansion of the product lines. In applying these factors, the court has cautioned that they 'imply no mathematical precision, but are simply a guide to help determine whether confusion is likely.' Given the fact-specific nature of trademark infringement actions, not all of the eight factors will be relevant in every case. In every case, '[t]he ultimate question remains whether relevant consumers are likely to believe that the products or services offered by the parties are affiliated in some way.' [¶] In reviewing the district court's decision on the issue of a likelihood of confusion following a bench trial, we examine any relevant factual findings for clear error. Whether a likelihood of confusion exists is a mixed question of law and fact subject to *de novo* review. That is, 'the determination of what is the state of affairs regarding each factor is a finding of fact reviewed on the clearly erroneous standard, but the further determination of the likelihood of confusion based on those factors is a legal conclusion.'" *See also* ***George & Co. v. Imagination Entm't Ltd.***, 575 F.3d 383, 393 (4th Cir. 2009) (nine factors); ***Vail Assocs. v. Vend-Tel-Co., Ltd.***, 516 F.3d 853, 863 (10th Cir.2008) (six factors); ***Au-Tomotive Gold, Inc. v. Volkswagen, Inc.***, 457 F.3d 1062, 1075-76 (9th Cir.2006) (eight factors); ***Davis v. Walt Disney Co.***, 430 F.3d 901, 903 (8th Cir.2005) (six factors); ***Brennan's, Inc. v. Brennan's Rest.***, 360 F.3d 125, 130 (2d Cir.2004) (eight factors); ***Frehling Enters. v. International Select Grp.***, 192 F.3d 1330, 1335 (11th Cir.1999) (seven factors); ***Equine Tech. v. Equitechnology, Inc.***, 68 F.3d 542, 546 (1st Cir.1995) (eight factors); ***McGraw-Edison Co. v. Walt Disney Prod.***, 787 F.2d 1163, 1167-68 (7th Cir.1986) (seven factors); ***Interpace Corp. v. Lapp, Inc.***, 721 F.2d 460, 463 (3d Cir.1983) (16 factors).

General Motors Corp. v. Keystone Auto. Indus., 453 F.3d 351, 355 (6th Cir.2006). "This Court has joined the vast majority of courts in extending the likelihood of confusion inquiry beyond only the point of sale. [¶] Likelihood of confusion at the point of sale involves a purchaser's confusion as to a product's origin or sponsorship occurring at the time of purchase. [¶] There can be no likelihood of confusion at the point of sale where a defendant conspicuously and unequivocally informs buyers that the defendant, and not the plaintiff, is the source of the product. [C]ustomers knowing they are purchasing a knockoff designer purse or Rolex watch simply do not confuse the counterfeit with the original. *At 356:* In addition to point-of-sale confusion, the Sixth Circuit recognizes that a likelihood of downstream confusion, also called 'post-sale' confusion, is actionable.... Thus, injection of knockoffs into the stream of commerce may lead to a likelihood of confusion among the general public. To assess the likelihood of downstream confusion, we first apply the eight-factor test and then discuss the potential harm from the influx of [D's] grilles into the stream of commerce."

Scott Fetzer Co. v. House of Vacuums Inc., 381 F.3d 477, 483 (5th Cir.2004). "A 'likelihood of confusion' means that confusion is not just possible, but probable."

Taubman Co. v. Webfeats, 319 F.3d 770, 776 (6th Cir.2003). "[T]he only important question is whether there is a likelihood of confusion *between the parties' goods or services*. Under Lanham Act jurisprudence, it is irrelevant whether customers would be confused as to the origin of the websites, unless there is confusion as to the origin of the respective products." *See also* ***Brookfield Comms. v. West Coast Entm't Corp.***, 174 F.3d 1036, 1055 (9th Cir.1999).

Lone Star Steakhouse & Saloon, Inc. v. Alpha, Inc., 43 F.3d 922, 933 (4th Cir.1995). "This Court has added [to the likelihood-of-confusion test the determination] that an unauthorized use of a trademark infringes the trademark holder's rights if it is likely to confuse an ordinary consumer as to the source or sponsorship of the goods. Given the fact that the likelihood of confusion depends on varying human reactions to situations incapable of exact appraisement, ... this Court has concluded that determining the likelihood of confusion is an inherently factual issue that depends on the facts and circumstances in each case." (Internal quotes omitted.) *See also* ***Scott Fetzer Co. v. House of Vacuums Inc.***, 381 F.3d 477, 483 (5th Cir.2004).

Burger King Corp. v. Mason, 710 F.2d 1480, 1493 (11th Cir.1983). Many "courts have held that continued trademark use by one whose trademark license has been cancelled satisfies the likelihood of confusion test and constitutes trademark infringement."

Sun Banks, Inc. v. Sun Fed. S&L Ass'n, 651 F.2d 311, 314 (5th Cir.1981). "In assessing whether there is a likelihood of confusion with respect to service marks, we weigh several objective factors: type of service mark, similarity of design, similarity of service, identity of service facilities and customers, similarity of advertising media used, defendant's intent and actual confusion."

§1114(1)—Likelihood of Confusion—Initial-Interest Confusion

Network Automation, Inc. v. Advanced Sys. Concepts, Inc., 638 F.3d 1137, 1148 (9th Cir.2011). "[W]e consider whether the use of another's trademark as a search engine keyword to trigger one's own product advertisement violates the Lanham Act. We begin by examining the [likelihood-of-confusion] factors that are most relevant to the determination whether the use is likely to cause initial interest confusion. While the district court analyzed each of the [likelihood-of-confusion] factors, it identified the three most important factors as (1) the similarity of the marks, (2) the relatedness of the goods or services, and (3) the simultaneous use of the Web as a marketing channel, for any case addressing trademark infringement on the Internet. [¶] However, we did not intend ... to forever enshrine these three factors—now often referred to as the 'Internet trinity' or 'Internet troika'—as the test for trademark infringement on the Internet. ... Depending on the facts of each specific case arising on the Internet, other factors may emerge as more illuminating on the question of consumer confusion. [W]e used the 'troika' factors to analyze the risk of source confusion generated by similar domain names, but we did not wholesale adopt them in the metatag analysis. [¶] Given the multifaceted nature of the Internet and the ever-expanding ways in which we all use the technology, however, it makes no sense to prioritize the same three factors for every type of potential online commercial activity. *At 1149:* In determining the proper inquiry for this particular trademark infringement claim, we adhere to two long stated principles: the [likelihood-of-confusion] factors (1) are non-exhaustive, and (2) should be applied flexibly, particularly in the context of Internet commerce. Finally, because the *sine qua non* of trademark infringement is consumer confusion, when we examine initial interest confusion, the owner of the mark must demonstrate likely confusion, not mere diversion. *At 1153-54:* In the keyword advertising context the 'likelihood of confusion will ultimately turn on what the consumer saw on the screen and reasonably believed, given the context.' [W]e [have] found it important that the consumers saw banner advertisements that were 'confusingly labeled or not labeled at all.' We noted that clear labeling 'might eliminate the likelihood of initial interest confusion….'"

Australian Gold, Inc. v. Hatfield, 436 F.3d 1228, 1238-39 (10th Cir.2006). "Initial interest confusion results when a consumer seeks a particular trademark holder's product and instead is lured to the product of a competitor by the competitor's use of the same or a similar mark. Even though the consumer eventually may realize that the product is not the one originally sought, he or she may stay with the competitor. In that way, the competitor has captured the trademark holder's potential visitors or customers. *At 1241:* [T]he first sale doctrine does not protect resellers who use other entities' trademarks to give the impression that they are favored or authorized dealers for a product when in fact they are not. [D's] use of [P's] trademarks on the internet was such an act. [D's] intentional use of [P's] trademarks on [D's] Web sites, in the metatags for the Web sites, and with [search-engine marketing website] constitutes more than merely displaying and stocking trademarked items. Thus, [D's] actions were indicative of an intent to cause consumer confusion, and are not shielded by the first sale doctrine." Held: The court found initial-interest confusion. *See also* ***Vail Assocs. v. Vend-Tel-Co., Ltd.***, 516 F.3d 853, 872 (10th Cir.2008).

Gibson Guitar Corp. v. Paul Reed Smith Guitars, LP, 423 F.3d 539, 549 (6th Cir.2005). "[P] argues that despite the lack of actual confusion at the point of sale, the district court's decision can be affirmed under a theory of either initial-interest confusion (the theory relied on by the district court), post-sale confusion, or some combination of the two. Initial-interest confusion takes place when a manufacturer improperly uses a trademark to create initial customer interest in a product, even if the customer realizes, prior to purchase, that the product was not actually manufactured by the trademark-holder. Post-sale confusion occurs when use of a trademark leads individuals (other than the purchaser) mistakenly to believe that a product was manufactured by the trademark-holder. *At 550 n.15:* [T]he applicability of the initial-interest-confusion doctrine outside of the Internet context is an issue of first impression in our circuit. Although other circuits have applied the initial-interest-confusion doctrine to find trademark infringement based on use of a deliberately deceptive name or logo, we are not aware of any circuit that has applied the initial-interest-confusion doctrine to a trademark on a product's shape." *See also* ***PACCAR Inc. v. TeleScan Techs.***, 319 F.3d 243, 253 (6th Cir. 2003), *overruled on other grounds*, ***KP Permanent Make-Up, Inc. v. Lasting Impression I, Inc.***, 543 U.S. 111 (2004); ***Promatek Indus. v. Equitrac Corp.***, 300 F.3d 808, 812 (7th Cir.2002); ***Brookfield Comms. v. West Coast Entm't Corp.***, 174 F.3d 1036, 1055-56 (9th Cir.1999). *But see* ***Lamparello v. Falwell***, 420 F.3d 309, 315-17 (4th Cir.2005) (refusing to adopt initial-interest-confusion doctrine).

Brookfield Comms. v. West Coast Entm't Corp., 174 F.3d 1036, 1062 (9th Cir.1999). "[M]etatags will … result in what is known as initial interest confusion. … Although there is no source confusion in the sense that consumers know they are patronizing [competitor] rather than [P], there is nevertheless initial interest confusion in the sense that, by using [trademark] to divert people looking for [P's] web site, [competitor] improperly benefits from the goodwill that [P] developed in its mark." *But see* ***Tiffany (NJ) Inc. v. eBay, Inc.***, this page.

Tiffany (NJ) Inc. v. eBay, Inc., 576 F.Supp.2d 463, 499 (S.D.N.Y.2008), *rev'd in part on other grounds*, 600 F.3d 93 (2d Cir.2010). "Courts in this Circuit … have routinely held that the use of a trademark in keywords and metatags, where the use is strictly internal and not communicated to the public, does not constitute 'use' under the Lanham Act and thus does not support a Lanham Act claim." *But see* ***Brookfield Comms. v. West Coast Entm't Corp.***, this page.

§1114(1)—Likelihood of Confusion—Parody

Louis Vuitton Malletier S.A. v. Haute Diggity Dog, LLC, 507 F.3d 252, 260 (4th Cir.2007). "For trademark purposes, a parody is defined as a simple form of entertainment conveyed by juxtaposing the irreverent representation of the trademark with the idealized image created by the mark's owner. A parody must convey two simultaneous—and contradictory—messages: that it is the original, but also that it is *not* the original and is instead a parody. This second message must not only differentiate the alleged parody from the original but must also communicate some articulable element of satire, ridicule, joking, or amusement. Thus, a parody relies upon a difference from the original mark, presumably a humorous difference, in order to produce its desired effect. *At 261:* [T]he 'Chewy Vuiton' dog toys convey just enough of the original design to allow the consumer to appreciate the point of the parody, but stop well short of appropriating the entire marks that [D] claims." (Internal quotes omitted.) *See also* ***People for the Ethical Treatment of Animals v. Doughney***, 263 F.3d 359, 366 (4th Cir.2001).

§1114(1)—Likelihood of Confusion—
Reverse Confusion

Marketquest Grp. v. BIC Corp., 862 F.3d 927, 932 (9th Cir.2017). "Our circuit has not previously addressed the pleading standard required to state a cause of action for trademark infringement under a reverse confusion theory. We now hold that reverse confusion is not a separate claim that must be specifically pleaded, but instead is a theory of likely confusion that may be alleged by itself or in addition to forward confusion. Thus, when reverse confusion is compatible with the theory of infringement alleged in the complaint, a plaintiff need not specifically plead it. *At 934-35:* [W]hen a court applies ***Sleekcraft*** in a case that presents reverse confusion, and the intent factor is relevant, it may consider several indicia of intent. At one extreme, intent could be shown through evidence that a defendant deliberately intended to push the plaintiff out of the market by flooding the market with advertising to create reverse confusion. Intent could also be shown by evidence that, for example, the defendant knew of the mark, should have known of the mark, intended to copy the plaintiff, failed to conduct a reasonably adequate trademark search, or otherwise culpably disregarded the risk of reverse confusion. The tenor of the intent inquiry shifts when considering reverse confusion due to the shift in the theory of confusion, but no specific type of evidence is necessary to establish intent, and the importance of intent and evidence presented will vary by case."

Fortres Grand Corp. v. Warner Bros. Entm't Inc., 763 F.3d 696, 701 (7th Cir.2014). "In reverse confusion, the *senior user's* products are mistaken as originating from (or being affiliated with or sponsored by) the *junior user*. This situation often occurs when the junior user is a well-known brand which can quickly swamp the marketplace and overwhelm a small senior user. The harm from this kind of confusion is that 'the senior user loses the value of the trademark—its product identity, corporate identity, control over its goodwill and reputation, and ability to move into new markets.'" *See also* ***JL Bev. Co. v. Jim Beam Brands Co.***, 828 F.3d 1098, 1107 (9th Cir.2016).

Freedom Card, Inc. v. JPMorgan Chase & Co., 432 F.3d 463, 472 (3d Cir.2005). "[I]n a typical case alleging reverse confusion, as in a case of direct confusion, a court should apply the ***Lapp*** factors in assessing likelihood of confusion. However, economic reality and common sense require that some of the ***Lapp*** factors be analyzed differently when reverse discrimination is at issue. Thus, the strength of the parties' marks[,] the intent in adopting the marks[,] and the evidence of actual confusion ... are analyzed differently from the method employed in a typical direct confusion case."

DeCosta v. Viacom Int'l, 981 F.2d 602, 608 (1st Cir. 1992). 15 U.S.C. §1114(1), Lanham Act §32(1), "protects the holder from the harm that confusion might cause, without specifying whether that harm flows from a copier taking advantage of the holder's 'good will,' or from the copier potentially reducing the value of the mark, say by associating the holder with the copier's own 'bad' name. The leading case on the subject, ***Big O Tire Dealers, Inc. v. Goodyear Tire & Rubber Co.***, 561 F.2d 1365 ... (10th Cir.1977), ... made absolutely clear that a trademark holder could base a claim on such 'reverse confusion.'"

§1114(1)—Likelihood of Confusion—Factor—
Actual Confusion

Streamline Prod. Sys. v. Streamline Mfg., 851 F.3d 440, 457 (5th Cir.2017). "A plaintiff may show actual confusion using anecdotal instances of consumer confusion, systematic consumer surveys, or both. We have set a low bar for this showing, stating that a plaintiff need provide 'very little proof of actual confusion ... to prove likelihood of confusion.' Even if the anecdotes are minor and isolated, 'courts may not ignore competent evidence of actual confusion.' Testimony of a single known incident of actual confusion by a consumer has been found to be sufficient evidence to support the district court's finding of actual confusion. And, if the plaintiff provides proof of actual confusion, the defendant must provide 'an almost overwhelming amount of proof ... to refute such proof.' However, not all confusion counts: evidence of actual confusion must show 'more than a fleeting mix-up of names'; rather it must show that '[t]he confusion was caused by the trademarks employed and it swayed consumer purchases.' We have rejected anecdotal evidence of actual confusion when the proponent did not show that 'a misleading representation by [the defendant], as opposed to some other source, caused a likelihood of confusion.'"

Sovereign Military Hospitaller Order v. Florida Priory of the Knights Hospitallers, 809 F.3d 1171, 1189 (11th Cir.2015). "The 'best evidence' that the parties' marks are likely to be confused is evidence that the marks actually have been confused. Evidence of actual confusion is 'not necessary' for the plaintiff to prevail on a claim of infringement, ... but even a 'very little' amount of it is highly probative.... The strength of such evidence depends on 'the number of instances of confusion,' 'the kinds of persons confused,' and the 'degree of confusion.'"

George & Co. v. Imagination Entm't Ltd., 575 F.3d 383, 398 (4th Cir.2009). "Actual confusion can be demonstrated by both anecdotal and survey evidence. Evidence of only a small number of instances of actual confusion may be dismissed as *de minimis*." *See also* ***Water Pik, Inc. v. Med-Sys.***, 726 F.3d 1136, 1144 (10th Cir.2013).

Jada Toys, Inc. v. Mattel, Inc., 518 F.3d 628, 633 (9th Cir.2008). "In the context of two subjectively dissimilar marks, evidence of actual confusion and evidence defining the context in which the goods are sold is particularly relevant."

Leelanau Wine Cellars, Ltd. v. Black & Red, Inc., 502 F.3d 504, 518 (6th Cir.2007). "Where a survey presented on the issue of actual confusion reflects methodological errors, a court may choose to limit the importance it accords the study in its likelihood of confusion analysis."

Audi AG v. D'Amato, 469 F.3d 534, 543 (6th Cir. 2006). "In evaluating ... evidence of actual confusion, we have noted that although such evidence is the best indicator of likelihood of confusion, the absence of actual confusion evidence is inconsequential. *At 546:* [D] contends that any proof of consumer confusion is rebutted by a disclaimer on his website which stated, '[t]his page is not associated with Audi GmbH or Audi USA in any way.' First, such a disclaimer does not absolve [D] of liability for his unlawful use of marks identical to [P's] trademarks. In addition, [a]n infringing domain name has the potential to misdirect consumers as they search for web sites associated with the owner of a trademark. A disclaimer disavowing affiliation with the trademark owner read by a consumer after reaching the web site comes too late. This initial interest confusion is recognized as an infringement under the Lanham Act." (Internal quotes omitted.) *See also* ***Au-Tomotive Gold, Inc. v. Volkswagen, Inc.***, 457 F.3d 1062, 1077-78 (9th Cir.2006).

Surfvivor Media, Inc. v. Survivor Prods., 406 F.3d 625, 633 (9th Cir.2005). "In analyzing [actual confusion], we may consider whether merchants and nonpurchasing members of the public, as well as actual consumers, were confused."

§1114(1)—Likelihood of Confusion—Factor—Consumer Care

Network Automation, Inc. v. Advanced Sys. Concepts, Inc., 638 F.3d 1137, 1152 (9th Cir.2011). "[T]he default degree of consumer care is becoming more heightened as the novelty of the Internet evaporates and online commerce becomes commonplace. *At 1153:* [W]e expect consumers searching for expensive products online to be even more sophisticated."

AutoZone, Inc. v. Strick, 543 F.3d 923, 932-33 (7th Cir.2008). "In assessing whether this factor favors finding a likelihood of confusion, ... '[t]he more widely accessible and inexpensive the products and services, the more likely that consumers will exercise a lesser degree of care and discrimination in their purchases.'" *See also* ***Audi AG v. D'Amato***, 469 F.3d 534, 544 (6th Cir.2006).

General Motors Corp. v. Keystone Auto. Indus., 453 F.3d 351, 357 (6th Cir.2006). "This factor involves assessing (1) the type of goods at issue, and (2) the level of sophistication of the purchaser. As to the first inquiry, 'when services are expensive or unusual, the buyer can be expected to exercise greater care in her purchases,' and there is accordingly less likelihood of confusion. A sophisticated purchaser exercises a high degree of care and is less likely to be confused as to a product's origin. This factor also focuses on the point of sale and is, therefore, generally inapplicable to downstream confusion." *See also* ***Streamline Prod. Sys. v. Streamline Mfg.***, 851 F.3d 440, 458 (5th Cir.2017); ***AuTomotive Gold, Inc. v. Volkswagen, Inc.***, 457 F.3d 1062, 1076 (9th Cir.2006).

Surfvivor Media, Inc. v. Survivor Prods., 406 F.3d 625, 634 (9th Cir.2005). "In analyzing the degree of care that a consumer might exercise in purchasing the parties' goods, the question is whether a 'reasonably prudent consumer' would take the time to distinguish between the two product lines. [¶] No clear standard exists for analyzing moderately priced goods, such as non-designer clothing. [¶] With respect to small, inexpensive goods ..., the consumer is likely to exercise very little care."

§1114(1)—Likelihood of Confusion—Factor—Defendant's Intent

Sovereign Military Hospitaller Order v. Florida Priory of the Knights Hospitallers, 809 F.3d 1171, 1188 (11th Cir.2015). This "factor asks whether the defendant adopted its mark with the intent of deriving benefit from the reputation of the plaintiff. Bad faith in the adoption and use of a trademark normally involves efforts by a party to 'pass off' its product as that of another. Intent can be proven with direct or circumstantial evidence. When intent is present, it can justify the inference that there is confusing similarity. But it is neither a necessary nor sufficient condition for determining the ultimate legal fact of the likelihood of confusion." (Internal quotes omitted.) *See also* ***Streamline Prod. Sys. v. Streamline Mfg.***, 851 F.3d 440, 455-56 (5th Cir.2017).

Water Pik, Inc. v. Med-Sys., 726 F.3d 1136, 1157 (10th Cir.2013). "When we have said that evidence of intent to copy may justify an inference of likelihood of confusion, we have been referring to copying a particular *mark*, not copying a competitor's product. And more specifically, the intent in copying the mark should be 'the intent to derive benefit from the reputation or goodwill of plaintiff.'"

Network Automation, Inc. v. Advanced Sys. Concepts, Inc., 638 F.3d 1137, 1153 (9th Cir.2011). "'[L]iability for infringement may not be imposed for using a registered trademark in connection with truthful comparative advertising.'"

AutoZone, Inc. v. Strick, 543 F.3d 923, 934 (7th Cir. 2008). "In some circumstances, an intent to confuse may be reasonably inferred from the similarity of the marks where the senior mark has attained great notoriety. If the marketing and business presence of the senior mark ... is nearly ubiquitous in the geographic area where the junior mark competes, a trier of fact can easily conclude that the creator of a strikingly similar junior mark intended to confuse."

Louis Vuitton Malletier S.A. v. Haute Diggity Dog, LLC, 507 F.3d 252, 263 (4th Cir.2007). "'An intent to parody is not an intent to confuse the public.' Despite [D's] obvious intent to profit from its use of parodies, this action does not amount to a bad faith intent to create consumer confusion. To the contrary, the intent is to do just the opposite—to evoke a humorous, satirical association that *distinguishes* the products."

Audi AG v. D'Amato, 469 F.3d 534, 544 (6th Cir. 2006). "'[T]he intent of [Ds] in adopting [their mark] is a critical factor, since if the mark was adopted with the intent of deriving benefit from the reputation of [P], that fact alone may be sufficient to justify the inference that there is confusing similarity.' [I]ntent need not be proved by direct evidence of intentional copying. Intent may be inferred. 'First, the use of a contested mark with knowledge of the protected mark at issue can support a finding of intentional copying.... Second, the nature of [D's] use of the marks on its web sites, such as including the marks in its domain names, repeating the marks in watermarks, and mimicking the distinctive scripts of the marks, indicates an intent to create the impression that the web sites are sponsored or affiliated with [P].' *At 546:* [E]ven if [D's] intention was in fact non-commercial (which it does not appear to be), the issue is whether his actions had a commercial *effect.* We have stated that 'the proper inquiry is not one of intent.... If consumers are confused by an infringing mark, the offender's motives are largely irrelevant.' Even 'minimal' advertisements constitute use of the owner's trademark in connection with the advertising of the goods, which the Lanham Act proscribes."

Lorillard Tobacco Co. v. Amouri's Grand Foods, Inc., 453 F.3d 377, 381 (6th Cir.2006). "While a 'defendant's intent' is one of the eight factors ..., it is considered only in the sense that its existence can 'strengthen[ ] the likelihood of confusion.' Its absence, on the other hand, does not preclude such likelihood."

General Motors Corp. v. Keystone Auto. Indus., 453 F.3d 351, 357 (6th Cir.2006). "Intent can be proven by direct or circumstantial evidence." *See also* ***Au-Tomotive Gold, Inc. v. Volkswagen, Inc.***, 457 F.3d 1062, 1076 (9th Cir.2006).

Boston Athletic Ass'n v. Sullivan, 867 F.2d 22, 35 (1st Cir.1989). When "a manufacturer intentionally uses another's mark as a means of establishing a link in consumers' minds with the other's enterprise, and directly profits from that link, there is an unmistakable aura of deception. Such a use is, by its very nature, 'likely to cause confusion, or to cause mistake, or to deceive.' Unless the defendant can show that there is in fact no likelihood of such confusion or deception about the product's connection to the trademark holder, such a use can be enjoined." *See also* ***George & Co. v. Imagination Entm't Ltd.***, 575 F.3d 383, 397 (4th Cir. 2009).

§1114(1)—Likelihood of Confusion—Factor—Expansion of Product

Network Automation, Inc. v. Advanced Sys. Concepts, Inc., 638 F.3d 1137, 1153 (9th Cir.2011). "Where two companies are direct competitors, this factor is unimportant."

General Motors Corp. v. Keystone Auto. Indus., 453 F.3d 351, 357-58 (6th Cir.2006). "[A] strong possibility that either party will expand his business to compete with the other or be marketed to the same consumers will weigh in favor of finding that the present use is infringing. Expansion could be geographic or an increase in products or services." (Internal quotes omitted.)

Surfvivor Media, Inc. v. Survivor Prods., 406 F.3d 625, 634 (9th Cir.2005). "To resolve [likelihood of expansion], we must determine whether existence of the allegedly infringing mark is hindering the plaintiff's expansion plans."

§1114(1)—Likelihood of Confusion—Factor—Marketing Channels

Sovereign Military Hospitaller Order v. Florida Priory of the Knights Hospitallers, 809 F.3d 1171, 1187-88 (11th Cir.2015). This "factor—similarity of the parties' sales methods—and the [similar] factor—similarity of the parties' advertising methods—merge in this case. The former focuses on 'where, how, and [with] whom' the parties do business. 'Dissimilarities between the retail outlets for and the predominant consumers of plaintiff's and defendants' goods lessen the possibility of confusion....' The latter compares the parties' advertisements and the audiences they reach. 'The greater the similarity ..., the greater the likelihood of confusion.'"

Network Automation, Inc. v. Advanced Sys. Concepts, Inc., 638 F.3d 1137, 1151 (9th Cir.2011). "'Convergent marketing channels increase the likelihood of confusion.' ... However, this factor becomes less important when the marketing channel is less obscure. Today, it would be the rare commercial retailer that did not advertise online, and the shared use of a ubiquitous marketing channel does not shed much light on the likelihood of consumer confusion."

Audi AG v. D'Amato, 469 F.3d 534, 543-44 (6th Cir. 2006). "[W]e consider 'the similarities or differences between the predominant customers of the parties' respective goods or services,' and 'whether the marketing approaches employed by each party resemble each other.' The same group of individuals—namely, those interested in purchasing goods and services displaying the Audi brand—would be the predominant customers to either Audi's or *www.audisport.com*'s goods. In addition, both [P] and [D] used the internet in marketing. '[S]imultaneous use of the Internet as a marketing tool exacerbates the likelihood of confusion,' given the fact that 'entering a web site takes little effort—usually one click from a linked site or a search engine's list; thus, Web surfers are more likely to be confused as to the ownership of a web site than traditional patrons of a brick-and-mortar store would be of a store's ownership.'"

General Motors Corp. v. Keystone Auto. Indus., 453 F.3d 351, 357 (6th Cir.2006). "'This factor ... consists of considerations of how and to whom the respective goods or services of the parties are sold.' This factor involves two considerations: (1) whether the parties use the same means to market the product, and (2) whether the 'predominant customers' are the same. There is less likelihood of confusion 'if the services of one party are sold through different marketing media in a different marketing context than those of another seller.' The same is true '[i]f one mark user sells exclusively at retail and the other exclusively to commercial buyers ... since no one buyer ever buys both products.' Since this factor focuses on the point of sale, it has little bearing on the question of downstream confusion."

§1114(1)—Likelihood of Confusion—Factor—Relatedness of Goods

Streamline Prod. Sys. v. Streamline Mfg., 851 F.3d 440, 454 (5th Cir.2017). "'The greater the similarity between the products and services, the greater the likelihood of confusion.'"

Network Automation, Inc. v. Advanced Sys. Concepts, Inc., 638 F.3d 1137, 1150 (9th Cir.2011). "'Related goods are generally more likely than unrelated goods to confuse the public as to the producers of the goods.' ... The proximity of goods is measured by whether the products are: (1) complementary; (2) sold to the same class of purchasers; and (3) similar in use and function." *See also* ***Florida Int'l Univ. Bd. of Trs. v. Florida Nat'l Univ., Inc.***, 830 F.3d 1242, 1261 (11th Cir.2016).

AutoZone, Inc. v. Strick, 543 F.3d 923, 931 (7th Cir. 2008). "Like the ... factor comparing the similarity of the marks, our inquiry in comparing the two products is not whether they are interchangeable, but whether the parties' products are the kind the public might very well attribute to a single source (the plaintiff). The rights of an owner of a registered trademark extend to any goods or services that, in the minds of consumers, might be put out by a single producer. Thus, a likelihood of confusion may exist even if the parties are not in direct competition, or their products and services are not identical." (Internal quotes omitted.) *See also* ***George & Co. v. Imagination Entm't Ltd.***, 575 F.3d 383, 397 (4th Cir.2009).

Leelanau Wine Cellars, Ltd. v. Black & Red, Inc., 502 F.3d 504, 516 (6th Cir.2007). "The Sixth Circuit evaluates the relatedness of goods by assigning the dispute in question to a place within a 'tripartite system.' If the parties are in direct competition, 'confusion is likely if the marks are sufficiently similar.' If the goods are 'somewhat related, but not competitive,' the likelihood of confusion determination will turn on one of the other seven factors. If the products are unrelated, a likelihood of confusion is 'highly unlikely.' 'Services and goods are related not because they coexist in the same broad industry, but are related if the services are marketed and consumed such that buyers are likely to believe that the services, similarly marked, come from the same source, or are somehow connected with or sponsored by a common company.'"

Louis Vuitton Malletier v. Burlington Coat Factory Whs. Corp., 426 F.3d 532, 538 (2d Cir.2005). "While a district court's simultaneous comparison of two products is not an inappropriate heuristic means of investigating similarities and differences in their respective designs on the way to an ultimate conclusion as to whether the products are likely to leave similar impressions on consumers, district courts must be careful to maintain a focus on the ultimate issue of the likelihood of consumer confusion. As a result, the Lanham Act requires a court to analyze the similarity of the products in light of the way in which the marks are actually displayed in their purchasing context. Whether simultaneous viewing by consumers is likely to result in confusion is not relevant when it is serial viewing that is at issue given the market context or the type of confusion claimed. In such a case, a district court must ask not whether differences are easily discernable on simultaneous viewing, but whether they are likely to be memorable enough to dispel confusion on serial viewing. *At 539:* [C]ourts must evaluate the likely effect on consumers of the marks' similar and dissimilar features *with a focus on market conditions*, even if the products appear to be adequately different in a non-marketplace setting."

Surfvivor Media, Inc. v. Survivor Prods., 406 F.3d 625, 633 (9th Cir.2005). "The standard for deciding whether the parties' goods or services are 'related' is whether customers are 'likely to associate' the two product lines. We must also consider whether the buying public could reasonably conclude that the products came from the same source."

Brennan's, Inc. v. Brennan's Rest., 360 F.3d 125, 134 (2d Cir.2004). "The proximity inquiry asks to what extent the two products compete with each other. In assessing product proximity we look at 'the nature of the products themselves and the structure of the relevant market.' [¶] The competitive proximity factor has two elements, market proximity and geographic proximity. Market proximity asks whether the two products are in related areas of commerce and geographic proximity looks to the geographic separation of the products. Both elements seek to determine whether the two products have an overlapping client base that creates a potential for confusion."

§1114(1)—Likelihood of Confusion—Factor—Similarity of Marks—Composite Marks

George & Co. v. Imagination Entm't Ltd., 575 F.3d 383, 396 (4th Cir.2009). "In assessing the similarity of the marks ..., we focus on the dominant portions of the parties' marks. In other words, we focus on whether there exists a similarity in sight, sound, and meaning which would result in confusion." *See also* ***Water Pik, Inc. v. Med-Sys.***, 726 F.3d 1136, 1155 (10th Cir.2013).

AutoZone, Inc. v. Strick, 543 F.3d 923, 929-30 (7th Cir.2008). "To determine whether two marks are similar, we view the marks as a whole. We must compare the marks 'in light of what happens in the marketplace and not merely by looking at the two marks side-by-side.' '[T]he test is not whether the public would confuse the *marks*, but whether the viewer of an accused mark would be likely to associate the product or service with which it is connected with the source of products or services with which an earlier mark is connected.' The court should therefore 'consider whether the customer would believe that the trademark owner sponsored, endorsed or was otherwise affiliated with the product.'" *See also* ***Reno Air Racing Ass'n v. McCord***, 452 F.3d 1126, 1136-37 (9th Cir.2006).

Louis Vuitton Malletier S.A. v. Haute Diggity Dog, LLC, 507 F.3d 252, 262 (4th Cir.2007). "[D] concedes that its marks are and were designed to be somewhat similar to [P's] marks. But that is the essence of a parody—the invocation of a famous mark in the consumer's mind, so long as the distinction between the marks is also readily recognized. While a trademark parody necessarily copies enough of the original design to bring it to mind as a target, a successful parody also distinguishes itself and, because of the implicit message communicated by the parody, allows the consumer to appreciate it."

Audi AG v. D'Amato, 469 F.3d 534, 543 (6th Cir. 2006). "'[W]hen analyzing similarity, courts should examine the pronunciation, appearance, and verbal translation of conflicting marks.' [W]e have held that with respect to domain names, addition of characters along with the mark 'does not eliminate the likelihood of confusion.'"

Opticians Ass'n v. Independent Opticians, 920 F.2d 187, 195 (3d Cir.1990). "Generally, if the overall impression created by marks is essentially the same, 'it is very probable that the marks are confusingly similar.' Where the owner of the trademark and the infringer 'deal in competing goods or services, the court need rarely look beyond the mark itself. In those cases the court will generally examine the registered mark ... and compare it against the challenged mark.' Proof of actual confusion is not necessary; likelihood is all that need be shown."

§1114(1)—Likelihood of Confusion—Factor—Similarity of Marks—Word Marks

Sovereign Military Hospitaller Order v. Florida Priory of the Knights Hospitallers, 809 F.3d 1171, 1186 (11th Cir.2015). This "factor for confusion—the similarity of marks—requires the factfinder to compare the plaintiff's marks with the defendant's marks and measure their similarity. '[T]he greater the similarity ..., the greater the likelihood of confusion.' Similarity must be determined 'by considering the overall impression created by the mark as a whole rather than simply comparing individual features of the marks.' Relevant points of comparison include 'the appearance, sound and meaning of the marks, as well as the manner in which the marks are used.'"

Hornady Mfg. Co. v. DoubleTap, Inc., 746 F.3d 995, 1001 (10th Cir.2014). "Similarity is gauged on three levels: 'sight, sound, and meaning.' Similarities in the marks get 'more weight than the differences.' In comparing marks, 'we do not independently examine each syllable of the marks but consider the mark as a whole as they are encountered by consumers in the marketplace.' We therefore compare the full marks, not just their components. *At 1002:* First, the court is not free to give dispositive weight to any one component of the marks, such as a shared syllable. [¶] Second, in its comparison of the marks, the court is 'not free to focus solely on name similarity.' The court must consider the effect of marketplace presentation, including 'lettering styles, logos and coloring schemes.' This includes the effect packaging has on consumers' ability to recognize a particular mark." *See also* ***Streamline Prod. Sys. v. Streamline Mfg.***, 851 F.3d 440, 454 (5th Cir.2017).

CareFirst v. First Care, P.C., 434 F.3d 263, 271 (4th Cir.2006). "If one of two similar marks is commonly paired with other material, that pairing will serve to lessen any confusion that might otherwise be caused by the textual similarity between the two marks. This effect is most significant when ... the allegedly infringed mark ... has little independent strength."

Surfvivor Media, Inc. v. Survivor Prods., 406 F.3d 625, 633 (9th Cir.2005). "In considering the degree of similarity between the two marks, courts should analyze each mark within the context of other identifying features. We also ask whether the marks are similar in sight, sound, and meaning."

Bell v. Starbucks U.S. Brands Corp., 389 F.Supp.2d 766, 777 (S.D.Tex.2005), *aff'd*, 205 Fed.Appx. 289 (5th Cir.2006). "The words 'Starbock' or 'Star Bock' and 'Starbucks' are remarkably similar in sight and sound. [¶] [P's] logo is sufficiently different from [D's] mark. But the Court's finding *only* applies to [P's] current use of this logo on beer and a small amount of promotional items available *only* at his bar (or any subsequent *local* establishment owned or operated by [P])...."

§1114(1)—Likelihood of Confusion—Factor—Strength of Mark

For more annotations on this topic, see 15 U.S.C. §1052, *Generally*, p. 10.

Sovereign Military Hospitaller Order v. Florida Priory of the Knights Hospitallers, 809 F.3d 1171, 1183 (11th Cir.2015). "In this Circuit, [a]n incontestable mark is 'presumed to be at least descriptive with secondary meaning, and therefore a relatively strong mark.' [¶] The majority of circuits to consider the question have held that incontestability does not affect the strength of a mark for purposes of confusion. The [TTAB] agrees with the majority view. As do the leading treatises. [¶] The law in this Circuit is almost certainly incorrect. *At 1184:* Nevertheless, 'one panel of this Court cannot disregard the precedent set by a prior panel, even though it conceives error in the precedent.'" *See also* ***Wynn Oil Co. v. American Way Serv.***, 943 F.2d 595, 600 (6th Cir.1991) (agreeing with 11th Circuit). *But see* ***Hornady Mfg. Co. v. DoubleTap, Inc.***, 746 F.3d 995, 1008 n.13 (10th Cir.2014) (incontestability does not affect strength of mark for purposes of confusion); ***Lone Star Steakhouse & Saloon, Inc. v. Alpha, Inc.***, 43 F.3d 922, 935 (4th Cir.1995) (same); ***Munters Corp. v. Matsui Am., Inc.***, 909 F.2d 250, 252 (7th Cir.1990) (same); ***Miss World (UK) Ltd. v. Mrs. Am. Pageants, Inc.***, 856 F.2d 1445, 1449 (9th Cir.1988) (same), *abrogated on other grounds*, ***Eclipse Assocs. v. Data Gen. Corp.***, 894 F.2d 1114 (9th Cir.1990); ***Oreck Corp. v. U.S. Floor Sys.***, 803 F.2d 166, 171 (5th Cir. 1986) (same).

Network Automation, Inc. v. Advanced Sys. Concepts, Inc., 638 F.3d 1137, 1149-50 (9th Cir.2011). "'The stronger a mark—meaning the more likely it is to be remembered and associated in the public mind with the mark's owner—the greater the protection it is accorded by the trademark laws.' Two relevant measurements are conceptual strength and commercial strength. Conceptual strength involves classification of a mark 'along a spectrum of generally increasing inherent distinctiveness as generic, descriptive, suggestive, arbitrary, or fanciful.' 'A mark's conceptual strength depends largely on the obviousness of its connection to the good or service to which it refers.' Federal trademark '[r]egistration alone may be sufficient in an appropriate case to satisfy a determination of distinctiveness.' However, 'while the registration adds something on the scales, we must come to grips with an assessment of the mark itself.' Commercial strength is based on 'actual marketplace recognition,' and thus 'advertising expenditures can transform a suggestive mark into a strong mark.' [¶] This factor is probative of confusion here because a consumer searching [the Internet] for a generic term is more likely to be searching for a product category. That consumer is more likely to expect to encounter links and advertisements from a variety of sources. By contrast, a user searching for a distinctive term is more likely to be looking for a particular product, and therefore could be more susceptible to confusion when sponsored links appear that advertise a similar product from a different source. On the other hand, if the ordinary consumers of this particular product are particularly sophisticated and knowledgeable, they might also be aware that [D] is the source of [marked goods] and not be confused at all." *See also* ***Streamline Prod. Sys. v. Streamline Mfg.***, 851 F.3d 440, 453-54 (5th Cir.2017); ***Water Pik, Inc. v. Med-Sys.***, 726 F.3d 1136, 1151-53 (10th Cir. 2013); ***CareFirst v. First Care, P.C.***, 434 F.3d 263, 269 (4th Cir.2006).

Lahoti v. Vericheck, Inc., 586 F.3d 1190, 1195 (9th Cir.2009). "[A] district court's classification of a trademark's strength is a factual determination to which we apply clear error review. *At 1196:* Under the clear error standard, we defer to the lower court's determination unless, based on the entire evidence, we are possessed of a definite and firm conviction that a mistake has been committed. [¶] When reviewing for clear error, we do not defer to a district court's categorization of a mark if its decision is based on incorrect law. Although we may affirm on any ground supported by the record, even if it differs from the district court's rationale, ... where it is unclear whether the district court relied on proper law, we may vacate the judgment and remand with instructions to apply the correct legal standard." (Internal quotes omitted.)

George & Co. v. Imagination Entm't Ltd., 575 F.3d 383, 395 (4th Cir.2009). "Our strength of the mark analysis does not end [with classification]. The placement of a mark in either the descriptive or suggestive category simply is the first step. The second step considers the mark's commercial strength, a concept similar to the 'secondary meaning' inquiry considered in evaluating a mark's validity. Proof of secondary meaning entails a rigorous evidentiary standard. [W]e set forth six factors for a court to consider in assessing the acquisition of secondary meaning. They are: (1) the plaintiff's advertising expenditures; (2) consumer studies linking the mark to a source; (3) the plaintiff's record of sales success; (4) unsolicited media coverage of the plaintiff's business; (5) attempts to plagiarize the mark; and (6) the length and exclusivity of the plaintiff's use of the mark." *See also* ***Christian Louboutin S.A. v. Yves Saint Laurent Am. Holding, Inc.***, 696 F.3d 206, 226 (2d Cir.2012).

AutoZone, Inc. v. Strick, 543 F.3d 923, 933 (7th Cir. 2008). "'The stronger the mark, the more likely it is that encroachment on it will produce confusion.' The strength of a mark usually corresponds to its economic and marketing strength."

Louis Vuitton Malletier S.A. v. Haute Diggity Dog, LLC, 507 F.3d 252, 261 (4th Cir.2007). "While it is true that finding a mark to be strong and famous usually favors the plaintiff in a trademark infringement case, the opposite may be true when a legitimate claim of parody is involved. [¶] It is a matter of common sense that the strength of a famous mark allows consumers immediately to perceive the target of the parody, while simultaneously allowing them to recognize the changes to the mark that make the parody funny or biting."

Surfvivor Media, Inc. v. Survivor Prods., 406 F.3d 625, 631-32 (9th Cir.2005). "The purpose of examining the strength of the plaintiff's mark is to determine the scope of trademark protection to which the mark is entitled. The more unique the mark, the greater the degree of protection. [¶] Trademarks are divided into five categories. The two strongest sets of marks are 'arbitrary' and 'fanciful' marks, which trigger the highest degree of trademark protection. 'Arbitrary' marks are common words that have no connection with the actual product—for example, 'Dutch Boy' paint. 'Fanciful' marks consist of 'coined phrases' that also have no commonly known connection with the product at hand. Examples of fanciful marks include 'Kodak' cameras or 'Aveda' skin care products. [¶] 'Suggestive' marks do not 'describe the product's features but suggest[] them.' The exercise of some imagination is required to associate a suggestive mark with the product. Examples include 'Slickcraft' boats or 'Air Care,' for a service that maintains medical equipment for administering oxygen. [¶] The fourth category of marks is referred to as 'descriptive.' These marks define a particular characteristic of the product in a way that does not require any exercise of the imagination. An example of a descriptive mark is 'Honey Roasted' for nuts roasted with honey. Because these marks merely describe a characteristic of the product, they do not receive any trademark protection unless they acquire sufficient 'secondary meaning' to create an association between the mark and the product. [¶] The final category of marks consists of 'generic' marks, which describe the product in its entirety, and which are not entitled to trademark protection. Examples include 'Liquid controls' for equipment that dispenses liquid, or 'Multistate Bar Examination' for a bar examination that may be taken across multiple states. [¶] [T]he mere fact that a mark consists of a coined term does not automatically render that mark fanciful. Fanciful marks have no commonly known connotation to the product at hand." *See also* ***Florida Int'l Univ. Bd. of Trs. v. Florida Nat'l Univ., Inc.***, 830 F.3d 1242, 1256-57 (11th Cir.2016); ***George & Co. v. Imagination Entm't Ltd.***, 575 F.3d 383, 393-94 (4th Cir.2009). *But see* ***Amazing Spaces, Inc. v. Metro Mini Storage***, p. 11 (forsaking distinctiveness categories to analyze symbols and designs in favor of ***Seabrook Foods*** test).

§1114(1)—Public-Use Doctrine

George & Co. v. Imagination Entm't Ltd., 575 F.3d 383, 403 (4th Cir.2009). "The Public Use doctrine, which is extremely limited in scope, states that abbreviations or nicknames used only by the public can give rise to protectable trademark rights to the owner of a mark which the public has modified. 'Such public use by others inures to the claimant's benefit and, where this occurs, public use can reasonably be deemed use by that party in the sense of a use on its behalf.' The Public Use doctrine was developed because 'Americans are prone to abbreviate recognized trademarks and to use nicknames.' Examples of nicknames held protectable as trademarks include Coke for Coca-Cola, ... and Bud for Budweiser beer.... [¶] [T]he Public Use doctrine generally is confined to instances in which the public modifies a well-known brand into a nickname or abbreviation."

§1114(1)—Registrant

Silverstar Enters. v. Aday, 537 F.Supp. 236, 239 (S.D.N.Y.1982). "Although the language of [15 U.S.C. §1114, Lanham Act §32,] speaks of an action by the 'registrant,' [15 U.S.C. §1127, Lanham Act §45,] further defines that term to include the legal representatives, predecessors, successors and assigns of the registrant."

§1114(2)(A)

Gucci, Inc. v. Hall & Assocs., 135 F.Supp.2d 409, 419-20 (S.D.N.Y.2001). "Although the phrase 'innocent infringer' is not defined in [15 U.S.C. §1114(2)(A), Lanham Act §32(2)(A)], it has been construed to embrace the actual malice standard set forth in ***New York Times v. Sullivan***, 376 U.S. 254 (1964), i.e. an infringer is innocent unless it acted either (1) with knowledge of the infringement or (2) with reckless disregard as to whether the material infringed the trademark owner's rights." (Internal quotes omitted.)

§1114(2)(B)

Century 21 Real Estate Corp. v. R. M. Post Inc., 8 U.S.P.Q.2d 1614, 1617 (N.D.Ill.1988). 15 U.S.C. §1114(2)(B), Lanham Act §32(2)(B), "does not limit liability to the advertisement of only one's own goods or services. In order to be liable for unlawful reproduction of a trademark, the reproduction must have been made with the knowledge that the imitation 'is intended to be used to cause confusion, or to cause mistake, or to deceive.'"

§1114(2)(D)

Hawes v. Network Solutions, Inc., 337 F.3d 377, 383-84 (4th Cir.2003). Section 1114(2)(D)(i)(II)(bb), Lanham Act §32(2)(D)(i)(II)(bb), "exposes a [domain name] registrar to liability ... by providing an exception to a registrar's general exemption from liability under the Act ... when the registrar, without court permission, transfers a domain name 'during the pendency of [an] action.' [¶] The [ACPA] creates a cause of action for cybersquatting against anyone who registers, traffics in, or uses a domain name that is identical or confusingly similar to a trademark with the bad-faith intent to profit from the good will associated with the trademark. It also creates a cause of action for reverse domain name hijacking against trademark owners who misuse or abuse their rights in bringing a cybersquatting action. The ACPA thus protects both trademark owners and domain name registrants. In creating these causes of action, Congress intended expressly to limit the liability of domain name registrars under the Act as long as the domain name registrars comply with the conditions stated in §1114(2)(D)(i). ... Section 1114(2)(D)(i) ... generally exempts domain name registrars from the liability imposed by the Act for cybersquatting or reverse domain name hijacking. Because the provisions conditioning the limitation of liability in §1114(2)(D)(i) relate to liability imposed by the Lanham Act as amended by the ACPA, cooperating conduct by registrars with respect to foreign courts under foreign law is given no relevance in interpreting §1114(2)(D)(i)(II)(bb) insofar as it requires the pendency of an 'action.' *At 386:* Adjudication of an action brought under §1114(2)(D)(v) involves neither appellate-like review of, nor deference to, any simultaneously pending actions in foreign jurisdictions.... *At 387:* Although a §1114(2)(D)(v) cause of action may be brought in a U.S. court and requires application of only U.S. law, this fact does not leave the foreign trademark owner bereft of protection. The trademark owner remains free to file a counterclaim or counterclaims, ... asserting any rights that it may have under U.S. law."

Barcelona.com, Inc. v. Excelentisimo Ayuntamiento, 330 F.3d 617, 624-25 (4th Cir.2003). "Although the [ACPA] was enacted primarily to redress cyberpiracy or 'cybersquatting,' it also provides limited liability for trademark infringement by [domain-name] registrars who participate in the administration of the registration, transfer, and cancellation of domain names pursuant to a 'reasonable policy' that is consistent with the purposes of the trademark laws. [¶] [W]hile a decision by an [Internet Corporation for Assigned Names and Numbers]-recognized panel might be a condition of, indeed the reason for, bringing an action under 15 U.S.C. §1114(2)(D)(v) [Lanham Act §32(2)(D)(v)], its recognition *vel non* is not jurisdictional. Jurisdiction to hear trademark matters is conferred on federal courts by 28 U.S.C. §§1331 and 1338, and a claim brought under the ACPA, which amended the Lanham Act, is a trademark matter over which federal courts have subject matter jurisdiction."

Sallen v. Corinthians Licenciamentos LTDA, 273 F.3d 14, 25 (1st Cir.2001). "[W]e do not read [15 U.S.C. §1114(2)(D)(v), Lanham Act §32(2)(D)(V),] as granting federal jurisdiction over mere abstract claims of federal right where no [U.S. Const.] art. 3 case exists. Although [D] has stated that it has no intent to sue [P] under the ACPA for his past actions related to [domain name], there is indeed a controversy between [P] and [D]: [P] asserts that he has rights to [domain name,] and [D] asserts that it has mutually exclusive rights to the same domain name. *At 28:* [S]ection 1114(2)(D)(v) provides disappointed administrative dispute resolution participants with a chance to have *any* unfavorable [Uniform Domain Name Dispute Resolution Policy] decision reviewed in a U.S. court. We think this provision means that a federal court's decision that [P] was in compliance with the ACPA necessarily contradicts the WIPO panel's finding that [P] lacked a legitimate interest in [domain name]. Congress has defined in the ACPA what it means to lack a legitimate interest in a domain name under U.S. law. For that reason, should a federal court declare that [P] is in compliance with the ACPA, that declaration would undercut the rationale of the WIPO panel decision."

Frayne v. Chicago 2016, No. 08 C 5290 (N.D.Ill. 2009) (memo op.; 1-8-09). "Nothing in the language of [15 U.S.C. §1114(2)(D)(v), Lanham Act §32(2)(D)(v),] creates a cause of action against a party that attempts to suspend, disable, or transfer a domain name but fails to actually do so." Held: There is no cause of action for attempted reverse-domain-name hijacking.

§1115. REGISTRATION ON PRINCIPAL REGISTER AS EVIDENCE OF EXCLUSIVE RIGHT TO USE MARK; DEFENSES

[LANHAM ACT §33]

(a) Evidentiary value; defenses.—Any registration issued under the Act of March 3, 1881, or the Act of February 20, 1905, or of a mark registered on the principal register provided by this chapter and owned by a party to an action shall be admissible in evidence and shall be prima facie evidence of the validity of the registered mark and of the registration of the mark, of the registrant's ownership of the mark, and of the registrant's exclusive right to use the registered mark in commerce on or in connection with the goods or services specified in the registration subject to any conditions or limitations stated therein, but shall not preclude another person from proving any legal or equitable defense or defect, including those set forth in subsection (b) of this section, which might have been asserted if such mark had not been registered.

(b) Incontestability; defenses.—To the extent that the right to use the registered mark has become incontestable under section 1065 of title 15, the registration shall be conclusive evidence of the validity of the registered mark and of the registration of the mark, of the registrant's ownership of the mark, and of the registrant's exclusive right to use the registered mark in commerce. Such conclusive evidence shall relate to the exclusive right to use the mark on or in connection with the goods or services specified in the affidavit filed under the provisions of section 1065 of title 15, or in the renewal application filed under the provisions of section 1059 of title 15 if the goods or services specified in the renewal are fewer in number, subject to any conditions or limitations in the registration or in such affidavit or renewal application. Such conclusive evidence of the right to use the registered mark shall be subject to proof of infringement as defined in section 1114 of title 15, and shall be subject to the following defenses or defects:

(1) That the registration or the incontestable right to use the mark was obtained fraudulently; or

(2) That the mark has been abandoned by the registrant; or

(3) That the registered mark is being used by or with the permission of the registrant or a person in privity with the registrant, so as to misrepresent the source of the goods or services on or in connection with which the mark is used; or

(4) That the use of the name, term, or device charged to be an infringement is a use, otherwise than as a mark, of the party's individual name in his own business, or of the individual name of anyone in privity with such party, or of a term or device which is descriptive of and used fairly and in good faith only to describe the goods or services of such party, or their geographic origin; or

(5) That the mark whose use by a party is charged as an infringement was adopted without knowledge of the registrant's prior use and has been continuously used by such party or those in privity with him from a date prior to (A) the date of constructive use of the mark established pursuant to section 1057(c) of title 15,

(B) the registration of the mark under this chapter if the application for registration is filed before the effective date of the Trademark Law Revision Act of 1988, or (C) publication of the registered mark under subsection (c) of section 1062(c) of title 15: *Provided, however*, That this defense or defect shall apply only for the area in which such continuous prior use is proved; or

(6) That the mark whose use is charged as an infringement was registered and used prior to the registration under this chapter or publication under subsection (c) of section 1062(c) of title 15 of the registered mark of the registrant, and not abandoned: *Provided, however*, That this defense or defect shall apply only for the area in which the mark was used prior to such registration or such publication of the registrant's mark; or

(7) That the mark has been or is being used to violate the antitrust laws of the United States; or

(8) That the mark is functional; or

(9) That equitable principles, including laches, estoppel, and acquiescence, are applicable.

History of 15 U.S.C. §1115: July 5, 1946, ch. 540, §33, 60 Stat. 438; Oct. 9, 1962, P.L. 87-772, §18, 76 Stat. 774; Nov. 16, 1988, P.L. 100-667, §128(a), 102 Stat. 3944; Oct. 30, 1998, P.L. 105-330, §201(a)(9), 112 Stat. 3070; Nov. 2, 2002, P.L. 107-273, §13207(b)(7), 116 Stat. 1908.

Treatise Cross-References

McCarthy on Trademark & Unfair Competition

Ch. 5, *Historical Basis of Trademarks & Legislative History*, §5:4
Ch. 11, *The Spectrum of Distinctiveness of Marks*, §§11:43; 11:44; 11:49
Ch. 16, *Acquisition & Priority of Trademark Rights*, §§16:18.50; 16:19
Ch. 17, *Loss of Trademark Rights*, §17:4
Ch. 18, *Assignment & Licensing of Trademarks*, §18:48
Ch. 19, *Federal Registration of Marks*, §19:36
Ch. 24, *Infringement by Use of Mark on Noncompetitive Goods or Services*, §§24:65; 24:124
Ch. 26, *The Territorial Extent of Trademark Rights*, §§26:31; 26:38; 26:43-26:53
Ch. 27, *Lanham Act §43(a) & False Advertising*, §27:19
Ch. 32, *Procedure in Trademark Infringement & Unfair Competition Litigation*, §§32:134-32:136; 32:139-32:141; 32:145; 32:147-32:149; 32:152-32:157

ANNOTATIONS

§1115(a)

Amazing Spaces, Inc. v. Metro Mini Storage, 608 F.3d 225, 237 (5th Cir.2010). The "presumption of validity may be rebutted by establishing that the mark is not inherently distinctive. *At 239:* [D's] introduction of evidence that the [mark] is not distinctive has reduced the presumption of validity to evidence that the PTO is of the opinion that the [mark] is sufficiently distinctive to be legally protectable as a mark. *At 240:* [A] mark is inherently distinctive if its intrinsic nature serves to identify a particular source. Inherent distinctiveness is attributable to a mark when the mark almost *automatically* tells a customer that it refers to a brand and immediately signals a brand or a product source." (Internal quotes omitted.)

Central Mfg. v. Brett, 492 F.3d 876, 881 (7th Cir. 2007). "Registration provides prima facie evidence of ownership, but this can be rebutted by competent evidence. Ultimately, it is not the fact of registration that matters so much as the use of the mark in commerce; '[b]y insisting that firms use marks to obtain rights in them, the law prevents entrepreneurs from reserving brand names in order to make their rivals' marketing more costly.' Established use by a nonregistrant is a valid defense to a registrant's infringement claim."

Colt Defense LLC v. Bushmaster Firearms, Inc., 486 F.3d 701, 705-06 (1st Cir.2007). "Where ... the party claiming infringement has registered the term on the Principal Register, the registration establishes a rebuttable presumption that the term is not generic. This presumption may be overcome where the alleged infringer demonstrates genericness by a preponderance of the evidence. 'In deciding genericness, evidence of the relevant public's understanding of a term may be obtained from any competent source.' Such sources include consumer surveys, the use of the term in media publications, use of the term by competitors in the industry, purchaser testimony concerning the term, and the plaintiff's use of the term. *At 707:* Generic use by the party seeking trademark protection is relevant because '[a] kind of estoppel arises when the proponent of [a] trademark use is proven to have itself used the term before the public as a generic name....'"

Custom Vehicles, Inc. v. Forest River, Inc., 476 F.3d 481, 485 (7th Cir.2007). "[A] trademark, like a patent, carries a presumption of validity. In the case of a registered descriptive mark, therefore, the presumption is that it has acquired secondary meaning. But the act of registration merely begins the process that leads to the presumption. Bare registration is not enough. ... You must certify that the product is in use in commerce—defined as 'the bona fide use of a mark in the ordinary course of trade, and not made merely to reserve a right in a mark[ ]' ...—within six months after the trademark was registered. Within those six months [P] sold a grand total of one van, and the trademark was not used in the sale. Even if it had been, that would not have been enough to place the trademark in the 'ordinary course of trade.'" *But see* ***Department of Parks & Recreation for the State of Cal. v. Bazaar del Mundo Inc.***, this page (single sale may be enough to establish use in commerce).

Department of Parks & Recreation for the State of Cal. v. Bazaar del Mundo Inc., 448 F.3d 1118, 1124 (9th Cir.2006). Respondent's "federal registration of the marks is prima facie evidence of its ownership of the marks. [Petitioner], however, may rebut the presumption of ownership with evidence establishing its own prior use in commerce of the registered mark. *At 1125-26:* To demonstrate priority of use, [petitioner] must prove (1) that it actually adopted and used the marks in commerce prior to [respondent's] registration in such a manner that sufficiently associated the marks with [petitioner's] services; and (2) that its use of the marks was continuous and not interrupted. Ownership of a mark requires both appropriation and use in trade; and ownership of a mark and the exclusive right to a mark belongs to the one who first uses the mark on goods placed on the market. While the first use need not be extensive, the use must be bona fide and commercial in character: A single sale or shipment may be sufficient to support an application to register the mark, providing that this shipment or sale has the color of a bona fide transaction and is accompanied or followed by activities which would tend to indicate a continuing effort or intent to continue such use and place the product on the market on a commercial scale within a time demonstrated to be reasonable in the particular trade. [Petitioner] cannot rely on a few instances of use of the marks in the distant past that were casual or had little importance apparently attached to them. To the contrary, the litigant attempting to establish priority of commercial use must demonstrate both adoption of the marks and use in a way sufficiently public to identify or distinguish the marked goods in an appropriate segment of the public mind as those of the adopter of the mark. Although mere advertising by itself may not establish priority of use, advertising combined with other non-sales activity, under our totality of the circumstances test, can constitute prior use in commerce." (Internal quotes omitted.) *But see* ***Custom Vehicles, Inc. v. Forest River, Inc.***, p. 81 (single sale not enough to establish use in commerce).

MTS Inc. v. Red Tower Records, Tapes & Video, 17 U.S.P.Q.2d 1441, 1446 (N.D.Ill.1990). "[W]hen the registrant's right is contestable, [15 U.S.C. §1115(a), Lanham Act §33(a),] allows for a [broad] range of defenses to infringement, namely 'any legal or equitable defense or defect which might have been asserted if [the] mark had not been registered.' All of the defenses in §1115(b) fall into this category, and thus if a defendant can prove all of the elements of [a] §1115(b) defense, that defense is valid under §1115(a) as well."

Standard Oil v. Osage Oil & Transp., 10 U.S.P.Q.2d 1554, 1557 (N.D.Okla.1988). "As the federal registrant of the ... marks on the Principal Register, [P] is entitled to exclusive use of the mark throughout the U.S. An exception to this rule is a subsequent user who prior to the registration or publication of a mark, adopts a mark in good faith and without knowledge of its prior use. A subsequent user may continue to use the mark only in specific geographic areas in which it had adopted the mark prior to the registration date of the mark, and continues to use the mark from this prior adoption to the present time *so long as* there is no confusion as to source."

§1115(b)

Park'N Fly, Inc. v. Dollar Park & Fly, Inc., 469 U.S. 189, 196 (1985). 15 U.S.C. §1115(a), Lanham Act §33(a), "would have allowed respondent to challenge petitioner's mark as merely descriptive if the mark had not become incontestable. With respect to incontestable marks, however, §33(b) provides that registration is *conclusive* evidence of the registrant's exclusive right to use the mark, subject to the conditions of [15 U.S.C. §1065, Lanham Act §15,] and the seven [now eight] defenses enumerated in §33(b) itself. Mere descriptiveness is not recognized by either §15 or §33(b) as a basis for challenging an incontestable mark."

Texas Pig Stands, Inc. v. Hard Rock Cafe Int'l, 951 F.2d 684, 690 (5th Cir.1992). "Prior use by a third party that does not continuously extend up until the time of trial does not fall within one of the enumerated defenses [in 15 U.S.C. §1115(b), Lanham Act §33(b)]."

Coherent, Inc. v. Coherent Tech., 935 F.2d 1122, 1125 (10th Cir.1991). "Congress amended [15 U.S.C. §1115(b), Lanham Act §33(b),] in 1988, adding the clause, '[s]uch conclusive evidence of the right to use the [incontestable] registered mark shall be subject to proof of infringement as defined in [15 U.S.C. §1114, Lanham Act §32].' The revision clarified that 'incontestability does not relieve the owner of an incontestable registration from the burden of proving likelihood of confusion.'"

Opticians Ass'n v. Independent Opticians, 920 F.2d 187, 192 n.7 (3d Cir.1990). "The term 'incontestable' is obviously somewhat misleading, since there are as many as 21 possible exceptions/defenses to the general rule of incontestability. [Lanham Act] §33(b) ..., 15 U.S.C. §1115(b)[,] lists eight exceptions to incontestability, and incorporates the exceptions of [Lanham Act] §15, 15 U.S.C. §1065. Section 15, in turn, incorporates [Lanham Act] §14(3) and (5) [15 U.S.C. §1064(3) and (5)] by reference while §14(3) incorporates the protections in [Lanham Act §§2(a)-(c) and 4, 15 U.S.C. §§1052(a)-(c) and 1054]."

Lindy Pen Co. v. Bic Pen Corp., 725 F.2d 1240, 1247 (9th Cir.1984). "[P] renews on appeal its argument that the incontestable status of its mark entitles it to an injunction in order to preserve its exclusive right to use its mark. ... The law of this circuit is otherwise. Incontestability of a mark may protect the registrant's mark from cancellation, but is of no offensive use."

§1115(b)(2)

For more annotations on this topic, see 15 U.S.C. §1064, *§1064(3)—Abandoned*, p. 41, and 15 U.S.C. §1127, *Abandoned*, p. 169.

Eva's Bridal Ltd. v. Halanick Enters., 639 F.3d 788, 790-91 (7th Cir.2011). "This argument that licensors may relinquish all control of licensees that operate 'high quality' businesses misunderstands what judicial decisions and the *Restatement* [*(Third) of Unfair Competition*] mean when they speak about 'quality.' There is no rule that trademark proprietors must ensure 'high quality' goods—or that 'high quality' permits unsupervised licensing. ... The sort of supervision required for a trademark license is the sort that produces *consistent* quality. 'Trademarks [are] indications of consistent and predictable quality assured through the trademark owner's control over the use of the designation.' [¶] How much control is enough? The licensor's self-interest largely determines the answer. Courts are apt to ask whether 'the control retained by the licensor [is] sufficient under the circumstances to insure that the licensee's goods or services would meet the expectations created by the presence of the trademark.' It isn't necessary to be more specific here, because [Ps] did not retain *any* control—not via the license agreement, not via course of performance. [¶] Trademark law requires that 'decisionmaking authority over quality remains with the owner of the mark.' How much authority is enough can't be answered generally; the nature of the business, and customers' expectations, both matter. Ours is the extreme case: [Ps] had, and exercised, *no* authority over the appearance and operations of [Ds'] business, or even over what inventory to carry or avoid. That is the paradigm of a naked license."

Grocery Outlet Inc. v. Albertson's Inc., 497 F.3d 949, 951 (9th Cir.2007). "Abandonment is a defense to a claim of infringement of a registered trademark. The Lanham Act provides for two ways that a trademark may be abandoned, namely, through (1) nonuse, or (2) the mark becoming generic. To show abandonment by nonuse, the party claiming abandonment must prove both the trademark owner's (1) 'discontinuance of trademark use' and (2) 'intent not to resume such use.'"

ITC Ltd. v. Punchgini, Inc., 482 F.3d 135, 147 (2d Cir.2007). "Once abandoned, a mark returns to the public domain and may, in principle, be appropriated for use by other actors in the marketplace, in accordance with the basic rules of trademark priority. [¶] The party asserting abandonment bears the burden of persuasion with respect to two facts: (1) non-use of the mark by the legal owner, and (2) lack of intent by that owner to resume use of the mark in the reasonably foreseeable future. [¶] The Lanham Act expressly states that nonuse of a mark for three consecutive years shall be prima facie evidence of abandonment. This court has explained that the term prima facie evidence in this context means a rebuttable presumption of abandonment. *At 150:* [T]o rebut a presumption of abandonment on a motion for summary judgment, the mark owner must come forward with evidence with respect to what outside events occurred from which an intent to resume use during the nonuse period may reasonably be inferred. *At 153:* [W]e conclude that [P's] continued foreign use of the ... mark for restaurants does not raise a material issue of fact regarding its intent to resume similar use of the mark in the U.S." (Internal quotes omitted.) *See also* ***Natural Answers, Inc. v. SmithKline Beecham Corp.***, 529 F.3d 1325, 1329-30 (11th Cir.2008); ***Levi Strauss & Co. v. GTFM, Inc.***, 196 F.Supp.2d 971, 976 (N.D.Cal.2002).

Emergency One, Inc. v. American FireEagle, Ltd., 228 F.3d 531, 535-36 (4th Cir.2000). "[A] party claiming that a mark has been abandoned must show 'non-use of the name by the legal owner and no intent by that person or entity to resume use in the reasonably foreseeable future.' Non-use for three consecutive years alone, however, constitutes prima facie evidence of abandonment. Proof of three consecutive years of non-use thus creates a presumption—a mandatory inference of intent not to resume use. [¶] [N]either promotional use of the mark on goods in a different course of trade nor mere token use constitute 'use' under the Lanham Act." *See also* ***Marshak v. Treadwell***, 240 F.3d 184, 198 (3d Cir.2001). *But see* ***Burgess v. Gilman***, 475 F.Supp.2d 1051, 1059-60 (D.Nev.2007), *aff'd*, 316 Fed.Appx. 542 (9th Cir.2008) (rejecting "preponderance of the evidence" standard and adopting "strictly proved" standard to prove intent).

Exxon Corp. v. Oxxford Clothes, Inc., 109 F.3d 1070, 1075 (5th Cir.1997). "A naked license is a trademark licensor's grant of permission to use its mark without attendant provisions to protect the quality of the goods or services provided under the licensed mark. *At 1078:* [D's] naked licensing defense, which as we have noted has ultimate relevance only to 'abandonment,' is authorized by 15 U.S.C. §1115(b)(2) [Lanham Act §33(b)(2)]. *At 1079:* The [second] definition of 'abandonment' set forth in [15 U.S.C. §1127, Lanham Act §45,] is the specific statutory explication of unintentional abandonment, including abandonment due to naked licensing."

Chere Amie, Inc. v. Windstar Apparel Corp., 191 F.Supp.2d 343, 349 (S.D.N.Y.2001). "A defense of abandonment must be proven by clear and convincing evidence."

§1115(b)(3)

Exxon Corp. v. Oxxford Clothes, Inc., 109 F.3d 1070, 1078 n.11 (5th Cir.1997). "A review of the jurisprudence construing [15 U.S.C. §1115(b)(3), Lanham Act §33(b)(3),] reveals that it is a defense of 'unclean hands,' only applicable when the origin or source of goods distributed under the subject mark is misrepresented."

§1115(b)(4)—Fair Use

Marketquest Grp. v. BIC Corp., 862 F.3d 927, 935-36 (9th Cir.2017). "A fair use must be a use other than as a trademark. ... To determine whether a term is being used as a mark, we look for indications that the term is being used to associate it with a manufacturer, and whether the term is used as a symbol to attract public attention. We also consider whether the allegedly infringing user undertook precautionary measures to minimize the risk that the term will be understood in its trademark sense. [¶] To prevail on fair use, a defendant must show that it used the mark in its primary, descriptive sense. While we accept some flexibility in what counts as descriptive, ... the scope of the fair use defense varies with the descriptive purity of the defendant's use and whether there are other words available to do the describing. Even when there is some evidence of descriptive use, a jury could still reasonably conclude that a defendant's lack of 'precautionary measures' outweighs such evidence. *At 937-38:* A defendant asserting fair use must also show that it used the mark in good faith. When considering forward confusion, this element involves the same issue as the intent factor in the likelihood of confusion analysis; that is, whether defendant in adopting its mark intended to capitalize on plaintiff's good will. ... In fair use, good faith is an element of the defense, not merely a factor to consider when it is relevant in a given case. [¶] As with intent in ***Sleekcraft***, there is no bright-line rule or required piece of evidence to establish good or bad faith. While the focus may differ when considering forward or reverse confusion, generally the same types of evidence will be relevant to this inquiry. This includes evidence such as whether the defendant intended to create confusion, whether forward or reverse; intended to push the plaintiff out of the market; remained ignorant of the plaintiff's mark when it reasonably should have known of the mark; knew of the mark and showed bad faith in its disregard of the plaintiff's rights; or any other evidence relevant to whether the defendant's claimed 'objectively fair' use of the mark was done in good faith. [¶] The fair use defense only comes into play once the party alleging infringement has shown by a preponderance of the evidence that confusion is likely. ... After the plaintiff meets the threshold showing, in the fair use analysis the degree of customer confusion is a factor to consider. However, a defendant raising the defense does not have the burden to negate any likelihood of consumer confusion. Some consumer confusion is compatible with fair use, and when a plaintiff chooses to identify its product with a mark that uses a well known descriptive phrase it assumes the risk of some confusion. [¶] We emphasize that the degree of consumer confusion is a *factor* in the fair use analysis, not an *element* of fair use. This factor is useful in considering whether, overall, the use was objectively fair. A use that is likely to confuse consumers, or that has caused actual confusion, is less likely to be objectively fair (although some confusion is permissible). The ***Sleekcraft*** factors and additional factors that we identified as relevant in ***KP Permanent II*** may also be relevant in a given case where fair use is at issue. A court is not required in every case to recite and analyze all the factors identified in ***Sleekcraft*** and ***KP Permanent II*** one-by-one for a fair use analysis to be complete. A court *may* do so, but these are merely factors to facilitate a court's analysis, to the degree they are relevant in a given case." (Internal quotes omitted.)

Fortune Dynamic, Inc. v. Victoria's Secret Stores Brand Mgmt., 618 F.3d 1025, 1031 (9th Cir. 2010). "We have recognized a nominative fair use defense and a classic fair use defense. Nominative fair use applies 'where a defendant has used the plaintiff's mark to describe the *plaintiff's product*,' ... whereas classic fair use—the only defense at issue here—involves a defendant's use of a descriptive term 'in its primary, descriptive sense'...."

Hensley Mfg. v. ProPride, Inc., 579 F.3d 603, 612 (6th Cir.2009). "Under the fair use doctrine, the holder of a trademark cannot prevent others from using the word that forms the trademark in its primary or descriptive sense. Rather, the only right of exclusion that trademark law creates in a descriptive word is in the secondary, new, 'trademark' meaning of the word that plaintiff has created. The original, descriptive primary meaning is always available for use by others to describe their goods, in the interest of free competition. [¶] In evaluating a defendant's fair use defense, a court must consider whether [the] defendant has used the mark: (1) in its descriptive sense; and (2) in good faith." (Internal quotes omitted.)

JA Apparel Corp. v. Abboud, 568 F.3d 390, 400 (2d Cir.2009). "Assessment of [fair use] requires analysis of whether a given use was '(1) other than as a mark, (2) in a descriptive sense, and (3) in good faith.' In making these assessments, the court focuses on the actual or proposed uses themselves. [¶] With respect to the first element, we have equated 'use ... as a mark' with 'the use of [a] term as a symbol to attract public attention.' *At 401:* With respect to the third element ..., the inquiry into the defendant's good faith 'concerns the question whether the user of a mark intended to create consumer confusion as to source or sponsorship.'" *See also* ***Cairns v. Franklin Mint Co.***, 292 F.3d 1139, 1151 (9th Cir.2002); ***Sugar Busters LLC v. Brennan***, 177 F.3d 258, 270-71 (5th Cir.1999); ***Beer Nuts, Inc. v. Clover Club Foods Co.***, 711 F.2d 934, 937 (10th Cir.1983).

E.S.S. Entm't 2000, Inc. v. Rock Star Videos, Inc., 547 F.3d 1095, 1099 (9th Cir.2008). "[D's] defense asks us to consider the intersection of trademark law and the First Amendment. ... We have adopted the Second Circuit's approach from ***Rogers v. Grimaldi***, [875 F.2d 994 (2d Cir.1989),] which requires courts to construe the Lanham Act to apply to artistic works only where the public interest in avoiding consumer confusion outweighs the public interest in free expression. The specific test contains two prongs. An artistic work's use of a trademark that otherwise would violate the Lanham Act is not actionable unless the use of the mark has no artistic relevance to the underlying work whatsoever, or, if it has some artistic relevance, unless it explicitly misleads as to the source or the content of the work. Although this test traditionally applies to uses of a trademark in the title of an artistic work, there is no principled reason why it ought not also apply to the use of a trademark in the body of the work. *At 1100:* [T]he level of relevance [in the first prong] merely must be above zero. [¶] [The second] prong of the test points directly at the purpose of trademark law, namely to avoid confusion in the marketplace by allowing a trademark owner to prevent others from duping consumers into buying a product they mistakenly believe is sponsored by the trademark owner. The relevant question, therefore, is whether [product] would confuse its [purchasers] into thinking that [P] is somehow behind [alleged infringement] or that it sponsors [D's] product." (Internal quotes omitted.) *See also* ***University of Ala. Bd. of Trs. v. New Life Art, Inc.***, 683 F.3d 1266, 1278 (11th Cir.2012).

International Stamp Art Inc. v. U.S. Postal Serv., 456 F.3d 1270, 1274-75 (11th Cir.2006). "We have not yet established a legal standard for good faith for purposes of a fair-use defense in the context of trademark infringement. In addressing this question, other circuits have concluded that the standard for good faith for fair use is the same as the legal standard for good faith in any other trademark infringement context and that that standard asks whether the alleged infringer intended to trade on the good will of the trademark owner by creating confusion as to the source of the goods or services. [W]e agree that this is the appropriate standard to use. *At 1276:* [P] asserts that [D] had a non-infringing, commercially viable alternative. Failure to employ a non-infringing, commercially viable alternative can raise a genuine issue of material fact.

[P] suggests that [D] could produce cards depicting the art upon which its stamp designs was based, rather than the stamps themselves, and points out that [D] has already done this on multiple occasions. This, however, is not an alternative manner of depicting the stamps, but rather a choice not to depict stamps."

Brother Records, Inc. v. Jardine, 318 F.3d 900, 905 (9th Cir.2003). "[T]he classic fair use defense, codified in ... 15 U.S.C. §1115(b)(4) [Lanham Act §33(b)(4)] applies only to marks that possess both a primary meaning and a secondary meaning—and only when the mark is used in its primary descriptive sense rather than its secondary trademark sense. *At 907:* We similarly have allowed classic fair use of a suggestive mark, which carries both an unprotectable primary meaning and a protected secondary meaning."

New Kids on the Block v. News Am. Publ'g, 971 F.2d 302, 306 (9th Cir.1992). "The fair-use defense, in essence, forbids a trademark registrant to appropriate a descriptive term for his exclusive use and so prevent others from accurately describing a characteristic of their goods." (Internal quotes omitted.)

§1115(b)(4)—Geographic Descriptiveness

KP Permanent Make-up, Inc. v. Lasting Impression I, Inc., 543 U.S. 111, 112 (2004). "[A] plaintiff claiming infringement of an incontestable mark must show likelihood of consumer confusion as part of the prima facie case, while the defendant has no independent burden to negate the likelihood of any confusion in raising the affirmative defense that a term is used descriptively, not as a mark, fairly, and in good faith."

Leelanau Wine Cellars, Ltd. v. Black & Red, Inc., 502 F.3d 504, 512-13 (6th Cir.2007). "Only those marks that are 'distinctive' as a matter of law are accorded trademark protection. Certain marks, described as 'arbitrary,' 'fanciful,' or 'suggestive' are 'inherently distinctive' and protectable. A so-called 'generic' mark may never qualify for trademark protection. Between these two poles lie 'descriptive' marks. Marks that are descriptive are not inherently distinctive but may enjoy the benefit of protection if they develop a 'secondary meaning.' This rule applies equally to phrases or terms that are 'descriptive of the geographic origin of a product.' A descriptive mark achieves secondary meaning when 'in the minds of the public, the primary significance of a product feature or term is to identify the source of the product rather than the product.' A geographically descriptive mark that has acquired secondary meaning 'no longer causes the public to associate the goods [at issue] with a particular place but to associate the goods with a particular source.'"

§1115(b)(4)—Nominative Fair Use

International Info. Sys. Sec. Certification Consortium, Inc. v. Security Univ., LLC, 823 F.3d 153, 156 (2d Cir.2016). "[W]e hold that nominative fair use is not an affirmative defense to a claim of infringement under the Lanham Act. We further hold that in cases involving nominative use, in addition to considering the ***Polaroid*** factors, courts are to consider (1) whether the use of the plaintiff's mark is necessary to describe both the plaintiff's product or service and the defendant's product or service, that is, whether the product or service is not readily identifiable without use of the mark; (2) whether the defendant uses only so much of the plaintiff's mark as is necessary to identify the product or service; and (3) whether the defendant did anything that would, in conjunction with the mark, suggest sponsorship or endorsement by the plaintiff holder, that is, whether the defendant's conduct or language reflects the true or accurate relationship between plaintiff's and defendant's products or services. When considering these factors, courts must be mindful of the different types of confusion relevant to infringement claims, including confusion as to sponsorship, affiliation, or connection, as well as, when considering a certification mark, the various ways such a mark can be infringed. *At 160:* The [***Polaroid***] factors are: (1) strength of the trademark; (2) similarity of the marks; (3) proximity of the products and their competitiveness with one another; (4) evidence that the senior user may 'bridge the gap' by developing a product for sale in the market of the alleged infringer's product; (5) evidence of actual consumer confusion; (6) evidence that the imitative mark was adopted in bad faith; (7) respective quality of the products; and (8) sophistication of consumers in the relevant market. *At 165:* Nominative use is a use of another's trademark to identify, not the defendant's goods or services, but the plaintiff's goods or services. It is called 'nominative' use because it 'names' the real owner of the mark. The doctrine of nominative fair use allows a defendant to use a plaintiff's trademark to identify the plaintiff's goods so long as there is no likelihood of confusion about the source of the defendant's product or the mark-holder's sponsorship or affiliation. Because the ***Polaroid*** factors—or their analogues in other circuits—are not easily applied in cases of nominative use, various courts have created new tests to apply in such circumstances. *At 166:* In the Ninth Circuit, nominative fair use is not an affirmative defense because it does not protect a defendant from liability if there is, in fact, a likelihood of consumer confusion. Rather, the nominative fair use test replaces the multi-factor test that the Ninth Circuit typically employs to determine consumer confusion, i.e., it replaces the Ninth Circuit's analogue to the ***Polaroid*** test. [¶] By contrast, the Third Circuit, another court to have developed a nominative fair use doctrine, affords defendants broader protection. The Third Circuit treats nominative fair use as an affirmative defense that may be asserted by the defendant despite a likelihood of consumer confusion. *At 167:* [W]e reject the Third Circuit's treatment of nominative fair use as an affirmative defense. *At 168:* Because we believe that the nominative fair use factors will be helpful to a district court's analysis, we hold that, in nominative use cases, district courts are to consider the Ninth Circuit and Third Circuit's nominative fair use factors, in addition to the ***Polaroid*** factors. [¶] When assessing the second nominative fair use factor, courts are to consider whether the alleged infringer stepped over the line into a likelihood of confusion by using the senior user's mark too prominently or too often, in terms of size, emphasis, or repetition. *At 169:* Additionally, when considering the third nominative fair use factor, courts must not, as the district court did here, consider only source confusion, but rather must consider confusion regarding affiliation, sponsorship, or endorsement by the mark holder." (Internal quotes omitted.)

Toyota Motor Sales, U.S.A., Inc. v. Tabari, 610 F.3d 1171, 1175-76 (9th Cir.2010). "[T]he ***Sleekcraft*** [likelihood-of-confusion] analysis doesn't apply where a defendant uses the mark to refer to the trademarked good itself. [¶] In cases where a nominative fair use defense is raised, we ask whether (1) the product was 'readily identifiable' without use of the mark; (2) defendant used more of the mark than necessary; or (3) defendant falsely suggested he was sponsored or endorsed by the trademark holder. This test 'evaluates the likelihood of confusion in nominative use cases.' ... The third factor speaks directly to the risk of ... confusion, and the others do so indirectly: Consumers may reasonably infer sponsorship or endorsement if a company uses an unnecessary trademark or 'more' of a mark than necessary. But if the nominative use satisfies the three-factor ... test, it doesn't infringe. If the nominative use does not satisfy all the ... factors, the district court may order defendants to modify their use of the mark so that all three factors are satisfied; it may not enjoin nominative use of the mark altogether. [¶] The injunction here is plainly overbroad ... because it prohibits domain names that on their face dispel any confusion as to sponsorship or endorsement. [Ds] are prohibited from doing business at sites like independent-lexus-broker.com and we-are-definitely-not-lexus.com, although a reasonable consumer wouldn't believe [P] sponsors the websites using those domains. *At 1177:* When a domain name consists *only* of the trademark followed by .com, or some other suffix like .org or .net, it will typically suggest sponsorship or endorsement by the trademark holder. *At 1179:* Of course a domain name containing a mark cannot be nominative fair use if it suggests sponsorship or endorsement by the trademark holder. ... Sites like trademark-USA.com, trademark-of-glendale.com or e-trademark.com will also generally suggest sponsorship or endorsement by the trademark holder; the addition of 'e' merely indicates the electronic version of a brand, and a location modifier following a trademark indicates that consumers can expect to find the brand's local subsidiary, franchise or affiliate. For even more obvious reasons, domains like official-trademark-site.com or we-are-trademark.com affirmatively suggest sponsorship or endorsement by the trademark holder and are not nominative fair use. But the district court's injunction is not limited to this narrow class of cases and, indeed, [Ds'] domain names do not fall within it." *See also* ***Swarovski A.G. v. Building #19, Inc.***, 704 F.3d 44, 52-53 (1st Cir.2013) (discussing whether nominative fair use should be P's cause of action or affirmative defense but declining to decide question).

Louisiana State Univ. v. Smack Apparel Co., 550 F.3d 465, 489 (5th Cir.2008). "[A] court ordinarily should consider a nominative fair use claim in conjunction with its likelihood-of-confusion analysis in order to avoid lowering the standard for confusion. [W]e have declined to require any particular method for the consideration [of nominative fair use] in cases where the nominative use is not a significant factor in the liability determination."

Century 21 Real Estate Corp. v. Lendingtree, Inc., 425 F.3d 211, 222 (3d Cir.2005). "Today we adopt a two-step approach in nominative fair use cases. The plaintiff must first prove that confusion is likely due to the defendant's use of plaintiff's mark. [B]ecause our traditional likelihood of confusion test does not apply neatly to nominative fair use cases, we suggest eliminating those factors used to establish confusion in other trademark infringement cases that do not 'fit' in the nominative use context. Once plaintiff has met its burden of proving that confusion is likely, the burden then shifts to defendant to show that its nominative use of plaintiff's mark is nonetheless fair. To demonstrate fairness, the defendant must satisfy a three-pronged nominative fair use test.... [A] defendant must show: (1) that the use of plaintiff's mark is necessary to describe both the plaintiff's product or service and the defendant's product or service; (2) that the defendant uses only so much of the plaintiff's mark as is necessary to describe plaintiff's product; and (3) that the defendant's conduct or language reflect the true and accurate relationship between plaintiff and defendant's products or services. *At 225:* The [similarity-of-marks factor] does not leave any room for the consideration of the context of the use—i.e., that the mark is being used to describe the plaintiff's own product. Therefore, it is not appropriate for analysis in a nominative use case. [¶] We find that all of the other [likelihood-of-confusion] factors ... could be analyzed in future nominative use cases, depending on the factual situation. *At 231-32:* [W]e hold today that the ***Lapp*** test for likelihood of confusion still has an important place in a trademark infringement case in which the defendant asserts the nominative fair use defense. In this case, the test should focus on the four relevant factors: (1) the price of the goods and other factors indicative of the care and attention expected of consumers when making a purchase; (2) the length of time the defendant has used the mark without evidence of actual confusion; (3) the intent of the defendant in adopting the mark; and (4) the evidence of actual confusion." *See also* ***Louisiana State Univ. v. Smack Apparel Co.***, 550 F.3d 465, 488-89 (5th Cir.2008). *But see* ***Toyota Motor Sales, U.S.A., Inc. v. Tabari***, p. 87 (three-pronged nominative-fair-use test replaces likelihood-of-confusion test); ***Health Grades, Inc. v. Robert Wood Johnson Univ. Hosp., Inc.***, 634 F.Supp.2d 1226, 1241-42 (D.Colo.2009) (nominative fair use is not affirmative defense, but rather goes to P's proof of likelihood-of-confusion element of its claim).

§1115(b)(5)

Stone Creek, Inc. v. Omnia Italian Design, Inc., 875 F.3d 426, 436 (9th Cir.2017). "The *Tea Rose-Rectanus* doctrine is an affirmative defense separate and apart from the underlying infringement claim. [¶] The *Tea Rose-Rectanus* doctrine has its roots in the common law: it is named for a pair of Supreme Court cases, ***Hanover Star Milling Co. v. Metcalf***, 240 U.S. 403 ... (1916) ('*Tea Rose*'), and ***United Drug Co. v. Theodore Rectanus Co.***, 248 U.S. 90 ... (1918). The central proposition underlying the two cases is that common-law trademark rights extend only to the territory where a mark is known and recognized, so a later user may sometimes acquire rights in pockets geographically remote from the first user's territory. The question we address is whether [D] acquired common-law rights in the Midwest under the *Tea Rose-Rectanus* doctrine. [¶] [D's] common-law rights, if they exist, are not wiped out merely because [P] later filed a federal registration. Although federal registration presumptively entitles the senior user to nationwide protection, ... the Lanham Act preserves legal and equitable defenses that could have been asserted prior to registration.... Under this rule, already-established common-law rights are carved out of the registrant's scope of protection. ... Because [D] began using the mark in 2008, well before [P's] federal registration in 2012, the *Tea Rose-Rectanus* defense is available to [D] if it is applicable. [¶] To take advantage of the *Tea Rose-Rectanus* doctrine, the junior user must establish good faith use in a geographically remote area. *At 437:* The varying descriptions of good faith in the leading Supreme Court cases have spawned a circuit split, and our circuit has not yet weighed in. On one side, some circuits have held that the junior user's knowledge of the senior user's prior use of the mark destroys good faith. In contrast, other circuits have held that knowledge is a factor informing good faith, but the 'focus is on whether the [junior] user had the intent to benefit from the reputation or goodwill of the [senior] user.' We conclude that the better view is that there is no good faith if the junior user had knowledge of the senior user's prior use. *At 439:* [O]ne major change affected by the Lanham Act is that securing federal registration affords nationwide rights regardless of where the registrant has used the mark, a result accomplished by a provision that puts would-be users on constructive notice. In other words, the Lanham Act displaces the *Tea Rose-Rectanus* defense by charging later users with knowledge of a mark listed on the federal register. If constructive notice is sufficient to defeat good faith, it follows that actual notice should be enough too."

Quiksilver, Inc. v. Kymsta Corp., 466 F.3d 749, 761 (9th Cir.2006). "To establish innocent use, [D] had the burden to prove that it (1) adopted the 'ROXYWEAR' mark without actual or constructive knowledge of [P's] prior use of 'QUIKSILVER ROXY' and 'ROXY,' (2) used 'ROXYWEAR' before [P] filed its trademark applications for the 'QUIKSILVER ROXY' and 'ROXY' marks, and (3) continuously used the 'ROXYWEAR' mark after [P] filed its applications. [¶] According to [P], there is or should be a fourth element to this defense: remoteness, which is an element of the common law innocent-use defense. A remoteness element would require [D] to prove that neither 'QUIKSILVER ROXY' nor 'ROXY' was known in the geographical and trade area where [D] first used 'ROXYWEAR.' However, we hold that remoteness is not an element of the innocent-use defense under 15 U.S.C. §1115(b)(5) [Lanham Act §33(b)(5)]. *At 762:* Absent a remoteness element, [P's] remaining challenge is to the 'continuous use' element of the innocent-use defense. This element includes a 'zone of reputation' component and a 'continuous use' component. When [P] filed its trademark applications, [D's] trade area for 'ROXYWEAR' was frozen; [D's] continuous use assertion is limited to those areas where 'ROXYWEAR' then enjoyed recognition based on its reputation, advertising, and sales. [¶] To maintain its trademark rights in the operative areas, [D] also had to establish that it continuously used 'ROXYWEAR' from the time [P] filed its trademark applications through the time of trial. Where usage is interrupted, the innocent-use defense 'dries up,' precluding the innocent user from asserting trademark rights in those areas." *See also* ***Emergency One, Inc. v. American Fire Eagle Engine Co.***, 332 F.3d 264, 272 (4th Cir.2003).

Allard Enters. v. Advanced Programming Res., 146 F.3d 350, 361 (6th Cir.1998). This good-faith prior-user "defense is available only if the following three elements are satisfied: '(1) that the junior user ... adopted its mark before the senior user's ... registration under the Lanham Act, and without knowledge of the senior user's prior use; (2) that the trade area in which the junior user used the mark prior to the senior user's registration was limited in extent; and (3) that the junior user has continuously used the mark in the preregistration trade area.'" *See also* ***Foxtrap, Inc. v. Foxtrap, Inc.***, 671 F.2d 636, 640 (D.C.Cir.1982); ***Davidoff Extension S.A. v. Davidoff Comercio E Industria Ltda.***, 747 F.Supp. 122, 128-29 (D.P.R.1990).

Thrifty Rent-a-Car Sys. v. Thrift Cars, Inc., 831 F.2d 1177, 1181 (1st Cir.1987). "[T]he scope of protection afforded by [15 U.S.C. §1115(b)(5), Lanham Act §33(b)(5),] is limited. A pre-existing good faith user's rights are frozen to the geographical location where the user has established a market penetration as of the date of registration. Such users are unable thereafter to acquire additional protection superior to that obtained by the federal registrant. *At 1182-83:* Continuous activity within the meaning of the statute is dependent on a threshold level of geographical market penetration. ... To what extent these areas are within plaintiff's effective market area ... presents a *genuine factual issue.* [¶] Under §1115(b)(5), the junior user must show that it has made continuous use of the mark prior to the issuance of the senior user's registration and must further prove continued use up until trial."

Wrist-Rocket Mfg. v. Saunders Archery Co., 578 F.2d 727, 731 (8th Cir.1978). "The courts have held that a common-law owner whose use antedated the registration but post-dated the registrant's use in other areas has exclusive rights in the area preempted by the common-law owner. Those cases involved the application of 15 U.S.C. §1115(b)(5) [Lanham Act §33(b)(5)]. We can conceive of no reason to reach a different result in this case, where the common-law owner's use antedated the registrant's use. Therefore, geographically defined areas of exclusive use are required for each party in this situation to effectuate the will of Congress and meet the needs of business and the public."

§1115(b)(6)

Sovereign Military Hospitaller Order v. Florida Priory of the Knights Hospitallers, 809 F.3d 1171, 1191-92 (11th Cir.2015). "The district court misinterpreted [15 U.S.C.] §1115(b)(5) and (b)(6) [Lanham Act §33(b)(5) and (6)] as providing complete defenses on the merits. The defenses in §1115(b) rebut the conclusive presumption of validity that comes with incontestability. When that presumption is rebutted, however, the defendant does not automatically prevail. Rebuttal reduces the conclusive presumption of validity to a prima facie presumption of validity. The defendant must still identify some additional reason why the plaintiff's marks are invalid. [¶] Of course, prior use *can* be a defense on the merits, but … any such defense would go beyond our mandate. Under the common law, prior use can defeat the validity of a plaintiff's mark. [¶] In short, the district court erred when it held that [D's] defenses of prior use defeat [P's] claims of infringement for its incontestable marks. The defenses in §1115(b)(5) and (b)(6) … are not complete defenses on the merits. Those defenses, when they apply, only lower the presumption of validity afforded to incontestable marks."

Patsy's Italian Rest., Inc. v. Banas, 658 F.3d 254, 267 (2d Cir.2011). "[P]rior use as a defense against a trademark infringement suit does not require use in commerce. Indeed, … even [D's] local rights would be sufficient to warrant cancellation of [Ps'] marks due to a likelihood of confusion."

§1115(b)(7)

Park'N Fly, Inc. v. Dollar Park & Fly, Inc., 469 U.S. 189, 201-02 (1985). "[I]f 'monopolization' of an incontestable mark threatens economic competition, [Lanham Act] §33(b)(7) [15 U.S.C. §1115(b)(7)] provides a defense on the grounds that the mark is being used to violate federal antitrust laws."

Union Carbide Corp. v. Ever-Ready Inc., 531 F.2d 366, 389 (7th Cir.1976). "A fair reading of the antitrust affirmative defense [15 U.S.C. §1115(b)(7), Lanham Act §33(b)(7),] would indicate that it is sufficiently broad as to include a claim for equitable denial of enforcement of the trademarks on the basis of their claimed use in violation of the antitrust laws aside from the specific defense to incontestability."

§1115(b)(8)

TrafFix Devices, Inc. v. Marketing Displays, Inc., 532 U.S. 23, 32-33 (2001). "[A] functional feature is one the 'exclusive use of [which] would put competitors at a significant non-reputation-related disadvantage.' The Court of Appeals in the instant case seemed to interpret this language to mean that the necessary test for functionality is 'whether the particular product configuration is a competitive necessity.' … This was incorrect as a comprehensive definition. [A] feature is also functional when it is essential to the use or purpose of the device or when it affects the cost or quality of the device."

Christian Louboutin S.A. v. Yves Saint Laurent Am. Holding, Inc., 696 F.3d 206, 218-19 (2d Cir.2012). "[F]unctional features can be protected only through the patent system, which grants a limited monopoly over such features until they are released into general use (typically after either 14 or 20 years, depending on the type of patent). [¶] [T]wo forms of the functionality doctrine are relevant to us today: 'traditional' or 'utilitarian' functionality, and 'aesthetic' functionality. Both forms serve as an affirmative defense to a trademark infringement claim. [¶] According to our traditional understanding of functionality, a product feature is considered to be 'functional' in a utilitarian sense if it is (1) essential to the use or purpose of the article, or if it (2) affects the cost or quality of the article. A feature is essential if it is dictated by the functions to be performed by the article. It affects the cost or quality of the article where it permits the article to be manufactured at a lower cost or constitutes an improvement in the operation of the goods. A finding that a product feature is functional according to the ***Inwood*** [***Labs. v. Ives Labs.***, 456 U.S. 844 (1982),] test will ordinarily render the feature ineligible for trademark protection. *At 220:* [T]he test for aesthetic functionality is threefold: At the start, we address the two prongs of the ***Inwood*** test, asking whether the design feature is either essential to the use or purpose or affects the cost or quality of the product at issue. Next, if necessary, we turn to a third prong, which is the competition inquiry set forth in ***Qualitex*** [***Co. v. Jacobson Prods. Co.***, 514 U.S. 159 (1995)]. In other words, if a design feature would, from a traditional utilitarian perspective, be considered essential to the use or purpose of the article, or to affect its cost or quality, then the design feature is functional under ***Inwood*** and our inquiry ends. But if the design feature is not 'functional' from a traditional perspective, it must still pass the fact-intensive ***Qualitex*** test and be shown not to have a significant effect on competition in order to receive trademark protection. *At 221:* In 1995, the Supreme Court in ***Qualitex*** gave its imprimatur to the aesthetic functionality doctrine, holding that the ultimate test of aesthetic functionality is whether the recognition of trademark rights in an aesthetic design feature would significantly hinder competition. Six years later, reiterating its ***Qualitex*** analysis, the Supreme Court in ***TrafFix*** declared that where aesthetic functionality is the central question, courts must inquire as to whether recognizing the trademark would put competitors at a significant non-reputation-related disadvantage. *At 222:* On the one hand, where an ornamental feature is claimed as a trademark and trademark protection would significantly hinder competition by limiting the range of adequate alternative designs, the aesthetic functionality doctrine denies such protection. But on the other hand, distinctive and arbitrary arrangements of predominantly ornamental features that do *not* hinder potential competitors from entering the same market with differently dressed versions of the product are non-functional, and are hence eligible for trademark protection. [¶] In short, a mark is aesthetically functional, and therefore ineligible for protection under the Lanham Act, where protection of the mark *significantly* undermines competitors' ability to compete in the relevant market. In making this determination, courts must carefully weigh the competitive benefits of protecting the source-identifying aspects of a mark against the competitive costs of precluding competitors from using the feature. [¶] Finally, we note that a product feature's successful source indication can sometimes be difficult to distinguish from the feature's aesthetic function, if any. Therefore, in determining whether a mark has an aesthetic function so as to preclude trademark protection, we take care to ensure that the mark's very success in denoting (and promoting) its source does not itself defeat the markholder's right to protect that mark. [¶] Because aesthetic function and branding success can sometimes be difficult to distinguish, the aesthetic functionality analysis is highly fact-specific. In conducting this inquiry, courts must consider both the markholder's right to enjoy the benefits of its effort to distinguish its product and the public's right to the vigorously competitive market protected by the Lanham Act, which an overly broad trademark might hinder. In sum, courts must avoid jumping to the conclusion that an aesthetic feature is functional merely because it denotes the product's desirable source." (Internal quotes omitted.) *See also* ***Maker's Mark Distillery, Inc. v. Diageo N. Am., Inc.***, 679 F.3d 410, 418 (6th Cir.2012) (discussing "comparable alternatives" and "effective competition" tests for aesthetic-functionality doctrine, but declining to adopt either); ***Rosetta Stone Ltd. v. Google, Inc.***, 676 F.3d 144, 161 (4th Cir.2012) (discussing ***Inwood*** test); ***Au-Tomotive Gold, Inc. v. Volkswagen, Inc.***, 457 F.3d 1062, 1072 (9th Cir.2006) (stating test for aesthetic functionality).

Jay Franco & Sons, Inc. v. Franek, 615 F.3d 855, 857 (7th Cir.2010). "[I]f a design enables a product to operate, or improves on a substitute design in some way (such as by making the product cheaper, faster, lighter, or stronger), then the design cannot be trademarked; it is functional because consumers would pay to have it rather than be indifferent toward or pay to avoid it. A qualification is that any pleasure a customer derives from the design's identification of the product's source—the joy of buying a marked good over an identical generic version because the consumer prefers the status conferred by the mark—doesn't count. That broad a theory of functionality would penalize companies for developing brands with cachet to distinguish themselves from competitors, which is the very purpose of trademark law. In short, a design that produces a benefit other than source identification is functional. [¶] Figuring out which designs meet this criterion can be tricky. Utility patents serve as excellent cheat sheets because any design claimed in a patent is supposed to be useful. For this reason, ***TrafFix*** held that expired utility patents provide 'strong evidence that the features therein claimed are functional.' *At 858:* Proving patent infringement can be *sufficient* to show that a trademarked design is useful, as it means that the infringing design is quite similar to a useful invention. But such proof is unnecessary. Functionality is determined by a feature's usefulness, not its patentability or its infringement of a patent. … If an invention is too useless to be patentable, or too dissimilar to a design to shed light on its functions, then the lack of proof of patent infringement is meaningful. Otherwise it is irrelevant. A design may not infringe a patented invention because the invention is obvious or taught by prior art, … but those and other disqualifiers do not mean that the design is not useful. *At 860:* The chief difficulty is distinguishing between designs that are fashionable enough to be functional and those that are merely pleasing to the eye. Only the latter group can be protected.… The Supreme Court broached the subject in ***Qualitex*** when it discussed the functionality of the green-gold color of the dry cleaning pad. Unwilling to say that the pad required a green-gold hue or was improved by it, the Court still thought that the color would be functional if its exclusive use by a single designer 'would put competitors at a significant non-reputation-related disadvantage.'"

Fuji Kogyo Co. v. Pacific Bay Int'l, 461 F.3d 675, 681 (6th Cir.2006). "Functionality [in a trademark case] is a factual determination reviewed only for clear error. *At 685:* Where the design is functional under the ***Inwood*** [***Labs. v. Ives Labs.***, 456 U.S. 844 (1982),] formulation there is no need to proceed further to consider if there is a competitive necessity for the feature. The Federal Circuit maintains a helpful doctrine of de jure versus de facto functionality: Our decisions distinguish de facto functional features, which may be entitled to trademark protection, from de jure functional features, which are not. In essence, de facto functional means that the design of a product has a function, i.e., a bottle of any design holds fluid. De facto functionality does not necessarily defeat registrability. De jure functionality means that the product has a particular shape because it works better in this shape. To determine whether a particular product design is de jure functional, we have applied the [***In re Morton-Norwich Prods.***, 671 F.2d 1332 (C.C.P.A.1982),] factors: (1) the existence of a utility patent disclosing the utilitarian advantages of the design; (2) advertising materials in which the originator of the design touts the design's utilitarian advantages; (3) the availability to competitors of functionally equivalent designs; and (4) facts indicating that the design results in a comparatively simple or cheap method of manufacturing the product." (Internal quotes omitted.)

§1115(b)(9)—Generally

Exxon Corp. v. Oxxford Clothes, Inc., 109 F.3d 1070, 1078 n.11 (5th Cir.1997). Acquiescence, "estoppel, and the other equitable defenses listed in [15 U.S.C. §1115(b)(9), Lanham Act §33(b)(9),] are personal defenses, based upon the trademark owner's conduct *vis-a-vis* the defendant, and thus also do not speak to the wholesale loss of rights in the mark remarked upon by naked licensing jurisprudence."

Levi Strauss & Co. v. GTFM, Inc., 196 F.Supp.2d 971, 983 (N.D.Cal.2002). "[T]he court finds that [15 U.S.C.] §1115(b)(9) [Lanham Act §33(b)(9)] does not provide a mechanism for importing a 'phantom mark' exception to incontestability."

§1115(b)(9)—Acquiescence

Covertech Fabricating, Inc. v. TVM Bldg. Prods., 855 F.3d 163, 175-76 (3d Cir.2017). "Once use becomes infringing, the relevant date for quantifying the 'delay' is when the trademark owner either knew or should have known of the existence of a provable claim of infringement, and an owner's claim does not ripen until the defendant's infringement is sufficiently far-reaching to create a likelihood of confusion."

Hyson USA, Inc. v. Hyson 2U, Ltd., 821 F.3d 935, 939-40 (7th Cir.2016). "If a trademark owner acquiesces to another's use of his mark ... then the mark's original source-identifying power is weakened and the owner may be estopped from obtaining relief in an infringement action against the junior user. Thus, acquiescence is an affirmative defense in an action for trademark infringement under the Lanham Act. [¶] Generally speaking, acquiescence is an equitable doctrine that permits the court to deny relief in an action for trademark infringement if the evidence shows that the owner of the mark has, through his words or conduct, conveyed his consent to the defendant's use of the mark. The defense prevents the trademark owner from impliedly permitting another's use of his mark and then attempting to enjoin that use *after* the junior user has invested substantial resources to develop the mark's goodwill. [¶] '[W]hereas laches is a negligent, unintentional failure to protect trademark rights, [a]cquiescence is associated with *intentional* abandonment.' It requires an '*affirmative* word or deed' that conveys the trademark owner's implied consent to the junior user's use of his marks. [¶] In short, although our cases sometimes blend the doctrines of acquiescence and laches, they are formally distinct and should be analyzed separately. *At 941:* [A]n equitable defense like acquiescence is not ordinarily susceptible to resolution at the pleading stage. The defense requires a qualitative examination of the parties' words and conduct and an equitable evaluation of the length of the delay and the degree of prejudice to the defendant if the trademark owner's rights are enforced. That kind of analysis generally requires a factual record."

University of Ala. Bd. of Trs. v. New Life Art, Inc., 683 F.3d 1266, 1281 (11th Cir.2012). "'The defense of acquiescence requires proof of three elements: (1) the plaintiff actively represented it would not assert a right or claim; (2) the delay between the active representation and assertion of the right or claim was not excusable; and (3) the delay caused the defendant undue prejudice.' 'The difference between acquiescence and laches is that laches denotes passive consent and acquiescence denotes active consent.' *At 1282:* 'Active consent' does not necessarily mean an explicit promise not to sue. It only requires 'conduct on the plaintiff's part that amounted to an assurance to the defendant, express or implied, that plaintiff would not assert his trademark rights against the defendant.'" *See also*

What-A-Burger, Inc. v. Whataburger, Inc., 357 F.3d 441, 452 (4th Cir.2004); ***Masters v. UHS of Del., Inc.***, 631 F.3d 464, 469 (8th Cir.2011).

§1115(b)(9)—Collateral Estoppel

Jean Alexander Cosmetics, Inc. v. L'Oreal USA, Inc., 458 F.3d 244, 250-51 (3d Cir.2006). "[T]he case could have been resolved without the [TTAB's] determination that there was no likelihood of confusion between [P's and D's marks]. We must determine whether a finding that is an alternate, but independently sufficient, basis for a judgment should be deemed necessary to a decision for purposes of collateral estoppel. *At 255:* [W]e will follow the traditional view that independently sufficient alternative findings should be given preclusive effect."

Santos v. Hecht, 82 U.S.P.Q.2d 1542, 1543 (E.D.N.Y. 2006). "[P] filed the complaint in this case … alleging [D] violated the law of unfair competition and false designation of origin…. [D] moved to dismiss the complaint, contending that the TTAB's default judgment decision [to cancel P's mark] bars [P] from pursuing this action. *At 1544:* This argument is rejected for several reasons. [¶] [T]here is no res judicata effect of a cancellation proceeding, such as the TTAB proceeding here, on a subsequent federal lawsuit alleging unfair competition and trademark infringement. [¶] [B]ecause the TTAB proceeding was not decided on the merits, collateral estoppel is inapplicable to this case."

§1115(b)(9)—Estoppel

Nguyen v. Biondo, 508 Fed.Appx. 932, 935 (11th Cir.2013). "The district court did not err in rejecting [D's] affirmative defense of abandonment. An owner of a trademark may abandon his mark through 'naked licensing,' or the failure to properly supervise his licensee's use of the mark, … but a claim of abandonment turns on when the lack of supervision occurred. A licensee is estopped to contest the validity of the licensor's title during the course of the licensing arrangement, but after its expiration, the licensee may challenge the licensor's title on facts which arose after the contract has expired. [D] argued that [P] abandoned the … mark between 2008 and early 2010, but when [D] later signed the sales agreement on March 11, 2010, he expressly recognized that [P] owned the mark. After the agreement expired, [P] sued [D] for trademark infringement. [D's] defense of abandonment fails." (Internal quotes omitted.)

Boston Duck Tours, LP v. Super Duck Tours, LLC, 531 F.3d 1, 22-23 (1st Cir.2008). "[D] is not foreclosed from arguing now that the term 'duck' or the phrase 'duck tours' is generic because it argued to the contrary several years ago in front of the PTO. That contrary argument is simply another factor in the evidentiary mix."

General Motors Corp. v. Lanard Toys, Inc., 468 F.3d 405, 420 (6th Cir.2006). "To demonstrate a valid estoppel claim, [D] 'must show that it had been misled by [P] through actual misrepresentations, affirmative acts of misconduct, intentional misleading silence, or conduct amounting to virtual abandonment of the trademark.'" *See also* ***Masters v. UHS of Del., Inc.***, 631 F.3d 464, 469 (8th Cir.2011).

§1115(b)(9)—First Sale

Au-Tomotive Gold Inc. v. Volkswagen of Am., Inc., 603 F.3d 1133, 1135-36 (9th Cir.2010). "[P] argues that because it purchased actual VW badges from a Volkswagen dealer for use on the marquee license plates, the 'first sale' doctrine protects the sale of the plates. We hold that the 'first sale' doctrine does not provide a defense because the plates create a likelihood of confusion as to their origin. We do not base our holding on a likelihood of confusion among purchasers of the plates. Rather, we base it on the likelihood of post-purchase confusion among observers who see the plates on purchasers' cars. *At 1138:* Post-purchase confusion creates a free-rider problem. [P] contends that in 'first sale' cases the element of 'free-riding' present in other post-purchase confusion cases disappears because the producer has paid the price asked by the trademark owner for the 'ride.' This contention misses the point. When a producer purchases a trademarked product, that producer is not purchasing the trademark. Rather, the producer is purchasing a product that has been trademarked. If a producer profits from a trademark because of post-purchase confusion about the product's origin, the producer is, to that degree, a free-rider." (Internal quotes omitted.)

Australian Gold, Inc. v. Hatfield, 436 F.3d 1228, 1240-41 (10th Cir.2006). "Because in general the right of a producer to control distribution of its trademarked product does not extend beyond the first sale of the product, resale by the first purchaser of the original article under the producer's trademark is neither trademark infringement nor unfair competition. It is the essence of the first sale doctrine that a purchaser who does no more than stock, display, and resell a producer's product under the producer's trademark violates no right conferred upon the producer by the Lanham Act. When a purchaser resells a trademarked article under the producer's trademark, and nothing more, there is no actionable misrepresentation under the statute. [¶] However, the first sale doctrine does not protect resellers who use other entities' trademarks to give the impression that they are favored or authorized dealers for a product when in fact they are not." (Internal quotes omitted.)

§1115(b)(9)—Laches

La Quinta Worldwide LLC v. Q.R.T.M., S.A. de C.V., 762 F.3d 867, 878 (9th Cir.2014). "We analyze the laches defense with a two-step process. First, we determine whether the limitations period for laches has expired. If the period has not expired before suit was filed, there is a strong presumption against the laches defense. That presumption is reversed if the laches period expired before the suit was filed. ... Second, if the laches period expired before suit was filed, we apply [six] factors ... to determine whether the trademark owner's delay in filing suit was unreasonable and, therefore, barred.... [¶] To prove that a delay in filing was unwarranted, the party asserting a laches defense must show that the following six factors weigh in its favor: (1) strength and value of trademark rights asserted; (2) plaintiff's diligence in enforcing mark; (3) harm to senior user if relief denied; (4) good faith ignorance by junior user; (5) competition between senior and junior users; and (6) extent of harm suffered by junior user because of senior user's delay. To benefit from this equitable defense, the party asserting laches must demonstrate that it has suffered prejudice as a result of plaintiff's unreasonable delay in filing suit." (Internal quotes omitted.)

Abraham v. Alpha Chi Omega, 708 F.3d 614, 626-27 (5th Cir.2013). "'A finding of laches alone ordinarily will not bar ... injunctive relief, although it typically will foreclose a demand for an accounting or damages.' This is because 'courts construe [a trademark owner's] unreasonable delay to imply consent to the [infringer's] conduct, which amounts to nothing more than a revocable license; the license is revoked once the plaintiff objects to the [infringer's] infringement.' ... 'There is no doubt that laches may defeat claims for injunctive relief as well as claims for an accounting.' [¶] Therefore, a finding of laches or acquiescence may bar injunctive relief if the trademark owner conducted itself in a way that induced the infringer's reliance or if an injunction would result in 'substantial prejudice' to the infringer. [¶] '[C]ourts consistently focus on the degree of prejudice the defendant would suffer in the event the infringing use is enjoined[.]'"

Ray Comms. v. Clear Channel Comms., 673 F.3d 294, 300-01 (4th Cir.2012). "Courts apply laches to address the inequities created, by a trademark owner who, despite having a colorable infringement claim, has unreasonably delayed in seeking redress to the detriment of the defendant. In determining whether laches operates as a defense to a trademark infringement claim, we consider at least the following factors: (1) whether the owner of the mark knew of the infringing use; (2) whether the owner's delay in challenging the infringement of the mark was inexcusable or unreasonable; and (3) whether the infringing user has been unduly prejudiced by the owner's delay. [¶] The question whether a trademark owner knew or should have known that it had a viable claim for infringement is determined by an objective standard. [¶] Logic dictates that 'unreasonable delay' does not include any period of time before the owner is able to pursue a claim for infringement—otherwise, a trademark owner could be punished for not bringing a claim he had no right to bring. [¶] [I]n the laches context, (1) delay is measured from the time at which the owner knew of an infringing use sufficient to require legal action; and (2) legal action is not required until there is a real likelihood of confusion. *At 304:* With respect to the second prong of the laches defense, whether the trademark owner unreasonably or inexcusably delayed, we reiterate that delay must be measured from the period at which the trademark owner knew or should have known of an infringing use. *At 305:* With respect to the third prong of the laches defense, whether the trademark owner's delay has resulted in undue prejudice to the defendant, the district court determined that [D] has suffered both economic and evidentiary prejudice. [¶] A defendant suffers economic prejudice when it relies on the trademark owner's inaction by developing a valuable business around the trademark. Evidentiary prejudice encompasses such things as lost, stale or degraded evidence or witnesses whose memories have faded or who have died. *At 307-08:* [L]aches *may* act as a bar to both monetary and injunctive relief under certain circumstances, but ... this result is not automatic.

[I]n consideration of the public interest, estoppel by laches may not be invoked to deny injunctive relief if it is apparent that the infringing use is likely to cause confusion. [¶] [C]ases involving the denial of injunctive relief usually present one or more aggravating factors, causing the balance of the equities (which has, at that point, favored the defendant by virtue of the delay-and-prejudice analysis) to shift even further to the defendant's advantage. These factors include: (1) delay during which the mark passed into use as a generic name, (2) a grossly long period of delay, (3) dubious proof of likelihood of confusion, (4) doubt as to the plaintiff's title to the mark, (5) prior business dealings between the parties that result in the plaintiff impliedly consenting to the defendant's infringement, and (6) the defendant's good-faith development of a specific territorial area." (Internal quotes omitted.) *See also* ***American Rice, Inc. v. Producers Rice Mill, Inc.***, 518 F.3d 321, 334 (5th Cir.2008); ***Miller v. Glenn Miller Prods.***, 454 F.3d 975, 997 (9th Cir.2006).

Roederer v. J. Garcia Carrion, S.A., 569 F.3d 855, 859 (8th Cir.2009). "[I]n trademark suits, courts consider two additional factors when evaluating the merits of a laches defense: (1) the doctrine of progressive encroachment, and (2) notice to the defendant of the plaintiff's objections to the potentially infringing mark. First, under the doctrine of progressive encroachment, the time of delay is to be measured not from when the plaintiff first learned of the potentially infringing mark, but from when such infringement became actionable and provable. [¶] Second, courts tend to reject a defendant's assertion of the laches defense when the defendant knew that the plaintiff objected to the use of the mark. This rule can be understood either as an analogue to assumption of risk, or as a factor that prevents the defendant from suffering undue prejudice. In either event, forewarning of a plaintiff's objections generally prevents a defendant from making a laches defense." *See also* ***Tillamook Country Smoker, Inc. v. Tillamook Cty. Creamery Ass'n***, 465 F.3d 1102, 1110 (9th Cir.2006).

Internet Specialties W., Inc. v. Milon-DiGiorgio Enters., 559 F.3d 985, 991 (9th Cir.2009). "In our circuit, we apply a 'hybrid' standard of review ..., reviewing de novo whether laches is a valid defense to a particular action, but reviewing the district court's application of the laches factors for abuse of discretion." Held: Laches did not apply. P's evidence of promotional expenses failed to prove that the use of the mark identified P's business. Because the mark did not identify P's business, prejudice was not proved.

Louisiana State Univ. v. Smack Apparel Co., 550 F.3d 465, 489 (5th Cir.2008). "[T]he record establishes the substantive and knowing bad faith necessary to foreclose [laches because D] admitted that it intentionally incorporated [P's] color schemes and other indicia in order to specifically call [P] to the public's mind, thus deriving a benefit from [P's] reputation."

Reno Air Racing Ass'n v. McCord, 452 F.3d 1126, 1138-39 (9th Cir.2006). "'While laches and the statute of limitations are distinct defenses [i]f the plaintiff filed suit within the analogous limitations period, the strong presumption is that laches is inapplicable.' If the plaintiff filed suit outside this analogous period, 'courts have often presumed that laches is applicable.' Because the Lanham Act contains no explicit statute of limitation, courts 'borrow' the analogous state time period.... [¶] 'In determining the presumption for laches, the limitations period runs from the time the plaintiff knew or should have known about his ... cause of action.'"

§1115(b)(9)—Res Judicata

Marcel Fashions Grp. v. Lucky Brand Dungarees, Inc., 779 F.3d 102, 107-08 (2d Cir.2015). "The term *res judicata*, which means essentially that the matter in controversy has already been adjudicated, encompasses two significantly different doctrines: claim preclusion and issue preclusion. Under *claim preclusion*, 'a final judgment forecloses successive litigation of the very same claim, whether or not relitigation of the claim raises the same issues as the earlier suit.' The doctrine precludes not only litigation of claims raised and adjudicated in a prior litigation between the parties (and their privies), but also of claims that might have been raised in the prior litigation but were not. The doctrine of *issue preclusion*, in contrast, 'bars successive litigation of an issue of fact or law actually litigated and resolved in a valid court determination essential to the prior judgment, even if the issue recurs in the context of a different claim.' [¶] Preclusion of a claim under this doctrine requires a showing that '(1) the previous action involved an adjudication on the merits; (2) the previous action involved the [same adverse parties] or those in privity with them; and (3) the claims asserted in the subsequent action were, or could have been, raised in the prior action.'"

Liberto v. D.F. Stauffer Biscuit Co., 441 F.3d 318, 326 (5th Cir.2006). "*Res judicata* applies only where (1) parties to the respective actions are identical; (2) the prior judgment was rendered by a court of competent jurisdiction; (3) the prior action resulted in a final judgment on the merits; and (4) the same cause of action is involved in both cases."

§1115(b)(9)—Unclean Hands

1-800 Contacts, Inc. v. Lens.com, Inc., 722 F.3d 1229, 1255 (10th Cir.2013). "[T]he doctrine of unclean hands 'does not empower a court of equity to deny relief for any and all inequitable conduct on the part of the plaintiff.' Rather, a plaintiff's unclean hands will bar recovery for trademark infringement only if the inequitable conduct is 'related to the plaintiff's cause of action.' We said that courts have found such a relationship in two situations: First, there is such a relationship when the plaintiff has engaged in inequitable conduct toward the public, such as 'deception in or misuse of the trademark itself, resulting in harm to the public such that it would be wrong for a court of equity to reward the plaintiff's conduct by granting relief.' Second, the plaintiff's misconduct is sufficiently related to the cause of action 'when the plaintiff has acted inequitably toward the defendant *in relation to the trademark*.' [D] does not claim that the first situation is present here. As for the second, [D] improperly refers to conduct relating to trademarks other than the one that it allegedly infringed. As one authority explains: 'The plaintiff's alleged infringement of a different trademark does not furnish grounds for an unclean hands defense. For example, if A sues B for infringement of A's trademark ALPHA, can B deflect the lawsuit by claiming that A has unclean hands, alleging that A is infringing B's trademark BETA? The answer is that this is *not* unclean hands because A's alleged infringement of the trademark BETA is not relevant to the subject matter of the litigation concerning B's alleged infringement of the trademark ALPHA. The plaintiff's alleged infringement of another's mark is actually a form of the defense of *jus tertii*, which is uniformly rejected by the courts.'"

Perfumebay.com Inc. v. eBay Inc., 506 F.3d 1165, 1177 (9th Cir.2007). "'Unclean hands is a defense to a Lanham Act infringement suit.' 'Trademark law's unclean hands defense springs from the rationale that it is essential that the plaintiff should not in his trade mark, or in his advertisements and business, be himself guilty of any false or misleading representation.' 'To show that a trademark plaintiff's conduct is inequitable, defendant must show that plaintiff used the trademark to deceive consumers.' 'Bad intent is the essence of the defense of unclean hands.'"

§1116. INJUNCTIVE RELIEF [LANHAM ACT §34]

(a) Jurisdiction; service.—The several courts vested with jurisdiction of civil actions arising under this chapter shall have power to grant injunctions, according to the principles of equity and upon such terms as the court may deem reasonable, to prevent the violation of any right of the registrant of a mark registered in the Patent and Trademark Office or to prevent a violation under subsection (a), (c), or (d) of section 1125 of title 15. Any such injunction may include a provision directing the defendant to file with the court and serve on the plaintiff within thirty days after the service on the defendant of such injunction, or such extended period as the court may direct, a report in writing under oath setting forth in detail the manner and form in which the defendant has complied with the injunction. Any such injunction granted upon hearing, after notice to the defendant, by any district court of the United States, may be served on the parties against whom such injunction is granted anywhere in the United States where they may be found, and shall be operative and may be enforced by proceedings to punish for contempt, or otherwise, by the court by which such injunction was granted, or by any other United States district court in whose jurisdiction the defendant may be found.

(b) Transfer of certified copies of court papers.—The said courts shall have jurisdiction to enforce said injunction, as provided in this chapter, as fully as if the injunction had been granted by the district court in which it is sought to be enforced. The clerk of the court or judge granting the injunction shall, when required to do so by the court before which application to enforce said injunction is made, transfer without delay to said court a certified copy of all papers on file in his office upon which said injunction was granted.

(c) Notice to Director.—It shall be the duty of the clerks of such courts within one month after the filing of any action, suit, or proceeding involving a mark registered under the provisions of this chapter to give notice thereof in writing to the Director setting forth in order so far as known the names and addresses of the litigants and the designating number or numbers of the registration or registrations upon which the action, suit, or proceeding has been brought, and in the event any other registration be subsequently included in the action, suit, or proceeding by amendment, answer, or other pleading, the clerk shall give like notice thereof to the Director, and within one month after the judgment is entered or an appeal is taken the clerk of the court shall give notice thereof to the Director, and it shall be the duty of the Director on receipt of such notice forthwith to endorse the same upon the file wrapper of the said registration or registrations and to incorporate the same as a part of the contents of said file wrapper.

(d) Civil actions arising out of use of counterfeit marks—

(1)(A) In the case of a civil action arising under section 1114(1)(a) of title 15 or section 220506 of title 36 with respect to a violation that consists of using a counterfeit mark in connection with the sale, offering for sale, or distribution of goods or services, the court may, upon ex parte application, grant an order under subsection (a) of this section pursuant to this subsection providing for the seizure of goods and counterfeit marks involved in such violation and the means of making such marks, and records documenting the manufacture, sale, or receipt of things involved in such violation.

(B) As used in this subsection the term "counterfeit mark" means—

(i) a counterfeit of a mark that is registered on the principal register in the United States Patent and Trademark Office for such goods or services sold, offered for sale, or distributed and that is in use, whether or not the person against whom relief is sought knew such mark was so registered; or

(ii) a spurious designation that is identical with, or substantially indistinguishable from, a designation as to which the remedies of this chapter are made available by reason of section 220506 of title 36;

but such term does not include any mark or designation used on or in connection with goods or services of which the manufacture[1] or producer was, at the time of the manufacture or production in question authorized to use the mark or designation for the type of goods or services so manufactured or produced, by the holder of the right to use such mark or designation.

(2) The court shall not receive an application under this subsection unless the applicant has given such notice of the application as is reasonable under the circumstances to the United States attorney for the judicial district in which such order is sought. Such attorney may participate in the proceedings arising under such application if such proceedings may affect evidence of an offense against the United States. The court may deny such application if the court determines that the public interest in a potential prosecution so requires.

(3) The application for an order under this subsection shall—

(A) be based on an affidavit or the verified complaint establishing facts sufficient to support the findings of fact and conclusions of law required for such order; and

(B) contain the additional information required by paragraph (5) of this subsection to be set forth in such order.

(4) The court shall not grant such an application unless—

(A) the person obtaining an order under this subsection provides the security determined adequate by the court for the payment of such damages as any person may be entitled to recover as a result of a wrongful seizure or wrongful attempted seizure under this subsection; and

(B) the court finds that it clearly appears from specific facts that—

(i) an order other than an ex parte seizure order is not adequate to achieve the purposes of section 1114 of title 15;

(ii) the applicant has not publicized the requested seizure;

(iii) the applicant is likely to succeed in showing that the person against whom seizure would be ordered used a counterfeit mark in connection with the sale, offering for sale, or distribution of goods or services;

(iv) an immediate and irreparable injury will occur if such seizure is not ordered;

(v) the matter to be seized will be located at the place identified in the application;

(vi) the harm to the applicant of denying the application outweighs the harm to the legitimate interests of the person against whom seizure would be ordered of granting the application; and

(vii) the person against whom seizure would be ordered, or persons acting in concert with such person, would destroy, move, hide, or otherwise make such matter inaccessible to the court, if the applicant were to proceed on notice to such person.

(5) An order under this subsection shall set forth—

(A) the findings of fact and conclusions of law required for the order;

(B) a particular description of the matter to be seized, and a description of each place at which such matter is to be seized;

(C) the time period, which shall end not later than seven days after the date on which such order is issued, during which the seizure is to be made;

(D) the amount of security required to be provided under this subsection; and

(E) a date for the hearing required under paragraph (10) of this subsection.

(6) The court shall take appropriate action to protect the person against whom an order under this subsection is directed from publicity, by or at the behest of the plaintiff, about such order and any seizure under such order.

(7) Any materials seized under this subsection shall be taken into the custody of the court. For seizures made under this section, the court shall enter an appropriate protective order with respect to discovery and use of any records or information that has been seized. The protective order shall provide for appropriate procedures to ensure that confidential, private, proprietary, or privileged information contained in such records is not improperly disclosed or used.

(8) An order under this subsection, together with the supporting documents, shall be sealed until the person against whom the order is directed has an opportunity to contest such order, except that any person against whom such order is issued shall have access to such order and supporting documents after the seizure has been carried out.

(9) The court shall order that service of a copy of the order under this subsection shall be made by a Federal law enforcement officer (such as a United States marshal or an officer or agent of the United States Customs Service, Secret Service, Federal Bureau of Investigation, or Post Office) or may be made by a State or local law enforcement officer, who, upon making service, shall carry out the seizure under the order. The court shall issue orders, when appropriate, to protect the defendant from undue damage from the disclosure of trade secrets or other confidential information during the course of the seizure, including, when appropriate, orders restricting the access of the applicant (or any agent or employee of the applicant) to such secrets or information.

(10)(A) The court shall hold a hearing, unless waived by all the parties, on the date set by the court in the order of seizure. That date shall be not sooner than ten days after the order is issued and not later than fifteen days after the order is issued, unless the applicant for the order shows good cause for another date or unless the party against whom such order is directed consents to another date for such hearing. At such hearing the party obtaining the order shall have the burden to prove that the facts supporting findings of fact and conclusions of law necessary to support such order are still in effect. If that party fails to meet that burden, the seizure order shall be dissolved or modified appropriately.

(B) In connection with a hearing under this paragraph, the court may make such orders modifying the time limits for discovery under the Rules of Civil Procedure as may be necessary to prevent the frustration of the purposes of such hearing.

(11) A person who suffers damage by reason of a wrongful seizure under this subsection has a cause of action against the applicant for the order under which such seizure was made, and shall be entitled to recover such relief as may be appropriate, including damages for lost profits, cost of materials, loss of good will, and punitive damages in instances where the seizure was sought in bad faith, and, unless the court finds extenuating circumstances, to recover a reasonable attorney's fee. The court in its discretion may award prejudgment interest on relief recovered under this paragraph, at an annual interest rate established under section 6621(a)(2) of title 26, commencing on the date of service of the claimant's pleading setting forth the claim under this paragraph and ending on the date such recovery is granted, or for such shorter time as the court deems appropriate.

1. **Editor's note:** Probably should be "manufacturer."

History of 15 U.S.C. §1116: July 5, 1946, ch. 540, §34, 60 Stat. 439; Jan. 2, 1975, P.L. 93-596, §1, 88 Stat. 1949; Oct. 12, 1984, P.L. 98-473, §1503(1), 98 Stat. 2179; Nov. 16, 1988, P.L. 100-667, §128(c)-(e), 102 Stat. 3945; July 2, 1996, P.L.

104-153, §6, 110 Stat. 1388; Aug. 5, 1999, P.L. 106-43, §3(a)(1), 113 Stat. 218; Nov. 29, 1999, P.L. 106-113, §1000(a)(9), 113 Stat. 1536; Nov. 2, 2002, P.L. 107-273, §13207(b)(8)-(10), 116 Stat. 1908; Oct. 13, 2008, P.L. 110-403, §102(b), 122 Stat. 4258.

See also FRCP 65.

Treatise Cross-References

McCarthy on Trademark & Unfair Competition

Ch. 5, *Historical Basis of Trademarks & Legislative History*, §5:7
Ch. 19, *Federal Registration of Marks*, §§19:26; 19:144
Ch. 25, *Types of Trademark Infringement*, §25:15
Ch. 30, *Remedies for Trademark Infringement & Unfair Competition*, §§30:1; 30:3; 30:17; 30:35-30:38; 30:44; 30:47; 30:55; 30:94

ANNOTATIONS

Generally

Paulsson Geophysical Servs. v. Sigmar, 529 F.3d 303, 308-09 (5th Cir.2008). Held: Because P, a U.S. company, had significant contracts and financial transactions that had a substantial effect on U.S. commerce, the district court had subject-matter jurisdiction over the Lanham Act claim and was able to issue an injunction against activities of infringement consummated outside the U.S. under ***Steele v. Bulova Watch Co.***, 344 U.S. 280 (1952), and ***American Rice, Inc. v. Arkansas Rice Growers Coop.***, 701 F.2d 408 (5th Cir. 1983).

Starter Corp. v. Converse, Inc., 170 F.3d 286, 300 (2d Cir.1999). "We find that the district court abused its discretion by enjoining the use of [P's mark] on all footwear when 'in combination with any other words or designs.' First, the jury's findings went only to the use of [mark] when used alone; the jury reached no conclusion as to the use of the marks in combination with other designs. Yet the language of the injunction, proposed by [D] and ordered by the district court, is broad enough to bar the continued use of [mark] when used in combination with other [shoe] designs.... This result is clearly wrong since [D's] witnesses testified that [P's] use of its Mark [on its other] shoe was not at issue in this litigation and its attorneys so agreed. We have vacated injunctions in other trademark cases that have gone beyond the scope of issues tried in the case."

Pebble Beach Co. v. Tour 18 I Ltd., 155 F.3d 526, 550 (5th Cir.1998), *overruled on other grounds*, ***TrafFix Devices, Inc. v. Marketing Displays, Inc.***, 532 U.S. 23 (2001). "We review the district court's decision whether to grant or deny an injunction and the scope and form of the injunction for an abuse of discretion. In reviewing the injunction, it is important to note that, in fashioning relief against a party who has transgressed the governing legal standards, a court of equity is free to proscribe activities that, standing alone, would have been unassailable." (Internal quotes omitted.)

American Bd. of Psychiatry & Neurology v. Johnson-Powell, 129 F.3d 1, 4-5 (1st Cir.1997). "[T]here was ample evidence here of past infringing conduct, not to mention conduct indicative of bad faith. [S]uch evidence, if not rebutted, may give rise to a strong inference that further infringing acts will occur in the future. Even so, we cannot say that a defendant can never take actions and provides assurances sufficient, in the face of such evidence, to convince a court that she will not commit future violations. Our system leaves it primarily in the hands of the district court to ascertain whether the danger of future harm has been adequately established so as to warrant the protection of an injunction."

Reebok Int'l v. Marnatech Enters., 970 F.2d 552, 554 (9th Cir.1992). "[T]he Lanham Act provides a 'broad jurisdictional grant.' 'The Lanham Act's coverage of foreign activities may be analyzed under the test for extraterritorial application of the federal antitrust laws set forth in ***Timberlane Lumber Co. v. Bank of Am. Nat'l Trust & Sav. Ass'n***, 549 F.2d 597 (9th Cir.1976). [F]irst, there must be some effect on American foreign commerce; second, the effect must be sufficiently great to present a cognizable injury to plaintiffs under the federal statute; and third, the interests of and links to American foreign commerce must be sufficiently strong in relation to those of other nations to justify an assertion of extraterritorial authority.'" *But see* ***McBee v. Delica Co.***, 417 F.3d 107, 120-21 (1st Cir.2005) (using federal antitrust laws to determine extraterritorial jurisdiction).

§1116(a)

Guthrie Healthcare Sys. v. ContextMedia, Inc., 826 F.3d 27, 46 (2d Cir.2016). "It is correct that a senior user must prove a probability of confusion in order to win an injunction. But it does not follow that the injunction may extend only into areas for which the senior user has shown probability of confusion. It is not as if the senior user must prove a new claim of infringement for each geographic area in which it seeks injunctive relief. Once the senior user has proven entitlement to an injunction, the scope of the injunction should be governed by a variety of equitable factors—the principal concern ordinarily being providing the injured senior user with reasonable protection from the junior user's infringement. Of course, if the junior user demonstrates that in a particular geographic area there is no likelihood of confusion, ordinarily no useful purpose would be served by extending the injunction into that area, potentially inflicting great harm on the junior user without meaningful justification."

CFE Racing Prods. v. BMF Wheels, Inc., 793 F.3d 571, 595 (6th Cir.2015). "We review the scope of injunctive relief in a trademark case for abuse of discretion. The factual findings of the district court are reviewed for clear error, and the legal conclusions are considered *de novo*. [¶] In a trademark case, a court determines the scope of an injunction depending upon: the manner in which the plaintiff is harmed, the ways in which the harm can be avoided, the viability of the defendant's defenses, the burden that would be placed on the defendant and the potential effect upon lawful competition between the parties. *At 596:* [H]arm is not negated by the absence of damages. For the purpose of an injunction, irreparable harm exists in a trademark case when the party seeking the injunction shows that it will lose control over the reputation of its trademark because loss of control over one's reputation is neither calculable nor precisely compensable." (Internal quotes omitted.)

Georgia-Pac. Consumer Prods. v. Von Drehle Corp., 781 F.3d 710, 715 (4th Cir.2015). "[T]he district court entered a permanent, nationwide injunction prohibiting [D] 'from interfering directly or indirectly with [P's] trademark rights[]'.... [D] contends that the district court should not have issued a nationwide injunction that 'conflict[s] with the decisions of other circuits' and that 'undermine[s] the prerogatives of courts of appeals that have yet to address the relevant legal issues.' [B]oth the Eighth and the Sixth Circuits have concluded that [P] may not enforce its ... mark [against D]. *At 716:* As a matter of comity, ... we conclude that the district court abused its discretion in extending the injunction to those jurisdictions, and accordingly we will not authorize its enforcement within the Eighth and Sixth Circuits. [¶] The question remains whether we should nonetheless authorize the injunction to operate within those circuits that have not yet had occasion to consider these issues. *At 717:* [F]or the sake of comity, we require, under the unique circumstances of this case, that the injunction be limited geographically to the States in this circuit. We therefore vacate the injunction granted by the district court and remand with instructions to modify it in accordance with this opinion."

Herb Reed Enters. v. Florida Entm't Mgmt., 736 F.3d 1239, 1242 (9th Cir.2013). "We consider an issue of first impression in our circuit: whether the likelihood of irreparable harm must be established—rather than presumed, as under prior Ninth Circuit precedent—by a plaintiff seeking injunctive relief in the trademark context. In light of Supreme Court precedent, the answer is yes, and we reverse the district court's order granting the preliminary injunction." *See also* ***Ferring Pharms. v. Watson Pharms.***, 765 F.3d 205, 206 (3d Cir. 2014); ***North Am. Med. Corp. v. Axiom Worldwide, Inc.***, 522 F.3d 1211, 1227-28 (11th Cir.2008); ***Audi AG v. D'Amato***, 469 F.3d 534, 550 (6th Cir.2006).

Abraham v. Alpha Chi Omega, 708 F.3d 614, 626 (5th Cir.2013). "An injunction against future infringement in a particular locale when laches and acquiescence have been found ... is properly denied if the plaintiff's delay or other conduct either induced reliance on the defendant's part or will result in substantial prejudice to the defendant if the plaintiff is permitted to enforce its rights in the trademark. Whether phrased as 'reliance' or 'prejudice,' the effect is the same—the defendant has done something it otherwise would not have done absent the plaintiff's conduct. [¶] The result is different, however, when the asserted future infringement would occur in a geographical area other than the one in which the plaintiff waived its right to protect its mark. In the new geographical area where the defendant has not yet expanded its business, the defendant is hard pressed to demonstrate how it could have relied to its detriment upon the plaintiff's inactivity or other conduct. Stated simply, the defendant at best can show only that the plaintiff acquiesced or unreasonably delayed in protecting its mark in the local area. *At 628:* [T]he district court did not abuse its discretion by not ordering disclaimers in lieu of a ban." (Internal quotes omitted.)

Toyota Motor Sales, U.S.A., Inc. v. Tabari, 610 F.3d 1171, 1176 (9th Cir.2010). "A trademark injunction, particularly one involving nominative fair use, can raise serious First Amendment concerns because it can interfere with truthful communication between buyers and sellers in the marketplace. Accordingly, we must ensure that the injunction is tailored to eliminate only the specific harm alleged. To uphold the broad injunction entered in this case, we would have to be convinced that consumers are likely to believe a site is sponsored or endorsed by a trademark holder whenever the domain name contains the string of letters that make up the trademark. [¶] In performing this analysis, our focus must be on the 'reasonably prudent consumer' in the marketplace. The relevant marketplace [in this case] is the online marketplace, and the relevant consumer is a reasonably prudent consumer accustomed to shopping online.... Unreasonable, imprudent and inexperienced web-shoppers are not relevant. [¶] The injunction here is plainly overbroad ... because it prohibits domain names that on their face dispel any confusion as to sponsorship or endorsement. [Ds] are prohibited from doing business at sites like independent-lexus-broker.com and we-are-definitely-not-lexus.com, although a reasonable consumer wouldn't believe [P] sponsors the websites using those domains. *At 1177:* Even if we were to modify the injunction to exclude domain names that expressly disclaim sponsorship or endorsement (like the examples above), the injunction would still be too broad. [Ds] may not do business at lexus-broker.com, even though that's the most straightforward, obvious and truthful way to describe their business. The nominative fair use doctrine allows such truthful use of a mark, even if the speaker fails to expressly disavow association with the trademark holder, so long as it's unlikely to cause confusion as to sponsorship or endorsement. ... Speakers are under no obligation to provide a disclaimer as a condition for engaging in truthful, non-misleading speech." (Internal quotes omitted.)

Zino Davidoff SA v. CVS Corp., 571 F.3d 238, 244 (2d Cir.2009). "[A] trademark holder is entitled to an injunction against one who would subvert its quality control measures upon a showing that (i) the asserted quality control procedures are established, legitimate, substantial, and nonpretextual, (ii) it abides by these procedures, and (iii) sales of products that fail to conform to these procedures will diminish the value of the mark."

John Allan Co. v. Craig Allen Co., 540 F.3d 1133, 1142 (10th Cir.2008). "[P] invokes the 'safe distance rule,' which was created to protect against defendants, found to have infringed upon a trademark from 'preserv[ing] ... good will acquired through fraud. The due protection of [trademark] and similar rights requires that a competitive business, once convicted of unfair competition in a given particular, should thereafter be required to keep a safe distance away from the margin line—even if that requirement involves a handicap as compared with those who have not disqualified themselves.' Like the original infringement itself, the safe distance rule is 'founded on a likelihood of confusion standard.' Where confusion lingers, the infringer must 'not only[] secure a new non-infringing name (or other infringing characteristic) for his product, but [choose] one so far removed from any characteristic of the plaintiff so as to put the public on notice that the two are not related.' [¶] [P] misperceives the safe distance rule. Even if the rule is applicable, it does not create a legal duty under which [D] is obligated to act. Although a district court may require a prior infringer to choose a mark that avoids all possibilities of confusion, it is 'not required as a matter of law to do so.'"

Paulsson Geophysical Servs. v. Sigmar, 529 F.3d 303, 312 (5th Cir.2008). "'Federal courts have long recognized that, when the threatened harm is more than de minimis, it is not so much the magnitude but the irreparability that counts for purposes of a preliminary injunction.... [A]n injury is irreparable only if it cannot be undone through monetary remedies.... The absence of an available remedy by which the movant can later recover monetary damages ... may ... be sufficient to show irreparable injury.'"

Time Warner Cable, Inc. v. DIRECTV, Inc., 497 F.3d 144, 161-62 (2d Cir.2007). "A plaintiff seeking a preliminary injunction under the Lanham Act must persuade a court not only that it is likely to succeed on the merits, but also that it is likely to suffer irreparable harm in the absence of immediate relief. Because '[i]t is virtually impossible to prove that so much of one's sales will be lost or that one's goodwill will be damaged as a direct result of a competitor's advertisement,' we have resolved that a plaintiff 'need not ... point to an actual loss or diversion of sales' to satisfy this requirement. At the same time, 'something more than a plaintiff's mere subjective belief that [it] is injured or likely to be damaged is required before [it] will be entitled even to injunctive relief.' The rule in this Circuit, therefore, is that a plaintiff 'must submit proof which provides a reasonable basis' for believing that the false advertising will likely cause it injury. [¶] In general, '[t]he likelihood of injury and causation will not be presumed, but must be demonstrated in some manner.' We have held, however, that these elements may be presumed 'where [the] plaintiff demonstrates a likelihood of success in showing literally false [the] defendant's comparative advertisement which mentions [the] plaintiff's product by name.' [I]n the case of a 'misleading, non-comparative commercial[] which tout[s] the benefits of the product advertised but ma[kes] no direct reference to any competitor's product,' the injury 'accrues equally to all competitors; none is more likely to suffer from the offending broadcasts than any other.' Thus, 'some indication of actual injury and causation' is necessary 'to satisfy Lanham Act standing requirements and to ensure [the] plaintiff's injury [is] not speculative.' By contrast, where the case presents a false comparative advertising claim, 'the concerns ... regarding speculative injury do not arise.' This is because a false 'comparison to a specific competing product necessarily diminishes that product's value in the minds of the consumer.' Accordingly, no proof of likely injury is necessary."

Lorillard Tobacco Co. v. Amouri's Grand Foods, Inc., 453 F.3d 377, 380 (6th Cir.2006). "In addressing a motion for preliminary injunction the district court should consider (1) the likelihood that the movant will succeed on the merits, (2) whether the movant will suffer irreparable harm without the injunction, (3) the probability that granting the injunction will cause substantial harm to others and (4) whether the public interest will be advanced by issuing the injunction. In making its determination the 'district court is required to make specific findings concerning each of the four factors, unless fewer factors are dispositive of the issue.'" *See also* ***Voice of the Arab World, Inc. v. MDTV Med. News Now, Inc.***, 645 F.3d 26, 32 (1st Cir. 2011); ***Network Automation, Inc. v. Advanced Sys. Concepts, Inc.***, 638 F.3d 1137, 1144 (9th Cir.2011); ***Beltronics USA, Inc. v. Midwest Inventory Distrib.***, 562 F.3d 1067, 1070 (10th Cir.2009); ***Paulsson Geophysical Servs. v. Sigmar***, 529 F.3d 303, 309 (5th Cir. 2008); ***Estate of Coll-Monge v. Inner Peace Movement***, 524 F.3d 1341, 1349 (D.C.Cir.2008); ***North Am. Med. Corp. v. Axiom Worldwide, Inc.***, 522 F.3d 1211, 1217 (11th Cir.2008); ***McNeil Nutritionals, LLC v. Heartland Sweeteners, LLC***, 511 F.3d 350, 356-57 (3d Cir.2007); ***Louis Vuitton Malletier v. Burlington Coat Factory Whs. Corp.***, 426 F.3d 532, 537 (2d Cir. 2005).

Reno Air Racing Ass'n v. McCord, 452 F.3d 1126, 1137-38 (9th Cir.2006). "[D]istrict courts should apply 'traditional equitable principles' in deciding whether to grant permanent injunctive relief, and the decision is 'an act of equitable discretion by the district court, reviewable on appeal for abuse of discretion.' *At 1137 n.11:* According to these equitable principles, a plaintiff seeking a permanent injunction must demonstrate: (1) that it has suffered an irreparable injury; (2) that remedies available at law, such as monetary damages, are inadequate to compensate for that injury; (3) that, considering the balance of hardships between the plaintiff and defendant, a remedy in equity is warranted; and (4) that the public interest would not be disserved by a permanent injunction." *See also* ***Angel Flight v. Angel Flight Am., Inc.***, 522 F.3d 1200, 1208 (11th Cir.2008); ***Audi AG v. D'Amato***, 469 F.3d 534, 550 (6th Cir.2006); ***Dakota Indus. v. Dakota Sportswear, Inc.***, 988 F.2d 61, 64 (8th Cir.1993).

Australian Gold, Inc. v. Hatfield, 436 F.3d 1228, 1243 (10th Cir.2006). "Although courts have found disclaimers to be adequate alternatives to injunctions in certain cases, 'each case must be judged by considering the circumstances of the relevant business and its consumers.' The proponent of a disclaimer bears a 'heavy burden ... to come forward with evidence sufficient to demonstrate that any proposed materials would significantly reduce the likelihood of consumer confusion.'" *See also* ***Weight Watchers Int'l v. Luigino's, Inc.***, 423 F.3d 137, 143-44 (2d Cir.2005).

Slazengers Ltd. v. Stoller, 16 U.S.P.Q.2d 2007, 2013 (N.D.Ill.1989). "*Where procedures set forth in [FRCP] 65 are inconsistent with the dictates of [15 U.S.C. §1116(a), Lanham Act §34(a),] courts should rely on §1116....* However, in those cases where §1116 is silent, and for precedential value, the courts should look to Rule 65 and to general principles of equity." *See also* ***Fishing Hot Spots, Inc. v. Simon & Schuster***, 720 F.Supp. 746, 747-48 (E.D.Wis.1989).

§1116(d)(1)

All Star Championship Racing, Inc. v. O'Reilly Auto. Stores, 940 F.Supp.2d 850, 866-67 (C.D.Ill.2013). "[T]he use of a counterfeit mark in the context of the Lanham Act is not, in and of itself, a cause of action. Rather, in a civil action arising under [15 U.S.C.] §1114 [Lanham Act §32], a finding that a counterfeit mark was used permits certain additional remedies, including seizure of the goods so marked, [15 U.S.C.] §1116(d)(1)(A) [Lanham Act §34(d)(1)(A)]; treble damages, [15 U.S.C.] §1117(b) [Lanham Act §35(b)]; the awarding of statutory damages, [15 U.S.C.]

§1117(c) [Lanham Act §35(c)]; and attorney's fees, [15 U.S.C.] §1117(a) [Lanham Act §35(a)]. [¶] [T]he elements of a counterfeit mark enhancement are: (1) a spurious mark which is identical with, or substantially indistinguishable from, a registered mark, 15 U.S.C. §1127 [Lanham Act §43]; (2) that is registered with the [PTO's] principal register for use on the same goods or services for which the defendant uses the mark; and (3) the defendant must not have been authorized to use the mark at the time the goods or services were manufactured or produced. While the first two elements are self-explanatory, the third is aided by some context. The third element's exception was intended to refer to overrun goods, which is when a licensed manufacturer makes more products than are authorized under the provision of the agreement. [¶] The question of whether a holdover licensee's use of a formerly-licensed mark denoting a sponsorship constitutes the use of 'counterfeit mark' appears to be a matter of first impression in this Circuit, and, perhaps, the Federal judiciary. This court holds that it does if and only if the incident or product alleged to be infringing occurred or was manufactured after the alleged infringer no longer had authorization to use the mark."

§1116(d)(4)

Louis Vuitton v. White, 945 F.2d 569, 575 (3d Cir. 1991). "We recognize that [15 U.S.C. §1116(d), Lanham Act §34(d),] requires both a finding that notice will thwart effective relief *and* a finding that a temporary restraining order would be ineffective. Nevertheless, where ... the district court finds that notice will cause [Ds] to conceal or destroy the counterfeit merchandise and the undisputed facts show that counterfeit merchandise is being sold despite an outstanding permanent injunction against some of [Ds], it is an abuse of discretion for the court to deny §1116(d) relief without explaining how an ex parte restraining order can be expected to effectively alter [Ds'] behavior."

Major League Baseball Promotion Corp. v. Colour-Tex, Inc., 729 F.Supp. 1035, 1050 (D.N.J.1990). "Due to the specificity with which [15 U.S.C. §1116(d), Lanham Act §34(d),] apparently requires a completed and actual seizure to have occurred, the reference to 'wrongful attempted seizure' in the bond provision, §1116(d)(4)(A), does not affect the interpretation of the term 'wrongful seizure' in §1116(d)(11). Section 1116(d)(4)(A) is a general provision that provides security to a defendant for any damages recoverable due to the ex parte seizure process, not just for damages recoverable through a statutory cause of action under §1116(d)(11)."

§1116(d)(11)

Waco Int'l v. KHK Scaffolding Inc., 278 F.3d 523, 531-32 (5th Cir.2002). "The *ex parte* seizure remedy must be narrowly construed, and is *not* coextensive with liability for any Lanham Act claim. Thus, even if [P] ultimately had prevailed at trial on its trademark infringement claim, its application for *ex parte* seizure still could be found wrongful. *At 533:* [T]he [15 U.S.C. §1116(d)(4), Lanham Act §34(d)(4),] factors a court looks to in determining whether to grant a seizure order are not determinative of whether the seizure was in fact 'wrongful' under §1116(d)(11). Nevertheless, there is nothing in the statute that precludes the absence of a particular factor from supporting a finding that the petition was baseless and therefore brought in 'bad faith.'"

Electronic Lab. Sup. v. Cullen, 977 F.2d 798, 802 (3d Cir.1992). "The narrow issue before us ... is whether the term 'applicant' is used in a context in [15 U.S.C. §1116(d)(11), Lanham Act §34(d)(11),] which clearly indicates that it does not refer to the attorneys of parties who seek *ex parte* seizure orders. *At 803:* Because these two subsections are obvious counterparts to one another, we conclude that the terms 'person obtaining an order' in §1116(d)(4)(A) and 'applicant' in §1116(d)(11) refer to the same person. The applicant for the *ex parte* seizure order must therefore post a security bond. [¶] [T]he use of the term 'applicant' in §1116(d)(4)(B)(iii) indicates that Congress considered the applicant for the seizure order to be a party, and not a party's attorney. *At 804:* The term 'applicant' in §1116(d)(4)(B)(vi) clearly refers only to a party, and not to an attorney. If a lawyer were an 'applicant,' a district court could never grant an *ex parte* seizure order 'unless it clearly appeared from specific facts' that the lawyer would suffer greater injury than the defendant. Congress could not have intended to require district courts to make such an illogical finding. *At 805:* In the usual case of wrongful seizure, the party whose goods were seized (the defendant) will sue the applicant (the plaintiff) under §1116(d)(11), and then the applicant may implead his attorney for legal malpractice."

Clorox Co. v. Inland Empire Wholesale Grocers, 874 F.Supp. 1065, 1071 (C.D.Cal.1994). 15 U.S.C. §1116(d)(11), Lanham Act §34(d)(11), "provides for a cause of action for wrongful seizure, but the statute does not state that opposing the seizure order at the hearing is a prerequisite to filing suit under §1116(d)(11)."

Major League Baseball Promotion Corp. v. Colour-Tex, Inc., 729 F.Supp. 1035, 1051 (D.N.J.1990). "The import of the omission of the term 'wrongful attempted seizure' in [15 U.S.C.] §1116(d)(11) [Lanham Act §34(d)(11)] is clear. If Congress had intended the conduct described in §1116(d)(11) to be defined as broadly as the conduct described in §1116(d)(4)(A), it would have included both the terms 'wrongful seizure' and 'wrongful attempted seizure' in §1116(d)(11), just as it had done in §1116(d)(4)(A). Accordingly, [Ds'] argument for a broader definition of wrongful seizure under §1116(d)(11) ... is unpersuasive."

§1117. RECOVERY FOR VIOLATION OF RIGHTS

[LANHAM ACT §35]

(a) Profits; damages and costs; attorney fees.—When a violation of any right of the registrant of a mark registered in the Patent and Trademark Office, a violation under section 1125(a) or (d) of title 15, or a willful violation under section 1125(c) of title 15, shall have been established in any civil action arising under this chapter, the plaintiff shall be entitled, subject to the provisions of sections 1111 and 1114 of title 15, and subject to the principles of equity, to recover (1) defendant's profits, (2) any damages sustained by the plaintiff, and (3) the costs of the action. The court shall assess such profits and damages or cause the same to be assessed under its direction. In assessing profits the plaintiff shall be required to prove defendant's sales only; defendant must prove all elements of cost or deduction claimed. In assessing damages the court may enter judgment, according to the circumstances of the case, for any sum above the amount found as actual damages, not exceeding three times such amount. If the court shall find that the amount of the recovery based on profits is either inadequate or excessive the court may in its discretion enter judgment for such sum as the court shall find to be just, according to the circumstances of the case. Such sum in either of the above circumstances shall constitute compensation and not a penalty. The court in exceptional cases may award reasonable attorney fees to the prevailing party.

(b) Treble damages for use of counterfeit mark.—In assessing damages under subsection (a) for any violation of section 1114(1)(a) of title 15 or section 220506 of title 36, United States Code, in a case involving use of a counterfeit mark or designation (as defined in section 1116(d) of title 15), the court shall, unless the court finds extenuating circumstances, enter judgment for three times such profits or damages, whichever amount is greater, together with a reasonable attorney's fee, if the violation consists of—

(1) intentionally using a mark or designation, knowing such mark or designation is a counterfeit mark (as defined in section 1116(d) of title 15), in connection with the sale, offering for sale, or distribution of goods or services; or

(2) providing goods or services necessary to the commission of a violation specified in paragraph (1), with the intent that the recipient of the goods or services would put the goods or services to use in committing the violation.

In such a case, the court may award prejudgment interest on such amount at an annual interest rate established under section 6621(a)(2) of title 26, beginning on the date of the service of the claimant's pleadings setting forth the claim for such entry of judgment and ending on the date such entry is made, or for such shorter time as the court considers appropriate.

(c) Statutory damages for use of counterfeit marks.—In a case involving the use of a counterfeit mark (as defined in section 1116(d) of title 15) in connection with the sale, offering for sale, or distribution of goods or services, the plaintiff may elect, at any time before final judgment is rendered by the trial court, to recover, instead of actual damages and profits under subsection (a) of this section, an award of statutory damages for any such use in connection with the sale, offering for sale, or distribution of goods or services in the amount of—

(1) not less than $1,000 or more than $200,000 per counterfeit mark per type of goods or services sold, offered for sale, or distributed, as the court considers just; or

(2) if the court finds that the use of the counterfeit mark was willful, not more than $2,000,000 per counterfeit mark per type of goods or services sold, offered for sale, or distributed, as the court considers just.

(d) Statutory damages for violation of section 1125(d)(1).—In a case involving a violation of section 1125(d)(1) of title 15, the plaintiff may elect, at any time before final judgment is rendered by the trial court, to recover, instead of actual damages and profits, an award of statutory damages in the amount of not less than $1,000 and not more than $100,000 per domain name, as the court considers just.

(e) Rebuttable presumption of willful violation.—In the case of a violation referred to in this section, it shall be a rebuttable presumption that the violation is willful for purposes of determining relief if the violator, or a person acting in concert with the violator, knowingly provided or knowingly caused to be provided materially false contact information to a domain name registrar, domain name registry, or other domain name registration authority in registering, maintaining, or renewing a domain name used in connection with the violation. Nothing in this subsection limits what may be considered a willful violation under this section.

History of 15 U.S.C. §1117: July 5, 1946, ch. 540, §35, 60 Stat. 439; Oct. 9, 1962, P.L. 87-772, §19, 76 Stat. 774; Jan. 2, 1975, P.L. 93-596, §1, 88 Stat. 1949; Jan. 2, 1975, P.L. 93-600, §3, 88 Stat. 1955; Oct. 12, 1984, P.L. 98-473, §1503(2), 98 Stat. 2182; Nov. 16, 1988, P.L. 100-667, §129, 102 Stat. 3945; July 2, 1996, P.L. 104-153, §7, 110 Stat. 1388; Aug. 5, 1999, P.L. 106-43, §3(b), 113 Stat. 219; Nov. 29, 1999, P.L. 106-113, §1000(a)(9), 113 Stat. 1536; Nov. 2, 2002, P.L. 107-273, §13207(a), (b)(11), 116 Stat. 1906, 1908; Dec. 23, 2004, P.L. 108-482, §202, 118 Stat. 3916; Oct. 13, 2008, P.L. 110-403, §§103, 104, 122 Stat. 4259.

See also 18 U.S.C. §2320; 19 U.S.C. §1526.

Treatise Cross-References

McCarthy on Trademark & Unfair Competition

Ch. 5, *Historical Basis of Trademarks & Legislative History*, §5:7
Ch. 19, *Federal Registration of Marks*, §19:144
Ch. 24, *Infringement by Use of Mark on Noncompetitive Goods or Services*, §24:132
Ch. 25, *Types of Trademark Infringement*, §25:15
Ch. 27, *Lanham Act §43(a) & False Advertising*, §§27:23; 27:40
Ch. 30, *Remedies for Trademark Infringement & Unfair Competition*, §§30:36; 30:59; 30:88-30:95; 30:97-30:100; 30:104; 30:107
Ch. 31, *Defenses to Infringement of Trademarks*, §31:33

ANNOTATIONS

Generally

Fishman Transducers, Inc. v. Paul, 684 F.3d 187, 191 (1st Cir.2012). "While damages in trademark or false advertising cases can be awarded without any special showing of scienter or equitable factors, ... our cases usually require willfulness ... to allow either (1) more than single damages or (2) a recovery of the defendant's profits. *At 192:* The ordinary rule in civil cases is proof by a preponderance of the evidence, ... and the text of [15 U.S.C.] §1117 [Lanham Act §35] does not prescribe a different burden of proof. *At 193:* Authority in other circuits is divided on whether in Lanham Act cases to equate fraud or willfulness with a heightened standard of proof, but [we use] the ordinary preponderance standard where ... the statutory language does not call for more. The omission of the term willful in the relevant portion of §1117 contrasts with its explicit use elsewhere in §1117. So, as a matter of first impression in this circuit, we think preponderance the proper standard." *See also* ***Harrods Ltd. v. Sixty Internet Domain Names***, 302 F.3d 214, 227 (4th Cir.2002) (preponderance-of-the-evidence standard for bad-faith requirement in Lanham Act's cyberpiracy provision). *But see* ***Versa Prods. Co. v. Bifold Co.***, 50 F.3d 189, 207-08 (3d Cir.1995) (heightened burden of proof of intent to confuse or deceive in trade-dress infringement cases).

Dial One, Inc. v. Bellsouth Telecomms., Inc., 401 F.3d 603, 609 (5th Cir.2005). "The limits to [the district court's] authority [in awarding damages] are, primarily, two: it may not provide for punitive damages, and the award must not be inequitable. The district court's decision to award damage is reviewed for plain error only."

Rickard v. Auto Publ'r, 735 F.2d 450, 455 (11th Cir. 1984). Under "the 'plain-meaning' rule of statutory construction, [15 U.S.C. §1117, Lanham Act §35,] is, arguably, limited to infringement of a federally registered trademark."

Gucci, Inc. v. Accents, 994 F.Supp. 538, 540 (S.D. N.Y.1998). Even "where there have been findings of willful deceptiveness or intentional counterfeiting, [15 U.S.C. §1117, Lanham Act §35,] provides that the Court may still exercise discretion to deny recovery beyond actual damages, either (in the case of defendants' profits) pursuant to general 'principles of equity,' under §1117(a), or (in the case of trebling the entire recovery) by finding 'extenuating circumstances' under §1117(b). But this in no way alters the conclusion that the threshold determinations of willful deceptiveness and intentional counterfeiting ... are for the jury. [¶] By contrast, determination of the actual amount of defendants' profits ..., being more akin to a determination of a fixed amount after liability has been established, does not so clearly impinge on the historical prerogatives of the jury. *At 541:* [Section] 1117(a) simply provides that '[t]he court shall assess such profits and damages or cause the same to be assessed under its direction.' This clearly empowers a court, in the exercise of its discretion, to leave the assessment of the amount of such profits to the same jury that will be determining whether there is willful deceptiveness."

§1117(a)—Generally

Masters v. UHS of Del., Inc., 631 F.3d 464, 474 (8th Cir.2011). "[D] contends that [P] was ineligible to recover profits because the jury answered 'none' to the specific interrogatory asking it to fix [P's] damages. An award of monetary relief under the Lanham Act must be compensatory, not a penalty. It does not follow, however, that a finding of damages is a precondition of any monetary award."

Santana Prods. v. Bobrick Washroom Equip., Inc., 401 F.3d 123, 135 (3d Cir.2005). "The Lanham Act does not contain a statute of limitations. Instead, the Act subjects all claims to 'the principles of equity.'"

Thompson v. Haynes, 305 F.3d 1369, 1380 (Fed.Cir. 2002). "By the terms of the statute, 'damages' are to be treated separately from 'profits.' As for damages, the court may award up to three times actual damages, depending on the circumstances of the case. As for profits, however, the court is not authorized to award up to three times the amount proved. For profits, the court is constrained to award the amount proved, subject only to an adjustment, up or down, where the recovery would be otherwise unjust. The court may not ... simply lump profits together with damages and apply the same measure of enhancement to both. In its consideration of an award of profits on remand, the court must treat the enhancement of damages and profits separately, as specified by the statute, keeping in mind the further statutory instruction that the sum awarded 'constitute compensation and not a penalty.'" *See also* ***Ideal World Mktg., Inc. v. Duracell, Inc.***, 997 F.Supp. 334, 339-40 (E.D.N.Y.1998), *aff'd*, 182 F.3d 900 (2d Cir.1999) (table case).

Reebok Int'l v. Marnatech Enters., 970 F.2d 552, 559 (9th Cir.1992). "Although the relief provided by [15 U.S.C. §1117, Lanham Act §35,] is explicitly 'subject to the principles of equity,' we have held that it is a *per se* abuse of discretion to fail to award relief under §1117 that is adequate to make willful trademark infringement unprofitable. It is possible, therefore, that [15 U.S.C. §1116(a), Lanham Act §34(a),] might authorize a prejudgment freeze of a defendant's assets if such an action were necessary to protect a plaintiff's right to recovery of §1117 profits and damages and to ensure that a defendant may not benefit by willfully engaging in illegal trademark activity."

§1117(a)—Attorney Fees

Fair Wind Sailing, Inc. v. Dempster, 764 F.3d 303, 314-15 (3d Cir.2014). "While this action was on appeal, the Supreme Court handed down ***Octane Fitness, LLC v. Icon Health & Fitness, Inc.***, ___ U.S. ___, 134 S.Ct. 1749 ... (2014), analyzing when a district Court may award fees under §285 of the Patent Act [35 U.S.C. §285]. Like §35(a) of the Lanham Act [15 U.S.C. §1117(a)], §285 provides that '[t]he court in exceptional cases may award reasonable attorney fees to the prevailing party.' [¶] While ***Octane Fitness*** directly concerns the scope of a district court's discretion to award fees for 'exceptional' case[s] under §285 of the Patent Act, the case controls our interpretation of §35(a) of the Lanham Act. Not only is §285 identical to §35(a), but Congress referenced §285 in passing §35(a). [¶] We therefore import ***Octane Fitness***'s definition of 'exceptionality' into our interpretation of §35(a) of the Lanham Act. Under ***Octane Fitness***, a district court may find a case 'exceptional,' and therefore award fees to the prevailing party, when (a) there is an unusual discrepancy in the merits of the positions taken by the parties or (b) the losing party has litigated the case in an 'unreasonable manner.' Whether litigation positions or litigation tactics are 'exceptional' enough to merit attorneys' fees must be determined by district courts 'in the case-by-case exercise of their discretion, considering the totality of the circumstances.' Importantly, that discretion is not cabined by a threshold requirement that the losing party acted culpably. The losing party's blameworthiness may well play a role in a district court's analysis of the 'exceptionality' of a case, but ***Octane Fitness*** has eliminated the first step in our two-step test for awarding fees under §35(a) of the Lanham Act." *See also* ***Romag Fasteners, Inc. v. Fossil, Inc.***, 866 F.3d 1330, 1336 (Fed.Cir.2017) (holding that 2d Circuit would follow ***Octane Fitness***); ***SunEarth, Inc. v. Sun Earth Solar Power Co.***, 839 F.3d 1179, 1180-81 (9th Cir.2016); ***Baker v. DeShong***, 821 F.3d 620, 624-25 (5th Cir.2016); ***Slep-Tone Entm't Corp. v. Karaoke Kandy Store, Inc.***, 782 F.3d 313, 317-18 (6th Cir.2015); ***Georgia-Pac. Consumer Prods. v. Von Drehle Corp.***, 781 F.3d 710, 721 (4th Cir.2015).

Louis Vuitton Malletier S.A. v. LY USA, Inc., 676 F.3d 83, 87 (2d Cir.2012). "We ... conclude that a plaintiff electing statutory damages pursuant to 15 U.S.C. §1117(c) [Lanham Act §35(c)] may recover attorney's fees pursuant to 15 U.S.C. §1117(a), and that the district court did not abuse its discretion either in awarding attorney's fees and costs in this case or in determining their amount."

Secalt, S.A. v. Wuxi Shenxi Constr. Mach. Co., 668 F.3d 677, 689 (9th Cir.2012). "We [have] outlined the path for fee calculation ...: When it sets a fee, the district court must first determine the presumptive lodestar figure by multiplying the number of hours reasonably expended on the litigation by the reasonable hourly rate. Next, in appropriate cases, the district court may adjust the presumptively reasonable lodestar figure based upon the factors listed in ***Kerr v. Screen Extras Guild, Inc.***, 526 F.2d 67 ... (9th Cir.1975), that have not been subsumed in the lodestar calculation. *At 690:* [A]ttorney's fees under the Lanham Act may also include reasonable costs that the party cannot recover as the 'prevailing party.'" (Internal quotes omitted.)

Lorillard Tobacco Co. v. Engida, 611 F.3d 1209, 1215 (10th Cir.2010). "[P] argues that [D] was not a prevailing party because [P] voluntarily dismissed the case without prejudice and without a court order under [FRCP] 41(a)(1)(A)(i). Under the facts of this case, we agree. 'Under Rule 41(a)(1)(A)(i)[,] a plaintiff may dismiss an action voluntarily before the defendant files an answer or a motion for summary judgment.' Voluntary dismissal of an action ordinarily does not create a prevailing party because in order to create a prevailing party there must be a 'judicially sanctioned change in the legal relationship of the parties.' [¶] We have previously made clear that '[a] preliminary injunction that does not provide a plaintiff with relief on the merits of [his] claim cannot serve as the basis for prevailing party status.' If a plaintiff who is *granted* a non-merits-based injunction cannot be a prevailing party, ... it logically and ineluctably follows that a defendant who *defeats* an injunction cannot be a prevailing party if the denial similarly is based on non-merits grounds."

Derek Andrew, Inc. v. Poof Apparel Corp., 528 F.3d 696, 702 (9th Cir.2008). "The district court entered default and [D] concedes that its default occurred with respect to a complaint that pled wilfulness. Thus, all factual allegations in the complaint are deemed true, including the allegation of [D's] willful infringement of [P's] trademarks. This default sufficiently establishes [P's] entitlement to attorneys' fees under the Lanham Act. Because [D] does not contest the amount of fees, the district court's award of fees under the Lanham Act is affirmed."

Attrezzi, LLC v. Maytag Corp., 436 F.3d 32, 41 (1st Cir.2006). "[T]he Lanham Act does not in general preclude state unfair competition statutes from operating.... *At 42:* Congress did not prohibit state unfair competition statutes that might have *substantive* terms somewhat more favorable to plaintiffs than the Lanham Act. [¶] If state substantive regimes are (ordinarily) not preempted by the Lanham Act, neither is New Hampshire's tinkering with the remedial components." Held: P was allowed to recover attorney fees under New Hampshire's more lenient standard for state trademark law.

Proctor & Gamble Co. v. Amway Corp., 280 F.3d 519, 527 (5th Cir.2002). "Several courts have held that a party can recover under [15 U.S.C. §1117(a), Lanham Act §35(a),] only for work performed in connection with claims filed under the Lanham Act. A court should permit recovery for work on non-Lanham Act claims only if 'the Lanham Act and non-Lanham Act claims are so intertwined that it is *impossible to differentiate* between work done on claims.' *At 528 n.12:* Only the Second Circuit has endorsed [the Fifth Circuit case's] holding that to recover fees under §1117(a), the defendant must prove the plaintiff brought the action in bad faith."

Gilbert/Robinson, Inc. v. Carrie Bev.-Mo., Inc., 989 F.2d 985, 991 n.5 (8th Cir.1993), *overruled on other grounds*, ***Lexmark Int'l v. Static Control Components, Inc.***, ___ U.S. ___, 134 S.Ct. 1377 (2014). "A [15 U.S.C. §1120, Lanham Act §38,] damage claim may not supplant the court's carefully circumscribed discretion to award [attorney] fees under [15 U.S.C. §1117, Lanham Act §35]."

§1117(a)—Attorney Fees—Standard of Review

Lorillard Tobacco Co. v. Engida, 611 F.3d 1209, 1213 (10th Cir.2010). "'[W]e review a district court's decision on whether to award attorney fees [under the Lanham Act] for abuse of discretion, but we review de novo the district court's application of the legal principles underlying that decision.' [¶] 'Under the abuse of discretion standard, a trial court's decision will not be disturbed unless the appellate court has a definite and firm conviction that the lower court made a clear error of judgment or exceeded the bounds of permissible choice in the circumstances.' Elaborating on that standard, we have stated: 'A district court abuses its discretion where it commits a legal error or relies on clearly erroneous factual findings, or where there is no rational basis in the evidence for its ruling.'" *See also* ***Louis Vuitton Malletier S.A. v. LY USA, Inc.***, 676 F.3d 83, 105 (2d Cir.2012); ***Secalt, S.A. v. Wuxi Shenxi Constr. Mach. Co.***, 668 F.3d 677, 687 (9th Cir.2012); ***Community of Christ Copyright Corp. v. Devon Park Restoration Branch of Jesus Christ's Ch.***, 634 F.3d 1005, 1013 (8th Cir.2011); ***Venture Tape Corp. v. McGills Glass Whs.***, 540 F.3d 56, 64 (1st Cir.2008); ***Schlotzsky's, Ltd. v. Sterling Purchasing & Nat'l Distrib.***, 520 F.3d 393, 402 (5th Cir.2008).

§1117(a)—Damages

Streamline Prod. Sys. v. Streamline Mfg., 851 F.3d 440, 459 (5th Cir.2017). "While not explicitly provided for in the Lanham Act, we have permitted trademark infringement damages on the basis of the royalty rate normally charged for licensing the unauthorized use of the mark, on the logic that the plaintiff sustained damages equal to the profit they could have made from such a license. 'Usually, when the courts have awarded a royalty for past acts of infringement, it was for continued use of a mark after a license ended and damages were measured by the royalty rate the parties had agreed on.' *At 461:* Because we conclude there is insufficient evidence to support the royalty award, we need not address whether a royalty-based award can be based on a hypothetical negotiation between the parties. [¶] A royalty-based damages award must be rationally related to the scope of the defendant's infringement."

Fishman Transducers, Inc. v. Paul, 684 F.3d 187, 194 (1st Cir.2012). "Single damages can be awarded without a finding of willfulness. But damages awards turn out to be comparatively rare in trademark cases primarily, it appears, because of the difficulty of proving them. Various damage theories are available, but proving causation and amount are very difficult unless the two products directly compete ..., and most cases that go beyond injunctive relief involve an attempt to recoup the infringer's profits. [¶] The problem ... is not theory but proof. The most straightforward theory of damages would be that the infringement had diverted specific sales away from [P]."

Skydive Ariz., Inc. v. Quattrocchi, 673 F.3d 1105, 1114 (9th Cir.2012). "[A]lthough a judge or jury may award up to triple the amount of lost profits, actual damages and costs to compensate a mark holder, the Lanham Act has been construed to expressly forbid the award of damages to punish an infringer."

TrafficSchool.com, Inc. v. Edriver Inc., 653 F.3d 820, 831 (9th Cir.2011). "Nothing in the Lanham Act conditions an award of profits on plaintiff's proof of harm, and we've held that profits may be awarded in the absence of such proof. But an award of profits with no proof of harm is an uncommon remedy in a false advertising suit. It's appropriate in false *comparative* advertising cases, where it's reasonable to presume that every dollar defendant makes has come directly out of plaintiff's pocket. It's also appropriate where ordinary damages won't deter unlawful conduct: for example, when defendant associates its product with plaintiff's noncompetitive product to appropriate good will or brand value. The reason there is that plaintiff is unlikely to have lost any sales or sale contracts to defendant, and the damages must be measured by defendant's gains from the illicit use. [¶] But neither the comparative advertising nor good will cases are relevant here, where [Ps] claim that '[Ds] advertised a different (and allegedly better) product than they delivered.' The Lanham Act allows an award of profits only to the extent the award 'shall constitute compensation and not a penalty.' But 'when advertising does not directly compare defendant's and plaintiff's products,' the injury to plaintiff 'may be a small fraction of the defendant's sales, profits, or advertising expenses.' [Ps] didn't produce *any* proof of past injury or causation, so the district court had no way to determine with any degree of certainty what award would be compensatory."

La Quinta Corp. v. Heartland Props. LLC, 603 F.3d 327, 342-43 (6th Cir.2010). "The general proof and measure of damages in a trademark action is governed by the law of damages of tort actions. Under general tort principles the infringer/tortfeasor is liable for all injuries caused to plaintiff by the wrongful act, whether or not actually anticipated or contemplated by the defendant when it performed the acts of infringement. Damages are not permitted which are remote and speculative in nature. In trademark cases courts draw a sharp distinction between proof of the *fact* of damage and proof of the *amount* of damage. Thus, the plaintiff is held to a lower standard of proof in ascertaining the exact amount of damages, and, once the existence of damages has been shown, all that an award requires is substantial evidence in the record to permit a factfinder to draw reasonable inferences and make a fair and reasonable assessment of the amount of damages. [¶] Certainly, ... the Lanham Act expressly prohibits levying damages that may be classified as a penalty. Generally, if a sum of money is to be recovered by a third person for violation of a statute instead of a person injured, or *if the sum exacted is greatly disproportionate to the actual loss, it constitutes a penalty rather than damages*." (Internal quotes omitted.) *See also* ***Skydive Ariz., Inc. v. Quattrocchi***, 673 F.3d 1105, 1112 (9th Cir.2012); ***Australian Gold, Inc. v. Hatfield***, 436 F.3d 1228, 1241 (10th Cir.2006).

Synergistic Int'l v. Korman, 470 F.3d 162, 175-76 (4th Cir.2006). "In making a damages award under the Lanham Act, the Third and the Fifth Circuits have identified six factors to guide the process. As those courts have spelled out, these factors include: '(1) whether the defendant had the intent to confuse or deceive, (2) whether sales have been diverted, (3) the adequacy of other remedies, (4) any unreasonable delay by the plaintiff in asserting his rights, (5) the public interest in making the misconduct unprofitable, and (6) whether it is a case of palming off.' [¶] The first [factor]—whether the defendant had an intent to confuse or deceive—addresses whether there has been a willful infringement on the trademark rights of the plaintiff, or whether the defendant has acted in bad faith. [A] lack of willfulness or bad faith should weigh against an award of damages being made, but does not necessarily preclude such an award. [¶] The second factor ...—whether sales have been diverted—involves the issue of whether the plaintiff lost sales as a result of the defendant's trademark infringement activities, and the extent to which the plaintiff had entered the market area where the infringement occurred. ... The fact that a plaintiff had not entered the relevant marketplace when the infringement was ongoing, in combination with the fact that no sales were diverted, should weigh against an award being made. [¶] The third of the six factors—the adequacy of other remedies—addresses whether another remedy, such as an injunction, might more appropriately correct any injury the plaintiff suffered from the defendant's infringement activities. [¶] The fourth factor—unreasonable delay by the plaintiff in asserting its rights—addresses the temporal issue of whether the plaintiff waited too long, after the infringement activities began, before seeking court relief. A substantial delay between the commencement of infringement activities and the plaintiff seeking judicial relief should weigh against an award of damages. The fifth factor—the public interest in making the infringing misconduct unprofitable—addresses the balance that a court should strike between a plaintiff's right to be compensated for the defendant's trademark infringement activities, and the statutory right of the defendant to not be assessed a penalty. [¶] The sixth and final factor—whether the situation involved a case of 'palming off'—involves the issue of whether the defendant used its infringement of the plaintiff's mark to sell its products, misrepresenting to the public that the defendant's products were really those of the plaintiff. We agree that, if 'palming off' is shown, such activity should weigh in favor of a damages award. [¶] [A] trial court, in assessing the issue of damages under [15] U.S.C. §1117(a) [Lanham Act §35(a)], should weigh the equities of the dispute and exercise its discretion on whether an award is appropriate and, if so, the amount thereof. In each instance, of course, the court should explain its reasoning and the impact of the relevant factors. And, although each trademark dispute is fact specific, the foregoing factors, as well as others that may be relevant in the circumstances, should guide a court's consideration of the damages issue." *See also* ***La Quinta Corp. v. Heartland Props. LLC***, 603 F.3d 327, 343 (6th Cir.2010); ***American Rice, Inc. v. Producers Rice Mill, Inc.***, 518 F.3d 321, 338 (5th Cir. 2008). *But see* ***Western Diversified Servs. v. Hyundai Motor Am., Inc.***, p. 112 (finding of willfulness necessary before profits awarded).

Bandag, Inc. v. Al Bolser's Tire Stores, 750 F.2d 903, 920 (Fed.Cir.1984). Any "royalty-based measure of damages must exhibit a strictly rational correlation between the rights appropriated and the measure of damages applied. '[R]oyalties normally received for the use of a mark are [not] *the* proper measure of damages for misuse of those marks.'"

Lifted Research Grp. v. Behdad, Inc., No. 08-390 (CKK) (D.D.C.2010) (memo op.; 6-30-10). "[T]he Court agrees that '[a] plaintiff may be awarded statutory damages under both the Copyright Act and the Lanham Act where the defendant's act simultaneously infringed the plaintiff's copyright and its trademark ... because the two statutory schemes serve different public policies, and protect against and remedy different injuries.'" *See also* ***Nintendo of Am., Inc. v. Dragon Pac. Int'l***, 40 F.3d 1007, 1010-11 (9th Cir.1994); ***Microsoft Corp. v.***

Nop, 549 F.Supp.2d 1233, 1238-39 (E.D.Cal.2008); ***Microsoft Corp. v. McGee***, 490 F.Supp.2d 874, 881-82 (S.D.Ohio 2007); ***Microsoft Corp. v. Sellers***, 411 F.Supp.2d 913, 920-21 (E.D.Tenn.2006).

§1117(a)—Damages—Standard of Review

Skydive Ariz., Inc. v. Quattrocchi, 673 F.3d 1105, 1112 (9th Cir.2012). "In reviewing a jury's award of actual damages for intentional infringement, we accept crude measures of damages based upon reasonable inferences so long as those inferences are neither inexorable nor fanciful. [¶] To support a jury's actual damages award, there need only be substantial evidence to permit the jury to draw *reasonable inferences* and make a *fair and reasonable assessment. At 1115:* A verdict based on the bias, passion, or sympathy of the jury cannot be permitted to stand. Beyond obvious bias or passion, a verdict will also not be sustained on appeal if it is grossly excessive or monstrous. However, in assessing whether a damages award is grossly excessive, the fact that the jury may have agreed with the plaintiff's expert and rejected the defendant's contentions does not render the verdict grossly excessive or monstrous." (Internal quotes omitted.)

La Quinta Corp. v. Heartland Props. LLC, 603 F.3d 327, 342 (6th Cir.2010). "We review the district court's award of damages under the Lanham Act for an abuse of discretion."

§1117(a)—Prejudgment Interest

Merck Eprova AG v. Gnosis S.p.A., 760 F.3d 247, 263-64 (2d Cir.2014). "[D] contends that the court's award of prejudgment interest to [P] was reversible error[ ] because the award of trebled profits already compensated [P] for the loss of the use of any money. [¶] Although [15 U.S.C.] §1117(a) [Lanham Act §35] does not provide for prejudgment interest, such an award is within the discretion of the trial court and is normally reserved for exceptional cases. [¶] There was no abuse of discretion here. The district court's opinion reiterates the exceptional nature of this case throughout, highlighting [D's] willfulness and bad faith, as well as the fact that [P] was the only manufacturer of the [product] at the time [D] entered the market with its intentionally mislabeled [product]. Certainly, it would have been preferable for the district court to explicitly state its reasons for awarding prejudgment interest. However, the factual record readily supports the district court's findings of willfulness and bad faith, and the conclusion that this is such an exceptional case as to warrant an award of prejudgment interest pursuant to §1117(a) is therefore affirmed." (Internal quotes omitted.)

Sands, Taylor & Wood v. Quaker Oats Co., 978 F.2d 947, 963 (7th Cir.1992). "[T]he Lanham Act is silent with respect to prejudgment interest. The court nevertheless decided to award such interest, relying on this Circuit's rule that 'prejudgment interest should be presumptively available to victims of federal law violations. Without it, compensation is incomplete and the defendant has an incentive to delay.'" *See also* ***Masters v. UHS of Del., Inc.***, 631 F.3d 464, 475 (8th Cir.2011).

§1117(a)—Profits

Covertech Fabricating, Inc. v. TVM Bldg. Prods., 855 F.3d 163, 177 (3d Cir.2017). "[W]here a district court endeavors to calculate damages under the Lanham Act on the basis of the defendant's actual profits, rather than awarding statutory damages, it must ground its estimate in the record—*e.g.*, business records, credible witness testimony, expert testimony, or industry data—in order to pass muster as a reasonable estimate and an appropriate exercise of discretion. Conversely, where the court lacks a sound basis for extrapolating actual profits, it abuses its discretion by resorting to guesswork. For just such situations, the Lanham Act provides for statutory damages in the alternative, and it is on that provision that the court must rely."

Romag Fasteners, Inc. v. Fossil, Inc., 817 F.3d 782, 788-89 (Fed.Cir.2016), *judgm't vacated*, ___ U.S. ___, 137 S.Ct. 1373 (2017), *opinion reinstated*, 686 Fed.Appx. 889 (Fed.Cir.2017). Held: The Second Circuit still requires a finding of willfulness to award D's profits despite the 1999 amendment to §1117(a). However, the Third, Fourth, and Fifth Circuits no longer require a finding of willfulness. *See also* ***Stone Creek, Inc. v. Omnia Italian Design, Inc.***, 875 F.3d 426, 441 (9th Cir. 2017). *But see* ***Synergistic Int'l v. Korman***, 470 F.3d 162, 175 (4th Cir.2006) (willfulness is one piece of recovery of profits); ***Quick Techs. v. Sage Grp. PLC***, 313 F.3d 338, 347-49 (5th Cir.2002) (same).

Gucci Am., Inc. v. Bank of China, 768 F.3d 122, 131-32 (2d Cir.2014). "[Ps] are seeking an *accounting* of [Ds'] profits, in addition to injunctive relief and monetary damages, under the Lanham Act. And as [Ps] correctly contend, the common law action of 'account' is one of the earliest examples of a restitutionary action in equity, imposing on a defendant the obligation to disclose and return profits from the use of the plaintiff's property, ... and founded in the Chancellor's equitable power to compel an accounting of wrongly gained assets. [¶] The Supreme Court, in ***Hamilton Brown Shoe Co. v. Wolf Bros. & Co.***, 240 U.S. 251 ... (1916), has explained that a trademark infringer is required *in equity to account* for and yield up his gains to the true owner, and profits are then allowed as an *equitable* measure of compensation. This Court, moreover, has expressly attested to the ancient roots of this remedy, explaining that the ancient remedies of accounting, constructive trust, and restitution have compelled wrongdoers to disgorge—*i.e.*, account for and surrender—their ill-gotten gains for centuries. [¶] Given the weight of this authority, it is not surprising that all three of our sister circuits to have considered the issue have unanimously held that district courts have the authority to issue a prejudgment asset restraint injunction in favor of plaintiffs seeking an accounting against allegedly infringing defendants in Lanham Act cases. Countless district courts, moreover, have determined that after ***Grupo Mexicano [de Desarollo, S.A. v. Alliance Bond Fund, Inc.***, 527 U.S. 308 (1999),] they maintain the authority to issue preliminary injunctions freezing the assets of defendants in this context. *At 133:* We conclude ... that the district court had the equitable authority to issue the Asset Freeze Injunction and that [D's] argument to the contrary is without merit." (Internal quotes omitted.)

Fishman Transducers, Inc. v. Paul, 684 F.3d 187, 196 (1st Cir.2012). "[I]f the two companies are in the same line of business, defendant's profits may be presumptively similar to what plaintiff would have earned on the sale."

Masters v. UHS of Del., Inc., 631 F.3d 464, 471 (8th Cir.2011). "We have recognized that upon proof of willful infringement, 'an accounting of profits may be based upon (1) unjust enrichment, (2) damages, or (3) deterrence of a willful infringer.'"

Visible Sys. v. Unisys Corp., 551 F.3d 65, 68 (1st Cir.2008). "[P's] primary argument is that the trial judge erred in not granting it a jury trial under both the Lanham Act and the Seventh Amendment on its claim for an accounting of [D's] profits. This court has not considered before the question of whether there is a jury trial right on such a claim." Held: P was not entitled to have a jury decide the accounting of profits in this reverse-confusion case. *See also* ***Fifty-Six Hope Road Music, Ltd. v. A.V.E.L.A., Inc.***, 778 F.3d 1059, 1074-75 (9th Cir.2015).

WMS Gaming Inc. v. WPC Prods., 542 F.3d 601, 606 (7th Cir.2008). "[B]ecause this was a default judgment, the usual rule that a party should be given the relief to which it is entitled whether or not it has requested that relief does not apply. Instead, [FRCP] 54(c) stipulates that '[a] default judgment must not differ in kind from, or exceed in amount, what is demanded in the pleadings.' [P's] pleadings thus are more important, for purposes of relief, than they would have been had [D] appeared and contested the case. [¶] [W]e find it clear from [P's] filings in the district court that, contrary to the assumption in the district court's orders [P] has throughout this litigation requested an equitable accounting of profits, rather than—or at least in addition to—actual damages. *At 608:* The burden was therefore on [D] to show that certain portions of its revenues—which for purposes of the award after its default judgment [P] established by using [D's] own public financial statements and reports—were not obtained through its infringement of [P's] marks. *At 609:* Courts consistently find that when a trademark plaintiff offers evidence of infringing sales and the infringer fails to carry its statutory burden to offer evidence of deductions, the plaintiff's entitlement to profits under the Lanham Act is equal to the infringer's gross sales."

Venture Tape Corp. v. McGills Glass Whs., 540 F.3d 56, 63 (1st Cir.2008). "When a mark owner cannot prove actual damages attributable to the infringer's misconduct (e.g., specific instances of lost sales), its recovery of an equitable share of the infringer's profits serves, *inter alia*, as a 'rough measure' of the likely harm that the mark owner incurred because of the infringement, while also preventing the infringer's unjust enrichment and deterring further infringement. *At 64:* '[O]nce the plaintiff has shown direct competition and infringement, the statute places the burden on the infringer to show the limits of the direct competition.'"

American Rice, Inc. v. Producers Rice Mill, Inc., 518 F.3d 321, 339-40 (5th Cir.2008). "Cooperatives like [D], partnerships, and subchapter 'S' corporations are all flow-through entities for tax purposes. We have been able to locate no cases addressing the disgorgement of profits of cooperatives under the Lanham Act. Additionally, we have found no authority for excusing any kind of flow-through entities from disgorgement due to their flow-through character, though we have found analogous cases in which partnerships and subchapter 'S' corporations have had profits disgorged pursuant to the Act. We see no reason to treat cooperatives such as [D] differently. We conclude, therefore, that profits earned by [D] are [D's] profits for purposes of the Lanham Act, regardless of how such profits are passed on or how they are taxed."

Aero Prods. v. Intex Recreation Corp., 466 F.3d 1000, 1019 (Fed.Cir.2006). "[T]he record demonstrates that [P] based both its patent and trademark damages solely on sales of the accused [D's goods]. [P] did not rely on any other evidence in support of its trademark damages. ... In short, all of the damages awarded to [P] flowed from the same operative facts: sales of the infringing [D's goods]. [P] was fully compensated for [D's] patent infringement when it was awarded a reasonable royalty for patent infringement based on sales of the infringing [D's goods]. It could not also be awarded [D's] profits for trademark infringement based on the same sales of the same accused devices."

Western Diversified Servs. v. Hyundai Motor Am., Inc., 427 F.3d 1269, 1272-73 (10th Cir.2005). "An accounting of profits is not automatically granted upon a showing of infringement. As the statute makes clear, any award of profits is 'subject to the principles of equity.' However, it is not required that the plaintiff demonstrate actual damages to sustain a profit award. [¶] An award of profits in the absence of actual damages is usually predicated on one of two theories: (1) unjust enrichment; or (2) deterrence. [¶] Whatever the theory that motivates the rule, 'a finding of actual damage remains an important factor in determining whether an award of profits is appropriate.' [W]e require a showing that [D's] actions were willful to support an award of profits under 15 U.S.C. §1117(a) [Lanham Act §35(a)]. *At 1273 n.1:* This standard is not universally applied among the circuit courts. While most courts basically agree that an award of profits in the absence of actual damages requires some kind of 'intent' on the defendant's part, the precise articulation of the required state of mind varies from deliberate and knowing to willful and fraudulent. *At 1273-74:* [A]n award of profits involves a two-step process: (1) a finding of willfulness or bad faith; and (2) a weighing of the equities. [¶] [A] court evaluating an award of profits claim at the summary judgment stage must confine its analysis to the first step: whether a genuine factual issue exists as to willful infringement. [¶] [T]o support an award of profits under the Lanham Act in the absence of actual damages, a plaintiff must ordinarily show that the defendant intended to benefit from the goodwill or reputation of the trademark holder. [¶] However, the standard we adopt today does not categorically preclude all other possibilities. Because an award of profits under the Lanham Act is grounded in equity, there may be other situations that constitute willful infringement even though the defendant does not intend to derive any benefit from the plaintiff's goodwill or reputation. For example, if the defendant deceives the plaintiff into thinking he has ceased infringing the trademark when in fact the illegal action continues, a finding of willfulness might be appropriate. Similarly, misrepresentation to the courts might constitute willful infringement. Finally, if the wrongdoer uses its own economic muscle to weaken a plaintiff who has threatened an infringement action, a finding of willfulness might be justified." *See also* ***Lindy Pen Co. v. Bic Pen Corp.***, 982 F.2d 1400, 1406 (9th Cir.1993); ***Malletier v. Dooney & Bourke, Inc.***, 500 F.Supp.2d 276, 280 & n.22 (S.D.N.Y. 2007). *But see* ***Synergistic Int'l v. Korman***, p. 109 (willfulness is a factor in awarding damages, but not necessary); ***Seatrax, Inc. v. Sonbeck Int'l***, p. 113 (not listing willfulness as a factor for profits).

Tamko Roofing Prods. v. Ideal Roofing Co., 282 F.3d 23, 35 (1st Cir.2002). "If injunctive relief provides a complete and adequate remedy, then the equities of the case may not require an accounting of profits. For example, injunctive relief may be adequate if there has been no fraud or palming off and there is little likelihood of actual damage to the plaintiff or profit to the defendant. *At 36:* [D's] most cogent argument is that it did not directly compete against [P] in all the markets in which it profited from use of the mark, and so all of its profits should not go to [P]. [¶] We reject any such limitation for an accounting of profits award, once there has been a finding of direct competition, for three reasons, each articulated in the Lanham Act [§35(a)], 15 U.S.C. §1117(a). First, the limitation misplaces the burdens, in assuming plaintiffs must meet such a test as to remedy, once infringement and direct competition are established. The burden of showing that not all profits should be awarded is more akin to the burden of showing the amount of costs to be deducted from profits, which the Act places on defendant. Second, such a test ignores the three rationales for the remedy of accounting of profits. Third, the test is inconsistent with the inherent equitable power of the district court and the Lanham Act's designation of an accounting of defendant's profits as an equitable remedy. *At 38:* The rule that where there is willful infringement, an accounting of profits is not necessarily restricted to the particular area of direct competition is reinforced by the intention of the Lanham Act to provide *nationwide* protection of a mark, in contrast to the more limited geographic protection afforded by the common law." *See also* ***Health Indus. v. European Health Spas***, 489 F.Supp. 860, 869 (D.S.D.1980).

Logan v. Burgers Ozark Country Cured Hams Inc., 263 F.3d 447, 464-65 (5th Cir.2001). "[W]e hold that where a plaintiff who has brought a Lanham Act claim for false advertising has failed to present evidence that the defendant benefitted from the alleged false advertising, the plaintiff will not be permitted to recover any of the defendant's profits under 15 U.S.C. §1117(a) [Lanham Act §35(a)]."

Seatrax, Inc. v. Sonbeck Int'l, 200 F.3d 358, 369 (5th Cir.2000). "An award of the defendant's profits is not automatic. We have identified a non-exhaustive list of factors to determine when a plaintiff is entitled to an accounting of the defendant's profits under [15 U.S.C. §1117(a), Lanham Act §35(a)]: (1) whether the defendant intended to confuse or deceive; (2) whether sales have been diverted; (3) the adequacy of other remedies; (4) any unreasonable delay by the plaintiff in asserting her rights; (5) the public interest in making the conduct unprofitable, and (6) whether it is a case of palming off." *See also* ***Banjo Buddies, Inc. v. Renosky***, 399 F.3d 168, 174-75 (3d Cir.2005); ***Quick Techs. v. Sage Grp. PLC***, 313 F.3d 338, 349 (5th Cir.2002). *But see* ***Western Diversified Servs. v. Hyundai Motor Am., Inc.***, p. 112 (finding of willfulness necessary before profits awarded).

Wynn Oil Co. v. American Way Serv., 943 F.2d 595, 605 (6th Cir.1991). "It is not the plaintiff's burden to prove the profits with exactness because the statute places the burden on the defendant once the plaintiff comes forward with proof of the defendant's gross sales."

Aris Isotoner Inc. v. Dong Jin Trading Co., 17 U.S.P.Q.2d 1017, 1022 (S.D.N.Y.1989). "[I]f the actual sales cannot be precisely determined, the court may resolve any doubts against the defendant in calculating profits, particularly if the uncertainty is due to the defendant's inadequate recordkeeping or failure to produce documentary evidence. Indeed, in such a situation it is permissible to award the highest reasonably ascertainable amount of profits."

§1117(a)—Profits—Standard of Review

Skydive Ariz., Inc. v. Quattrocchi, 673 F.3d 1105, 1113 (9th Cir.2012). "In reviewing an award of lost profits, we do not ask whether the substance of the evidence presented to the jury was correct or even credible; we only ascertain whether the award was based on reasonable inferences and fair assessments of the evidence in the record."

§1117(a)—Treble Damages

Merck Eprova AG v. Gnosis S.p.A., 760 F.3d 247, 262-63 (2d Cir.2014). "[T]he [lower] court concluded that enhanced damages were warranted, not as a punishment or penalty—which are not permitted under the Lanham Act ...—but to 'reflect the intangible benefits that accrued to [D] as a result of its false advertising,' and in particular, '[D's] usurpation of [P's] market share.' We hold that the Lanham Act permits enhanced damages in such a situation, and find no abuse of discretion in the court's decision to enhance the damages awarded to [P]."

H-D Inc. v. Bikers Dream, Inc., 48 U.S.P.Q.2d 1108, 1116 (C.D.Cal.1998), *rev'd in part on other grounds*, 230 F.3d 1366 (9th Cir.2000) (table case). "The Sixth Circuit appears to interpret the words 'not exceeding' to modify the phrase 'above the amount,' so that the amount of the increase cannot exceed three times the amount of actual damages. The Court disagrees. Removing the language which grants the Court discretion to modify the award 'according to the circumstances of the case,' the statute reads that the *judgment* may be 'for any sum above the amount found as actual damages not exceeding three times such amount.' The words 'not exceeding' thus modify 'judgment,' implying that the Court's power is limited to making a total award of up to three times the actual amount."

§1117(b)

Lorillard Tobacco Co. v. A&E Oil, Inc., 503 F.3d 588, 591-92 (7th Cir.2007), *overruled on other grounds*, ***McCarter v. Retirement Plan for Dist. Mgrs. of the Am. Family Ins. Grp.***, 540 F.3d 649 (7th Cir.2008). "Because the award of attorneys' fees follows from an application of statutory language, we review the district court's application of [15 U.S.C. §1117(b), Lanham Act §35(b),] de novo as a question of law. [¶] To prove knowledge of the counterfeiting, [P] was not required to prove [Ds'] actual knowledge; knowledge includes a willful blindness or a failure to investigate because one 'was afraid of what the inquiry would yield.' If willful blindness occurs, an award of attorneys' fees is required by the statutory language absent extenuating circumstances." *See also* ***Louis Vuitton S.A. v. Lee***, 875 F.2d 584, 590 (7th Cir.1989).

Vector Prods. v. Hartford Fire Ins., 397 F.3d 1316, 1320 n.2 (11th Cir.2005). "[T]o be eligible for Lanham Act treble damages, the plaintiff must prove that the defendant's conduct was intentional. Thus, [P] was required to plead intent or knowledge of falsity in order to seek the treble damages remedy."

Hunting World, Inc. v. Reboans, Inc., 33 U.S.P.Q.2d 1780, 1785 (N.D.Cal.1994). Because "remedies under [15 U.S.C.] §1117(b) [Lanham Act §35(b)] are 'penalties,' defendants have no absolute right to a jury for determination of the amount of penalties authorized by that section."

§1117(c)

Louis Vuitton Malletier, S.A. v. Akanoc Solutions, Inc., 658 F.3d 936, 944-45 (9th Cir.2011). "[Ds] assert that statutory damages cannot be awarded against contributory infringers because the statute defines infringement in terms of the unauthorized 'use' of a counterfeit mark. But [15 U.S.C.] §1117(c) [Lanham Act §35(c)] does not require defendants to 'use ... [the] counterfeit mark.' It applies so long as the 'case *involves* such use.' At bottom, [Ds] urge us to hold that a defendant may avoid the consequences of contributory liability (i.e., statutory damages) simply by claiming that the infringing acts (the unauthorized uses) were committed by others. But holding a defendant liable for the unauthorized acts of another is a primary purpose of the doctrine of contributory trademark liability."

Gabbanelli Accordions & Imps., L.L.C. v. Gabbanelli, 575 F.3d 693, 698 (7th Cir.2009). "It is true that if there are separate violations, the fact that they are charged in the same case does not preclude an award of compensatory damages for some of the violations and statutory damages for others as to which compensatory damages can't be ascertained or are too slight to warrant the expense of determining but in which deterrence would be served by a money judgment."

K&N Eng'g v. Bulat, 510 F.3d 1079, 1082 (9th Cir. 2007). "[P] elected to recover statutory damages under [15 U.S.C.] §1117(c) [Lanham Act §35(c)]. Because of [P's] election, the court did not assess or award [P] actual damages or profits under §1117(a). Therefore, there is no statutory basis to award [P] attorney's fees under §1117(b)."

State of Idaho Potato Comm'n v. G&T Terminal Packaging, Inc., 425 F.3d 708, 721 (9th Cir.2005). "In order to invoke [15 U.S.C.] §1117's [Lanham Act §35's] special civil monetary remedies against counterfeiting, [P] must establish that: (1) [D] intentionally used a counterfeit mark in commerce; (2) knowing the mark was counterfeit; (3) in connection with the sale, offering for sale, or distribution of goods; and (4) its use was likely to confuse or deceive. In this context, the mark used by [D] was counterfeit if: (1) it was a non-genuine mark identical to [P's] mark; (2) [P's] mark was registered on the Principal Register for use on the same goods to which [D] applied the mark; (3) [P's] mark was in use; and (4) [D] was not authorized to use [P's] mark on [the goods]."

§1117(d)

GoPets Ltd. v. Hise, 657 F.3d 1024, 1034 (9th Cir. 2011). 15 U.S.C. §1117(d), Lanham Act §35(d), "does not provide for a jury trial on damages. [¶] [W]e hold that there is no right to a jury trial when a judge awards the minimum statutory damages."

Newport News Holdings Corp. v. Virtual City Vision, Inc., 650 F.3d 423, 441-42 (4th Cir.2011). "Our analysis of ACPA statutory damages is guided, in part, by their similarity to statutory damages under the Federal Copyright Act.... [L]ike the Copyright Act, the ACPA reflects a Congressional intent to deter offenders. ... Because these damages 'serve[] as a sanction to deter wrongful conduct,' ... a district court may properly weigh the seriousness of the conduct in determining the amount of the award."

Ford Motor Co. v. Catalanotte, 342 F.3d 543, 546 (6th Cir.2003). "The ACPA applies to 'all domain names registered before, on, or after the date of the enactment' of the ACPA, but actual and statutory damages are not 'available with respect to the registration, trafficking, or use of a domain name that [occurred] before the date of the enactment.'"

Shields v. Zuccarini, 254 F.3d 476, 487 (3d Cir. 2001). "Under the statute, the court has the discretion to award statutory damages that it 'considers just' within a range from $1,000 to $100,000 per infringing domain name. There is nothing in the statute that requires that the court consider the duration of the infringement when calculating statutory damages."

§1118. DESTRUCTION OF INFRINGING ARTICLES

[LANHAM ACT §36]

In any action arising under this chapter, in which a violation of any right of the registrant of a mark registered in the Patent and Trademark Office, a violation under section 1125(a) of title 15, or a willful violation under section 1125(c) of title 15, shall have been established, the court may order that all labels, signs, prints, packages, wrappers, receptacles, and advertisements in the possession of the defendant, bearing the registered mark or, in the case of a violation of section 1125(a) of title 15 or a willful violation under section 1125(c) of title 15, the word, term, name, symbol, device, combination thereof, designation, description, or representation that is the subject of the violation, or any reproduction, counterfeit, copy, or colorable imitation thereof, and all plates, molds, matrices, and other means of making the same, shall be delivered up and destroyed. The party seeking an order under this section for destruction of articles seized under section 1116(d) of title 15 shall give ten days' notice to the United States attorney for the judicial district in which such order is sought (unless good cause is shown for lesser notice) and such United States attorney may, if such destruction may affect evidence of an offense against the United States, seek a hearing on such destruction or participate in any hearing otherwise to be held with respect to such destruction.

History of 15 U.S.C. §1118: July 5, 1946, ch. 540, §36, 60 Stat. 440; Jan. 2, 1975, P.L. 93-596, §1, 88 Stat. 1949; Oct. 12, 1984, P.L. 98-473, §1503(3), 98 Stat. 2182; Nov. 16, 1988, P.L. 100-667, §130, 102 Stat. 3945; Aug. 5, 1999, P.L. 106-43, §3(c), 113 Stat. 219.

See also 18 U.S.C. §§2320, 2323; 19 U.S.C. §1526.

Treatise Cross-References

McCarthy on Trademark & Unfair Competition

Ch. 5, *Historical Basis of Trademarks & Legislative History*, §5:7
Ch. 25, *Types of Trademark Infringement*, §25:15
Ch. 30, *Remedies for Trademark Infringement & Unfair Competition*, §30:36

§1119. POWER OF COURT OVER REGISTRATION

[LANHAM ACT §37]

In any action involving a registered mark the court may determine the right to registration, order the cancelation of registrations, in whole or in part, restore canceled registrations, and otherwise rectify the register with respect to the registrations of any party to the action. Decrees and orders shall be certified by the court to the Director, who shall make appropriate entry upon the records of the Patent and Trademark Office, and shall be controlled thereby.

History of 15 U.S.C. §1119: July 5, 1946, ch. 540, §37, 60 Stat. 440; Jan. 2, 1975, P.L. 93-596, §1, 88 Stat. 1949; Nov. 29, 1999, P.L. 106-113, §1000(a)(9), 113 Stat. 1536.

Treatise Cross-References

McCarthy on Trademark & Unfair Competition

Ch. 20, *Inter Partes Trademark Proceedings in the Patent & Trademark Office*, §20:44
Ch. 30, *Remedies for Trademark Infringement & Unfair Competition*, §§30:108-30:112; 30:113.50
Ch. 32, *Procedure in Trademark Infringement & Unfair Competition Litigation*, §§32.54-32.56

ANNOTATIONS

Already, LLC v. Nike, Inc., 568 U.S. 85, 88 (2013). "The question is whether a covenant not to enforce a trademark against a competitor's existing products and any future 'colorable imitations' moots the competitor's action to have the trademark declared invalid. *At 91:* [O]ur cases have explained that 'a defendant claiming that its voluntary compliance moots a case bears the formidable burden of showing that it is absolutely clear the allegedly wrongful behavior could not reasonably be expected to recur.' *At 92:* [P] dismissed its claims with prejudice and issued its covenant, calling into question the existence of any continuing case or controversy. [¶] [I]t was [P's] burden to show that it 'could not reasonably be expected' to resume its enforcement efforts against [D]." Held: P's covenant complied with the voluntary-cessation doctrine and mooted the controversy.

East Iowa Plastics, Inc. v. PI, Inc., 832 F.3d 899, 903-04 (8th Cir.2016). "[P's] standing to seek cancellation of the trademark under ... 15 U.S.C. §1119 [Lanham Act §37] was dependent on its [15 U.S.C. §1120, Lanham Act §38,] claim, because [§1119] only provides a remedy for some other violation of the trademark laws, not an independent cause of action. Once the district court had determined that [P] did not suffer any damages from [D's] violation of [§1120], there was no further basis for [P] to have standing to seek cancellation of the [mark] registrations. In so holding, we do not mean to suggest that monetary damages are the only possible basis for [P's] standing. But we see no evidence even of non-monetary injuries to [P]."

CFE Racing Prods. v. BMF Wheels, Inc., 793 F.3d 571, 593-94 (6th Cir.2015). "'[A] district court's determination to grant relief pursuant to 15 U.S.C. §1119 [Lanham Act §37] is reviewed for an abuse of discretion.' [¶] A request for cancellation under §1119 must be supported by a showing that (1) the party 'has standing to petition for cancellation because it is likely to be damaged,' and (2) 'there are valid grounds for discontinuing registration.' Appellate courts have found an abuse of the discretionary authority granted by §1119 where district courts 'refus[e] to order the cancellation of registrations for claimed marks found to be incapable of serving as valid marks.' As the Seventh Circuit explained, because the judgment of a court 'may raise doubts about the validity of a trademark registration, §1119 arms the court with the power to update the federal trademark register to account for a mark's actual legal status (or lack thereof) after it has been adjudicated, thereby reducing the potential for future uncertainty over the rights in a particular mark.' Where a jury's verdict establishes that one of the party's registered trademarks is invalid, then 'cancellation is not merely appropriate, it is the best course.'"

Empresa Cubana del Tabaco v. Culbro Corp., 541 F.3d 476, 478-79 (2d Cir.2008). "[D] did not request [15 U.S.C.] §1119 [Lanham Act §37] relief as a counterclaim, but only as part of its ... motion, following the adjudication of the underlying trademark dispute and the district court's dismissal of the action. [¶] [W]e review the district court's decision in this case not to amend the judgment to include §1119 relief for an abuse of discretion. [¶] A request for dismissal of a cancellation proceeding pursuant to §1119 ordinarily is made as a counterclaim in an infringement action. [W]hen such a request is made for the first time after the underlying trademark dispute has been adjudicated, it is properly construed as being based on an estoppel theory. That is, a request for §1119 relief made for the first time after judgment essentially amounts to a claim that because the district court adjudicated a trademark case in a certain way, there is nothing left for the PTO to decide, and so it ought to be instructed to follow the court's lead for the sake of efficiency and consistency. [W]e see no reason why it was an abuse of discretion for the district court simply to tell [D] to raise its estoppel claim before the PTO and let the agency decide, subject to review by the Federal Circuit, what preclusive effect should be given to our decision in [***Empresa Cubana del Tabaco v. Culbro Corp.***, 399 F.3d 462 (2d Cir.2005)], if any."

E.T. Browne Drug Co. v. Cococare Prods., 538 F.3d 185, 201 (3d Cir.2008). "'[A] controversy as to the validity of or interference with a registered mark must exist before a district court has jurisdiction to grant the cancellation remedy.' *At 202:* [E]ven if [D] will not benefit from [a] disclaimer, we should not allow the absence of a disclaimer on the principal register to confuse a future business into believing that it may not use the term 'Cocoa Butter Formula.' As such, on remand the District Court should order that an appropriate disclaimer should be entered on the principal register."

Central Mfg. v. Brett, 492 F.3d 876, 883 (7th Cir. 2007). "Invoking the authority granted by 15 U.S.C. §1119 [Lanham Act §37], [trial judge] ordered the cancellation of [P's] 2005 registration of [mark]. We find no error in this decision, which we review for abuse of discretion. [D] could have asserted its rights earlier by petitioning the PTO for cancellation, but nothing in §1119 requires such a step. Instead, the provision arms courts with the power to effectively put the public on notice of its trademark-related judgments. Because a court's decision may raise doubts about the validity of a trademark registration, §1119 arms the court with the power to update the federal trademark register to account for a mark's actual legal status (or lack thereof) after it has been adjudicated, thereby reducing the potential for future uncertainty over the rights in a particular mark. Where, as here, a registrant's asserted rights to a mark are shown to be invalid, cancellation is not merely appropriate, it is the best course." *See also* ***Marshak v. Treadwell***, 240 F.3d 184, 193 (3d Cir. 2001).

Shakespeare Co. v. Silstar Corp., 9 F.3d 1091, 1092 (4th Cir.1993). "We hold that Congress adopted 15 U.S.C. §1119 [Lanham Act §37] to give the district court power concurrent with, but not in excess of, the Patent and Trademark Review Board and that the district court is also limited by the language of the statutes controlling the Board. *At 1097:* If the power of the district court under §1119 is implicitly constrained by the specific provisions of [15 U.S.C. §1115(b), Lanham Act §33(b)], it is reasonable to conclude that it is limited by another related subsection, [15 U.S.C.] §1064 [Lanham Act §14]. The [Supreme Court in ***Park'N Fly, Inc. v. Dollar Park & Fly, Inc.***, 469 U.S. 189 (1985),] states that §1064 does limit cancellation of a registration more than five years old and this would be cancellation pursuant to §1119 because the Court's inquiry was rooted in that context." *But see* ***Wilhelm Pudenz, GmbH v. Littlefuse, Inc.***, 177 F.3d 1204, 1209-10 (11th Cir.1999) (in contrast to Fourth Circuit, court holds functionality is a ground for cancellation even though not specifically mentioned in 15 U.S.C. §1064).

Durox Co. v. Duron Paint Mfg., 320 F.2d 882, 887 (4th Cir.1963). "[T]he question is whether 15 U.S.C. §1119 [Lanham Act §37] is applicable to a case following the route of the administrative process or whether it relates only to civil actions for infringement or declaratory judgment involving trademark registrations begun in the district courts. In other words, is the administrative process exclusive (except as to the judicial review provided under [Lanham Act] §21 [15 U.S.C. §1071]) over *applications* for registrations? We do not find this point discussed in the cases. There are no apparent reasons of legislative history which would require the limiting of the plain words of ... §1119 in such a way. We note too that the nature of the review provided under §21 is de novo, with the right to introduce evidence not before the [PTO], rather than a review limited to the record. It would do no violence to the administrative process under the circumstances, and would result in a substantial savings of time and determine the matter in one proceeding, to allow the district court to modify a [PTO] determination in the light of all the evidence."

Johnny Blastoff, Inc. v. Los Angeles Rams Football Co., 48 U.S.P.Q.2d 1385, 1393 (W.D.Wis.1998), *aff'd*, 188 F.3d 427 (7th Cir.1999). "Several cases hold that [15 U.S.C. §1119, Lanham Act §37,] authorizes federal courts to determine the registerability of an as-yet unregistered mark in an action in which a registered mark is involved as well. ... Even if these cases were controlling, they read §1119 to allow intrusion into trademark application proceedings only when there is a sufficient nexus between the application proceeding and the dispute involving the registered mark. [¶] In virtually every case in which a federal court has found authorization to determine the initial registerability of a mark under §1119, that registerability determination was tied directly to a challenge to an existing competing registration or a claim of infringement based on an existing registration."

§1120. CIVIL LIABILITY FOR FALSE OR FRAUDULENT REGISTRATION

[LANHAM ACT §38]

Any person who shall procure registration in the Patent and Trademark Office of a mark by a false or fraudulent declaration or representation, oral or in writing, or by any false means, shall be liable in a civil action by any person injured thereby for any damages sustained in consequence thereof.

History of 15 U.S.C. §1120: July 5, 1946, ch. 540, §38, 60 Stat. 440; Jan. 2, 1975, P.L. 93-596, §1, 88 Stat. 1949.

Treatise Cross-References

McCarthy on Trademark & Unfair Competition

Ch. 31, *Defenses to Infringement of Trademarks*, §§31:85-31:89

ANNOTATIONS

Lorenzana v. South Am. Rests. Corp., 799 F.3d 31, 35 (1st Cir.2015). "[A] claim under [15 U.S.C. §1120, Lanham Act §38,] must sufficiently plead: (1) that the registrant ... made a false representation to the USPTO regarding a material fact; (2) that the petitioner knew or should have known the representation was false; (3) that the petitioner intended to induce the USPTO to act or refrain from acting based upon such representation; (4) that the USPTO reasonably relied on the misrepresentation; and (5) that some damage was proximately caused by the USPTO's reliance on the false material fact." *See also* ***Patsy's Italian Rest., Inc. v. Banas***, 658 F.3d 254, 270-71 (2d Cir.2011); ***Robi v. Five Platters, Inc.***, 918 F.2d 1439, 1444 (9th Cir.1990); ***San Juan Prods. v. San Juan Pools***, 849 F.2d 468, 473 (10th Cir.1988).

Santander Consumer USA Inc. v. Walsh, 762 F.Supp.2d 217, 234 (D.Mass.2010). "Entitlement to attorneys' fees or other litigation costs as an element of recoverable damages under [15 U.S.C.] §1120 [Lanham Act §38] is an issue of first impression in this circuit. Other circuits addressing the issue uniformly deny litigation costs and attorneys' fees as recoverable damages under §1120. Accordingly, [Ds] are not entitled to recover attorneys' fees or defense costs directly under §1120." *See also* ***Aromatique, Inc. v. Gold Seal, Inc.***, 28 F.3d 863, 876 (8th Cir.1994); ***Exxon Corp. v. Exxene Corp.***, 696 F.2d 544, 550 (7th Cir.1982).

§1121. JURISDICTION OF FEDERAL COURTS; STATE & LOCAL REQUIREMENTS THAT REGISTERED TRADEMARKS BE ALTERED OR DISPLAYED DIFFERENTLY; PROHIBITION

[LANHAM ACT §39]

(a) The district and territorial courts of the United States shall have original jurisdiction and the courts of appeal of the United States (other than the United States Court of Appeals for the Federal Circuit) shall have appellate jurisdiction, of all actions arising under this chapter, without regard to the amount in controversy or to diversity or lack of diversity of the citizenship of the parties.

(b) No State or other jurisdiction of the United States or any political subdivision or any agency thereof may require alteration of a registered mark, or require that additional trademarks, service marks, trade names, or corporate names that may be associated with or incorporated into the registered mark be displayed in the mark in a manner differing from the display of such additional trademarks, service marks, trade names, or corporate names contemplated by the registered mark as exhibited in the certificate of registration issued by the United States Patent and Trademark Office.

History of 15 U.S.C. §1121: July 5, 1946, ch. 540, §39 [§§39, 39a], 60 Stat. 440; June 25, 1948, ch. 646, §32, 62 Stat. 907; May 24, 1949, ch. 139, §127, 63 Stat. 107; Apr. 2, 1982, P.L. 97-164, §148, 96 Stat. 46; Oct. 12, 1982, P.L. 97-296, 96 Stat. 1316; Nov. 16, 1988, P.L. 100-667, §131, 102 Stat. 3946; Oct. 30, 1998, P.L. 105-330, §201(a)(10), 112 Stat. 3070.

See also 28 U.S.C. §§1295, 1338; 48 U.S.C. §1405q.

Treatise Cross-References

McCarthy on Trademark & Unfair Competition

Ch. 22, *State Protection & Registration of Marks*, §22:4

Ch. 30, *Remedies for Trademark Infringement & Unfair Competition*, §30:110

Ch. 32, *Procedure in Trademark Infringement & Unfair Competition Litigation*, §32:2

ANNOTATIONS

Generally

Philip Morris USA, Inc. v. King Mountain Tobacco Co., 569 F.3d 932, 934 (9th Cir.2009). "The precise question presented is whether there is colorable tribal court jurisdiction over a nonmember's federal trademark and related state law claims against tribal defendants for alleged passing off of cigarettes on the Internet, on the reservation of another tribe, and elsewhere. *At 935:* [W]e conclude that the Tribal Court does not have colorable jurisdiction over nonmember [P's] federal and state claims for trademark infringement on the Internet and beyond the reservation."

Rhoades v. Avon Prods., 504 F.3d 1151, 1165 (9th Cir.2007). "[W]e hold that the district court abused its discretion in declining to hear [P's] action. We agree with the Second Circuit that some situations might justify deferring a declaratory judgment case when related TTAB proceedings are pending; specifically, where the 'district court action involves only the issue of whether a mark is entitled to registration,' it might make more sense to resolve the registration claims at the TTAB first. On the other hand, if, as here, a potential infringement claim 'requires the district court to resolve much or all of [the registration issues], it would waste everyone's time not to settle the registration issue now[, in district court].' The deciding factor should be efficiency; the district court should exercise jurisdiction 'if this course is more efficient; otherwise, not.'"

Country Mut. Ins. v. American Farm Bur. Fed'n, 876 F.2d 599, 601 (7th Cir.1989). "Any error the PTO makes may be reviewed later, on the authority of [Lanham Act] §39, 15 U.S.C. §1121."

WSM, Inc. v. Wheeler Media Servs., 810 F.2d 113, 117 (6th Cir.1987). "'[I]n a trademark infringement action a federal district court has jurisdiction over an action arising under the Lanham Act [§39], 15 U.S.C. §1121 and 28 U.S.C. §1338, only if the plaintiff has a registered mark.... Absent federal registration, jurisdiction of this Court over common law trademarks or other trademarks not registered exist [sic] only if there is a complete diversity of citizenship even if in determining common law rights the court refers to the federal statute.'"

Vitarroz Corp. v. Borden, Inc., 644 F.2d 960, 963-64 (2d Cir.1981). "If a trademark claim arises under federal law, federal jurisdiction also is available for a related unfair competition claim, and pendent jurisdiction may appropriately be exercised over a related state law claim concerning trademark dilution."

Moser Pilon Nelson Architects, LLC v. HNTB Corp., 80 U.S.P.Q.2d 1085, 1095 (D.Conn.2006). "[C]opying of creative content like [architectural plans] is not protected by the 'origin of work' provision of the Lanham Act, which covers only 'the producer of the tangible goods that are offered for sale, and not ... the author of any idea, concept, or communication embodied in those goods.' ... It appears to the Court that ***Dastar*** [***v. Twentieth Century Fox Film Corp.***, 539 U.S. 23 (2003),] applies with equal force to architectural works and that [Ps'] claim under the Lanham Act therefore fails. [¶] [Ps'] claim under the Lanham Act is preempted by the Copyright Act...." *See also* ***Beckwith Builders, Inc. v. Depietri***, 81 U.S.P.Q.2d 1302, 1307 (D.N.H.2006).

Extraterritorial Jurisdiction

Steele v. Bulova Watch Co., 344 U.S. 280, 289 (1952). "Where ... there can be no interference with the sovereignty of another nation, the District Court in exercising its equity powers may command persons properly before it to cease or perform acts outside its territorial jurisdiction."

Trader Joe's Co. v. Hallatt, 835 F.3d 960, 966 (9th Cir.2016). "We resolve two questions to decide whether the Lanham Act reaches [D's] allegedly infringing conduct, much of which occurred in Canada: First, is the extraterritorial application of the Lanham Act an issue that implicates federal courts' subject-matter jurisdiction? Second, did [P] allege that [D's] conduct impacted American commerce in a manner sufficient to invoke the Lanham Act's protections? [W]e answer 'no' to the first question but 'yes' to the second.... *At 968:* We hold that the extraterritorial reach of the Lanham Act is a merits question that does not implicate federal courts' subject-matter jurisdiction, and that the district court erred as a matter of law when it decided otherwise. *At 969:* We next consider the limits, if any, Congress imposed on the Act's extraterritorial application. In 15 U.S.C. §1127, Congress directed that the Lanham Act applies to 'all commerce which may lawfully be regulated by Congress.' Whether this provision sweeps foreign activities into the Act's proscriptive reach depends on a three-part test we originally applied to the Sherman Act in [***Timberlane Lumber Co. v. Bank of Am. Nat'l Trust & Sav. Ass'n***], 549 F.2d 597 (9th Cir.1976). [¶] ***Timberlane***'s first two prongs require [P] to allege that [D] infringes its trademarks (1) in a way that affects American foreign commerce, and (2) causes [P] a cognizable injury under the Lanham Act. A defendant's foreign activities need not have a substantial or even significant effect on American commerce, rather, 'some effect' may be sufficient. [¶] Plaintiffs usually satisfy ***Timberlane***'s first and second prongs by alleging that infringing goods, though sold initially in a foreign country, flowed into American domestic markets. *At 972-73:* The third ***Timberlane*** prong considers international comity, ... and gives effect to the 'rule that we construe statutes to avoid unreasonable interference with other nations' sovereign authority where possible[ ]'.... This prong involves weighing seven factors: '(1) the degree of conflict with foreign law or policy, (2) the nationality or allegiance of the parties and the locations or principal places of business of corporations, (3) the extent to which enforcement by either state can be expected to achieve compliance, (4) the relative significance of effects on the U.S. as compared with those elsewhere, (5) the extent to which there is explicit purpose to harm or affect American commerce, (6) the foreseeability of such effect, and (7) the relative importance to the violations charged of conduct within the U.S. as compared with conduct abroad.' No one factor is dispositive; each factor 'is just one consideration to be balanced.'" *But see* ***McBee v. Delica Co.***, this page.

Tire Eng'g & Distrib. v. Shandong Linglong Rubber Co., 682 F.3d 292, 310-11 (4th Cir.2012). "[W]e have reasoned that the archetypal injury contemplated by the [Lanham] Act is harm to [P's] 'trade reputation in U.S. markets.' [¶] Other circuits have posited that the Lanham Act's significant-effect requirement may be satisfied by extraterritorial conduct even when that conduct will not cause confusion among U.S. consumers. Under this diversion-of-sales theory, courts find a significant effect on U.S. commerce where sales to foreign consumers would jeopardize the income of an American company. The doctrine is narrowly applied, however, because the injury in this context—harm to a U.S. business's income absent confusion among U.S. consumers—'is less tightly tied to the interests that the Lanham Act intends to protect, since there is no U.S. interest in protecting [*foreign*] *consumers*.' Thus courts invoking the diversion-of-sales theory have required the defendants to be U.S. corporations that conducted operations—including at least some of the infringing activity—within the U.S. Only in such instances is there a sufficient nexus between U.S. commerce and the infringing activity. [¶] Courts upholding liability under the Lanham Act based solely on harm to a U.S. company's income from foreign infringement have stressed that the defendants in those cases were U.S. companies that conducted substantial domestic business activity. Here, in contrast, [Ds] are not U.S. corporations and they lack a pervasive system of domestic operations. Thus we cannot conclude that the extraterritorial conduct—exclusively foreign sales of infringing tires—has a significant effect on U.S. commerce as required by the dictates of the Lanham Act...."

McBee v. Delica Co., 417 F.3d 107, 110 (1st Cir. 2005). "This case ... requires us ... to lay out a framework for determining when ... extraterritorial use of the Lanham Act is proper. *At 116:* By extraterritorial application of the Lanham Act, we mean application of the Act to activity (such as sales) of a defendant outside of the territorial boundaries of the U.S. *At 120-21:* We hold that the Lanham Act grants subject matter jurisdiction over extraterritorial conduct by foreign defendants only where the conduct has a substantial effect on U.S. commerce. [¶] The substantial effects test requires that there be evidence of impacts within the U.S., and these impacts must be of a sufficient character and magnitude to give the U.S. a reasonably strong interest in the litigation. The 'substantial effects' test must be applied in light of the core purposes of the Lanham Act, which are both to protect the ability of American consumers to avoid confusion and to help assure a trademark's owner that it will reap the financial and reputational rewards associated with having a desirable name or product. [¶] If the substantial effects test is met, then the court should proceed, in appropriate cases, to consider comity. [C]omity considerations are properly analyzed not as questions of whether there is subject matter jurisdiction, but as prudential questions of whether that jurisdiction should be exercised." *But see* ***Trader Joe's Co. v. Hallatt***, p. 119.

International Café, S.A.L. v. Hard Rock Café Int'l, 252 F.3d 1274, 1278 (11th Cir.2001). "[T]he Lanham Act confer[s] jurisdiction over extraterritorial disputes involving trademark infringement and unfair competition when: (1) Defendant is a U.S. corporation; (2) the foreign activity had substantial effects in the U.S.; and (3) exercising jurisdiction would not interfere with the sovereignty of another nation." *See also* ***Nintendo, Inc. v. Aeropower Co.***, 34 F.3d 246, 250-51 (4th Cir.1994); ***Vanity Fair Mills, Inc. v. T. Eaton Co.***, 234 F.2d 633, 642 (2d Cir.1956).

American Rice, Inc. v. Arkansas Rice Growers Coop., 701 F.2d 408, 414 (5th Cir.1983). "[C]ertain factors are relevant in determining whether the contacts and interests of the U.S. are sufficient to support the exercise of extraterritorial jurisdiction. These include the citizenship of the defendant, the effect on U.S. commerce, and the existence of a conflict with foreign law. The absence of any one of these is not dispositive. Nor should a court limit its inquiry exclusively to these considerations. Rather, these factors will necessarily be the primary elements in any balancing analysis. *At 414 n.8:* [T]he Second Circuit ... stated that the degree of effect on U.S. commerce must be 'substantial' before the contacts and interests of the U.S. are sufficient to support the exercise of extraterritorial jurisdiction. ... We agree with the Ninth Circuit ... that *some* effect may be sufficient. *At 416:* 'No principle of international law bars the U.S. from governing the conduct of its own citizens upon the high seas or even in foreign countries when the rights of other nations are not infringed.'"

§1121(a)

La Quinta Worldwide LLC v. Q.R.T.M., S.A. de C.V., 762 F.3d 867, 872 (9th Cir.2014). "[D] argues that we lack subject-matter jurisdiction because its expressions of intent to open a hotel are not sufficient to show a 'use in commerce' under the Lanham Act. The 'use in commerce' requirement that [D] relies on is found in §§32 and 43(a) of the Lanham Act [15 U.S.C. §§1114 and 1125(a)], which both lay out claims for infringement. We hold that the 'use in commerce' element of Lanham Act §§32 and 43(a) claims is not a jurisdictional requirement, and we have subject-matter jurisdiction under 15 U.S.C. §1121(a) [Lanham Act §39(a)]."

Facenda v. NFL Films, Inc., 542 F.3d 1007, 1013-14 (3d Cir.2008). "We review the District Court's legal conclusions *de novo*, reading all facts in the light most favorable to the party that did not move for summary judgment.... [¶] 'Failure to strictly observe the principles governing summary judgment becomes particularly significant in a trademark or tradename action, where summary judgments are the exception.' On a summary judgment motion, the District Court must not find facts. Rather, it should identify undisputed facts and resolve the remaining disputed facts in favor of the non-movant. For example, '[c]redibility determinations that underlie findings of fact are appropriate to a bench verdict,' but '[t]hey are inappropriate to the legal conclusions necessary to a ruling on summary judgment.' When considering the District Court's grant of summary judgment to [P] on a particular claim, 'the sole question before [our] Court is whether plaintiff met its burden of demonstrating that it was entitled to judgment as a matter of law.'"

Pebble Beach Co. v. Caddy, 453 F.3d 1151, 1158 (9th Cir.2006), *overruled on other grounds*, ***TrafFix Devices, Inc. v. Marketing Displays, Inc.***, 532 U.S. 23 (2001). "[T]here can be no doubt that we still require 'something more' than just a foreseeable effect to conclude that personal jurisdiction is proper. [A]n internet domain name and passive website alone are not 'something more,' and, therefore, alone are not enough to subject a party to jurisdiction." Held: Noninteractive website, www.pebblebeach-uk.com, was not a purposeful availment of activities toward California, even though D once resided there.

Kentucky Fried Chicken Corp. v. Diversified Packaging Corp., 549 F.2d 368, 392 (5th Cir.1977). "When these statutes [including 15 U.S.C. §1121, Lanham Act §39,] confer subject matter jurisdiction, they do so simultaneously for all federal district courts. The choice among courts is a matter of venue, not jurisdiction."

Holiday Inns, Inc. v. Holiday Motel, Inc., 200 U.S.P.Q. 360, 363 (D.Mont.1978). Since "diversity is not necessary to jurisdiction under 15 U.S.C. §1121 [Lanham Act §39] and 28 U.S.C. §1338, joinder can have no impact on jurisdiction."

§1121(b)

Lisa's Party City, Inc. v. Town of Henrietta, 185 F.3d 12, 15 (2d Cir.1999). "The statutory language of [15 U.S.C. §1121(b), Lanham Act §39(b),] bars state or local regulations from requiring 'alteration' of a federally-registered trademark. [Subsection (b) allows] a local government to restrict businesses in a narrowly circumscribed location from using exterior signs in any color other than red. Such regulation does not compel a businesses to alter their trademark, since they remain free to use their trademarks without alteration in every manifestation other than the exterior sign at the covered location—on letterhead, leaflets, billboards, magazines, newspapers, television and Internet advertising, point-of-sale displays inside the store, and external signs at other locations. Under this narrower construction of §1121(b), a restriction on external signs in a narrowly circumscribed locality would not come within the statute's prohibition on requiring businesses to alter their trademarks. [¶] We think the more plausible interpretation of §1121(b) reads its use of the term 'alteration' 'to describe state-mandated changes in the mark itself, which are, of necessity, reflected in every subsequent display of that mark within the relevant jurisdiction.'" *See also* ***Blockbuster Videos, Inc. v. City of Tempe***, 141 F.3d 1295, 1299 (9th Cir.1998).

§1121a. TRANSFERRED

Transferred to §1121(b) by P.L. 100-667, §131(b)(1), 102 Stat. 3946, eff. Nov. 16, 1988.

§1122. LIABILITY OF UNITED STATES & STATES, & INSTRUMENTALITIES & OFFICIALS THEREOF

[LANHAM ACT §40]

(a) Waiver of sovereign immunity by the United States.—The United States, all agencies and instrumentalities thereof, and all individuals, firms, corporations, other persons acting for the United States and with the authorization and consent of the United States, shall not be immune from suit in Federal or State court by any person, including any governmental or nongovernmental entity, for any violation under this chapter.

(b) Waiver of sovereign immunity by States.—Any State, instrumentality of a State or any officer or employee of a State or instrumentality of a State acting in his or her official capacity, shall not be immune, under the eleventh amendment of the Constitution of the United States or under any other doctrine of sovereign immunity, from suit in Federal court by any person, including any governmental or nongovernmental entity for any violation under this chapter.

(c) Remedies.—In a suit described in subsection (a) or (b) of this section for a violation described therein, remedies (including remedies both at law and in equity) are available for the violation to the same extent as such remedies are available for such a violation in a suit against any person other than the United States or any agency or instrumentality thereof, or any individual, firm, corporation, or other person acting for the United States and with authorization and consent of the United States, or a State, instrumentality of a State, or officer or employee of a State or instrumentality of a State acting in his or her official capacity. Such remedies include injunctive relief under section 1116 of title 15, actual damages, profits, costs and attorney's fees under section 1117 of title 15, destruction of infringing articles under section 1118 of title 15, the remedies provided for under sections 1114, 1119, 1120, 1124, and 1125 of title 15 and for any other remedies provided under this chapter.

History of 15 U.S.C. §1122: July 5, 1946, ch. 540, §40, as added Oct. 27, 1992, P.L. 102-542, §3(b), 106 Stat. 3567; Aug. 5, 1999, P.L. 106-43, §4(b), 113 Stat. 219.

§1123. RULES & REGULATIONS FOR CONDUCT OF PROCEEDINGS IN PATENT & TRADEMARK OFFICE

[LANHAM ACT §41]

The Director shall make rules and regulations, not inconsistent with law, for the conduct of proceedings in the Patent and Trademark Office under this chapter.

History of 15 U.S.C. §1123: July 5, 1946, ch. 540, §41, 60 Stat. 440; Jan. 2, 1975, P.L. 93-596, §1, 88 Stat. 1949; Nov. 29, 1999, P.L. 106-113, §1000(a)(9), 113 Stat. 1536.

See also 37 C.F.R. pt. 11.

§1124. IMPORTATION OF GOODS BEARING INFRINGING MARKS OR NAMES FORBIDDEN

[LANHAM ACT §42]

Except as provided in section 1526(d) of title 19, no article of imported merchandise which shall copy or simulate the name of any domestic manufacture, or manufacturer, or trader, or of any manufacturer or trader located in any foreign country which, by treaty, convention, or law affords similar privileges to citizens of the United States, or which shall copy or simulate a trademark registered in accordance with the provisions of this chapter or shall bear a name or mark calculated to induce the public to believe that the article is manufactured in the United States, or that it is manufactured in any foreign country or locality other than the country or locality in which it is in fact manufactured, shall be admitted to entry at any customhouse of the United States; and, in order to aid the officers of the customs in enforcing this prohibition, any domestic manufacturer or trader, and any foreign manufacturer or trader, who is entitled under the provisions of a treaty, convention, declaration, or agreement between the United States and any foreign country to the advantages afforded by law to citizens of the United States in respect to trademarks and commercial names, may require his name and residence, and the name of the locality in which his goods are manufactured, and a copy of the certificate of registration of his trademark, issued in accordance with the provisions of this chapter, to be recorded in books which shall be kept for this purpose in the Department of the Treasury, under such regulations as the Secretary of the Treasury shall prescribe, and may furnish to the Department facsimiles of his name, the name of the locality in which his goods are manufactured, or of his registered trademark, and thereupon the Secretary of the Treasury shall cause one or more copies of the same to be transmitted to each collector or other proper officer of customs.

History of 15 U.S.C. §1124: July 5, 1946, ch. 540, §42, 60 Stat. 440; Oct. 3, 1978, P.L. 95-410, §211(b), 92 Stat. 903; Oct. 30, 1998, P.L. 105-330, §201(a)(11), (12), 112 Stat. 3070; Aug. 5, 1999, P.L. 106-43, §6(b), 113 Stat. 220.

See also 19 U.S.C. §§1337, 1595a; 48 U.S.C. §1643.

Treatise Cross-References

McCarthy on Trademark & Unfair Competition

Ch. 19, *Federal Registration of Marks*, §19:92.50

Ch. 29, *International Aspects of Trademark Law*, §§29:37; 29:39; 29:48; 29:50; 29:50.50; 29:51.75; 29:54

ANNOTATIONS

K Mart Corp. v. Cartier, Inc., 486 U.S. 281, 285 (1988). "A gray-market good is a foreign-manufactured good, bearing a valid U.S. trademark, that is imported without the consent of the U.S. trademark holder."

Hokto Kinoko Co. v. Concord Farms, Inc., 738 F.3d 1085, 1092-94 (9th Cir.2013). "Some commentators apply the term 'gray market' only where both the trademark owner and the alleged infringer import their product from foreign countries, ... or only where the U.S. trademark owner also owns foreign rights in the disputed mark.... Regardless of whether we categorize the [goods] here as gray-market goods, however, the fundamental nature of the infringement claim is the same as that in gray-market cases: [P] alleges that [D] violated its trademarks by importing legitimately produced goods sold under those same marks. [¶] In general, the sale of gray-market goods may infringe on the U.S. trademark holder's rights, subject to the consumer confusion analysis that generally governs trademark infringement claims. An exception to this rule, however, is that trademark law does not extend to the sale of 'genuine goods.' [¶] We have approached the 'genuine good' inquiry both as a threshold question for the applicability of trademark law, and as part of the test for consumer confusion. Here, because we confront a classic gray-market case, we must analyze the genuine goods question as a threshold matter, for if [D's goods] are 'genuine,' it is not subject to liability for trademark infringement. [¶] 'Genuine,' in the trademark context, is a term of art: a gray-market good is 'genuine' only if it does not materially differ from the U.S. trademark owner's product. [¶] Because the likelihood of confusion increases as the differences between products become more subtle, the threshold for determining a material difference is low. The key question is whether a consumer is likely to consider a difference relevant when purchasing a product. Courts have found a wide range of differences 'material' in this context. [D]ifferences in language, quality control, and packaging may each be sufficiently material to render imported goods not 'genuine.'"

R.J. Reynolds Tobacco Co. v. Cigarettes Cheaper!, 462 F.3d 690, 700 (7th Cir.2006). "The Lanham Act does not block the reimportation and sale of genuine articles under their real trademarks. But this principle does not apply if the domestic and foreign products are materially different, for then sale of the foreign product in the U.S. under the domestic marks has a potential to mislead or confuse consumers about the nature or quality of the product they are buying; they will assume it to be the same as the normal domestic product and be disappointed."

Acadia Tech. v. U.S., 458 F.3d 1327, 1332 (Fed.Cir. 2006). "The government's seizure, retention, and damaging of the property did not give rise to an actionable claim for a taking ... because items properly seized by the government under its police power are not seized for public use within the meaning of the Fifth Amendment. [¶] A Customs seizure of goods suspected of bearing counterfeit marks is a classic example of the government's exercise of the police power to condemn contraband or noxious goods, an exercise that has not been regarded as a taking for public use for which compensation must be paid." (Internal quotes omitted.)

SKF USA, Inc. v. ITC, 423 F.3d 1307, 1312-13 (Fed. Cir.2005). "The ... issue we address is whether the distinction between domestic goods and gray market goods must be physical in nature in order to satisfy the 'material difference' test, an issue of first impression for this court. [¶] We ... hold that physical material differences are not required to establish trademark infringement involving gray market goods. That is because trademarked goods originating from the trademark owner may have nonphysical characteristics associated with them, including services, such that similar goods lacking those associated characteristics may be believed by consumers to have originated from the trademark owner and, lacking such traits, may mislead the consumer and damage the owner's goodwill. [¶] 'The principle of gray market law is that the importation of a product that was produced by the owner of the U.S. trademark or with its consent, but not authorized for sale in the U.S., may, in appropriate cases, infringe the U.S. trademark.'"

Lever Bros. v. U.S., 981 F.2d 1330, 1338-39 (D.C.Cir. 1993). "Lanham Act [§42], 15 U.S.C. §1124, bars the importation of physically different foreign goods bearing a trademark identical to a valid U.S. trademark, regardless of the trademark's genuine character abroad or affiliation between the producing firms." *See also* ***Olympus Corp. v. U.S.***, 792 F.2d 315, 321 (2d Cir.1986).

NEC Elecs. v. CAL Circuit ABCO, 810 F.2d 1506, 1510 (9th Cir.1988). "Lanham Act [§42], 15 U.S.C. §1124, barring importation of goods that 'copy or simulate' a trademark, [does] not apply to genuine goods except in cases presenting the same 'equities' as [***A. Bourjois & Co. v. Katzel***, 260 U.S. 689 (1923)]."

Vivitar Corp. v. U.S., 761 F.2d 1552, 1569 (Fed.Cir. 1985). "Regardless of whether Customs excludes or does not exclude particular imports, the courts must independently determine whether the importation is or is not precluded by the statute. ... Customs' decision, as expressed in the subject regulations, not to exclude grey market goods does not control on the question of whether particular goods should or should not be excluded. *At 1569 n.23:* If we turn to regulations of Customs related to other statutory exclusions, the non-legislative nature of all of these regulations becomes readily apparent. Trade names (i.e., company names) may be recorded only if used for six months. Nothing in 15 U.S.C. §1124 [Lanham Act §42] establishes this requirement."

U.S. v. 10,510 Packaged Computer Towers, 152 F.Supp.2d 1189, 1195 (N.D.Cal.2001). "[T]he seizure and forfeiture statute [19 U.S.C. §1526(e)] expressly extends protection to merchandise 'imported into the U.S. in violation of the provisions of [15 U.S.C.] §1124 [Lanham Act §42].' Thus, the question *whether a violation has occurred* should be analyzed with respect to ... §1124, but *the protection authorized* in case of a violation is governed by the seizure and forfeiture statute. *At 1196:* [I]mportation of goods bearing copied or simulated trademarks[] would violate ... §1124."

U.S. v. Watches, Watch Parts, Calculators & Misc. Parts, 692 F.Supp. 1317, 1321 (S.D.Fla.1988). "[C]ourts, when considering the question of importation more recently, have stated: imported merchandise is merchandise that has been brought within the limits of a port of entry from a foreign country with intention of unlade, and the word 'importation' as used in tariff statutes, unless otherwise limited, means merchandise in which that condition has attached. *At 1322:* [T]he use of the word 'entry' in 15 U.S.C. §1124 [Lanham Act §42] should not be limited to the definition in 19 C.F.R. §141.0a, but rather [should be] given its much broader meaning encompassing every type of entry used throughout the customs regulations." (Internal quotes omitted.)

International Armament Corp. v. Matra Manurhin Int'l, 630 F.Supp. 741, 746 (E.D.Va.1986). "15 U.S.C. §1124 [Lanham Act §42] and 19 U.S.C. §1526[] allow the owners of a U.S. trademark to prevent imports where marks on the goods are confusingly similar to those owned by the U.S. owner or where the marks are owned by U.S. companies. That the assignments here were made to exclude import of goods made by a foreign manufacturer and licensee ... of the foreign holder of the trademarks ... is irrelevant. Ownership of the marks is a matter of agreement between the foreign owner and the U.S. distributor."

§1125. FALSE DESIGNATIONS OF ORIGIN, FALSE DESCRIPTIONS & DILUTION FORBIDDEN

[LANHAM ACT §43]

(a) Civil action—

(1) Any person who, on or in connection with any goods or services, or any container for goods, uses in commerce any word, term, name, symbol, or device, or any combination thereof, or any false designation of origin, false or misleading description of fact, or false or misleading representation of fact, which—

(A) is likely to cause confusion, or to cause mistake, or to deceive as to the affiliation, connection, or association of such person with another person, or as to the origin, sponsorship, or approval of his or her goods, services, or commercial activities by another person, or

(B) in commercial advertising or promotion, misrepresents the nature, characteristics, qualities, or geographic origin of his or her or another person's goods, services, or commercial activities,

shall be liable in a civil action by any person who believes that he or she is or is likely to be damaged by such act.

(2) As used in this subsection, the term "any person" includes any State, instrumentality of a State or employee of a State or instrumentality of a State acting in his or her official capacity. Any State, and any such instrumentality, officer, or employee, shall be subject to the provisions of this chapter in the same manner and to the same extent as any nongovernmental entity.

(3) In a civil action for trade dress infringement under this chapter for trade dress not registered on the principal register, the person who asserts trade dress protection has the burden of proving that the matter sought to be protected is not functional.

(b) Importation.—Any goods marked or labeled in contravention of the provisions of this section shall not be imported into the United States or admitted to entry at any customhouse of the United States. The owner, importer, or consignee of goods refused entry at any customhouse under this section may have any recourse by protest or appeal that is given under the customs revenue laws or may have the remedy given by this chapter in cases involving goods refused entry or seized.

(c) Dilution by blurring; dilution by tarnishment—

(1) Injunctive relief.—Subject to the principles of equity, the owner of a famous mark that is distinctive, inherently or through acquired distinctiveness, shall be entitled to an injunction against another person who, at any time after the owner's mark has become famous, commences use of a mark or trade name in commerce that is likely to cause dilution by blurring or dilution by tarnishment of the famous mark, regardless of the presence or absence of actual or likely confusion, of competition, or of actual economic injury.

(2) Definitions—

(A) For purposes of paragraph (1), a mark is famous if it is widely recognized by the general consuming public of the United States as a designation of source of the goods or services of the mark's owner. In determining whether a mark possesses the requisite degree of recognition, the court may consider all relevant factors, including the following:

(i) The duration, extent, and geographic reach of advertising and publicity of the mark, whether advertised or publicized by the owner or third parties.

(ii) The amount, volume, and geographic extent of sales of goods or services offered under the mark.

(iii) The extent of actual recognition of the mark.

(iv) Whether the mark was registered under the Act of March 3, 1881, or the Act of February 20, 1905, or on the principal register.

(B) For purposes of paragraph (1), "dilution by blurring" is association arising from the similarity between a mark or trade name and a famous mark that impairs the distinctiveness of the famous mark. In determining whether a mark or trade name is likely to cause dilution by blurring, the court may consider all relevant factors, including the following:

(i) The degree of similarity between the mark or trade name and the famous mark.

(ii) The degree of inherent or acquired distinctiveness of the famous mark.

(iii) The extent to which the owner of the famous mark is engaging in substantially exclusive use of the mark.

(iv) The degree of recognition of the famous mark.

(v) Whether the user of the mark or trade name intended to create an association with the famous mark.

(vi) Any actual association between the mark or trade name and the famous mark.

(C) For purposes of paragraph (1), "dilution by tarnishment" is association arising from the similarity between a mark or trade name and a famous mark that harms the reputation of the famous mark.

(3) Exclusions.—The following shall not be actionable as dilution by blurring or dilution by tarnishment under this subsection:

(A) Any fair use, including a nominative or descriptive fair use, or facilitation of such fair use, of a famous mark by another person other than as a designation of source for the person's own goods or services, including use in connection with—

(i) advertising or promotion that permits consumers to compare goods or services; or

(ii) identifying and parodying, criticizing, or commenting upon the famous mark owner or the goods or services of the famous mark owner.

(B) All forms of news reporting and news commentary.

(C) Any noncommercial use of a mark.

(4) Burden of proof.—In a civil action for trade dress dilution under this chapter for trade dress not registered on the principal register, the person who asserts trade dress protection has the burden of proving that—

(A) the claimed trade dress, taken as a whole, is not functional and is famous; and

(B) if the claimed trade dress includes any mark or marks registered on the principal register, the unregistered matter, taken as a whole, is famous separate and apart from any fame of such registered marks.

(5) Additional remedies.—In an action brought under this subsection, the owner of the famous mark shall be entitled to injunctive relief as set forth in section 1116 of title 15. The owner of the famous mark shall also be entitled to the remedies set forth in sections 1117(a) and 1118 of title 15, subject to the discretion of the court and the principles of equity if—

(A) the mark or trade name that is likely to cause dilution by blurring or dilution by tarnishment was first used in commerce by the person against whom the injunction is sought after October 6, 2006; and

(B) in a claim arising under this subsection—

(i) by reason of dilution by blurring, the person against whom the injunction is sought willfully intended to trade on the recognition of the famous mark; or

(ii) by reason of dilution by tarnishment, the person against whom the injunction is sought willfully intended to harm the reputation of the famous mark.

(6) Ownership of valid registration a complete bar to action.—The ownership by a person of a valid registration under the Act of March 3, 1881, or the Act of February 20, 1905, or on the principal register under this chapter shall be a complete bar to an action against that person, with respect to that mark, that—

(A) is brought by another person under the common law or a statute of a State; and

(B)(i) seeks to prevent dilution by blurring or dilution by tarnishment; or

(ii) asserts any claim of actual or likely damage or harm to the distinctiveness or reputation of a mark, label, or form of advertisement.

(7) Savings clause.—Nothing in this subsection shall be construed to impair, modify, or supersede the applicability of the patent laws of the United States.

(d) Cyberpiracy prevention—

(1)(A) A person shall be liable in a civil action by the owner of a mark, including a personal name which is protected as a mark under this section, if, without regard to the goods or services of the parties, that person—

(i) has a bad faith intent to profit from that mark, including a personal name which is protected as a mark under this section; and

(ii) registers, traffics in, or uses a domain name that—

(I) in the case of a mark that is distinctive at the time of registration of the domain name, is identical or confusingly similar to that mark;

(II) in the case of a famous mark that is famous at the time of registration of the domain name, is identical or confusingly similar to or dilutive of that mark; or

(III) is a trademark, word, or name protected by reason of section 706 of title 18 or section 220506 of title 36.

(B)(i) In determining whether a person has a bad faith intent described under subparagraph (A), a court may consider factors such as, but not limited to—

(I) the trademark or other intellectual property rights of the person, if any, in the domain name;

(II) the extent to which the domain name consists of the legal name of the person or a name that is otherwise commonly used to identify that person;

(III) the person's prior use, if any, of the domain name in connection with the bona fide offering of any goods or services;

(IV) the person's bona fide noncommercial or fair use of the mark in a site accessible under the domain name;

(V) the person's intent to divert consumers from the mark owner's online location to a site accessible under the domain name that could harm the goodwill represented by the mark, either for commercial gain or with the intent to tarnish or disparage the mark, by creating a likelihood of confusion as to the source, sponsorship, affiliation, or endorsement of the site;

(VI) the person's offer to transfer, sell, or otherwise assign the domain name to the mark owner or any third party for financial gain without having used, or having an intent to use, the domain name in the bona fide offering of any goods or services, or the person's prior conduct indicating a pattern of such conduct;

(VII) the person's provision of material and misleading false contact information when applying for the registration of the domain name, the person's intentional failure to maintain accurate contact information, or the person's prior conduct indicating a pattern of such conduct;

(VIII) the person's registration or acquisition of multiple domain names which the person knows are identical or confusingly similar to marks of others that are distinctive at the time of registration of such domain names, or dilutive of famous marks of others that are famous at the time of registration of such domain names, without regard to the goods or services of the parties; and

(IX) the extent to which the mark incorporated in the person's domain name registration is or is not distinctive and famous within the meaning of subsection (c).

(ii) Bad faith intent described under subparagraph (A) shall not be found in any case in which the court determines that the person believed and had reasonable grounds to believe that the use of the domain name was a fair use or otherwise lawful.

(C) In any civil action involving the registration, trafficking, or use of a domain name under this paragraph, a court may order the forfeiture or cancellation of the domain name or the transfer of the domain name to the owner of the mark.

(D) A person shall be liable for using a domain name under subparagraph (A) only if that person is the domain name registrant or that registrant's authorized licensee.

(E) As used in this paragraph, the term "traffics in" refers to transactions that include, but are not limited to, sales, purchases, loans, pledges, licenses, exchanges of currency, and any other transfer for consideration or receipt in exchange for consideration.

(2)(A) The owner of a mark may file an in rem civil action against a domain name in the judicial district in which the domain name registrar, domain name registry, or other domain name authority that registered or assigned the domain name is located if—

(i) the domain name violates any right of the owner of a mark registered in the Patent and Trademark Office, or protected under subsection (a) or (c); and

(ii) the court finds that the owner—

(I) is not able to obtain in personam jurisdiction over a person who would have been a defendant in a civil action under paragraph (1); or

(II) through due diligence was not able to find a person who would have been a defendant in a civil action under paragraph (1) by—

(aa) sending a notice of the alleged violation and intent to proceed under this paragraph to the registrant of the domain name at the postal and e-mail address provided by the registrant to the registrar; and

(bb) publishing notice of the action as the court may direct promptly after filing the action.

(B) The actions under subparagraph (A)(ii) shall constitute service of process.

(C) In an in rem action under this paragraph, a domain name shall be deemed to have its situs in the judicial district in which—

(i) the domain name registrar, registry, or other domain name authority that registered or assigned the domain name is located; or

(ii) documents sufficient to establish control and authority regarding the disposition of the registration and use of the domain name are deposited with the court.

(D)(i) The remedies in an in rem action under this paragraph shall be limited to a court order for the forfeiture or cancellation of the domain name or the transfer of the domain name to the owner of the mark. Upon receipt of written notification of a filed, stamped copy of a complaint filed by the owner of a mark in a United States district court under this paragraph, the domain name registrar, domain name registry, or other domain name authority shall—

(I) expeditiously deposit with the court documents sufficient to establish the court's control and authority regarding the disposition of the registration and use of the domain name to the court; and

(II) not transfer, suspend, or otherwise modify the domain name during the pendency of the action, except upon order of the court.

(ii) The domain name registrar or registry or other domain name authority shall not be liable for injunctive or monetary relief under this paragraph except in the case of bad faith or reckless disregard, which includes a willful failure to comply with any such court order.

(3) The civil action established under paragraph (1) and the in rem action established under paragraph (2), and any remedy available under either such action, shall be in addition to any other civil action or remedy otherwise applicable.

(4) The in rem jurisdiction established under paragraph (2) shall be in addition to any other jurisdiction that otherwise exists, whether in rem or in personam.

History of 15 U.S.C. §1125: July 5, 1946, ch. 540, §43, 60 Stat. 441; Nov. 16, 1988, P.L. 100-667, §132, 102 Stat. 3946; Oct. 27, 1992, P.L. 102-542, §3(c), 106 Stat. 3568; Jan. 16, 1996, P.L. 104-98, §3(a), 109 Stat. 985; Aug. 5, 1999, P.L. 106-43, §§3(a)(2), 5, 113 Stat. 219, 220; Nov. 29, 1999, P.L. 106-113, §1000(a)(9), 113 Stat. 1536; Oct. 6, 2006, P.L. 109-312, §2, 120 Stat. 1730; Oct. 5, 2012, P.L. 112-190, §1(a), 126 Stat. 1436.

See also 15 U.S.C. §70b; NAFTA art. 1712; Paris Convention art. 6bis; TRIPs pt. II, §3.

Treatise Cross-References

McCarthy on Trademark & Unfair Competition

Ch. 1, *Basic Principles of Unfair Competition*, §§1:11; 1:18; 1:19
Ch. 5, *Historical Basis of Trademarks & Legislative History*, §§5:9; 5:10
Ch. 6, *Trademarks Compared to Patents & Copyrights*, §§6:14; 6:27; 6:29
Ch. 7, *Trademark & Trade Dress Formats*, §§7:23; 7:25; 7:54; 7:59; 7:69; 7:72; 7:76; 7:89.30; 7:91; 7:94; 7:96; 7:100; 7:103
Ch. 8, *Trade Dress*, §§8:1; 8:6; 8:6.50; 8:7; 8:8; 8:11; 8:12; 8:21
Ch. 9, *Corporation & Organization Trade Names*, §§9:4; 9:6
Ch. 10, *Literary, Artistic & Entertainment Rights*, §§10:4; 10:4.10; 10:15; 10:19; 10:26.10; 10:27; 10:28; 10:30; 10:31; 10:35; 10:39; 10:40; 10:42; 10:44
Ch. 11, *The Spectrum of Distinctiveness of Marks*, §11:49
Ch. 14, *Geographic Term Marks*, §14:23
Ch. 15, *Secondary Meaning*, §15:9
Ch. 16, *Acquisition & Priority of Trademark Rights*, §16:48
Ch. 18, *Assignment & Licensing of Trademarks*, §18:63
Ch. 19, *Federal Registration of Marks*, §§19:8; 19:26; 19:104; 19:117; 19:118; 19:144; 19:146
Ch. 20, *Inter Partes Trademark Proceedings in the Patent & Trademark Office*, §§20:20.50; 20:53.50
Ch. 23, *Likelihood of Confusion: The Test of Trademark Infringement*, §§23:1; 23:10; 23:11.50; 23:12; 23:53; 23:107
Ch. 24, *Infringement by Use of Mark on Noncompetitive Goods or Services*, §§24:74; 24:80; 24:83; 24:89; 24:94-24:96; 24:99-24:106; 24:111; 24:112; 24:117; 24:118; 24:120-24:132; 24:134
Ch. 25, *Types of Trademark Infringement*, §§25:3; 25:6-25:9; 25:19; 25:21.25; 25:21.75; 25:29; 25:59; 25:65-25:67
Ch. 26, *The Territorial Extent of Trademark Rights*, §§26:4; 26:52
Ch. 27, *Lanham Act §43(a) & False Advertising*, §§27:6-27:21; 27:23-27:28; 27:30-27:32; 27:36; 27:38-27:49; 27:51-27:53; 27:56; 27:59-27:68; 27:70-27:79; 27:81-27:91; 27:100; 27:109; 27:118; 27:119
Ch. 28, *False Endorsement & the Right of Publicity*, §28:15
Ch. 29, *International Aspects of Trademark Law*, §§29:4; 29:33; 29:39; 29:53; 29:54
Ch. 30, *Remedies for Trademark Infringement & Unfair Competition*, §§30:10; 30:36; 30:74; 30:88; 30:89; 30:97; 30:104; 30:107
Ch. 31, *Defenses to Infringement of Trademarks*, §§31:23; 31:60; 31:65; 31:141
Ch. 32, *Procedure in Trademark Infringement & Unfair Competition Litigation*, §§32:3; 32:10-32:13; 32:16; 32:18; 32:57; 32:131

ANNOTATIONS

Generally

College Sav. Bank v. Florida Prepaid Postsecondary Educ. Expense Bd., 527 U.S. 666, 669 (1999). "The question presented in this case is whether [15 U.S.C. §1125(a), Lanham Act §43(a),] is effective to permit suit against a State for its alleged misrepresentation of its own product—either because the [Trademark Remedy Clarification Act (TRCA)] effects a constitutionally permissible abrogation of state sovereign immunity, or because the TRCA operates as an invitation to waiver of such immunity which is automatically accepted by a State's engaging in the activities regulated by the Lanham Act. *At 691:* [Because] the sovereign immunity of the [state] was neither validly abrogated by the [TRCA], nor voluntarily waived by the State's activities in interstate commerce, we hold that the federal courts are without jurisdiction to entertain this suit against an arm of the [state]."

Fleischer Studios, Inc. v. A.V.E.L.A., Inc., 654 F.3d 958, 966-67 (9th Cir.2011). "[P's] failure to provide timely evidence of a federal registration [of mark], while detrimental to [P's] trademark claim, does not completely resolve it. Under §43(a) of the Lanham Act [15 U.S.C. §1125], ... a claimant may still prove the validity of an unregistered mark. Without a federal registration, however, the claimant loses out on the presumption of validity that registration confers."

Fortune Dynamic, Inc. v. Victoria's Secret Stores Brand Mgmt., 618 F.3d 1025, 1031 (9th Cir. 2010). "'[B]ecause of the intensely factual nature of trademark disputes, summary judgment is generally disfavored in the trademark arena.'"

Exxon Corp. v. Humble Expl. Co., 695 F.2d 96, 103 (5th Cir.1983). "While [15 U.S.C. §1125, Lanham Act §43,] has a broader reach than [15 U.S.C. §1114, Lanham Act §32], and claims under it can be maintained by plaintiffs who are not owners of a trademark, when a claim is based on alleged ownership of a mark, the two sections must be applied in a parallel manner. Otherwise stated, the §1125 claim rises or falls on the issue of abandonment for the reason that the only basis for the trial court's holding that §1125 was violated was the use by appellant of the mark, a use not faulted if the mark has been abandoned."

Whitney Information Network, Inc. v. Verio, Inc., 79 U.S.P.Q.2d 1606, 1607-08 (M.D.Fla.2006). Held: Offensive statements on an interactive website did not provide basis for an alleged violation under 15 U.S.C. §1125(a), Lanham Act §43(a), because website operator was immune from suit under safe harbor provided by Communications Decency Act of 1966 §230, 47 U.S.C. §230, which states: "No provider or user of an interactive computer service shall be treated as the publisher or speaker of any information provided by another information content provider." In dismissing the case, the court applied the three-part test in ***Corbis Corp. v. Amazon.com***, 351 F.Supp.2d 1090 (W.D. Wash.2004): (1) whether D is a service provider or user of an interactive computer service, (2) whether the cause of action treats D as a publisher or speaker of information, and (3) whether the statement on which the action is based was provided by a third party.

§1125(a)(1)—Generally

Eastman Chem. Co. v. PlastiPure, Inc., 775 F.3d 230, 234 (5th Cir.2014). "Essential to any claim under §43(a) of the Lanham Act [15 U.S.C. §1125(a)] is a determination of whether the challenged statement is one of fact—actionable under §43(a)—or one of general opinion—not actionable under §43(a). *At 235:* We have held that a statement of fact is one that (1) admits of being adjudged true or false in a way that (2) admits of empirical verification. Similarly, we have said that the challenged statement must make a specific and measurable claim, capable of being proved false or of being reasonably interpreted as a statement of objective fact. In contrast, bald assertions of superiority and exaggerated, blustering, and boasting statements are non-actionable opinions. Predictions of future events are also non-actionable expressions of opinion. [¶] [Ds] argue that commercial statements relating to live scientific controversies should be treated as opinions for Lanham Act purposes. According to [Ds], enjoining statements that embrace one side of an open scientific debate would stifle academic freedom and inhibit the free flow of scientific ideas, contrary to the principles undergirding the First Amendment. *At 236-37:* Given the applicable binding precedent, it is of no moment that the commercial speech in this case concerned a topic of scientific debate. Advertisements do not become immune from Lanham Act scrutiny simply because their claims are open to scientific or public debate. Otherwise, the Lanham Act would hardly ever be enforceable—many, if not most, products may be tied to public concerns with the environment, energy, economic policy, or individual health and safety. The Supreme Court has made clear that advertising which links a product to a current public debate is not thereby entitled to the constitutional protection afforded noncommercial speech. The First Amendment ensures a robust discourse in the pages of academic journals, but it does not immunize false or misleading commercial claims." (Internal quotes omitted.)

La Quinta Worldwide LLC v. Q.R.T.M., S.A. de C.V., 762 F.3d 867, 872 (9th Cir.2014). "[D] argues that we lack subject-matter jurisdiction because its expressions of intent to open a hotel are not sufficient to show a 'use in commerce' under the Lanham Act. The 'use in commerce' requirement that [D] relies on is found in §§32 and 43(a) of the Lanham Act [15 U.S.C. §§1114 and 1125(a)], which both lay out claims for infringement. We hold that the 'use in commerce' element of Lanham Act §§32 and 43(a) claims is not a jurisdictional requirement, and we have subject-matter jurisdiction under 15 U.S.C. §1121(a) [Lanham Act §39(a)]."

Facenda v. NFL Films, Inc., 542 F.3d 1007, 1021 (3d Cir.2008). "The statutory text of [15 U.S.C. §1125(a)(1)(A) and (a)(1)(B), Lanham Act

§43(a)(1)(A) and (a)(1)(B),] differs; only subsection (a)(1)(A) includes the phrase 'likely to cause confusion.' The case law also differs; our Court has long applied the ***Lapp*** factors in (a)(1)(A) cases but not in (a)(1)(B) cases. The leading treatise on trademark law explains that plaintiffs *could* bring false endorsement claims under either (a)(1)(A) or (a)(1)(B). But that does not mean that plaintiffs *must* bring claims under both subsections. Nor does it mean that the elements of (a)(1)(A) claims and (a)(1)(B) claims are the same, as [D] alleges. In fact, (a)(1)(A) requires only a likelihood of confusion whereas claims of impliedly false statements under (a)(1)(B) require showing actual confusion or misleading statements." *See also* ***Rosco, Inc. v. Mirror Lite Co.***, 304 F.3d 1373, 1383 (Fed.Cir. 2002); ***Fisons Horticulture, Inc. v. Vigoro Indus.***, 30 F.3d 466, 472 n.8 (3d Cir.1994).

Judkins v. HT Window Fashion Corp., 529 F.3d 1334, 1338-39 (Fed.Cir.2008). "To prevail on an unfair-competition claim under [Lanham Act] §43(a) [15 U.S.C. §1125(a)] stemming from a patentee's marketplace activity in support of his patent, the claimant must first establish that the activity was undertaken in bad faith. '[A] patentee has a right to inform potential infringers of a patent and potentially infringing activity unless the communication is made in bad faith.' Although bad faith in this context has both objective and subjective elements, the former is a threshold requirement: 'a bad faith standard cannot be satisfied in the absence of a showing that the claims asserted were objectively baseless,' meaning no reasonable litigant could realistically expect to prevail in a dispute over infringement of the patent. If a district court weighing a motion to enjoin a patentee from communicating its rights [in an unfair-competition action under §1125(a)(1)] determines the patent in question is not necessarily invalid or unenforceable, the objective baselessness requirement is not met, and no injunction should issue. [O]nce the court concludes that the claims of infringement are objectively baseless, the court must then consider whether the claims were made in subjective bad faith." *See also* ***Fisher Tool Co. v. Gillet Outillage***, 530 F.3d 1063, 1068 (9th Cir.2008).

Utah Lighthouse Ministry v. Foundation for Apologetic Info. & Research, 527 F.3d 1045, 1054 (10th Cir.2008). "It is important to distinguish between the merely jurisdictional 'in commerce' requirement, ... and the 'in connection with any goods and services' requirement that establishes a violation of [15 U.S.C. §1125(a), Lanham Act §43(a)]. [T]he Internet is generally an instrumentality of interstate commerce, ... and thus ... the jurisdiction of the Lanham Act constitutionally extends to unauthorized uses of trademarks on the Internet. However, this does not mean that any use of the Internet is necessarily commercial for the purposes of the Lanham Act, as [P] advocates. ... We therefore decline to adopt [P's] proposed rule that any use of a trademark on the Internet is a use 'in connection with goods or services.'"

Schlotzsky's, Ltd. v. Sterling Purchasing & Nat'l Distrib., 520 F.3d 393, 401 (5th Cir.2008). "[T]he injury requirement under [Lanham Act] §43(a) [15 U.S.C. §1125(a)] can be satisfied even though a party fails to establish a specific amount of actual loss. [¶] The district court did not err in awarding injunctive relief without finding a precise measure of monetary damages."

Test Masters Educ. Servs. v. Singh, 428 F.3d 559, 572 (5th Cir.2005). "Although [the previous action and the current action both] involve potential customer confusion stemming from [D's] website, the operative facts between the current litigation and the previous litigation are not the same. The current action does not involve the legitimacy of [D's] use of [P's mark in a] domain name, which was the central dispute in the previous litigation. Moreover, the nucleus of facts in the current action concerns allegations of intentional fraud and malice that did not occur at the time of the previous action. [P's] action is not estopped by res judicata or claim preclusion. *At 576:* [Collateral estoppel does not apply because] although [P] has presented evidence that his ... company has become more successful since the prior judgment, that success is not dispositive of the question of secondary meaning. [P] has alleged no set of facts that would suggest that there has been a change in the minds of the public in the relevant geographic area such that they could immediately associate the 'TESTMASTERS' mark with his test preparation corporation."

Bosley Med. Inst. v. Kremer, 403 F.3d 672, 677 (9th Cir.2005). "As a matter of First Amendment law, commercial speech may be regulated in ways that would be impermissible if the same regulation were applied to noncommercial expressions. 'The First Amendment may offer little protection for a competitor who labels its commercial good with a confusingly similar mark, but trademark rights do not entitle the owner to quash an unauthorized use of the mark by another who is communicating ideas or expressing points of view.'" *See also* ***Radiance Found. v. NAACP***, 786 F.3d 316, 321-22 (4th Cir.2015); ***Farah v. Esquire Mag.***, 736 F.3d 528, 541 (D.C.Cir.2013); ***Utah Lighthouse Ministry v. Foundation for Apologetic Info. & Research***, 527 F.3d 1045, 1052-53 (10th Cir.2008); ***Taubman Co. v. Webfeats***, 319 F.3d 770, 778 (6th Cir.2003).

Tumblebus Inc. v. Cranmer, 399 F.3d 754, 760-61 (6th Cir.2005). "Lanham Act [§43(a)], 15 U.S.C. §1125(a), provides a federal cause of action for infringement of marks and trade dress that have not obtained federal registration. *At 761 n.4:* 'Section 43(a) prohibits a broader range of practices than does [15 U.S.C. §1114, Lanham Act §32], which applies to registered marks, but it is common ground that §43(a) protects qualifying unregistered trademarks and that the general principles qualifying a mark for registration under [Lanham Act] §2 [15 U.S.C. §1052] are for the most part applicable in determining whether an unregistered mark is entitled to protection under §43(a).'"

Electronic Lab. Sup. v. Cullen, 977 F.2d 798, 807 (3d Cir.1992). "[A] corporate officer who actually and substantially participates in the corporation's act of trademark infringement is personally liable under [15 U.S.C. §1125(a), Lanham Act §43(a)], even though he acted as an agent of the corporation rather than on his own behalf."

GTE Corp. v. Williams, 904 F.2d 536, 542 (10th Cir. 1990). When 15 U.S.C. §1125(a), Lanham Act §43(a), "'is used as the basis for an alternative count along with a count for infringement of a registered mark, a good faith remote use defense good against the registration should be good against the §43(a) count as well.'"

§1125(a)(1)—Cause of Action

Parks LLC v. Tyson Foods, Inc., 863 F.3d 220, 225 (3d Cir.2017). Section 1125(a) "creates 'two distinct bases of liability: false association ... and false advertising.' *At 226:* False advertising claims do not require proof of secondary meaning, so litigants may be tempted to frame a false association claim as a false advertising claim, to ease their evidentiary burden. That is what seems to have happened here, and we take this opportunity to clarify the distinction between claims brought under §1125(a)(1)(A) and §1125(a)(1)(B). [¶] [T]he statement at issue in a false advertising claim must 'misrepresent[] the nature, characteristics, qualities, or geographic origin' of a product. *At 228-29:* Section 1125(a)(1)(B) focuses specifically on statements that are false with regard to 'geographic origin' and not other types of 'false designation[s] of origin[]'.... So, §1125(a)(1)(B) can be the proper vehicle for bringing a challenge to, for example, a Swiss army knife not made in Switzerland, Black Hills gold jewelry that is not made in the Black Hills, or Scotch whiskey not manufactured in Scotland. But that subsection is not the right vehicle for addressing claims of false designation of origin that are not concerned specifically with geographic origin. [W]e conclude that the term 'geographic origin' refers solely to the place of origin and not to the creator, manufacturer, or any broader conception of the term 'origin.' *At 230 n.14:* To be clear, we are not opining that a mark must be a 'geographically distinctive trademark' before a manufacturer may be found liable for falsely advertising the geographic origin of its goods. ... We only hold that the term 'geographic origin' must refer, at the very least, to the place of the origin of goods and that PARK'S FINEST does not meet that requirement. *At 230:* The elements of a false association trademark claim under the Lanham Act track the elements of a common law trademark infringement claim: a plaintiff must prove that '(1) the marks are valid and legally protectable; (2) the marks are owned by the plaintiff; and (3) the defendant's use of the marks to identify goods or services is likely to create confusion concerning the origin of the goods or services.' Even when those elements are satisfied, relief is limited in scope to where 'market penetration is significant enough to pose the real likelihood of confusion among the consumers in that area.' *At 231:* Trademarks based on the surname of a founder are not inherently distinctive. [¶] [P] was therefore required to demonstrate that the mark had secondary meaning at the time that [D] began to use the name PARK'S FINEST. ... In assessing secondary meaning, we have relied on the following factors, to the extent relevant: '(1) the extent of sales and advertising leading to buyer association; (2) length of use; (3) exclusivity of use; (4) the fact of copying; (5) customer surveys; (6) customer testimony; (7) the use of the mark in trade journals; (8) the size of the company; (9) the number of sales; (10) the number of customers; and, (11) actual confusion.' [¶] Secondary meaning is generally 'established through extensive advertising which creates in the minds of consumers an association between the mark and the provider of the [products or] services advertised under the mark.' Use of a mark 'for a long period of time in a prevalent advertising campaign' can 'create a reasonable inference' of secondary meaning. *At 232:* Merely proving length and exclusivity of use does not prove widespread familiarity."

International Info. Sys. Sec. Certification Consortium, Inc. v. Security Univ., LLC, 823 F.3d 153, 160 (2d Cir.2016). "To prevail on a claim of certification mark infringement, 'a plaintiff must show, first, that its mark merits protection, and, second, that the defendant's use of a similar mark is likely to cause consumer confusion.' *At 163:* There are numerous ways in which a certification mark can be infringed. Two of the most well-established '[e]xamples of infringement of a certification mark are: the use of the mark in a resume of a professional who is in fact not certified by the organization that is the owner of the mark; and the use of the mark on goods that have not in fact been certified.' In addition, it is clear that a competing certifier may infringe a certification mark by using a certification mark confusingly similar to the certification mark of another certifying body. *At 164:* [A]lthough a person who is not certified can infringe a certification mark by engaging in unlicensed use of the mark, this is not the only manner of misusing a certification mark that is cognizable in an infringement suit."

Crystal Entm't & Filmworks, Inc. v. Jurado, 643 F.3d 1313, 1320 (11th Cir.2011). "To establish a prima facie case under [Lanham Act] §43(a) [15 U.S.C. §1125], a plaintiff must show (1) that the plaintiff had enforceable rights in the mark or name, and (2) that the defendant made unauthorized use of it such that consumers were likely to confuse the two. *At 1321:* Common-law trademark rights are appropriated only through actual prior use in commerce. The use of a mark in commerce must be sufficient to establish *ownership rights* for a plaintiff to recover against subsequent users under §43(a). [P] bore the burden of proving its prior use. [¶] We have applied a two-part test to determine whether a party has proved prior use of a mark sufficient to establish ownership: Evidence showing, first, adoption, and, second, use in a way sufficiently public to identify or distinguish the marked goods in an appropriate segment of the public mind as those of the adopter of the mark. [¶] [T]rademark law permits a corporate entity to own the right to the name of a musical group, and the public need not associate the mark with the name of the corporate entity.... *At 1322:* Because [P] failed to prove that it first appropriated the ... mark, the district court was required to determine the owner of the mark where prior ownership by one of several claimants cannot be established. [This is] a case of joint endeavors. We have yet to address a trademark dispute of this type, but other courts have consistently resolved such disputes by awarding trademark rights to the claimant who controls the nature and quality of the services performed under the mark. [¶] [There is] a two-step approach in this circumstance: To determine ownership in a case of this kind, a court must first identify that quality or characteristic for which the group is known by the public. It then may proceed to the second step of the ownership inquiry, namely, who controls that quality or characteristic." (Internal quotes omitted.) *See also* ***1-800 Contacts, Inc. v. Lens.com, Inc.***, 722 F.3d 1229, 1238 (10th Cir.2013) (factors court considers to establish likelihood of confusion); ***Community of Christ Copyright Corp. v. Devon Park Restoration Branch of Jesus Christ's Ch.***, 634 F.3d 1005, 1009 (8th Cir.2011) (same); ***In re Polar Music Int'l***, 714 F.2d 1567, 1571 (Fed.Cir.1983) (no need to associate mark with manufacturer).

Lamparello v. Falwell, 420 F.3d 309, 313 (4th Cir. 2005). "Both infringement and false designation of origin have five elements. To prevail under either cause of action, the trademark holder must prove: (1) that it possesses a mark; (2) that the opposing party used the mark; (3) that the opposing party's use of the mark occurred 'in commerce'; (4) that the opposing party used the mark in connection with the sale, offering for sale, distribution, or advertising of goods or services; and (5) that the opposing party used the mark in a manner likely to confuse consumers." (Internal quotes omitted.)

Virgin Enters. v. Nawab, 335 F.3d 141, 146 (2d Cir. 2003). "A claim of trademark infringement, whether brought under 15 U.S.C. §1114(1) [Lanham Act §32(1)] (for infringement of a registered mark) or 15 U.S.C. §1125(a) [Lanham Act §43(a)] (for infringement of rights in a mark acquired by use), is analyzed under the familiar two-prong test described in ***Gruner + Jahr USA Publ'g v. Meredith Corp.***, 991 F.2d 1072 (2d Cir.1993). The test looks first to whether the plaintiff's mark is entitled to protection, and second to whether defendant's use of the mark is likely to cause consumers confusion as to the origin or sponsorship of the defendant's goods." *See also* ***Tana v. Dantanna's***, 611 F.3d 767, 773 (11th Cir.2010).

§1125(a)(1)—Possible Causes of Action

Brown v. Electronic Arts, Inc., 724 F.3d 1235, 1239 (9th Cir.2013). "Although claims under [Lanham Act] §43(a) [15 U.S.C. §1125(a)] generally relate to the use of trademarks or trade dress to cause consumer confusion over affiliation or endorsement, we have held that claims can also be brought under §43(a) relating to the use of a public figure's persona, likeness, or other uniquely distinguishing characteristic to cause such confusion."

Schlotzsky's, Ltd. v. Sterling Purchasing & Nat'l Distrib., 520 F.3d 393, 399-400 (5th Cir.2008). "[P's] claim is that [D] damaged its goodwill and profited by misrepresenting that it was solely authorized to act on behalf of the franchisor in relevant respects. [D's] action threatened the goodwill of [P's] brand with suppliers, some of whom already had the authority to manufacture and distribute [P's] products. It caused confusion with franchisees concerning the details of the association [D] had with [P]. As middleman between suppliers and franchisees, [D] deceptively used [P's] brand name in an effort to further [D's] position in the marketplace. These actions violate the prohibition against representations of fact that are 'likely to cause confusion, or to cause mistake, or to deceive as to the affiliation, connection, or association of such person with another….' [¶] The reach of [Lanham Act] §43(a) [15 U.S.C. §1125(a)] is sufficient to encompass [D's] deceptions." *See also* ***Gnesys, Inc. v. Greene***, 437 F.3d 482, 488-89 (6th Cir.2005) (§1125(a) concerns false representation by those engaged in commerce and is clearly not limited to trademark issues); ***Empresa Cubana del Tabaco v. Culbro Corp.***, 399 F.3d 462, 478 (2d Cir.2005) (§1125(a) includes causes of action grounded in allegations of false or misleading description or representation of fact).

Sybersound Records, Inc. v. UAV Corp., 517 F.3d 1137, 1141 (9th Cir.2008). "In this appeal, we determine whether a party lacking standing to bring a copyright infringement suit under the Copyright Act, but who complains of competitive injury stemming from acts of alleged infringement, may bring a Lanham Act claim, Racketeer Influenced and Corrupt Organizations Act (RICO) claim, or related state law unfair competition claims, whose successful prosecution would require the litigation of the underlying infringement claim. We hold that it cannot."

§1125(a)(1)—Protectability of Mark

Tana v. Dantanna's, 611 F.3d 767, 773 (11th Cir. 2010). "To satisfy the first element of [Lanham Act] §43(a) [15 U.S.C. §1125(a)]—proof of a valid trademark—a plaintiff need not have a registered mark. We have recognized that 'the use of another's unregistered, i.e., common law, trademark can constitute a violation of §43(a) where the alleged unregistered trademarks used by the plaintiff are so associated with its goods that the use of the same or similar marks by another company constitutes a false representation that its goods came from the same source.' However, only those marks that are capable of distinguishing the owner's goods from those of others, i.e., that are sufficiently 'distinctive,' are eligible for federal registration or protection as common law marks under the Lanham Act. *At 774:* Our circuit recognizes four categories of distinctiveness, listed in ascending order of strength: '(1) generic—marks that suggest the basic nature of the product or service; (2) descriptive—marks that identify the characteristic or quality of a product or service; (3) suggestive—marks that suggest characteristics of the product or service and require an effort of the imagination by the consumer in order to be understood as descriptive; and (4) arbitrary or fanciful—marks that bear no relationship to the product or service, and the strongest category of trademarks.' Suggestive and arbitrary or fanciful marks are deemed 'inherently distinctive' because 'their intrinsic nature serves to identify a particular source of a product' and are generally entitled to trademark protection. Generic marks, on the other hand, are generally incapable of receiving trademark protection and may never be registered as trademarks under the Lanham Act. Descriptive marks, though not inherently distinctive, may become sufficiently distinctive to enjoy trademark protection by acquiring 'secondary meaning.' 'A name has acquired secondary meaning when the primary significance of the term in the minds of the consuming public is not the product but the producer.' [¶] 'Names—both surnames and first names—are regarded as descriptive terms and therefore one who claims federal trademark rights in a name must prove that the name has acquired a secondary meaning.'" *See also* ***Miller's Ale House, Inc. v. Boynton Carolina Ale House, LLC***, 702

F.3d 1312, 1317 (11th Cir.2012); ***Yellow Cab Co. v. Yellow Cab, Inc.***, 419 F.3d 925, 927 (9th Cir.2005). *But see* ***Amazing Spaces, Inc. v. Metro Mini Storage***, 608 F.3d 225, 243-45 (5th Cir.2010) (forsaking distinctiveness categories to analyze symbols and designs in favor of ***Seabrook Foods*** test).

Utah Lighthouse Ministry v. Foundation for Apologetic Info. & Research, 527 F.3d 1045, 1051 (10th Cir.2008). "The number of search engine hits, standing alone, is inadequate to demonstrate that consumers associate the mark with a particular product or producer, or perceive UTAH LIGHTHOUSE as a distinctive mark. [T]he number of search engine 'hits' would support [P's] claim of secondary meaning only if accompanied by some kind of evidence that the relevant market of consumers has visited the websites containing these hits."

Welding Servs. v. Forman, 509 F.3d 1351, 1359 (11th Cir.2007). "Abbreviations of generic words may become protectable if the party claiming protection for such an abbreviation shows that the abbreviation has a meaning distinct from the underlying words in the mind of the public."

Louis Vuitton Malletier v. Dooney & Bourke, Inc., 454 F.3d 108, 116 (2d Cir.2006). "Basic geometric shapes, basic letters, and single colors are not protectable as inherently distinctive. These symbols may be protected only upon a showing of secondary meaning. However, stylized letters or shapes are not basic, and are protectable when original within the relevant market." (Internal quotes omitted.)

Yellow Cab Co. v. Yellow Cab, Inc., 419 F.3d 925, 926 (9th Cir.2005). "[T]he burden of proof as to validity and protectability of an unregistered mark lies with the party claiming trademark protection. *At 927:* When a plaintiff pursues a trademark action involving a properly registered mark, that mark is presumed valid, and the burden of proving that the mark is generic rests upon the defendant. However, if the disputed term has not been federally registered, and the defendant asserts genericness as a defense, the burden shifts to the plaintiff to show that the mark is nongeneric. *At 930:* To determine whether a descriptive mark has secondary meaning, a finder of fact considers: '(1) whether actual purchasers of the product bearing the claimed trademark associate the trademark with the producer, (2) the degree and manner of advertising under the claimed trademark, (3) the length and manner of use of the claimed trademark, and (4) whether use of the claimed trademark has been exclusive.'"

§1125(a)(1)—Standing

Lexmark Int'l v. Static Control Components, Inc., ___ U.S. ___, 134 S.Ct. 1377, 1388 (2014). "[T]his case presents a straightforward question of statutory interpretation: Does the cause of action in [15 U.S.C.] §1125(a) [Lanham Act §43(a)] extend to plaintiffs [who claim to be damaged by a defendant's false advertising]? [¶] First, we presume that a statutory cause of action extends only to plaintiffs whose interests 'fall within the zone of interests protected by the law invoked.' *At 1390:* We … hold that to come within the zone of interests in a suit for false advertising under §1125(a), a plaintiff must allege an injury to a commercial interest in reputation or sales. A consumer who is hoodwinked into purchasing a disappointing product may well have an injury-in-fact cognizable under [U.S. Const.] Art. 3, but he cannot invoke the protection of the Lanham Act.… Even a business misled by a supplier into purchasing an inferior product is, like consumers generally, not under the Act's aegis. [¶] Second, we generally presume that a statutory cause of action is limited to plaintiffs whose injuries are proximately caused by violations of the statute. *At 1391:* We thus hold that a plaintiff suing under §1125(a) ordinarily must show economic or reputational injury flowing directly from the deception wrought by the defendant's advertising; and that that occurs when deception of consumers causes them to withhold trade from the plaintiff. That showing is generally not made when the deception produces injuries to a fellow commercial actor that in turn affect the plaintiff. For example, while a competitor who is forced out of business by a defendant's false advertising generally will be able to sue for its losses, the same is not true of the competitor's landlord, its electric company, and other commercial parties who suffer merely as a result of the competitor's 'inability to meet [its] financial obligations.' [¶] We hold instead that a direct application of the zone-of-interests test and the proximate-cause requirement supplies the relevant limits on who may sue. *At 1392:* It is … a mistake to infer that because the Lanham Act treats false advertising as a form of unfair competition, it can protect *only* the false-advertiser's direct competitors."

Editor's note: The Court goes on to dismiss the five-factor balancing test from ***Conte Bros. Auto., Inc. v. Quaker State-Slick 50, Inc.***, 165 F.3d 221 (3d Cir.1998), the direct-competitor test, and the reasonable-interest test for false-advertising standing.

Belmora LLC v. Bayer Consumer Care AG, 819 F.3d 697, 701 (4th Cir.2016). "In this unfair competition case, we consider whether the Lanham Act permits the owner of a foreign trademark and its sister company to pursue false association, false advertising, and trademark cancellation claims against the owner of the same mark in the U.S. *At 706:* [T]he plain language of [15 U.S.C. §1125(a), Lanham Act §43(a),] does not require that a plaintiff possess or have used a trademark in U.S. commerce as an element of the cause of action. Section [1125(a)] stands in sharp contrast to [15 U.S.C. §1114, Lanham Act §32], which is titled as and expressly addresses 'infringement.' *At 710:* [T]he Lanham Act's plain language contains no unstated requirement that a [§1125(a)] plaintiff have used a U.S. trademark in U.S. commerce to bring a Lanham Act unfair competition claim. [¶] As [P] is not barred from making a [§1125(a)] claim, the proper ***Lexmark*** inquiry is twofold. Did the alleged acts of unfair competition fall within the Lanham Act's protected zone of interests? And if so, did [P] plead proximate causation of a cognizable injury?"

Made in the USA Found. v. Phillips Foods, Inc., 365 F.3d 278, 281 (4th Cir.2004). "[A] consumer does not have standing under the Lanham Act to sue for false advertising."

§1125(a)(1)(A)—Generally

For more annotations on this topic, see 15 U.S.C. §1115, *§1115(b)(4)—Nominative Fair Use*, p. 86.

Dastar Corp. v. Twentieth Century Fox Film Corp., 539 U.S. 23, 37 (2003). "[T]he phrase ['origin of the goods'] refers to the producer of the tangible goods that are offered for sale, and not to the author of any idea, concept, or communication embodied in those goods."

Gensler v. Strabala, 764 F.3d 735, 736 (7th Cir. 2014). "The district court read ***Dastar Corp. v. Twentieth Century Fox Film Corp.***, 539 U.S. 23 … (2003), to limit [Lanham Act] §43(a) [15 U.S.C. §1125(a)] to false designations of goods' origin—and since [P's] claim concerns services rather than goods, the court held that [P] cannot invoke the Lanham Act. That conclusion misreads ***Dastar***. True enough, it held that the absence of a false or misleading designation of goods' origin nixed a Lanham Act claim, but that was because the suit involved only goods. The Supreme Court did not read 'services' out of the Lanham Act. Nor did it hold that a false claim of origin is the only way to violate §43(a). *At 737:* [P] contends [D] made a 'false or misleading representation of fact' (his role in designing the five buildings) that is 'likely to … deceive as to the … connection[] or association of such person [D] with another person [P]' and to deceive clients about the 'origin' of the designs. Nothing in ***Dastar*** forecloses such a claim."

Optimum Techs. v. Henkel Consumer Adhesives, Inc., 496 F.3d 1231, 1248 (11th Cir.2007). "[A] passing off claim requires a showing that the defendant falsely represented that the plaintiff was the 'source' of the goods when it was not, that is, that it falsely suggested that the plaintiff was 'the producer of the tangible product sold in the marketplace.'"

ITC Ltd. v. Punchgini, Inc., 482 F.3d 135, 154 (2d Cir.2007). "To succeed on a [§1125(a)(1)(A)] claim, a plaintiff must prove (1) that the mark or dress is distinctive as to the source of the good or service at issue, and (2) that there is the likelihood of confusion between the plaintiff's good or service and that of the defendant. Preliminary to making this showing, however, a plaintiff must demonstrate its own right to use the mark or dress in question. [¶] To clear this hurdle, [P] invokes the famous marks doctrine. [¶] To explain why we disagree, we begin by discussing the principle of trademark territoriality. *At 155-56:* Precisely because a trademark has a separate legal existence under each country's laws, ownership of a mark in one country does not automatically confer upon the owner the exclusive right to use that mark in another country. Rather, a mark owner must take the proper steps to ensure that its rights to that mark are recognized in any country in which it seeks to assert them. [¶] The territoriality principle requires [prior] use to be in the U.S. for the owner to assert priority rights to the mark under the Lanham Act. Thus, absent some use of its mark in the U.S., a foreign mark holder generally may not assert priority rights under federal law, even if a U.S. competitor has knowingly appropriated that mark for his own use. [¶] [P] urges us to recognize an exception to the territoriality principle for those foreign marks that, even if not used in the U.S. by their owners, have achieved a certain measure of fame within this country. *At 159:* To date, the Ninth Circuit Court of Appeals is the only federal appeals court to have recognized the famous marks doctrine as a matter of federal law." Held: The famous-marks doctrine is not an exception to trademark territoriality. *See also* ***H-D Mich., Inc. v. Top Quality Serv.***, 496 F.3d 755, 759 (7th Cir.2007).

Pebble Beach Co. v. Tour 18 I Ltd., 155 F.3d 526, 545-46 (5th Cir.1998), *overruled on other grounds*, ***TrafFix Devices, Inc. v. Marketing Displays, Inc.***, 532 U.S. 23 (2001). "[O]ne who has lawfully copied another's product can tell the public what he has copied. ... This right to use a mark to identify the markholder's products—a nominative use—however, is limited in that the use cannot be one that creates a likelihood of confusion as to source, sponsorship, affiliation, or approval. [¶] [W]here a nominative use of a mark occurs without any implication of affiliation, sponsorship, or endorsement—i.e., a likelihood of confusion—the use 'lies outside the strictures of trademark law.' In order to avail itself of the shield of nominative use, the defendant (1) may only use so much of the mark as necessary to identify the product or service and (2) may not do anything that suggests affiliation, sponsorship, or endorsement by the markholder. By definition, the defendant cannot use the mark to identify its goods because this would not be a nominative use, and it would also suggest affiliation, sponsorship, or endorsement." *But see* ***Health Grades, Inc. v. Robert Wood Johnson Univ. Hosp., Inc.***, 634 F.Supp.2d 1226, 1241 (D.Colo. 2009) (most circuits consider nominative fair use in the multifactor likelihood-of-confusion analysis rather than in a separate test).

Waits v. Frito-Lay, Inc., 978 F.2d 1093, 1107 (9th Cir.1992), *overruled on other grounds*, ***Lexmark Int'l v. Static Control Components, Inc.***, ___ U.S. ___, 134 S.Ct. 1377 (2014). "[W]e read the amended language [of 15 U.S.C. §1125(a), Lanham Act §43(a),] to codify case law interpreting §43(a) to encompass false endorsement claims. Section 43(a) now expressly prohibits, *inter alia*, the use of any symbol or device which is likely to deceive consumers as to the association, sponsorship, or approval of goods or services by another person."

Moser Pilon Nelson Architects, LLC v. HNTB Corp., 80 U.S.P.Q.2d 1085, 1095 (D.Conn.2006). "[C]opying of creative content like [architectural plans] is not protected by the 'origin of work' provision of the Lanham Act, which covers only 'the producer of the tangible goods that are offered for sale, and not ... the author of any idea, concept, or communication embodied in those goods.' ... It appears to the Court that ***Dastar*** [***v. Twentieth Century Fox Film Corp.***, 539 U.S. 23 (2003),] applies with equal force to architectural works and that [Ps'] claim under the Lanham Act therefore fails. [¶] [Ps'] claim under the Lanham Act is preempted by the Copyright Act...." *See also* ***Beckwith Builders, Inc. v. Depietri***, 81 U.S.P.Q.2d 1302, 1307 (D.N.H.2006).

Curcio Webb LLC v. National Benefit Programs Agency, Inc., 79 U.S.P.Q.2d 1119, 1126-27 (S.D.Ohio 2006). Held: P, an employee-benefits consultant, developed a "Request for Proposal" (RFP) for a customer's employee-benefits program that contained confidential information and a notice of confidentiality. After the RFP was sent to service providers for bids, one of them, D, used the RFP as its own and changed P's e-mail address, but failed to change the embedded code, which resulted in D's completed forms being sent to P. There was no likelihood of confusion under §1125(a) because the presence of one e-mail address in a multi-page document would not cause likelihood of confusion given the sophistication of the customers involved.

§1125(a)(1)(A)—Expressive Works

Twentieth Century Fox TV v. Empire Distrib., 875 F.3d 1192, 1196-97 (9th Cir.2017). "In general, claims of trademark infringement under the Lanham Act are governed by a likelihood-of-confusion test. When the allegedly infringing use is in the title of an expressive work, however, we instead apply a test developed by the Second Circuit in ***Rogers v. Grimaldi***, 875 F.2d 994 (2d Cir.1989), to determine whether the Lanham Act applies. [¶] Under the ***Rogers*** test, the title of an expressive work does not violate the Lanham Act unless the title has no artistic relevance to the underlying work whatsoever, or, if it has some artistic relevance, unless the title explicitly misleads as to the source or the content of the work. We have extended this test from titles to allegedly infringing uses within the body of an expressive work. [¶] Although it is true that ... promotional efforts technically fall outside the title or body of an expressive work, it requires only a minor logical extension of the reasoning of ***Rogers*** to hold that works protected under its test may be advertised and marketed by name, and we so hold. *At 1199:* This is how a work fails the first prong of the ***Rogers*** test: by bearing a title which has no artistic relevance to the work. A title may have artistic relevance by linking the work to another mark, as with 'Barbie Girl,' or it may have artistic relevance by supporting the themes and geographic setting of the work, as with *Empire*. Reference to another work may be a component of artistic relevance, but it is not a prerequisite. Accordingly, the relevance of the word 'empire' to [P's] expressive work is sufficient to satisfy the first prong of the ***Rogers*** test. [¶] If the use of a mark is artistically relevant to the underlying work, the Lanham Act does not apply unless the title explicitly misleads as to the source or the content of the work. [¶] To fail the second prong of the ***Rogers*** test, it is key that the creator must *explicitly* mislead consumers. We must ask not only about the likelihood of consumer confusion but also whether there was an explicit indication, overt claim, or explicit misstatement that caused such consumer confusion. As the use of a mark alone is not enough to satisfy this prong of the ***Rogers*** test, [P's] *Empire* show, which contains no overt claims or explicit references to Empire Distribution, is not explicitly misleading, and it satisfies the second ***Rogers*** prong." (Internal quotes omitted.) *See also* ***Bosley Med. Inst. v. Kremer***, 403 F.3d 672, 676-77 (9th Cir.2005).

§1125(a)(1)(A)—False Endorsement

Fifty-Six Hope Road Music, Ltd. v. A.V.E.L.A., Inc., 778 F.3d 1059, 1067 (9th Cir.2015). "This case presents a question that is familiar in our circuit: when does the use of a celebrity's likeness or persona in connection with a product constitute false endorsement that is actionable under the Lanham Act? We conclude that the evidence presented at trial was sufficient for a jury to find [Ds] violated the Lanham Act by using [celebrity's] likeness. Our narrow holding relies on the familiar principles that underlie celebrity false endorsement claims, and we reject [Ds'] contention that the application of those principles results in a federal right of publicity. *At 1068:* Our jurisprudence recognizes a [15 U.S.C.] §1125(a) [Lanham Act §43(a)] claim for misuse of a celebrity's persona. '[A] celebrity whose endorsement of a product is implied through the imitation of a distinctive attribute of the celebrity's identity, has standing to sue for false endorsement under §43(a) of the Lanham Act.' *At 1072:* [Ds] argue that the ... §1125(a) claim fails, because [celebrity's] image needed to have been used in connection with a separate product or service to constitute an 'endorsement.' As [Ps] point out, the statute does not mention 'endorsement.' Rather, we commonly call §1125(a) claims 'false endorsement claims' because they often involve likelihood of confusion as to a plaintiff's 'sponsorship or approval' of the defendant's product. [¶] Rather than the lack of the word 'endorsement,' it is the statutory phrase referring to a defendant's use of the mark '*on* ... any goods[ ]' ... that requires us to reject [Ds'] argument. The 'goods' in the phrase 'on any goods' refers to the goods consumers may mistakenly think are approved by the owner of the mark. Thus, the plain text of the statute establishes that a viable false endorsement claim does not require that the mark be used *in connection* with separate goods to promote the purchase of those separate goods—but may be used directly *on* the defendant's goods. [¶] Here, the fact that [celebrity's] image appears directly on [Ds'] merchandise does not preclude relief under §1125(a). Instead, as in any §1125(a) claim, the particular use and placement of the mark is probative of likelihood of confusion. [T]he jury found [Ds'] use was likely to confuse, and we may not disturb that finding."

Facenda v. NFL Films, Inc., 542 F.3d 1007, 1014 (3d Cir.2008). "To prove a violation of [Lanham Act] §43(a)(1)(A) [15 U.S.C. §1125(a)(1)(A)] in a false endorsement case, a plaintiff must show that: (1) its mark is legally protectable; (2) it owns the mark; and (3) the defendant's use of the mark to identify its goods or services is likely to create confusion concerning the plaintiff's sponsorship or approval of those goods or services. *At 1014 n.3:* The phrase 'another person' in §43(a)(1)(A) indicates that Congress selected language broad enough to encompass a claim by a deceased celebrity's estate or by any celebrity's assignee. *At 1014:* [D] does not deny that courts broadly interpret the terms 'name, symbol, or device' in §43(a)(1) to include other indicia of identity, such as a person's voice. Nor does [D] deny that [P's] voice is distinctive and generally protectable as an unregistered mark. Thus, [P] has satisfied the first prong of a §43(a) claim. [D] also declines to contest the second prong—that the mark is owned by [P]. [¶] Our case thus focuses on the third prong: whether [D's] use of [P's] voice was likely to cause confusion among consumers by suggesting that [P] has an affiliation, connection, or association with [product] implying that [P] sponsors or approves of that product. *At 1015:* [D] argues that its production constitutes informational expression, artistic expression, or both, and is thus protected by the First Amendment. *At 1017:* [P] contends that the program is commercial speech, and we agree. Our Court has three factors to consider in deciding whether speech is commercial: (1) is the speech an advertisement; (2) does the speech refer to a specific product or service; and (3) does the speaker have an economic motivation for the speech. An affirmative answer to all three questions provides strong support for the conclusion that the speech is commercial. This inquiry involves making a commonsense distinction between speech proposing a commercial transaction and other varieties of speech. *At 1019:* Our Court evaluates §43(a)(1)(A) claims under the ten-factor test outlined in ***Interpace Corp. v. Lapp, Inc.***, 721 F.2d 460 (3d Cir.1983).... We subsequently adapted ***Lapp*** slightly to accommodate cases involving either directly competing or non-competing goods. Applying ***Lapp***, we consider the following ten factors: (1) the degree of similarity between the owner's mark and the alleged infringing mark; (2) the strength of the owner's mark; (3) the price of the goods and other factors indicative of the care and attention expected of consumers when making a purchase; (4) the length of time the defendant has used the mark without evidence of actual confusion arising; (5) the intent of the defendant in adopting the mark; (6) the evidence of actual confusion; (7) whether the goods, competing or not competing, are marketed through the same channels of trade and advertised through the same media; (8) the extent to which the targets of the parties' sales efforts are the same; (9) the relationship of the goods in the minds of consumers, whether because of the near-identity of the products, the similarity of function, or other factors; and (10) other facts suggesting that the consuming public might expect the prior owner to manufacture both products, or expect the prior owner to manufacture a product in the defendant's market, or expect that the prior owner is likely to expand into the defendant's market. [¶] [T]he District Court concluded that under §43(a)(1)(A) the traditional ***Lapp*** factors apply in a modified form specifically crafted for false-endorsement cases by the Ninth Circuit Court of Appeals: (1) the level of recognition that the plaintiff has among the segment of the society for whom the defendant's product is intended; (2) the relatedness of the fame or success of the plaintiff to the defendant's product; (3) the similarity of the likeness used by the defendant to the actual plaintiff; (4) evidence of actual confusion; (5) marketing channels used; (6) likely degree of purchaser care; (7) defendant's intent [in] selecting the plaintiff; and (8) likelihood of expansion of the product lines. *At 1020:* We substantially agree with the District Court's approach to tailoring the ***Lapp*** factors.... [W]e modify the fourth [modified] factor ... by adding the words 'and the length of time the defendant employed the allegedly infringing work before any evidence of actual confusion arose.' This accounts for the fourth ***Lapp*** factor.... Otherwise, we hold that the [modified] factors retain the substance of ***Lapp*** while appropriately tailoring the language to false endorsement claims. *At 1024:* [L]ikelihood of confusion is a question of fact." (Internal quotes omitted.)

§1125(a)(1)(A)—Likelihood of Confusion—Generally

For more annotations on this topic, see 15 U.S.C. §1052(d), *§1052(d)—Likelihood of Confusion*, p. 15, and 15 U.S.C. §1114(1), *§1114(1)—Likelihood of Confusion—Generally*, p. 68.

Hensley Mfg. v. ProPride, Inc., 579 F.3d 603, 610 (6th Cir.2009). "[T]he likelihood of confusion analysis ... involves a preliminary question: whether the defendants are using the challenged mark in a way that identifies the source of their goods. If they are not, then the mark is being used in a non-trademark way and trademark infringement laws, along with the eight-factor analysis, do not even apply." (Internal quotes omitted.) *But see* ***Kelly-Brown v. Winfrey***, 717 F.3d 295, 307-08 (2d Cir.2013) (declining to adopt Sixth Circuit's threshold requirement that allegedly infringing content is being used "as a mark" before applying likelihood-of-confusion test; instead, finding that test applies as long as mark is actually used).

Audi AG v. D'Amato, 469 F.3d 534, 542 (6th Cir. 2006). "[W]e use the same test to decide whether there has been trademark infringement, unfair competition, or false designation of origin: the likelihood of confusion between the two marks. [D] argues that the district court's finding of a likelihood of confusion should be reversed because [P] did not offer evidence demonstrating *actual* confusion. However, although proof that the buying public was actually deceived is necessary in order to recover *statutory damages* under the Lanham Act, only a 'likelihood of confusion' must be shown in order to obtain *equitable relief*, which is at issue in this appeal." *But see* ***Masters v. UHS of Del., Inc.***, 631 F.3d 464, 472 (8th Cir.2011) (proof of actual confusion is not necessary to recover monetary relief, e.g., profits).

Freedom Card, Inc. v. JPMorgan Chase & Co., 432 F.3d 463, 470-71 (3d Cir.2005). "In deciding whether similar marks create a likelihood of confusion, we have adopted a non-exhaustive test using ten factors that have come to be known as the '*Lapp* factors,' for determining the likelihood of confusion between two marks where direct confusion is alleged. Pursuant to that analysis, we examine: (1) the degree of similarity between the owner's mark and the alleged infringing mark; (2) the strength of the owner's mark; (3) the price of the goods and other factors indicative of the care and attention expected of consumers when making a purchase; (4) the length of time the defendant has used the mark without evidence of actual confusion arising; (5) the intent of the defendant in adopting the mark; (6) the evidence of actual confusion; (7) whether the goods, though not competing, are marketed through the same channels of trade and advertised through the same media; (8) the extent to which the targets of the parties' sales efforts are the same; (9) the relationship of the goods in the minds of consumers because of the similarity of function; (10) other factors suggesting that the consuming public might expect the prior owner to manufacture a product in the defendant's market, or that he is likely to expand into that market. [T]he *Lapp* factors should be used for both competing and non-competing goods. '[T]he *Lapp* test is a qualitative inquiry. Not all factors will be relevant in all cases; further, the different factors may properly be accorded different weights depending on the particular factual setting. A district court should utilize the factors that seem appropriate to a given situation.'" *See also* ***John Allan Co. v. Craig Allen Co.***, 540 F.3d 1133, 1138 (10th Cir.2008) (six factors); ***Paulsson Geophysical Servs. v. Sigmar***, 529 F.3d 303, 310 (5th Cir.2008) (eight factors); ***Welding Servs. v. Forman***, 509 F.3d 1351, 1360 (11th Cir.2007) (seven factors); ***Custom Mfg. & Eng'g v. Midway Servs.***, 508 F.3d 641, 648 (11th Cir.2007) (same); ***Louis Vuitton Malletier v. Dooney & Bourke, Inc.***, 454 F.3d 108, 116 (2d Cir. 2006) (eight factors); ***Davis v. Walt Disney Co.***, 430 F.3d 901, 903 (8th Cir.2005) (six factors); ***M2 Software, Inc. v. Madacy Entm't***, 421 F.3d 1073, 1080 (9th Cir.2005) (eight factors); ***Lamparello v. Falwell***, 420 F.3d 309, 315 (4th Cir.2005) (seven factors); ***Beacon Mut. Ins. v. OneBeacon Ins.***, 376 F.3d 8, 15 (1st Cir.2004) (eight factors); ***Holiday Inns, Inc. v. 800 Reservation, Inc.***, 86 F.3d 619, 623 (6th Cir.1996) (same).

Beacon Mut. Ins. v. OneBeacon Ins., 376 F.3d 8, 10 (1st Cir.2004). "We hold that the type of commercial injury actionable under [Lanham Act] §43(a) ..., 15 U.S.C. §1125(a), is not restricted to the loss of sales to actual and prospective buyers of the product in question. Confusion is relevant when it exists in the minds of persons in a position to influence the purchasing decision or persons whose confusion presents a significant risk to the sales, goodwill, or reputation of the trademark owner. This holding is consistent with our existing case law, under which post-sale confusion is actionable. We also hold that relevant commercial injury includes not only loss of sales but also harm to the trademark holder's goodwill and reputation. *At 16-17:* We also hold that the likelihood of confusion inquiry is not limited to actual or potential purchasers, but also includes others whose confusion threatens the trademark owner's commercial interest in its mark. Actual and potential customers of the trademark owner are the most obvious relevant persons, but other persons might be relevant if their confusion threatens the commercial interests of the owner of the mark. Relevant confusion among non-purchasers may well extend beyond the confusion of those persons positioned to influence directly the decisions of purchasers." (Internal quotes omitted.) *See also* ***Eli Lilly & Co. v. Natural Answers, Inc.***, 233 F.3d 456, 462 (7th Cir.2000).

Register.com, Inc. v. Verio, Inc., 356 F.3d 393, 441-42 (2d Cir.2004). A likelihood of confusion is "defined as a likelihood that an appreciable number of ordinarily prudent purchasers are likely to be misled, or indeed simply confused, as to the source of the goods in question, or ... confusion as to plaintiff's sponsorship or endorsement of the defendant's goods or services." (Internal quotes omitted.)

People for the Ethical Treatment of Animals v. Doughney, 263 F.3d 359, 366 (4th Cir.2001). D asserts parody as a defense to likelihood of confusion. "A 'parody' is defined as a 'simple form of entertainment conveyed by juxtaposing the irreverent representation of the trademark with the idealized image created by the mark's owner.' A parody must 'convey two simultaneous—and contradictory—messages: that it is the original, but also that it is not the original and is instead a parody.' To the extent that an alleged parody conveys only the first message, 'it is not only a poor parody but also vulnerable under trademark law, since the customer will be confused.' While a parody necessarily must engender some initial confusion, an effective parody will diminish the risk of consumer confusion 'by conveying [only] just enough of the original design to allow the consumer to appreciate the point of parody.'"

§1125(a)(1)(A)—Likelihood of Confusion—Factor—Actual Confusion

Parks LLC v. Tyson Foods, Inc., 863 F.3d 220, 232-33 (3d Cir.2017). "There are two predominant formats of consumer surveys used in trademark litigation to show a likelihood of confusion. The first, the ***Ever-Ready*** survey, named after the case of ***Union Carbide Corp. v. Ever-Ready, Inc.***, 531 F.2d 366, 385-88 (7th Cir.1976), ... involves showing consumers only the potentially-infringing product and asking open-ended questions to determine whether they believe the product is associated with the senior mark. Even though that survey design is most helpful for illustrating a likelihood of confusion, it can also indicate secondary meaning by showing a high degree of familiarity with the senior mark. [¶] An ***Ever-Ready*** survey is usually employed by owners of commercially strong marks. Holders of weaker marks more frequently employ a ***Squirt*** survey, named after the type used in ***SquirtCo v. Seven-Up Co.***, 628 F.2d 1086, 1089 n.4 (8th Cir. 1980). ... In a ***Squirt*** survey, two products are placed side by side, often with other products that serve as controls, and participants are asked questions to determine if confusion exists as to the source of the products. Courts have sometimes criticized ***Squirt*** surveys for utilizing closed-ended questions that can lead participants to the desired answer. Nevertheless, a well-designed ***Squirt*** survey may show a likelihood of confusion. What it does not do or even purport to do, however, is prove secondary meaning."

Kibler v. Hall, 843 F.3d 1068, 1078 (6th Cir.2016). "Evidence of actual confusion is the strongest proof of likely confusion. So any such evidence favors the nonmovant. But the weight we give that evidence depends on the amount and type of confusion. On one end of the spectrum are persistent mistakes and confusion by actual customers. On the other are relatively few instances of confusion and inquiries rather than purchases. The analysis is, above all, contextual."

Oriental Fin. Grp. v. Cooperativa de Ahorro y Crédito Oriental, 832 F.3d 15, 30-31 (1st Cir.2016). "'Evidence of actual confusion is not invariably necessary to prove likelihood of confusion; on the other hand, absent evidence of actual confusion, when the marks have been in the same market, side by side, for a substantial period of time, there is a strong presumption that there is little likelihood of confusion.' We have said that a lack of evidence of actual confusion weighs against a finding of likely confusion when competing marks have competed in the same market for six years, ... four years, ... or as little as three and a half years...."

Fortune Dynamic, Inc. v. Victoria's Secret Stores Brand Mgmt., 618 F.3d 1025, 1036 (9th Cir. 2010). "[S]urvey evidence [used to prove actual confusion] should be admitted 'as long as [it is] conducted according to accepted principles and [is] relevant.' Furthermore, we have made clear that 'technical inadequacies' in a survey, 'including the format of the questions or the manner in which it was taken, bear on the weight of the evidence, not its admissibility.'" *See also* ***1-800 Contacts, Inc. v. Lens.com, Inc.***, 722 F.3d 1229, 1246 (10th Cir.2013).

Caliber Auto. Liquidators, Inc. v. Premier Chrysler, Jeep, Dodge, LLC, 605 F.3d 931, 936-37 (11th Cir.2010). "'[P]erhaps as important as ... the number of instances of confusion are the kinds of persons confused and degree of confusion. Short-lived confusion or confusion of individuals casually acquainted with a business is worthy of little weight while confusion of actual customers of a business is worthy of substantial weight.' [¶] We have specified that '[a]ctual *consumer* confusion is the best evidence of likelihood of confusion.' This circuit's caselaw makes plain that the consumers of the relevant product or service, especially the mark holder's customers, turn the key. All potential consumers of the relevant product or service, including middlemen, can inform the inquiry, and the ultimate consumers deserve special attention."

John Allan Co. v. Craig Allen Co., 540 F.3d 1133, 1140 (10th Cir.2008). "'Actual confusion in the marketplace is often considered the best of evidence of likelihood of confusion.' A plaintiff, however, 'need not set forth evidence of actual confusion to prevail in a trademark infringement action.' A court may disregard as *de minimis* isolated instances of actual confusion." *See also* ***Grubbs v. Sheakley Grp.***, 807 F.3d 785, 796 (6th Cir.2015); ***Sensient Techs. v. SensoryEffects Flavor Co.***, 613 F.3d 754, 768 (8th Cir.2010).

McNeil Nutritionals, LLC v. Heartland Sweeteners, LLC, 511 F.3d 350, 366 (3d Cir.2007). "[I]t takes very little evidence to establish the existence of the actual confusion factor ..., but a district court may weigh the [actual-confusion] factor in favor of a defendant when it concludes that the evidence of actual confusion was isolated and idiosyncratic. Further, as to those few customers who do not care about brands and do not pay any attention to them, such brand indifferent customers do not count in the equation of likelihood of confusion." (Internal quotes omitted.)

Frosty Treats, Inc. v. Sony Computer Entm't Am., Inc., 426 F.3d 1001, 1010 (8th Cir.2005). "'Confusion' means more than that the junior user's mark merely 'calls to mind' the senior user's mark. ... While the junior user's mark may call to mind the senior user's famous mark, this alone is not sufficient for a likelihood of confusion. The survey fails to address the relevant inquiry, which is whether consumers are confused as to existence of any sponsorship of or affiliation or association with [D's product] by [P]." (Internal quotes omitted.)

§1125(a)(1)(A)—Likelihood of Confusion—Factor—Consumer Sophistication

Kibler v. Hall, 843 F.3d 1068, 1080 (6th Cir.2016). "When consumers are more likely to exercise caution in purchasing items, they are less likely to confuse their origins. This happens when consumers have expertise in the items and when the items are particularly expensive."

Sensient Techs. v. SensoryEffects Flavor Co., 613 F.3d 754, 769 (8th Cir.2010). "This factor is 'more important in confusion-of-source cases where the degree of care that the purchaser exercises in purchasing a product can eliminate the confusion that might otherwise exist.'"

Star Indus. v. Bacardi & Co., 412 F.3d 373, 390 (2d Cir.2005). "Our analysis of consumer sophistication 'consider[s] the general impression of the ordinary purchaser, buying under the normally prevalent conditions of the market and giving the attention such purchasers usually give in buying that class of goods.' Consumer sophistication may be proved by direct evidence such as expert opinions or surveys. In addition, in some cases a court is entitled to reach a conclusion about consumer sophistication based solely on the nature of the product or its price."

Versa Prods. Co. v. Bifold Co., 50 F.3d 189, 204-05 (3d Cir.1995). "The following non-exhaustive considerations should guide a court's determination of the standard of ordinary care for a particular product. Inexpensive goods require consumers to exercise less care in their selection than expensive ones. The more important the use of a product, the more care that must be exercised in its selection. In addition, 'the degree of caution used ... depends on the relevant buying class. That is, some buyer classes, for example, professional buyers ... will be held to a higher standard of care than others. Where the buyer class consists of both professional buyers and consumers, ... the standard of care to be exercised by the reasonably prudent purchaser will be equal to that of the least sophisticated consumer in the class.'" *See also* ***Fortune Dynamic, Inc. v. Victoria's Secret Stores Brand Mgmt.***, 618 F.3d 1025, 1038 (9th Cir.2010); ***Xtreme Lashes, LLC v. Xtended Beauty, Inc.***, 576 F.3d 221, 231 (5th Cir.2009).

§1125(a)(1)(A)—Likelihood of Confusion—Factor—Defendant's Intent

Kibler v. Hall, 843 F.3d 1068, 1081 (6th Cir.2016). "This court may infer a likelihood of confusion from evidence that [D] chose its mark to confuse consumers about the source of the parties' products. The standard assumes that [D] itself believed that using the mark would divert business from [P]. Circumstantial evidence of intent is sufficient when direct evidence is unavailable (as it often is). And evidence that [D] knew of [P's] trademark while using its mark constitutes such circumstantial evidence."

Sensient Techs. v. SensoryEffects Flavor Co., 613 F.3d 754, 766 (8th Cir.2010). "While proof of bad intent is not required for success in an infringement or unfair competition claim, 'the absence of such intent is a factor to be considered.' 'Knowledge of another's product and an intent to compete with that product is not ... equivalent to an intent by a new entrant to a market to mislead and to cause consumer confusion.'"

Starbucks Corp. v. Wolfe's Borough Coffee, Inc., 588 F.3d 97, 117-18 (2d Cir.2009). "[T]he 'only relevant intent is intent to confuse. There is a considerable difference between an intent to copy and an intent to deceive.' Although deliberate copying may indicate that the defendant acted in bad faith, ... the District Court is not required to draw that inference where there is evidence to the contrary."

John Allan Co. v. Craig Allen Co., 540 F.3d 1133, 1139 (10th Cir.2008). "'Evidence that the alleged infringer chose a mark with the intent to copy, rather than randomly or by accident, typically supports an inference of likelihood of confusion.' The focus is on whether the defendant sought 'to derive benefit from the reputation or goodwill of the plaintiff.' *At 1139 n.4:* Evidence of intent to copy does not create a rebuttable presumption of likelihood of confusion, thereby shifting the burden to the defendant, as [P] argues. Instead, the intent of the alleged infringer remains but one factor in our analysis. A finding that the infringer intended to copy may lead to an inference of confusion, even a strong inference, but the inference is a permissive one." *See also* ***Grubbs v. Sheakley Grp.***, 807 F.3d 785, 797 (6th Cir.2015); ***Caliber Auto. Liquidators, Inc. v. Premier Chrysler, Jeep, Dodge, LLC***, 605 F.3d 931, 940 (11th Cir.2010).

Star Indus. v. Bacardi & Co., 412 F.3d 373, 388 (2d Cir.2005). "Bad faith generally refers to an attempt by a junior user of a mark to exploit the good will and reputation of a senior user by adopting the mark with the intent to sow confusion between the two companies' products. 'Selection of a mark that reflects the product's characteristics, request for a trademark search and reliance on the advice of counsel are factors that support a finding of good faith.' [¶] This Court has never held adoption of a mark with no knowledge of a prior similar mark to be in bad faith even in the total absence of a trademark search, much less on the basis of an allegedly flawed trademark search. Furthermore, in some cases even where a trademark search resulted in knowledge of the earlier mark, in the absence of additional evidence indicating an intent to promote confusion or exploit good will or reputation, this Court has found the junior user to be in good faith. *At 389:* Bad faith may be inferred from the junior user's actual or constructive knowledge of the senior user's mark."

§1125(a)(1)(A)—Likelihood of Confusion—Factor—Expansion of Product Line

Kibler v. Hall, 843 F.3d 1068, 1082 (6th Cir.2016). "A strong possibility that either party will expand its business to compete with the other's increases the likelihood of consumers confusing the sources of the parties' products. As with intent, a finding that neither party will expand its business is irrelevant in determining the likelihood of confusion." *See also* ***M2 Software, Inc. v. Madacy Entm't***, 421 F.3d 1073, 1085 (9th Cir. 2005).

§1125(a)(1)(A)—Likelihood of Confusion—Factor—Geographical Proximity

Tana v. Dantanna's, 611 F.3d 767, 780-81 (11th Cir. 2010). "Our circuit has recognized that 'new factors may merit consideration' in determining whether there is a likelihood of confusion. And our case law already establishes that geographic considerations may be relevant to the likelihood-of-confusion analysis, even where we have not articulated this consideration as a separate factor. [¶] Where the secondary meaning acquired by a descriptive mark dictates its strength and distinctiveness, ... the geographic remoteness of a mark's use may be relevant to the likelihood-of-confusion inquiry. Because [P] seeks to establish a likelihood of confusion with a restaurant in Atlanta, the geographically remote use of his mark in West Hollywood weighs against a finding of nationwide secondary meaning, leaving him with only a weak mark unlikely to cause a likelihood of confusion in Atlanta. [¶] Geographic considerations are also particularly relevant where a plaintiff holds only common-law trademark rights in a mark because it is well-established that the scope of protection accorded his mark is coextensive only with the territory throughout which it is known and from which it has drawn its trade. The owner of a registered mark, in contrast, enjoys the unlimited right to use the mark nationwide, and federal registration affords the registrant priority over all future users of confusingly similar marks. Therefore, a Lanham Act plaintiff asserting common-law trademark rights under [§1125(a)] against the owner of a registered mark ... bears the burden of establishing the right to use its mark by actual use in a given territory. And because registration constitutes constructive nationwide notice of the registrant's priority of use of a mark, ... only actual use occurring prior to such registration gives rise to enforceable common-law trademark rights.... Thus, federal registration has the practical effect of freezing a prior user's enforceable trademark rights thereby terminating any right to future expansion beyond the user's existing territory."

§1125(a)(1)(A)—Likelihood of Confusion—Factor—Marketing Channels

Kibler v. Hall, 843 F.3d 1068, 1079 (6th Cir.2016). "The marketing channels factor requires us to compare both how the parties market their products and their main customers. The more channels and buyers overlap, the greater the likelihood that relevant consumers will confuse the sources of the parties' products. The reverse is true too. [¶] Today, most parties advertise online. We consider the following in deciding whether certain online marketing could support a finding of likely confusion. First, do the parties use the internet as a substantial marketing channel? Second, are the parties' marks used with web-based products? Third, do the parties' marketing channels overlap in any other way? Only one case has conducted this analysis and there it was straightforward: the plaintiff did not produce web-based products or market them online."

Grubbs v. Sheakley Grp., 807 F.3d 785, 796 (6th Cir.2015). "This factor requires us to consider 'how and to whom the respective goods or services of the parties are sold.' In essence, this part of the test asks us to evaluate the similarity in the customers for the goods and services as well as in the 'marketing efforts' employed by each party."

§1125(a)(1)(A)—Likelihood of Confusion—Factor—Nonconsumer Confusion

Rearden LLC v. Rearden Commerce, Inc., 683 F.3d 1190, 1214 (9th Cir.2012). "[L]itigants usually satisfy the 'likelihood of confusion' test by providing direct evidence of consumer confusion. Nevertheless, we conclude that non-consumer confusion may also be relevant to the 'likelihood of confusion' inquiry in three specific and overlapping circumstances—namely where there is confusion on the part of: (1) potential consumers; (2) non-consumers whose confusion could create an inference that consumers are likely to be confused; and (3) non-consumers whose confusion could influence consumers. In all three instances, the non-consumer confusion bears a relationship to the existence of confusion on the part of consumers themselves. *At 1216:* Recognizing the potential relevance of non-consumer confusion accords with this Circuit's precedent, which reflects a flexible approach to assessing 'likelihood of confusion,' as embodied in the highly fact-specific [likelihood-of-confusion] analysis. In addition, it appears to be a matter of basic common sense to recognize the very real possibility that confusion on the part of at least certain non-consumers could either: (1) turn into actual consumer confusion (i.e., potential consumers); (2) serve as an adequate proxy or substitute for evidence of actual consumer confusion (i.e., non-consumers whose confusion could create an inference of consumer confusion); or (3) otherwise contribute to confusion on the part of the consumers themselves (i.e., non-consumers whose confusion could influence consumer perceptions and decision-making)."

§1125(a)(1)(A)—Likelihood of Confusion—Factor—Relatedness of Goods

Kibler v. Hall, 843 F.3d 1068, 1076-77 (6th Cir. 2016). "This court uses the following test to decide whether relatedness favors either party: (1) if the parties' products compete directly with each other, consumer confusion is likely if the parties' marks are sufficiently similar; (2) if the products are somewhat related, but do not compete directly, the likelihood of confusion will depend on other factors; (3) if the products are completely unrelated, confusion is unlikely. [¶] Products belonging to the same industry are not necessarily related. To be related, they must be marketed and consumed in ways that lead buyers to believe they come from the same source." *See also* ***M2 Software, Inc. v. Madacy Entm't***, 421 F.3d 1073, 1081-82 (9th Cir.2005).

Caliber Auto. Liquidators, Inc. v. Premier Chrysler, Jeep, Dodge, LLC, 605 F.3d 931, 939-40 (11th Cir.2010). "Analyzing the similarity of the products the marks represent 'requires a determination as to whether the products are the kind that the public attributes to a single source, not whether or not the purchasing public can readily distinguish between the products of the respective parties.'"

§1125(a)(1)(A)—Likelihood of Confusion—Factor—Similarity of Marks—Composite Marks

Sensient Techs. v. SensoryEffects Flavor Co., 613 F.3d 754, 764 (8th Cir.2010). "'Rather than consider the similarities between the component parts of the marks, we must evaluate the impression that each mark in its entirety is likely to have on a purchaser exercising the attention usually given by purchasers of such products.' 'The use of identical, even dominant, words in common does not automatically mean that two marks are similar.' 'We may consider the marks' visual, aural, and definitional attributes and compare the trade dress of the products in determining whether the total effect conveyed by the two marks is confusingly similar.' *At 765:* We have continually held the use of identical dominant words does not automatically equate to similarity between marks. [¶] [P] contends the visual appearance of the marks is irrelevant because the point of contact between the companies and the customers generally occurs via telephone, and thus the auditory similarities should be given priority. [P's] suggestion to place particular emphasis on the verbal effect of the marks is not without merit. However, we agree with the district court that the composite marks maintain a distinct auditory difference."

Xtreme Lashes, LLC v. Xtended Beauty, Inc., 576 F.3d 221, 228 (5th Cir.2009). "Mark similarity 'is determined by comparing the marks' appearance, sound, and meaning.' 'Similarity of appearance is determined on the basis of the total effect of the designation, rather than on a comparison of individual features.' Nevertheless, courts should give more attention to the dominant features of a mark. Even if two marks are distinguishable, we ask whether, under the circumstances of use, the marks are similar enough that a reasonable person could believe the two products have a common origin or association. To determine the 'meaning and connotation' of the marks, we consider the context of use, such as labels, packaging, and advertising. 'The two marks must bear some threshold resemblance in order to trigger inquiry into extrinsic factors, but this threshold is considerably lower than the degree of similarity required where the plaintiff presents little or no evidence on extrinsic factors supporting infringement.'" *See also* ***M2 Software, Inc. v. Madacy Entm't***, 421 F.3d 1073, 1082 (9th Cir.2005).

Boston Duck Tours, LP v. Super Duck Tours, LLC, 531 F.3d 1, 29 (1st Cir.2008). "As with word marks, when comparing design marks 'similarity is determined on the basis of the total effect of the designation, rather than a comparison of individual features.' Even if elements of each party's mark overlap, or are visually similar, the marks as a whole may still create a distinct commercial impression, especially if the similarities are limited to generic or descriptive elements. Further, the marks should be viewed 'sequentially [as if one were] in the context of the marketplace' rather than 'in a side-by-side comparison.'" *See also* ***Louis Vuitton Malletier v. Burlington Coat Factory Whs. Corp.***, 426 F.3d 532, 538-39 (2d Cir.2005).

§1125(a)(1)(A)—Likelihood of Confusion—Factor—Similarity of Marks—Word Marks

Kibler v. Hall, 843 F.3d 1068, 1077 (6th Cir.2016). "The more similar the marks are, the more likely it is that relevant consumers will confuse their sources. We determine the similarity of marks by considering whether either mark would confuse a consumer who did not have both marks before her and had only a vague impression of the other mark. We consider the marks' pronunciation, appearance, and verbal translation. [¶] The anti-dissection rule requires us not to dwell on the prominent features of a mark and instead consider it as a whole."

Oriental Fin. Grp. v. Cooperativa de Ahorro y Crédito Oriental, 832 F.3d 15, 28-29 (1st Cir.2016). "Where two marks share their most salient word, that fact weighs strongly in favor of similarity. The 'addition of a suggestive or descriptive element' to the dominant word in a mark 'is generally not sufficient to avoid confusion.' [¶] As further evidence of salience, the shared word ORIENTAL is the 'surname in Oriental's family of marks.' The family is 'a group of marks having a recognizable common characteristic, wherein the marks are composed and used in such a way that the public associates not only the individual marks, but the common characteristic of the family, with the trademark owner.' '[T]he purchasing public recognizes that the common characteristic,' the word ORIENTAL, 'is indicative of a common origin of the goods.' This public association between ORIENTAL and Oriental Group is further support for the proposition that ORIENTAL is the most salient, and the most source-identifying, element in the marks."

Fortune Dynamic, Inc. v. Victoria's Secret Stores Brand Mgmt., 618 F.3d 1025, 1031-32 (9th Cir. 2010). "Although some of the ***Sleekcraft*** factors will not always be helpful in assessing the likelihood of confusion, 'the similarity of the marks ... has always been considered a critical question in the likelihood-of-confusion analysis.' Three general principles help determine whether marks are similar. First, '[s]imilarity is best adjudged by appearance, sound, and meaning.' Second, the 'marks must be considered in their entirety and as they appear in the marketplace.' Third, 'similarities are weighed more heavily than differences.'"

Boston Duck Tours, LP v. Super Duck Tours, LLC, 531 F.3d 1, 24 (1st Cir.2008). "The degree of similarity between two marks ... is determined by analyzing their sight, sound, and meaning. Although 'similarity is determined on the basis of the total effect of the designation, rather than a comparison of individual features,' ... we give less weight to the generic portions of the parties' respective, composite marks. Accordingly, we compare 'the nongeneric components of a mark ... in the context of the overall composite mark.'" *See also*

Caliber Auto. Liquidators, Inc. v. Premier Chrysler, Jeep, Dodge, LLC, 605 F.3d 931, 939 (11th Cir.2010).

§1125(a)(1)(A)—Likelihood of Confusion—Factor—Similarity of Marks—Trade Dress

McNeil Nutritionals, LLC v. Heartland Sweeteners, LLC, 511 F.3d 350, 359-60 (3d Cir.2007). "'The proper test is not side-by-side comparison but whether the [trade dresses] create the same overall impression when viewed separately.' However, if buyers typically see the two products side-by-side, ... then a side-by-side comparison may be appropriate. [¶] [F]orceful and distinctive design features should be weighed more heavily because they are more likely to impact the overall impression regardless of whether they happen to be similarities or differences. [¶] Further, although it is legal error to engage in a 'detailed analysis of the differences in the marks rather than focusing on the overall impression created by them,' ... it likewise would be legal error to engage in a skewed analysis of the similarities in the trade dresses rather than focusing on the overall impressions they create. *At 361:* [W]e do not suggest that the prominent presence of another well-known mark is an affirmative defense to every trade dress infringement action. But this fact unquestionably plays a role in a district court's analysis of the [similarity-of-trade-dress] factor, such that it may cause the overall impressions created by two trade dresses to be different enough for [this] factor to be weighed in a defendant's favor. When it is relevant, district courts should consider this fact as part of its analysis of the degree of similarity ... as opposed to some sort of independent defense."

§1125(a)(1)(A)—Likelihood of Confusion—Factor—Strength of Mark

For more annotations on this topic, see 15 U.S.C. §1052, *Generally*, p. 10.

Kibler v. Hall, 843 F.3d 1068, 1073 (6th Cir.2016). "The stronger a mark is, the greater the risk of confusion. A mark cannot be strong unless it is both conceptually and commercially strong. And it cannot be conceptually strong unless it is inherently distinctive. *At 1074:* But a mark can be conceptually strong without being commercially strong, and thus weak under [***Frisch's Rest., Inc. v. Shoney's Inc.***, 759 F.2d 1261 (6th Cir.1985)]. A mark's commercial strength depends on public recognition, the extent to which people associate the mark with the product it announces. [¶] Survey evidence is not a prerequisite for establishing public recognition, but it is the most persuasive evidence of it. Proof of marketing is not a prerequisite either. But plaintiffs lacking such proof must provide other evidence of 'broad public recognition.' [¶] Conversely, proof that third parties have extensively used a trademark or similar trademarks in the relevant market indicates the trademark is commercially weak."

Fortune Dynamic, Inc. v. Victoria's Secret Stores Brand Mgmt., 618 F.3d 1025, 1032-34 (9th Cir. 2010). "A mark's conceptual strength depends largely on the obviousness of its connection to the good or service to which it refers. The less obvious the connection, the stronger the mark, and vice versa. Using a list originally formulated by Judge Friendly [in ***Abercrombie***,] marks are placed in one of five categories, ranging from weakest to strongest: generic, descriptive, suggestive, arbitrary, and fanciful.... At one end of the spectrum, generic marks 'refer[] to the genus of which the particular product is a species,' such as 'bread' or 'door,' and 'are not registerable' as trademarks. At the other end of the spectrum are arbitrary marks—actual words with no connection to the product—such as Apple computers and Camel cigarettes, and fanciful marks—made-up words with no discernable meaning—such as Kodak film and Sony electronics that are inherently distinctive and therefore receive 'maximum trademark protection.' In the middle are descriptive marks, which 'describe[] the qualities or characteristics of a good or service' and only receive protection if they acquire secondary meaning, ... and suggestive marks, which require a consumer to 'use imagination or any type of multistage reasoning to understand the mark's significance' and automatically receive protection.... [¶] Far from being neatly distinct and discrete, trademark categories often 'blur at the edges and merge together.' 'The labels are more advisory than definitional, more like guidelines than pigeonholes. Not surprisingly, they are somewhat difficult to articulate and to apply.' The line between descriptive and suggestive marks is nearly incapable of precise description. [¶] 'A suitable starting place' for attempting to draw the line between a suggestive and a descriptive mark 'is the dictionary.' With that in mind, two tests help distinguish between a descriptive and a suggestive mark. First, a mark is more likely suggestive if it passes the imagination test, which asks whether the mark 'requires a mental leap from the mark to the product.' '[T]he imagination test is [the] primary criterion for evaluating' whether a mark is suggestive. Second, a mark is more likely suggestive if it passes the competitor test, which asks whether 'the suggestion made by the mark is so remote and subtle that it is really not likely to be needed by competitive sellers to describe their goods.'" *See also* ***Sensient Techs. v. SensoryEffects Flavor Co.***, 613 F.3d 754, 763 (8th Cir.2010).

Lahoti v. Vericheck, Inc., 586 F.3d 1190, 1195 (9th Cir.2009). "[A] district court's classification of a trademark's strength is a factual determination to which we apply clear error review. *At 1196:* Under the clear error standard, we defer to the lower court's determination unless, based on the entire evidence, we are possessed of a definite and firm conviction that a mistake has been committed. [¶] When reviewing for clear error, we do not defer to a district court's categorization of a mark if its decision is based on incorrect law. Although we may affirm on any ground supported by the record, even if it differs from the district court's rationale, … where it is unclear whether the district court relied on proper law, we may vacate the judgment and remand with instructions to apply the correct legal standard." (Internal quotes omitted.)

Boston Duck Tours, LP v. Super Duck Tours, LLC, 531 F.3d 1, 16-17 (1st Cir.2008). "The district court was correct in analyzing both the conceptual and commercial strength of [P's] mark in this case. Although we have tended to focus our strength analysis on 'practical matters [related to a mark's perception in the marketplace] and not the legal classification of the mark,' … even going so far as to say that consideration of the inherent distinctiveness of a mark was 'a proposition [not] supported by any First Circuit case law and its logic is not apparent to us,' … the conceptual strength of the overall mark, and its components, is indeed relevant where a composite mark contains an arguably generic phrase. If we were to measure BOSTON DUCK TOURS' strength only on the basis of practical, commercial factors, we would risk affording greater protection to the mark than is warranted. Specifically, we would risk recognizing commercial strength that is the result of the descriptive force of the unprotectable generic element 'duck tours.' For this reason, our statement in ***Attrezzi**[, **LLC v. Maytag Corp.***, 436 F.3d 32 (1st Cir.2006),] where we determined the strength of a protectable, unitary mark, does not apply to this case. *At 17 n.19:* Genericism was the focus of the parties' arguments below and on appeal. We think that focus was appropriate. We respectfully disagree with the concurrence's reading of ***Attrezzi*** that would foreclose in all cases any consideration of genericism when evaluating the strength of a mark, composite or otherwise, as part of the likelihood of confusion analysis. *At 18-19:* In undertaking the genericism analysis, the court overlooked relevant evidence in the record on the genericism question. Tasked with determining the 'primary significance' of the phrase at issue 'to the relevant public,' the law instructs courts to consider several factors when undertaking this analysis: (1) consumer surveys; (2) the use of the term in media publications, (3) use of the term by competitors in the industry, (4) purchaser testimony concerning the term; and (5) the plaintiff's use of the term. … Although the presence or absence of a word in the dictionary, and its corresponding meaning(s), is evidence of how the public perceives a term, … it is only one of many factors to consider. The touchstone of the analysis remains the phrase's primary significance to the relevant public. [¶] In addition, the district court focused on the separate terms 'duck' and 'tours,' not the entire phrase. Rather than analyzing each word separately, thereby altering the context of the inquiry, the court should have considered 'duck tours' as a unified phrase. As courts have found in related contexts, a complete phrase may signify something different than the sum of its parts."

M2 Software, Inc. v. Madacy Entm't, 421 F.3d 1073, 1081 (9th Cir.2005). "A mark's overall strength is relative and cannot be determined by mechanistically assessing its conceptual or commercial strengths. Our court has previously recognized that a suggestive or descriptive mark, which is conceptually weak, can have its overall strength as a mark bolstered by its commercial success. But we have never held that an arbitrary or fanciful mark (i.e., a conceptually strong mark) can have its overall strength diminished by feeble commercial success. [A] lack of commercial strength cannot diminish the overall strength of a conceptually strong mark so as to render it undeserving of protection."

§1125(a)(1)(A)—Likelihood of Confusion—
Initial-Interest Confusion

For more annotations on this topic, see 15 U.S.C. §1114, *§1114(1)—Likelihood of Confusion—Initial-Interest Confusion*, p. 69.

Multi Time Mach., Inc. v. Amazon.com, Inc., 804 F.3d 930, 932 (9th Cir.2015). "[W]e must decide whether the following scenario constitutes trademark infringement: A customer goes online to [D's website] looking for a certain military-style wristwatch—specifically the 'MTM Special Ops'—marketed and manufactured by [P]. The customer types 'mtm special ops' in the search box and presses enter. Because [D] does not sell the MTM Special Ops watch, what the search produces is a list, with photographs, of several other brands of military style watches that [D] *does* carry, specifically identified by their brand names.... *At 933:* [P] contends that [D's] search results page creates a likelihood of confusion, even though there is no evidence of any actual confusion and even though the other brands are clearly identified by name. *At 937:* [T]he confusion is not caused by the design of the competitor's mark, but by the design of the web page that is displaying the competing mark and offering the competing products for sale. [T]he ultimate test for determining likelihood of confusion is whether a 'reasonably prudent consumer' in the marketplace is likely to be confused as to the origin of the goods. [T]he case will turn on the answers to the following two questions: (1) Who is the relevant reasonable consumer?; and (2) What would he reasonably believe based on what he saw on the screen? [¶] Turning to the first question, we have explained that the nature of the goods and the type of consumer is highly relevant to determining the likelihood of confusion in the keyword advertising context. In evaluating this factor, we consider the typical buyer exercising ordinary caution. Confusion is less likely where buyers exercise care and precision in their purchases, such as for expensive or sophisticated items. Moreover, the default degree of consumer care is becoming more heightened as the novelty of the Internet evaporates and online commerce becomes commonplace. [¶] The goods in the present case are expensive. ... Therefore, the relevant consumer in the present case is a reasonably prudent consumer accustomed to shopping online. [¶] Turning to the second question, ... the labeling and appearance of the products for sale on [D's] web page is the most important factor in this case ... because ... clear labeling can eliminate the likelihood of initial interest confusion in cases involving Internet search terms. Indeed, [P] itself argues: The common thread of [Ninth Circuit case law] is that liability under the Lanham Act can only be avoided as a matter of law where there is clear labeling to avoid the possibility of confusion—including initial interest confusion—resulting from the use of another's trademark. Thus, [P] agrees that summary judgment of its trademark claims is appropriate if there is clear labeling that avoids likely confusion. *At 938:* In light of the clear labeling [D] uses on its search results page, no reasonable trier of fact could conclude that [D's] search results page would likely confuse a reasonably prudent consumer accustomed to shopping online as to the source of the goods being offered." (Internal quotes omitted.)

McNeil Nutritionals, LLC v. Heartland Sweeteners, LLC, 511 F.3d 350, 358 (3d Cir.2007). "Whether a plaintiff alleges initial interest or point-of-sale confusion or both, a district court should employ the [likelihood-of-confusion] factors ... to decide whether there is a likelihood of confusion."

Australian Gold, Inc. v. Hatfield, 436 F.3d 1228, 1239-40 (10th Cir.2006). "[Ds] used [Ps'] trademarks on [Ds'] Web sites. [Ds] also placed [Ps'] trademarks in the metatags of [Ds'] Web sites. Further, [Ds] paid [search-engine marketing website] to list [Ds] in a preferred position whenever a computer user searched for [Ps'] trademarks. All of these actions were attempts to divert traffic to [Ds'] Web sites. [¶] We evaluate [Ps'] claim for initial interest confusion according to the six-prong test.... We look at (1) the degree of similarity between the marks; (2) the intent of the alleged infringer in adopting the mark; (3) evidence of actual confusion; (4) similarity of products and manner of marketing; (5) the degree of care likely to be exercised by purchasers; and (6) the strength or weakness of the marks. No one factor is dispositive, and likelihood of confusion is a question of fact. [¶] '[A] defendant's website disclaimer, proclaiming its real source and disavowing any connection with its competitor, cannot prevent damage of initial interest confusion, which will already have been done by the misdirection of consumers looking for [Ps'] websites.'"

Lamparello v. Falwell, 420 F.3d 309, 315-16 (4th Cir.2005). "[P] argues that he is entitled to prevail under the 'initial interest confusion' doctrine. This relatively new and sporadically applied doctrine holds that 'the Lanham Act forbids a competitor from luring potential customers away from a producer by initially passing off its goods as those of the producer's, even if confusion as to the source of the goods is dispelled by the time any sales are consummated.' *At 317:* Profiting financially from initial interest confusion is ... a key element for imposition of liability under this theory. When an alleged infringer does not compete with the markholder for sales, 'some initial confusion will not likely facilitate free riding on the goodwill of another mark, or otherwise harm the user claiming infringement. Where confusion has little or no meaningful effect in the marketplace, it is of little or no consequence in our analysis.'" Held: The Fourth Circuit has not adopted the initial-interest-confusion doctrine. Rather, the Fourth Circuit holds that to determine whether a likelihood of confusion exists as to the source of a gripe (website), a court must look not only to the allegedly infringing domain name, but also to the underlying content of the website. *See also* ***McNeil Nutritionals, LLC v. Heartland Sweeteners, LLC***, 511 F.3d 350, 357-58 (3d Cir.2007); ***Playboy Enters. v. Netscape Comms.***, 354 F.3d 1020, 1025 (9th Cir.2004); ***PACCAR Inc. v. TeleScan Techs.***, 319 F.3d 243, 253 (6th Cir.2003), *overruled on other grounds*, ***KP Permanent Make-Up, Inc. v. Lasting Impression I, Inc.***, 543 U.S. 111 (2004); ***Promatek Indus. v. Equitrac Corp.***, 300 F.3d 808, 812 (7th Cir.2002); ***Brookfield Comms. v. West Coast Entm't Corp.***, 174 F.3d 1036, 1055-56 (9th Cir. 1999).

§1125(a)(1)(A)—Likelihood of Confusion—Reverse Confusion

Syngenta Seeds, Inc. v. Delta Cotton Co-op., 457 F.3d 1269, 1277 (Fed.Cir.2006). "The Supreme Court has defined reverse passing off—also known as reverse palming off—as occurring when a person misrepresents someone else's goods or services as his own and has held that it is actionable under §1125(a). In order to recover on a Lanham Act claim for reverse palming off, a plaintiff must prove: (1) that the work at issue originated with the plaintiff; (2) that origin of the work was falsely designated by the defendant; (3) that the false designation of origin was likely to cause consumer confusion; and (4) that the plaintiff was harmed by the defendant's false designation of origin. *At 1277 n.3:* Reverse palming off exists in contradistinction to the palming off theory recognized by the Supreme Court ... in which a seller attempts to pass off his own goods as another's. *At 1278:* [T]he gravamen of the injury in a reverse passing off case is that the originator of the misidentified product is involuntarily deprived of the advertising value of its name and of the goodwill that otherwise would stem from public knowledge of the true source of the satisfactory product." (Internal quotes omitted.) *See also* ***Universal Furniture Int'l v. Collezione Europa USA, Inc.***, 618 F.3d 417, 438 (4th Cir.2010); ***Visible Sys. v. Unisys Corp.***, 551 F.3d 65, 72 (1st Cir.2008); ***Societe des Hotels Meridien v. Lasalle Hotel Oper. Prtshp.***, 380 F.3d 126, 131 (2d Cir.2004); ***General Univ'l Sys. v. Lee***, 379 F.3d 131, 148 n.41 (5th Cir.2004); ***John G. Danielson, Inc. v. Winchester-Conant Props., Inc.***, 322 F.3d 26, 45 (1st Cir.2003).

Freedom Card, Inc. v. JPMorgan Chase & Co., 432 F.3d 463, 470 (3d Cir.2005). "There are two types of 'likelihood of confusion' claims—'direct confusion' claims and 'reverse confusion' claims. [¶] The essence of a direct confusion claim is that a junior user of a mark attempts to free-ride on the reputation and goodwill of the senior user by adopting a similar or identical mark. *At 471:* 'Reverse confusion occurs when a larger, more powerful company uses the trademark of a smaller, less powerful senior owner and thereby causes likely confusion as to the source of the senior user's goods or services.' Thus, the 'junior' user is junior in time but senior in market dominance or size. [¶] In reverse confusion, the junior user saturates the market with a similar trademark and overwhelms the senior user. The public comes to assume the senior user's products are really the junior user's or that the former has become somehow connected to the latter. *At 472:* [I]n a typical case alleging reverse confusion, as in a case of direct confusion, a court should apply the ***Lapp*** factors in assessing likelihood of confusion. However, economic reality and common sense require that some of the ***Lapp*** factors be analyzed differently when reverse discrimination is at issue. Thus, the strength of the parties' marks[,] the intent in adopting the marks[,] and the evidence of actual confusion ... are analyzed differently from the method employed in a typical direct confusion case. *At 473-74:* '[I]n the typical case in which there is a claim of reverse confusion, a court should examine the following factors [in determining] whether or not there is a likelihood of confusion: (1) the degree of similarity between the owner's mark and the alleged infringing mark; (2) the strength of the two marks, weighing both a commercially strong junior user's mark and a conceptually strong senior user's mark in the senior user's favor; (3) the price of the goods and other factors indicative of the care and attention expected of consumers when making a purchase; (4) the length of time the defendant has used the mark without evidence of actual confusion arising; (5) the intent of the defendant in adopting the mark; (6) the evidence of actual confusion; (7) whether the goods, competing or not competing, are marketed through the same channels of trade and advertised through the same media; (8) the extent to which the targets of the parties' sales efforts are the same; (9) the relationship of the goods in the minds of consumers, whether because of the near-identity of the products, the similarity of function, or other factors; (10) other facts suggesting that the consuming public might expect the larger, more powerful company to manufacture both products, or expect the larger company to manufacture a product in the plaintiff's market, or expect that the larger company is likely to expand into the plaintiff's market. '[N]o one factor is dispositive.' The weight given each factor can vary with the circumstances of a particular case."

Bretford Mfg. v. Smith Sys. Mfg., 419 F.3d 576, 580 (7th Cir.2005). "[T]he Supreme Court said in ***Dastar [v. Twentieth Century Fox Film Corp.***, 539 U.S. 23 (2003),] that 'reverse passing off' can violate the Lanham Act if a misdescription of goods' origin causes commercial injury. *At 581:* [T]he right question [to ask in determining if there is confusion about a good's origin] is whether the consumer knows who has produced the finished product." Held: Although D used hardware from P's table in making a sample and then copied the design, there was no reverse passing off because, as far as the customer was concerned, the table's "origin" was D.

§1125(a)(1)(B)—False Advertising

POM Wonderful LLC v. Coca-Cola Co., ___ U.S. ___, 134 S.Ct. 2228, 2236 (2014). "This Court granted certiorari to consider whether a private party may bring a Lanham Act claim challenging a food label that is regulated by the FDCA [Food, Drug, and Cosmetic Act, 21 U.S.C. §§331, 343]. *At U.S. ___, S.Ct. 2241:* Congress did not intend the FDCA to preclude Lanham Act suits like [P's]." *See also* ***Church & Dwight Co. v. SPD Swiss Precision Diagnostics, GmbH***, 843 F.3d 48, 62-63 (2d Cir.2016) (labeling requirement of FDCA did not preclude Lanham Act claim because statutes serve different purposes).

Tobinick v. Novella, 848 F.3d 935, 950 (11th Cir. 2017). "Commercial advertising or promotion includes (1) commercial speech; (2) by a defendant who is in commercial competition with plaintiff; (3) for the purpose of influencing consumers to buy defendant's goods or services; and (4) the representations must be disseminated sufficiently to the relevant purchasing public to constitute 'advertising' or 'promotion' within that industry. [¶] Commercial speech is expression related solely to the economic interests of the speaker and its audience. The 'core notion' of commercial speech extends to speech that proposes a commercial transaction. The Supreme Court has identified three factors in looking beyond the core notion of commercial speech: (1) that the material was conceded to be advertisements, (2) it contained a reference to a specific product, and (3) the speaker has an economic motivation for distributing the material. No one factor is dispositive. The combination of all three characteristics, however, provides strong support for the conclusion that the material is properly characterized as commercial speech. But, speech is not rendered commercial by the mere fact that it relates to an advertisement. *At 952:* [M]agazines and newspapers often have commercial purposes, but those purposes do not convert the individual articles within these editorial sources into commercial speech subject to Lanham Act liability." (Internal quotes omitted.) *See also* ***Newcal Indus. v. Ikon Office Solution***, 513 F.3d 1038, 1054 (9th Cir.2008); ***Proctor & Gamble Co. v. Haugen***, 222 F.3d 1262, 1273-74 (10th Cir.2000). *But see* ***Grubbs v. Sheakley Grp.***, this page.

Grubbs v. Sheakley Grp., 807 F.3d 785, 798 (6th Cir.2015). "This Court has established a five-part test for establishing a false advertising claim: (1) the defendant has made false or misleading statements of fact concerning his own product or another's; (2) the statement actually deceives or tends to deceive a substantial portion of the intended audience; (3) the statement is material in that it will likely influence the deceived consumer's purchasing decisions; (4) the advertisements were introduced into interstate commerce; (5) there is some causal link between the challenged statements and harm to the plaintiff. The statements need not have appeared in a format resembling traditional advertising. [¶] [T]he court below used a different test first developed by the Southern District of New York in ***Gordon & Breach Sci. Publ'rs S.A. v. Am. Inst. of Physics***, 859 F.Supp. 1521, 1536 (S.D.N.Y.1994), which is employed in many other circuits to determine whether a statement is made in 'commercial advertising or promotion.' The statement must be: (1) commercial speech; (2) by a defendant who is in commercial competition with the plaintiff; (3) for the purpose of influencing customers to buy the defendant's goods or services; (4) *that is disseminated sufficiently to the relevant purchasing public to constitute advertising or promotion within that industry. At 799:* In some cases, it may be obvious whether statements were made in 'advertising or promotion.' Yet, ... communications need not necessarily resemble traditional television, radio, print, or Internet advertisements to fall within the purview of the Lanham Act. *At 800:* Like the Second Circuit, we readily adopt the first and third requirements of the ***Gordon & Breach*** test: namely, that 'commercial advertising or promotion' must consist of 'commercial speech' that is made for the purpose of influencing the purchasing decisions of the consuming public. These criteria add only an intent requirement to the [five-element] test, which requires plaintiffs to show that the supposed advertisements will likely influence the deceived consumer's purchasing decisions. [¶] We further agree with the Second Circuit that the touchstone of whether a defendant's actions may be considered 'commercial advertising or promotion' under the Lanham Act is that the contested representations are part of an organized campaign to penetrate the relevant market. *At 801:* We therefore define 'commercial advertising or promotion' as: (1) commercial speech; (2) for the purpose of influencing customers to buy the defendant's goods or services; (3) that is disseminated either widely enough to the relevant purchasing public to constitute advertising or promotion within that industry or to a substantial portion of the plaintiff's or defendant's existing customer or client base. [¶] We decline to adopt the requirement that the parties be in competition. *At 802:* Plaintiffs seeking damages for false advertising must present evidence that a 'significant portion' of the consumer population was deceived. ... Where false advertising cases have involved only mass mailings ... this Court has treated the intended audience as the recipients of the letters." (Internal quotes omitted.) *But see* ***Tobinick v. Novella***, p. 148.

Duty Free Americas, Inc. v. Estée Lauder Cos., 797 F.3d 1248, 1274 (11th Cir.2015). "Whether [Lanham Act] §43(a) [15 U.S.C. §1125(a)] includes within its ambit a claim for false advertising based on contributory liability is a question of first impression. *At 1277-78:* [W]e hold that a plaintiff may bring a claim for contributory false advertising under §43(a).... [¶] What, then, must a plaintiff establish in order to state a contributory false advertising claim? First, the plaintiff must show that a third party in fact directly engaged in false advertising that injured the plaintiff. Second, the plaintiff must allege that the defendant contributed to that conduct either by knowingly inducing or causing the conduct, or by materially participating in it. [¶] In order to establish that a third party engaged in false advertising, the plaintiff 'must plead (and ultimately prove) an injury to a commercial interest in sales or business reputation proximately caused by the ... misrepresentations.' To prove that the third party's statements caused the requisite injury, we have held that the plaintiff must show: '(1) the ... statements were false or misleading; (2) the statements deceived, or had the capacity to deceive, consumers; (3) the deception had a material effect on the consumers' purchasing decision; (4) the misrepresented service affects interstate commerce; and (5) [the plaintiff] has been, or likely will be, injured as a result of the false or misleading statement.' [¶] Once the plaintiff establishes the elements of a direct false advertising claim against a third party, it must allege that the defendant contributed to that conduct. This means that the plaintiff must allege that the defendant had the necessary state of mind—in other words that it 'intended to participate in' or 'actually knew about' the false advertising. The plaintiff must also allege that the defendant actively and materially furthered the unlawful conduct—either by inducing it, causing it, or in some other way working to bring it about. [¶] Analogies from trademark infringement, in which contributory liability is more developed, can be instructive. Thus, for example, a plaintiff may be able to make out the participation prong of a contributory false advertising claim by alleging that the defendant directly controlled or monitored the third party's false advertising. It is also conceivable that there could be circumstances under which the provision of a necessary product or service, without which the false advertising would not be possible, could support a theory of contributory liability. In determining whether a plaintiff has adequately alleged facts to support such a claim, we look to whether the complaint suggests a plausible inference of knowing or intentional participation, examining 'the nature and extent of the communication' between the third party and the defendant regarding the false advertising; 'whether or not the [defendant] explicitly or implicitly encouraged' the false advertising; whether the false advertising 'is serious and widespread,' making it more likely that the defendant 'kn[ew] about and condone[d] the acts'; and whether the defendant engaged in 'bad faith refusal to exercise a clear contractual power to halt' the false advertising."

Merck Eprova AG v. Gnosis S.p.A., 760 F.3d 247, 251 (2d Cir.2014). "This appeal requires our Court to clarify certain aspects of our false advertising jurisprudence. We conclude that where, as here, the parties operate in the context of a two-player market and literal falsity and deliberate deception have been proved, it is appropriate to utilize legal presumptions of consumer confusion and injury for the purposes of finding liability in a false advertising case brought under the Lanham Act. We further hold that in a case where willful deception is proved, a presumption of injury may be used to award a plaintiff damages in the form of defendant's profits, and may, in circumstances such as those present here, warrant enhanced damages. *At 256:* [I]n cases of *implied falsity*, where a plaintiff adequately demonstrates that a defendant has intentionally set out to deceive the public, and the defendant's deliberate conduct in this regard is of an egregious nature, a presumption arises that consumers are, in fact, being deceived. In such a case, once a plaintiff establishes deceptive intent, the burden shifts to the defendant to demonstrate the absence of consumer confusion." (Internal quotes omitted.)

Pernod Ricard USA, LLC v. Bacardi U.S.A., Inc., 653 F.3d 241, 253 (3d Cir.2011). "[E]ven if the words 'Havana Club,' taken in isolation, may be understood as indicating a product's geographic origin in Havana, Cuba, those same words cannot mislead a reasonable consumer who is told in no uncertain terms that 'Havana Club' is a brand of rum made in Puerto Rico. [¶] Under these circumstances, a district court can properly disregard survey evidence as immaterial, because, by definition, [Lanham Act] §43(a)(1) [15 U.S.C. §1125] does not forbid language that reasonable people would have to acknowledge is not false or misleading. *At 254-55:* A word of caution is nevertheless in order.... Before a defendant or a district judge decides that an advertisement could not mislead a reasonable person, serious care must be exercised to avoid the temptation of thinking, 'my way of seeing this is naturally the only reasonable way.' Thoughtful reflection on potential ambiguities in an advertisement, which can be revealed by surveys and will certainly be pointed out by plaintiffs, will regularly make it the wisest course to consider survey evidence."

Osmose, Inc. v. Viance, LLC, 612 F.3d 1298, 1308-09 (11th Cir.2010). "In order to establish the requisite likelihood of success on a false advertising claim, the movant must establish that: '(1) the ads of the opposing party were false or misleading, (2) the ads deceived, or had the capacity to deceive, consumers, (3) the deception had a material effect on purchasing decisions, (4) the misrepresented product or service affects interstate commerce, and (5) the movant has been—or is likely to be—injured as a result of the false advertising.' [¶] The first element of a false advertising claim is 'satisfied if the challenged advertisement is literally false, or if the challenged advertisement is literally true, but misleading.' When determining whether an advertisement is literally false or misleading, courts 'must analyze the message conveyed in full context,' and 'must view the face of the statement in its entirety....' The distinction between literally false and merely misleading statements is often a 'fine line.' The ambiguity of the statement at issue, or the lack thereof, is significant. Statements that have an unambiguous meaning, either facially or considered in context, may be classified as literally false. As the meaning of a statement becomes less clear, however, and it becomes susceptible to multiple meanings, the statement is more likely to be merely misleading. Literal falsity is a finding of fact reviewed for clear error. [¶] The district court construed the various statements in the advertisements as 'tests prove' or 'establishment' claims, placing the burden on [P] to demonstrate that [D's] tests do not establish the proposition for which they are cited. [T]he 'plaintiff's burden in proving an advertisement to be literally false should depend on whether the defendant's advertisement cites consumer testing.' Advertising that cites such testing is classified as an 'establishment' claim. In order to prove the literal falsity of such a claim, the plaintiff must prove only that the tests did not establish the proposition for which they were cited. *At 1318-19:* The classification of an advertisement as literally false or true but misleading affects the movant's burden with respect to the element of consumer deception. If the court deems an advertisement to be literally false, then the movant is not required to present evidence of consumer deception. If, on the other hand, the court deems the advertisement to be true but misleading, then the movant is required to present evidence of deception. [¶] Even if an advertisement is literally false, the plaintiff must still establish materiality. In order to establish materiality, the plaintiff must demonstrate that 'the defendant's deception is likely to influence the purchasing decision.' A plaintiff may demonstrate this by showing that 'the defendants misrepresented an inherent quality or characteristic of the product.'" *See also* ***Wells Fargo & Co. v. ABD Ins. & Fin. Servs.***, 758 F.3d 1069, 1071 (9th Cir. 2014) (five elements; same as annotation); ***Groupe SEB USA, Inc. v. Euro-Pro Oper., LLC***, 774 F.3d 192, 198 (3d Cir.2014) (five elements; same as annotation); ***PBM Prods. v. Mead Johnson & Co.***, 639 F.3d 111, 120 (4th Cir.2011) (five elements; same as annotation); ***Schlotzsky's, Ltd. v. Sterling Purchasing & Nat'l Distrib.***, 520 F.3d 393, 400 (5th Cir.2008) (five elements; same as annotation); ***Newcal Indus. v. Ikon Office Solution***, 513 F.3d 1038, 1052 (9th Cir.2008) (six elements; additional showing that false statement was made in commercial advertisement or promotion); ***Time Warner Cable, Inc. v. DIRECTV, Inc.***, 497 F.3d 144, 153 (2d Cir.2007) (literally false v. misleading); ***Allsup, Inc. v. Advantage 2000 Consultants Inc.***, 428 F.3d 1135, 1138 (8th Cir.2005) (five elements; same as annotation); ***Rhone-Poulenc Rorer Pharms. v. Marion Merrell Dow, Inc.***, 93 F.3d 511, 514-15 (8th Cir.1996) ("tests prove" claims).

Schering-Plough Healthcare Prods. v. Schwarz Pharma, Inc., 586 F.3d 500, 512 (7th Cir.2009). "Many literally false statements are not deceptive. ... The cases that reject liability do so in the name of 'puffery'—meaningless superlatives—but the principle cuts deeper; if no one is or could be fooled, no one is or could be hurt. [¶] The other side of this coin is that a representation may be so obviously misleading that there is no need to gather evidence that anyone was confused. And it is often clearer that a claim is misleading than that it is literally false, because what is 'literally' false is often a semantic question. [¶] What the cases mean when they say that proof of literal falsity allows the plaintiff to dispense with evidence that anyone was misled or likely to be misled is that the seller who places an indisputably false statement in his advertising or labeling probably did so for a malign purpose, namely to sell his product by lies, and if the statement is false probably at least some people were misled, and since it was a lie why waste time on costly consumer surveys?" *See also* ***Hall v. Bed Bath & Beyond, Inc.***, 705 F.3d 1357, 1368 (Fed.Cir.2013); ***York Grp. v. Horizon Casket Grp.***, 459 F.Supp.2d 567, 576 (S.D.Tex. 2006).

Newcal Indus. v. Ikon Office Solution, 513 F.3d 1038, 1053 (9th Cir.2008). "[T]he determination of whether an alleged misrepresentation 'is a statement of fact' or is instead 'mere puffery' is a legal question that may be resolved on [an FRCP] 12(b)(6) motion. A statement is considered puffery if the claim is extremely unlikely to induce consumer reliance. Ultimately, the difference between a statement of fact and mere puffery rests in the specificity or generality of the claim. 'The common theme that seems to run through cases considering puffery in a variety of contexts is that consumer reliance will be induced by specific rather than general assertions.' Thus, a statement that is quantifiable, that makes a claim as to the 'specific or absolute characteristics of a product,' may be an actionable statement of fact while a general, subjective claim about a product is non-actionable puffery."

Time Warner Cable, Inc. v. DIRECTV, Inc., 497 F.3d 144, 148 (2d Cir.2007). "This appeal requires us to clarify certain aspects of our false advertising doctrine. We make three clarifications in particular. First, we hold that an advertisement can be literally false even though it does not explicitly make a false assertion, if the words or images, considered in context, necessarily and unambiguously imply a false message. Second, we decide that the category of non-actionable 'puffery' encompasses visual depictions that, while factually inaccurate, are so grossly exaggerated that no reasonable consumer would rely on them in navigating the marketplace. Third, we conclude that the likelihood of irreparable harm may be presumed where the plaintiff demonstrates a likelihood of success in showing that the defendant's comparative advertisement is literally false and that given the nature of the market, it would be obvious to the viewing audience that the advertisement is targeted at the plaintiff, even though the plaintiff is not identified by name. *At 158:* [We now] adopt what is known in other circuits as the 'false by necessary implication' doctrine. Under this doctrine, a district court evaluating whether an advertisement is literally false 'must analyze the message conveyed in full context,' ... *i.e.*, it 'must consider the advertisement in its entirety and not ... engage in disputatious dissection[]'.... If the words or images, considered in context, necessarily imply a false message, the advertisement is literally false and no extrinsic evidence of consumer confusion is required. However, 'only an *unambiguous* message can be literally false.' Therefore, if the language or graphic is susceptible to more than one reasonable interpretation, the advertisement cannot be literally false. There may still be a 'basis for a claim that the advertisement is misleading,' ... but to resolve such a claim, the district court must look to consumer data to determine what 'the person to whom the advertisement is addressed find[s] to be the message[ ]'.... In short, where the advertisement does not unambiguously make a claim, 'the court's reaction is at best not determinative and at worst irrelevant.'" *See also* ***Santana Prods. v. Bobrick Washroom Equip., Inc.***, 401 F.3d 123, 136 (3d Cir.2005); ***Clorox Co. v. Proctor & Gamble Commercial Co.***, 228 F.3d 24, 33 (1st Cir. 2000).

Everest Capital Ltd. v. Everest Funds Mgmt., 393 F.3d 755, 764 (8th Cir.2005). "We reject as contrary to law [P's] contention that the district court abused its discretion by refusing to instruct the jury that a 'literally false' statement is presumed to be likely to deceive."

American Italian Pasta Co. v. New World Pasta Co., 371 F.3d 387, 390-91 (8th Cir.2004). "[A] category of non-actionable statements exists. Many statements fall into this category, popularly known as puffery. Puffery exists in two general forms: (1) exaggerated statements of bluster or boast upon which no reasonable consumer would rely; and (2) vague or highly subjective claims of product superiority, including bald assertions of superiority."

C.B. Fleet Co. v. SmithKline Beecham Consumer Healthcare, L.P., 131 F.3d 430, 434 (4th Cir.1997). "[B]oth false advertising of a competitor's products and false advertising of one's own products are actionable."

§1125(a)(3)—Trade Dress

TrafFix Devices, Inc. v. Marketing Displays, Inc., 532 U.S. 23, 29-30 (2001). "A prior patent ... has vital significance in resolving [a] trade dress [infringement] claim. A utility patent is strong evidence that the features therein claimed are functional. If trade dress protection is sought for those features the strong evidence of functionality based on the previous patent adds great weight to the statutory presumption that features are deemed functional until proved otherwise by the party seeking trade dress protection. Where the expired patent claimed the features in question, one who seeks to establish trade dress protection must carry the heavy burden of showing that the feature is not functional, for instance by showing that it is merely an ornamental, incidental, or arbitrary aspect of the device." *See also* ***Fuji Kogyo Co. v. Pacific Bay Int'l***, 461 F.3d 675, 683 (6th Cir.2006).

Wal-Mart Stores v. Samara Bros., 529 U.S. 205, 216 (2000). "We hold that, in an action for infringement of unregistered trade dress under [Lanham Act] §43(a) [15 U.S.C. §1125(a)], a product's design is distinctive, and therefore [protectable], only upon a showing of secondary meaning."

Two Pesos, Inc. v. Taco Cabana, Inc., 505 U.S. 763, 776 (1992). Proof "of secondary meaning is not required to prevail on a claim under [15 U.S.C. §1125(a), Lanham Act §43(a),] where the trade dress at issue is inherently distinctive...." *See also* ***Antioch Co. v. Western Trimming Corp.***, 347 F.3d 150, 154 (6th Cir. 2003).

Leapers, Inc. v. SMTS, LLC, 879 F.3d 731, 735 (6th Cir.2018). "In order to prevail on a claim for trade dress infringement based on a product's design, a plaintiff must show that its design is (1) nonfunctional, (2) has acquired a secondary meaning, and (3) is confusingly similar to the allegedly infringing design. *At 736-37:* The burden of proving nonfunctionality is unusual because it requires a party to introduce affirmative evidence that a quality is *not* present—to introduce 'evidence of an absence' rather than merely an absence of evidence. Evidence that a product design is purely 'ornamental, incidental, or arbitrary' can be evidence of an absence of functionality. [¶] Evidence of aesthetic intent—that the product was designed for an aesthetic purpose—tends to show that a product's design is purely ornamental, incidental, or arbitrary. Intent, however, is not conclusive; not every design created for an aesthetic purpose will turn out to be nonfunctional. Indeed, a design might turn out to have functional value despite any original aesthetic intent if the design becomes 'essential to the use or purpose of the article' or if it turns out to 'affect[ ] the cost or quality of the article.' For example, a new windshield designed solely for the purpose of making a sedan more visually appealing will nevertheless be deemed functional if the windshield turns out to be more aerodynamic or cheaper to produce than other designs. Thus, proof of aesthetic intent alone cannot establish nonfunctionality due to the possibility of incidental functionality. [¶] Aesthetic intent alone is also insufficient because some products function based on their aesthetic properties through so-called 'aesthetic functionality.' A design has aesthetic functionality when it communicates the use, purpose, cost, or quality of the product in a way that competitors cannot avoid replicating without incurring costs 'not to copy but to design around.' But 'there are few aesthetic designs that are so fundamental to an industry that competitors cannot fairly compete without free use of [them].' Thus, a party's initial burden to show that a design lacks aesthetic functionality is not substantial; the plaintiff need only show that the design is not a competitive necessity such that 'exclusive use ... would put competitors at a significant non-reputation related disadvantage.' *At 738:* [A]n aesthetic design that merely communicates the *source* of the article—rather than anything about the article's use, purpose, cost, or quality—is not functional."

Arlington Specialties, Inc. v. Urban Aid, Inc., 847 F.3d 415, 418 (7th Cir.2017). "The doctrine of functionality imposes a critical limit on trade dress rights because 'product design almost invariably serves purposes other than source identification.' Because trademark protection for trade dress has no time limit, giving one competitor a perpetual and exclusive right to a useful product feature would result in a perpetual competitive advantage. 'The Lanham Act does not exist to reward manufacturers for their innovation in creating a particular device; that is the purpose of the patent law and its [limited] period of exclusivity.' When the trade dress is unregistered (as [P's] is), the party seeking protection has the burden to show it is not functional. *At 419-20:* In ***TrafFix Devices***, the Supreme Court embraced two tests for functionality from its precedents. A product feature is functional, the Court said, 'if it is essential to the use or purpose of the article or if it affects the cost or quality of the article.' Even if a product feature does not satisfy that definition, it can still be functional if it is a 'competitive necessity,' that is, if its exclusive use 'would put competitors at a significant non-reputation-related disadvantage.' [¶] In an effort to narrow the doctrine of functionality, [P] emphasizes the latter verbal formulation using the concept of necessity. [P] argues that summary judgment can be affirmed only if its competitors 'must' be able to use its claimed trade dress to compete. In ***TrafFix Devices***, however, the Supreme Court rejected exclusive reliance on that definition. The Court explained (a) that competitive necessity is 'incorrect as a comprehensive definition' of functionality and (b) that a feature is functional when it 'affects the cost or quality of the device.' [¶] [A] design need not be 'the only way to do things' to be functional; it need only 'represent[] one of many solutions to a problem.' [¶] Functionality is a factual question, ... but the bar for functionality is so low that it can often be decided as a matter of law, as in this case. [¶] The question is not ... whether the claimed trade dress has 'less utility' than alternatives. ... Under ***TrafFix Devices***, ***Specialized Seating*** [***Inc. v. Greenwich Indus.***, 616 F.3d 722 (7th Cir.2010)], and ***Georgia-***[***Pac. Consumer Prods. v. Kimberly-Clark Corp.***, 647 F.3d 723 (7th Cir.2011)], the right question is whether the design feature affects product quality or cost or is 'merely ornamental.' Here, the undisputed evidence shows that the claimed design features affect product quality, so we need not consider the availability of alternative designs for competitors."

Forney Indus. v. Daco of Mo., Inc., 835 F.3d 1238, 1248 (10th Cir.2016). "In light of the Supreme Court's directive that a product's color cannot be inherently distinctive and its concern that inherent distinctiveness not be the subject of excessive litigation, we hold that the use of color in product packaging can be inherently distinctive (so that it is unnecessary to show secondary meaning) only if specific colors are used in combination with a well-defined shape, pattern, or other distinctive design. *At 1253:* Trade dress is said to have developed secondary meaning 'when in the minds of the public, the primary significance of the mark is to identify the source of the product rather than the product itself.' ... Secondary meaning can be established through 'direct evidence, such as consumer surveys or testimony from consumers.' But a plaintiff can also rely on circumstantial evidence, such as: '(1) the length and manner of the trade dress's use; (2) the nature and extent of advertising and promotion of the trade dress; (3) the efforts made in the direction of promoting a conscious connection, in the public's mind, between the trade dress and a particular product or venture; (4) actual consumer confusion; (5) proof of intentional copying; or (6) evidence of sales volume.' [¶] We agree that advertising can be strongly probative. *At 1254:* But advertising alone is typically unhelpful to prove secondary meaning when it is not directed at highlighting the trade dress. [¶] [P's] evidence of sales data is similarly unavailing. It provides total sales volume but gives no indication of how those sales relate to the color mark."

Groeneveld Transp. Efficiency, Inc. v. Lubecore Int'l, 730 F.3d 494, 500 (6th Cir.2013). "The key issue in this case is whether a company can use trade-dress law to protect its functional product design from competition with a 'copycat' design made by another company where there is no reasonable likelihood that consumers would confuse the two companies' products as emanating from a single source. We hold that it cannot. In so holding, we reaffirm that trademark law is designed to promote brand recognition, not to insulate product manufacturers from lawful competition."

Secalt, S.A. v. Wuxi Shenxi Constr. Mach. Co., 668 F.3d 677, 683 (9th Cir.2012). "In conducting the functionality analysis, which is a question of fact, we must be mindful that for an overall product configuration to be recognized as a trademark, the entire design must be nonfunctional. 'De facto' functionality means that the design of a product has a function, i.e., a bottle of any design holds fluid, whereas 'de jure' functionality means that the product is in its particular shape *because it works better in this shape*. Before an overall product configuration can be recognized as a trademark, the entire design must be arbitrary or non de jure functional. *At 685:* Courts have uniformly held that a design patent, without more, is insufficient to prove that a design is nonfunctional. At best, a design patent can only help rebut the functionality defense; it cannot do the whole job of proving inherent distinctiveness. The plaintiff still needs to show that, in its market at the time of the alleged infringement, the design is both ornamental and deserving of trade dress protection. [¶] [We have used four] factors in analyzing functionality: (1) whether the design yields a utilitarian advantage, (2) whether alternative designs are available, (3) whether advertising touts the utilitarian advantages of the design, and (4) whether the particular design results from a comparatively simple or inexpensive method of manufacture." (Internal quotes omitted.)

In re Chippendales USA, Inc., 622 F.3d 1346, 1351 (Fed.Cir.2010). "This court applies a four-part test for determining the inherent distinctiveness of trade dress. This four-part test is set forth in our decision in ***Seabrook Foods*** as follows: (1) whether it was a 'common' basic shape or design, (2) whether it was not unique or unusual in the particular field, (3) whether it was a mere refinement of a commonly-adopted and well-known form of ornamentation for a particular class of goods viewed by the public as a dress or ornamentation for the goods, or (4) whether it was capable of creating a commercial impression distinct from the accompanying words. If a mark satisfies any of the first three tests, it is not inherently distinctive. *At 1352:* Inherent distinctiveness does not depend on a showing that consumers *actually* identify the particular mark with the particular business; this is a question of acquired distinctiveness, or secondary meaning. [U]ltimately the focus of the inherent distinctiveness inquiry is whether or not the trade dress is of such a design that a buyer will immediately rely on it to differentiate the product from those of competing manufacturers; if so, it is inherently distinctive. Thus, if the mark is inherently distinctive, it is presumed that consumers will view it as a source identifier. If the mark is not inherently distinctive, it is unfair to others in the industry to allow what is in essence in the public domain to be registered and appropriated, absent a showing of secondary meaning. The policy here is basically the same as the prohibition against registering generic word marks, or descriptive marks that have not acquired secondary meaning. *At 1354:* We agree with the PTO's argument on appeal that the proper time for measuring inherent distinctiveness is at the time of registration. [¶] Judging inherent distinctiveness at the time of first use would be fundamentally unfair. As we have noted, trademark rights are not static. The test for inherent distinctiveness depends on whether the mark, or a variation thereof, has been in common use in general or in the particular field. A term or device that was once inherently distinctive may lose its distinguishing characteristics over time." (Internal quotes omitted.) *See also* ***Miller's Ale House, Inc. v. Boynton Carolina Ale House, LLC***, 702 F.3d 1312, 1323-24 (11th Cir. 2012).

Art Attacks Ink, LLC v. MGA Entm't Inc., 581 F.3d 1138, 1146 (9th Cir.2009). "To demonstrate secondary meaning based on advertising, the advertising must be of a 'nature and extent to create an association' with the advertiser's goods. The 'true test of secondary meaning' is the effectiveness of the advertising effort. [¶] Other circuits have explicitly held that extensive use alone cannot establish secondary meaning. Our own cases have suggested that secondary meaning requires more than extensive use alone."

General Motors Corp. v. Urban Gorilla, LLC, 500 F.3d 1222, 1226 (10th Cir.2007). "A product's trade dress 'is its overall image and appearance, and may include features such as size, shape, color or color combinations, texture, graphics, and even particular sales techniques.'"

General Motors Corp. v. Lanard Toys, Inc., 468 F.3d 405, 414 (6th Cir.2006). "A party seeking to recover for trade dress infringement must prove by a preponderance of the evidence that (1) the trade dress is not functional; (2) the trade dress is distinctive in the marketplace and has acquired secondary meaning, thereby indicating the source of the goods; and (3) the trade dress of the accused product is confusingly similar. *At 415:* It will not do to solely identify in litigation a combination as the trade dress. Rather, the discrete elements which make up that combination should be separated out and identified in a list. [F]ocus on the overall look of a product does not permit a plaintiff to dispense with an articulation of the specific elements which comprise its distinct dress. [¶] In the end, the question is whether or not the court and the parties coherently define exactly what the trade dress consists of and determine whether that trade dress is valid and if what the accused is doing is an infringement. *At 416:* A trade dress's nonfunctional nature must be proven by the party asserting the trade dress protection. A product feature is functional, and cannot serve as a trademark, if it is essential to the use or purpose of the article or if it affects the cost or quality of the article, that is, if exclusive use of the feature would put competitors at a significant non-reputation-related disadvantage. If a trade dress is found to be functional, the mere fact that there are other non-infringing designs which would serve the same functional purpose is no defense to functionality. *At 417-18:* [P] bears the burden of proof on the issue of secondary meaning. To demonstrate secondary meaning, the evidence must show that in the minds of the public, the primary significance of the trade dress is to identify the source of the product rather than the product itself. This Court applies a seven-factor test to determine whether secondary meaning exists in a trade dress: (1) direct consumer testimony, (2) consumer surveys, (3) exclusivity, length, and manner of use, (4) amount and manner of advertising, (5) amount of sales and number of customers, (6) established place in the market, and (7) proof of intentional copying. *At 419:* This Court has historically favored the use of consumer surveys as proof of secondary meaning. However, the question remains whether we should ignore all survey evidence conducted post-infringement or accept the evidence with the understanding that the survey does not reflect a pre-infringement world. A court may easily take into consideration the strength of recognition at the time of the survey in light of the amount of time passed between that date and the date of infringement." (Internal quotes omitted.) *See also* ***Amazing Spaces, Inc. v. Metro Mini Storage***, 608 F.3d 225, 248 (5th Cir.2010); ***Art Attacks Ink, LLC v. MGA Entm't Inc.***, 581 F.3d 1138, 1145 (9th Cir.2009); ***McNeil Nutritionals, LLC v. Heartland Sweeteners, LLC***, 511 F.3d 350, 359-60 (3d Cir.2007); ***Dippin' Dots, Inc. v. Frosty Bites Distrib.***, 369 F.3d 1197, 1202 (11th Cir.2004); ***OddzOn Prods. v. Just Toys, Inc.***, 122 F.3d 1396, 1407-08 (Fed. Cir.1997); ***Insty*Bit, Inc. v. Poly-Tech Indus.***, 95 F.3d 663, 667 (8th Cir.1996); ***Dorr-Oliver, Inc. v. Fluid-Quip, Inc.***, 94 F.3d 376, 380 (7th Cir.1996), *aff'd*, 132 F.3d 36 (7th Cir.1997).

Fun-Damental Too, Ltd. v. Gemmy Indus., 111 F.3d 993, 999 (2d Cir.1997). "The concept of trade dress encompasses the design and appearance of the product together with all the elements making up the overall image that serves to identify the product presented to the consumer. These other elements include 'the appearance of labels, wrappers, and containers used in packaging a product as well as displays and other materials used in presenting the product to prospective purchasers.'"

Insty*Bit, Inc. v. Poly-Tech Indus., 95 F.3d 663, 672 (8th Cir.1996). "Although [Lanham Act] §32 [15 U.S.C. §1114] protects registered trademarks, rather than trade dress, the Supreme Court's holding ... that the same analyses apply to the protection of trademarks and trade dress under [Lanham Act] §43(a) [15 U.S.C. §1125(a)] leads us to conclude that the likelihood of post-sale confusion may be considered in trade dress infringement actions."

Parker Waichman LLP v. Gilman Law LLP, No. 12-CV-4784(JS)(AKT) (E.D.N.Y.2013) (memo op.; 7-24-13). Held: Trade-dress protection for a website is a novel concept that must be supported by explaining how a website's elements synthesize to create the website's protectable "look and feel." *See also* ***Blue Nile, Inc. v. Ice.com, Inc.***, 478 F.Supp.2d 1240, 1246 & n.8 (W.D.Wash.2007).

§1125(c)

National Bus. Forms & Printing, Inc. v. Ford Motor Co., 671 F.3d 526, 536 (5th Cir.2012). "The issue here is essentially whether a commercial printer 'uses' a trademark under §1125(c)(1) when it reproduces or offers to reproduce the mark for customers as part of its printing business. This issue is one of first impression in this circuit. The district court found that [P] did not make use of the [D's] marks as envisioned by §1125(c)(1) because [P] had not appropriated [D's] marks as its own. [¶] We agree with the district court that [P] did not 'use' [D's] marks (as the [Trademark Dilution Revision Act] contemplates that term) in identifying or distinguishing its own goods or services merely by reproducing them for customers as part of its commercial printing business."

Coach Servs. v. Triumph Learning LLC, 668 F.3d 1356, 1372 (Fed.Cir.2012). "A threshold question in a federal dilution claim is whether the mark at issue is 'famous.' Under the [Trademark Dilution Revision Act (TDRA)], a mark is famous if it 'is widely recognized by the general consuming public of the U.S. as a designation of source of the goods or services of the mark's owner.' By using the 'general consuming public' as the benchmark, the TDRA eliminated the possibility of 'niche fame,' which some courts had recognized under the previous version of the statute. *At 1373:* Fame for likelihood of confusion and fame for dilution are distinct concepts, and dilution fame requires a more stringent showing. While fame for dilution 'is an either/or proposition'—it either exists or does not—fame for likelihood of confusion is a matter of degree along a continuum. Accordingly, a mark can acquire 'sufficient public recognition and renown to be famous for purposes of likelihood of confusion without meeting the more stringent requirement for dilution fame.' [¶] It is well-established that dilution fame is difficult to prove. This is particularly true where ... the mark is a common English word that has different meanings in different contexts. Importantly, the owner of the allegedly famous mark must show that its mark became famous 'prior to the filing date of the trademark application or registration against which it intends to file an opposition or cancellation proceeding.' [¶] [F]ame for dilution requires widespread recognition by the general public. To establish the requisite level of fame, the 'mark's owner must demonstrate that the common or proper noun uses of the term and third-party uses of the mark are now eclipsed by the owner's use of the mark.' An opposer must show that, when the general public encounters the mark 'in almost any context, it associates the term, at least initially, with the mark's owner.'"

Audi AG v. D'Amato, 469 F.3d 534, 547 (6th Cir. 2006). "'Dilution law, unlike traditional trademark infringement law[,] is not based on a likelihood of confusion standard, but only exists to protect the quasi-property rights a holder has in maintaining the integrity and distinctiveness of his mark.' We use a five-point test to determine whether a plaintiff will succeed in a federal dilution claim. [P] must show that its trademark is (1) famous and (2) distinctive, and that [D's] use of the mark (3) was in commerce, (4) began after [P's] mark became famous, and (5) 'cause[d] dilution of the distinctive quality' of [P's] mark." *See also* ***CareFirst v. First Care, P.C.***, 434 F.3d 263, 274 (4th Cir. 2006); ***Everest Capital Ltd. v. Everest Funds Mgmt.***, 393 F.3d 755, 762 (8th Cir.2005).

Scott Fetzer Co. v. House of Vacuums Inc., 381 F.3d 477, 489 (5th Cir.2004). "Trademark dilution is the weakening of the ability of a mark to clearly and unmistakably distinguish the source of a product. Dilution may occur through blurring or tarnishing. Blurring involves a diminution in the uniqueness or individuality of a mark because of its use on unrelated goods. Tarnishing occurs when a trademark is linked to products of shoddy quality, or is portrayed in an unwholesome or unsavory context, with the result that the public will associate the lack of quality or lack of prestige in the defendant's goods with the plaintiff's unrelated goods." (Internal quotes omitted.)

AM Gen. Corp. v. DaimlerChrysler Corp., 311 F.3d 796, 811-12 (7th Cir.2002). "The [Federal Trademark Dilution] Act [15 U.S.C. §§1125(c) and 1127, Lanham Act §§43(c) and 45,] protects non-functional product configuration against dilution to the same extent as any other trademark."

Derminer v. Kramer, 406 F.Supp.2d 756, 758 (E.D. Mich.2005). "[U]nder the plain meaning of the statute, an action between co-owners of a trademark for dilution of that mark under 15 U.S.C. §1125(c) [Lanham Act §43(c)] is not permitted. Like an action for trademark infringement by a co-owner, the claim is best understood as an action for an accounting that arises under state contract law, not under the Lanham Act."

§1125(c)(1)

Nola Spice Designs, L.L.C. v. Haydel Enters., 783 F.3d 527, 548 (5th Cir.2015). "To state a dilution claim under the Lanham Act, [P] must show that (1) it owns a famous and distinctive mark; (2) [D] has commenced using a mark in commerce that is diluting

[P's] mark; (3) the similarity between [D's] mark and [P's] mark gives rise to an association between the marks; and (4) the association is likely to impair the distinctiveness of [P's] mark or harm the reputation of [P's] mark." *See also* ***Radiance Found. v. NAACP***, 786 F.3d 316, 330 (4th Cir.2015).

§1125(c)(2)(A)

Kibler v. Hall, 843 F.3d 1068, 1083 (6th Cir.2016). "Courts have interpreted the [Federal Trademark Dilution Act] to require the mark to be a 'household name.' That is, 'when the general public encounters the mark in almost any context, it associates the term, at least initially, with the mark's owner.' It is difficult to establish fame under the Act sufficient to show trademark dilution."

§1125(c)(2)(B)—Blurring

Levi Strauss & Co. v. Abercrombie & Fitch Trading Co., 633 F.3d 1158, 1172 (9th Cir.2011). "[T]he plain language of ... §1125(c) does not require that a plaintiff establish that the junior mark is identical, nearly identical or substantially similar to the senior mark in order to obtain injunctive relief. Rather, a plaintiff must show, based on the factors set forth in §1125(c)(2)(B), including the degree of similarity, that a junior mark is likely to impair the distinctiveness of the famous mark." *See also* ***General Motors Co. v. Urban Gorilla, LLC***, No. 2:06-CV-00133 BSJ (D.Utah 2010) (memo op.; 12-27-10).

Tiffany (NJ) Inc. v. eBay Inc., 600 F.3d 93, 111 (2d Cir.2010). "Some classic examples of blurring include hypothetical anomalies as Dupont shoes, Buick aspirin tablets, Schlitz varnish, Kodak pianos, Bulova gowns, and so forth. It is not a question of confusion; few consumers would likely confuse the source of a Kodak camera with the source of a Kodak piano. Dilution by blurring refers instead to the whittling away of the established trademark's selling power and value through its unauthorized use by others." (Internal quotes omitted.)

Starbucks Corp. v. Wolfe's Borough Coffee, Inc., 588 F.3d 97, 109 (2d Cir.2009). "The determination of an 'intent to associate,' ... does not require the additional consideration of whether bad faith corresponded with that intent. ... Thus, where, as here, the allegedly diluting mark was created with an intent to associate with the famous mark, this factor favors a finding of a likelihood of dilution."

Louis Vuitton Malletier S.A. v. Haute Diggity Dog, LLC, 507 F.3d 252, 265 (4th Cir.2007). "In the context of blurring, distinctiveness refers to the ability of the famous mark uniquely to identify a single source and thus maintain its selling power. *At 266:* The [Trademark Dilution Revision Act] prohibits a person from using a junior mark that is likely to dilute (by blurring) the famous mark, and blurring is defined to be an impairment to the famous mark's distinctiveness. 'Distinctiveness' in turn refers to the public's recognition that the famous mark identifies a single source of the product using the famous mark. [¶] Not every factor [in §1125(c)(2)(B)] will be relevant in every case, and not every blurring claim will require extensive discussion of the factors. But a trial court must offer a sufficient indication of which factors it has found persuasive and explain why they are persuasive so that the court's decision can be reviewed."

Autozone, Inc. v. Tandy Corp., 373 F.3d 786, 802 (6th Cir.2004). "The extent of [P's] use of the mark, the pervasive and geographically widespread advertising of the mark, the high recognition of the mark, and [P's] registration of its mark, which entitles [P] to a presumption of distinctiveness, all highlight the distinctive nature of the ... mark. However, a finding that the mark was distinctive does not address the degree of distinctiveness, which is part of the test for determining whether the use of a junior mark causes dilution. [¶] The ten [dilution] factors are: 'distinctiveness; similarity of the marks; proximity of the products and the likelihood of bridging the gap; interrelationship among the distinctiveness of the senior mark, the similarity of the junior mark, and the proximity of the products; shared consumers and geographic limitations; sophistication of consumers; actual confusion; adjectival or referential quality of the junior use; harm to the junior user and delay by the senior user; and the effect of [the] senior's prior laxity in protecting the mark.'" *See also* ***Luigino's, Inc. v. Stouffer Corp.***, 170 F.3d 827, 830 (8th Cir.1999).

TCPIP Holding Co. v. Haar Comms., 244 F.3d 88, 98 (2d Cir.2001). "We ... understand [15 U.S.C. §1125(c)(1)(A), now §1125(c)(2)(B)(ii)(A), Lanham Act §43(c)(2)(B)(ii)(A),] to invite two inquiries: (1) Has the plaintiff's mark achieved a sufficient degree of consumer recognition ('acquired distinctiveness') to satisfy the [Lanham] Act's requirement of fame? (2) Does the mark possess a sufficient degree of 'inherent distinctiveness' to satisfy the Act's requirement of 'distinctive quality.' The latter requirement cannot be satisfied by the mere fact that the public has come to associate the mark with the source. Thus, weak, non-distinctive, descriptive marks do not qualify for the Act's protection, even if famous."

§1125(c)(2)(C)—Tarnishment

Radiance Found. v. NAACP, 786 F.3d 316, 330-32 (4th Cir.2015). "The law provides three broad, overlapping categories within which any use of a famous mark, even if likely to cause harm or blurring, is not actionable: fair use; news reporting and news commentary; and noncommercial use. [¶] The first exclusion covers '[a]ny fair use, including a nominative or descriptive fair use,' and 'including use in connection with,' among other things, '*identifying and parodying, criticizing, or commenting upon* the famous mark owner or the goods or services of the famous mark owner.' A descriptive fair use 'applies when the ... defendant is using a trademark in its primary, descriptive sense to describe the defendant's goods or services,' whereas 'nominative fair use comes into play when the defendant uses the famous mark to identify or compare the trademark owner's product.' No use may be 'a designation of source for the [user's] own goods or services.' That is, the fair use exclusion does not provide a safe harbor for one who uses another's famous mark as a trademark. Finally, good faith is a 'common component' of fair use analysis. [¶] In determining whether speech is commercial, we consider several factors: (1) whether the speech is an advertisement; (2) whether [the] speech refers to specific products or services; (3) whether the speaker has an economic motivation for the speech; and (4) 'the viewpoint of the listener,' i.e. whether the listener would perceive the speech as proposing a transaction. The factors are cumulative, but, again, the absence of any particular element does not necessarily render the speech noncommercial."

Starbucks Corp. v. Wolfe's Borough Coffee, Inc., 588 F.3d 97, 110 (2d Cir.2009). "'A trademark may be tarnished when it is linked to products of shoddy quality, or is portrayed in an unwholesome or unsavory context, with the result that the public will associate the lack of quality or lack of prestige in the defendant's goods with the plaintiff's unrelated goods.' A trademark may also be diluted by tarnishment if the mark loses its ability to serve as a 'wholesome identifier' of plaintiff's product."

§1125(c)(3)

Rosetta Stone Ltd. v. Google, Inc., 676 F.3d 144, 168 (4th Cir.2012). "We view §1125(c)(3)(A) as affording a fair use *defense* to defendants in dilution actions. *At 169:* Although the [Federal Trademark Dilution Act (FTDA)] does not expressly define 'fair use,' the classic concept of 'fair use' is well-established and incorporated as an affirmative defense to a claim of trademark infringement. The contours of the fair-use defense in the infringement context are therefore instructive on the classic or descriptive fair-use defense to a dilution claim. [¶] Descriptive, or classic, fair use applies when the defendant is using a trademark 'in its primary, descriptive sense' to *describe* the defendant's goods or services. The FTDA also expressly includes 'nominative' fair use as a defense. Typically, nominative fair use comes into play when the defendant uses the famous mark to identify or compare *the trademark owner's* product. Regardless of the type of fair use claimed by a defendant, a common component of fair use is good faith."

Louis Vuitton Malletier S.A. v. Haute Diggity Dog, LLC, 507 F.3d 252, 266-67 (4th Cir.2007). "[P]arody is not automatically a complete *defense* to a claim of dilution by blurring where the defendant uses the parody as its own designation of source, i.e., *as a trademark*. Although the [Trademark Dilution Revision Act (TDRA)] does provide that fair use is a complete defense and allows that a parody can be considered fair use, it does not extend the fair use defense to parodies used as a trademark. [¶] Under the statute's plain language, parodying a famous mark is protected by the fair use defense only if the parody is *not* 'a designation of source for the person's own goods or services.' [¶] The TDRA, however, does not require a court to ignore the existence of a parody that is used as a trademark, and it does not preclude a court from considering parody as part of the circumstances to be considered for determining whether the plaintiff has made out a claim for dilution by blurring. Indeed, the statute permits a court to consider 'all relevant factors,' including the six factors supplied in §1125(c)(2)(B). [¶] Thus, it would appear that a defendant's use of a mark as a parody is relevant to the overall question of whether the defendant's use is likely to impair the famous mark's distinctiveness. Moreover, the fact that the defendant uses its marks as a parody is specifically relevant to several of the listed factors. For example, factor (v) (whether the defendant intended to create an association with the famous mark) and factor (vi) (whether there exists an actual association between the defendant's mark and the famous mark) directly invite inquiries into the defendant's intent in using the parody, the defendant's actual use of the parody, and the effect that its use has on the famous mark. While a parody intentionally creates an association with the famous mark in order to be a parody, it also intentionally communicates, if it is successful, that it is *not* the famous mark, but rather a satire of the famous mark. That the defendant is using its mark as a parody is therefore relevant in the consideration of these statutory factors. [¶] Similarly, factors (i), (ii), and (iv)—the degree of similarity between the two marks, the degree of distinctiveness of the famous mark, and its recognizability—are directly implicated by consideration of the fact that the defendant's mark is a successful parody. Indeed, by making the famous mark an object of the parody, a successful parody might actually enhance the famous mark's distinctiveness by making it an icon. The brunt of the joke becomes yet more famous. [¶] Even as [D's] parody mimics the famous mark, it communicates simultaneously that it is not the famous mark, but is only satirizing it. And because the famous mark is particularly strong and distinctive, it becomes more likely that a parody will not impair the distinctiveness of the mark. In short, as [D's] 'Chewy Vuiton' marks are a successful parody, we conclude that they will not blur the distinctiveness of the famous mark as a unique identifier of its source."

Bosley Med. Inst. v. Kremer, 403 F.3d 672, 677 (9th Cir.2005). "[P] argues that it has met the commercial use requirement in three ways. First, it argues that a mark used in an otherwise noncommercial website or as a domain name for an otherwise noncommercial website is nonetheless used in connection with goods and services where a user can click on a link available on that website to reach a commercial site. *At 678:* [D's] website contains no commercial links, but rather contains links to a discussion group, which in turn contains advertising. This roundabout path to the advertising of others is too attenuated to render [D's] site commercial. [¶] [P's] second argument ... is that [D] created his website to enable an extortion scheme in an attempt to profit from registering [website]. [¶] [T]here is no evidence that [D] was trying to sell the domain name itself. [¶] [P's] third ... argument ... is that [D's] use of [P's] trademark was ... 'in connection with goods and services' because [D] prevented users from obtaining [P's] goods and services. *At 679:* [T]he ... inquiry is whether [D] offers *competing* services to the public. [D] is not [P's] competitor; he is their critic. His use of [P's] mark is not in connection with a sale of goods or services—it is in connection with the expression of his opinion *about* [P's] goods and services." *But see* ***People for the Ethical Treatment of Animals v. Doughney***, 263 F.3d 359, 365-66 (4th Cir.2001) (commercial-use requirement met because D's website had links to commercial websites).

Nissan Motor Co. v. Nissan Computer Corp., 378 F.3d 1002, 1016-17 (9th Cir.2004). "The [Federal Trademark Dilution Act] anticipates the constitutional problem where the speech is not commercial but is potentially dilutive by including an exception for noncommercial use of a mark. [¶] Although the boundary between commercial and non-commercial speech has yet to be clearly delineated, the core notion of commercial speech is that it does no more than propose a commercial transaction. If speech is not purely commercial—that is, if it does more than propose a commercial transaction—then it is entitled to full First Amendment protection." (Internal quotes omitted.)

§1125(c)(5)

Everest Capital Ltd. v. Everest Funds Mgmt., 393 F.3d 755, 762 n.4 (8th Cir.2005). "Courts have rejected demands for jury trials when there is insufficient evidence of willful intent or actual damages. [E]ven when there is no right to a jury trial, if a dilution claim is tried with other claims that must be submitted to the jury, the court has discretion to submit the dilution claim to the jury on an advisory basis."

§1125(d)—Generally

Petroliam Nasional Berhad v. GoDaddy.com, Inc., 737 F.3d 546, 550 (9th Cir.2013). "We hold that the ACPA does not include a cause of action for contributory cybersquatting because: (1) the text of the Act does not apply to the conduct that would be actionable under such a theory; (2) Congress did not intend to implicitly include common law doctrines applicable to trademark infringement because the ACPA created a new cause of action that is distinct from traditional trademark remedies; and (3) allowing suits against registrars for contributory cybersquatting would not advance the goals of the statute."

GoPets Ltd. v. Hise, 657 F.3d 1024, 1030 (9th Cir. 2011). "ACPA applies to all domain names, whether registered before or after the enactment of the statute."

Bosley Med. Inst. v. Kremer, 403 F.3d 672, 680 (9th Cir.2005). "[D] argues that the 'noncommercial use' proviso [in §1125(c)(4)(B), now §1125(c)(3)(C),] that appears in the dilution portion of §1125 applies to cybersquatting claims [under §1125(d)] with equal force. Admittedly, the language in §1125 is confusing. [D] asserts that by using the word 'section' [in §1125(c)(4)], rather than the more precise term 'subsection,' Congress meant for the proviso to apply to all of §1125, as opposed to subsection (c). [¶] This argument fails…."

Daimler-Chrysler v. Net, Inc., 388 F.3d 201, 204 (6th Cir.2004). "A trademark owner asserting a claim under the ACPA must establish the following: (1) it has a valid trademark entitled to protection; (2) its mark is distinctive or famous; (3) the defendant's domain name is identical or confusingly similar to, or in the case of famous marks, dilutive of, the owner's mark; and (4) the defendant used, registered, or trafficked in the domain name (5) with a bad faith intent to profit. *At 205:* A trademark need not be registered to be entitled to protection under the ACPA. Rather, 'the general principles qualifying a mark for registration under [the act] are for the most part applicable in determining whether an unregistered mark is entitled to protection.'"

Hawes v. Network Solutions, Inc., 337 F.3d 377, 383-84 (4th Cir.2003). "The ACPA creates a cause of action for cybersquatting against anyone who registers, traffics in, or uses a domain name that is identical or confusingly similar to a trademark with the bad-faith intent to profit from the good will associated with the trademark. It also creates a cause of action for reverse domain name hijacking against trademark owners who misuse or abuse their rights in bringing a cybersquatting action. The ACPA thus protects both trademark owners and domain name registrants. In creating these causes of action, Congress intended expressly to limit the liability of domain name registrars under the Act as long as the domain name registrars comply with the conditions stated in [15 U.S.C. §1114(2)(D)(i), Lanham Act §32(2)(D)(i)]. … Without such limitation of liability, all registrars would potentially have been exposed to the offense of cybersquatting because they register and traffic in domain names that could be infringing or diluting trademarks protected by the Lanham Act." *See also* ***Bird v. Parsons***, 289 F.3d 865, 878 (6th Cir.2002).

Porsche Cars N. Am., Inc. v. Porsche.Net, 302 F.3d 248, 258 (4th Cir.2002). "[T]he ACPA … indicates far more clearly than the diversity statute that once the action is filed and the finding is made, in rem jurisdiction is ordinarily complete. *At 261:* In [enacting 15 U.S.C. §1125(d)(4), Lanham Act §43(d)(4)], Congress took no position on whether in rem jurisdiction under [28 U.S.C.] §1655 'otherwise exists' for trademark-dilution claims under §1125(c)."

Christensen Firm v. Chameleon Data Corp., 83 U.S.P.Q.2d 1856, 1859 (W.D.Wash.2006). D, an information-technology-services company, "argues that it did not 'register' the domain name [by transferring the name to itself], but merely changed the name of the account holder. It argues that ownership never changed, and that its actions did not constitute 'registration' of the domain names in question. However, [D] ignores the import of its actions: transferring the domain name is the 'registration' of that domain name for purposes of the ACPA. … Before [D] transferred the domain names, they were registered to (i.e., owned by) [P]. After it transferred the domain names, they were registered to (i.e., owned by) [D]. The Court concludes as a matter of law that [D] did register the disputed domain names."

Graham & Buffet, Ltd. v. www.vilcabamba.com, 80 U.S.P.Q.2d 1218, 1221 (W.D.Wash.2006). Held: An answer filed by the owner of a domain name divests the trial court of *in rem* jurisdiction over the domain name even though the owner failed to return phone calls, used a post office for an address, and was difficult to find.

§1125(d)(1)

GoPets Ltd. v. Hise, 657 F.3d 1024, 1026 (9th Cir. 2011). "The prohibition contained in §1125(d)(1) applies when a domain name is identical or confusingly similar to a mark that is distinctive 'at the time of registration of the domain name.' The primary question before us is whether the term 'registration' applies only to the initial registration of the domain name, or whether it also applies to a re-registration of a currently registered domain name by a new registrant. We hold that such re-registration is not a 'registration' within the meaning of §1125(d)(1)." *But see* ***Jysk Bed'N Linen v. Dutta-Roy***, 810 F.3d 767, 774 (11th Cir.

2015) (re-registration is a 'registration' within the meaning of §1125(d)(1)); ***Schmidheiny v. Weber***, 319 F.3d 581, 582 (3d Cir.2003) (same).

DSPT Int'l v. Nahum, 624 F.3d 1213, 1219-20 (9th Cir.2010). "[D] argues that the statute applies only to one who registers a well-known trademark as a domain name, and then attempts to profit in bad faith by either (1) selling the domain name back to the trademark holder, or (2) using the domain name to divert business from the trademark holder. He argues that he cannot owe damages under the statute because the evidence shows only that he used [P's] mark to gain leverage over [P] in bargaining for money he claimed he was owed, not to sell under [P's] mark or sell the mark to [P]. He argues that even if in some sense he had a bad-faith intent to profit, any 'intent to profit' under the act must be an intent to profit from the goodwill associated with the mark rather than to gain some other benefit. The core of his argument is that he did not register the domain name in bad faith, and used it only to get what he was entitled to. [¶] His arguments are not implausible, but we conclude that they are mistaken. [¶] Though there was no evidence of anything wrong with [D's] registration of the domain name to himself, the evidence supported a verdict that [D] subsequently, years later, used the domain name to get leverage for his claim for commissions. The statute says 'registers, traffics in, or uses,' with 'or' between the terms, so use alone is enough to support a verdict, even in the absence of violative registration or trafficking. [¶] As for whether use to get leverage in a business dispute can establish a violation, the statutory factors for 'bad faith intent' establish that it can. *At 1224:* Even if a domain name was put up innocently and used properly for years, a person is liable under ... §1125(d) if he subsequently uses the domain name with a bad faith intent to profit from the protected mark by holding the domain name for ransom."

Lahoti v. Vericheck, Inc., 586 F.3d 1190, 1202 (9th Cir.2009). "A finding of 'bad faith' is an essential prerequisite to finding an ACPA violation, though it is not required for general trademark liability. Evidence of bad faith may arise well after registration of the domain name. [¶] Congress has enumerated nine nonexclusive factors for courts to consider in determining whether bad faith exists. We need not, however, march through the nine factors seriatim because the ACPA itself notes that use of the listed criteria is permissive. Instead, the most important grounds for finding bad faith are the unique circumstances of the case. Congress has said that in evaluating bad faith, courts may consider a person's prior cybersquatting activities." (Internal quotes omitted.) *See also* ***Southern Grouts & Mortars, Inc. v. 3M Co.***, 575 F.3d 1235, 1246-47 (11th Cir.2009).

Audi AG v. D'Amato, 469 F.3d 534, 551 (6th Cir. 2006). "A finding of bad faith under the ACPA does not necessarily compel a court to find 'malicious, fraudulent, willful or deliberate' conduct. However, a court would be well within its discretion in determining that bad faith under the ACPA supports finding such conduct." Held: Enough of the ACPA's nine factors for bad faith were established to show bad faith, including that D did not have any prior relationship to the marks and his use of the marks did not constitute noncommercial or fair use.

Lamparello v. Falwell, 420 F.3d 309, 319-20 (4th Cir.2005). "'The first four [factors under §1125(d)(1)(B)(i)] suggest circumstances that may tend to indicate an absence of bad-faith intent to profit from the goodwill of a mark, and the others suggest circumstances that may tend to indicate that such bad-faith intent exists.' However, '[t]here is no simple formula for evaluating and weighing these factors. For example, courts do not simply count up which party has more factors in its favor after the evidence is in.' In fact, because use of these listed factors is permissive, '[w]e need not ... march through' them all in every case. 'The factors are given to courts as a guide, not as a substitute for careful thinking about whether the conduct at issue is motivated by a bad faith intent to profit.'"

Coca-Cola Co. v. Purdy, 382 F.3d 774, 783 (8th Cir. 2004). "The question under the ACPA is not whether the domain names which [D] registered are likely to be confused with a plaintiff's *domain name*, but whether they are identical or confusingly similar to a plaintiff's *mark*. The inquiry under the ACPA is ... narrower than the traditional multifactor likelihood of confusion test for trademark infringement. The fact that confusion about a website's source or sponsorship could be resolved by visiting the website is not relevant to whether the domain name itself is identical or confusingly similar to a plaintiff's mark. *At 786:* A proposal to exchange domain names for valuable consideration is not insignificant in respect to the issue of bad faith intent to profit. ... Profit includes an attempt to procure an 'advantageous gain or return.'" *See also* ***Newport News Holdings Corp. v. Virtual City Vision, Inc.***, 650 F.3d 423, 436-37 (4th Cir.2011).

TMI, Inc. v. Maxwell, 368 F.3d 433, 437 (5th Cir.2004). "When defining commercial use [in §1125(d)(1)(B)(i)(IV)], courts have examined several different aspects of the defendant's use. The Ninth Circuit has emphasized that commercial use in commerce 'refers to a use of a famous and distinctive mark to sell goods other than those produced or authorized by the mark's owner[]' ... and that the phrase 'requires the defendant to be using the trademark as a trademark, capitalizing on its trademark status.' ... This Court has provided a similar definition, determining ... that the defendant's business of selling domain names containing marks satisfied the commercial use requirement. Other courts have emphasized the content of the website. For example, ... the Sixth Circuit concluded that so long as the defendant's fan website contained no links to commercial sites, and contained no advertising or other specifically commercial content, his site was not commercial."

Storey v. Cello Holdings, L.L.C., 347 F.3d 370, 387 (2d Cir.2003). "In cases where the merits of the first action were actually litigated and resolved in the domain-name registrant's favor, *collateral estoppel* may apply to bar relitigation of the confusion issue in §1125(d)(1)(A)(ii), even if *res judicata* does not apply to bar the entire claim." *See also* ***Interstellar Starship Servs. v. Epix, Inc.***, 304 F.3d 936, 946-47 (9th Cir. 2002).

Sporty's Farm L.L.C. v. Sportsman's Mkt., Inc., 202 F.3d 489, 497-98 (2d Cir.2000). Apostrophes "cannot be used in domain names. As a result, the secondary domain name in this case (sportys) is indistinguishable from the ... trademark (*sporty's*). We therefore conclude that, although the domain name sportys .com is not precisely identical to the *sporty's* mark, it is certainly 'confusingly similar' to the protected mark under [15 U.S.C. §1125(d)(1)(A)(ii)(I), Lanham Act §43(d)(1)(A)(ii)(I)]."

Tillery v. Leonard & Sciolla, LLP, 437 F.Supp.2d 312, 320-21 (E.D.Pa.2006). Held: Attorney could not enjoin his former firm to surrender its Internet domain name comprised of his name, because attorney did not present sufficient evidence that he had trademark rights in his name. Attorney had no likelihood of success on the merits because personal names are descriptive and protected under the trademark laws only if they have acquired distinctiveness through evidence of secondary meaning. This was not the case here because attorney did not show that his name was so well known that strangers sought his services, no likelihood of confusion was demonstrated, and there was no evidence of bad faith by Ds.

§1125(d)(2)

Mattel, Inc. v. Barbie-Club.Com, 310 F.3d 293, 300 (2d Cir.2002). "[T]he arrangement of §1125(d)(2) separates, conceptually and chronologically, the prescriptive jurisdiction-granting language of subsection (d)(2)(A) from the descriptive language of legal situs in subsection (d)(2)(C). *At 301:* [B]oth the language of the statute and its legislative history indicate that *in rem* jurisdiction is a preexisting fact determined by the location of the disputed domain name's registrar or a similar authority, and that the subsequent deposit of sufficient documents with a court of appropriate jurisdiction confirms the domain name's legal situs as being in that judicial district for purposes of the litigation. *At 305:* No scenario consistent with this statutory scheme ... would permit an ACPA plaintiff to establish in rem jurisdiction by filing a complaint in a judicial district not contemplated by subsection (d)(2)(A) and then unilaterally seeking to effect a transfer of legal situs to that district."

Harrods Ltd. v. Sixty Internet Domain Names, 302 F.3d 214, 247 (4th Cir.2002). "[W]e hold that 15 U.S.C. §1125(d)(2) [Lanham Act §43(d)(2)] authorizes an in rem action against domain names based on claims of infringement and dilution as well as bad faith registration."

Yahoo!, Inc. v. Yahooahtos.com, 82 U.S.P.Q.2d 1361, 1362-63 (E.D.Va.2006). Held: Acknowledging disagreement among courts within the district, the court held that the publication requirement under the ACPA may be waived if the domain-name registrant has received actual notice of the action. The court found that the word "may" in 15 U.S.C. §1125(d)(2)(A)(II)(bb), Lanham Act §43(d)(2)(A)(II)(bb), made the act ambiguous as to whether publication was mandatory regardless of personal service. *But see* ***INVESTools, Inc. v. investtools.com***, this page.

INVESTools, Inc. v. investtools.com, 81 U.S.P.Q.2d 2019, 2020-21 (E.D.Va.2006). Held: Service for an *in rem* action under the ACPA can only be perfected when all four requirements ((1) jurisdiction is proper, (2) P is unable to obtain *in personam* jurisdiction, (3) service has been perfected under 15 U.S.C. §1125(d)(2)(A)(II), Lanham Act §43(d)(2)(A)(II), and (4) P establishes the elements of trademark infringement or dilution) are satisfied, including publishing a notice of the action. Publication must be demonstrated to the court even though the registrant received actual notice of the action. *But see* ***Yahoo!, Inc. v. Yahooahtos.com***, p. 162.

§1125(d)(3)

St. Luke's Cataract & Laser Inst. v. Sanderson, 573 F.3d 1186, 1203-05 (11th Cir.2009). "[W]e conclude that the district court erred in determining that [P] could not recover damages under both the ACPA and the Lanham Act for several reasons. First, the statutory text of the ACPA explicitly states that a cyberpiracy damages award is 'in addition to' any other civil remedies otherwise available. [¶] An ACPA-cyberpiracy claim, unlike a service mark infringement claim, requires a showing of a 'bad faith intent to profit' from a protected domain name. ... The statutory damages on [P's] ACPA-cyberpiracy claim thus served to sanction or punish [D] for his bad faith conduct in order to deter future violations of the ACPA by him. In contrast, the actual damages on its service mark infringement claim compensated [P] for its own injuries and losses."

§1126. INTERNATIONAL CONVENTIONS

[LANHAM ACT §44]

(a) Register of marks communicated by international bureaus.—The Director shall keep a register of all marks communicated to him by the international bureaus provided for by the conventions for the protection of industrial property, trademarks, trade and commercial names, and the repression of unfair competition to which the United States is or may become a party, and upon the payment of the fees required by such conventions and the fees required in this chapter may place the marks so communicated upon such register. This register shall show a facsimile of the mark or trade or commercial name; the name, citizenship, and address of the registrant; the number, date, and place of the first registration of the mark, including the dates on which application for such registration was filed and granted and the term of such registration; a list of goods or services to which the mark is applied as shown by the registration in the country of origin, and such other data as may be useful concerning the mark. This register shall be a continuation of the register provided in section 1(a) of the Act of March 19, 1920.

(b) Benefits of section to persons whose country of origin is party to convention or treaty.—Any person whose country of origin is a party to any convention or treaty relating to trademarks, trade or commercial names, or the repression of unfair competition, to which the United States is also a party, or extends reciprocal rights to nationals of the United States by law, shall be entitled to the benefits of this section under the conditions expressed herein to the extent necessary to give effect to any provision of such convention, treaty or reciprocal law, in addition to the rights to which any owner of a mark is otherwise entitled by this chapter.

(c) Prior registration in country of origin; country of origin defined.—No registration of a mark in the United States by a person described in subsection (b) of this section shall be granted until such mark has been registered in the country of origin of the applicant, unless the applicant alleges use in commerce.

For the purposes of this section, the country of origin of the applicant is the country in which he has a bona fide and effective industrial or commercial establishment, or if he has not such an establishment the country in which he is domiciled, or if he has not a domicile in any of the countries described in subsection (b) of this section, the country of which he is a national.

(d) Right of priority.—An application for registration of a mark under section 1051, 1053, 1054, or 1091 of title 15 or under subsection (e) of this section, filed by a person described in subsection (b) of this section who has previously duly filed an application for registration of the same mark in one of the countries described in subsection (b) shall be accorded the same force and effect as would be accorded to the same application if filed in the United States on the same date on which the application was first filed in such foreign country: *Provided*, That—

(1) the application in the United States is filed within six months from the date on which the application was first filed in the foreign country;

(2) the application conforms as nearly as practicable to the requirements of this chapter, including a statement that the applicant has a bona fide intention to use the mark in commerce;

(3) the rights acquired by third parties before the date of the filing of the first application in the foreign country shall in no way be affected by a registration obtained on an application filed under this subsection;

(4) nothing in this subsection shall entitle the owner of a registration granted under this section to sue for acts committed prior to the date on which his mark was registered in this country unless the registration is based on use in commerce.

In like manner and subject to the same conditions and requirements, the right provided in this section may be based upon a subsequent regularly filed application in the same foreign country, instead of the first filed foreign application: *Provided*, That any foreign application filed prior to such subsequent application has been withdrawn, abandoned, or otherwise disposed of, without having been laid open to public inspection and without leaving any rights outstanding, and has not served, nor thereafter shall serve, as a basis for claiming a right of priority.

(e) Registration on principal or supplemental register; copy of foreign registration.—A mark duly registered in the country of origin of the foreign applicant may be registered on the principal register if eligible, otherwise on the supplemental register in this chapter provided. Such applicant shall submit, within such time period as may be prescribed by the Director, a true copy, a photocopy, a certification, or a certified copy of the registration in the country of origin of the applicant. The application must state the applicant's bona fide intention to use the mark in commerce, but use in commerce shall not be required prior to registration.

(f) Domestic registration independent of foreign registration.—The registration of a mark under the provisions of subsections (c), (d), and (e) of this section by a person described in subsection (b) of this section shall be independent of the registration in the country of origin and the duration, validity, or transfer in the United States of such registration shall be governed by the provisions of this chapter.

(g) Trade or commercial names of foreign nationals protected without registration.—Trade names or commercial names of persons described in subsection (b) of this section shall be protected without the obligation of filing or registration whether or not they form parts of marks.

(h) Protection of foreign nationals against unfair competition.—Any person designated in subsection (b) of this section as entitled to the benefits and subject to the provisions of this chapter shall be entitled to effective protection against unfair competition, and the remedies provided in this chapter for infringement of marks shall be available so far as they may be appropriate in repressing acts of unfair competition.

(i) Citizens or residents of United States entitled to benefits of section.—Citizens or residents of the United States shall have the same benefits as are granted by this section to persons described in subsection (b) of this section.

History of 15 U.S.C. §1126: July 5, 1946, ch. 540, §44, 60 Stat. 441; Oct. 3, 1961, P.L. 87-333, §2, 75 Stat. 748; Oct. 9, 1962, P.L. 87-772, §20, 76 Stat. 774; Nov. 16, 1988, P.L. 100-667, §133, 102 Stat. 3946; Oct. 30, 1998, P.L. 105-330, §108, 112 Stat. 3068; Aug. 5, 1999, P.L. 106-43, §6(b), 113 Stat. 220; Nov. 29, 1999, P.L. 106-113, §1000(a)(9), 113 Stat. 1536; Nov. 2, 2002, P.L. 107-273, §13207(b)(12), 116 Stat. 1908.

See also Paris Convention arts. 6-10ter; TRIPs pt. II, §§2, 3.

Treatise Cross-References

McCarthy on Trademark & Unfair Competition

Ch. 16, *Acquisition & Priority of Trademark Rights*, §16:21

Ch. 19, *Federal Registration of Marks*, §§19:1; 19:2; 19:5; 19:26; 19:27; 19:31.30; 19:34; 19:46; 19:73; 19:120

Ch. 20, *Inter Partes Trademark Proceedings in the Patent & Trademark Office*, §20:13

Ch. 24, *Infringement by Use of Mark on Noncompetitive Goods or Services*, §24:100

Ch. 26, *The Territorial Extent of Trademark Rights*, §§26:37; 26:38; 26:40

Ch. 27, *Lanham Act §43(a) & False Advertising*, §27:7

Ch. 29, *International Aspects of Trademark Law*, §§29:2; 29:4; 29:10-29:22; 29:25; 29:33

Ch. 32, *Procedure in Trademark Infringement & Unfair Competition Litigation*, §§32:15; 32:16

ANNOTATIONS

Generally

Barcelona.com, Inc. v. Excelentisimo Ayuntamiento, 330 F.3d 617, 628 (4th Cir.2003). "Lanham Act [§44], 15 U.S.C. §1126, incorporates the Paris Convention into U.S. law, but only to provide foreign nationals with rights under U.S. law which are coextensive with the substantive provisions of the treaty involved. The relevant substantive provision in this case is art. 6(3) of the Paris Convention, which implements the doctrine of territoriality by providing that a mark duly registered in a country of the Paris Union shall be regarded as independent of marks registered in the other countries of the Union, including the country of origin. [T]he Paris Convention creates nothing that even remotely resembles a world mark or an international registration. Rather, it recognizes the principle of the territoriality of trademarks in the sense that a mark exists only under the laws of each sovereign nation." (Internal quotes omitted.) *See also* ***Scotch Whisky Ass'n v. Majestic Distilling Co.***, 958 F.2d 594, 597 (4th Cir.1992).

§1126(b)

ITC Ltd. v. Punchgini, Inc., 482 F.3d 135, 163 (2d Cir.2007). "[W]e do not ourselves discern in the plain language of [Lanham Act] §44(b) and (h) [15 U.S.C. §1126(b) and (h)] a clear congressional intent to incorporate a famous marks exception into federal unfair competition law. Section 44(b) guarantees foreign mark holders only 'the benefits of this section ... to the extent necessary to give effect to any ... convention, treaty or reciprocal law,' as well as the 'rights to which any owner of a mark is otherwise entitled by this chapter.' In short, whatever protections [Paris Convention] Arts. 6*bis* and ... 16(2) might contemplate for famous marks, §44(b) grants foreign mark holders covered by these treaties only those protections of U.S. law already specified in the Lanham Act."

Grupo Gigante S.A. v. Dallo & Co., 391 F.3d 1088, 1099 (9th Cir.2004). 15 U.S.C. §1126, Lanham Act §44, "implements Art. 10*bis* [of the Paris Convention] by extending Lanham Act protection to foreign nationals to the extent necessary to satisfy the U.S.'s treaty obligations.... [¶] [P] uses the phrase 'in addition to the rights to which any owner of a mark is otherwise entitled to by this chapter' to argue that §44 ... implements certain additional substantive rights created by international treaties. Although that may be true as a general matter, Art. 10*bis* itself does not create additional substantive rights. Rather, the Paris Convention ensures that foreign nationals should be given the same treatment in each of the member countries as that country makes available to its own citizens as to trademark and related rights. *At 1100:* [T]he Paris Convention was not intended to define the substantive law in the area of unfair competition of the signatory countries. More recently, we concluded that the interaction between §44 ... and Art. 10*bis* ... simply results in equal treatment of foreign and domestic parties in trademark disputes...." (Internal quotes omitted.)

§1126(d)

Empresa Cubana del Tabaco v. Culbro Corp., 399 F.3d 462, 483 (2d Cir.2005). "Foreign entities are entitled to [the] benefit [of priority] regardless of whether a domestic registrant or user had knowledge of the prior foreign registration or use."

In re Hacot-Colombier, 105 F.3d 616, 618 (Fed.Cir. 1997). 15 U.S.C. §1126(d), Lanham Act §44(d), "grants a priority in filing date based on a foreign filing, if a qualified applicant files a U.S. application within six months of filing the same mark in a treaty country. Under this law, the U.S. application receives an effective filing date that is the same as the foreign filing date. To qualify, however, an applicant must include a drawing of the mark with the trademark application."

In re Mastic Inc., 829 F.2d 1114, 1115 (Fed.Cir. 1987). An applicant under 15 U.S.C. §1126, Lanham Act §44, "is excused from the statutory requirement that a mark must be used in commerce in or with the U.S. before such application is filed. An application under §44 must, however, satisfy all other provisions of the Act including ... the requirement that the mark is not likely to cause confusion with a registered mark."

Crocker Nat'l Bank v. Canadian Imperial Bank of Commerce, 223 U.S.P.Q. 909, 924 (T.T.A.B.1984). "[T]he only proper construction of [Lanham Act] §44(c), (d) and (e) [15 U.S.C. §1126(c)-(e)] is that a foreign national qualified under §44(b) is entitled to an alternative basis for registration of a trademark registered in its country of origin without regard to whether such mark is in use prior to the application's filing date. Based on this interpretation, the two requirements imposed in the instant case, i.e., an allegation of use somewhere and specimens demonstrating such use, are contrary to the statute."

§1126(e)

In re Rath, 402 F.3d 1207, 1214 (Fed.Cir.2005). "[W]hile [Lanham Act] §44(e) [15 U.S.C. §1126(e)], like §44(d) [§1126(d)], affects U.S. priority or prior use rules, it is impossible to read §44(e) to require the registration of foreign marks that fail to meet U.S. requirements for eligibility. Section 44 applications are subject to the [Lanham Act §2, 15 U.S.C. §1052,] bars to registration, of which the surname rule is one."

Ocean Garden, Inc. v. Marktrade Co., 953 F.2d 500, 505-06 (9th Cir.1991). 15 U.S.C. §1126, Lanham Act §44, "allows a foreign national to register a mark even though the mark has never been used in U.S. commerce. It is *necessary*, however, for the foreign registrant to use the mark in U.S. commerce within a reasonable time or it is deemed abandoned." *See also* ***Imperial Tobacco Ltd. v. Philip Morris, Inc.***, 899 F.2d 1575, 1578-79 (Fed.Cir.1990).

Imperial Tobacco Ltd. v. Philip Morris, Inc., 899 F.2d 1575, 1578 n.3 (Fed.Cir.1990). "[A] declaration of intent-to-use must now be made in connection with [15 U.S.C. §1126, Lanham Act §44,] applications, but such registration may issue without actual use."

§1126(h)

ITC Ltd. v. Punchgini, Inc., 482 F.3d 135, 164 (2d Cir.2007). "To the extent [Lanham Act] §44(h) [15 U.S.C. §1126(h)] references an 'entitle[ment] to effective protection against unfair competition,' our precedent precludes us from construing this phrase to afford foreign mark holders any rights beyond those specified in §44(b)."

Toho Co. v. Sears, Roebuck & Co., 645 F.2d 788, 793 (9th Cir.1981). 15 U.S.C. §1126(h), Lanham Act §44(h), "requires only that [foreign company] be granted [protection against infringement, passing off, and state-law unfair competition] because it extends only as far as is necessary to give effect to the treaty. Thus, the practical effect of §44 and [the Treaty of Friendship, Commerce and Navigation] is to provide a federal forum in which [a foreign company] can pursue its state claims."

International Bancorp, L.L.C. v. Societe des Bains de Mer, 192 F.Supp.2d 467, 487-88 (E.D.Va. 2002), *aff'd*, 329 F.3d 359 (4th Cir.2003). "[W]hen read with [15 U.S.C. §1126(b), Lanham Act §44(b)], §1126(h) 'provide[s] foreign nationals with rights under U.S. law which are coextensive with the substantive provisions of the treaty involved.' [T]he Paris Convention ... creates no substantive rights beyond those independently provided in the Lanham Act. Given this, there is no occasion here for the operation of §1126(h)."

Magna Pictures Corp. v. Paramount Pictures Corp., 265 F.Supp. 144, 152 (C.D.Cal.1967). 15 U.S.C. §1126, Lanham Act §44, "clearly gives the right of action—then provides—that the remedies shall be the same (where appropriate) as the remedies for infringement of trade marks, i.e., injunction and/or damages."

§1126(i)

Mattel, Inc. v. MCA Records, Inc., 296 F.3d 894, 907-08 (9th Cir.2002). 15 U.S.C. §1126(i), Lanham Act §44(i), "does not create a federal cause of action where §44(h) would not, because it provides only that U.S. citizens shall have the same benefits as are granted by this section to persons described in subsection (b) of this section. And, so far as concerns unfair competition, those benefits are limited to such as may be found in some convention or treaty relating to ... the repression of unfair competition. The purpose of §44(i) ... is no more than to extend to citizens and residents those benefits that any convention or treaty gives to aliens, including the same remedies for protection against unfair competition that subsection (h) gives to aliens. The only protection against unfair competition that §44(h) grants to foreign nationals, and that §44(i) therefore grants to American citizens, is that necessary to give effect to any provisions of trademark treaties." (Internal quotes omitted.)

General Motors Corp. v. Ignacio Lopez de Arriortua, 948 F.Supp. 684, 687 (E.D.Mich.1996). Lanham Act §44(i), 15 U.S.C. §1126(i), "specifically provides ... that U.S. citizens shall have the same rights as foreigners."

§1127. CONSTRUCTION & DEFINITIONS; INTENT OF CHAPTER

[LANHAM ACT §45]

In the construction of this chapter, unless the contrary is plainly apparent from the context—

The United States includes and embraces all territory which is under its jurisdiction and control.

The word "commerce" means all commerce which may lawfully be regulated by Congress.

The term "principal register" refers to the register provided for by sections 1051 to 1072 of title 15, and the term "supplemental register" refers to the register provided for by sections 1091 to 1096 of title 15.

The term "person" and any other word or term used to designate the applicant or other entitled to a benefit or privilege or rendered liable under the provisions of this chapter includes a juristic person as well as a natural person. The term "juristic person" includes a firm, corporation, union, association, or other organization capable of suing and being sued in a court of law.

The term "person" also includes the United States, any agency or instrumentality thereof, or any individual, firm, or corporation acting for the United States and with the authorization and consent of the United States. The United States, any agency or instrumentality thereof, and any individual, firm, or corporation acting for the United States and with the authorization and consent of the United States, shall be subject to the provisions of this chapter in the same manner and to the same extent as any nongovernmental entity.

The term "person" also includes any State, any instrumentality of a State, and any officer or employee of a State or instrumentality of a State acting in his or her official capacity. Any State, and any such instrumentality, officer, or employee, shall be subject to the provisions of this chapter in the same manner and to the same extent as any nongovernmental entity.

The terms "applicant" and "registrant" embrace the legal representatives, predecessors, successors and assigns of such applicant or registrant.

The term "Director" means the Under Secretary of Commerce for Intellectual Property and Director of the United States Patent and Trademark Office.

The term "related company" means any person whose use of a mark is controlled by the owner of the mark with respect to the nature and quality of the goods or services on or in connection with which the mark is used.

The terms "trade name" and "commercial name" mean any name used by a person to identify his or her business or vocation.

The term "trademark" includes any word, name, symbol, or device, or any combination thereof—

(1) used by a person, or

(2) which a person has a bona fide intention to use in commerce and applies to register on the principal register established by this chapter,

to identify and distinguish his or her goods, including a unique product, from those manufactured or sold by others and to indicate the source of the goods, even if that source is unknown.

The term "service mark" means any word, name, symbol, or device, or any combination thereof—

(1) used by a person, or

(2) which a person has a bona fide intention to use in commerce and applies to register on the principal register established by this chapter,

to identify and distinguish the services of one person, including a unique service, from the services of others and to indicate the source of the services, even if that source is unknown. Titles, character names, and other distinctive features of radio or television programs may be registered as service marks notwithstanding that they, or the programs, may advertise the goods of the sponsor.

The term "certification mark" means any word, name, symbol, or device, or any combination thereof—

(1) used by a person other than its owner, or

(2) which its owner has a bona fide intention to permit a person other than the owner to use in commerce and files an application to register on the principal register established by this chapter,

to certify regional or other origin, material, mode of manufacture, quality, accuracy, or other characteristics of such person's goods or services or that the work or labor on the goods or services was performed by members of a union or other organization.

The term "collective mark" means a trademark or service mark—

(1) used by the members of a cooperative, an association, or other collective group or organization, or

(2) which such cooperative, association, or other collective group or organization has a bona fide intention to use in commerce and applies to register on the principal register established by this chapter,

and includes marks indicating membership in a union, an association, or other organization.

The term "mark" includes any trademark, service mark, collective mark, or certification mark.

The term "use in commerce" means the bona fide use of a mark in the ordinary course of trade, and not made merely to reserve a right in a mark. For purposes of this chapter, a mark shall be deemed to be in use in commerce—

(1) on goods when—

(A) it is placed in any manner on the goods or their containers or the displays associated therewith or on the tags or labels affixed thereto, or if the nature of the goods makes such placement impracticable, then on documents associated with the goods or their sale, and

(B) the goods are sold or transported in commerce, and

(2) on services when it is used or displayed in the sale or advertising of services and the services are rendered in commerce, or the services are rendered in more than one State or in the United States and a foreign country and the person rendering the services is engaged in commerce in connection with the services.

A mark shall be deemed to be "abandoned" if either of the following occurs:

(1) When its use has been discontinued with intent not to resume such use. Intent not to resume may be inferred from circumstances. Nonuse for 3 consecutive years shall be prima facie evidence of abandonment. "Use" of a mark means the bona fide use of such mark made in the ordinary course of trade, and not made merely to reserve a right in a mark.

(2) When any course of conduct of the owner, including acts of omission as well as commission, causes the mark to become the generic name for the goods or services on or in connection with which it is used or otherwise to lose its significance as a mark. Purchaser motivation shall not be a test for determining abandonment under this paragraph.

The term "colorable imitation" includes any mark which so resembles a registered mark as to be likely to cause confusion or mistake or to deceive.

The term "registered mark" means a mark registered in the United States Patent and Trademark Office under this chapter or under the Act of March 3, 1881, or the Act of February 20, 1905, or the Act of March 19, 1920. The phrase "marks registered in the Patent and Trademark Office" means registered marks.

The term "Act of March 3, 1881," "Act of February 20, 1905," or "Act of March 19, 1920," means the respective Act as amended.

A "counterfeit" is a spurious mark which is identical with, or substantially indistinguishable from, a registered mark.

The term "domain name" means any alphanumeric designation which is registered with or assigned by any domain name registrar, domain name registry, or other domain name registration authority as part of an electronic address on the Internet.

The term "Internet" has the meaning given that term in section 230(f)(1) of title 47.

Words used in the singular include the plural and vice versa.

The intent of this chapter is to regulate commerce within the control of Congress by making actionable the deceptive and misleading use of marks in such commerce; to protect registered marks used in such commerce from interference by State, or territorial legislation; to protect persons engaged in such commerce against unfair competition; to prevent fraud and deception in such commerce by the use of reproductions, copies, counterfeits, or colorable imitations of registered marks; and to provide rights and remedies stipulated by treaties and conventions respecting trademarks, trade names, and unfair competition entered into between the United States and foreign nations.

History of 15 U.S.C. §1127: July 5, 1946, ch. 540, §45, 60 Stat. 443; Oct. 9, 1962, P.L. 87-772, §21, 76 Stat. 774; Jan. 2, 1975, P.L. 93-596, §1, 88 Stat. 1949; Nov. 8, 1984, P.L. 98-620, §103, 98 Stat. 3335; Nov. 16, 1988, P.L. 100-667, §134, 102 Stat. 3946; Oct. 27, 1992, P.L. 102-542, §3(d), 106 Stat. 3568; Dec. 8, 1994, P.L. 103-465, §521, 108 Stat. 4981; Jan. 16, 1996, P.L. 104-98, §4, 109 Stat. 986; Aug. 5, 1999, P.L. 106-43, §§4(c), 6(b), 113 Stat. 219, 220; Nov. 29, 1999, P.L. 106-113, §1000(a)(9), 113 Stat. 1536; Oct. 6, 2006, P.L. 109-312, §3(e), 120 Stat. 1732.

See also TRIPs pt. II, §§2, 3.

Treatise Cross-References

McCarthy on Trademark & Unfair Competition

Ch. 3, *The Functions of Trademarks*, §3:1
Ch. 4, *Explaining Terms of Art in Trademark & Unfair Competition Law*, §§4:10; 4:12
Ch. 5, *Historical Basis of Trademarks & Legislative History*, §§5:8; 5:9
Ch. 6, *Trademarks Compared to Patents & Copyrights*, §6:11
Ch. 7, *Trademark & Trade Dress Formats*, §7:54
Ch. 9, *Corporation & Organization Trade Names*, §9:13
Ch. 10, *Literary, Artistic & Entertainment Rights*, §10:38
Ch. 12, *Generic Terms*, §12:56
Ch. 15, *Secondary Meaning*, §15:8
Ch. 16, *Acquisition & Priority of Trademark Rights*, §§16:23; 16:27; 16:33; 16:41
Ch. 17, *Loss of Trademark Rights*, §§17:5; 17:9; 17:11; 17:17; 17:18; 17:21
Ch. 18, *Assignment & Licensing of Trademarks*, §§18:15; 18:48; 18:49; 18:51; 18:53
Ch. 19, *Federal Registration of Marks*, §§19:1.25; 19:16; 19:80; 19:90; 19:98; 19:103; 19:103.50; 19:108; 19:109; 19:115; 19:117; 19:118
Ch. 23, *Likelihood of Confusion: The Test of Trademark Infringement*, §§23:1; 23:11.50; 23:76
Ch. 24, *Infringement by Use of Mark on Noncompetitive Goods or Services*, §24:102
Ch. 25, *Types of Trademark Infringement*, §§25:10; 25:11; 25:15; 25:53
Ch. 27, *Lanham Act §43(a) & False Advertising*, §27:6

ANNOTATIONS

Generally

International Franchise Ass'n v. City of Seattle, 803 F.3d 389, 409 (9th Cir.2015). "As the Lanham Act does not expressly preempt state law, … and courts have said that it does not occupy the field, [state or local law] can only be preempted if it conflicts with the Lanham Act.…"

Topps Co. v. Cadbury Stani S.A.I.C., 526 F.3d 63, 70 (2d Cir.2008). "The principle of territoriality is fundamental to trademark law. A trademark has a separate legal existence under each country's laws, and trademark rights exist in each country solely according to that nation's laws."

Abandoned

For more annotations on this topic, see 15 U.S.C. §1064, *§1064(3)—Abandoned*, p. 41, and 15 U.S.C. §1115, *§1115(b)(2)*, p. 83.

Specht v. Google Inc., 747 F.3d 929, 934-35 (7th Cir.2014). "Under the Lanham Act, '[n]onuse for three consecutive years shall be prima facie evidence of abandonment[ ]'.... A prima facie showing of abandonment may be rebutted with evidence excusing the nonuse or demonstrating an intent to resume use. But the intent to resume use in commerce must be formulated within the three years of nonuse. Furthermore, the use must pertain to the sale of goods or provision of services. [¶] [P] points out that [P's] website was operating until 2005, and a website that bears a trademark may constitute a bona fide use in commerce. But [P] did not identify any goods or services [P's company] could have provided through or in connection with the website after 2002. As such, the website was not a use in commerce. [P] maintains that his two sales efforts in 2007 (the mass mailing and his failed bid to license software to a healthcare firm) are evidence of commercial use of the mark. But these two efforts were isolated and not sustained; sporadic attempts to solicit business are not a 'use in commerce' meriting the protection of the Lanham Act."

Patsy's Italian Rest., Inc. v. Banas, 658 F.3d 254, 264-65 (2d Cir.2011). "Although some forms of trademark abandonment may result in a loss of all rights in the mark, ... abandonment of a mark through naked licensing has different effects on the validity of the mark in different markets. For example, if a restaurant operates in both New York and California, but engages in naked licensing only in California, the restaurant's registered mark may lose its significance in California while retaining its significance in New York. Thus, naked licensing will lead to an abandonment of a mark only where the mark loses its significance."

ITC Ltd. v. Punchgini, Inc., 482 F.3d 135, 147 (2d Cir.2007). "The Lanham Act expressly states that '[n]onuse' of a mark 'for three consecutive years shall be prima facie evidence of abandonment.' This court has explained that the term 'prima facie evidence' in this context means 'a rebuttable presumption of abandonment.' *At 148:* [T]he statutory presumption of abandonment requires that one fact, i.e., abandonment, be inferred from another fact, i.e., nonuse of the mark for three years or more. The significance of a presumption of abandonment is to shift the burden of production to the mark owner to come forward with evidence indicating that, despite three years of nonuse, it intended to resume use of the mark within a reasonably foreseeable time. The ultimate burden of persuasion on the issue of abandonment, however, remains at all times with the alleged infringer." *See also* ***George & Co. v. Imagination Entm't Ltd.***, 575 F.3d 383, 400-01 (4th Cir.2009); ***Burgess v. Gilman***, 475 F.Supp.2d 1051, 1059-60 (D.Nev.2007), *aff'd*, 316 Fed.Appx. 542 (9th Cir.2008) (explaining that Ninth Circuit follows Second Circuit, but there is a circuit split over shifting burdens).

Electro Source, LLC v. Brandess-Kalt-Aetna Grp., 458 F.3d 931, 933 (9th Cir.2006). "Is a summary judgment determination of abandonment appropriate when the record supports an inference that the trademark holder—a small, troubled business—continued to transport and sell trademarked goods in the ordinary course of trade as part of a good faith effort to deplete inventory? The answer is no, because the trademark law requires both discontinuance of all bona fide trademark use in the ordinary course of trade and an intent not to resume such use. Legitimate commercial transport or sales of trademarked goods, even for a failing business, are sufficient to defeat a claim of abandonment. *At 937 n.4:* In cases where there is a presumption of abandonment from nonuse, ... a mere statement declaring an intent not to abandon, or an intent to resume, use is not dispositive. *At 938:* Even a single instance of use is sufficient against a claim of abandonment of a mark if such use is made in good faith. *At 938 n.5:* [U]se in commerce appears to contemplate a trading upon the goodwill of or association with the trademark holder. This requirement attempts to distinguish activities that may be made in good faith, but nonetheless do not constitute a trademark use. The question is whether the transaction was one that could trade upon the goodwill or association with the trademark. *At 939:* Good faith nominal or limited commercial sales of trademarked goods are sufficient, we held, to avoid abandonment, where the circumstances legitimately explained the paucity of the sales. *At 939 n.6:* In contrast, a trademark maintenance program obviously cannot in itself justify a minimal sales effort, or the requirement of good faith commercial use would be read out of the trademark law altogether. Similarly, the sale of a trademarked item cannot be a trademark use if not made in the ordinary course of trade. *At 940:* Because the abandonment inquiry is tied to the unique circumstances of each case, it is appropriate to look at the totality of the circumstances to determine if genuine, albeit limited, usage of the mark qualifies a trademark use in the ordinary course of trade under §1127. The factors that guide courts in examining trademark use in the context of trademark registration are instructive: In applying this approach, the district courts should be guided in their consideration by factors such as the genuineness and commercial character of the activity, the determination of whether the mark was sufficiently public to identify or distinguish the marked service or product in an appropriate segment of the public mind as those of the holder of the mark, the scope of the trademark activity relative to what would be a commercially reasonable attempt to market the service or product, the degree of ongoing activity of the holder to conduct the business using the mark, the amount of business transacted, and other similar factors which might distinguish whether a service or product has actually been rendered in commerce." (Internal quotes omitted.) *See also* ***Central Mfg. v. Brett***, 78 U.S.P.Q.2d 1662, 1669 (N.D.Ill.2005), *aff'd*, 492 F.3d 876 (7th Cir.2007).

Tumblebus Inc. v. Cranmer, 399 F.3d 754, 764 (6th Cir.2005). "One method by which a mark may be abandoned is through 'naked licensing,' which occurs '[w]hen a trademark owner fails to exercise reasonable control over the use of a mark by a licensee,' such that 'the presence of the mark on the licensee's goods or services misrepresents their connection with the trademark owner since the mark no longer identifies goods or services that are under the control of the owner of the mark' and the mark can no longer provide 'a meaningful assurance of quality.'" *See also* ***Doeblers' Pa. Hybrids, Inc. v. Doebler***, 442 F.3d 812, 823-24 (3d Cir.2006).

interState Net Bank v. NetB@nk, Inc., 348 F.Supp.2d 340, 352 (D.N.J.2004). "[T]he effect of the invalid assignment of the trademark registration from Software Agents to Net.B@nk is that the rights revert to Software Agents, the original registrant. Software Agents, however, ceased any use of the term NETBANK as of April 1998. Since this cessation of use occurred more than three years ago, prima facie evidence of abandonment exists and in the absence here of anything in the record to support an inference that Software Agents intends to resume any use, cancellation of the registration is appropriate."

EH Yacht, LLC v. Egg Harbor, LLC, 84 F.Supp.2d 556, 566 (D.N.J.2000). Congress's "use in [15 U.S.C. §1127, Lanham Act §45,] of the term 'deemed'—a term that suggests an objective finding of abandonment by a factfinder—shows Congress's intent that a determination of intent not to resume use should be based on the totality of objective evidence of intent to resume use, not simply the intent of the registered trademark owner. Under this standard, so long as there is power to do so, *any* valid intent to resume use within a reasonable time becomes relevant. Thus, the Court holds that ... the party wishing to show intent not to resume use ... must point to objective evidence that clearly and convincingly establishes that, among those that had an interest and right to do so, there was no intent to resume use of the ... name within a reasonable time."

Collective Mark

National Cable TV Ass'n v. American Cinema Editors, Inc., 937 F.2d 1572, 1574 (Fed.Cir.1991). "Members [of D-corporation] are entitled to display the acronym 'A.C.E.' after their names which appear ... in the screen credits appended to television programs and motion picture films. A mark so used by members of an organization is known as a 'collective mark.'"

Opticians Ass'n v. Independent Opticians, 920 F.2d 187, 193 n.8 (3d Cir.1990). "The Lanham Act definition of collective marks includes two types. The first is the collective membership mark, which is 'used by members to indicate that they are members of a union, association or another organization[.] They are used to signify membership of an individual.' The second type of collective mark is the collective trade- or service mark, 'used only by members of an organization to identify and distinguish *their* goods or services. The collective organization itself neither sells goods nor performs services under the mark, but may advertise or promote goods or services sold by its members under the mark.'"

Commerce

For more annotations on this topic, see 15 U.S.C. §1114, *§1114(1)—Commerce*, p. 64.

McBee v. Delica Co., 417 F.3d 107, 120 (1st Cir. 2005). "The substantial effects test requires that there be evidence of impacts within the U.S., and these impacts must be of a sufficient character and magnitude to give the U.S. a reasonably strong interest in the litigation. *At 122:* Since sales in the U.S. are domestic acts, [P] need not satisfy the 'substantial effect on U.S. commerce' test for this claim; jurisdiction exists because, under the ordinary domestic test, the $2,500 worth of goods sold by [D] to [P's] investigators in the U.S. were in U.S. commerce.... *At 123:* [D's] website, although hosted from Japan and written in Japanese, happens to be reachable from the U.S. just as it is reachable from other countries. *At 124:* [T]he mere existence of a website that is visible in a forum and that gives information about a company and its products is not enough, by itself, to subject a defendant to personal jurisdiction in that forum. [¶] Something more is necessary, such as interactive features which allow the successful online ordering of the defendant's products. *At 125:* [P's] claim for damages due to [D's] sales in Japan fares no better, because these sales as well have no substantial effect on commerce in the U.S."

Shatel Corp. v. Mao Ta Lumber & Yacht Corp., 697 F.2d 1352, 1356 (11th Cir.1983). "'Commerce' ... includes commerce between citizens of the U.S. and citizens and subjects of foreign nations. Commerce within the power of Congress to control 'is not confined to transportation from one State to another, but comprehends all commercial intercourse between different States and all the component parts of that intercourse.' Advertising that affects interstate commerce and solicitation of sales across state lines or between citizens of the U.S. and citizens and subjects of a foreign nation is therefore commerce within the meaning of the Lanham Act."

Cable News Network L.P. v. cnnews.com, 177 F.Supp.2d 506, 517 (E.D.Va.2001), *vacated in part on other grounds*, 56 Fed.Appx. 599 (4th Cir.2003). "[I]t is clear that the provision of news and information services on the Internet constitutes 'commerce' under the [Lanham] Act. But this does not end the analysis, as it is less clear whether the 'use in [U.S.] commerce' requirement is met where, as here, a website ostensibly directed solely at internet users outside the U.S. can satisfy the requirement."

Domain Name

State Auto Prop. & Cas. Ins. v. Travelers Indem. Co., 343 F.3d 249, 252 n.4 (4th Cir.2003). "A domain name is an electronic address that directs Internet users to a website." *See also* ***Virtual Countries, Inc. v. Republic of S. Africa***, 300 F.3d 230, 233 n.2 (2d Cir. 2002).

Porsche Cars N. Am., Inc. v. Porsche.Net, 302 F.3d 248, 252 (4th Cir.2002). "Also known colloquially as a 'Web address,' a domain name is a combination of characters that a person types into a computer software program called a browser, in order to gain access to a Web site, a set of computer files through which another person provides information over the Internet."

Registrant

Federal Treasury Enter. Sojuzplodoimport v. SPI Spirits Ltd., 726 F.3d 62, 79 (2d Cir.2013). "The interpretation of the phrase 'legal representative' in the Lanham Act context appears to present a question of first impression in the federal courts of appeal. *At 82:* We ... conclude that to serve as a 'legal representative' entitled to bring suit under [Lanham Act] §32(1) [15 U.S.C. §1114(1)] on behalf of a trademark holder, a putative plaintiff must demonstrate *both* its legal authority to represent the owner and that the trademark holder is legally incapable of representing itself."

Related Company

First Interstate Bancorp v. Stenquist, 16 U.S.P.Q.2d 1704, 1706 (N.D.Cal.1990). Where "a trademark owner engages in naked licensing, without any control over the quality of goods produced by the licensee, such a practice is inherently deceptive and constitutes abandonment of any rights to the trademark by the licensor."

Huntington Nat'l Mattress Co. v. Celanese Corp., 201 F.Supp. 938, 945 (D.Md.1962). "Even if the affiliated companies are so controlled by [P] as to be 'related companies' within the meaning of the statute, there is a duty on [P], as the owner and licensor of the registered mark ..., to take reasonable means to detect and prevent misleading uses of its mark by the affiliated companies. The only effective way to protect the public, where a trademark is used by licensees, is to place on the owner the affirmative duty of policing in a reasonable manner the activities of his licensees to assure that the licensee will apply the mark to a product of substantially the same quality that the public has in the past associated with it."

Service Mark

Radiance Found. v. NAACP, 786 F.3d 316, 323-24 (4th Cir.2015). "A service is [an] amorphous concept, 'denot[ing] an intangible commodity in the form of human effort, such as labor, skill, or advice.' Because Congress intended the Lanham Act to protect consumers from confusion in the marketplace, it is probable that the Act is meant to cover a wide range of products, whether 'goods' or 'services.'"

Trademark

Qualitex Co. v. Jacobson Prods. Co., 514 U.S. 159, 160-61 (1995). "The question in this case is whether the Trademark Act ... (Lanham Act) ... permits the registration of a trademark that consists, purely and simply, of a color. We conclude that, sometimes, a color will meet ordinary legal trademark requirements. And, when it does so, no special legal rule prevents color alone from serving as a trademark." *See also* ***Sunrise Jewelry Mfg. v. Fred S.A.***, 175 F.3d 1322, 1325 (Fed. Cir.1999).

Radiance Found. v. NAACP, 786 F.3d 316, 323 (4th Cir.2015). "A 'good' is best understood as a valuable product, physical or otherwise, that the consumer may herself employ."

Fortune Dynamic, Inc. v. Victoria's Secret Stores Brand Mgmt., 618 F.3d 1025, 1040 (9th Cir. 2010). "To determine whether a term is being used as a mark, we look for indications that the term is being used to 'associate it with a manufacturer.' Indications of trademark use include whether the term is used as a 'symbol to attract public attention,' ... which can be demonstrated by 'the lettering, type style, size and visual placement and prominence of the challenged words'.... Another indication of trademark use is whether the allegedly infringing user undertook 'precautionary measures such as labeling or other devices designed to minimize the risk that the term will be understood in its trademark sense.'"

ETW Corp. v. Jireh Publ'g, 332 F.3d 915, 921-22 (6th Cir.2003). "The essence of a trademark is a designation in the form of a distinguishing name, symbol or device which is used to identify a person's goods and distinguish them from the goods of another. Not every word, name, symbol or device qualifies as a protectable mark; rather, it must be proven that it performs the job of identification, *i.e.*, to identify one source and to distinguish it from other sources. If it does not do this, then it is not protectable as a trademark."

Oliveira v. Frito-Lay, Inc., 251 F.3d 56, 61 (2d Cir. 2001). "We can see no reason why a musical composition should be ineligible to serve as a symbol or device to identify a person's goods or services."

Blockbuster Videos, Inc. v. City of Tempe, 141 F.3d 1295, 1300 (9th Cir.1998). "In order for a trademark to be a symbol that customers will recognize, it must have a uniform appearance, not only in design, but also in color. The Supreme Court has recognized that color is so important to customer recognition that, in some instances, the color itself can be registered as a trademark because customers identify a particular brand by its color."

In re Marriott Corp., 459 F.2d 525, 527 (C.C.P.A. 1972). "The 1946 Trademark Act created an innovation in making use of the mark on displays associated with the goods a trademark usage, although there had previously been limited recognition of such use. A distinction is drawn between a display *per se* as a trademark and a display which exhibits the mark thereon. The latter would be a poster or the like on, or in, the showcase for the goods, or conceivably even on the window of the store in which the goods were sold, which poster exhibited the word, name, symbol or device and would be a use within the terms of the statute of the word, name, symbol or device." (Internal quotes omitted.)

Use in Commerce

For more annotations on this topic, see 15 U.S.C. §1051, *§1051(a)—Use in Commerce*, p. 6, and 15 U.S.C. §1114, *§1114(1)—Commerce*, p. 64.

Lyons v. American Coll. of Vet. Sports Med. & Rehab., 859 F.3d 1023, 1028 (Fed.Cir.2017). "[T]o meet the use requirement for a service mark, an applicant must use the mark in *advertising or sale* of a service, and show that the service was *actually rendered* in interstate commerce or in more than one state, or in this and a foreign country, by a person engaged in commerce." *See also* ***Sensient Techs. v. SensoryEffects Flavor Co.***, 613 F.3d 754, 759-63 (8th Cir.2010); ***International Bancorp, LLC v. Societe des Bains de Mer***, 329 F.3d 359, 361-66 (4th Cir.2003); ***Buti v. Impressa Perosa, S.R.L.***, 139 F.3d 98, 101-03 (2d Cir.1998).

FN Herstal SA v. Clyde Armory Inc., 838 F.3d 1071, 1081 (11th Cir.2016). "The typical evidence of use in commerce is the sale of goods bearing the mark. However, in the absence of actual sales, advertising, publicity, and solicitation can sufficiently meet the public identification prong of the test. The district court and the parties use the term 'analogous use' to describe these promotional efforts, which is derived from other courts' analysis of this issue. However, 'activities claimed to constitute analogous use must have substantial impact on the purchasing public.' 'At the very least analogous use must be use that is open and notorious [or] of such a nature and extent that the mark has become popularized in the public mind so that the relevant segment of the public identifies the marked goods with the mark's adopter.' The promotional activities must also occur within a commercially reasonable period of time prior to actual use of the mark to be considered analogous use of the mark." *See also* ***Rearden LLC v. Rearden Commerce, Inc.***, 683 F.3d 1190, 1205-06 (9th Cir.2012).

Christian Faith Fellowship Ch. v. adidas AG, 841 F.3d 986, 992-93 (Fed.Cir.2016). "[T]he [registrant's] sale of two 'ADD A ZERO'-marked hats to an out-of-state resident is regulable by Congress under the Commerce Clause and, therefore, constitutes 'use in commerce' under the Lanham Act. [I]t cannot be doubted that the transaction at issue—the private sale of goods, particularly apparel, to an out-of-state resident—is 'quintessentially economic.' This transaction, taken in the aggregate, would cause a substantial effect on interstate commerce and thus it falls under Congress's Commerce Clause powers. The [registrant] did not need to present evidence of an actual and specific effect that its sale of hats to an out-of-state resident had on interstate commerce. Nor did it need to make a particularized showing that the hats themselves were destined to travel out of state. [¶] '[T]he *de minimis* character of individual instances' arising under a valid statute enacted under the Commerce Clause 'is of no consequence.' '[I]t makes no difference under our cases that any actual or threatened effect on commerce in a particular case is minimal.' [Opposer's] argument that [registrant] must present actual proof that its sale to [third party] directly affected commerce also contradicts precedent. '[P]roof that the defendant's conduct in and of itself affected or threatened commerce is not needed. All that is needed is proof that the defendant's conduct fell within a category of conduct that, in the aggregate, had the requisite effect.'"

Lens.com, Inc. v. 1-800 Contacts, Inc., 686 F.3d 1376, 1380 (Fed.Cir.2012). "[T]he actual sale of goods is not required to satisfy §1127's 'use in commerce' requirement, provided that the goods are 'transported' in commerce. However, 'not every transport of a good is sufficient to establish ownership rights in a mark.' 'In assessing rights stemming from transportation, courts and commentators have required an element of public awareness of the use.' [¶] The focus of the appeal is ... whether [petitioner's website] software is a 'good' that is 'transported in commerce.' Our predecessor court established that an article does not qualify as a good in trade when that article is 'simply the conduit through which [the applicant] renders services,' i.e., is 'the essence or gist of [the applicant's] services.' It is also well established that when an article 'has no independent value apart from the services,' such article is not likely to be an independent good in trade. *At 1381-82:* While we agree with the 11th Circuit that the distribution of Software over the internet *can* satisfy the jurisdictional predicate for 'use in commerce[,]' ... whether consumers actually associate a mark with *software*, as opposed to other *services*, is a factual determination that must be conducted on a case-by-case basis. Relevant factors to consider include whether the software: (1) is simply the conduit or necessary tool useful only to obtain applicant's services; (2) is so inextricably tied to and associated with the service as to have no viable existence apart therefrom; and (3) is neither sold separately from nor has any independent value apart from the services. None of these factors need necessarily be dispositive, but each may shed light on whether an applicant's software is an independent *good* being 'sold or transported in commerce.' *At 1383:* [T]his court concludes that the Board properly determined that the mark ... is not in 'use in commerce' in association with software. The Board's decision on the issue of abandonment is ... affirmed."

Network Automation, Inc. v. Advanced Sys. Concepts, Inc., 638 F.3d 1137, 1144-45 (9th Cir.2011). "We note that the district court correctly found the prerequisite 'use in commerce' in [D's] use of the mark to purchase key-words to advertise its products for sale on the Internet. Previously we have assumed, without expressly deciding, that the use of a trademark as a search engine keyword that triggers the display of a competitor's advertisement is a 'use in commerce' under the Lanham Act. We now agree with the Second Circuit that such use is a 'use in commerce' under the Lanham Act." *See also* ***Rescuecom Corp. v. Google Inc.***, 562 F.3d 123, 127 (2d Cir.2009).

Sensient Techs. v. SensoryEffects Flavor Co., 613 F.3d 754, 762 (8th Cir.2010). "[P] attempts to satisfy [use in commerce] by pointing to [subsidiary's] efforts to advertise and market its goods through two customer presentations, a press release, an announcement, and a website. [¶] [P's] argument conflates the distinction between goods and services provided under [§1127]. ***Rescuecom*** and the other cases [P] relies upon involved an alleged infringer's services, not goods, and therefore the courts applied the separate definition ... for determining whether the services were 'used in commerce.' Even in cases applying the services definition, many courts have held mere advertising is not enough to constitute 'use in commerce' because 'a mark is used in commerce only if it accompanies services rendered in commerce.' [¶] [P] fails to show evidence of any sale or transport of any goods bearing [subsidiary's] mark."

Rescuecom Corp. v. Google Inc., 562 F.3d 123, 130 (2d Cir.2009). "[A] defendant must do more than use another's mark in commerce to violate the Lanham Act. The gist of a Lanham Act violation is an unauthorized use, which 'is likely to cause confusion, ... mistake, or to deceive as to the affiliation, ... or as to the origin, sponsorship, or approval of ... goods [or] services.'"

Editor's note: Appendix to opinion is an explanation of the history and meaning of "use in commerce" and an observation that the court's opinion assumed the requirements of the second sentence of the definition of "use in commerce" in §1127 apply to infringing conduct and found use in commerce was adequately pleaded. The Northern District of Texas elaborated on ***Rescuecom***'s discussion and noted that the circuits are split on whether §1127's definition of "use in commerce" applies to infringement claims, finally concluding that the Fifth Circuit uses the definition but dispenses with the "bona fide use" requirement. ***GoForIt Entm't, LLC v. DigiMedia.com L.P.***, 750 F.Supp.2d 712, 726 n.10 (N.D.Tex.2010).

Aycock Eng'g v. Airflite, Inc., 560 F.3d 1350, 1355 (Fed.Cir.2009). "A prerequisite to deciding the use requirement issue ... involves defining the recitation of services in the application. *At 1357:* [The] 'bona fide use' language was intended to eliminate 'token uses,' which occurred when applicants used marks in conjunction with selling goods or offering services for the sole purpose of obtaining registration, and with no intention of legitimately using the mark in commerce until a later date." *See also* ***Allard Enters. v. Advanced Programming Res.***, 146 F.3d 350, 357 (6th Cir.1998); ***Personal Publ'ns v. Sagittarius Broad. Corp.***, 42 U.S.P.Q.2d 1089, 1091 (S.D.N.Y.1996).

1-800 Contacts, Inc. v. WhenU.Com, Inc., 414 F.3d 400, 403 (2d Cir.2005). "We hold that, as a matter of law, [D] does not 'use' [P's] trademarks within the meaning of the Lanham Act when it (1) includes [P's] website address, which is almost identical to [P's] trademark, in an unpublished directory of terms that trigger delivery of [D's] contextually relevant advertising to [computer users]; or (2) causes separate, branded pop-up ads to appear on a [computer user's] computer screen either above, below, or along the bottom edge of [P's] website window." Held: The use of a trademark owner's Internet address in an unpublished internal directory to trigger pop-up advertising was not a trademark "use" in commerce because such an internal use "is analogous to an individual's private thoughts about a trademark." *See also* ***Merck & Co. v. Mediplan Health Consulting, Inc.***, 425 F.Supp.2d 402, 415 (S.D.N.Y.2006). *But see* ***Australian Gold, Inc. v. Hatfield***, 436 F.3d 1228, 1239 (10th Cir.2006) (use of trademark in metatags was trademark violation); ***800-JR Cigar, Inc. v. GoTo.com, Inc.***, p. 175.

General Healthcare Ltd. v. Qashat, 364 F.3d 332, 335 (1st Cir.2004). "'[N]ot every transport of a good is sufficient to establish ownership rights in a mark.' In assessing rights stemming from transportation, courts and commentators have required an element of public awareness of the use."

International Bancorp, LLC v. Societe des Bains de Mer, 329 F.3d 359, 373 (4th Cir.2003). 15 U.S.C. §1127, Lanham Act §45, "defines the term 'use in commerce' with respect to services as being when a mark is 'used or displayed in the sale or advertising of services *and* the services are rendered in commerce.' As a consequence of the *conjunctive* command, it is not enough for a mark owner simply to render services in foreign commerce for it to be eligible for trademark protection. Nor is it enough for a mark owner simply to use or display a mark in the sale or advertising of services to U.S. consumers. *Both* elements are required, and *both* elements must be distinctly analyzed." *But see* ***Kerzner Int'l v. Monarch Casino & Resort, Inc.***, 675 F.Supp.2d 1029, 1038-39 (D.Nev.2009) (predicting Ninth Circuit will decline to adopt ***International Bancorp***'s exception to territoriality principle).

Karl Storz Endoscopy, Inc. v. Surgical Tech., 285 F.3d 848, 855 (9th Cir.2002). "The 'or transported' language of 15 U.S.C. §1127 [Lanham Act §45] makes it clear that a 'use in commerce' under the Lanham Act is not limited to sales. The sending of a product from Los Angeles to New York with its label attached so that its trademark could be registered has been considered transportation in commerce. Further, nothing in the language of the statute itself expressly precludes a repair or reconstruction from constituting a 'use in commerce.' However, 'use in commerce' appears to contemplate a trading upon the goodwill of or association with the trademark holder. Therefore, a mere repair of a trademarked good, followed by return of the good to the same owner who requested the repair or rebuild, does not constitute a 'use in commerce' of the trademark under the Lanham Act."

New England Duplicating Co. v. Mendes, 190 F.2d 415, 418 (1st Cir.1951). "It seems to us that although evidence of sales is highly persuasive, the question of use [in commerce] adequate to establish appropriation remains one to be decided on the facts of each case, and that evidence showing, first, adoption, and, second, use in a way sufficiently public to identify or distinguish the marked goods in an appropriate segment of the public mind as those of the adopter of the mark, is competent to establish ownership, even without evidence of actual sales."

800-JR Cigar, Inc. v. GoTo.com, Inc., 437 F.Supp.2d 273, 285 (D.N.J.2006). "[T]he pop-up advertising context, where the use of trademarks in internal computer coding is neither communicated to the public nor for sale to the highest bidder, [is different from D's use of P's marks]. [¶] Here, [D] makes trademark use of [P's] marks in three ways. First, by accepting bids from those competitors of [P] desiring to pay for prominence in search results, [D] trades on the value of the marks. Second, by ranking its paid advertisers before any 'natural' listings in a search results list, [D] has injected itself into the marketplace, acting as a conduit to steer potential customers away from [P] to [P's] competitors. Finally, through the Search Term Suggestion Tool, [D] identifies those of [P's] marks which are effective search terms and markets them to [P's] competitors." Held: D uses P's marks in commerce. *See also* ***Playboy Enters. v. Netscape Comms.***, 354 F.3d 1020, 1024 (9th Cir.2004); ***Boston Duck Tours, LP v. Super Duck Tours, LLC***, 527 F.Supp.2d 205, 207 (D.Mass.2007) (use of mark to sell "sponsored links" advertising is commercial use). *But see* ***1-800 Contacts, Inc. v. WhenU.Com, Inc.***, p. 174.

Cable News Network L.P. v. cnnews.com, 177 F.Supp.2d 506, 517 (E.D.Va.2001), *vacated in part on other grounds*, 56 Fed.Appx. 599 (4th Cir.2003). "[I]t is clear that the provision of news and information services on the Internet constitutes 'commerce' under the [Lanham] Act. But this does not end the analysis, as it is less clear whether the 'use in [U.S.] commerce' requirement is met where, as here, a website ostensibly directed solely at internet users outside the U.S. can satisfy the requirement."

Aluminum Fabricating Co. v. Season-All Window Corp., 160 F.Supp. 41, 45 (S.D.N.Y.1957), *aff'd*, 259 F.2d 314 (2d Cir.1958). A trademark "is used in commerce 'on goods when it is placed in any manner on the goods or their containers or the displays associated therewith ... *and* the goods are sold or transported in commerce....' The use of the conjunction 'and' implies that the display and sale need not be contemporaneous."

§1128. REPEALED

[LANHAM ACT §46]

Repealed Oct. 13, 2008, P.L. 110-403, §305(a)(1), 122 Stat. 4270.

§1129. TRANSFERRED

[LANHAM ACT §47]

Transferred to 15 U.S.C. §8131.

Sections 1129-1140 reserved for expansion

SUBCHAPTER IV. THE MADRID PROTOCOL

§1141. DEFINITIONS

[LANHAM ACT §60]

In this subchapter:

(1) Basic application.—The term "basic application" means the application for the registration of a mark that has been filed with an Office of a Contracting Party and that constitutes the basis for an application for the international registration of that mark.

(2) Basic registration.—The term "basic registration" means the registration of a mark that has been granted by an Office of a Contracting Party and that constitutes the basis for an application for the international registration of that mark.

(3) Contracting party.—The term "Contracting Party" means any country or inter-governmental organization that is a party to the Madrid Protocol.

(4) Date of recordal.—The term "date of recordal" means the date on which a request for extension of protection, filed after an international registration is granted, is recorded on the International Register.

(5) Declaration of bona fide intention to use the mark in commerce.—The term "declaration of bona fide intention to use the mark in commerce" means a declaration that is signed by the applicant for, or holder of, an international registration who is seeking extension of protection of a mark to the United States and that contains a statement that—

(A) the applicant or holder has a bona fide intention to use the mark in commerce;

(B) the person making the declaration believes himself or herself, or the firm, corporation, or association in whose behalf he or she makes the declaration, to be entitled to use the mark in commerce; and

(C) no other person, firm, corporation, or association, to the best of his or her knowledge and belief, has the right to use such mark in commerce either in the identical form of the mark or in such near resemblance to the mark as to be likely, when used on or in connection with the goods of such other person, firm, corporation, or association, to cause confusion, mistake, or deception.

(6) Extension of protection.—The term "extension of protection" means the protection resulting from an international registration that extends to the United States at the request of the holder of the international registration, in accordance with the Madrid Protocol.

(7) Holder of an international registration.—A "holder" of an international registration is the natural or juristic person in whose name the international registration is recorded on the International Register.

(8) International application.—The term "international application" means an application for international registration that is filed under the Madrid Protocol.

(9) International Bureau.—The term "International Bureau" means the International Bureau of the World Intellectual Property Organization.

(10) International Register.—The term "International Register" means the official collection of data concerning international registrations maintained by the International Bureau that the Madrid Protocol or its implementing regulations require or permit to be recorded.

(11) International registration.—The term "international registration" means the registration of a mark granted under the Madrid Protocol.

(12) International registration date.—The term "international registration date" means the date assigned to the international registration by the International Bureau.

(13) Madrid Protocol.—The term "Madrid Protocol" means the Protocol Relating to the Madrid Agreement Concerning the International Registration of Marks, adopted at Madrid, Spain, on June 27, 1989.

(14) Notification of refusal.—The term "notification of refusal" means the notice sent by the United States Patent and Trademark Office to the International Bureau declaring that an extension of protection cannot be granted.

(15) Office of a Contracting Party.—The term "Office of a Contracting Party" means—

(A) the office, or governmental entity, of a Contracting Party that is responsible for the registration of marks; or

(B) the common office, or governmental entity, of more than 1 Contracting Party that is responsible for the registration of marks and is so recognized by the International Bureau.

(16) Office of origin.—The term "office of origin" means the Office of a Contracting Party with which a basic application was filed or by which a basic registration was granted.

(17) Opposition period.—The term "opposition period" means the time allowed for filing an opposition in the United States Patent and Trademark Office, including any extension of time granted under section 1063 of title 15.

History of 15 U.S.C. §1141: July 5, 1946, ch. 540, §60, as added Nov. 2, 2002, P.L. 107-273, §13402, 116 Stat. 1913.

See also 37 C.F.R. pt. 7; Madrid Protocol.

Treatise Cross-References

McCarthy on Trademark & Unfair Competition

Ch. 19, *Federal Registration of Marks*, §§19:31.20; 19:31.55; 19:31.60

§1141a. INTERNATIONAL APPLICATIONS BASED ON UNITED STATES APPLICATIONS OR REGISTRATIONS

[LANHAM ACT §61]

(a) In general.—The owner of a basic application pending before the United States Patent and Trademark Office, or the owner of a basic registration granted by the United States Patent and Trademark Office may file an international application by submitting to the United States Patent and Trademark Office a written application in such form, together with such fees, as may be prescribed by the Director.

(b) Qualified owners.—A qualified owner, under subsection (a) of this section, shall—

(1) be a national of the United States;

(2) be domiciled in the United States; or

(3) have a real and effective industrial or commercial establishment in the United States.

History of 15 U.S.C. §1141a: July 5, 1946, ch. 540, §61, as added Nov. 2, 2002, P.L. 107-273, §13402, 116 Stat. 1915.

Treatise Cross-References

McCarthy on Trademark & Unfair Competition

Ch. 19, *Federal Registration of Marks*, §19:31.40

§1141b. CERTIFICATION OF THE INTERNATIONAL APPLICATION

[LANHAM ACT §62]

(a) Certification procedure.—Upon the filing of an application for international registration and payment of the prescribed fees, the Director shall examine the international application for the purpose of certifying that the information contained in the international application corresponds to the information contained in the basic application or basic registration at the time of the certification.

(b) Transmittal.—Upon examination and certification of the international application, the Director shall transmit the international application to the International Bureau.

History of 15 U.S.C. §1141b: July 5, 1946, ch. 540, §62, as added Nov. 2, 2002, P.L. 107-273, §13402, 116 Stat. 1915.

See also Madrid Protocol arts. 3, 5bis, 8.

§1141c. RESTRICTION, ABANDONMENT, CANCELLATION, OR EXPIRATION OF A BASIC APPLICATION OR BASIC REGISTRATION

[LANHAM ACT §63]

With respect to an international application transmitted to the International Bureau under section 1141b of title 15, the Director shall notify the International Bureau whenever the basic application or basic registration which is the basis for the international application has been restricted, abandoned, or canceled, or has expired, with respect to some or all of the goods and services listed in the international registration—

(1) within 5 years after the international registration date; or

(2) more than 5 years after the international registration date if the restriction, abandonment, or cancellation of the basic application or basic registration resulted from an action that began before the end of that 5-year period.

History of 15 U.S.C. §1141c: July 5, 1946, ch. 540, §63, as added Nov. 2, 2002, P.L. 107-273, §13402, 116 Stat. 1915.

See also Madrid Protocol arts. 6-8.

§1141d. REQUEST FOR EXTENSION OF PROTECTION SUBSEQUENT TO INTERNATIONAL REGISTRATION

[LANHAM ACT §64]

The holder of an international registration that is based upon a basic application filed with the United States Patent and Trademark Office or a basic registration granted by the Patent and Trademark Office may request an extension of protection of its international registration by filing such a request—

(1) directly with the International Bureau; or

(2) with the United States Patent and Trademark Office for transmittal to the International Bureau, if the request is in such form, and contains such transmittal fee, as may be prescribed by the Director.

History of 15 U.S.C. §1141d: July 5, 1946, ch. 540, §64, as added Nov. 2, 2002, P.L. 107-273, §13402, 116 Stat. 1916.

See also Madrid Protocol art. 3ter.

§1141e. EXTENSION OF PROTECTION OF AN INTERNATIONAL REGISTRATION TO THE UNITED STATES UNDER THE MADRID PROTOCOL

[LANHAM ACT §65]

(a) In general.—Subject to the provisions of section 1141h of title 15, the holder of an international registration shall be entitled to the benefits of extension of protection of that international registration to the United States to the extent necessary to give effect to any provision of the Madrid Protocol.

(b) If the United States is office of origin.—Where the United States Patent and Trademark Office is the office of origin for a trademark application or registration, any international registration based on such application or registration cannot be used to obtain the benefits of the Madrid Protocol in the United States.

History of 15 U.S.C. §1141e: July 5, 1946, ch. 540, §65, as added Nov. 2, 2002, P.L. 107-273, §13402, 116 Stat. 1916.

See also Madrid Protocol.

§1141f. EFFECT OF FILING A REQUEST FOR EXTENSION OF PROTECTION OF AN INTERNATIONAL REGISTRATION TO THE UNITED STATES

[LANHAM ACT §66]

(a) Requirement for request for extension of protection.—A request for extension of protection of an international registration to the United States that the International Bureau transmits to the United States Patent and Trademark Office shall be deemed to be properly filed in the United States if such request, when received by the International Bureau, has attached to it a declaration of bona fide intention to use the mark in commerce that is verified by the applicant for, or holder of, the international registration.

(b) Effect of proper filing.—Unless extension of protection is refused under section 1141h of title 15, the proper filing of the request for extension of protection under subsection (a) of this section shall constitute constructive use of the mark, conferring the same rights as those specified in section 1057(c) of title 15, as of the earliest of the following:

(1) The international registration date, if the request for extension of protection was filed in the international application.

(2) The date of recordal of the request for extension of protection, if the request for extension of protection was made after the international registration date.

(3) The date of priority claimed pursuant to section 1141g of title 15.

History of 15 U.S.C. §1141f: July 5, 1946, ch. 540, §66, as added Nov. 2, 2002, P.L. 107-273, §13402, 116 Stat. 1916.

See also Madrid Protocol arts. 4-5.

Treatise Cross-References

McCarthy on Trademark & Unfair Competition

Ch. 19, *Federal Registration of Marks*, §§19:1; 19:31.30; 19:31.60
Ch. 20, *Inter Partes Trademark Proceedings in the Patent & Trademark Office*, §20:13

§1141g. RIGHT OF PRIORITY FOR REQUEST FOR EXTENSION OF PROTECTION TO THE UNITED STATES

[LANHAM ACT §67]

The holder of an international registration with a request for an extension of protection to the United States shall be entitled to claim a date of priority based on a right of priority within the meaning of Article 4 of the Paris Convention for the Protection of Industrial Property if—

(1) the request for extension of protection contains a claim of priority; and

(2) the date of international registration or the date of the recordal of the request for extension of protection to the United States is not later than 6 months after the date of the first regular national filing (within the meaning of Article 4(A)(3) of the Paris Convention for the Protection of Industrial Property) or a subsequent application (within the meaning of Article 4(C)(4) of the Paris Convention for the Protection of Industrial Property).

History of 15 U.S.C. §1141g: July 5, 1946, ch. 540, §67, as added Nov. 2, 2002, P.L. 107-273, §13402, 116 Stat. 1917.

See also Madrid Protocol arts. 4, 9quinquies; Paris Convention art. 4.

Treatise Cross-References

McCarthy on Trademark & Unfair Competition

Ch. 19, *Federal Registration of Marks*, §19:31.60

§1141h. EXAMINATION OF & OPPOSITION TO REQUEST FOR EXTENSION OF PROTECTION; NOTIFICATION OF REFUSAL

[LANHAM ACT §68]

(a) Examination and opposition—

(1) A request for extension of protection described in section 1141f(a) of title 15 shall be examined as an application for registration on the Principal Register under this chapter, and if on such examination it appears that the applicant is entitled to extension of protection under this subchapter, the Director shall cause the mark to be published in the Official Gazette of the United States Patent and Trademark Office.

(2) Subject to the provisions of subsection (c) of this section, a request for extension of protection under this subchapter shall be subject to opposition under section 1063 of title 15.

(3) Extension of protection shall not be refused on the ground that the mark has not been used in commerce.

(4) Extension of protection shall be refused to any mark not registrable on the Principal Register.

(b) Notification of refusal.—If,[1] a request for extension of protection is refused under subsection (a) of this section, the Director shall declare in a notification of refusal (as provided in subsection (c) of this section) that the extension of protection cannot be granted, together with a statement of all grounds on which the refusal was based.

(c) Notice to International Bureau—

(1) Within 18 months after the date on which the International Bureau transmits to the Patent and Trademark Office a notification of a request for extension of protection, the Director shall transmit to the International Bureau any of the following that applies to such request:

(A) A notification of refusal based on an examination of the request for extension of protection.

(B) A notification of refusal based on the filing of an opposition to the request.

(C) A notification of the possibility that an opposition to the request may be filed after the end of that 18-month period.

(2) If the Director has sent a notification of the possibility of opposition under paragraph (1)(C), the Director shall, if applicable, transmit to the International Bureau a notification of refusal on the basis of the opposition, together with a statement of all the grounds for the opposition, within 7 months after the beginning of the opposition period or within 1 month after the end of the opposition period, whichever is earlier.

(3) If a notification of refusal of a request for extension of protection is transmitted under paragraph (1) or (2), no grounds for refusal of such request other than those set forth in such notification may be transmitted to the International Bureau by the Director after the expiration of the time periods set forth in paragraph (1) or (2), as the case may be.

(4) If a notification specified in paragraph (1) or (2) is not sent to the International Bureau within the time period set forth in such paragraph, with respect to a request for extension of protection, the request for extension of protection shall not be refused and the Director shall issue a certificate of extension of protection pursuant to the request.

(d) Designation of agent for service of process.—In responding to a notification of refusal with respect to a mark, the holder of the international registration of the mark may designate, by a document filed in the United States Patent and Trademark Office, the name and address of a person residing in the United States on whom notices or process in proceedings affecting the mark may be served. Such notices or process may be served upon the person designated by leaving with that person, or mailing to that person, a copy thereof at the address specified in the last designation filed. If the person designated cannot be found at the address given in the last designation, or if the holder does not designate by a document filed in the United States Patent and Trademark Office the name and address of a person residing in the United States for service of notices or process in proceedings affecting the mark, the notice or process may be served on the Director.

1. **Editor's note:** The comma probably should not appear.

History of 15 U.S.C. §1141h: July 5, 1946, ch. 540, §68, as added Nov. 2, 2002, P.L. 107-273, §13402, 116 Stat. 1917.

See also Madrid Protocol arts. 4, 5.

Treatise Cross-References

McCarthy on Trademark & Unfair Competition

Ch. 19, *Federal Registration of Marks*, §19:31.60

§1141i. Effect of Extension of Protection

[Lanham Act §69]

(a) Issuance of extension of protection.—Unless a request for extension of protection is refused under section 1141h of title 15, the Director shall issue a certificate of extension of protection pursuant to the request and shall cause notice of such certificate of extension of protection to be published in the Official Gazette of the United States Patent and Trademark Office.

(b) Effect of extension of protection.—From the date on which a certificate of extension of protection is issued under subsection (a) of this section—

(1) such extension of protection shall have the same effect and validity as a registration on the Principal Register; and

(2) the holder of the international registration shall have the same rights and remedies as the owner of a registration on the Principal Register.

History of 15 U.S.C. §1141i: July 5, 1946, ch. 540, §69, as added Nov. 2, 2002, P.L. 107-273, §13402, 116 Stat. 1918.

See also Madrid Protocol arts. 3ter, 4, 8.

§1141j. Dependence of Extension of Protection to the United States on the Underlying International Registration

[Lanham Act §70]

(a) Effect of cancellation of international registration.—If the International Bureau notifies the United States Patent and Trademark Office of the cancellation of an international registration with respect to some or all of the goods and services listed in the international registration, the Director shall cancel any extension of protection to the United States with respect to such goods and services as of the date on which the international registration was canceled.

(b) Effect of failure to renew international registration.—If the International Bureau does not renew an international registration, the corresponding extension of protection to the United States shall cease to be valid as of the date of the expiration of the international registration.

(c) Transformation of an extension of protection into a United States application.—The holder of an international registration canceled in whole or in part by the International Bureau at the request of the office of origin, under article 6(4) of the Madrid Protocol, may file an application, under section 1051 or 1126 of this title, for the registration of the same mark for any of the goods and services to which the cancellation applies that were covered by an extension of protection to the United States based on that international registration. Such an application shall be treated as if it had been filed on the international registration date or the date of recordal of the request for extension of protection with the International Bureau, whichever date applies, and, if the extension of protection enjoyed priority under section 1141g of this title, shall enjoy the same priority. Such an application shall be entitled to the benefits conferred by this subsection only if the application is filed not later than 3 months after the date on which the international registration was canceled, in whole or in part, and only if the application complies with all the requirements of this chapter which apply to any application filed pursuant to section 1051 or 1126 of this title.

History of 15 U.S.C. §1141j: July 5, 1946, ch. 540, §69, as added Nov. 2, 2002, P.L. 107-273, §13402, 116 Stat. 1918.

See also Madrid Protocol arts. 6, 7.

Treatise Cross-References

McCarthy on Trademark & Unfair Competition

Ch. 19, *Federal Registration of Marks*, §§19:1; 19:31.65

§1141k. DURATION, AFFIDAVITS & FEES

[LANHAM ACT §71]

(a) Time periods for required affidavits.—Each extension of protection for which a certificate has been issued under section 1141i of title 15 shall remain in force for the term of the international registration upon which it is based, except that the extension of protection of any mark shall be canceled by the Director unless the holder of the international registration files in the United States Patent and Trademark Office affidavits that meet the requirements of subsection (b), within the following time periods:

(1) Within the 1-year period immediately preceding the expiration of 6 years following the date of issuance of the certificate of extension of protection.

(2) Within the 1-year period immediately preceding the expiration of 10 years following the date of issuance of the certificate of extension of protection, and each successive 10-year period following the date of issuance of the certificate of extension of protection.

(3) The holder may file the affidavit required under this section within a grace period of 6 months after the end of the applicable time period established in paragraph (1) or (2), together with the fee described in subsection (b) and the additional grace period surcharge prescribed by the Director.

(b) Requirements for affidavit.—The affidavit referred to in subsection (a) shall—

(1)(A) state that the mark is in use in commerce;

(B) set forth the goods and services recited in the extension of protection on or in connection with which the mark is in use in commerce;

(C) be accompanied by such number of specimens or facsimiles showing current use of the mark in commerce as may be required by the Director; and

(D) be accompanied by the fee prescribed by the Director; or

(2)(A) set forth the goods and services recited in the extension of protection on or in connection with which the mark is not in use in commerce;

(B) include a showing that any nonuse is due to special circumstances which excuse such nonuse and is not due to any intention to abandon the mark; and

(C) be accompanied by the fee prescribed by the Director.

(c) Deficient affidavit.—If any submission filed within the period set forth in subsection (a) is deficient, including that the affidavit was not filed in the name of the holder of the international registration, the deficiency may be corrected after the statutory time period, within the time prescribed after notification of the deficiency. Such submission shall be accompanied by the additional deficiency surcharge prescribed by the Director.

(d) Notice of requirement.—Special notice of the requirement for such affidavit shall be attached to each certificate of extension of protection.

(e) Notification of acceptance or refusal.—The Director shall notify the holder of the international registration who files any affidavit required by this section of the Director's acceptance or refusal thereof and, in the case of a refusal, the reasons therefor.

(f) Designation of resident for service of process and notices.—If the holder of the international registration of the mark is not domiciled in the United States, the holder may designate, by a document filed in the United States Patent and Trademark Office, the name and address of a person resident in the United States on whom may be served notices or process in proceedings affecting the mark. Such notices or process may be served upon the person so designated by leaving with that person or mailing to that person a copy thereof at the address specified in the last designation so filed. If the person so designated cannot be found at the last designated address, or if the holder does not designate by a document filed in the United States Patent and Trademark Office the name and address of a person resident in the United States on whom may be served notices or process in proceedings affecting the mark, such notices or process may be served on the Director.

History of 15 U.S.C. §1141k: July 5, 1946, ch. 540, §71, as added Nov. 2, 2002, P.L. 107-273, §13402, 116 Stat. 1919; Mar. 17, 2010, P.L. 111-146, §3(d)(2), 124 Stat. 68.

See also Madrid Protocol arts. 6-8.

Treatise Cross-References

McCarthy on Trademark & Unfair Competition

Ch. 19, *Federal Registration of Marks*, §19:31.60

§1141*l*. ASSIGNMENT OF AN EXTENSION OF PROTECTION

[LANHAM ACT §72]

An extension of protection may be assigned, together with the goodwill associated with the mark, only to a person who is a national of, is domiciled in, or has a bona fide and effective industrial or commercial establishment either in a country that is a Contracting Party or in a country that is a member of an intergovernmental organization that is a Contracting Party.

History of 15 U.S.C. §1141*l*: July 5, 1946, ch. 540, §72, as added Nov. 2, 2002, P.L. 107-273, §13402, 116 Stat. 1920.

See also Madrid Protocol art. 9.

§1141m. INCONTESTABILITY

[LANHAM ACT §73]

The period of continuous use prescribed under section 1065 of title 15 for a mark covered by an extension of protection issued under this subchapter may begin no earlier than the date on which the Director issues the certificate of the extension of protection under section 1141i of title 15, except as provided in section 1141n of title 15.

History of 15 U.S.C. §1141m: July 5, 1946, ch. 540, §73, as added Nov. 2, 2002, P.L. 107-273, §13402, 116 Stat. 1920.

See also Madrid Protocol.

§1141n. RIGHTS OF EXTENSION OF PROTECTION

[LANHAM ACT §74]

When a United States registration and a subsequently issued certificate of extension of protection to the United States are owned by the same person, identify the same mark, and list the same goods or services, the extension of protection shall have the same rights that accrued to the registration prior to issuance of the certificate of extension of protection.

History of 15 U.S.C. §1141n: July 5, 1946, ch. 540, §74, as added Nov. 2, 2002, P.L. 107-273, §13402, 116 Stat. 1920.

See also Madrid Protocol art. 4.

Treatise Cross-References

McCarthy on Trademark & Unfair Competition

Ch. 19, *Federal Registration of Marks*, §19:31.60

TITLE 17. COPYRIGHTS

TABLE OF CONTENTS

TITLE 17. COPYRIGHTS

TITLE 17. COPYRIGHTS

TABLE OF CONTENTS

TITLE 17. COPYRIGHTS

CHAPTER 1. SUBJECT MATTER & SCOPE OF COPYRIGHT

§101. DEFINITIONS

Except as otherwise provided in this title, as used in this title, the following terms and their variant forms mean the following:

An "anonymous work" is a work on the copies or phonorecords of which no natural person is identified as author.

An "architectural work" is the design of a building as embodied in any tangible medium of expression, including a building, architectural plans, or drawings. The work includes the overall form as well as the arrangement and composition of spaces and elements in the design, but does not include individual standard features.

"Audiovisual works" are works that consist of a series of related images which are intrinsically intended to be shown by the use of machines, or devices such as projectors, viewers, or electronic equipment, together with accompanying sounds, if any, regardless of the nature of the material objects, such as films or tapes, in which the works are embodied.

The "Berne Convention" is the Convention for the Protection of Literary and Artistic Works, signed at Berne, Switzerland, on September 9, 1886, and all acts, protocols, and revisions thereto.

The "best edition" of a work is the edition, published in the United States at any time before the date of deposit, that the Library of Congress determines to be most suitable for its purposes.

A person's "children" are that person's immediate offspring, whether legitimate or not, and any children legally adopted by that person.

A "collective work" is a work, such as a periodical issue, anthology, or encyclopedia, in which a number of contributions, constituting separate and independent works in themselves, are assembled into a collective whole.

A "compilation" is a work formed by the collection and assembling of preexisting materials or of data that are selected, coordinated, or arranged in such a way that the resulting work as a whole constitutes an original work of authorship. The term "compilation" includes collective works.

A "computer program" is a set of statements or instructions to be used directly or indirectly in a computer in order to bring about a certain result.

"Copies" are material objects, other than phonorecords, in which a work is fixed by any method now known or later developed, and from which the work can be perceived, reproduced, or otherwise communicated, either directly or with the aid of a machine or device. The term "copies" includes the material object, other than a phonorecord, in which the work is first fixed.

"Copyright owner," with respect to any one of the exclusive rights comprised in a copyright, refers to the owner of that particular right.

A "Copyright Royalty Judge" is a Copyright Royalty Judge appointed under section 802 of this title, and includes any individual serving as an interim Copyright Royalty Judge under such section.

A work is "created" when it is fixed in a copy or phonorecord for the first time; where a work is prepared over a period of time, the portion of it that has been fixed at any particular time constitutes the work as of that time, and where the work has been prepared in different versions, each version constitutes a separate work.

A "derivative work" is a work based upon one or more preexisting works, such as a translation, musical arrangement, dramatization, fictionalization, motion picture version, sound recording, art reproduction, abridgment, condensation, or any other form in which a work may be recast, transformed, or adapted. A work consisting of editorial revisions, annotations, elaborations, or other modifications which, as a whole, represent an original work of authorship, is a "derivative work."

A "device," "machine," or "process" is one now known or later developed.

A "digital transmission" is a transmission in whole or in part in a digital or other non-analog format.

To "display" a work means to show a copy of it, either directly or by means of a film, slide, television image, or any other device or process or, in the case of a motion picture or other audiovisual work, to show individual images nonsequentially.

An "establishment" is a store, shop, or any similar place of business open to the general public for the primary purpose of selling goods or services in which the majority of the gross square feet of space that is nonresidential is used for that purpose, and in which nondramatic musical works are performed publicly.

The term "financial gain" includes receipt, or expectation of receipt, of anything of value, including the receipt of other copyrighted works.

A work is "fixed" in a tangible medium of expression when its embodiment in a copy or phonorecord, by or under the authority of the author, is sufficiently permanent or stable to permit it to be perceived, reproduced, or otherwise communicated for a period of more than transitory duration. A work consisting of sounds, images, or both, that are being transmitted, is "fixed" for purposes of this title if a fixation of the work is being made simultaneously with its transmission.

A "food service or drinking establishment" is a restaurant, inn, bar, tavern, or any other similar place of business in which the public or patrons assemble for the primary purpose of being served food or drink, in which the majority of the gross square feet of space that is nonresidential is used for that purpose, and in which nondramatic musical works are performed publicly.

The "Geneva Phonograms Convention" is the Convention for the Protection of Producers of Phonograms Against Unauthorized Duplication of Their Phonograms, concluded at Geneva, Switzerland, on October 29, 1971.

The "gross square feet of space" of an establishment means the entire interior space of that establishment, and any adjoining outdoor space used to serve patrons, whether on a seasonal basis or otherwise.

The terms "including" and "such as" are illustrative and not limitative.

An "international agreement" is—

(1) the Universal Copyright Convention;

(2) the Geneva Phonograms Convention;

(3) the Berne Convention;

(4) the WTO Agreement;

(5) the WIPO Copyright Treaty;

(6) the WIPO Performances and Phonograms Treaty; and

(7) any other copyright treaty to which the United States is a party.

A "joint work" is a work prepared by two or more authors with the intention that their contributions be merged into inseparable or interdependent parts of a unitary whole.

"Literary works" are works, other than audiovisual works, expressed in words, numbers, or other verbal or numerical symbols or indicia, regardless of the nature of the material objects, such as books, periodicals, manuscripts, phonorecords, film, tapes, disks, or cards, in which they are embodied.

The term "motion picture exhibition facility" means a movie theater, screening room, or other venue that is being used primarily for the exhibition of a copyrighted motion picture, if such exhibition is open to the public or is made to an assembled group of viewers outside of a normal circle of a family and its social acquaintances.

"Motion pictures" are audiovisual works consisting of a series of related images which, when shown in succession, impart an impression of motion, together with accompanying sounds, if any.

To "perform" a work means to recite, render, play, dance, or act it, either directly or by means of any device or process or, in the case of a motion picture or other audiovisual work, to show its images in any sequence or to make the sounds accompanying it audible.

A "performing rights society" is an association, corporation, or other entity that licenses the public performance of nondramatic musical works on behalf of copyright owners of such works, such as the American Society of Composers, Authors and Publishers (ASCAP), Broadcast Music, Inc. (BMI), and SESAC, Inc.

"Phonorecords" are material objects in which sounds, other than those accompanying a motion picture or other audiovisual work, are fixed by any method now known or later developed, and from which the sounds can be perceived, reproduced, or otherwise communicated, either directly or with the aid of a machine or device. The term "phonorecords" includes the material object in which the sounds are first fixed.

"Pictorial, graphic, and sculptural works" include two-dimensional and three-dimensional works of fine, graphic, and applied art, photographs, prints and art reproductions, maps, globes, charts, diagrams, models, and technical drawings, including architectural plans. Such works shall include works of artistic craftsmanship insofar as their form but not their mechanical or utilitarian aspects are concerned; the design of a useful article, as defined in this section, shall be considered a pictorial, graphic, or sculptural work only if, and only to the extent that, such design incorporates pictorial, graphic, or sculptural features that can be identified separately from, and are capable of existing independently of, the utilitarian aspects of the article.

For purposes of section 513, a "proprietor" is an individual, corporation, partnership, or other entity, as the case may be, that owns an establishment or a food service or drinking establishment, except that no owner or operator of a radio or television station licensed by the Federal Communications Commission, cable system or satellite carrier, cable or satellite carrier service or programmer, provider of online services or network access or the operator of facilities therefor, telecommunications company, or any other such audio or audiovisual service or programmer now known or as may be developed in the future, commercial subscription music service, or owner or operator of any other transmission service, shall under any circumstances be deemed to be a proprietor.

A "pseudonymous work" is a work on the copies or phonorecords of which the author is identified under a fictitious name.

"Publication" is the distribution of copies or phonorecords of a work to the public by sale or other transfer of ownership, or by rental, lease, or lending. The offering to distribute copies or phonorecords to a group of persons for purposes of further distribution, public performance, or public display, constitutes publication. A public performance or display of a work does not of itself constitute publication.

To perform or display a work "publicly" means—

(1) to perform or display it at a place open to the public or at any place where a substantial number of persons outside of a normal circle of a family and its social acquaintances is gathered; or

(2) to transmit or otherwise communicate a performance or display of the work to a place specified by clause (1) or to the public, by means of any device or process, whether the members of the public capable of receiving the performance or display receive it in the same place or in separate places and at the same time or at different times.

"Registration," for purposes of sections 205(c)(2), 405, 406, 410(d), 411, 412, and 506(e), means a registration of a claim in the original or the renewed and extended term of copyright.

"Sound recordings" are works that result from the fixation of a series of musical, spoken, or other sounds, but not including the sounds accompanying a motion picture or other audiovisual work, regardless of the nature of the material objects, such as disks, tapes, or other phonorecords, in which they are embodied.

"State" includes the District of Columbia and the Commonwealth of Puerto Rico, and any territories to which this title is made applicable by an Act of Congress.

A "transfer of copyright ownership" is an assignment, mortgage, exclusive license, or any other conveyance, alienation, or hypothecation of a copyright or of any of the exclusive rights comprised in a copyright, whether or not it is limited in time or place of effect, but not including a nonexclusive license.

A "transmission program" is a body of material that, as an aggregate, has been produced for the sole purpose of transmission to the public in sequence and as a unit.

To "transmit" a performance or display is to communicate it by any device or process whereby images or sounds are received beyond the place from which they are sent.

A "treaty party" is a country or intergovernmental organization other than the United States that is a party to an international agreement.

The "United States," when used in a geographical sense, comprises the several States, the District of Columbia and the Commonwealth of Puerto Rico, and the organized territories under the jurisdiction of the United States Government.

For purposes of section 411, a work is a "United States work" only if—

(1) in the case of a published work, the work is first published—

(A) in the United States;

(B) simultaneously in the United States and another treaty party or parties, whose law grants a term of copyright protection that is the same as or longer than the term provided in the United States;

(C) simultaneously in the United States and a foreign nation that is not a treaty party; or

(D) in a foreign nation that is not a treaty party, and all of the authors of the work are nationals, domiciliaries, or habitual residents of, or in the case of an audiovisual work legal entities with headquarters in, the United States;

(2) in the case of an unpublished work, all the authors of the work are nationals, domiciliaries, or habitual residents of the United States, or, in the case of an unpublished audiovisual work, all the authors are legal entities with headquarters in the United States; or

(3) in the case of a pictorial, graphic, or sculptural work incorporated in a building or structure, the building or structure is located in the United States.

A "useful article" is an article having an intrinsic utilitarian function that is not merely to portray the appearance of the article or to convey information. An article that is normally a part of a useful article is considered a "useful article."

The author's "widow" or "widower" is the author's surviving spouse under the law of the author's domicile at the time of his or her death, whether or not the spouse has later remarried.

The "WIPO Copyright Treaty" is the WIPO Copyright Treaty concluded at Geneva, Switzerland, on December 20, 1996.

The "WIPO Performances and Phonograms Treaty" is the WIPO Performances and Phonograms Treaty concluded at Geneva, Switzerland, on December 20, 1996.

A "work of visual art" is—

(1) a painting, drawing, print, or sculpture, existing in a single copy, in a limited edition of 200 copies or fewer that are signed and consecutively numbered by the author, or, in the case of a sculpture, in multiple cast, carved, or fabricated sculptures of 200 or fewer that are consecutively numbered by the author and bear the signature or other identifying mark of the author; or

(2) a still photographic image produced for exhibition purposes only, existing in a single copy that is signed by the author, or in a limited edition of 200 copies or fewer that are signed and consecutively numbered by the author.

A work of visual art does not include—

(A)(i) any poster, map, globe, chart, technical drawing, diagram, model, applied art, motion picture or other audiovisual work, book, magazine, newspaper, periodical, data base, electronic information service, electronic publication, or similar publication;

(ii) any merchandising item or advertising, promotional, descriptive, covering, or packaging material or container;

(iii) any portion or part of any item described in clause (i) or (ii);

(B) any work made for hire; or

(C) any work not subject to copyright protection under this title.

A "work of the United States Government" is a work prepared by an officer or employee of the United States Government as part of that person's official duties.

A "work made for hire" is—

(1) a work prepared by an employee within the scope of his or her employment; or

(2) a work specially ordered or commissioned for use as a contribution to a collective work, as a part of a motion picture or other audiovisual work, as a translation, as a supplementary work, as a compilation, as an instructional text, as a test, as answer material for a test, or as an atlas, if the parties expressly agree in a written instrument signed by them that the work shall be considered a work made for hire. For the purpose of the foregoing sentence, a "supplementary work" is a work prepared for publication as a secondary adjunct to a work by another author for the purpose of introducing, concluding, illustrating, explaining, revising, commenting upon, or assisting in the use of the other work, such as forewords, afterwords, pictorial illustrations, maps, charts, tables, editorial notes, musical arrangements, answer material for tests, bibliographies, appendixes, and indexes, and an "instructional text" is a literary, pictorial, or graphic work prepared for publication and with the purpose of use in systematic instructional activities.

In determining whether any work is eligible to be considered a work made for hire under paragraph (2), neither the amendment contained in section 1011(d) of the Intellectual Property and Communications Omnibus Reform Act of 1999, as enacted by section 1000(a)(9) of Public Law 106-113, nor the deletion of the words added by that amendment—

(A) shall be considered or otherwise given any legal significance, or

(B) shall be interpreted to indicate congressional approval or disapproval of, or acquiescence in, any judicial determination,

by the courts or the Copyright Office. Paragraph (2) shall be interpreted as if both section 2(a)(1) of the Work Made For Hire and Copyright Corrections Act of 2000 and section 1011(d) of the Intellectual Property and Communications Omnibus Reform Act of 1999, as enacted by section 1000(a)(9) of Public Law 106-113, were never enacted, and without regard to any inaction or awareness by the Congress at any time of any judicial determinations.

The terms "WTO Agreement" and "WTO member country" have the meanings given those terms in paragraphs (9) and (10), respectively, of section 3501 of title 19.

History of 17 U.S.C. §101: Oct. 19, 1976, P.L. 94-553, §101, 90 Stat. 2541; Dec. 12, 1980, P.L. 96-517, §10(a), 94 Stat. 3028; Oct. 31, 1988, P.L. 100-568, §4(a)(1), 102 Stat. 2854; Dec. 1, 1990, P.L. 101-650, §§602, 702, 104 Stat. 5128, 5133; June 26, 1992, P.L. 102-307, §102(b)(2), 106 Stat. 266; Oct. 28, 1992, P.L. 102-563, §3(b), 106 Stat. 4248; Nov. 1, 1995, P.L. 104-39, §5(a), 109 Stat. 348; Nov. 13, 1997, P.L. 105-80, §12(a)(3), 111 Stat. 1534; Dec. 16, 1997, P.L. 105-147, §2(a), 111 Stat. 2678; Oct. 27, 1998, P.L. 105-298, §205, 112 Stat. 2833; Oct. 28, 1998, P.L. 105-304, §102(a), 112 Stat. 2861; Aug. 5, 1999, P.L. 106-44, §1(g)(1), 113 Stat. 222; Nov. 29, 1999, P.L. 106-113, §1000(a)(9), 113 Stat. 1536; Oct. 27, 2000, P.L. 106-379, §2(a), 114 Stat. 1444; Nov. 2, 2002, P.L. 107-273, §13210(5), 116 Stat. 1909; Apr. 27, 2005, P.L. 109-9, §102(c), 119 Stat. 220; May 30, 2005, P.L. 108-419, §4, 118 Stat. 2361; Dec. 9, 2010, P.L. 111-295, §6(a), 124 Stat. 3181.

See also Berne Convention; WIPO Copyright Treaty; WIPO Performances & Phonograms Treaty.

ANNOTATIONS

Architectural Work

T-Peg, Inc. v. Vermont Timber Works, Inc., 459 F.3d 97, 109 (1st Cir.2006). "The definition of an 'architectural work' … has three main components. First, an 'architectural work' is the 'design of a building as embodied in any tangible medium of expression.' The definition provides three exemplars of such a tangible medium of expression—'a building, architectural plans, or drawings'—although these are not the only possible media of expression. *At 110:* The second component of the definition is that an architectural work 'includes the overall form as well as the arrangement and composition of spaces and elements in the design.' According to the legislative history, '[t]he phrase arrangement and composition of spaces and elements' recognizes that: (1) creativity in architecture frequently takes the form of a selection, coordination, or arrangement of unprotectible elements into an original, protectible whole; (2) an architect may incorporate new, protectible design elements into otherwise standard, unprotectible building features; and (3) interior architecture may be protected. [¶] Finally, the definition excludes from the protectable 'architectural work' 'individual standard features.' The legislative history provides examples of such individual standard features: 'common windows, doors, and other staple building components.' Nonstandard individual features reflecting some amount of originality are not necessarily excluded from copyright protection. Furthermore, while individual standard features may not be individually copyrightable, as the quoted legislative history above confirms, the combination of such standard features may be copyrightable."

Audiovisual Works

Lulirama Ltd. v. Axcess Broad. Servs., 128 F.3d 872, 878 (5th Cir.1997). "To conclude that an 'image' within the [Copyright] Act's definition of 'audiovisual works' need not contain a visual component would render the reference to 'accompanying sounds' in the definition superfluous because 'accompanying sounds' would be subsumed by the term 'images.' Such a statutory construction would violate the long-settled principle that each word in a statutory scheme must be given meaning."

Collective Work

New York Times Co. v. Tasini, 533 U.S. 483, 493-94 (2001). "When … a freelance author has contributed an article to a 'collective work' such as a newspaper or magazine, the statute recognizes two distinct copyrighted works: 'Copyright in *each separate contribution to a collective work* is distinct from copyright in *the collective work as a whole*....' Copyright in the separate contribution 'vests initially in the author of the contribution' (here, the freelancer). Copyright in the collective work vests in the collective author (here, the newspaper or magazine publisher) and extends only to the creative material contributed by that author, not to 'the preexisting material employed in the work.'" *See also* ***North Am. Thought Combine, Inc. v. Kelly***, 66 U.S.P.Q.2d 1158, 1159 n.2 (S.D.N.Y.2003).

O'Well Novelty Co. v. Offenbacher, Inc., 49 U.S.P.Q.2d 1576, 1580 (D.Md.1998), *aff'd*, 255 F.3d 655 (4th Cir.2000). Collective work "is a term of art describing a variety of items within a collective whole."

Compilation

Schoolhouse, Inc. v. Anderson, 275 F.3d 726, 728-29 (8th Cir.2002). "Because copyright law protects only expression, and not ideas or facts, copyright protection for a factual compilation is 'thin.' As applied to a factual compilation, copyright law protects an author's original selection and arrangement of facts, but the facts and ideas within the compilation are free for the taking."

Inkadinkado, Inc. v. Meyer, 68 U.S.P.Q.2d 1540, 1542 (D.Mass.2003). "The threshold of originality is quite low for compilations. But the copyright protection provided is correspondingly thin, guarding against only 'virtually identical copying' of the artist's original contribution to ideas already in the public domain."

Computer Program

Syntek Semiconductor Co. v. Microchip Tech., 307 F.3d 775, 779 (9th Cir.2002). "'For registration purposes, the claim is in the computer program rather than in any particular representation of the program.' However, source code created by decompiling object code will not necessarily be identical to the source code that was compiled to create the object code."

Sega Enters. v. Accolade, Inc., 977 F.2d 1510, 1520 (9th Cir.1992). "The statutory language, read together with the [National Commission on New Technological Uses of Copyrighted Works] report, leads inexorably to the conclusion that the copyright in a computer program extends to the object code version of the program. *At 1526:* If disassembly of copyrighted object code is *per se* an unfair use, the owner of the copyright gains a *de facto* monopoly over the functional aspects of his work—aspects that were expressly denied copyright protection by Congress." *See also* ***DSC Comms. v. DGI Techs.***, 898 F.Supp. 1183, 1189 (N.D.Tex.1995), *aff'd*, 81 F.3d 597 (5th Cir.1996).

Derivative Work

Authors Guild v. Google, Inc., 804 F.3d 202, 225 (2d Cir.2015). The definition of "derivative work," "while imprecise, strongly implies that derivative works over which the author of the original enjoys exclusive rights ordinarily are those that represent the protected aspects of the original work, *i.e.*, its expressive content, converted into an altered form, such as the conversion of a novel into a film, the translation of a writing into a different language, the reproduction of a painting in the form of a poster or post card, recreation of a cartoon character in the form of a three-dimensional plush toy, adaptation of a musical composition for different instruments, or other similar conversions."

Atkins v. Fischer, 331 F.3d 988, 993-94 (D.C.Cir. 2003). "The Copyright Act defines derivative works as those 'based upon' the copyrighted work. Courts interpret the Act to mandate that derivative work that is 'substantially similar' to the original work upon which it is based is an infringement. Because substantial similarity is an extremely close question of fact, summary judgment has traditionally been frowned upon. The question is whether 'an average lay observer would recognize the alleged copy as having been appropriated from the copyrighted work.' ... Although all derivative works have differences from the original, it is the similarities, rather than the differences, that inform whether the 'total concept and feel' of the works and their 'aesthetic appeal' is the same."

Ty, Inc. v. Publications Int'l, 292 F.3d 512, 520-21 (7th Cir.2002). "A derivative work ... must either be in one of the forms named or be 'recast, transformed, or adapted.' The textual portions of a collectors' guide to copyrighted works are not among the examples of derivative works listed in the statute, and guides don't recast, transform, or adapt the things to which they are guides. A guide to Parisian restaurants is not a recasting, transforming, or adapting of Parisian restaurants. Indeed, a collectors' guide is very much like a book review, which is a guide to a book and which no one supposes is a derivative work."

Shoptalk, Ltd. v. Concorde-New Horizons Corp., 168 F.3d 586, 591 (2d Cir.1999). When "the author consents to the inclusion of his work in a derivative work, the publication of the derivative work, to the extent that it discloses the original work, also constitutes publication of that underlying work."

Entertainment Research Grp. v. Genesis Creative Grp., 122 F.3d 1211, 1222 (9th Cir.1997). Because "any utilitarian, functional or mechanical aspects of a derivative work will not be copyrightable in the long run, any differences in appearance between a derivative work and the preexisting work which are not conceptually separable from any utilitarian, functional or mechanical purposes should not be considered by a court in determining whether sufficient artistic differences exist to constitute 'originality.'"

Lewis Galoob Toys, Inc. v. Nintendo, Inc., 964 F.2d 965, 968 (9th Cir.1992). "A derivative work must be fixed to be *protected* under the [Copyright] Act, but not to *infringe*."

Liu v. Price Waterhouse L.L.P., 182 F.Supp.2d 666, 672 n.1 (N.D.Ill.2001), *aff'd*, 302 F.3d 749 (7th Cir.2002). "A derivative work, by definition, is a work based upon a preexisting work, and the author of a derivative work must either have or acquire the right to use the original preexisting work. A work for hire, by contrast, is composed of original material and could be independently created and copyrighted by the author. As such, it makes sense to require an explicit transfer of ownership in works made for hire to protect the true author's rights in his or her work. A derivative work author, by contrast, is by definition working within the confines of his or her license to create that work and is bound not to infringe the rights of the original work's owner by exceeding the scope of that license."

Display

Society of the Holy Transfiguration Monastery, Inc. v. Gregory, 689 F.3d 29, 55 (1st Cir.2012). "[D] 'display[ed]' the Works publicly ... when he posted the Works on his website. Although the question of whether a computer has 'displayed' a copyrighted work may be a difficult one in other contexts, ... it is beyond question here that [D] has 'displayed' the Works on his website. We need not delineate the outer bounds of the scope of the term 'display' where ... the fact that the Works were 'displayed' on [D's] website is undisputed."

Fixed

Cartoon Network LP v. CSC Holdings, Inc., 536 F.3d 121, 127 (2d Cir.2008). "We believe [the definition of 'fixed'] plainly imposes two distinct but related requirements: the work must be embodied in a medium, i.e., placed in a medium such that it can be perceived, reproduced, etc., from that medium (the 'embodiment requirement'), and it must remain thus embodied 'for a period of more than transitory duration' (the 'duration requirement'). Unless both requirements are met, the work is not 'fixed' in the buffer, and, as a result, the buffer data is not a 'copy' of the original work whose data is buffered. *At 129:* [T]o determine whether a work is 'fixed' in a given medium, the statutory language directs us to ask not only (1) whether a work is 'embodied' in that medium, but also (2) whether it is embodied in the medium 'for a period of more than transitory duration.' According to the Copyright Office [in its 2001 DMCA Report], if the work is capable of being copied from that medium *for any amount of time*, the answer to both questions is 'yes.' The problem with this interpretation is that it reads the 'transitory duration' language out of the statute. [¶] [N]o case law or other authority dissuades us from concluding that the definition of 'fixed' imposes both an embodiment requirement and a duration requirement." *See also* ***Society of the Holy Transfiguration Monastery, Inc. v. Gregory***, 689 F.3d 29, 55 (1st Cir.2012).

Toney v. L'Oreal USA, Inc., 406 F.3d 905, 910 (7th Cir.2005). "[W]e find that [P's] identity is not fixed in a tangible medium of expression. ... A person's likeness—her persona—is not authored and it is not fixed."

U.S. v. Moghadam, 175 F.3d 1269, 1280-81 (11th Cir.1999). "If a live performance is broadcast, e.g., by radio or television, and simultaneously recorded by the performer, any unauthorized recording by a person receiving the broadcast constitutes copyright infringement of the sound recording or motion picture, notwithstanding that the infringer actually copied the live performance directly, and not the fixation thereof. This result is based upon the last sentence of the definition of 'fixed' in ... §101. ... This definition creates a legal fiction that the simultaneous fixation occurs before the transmission and the unauthorized recording. While we are aware that the constitutionality of this aspect of the statute has never been tested, the ease with which it has been incorporated into the prior copyright law suggests that fixation, as a constitutional concept, is something less than a rigid, inflexible barrier to Congressional power. Indeed, if a performer under the prior law could effectively protect a live musical performance, circumventing the fixation requirement, simply by the device of simultaneous recordation, the antibootlegging law seems to us like more of an incremental change than a constitutional breakthrough. Common sense does not indicate that extending copyright-like protection to a live performance is fundamentally inconsistent with the Copyright Clause." *See also* ***National Basketball Ass'n v. Motorola, Inc.***, 105 F.3d 841, 847 (2d Cir.1997).

Matthew Bender & Co. v. West Publ'g, 158 F.3d 693, 702 (2d Cir.1998). "The Copyright Act establishes a 'fundamental distinction' between the original work of authorship and the material object in which that work is 'fixed.' The sole purpose of §101's definitions of the words 'copies' and 'fixed' is to explicate the 'fixation' requirement, i.e., to define the material objects in which copyrightable and infringing works may be embedded and to describe the requisite fixed nature of that work within the material object. Under §101's definition of 'copies,' a work satisfies the fixation requirement when it is fixed in a material object from which it can be perceived or communicated directly or with the aid of a machine."

Triad Sys. v. Southeastern Express Co., 31 U.S.P.Q.2d 1239, 1243 (N.D.Cal.1994). "[T]he copyright law is not so much concerned with the temporal 'duration' of a copy as it is with what that copy does, and what it is capable of doing, while it exists. 'Transitory duration' is a relative term that must be interpreted and applied in context. This concept is particularly important in cases involving computer technology where the speed and complexity of machines and software is rapidly advancing, and where the diversity of computer architecture and software design is expanding at an ever-increasing rate."

Joint Work

Greene v. Ablon, 794 F.3d 133, 150-51 (1st Cir. 2015). "'Inseparable' contributions 'have little or no independent meaning standing alone,' as might frequently be the case with collaboration on a written text like a play or a novel. 'Interdependent' contributions, on the other hand, 'have some meaning standing alone but achieve their primary significance because of their combined effect, as in the case of the words and music of a song.' For a work to be 'joint,' the authors must have intended, 'at the time the writing is done,' that their contributions be merged into 'an integrated unit.' It is not necessary that the authors' contributions be quantitatively or qualitatively equal, only that each author's contribution be more than de minimis."

Janky v. Lake Cty. Convention & Visitors Bur., 576 F.3d 356, 362 (7th Cir.2009). A joint work is created by "(1) intent to create a joint work; and (2) contribution of independently copyrightable material. With respect to the first element, ... the intent prong does not have to do with the collaborators' intent to recognize each other as co-authors for purposes of copyright law; the focus is on the parties' intent to work together in the creation of a single product, not on the legal consequences of that collaboration. [B]illing or credit may be evidence of intent to create a joint work. As to the second element, we reject[] Professor Nimmer's de minimis test, which posits that a joint work exists whenever there is more than a de minimis contribution by each author. The standard we embrace[] requires more than that: a contribution that is independently copyrightable. Measured against this standard, ... the putative joint author of a play [is] not a joint author where his contributions were limited to ideas, refinements, and suggestions. Standing alone ... these contributions [are] not the subject of copyright." (Internal quotes omitted.) *See also* ***Visitor Indus. Publ'ns, Inc. v. NOPG, L.L.C.***, 91 F.Supp.2d 910, 914-15 (E.D.La.2000); ***Bencich v. Hoffman***, 84 F.Supp.2d 1053, 1055 (D.Ariz. 2000); ***Maurizio v. Goldsmith***, 84 F.Supp.2d 455, 465 (S.D.N.Y.2000), *aff'd*, 230 F.3d 518 (2d Cir.2000).

Aalmuhammed v. Lee, 202 F.3d 1227, 1232 (9th Cir.2000). "We hold that authorship is required under the statutory definition of a joint work, and that authorship is not the same thing as making a valuable and copyrightable contribution. We recognize that a contributor of an expression may be deemed to be the 'author' of that expression for purposes of determining whether it is independently copyrightable. The issue we deal with is a different and larger one: is the contributor an author of the joint work within the meaning of ... §101. *At 1233-34:* [The Second and Seventh Circuits] have held that a person claiming to be an author of a joint work must prove that both parties intended each other to be joint authors. In determining whether the parties have the intent to be joint authors, the Second Circuit looks at who has decision making authority, how the parties bill themselves, and other evidence. [¶] [S]everal factors suggest themselves as among the criteria for joint authorship, in the absence of contract. First, an author 'superintend[s]' the work by exercising control. This will likely be a person 'who has actually formed the picture by putting the persons in position, and arranging the place where the people are to be—the man who is the effective cause of that,' or 'the inventive or master mind' who 'creates, or gives effect to the idea.' Second, putative coauthors make objective manifestations of a shared intent to be coauthors.... We say objective manifestations because, were the mutual intent to be determined by subjective intent, it could become an instrument of fraud, were one coauthor to hide from the other an intention to take sole credit for the work. Third, the audience appeal of the work turns on both contributions and 'the share of each in its success cannot be appraised.' Control in many cases will be the most important factor." Held: Ninth Circuit agrees with and elaborates on opinions from Second and Seventh Circuits. *But see* ***Childress v. Taylor***, 945 F.2d 500, 507 (2d Cir.1991) (authorship in joint work requires contribution of independently copyrightable work).

Clogston v. American Acad. of Orthopaedic Surgeons, 40 U.S.P.Q.2d 1125, 1127 (W.D.Tex.1996). "Parts of a unitary whole are considered 'inseparable' when they have little or no meaning standing alone."

Literary Works

Leadsinger, Inc. v. BMG Music Publ'g, 512 F.3d 522, 527 (9th Cir.2008). "Song lyrics are copyrightable as a literary work and, therefore, enjoy separate protection under the Copyright Act."

Perform

U.S. v. American Soc'y of Composers, Authors & Publ'rs, 627 F.3d 64, 72 (2d Cir.2010). "The ordinary sense of the words 'recite,' 'render,' and 'play' refer[s] to actions that can be perceived contemporaneously. *At 73:* The fact that the statute defines performance in the audio-visual context as 'show[ing]' the work or making it 'audible' reinforces the conclusion that 'to perform' a musical work entails contemporaneous perceptibility. [¶] The downloads at issue in this appeal are not musical performances that are contemporaneously perceived by the listener. They are simply transfers of electronic files containing digital copies from an on-line server to a local hard drive. The downloaded songs are not performed in any perceptible manner during the transfers; the user must take some further action to play the songs after they are downloaded. Because the electronic download itself involves no recitation, rendering, or playing of the musical work encoded in the digital transmission, we hold that such a download is not a performance of that work, as defined by §101. [¶] '[W]hen Congress speaks of transmitting a performance to the public, it refers to the performance created by the act of transmission,' not simply to transmitting a recording of a performance."

Video Pipeline, Inc. v. Buena Vista Home Entm't, Inc., 192 F.Supp.2d 321, 331 (D.N.J.2002), *aff'd*, 342 F.3d 191 (3d Cir.2002). "An individual is performing a work 'whenever he does anything by which the work is transmitted, repeated, or made to recur.' *At 332:* Internet transmission of copyrighted photographs constituted a 'public display' even though it was limited to subscribers."

Phonorecords

Woods v. Bourne Co., 60 F.3d 978, 986 n.3 (2d Cir. 1995). A sound recording "is distinct from a phonorecord, which is the tangible thing on which the sounds (other than sounds accompanying an audiovisual work) are fixed. The term 'phonorecords' thus includes records and cassettes, etc."

Pictorial, Graphic & Sculptural Works

Star Athletica, L.L.C. v. Varsity Brands, Inc., ___ U.S. ___, 137 S.Ct. 1002, 1007 (2017). "We granted certiorari to resolve widespread disagreement over the proper test for implementing §101's separate-identification and independent-existence requirements. We hold that a feature incorporated into the design of a useful article is eligible for copyright protection only if the feature (1) can be perceived as a two- or three-dimensional work of art separate from the useful article and (2) would qualify as a protectable pictorial, graphic, or sculptural work—either on its own or fixed in some other tangible medium of expression—if it were imagined separately from the useful article into which it is incorporated. *At U.S. ___, S.Ct. 1009:* [Section 101] requires separability analysis for any 'pictorial, graphic, or sculptural features' incorporated into the 'design of a useful article.' 'Design' refers here to 'the combination' of 'details' or 'features' that 'go to make up' the useful article. Furthermore, the words 'pictorial' and 'graphic' include, in this context, two-dimensional features such as pictures, paintings, or drawings. And the statute expressly defines '[p]ictorial, graphical, and sculptural works' to include 'two-dimensional ... works of ... art.' The statute thus provides that the 'design of a useful article' can include two-dimensional 'pictorial' and 'graphic' features, and separability analysis applies to those features just as it does to three-dimensional 'sculptural' features. *At U.S. ___, S.Ct. 1010:* The first requirement—separate identification—is not onerous. The decisionmaker need only be able to look at the useful article and spot some two- or three-dimensional element that appears to have pictorial, graphic, or sculptural qualities. [¶] The independent-existence requirement is ordinarily more difficult to satisfy. The decisionmaker must determine that the separately identified feature has the capacity to exist apart from the utilitarian aspects of the article. In other words, the feature must be able to exist as its own pictorial, graphic, or sculptural work as defined in §101 once it is imagined apart from the useful article. If the feature is not capable of existing as a pictorial, graphic, or sculptural work once separated from the useful article, then it was not a pictorial, graphic, or sculptural feature of that article, but rather one of its utilitarian aspects. *At U.S. ___, S.Ct. 1014:* [W]e ... abandon the distinction between 'physical' and 'conceptual' separability, which some courts and commentators have adopted based on the Copyright Act's legislative history. [¶] Because separability does not require the underlying useful article to remain, the physical-conceptual distinction is unnecessary."

Publication

Kernel Records Oy v. Mosley, 694 F.3d 1294, 1303 (11th Cir.2012). "Publication ... occurs 'when an authorized offer is made to dispose of the work in any such manner[,] even if a sale or other such disposition does not in fact occur.' Further, when copies are 'given away' to the general public, a sufficient transfer of ownership has occurred. Thus, proof of distribution or an offer of distribution is necessary to prove publication. [¶] However, proof of distribution or an offer to distribute, alone, is insufficient to prove publication. Central to the determination of publication is the method, extent, and purpose of distribution. Most publication disputes concern whether distribution of the subject work was sufficiently broad, or whether the purpose of the distribution included a transfer of the right of diffusion, reproduction, distribution, or sale."

Agee v. Paramount Comm., 59 F.3d 317, 325 (2d Cir.1995). "It is clear that merely transmitting a sound recording to the public on the airwaves does not constitute a 'distribution'; otherwise, sound recording copyright owners would have the performance rights expressly denied to them under the statute. For this reason, distribution is generally thought to require transmission of a 'material object' in which the sound recording is fixed: a work that is of 'more than transitory duration.'"

ABC, Inc. v. Primetime 24, Jt.V., 67 F.Supp.2d 558, 562 (M.D.N.C.1999), *aff'd*, 232 F.3d 886 (4th Cir.2000) (table case). "Just as it is clear that mere broadcast does not constitute publication, it is also clear that 'the distribution of copies of a motion picture to television stations for broadcast purposes constitutes an act of publication.'"

Publicly

American Broad. Cos. v. Aereo, Inc., ___ U.S. ___, 134 S.Ct. 2498, 2509-11 (2014). "[A]n entity may transmit a performance through multiple, discrete transmissions. That is because one can 'transmit' or 'communicate' something through a *set* of actions. [¶] The fact that a singular noun ('a performance') follows the words 'to transmit' does not suggest the contrary. One can sing a song to his family, whether he sings the same song one-on-one or in front of all together. ... By the same principle, an entity may transmit a performance through one or several transmissions, where the performance is of the same work. [¶] The Transmit Clause must permit this interpretation, for it provides that one may transmit a performance to the public 'whether the members of the public capable of receiving the performance ... receive it ... at the same time or at different times.' Were the words 'to transmit ... a performance' limited to a single act of communication, members of the public could not receive the performance communicated 'at different times.' Therefore, in light of the purpose and text of the Clause, we conclude that when an entity communicates the same contemporaneously perceptible images and sounds to multiple people, it transmits a performance to them regardless of the number of discrete communications it makes. [¶] We do not see how the fact that [D] transmits via personal copies of programs could make a difference. The [Copyright] Act applies to transmissions 'by means of any device or process.' And retransmitting a television program using user-specific copies is a 'process' of transmitting a performance. A 'cop[y]' of a work is simply a 'material objec[t] ... in which a work is fixed ... and from which the work can be perceived, reproduced, or otherwise communicated.' So whether [D] transmits from the same or separate copies, it performs the same work; it shows the same images and makes audible the same sounds. Therefore, when [D] streams the same television program to multiple subscribers, it 'transmit[s] ... a performance' to all of them. [¶] Moreover, the subscribers to whom [D] transmits television programs constitute 'the public.' [D] communicates the same contemporaneously perceptible images and sounds to a large number of people who are unrelated and unknown to each other. This matters because, although the Act does not define 'the public,' it specifies that an entity performs publicly when it performs at 'any place where a substantial number of persons outside of a normal circle of a family and its social acquaintances is gathered.' The Act thereby suggests that 'the public' consists of a large group of people outside of a family and friends. [¶] [W]hen an entity performs to a set of people, whether they constitute 'the public' often depends upon their relationship to the underlying work. [A]n entity that transmits a performance to individuals in their capacities as owners or possessors does not perform to 'the public,' whereas an entity like [D] that transmits to large numbers of paying subscribers who lack any prior relationship to the works does so perform. [¶] [W]e have interpreted the term 'the public' to apply to a group of individuals acting as ordinary members of the public who pay primarily to watch broadcast television programs, many of which are copyrighted. We have said that it does not extend to those who act as owners or possessors of the relevant product. And we have not considered whether the public performance right is infringed when the user of a service pays primarily for something other than the transmission of copyrighted works, such as the remote storage of content. In addition, an entity does not transmit to the public if it does not transmit to a substantial number of people outside of a family and its social circle."

U.S. v. American Soc'y of Composers, Authors & Publ'rs, 627 F.3d 64, 74 (2d Cir.2010). "[A] 'transmittal of a work' is distinct from a transmittal of 'a performance'—the former being a transmittal of the underlying work and the latter being a transmittal that is itself a performance of the underlying work. [¶] The Internet Companies' stream transmissions, which all parties agree constitute public performances, illustrate why a download is not a public performance. A stream is an electronic transmission that renders the musical work audible as it is received by the client-computer's temporary memory. This transmission, like a television or radio broadcast, is a performance because there is a playing of the song that is perceived simultaneously with the transmission. In contrast, downloads do not immediately produce sound; only after a file has been downloaded on a user's hard drive can he perceive a performance by playing the downloaded song. Unlike musical works played during radio broadcasts and stream transmissions, downloaded musical works are transmitted at one point in time and performed at another. Transmittal without a performance does not constitute a 'public performance.'"

National Football League v. PrimeTime 24 Jt.V., 211 F.3d 10, 13 (2d Cir.2000). "[A] public performance or display includes 'each step in the process by which a protected work wends its way to its audience.' Under that analysis, it is clear that [D's] uplink transmission of signals captured in the U.S. is a step in the process by which [P's] protected work wends its way to a public audience. In short, [D] publicly displayed or performed material in which [P] owns the copyright."

Bagdadi v. Nazar, 84 F.3d 1194, 1199 (9th Cir. 1996). "One of the principal purposes of the definition [of 'publicly' in §101] was to make clear that ... performances in semi-public places such as clubs, lodges, factories, summer camps, and schools are public performances subject to copyright control." (Internal quotes omitted.)

Transfer of Copyright Ownership

Gardner v. Nike, Inc., 279 F.3d 774, 778 (9th Cir. 2002). The "definition [of 'transfer of copyright ownership'] calls into question the distinctions that were previously drawn between an assignment and an exclusive license under the indivisibility doctrine. *At 780:* This explicit language limits the rights afforded to an owner of exclusive rights. Based on basic principles of statutory construction, the specific language of [17 U.S.C.] §201(d)(2) is given precedence over the more general language of [17 U.S.C.] §§101 and 201(d)(1)." *But see* ***Traicoff v. Digital Media, Inc.***, 439 F.Supp.2d 872, 877-78 (S.D.Ind.2006) (exclusive licensees are free to sublicense their rights).

Transmit

Bonneville Int'l v. Peters, 347 F.3d 485, 491 n.10 (3d Cir.2003). Legislative "history makes clear that 'transmit' is to be interpreted very broadly."

United States Work

Kernel Records Oy v. Mosley, 694 F.3d 1294, 1304 (11th Cir.2012). "Because the statutory definition of 'United States work' contains strict temporal and geographic requirements (e.g., 'first,' 'simultaneously,' 'in the United States,' 'foreign nation,' and 'treaty party'), ... a determination that a work was first published abroad requires both: (1) an examination of the method, extent, and purpose of the alleged distribution to determine whether that distribution was sufficient for publication, and (2) an examination of both the timing and geographic extent of the first publication to determine whether the work was published abroad. [¶] For example, a free pamphlet distributed by mail to every household on the continent of North America would undoubtedly meet the statutory definition of 'publication.' However, to determine whether the very same pamphlet was first published abroad, the exact timing and geographic extent of the first publication must be known. Was the pamphlet first mailed to every household in Mexico, followed a week later by a separate mailing to the rest of the continent? If so, the pamphlet is a foreign work, first published abroad, and is *not* subject to the registration requirement. Or was the pamphlet first mailed to households in the U.S. and Mexico, followed a week later by a separate mailing to the rest of the continent? If so, the pamphlet was first published in the U.S. and a treaty party whose law grants a term of copyright protection longer than the U.S., making the work a United States work that is subject to the registration requirement. [¶] Of course, if a distribution is insufficient to establish publication, the timing and geographic extent of the deficient distribution is immaterial. *At 1305-06:* Although 'online' and 'Internet' are largely synonymous terms, the Internet consists of distribution methods of significantly different types. Thus, an 'online' activity may occur through public websites, restricted websites, peer-to-peer networks, e-mail, or other less common methods. Although it may be possible to presume simultaneous worldwide availability of a public website, ... such a presumption could not apply to restricted websites, peer-to-peer networks, and e-mail. A restricted website is only available to those willing to pay a fee or who meet specified criteria; a peer-to-peer network is only available to those who have downloaded the required software; and an e-mail only goes to the addresses input by the sender. Thus, unlike public websites on the World Wide Web, each of these other methods of online distribution would be inconsistent with a presumption of simultaneous worldwide availability. [¶] Throughout this case, the district court (as well as the parties) confounded 'the Internet' and 'online' with 'World Wide Web' and 'website.' Because of the strict temporal and geographic requirements contained in the statutory definition of 'United States work,' conflating these terms had a profound impact on the district court's evidentiary analysis. By confounding 'Internet' with 'website,' the district court erroneously assumed that all 'Internet publication' must occur on the 'World Wide Web' or a 'website.' The district court then erroneously assumed all 'Internet publication' results in simultaneous, worldwide distribution."

Useful Article

Chosun Int'l v. Chrisha Creations, Ltd., 413 F.3d 324, 328 (2d Cir.2005). "[I]f a useful article incorporates a design element that is physically or conceptually separable from the underlying product, the element is eligible for copyright protection. For this reason, one may not copyright the general shape of a lamp, because its overall shape contributes to its ability to illuminate the reaches of a room. But one can copyright the fanciful designs imprinted on, or carved into, the lamp's base, so long as those designs are unrelated to the lamp's utilitarian function as a device used to combat darkness. [¶] [A]rticles of clothing have been identified as 'useful' items and, hence, excluded from copyright eligibility." *See also* ***Baby Buddies, Inc. v. Toys "R" Us, Inc.***, 611 F.3d 1308, 1315-16 (11th Cir.2010); ***Langman Fabrics v. Graff Californiawear, Inc.***, 160 F.3d 106, 114 (2d Cir.1998), *amended*, 169 F.3d 782 (2d Cir.1998); ***Celebration Int'l v. Chosun Int'l***, 234 F.Supp.2d 905, 912 (S.D.Ind.2002).

Pivot Point Int'l v. Charlene Prods., 372 F.3d 913, 931 (7th Cir.2004). "Conceptual separability exists ... when the artistic aspects of an article can be 'conceptualized as existing independently of their utilitarian function.' This independence is necessarily informed by 'whether the design elements can be identified as reflecting the designer's artistic judgment exercised independently of functional influences.' If the elements do reflect the independent, artistic judgment of the designer, conceptual separability exists. Conversely, when the design of a useful article is 'as much the result of utilitarian pressures as aesthetic choices,' ...

the useful and aesthetic elements are not conceptually separable." *See also* ***Universal Furniture Int'l v. Collezione Europa USA, Inc.***, 618 F.3d 417, 432-33 (4th Cir.2010).

Work Made for Hire

Community for Creative Non-Violence v. Reid, 490 U.S. 730, 743 (1989). "[A] work for hire can arise through one of two mutually exclusive means, one for employees and one for independent contractors, and ... the classification of a particular hired party should be made with reference to agency law. *At 751-52:* In determining whether a hired party is an employee under the general common law of agency, we consider the hiring party's right to control the manner and means by which the product is accomplished. Among the other factors relevant to this inquiry are the skill required; the source of the instrumentalities and tools; the location of the work; the duration of the relationship between the parties; whether the hiring party has the right to assign additional projects to the hired party; the extent of the hired party's discretion over when and how long to work; the method of payment; the hired party's role in hiring and paying assistants; whether the work is part of the regular business of the hiring party; whether the hiring party is in business; the provision of employee benefits; and the tax treatment of the hired party. No one of these factors is determinative."

Urbont v. Sony Music Entm't, 831 F.3d 80, 88 (2d Cir.2016). "[T]hird parties to an alleged employer-employee relationship have standing to raise a 'work for hire' defense against a claim of copyright infringement." *But see* ***Jules Jordan Video, Inc. v. 144942 Canada Inc.***, 617 F.3d 1146, 1157 (9th Cir.2010) (rejecting third-party standing under work-for-hire doctrine when both potential copyright owners are parties to lawsuit and issue of ownership is undisputed between them).

U.S. Auto Parts Network, Inc. v. Parts Geek, LLC, 692 F.3d 1009, 1015 (9th Cir.2012). "[C]ourts have ... adopted [the Restatement (2d) of Agency] §228's three-prong test for determining when a work is made by an employee 'within the scope' of employment: '(a) it is of the kind [the employee] is employed to perform; (b) it occurs substantially within the authorized time and space limits; [and] (c) it is actuated, at least in part, by a purpose to serve the [employer].' [¶] We join our sister circuits in adopting this approach."

Gaiman v. McFarlane, 360 F.3d 644, 650 (7th Cir. 2004). "[A] commissioned work not falling under [subsection (2) of the 'work made for hire' definition] may be deemed a work for hire under [subsection (1) of the 'work made for hire' definition] if, for example, the commissioning party pays the author a monthly stipend, pays health and other fringe benefits during the time the author works on the project, and exercises overall though not necessarily daily supervision. The work for hire concept isn't limited to formal employment because a functionally identical relationship can be created by skillful drafting of contracts that purport to treat the (de facto) employee as an independent contractor."

Estate of Burne Hogarth v. Edgar Rice Burroughs, Inc., 342 F.3d 149, 156 (2d Cir.2003). With "respect to works made for hire, the employer is legally regarded as the 'author,' as distinguished from the creator of the work...."

Warren v. Fox Family Worldwide, Inc., 328 F.3d 1136, 1140 n.4 (9th Cir.2003). "Because the parties are not in an employer-employee relationship, the Copyright Act requires not only that the work be specially commissioned pursuant to a written agreement, but that the work come within one of the enumerated categories listed in [subsection (2) of the 'work made for hire' definition]." *See also* ***Billy-Bob Teeth, Inc. v. Novelty, Inc.***, 329 F.3d 586, 590-91 (7th Cir.2003).

Merkos L'Inyonei Chinuch, Inc. v. Otsar Sifrei Lubavitch, Inc., 312 F.3d 94, 98 (2d Cir.2002). "Under the 1976 [Copyright] Act, the absence of a written agreement between [P] and [creator of work] will require [P] to satisfy the multifactored test [for agency] of ***Community for Creative Non-Violence v. Reid***, 490 U.S. 730 ... (1989), for demonstrating that [creator of work] prepared the translation 'within the scope of his or her employment.' Under the 1909 [Copyright] Act, [P] would face the lower threshold of demonstrating that the work was prepared at its 'instance and expense.'"

Playboy Enters. v. Dumas, 53 F.3d 549, 559 (2d Cir. 1995). The "writing requirement was created, in part, to make the ownership of intellectual property rights clear and definite. [¶] In the fact pattern of this case, we will assume that the writing requirement of §101(2) can be met by a writing executed after the work is created, if the writing confirms a prior agreement, either explicit or implicit, made before the creation of the work." Held: Absence of phrase "work made for hire" does not satisfy writing requirement.

In re Napster, Inc., 191 F.Supp.2d 1087, 1097 (N.D. Cal.2002). "Sound recordings are not one of the nine listed works. This glaring omission in the statutory requirements suggests that [Ps'] works cannot be 'specially commissioned' works for hire."

Work of Visual Art

Cheffins v. Stewart, 825 F.3d 588, 594 (9th Cir. 2016). "We … hold that an object constitutes a piece of 'applied art'—as opposed to a 'work of visual art'—where the object initially served a utilitarian function and the object continues to serve such a function after the artist made embellishments or alterations to it. This test embraces the circumstances both where a functional object incorporates a decorative design in its initial formulation, and where a functional object is decorated after manufacture but continues to serve a practical purpose. Conversely, 'applied art' would not include a piece of art whose function is purely aesthetic or a utilitarian object which is so transformed through the addition of artistic elements that its utilitarian functions cease. *At 594 n.6:* With recognition that nearly every object on which art is installed will be in some sense 'utilitarian,' we caution that the utilitarian function must be something other than mere display of the work in question. *At 594 n.7:* For example, we have explained that the 'transformation from utilitarian object to work of art,' … occurs where an object's *utilitarian functions cease*. We can leave for another case whether there might be some de minimis exception to this standard, where an object continues to serve only the most trivial of utilitarian functions. Further, we have explained that our focus is on objects that *in fact* continue to serve real utilitarian functions (as opposed to those which may retain the ability to serve utilitarian functions, or those which at one point in history served such functions …). *At 595:* Under the definition we adopt today, [work] plainly was 'applied art.' It began as a rudimentary utilitarian object, and despite being visually transformed through elaborate artistry, it continued to serve a significant utilitarian function upon its completion." *See also* ***Carter v. Helmsley-Spear, Inc.***, 71 F.3d 77, 84-85 (2d Cir.1995).

Phillips v. Pembroke Real Estate, Inc., 459 F.3d 128, 129 (1st Cir.2006). "This case raises important questions about the application of the [VARA] to 'site-specific art,' which is a subset of 'integrated art.' A work of 'integrated art' is comprised of two or more physical objects that must be presented together as the artist intended for the work to retain its meaning and integrity. In a work of 'site-specific art,' one of the component physical objects is the location of the art. To remove a work of site-specific art from its original site is to destroy it. *At 133:* 'VARA grants three rights: the right of attribution, the right of integrity and, in the case of works of visual art of recognized stature, the right to prevent destruction.' [¶] The right of attribution generally consists of the right of an artist to be recognized by name as the author of his work or to publish anonymously or pseudonymously, the right to prevent the author's work from being attributed to someone else, and to prevent the use of the author's name on works created by others, including distorted editions of the author's original work. The right of integrity allows the author to prevent any deforming or mutilating changes to his work, even after title in the work has been transferred. In other words, these moral rights protect what an artist retains after relinquishing ownership (and/or copyright) of the tangible object that the artist has created. *At 143:* [T]he plain language of VARA does not protect site-specific art."

Carter v. Helmsley-Spear, Inc., 71 F.3d 77, 84 (2d Cir.1995). "A 'work of visual art' is defined by the [VARA] in terms both positive (what it is) and negative (what it is not). In relevant part VARA defines a work of visual art as 'a painting, drawing, print, or sculpture, existing in a single copy' or in a limited edition of 200 copies or fewer. Although [Ds] aver that elements of the work are not visual art, their contention is foreclosed by the factual finding that the work is a single, indivisible whole. Concededly, considered as a whole, the work is a sculpture and exists only in a single copy. Therefore, the work satisfies the Act's positive definition of a work of visual art. We next turn to the second part of the statutory definition—what is not a work of visual art. [¶] The definition of visual art excludes 'any poster, map, globe, chart, technical drawing, diagram, model, applied art, motion picture or other audio-visual work.' Congress meant to distinguish works of visual art from other media, such as audio-visual works and motion pictures, due to the different circumstances surrounding how works of each genre are created and disseminated."

Lilley v. Stout, 384 F.Supp.2d 83, 87 (D.D.C.2005). "[B]oth photographic negatives and prints fit the definition of a 'still photographic image.' [T]he term 'for exhibition purposes only' cannot be limited to the author's 'purpose' at the moment she clicks the camera's shutter. [I]t seems more reasonable that the intent or purpose of the author be examined as of the time the unique work in question is 'produced.' *At 88:* [P's] intent when clicking the shutter of his camera and creating the negatives is irrelevant to his claim. His probably different purpose in developing the negatives to produce the prints is the real issue. Were they 'produced for exhibition purposes only?'" Held: No, they were not.

§102. SUBJECT MATTER OF COPYRIGHT: IN GENERAL

(a) Copyright protection subsists, in accordance with this title, in original works of authorship fixed in any tangible medium of expression, now known or later developed, from which they can be perceived, reproduced, or otherwise communicated, either directly or with the aid of a machine or device. Works of authorship include the following categories:

(1) literary works;

(2) musical works, including any accompanying words;

(3) dramatic works, including any accompanying music;

(4) pantomimes and choreographic works;

(5) pictorial, graphic, and sculptural works;

(6) motion pictures and other audiovisual works;

(7) sound recordings; and

(8) architectural works.

(b) In no case does copyright protection for an original work of authorship extend to any idea, procedure, process, system, method of operation, concept, principle, or discovery, regardless of the form in which it is described, explained, illustrated, or embodied in such work.

History of 17 U.S.C. §102: Oct. 19, 1976, P.L. 94-553, §101, 90 Stat. 2544; Dec. 1, 1990, P.L. 101-650, §703, 104 Stat. 5133.

See also 48 U.S.C. §1421n; 37 C.F.R. §202.1.

ANNOTATIONS

Generally

Baker v. Selden, 101 U.S. 99, 105 (1880). "The description of the art in a book, though entitled to the benefit of copyright, lays no foundation for an exclusive claim to the art itself. The object of the one is explanation; the object of the other is use."

Southco, Inc. v. Kanebridge Corp., 390 F.3d 276, 285 (3d Cir.2004). "Since at least 1899, it has been the practice of the Copyright Office to deny registration to 'words and phrases.' *At 287:* We ... believe that [the practice] logically extends to part numbers."

Gaiman v. McFarlane, 360 F.3d 644, 648 (7th Cir.2004). "We have found only a handful of appellate cases addressing the issue [of the copyright-infringement defense of uncopyrightability], and they are split. ***Matthew Bender & Co. v. West Publ'g***, 158 F.3d 674 ... (2d Cir.1998), and ***North Coast Indus. v. Jason Maxwell, Inc.***, 972 F.2d 1031 ... (9th Cir.1992), hold that copyrightability is a mixed question of law and fact, at least when it depends (as it usually does) on originality, and that it is therefore an issue for the jury or other factfinder. But ***Yankee Candle Co. v. Bridgewater Candle Co.***, 259 F.3d 25 ... (1st Cir.2001), and our own ***Publications Int'l v. Meredith Corp.***, 88 F.3d 473 ... (7th Cir.1996), along with a number of district court cases, e.g., ***Collezione Europa U.S.A., Inc. v. Hillsdale House, Ltd.***, 243 F.Supp.2d 444 ... (M.D.N.C.2003); ***Newton v. Diamond***, 204 F.Supp.2d 1244 ... (C.D.Cal.2002), hold that copyrightability is always an issue of law."

Montgomery v. Noga, 168 F.3d 1282, 1288 (11th Cir.1999). "For original computer programs and other original works of authorship created after 1977, copyright automatically inheres in the work at the moment it is created without regard to whether it is ever registered."

§102(a)—Authorship

16 Casa Duse, LLC v. Merkin, 791 F.3d 247, 254 (2d Cir.2015). "This case requires us to answer a question of first impression in this Circuit: May a contributor to a creative work whose contributions are inseparable from, and integrated into, the work maintain a copyright interest in his or her contributions alone? We conclude that, at least on the facts of the present case, he or she may not. *At 256-57:* The Copyright Act does not define the term 'works of authorship.' Section 102 ..., however, lists examples of categories of 'works of authorship,' including 'literary works,' ... 'musical works,' ... and—most relevant here—'motion pictures and other audiovisual works[ ]'.... This list is not exhaustive, but as we have previously observed, categories of creative efforts that are not 'similar [ ]or analogous to any of the listed categories' are unlikely to fall within the subject matter of federal copyright protection. Motion pictures, like 'pantomimes,' ... and 'dramatic works,' ... are works that may be expected to contain contributions from multiple individuals. But the Act lists none of the constituent parts of any of these kinds of works as 'works of authorship.' This uniform absence of explicit protection suggests that non-free-standing contributions to works of authorship are not ordinarily themselves works of authorship." *See also* ***Garcia v. Google, Inc.***, 786 F.3d 733, 740-41 (9th Cir. 2015).

Andrien v. Southern Ocean Cty. Chamber of Commerce, 927 F.2d 132, 134-35 (3d Cir.1991). The "definition of an author [is] the party who actually creates the work, that is, the person who translates an idea into an expression that is embodied in a copy by himself or herself, or who authorizes another to embody the expression in a copy. The definition, however, has limits. When one authorizes embodiment, that process must be rote or mechanical transcription that does not require intellectual modification or highly technical enhancement.... [¶] Poets, essayists, novelists, and the like may have copyrights even if they do not run the printing presses or process the photographic plates necessary to fix the writings into book form. These writers are entitled to copyright protection even if they do not perform with their own hands the mechanical tasks of putting the material into the form distributed to the public." Held: Compiler of maps was author, even though he gave compilation to printer to make composite.

§102(a)—Originality

Feist Publ'ns, Inc. v. Rural Tel. Serv., 499 U.S. 340, 345 (1991). "The *sine qua non* of copyright is originality. To qualify for copyright protection, a work must be original to the author. Original, as the term is used in copyright, means only that the work was independently created by the author (as opposed to copied from other works), and that it possesses at least some minimal degree of creativity. To be sure, the requisite level of creativity is extremely low; even a slight amount will suffice. The vast majority of works make the grade quite easily, as they possess some creative spark, 'no matter how crude, humble or obvious' it might be. Originality does not signify novelty; a work may be original even though it closely resembles other works, so long as the similarity is fortuitous, not the result of copying." *See also* ***Medforms, Inc. v. Healthcare Mgmt. Solutions***, 290 F.3d 98, 107 (2d Cir.2002).

Oracle Am., Inc. v. Google, Inc., 750 F.3d 1339, 1362 (Fed.Cir.2014). "The district court is correct that '[w]ords and short phrases such as names, titles, and slogans' are not subject to copyright protection. The court failed to recognize, however, that the relevant question for copyrightability purposes is not whether the work at issue contains short phrases—as literary works often do—but, rather, whether those phrases are creative. And, by dissecting the individual lines of declaring code at issue into short phrases, the district court further failed to recognize that an original *combination* of elements can be copyrightable. *At 1367:* [W]e conclude that a set of commands to instruct a computer to carry out desired operations may contain expression that is eligible for copyright protection. We agree with [P] that, under Ninth Circuit law, an original work—even one that serves a function—is entitled to copyright protection as long as the author had multiple ways to express the underlying idea."

Schrock v. Learning Curve Int'l, 586 F.3d 513, 519 (7th Cir.2009). "Federal courts have historically applied a generous standard of originality in evaluating photographic works for copyright protection. In some cases, the original expression may be found in the staging and creation of the scene depicted in the photograph. But in many cases, the photographer does not invent the scene or create the subject matter depicted in it. Rather, the original expression he contributes lies in the *rendition* of the subject matter—that is, the effect created by the combination of his choices of perspective, angle, lighting, shading, focus, lens, and so on. Most photographs contain at least some originality in their rendition, ... except perhaps for a very limited class of photographs that can be characterized as 'slavish copies' of an underlying work...."

Situation Mgmt. Sys. v. ASP. Consulting LLC, 560 F.3d 53, 60 (1st Cir.2009). "[A] work's entitlement to copyright protection does not depend in any way upon the court's subjective assessment of its creative worth."

Meshwerks, Inc. v. Toyota Motor Sales U.S.A., Inc., 528 F.3d 1258, 1268 (10th Cir.2008). "[I]n assessing the originality of a work for which copyright protection is sought, we look only at the final *product*, not the process, and the fact that intensive, skillful, and even creative labor is invested in the process of creating a product does not guarantee its copyrightability. *At 1269-70:* Digital modeling can be, surely is being, and no doubt increasingly will be used to create copyrightable expressions. Yet, just as photographs *can be*, but are not *per se*, copyrightable, the same holds true for digital models."

ATC Distrib. Grp. v. Whatever It Takes Transmissions & Parts, Inc., 402 F.3d 700, 706 (6th Cir. 2005). "Classification schemes can in principle be creative enough to satisfy the originality requirement of copyright protection. *At 712:* A reproduction of a work of art or photograph in a different medium is copyrightable in principle, if it involves 'great skill and originality,' … or 'substantial variation, not merely a trivial variation such as might occur in the translation to a different medium.' Mere 'sweat of the brow,' however, is insufficient to render a copy eligible for copyright protection. Nor is the mere demonstration of physical skill or special training." *See also* ***Waldman Publ'g v. Landoll, Inc.***, 43 F.3d 775, 782 (2d Cir.1994).

Satava v. Lowry, 323 F.3d 805, 810 (9th Cir.2003). "Any copyrighted expression must be 'original.' Although the amount of creative input by the author required to meet the originality standard is low, it is not negligible. There must be something more than a 'merely trivial' variation, something recognizably the artist's own."

Bellsouth Adver. & Publ'g v. Donnelley Info. Publ'g, 999 F.2d 1436, 1441 (11th Cir.1993). "The protection of copyright must inhere in a creatively original *selection* of facts to be reported and not in the creative means used to discover those facts."

Atari, Inc. v. North Am. Philips Consumer Elecs. Corp., 672 F.2d 607, 615-16 (7th Cir.1982). "[A] relatively minimal artistic expression, if original, would render copyrightable … the pattern or design of game boards and playing cards as pictorial or graphic works. Recognizing this principle, the Second Circuit has held copyrightable as an audiovisual work the repetitive sequence of a substantial portion of the sights and sounds of a video game…. [¶] In ***Nichols v. Universal Pictures Corp.***, 45 F.2d 119 … (2d Cir.1930), [judge] articulated what is now known as the 'abstractions test': Upon any work[,] a great number of patterns of increasing generality will fit equally well, as more and more of the incident is left out…. [T]here is a point in this series of abstractions where they are no longer protected, since otherwise the playwright could prevent the use of his ideas, to which, apart from their expression, his property is never extended. Nobody has ever been able to fix that boundary, and nobody ever can. … As respects plays, the controversy chiefly centers upon the characters and sequence of incident, these being the substance. This test has proven useful in analyzing dramatic works, literary works, and motion pictures, where the recurring patterns can readily be abstracted into very general themes." (Internal quotes omitted.) Held: Seventh Circuit agrees with Second Circuit.

Adobe Sys. v. Southern Software, Inc., 45 U.S.P.Q.2d 1827, 1830 (N.D.Cal.1998). "[T]he fact that a computer program produces unprotectable typefaces does not make the computer program itself unprotectable."

Raffoler, Ltd. v. Peabody & Wright, Ltd., 671 F.Supp. 947, 950-51 (E.D.N.Y.1987). "Advertisements are generally capable of receiving copyright protection, provided that their material is otherwise copyrightable and falls within one of the categories of copyrightable subject matter set forth in … §102. Dissection of the material to determine its copyrightability is inappropriate; that determination must be made by an assessment of the work as a whole, not of its component parts, since there is no requirement that each part be capable of individual copyright protection."

§102(a)—Uncopyrightable

Lorenzana v. South Am. Rests. Corp., 799 F.3d 31, 34 (1st Cir.2015). "[A] chicken sandwich is not eligible for copyright protection. … A recipe—or any instructions—listing the combination of chicken, lettuce, tomato, cheese, and mayonnaise on a bun to create a sandwich is quite plainly not a copyrightable work."

Downing v. Abercrombie & Fitch, 265 F.3d 994, 1004 (9th Cir.2001). "A person's name or likeness is not a work of authorship within the meaning of … §102."

Brown v. Ames, 201 F.3d 654, 658 (5th Cir.2000). "A *persona* does not fall within the subject matter of copyright—it does not consist of a writing of an author within the meaning of the Copyright Clause of the Constitution." (Internal quotes omitted.) *See also* ***Waits v. Frito-Lay, Inc.***, 978 F.2d 1093, 1100 (9th Cir.1992) (vocal style is not copyrightable), *overruled on other grounds*, ***Lexmark Int'l v. Static Control Components, Inc.***, ___ U.S. ___, 134 S.Ct. 1377 (2014).

U.S. v. Moghadam, 175 F.3d 1269, 1273 (11th Cir. 1999). "Congress could have amended … §102 to include live musical performances in the list of protectable subject matter, but it did not do so. Likewise, it is unclear whether longstanding concepts generally applicable to copyright law such as fair use, the work-for-hire doctrine, limited duration, and the statute of limitations, carry over to the anti-bootlegging provisions."

Beal v. Paramount Pictures Corp., 20 F.3d 454, 459 (11th Cir.1994). "Material that is not original cannot be copyrighted. In addition to broad ideas, noncopyrightable material includes 'scenes a faire'—stock scenes that naturally flow from a common theme."

Madrid v. Chronicle Books, 209 F.Supp.2d 1227, 1241 (D.Wyo.2002). "The feel, essence and reaction by the reader that [P] mentions are likewise unprotectable under copyright law, as they are merely amorphous concepts and do not meet the requirements of ... §102(a).... Feelings and reactions are not fixed, and can vary in accordance with many factors, none of which relate to [P's] copyrighted work—which, it is essential to remember—consists only of the poem in its entirety. It seems that [P] would have the Court believe that every element of the poem is protected, but this is not the case."

§102(a)(1)

Hutchinson Tel. Co. v. Fronteer Directory Co., 770 F.2d 128, 131 (8th Cir.1985). "The legislative history of §102(a)(1) states that the term 'literary works' does not connote any criterion of literary merit or qualitative value: it includes catalogs, *directories* and similar factual, reference or instructional works and compilations of data. It thus appears that Congress intended that directories be copyrightable, thereby ratifying an unbroken line of cases holding telephone directories to be copyrightable. *At 132:* We hold ... that [P's] telephone directory is an original work of authorship and therefore is copyrightable under the provisions of ... §102." (Internal quotes omitted.) *But see* ***Feist Publ'ns, Inc. v. Rural Tel. Serv.***, 499 U.S. 340, 362-63 (1991) (white-pages directory lacked originality).

Berkic v. Crichton, 761 F.2d 1289, 1293 (9th Cir. 1985). "No one can own the basic idea for a story. General plot ideas are not protected by copyright law; they remain forever the common property of artistic mankind."

§102(a)(2)

Swirsky v. Carey, 376 F.3d 841, 851-52 (9th Cir. 2004). "No federal court has stated that a musical motive is not protectable because it is an idea. Nor does the 'musical idea' of the first measure of [P's] chorus lack protection because of its brevity. Although it is true that a single musical note would be too small a unit to attract copyright protection ..., an arrangement of a limited number of notes can garner copyright protection. This Court has stated that '[e]ven if a copied portion be relatively small in proportion to the entire work, if qualitatively important, the finder of fact may properly find substantial similarity.'"

§102(a)(4)

Conrad v. AM Cmty. Credit Un., 750 F.3d 634, 636 (7th Cir.2014). "[Ds] had hired [P] to perform a 'singing telegram' at a credit union trade association event. [¶] The performance itself was not copyrighted or even copyrightable, not being 'fixed in any tangible medium of expression.' To comply with the requirement of fixity[, P] would have had either to have recorded the performance or to have created a written 'dance notation' of it. She did neither."

§102(a)(5)

Star Athletica, L.L.C. v. Varsity Brands, Inc., ___ U.S. ___, 137 S.Ct. 1002, 1007 (2017). "We granted certiorari to resolve widespread disagreement over the proper test for implementing [17 U.S.C.] §101's separate-identification and independent-existence requirements. We hold that a feature incorporated into the design of a useful article is eligible for copyright protection only if the feature (1) can be perceived as a two- or three-dimensional work of art separate from the useful article and (2) would qualify as a protectable pictorial, graphic, or sculptural work—either on its own or fixed in some other tangible medium of expression—if it were imagined separately from the useful article into which it is incorporated."

DC Comics v. Towle, 802 F.3d 1012, 1015 (9th Cir. 2015). "We are asked to decide whether [D] infringed [P's] exclusive rights under a copyright when he built and sold replicas of the Batmobile.... *At 1019:* Courts have recognized that copyright protection extends not only to an original work as a whole, but also to 'sufficiently distinctive' elements, like comic book characters, contained within the work. Although comic book characters are not listed in the Copyright Act, we have long held that such characters are afforded copyright protection. [¶] Not every comic book, television, or motion picture character is entitled to copyright protection. We have held that copyright protection is available only for characters that are especially distinctive. To meet this standard, a character must be 'sufficiently delineated' and display consistent, widely identifiable traits. A masked magician dressed in standard magician garb whose role is limited to performing and revealing the magic tricks, for example, is not an 'especially distinct' character differing from an ordinary magician in a manner that warrants copyright protection. Further, characters that have been 'lightly sketched' and lack descriptions may not merit copyright protection. [¶] We have previously determined that an automotive character can be copyrightable. *At 1020:* [A] character may be protectable if it has distinctive character traits and attributes, even if the character does not maintain the same physical appearance in every context. [T]he presence of distinctive qualities apart from visual appearance can diminish or even negate the need for consistent visual appearance. [¶] Similarly, district courts have determined that James Bond, Batman, and Godzilla are characters protected by copyright, despite their changes in appearance. In each instance, courts have deemed the persistence of a character's traits and attributes to be key to determining whether the character qualifies for copyright protection. *At 1021:* We read these precedents as establishing a three-part test for determining whether a character in a comic book, television program, or motion picture is entitled to copyright protection. First, the character must generally have physical as well as conceptual qualities. Second, the character must be 'sufficiently delineated' to be recognizable as the same character whenever it appears. Considering the character as it has appeared in different productions, it must display consistent, identifiable character traits and attributes, although the character need not have a consistent appearance. Third, the character must be 'especially distinctive' and contain some unique elements of expression. It cannot be a stock character such as a magician in standard magician garb. Even when a character lacks sentient attributes and does not speak (like a car), it can be a protectable character if it meets this standard. *At 1022:* [W]e conclude that the Batmobile is a character that qualifies for copyright protection." (Internal quotes omitted.)

Coquico, Inc. v. Rodriguez-Miranda, 562 F.3d 62, 66 (1st Cir.2009). "Copyright protection can subsist in original plush-toy designs."

Kay Berry, Inc. v. Taylor Gifts, Inc., 421 F.3d 199, 207 (3d Cir.2005). "A sculptural work's creativity derives from the combination of texture, color, size, and shape, as well as the particular verse inscribed and the way the verse is presented. It means nothing that these elements may not be individually entitled to protection; all creative works draw on the common wellspring that is the public domain. In this pool are not only elemental raw materials, like colors, letters, descriptive facts, and the catalogue of standard geometric forms, but also earlier works of art that, due to the passage of time or for other reasons, are no longer copyright protected. When an author combines these elements and adds his or her own imaginative spark, creation occurs, and the author is entitled to protection for the result." (Internal quotes omitted.)

Leigh v. Warner Bros., 212 F.3d 1210, 1214 (11th Cir.2000). "[C]opyright law protects only original expression, not ideas. *At 1215:* Thus, the district court correctly identified the elements of artistic craft protected by [P's] copyright [of the photograph] as the selection of lighting, shading, timing, angle, and film. [¶] Although some cases have evaluated the 'mood' of a work independently, ... in this case it is safest to focus on the more concrete elements of the photographer's craft."

Masquerade Novelty, Inc. v. Unique Indus., 912 F.2d 663, 670 (3d Cir.1990). "If a sculptural work is not a 'useful article' because its sole 'utilitarian function ... is ... to portray the appearance of the article,' then it remains copyrightable under ... §102(a)(5) and a court need not analyze whether its utilitarian function is separable from the work's sculptural elements."

Robert R. Jones Assocs. v. Nino Homes, 858 F.2d 274, 278 (6th Cir.1988). Section 102(a)(5) has "been interpreted to include architectural drawings."

Weindling Int'l v. Kobi Katz, Inc., 56 U.S.P.Q.2d 1763, 1766 (S.D.N.Y.2000). The artistic design at the heart of the jewelry business "is why this Court respectfully disagrees with ***DBC, Inc. v. Merit Diamond Corp.***, 768 F.Supp. 414 (S.D.N.Y.1991)[,] which treated diamond rings as utilitarian articles, whereas in fact they are chiefly works of art, or more precisely ornamental sculpture, even if mass-produced. Just as any artist's painting of a bridge, if not slavishly copied from some other artist's painting, is entitled to copyright protection, so too [D's] original bridge ring design is likewise entitled to copyright."

§102(a)(6)

Lulirama Ltd. v. Axcess Broad. Servs., 128 F.3d 872, 878 (5th Cir.1997). "That Congress chose to create [the 'motion pictures and other audiovisual works' and 'sound recordings' categories] indicates that it recognized a distinction between audiovisual and purely audio works."

§102(a)(8)

Home Design Servs. v. Turner Heritage Homes, Inc., 825 F.3d 1314, 1322-23 (11th Cir.2016). "The Second Circuit's critique of ***Intervest*** demonstrates a difference between how we have described our copyright-infringement doctrine versus how they do. In the Second Circuit, a court can rule out copyright infringement as a matter of law 'either because the similarity between two works concerns only non-copyrightable elements of the plaintiff's work, or because no reasonable jury, properly instructed, could find that the two works are substantially similar.' But the 11th Circuit declined to adopt a similar two-part framework in ***Oravec***, on grounds that the formulation was 'not useful in [***Oravec***] because the two [parts] ultimately merge into a single inquiry: whether a reasonable jury could find the competing designs substantially similar at the level of protected expression.' In ***Intervest***, we framed our holding in terms of the merged inquiry from ***Oravec***. When recounting ***Intervest*** in ***Zalewski***, however, the Second Circuit used terminology from the first part of its two-part framework. According to the Second Circuit, we 'intuit[ed] that there was no copying of the [protected] arrangement,' in other words 'that any copying of the plaintiff's house designs went only to standard architectural features arranged in standard ways.' *At 1324:* We agree with both the reasoning and outcome of ***Zalewski***. If 'the similarity between two works concerns only non-copyrightable elements,' then there can be no copyright infringement as a matter of law. Customary styles and efficiency- or expectation-driven industry standards are not susceptible to copyright. And when floor plans are drawn in a customary style and to industry standards, even 'subtle differences' like those in ***Zalewski*** can indicate that there is no copyright infringement. After all, customary styles and industry standards, though not themselves copyrightable, often control room placement and features. [¶] We also agree that ***Intervest*** is best couched as holding that there was no copyright infringement because the floor plans at issue were similar only with respect to their noncopyrightable elements. Although the ***Intervest*** floor plans shared the same overall layout, the layout was not copyrightable in that case. ... Because the layouts were noncopyrightable, and because the floor plans differed in terms of dimensions, wall placement, and the presence and arrangement of particular features (or use of slightly varied features), we held that the similarities between the plans concerned only their noncopyrightable elements. There was therefore no copyright infringement. *At 1324 n.7:* It is important to frame ***Intervest*** as holding only that there is no copyright infringement when floor plans with the same *noncopyrightable* layouts also boast modest differences such as those in ***Intervest***. A more expansive reading would nearly eliminate copyright protection for architectural works. Specifically, if ***Intervest*** is read as holding that modest differences between floor plans always preclude copyright infringement, then even a plan with an entirely original layout would receive no copyright protection so long as the copying plan bore some superficial differences. That is not the correct result. The Copyright Act protects 'original works of authorship,' including 'architectural works.' [¶] Also, although we agree with the Second Circuit that ***Intervest*** is best framed under the first part of the Second Circuit's two-part framework, we do not abandon the merged inquiry from ***Oravec*** as a general matter. In many, perhaps most, copyright-infringement cases, sorting out the copyrightable and uncopyrightable elements of floor plans will be unnecessary because the floor plans will be so obviously different (in terms of overall layout or otherwise) that no reasonable jury could find the floor plans substantially similar at the level of protected expression. *At 1325:* Taken together, ***Intervest*** and ***Zalewski*** also support the proposition that courts are best-situated to determine whether similarity between two architectural works concerns only their noncopyrightable elements. In ***Intervest***, we held that 'separat[ing] protectable expression from non-protectable expression is ... a question of law or, at the very least, a mixed question of law and fact.' ***Zalewski*** effectuated the ***Intervest*** holding insofar as the Second Circuit took it upon itself not only to partially define noncopyrightable expression (customary styles, industry standards), but also to hold that in light of the floor plans' shared colonial style, subtle differences demonstrated the absence of copyright infringement."

Zalewski v. Cicero Builder Dev., Inc., 754 F.3d 95, 103 (2d Cir.2014). In ***Intervest Constr., Inc. v. Canterbury Estate Homes, Inc.***, 554 F.3d 914 (11th Cir.2008), the 11th Circuit "held that all copyrighted works are either 'creative, derivative, [or] compiled,' that is original, variations on an original, or compilations of unoriginal material. According to ***Intervest***, each kind of work gets varying levels of protection. The court then relied on the similarity between the statutory definitions of 'compilation' and 'architectural work' to conclude that architectural works fall into the 'compiled' category, and are thus entitled to only a 'thin' copyright based solely on their 'arrangement and coordination' of unoriginal and uncopyrightable elements. On facts similar to those here, the ***Intervest*** court held that any copying of the plaintiff's house designs went only to standard architectural features arranged in standard ways. In other words, any copying was not wrongful. [¶] While we agree with the outcome in ***Intervest***, we disagree with its reasoning. 'Creative,' 'derivative,' and 'compiled' may be useful concepts in some cases, but we reject the idea that works always fall neatly into one of these categories. *At 104:* Moreover, we see little support in [17 U.S.C. §101] for ***Intervest***'s use of categories. Although the statutory definitions of 'compilations' and 'architectural works' both speak of an 'arrangement' or 'to arrange' and refer to 'standard features' or 'preexisting material,' architectural works and compilations are not the only works that are defined with reference to their discrete—and perhaps uncopyrightable—elements. [¶] Labeling architecture a compilation obscures the real issue. Every work of art will have some standard elements, which taken in isolation are uncopyrightable, but many works will have original elements—or original arrangements of elements. The challenge in adjudicating copyright cases is not to determine whether a work is a creative work, a derivative work, or a compilation, but to determine what in it originated with the author and what did not. ***Intervest*** fails to do this. [¶] Courts should treat architectural copyrights no differently than other copyrights. *At 105-06:* Any design elements attributable to building codes, topography, structures that already exist on the construction site, or engineering necessity should therefore get no protection. [¶] There are scenes-a-faire in architecture. Neoclassical government buildings, colonial houses, and modern high-rise office buildings are all recognized styles from which architects draw. Elements taken from these styles should get no protection. Likewise, there are certain market expectations for homes or commercial buildings. Design features used by all architects, because of consumer demand, also get no protection. [¶] [W]e [have] recognized that 'generalized notions of where to place functional elements, how to route the flow of traffic, and ... methods of construction' are un-protectable. [¶] [M]any of the similarities [in this case] are a function of consumer expectations and standard house design generally. [P] can get no credit for putting a closet in every bedroom, a fireplace in the middle of an exterior wall, and kitchen counters against the kitchen walls. Furthermore, the overall footprint of the house and the size of the rooms are 'design parameters' dictated by consumer preferences and the lot the house will occupy, not the architect. *At 107:* Although he undoubtedly spent many hours on his designs, and although there is certainly something of [P's] own expression in his work, as long as [P] adhered to a pre-existing style his original contribution was slight—his copyright very thin. Only very close copying would have taken whatever actually belonged to [P]." *See also* ***Design Basics, LLC v. Lexington Homes, Inc.***, 858 F.3d 1093, 1102-03 (7th Cir.2017).

T-Peg, Inc. v. Vermont Timber Works, Inc., 459 F.3d 97, 109-10 (1st Cir.2006). "[T]he holder of a copyright in an architectural plan ... has two forms of protection, one under the provision for an 'architectural work' under ... §102(a)(8), and another under the provision for a 'pictorial, graphical, or sculptural work' under ... §102(a)(5). [¶] The requirement that the protectable elements of a pictorial, graphic, or sculptural work be separated from the 'utilitarian aspects' of the work under ... §102(a)(5) is known as the 'separability test.' By contrast, there is no separability test for an architectural work. *At 115:* Copyright protection exists not only in the architectural work taken as a whole (which includes a particular floor plan and arrangement of external features), but also in protectable portions of the work."

John Alden Homes, Inc. v. Kangas, 142 F.Supp.2d 1338, 1343 (M.D.Fla.2001), *aff'd*, 37 F.App'x 979 (11th Cir.2002) (table case). "The 11th Circuit has consistently held that original floor plans and construction drawings for single family houses can be protected under the copyright laws."

§102(b)—Generally

Feist Publ'ns, Inc. v. Rural Tel. Serv., 499 U.S. 340, 347 (1991). "'No one may claim originality as to facts.' This is because facts do not owe their origin to an act of authorship. The distinction is one between creation and discovery: the first person to find and report a particular fact has not created the fact; he or she has merely discovered its existence." *See also* ***Anti-Monopoly, Inc. v. General Mills Fun Grp.***, 611 F.2d 296, 300 n.1 (9th Cir.1979) (business ideas, such as a game concept, cannot be copyrighted); ***Torah Soft Ltd. v. Drosnin***, 136 F.Supp.2d 276, 291 (S.D.N.Y.2001) (algorithm is clearly method of operation that cannot be protected); ***Taggart v. WMAQ***, 57 U.S.P.Q.2d 1083, 1087 (S.D.Ill.2000) (utterances made during an interview are simply an idea, and thus not subject to copyright protection).

Harper & Row, Publ'rs v. Nation Enters., 471 U.S. 539, 556 (1985). Copyright's "idea/expression dichotomy 'strike[s] a definitional balance between the First Amendment and the Copyright Act by permitting free communication of facts while still protecting an author's expression.' No author may copyright his ideas or the facts he narrates." *See also* ***Mazer v. Stein***, 347 U.S. 201, 217 (1954).

Bikram's Yoga Coll. of India, L.P. v. Evolation Yoga, LLC, 803 F.3d 1032, 1039-40 (9th Cir.2015). "[P] attempts to secure copyright protection for a healing art [(yoga)]: a system designed to yield physical benefits and a sense of well-being. Simply put, this attempt is precluded by copyright's idea/expression dichotomy, codified by §102(b). [T]he copyright for a book describing how to perform a complicated surgery does not give the holder the exclusive right to perform the surgery. [P's] healing methodology is not eligible for protection by copyright. Indeed, if it is entitled to protection at all, that protection is more properly sought through the patent process."

Oracle Am., Inc. v. Google, Inc., 750 F.3d 1339, 1363 (Fed.Cir.2014). "The scenes a faire doctrine, which is related to the merger doctrine, operates to bar certain otherwise creative expression from copyright protection. It provides that expressive elements of a work of authorship are not entitled to protection against infringement if they are standard, stock, or common to a topic, or if they necessarily follow from a common theme or setting. Under this doctrine, when certain commonplace expressions are indispensable and naturally associated with the treatment of a given idea, those expressions are treated like ideas and therefore are not protected by copyright. In the computer context, the scene a faire doctrine denies protection to program elements that are dictated by external factors such as the mechanical specifications of the computer on which a particular program is intended to run or widely accepted programming practices within the computer industry. *At 1364:* [L]ike merger, in the Ninth Circuit, the scenes a faire doctrine is a component of the infringement analysis. Similarity of expression, whether literal or non-literal, which necessarily results from the fact that the common idea is only capable of expression in more or less stereotyped form, will preclude a finding of actionable similarity. Thus, the expression is not excluded from copyright protection; it is just that certain copying is forgiven as a necessary incident of *any* expression of the underlying idea. [¶] Like merger, the focus of the scenes a faire doctrine is on the circumstances presented to the creator, not the copier. The court's analytical focus must be upon the external factors that dictated [the creator's] selection of classes, methods, and code—not upon what [D] encountered at the time it chose to copy those groupings and that code. The scenes a faire doctrine identifies and excludes from protection against infringement expression whose creation flowed naturally from considerations external to the author's creativity." (Internal quotes omitted.) *See also* ***Miracle Blade, LLC v. Ebrands Commerce Grp.***, 207 F.Supp.2d 1136, 1151 (D.Nev.2002) (telemarketing script was *scene a faire*); ***Taylor Corp. v. Four Seasons Greetings LLC***, 171 F.Supp.2d 970, 973-74 (D.Minn.2001) (greeting-card designs were not *scenes a faire*), *aff'd*, 315 F.3d 1039 (8th Cir.2003).

Blehm v. Jacobs, 702 F.3d 1193, 1201 (10th Cir. 2012). "Because no principle can be stated as to when an imitator has gone beyond copying the idea, and has borrowed its expression, decisions must therefore inevitably be ad hoc." (Internal quotes omitted.)

Oravec v. Sunny Isles Luxury Ventures, L.C., 527 F.3d 1218, 1224 (11th Cir.2008). "In identifying the protected elements of a plaintiff's work, the court must be mindful of the fundamental axiom that copyright protection does not extend to ideas but only to particular expressions of ideas. This distinction—known as the idea/expression dichotomy—can be difficult to apply, as there is no bright line separating the ideas conveyed by a work from the specific expression of those ideas. *At 1225:* Nevertheless, in attempting to distinguish between ideas and expression, it is useful to note the policy purposes served by the distinction. The idea/expression dichotomy seeks to achieve a proper balance between competing societal interests: that of encouraging the creation of original works on the one hand, and that of promoting the free flow of ideas and information on the other. Therefore, in defining protectable expression, the court should neither draw the line so narrowly that authors, composers and artists will have no incentive to produce original literary, musical and artistic works, nor should the court draw it so broadly that future authors, composers and artists will find a diminished store of ideas on which to build their works." (Internal quotes omitted.)

BUC Int'l v. International Yacht Council Ltd., 489 F.3d 1129, 1141 (11th Cir.2007). "'[A] compiler's *selection, arrangement and coordination*, if original, are the only protectable elements of a factual compilation.' [¶] In terms of selection, we [distinguish] between 'a creatively original *selection* of facts' and 'the creative means used to discover those facts.' While the former is protected as an original work of authorship, the latter, i.e., methods used to discover facts and/or collect data, are not."

Tufenkian Imp./Exp. Ventures v. Einstein Moomjy, Inc., 338 F.3d 127, 132 n.4 (2d Cir.2003). The "copyright on a work whose design reflects the artist's original advance in technique does not extend to the technical development itself."

ETS-Hokin v. Skyy Spirits, Inc., 225 F.3d 1068, 1082 (9th Cir.2000). "Under the merger doctrine, courts will not protect a copyrighted work from infringement if the idea underlying the copyrighted work can be expressed in only one way, lest there be a monopoly on the underlying idea. In such an instance, it is said that the work's idea and expression 'merge.'" *See also* ***Oracle Am., Inc. v. Google, Inc.***, 750 F.3d 1339, 1359-60 (Fed.Cir.2014); ***R.W. Beck, Inc. v. E3 Consulting, LLC***, 577 F.3d 1133, 1144-45 (10th Cir.2009); ***New York Mercantile Exch., Inc. v. IntercontinentalExchange, Inc.***, 497 F.3d 109, 118 (2d Cir.2007) (end-of-day settlement price for commodities market is a merger of the expression of the price and the idea of the settlement price; therefore, settlement prices are uncopyrightable); ***Kay Berry, Inc. v. Taylor Gifts, Inc.***, 421 F.3d 199, 209 (3d Cir.2005); ***John G. Danielson, Inc. v. Winchester-Conant Props., Inc.***, 322 F.3d 26, 42-43 (1st Cir.2003); ***Veeck v. Southern Bldg. Code Cong. Int'l***, 293 F.3d 791, 801-02 (5th Cir.2002); ***Yurman Design, Inc. v. Paj, Inc.***, 262 F.3d 101, 111-12 (2d Cir.2001).

Mitel, Inc. v. Iqtel, Inc., 124 F.3d 1366, 1371 (10th Cir.1997). "Section 102(b) codifies one of copyright law's fundamental distinctions—copyright protection extends to an 'author's original expression and not to the ideas embodied in that expression.' Thus, when considering whether a defendant copied protectable elements of a copyrighted work, we must determine whether or to what extent the copied portions constitute ideas, processes, systems, or methods of operation, on one hand, or protectable expression, on the other. [¶] [T]his court has relied increasingly upon the conceptual framework known as abstraction-filtration-comparison to aid in separating idea from expression and identifying protectable expression. We utilize this approach as follows: 'First, in order to provide a framework for analysis, ... a court should dissect the [work] according to its varying levels of generality as provided in the abstractions test. Second, poised with this framework, the court should examine each level of abstraction in order to filter out those elements of the [work] which are unprotectable. Filtration should eliminate from comparison the unprotectable elements of ideas, processes, facts, public domain information, merger material, scenes a faire material, and other unprotectable elements suggested by the particular facts of the program under examination. Third, the court should then compare the remaining protectable elements with the allegedly infringing [work] to determine whether the defendants have misappropriated substantial elements of the plaintiff's [work].' Although abstraction-filtration-comparison analysis is particularly useful in cases involving copyright in computer programs, we recently noted that the approach merits application in cases that extend well beyond that narrow context. *At 1372:* We conclude that although an element of a work may be characterized as a method of operation, that element may nevertheless contain expression that is eligible for copyright protection. Section 102(b) does not extinguish the protection accorded a particular expression of an idea merely because that expression is embodied in a method of operation at a higher level of abstraction. Rather, §102(a) & (b) interact to secure ideas for public domain and to set apart an author's particular expression for further scrutiny to ensure that copyright protection will 'promote the ... useful Arts.' Our abstraction-filtration-comparison approach is directed to achieving this balance. Thus, we ... continue to adhere to our abstraction-filtration-comparison approach." *See also* ***Oracle Am., Inc. v. Google, Inc.***, 750 F.3d 1339, 1357-58 (Fed.Cir.2014); ***Seng-Tiong Ho v. Taflove***, 648 F.3d 489, 497-98 (7th Cir.2011). *But see* ***Lotus Dev. Corp. v. Borland Int'l***, this page.

Lotus Dev. Corp. v. Borland Int'l, 49 F.3d 807, 815 (1st Cir.1995), *aff'd by equally divided court*, 516 U.S. 233 (1996). "We think that 'method of operation,' as that term is used in §102(b), refers to the means by which a person operates something, whether it be a car, a food processor, or a computer. Thus a text describing how to operate something would not extend copyright protection to the method of operation itself; other people would be free to employ that method and to describe it in their own words. Similarly, if a new method of operation is used rather than described, other people would still be free to employ or describe that method. *At 818:* Our holding that methods of operation are not limited to abstractions goes against ... the Tenth Circuit[, which] rejected [D's] argument that the keying procedure used in a computer program was an uncopyrightable 'procedure' or 'method of operation' under §102(b)." *But see* ***Mitel, Inc. v. Iqtel, Inc.***, p. 207.

Atari Games Corp. v. Nintendo Inc., 975 F.2d 832, 842 (Fed.Cir.1992). "An author cannot acquire patent-like protection by putting an idea, process, or method of operation in an unintelligible format and asserting copyright infringement against those who try to understand that idea, process, or method of operation."

Broderbund Software, Inc. v. Unison World, Inc., 648 F.Supp. 1127, 1132 (N.D.Cal.1986). The Ninth Circuit "held that the idea of a jewel-encrusted bee pin could not be distinguished from the expression of that idea. As long as more than one manufacturer produced jewel-encrusted bee pins, the court found, it was inevitable that there would be a substantial similarity between the two forms of expression. In other words, the number of ways in which one can design a jewel-encrusted bee pin is strictly limited. Under such circumstances, to give one manufacturer a copyright on its bee pin would be to give that manufacturer a monopoly on the jewel-encrusted bee pin market because no other manufacturer could possibly conceive of a substantially different jewel-encrusted bee pin." *See also* ***Herbert Rosenthal Jewelry Corp. v. Kalpakian***, 446 F.2d 738, 741-42 (9th Cir.1971).

§102(b)—Specific Examples

Rentmeester v. Nike, Inc., 883 F.3d 1111, 1119 (9th Cir.2018). "[P]hotos can be broken down into objective elements that reflect the various creative choices the photographer made in composing the image—choices related to subject matter, pose, lighting, camera angle, depth of field, and the like. But none of those elements is subject to copyright protection when viewed in isolation. For example, a photographer who produces a photo using a highly original lighting technique or a novel camera angle cannot prevent other photographers from using those same techniques to produce new images of their own, provided the new images are not substantially similar to the earlier, copyrighted photo. With respect to a photograph's subject matter, no photographer can claim a monopoly on the right to photograph a particular subject just because he was the first to capture it on film. A subsequent photographer is free to take her own photo of the same subject, again so long as the resulting image is not substantially similar to the earlier photograph. [¶] That remains true even if, as here, a photographer creates wholly original subject matter by having someone pose in an unusual or distinctive way. [¶] Without gainsaying the originality of the pose [P] created, he cannot copyright the pose itself and thereby prevent others from photographing a person in the same pose. He is entitled to protection only for the way the pose is expressed in his photograph, a product of not just the pose but also the camera angle, timing, and shutter speed [P] chose. [¶] What *is* protected by copyright is the photographer's selection and arrangement of the photo's otherwise unprotected elements. If sufficiently original, the combination of subject matter, pose, camera angle, etc., receives protection, not any of the individual elements standing alone." *See also* ***Harney v. Sony Pictures TV, Inc.***, 704 F.3d 173, 180-81 (1st Cir. 2013).

Oracle Am., Inc. v. Google, Inc., 750 F.3d 1339, 1355-56 (Fed.Cir.2014). "[C]opyright protection can extend to both literal and non-literal elements of a computer program. The literal elements of a computer program are the source code and object code. Courts have defined source code as 'the spelled-out program commands that humans can read.' Object code refers to 'the binary language comprised of zeros and ones through which the computer directly receives its instructions.' Both source and object code 'are consistently held protected by a copyright on the program.' [¶] The non-literal components of a computer program include, among other things, the program's sequence, structure, and organization, as well as the program's user interface. [W]hether the non-literal elements of a program 'are protected depends on whether, on the particular facts of each case, the component in question qualifies as an expression of an idea, or an idea itself.'"

Seng-Tiong Ho v. Taflove, 648 F.3d 489, 498 (7th Cir.2011). "[Ps'] Model is an idea. ... That is, the Model attempts to represent and describe reality for scientific purposes. This scientific reality was not created by [Ps]. Rather, the Model embodies certain newly discovered scientific principles. *At 499:* [Ps] do not contend that [Ds] appropriated their creative presentation of the Model through copying such aspects as the color or font employed by [Ps]. Rather, [Ps] contend that [Ds] copied the *substance* of the equations, figures and text. [Ps] claim a copyright interest in the substance—not presentation—of the equations, figures and text. [¶] Equations and figures are common components of mathematical science used to depict ideas. Although equations can be rearranged through the laws of mathematics, the substance of the equation nevertheless remains the same. Without any evidence that the Model could be expressed by equations and figures other than those used by [Ps], we conclude that these equations and figures are '*required* by' the Model, ... and as such, are not subject to copyright."

Situation Mgmt. Sys. v. ASP. Consulting LLC, 560 F.3d 53, 61 (1st Cir.2009). "[*D*]*escriptions* of a process or system are copyrightable, but the underlying process or system itself is not. At least one circuit court has rejected as 'absurd' the argument that management training materials contain no protectable expression because they teach a noncopyrightable process."

Sony Computer Entm't, Inc. v. Connectix Corp., 203 F.3d 596, 602 (9th Cir.2000). "The object code of a program may be copyrighted as expression, but it also contains ideas and performs functions that are not entitled to copyright protection. *At 606:* The expressive element of software lies as much in the organization and structure of the object code that runs the computer as it does in the visual expression of that code that appears on a computer screen." Held: Fair use for D to copy P's computer program to gain access to noncopyrightable elements. *See also* ***Sega Enters. v. Accolade, Inc.***, 977 F.2d 1510, 1520 (9th Cir.1992).

National Basketball Ass'n v. Motorola, Inc., 105 F.3d 841, 847 (2d Cir.1997). Recorded "broadcasts of NBA games—as opposed to the games themselves—are ... entitled to copyright protection. [¶] Although the broadcasts are protected under copyright law, the district court correctly held that [Ds] did not infringe [P's] copyright because they reproduced only facts [i.e., game scores and statistics] from the broadcasts [on Ds' pagers], not the expression or description of the game that constitutes the broadcast."

Publications Int'l v. Meredith Corp., 88 F.3d 473, 481 (7th Cir.1996). "The recipes at issue here describe a procedure by which the reader may produce many dishes featuring ... yogurt. As such, they are excluded from copyright protection as either a 'procedure, process, [or] system.'" *See also* ***Barbour v. Head***, 178 F.Supp.2d 758, 762-63 (S.D.Tex.2001) (recipes that contain more than mechanical listings of ingredients and cooking directions may be copyrightable).

Wildlife Express Corp. v. Carol Wright Sales, Inc., 18 F.3d 502, 508 (7th Cir.1994). "[I]n a video game, ... the original manner of expressing ideas is found in the 'shapes, sizes, colors, sequences, arrangements and sounds.'"

Computer Assocs. Int'l v. Altai, Inc., 982 F.2d 693, 704 (2d Cir.1992). "In order to describe both computational processes and abstract ideas, [a computer program's] content 'combines creative and technical expression.' The variations of expression found in purely creative compositions, as opposed to those contained in utilitarian works, are not directed towards practical application. For example, a narration of Humpty Dumpty's demise, which would clearly be a creative composition, does not serve the same ends as, say, a recipe for scrambled eggs—which is a more process oriented text. Thus, compared to aesthetic works, computer programs hover even more closely to the elusive boundary line described in §102(b)."

§103. SUBJECT MATTER OF COPYRIGHT: COMPILATIONS & DERIVATIVE WORKS

(a) The subject matter of copyright as specified by section 102 includes compilations and derivative works, but protection for a work employing preexisting material in which copyright subsists does not extend to any part of the work in which such material has been used unlawfully.

(b) The copyright in a compilation or derivative work extends only to the material contributed by the author of such work, as distinguished from the preexisting material employed in the work, and does not imply any exclusive right in the preexisting material. The copyright in such work is independent of, and does not affect or enlarge the scope, duration, ownership, or subsistence of, any copyright protection in the preexisting material.

History of 17 U.S.C. §103: Oct. 19, 1976, P.L. 94-553, §101, 90 Stat. 2545.

ANNOTATIONS

Generally

ETS-Hokin v. Skyy Spirits, Inc., 225 F.3d 1068, 1078-79 (9th Cir.2000). "A comparison of how the Copyright Act defines 'derivative works' and 'compilations' provides an explanation for the use of the term 'preexisting material' in §103 as well as further support for the proposition that the underlying 'preexisting work' must be copyrightable."

Compilations

Feist Publ'ns, Inc. v. Rural Tel. Serv., 499 U.S. 340, 348 (1991). "Factual compilations ... may possess the requisite originality. The compilation author typically chooses which facts to include, in what order to place them, and how to arrange the collected data so that they may be used effectively by readers. These choices as to selection and arrangement, so long as they are made independently by the compiler and entail a minimal degree of creativity, are sufficiently original that Congress may protect such compilations through the copyright laws. Thus, even a directory that contains absolutely no protectible written expression, only facts, meets the constitutional minimum for copyright protection if it features an original selection or arrangement. [¶] This protection is subject to an important limitation. The mere fact that a work is copyrighted does not mean that every element of the work may be protected. ... Thus, if the compilation author clothes facts with an original collocation of words, he or she may be able to claim a copyright in this written expression. Others may copy the underlying facts from the publication, but not the precise words used to present them."

Bikram's Yoga Coll. of India, L.P. v. Evolation Yoga, LLC, 803 F.3d 1032, 1041 (9th Cir.2015). 17 U.S.C. §103 "complements [17 U.S.C.] §102. Thus, while a compilation may be eligible for copyright protection, it must nevertheless satisfy the requirements of §102. A compilation must, in other words, represent an 'original work[ ] of authorship,' and '[i]n no case' may copyright protection 'extend to any idea, procedure, process, [or] system.' The availability of copyright protection for compilations, therefore, does not eliminate §102's categorical bar on copyright protection for ideas."

MyWebGrocer, LLC v. HomeTown Info, Inc., 375 F.3d 190, 193 (2d Cir.2004). "A compilation of non-protectible facts is copyrightable if it 'features an original selection or arrangement of facts,' so that the selection or arrangement 'possesses at least some minimal degree of creativity.' 'Selection implies the exercise of judgment in choosing which facts from a given body of data to include in a compilation.' '[I]f the selection process imbues a compilation with the requisite creative spark, the compilation may be protected so long as there are indicia that principles of selection (other than all-inclusiveness) have been employed.'" *See also* ***Society of the Holy Transfiguration Monastery, Inc. v. Gregory***, 689 F.3d 29, 47 (1st Cir.2012); ***Silverstein v. Penguin Putnam, Inc.***, 368 F.3d 77, 82-83 (2d Cir.2004).

Derivative Works

Keeling v. Hars, 809 F.3d 43, 44-45 (2d Cir.2015). "The primary question presented is whether an unauthorized work that makes 'fair use' of its source material may itself be protected by copyright. [¶] We hold ... that, if the creator of an unauthorized work stays within the bounds of fair use and adds sufficient originality, she may claim protection under ... §103 ... for her original contributions."

Greene v. Ablon, 794 F.3d 133, 152 (1st Cir.2015). "'[T]he copyright in a ... derivative work extends only to the material contributed by the author of such work, as distinguished from the preexisting material employed in the work....' With respect to that preexisting work, '[a]ny elements that the author of the derivative work borrowed from the underlying work ... remain protected by the copyrights in the underlying work.' *At 153:* When the authors of a derivative work are joint authors, they share equally in the copyright to the derivative work, regardless of who penned the new material."

U.S. Auto Parts Network, Inc. v. Parts Geek, LLC, 692 F.3d 1009, 1016 (9th Cir.2012). "We have adopted the Second Circuit's test for ascertaining whether a derivative work meets copyright law's fundamental requirement of originality. In order to be copyrightable, (1) 'the original aspects of a derivative work must be more than trivial' and (2) 'the original aspects of a derivative work must reflect the degree to which it relies on preexisting material and must not in any way affect the scope of any copyright protection in that preexisting material.' This ... test establishes two ways of asking the same underlying question: whether the derivative work meets the 'constitutional requirement' of originality enunciated in ***Feist*** [***Publ'ns, Inc. v. Rural Tel. Serv.***, 499 U.S. 340 (1991)]."

Schrock v. Learning Curve Int'l, 586 F.3d 513, 518 (7th Cir.2009). "The Copyright Act specifically grants the author of a derivative work copyright protection in the incremental original expression he contributes as long as the derivative work does not infringe the underlying work."

Mulcahy v. Cheetah Learning L.L.C., 386 F.3d 849, 852 (8th Cir.2004). "A derivative work may itself be copyrighted if it has the requisite originality. However, 'the copyright is limited to the features that the derivative work adds to the original.' Moreover, because the owner of the original copyright has the exclusive right to prepare derivative works, the creator of an original derivative work is only entitled to a copyright if she had permission to use the underlying copyrighted work. *At 853-54:* [A] work may be found to be derivative even if it has 'a different total concept and feel from the original work.'" *See also* ***Palladium Music, Inc. v. EatSleepMusic, Inc.***, 398 F.3d 1193, 1197 (10th Cir. 2005).

Gaiman v. McFarlane, 360 F.3d 644, 661 (7th Cir. 2004). "The purpose of requiring that a derivative work to be copyrightable be significantly different from the copyrighted original is twofold: to avoid the confusion that would be created if two indistinguishable works were copyrighted and to prevent a copyright owner from extending his copyright beyond the statutory period by making an identical work as the statutory period was nearing its end, calling it a derivative work, and copyrighting it."

§104. SUBJECT MATTER OF COPYRIGHT: NATIONAL ORIGIN

(a) Unpublished works.—The works specified by sections 102 and 103, while unpublished, are subject to protection under this title without regard to the nationality or domicile of the author.

(b) Published works.—The works specified by sections 102 and 103, when published, are subject to protection under this title if—

(1) on the date of first publication, one or more of the authors is a national or domiciliary of the United States, or is a national, domiciliary, or sovereign authority of a treaty party, or is a stateless person, wherever that person may be domiciled; or

(2) the work is first published in the United States or in a foreign nation that, on the date of first publication, is a treaty party; or

(3) the work is a sound recording that was first fixed in a treaty party; or

(4) the work is a pictorial, graphic, or sculptural work that is incorporated in a building or other structure, or an architectural work that is embodied in a building and the building or structure is located in the United States or a treaty party; or

(5) the work is first published by the United Nations or any of its specialized agencies, or by the Organization of American States; or

(6) the work comes within the scope of a Presidential proclamation. Whenever the President finds that a particular foreign nation extends, to works by authors who are nationals or domiciliaries of the United States or to works that are first published in the United States, copyright protection on substantially the same basis as that on which the foreign nation extends protection to works of its own nationals and domiciliaries and works first published in that nation, the President may by proclamation extend protection under this title to works of which one or more of the authors is, on the date of first publication, a national, domiciliary, or sovereign authority of that nation, or which was first published in that nation. The President may revise, suspend, or revoke any such proclamation or impose any conditions or limitations on protection under a proclamation.

For purposes of paragraph (2), a work that is published in the United States or a treaty party within 30 days after publication in a foreign nation that is not a treaty party shall be considered to be first published in the United States or such treaty party, as the case may be.

(c) Effect of Berne Convention.—No right or interest in a work eligible for protection under this title may be claimed by virtue of, or in reliance upon, the provisions of the Berne Convention, or the adherence of the United States thereto. Any rights in a work eligible for protection under this title that derive from this title, other Federal or State statutes, or the common law, shall not be expanded or reduced by virtue of, or in reliance upon, the provisions of the Berne Convention, or the adherence of the United States thereto.

(d) Effect of phonograms treaties.—Notwithstanding the provisions of subsection (b), no works other than sound recordings shall be eligible for protection under this title solely by virtue of the adherence of the United States to the Geneva Phonograms Convention or the WIPO Performances and Phonograms Treaty.

History of 17 U.S.C. §104: Oct. 19, 1976, P.L. 94-553, §101, 90 Stat. 2545; Oct. 31, 1988, P.L. 100-568, §4(a)(2), (3), 102 Stat. 2855; Oct. 28, 1998, P.L. 105-304, §102(b), 112 Stat. 2862.

See also Berne Convention; WIPO Copyright Treaty; WIPO Performances & Phonograms Treaty.

§104A. COPYRIGHT IN RESTORED WORKS

(a) Automatic protection and term—

(1) Term—

(A) Copyright subsists, in accordance with this section, in restored works, and vests automatically on the date of restoration.

(B) Any work in which copyright is restored under this section shall subsist for the remainder of the term of copyright that the work would have otherwise been granted in the United States if the work never entered the public domain in the United States.

(2) Exception.—Any work in which the copyright was ever owned or administered by the Alien Property Custodian and in which the restored copyright would be owned by a government or instrumentality thereof, is not a restored work.

(b) Ownership of restored copyright.—A restored work vests initially in the author or initial rightholder of the work as determined by the law of the source country of the work.

(c) Filing of notice of intent to enforce restored copyright against reliance parties.—On or after the date of restoration, any person who owns a copyright in a restored work or an exclusive right therein may file with the Copyright Office a notice of intent to enforce that person's copyright or exclusive right or may serve such a notice directly on a reliance party. Acceptance of a notice by the Copyright Office is effective as to any reliance parties but shall not create a presumption of the validity of any of the facts stated therein. Service on a reliance party is effective as to that reliance party and any other reliance parties with actual knowledge of such service and of the contents of that notice.

(d) Remedies for infringement of restored copyrights—

(1) Enforcement of copyright in restored works in the absence of a reliance party.—As against any party who is not a reliance party, the remedies provided in chapter 5 of this title shall be available on or after the date of restoration of a restored copyright with respect to an act of infringement of the restored copyright that is commenced on or after the date of restoration.

(2) Enforcement of copyright in restored works as against reliance parties.—As against a reliance party, except to the extent provided in paragraphs (3) and (4), the remedies provided in chapter 5 of this title shall be available, with respect to an act of infringement of a restored copyright, on or after the date of restoration of the restored copyright if the requirements of either of the following subparagraphs are met:

(A)(i) The owner of the restored copyright (or such owner's agent) or the owner of an exclusive right therein (or such owner's agent) files with the Copyright Office, during the 24-month period beginning on the date of restoration, a notice of intent to enforce the restored copyright; and

(ii)(I) the act of infringement commenced after the end of the 12-month period beginning on the date of publication of the notice in the Federal Register;

(II) the act of infringement commenced before the end of the 12-month period described in subclause (I) and continued after the end of that 12-month period, in which case remedies shall be available only for infringement occurring after the end of that 12-month period; or

(III) copies or phonorecords of a work in which copyright has been restored under this section are made after publication of the notice of intent in the Federal Register.

(B)(i) The owner of the restored copyright (or such owner's agent) or the owner of an exclusive right therein (or such owner's agent) serves upon a reliance party a notice of intent to enforce a restored copyright; and

(ii)(I) the act of infringement commenced after the end of the 12-month period beginning on the date the notice of intent is received;

(II) the act of infringement commenced before the end of the 12-month period described in subclause (I) and continued after the end of that 12-month period, in which case remedies shall be available only for the infringement occurring after the end of that 12-month period; or

(III) copies or phonorecords of a work in which copyright has been restored under this section are made after receipt of the notice of intent.

In the event that notice is provided under both subparagraphs (A) and (B), the 12-month period referred to in such subparagraphs shall run from the earlier of publication or service of notice.

(3) Existing derivative works—

(A) In the case of a derivative work that is based upon a restored work and is created—

(i) before December 8, 1994, if the source country of the restored work is an eligible country on such date, or

(ii) before the date on which the source country of the restored work becomes an eligible country, if that country is not an eligible country on December 8, 1994,

a reliance party may continue to exploit that derivative work for the duration of the restored copyright if the reliance party pays to the owner of the restored copyright reasonable compensation for conduct which would be subject to a remedy for infringement but for the provisions of this paragraph.

(B) In the absence of an agreement between the parties, the amount of such compensation shall be determined by an action in United States district court, and shall reflect any harm to the actual or potential market for or value of the restored work from the reliance party's continued exploitation of the work, as well as compensation for the relative contributions of expression of the author of the restored work and the reliance party to the derivative work.

(4) Commencement of infringement for reliance parties.—For purposes of section 412, in the case of reliance parties, infringement shall be deemed to have commenced before registration when acts which would have constituted infringement had the restored work been subject to copyright were commenced before the date of restoration.

(e) Notices of intent to enforce a restored copyright—

(1) Notices of intent filed with the copyright office—

(A)(i) A notice of intent filed with the Copyright Office to enforce a restored copyright shall be signed by the owner of the restored copyright or the owner of an exclusive right therein, who files the notice under subsection (d)(2)(A)(i) (hereafter in this paragraph referred to as the "owner"), or by the owner's agent, shall identify the title of the restored work, and shall include an English translation of the title and any other alternative titles known to the owner by which the restored work may be identified, and an address and telephone number at which the owner may be contacted. If the notice is signed by an agent, the agency relationship must have been constituted in a writing signed by the owner before the filing of the notice. The Copyright Office may specifically require in regulations other information to be included in the notice, but failure to provide such other information shall not invalidate the notice or be a basis for refusal to list the restored work in the Federal Register.

(ii) If a work in which copyright is restored has no formal title, it shall be described in the notice of intent in detail sufficient to identify it.

(iii) Minor errors or omissions may be corrected by further notice at any time after the notice of intent is filed. Notices of corrections for such minor errors or omissions shall be accepted after the period established in subsection (d)(2)(A)(i). Notices shall be published in the Federal Register pursuant to subparagraph (B).

(B)(i) The Register of Copyrights shall publish in the Federal Register, commencing not later than 4 months after the date of restoration for a particular nation and every 4 months thereafter for a period of 2 years, lists identifying restored works and the ownership thereof if a notice of intent to enforce a restored copyright has been filed.

(ii) Not less than 1 list containing all notices of intent to enforce shall be maintained in the Public Information Office of the Copyright Office and shall be available for public inspection and copying during regular business hours pursuant to sections 705 and 708.

(C) The Register of Copyrights is authorized to fix reasonable fees based on the costs of receipt, processing, recording, and publication of notices of intent to enforce a restored copyright and corrections thereto.

(D)(i) Not later than 90 days before the date the Agreement on Trade-Related Aspects of Intellectual Property referred to in section 3511(d)(15) of title 19 enters into force with respect to the United States, the Copyright Office shall issue and publish in the Federal Register regulations governing the filing under this subsection of notices of intent to enforce a restored copyright.

(ii) Such regulations shall permit owners of restored copyrights to file simultaneously for registration of the restored copyright.

(2) Notices of intent served on a reliance party—

(A) Notices of intent to enforce a restored copyright may be served on a reliance party at any time after the date of restoration of the restored copyright.

(B) Notices of intent to enforce a restored copyright served on a reliance party shall be signed by the owner or the owner's agent, shall identify the restored work and the work in which the restored work is used, if any, in detail sufficient to identify them, and shall include an English translation of the title, any other alternative titles known to the owner by which the work may be identified, the use or uses to which the owner objects, and an address and telephone number at which the reliance party may contact the owner. If the notice is signed by an agent, the agency relationship must have been constituted in writing and signed by the owner before service of the notice.

(3) Effect of material false statements.—Any material false statement knowingly made with respect to any restored copyright identified in any notice of intent shall make void all claims and assertions made with respect to such restored copyright.

(f) Immunity from warranty and related liability—

(1) In general.—Any person who warrants, promises, or guarantees that a work does not violate an exclusive right granted in section 106 shall not be liable for legal, equitable, arbitral, or administrative relief if the warranty, promise, or guarantee is breached by virtue of the restoration of copyright under this section, if such warranty, promise, or guarantee is made before January 1, 1995.

(2) Performances.—No person shall be required to perform any act if such performance is made infringing by virtue of the restoration of copyright under the provisions of this section, if the obligation to perform was undertaken before January 1, 1995.

(g) Proclamation of copyright restoration.—Whenever the President finds that a particular foreign nation extends, to works by authors who are nationals or domiciliaries of the United States, restored copyright protection on substantially the same basis as provided under this section, the President may by proclamation extend restored protection provided under this section to any work—

(1) of which one or more of the authors is, on the date of first publication, a national, domiciliary, or sovereign authority of that nation; or

(2) which was first published in that nation.

The President may revise, suspend, or revoke any such proclamation or impose any conditions or limitations on protection under such a proclamation.

(h) Definitions.—For purposes of this section and section 109(a):

(1) The term "date of adherence or proclamation" means the earlier of the date on which a foreign nation which, as of the date the WTO Agreement enters into force with respect to the United States, is not a nation adhering to the Berne Convention or a WTO member country, becomes—

(A) a nation adhering to the Berne Convention;

(B) a WTO member country;

(C) a nation adhering to the WIPO Copyright Treaty;

(D) a nation adhering to the WIPO Performances and Phonograms Treaty; or

(E) subject to a Presidential proclamation under subsection (g).

(2) The "date of restoration" of a restored copyright is—

(A) January 1, 1996, if the source country of the restored work is a nation adhering to the Berne Convention or a WTO member country on such date, or

(B) the date of adherence or proclamation, in the case of any other source country of the restored work.

(3) The term "eligible country" means a nation, other than the United States, that—

(A) becomes a WTO member country after December 8, 1994;

(B) on December 8, 1994, or after December 8, 1994 becomes, a nation adhering to the Berne Convention;

(C) adheres to the WIPO Copyright Treaty;

(D) adheres to the WIPO Performances and Phonograms Treaty; or

(E) after December 8, 1994 becomes subject to a proclamation under subsection (g).

(4) The term "reliance party" means any person who—

(A) with respect to a particular work, engages in acts, before the source country of that work becomes an eligible country, which would have violated section 106 if the restored work had been subject to copyright protection, and who, after the source country becomes an eligible country, continues to engage in such acts;

(B) before the source country of a particular work becomes an eligible country, makes or acquires 1 or more copies or phonorecords of that work; or

(C) as the result of the sale or other disposition of a derivative work covered under subsection (d)(3), or significant assets of a person described in subparagraph (A) or (B), is a successor, assignee, or licensee of that person.

(5) The term "restored copyright" means copyright in a restored work under this section.

(6) The term "restored work" means an original work of authorship that—

(A) is protected under subsection (a);

(B) is not in the public domain in its source country through expiration of term of protection;

(C) is in the public domain in the United States due to—

(i) noncompliance with formalities imposed at any time by United States copyright law, including failure of renewal, lack of proper notice, or failure to comply with any manufacturing requirements;

(ii) lack of subject matter protection in the case of sound recordings fixed before February 15, 1972; or

(iii) lack of national eligibility;

(D) has at least one author or rightholder who was, at the time the work was created, a national or domiciliary of an eligible country, and if published, was first published in an eligible country and not published in the United States during the 30-day period following publication in such eligible country; and

(E) if the source country for the work is an eligible country solely by virtue of its adherence to the WIPO Performances and Phonograms Treaty, is a sound recording.

(7) The term "rightholder" means the person—

(A) who, with respect to a sound recording, first fixes a sound recording with authorization, or

(B) who has acquired rights from the person described in subparagraph (A) by means of any conveyance or by operation of law.

(8) The "source country" of a restored work is—

(A) a nation other than the United States;

(B) in the case of an unpublished work—

(i) the eligible country in which the author or rightholder is a national or domiciliary, or, if a restored work has more than 1 author or rightholder, of which the majority of foreign authors or rightholders are nationals or domiciliaries; or

(ii) if the majority of authors or rightholders are not foreign, the nation other than the United States which has the most significant contacts with the work; and

(C) in the case of a published work—

(i) the eligible country in which the work is first published, or

(ii) if the restored work is published on the same day in 2 or more eligible countries, the eligible country which has the most significant contacts with the work.

History of 17 U.S.C. §104A: Dec. 8, 1993, P.L. 103-182, §334(a), 107 Stat. 2115; Dec. 8, 1994, P.L. 103-465, §514(a), 108 Stat. 4976; Oct. 11, 1996, P.L. 104-295, §20(e)(2), 110 Stat. 3529; Nov. 13, 1997, P.L. 105-80, §2, 111 Stat. 1530; Oct. 28, 1998, P.L. 105-304, §102(c), 112 Stat. 2862.

See also 37 C.F.R. §§201.33, 201.34, 202.12; Berne Convention; NAFTA arts. 1705, 1706, annex 1705.7; TRIPs pt. II, §1; WIPO Copyright Treaty; WIPO Performances & Phonograms Treaty.

ANNOTATIONS

Golan v. Holder, 565 U.S. 302, 307, 101 U.S.P.Q.2d 1297, 1300 (2012). "Congress, in 1994, gave works enjoying copyright protection abroad the same full term of protection available to U.S. works. Congress did so in §514 of the Uruguay Round Agreements Act ..., which grants copyright protection to preexisting works of Berne member countries, protected in their country of origin, but lacking protection in the U.S. for any of three reasons: The U.S. did not protect works from the country of origin at the time of publication; the U.S. did not protect sound recordings fixed before 1972; or the author had failed to comply with U.S. statutory formalities (formalities Congress no longer requires as prerequisites to copyright protection). *At U.S. 308, U.S.P.Q.2d 1301:* Neither the Copyright and Patent Clause nor the First Amendment [of the U.S. Constitution], we hold, makes the public domain, in any and all cases, a territory that works may never exit."

Troll Co. v. Uneeda Doll Co., 483 F.3d 150, 156-57 (2d Cir.2007). "Much of §104A concerns the enforcement of restored copyrights against parties that were legitimately exploiting works in reliance on their public domain status. The statute creates a category of prior exploiters called 'reliance parties,' who may continue to exploit the work until the owner of the restored copyright makes known its intent to enforce its copyright. The statute creates three categories of reliance parties [in §104A(h)(4)]. Thus, [§104A(h)(4)(A) and (B)] make the status of a reliance party turn on whether a person took certain actions with respect to a work prior to the date that the source country of that work became an eligible country. [¶] An owner of a restored copyright may not enforce its copyright against a reliance party without first giving notice, either constructive or actual, of its intent to enforce the copyright. ... After receiving actual or constructive notice of intent to enforce, a reliance party must cease making copies of the protected work. However, the reliance party is entitled to a 12-month grace period in which to sell off its already existing copies. *At 159:* We therefore construe §104A(h)(4)(A) to confer reliance party status only on persons whose infringement is ongoing and without more than trivial interruption. *At 160:* [W]e conclude that Congress intended to limit the benefit of reliance party status under §104A(h)(4)(B) only to those copies made or acquired before the [Uruguay Round Agreements Act's (URAA)] enactment. [¶] Because [D] intends to sell recently manufactured [works in the public domain] and does not claim to be disposing of [works in the public domain] made by [D's predecessor] before the URAA's enactment, it is not entitled to reliance party status as [a] successor under §104A(h)(4)(B)-(C)."

Capitol Records, Inc. v. Naxos, Inc., 372 F.3d 471, 480 (2d Cir.2004). "The restoration provision of §104A extends federal protection to otherwise unprotected works within its coverage; it does not deny protection to works protected by common law copyright."

Alameda Films v. Authors Rights Restoration Corp., 331 F.3d 472, 477 (5th Cir.2003). "The [Uruguay Round Agreements Act (URAA)] provides that a '[c]opyright subsists ... in restored works, and vests automatically on the date of restoration.' The copyright in a restored work 'vests initially in the *author* or *initial rightholder* of the work as determined by the law of the source country of the work.' The URAA thus establishes two categories for foreign copyright owners whose U.S. copyrights can be restored: (1) authors, and (2) initial rightholders. The class of 'initial rightholders' includes only owners of a copyright in a 'sound recording,' e.g., music composers; whereas, the class of 'authors' includes all other creators of works originally copyrighted in foreign jurisdictions. *At 479:* Following the threshold determination whether one who claims a restored copyright is an 'author' under the source country's law, the URAA predicates restoration of the work's U.S. copyright on its meeting three requirements: The work (1) is not in the public domain in the source country, (2) is in the public domain in the U.S. because of noncompliance with copyright formalities, lack of subject matter protection, or lack of national eligibility, and (3) was first published in the source country and was not published in the U.S. within 30 days after its initial foreign publication."

Dam Things from Denmark v. Russ Berrie & Co., 290 F.3d 548, 563 (3d Cir.2002). "An author's right to protection of the derivative work only extends to the elements that he has added to the work; he cannot receive protection for the underlying work. Furthermore, if the underlying work is itself protected by copyright, then he will receive no protection at all; on the contrary, he is a copyright infringer, because in order to create his work he has copied the underlying work. However, §104A obviously creates an exception to this rule and even though the foreign author has a restored copyright, the creator of the derivative work is given special dispensation and is not considered an infringer, and is instead treated as a licensee."

§105. SUBJECT MATTER OF COPYRIGHT: UNITED STATES GOVERNMENT WORKS

Copyright protection under this title is not available for any work of the United States Government, but the United States Government is not precluded from receiving and holding copyrights transferred to it by assignment, bequest, or otherwise.

History of 17 U.S.C. §105: Oct. 19, 1976, P.L. 94-553, §101, 90 Stat. 2546.

ANNOTATIONS

County of Suffolk v. First Am. Real Estate Solutions, 261 F.3d 179, 187 (2d Cir.2001). "Although the federal government does not possess a statutory right to obtain copyright protection for its works, the Copyright Act is silent as to the rights of states or their subdivisions. Nor is there an indication in the statute that copyright ownership is limited to private persons. By specifying a limitation on ownership solely against the federal government, the Copyright Act implies that states and their subdivisions are not excluded from protection under the Act." *See also* ***National Conf. of Bar Exam'rs v. Multistate Legal Studies, Inc.***, 495 F.Supp. 34, 35 (N.D.Ill.1980), *rev'd in part on other grounds*, 692 F.2d 478 (7th Cir.1982).

§106. EXCLUSIVE RIGHTS IN COPYRIGHTED WORKS

Subject to sections 107 through 122, the owner of copyright under this title has the exclusive rights to do and to authorize any of the following:

(1) to reproduce the copyrighted work in copies or phonorecords;

(2) to prepare derivative works based upon the copyrighted work;

(3) to distribute copies or phonorecords of the copyrighted work to the public by sale or other transfer of ownership, or by rental, lease, or lending;

(4) in the case of literary, musical, dramatic, and choreographic works, pantomimes, and motion pictures and other audiovisual works, to perform the copyrighted work publicly;

(5) in the case of literary, musical, dramatic, and choreographic works, pantomimes, and pictorial, graphic, or sculptural works, including the individual images of a motion picture or other audiovisual work, to display the copyrighted work publicly; and

(6) in the case of sound recordings, to perform the copyrighted work publicly by means of a digital audio transmission.

History of 17 U.S.C. §106: Oct. 19, 1976, P.L. 94-553, §101, 90 Stat. 2546; July 3, 1990, P.L. 101-318, §3(d), 104 Stat. 288; Dec. 1, 1990, P.L. 101-650, §704(b)(2), 104 Stat. 5134; Nov. 1, 1995, P.L. 104-39, §2, 109 Stat. 336; Aug. 5, 1999, P.L. 106-44, §1(g)(2), 113 Stat. 222; Nov. 2, 2002, P.L. 107-273, §13210(4)(A), 116 Stat. 1909.

See also Berne Convention; NAFTA arts. 1705, 1706; WIPO Copyright Treaty art. 6; WIPO Performances & Phonograms Treaty arts. 6-14.

ANNOTATIONS

Generally

New York Times Co. v. Tasini, 533 U.S. 483, 495 (2001). "The 1976 [Copyright] Act rejected the doctrine of indivisibility, recasting the copyright as a bundle of discrete 'exclusive rights'...."

Dowling v. U.S., 473 U.S. 207, 217 (1985). The bundle of exclusive rights of a copyright owner "'has never accorded the copyright owner complete control over all possible uses of his work.'"

Harper & Row, Publ'rs v. Nation Enters., 471 U.S. 539, 546-47 (1985). 17 U.S.C. §106 "confers a bundle of exclusive rights to the owner of the copyright. Under the Copyright Act, these rights—to publish, copy, and distribute the author's work—vest in the author of an original work from the time of its creation. In practice, the author commonly sells his rights to publishers who offer royalties in exchange for their services in producing and marketing the author's work. The copyright owner's rights, however, are subject to certain statutory exceptions. Among these is [17 U.S.C.] §107 which codifies the traditional privilege of other authors to make 'fair use' of an earlier writer's work. In addition, no author may copyright facts or ideas. The copyright is limited to those aspects of the work—termed 'expression'—that display the stamp of the author's originality."

Sony Corp. v. Universal City Studios, Inc., 464 U.S. 417, 447 (1984). 17 U.S.C. §§107-118 "describe a variety of uses of copyrighted material that 'are not infringements of copyright' 'notwithstanding the provisions of [17 U.S.C.] §106.' The most pertinent in this case is §107, the legislative endorsement of the doctrine of 'fair use.'"

Geophysical Serv. v. TGS-NOPEC Geophysical Co., 850 F.3d 785, 799 (5th Cir.2017). "The phrase 'to authorize' appears in the preamble to the list of exclusive rights alongside 'to do.' We believe that this structure supports the conclusion that 'to do' and 'to authorize' refer to direct and contributory infringement, respectively, but that infringement in either case must be predicated on one of the listed exclusive rights. So codified, the doctrine of contributory infringement requires that the underlying direct infringement upon which it is predicated be actionable under the Copyright Act."

Foley v. Luster, 249 F.3d 1281, 1286 (11th Cir. 2001). "The [Copyright] Act establishes a comprehensive set of rights and remedies to protect copyrights, and preempts most state actions so that the rights and remedies will be consistent for all copyright holders. The indemnity case before us, however, *does not concern the rights of a copyright holder*. Rather, it concerns the *allocation of responsibility between copyright infringers. At 1287:* It is evident that the congressional intent in §106 was to protect the rights of copyright holders, not to govern cases between infringers."

DSC Comms. v. Pulse Comms., 170 F.3d 1354, 1361 (Fed.Cir.1999). The 17 U.S.C. §106 "rights are expressly limited ... by [17 U.S.C.] §§107 through 120.... Of particular importance are the limitations of §§109 and 117. As we have seen, §117 limits the copyright owner's exclusive rights by allowing an owner of a copy of a computer program to reproduce or adapt the program if reproduction or adaptation is necessary for the program to be used in conjunction with a machine. Section 109, which embodies the 'first sale' doctrine, limits the copyright owner's otherwise exclusive right of distribution...."

Broadcast Music, Inc. v. Hirsch, 104 F.3d 1163, 1166 (9th Cir.1997). "Assignments of interests in royalties have no relationship to the existence, scope, duration or identification of a copyright, nor to 'rights under a copyright.'"

La Salle Music Publ'rs v. Highfill, 3 U.S.P.Q.2d 1849, 1851 (8th Cir.1987). "[A] 'not for profit' defense is included in 17 U.S.C. §110 among the exemptions from the protections of [17 U.S.C.] §106. Both the language and structure of these two statutory provisions make clear that performance 'for profit' is not an element of the prima facie case for copyright infringement."

Baltimore Orioles, Inc. v. Major League Baseball Players Ass'n, 805 F.2d 663, 677 (7th Cir.1986). "[A] right is equivalent to one of the rights comprised by a copyright if it 'is infringed by the mere act of reproduction, performance, distribution or display.'"

Donald Frederick Evans & Assocs. v. Continental Homes, Inc., 785 F.2d 897, 901 n.7 (11th Cir.1986). "Public display of a model home must be distinguished from publication of architectural drawings when analyzing the protection afforded by the Copyright Act to the owner of a copyright in the architectural drawings. The copyright owner is vested with certain exclusive rights in the drawings as listed in ... §106, including reproduction of, and preparation of derivative works therefrom 'so as to instruct a would-be builder on how to proceed to construct the dwelling pictured.'"

Columbia Pictures Indus. v. Redd Horne, Inc., 749 F.2d 154, 158 (3d Cir.1984). "Since the rights granted by §106 are separate and distinct, and are severable from one another, the grant of one does not waive any of the other exclusive rights."

Pacific & S. Co. v. Duncan, 744 F.2d 1490, 1495 (11th Cir.1984). "Where strict enforcement of the rights of a copyright holder under ... §106 would conflict with the purpose of copyright law or with some other important societal value, courts should be free to fashion an appropriate fair use exemption."

R&R Recreation Prods. v. Joan Cook Inc., 25 U.S.P.Q.2d 1781, 1785 (S.D.N.Y.1992). "Section 106 lists the exclusive rights in a copyrighted work. The right to sue on accrued claims is not among them."

Contributory Infringement

Metro-Goldwyn-Mayer Studios Inc. v. Grokster, Ltd., 545 U.S. 913, 916 (2005). "The question is under what circumstances the distributor of a product capable of both lawful and unlawful use is liable for acts of copyright infringement by third parties using the product. We hold that one who distributes a device with the object of promoting its use to infringe copyright, as shown by clear expression or other affirmative steps taken to foster infringement, is liable for the resulting acts of infringement by third parties."

Geophysical Serv. v. TGS-NOPEC Geophysical Co., 850 F.3d 785, 789 (5th Cir.2017). "We must ... decide whether the inapplicability of the Copyright Act to extraterritorial conduct bars a contributory infringement claim based on the domestic authorization of entirely extraterritorial conduct. We hold that it does. *At 799:* [W]e follow the holding of the Ninth Circuit in ***Subafilms***. Where a copyright plaintiff claims contributory infringement predicated on direct infringement that occurred entirely extraterritorially, the plaintiff has stated no claim."

Ellison v. Robertson, 357 F.3d 1072, 1076 (9th Cir. 2004). "One who, with knowledge of the infringing activity, induces, causes or materially contributes to the infringing conduct *of another* may be liable as a contributory [copyright] infringer. We have interpreted the knowledge requirement for contributory copyright infringement to include both those with *actual knowledge* and those who *have reason to know* of direct infringement." (Internal quotes omitted.) *See also* ***Bridgeport Music, Inc. v. Rhyme Syndicate Music***, 376 F.3d 615, 621 (6th Cir.2004).

Subafilms, Ltd. v. MGM-Pathe Comms., 24 F.3d 1088, 1092 (9th Cir.1994). When "a party authorizes an activity *not* proscribed by one of the five §106 clauses, the authorizing party cannot be held liable as an infringer. *At 1093:* The exclusive rights accorded to a copyright owner under §106 are to do and to authorize any of the activities specified in the five numbered clauses. *Use of the phrase 'to authorize' is intended to avoid any questions as to the liability of contributory infringers.* For example, a person who lawfully acquires an authorized copy of a motion picture would be an infringer if he or she engages in the business of renting it to others for purposes of unauthorized public performance. *At 1094:* In light of our above conclusion that the authorization right refers to the doctrine of contributory infringement, which requires that the authorized act *itself* could violate one of the exclusive rights listed in §106(1)-(5), we believe that it is simply not possible to draw a principled distinction between an act that does not violate a copyright because it is not the type of conduct proscribed by §106, and one that does not violate §106 because the illicit act occurs overseas. In both cases, the authorized conduct could not violate the exclusive rights guaranteed by §106. In both cases, therefore, there can be no liability for authorizing such conduct." (Internal quotes omitted.) *See also* ***Venegas-Hernández v. Asociación de Compositores y Editores de Música Latinoamericana***, 424 F.3d 50, 58 (1st Cir.2005). *But see* ***Expediters Int'l v. Direct Line Cargo Mgmt. Servs.***, 995 F.Supp. 468, 477 (D.N.J.1998) (authorization of infringing acts abroad is direct, actionable infringement).

SBK Catalogue Prtshp. v. Orion Pictures Corp., 723 F.Supp. 1053, 1064-65 (D.N.J.1989). "Under the Copyright Act of 1976, the language of §106 was amended to include the right 'to authorize' use of the copyrighted work among the 'bundle of exclusive rights' granted to a copyright holder under the Act. The inclusion of the words 'to authorize' was intended to clear up the confusion surrounding a party's liability under the doctrine of contributory infringement. The doctrine of 'contributory infringement' has been applied in those cases in which there was an ongoing relationship between the direct infringer and the 'contributory' infringer at the time the infringement took place. Thus, where direct infringement was induced by a party who was in a position to control the use of copyrighted works by others, and who had authorized the use of those works without permission from the copyright owner, that party was found liable as a 'contributory' infringer. Prior to the enactment of the amended version of §106, the courts were split on how much involvement in the infringing conduct was necessary to subject a defendant to liability for contributory infringement; however, under the new law, mere authorization of the use is sufficient."

§106(1)

Harper & Row, Publ'rs v. Nation Enters., 471 U.S. 539, 552 (1985). "Respondents contend … that Congress, in including first publication among the rights enumerated in [17 U.S.C.] §106, which are expressly subject to fair use under [17 U.S.C.] §107, intended that fair use would apply *in pari materia* to published and unpublished works. The Copyright Act does not support this proposition."

Cartoon Network LP v. CSC Holdings, Inc., 536 F.3d 121, 127 (2d Cir.2008). "It is undisputed that [D], not any customer or other entity, takes the content from one stream of programming, after the split, and stores it, one small piece at a time, in the BMR buffer and the primary ingest buffer. As a result, the information is buffered before any customer requests a recording, and would be buffered even if no such request were made. The question is whether, by buffering the data that make up a given work, [D] 'reproduce[s]' that work 'in copies,' … and thereby infringes the copyright holder's reproduction right." Held: Because data is not fixed in buffer for more than transitory time, copy is not made that results in infringement.

Worldwide Ch. of God v. Philadelphia Ch. of God, Inc., 227 F.3d 1110, 1115 (9th Cir.2000). Copyright owner's exclusive right to reproduce and distribute copies "is not diminished or qualified by the fact that [copyright owner] is a not-for-profit organization and does not realize monetary benefit from the use of the copyrighted work. Nor is that right affected by the religious nature of its activity…."

ABKCO Music, Inc. v. Stellar Records, Inc., 96 F.3d 60, 62-63 n.4 (2d Cir.1996). "The 'synch' right is a right exclusively enjoyed by the copyright owner. The Copyright Act does not explicitly confer synchronization rights, but courts have held that the synch right is derived from the exclusive right of a copyright owner, under … §106(1), to reproduce his work. *At 64:* Thus, while a compulsory license permits the recording of a 'cover' version of a song, it does not permit the inclusion of a copy of the lyrics. That requires the separate permission of the copyright holder."

American Geophysical Un. v. Texaco Inc., 60 F.3d 913, 930 (2d Cir.1994). "Since the Copyright Act explicitly provides that copyright holders have the 'exclusive rights' to 'reproduce' and 'distribute copies' of their works, and since there currently exists a viable market for licensing these rights for individual journal articles, it is appropriate that potential licensing revenues for photocopying be considered in a fair use analysis."

§106(2)

Schrock v. Learning Curve Int'l, 586 F.3d 513, 515-16 (7th Cir.2009). "As long as [P] was authorized to make the photos ([P] was), [P] owned the copyright in the photos to the extent of their incremental original expression. [C]opyright in a derivative work arises by operation of law—not through authority from the owner of the copyright in the underlying work—although the parties may alter this default rule by agreement. *At 521:* [T]he following general principles [apply to the copyrightability of a derivative work]: (1) the originality requirement for derivative works is not more demanding than the originality requirement for other works; and (2) the key inquiry is whether there is sufficient non-trivial expressive variation in the derivative work to make it distinguishable from the underlying work in some meaningful way. This focus on the presence of nontrivial 'distinguishable variation' adequately captures the concerns articulated in ***Gracen*** [***v. Bradford Exchange***, 698 F.2d 300 (7th Cir.1983),] without unduly narrowing the copyrightability of derivative works. It is worth repeating that the copyright in a derivative work is thin, extending only to the incremental original expression contributed by the author of the derivative work."

Facenda v. NFL Films, Inc., 542 F.3d 1007, 1026 (3d Cir.2008). "By using the sound clips of [P's] voice in [program], [D] was exercising its exclusive right to make derivative works of those sound clips under §106(2). In effect, it was 'sampling' itself, making a collage, taking a small piece of an old work and using it in a new work—as when a hip-hop group samples the drum part from James Brown's 'Funky Drummer.' It is well-established that copyrights extend to samples, even brief samples."

ETS-Hokin v. Skyy Spirits, Inc., 225 F.3d 1068, 1078 (9th Cir.2000). "The statute … presupposes that the preexisting work—that is, the work that underlies the derivative work—is copyrightable."

Lee v. A.R.T. Co., 125 F.3d 580, 581 (7th Cir.1997). "No one believes that a museum violates [17 U.S.C.] §106(2) every time it changes the frame of a painting that is still under copyright, although the choice of frame or glazing affects the impression the art conveys, and many artists specify frames (or pedestals for sculptures) in detail. [The Ninth Circuit] acknowledge[s] that framing and other traditional means of mounting and displaying art do not infringe authors' exclusive right to make derivative works. Nonetheless, the ninth circuit held, what [D] does creates a derivative work because the epoxy resin bonds the art to the tile. Our district judge thought this a distinction without a difference, and we agree. If changing the way in which a work of art will be displayed creates a derivative work, and if [P] is right about what 'prepared' means, then the derivative work is 'prepared' when the art is mounted; what happens later is not relevant, because the violation of the §106(2) right has already occurred. If the framing process does not create a derivative work, then mounting art on a tile, which serves as a flush frame, does not create a derivative work. What is more, the ninth circuit erred in assuming that normal means of mounting and displaying art are easily reversible. A painting is placed in a wooden 'stretcher' as part of the framing process; this leads to some punctures (commonly tacks or staples), may entail trimming the edges of the canvas, and may affect the surface of the painting as well. *At 582-83:* If [the Ninth Circuit is] right about what counts as a derivative work, then the U.S. has established through the back door an extraordinarily broad version of authors' moral rights, under which artists may block any modification of their works of which they disapprove. … What is more, [17 U.S.C.] §106A applies only to a 'work of visual art,' a new term defined in [17 U.S.C.] §101 to mean either a unique work or part of a limited edition (200 copies or fewer) that has been 'signed and consecutively numbered by the author.' … It would not be sound to use §106(2) to provide artists with exclusive rights deliberately omitted from the [VARA]. We therefore decline to follow [the Ninth Circuit]."

Litchfield v. Spielberg, 736 F.2d 1352, 1357 (9th Cir.1984). "To constitute a violation of §106(2) the infringing work must incorporate in some form a portion of the copyrighted work."

Rogers v. Koons, 751 F.Supp. 474, 477 (S.D.N.Y. 1990), *amended*, 777 F.Supp. 1 (S.D.N.Y.1991), *aff'd*, 960 F.2d 301 (2d Cir.1992). "Under the [17 U.S.C. §101 definition of 'derivative work'], [D's] sculpture is a derivative work based upon [P's] photograph; and [P] as copyright owner had the exclusive right to authorize derivative work. It is well settled that a photographer's originality in photographic expression is entitled to full copyright protection."

Anderson v. Stallone, 11 U.S.P.Q.2d 1161, 1169 (C.D.Cal.1989). 17 U.S.C. §103(a) "was not intended to arm an infringer and limit the applicability of [17 U.S.C.] §106(2) on unified derivative works. [S]ection 106(2) most certainly precludes the author of an unauthorized infringing derivative work from suing the author of the work which he had already infringed."

§106(3)

Quality King Distribs. v. L'anza Research Int'l, 523 U.S. 135, 144 (1998). "The introductory language in [17 U.S.C.] §106 expressly states that all of the exclusive rights granted by that section—including ... the distribution right granted by subsection (3)—are limited by the provisions of [17 U.S.C.] §§107 through 120. One of those limitations ... is provided by the terms of §109(a), which expressly permit the owner of a lawfully made copy to sell that copy '[n]otwithstanding the provisions of §106(3).' *At 150-51:* [T]he §106 rights are subject not only to the first sale defense in §109(a), but also to all of the other provisions of '§§107 through 120.' If [17 U.S.C.] §602(a) functioned independently, none of those sections would limit its coverage. For example, the 'fair use' defense embodied in §107 would be unavailable to importers if §602(a) created a separate right not subject to the limitations on the §106(3) distribution right. Under [P's incorrect] interpretation of the [Copyright] Act, it presumably would be unlawful for a distributor to import copies of a British newspaper that contained a book review quoting excerpts from an American novel protected by a U.S. copyright."

Harper & Row, Publ'rs v. Nation Enters., 471 U.S. 539, 553 (1985). "The right of first publication implicates a threshold decision by the author whether and in what form to release his work. First publication is inherently different from other §106 rights in that only one person can be the first publisher; ... the commercial value of the right lies primarily in exclusivity. Because the potential damage to the author from judicially enforced 'sharing' of the first publication right with unauthorized users of his manuscript is substantial, the balance of equities in evaluating such a claim of fair use inevitably shifts. *At 564:* The right of first publication encompasses not only the choice whether to publish at all, but also the choices of when, where, and in what form first to publish a work." *See also* ***Perfect 10, Inc. v. Amazon.com, Inc.***, 508 F.3d 1146, 1167 (9th Cir.2007).

Litecubes, LLC v. Northern Light Prods., 523 F.3d 1353, 1371 (Fed.Cir.2008). "We agree that the term 'sale' should be interpreted consistently in copyright and patent law.... [¶] [T]he Copyright Act does not explicitly require that sales be 'in the U.S.,' and courts have generally held that the Copyright Act only does not reach activities that 'that take place *entirely* abroad.'"

Perfect 10, Inc. v. Amazon.com, Inc., 508 F.3d 1146, 1162 (9th Cir.2007). "[D]istribution requires an 'actual dissemination' of a copy. Because [D] did not communicate the full-size images to the user's computer, [D] did not distribute these images. [¶] [D's] search engine communicates HTML instructions that tell a user's browser where to find full-size images on a website publisher's computer, but [D] does not itself distribute copies of the infringing photographs. It is the website publisher's computer that distributes copies of the images by transmitting the photographic image electronically to the user's computer."

Hotaling v. Church of Jesus Christ of Latter-Day Saints, 118 F.3d 199, 203 (4th Cir.1997). Distributing "unlawful copies of a copyrighted work does violate the copyright owner's distribution right and, as a result, constitutes copyright infringement. In order to establish 'distribution' of a copyrighted work, a party must show that an unlawful copy was disseminated 'to the public.'" Held: Although infringing work never made it into the hands of the public, D infringed P's distribution right by making infringing work available. *But see* ***Elektra Entm't Grp. v. Barker***, 551 F.Supp.2d 234, 244-45 (S.D.N.Y.2008) (to infringe distribution right, D must do more than "make available"; D must at least offer to distribute work).

National Car Rental Sys. v. Computer Assocs., 991 F.2d 426, 430 (8th Cir.1993). "The exclusive right to lease a copyrighted work is derivative of the right to distribute, which ... is the right to distribute copies. Allegations of a lease agreement thus cannot expand that distribution right; the right to lease must be the right to lease a copy. Because the pleadings cannot properly be read to allege distribution of a copy, neither can they be read to allege a lease of a copy."

Ford Motor Co. v. Summit Motor Prods., 930 F.2d 277, 299 (3d Cir.1991). Counterclaiming D "contends that a one-time gift to another person does not implicate §106(3). We disagree. ... The term 'other transfer of ownership' is broad enough to encompass gifts. [¶] [Counterclaiming D] also claims that §106(3) is inapplicable because the gift to [co-D corporation's president] was not a distribution to the 'public.' This argument fails because even one person can be the public for the purposes of §106(3). The term 'public' is not defined in the Copyright Act. Thus, we need to look elsewhere for a definition. Our search commences with the observation that the right protected by §106(3) is generally referred to as that of publication. ... 'Publication' and the exclusive right protected by §106(3) ... are for all practical purposes, synonymous. *At 300:* [B]ecause 'publication' and the right protected by §106(3) are the same, and because a 'publication' can occur when only one member of the public receives a copyrighted work, it follows that a violation of §106(3) can also occur when illicit copies of a copyrighted work are only distributed to one person. [¶] Given this construction of §106(3), there is no doubt that [counterclaiming D's] one-time gift to [co-D corporation's president] of the plastic bags, however innocent, clearly falls within the scope of that section."

Peer Int'l v. Pausa Records, Inc., 909 F.2d 1332, 1337 (9th Cir.1990). Once "the owner of a copyright in a nondramatic musical work distributes phonorecords of that work to the public, any other person may obtain a compulsory license from the U.S. Copyright Office to make and distribute that work simply by giving the copyright owner notice of his intention to do so."

§106(4)

American Broad. Cos. v. Aereo, Inc., ___ U.S. ___, 134 S.Ct. 2498, 2503 (2014). "We must decide whether [D] infringes [on the right to perform a work publicly] by selling its subscribers a technologically complex service that allows them to watch television programs over the Internet at about the same time as the programs are broadcast over the air. We conclude that it does."

U.S. v. American Soc'y of Composers, Authors & Publ'rs, 627 F.3d 64, 68 (2d Cir.2010). "This case presents [a] distinct question[] that arise[s] from the transmittal of musical works over the Internet: [W]hether a download of a digital file containing a musical work constitutes a public performance of that musical work.... [¶] [W]e affirm the district court's ruling that a download of a musical work does not constitute a public performance of that work...."

Cartoon Network LP v. CSC Holdings, Inc., 536 F.3d 121, 134 (2d Cir.2008). "[Ps'] theory is that [D] will violate the Copyright Act by engaging in unauthorized public performances of their works through the playback of [off-site DVR] copies [that were made by D's customers]. [¶] No one disputes that [off-site DVR] playback results in the transmission of a performance of a work—the transmission from [D's server] to the customer's television set. [D] contends that (1) [off-site DVR] customer, rather than [D], does the transmitting and thus the performing and (2) the transmission is not 'to the public' under the transmit clause. [¶] [W]e find that [off-site DVR] playback, as described here, does not involve the transmission of a performance 'to the public.' *At 139:* [W]e find that the transmit clause directs us to identify the potential audience of a given transmission, i.e., the persons 'capable of receiving' it, to determine whether that transmission is made 'to the public.' Because each [off-site DVR] playback transmission is made to a single subscriber using a single unique copy produced by that subscriber, we conclude that such transmissions are not performances 'to the public,' and therefore do not infringe any exclusive right of public performance. We base this decision on the application of undisputed facts; thus, [D] is entitled to summary judgment on this point."

Leadsinger, Inc. v. BMG Music Publ'g, 512 F.3d 522, 527 (9th Cir.2008). "[C]ourts have recognized a copyright holder's right to control the synchronization of musical compositions with the content of audiovisual works and have required parties to obtain synchronization licenses from copyright holders."

Bridgeport Music, Inc. v. Rhyme Syndicate Music, 376 F.3d 615, 623 (6th Cir.2004). "A claim for infringement of [the §106(4)] right requires proof that the composition was publicly performed without having obtained permission." *See also* ***Lodge Hall Music, Inc. v. Waco Wrangler Club, Inc.***, 831 F.2d 77, 78 (5th Cir. 1987).

Broadcast Music, Inc. v. Claire's Boutiques, Inc., 949 F.2d 1482, 1486 (7th Cir.1991). "One obvious example of a public performance is a live musical concert before a substantial paying audience. A live concert, then, is an infringement unless it is licensed or unless an exemption applies. On the other hand, a rendition of a copyrighted song in the shower is not a public performance and therefore not an infringement, so that there is no need to obtain a license or search for an exemption."

National Ass'n of Broadcasters v. Copyright Royalty Tribunal, 809 F.2d 172, 179 n.9 (2d Cir.1986). "Cable retransmissions are recognized as public performances under §106(4)."

Columbia Pictures Indus. v. Redd Horne, Inc., 749 F.2d 154, 160 (3d Cir.1984). "The transfer of the video cassettes to [Ds] did not result in the forfeiture or waiver of all of the exclusive rights found in §106. The copyright owner's exclusive right 'to perform the copyrighted work publicly' has not been affected; only its distribution right as to the transferred copy has been circumscribed."

§106(5)

Perfect 10, Inc. v. Amazon.com, Inc., 508 F.3d 1146, 1160-61 (9th Cir.2007). "[A] person displays a photographic image by using a computer to fill a computer screen with a copy of the photographic image fixed in the computer's memory. There is no dispute that [D's] computers store thumbnail versions of [P's] copyrighted images and communicate copies of those thumbnails to [D's] users. Therefore, [P] has made a prima facie case [of infringement] that [D's] communication of its stored thumbnail images directly infringes [P's] display right. [¶] [D] does not, however, display a copy of full-size infringing photographic images for purposes of the Copyright Act when [D] frames in-line linked images that appear on a user's computer screen. Because [D's] computers do not store the photographic images, [D] does not have a copy of the images for purposes of the Copyright Act. In other words, [D] does not have any 'material objects ... in which a work is fixed ... and from which the work can be perceived, reproduced, or otherwise communicated' and thus cannot communicate a copy. [¶] Instead of communicating a copy of the image, [D] provides HTML instructions that direct a user's browser to a website publisher's computer that stores the full-size photographic image. Providing these HTML instructions is not equivalent to showing a copy."

§106(6)

Recording Indus. Ass'n v. Librarian of Congress, 176 F.3d 528, 530 (D.C.Cir.1999). The "Digital Performance Right in Sound Recordings Act of 1995 ... afforded copyright owners a separate right to the performance of sound recordings via digital audio transmissions. This meant that certain digital music services would be required to pay recording companies and recording artists when they transmitted sound recordings. Although copyright owners now have protected interests under the 1995 law, they are nonetheless *required* to give licenses to those who seek to transmit sound recordings."

§106A. RIGHTS OF CERTAIN AUTHORS TO ATTRIBUTION & INTEGRITY

(a) Rights of attribution and integrity.—Subject to section 107 and independent of the exclusive rights provided in section 106, the author of a work of visual art—

(1) shall have the right—

(A) to claim authorship of that work, and

(B) to prevent the use of his or her name as the author of any work of visual art which he or she did not create;

(2) shall have the right to prevent the use of his or her name as the author of the work of visual art in the event of a distortion, mutilation, or other modification of the work which would be prejudicial to his or her honor or reputation; and

(3) subject to the limitations set forth in section 113(d), shall have the right—

(A) to prevent any intentional distortion, mutilation, or other modification of that work which would be prejudicial to his or her honor or reputation, and any intentional distortion, mutilation, or modification of that work is a violation of that right, and

(B) to prevent any destruction of a work of recognized stature, and any intentional or grossly negligent destruction of that work is a violation of that right.

(b) Scope and exercise of rights.—Only the author of a work of visual art has the rights conferred by subsection (a) in that work, whether or not the author is the copyright owner. The authors of a joint work of visual art are coowners of the rights conferred by subsection (a) in that work.

(c) Exceptions—

(1) The modification of a work of visual art which is a result of the passage of time or the inherent nature of the materials is not a distortion, mutilation, or other modification described in subsection (a)(3)(A).

(2) The modification of a work of visual art which is the result of conservation, or of the public presentation, including lighting and placement, of the work is not a destruction, distortion, mutilation, or other modification described in subsection (a)(3) unless the modification is caused by gross negligence.

(3) The rights described in paragraphs (1) and (2) of subsection (a) shall not apply to any reproduction, depiction, portrayal, or other use of a work in, upon, or in any connection with any item described in subparagraph (A) or (B) of the definition of "work of visual art" in section 101, and any such reproduction, depiction, portrayal, or other use of a work is not a destruction, distortion, mutilation, or other modification described in paragraph (3) of subsection (a).

(d) Duration of rights—

(1) With respect to works of visual art created on or after the effective date set forth in section 610(a) of the Visual Artists Rights Act of 1990, the rights conferred by subsection (a) shall endure for a term consisting of the life of the author.

(2) With respect to works of visual art created before the effective date set forth in section 610(a) of the Visual Artists Rights Act of 1990, but title to which has not, as of such effective date, been transferred from the author, the rights conferred by subsection (a) shall be coextensive with, and shall expire at the same time as, the rights conferred by section 106.

(3) In the case of a joint work prepared by two or more authors, the rights conferred by subsection (a) shall endure for a term consisting of the life of the last surviving author.

(4) All terms of the rights conferred by subsection (a) run to the end of the calendar year in which they would otherwise expire.

(e) Transfer and waiver—

(1) The rights conferred by subsection (a) may not be transferred, but those rights may be waived if the author expressly agrees to such waiver in a written instrument signed by the author. Such instrument shall specifically identify the work, and uses of that work, to which the waiver applies, and the waiver shall apply only to the work and uses so identified. In the case of a joint work prepared by two or more authors, a waiver of rights under this paragraph made by one such author waives such rights for all such authors.

(2) Ownership of the rights conferred by subsection (a) with respect to a work of visual art is distinct from ownership of any copy of that work, or of a copyright or any exclusive right under a copyright in that work. Transfer of ownership of any copy of a work of visual art, or of a copyright or any exclusive right under a copyright, shall not constitute a waiver of the rights conferred by subsection (a). Except as may otherwise be agreed by the author in a written instrument signed by the author, a waiver of the rights conferred by subsection (a) with respect to a work of visual art shall not constitute a transfer of ownership of any copy of that work, or of ownership of a copyright or of any exclusive right under a copyright in that work.

History of 17 U.S.C. §106A: Dec. 1, 1990, P.L. 101-650, §603(a), 104 Stat. 5128.

See also Berne Convention.

ANNOTATIONS

Dastar Corp. v. Twentieth Century Fox Film Corp., 539 U.S. 23, 34-35 (2003). "The [VARA] provides that the author of an artistic work 'shall have the right ... to claim authorship of that work.' That express right of attribution is carefully limited and focused: It attaches only to specified 'work[s] of visual art,' is personal to the artist, and endures only for 'the life of the author.' Recognizing in [15 U.S.C. §1125(a)] a cause of action for misrepresentation of authorship of noncopyrighted works (visual or otherwise) would render these limitations superfluous."

Quality King Distribs. v. L'anza Research Int'l, 523 U.S. 135, 149 (1998). The "text of [17 U.S.C.] §602(a) itself unambiguously states that the prohibited importation is an infringement of the exclusive distribution right 'under [17 U.S.C.] §106, actionable under [17 U.S.C.] §501.' Unlike that phrase, which identifies §602 violations as a species of §106 violations, the text of [17 U.S.C.] §106A, which is also cross-referenced in §501, uses starkly different language. It states that the author's right protected by §106A is 'independent of the exclusive rights provided in §106.' The contrast between the relevant language in §602 and that in §106A strongly implies that only the latter describes an independent right."

Cheffins v. Stewart, 825 F.3d 588, 592 (9th Cir. 2016). "The purpose of VARA is to protect two 'moral rights' of artists—the rights of 'integrity' and 'attribution.' The right of integrity allows the artist to prevent any deforming or mutilating changes to his work, even after the title in the work has been transferred. The right of attribution allows the artist to be recognized by name as the creator of a work." (Internal quotes omitted.)

Kelley v. Chicago Park Dist., 635 F.3d 290, 292 (7th Cir.2011). "[F]or reasons relating to copyright's requirements of expressive authorship and fixation, a living garden like [P's work] is not copyrightable. *At 296:* Moral rights are generally grouped into two categories: rights of attribution and rights of integrity. 'Rights of attribution' generally include the artist's right to be recognized as the author of his work, to publish anonymously and pseudonymously, to prevent attribution of his name to works he did not create, and to prevent his work from being attributed to other artists. 'Rights of integrity' include the artist's right to prevent the modification, mutilation, or distortion of his work, and in some cases (if the work is of recognized stature), to prevent its destruction. *At 298:* The statutory coverage is limited to paintings, drawings, prints, sculptures, and photographs created for exhibition existing in a single copy or a limited edition of 200 or less. The rights conferred by the statute exist independently of property rights; the artist retains them even after he no longer holds title to his work. *At 300-01:* Copyright's broad general coverage extends to 'original works of authorship,' and this includes 'pictorial, graphic, and sculptural works.' The use of the adjectives 'pictorial' and 'sculptural' suggests flexibility and breadth in application. In contrast VARA uses the specific nouns 'painting' and 'sculpture.' To qualify for moral-rights protection under VARA, [P's work] cannot just be 'pictorial' or 'sculptural' in some aspect or effect, it must actually *be* a 'painting' or a 'sculpture.' Not metaphorically or by analogy, but *really*. [¶] Even assuming a generous stance on what qualifies [as a 'painting' or a 'sculpture'], ... the terms cannot be read coextensively with the broader categories of 'pictorial' and 'sculptural' works that are generally eligible for copyright under [17 U.S.C.] §102(a)(5). If a living garden like [P's work] really counts as both a painting and a sculpture, then these terms do no limiting work at all. *At 304:* Simply put, gardens are planted and cultivated, not authored. A garden's constituent elements are alive and inherently changeable, not fixed. Most of what we see and experience in a garden—the colors, shapes, textures, and scents of the plants—originates in nature, not in the mind of the gardener. *At 305:* In contrast, when a landscape designer conceives of a plan for a garden and puts it in writing—records it in text, diagrams, or drawings on paper or on a digital-storage device—we can say that his intangible intellectual property has been embodied in a fixed and tangible 'copy.' This writing is a sufficiently permanent and stable copy of the designer's intellectual expression and is vulnerable to infringing copying, giving rise to the designer's right to claim copyright. The same cannot be said of a garden, which is not a fixed copy of the gardener's intellectual property. [¶] We are not suggesting that copyright attaches *only* to works that are static or fully permanent (no medium of expression lasts forever), or that artists who incorporate natural or living elements in their work can *never* claim copyright. *At 306:* Because [P's work] is neither 'authored' nor 'fixed' in the senses required for basic copyright, it cannot qualify for moral-rights protection under VARA." *See also* ***Massachusetts Museum of Contemporary Art Found. v. Büchel***, 593 F.3d 38, 47-48 (1st Cir.2010).

Massachusetts Museum of Contemporary Art Found. v. Büchel, 593 F.3d 38, 52 (1st Cir.2010). "We ... hold that VARA protects the moral rights of artists who have 'created' works of art within the meaning of the Copyright Act even if those works are not yet complete. *At 54:* [W]e conclude that Congress intended the prejudice requirement [in 17 U.S.C. §106A(a)(3)(A)] to apply to the right of integrity whether the remedy sought is injunctive relief or damages. [¶] Relying on dictionary definitions of prejudice, honor and reputation, the district court in ***Carter*** concluded that it should 'consider whether [the proposed] alteration would cause injury or damage to plaintiffs' good name, public esteem, or reputation in the artistic community.' We think this a useful approach, but emphasize that the focus is on the artist's reputation in relation to the altered work of art; the artist need not have public stature beyond the context of the creation at issue. *At 55:* The right of attribution [in subsections (a)(1) and (2)] gives an artist a claim for injunctive relief to, inter alia, assert or disclaim authorship of a work. [¶] VARA does not provide a damages remedy for an attribution violation. *At 62:* [D] maintains that, even aside from the alleged modifications to [work], merely exhibiting the work of art in its unfinished state, without the artist's consent, constitutes a distortion. We reject this claim. A separate moral right of disclosure (also known as the right of divulgation) protects an author's authority to 'prevent third parties from disclosing [his or her] work to the public without the author's consent,' and is not covered by VARA. *At 63:* [T]he moral rights granted to specific artists under VARA are separate and independent from the economic rights guaranteed by [17 U.S.C.] §106. Thus, the inadequacy of claims under VARA does not, on its own, signify the inadequacy of more traditional copyright claims."

Phillips v. Pembroke Real Estate, Inc., 459 F.3d 128, 129 (1st Cir.2006). "This case raises important questions about the application of the [VARA] to 'site-specific art,' which is a subset of 'integrated art.' A work of 'integrated art' is comprised of two or more physical objects that must be presented together as the artist intended for the work to retain its meaning and integrity. In a work of 'site-specific art,' one of the component physical objects is the location of the art. To remove a work of site-specific art from its original site is to destroy it. *At 143:* [T]he plain language of VARA does not protect site-specific art."

Carter v. Helmsley-Spear, Inc., 71 F.3d 77, 83 (2d Cir.1995). "For works created on or after June 1, 1991—the effective date of the [VARA]—the rights provided for endure for the life of the author or, in the case of a joint work, the life of the last surviving author. The rights cannot be transferred, but may be waived by a writing signed by the author. Copyright registration is not required to bring an action for infringement of the rights granted under VARA, or to secure statutory damages and attorney's fees. All remedies available under copyright law, other than criminal remedies, are available in an action for infringement of moral rights." *See also* ***Massachusetts Museum of Contemporary Art Found. v. Büchel***, 593 F.3d 38, 49 (1st Cir.2010); ***Martin v. City of Indianapolis***, 192 F.3d 608, 611-12 (7th Cir.1999).

Flack v. Friends of Queen Catherine Inc., 139 F.Supp.2d 526, 534 (S.D.N.Y.2001). "VARA does not provide a means of enjoining or obtaining damages due to modifications resulting from 'the passage of time or the inherent nature of the materials.' This is true even if the modification is caused by gross negligence."

Carter v. Helmsley-Spear, Inc., 861 F.Supp. 303, 325 (S.D.N.Y.1994), *rev'd in part on other grounds*, 71 F.3d 77 (2d Cir.1995). "The recognized stature requirement must be interpreted in such a manner as to maintain the preservative purpose of ... §106A(a)(3)(B) and in light of this Section's plain meaning. Thus, for a work of visual art to be protected under this Section, a plaintiff must make a two-tiered showing: (1) that the visual art in question has 'stature,' *i.e.* is viewed as meritorious, and (2) that this stature is 'recognized' by art experts, other members of the artistic community, or by some cross-section of society. In making this showing, plaintiffs generally, but not inevitably, will need to call expert witnesses to testify before the trier of fact. Finally, in order to be entitled to injunctive relief, a plaintiff must show that the defendant has commenced destruction of, or intends to destroy, the subject art work."

§107. LIMITATIONS ON EXCLUSIVE RIGHTS: FAIR USE

Notwithstanding the provisions of sections 106 and 106A, the fair use of a copyrighted work, including such use by reproduction in copies or phonorecords or by any other means specified by that section, for purposes such as criticism, comment, news reporting, teaching (including multiple copies for classroom use), scholarship, or research, is not an infringement of copyright. In determining whether the use made of a work in any particular case is a fair use the factors to be considered shall include—

(1) the purpose and character of the use, including whether such use is of a commercial nature or is for nonprofit educational purposes;

(2) the nature of the copyrighted work;

(3) the amount and substantiality of the portion used in relation to the copyrighted work as a whole; and

(4) the effect of the use upon the potential market for or value of the copyrighted work.

The fact that a work is unpublished shall not itself bar a finding of fair use if such finding is made upon consideration of all the above factors.

History of 17 U.S.C. §107: Oct. 19, 1976, P.L. 94-553, §101, 90 Stat. 2546; Dec. 1, 1990, P.L. 101-650, §607, 104 Stat. 5132; Oct. 24, 1992, P.L. 102-492, 106 Stat. 3145.

ANNOTATIONS

Generally

Quality King Distribs. v. L'anza Research Int'l, 523 U.S. 135, 150-51 (1998). The "'fair use' defense embodied in [17 U.S.C.] §107 would be unavailable to importers if [17 U.S.C.] §602(a) created a separate right not subject to the limitations on the [17 U.S.C.] §106(3) distribution right. ... Given the importance of the fair use defense to publishers of scholarly works, as well as to publishers of periodicals, it is difficult to believe that Congress intended to impose an absolute ban on the importation of all such works containing any copying of material protected by a U.S. copyright. [¶]

In the context of this case, involving copyrighted labels, it seems unlikely that an importer could defend an infringement as a 'fair use' of the label. In construing the statute, however, we must remember that its principal purpose was to promote the progress of the 'useful Arts' by rewarding creativity, and its principal function is the protection of original works, rather than ordinary commercial products that use copyrighted material as a marketing aid. It is therefore appropriate to take into account the impact of the denial of the fair use defense for the importer of foreign publications. As applied to such publications, [P's] construction of §602 'would merely inhibit access to ideas without any countervailing benefit.'"

Stewart v. Abend, 495 U.S. 207, 236 (1990). "At common law, the property of the author in his intellectual creation was absolute until he voluntarily parted with the same. The fair use doctrine ... evolved in response to this absolute rule. The doctrine is an equitable rule of reason, ... which permits courts to avoid rigid application of the copyright statute when, on occasion, it would stifle the very creativity which that law is designed to foster." (Internal quotes omitted.)

Harper & Row, Publ'rs v. Nation Enters., 471 U.S. 539, 549 (1985). "Fair use was traditionally defined as 'a privilege in others than the owner of the copyright to use the copyrighted material in a reasonable manner without his consent.' The statutory formulation of the defense of fair use in the Copyright Act reflects the intent of Congress to codify the common-law doctrine. Section 107 requires a case-by-case determination whether a particular use is fair, and the statute notes four nonexclusive factors to be considered. This approach was 'intended to restate the [pre-existing] judicial doctrine of fair use, not to change, narrow, or enlarge it in any way.'" *See also* ***Latimer v. Roaring Toyz, Inc.***, 601 F.3d 1224, 1239 (11th Cir.2010) (fair use must be pleaded as an affirmative defense).

Sony Corp. v. Universal City Studios, Inc., 464 U.S. 417, 432-33 (1984). "Copyright protection 'subsists ... in original works of authorship fixed in any tangible medium of expression.' This protection has never accorded the copyright owner complete control over all possible uses of his work. Rather, the Copyright Act grants the copyright holder 'exclusive' rights to use and to authorize the use of his work in five qualified ways, including reproduction of the copyrighted work in copies. All reproductions of the work, however, are not within the exclusive domain of the copyright owner; some are in the public domain. Any individual may reproduce a copyrighted work for a 'fair use'; the copyright owner does not possess the exclusive right to such a use."

Cambridge Univ. Press v. Patton, 769 F.3d 1232, 1258 (11th Cir.2014). "[T]he proper scope of the fair use doctrine in a given case boils down to an evidentiary question. As a conceptual matter, in making fair use determinations, we must conjure up a hypothetical, perfect market for the work in question, consisting of the whole universe of those who might buy it, in which everyone involved has perfect knowledge of the value of the work to its author and to potential buyers, and excluding for the moment any potential fair uses of the work. Then, keeping in mind the purposes animating copyright law—the fostering of learning and the creation of new works—we must determine how much of that value the implied licensee-fair users can capture before the value of the remaining market is so diminished that it no longer makes economic sense for the author—or a subsequent holder of the copyright—to propagate the work in the first place. [¶] In most instances, licensors (authors and copyright holders) and licensees (both paying licensees, and implied-by-law fair use licensees) will independently perform some version of this analysis in order to reach a mutually equitable arrangement. Ideally, a copyright holder will sell his or her works to buyers who pay the price that the market will bear and will routinely tolerate secondary uses which do not adversely impact that market. However, in the event of a disagreement, the copyright holder can file an infringement suit and the secondary user may invoke the fair use defense. In so doing the parties essentially turn to a court to make a determination for them as to the appropriate boundaries of the secondary user's implied license. *At 1259-60:* [Ps] contend that the District Court erred by performing a work-by-work analysis which focused on whether the use of each individual work was fair use rather than on the broader context of ongoing practices at [university]. We disagree. [W]e find that the District Court's work-by-work approach—in which the District Court considered whether the fair use defense excused a representative sample of instances of alleged infringement in order to determine the need for injunctive relief—was the proper one. [¶] [Ps] argue that the District Court erred in giving each of the four factors equal weight, essentially taking a mechanical 'add up the factors' approach, finding fair use if three factors weighed in favor of fair use and one against and vice versa, and only performing further analysis in case of a 'tie.' We agree that the District Court's arithmetic approach was improper."

Authors Guild, Inc. v. HathiTrust, 755 F.3d 87, 90-91 (2d Cir.2014). "This appeal requires us to decide whether [D-digital library's] use of copyrighted material is protected against a claim of copyright infringement under the doctrine of fair use. *At 95-96:* Under the fair-use doctrine, a book reviewer may, for example, quote from an original work in order to illustrate a point and substantiate criticisms, ... and a biographer may quote from unpublished journals and letters for similar purposes.... An artist may employ copyrighted photographs in a new work that uses a fundamentally different artistic approach, aesthetic, and character from the original. An internet search engine can display low-resolution versions of copyrighted images in order to direct the user to the website where the original could be found. A newspaper can publish a copyrighted photograph (taken for a modeling portfolio) in order to inform and entertain the newspaper's readership about a news story. A viewer can create a recording of a broadcast television show in order to view it at a later time. And a competitor may create copies of copyrighted software for the purpose of analyzing that software and discovering how it functions (a process called 'reverse engineering'). [¶] The doctrine is generally subject to an important proviso: A fair use must not excessively damage the market for the original by providing the public with a substitute for that original work. Thus, a book review may fairly quote a copyrighted book 'for the purposes of fair and reasonable criticism,' ... but the review may not quote extensively from the 'heart' of a forthcoming memoir in a manner that usurps the right of first publication and serves as a substitute for purchasing the memoir.... *At 97:* It is not disputed that, in order to perform a full-text search of books, the Libraries must first create digital copies of the entire books. Importantly, ... the [digital library] does not allow users to view any portion of the books they are searching. Consequently, in providing this service, the [digital library] does not add into circulation any new, human-readable copies of any books. Instead, the [digital library] simply permits users to 'word search'—that is, to locate where specific words or phrases appear in the digitized books. Applying the relevant factors, we conclude that this use is a fair use. *At 101:* The [digital library] also provides print-disabled patrons with versions of all of the works contained in its digital archive in formats accessible to them. In order to obtain access to the works, a patron must submit documentation from a qualified expert verifying that the disability prevents him or her from reading printed materials, and the patron must be affiliated with [a digital-library] member that has opted-into the program. Currently, ... only [one] member institution ... has opted-in. We conclude that this use is also protected by the doctrine of fair use."

Peter Letterese & Assocs. v. World Inst. of Scientology Enters., 533 F.3d 1287, 1308 (11th Cir.2008). "[T]he existence of actual consent negates the necessity of conducting a fair use analysis in the first place, as the existence of a license is an independent affirmative defense to a claim of copyright infringement."

Bill Graham Archives v. Dorling Kindersley Ltd., 448 F.3d 605, 608 (2d Cir.2006). "Although the issue of fair use is a mixed question of law and fact, the court may resolve issues of fair use at the summary judgment stage where there are no genuine issues of material fact as to such issues."

Wall Data Inc. v. Los Angeles Cty. Sheriff's Dept., 447 F.3d 769, 778 (9th Cir.2006). "As we balance these factors, we bear in mind that fair use is appropriate where a 'reasonable copyright owner' would have consented to the use, i.e., where the 'custom or public policy' at the time would have defined the use as reasonable."

NXIVM Corp. v. Ross Inst., 364 F.3d 471, 476-77 (2d Cir.2004). "Although defendants bear the burden of proving that their use was fair, they need not establish that each of the factors set forth in §107 weigh in their favor. Instead, all factors must be explored and the results weighed together in light of the purposes of copyright and the fair use defense."

Sega Enters. v. Accolade, Inc., 977 F.2d 1510, 1521 (9th Cir.1992). "Nothing in the language or the legislative history of [17 U.S.C.] §117, or in the [National Commission on New Technological Uses of Copyrighted Works] Report, suggests that §117 was intended to preclude the assertion of a fair use defense with respect to uses of computer programs that are not covered by §117, nor has [17 U.S.C.] §107 been amended to exclude computer programs from its ambit.

[¶] Moreover, §§107 and 117 serve entirely different functions. Section 117 defines a narrow category of copying that is lawful *per se*. Section 107, by contrast, establishes a *defense* to an otherwise valid claim of copyright infringement. It provides that particular instances of copying that otherwise would be actionable are lawful, and sets forth the factors to be considered in determining whether the defense applies. The fact that Congress has not chosen to provide a *per se* exemption to [17 U.S.C.] §106 for disassembly does not mean that particular instances of disassembly may not constitute fair use."

Lewis Galoob Toys, Inc. v. Nintendo, Inc., 964 F.2d 965, 969 (9th Cir.1992). "'The doctrine of fair use allows a holder of the privilege to use copyrighted material in a reasonable manner without the consent of the copyright owner.'"

United Video, Inc. v. F.C.C., 890 F.2d 1173, 1191-92 (D.C.Cir.1989). Petitioner "notes that copyright law 'builds in protection of the non-copyright holder's free speech rights through the fair use doctrine,' whereas syndex does not. This argument lacks force in the context of the present case, because the use to which the cable companies wish to put the copyrighted signals of others could never be considered fair use. The cable companies wish to make their own commercial profit by simply retransmitting the whole of another's copyrighted work in a way that, as the Commission found, diminishes the potential value of that work. This is not fair use."

Newport-Mesa Unified Sch. Dist. v. State of Cal. Dept. of Educ., 371 F.Supp.2d 1170, 1175 (C.D.Cal. 2005). "The small body of law on the topic of fair use of tests has uniformly indicated copying or distribution of copyrighted standardized tests is not 'fair use' under federal copyright law. [¶] However, these cases involved standardized competitive admission testing where future test-takers were given access to the tests before taking them. *At 1176:* The Court finds giving a copy of the test protocols to parents of special education students falls within … §107…."

Preamble

Campbell v. Acuff-Rose Music, Inc., 510 U.S. 569, 577-78 (1994). "The task [of determining fair use] is not to be simplified with bright-line rules, for the statute, like the doctrine it recognizes, calls for case-by-case analysis. The text employs the terms 'including' and 'such as' in the preamble paragraph to indicate the 'illustrative and not limitative' function of the examples given which thus provide only general guidance about the sorts of copying that courts and Congress most commonly had found to be fair uses. Nor may the four statutory factors be treated in isolation, one from another. All are to be explored, and the results weighed together, in light of the purposes of copyright. [¶] The enquiry here may be guided by the examples given in the preamble to §107, looking to whether the use is for criticism, or comment, or news reporting, and the like. The central purpose of this investigation is to see … whether the new work merely 'supersede[s] the objects' of the original creation, or instead adds something new, with a further purpose or different character, altering the first with new expression, meaning, or message; it asks, in other words, whether and to what extent the new work is 'transformative.' Although such transformative use is not absolutely necessary for a finding of fair use, the goal of copyright, to promote science and the arts, is generally furthered by the creation of transformative works…. [T]he more transformative the new work, the less will be the significance of other factors, like commercialism, that may weigh against a finding of fair use." *See also* ***Bill Graham Archives v. Dorling Kindersley Ltd.***, 448 F.3d 605, 608 (2d Cir. 2006).

Harper & Row, Publ'rs v. Nation Enters., 471 U.S. 539, 561 (1985). "News reporting is one of the examples enumerated in §107 to 'give some idea of the sort of activities the courts might regard as fair use under the circumstances.' This listing was not intended to be exhaustive, or to single out any particular use as presumptively a 'fair' use. The drafters … structured the provision as an affirmative defense requiring a case-by-case analysis. '[W]hether a use referred to in the first sentence of §107 is a fair use in a particular case will depend upon the application of the determinative factors, including those mentioned in the second sentence.' The fact that an article arguably is 'news' and therefore a productive use is simply one factor in a fair use analysis."

Monge v. Maya Mags., Inc., 688 F.3d 1164, 1173 (9th Cir.2012). "[F]air use has bounds even in news reporting, and no per se 'public interest' exception exists. *At 1174:* [D]espite the newsworthiness of [news] videos …, their mere rebroadcast was not in itself transformative…. Minor changes, such as placing 'voice-overs' on video clips, do not 'necessarily transform a work.' [¶] Arrangement of a work in a photo montage, however, can be transformative where copyrighted material is incorporated into other material."

Video Pipeline, Inc. v. Buena Vista Home Entm't, Inc., 342 F.3d 191, 197 (3d Cir.2003). "A fair use, although not specifically defined by the statute, is one made 'for purposes such as criticism, comment, news reporting, teaching ..., scholarship, or research.' It is an affirmative defense for which the alleged infringer bears the burden of proof."

Twin Peaks Prods. v. Publications Int'l, 996 F.2d 1366, 1374 (2d Cir.1993). "We agree with the appellants that the Book serves one or more of the non-exclusive purposes that §107 identifies as examples of purposes for which a protected fair use may be made. ... It is a work of and about pop culture, but that does not remove it from the scope of §107. Courts must be alert to the risk of permitting subjective judgments about quality to tilt the scales on which the fair use balance is made. ... And the defense will be available whether the comment makes some erudite point appreciated mainly by students of literature or a more prosaic point of interest to average television viewers. The issue in either case will ultimately be whether the comment, in borrowing the protected expression of the original work, does so for purposes that advance the interests sought to be promoted by the copyright law. Determination of that issue turns on careful consideration of the four statutory factors."

Factor 1

Campbell v. Acuff-Rose Music, Inc., 510 U.S. 569, 578-79 (1994). "This factor draws on Justice Story's formulation, 'the nature and objects of the selections made.' The enquiry here may be guided by the examples given in the preamble to §107, looking to whether the use is for criticism, or comment, or news reporting, and the like. ... The central purpose of this investigation is to see ... whether the new work merely 'supersede[s] the objects' of the original creation ... or instead adds something new, with a further purpose or different character, altering the first with new expression, meaning, or message; it asks, in other words, whether and to what extent the new work is 'transformative.' *At 579 n.11:* The obvious statutory exception to this focus on transformative uses is the straight reproduction of multiple copies for classroom distribution. *At 579:* [P]arody, like other comment or criticism, may claim fair use under §107. *At 580-81:* For the purposes of copyright law, the nub of the definitions, and the heart of any parodist's claim to quote from existing material, is the use of some elements of a prior author's composition to create a new one that, at least in part, comments on that author's works. If, on the contrary, the commentary has no critical bearing on the substance or style of the original composition, which the alleged infringer merely uses to get attention or to avoid the drudgery in working up something fresh, the claim to fairness in borrowing from another's work diminishes accordingly (if it does not vanish), and other factors, like the extent of its commerciality, loom larger. Parody needs to mimic an original to make its point, and so has some claim to use the creation of its victim's (or collective victims') imagination, whereas satire can stand on its own two feet and so requires justification for the very act of borrowing. *At 582:* The threshold question when fair use is raised in defense of parody is whether a parodic character may reasonably be perceived. Whether, going beyond that, parody is in good taste or bad does not and should not matter to fair use. *At 584:* The language of the statute makes clear that the commercial or nonprofit educational purpose of a work is only one element of the first factor enquiry into its 'purpose and character.' Congress resisted attempts to narrow the ambit of this traditional enquiry by adopting categories of presumptively fair use, and it urged courts to preserve the breadth of their traditionally ample view of the universe of relevant evidence. Accordingly, the mere fact that a use is educational and not for profit does not insulate it from a finding of infringement, any more than the commercial character of a use bars a finding of fairness." *See also* ***Zomba Enters. v. Panorama Records, Inc.***, 491 F.3d 574, 582 (6th Cir.2007); ***Mattel Inc. v. Walking Mountain Prods.***, 353 F.3d 792, 800-01 (9th Cir.2003); ***Suntrust Bank v. Houghton Mifflin Co.***, 268 F.3d 1257, 1269 (11th Cir.2001).

Harper & Row, Publ'rs v. Nation Enters., 471 U.S. 539, 562 (1985). "The fact that a publication was commercial as opposed to nonprofit is a separate factor that tends to weigh against a finding of fair use. '[E]very commercial use of copyrighted material is presumptively an unfair exploitation of the monopoly privilege that belongs to the owner of the copyright.' ... The crux of the profit/nonprofit distinction is not whether the sole motive of the use is monetary gain but whether the user stands to profit from exploitation of the copyrighted material without paying the customary price."

Sony Corp. v. Universal City Studios, Inc., 464 U.S. 417, 451 (1984). "A challenge to a noncommercial use of a copyrighted work requires proof either that the particular use is harmful, or that if it should become widespread, it would adversely affect the potential market for the copyrighted work. Actual present harm need not be shown; such a requirement would leave the copyright holder with no defense against predictable damage. Nor is it necessary to show with certainty that future harm will result. What is necessary is a showing by a preponderance of the evidence that *some* meaningful likelihood of future harm exists. If the intended use is for commercial gain, that likelihood may be presumed. But if it is for a noncommercial purpose, the likelihood must be demonstrated. *At 455-56 n.40:* Congress has plainly instructed us that fair use analysis calls for a sensitive balancing of interests. The distinction between 'productive' and 'unproductive' uses may be helpful in calibrating the balance, but it cannot be wholly determinative. Although copying to promote a scholarly endeavor certainly has a stronger claim to fair use than copying to avoid interrupting a poker game, the question is not simply two-dimensional. [¶] Making a copy of a copyrighted work for the convenience of a blind person is expressly identified by the House Committee Report as an example of fair use, with no suggestion that anything more than a purpose to entertain or to inform need motivate the copying. In a hospital setting, using a [videotape recorder] to enable a patient to see programs he would otherwise miss has no productive purpose other than contributing to the psychological well-being of the patient. Virtually any time-shifting that increases viewer access to television programming may result in a comparable benefit. The statutory language does not identify any dichotomy between productive and nonproductive time-shifting, but does require consideration of the economic consequences of copying."

TCA TV Corp. v. McCollum, 839 F.3d 168, 180 (2d Cir.2016). "[T]he focus of inquiry is not simply on the new work, i.e., on whether that work serves a purpose or conveys an overall expression, meaning, or message different from the copyrighted material it appropriates. Rather, the critical inquiry is whether the new work uses the copyrighted material itself for a purpose, or imbues it with a character, different from that for which it was created. Otherwise, any play that needed a character to sing a song, tell a joke, or recite a poem could use unaltered copyrighted material with impunity, so long as the purpose or message of the play was different from that of the appropriated material."

Authors Guild v. Google, Inc., 804 F.3d 202, 215-17 (2d Cir.2015). "'[P]aradigmatic examples of derivative works include the translation of a novel into another language, the adaptation of a novel into a movie or play, or the recasting of a novel as an e-book or an audiobook.' While such changes can be described as transformations, they do not involve the kind of transformative purpose that favors a fair use finding. The statutory definition suggests that derivative works generally involve transformations in the nature of *changes of form*. By contrast, copying from an original for the purpose of criticism or commentary on the original or provision of information about it, tends most clearly to satisfy ***Campbell***'s notion of the 'transformative' purpose involved in the analysis of Factor One. [¶] We have no difficulty concluding that [D's] making of a digital copy of [Ps'] books for the purpose of enabling a search for identification of books containing a term of interest to the searcher involves a highly transformative purpose, in the sense intended by ***Campbell***. *At 218:* [D's] division of the page into tiny snippets is designed to show the searcher just enough context surrounding the searched term to help her evaluate whether the book falls within the scope of her interest (without revealing so much as to threaten the author's copyright interests). Snippet view thus adds importantly to the highly transformative purpose of identifying books of interest to the searcher. With respect to the first factor test, it favors a finding of fair use (unless the value of its transformative purpose is overcome by its providing text in a manner that offers a competing substitute for [Ps'] books …)."

Cambridge Univ. Press v. Patton, 769 F.3d 1232, 1267 (11th Cir.2014). "Congress devoted extensive effort to ensure that fair use would allow for educational copying under the proper circumstances and was sufficiently determined to achieve this goal that it amended the text of [§107] at the eleventh hour in order to expressly state it. Furthermore, … allowing latitude for educational fair use promotes the goals of copyright. Thus, we are persuaded that, despite the recent focus on transformativeness under the first factor, use for teaching purposes by a nonprofit, educational institution such as [Ds'] favors a finding of fair use under the first factor, despite the nontransformative nature of the use." *See also* ***Richard Anderson Photography v. Brown***, 852 F.2d 114, 119 (4th Cir.1988).

Seltzer v. Green Day, Inc., 725 F.3d 1170, 1177 (9th Cir.2013). "In the typical 'non-transformative' case, the use is one which makes no alteration to the *expressive content or message* of the original work. [¶] In contrast, an allegedly infringing work is typically viewed as transformative as long as new expressive content or message is apparent. This is so even where ... the allegedly infringing work makes few physical changes to the original or fails to comment on the original."

Cariou v. Prince, 714 F.3d 694, 698 (2d Cir.2013). "[T]he law does not require that a secondary use comment on the original artist or work, or popular culture.... *At 707:* It is not surprising that, when transformative use is at issue, the alleged infringer would go to great lengths to explain and defend his use as transformative. [D] did not do so here. However, the fact that [D] did not provide those sorts of explanations in his deposition—which might have lent strong support to his defense—is not dispositive. What is critical is how the work in question appears to the reasonable observer, not simply what an artist might say about a particular piece or body of work. [D's] work could be transformative even without commenting on [P's] work or on culture, and even without [D's] stated intention to do so. Rather than confining our inquiry to [D's] explanations of his artworks, we instead examine how the artworks may 'reasonably be perceived' in order to assess their transformative nature." *But see* ***Kienitz v. Sconnie Nation LLC***, 766 F.3d 756, 758 (7th Cir.2014) (asking exclusively if something is "transformative" not only replaces list in 17 U.S.C. §107, it also could override 17 U.S.C. §106(2)).

Perfect 10, Inc. v. Amazon.com, Inc., 508 F.3d 1146, 1165 (9th Cir.2007). "[D's] use of thumbnails [of copyrighted images] is highly transformative. ... Although an image may have been created originally to serve an entertainment, aesthetic, or informative function, a search engine transforms the image into a pointer directing a user to a source of information. Just as a 'parody has an obvious claim to transformative value' because 'it can provide social benefit, by shedding light on an earlier work, and, in the process, creating a new one,' a search engine provides social benefit by incorporating an original work into a new work, namely, an electronic reference tool. *At 1166:* In conducting our case-specific analysis of fair use in light of the purposes of copyright, we must weigh [D's] superseding and commercial uses of thumbnail images against [D's] significant transformative use, as well as the extent to which [D's] search engine promotes the purposes of copyright and serves the interests of the public. *At 1167:* [W]e conclude that the transformative nature of [D's] use is more significant than any incidental superseding use or the minor commercial aspects of [D's] search engine and website."

Wall Data Inc. v. Los Angeles Cty. Sheriff's Dept., 447 F.3d 769, 779 (9th Cir.2006). "'[R]epeated and exploitative copying of copyrighted works, even if the copies are not offered for sale, may constitute a commercial use.' A commercial use is demonstrated by a showing that repeated and exploitative unauthorized copies of copyrighted works were made to save the expense of purchasing authorized copies."

NXIVM Corp. v. Ross Inst., 364 F.3d 471, 477 (2d Cir.2004). There "'is a strong presumption that factor one favors the defendant if the allegedly infringing work fits the description of uses described in §107.' [¶] This presumption ... is not necessarily rebutted by a concurrent commercial purpose on a defendant's part.... The Supreme Court in ***Campbell*** rejected the notion that the commercial nature of the use could by itself be a dispositive consideration. ... The commercial objective of the secondary work is only a subfactor within the first factor. '[T]he more transformative the new work, the less will be the significance of other factors, like commercialism, that may weigh against a finding of fair use.' *At 479:* [W]e believe that the bad faith of a defendant is not dispositive of a fair use defense."

Twin Peaks Prods. v. Publications Int'l, 996 F.2d 1366, 1374 (2d Cir.1993). "'Purpose' in fair use analysis is not an all-or-nothing matter. The issue is not simply whether a challenged work serves one of the non-exclusive purposes identified in §107, such as comment or criticism, but whether it does so to an insignificant or a substantial extent. The weight ascribed to the 'purpose' factor involves a more refined assessment than the initial, fairly easy decision that a work serves a purpose illustrated by the categories listed in §107."

Sega Enters. v. Accolade, Inc., 977 F.2d 1510, 1520 (9th Cir.1992). "Where there is good reason for studying or examining the unprotected aspects of a copyrighted computer program, disassembly for purposes of such study or examination constitutes a fair use."

Atari Games Corp. v. Nintendo Inc., 975 F.2d 832, 843 (Fed.Cir.1992). "Fair use to discern a work's ideas ... does not justify extensive efforts to profit from replicating protected expression. Subparagraphs 1 and 4 of §107 clarify that the fair use in intermediate copying does not extend to commercial exploitation of protected expression. The fair use reproductions of a computer program must not exceed what is necessary to understand the unprotected elements of the work. This limited exception is not an invitation to misappropriate protectable expression. Any reproduction of protectable expression must be strictly necessary to ascertain the bounds of protected information within the work."

Wright v. Warner Books, Inc., 953 F.2d 731, 736-37 (2d Cir.1991). The "book is a scholarly biography. As such, it fits comfortably within several of the statutory categories of uses that Congress has indicated may be fair—criticism, scholarship, and research. The analytic research contained in [the book] furthers the goals of the copyright laws by adding value to prior intellectual labor. Moreover, there is a strong presumption that factor one favors the defendant if the allegedly infringing work fits the description of uses described in §107. If a book falls into one of these categories[,] i.e., criticism, scholarship or research, assessment of the first fair use factor should be at an end, even though, as will often be the case, the biographer and publisher anticipate profits." (Internal quotes omitted.)

Factor 2

Campbell v. Acuff-Rose Music, Inc., 510 U.S. 569, 586 (1994). "The second statutory factor, 'the nature of the copyrighted work,' draws on [the] expression, the 'value of the materials used.' This factor calls for recognition that some works are closer to the core of intended copyright protection than others, with the consequence that fair use is more difficult to establish when the former works are copied." *See also* ***Dr. Seuss Enters. v. Penguin Books, Inc.***, 109 F.3d 1394, 1402 (9th Cir.1997).

Harper & Row, Publ'rs v. Nation Enters., 471 U.S. 539, 552 (1985). "Though the right of first publication, like the other rights enumerated in [17 U.S.C.] §106, is expressly made subject to the fair use provision of [17 U.S.C.] §107, fair use analysis must always be tailored to the individual case. *At 553:* If the work is out of print and unavailable for purchase through normal channels, the user may have more justification for reproducing it.... The applicability of the fair use doctrine to unpublished works is narrowly limited since, although the work is unavailable, this is the result of a deliberate choice on the part of the copyright owner. Under ordinary circumstances, the copyright owner's right of first publication would outweigh any needs of reproduction for classroom purposes. *At 563:* The law generally recognizes a greater need to disseminate factual works than works of fiction or fantasy. [Even] within the field of fact works, there are gradations as to the relative proportion of fact and fancy. One may move from sparsely embellished maps and directories to elegantly written biography. The extent to which one must permit expressive language to be copied, in order to assure dissemination of the underlying facts, will thus vary from case to case. *At 564:* The fact that a work is unpublished is a critical element of its nature. Our prior discussion establishes that the scope of fair use is narrower with respect to unpublished works. While even substantial quotations might qualify as fair use in a review of a published work or a news account of a speech that had been delivered to the public or disseminated to the press, the author's right to control the first public appearance of his expression weighs against such use of the work before its release. The right of first publication encompasses not only the choice whether to publish at all, but also the choices of when, where, and in what form first to publish a work. [¶] In the case of [the] manuscript, the copyright holders' interest in confidentiality is irrefutable; the copyright holders had entered into a contractual undertaking to keep the manuscript confidential and required that all those to whom the manuscript was shown also sign an agreement to keep the manuscript confidential. ... A use that so clearly infringes the copyright holder's interests in confidentiality and creative control is difficult to characterize as fair." (Internal quotes omitted.)

Authors Guild v. Google, Inc., 804 F.3d 202, 219 (2d Cir.2015). "While we recognize that in some circumstances, a commercial motivation on the part of the secondary user will weigh against her, especially, as the Supreme Court suggested, when a persuasive transformative purpose is lacking, ... we see no reason in this case why [D's] overall profit motivation should prevail as a reason for denying fair use over its highly convincing transformative purpose, together with the absence of significant substitutive competition, as reasons for granting fair use. Many of the most universally accepted forms of fair use, such as news reporting and commentary, quotation in historical or analytic books, reviews of books, and performances, as well as parody, are all normally done commercially for profit. *At 220:* While each of the three [Ps'] books in this case is factual, we do not consider that as a boost to [D's] claim of fair use. If one (or all) of [Ps'] works were fiction, we do not think that would change in any way our appraisal. Nothing in this case influences us one way or the other with respect to the second factor considered in isolation. To the extent that the 'nature' of the original copyrighted work necessarily combines with the 'purpose and character' of the secondary work to permit assessment of whether the secondary work uses the original in a 'transformative' manner, as the term is used in ***Campbell***, the second factor favors fair use not because [Ps'] works are factual, but because the secondary use transformatively provides valuable information about the original, rather than replicating protected expression in a manner that provides a meaningful substitute for the original."

Peter Letterese & Assocs. v. World Inst. of Scientology Enters., 533 F.3d 1287, 1312 (11th Cir.2008). "The second factor 'recognizes that there is a hierarchy of copyright protection' depending upon the nature of the copyrighted work. Works that are 'closer to the core of intended copyright protection,' and thus merit greater protection, include original as opposed to derivative works; creative as opposed to factual works; and unpublished as opposed to published works. *At 1313:* The law provides greater copyright protection for unpublished works in recognition of the author's property interest in the 'commercially valuable right of first publication,' including the 'exploitation of prepublication rights, which are valuable in themselves and serve as a valuable adjunct to publicity and marketing,' ... and because of the author's 'personal interest' in 'creative or quality control'.... By contrast, out-of-print works are generally accorded less copyright protection. The relevant fact is not simply that the work is unavailable for purchase through normal channels. 'Any copyright infringer may claim to benefit the public by increasing public access to the copyrighted work.' Rather, that fair use is more likely to apply in the standard scenario of an out-of-print work reflects in large part the assumption that no market harm to the owner will come of the use, as presumably it was lack of demand for the work that led to its demise. Moreover, as it was the market mechanism that caused the work to become unavailable, the countervailing personal interest of the author is not implicated; the author presumably would wish for the work's continued dissemination. Neither the personal nor the property interests of the author are thus strongly implicated with respect to the typical out-of-print work."

Bill Graham Archives v. Dorling Kindersley Ltd., 448 F.3d 605, 612 (2d Cir.2006). "To resolve this inquiry the court considers 'the protection of the reasonable expectations of one who engages in the kinds of creation/authorship that the copyright seeks to encourage.' [¶] [T]he second factor may be of limited usefulness where the creative work of art is being used for a transformative purpose."

Wall Data Inc. v. Los Angeles Cty. Sheriff's Dept., 447 F.3d 769, 780 (9th Cir.2006). "Our sister circuits have also considered, under this factor, whether the copyrighted work represents 'substantial investment of time and labor ... in anticipation of a financial return.'"

Mattel Inc. v. Walking Mountain Prods., 353 F.3d 792, 803 (9th Cir.2003). "The second factor in the fair use analysis recognizes that creative works are closer to the core of intended copyright protection than informational and functional works. ... As we have recognized in the past, this [nature of the copyrighted work] factor typically has not been terribly significant in the overall fair use balancing." (Internal quotes omitted.) *See also* ***Video Pipeline, Inc. v. Buena Vista Home Entm't, Inc.***, 342 F.3d 191, 200-01 (3d Cir.2003); ***Sundeman v. Seajay Soc'y, Inc.***, 142 F.3d 194, 204 (4th Cir.1998).

Sony Computer Entm't, Inc. v. Bleem, L.L.C., 214 F.3d 1022, 1028 (9th Cir.2000). The second "factor is of most relevance to the fair use analysis when the original material and the copy are of a different nature. For instance, 'if the copyrighted work is out of print and cannot be purchased, a user may be more likely to prevail on a fair use defense.' On the other hand, if the copyrighted material is unpublished and creative while the copy is a commercial publication, courts would be less receptive to the defense of fair use. In this case, the copyrighted work and the copies are both commercial video game products; although the copyrighted work is creative in nature generally, a screen shot is not necessarily. A screen shot is merely an inanimate sliver of the game."

Warner Bros. v. American Broad. Cos., 720 F.2d 231, 242 (2d Cir.1983). "An entirely separate issue of infringement ... concerns what Professor Nimmer calls 'fragmented literal similarity,' duplicating the exact or nearly exact wording of a fragment of the protected work. With respect to such claims, courts have invoked two distinct doctrines. First, a *de minimis* rule has been applied, allowing the literal copying of a small and usually insignificant portion of the plaintiff's work. Second, under the 'fair use' doctrine, codified in ... §107(2), courts have allowed the taking of words or phrases when adapted for use as commentary or parody."

Factor 3

Campbell v. Acuff-Rose Music, Inc., 510 U.S. 569, 588 (1994). "When parody takes aim at a particular original work, the parody must be able to 'conjure up' at least enough of that original to make the object of its critical wit recognizable. What makes for this recognition is quotation of the original's most distinctive or memorable features, which the parodist can be sure the audience will know. Once enough has been taken to assure identification, how much more is reasonable will depend, say, on the extent to which the song's overriding purpose and character is to parody the original or, in contrast, the likelihood that the parody may serve as a market substitute for the original. But using some characteristic features cannot be avoided. *At 589:* This is not, of course, to say that anyone who calls himself a parodist can skim the cream and get away scot free. In parody, as in news reporting, context is everything, and the question of fairness asks what else the parodist did besides go to the heart of the original. ... This is not a case, then, where 'a substantial portion' of the parody itself is composed of a 'verbatim' copying of the original. It is not, that is, a case where the parody is so insubstantial, as compared to the copying, that the third factor must be resolved as a matter of law against the parodists." *See also* ***Suntrust Bank v. Houghton Mifflin Co.***, 268 F.3d 1257, 1271 (11th Cir.2001).

Harper & Row, Publ'rs v. Nation Enters., 471 U.S. 539, 565 (1985). "As the statutory language indicates, a taking may not be excused merely because it is insubstantial with respect to the *infringing* work. '[N]o plagiarist can excuse the wrong by showing how much of his work he did not pirate.' Conversely, the fact that a substantial portion of the infringing work was copied verbatim is evidence of the qualitative value of the copied material, both to the originator and to the plagiarist who seeks to profit from marketing someone else's copyrighted expression."

Sony Corp. v. Universal City Studios, Inc., 464 U.S. 417, 449-50 (1984). "If [recording device] were used to make copies for a commercial or profitmaking purpose, such use would presumptively be unfair. The contrary presumption is appropriate here, however, because the District Court's findings plainly establish that time-shifting for private home use must be characterized as a noncommercial, nonprofit activity. Moreover, when one considers the nature of a televised copyrighted audiovisual work, and that time-shifting merely enables a viewer to see such a work which he had been invited to witness in its entirety free of charge, the fact that the entire work is reproduced does not have its ordinary effect of militating against a finding of fair use."

Authors Guild v. Google, Inc., 804 F.3d 202, 221-22 (2d Cir.2015). "The clear implication of the third factor is that a finding of fair use is more likely when small amounts, or less important passages, are copied than when the copying is extensive, or encompasses the most important parts of the original. The obvious reason for this lies in the relationship between the third and the fourth factors. The larger the amount, or the more important the part, of the original that is copied, the greater the likelihood that the secondary work might serve as an effectively competing substitute for the original, and might therefore diminish the original rights holder's sales and profits. [¶] [C]ourts have rejected any categorical rule that a copying of the entirety cannot be a fair use. [¶] While [D] *makes* an unauthorized digital copy of the entire book, it does not reveal that digital copy to the public. The copy is made to enable the search functions to reveal limited, important information about the books. [¶] Without doubt, enabling searchers to see portions of the copied texts could have determinative effect on the fair use analysis. The larger the quantity of the copyrighted text the searcher can see and the more control the searcher can exercise over what part of the text she sees, the greater the likelihood that those revelations could serve her as an effective, free substitute for the purchase of the plaintiff's book. We nonetheless conclude that, at least as presently structured by [D], the snippet view does not reveal matter that offers the marketplace a significantly competing substitute for the copyrighted work."

Peter Letterese & Assocs. v. World Inst. of Scientology Enters., 533 F.3d 1287, 1314-15 (11th Cir. 2008). "[T]he amount and substantiality of the portion used is measured with respect to the copyrighted work as a whole, not to the putatively infringing work. ... A taking may not be excused merely because it is insubstantial with respect to the *infringing* work. No plagiarist can excuse the wrong by showing how much of his work he did not pirate. [¶] [I]n analyzing the amount and substantiality of the portion used, a court considers not only the quantity of the materials used, but their quality and importance, too. Quantitatively, the amount of verbatim copying or paraphrasing appears to be a small portion of [work]. But the amount taken may be substantial from a qualitative perspective if the defendant has copied the heart of the book." (Internal quotes omitted.) *See also* ***NXIVM Corp. v. Ross Inst.***, 364 F.3d 471, 480 (2d Cir.2004); ***Sundeman v. Seajay Soc'y, Inc.***, 142 F.3d 194, 205 (4th Cir.1998).

Wright v. Warner Books, Inc., 953 F.2d 731, 738 (2d Cir.1991). "Both direct quotes and close paraphrases count as being 'used.'"

Hustler Mag., Inc. v. Moral Majority, Inc., 796 F.2d 1148, 1153 (9th Cir.1986). An "individual in rebutting a copyrighted work containing derogatory information about himself may copy such parts of the work as are necessary to permit understandable comment. [D] did not use more than was reasonably necessary to make an understandable comment when he copied the entire parody from the magazine. Therefore, the public interest in allowing an individual to defend himself against such derogatory personal attacks serves to rebut the presumption of unfairness."

Factor 4

Campbell v. Acuff-Rose Music, Inc., 510 U.S. 569, 590 (1994). The fourth factor "requires courts to consider not only the extent of market harm caused by the particular actions of the alleged infringer, but also 'whether unrestricted and widespread conduct of the sort engaged in by the defendant ... would result in a substantially adverse impact on the potential market' for the original. The enquiry 'must take account not only of harm to the original but also of harm to the market for derivative works.' *At 591-92:* We do not ... suggest that a parody may not harm the market at all, but when a lethal parody, like a scathing theater review, kills demand for the original, it does not produce a harm cognizable under the Copyright Act. Because 'parody may quite legitimately aim at garroting the original, destroying it commercially as well as artistically,' the role of the courts is to distinguish between '[b]iting criticism [that merely] suppresses demand [and] copyright infringement[, which] usurps it.'" *See also* ***Davis v. Gap, Inc.***, 246 F.3d 152, 175 (2d Cir.2001).

Harper & Row, Publ'rs v. Nation Enters., 471 U.S. 539, 566-67 (1985). "'Fair use, when properly applied, is limited to copying by others which does not materially impair the marketability of the work which is copied.' *At 569:* Any copyright infringer may claim to benefit the public by increasing public access to the copyrighted work. But Congress has not designed, and we see no warrant for judicially imposing, a 'compulsory license' permitting unfettered access to the unpublished copyrighted expression of public figures." *See also* ***Stewart v. Abend***, 495 U.S. 207, 238 (1990).

TCA TV Corp. v. McCollum, 839 F.3d 168, 186 (2d Cir.2016). "[I]n assessing harm posed to a licensing market, a court's focus is not on possible lost licensing fees from defendants' challenged use. Rather, a court properly considers the challenged use's 'impact on potential licensing revenues for traditional, reasonable, or likely to be developed markets.'"

Authors Guild v. Google, Inc., 804 F.3d 202, 223-24 (2d Cir.2015). "Even if the *purpose* of the copying is for a valuably transformative purpose, such copying might nonetheless harm the value of the copyrighted original if done in a manner that results in widespread revelation of sufficiently significant portions of the original as to make available a significantly competing substitute. The question for us is whether snippet view, notwithstanding its transformative purpose, does that. We conclude that, at least as snippet view is presently constructed, it does not. [¶] Especially in view of the fact that the normal purchase price of a book is relatively low in relation to the cost of manpower needed to secure an arbitrary assortment of randomly scattered snippets, we conclude that the snippet function does not give searchers access to effectively competing substitutes. Snippet view, at best and after a large commitment of manpower, produces discontinuous, tiny fragments, amounting in the aggregate to no more than 16% of a book. This does not threaten the rights holders with any significant harm to the value of their copyrights or diminish their harvest of copyright revenue.

[¶] We recognize that the snippet function can cause *some* loss of sales. There are surely instances in which a searcher's need for access to a text will be satisfied by the snippet view, resulting in either the loss of a sale to that searcher, or reduction of demand on libraries for that title, which might have resulted in libraries purchasing additional copies. But the possibility, or even the probability or certainty, of some loss of sales does not suffice to make the copy an effectively competing substitute that would tilt the weighty fourth factor in favor of the rights holder in the original. There must be a meaningful or significant effect 'upon the potential market for or value of the copyrighted work.'"

Cambridge Univ. Press v. Patton, 769 F.3d 1232, 1276 (11th Cir.2014). "The central question under the fourth factor is not whether [Ds'] use of [Ps'] works caused [Ps] to lose some potential revenue. Rather, it is whether [Ds'] use—taking into account the damage that might occur if 'everybody did it'—would cause *substantial* economic harm such that allowing it would frustrate the purposes of copyright by materially impairing [P's] incentive to publish the work. *At 1277:* [A]bsent evidence to the contrary, if a copyright holder has not made a license available to use a particular work in a particular manner, the inference is that the author or publisher did not think that there would be enough such use to bother making a license available. In such a case, there is little damage to the publisher's market when someone makes use of the work in that way without obtaining a license, and hence the fourth factor should generally weigh in favor of fair use. This is true of [Ps'] works for which no license for a digital excerpt was available. *At 1279-80:* Fair use is an affirmative defense, and the evidentiary burden on all four of its factors rests on the alleged infringer. However, [Ps]—as publishers—can reasonably be expected to have the evidence as to availability of licenses for their own works. It is therefore reasonable to place on [Ps] the burden of going forward with the evidence on this question. [¶] In effect, this creates a presumption that no market for digital permissions exists for a particular work. This is reasonable, because if a license was available during the relevant time period, [Ps] can rebut the presumption of no market by going forward with evidence of license availability. If there is evidence of a potential, future market, [Ps] can rebut the presumption by going forward with that. Then, [Ds]—retaining the overall burden of persuasion on the fourth factor—must demonstrate that their use does not materially impair the existing or potential market in order to prevail."

Perfect 10, Inc. v. Amazon.com, Inc., 508 F.3d 1146, 1168 (9th Cir.2007). "[P] argues ... the likelihood of market harm may be presumed if the intended use of an image is for commercial gain. However, this presumption does not arise when a work is transformative because 'market substitution is at least less certain, and market harm may not be so readily inferred.' [D's] use of thumbnails for search engine purposes is highly transformative, and so market harm cannot be presumed."

Bill Graham Archives v. Dorling Kindersley Ltd., 448 F.3d 605, 614-15 (2d Cir.2006). "In order to establish a traditional license market, [P] points to the fees paid to other copyright owners for the reproduction of their images in [allegedly infringing work]. Moreover, [P] asserts that it established a market for licensing its images, and in this case expressed a willingness to license images to [D]. Neither of these arguments shows impairment to a traditional, as opposed to a transformative market. [¶] [W]e hold that [D's] use of [P's] images is transformatively different from their original expressive purpose. In a case such as this, a copyright holder cannot prevent others from entering fair use markets merely 'by developing or licensing a market for parody, news reporting, educational or other transformative uses of its own creative work.' '[C]opyright owners may not preempt exploitation of transformative markets....' Moreover, a publisher's willingness to pay license fees for reproduction of images does not establish that the publisher may not, in the alternative, make fair use of those images. Since [D's] use of [P's] images falls within a transformative market, [P] does not suffer market harm due to the loss of license fees."

Mattel Inc. v. Walking Mountain Prods., 353 F.3d 792, 805 (9th Cir.2003). "We recognize ... that critical works may have another dimension beyond their critical aspects that may have effects on potential markets for the copyrighted work. Thus, we look more generally, not only to the critical aspects of a work, but to the type of work itself in determining market harm."

Ty, Inc. v. Publications Int'l, 292 F.3d 512, 522 (7th Cir.2002). "Factor (4) at least glances at the distinction ... between substitute and complementary copying, since the latter does not impair the potential market or value of the copyrighted work except insofar as it criticizes the work, which is the opposite of taking a free ride on its value."

Sundeman v. Seajay Soc'y, Inc., 142 F.3d 194, 206 (4th Cir.1998). "A use that does not materially impair the marketability of the copyrighted work generally will be deemed fair. *At 207:* Another key element of the fourth enquiry is whether the allegedly infringing work is a market substitute for the copyrighted work. [¶] A final element of the fourth factor is the impact the allegedly infringing uses may have on the market for derivatives of the copyrighted work. The market for potential derivatives includes those uses that the copyright holder of the original work would develop or license others to develop. As the Supreme Court declared, however, there is no protectible derivative market for criticism. If there were a protectible derivative market for critical works, copyright holders would only license to those who would render favorable comment. The copyright holder cannot control the dissemination of criticism." (Internal quotes omitted.)

§108. LIMITATIONS ON EXCLUSIVE RIGHTS: REPRODUCTION BY LIBRARIES & ARCHIVES

(a) Except as otherwise provided in this title and notwithstanding the provisions of section 106, it is not an infringement of copyright for a library or archives, or any of its employees acting within the scope of their employment, to reproduce no more than one copy or phonorecord of a work, except as provided in subsections (b) and (c), or to distribute such copy or phonorecord, under the conditions specified by this section, if—

(1) the reproduction or distribution is made without any purpose of direct or indirect commercial advantage;

(2) the collections of the library or archives are (i) open to the public, or (ii) available not only to researchers affiliated with the library or archives or with the institution of which it is a part, but also to other persons doing research in a specialized field; and

(3) the reproduction or distribution of the work includes a notice of copyright that appears on the copy or phonorecord that is reproduced under the provisions of this section, or includes a legend stating that the work may be protected by copyright if no such notice can be found on the copy or phonorecord that is reproduced under the provisions of this section.

(b) The rights of reproduction and distribution under this section apply to three copies or phonorecords of an unpublished work duplicated solely for purposes of preservation and security or for deposit for research use in another library or archives of the type described by clause (2) of subsection (a), if—

(1) the copy or phonorecord reproduced is currently in the collections of the library or archives; and

(2) any such copy or phonorecord that is reproduced in digital format is not otherwise distributed in that format and is not made available to the public in that format outside the premises of the library or archives.

(c) The right of reproduction under this section applies to three copies or phonorecords of a published work duplicated solely for the purpose of replacement of a copy or phonorecord that is damaged, deteriorating, lost, or stolen, or if the existing format in which the work is stored has become obsolete, if—

(1) the library or archives has, after a reasonable effort, determined that an unused replacement cannot be obtained at a fair price; and

(2) any such copy or phonorecord that is reproduced in digital format is not made available to the public in that format outside the premises of the library or archives in lawful possession of such copy.

For purposes of this subsection, a format shall be considered obsolete if the machine or device necessary to render perceptible a work stored in that format is no longer manufactured or is no longer reasonably available in the commercial marketplace.

(d) The rights of reproduction and distribution under this section apply to a copy, made from the collection of a library or archives where the user makes his or her request or from that of another library or archives, of no more than one article or other contribution to a copyrighted collection or periodical issue, or to a copy or phonorecord of a small part of any other copyrighted work, if—

(1) the copy or phonorecord becomes the property of the user, and the library or archives has had no notice that the copy or phonorecord would be used for any purpose other than private study, scholarship, or research; and

(2) the library or archives displays prominently, at the place where orders are accepted, and includes on its order form, a warning of copyright in accordance with requirements that the Register of Copyrights shall prescribe by regulation.

(e) The rights of reproduction and distribution under this section apply to the entire work, or to a substantial part of it, made from the collection of a library or archives where the user makes his or her request or from that of another library or archives, if the library or archives has first determined, on the basis of a reasonable investigation, that a copy or phonorecord of the copyrighted work cannot be obtained at a fair price, if—

(1) the copy or phonorecord becomes the property of the user, and the library or archives has had no notice that the copy or phonorecord would be used for any purpose other than private study, scholarship, or research; and

(2) the library or archives displays prominently, at the place where orders are accepted, and includes on its order form, a warning of copyright in accordance with requirements that the Register of Copyrights shall prescribe by regulation.

(f) Nothing in this section—

(1) shall be construed to impose liability for copyright infringement upon a library or archives or its employees for the unsupervised use of reproducing equipment located on its premises: *Provided*, That such equipment displays a notice that the making of a copy may be subject to the copyright law;

(2) excuses a person who uses such reproducing equipment or who requests a copy or phonorecord under subsection (d) from liability for copyright infringement for any such act, or for any later use of such copy or phonorecord, if it exceeds fair use as provided by section 107;

(3) shall be construed to limit the reproduction and distribution by lending of a limited number of copies and excerpts by a library or archives of an audiovisual news program, subject to clauses (1), (2), and (3) of subsection (a); or

(4) in any way affects the right of fair use as provided by section 107, or any contractual obligations assumed at any time by the library or archives when it obtained a copy or phonorecord of a work in its collections.

(g) The rights of reproduction and distribution under this section extend to the isolated and unrelated reproduction or distribution of a single copy or phonorecord of the same material on separate occasions, but do not extend to cases where the library or archives, or its employee—

(1) is aware or has substantial reason to believe that it is engaging in the related or concerted reproduction or distribution of multiple copies or phonorecords of the same material, whether made on one occasion or over a period of time, and whether intended for aggregate use by one or more individuals or for separate use by the individual members of a group; or

(2) engages in the systematic reproduction or distribution of single or multiple copies or phonorecords of material described in subsection (d): *Provided*, That nothing in this clause prevents a library or archives from participating in interlibrary arrangements that do not have, as their purpose or effect, that the library or archives receiving such copies or phonorecords for distribution does so in such aggregate quantities as to substitute for a subscription to or purchase of such work.

(h)(1) For purposes of this section, during the last 20 years of any term of copyright of a published work, a library or archives, including a nonprofit educational institution that functions as such, may reproduce, distribute, display, or perform in facsimile or digital form a copy or phonorecord of such work, or portions thereof, for purposes of preservation, scholarship, or research, if such library or archives has first determined, on the basis of a reasonable investigation, that none of the conditions set forth in subparagraphs (A), (B), and (C) of paragraph (2) apply.

(2) No reproduction, distribution, display, or performance is authorized under this subsection if—

(A) the work is subject to normal commercial exploitation;

(B) a copy or phonorecord of the work can be obtained at a reasonable price; or

(C) the copyright owner or its agent provides notice pursuant to regulations promulgated by the Register of Copyrights that either of the conditions set forth in subparagraphs (A) and (B) applies.

(3) The exemption provided in this subsection does not apply to any subsequent uses by users other than such library or archives.

(i) The rights of reproduction and distribution under this section do not apply to a musical work, a pictorial, graphic or sculptural work, or a motion picture or other audiovisual work other than an audiovisual work dealing with news, except that no such limitation shall apply with respect to rights granted by subsections (b), (c), and (h), or with respect to pictorial or graphic works published as illustrations, diagrams, or similar adjuncts to works of which copies are reproduced or distributed in accordance with subsections (d) and (e).

History of 17 U.S.C. §108: Oct. 19, 1976, P.L. 94-553, §101, 90 Stat. 2546; June 26, 1992, P.L. 102-307, §301, 106 Stat. 272; Nov. 13, 1997, P.L. 105-80, §12(a)(4), 111 Stat. 1534; Oct. 27, 1998, P.L. 105-298, §104, 112 Stat. 2829; Oct. 28, 1998, P.L. 105-304, §404, 112 Stat. 2889; Apr. 27, 2005, P.L. 109-9, §402, 119 Stat. 227.

See also 37 C.F.R. §§201.14, 201.39.

§109. LIMITATIONS ON EXCLUSIVE RIGHTS: EFFECT OF TRANSFER OF PARTICULAR COPY OR PHONORECORD

(a) Notwithstanding the provisions of section 106(3), the owner of a particular copy or phonorecord lawfully made under this title, or any person authorized by such owner, is entitled, without the authority of the copyright owner, to sell or otherwise dispose of the possession of that copy or phonorecord. Notwithstanding the preceding sentence, copies or phonorecords of works subject to restored copyright under section 104A that are manufactured before the date of restoration of copyright or, with respect to reliance parties, before publication or service of notice under section 104A(e), may be sold or otherwise disposed of without the authorization of the owner of the restored copyright for purposes of direct or indirect commercial advantage only during the 12-month period beginning on—

(1) the date of the publication in the Federal Register of the notice of intent filed with the Copyright Office under section 104A(d)(2)(A), or

(2) the date of the receipt of actual notice served under section 104A(d)(2)(B), whichever occurs first.

(b)(1)(A) Notwithstanding the provisions of subsection (a), unless authorized by the owners of copyright in the sound recording or the owner of copyright in a computer program (including any tape, disk, or other medium embodying such program), and in the case of a sound recording in the musical works embodied therein, neither the owner of a particular phonorecord nor any person in possession of a particular copy of a computer program (including any tape, disk, or other medium embodying such program), may, for the purposes of direct or indirect commercial advantage, dispose of, or authorize the disposal of, the possession of that phonorecord or computer program (including any tape, disk, or other medium embodying such program) by rental, lease, or lending, or by any other act or practice in the nature of rental, lease, or lending. Nothing in the preceding sentence shall apply to the rental, lease, or lending of a phonorecord for nonprofit purposes by a nonprofit library or nonprofit educational institution. The transfer of possession of a lawfully made copy of a computer program by a nonprofit educational institution to another nonprofit educational institution or to faculty, staff, and students does not constitute rental, lease, or lending for direct or indirect commercial purposes under this subsection.

(B) This subsection does not apply to—

(i) a computer program which is embodied in a machine or product and which cannot be copied during the ordinary operation or use of the machine or product; or

(ii) a computer program embodied in or used in conjunction with a limited purpose computer that is designed for playing video games and may be designed for other purposes.

(C) Nothing in this subsection affects any provision of chapter 9 of this title.

(2)(A) Nothing in this subsection shall apply to the lending of a computer program for nonprofit purposes by a nonprofit library, if each copy of a computer program which is lent by such library has affixed to the packaging containing the program a warning of copyright in accordance with requirements that the Register of Copyrights shall prescribe by regulation.

(B) Not later than three years after December 1, 1990, and at such times thereafter as the Register of Copyrights considers appropriate, the Register of Copyrights, after consultation with representatives of copyright owners and librarians, shall submit to the Congress a report stating whether this paragraph has achieved its intended purpose of maintaining the integrity of the copyright system while providing nonprofit libraries the capability to fulfill their function. Such report shall advise the Congress as to any information or recommendations that the Register of Copyrights considers necessary to carry out the purposes of this subsection.

(3) Nothing in this subsection shall affect any provision of the antitrust laws. For purposes of the preceding sentence, "antitrust laws" has the meaning given that term in section 12 of title 15 and includes section

45 of title 15 to the extent that section relates to unfair methods of competition.

(4) Any person who distributes a phonorecord or a copy of a computer program (including any tape, disk, or other medium embodying such program) in violation of paragraph (1) is an infringer of copyright under section 501 of this title and is subject to the remedies set forth in sections 502, 503, 504, and 505. Such violation shall not be a criminal offense under section 506 or cause such person to be subject to the criminal penalties set forth in section 2319 of title 18.

(c) Notwithstanding the provisions of section 106(5), the owner of a particular copy lawfully made under this title, or any person authorized by such owner, is entitled, without the authority of the copyright owner, to display that copy publicly, either directly or by the projection of no more than one image at a time, to viewers present at the place where the copy is located.

(d) The privileges prescribed by subsections (a) and (c) do not, unless authorized by the copyright owner, extend to any person who has acquired possession of the copy or phonorecord from the copyright owner, by rental, lease, loan, or otherwise, without acquiring ownership of it.

(e) Notwithstanding the provisions of sections 106(4) and 106(5), in the case of an electronic audiovisual game intended for use in coin-operated equipment, the owner of a particular copy of such a game lawfully made under this title, is entitled, without the authority of the copyright owner of the game, to publicly perform or display that game in coin-operated equipment, except that this subsection shall not apply to any work of authorship embodied in the audiovisual game if the copyright owner of the electronic audiovisual game is not also the copyright owner of the work of authorship.

History of 17 U.S.C. §109: Oct. 19, 1976, P.L. 94-553, §101, 90 Stat. 2548; Oct. 4, 1984, P.L. 98-450, §2, 98 Stat. 1727; Nov. 5, 1988, P.L. 100-617, §2, 102 Stat. 3194; Dec. 1, 1990, P.L. 101-650, §§802, 803, 104 Stat. 5134, 5135; Dec. 8, 1994, P.L. 103-465, §514(b), 108 Stat. 4981; Nov. 13, 1997, P.L. 105-80, §12(a)(5), 111 Stat. 1534; Oct. 13, 2008, P.L. 110-403, §209(a)(1), 122 Stat. 4264.

See also 37 C.F.R. §201.24; TRIPs pt. II, §1.

ANNOTATIONS

§109(a)

Kirtsaeng v. John Wiley & Sons, Inc., 568 U.S. 519, 524 (2013). "[E]ven though [17 U.S.C.] §106(3) forbids distribution of a copy of [a novel, for example,] without the copyright owner's permission, [17 U.S.C.] §109(a) adds that, once a copy of [the novel] has been lawfully sold (or its ownership otherwise lawfully transferred), the buyer of *that copy* and subsequent owners are free to dispose of it as they wish. In copyright jargon, the 'first sale' has 'exhausted' the copyright owner's §106(3) exclusive distribution right. [¶] What, however, if the copy of [the novel] was printed abroad and then initially sold with the copyright owner's permission? Does the 'first sale' doctrine still apply? Is the buyer, like the buyer of a domestically manufactured copy, free to bring the copy into the U.S. and dispose of it as he or she wishes? *At 525:* This case is like ***Quality King*** but for one important fact. The copies at issue here were manufactured abroad. That fact is important because §109(a) says that the 'first sale' doctrine applies to 'a particular copy or phonorecord *lawfully made under this title*.' And we must decide here whether the five words, 'lawfully made under this title,' make a critical legal difference. [¶] [W]e ask whether the 'first sale' doctrine applies to protect a buyer or other lawful owner of a copy (of a copyrighted work) lawfully manufactured abroad. Can that buyer bring that copy into the U.S. (and sell it or give it away) without obtaining permission to do so from the copyright owner? Can, for example, someone who purchases, say at a used bookstore, a book printed abroad subsequently resell it without the copyright owner's permission? [¶] In our view, the answers to these questions are, yes. We hold that the 'first sale' doctrine applies to copies of a copyrighted work lawfully made abroad."

Quality King Distribs. v. L'anza Research Int'l, 523 U.S. 135, 145 (1998). "After the first sale of a copyrighted item 'lawfully made under this title,' any subsequent purchaser, whether from a domestic or from a foreign reseller, is obviously an 'owner' of that item. Read literally, [17 U.S.C.] §109(a) unambiguously states that such an owner 'is entitled, without the authority of the copyright owner, to sell' that item. Moreover, since [17 U.S.C.] §602(a) merely provides that unauthorized importation is an infringement of an exclusive right 'under [17 U.S.C.] §106,' and since that limited right does not encompass resales by lawful owners, the literal text of §602(a) is simply inapplicable to both domestic and foreign owners of [copyright owner's] products who decide to import them and resell them in the U.S. *At 146-47:* [B]ecause the protection afforded by §109(a) is available only to the 'owner' of a lawfully made copy (or someone authorized by the owner), the first sale doctrine would not provide a defense to a §602(a) action against any non-owner such as a bailee, a licensee, a consignee, or one whose possession of the copy was unlawful. *At 148:* If the author of the work gave the exclusive U.S. distribution rights … to the publisher of the U.S. edition and the exclusive British distribution rights to the publisher of the British edition … presumably only those made by the publisher of the U.S. edition would be 'lawfully made under this title' within the meaning of §109(a). The first sale doctrine would not provide the publisher of the British edition who decided to sell in the American market with a defense to an action under §602(a) (or, for that matter, to an action under §106(3), if there was a distribution of the copies)."

Geophysical Serv. v. TGS-NOPEC Geophysical Co., 850 F.3d 785, 789 (5th Cir.2017). "We are called upon to determine whether the act of state doctrine forbids a U.S. court from considering the applicability of copyright's first sale doctrine to foreign-made copies when the foreign copier was a government agency. We hold that it does not. *At 794:* The doctrine of 'first sale' is somewhat of a misnomer. The limitation embodied in [17 U.S.C.] §109 does not depend on whether the copyright owner's initial disposition was by sale; the only prerequisite is that the copy or phonorecord in question be 'lawfully made.' Accordingly, nations elsewhere in the world with similar copyright regimes refer to the principle as the 'exhaustion doctrine,' reflecting the notion that the copyright owner 'exhausts' his distribution right in a copy or phonorecord upon first transfer of that copy or phonorecord. [¶] [17 U.S.C.] §602 … establishes that unauthorized importation into the U.S. of copies or phonorecords acquired outside the U.S. is infringement of the [17 U.S.C.] §106(3) exclusive right to distribute. Because this 'importation right' is merely a corollary of the distribution right, it is similarly limited by the first sale doctrine. Accordingly, importation into the U.S. of lawfully made copies or phonorecords, even where the copyright holder has not authorized such importation, is protected by §109. *At 796-97:* The act of state doctrine 'limits, for prudential rather than jurisdictional reasons, the adjudication in American courts of the validity of a foreign sovereign's public acts.' The doctrine applies to bar an action when 'the relief sought or the defense interposed would have required a court in the U.S. to declare invalid the official act of a foreign sovereign performed within its own territory.' … 'Act of state issues only arise when a court *must decide*—that is, when the outcome of the case turns upon—the effect of official action by a foreign sovereign.' It can apply 'even if the defendant is a private party, not an instrumentality of a foreign state, and even if the suit is not based specifically on a sovereign act.' [¶] We find that the question presented by the first sale doctrine, whether imported copies were 'lawfully made,' is different in kind from the question whether the copy-maker acted illegally or invalidly. Hence, the first sale question is outside the scope of the act of state doctrine even when the foreign copy-maker is a government agency."

Adobe Sys. v. Christenson, 809 F.3d 1071, 1073 (9th Cir.2015). "This appeal, which arises in the context of software licenses, requires us to address the burden of proof applicable to the first sale defense to a copyright infringement claim. *At 1074:* While the copyright holder bears the ultimate burden of establishing copyright infringement, the party raising a first sale defense bears an initial burden with respect to the defense. At the summary judgment stage, this burden is discharged by producing evidence sufficient for a jury to find that the alleged infringer lawfully acquired ownership of genuine copies of the copyrighted software. Once this initial burden is satisfied, the burden shifts back to the copyright owner to establish the absence of a *first* sale, because of a licensing or other non-ownership-transferring arrangement when the copy first changed hands. *At 1077:* In digital copyright cases, the distinction between a 'sale' and a 'license' has become central. *At 1078:* [B]ecause 'the first sale doctrine does not apply to a licensee,' … licensing arrangements enable software companies to restrict initial licensees of software from selling their licensed copies of the software to downstream users. [¶] Broadly construed, the licensing exception in the software context could swallow the statutory first sale defense. We have recognized, however, that some purported software licensing agreements may actually create a sale. To determine whether there is a legitimate license, we examine whether 'the copyright owner (1) specifies that the user is granted a license; (2) significantly restricts the user's ability to transfer the software; and (3) imposes notable use restrictions.' Where these factors aren't satisfied, the upshot is that the copyright holder has sold its software to the user, and the user can assert the first sale defense. *At 1079:* To the extent that the copyright holder claims that the alleged infringer could not acquire title or ownership because the software was never sold, only licensed, the burden shifts back to the copyright holder to establish such a license or the absence of a sale."

UMG Recordings, Inc. v. Augusto, 628 F.3d 1175, 1179 (9th Cir.2011). "Notwithstanding its distinctive name, the [first-sale] doctrine applies not only when a copy is first sold, but when a copy is given away or title is otherwise transferred without the accouterments of a sale. *At 1180:* We conclude that, under all the circumstances of the CDs' distribution, the recipients were entitled to use or dispose of them in any manner they saw fit, and [P] did not enter a license agreement for the CDs with the recipients. Accordingly, [P] transferred title to the particular copies of its promotional CDs and cannot maintain an infringement action against [D] for his subsequent sale of those copies. [¶] We also hold that, because the CDs were unordered merchandise, the recipients were free to dispose of them as they saw fit under the Unordered Merchandise Statute, 39 U.S.C. §3009…." *See also* ***Walt Disney Prods. v. Basmajian***, 600 F.Supp. 439, 442 (S.D.N.Y. 1984) (title may be transferred by gift).

Vernor v. Autodesk, Inc., 621 F.3d 1102, 1111 (9th Cir.2010). "We hold today that a software user is a licensee rather than an owner of a copy where the copyright owner (1) specifies that the user is granted a license; (2) significantly restricts the user's ability to transfer the software; and (3) imposes notable use restrictions. Applying our holding to [copyright owner's license], we conclude that [original software purchaser] was a licensee rather than an owner of copies of [software] and thus was not entitled to invoke the first sale doctrine or the essential step defense."

Mirage Editions, Inc. v. Albuquerque A.R.T. Co., 856 F.2d 1341, 1344 (9th Cir.1988). Under "the 'first sale' doctrine as enunciated at … §109(a) …, appellant can purchase a copy of the … book and subsequently alienate its ownership in that book. However, the right to transfer applies only to the particular copy of the book which appellant has purchased and nothing else. The mere sale of the book to the appellant without a specific transfer by the copyright holder of its exclusive right to prepare derivative works, does not transfer that right to appellant. The derivative works right[] remains unimpaired and with the copyright proprietors…."

U.S. v. Goss, 803 F.2d 638, 644 (11th Cir.1986). We "hold that in a criminal copyright case involving unauthorized distribution of copies, §109(a) is a defense. If a defendant presents any evidence that the copies were legally made and that he or she owned them, this is sufficient to create a jury issue with respect to the §109(a) defense. When the defendant makes such a showing, the burden shifts to the government to demonstrate beyond a reasonable doubt that the pertinent copies were either not legally made or not owned by the defendant."

Columbia Pictures Indus. v. Aveco, Inc., 800 F.2d 59, 63-64 (3d Cir.1986). "The first sale doctrine, codified at … §109(a), prevents the copyright owner from controlling future transfers of a particular copy of a copyrighted work after he has transferred its 'material ownership' to another. When a copyright owner parts with title to a particular copy of his copyrighted work, he thereby divests himself of his exclusive right to vend that particular copy. Accordingly, under the first sale doctrine, [copyright owners] cannot claim that [D's] rentals or sales of lawfully acquired video cassettes infringe on their exclusive rights to vend those cassettes." *See also* ***Columbia Pictures Indus. v. Redd Horne, Inc.***, 749 F.2d 154, 159-60 (3d Cir.1984).

Peker v. Masters Collection, 96 F.Supp.2d 216, 219 (E.D.N.Y.2000). "[D] argues that it did not engage in unauthorized 'reproduction' because (1) its replication process requires the purchase and use of one poster for each replica and (2) the 'first sale doctrine,' … protects its use and sale of each lawfully acquired poster. [¶] Neither of these arguments apply to this case. [D] is not reselling a poster. It is selling a painting that uses the poster as one ingredient. The 'first sale' of the poster gives [D] the right to sell the poster in whatever fancy frame or other setting [D] chooses. What that 'first sale' of the poster does not sanctify is [D's] transmogrification of that poster by adding paint into what [D] describes as a 'virtually indistinguishable' copy of the 'original oil painting.'"

Microsoft Corp. v. Harmony Computers & Elecs., Inc., 846 F.Supp. 208, 212 (E.D.N.Y.1994). "Although a sale of a copyrighted work by a party authorized by the copyright holder may constitute a 'first sale' for purposes of the first sale doctrine, [Ds] have the burden of tracing the chain of title to show that their authority to sell [copyright owner's products] flows from the copyright holder."

§109(b)

Action Tapes, Inc. v. Mattson, 462 F.3d 1010, 1014 (8th Cir.2006). "A computer program copyright protects the instructions that cause a computer 'to bring about a certain result,' here, the stitching of a design by a computerized sewing machine. A visual arts copyright protects the result, here, the original design embedded in the memory card and then stitched on the fabric. The Rental Amendments Act [§109(b)] protects the owners of computer program copyrights from competition from customer leasing, but not the owners of copyrights in the design results."

§110. LIMITATIONS ON EXCLUSIVE RIGHTS: EXEMPTION OF CERTAIN PERFORMANCES & DISPLAYS

Notwithstanding the provisions of section 106, the following are not infringements of copyright:

(1) performance or display of a work by instructors or pupils in the course of face-to-face teaching activities of a nonprofit educational institution, in a classroom or similar place devoted to instruction, unless, in the case of a motion picture or other audiovisual work, the performance, or the display of individual images, is given by means of a copy that was not lawfully made under this title, and that the person responsible for the performance knew or had reason to believe was not lawfully made;

(2) except with respect to a work produced or marketed primarily for performance or display as part of mediated instructional activities transmitted via digital networks, or a performance or display that is given by means of a copy or phonorecord that is not lawfully made and acquired under this title, and the transmitting government body or accredited nonprofit educational institution knew or had reason to believe was not lawfully made and acquired, the performance of a nondramatic literary or musical work or reasonable and limited portions of any other work, or display of a work in an amount comparable to that which is typically displayed in the course of a live classroom session, by or in the course of a transmission, if—

(A) the performance or display is made by, at the direction of, or under the actual supervision of an instructor as an integral part of a class session offered as a regular part of the systematic mediated instructional activities of a governmental body or an accredited nonprofit educational institution;

(B) the performance or display is directly related and of material assistance to the teaching content of the transmission;

(C) the transmission is made solely for, and, to the extent technologically feasible, the reception of such transmission is limited to—

(i) students officially enrolled in the course for which the transmission is made; or

(ii) officers or employees of governmental bodies as a part of their official duties or employment; and

(D) the transmitting body or institution—

(i) institutes policies regarding copyright, provides informational materials to faculty, students, and relevant staff members that accurately describe, and promote compliance with, the laws of the United States relating to copyright, and provides notice to students that materials used in connection with the course may be subject to copyright protection; and

(ii) in the case of digital transmissions—

(I) applies technological measures that reasonably prevent—

(aa) retention of the work in accessible form by recipients of the transmission from the transmitting body or institution for longer than the class session; and

(bb) unauthorized further dissemination of the work in accessible form by such recipients to others; and

(II) does not engage in conduct that could reasonably be expected to interfere with technological measures used by copyright owners to prevent such retention or unauthorized further dissemination;

(3) performance of a nondramatic literary or musical work or of a dramatico-musical work of a religious nature, or display of a work, in the course of services at a place of worship or other religious assembly;

(4) performance of a nondramatic literary or musical work otherwise than in a transmission to the public, without any purpose of direct or indirect commercial advantage and without payment of any fee or other compensation for the performance to any of its performers, promoters, or organizers, if—

(A) there is no direct or indirect admission charge; or

(B) the proceeds, after deducting the reasonable costs of producing the performance, are used exclusively for educational, religious, or charitable purposes and not for private financial gain, except where the copyright owner has served notice of objection to the performance under the following conditions:

(i) the notice shall be in writing and signed by the copyright owner or such owner's duly authorized agent; and

(ii) the notice shall be served on the person responsible for the performance at least seven days before the date of the performance, and shall state the reasons for the objection; and

(iii) the notice shall comply, in form, content, and manner of service, with requirements that the Register of Copyrights shall prescribe by regulation;

(5)(A) except as provided in subparagraph (B), communication of a transmission embodying a performance or display of a work by the public reception of the transmission on a single receiving apparatus of a kind commonly used in private homes, unless—

(i) a direct charge is made to see or hear the transmission; or

(ii) the transmission thus received is further transmitted to the public;

(B) communication by an establishment of a transmission or retransmission embodying a performance or display of a nondramatic musical work intended to be received by the general public, originated by a radio or television broadcast station licensed as such by the Federal Communications Commission, or, if an audiovisual transmission, by a cable system or satellite carrier, if—

(i) in the case of an establishment other than a food service or drinking establishment, either the establishment in which the communication occurs has less than 2,000 gross square feet of space (excluding space used for customer parking and for no other purpose), or the establishment in which the communication occurs has 2,000 or more gross square feet of space (excluding space used for customer parking and for no other purpose) and—

(I) if the performance is by audio means only, the performance is communicated by means of a total of not more than 6 loudspeakers, of which not more than 4 loudspeakers are located in any 1 room or adjoining outdoor space; or

(II) if the performance or display is by audiovisual means, any visual portion of the performance or display is communicated by means of a total of not more than 4 audiovisual devices, of which not more than 1 audiovisual device is located in any 1 room, and no such audiovisual device has a diagonal screen size greater than 55 inches, and any audio portion of the performance or display is communicated by means of a total of not more than 6 loudspeakers, of which not more than 4 loudspeakers are located in any 1 room or adjoining outdoor space;

(ii) in the case of a food service or drinking establishment, either the establishment in which the communication occurs has less than 3,750 gross square feet of space (excluding space used for customer parking and for no other purpose), or the establishment in which the communication occurs has 3,750 gross square feet of space or more (excluding space used for customer parking and for no other purpose) and—

(I) if the performance is by audio means only, the performance is communicated by means of a total of not more than 6 loudspeakers, of which not more than 4 loudspeakers are located in any 1 room or adjoining outdoor space; or

(II) if the performance or display is by audiovisual means, any visual portion of the performance or display is communicated by means of a total of not more than 4 audiovisual devices, of which not more than one audiovisual device is located in any 1 room, and no such audiovisual device has a diagonal screen size greater than 55 inches, and any audio portion of the performance or display is communicated by means of a total of not more than 6 loudspeakers, of which not more than 4 loudspeakers are located in any 1 room or adjoining outdoor space;

(iii) no direct charge is made to see or hear the transmission or retransmission;

(iv) the transmission or retransmission is not further transmitted beyond the establishment where it is received; and

(v) the transmission or retransmission is licensed by the copyright owner of the work so publicly performed or displayed;

(6) performance of a nondramatic musical work by a governmental body or a nonprofit agricultural or horticultural organization, in the course of an annual agricultural or horticultural fair or exhibition conducted by such body or organization; the exemption provided by this clause shall extend to any liability for copyright infringement that would otherwise be imposed on such

body or organization, under doctrines of vicarious liability or related infringement, for a performance by a concessionaire, business establishment, or other person at such fair or exhibition, but shall not excuse any such person from liability for the performance;

(7) performance of a nondramatic musical work by a vending establishment open to the public at large without any direct or indirect admission charge, where the sole purpose of the performance is to promote the retail sale of copies or phonorecords of the work, or of the audiovisual or other devices utilized in such performance, and the performance is not transmitted beyond the place where the establishment is located and is within the immediate area where the sale is occurring;

(8) performance of a nondramatic literary work, by or in the course of a transmission specifically designed for and primarily directed to blind or other handicapped persons who are unable to read normal printed material as a result of their handicap, or deaf or other handicapped persons who are unable to hear the aural signals accompanying a transmission of visual signals, if the performance is made without any purpose of direct or indirect commercial advantage and its transmission is made through the facilities of: (i) a governmental body; or (ii) a noncommercial educational broadcast station (as defined in section 397 of title 47); or (iii) a radio subcarrier authorization (as defined in 47 CFR 73.293-73.295 and 73.593-73.595); or (iv) a cable system (as defined in section 111(f));

(9) performance on a single occasion of a dramatic literary work published at least ten years before the date of the performance, by or in the course of a transmission specifically designed for and primarily directed to blind or other handicapped persons who are unable to read normal printed material as a result of their handicap, if the performance is made without any purpose of direct or indirect commercial advantage and its transmission is made through the facilities of a radio subcarrier authorization referred to in clause (8)(iii), *Provided*, That the provisions of this clause shall not be applicable to more than one performance of the same work by the same performers or under the auspices of the same organization;

(10) notwithstanding paragraph (4), the following is not an infringement of copyright: performance of a nondramatic literary or musical work in the course of a social function which is organized and promoted by a nonprofit veterans' organization or a nonprofit fraternal organization to which the general public is not invited, but not including the invitees of the organizations, if the proceeds from the performance, after deducting the reasonable costs of producing the performance, are used exclusively for charitable purposes and not for financial gain. For purposes of this section the social functions of any college or university fraternity or sorority shall not be included unless the social function is held solely to raise funds for a specific charitable purpose; and

(11) the making imperceptible, by or at the direction of a member of a private household, of limited portions of audio or video content of a motion picture, during a performance in or transmitted to that household for private home viewing, from an authorized copy of the motion picture, or the creation or provision of a computer program or other technology that enables such making imperceptible and that is designed and marketed to be used, at the direction of a member of a private household, for such making imperceptible, if no fixed copy of the altered version of the motion picture is created by such computer program or other technology.

The exemptions provided under paragraph (5) shall not be taken into account in any administrative, judicial, or other governmental proceeding to set or adjust the royalties payable to copyright owners for the public performance or display of their works. Royalties payable to copyright owners for any public performance or display of their works other than such performances or displays as are exempted under paragraph (5) shall not be diminished in any respect as a result of such exemption.

In paragraph (2), the term "mediated instructional activities" with respect to the performance or display of a work by digital transmission under this section refers to activities that use such work as an integral part of the class experience, controlled by or under the actual supervision of the instructor and analogous to the type of performance or display that would take place in a live classroom setting. The term does not refer to activities that use, in 1 or more class sessions of a single course, such works as textbooks, course packs, or other material in any media, copies or phonorecords of which are typically purchased or acquired by the students in higher education for their independent use and retention or are typically purchased or acquired for elementary and secondary students for their possession and independent use.

For purposes of paragraph (2), accreditation—

(A) with respect to an institution providing post-secondary education, shall be as determined by a regional or national accrediting agency recognized by the Council on Higher Education Accreditation or the United States Department of Education; and

(B) with respect to an institution providing elementary or secondary education, shall be as recognized by the applicable state certification or licensing procedures.

For purposes of paragraph (2), no governmental body or accredited nonprofit educational institution shall be liable for infringement by reason of the transient or temporary storage of material carried out through the automatic technical process of a digital transmission of the performance or display of that material as authorized under paragraph (2). No such material stored on the system or network controlled or operated by the transmitting body or institution under this paragraph shall be maintained on such system or network in a manner ordinarily accessible to anyone other than anticipated recipients. No such copy shall be maintained on the system or network in a manner ordinarily accessible to such anticipated recipients for a longer period than is reasonably necessary to facilitate the transmissions for which it was made.

For purposes of paragraph (11), the term "making imperceptible" does not include the addition of audio or video content that is performed or displayed over or in place of existing content in a motion picture.

Nothing in paragraph (11) shall be construed to imply further rights under section 106 of this title, or to have any effect on defenses or limitations on rights granted under any other section of this title or under any other paragraph of this section.

History of 17 U.S.C. §110: Oct. 19, 1976, P.L. 94-553, §101, 90 Stat. 2549; Oct. 15, 1982, P.L. 97-366, §3, 96 Stat. 1759; Nov. 13, 1997, P.L. 105-80, §12(a)(6), 111 Stat. 1534; Oct. 27, 1998, P.L. 105-298, §202, 112 Stat. 2830; Aug. 5, 1999, P.L. 106-44, §1(a), 113 Stat. 221; Nov. 2, 2002, P.L. 107-273, §§13210(6), 13301(b), 116 Stat. 1909, 1910; Apr. 27, 2005, P.L. 109-9, §202(a), 119 Stat. 223.

See also 37 C.F.R. §201.13.

ANNOTATIONS

§110(2)

Richard Anderson Photography v. Brown, 852 F.2d 114, 119 (4th Cir.1988). "[P] argues that [17 U.S.C. §107] is superfluous if state schools are to be considered immune from suit. This argument is without merit not only because ... a teacher's immunity from suit is not coextensive with that of the state, but also because the limitations in §107 can be read as applying to teachers in local school districts that might not, in any event, share the states' 11th amendment immunity. Likewise, the explicit limitations on a copyright holder's exclusive rights pertaining to use of the copyrighted work by 'libraries and archives' found in [17 U.S.C.] §108, can be read as applicable to private and local institutions and therefore are not superfluous absent congressional abrogation of the states' 11th amendment immunity. [¶] We conclude ... that the phrase 'governmental bodies' in this context has the same ambiguity for the purpose at hand as do the provisions in §§107-108. Clearly the phrase could be read as applicable only to local governments or to actions by government officials so that the states' continued immunity would not render [17 U.S.C.] §110(2) superfluous."

§110(4)

Bourne Co. v. Speeks, 670 F.Supp. 777, 779 (E.D. Tenn.1987). "Whether the use of copyrighted material is in fact a financial success is not the deciding factor in determining the exemption under §110(4). The language of §110(4) requires that to be exempt the performance must be 'without any purpose of direct or indirect commercial advantage.' ... There was an admission charge to [D's theater]. The band members were paid a nominal fee. The occasional charitable use of [D's theater] does not meet the mandate of §110(4)(B) that the proceeds are to be used exclusively for educational, religious, or charitable purposes and not for private financial gain. For all of these reasons, the court finds that [D] is not entitled to the exemption claimed under §110(4)."

§110(5)

Edison Bros. Stores v. Broadcast Music, Inc., 954 F.2d 1419, 1425 (8th Cir.1992). "We hold that ... §110(5) does not require that the square footage of a qualifying establishment be less than 1055, with fewer than 620 square feet open to the public; nor does it require that the entity's ability to pay for a commercial background music service be considered. The focus of the statute is on the equipment in use, and as each of [D's] unlicensed stores uses only homestyle equipment each qualifies for the homestyle exemption."

Broadcast Music, Inc. v. Claire's Boutiques, Inc., 949 F.2d 1482, 1489 (7th Cir.1991). "On the face of the statute, the exemption is available only if (1) a single receiving apparatus is used, (2) the single receiving apparatus is of a kind commonly used in private homes, (3) the transmission is provided free of charge, and (4) the transmission is not 'further transmitted' to the public. *At 1496 n.13:* Although we agree that the *financial* size of an establishment is irrelevant, we disagree with the district court's conclusion that the *physical* size of the establishment is not a relevant concern under §110(5). [T]his consideration does not bring into play a contradictory rule but rather gives content to what Congress meant by the term 'receiving apparatus of a kind commonly used in private homes.' *At 1493:* Because we examine the entire stereo system, there are two ways a company can fall out of the §110(5) exemption for failure to use a home-type system. If the company uses any non-home-type components in its stereo system, then the system is not home-type. Analysis does not end, however, if all the components are home-type. The company also may not claim the exemption if it configures and uses home-type components in a manner not commonly found in a home. *At 1495:* [T]he statute uses the term 'receiving apparatus,' which ... encompasses not just the receiver but all the components of an integrated music system. It is sensible to consider that the entire receiving apparatus, and not just the receiver, 'receives' the performance." *See also* ***Cass Cty. Music Co. v. Muedini***, 55 F.3d 263, 267-69 (7th Cir.1995).

Blue Seas Music, Inc. v. Fitness Surveys, Inc., 831 F.Supp. 863, 865 (N.D.Ga.1993). "[Ds] cannot benefit from [the] 'home system defense [of §110(5)].' First, there is a direct charge to enter the workout area at [D's business]. Second, the system utilized by [Ds] is not a small 'home-type' sound system; it includes 13 recessed ceiling speakers and several floor speakers. Finally, the system does 'further transmit' the copyrighted works throughout the facility." *See also* ***Gnossos Music v. DiPompo***, 13 U.S.P.Q.2d 1539, 1541-42 (D.Me.1989).

Merrill v. Bill Miller's Bar-B-Q Enters., 688 F.Supp. 1172, 1175 (W.D.Tex.1988). "[Ds] do not employ in their restaurants 'a single receiving apparatus of a kind commonly used in private homes.' The fact that individual components of the entire apparatus may be 'home-type' does not make the entire apparatus 'home-type.' Rather, all the features of the complete apparatus must be considered in determining whether it is 'home-type,' including, for example, whether the wiring is hidden, the distance between the speakers, and the mounting of the speakers. *At 1176:* [T]he radio broadcasts received by [Ds] were 'further transmitted' to the public because the broadcasts were initially received in a room or area without speakers and were sent to a separate room with speakers via some 40 feet of wiring. [¶] [Ds'] chain operation is 'of a sufficient size to justify, as a practical matter, a subscription to a commercial background music service.' It is clearly 'practical' for a chain of restaurants, each restaurant having 1000 to 1500 square feet of public dining area and grossing well over $500,000 annually, to subscribe to a commercial background music service. [Ds'] prior subscription to a commercial background music service further establishes the inapplicability of the exemption to [Ds'] performances of copyrighted musical compositions." *See also* ***Little Mole Music v. Mavar's Supermarket***, 12 U.S.P.Q.2d 1209, 1213-14 (N.D.Ohio 1989); ***Merrill v. County Stores, Inc.***, 669 F.Supp. 1164, 1170 (D.N.H.1987).

Rodgers v. Eighty Four Lumber Co., 617 F.Supp. 1021, 1022 (W.D.Pa.1985). "[D] is ... arguing that since its primary purpose for using the music was to muffle industrial noise for the benefit of employees and not to attract the public to its stores, it should be exempt. We have no doubt that §110(5) provides no such exemption, and that the purpose for which the music was used is irrelevant to the question of infringement in this case."

§111. LIMITATIONS ON EXCLUSIVE RIGHTS: SECONDARY TRANSMISSIONS OF BROADCAST PROGRAMMING BY CABLE

(a) Certain Secondary Transmissions Exempted.—The secondary transmission of a performance or display of a work embodied in a primary transmission is not an infringement of copyright if—

(1) the secondary transmission is not made by a cable system, and consists entirely of the relaying, by the management of a hotel, apartment house, or similar establishment, of signals transmitted by a broadcast station licensed by the Federal Communications Commission, within the local service area of such station, to the private lodgings of guests or residents of such establishment, and no direct charge is made to see or hear the secondary transmission; or

(2) the secondary transmission is made solely for the purpose and under the conditions specified by paragraph (2) of section 110; or

(3) the secondary transmission is made by any carrier who has no direct or indirect control over the content or selection of the primary transmission or over the particular recipients of the secondary transmission, and whose activities with respect to the secondary transmission consist solely of providing wires, cables, or other communications channels for the use of others: *Provided*, That the provisions of this paragraph extend only to the activities of said carrier with respect to secondary transmissions and do not exempt from liability the activities of others with respect to their own primary or secondary transmissions;

(4) the secondary transmission is made by a satellite carrier pursuant to a statutory license under section 119 or section 122;

(5) the secondary transmission is not made by a cable system but is made by a governmental body, or other nonprofit organization, without any purpose of direct or indirect commercial advantage, and without charge to the recipients of the secondary transmission other than assessments necessary to defray the actual and reasonable costs of maintaining and operating the secondary transmission service.

(b) Secondary Transmission of Primary Transmission to Controlled Group.—Notwithstanding the provisions of subsections (a) and (c), the secondary transmission to the public of a performance or display of a work embodied in a primary transmission is actionable as an act of infringement under section 501, and is fully subject to the remedies provided by sections 502 through 506, if the primary transmission is not made for reception by the public at large but is controlled and limited to reception by particular members of the public: *Provided, however*, That such secondary transmission is not actionable as an act of infringement if—

(1) the primary transmission is made by a broadcast station licensed by the Federal Communications Commission; and

(2) the carriage of the signals comprising the secondary transmission is required under the rules, regulations, or authorizations of the Federal Communications Commission; and

(3) the signal of the primary transmitter is not altered or changed in any way by the secondary transmitter.

(c) Secondary Transmissions by Cable Systems—

(1) Subject to the provisions of paragraphs (2), (3), and (4) of this subsection and section 114(d), secondary transmissions to the public by a cable system of a performance or display of a work embodied in a primary transmission made by a broadcast station licensed by the Federal Communications Commission or by an appropriate governmental authority of Canada or Mexico shall be subject to statutory licensing upon compliance with the requirements of subsection (d) where the carriage of the signals comprising the secondary transmission is permissible under the rules, regulations, or authorizations of the Federal Communications Commission.

(2) Notwithstanding the provisions of paragraph (1) of this subsection, the willful or repeated secondary transmission to the public by a cable system of a primary transmission made by a broadcast station licensed by the Federal Communications Commission or by an appropriate governmental authority of Canada or Mexico and embodying a performance or display of a work is actionable as an act of infringement under section 501, and is fully subject to the remedies provided by sections 502 through 506, in the following cases:

(A) where the carriage of the signals comprising the secondary transmission is not permissible under the rules, regulations, or authorizations of the Federal Communications Commission; or

(B) where the cable system has not deposited the statement of account and royalty fee required by subsection (d).

(3) Notwithstanding the provisions of paragraph (1) of this subsection and subject to the provisions of subsection (e) of this section, the secondary transmission to the public by a cable system of a performance or display of a work embodied in a primary transmission made by a broadcast station licensed by the Federal Communications Commission or by an appropriate governmental authority of Canada or Mexico is actionable as an act of infringement under section 501, and is fully subject to the remedies provided by sections 502 through 506 and section 510, if the content of the particular program in which the performance or display is embodied, or any commercial advertising or station announcements transmitted by the primary transmitter during, or immediately before or after, the transmission of such program, is in any way willfully altered by the cable system through changes, deletions, or additions, except for the alteration, deletion, or substitution of commercial advertisements performed by those engaged in television commercial advertising market research: *Provided*, That the research company has obtained the prior consent of the advertiser who has purchased the original commercial advertisement, the television station broadcasting that commercial advertisement, and the cable system performing the secondary transmission: And provided further, That such commercial alteration, deletion, or substitution is not performed for the purpose of deriving income from the sale of that commercial time.

(4) Notwithstanding the provisions of paragraph (1) of this subsection, the secondary transmission to the public by a cable system of a performance or display of a work embodied in a primary transmission made by a broadcast station licensed by an appropriate governmental authority of Canada or Mexico is actionable as an act of infringement under section 501, and is fully subject to the remedies provided by sections 502 through 506, if (A) with respect to Canadian signals, the community of the cable system is located more than 150 miles from the United States-Canadian border and is also located south of the forty-second parallel of latitude, or (B) with respect to Mexican signals, the secondary transmission is made by a cable system which received the primary transmission by means other than direct interception of a free space radio wave emitted by such broadcast television station, unless prior to April 15, 1976, such cable system was actually carrying, or was specifically authorized to carry, the signal of such foreign station on the system pursuant to the rules, regulations, or authorizations of the Federal Communications Commission.

(d) Statutory License for Secondary Transmissions by Cable Systems—

(1) Statement of account and royalty fees.—Subject to paragraph (5), a cable system whose secondary transmissions have been subject to statutory licensing under subsection (c) shall, on a semiannual basis, deposit with the Register of Copyrights, in accordance with requirements that the Register shall prescribe by regulation the following:

(A) A statement of account, covering the six months next preceding, specifying the number of channels on which the cable system made secondary transmissions to its subscribers, the names and locations of all primary transmitters whose transmissions were further transmitted by the cable system, the total number of subscribers, the gross amounts paid to the cable system for the basic service of providing secondary transmissions of primary broadcast transmitters, and such other data as the Register of Copyrights may from time to time prescribe by regulation. In determining the total number of subscribers and the gross amounts paid to the cable system for the basic service of providing secondary transmissions of primary broadcast transmitters, the system shall not include subscribers and amounts collected from subscribers receiving secondary transmissions pursuant to section 119. Such statement shall also include a special statement of account covering any non-network television programming that was carried by the cable system in whole or in part beyond the local service area of the primary transmitter, under rules, regulations, or authorizations of the Federal Communications Commission permitting the substitution or addition of signals under certain circumstances, together with logs showing the times, dates, stations, and programs involved in such substituted or added carriage.

(B) Except in the case of a cable system whose royalty fee is specified in subparagraph (E) or (F), a total royalty fee payable to copyright owners pursuant to paragraph (3) for the period covered by the statement, computed on the basis of specified percentages of the gross receipts from subscribers to the cable service during such period for the basic service of providing secondary transmissions of primary broadcast transmitters, as follows:

(i) 1.064 percent of such gross receipts for the privilege of further transmitting, beyond the local service area of such primary transmitter, any non-network programming of a primary transmitter in whole or in part, such amount to be applied against the fee, if any, payable pursuant to clauses (ii) through (iv);

(ii) 1.064 percent of such gross receipts for the first distant signal equivalent;

(iii) 0.701 percent of such gross receipts for each of the second, third, and fourth distant signal equivalents; and

(iv) 0.330 percent of such gross receipts for the fifth distant signal equivalent and each distant signal equivalent thereafter.

(C) In computing amounts under clauses (ii) through (iv) of subparagraph (B)—

(i) any fraction of a distant signal equivalent shall be computed at its fractional value;

(ii) in the case of any cable system located partly within and partly outside of the local service area of a primary transmitter, gross receipts shall be limited to those gross receipts derived from subscribers located outside of the local service area of such primary transmitter; and

(iii) if a cable system provides a secondary transmission of a primary transmitter to some but not all communities served by that cable system—

(I) the gross receipts and the distant signal equivalent values for such secondary transmission shall be derived solely on the basis of the subscribers in those communities where the cable system provides such secondary transmission; and

(II) the total royalty fee for the period paid by such system shall not be less than the royalty fee calculated under subparagraph (B)(i) multiplied by the gross receipts from all subscribers to the system.

(D) A cable system that, on a statement submitted before May 27, 2010, computed its royalty fee consistent with the methodology under subparagraph (C)(iii), or that amends a statement filed before such date of enactment to compute the royalty fee due using such methodology, shall not be subject to an action for infringement, or eligible for any royalty refund or offset, arising out of its use of such methodology on such statement.

(E) If the actual gross receipts paid by subscribers to a cable system for the period covered by the statement for the basic service of providing secondary transmissions of primary broadcast transmitters are $263,800 or less—

(i) gross receipts of the cable system for the purpose of this paragraph shall be computed by subtracting from such actual gross receipts the amount by which $263,800 exceeds such actual gross receipts, except that in no case shall a cable system's gross receipts be reduced to less than $10,400; and

(ii) the royalty fee payable under this paragraph to copyright owners pursuant to paragraph (3) shall be 0.5 percent, regardless of the number of distant signal equivalents, if any.

(F) If the actual gross receipts paid by subscribers to a cable system for the period covered by the statement for the basic service of providing secondary transmissions of primary broadcast transmitters are more than $263,800 but less than $527,600, the royalty fee payable under this paragraph to copyright owners pursuant to paragraph (3) shall be—

(i) 0.5 percent of any gross receipts up to $263,800, regardless of the number of distant signal equivalents, if any; and

(ii) 1 percent of any gross receipts in excess of $263,800, but less than $527,600, regardless of the number of distant signal equivalents, if any.

(G) A filing fee, as determined by the Register of Copyrights pursuant to section 708(a).

(2) Handling of fees.—The Register of Copyrights shall receive all fees (including the filing fee specified in paragraph (1)(G)) deposited under this section and, after deducting the reasonable costs incurred by the Copyright Office under this section, shall deposit the balance in the Treasury of the United States, in such manner as the Secretary of the Treasury directs. All funds held by the Secretary of the Treasury shall be invested in interest-bearing United States securities for later distribution with interest by the Librarian of Congress upon authorization by the Copyright Royalty Judges.

(3) Distribution of royalty fees to copyright owners.—The royalty fees thus deposited shall, in accordance with the procedures provided by paragraph (4), be distributed to those among the following copyright owners who claim that their works were the subject of secondary transmissions by cable systems during the relevant semiannual period:

(A) Any such owner whose work was included in a secondary transmission made by a cable system of a non-network television program in whole or in part beyond the local service area of the primary transmitter.

(B) Any such owner whose work was included in a secondary transmission identified in a special statement of account deposited under paragraph (1)(A).

(C) Any such owner whose work was included in non-network programming consisting exclusively of aural signals carried by a cable system in whole or in part beyond the local service area of the primary transmitter of such programs.

(4) Procedures for royalty fee distribution.—The royalty fees thus deposited shall be distributed in accordance with the following procedures:

(A) During the month of July in each year, every person claiming to be entitled to statutory license fees for secondary transmissions shall file a claim with the Copyright Royalty Judges, in accordance with requirements that the Copyright Royalty Judges shall prescribe by regulation. Notwithstanding any provisions of the antitrust laws, for purposes of this clause any claimants may agree among themselves as to the proportionate division of statutory licensing fees among them, may lump their claims together and file them jointly or as a single claim, or may designate a common agent to receive payment on their behalf.

(B) After the first day of August of each year, the Copyright Royalty Judges shall determine whether there exists a controversy concerning the distribution of royalty fees. If the Copyright Royalty Judges determine that no such controversy exists, the Copyright Royalty Judges shall authorize the Librarian of Congress to proceed to distribute such fees to the copyright owners entitled to receive them, or to their designated agents, subject to the deduction of reasonable administrative costs under this section. If the Copyright Royalty Judges find the existence of a controversy, the Copyright Royalty Judges shall, pursuant to chapter 8 of this title, conduct a proceeding to determine the distribution of royalty fees.

(C) During the pendency of any proceeding under this subsection, the Copyright Royalty Judges shall have the discretion to authorize the Librarian of Congress to proceed to distribute any amounts that are not in controversy.

(5) 3.75 percent rate and syndicated exclusivity surcharge not applicable to multicast streams.—The royalty rates specified in sections 256.2(c) and 256.2(d) of title 37, Code of Federal Regulations (commonly referred to as the "3.75 percent rate" and the "syndicated exclusivity surcharge," respectively), as in effect on May 27, 2010, as such rates may be adjusted, or such sections redesignated, thereafter by the Copyright Royalty Judges, shall not apply to the secondary transmission of a multicast stream.

(6) Verification of accounts and fee payments.—The Register of Copyrights shall issue regulations to provide for the confidential verification by copyright owners whose works were embodied in the secondary transmissions of primary transmissions pursuant to this section of the information reported on the semiannual statements of account filed under this subsection for accounting periods beginning on or after January 1, 2010, in order that the auditor designated under subparagraph (A) is able to confirm the correctness of the calculations and royalty payments reported therein. The regulations shall—

(A) establish procedures for the designation of a qualified independent auditor—

(i) with exclusive authority to request verification of such a statement of account on behalf of all copyright owners whose works were the subject of secondary transmissions of primary transmissions by the cable system (that deposited the statement) during the accounting period covered by the statement; and

(ii) who is not an officer, employee, or agent of any such copyright owner for any purpose other than such audit;

(B) establish procedures for safeguarding all nonpublic financial and business information provided under this paragraph;

(C)(i) require a consultation period for the independent auditor to review its conclusions with a designee of the cable system;

(ii) establish a mechanism for the cable system to remedy any errors identified in the auditor's report and to cure any underpayment identified; and

(iii) provide an opportunity to remedy any disputed facts or conclusions;

(D) limit the frequency of requests for verification for a particular cable system and the number of audits that a multiple system operator can be required to undergo in a single year; and

(E) permit requests for verification of a statement of account to be made only within 3 years after the last day of the year in which the statement of account is filed.

(7) Acceptance of additional deposits.—Any royalty fee payments received by the Copyright Office from cable systems for the secondary transmission of primary transmissions that are in addition to the payments calculated and deposited in accordance with this subsection shall be deemed to have been deposited for the particular accounting period for which they are received and shall be distributed as specified under this subsection.

(e) Nonsimultaneous Secondary Transmissions by Cable Systems—

(1) Notwithstanding those provisions of the subsection (f)(2) relating to nonsimultaneous secondary transmissions by a cable system, any such transmissions are actionable as an act of infringement under section 501, and are fully subject to the remedies provided by sections 502 through 506, and section 510, unless—

(A) the program on the videotape is transmitted no more than one time to the cable system's subscribers;

(B) the copyrighted program, episode, or motion picture videotape, including the commercials contained within such program, episode, or picture, is transmitted without deletion or editing;

(C) an owner or officer of the cable system (i) prevents the duplication of the videotape while in the possession of the system, (ii) prevents unauthorized duplication while in the possession of the facility making the videotape for the system if the system owns or controls the facility, or takes reasonable precautions to prevent such duplication if it does not own or control the facility, (iii) takes adequate precautions to prevent duplication while the tape is being transported, and (iv) subject to paragraph (2), erases or destroys, or causes the erasure or destruction of, the videotape;

(D) within forty-five days after the end of each calendar quarter, an owner or officer of the cable system executes an affidavit attesting (i) to the steps and precautions taken to prevent duplication of the videotape, and (ii) subject to paragraph (2), to the erasure or destruction of all videotapes made or used during such quarter;

(E) such owner or officer places or causes each such affidavit, and affidavits received pursuant to paragraph (2)(C), to be placed in a file, open to public inspection, at such system's main office in the community where the transmission is made or in the nearest community where such system maintains an office; and

(F) the nonsimultaneous transmission is one that the cable system would be authorized to transmit under the rules, regulations, and authorizations of the Federal Communications Commission in effect at the time of the nonsimultaneous transmission if the transmission had been made simultaneously, except that this subparagraph shall not apply to inadvertent or accidental transmissions.

(2) If a cable system transfers to any person a videotape of a program nonsimultaneously transmitted by it, such transfer is actionable as an act of infringement under section 501, and is fully subject to the remedies provided by sections 502 through 506, except that, pursuant to a written, nonprofit contract providing for the equitable sharing of the costs of such videotape and its transfer, a videotape nonsimultaneously transmitted by it, in accordance with paragraph (1), may be transferred by one cable system in Alaska to another system in Alaska, by one cable system in Hawaii permitted to make such nonsimultaneous transmissions to another such cable system in Hawaii, or by one cable system in Guam, the Northern Mariana Islands, the Federated States of Micronesia, the Republic of Palau, or the Republic of the Marshall Islands, to another cable system in any of those five entities, if—

(A) each such contract is available for public inspection in the offices of the cable systems involved, and a copy of such contract is filed, within thirty days after such contract is entered into, with the Copyright Office (which Office shall make each such contract available for public inspection);

(B) the cable system to which the videotape is transferred complies with paragraph (1)(A), (B), (C)(i), (iii), and (iv), and (D) through (F); and

(C) such system provides a copy of the affidavit required to be made in accordance with paragraph (1)(D) to each cable system making a previous nonsimultaneous transmission of the same videotape.

(3) This subsection shall not be construed to supersede the exclusivity protection provisions of any existing agreement, or any such agreement hereafter entered into, between a cable system and a television broadcast station in the area in which the cable system is located, or a network with which such station is affiliated.

(4) As used in this subsection, the term "videotape" means the reproduction of the images and sounds of a program or programs broadcast by a television broadcast station licensed by the Federal Communications Commission, regardless of the nature of the material objects, such as tapes or films, in which the reproduction is embodied.

(f) Definitions.—As used in this section, the following terms mean the following:

(1) Primary transmission.—A "primary transmission" is a transmission made to the public by a transmitting facility whose signals are being received and further transmitted by a secondary transmission service, regardless of where or when the performance or display was first transmitted. In the case of a television broadcast station, the primary stream and any multicast streams transmitted by the station constitute primary transmissions.

(2) Secondary transmission.—A "secondary transmission" is the further transmitting of a primary transmission simultaneously with the primary transmission, or nonsimultaneously with the primary transmission if by a cable system not located in whole or in part within the boundary of the forty-eight contiguous States, Hawaii, or Puerto Rico: *Provided, however*, That a nonsimultaneous further transmission by a cable system located in Hawaii of a primary transmission shall be deemed to be a secondary transmission if the carriage of the television broadcast signal comprising such further transmission is permissible under the rules, regulations, or authorizations of the Federal Communications Commission.

(3) Cable system.—A "cable system" is a facility, located in any State, territory, trust territory, or possession of the United States, that in whole or in part receives signals transmitted or programs broadcast by one or more television broadcast stations licensed by the Federal Communications Commission, and makes secondary transmissions of such signals or programs by wires, cables, microwave, or other communications channels to subscribing members of the public who pay for such service. For purposes of determining the royalty fee under subsection (d)(1), two or more cable systems in contiguous communities under common ownership or control or operating from one headend shall be considered as one system.

(4) Local service area of a primary transmitter.—The "local service area of a primary transmitter," in the case of both the primary stream and any multicast streams transmitted by a primary transmitter that is a television broadcast station, comprises the area where such primary transmitter could have insisted upon its signal being retransmitted by a cable system pursuant to the rules, regulations, and authorizations of the Federal Communications Commission in effect on April 15, 1976, or such station's television market as defined in section 76.55(e) of title 47, Code of Federal Regulations (as in effect on September 18, 1993), or any modifications to such television market made, on or after September 18, 1993, pursuant to section 76.55(e) or 76.59 of title 47, Code of Federal Regulations, or within the noise-limited contour as defined in 73.622(e)(1) of title 47, Code of Federal Regulations, or in the case of a television broadcast station licensed by an appropriate governmental authority of Canada or Mexico, the area in which it would be entitled to insist upon its signal being retransmitted if it were a television broadcast station subject to such rules, regulations, and authorizations. In the case of a low power television station, as defined by the rules and regulations of the Federal Communications Commission, the "local service area of a primary transmitter" comprises the designated market area, as defined in section 122(j)(2)(C), that encompasses the community of license of such station and any community that is located outside such designated market area that is either wholly or partially within 35 miles of the transmitter site or, in the case of such a station located in a standard metropolitan statistical area which has one of the 50 largest populations of all standard metropolitan statistical areas (based on the 1980 decennial census of population taken by the Secretary of Commerce), wholly or partially within 20 miles of such transmitter site. The "local service area of a primary transmitter," in the case of a radio broadcast station, comprises the primary service area of such station, pursuant to the rules and regulations of the Federal Communications Commission.

(5) Distant signal equivalent—

(A) In general.—Except as provided under subparagraph (B), a "distant signal equivalent"—

(i) is the value assigned to the secondary transmission of any non-network television programming carried by a cable system in whole or in part beyond the local service area of the primary transmitter of such programming; and

(ii) is computed by assigning a value of one to each primary stream and to each multicast stream (other than a simulcast) that is an independent station, and by assigning a value of one-quarter to each primary stream and to each multicast stream (other than a simulcast) that is a network station or a noncommercial educational station.

(B) Exceptions.—The values for independent, network, and noncommercial educational stations specified in subparagraph (A) are subject to the following:

(i) Where the rules and regulations of the Federal Communications Commission require a cable system to omit the further transmission of a particular program and such rules and regulations also permit the substitution of another program embodying a performance or display of a work in place of the omitted transmission, or where such rules and regulations in effect on the date of the enactment of the Copyright Act of 1976 permit a cable system, at its election, to effect such omission and substitution of a nonlive program or to carry additional programs not transmitted by primary transmitters within whose local service area the cable system is located, no value shall be assigned for the substituted or additional program.

(ii) Where the rules, regulations, or authorizations of the Federal Communications Commission in effect on the date of the enactment of the Copyright Act of 1976 permit a cable system, at its election, to omit the further transmission of a particular program and such rules, regulations, or authorizations also permit the substitution of another program embodying a performance or display of a work in place of the omitted transmission, the value assigned for the substituted or additional program shall be, in the case of a live program, the value of one full distant signal equivalent multiplied by a fraction that has as its numerator the number of days in the year in which such substitution occurs and as its denominator the number of days in the year.

(iii) In the case of the secondary transmission of a primary transmitter that is a television broadcast station pursuant to the late-night or specialty programming rules of the Federal Communications Commission, or the secondary transmission of a primary transmitter that is a television broadcast station on a part-time basis where full-time carriage is not possible because the cable system lacks the activated channel capacity to retransmit on a full-time basis all signals that it is authorized to carry, the values for independent, network, and noncommercial educational stations set forth in subparagraph (A), as the case may be, shall be multiplied by a fraction that is equal to the ratio of the broadcast hours of such primary transmitter retransmitted by the cable system to the total broadcast hours of the primary transmitter.

(iv) No value shall be assigned for the secondary transmission of the primary stream or any multicast streams of a primary transmitter that is a television broadcast station in any community that is within the local service area of the primary transmitter.

(6) Network station—

(A) Treatment of primary stream.—The term "network station" shall be applied to a primary stream of a television broadcast station that is owned or operated by, or affiliated with, one or more of the television networks in the United States providing nationwide transmissions, and that transmits a substantial part of the programming supplied by such networks for a substantial part of the primary stream's typical broadcast day.

(B) Treatment of multicast streams.—The term "network station" shall be applied to a multicast stream on which a television broadcast station transmits all or substantially all of the programming of an interconnected program service that—

(i) is owned or operated by, or affiliated with, one or more of the television networks described in subparagraph (A); and

(ii) offers programming on a regular basis for 15 or more hours per week to at least 25 of the affiliated television licensees of the interconnected program service in 10 or more States.

(7) Independent station.—The term "independent station" shall be applied to the primary stream or a multicast stream of a television broadcast station that is not a network station or a noncommercial educational station.

(8) Noncommercial educational station.—The term "noncommercial educational station" shall be applied to the primary stream or a multicast stream of a television broadcast station that is a noncommercial educational broadcast station as defined in section 397 of the Communications Act of 1934, as in effect on May 27, 2010.

(9) Primary stream.—A "primary stream" is—

(A) the single digital stream of programming that, before June 12, 2009, was substantially duplicating the programming transmitted by the television broadcast station as an analog signal; or

(B) if there is no stream described in subparagraph (A), then the single digital stream of programming transmitted by the television broadcast station for the longest period of time.

(10) Primary transmitter.—A "primary transmitter" is a television or radio broadcast station licensed by the Federal Communications Commission, or by an appropriate governmental authority of Canada or Mexico, that makes primary transmissions to the public.

(11) Multicast stream.—A "multicast stream" is a digital stream of programming that is transmitted by a television broadcast station and is not the station's primary stream.

(12) Simulcast.—A "simulcast" is a multicast stream of a television broadcast station that duplicates the programming transmitted by the primary stream or another multicast stream of such station.

(13) Subscriber; subscribe—

(A) Subscriber.—The term "subscriber" means a person or entity that receives a secondary transmission service from a cable system and pays a fee for the service, directly or indirectly, to the cable system.

(B) Subscribe.—The term "subscribe" means to elect to become a subscriber.

History of 17 U.S.C. §111: Oct. 19, 1976, P.L. 94-553, §101, 90 Stat. 2550; Aug. 27, 1986, P.L. 99-397, §§1, 2(a), (b), 100 Stat. 848; Nov. 16, 1988, P.L. 100-667, §202(1), 102 Stat. 3949; July 3, 1990, P.L. 101-318, §3(a), 104 Stat. 288; Dec. 17, 1993, P.L. 103-198, §6(a), 107 Stat. 2311; Oct. 18, 1994, P.L. 103-369, §3, 108 Stat. 3480; Nov. 1, 1995, P.L. 104-39, §5(b), 109 Stat. 348; Nov. 29, 1999, P.L. 106-13, §1011(a)(1), (2), (b)(1), 113 Stat. 1536, 1501A-543; Dec. 8, 2004, P.L. 108-447, §107(b), 118 Stat. 3406; May 30, 2005, P.L. 108-419, §5(a), 118 Stat. 2361; May 30, 2005, P.L. 109-303, §4(a), 120 Stat. 1481; May 8, 2008, P.L. 110-229, §807, 122 Stat. 874; Oct. 13, 2008, P.L. 110-403, §209(a)(2), 122 Stat. 4264; May 27, 2010, P.L. 111-175, §104(a)(1), (b), (c), (e), (g), 124 Stat. 1231-1238; Dec. 4, 2014, P.L. 113-200, §§201(1), 203, 128 Stat. 2066, 2067.

See also 17 U.S.C. §801; 37 C.F.R. §§201.17, 360.1-360.32, 387.1, 387.2.

ANNOTATIONS

§111(a)

National Football League v. PrimeTime 24 Jt.V., 211 F.3d 10, 12 (2d Cir.2000). If "a copyrighted signal is publicly performed or displayed only when received by viewers, there would be no need for a passive carrier exemption because these passive intermediate carriers 'do not transmit directly to the public.'"

WGN Cont'l Broad. Co. v. United Video, Inc., 693 F.2d 622, 624-25 (7th Cir.1982). "The [§111(a)(3)] exemption ... allows carriers such as [D] to act as purely passive intermediaries between broadcasters and the cable systems that carry the broadcast signals into the home, without incurring any copyright liability. The cable system selects the signals it wants to retransmit, pays the copyright owners for the right to retransmit their programs, and pays the intermediate carrier a fee for getting the signal from the broadcast station to the cable system. The intermediate carrier pays the copyright owners nothing, provided it really is passive in relation to what it transmits, like a telephone company. It may not even delete commercials; an important part of the scheme set up in §111 is the requirement that any cable system that wants to retransmit a broadcast signal without negotiating with the broadcast station or copyright owner transmit intact any commercials it receives from that station. *At 628:* We want to make clear, however, that our holding is not that [P] 'owns' the vertical blanking interval in the programs that it has copyrighted. The copyright is in the programming rather than in the method by which it is transmitted. If [P] devised a teletext that was not intended to be viewed in conjunction with the nine o'clock news—a cartoon show for preschoolers, for example—the fact that it used the vertical blanking intervals in the signal transmitting that news to encode the teletext would not give the teletext copyright protection as part of the nine o'clock news."

Infinity Broad. Corp. v. Kirkwood, 63 F.Supp.2d 420, 420 (S.D.N.Y.1999). "The issue before the Court is whether the passive carrier exemption provided by §111(a)(3) ... protects [D], which operates a dial-up 'listen line' service for monitoring copyrighted radio broadcasts in locations remote from that of the caller, from liability for copyright infringement. *At 425:* The question is whether [D] is the sort of passive agent whose activities ... are within the intended scope of the exemption. *At 426:* [T]he Court holds that [D], whose entire business consists of the retransmission of copyrighted or frequently copyrighted material, is not a carrier within the meaning of the statute."

Religious Tech. Ctr. v. Netcom On-Line Comm., 907 F.Supp. 1361, 1369 n.12 (N.D.Cal.1995). Section 111 "codifies the exemption for passive carriers who are otherwise liable for a secondary transmission. However, the carrier must not have any direct or indirect control over the content or selection of the primary transmission. In any event, common carriers are granted statutory exemptions for liability that might otherwise exist. Here, [D-usenet server] does not fall under this statutory exemption, and thus faces the usual strict liability scheme that exists for copyright."

§111(b)

Hubbard Broad., Inc. v. Southern Satellite Sys., 777 F.2d 393, 399-400 (8th Cir.1985). "At issue here is whether [TV station's] microwave signal[, broadcast simultaneously with its UHF signal,] 'is not made for reception by the public at large but is controlled and limited to reception by particular members of the public....' [¶] In our view, §111(b) is not intended to regulate the method of transmission but rather is intended to apply in those situations in which the primary transmitter itself seeks to limit the reception of its signal to 'particular members of the public.' Examples of situations in which §111(b) would be applicable include among others, closed circuit television, pay television, and pay cable. Central to each of these examples is the primary transmitter's specific intent and actual attempt to narrow the reception of its signal to an identifiable and distinct segment of the general public who generally will either subscribe to or purchase the service provided. Thus, if a secondary transmitter picks up this type of 'controlled' signal, §111(b) protects the primary transmitter and provides it with a remedy against the secondary transmitter even though the secondary transmitter might otherwise fit within the carrier exemption of §111(a)(3) or the compulsory licensing provision of §111(c)(1). *At 404:* [B]oth [D1] and the cable systems retransmit intact any commercials they receive from [D2] on [TV station's] signal. Thus, under the literal language of §111(c)(3), no infringement based upon commercial substitution has occurred. [¶] Additionally, we conclude that none of the concerns raised by Congress in adopting §111(c)(3) are implicated by [D2's] practices. [TV station], in placing only national advertising on the microwave signal, seeks to and in fact can economically address only the national advertising market. [D2] cannot effectively address the local advertising markets served by [P]. Thus, [D2] does not compete with [P] for local advertising dollars."

§111(c)

Fox TV Stations, Inc. v. AereoKiller, LLC, 851 F.3d 1002, 1006 (9th Cir.2017). "We must decide whether a service that captures copyrighted works broadcast over the air, and then retransmits them to paying subscribers over the Internet without the consent of the copyright holders, is a 'cable system' eligible for a compulsory license under the Copyright Act. [¶] Under §111 ..., a 'cable system' is eligible for a so-called compulsory license that allows it to retransmit 'a performance or display of a work' that had originally been broadcast by someone else—even if such material is copyrighted—without having to secure the consent of the copyright holder. So long as the cable system pays a statutory fee to the Copyright Office and complies with certain other regulations, it is protected from infringement liability. *At 1015:* [D] and other Internet-based retransmission services are neither clearly eligible nor clearly ineligible for the compulsory license §111 makes available to 'cable systems.' The Copyright Office says they are not eligible. Because the Office's views are persuasive, and because they are reasonable, we defer to them. The judgment of the district court is therefore [reversed]." *But see* ***WPIX, Inc. v. IVI, Inc.***, below.

WPIX, Inc. v. IVI, Inc., 691 F.3d 275, 282 (2d Cir. 2012). "[W]e conclude that Congress did not intend for §111's compulsory license to extend to Internet retransmissions." *But see* ***Fox TV Stations, Inc. v. AereoKiller, LLC***, above.

United Video, Inc. v. F.C.C., 890 F.2d 1173, 1184 (D.C.Cir.1989). 17 U.S.C. §111(c) "explicitly withholds a compulsory license from cable companies in cases where the FCC forbids the cable companies' transmissions. *At 1187 n.10:* [P]etitioners ... claim that [the FCC's syndicated exclusivity rules are] impermissible because of the Copyright Act's preemption [17 U.S.C. §301], which provides that all rights equivalent to exclusive rights within the general scope of copyright are governed exclusively by Title 17. However, §111, which is part of Title 17, specifically incorporates FCC regulations as part of the requirements governing the availability of compulsory licenses. The very act that incorporates FCC regulations cannot preempt those same regulations."

National Broad. Co. v. Copyright Royalty Tribunal, 848 F.2d 1289, 1293 (D.C.Cir.1988). "In order fully to effectuate the intent of Congress in passing §111, private orderings of ownership must be honored, so that those actually directly harmed by retransmissions are those who receive cable royalties. In short, determining that a party owns *a* copyright may be insufficient [for purposes of royalty distribution], for ... there may be more than one party able to claim the benefits of a copyright for portions of the property in question. *At 1296:* The [Copyright Royalty Tribunal (CRT)] determined that the directly affected party will *typically* be the exclusive syndicator, and that the CRT will therefore as a general rule always distribute royalties initially to the syndicator. This presumption by the CRT, in the face of congressional silence, is a permissible interpretation of the statute, to which we defer."

§111(d)

Independent Producers Grp. v. Librarian of Congress, 792 F.3d 132, 135 (D.C.Cir.2015). "Royalty fee distribution proceedings have two phases. During Phase I, claimants may group themselves into categories based on the kind of programming that they own. Using evidence supplied by the claimants, the [Copyright Royalty] Board calculates the marketplace value of each category. It then assigns a percentage of the total royalty fee fund to each category based on its value relative to other categories. During Phase II, the Board subdivides the fees allotted to each category among the individual claimants within that category. [¶] Phase I and Phase II proceedings follow the same set of procedures. First, the Board publishes a notice of the proceeding in the Federal Register. Claimants then petition to participate in the proceeding. A three-month voluntary negotiation period ensues, during which the participating claimants attempt to reach an agreement without assistance from the Board. *At 136:* At the end of the voluntary negotiation period, if any disputes remain, the Board plays a more active role in the process. The Board accepts written statements from the participating claimants, allows the participating claimants to conduct discovery, and orders a post-discovery settlement conference. If the participating claimants are still unable to resolve their differences, the Board then conducts a hearing and issues a final determination. Finally, the Librarian of Congress publishes the Board's determination in the Federal Register and distributes the royalty fees." *See also* ***Program Suppliers v. Librarian of Congress***, 409 F.3d 395, 397 (D.C.Cir.2005).

Universal City Studios LLLP v. Peters, 402 F.3d 1238, 1244 (D.C.Cir.2005). "The studios assume that they are entitled to royalties if they can prove they mailed their claims in July, but this 'misconstrues the Copyright Act and its regulations by equating mailing with filing.' ... Under the regulations, the studios are not entitled to royalties on a claim that arrives in August without a July U.S. postmark or a stamped postal receipt, regardless of how compelling the proof may be that the claim was mailed in July."

Barris Indus. v. Worldvision Enters., 875 F.2d 1446, 1449 n.1 (9th Cir.1989). "While we hold that [copyright owner] owns 100% of the royalties, we do not reach the issue of whether it is appropriate for the [Copyright Royalty Tribunal] to distribute royalties to [copyright owner] in the first instance. *At 1449:* [Distributor] urges us to conclude ... that a general rule exists that where the copyright is divided among two or more parties, the distributor of the program to over-the-air television is entitled to retain the statutory cable royalties under §111. [However,] the general rule favoring syndicators should not be seen as determinative of ownership. Ownership of the relevant copyright instead is a matter to be determined from the parties' contract. ... We agree with the D.C. Circuit that 'ownership is itself dependent on the contractual terms; it cannot be settled without reference to those terms.' We therefore reject [distributor's] contention that its position as distributor entitles it to statutory cable royalties as a matter of law."

Cablevision Sys. Dev. Co. v. Motion Picture Ass'n, 836 F.2d 599, 611 (D.C.Cir.1988). The "reasonableness of the regulatory requirement that all revenues from a tier containing one retransmitted broadcast signal be included in gross receipts cannot be attacked for its failure to allow cable systems to attribute a value to nonbroadcast programs and to subtract that value from gross receipts. We find no requirement in the statute or its history that the fee paid by a cable system reflect precisely the value it received from retransmissions—indeed, as we have shown, in many cases the relationship is skewed considerably. Congress instead chose an easily calculable revenue base and used the [distant signal equivalents] to approximate the value received by the cable companies."

National Ass'n of Broadcasters v. Copyright Royalty Tribunal, 809 F.2d 172, 175 (2d Cir.1986). "A cable system is protected from copyright liability when it carries only those signals and programs designated under the rules of the [FCC], and deposits semi-annual royalty payments into a central fund...."

Eastern Microwave, Inc. v. Doubleday Sports, Inc., 691 F.2d 125, 129 (2d Cir.1982). The retransmitting communication receiver "is entitled to the 'carrier' exemption if its activities are passive, merely retransmitting exactly what it receives, if it exercises no control over the content or selection of the primary transmission, or over the particular recipients of its transmission, and if its retransmission activities consist solely of providing wires, cables, or other communications channels for the use of others. *At 130:* The first question presented is thus whether [retransmitting communications carrier] exercised 'control over selection of the primary transmission' when it chose to retransmit [TV station] signal via satellite. *At 133:* It is undisputed that if each [cable television] system had its own string of microwave repeaters or satellite transponder it would be liable through the Tribunal to a copyright owner for only the one established royalty fee when and if it publicly performed the copyrighted work by making it available to its subscribers; and that such an integrated [cable television] system would not be liable for a second royalty fee for having itself retransmitted the original broadcast signal to its headend. We are unpersuaded by counsel's urging that a different result should obtain when a separate entity, e.g. [retransmitting communications carrier], supplies the retransmission service. That [retransmitting communications carrier] is a separate entity supplies no justification for subjecting [retransmitting communications carrier] to copyright liability when those same activities would not result in copyright liability if carried out by the [cable television] systems served by [retransmitting communications carrier]."

§111(f)

Satellite Broad. & Comms. v. Oman, 17 F.3d 344, 348 (11th Cir.1994). The "Copyright Office's construction of 'cable system' to exclude satellite carriers is neither arbitrary, capricious, nor contrary to the statute's 'clear meaning.' [T]he Copyright Office's exclusion of satellite carriers from the definition of 'cable systems' is an interpretation based on reasonable inferences drawn from statutory scheme and policy."

§112. LIMITATIONS ON EXCLUSIVE RIGHTS: EPHEMERAL RECORDINGS

(a)(1) Notwithstanding the provisions of section 106, and except in the case of a motion picture or other audiovisual work, it is not an infringement of copyright for a transmitting organization entitled to transmit to the public a performance or display of a work, under a license, including a statutory license under section 114(f), or transfer of the copyright or under the limitations on exclusive rights in sound recordings specified by section 114(a), or for a transmitting organization that is a broadcast radio or television station licensed as such by the Federal Communications Commission and that makes a broadcast transmission of a performance of a sound recording in a digital format on a nonsubscription basis, to make no more than one copy or phonorecord of a particular transmission program embodying the performance or display, if—

(A) the copy or phonorecord is retained and used solely by the transmitting organization that made it, and no further copies or phonorecords are reproduced from it; and

(B) the copy or phonorecord is used solely for the transmitting organization's own transmissions within its local service area, or for purposes of archival preservation or security; and

(C) unless preserved exclusively for archival purposes, the copy or phonorecord is destroyed within six months from the date the transmission program was first transmitted to the public.

(2) In a case in which a transmitting organization entitled to make a copy or phonorecord under paragraph (1) in connection with the transmission to the public of a performance or display of a work is prevented from making such copy or phonorecord by reason of the application by the copyright owner of technical measures that prevent the reproduction of the work, the copyright owner shall make available to the transmitting organization the necessary means for permitting the making of such copy or phonorecord as permitted under that paragraph, if it is technologically feasible and economically reasonable for the copyright owner to do so. If the copyright owner fails to do so in a timely manner in light of the transmitting organization's reasonable business requirements, the transmitting organization shall not be liable for a violation of section 1201(a)(1) of this title for engaging in such activities as are necessary to make such copies or phonorecords as permitted under paragraph (1) of this subsection.

(b) Notwithstanding the provisions of section 106, it is not an infringement of copyright for a governmental body or other nonprofit organization entitled to transmit a performance or display of a work, under section 110(2) or under the limitations on exclusive rights in sound recordings specified by section 114(a), to make no more than thirty copies or phonorecords of a particular transmission program embodying the performance or display, if—

(1) no further copies or phonorecords are reproduced from the copies or phonorecords made under this clause; and

(2) except for one copy or phonorecord that may be preserved exclusively for archival purposes, the copies or phonorecords are destroyed within seven years from the date the transmission program was first transmitted to the public.

(c) Notwithstanding the provisions of section 106, it is not an infringement of copyright for a governmental body or other nonprofit organization to make for distribution no more than one copy or phonorecord, for each transmitting organization specified in clause (2) of this subsection, of a particular transmission program embodying a performance of a nondramatic musical work of a religious nature, or of a sound recording of such a musical work, if—

(1) there is no direct or indirect charge for making or distributing any such copies or phonorecords; and

(2) none of such copies or phonorecords is used for any performance other than a single transmission to the public by a transmitting organization entitled to transmit to the public a performance of the work under a license or transfer of the copyright; and

(3) except for one copy or phonorecord that may be preserved exclusively for archival purposes, the copies or phonorecords are all destroyed within one year from the date the transmission program was first transmitted to the public.

(d) Notwithstanding the provisions of section 106, it is not an infringement of copyright for a governmental body or other nonprofit organization entitled to transmit a performance of a work under section 110(8) to make no more than ten copies or phonorecords embodying the performance, or to permit the use of any such copy or phonorecord by any governmental body or nonprofit organization entitled to transmit a performance of a work under section 110(8), if—

(1) any such copy or phonorecord is retained and used solely by the organization that made it, or by a governmental body or nonprofit organization entitled to transmit a performance of a work under section 110(8), and no further copies or phonorecords are reproduced from it; and

(2) any such copy or phonorecord is used solely for transmissions authorized under section 110(8), or for purposes of archival preservation or security; and

(3) the governmental body or nonprofit organization permitting any use of any such copy or phonorecord by any governmental body or nonprofit organization under this subsection does not make any charge for such use.

(e) Statutory license—

(1) A transmitting organization entitled to transmit to the public a performance of a sound recording under the limitation on exclusive rights specified by section 114(d)(1)(C)(iv) or under a statutory license in accordance with section 114(f) is entitled to a statutory license, under the conditions specified by this subsection, to make no more than 1 phonorecord of the sound recording (unless the terms and conditions of the statutory license allow for more), if the following conditions are satisfied:

(A) The phonorecord is retained and used solely by the transmitting organization that made it, and no further phonorecords are reproduced from it.

(B) The phonorecord is used solely for the transmitting organization's own transmissions originating in the United States under a statutory license in accordance with section 114(f) or the limitation on exclusive rights specified by section 114(d)(1)(C)(iv).

(C) Unless preserved exclusively for purposes of archival preservation, the phonorecord is destroyed within 6 months from the date the sound recording was first transmitted to the public using the phonorecord.

(D) Phonorecords of the sound recording have been distributed to the public under the authority of the copyright owner or the copyright owner authorizes the transmitting entity to transmit the sound recording, and the transmitting entity makes the phonorecord under this subsection from a phonorecord lawfully made and acquired under the authority of the copyright owner.

(2) Notwithstanding any provision of the antitrust laws, any copyright owners of sound recordings and any transmitting organizations entitled to a statutory license under this subsection may negotiate and agree upon royalty rates and license terms and conditions for making phonorecords of such sound recordings under this section and the proportionate division of fees paid among copyright owners, and may designate common agents to negotiate, agree to, pay, or receive such royalty payments.

(3) Proceedings under chapter 8 shall determine reasonable rates and terms of royalty payments for the activities specified by paragraph (1) during the 5-year period beginning on January 1 of the second year following the year in which the proceedings are to be commenced, or such other period as the parties may agree. Such rates shall include a minimum fee for each type of service offered by transmitting organizations. Any copyright owners of sound recordings or any transmitting organizations entitled to a statutory license under this subsection may submit to the Copyright Royalty Judges licenses covering such activities with respect to such sound recordings. The parties to each proceeding shall bear their own costs.

(4) The schedule of reasonable rates and terms determined by the Copyright Royalty Judges shall, subject to paragraph (5), be binding on all copyright owners of sound recordings and transmitting organizations entitled to a statutory license under this subsection during the 5-year period specified in paragraph (3), or such other period as the parties may agree. Such rates shall include a minimum fee for each type of service offered by transmitting organizations. The Copyright Royalty Judges shall establish rates that most clearly represent the fees that would have been negotiated in the marketplace between a willing buyer and a willing seller. In determining such rates and terms, the Copyright Royalty Judges shall base their decision on economic, competitive, and programming information presented by the parties, including—

(A) whether use of the service may substitute for or may promote the sales of phonorecords or otherwise interferes with or enhances the copyright owner's traditional streams of revenue; and

(B) the relative roles of the copyright owner and the transmitting organization in the copyrighted work and the service made available to the public with respect to relative creative contribution, technological contribution, capital investment, cost, and risk.

In establishing such rates and terms, the Copyright Royalty Judges may consider the rates and terms under voluntary license agreements described in paragraphs (2) and (3). The Copyright Royalty Judges shall also establish requirements by which copyright owners may receive reasonable notice of the use of their sound recordings under this section, and under which records of such use shall be kept and made available by transmitting organizations entitled to obtain a statutory license under this subsection.

(5) License agreements voluntarily negotiated at any time between 1 or more copyright owners of sound recordings and 1 or more transmitting organizations entitled to obtain a statutory license under this subsection shall be given effect in lieu of any decision by the Librarian of Congress or determination by the Copyright Royalty Judges.

(6)(A) Any person who wishes to make a phonorecord of a sound recording under a statutory license in accordance with this subsection may do so without infringing the exclusive right of the copyright owner of the sound recording under section 106(1)—

(i) by complying with such notice requirements as the Copyright Royalty Judges shall prescribe by regulation and by paying royalty fees in accordance with this subsection; or

(ii) if such royalty fees have not been set, by agreeing to pay such royalty fees as shall be determined in accordance with this subsection.

(B) Any royalty payments in arrears shall be made on or before the 20th day of the month next succeeding the month in which the royalty fees are set.

(7) If a transmitting organization entitled to make a phonorecord under this subsection is prevented from making such phonorecord by reason of the application by the copyright owner of technical measures that prevent the reproduction of the sound recording, the copyright owner shall make available to the transmitting organization the necessary means for permitting the making of such phonorecord as permitted under this subsection, if it is technologically feasible and economically reasonable for the copyright owner to do so. If the copyright owner fails to do so in a timely manner in light of the transmitting organization's reasonable business requirements, the transmitting organization shall not be liable for a violation of section 1201(a)(1) of this title for engaging in such activities as are necessary to make such phonorecords as permitted under this subsection.

(8) Nothing in this subsection annuls, limits, impairs, or otherwise affects in any way the existence or value of any of the exclusive rights of the copyright owners in a sound recording, except as otherwise provided in this subsection, or in a musical work, including the exclusive rights to reproduce and distribute a sound recording or musical work, including by means of a digital phonorecord delivery, under sections 106(1), 106(3), and 115, and the right to perform publicly a sound recording or musical work, including by means of a digital audio transmission, under sections 106(4) and 106(6).

(f)(1) Notwithstanding the provisions of section 106, and without limiting the application of subsection (b), it is not an infringement of copyright for a governmental body or other nonprofit educational institution entitled under section 110(2) to transmit a performance or display to make copies or phonorecords of a work that is in digital form and, solely to the extent permitted in paragraph (2), of a work that is in analog form, embodying the performance or display to be used for making transmissions authorized under section 110(2), if—

(A) such copies or phonorecords are retained and used solely by the body or institution that made them, and no further copies or phonorecords are reproduced from them, except as authorized under section 110(2); and

(B) such copies or phonorecords are used solely for transmissions authorized under section 110(2).

(2) This subsection does not authorize the conversion of print or other analog versions of works into digital formats, except that such conversion is permitted hereunder, only with respect to the amount of such works authorized to be performed or displayed under section 110(2), if—

(A) no digital version of the work is available to the institution; or

(B) the digital version of the work that is available to the institution is subject to technological protection measures that prevent its use for section 110(2).

(g) The transmission program embodied in a copy or phonorecord made under this section is not subject to protection as a derivative work under this title except with the express consent of the owners of copyright in the preexisting works employed in the program.

History of 17 U.S.C. §112: Oct. 19, 1976, P.L. 94-553, §101, 90 Stat. 2558; Oct. 28, 1998, P.L. 105-304, §§402, 405(b), 112 Stat. 2888; Aug. 5, 1999, P.L. 106-44, §1(b), 113 Stat. 221; Nov. 2, 2002, P.L. 107-273, §13301(c)(1), 116 Stat. 1912; May 30, 2005, P.L. 108-419, §5(b), 118 Stat. 2361.

See also 37 C.F.R. §§380.30-380.37, 382.1-382.8, 382.10-382.17, 383.1-383.4, 384.1-384.8.

§113. SCOPE OF EXCLUSIVE RIGHTS IN PICTORIAL, GRAPHIC, & SCULPTURAL WORKS

(a) Subject to the provisions of subsections (b) and (c) of this section, the exclusive right to reproduce a copyrighted pictorial, graphic, or sculptural work in copies under section 106 includes the right to reproduce the work in or on any kind of article, whether useful or otherwise.

(b) This title does not afford, to the owner of copyright in a work that portrays a useful article as such, any greater or lesser rights with respect to the making, distribution, or display of the useful article so portrayed than those afforded to such works under the law, whether title 17 or the common law or statutes of a State, in effect on December 31, 1977, as held applicable and construed by a court in an action brought under this title.

(c) In the case of a work lawfully reproduced in useful articles that have been offered for sale or other distribution to the public, copyright does not include any right to prevent the making, distribution, or display of pictures or photographs of such articles in connection with advertisements or commentaries related to the distribution or display of such articles, or in connection with news reports.

(d)(1) In a case in which—

(A) a work of visual art has been incorporated in or made part of a building in such a way that removing the work from the building will cause the destruction, distortion, mutilation, or other modification of the work as described in section 106A(a)(3), and

(B) the author consented to the installation of the work in the building either before the effective date set forth in section 610(a) of the Visual Artists Rights Act of 1990, or in a written instrument executed on or after such effective date that is signed by the owner of the building and the author and that specifies that installation of the work may subject the work to destruction, distortion, mutilation, or other modification, by reason of its removal,

then the rights conferred by paragraphs (2) and (3) of section 106A(a) shall not apply.

(2) If the owner of a building wishes to remove a work of visual art which is a part of such building and which can be removed from the building without the destruction, distortion, mutilation, or other modification of the work as described in section 106A(a)(3), the author's rights under paragraphs (2) and (3) of section 106A(a) shall apply unless—

(A) the owner has made a diligent, good faith attempt without success to notify the author of the owner's intended action affecting the work of visual art, or

(B) the owner did provide such notice in writing and the person so notified failed, within 90 days after receiving such notice, either to remove the work or to pay for its removal.

For purposes of subparagraph (A), an owner shall be presumed to have made a diligent, good faith attempt to send notice if the owner sent such notice by registered mail to the author at the most recent address of the author that was recorded with the Register of Copyrights pursuant to paragraph (3). If the work is removed at the expense of the author, title to that copy of the work shall be deemed to be in the author.

(3) The Register of Copyrights shall establish a system of records whereby any author of a work of visual art that has been incorporated in or made part of a building, may record his or her identity and address with the Copyright Office. The Register shall also establish procedures under which any such author may update the information so recorded, and procedures under which owners of buildings may record with the

Copyright Office evidence of their efforts to comply with this subsection.

History of 17 U.S.C. §113: Oct. 19, 1976, P.L. 94-553, §101, 90 Stat. 2560; Dec. 1, 1990, P.L. 101-650, §604, 104 Stat. 5130.

See also 37 C.F.R. §201.25.

§114. SCOPE OF EXCLUSIVE RIGHTS IN SOUND RECORDINGS

(a) The exclusive rights of the owner of copyright in a sound recording are limited to the rights specified by clauses (1), (2), (3) and (6) of section 106, and do not include any right of performance under section 106(4).

(b) The exclusive right of the owner of copyright in a sound recording under clause (1) of section 106 is limited to the right to duplicate the sound recording in the form of phonorecords or copies that directly or indirectly recapture the actual sounds fixed in the recording. The exclusive right of the owner of copyright in a sound recording under clause (2) of section 106 is limited to the right to prepare a derivative work in which the actual sounds fixed in the sound recording are rearranged, remixed, or otherwise altered in sequence or quality. The exclusive rights of the owner of copyright in a sound recording under clauses (1) and (2) of section 106 do not extend to the making or duplication of another sound recording that consists entirely of an independent fixation of other sounds, even though such sounds imitate or simulate those in the copyrighted sound recording. The exclusive rights of the owner of copyright in a sound recording under clauses (1), (2), and (3) of section 106 do not apply to sound recordings included in educational television and radio programs (as defined in section 397 of title 47) distributed or transmitted by or through public broadcasting entities (as defined by section 118(f)): *Provided*, That copies or phonorecords of said programs are not commercially distributed by or through public broadcasting entities to the general public.

(c) This section does not limit or impair the exclusive right to perform publicly, by means of a phonorecord, any of the works specified by section 106(4).

(d) Limitations on exclusive right.—Notwithstanding the provisions of section 106(6)—

(1) Exempt transmissions and retransmissions.—The performance of a sound recording publicly by means of a digital audio transmission, other than as a part of an interactive service, is not an infringement of section 106(6) if the performance is part of—

(A) a nonsubscription broadcast transmission;

(B) a retransmission of a nonsubscription broadcast transmission: *Provided*, That, in the case of a retransmission of a radio station's broadcast transmission—

(i) the radio station's broadcast transmission is not willfully or repeatedly retransmitted more than a radius of 150 miles from the site of the radio broadcast transmitter, however—

(I) the 150 mile limitation under this clause shall not apply when a nonsubscription broadcast transmission by a radio station licensed by the Federal Communications Commission is retransmitted on a nonsubscription basis by a terrestrial broadcast station, terrestrial translator, or terrestrial repeater licensed by the Federal Communications Commission; and

(II) in the case of a subscription retransmission of a nonsubscription broadcast retransmission covered by subclause (I), the 150 mile radius shall be measured from the transmitter site of such broadcast retransmitter;

(ii) the retransmission is of radio station broadcast transmissions that are—

(I) obtained by the retransmitter over the air;

(II) not electronically processed by the retransmitter to deliver separate and discrete signals; and

(III) retransmitted only within the local communities served by the retransmitter;

(iii) the radio station's broadcast transmission was being retransmitted to cable systems (as defined in section 111(f)) by a satellite carrier on January 1, 1995, and that retransmission was being retransmitted by cable systems as a separate and discrete signal, and the satellite carrier obtains the radio station's broadcast transmission in an analog format: *Provided*, That the broadcast transmission being retransmitted may embody the programming of no more than one radio station; or

(iv) the radio station's broadcast transmission is made by a noncommercial educational broadcast station funded on or after January 1, 1995, under section 396(k) of the Communications Act of 1934 (47 U.S.C. 396(k)), consists solely of noncommercial educational and cultural radio programs, and the retransmission, whether or not simultaneous, is a nonsubscription terrestrial broadcast retransmission; or

(C) a transmission that comes within any of the following categories—

(i) a prior or simultaneous transmission incidental to an exempt transmission, such as a feed received by and then retransmitted by an exempt transmitter: *Provided*, That such incidental transmissions do not include any subscription transmission directly for reception by members of the public;

(ii) a transmission within a business establishment, confined to its premises or the immediately surrounding vicinity;

(iii) a retransmission by any retransmitter, including a multichannel video programming distributor as defined in section 602(12) of the Communications Act of 1934 (47 U.S.C. 522(12)), of a transmission by a transmitter licensed to publicly perform the sound recording as a part of that transmission, if the retransmission is simultaneous with the licensed transmission and authorized by the transmitter; or

(iv) a transmission to a business establishment for use in the ordinary course of its business: *Provided*, That the business recipient does not retransmit the transmission outside of its premises or the immediately surrounding vicinity, and that the transmission does not exceed the sound recording performance complement. Nothing in this clause shall limit the scope of the exemption in clause (ii).

(2) Statutory licensing of certain transmissions.—The performance of a sound recording publicly by means of a subscription digital audio transmission not exempt under paragraph (1), an eligible nonsubscription transmission, or a transmission not exempt under paragraph (1) that is made by a preexisting satellite digital audio radio service shall be subject to statutory licensing, in accordance with subsection (f) if—

(A)(i) the transmission is not part of an interactive service;

(ii) except in the case of a transmission to a business establishment, the transmitting entity does not automatically and intentionally cause any device receiving the transmission to switch from one program channel to another; and

(iii) except as provided in section 1002(e), the transmission of the sound recording is accompanied, if technically feasible, by the information encoded in that sound recording, if any, by or under the authority of the copyright owner of that sound recording, that identifies the title of the sound recording, the featured recording artist who performs on the sound recording, and related information, including information concerning the underlying musical work and its writer;

(B) in the case of a subscription transmission not exempt under paragraph (1) that is made by a preexisting subscription service in the same transmission medium used by such service on July 31, 1998, or in the case of a transmission not exempt under paragraph (1) that is made by a preexisting satellite digital audio radio service—

(i) the transmission does not exceed the sound recording performance complement; and

(ii) the transmitting entity does not cause to be published by means of an advance program schedule or prior announcement the titles of the specific sound recordings or phonorecords embodying such sound recordings to be transmitted; and

(C) in the case of an eligible nonsubscription transmission or a subscription transmission not exempt under paragraph (1) that is made by a new subscription service or by a preexisting subscription service other than in the same transmission medium used by such service on July 31, 1998—

(i) the transmission does not exceed the sound recording performance complement, except that this requirement shall not apply in the case of a retransmission of a broadcast transmission if the retransmission is made by a transmitting entity that does not have the right or ability to control the programming of the broadcast station making the broadcast transmission, unless—

(I) the broadcast station makes broadcast transmissions—

(aa) in digital format that regularly exceed the sound recording performance complement; or

(bb) in analog format, a substantial portion of which, on a weekly basis, exceed the sound recording performance complement; and

(II) the sound recording copyright owner or its representative has notified the transmitting entity in writing that broadcast transmissions of the copyright owner's sound recordings exceed the sound recording performance complement as provided in this clause;

(ii) the transmitting entity does not cause to be published, or induce or facilitate the publication, by means of an advance program schedule or prior announcement, the titles of the specific sound recordings to be transmitted, the phonorecords embodying such sound recordings, or, other than for illustrative purposes, the names of the featured recording artists, except that this clause does not disqualify a transmitting entity that makes a prior announcement that a particular artist will be featured within an unspecified future time period, and in the case of a retransmission of a broadcast transmission by a transmitting entity that does not have the right or ability to control the programming of the broadcast transmission, the requirement of this clause shall not apply to a prior oral announcement by the broadcast station, or to an advance program schedule published, induced, or facilitated by the broadcast station, if the transmitting entity does not have actual knowledge and has not received written notice from the copyright owner or its representative that the broadcast station publishes or induces or facilitates the publication of such advance program schedule, or if such advance program schedule is a schedule of classical music programming published by the broadcast station in the same manner as published by that broadcast station on or before September 30, 1998;

(iii) the transmission—

(I) is not part of an archived program of less than 5 hours duration;

(II) is not part of an archived program of 5 hours or greater in duration that is made available for a period exceeding 2 weeks;

(III) is not part of a continuous program which is of less than 3 hours duration; or

(IV) is not part of an identifiable program in which performances of sound recordings are rendered in a predetermined order, other than an archived or continuous program, that is transmitted at—

(aa) more than 3 times in any 2-week period that have been publicly announced in advance, in the case of a program of less than 1 hour in duration, or

(bb) more than 4 times in any 2-week period that have been publicly announced in advance, in the case of a program of 1 hour or more in duration,

except that the requirement of this subclause shall not apply in the case of a retransmission of a broadcast transmission by a transmitting entity that does not have the right or ability to control the programming of the broadcast transmission, unless the transmitting entity is given notice in writing by the copyright owner of the sound recording that the broadcast station makes broadcast transmissions that regularly violate such requirement;

(iv) the transmitting entity does not knowingly perform the sound recording, as part of a service that offers transmissions of visual images contemporaneously with transmissions of sound recordings, in a manner that is likely to cause confusion, to cause mistake, or to deceive, as to the affiliation, connection, or association of the copyright owner or featured recording artist with the transmitting entity or a particular product or service advertised by the transmitting entity, or as to the origin, sponsorship, or approval by the copyright owner or featured recording artist of the activities of the transmitting entity other than the performance of the sound recording itself;

(v) the transmitting entity cooperates to prevent, to the extent feasible without imposing substantial costs or burdens, a transmission recipient or any other person or entity from automatically scanning the transmitting entity's transmissions alone or together with transmissions by other transmitting entities in order to select a particular sound recording to be transmitted to the transmission recipient, except that the requirement of this clause shall not apply to a satellite digital audio service that is in operation, or that is licensed by the Federal Communications Commission, on or before July 31, 1998;

(vi) the transmitting entity takes no affirmative steps to cause or induce the making of a phonorecord by the transmission recipient, and if the technology used by the transmitting entity enables the transmitting entity to limit the making by the transmission recipient of phonorecords of the transmission directly in a digital format, the transmitting entity sets such technology to limit such making of phonorecords to the extent permitted by such technology;

(vii) phonorecords of the sound recording have been distributed to the public under the authority of the copyright owner or the copyright owner authorizes the transmitting entity to transmit the sound recording, and the transmitting entity makes the transmission from a phonorecord lawfully made under the authority of the copyright owner, except that the requirement of this clause shall not apply to a retransmission of a broadcast transmission by a transmitting entity that does not have the right or ability to control the programming of the broadcast transmission, unless the transmitting entity is given notice in writing by the copyright owner of the sound recording that the broadcast station makes broadcast transmissions that regularly violate such requirement;

(viii) the transmitting entity accommodates and does not interfere with the transmission of technical measures that are widely used by sound recording copyright owners to identify or protect copyrighted works, and that are technically feasible of being transmitted by the transmitting entity without imposing substantial costs on the transmitting entity or resulting in perceptible aural or visual degradation of the digital signal, except that the requirement of this clause shall not apply to a satellite digital audio service that is in operation, or that is licensed under the authority of the Federal Communications Commission, on or before July 31, 1998, to the extent that such service has designed, developed, or made commitments to procure equipment or technology that is not compatible with such technical measures before such technical measures are widely adopted by sound recording copyright owners; and

(ix) the transmitting entity identifies in textual data the sound recording during, but not before, the time it is performed, including the title of the sound recording, the title of the phonorecord embodying such sound recording, if any, and the featured recording artist, in a manner to permit it to be displayed to the transmission recipient by the device or technology intended for receiving the service provided by the transmitting entity, except that the obligation in this clause shall not take effect until 1 year after Oct. 28, 1998 and shall not apply in the case of a retransmission of a broadcast transmission by a transmitting entity that does not have the right or ability to control the programming of the broadcast transmission, or in the case in which devices or technology intended for receiving the service provided by the transmitting entity that have the capability to display such textual data are not common in the marketplace.

(3) Licenses for transmissions by interactive services—

(A) No interactive service shall be granted an exclusive license under section 106(6) for the performance of a sound recording publicly by means of digital audio transmission for a period in excess of 12 months, except that with respect to an exclusive license granted to an interactive service by a licensor that holds the copyright to 1,000 or fewer sound recordings, the period of such license shall not exceed 24 months: *Provided, however*, That the grantee of such exclusive license shall be ineligible to receive another exclusive license for the performance of that sound recording for a period of 13 months from the expiration of the prior exclusive license.

(B) The limitation set forth in subparagraph (A) of this paragraph shall not apply if—

(i) the licensor has granted and there remain in effect licenses under section 106(6) for the public performance of sound recordings by means of digital audio transmission by at least 5 different interactive services: *Provided, however*, That each such license must be for a minimum of 10 percent of the copyrighted sound recordings owned by the licensor that have been licensed to interactive services, but in no event less than 50 sound recordings; or

(ii) the exclusive license is granted to perform publicly up to 45 seconds of a sound recording and the sole purpose of the performance is to promote the distribution or performance of that sound recording.

(C) Notwithstanding the grant of an exclusive or nonexclusive license of the right of public performance under section 106(6), an interactive service may not publicly perform a sound recording unless a license has been granted for the public performance of any copyrighted musical work contained in the sound recording: *Provided*, That such license to publicly perform the copyrighted musical work may be granted either by a performing rights society representing the copyright owner or by the copyright owner.

(D) The performance of a sound recording by means of a retransmission of a digital audio transmission is not an infringement of section 106(6) if—

(i) the retransmission is of a transmission by an interactive service licensed to publicly perform the sound recording to a particular member of the public as part of that transmission; and

(ii) the retransmission is simultaneous with the licensed transmission, authorized by the transmitter, and limited to that particular member of the public intended by the interactive service to be the recipient of the transmission.

(E) For the purposes of this paragraph—

(i) a "licensor" shall include the licensing entity and any other entity under any material degree of common ownership, management, or control that owns copyrights in sound recordings; and

(ii) a "performing rights society" is an association or corporation that licenses the public performance of nondramatic musical works on behalf of the copyright owner, such as the American Society of Composers, Authors and Publishers, Broadcast Music, Inc., and SESAC, Inc.

(4) Rights not otherwise limited—

(A) Except as expressly provided in this section, this section does not limit or impair the exclusive right to perform a sound recording publicly by means of a digital audio transmission under section 106(6).

(B) Nothing in this section annuls or limits in any way—

(i) the exclusive right to publicly perform a musical work, including by means of a digital audio transmission, under section 106(4);

(ii) the exclusive rights in a sound recording or the musical work embodied therein under sections 106(1), 106(2) and 106(3); or

(iii) any other rights under any other clause of section 106, or remedies available under this title, as such rights or remedies exist either before or after Nov. 1, 1995.

(C) Any limitations in this section on the exclusive right under section 106(6) apply only to the exclusive right under section 106(6) and not to any other exclusive rights under section 106. Nothing in this section shall be construed to annul, limit, impair or otherwise affect in any way the ability of the owner of a copyright in a sound recording to exercise the rights under sections 106(1), 106(2) and 106(3), or to obtain the remedies available under this title pursuant to such rights, as such rights and remedies exist either before or after Nov. 1, 1995.

(e) Authority for negotiations—

(1) Notwithstanding any provision of the antitrust laws, in negotiating statutory licenses in accordance with subsection (f), any copyright owners of sound recordings and any entities performing sound recordings affected by this section may negotiate and agree upon the royalty rates and license terms and conditions for the performance of such sound recordings and the proportionate division of fees paid among copyright owners, and may designate common agents on a nonexclusive basis to negotiate, agree to, pay, or receive payments.

(2) For licenses granted under section 106(6), other than statutory licenses, such as for performances by interactive services or performances that exceed the sound recording performance complement—

(A) copyright owners of sound recordings affected by this section may designate common agents to act on their behalf to grant licenses and receive and remit royalty payments: *Provided*, That each copyright owner shall establish the royalty rates and material license terms and conditions unilaterally, that is, not in agreement, combination, or concert with other copyright owners of sound recordings; and

(B) entities performing sound recordings affected by this section may designate common agents to act on their behalf to obtain licenses and collect and pay royalty fees: *Provided*, That each entity performing sound recordings shall determine the royalty rates and material license terms and conditions unilaterally, that is, not in agreement, combination, or concert with other entities performing sound recordings.

(f) Licenses for certain nonexempt transmissions—

(1)(A) Proceedings under chapter 8 shall determine reasonable rates and terms of royalty payments for subscription transmissions by preexisting subscription services and transmissions by preexisting satellite digital audio radio services specified by subsection (d)(2) during the 5-year period beginning on January 1 of the second year following the year in which the proceedings are to be commenced, except in the case of a different transitional period provided under section 6(b)(3) of the Copyright Royalty and Distribution Reform Act of 2004, or such other period as the parties may agree. Such terms and rates shall distinguish among the different types of digital audio transmission services then in operation. Any copyright owners of sound recordings, preexisting subscription services, or preexisting satellite digital audio radio services may submit to the Copyright Royalty Judges licenses covering such subscription transmissions with respect to such sound recordings. The parties to each proceeding shall bear their own costs.

(B) The schedule of reasonable rates and terms determined by the Copyright Royalty Judges shall, subject to paragraph (3), be binding on all copyright owners of sound recordings and entities performing sound recordings affected by this paragraph during the 5-year period specified in subparagraph (A), a transitional period provided under section 6(b)(3) of the Copyright Royalty and Distribution Reform Act of 2004, or such other period as the parties may agree. In establishing rates and terms for preexisting subscription services and preexisting satellite digital audio radio services, in addition to the objectives set forth in section 801(b)(1), the Copyright Royalty Judges may consider the rates and terms for comparable types of subscription digital audio transmission services and comparable circumstances under voluntary license agreements described in subparagraph (A).

(C) The procedures under subparagraphs (A) and (B) also shall be initiated pursuant to a petition filed by any copyright owners of sound recordings, any preexisting subscription services, or any preexisting satellite digital audio radio services indicating that a new type of subscription digital audio transmission service on which sound recordings are performed is or is about to become operational, for the purpose of determining reasonable terms and rates of royalty payments with respect to such new type of transmission service for the period beginning with the inception of such new type of service and ending on the date on which the royalty rates and terms for subscription digital audio transmission services most recently determined under subparagraph (A) or (B) and chapter 8 expire, or such other period as the parties may agree.

(2)(A) Proceedings under chapter 8 shall determine reasonable rates and terms of royalty payments for public performances of sound recordings by means of eligible nonsubscription transmission services and new subscription services specified by subsection (d)(2) during the 5-year period beginning on January 1 of the second year following the year in which the proceedings are to be commenced, except in the case of a different transitional period provided under section 6(b)(3) of the Copyright Royalty and Distribution Reform Act of 2004, or such other period as the parties may agree. Such rates and terms shall distinguish among the different types of eligible nonsubscription transmission services and new subscription services then in operation and shall include a minimum fee for each such type of service. Any copyright owners of sound recordings or any entities performing sound recordings affected by this paragraph may submit to the Copyright Royalty Judges licenses covering such eligible nonsubscription transmissions and new subscription services with respect to such sound recordings. The parties to each proceeding shall bear their own costs.

(B) The schedule of reasonable rates and terms determined by the Copyright Royalty Judges shall, subject to paragraph (3), be binding on all copyright owners of sound recordings and entities performing sound recordings affected by this paragraph during the 5-year period specified in subparagraph (A), a transitional period provided under section 6(b)(3) of the Copyright Royalty and Distribution Act[1] of 2004, or such other period as the parties may agree. Such rates and terms shall distinguish among the different types of eligible nonsubscription transmission services then in operation and shall include a minimum fee for each such type of service, such differences to be based on criteria including, but not limited to, the quantity and nature of the use of sound recordings and the degree to which use of the service may substitute for or may promote the purchase of phonorecords by consumers. In establishing rates and terms for transmissions by eligible nonsubscription services and new subscription services, the Copyright Royalty Judges shall establish rates and terms that most clearly represent the rates and terms that would have been negotiated in the marketplace between a willing buyer and a willing seller. In determining such rates and terms, the Copyright Royalty Judges shall base their decision on economic, competitive and programming information presented by the parties, including—

(i) whether use of the service may substitute for or may promote the sales of phonorecords or otherwise may interfere with or may enhance the sound recording copyright owner's other streams of revenue from its sound recordings; and

(ii) the relative roles of the copyright owner and the transmitting entity in the copyrighted work and the service made available to the public with respect to relative creative contribution, technological contribution, capital investment, cost, and risk.

In establishing such rates and terms, the Copyright Royalty Judges may consider the rates and terms for comparable types of digital audio transmission services and comparable circumstances under voluntary license agreements described in subparagraph (A).

(C) The procedures under subparagraphs (A) and (B) shall also be initiated pursuant to a petition filed by any copyright owners of sound recordings or any eligible nonsubscription service or new subscription service indicating that a new type of eligible nonsubscription service or new subscription service on which sound recordings are performed is or is about to become operational, for the purpose of determining reasonable terms and rates of royalty payments with respect to such new type of service for the period beginning with the inception of such new type of service and ending on the date on which the royalty rates and terms for eligible nonsubscription services and new subscription services, as the case may be, most recently determined under subparagraph (A) or (B) and chapter 8 expire, or such other period as the parties may agree.

(3) License agreements voluntarily negotiated at any time between 1 or more copyright owners of sound recordings and 1 or more entities performing sound recordings shall be given effect in lieu of any decision by the Librarian of Congress or determination by the Copyright Royalty Judges.

(4)(A) The Copyright Royalty Judges shall also establish requirements by which copyright owners may receive reasonable notice of the use of their sound recordings under this section, and under which records of such use shall be kept and made available by entities performing sound recordings. The notice and recordkeeping rules in effect on the day before the effective date of the Copyright Royalty and Distribution Reform Act of 2004 shall remain in effect unless and until new regulations are promulgated by the Copyright Royalty Judges. If new regulations are promulgated under this subparagraph, the Copyright Royalty Judges shall take into account the substance and effect of the rules in effect on the day before the effective date of the Copyright Royalty and Distribution Reform Act of 2004 and shall, to the extent practicable, avoid significant disruption of the functions of any designated agent authorized to collect and distribute royalty fees.

(B) Any person who wishes to perform a sound recording publicly by means of a transmission eligible for statutory licensing under this subsection may do so without infringing the exclusive right of the copyright owner of the sound recording—

(i) by complying with such notice requirements as the Copyright Royalty Judges shall prescribe by regulation and by paying royalty fees in accordance with this subsection; or

(ii) if such royalty fees have not been set, by agreeing to pay such royalty fees as shall be determined in accordance with this subsection.

(C) Any royalty payments in arrears shall be made on or before the twentieth day of the month next succeeding the month in which the royalty fees are set.

(5)(A) Notwithstanding section 112(e) and the other provisions of this subsection, the receiving agent may enter into agreements for the reproduction and performance of sound recordings under section 112(e) and this section by any 1 or more commercial webcasters or noncommercial webcasters for a period of not more than 11 years beginning on January 1, 2005, that, once published in the Federal Register pursuant to subparagraph (B), shall be binding on all copyright owners of sound recordings and other persons entitled to payment under this section, in lieu of any determination by the Copyright Royalty Judges. Any such agreement for commercial webcasters may include provisions for payment of royalties on the basis of a percentage of revenue or expenses, or both, and include a minimum fee. Any such agreement may include other terms and conditions, including requirements by which copyright owners may receive notice of the use of their sound recordings and under which records of such use shall be kept and made available by commercial webcasters or noncommercial webcasters. The receiving agent shall be under no obligation to negotiate any such agreement. The receiving agent shall have no obligation to any copyright owner of sound recordings or any other person entitled to payment under this section in negotiating any such agreement, and no liability to any copyright owner of sound recordings or any other person entitled to payment under this section for having entered into such agreement.

(B) The Copyright Office shall cause to be published in the Federal Register any agreement entered into pursuant to subparagraph (A). Such publication shall include a statement containing the substance of subparagraph (C). Such agreements shall not be included in the Code of Federal Regulations. Thereafter, the terms of such agreement shall be available, as an option, to any commercial webcaster or noncommercial webcaster meeting the eligibility conditions of such agreement.

(C) Neither subparagraph (A) nor any provisions of any agreement entered into pursuant to subparagraph (A), including any rate structure, fees, terms, conditions, or notice and recordkeeping requirements set forth therein, shall be admissible as evidence or otherwise taken into account in any administrative, judicial, or other government proceeding involving the setting or adjustment of the royalties payable for the public performance or reproduction in ephemeral phonorecords or copies of sound recordings, the determination of terms or conditions related thereto, or the establishment of notice or recordkeeping requirements by the Copyright Royalty Judges under paragraph (4) or section 112(e)(4). It is the intent of Congress that any royalty rates, rate structure, definitions, terms, conditions, or notice and recordkeeping requirements, included in such agreements shall be considered as a compromise motivated by the unique business, economic and political circumstances of webcasters, copyright owners, and performers rather than as matters that would have been negotiated in the marketplace between a willing buyer and a willing seller, or otherwise meet the objectives set forth in section 801(b). This subparagraph shall not apply to the extent that the receiving agent and a webcaster that is party to an agreement entered into pursuant to subparagraph (A) expressly authorize the submission of the agreement in a proceeding under this subsection.

(D) Nothing in the Webcaster Settlement Act of 2008, the Webcaster Settlement Act of 2009, or any agreement entered into pursuant to subparagraph (A) shall be taken into account by the United States Court of Appeals for the District of Columbia Circuit in its review of the determination by the Copyright Royalty Judges of May 1, 2007, of rates and terms for the digital performance of sound recordings and ephemeral recordings, pursuant to sections 112 and 114.

(E) As used in this paragraph—

(i) the term "noncommercial webcaster" means a webcaster that—

(I) is exempt from taxation under section 501 of the Internal Revenue Code of 1986 (26 U.S.C. 501);

(II) has applied in good faith to the Internal Revenue Service for exemption from taxation under section 501 of title 26 and has a commercially reasonable expectation that such exemption shall be granted; or

(III) is operated by a State or possession or any governmental entity or subordinate thereof, or by the United States or District of Columbia, for exclusively public purposes;

(ii) the term "receiving agent" shall have the meaning given that term in section 261.2 of title 37, Code of Federal Regulations, as published in the Federal Register on July 8, 2002; and

(iii) the term "webcaster" means a person or entity that has obtained a compulsory license under section 112 or 114 and the implementing regulations therefor.

(F) The authority to make settlements pursuant to subparagraph (A) shall expire at 11:59 p.m. Eastern time on the 30th day after June 30, 2009.

(g) Proceeds from licensing of transmissions—

(1) Except in the case of a transmission licensed under a statutory license in accordance with subsection (f) of this section—

(A) a featured recording artist who performs on a sound recording that has been licensed for a transmission shall be entitled to receive payments from the copyright owner of the sound recording in accordance with the terms of the artist's contract; and

(B) a nonfeatured recording artist who performs on a sound recording that has been licensed for a transmission shall be entitled to receive payments from the copyright owner of the sound recording in accordance with the terms of the nonfeatured recording artist's applicable contract or other applicable agreement.

(2) An agent designated to distribute receipts from the licensing of transmissions in accordance with subsection (f) shall distribute such receipts as follows:

(A) 50 percent of the receipts shall be paid to the copyright owner of the exclusive right under section 106(6) of this title to publicly perform a sound recording by means of a digital audio transmission.

(B) 2½ percent of the receipts shall be deposited in an escrow account managed by an independent administrator jointly appointed by copyright owners of sound recordings and the American Federation of Musicians (or any successor entity) to be distributed to nonfeatured musicians (whether or not members of the American Federation of Musicians) who have performed on sound recordings.

(C) 2½ percent of the receipts shall be deposited in an escrow account managed by an independent administrator jointly appointed by copyright owners of sound recordings and the American Federation of Television and Radio Artists (or any successor entity) to be distributed to nonfeatured vocalists (whether or not members of the American Federation of Television and Radio Artists) who have performed on sound recordings.

(D) 45 percent of the receipts shall be paid, on a per sound recording basis, to the recording artist or artists featured on such sound recording (or the persons conveying rights in the artists' performance in the sound recordings).

(3) A nonprofit agent designated to distribute receipts from the licensing of transmissions in accordance with subsection (f) may deduct from any of its receipts, prior to the distribution of such receipts to any person or entity entitled thereto other than copyright owners and performers who have elected to receive royalties from another designated agent and have notified such nonprofit agent in writing of such election, the reasonable costs of such agent incurred after November 1, 1995, in—

(A) the administration of the collection, distribution, and calculation of the royalties;

(B) the settlement of disputes relating to the collection and calculation of the royalties; and

(C) the licensing and enforcement of rights with respect to the making of ephemeral recordings and performances subject to licensing under section 112 and this section, including those incurred in participating in negotiations or arbitration proceedings under section 112 and this section, except that all costs incurred relating to the section 112 ephemeral recordings right may only be deducted from the royalties received pursuant to section 112.

(4) Notwithstanding paragraph (3), any designated agent designated to distribute receipts from the licensing of transmissions in accordance with subsection (f) may deduct from any of its receipts, prior to the distribution of such receipts, the reasonable costs identified in paragraph (3) of such agent incurred after November 1, 1995, with respect to such copyright owners and performers who have entered with such agent a contractual relationship that specifies that such costs may be deducted from such royalty receipts.

(h) Licensing to affiliates.—

(1) If the copyright owner of a sound recording licenses an affiliated entity the right to publicly perform a sound recording by means of a digital audio transmission under section 106(6), the copyright owner shall make the licensed sound recording available under section 106(6) on no less favorable terms and conditions to all bona fide entities that offer similar services, except that, if there are material differences in the scope of the requested license with respect to the type of service, the particular sound recordings licensed, the frequency of use, the number of subscribers served, or the duration, then the copyright owner may establish different terms and conditions for such other services.

(2) The limitation set forth in paragraph (1) of this subsection shall not apply in the case where the copyright owner of a sound recording licenses—

(A) an interactive service; or

(B) an entity to perform publicly up to 45 seconds of the sound recording and the sole purpose of the performance is to promote the distribution or performance of that sound recording.

(i) No effect on royalties for underlying works.—License fees payable for the public performance of sound recordings under section 106(6) shall not be taken into account in any administrative, judicial, or other governmental proceeding to set or adjust the royalties payable to copyright owners of musical works for the public performance of their works. It is the intent of Congress that royalties payable to copyright owners of musical works for the public performance of their works shall not be diminished in any respect as a result of the rights granted by section 106(6).

(j) Definitions.—As used in this section, the following terms have the following meanings:

(1) An "affiliated entity" is an entity engaging in digital audio transmissions covered by section 106(6), other than an interactive service, in which the licensor has any direct or indirect partnership or any ownership interest amounting to 5 percent or more of the outstanding voting or non-voting stock.

(2) An "archived program" is a predetermined program that is available repeatedly on the demand of the transmission recipient and that is performed in the same order from the beginning, except that an archived program shall not include a recorded event or broadcast transmission that makes no more than an incidental use of sound recordings, as long as such recorded event or broadcast transmission does not contain an entire sound recording or feature a particular sound recording.

(3) A "broadcast" transmission is a transmission made by a terrestrial broadcast station licensed as such by the Federal Communications Commission.

(4) A "continuous program" is a predetermined program that is continuously performed in the same order and that is accessed at a point in the program that is beyond the control of the transmission recipient.

(5) A "digital audio transmission" is a digital transmission as defined in section 101, that embodies the transmission of a sound recording. This term does not include the transmission of any audiovisual work.

(6) An "eligible nonsubscription transmission" is a noninteractive nonsubscription digital audio transmission not exempt under subsection (d)(1) that is made as part of a service that provides audio programming consisting, in whole or in part, of performances of sound recordings, including retransmissions of broadcast transmissions, if the primary purpose of the service is to provide to the public such audio or other entertainment programming, and the primary purpose of the service is not to sell, advertise, or promote particular products or services other than sound recordings, live concerts, or other music-related events.

(7) An "interactive service" is one that enables a member of the public to receive a transmission of a program specially created for the recipient, or on request, a transmission of a particular sound recording, whether or not as part of a program, which is selected by or on behalf of the recipient. The ability of individuals to request that particular sound recordings be performed for reception by the public at large, or in the case of a subscription service, by all subscribers of the service, does not make a service interactive, if the programming on each channel of the service does not substantially consist of sound recordings that are performed within 1 hour of the request or at a time designated by either the transmitting entity or the individual making such request. If an entity offers both interactive and noninteractive services (either concurrently or at different times), the noninteractive component shall not be treated as part of an interactive service.

(8) A "new subscription service" is a service that performs sound recordings by means of noninteractive subscription digital audio transmissions and that is not a preexisting subscription service or a preexisting satellite digital audio radio service.

(9) A "nonsubscription" transmission is any transmission that is not a subscription transmission.

(10) A "preexisting satellite digital audio radio service" is a subscription satellite digital audio radio service provided pursuant to a satellite digital audio radio service license issued by the Federal Communications Commission on or before July 31, 1998, and any renewal of such license to the extent of the scope of the original license, and may include a limited number of sample channels representative of the subscription service that are made available on a nonsubscription basis in order to promote the subscription service.

(11) A "preexisting subscription service" is a service that performs sound recordings by means of noninteractive audio-only subscription digital audio transmissions, which was in existence and was making such transmissions to the public for a fee on or before July 31, 1998, and may include a limited number of sample channels representative of the subscription service that are made available on a nonsubscription basis in order to promote the subscription service.

(12) A "retransmission" is a further transmission of an initial transmission, and includes any further retransmission of the same transmission. Except as provided in this section, a transmission qualifies as a "retransmission" only if it is simultaneous with the initial transmission. Nothing in this definition shall be construed to exempt a transmission that fails to satisfy a separate element required to qualify for an exemption under section 114(d)(1).

(13) The "sound recording performance complement" is the transmission during any 3-hour period, on a particular channel used by a transmitting entity, of no more than—

(A) 3 different selections of sound recordings from any one phonorecord lawfully distributed for public performance or sale in the United States, if no more than 2 such selections are transmitted consecutively; or

(B) 4 different selections of sound recordings—

(i) by the same featured recording artist; or

(ii) from any set or compilation of phonorecords lawfully distributed together as a unit for public performance or sale in the United States,

if no more than three such selections are transmitted consecutively:

Provided, That the transmission of selections in excess of the numerical limits provided for in clauses (A) and (B) from multiple phonorecords shall nonetheless qualify as a sound recording performance complement if the programming of the multiple phonorecords was not willfully intended to avoid the numerical limitations prescribed in such clauses.

(14) A "subscription" transmission is a transmission that is controlled and limited to particular recipients, and for which consideration is required to be paid or otherwise given by or on behalf of the recipient to receive the transmission or a package of transmissions including the transmission.

(15) A "transmission" is either an initial transmission or a retransmission.

1. **Editor's note:** Probably should be "Copyright Royalty and Distribution Reform Act."

History of 17 U.S.C. §114: Oct. 19, 1976, P.L. 94-553, §101, 90 Stat. 2560; Nov. 1, 1995, P.L. 104-39, §3, 109 Stat. 336; Nov. 13, 1997, P.L. 105-80, §3, 111 Stat. 1531; Oct. 28, 1998, P.L. 105-304, §405(a)(1)-(4), 112 Stat. 2890; Dec. 4, 2002, P.L. 107-321, §§4, 5(b), (c), 116 Stat. 2781, 2784; May 30, 2005, P.L. 108-419, §5(c), 118 Stat. 2362; May 30, 2005, P.L. 109-303, §4(b), 120 Stat. 1481; Oct. 16, 2008, P.L. 110-435, §2, 122 Stat. 4974; June 30, 2009, P.L. 111-36, §2, 123 Stat. 1926; Dec. 9, 2010, P.L. 111-295, §§5(b), 6(b), (f)(1), 124 Stat. 3181.

See also 37 C.F.R. §§380.30-380.37, 382.1-382.8, 382.10-382.17, 383.1-383.4, 384.1-384.8.

ANNOTATIONS

§114(b)

VMG Salsoul, LLC v. Ciccone, 824 F.3d 871, 874 (9th Cir.2016). "We ... reject [P's] argument that Congress eliminated the 'de minimis' exception to claims alleging infringement of a sound recording. We recognize that the Sixth Circuit held to the contrary in ***Bridgeport Music, Inc. v. Dimension Films***, 410 F.3d 792 (6th Cir.2005), but—like the leading copyright treatise and several district courts—we find ***Bridgeport***'s reasoning unpersuasive. We hold that the 'de minimis' exception applies to infringement actions concerning copyrighted sound recordings, just as it applies to all other copyright infringement actions. *At 878:* A 'use is de minimis only if the average audience would not recognize the appropriation.' *At 886:* Because we conclude that Congress intended to maintain the 'de minimis' exception for copyrights to sound recordings, we take the unusual step of creating a circuit split by disagreeing with the Sixth Circuit's contrary holding in ***Bridgeport***. *At 887:* We hold that the 'de minimis' exception applies to actions alleging infringement of a copyright to sound recordings." *See also* ***Newton v. Diamond***, 388 F.3d 1189, 1192-93 (9th Cir.2004) (sampling was trivial and noninfringing); ***Saregama India Ltd. v. Mosley***, 687 F.Supp.2d 1325, 1340 (S.D.Fla. 2009) (D's recording infringes on P's recording if D (1) samples any sound from P's recording and (2) imitates or simulates P's recording), *aff'd*, 635 F.3d 1284 (11th Cir.2011).

§114(d)

Bonneville Int'l v. Peters, 347 F.3d 485, 500 (3d Cir.2003). "Section 114(d)(1)(A)'s non-subscription broadcast transmission's exemption implicates only over-the-air radio broadcast transmissions, and does not cover the internet streaming of AM/FM broadcast signals."

§114(f)

Intercollegiate Broad. Sys. v. Copyright Royalty Bd., 796 F.3d 111, 128-29 (D.C.Cir.2015). Section 114(f)(2)(B) "requires the [Copyright Royalty] Board to impose a 'minimum fee for each such *type* of service,' ... not for each individual webcaster. [T]he Board must [also] set a fee that both a willing buyer *and* a willing seller would negotiate, not just one that is acceptable to the buyer (the webcaster). The Act does not permit [petitioner] to veto a fee simply by objecting."

Intercollegiate Broad. Sys. v. Copyright Royalty Bd., 574 F.3d 748, 757 (D.C.Cir.2009). Section 114(f)(2)(B) "does not require that the market assumed by the Judges achieve metaphysical perfection in competitiveness. *At 761:* [I]t was not error for the Judges to reject the small commercial webcasters' pleas that paying per performance would wreck their inefficient business models. The Judges made clear they could not 'guarantee a profitable business to every market entrant.' The Judges are not required to preserve the business of every participant in a market. They are required to set rates and terms that 'most clearly represent the rates and terms that would have been negotiated in the marketplace between a willing buyer and a willing seller.' If small commercial webcasters cannot pay the same rate as other willing buyers and still earn a profit, then the Judges are not required to accommodate them."

§114(j)

SoundExchange, Inc. v. Muzak LLC, 854 F.3d 713, 716 (D.C.Cir.2017). "The parties quarrel over the meaning of the phrase 'such transmissions.' [D] argues that 'such transmissions' refers to the general category of transmissions identified in the preceding part of the definition [for 'preexisting subscription service']: noninteractive audio-only subscription digital audio transmissions made by an entity that was in existence and making that category of transmissions on or before July 31, 1998. [¶] [D's] reading of 'such transmissions' is the more persuasive. But we do not think the crucial phrase is 'such transmissions.' Rather, it is the term 'service,' which is also disputed. Does 'service' refer only to the business entity, or does it also include the original program offerings? Put differently, does the grandfather rate inhere in the business or the product? [¶] Unfortunately, the statute is quite unclear. It uses the word 'service' in both senses.

At 719: [A]lthough the Register did not decide our issue, she did emphasize that the grandfather clause should be interpreted narrowly. [¶] The grandfather provisions were intended to protect prior investments the three business entities had made during a more favorable pre-1998 rate-setting regulatory climate. '[D] was [a] pioneer music service that incurred both the benefits and risks that came with its investment[ ]'.... But when [D] expands its operations and provides additional transmissions to subscribers to a different 'service,' ... this is an entirely new investment. [¶] We conclude ... that the better interpretation of the statute is that the term 'service' contemplates a double limitation; both the business and the program offering must qualify before the transmissions are eligible for the favorable rate."

Arista Records, LLC v. Launch Media, Inc., 578 F.3d 148, 149-50 (2d Cir.2009). "We are the first federal appellate court called upon to determine whether a webcasting service that provides users with individualized internet radio stations—the content of which can be affected by users' ratings of songs, artists, and albums—is an interactive service within the meaning of ... §114(j)(7). If it is an interactive service, the webcasting service would be required to pay individual licensing fees to those copyright holders of the sound recordings of songs the webcasting service plays for its users. If it is not an interactive service, the webcasting service must only pay a statutory licensing fee set by the Copyright Royalty Board. [T]he webcasting service is not an interactive service as a matter of law."

§115. SCOPE OF EXCLUSIVE RIGHTS IN NONDRAMATIC MUSICAL WORKS: COMPULSORY LICENSE FOR MAKING & DISTRIBUTING PHONORECORDS

In the case of nondramatic musical works, the exclusive rights provided by clauses (1) and (3) of section 106, to make and to distribute phonorecords of such works, are subject to compulsory licensing under the conditions specified by this section.

(a) Availability and scope of compulsory license—

(1) When phonorecords of a nondramatic musical work have been distributed to the public in the United States under the authority of the copyright owner, any other person, including those who make phonorecords or digital phonorecord deliveries, may, by complying with the provisions of this section, obtain a compulsory license to make and distribute phonorecords of the work. A person may obtain a compulsory license only if his or her primary purpose in making phonorecords is to distribute them to the public for private use, including by means of a digital phonorecord delivery. A person may not obtain a compulsory license for use of the work in the making of phonorecords duplicating a sound recording fixed by another, unless: (i) such sound recording was fixed lawfully; and (ii) the making of the phonorecords was authorized by the owner of copyright in the sound recording or, if the sound recording was fixed before February 15, 1972, by any person who fixed the sound recording pursuant to an express license from the owner of the copyright in the musical work or pursuant to a valid compulsory license for use of such work in a sound recording.

(2) A compulsory license includes the privilege of making a musical arrangement of the work to the extent necessary to conform it to the style or manner of interpretation of the performance involved, but the arrangement shall not change the basic melody or fundamental character of the work, and shall not be subject to protection as a derivative work under this title, except with the express consent of the copyright owner.

(b) Notice of intention to obtain compulsory license—

(1) Any person who wishes to obtain a compulsory license under this section shall, before or within thirty days after making, and before distributing any phonorecords of the work, serve notice of intention to do so on the copyright owner. If the registration or other public records of the Copyright Office do not identify the copyright owner and include an address at which notice can be served, it shall be sufficient to file the notice of intention in the Copyright Office. The notice shall comply, in form, content, and manner of service, with requirements that the Register of Copyrights shall prescribe by regulation.

(2) Failure to serve or file the notice required by clause (1) forecloses the possibility of a compulsory license and, in the absence of a negotiated license, renders the making and distribution of phonorecords actionable as acts of infringement under section 501 and fully subject to the remedies provided by sections 502 through 506 and 509.

(c) Royalty payable under compulsory license—

(1) To be entitled to receive royalties under a compulsory license, the copyright owner must be identified in the registration or other public records of the Copyright Office. The owner is entitled to royalties for phonorecords made and distributed after being so identified, but is not entitled to recover for any phonorecords previously made and distributed.

(2) Except as provided by clause (1), the royalty under a compulsory license shall be payable for every phonorecord made and distributed in accordance with the license. For this purpose, and other than as provided in paragraph (3), a phonorecord is considered "distributed" if the person exercising the compulsory license has voluntarily and permanently parted with its possession. With respect to each work embodied in the phonorecord, the royalty shall be either two and three-fourths cents, or one-half of one cent per minute of playing time or fraction thereof, whichever amount is larger.

(3)(A) A compulsory license under this section includes the right of the compulsory licensee to distribute or authorize the distribution of a phonorecord of a nondramatic musical work by means of a digital transmission which constitutes a digital phonorecord delivery, regardless of whether the digital transmission is also a public performance of the sound recording under section 106(6) of this title or of any nondramatic musical work embodied therein under section 106(4) of this title. For every digital phonorecord delivery by or under the authority of the compulsory licensee—

(i) on or before December 31, 1997, the royalty payable by the compulsory licensee shall be the royalty prescribed under paragraph (2) and chapter 8 of this title; and

(ii) on or after January 1, 1998, the royalty payable by the compulsory licensee shall be the royalty prescribed under subparagraphs (B) through (E) and chapter 8 of this title.

(B) Notwithstanding any provision of the antitrust laws, any copyright owners of nondramatic musical works and any persons entitled to obtain a compulsory license under subsection (a)(1) may negotiate and agree upon the terms and rates of royalty payments under this section and the proportionate division of fees paid among copyright owners, and may designate common agents on a nonexclusive basis to negotiate, agree to, pay or receive such royalty payments. Such authority to negotiate the terms and rates of royalty payments includes, but is not limited to, the authority to negotiate the year during which the royalty rates prescribed under this subparagraph and subparagraphs (C) through (E) and chapter 8 of this title shall next be determined.

(C) Proceedings under chapter 8 shall determine reasonable rates and terms of royalty payments for the activities specified by this section during the period beginning with the effective date of such rates and terms, but not earlier than January 1 of the second year following the year in which the petition requesting the proceeding is filed, and ending on the effective date of successor rates and terms, or such other period as the parties may agree. Such terms and rates shall distinguish between (i) digital phonorecord deliveries where the reproduction or distribution of a phonorecord is incidental to the transmission which constitutes the digital phonorecord delivery, and (ii) digital phonorecord deliveries in general. Any copyright owners of nondramatic musical works and any persons entitled to obtain a compulsory license under subsection (a)(1) may submit to the Copyright Royalty Judges licenses covering such activities. The parties to each proceeding shall bear their own costs.

(D) The schedule of reasonable rates and terms determined by the Copyright Royalty Judges shall, subject to subparagraph (E), be binding on all copyright owners of nondramatic musical works and persons entitled to obtain a compulsory license under subsection (a)(1) during the period specified in subparagraph (C), such other period as may be determined pursuant to subparagraphs (B) and (C), or such other period as the parties may agree. Such terms and rates shall distinguish between (i) digital phonorecord deliveries where the reproduction or distribution of a phonorecord is incidental to the transmission which constitutes the digital phonorecord delivery, and (ii) digital phonorecord deliveries in general. In addition to the objectives set forth in section 801(b)(1), in establishing such rates and terms, the Copyright Royalty Judges may consider rates and terms under voluntary license agreements described in subparagraphs (B) and (C). The royalty rates payable for a compulsory license for a digital phonorecord delivery under this section shall be established de novo and no precedential effect shall be given to the amount of the royalty payable by a compulsory licensee for digital phonorecord deliveries on or before December 31, 1997. The Copyright Royalty Judges shall also establish requirements by which copyright owners may receive reasonable notice of the use of their works under this section, and under which records of such use shall be kept and made available by persons making digital phonorecord deliveries.

(E)(i) License agreements voluntarily negotiated at any time between one or more copyright owners of nondramatic musical works and one or more persons entitled to obtain a compulsory license under subsection (a)(1) shall be given effect in lieu of any determination by the Librarian of Congress and Copyright Royalty Judges. Subject to clause (ii), the royalty rates determined pursuant to subparagraph (C) and (D) shall be given effect as to digital phonorecord deliveries in lieu of any contrary royalty rates specified in a contract pursuant to which a recording artist who is the author of a nondramatic musical work grants a license under that person's exclusive rights in the musical work under paragraphs (1) and (3) of section 106 or commits another person to grant a license in that musical work under paragraphs (1) and (3) of section 106, to a person desiring to fix in a tangible medium of expression a sound recording embodying the musical work.

(ii) The second sentence of clause (i) shall not apply to—

(I) a contract entered into on or before June 22, 1995, and not modified thereafter for the purpose of reducing the royalty rates determined pursuant to subparagraph (C) and (D) or of increasing the number of musical works within the scope of the contract covered by the reduced rates, except if a contract entered into on or before June 22, 1995, is modified thereafter for the purpose of increasing the number of musical works within the scope of the contract, any contrary royalty rates specified in the contract shall be given effect in lieu of royalty rates determined pursuant to subparagraph (C) and (D) for the number of musical works within the scope of the contract as of June 22, 1995; and

(II) a contract entered into after the date that the sound recording is fixed in a tangible medium of expression substantially in a form intended for commercial release, if at the time the contract is entered into, the recording artist retains the right to grant licenses as to the musical work under paragraphs (1) and (3) of section 106.

(F) Except as provided in section 1002(e) of this title, a digital phonorecord delivery licensed under this paragraph shall be accompanied by the information encoded in the sound recording, if any, by or under the authority of the copyright owner of that sound recording, that identifies the title of the sound recording, the featured recording artist who performs on the sound recording, and related information, including information concerning the underlying musical work and its writer.

(G)(i) A digital phonorecord delivery of a sound recording is actionable as an act of infringement under section 501, and is fully subject to the remedies provided by sections 502 through 506, unless—

(I) the digital phonorecord delivery has been authorized by the copyright owner of the sound recording; and

(II) the owner of the copyright in the sound recording or the entity making the digital phonorecord delivery has obtained a compulsory license under this section or has otherwise been authorized by the copyright owner of the musical work to distribute or authorize the distribution, by means of a digital phonorecord delivery, of each musical work embodied in the sound recording.

(ii) Any cause of action under this subparagraph shall be in addition to those available to the owner of the copyright in the nondramatic musical work under subsection (c)(6) and section 106(4) and the owner of the copyright in the sound recording under section 106(6).

(H) The liability of the copyright owner of a sound recording for infringement of the copyright in a nondramatic musical work embodied in the sound recording shall be determined in accordance with applicable law, except that the owner of a copyright in a sound recording shall not be liable for a digital phonorecord delivery by a third party if the owner of the copyright in the sound recording does not license the distribution of a phonorecord of the nondramatic musical work.

(I) Nothing in section 1008 shall be construed to prevent the exercise of the rights and remedies allowed by this paragraph, paragraph (6), and chapter 5 in the event of a digital phonorecord delivery, except that no action alleging infringement of copyright may be brought under this title against a manufacturer, importer or distributor of a digital audio recording device, a digital audio recording medium, an analog recording device, or an analog recording medium, or against a consumer, based on the actions described in such section.

(J) Nothing in this section annuls or limits (i) the exclusive right to publicly perform a sound recording or the musical work embodied therein, including by means of a digital transmission, under sections 106(4) and 106(6), (ii) except for compulsory licensing under the conditions specified by this section, the exclusive rights to reproduce and distribute the sound recording and the musical work embodied therein under sections 106(1) and 106(3), including by means of a digital phonorecord delivery, or (iii) any other rights under any other provision of section 106, or remedies available under this title, as such rights or remedies exist either before or after Nov. 1, 1995.

(K) The provisions of this section concerning digital phonorecord deliveries shall not apply to any exempt transmissions or retransmissions under section 114(d)(1). The exemptions created in section 114(d)(1) do not expand or reduce the rights of copyright owners under section 106 (1) through (5) with respect to such transmissions and retransmissions.

(4) A compulsory license under this section includes the right of the maker of a phonorecord of a nondramatic musical work under subsection (a)(1) to distribute or authorize distribution of such phonorecord by rental, lease, or lending (or by acts or practices in the nature of rental, lease, or lending). In addition to any royalty payable under clause (2) and chapter 8 of this title, a royalty shall be payable by the compulsory licensee for every act of distribution of a phonorecord by or in the nature of rental, lease, or lending, by or under the authority of the compulsory licensee. With respect to each nondramatic musical work embodied in the phonorecord, the royalty shall be a proportion of the revenue received by the compulsory licensee from every such act of distribution of the phonorecord under this clause equal to the proportion of the revenue received by the compulsory licensee from distribution of the phonorecord under clause (2) that is payable by a compulsory licensee under that clause and under chapter 8. The Register of Copyrights shall issue regulations to carry out the purpose of this clause.

(5) Royalty payments shall be made on or before the twentieth day of each month and shall include all royalties for the month next preceding. Each monthly payment shall be made under oath and shall comply with requirements that the Register of Copyrights shall prescribe by regulation. The Register shall also prescribe regulations under which detailed cumulative annual statements of account, certified by a certified public accountant, shall be filed for every compulsory license under this section. The regulations covering both the monthly and the annual statements of account shall prescribe the form, content, and manner of certification with respect to the number of records made and the number of records distributed.

(6) If the copyright owner does not receive the monthly payment and the monthly and annual statements of account when due, the owner may give written notice to the licensee that, unless the default is remedied within thirty days from the date of the notice, the compulsory license will be automatically terminated. Such termination renders either the making or the distribution, or both, of all phonorecords for which the royalty has not been paid, actionable as acts of infringement under section 501 and fully subject to the remedies provided by sections 502 through 506.

(d) Definition.—As used in this section, the following term has the following meaning: A "digital phonorecord delivery" is each individual delivery of a phonorecord by digital transmission of a sound recording which results in a specifically identifiable reproduction by or for any transmission recipient of a phonorecord of that sound recording, regardless of whether the digital transmission is also a public performance of the sound recording or any nondramatic musical work embodied therein. A digital phonorecord delivery does not result from a real-time, non-interactive subscription transmission of a sound recording where no reproduction of the sound recording or the musical work embodied therein is made from the inception of the transmission through to its receipt by the transmission recipient in order to make the sound recording audible.

History of 17 U.S.C. §115: Oct. 19, 1976, P.L. 94-553, §101, 90 Stat. 2561; Oct. 4, 1984, P.L. 98-450, §3, 98 Stat. 1727; Nov. 1, 1995, P.L. 104-39, §4, 109 Stat. 344; Nov. 13, 1997, P.L. 105-80, §§4, 10, 12(a)(7), 111 Stat. 1531, 1534; May 30, 2005, P.L. 108-419, §5(d), 118 Stat. 2364; May 30, 2005, P.L. 109-303, §4(c), 120 Stat. 1482; Oct. 13, 2008, P.L. 110-403, §209(a)(3), 122 Stat. 4264.

See also 37 C.F.R. §§201.18, 385.1-385.26.

ANNOTATIONS

Recording Indus. Ass'n v. Librarian of Congress, 608 F.3d 861, 863-64 (D.C.Cir.2010). "By law, the Copyright Royalty Board sets the terms and rates for copyright royalties when copyright owners and licensees fail to negotiate terms and rates themselves. [¶] Section 115 ... allows an individual to make and distribute phonorecords (that is, sound recordings) of a copyrighted musical work without reaching any kind of agreement with the copyright owner. That right does not include authorization to make exact copies of an existing sound recording and distribute it; if a musical work has been recorded and copyrighted by another artist, a licensee 'may exercise his rights under the [§115] license only by assembling his own musicians, singers, recording engineers and equipment, etc. for the purpose of recording anew the musical work that is the subject of the [§115] license.' [¶] The §115 licensing regime operates in a fairly straightforward manner. When a copyright owner distributes work 'to the public,' §115's provisions are triggered. Once that occurs, anyone may 'obtain a compulsory license to make and distribute phonorecords of the work' under §115 so long as the 'primary purpose in making [the] phonorecords is to distribute them to the public for private use.' Assuming the copyright has been registered with the Copyright Office, the licensee owes the copyright owner a royalty for every phonorecord 'made and distributed in accordance with the [§115] license.' For purposes of the Copyright Act, a phonorecord is 'distributed'—and an obligation to pay the copyright owner a royalty created—when 'the person exercising the [§115] license has voluntarily and permanently parted with' the phonorecord. In other words, the licensee's sale of its recording of the copyright owner's work triggers the royalty payment obligation."

Leadsinger, Inc. v. BMG Music Publ'g, 512 F.3d 522, 526 (9th Cir.2008). Section 115's "compulsory licensing scheme does not apply to audiovisual works. *At 527:* The definition of phonorecords is explicit ... that audiovisual works are not phonorecords and are excluded from §115's compulsory licensing scheme. [P's] karaoke device meets each element of the statutory definition of audiovisual works and, therefore, cannot be a phonorecord. *At 529:* [P] also is not entitled to a declaration that compulsory mechanical licenses under §115 allow it to reprint lyrics in booklets that accompany its karaoke products. [L]yrics are separately copyrightable as literary works. Section 115 covers only the right to 'make and distribute phonorecords.' Though these phonorecords may include oral renditions of song lyrics, the reproduction of song lyrics on paper is not within the scope of §115. [¶] We hold that [P's] karaoke machine falls within the definition of an audiovisual work. As a result, in addition to any §115 compulsory licenses necessary to make and distribute phonorecords and reprint licenses necessary to reprint song lyrics, [P] is also required to secure synchronization licenses to display images of song lyrics in timed relation with recorded music."

Palladium Music, Inc. v. EatSleepMusic, Inc., 398 F.3d 1193, 1199 (10th Cir.2005). "Under §115, a party intending to make and distribute a sound recording of a previously published musical work may obtain a compulsory license in that work simply by complying with the statutory requirements, including timely and sufficient notice to the owner of the copyright in the musical work and payment of statutory, or otherwise negotiated, royalties. Thus, the exclusive rights of copyright owners of previously published musical works are limited only in that they are required (hence the term 'compulsory') to license the work to a party who has complied with §115. *At 1200:* [P's] sound recordings are derivative works, and its copyrights in the sound recordings are invalid and unenforceable because it has failed to obtain compulsory or consensual licenses from the copyright owners of the underlying musical compositions as required by ... §115. Further, [P's] argument [that the sound recordings were distributed only on a wholesale basis and not retail or 'directly to the public' as required by §115(a)(1)] has no application to the 'distributed to the public' reference in §115(a)(1)."

U.S. v. ASCAP, 485 F.Supp.2d 438, 447 (S.D.N.Y. 2007), *aff'd*, 627 F.3d 64 (2d Cir.2010). "[T]he delivery of a music file to a purchaser via a download constitutes a mechanical reproduction of the copyrighted work in the form of a 'digital phonorecord delivery' as set forth in ... §115(d)."

§116. NEGOTIATED LICENSES FOR PUBLIC PERFORMANCES BY MEANS OF COIN-OPERATED PHONORECORD PLAYERS

(a) Applicability of section.—This section applies to any nondramatic musical work embodied in a phonorecord.

(b) Negotiated licenses—

(1) Authority for negotiations.—Any owners of copyright in works to which this section applies and any operators of coin-operated phonorecord players may negotiate and agree upon the terms and rates of royalty payments for the performance of such works and the proportionate division of fees paid among copyright owners, and may designate common agents to negotiate, agree to, pay, or receive such royalty payments.

(2) Chapter 8 proceeding.—Parties not subject to such a negotiation may have the terms and rates and the division of fees described in paragraph (1) determined in a proceeding in accordance with the provisions of chapter 8.

(c) License agreements superior to determinations by Copyright Royalty Judges.—License agreements between one or more copyright owners and one or more operators of coin-operated phonorecord players, which are negotiated in accordance with subsection (b), shall be given effect in lieu of any otherwise applicable determination by the Copyright Royalty Judges.

(d) Definitions.—As used in this section, the following terms mean the following:

(1) A "coin-operated phonorecord player" is a machine or device that—

(A) is employed solely for the performance of nondramatic musical works by means of phonorecords upon being activated by the insertion of coins, currency, tokens, or other monetary units or their equivalent;

(B) is located in an establishment making no direct or indirect charge for admission;

(C) is accompanied by a list which is comprised of the titles of all the musical works available for performance on it, and is affixed to the phonorecord player or posted in the establishment in a prominent position where it can be readily examined by the public; and

(D) affords a choice of works available for performance and permits the choice to be made by the patrons of the establishment in which it is located.

(2) An "operator" is any person who, alone or jointly with others—

(A) owns a coin-operated phonorecord player;

(B) has the power to make a coin-operated phonorecord player available for placement in an establishment for purposes of public performance; or

(C) has the power to exercise primary control over the selection of the musical works made available for public performance on a coin-operated phonorecord player.

(e) to (g) Repealed.

History of 17 U.S.C. §116: Oct. 31, 1988, P.L. 100-568, §4(a)(4), 102 Stat. 2855; Dec. 17, 1993, P.L. 103-198, §3(b)(1), 107 Stat. 2309; Nov. 13, 1997, P.L. 105-80, §5, 111 Stat. 1531; May 30, 2005, P.L. 108-419, §5(e), 118 Stat. 2365.

See also 37 C.F.R. §§388.1-388.3; Berne Convention.

§117. LIMITATIONS ON EXCLUSIVE RIGHTS: COMPUTER PROGRAMS

(a) Making of additional copy or adaptation by owner of copy.—Notwithstanding the provisions of section 106, it is not an infringement for the owner of a copy of a computer program to make or authorize the making of another copy or adaptation of that computer program provided:

(1) that such a new copy or adaptation is created as an essential step in the utilization of the computer program in conjunction with a machine and that it is used in no other manner, or

(2) that such new copy or adaptation is for archival purposes only and that all archival copies are destroyed in the event that continued possession of the computer program should cease to be rightful.

(b) Lease, sale, or other transfer of additional copy or adaptation.—Any exact copies prepared in accordance with the provisions of this section may be leased, sold, or otherwise transferred, along with the copy from which such copies were prepared, only as part of the lease, sale, or other transfer of all rights in the program. Adaptations so prepared may be transferred only with the authorization of the copyright owner.

(c) Machine maintenance or repair.—Notwithstanding the provisions of section 106, it is not an infringement for the owner or lessee of a machine to make or authorize the making of a copy of a computer program if such copy is made solely by virtue of the activation of a machine that lawfully contains an authorized copy of the computer program, for purposes only of maintenance or repair of that machine, if—

(1) such new copy is used in no other manner and is destroyed immediately after the maintenance or repair is completed; and

(2) with respect to any computer program or part thereof that is not necessary for that machine to be activated, such program or part thereof is not accessed or used other than to make such new copy by virtue of the activation of the machine.

(d) Definitions.—For purposes of this section—

(1) the "maintenance" of a machine is the servicing of the machine in order to make it work in accordance with its original specifications and any changes to those specifications authorized for that machine; and

(2) the "repair" of a machine is the restoring of the machine to the state of working in accordance with its original specifications and any changes to those specifications authorized for that machine.

History of 17 U.S.C. §117: Oct. 19, 1976, P.L. 94-553, §101, 90 Stat. 2565; Dec. 12, 1980, P.L. 96-517, §10(b), 94 Stat. 3028; Oct. 28, 1998, P.L. 105-304, §302, 112 Stat. 2887.

See also WIPO Copyright Treaty arts. 4, 7.

ANNOTATIONS

Vernor v. Autodesk, Inc., 621 F.3d 1102, 1109 (9th Cir.2010). "Congress enacted the **essential step defense** to codify that a software user who is the 'owner of a copy' of a copyrighted software program does not infringe by making a copy of the computer program, if the new copy is 'created as an essential step in the utilization of the computer program in conjunction with a machine and ... is used in no other manner.' *At 1111:* We hold today that a software user is a licensee rather than an owner of a copy where the copyright owner (1) specifies that the user is granted a license; (2) significantly restricts the user's ability to transfer the software; and (3) imposes notable use restrictions. Applying our holding to [copyright owner's license], we conclude that [original software purchaser] was a licensee rather than an owner of copies of [software] and thus was not entitled to invoke the first sale doctrine or the essential step defense. *At 1112:* Because [D] was not an owner, his customers are also not owners of [software] copies. Therefore, when they install [software] on their computers, the copies of the software that they make during installation infringe [copyright owner's] exclusive reproduction right because they too are not entitled to the benefit of the essential step defense. *At 1113:* Although ***DSC*** is ... narrower than ***MAI***, it does not conflict with our holding today that a software customer bound by a restrictive license agreement may be a licensee of a copy not entitled to the first sale doctrine or the essential step defense."

Wall Data Inc. v. Los Angeles Cty. Sheriff's Dept., 447 F.3d 769, 785 (9th Cir.2006). "[I]f a software developer retains ownership of every copy of software, and merely licenses the use of those copies, §117 does not apply." *But see* ***DSC Comms. v. Pulse Comms.***, this page.

Storage Tech. v. Custom Hardware Eng'g & Consulting, Inc., 421 F.3d 1307, 1312 (Fed.Cir.2005). "The requirement in §117(c)(1) that the new copy of the computer program be destroyed after maintenance or repair is completed can be achieved in most cases by turning off the machine, which erases the copy from RAM. [¶] The term 'repair' denotes fixing a broken machine that is no longer 'working in accordance with its original specifications.' That term would apply whenever there is a discrete problem with the machine, e.g., when there are 'worn or defective components such as memory chips, circuit boards, and hard drives' that need to be replaced. Once the machine is 'restored' to its original working condition, the new copy of the program would have to be destroyed immediately in order for §117(c) to apply. In contrast, the term 'maintenance' has a much broader temporal connotation. [M]aintenance, or 'servicing,' was meant to encompass monitoring systems for problems, not simply fixing a single, isolated malfunction. *At 1313:* [T]he protection of §117 does not cease simply by virtue of the passage of time. Rather, it ceases only when that maintenance ends. *At 1314:* [T]he service provider must be able to cause the machine to boot up in order to determine if it 'works in accordance with its original specifications.' Accessing software programs, such as freestanding diagnosis and utility programs, that are not needed to boot up the computer and make that determination, goes too far because access to those programs is not strictly necessary to verify that the computer is 'working in accordance with its original specifications.' [¶] [T]he phrase 'necessary for the machine to be activated' refers to the portion of code that must be copied in order for the machine 'to be turned on.' In this case, copying the maintenance code into RAM is indispensable for the machine to be turned on or activated; its functionality (or lack thereof) after bootup is moot." *See also* ***Sony Computer Entm't, Inc. v. Connectix Corp.***, 203 F.3d 596, 600 n.1 (9th Cir.2000).

Krause v. Titleserv, Inc., 402 F.3d 119, 124 (2d Cir. 2005). "[F]ormal title in a program copy is not an absolute prerequisite to qualifying for §117(a)'s affirmative defense. Instead, courts should inquire into whether the party exercises sufficient incidents of ownership over a copy of the program to be sensibly considered the owner of the copy for purposes of §117(a). The presence or absence of formal title may of course be a factor in this inquiry, but the absence of formal title may be outweighed by evidence that the possessor of the copy enjoys sufficiently broad rights over it to be sensibly considered its owner. *At 129:* Whether a questioned use is a use in another manner [under §117(a)(1)] seems to us to depend on the type of use envisioned in the creation of the program. *At 130:* [W]hether a questioned use of an adaptation violates the requirement of 'use in no other manner' depends on the facts of the particular case."

DSC Comms. v. Pulse Comms., 170 F.3d 1354, 1360 (Fed.Cir.1999). "Plainly, a party who purchases copies of software from the copyright owner can hold a license under a copyright while still being an 'owner' of a copy of the copyrighted software for purposes of §117. We therefore do not adopt the Ninth Circuit's characterization of all licensees as non-owners. *At 1362:* In light of the restrictions on [licensees'] rights in the copies of the ... software, we hold that it was improper for the court to conclude, as a matter of law, that [licensees] were 'owners' under §117 of the copies of [P's] software that were in their possession. [S]ection 117 [did not give licensees] the right to copy the ... software when using [D's software interface] cards without violating [P's] copyright in the software[, thereby making D liable for contributory infringement]. *At 1363:* With respect to [D's] activities in creating copies of the ... software with its own [hardware] systems, we reach a different conclusion. [D] obtained its [hardware] systems on the open market. It was thus an owner of those systems and the associated software, and it was not subject to any restriction on its ownership interest through a licensing agreement or otherwise. As such, it was entitled, under ... §117, to make such copies of the ... software as were necessary to operate the systems. To the extent that [P's] direct infringement claim is directed at [D's] conduct in making copies of the ... software during the operation of its own [hardware] systems, [P] has no valid claim...." *But see* ***Wall Data Inc. v. Los Angeles Cty. Sheriff's Dept.***, p. 280.

Alcatel, Inc. v. DGI Tech., 166 F.3d 772, 791 (5th Cir.1999). "[D] engaged in contributory infringement as a matter of law. The evidence shows that each time [D's] microprocessor card is booted up, it downloads (makes a copy of) [P's] operating system. By selling its [microprocessor] card, therefore, [D] knowingly induces and causes its customers ... to violate [P's] exclusive right to reproduce its software. Under §117 ..., [D] could have avoided liability for contributory infringement by proving that its customers *owned* copies of [P's] operating system software, and were therefore *authorized* to make additional copies, provided such reproduction was 'an essential step in the utilization of the computer program.'"

ProCD, Inc. v. Zeidenberg, 86 F.3d 1447, 1448-49 (7th Cir.1996). "Must buyers of computer software obey the terms of shrinkwrap licenses? ... Shrinkwrap licenses are enforceable unless their terms are objectionable on grounds applicable to contracts in general (for example, if they violate a rule of positive law, or if they are unconscionable)."

MAI Sys. v. Peak Computer, Inc., 991 F.2d 511, 519 (9th Cir.1993). Since "we find that the copy created in the RAM can be 'perceived, reproduced, or otherwise communicated,' we hold that the loading of software into the RAM creates a copy under the Copyright Act."

Sega Enters. v. Accolade, Inc., 977 F.2d 1510, 1520 (9th Cir.1992). The "copyright in a computer program extends to the object code version of the program. [¶] [17 U.S.C. §117] does not purport to protect a user who disassembles object code, converts it from assembly into source code, and makes printouts and photocopies of the refined source code version. *At 1521:* Section 117 defines a narrow category of copying that is lawful *per se.* [17 U.S.C. §107], by contrast, establishes a *defense* to an otherwise valid claim of copyright infringement. It provides that particular instances of copying that otherwise would be actionable are lawful, and sets forth the factors to be considered in determining whether the defense applies. The fact that Congress has not chosen to provide a *per se* exemption to [17 U.S.C.] §106 for disassembly does not mean that particular instances of disassembly may not constitute fair use."

Vault Corp. v. Quaid Software Ltd., 847 F.2d 255, 261 (5th Cir.1988). "Congress recognized that a computer program cannot be used unless it is first copied into a computer's memory, and thus provided the §117(1) exception to permit copying for this essential purpose. [P] contends that, due to the inclusion of the phrase 'and that it is used in no other manner,' this exception should be interpreted to permit only the copying of a computer program for the purpose of using it for *its intended purpose*. Because [D] copied [P's] program into its computer's memory for the express purpose of devising a means of defeating its protective function, [P] contends that §117(1) is not applicable. [¶] We decline to construe §117(1) in this manner. ... Section 117(1) contains no language to suggest that the copy it permits must be employed for a use intended by the copyright owner, and, absent clear congressional guidance to the contrary, we refuse to read such limiting language into this exception. *At 267:* An owner of a program is entitled, under §117(2), to make an archival copy of that program in order to guard against *all* types of risks, including physical and human mishap as well as mechanical and electrical failure."

§118. SCOPE OF EXCLUSIVE RIGHTS: USE OF CERTAIN WORKS IN CONNECTION WITH NONCOMMERCIAL BROADCASTING

(a) The exclusive rights provided by section 106 shall, with respect to the works specified by subsection (b) and the activities specified by subsection (d),[1] be subject to the conditions and limitations prescribed by this section.

(b) Notwithstanding any provision of the antitrust laws, any owners of copyright in published nondramatic musical works and published pictorial, graphic, and sculptural works and any public broadcasting entities, respectively, may negotiate and agree upon the terms and rates of royalty payments and the proportionate division of fees paid among various copyright owners, and may designate common agents to negotiate, agree to, pay, or receive payments.

(1) Any owner of copyright in a work specified in this subsection or any public broadcasting entity may submit to the Copyright Royalty Judges proposed licenses covering such activities with respect to such works.

(2) License agreements voluntarily negotiated at any time between one or more copyright owners and one or more public broadcasting entities shall be given effect in lieu of any determination by the Librarian of Congress or the Copyright Royalty Judges, if copies of such agreements are filed with the Copyright Royalty Judges within 30 days of execution in accordance with regulations that the Copyright Royalty Judges shall issue.

(3) Voluntary negotiation proceedings initiated pursuant to a petition filed under section 804(a) for the purpose of determining a schedule of terms and rates of royalty payments by public broadcasting entities to owners of copyright in works specified by this subsection and the proportionate division of fees paid among various copyright owners shall cover the 5-year period beginning on January 1 of the second year following the year in which the petition is filed. The parties to each negotiation proceeding shall bear their own costs.

(4) In the absence of license agreements negotiated under paragraph (2) or (3), the Copyright Royalty Judges shall, pursuant to chapter 8, conduct a proceeding to determine and publish in the Federal Register a schedule of rates and terms which, subject to paragraph (2), shall be binding on all owners of copyright in works specified by this subsection and public broadcasting entities, regardless of whether such copyright owners have submitted proposals to the Copyright Royalty Judges. In establishing such rates and terms the Copyright Royalty Judges may consider the rates for comparable circumstances under voluntary license agreements negotiated as provided in paragraph (2) or (3). The Copyright Royalty Judges shall also establish requirements by which copyright owners may receive reasonable notice of the use of their works under this section, and under which records of such use shall be kept by public broadcasting entities.

(c) Subject to the terms of any voluntary license agreements that have been negotiated as provided by subsection (b)(2) or (3), a public broadcasting entity may, upon compliance with the provisions of this section, including the rates and terms established by the Copyright Royalty Judges under subsection (b)(4), engage in the following activities with respect to published nondramatic musical works and published pictorial, graphic, and sculptural works:

(1) performance or display of a work by or in the course of a transmission made by a noncommercial educational broadcast station referred to in subsection (f); and

(2) production of a transmission program, reproduction of copies or phonorecords of such a transmission program, and distribution of such copies or phonorecords, where such production, reproduction, or distribution is made by a nonprofit institution or organization solely for the purpose of transmissions specified in paragraph (1); and

(3) the making of reproductions by a governmental body or a nonprofit institution of a transmission program simultaneously with its transmission as specified in paragraph (1), and the performance or display of the contents of such program under the conditions specified by paragraph (1) of section 110, but only if the reproductions are used for performances or displays for a period of no more than seven days from the date of the transmission specified in paragraph (1), and are destroyed before or at the end of such period. No person supplying, in accordance with paragraph (2), a reproduction of a transmission program to governmental bodies or nonprofit institutions under this paragraph shall have any liability as a result of failure of such body or institution to destroy such reproduction: *Provided*, That it shall have notified such body or institution of the requirement for such destruction pursuant to this paragraph: And provided further, That if such body or institution itself fails to destroy such reproduction it shall be deemed to have infringed.

(d) Except as expressly provided in this subsection, this section shall have no applicability to works other than those specified in subsection (b). Owners of copyright in nondramatic literary works and public broadcasting entities may, during the course of voluntary negotiations, agree among themselves, respectively, as to the terms and rates of royalty payments without liability under the antitrust laws. Any such terms and rates of royalty payments shall be effective upon filing with the Copyright Royalty Judges, in accordance with regulations that the Copyright Royalty Judges shall prescribe as provided in section 803 (b)(6).

(e) Nothing in this section shall be construed to permit, beyond the limits of fair use as provided by section 107, the unauthorized dramatization of a nondramatic musical work, the production of a transmission program drawn to any substantial extent from a published compilation of pictorial, graphic, or sculptural works, or the unauthorized use of any portion of an audiovisual work.

(f) As used in this section, the term "public broadcasting entity" means a noncommercial educational broadcast station as defined in section 397 of title 47 and any nonprofit institution or organization engaged in the activities described in paragraph (2) of subsection (c).

1. **Editor's note:** Subsection (d) was relettered subsection (c) by P.L. 108-419, §5(f)(2), eff. Nov. 30, 2004.

History of 17 U.S.C. §118: Oct. 19, 1976, P.L. 94-553, §101, 90 Stat. 2565; Dec. 17, 1993, P.L. 103-198, §4, 107 Stat. 2309; Aug. 5, 1999, P.L. 106-44, §1(g)(3), 113 Stat. 222; Nov. 2, 2002, P.L. 107-273, §13210(7), 116 Stat. 1909; May 30, 2005, P.L. 108-419, §5(f), 118 Stat. 2365; May 30, 2005, P.L. 109-303, §4(d), 120 Stat. 1482.

See also 37 C.F.R. §§381.1-381.11.

§119. LIMITATIONS ON EXCLUSIVE RIGHTS: SECONDARY TRANSMISSIONS OF DISTANT TELEVISION PROGRAMMING BY SATELLITE

(a) Secondary transmissions by satellite carriers—

(1) Non-network stations.—Subject to the provisions of paragraphs (4), (5), and (7) of this subsection and section 114(d), secondary transmissions of a performance or display of a work embodied in a primary transmission made by a non-network station shall be subject to statutory licensing under this section if the secondary transmission is made by a satellite carrier to the public for private home viewing or for viewing in a commercial establishment, with regard to secondary transmissions the satellite carrier is in compliance with the rules, regulations, or authorizations of the Federal Communications Commission governing the carriage of television broadcast station signals, and the carrier makes a direct or indirect charge for each retransmission service to each subscriber receiving the secondary transmission or to a distributor that has contracted with the carrier for direct or indirect delivery of the secondary transmission to the public for private home viewing or for viewing in a commercial establishment.

(2) Network stations—

(A) In general.—Subject to the provisions of subparagraph (B) of this paragraph and paragraphs (4), (5), (6), and (7) of this subsection and section 114(d), secondary transmissions of a performance or display of a work embodied in a primary transmission made by a network station shall be subject to statutory licensing under this section if the secondary transmission is made by a satellite carrier to the public for private home viewing, with regard to secondary transmissions the satellite carrier is in compliance with the rules, regulations, or authorizations of the Federal Communications Commission governing the carriage of television broadcast station signals, and the carrier makes a direct or indirect charge for such retransmission service to each subscriber receiving the secondary transmission.

(B) Secondary transmissions to unserved households—

(i) In general.—The statutory license provided for in subparagraph (A) shall be limited to secondary transmissions of the signals of no more than two network stations in a single day for each television network to persons who reside in unserved households.

(ii) Accurate determinations of eligibility—

(I) Accurate predictive model.—In determining presumptively whether a person resides in an unserved household under subsection (d)(10)(A), a court shall rely on the Individual Location Longley-Rice model set forth by the Federal Communications Commission in Docket No. 98-201, as that model may be amended by the Commission over time under section 339(c)(3) of title 47 to increase the accuracy of that model.

(II) Accurate measurements.—For purposes of site measurements to determine whether a person resides in an unserved household under subsection (d)(10)(A), a court shall rely on section 339(c)(4) of title 47.

(III) Accurate predictive model with respect to digital signals.—Notwithstanding subclause (I), in determining presumptively whether a person resides in an unserved household under subsection (d)(10)(A) with respect to digital signals, a court shall rely on a predictive model set forth by the Federal Communications Commission pursuant to a rulemaking as provided in section 339(c)(3) of the Communications Act of 1934 (47 U.S.C. 339(c)(3)), as that model may be amended by the Commission over time under such section to increase the accuracy of that model. Until such time as the Commission sets forth such model, a court shall rely on the predictive model as recommended by the Commission with respect to digital signals in its Report to Congress in ET Docket No. 05-182, FCC 05-199 (released December 9, 2005).

(iii) C-band exemption to unserved households—

(I) In general.—The limitations of clause (i) shall not apply to any secondary transmissions by C-band services of network stations that a subscriber to C-band service received before any termination of such secondary transmissions before October 31, 1999.

(II) Definition.—In this clause, the term "C-band service" means a service that is licensed by the Federal Communications Commission and operates in the Fixed Satellite Service under part 25 of title 47, Code of Federal Regulations.

(C) Submission of subscriber lists to networks—

(i) Initial lists.—A satellite carrier that makes secondary transmissions of a primary transmission made by a network station pursuant to subparagraph (A) shall, not later than 90 days after commencing such secondary transmissions, submit to the network that owns or is affiliated with the network station a list identifying (by name and address, including street or rural route number, city, State, and 9-digit zip code) all subscribers to which the satellite carrier makes secondary transmissions of that primary transmission to subscribers in unserved households.

(ii) Monthly lists.—After the submission of the initial lists under clause (i), the satellite carrier shall, not later than the 15th of each month, submit to the network a list, aggregated by designated market area, identifying (by name and address, including street or rural route number, city, State, and 9-digit zip code) any persons who have been added or dropped as subscribers under clause (i) since the last submission under this subparagraph.

(iii) Use of subscriber information.—Subscriber information submitted by a satellite carrier under this subparagraph may be used only for purposes of monitoring compliance by the satellite carrier with this subsection.

(iv) Applicability.—The submission requirements of this subparagraph shall apply to a satellite carrier only if the network to which the submissions are to be made places on file with the Register of Copyrights a document identifying the name and address of the person to whom such submissions are to be made. The Register shall maintain for public inspection a file of all such documents.

(3) Statutory license where retransmissions into local market available—

(A) Rules for subscribers to signals under subsection (e)—

(i) For those receiving distant signals.—In the case of a subscriber of a satellite carrier who is eligible to receive the secondary transmission of the primary transmission of a network station solely by reason of subsection (e) (in this subparagraph referred to as a "distant signal"), and who, as of October 1, 2004, is receiving the distant signal of that network station, the following shall apply:

(I) In a case in which the satellite carrier makes available to the subscriber the secondary transmission of the primary transmission of a local network station affiliated with the same television network pursuant to the statutory license under section 122, the statutory license under paragraph (2) shall apply only to secondary transmissions by that satellite carrier to that subscriber of the distant signal of a station affiliated with the same television network—

(aa) if, within 60 days after receiving the notice of the satellite carrier under section 338(h)(1) of title 47, the subscriber elects to retain the distant signal; but

(bb) only until such time as the subscriber elects to receive such local signal.

(II) Notwithstanding subclause (I), the statutory license under paragraph (2) shall not apply with respect to any subscriber who is eligible to receive the distant signal of a television network station solely by reason of subsection (e), unless the satellite carrier, within 60 days after December 8, 2004, submits to that television network a list, aggregated by designated market area (as defined in section 122(j)(2)(C)), that—

(aa) identifies that subscriber by name and address (street or rural route number, city, State, and zip code) and specifies the distant signals received by the subscriber; and

(bb) states, to the best of the satellite carrier's knowledge and belief, after having made diligent and good faith inquiries, that the subscriber is eligible under subsection (e) to receive the distant signals.

(ii) For those not receiving distant signals.—In the case of any subscriber of a satellite carrier who is eligible to receive the distant signal of a network station solely by reason of subsection (e) and who did not receive a distant signal of a station affiliated with the same network on October 1, 2004, the statutory license under paragraph (2) shall not apply to secondary transmissions by that satellite carrier to that subscriber of the distant signal of a station affiliated with the same network.

(B) Rules for lawful subscribers as of date of enactment of 2010 act.—In the case of a subscriber of a satellite carrier who, on the day before the date of the enactment of the Satellite Television Extension and Localism Act of 2010, was lawfully receiving the secondary transmission of the primary transmission of a network station under the statutory license under paragraph (2) (in this subparagraph referred to as the "distant signal"), other than subscribers to whom subparagraph (A) applies, the statutory license under paragraph (2) shall apply to secondary transmissions by that satellite carrier to that subscriber of the distant signal of a station affiliated with the same television network, and the subscriber's household shall continue to be considered to be an unserved household with respect to such network, until such time as the subscriber elects to terminate such secondary transmissions, whether or not the subscriber elects to subscribe to receive the secondary transmission of the primary transmission of a local network station affiliated with the same network pursuant to the statutory license under section 122.

(C) Future applicability—

(i) When local signal available at time of subscription.—The statutory license under paragraph (2) shall not apply to the secondary transmission by a satellite carrier of the primary transmission of a network station to a person who is not a subscriber lawfully receiving such secondary transmission as of May 27, 2010, and, at the time such person seeks to subscribe to receive such secondary transmission, resides in a local market where the satellite carrier makes available to that person the secondary transmission of the primary transmission of a local network station affiliated with the same network pursuant to the statutory license under section 122.

(ii) When local signal available after subscription.—In the case of a subscriber who lawfully subscribes to and receives the secondary transmission by a satellite carrier of the primary transmission of a network station under the statutory license under paragraph (2) (in this clause referred to as the "distant signal") on or after May 27, 2010, the statutory license under paragraph (2) shall apply to secondary transmissions by that satellite carrier to that subscriber of the distant signal of a station affiliated with the same television network, and the subscriber's household shall continue to be considered to be an unserved household with respect to such network, until such time as the subscriber elects to terminate such secondary transmissions, but only if such subscriber subscribes to the secondary transmission of the primary transmission of a local network station affiliated with the same network within 60 days after the satellite carrier makes available to the subscriber such secondary transmission of the primary transmission of such local network station.

(D) Other provisions not affected.—This paragraph shall not affect the applicability of the statutory license to secondary transmissions to unserved households included under paragraph (11).

(E) Waiver.—A subscriber who is denied the secondary transmission of a network station under subparagraph (B) or (C) may request a waiver from such denial by submitting a request, through the subscriber's satellite carrier, to the network station in the local market affiliated with the same network where the subscriber is located. The network station shall accept or reject the subscriber's request for a waiver within 30 days after receipt of the request. If the network station fails to accept or reject the subscriber's request for a waiver within that 30-day period, that network station shall be deemed to agree to the waiver request. Unless specifically stated by the network station, a waiver that was granted before Dec. 8, 2004 under section 339(c)(2) of title 47 shall not constitute a waiver for purposes of this subparagraph.

(F) Available defined.—For purposes of this paragraph, a satellite carrier makes available a secondary transmission of the primary transmission of a local station to a subscriber or person if the satellite carrier offers that secondary transmission to other subscribers who reside in the same 9-digit zip code as that subscriber or person.

(4) Noncompliance with reporting and payment requirements.—Notwithstanding the provisions of paragraphs (1) and (2), the willful or repeated secondary transmission to the public by a satellite carrier of a primary transmission made by a non-network station or a network station and embodying a performance or display of a work is actionable as an act of infringement under section 501, and is fully subject to the remedies provided by sections 502 through 506, where the satellite carrier has not deposited the statement of account and royalty fee required by subsection (b), or has failed to make the submissions to networks required by paragraph (2)(C).

(5) Willful alterations.—Notwithstanding the provisions of paragraphs (1) and (2), the secondary transmission to the public by a satellite carrier of a performance or display of a work embodied in a primary transmission made by a non-network station or a network station is actionable as an act of infringement under section 501, and is fully subject to the remedies provided by sections 502 through 506 and section 510, if the content of the particular program in which the performance or display is embodied, or any commercial advertising or station announcement transmitted by the primary transmitter during, or immediately before or after, the transmission of such program, is in any way willfully altered by the satellite carrier through changes, deletions, or additions, or is combined with programming from any other broadcast signal.

(6) Violation of territorial restrictions on statutory license for network stations—

(A) Individual violations.—The willful or repeated secondary transmission by a satellite carrier of a primary transmission made by a network station and embodying a performance or display of a work to a subscriber who is not eligible to receive the transmission under this section is actionable as an act of infringement under section 501 and is fully subject to the remedies provided by sections 502 through 506, except that—

(i) no damages shall be awarded for such act of infringement if the satellite carrier took corrective action by promptly withdrawing service from the ineligible subscriber, and

(ii) any statutory damages shall not exceed $250 for such subscriber for each month during which the violation occurred.

(B) Pattern of violations.—If a satellite carrier engages in a willful or repeated pattern or practice of delivering a primary transmission made by a network station and embodying a performance or display of a work to subscribers who are not eligible to receive the transmission under this section, then in addition to the remedies set forth in subparagraph (A)—

(i) if the pattern or practice has been carried out on a substantially nationwide basis, the court shall order a permanent injunction barring the secondary transmission by the satellite carrier, for private home viewing, of the primary transmissions of any primary network station affiliated with the same network, and the court may order statutory damages of not to exceed $2,500,000 for each 3-month period during which the pattern or practice was carried out; and

(ii) if the pattern or practice has been carried out on a local or regional basis, the court shall order a permanent injunction barring the secondary transmission, for private home viewing in that locality or region, by the satellite carrier of the primary transmissions of any primary network station affiliated with the same network, and the court may order statutory damages of not to exceed $2,500,000 for each 6-month period during which the pattern or practice was carried out.

(C) Previous subscribers excluded.—Subparagraphs (A) and (B) do not apply to secondary transmissions by a satellite carrier to persons who subscribed to receive such secondary transmissions from the satellite carrier or a distributor before November 16, 1988.

(D) Burden of proof.—In any action brought under this paragraph, the satellite carrier shall have the burden of proving that its secondary transmission of a primary transmission by a network station is to a subscriber who is eligible to receive the secondary transmission under this section.

(E) Exception.—The secondary transmission by a satellite carrier of a performance or display of a work embodied in a primary transmission made by a network station to subscribers who do not reside in unserved households shall not be an act of infringement if—

(i) the station on May 1, 1991, was retransmitted by a satellite carrier and was not on that date owned or operated by or affiliated with a television network that offered interconnected program service on a regular basis for 15 or more hours per week to at least 25 affiliated television licensees in 10 or more States;

(ii) as of July 1, 1998, such station was retransmitted by a satellite carrier under the statutory license of this section; and

(iii) the station is not owned or operated by or affiliated with a television network that, as of January 1, 1995, offered interconnected program service on a regular basis for 15 or more hours per week to at least 25 affiliated television licensees in 10 or more States.

The court shall direct one half of any statutory damages ordered under clause (i) to be deposited with the Register of Copyrights for distribution to copyright owners pursuant to subsection (b). The Copyright Royalty Judges shall issue regulations establishing procedures for distributing such funds, on a proportional basis, to copyright owners whose works were included in the secondary transmissions that were the subject of the statutory damages.

(7) Discrimination by a satellite carrier.—Notwithstanding the provisions of paragraph (1), the willful or repeated secondary transmission to the public by a satellite carrier of a performance or display of a work embodied in a primary transmission made by a non-network station or a network station is actionable as an act of infringement under section 501, and is fully subject to the remedies provided by sections 502 through 506, if the satellite carrier unlawfully discriminates against a distributor.

(8) Geographic limitation on secondary transmissions.—The statutory license created by this section shall apply only to secondary transmissions to households located in the United States.

(9) Loser pays for signal intensity measurement; recovery of measurement costs in a civil action.—In any civil action filed relating to the eligibility of subscribing households as unserved households—

(A) a network station challenging such eligibility shall, within 60 days after receipt of the measurement results and a statement of such costs, reimburse the satellite carrier for any signal intensity measurement that is conducted by that carrier in response to a challenge by the network station and that establishes the household is an unserved household; and

(B) a satellite carrier shall, within 60 days after receipt of the measurement results and a statement of such costs, reimburse the network station challenging such eligibility for any signal intensity measurement that is conducted by that station and that establishes the household is not an unserved household.

(10) Inability to conduct measurement.—If a network station makes a reasonable attempt to conduct a site measurement of its signal at a subscriber's household and is denied access for the purpose of conducting the measurement, and is otherwise unable to conduct a measurement, the satellite carrier shall within 60 days notice thereof, terminate service of the station's network to that household.

(11) Service to recreational vehicles and commercial trucks—

(A) Exemption—

(i) In general.—For purposes of this subsection, and subject to clauses (ii) and (iii), the term "unserved household" shall include—

(I) recreational vehicles as defined in regulations of the Secretary of Housing and Urban Development under section 3282.8 of title 24, Code of Federal Regulations; and

(II) commercial trucks that qualify as commercial motor vehicles under regulations of the Secretary of Transportation under section 383.5 of title 49, Code of Federal Regulations.

(ii) Limitation.—Clause (i) shall apply only to a recreational vehicle or commercial truck if any satellite carrier that proposes to make a secondary transmission of a network station to the operator of such a recreational vehicle or commercial truck complies with the documentation requirements under subparagraphs (B) and (C).

(iii) Exclusion.—For purposes of this subparagraph, the terms "recreational vehicle" and "commercial truck" shall not include any fixed dwelling, whether a mobile home or otherwise.

(B) Documentation requirements.—A recreational vehicle or commercial truck shall be deemed to be an unserved household beginning 10 days after the relevant satellite carrier provides to the network that owns or is affiliated with the network station that will be secondarily transmitted to the recreational vehicle or commercial truck the following documents:

(i) Declaration.—A signed declaration by the operator of the recreational vehicle or commercial truck that the satellite dish is permanently attached to the recreational vehicle or commercial truck, and will not be used to receive satellite programming at any fixed dwelling.

(ii) Registration.—In the case of a recreational vehicle, a copy of the current State vehicle registration for the recreational vehicle.

(iii) Registration and license.—In the case of a commercial truck, a copy of—

(I) the current State vehicle registration for the truck; and

(II) a copy of a valid, current commercial driver's license, as defined in regulations of the Secretary of Transportation under section 383 of title 49, Code of Federal Regulations, issued to the operator.

(C) Updated documentation requirements.—If a satellite carrier wishes to continue to make secondary transmissions to a recreational vehicle or commercial truck for more than a 2-year period, that carrier shall provide each network, upon request, with updated documentation in the form described under subparagraph (B) during the 90 days before expiration of that 2-year period.

(12) Statutory license contingent on compliance with FCC rules and remedial steps.—Notwithstanding any other provision of this section, the willful or repeated secondary transmission to the public by a satellite carrier of a primary transmission embodying a performance or display of a work made by a broadcast station licensed by the Federal Communications Commission is actionable as an act of infringement under section 501, and is fully subject to the remedies provided by sections 502 through 506, if, at the time of such transmission, the satellite carrier is not in compliance with the rules, regulations, and authorizations of the Federal Communications Commission concerning the carriage of television broadcast station signals.

(13) Waivers.—A subscriber who is denied the secondary transmission of a signal of a network station under subsection (a)(2)(B) may request a waiver from such denial by submitting a request, through the subscriber's satellite carrier, to the network station asserting that the secondary transmission is prohibited. The network station shall accept or reject a subscriber's request for a waiver within 30 days after receipt of the request. If a television network station fails to accept or reject a subscriber's request for a waiver within the 30-day period after receipt of the request, that station shall be deemed to agree to the waiver request and have filed such written waiver. Unless specifically stated by the network station, a waiver that was granted before December 8, 2004 under section 339(c)(2) of title 47, and that was in effect on December 8, 2004, shall constitute a waiver for purposes of this paragraph.

(14) Restricted transmission of out-of-State distant network signals into certain markets—

(A) Out-of-state network affiliates.—Notwithstanding any other provision of this title, the statutory license in this subsection and subsection (b) shall not apply to any secondary transmission of the primary transmission of a network station located outside of the State of Alaska to any subscriber in that State to whom the secondary transmission of the primary transmission of a television station located in that State is made available by the satellite carrier pursuant to section 122.

(B) Exception.—The limitation in subparagraph (A) shall not apply to the secondary transmission of the primary transmission of a digital signal of a network station located outside of the State of Alaska if at the time that the secondary transmission is made, no television station licensed to a community in the State and affiliated with the same network makes primary transmissions of a digital signal.

(b) Deposit of statements and fees; verification procedures—

(1) Deposits with the Register of Copyrights.—A satellite carrier whose secondary transmissions are subject to statutory licensing under subsection (a) shall, on a semiannual basis, deposit with the Register of Copyrights, in accordance with requirements that the Register shall prescribe by regulation—

(A) a statement of account, covering the preceding 6-month period, specifying the names and locations of all non-network stations and network stations whose signals were retransmitted, at any time during that period, to subscribers as described in subsections (a)(1) and (a)(2), the total number of subscribers that received such retransmissions, and such other data as the Register of Copyrights may from time to time prescribe by regulation;

(B) a royalty fee payable to copyright owners pursuant to paragraph (4) for that 6-month period, computed by multiplying the total number of subscribers receiving each secondary transmission of a primary stream or multicast stream of each non-network station or network station during each calendar year month by the appropriate rate in effect under this subsection; and

(C) a filing fee, as determined by the Register of Copyrights pursuant to section 708(a).

(2) Verification of accounts and fee payments.—The Register of Copyrights shall issue regulations to permit interested parties to verify and audit the statements of account and royalty fees submitted by satellite carriers under this subsection.

(3) Investment of fees.—The Register of Copyrights shall receive all fees (including the filing fee specified in paragraph (1)(C)) deposited under this section and, after deducting the reasonable costs incurred by the Copyright Office under this section (other than the costs deducted under paragraph (5)), shall deposit the balance in the Treasury of the United States, in such manner as the Secretary of the Treasury directs. All funds held by the Secretary of the Treasury shall be invested in interest-bearing securities of the United States for later distribution with interest by the Librarian of Congress as provided by this title.

(4) Persons to whom fees are distributed.—The royalty fees deposited under paragraph (3) shall, in accordance with the procedures provided by paragraph (5), be distributed to those copyright owners whose works were included in a secondary transmission made by a satellite carrier during the applicable 6-month accounting period and who file a claim with the Copyright Royalty Judges under paragraph (5).

(5) Procedures for distribution.—The royalty fees deposited under paragraph (3) shall be distributed in accordance with the following procedures:

(A) Filing of claims for fees.—During the month of July in each year, each person claiming to be entitled to statutory license fees for secondary transmissions shall file a claim with the Copyright Royalty Judges, in accordance with requirements that the Copyright Royalty Judges shall prescribe by regulation. For purposes of this paragraph, any claimants may agree among themselves as to the proportionate division of statutory license fees among them, may lump their claims together and file them jointly or as a single claim, or may designate a common agent to receive payment on their behalf.

(B) Determination of controversy; distributions.—After the first day of August of each year, the Copyright Royalty Judges shall determine whether there exists a controversy concerning the distribution of royalty fees. If the Copyright Royalty Judges determine that no such controversy exists, the Copyright Royalty Judges shall authorize the Librarian of Congress to proceed to distribute such fees to the copyright owners entitled to receive them, or to their designated agents, subject to the deduction of reasonable administrative costs under this section. If the Copyright Royalty Judges find the existence of a controversy, the Copyright Royalty Judges shall, pursuant to chapter 8 of this title, conduct a proceeding to determine the distribution of royalty fees.

(C) Withholding of fees during controversy.—During the pendency of any proceeding under this subsection, the Copyright Royalty Judges shall have the discretion to authorize the Librarian of Congress to proceed to distribute any amounts that are not in controversy.

(c) Adjustment of royalty fees—

(1) Applicability and determination of royalty fees for signals—

(A) Initial fee.—The appropriate fee for purposes of determining the royalty fee under subsection (b)(1)(B) for the secondary transmission of the primary transmissions of network stations and non-network stations shall be the appropriate fee set forth in part 258 of title 37, Code of Federal Regulations, as in effect on July 1, 2009, as modified under this paragraph.

(B) Fee set by voluntary negotiation.—On or before June 1, 2010, the Copyright Royalty Judges shall cause to be published in the Federal Register of the initiation of voluntary negotiation proceedings for the purpose of determining the royalty fee to be paid by satellite carriers for the secondary transmission of the primary transmission of network stations and non-network stations under subsection (b)(1)(B).

(C) Negotiations.—Satellite carriers, distributors, and copyright owners entitled to royalty fees under this section shall negotiate in good faith in an effort to reach a voluntary agreement or agreements for the payment of royalty fees. Any such satellite carriers, distributors and copyright owners may at any time negotiate and agree to the royalty fee, and may designate common agents to negotiate, agree to, or pay such fees. If the parties fail to identify common agents, the Copyright Royalty Judges shall do so, after requesting recommendations from the parties to the negotiation proceeding. The parties to each negotiation proceeding shall bear the cost thereof.

(D) Agreements binding on parties; filing of agreements; public notice—

(i) Voluntary agreements; filing.—Voluntary agreements negotiated at any time in accordance with this paragraph shall be binding upon all satellite carriers, distributors, and copyright owners that are parties thereto. Copies of such agreements shall be filed with the Copyright Office within 30 days after execution in accordance with regulations that the Register of Copyrights shall prescribe.

(ii) Procedure for adoption of fees—

(I) Publication of notice.—Within 10 days after publication in the Federal Register of a notice of the initiation of voluntary negotiation proceedings, parties who have reached a voluntary agreement may request that the royalty fees in that agreement be applied to all satellite carriers, distributors, and copyright owners without convening a proceeding under subparagraph (F).

(II) Public notice of fees.—Upon receiving a request under subclause (I), the Copyright Royalty Judges shall immediately provide public notice of the royalty fees from the voluntary agreement and afford parties an opportunity to state that they object to those fees.

(III) Adoption of fees.—The Copyright Royalty Judges shall adopt the royalty fees from the voluntary agreement for all satellite carriers, distributors, and copyright owners without convening the proceeding under subparagraph (F) unless a party with an intent to participate in that proceeding and a significant interest in the outcome of that proceeding objects under subclause (II).

(E) Period agreement is in effect.—The obligation to pay the royalty fees established under a voluntary agreement which has been filed with the Copyright Royalty Judges in accordance with this paragraph shall become effective on the date specified in the agreement, and shall remain in effect until December 31, 2019, or in accordance with the terms of the agreement, whichever is later.

(F) Fee set by Copyright Royalty Judges proceeding—

(i) Notice of initiation of the proceeding.—On or before September 1, 2010, the Copyright Royalty Judges shall cause notice to be published in the Federal Register of the initiation of a proceeding for the purpose of determining the royalty fees to be paid for the secondary transmission of the primary transmissions of network stations and non-network stations under subsection (b)(1)(B) by satellite carriers and distributors—

(I) in the absence of a voluntary agreement filed in accordance with subparagraph (D) that establishes royalty fees to be paid by all satellite carriers and distributors; or

(II) if an objection to the fees from a voluntary agreement submitted for adoption by the Copyright Royalty Judges to apply to all satellite carriers, distributors, and copyright owners is received under subparagraph (D) from a party with an intent to participate in the proceeding and a significant interest in the outcome of that proceeding.

Such proceeding shall be conducted under chapter 8.

(ii) Establishment of royalty fees.—In determining royalty fees under this subparagraph, the Copyright Royalty Judges shall establish fees for the secondary transmissions of the primary transmissions of network stations and non-network stations that most clearly represent the fair market value of secondary transmissions, except that the Copyright Royalty Judges shall adjust royalty fees to account for the obligations of the parties under any applicable voluntary agreement filed with the Copyright Royalty Judges in accordance with subparagraph (D). In determining the fair market value, the Judges shall base their decision on economic, competitive, and programming information presented by the parties, including—

(I) the competitive environment in which such programming is distributed, the cost of similar signals in similar private and compulsory license marketplaces, and any special features and conditions of the retransmission marketplace;

(II) the economic impact of such fees on copyright owners and satellite carriers; and

(III) the impact on the continued availability of secondary transmissions to the public.

(iii) Effective date for decision of Copyright Royalty Judges.—The obligation to pay the royalty fees established under a determination that is made by the Copyright Royalty Judges in a proceeding under this paragraph shall be effective as of January 1, 2010.

(iv) Persons subject to royalty fees.—The royalty fees referred to in clause (iii) shall be binding on all satellite carriers, distributors and copyright owners, who are not party to a voluntary agreement filed with the Copyright Office under subparagraph (D).

(2) Annual royalty fee adjustment.—Effective January 1 of each year, the royalty fee payable under subsection (b)(1)(B) for the secondary transmission of the primary transmissions of network stations and non-network stations shall be adjusted by the Copyright Royalty Judges to reflect any changes occurring in the cost of living as determined by the most recent Consumer Price Index (for all consumers and for all items) published by the Secretary of Labor before December 1 of the preceding year. Notification of the adjusted fees shall be published in the Federal Register at least 25 days before January 1.

(d) Definitions.—As used in this section—

(1) Distributor.—The term "distributor" means an entity that contracts to distribute secondary transmissions from a satellite carrier and, either as a single channel or in a package with other programming, provides the secondary transmission either directly to individual subscribers or indirectly through other program distribution entities in accordance with the provisions of this section.

(2) Network station.—The term "network station" means—

(A) a television station licensed by the Federal Communications Commission, including any translator station or terrestrial satellite station that rebroadcasts all or substantially all of the programming broadcast by a network station, that is owned or operated by, or affiliated with, one or more of the television networks in the United States that offer an interconnected program service on a regular basis for 15 or more hours per week to at least 25 of its affiliated television licensees in 10 or more States; or

(B) a noncommercial educational broadcast station (as defined in section 397 of title 47); except that the term does not include the signal of the Alaska Rural Communications Service, or any successor entity to that service.

(3) Primary network station.—The term "primary network station" means a network station that broadcasts or rebroadcasts the basic programming service of a particular national network.

(4) Primary transmission.—The term "primary transmission" has the meaning given that term in section 111(f) of this title.

(5) Private home viewing.—The term "private home viewing" means the viewing, for private use in a household by means of satellite reception equipment that is operated by an individual in that household and that serves only such household, of a secondary transmission delivered by a satellite carrier of a primary transmission of a television station licensed by the Federal Communications Commission.

(6) Satellite carrier.—The term "satellite carrier" means an entity that uses the facilities of a satellite or satellite service licensed by the Federal Communications Commission and operates in the Fixed-Satellite Service under part 25 of title 47, Code of Federal Regulations, or the Direct Broadcast Satellite Service under part 100 of title 47, Code of Federal Regulations, to establish and operate a channel of communications for point-to-multipoint distribution of television station signals, and that owns or leases a capacity or service on a satellite in order to provide such point-to-multipoint distribution, except to the extent that such entity provides such distribution pursuant to tariff under the Communications Act of 1934, other than for private home viewing pursuant to this section.

(7) Secondary transmission.—The term "secondary transmission" has the meaning given that term in section 111(f) of this title.

(8) Subscriber; subscribe—

(A) Subscriber.—The term "subscriber" means a person or entity that receives a secondary transmission service from a satellite carrier and pays a fee for the service, directly or indirectly, to the satellite carrier or to a distributor.

(B) Subscribe.—The term "subscribe" means to elect to become a subscriber.

(9) Non-network station.—The term "non-network station" means a television station, other than a network station, licensed by the Federal Communications Commission, that is secondarily transmitted by a satellite carrier.

(10) Unserved household.—The term "unserved household," with respect to a particular television network, means a household that—

(A) cannot receive, through the use of an antenna, an over-the-air signal containing the primary stream, or, on or after the qualifying date, the multicast stream, originating in that household's local market and affiliated with that network of—

(i) if the signal originates as an analog signal, Grade B intensity as defined by the Federal Communications Commission in section 73.683(a) of title 47, Code of Federal Regulations, as in effect on January 1, 1999; or

(ii) if the signal originates as a digital signal, intensity defined in the values for the digital television noise-limited service contour, as defined in regulations issued by the Federal Communications Commission (section 73.622(e) of title 47, Code of Federal Regulations), as such regulations may be amended from time to time;

(B) is subject to a waiver that meets the standards of subsection (a)(13) whether or not the waiver was granted before May 27, 2010;

(C) is a subscriber to whom subsection (e) applies;

(D) is a subscriber to whom subsection (a)(11) applies; or

(E) is a subscriber to whom the exemption under subsection (a)(2)(B)(iii) applies.

(11) Local market.—The term "local market" has the meaning given such term under section 122(j).

(12) Commercial establishment.—The term "commercial establishment"—

(A) means an establishment used for commercial purposes, such as a bar, restaurant, private office, fitness club, oil rig, retail store, bank or other financial institution, supermarket, automobile or boat dealership, or any other establishment with a common business area; and

(B) does not include a multi-unit permanent or temporary dwelling where private home viewing occurs, such as a hotel, dormitory, hospital, apartment, condominium, or prison.

(13) Qualifying date.—The term "qualifying date", for purposes of paragraph (10)(A), means—

(A) October 1, 2010, for multicast streams that exist on March 31, 2010; and

(B) January 1, 2011, for all other multicast streams.

(14) Multicast stream.—The term "multicast stream" means a digital stream containing programming and program-related material affiliated with a television network, other than the primary stream.

(15) Primary stream.—The term "primary stream" means—

(A) the single digital stream of programming as to which a television broadcast station has the right to mandatory carriage with a satellite carrier under the rules of the Federal Communications Commission in effect on July 1, 2009; or

(B) if there is no stream described in subparagraph (A), then either—

(i) the single digital stream of programming associated with the network last transmitted by the station as an analog signal; or

(ii) if there is no stream described in clause (i), then the single digital stream of programming affiliated with the network that, as of July 1, 2009, had been offered by the television broadcast station for the longest period of time.

(e) Moratorium on copyright liability.—Until December 31, 2019, a subscriber who does not receive a signal of Grade A intensity (as defined in the regulations of the Federal Communications Commission under section 73.683(a) of title 47, Code of Federal Regulations, as in effect on January 1, 1999, or predicted by the Federal Communications Commission using the Individual Location Longley-Rice methodology described by the Federal Communications Commission in Docket No. 98-201) of a local network television broadcast station shall remain eligible to receive signals of network stations affiliated with the same network, if that subscriber had satellite service of such network signal terminated after July 11, 1998, and before October 31, 1999, as required by this section, or received such service on October 31, 1999.

(f) Expedited consideration by Justice Department of voluntary agreements to provide satellite secondary transmissions to local markets—

(1) In general.—In a case in which no satellite carrier makes available, to subscribers located in a local market, as defined in section 122(j)(2), the secondary transmission into that market of a primary transmission of one or more television broadcast stations licensed by the Federal Communications Commission, and two or more satellite carriers request a business review letter in accordance with section 50.6 of title 28, Code of Federal Regulations (as in effect on July 7, 2004), in order to assess the legality under the antitrust laws of proposed business conduct to make or carry out an agreement to provide such secondary transmission into such local market, the appropriate official of the Department of Justice shall respond to the request no later than 90 days after the date on which the request is received.

(2) Definition.—For purposes of this subsection, the term "antitrust laws"—

(A) has the meaning given that term in subsection (a) of the first section of the Clayton Act (15 U.S.C. 12(a)), except that such term includes section 5 of the Federal Trade Commission Act (15 U.S.C. 45) to the extent such section 5 applies to unfair methods of competition; and

(B) includes any State law similar to the laws referred to in paragraph (1).

(g) Certain waivers granted to providers of local-into-local service to all DMAs—

(1) Injunction waiver.—A court that issued an injunction pursuant to subsection (a)(7)(B) before May 27, 2010, shall waive such injunction if the court recognizes the entity against which the injunction was issued as a qualified carrier.

(2) Limited temporary waiver—

(A) In general.—Upon a request made by a satellite carrier, a court that issued an injunction against such carrier under subsection (a)(7)(B) before May 27, 2010, shall waive such injunction with respect to the statutory license provided under subsection (a)(2) to the extent necessary to allow such carrier to make secondary transmissions of primary transmissions made by a network station to unserved households located in short markets in which such carrier was not providing local service pursuant to the license under section 122 as of December 31, 2009.

(B) Expiration of temporary waiver.—A temporary waiver of an injunction under subparagraph (A) shall expire after the end of the 120-day period beginning on the date such temporary waiver is issued unless extended for good cause by the court making the temporary waiver.

(C) Failure to provide local-into-local service to all DMAs—

(i) Failure to act reasonably and in good faith.—If the court issuing a temporary waiver under subparagraph (A) determines that the satellite carrier that made the request for such waiver has failed to act reasonably or has failed to make a good faith effort to provide local-into-local service to all DMAs, such failure—

(I) is actionable as an act of infringement under section 501 and the court may in its discretion impose the remedies provided for in sections 502 through 506 and subsection (a)(6)(B) of this section; and

(II) shall result in the termination of the waiver issued under subparagraph (A).

(ii) Failure to provide local-into-local service.—If the court issuing a temporary waiver under subparagraph (A) determines that the satellite carrier that made the request for such waiver has failed to provide local-into-local service to all DMAs, but determines that the carrier acted reasonably and in good faith, the court may in its discretion impose financial penalties that reflect—

(I) the degree of control the carrier had over the circumstances that resulted in the failure;

(II) the quality of the carrier's efforts to remedy the failure; and

(III) the severity and duration of any service interruption.

(D) Single temporary waiver available.—An entity may only receive one temporary waiver under this paragraph.

(E) Short market defined.—For purposes of this paragraph, the term "short market" means a local market in which programming of one or more of the four most widely viewed television networks nationwide as measured on May 27, 2010, is not offered on the primary stream transmitted by any local television broadcast station.

(3) Establishment of qualified carrier recognition—

(A) Statement of eligibility.—An entity seeking to be recognized as a qualified carrier under this subsection shall file a statement of eligibility with the court that imposed the injunction. A statement of eligibility must include—

(i) an affidavit that the entity is providing local-into-local service to all DMAs;

(ii) a motion for a waiver of the injunction;

(iii) a motion that the court appoint a special master under Rule 53 of the Federal Rules of Civil Procedure;

(iv) an agreement by the carrier to pay all expenses incurred by the special master under paragraph (4)(B)(ii); and

(v) a certification issued pursuant to section 342(a) of Communications Act of 1934.

(B) Grant of recognition as a qualified carrier.—Upon receipt of a statement of eligibility, the court shall recognize the entity as a qualified carrier and issue the waiver under paragraph (1). Upon motion pursuant to subparagraph (A)(iii), the court shall appoint a special master to conduct the examination and provide a report to the court as provided in paragraph (4)(B).

(C) Voluntary termination.—At any time, an entity recognized as a qualified carrier may file a statement of voluntary termination with the court certifying that it no longer wishes to be recognized as a qualified carrier. Upon receipt of such statement, the court shall reinstate the injunction waived under paragraph (1).

(D) Loss of recognition prevents future recognition.—No entity may be recognized as a qualified carrier if such entity had previously been recognized as a qualified carrier and subsequently lost such recognition or voluntarily terminated such recognition under subparagraph (C).

(4) Qualified carrier obligations and compliance—

(A) Continuing obligations—

(i) In general.—An entity recognized as a qualified carrier shall continue to provide local-into-local service to all DMAs.

(ii) Cooperation with compliance examination.—An entity recognized as a qualified carrier shall fully cooperate with the special master appointed by the court under paragraph (3)(B) in an examination set forth in subparagraph (B).

(B) Qualified carrier compliance examination—

(i) Examination and report.—A special master appointed by the court under paragraph (3)(B) shall conduct an examination of, and file a report on, the qualified carrier's compliance with the royalty payment and household eligibility requirements of the license under this section. The report shall address the qualified carrier's conduct during the period beginning on the date on which the qualified carrier is recognized as such under paragraph (3)(B) and ending on April 30, 2012.

(ii) Records of qualified carrier.—Beginning on the date that is one year after the date on which the qualified carrier is recognized as such under paragraph (3)(B), but not later than December 1, 2011, the qualified carrier shall provide the special master with all records that the special master considers to be directly pertinent to the following requirements under this section:

(I) Proper calculation and payment of royalties under the statutory license under this section.

(II) Provision of service under this license to eligible subscribers only.

(iii) Submission of report.—The special master shall file the report required by clause (i) not later than July 24, 2012, with the court referred to in paragraph (1) that issued the injunction, and the court shall transmit a copy of the report to the Register of Copyrights, the Committees on the Judiciary and on Energy and Commerce of the House of Representatives, and the Committees on the Judiciary and on Commerce, Science, and Transportation of the Senate.

(iv) Evidence of infringement.—The special master shall include in the report a statement of whether the examination by the special master indicated that there is substantial evidence that a copyright holder could bring a successful action under this section against the qualified carrier for infringement.

(v) Subsequent examination.—If the special master's report includes a statement that its examination indicated the existence of substantial evidence that a copyright holder could bring a successful action under this section against the qualified carrier for infringement, the special master shall, not later than 6 months after the report under clause (i) is filed, initiate another examination of the qualified carrier's compliance with the royalty payment and household eligibility requirements of the license under this section since the last report was filed under clause (iii). The special master shall file a report on the results of the examination conducted under this clause with the court referred to in paragraph (1) that issued the injunction, and the court shall transmit a copy to the Register of Copyrights, the Committees on the Judiciary and on Energy and Commerce of the House of Representatives, and the Committees on the Judiciary and on Commerce, Science, and Transportation of the Senate. The report shall include a statement described in clause (iv).

(vi) Compliance.—Upon motion filed by an aggrieved copyright owner, the court recognizing an entity as a qualified carrier shall terminate such designation upon finding that the entity has failed to cooperate with an examination required by this subparagraph.

(vii) Oversight.—During the period of time that the special master is conducting an examination under this subparagraph, the Comptroller General shall monitor the degree to which the entity seeking to be recognized or recognized as a qualified carrier under paragraph (3) is complying with the special master's examination. The qualified carrier shall make available to the Comptroller General all records and individuals that the Comptroller General considers necessary to meet the Comptroller General's obligations under this clause. The Comptroller General shall report the results of the monitoring required by this clause to the Committees on the Judiciary and on Energy and Commerce of the House of Representatives and the Committees on the Judiciary and on Commerce, Science, and Transportation of the Senate at intervals of not less than six months during such period.

(C) Affirmation.—A qualified carrier shall file an affidavit with the district court and the Register of Copyrights 30 months after such status was granted stating that, to the best of the affiant's knowledge, it is in compliance with the requirements for a qualified carrier. The qualified carrier shall attach to its affidavit copies of all reports or orders issued by the court, the special master, and the Comptroller General.

(D) Compliance determination.—Upon the motion of an aggrieved television broadcast station, the court recognizing an entity as a qualified carrier may make a determination of whether the entity is providing local-into-local service to all DMAs.

(E) Pleading requirement.—In any motion brought under subparagraph (D), the party making such motion shall specify one or more designated market areas (as such term is defined in section 122(j)(2)(C)) for which the failure to provide service is being alleged, and, for each such designated market area, shall plead with particularity the circumstances of the alleged failure.

(F) Burden of proof.—In any proceeding to make a determination under subparagraph (D), and with respect to a designated market area for which failure to provide service is alleged, the entity recognized as a qualified carrier shall have the burden of proving that the entity provided local-into-local service with a good quality satellite signal to at least 90 percent of the households in such designated market area (based on the most recent census data released by the United States Census Bureau) at the time and place alleged.

(5) Failure to provide service—

(A) Penalties.—If the court recognizing an entity as a qualified carrier finds that such entity has willfully failed to provide local-into-local service to all DMAs, such finding shall result in the loss of recognition of the entity as a qualified carrier and the termination of the waiver provided under paragraph (1), and the court may, in its discretion—

(i) treat such failure as an act of infringement under section 501, and subject such infringement to the remedies provided for in sections 502 through 506 and subsection (a)(6)(B) of this section; and

(ii) impose a fine of not less than $250,000 and not more than $5,000,000.

(B) Exception for nonwillful violation.—If the court determines that the failure to provide local-into-local service to all DMAs is nonwillful, the court may in its discretion impose financial penalties for noncompliance that reflect—

(i) the degree of control the entity had over the circumstances that resulted in the failure;

(ii) the quality of the entity's efforts to remedy the failure and restore service; and

(iii) the severity and duration of any service interruption.

(6) Penalties for violations of license.—A court that finds, under subsection (a)(6)(A), that an entity recognized as a qualified carrier has willfully made a secondary transmission of a primary transmission made by a network station and embodying a performance or display of a work to a subscriber who is not eligible to receive the transmission under this section shall reinstate the injunction waived under paragraph (1), and the court may order statutory damages of not more than $2,500,000.

(7) Local-into-local service to all DMAs defined.—For purposes of this subsection:

(A) In general.—An entity provides "local-into-local service to all DMAs" if the entity provides local service in all designated market areas (as such term is defined in section 122(j)(2)(C)) pursuant to the license under section 122.

(B) Household coverage.—For purposes of subparagraph (A), an entity that makes available local-into-local service with a good quality satellite signal to at least 90 percent of the households in a designated market area based on the most recent census data released by the United States Census Bureau shall be considered to be providing local service to such designated market area.

(C) Good quality satellite signal defined.—The term "good quality satellite signal" has the meaning given such term under section 342(e)(2) of Communications[1] Act of 1934.

(h) Termination of license.—This section shall cease to be effective on December 31, 2019.

1. **Editor's note:** Probably should be "of the Communication."

History of 17 U.S.C. §119: Nov. 16, 1988, P.L. 100-667, §202(2), 102 Stat. 3949; Dec. 17, 1993, P.L. 103-198, §5, 107 Stat. 2310; Oct. 18, 1994, P.L. 103-369, §2, 108 Stat. 3477; Nov. 1, 1995, P.L. 104-39, §5(c), 109 Stat. 348; Nov. 13, 1997, P.L. 105-80, §§1, 12(a)(8), 111 Stat. 1529, 1535; Aug. 5, 1999, P.L. 106-44, §1(g)(4), 113 Stat. 222; Nov. 29, 1999, P.L. 106-113, §1000(a)(9), 113 Stat. 1536; Nov. 2, 2002, P.L. 107-273, §§13209, 13210(1), (8), 116 Stat. 1908, 1909; Dec. 8, 2004, P.L. 108-447, §§101(b)-105, 107(a), 108, 111(a), 118 Stat. 3394-3405, 3406, 3407, 3408; May 30, 2005, P.L. 108-419, §5(g), (h), 118 Stat. 2367; May 30, 2005, P.L. 109-303, §4(e), 120 Stat. 1482; Oct. 13, 2008, P.L. 110-403, §209(a)(4), 122 Stat. 4264; Mar. 2, 2010, P.L. 111-144, §10(a)(1), 124 Stat. 47; Mar. 25, 2010, P.L. 111-151, §2(a), 124 Stat. 1027; Apr. 15, 2010, P.L. 111-157, §9(a)(1), 124 Stat. 1119; May 27, 2010, P.L. 111-175, §§102(a)(1), (b)-(k), 105, 124 Stat. 1219-1226, 1239; Dec. 9, 2010, P.L. 111-295, §6(c), 124 Stat. 3181; Dec. 4, 2014, P.L. 113-200, §§201(2), 202(a), 128 Stat. 2066.

See also 37 C.F.R. §§201.11, 360.1-360.32, 386.1, 386.2.

ANNOTATIONS

Generally

EchoStar Satellite L.L.C. v. FCC, 457 F.3d 31, 33 (D.C.Cir.2006). "A network television broadcaster generally has 'exclusive rights,' pursuant to [17 U.S.C. §106(5)], to authorize the public display of its copyrighted content, including the retransmission of its broadcast signal. In the Satellite Home Viewer Act of 1998 ..., the Congress, in order to make network programming available to households outside the broadcast range of a local network affiliate, gave satellite carriers a 'statutory license,' that is, a compulsory license subject to payment of a prescribed royalty, to retransmit to 'unserved households' the signals of no more than two distant network television stations. An unserved household is, with respect to a particular television network, one that is unable to receive by way of a conventional rooftop antenna a Grade B signal, as defined by the Commission, from one of that network's affiliates."

§119(a)(2)

EchoStar Satellite L.L.C. v. FCC, 457 F.3d 31, 37 (D.C.Cir.2006). "The statutory directives in ... 47 U.S.C. §339(c)(3) to ensure land cover is taken into account and to establish procedures for the 'continued refinement' of the [Individual Location Longley-Rice (ILLR)] model are subordinate to the anterior and more fundamental mandate to design a model that 'reliably' predicts signal strength. Only in the context of 'prescribing such [a] model' is the Commission directed to ensure land cover is 'take[n] into account.' Moreover, [§339(c)(3)] should be read in tandem with [17 U.S.C. §119(a)(2)(B)(ii)(I)]. The latter provision amended the Copyright Act to require courts, in copyright disputes between broadcasters and satellite carriers, to rely upon the ILLR model 'as that model may be amended by the Commission over time under [§339(c)(3)] to increase the accuracy of that model.' Section [119(a)(2)(B)(ii)(I)] plainly contemplates any revision to the ILLR model adopted pursuant to [§339(c)(3)] will 'increase,' not decrease, the accuracy of that model. Therefore, when the Commission determined, with respect to VHF stations, that the proposed adjustments would 'make the ILLR model less accurate,' it lawfully set the clutter loss value to zero. *At 41:* [A] prediction of the ILLR model presumptively establishes whether a household is unserved, ... and §339(c)(2) and (4) lay[s] out an elaborate procedure for requesting a waiver from a denial of service based upon, and for testing the result of, that prediction. Moreover, we note that [petitioner's] claim that it may circumvent the procedures in §339 so long as it pays for an on-site measurement by an independent tester, because its right to do so pre-dates and survives the [Satellite Home Viewer Improvement Act], does not square with ... §119(a)(2)(B)(ii)(II). That provision directs that for 'purposes of site measurements to determine whether a person resides in an unserved household under [§119(d)(10)(A)], a court shall rely on [§339(c)(4)],' which is the very provision that prescribes what [petitioner] calls the 'unnecessarily inefficient and burdensome' process for testing that it seeks to avoid. [Petitioner] points to nothing in the statute to support its conclusion that it may bypass the procedures in §339 by conducting its own on-site testing; nor do we see how one can square the above-referenced instruction to courts with any procedure other than that in §339." *See also* ***CBS Broad., Inc. v. EchoStar Comms.***, 450 F.3d 505, 508 (11th Cir.2006).

CBS Broad., Inc. v. EchoStar Comms., 450 F.3d 505, 508 n.1 (11th Cir.2006). "Distant network signals are network stations from outside a subscriber's market area. For example, a person who lives in Fort Lauderdale but receives an ABC, CBS, Fox or NBC network station from New York City is receiving 'distant network programming' or 'distant network stations.' *At 510-11:* Congress, as part of the [Satellite Home Viewer Improvement Act] amendment, instructed that the courts may use two methods to resolve the issue [of how to determine if a household is served or unserved]: the 'Accurate measurements' method and the 'Accurate predictive model.' The 'Accurate measurements' method requires actual physical measurements to determine the strength of the television station's signal at the subscriber's residence. These measurements must follow the procedures elaborated in 47 U.S.C. §339 and 47 C.F.R. §73.686, including measuring the signal intensity at a 'minimum of five locations as close as possible to the specific site where the site's receiving antenna is located.' The 'Accurate predictive model' for determining signal intensity is 'the Individual Location Longley-Rice [(ILLR)] model set forth by the Federal Communications Commission.' If used, the ILLR model permits the satellite carrier to avoid having to make time-consuming physical measurements of the signal intensity at a subscriber's residence by allowing the carrier to establish presumptively that a household cannot receive at least a Grade B signal and is therefore unserved."

§119(a)(6)

CBS Broad., Inc. v. EchoStar Comms., 450 F.3d 505, 511-12 (11th Cir.2006). Collectively, the Satellite Home Viewer Act (SHVA) of 1998 and the Satellite Home Viewer Improvement Act of 1999 make "abundantly clear that it is the satellite carrier who bears the burden of proving that its subscribers are, in fact, unserved. Plaintiff network stations have no obligation to put on any evidence demonstrating a violation of the terms of the statutory license. To the extent networks put on affirmative evidence of ineligibility, a satellite carrier cannot simply rebut or impeach that evidence. The satellite carrier must provide additional evidence that its challenged subscribers are unserved. Thus, a satellite carrier may be found to have violated the Act even if a court does not find that its subscribers are 'served.' A violation occurs so long as a carrier does not satisfy its burden of proving that its subscribers are 'unserved.' [¶] The Act contemplates two categories of violations as it relates to the secondary transmission of distant network service to served households: 'Individual violations' and 'Pattern[s] of violations.' An 'Individual violation' occurs where there is a 'willful or repeated secondary transmission … to a subscriber who is not eligible to receive the transmission under this section.' A district court has broad discretion to remedy such violation(s). A 'Pattern of violations' arises where 'a satellite carrier engages in a willful or repeated pattern or practice of delivering [distant network service] to subscribers who are not eligible to receive the transmission under this section.' The Act grants a court no discretion in its choice of remedy for a 'pattern or practice' of violations. *At 512 n.11:* The scope of the permanent injunction [under §119(a)(6)(B)(i)] depends on the scope of the 'pattern or practice' of violations. Where the 'pattern or practice' has been carried out on a 'substantially nationwide basis,' the Act mandates a nationwide injunction. A local or regional 'pattern or practice' results in a permanent injunction limited to 'that locality or region.' *At 520:* [T]he use of any [Individual Location Longley-Rice (ILLR)] method that does not comply with the specific procedures the FCC establishes for the model cannot be said to conform to the Act's requirements. *At 521:* So long as a satellite carrier uses vendors whose models comply with the FCC's ILLR guidelines, the carrier may utilize as many different vendors as it would like. We note, however, that the ILLR model is only a presumptive determination of eligibility, and the satellite carrier bears the ultimate burden of proving that a household is unserved. Unless there is evidence that one model is more accurate than another … when the models produce conflicting results, it would be difficult to conclude that a satellite carrier has satisfied its burden of proof. In such circumstances it would likely be necessary to obtain an accurate measurement pursuant to §119(a)(2)(B)(ii)(II) to demonstrate subscriber eligibility. *At 522-23:* [W]e conclude that the Act imposes a requirement that a household be presently unserved, not unserved solely at sign-up, as [D] suggests. *At 524:* [W]hile the statute itself does not automatically impose 'pattern or practice' liability where the 20% threshold is met, nor does it preclude a finding of 'pattern or practice' where the threshold is not reached, we believe the 20% ineligibility proportion to be a relevant marker for 'pattern or practice' analysis. [¶] [W]e read the statute as imposing liability '[i]f a satellite carrier [*ever*] engages in a willful or repeated pattern or practice' of statutory violations. The moment a satellite carrier engages in what can be said to be a 'pattern or practice' of violations, it makes itself eligible for the specified remedy, regardless of when it is found to have been doing so. [¶] [W]e presume, for the purpose of evaluating 'pattern or practice' liability, that a finding that a satellite carrier failed to carry its burden of establishing eligibility is tantamount to a finding of ineligibility. Section [119(a)(6)(B)] liability is triggered whenever a satellite carrier fails to carry its burden of proving eligibility on a sufficient scale, and to a sufficient degree, such that we can presume that the satellite carrier is engaging in a 'pattern or practice' of serving ineligible subscribers. *At 527:* [W]e find that Congress unequivocally stated a purpose to restrict the courts' traditional equitable authority upon a finding of a 'pattern or practice.' Because, as discussed, we come to the unavoidable conclusion that [D] engaged in a 'pattern or practice' of SHVA violations, we hold that the district court is required to issue a nationwide permanent injunction barring the provision of distant network programming pursuant to the Act's statutory license." *See also* ***CBS Broad., Inc. v. EchoStar Comms.***, 532 F.3d 1294, 1302 (11th Cir.2008).

§119(d)(6)

CBS Broad., Inc. v. EchoStar Comms., 532 F.3d 1294, 1300 (11th Cir.2008). "[Ps] argue that the injunction, which enjoins a satellite carrier's secondary transmissions of distant network programming, prohibits the Lease Agreement because [D], even in its passive role, continues to act as a satellite carrier engaged in such retransmissions. [¶] The parties' disagreement is centered on whether [D], despite its passive role, continues to *use* the facilities of the satellite for the purpose of *establishing* and *operating* a channel of communications for point-to-multipoint distribution of television station signals. *At 1301-02:* [Ps] fail to convince us that [D] is 'us[ing] the facilities of a satellite ... to establish and operate a channel of communications for point to multipoint distribution.' Importantly, the verbs are in the present tense. The satellite carrier must be in the continuing enterprise of *establishing* and *operating* the 'channel of communications for point-to-multipoint distribution.' [Ps] point out that [D] continues to have operational control over the transmission infrastructure of the satellite because [third party] is without the requisite license to operate an apparatus for the transmission of satellite television broadcasts under 47 U.S.C. §301. [Ps], however, fail to provide any detail on the intricacies and scope of [D's] operational control over the transmission infrastructure. [¶] The ... definition of 'satellite carrier' clearly contemplates a satellite owner leasing out its capacity (i.e., transponder and other equipment). [D] tells us that the leasehold arrangement is common in the industry and we are given no reason to disbelieve them. In such a leasing arrangement, [17 U.S.C. §119(d)(6)] makes clear that lessee becomes a satellite carrier. [¶] From this premise, it follows that the lessor cannot be a satellite carrier engaging in the retransmission of distant network programming simultaneously with the lessee's own retransmissions of the same kind. [¶] We conclude ... that [D], as a passive lessor of its satellite equipment, does not qualify as a satellite carrier with respect to [third party's] retransmissions of distant network programming."

§120. SCOPE OF EXCLUSIVE RIGHTS IN ARCHITECTURAL WORKS

(a) Pictorial representations permitted.—The copyright in an architectural work that has been constructed does not include the right to prevent the making, distributing, or public display of pictures, paintings, photographs, or other pictorial representations of the work, if the building in which the work is embodied is located in or ordinarily visible from a public place.

(b) Alterations to and destruction of buildings.—Notwithstanding the provisions of section 106(2), the owners of a building embodying an architectural work may, without the consent of the author or copyright owner of the architectural work, make or authorize the making of alterations to such building, and destroy or authorize the destruction of such building.

History of 17 U.S.C. §120: Dec. 1, 1990, P.L. 101-650, §704(a), 104 Stat. 5133.

§121. LIMITATIONS ON EXCLUSIVE RIGHTS: REPRODUCTION FOR BLIND OR OTHER PEOPLE WITH DISABILITIES

(a) Notwithstanding the provisions of section 106, it is not an infringement of copyright for an authorized entity to reproduce or to distribute copies or phonorecords of a previously published, nondramatic literary work if such copies or phonorecords are reproduced or distributed in specialized formats exclusively for use by blind or other persons with disabilities.

(b)(1) Copies or phonorecords to which this section applies shall—

(A) not be reproduced or distributed in a format other than a specialized format exclusively for use by blind or other persons with disabilities;

(B) bear a notice that any further reproduction or distribution in a format other than a specialized format is an infringement; and

(C) include a copyright notice identifying the copyright owner and the date of the original publication.

(2) The provisions of this subsection shall not apply to standardized, secure, or norm-referenced tests and related testing material, or to computer programs, except the portions thereof that are in conventional human language (including descriptions of pictorial works) and displayed to users in the ordinary course of using the computer programs.

(c) Notwithstanding the provisions of section 106, it is not an infringement of copyright for a publisher of print instructional materials for use in elementary or secondary schools to create and distribute to the National Instructional Materials Access Center copies of the electronic files described in sections 612(a)(23)(C), 613(a)(6), and section 674(e) of the Individuals with Disabilities Education Act that contain the contents of print instructional materials using the National Instructional Material Accessibility Standard (as defined in section 674(e)(3) of that Act), if—

(1) the inclusion of the contents of such print instructional materials is required by any State educational agency or local educational agency;

(2) the publisher had the right to publish such print instructional materials in print formats; and

(3) such copies are used solely for reproduction or distribution of the contents of such print instructional materials in specialized formats.

(d) For purposes of this section, the term—

(1) "authorized entity" means a nonprofit organization or a governmental agency that has a primary mission to provide specialized services relating to training, education, or adaptive reading or information access needs of blind or other persons with disabilities;

(2) "blind or other persons with disabilities" means individuals who are eligible or who may qualify in accordance with the Act entitled "An Act to provide books for the adult blind," approved March 3, 1931 (2 U.S.C. 135a; 46 Stat. 1487) to receive books and other publications produced in specialized formats;

(3) "print instructional materials" has the meaning given under section 674(e)(3)(C) of the Individuals with Disabilities Education Act; and

(4) "specialized formats" means—

(A) braille, audio, or digital text which is exclusively for use by blind or other persons with disabilities; and

(B) with respect to print instructional materials, includes large print formats when such materials are distributed exclusively for use by blind or other persons with disabilities.

History of 17 U.S.C. §121: Sept. 16, 1996, P.L. 104-197, §316(a), 110 Stat. 2416; Oct. 27, 2000, P.L. 106-379, §3(b), 114 Stat. 1445; Nov. 2, 2002, P.L. 107-273, §13210(3)(A), 116 Stat. 1909; Dec. 3, 2004, P.L. 108-446, §306, 118 Stat. 2807.

§122. LIMITATIONS ON EXCLUSIVE RIGHTS: SECONDARY TRANSMISSIONS OF LOCAL TELEVISION PROGRAMMING BY SATELLITE

(a) Secondary transmissions into local markets—

(1) Secondary transmissions of television broadcast stations within a local market.—A secondary transmission of a performance or display of a work embodied in a primary transmission of a television broadcast station into the station's local market shall be subject to statutory licensing under this section if—

(A) the secondary transmission is made by a satellite carrier to the public;

(B) with regard to secondary transmissions, the satellite carrier is in compliance with the rules, regulations, or authorizations of the Federal Communications Commission governing the carriage of television broadcast station signals; and

(C) the satellite carrier makes a direct or indirect charge for the secondary transmission to—

(i) each subscriber receiving the secondary transmission; or

(ii) a distributor that has contracted with the satellite carrier for direct or indirect delivery of the secondary transmission to the public.

(2) Significantly viewed stations—

(A) In general.—A secondary transmission of a performance or display of a work embodied in a primary transmission of a television broadcast station to subscribers who receive secondary transmissions of primary transmissions under paragraph (1) shall be subject to statutory licensing under this paragraph if the secondary transmission is of the primary transmission of a network station or a non-network station to a subscriber who resides outside the station's local market but within a community in which the signal has been determined by the Federal Communications Commission to be significantly viewed in such community, pursuant to the rules, regulations, and authorizations of the Federal Communications Commission in effect on April 15, 1976, applicable to determining with respect to a cable system whether signals are significantly viewed in a community.

(B) Waiver.—A subscriber who is denied the secondary transmission of the primary transmission of a network station or a non-network station under subparagraph (A) may request a waiver from such denial by submitting a request, through the subscriber's satellite carrier, to the network station or non-network station in the local market affiliated with the same network or non-network where the subscriber is located. The network station or non-network station shall accept or reject the subscriber's request for a waiver within 30 days after receipt of the request. If the network station or non-network station fails to accept or reject the subscriber's request for a waiver within that 30-day period, that network station or non-network station shall be deemed to agree to the waiver request.

(3) Secondary transmission of low power programming—

(A) In general.—Subject to subparagraphs (B) and (C), a secondary transmission of a performance or display of a work embodied in a primary transmission of a television broadcast station to subscribers who receive secondary transmissions of primary transmissions under paragraph (1) shall be subject to statutory licensing under this paragraph if the secondary transmission is of the primary transmission of a television broadcast station that is licensed as a low power television station, to a subscriber who resides within the same designated market area as the station that originates the transmission.

(B) No applicability to repeaters and translators.—Secondary transmissions provided for in subparagraph (A) shall not apply to any low power television station that retransmits the programs and signals of another television station for more than 2 hours each day.

(C) No impact on other secondary transmissions obligations.—A satellite carrier that makes secondary transmissions of a primary transmission of a low power television station under a statutory license provided under this section is not required, by reason of such secondary transmissions, to make any other secondary transmissions.

(4) Special exceptions.—A secondary transmission of a performance or display of a work embodied in a primary transmission of a television broadcast station to subscribers who receive secondary transmissions of primary transmissions under paragraph (1) shall, if the secondary transmission is made by a satellite carrier that complies with the requirements of paragraph (1), be subject to statutory licensing under this paragraph as follows:

(A) States with single full-power network station.—In a State in which there is licensed by the Federal Communications Commission a single full-power station that was a network station on January 1, 1995, the statutory license provided for in this paragraph shall apply to the secondary transmission by a satellite carrier of the primary transmission of that station to any subscriber in a community that is located within that State and that is not within the first 50 television markets as listed in the regulations of the Commission as in effect on such date (47 C.F.R. 76.51).

(B) States with all network stations and non-network stations in same local market.—In a State in which all network stations and non-network stations licensed by the Federal Communications Commission within that State as of January 1, 1995, are assigned to the same local market and that local market does not encompass all counties of that State, the statutory license provided under this paragraph shall apply to the secondary transmission by a satellite carrier of the primary transmissions of such station to all subscribers in the State who reside in a local market that is within the first 50 major television markets as listed in the regulations of the Commission as in effect on such date (section 76.51 of title 47, Code of Federal Regulations).

(C) Additional stations.—In the case of that State in which are located 4 counties that—

(i) on January 1, 2004, were in local markets principally comprised of counties in another State, and

(ii) had a combined total of 41,340 television households, according to the U.S. Television Household Estimates by Nielsen Media Research for 2004,

the statutory license provided under this paragraph shall apply to secondary transmissions by a satellite carrier to subscribers in any such county of the primary transmissions of any network station located in that State, if the satellite carrier was making such secondary transmissions to any subscribers in that county on January 1, 2004.

(D) Certain additional stations.—If 2 adjacent counties in a single State are in a local market comprised principally of counties located in another State, the statutory license provided for in this paragraph shall apply to the secondary transmission by a satellite carrier to subscribers in those 2 counties of the primary transmissions of any network station located in the capital of the State in which such 2 counties are located, if—

(i) the 2 counties are located in a local market that is in the top 100 markets for the year 2003 according to Nielsen Media Research; and

(ii) the total number of television households in the 2 counties combined did not exceed 10,000 for the year 2003 according to Nielsen Media Research.

(E) Networks of noncommercial educational broadcast stations.—In the case of a system of three or more noncommercial educational broadcast stations licensed to a single State, public agency, or political, educational, or special purpose subdivision of a State, the statutory license provided for in this paragraph shall apply to the secondary transmission of the primary transmission of such system to any subscriber in any county or county equivalent within such State, if such subscriber is located in a designated market area that is not otherwise eligible to receive the secondary transmission of the primary transmission of a noncommercial educational broadcast station located within the State pursuant to paragraph (1).

(5) Applicability of royalty rates and procedures.—The royalty rates and procedures under section 119(b) shall apply to the secondary transmissions to which the statutory license under paragraph (4) applies.

(b) Reporting requirements—

(1) Initial lists.—A satellite carrier that makes secondary transmissions of a primary transmission made by a network station under subsection (a) shall, within 90 days after commencing such secondary transmissions, submit to the network that owns or is affiliated with the network station—

(A) a list identifying (by name in alphabetical order and street address, including county and 9-digit zip code) all subscribers to which the satellite carrier makes secondary transmissions of that primary transmission under subsection (a); and

(B) a separate list, aggregated by designated market area (by name and address, including street or rural route number, city, State, and 9-digit zip code), which shall indicate those subscribers being served pursuant to paragraph (2) of subsection (a).

(2) Subsequent lists.—After the list is submitted under paragraph (1), the satellite carrier shall, on the 15th of each month, submit to the network—

(A) a list identifying (by name in alphabetical order and street address, including county and 9-digit zip code) any subscribers who have been added or dropped as subscribers since the last submission under this subsection; and

(B) a separate list, aggregated by designated market area (by name and street address, including street or rural route number, city, State, and 9-digit zip code), identifying those subscribers whose service pursuant to paragraph (2) of subsection (a) has been added or dropped since the last submission under this subsection.

(3) Use of subscriber information.—Subscriber information submitted by a satellite carrier under this subsection may be used only for the purposes of monitoring compliance by the satellite carrier with this section.

(4) Requirements of networks.—The submission requirements of this subsection shall apply to a satellite carrier only if the network to which the submissions are to be made places on file with the Register of Copyrights a document identifying the name and address of the person to whom such submissions are to be made. The Register of Copyrights shall maintain for public inspection a file of all such documents.

(c) No royalty fee required for certain secondary transmissions.—A satellite carrier whose secondary transmissions are subject to statutory licensing under paragraphs (1), (2), and (3) of subsection (a) shall have no royalty obligation for such secondary transmissions.

(d) Noncompliance with reporting and regulatory requirements.—Notwithstanding subsection (a), the willful or repeated secondary transmission to the public by a satellite carrier into the local market of a television broadcast station of a primary transmission embodying a performance or display of a work made by that television broadcast station is actionable as an act of infringement under section 501, and is fully subject to the remedies provided under sections 502 through 506, if the satellite carrier has not complied with the reporting requirements of subsection (b) or with the rules, regulations, and authorizations of the Federal Communications Commission concerning the carriage of television broadcast signals.

(e) Willful alterations.—Notwithstanding subsection (a), the secondary transmission to the public by a satellite carrier into the local market of a television broadcast station of a performance or display of a work embodied in a primary transmission made by that television broadcast station is actionable as an act of infringement under section 501, and is fully subject to the remedies provided by sections 502 through 506 and section 510, if the content of the particular program in which the performance or display is embodied, or any commercial advertising or station announcement transmitted by the primary transmitter during, or immediately before or after, the transmission of such program, is in any way willfully altered by the satellite carrier through changes, deletions, or additions, or is combined with programming from any other broadcast signal.

(f) Violation of territorial restrictions on statutory license for television broadcast stations—

(1) Individual violations.—The willful or repeated secondary transmission to the public by a satellite carrier of a primary transmission embodying a performance or display of a work made by a television broadcast station to a subscriber who does not reside in that station's local market, and is not subject to statutory licensing under section 119, subject to statutory licensing by reason of paragraph (2)(A), (3), or (4) of subsection (a), or subject to a private licensing agreement, is actionable as an act of infringement under section 501 and is fully subject to the remedies provided by sections 502 through 506, except that—

(A) no damages shall be awarded for such act of infringement if the satellite carrier took corrective action by promptly withdrawing service from the ineligible subscriber; and

(B) any statutory damages shall not exceed $250 for such subscriber for each month during which the violation occurred.

(2) Pattern of violations.—If a satellite carrier engages in a willful or repeated pattern or practice of secondarily transmitting to the public a primary transmission embodying a performance or display of a work made by a television broadcast station to subscribers who do not reside in that station's local market, and are not subject to statutory licensing under section 119, subject to statutory licensing by reason of paragraph (2)(A), (3), or (4) of subsection (a), or subject to a private licensing agreement, then in addition to the remedies under paragraph (1)—

(A) if the pattern or practice has been carried out on a substantially nationwide basis, the court—

(i) shall order a permanent injunction barring the secondary transmission by the satellite carrier of the primary transmissions of that television broadcast station (and if such television broadcast station is a network station, all other television broadcast stations affiliated with such network); and

(ii) may order statutory damages not exceeding $2,500,000 for each 6-month period during which the pattern or practice was carried out; and

(B) if the pattern or practice has been carried out on a local or regional basis with respect to more than one television broadcast station, the court—

(i) shall order a permanent injunction barring the secondary transmission in that locality or region by the satellite carrier of the primary transmissions of any television broadcast station; and

(ii) may order statutory damages not exceeding $2,500,000 for each 6-month period during which the pattern or practice was carried out.

(g) Burden of proof.—In any action brought under subsection (f), the satellite carrier shall have the burden of proving that its secondary transmission of a primary transmission by a television broadcast station is made only to subscribers located within that station's local market or subscribers being served in compliance with section 119, paragraph (2)(A), (3), or (4) of subsection (a), or a private licensing agreement.

(h) Geographic limitations on secondary transmissions.—The statutory license created by this section shall apply to secondary transmissions to locations in the United States.

(i) Exclusivity with respect to secondary transmissions of broadcast stations by satellite to members of the public.—No provision of section 111 or any other law (other than this section and section 119) shall be construed to contain any authorization, exemption, or license through which secondary transmissions by satellite carriers of programming contained in a primary transmission made by a television broadcast station may be made without obtaining the consent of the copyright owner.

(j) Definitions.—In this section—

(1) Distributor.—The term "distributor" means an entity that contracts to distribute secondary transmissions from a satellite carrier and, either as a single channel or in a package with other programming, provides the secondary transmission either directly to individual subscribers or indirectly through other program distribution entities.

(2) Local market—

(A) In general.—The term "local market," in the case of both commercial and noncommercial television broadcast stations, means the designated market area in which a station is located, and—

(i) in the case of a commercial television broadcast station, all commercial television broadcast stations licensed to a community within the same designated market area are within the same local market; and

(ii) in the case of a noncommercial educational television broadcast station, the market includes any station that is licensed to a community within the same designated market area as the noncommercial educational television broadcast station.

(B) County of license.—In addition to the area described in subparagraph (A), a station's local market includes the county in which the station's community of license is located.

(C) Designated market area.—For purposes of subparagraph (A), the term "designated market area" means a designated market area, as determined by Nielsen Media Research and published in the 1999-2000 Nielsen Station Index Directory and Nielsen Station Index United States Television Household Estimates or any successor publication.

(D) Certain areas outside of any designated market area.—Any census area, borough, or other area in the State of Alaska that is outside of a designated market area, as determined by Nielsen Media Research, shall be deemed to be part of one of the local markets in the State of Alaska. A satellite carrier may determine which local market in the State of Alaska will be deemed to be the relevant local market in connection with each subscriber in such census area, borough, or other area.

(E) Market determinations.—The local market of a commercial television broadcast station may be modified by the Federal Communications Commission in accordance with section 338(*l*) of the Communications Act of 1934 (47 U.S.C. 338).

(3) Low power television station.—The term "low power television station" means a low power TV station as defined in section 74.701(f) of title 47, Code of Federal Regulations, as in effect on June 1, 2004. For purposes of this paragraph, the term "low power television station" includes a low power television station that has been accorded primary status as a Class A television licensee under section 73.6001(a) of title 47, Code of Federal Regulations.

(4) Network station; non-network station; satellite carrier; secondary transmission.—The terms "network station," "non-network station," "satellite carrier," and "secondary transmission" have the meanings given such terms under section 119(d).

(5) Noncommercial educational broadcast station.—The term "noncommercial educational broadcast station" means a television broadcast station that is a noncommercial educational broadcast station as defined in section 397 of the Communications Act of 1934, as in effect on May 27, 2010.

(6) Subscriber.—The term "subscriber" means a person or entity that receives a secondary transmission service from a satellite carrier and pays a fee for the service, directly or indirectly, to the satellite carrier or to a distributor.

(7) Television broadcast station.—The term "television broadcast station"—

(A) means an over-the-air, commercial or noncommercial television broadcast station licensed by the Federal Communications Commission under subpart E of part 73 of title 47, Code of Federal Regulations, except that such term does not include a low-power or translator television station; and

(B) includes a television broadcast station licensed by an appropriate governmental authority of Canada or Mexico if the station broadcasts primarily in the English language and is a network station as defined in section 119(d)(2)(A).

History of 17 U.S.C. §122: Nov. 29, 1999, P.L. 106-113, §1000(a)(9), 113 Stat. 1536; Nov. 2, 2002, P.L. 107-273, §13210(2)(A), 116 Stat. 1909; Dec. 8,

2004, P.L. 108-447, §111(b), 118 Stat. 3409; Oct. 13, 2008, P.L. 110-403, §209(a)(5), 122 Stat. 4264; May 27, 2010, P.L. 111-175, §103(a)(1), (b)-(f), 124 Stat. 1227-1230; Dec. 4, 2014, P.L. 113-200, §204, 128 Stat. 2067.

CHAPTER 2. COPYRIGHT OWNERSHIP & TRANSFER

§201. OWNERSHIP OF COPYRIGHT

(a) Initial ownership.—Copyright in a work protected under this title vests initially in the author or authors of the work. The authors of a joint work are coowners of copyright in the work.

(b) Works made for hire.—In the case of a work made for hire, the employer or other person for whom the work was prepared is considered the author for purposes of this title, and, unless the parties have expressly agreed otherwise in a written instrument signed by them, owns all of the rights comprised in the copyright.

(c) Contributions to collective works.—Copyright in each separate contribution to a collective work is distinct from copyright in the collective work as a whole, and vests initially in the author of the contribution. In the absence of an express transfer of the copyright or of any rights under it, the owner of copyright in the collective work is presumed to have acquired only the privilege of reproducing and distributing the contribution as part of that particular collective work, any revision of that collective work, and any later collective work in the same series.

(d) Transfer of ownership—

(1) The ownership of a copyright may be transferred in whole or in part by any means of conveyance or by operation of law, and may be bequeathed by will or pass as personal property by the applicable laws of intestate succession.

(2) Any of the exclusive rights comprised in a copyright, including any subdivision of any of the rights specified by section 106, may be transferred as provided by clause (1) and owned separately. The owner of any particular exclusive right is entitled, to the extent of that right, to all of the protection and remedies accorded to the copyright owner by this title.

(e) Involuntary transfer.—When an individual author's ownership of a copyright, or of any of the exclusive rights under a copyright, has not previously been transferred voluntarily by that individual author, no action by any governmental body or other official or organization purporting to seize, expropriate, transfer, or exercise rights of ownership with respect to the copyright, or any of the exclusive rights under a copyright, shall be given effect under this title, except as provided under title 11.

History of 17 U.S.C. §201: Oct. 19, 1976, P.L. 94-553, §101, 90 Stat. 2568; Nov. 6, 1978, P.L. 95-598, §313, 92 Stat. 2676.

See also 11 U.S.C. §365(n); 26 U.S.C. §1249; 28 U.S.C. §4001.

ANNOTATIONS

§201(a)

Community for Creative Non-Violence v. Reid, 490 U.S. 730, 737 (1989). "As a general rule, the author is the party who actually creates the work, that is, the person who translates an idea into a fixed, tangible expression entitled to copyright protection."

Brownstein v. Lindsay, 742 F.3d 55, 64-65 (3d Cir. 2014). "When two or more people create a 'joint work,' they become co-authors and co-owners of the work, each entitled to 'undivided ownership in the entire work.' This ownership interest vests from the act of creating the work, rather than from any sort of agreement between the authors or any act of registration with the Copyright Office. [¶] For two or more people to become co-authors, each author must contribute some non-trivial amount of creative, original, or intellectual expression to the work and both must intend that their contributions be combined. The components must also be 'inseparable or interdependent' parts of a whole but each co-author's contribution need not be equal for them to have an equal stake in the work as a whole. Thus, if Person A writes lyrics to a song and intends for a composer to write the score, Person B who writes the score becomes a co-author in the work." *See also* ***Gaylord v. U.S.***, 595 F.3d 1364, 1376-77 (Fed.Cir.2010); ***Janky v. Lake Cty. Convention & Visitors Bur.***, 576 F.3d 356, 361 (7th Cir.2009).

Saregama India Ltd. v. Mosley, 635 F.3d 1284, 1290 (11th Cir.2011). "'Initial ownership of a copyrighted work is determined by the laws in the work's country of origin.'"

Universal Furniture Int'l v. Collezione Europa USA, Inc., 618 F.3d 417, 428 (4th Cir.2010). "A certificate of registration issued by the Copyright Office [under 17 U.S.C. §410(c)] is 'prima facie evidence of the validity of the copyright and of the facts stated in the certificate,' such as ownership. When such a certificate exists, the burden shifts to the defendant to prove that the claimed copyrights are invalid. However, the Copyright Office's practice of summarily issuing registrations (perhaps even the day of filing the application, as in this case) counsels against placing too much weight on registrations as proof of a valid copyright. Accordingly, a reviewing court should assess other relevant indicia of ownership, such as the parties' intent and the terms of transfer agreements and other documents establishing a chain of title."

Warren Freedenfeld Assocs. v. McTigue, 531 F.3d 38, 47-48 (1st Cir.2008). "Under the Copyright Act, no copyright infringement action lies as between joint owners of the same copyright. Each co-owner of a copyright is akin to a tenant in common and each owns a share of an undivided whole. It follows inexorably that the co-owner of a copyright is incapable of infringing that copyright vis-à-vis his counterpart co-owner. *At 48 n.5:* This is not to say that an aggrieved co-owner of a copyright is without recourse if his counterpart co-owner acts wrongfully. The aggrieved co-owner may, for example, be able to bring a declaratory action to determine his ownership rights. Alternatively, he may be able to bring a state-law claim for an accounting."

Davis v. Blige, 505 F.3d 90, 99 (2d Cir.2007). "[A] joint owner is not required to join his other co-owners in an action for infringement."

Rodrigue v. Rodrigue, 218 F.3d 432, 436 (5th Cir. 2000). "We agree with [wife claiming interest in copyright] that, in and of itself, 'vesting' of the copyright and its five (and five only) statutorily delineated attributes in one spouse does not preclude classification of other attributes of ownership of a copyright as community property. Moreover, by its very title, [17 U.S.C.] §201(a) addresses only *initial*—not *permanent*—vesting of the copyright in the author. And, even though the author's copyright arises at the moment of creation of the work, the [Copyright] Act explicitly allows for subsequent vesting in non-authors, either jointly with the author or subsequent to him by virtue of transfer of all or lesser portions of the copyright. [¶] We ... conclude ... that the language of §201(a), providing that a bundle of but five specific rights, those listed in [17 U.S.C.] §106, 'vests initially' in the author, does not ineluctably conflict with any provision of Louisiana matrimonial property law that would recognize that [wife] does have an economic interest in [husband's] copyrights. *At 441 n.47:* Even though the Act explicitly prohibits involuntary transfers by any governmental body or other official or organization, it specifies that '[t]raditional legal actions that may involve transfer of ownership, such as bankruptcy proceedings and mortgage foreclosures, are not within the scope of [the involuntary transfer] subsection.' These other types of transfer, like contractual conveyance and inheritance, are subject to varying state laws, yet Congress has not perceived any inherent obstruction of federal interests in such additional modes of alienation, and neither do we."

Seshadri v. Kasraian, 130 F.3d 798, 803 (7th Cir. 1997). "To be a joint author, an assistant or collaborator must contribute significant copyrightable material. [¶] This is merely a default rule; by contract the sole creator of a work can transfer 'authorship' in whole or part to another. But it is a sensible rule, because ordinarily the person who does not contribute significant copyrightable work does not expect to have a copyright interest, and one who does does."

Childress v. Taylor, 945 F.2d 500, 508-09 (2d Cir. 1991). "Joint authorship entitles the co-authors to equal undivided interests in the work. That equal sharing of rights should be reserved for relationships in which all participants fully intend to be joint authors. The sharing of benefits in other relationships involving assistance in the creation of a copyrightable work can be more precisely calibrated by the participants in their contract negotiations regarding division of royalties or assignment of shares of ownership of the copyright."

Young Money Entm't, LLC v. Digerati Holdings, LLC, No. 2:12-cv-07663-ODW(JCx) (C.D.Cal.2012) (order; 11-15-12). "Whether co-owners of a copyright can be held in privity for purposes of collateral estoppel and res judicata is ... a matter of first impression for this Court. [¶] [C]o-owners in copyright are generally considered similar to tenants in common. But typically a tenancy in common does not create privity sufficient to make a judgment 'for or against one operate as an estoppel for or against others.' [¶] Co-owners in copyright have a duty to account to one another for profits derived from the use of that copyright. If one tenant in common licenses the copyright to a third party, the other tenant in common can seek the profits from the licensor. [¶] Applying collateral estoppel here would effectively allow one co-owner to rob another co-owner's own right to sue for an accrued cause of action by being the first to the courthouse steps."

BTE v. Bonnecaze, 49 U.S.P.Q.2d 1153, 1154 (E.D. La.1998). "Parts of a unitary whole are considered 'inseparable' when they have little or no meaning standing alone. For example, when two authors collaborate to produce one written text their contributions are inseparable. Parts of a unitary whole are considered 'interdependent' when 'they have some meaning standing alone but achieve their primary significance because of their combined effect.' The lyrics and music of a song are often ... interdependent parts. The authors of a joint work are co-owners of the copyright in that work."

§201(b)

Community for Creative Non-Violence v. Reid, 490 U.S. 730, 737 (1989). "The [Copyright] Act carves out an important exception ... for 'works made for hire.' If the work is for hire, 'the employer or other person for whom the work was prepared is considered the author' and owns the copyright, unless there is a written agreement to the contrary. Classifying a work as 'made for hire' determines not only the initial ownership of its copyright, but also the copyright's duration, and the owners' renewal rights, termination rights, and right to import certain goods bearing the copyright. *At 742-43:* The structure of [17 U.S.C.] §101 indicates that a work for hire can arise through one of two mutually exclusive means, one for employees and one for independent contractors, and ordinary cannons of statutory interpretation indicate that the classification of a particular hired party should be made with reference to agency law." *See also* ***Lulirama Ltd. v. Axcess Broad. Servs.***, 128 F.3d 872, 876 (5th Cir.1997).

Pritchett v. Pound, 473 F.3d 217, 219 (5th Cir. 2006). "We agree with the district judge that [employer] was the sole owner of the books. The employment agreement governing [employee's] employment with [employer] specifically provided that all written materials created by [employee] in his employment were to be exclusive property of the employer. The books were therefore made for hire because [employer] and [employee] did not expressly agree otherwise by written instrument signed by them. While [copyright] registration form, if standing alone, would be evidence of joint ownership, it is not a written agreement changing the employment relationship that the statute requires." *See also* ***LaJoie v. Pavcon, Inc.***, 146 F.Supp.2d 1240, 1246 n.5 (M.D.Fla.2000).

Metcalf v. Bochco, 294 F.3d 1069, 1072-73 (9th Cir. 2002). "In the absence of a written agreement, to determine whether the writer of a work is an employee who does not own the work, or instead an independent contractor who does, we apply 'principles of general common law of agency.'"

Cleary v. News Corp., 30 F.3d 1255, 1259-60 (9th Cir.1994). Because "employer is considered the author of the work, once authorship rights are relinquished through a work for hire contract provision, the right to attribution is also relinquished unless that right is reserved explicitly in the contract."

Liu v. Price Waterhouse L.L.P., 182 F.Supp.2d 666, 672 n.1 (N.D.Ill.2001), *aff'd*, 302 F.3d 749 (7th Cir.2002). "The difference between the work for hire doctrine, under which the party creating the work (if not an employee) must explicitly assign his or her rights to the party commissioning its creation, and derivative work licenses, is that the author of a derivative work must get permission to create the derivative work. [I]t makes sense to require an explicit transfer of ownership in works made for hire to protect the true author's rights in his or her work. A derivative work author, by contrast, is by definition working within the confines of his or her license to create that work and is bound not to infringe the rights of the original work's owner by exceeding the scope of that license."

Manning v. Parkland Coll., 109 F.Supp.2d 976, 980 (C.D.Ill.2000). "By the terms of [§201(b)], the agreement must be in writing and must be signed by both parties. The statutory language is 'signed by them,' that is, by both parties, and it means what it says. [T]here must be a sufficient writing to rebut the presumption that the employer retains the copyright in a work made for hire. It is the employee's burden to show the existence of a writing granting the employee the copyright in any work made for hire. Unwritten understandings or writings not containing the signatures of both parties are insufficient to rebut the presumption."

§201(c)

New York Times Co. v. Tasini, 533 U.S. 483, 487 (2001). "Under agreements with the periodicals' publishers, but without the freelancers' consent, two computer database companies [electronic publishers] placed copies of the freelancers' articles—along with all other articles from the periodicals in which the freelancers' work appeared—into three databases. Whether written by a freelancer or staff member, each article is presented to, and retrievable by, the user in isolation, clear of the context the original print publication presented. *At 488:* [W]e hold that §201(c) does not authorize the copying at issue here. The publishers are not sheltered by §201(c), we conclude, because the databases reproduce and distribute articles standing alone and not in context, not 'as part of that particular collective work' to which the author contributed, 'as part of ... any revision' thereof, or 'as part of ... any later collective work in the same series.'"

Greenberg v. National Geographic Soc'y, 533 F.3d 1244, 1251 (11th Cir.2008). "[T]he teachings of ***Tasini*** are twofold. First, the concept of 'revision' necessarily includes some element of novelty or 'newness' as defined by the Court, and second, consideration of the context in which the contributions are presented is critical in determining whether that novelty is sufficient to defeat the publisher's §201(c) privilege."

Faulkner v. National Geographic Enters., 409 F.3d 26, 38 (2d Cir.2005). "[W]e hold that, because the original context of the Magazines is omnipresent in [digital collection] and because it is a new version of the Magazine, [digital collection] is a privileged revision. [¶] Revision denotes a new version, and a version is, in this setting, a distinct form of something regarded by its creator or others as one work. In determining whether [underlying works] have been reproduced and distributed as part of a revision of the collective works in issue, we focus on [underlying works] as presented to, and perceptible by, the user of [digital collection]. *At 39:* [I]t is more than reasonable to read §201(c) and §201(d) together to render the publisher's limited privilege under §201(c) to be transferrable under §201(d). [¶] [P]ublishers may transfer any subdivision of a copyright that they acquire." (Internal quotes omitted.)

Gaiman v. McFarlane, 360 F.3d 644, 654 (7th Cir. 2004). "The compiler's copyright entitles him to reprint the contents of the compilation in future editions of the compilation. But all the other rights of copyright remain in the authors of the contributions, provided the contributions satisfy the criteria of copyrightability. Therefore the compiler's copyright notice is not adverse to the contributors' copyrights and so does not put them on notice that their rights are being challenged. On the contrary, 'a single copyright notice applicable to the collective work as a whole serves to indicate protection for all the contributions in the collective work, except for advertisements, regardless of the ownership of copyright in the individual contributions and whether they have been published previously.'"

Tasini v. New York Times Co., 206 F.3d 161, 168 (2d Cir.2000), *aff'd*, 533 U.S. 483 (2001). "The aspects of a collective work that make it 'an original work of authorship' are the selection, coordination, and arrangement of the preexisting materials." *See also* ***Greenberg v. National Geographic Soc'y***, 533 F.3d 1244, 1258 (11th Cir.2008).

Ryan v. Carl Corp., 23 F.Supp.2d 1146, 1150 (N.D. Cal.1998). When "in doubt, courts should construe the rights of publishers narrowly rather than broadly in relation to those of authors. [Section 201(c)] expressly states that the holder of the copyright in the collective work is presumed 'only' the enumerated rights. [¶] [I]t makes more sense to allocate the right of reproduction to publishers, because publishers are easier to locate."

§201(d)—Generally

Brownstein v. Lindsay, 742 F.3d 55, 68 (3d Cir. 2014). "With respect to licensing a joint work, each co-author is entitled to convey non-exclusive rights to the joint work without the consent of his co-author. The only caveat is that the licensing author must account to his co-author for his fair share of profits from any non-exclusive license. If a co-author attempts to convey exclusive rights, his co-author can convey the same exclusive rights—in effect, such an exclusive license becomes a non-exclusive license. Accordingly, the only way for truly exclusive rights to be conveyed to a joint work is for all co-authors to consent to such an exclusive conveyance. As with tenants in common of real property, a co-author can transfer or assign the rights to his ownership interest in the joint work, but this does not affect the ownership rights of his co-author. [¶] With respect to transferring the ownership of a joint work, a co-author cannot transfer the ownership interest of his co-author. The Copyright Act's 'statute of frauds' requires that any transfer of an ownership interest must be signed and in writing."

Cincom Sys. v. Novelis Corp., 581 F.3d 431, 436 (6th Cir.2009). "Federal common law governs 'questions with respect to the assignability of a patent [or copyright] license.' *At 437:* Despite the federal common law rule that copyright licenses are unassignable absent express language to the contrary, '[s]tate law is not displaced merely because the contract relates to intellectual property.' The states are thus 'free to regulate the use of ... intellectual property in any manner not inconsistent with federal law.' Applying these principles, state contract law will govern the interpretation of a license because a license is merely a type of contract. As there is no general federal corporate law, state law will also determine whether a merger results in the transfer of an intellectual property license. However, where state law would allow for the transfer of a license absent express authorization, state law must yield to the federal common law rule prohibiting such unauthorized transfers. [¶] [P] granted [D] a non-exclusive and non-transferrable license. [T]he license issued to [D] also required the express written approval of the grantor prior to any transfer of the license. *At 440:* When [D's predecessor] merged with [D's subsidiary], the license granted by [P] solely to [D's predecessor] transferred to the surviving corporation, now known as [D]. Because [D] did not abide by the express terms of [P's] license and gain [P's] prior written approval, [D] infringed [P's] copyright."

Roger Miller Music, Inc. v. Sony/ATV Publ'g, 477 F.3d 383, 391-92 (6th Cir.2007). "The renewal term of a copyrighted work is distinct from the original copyright term and can therefore be transferred independently of the original copyright. There is a strong presumption against the conveyance of renewal-copyright interests simultaneous with the conveyance of the original-copyright interest. Therefore, a valid transfer or assignment of a renewal-copyright interest must expressly grant rights in the renewal copyright. An assignment by an author that merely references his 'copyright' in general terms, without mentioning the renewal rights, does not include a conveyance of the author's renewal interests. [¶] Nevertheless, '[s]o long as the parties' intent is clear, a transfer of copyright need not include any particular language.' General words of assignment, such as 'forever,' 'perpetual,' and 'hereafter,' can be sufficient to transfer renewal rights if a court concludes that a transfer comports with the parties' intent. [¶] An author of a copyrighted work can assign the right to the renewal copyright before the renewal period commences: 'An assignment by an author of his renewal rights made before the original copyright expires is valid against the world, if the author is alive at the commencement of the renewal period.' An author, therefore, has the freedom to assign both his original and renewal-copyright interests at the same time, even if the renewal-copyright interest has not yet vested. If the author assigns his renewal copyrights and the renewal copyright term begins during the author's lifetime, the author is bound by the assignment. If, however, the author dies before vesting of the renewal copyright, the party to whom the renewal-copyright interest was conveyed loses the entitlement to that interest."

Thompkins v. Lil' Joe Records, Inc., 476 F.3d 1294, 1297-98 (11th Cir.2007). "[P] sold copyrights in his works to a music recording company in exchange for a recording contract that entitled the artist to future royalties. The recording company later went bankrupt, becoming the debtor-in-possession. In confirming the debtor's reorganization plan, the bankruptcy court ordered that all of the debtor's contracts with [P] be rejected under the bankruptcy code and the copyrights sold to a rival recording company and its owner, [Ds]. [¶] [P] sued [Ds], alleging that they did not actually gain ownership of the copyrights through the bankruptcy, or if they did, they now owe him royalties." Held: Ds were legal owners of copyrights.

TVT Records v. Island Def Jam Music Grp., 412 F.3d 82, 92-93 (2d Cir.2005). "[W]e hold that the District Court mistakenly concluded that '[a] fraudulently induced copyright license is invalid' ipso facto. This conclusion overlooks the fact that the license must formally be rescinded before an infringement action based on fraudulent inducement of a copyright license can proceed."

Video Views, Inc. v. Studio 21, Ltd., 925 F.2d 1010, 1018 (7th Cir.1991), *overruled on other grounds*, ***Fogerty v. Fantasy, Inc.***, 510 U.S. 517 (1994). "It is clear that a licensing agreement cannot *create* property rights enforceable under the copyright laws. A licensing agreement is an assignment of preexisting property rights ... created under the Copyright Act of 1976. Any other obligations or liabilities created by the licensing agreement exist only between the parties to that agreement...."

Warner Bros. v. Wilkinson, 533 F.Supp. 105, 108 (D.Utah 1981), *appeal dism'd*, 782 F.2d 136 (10th Cir.1985). "The right to transfer or license copyrighted material for use by others under [17 U.S.C.] §§106 and 201 *et seq.* ... has never encompassed a right to transfer the work at all times and at all places free and clear of all regulation; it has meant that the copyright owner has the exclusive right to transfer the material for a consideration to others."

§201(d)—Exclusive License

HyperQuest, Inc. v. N'Site Solutions, Inc., 632 F.3d 377, 382 (7th Cir.2011). "[I]f the exclusive right to reproduce (meaning exclusive of the grantor as well as all third parties) were transferred to A, the exclusive right to prepare derivative works were given to B, and the exclusive right to distribute copies to the public were granted to C, each transferee would be entitled to sue for infringement of its particular right. The corollary to this rule is that a person holding a non-exclusive license is not entitled to complain about any alleged infringement of the copyright. *At 383:* We must read [the] agreement ... as a whole. The fact that it uses the phrase 'exclusive license' or its equivalent from time to time is something of which we take note, but it is not dispositive. It is the substance of the agreement, not the labels that it uses, that controls our analysis." *See also* ***Sybersound Records, Inc. v. UAV Corp.***, 517 F.3d 1137, 1146 (9th Cir.2008) (all co-owners must transfer a copyright interest to an assignee; otherwise assignee has only a nonexclusive license).

Gardner v. Nike, Inc., 279 F.3d 774, 780 (9th Cir. 2002). We "hold that the 1976 [Copyright] Act does not allow a copyright licensee to transfer its rights under an exclusive license, without the consent of the original licensor." *But see* ***Traicoff v. Digital Media, Inc.***, 439 F.Supp.2d 872, 876-77 (S.D.Ind.2006) (exclusive licensees are free to transfer their rights).

Morris v. Business Concepts, Inc., 259 F.3d 65, 70 (2d Cir.2001), *overruled on other grounds*, ***Reed Elsevier, Inc. v. Muchnick***, 559 U.S. 154 (2010). "[W]e think that [17 U.S.C.] §101's definition reflects the fact that exclusive licensees are treated as copyright owners for the purpose of protection and remedy pursuant to [17 U.S.C.] §201(d)(2)."

Library Publ'ns, Inc. v. Medical Econ. Co., 548 F.Supp. 1231, 1233-34 (E.D.Pa.1982), *aff'd*, 714 F.2d 123 (3d Cir.1983) (table case). An "exclusive license can be limited to given rights at a particular time. For example, a local broadcasting station can hold an exclusive license to transmit a particular work within a particular geographic area for a particular time. Furthermore, there appears to be no limit on how narrow the scope of exclusive rights can be yet still constitute a 'transfer of ownership,' provided the licensed rights are exclusive. An exclusive license to a newsstand dealer to distribute a given edition of a given newspaper at a designated corner on a particular afternoon, for example, gives the dealer 'ownership' of that right."

§201(d)—Exclusive License v. Nonexclusive License

Davis v. Blige, 505 F.3d 90, 99-101 (2d Cir.2007). "An owner may not ... convey the interests of his fellow co-owners without their express written consent, even if the transferee has no notice of the non-consenting owners' interest. A co-owner's ability to grant licenses to third parties unilaterally will therefore depend on the type of licenses granted. There are two general categories of licenses: non-exclusive licenses, which permit licensees to use the copyrighted material and may be granted to multiple licensees; and exclusive licenses, which grant to the licensee the exclusive right—superior even to copyright owners' rights—to use the copyrighted material in a manner as specified by the license agreement. A valid license of either sort immunizes the licensee from a charge of copyright infringement, provided that the licensee uses the copyright as agreed with the licensor. [¶] A co-owner may grant a *non-exclusive* license to use the work unilaterally, because his co-owners may also use the work or grant similar licenses to other users and because the non-exclusive license presumptively does not diminish the value of the copyright to the co-owners. In any event, a co-owner who grants a non-exclusive license is accountable to his co-owner for income gained by the grant of the license. However, a licensee is not liable to a non-licensing co-owner for use authorized by the license, because the licensee's rights rest on the license conveyed by the licensing co-owner. Likewise, a licensee need not pay any royalties or other consideration to the co-owners who are not parties to the license agreement. ... Accordingly an exclusive licensee may sue others for infringement, including the licensor if the licensor infringes on the exclusive right he granted the licensee. Because no one other than the exclusive licensee may exercise the right specified by the exclusive license agreement, the interests of the other co-owners to use or grant non-exclusive licenses to the work are necessarily impaired. An exclusive license thus destroys the value of a copyright to the copyright owners, to the extent that the licensed rights cannot be used or exploited by the copyright owners. Unlike a transfer of one co-owner's copyright interest to another person, which conveys only the co-owner's share of that interest, an exclusive license grants all co-owners' shares of a particular copyright interest to the exclusive licensee. Accordingly, a co-owner cannot unilaterally grant an exclusive license. *At 103:* A retroactive license or assignment that purports to eliminate the accrued causes of action for infringement held by a co-owner who is not party to the license or agreement also violates the fundamental principle of contract law prohibiting the parties to a contract from binding nonparties. Moreover, a co-owner who purports to convey not only his right to prosecute past infringements but also his co-owners' right to prosecute past infringements violates the basic rule that an owner cannot convey more than he owns. *At 104:* An owner who wishes to release unilaterally his own accrued claims may do so using whatever language he chooses—including by calling the negotiated settlement the proverbial 'banana'—but such an agreement cannot have the effect of eviscerating a co-owner's claims based on past copyright infringement, nor can it settle accrued claims held by co-owners who are not themselves parties to the agreement. Accordingly, we hold that a license or assignment in copyright can only act prospectively." *See also* ***Minden Pictures, Inc. v. John Wiley & Sons, Inc.***, 795 F.3d 997, 1002-03 (9th Cir.2015); ***U.S. v. Board of Trs. of the Univ. of Ala.***, 104 F.3d 1453, 1461 (4th Cir.1997); ***Erickson v. Trinity Theatre, Inc.***, 13 F.3d 1061, 1068 (7th Cir.1994).

§201(d)—Implied License

Estate of Hevia v. Portrio Corp., 602 F.3d 34, 40-41 (1st Cir.2010). "Short of a transfer of ownership, a nonexclusive right to use a copyright may be granted by the copyright owner. This may occur by the granting of a written license. It also may occur without any particular formality, as by conduct manifesting the owner's intent. This kind of implied license is, by definition, of limited scope; it 'simply permits the use of a copyrighted work in a particular manner.' Uses of a copyrighted work that stay within the bounds of an implied license do not infringe the copyright. [¶] We do not mean to suggest that implied licenses are an everyday occurrence in copyright matters. The opposite is true: implied licenses are found only in narrow circumstances. When, as in this case, an implied license is asserted as a defense to infringement, the burden of proving its existence rests on the proponent. *At 44-45:* When ... there is no indication that a license-granting copyright owner has restricted the licensee's ability to use third parties in implementing the license, the license is generally construed to allow such delegation."

Asset Mktg. Sys. v. Gagnon, 542 F.3d 748, 754-55 (9th Cir.2008). "Though exclusive licenses must be in writing, ... grants of nonexclusive licenses need not be in writing, and may be granted orally or by implication. [¶] [W]e have held that an implied license is granted when '(1) a person (the licensee) requests the creation of a work, (2) the creator (the licensor) makes that particular work and delivers it to the licensee who requested it, and (3) the licensor intends that the licensee-requestor copy and distribute his work.' ... The last prong ..., however, is not limited to copying and distribution; instead we look at the protected right at issue—here, whether [D] intended that [P] use, retain, and modify the programs. *At 755 n.4:* Though delivery of a copy of software does not compel the conclusion that [D] granted [P] a license, it is a relevant factor that we may consider. *At 756:* The relevant intent is the licensor's objective intent at the time of the creation and delivery of the software as manifested by the parties' conduct. The First and Fourth Circuits consider the following factors to determine such an intent: (1) whether the parties were engaged in a short-term discrete transaction as opposed to an ongoing relationship; (2) whether the creator utilized written contracts ... providing that copyrighted materials could only be used with the creator's future involvement or express permission; and (3) whether the creator's conduct during the creation or delivery of the copyrighted material indicated that use of the material without the creator's involvement or consent was permissible. *At 757:* [W]e hold that [D] granted [P] an unlimited, nonexclusive license to retain, use, and modify the software. Furthermore, because [P] paid consideration, this license is irrevocable. ... If an implied license accompanied by consideration were revocable at will, the contract would be illusory." *See also* ***Muhammad-Ali v. Final Call, Inc.***, 832 F.3d 755, 762 (7th Cir.2016) (creation of implied license); ***Estate of Hevia v. Portrio Corp.***, 602 F.3d 34, 41 (1st Cir.2010) (intent); ***Latimer v. Roaring Toyz, Inc.***, 601 F.3d 1224, 1235 (11th Cir.2010) (creation of implied license); ***Nelson-Salabes, Inc. v. Morningside Dev., LLC***, 284 F.3d 505, 516 (4th Cir. 2002) (intent); ***Walthal v. Rusk***, 172 F.3d 481, 484 (7th Cir.1999) (oral transfer).

§201(d)—Nonexclusive License

Vernor v. Autodesk, Inc., 621 F.3d 1102, 1111 (9th Cir.2010). "We hold today that a software user is a licensee rather than an owner of a copy where the copyright owner (1) specifies that the user is granted a license; (2) significantly restricts the user's ability to transfer the software; and (3) imposes notable use restrictions. Applying our holding to [copyright owner's license], we conclude that [original software purchaser] was a licensee rather than an owner of copies of [software] and thus was not entitled to invoke the first sale doctrine or the essential step defense."

F.B.T. Prods. v. Aftermath Records, 621 F.3d 958, 965 (9th Cir.2010). "[W]here a copyright owner transfers a copy of copyrighted material, retains title, limits the uses to which the material may be put, and is compensated periodically based on the transferee's exploitation of the material, the transaction is a license."

§201(e)

Hendricks & Lewis PLLC v. Clinton, 766 F.3d 991, 997 (9th Cir.2014). "The stated purpose of [§201(e)] was to protect foreign authors against laws and decrees purporting to divest them of their rights under the U.S. copyright statute, and would protect authors within the foreign country who choose to resist such covert pressures. ... The legislative history of §201(e) explains that the purpose of this subsection is to reaffirm the basic principle that the U.S. copyright of an individual author shall be secured to that author, and cannot be taken away by any involuntary transfer. *At 998:* [Section] 201(e) is of no help to [D,] whether or not he is the author of [musical work]. Section 201(e) protection does not apply where a copyright was previously transferred voluntarily by that individual author. There is no question that [D] transferred any interest that he had in [musical work] to [producer], and, as part of a settlement arising from unrelated litigation, [producer] subsequently agreed to transfer ownership back to [D]. These voluntary transfers are a sufficient basis for rejecting [D's] argument that he enjoys §201(e) protection as the author of the master sound recordings." (Internal quotes omitted.)

§202. OWNERSHIP OF COPYRIGHT AS DISTINCT FROM OWNERSHIP OF MATERIAL OBJECT

Ownership of a copyright, or of any of the exclusive rights under a copyright, is distinct from ownership of any material object in which the work is embodied. Transfer of ownership of any material object, including the copy or phonorecord in which the work is first fixed, does not of itself convey any rights in the copyrighted work embodied in the object; nor, in the absence of an agreement, does transfer of ownership of a copyright or of any exclusive rights under a copyright convey property rights in any material object.

History of 17 U.S.C. §202: Oct. 19, 1976, P.L. 94-553, §101, 90 Stat. 2568.

§203. TERMINATION OF TRANSFERS & LICENSES GRANTED BY THE AUTHOR

(a) Conditions for termination.—In the case of any work other than a work made for hire, the exclusive or nonexclusive grant of a transfer or license of copyright or of any right under a copyright, executed by the author on or after January 1, 1978, otherwise than by will, is subject to termination under the following conditions:

(1) In the case of a grant executed by one author, termination of the grant may be effected by that author or, if the author is dead, by the person or persons who, under clause (2) of this subsection, own and are entitled to exercise a total of more than one-half of that author's termination interest. In the case of a grant executed by two or more authors of a joint work, termination of the grant may be effected by a majority of the authors who executed it; if any of such authors is dead, the termination interest of any such author may be exercised as a unit by the person or persons who, under clause (2) of this subsection, own and are entitled to exercise a total of more than one-half of that author's interest.

(2) Where an author is dead, his or her termination interest is owned, and may be exercised, as follows:

(A) The widow or widower owns the author's entire termination interest unless there are any surviving children or grandchildren of the author, in which case the widow or widower owns one-half of the author's interest.

(B) The author's surviving children, and the surviving children of any dead child of the author, own the author's entire termination interest unless there is a widow or widower, in which case the ownership of one-half of the author's interest is divided among them.

(C) The rights of the author's children and grandchildren are in all cases divided among them and exercised on a per stirpes basis according to the number of such author's children represented; the share of the children of a dead child in a termination interest can be exercised only by the action of a majority of them.

(D) In the event that the author's widow or widower, children, and grandchildren are not living, the author's executor, administrator, personal representative, or trustee shall own the author's entire termination interest.

(3) Termination of the grant may be effected at any time during a period of five years beginning at the end of thirty-five years from the date of execution of the grant; or, if the grant covers the right of publication of the work, the period begins at the end of thirty-five years from the date of publication of the work under the grant or at the end of forty years from the date of execution of the grant, whichever term ends earlier.

(4) The termination shall be effected by serving an advance notice in writing, signed by the number and proportion of owners of termination interests required under clauses (1) and (2) of this subsection, or by their duly authorized agents, upon the grantee or the grantee's successor in title.

(A) The notice shall state the effective date of the termination, which shall fall within the five-year period specified by clause (3) of this subsection, and the notice shall be served not less than two or more than ten years before that date. A copy of the notice shall be recorded in the Copyright Office before the effective date of termination, as a condition to its taking effect.

(B) The notice shall comply, in form, content, and manner of service, with requirements that the Register of Copyrights shall prescribe by regulation.

(5) Termination of the grant may be effected notwithstanding any agreement to the contrary, including an agreement to make a will or to make any future grant.

(b) Effect of termination.—Upon the effective date of termination, all rights under this title that were covered by the terminated grants revert to the author, authors, and other persons owning termination interests under clauses (1) and (2) of subsection (a), including those owners who did not join in signing the notice of termination under clause (4) of subsection (a), but with the following limitations:

(1) A derivative work prepared under authority of the grant before its termination may continue to be utilized under the terms of the grant after its termination, but this privilege does not extend to the preparation after the termination of other derivative works based upon the copyrighted work covered by the terminated grant.

(2) The future rights that will revert upon termination of the grant become vested on the date the notice of termination has been served as provided by clause (4) of subsection (a). The rights vest in the author, authors, and other persons named in, and in the proportionate shares provided by, clauses (1) and (2) of subsection (a).

(3) Subject to the provisions of clause (4) of this subsection, a further grant, or agreement to make a further grant, of any right covered by a terminated grant is valid only if it is signed by the same number and proportion of the owners, in whom the right has vested under clause (2) of this subsection, as are required to terminate the grant under clauses (1) and (2) of subsection (a). Such further grant or agreement is effective with respect to all of the persons in whom the right it covers has vested under clause (2) of this subsection, including those who did not join in signing it. If any person dies after rights under a terminated grant have vested in him or her, that person's legal representatives, legatees, or heirs at law represent him or her for purposes of this clause.

(4) A further grant, or agreement to make a further grant, of any right covered by a terminated grant is valid only if it is made after the effective date of the termination. As an exception, however, an agreement for such a further grant may be made between the persons provided by clause (3) of this subsection and the original grantee or such grantee's successor in title, after the notice of termination has been served as provided by clause (4) of subsection (a).

(5) Termination of a grant under this section affects only those rights covered by the grants that arise under this title, and in no way affects rights arising under any other Federal, State, or foreign laws.

(6) Unless and until termination is effected under this section, the grant, if it does not provide otherwise, continues in effect for the term of copyright provided by this title.

History of 17 U.S.C. §203: Oct. 19, 1976, P.L. 94-553, §101, 90 Stat. 2569; Oct. 27, 1998, P.L. 105-298, §103, 112 Stat. 2829; Nov. 2, 2002, P.L. 107-273, §13210(9), 116 Stat. 1909.

See also 11 U.S.C. §365; 37 C.F.R. §201.10.

ANNOTATIONS

Baldwin v. EMI Feist Catalog, Inc., 805 F.3d 18, 25 (2d Cir.2015). Section 203 "termination rights are not available against pre-1978 grants [of rights]."

Ray Charles Found. v. Robinson, 795 F.3d 1109, 1112-13 (9th Cir.2015). 17 U.S.C. §§203 and 304 "govern termination of copyright grants. [¶] Section 203 pertains to grants and transfers made after 1978.... Under this statute, termination of a copyright grant may be effected at any time during a five-year period, starting 35 years after the execution of the grant. Because the 35-year period began with grants made in 1978, opportunities to execute termination notices under §203 started to accrue 'for the first time on January 1, 2013.' [¶] Subsection 304(c) covers grants made before 1978.... The subsection is 'a close but not exact counterpart of §203.' Under §304(c), terminations may be effected during a five-year period starting 56 years from the date the copyright was secured, or January 1, 1978, whichever is later. Most existing case law on copyright termination pertains to §304(c) because opportunities to terminate copyright grants became ripe under this statute earlier than grants subject to §203. [¶] Both §203 and §304(c) are silent on who may challenge the validity of termination notices. *At 1122:* The Copyright Act does not expressly provide for a private right of action under §203 and §304(c), but we conclude that an implied private cause of action exists under the termination provisions."

§204. EXECUTION OF TRANSFERS OF COPYRIGHT OWNERSHIP

(a) A transfer of copyright ownership, other than by operation of law, is not valid unless an instrument of conveyance, or a note or memorandum of the transfer, is in writing and signed by the owner of the rights conveyed or such owner's duly authorized agent.

(b) A certificate of acknowledgement is not required for the validity of a transfer, but is prima facie evidence of the execution of the transfer if—

(1) in the case of a transfer executed in the United States, the certificate is issued by a person authorized to administer oaths within the United States; or

(2) in the case of a transfer executed in a foreign country, the certificate is issued by a diplomatic or consular officer of the United States, or by a person authorized to administer oaths whose authority is proved by a certificate of such an officer.

History of 17 U.S.C. §204: Oct. 19, 1976, P.L. 94-553, §101, 90 Stat. 2570. See also 11 U.S.C. §365.

ANNOTATIONS

DRK Photo v. McGraw-Hill Global Educ. Holdings, LLC, 870 F.3d 978, 986 (9th Cir.2017). "Although a third party may not raise noncompliance with ... §204(a)'s writing requirement as a defense to a copyright transfer where the parties to the transfer do not dispute its existence, ... a third party is not foreclosed from challenging a plaintiff's ownership for purposes of standing.... Indeed, it is the plaintiff who has the burden of establishing a qualifying ownership interest both as a substantive element of the infringement claim, ... and as a necessary predicate for standing to bring the claim...."

Metropolitan Reg'l Info. Sys. v. American Home Rlty. Network, Inc., 722 F.3d 591, 601 (4th Cir.2013). "The issue we must ... resolve is whether a subscriber, who 'clicks yes' in response to [a website's terms of use] prior to uploading copyrighted photographs, has *signed* a *written* transfer of the exclusive rights of copyright ownership in those photographs consistent with [17 U.S.C.] §204(a). *At 602:* To invalidate copyright transfer agreements solely because they were made electronically would thwart the clear congressional intent embodied in the E-Sign Act [15 U.S.C. §§7001-7006, 7021, 7031]. We therefore hold that an electronic agreement may effect a valid transfer of copyright interests under §204...."

Barefoot Architect, Inc. v. Bunge, 632 F.3d 822, 827 (3d Cir.2011). "Section 204(a)—frequently referred to as the Copyright Act's 'statute of frauds'—specifically contemplates a post-hoc 'note or memorandum of the transfer,' as distinct from an 'instrument of conveyance,' as a permissible means of satisfying the Act's writing requirement. The 'note or memorandum' does not itself constitute the transfer; rather, the writing renders valid and enforceable in court a change in ownership that has already taken place. Under the statute's plain terms it is clear that an oral transfer can be given legal effect by a subsequent signed writing. *At 830:* [W]here there is no dispute between transferor and transferee regarding the ownership of a copyright, there is little reason to demand that a validating written instrument be drafted and signed contemporaneously with the transferring event. [W]e hold that a third-party infringer in such a case cannot evade liability by invoking §204(a) and demanding a contemporaneously-drafted instrument." *See also* ***Billy-Bob Teeth, Inc. v. Novelty, Inc.***, 329 F.3d 586, 592-93 (7th Cir. 2003); ***Magnuson v. Video Yesteryear***, 85 F.3d 1424, 1429 (9th Cir.1996); ***Imperial Residential Design, Inc. v. Palms Dev. Grp.***, 70 F.3d 96, 99 (11th Cir.1995);

Eden Toys, Inc. v. Florelee Undergarment Co., 697 F.2d 27, 36 (2d Cir.1982).

Latin Am. Music Co. v. American Soc'y of Composers, Authors & Publ'rs, 593 F.3d 95, 100 (1st Cir. 2010). "Section 204, which requires a writing signed by the transferor, … applies to the transfer or grant of copyright ownership, *not* to the termination of such a transfer or grant." Held: Unless 17 U.S.C. §203 applies, state law governs termination of transfers and grants.

SCO Grp. v. Novell, Inc., 578 F.3d 1201, 1212-13 (10th Cir.2009). "[S]ome courts have understood §204(a) to impose requirements similar to that necessary to satisfy the statute of frauds. [¶] In the absence of any support from the language or legislative history, we are unwilling to read into §204 such an onerous restraint on the alienability of copyrights. … Where ambiguity persists in the language of a parties' shared agreement concerning a copyright transfer, the transfer is not invalidated; instead, we look to parol evidence to construe the terms of the agreement. [¶] We think that §204's writing requirement is best understood as a means of ensuring that parties intend to transfer copyrights themselves, as opposed to other categories of rights. But when it is clear that the parties contemplated that copyrights transfer, we do not think that a linguistic ambiguity concerning which particular copyrights transferred creates an insuperable barrier invalidating the transaction. [¶] [A] written asset transfer agreement may satisfy §204(a) even when it does not mention the word copyright itself. And when a party acquires all rights and ownership in a set of items, as was the case here, courts have generally found such language sufficient to satisfy §204(a) in the absence of language excepting copyrights or other special circumstances. *At 1214:* We also do not see why the absence of a Bill of Sale is fatal to an alleged transfer under the Copyright Act. Section 204 makes clear that the writing requirement can be satisfied not only by an instrument of conveyance but also by a note or memorandum of the transfer." (Internal quotes omitted.)

Martha Graham Sch. & Dance Found. v. Martha Graham Ctr. of Contemporary Dance, Inc., 380 F.3d 624, 643 (2d Cir.2004). "A valid assignment of statutory copyright must be in writing. However, we have ruled that assignments of common law copyright need not be in writing."

§205. RECORDATION OF TRANSFERS & OTHER DOCUMENTS

(a) Conditions for recordation.—Any transfer of copyright ownership or other document pertaining to a copyright may be recorded in the Copyright Office if the document filed for recordation bears the actual signature of the person who executed it, or if it is accompanied by a sworn or official certification that it is a true copy of the original, signed document. A sworn or official certification may be submitted to the Copyright Office electronically, pursuant to regulations established by the Register of Copyrights.

(b) Certificate of recordation.—The Register of Copyrights shall, upon receipt of a document as provided by subsection (a) and of the fee provided by section 708, record the document and return it with a certificate of recordation.

(c) Recordation as constructive notice.—Recordation of a document in the Copyright Office gives all persons constructive notice of the facts stated in the recorded document, but only if—

(1) the document, or material attached to it, specifically identifies the work to which it pertains so that, after the document is indexed by the Register of Copyrights, it would be revealed by a reasonable search under the title or registration number of the work; and

(2) registration has been made for the work.

(d) Priority between conflicting transfers.—As between two conflicting transfers, the one executed first prevails if it is recorded, in the manner required to give constructive notice under subsection (c), within one month after its execution in the United States or within two months after its execution outside the United States, or at any time before recordation in such manner of the later transfer. Otherwise the later transfer prevails if recorded first in such manner, and if taken in good faith, for valuable consideration or on the basis of a binding promise to pay royalties, and without notice of the earlier transfer.

(e) Priority between conflicting transfer of ownership and nonexclusive license.—A nonexclusive license, whether recorded or not, prevails over a conflicting transfer of copyright ownership if the license is evidenced by a written instrument signed by the owner of the rights licensed or such owner's duly authorized agent, and if—

(1) the license was taken before execution of the transfer; or

(2) the license was taken in good faith before recordation of the transfer and without notice of it.

(f) Redesignated.

History of 17 U.S.C. §205: Oct. 19, 1976, P.L. 94-553, §101, 90 Stat. 2571; Oct. 31, 1988, P.L. 100-568, §5, 102 Stat. 2857; Dec. 9, 2010, P.L. 111-295, §3(b), 124 Stat. 3180.

See also 37 C.F.R. §§201.4, 201.26; Berne Convention.

ANNOTATIONS

§205(c)

Gaiman v. McFarlane, 360 F.3d 644, 655 (7th Cir. 2004). It "is no more the purpose of registration to start statutes of limitations running than it is the purpose of the copyright notice itself to do so. [¶] [T]he court was wrong to say that registration gives constructive notice. What the [Copyright] Act actually says is that recording a document in the Copyright Office gives constructive notice of the facts in the document if the document identifies a registered work. The purpose is to establish priority in the event of disputes, in bankruptcy court or elsewhere, over creditors' rights. A creditor who wants to know whether he can seize a debtor's copyright consults the register; a co-author does not."

§205(d)

Latin Am. Music Co. v. Archdiocese of San Juan of the Roman Catholic & Apostolic Ch., 499 F.3d 32, 40-41 (1st Cir.2007). "To meet the §205(d) requirements and prevail on summary judgment as the first to record [a transfer of ownership], [P] had to provide undisputed facts that they recorded the transfer from [composer] in good faith and without notice of the earlier transfer to [publisher 1]. It is undisputed, however, that [publisher 1] obtained a certificate of copyright registration for [song] in September of 1985, days before [composer] entered an agreement with [publisher 2] transferring rights to the song, and almost two years before [publisher 2] and [P] obtained a copyright registration for the song. At the time [P] entered into their transfer agreement with [composer], a review of the Copyright Office register would have revealed that [publisher 1] was listed as the copyright owner. [Publisher 1's] registration certification for [song], therefore, provided notice that prior transactions existed relating to the copyright for [song], regardless of what entity currently might claim those rights."

CHAPTER 3. DURATION OF COPYRIGHT

§301. PREEMPTION WITH RESPECT TO OTHER LAWS

(a) On and after January 1, 1978, all legal or equitable rights that are equivalent to any of the exclusive rights within the general scope of copyright as specified by section 106 in works of authorship that are fixed in a tangible medium of expression and come within the subject matter of copyright as specified by sections 102 and 103, whether created before or after that date and whether published or unpublished, are governed exclusively by this title. Thereafter, no person is entitled to any such right or equivalent right in any such work under the common law or statutes of any State.

(b) Nothing in this title annuls or limits any rights or remedies under the common law or statutes of any State with respect to—

(1) subject matter that does not come within the subject matter of copyright as specified by sections 102 and 103, including works of authorship not fixed in any tangible medium of expression; or

(2) any cause of action arising from undertakings commenced before January 1, 1978;

(3) activities violating legal or equitable rights that are not equivalent to any of the exclusive rights within the general scope of copyright as specified by section 106; or

(4) State and local landmarks, historic preservation, zoning, or building codes, relating to architectural works protected under section 102(a)(8).

(c) With respect to sound recordings fixed before February 15, 1972, any rights or remedies under the common law or statutes of any State shall not be annulled or limited by this title until February 15, 2067. The preemptive provisions of subsection (a) shall apply to any such rights and remedies pertaining to any cause of action arising from undertakings commenced on and after February 15, 2067. Notwithstanding the provisions of section 303, no sound recording fixed before February 15, 1972, shall be subject to copyright under this title before, on, or after February 15, 2067.

(d) Nothing in this title annuls or limits any rights or remedies under any other Federal statute.

(e) The scope of Federal preemption under this section is not affected by the adherence of the United

States to the Berne Convention or the satisfaction of obligations of the United States thereunder.

(f)(1) On or after the effective date set forth in section 106A of this title, all legal or equitable rights that are equivalent to any of the rights conferred by section 106A with respect to works of visual art to which the rights conferred by section 106A apply are governed exclusively by section 106A and section 113(d) and the provisions of this title relating to such sections. Thereafter, no person is entitled to any such right or equivalent right in any work of visual art under the common law or statutes of any State.

(2) Nothing in paragraph (1) annuls or limits any rights or remedies under the common law or statutes of any State with respect to—

(A) any cause of action from undertakings commenced before the effective date set forth in section 610(a) of the Visual Artists Rights Act of 1990;

(B) activities violating legal or equitable rights that are not equivalent to any of the rights conferred by section 106A with respect to works of visual art; or

(C) activities violating legal or equitable rights which extend beyond the life of the author.

History of 17 U.S.C. §301: Oct. 19, 1976, P.L. 94-553, §101, 90 Stat. 2572; Oct. 31, 1988, P.L. 100-568, §6, 102 Stat. 2857; Dec. 1, 1990, P.L. 101-650, §§605, 705, 104 Stat. 5131, 5134; Oct. 27, 1998, P.L. 105-298, §102(a), 112 Stat. 2827.

See also U.S. Const. art. 1, §8, cl. 8; Berne Convention.

ANNOTATIONS

GlobeRanger Corp. v. Software AG USA, Inc., 836 F.3d 477, 486 (5th Cir.2016). "Because trade secret law protects against not just copying but also any taking that occurs through breach of a confidential relationship or other improper means, all ten circuits that have considered trade secret misappropriation claims have found them not preempted by the Copyright Act. *At 488:* We ... conclude that [P's] trade secret misappropriation claim requires establishing an additional element than what is required to make out a copyright violation: that the protected information was taken via improper means or breach of a confidential relationship. Because the state tort provides substantially different protection than copyright law, it is not preempted." *See also* ***Seng-Tiong Ho v. Taflove***, 648 F.3d 489, 503-04 (7th Cir.2011); ***Stromback v. New Line Cinema***, 384 F.3d 283, 302-05 (6th Cir.2004); ***Dun & Bradstreet Software Servs. v. Grace Consulting, Inc.***, 307 F.3d 197, 217-18 (3d Cir.2002); ***DSC Comms. v. Pulse Comms.***, 170 F.3d 1354, 1365 (Fed.Cir.1999); ***Bateman v. Mnemonics, Inc.***, 79 F.3d 1532, 1549 (11th Cir. 1996); ***Data Gen. Corp. v. Grumman Sys. Support Corp.***, 36 F.3d 1147, 1164-65 (1st Cir.1994), *abrogated on other grounds*, ***Reed Elsevier, Inc. v. Muchnick***, 559 U.S. 154 (2010); ***Gates Rubber Co. v. Bando Chem. Indus.***, 9 F.3d 823, 847-48 (10th Cir.1993); ***Trandes Corp. v. Guy F. Atkinson Co.***, 996 F.2d 655, 658-60 (4th Cir.1993); ***Computer Assocs. Int'l v. Altai, Inc.***, 982 F.2d 693, 716-17 (2d Cir.1992); ***S.O.S., Inc. v. Payday, Inc.***, 886 F.2d 1081, 1090 n.13 (9th Cir. 1989).

Spear Mktg., Inc. v. BancorpSouth Bank, 791 F.3d 586, 595-97 (5th Cir.2015). "Looking to other circuits, we find a clear and lopsided split. The Second, Fourth, Sixth, and Seventh Circuit, as well as the Ninth Circuit en banc, all recognize that, for the purpose of preemption under [17 U.S.C.] §301(a), ideas fixed in tangible media fall within the subject matter of copyright. Only the 11th Circuit disagrees, holding that ideas are substantively ineligible for copyright protection and, therefore, are categorically excluded from the subject matter of copyright even if expressed in a tangible medium. [¶] The position of the majority of circuits clearly delineates between the purpose of federal copyright *preemption* and that of federal copyright *protection*. Congress intended the Copyright Act to protect some expressions but not others, and it wrote §301(a) to ensure that the states did not undo this decision: One function of §301(a) is to prevent states from giving special protection to works of authorship that Congress has decided should be in the public domain, which it can accomplish only if 'subject matter of copyright' includes all works of a type covered by [17 U.S.C.] §§102 and 103, even if federal law does not afford protection to them. Finding this reasoning is persuasive, we join the majority position and hold that state law claims based on ideas fixed in tangible media are preempted by §301(a)." (Internal quotes omitted.) *But see* ***Dunlap v. G&L Holding Grp.***, 381 F.3d 1285, 1295 (11th Cir.2004) (conversion of ideas expressed in tangible media not preempted by Copyright Act).

Forest Park Pictures v. Universal TV Network, Inc., 683 F.3d 424, 430-31 (2d Cir.2012). "Applying [the] 'extra element' test, we have held numerous categories of claims to be not preempted, including trade secret claims, in which the plaintiff must show the defendant breached a duty of trust through improper disclosure of confidential material ...; certain 'hot news' misappropriation claims, because the plaintiff must show time-sensitive factual information, free-riding by the defendant, and a threat to the very existence of the plaintiff's product ...; and breach of confidential relationship, in which the plaintiff must show an obligation not to disclose ideas revealed in confidence.... By contrast, we have found a state law claim preempted when the extra element changes the scope but not the fundamental nature of the right. [¶] A number of our sister circuits have ... concluded that at least some contract claims involving the subject matter of copyright do not contest rights that are the equivalent of rights under the Copyright Act, and thus are not preempted. *At 432:* As long as the elements of a contract are properly pleaded, there is no difference for preemption purposes between an express contract and an implied-in-fact contract. There is, however, a significant difference for preemption purposes between contracts implied-in-fact and contracts implied-in-law. Theories of implied-in-law contract, quasi-contract, or unjust enrichment differ significantly from breach of contract because the plaintiff need not allege the existence of an actual agreement between the parties. Under these quasi-contractual theories, the plaintiff need only prove that the defendant was unjustly enriched through the use of her idea or work. Such a claim is not materially different from a claim for copyright infringement that requires a plaintiff to prove that the defendant used, reproduced, copied, or displayed a copyrighted work. *At 433:* A claim for breach of a contract including a promise to pay is qualitatively different from a suit to vindicate a right included in the Copyright Act and is not subject to preemption."

Cambridge Literary Props., Ltd. v. W. Goebel Porzellanfabrik G.m.b.H., 510 F.3d 77, 86 (1st Cir. 2007). "All of the federal circuit courts of appeal that have addressed the issue, including this one, agree that a determination of copyright ownership based on a disputed allegation of co-authorship presents a federal question that arises under, and must be determined according to, the Copyright Act."

Santa-Rosa v. Combo Records, 471 F.3d 224, 227 (1st Cir.2006). "Because [P] seeks rescission of his contract, if we were to grant him the relief that he sought, we would be required to determine his ownership rights by reference to the Copyright Act. In such a case, there is little question that we would be merely determining whether [P] was entitled to compensation because of 'mere copying' or 'performance, distribution or display' of his recordings. As such, ... §301(a) preempts [P's] rescission claim. Once it is determined that [P's] rescission claim is preempted, his only remedy is a claim under the Copyright Act, and 'the court must then dismiss the [contract] claim for failing to state a cause of action.' Thus, we find no error in the dismissal of [P's] rescission claim."

Bucklew v. Hawkins, Ash, Baptie & Co., 329 F.3d 923, 934 (7th Cir.2003). "The copyright statute does not authorize [punitive] damages, ... and the statute's preemption clause forbids states to add sanctions for a wrongful act that is identical to a violation of the statute."

Wrench LLC v. Taco Bell Corp., 256 F.3d 446, 453 (6th Cir.2001). Under 17 U.S.C. §301, "a state common law or statutory claim is preempted if: (1) the work is within the scope of the 'subject matter of copyright,' as specified in 17 U.S.C. §§102, 103; and, (2) the rights granted under state law are equivalent to any exclusive rights within the scope of federal copyright as set out in 17 U.S.C. §106. Courts and commentators have described this preemption analysis as encompassing a 'subject matter requirement' and a 'general scope' or 'equivalency' requirement. *At 455:* [T]he scope of the Copyright Act's subject matter is broader than the scope of the Act's protections. [¶] The second prong of the preemption analysis ... augments the subject matter inquiry by asking whether the state common law or statutory action at issue asserts rights that are the same as those protected under §106.... *At 456:* Equivalency exists if the right defined by state law may be abridged by an act which in and of itself would infringe one of the exclusive rights. Conversely, if an extra element is required instead of or in addition to the acts of reproduction, performance, distribution or display in order to constitute a state-created cause of action, there is no preemption, provided that the extra element changes the nature of the action so that it is qualitatively different from a copyright infringement claim." *See also* ***SCO Grp. v. IBM Corp.***, 879 F.3d 1062, 1080 (10th Cir.2018) (same as annotation); ***Ray v. ESPN, Inc.***, 783 F.3d 1140, 1142 (8th Cir.2015) (same as annotation); ***Montz v. Pilgrim Films & TV, Inc.***, 649 F.3d 975, 977 (9th Cir.2011) (extra element of consideration for "use of concept" is not limited to money and can be in form of partnership interest); ***R.W. Beck, Inc. v. E3 Consulting, LLC***, 577 F.3d 1133, 1146-49 (10th Cir.

2009) (state-law claims of unfair competition and unjust enrichment preempted); ***Facenda v. NFL Films, Inc.***, 542 F.3d 1007, 1028-32 (3d Cir.2008) (right-of-publicity state-law claim not preempted because persona is outside scope of copyright subject matter when used in marketing); ***Carson v. Dynegy, Inc.***, 344 F.3d 446, 456 (5th Cir.2003) (conversion claim had extra element); ***Bowers v. Baystate Techs.***, 320 F.3d 1317, 1324 (Fed.Cir.2003) (not every extra element of state-law claim will establish qualitative variance); ***Dun & Bradstreet Software Servs. v. Grace Consulting, Inc.***, 307 F.3d 197, 218 (3d Cir.2002) (breach of duty of trust or confidence is extra element); ***Sturdza v. United Arab Emirates***, 281 F.3d 1287, 1303-04 (D.C. Cir.2002) (same as annotation); ***Lipscher v. LRP Publ'ns, Inc.***, 266 F.3d 1305, 1311-12 (11th Cir.2001) (same as annotation); ***Downing v. Abercrombie & Fitch***, 265 F.3d 994, 1003 (9th Cir.2001) (same as annotation); ***U.S. v. Board of Trs. of the Univ. of Ala.***, 104 F.3d 1453, 1463 (4th Cir.1997) (same as annotation); ***Valente-Kritzer Video v. Pinckney***, 881 F.2d 772, 776 (9th Cir.1989) (fraud not preempted because of extra element of misrepresentation).

Foley v. Luster, 249 F.3d 1281, 1287 (11th Cir. 2001). "Nothing in the language of [17 U.S.C.] §301 explicitly prohibits indemnity suits, nor is there a message in the structure of [17 U.S.C.] §§301 and 106 read together that implies a preemption of indemnity suits. Therefore, such suits are not explicitly preempted by the [Copyright] Act."

Rodrigue v. Rodrigue, 218 F.3d 432, 440 (5th Cir. 2000). "We discern nothing in the [Copyright] Act's plain wording or legislative history to indicate that Congress—fully aware of the existence of community property laws in a number of states—had any intention of preempting [state community property laws]. Our conclusion is buttressed by the explicit clarification in §301(b)(3) ... that the preemptive effect does not extend beyond the subject matter of the [Copyright] Act."

Corcoran v. Sullivan, 112 F.3d 836, 838 (7th Cir. 1997). "*Of course* federal copyright law does not preempt state criminal prosecutions for destroying noncopyrighted property that is commingled with a copyrighted work. Otherwise an author invited into the home of someone who had bought one of his books would have a legal privilege to tear up the book if he had retained the copyright in it."

ProCD, Inc. v. Zeidenberg, 86 F.3d 1447, 1453 (7th Cir.1996). "One function of [17 U.S.C.] §301(a) is to prevent states from giving special protection to works of authorship that Congress has decided should be in the public domain, which it can accomplish only if 'subject matter of copyright' includes all works of a *type* covered by [17 U.S.C.] §§102 and 103, even if federal law does not afford protection to them."

Allarcom Pay TV, Ltd. v. General Instr. Corp., 69 F.3d 381, 387 (9th Cir.1995). Federal "copyright law does not apply to extraterritorial acts of infringement. Accordingly, it does not preempt causes of action premised upon possible extraterritorial infringement."

Rosciszewski v. Arete Assocs., 1 F.3d 225, 229-30 (4th Cir.1993). "State-law claims that infringe one of the exclusive rights contained in [17 U.S.C.] §106 are preempted by [17 U.S.C.] §301(a) if the right defined by state law may be abridged by an act which, in and of itself, would infringe one of the exclusive rights. However, if an extra element is required instead of or in addition to the acts of reproduction, performance, distribution or display, in order to constitute a state-created cause of action, ... there is no preemption, provided that the extra element changes the nature of the action so that it is *qualitatively* different from a copyright infringement claim." (Internal quotes omitted.)

Trandes Corp. v. Guy F. Atkinson Co., 996 F.2d 655, 658 (4th Cir.1993). "As nothing more than a jurisdictional prerequisite, [17 U.S.C.] §411(a) does not affect the broad preemptive scope of [17 U.S.C.] §301. [P] cannot escape the preemptive effect of §301 merely by failing to register its copyright in a timely fashion."

Fantastic Fakes, Inc. v. Pickwick Int'l, 661 F.2d 479, 483 (5th Cir.1981). "A choice of law provision [in a licensing agreement] merely designates the state whose law is to be applied to the extent its use is not preempted by nor contrary to the policies of the 1909 and 1976 Copyright Acts."

WNET v. Aereo, Inc., 871 F.Supp.2d 281, 283 (S.D. N.Y.2012), *aff'd*, 712 F.3d 676 (2d Cir.2013). "[D's] motion turns exclusively on a question of statutory interpretation—apparently one of first impression—regarding the breadth of preemption under §301: does a state law unfair competition claim founded on the private performance [rather than a public performance] of copyrighted works seek to vindicate rights that fall into the general scope of the exclusive rights created by the Copyright Act?" Held: Claim is preempted.

Information Handling Servs. v. LRP Pubs., 54 U.S.P.Q.2d 1571, 1573 (E.D.Pa.2000). "A claim for unauthorized copying falls squarely within the scope of the rights specified in [17 U.S.C.] §106, and the vast weight of authority holds that state law misappropriation and unfair competition claims that are really claims for unauthorized copying are preempted."

Brode v. Tax Mgmt., 14 U.S.P.Q.2d 1195, 1203 (N.D.Ill.1990). "A right under state law is 'equivalent' to a right within the scope of copyright if it is violated by the exercise of any of the rights set forth in §106. Section 106 provides that a copyright owner has the exclusive right to reproduce (whether in original or derivative form), distribute, perform, and display the copyrighted work. If the state law right is infringed by one of the acts set forth in §106, or if a violation requires the plaintiff to establish additional elements, but the elements do not differ in kind from those necessary for copyright infringement, the state law claim is 'equivalent.' [¶] Because [P's] right of publicity was allegedly infringed when copies of his portfolio were distributed during the post-license period, [P's] right of publicity claim is 'equivalent' to at least one of the rights encompassed by copyright."

§302. DURATION OF COPYRIGHT: WORKS CREATED ON OR AFTER JANUARY 1, 1978

(a) In general.—Copyright in a work created on or after January 1, 1978, subsists from its creation and, except as provided by the following subsections, endures for a term consisting of the life of the author and 70 years after the author's death.

(b) Joint works.—In the case of a joint work prepared by two or more authors who did not work for hire, the copyright endures for a term consisting of the life of the last surviving author and 70 years after such last surviving author's death.

(c) Anonymous works, pseudonymous works, and works made for hire.—In the case of an anonymous work, a pseudonymous work, or a work made for hire, the copyright endures for a term of 95 years from the year of its first publication, or a term of 120 years from the year of its creation, whichever expires first. If, before the end of such term, the identity of one or more of the authors of an anonymous or pseudonymous work is revealed in the records of a registration made for that work under subsections (a) or (d) of section 408, or in the records provided by this subsection, the copyright in the work endures for the term specified by subsection (a) or (b), based on the life of the author or authors whose identity has been revealed. Any person having an interest in the copyright in an anonymous or pseudonymous work may at any time record, in records to be maintained by the Copyright Office for that purpose, a statement identifying one or more authors of the work; the statement shall also identify the person filing it, the nature of that person's interest, the source of the information recorded, and the particular work affected, and shall comply in form and content with requirements that the Register of Copyrights shall prescribe by regulation.

(d) Records relating to death of authors.—Any person having an interest in a copyright may at any time record in the Copyright Office a statement of the date of death of the author of the copyrighted work, or a statement that the author is still living on a particular date. The statement shall identify the person filing it, the nature of that person's interest, and the source of the information recorded, and shall comply in form and content with requirements that the Register of Copyrights shall prescribe by regulation. The Register shall maintain current records of information relating to the death of authors of copyrighted works, based on such recorded statements and, to the extent the Register considers practicable, on data contained in any of the records of the Copyright Office or in other reference sources.

(e) Presumption as to author's death.—After a period of 95 years from the year of first publication of a work, or a period of 120 years from the year of its creation, whichever expires first, any person who obtains from the Copyright Office a certified report that the records provided by subsection (d) disclose nothing to indicate that the author of the work is living, or died less than 70 years before, is entitled to the benefit of a presumption that the author has been dead for at least 70 years. Reliance in good faith upon this presumption shall be a complete defense to any action for infringement under this title.

History of 17 U.S.C. §302: Oct. 19, 1976, P.L. 94-553, §101, 90 Stat. 2572; Oct. 27, 1998, P.L. 105-298, §102(b), 112 Stat. 2827.

See also U.S. Const. art. 1, §8, cl. 8.

ANNOTATIONS

Dastar Corp. v. Twentieth Century Fox Film Corp., 539 U.S. 23, 33-34 (2003). "The right to copy, and to copy without attribution, once a copyright has expired, like 'the right to make [an article whose patent has expired]—including the right to make it in precisely the shape it carried when patented—passes to the public.' 'In general, unless an intellectual property right such as a patent or copyright protects an item, it will be subject to copying.' The rights of a patentee or copyright holder are part of a 'carefully crafted bargain,' under which, once the patent or copyright monopoly has expired, the public may use the invention or work at will and without attribution. Thus, in construing the Lanham Act, we have been 'careful to caution against misuse or over-extension' of trademark and related protections into areas traditionally occupied by patent or copyright."

§303. DURATION OF COPYRIGHT: WORKS CREATED BUT NOT PUBLISHED OR COPYRIGHTED BEFORE JANUARY 1, 1978

(a) Copyright in a work created before January 1, 1978, but not theretofore in the public domain or copyrighted, subsists from January 1, 1978, and endures for the term provided by section 302. In no case, however, shall the term of copyright in such a work expire before December 31, 2002; and, if the work is published on or before December 31, 2002, the term of copyright shall not expire before December 31, 2047.

(b) The distribution before January 1, 1978, of a phonorecord shall not for any purpose constitute a publication of any musical work, dramatic work, or literary work embodied therein.

History of 17 U.S.C. §303: Oct. 19, 1976, P.L. 94-553, §101, 90 Stat. 2573; Nov. 13, 1997, P.L. 105-80, §11, 111 Stat. 1534; Oct. 27, 1998, P.L. 105-298, §102(c), 112 Stat. 2827; Dec. 9, 2010, P.L. 111-295, §5(b), 124 Stat. 3181.

See also U.S. Const. art. 1, §8, cl. 8.

ANNOTATIONS

Societe Civile Succession Richard Guino v. Renoir, 549 F.3d 1182, 1187-88 (9th Cir.2008). "[T]he sculptures in this case were not in the public domain. The sculptures were published in France as Renoir works in 1917. The sculptures were published as Renoir-Guino works in 1974, in an exhibition held in Paris. Neither party asserts that the sculptures were published with notice of U.S. copyright either in 1917 or 1974. [¶] Because those publications were in a foreign country and without notice of U.S. copyright, they 'did not put the work in the public domain in the U.S.' [¶] Furthermore, because the sculptures were never published with copyright notice, ... the sculptures were not protected by copyright under the 1909 [Copyright] Act. For the years between 1917 and 1978, therefore, the sculptures were neither protected by copyright nor injected into the public domain. [¶] The sculptures would not be entitled to protection under [17 U.S.C. §104A] because ... the sculptures have not passed into the public domain as required by §104A(h)(6)(c) as they were published abroad without copyright notice. [¶] [17 U.S.C. §303(a)] of the 1976 [Copyright] Act applies because the sculptures were 'created before January 1, 1978, but not theretofore in the public domain or copyrighted.' The sculptures were created between 1913 and 1917. [T]he sculptures have not passed into the public domain, ... and were not protected by copyright after foreign publication without notice.... The sculptures were not copyrighted until 1984. Section 303(a) provides protection for the term provided by [17 U.S.C.] §302, which is a term 70 years after the death of the last surviving author. Because [coauthor] passed away in 1973, the sculptures are entitled to protection until 2043, which the district court properly held."

§304. DURATION OF COPYRIGHT: SUBSISTING COPYRIGHTS

(a) Copyrights in their first term on January 1, 1978—

(1)(A) Any copyright, the first term of which is subsisting on January 1, 1978, shall endure for 28 years from the date it was originally secured.

(B) In the case of—

(i) any posthumous work or of any periodical, cyclopedic, or other composite work upon which the copyright was originally secured by the proprietor thereof, or

(ii) any work copyrighted by a corporate body (otherwise than as assignee or licensee of the individual author) or by an employer for whom such work is made for hire,

the proprietor of such copyright shall be entitled to a renewal and extension of the copyright in such work for the further term of 67 years.

(C) In the case of any other copyrighted work, including a contribution by an individual author to a periodical or to a cyclopedic or other composite work—

(i) the author of such work, if the author is still living,

(ii) the widow, widower, or children of the author, if the author is not living,

(iii) the author's executors, if such author, widow, widower, or children are not living, or

(iv) the author's next of kin, in the absence of a will of the author,

shall be entitled to a renewal and extension of the copyright in such work for a further term of 67 years.

(2)(A) At the expiration of the original term of copyright in a work specified in paragraph (1)(B) of this subsection, the copyright shall endure for a renewed and extended further term of 67 years, which—

(i) if an application to register a claim to such further term has been made to the Copyright Office within 1 year before the expiration of the original term of copyright, and the claim is registered, shall vest, upon the beginning of such further term, in the proprietor of the copyright who is entitled to claim the renewal of copyright at the time the application is made; or

(ii) if no such application is made or the claim pursuant to such application is not registered, shall vest, upon the beginning of such further term, in the person or entity that was the proprietor of the copyright as of the last day of the original term of copyright.

(B) At the expiration of the original term of copyright in a work specified in paragraph (1)(C) of this subsection, the copyright shall endure for a renewed and extended further term of 67 years, which—

(i) if an application to register a claim to such further term has been made to the Copyright Office within 1 year before the expiration of the original term of copyright, and the claim is registered, shall vest, upon the beginning of such further term, in any person who is entitled under paragraph (1)(C) to the renewal and extension of the copyright at the time the application is made; or

(ii) if no such application is made or the claim pursuant to such application is not registered, shall vest, upon the beginning of such further term, in any person entitled under paragraph (1)(C), as of the last day of the original term of copyright, to the renewal and extension of the copyright.

(3)(A) An application to register a claim to the renewed and extended term of copyright in a work may be made to the Copyright Office—

(i) within 1 year before the expiration of the original term of copyright by any person entitled under paragraph (1)(B) or (C) to such further term of 67 years; and

(ii) at any time during the renewed and extended term by any person in whom such further term vested, under paragraph (2)(A) or (B), or by any successor or assign of such person, if the application is made in the name of such person.

(B) Such an application is not a condition of the renewal and extension of the copyright in a work for a further term of 67 years.

(4)(A) If an application to register a claim to the renewed and extended term of copyright in a work is not made within 1 year before the expiration of the original term of copyright in a work, or if the claim pursuant to such application is not registered, then a derivative work prepared under authority of a grant of a transfer or license of the copyright that is made before the expiration of the original term of copyright may continue to be used under the terms of the grant during the renewed and extended term of copyright without infringing the copyright, except that such use does not extend to the preparation during such renewed and extended term of other derivative works based upon the copyrighted work covered by such grant.

(B) If an application to register a claim to the renewed and extended term of copyright in a work is made within 1 year before its expiration, and the claim is registered, the certificate of such registration shall constitute prima facie evidence as to the validity of the copyright during its renewed and extended term and of the facts stated in the certificate. The evidentiary weight to be accorded the certificates of a registration of a renewed and extended term of copyright made after the end of that 1-year period shall be within the discretion of the court.

(b) Copyrights in their renewal term at the time of the effective date of the Sonny Bono Copyright Term Extension Act.—Any copyright still in its renewal term as of Oct. 27, 1998 shall have a copyright term of 95 years from the date copyright was originally secured.

(c) Termination of transfers and licenses covering extended renewal term.—In the case of any copyright subsisting in either its first or renewal term on January 1, 1978, other than a copyright in a work made for hire, the exclusive or nonexclusive grant of a transfer or license of the renewal copyright or any right under it, executed before January 1, 1978, by any of the persons designated by subsection (a)(1)(C) of this section, otherwise than by will, is subject to termination under the following conditions:

(1) In the case of a grant executed by a person or persons other than the author, termination of the grant may be effected by the surviving person or persons who executed it. In the case of a grant executed by one or more of the authors of the work, termination of the grant may be effected, to the extent of a particular author's share in the ownership of the renewal copyright, by the author who executed it or, if such author is dead, by the person or persons who, under clause (2) of this subsection, own and are entitled to exercise a total of more than one-half of that author's termination interest.

(2) Where an author is dead, his or her termination interest is owned, and may be exercised, as follows:

(A) The widow or widower owns the author's entire termination interest unless there are any surviving children or grandchildren of the author, in which case the widow or widower owns one-half of the author's interest.

(B) The author's surviving children, and the surviving children of any dead child of the author, own the author's entire termination interest unless there is a widow or widower, in which case the ownership of one-half of the author's interest is divided among them.

(C) The rights of the author's children and grandchildren are in all cases divided among them and exercised on a per stirpes basis according to the number of such author's children represented; the share of the children of a dead child in a termination interest can be exercised only by the action of a majority of them.

(D) In the event that the author's widow or widower, children, and grandchildren are not living, the author's executor, administrator, personal representative, or trustee shall own the author's entire termination interest.

(3) Termination of the grant may be effected at any time during a period of five years beginning at the end of fifty-six years from the date copyright was originally secured, or beginning on January 1, 1978, whichever is later.

(4) The termination shall be effected by serving an advance notice in writing upon the grantee or the grantee's successor in title. In the case of a grant executed by a person or persons other than the author, the notice shall be signed by all of those entitled to terminate the grant under clause (1) of this subsection, or by their duly authorized agents. In the case of a grant executed by one or more of the authors of the work, the notice as to any one author's share shall be signed by that author or his or her duly authorized agent or, if that author is dead, by the number and proportion of the owners of his or her termination interest required under clauses (1) and (2) of this subsection, or by their duly authorized agents.

(A) The notice shall state the effective date of the termination, which shall fall within the five-year period specified by clause (3) of this subsection, or, in the case of a termination under subsection (d), within the five-year period specified by subsection (d)(2), and the notice shall be served not less than two or more than ten years before that date. A copy of the notice shall be recorded in the Copyright Office before the effective date of termination, as a condition to its taking effect.

(B) The notice shall comply, in form, content, and manner of service, with requirements that the Register of Copyrights shall prescribe by regulation.

(5) Termination of the grant may be effected notwithstanding any agreement to the contrary, including an agreement to make a will or to make any future grant.

(6) In the case of a grant executed by a person or persons other than the author, all rights under this title that were covered by the terminated grant revert, upon the effective date of termination, to all of those entitled to terminate the grant under clause (1) of this subsection. In the case of a grant executed by one or more of the authors of the work, all of a particular author's rights under this title that were covered by the terminated grant revert, upon the effective date of termination, to that author or, if that author is dead, to the persons owning his or her termination interest under clause (2) of this subsection, including those owners who did not join in signing the notice of termination under clause (4) of this subsection. In all cases the reversion of rights is subject to the following limitations:

(A) A derivative work prepared under authority of the grant before its termination may continue to be utilized under the terms of the grant after its termination, but this privilege does not extend to the preparation after the termination of other derivative works based upon the copyrighted work covered by the terminated grant.

(B) The future rights that will revert upon termination of the grant become vested on the date the notice of termination has been served as provided by clause (4) of this subsection.

(C) Where the author's rights revert to two or more persons under clause (2) of this subsection, they shall vest in those persons in the proportionate shares provided by that clause. In such a case, and subject to the provisions of subclause (D) of this clause, a further grant, or agreement to make a further grant, of a particular author's share with respect to any right covered by a terminated grant is valid only if it is signed by the same number and proportion of the owners, in whom the right has vested under this clause, as are required to terminate the grant under clause (2) of this subsection. Such further grant or agreement is effective with respect to all of the persons in whom the right it covers has vested under this subclause, including those who did not join in signing it. If any person dies after rights under a terminated grant have vested in him or her, that person's legal representatives, legatees, or heirs at law represent him or her for purposes of this subclause.

(D) A further grant, or agreement to make a further grant, of any right covered by a terminated grant is valid only if it is made after the effective date of the termination. As an exception, however, an agreement for such a further grant may be made between the author or any of the persons provided by the first sentence of clause (6) of this subsection, or between the persons provided by subclause (C) of this clause, and the original grantee or such grantee's successor in title, after the notice of termination has been served as provided by clause (4) of this subsection.

(E) Termination of a grant under this subsection affects only those rights covered by the grant that arise under this title, and in no way affects rights arising under any other Federal, State, or foreign laws.

(F) Unless and until termination is effected under this subsection, the grant, if it does not provide otherwise, continues in effect for the remainder of the extended renewal term.

(d) Termination rights provided in subsection (c) which have expired on or before the effective date of the Sonny Bono Copyright Term Extension Act.—In the case of any copyright other than a work made for hire, subsisting in its renewal term as of October 27, 1998 for which the termination right provided in subsection (c) has expired by such date, where the author or owner of the termination right has not previously exercised such termination right, the exclusive or nonexclusive grant of a transfer or license of the renewal copyright or any right under it, executed before January 1, 1978, by any of the persons designated in subsection (a)(1)(C) of this section, other than by will, is subject to termination under the following conditions:

(1) The conditions specified in subsections (c)(1), (2), (4), (5), and (6) of this section apply to terminations of the last 20 years of copyright term as provided by the amendments made by the Sonny Bono Copyright Term Extension Act.

(2) Termination of the grant may be effected at any time during a period of 5 years beginning at the end of 75 years from the date copyright was originally secured.

History of 17 U.S.C. §304: Oct. 19, 1976, P.L. 94-553, §101, 90 Stat. 2573; June 26, 1992, P.L. 102-307, §102(a), (d), 106 Stat. 264, 266; Nov. 13, 1997, P.L. 105-80, §12(a)(9), 111 Stat. 1535; Oct. 27, 1998, P.L. 105-298, §§102(d)(1), 103, 112 Stat. 2827, 2829; Nov. 2, 2002, P.L. 107-273, §13210(10), 116 Stat. 1910.

See also U.S. Const. art. 1, §8, cl. 8; 37 C.F.R. §201.10.

ANNOTATIONS

§304(a)

Roger Miller Music, Inc. v. Sony/ATV Publ'g, 477 F.3d 383, 391-92 (6th Cir.2007). "The renewal term of a copyrighted work is distinct from the original copyright term and can therefore be transferred independently of the original copyright. There is a strong presumption against the conveyance of renewal-copyright interests simultaneous with the conveyance of the original-copyright interest. Therefore, a valid transfer or assignment of a renewal-copyright interest must expressly grant rights in the renewal copyright. An assignment by an author that merely references his 'copyright' in general terms, without mentioning the renewal rights, does not include a conveyance of the author's renewal interests. [¶] Nevertheless, '[s]o long as the parties' intent is clear, a transfer of copyright need not include any particular language.' General words of assignment, such as 'forever,' 'perpetual,' and 'hereafter,' can be sufficient to transfer renewal rights if a court concludes that a transfer comports with the parties' intent. [¶] An author of a copyrighted work can assign the right to the renewal copyright before the renewal period commences: 'An assignment by an author of his renewal rights made before the original copyright expires is valid against the world, if the author is alive at the commencement of the renewal period.' An author, therefore, has the freedom to assign both his original and renewal-copyright interests at the same time, even if the renewal-copyright interest has not yet vested. If the author assigns his renewal copyrights and the renewal copyright term begins during the author's lifetime, the author is bound by the assignment. If, however, the author dies before vesting of the renewal copyright, the party to whom the renewal-copyright interest was conveyed loses the entitlement to that interest." *See also* ***Gary Friedrich Enters. v. Marvel Characters, Inc.***, 716 F.3d 302, 312 (2d Cir.2013).

Broadcast Music, Inc. v. Roger Miller Music, Inc., 396 F.3d 762, 768 (6th Cir.2005). An "author's children and an author's surviving spouse may simultaneously hold ownership interests in renewed copyrights if the author is deceased at the time of renewal. *At 782:* [W]e interpret §304(a) as providing that, when the copyright to an author's work is renewed after the author's death and that author is survived by a spouse and children, the surviving spouse holds a 50% share in the renewal copyright and the surviving children hold equal divided shares in the remaining 50%." *See also* ***Venegas-Hernández v. Asociación de Compositores y Editores de Música Latinoamericana***, 424 F.3d 50, 54-55 (1st Cir.2005).

Stone v. Williams, 970 F.2d 1043, 1064 (2d Cir. 1992). "As to works copyrighted prior to January 1, 1978 but which did not come into their renewal term until after that date, the determination of whether one is a 'child' entitled to claim ... renewals under [17 U.S.C.] §304(a) involves somewhat different considerations [than determination of a 'child' under the 1909 Copyright Act]. Although §304(a), like §24 [of the 1909 Act], provides that an author's 'widow, widower or children' are entitled to copyright renewals, unlike the 1909 Act, [17 U.S.C.] §101 of the 1976 [Copyright] Act defines children.... [¶] We do not think §101 commands a uniform federal definition of 'children' for purposes of copyright renewals under §304(a). *At 1066:* We therefore hold that [P] is entitled to a share of copyright renewals under §24 of the 1909 Act and under §304(a) of the 1976 Act, despite having been [adopted after copyright-owner-parent's death], since 'children' for purposes of both sections is defined by state law."

Swan v. EMI Music Publ'g, 58 U.S.P.Q.2d 1089, 1091 (S.D.N.Y.2000). "In the case of co-authorship, if one co-author renews the original copyright solely in his own name, that renewal is held upon a constructive trust for the other authors or the other author's heirs."

§304(c)

Stewart v. Abend, 495 U.S. 207, 226-27 (1990). "Congress would not have stated explicitly in §304(c)(6)(A) that, at the end of the renewal term, the owner of the rights in the pre-existing work may not terminate use rights in existing derivative works unless Congress had assumed that the owner continued to hold the right to sue for infringement even after incorporation of the pre-existing work into the derivative work."

Mills Music, Inc. v. Snyder, 469 U.S. 153, 156 (1985). The "phrase 'under the terms of the grant' as it is used in §304(c)(6)(A) [is] the so-called 'derivative works exception' (the Exception) to the 'termination of transfer and licenses' provisions found in §304(c). *At 173-74:* The Exception in §304(c)(6)(A) was designed ... to exclude a specific category of grants—even if they were manifestly unfair to the author—from that broad objective. The purpose of the Exception was to 'preserve the right of the owner of a derivative work to exploit it, notwithstanding the reversion.' Therefore, even if a person acquired the right to exploit an already prepared derivative work by means of an unfavorable bargain with an author, that right was to be excluded from the bundle of rights that would revert to the author when he exercised his termination right. The critical point in determining whether the right to continue utilizing a derivative work survives the termination of a transfer of a copyright is whether it was 'prepared' before the termination. Pretermination derivative works—those prepared under the authority of the terminated grant—may continue to be utilized under the terms of the terminated grant. Derivative works prepared after the termination of the grant are not extended this exemption from the termination provisions. ... The scope of the duly authorized grant and the time the derivative work was prepared are what the statute makes relevant because these are the factors that determine which of the statute's two countervailing purposes should control."

Brumley v. Albert E. Brumley & Sons, Inc., 822 F.3d 926, 930 (6th Cir.2016). "The termination provision has two salient features. One is that, so long as the author never exercised the termination right, it survives him. His 'widow or widower owns the author's entire termination interest unless there are any surviving children or grandchildren of the author, in which case the widow or widower owns one-half of the author's interest' and 'the ownership of one-half of the author's interest is divided among the [surviving children and grandchildren].' When there is no surviving spouse, '[t]he author's surviving children, and the surviving children of any dead child of the author, own the author's entire termination interest.' In order to terminate, a group that is 'entitled to exercise a total of more than one-half of [the] author's termination interest' must agree to the termination, give advance notice of the termination, and file everything within one of two windows of time. [¶] The other key feature of the termination right is that, at a minimum, agreements predating 1978 that purport to bargain away all rights in a copyrighted work may not limit the termination right. Else, the purpose of transforming the 'renewal right' regime into a 'termination right' regime would be thwarted. In the words of the statute: 'Termination of the grant may be effected notwithstanding any agreement to the contrary, including an agreement to make a will or to make any future grant.'"

Baldwin v. EMI Feist Catalog, Inc., 805 F.3d 18, 26-27 (2d Cir.2015). "We will refer to the exception permitting pre-termination, post-notice agreements with the original grantee as the 'existing-grantee exception.' This existing-grantee exception was included in the 1976 Act to give the grantee 'some advantage over others in obtaining the terminated rights.' [¶] When an author or his statutory heirs serves a termination notice, the grantee's previously undivided copyright interest is effectively split into three pieces, one owned by the author or his statutory heirs and two owned by the grantee. The author (or his statutory heirs) holds a future interest in the copyright. This future interest, however (unlike an author's renewal right under the 1909 Act), 'become[s] vested on the date the notice of termination has been served,' ... which gives the grantee confidence, in negotiations under the existing-grantee exception, that the grantor actually has something to convey. [¶] Although an author's (or his statutory heirs') interest vests immediately upon service of a termination notice, it becomes possessory—i.e., it entitles the author (or his statutory heirs) to ownership of the copyright—only if the notice is recorded before the termination date. In other words, even after a notice is served, the interest that vests upon service may be divested if the notice is not recorded, and the grantee will continue to own the copyright through the end of the extended renewal term. So upon being served with a termination notice, the grantee—by virtue of the existing grant—holds both a present interest scheduled to terminate on the notice's effective date and a contingent future interest that will vest on that date and entitle the grantee to possession if the notice goes unrecorded. [¶] [I]n the prototypical agreement contemplated by the existing-grantee exception, the author or his statutory heirs convey only the future interest that vested in them upon service of the termination notice—that is, the only interest they hold at the time the notice is served."

Penguin Grp. v. Steinbeck, 537 F.3d 193, 198-99 (2d Cir.2008). "It is worth noting that [17 U.S.C.] §304(c), by its terms, does not apply to grants of a transfer or license of the renewal copyright made on or after January 1, 1978. Such grants are subject to the slightly different termination right provided at 17 U.S.C. §203, which, among other distinctions, applies only to grants made by the author rather than to grants made by either the author or other parties. [¶] Section 304(c) also provides only a limited five-year window of time ... during which termination rights may be exercised. If the termination right is not exercised during this window, the original grant remains in effect. So, for [book], the earliest work included in the 1938 Agreement, the termination right under §304(c) expired on August 2, 1990, and for [other book], the latest work, the right expired on April 14, 2000. It is undisputed, however, that no termination right under §304(c) was ever exercised with respect to the copyrights covered by the 1938 Agreement. [¶] When the length of the copyright term was extended in 1998, Congress provided an additional window of time corresponding to this extension, during which the same termination right could be, had it not already been, exercised. For pre-1978 grants whose §304(c) termination right, as of October 26, 1998, had expired without being exercised, termination could 'be effected at any time during a period of five years beginning at the end of 75 years from the date copyright was originally secured.' Section 304(d) otherwise incorporated the conditions specified in §304(c) including the statutory heirs of an author's termination right. The Notice of Termination issued in 2004 by [author's d]escendants purported to terminate the 1938 grants of copyright licenses within each work's §304(d) termination period. *At 202:* [N]othing in §304(c)(6)(D) prevents renegotiation of a prior grant where a notice of termination has not been served. Such a succeeding grant of rights would presumably take place with the parties' knowledge that the holder of a termination right *could* exercise that right if they failed to reach a new agreement. [¶] We do not read the phrase 'agreement to the contrary' so broadly that it would include any agreement that has the effect of eliminating a termination right. To do so would negate the effect of other provisions of the Copyright Act that explicitly contemplate the loss of termination rights. For example, §§304(c) and (d) require only the consent of a simple majority in interest for the exercise of a termination right. Once the termination right is extinguished, it is extinguished with respect to all parties holding a termination interest, whether or not they agreed to its exercise. Similarly, if a termination right expires without being exercised, the original grant is no longer subject to termination, and the Copyright Act specifically provides that in such a case a grant would 'continue[] in effect for the remainder of the extended renewal term.' If the holders of a majority of an author's termination interest were to agree that they would not exercise their termination rights, this would have the effect of eliminating a termination right as to the minority termination interests. Yet such an agreement could not be held ineffective as an 'agreement to the contrary' inasmuch as §304 itself contemplates elimination of termination rights in that manner. *At 204:* It should be noted that under our view, authors or their statutory heirs holding termination rights are still left with an opportunity to threaten (or to make good on a threat) to exercise termination rights and extract more favorable terms from early grants of an author's copyright. But nothing in the statute suggests that an author or an author's statutory heirs are entitled to more than one opportunity, between them, to use termination rights to enhance their bargaining power or to exercise them." *See also* ***Ray Charles Found. v. Robinson***, 795 F.3d 1109, 1112-13 (9th Cir. 2015); ***Classic Media, Inc. v. Mewborn***, 532 F.3d 978, 989 (9th Cir.2008), *overruled on other grounds*, ***Octane Fitness, LLC v. ICON Health & Fitness, Inc.***, ___ U.S. ___, 134 S.Ct. 1749 (2014).

Classic Media, Inc. v. Mewborn, 532 F.3d 978, 986 (9th Cir.2008), *overruled on other grounds*, ***Octane Fitness, LLC v. ICON Health & Fitness, Inc.***, ___ U.S. ___, 134 S.Ct. 1749 (2014). "[I]nsofar as [P] urges us to hold that the 1978 Assignment transferred the motion picture, television and radio rights subject to [D's] termination rights, we cannot so hold because such an assignment would be void as an 'agreement to the contrary' pursuant to §304(c)(5). Moreover, all that [D] had at the time of the 1978 Assignment was future rights that would revert upon termination of the grant and the 1978 Assignment does not purport to grant those rights."

Marvel Characters, Inc. v. Simon, 310 F.3d 280, 292 (2d Cir.2002). An "agreement made subsequent to a work's creation which retroactively deems it a 'work for hire' constitutes an 'agreement to the contrary' under §304(c)(5) of the 1976 [Copyright] Act."

Fred Ahlert Music Corp. v. Warner/Chappell Music, Inc., 155 F.3d 17, 25 (2d Cir.1998). When original copyright owner's "heirs terminated [copyright assignee 1's] domestic copyright interest in the Song pursuant to ... §304(c), the right to authorize new uses of the Song as embodied by [recording artist's] derivative reverted to the heirs, because that right is not within the 'terms of the grant' preserved by the Derivative Works Exception. The district court properly entered judgment in favor of [copyright assignee 2]."

Burroughs v. Metro-Goldwyn-Mayer, Inc., 683 F.2d 610, 622 (2d Cir.1982). "To be effective, a notice of termination under §304(c) must clearly identify 'the grant to which the notice of termination applies,' and must list the title, author, and date of original copyright for 'each work to which the notice of termination applies.' While we do not suggest that the omission of the five titles affected the efficacy of the notice to terminate the interest of [P] in such titles as *were* listed, it did leave [P's] interest in those five books ... intact."

Range Road Music, Inc. v. Music Sales Corp., 76 F.Supp.2d 375, 377 (S.D.N.Y.1999). Upon "the effective date of termination, the terminated copyright reverts back to the party that served the notice of termination. The reversionary interest created by the service of the notice of termination vests at the time the notice of termination has been served on the grantee. Furthermore, the reversionary interest ... is subject to several limitations.... Thus, an author may not ordinarily assign or grant the extended renewal term until after the effective date of termination, i.e. after the 56th year. An exception to this provision permits the author or his statutory successor to make a grant prior to the effective date of termination and after the notice of termination has been served, provided that the grant of the extended renewal term is made to the original grantee whose interest has been terminated."

§304(d)

Penguin Grp. v. Steinbeck, 537 F.3d 193, 200 (2d Cir.2008). "The Copyright Act provides a termination right for the grant of a transfer or license of copyright made by parties other than the author only if the grant was made prior to January 1, 1978. Our first inquiry, then, is whether the 1994 Agreement [between author's assignee and publisher] terminated and superseded the 1938 Agreement [between author and publisher]. We conclude that it did, leaving in effect no pre-1978 grants to which the termination rights provided by §304(d) could be applied. [¶] The language of the 1994 Agreement makes clear that the parties intended that the 1938 Agreement be terminated. Under New York law, 'parties to an agreement can mutually agree to terminate it by expressly assenting to its rescission while simultaneously entering into a new agreement dealing with the same subject matter.' Once terminated and superseded, the new contract provides all of the parties' obligations and remedies for breach."

§305. DURATION OF COPYRIGHT: TERMINAL DATE

All terms of copyright provided by sections 302 through 304 run to the end of the calendar year in which they would otherwise expire.

History of 17 U.S.C. §305: Oct. 19, 1976, P.L. 94-553, §101, 90 Stat. 2576.
See also U.S. Const. art. 1, §8, cl. 8.

CHAPTER 4. COPYRIGHT NOTICE, DEPOSIT, & REGISTRATION

§401. NOTICE OF COPYRIGHT: VISUALLY PERCEPTIBLE COPIES

(a) General provisions.—Whenever a work protected under this title is published in the United States or elsewhere by authority of the copyright owner, a notice of copyright as provided by this section may be placed on publicly distributed copies from which the work can be visually perceived, either directly or with the aid of a machine or device.

(b) Form of notice.—If a notice appears on the copies, it shall consist of the following three elements:

(1) the symbol © (the letter C in a circle), or the word "Copyright," or the abbreviation "Copr."; and

(2) the year of first publication of the work; in the case of compilations, or derivative works incorporating previously published material, the year date of first publication of the compilation or derivative work is sufficient. The year date may be omitted where a pictorial, graphic, or sculptural work, with accompanying text matter, if any, is reproduced in or on greeting cards, postcards, stationery, jewelry, dolls, toys, or any useful articles; and

(3) the name of the owner of copyright in the work, or an abbreviation by which the name can be recognized, or a generally known alternative designation of the owner.

(c) Position of notice.—The notice shall be affixed to the copies in such manner and location as to give reasonable notice of the claim of copyright. The Register of Copyrights shall prescribe by regulation, as examples, specific methods of affixation and positions of the notice on various types of works that will satisfy this requirement, but these specifications shall not be considered exhaustive.

(d) Evidentiary weight of notice.—If a notice of copyright in the form and position specified by this section appears on the published copy or copies to which a defendant in a copyright infringement suit had access, then no weight shall be given to such a defendant's interposition of a defense based on innocent infringement in mitigation of actual or statutory damages, except as provided in the last sentence of section 504(c)(2).

History of 17 U.S.C. §401: Oct. 19, 1976, P.L. 94-553, §101, 90 Stat. 2576; Oct. 31, 1988, P.L. 100-568, §7(a), 102 Stat. 2857.
See also 37 C.F.R. §202.2; Berne Convention.

ANNOTATIONS

§401(a)

Society of the Holy Transfiguration Monastery, Inc. v. Gregory, 689 F.3d 29, 44 (1st Cir.2012). "There were three paths under the common law pursuant to which a work could be exposed to the public or enter the public domain: (1) exhibition or performance of the work; (2) limited publication; and (3) general publication. Only one such path, however, would extinguish the creator's copyright in a work; the road to such loss was general publication. For the most part, the Copyright Act of 1976 abolished the common law of copyright, but even under the 1976 Act, general publication without notice could cause a work to enter the public domain if the copyright owner failed to register the work within five years of the date of first publication. The Berne Convention Implementation Act of 1988 transformed this legal landscape, and notice is no longer mandatory for works published after that Act's March 1, 1989 effective date. But the Berne Act does not apply to works published before 1989, so a work published without proper notice prior to 1989 would still become part of the public domain if the copyright owner failed to cure the defective notice in time. *At 45:* A general publication is 'when a work is made available to members of the public at large without regard to who they are or what they propose to do with it.' That is, a general publication consists of such a level of circulation within the public sphere that a work may be deemed 'dedicated to the public and rendered common property.' Conversely, a limited publication 'occurs when tangible copies of the work are distributed, but to a limited class of persons and for a limited purpose.' [¶] Delivery of [the] booklets to selected religious congregations for the circumscribed purpose of literary feedback rings more of a limited publication (distribution 'to a limited class of persons and for a limited purpose')—than of a general publication (distribution to 'the public at large without regard to who they are or what they propose to do with [the work]')." *See also* ***Norma Ribbon & Trimming, Inc. v. Little***, 51 F.3d 45, 48 (5th Cir.1995).

Donald Frederick Evans & Assocs. v. Continental Homes, Inc., 785 F.2d 897, 908 (11th Cir.1986). "[A] finding of forfeiture of copyright protection cannot be based on *unauthorized* distribution of the work without notice because the notice requirement applies only to copies of works published 'by authority of the copyright owner.'"

Hasbro Bradley, Inc. v. Sparkle Toys, Inc., 780 F.2d 189, 194-95 (2d Cir.1985). "According to [P], since it—not [Japanese toy designer]—is the copyright owner in the U.S., and since all of the toys sold by its authority in the U.S. and elsewhere have displayed proper copyright notice, it cannot be in violation of the notice requirement. The fallacy with this argument is that it starts by assuming the very point here in dispute: that [P] is the owner of valid copyrights in the U.S. [P's] copyrights initially had only such validity as [Japanese toy designer's]. For purposes of determining the validity in the U.S. of [Japanese toy designer's] copyrights at the time of assignment, [Japanese toy designer] is the relevant 'copyright owner' under [17 U.S.C.] §401(a). [Japanese toy designer's] violation of the notice requirement left [P] with only an incipient copyright, subject to cure. [¶] The issue ... becomes whether [P] has cured [Japanese toy designer's] omission of notice under [17 U.S.C.] §405(a)(2). There is no question that [P], as [Japanese toy designer's] assignee, is permitted to effect cure through its own efforts. The 'copyright claimant' entitled under the [Copyright] Act to register a copyright in the U.S. may be either the author of the work or his assignee, and any registration is of the work *per se* and redounds to the benefit of the assignor as well as the assignee. Not disputing this, [D] argues that [P] cannot effect cure under §405(a)(2) because [Japanese toy designer's] omission of notice was deliberate." Held: P-assignee may cure toy designer's omission of notice even though omission was deliberate.

§401(b)

Langman Fabrics v. Graff Californiawear, Inc., 160 F.3d 106, 115 (2d Cir.1998), *amended*, 169 F.3d 782 (2d Cir.1998). "The plain meaning of the statute and the implicit meaning of the Copyright Office's Compendium require a holding that fabric manufactured for the purpose of being made into clothing is a 'useful article' within the meaning of §401(b)(2). [D] did not invalidate its copyright by failing to include the year of first publication in its copyright notice."

Charles Garnier v. Andin Int'l, 36 F.3d 1214, 1217 n.2 (1st Cir.1994). "Copyright notice for jewelry consists of the copyright symbol or the word 'Copyright,' followed by the name of the owner of the copyright, 'affixed' to each copy in such a manner as 'to give reasonable notice of the claim of copyright.'"

Community for Creative Non-Violence v. Reid, 846 F.2d 1485, 1488 n.2 (D.C.Cir.1988), *aff'd*, 490 U.S. 730 (1989). "Beneath the title of the sculpture, which was molded into the human figure portion of the work, [sculptor] had placed a copyright notice: '© James Earl Reid, Sculptor 85.' This measure, which [sculptor] took before the creation was displayed in D.C. was unnecessary to secure any copyright protection to which [sculptor] might be entitled. Generally, a notice of copyright is required upon publication of copies of a copyrighted work. However, a public display is not a publication."

Shapiro & Son Bedspread Corp. v. Royal Mills Assocs., 764 F.2d 69, 72 (2d Cir.1985). "[P] jeopardized its present claim of copyright in [bedspread] design by publishing it without proper notice of copyright for the period October 1978 to April 1984, during which the only notice on the product was the words 'Design Copyrighted' which appeared on the flyer inserted into the bags containing the bedspreads. [P's] original notice was deficient in two respects: (1) it was not in the form specified by ... §401(b) ...; and (2) it was not 'affixed to' the work, as required by §401(c). In general, publication of a work without a proper notice of copyright affixed injects the work into the public domain." *See also* ***M. Kramer Mfg. v. Andrews***, 783 F.2d 421, 443 (4th Cir.1986).

Metzke v. May Dept. Stores, 878 F.Supp. 756, 759 (W.D.Pa.1995). "Notice is sufficient even where it is legible only to 'someone with excellent vision,' or if finding it requires 'close examination.'" *See also* ***Spectravest, Inc. v. Fleet St. Ltd.***, 13 U.S.P.Q.2d 1457, 1459 (N.D.Cal.1989).

Holland Fabrics, Inc. v. Delta Fabrics, Inc., 2 U.S.P.Q.2d 1157, 1158 (S.D.N.Y.1987). "The notation 'c.' is not the proper symbol for a copyright. Rather, the letter 'c' with a circle around it is acceptable, as is the word 'Copyright' or the abbreviation 'Copr.' As noted by [Ds], not only is the notation 'c.' by itself not recognizable as a copyright symbol, it is also ambiguous. The symbol 'c.' could be read as an abbreviation for the word company or color, or for a style or grade designation...."

§401(c)

Charles Garnier v. Andin Int'l, 36 F.3d 1214, 1227 (1st Cir.1994). Copyright "notice must be 'affixed' to each copy for which protection is desired. Failure to 'affix' a notice to the copy renders that notice legally deficient and defective. The legal consequences of a deficient notice are the same as those for an omitted notice. Accordingly, to cure an omission, the author must add legally proper notice to all copies."

Koontz v. Jaffarian, 787 F.2d 906, 909 (4th Cir. 1986). "[D] argues that he was free to copy from [copyright owner's] data compilation contained in the software because there was no copyright notice on the software as required by ... §401. [¶] Courts adhering to the unit publication doctrine hold that copyright notice affixed 'to one element of a publication containing various elements gives copyright protection to all elements of the publication.' ... In proper circumstances, linked elements of a publication should be collectively protected, and we agree with the district court that the unit publication doctrine should apply where ... the elements of the publication form a single commercial unit." *See also* ***Mitel, Inc. v. Iqtel, Inc.***, 896 F.Supp. 1050, 1054 (D.Colo.1995), *aff'd*, 124 F.3d 1366 (10th Cir.1997).

§401(d)

Matthew Bender & Co. v. West Publ'g, 240 F.3d 116, 123 (2d Cir.2001). 17 U.S.C. §§401(d) and 402(d) "prevent an alleged infringer from asserting an 'innocent infringement' defense if a notice of copyright appears on the material allegedly infringed."

Columbia Pictures Indus. v. Garcia, 996 F.Supp. 770, 771-72 (N.D.Ill.1998). "Since 'each and every videocassette seized [by marshals] bore a notice of copyright,' [Ps] reason that [distributor] may not raise the innocent infringer defense. [¶] We are uneasy with this interpretation and application of §401(d). The copyright notices at issue here appeared on the *seized* videotapes—the fakes—and §401(d) applies only where the notice appeared 'on the published copy or copies to which [D] had access.' The unauthorized duplicate videotapes obviously are not 'the published copy,' and we doubt that they are 'copies to which a defendant ... had access,' for if they are, then every defendant who infringes a copyright by distributing unauthorized duplicates has 'access' to the unauthorized duplicate that he's distributing. And if every distributor has 'access,' unlawful distribution can be innocent only when the unauthorized copies do *not* bear the copyright mark. Under this reasoning, if one unauthorized duplicate videotape was labeled with a believable reproduction of the original label (and thus bore a copyright mark) while another had a handwritten label (without a copyright mark), the distributor of the first videotape could not claim innocent infringement but the second could, despite the fact that it is the second distributor who has no credible claim of innocence. It seems unlikely that Congress intended such a perverse outcome."

Broderbund Software, Inc. v. Unison World, Inc., 648 F.Supp. 1127, 1135 (N.D.Cal.1986). "The Court finds that [Ps'] display of the copyright notice provided

[D] with reasonable warning that the audiovisual displays in 'Print Shop' were copyrighted. The general notice that appears on the 'boot up' screen implies that the copyright holder claims protection for as much of the work as is allowable under the copyright laws. It would be unreasonable to expect copyright holders to list on each copy of their works every single aspect or element of the work for which they claim protection. It would also be unreasonable to expect copyright holders to know at any given time the exact state of the law on the scope of copyright protection. [Ps'] copyright notice was adequate."

§402. NOTICE OF COPYRIGHT: PHONORECORDS OF SOUND RECORDINGS

(a) General provisions.—Whenever a sound recording protected under this title is published in the United States or elsewhere by authority of the copyright owner, a notice of copyright as provided by this section may be placed on publicly distributed phonorecords of the sound recording.

(b) Form of notice.—If a notice appears on the phonorecords, it shall consist of the following three elements:

(1) the symbol (P) (the letter P in a circle); and

(2) the year of first publication of the sound recording; and

(3) the name of the owner of copyright in the sound recording, or an abbreviation by which the name can be recognized, or a generally known alternative designation of the owner; if the producer of the sound recording is named on the phonorecord labels or containers, and if no other name appears in conjunction with the notice, the producer's name shall be considered a part of the notice.

(c) Position of notice.—The notice shall be placed on the surface of the phonorecord, or on the phonorecord label or container, in such manner and location as to give reasonable notice of the claim of copyright.

(d) Evidentiary weight of notice.—If a notice of copyright in the form and position specified by this section appears on the published phonorecord or phonorecords to which a defendant in a copyright infringement suit had access, then no weight shall be given to such a defendant's interposition of a defense based on innocent infringement in mitigation of actual or statutory damages, except as provided in the last sentence of section 504(c)(2).

History of 17 U.S.C. §402: Oct. 19, 1976, P.L. 94-553, §101, 90 Stat. 2577; Oct. 31, 1988, P.L. 100-568, §7(b), 102 Stat. 2857.

See also Berne Convention.

ANNOTATIONS

Maverick Recording Co. v. Harper, 598 F.3d 193, 199 (5th Cir.2010). "[D's] reliance on her own understanding of copyright law—or lack thereof—is irrelevant in the context of §402(d). The plain language of the statute shows that the infringer's knowledge or intent does not affect its application. Lack of legal sophistication cannot overcome a properly asserted §402(d) limitation to the innocent infringer defense."

BMG Music v. Gonzalez, 430 F.3d 888, 891-92 (7th Cir.2005). "[D] asked the district court to reduce the [17 U.S.C. §504(c) statutory damages] award under [17 U.S.C. §402(d)], but the judge concluded that §402(d) bars any reduction in the minimum award. ... It is undisputed that [P] gave copyright notice as required—'on the surface of the phonorecord, or on the phonorecord label or container.' It is likewise undisputed that [D] had 'access' to records and compact disks bearing the proper notice. She downloaded data rather than discs, and the data lacked copyright notices, but the statutory question is whether 'access' to legitimate works was available rather than whether infringers earlier in the chain attached copyright notices to the pirated works. [D] readily could have learned, had she inquired, that the music was under copyright."

Innovative Concepts in Entm't, Inc. v. Entertainment Enters., 576 F.Supp. 457, 460-61 (E.D.N.Y. 1983). "The legislative history indicates three reasons for the requirement of the special 'P' symbol: 'to avoid confusion between claims to copyright in the sound recording and in the musical or literary work embodied in it, [to distinguish] between copyright claims in the sound recording and in the printed text or art work appearing on the record label, album cover, liner notes,' and because the symbol has been adopted by the international 'Phonograms Convention.' The 'phonorecord' here is a computer chip which carries the standard '©' notice of copyright. As the recording in question is of crowd noises from an actual hockey game rather than of a separately copyrighted musical or literary work, [D] cannot claim to have been misled. Accordingly, the court finds that this omission will be cured pursuant to

17 U.S.C. §405(a)(2) ... if [P] henceforth affixes the notice required by [17 U.S.C.] §402."

§403. NOTICE OF COPYRIGHT: PUBLICATIONS INCORPORATING UNITED STATES GOVERNMENT WORKS

Sections 401(d) and 402(d) shall not apply to a work published in copies or phonorecords consisting predominantly of one or more works of the United States Government unless the notice of copyright appearing on the published copies or phonorecords to which a defendant in the copyright infringement suit had access includes a statement identifying, either affirmatively or negatively, those portions of the copies or phonorecords embodying any work or works protected under this title.

History of 17 U.S.C. §403: Oct. 19, 1976, P.L. 94-553, §101, 90 Stat. 2577; Oct. 31, 1988, P.L. 100-568, §7(c), 102 Stat. 2858.

See also Berne Convention.

ANNOTATIONS

Matthew Bender & Co. v. West Publ'g, 240 F.3d 116, 123 (2d Cir.2001). Section 403 "serves to reinstate the innocent infringement defense in certain circumstances. The section does not impose any affirmative obligation on a copyright holder, but rather simply states that, in the case of works consisting predominantly of government material, the failure to provide the specified form of notice allows an alleged infringer to assert an innocent infringement defense and to mitigate his damages. *At 124:* A plain reading of the section demonstrates that the sole consequence of failing to provide sufficient notice is that an alleged infringer may mitigate his actual or statutory damages by asserting the innocent infringement defense. [¶] The District Court's imposition of attorneys' fees on the basis of a 'violation' of §403 ... involves an application of the 'wrong legal standard.' Accordingly, we conclude that the District Court exceeded its allowable discretion in awarding fees on this basis."

§404. NOTICE OF COPYRIGHT: CONTRIBUTIONS TO COLLECTIVE WORKS

(a) A separate contribution to a collective work may bear its own notice of copyright, as provided by sections 401 through 403. However, a single notice applicable to the collective work as a whole is sufficient to invoke the provisions of section 401(d) or 402(d), as applicable with respect to the separate contributions it contains (not including advertisements inserted on behalf of persons other than the owner of copyright in the collective work), regardless of the ownership of copyright in the contributions and whether or not they have been previously published.

(b) With respect to copies and phonorecords publicly distributed by authority of the copyright owner before the effective date of the Berne Convention Implementation Act of 1988, where the person named in a single notice applicable to a collective work as a whole is not the owner of copyright in a separate contribution that does not bear its own notice, the case is governed by the provisions of section 406(a).

History of 17 U.S.C. §404: Oct. 19, 1976, P.L. 94-553, §101, 90 Stat. 2577; Oct. 31, 1988, P.L. 100-568, §7(d), 102 Stat. 2858.

See also Berne Convention.

ANNOTATIONS

New York Times Co. v. Tasini, 533 U.S. 483, 496 (2001). "Together, [17 U.S.C. §§201(c) and 404(a)] 'preserve the author's copyright in a contribution even if the contribution does not bear a separate notice in the author's name, and without requiring any unqualified transfer of rights to the owner of the collective work.'"

TransWestern Publ'g Co. v. Multimedia Mktg. Assocs., 133 F.3d 773, 781 (10th Cir.1998). "Treating the yellow pages advertising as creations that are something more than compilations of facts, we hold that under ... §404(a), the existence of a copyright notice on [P's] directory is insufficient to prohibit the copying of an advertisement from that directory, absent a copyright notice specific to the advertisement itself." *But see* ***Idearc Media Corp. v. Northwest Directories, Inc.***, 623 F.Supp.2d 1223, 1230 (D.Or.2008) (lack of copyright notice on ad affects presumption of innocent infringement, not enforceability of ad owner's rights).

Hustler Mag., Inc. v. Moral Majority, Inc., 796 F.2d 1148, 1154-55 (9th Cir.1986). "Although each component of a composite work is capable of individual copyright protection and need not bear a separate copyright notice, courts have not always evaluated a component of a copyrighted composite work as an 'entire work.' Rather courts consider the relationship of the copied component to the composite work to determine whether to analyze the work as an 'entire work.' [¶] [T]o determine whether the parody should be treated as an 'entire work,' we consider the relationship of the copied parody to the periodical as a whole. Unlike [a magazine cover], the inside pages of a magazine are not on public display. Moreover, the parody in this case ... represents the 'essence' of [magazine]. In addition, ... the parody is not an interwoven component of the magazine, but can stand totally alone. A creative work does not deserve less copyright protection just because it is part of a composite work. Therefore, in this case, we view [Ds] as having copied an entire work."

§405. NOTICE OF COPYRIGHT: OMISSION OF NOTICE ON CERTAIN COPIES & PHONORECORDS

(a) Effect of omission on copyright.—With respect to copies and phonorecords publicly distributed by authority of the copyright owner before the effective date of the Berne Convention Implementation Act of 1988, the omission of the copyright notice described in sections 401 through 403 from copies or phonorecords publicly distributed by authority of the copyright owner does not invalidate the copyright in a work if—

(1) the notice has been omitted from no more than a relatively small number of copies or phonorecords distributed to the public; or

(2) registration for the work has been made before or is made within five years after the publication without notice, and a reasonable effort is made to add notice to all copies or phonorecords that are distributed to the public in the United States after the omission has been discovered; or

(3) the notice has been omitted in violation of an express requirement in writing that, as a condition of the copyright owner's authorization of the public distribution of copies or phonorecords, they bear the prescribed notice.

(b) Effect of omission on innocent infringers.—Any person who innocently infringes a copyright, in reliance upon an authorized copy or phonorecord from which the copyright notice has been omitted and which was publicly distributed by authority of the copyright owner before the effective date of the Berne Convention Implementation Act of 1988, incurs no liability for actual or statutory damages under section 504 for any infringing acts committed before receiving actual notice that registration for the work has been made under section 408, if such person proves that he or she was misled by the omission of notice. In a suit for infringement in such a case the court may allow or disallow recovery of any of the infringer's profits attributable to the infringement, and may enjoin the continuation of the infringing undertaking or may require, as a condition for permitting the continuation of the infringing undertaking, that the infringer pay the copyright owner a reasonable license fee in an amount and on terms fixed by the court.

(c) Removal of notice.—Protection under this title is not affected by the removal, destruction, or obliteration of the notice, without the authorization of the copyright owner, from any publicly distributed copies or phonorecords.

History of 17 U.S.C. §405: Oct. 19, 1976, P.L. 94-553, §101, 90 Stat. 2578; Oct. 31, 1988, P.L. 100-568, §7(e), 102 Stat. 2858; Nov. 13, 1997, P.L. 105-80, §12(a)(10), 111 Stat. 1535.

See also Berne Convention; NAFTA annex 1705.7.

ANNOTATIONS

Generally

Norma Ribbon & Trimming, Inc. v. Little, 51 F.3d 45, 48 (5th Cir.1995). "Although since the Berne Convention Implementation Act of 1988 notice is no longer a prerequisite to copyright protection, the notice requirement remains in effect for works that predated that Act."

§405(a)

Harris Custom Builders, Inc. v. Hoffmeyer, 92 F.3d 517, 520 (7th Cir.1996). "How can a published work remain copyrighted based on its status as an unpublished work? The answer, at least on these facts, is that it cannot. Because ... the alleged owner of the copyright in the unpublished drawings, itself published, without notice, the brochure with the abbreviated drawings, it forfeited its right to protect that part of the drawings which were published. Under the 1976 [Copyright] Act while unpublished works are protected, if a published work is to be protected, it must have proper copyright notice or meet the cure provisions in §405(a). Otherwise, the protection of a copyright is forfeited. Forfeiture of a copyright under the 1976 Act can arise through a failure to meet the statutory formalities. A copyright can be forfeited whether or not the owner of the copyright intends that result."

Hardwick Airmasters, Inc. v. Lennox Indus., 78 F.3d 1332, 1336 (8th Cir.1996). "[P] argues that he reasonably believed he could wait up to five years to register the copyright and that he could continue during this five-year period to knowingly publish material without a copyright notice. [P] claims that his erroneous construction of §405 is a 'mistake of law,' and that as such, 'discovery' for the purposes of §405 did not occur until after he correctly understood §405's requirements. [¶] [P's] construction of §405(a)(2) is not permissible."

Charles Garnier v. Andin Int'l, 36 F.3d 1214, 1219 (1st Cir.1994). Effective "March 1, 1989, the attachment of notice of copyright is no longer required to gain copyright protection for creative works, although it is still encouraged through various incentives. *At 1221:* We ... conclude that deliberate omissions are potentially curable and can be discovered after the first copy of a work is published. *At 1222:* When an author makes a deliberate decision to forgo potential copyright protection of a work by failing to affix notice on copies, with the knowledge that copyright notice is normally required, that author becomes aware of the legal effect of its omission of notice and thus has discovered the omission for purposes of §405(a)(2). Discovery can occur upon the date of first publication if the author has this state of mind when the first copies are distributed. Finding that conscious decisions to forgo the expense of complying with the requirements for a copyright can result in an immediate discovery of the omission of notice under §405(a)(2) does no injustice to the legislative intent to provide notice of all omissions. No cure can be considered 'reasonable' in cases where the author simply sits back and waits to see whether his or her work will be a best-seller, before suddenly springing into action and deciding to claim copyright protection after a competitor invests significant time and resources in developing a competing product. *At 1226:* [W]e hold that §405(a) imposes a cure requirement for all copies of any work which was first published prior to the effective date of the [Berne Convention Implementation Act]. *At 1228:* Section 405(a)(2) requires reasonable efforts to add notice to 'all' copies. Where an author makes no legally cognizable effort to add notice to an identifiable group of copies which lack notice, and there are no significant obstacles hindering the author from adding notice to such copies, that author cannot be said to have taken reasonable efforts to cure as a matter of law. In the event that adding notice to retail inventories would have been burdensome, unduly costly, unavailing, futile or otherwise unreasonable, a prospective cure—that is adding notice only to new copies thereafter produced and distributed—by itself can be sufficient to constitute reasonable efforts to cure."

Princess Fabrics, Inc. v. CHF, Inc., 922 F.2d 99, 103 (2d Cir.1990). The "party seeking to cure the defect is required to make a reasonable effort to affix notice to copies in the possession of retail dealers as such copies are yet to be distributed to the public. What constitutes a reasonable effort is a question of fact." *See also* ***Shapiro & Son Bedspread Corp. v. Royal Mills Assocs.***, 764 F.2d 69, 73-74 (2d Cir.1985).

Lloyd v. Schlag, 884 F.2d 409, 415 (9th Cir.1989). "The burden of proof is on the copyright holder to show by a preponderance of the evidence that he made reasonable efforts."

Lifshitz v. Walter Drake & Sons, Inc., 806 F.2d 1426, 1434 (9th Cir.1986). "It seems reasonable to infer ... that when Congress used the phrase 'distributed to the public' and then required only 'reasonable efforts' to effect a cure despite its strong interest in encouraging the use of proper copyright notice, it was contemplating a situation where offending copies were scattered among the public and difficult if not impossible to correct. *At 1435:* Where a party has failed to comply with the provisions of §405(a) ... it cannot be permitted to assert liability merely because the infringement was willful."

Donald Frederick Evans & Assocs. v. Continental Homes, Inc., 785 F.2d 897, 910 (11th Cir.1986). "We agree that the question of what constitutes 'no more than a relatively small number of copies' cannot be answered merely by reference to an absolute number. ... The question must be answered on a case-by-case basis in light of the totality of the circumstances."

M. Kramer Mfg. v. Andrews, 783 F.2d 421, 444 (4th Cir.1986). "The holder of copyright has no duty ... to add a notice to copies that have already been distributed and therefore has no duty to send out replacement programs for games that have already been distributed to the public."

Hasbro Bradley, Inc. v. Sparkle Toys, Inc., 780 F.2d 189, 194-95 (2d Cir.1985). "The issue [is] whether [assignee] has cured [assignor's] omission of notice under §405(a)(2). There is no question that [assignee] is permitted to effect cure through its own efforts. The 'copyright claimant' entitled under the [Copyright] Act to register a copyright in the U.S. may be either the author of the work or his assignee, and any registration is of the work *per se* and redounds to the benefit of the assignor as well as the assignee. Not disputing this, [infringer] argues that [assignee] cannot effect cure under §405(a)(2) because [assignor's] omission of notice was deliberate. *At 196:* More important, the premise of the argument—namely, that a deliberate omission cannot be 'discovered'—is unsound. ... Similarly, a deliberate omission at a lower level of a corporate hierarchy might well be 'discovered,' in realistic terms, by someone at a higher level. Instances like these at least indicate that the 'discovered' language does not reveal a plain intent to exclude all deliberate omissions. [¶] At most, the 'discovered' language introduces an ambiguity. [T]he legislative history ... demonstrates that intentional as well as unintentional omissions were intended to be made curable. ... We ... conclude that the omission of notice from the toys, even if deliberate on [assignor's] part, was subject to cure under §405(a)(2)...."

Mitel, Inc. v. Iqtel, Inc., 896 F.Supp. 1050, 1054 (D. Colo.1995), *aff'd*, 124 F.3d 1366 (10th Cir.1997). "The unit publication doctrine provides that copyright notice affixed to one element of a publication containing various elements gives copyright protection to all elements of the publication. Here, the manual clearly contained a copyright notice. The abbreviated manuals and reference cards were simplified versions of the manual. These supplemental materials referenced the copyrighted materials. Thus, the supplemental material[s] were part of several elements consisting of one publication." *See also* ***Koontz v. Jaffarian***, 787 F.2d 906, 909 (4th Cir.1986).

NEC Corp. v. Intel Corp., 10 U.S.P.Q.2d 1177, 1180 (N.D.Cal.1989). "There appears to be no precise authoritative definition as to what constitutes 'a reasonable effort' under §405(a)(2). The matter must be considered on a case by case basis in which the efforts taken are viewed as a whole in order to determine whether they should be considered reasonable. In the present case, we shall take into account the following factors: When discovery of the failure to add the notice occurred; the time that elapsed between such discovery and the commencement of corrective action; the reasonable sufficiency of the corrective action; the extent of any follow-up to determine implementation by the licensees, and the quantity of copies distributed to the public between discovery and corrective action."

Videotronics, Inc. v. Bend Elec., 586 F.Supp. 478, 483 (D.Nev.1984). "Implicit in the concept of a 'reasonable effort' under §405(a)(2) is the exception that an expenditure of time and money over and above that required in the normal course of business will be made."

Schuchart & Assoc. v. Solo Serve Corp., 220 U.S.P.Q. 170, 181 (W.D.Tex.1983). "The Court finds that the words 'publicly distributed' as used in §405 have the same meaning as 'published' under the federal copyright statutes."

§405(b)

M. Kramer Mfg. v. Andrews, 783 F.2d 421, 446 (4th Cir.1986). "While it is true that under §405(b) an innocent infringer who relies on an omission of copyright notice is immune from damages accrued up to the time he received actual notice, the statute expressly requires the infringer to prove that he or she was misled by the omission of notice."

Canfield v. Ponchatoula Times, 759 F.2d 493, 498-99 (5th Cir.1985). "A publisher who reprints an unnoticed work which falls within one of the §405(a) exceptions has the burden, under §405(b), of proving good faith. But, the good faith requirement raised by §405(b) is triggered only in cases where a §405(a) exception applies."

Marobie-Fl, Inc. v. National Ass'n of Fire Equip. Distrib., 983 F.Supp. 1167, 1174 (N.D.Ill.1997). "[D] cannot qualify as an innocent infringer as a matter of law because the defense may be raised only when the infringer relied on an authorized copy that omitted the copyright notice. In this case, [D's employee] relied on unauthorized copies of [P's] clip art files."

Kleier Adver., Inc. v. Naegele Outdoor Adver., Inc., 676 F.Supp. 140, 143 (W.D.Ky.1987). "As we read 17 U.S.C. §405(b), there are five elements to an 'innocent infringer' defense. The party desiring this protection must show (1) innocent infringement (2) in reliance on (3) an authorized copy (4) which omitted the copyright notice, and (5) that the party was misled by the omission."

Videotronics, Inc. v. Bend Elec., 586 F.Supp. 478, 484 (D.Nev.1984). "[A] copyright notice that contains a technical deviation from the statutory requirements may still be found to serve the statutory purpose of informing the public of the existence of copyright."

§406. NOTICE OF COPYRIGHT: ERROR IN NAME OR DATE ON CERTAIN COPIES & PHONORECORDS

(a) Error in name.—With respect to copies and phonorecords publicly distributed by authority of the copyright owner before the effective date of the Berne Convention Implementation Act of 1988, where the person named in the copyright notice on copies or phonorecords publicly distributed by authority of the copyright owner is not the owner of copyright, the validity and ownership of the copyright are not affected. In such a case, however, any person who innocently begins an undertaking that infringes the copyright has a complete defense to any action for such infringement if such person proves that he or she was misled by the notice and began the undertaking in good faith under a purported transfer or license from the person named therein, unless before the undertaking was begun—

(1) registration for the work had been made in the name of the owner of copyright; or

(2) a document executed by the person named in the notice and showing the ownership of the copyright had been recorded.

The person named in the notice is liable to account to the copyright owner for all receipts from transfers or licenses purportedly made under the copyright by the person named in the notice.

(b) Error in date.—When the year date in the notice on copies or phonorecords distributed before the effective date of the Berne Convention Implementation Act of 1988 by authority of the copyright owner is earlier than the year in which publication first occurred, any period computed from the year of first publication under section 302 is to be computed from the year in the notice. Where the year date is more than one year later than the year in which publication first occurred, the work is considered to have been published without any notice and is governed by the provisions of section 405.

(c) Omission of name or date.—Where copies or phonorecords publicly distributed before the effective date of the Berne Convention Implementation Act of 1988 by authority of the copyright owner contain no name or no date that could reasonably be considered a part of the notice, the work is considered to have been published without any notice and is governed by the provisions of section 405 as in effect on the day before the effective date of the Berne Convention Implementation Act of 1988.

History of 17 U.S.C. §406: Oct. 19, 1976, P.L. 94-553, §101, 90 Stat. 2578; Oct. 31, 1988, P.L. 100-568, §7(f), 102 Stat. 2858.

See also Berne Convention.

§407. DEPOSIT OF COPIES OR PHONORECORDS FOR LIBRARY OF CONGRESS

(a) Except as provided by subsection (c), and subject to the provisions of subsection (e), the owner of copyright or of the exclusive right of publication in a work published in the United States shall deposit, within three months after the date of such publication—

(1) two complete copies of the best edition; or

(2) if the work is a sound recording, two complete phonorecords of the best edition, together with any printed or other visually perceptible material published with such phonorecords.

Neither the deposit requirements of this subsection nor the acquisition provisions of subsection (e) are conditions of copyright protection.

(b) The required copies or phonorecords shall be deposited in the Copyright Office for the use or disposition of the Library of Congress. The Register of Copyrights shall, when requested by the depositor and upon payment of the fee prescribed by section 708, issue a receipt for the deposit.

(c) The Register of Copyrights may by regulation exempt any categories of material from the deposit requirements of this section, or require deposit of only one copy or phonorecord with respect to any categories. Such regulations shall provide either for complete exemption from the deposit requirements of this section, or for alternative forms of deposit aimed at providing a satisfactory archival record of a work without imposing practical or financial hardships on the depositor, where the individual author is the owner of copyright in a pictorial, graphic, or sculptural work and (i) less than five copies of the work have been published, or (ii) the work has been published in a limited edition consisting of numbered copies, the monetary value of which would make the mandatory deposit of two copies of the best edition of the work burdensome, unfair, or unreasonable.

(d) At any time after publication of a work as provided by subsection (a), the Register of Copyrights may make written demand for the required deposit on any of the persons obligated to make the deposit under subsection (a). Unless deposit is made within three months after the demand is received, the person or persons on whom the demand was made are liable—

(1) to a fine of not more than $250 for each work; and

(2) to pay into a specially designated fund in the Library of Congress the total retail price of the copies or phonorecords demanded, or, if no retail price has been fixed, the reasonable cost to the Library of Congress of acquiring them; and

(3) to pay a fine of $2,500, in addition to any fine or liability imposed under clauses (1) and (2), if such person willfully or repeatedly fails or refuses to comply with such a demand.

(e) With respect to transmission programs that have been fixed and transmitted to the public in the United States but have not been published, the Register of Copyrights shall, after consulting with the Librarian of Congress and other interested organizations and officials, establish regulations governing the acquisition, through deposit or otherwise, of copies or phonorecords of such programs for the collections of the Library of Congress.

(1) The Librarian of Congress shall be permitted, under the standards and conditions set forth in such regulations, to make a fixation of a transmission program directly from a transmission to the public, and to reproduce one copy or phonorecord from such fixation for archival purposes.

(2) Such regulations shall also provide standards and procedures by which the Register of Copyrights may make written demand, upon the owner of the right of transmission in the United States, for the deposit of a copy or phonorecord of a specific transmission program. Such deposit may, at the option of the owner of the right of transmission in the United States, be accomplished by gift, by loan for purposes of reproduction, or by sale at a price not to exceed the cost of reproducing and supplying the copy or phonorecord. The regulations established under this clause shall provide reasonable periods of not less than three months for compliance with a demand, and shall allow for extensions of such periods and adjustments in the scope of the demand or the methods for fulfilling it, as reasonably warranted by the circumstances. Willful failure or refusal to comply with the conditions prescribed by such regulations shall subject the owner of the right of transmission in the United States to liability for an amount, not to exceed the cost of reproducing and supplying the copy or phonorecord in question, to be paid into a specially designated fund in the Library of Congress.

(3) Nothing in this subsection shall be construed to require the making or retention, for purposes of deposit, of any copy or phonorecord of an unpublished transmission program, the transmission of which occurs before the receipt of a specific written demand as provided by clause (2).

(4) No activity undertaken in compliance with regulations prescribed under clauses (1) or (2) of this subsection shall result in liability if intended solely to assist in the acquisition of copies or phonorecords under this subsection.

History of 17 U.S.C. §407: Oct. 19, 1976, P.L. 94-553, §101, 90 Stat. 2579; Oct. 31, 1988, P.L. 100-568, §8, 102 Stat. 2859; Nov. 13, 1997, P.L. 105-80, §12(a)(11), 111 Stat. 1535.

See also Berne Convention.

§408. COPYRIGHT REGISTRATION IN GENERAL

(a) Registration permissive.—At any time during the subsistence of the first term of copyright in any published or unpublished work in which the copyright was secured before January 1, 1978, and during the subsistence of any copyright secured on or after that date, the owner of copyright or of any exclusive right in the work may obtain registration of the copyright claim by delivering to the Copyright Office the deposit specified by this section, together with the application and fee specified by sections 409 and 708. Such registration is not a condition of copyright protection.

(b) Deposit for copyright registration.—Except as provided by subsection (c), the material deposited for registration shall include—

(1) in the case of an unpublished work, one complete copy or phonorecord;

(2) in the case of a published work, two complete copies or phonorecords of the best edition;

(3) in the case of a work first published outside the United States, one complete copy or phonorecord as so published;

(4) in the case of a contribution to a collective work, one complete copy or phonorecord of the best edition of the collective work.

Copies or phonorecords deposited for the Library of Congress under section 407 may be used to satisfy the deposit provisions of this section, if they are accompanied by the prescribed application and fee, and by any additional identifying material that the Register may, by regulation, require. The Register shall also prescribe regulations establishing requirements under which copies or phonorecords acquired for the Library of Congress under subsection (e) of section 407, otherwise than by deposit, may be used to satisfy the deposit provisions of this section.

(c) Administrative classification and optional deposit—

(1) The Register of Copyrights is authorized to specify by regulation the administrative classes into which works are to be placed for purposes of deposit and registration, and the nature of the copies or phonorecords to be deposited in the various classes specified. The regulations may require or permit, for particular classes, the deposit of identifying material instead of copies or phonorecords, the deposit of only one copy or phonorecord where two would normally be required, or a single registration for a group of related works. This administrative classification of works has no significance with respect to the subject matter of copyright or the exclusive rights provided by this title.

(2) Without prejudice to the general authority provided under clause (1), the Register of Copyrights shall establish regulations specifically permitting a single registration for a group of works by the same individual author, all first published as contributions to periodicals, including newspapers, within a twelve-month period, on the basis of a single deposit, application, and registration fee, under the following conditions:

(A) if the deposit consists of one copy of the entire issue of the periodical, or of the entire section in the case of a newspaper, in which each contribution was first published; and

(B) if the application identifies each work separately, including the periodical containing it and its date of first publication.

(C) Redesignated.

(3) As an alternative to separate renewal registrations under subsection (a) of section 304, a single renewal registration may be made for a group of works by the same individual author, all first published as contributions to periodicals, including newspapers, upon the filing of a single application and fee, under all of the following conditions:

(A) the renewal claimant or claimants, and the basis of claim or claims under section 304(a), is the same for each of the works; and

(B) the works were all copyrighted upon their first publication, either through separate copyright notice and registration or by virtue of a general copyright notice in the periodical issue as a whole; and

(C) the renewal application and fee are received not more than twenty-eight or less than twenty-seven years after the thirty-first day of December of the calendar year in which all of the works were first published; and

(D) the renewal application identifies each work separately, including the periodical containing it and its date of first publication.

(d) Corrections and amplifications.—The Register may also establish, by regulation, formal procedures for the filing of an application for supplementary registration, to correct an error in a copyright registration or to amplify the information given in a registration. Such application shall be accompanied by the fee provided by section 708, and shall clearly identify the registration to be corrected or amplified. The information contained in a supplementary registration augments but does not supersede that contained in the earlier registration.

(e) Published edition of previously registered work.—Registration for the first published edition of a work previously registered in unpublished form may be made even though the work as published is substantially the same as the unpublished version.

(f) Preregistration of works being prepared for commercial distribution—

(1) Rulemaking.—Not later than 180 days after April 27, 2005, the Register of Copyrights shall issue regulations to establish procedures for preregistration of a work that is being prepared for commercial distribution and has not been published.

(2) Class of works.—The regulations established under paragraph (1) shall permit preregistration for any work that is in a class of works that the Register determines has had a history of infringement prior to authorized commercial distribution.

(3) Application for registration.—Not later than 3 months after the first publication of a work preregistered under this subsection, the applicant shall submit to the Copyright Office—

(A) an application for registration of the work;

(B) a deposit; and

(C) the applicable fee.

(4) Effect of untimely application.—An action under this chapter for infringement of a work preregistered under this subsection, in a case in which the infringement commenced no later than 2 months after the first publication of the work, shall be dismissed if the items described in paragraph (3) are not submitted to the Copyright Office in proper form within the earlier of—

(A) 3 months after the first publication of the work; or

(B) 1 month after the copyright owner has learned of the infringement.

History of 17 U.S.C. §408: Oct. 19, 1976, P.L. 94-553, §101, 90 Stat. 2580; Oct. 31, 1988, P.L. 100-568, §9(a), 102 Stat. 2859; June 26, 1992, P.L. 102-307, §102(e), 106 Stat. 266; Apr. 27, 2005, P.L. 109-9, §104(a), 119 Stat. 221.

See also 37 C.F.R. pt. 202; Berne Convention; www.copyright.gov/registration.

ANNOTATIONS

Generally

Brownstein v. Lindsay, 742 F.3d 55, 58 (3d Cir. 2014). "The [issue] is whether courts have the authority to cancel copyright registrations. ... We ... hold that courts have no authority to cancel copyright registrations."

Kay Berry, Inc. v. Taylor Gifts, Inc., 421 F.3d 199, 205 (3d Cir.2005). "'Single Work' registration is separate and distinct from 'Group Registration.' The group registration provisions were enacted pursuant to ... §408(c)(1).... The single work registration provision, by contrast, was promulgated pursuant to the language of ... §408(a)...."

La Resolana Architects, PA v. Clay Realtors Angel Fire, 416 F.3d 1195, 1200 (10th Cir.2005), *overruled on other grounds*, ***Reed Elsevier, Inc. v. Muchnick***, 559 U.S. 154 (2010). "The most important step necessary before instituting an infringement action is registering one's copyright. Registration is satisfied by completing the following steps: (a) application and payment of fee, [17 U.S.C.] §408; (b) deposit of a copy of the copyrightable material, §408; (c) examination by the Register of Copyrights, [17 U.S.C.] §410; (d) registration (or refusal to register) by the Register, §410; (e) issuance of certificate of registration, §410."

Geoscan, Inc. v. Geotrace Tech., 226 F.3d 387, 393 (5th Cir.2000). "We have previously held that a plaintiff has complied with all statutory formalities for copyright registration when the Copyright office receives the plaintiff's application for registration, fee, and deposit. [¶] The Ninth Circuit has held that the registration deposit requirement permits 'bona fide copies of the original work only.' ... Thus, we hold that at the time of the filing of this suit in July 1998, although [P] had filed an application, paid a fee, and made a deposit with the Copyright Office, the deposit was not a complete copy of the original source code, thus [P] had not fulfilled all the statutory formalities necessary to register its copyright and have 'ownership' in its software for the purposes of a copyright infringement claim."

Olan Mills, Inc. v. Linn Photo Co., 23 F.3d 1345, 1349 (8th Cir.1994). "[A] copyright holder can register a copyright and file suit after infringement occurs. The timing of registration only determines whether the copyright holder can recover statutory as opposed to actual damages."

§408(a)

In re World Auxiliary Power Co., 303 F.3d 1120, 1125 (9th Cir.2002). "While an owner must register his copyright as a condition of seeking certain infringement remedies [e.g., action for infringement, statutory damages, and attorney fees], registration is permissive, not mandatory, and is not a condition for copyright protection. *At 1126:* Since an unregistered work doesn't have a title or registration number that would be 'revealed by a reasonable search,' recording a security interest in an unregistered copyright in the Copyright Office wouldn't give 'constructive notice' under the Copyright Act, and, because it wouldn't, it couldn't preserve a creditor's priority. There just isn't any way for a secured creditor to preserve a priority in an unregistered copyright by recording anything in the Copyright Office. And the secured party can't get around this problem by registering the copyright, because the secured party isn't the owner of the copyright, and the Copyright Act states that only 'the owner of copyright ... may obtain registration of the copyright claim....'"

Morris v. Business Concepts, Inc., 259 F.3d 65, 71-72 (2d Cir.2001), *overruled on other grounds*, ***Reed Elsevier, Inc. v. Muchnick***, 559 U.S. 154 (2010). "As the owner of the exclusive first right to publish [writer's] articles for a 90-day period, [publisher] falls within the scope of [17 U.S.C.] §408(a). It therefore had the right to register the copyrights in [writer's] articles. [¶] [Publisher's] registrations of [magazine] contained none of [the registration requirements of 17 U.S.C. §409] with respect to [writer's] articles: None of the registrations identified [writer] as the 'copyright claimant,' none of them specified [writer] as the author of the work, and none of them listed the titles of [writer's] articles. [¶] [Publisher's] registrations were not intended for [writer's] articles but, rather, for the issues of [magazine] as collective works. [Writer] cannot reasonably contend that the valid registrations of [magazine] were, in reality, error-laden registrations of her articles. [¶] [E]ven if we assume *arguendo* that [publisher's] registrations were intended for [writer's] articles, the errors contained in the registrations would be much more than ... minor 'technical misdescriptions' ...; these errors would render the registrations completely inaccurate. ... Accordingly, [publisher's] registrations cannot be viewed as valid copyright registrations under §408(a)."

Grundberg v. Upjohn Co., 137 F.R.D. 372, 385 (D.Utah 1991). "In order for the single collection provision to apply, all of the documents must be unpublished, authored by the same author, or a single author must have contributed copyrightable authorship to each document, and the claimant must be the same."

§408(b)

Unicolors, Inc. v. Urban Outfitters, Inc., 853 F.3d 980, 989 (9th Cir.2017). "An applicant does not need to list the names of the component works in a collection to register them as long as it holds the rights to the component works."

Nova Design Build, Inc. v. Grace Hotels, LLC, 652 F.3d 814, 817 (7th Cir.2011). "The copy submitted must be a *bona fide* copy—that is, virtually identical to the original and produced by directly referring to the original." (Internal quotes omitted.)

Coles v. Wonder, 283 F.3d 798, 802 (6th Cir.2002). "The [court's] rule permits an artist to protect an original song against potential infringement by registering the original work with the Copyright Office immediately after its creation by depositing either a recording of the song or a written version of it with the copyright application; by retaining a copy of a recording of the original song or written version of it that dates from the time of creation for deposit with a subsequent copyright application; or by making the copy for deposit by referring to a recording or written version of the original work."

Kodadek v. MTV Networks, Inc., 152 F.3d 1209, 1211 (9th Cir.1998). "In order to obtain a copyright registration, an applicant must deposit as a part of his application a 'copy' or 'copies' of the work. We have stated that the registration deposit requirement permits 'bona fide copies of the original work only....' We have not expressly defined the characteristics of 'bona fide copies,' but have distinguished them from 'reconstructions.' *At 1212:* While it may be possible for an artist to accurately reproduce his or her previous work from memory, for the purpose of certainty in obtaining copyright registration, such reproductions are simply insufficient. [A deposit of a bona fide copy] means that any 'copy' deposited as part of an application for a certificate of copyright registration must be virtually identical to the original and must have been produced by directly referring to the original. Once a bona fide copy is made in this manner, subsequent copies can be made by directly referring to that copy. For example, a photocopy or other electronic means of reproduction of an original drawing could suffice. Similarly, an accurate trace of an original drawing could suffice. In fact, a meticulous freehand redrawing of an original, made while the artist referred directly to the original, could suffice." *See also* ***Torres-Negrón v. J&N Records, LLC***, 504 F.3d 151, 157 (1st Cir.2007).

Data Gen. Corp. v. Grumman Sys. Support Corp., 36 F.3d 1147, 1161 (1st Cir.1994), *overruled on other grounds*, ***Reed Elsevier, Inc. v. Muchnick***, 559 U.S. 154 (2010). "[D] observes that the cases approving substantial compliance with registration requirements concern errors in the *application*, not the *deposit*, and suggests that we adopt a rule demanding strict compliance with the deposit requirement. Although a different rule for deposit errors might be warranted if the language and underlying purposes of the deposit requirement were of a significantly different character than that of the application requirement, we do not find that to be the case. [¶] In the first place, the registration application described in [17 U.S.C.] §409, as well as the deposit described in [17 U.S.C.] §408(b), are both equally mandatory components of the registration process outlined in §408(a). Likewise, just as §409 sets forth what an application '*shall* include,' ... §408(b) uses the same phrase to prescribe the contents of the deposit. There is nothing in this language that would prevent our interpreting both the application requirements and the deposit requirements in a consistent and practical manner. *At 1163:* We conclude that there is no support in law or reason for a rule that penalizes immaterial, inadvertent errors in a copyright deposit."

§408(c)

L.A. Printex Indus. v. Aeropostale, Inc., 676 F.3d 841, 853 (9th Cir.2012). "The Copyright Act permits the registration of multiple works as a single work. For purposes of registration as a single work, copyright regulations distinguish between published works and unpublished works. A published collection of works must be sold, distributed or offered for sale concurrently. For unpublished works, there is no such requirement. A group of unpublished works may be registered as a single work if it consists of all copyrightable elements that are otherwise recognizable as self-contained works, and are combined in a single unpublished collection." (Internal quotes omitted.)

Action Tapes, Inc. v. Mattson, 462 F.3d 1010, 1013 (8th Cir.2006). "[T]he Copyright Office has prescribed five categories for registration purposes—nondramatic literary works, works of the performing arts, works of the visual arts, sound recordings, and serials (periodicals). [¶] The Copyright Office classifies computer programs as nondramatic literary works because they can be expressed in words and numbers."

Kay Berry, Inc. v. Taylor Gifts, Inc., 421 F.3d 199, 204 (3d Cir.2005). Section 408(c)(1) "plainly does not grant to all copyright applicants a general right to register a group of works under a single registration. [T]he plain language of §408(c)(1) merely allows the Register of Copyrights to determine what types of works are eligible for group registration...."

Syntek Semiconductor Co. v. Microchip Tech., 307 F.3d 775, 779-80 (9th Cir.2002). "The Copyright Act allows the Register to 'require or permit ... the deposit of identifying material instead of copies' for particular types of works. The Register has enacted regulations which allow for the deposit of 'identifying portions,' rather than copies, for computer programs. The regulations define 'identifying portions' as '[t]he first and last 25 pages ... of the source code' or the entire source code if the program is 50 pages or less. The regulations do not explicitly provide for the deposit of object code. However, both Copyright Office Circular 61, Copyright Registration for Computer Programs, and Compendium II, the Compendium of Copyright Office Practices, allow for the deposit of object code instead of source code. Both of these publications provide that the deposit of object code leads to a rule of doubt registration, or a registration without the ordinary presumption of validity, because the deposit of object code does not allow the Register to determine the existence of copyrightable material."

National Conf. of Bar Exam'rs v. Multistate Legal Studies, Inc., 692 F.2d 478, 483 (7th Cir.1982). "We agree with the district court's view that the entire deposit may consist of excised copies and find that the 'complete copy' requirement of [17 U.S.C.] §408(b)(1) for unpublished works is inapplicable to secure tests [under 37 C.F.R. §207.20(c)] and is excepted under §408(c)(1) from normal deposit requirements."

Williams Elecs., Inc. v. Artic Int'l, 685 F.2d 870, 875 (3d Cir.1982). "The deposit of videotapes as a satisfactory method of complying with the statutory deposit requirement has been universally accepted in cases considering copyrights for the audiovisual works displayed in these video games." *See also* ***Atari, Inc. v. Amusement World, Inc.***, 547 F.Supp. 222, 227 (D.Md. 1981).

§409. APPLICATION FOR COPYRIGHT REGISTRATION

The application for copyright registration shall be made on a form prescribed by the Register of Copyrights and shall include—

(1) the name and address of the copyright claimant;

(2) in the case of a work other than an anonymous or pseudonymous work, the name and nationality or domicile of the author or authors, and, if one or more of the authors is dead, the dates of their deaths;

(3) if the work is anonymous or pseudonymous, the nationality or domicile of the author or authors;

(4) in the case of a work made for hire, a statement to this effect;

(5) if the copyright claimant is not the author, a brief statement of how the claimant obtained ownership of the copyright;

(6) the title of the work, together with any previous or alternative titles under which the work can be identified;

(7) the year in which creation of the work was completed;

(8) if the work has been published, the date and nation of its first publication;

(9) in the case of a compilation or derivative work, an identification of any preexisting work or works that it is based on or incorporates, and a brief, general statement of the additional material covered by the copyright claim being registered; and

(10) any other information regarded by the Register of Copyrights as bearing upon the preparation or identification of the work or the existence, ownership, or duration of the copyright.

If an application is submitted for the renewed and extended term provided for in section 304(a)(3)(A) and an original term registration has not been made, the Register may request information with respect to the existence, ownership, or duration of the copyright for the original term.

History of 17 U.S.C. §409: Oct. 19, 1976, P.L. 94-553, §101, 90 Stat. 2582; June 26, 1992, P.L. 102-307, §102(b)(1), 106 Stat. 266; Dec. 9, 2010, P.L. 111-295, §4(b)(2), 124 Stat. 3180.

See also 37 C.F.R. §202.3; www.copyright.gov/registration.

ANNOTATIONS

Metropolitan Reg'l Info. Sys. v. American Home Rlty. Network, Inc., 722 F.3d 591, 597-98 (4th Cir. 2013). "Lacking clear statutory guidance on the matter, courts have disagreed on how to apply the Copyright Act's registration requirement to collective works and their component parts. Some courts have barred infringement suits to protect copyrighted component works for failure to comply with §409's pre-suit registration requirement where the authors of those component works were not listed in the application to register the collective work. [¶] On the other hand, some courts have recognized collective work registrations as sufficient to permit an infringement action on behalf of component works, at least so long as the registrant owns the rights to the component works as well. [¶] We find this latter approach more consistent with the statutory and regulatory scheme." *See also* ***Alaska Stock, LLC v. Houghton Mifflin Harcourt Publ'g***, 747 F.3d 673, 683 (9th Cir.2014). *But see* ***Muench Photography, Inc. v. Houghton Mifflin Harcourt Publ'g***, 712 F.Supp.2d 84, 94-95 (S.D.N.Y.2010) (barring copyright-infringement suit when authors' names were unlisted in registration application).

Urantia Found. v. Maaherra, 114 F.3d 955, 963 (9th Cir.1997). Inadvertent "mistakes on registration certificates do not invalidate a copyright and thus do not bar infringement actions, unless ... the claimant intended to defraud the Copyright Office by making the misstatement."

§410. REGISTRATION OF CLAIM & ISSUANCE OF CERTIFICATE

(a) When, after examination, the Register of Copyrights determines that, in accordance with the provisions of this title, the material deposited constitutes copyrightable subject matter and that the other legal and formal requirements of this title have been met, the Register shall register the claim and issue to the applicant a certificate of registration under the seal of the Copyright Office. The certificate shall contain the information given in the application, together with the number and effective date of the registration.

(b) In any case in which the Register of Copyrights determines that, in accordance with the provisions of this title, the material deposited does not constitute copyrightable subject matter or that the claim is invalid for any other reason, the Register shall refuse registration and shall notify the applicant in writing of the reasons for such refusal.

(c) In any judicial proceedings the certificate of a registration made before or within five years after first publication of the work shall constitute prima facie evidence of the validity of the copyright and of the facts stated in the certificate. The evidentiary weight to be accorded the certificate of a registration made thereafter shall be within the discretion of the court.

(d) The effective date of a copyright registration is the day on which an application, deposit, and fee, which are later determined by the Register of Copyrights or by a court of competent jurisdiction to be acceptable for registration, have all been received in the Copyright Office.

History of 17 U.S.C. §410: Oct. 19, 1976, P.L. 94-553, §101, 90 Stat. 2582.

ANNOTATIONS

§410(a)

Jules Jordan Video, Inc. v. 144942 Canada Inc., 617 F.3d 1146, 1156 (9th Cir.2010). "[P] simply made a mistake in listing himself as the author on the copyright registration forms. That mistake does not constitute a basis to invalidate the copyright. Inadvertent mistakes on registration certificates do not invalidate a copyright and thus do not bar infringement actions, unless the alleged infringer has relied to its detriment on the mistake, or the claimant intended to defraud the Copyright Office by making the misstatement." (Internal quotes omitted.)

Masquerade Novelty, Inc. v. Unique Indus., 912 F.2d 663, 669 (3d Cir.1990). "Where ... the issue is whether particular articles with certain undisputed characteristics are copyrightable, the defendant need not introduce evidence but instead must show that the Copyright Office erroneously applied the copyright laws in registering plaintiff's articles."

§410(b)

Darden v. Peters, 488 F.3d 277, 283 (4th Cir.2007). "Because the Register's denial of a copyright registration application is, by the statute's plain terms, an action taken by the Register under the Copyright Act, the

[Administrative Procedure Act (APA)] governs judicial review. [T]he proper standard of review under the APA is the familiar 'abuse of discretion' standard whereby a reviewing court will 'set aside agency action, findings, and conclusions' that are 'arbitrary, capricious, an abuse of discretion, or otherwise not in accordance with law.'"

§410(c)

Varsity Brands, Inc. v. Star Athletica, LLC, 799 F.3d 468, 479 (6th Cir.2015), *aff'd*, ___ U.S. ___ (2017) (No. 15-866; 3-22-17). "We ... hold that the Copyright Office's determination that a design is protectable under the Copyright Act is entitled to ***Skidmore*** [***v. Swift & Co.***, 323 U.S. 134 (1944),] deference. Individual decisions about the copyrightability of works are not like 'rules carrying the force of law,' which command ***Chevron*** [***U.S.A. Inc. v. Natural Res. Def. Council, Inc.***, 467 U.S. 837 (1984),] deference. *At 480:* How much to defer to the determination to issue a copyright registration depends on the thoroughness evident in the agency's consideration, the validity of its reasoning, its consistency with earlier and later pronouncements, and all those factors which give it power to persuade, if lacking the power to control." (Internal quotes omitted.)

Three Boys Music Corp. v. Bolton, 212 F.3d 477, 488-89 (9th Cir.2000). "Registration is prima facie evidence of the validity of a copyright. This presumption can be rebutted by the defendant's showing that the plaintiff's work is not original. [The Ninth Circuit's] definition of originality is broad: All that is needed to satisfy both the Constitution and the statute is that the author contributed something more than a merely trivial variation, something recognizably his own. Originality in this context means little more than a prohibition of actual copying." (Internal quotes omitted.) *See also* ***Meshwerks, Inc. v. Toyota Motor Sales U.S.A., Inc.***, 528 F.3d 1258, 1262 (10th Cir.2008); ***Samara Bros. v. Wal-Mart Stores***, 165 F.3d 120, 132 (2d Cir.1998), *rev'd on other grounds*, 529 U.S. 205 (2000).

Langman Fabrics v. Graff Californiawear, Inc., 160 F.3d 106, 111 (2d Cir.1998), *amended*, 169 F.3d 782 (2d Cir.1988). "[P] is entitled to a statutory presumption of the validity of the facts stated in its copyright registration. [P's] registration stated that [P] was the author of the plume design by virtue of the work-for-hire rule. The statutory presumption is by no means irrebuttable, but it does order the burden of proof." *See also* ***SHL Imaging, Inc. v. Artisan House, Inc.***, 117 F.Supp.2d 301, 305 (S.D.N.Y.2000).

Entertainment Research Grp. v. Genesis Creative Grp., 122 F.3d 1211, 1217 (9th Cir.1997). "A certificate of copyright registration ... 'shifts to the defendant the burden to prove the invalidity of the plaintiff's copyrights.'" *See also* ***Latin Am. Music Co. v. Media Power Grp.***, 705 F.3d 34, 38 (1st Cir.2013).

Whimsicality, Inc. v. Rubie's Costume Co., 891 F.2d 452, 455 (2d Cir.1989), *abrogated on other grounds*, ***Fogerty v. Fantasy, Inc.***, 510 U.S. 517 (1994). "The presumption [of validity] generally is not overcome by an 'innocent misstatement.' It may be overcome, however, by proof of deliberate misrepresentation."

Seiler v. Lucasfilm, Ltd., 808 F.2d 1316, 1322 n.5 (9th Cir.1986). Section 410(c) "only makes the certificate prima facie evidence of the facts stated in the certificate. The trial court determined in a pre-trial hearing that [P] had lost or destroyed the originals in bad faith. That finding overcame any presumption of veracity of the attached work[, a reconstruction,] that might have come from the copyright certificate."

Sygma Photo News, Inc. v. High Soc'y Mag., Inc., 778 F.2d 89, 92 (2d Cir.1985). The "presumption of validity and of compliance with all formalities [under §410(c)] applies to an assignee ... who makes the first registration of a claim of statutory copyright in his name."

Lennon v. Seaman, 84 F.Supp.2d 522, 525 (S.D.N.Y. 2000). "A party seeking to establish a fraud on the Copyright Office, and thereby rebut the presumption of copyright validity, bears a heavy burden. The party asserting fraud must establish that the application for copyright registration is factually inaccurate, that the inaccuracies were willful or deliberate, and that the Copyright Office relied on those misrepresentations. Moreover, some courts have also required a party alleging fraud on the Copyright Office to prove that it has been prejudiced, or suffered some damage, as a result of the alleged fraud."

Apple Computer, Inc. v. Microsoft Corp., 759 F.Supp. 1444, 1453 (N.D.Cal.1991), *rev'd in part on other grounds*, 35 F.3d 1435 (9th Cir.1994). "The presumptive validity of a certificate of registration may be resolved on summary judgment. Furthermore, the presumption of copyright validity may not be overcome on the basis of fraud without proof that omissions in copyright application were intentional."

§410(d)

International Kitchen Exhaust Cleaning Ass'n v. Power Washers, 81 F.Supp.2d 70, 72 (D.D.C.2000). The Copyright "Act does not explicitly establish whether [the] 'effective date' [in §410(d)] is indeed effective upon filing or only once the filer has the copyright certification (or denial) in hand." *See also* ***Haan Crafts Corp. v. Craft Masters, Inc.***, 683 F.Supp. 1234, 1242 (N.D.Ind.1988).

§411. REGISTRATION & CIVIL INFRINGEMENT ACTIONS

(a) Except for an action brought for a violation of the rights of the author under section 106A(a), and subject to the provisions of subsection (b), no civil action for infringement of the copyright in any United States work shall be instituted until preregistration or registration of the copyright claim has been made in accordance with this title. In any case, however, where the deposit, application, and fee required for registration have been delivered to the Copyright Office in proper form and registration has been refused, the applicant is entitled to institute a civil action for infringement if notice thereof, with a copy of the complaint, is served on the Register of Copyrights. The Register may, at his or her option, become a party to the action with respect to the issue of registrability of the copyright claim by entering an appearance within sixty days after such service, but the Register's failure to become a party shall not deprive the court of jurisdiction to determine that issue.

(b)(1) A certificate of registration satisfies the requirements of this section and section 412, regardless of whether the certificate contains any inaccurate information, unless—

(A) the inaccurate information was included on the application for copyright registration with knowledge that it was inaccurate; and

(B) the inaccuracy of the information, if known, would have caused the Register of Copyrights to refuse registration.

(2) In any case in which inaccurate information described under paragraph (1) is alleged, the court shall request the Register of Copyrights to advise the court whether the inaccurate information, if known, would have caused the Register of Copyrights to refuse registration.

(3) Nothing in this subsection shall affect any rights, obligations, or requirements of a person related to information contained in a registration certificate, except for the institution of and remedies in infringement actions under this section and section 412.

(c) In the case of a work consisting of sounds, images, or both, the first fixation of which is made simultaneously with its transmission, the copyright owner may, either before or after such fixation takes place, institute an action for infringement under section 501, fully subject to the remedies provided by sections 502 through 505 and section 510, if, in accordance with requirements that the Register of Copyrights shall prescribe by regulation, the copyright owner—

(1) serves notice upon the infringer, not less than 48 hours before such fixation, identifying the work and the specific time and source of its first transmission, and declaring an intention to secure copyright in the work; and

(2) makes registration for the work, if required by subsection (a), within three months after its first transmission.

History of 17 U.S.C. §411: Oct. 19, 1976, P.L. 94-553, §101, 90 Stat. 2583; Oct. 31, 1988, P.L. 100-568, §9(b)(1), 102 Stat. 2859; Dec. 1, 1990, P.L. 101-650, §606(c)(1), 104 Stat. 5131; Nov. 13, 1997, P.L. 105-80, §6, 111 Stat. 1532; Oct. 28, 1998, P.L. 105-304, §102(d), 112 Stat. 2863; Apr. 27, 2005, P.L. 109-9, §104(b), 119 Stat. 222; Oct. 13, 2008, P.L. 110-403, §§101(a), 209(a)(6), 122 Stat. 4257, 4264.

See also 28 U.S.C. §1338; 37 C.F.R. §§201.22, 205.1-205.5, 205.11-205.13, 205.21-205.23; Berne Convention; WIPO Copyright Treaty; WIPO Performances & Phonograms Treaty.

ANNOTATIONS

§411(a)

Reed Elsevier, Inc. v. Muchnick, 559 U.S. 154, 157 (2010). "[T]he Court of Appeals for the Second Circuit held that a copyright holder's failure to comply with §411(a)'s registration requirement deprives a federal court of jurisdiction to adjudicate his copyright infringement claim. We disagree. Section 411(a)'s registration requirement is a precondition to filing a claim that does not restrict a federal court's subject-matter jurisdiction. *At 166:* Section 411(a) imposes a precondition to filing a claim that is not clearly labeled jurisdictional, is not located in a jurisdiction-granting provision, and admits of congressionally authorized exceptions. Section 411(a) thus imposes a type of precondition to suit that supports nonjurisdictional treatment under our precedents. *At 171:* We ... decline to address whether §411(a)'s registration requirement is a mandatory precondition to suit that ... district courts may or should enforce *sua sponte* by dismissing copyright infringement claims involving unregistered works." *See also* ***Roberts v. Gordy***, 877 F.3d 1024, 1028 (11th Cir.2017) (if failure to register does not eliminate subject-matter jurisdiction, improper registration would not either); ***Airframe Sys. v. L-3 Comms.***, 658 F.3d 100, 105 (1st Cir.2011) (post-***Reed Elsevier***, registration is an element of an infringement claim, rather than a jurisdictional bar); ***Cosmetic Ideas, Inc. v. IAC/InteractiveCorp***, 606 F.3d 612, 615 (9th Cir.2010) (same).

Oravec v. Sunny Isles Luxury Ventures, L.C., 527 F.3d 1218, 1231 (11th Cir.2008). "[C]ourts recognizing the effective registration doctrine have held that the registration of a derivative work satisfies the registration requirement for all aspects of the *registered* work, even the aspects copied from an unregistered preexisting work, so long as the owner of both copyrights is the same. But this theory only applies to aspects of the underlying work that are actually incorporated into the registered work. A plaintiff cannot use an effective registration theory to sue on aspects of unregistered preexisting works that are not included in the work he did register." *See also* **Christopher Phelps & Assocs. v. *Galloway***, 492 F.3d 532, 539 (4th Cir.2007); ***Streetwise Maps, Inc. v. VanDam, Inc.***, 159 F.3d 739, 747 (2d Cir. 1998).

Torres-Negrón v. J&N Records, LLC, 504 F.3d 151, 162 (1st Cir.2007). "[W]e conclude that omission of a proper deposit copy with a copyright application renders the registration invalid and eliminates the federal courts' subject matter jurisdiction over an infringement claim. As we have previously recognized, most errors or mistakes in a copyright registration application will be inadvertent or immaterial, and thus will not invalidate the application (or any resulting certificate). In the rare instances where a plaintiff's registration was procured through fraud or in the absence of a bona fide copy, such as occurred here, the registration becomes invalid and the federal courts lack jurisdiction over the case. *At 164:* Where the parties dispute whether the deposit copy was bona fide, or was an impermissible reconstruction, the district court should first determine whether that question implicates the merits of the case. If it does not, the court should weigh the evidence that is submitted and make a factual finding on the copy/reconstruction issue. If the jurisdictional facts and merits are intertwined, the court should treat a [FRCP] 12(b)(1) motion as a summary judgment motion and resolve it accordingly. Although [Ds] could have filed a 12(b)(1) motion and the district court could have resolved the disputed facts and dismissed the claims earlier, its ruling after trial was correct in light of the evidence presented."

Editor's note: Although the case above states §411(a) is "jurisdictional" in contradiction of ***Reed Elsevier, Inc. v. Muchnick***, p. 343, its analysis applies equally to registration as a "precondition" to suit.

Darden v. Peters, 488 F.3d 277, 286 (4th Cir.2007). "[I]t is not a foregone conclusion that courts owe no deference whatsoever to the Register's decision in the context of an infringement action under §411(a). Indeed, courts are split on this issue." *Compare* ***OddzOn Prods. v. Oman***, 924 F.2d 346, 348 (D.C.Cir.1991) (applying abuse-of-discretion standard to infringement claim), ***John Muller & Co. v. New York Arrows Soccer Team***, 802 F.2d 989, 990 (8th Cir.1986) (same), *and* ***Norris Indus. v. International Tel. & Tel. Corp.***, 696 F.2d 918, 922 (11th Cir.1983) (same), *with* ***Carol Barnhart, Inc. v. Economy Cover Corp.***, 773 F.2d 411, 414 (2d Cir.1985) (according no deference to Register's copyrightability conclusion).

La Resolana Architects, PA v. Clay Realtors Angel Fire, 416 F.3d 1195, 1197 (10th Cir.2005), *overruled on other grounds*, ***Reed Elsevier, Inc. v. Muchnick***, 559 U.S. 154 (2010). "Two conflicting interpretations of the [Copyright] Act's registration requirement have been upheld by circuit courts: (1) registration occurs when the copyright owner submits an application for registration to the copyright office, or, conversely (2) registration occurs when the copyright office actually approves or rejects the application. We hold that the second interpretation is correct. *At 1202-03:* [R]egistration is separate from the issuance of a registration certificate and ... a court's jurisdiction [over an infringement suit] does not turn on the existence of a paper certificate, but rather on the fact of registration, however it is demonstrated. *At 1207-08:* Our conclusion that suits for infringement can be brought only when the copyright is registered leaves open one question: how does a litigant demonstrate to a court that a copyright is registered? While 17 U.S.C. §410(c) states that 'the certificate of registration ... shall constitute prima facie evidence of the validity of the copyright,' it does not prohibit the use of other evidence to demonstrate validity. ... Adequate proof may come in the form of a certificate of registration from the copyright office. ... Even if the copyright owner cannot present a certificate, the owner can still attempt to prove registration through other means, such as testimony or other evidence from the copyright office. Such other evidence, however, does not entitle a copyright owner to the presumption of validity that §410 confers on a certificate. Upon proof of registration the copyright is valid and subject to the remedies set forth in Title 17. Once a copyright owner proves registration, absent other defects, the court has jurisdiction and the infringement suit can go forward." *See also* ***Fourth Estate Pub. Benefit Corp. v. Wall-Street.com, LLC***, 856 F.3d 1338, 1340-41 (11th Cir.2017); ***Asche & Spencer Music, Inc. v. Principato-Young Entm't, Inc.***, 147 F.Supp.3d 833, 835-36 (D.Minn.2015); ***Christians of Cal., Inc. v. Clive Christian N.Y., LLP***, No. 13 Civ. 0275 (KBF) (JCF) (S.D.N.Y.2014) (memo op.; 5-30-14) (consensus among district courts in 2d Cir. favors registration approach); ***Denenberg v. Berman***, 64 U.S.P.Q.2d 1054, 1056 (D.Neb.2002). *But see* ***Positive Black Talk Inc. v. Cash Money Records Inc.***, this page.

Editor's note: Although the case above states §411(a) is "jurisdictional" in contradiction of ***Reed Elsevier, Inc. v. Muchnick***, p. 343, its analysis applies equally to registration as a "precondition" to suit.

Positive Black Talk Inc. v. Cash Money Records Inc., 394 F.3d 357, 365 (5th Cir.2004), *overruled on other grounds*, ***Reed Elsevier, Inc. v. Muchnick***, 559 U.S. 154 (2010). "Although some circuits require that a plaintiff actually obtain a certificate from the Copyright Office before bringing suit, the Fifth Circuit requires only that the Copyright Office actually receive the application, deposit, and fee before a plaintiff files an infringement action. Here, [Ds] argue that [P] failed to comply with the statutory formality set forth in §411 (and that the district court therefore lacked jurisdiction over [P's] copyright infringement claim) because [P] filed suit four days before the Copyright Office received its application, deposit, and fee (all of which [P] had mailed on the same day it filed suit). [¶] We hold ... that the ultimate judgment is not rendered a nullity in this instance by the district court's refusal to dismiss [P's] suit for want of jurisdiction. Rather, we find that the jurisdictional defect was cured when the Copyright Office received [P's] application, deposit, and fee four days after [P] filed suit." *See also* ***Cosmetic Ideas, Inc. v. IAC/InteractiveCorp***, 606 F.3d 612, 621 (9th Cir. 2010); ***Chicago Bd. of Educ. v. Substance, Inc.***, 354 F.3d 624, 631 (7th Cir.2003); ***Secure Servs. Tech. v. Time & Space Processing, Inc.***, 722 F.Supp. 1354, 1363-64 (E.D.Va.1989). *But see* ***La Resolana Architects, PA v. Clay Realtors Angel Fire***, p. 344.

Editor's note: Although the case above states §411(a) is "jurisdictional" in contradiction of ***Reed Elsevier, Inc. v. Muchnick***, p. 343, its analysis applies equally to registration as a "precondition" to suit.

Gaiman v. McFarlane, 360 F.3d 644, 655 (7th Cir. 2004). It "is no more the purpose of registration to start statutes of limitations running than it is the purpose of the copyright notice itself to do so. [¶] [T]he court was wrong to say that registration gives constructive notice. What the [Copyright] Act actually says is that recording a document in the Copyright Office gives constructive notice of the facts in the document if the document identifies a registered work. The purpose is to establish priority in the event of disputes, in bankruptcy court or elsewhere, over creditors' rights. A creditor who wants to know whether he can seize a debtor's copyright consults the register; a co-author does not."

Morris v. Business Concepts, Inc., 283 F.3d 502, 505 (2d Cir.2002). "The distinction between those constituent parts of a collective work in which the author of the collective work owns all rights and those constituent parts in which the author does not own all rights is critical in determining whether a copyright registration in a collective work also registers a copyright claim in a particular constituent work. [I]f all rights in a constituent work have not been transferred to the claimant, a collective work registration will not apply to the constituent work. If, on the other hand, all rights have been transferred to the claimant, then the constituent work is included in the registration of the collective work. *At 506:* [W]e hold that unless the copyright owner of a collective work also owns all the rights in a constituent part, a collective work registration will not extend to a constituent part. [¶] We ... conclude that regardless whether [publisher] was a copyright owner of [P's] articles, its registration of the collective works in which they appeared do not satisfy §411(a)'s requirements with respect to [P]." *See also* ***Xoom, Inc. v. Imageline, Inc.***, 323 F.3d 279, 283 (4th Cir.2003), *overruled on other grounds*, ***Reed Elsevier, Inc. v. Muchnick***, 559 U.S. 154 (2010); ***Murray Hill Publ'ns, Inc. v. ABC Comm.***, 264 F.3d 622, 632 (6th Cir.2001), *overruled on other grounds*, ***Reed Elsevier, Inc. v. Muchnick***, 559 U.S. 154 (2010).

Moberg v. 33T LLC, 666 F.Supp.2d 415, 419-20 (D. Del.2009). "What appears to be a simple premise actually joins an issue of first impression not addressed by any court. [Ds] contend that [P's] photographs, which were created undisputably outside the U.S., are U.S. works because when they were posted on a German website, they were 'published' simultaneously in Germany and in the U.S. [Ds] argue that it is 'well settled that Internet publications are published everywhere simultaneously, regardless of the location of the server hosting the website.' Therefore, because the posting of a photograph on a website simultaneously 'publishes' the photograph 'everywhere,' including the U.S., it is a 'U.S. work,' and as such, it must be registered prior to filing suit for infringement. [¶] [P] does not dispute that he has never registered his photographs in the U.S. He contends, however, that [Ds'] premise is flawed because the posting of a photograph on a foreign country's website does not publish it simultaneously in the U.S. so as to transform the work into a 'U.S. work.' Because it is not a 'U.S. work' as contemplated by our law, [P] argues that he is not required to follow the registration requirement of §411(a) in order for this Court to have subject matter jurisdiction over his Copyright Act claims. The Court agrees with [P], because ... the acceptance of [Ds'] position would overextend and pervert the U.S. copyright laws, and would be contrary to the Berne Convention."

Joyce v. Renaissance Design Inc., 56 U.S.P.Q.2d 1541, 1543 n.2 (C.D.Cal.2000). "The two exceptions to the strict enforcement of 17 U.S.C. §411(a) involve actions for infringement of copyright in Berne Convention works whose country of origin is not the U.S. and actions brought for violation of the rights of an author under [17 U.S.C.] §106A(a) regarding visual arts. The Berne Convention allows foreigners, who have not registered, to sue for copyright infringements occurring after March 1, 1999. The visual arts exception allows sculptors and painters to bring an action based upon signed original works existing in either a single copy or consecutively numbered signed works of 200 copies or less."

Midway Mfg. v. Dirkschneider, 543 F.Supp. 466, 481 (D.Neb.1981). "[P's] failure to obtain copyright registrations on the computer programs underlying its audiovisual works does not preclude [P] from bringing a suit to prevent infringement of its [registered] audiovisual works."

§411(b)

Roberts v. Gordy, 877 F.3d 1024, 1029 (11th Cir. 2017). Section 411(b) "codifies the defense of Fraud on the Copyright Office. [Ds] assert that the 2008 amendment to the Copyright Act precludes reading 'fraud' into the statute.... They are wrong. [¶] Materiality hinges on whether the Copyright Office would have refused the application if the inaccuracy were known. In order to aid in the determination of materiality, the district court must make an inquiry to the Copyright Office. *At 1030:* [I]n order to invalidate a registration, (1) the application must contain inaccuracies, (2) the inaccuracies must be material, and (3) the applicant must have the required scienter of intentional or purposeful concealment. While the district court correctly found material inaccuracies in the registrations, it erred by not applying the appropriate scienter for Fraud on the Copyright Office. [¶] While error is not generally a strong legal argument, it is a sufficient counter to a claim of Fraud on the Copyright Office. *At 1031:* [Ps] are the undisputed authors of [song], and they should be afforded the opportunity to protect their copyright from what they view as an unlawful use. Their song was registered and re-registered and re-registered, but the good faith inaccuracies in those registrations should not preclude the undisputed authors from copyright protection." (Internal quotes omitted.)

DeliverMed Holdings, LLC v. Schaltenbrand, 734 F.3d 616, 625 (7th Cir.2013). "Although the statute appears to mandate that the Register get involved '[i]n any case in which inaccurate information [in an application for copyright registration] is alleged,' ... input need not be sought immediately after a party makes such a claim. Instead, courts can demand that the party seeking invalidation first establish that the other preconditions to invalidity are satisfied before obtaining the Register's advice on materiality. In other words, a litigant should demonstrate that (1) the registration application included inaccurate information; and (2) the registrant knowingly included the inaccuracy in his submission to the Copyright Office. Once these requirements are met, a court may question the Register as to whether the inaccuracy would have resulted in the application's refusal. Aside from minimizing the risk that parties would use this provision as a delay tactic, this approach has the added benefit of an endorsement from the Register. When faced with this situation in the future, courts should tread carefully and employ this mechanism only when necessary."

Urantia Found. v. Maaherra, 114 F.3d 955, 963 (9th Cir.1997). "[I]nadvertent mistakes on registration certificates do not invalidate a copyright and thus do not bar infringement actions, unless the alleged infringer has relied to its detriment on the mistake, or the claimant intended to defraud the Copyright Office by making the misstatement."

§411(c)

Georgia TV Co. v. TV News Clips, Inc., 718 F.Supp. 939, 946 (N.D.Ga.1989). "Pursuant to 17 U.S.C. §102 and [17 U.S.C.] §411(b) [now §411(c)], copyright protection subsists in these programs once they become 'fixed' in a tangible medium. In other words, copyright protection attaches to the broadcast feature only when the first copy of the transmission is made. [¶] [P] has informed the public of its copyright claims in its programs through broadcast of its notices of copyright at the conclusion of each program and has informed [Ds] in particular through service of advance notices of potential infringement. Moreover, [P] has filed with the Copyright Office formal applications for registration of its copyrights in the 27 programs at issue in this case, and one program has received registration on an expedited basis. [P] has a statutory right to institute an infringement action for both the program that received registration on an expedited basis and as-yet unregistered programs pursuant to … §411(b). *At 952:* Reports of news stories, particularly stories breaking near broadcast time, cannot be registered in the copyright office prior to their transmission on a news program. [P's] broadcasts, therefore, fall within the requirements of §411(b) of a 'work consisting of sound, images, or both, the first fixation of which is made simultaneously with its transmission.'"

KCNC-TV, Inc. v. Broadcast Info. Servs., 717 F.Supp. 1449, 1453 (D.Colo.1988). "Statutory damages and attorney's fees are available in any action instituted under §411(b) [now §411(c)]."

§412. REGISTRATION AS PREREQUISITE TO CERTAIN REMEDIES FOR INFRINGEMENT

In any action under this title, other than an action brought for a violation of the rights of the author under section 106A(a), an action for infringement of the copyright of a work that has been preregistered under section 408(f) before the commencement of the infringement and that has an effective date of registration not later than the earlier of 3 months after the first publication of the work or 1 month after the copyright owner has learned of the infringement, or an action instituted under section 411(c), no award of statutory damages or of attorney's fees, as provided by sections 504 and 505, shall be made for—

(1) any infringement of copyright in an unpublished work commenced before the effective date of its registration; or

(2) any infringement of copyright commenced after first publication of the work and before the effective date of its registration, unless such registration is made within three months after the first publication of the work.

History of 17 U.S.C. §412: Oct. 19, 1976, P.L. 94-553, §101, 90 Stat. 2583; Dec. 1, 1990, P.L. 101-650, §606(c)(2), 104 Stat. 5131; Apr. 27, 2005, P.L. 109-9, §104(c), 119 Stat. 222; Oct. 13, 2008, P.L. 110-403, §101(b)(1), 122 Stat. 4258.

ANNOTATIONS

Latin Am. Music Co. v. ASCAP, 642 F.3d 87, 90 (1st Cir.2011). "[T]here is nothing in [§412] that prohibits fee awards in cases … of *non* infringement. The reason is obvious: only copyright owners may register their copyright claims, the conduct incentivized by §412. A defendant accused of infringing someone else's copyright could not possibly comply with the statute's registration criterion. Section 412 thus does not, logically, apply to alleged infringers."

Derek Andrew, Inc. v. Poof Apparel Corp., 528 F.3d 696, 700-01 (9th Cir.2008). "Until now, we have not expressly addressed the issue presented; namely, whether §412 bars an award of statutory damages for post-registration infringements when the initial act of infringement occurred prior to the effective copyright registration date. Resolution of this issue necessarily depends upon our interpretation of the term 'commenced' as it is used in §412. In that regard, we examine the text of §412 and consider the purposes behind its enactment. [¶] Every court to consider the issue has held that infringement 'commences' for the purposes of §412 when the first act in a series of acts constituting continuing infringement occurs. [¶] [W]e join those circuits that addressed the issue before us and hold that *the first act of infringement* in a series of ongoing infringements of the same kind marks the commencement of one continuing infringement under §412. [¶] [D] began its infringing activity before the effective registration date, and it repeated the same act after that date each time it used the same copyrighted material. [¶] [D] simply engaged in an ongoing series of infringements that commenced with the first distribution in May 2005. Therefore, [P] is not entitled to statutory damages under the Copyright Act, and the court's award of $15,000 is REVERSED." (Internal quotes omitted.) *See also* ***Bouchat v. Bon-Ton Dept.***

Stores, 506 F.3d 315, 330 (4th Cir.2007); ***Troll Co. v. Uneeda Doll Co.***, 483 F.3d 150, 158 (2d Cir.2007); ***Johnson v. Jones***, 149 F.3d 494, 506 (6th Cir.1998); ***Mason v. Montgomery Data, Inc.***, 967 F.2d 135, 142-44 (5th Cir.1992).

Zito v. Steeplechase Films, Inc., 267 F.Supp.2d 1022, 1026 (N.D.Cal.2003). The "case law applying ... §412, while not directly addressing the issue, supports the inference that an act that commences infringement does not publish an otherwise unpublished work. In ***Harper & Row, Publishers, Inc. v. Nation Ent.***, for instance, holders of a copyright on unpublished and unregistered memoirs brought a copyright infringement action against the publishers of a weekly magazine in connection with an article quoting and paraphrasing from portions of the memoirs. Despite the fact that the magazine article made available portions of an unpublished work to the public, [Ps] were not entitled to statutory damages or attorney's fees pursuant to the plain meaning of §412."

Hernandez v. Sony, 66 U.S.P.Q.2d 1143, 1148 (D.P.R.2003). There "is no presumption in favor of awarding fees to a prevailing plaintiff under the statute."

Cook v. Jane Lyons Adver., Inc., 47 U.S.P.Q.2d 1147, 1150-51 n.5 (D.D.C.1998). "17 U.S.C. §412 acts a partial bar *only* to the recovery of statutory damages and attorneys' fees. 17 U.S.C. §505 characterizes attorneys' fees as part of costs. ... Because §412 only bars the award of the attorneys' fees portion of costs, [P's] request for those costs other than attorneys' fees is *not* stricken from the complaint."

Parfums Givenchy, Inc. v. C&C Beauty Sales, Inc., 832 F.Supp. 1378, 1394 (C.D.Cal.1993). Section 412 is "applicable to works of foreign and domestic origin alike."

Brode v. Tax Mgmt., 14 U.S.P.Q.2d 1195, 1200-01 (N.D.Ill.1990). "The statute does not address copyright assignments or indicate that an assignment in any way alters the effect of this provision. [A]n assignee is not required to 're-register' a copyright in order to preserve his right to statutory damages or as a prerequisite to instituting an action. The initial registration of the copyright is sufficient."

Singh v. Famous Overseas, Inc., 680 F.Supp. 533, 536 (E.D.N.Y.1988). The §412(2) "'exception is needed to take care of newsworthy or suddenly popular works which may be infringed almost as soon as they are published, before the copyright owner has had a reasonable opportunity to register his claim.'"

CHAPTER 5. COPYRIGHT INFRINGEMENT & REMEDIES

§501. INFRINGEMENT OF COPYRIGHT

(a) Anyone who violates any of the exclusive rights of the copyright owner as provided by sections 106 through 122 or of the author as provided in section 106A(a), or who imports copies or phonorecords into the United States in violation of section 602, is an infringer of the copyright or right of the author, as the case may be. For purposes of this chapter (other than section 506), any reference to copyright shall be deemed to include the rights conferred by section 106A(a). As used in this subsection, the term "anyone" includes any State, any instrumentality of a State, and any officer or employee of a State or instrumentality of a State acting in his or her official capacity. Any State, and any such instrumentality, officer, or employee, shall be subject to the provisions of this title in the same manner and to the same extent as any nongovernmental entity.

(b) The legal or beneficial owner of an exclusive right under a copyright is entitled, subject to the requirements of section 411, to institute an action for any infringement of that particular right committed while he or she is the owner of it. The court may require such owner to serve written notice of the action with a copy of the complaint upon any person shown, by the records of the Copyright Office or otherwise, to have or claim an interest in the copyright, and shall require that such notice be served upon any person whose interest is likely to be affected by a decision in the case. The court may require the joinder, and shall permit the intervention, of any person having or claiming an interest in the copyright.

(c) For any secondary transmission by a cable system that embodies a performance or a display of a work which is actionable as an act of infringement under subsection (c) of section 111, a television broadcast station holding a copyright or other license to transmit or perform the same version of that work shall, for purposes of subsection (b) of this section, be treated as a legal or beneficial owner if such secondary transmission occurs within the local service area of that television station.

(d) For any secondary transmission by a cable system that is actionable as an act of infringement pursuant to section 111(c)(3), the following shall also have standing to sue: (i) the primary transmitter whose transmission has been altered by the cable system; and (ii) any broadcast station within whose local service area the secondary transmission occurs.

(e) With respect to any secondary transmission that is made by a satellite carrier of a performance or display of a work embodied in a primary transmission and is actionable as an act of infringement under section 119(a)(5), a network station holding a copyright or other license to transmit or perform the same version of that work shall, for purposes of subsection (b) of this section, be treated as a legal or beneficial owner if such secondary transmission occurs within the local service area of that station.

(f)(1) With respect to any secondary transmission that is made by a satellite carrier of a performance or display of a work embodied in a primary transmission and is actionable as an act of infringement under section 122, a television broadcast station holding a copyright or other license to transmit or perform the same version of that work shall, for purposes of subsection (b) of this section, be treated as a legal or beneficial owner if such secondary transmission occurs within the local market of that station.

(2) A television broadcast station may file a civil action against any satellite carrier that has refused to carry television broadcast signals, as required under section 122(a)(2), to enforce that television broadcast station's rights under section 338(a) of the Communications Act of 1934.

History of 17 U.S.C. §501: Oct. 19, 1976, P.L. 94-553, §101, 90 Stat. 2584; Oct. 31, 1988, P.L. 100-568, §10(a), 102 Stat. 2860; Nov. 16, 1988, P.L. 100-667, §202(3), 102 Stat. 3957; Nov. 15, 1990, P.L. 101-553, §2(a)(1), 104 Stat. 2749; Dec. 1, 1990, P.L. 101-650, §606(a), 104 Stat. 5131; Aug. 5, 1999, P.L. 106-44, §1(g)(5), 113 Stat. 222; Nov. 29, 1999, P.L. 106-113, §1000(a)(9), 113 Stat. 1536; Nov. 2, 2002, P.L. 107-273, §13210(4)(B), 116 Stat. 1909.

See also 2 U.S.C. §170; 19 U.S.C. §1337; 28 U.S.C. §§1295, 1338, 1400, 1498; 44 U.S.C. §2117; 48 U.S.C. §§1405q, 1421n; Berne Convention.

CHARTS

See "Direct Copyright Infringement Under 17 U.S.C. §501(a)," p. 455.

ANNOTATIONS

Generally

Sony Corp. v. Universal City Studios, Inc., 464 U.S. 417, 433-34 (1984). "The Copyright Act provides the owner of a copyright with a potent arsenal of remedies against an infringer of his work, including an injunction to restrain the infringer from violating his rights, the impoundment and destruction of all reproductions of his work made in violation of his rights, a recovery of his actual damages and any additional profits realized by the infringer or a recovery of statutory damages, and attorney's fees."

VMG Salsoul, LLC v. Ciccone, 824 F.3d 871, 878 (9th Cir.2016). "When considering an infringement claim of a copyrighted musical composition, what matters is not how the musicians actually played the notes but, rather, a 'generic rendition of the composition.' That is, we must compare the written compositions of the two pieces. *At 879:* When considering a claimed infringement of a copyrighted sound recording, what matters is how the musicians *played* the notes, that is, how their rendition distinguishes the recording from a generic rendition of the same composition."

Luvdarts, LLC v. AT&T Mobility, LLC, 710 F.3d 1068, 1070 (9th Cir.2013). "We must decide whether the owners of mobile multimedia messaging networks can be held liable for copyright infringement that allegedly occurs on their networks." Held: P did not allege facts to state a cause of action under either contributory infringement or vicarious infringement.

Blueport Co. v. U.S., 533 F.3d 1374, 1379 (Fed.Cir. 2008). 28 U.S.C. §1498(b) "grants copyright owners a right of action for copyright infringement against the U.S., subject to three provisos. First, §1498(b) does not provide a Government employee a right of action 'where he was in a position to *order, influence, or induce* use of the copyrighted work by the Government.' Second, §1498(b) confers no right of action 'with respect to any copyrighted work prepared by a person while in the employment or service of the U.S., where the copyrighted work was prepared as a part of the *official functions* of the employee.' Third, §1498(b) confers no right of action 'with respect to any copyrighted work ... in the preparation of which *Government time, material, or facilities* were used.' *At 1380:* [W]e interpret the provisos of §1498(b) as carving out three classes of copyright infringement claims from the Government's general waiver of sovereign immunity for copyright infringement."

Corwin v. Walt Disney Co., 475 F.3d 1239, 1250-51 (11th Cir.2007). "[I]f an expert relies on uncopyrightable ideas rather than on expression of those ideas in analyzing alleged copyright infringement the report is excludable. [¶] [I]f an expert relies solely upon *scenes a faire* or other stock elements not protected by copyright, the report is excludable. Further, lists of similarities are 'inherently subjective and unreliable, particularly where the lists contain random similarities, and many such similarities could be found in very dissimilar works.'"

1mage Software, Inc. v. Reynolds & Reynolds Co., 459 F.3d 1044, 1050 (10th Cir.2006). "The Second Circuit's solution to [the] jurisdictional problem [of hybrid claims raising both federal (copyright) and state (contract) issues] was to establish a test that focused on whether and how a complaint implicates the Copyright Act. Thus, the analysis turns on what is alleged on the face of the complaint. Applying that test, a suit arises under the Copyright Act if: (1) The complaint is for a remedy expressly granted by the Act, e.g., a suit for infringement; or, (2) The complaint asserts a claim requiring construction of the Act. *At 1051:* We join a number of other circuits in adopting the Second Circuit's approach to this difficult jurisdictional issue." (Internal quotes omitted.) *See also* ***Automation by Design, Inc. v. Raybestos Prods.***, 463 F.3d 749, 753 (7th Cir.2006); ***Scandinavian Satellite Sys. v. Prime TV Ltd.***, 291 F.3d 839, 844 (D.C.Cir.2002); ***Bassett v. Mashantucket Pequot Tribe***, 204 F.3d 343, 349-51 (2d Cir.2000); ***MCA Television Ltd. v. Public Interest Corp.***, 171 F.3d 1265, 1269-70 (11th Cir.1999); ***Rano v. Sipa Press, Inc.***, 987 F.2d 580, 584 (9th Cir.1993); ***Royal v. Leading Edge Prods.***, 833 F.2d 1, 2 (1st Cir.1987); ***Goodman v. Lee***, 815 F.2d 1030, 1031 (5th Cir.1987).

General Univ'l Sys. v. Lee, 379 F.3d 131, 142-43 (5th Cir.2004). Computer "programs are entitled to copyright protection. This protection extends not only to the 'literal' elements of computer software—the source code and object code—but also to a program's nonliteral elements, including its structure, sequence, organization, user interface, screen displays, and menu structures. To assess a claim of software infringement, we have generally endorsed the 'abstraction-filtration-comparison' test.... The ... *test* deploys a three-step procedure to assess whether protectable expression has been improperly copied. First, at the abstraction stage, the court 'dissect[s] the allegedly copied program's structure and isolate[s] each level of abstraction contained within it.' Second, the court filters out unprotectable expression by examining the structural components at each level of abstraction to determine whether they can be protected by copyright. Copyright protection does not extend to ideas, processes, facts, elements dictated by considerations of efficiency, elements required by factors external to the program itself, or items taken from the public domain. With these nonprotectable elements filtered out, there remains a 'core of protectable expression,' and we must then 'determine whether the defendant's program misappropriated substantial portions of the plaintiff's program.' [¶] Although we have generally endorsed the ... test to evaluate claims that nonliteral software elements were copied, we have not explicitly addressed whether that test should be used to evaluate charges that a program's source or object code was copied." *See also* ***Lexmark Int'l v. Static Control Components, Inc.***, 387 F.3d 522, 533-35 (6th Cir.2004); ***MiTek Holdings, Inc. v. Arce Eng'g Co.***, 89 F.3d 1548, 1559 (11th Cir.1996); ***Gates Rubber Co. v. Bando Chem. Indus.***, 9 F.3d 823, 833-34 (10th Cir.1993); ***Sega Enters. v. Accolade, Inc.***, 977 F.2d 1510, 1524-25 (9th Cir.1992).

Personal Jurisdiction

Penguin Grp. v. American Buddha, 609 F.3d 30, 35 (2d Cir.2010). "In litigation arising under federal statutes that do not contain their own jurisdictional provisions, ... federal courts are to apply the personal jurisdiction rules of the forum state, ... provided that those rules are consistent with the requirements of Due Process.... Except where the long-arm statute permits jurisdiction to the extent permitted by principles of Due Process ... analysis under Due Process principles is not necessary unless there is long-arm jurisdiction under the applicable state statute."

Extraterritorial Jurisdiction

Geophysical Serv. v. TGS-NOPEC Geophysical Co., 850 F.3d 785, 791 (5th Cir.2017). "The Copyright Act does not express its limit on territorial reach. That limit arises from the background presumption that legislation reaches only domestic conduct. Because the domestic boundary is not 'clearly state[d]' to 'count as jurisdictional,' we 'treat the restriction as nonjurisdictional in character.' [¶] We are persuaded that bounding the reach of the Copyright Act to territorial conduct presents a question of the merits of the claim, not the jurisdiction of the court."

Tire Eng'g & Distrib. v. Shandong Linglong Rubber Co., 682 F.3d 292, 306 (4th Cir.2012). "We adopt the predicate-act doctrine, which posits that a plaintiff may collect damages from foreign violations of the Copyright Act so long as the foreign conduct stems from a domestic infringement. No court applying the doctrine has ascribed significance to the timeliness of domestic claims, and we decline to endorse [Ds'] proposal that we limit its application to cases where a domestic violation is not time barred. [¶] As a general matter, the Copyright Act is considered to have no extraterritorial reach. But courts have recognized a fundamental exception: 'when the type of infringement permits further reproduction abroad,' a plaintiff may collect damages flowing from the foreign conduct. *At 307:* Once a plaintiff demonstrates a domestic violation of the Copyright Act, then, it may collect damages from foreign violations that are directly linked to the U.S. infringement. *At 308:* [P]laintiffs may collect only those damages 'suffered during the statutory period for bringing claims, regardless of where they may have been incurred[ ]'...." *See also* ***L.A. News Serv. v. Reuters TV Int'l***, 149 F.3d 987, 990-92 (9th Cir.1998).

Palmer v. Braun, 376 F.3d 1254, 1258 (11th Cir. 2004). "[F]ederal copyright law has no extraterritorial effect, and cannot be invoked to secure relief for acts of infringement occurring outside the U.S. [¶] Where a person imports an infringing work into the U.S., the federal courts have jurisdiction over the action for infringement because: [17 U.S.C.] §106 ... grants the owner of a copyright the exclusive rights to do and to authorize certain acts, among which are the reproduction and distribution of the copyrighted work. The distribution right includes the right to import copies of the work." (Internal quotes omitted.) *See also* ***Datacarrier S.A. v. WOCCU Servs. Grp.***, 221 F.Supp.3d 1078, 1082 (W.D.Wis.2016) (whether extraterritoriality is jurisdictional or an element is an open question in 7th Circuit). *But see* ***Litecubes, LLC v. Northern Light Prods.***, 523 F.3d 1353, 1367-68 (Fed.Cir.2008) (extraterritoriality should be element of claim, not jurisdictional).

Shropshire v. Canning, 809 F.Supp.2d 1139, 1145 (N.D.Cal.2011). For "extraterritorial applicability of the Copyright Act, courts are split on whether the infringing act must occur wholly within the U.S. or if the infringing act only must not occur wholly outside of the U.S. Put differently, the dispute is whether all parts of the infringing act must take place in the U.S., or if it is sufficient that some part of the infringing acts take place in the U.S. ***Subafilms***[***, Ltd. v. MGM-Pathe Comms.***, 24 F.3d 1088 (9th Cir.1994),] and ***Litecubes***[***, LLC v. Northern Light Prods.***, 523 F.3d 1353 (Fed.Cir. 2008),] both articulate the latter approach, holding that the Copyright Act extends to all infringing acts that do not occur entirely abroad. On the other hand, [***L.A. News Serv. v. Reuters TV Int'l***], 149 F.3d 987 (9th Cir.1998), requires at least one act of infringement to take place entirely within the U.S. [***Allarcom Pay TV Ltd. v. General Instr. Corp.***], 69 F.3d 381 (9th Cir.1995) also requires that 'one alleged infringement must be completed entirely within the U.S.' [¶] Those cases holding that the Copyright Act requires at least one infringing act to occur entirely within the U.S. dealt with situations in which the infringing transmission was authorized or sent from within the U.S. but received and accessed abroad. In this case, however, we face the opposite scenario. *At 1146:* If acts beginning in the U.S. but culminating overseas are considered to be under the purview of the copyright laws in the country of destination, ... then it is reasonable to conclude, at least in the context of a motion to dismiss, that the allegedly infringing act here falls within the purview of the Copyright Act."

§501(a)—Generally

Sony Corp. v. Universal City Studios, Inc., 464 U.S. 417, 433 (1984). Anyone "who is authorized by the copyright owner to use the copyrighted work in a way specified in [17 U.S.C. §106] or who makes a fair use of the work is not an infringer of the copyright with respect to such use."

Dream Games v. PC Onsite, 561 F.3d 983, 988 (9th Cir.2009). "[A] claim of copyright infringement can be based on infringement of a combination of unprotected elements. [A] jury may find a combination of unprotectable elements to be protectable because the over-all impact and effect indicate substantial appropriation. To allow the possibility of such a finding, the jury must be allowed to see the complete work. [T]he unprotected elements [must] be identified to the jury." (Internal quotes omitted.)

Warren Freedenfeld Assocs. v. McTigue, 531 F.3d 38, 47-48 (1st Cir.2008). "Under the Copyright Act, no copyright infringement action lies as between joint owners of the same copyright. Each co-owner of a copyright is akin to a tenant in common and each owns a share of an undivided whole. It follows inexorably that the co-owner of a copyright is incapable of infringing that copyright vis-à-vis his counterpart co-owner. *At 48 n.5:* This is not to say that an aggrieved co-owner of a copyright is without recourse if his counterpart co-owner acts wrongfully. The aggrieved co-owner may, for example, be able to bring a declaratory action to determine his ownership rights. Alternatively, he may be able to bring a state-law claim for an accounting." *See also* ***Zuill v. Shanahan***, 80 F.3d 1366, 1369 (9th Cir. 1996).

Broadcast Music, Inc. v. Claire's Boutiques, Inc., 949 F.2d 1482, 1490 (7th Cir.1991). "'Anyone' ... includes both corporate entities and individual persons."

Hayes v. Carlin, Inc., 168 F.Supp.2d 154, 161 (S.D. N.Y.2001). "Since the right to receive royalties is not a copyright interest, collecting royalties unlawfully is not copyright infringement."

Carell v. Shubert Org., 104 F.Supp.2d 236, 247-48 (S.D.N.Y.2000). "Simply because certain designs are registered as a group does not prevent the alleged owner from bringing a claim for infringement as to individual designs."

§501(a)—Infringement—Elements

Feist Publ'ns, Inc. v. Rural Tel. Serv., 499 U.S. 340, 361 (1991). "To establish infringement, two elements must be proven: (1) ownership of a valid copyright, and (2) copying of constituent elements of the work that are original."

Rentmeester v. Nike, Inc., 883 F.3d 1111, 1117 (9th Cir.2018). "Although our cases have not always made this point explicit, the second element has two distinct components: 'copying' and 'unlawful appropriation.' Proof of copying by the defendant is necessary because independent creation is a complete defense to copyright infringement. No matter how similar the plaintiff's and the defendant's works are, if the defendant created his independently, without knowledge of or exposure to the plaintiff's work, the defendant is not liable for infringement. Proof of unlawful appropriation—that is, *illicit* copying—is necessary because copyright law does not forbid all copying. The Copyright Act provides that copyright protection does not 'extend to any idea, procedure, process, system, method of operation, concept, principle, or discovery, regardless of the form in which it is described, explained, illustrated, or embodied in [the copyrighted] work.' Thus, a defendant incurs no liability if he copies only the 'ideas' or 'concepts' used in the plaintiff's work. To infringe, the defendant must also copy enough of the plaintiff's expression of those ideas or concepts to render the two works 'substantially similar.' [¶] Unfortunately, we have used the same term—'substantial similarity'—to describe both the degree of similarity relevant to proof of copying and the degree of similarity necessary to establish unlawful appropriation. The term means different things in those two contexts. To prove copying, the similarities between the two works need not be extensive, and they need not involve protected elements of the plaintiff's work. They just need to be similarities one would not expect to arise if the two works had been created independently. To prove unlawful appropriation, on the other hand, the similarities between the two works must be 'substantial' and they must involve protected elements of the plaintiff's work."

Perfect 10, Inc. v. Giganews, Inc., 847 F.3d 657, 666 (9th Cir.2017). "To establish a prima facie case of direct infringement, a plaintiff must show ownership of the allegedly infringed material and demonstrate that the alleged infringers violated at least one exclusive right granted to copyright holders under 17 U.S.C. §106. In addition, direct infringement requires the plaintiff to show causation (also referred to as 'volitional conduct') by the defendant. [¶] We wish to emphasize that the word 'volition' in this context does not really mean an act of willing or choosing or an act of deciding, which is how the dictionary defines the term. Rather, as used by the court in ***Religious Tech. Ctr. v. Netcom On-Line [Comm. Servs.]***, 907 F.Supp. 1361 ... (N.D.Cal.1995), it simply stands for the unremarkable proposition that proximate causation historically underlines copyright infringement liability no less than other torts. As the district court cogently explained: The so-called 'volition' element of direct infringement is not a judicially-created element of intent or knowledge; it is a basic requirement of causation. As its name suggests, *direct* liability must be premised on conduct that can reasonably be described as the *direct cause* of the infringement. [¶] Contrary to [P's] contention, this requirement of causation remains an element of a direct infringement claim. [W]e [have] explained that infringement of the reproduction right requires copying *by* the defendant, which comprises a requirement that the defendant cause the copying. In using this language, we indicated that causation is an element of a direct infringement claim." (Internal quotes omitted.) *See also* ***BWP Media USA, Inc. v. T&S Software Assocs.***, 852 F.3d 436, 438-40 & n.1 (5th Cir.2017).

Broadcast Music, Inc. v. Evie's Tavern Ellenton, Inc., 772 F.3d 1254, 1257-58 (11th Cir.2014). "When a plaintiff is challenging the unauthorized public performance of a copyrighted musical composition, the plaintiff must show: '(1) the originality and authorship of the compositions involved; (2) compliance with all formalities required to secure a copyright under Title 17, [U.S.C.]; (3) that plaintiffs are the proprietors of the copyrights of the compositions involved in the action; (4) that the compositions were performed publicly by the defendant; and (5) that the defendant had not receive[d] permission from any of the plaintiffs or their representatives for such performance.'"

Zalewski v. Cicero Builder Dev., Inc., 754 F.3d 95, 100 (2d Cir.2014). "In order to make out a claim of copyright infringement for an architectural work—or any work—a plaintiff must establish three things: (1) that his work is protected by a valid copyright, (2) that the defendant copied his work, and (3) that the copying was wrongful. The second and third elements—copying and wrongful copying—are often confused. This confusion is understandable; in many cases *any* copying of a work is wrongful, and thus there is often no need to draw the distinction. Nonetheless, the distinction can be important. Not every portion or aspect of a copyrighted work is given copyright law's protection. Copying these aspects of a work is not wrongful, and thus not *all* copying is wrongful. *At 101:* When an original work contains many *un*protected elements, however, a close similarity between it and a copy may prove only copying, not wrongful copying. This is because the similarity may derive only from these unprotected elements. For clarity, the term 'substantial similarity' is properly reserved for similarity that exists between the protected elements of a work and another work. If two works are 'substantially similar,' any copying was wrongful. By contrast, similarity that relates to unprotected elements is probative only of copying—not wrongful copying—and is referred to as 'probative similarity.'"

Fitzgerald Publ'g v. Baylor Publ'g, 807 F.2d 1110, 1113 (2d Cir.1986). "Under §501(a) intent or knowledge is not an element of infringement. Innocence is only significant to a trial court when it fixes statutory damages, which is a remedy equitable in nature."

§501(a)—Infringement—Elements—Ownership

For annotations on this topic, see 17 U.S.C. §§201-205, p. 304.

§501(a)—Infringement—Elements—Valid Copyright

For more annotations on this topic, see 17 U.S.C. §101, p. 189; 17 U.S.C. §102, p. 199; 17 U.S.C. §410, p. 341; 17 U.S.C. §411, p. 343.

Coquico, Inc. v. Rodriguez-Miranda, 562 F.3d 62, 68 (1st Cir.2009). "The merger doctrine denies copyright protection when creativity merges with reality; that is, when there is only one way to express a particular idea. The doctrine of scènes à faire denies copyright protection to elements of a work that are for all practical purposes indispensable, or at least customary, in the treatment of a given subject matter." *See also* ***Stromback v. New Line Cinema***, 384 F.3d 283, 296 (6th Cir. 2004); ***MyWebGrocer, LLC v. HomeTown Info, Inc.***, 375 F.3d 190, 194 (2d Cir.2004).

Meshwerks, Inc. v. Toyota Motor Sales U.S.A., Inc., 528 F.3d 1258, 1262 (10th Cir.2008). "Because [P] obtained registration certificates for its models from the Copyright Office, we presume that it holds a valid copyright. At the same time, [Ds] may overcome this presumption by presenting evidence and legal argument sufficient to establish that the works in question were not entitled to copyright protection. [¶] [N]ot every work of authorship, let alone every aspect of every work of authorship, is protectable in copyright; only original expressions are protected. *At 1263:* What exactly does it mean for a work to qualify as 'original'? In ***Feist***, the Supreme Court clarified that the work must be 'independently created by the author (as opposed to copied from other works).' In addition, the work must 'possess[ ] at least some minimal degree of creativity,' ... though this is not to say that to count as containing a minimal degree of creativity a work must have aesthetic merit in the minds of judges.... *At 1264:* [T]he operative distinction is between, on the one hand, ideas or facts in the world, items that cannot be copyrighted, and a particular expression of that idea or fact, that can be. 'This principle, known as the idea/expression or fact/expression dichotomy, applies to all works of authorship. As applied to a factual compilation,' ... 'assuming the absence of original written expression, only the compiler's selection and arrangement may be protected; the raw facts may be copied at will. This result is neither unfair nor unfortunate. It is the means by which copyright advances the progress of science and art.'"

§501(a)—Infringement—Elements—Copying—Access to Work & Direct Evidence

Oracle USA, Inc. v. Rimini St., Inc., 879 F.3d 948, 953 (9th Cir.2018). "The ... dispute in this case is whether [D] copied [P's] software in a manner that infringed [P's] copyright. [A]t the highest level of generality, [D's] alleged copyright infringement included copying under [one customer's] license ... for work for other existing customers or for unknown or future customers, rather than restricting such copying to work for that particular customer. *At 957:* The licenses do not authorize [D] to 'develop products [D] could sell for [D's] financial gain.' Any work that [D] performs under color of a license held by a customer for other existing customers cannot be considered work in support of that particular customer. The same logic applies to work [D] performs for unknown, future customers. The licensees may hire a third party such as [D] to maintain their software for them, but nothing in the licenses permits them to grant a non-party to the license a general right to copy proprietary software."

DC Comics v. Towle, 802 F.3d 1012, 1026 (9th Cir. 2015). "While we ordinarily apply a two-part 'substantial similarity' test to determine whether a plaintiff has established 'copying of constituent elements of the work that are original,' ... we need not do so where ... 'the copying of the substance of the entire work' is admitted...."

Humphreys & Partners Architects, L.P. v. Lessard Design, Inc., 790 F.3d 532, 537 (4th Cir.2015). "'Direct evidence of copying ... includes evidence such as party admissions, witness accounts of the physical act of copying, and common errors in the works of plaintiffs and the defendants.' In ***M. Kramer [Mfg.] Co. v. Andrews***, 783 F.2d 421 (4th Cir.1986), for example, we found direct evidence of copying where '[t]he computer programs in the record [were] virtually identical' and the defendants' program, like plaintiff's, included 'a hidden legend that would appear only when the [program's] buttons were pressed in an abnormal sequence[]'.... Similarly, our sister circuits have found direct evidence of copying where a defendant 'gave ... explicit instruction that [a] work be copied,' ... and where the defendant admitted to copying the plaintiff's work...." *See also* ***Enterprise Mgmt. Ltd. v. Warrick***, 717 F.3d 1112, 1120 (10th Cir.2013) (D admitted copying); ***Society of the Holy Transfiguration Monastery, Inc. v. Gregory***, 689 F.3d 29, 49 (1st Cir.2012) (same); ***Rogers v. Koons***, 960 F.2d 301, 307 (2d Cir.1992) (specific instructions to copy).

Wall Data Inc. v. Los Angeles Cty. Sheriff's Dept., 447 F.3d 769, 773-74 (9th Cir.2006). "[D] purchased 3,663 licenses to [P's] computer software, but installed the software onto 6,007 computers. We are asked to determine whether [D's] conduct constituted copyright infringement. The wrinkle in this otherwise smooth question is that, although the software was installed onto 6,007 computers, the computers were configured such that the total number of workstations able to access the installed software did not exceed the total number of licenses [D] purchased. We ... hold that such copying constitutes copyright infringement despite [D's] configuration."

§501(a)—Infringement—Elements—Copying—Access to Work & Indirect Evidence

Design Basics, LLC v. Lexington Homes, Inc., 858 F.3d 1093, 1099-1100 (7th Cir.2017). "The access requirement is not onerous. For example, a plaintiff may satisfy the requirement by showing that the copyrighted work was 'sent directly to the defendant ... or a close associate of the defendant.' A plaintiff may also satisfy the requirement by showing that the copyrighted work was so widely disseminated that the defendant can be presumed to have seen or heard it. [¶] [I]n the rare case involving an uncanny resemblance for which copying the plaintiff's work is the only plausible explanation, further proof of access may not be required. But in general, to prove a circumstantial case of copyright infringement, the plaintiff must separately prove both access and similarity. In this case, [P's] proof falls short in both ways. *At 1106-07:* We have not previously considered whether an Internet presence, without more, can satisfy the access element of a copyright infringement claim. The Fourth Circuit rejected a similar argument in ***Building Graphics, Inc. v. Lennar Corp.***, 708 F.3d 573 (4th Cir.2013). [¶] The Fourth Circuit's analysis is persuasive. *At 1108:* We do not draw here a bright line as to the quantity or quality of evidence, in addition to a web presence, a plaintiff must offer to raise a genuine issue of fact concerning access. We decide only that the existence of the plaintiff's copyrighted materials on the Internet, even on a public and 'user-friendly' site, cannot by itself justify an inference that the defendant accessed those materials. It follows that a plaintiff who cannot show striking similarity and whose evidence of access reduces to the mere existence of a website cannot survive summary judgment on a copyright infringement claim."

Unicolors, Inc. v. Urban Outfitters, Inc., 853 F.3d 980, 987 (9th Cir.2017). "We conclude that a district court may grant summary judgment for plaintiffs on the issue of copying when the works are so overwhelmingly similar that the possibility of independent creation is precluded. The works at issue in this case meet this standard. The objective similarities between the works are stark: the shapes, motifs, arrangements, spacing, and colors of the images in each design are nearly identical. Because of the decisive objective overlap between the works, no reasonable juror could conclude under the intrinsic test that the works are not substantially similar in total concept and feel. [¶] Absent evidence of access, a 'striking similarity' between the works may give rise to a permissible inference of copying." (Internal quotes omitted.)

Loomis v. Cornish, 836 F.3d 991, 995-96 (9th Cir. 2016). "Proof of access requires an opportunity to view or to copy plaintiff's work. To prove access, a plaintiff must show a reasonable possibility, not merely a bare possibility, that an alleged infringer had the chance to view the protected work. Where there is no direct evidence of access, circumstantial evidence can be used to prove access either by (1) establishing a chain of events linking the plaintiff's work and the defendant's access, or (2) showing that the plaintiff's work has been widely disseminated. [¶] Evidence that a third party with whom both the plaintiff and defendant were dealing had possession of plaintiff's work is sufficient to establish access by the defendant. The dealings between the plaintiff and the intermediary and between the intermediary and the alleged copier must involve some overlap in subject matter to permit an inference of access. [¶] By contrast, multiple courts have held that a plaintiff cannot create a triable issue of access merely by showing 'bare corporate receipt' of her work by an individual who shares a common employer with the alleged copier. Rather, it must be reasonably possible that the paths of the infringer and the infringed work crossed. *At 997:* The evidence required to show widespread dissemination will vary from case to case. In most cases, the evidence of widespread dissemination centers on the degree of a work's commercial success and on its distribution through radio, television, and other relevant mediums. [¶] We have also recognized a doctrinal variant that focuses on saturation in a relevant market in which both the plaintiff and the defendant participate. [A] triable issue of access exist[s] where (1) the plaintiff's fabric design had saturated the fabric market for apparel vendors in Los Angeles over a four-year period, and (2) the defendant routinely participated in the Los Angeles fabric market during that period. This ... created a 'reasonable possibility' that [Ds] had an opportunity to view and copy [P's] design." (Internal quotes omitted.) *See also* ***Jones v. Blige***, 558 F.3d 485, 491-92 (6th Cir.2009); ***Jorgensen v. Epic/Sony Records***, 351 F.3d 46, 48 (2d Cir.2003); ***Towler v. Sayles***, 76 F.3d 579, 583 (4th Cir.1996).

Copeland v. Bieber, 789 F.3d 484, 490 (4th Cir. 2015). "[I]ntrinsic similarity is assessed from the perspective of a work's intended audience. That means that the first step in undertaking an analysis of intrinsic similarity is identifying the right audience. [¶] [W]e [have] clarified our intrinsic similarity analysis by introducing the 'intended audience' formulation. Because a primary purpose of copyright law is to 'protect[] a creator's market,' ... the intrinsic similarity inquiry should be keyed to the impressions of the intended audience for a creator's work—the impressions that count for purposes of marketability. So where the market for a given work consists of a discrete and specialized class, the reactions of a generic ordinary observer will not be particularly relevant. But in most cases, ... the general public is in fact the intended audience, and 'a court should be hesitant' to find otherwise. *At 492-94:* [W]hile genre may be relevant to intrinsic analysis of musical works, it cannot be dispositive under copyright law. For if a difference in genre were enough by itself to preclude intrinsic similarity, then nothing would prevent someone from translating, say, the Beatles' songbook into a different genre, and then profiting from an unlicensed reggae or heavy metal version of 'Hey Jude' on the ground that it is different in 'concept and feel' than the original. [¶] Even when quantitative majorities of two works bear little resemblance, courts routinely permit a finding of substantial similarity where the works share some especially significant sequence of notes or lyrics. And we think it is clear that when it comes to popular music, a song's chorus may be the kind of key sequence that can give rise to intrinsic similarity, even when works differ in other respects. [¶] It is the chorus—often termed the 'hook,' in recognition of its power to keep a listener coming back for more—that many listeners will recognize immediately or hear in their minds when a song title is mentioned. As the part of a song that is most often repeated and remembered, a chorus hook is important not only aesthetically but also commercially, where it may be central to a song's economic success."

Peters v. West, 692 F.3d 629, 632-34 (7th Cir.2012). "Satisfied that [P] has shown valid copyright ownership, we turn our attention to the question of copying. The standard for copying is surprisingly muddled. Where direct evidence, such as an admission of copying, is not available (as is typically the case ...), a plaintiff may prove copying by showing that the defendant had the opportunity to copy the original (often called 'access') and that the two works are 'substantially similar,' thus permitting an inference that the defendant actually did copy the original. The various efforts to define these two key concepts, however, have unfortunately had the unintended effect of obscuring rather than clarifying the issues. This court has said that substantial similarity can be shown by evidence of 'actual copying' and 'improper appropriation.' Thus, we permit copying to be proven by evidence of access, actual copying, and improper appropriation. [P] argues that we should adopt a hybrid of our own approach and the one that he argues prevails in the Second Circuit. That court, he contends, permits actual copying to be proven by 'access' and 'probative similarity' (which is distinct from substantial similarity). Putting these tests together, he seems to want us to require proof of access, improper appropriation, and actual copying by means of showing probative similarity and access (again). [¶] Other circuits have also had trouble expressing the test with any clarity. The First Circuit, for example, finds copying where the plaintiff has shown substantial similarity, access, and probative similarity. The formulation found in the Second Circuit requires proof of improper appropriation and actual copying; the latter is shown by proving access and probative similarity. The 11th Circuit takes still a different approach, requiring either 'striking similarity' or access and merely probative similarity. [¶] Despite all of this confusing nomenclature, this strikes us as a 'pseudo-conflict': despite the conflicting and confusing verbiage, the outcomes do not appear to differ. Fundamentally, proving the basic tort of infringement simply requires the plaintiff to show that the defendant had an actual opportunity to copy the original (this is because independent creation is a defense to copyright infringement), and that the two works share enough unique features to give rise to a breach of the duty not to copy another's work. Our analysis will follow this structure. [¶] [W]e must confront the differences among the circuits about the relation between proof of access and evidence of similarity. Some circuits follow an 'inverse ratio' rule, under which the strength of proof of similarity varies inversely with the proof of access (*i.e.*, strong proof of access allows for only weak proof of similarity, and vice versa). Other courts have rejected the inverse-ratio rule. After following that rule for several decades, the Second Circuit expressly rejected it in 1961, concluding that the rule 'confuses more than it clarifies.' [¶] This court's rule has not been so explicit, although we have occasionally endorsed something that comes close to this inverse approach. [W]e [have] held that 'degree of similarity required to establish an inference of access [should be] in an inverse ratio to the quantum of direct evidence adduced to establish access.' More recently, we noted that 'similarity that is so close as to be highly unlikely to have been an accident of independent creation is evidence of access.' Thus, ... we noted that evidence that two works are very similar can suggest that the alleged infringer had access to the original. *At 635:* Notably, however, we have never endorsed the other side of the inverse relation: the idea that a 'high degree of access' justifies a 'lower standard of proof' for similarity. As we explained above, evidence of access is required because independent creation is a defense to copyright infringement, and so a plaintiff must show that the defendant had an opportunity to copy her original work. This issue is independent of the question whether an alleged infringer breached his duty not to copy another's work. Once a plaintiff establishes that a defendant could have copied her work, she must separately prove—regardless of how good or restricted the opportunity was—that the allegedly infringing work is indeed a copy of her original."

Mag Jewelry Co. v. Cherokee, Inc., 496 F.3d 108, 117 (1st Cir.2007). "[P] is correct that reasonable opportunity is the applicable standard for evaluating access; a copyright owner need not demonstrate an alleged infringer's actual access to a protected work. However, evidence that only creates a bare possibility that the defendant had access is not sufficient." (Internal quotes omitted.)

BUC Int'l v. International Yacht Council Ltd., 489 F.3d 1129, 1148 (11th Cir.2007). "The 'substantial similarity' standard applies to actions for the infringement of factual compilations. The nuances of the 'substantial similarity' test vary, however, depending on the nature of the copyrighted work at issue. For example, in cases involving a compilation, 'substantial similarity' imparts a narrowed construction. '[T]he components of a compilation are generally in the public domain, and a finding of substantial similarity or even absolute identity as to matters in the public domain will not suffice to prove infringement. What must be shown is substantial similarity between those elements, and only those elements, that provide copyrightability to the allegedly infringed compilation.' [I]t is the original selection and arrangement of the collected data that bear legal significance for factual compilations. [¶] By comparison, the 'virtual identicality' standard calls for a greater degree of similarity between the copyrighted work and the allegedly infringing work than does 'substantial similarity.' 'Virtual identicality,' as adopted in this circuit, applies to 'claims of compilation copyright infringement of nonliteral elements of a computer program.'"

T-Peg, Inc. v. Vermont Timber Works, Inc., 459 F.3d 97, 108 (1st Cir.2006). "Proving copying of constituent elements of the work that are original (the second element of the *Feist* test) itself involves two steps: the plaintiff must show (a) that the defendant actually copied the work as a factual matter, either through direct evidence or through indirect means, ... and (b) that the defendant's copying of the copyrighted material was so extensive that it rendered the infringing and copyrighted works 'substantially similar.' [¶] In an infringement action, the burden is on the plaintiff to prove these elements. *At 111:* Copying may be proven through direct or circumstantial evidence. [¶] In the absence of direct evidence of copying[,] one of the ways to indirectly establish that the defendant copied the plaintiff's work is to provide evidence that (1) the defendant enjoyed access to the copyrighted work, and so had the opportunity to copy the work, and (2) a sufficient degree of similarity exists between the copyrighted work and the allegedly infringing work to give rise to an inference of actual copying. The similarity inquiry used to indirectly establish copying is referred to as *probative* similarity and is somewhat akin to, but different than, the requirement of substantial similarity that must be shown to prove copyright infringement. [¶] A trier of fact may impute access when there is evidence that a third party with whom both the plaintiff and defendant were dealing had possession of plaintiff's work, and the plaintiff's and defendant's dealings took place concurrently. *At 112:* As to whether there is a genuine issue of material fact as to probative similarity—whether a sufficient degree of similarity exists between the copyrighted work and the allegedly infringing work to give rise to an inference of actual copying—this analysis merges somewhat with the question of substantial similarity (although they are separate questions). [¶] The substantial similarity inquiry entails proof that the copying was so extensive that it rendered the works so similar that the later work represented a wrongful appropriation of expression. The inquiry focuses not on every aspect of the copyrighted work, but on those aspects of the plaintiff's work that are protectible under copyright laws and whether whatever copying took place appropriated those protected elements. Summary judgment on substantial similarity is unusual but can be warranted on the right set of facts. [¶] Substantial similarity can be measured by the 'ordinary observer' test. Under that test, two works will be said to be substantially similar if a reasonable, ordinary observer, upon examination of the two works, would conclude that the defendant unlawfully appropriated the plaintiff's protectable expression. The two works need not be exact copies to be substantially similar. Differences between the works have some effect on the inquiry, but the mere existence of differences is insufficient to end the matter in the defendant's favor. If the points of dissimilarity not only exceed the points of similarity, but indicate that the remaining points of similarity are, within the context of plaintiff's work, of minimal importance, either quantitatively or qualitatively, then no infringement results. *At 114 n.7:* The extent to which the copyrighted work contains protected expression is a matter of law, determined by the court. Once this determination is made, the question of whether two works are substantially similar (and corresponding application of the ordinary observer test) is a matter for the trier of fact unless summary judgment is proper." (Internal quotes omitted.) *See also* ***Design Basics, LLC v. Lexington Homes, Inc.***, 858 F.3d 1093, 1101 (7th Cir.2017) (discussing substantial-similarity standard); ***R.W. Beck, Inc. v. E3 Consulting, LLC***, 577 F.3d 1133, 1142 (10th Cir.2009) (same as annotation); ***Peter Letterese & Assocs. v. World Inst. of Scientology Enters.***, 533 F.3d 1287, 1300-01 (11th Cir.2008) (same); ***Kay Berry, Inc. v. Taylor Gifts, Inc.***, 421 F.3d 199, 207-08 (3d Cir.2005) (same); ***Johnson v. Gordon***, 409 F.3d 12, 17-18 (1st Cir.2005) (discussing difference between "substantial similarity" and "probative similarity"); ***Positive Black Talk Inc. v. Cash Money Records Inc.***, 394 F.3d 357, 367-68 (5th Cir.2004) (same), *overruled on other grounds*, ***Reed Elsevier, Inc. v. Muchnick***, 559 U.S. 154 (2010); ***Stromback v. New Line Cinema***, 384 F.3d 283, 293-94 (6th Cir.2004) (substantial similarity test consists of two steps); ***General Univ'l Sys. v. Lee***, 379 F.3d 131, 141-42 (5th Cir. 2004) (slightly different elements); ***Jorgensen v. Epic/Sony Records***, 351 F.3d 46, 51 (2d Cir.2003) (discussing "access"); ***Sturdza v. United Arab Emirates***, 281 F.3d 1287, 1295-96 (D.C.Cir.2002) (substantial similarity test consists of two steps); ***Castle Rock Entm't, Inc. v. Carol Publ'g***, 150 F.3d 132, 138 (2d Cir.1998) (discussing "substantial similarity").

Well-Made Toy Mfg. v. Goffa Int'l, 354 F.3d 112, 117 (2d Cir.2003), *overruled on other grounds*, ***Reed Elsevier, Inc. v. Muchnick***, 559 U.S. 154 (2010). Even "when one work is 'based upon' another, 'if the secondary work sufficiently transforms the expression of the original work such that the two works cease to be *substantially similar*, then the secondary work is not a derivative work and, for that matter, does not infringe the copyright of the original work.'"

Bridgmon v. Array Sys., 325 F.3d 572, 576 n.7 (5th Cir.2003). "'Probative similarity' and 'substantial similarity' are analytically distinct inquiries. *At 577 n.8:* [P] cites several cases from other jurisdictions where the phrase substantial similarity is used interchangeably in the two different inquiries. [W]ith respect to factual copying the test is 'probative similarity' (if relying on circumstantial evidence of copying) and that the test for actionable copying is 'substantial similarity.' While it is possible that the same evidence will satisfy both tests, the tests are not the same."

Olson v. National Broad. Co., 855 F.2d 1446, 1448-49 (9th Cir.1988). There is a "two-part test for determining whether one work is substantially similar to another. The extrinsic test, which is used to determine whether there is a substantial similarity in ideas, depends not on the responses of the trier of fact, but on specific criteria which can be listed and analyzed. The intrinsic test, which is used to compare forms of expression, depends on the response of the ordinary reasonable person. Although analytic dissection and expert testimony are appropriate under the extrinsic test, they are not appropriate under the intrinsic test. To demonstrate substantial similarity, [P] must prove both substantial similarity of general ideas under the extrinsic test and substantial similarity of the protectable expression of those ideas under the intrinsic test. *At 1450:* [The] specific analysis that is appropriate under the extrinsic test [is]: The test for substantial similarity of ideas compares, not the basic plot ideas for stories, but the actual concrete elements that make up the total sequence of events and the relationships between the major characters. The extrinsic test for similarity of ideas looks beyond the vague, abstracted idea of a general plot and instead focuses on the objective details of the works. The extrinsic test requires a comparison of plot, theme, dialogue, mood, setting, pace, and sequence." (Internal quotes omitted.) *See also* ***Universal Furniture Int'l v. Collezione Europa USA, Inc.***, 618 F.3d 417, 435-36 (4th Cir.2010); ***Frye v. YMCA Camp Kitaki***, 617 F.3d 1005, 1008 (8th Cir.2010); ***Swirsky v. Carey***, 376 F.3d 841, 844-49 (9th Cir.2004); ***Concrete Mach. Co. v. Classic Lawn Ornaments, Inc.***, 843 F.2d 600, 606 (1st Cir.1988), *overruled on other grounds*, ***eBay Inc. v. MercExchange, L.L.C.***, 547 U.S. 388 (2006); ***Chase-Riboud v. Dreamworks, Inc.***, 987 F.Supp. 1222, 1225-26 (C.D.Cal.1997).

Acuff-Rose Music, Inc. v. Jostens, Inc., 988 F.Supp. 289, 292 (S.D.N.Y.1997), *aff'd*, 155 F.3d 140 (2d Cir.1998). "A copier will be liable for copying [a] musical work in its entirety, that is, the composition's words and music together, as well as for copying just the music or the words alone."

RSO Records, Inc. v. Peri, 596 F.Supp. 849, 853 (S.D.N.Y.1984). "The question of whether the making of color separations of copyrighted graphics constitutes infringement leaves more room for dispute. Graphic works, too, are expressly granted copyright protection, but color separations are not exact reproductions of copyrighted graphics. While they do reproduce the copyrighted image, they split its color scheme into four parts and frequently portray the image in that distorted manner familiar from photographic negatives. ... Because the making of an accurate color separation is a crucial step in the process of record counterfeiting, those making the color separation may be held liable for infringement of the recording itself."

§501(a)—Infringement—Elements—Copying—Indirect Evidence—No Access to Work

Corwin v. Walt Disney Co., 475 F.3d 1239, 1253 (11th Cir.2007). "'Where a plaintiff cannot demonstrate access he may, nonetheless, establish copying by demonstrating that his original work and the putative infringing work are strikingly similar.' Striking similarity exists where the proof of similarity in appearance is 'so striking that the possibilities of independent creation, coincidence and prior common source are, as a practical matter, precluded.'" *See also* ***Jones v. Blige***, 558 F.3d 485, 490-91 (6th Cir.2009).

§501(a)—Infringement—Elements—Copying—Inverse-Relationship Doctrine

Positive Black Talk Inc. v. Cash Money Records Inc., 394 F.3d 357, 371-72 (5th Cir.2004), *overruled on other grounds*, ***Reed Elsevier, Inc. v. Muchnick***, 559 U.S. 154 (2010). "[Ds] are correct that this circuit has not expressly adopted the principle that there is an inverse relationship between the requisite proof of access and similarity, and there is no need to do so here. However, this doctrine finds support in other circuits. Thus, other courts have held that a plaintiff who shows a high degree of similarity may satisfy the factual copying requirement with a lesser showing of access, and, conversely, a plaintiff who shows a greater degree of access may satisfy the factual copying element with a lesser degree of probative similarity."

§501(a)—Infringement—FRCP 12(b)(6) Motion to Dismiss

Peter F. Gaito Architecture, LLC v. Simone Dev. Corp., 602 F.3d 57, 64 (2d Cir.2010). "[W]here ... the works in question are attached to a plaintiff's complaint, it is entirely appropriate for the district court to consider the similarity between those works in connection with a motion to dismiss, because the court has before it all that is necessary in order to make such an evaluation. If, in making that evaluation, the district court determines that the two works are 'not substantially similar as a matter of law,' ... the district court can properly conclude that the plaintiff's complaint, together with the works incorporated therein, do not 'plausibly give rise to an entitlement to relief.' *At 65:* [W]here ... the district court has before it all that is necessary to make a comparison of the works in question, we see no error in the district court's decision to resolve the question of substantial similarity as a matter of law on [an FRCP] 12(b)(6) motion to dismiss." *See also* ***Jacobsen v. Deseret Book Co.***, 287 F.3d 936, 941-42 (10th Cir.2002); ***Nelson v. PRN Prods.***, 873 F.2d 1141, 1143-44 (8th Cir.1989); ***Christianson v. West Publ'g***, 149 F.2d 202, 203 (9th Cir.1945).

§501(a)—Infringement—Summary Judgment

Intervest Constr., Inc. v. Canterbury Estate Homes, Inc., 554 F.3d 914, 920 (11th Cir.2008). "[W]e have approved the use of summary judgment particularly in cases where: (1) because access has been established, the crucial issue is substantial similarity; (2) there may be substantial similarity with respect to the non-copyrightable elements of the two works compared; and, (3) as to the protectable elements, there is substantial dissimilarity. In fact, when the crucial question in a dispute involving compilations is substantial similarity at the level of protectable expression, it is often more reliably and accurately resolved in a summary judgment proceeding. This is so because a judge is better able to separate original expression from the non-original elements of a work where the copying of the latter is not protectable and the copying of the former is protectable. The judge understands the concept of the idea/expression dichotomy and how it should be applied in the context of the works before him. ... Moreover, in examining compilations wherein only the arrangement and coordination of elements which by the nature of the work (here architectural floor plans) are sure to be common to each of the works and are not copyrightable themselves (spacial depictions of rooms, doors, windows, walls, etc.), the already difficult tasks may become even more nuanced. Because a judge will more readily understand that all copying is not infringement, particularly in the context of works that are compilations, the 'substantial-similarity' test is more often correctly administered by a judge rather than a jury—even one provided proper instruction." *See also*

T-Peg, Inc. v. Vermont Timber Works, Inc., 459 F.3d 97, 112 (1st Cir.2006).

§501(a)—Contributory Infringement

Metro-Goldwyn-Mayer Studios Inc. v. Grokster, Ltd., 545 U.S. 913, 916 (2005). "The question is under what circumstances the distributor of a product capable of both lawful and unlawful use is liable for acts of copyright infringement by third parties using the product. We hold that one who distributes a device with the object of promoting its use to infringe copyright, as shown by clear expression or other affirmative steps taken to foster infringement, is liable for the resulting acts of infringement by third parties." *See also **BMG Music v. Gonzalez***, 430 F.3d 888, 889 (7th Cir.2005).

Sony Corp. v. Universal City Studios, Inc., 464 U.S. 417, 442 (1984). "[T]he sale of copying equipment, like the sale of other articles of commerce, does not constitute contributory infringement if the product is widely used for legitimate, unobjectionable purposes. Indeed, it need merely be capable of substantial noninfringing uses."

Columbia Pictures Indus. v. Fung, 710 F.3d 1020, 1032 (9th Cir.2013). "***Grokster III*** ... enunciate[d] the 'inducement rule,' ... providing that 'one who distributes a device with the object of promoting its use to infringe copyright, as shown by clear expression or other affirmative steps taken to foster infringement, is liable for the resulting acts of infringement by third parties.' This inducement principle, as enunciated in ***Grokster III***, has four elements: (1) the distribution of a device or product, (2) acts of infringement, (3) an object of promoting its use to infringe copyright, and (4) causation. *At 1033:* Inducement liability is not limited, either logically or as articulated in ***Grokster III***, to those who distribute a 'device.' As a result, one can infringe a copyright through culpable actions resulting in the impermissible reproduction of copyrighted expression, whether those actions involve making available a device or product or providing some service used in accomplishing the infringement. *At 1034:* Both uploading and downloading copyrighted material are infringing acts. The former violates the copyright holder's right to distribution, the latter the right to reproduction. [¶] The third, usually dispositive, requirement for inducement liability is that the 'device' or service be distributed 'with the object of promoting its use to infringe copyright, as shown by clear expression or other affirmative steps taken to foster infringement.' *At 1037:* [I]f one provides a service that could be used to infringe copyrights, with the manifested intent that the service actually be used in that manner, that person is liable for the infringement that occurs through the use of the service. *At 1038:* We emphasize a few points in this regard. First, ... proper proof of the defendant's intent that its product or service be used to infringe copyrights is paramount. '[M]ere knowledge of infringing potential or of actual infringing uses' does not subject a product distributor or service provider to liability. When dealing with corporate or entity defendants, ... the relevant intent must be that of the entity itself, as defined by traditional agency law principles; liability cannot be premised on stray or unauthorized statements that cannot fairly be imputed to the entity. [¶] [P]roving that an entity had an unlawful purpose at a particular time in providing a product or service does not infinitely expand its liability in either temporal direction."

Flava Works, Inc. v. Gunter, 689 F.3d 754, 757 (7th Cir.2012). "A typical, and typically unhelpful, definition of 'contributory infringer' is one who, with knowledge of the infringing activity, induces, causes or materially contributes to the infringing conduct of another. Such a one may be held liable as a contributory infringer. But does '*may* be held liable' mean that a person who fits the definition of contributory infringer may nevertheless *not* be a contributory infringer after all? And what exactly does 'materially contribute' mean? And how does one materially contribute to something without causing or inducing it? And how does 'cause' differ from 'induce'? [¶] We ... prefer the succinct definition of contributory infringement [as] personal conduct that encourages or assists the infringement. *At 758:* As the record stands ..., [D] is not an infringer, at least in the form of copying or distributing copies of copyrighted work. The infringers are the uploaders of copyrighted work. There is no evidence that [D] is encouraging them, which would make it a contributory infringer." (Internal quotes omitted.)

Louis Vuitton Malletier, S.A. v. Akanoc Solutions, Inc., 658 F.3d 936, 943 (9th Cir.2011). "We have never held that an express finding of intent is necessary to support liability for contributory copyright infringement. To the contrary, we have held that 'intent may be imputed' as a result of 'a service provider's knowing failure to prevent infringing actions.' The district court was not required to instruct the jury ... to make a separate finding that [Ds'] knowing action evinced intent to contribute to copyright infringement. [Ds] also argue that the jury instructions should have required an express finding of material contribution. We disagree. [¶] Material contribution turns on whether the activity in question 'substantially assists' direct infringement. There is no question that providing direct infringers with server space satisfies that standard."

MDY Indus. v. Blizzard Entm't, Inc., 629 F.3d 928, 940 (9th Cir.2010). "To recover for copyright infringement based on breach of a license agreement, (1) the copying must exceed the scope of the defendant's license and (2) the copyright owner's complaint must be grounded in an exclusive right of copyright (e.g., unlawful reproduction or distribution). *At 941:* A [software-bot] user violates the covenants with [computer-game licensor], but does not thereby commit copyright infringement because [the software bot] does not infringe any of [computer-game licensor's] exclusive rights. For instance, the use does not alter or copy [computer game's] software. [¶] We conclude that for a licensee's violation of a contract to constitute copyright infringement, there must be a nexus between the condition and the licensor's exclusive rights of copyright." Held: Producer of software bot was not contributorily liable for infringement of computer-game licensor's software.

Cartoon Network LP v. CSC Holdings, Inc., 536 F.3d 121, 130 (2d Cir.2008). "[T]he core of the dispute is over the authorship of the infringing conduct. After an RS-DVR subscriber selects a program to record, and that program airs, a copy of the program—a copyrighted work—resides on the hard disks of [D's server], its creation unauthorized by the copyright holder. The question is *who* made this copy. If it is [D], [Ps'] theory of direct infringement succeeds; if it is the customer, [Ps'] theory fails because [D] would then face, at most, secondary liability, a theory of liability expressly disavowed by [Ps]. *At 131:* We do not believe that an RS-DVR customer is sufficiently distinguishable from a VCR user to impose liability as a direct infringer on a different party for copies that are made automatically upon that customer's command. *At 133:* We conclude only that on the facts of this case, copies produced by the RS-DVR system are 'made' by the RS-DVR customer, and [D's] contribution to this reproduction by providing the system does not warrant the imposition of direct liability."

CoStar Grp. v. LoopNet, Inc., 373 F.3d 544, 549 (4th Cir.2004). "While the Copyright Act does not require that the infringer know that he is infringing or that his conduct amount to a willful violation of the copyright owner's rights, it nonetheless requires conduct by a person who causes in some meaningful way an infringement. ... This, of course, does not mean that a manufacturer or owner of machines used for copyright violations could not have some indirect liability, such as contributory or vicarious liability. But such extensions of liability would require a showing of additional elements such as knowledge coupled with inducement or supervision coupled with a financial interest in the illegal copying. *At 555:* [W]e hold that [Internet-service providers (ISPs)], when passively storing material at the direction of users in order to make that material available to other users upon their request, do not 'copy' the material in direct violation of [17 U.S.C.] §106.... [W]e hold that the automatic copying, storage, and transmission of copyrighted materials, when instigated by others, does not render an ISP strictly liable for copyright infringement under [17 U.S.C.] §§501 and 106.... An ISP, however, can become liable indirectly upon a showing of additional involvement sufficient to establish a contributory or vicarious violation of the Act. In that case, the ISP could still look to the DMCA for a safe harbor if it fulfilled the conditions therein."

Ellison v. Robertson, 357 F.3d 1072, 1076 (9th Cir. 2004). "One who, with knowledge of the infringing activity, induces, causes or materially contributes to the infringing conduct *of another* may be liable as a contributory [copyright] infringer. We have interpreted the knowledge requirement for contributory copyright infringement to include both those with *actual knowledge* and those who *have reason to know* of direct infringement." (Internal quotes omitted.) *See also* ***EMI Christian Music Grp. v. MP3tunes, LLC***, 844 F.3d 79, 99-100 (2d Cir.2016); ***Leonard v. Stemtech Int'l***, 834 F.3d 376, 387 (3d Cir.2016); ***Diversey v. Schmidly***, 738 F.3d 1196, 1204 (10th Cir.2013); ***Perfect 10, Inc. v. Amazon.com, Inc.***, 508 F.3d 1146, 1172 (9th Cir.2007); ***Bridgeport Music, Inc. v. WB Music Corp.***, 508 F.3d 394, 398 (6th Cir.2007); ***Perfect 10, Inc. v. Visa Int'l Serv.***, 494 F.3d 788, 795 (9th Cir.2007).

§501(a)—Vicarious Infringement

Sony Corp. v. Universal City Studios, Inc., 464 U.S. 417, 434-35 (1984). "The Copyright Act does not expressly render anyone liable for infringement committed by another. In contrast, the Patent Act expressly brands anyone who 'actively induces infringement of a patent' as an infringer, and further imposes liability on certain individuals labeled 'contributory' infringers. The absence of such express language in the copyright statute does not preclude the imposition of liability for copyright infringements on certain parties who have not themselves engaged in the infringing activity. For vicarious liability is imposed in virtually all areas of the law, and the concept of contributory infringement is merely a species of the broader problem of identifying the circumstances in which it is just to hold one individual accountable for the actions of another."

Broadcast Music, Inc. v. Meadowlake, Ltd., 754 F.3d 353, 354 (6th Cir.2014). "A restaurant played live and recorded music without permission of the copyright holders. At stake is whether the Copyright Act imposes vicarious liability on the owners of the restaurant for the infringement. [¶] The one wrinkle in the case, and the key source of [D-owner's] appeal, is that he did not perform any of the copyrighted music. [¶] [D-owner] is vicariously liable for the pervasive copyright infringement at his restaurant. *At 355:* It makes no difference that [D-owner's son], not [D-owner], managed the restaurant from day to day. What matters is whether [D-owner] had 'the *right* and *ability*' to supervise the infringement, not whether he in fact supervised it. [¶] It makes no difference that [D-owner] claims to have known nothing about the infringing performances. A defendant's ignorance about the infringement or the performances does not blunt vicarious liability. [¶] What, finally, of the reality that [D-owner] owns the restaurant through a limited liability company? In one sense, the form of the business makes a difference. The legal structure of a business—corporation, limited liability company, partnership, what have you—may affect whether a defendant satisfies the test for vicarious liability in the first place. Business form might affect a defendant's right to police the infringement or his financial interest in the infringement. But this case involves none of these complications. [D-owner] does not suggest that the structure of his business sapped his authority over, or dulled his financial interest in, the prohibited performances. [¶] In another sense, however, the form of the business does not make a difference. Once a defendant meets the test for vicarious liability, the classification of his business does not (at least in general) exempt him from liability. It thus does not matter whether [state's] laws on limited liability companies would make [D-owner] personally liable for wrongs committed by or at his restaurant. Either way, [D-owner] profited from infringement at his restaurant while refusing to exercise his right to stop it. And so either way, [D-owner] remains vicariously liable."

Perfect 10, Inc. v. Amazon.com, Inc., 508 F.3d 1146, 1173 (9th Cir.2007). "[O]ne 'infringes vicariously by profiting from direct infringement while declining to exercise a right to stop or limit it.' [T]o succeed in imposing vicarious liability, a plaintiff must establish that the defendant exercises the requisite control over the direct infringer and that the defendant derives a direct financial benefit from the direct infringement. [T]he 'control' element of the vicarious liability test [is] the defendant's 'right and ability to supervise the direct infringer.' [A] defendant exercises control over a direct infringer when he has both a legal right to stop or limit the directly infringing conduct, as well as the practical ability to do so." *See also* ***EMI Christian Music Grp. v. MP3tunes, LLC***, 844 F.3d 79, 99, 121 U.S.P.Q.2d 1373, 1387 (2d Cir.2016); ***Leonard v. Stemtech Int'l***, 834 F.3d 376, 388 (3d Cir.2016); ***Diversey v. Schmidly***, 738 F.3d 1196, 1204 (10th Cir.2013); ***Bridgeport Music, Inc. v. WB Music Corp.***, 508 F.3d 394, 398 (6th Cir.2007).

Perfect 10, Inc. v. Visa Int'l Serv., 494 F.3d 788, 802 (9th Cir.2007). "Vicarious infringement is a concept related to, but distinct from, contributory infringement. Whereas contributory infringement is based on tort-law principles of enterprise liability and imputed intent, vicarious infringement's roots lie in the agency principles of *respondeat superior*. To state a claim for vicarious copyright infringement, a plaintiff must allege that the defendant has (1) the right and ability to supervise the infringing conduct and (2) a direct financial interest in the infringing activity. The Supreme Court has recently offered (in dictum) an alternate formulation of the test: 'One ... infringes vicariously by profiting from direct infringement while declining to exercise a right to stop or limit it.'"

§501(b)

John Wiley & Sons, Inc. v. DRK Photo, 882 F.3d 394, 414-15 (2d Cir.2018). "The statute does not define the phrase 'beneficial owner,' and the circumstances in which a person or entity becomes a beneficial owner with a cause of action for infringement have not been explored by our Court in much detail. The paradigmatic—and only—example of an approved 'beneficial owner' suit is set forth in the legislative history of the Copyright Act, which describes the term 'beneficial owner' as 'includ[ing], for example, an author who had parted with legal title to the copyright in exchange for percentage royalties based on sales or license fees.' Our Court has endorsed this example and explained that the beneficial ownership provision protects a person from having his or her equitable interest in a copyright 'diluted or lessened by a wrongdoer's infringement,' affording the holder of the equitable interest the right to seek damages under the Act. [¶] We have not had occasion to decide whether beneficial ownership may extend beyond the circumstance of an author transferring exclusive rights in exchange for royalty payments. ... At least one limit is readily supplied by the Act itself, which recognizes a cause of action only in the 'beneficial owner of an *exclusive right*.' Accordingly, at most, a person would become a 'beneficial owner' for purposes of §501(b) upon obtaining an equitable interest in an *exclusive* right under a copyright. It is therefore not enough that a putative beneficial owner obtains a mere interest in a copyright, even if that interest is valuable. The interest must be one that derives its value directly from another person's use of an exclusive right, such that the interest is necessarily 'diluted' by infringement."

Authors Guild, Inc. v. HathiTrust, 755 F.3d 87, 94 (2d Cir.2014). "[W]e consider whether [seven] authors' associations have standing to assert infringement claims on behalf of their members. [¶] [Section] 501 of 'the Copyright Act does not permit copyright holders to choose third parties to bring suits on their behalf.' Accordingly, we agree with the district court that [three] associations lack standing to bring suit on behalf of their members, and they were properly dismissed from the suit. [¶] The remaining four authors' associations ... assert that foreign law confers upon them certain exclusive rights to enforce the copyrights of their foreign members (an assertion that [Ds do] not contest on this appeal). These four associations do have standing to bring suit on behalf of their members."

Smith v. Casey, 741 F.3d 1236, 1238 (11th Cir. 2014). "At issue in this appeal is whether the author of a musical composition who assigned his rights in exchange for royalties may rely for purposes of standing to sue for infringement under the Copyright Act on a registration his publisher filed. *At 1241-42:* To our knowledge, each of our sister circuits to have confronted the situation has agreed that an author who assigns his legal rights to a work in exchange for royalties from its exploitation has a beneficial interest sufficient for statutory standing under §501(b). By contrast, an author who creates a work within the scope of her employment under a 'work for hire' agreement lacks statutory standing to maintain an infringement suit." Held: Yes, the author has standing to sue. *See also* ***Batiste v. Island Records Inc.***, 179 F.3d 217, 220 & n.2 (5th Cir.1999); ***Moran v. London Records, Ltd.***, 827 F.2d 180, 183 (7th Cir.1987); ***Cortner v. Israel***, 732 F.2d 267, 271 (2d Cir.1984).

Davis v. Blige, 505 F.3d 90, 99 (2d Cir.2007). "[I]t is a right that may be exercised independently of co-owners; a joint owner is not required to join his other co-owners in an action for infringement. [¶] An owner may also convey his interest in prosecuting accrued causes of action for infringement. [¶] An owner may not, however, convey the interests of his fellow co-owners without their express written consent, even if the transferee has no notice of the non-consenting owners' interest." *But see* ***Silvers v. Sony Pictures Entm't, Inc.***, this page.

Silvers v. Sony Pictures Entm't, Inc., 402 F.3d 881, 890 (9th Cir.2005). "The bare assignment of an accrued cause of action is impermissible under ... §501(b). Because that is all [copyright owner] conveyed to [P], [P] was not entitled to institute and may not maintain this action against [D] for alleged infringement of the copyright...." *See also* ***John Wiley & Sons, Inc. v. DRK Photo***, 882 F.3d 394, 413-14 (2d Cir. 2018) (conveyance of interest in images for registration purposes coupled with bare right to sue for infringement is insufficient legal ownership to maintain infringement action); ***DRK Photo v. McGraw-Hill Global Educ. Holdings, LLC***, 870 F.3d 978, 985 (9th Cir.2017) (purported transfer of legal title coupled with transfer of accrued claims does not confer standing when transaction, in substance and effect, merely transfers bare right to sue). *But see* ***Davis v. Blige***, this page.

Warren v. Fox Family Worldwide, Inc., 328 F.3d 1136, 1144 (9th Cir.2003). "Only the Seventh Circuit has addressed [the] specific issue [of payment of royalties in a work-for-hire relationship], finding that, absent an express grant of rights, a creator of a work for

17 U.S.C. §501

hire *cannot* be a beneficial owner. … The [Seventh Circuit] held that the legislative history indicating beneficial ownership where an assignment is made in exchange for royalties has no bearing on the work-for hire situation where no 'assignment' takes place. Therefore, that the legislative history to the [Copyright] Act mentioned only the 'assignment' example 'supports the conclusion that Congress did not intend to extend the concept of beneficial ownership to include an employee in a work-made-for-hire arrangement.' [¶] We conclude that the statutory language of the Act supports the Seventh Circuit's analysis."

Yount v. Acuff Rose-Opryland, 103 F.3d 830, 834 (9th Cir.1996). "[P] points to [§501(b)] which allows beneficial owners of a right under a copyright to sue for its infringement and says that the provision indicates that Congress intended to protect authors' royalty interests. However, that provision only indicates an intent to allow every beneficial owner to protect his interests, just in case the legal owner is not doing so. In other words, because an infringer may well injure those who have rights to royalties, standing has been conferred upon them. That, however, has no special reference to authors. It protects anyone who may own a right to royalties, but a determination of who those individuals may be in a given case is … a question of state law."

Bandai Inc. v. Bally Midway Mfg., 775 F.2d 70, 74 (3d Cir.1985). An "assignee [is] the legal owner, and ha[s] standing in this capacity despite the beneficial owner's right to have legal ownership reassigned." *See also* ***Itar-Tass Russian News Agency v. Russian Kurier, Inc.***, 42 U.S.P.Q.2d 1810, 1816 (S.D.N.Y.1997), *rev'd in part on other grounds*, 153 F.3d 82 (2d Cir.1998).

Motta v. Samuel Weiser, Inc., 768 F.2d 481, 484 (1st Cir.1985). "If a plaintiff is not the author of the copyrighted work then he or she must establish a proprietary right through the chain of title in order to support a valid claim to the copyright. Absent this showing, a plaintiff does not have standing to bring an action under the Copyright Act."

Fisher v. United Feature Syndicate, Inc., 37 F.Supp.2d 1213, 1217 (D.Colo.1999), *aff'd*, 203 F.3d 834 (10th Cir.2000). "'[A] copyright owner can assign its copyright but, if the accrued causes of action are not expressly included in the assignment, the assignee will not be able to prosecute them.'"

Ocasek v. Hegglund, 116 F.R.D. 154, 157 (D.Wyo. 1987). While "ASCAP bears the primary responsibility for enforcing its members' copyrights and has authority to bring enforcing lawsuits on behalf of its members, it must remain a non-exclusive licensee and, therefore, cannot bring the suit in its own name." *See also* ***Bourne Co. v. Hunter Country Club, Inc.***, 990 F.2d 934, 937 (7th Cir.1993).

Broadcast Music, Inc. v. Peppermint Club, Inc., 229 U.S.P.Q. 534, 537 (N.D.Ohio 1985). "There is no requirement in §501 that a plaintiff must sue all infringers who may be liable. It is evident that a copyright infringement action is akin to a tort action in that all infringers may be jointly and severally liable. *At 538:* 'A well established principle of copyright law is that a person who violates any of the exclusive rights of the copyright owner is an infringer, including persons who can be considered related or vicarious infringers….'"

Hayt v. U.S., 27 U.S.P.Q.2d 1386, 1390 (Fed.Cl. 1993). "Because Congress did not, although it clearly could have, include *both* legal and beneficial owners in the definition of 'owner' in [28 U.S.C.] §1498(b), as it did in 17 U.S.C. §501(b), this court cannot of its own volition read in the additional term, particularly not if this would extend the government's waiver of sovereign immunity."

Defense—Copyright Misuse

Apple Inc. v. Psystar Corp., 658 F.3d 1150, 1154-55 (9th Cir.2011). "[D's] main contention of misuse is aimed at [P's] requirement that licensees of [software] run their copies only on [P's] computers. [D] contends that this language barring use of [P's] software on non-[P] computers impermissibly extends the reach of [P's] copyright and constitutes misuse. We conclude that the district court correctly ruled that [P] had not engaged in copyright misuse. [T]his is principally because its licensing agreement was intended to require the operating system to be used on the computer it was designed to operate, and it did not prevent others from developing their own computer or operating systems. These licensing agreements were thus appropriately used to prevent infringement and control use of the copyrighted material. *At 1157:* Copyright misuse is a judicially crafted affirmative defense to copyright infringement, derived from the longstanding existence of such a defense in patent litigation. The patent misuse defense was originally recognized by the Supreme Court in 1942, in holding that the owner of the patent on a salt tablet machine could not require licensees to use only unpatented salt tablets sold by the patent owner. The Court held that this improper tying of a patented product and an unpatented product constituted misuse, and prohibited the patent holder from maintaining infringement actions until the patent holder ceased misuse of the patent. [¶] We have … applied the [copyright-misuse] doctrine sparingly. The doctrine did not apply … when there had been no allegation of copyright infringement. [W]e [have also] observed that the plaintiffs who sought to enjoin unlicensed use of copyrighted works were entitled to do so because they were not seeking to extend a copyright monopoly to other products or works. We described the purpose of the defense as preventing holders of copyrights 'from leveraging their limited monopoly to allow them control of areas outside the monopoly.' *At 1159:* While copyright owners may choose to simply exclude others from their work, i.e. not to transfer their rights, … courts have long held that copyright holders may also use their limited monopoly to leverage the right to use their work on the acceptance of specific conditions…. [¶] The copyright misuse doctrine does not prohibit using conditions to control use of copyrighted material, but it does prevent copyright holders from using the conditions to stifle competition." *See also* ***Lasercomb Am., Inc. v. Reynolds***, 911 F.2d 970, 976-77 (4th Cir.1990).

Defense—Illegal Use

Dream Games v. PC Onsite, 561 F.3d 983, 991-92 (9th Cir.2009). "[I]llegal operation of a copyrightable work neither deprives the work of copyright protection nor precludes generally available remedies. If work that contains illegal content is copyrightable, then a work that contains legal content, but which may be used for illegal purposes is surely copyrightable. The same holds true for works that are capable of illegal uses in geographically limited areas. [¶] Thus, illegal operation of an otherwise copyrightable work does not deprive the work of copyright protection, nor is it a defense to infringement."

Defense—Independent Creation

JCW Invs. v. Novelty, Inc., 482 F.3d 910, 915-16 (7th Cir.2007). "If the inference of copying is drawn from proof of access and substantial similarity, it can be rebutted if the alleged copier can show that she instead independently created the allegedly infringing work. A defendant independently created a work if it created its own work without copying anything or if it copied something other than the plaintiff's copyrighted work. [¶] [A] reasonable possibility of access can be established under the corporate receipt doctrine, under which: if the defendant is a corporation, the fact that one employee of the corporation has possession of plaintiff's work should warrant a finding that another employee (who composed defendant's work) had access to plaintiff's work, where by reason of the physical propinquity between the employees the latter has the opportunity to view the work in the possession of the former." (Internal quotes omitted.) *See also* ***Jones v. Blige***, 558 F.3d 485, 492-93 (6th Cir.2009).

§502. REMEDIES FOR INFRINGEMENT: INJUNCTIONS

(a) Any court having jurisdiction of a civil action arising under this title may, subject to the provisions of section 1498 of title 28, grant temporary and final injunctions on such terms as it may deem reasonable to prevent or restrain infringement of a copyright.

(b) Any such injunction may be served anywhere in the United States on the person enjoined; it shall be operative throughout the United States and shall be enforceable, by proceedings in contempt or otherwise, by any United States court having jurisdiction of that person. The clerk of the court granting the injunction shall, when requested by any other court in which enforcement of the injunction is sought, transmit promptly to the other court a certified copy of all the papers in the case on file in such clerk's office.

History of 17 U.S.C. §502: Oct. 19, 1976, P.L. 94-553, §101, 90 Stat. 2584. See also FRCP 65.

ANNOTATIONS

Generally

Suntrust Bank v. Houghton Mifflin Co., 268 F.3d 1257, 1265 (11th Cir.2001). "While injunctive relief may be particularly appropriate in cases involving simple copying or 'piracy' of a copyrighted work, the Supreme Court has cautioned that such relief may not be consistent with the goals of copyright law in cases in which the alleged infringer of the copyright has a colorable fair-use defense."

Olan Mills, Inc. v. Linn Photo Co., 23 F.3d 1345, 1349 (8th Cir.1994). "The power to grant injunctive relief is not limited to registered copyrights, or even to those copyrights which give rise to an infringement action."

Modtech Inc. v. Designed Facilities Constr. Inc., 51 U.S.P.Q.2d 1206, 1207 (C.D.Cal.1999). Held: Plaintiff may enjoin infringement of derivative works under §502.

Georgia TV Co. v. TV News Clips, Inc., 718 F.Supp. 939, 945 (N.D.Ga.1989). "The fact that [P's] future news broadcasts are not presently created does not preclude injunctive relief against [Ds] videotaping these copyrighted broadcasts because ... §502(a) provides for injunctions to prevent infringement of a copyright and not necessarily the registered copyright that gives rise to the action."

Permanent

Capitol Records, Inc. v. Thomas-Rasset, 692 F.3d 899, 906 (8th Cir.2012). "[Ps] urged the district court to amend the judgment to enjoin [D] from making any of their sound recordings available for distribution to the public through an online media distribution system. The district court declined to do so on the ground that the Copyright Act does not provide an exclusive right to making recordings available. [¶] [A] district court has authority to issue a broad injunction in cases where 'a proclivity for unlawful conduct has been shown.' The district court is even permitted to 'enjoin certain otherwise lawful conduct' where 'the defendant's conduct has demonstrated that prohibiting only unlawful conduct would not effectively protect the plaintiff's rights against future encroachment.' [¶] [D's] willful infringement and subsequent efforts to conceal her actions certainly show 'a proclivity for unlawful conduct.' *At 907:* [W]e conclude that the district court erred ... by concluding that the broader injunction requested by [Ps] was impermissible as a matter of law. An injunction against making recordings available was lawful and appropriate under the circumstances, even accepting the district court's interpretation of the Copyright Act."

Bridgeport Music, Inc. v. Justin Combs Publ'g, 507 F.3d 470, 492 (6th Cir.2007). "When a district court grants a permanent injunction, this court reviews its factual findings for clear error, legal conclusions de novo, and the scope of injunctive relief for an abuse of discretion."

Christopher Phelps & Assocs. v. Galloway, 492 F.3d 532, 543 (4th Cir.2007). "In ***eBay*** [***Inc. v. MercExchange, L.L.C.***, 547 U.S. 388 (2006)], the Supreme Court rejected any notion that 'an injunction automatically follows a determination that a copyright has been infringed.' The Supreme Court reaffirmed the traditional showing that a plaintiff must make to obtain a permanent injunction in any type of case, including a patent or copyright case: 'A plaintiff must demonstrate: (1) that it has suffered an irreparable injury; (2) that remedies available at law, such as monetary damages, are inadequate to compensate for that injury; (3) that, considering the balance of hardships between the plaintiff and defendant, a remedy in equity is warranted; and (4) that the public interest would not be disserved by a permanent injunction.' Moreover, the Court reiterated that even upon this showing, whether to grant the injunction still remains in the 'equitable discretion' of the court. *At 545:* [W]ith respect to [D's] house as one manifestation of [P's] design, arising from a single infringing transaction, [P] is limited to the other relief provided in this case [in lieu of a permanent injunction against the sale of the house]. Upon satisfaction of that relief, [D] will be entitled to peaceful ownership of the house, with good and marketable title." *See also* ***CoxCom, Inc. v. Chaffee***, 536 F.3d 101, 112 (1st Cir.2008); ***Peter Letterese & Assocs. v. World Inst. of Scientology Enters.***, 533 F.3d 1287, 1323 (11th Cir.2008).

Preliminary

Salinger v. Colting, 607 F.3d 68, 77 (2d Cir.2010). "'According to well-established principles of equity, a plaintiff seeking a permanent injunction must satisfy a four-factor test before a court may grant such relief. A plaintiff must demonstrate: (1) that it has suffered an irreparable injury; (2) that remedies available at law, such as monetary damages, are inadequate to compensate for that injury; (3) that, considering the balance of hardships between the plaintiff and defendant, a remedy in equity is warranted; and (4) that the public interest would not be disserved by a permanent injunction.' [¶] We hold today that [***eBay Inc. v. MercExchange, L.L.C.***, 547 U.S. 388 (2006),] applies with equal force (a) to preliminary injunctions (b) that are issued for alleged copyright infringement." *See also* ***Flava Works, Inc. v. Gunter***, 689 F.3d 754, 755 (7th Cir.2012); ***Flexible Lifeline Sys. v. Precision Lift, Inc.***, 654 F.3d 989, 996-98 (9th Cir.2011). *But see* ***Mercado-Salinas v. Bart Enters. Int'l***, 671 F.3d 12, 19 & n.7 (1st Cir.2011) (using likelihood of success on the merits and discussing, but not deciding, whether presumption of irreparable harm survives post-***eBay***); ***Kern River Gas Transmission Co. v. Coastal Corp.***, 899 F.2d 1458,

1462 (5th Cir.1990) (four-factor test under §502 requires P to establish substantial likelihood of success on the merits); ***Microsoft Corp. v. Action Software***, 136 F.Supp.2d 735, 738-39 (N.D.Ohio 2001) (because injunction against infringing activity is authorized by statute, P need only show strong likelihood of success on the merits).

§503. REMEDIES FOR INFRINGEMENT: IMPOUNDING & DISPOSITION OF INFRINGING ARTICLES

(a)(1) At any time while an action under this title is pending, the court may order the impounding, on such terms as it may deem reasonable—

(A) of all copies or phonorecords claimed to have been made or used in violation of the exclusive right of the copyright owner;

(B) of all plates, molds, matrices, masters, tapes, film negatives, or other articles by means of which such copies or phonorecords may be reproduced; and

(C) of records documenting the manufacture, sale, or receipt of things involved in any such violation, provided that any records seized under this subparagraph shall be taken into the custody of the court.

(2) For impoundments of records ordered under paragraph (1)(C), the court shall enter an appropriate protective order with respect to discovery and use of any records or information that has been impounded. The protective order shall provide for appropriate procedures to ensure that confidential, private, proprietary, or privileged information contained in such records is not improperly disclosed or used.

(3) The relevant provisions of paragraphs (2) through (11) of section 34(d) of the Trademark Act (15 U.S.C. 1116(d)(2) through (11)) shall extend to any impoundment of records ordered under paragraph (1)(C) that is based upon an ex parte application, notwithstanding the provisions of rule 65 of the Federal Rules of Civil Procedure. Any references in paragraphs (2) through (11) of section 34(d) of the Trademark Act to section 32 of such Act shall be read as references to section 501 of this title, and references to use of a counterfeit mark in connection with the sale, offering for sale, or distribution of goods or services shall be read as references to infringement of a copyright.

(b) As part of a final judgment or decree, the court may order the destruction or other reasonable disposition of all copies or phonorecords found to have been made or used in violation of the copyright owner's exclusive rights, and of all plates, molds, matrices, masters, tapes, film negatives, or other articles by means of which such copies or phonorecords may be reproduced.

History of 17 U.S.C. §503: Oct. 19, 1976, P.L. 94-553, §101, 90 Stat. 2585; Oct. 13, 2008, P.L. 110-403, §102(a), 122 Stat. 4258; Dec. 9, 2010, P.L. 111-295, §6(d), 124 Stat. 3181.

ANNOTATIONS

First Tech. Safety Sys. v. Depinet, 11 F.3d 641, 647 (6th Cir.1993). "The Copyright Act does not provide a standard for the district court's decision to grant an order of impoundment; rather, [17 U.S.C.] §503 leaves this decision to the discretion of the district court.... *At 649:* The parts of the district court's order allowing [P] to seize [Ds'] business records were not authorized by ... §503(a). The language of §503(a) only authorizes the impoundment of goods that infringe plaintiff's copyrights and articles that can be used to copy those infringing goods. ... Moreover, §503 was not meant to give the copyright holder a means to preserve evidence generally. *At 652:* [T]he district court abused its discretion in issuing the ex parte order of inventory and impoundment. The court was required to apply the standard provided in [FRCP] 65(b) for granting ex parte relief, because neither ... §503(a) nor the Copyright Rules authorizes the copying of business records, which the district court's order permitted." *See also* ***Warner Bros. v. Dae Rim Trading, Inc.***, 877 F.2d 1120, 1126 (2d Cir.1989).

Rogers v. Koons, 960 F.2d 301, 313 (2d Cir.1992). "[T]he turn-over order of the artist's copy is an equitable remedy issued under the broad powers vested in a trial judge under ... §503(b). ... We see no abuse of the district court's discretion in directing turn-over and ... the contempt order for the direct violation of the turn-over order was entirely proper."

Century Home Entm't, Inc. v. Laser Beat, Inc., 859 F.Supp. 636, 638 (E.D.N.Y.1994). It "is the norm in this district that where a danger of destruction or hiding of the evidence exists to grant *ex parte* orders of seizure."

Paramount Pictures Corp. v. Doe, 821 F.Supp. 82, 85 (E.D.N.Y.1993). The "impoundment may in appropriate circumstances occur at the commencement of an action for copyright infringement. *At 86:* Because any impoundment necessarily entails a seizure of property and invasion of privacy ..., the invocation of this Court's discretionary powers under §503(a) must involve appropriate safeguards for a defendant's constitutional rights. *At 87 n.4:* Read together, the rules are inconsistent with the right to impoundment described in §503: the rules describe preliminary impoundment as a mandatory right conditioned only on compliance with the rules, while §503 clearly states that the right to impoundment is left to the sound discretion of the court. Since the right to impoundment is a substantive right and not simply a matter of procedure the standard set forth by statutory law governs. *At 87:* [C]ompliance with the Supreme Court [Copyright Rules] is not a sufficient basis on which to justify an ex parte impoundment under §503(a)."

§504. REMEDIES FOR INFRINGEMENT: DAMAGES & PROFITS

(a) In general.—Except as otherwise provided by this title, an infringer of copyright is liable for either—

(1) the copyright owner's actual damages and any additional profits of the infringer, as provided by subsection (b); or

(2) statutory damages, as provided by subsection (c).

(b) Actual damages and profits.—The copyright owner is entitled to recover the actual damages suffered by him or her as a result of the infringement, and any profits of the infringer that are attributable to the infringement and are not taken into account in computing the actual damages. In establishing the infringer's profits, the copyright owner is required to present proof only of the infringer's gross revenue, and the infringer is required to prove his or her deductible expenses and the elements of profit attributable to factors other than the copyrighted work.

(c) Statutory damages—

(1) Except as provided by clause (2) of this subsection, the copyright owner may elect, at any time before final judgment is rendered, to recover, instead of actual damages and profits, an award of statutory damages for all infringements involved in the action, with respect to any one work, for which any one infringer is liable individually, or for which any two or more infringers are liable jointly and severally, in a sum of not less than $750 or more than $30,000 as the court considers just. For the purposes of this subsection, all the parts of a compilation or derivative work constitute one work.

(2) In a case where the copyright owner sustains the burden of proving, and the court finds, that infringement was committed willfully, the court in its discretion may increase the award of statutory damages to a sum of not more than $150,000. In a case where the infringer sustains the burden of proving, and the court finds, that such infringer was not aware and had no reason to believe that his or her acts constituted an infringement of copyright, the court in its discretion may reduce the award of statutory damages to a sum of not less than $200. The court shall remit statutory damages in any case where an infringer believed and had reasonable grounds for believing that his or her use of the copyrighted work was a fair use under section 107, if the infringer was: (i) an employee or agent of a nonprofit educational institution, library, or archives acting within the scope of his or her employment who, or such institution, library, or archives itself, which infringed by reproducing the work in copies or phonorecords; or (ii) a public broadcasting entity which or a person who, as a regular part of the nonprofit activities of a public broadcasting entity (as defined in section 118(f)) infringed by performing a published nondramatic literary work or by reproducing a transmission program embodying a performance of such a work.

(3)(A) In a case of infringement, it shall be a rebuttable presumption that the infringement was committed willfully for purposes of determining relief if the violator, or a person acting in concert with the violator, knowingly provided or knowingly caused to be provided materially false contact information to a domain name registrar, domain name registry, or other domain name registration authority in registering, maintaining, or renewing a domain name used in connection with the infringement.

(B) Nothing in this paragraph limits what may be considered willful infringement under this subsection.

(C) For purposes of this paragraph, the term "domain name" has the meaning given that term in section 45 of the Act entitled "An Act to provide for the registration and protection of trademarks used in commerce, to carry out the provisions of certain international conventions, and for other purposes" approved July 5, 1946 (commonly referred to as the "Trademark Act of 1946"; 15 U.S.C. 1127).

(d) Additional damages in certain cases.—In any case in which the court finds that a defendant proprietor of an establishment who claims as a defense that its activities were exempt under section 110(5) did not have reasonable grounds to believe that its use of a copyrighted work was exempt under such section, the plaintiff shall be entitled to, in addition to any award of damages under this section, an additional award of two times the amount of the license fee that the proprietor of the establishment concerned should have paid the plaintiff for such use during the preceding period of up to 3 years.

History of 17 U.S.C. §504: Oct. 19, 1976, P.L. 94-553, §101, 90 Stat. 2585; Oct. 31, 1988, P.L. 100-568, §10(b), 102 Stat. 2860; Nov. 13, 1997, P.L. 105-80, §12(a)(13), 111 Stat. 1535; Oct. 27, 1998, P.L. 105-298, §204, 112 Stat. 2833; Dec. 9, 1999, P.L. 106-160, §2, 113 Stat. 1774; Dec. 23, 2004, P.L. 108-482, §203, 118 Stat. 3916; Dec. 9, 2010, P.L. 111-295, §6(f)(2), 124 Stat. 3181.

ANNOTATIONS

Generally

BUC Int'l v. International Yacht Council Ltd., 517 F.3d 1271, 1276 (11th Cir.2008). "[Ds] argue on appeal that they are entitled to credit against the ... award against them for the settlement amounts ... paid by the settling defendants. [Ds] predicate their request on the one-satisfaction rule.... The rule generally provides that a plaintiff is entitled to only one satisfaction for a single injury, such that amounts received in settlement from an alleged tortfeasor are credited against judgments for the same injury against non-settling tortfeasors. *At 1277:* [Ds] are not seeking contribution by invoking the one-satisfaction rule. A right of 'contribution' allows a defendant 'to demand that another who is jointly responsible for a third party's injury supply part of what is required to compensate the third party.' ... The one-satisfaction rule, by contrast, operates to prevent double recovery, or the overcompensation of a plaintiff for a single injury. Although similar, the theories do not always overlap. For example, the one-satisfaction rule has been applied even where a right to contribution does not lie. ... The one-satisfaction rule operates against plaintiffs and requires nothing of joint tortfeasors, whereas the right to contribution requires actual, and not just potential, joint tortfeasors to share liability. *At 1278:* [W]e join the Second Circuit in holding that the rule does indeed apply to infringement actions under the Copyright Act."

Ortiz-Gonzalez v. Fonovisa, 277 F.3d 59, 64 (1st Cir.2002). "Discretion as to the judgment or the need for a hearing on damages is vested with the district court."

Lifted Research Grp. v. Behdad, Inc., No. 08-390 (CKK) (D.D.C.2010) (memo op.; 6-30-10). "[T]he Court agrees that '[a] plaintiff may be awarded statutory damages under both the Copyright Act and the Lanham Act where the defendant's act simultaneously infringed the plaintiff's copyright and its trademark ... because the two statutory schemes serve different public policies, and protect against and remedy different injuries.'" *See also* ***Nintendo of Am., Inc. v. Dragon Pac. Int'l***, 40 F.3d 1007, 1010-11 (9th Cir.1994); ***Microsoft Corp. v. Nop***, 549 F.Supp.2d 1233, 1238-39 (E.D.Cal.2008); ***Microsoft Corp. v. McGee***, 490 F.Supp.2d 874, 881-82 (S.D.Ohio 2007); ***Microsoft Corp. v. Sellers***, 411 F.Supp.2d 913, 921-22 (E.D.Tenn.2006).

Spooner v. EEN, Inc., No. 08-cv-262-P-S (D.Me. 2010) (slip op.; 5-11-10). "[I]n the context of awarding statutory damages, courts have declared that separate copyrights are not distinct works unless they can live their own copyright life. In determining whether a work lives its own copyright life, the salient question is whether each expression has an independent economic value and is, in itself, viable. [¶] In arguing that he is entitled to two statutory damage awards because [D's] commercial simultaneously infringed on the ... sound recording and musical composition, [P] has acknowledged that this case is unusual and presents an issue of first impression for the courts of this district. Notably, [P] has been unable to point the Court to any case in which a single plaintiff has received the type of doubled statutory award for a sound recording infringement that he now seeks. ... In the situation presented here in which the same person holds the copyright to both the sound recording and musical composition at issue, this type of per work doubling of damages seems illogical. [¶] [D's] infringement of the ... sound recordings involved overlapping copyrights but infringed on only one work for purposes of statutory damages under ... §504(c)(1)." (Internal quotes omitted.)

§504(a)

Gaylord v. U.S., 678 F.3d 1339, 1342 (Fed.Cir.2012). "[P] argues that the trial court erred as a matter of law by holding that royalty damages are not available in copyright cases. *At 1343:* We conclude that the methods used to determine 'actual damages' under the copyright damages statute ... are appropriate for measuring the copyright owner's loss. When ... the plaintiff cannot show 'lost sales, lost opportunities to license, or diminution in the value of the copyright,' many circuits award actual damages based on 'the fair market value of a license covering the defendant's use.' The value of this license should be calculated based on a hypothetical, arms-length negotiation between the parties.

At 1344: The trial court legally erred in this case by failing to calculate the fair market value of a license based on a hypothetical negotiation between [P] and [D]. In applying the so-called 'zone of reasonableness' test, the court improperly limited its inquiry to [D's] past licenses and, as a result, erroneously capped [P's] maximum damages without considering other evidence supporting a higher award."

Bucklew v. Hawkins, Ash, Baptie & Co., 329 F.3d 923, 931 (7th Cir.2003). "A copyright owner can sue for his losses or for the infringer's profits, but not for the sum of the two amounts. That would be double counting. ... The copyright owner is allowed to waive damages (lost profits) and sue for the infringer's gain. Copyright infringement unlike patent infringement is an intentional tort, and by forcing the infringer to disgorge his profit should it exceed the copyright owner's loss the law discourages infringement and encourages the would-be infringer to transact with the copyright owner rather than 'steal' the copyrighted work. But there is no basis in the law for requiring the infringer to give up more than his gain when it exceeds the copyright owners' loss."

Davis v. Gap, Inc., 246 F.3d 152, 159 (2d Cir.2001). "Section 504 imposes two categories of compensatory damages. Taking care to specify that double recovery is not permitted where the two categories overlap, the statute provides for the recovery of both the infringer's profits and the copyright owner's 'actual damages.' It is important that these two categories of compensation have different justifications and are based on different financial data. The award of the infringer's profits examines the facts only from the infringer's point of view. If the infringer has earned a profit, this award makes him disgorge the profit to insure that he not benefit from his wrongdoing. The award of the owner's actual damages looks at the facts from the point of view of [the] copyright owner; it undertakes to compensate the owner for any harm he suffered by reason of the infringer's illegal act." *See also* ***Deltak, Inc. v. Advanced Sys.***, 767 F.2d 357, 363 (7th Cir.1985).

§504(b)—Actual Damages

Leonard v. Stemtech Int'l, 834 F.3d 376, 392 (3d Cir.2016). Expert "testified that a 'premium' or multiplier of three to five times the benchmark [damages] figure was warranted to account for the scarcity, and a multiplier of 3.75 to 8.75 times the benchmark was appropriate to account for the exclusivity of [P's] images during the infringement period.... *At 393:* The few district courts to consider the use of punitive multipliers have concluded that such use is improper under the Copyright Act because the value of what was illegally taken is not determined by multiplying it. These courts rejected the use of a multiplier or 'fee for unauthorized usage' over and above what would otherwise represent a fair and reasonable licensing fee for the infringed material as a component of the actual damages calculation. We agree with the reasoning of these district courts that, under the Copyright Act, an actual damages award may not include such a punitive component. We also agree with [P] that this case does not involve the use of a multiplier to penalize unauthorized use. Rather, the record demonstrates that the multiplier here was used to calculate fair market value. [¶] [Expert's] fair market value calculation in this case had two components: the stock agency quotes and the adjustments to reflect the uniqueness of the images and the impact of [D's] usage. The multipliers here reflected a premium that, according to [expert], the market would find acceptable given the scarcity and exclusivity of the images as compared to the images for which he had secured rates for comparative purposes. The unrebutted evidence here showed that the fair market value calculation was complete only after these additional factors were applied. *At 394:* Because there is no evidence that the scarcity and exclusivity multipliers were punitive rather than valid factors for calculating fair market value, we cannot say that the verdict is based upon an improper consideration." (Internal quotes omitted.)

Bell v. Taylor, 827 F.3d 699, 709-10 (7th Cir.2016). "Without additional evidence, [P's] subjective belief as to the fair market value of his photo is not enough to prove damages. [¶] Likewise, the price that [P] listed on his website is not sufficiently concrete to show the fair market value of his photo. [P] never produced any evidence supporting his assertion that he has sold the photo for $200. [¶] [P] argues that [Ds] did not present any evidence contradicting [P's] affidavit or price listing. However, it was [P's] burden to prove damages, and [Ds] were not required to produce any evidence showing a lack of damages."

Gaylord v. U.S., 777 F.3d 1363, 1367-68 (Fed.Cir. 2015). "[T]he methods used to determine actual damages under the copyright damages statute, 17 U.S.C.

§504, are appropriate for measuring the copyright owner's loss under [28 U.S.C.] §1498(b). Consistent with the conclusions of other circuits that have considered the issue, we held that actual damages for copyright infringement may be based on a reasonable royalty representing the fair market value of a license covering the defendant's use. [¶] To calculate the fair market value, a court deciding a copyright case may use a tool familiar from patent law, without necessarily following every aspect of patent law's use of that tool. It may hypothesize a negotiation between the parties before the infringement occurred and determine the reasonable license fee on which a willing buyer and a willing seller would have agreed for the use taken by the infringer. Several cases have stressed the use of objective considerations in the determination of a copyrighted work's market value using that method. The court is not constrained to accept particular practices of the parties on either side—either to allow owners to charge what they would like to have charged if unconstrained by reality, ... or to shield infringers from paying fair market value for what they took.... [¶] Determining a reasonable royalty does not require mathematical exactness, but a reasonable approximation under the circumstances of a given case. Other circuits have recognized the often unavoidable uncertainties in establishing the fair market value of a reasonable license fee as well as the importance of avoiding undue speculation. Some difficulty in quantifying the damages attributable to the infringement should not bar recovery. [¶] The hypothetical-negotiation determination must be tied to the particular work at issue and its marketplace value—much as, in patent law, the determination must be tied to the particular patented technology and its footprint in the market. Different kinds of evidence may be relevant, as long as it is viewed for what it says about the work-specific value. For example, past arms-length licensing practices by the copyright owner or the infringer for similar uses and benchmark licenses by others in the industry may be useful. But the use of past licenses as evidence must always take account of economically relevant differences between the circumstances of those licenses and the circumstances of the matter in litigation—as we have said in the related patent-law context. Thus, in the copyright context, the unique features of a particular work (including its recognized stature and symbolic value) may be important in assessing the ultimate significance of past practices in licensing other works." (Internal quotes omitted.)

Oracle Corp. v. SAP AG, 765 F.3d 1081, 1088 (9th Cir.2014). "[W]e hold that a copyright plaintiff's unwillingness to grant a license to use its copyrighted work does not defeat its ability to recover hypothetical-license damages. *At 1093:* Although a copyright plaintiff need not demonstrate that it would have reached a licensing agreement with the infringer or present evidence of 'benchmark' agreements in order to recover hypothetical-license damages, it may be difficult for a plaintiff to establish the amount of such damages without undue speculation in the absence of such evidence. Here, because [P] has no history of granting similar licenses, and has not presented evidence of 'benchmark' licenses in the industry approximating the hypothetical license in question here, [P] faced an uphill battle. [¶] [P] bore the burden of proving the fair market value of the hypothetical license in question. We agree with the district court that [P] failed to provide sufficient objective evidence of the market value of the hypothetical license underpinning the jury's damages award."

Dash v. Mayweather, 731 F.3d 303, 312 (4th Cir. 2013). "Generally, the term 'actual damages' is 'broadly construed to favor victims of infringement.' [¶] Consistent with this approach, courts have recognized several methods for calculating the compensable loss suffered by a copyright owner as a result of infringement. It is generally accepted that 'the primary measure of recovery is the extent to which the market value of the copyrighted work at the time of the infringement has been injured or destroyed by the infringement.' The fair market value of a copyrighted work is derived from an objective, not a subjective, inquiry. [¶] Injury to a copyrighted work's market value can be measured in a variety of ways. The first possible measure is the amount of revenue that the copyright holder lost as a result of infringement, such as his own lost sales of the work. Another cognizable measure is the fair market value of the licensing 'fee the owner was entitled to charge for [the infringer's] use' of his copyrighted work. 'In order to make out his claim that he suffered actual damage because of the infringer's failure to pay the fee, the owner must show that the thing taken had a fair market value.' *At 313:* Regardless of the measure or combination of measures used to establish actual damages, a copyright holder asserting such damages 'must prove the existence of a causal connection between the alleged infringement and some loss of anticipated revenue.' Although the nature of actual damages will often require a court to 'engage in some degree of speculation,' ... the amount of damages sought cannot be based on 'undue speculation[]'.... In the summary judgment context, once a defendant has properly supported his claim that there are no actual damages resulting from infringement, the plaintiff must respond with nonspeculative evidence that such damages do, in fact, exist. [¶] Under the lost licensing fee theory, actual damages are generally calculated based on 'what a willing buyer would have been reasonably required to pay to a willing seller for [the] plaintiffs' work.' 'The question is not what the owner would have charged,' nor what the infringer might have been willing to pay. Rather, the objective inquiry focuses on the fair market value of the work as 'negotiat[ed] between a willing buyer and a willing seller' contemplating the use the infringer made. *At 316:* Like any other evidence, expert testimony ... will not preclude summary judgment unless it raises a genuine dispute concerning a material fact. By referencing [the work's] maximal value—without any actual mention of a minimum value—the [expert report] failed to satisfy this burden. *At 318:* Evidence of the owner's prior sale or licensing of copyrighted work will satisfy this burden [of showing fair-market value] when it is 'sufficiently concrete.' *At 319:* Although evidence of a copyright holder's own prior sale or licensing of copyrighted work can support the existence of actual damages under §504(b), such evidence is not required to defeat a motion for summary judgment. Otherwise, first-time copyright owners would never be able to overcome summary judgment of an actual damages claim. Rather, evidence of an owner's prior sales is but one way of measuring 'what a willing buyer would have been reasonably required to pay a willing seller' for the use that the infringer made. Evidence of licensing fees paid to other artists for the use of other works may, in some cases, be sufficient to support the conclusion that a copyright holder would have been entitled to such a fee for the use of his work; however, such evidence may properly be rejected as a measure of damages if it is too speculative." *See also* ***Leonard v. Stemtech Int'l***, 834 F.3d 376, 390-91 (3d Cir. 2016); ***Oracle Corp. v. SAP AG***, 765 F.3d 1081, 1087 (9th Cir.2014); ***McRoberts Software, Inc. v. Media 100, Inc.***, 329 F.3d 557, 566 (7th Cir.2003); ***Data Gen. Corp. v. Grumman Sys. Support Corp.***, 36 F.3d 1147, 1170 (1st Cir.1994), *overruled on other grounds*, ***Reed Elsevier, Inc. v. Muchnick***, 559 U.S. 154 (2010).

Thoroughbred Software Int'l v. Dice Corp., 488 F.3d 352, 358 (6th Cir.2007). "A plaintiff seeking actual damages 'must prove the existence of a causal connection between the ... alleged infringement and some loss of anticipated revenue.' *At 359-60:* [T]he causal connection between the unused infringing software and [P's] actual damages is that, under the Dealer Agreement, [D] should have paid [P] a license fee for each copy of the software. Thus, [D] is liable for the unpaid license fees for all the unauthorized copies it made, regardless of whether these copies were accessible to or used by [D's] customers. Consequently, the district court's finding that there were no actual damages for the copies that were unused and/or inaccessible to [D's] customers was erroneous. [¶] The lost license fee that the district court used to measure actual damages for the used software copies is also the proper measure of actual damages for the unused copies." *See also* ***MGE UPS Sys. v. GE Consumer & Indus.***, 622 F.3d 361, 366-67 (5th Cir.2010).

Polar Bear Prods. v. Timex Corp., 384 F.3d 700, 708 (9th Cir.2004). "Under §504(b), actual damages must be suffered 'as a result of the infringement,' and recoverable profits must be 'attributable to the infringement.' From the statutory language, it is apparent that a causal link between the infringement and the monetary remedy sought is a predicate to recovery of both actual damages and profits. [A] plaintiff in a §504(b) action must establish this causal connection, and that this requirement is akin to tort principles of causation and damages." *See also* ***MGE UPS Sys. v. GE Consumer & Indus.***, 622 F.3d 361, 366-67 (5th Cir. 2010).

§504(b)—Deductions

Three Boys Music Corp. v. Bolton, 212 F.3d 477, 487 (9th Cir.2000). "The Supreme Court held [in ***L.P. Larson, Jr., Co. v. Wm. Wrigley, Jr., Co.***, 277 U.S. 97 (1928),] that willful infringers could not deduct income taxes, but it left open the possibility that non-willful infringers could deduct their income taxes from the infringing profits. The circuits are split over whether non-willful infringers ... can deduct income taxes from their infringing profits. *At 488:* We uphold the district court's decision to allow non-willful infringers to deduct income taxes, but not [Net Operating Loss

(NOL)]. ... No court has ever found that NOL is a deductible expense under §504(b)."

In Design v. K-Mart Apparel Corp., 13 F.3d 559, 563 (2d Cir.1994). "Since the term 'profit' is not defined in the Copyright Act, the word has been assigned its usual meaning, such as the excess of return over expenditures realized from the conduct of a business or the gain derived from an investment represented by the difference between its selling price above its cost. *At 567:* [W]e include income tax expenses in the deductible overhead in determining a defendant's net profit."

New York Chinese TV Programs v. U.E. Enters., 19 U.S.P.Q.2d 1801, 1803 (S.D.N.Y.1991), *aff'd*, 954 F.2d 847 (2d Cir.1992). "The infringer may deduct only those expenses that he can show relate specifically to the infringing work. For example, overhead that is not directly attributable to the production of the infringing goods may not be subtracted from the infringer's profits. Moreover, 'when a defendant infringer's own failure to keep records results in uncertainty, all doubt must be resolved in favor of the plaintiff.'"

§504(b)—Prejudgment Interest

William A. Graham Co. v. Haughey, 646 F.3d 138, 145-46 (3d Cir.2011). "[Ds'] insistence that a plaintiff seeking to recover an infringer's profits ... should not receive interest because he 'has suffered no loss *at all*' is ... unpersuasive, for interest is just as appropriate to achieve full disgorgement as to ensure just compensation. [¶] We ... hold that prejudgment interest is available in copyright cases at the District Court's discretion, exercised in light of 'considerations of fairness.' *At 150-51:* We hold that the 'accrual' of a cause of action occurs at the moment at which each of its component elements has come into being as a matter of objective reality, such that an attorney with knowledge of all the facts could get it past a motion to dismiss for failure to state a claim. The federal discovery rule then operates in applicable cases to toll the running of the limitations period. Prejudgment interest, however, may be awarded in appropriate cases from the initial accrual date."

Bridgeport Music, Inc. v. Justin Combs Publ'g, 507 F.3d 470, 484-85 (6th Cir.2007). "The amount of compensatory damages that the jury awarded ... mistakenly included compounded, prejudgment interest. This Circuit has determined a jury verdict should not be remitted by a court unless it is beyond the maximum damages that the jury reasonably could find to be compensatory for a party's loss. An award must fall if, for example, it is beyond the range supportable by proof or is the result of a mistake. Here, it is evident that the jury award was the result of a mistake. ... Because [Ps] mistakenly asked for a damages award that included compounded prejudgment interest, and the jury mistakenly awarded [Ps] just that, we reverse this portion of the district court's order and remand so that the district court may offer [P] a remittitur in the amount of damages excluding compounded prejudgment interest." (Internal quotes omitted.)

Polar Bear Prods. v. Timex Corp., 384 F.3d 700, 716 (9th Cir.2004). We "conclude that prejudgment interest is available under the Copyright Act of 1976." *See also* ***Gaylord v. U.S.***, 678 F.3d 1339, 1345 (Fed.Cir. 2012).

§504(b)—Profits

Harper & Row, Publ'rs v. Nation Enters., 471 U.S. 539, 567 (1985). "With respect to apportionment of profits flowing from a copyright infringement, this Court has held that an infringer who commingles infringing and noninfringing elements 'must abide the consequences, unless he can make a separation of the profits so as to assure to the injured party all that justly belongs to him.' Similarly, once a copyright holder establishes with reasonable probability the existence of a causal connection between the infringement and a loss of revenue, the burden properly shifts to the infringer to show that this damage would have occurred had there been no taking of copyrighted expression." *See also* ***Montgomery v. Noga***, 168 F.3d 1282, 1294 (11th Cir.1999).

Dash v. Mayweather, 731 F.3d 303, 326 (4th Cir. 2013). "[W]hen the infringement occurs as a small part of a much larger work, the fact finder properly focuses not on the profit of the work overall, but only on the profit that the infringement contributes. *At 329-31:* [W]hether at the summary judgment stage or at trial, a plaintiff seeking profit damages has an affirmative duty to prove the defendant's gross revenue reasonably related to the infringement. This requires the plaintiff to prove (1) the amount of the claimed revenue streams, and (2) that there is some reasonable relationship between the infringement and those particular profit streams. Proving that the claimed profit streams are reasonably related to the infringement requires the plaintiff to (1) allege a conceivable connection between the infringement and the claimed revenues, and (2) offer nonspeculative evidence that a causal link exists. [¶] The first step, alleging a conceivable connection, is not an exacting standard. A proffered connection will be considered conceivable even if it is highly unlikely that the infringement actually contributed to the claimed revenues. However, in order for a conceivable connection to exist, the connection between the infringement and the revenues must be at least hypothetically possible. [¶] The plaintiff must also prove the existence of a causal link between the infringement and the level of the defendant's revenues. Once he has done so, the burden then shifts to the defendant to prove that those revenues are not actually attributable to the infringing aspects of the work. [¶] In the summary judgment context, a defendant can challenge the relationship between the claimed revenues and the infringement in any or all of three ways. First, the defendant can argue that the plaintiff cannot state a conceivable connection between the infringement and the claimed revenues. The plaintiff must respond to this challenge by arguing that some such connection exists. A defendant will be granted summary judgment on this basis only if it is not even hypothetically possible that the infringement could have affected the revenues, such as when the revenues were determined prior to the infringement. [¶] The second method by which a defendant can challenge the connection between the infringement and the claimed revenues on summary judgment is to argue that, although there may be a conceivable connection, the plaintiff has not presented sufficient evidence of a causal link between the infringement and the claimed revenues. If a defendant makes this argument, the plaintiff must respond by providing some non-speculative evidence that would suggest a link between the infringement and the defendant's supposedly enhanced revenues. The plaintiff is not required at this step to show that the infringement was the primary cause of the defendant's revenues, and a fair degree of inference is allowed. However, the link provided by the plaintiff must be reasonable in light of the evidence. [¶] As a third option, a defendant can seek summary judgment on the basis that all of the claimed revenues are attributable to factors other than the infringement. Although the defendant bears the statutory burden of proof on this issue, it can still raise a proper motion for summary judgment if it submits evidence that no reasonable jury could find that any portion of the claimed revenues is attributable to the infringement. If the defendant's motion is properly supported, the plaintiff must respond with evidence showing that reasonable minds could differ on a material point, or summary judgment may be entered. [¶] It is important to emphasize the distinction between what must be shown to demonstrate a causal link and what must be shown to rebut a defendant's argument that the revenues are not attributable to the infringement. In order to demonstrate a causal link, the plaintiff must show that the infringement could reasonably be viewed as one of the causes of the claimed revenues. In order to rebut a defendant's evidence that the claimed revenues are not attributable to the infringement, the plaintiff must show that at least some portion of the revenues was actually generated by the infringement, rather than by other factors. If the revenues have *some* reasonable causal link to the infringement, but the evidence shows that they are attributable to other factors, the plaintiff will have satisfied his burden of demonstrating a causal link but failed to rebut the defendants' evidence that the revenues are not attributable to the infringement." (Internal quotes omitted.) *See also* ***William A. Graham Co. v. Haughey***, 568 F.3d 425, 442 (3d Cir.2009); ***Polar Bear Prods. v. Timex Corp.***, 384 F.3d 700, 711 (9th Cir.2004).

Mackie v. Rieser, 296 F.3d 909, 914 (9th Cir.2002). "On its face, §504(b) does not differentiate between 'direct profits'—those that are generated by selling an infringing product—and 'indirect profits'—revenue that has a more attenuated nexus to the infringement. Nor does it discuss whether tort principles, such as causation, should play a role in determining whether the infringer's profits were a result of the infringing act. *At 915-16:* [W]e hold that to survive summary judgment on a demand for indirect profits pursuant to §504(b), a copyright holder must proffer sufficient nonspeculative evidence to support a causal relationship between the infringement and the profits generated indirectly from such an infringement." *See also* ***Bruce v. Weekly World News, Inc.***, 310 F.3d 25, 31 (1st Cir. 2002).

Gaste v. Kaiserman, 863 F.2d 1061, 1069 (2d Cir. 1988). "An infringing defendant is entitled to an apportionment of profits to account for his independent contributions only when 'the evidence is sufficient to provide a fair basis of division so as to give the copyright proprietor all the profits that can be deemed to have resulted from the use of what belonged to him.'"

Associated Residential Design, L.L.C., v. Molotky, 226 F.Supp.2d 1251, 1256 (D.Nev.2002). "At trial, if it is clear that not all of the infringer's profits derived from the infringement, then the court must make some apportionment."

§504(c)—Generally

Feltner v. Columbia Pictures TV, Inc., 523 U.S. 340, 342 (1998). "In this case, we consider whether §504(c) or the Seventh Amendment grants a right to a jury trial when a copyright owner elects to recover statutory damages. We hold that although the statute is silent on the point, the Seventh Amendment provides a right to a jury trial, which includes a right to a jury determination of the amount of statutory damages."

EMI Christian Music Grp. v. MP3tunes, LLC, 844 F.3d 79, 94 (2d Cir.2016). "[T]he District Court held that [Ps] could recover only one statutory damages award for a musical composition and its corresponding sound recording, even where the composition and the recording were owned by separate [Ps]. In doing so, it agreed with those district courts that have concluded that infringement of a musical composition and its corresponding sound recording entitles a plaintiff to only one statutory damages award. [¶] A plain reading of the Copyright Act's text supports the District Court's conclusion."

Friedman v. Live Nation Merch., Inc., 833 F.3d 1180, 1190 (9th Cir.2016). "Our question is whether [P] is entitled under the statute to 104 separate awards, because the retailers were each jointly and severally liable with [D] but not collectively jointly and severally liable for the infringement of any one work. *At 1192:* We ... hold that §504(c)(1)'s provision of separate statutory damage awards for the infringement of each work 'for which any two or more infringers are liable jointly and severally' applies only to parties who have been determined jointly and severally liable in the course of the liability determinations in the case for the infringements adjudicated in the action. A plaintiff seeking separate damages awards on the basis of downstream infringement must join the alleged downstream infringers in the action and prove their liability for infringement. Because [P] did not join any of his alleged downstream infringers as defendants in this case, the district court correctly held that he was limited to one award per work infringed by [D]."

Broadcast Music, Inc. v. Evie's Tavern Ellenton, Inc., 772 F.3d 1254, 1260-61 (11th Cir.2014). "[Ds'] argument that the disputed fact of whether or not they were innocent infringers was sufficient to survive a motion for summary judgment is misplaced. The district court did not need to make a finding as to whether [Ds'] infringement was innocent or willful to grant summary judgment or to award statutory damages within the default range. The district court did not specifically find that [Ds] acted willfully, rather it exercised its discretion in refusing to reduce the statutory damages below the normally applicable minimum. The courts have wide discretion in awarding damages within the statutory range provided in §504(c), and here the district court's imposition of damages was not an abuse of discretion."

Bryant v. Media Right Prods., 603 F.3d 135, 140-42 (2d Cir.2010). "An album falls within the Act's expansive definition of compilation. ... Based on a plain reading of the statute, therefore, infringement of an album should result in only one statutory damage award. The fact that each song may have received a separate copyright is irrelevant to this analysis. [¶] Here, it is the copyright holders who issued their works as 'compilations'; they chose to issue Albums. In this situation, the plain language of the Copyright Act limits the copyright holders' statutory damage award to one for each Album. [¶] [Ps] argue that the District Court should have allowed a statutory damage award for each song, because each song has 'independent economic value': internet customers could listen to and purchase copies of each song, each of which [Ps] claim was independently copyrighted. [Ps] point to a decision from the First Circuit ... in which the Court held that a work that is part of a multi-part product can constitute a separate work for the purposes of statutory damages if it has 'independent economic value and ... is viable.' Applying what that court described as a 'functional' test, the court held that each episode of a television show, although released on videotape as part of a complete series, could be the subject of a separate statutory damage award because each episode *could* be rented and viewed separately. At least three other circuits have adopted the 'independent economic value' test, although to date none has applied the test to an album of music. [Ps] argue that it is particularly appropriate to apply the 'independent economic value' test to music albums, because music is increasingly available in digital form, which has made it easier for infringers to break apart albums and sell the album's songs individually, as [Ds] did here. [¶] This Court has never adopted the independent economic value test, and we decline to do so in this case. *At 144:* When determining the amount of statutory damages to award for copyright infringement, courts consider: (1) the infringer's state of mind; (2) the expenses saved, and profits earned, by the infringer; (3) the revenue lost by the copyright holder; (4) the deterrent effect on the infringer and third parties; (5) the infringer's cooperation in providing evidence concerning the value of the infringing material; and (6) the conduct and attitude of the parties." *See also* ***Roeslin v. District of Columbia***, 921 F.Supp. 793, 799-800 (D.D.C.1995) (factors for statutory damages); ***Cross Keys Publ'g v. LL Bar T Land & Cattle Co.***, 887 F.Supp. 219, 224 (E.D.Mo.1995) (same); ***Sailor Music v. Mai Kai, Inc.***, 640 F.Supp. 629, 635 (D.N.H. 1986) (same). *But see* ***Columbia Pictures TV v. Krypton Broad.***, 106 F.3d 284, 295 (9th Cir.1997) (applying independent-economic-value test), *rev'd on other grounds sub nom.* ***Feltner v. Columbia Pictures TV, Inc.***, 523 U.S. 340 (1998); ***MCA TV Ltd. v. Feltner***, 89 F.3d 766, 769 (11th Cir.1996) (same); ***Gamma Audio & Video, Inc. v. Ean-Chea***, 11 F.3d 1106, 1116-18 (1st Cir.1993) (same); ***Walt Disney Co. v. Powell***, 897 F.2d 565, 569-70 (D.C.Cir.1990) (same).

WB Music Corp. v. RTV Comm. Grp., 445 F.3d 538, 539 (2d Cir.2006). "We hold that, for purposes of statutory damages under §504(c), a compilation created [by D] without authorization from the owners of the separate, infringed copyrights in its constituent parts is not a compilation contemplated by the last sentence of §504(c)(1), which states that '[f]or the purposes of this subsection, all the parts of a compilation or derivative work constitute one work.'"

BMG Music v. Gonzalez, 430 F.3d 888, 892-93 (7th Cir.2005). "We read ***Feltner*** as establishing no more (and no less) than that cases under §504(c) are normal civil actions subject to the normal allocation of functions between judge and jury. When there is a material dispute of fact to be resolved or discretion to be exercised in selecting a financial award, then either side is entitled to a jury; if there is no material dispute and a rule of law eliminates discretion in selecting the remedy, then summary judgment is permissible."

Columbia Pictures TV, Inc. v. Krypton Broad., Inc., 259 F.3d 1186, 1194-95 (9th Cir.2001). "A plaintiff may elect statutory damages regardless of the adequacy of the evidence offered as to his actual damages and the amount of the defendant's profits. If statutory damages are elected, the court has wide discretion in determining the amount of statutory damages to be awarded, constrained only by the specified maxima and minima. ... We will uphold a jury's finding of willful infringement if it is supported by substantial evidence." (Internal quotes omitted.)

Lyons Prtshp. v. Morris Costumes, Inc., 243 F.3d 789, 799 (4th Cir.2001), *overruled on other grounds*, ***Petrella v. MGM, Inc.***, ___ U.S. ___, 134 S.Ct. 1962 (2014). "The election for statutory damages must be made before final judgment is rendered."

Cass Cty. Music Co. v. C.H.L.R., Inc., 88 F.3d 635, 642-43 (8th Cir.1996). The "amount of statutory damages assessed may go beyond literal restitution, given that statutory damages are by definition a substitute for unproven or unprovable actual damages, statutory damages are arguably the quintessential equitable remedy, invoked when the legal remedy is inadequate."

Nintendo of Am., Inc. v. Dragon Pac. Int'l, 40 F.3d 1007, 1012 (9th Cir.1994). Apportionment "is simply not an option when statutory damages are elected. Section 504(c), the provision governing statutory damages, makes no mention of apportionment."

Mason v. Montgomery Data, Inc., 967 F.2d 135, 143-44 (5th Cir.1992). "Under [17 U.S.C. §504(c)], the total number of 'awards' of statutory damages ... that a plaintiff may recover in any given action depends on the number of *works* that are infringed and the number of individually liable *infringers*, regardless of the number of *infringements* of those works. So if a plaintiff proves that *one* defendant committed *five* separate infringements of *one* copyrighted work, that plaintiff is entitled to only one award of statutory damages. ... And if a plaintiff proves that *two* different defendants each committed *five* separate infringements of *five* different works, the plaintiff is entitled to ten awards, not 50. It would be inconsistent to read §504 to include all of one defendant's infringements of one work within 'an award of statutory damages,' and then read [17 U.S.C.] §412 to treat each infringement separately for purposes of barring that award. [¶] '[A]n award of statutory damages'—which §504 giveth and §412 taketh away—encompasses *all* of one defendant's infringements of one work." *See also* ***Louis Vuitton Malletier, S.A. v. Akanoc Solutions, Inc.***, 658 F.3d 936, 946-47 (9th Cir. 2011); ***Venegas-Hernandez v. Sonolux Records***, 370

F.3d 183, 194 (1st Cir.2004); ***Gamma Audio & Video, Inc. v. Ean-Chea***, 11 F.3d 1106, 1117 n.8 (1st Cir.1993).

D.C. Comics Inc. v. Mini Gift Shop, 912 F.2d 29, 35-36 (2d Cir.1990). "The level of sophistication of the defendant in business is an entirely proper means of determining whether or not his infringement was innocent. [¶] The district court correctly found that the lack of business sophistication and the absence of a copyright notice on the infringing goods formed a proper basis for a determination of innocent infringement and explained the failure of defendants to inquire as to the source of the goods."

§504(c)—Willful

Zomba Enters. v. Panorama Records, Inc., 491 F.3d 574, 584-85 (6th Cir.2007). "[O]ne who has been notified that his conduct constitutes copyright infringement, but who reasonably and in good faith believes the contrary, is not willful for these purposes. This belief must be both (1) reasonable *and* (2) held in good faith. [¶] [T]he issue is not so much whether [D] held in good faith its belief that its copying was fair use (although we have serious misgivings on this matter), but whether [D] *reasonably* believed that its conduct did not amount to copyright infringement. To decide this issue, we must determine whether the copyright law supported the plaintiffs' position so clearly that the defendants must be deemed as a matter of law to have exhibited a reckless disregard of the plaintiffs' property rights. We review de novo this narrow issue, but we note that other circuits have reviewed for clear error district courts' conclusions on the broader issue of willfulness. [¶] In copyright cases, it is unreasonable to rely on a defense to infringement after a court rejects it on the merits." (Internal quotes omitted.) *See also* ***Peer Int'l v. Pausa Records, Inc.***, 909 F.2d 1332, 1336 (9th Cir.1990); ***RCA/Ariola Int'l v. Thomas & Grayston***, 845 F.2d 773, 779 (8th Cir.1988).

Island Software & Computer Serv. v. Microsoft Corp., 413 F.3d 257, 263 (2d Cir.2005). "To prove 'willfulness' under the Copyright Act, the plaintiff must show (1) that the defendant was actually aware of the infringing activity, or (2) that the defendant's actions were the result of 'reckless disregard' for, or 'willful blindness' to, the copyright holder's rights. *At 264:* [E]ven in the absence of evidence establishing the infringer's actual knowledge of infringement, a plaintiff can still prove willfulness by proffering circumstantial evidence that gives rise to an inference of willful conduct. [W]here the non-moving party [in a summary judgment] does not traverse the evidence suggesting constructive knowledge of infringement, but only disputes the inferences to be drawn from that evidence, our standard of review requires that we decide in favor of the non-moving party." *See also* ***Louis Vuitton Malletier, S.A. v. Akanoc Solutions, Inc.***, 658 F.3d 936, 944 (9th Cir.2011); ***MCA TV Ltd. v. Feltner***, 89 F.3d 766, 768 (11th Cir.1996); ***Lipton v. Nature Co.***, 71 F.3d 464, 472 (2d Cir.1995).

Davis v. Gap, Inc., 246 F.3d 152, 172 (2d Cir.2001). "As a general rule, punitive damages are not awarded in a statutory copyright infringement action. The purpose of punitive damages—to punish and prevent malicious conduct—is generally achieved under the Copyright Act through the provisions of 17 U.S.C. §504(c)(2), which allow increases to an award of statutory damages in cases of willful infringement."

Fitzgerald Publ'g v. Baylor Publ'g, 807 F.2d 1110, 1117 (2d Cir.1986). Section 504(c) "provides two opportunities for a defendant to escape the full measure of joint and several liability with a more culpable defendant. It can establish that it was an innocent infringer under §504(c)(2), or it may successfully oppose the plaintiff's contention that it willfully infringed plaintiff's copyright. Nevertheless, when the copyright owner has successfully established that two or more defendants were willful infringers, §504(c)(2) is unconcerned about gradations in blameworthiness. The statute does not distinguish between those who maliciously infringe another's copyright or those who simply act knowing that they are infringing upon the copyright."

§504(c)—Standard of Review

Yellow Pages Photos, Inc. v. Ziplocal, LP, 795 F.3d 1255, 1277 (11th Cir.2015). "This Court has not previously determined the standard by which it reviews a district court's determination of what constitutes a work for statutory damages purposes under the Copyright Act. At least one other circuit has concluded that the review is *de novo*. We hold that this issue is a mixed question of law and fact, and we review the district court's application of the law to the facts *de novo*."

Curet-Velazquez v. ACEMLA, 656 F.3d 47, 58 (1st Cir.2011). "Our review of a trier of fact's decision as to the amount of a statutory damages award is 'extremely narrow.' 'The employment of the statutory yardstick, within set limits, is committed solely to the court which hears the case, and this fact takes the matter out of the ordinary rule with respect to abuse of discretion.' Other circuit courts agree that an appellate court's review of a district court's award of statutory damages is extremely limited." *See also* ***Superior Form Builders, Inc. v. Dan Chase Taxidermy Sup.***, 74 F.3d 488, 496 (4th Cir. 1996).

§505. REMEDIES FOR INFRINGEMENT: COSTS & ATTORNEY'S FEES

In any civil action under this title, the court in its discretion may allow the recovery of full costs by or against any party other than the United States or an officer thereof. Except as otherwise provided by this title, the court may also award a reasonable attorney's fee to the prevailing party as part of the costs.

History of 17 U.S.C. §505: Oct. 19, 1976, P.L. 94-553, §101, 90 Stat. 2586.

ANNOTATIONS

Attorney Fees

Fogerty v. Fantasy, Inc., 510 U.S. 517, 534 (1994). We "reject both the 'dual standard' ... and petitioner's claim that §505 enacted the British Rule for automatic recovery of attorney's fees by the prevailing party. Prevailing plaintiffs and prevailing defendants are to be treated alike, but attorney's fees are to be awarded to prevailing parties only as a matter of the court's discretion. 'There is no precise rule or formula for making these determinations,' but instead equitable discretion should be exercised 'in light of the considerations [hours x rate and results obtained] we have identified.' *At 534 n.19:* [T]he Third Circuit has listed several nonexclusive factors that courts should consider in making awards of attorney's fees to any prevailing party. These factors include 'frivolousness, motivation, objective unreasonableness (both in the factual and in the legal components of the case) and the need in particular circumstances to advance considerations of compensation and deterrence.' We agree that such factors may be used to guide courts' discretion, so long as such factors are faithful to the purposes of the Copyright Act and are applied to prevailing plaintiffs and defendants in an evenhanded manner." *See also* ***Perfect 10, Inc. v. Giganews, Inc.***, 847 F.3d 657, 675 (9th Cir.2017) (additional considerations are degree of success obtained, purposes of Copyright Act, and whether chilling effect of attorney fees may be too great or impose inequitable burden on indigent P); ***Eagle Servs. v. H2O Indus. Servs.***, 532 F.3d 620, 624 (7th Cir.2008); ***Bridgeport Music, Inc. v. WB Music Corp.***, 520 F.3d 588, 593 (6th Cir.2008) (although P's claim was objectively reasonable, its conduct allowed trial court to award fees to prevailing D); ***García-Goyco v. Law Envtl. Consultants, Inc.***, 428 F.3d 14, 20 (1st Cir.2005); ***King Records, Inc. v. Bennett***, 438 F.Supp.2d 812, 868-69 (M.D.Tenn.2006) (prevailing party denied attorney fees because of its discovery misconduct).

Ryan v. Editions Ltd. W., Inc., 786 F.3d 754, 757 (9th Cir.2015). "Does the Copyright Act of 1976 preclude enforcement of a contractual attorney fees provision in copyright-based litigation? [¶] We conclude the Copyright Act does not bar an award of attorney fees under the circumstances but hold that the district court abused its discretion by categorically excluding the majority of [P's] requested fees without adequate explanation. Therefore, we vacate the district court's order awarding [P] attorney fees…."

Klinger v. Conan Doyle Estate, Ltd., 761 F.3d 789, 791 (7th Cir.2014). "[T]he two most important considerations in deciding whether to award fees 'are the strength of the prevailing party's case and the amount of damages or other relief the party obtained. If the case was a toss-up and the prevailing party obtained generous damages, or injunctive relief of substantial monetary value, there is no urgent need to add an award of attorneys' fees. But if at the other extreme the claim or defense was frivolous and the prevailing party obtained no relief at all, the case for awarding attorneys' fees is compelling'…. We said that as a consequence of the successful defense of an infringement suit the defendant is entitled to a 'very strong' presumption in favor of receiving attorneys' fees, in order to ensure that an infringement defendant does not abandon a meritorious defense in situations in which 'the cost of vindication exceeds the private benefit to the party.' 'For without the prospect of such an award, [an infringement defendant] might be forced into a nuisance settlement or deterred altogether from exercising [its] rights.'"

Spooner v. EEN, Inc., 644 F.3d 62, 67-68 (1st Cir. 2011). "When a statute specifies that attorneys' fees are a part of costs in a particular class of cases, an inquiring court must honor that directive. This taxonomy has practical consequences, one of which is that as long as the overall question of costs remains unresolved, an award of attorneys' fees—itself a component of the total recoverable costs—does not constitute a final and appealable order. [¶] [W]e first describe the conventional framework that courts use in fashioning fee awards: the lodestar method. This approach requires the district court to ascertain the number of hours productively expended and multiply that time by reasonable hourly rates. The obligation to support both the time and rate components rests with the party seeking the award, … but the opposing party may proffer countervailing evidence…. Appropriate supporting documentation includes counsel's contemporaneous time and billing records and information establishing the usual and customary rates in the marketplace for comparably credentialed counsel. [¶] Once the parties have made their submissions, the court determines how much compensable time counsel spent on the case, deleting any 'duplicative, unproductive, or excessive hours.' The court then applies prevailing rates in the community to arrive at the lodestar. Although the lodestar amount 'represents a presumptively reasonable fee,' … the court may adjust it up or down for other factors, say, a significant gap between the relief requested and the result obtained."

HyperQuest, Inc. v. N'Site Solutions, Inc., 632 F.3d 377, 387 (7th Cir.2011). "The Copyright Act gives the district court discretionary authority to grant attorneys' fees in favor of the prevailing party. Following the Supreme Court's decision in [***Buckhannon Bd. & Care Home, Inc. v. West Va. Dept. of Health & Human Res.***,] 532 U.S. 598 (2001), we have held that a litigant prevails (for the purpose of fee-shifting statutes) when it obtains a material alteration of the legal relationship of the parties." (Internal quotes omitted.)

Cadkin v. Loose, 569 F.3d 1142, 1144 (9th Cir. 2009). "This appeal concerns whether a defendant is entitled to attorney's fees as a prevailing party under §505 … when a plaintiff voluntarily dismisses without prejudice a lawsuit containing copyright claims. *At 1145:* Because [Ps] in this lawsuit remained free to refile their copyright claims against [Ds] in federal court following their voluntary dismissal of the complaint, we hold [Ds] are not prevailing parties and thus not entitled to the attorney's fees the district court awarded them." *See also* ***Newport News Holdings Corp. v. Virtual City Vision, Inc.***, 650 F.3d 423, 444 (4th Cir.2011); ***Latin Am. Music Co. v. ASCAP***, 642 F.3d 87, 91 (1st Cir.2011).

Riviera Distribs., Inc. v. Jones, 517 F.3d 926, 928 (7th Cir.2008). "[A] litigant 'prevails' … when it obtains a 'material alteration of the legal relationship of the parties.' A judgment in a party's favor has such an effect, which is why a consent decree confers prevailing-party status even though everyone denies liability as part of the underlying settlement, and the judge takes no position on the merits. [¶] [D] obtained a favorable judgment. That this came about when [P] threw in the towel [and the trial court dismissed with prejudice] does not make [D] less the victor than it would have been had the judge granted summary judgment or a jury returned a verdict in its favor. [P] sued; [D] won; no more is required."

Wall Data Inc. v. Los Angeles Cty. Sheriff's Dept., 447 F.3d 769, 787 (9th Cir.2006). "We review a district court's decision regarding the award of attorneys' fees under the Copyright Act for an abuse of discretion." *See also* ***Spooner v. EEN, Inc.***, 644 F.3d 62, 66 (1st Cir.2011).

Bridgeport Music, Inc. v. Dimension Films, 410 F.3d 792, 807 (6th Cir.2005). "There is no precise rule or formula for making [determinations to award attorney fees consistent with the purposes of the Copyright Act], but instead equitable discretion should be exercised in light of the considerations we have identified. *At 808 n.23:* Those considerations include: the primary objective of the Copyright Act to encourage the production of original literary, artistic, and musical expression for the good of the public; the fact that defendants as well as plaintiffs may hold copyrights and run the gamut from large corporations to starving artists; the need to encourage defendants who seek to advance a variety of meritorious copyright defenses … to litigate them to the same extent that plaintiffs are encouraged to litigate meritorious claims of infringement; and the fact that a successful defense of a copyright infringement action may further the policies of the Copyright Act every bit as much as a successful prosecution of an infringement claim by the holder of a copyright." (Internal quotes omitted.)

Assessment Tech. v. WireDATA, Inc., 361 F.3d 434, 438 (7th Cir.2004). "The courts of appeals have split three ways on the question of the weight to be given to the terms of the contract between the party and his lawyer in determining an award of attorneys' fees in a copyright case. [W]e think the Third Circuit has it right [that the contract has controlling weight in the sense that the contract places a ceiling on what the court can award the lawyer]. The best evidence of the value of the lawyer's services is what the client agreed to pay him." *See also* ***Crescent Publ'g v. Playboy Enters.***, 246 F.3d 142, 151 (2d Cir.2001) (contract is significant, though not controlling, factor in determining reasonable fee); ***Pinkham v. Camex, Inc.***, 84 F.3d 292, 294 (8th Cir.1996) (no weight).

McRoberts Software, Inc. v. Media 100, Inc., 329 F.3d 557, 571 (7th Cir.2003). "A showing of bad faith or frivolousness is no longer required to receive attorney's fees." *See also* ***Latin Am. Music Co. v. ASCAP***, 642 F.3d 87, 91 (1st Cir.2011).

Gonzales v. Transfer Tech., 301 F.3d 608, 609 (7th Cir.2002). Courts of appeals "insist that the judge explain the grounds for his decision in sufficient depth to enable their reasonableness to be determined; otherwise there would be no appellate control at all over such decisions. And so we have not hesitated in the past to remand §505 determinations when the district judge had not supplied us with sufficient indication of his reasoning process to enable us to decide whether the determination was reasonable."

Utility Automation 2000, Inc. v. Choctawhatchee Elec. Coop., 298 F.3d 1238, 1246 n.6 (11th Cir. 2002). This "Court [has] held that a plaintiff who prevailed, but for less than the [FRCP] 68 offer amount, *automatically* had to pay the defendant's fees, because the underlying statute (the Copyright Act, 17 U.S.C. §505) defined fees as costs, and notwithstanding that the Copyright Act grants attorneys' fees only to the 'prevailing party.' In contrast, the D.C., First, Fourth, Fifth, Seventh, Eighth, and Ninth Circuits have held that when a plaintiff rejects an offer and ultimately receives less than the offer amount in a suit brought under a statute that awards attorneys' fees as part of costs to a prevailing party, [FRCP] 68's cost-shifting provision will not shift the defendant's post-offer attorneys' fees to the plaintiff because the defendant has not 'prevailed' under the statute (although the cost-shifting provision will shift the defendant's other post-offer *costs* to the plaintiff)." *See also* ***Harbor Motor Co. v. Arnell Chevrolet-Geo, Inc.***, 265 F.3d 638, 645-46 (7th Cir.2001).

Maljack Prod. v. Palisades Entm't, 36 U.S.P.Q.2d 1281, 1283 (C.D.Cal.1995). "The prevailing party bears the burden of demonstrating the time spent [by the attorney] and that it was reasonably necessary."

Costs

Twentieth Century Fox Film Corp. v. Entertainment Distrib., 429 F.3d 869, 884 (9th Cir.2005). "[D] argues that the district court erred in awarding non-taxable costs under [17 U.S.C.] §505 because only costs specified as taxable costs in 28 U.S.C. §1920 can be included in an attorneys' fee award. On this ... point we again disagree with [D]. *At 885:* [O]ur brethren who have addressed the issue are split. [T]he Eighth Circuit concluded that §505 did not clearly evidence congressional intent that it exceeded the scope of costs authorized by §1920. On the other hand, the Seventh Circuit has suggested that non-taxable costs, outside the gambit of those available under §1920, may be awarded under §505. [¶] [W]e hold that district courts may award otherwise non-taxable costs, including those that lie outside the scope of §1920, under §505." *See also* ***Susan Wakeen Doll Co. v. Ashton-Drake Galleries***, 272 F.3d 441, 458 (7th Cir.2001). *But see* ***Artisan Contractors Ass'n v. Frontier Ins.***, 275 F.3d 1038, 1039-40 (11th Cir.2001) (party may recover only costs taxable under 28 U.S.C. §1920); ***Pinkham v. Camex, Inc.***, 84 F.3d 292, 295 (8th Cir.1996) (same).

InvesSys, Inc. v. McGraw-Hill Cos., 369 F.3d 16, 22-23 (1st Cir.2004). Computer-assisted "research should be treated similarly and reimbursed under attorney's fee statutes like §505, so long as the research cost is in fact paid by the firm to a third-party provider and is customarily charged by the firm to its clients as a separate disbursement. If it saves attorney time to do research this way, probably the hours billed are fewer, and in any event [computer-assisted research is] now as much part of legal service as a lawyer's taxi to the courthouse." *But see* ***King v. JCS Enters.***, 325 F.Supp.2d 162, 172 & n.12 (E.D.N.Y.2004) (electronic-research costs should be included in lodestar attorney-fees calculation, not determined separately).

§506. CRIMINAL OFFENSES

(a) Criminal infringement—

(1) In general.—Any person who willfully infringes a copyright shall be punished as provided under section 2319 of title 18, if the infringement was committed—

(A) for purposes of commercial advantage or private financial gain;

(B) by the reproduction or distribution, including by electronic means, during any 180-day period, of 1 or more copies or phonorecords of 1 or more copyrighted works, which have a total retail value of more than $1,000; or

(C) by the distribution of a work being prepared for commercial distribution, by making it available on a computer network accessible to members of the public, if such person knew or should have known that the work was intended for commercial distribution.

(2) Evidence.—For purposes of this subsection, evidence of reproduction or distribution of a copyrighted work, by itself, shall not be sufficient to establish willful infringement of a copyright.

(3) Definition.—In this subsection, the term "work being prepared for commercial distribution" means—

(A) a computer program, a musical work, a motion picture or other audiovisual work, or a sound recording, if, at the time of unauthorized distribution—

(i) the copyright owner has a reasonable expectation of commercial distribution; and

(ii) the copies or phonorecords of the work have not been commercially distributed; or

(B) a motion picture, if, at the time of unauthorized distribution, the motion picture—

(i) has been made available for viewing in a motion picture exhibition facility; and

(ii) has not been made available in copies for sale to the general public in the United States in a format intended to permit viewing outside a motion picture exhibition facility.

(b) Forfeiture, destruction, and restitution.—Forfeiture, destruction, and restitution relating to this section shall be subject to section 2323 of title 18, to the extent provided in that section, in addition to any other similar remedies provided by law.

(c) Fraudulent copyright notice.—Any person who, with fraudulent intent, places on any article a notice of copyright or words of the same purport that such person knows to be false, or who, with fraudulent intent, publicly distributes or imports for public distribution any article bearing such notice or words that such person knows to be false, shall be fined not more than $2,500.

(d) Fraudulent removal of copyright notice.—Any person who, with fraudulent intent, removes or alters any notice of copyright appearing on a copy of a copyrighted work shall be fined not more than $2,500.

(e) False representation.—Any person who knowingly makes a false representation of a material fact in the application for copyright registration provided for by section 409, or in any written statement filed in connection with the application, shall be fined not more than $2,500.

(f) Rights of attribution and integrity.—Nothing in this section applies to infringement of the rights conferred by section 106A(a).

History of 17 U.S.C. §506: Oct. 19, 1976, P.L. 94-553, §101, 90 Stat. 2586; May 24, 1982, P.L. 97-180, §5, 96 Stat. 93; Dec. 1, 1990, P.L. 101-650, §606(b), 104 Stat. 5131; Dec. 16, 1997, P.L. 105-147, §2(b), 111 Stat. 2678; Apr. 27, 2005, P.L. 109-9, §103(a), 119 Stat. 220; Oct. 13, 2008, P.L. 110-403, §201(a), 122 Stat. 4260.

See also 18 U.S.C. §§545, 2318-2320.

ANNOTATIONS

U.S. v. Liu, 731 F.3d 982, 985 (9th Cir.2013). "We hold that the term 'willfully' requires the government to prove that a defendant knew he was acting illegally rather than simply that he knew he was making copies."

U.S. v. Armstead, 524 F.3d 442, 445 (4th Cir.2008). "'[R]etail value' refers to the greatest of any face value, par value, or market value of commodities or goods in reference to actual or potential sales to ultimate consumers. Thus, while market value—a value determined by the price that a willing buyer would pay a willing seller—is included in the class of values defined as 'retail value,' it is not the exclusive determinant. It follows that if a manufacturer of DVDs sells its DVDs at wholesale with a suggested retail price of $29 and the retailer actually sells the DVDs to the consumer at the discounted price of $19, the 'retail value' as used in [18 U.S.C.] §2319(b)(1) refers to the greater of the two numbers, or $29 per DVD."

U.S. v. Cross, 861 F.2d 297, 301 (7th Cir.1987). "A conviction under ... §506(a) does not require that a defendant actually realize either a commercial advantage or private financial gain. It is only necessary that the activity be for the purpose of financial gain or benefit."

§507. LIMITATIONS ON ACTIONS

(a) Criminal proceedings.—Except as expressly provided otherwise in this title, no criminal proceeding shall be maintained under the provisions of this title unless it is commenced within 5 years after the cause of action arose.

(b) Civil actions.—No civil action shall be maintained under the provisions of this title unless it is commenced within three years after the claim accrued.

History of 17 U.S.C. §507: Oct. 19, 1976, P.L. 94-553, §101, 90 Stat. 2586; Dec. 16, 1997, P.L. 105-147, §2(c), 111 Stat. 2678; Oct. 28, 1998, P.L. 105-304, §102(e), 112 Stat. 2863.

ANNOTATIONS

Generally

Petrella v. MGM, Inc., ___ U.S. ___, 134 S.Ct. 1962, 1969-70 (2014). "To comprehend how the Copyright Act's limitations period works, one must understand when a copyright infringement claim accrues. [¶] A claim ordinarily accrues 'when [a] plaintiff has a complete and present cause of action.' In other words, the limitations period generally begins to run at the point when 'the plaintiff can file suit and obtain relief.' A copyright claim thus arises or 'accrue[s]' when an infringing act occurs. [¶] It is widely recognized that the separate-accrual rule attends the copyright statute of limitations. Under that rule, when a defendant commits successive violations, the statute of limitations runs separately from each violation. Each time an infringing work is reproduced or distributed, the infringer commits a new wrong. Each wrong gives rise to a discrete 'claim' that 'accrue[s]' at the time the wrong occurs. In short, each infringing act starts a new limitations period. [¶] Under the Act's three-year provision, an infringement is actionable within three years, and only three years, of its occurrence. And the infringer is insulated from liability for earlier infringements of the same work. Thus, when a defendant has engaged (or is alleged to have engaged) in a series of discrete infringing acts, the copyright holder's suit ordinarily will be timely under §507(b) with respect to more recent acts of infringement (*i.e.*, acts within the three-year window), but untimely with respect to prior acts of the same or similar kind."

Chicago Bldg. Design, P.C. v. Mongolian House, Inc., 770 F.3d 610, 616 (7th Cir.2014). "[I]n light of ***Petrella***, we now know that the right question to ask in copyright cases is whether the complaint contains allegations of infringing acts that occurred within the three-year look-back period from the date on which the suit was filed. *At 618:* A final word on the statute-of-limitations: If on remand [P] continues to claim a right to recover for infringing acts that occurred … outside the three-year look-back period, the parties will need to address whether ***Petrella*** abrogates the discovery rule in copyright cases. We express no opinion on that question today."

Brownstein v. Lindsay, 742 F.3d 55, 58 (3d Cir. 2014). "The [issue] is when a joint authorship claim under the Copyright Act arises and accrues…. [W]e hold that an authorship claim arises and accrues when a plaintiff's authorship has been 'expressly repudiated.'"

Welles v. Turner Entm't Co., 503 F.3d 728, 734 (9th Cir.2007). "A claim for copyright ownership is barred three years from the 'plain and express repudiation' of copyright ownership. [¶] [Ds] point to no evidence that, before this litigation commenced, they plainly and expressly repudiated [P's] claim to ownership of the home video rights to [movie]. The evidence [Ds] cite as notice that they were exploiting home video rights in [movie] is correspondence between [original copyright holder] and [Ds] regarding the inclusion of [movie] screenplay in a 'home video collector's edition gift set.' While this might have informed [P] that [Ds] were distributing [movie] on home video, it is not the plain and express repudiation of copyright ownership that our case law requires for the statute of limitations on a copyright ownership claim to begin running. [P's] claim is not time barred." *See also* ***Cooper v. NCS Pearson, Inc.***, 733 F.3d 1013, 1015-16 (10th Cir.2013); ***Gary Friedrich Enters. v. Marvel Characters, Inc.***, 716 F.3d 302, 316-17 (2d Cir.2013).

Roger Miller Music, Inc. v. Sony/ATV Publ'g, 477 F.3d 383, 390 (6th Cir.2007). "A copyright ownership claim 'accrues only once, and if an action is not brought within three years of accrual, it is forever barred.' In contrast, a claim for copyright infringement can accrue more than once because each infringement is a distinct harm. [¶] A copyright-infringement claim 'accrues when a plaintiff knows of the potential violation or is chargeable with such knowledge.' '[B]ecause each act of infringement is a distinct harm, the statute of limitations bars infringement claims that accrued more than three years before suit was filed, but does not preclude infringement claims that accrued within the statutory period.'" *See also* ***Diversey v. Schmidly***, 738 F.3d 1196, 1198 (10th Cir.2013); ***Kwan v. Schlein***, 634 F.3d 224, 228 (2d Cir.2011).

Hotaling v. Church of Jesus Christ of Latter-Day Saints, 118 F.3d 199, 202 (4th Cir.1997). "A party does not waive the right to sue for infringements that accrue within three years of filing by not asserting related claims that accrued beyond three years. In addition, under the prevailing view, a party cannot reach back, based on acts of infringement that accrued within the limitations period, and recover for claims that accrued outside the limitations period."

Continuing Infringement

Diversey v. Schmidly, 738 F.3d 1196, 1200-01 (10th Cir.2013). "First, the statute itself says nothing to support a special limitation rule for 'continuing wrongs.' Second, although the minority view seems intended to ensure copyright infringers do not escape liability when their infringing acts are obfuscated by the stream of commerce, the majority accrual rule and tolling principles adequately protect copyright owners' rights in such situations. The limitation period never begins to run until the plaintiff knows or has reason to know of the infringement. Moreover, when an infringer's actions are calculated to deceive the plaintiff, the accrual may be tolled even further. Indeed, this tolling principle alone would have been sufficient to allow the ***Taylor*** plaintiff relief from the statute of limitations. Accordingly, we reject as unnecessary the 'continuing wrong' doctrine in the copyright infringement context and adopt the majority view." *See also* ***Makedwde Publ'g v. Johnson***, 37 F.3d 180, 181-82 (5th Cir.1994). *But see* ***Taylor v. Meirick***, this page.

Kwan v. Schlein, 634 F.3d 224, 228 (2d Cir.2011). "[A]n infringement action may be commenced within three years *of any* infringing act, regardless of any prior acts of infringement; we have applied the three-year limitations period to bar only recovery for infringing acts occurring outside the three-year period."

Roley v. New World Pictures, Ltd., 19 F.3d 479, 481 (9th Cir.1994). "In a case of continuing copyright infringements, an action may be brought for all acts that accrued within the three years preceding the filing of the suit."

Taylor v. Meirick, 712 F.2d 1112, 1117 (7th Cir. 1983). Knowing "that he had placed infringing copies in the hands of his dealers[, D] could not sit on his hands while they sold them. A tortfeasor has a duty to assist his victim. The initial injury creates a duty of aid and the breach of the duty is an independent tort. This principle applies to a statutory tort such as copyright infringement. So if [D] failed to take reasonable steps to prevent infringement by his dealers he became a participant in their infringements. *At 1118:* [T]he copyright statute of limitations is tolled by 'fraudulent concealment' of the infringement. *At 1119:* [D's] infringement was a continuing wrong. He copied [P's] maps in 1976 and 1977 and either sold copies till 1979, which was well within three years of the bringing of this suit, or at least became party to infringements by his dealers which continued till after the suit was filed." *But see* ***Diversey v. Schmidly***, this page.

Discovery Rule

Psihoyos v. John Wiley & Sons, Inc., 748 F.3d 120, 124-25 (2d Cir.2014). "This Circuit has previously employed a discovery rule for copyright claims under ... §507(b). [D] strives to distinguish the cases in which we have done so on the ground that they involved co-ownership claims. We reject [D's] suggestion that we apply different accrual rules for ownership and infringement claims, both of which are governed by ... §507(b). In doing so, we join every Circuit to have considered the issue of claim accrual in the context of infringement claims. [¶] We agree with our sister Circuits that the text and structure of the Copyright Act ... evince Congress's intent to employ the discovery rule, not the injury rule. [C]opyright infringement claims do not accrue until actual or constructive discovery of the relevant infringement and that the Act's statute of limitations did not bar any of [P's] infringement claims." *See also* ***Diversey v. Schmidly***, 738 F.3d 1196, 1200-01 (10th Cir.2013); ***William A. Graham Co. v. Haughey***, 568 F.3d 425, 433-37 (3d Cir.2009); ***Warren Freedenfeld Assocs. v. McTigue***, 531 F.3d 38, 44 (1st Cir.2008); ***Comcast of Ill. X. v. Multi-Vision Elecs., Inc.***, 491 F.3d 938, 944 (8th Cir.2007); ***Roger Miller Music, Inc. v. Sony/ATV Publ'g***, 477 F.3d 383, 390 (6th Cir.2007); ***Polar Bear Prods. v. Timex Corp.***, 384 F.3d 700, 705-07 (9th Cir.2004); ***Gaiman v. McFarlane***, 360 F.3d 644, 653 (7th Cir.2004); ***Lyons Prtshp. v. Morris Costumes, Inc.***, 243 F.3d 789, 796 (4th Cir.2001), *overruled on other grounds*, ***Petrella v. MGM, Inc.***, ___ U.S. ___, 134 S.Ct. 1962 (2014).

Brownstein v. Lindsay, 742 F.3d 55, 70 (3d Cir. 2014). "The Ninth Circuit, Seventh Circuit, and Second Circuit have adopted an 'express repudiation' rule, such that a joint authorship claim arises and an author is alerted to the potential violation of his rights when his authorship has been expressly repudiated by his co-author. Thus, in assessing the accrual of a joint authorship claim, we will apply the discovery rule to the express repudiation rule. Fusing these two concepts, the discovery rule will only apply once a plaintiff's authorship has been expressly repudiated since he can only be on inquiry notice once his rights have been violated. [¶] Similar to the discovery rule, the express repudiation rule looks for evidence that a co-author has acted adversely to the plaintiff's status as a co-author. *At 71:*

The act of registering a copyright does not repudiate co-authorship; put differently, the way to expressly repudiate your co-author's authorship is not to register the copyright in your name." *See also* ***Gary Friedrich Enters. v. Marvel Characters, Inc.***, 716 F.3d 302, 317-18 (2d Cir.2013); ***Gaiman v. McFarlane***, 360 F.3d 644, 653 (7th Cir.2004); ***Zuill v. Shanahan***, 80 F.3d 1366, 1370-71 (9th Cir.1996).

Gary Friedrich Enters. v. Marvel Characters, Inc., 716 F.3d 302, 317 (2d Cir.2013). "[A] claim can accrue: when a book is published without the alleged co-author's name on it, ... when alleged co-authors are presented with a contract identifying the defendant as the 'sole owner and copyright holder,' ... or when alleged co-owners learn they are entitled to royalties that they are not receiving...."

William A. Graham Co. v. Haughey, 646 F.3d 138, 147 (3d Cir.2011). "Accrual ... occurs once events satisfying all the elements of a cause of action have taken place. At that point, the period prescribed by the applicable statute of limitations ordinarily begins to run—time begins to count against the plaintiff, such that if enough of it goes past he can no longer obtain relief. *At 148:* The discovery rule has been characterized both as delaying the accrual of a cause of action and as tolling the running of the limitations period. The distinction between the two concepts is 'often confusing,' ... but because it makes no difference for purposes of deciding whether a claim survives a statute-of-limitations defense, the question has rarely been analyzed with semantic precision. *At 149:* [A]ccrual is defined in terms of the objective existence of a viable cause of action, not in terms of whether the limitations clock has started. It happens to be the case that the limitations period generally commences once a claim exists, but a running clock is not the sine qua non of accrual. *At 150-51:* [W]e do not think the discovery rule should be read to alter the date on which a cause of action accrues. [¶] Since it cannot be an accrual doctrine, the discovery rule must instead be one of those legal precepts that operate to toll the running of the limitations period after a cause of action has accrued.... This conclusion fits with the usual definitions of 'toll' and 'accrue,' ... but its appeal does not end there. [¶] We hold that the 'accrual' of a cause of action occurs at the moment at which each of its component elements has come into being as a matter of objective reality, such that an attorney with knowledge of all the facts could get it past a motion to dismiss for failure to state a claim. The federal discovery rule then operates in applicable cases to toll the running of the limitations period. Prejudgment interest, however, may be awarded in appropriate cases from the initial accrual date."

Warren Freedenfeld Assocs. v. McTigue, 531 F.3d 38, 44 (1st Cir.2008). The "date of accrual is not always determined mechanically; in certain circumstances, accrual contemplates application of the so-called discovery rule. Under the aegis of this rule, a claim accrues only when a plaintiff knows or has sufficient reason to know of the conduct upon which the claim is grounded. [¶] The easy cases are those involving actual knowledge of an act of infringement. There, accrual begins with the acquisition of that knowledge; thus, computing the limitations period is simply a matter of checking the passage of time. [¶] In the absence of actual knowledge—and there is no allegation of such knowledge in the complaint—the question becomes when a reasonably prudent person in the plaintiff's shoes would have discovered (that is, would have acquired an awareness of) the putative infringement. [¶] It stands to reason that determining when a reasonable person would have become aware of a copyright infringement is a fact-sensitive enterprise. Common sense suggests, therefore, that an inquiring court must explore the idiosyncratic circumstances of each individual case. One thing is clear, however: the reasonable person standard incorporates a duty of diligence. It is not a barrier to accrual that a plaintiff has failed to discover a cause of action if a reasonably diligent person, similarly situated, would have made such a discovery. In other words, a plaintiff can be charged with inquiry notice, sufficient to start the limitations clock, once he possesses information fairly suggesting some reason to investigate whether he may have suffered an injury at the hands of a putative infringer. *At 45:* But the duty to investigate is not always in the wind. Typically, inquiry notice must be triggered by some event or series of events that comes to the attention of the aggrieved party." *See also* ***Polar Bear Prods. v. Timex Corp.***, 384 F.3d 700, 706 (9th Cir. 2004).

Equitable Estoppel

Bridgeport Music, Inc. v. Diamond Time, Ltd., 371 F.3d 883, 891 (6th Cir.2004). "Equitable estoppel, sometimes referred to as fraudulent concealment, is invoked in cases where the defendant takes active steps to prevent the plaintiff from suing in time, such as by hiding evidence or promising not to plead the statute of limitations. Application of equitable estoppel should be premised on a defendant's improper conduct as well as a plaintiff's actual and reasonable reliance thereon." (Internal quotes omitted.)

Laches

Petrella v. MGM, Inc., ___ U.S. ___, 134 S.Ct. 1962, 1967 (2014). "This case presents the question [of] whether the equitable defense of laches (unreasonable, prejudicial delay in commencing suit) may bar relief on a copyright infringement claim brought within §507(b)'s three-year limitations period. Section 507(b), it is undisputed, bars relief of any kind for conduct occurring prior to the three-year limitations period. To the extent that an infringement suit seeks relief solely for conduct occurring within the limitations period, however, courts are not at liberty to jettison Congress' judgment on the timeliness of suit. Laches, we hold, cannot be invoked to preclude adjudication of a claim for damages brought within the three-year window. As to equitable relief, in extraordinary circumstances, laches may bar at the very threshold the particular relief requested by the plaintiff. And a plaintiff's delay can always be brought to bear at the remedial stage, in determining appropriate injunctive relief, and in assessing the 'profits of the infringer ... attributable to the infringement.' *At U.S. ___, S.Ct. 1973:* [A] successful plaintiff can gain retrospective relief only three years back from the time of suit. No recovery may be had for infringement in earlier years. Profits made in those years remain the defendant's to keep. [¶] Moreover, if infringement within the three-year look-back period is shown, the [Copyright] Act allows the defendant to prove and offset against profits made in that period 'deductible expenses' incurred in generating those profits."

Peter Letterese & Assocs. v. World Inst. of Scientology Enters., 533 F.3d 1287, 1320 (11th Cir.2008). "In answering the question of whether the defense of laches may be interposed in a copyright infringement suit, ... we cannot agree with the conclusion of the Fourth Circuit, which is an unqualified 'no.' ... However, we remain mindful of the Fourth Circuit's invocation of separation of powers principles which counsel against the use of 'the judicially created doctrine of laches to bar a federal statutory claim that has been timely filed under an express statute of limitations.' We therefore answer this question with a presumptive 'no'; there is a strong presumption that a plaintiff's suit is timely if it is filed before the statute of limitations has run. Only in the most extraordinary circumstances will laches be recognized as a defense. *At 1321:* Even where such extraordinary circumstances exist, however, laches serves as a bar only to the recovery of retrospective damages, not to prospective relief." *See also* ***Jacobsen v. Deseret Book Co.***, 287 F.3d 936, 950 (10th Cir. 2002).

Chirco v. Crosswinds Cmty., Inc., 474 F.3d 227, 229 (6th Cir.2007). "[T]he dispositive question is whether the equitable doctrine of laches can be held to trump the statutorily-prescribed period for filing suit under §507(b). To the extent that [Ps] are seeking only monetary damages and injunctive relief, we give effect to the Sixth Circuit's presumption that the statute of limitations must prevail. However, to the extent that the relief sought is destruction of the condominium complex that allegedly infringes [Ps'] copyright, the facts before us suggest that this is indeed the extraordinary case in which the defense of laches is properly interposed." Held: Court allowed suit and damages for infringed architectural plans, but applied laches to prohibit destruction of building built according to plans.

Suit on Copyright Ownership

Consumer Health Info. Corp. v. Amylin Pharms., 819 F.3d 992, 997 (7th Cir.2016). "We're persuaded by the unanimous line of cases from our sister circuits and now hold that when the gravamen of a copyright suit is a question of copyright ownership, the claim accrues when the ownership dispute becomes explicit—that is, when the claimant has notice that his claim of ownership is repudiated or contested." *See also* ***Stan Lee Media, Inc. v. Walt Disney Co.***, 774 F.3d 1292, 1300 n.4 (10th Cir.2014); ***Kwan v. Schlein***, 634 F.3d 224, 229 (2d Cir.2011); ***Ritchie v. Williams***, 395 F.3d 283, 288 n.5 (6th Cir.2005).

Seven Arts Filmed Entm't Ltd. v. Content Media Corp. PLC, 733 F.3d 1251, 1254-55 (9th Cir.2013). "We must decide ... whether a claim for copyright infringement in which ownership is the disputed issue is time-barred if a freestanding ownership claim would be barred. [¶] Although this is an issue of first impression in our circuit, we are guided by the Second and Sixth Circuits. Our sister circuits have held that, where the gravamen of a copyright infringement suit is ownership, and a freestanding ownership claim would be time-barred, any infringement claims are also barred.

'When claims for both infringement and ownership are alleged,' according to the Sixth Circuit, 'the infringement claim is timely only if the corresponding ownership claim is also timely.' Or, as the Second Circuit puts it, '[w]here ... the ownership claim is time-barred, and ownership is the dispositive issue, any attendant infringement claims must fail.'" *See also* ***Kwan v. Schlein***, 634 F.3d 224, 229-30 (2d Cir.2011); ***Ritchie v. Williams***, 395 F.3d 283, 288 n.5 (6th Cir.2005).

§508. NOTIFICATION OF FILING & DETERMINATION OF ACTIONS

(a) Within one month after the filing of any action under this title, the clerks of the courts of the United States shall send written notification to the Register of Copyrights setting forth, as far as is shown by the papers filed in the court, the names and addresses of the parties and the title, author, and registration number of each work involved in the action. If any other copyrighted work is later included in the action by amendment, answer, or other pleading, the clerk shall also send a notification concerning it to the Register within one month after the pleading is filed.

(b) Within one month after any final order or judgment is issued in the case, the clerk of the court shall notify the Register of it, sending with the notification a copy of the order or judgment together with the written opinion, if any, of the court.

(c) Upon receiving the notifications specified in this section, the Register shall make them a part of the public records of the Copyright Office.

History of 17 U.S.C. §508: Oct. 19, 1976, P.L. 94-553, §101, 90 Stat. 2586.

§509. REPEALED

Repealed Oct. 13, 2008, P.L. 110-403, §201(b)(1), 122 Stat. 4260. Recodified as 19 U.S.C. §1595a.

§510. REMEDIES FOR ALTERATION OF PROGRAMMING BY CABLE SYSTEMS

(a) In any action filed pursuant to section 111(c)(3), the following remedies shall be available:

(1) Where an action is brought by a party identified in subsections (b) or (c) of section 501, the remedies provided by sections 502 through 505, and the remedy provided by subsection (b) of this section; and

(2) When an action is brought by a party identified in subsection (d) of section 501, the remedies provided by sections 502 and 505, together with any actual damages suffered by such party as a result of the infringement, and the remedy provided by subsection (b) of this section.

(b) In any action filed pursuant to section 111(c)(3), the court may decree that, for a period not to exceed thirty days, the cable system shall be deprived of the benefit of a statutory license for one or more distant signals carried by such cable system.

History of 17 U.S.C. §510: Oct. 19, 1976, P.L. 94-553, §101, 90 Stat. 2587; Nov. 29, 1999, P.L. 106-113, §1000(a)(9), 113 Stat. 1536.

§511. LIABILITY OF STATES, INSTRUMENTALITIES OF STATES, & STATE OFFICIALS FOR INFRINGEMENT OF COPYRIGHT

(a) In general.—Any State, any instrumentality of a State, and any officer or employee of a State or instrumentality of a State acting in his or her official capacity, shall not be immune, under the Eleventh Amendment of the Constitution of the United States or under any other doctrine of sovereign immunity, from suit in Federal court by any person, including any governmental or nongovernmental entity, for a violation of any of the exclusive rights of a copyright owner provided by sections 106 through 122, for importing copies of phonorecords in violation of section 602, or for any other violation under this title.

(b) Remedies.—In a suit described in subsection (a) for a violation described in that subsection, remedies (including remedies both at law and in equity) are available for the violation to the same extent as such remedies are available for such a violation in a suit against any public or private entity other than a State, instrumentality of a State, or officer or employee of a State acting in his or her official capacity. Such remedies include impounding and disposition of infringing articles under section 503, actual damages and profits and statutory damages under section 504, costs and attorney's fees under section 505, and the remedies provided in section 510.

History of 17 U.S.C. §511: Nov. 15, 1990, P.L. 101-553, §2(a)(2), 104 Stat. 2749; Aug. 5, 1999, P.L. 106-44, §1(g)(6), 113 Stat. 222; Nov. 2, 2002, P.L. 107-273, §13210(4)(C), 116 Stat. 1909.

ANNOTATIONS

National Ass'n of Bds. of Pharm. v. Board of Regents, 633 F.3d 1297, 1315 (11th Cir.2011). "We hold that Congress may not abrogate the States' sovereign immunity pursuant to the Copyright and Patent Clause; therefore, [P] cannot rely on that clause to support its claim for damages under [17 U.S.C. §511]. [¶] [P] argues that §5 of the 14th Amendment supports Congress' abrogation of the States' sovereign immunity in [§511]. *At 1316:* The district court held (1) that [P] did not allege an actual violation of the Due Process Clause of the 14th Amendment, and (2) that [§511] does not constitute valid prophylactic legislation under §5 of the 14th Amendment, such that [P's] claim for [§511] damages may be maintained. [P] only challenges the court's first holding, that the copyright infringement complained of amounts to a violation of the Due Process Clause. *At 1319:* [P] could only establish an actual due process violation if it sufficiently alleged that the State failed to provide adequate post-deprivation remedies. But [P] does not argue on appeal that [state's] post-deprivation remedies are inadequate. [¶] [W]e hold that the amended complaint failed to allege a due process violation and consequently did not allege a damages claim that may be brought under [§511].

§512. LIMITATIONS ON LIABILITY RELATING TO MATERIAL ONLINE

(a) Transitory digital network communications.—A service provider shall not be liable for monetary relief, or, except as provided in subsection (j), for injunctive or other equitable relief, for infringement of copyright by reason of the provider's transmitting, routing, or providing connections for, material through a system or network controlled or operated by or for the service provider, or by reason of the intermediate and transient storage of that material in the course of such transmitting, routing, or providing connections, if—

(1) the transmission of the material was initiated by or at the direction of a person other than the service provider;

(2) the transmission, routing, provision of connections, or storage is carried out through an automatic technical process without selection of the material by the service provider;

(3) the service provider does not select the recipients of the material except as an automatic response to the request of another person;

(4) no copy of the material made by the service provider in the course of such intermediate or transient storage is maintained on the system or network in a manner ordinarily accessible to anyone other than anticipated recipients, and no such copy is maintained on the system or network in a manner ordinarily accessible to such anticipated recipients for a longer period than is reasonably necessary for the transmission, routing, or provision of connections; and

(5) the material is transmitted through the system or network without modification of its content.

(b) System caching—

(1) Limitation on liability.—A service provider shall not be liable for monetary relief, or, except as provided in subsection (j), for injunctive or other equitable relief, for infringement of copyright by reason of the intermediate and temporary storage of material on a system or network controlled or operated by or for the service provider in a case in which—

(A) the material is made available online by a person other than the service provider;

(B) the material is transmitted from the person described in subparagraph (A) through the system or network to a person other than the person described in subparagraph (A) at the direction of that other person; and

(C) the storage is carried out through an automatic technical process for the purpose of making the material available to users of the system or network who, after the material is transmitted as described in subparagraph (B), request access to the material from the person described in subparagraph (A),

if the conditions set forth in paragraph (2) are met.

(2) Conditions.—The conditions referred to in paragraph (1) are that—

(A) the material described in paragraph (1) is transmitted to the subsequent users described in paragraph (1)(C) without modification to its content from the manner in which the material was transmitted from the person described in paragraph (1)(A);

(B) the service provider described in paragraph (1) complies with rules concerning the refreshing, reloading, or other updating of the material when specified by the person making the material available online in accordance with a generally accepted industry standard data communications protocol for the system or network through which that person makes the material available, except that this subparagraph applies only if those rules are not used by the person described in paragraph (1)(A) to prevent or unreasonably impair the intermediate storage to which this subsection applies;

(C) the service provider does not interfere with the ability of technology associated with the material to return to the person described in paragraph (1)(A) the information that would have been available to that person if the material had been obtained by the subsequent users described in paragraph (1)(C) directly from that person, except that this subparagraph applies only if that technology—

(i) does not significantly interfere with the performance of the provider's system or network or with the intermediate storage of the material;

(ii) is consistent with generally accepted industry standard communications protocols; and

(iii) does not extract information from the provider's system or network other than the information that would have been available to the person described in paragraph (1)(A) if the subsequent users had gained access to the material directly from that person;

(D) if the person described in paragraph (1)(A) has in effect a condition that a person must meet prior to having access to the material, such as a condition based on payment of a fee or provision of a password or other information, the service provider permits access to the stored material in significant part only to users of its system or network that have met those conditions and only in accordance with those conditions; and

(E) if the person described in paragraph (1)(A) makes that material available online without the authorization of the copyright owner of the material, the service provider responds expeditiously to remove, or disable access to, the material that is claimed to be infringing upon notification of claimed infringement as described in subsection (c)(3), except that this subparagraph applies only if—

(i) the material has previously been removed from the originating site or access to it has been disabled, or a court has ordered that the material be removed from the originating site or that access to the material on the originating site be disabled; and

(ii) the party giving the notification includes in the notification a statement confirming that the material has been removed from the originating site or access to it has been disabled or that a court has ordered that the material be removed from the originating site or that access to the material on the originating site be disabled.

(c) Information residing on systems or networks at direction of users—

(1) In general.—A service provider shall not be liable for monetary relief, or, except as provided in subsection (j), for injunctive or other equitable relief, for infringement of copyright by reason of the storage at the direction of a user of material that resides on a system or network controlled or operated by or for the service provider, if the service provider—

(A)(i) does not have actual knowledge that the material or an activity using the material on the system or network is infringing;

(ii) in the absence of such actual knowledge, is not aware of facts or circumstances from which infringing activity is apparent; or

(iii) upon obtaining such knowledge or awareness, acts expeditiously to remove, or disable access to, the material;

(B) does not receive a financial benefit directly attributable to the infringing activity, in a case in which the service provider has the right and ability to control such activity; and

(C) upon notification of claimed infringement as described in paragraph (3), responds expeditiously to remove, or disable access to, the material that is claimed to be infringing or to be the subject of infringing activity.

(2) Designated agent.—The limitations on liability established in this subsection apply to a service provider only if the service provider has designated an agent to receive notifications of claimed infringement described in paragraph (3), by making available through its service, including on its website in a location accessible to the public, and by providing to the Copyright Office, substantially the following information:

(A) the name, address, phone number, and electronic mail address of the agent.

(B) other contact information which the Register of Copyrights may deem appropriate.

The Register of Copyrights shall maintain a current directory of agents available to the public for inspection, including through the Internet, and may require payment of a fee by service providers to cover the costs of maintaining the directory.

(3) Elements of notification—

(A) To be effective under this subsection, a notification of claimed infringement must be a written communication provided to the designated agent of a service provider that includes substantially the following:

(i) A physical or electronic signature of a person authorized to act on behalf of the owner of an exclusive right that is allegedly infringed.

(ii) Identification of the copyrighted work claimed to have been infringed, or, if multiple copyrighted works at a single online site are covered by a single notification, a representative list of such works at that site.

(iii) Identification of the material that is claimed to be infringing or to be the subject of infringing activity and that is to be removed or access to which is to be disabled, and information reasonably sufficient to permit the service provider to locate the material.

(iv) Information reasonably sufficient to permit the service provider to contact the complaining party, such as an address, telephone number, and, if available, an electronic mail address at which the complaining party may be contacted.

(v) A statement that the complaining party has a good faith belief that use of the material in the manner complained of is not authorized by the copyright owner, its agent, or the law.

(vi) A statement that the information in the notification is accurate, and under penalty of perjury, that the complaining party is authorized to act on behalf of the owner of an exclusive right that is allegedly infringed.

(B)(i) Subject to clause (ii), a notification from a copyright owner or from a person authorized to act on behalf of the copyright owner that fails to comply substantially with the provisions of subparagraph (A) shall not be considered under paragraph (1)(A) in determining whether a service provider has actual knowledge or is aware of facts or circumstances from which infringing activity is apparent.

(ii) In a case in which the notification that is provided to the service provider's designated agent fails to comply substantially with all the provisions of subparagraph (A) but substantially complies with clauses (ii), (iii), and (iv) of subparagraph (A), clause (i) of this subparagraph applies only if the service provider promptly attempts to contact the person making the notification or takes other reasonable steps to assist in the receipt of notification that substantially complies with all the provisions of subparagraph (A).

(d) Information location tools.—A service provider shall not be liable for monetary relief, or, except as provided in subsection (j), for injunctive or other equitable relief, for infringement of copyright by reason of the provider referring or linking users to an online location containing infringing material or infringing activity, by using information location tools, including a directory, index, reference, pointer, or hypertext link, if the service provider—

(1)(A) does not have actual knowledge that the material or activity is infringing;

(B) in the absence of such actual knowledge, is not aware of facts or circumstances from which infringing activity is apparent; or

(C) upon obtaining such knowledge or awareness, acts expeditiously to remove, or disable access to, the material;

(2) does not receive a financial benefit directly attributable to the infringing activity, in a case in which the service provider has the right and ability to control such activity; and

(3) upon notification of claimed infringement as described in subsection (c)(3), responds expeditiously to remove, or disable access to, the material that is claimed to be infringing or to be the subject of infringing activity, except that, for purposes of this paragraph, the information described in subsection (c)(3)(A)(iii) shall be identification of the reference or link, to material or activity claimed to be infringing, that is to be removed or access to which is to be disabled, and information reasonably sufficient to permit the service provider to locate that reference or link.

(e) Limitation on liability of nonprofit educational institutions—

(1) When a public or other nonprofit institution of higher education is a service provider, and when a faculty member or graduate student who is an employee of such institution is performing a teaching or research function, for the purposes of subsections (a) and (b) such faculty member or graduate student shall be considered to be a person other than the institution, and for the purposes of subsections (c) and (d) such faculty member's or graduate student's knowledge or awareness of his or her infringing activities shall not be attributed to the institution, if—

(A) such faculty member's or graduate student's infringing activities do not involve the provision of online access to instructional materials that are or were required or recommended, within the preceding 3-year period, for a course taught at the institution by such faculty member or graduate student;

(B) the institution has not, within the preceding 3-year period, received more than two notifications described in subsection (c)(3) of claimed infringement by such faculty member or graduate student, and such notifications of claimed infringement were not actionable under subsection (f); and

(C) the institution provides to all users of its system or network informational materials that accurately describe, and promote compliance with, the laws of the United States relating to copyright.

(2) For the purposes of this subsection, the limitations on injunctive relief contained in subsections (j)(2) and (j)(3), but not those in (j)(1), shall apply.

(f) Misrepresentations.—Any person who knowingly materially misrepresents under this section—

(1) that material or activity is infringing, or

(2) that material or activity was removed or disabled by mistake or misidentification,

shall be liable for any damages, including costs and attorneys' fees, incurred by the alleged infringer, by any copyright owner or copyright owner's authorized licensee, or by a service provider, who is injured by such misrepresentation, as the result of the service provider relying upon such misrepresentation in removing or disabling access to the material or activity claimed to be infringing, or in replacing the removed material or ceasing to disable access to it.

(g) Replacement of removed or disabled material and limitation on other liability—

(1) No liability for taking down generally.—Subject to paragraph (2), a service provider shall not be liable to any person for any claim based on the service provider's good faith disabling of access to, or removal of, material or activity claimed to be infringing or based on facts or circumstances from which infringing activity is apparent, regardless of whether the material or activity is ultimately determined to be infringing.

(2) Exception.—Paragraph (1) shall not apply with respect to material residing at the direction of a subscriber of the service provider on a system or network controlled or operated by or for the service provider that is removed, or to which access is disabled by the service provider, pursuant to a notice provided under subsection (c)(1)(C), unless the service provider—

(A) takes reasonable steps promptly to notify the subscriber that it has removed or disabled access to the material;

(B) upon receipt of a counter notification described in paragraph (3), promptly provides the person who provided the notification under subsection (c)(1)(C) with a copy of the counter notification, and informs that person that it will replace the removed material or cease disabling access to it in 10 business days; and

(C) replaces the removed material and ceases disabling access to it not less than 10, nor more than 14, business days following receipt of the counter notice, unless its designated agent first receives notice from the person who submitted the notification under subsection (c)(1)(C) that such person has filed an action seeking a court order to restrain the subscriber from engaging in infringing activity relating to the material on the service provider's system or network.

(3) Contents of counter notification.—To be effective under this subsection, a counter notification must be a written communication provided to the service provider's designated agent that includes substantially the following:

(A) A physical or electronic signature of the subscriber.

(B) Identification of the material that has been removed or to which access has been disabled and the location at which the material appeared before it was removed or access to it was disabled.

(C) A statement under penalty of perjury that the subscriber has a good faith belief that the material was removed or disabled as a result of mistake or misidentification of the material to be removed or disabled.

(D) The subscriber's name, address, and telephone number, and a statement that the subscriber consents to the jurisdiction of Federal District Court for the judicial district in which the address is located, or if the subscriber's address is outside of the United States, for any judicial district in which the service provider may be found, and that the subscriber will accept service of process from the person who provided notification under subsection (c)(1)(C) or an agent of such person.

(4) Limitation on other liability.—A service provider's compliance with paragraph (2) shall not subject the service provider to liability for copyright infringement with respect to the material identified in the notice provided under subsection (c)(1)(C).

(h) Subpoena to identify infringer—

(1) Request.—A copyright owner or a person authorized to act on the owner's behalf may request the clerk of any United States district court to issue a subpoena to a service provider for identification of an alleged infringer in accordance with this subsection.

(2) Contents of request.—The request may be made by filing with the clerk—

(A) a copy of a notification described in subsection (c)(3)(A);

(B) a proposed subpoena; and

(C) a sworn declaration to the effect that the purpose for which the subpoena is sought is to obtain the identity of an alleged infringer and that such information will only be used for the purpose of protecting rights under this title.

(3) Contents of subpoena.—The subpoena shall authorize and order the service provider receiving the notification and the subpoena to expeditiously disclose to the copyright owner or person authorized by the copyright owner information sufficient to identify the alleged infringer of the material described in the notification to the extent such information is available to the service provider.

(4) Basis for granting subpoena.—If the notification filed satisfies the provisions of subsection (c)(3)(A), the proposed subpoena is in proper form, and the accompanying declaration is properly executed, the clerk shall expeditiously issue and sign the proposed subpoena and return it to the requester for delivery to the service provider.

(5) Actions of service provider receiving subpoena.—Upon receipt of the issued subpoena, either accompanying or subsequent to the receipt of a notification described in subsection (c)(3)(A), the service provider shall expeditiously disclose to the copyright owner or person authorized by the copyright owner the information required by the subpoena, notwithstanding any other provision of law and regardless of whether the service provider responds to the notification.

(6) Rules applicable to subpoena.—Unless otherwise provided by this section or by applicable rules of the court, the procedure for issuance and delivery of the subpoena, and the remedies for noncompliance with the subpoena, shall be governed to the greatest extent practicable by those provisions of the Federal Rules of Civil Procedure governing the issuance, service, and enforcement of a subpoena duces tecum.

(i) Conditions for eligibility—

(1) Accommodation of technology.—The limitations on liability established by this section shall apply to a service provider only if the service provider—

(A) has adopted and reasonably implemented, and informs subscribers and account holders of the service provider's system or network of, a policy that provides for the termination in appropriate circumstances of subscribers and account holders of the service provider's system or network who are repeat infringers; and

(B) accommodates and does not interfere with standard technical measures.

(2) Definition.—As used in this subsection, the term "standard technical measures" means technical measures that are used by copyright owners to identify or protect copyrighted works and—

(A) have been developed pursuant to a broad consensus of copyright owners and service providers in an open, fair, voluntary, multi-industry standards process;

(B) are available to any person on reasonable and nondiscriminatory terms; and

(C) do not impose substantial costs on service providers or substantial burdens on their systems or networks.

(j) Injunctions.—The following rules shall apply in the case of any application for an injunction under section 502 against a service provider that is not subject to monetary remedies under this section:

(1) Scope of relief—

(A) With respect to conduct other than that which qualifies for the limitation on remedies set forth in subsection (a), the court may grant injunctive relief with respect to a service provider only in one or more of the following forms:

(i) An order restraining the service provider from providing access to infringing material or activity residing at a particular online site on the provider's system or network.

(ii) An order restraining the service provider from providing access to a subscriber or account holder of the service provider's system or network who is engaging in infringing activity and is identified in the order, by terminating the accounts of the subscriber or account holder that are specified in the order.

(iii) Such other injunctive relief as the court may consider necessary to prevent or restrain infringement of copyrighted material specified in the order of the court at a particular online location, if such relief is the least burdensome to the service provider among the forms of relief comparably effective for that purpose.

(B) If the service provider qualifies for the limitation on remedies described in subsection (a), the court may only grant injunctive relief in one or both of the following forms:

(i) An order restraining the service provider from providing access to a subscriber or account holder of the service provider's system or network who is using the provider's service to engage in infringing activity and is identified in the order, by terminating the accounts of the subscriber or account holder that are specified in the order.

(ii) An order restraining the service provider from providing access, by taking reasonable steps specified in the order to block access, to a specific, identified, online location outside the United States.

(2) Considerations.—The court, in considering the relevant criteria for injunctive relief under applicable law, shall consider—

(A) whether such an injunction, either alone or in combination with other such injunctions issued against the same service provider under this subsection, would significantly burden either the provider or the operation of the provider's system or network;

(B) the magnitude of the harm likely to be suffered by the copyright owner in the digital network environment if steps are not taken to prevent or restrain the infringement;

(C) whether implementation of such an injunction would be technically feasible and effective, and would not interfere with access to noninfringing material at other online locations; and

(D) whether other less burdensome and comparably effective means of preventing or restraining access to the infringing material are available.

(3) Notice and ex parte orders.—Injunctive relief under this subsection shall be available only after notice to the service provider and an opportunity for the service provider to appear are provided, except for orders ensuring the preservation of evidence or other orders having no material adverse effect on the operation of the service provider's communications network.

(k) Definitions—

(1) Service provider—

(A) As used in subsection (a), the term "service provider" means an entity offering the transmission, routing, or providing of connections for digital online communications, between or among points specified by a user, of material of the user's choosing, without modification to the content of the material as sent or received.

(B) As used in this section, other than subsection (a), the term "service provider" means a provider of online services or network access, or the operator of facilities therefor, and includes an entity described in subparagraph (A).

(2) Monetary relief.—As used in this section, the term "monetary relief" means damages, costs, attorneys' fees, and any other form of monetary payment.

(*l*) Other defenses not affected.—The failure of a service provider's conduct to qualify for limitation of liability under this section shall not bear adversely upon the consideration of a defense by the service provider that the service provider's conduct is not infringing under this title or any other defense.

(m) Protection of privacy.—Nothing in this section shall be construed to condition the applicability of subsections (a) through (d) on—

(1) a service provider monitoring its service or affirmatively seeking facts indicating infringing activity, except to the extent consistent with a standard technical measure complying with the provisions of subsection (i); or

(2) a service provider gaining access to, removing, or disabling access to material in cases in which such conduct is prohibited by law.

(n) Construction.—Subsections (a), (b), (c), and (d) describe separate and distinct functions for purposes of applying this section. Whether a service provider qualifies for the limitation on liability in any one of those subsections shall be based solely on the criteria in that subsection, and shall not affect a determination of whether that service provider qualifies for the limitations on liability under any other such subsection.

History of 17 U.S.C. §512: Oct. 28, 1998, P.L. 105-304, §202(a), 112 Stat. 2877; Aug. 5, 1999, P.L. 106-44, §1(d), 113 Stat. 222; Dec. 9, 2010, P.L. 111-295, §3(a), 124 Stat. 3180.

See also 37 C.F.R. §201.38; WIPO Copyright Treaty; WIPO Performances & Phonograms Treaty.

ANNOTATIONS

Generally

Perfect 10, Inc. v. Amazon.com, Inc., 508 F.3d 1146, 1175 (9th Cir.2007). "[T]he limitations on liability contained in … §512 protect secondary infringers as well as direct infringers."

§512(a)

In re Charter Comms., 393 F.3d 771, 776-77 (8th Cir.2005). The "safe harbor provision implicated here is §512(a), which limits the liability of an [Internet-service provider (ISP)] when it merely acts as a conduit for infringing material without storing, caching, or providing links to copyrighted material. Section 512(a) does not reference the notification provision of §512(c)(3)(A), nor does it contain the remove-or-disable-access provision found in the three safe harbors created for the storage, caching, and linking functions of an ISP. The absence of the remove-or-disable-access provision (and the concomitant notification provision) makes sense where an ISP merely acts as a conduit for infringing material—rather than directly storing, caching, or linking to infringing material—because the ISP has no ability to remove the infringing material from its system or disable access to the infringing material. [¶] [Subpoenaed ISP] argues §512(h) does not allow a copyright owner to request a subpoena for an ISP which merely acts as a conduit for data transferred between two internet users. ... We agree." *See also* ***Recording Indus. Ass'n of Am., Inc. v. Verizon Internet Servs.***, 351 F.3d 1229, 1232 (D.C.Cir.2003).

§512(c)

Mavrix Photographs, LLC v. LiveJournal, Inc., 873 F.3d 1045, 1054 (9th Cir.2017). "We ... have little difficulty holding that common law agency principles apply to the analysis of whether a service provider like [D] is liable for the acts of the [webgroup] moderators. *At 1057:* If [D] shows that it meets the threshold requirement for the §512(c) safe harbor because the photographs were stored at the direction of the user, [D] must then show that it lacked both actual and red flag knowledge of the infringements. Actual knowledge refers to whether the service provider had subjective knowledge, while red flag knowledge turns on whether a reasonable person would objectively know of the infringements. Both actual and red flag knowledge refer to knowledge of the specific infringement alleged. [¶] A copyright holder's failure to notify the service provider of infringement through the notice and takedown procedure, as [P] failed to do here, strips it of the most powerful evidence of actual knowledge. *At 1058:* [I]f the fact finder determines that [D] met the §512(c) safe harbor threshold requirement (i.e., that the photographs were stored at the direction of the user, ... and that [D] lacked knowledge of the infringements ...), then the fact finder should determine whether [D] showed that it did not financially benefit from infringements that it had the right and ability to control. [¶] [T]he fact finder should consider the service provider's procedures that existed at the time of the infringements when assessing the service provider's right and ability to control the infringements. The fact finder should consider the service provider's general practices, not its conduct with respect to the specific infringements. [¶] Right and ability to control involves something more than the ability to remove or block access to materials posted on a service provider's website. The service provider does something more when it exerts high levels of control over activities of users. The service provider exerts high levels of control, for example, when it[] prescreens sites, gives them extensive advice, prohibits the proliferation of identical sites, provides detailed instructions regarding issues of layout, appearance, and content, and ensures that celebrity images do not oversaturate the content. *At 1059:* In determining whether the financial benefit criterion is satisfied, courts should take a common-sense, fact-based approach, not a formalistic one. The financial benefit need not be substantial or a large proportion of the service provider's revenue." (Internal quotes omitted.)

BWP Media USA, Inc. v. T&S Software Assocs., 852 F.3d 436, 443 (5th Cir.2017). "[D] does not qualify for §512(c)'s safe harbor, as it never designated an agent."

Capitol Records, LLC v. Vimeo, LLC, 826 F.3d 78, 99 (2d Cir.2016). "We conclude: (1) The safe harbor of §512(c) of the DMCA does apply to pre-1972 sound recordings, and therefore protects service providers against liability for copyright infringement under state law with respect to pre-1972 sound recordings, as well as under the federal copyright law for post-1972 recordings. ... (2) The various factual issues that arise in connection with a service provider's claim of the safe harbor of §512(c) are subject to shifting burdens of proof.... [O]n a defendant's claim of the safe harbor of §512(c), the burden of showing facts supporting a finding of red flag knowledge shifts to the plaintiff...."

BWP Media USA, Inc. v. Clarity Digital Grp., 820 F.3d 1175, 1179 (10th Cir.2016). "The word 'user' in the DMCA is straightforward and unambiguous. Simply put, a 'user' is 'one that uses.' In the DMCA context, we agree with the district court that the term 'user' describes a person or entity who avails itself of the service provider's system or network to store material. *At 1181:* The key to limiting the safe harbor provision and preventing the creation of the lawless no-man's-land, ... is to look to the language constraining the word 'user.' The relevant question isn't who is the 'user,' but rather, who directed the storage of the infringing content? Key to this provision is control. There is no protection under §512 when the infringing material is on the system or network as a result of the [Internet-Service Provider's (ISP)] own acts or decisions. When an ISP actively encourages infringement, by urging its users to both upload and download particular copyrighted works, it will not reap the benefits of §512's safe harbor. However, if the infringing content has merely gone through a screening or automated process, the ISP will generally benefit from the safe harbor's protection." (Internal quotes omitted.)

Lenz v. Universal Music Corp., 815 F.3d 1145, 1151 (9th Cir.2016). "We must first determine whether 17 U.S.C. §512(c)(3)(A)(v) requires copyright holders to consider whether the potentially infringing material is a fair use of a copyright under 17 U.S.C. §107 before issuing a takedown notification. ... We agree with the district court and hold that the statute unambiguously contemplates fair use as a use authorized by the law. *At 1153:* We conclude that because ... §107 created a type of non-infringing use, fair use is 'authorized by the law' and a copyright holder must consider the existence of fair use before sending a takedown notification under §512(c). *At 1155:* We hold the willful blindness doctrine may be used to determine whether a copyright holder 'knowingly materially misrepresent[ed]' that it held a 'good faith belief' the offending activity was not a fair use. '[T]he willful blindness doctrine may be applied, in appropriate circumstances, to demonstrate knowledge or awareness of specific instances of infringement under the DMCA.' [¶] To demonstrate willful blindness a plaintiff must establish two factors: '(1) the defendant must subjectively believe that there is a high probability that a fact exists and (2) the defendant must take deliberate actions to avoid learning of that fact.' 'Under this formulation, a willfully blind defendant is one who takes deliberate actions to avoid confirming a high probability of wrongdoing and who can almost be said to have actually known the critical facts.' *At 1156:* We hold a plaintiff may seek recovery of nominal damages for an injury incurred as a result of a §512(f) misrepresentation. [¶] [D] incorrectly asserts that [P] must demonstrate she incurred 'actual monetary loss.' Section 512(k) provides a definition for 'monetary relief' as 'damages, costs, attorneys['] fees, and any other form of monetary payment.' The term 'monetary relief' appears in §512(a), (b)(1), (c)(1), and (d), but is notably absent from §512(f). As a result, the damages an alleged infringer may recover under §512(f) from 'any person' are broader than monetary relief."

UMG Recordings, Inc. v. Shelter Capital Partners, 718 F.3d 1006, 1016 (9th Cir.2013). "[T]he phrase 'by reason of the storage at the direction of the user' is broader causal language than [P] contends, 'clearly meant to cover more than mere electronic storage lockers.' We hold that the language and structure of the statute, as well as the legislative intent that motivated its enactment, clarify that §512(c) encompasses the access-facilitating processes that automatically occur when a user uploads a video to [D's website]. *At 1022-23:* We ... hold that merely hosting a category of copyrightable content, such as music videos, with the general knowledge that one's services could be used to share infringing material, is insufficient to meet the actual knowledge requirement under §512(c)(1)(A)(i). [¶] We reach the same conclusion with regard to the §512(c)(1)(A)(ii) inquiry into whether a service provider is 'aware of facts or circumstances from which infringing activity is apparent.' [¶] Of course, a service provider cannot willfully bury its head in the sand to avoid obtaining such specific knowledge. *At 1030:* We agree with the Second Circuit and hold that, in order to have the 'right and ability to control,' the service provider must 'exert[] substantial influence on the activities of users.' 'Substantial influence' may include ... high levels of control over activities of users.... Or it may include purposeful conduct...."

Viacom Int'l v. YouTube, Inc., 676 F.3d 19, 36 (2d Cir.2012). "[W]e hold that the District Court erred by importing a specific knowledge requirement into the control and benefit provision [§512(c)(1)(B)]. *At 38:* [W]e conclude that the 'right and ability to control' infringing activity under §512(c)(1)(B) 'requires something more than the ability to remove or block access to materials posted on a service provider's website.' The remaining—and more difficult—question is how to define the 'something more' that is required. [¶] In light of our holding that §512(c)(1)(B) does not include a specific knowledge requirement, we think it prudent to remand to the District Court to consider in the first instance whether [Ps] have adduced sufficient evidence to allow a reasonable jury to conclude that [D] had the right and ability to control the infringing activity and received a financial benefit directly attributable to that activity."

Perfect 10, Inc. v. CCBill LLC, 488 F.3d 1102, 1117 (9th Cir.2007). "[W]e hold that 'direct financial benefit' [in §512(c)(1)(B)] should be interpreted consistent with the similarly-worded common law standard for vicarious copyright liability. Thus, the relevant inquiry is 'whether the infringing activity constitutes a draw for subscribers, not just an added benefit.'"

Rossi v. Motion Picture Ass'n of Am., Inc., 391 F.3d 1000, 1004 (9th Cir.2004). The "'good faith belief' requirement in §512(c)(3)(A)(v) encompasses a subjective, rather than objective, standard."

ALS Scan, Inc. v. RemarQ Cmty., Inc., 239 F.3d 619, 623 (4th Cir.2001). To "qualify for this safe harbor protection, the Internet service provider must demonstrate that it has met all three of the safe harbor requirements [of §512(c)(1)], and a showing under the first prong—the lack of actual or constructive knowledge—is prior to and separate from the showings that must be made under the second and third prongs. *At 625:* The DMCA's protection of an innocent service provider disappears at the moment the service provider loses its innocence, i.e., at the moment it becomes aware that a third party is using its system to infringe. At that point, the Act shifts responsibility to the service provider to disable the infringing matter.... [T]he DMCA requires that a copyright owner put the service provider on notice in a detailed manner but allows notice by means that comport with the prescribed format only 'substantially,' rather than perfectly. [Section 512(c)(3)] specifying the requirements of a notification does not seek to burden copyright holders with the responsibility of identifying every infringing work—or even most of them—when multiple copyrights are involved. Instead, the requirements are written so as to reduce the burden of holders of multiple copyrights who face extensive infringement of their works. Thus, when a letter provides notice equivalent to a list of representative works that can be easily identified by the service provider, the notice substantially complies with the notification requirements." *See also* ***In re Aimster***, 334 F.3d 643, 655 (7th Cir.2003).

Ellison v. Robertson, 189 F.Supp.2d 1051, 1063-64 (C.D.Cal.2002), *rev'd in part on other grounds*, 357 F.3d 1072 (9th Cir.2004). "In determining whether the financial benefit criterion [of §512(c)(1)(B)] is satisfied, courts should take a common-sense, fact-based approach, not a formalistic one. In general, a service provider conducting a legitimate business would not be considered to receive a financial benefit directly attributable to the infringing activity where the infringer makes the same kind of payment as non-infringing users of the provider's service." (Internal quotes omitted.)

Hendrickson v. eBay Inc., 165 F.Supp.2d 1082, 1089-90 (C.D.Cal.2001). "[P's] pre-suit 'cease and desist' letter and e-mails to [D] do not include several of the key elements for proper notice required by [§512(c)(3)]. Additionally, none of these writings includes a written statement that [P] 'has a good faith belief that use of the material in the manner complained of is not authorized.' The complete failure to include these key elements in his written communications to [D], even after [D] specifically asked for these items, renders [P's] notification of claimed infringement deficient under §512(c)(3)."

§512(f)

Lenz v. Universal Music Corp., 815 F.3d 1145, 1148 (9th Cir.2016). "[P] alleges [D] misrepresented in a takedown notification that her 29-second home video (the 'video') constituted an infringing use of a portion of a [protected] composition.... Her claim boils down to a question of whether copyright holders have been abusing the extrajudicial takedown procedures provided for in the DMCA by declining to first evaluate whether the content qualifies as fair use. We hold that the statute requires copyright holders to consider fair use before sending a takedown notification, and that [failure to do so] raises a triable issue as to whether the copyright holder formed a subjective good faith belief that the use was not authorized by law. *At 1154:* To be clear, if a copyright holder ignores or neglects our unequivocal holding that it must consider fair use before sending a takedown notification, it is liable for damages under §512(f). If, however, a copyright holder forms a subjective *good faith* belief the allegedly infringing material does not constitute fair use, we are in no position to dispute the copyright holder's belief even if we would have reached the opposite conclusion. A copyright holder who pays lip service to the consideration of fair use by claiming it formed a good faith belief when there is evidence to the contrary is still subject to §512(f) liability."

§512(h)

In re Subpoena Issued to Birch Comms., No. 1:14-cv-3904-WSD (N.D.Ga.2015) (order; 5-5-15). "Although the 11th Circuit has not considered the issue, the Courts of Appeals for the District of Columbia Circuit and the Eighth Circuit have held ... that §512(h) does not authorize issuance of a subpoena to a §512(a) [Internet-service provider] that acts as a conduit for data transfer between two users, but does not store any material on its servers." *See also* ***In re Charter Comms.***, 393 F.3d 771, 777 (8th Cir.2005); ***Recording Indus. Ass'n of Am., Inc. v. Verizon Internet Servs.***, 351 F.3d 1229, 1235-36 (D.C.Cir.2003).

§512(i)

EMI Christian Music Grp. v. MP3tunes, LLC, 844 F.3d 79, 89 (2d Cir.2016). "[T]he DMCA does not itself define 'repeat infringers.' [W]e take 'repeat' to mean 'a person who does something ... again or repeatedly,' ... while an 'infringer' is '[s]omeone who interferes with one of the exclusive rights of a ... copyright[ ]'.... In the context of this case, all it took to be a 'repeat infringer' was to repeatedly sideload copyrighted material for personal use. *At 90:* [T]he legislative history of the DMCA indicates that a 'repeat infringer' does not need to know of the infringing nature of its online activities." *See also* ***BMG Rights Mgmt. (US) LLC v. Cox Comms.***, 881 F.3d 293, 302-03 (4th Cir.2018).

Perfect 10, Inc. v. CCBill LLC, 488 F.3d 1102, 1109 (9th Cir.2007). Section 512(i)(1)(A) "does not define 'reasonably implemented.' We hold that a service provider 'implements' a policy if it has a working notification system, a procedure for dealing with DMCA-compliant notifications, and if it does not actively prevent copyright owners from collecting information needed to issue such notifications. [A]n implementation is reasonable if, under 'appropriate circumstances,' the service provider terminates users who repeatedly or blatantly infringe copyright. *At 1110:* [A] substantial failure to record webmasters associated with allegedly infringing websites may raise a genuine issue of material fact as to the implementation of the service provider's repeat infringer policy. *At 1111:* A service provider reasonably implements its repeat infringer policy if it terminates users when 'appropriate.' [¶] To identify and terminate repeat infringers, a service provider need not affirmatively police its users for evidence of repeat infringement. *At 1112:* [S]ubstantial compliance [under §512(c)(3)(B)(ii)] means substantial compliance with *all* of §512(c)(3)'s clauses, not just some of them. *At 1113:* [D's] actions towards copyright holders who are not a party to the litigation are relevant in determining whether [Ds] reasonably implemented their repeat infringer policy. Section 512(i)(1)(A) requires an assessment of the service provider's 'policy,' not how the service provider treated a particular copyright holder. *At 1114:* [I]n order for a website to qualify as a 'red flag' of infringement [under §512(c)(1)(A)(ii)], it would need to be apparent that the website instructed or enabled users to infringe another's copyright. We find that the burden of determining whether passwords on a website enabled infringement is not on the service provider. ... Password-hacking websites are thus not *per se* 'red flags' of infringement." *See also* ***BMG Rights Mgmt. (US) LLC v. Cox Comms.***, 881 F.3d 293, 305 (4th Cir.2018).

§512(l)

CoStar Grp. v. LoopNet, Inc., 373 F.3d 544, 552 (4th Cir.2004). Section 512(*l*) "specifically provides that despite a failure to meet the safe-harbor conditions in §512(c) and (i), an [Internet-service provider] is still entitled to all other arguments under the law—whether by way of an affirmative defense or through an argument that conduct simply does not constitute a prima facie case of infringement under the Copyright Act." *See also* ***BWP Media USA, Inc. v. T&S Software Assocs.***, 852 F.3d 436, 443-44 (5th Cir.2017).

§512(m)

Viacom Int'l v. YouTube, Inc., 676 F.3d 19, 34 (2d Cir.2012). "[Ps] argue that the District Court erred in granting summary judgment to [Ds] despite evidence that [D] was 'willfully blind' to specific infringing activity. On this issue of first impression, we consider the application of the common law willful blindness doctrine in the DMCA context. *At 35:* A person is 'willfully blind' or engages in 'conscious avoidance' amounting to knowledge where the person was aware of a high probability of the fact in dispute and consciously avoided confirming that fact. [¶] Section 512(m) is explicit: DMCA safe harbor protection cannot be conditioned on affirmative monitoring by a service provider. For that reason, §512(m) is incompatible with a broad common law duty to monitor or otherwise seek out infringing activity based on general awareness that infringement may be occurring. That fact does not, however, dispose of the abrogation inquiry; ... willful blindness cannot be defined as an affirmative duty to monitor. Because the statute does not speak directly to the willful blindness doctrine, §512(m) limits—but does not abrogate—the doctrine. Accordingly, we hold that the willful blindness doctrine may be applied, in appropriate circumstances, to demonstrate knowledge or awareness of specific instances of infringement under the DMCA." (Internal quotes omitted.)

§513. DETERMINATION OF REASONABLE LICENSE FEES FOR INDIVIDUAL PROPRIETORS

In the case of any performing rights society subject to a consent decree which provides for the determination of reasonable license rates or fees to be charged by the performing rights society, notwithstanding the provisions of that consent decree, an individual proprietor who owns or operates fewer than 7 non-publicly traded establishments in which nondramatic musical works are performed publicly and who claims that any license agreement offered by that performing rights society is unreasonable in its license rate or fee as to that individual proprietor, shall be entitled to determination of a reasonable license rate or fee as follows:

(1) The individual proprietor may commence such proceeding for determination of a reasonable license rate or fee by filing an application in the applicable district court under paragraph (2) that a rate disagreement exists and by serving a copy of the application on the performing rights society. Such proceeding shall commence in the applicable district court within 90 days after the service of such copy, except that such 90-day requirement shall be subject to the administrative requirements of the court.

(2) The proceeding under paragraph (1) shall be held, at the individual proprietor's election, in the judicial district of the district court with jurisdiction over the applicable consent decree or in that place of holding court of a district court that is the seat of the Federal circuit (other than the Court of Appeals for the Federal Circuit) in which the proprietor's establishment is located.

(3) Such proceeding shall be held before the judge of the court with jurisdiction over the consent decree governing the performing rights society. At the discretion of the court, the proceeding shall be held before a special master or magistrate judge appointed by such judge. Should that consent decree provide for the appointment of an advisor or advisors to the court for any purpose, any such advisor shall be the special master so named by the court.

(4) In any such proceeding, the industry rate shall be presumed to have been reasonable at the time it was agreed to or determined by the court. Such presumption shall in no way affect a determination of whether the rate is being correctly applied to the individual proprietor.

(5) Pending the completion of such proceeding, the individual proprietor shall have the right to perform publicly the copyrighted musical compositions in the repertoire of the performing rights society by paying an interim license rate or fee into an interest bearing escrow account with the clerk of the court, subject to retroactive adjustment when a final rate or fee has been determined, in an amount equal to the industry rate, or, in the absence of an industry rate, the amount of the most recent license rate or fee agreed to by the parties.

(6) Any decision rendered in such proceeding by a special master or magistrate judge named under paragraph (3) shall be reviewed by the judge of the court with jurisdiction over the consent decree governing the performing rights society. Such proceeding, including such review, shall be concluded within 6 months after its commencement.

(7) Any such final determination shall be binding only as to the individual proprietor commencing the proceeding, and shall not be applicable to any other proprietor or any other performing rights society, and the performing rights society shall be relieved of any obligation of nondiscrimination among similarly situated music users that may be imposed by the consent decree governing its operations.

(8) An individual proprietor may not bring more than one proceeding provided for in this section for the determination of a reasonable license rate or fee under any license agreement with respect to any one performing rights society.

(9) For purposes of this section, the term "industry rate" means the license fee a performing rights society has agreed to with, or which has been determined by the court for, a significant segment of the music user industry to which the individual proprietor belongs.

History of 17 U.S.C. §513: Oct. 27, 1998, P.L. 105-298, §203(a), 112 Stat. 2831; Aug. 5, 1999, P.L. 106-44, §1(c)(1), 113 Stat. 221.

CHAPTER 6. IMPORTATION & EXPORTATION

§601. REPEALED

Repealed Dec. 9, 2010, P.L. 111-295, §4(a), 124 Stat. 3180.

§602. INFRINGING IMPORTATION OR EXPORTATION OF COPIES OR PHONORECORDS

(a) Infringing importation or exportation—

(1) Importation.—Importation into the United States, without the authority of the owner of copyright under this title, of copies or phonorecords of a work that have been acquired outside the United States is an infringement of the exclusive right to distribute copies or phonorecords under section 106, actionable under section 501.

(2) Importation or exportation of infringing items.—Importation into the United States or exportation from the United States, without the authority of the owner of copyright under this title, of copies or phonorecords, the making of which either constituted an infringement of copyright, or which would have constituted an infringement of copyright if this title had been applicable, is an infringement of the exclusive right to distribute copies or phonorecords under section 106, actionable under sections 501 and 506.

(3) Exceptions.—This subsection does not apply to—

(A) importation or exportation of copies or phonorecords under the authority or for the use of the Government of the United States or of any State or political subdivision of a State, but not including copies or phonorecords for use in schools, or copies of any audiovisual work imported for purposes other than archival use;

(B) importation or exportation, for the private use of the importer or exporter and not for distribution, by any person with respect to no more than one copy or phonorecord of any one work at any one time, or by any person arriving from outside the United States or departing from the United States with respect to copies or phonorecords forming part of such person's personal baggage; or

(C) importation by or for an organization operated for scholarly, educational, or religious purposes and not for private gain, with respect to no more than one copy of an audiovisual work solely for its archival purposes, and no more than five copies or phonorecords of any other work for its library lending or archival purposes, unless the importation of such copies or phonorecords is part of an activity consisting of systematic reproduction or distribution, engaged in by such organization in violation of the provisions of section 108(g)(2).

(b) Import prohibition.—In a case where the making of the copies or phonorecords would have constituted an infringement of copyright if this title had been applicable, their importation is prohibited. In a case where the copies or phonorecords were lawfully made, United States Customs and Border Protection has no authority to prevent their importation. In either case, the Secretary of the Treasury is authorized to prescribe, by regulation, a procedure under which any person claiming an interest in the copyright in a particular work may, upon payment of a specified fee, be entitled to notification by United States Customs and Border Protection of the importation of articles that appear to be copies or phonorecords of the work.

History of 17 U.S.C. §602: Oct. 19, 1976, P.L. 94-553, §101, 90 Stat. 2589; Oct. 13, 2008, P.L. 110-403, §105(b), (c)(1), 122 Stat. 4259, 4260; Dec. 9, 2010, P.L. 111-295, §4(b)(1), (c), 124 Stat. 3180, 3181.

See also 19 U.S.C. §1337.

ANNOTATIONS

Quality King Distribs. v. L'anza Research Int'l, 523 U.S. 135, 145 (1998). "After the first sale of a copyrighted item 'lawfully made under this title,' any subsequent purchaser, whether from a domestic or from a foreign reseller, is obviously an 'owner' of that item. Read literally, [17 U.S.C.] §109(a) unambiguously states that such an owner 'is entitled, without the authority of the copyright owner, to sell' that item. Moreover, since [17 U.S.C.] §602(a) merely provides that unauthorized importation is an infringement of an exclusive right 'under [17 U.S.C.] §106,' and since that limited right does not encompass resales by lawful owners, the literal text of §602(a) is simply inapplicable to both domestic and foreign owners of [P's] products who decide to import and resell them in the U.S." Held: 'First sale' doctrine in §109(a) is applicable to imported copies. *See also* ***Enesco Corp. v. Jan Bell Mktg., Inc.***, 992 F.Supp. 1021, 1023 (N.D.Ill.1998).

Geophysical Serv. v. TGS-NOPEC Geophysical Co., 850 F.3d 785, 792 (5th Cir.2017). "Unauthorized importation of copyrighted work is a statutorily established method of demonstrating infringement of one of the exclusive rights afforded by [17 U.S.C.] §106 ... and is not itself a separate claim that must be separately pleaded."

Litecubes, LLC v. Northern Light Prods., 523 F.3d 1353, 1366 (Fed.Cir.2008). "The question raised here, whether the lack of extraterritorial reach of the Copyright Act limits the subject matter jurisdiction of the federal courts, implicates the substance of the Copyright Act but is ultimately a question of our jurisdiction. *At 1367:* Both parties stated at oral argument that the Patent Act and the Copyright Act should be interpreted consistently, and thus that if the Patent Act's requirement that the infringing act take place in the U.S. is not a jurisdictional requirement, the exclusion from the Copyright Act of acts taking place entirely abroad should also not be jurisdictional. We agree. [¶] [W]hether the territorial limitation is explicit in the statute, as in the Patent Act, or implied based on the presumption that Congress does not intend its acts to have extraterritorial effect, as in the Copyright Act, the limit on the extraterritorial reach of a statute is a question of statutory interpretation—what did Congress intend the scope of its exercise of prescriptive jurisdiction to be—not an independent limitation on the federal court's authority. And ***Arbaugh***'s bright-line rule applies. That is, whether an accused action is within the extraterritorial limitation should be treated as an element of the claim, not a predicate for subject matter jurisdiction, unless Congress has clearly provided that the limitation is jurisdictional."

Denbicare Inc. v. Toys "R" Us, Inc., 84 F.3d 1143, 1149 (9th Cir.1996), *abrogated on other grounds*, ***Kirtsaeng v. John Wiley & Sons, Inc.***, 568 U.S. 519 (2013). "Given the 1976 [Copyright] Act's definition of the term 'United States,' it seems highly improbable that Congress intended ... that Foreign Trade Zones on the geographic and political territory of the U.S. be considered 'outside the U.S.' for purposes of the acquisition required for a violation of §602 by importation. ... Because the diapers were already in the U.S. [in a Foreign Trade Zone], [D] did not violate [P's] exclusive distribution right under §602."

Subafilms, Ltd. v. MGM-Pathe Comms., 24 F.3d 1088, 1096 (9th Cir.1994). "Congress chose in 1976 to expand one specific 'extraterritorial' application of the [Copyright] Act by declaring that the unauthorized importation of copyrighted works constitutes infringement even when the copies lawfully were made abroad. Had Congress been inclined to overturn the preexisting doctrine that infringing acts that take place wholly outside the U.S. are not actionable under the Copyright Act, it knew how to do so." Held: Federal copyright law does not apply to extraterritorial acts of infringement. *But see* ***Expediters Int'l v. Direct Line Cargo Mgmt. Servs.***, 995 F.Supp. 468, 477 (D.N.J.1998) (authorization of infringing acts abroad is direct, actionable infringement).

Richard Anderson Photography v. Brown, 852 F.2d 114, 120 (4th Cir.1988). The "exception [in §602(a)(1)] can most logically ... be read as exempting from liability only those private persons or public officials acting in their individual capacity who import copyright materials under governmental authority or for governmental use."

§603. IMPORTATION PROHIBITIONS: ENFORCEMENT & DISPOSITION OF EXCLUDED ARTICLES

(a) The Secretary of the Treasury and the United States Postal Service shall separately or jointly make regulations for the enforcement of the provisions of this title prohibiting importation.

(b) These regulations may require, as a condition for the exclusion of articles under section 602—

(1) that the person seeking exclusion obtain a court order enjoining importation of the articles; or

(2) that the person seeking exclusion furnish proof, of a specified nature and in accordance with prescribed procedures, that the copyright in which such person claims an interest is valid and that the importation would violate the prohibition in section 602; the person seeking exclusion may also be required to post a surety bond for any injury that may result if the detention or exclusion of the articles proves to be unjustified.

(c) Articles imported in violation of the importation prohibitions of this title are subject to seizure and forfeiture in the same manner as property imported in violation of the customs revenue laws. Forfeited articles shall be destroyed as directed by the Secretary of the Treasury or the court, as the case may be.

History of 17 U.S.C. §603: Oct. 19, 1976, P.L. 94-553, §101, 90 Stat. 2590; July 2, 1996, P.L. 104-153, §8, 110 Stat. 1388.

See also 19 U.S.C. §§1337, 1595a.

CHAPTER 7. COPYRIGHT OFFICE

§701. THE COPYRIGHT OFFICE: GENERAL RESPONSIBILITIES & ORGANIZATION

(a) All administrative functions and duties under this title, except as otherwise specified, are the responsibility of the Register of Copyrights as director of the Copyright Office of the Library of Congress. The Register of Copyrights, together with the subordinate officers and employees of the Copyright Office, shall be appointed by the Librarian of Congress, and shall act under the Librarian's general direction and supervision.

(b) In addition to the functions and duties set out elsewhere in this chapter, the Register of Copyrights shall perform the following functions:

(1) Advise Congress on national and international issues relating to copyright, other matters arising under this title, and related matters.

(2) Provide information and assistance to Federal departments and agencies and the Judiciary on national and international issues relating to copyright, other matters arising under this title, and related matters.

(3) Participate in meetings of international intergovernmental organizations and meetings with foreign government officials relating to copyright, other matters arising under this title, and related matters, including as a member of United States delegations as authorized by the appropriate Executive branch authority.

(4) Conduct studies and programs regarding copyright, other matters arising under this title, and related matters, the administration of the Copyright Office, or any function vested in the Copyright Office by law, including educational programs conducted cooperatively with foreign intellectual property offices and international intergovernmental organizations.

(5) Perform such other functions as Congress may direct, or as may be appropriate in furtherance of the functions and duties specifically set forth in this title.

(c) The Register of Copyrights shall adopt a seal to be used on and after January 1, 1978, to authenticate all certified documents issued by the Copyright Office.

(d) The Register of Copyrights shall make an annual report to the Librarian of Congress of the work and accomplishments of the Copyright Office during the previous fiscal year. The annual report of the Register of Copyrights shall be published separately and as a part of the annual report of the Librarian of Congress.

(e) Except as provided by section 706(b) and the regulations issued thereunder, all actions taken by the Register of Copyrights under this title are subject to the provisions of the Administrative Procedure Act of June 11, 1946, as amended (c. 324, 60 Stat. 237, Title 5, United States Code, Chapter 5, Subchapter II and Chapter 7).

(f) The Register of Copyrights shall be compensated at the rate of pay in effect for level III of the Executive Schedule under section 5314 of title 5. The Librarian of Congress shall establish not more than four positions for Associate Registers of Copyrights, in accordance with the recommendations of the Register of Copyrights. The Librarian shall make appointments to such positions after consultation with the Register of Copyrights. Each Associate Register of Copyrights shall be paid at a rate not to exceed the maximum annual rate of basic pay payable for GS-18 of the General Schedule under section 5332 of title 5.

History of 17 U.S.C. §701: Oct. 19, 1976, P.L. 94-553, §101, 90 Stat. 2591; July 3, 1990, P.L. 101-319, §2(b), 104 Stat. 290; Oct. 28, 1998, P.L. 105-304, §401(a)(2), (b), 112 Stat. 2887.

See also 2 U.S.C. §§170, 1703; 37 C.F.R. §§201.1-201.40, 204.1-204.9.

§702. COPYRIGHT OFFICE REGULATIONS

The Register of Copyrights is authorized to establish regulations not inconsistent with law for the administration of the functions and duties made the responsibility of the Register under this title. All regulations established by the Register under this title are subject to the approval of the Librarian of Congress.

History of 17 U.S.C. §702: Oct. 19, 1976, P.L. 94-553, §101, 90 Stat. 2591.

§703. EFFECTIVE DATE OF ACTIONS IN COPYRIGHT OFFICE

In any case in which time limits are prescribed under this title for the performance of an action in the Copyright Office, and in which the last day of the prescribed period falls on a Saturday, Sunday, holiday, or other nonbusiness day within the District of Columbia or the Federal Government, the action may be taken on the next succeeding business day, and is effective as of the date when the period expired.

History of 17 U.S.C. §703: Oct. 19, 1976, P.L. 94-553, §101, 90 Stat. 2591.

§704. RETENTION & DISPOSITION OF ARTICLES DEPOSITED IN COPYRIGHT OFFICE

(a) Upon their deposit in the Copyright Office under sections 407 and 408, all copies, phonorecords, and identifying material, including those deposited in connection with claims that have been refused registration, are the property of the United States Government.

(b) In the case of published works, all copies, phonorecords, and identifying material deposited are available to the Library of Congress for its collections, or for exchange or transfer to any other library. In the case of unpublished works, the Library is entitled, under regulations that the Register of Copyrights shall prescribe, to select any deposits for its collections or for transfer to the National Archives of the United States or to a Federal records center, as defined in section 2901 of title 44.

(c) The Register of Copyrights is authorized, for specific or general categories of works, to make a facsimile reproduction of all or any part of the material deposited under section 408, and to make such reproduction a part of the Copyright Office records of the registration, before transferring such material to the Library of Congress as provided by subsection (b), or before destroying or otherwise disposing of such material as provided by subsection (d).

(d) Deposits not selected by the Library under subsection (b), or identifying portions or reproductions of them, shall be retained under the control of the Copyright Office, including retention in Government storage facilities, for the longest period considered practicable and desirable by the Register of Copyrights and the Librarian of Congress. After that period it is within the joint discretion of the Register and the Librarian to order their destruction or other disposition; but, in the case of unpublished works, no deposit shall be knowingly or intentionally destroyed or otherwise disposed of during its term of copyright unless a facsimile reproduction of the entire deposit has been made a part of the Copyright Office records as provided by subsection (c).

(e) The depositor of copies, phonorecords, or identifying material under section 408, or the copyright owner of record, may request retention, under the control of the Copyright Office, of one or more of such articles for the full term of copyright in the work. The Register of Copyrights shall prescribe, by regulation, the conditions under which such requests are to be made and granted, and shall fix the fee to be charged under section 708(a) if the request is granted.

History of 17 U.S.C. §704: Oct. 19, 1976, P.L. 94-553, §101, 90 Stat. 2591; July 3, 1990, P.L. 101-318, §2(c), 104 Stat. 288; Dec. 9, 2010, P.L. 111-295, §6(e), 124 Stat. 3181.

See also 37 C.F.R. §201.23.

§705. COPYRIGHT OFFICE RECORDS: PREPARATION, MAINTENANCE, PUBLIC INSPECTION, & SEARCHING

(a) The Register of Copyrights shall ensure that records of deposits, registrations, recordations, and other actions taken under this title are maintained, and that indexes of such records are prepared.

(b) Such records and indexes, as well as the articles deposited in connection with completed copyright registrations and retained under the control of the Copyright Office, shall be open to public inspection.

(c) Upon request and payment of the fee specified by section 708, the Copyright Office shall make a search of its public records, indexes, and deposits, and shall furnish a report of the information they disclose with respect to any particular deposits, registrations, or recorded documents.

History of 17 U.S.C. §705: Oct. 19, 1976, P.L. 94-553, §101, 90 Stat. 2592; Oct. 27, 2000, P.L. 106-379, §3(a)(2), 114 Stat. 1445.

§706. COPIES OF COPYRIGHT OFFICE RECORDS

(a) Copies may be made of any public records or indexes of the Copyright Office; additional certificates of copyright registration and copies of any public records or indexes may be furnished upon request and payment of the fees specified by section 708.

(b) Copies or reproductions of deposited articles retained under the control of the Copyright Office shall be authorized or furnished only under the conditions specified by the Copyright Office regulations.

History of 17 U.S.C. §706: Oct. 19, 1976, P.L. 94-553, §101, 90 Stat. 2592.

§707. COPYRIGHT OFFICE FORMS & PUBLICATIONS

(a) Catalog of copyright entries.—The Register of Copyrights shall compile and publish at periodic intervals catalogs of all copyright registrations. These catalogs shall be divided into parts in accordance with the various classes of works, and the Register has discretion to determine, on the basis of practicability and usefulness, the form and frequency of publication of each particular part.

(b) Other publications.—The Register shall furnish, free of charge upon request, application forms for copyright registration and general informational material in connection with the functions of the Copyright Office. The Register also has the authority to publish compilations of information, bibliographies, and other material he or she considers to be of value to the public.

(c) Distribution of publications.—All publications of the Copyright Office shall be furnished to depository libraries as specified under section 1905 of title 44, and, aside from those furnished free of charge, shall be offered for sale to the public at prices based on the cost of reproduction and distribution.

History of 17 U.S.C. §707: Oct. 19, 1976, P.L. 94-553, §101, 90 Stat. 2592.

§708. COPYRIGHT OFFICE FEES

(a) Fees.—Fees shall be paid to the Register of Copyrights—

(1) on filing each application under section 408 for registration of a copyright claim or for a supplementary registration, including the issuance of a certificate of registration if registration is made;

(2) on filing each application for registration of a claim for renewal of a subsisting copyright under section 304(a), including the issuance of a certificate of registration if registration is made;

(3) for the issuance of a receipt for a deposit under section 407;

(4) for the recordation, as provided by section 205, of a transfer of copyright ownership or other document;

(5) for the filing, under section 115(b), of a notice of intention to obtain a compulsory license;

(6) for the recordation, under section 302(c), of a statement revealing the identity of an author of an anonymous or pseudonymous work, or for the recordation, under section 302(d), of a statement relating to the death of an author;

(7) for the issuance, under section 706, of an additional certificate of registration;

(8) for the issuance of any other certification;

(9) for the making and reporting of a search as provided by section 705, and for any related services;

(10) on filing a statement of account based on secondary transmissions of primary transmissions pursuant to section 119 or 122; and

(11) on filing a statement of account based on secondary transmissions of primary transmissions pursuant to section 111.

The Register is authorized to fix fees for other services, including the cost of preparing copies of Copyright Office records, whether or not such copies are certified, based on the cost of providing the service. Fees established under paragraphs (10) and (11) shall be reasonable and may not exceed one-half of the cost necessary to cover reasonable expenses incurred by the Copyright Office for the collection and administration of the statements of account and any royalty fees deposited with such statements.

(b) Adjustment of fees.—The Register of Copyrights may, by regulation, adjust the fees for the services specified in paragraphs (1) through (9) of subsection (a) in the following manner:

(1) The Register shall conduct a study of the costs incurred by the Copyright Office for the registration of claims, the recordation of documents, and the provision of services. The study shall also consider the timing of any adjustment in fees and the authority to use such fees consistent with the budget.

(2) The Register may, on the basis of the study under paragraph (1), and subject to paragraph (5), adjust fees to not more than that necessary to cover the reasonable costs incurred by the Copyright Office for the services described in paragraph (1), plus a reasonable inflation adjustment to account for any estimated increase in costs.

(3) Any fee established under paragraph (2) shall be rounded off to the nearest dollar, or for a fee less than $12, rounded off to the nearest 50 cents.

(4) Fees established under this subsection shall be fair and equitable and give due consideration to the objectives of the copyright system.

(5) If the Register determines under paragraph (2) that fees should be adjusted, the Register shall prepare a proposed fee schedule and submit the schedule with the accompanying economic analysis to the Congress. The fees proposed by the Register may be instituted after the end of 120 days after the schedule is submitted to the Congress unless, within that 120-day period, a law is enacted stating in substance that the Congress does not approve the schedule.

(c) The fees prescribed by or under this section are applicable to the United States Government and any of its agencies, employees, or officers, but the Register of Copyrights has discretion to waive the requirement of this subsection in occasional or isolated cases involving relatively small amounts.

(d)(1) Except as provided in paragraph (2), all fees received under this section shall be deposited by the Register of Copyrights in the Treasury of the United States and shall be credited to the appropriations for necessary expenses of the Copyright Office. Such fees that are collected shall remain available until expended. The Register may, in accordance with regulations that he or she shall prescribe, refund any sum paid by mistake or in excess of the fee required by this section.

(2) In the case of fees deposited against future services, the Register of Copyrights shall request the Secretary of the Treasury to invest in interest-bearing securities in the United States Treasury any portion of the fees that, as determined by the Register, is not required to meet current deposit account demands. Funds from such portion of fees shall be invested in securities that permit funds to be available to the Copyright Office at all times if they are determined to be necessary to meet current deposit account demands. Such investments shall be in public debt securities with maturities suitable to the needs of the Copyright Office, as determined by the Register of Copyrights, and bearing interest at rates determined by the Secretary of the Treasury, taking into consideration current market yields on outstanding marketable obligations of the United States of comparable maturities.

(3) The income on such investments shall be deposited in the Treasury of the United States and shall be credited to the appropriations for necessary expenses of the Copyright Office.

History of 17 U.S.C. §708: Oct. 19, 1976, P.L. 94-553, §101, 90 Stat. 2593; Aug. 5, 1977, P.L. 95-94, §406(b), 91 Stat. 682; Oct. 15, 1982, P.L. 97-366, §1, 96 Stat. 1759; July 3, 1990, P.L. 101-318, §2, 104 Stat. 287; June 26, 1992, P.L. 102-307, §102(f), 106 Stat. 266; Nov. 13, 1997, P.L. 105-80, §7, 111 Stat. 1532; Oct. 27, 2000, P.L. 106-379, §3(a)(3), 114 Stat. 1445; May 27, 2010, P.L. 111-175, §106, 124 Stat. 1244.

See also 37 C.F.R. §201.3.

§709. DELAY IN DELIVERY CAUSED BY DISRUPTION OF POSTAL OR OTHER SERVICES

In any case in which the Register of Copyrights determines, on the basis of such evidence as the Register may by regulation require, that a deposit, application, fee, or any other material to be delivered to the Copyright Office by a particular date, would have been received in the Copyright Office in due time except for a general disruption or suspension of postal or other transportation or communications services, the actual receipt of such material in the Copyright Office within one month after the date on which the Register determines that the disruption or suspension of such services has terminated, shall be considered timely.

History of 17 U.S.C. §709: Oct. 19, 1976, P.L. 94-553, §101, 90 Stat. 2594.

§710. REPEALED

Repealed Oct. 27, 2000, P.L. 106-379, §3(a)(1), 114 Stat. 1445.

CHAPTER 8. PROCEEDINGS BY COPYRIGHT ROYALTY JUDGES

§801. COPYRIGHT ROYALTY JUDGES; APPOINTMENT & FUNCTIONS

(a) Appointment.—The Librarian of Congress shall appoint 3 full-time Copyright Royalty Judges, and shall appoint 1 of the 3 as the Chief Copyright Royalty Judge. The Librarian shall make appointments to such positions after consultation with the Register of Copyrights.

(b) Functions.—Subject to the provisions of this chapter, the functions of the Copyright Royalty Judges shall be as follows:

(1) To make determinations and adjustments of reasonable terms and rates of royalty payments as provided in sections 112(e), 114, 115, 116, 118, 119, and 1004. The rates applicable under sections 114(f)(1)(B), 115, and 116 shall be calculated to achieve the following objectives:

(A) To maximize the availability of creative works to the public.

(B) To afford the copyright owner a fair return for his or her creative work and the copyright user a fair income under existing economic conditions.

(C) To reflect the relative roles of the copyright owner and the copyright user in the product made available to the public with respect to relative creative contribution, technological contribution, capital investment, cost, risk, and contribution to the opening of new markets for creative expression and media for their communication.

(D) To minimize any disruptive impact on the structure of the industries involved and on generally prevailing industry practices.

(2) To make determinations concerning the adjustment of the copyright royalty rates under section 111 solely in accordance with the following provisions:

(A) The rates established by section 111(d)(1)(B) may be adjusted to reflect—

(i) national monetary inflation or deflation; or

(ii) changes in the average rates charged cable subscribers for the basic service of providing secondary transmissions to maintain the real constant dollar level of the royalty fee per subscriber which existed as of the date of October 19, 1976, except that—

(I) if the average rates charged cable system subscribers for the basic service of providing secondary transmissions are changed so that the average rates exceed national monetary inflation, no change in the rates established by section 111(d)(1)(B) shall be permitted; and

(II) no increase in the royalty fee shall be permitted based on any reduction in the average number of distant signal equivalents per subscriber.

The Copyright Royalty Judges may consider all factors relating to the maintenance of such level of payments, including, as an extenuating factor, whether the industry has been restrained by subscriber rate regulating authorities from increasing the rates for the basic service of providing secondary transmissions.

(B) In the event that the rules and regulations of the Federal Communications Commission are amended at any time after April 15, 1976, to permit the carriage by cable systems of additional television broadcast signals beyond the local service area of the primary transmitters of such signals, the royalty rates established by section 111(d)(1)(B) may be adjusted to ensure that the rates for the additional distant signal equivalents resulting from such carriage are reasonable in the light of the changes effected by the amendment to such rules and regulations. In determining the reasonableness of rates proposed following an amendment of Federal Communications Commission rules and regulations, the Copyright Royalty Judges shall consider, among other factors, the economic impact on copyright owners and users; except that no adjustment in royalty rates shall be made under this subparagraph with respect to any distant signal equivalent or fraction thereof represented by—

(i) carriage of any signal permitted under the rules and regulations of the Federal Communications Commission in effect on April 15, 1976, or the carriage of a signal of the same type (that is, independent, network, or noncommercial educational) substituted for such permitted signal; or

(ii) a television broadcast signal first carried after April 15, 1976, pursuant to an individual waiver of the rules and regulations of the Federal Communications Commission, as such rules and regulations were in effect on April 15, 1976.

(C) In the event of any change in the rules and regulations of the Federal Communications Commission with respect to syndicated and sports program exclusivity after April 15, 1976, the rates established by section 111(d)(1)(B) may be adjusted to assure that such rates are reasonable in light of the changes to such rules and regulations, but any such adjustment shall apply only to the affected television broadcast signals carried on those systems affected by the change.

(D) The gross receipts limitations established by section 111(d)(1) (C) and (D) shall be adjusted to reflect national monetary inflation or deflation or changes in the average rates charged cable system subscribers for the basic service of providing secondary transmissions to maintain the real constant dollar value of the exemption provided by such section, and the royalty rate specified therein shall not be subject to adjustment.

(3)(A) To authorize the distribution, under sections 111, 119, and 1007, of those royalty fees collected under sections 111, 119, and 1005, as the case may be, to the extent that the Copyright Royalty Judges have found that the distribution of such fees is not subject to controversy.

(B) In cases where the Copyright Royalty Judges determine that controversy exists, the Copyright Royalty Judges shall determine the distribution of such fees, including partial distributions, in accordance with section 111, 119, or 1007, as the case may be.

(C) Notwithstanding section 804(b)(8), the Copyright Royalty Judges, at any time after the filing of claims under section 111, 119, or 1007, may, upon motion of one or more of the claimants and after publication in the Federal Register of a request for responses to the motion from interested claimants, make a partial distribution of such fees, if, based upon all responses received during the 30-day period beginning on the date of such publication, the Copyright Royalty Judges conclude that no claimant entitled to receive such fees has stated a reasonable objection to the partial distribution, and all such claimants—

(i) agree to the partial distribution;

(ii) sign an agreement obligating them to return any excess amounts to the extent necessary to comply with the final determination on the distribution of the fees made under subparagraph (B);

(iii) file the agreement with the Copyright Royalty Judges; and

(iv) agree that such funds are available for distribution.

(D) The Copyright Royalty Judges and any other officer or employee acting in good faith in distributing funds under subparagraph (C) shall not be held liable for the payment of any excess fees under subparagraph (C). The Copyright Royalty Judges shall, at the time the final determination is made, calculate any such excess amounts.

(4) To accept or reject royalty claims filed under sections 111, 119, and 1007, on the basis of timeliness or the failure to establish the basis for a claim.

(5) To accept or reject rate adjustment petitions as provided in section 804 and petitions to participate as provided in section 803(b) (1) and (2).

(6) To determine the status of a digital audio recording device or a digital audio interface device under sections 1002 and 1003, as provided in section 1010.

(7)(A) To adopt as a basis for statutory terms and rates or as a basis for the distribution of statutory royalty payments, an agreement concerning such matters reached among some or all of the participants in a proceeding at any time during the proceeding, except that—

(i) the Copyright Royalty Judges shall provide to those that would be bound by the terms, rates, or other determination set by any agreement in a proceeding to determine royalty rates an opportunity to comment on the agreement and shall provide to participants in the proceeding under section 803(b)(2) that would be bound by the terms, rates, or other determination set by the agreement an opportunity to comment on the agreement and object to its adoption as a basis for statutory terms and rates; and

(ii) the Copyright Royalty Judges may decline to adopt the agreement as a basis for statutory terms and rates for participants that are not parties to the agreement, if any participant described in clause (i) objects to the agreement and the Copyright Royalty Judges conclude, based on the record before them if one exists, that the agreement does not provide a reasonable basis for setting statutory terms or rates.

(B) License agreements voluntarily negotiated pursuant to section 112(e)(5), 114(f)(3), 115(c)(3)(E)(i), 116(c), or 118(b)(2) that do not result in statutory terms and rates shall not be subject to clauses (i) and (ii) of subparagraph (A).

(C) Interested parties may negotiate and agree to, and the Copyright Royalty Judges may adopt, an agreement that specifies as terms notice and recordkeeping requirements that apply in lieu of those that would otherwise apply under regulations.

(8) To perform other duties, as assigned by the Register of Copyrights within the Library of Congress, except as provided in section 802(g), at times when Copyright Royalty Judges are not engaged in performing the other duties set forth in this section.

(c) Rulings.—The Copyright Royalty Judges may make any necessary procedural or evidentiary rulings in any proceeding under this chapter and may, before commencing a proceeding under this chapter, make any such rulings that would apply to the proceedings conducted by the Copyright Royalty Judges.

(d) Administrative support.—The Librarian of Congress shall provide the Copyright Royalty Judges with the necessary administrative services related to proceedings under this chapter.

(e) Location in Library of Congress.—The offices of the Copyright Royalty Judges and staff shall be in the Library of Congress.

(f) Effective Date of Actions.—On and after May 30, 2005, in any case in which time limits are prescribed under this title for performance of an action with or by the Copyright Royalty Judges, and in which the last day of the prescribed period falls on a Saturday, Sunday, holiday, or other nonbusiness day within the District of Columbia or the Federal Government, the action may be taken on the next succeeding business day, and is effective as of the date when the period expired.

History of 17 U.S.C. §801: May 30, 2005, P.L. 108-419, §3(a), 118 Stat. 2341; May 30, 2005, P.L. 109-303, §3(1), (2), 120 Stat. 1478; Oct. 6, 2006, P.L. 109-303, §5, 120 Stat. 1483.

History of Former 17 U.S.C. §801: Oct. 19, 1976, P.L. 94-553, §101, 90 Stat. 2594; Aug. 27, 1986, P.L. 99-397, §2(c), (d), 100 Stat. 848; Oct. 31, 1988, P.L. 100-568, §11(1), 102 Stat. 2860; Nov. 16, 1988, P.L. 100-667, §202(4), 102 Stat. 3958; July 3, 1990, P.L. 101-318, §3(b), 104 Stat. 288; Oct. 28, 1992, P.L. 102-563,

§3(a)(1), 106 Stat. 4247; Dec. 17, 1993, P.L. 103-198, §2(a), 107 Stat. 2304; Nov. 1, 1995, P.L. 104-39, §5(d)(1), 109 Stat. 348; Nov. 13, 1997, P.L. 105-80, §§8(a), 12(a)(19), 111 Stat. 1533, 1535; Oct. 28, 1998, P.L. 105-304, §405(e)(1), 112 Stat. 2902.

See also 37 C.F.R. §§301.1-360.32, 387.1, 387.2; Berne Convention.

ANNOTATIONS

Music Choice v. Copyright Royalty Bd., 774 F.3d 1000, 1012 (D.C.Cir.2014). "[N]othing in the statute requires the Judges to rely on market rates or agreements when setting [17 U.S.C.] §114 rates. *At 1013:* We have previously rejected the notion that the rate-maker must first determine the range of market rates that are appropriate and then select a rate from within the range of fair market rates that meets the objectives of [17 U.S.C.] §801(b)(1)(A)-(D). The Copyright Act does not clearly *require* the use of 'market rates.' Instead, 'reasonable rates' are those that are calculated with reference to the four statutory criteria." (Internal quotes omitted.)

Recording Indus. Ass'n v. Librarian of Congress, 608 F.3d 861, 866 (D.C.Cir.2010). "[T]he Board 'may consider rates and terms under voluntary license agreements' in addition to the mandatory 'objectives set forth in [17 U.S.C.] §801(b)(1)' when setting the terms of the [17 U.S.C.] §115 license. [T]he Librarian [of Congress] has interpreted a Seventh Circuit 'precedent to mean that marketplace analogies, along with other evidence, must be considered,' which we held to be 'a reasonable interpretation of the precedent.' At most, then, the Board must 'consider[ ]' the existing market for voluntary licenses. [¶] The Board did so here, explaining that a late fee would correspond with the practices in other similar markets—in particular, the closely related webcasting and satellite digital radio industries. *At 867:* In short, the Board appropriately took market evidence into account when imposing the late fee. [¶] [A] copyright owner's ability to terminate a §115 license [under §115(c)(6)] in no ways bars the imposition of a late fee."

§802. COPYRIGHT ROYALTY JUDGESHIPS; STAFF

(a) Qualifications of Copyright Royalty Judges—

(1) In general.—Each Copyright Royalty Judge shall be an attorney who has at least 7 years of legal experience. The Chief Copyright Royalty Judge shall have at least 5 years of experience in adjudications, arbitrations, or court trials. Of the other 2 Copyright Royalty Judges, 1 shall have significant knowledge of copyright law, and the other shall have significant knowledge of economics. An individual may serve as a Copyright Royalty Judge only if the individual is free of any financial conflict of interest under subsection (h).

(2) Definition.—In this subsection, the term "adjudication" has the meaning given that term in section 551 of title 5, but does not include mediation.

(b) Staff.—The Chief Copyright Royalty Judge shall hire 3 full-time staff members to assist the Copyright Royalty Judges in performing their functions.

(c) Terms.—The individual first appointed as the Chief Copyright Royalty Judge shall be appointed to a term of 6 years, and of the remaining individuals first appointed as Copyright Royalty Judges, 1 shall be appointed to a term of 4 years, and the other shall be appointed to a term of 2 years. Thereafter, the terms of succeeding Copyright Royalty Judges shall each be 6 years. An individual serving as a Copyright Royalty Judge may be reappointed to subsequent terms. The term of a Copyright Royalty Judge shall begin when the term of the predecessor of that Copyright Royalty Judge ends. When the term of office of a Copyright Royalty Judge ends, the individual serving that term may continue to serve until a successor is selected.

(d) Vacancies or incapacity—

(1) Vacancies.—If a vacancy should occur in the position of Copyright Royalty Judge, the Librarian of Congress shall act expeditiously to fill the vacancy, and may appoint an interim Copyright Royalty Judge to serve until another Copyright Royalty Judge is appointed under this section. An individual appointed to fill the vacancy occurring before the expiration of the term for which the predecessor of that individual was appointed shall be appointed for the remainder of that term.

(2) Incapacity.—In the case in which a Copyright Royalty Judge is temporarily unable to perform his or her duties, the Librarian of Congress may appoint an interim Copyright Royalty Judge to perform such duties during the period of such incapacity.

(e) Compensation—

(1) Judges.—The Chief Copyright Royalty Judge shall receive compensation at the rate of basic pay payable for level AL-1 for administrative law judges pursuant to section 5372(b) of title 5, and each of the other two Copyright Royalty Judges shall receive compensation at the rate of basic pay payable for level AL-2 for administrative law judges pursuant to such section. The compensation of the Copyright Royalty Judges shall not be subject to any regulations adopted by the Office of Personnel Management pursuant to its authority under section 5376(b)(1) of title 5.

(2) Staff members.—Of the staff members appointed under subsection (b)—

(A) the rate of pay of 1 staff member shall be not more than the basic rate of pay payable for level 10 of GS-15 of the General Schedule;

(B) the rate of pay of 1 staff member shall be not less than the basic rate of pay payable for GS-13 of the General Schedule and not more than the basic rate of pay payable for level 10 of GS-14 of such Schedule; and

(C) the rate of pay for the third staff member shall be not less than the basic rate of pay payable for GS-8 of the General Schedule and not more than the basic rate of pay payable for level 10 of GS-11 of such Schedule.

(3) Locality pay.—All rates of pay referred to under this subsection shall include locality pay.

(f) Independence of Copyright Royalty Judge—

(1) In making determinations—

(A) In general—

(i) Subject to subparagraph (B) and clause (ii) of this subparagraph, the Copyright Royalty Judges shall have full independence in making determinations concerning adjustments and determinations of copyright royalty rates and terms, the distribution of copyright royalties, the acceptance or rejection of royalty claims, rate adjustment petitions, and petitions to participate, and in issuing other rulings under this title, except that the Copyright Royalty Judges may consult with the Register of Copyrights on any matter other than a question of fact.

(ii) One or more Copyright Royalty Judges may, or by motion to the Copyright Royalty Judges, any participant in a proceeding may, request from the Register of Copyrights an interpretation of any material questions of substantive law that relate to the construction of provisions of this title and arise in the course of the proceeding. Any request for a written interpretation shall be in writing and on the record, and reasonable provision shall be made to permit participants in the proceeding to comment on the material questions of substantive law in a manner that minimizes duplication and delay. Except as provided in subparagraph (B), the Register of Copyrights shall deliver to the Copyright Royalty Judges a written response within 14 days after the receipt of all briefs and comments from the participants. The Copyright Royalty Judges shall apply the legal interpretation embodied in the response of the Register of Copyrights if it is timely delivered, and the response shall be included in the record that accompanies the final determination. The authority under this clause shall not be construed to authorize the Register of Copyrights to provide an interpretation of questions of procedure before the Copyright Royalty Judges, the ultimate adjustments and determinations of copyright royalty rates and terms, the ultimate distribution of copyright royalties, or the acceptance or rejection of royalty claims, rate adjustment petitions, or petitions to participate in a proceeding.

(B) Novel questions—

(i) In any case in which a novel material question of substantive law concerning an interpretation of those provisions of this title that are the subject of the proceeding is presented, the Copyright Royalty Judges shall request a decision of the Register of Copyrights, in writing, to resolve such novel question. Reasonable provision shall be made for comment on such request by the participants in the proceeding, in such a way as to minimize duplication and delay. The Register of Copyrights shall transmit his or her decision to the Copyright Royalty Judges within 30 days after the Register of Copyrights receives all of the briefs or comments of the participants. Such decision shall be in writing and included by the Copyright Royalty Judges in the record that accompanies their final determination. If such a decision is timely delivered to the Copyright Royalty Judges, the Copyright Royalty Judges shall apply the legal determinations embodied in the decision of the Register of Copyrights in resolving material questions of substantive law.

(ii) In clause (i), a "novel question of law" is a question of law that has not been determined in prior decisions, determinations, and rulings described in section 803(a).

(C) Consultation.—Notwithstanding the provisions of subparagraph (A), the Copyright Royalty Judges shall consult with the Register of Copyrights with respect to any determination or ruling that would require that any act be performed by the Copyright Office, and any such determination or ruling shall not be binding upon the Register of Copyrights.

(D) Review of legal conclusions by the Register of Copyrights.—The Register of Copyrights may review for legal error the resolution by the Copyright Royalty Judges of a material question of substantive law under this title that underlies or is contained in a final determination of the Copyright Royalty Judges. If the Register of Copyrights concludes, after taking into consideration the views of the participants in the proceeding, that any resolution reached by the Copyright Royalty Judges was in material error, the Register of Copyrights shall issue a written decision correcting such legal error, which shall be made part of the record of the proceeding. The Register of Copyrights shall issue such written decision not later than 60 days after the date on which the final determination by the Copyright Royalty Judges is issued. Additionally, the Register of Copyrights shall cause to be published in the Federal Register such written decision, together with a specific identification of the legal conclusion of the Copyright Royalty Judges that is determined to be erroneous. As to conclusions of substantive law involving an interpretation of the statutory provisions of this title, the decision of the Register of Copyrights shall be binding as precedent upon the Copyright Royalty Judges in subsequent proceedings under this chapter. When a decision has been rendered pursuant to this subparagraph, the Register of Copyrights may, on the basis of and in accordance with such decision, intervene as of right in any appeal of a final determination of the Copyright Royalty Judges pursuant to section 803(d) in the United States Court of Appeals for the District of Columbia Circuit. If, prior to intervening in such an appeal, the Register of Copyrights gives notification to, and undertakes to consult with, the Attorney General with respect to such intervention, and the Attorney General fails, within a reasonable period after receiving such notification, to intervene in such appeal, the Register of Copyrights may intervene in such appeal in his or her own name by any attorney designated by the Register of Copyrights for such purpose. Intervention by the Register of Copyrights in his or her own name shall not preclude the Attorney General from intervening on behalf of the United States in such an appeal as may be otherwise provided or required by law.

(E) Effect on judicial review.—Nothing in this section shall be interpreted to alter the standard applied by a court in reviewing legal determinations involving an interpretation or construction of the provisions of this title or to affect the extent to which any construction or interpretation of the provisions of this title shall be accorded deference by a reviewing court.

(2) Performance appraisals—

(A) In general.—Notwithstanding any other provision of law or any regulation of the Library of Congress, and subject to subparagraph (B), the Copyright Royalty Judges shall not receive performance appraisals.

(B) Relating to sanction or removal.—To the extent that the Librarian of Congress adopts regulations under subsection (h) relating to the sanction or removal of a Copyright Royalty Judge and such regulations require documentation to establish the cause of such sanction or removal, the Copyright Royalty Judge may receive an appraisal related specifically to the cause of the sanction or removal.

(g) Inconsistent duties barred.—No Copyright Royalty Judge may undertake duties that conflict with his or her duties and responsibilities as a Copyright Royalty Judge.

(h) Standards of conduct.—The Librarian of Congress shall adopt regulations regarding the standards of conduct, including financial conflict of interest and restrictions against ex parte communications, which shall govern the Copyright Royalty Judges and the proceedings under this chapter.

(i) Removal or sanction.—The Librarian of Congress may sanction or remove a Copyright Royalty Judge for violation of the standards of conduct adopted under subsection (h), misconduct, neglect of duty, or any disqualifying physical or mental disability. Any such sanction or removal may be made only after notice and opportunity for a hearing, but the Librarian of Congress may suspend the Copyright Royalty Judge during the pendency of such hearing. The Librarian shall appoint an interim Copyright Royalty Judge during the period of any such suspension.

History of 17 U.S.C. §802: May 30, 2005, P.L. 108-419, §3(a), 118 Stat. 2345; May 30, 2005, P.L. 109-303, §3(3), (4), 120 Stat. 1478, 1479.

History of Former 17 U.S.C. §802: Oct. 19, 1976, P.L. 94-553, §101, 90 Stat. 2596; July 3, 1990, P.L. 101-319, §2(a), 104 Stat. 290; Dec. 17, 1993, P.L. 103-198, §2(b), 107 Stat. 2305; Nov. 1, 1995, P.L. 104-39, §5(d)(2)-(4), 109 Stat. 349; Nov. 13, 1997, P.L. 105-80, §8(b), 111 Stat. 1533; Oct. 28, 1998, P.L. 105-304, §405(d), (e)(2)-(4), 112 Stat. 2902; Nov. 2, 2002, P.L. 107-273, §13301(c)(2), 116 Stat. 1912.

See also 37 C.F.R. §§301.1-360.32.

ANNOTATIONS

Intercollegiate Broad. Sys. v. Copyright Royalty Bd., 684 F.3d 1332, 1336-37 (D.C.Cir.2012). "[P] argues that the Copyright Royalty Board as currently structured violates the Constitution's Appointments Clause, art. 2, §2, cl. 2, on two grounds: (1) the Judges' exercise of significant ratemaking authority, without any effective means of control by a superior (such as unrestricted removability), qualifies them as 'principal' officers who must be appointed by the President with Senate confirmation; and (2) even if the Judges are 'inferior' officers, the Librarian of Congress is not a 'Head of Department' in whom Congress may vest appointment power. [W]e agree with [P] on the first claim but not the second, and accordingly provide a remedy that cures the constitutional defect with as little disruption as possible. *At 1340-41:* [W]e find unconstitutional all of the language in 17 U.S.C. §802(i) following 'The Librarian of Congress may sanction or remove a Copyright Royalty Judge [(CRJ)].' Without this restriction, we are confident that (so long as the Librarian is a Head of Department ...) the CRJs will be inferior rather than principal officers. With unfettered removal power, the Librarian will have the direct ability to 'direct,' 'supervise,' and exert some 'control' over the Judges' decisions. Although individual CRJ decisions will still not be directly reversible, the Librarian would be free to provide substantive input on non-factual issues via the Register, whom the Judges are free to consult.... This, coupled with the threat of removal satisfies us that the CRJs' decisions will be constrained to a significant degree by a principal officer (the Librarian). We further conclude that free removability constrains their power enough to outweigh the extent to which the scope of their duties exceeds that of the special counsel in *Morrison*."

§803. PROCEEDINGS OF COPYRIGHT ROYALTY JUDGES

(a) Proceedings—

(1) In general.—The Copyright Royalty Judges shall act in accordance with this title, and to the extent not inconsistent with this title, in accordance with subchapter II of chapter 5 of title 5, in carrying out the purposes set forth in section 801. The Copyright Royalty Judges shall act in accordance with regulations issued by the Copyright Royalty Judges and the Librarian of Congress, and on the basis of a written record, prior determinations and interpretations of the Copyright Royalty Tribunal, Librarian of Congress, the Register of Copyrights, copyright arbitration royalty panels (to the extent those determinations are not inconsistent with a decision of the Librarian of Congress or the Register of Copyrights), and the Copyright Royalty Judges (to the extent those determinations are not inconsistent with a decision of the Register of Copyrights that was timely delivered to the Copyright Royalty Judges pursuant to section 802(f)(1) (A) or (B), or with a decision of the Register of Copyrights pursuant to section 802(f)(1)(D)), under this chapter, and decisions of the court of appeals under this chapter before, on, or after the effective date of the Copyright Royalty and Distribution Reform Act of 2004.

(2) Judges acting as panel and individually.—The Copyright Royalty Judges shall preside over hearings in proceedings under this chapter en banc. The Chief Copyright Royalty Judge may designate a Copyright Royalty Judge to preside individually over such collateral and administrative proceedings, and over such proceedings under paragraphs (1) through (5) of subsection (b), as the Chief Judge considers appropriate.

(3) Determinations.—Final determinations of the Copyright Royalty Judges in proceedings under this chapter shall be made by majority vote. A Copyright Royalty Judge dissenting from the majority on any determination under this chapter may issue his or her dissenting opinion, which shall be included with the determination.

(b) Procedures—

(1) Initiation—

(A) Call for petitions to participate—

(i) The Copyright Royalty Judges shall cause to be published in the Federal Register notice of commencement of proceedings under this chapter, calling for the filing of petitions to participate in a proceeding under this chapter for the purpose of making the relevant determination under section 111, 112, 114, 115, 116, 118, 119, 1004, or 1007, as the case may be—

(I) promptly upon a determination made under section 804(a);

(II) by no later than January 5 of a year specified in paragraph (2) of section 804(b) for the commencement of proceedings;

(III) by no later than January 5 of a year specified in subparagraph (A) or (B) of paragraph (3) of section 804(b) for the commencement of proceedings, or as otherwise provided in subparagraph (A) or (C) of such paragraph for the commencement of proceedings;

(IV) as provided under section 804(b)(8); or

(V) by no later than January 5 of a year specified in any other provision of section 804(b) for the filing of petitions for the commencement of proceedings, if a petition has not been filed by that date, except that the publication of notice requirement shall not apply in the case of proceedings under section 111 that are scheduled to commence in 2005.

(ii) Petitions to participate shall be filed by no later than 30 days after publication of notice of commencement of a proceeding under clause (i), except that the Copyright Royalty Judges may, for substantial good cause shown and if there is no prejudice to the participants that have already filed petitions, accept late petitions to participate at any time up to the date that is 90 days before the date on which participants in the proceeding are to file their written direct statements. Notwithstanding the preceding sentence, petitioners whose petitions are filed more than 30 days after publication of notice of commencement of a proceeding are not eligible to object to a settlement reached during the voluntary negotiation period under paragraph (3), and any objection filed by such a petitioner shall not be taken into account by the Copyright Royalty Judges.

(B) Petitions to participate.—Each petition to participate in a proceeding shall describe the petitioner's interest in the subject matter of the proceeding. Parties with similar interests may file a single petition to participate.

(2) Participation in general.—Subject to paragraph (4), a person may participate in a proceeding under this chapter, including through the submission of briefs or other information, only if—

(A) that person has filed a petition to participate in accordance with paragraph (1) (either individually or as a group under paragraph (1)(B));

(B) the Copyright Royalty Judges have not determined that the petition to participate is facially invalid;

(C) the Copyright Royalty Judges have not determined, sua sponte or on the motion of another participant in the proceeding, that the person lacks a significant interest in the proceeding; and

(D) the petition to participate is accompanied by either—

(i) in a proceeding to determine royalty rates, a filing fee of $150; or

(ii) in a proceeding to determine distribution of royalty fees—

(I) a filing fee of $150; or

(II) a statement that the petitioner (individually or as a group) will not seek a distribution of more than $1000, in which case the amount distributed to the petitioner shall not exceed $1000.

(3) Voluntary negotiation period—

(A) Commencement of proceedings—

(i) Rate adjustment proceeding.—Promptly after the date for filing of petitions to participate in a proceeding, the Copyright Royalty Judges shall make available to all participants in the proceeding a list of such participants and shall initiate a voluntary negotiation period among the participants.

(ii) Distribution proceeding.—Promptly after the date for filing of petitions to participate in a proceeding to determine the distribution of royalties, the Copyright Royalty Judges shall make available to all participants in the proceeding a list of such participants. The initiation of a voluntary negotiation period among the participants shall be set at a time determined by the Copyright Royalty Judges.

(B) Length of proceedings.—The voluntary negotiation period initiated under subparagraph (A) shall be 3 months.

(C) Determination of subsequent proceedings.—At the close of the voluntary negotiation proceedings, the Copyright Royalty Judges shall, if further proceedings under this chapter are necessary, determine whether and to what extent paragraphs (4) and (5) will apply to the parties.

(4) Small claims procedure in distribution proceedings—

(A) In general.—If, in a proceeding under this chapter to determine the distribution of royalties, the contested amount of a claim is $10,000 or less, the Copyright Royalty Judges shall decide the controversy on the basis of the filing of the written direct statement by the participant, the response by any opposing participant, and 1 additional response by each such party.

(B) Bad faith inflation of claim.—If the Copyright Royalty Judges determine that a participant asserts in bad faith an amount in controversy in excess of $10,000 for the purpose of avoiding a determination under the procedure set forth in subparagraph (A), the Copyright Royalty Judges shall impose a fine on that participant in an amount not to exceed the difference between the actual amount distributed and the amount asserted by the participant.

(5) Paper proceedings.—The Copyright Royalty Judges in proceedings under this chapter may decide, sua sponte or upon motion of a participant, to determine issues on the basis of the filing of the written direct statement by the participant, the response by any opposing participant, and one additional response by each such participant. Prior to making such decision to proceed on such a paper record only, the Copyright Royalty Judges shall offer to all parties to the proceeding the opportunity to comment on the decision. The procedure under this paragraph—

(A) shall be applied in cases in which there is no genuine issue of material fact, there is no need for evidentiary hearings, and all participants in the proceeding agree in writing to the procedure; and

(B) may be applied under such other circumstances as the Copyright Royalty Judges consider appropriate.

(6) Regulations—

(A) In general.—The Copyright Royalty Judges may issue regulations to carry out their functions under this title. All regulations issued by the Copyright Royalty Judges are subject to the approval of the Librarian of Congress and are subject to judicial review pursuant to chapter 7 of title 5, except as set forth in subsection (d). Not later than 120 days after Copyright Royalty Judges or interim Copyright Royalty Judges, as the case may be, are first appointed after the enactment of the Copyright Royalty and Distribution Reform Act of 2004, such judges shall issue regulations to govern proceedings under this chapter.

(B) Interim regulations.—Until regulations are adopted under subparagraph (A), the Copyright Royalty Judges shall apply the regulations in effect under this chapter on the day before the effective date of the Copyright Royalty and Distribution Reform Act of 2004, to the extent such regulations are not inconsistent with this chapter, except that functions carried out under such regulations by the Librarian of Congress, the Register of Copyrights, or copyright arbitration royalty panels that, as of such date of enactment, are to be carried out by the Copyright Royalty Judges under this chapter, shall be carried out by the Copyright Royalty Judges under such regulations.

(C) Requirements.—Regulations issued under subparagraph (A) shall include the following:

(i) The written direct statements and written rebuttal statements of all participants in a proceeding under paragraph (2) shall be filed by a date specified by the Copyright Royalty Judges, which, in the case of written direct statements, may be not earlier than 4 months, and not later than 5 months, after the end of the voluntary negotiation period under paragraph (3). Notwithstanding the preceding sentence, the Copyright Royalty Judges may allow a participant in a proceeding to file an amended written direct statement based on new information received during the discovery process, within 15 days after the end of the discovery period specified in clause (iv).

(ii)(I) Following the submission to the Copyright Royalty Judges of written direct statements and written rebuttal statements by the participants in a proceeding under paragraph (2), the Copyright Royalty Judges, after taking into consideration the views of the participants in the proceeding, shall determine a schedule for conducting and completing discovery.

(II) In this chapter, the term "written direct statements" means witness statements, testimony, and exhibits to be presented in the proceedings, and such other information that is necessary to establish terms and rates, or the distribution of royalty payments, as the case may be, as set forth in regulations issued by the Copyright Royalty Judges.

(iii) Hearsay may be admitted in proceedings under this chapter to the extent deemed appropriate by the Copyright Royalty Judges.

(iv) Discovery in connection with written direct statements shall be permitted for a period of 60 days, except for discovery ordered by the Copyright Royalty Judges in connection with the resolution of motions, orders, and disputes pending at the end of such period. The Copyright Royalty Judges may order a discovery schedule in connection with written rebuttal statements.

(v) Any participant under paragraph (2) in a proceeding under this chapter to determine royalty rates may request of an opposing participant nonprivileged documents directly related to the written direct statement or written rebuttal statement of that participant. Any objection to such a request shall be resolved by a motion or request to compel production made to the Copyright Royalty Judges in accordance with regulations adopted by the Copyright Royalty Judges. Each motion or request to compel discovery shall be determined by the Copyright Royalty Judges, or by a Copyright Royalty Judge when permitted under subsection (a)(2). Upon such motion, the Copyright Royalty Judges may order discovery pursuant to regulations established under this paragraph.

(vi)(I) Any participant under paragraph (2) in a proceeding under this chapter to determine royalty rates may, by means of written motion or on the record, request of an opposing participant or witness other relevant information and materials if, absent the discovery sought, the Copyright Royalty Judges' resolution of the proceeding would be substantially impaired. In determining whether discovery will be granted under this clause, the Copyright Royalty Judges may consider—

(aa) whether the burden or expense of producing the requested information or materials outweighs the likely benefit, taking into account the needs and resources of the participants, the importance of the issues at stake, and the probative value of the requested information or materials in resolving such issues;

(bb) whether the requested information or materials would be unreasonably cumulative or duplicative, or are obtainable from another source that is more convenient, less burdensome, or less expensive; and

(cc) whether the participant seeking discovery has had ample opportunity by discovery in the proceeding or by other means to obtain the information sought.

(II) This clause shall not apply to any proceeding scheduled to commence after December 31, 2010.

(vii) In a proceeding under this chapter to determine royalty rates, the participants entitled to receive royalties shall collectively be permitted to take no more than 10 depositions and secure responses to no more than 25 interrogatories, and the participants obligated to pay royalties shall collectively be permitted to take no more than 10 depositions and secure responses to no more than 25 interrogatories. The Copyright Royalty Judges shall resolve any disputes among similarly aligned participants to allocate the number of depositions or interrogatories permitted under this clause.

(viii) The rules and practices in effect on the day before the effective date of the Copyright Royalty and Distribution Reform Act of 2004, relating to discovery in proceedings under this chapter to determine the distribution of royalty fees, shall continue to apply to such proceedings on and after such effective date.

(ix) In proceedings to determine royalty rates, the Copyright Royalty Judges may issue a subpoena commanding a participant or witness to appear and give testimony, or to produce and permit inspection of documents or tangible things, if the Copyright Royalty Judges' resolution of the proceeding would be substantially impaired by the absence of such testimony or production of documents or tangible things. Such subpoena shall specify with reasonable particularity the materials to be produced or the scope and nature of the required testimony. Nothing in this clause shall preclude the Copyright Royalty Judges from requesting the production by a nonparticipant of information or materials relevant to the resolution by the Copyright Royalty Judges of a material issue of fact.

(x) The Copyright Royalty Judges shall order a settlement conference among the participants in the proceeding to facilitate the presentation of offers of settlement among the participants. The settlement conference shall be held during a 21-day period following the 60-day discovery period specified in clause (iv) and shall take place outside the presence of the Copyright Royalty Judges.

(xi) No evidence, including exhibits, may be submitted in the written direct statement or written rebuttal statement of a participant without a sponsoring witness, except where the Copyright Royalty Judges have taken official notice, or in the case of incorporation by reference of past records, or for good cause shown.

(c) Determination of Copyright Royalty Judges—

(1) Timing.—The Copyright Royalty Judges shall issue their determination in a proceeding not later than 11 months after the conclusion of the 21-day settlement conference period under subsection (b)(6)(C)(x), but, in the case of a proceeding to determine successors to rates or terms that expire on a specified date, in no event later than 15 days before the expiration of the then current statutory rates and terms.

(2) Rehearings—

(A) In general.—The Copyright Royalty Judges may, in exceptional cases, upon motion of a participant in a proceeding under subsection (b)(2), order a rehearing, after the determination in the proceeding is issued under paragraph (1), on such matters as the Copyright Royalty Judges determine to be appropriate.

(B) Timing for filing motion.—Any motion for a rehearing under subparagraph (A) may only be filed within 15 days after the date on which the Copyright Royalty Judges deliver to the participants in the proceeding their initial determination.

(C) Participation by opposing party not required.—In any case in which a rehearing is ordered, any opposing party shall not be required to participate in the rehearing, except that nonparticipation may give rise to the limitations with respect to judicial review provided for in subsection (d)(1).

(D) No negative inference.—No negative inference shall be drawn from lack of participation in a rehearing.

(E) Continuity of rates and terms—

(i) If the decision of the Copyright Royalty Judges on any motion for a rehearing is not rendered before the expiration of the statutory rates and terms that were previously in effect, in the case of a proceeding to determine successors to rates and terms that expire on a specified date, then—

(I) the initial determination of the Copyright Royalty Judges that is the subject of the rehearing motion shall be effective as of the day following the date on which the rates and terms that were previously in effect expire; and

(II) in the case of a proceeding under section 114(f)(1)(C) or 114(f)(2)(C), royalty rates and terms shall, for purposes of section 114(f)(4)(B), be deemed to have been set at those rates and terms contained in the initial determination of the Copyright Royalty Judges that is the subject of the rehearing motion, as of the date of that determination.

(ii) The pendency of a motion for a rehearing under this paragraph shall not relieve persons obligated to make royalty payments who would be affected by the determination on that motion from providing the statements of account and any reports of use, to the extent required, and paying the royalties required under the relevant determination or regulations.

(iii) Notwithstanding clause (ii), whenever royalties described in clause (ii) are paid to a person other than the Copyright Office, the entity designated by the Copyright Royalty Judges to which such royalties are paid by the copyright user (and any successor thereto) shall, within 60 days after the motion for rehearing is resolved or, if the motion is granted, within 60 days after the rehearing is concluded, return any excess amounts previously paid to the extent necessary to comply with the final determination of royalty rates by the Copyright Royalty Judges. Any underpayment of royalties resulting from a rehearing shall be paid within the same period.

(3) Contents of determination.—A determination of the Copyright Royalty Judges shall be supported by the written record and shall set forth the findings of fact relied on by the Copyright Royalty Judges. Among other terms adopted in a determination, the Copyright Royalty Judges may specify notice and recordkeeping requirements of users of the copyrights at issue that apply in lieu of those that would otherwise apply under regulations.

(4) Continuing jurisdiction.—The Copyright Royalty Judges may issue an amendment to a written determination to correct any technical or clerical errors in the determination or to modify the terms, but not the rates, of royalty payments in response to unforeseen circumstances that would frustrate the proper implementation of such determination. Such amendment shall be set forth in a written addendum to the determination that shall be distributed to the participants of the proceeding and shall be published in the Federal Register.

(5) Protective order.—The Copyright Royalty Judges may issue such orders as may be appropriate to protect confidential information, including orders excluding confidential information from the record of the determination that is published or made available to the public, except that any terms or rates of royalty payments or distributions may not be excluded.

(6) Publication of determination.—By no later than the end of the 60-day period provided in section 802(f)(1)(D), the Librarian of Congress shall cause the determination, and any corrections thereto, to be published in the Federal Register. The Librarian of Congress shall also publicize the determination and corrections in such other manner as the Librarian considers appropriate, including, but not limited to, publication on the Internet. The Librarian of Congress shall also make the determination, corrections, and the accompanying record available for public inspection and copying.

(7) Late payment.—A determination of the Copyright Royalty Judges may include terms with respect to late payment, but in no way shall such terms prevent the copyright holder from asserting other rights or remedies provided under this title.

(d) Judicial review—

(1) Appeal.—Any determination of the Copyright Royalty Judges under subsection (c) may, within 30 days after the publication of the determination in the

Federal Register, be appealed, to the United States Court of Appeals for the District of Columbia Circuit, by any aggrieved participant in the proceeding under subsection (b)(2) who fully participated in the proceeding and who would be bound by the determination. Any participant that did not participate in a rehearing may not raise any issue that was the subject of that rehearing at any stage of judicial review of the hearing determination. If no appeal is brought within that 30-day period, the determination of the Copyright Royalty Judges shall be final, and the royalty fee or determination with respect to the distribution of fees, as the case may be, shall take effect as set forth in paragraph (2).

(2) Effect of rates—

(A) Expiration on specified date.—When this title provides that the royalty rates and terms that were previously in effect are to expire on a specified date, any adjustment or determination by the Copyright Royalty Judges of successor rates and terms for an ensuing statutory license period shall be effective as of the day following the date of expiration of the rates and terms that were previously in effect, even if the determination of the Copyright Royalty Judges is rendered on a later date. A licensee shall be obligated to continue making payments under the rates and terms previously in effect until such time as rates and terms for the successor period are established. Whenever royalties pursuant to this section are paid to a person other than the Copyright Office, the entity designated by the Copyright Royalty Judges to which such royalties are paid by the copyright user (and any successor thereto) shall, within 60 days after the final determination of the Copyright Royalty Judges establishing rates and terms for a successor period or the exhaustion of all rehearings or appeals of such determination, if any, return any excess amounts previously paid to the extent necessary to comply with the final determination of royalty rates. Any underpayment of royalties by a copyright user shall be paid to the entity designated by the Copyright Royalty Judges within the same period.

(B) Other cases.—In cases where rates and terms have not, prior to the inception of an activity, been established for that particular activity under the relevant license, such rates and terms shall be retroactive to the inception of activity under the relevant license covered by such rates and terms. In other cases where rates and terms do not expire on a specified date, successor rates and terms shall take effect on the first day of the second month that begins after the publication of the determination of the Copyright Royalty Judges in the Federal Register, except as otherwise provided in this title, or by the Copyright Royalty Judges, or as agreed by the participants in a proceeding that would be bound by the rates and terms. Except as otherwise provided in this title, the rates and terms, to the extent applicable, shall remain in effect until such successor rates and terms become effective.

(C) Obligation to make payments—

(i) The pendency of an appeal under this subsection shall not relieve persons obligated to make royalty payments under section 111, 112, 114, 115, 116, 118, 119, or 1003, who would be affected by the determination on appeal, from—

(I) providing the applicable statements of account and reports of use; and

(II) paying the royalties required under the relevant determination or regulations.

(ii) Notwithstanding clause (i), whenever royalties described in clause (i) are paid to a person other than the Copyright Office, the entity designated by the Copyright Royalty Judges to which such royalties are paid by the copyright user (and any successor thereto) shall, within 60 days after the final resolution of the appeal, return any excess amounts previously paid (and interest thereon, if ordered pursuant to paragraph (3)) to the extent necessary to comply with the final determination of royalty rates on appeal. Any underpayment of royalties resulting from an appeal (and interest thereon, if ordered pursuant to paragraph (3)) shall be paid within the same period.

(3) Jurisdiction of court.—Section 706 of title 5 shall apply with respect to review by the court of appeals under this subsection. If the court modifies or vacates a determination of the Copyright Royalty Judges, the court may enter its own determination with respect to the amount or distribution of royalty fees and costs, and order the repayment of any excess fees, the payment of any underpaid fees, and the payment of interest pertaining respectively thereto, in accordance with its final judgment. The court may also vacate the determination of the Copyright Royalty Judges and remand the case to the Copyright Royalty Judges for further proceedings in accordance with subsection (a).

(e) Administrative matters—

(1) Deduction of costs of Library of Congress and Copyright Office from filing fees—

(A) Deduction from filing fees.—The Librarian of Congress may, to the extent not otherwise provided under this title, deduct from the filing fees collected under subsection (b) for a particular proceeding under this chapter the reasonable costs incurred by the Librarian of Congress, the Copyright Office, and the Copyright Royalty Judges in conducting that proceeding, other than the salaries of the Copyright Royalty Judges and the 3 staff members appointed under section 802(b).

(B) Authorization of appropriations.—There are authorized to be appropriated such sums as may be necessary to pay the costs incurred under this chapter not covered by the filing fees collected under subsection (b). All funds made available pursuant to this subparagraph shall remain available until expended.

(2) Positions required for administration of compulsory licensing.—Section 307 of the Legislative Branch Appropriations Act, 1994, shall not apply to employee positions in the Library of Congress that are required to be filled in order to carry out section 111, 112, 114, 115, 116, 118, or 119 or chapter 10.

History of 17 U.S.C. §803: May 30, 2005, P.L. 108-419, §3(a), 118 Stat. 2348; Dec. 8, 2004, P.L. 108-447, §112, 118 Stat. 3409; May 30, 2005, P.L. 109-303, §3(5)-(11), 120 Stat. 1479-1481; Dec. 9, 2010, P.L. 111-295, §5(b), 124 Stat. 3181.

History of Former 17 U.S.C. §803: Oct. 19, 1976, P.L. 94-553, §101, 90 Stat. 2597; Oct. 31, 1988, P.L. 100-568, §11(2), 102 Stat. 2860; Nov. 16, 1988, P.L. 100-667, §202(5), 102 Stat. 3958; July 3, 1990, P.L. 101-318, §3(c), 104 Stat. 288; Oct. 28, 1992, P.L. 102-563, §3(a)(2), 106 Stat. 4248; Dec. 17, 1993, P.L. 103-198, §2(d), 107 Stat. 2307; Nov. 1, 1995, P.L. 104-39, §5(d)(5)-(7), 109 Stat. 349; Nov. 13, 1997, P.L. 105-80, §12(a)(20), 111 Stat. 1535; Oct. 28, 1998, P.L. 105-304, §405(e)(5), (6), 112 Stat. 2902.

See also 37 C.F.R. §§351.1-353.5.

ANNOTATIONS

Independent Producers Grp. v. Library of Congress, 759 F.3d 100, 102-03 (D.C.Cir.2014). "When a controversy arises, the Royalty Judges publish a notice of commencement of dispute proceedings in the Federal Register, ... at which point interested claimants must file petitions to participate.... Once the time to file petitions expires, ... the Royalty Judges send each petitioner a list of all the other petitioners, which marks the start of a three-month long 'voluntary negotiation period.' [¶] For claims still in dispute after the negotiation period, the Royalty Judges accept written submissions, supervise a 60-day discovery period, and order a 21-day settlement conference period. Only after those time-periods for voluntary resolution pass may the Royalty Judges resolve the dispute. Their decision must be in writing, 'supported by the written record,' and must 'set forth the findings of fact relied on by the Copyright Royalty Judges.' The Register of Copyrights then has 60 days to review that determination for 'legal error' in the resolution 'of a material question of substantive law[.]' The final determination is published in the Federal Register. [¶] Not every decision the Royalty Judges make is subject to judicial review. Instead, Congress provided that '[a]ny determination of the Copyright Royalty Judges *under subsection (c)*'—that is, 17 U.S.C. §803(c)'s controversy-resolution process—'may, within 30 days after the publication of the determination in the Federal Register, be appealed, to the U.S. Court of Appeals for the District of Columbia Circuit[.]' *At 105-06:* Section 803(d) does not authorize judicial review of just any objection to any decision made by the Royalty Judges. Instead, appeals may be taken only by an 'aggrieved participant in the proceeding under subsection (b)(2) who fully participated in the proceeding and who would be bound by the determination.' Thus, one precondition for judicial review is that there be a 'proceeding' conducted by the Royalty Judges 'under subsection (b)(2).' And subsection (b)(2), in turn, governs petitions by parties to participate following the Royalty Judges' formal notice in the Federal Register that a contested proceeding will be conducted.... The 2003 determination that no controversy remained involving the devotional programming category, and the Royalty Judges' reliance on that decision here, did not involve any controversy 'proceeding' 'under subsection (b)(2).' [¶] Moreover, a right to appeal does not arise unless the Royalty Judges conduct the type of controversy proceeding in which parties may 'fully participate[]' and which results in binding determinations. Resolution of a disputed controversy through formal proceedings fits that bill; the decision in this case that no controversy exists and thus that no proceedings are needed does not. [¶] Likewise, Congress set a time limit on appeals, requiring that they be filed 'within 30 days after the publication of the [Royalty Judges'] determination in the Federal Register.' That timeframe works when a contested determination results in a final written decision by the Royalty Judges, which, by statute, must be published in the Federal Register. But a determination of no controversy and a distribution pursuant to private settlement, as occurred here, make no appearance in the Federal Register. The time to appeal from the type of non-controversy determination at issue here, if an appeal were permitted, would never begin or end. *At 107:* There are, in short, two different kinds of decisions that arise in the Copyright Act's royalty distribution process: (1) a determination under Chapter 8 in which the Royalty Judges decide who gets what, subject to direct review in this court; and (2) a mechanical distribution under Chapter 1 in which the parties themselves decide who gets what and the Royalty Judges simply give effect to that uncontroverted division of the pie, with no direct review in this court ensuing. When the parties bypass the controversy process by settling their dispute, they forgo the particular opportunity for judicial review in this court authorized by … §803(d)(1)."

Recording Indus. Ass'n v. Librarian of Congress, 608 F.3d 861, 865 (D.C.Cir.2010). "'To the extent that the statutory objectives determine a range of reasonable royalty rates that would serve all [the] objectives adequately but to differing degrees, the [Board] is free to choose among those rates, and courts are without authority to set aside the particular rate chosen by the [Board] if it lies within a zone of reasonableness.'"

Intercollegiate Broad. Sys. v. Copyright Royalty Bd., 574 F.3d 748, 755 (D.C.Cir.2009). "We review determinations of the Judges under the familiar standard of the Administrative Procedure Act ('APA'). Under the APA, we uphold the results of adversarial agency proceedings unless they are arbitrary, capricious, contrary to law, or not supported by substantial evidence. Review of administratively determined rates is 'particularly deferential' because of their 'highly technical' nature."

§804. INSTITUTION OF PROCEEDINGS

(a) Filing of petition.—With respect to proceedings referred to in paragraphs (1) and (2) of section 801(b) concerning the determination or adjustment of royalty rates as provided in sections 111, 112, 114, 115, 116, 118, 119, and 1004, during the calendar years specified in the schedule set forth in subsection (b), any owner or user of a copyrighted work whose royalty rates are specified by this title, or are established under this chapter before or after the enactment of the Copyright Royalty and Distribution Reform Act of 2004, may file a petition with the Copyright Royalty Judges declaring that the petitioner requests a determination or adjustment of the rate. The Copyright Royalty Judges shall make a determination as to whether the petitioner has such a significant interest in the royalty rate in which a determination or adjustment is requested. If the Copyright Royalty Judges determine that the petitioner has such a significant interest, the Copyright Royalty Judges shall cause notice of this determination, with the reasons for such determination, to be published in the Federal Register, together with the notice of commencement of proceedings under this chapter. With respect to proceedings under paragraph (1) of section 801(b) concerning the determination or adjustment of royalty rates as provided in sections 112 and 114, during the calendar years specified in the schedule set forth in subsection (b), the Copyright Royalty Judges shall cause notice of commencement of proceedings under this chapter to be published in the Federal Register as provided in section 803(b)(1)(A).

(b) Timing of proceedings—

(1) Section 111 proceedings—

(A) A petition described in subsection (a) to initiate proceedings under section 801(b)(2) concerning the adjustment of royalty rates under section 111 to which subparagraph (A) or (D) of section 801(b)(2) applies may be filed during the year 2015 and in each subsequent fifth calendar year.

(B) In order to initiate proceedings under section 801(b)(2) concerning the adjustment of royalty rates under section 111 to which subparagraph (B) or (C) of section 801(b)(2) applies, within 12 months after an event described in either of those subsections, any owner or user of a copyrighted work whose royalty rates are specified by section 111, or by a rate established under this chapter before or after the enactment of the Copyright Royalty and Distribution Reform Act of 2004, may file a petition with the Copyright Royalty Judges declaring that the petitioner requests an adjustment of the rate. The Copyright Royalty Judges shall then proceed as set forth in subsection (a) of this section. Any change in royalty rates made under this chapter pursuant to this subparagraph may be reconsidered in the year 2015, and each fifth calendar year thereafter, in accordance with the provisions in section 801(b)(2)(B) or (C), as the case may be. A petition for adjustment of rates established by section 111(d)(1)(B) as a result of a change in the rules and regulations of the Federal Communications Commission shall set forth the change on which the petition is based.

(C) Any adjustment of royalty rates under section 111 shall take effect as of the first accounting period commencing after the publication of the determination of the Copyright Royalty Judges in the Federal Register, or on such other date as is specified in that determination.

(2) Certain section 112 proceedings.—Proceedings under this chapter shall be commenced in the year 2007 to determine reasonable terms and rates of royalty payments for the activities described in section 112(e)(1) relating to the limitation on exclusive rights specified by section 114(d)(1)(C)(iv), to become effective on January 1, 2009. Such proceedings shall be repeated in each subsequent fifth calendar year.

(3) Section 114 and corresponding 112 proceedings—

(A) For eligible nonsubscription services and new subscription services.—Proceedings under this chapter shall be commenced as soon as practicable after the date of enactment of the Copyright Royalty and Distribution Reform Act of 2004 to determine reasonable terms and rates of royalty payments under sections 114 and 112 for the activities of eligible nonsubscription transmission services and new subscription services, to be effective for the period beginning on January 1, 2006, and ending on December 31, 2010. Such proceedings shall next be commenced in January 2009 to determine reasonable terms and rates of royalty payments, to become effective on January 1, 2011. Thereafter, such proceedings shall be repeated in each subsequent fifth calendar year.

(B) For preexisting subscription and satellite digital audio radio services.—Proceedings under this chapter shall be commenced in January 2006 to determine reasonable terms and rates of royalty payments under sections 114 and 112 for the activities of preexisting subscription services, to be effective during the period beginning on January 1, 2008, and ending on December 31, 2012, and preexisting satellite digital audio radio services, to be effective during the period beginning on January 1, 2007, and ending on December 31, 2012. Such proceedings shall next be commenced in 2011 to determine reasonable terms and rates of royalty payments, to become effective on January 1, 2013. Thereafter, such proceedings shall be repeated in each subsequent fifth calendar year.

(C)(i) Notwithstanding any other provision of this chapter, this subparagraph shall govern proceedings commenced pursuant to section 114(f)(1)(C) and 114(f)(2)(C) concerning new types of services.

(ii) Not later than 30 days after a petition to determine rates and terms for a new type of service is filed by any copyright owner of sound recordings, or such new type of service, indicating that such new type of service is or is about to become operational, the Copyright Royalty Judges shall issue a notice for a proceeding to determine rates and terms for such service.

(iii) The proceeding shall follow the schedule set forth in subsections (b), (c), and (d) of section 803, except that—

(I) the determination shall be issued by not later than 24 months after the publication of the notice under clause (ii); and

(II) the decision shall take effect as provided in subsections (c)(2) and (d)(2) of section 803 and section 114(f)(4)(B)(ii) and (C).

(iv) The rates and terms shall remain in effect for the period set forth in section 114(f)(1)(C) or 114(f)(2)(C), as the case may be.

(4) Section 115 proceedings.—A petition described in subsection (a) to initiate proceedings under section 801(b)(1) concerning the adjustment or determination of royalty rates as provided in section 115 may be filed in the year 2006 and in each subsequent fifth calendar year, or at such other times as the parties have agreed under section 115(c)(3) (B) and (C).

(5) Section 116 proceedings—

(A) A petition described in subsection (a) to initiate proceedings under section 801(b) concerning the determination of royalty rates and terms as provided in section 116 may be filed at any time within 1 year after negotiated licenses authorized by section 116 are terminated or expire and are not replaced by subsequent agreements.

(B) If a negotiated license authorized by section 116 is terminated or expires and is not replaced by another such license agreement which provides permission to use a quantity of musical works not substantially smaller than the quantity of such works performed on coin-operated phonorecord players during the 1-year period ending March 1, 1989, the Copyright Royalty Judges shall, upon petition filed under paragraph (1) within 1 year after such termination or expiration, commence a proceeding to promptly establish an interim royalty rate or rates for the public performance by means of a coin-operated phonorecord player of nondramatic musical works embodied in phonorecords which had been subject to the terminated or expired negotiated license agreement. Such rate or rates shall be the same as the last such rate or rates and shall remain in force until the conclusion of proceedings by the Copyright Royalty Judges, in accordance with section 803, to adjust the royalty rates applicable to such works, or until superseded by a new negotiated license agreement, as provided in section 116(b).

(6) Section 118 proceedings.—A petition described in subsection (a) to initiate proceedings under section 801(b)(1) concerning the determination of reasonable terms and rates of royalty payments as provided in section 118 may be filed in the year 2006 and in each subsequent fifth calendar year.

(7) Section 1004 proceedings.—A petition described in subsection (a) to initiate proceedings under section 801(b)(1) concerning the adjustment of reasonable royalty rates under section 1004 may be filed as provided in section 1004(a)(3).

(8) Proceedings concerning distribution of royalty fees.—With respect to proceedings under section 801(b)(3) concerning the distribution of royalty fees in certain circumstances under section 111, 119, or 1007, the Copyright Royalty Judges shall, upon a determination that a controversy exists concerning such distribution, cause to be published in the Federal Register notice of commencement of proceedings under this chapter.

History of 17 U.S.C. §804: May 30, 2005, P.L. 108-419, §3(a), 118 Stat. 2357; May 30, 2005, P.L. 109-303, §3(12), (13), 120 Stat. 1481; May 27, 2010, P.L. 111-175, §104(f), 124 Stat. 1238.

History of Former 17 U.S.C. §804: Oct. 28, 1992, P.L. 102-563, §3(a)(2), 106 Stat. 4248. Renumbered as §803 and amended Dec. 17, 1993, P.L. 103-198, §2(d), 107 Stat. 2307. Nov. 1, 1995, P.L. 104-39, §5(d)(5)-(7), 109 Stat. 349; Nov. 13, 1997, P.L. 105-80, §12(a)(20), 111 Stat. 1535; Oct. 28, 1998, P.L. 105-304, §405(e)(5), (6), 112 Stat. 2902.

See also 37 C.F.R. §§351.1-351.15.

§805. GENERAL RULE FOR VOLUNTARILY NEGOTIATED AGREEMENTS

Any rates or terms under this title that—

(1) are agreed to by participants to a proceeding under section 803(b)(3),

(2) are adopted by the Copyright Royalty Judges as part of a determination under this chapter, and

(3) are in effect for a period shorter than would otherwise apply under a determination pursuant to this chapter, shall remain in effect for such period of time as would otherwise apply under such determination, except that the Copyright Royalty Judges shall adjust the rates pursuant to the voluntary negotiations to reflect national monetary inflation during the additional period the rates remain in effect.

History of 17 U.S.C. §805: May 30, 2005, P.L. 108-419, §3(a), 118 Stat. 2360.

History of Former 17 U.S.C. §805: Oct. 19, 1976, P.L. 94-553, §101, 90 Stat. 2598; Dec. 17, 1993, P.L. 103-198, §2(e), 107 Stat. 2308.

See also 37 C.F.R. §§351.2, 351.3.

CHAPTER 9. PROTECTION OF SEMICONDUCTOR CHIP PRODUCTS

§901. DEFINITIONS

(a) As used in this chapter—

(1) a "semiconductor chip product" is the final or intermediate form of any product—

(A) having two or more layers of metallic, insulating, or semiconductor material, deposited or otherwise placed on, or etched away or otherwise removed from, a piece of semiconductor material in accordance with a predetermined pattern; and

(B) intended to perform electronic circuitry functions;

(2) a "mask work" is a series of related images, however fixed or encoded—

(A) having or representing the predetermined, three-dimensional pattern of metallic, insulating, or semiconductor material present or removed from the layers of a semiconductor chip product; and

(B) in which series the relation of the images to one another is that each image has the pattern of the surface of one form of the semiconductor chip product;

(3) a mask work is "fixed" in a semiconductor chip product when its embodiment in the product is sufficiently permanent or stable to permit the mask work to be perceived or reproduced from the product for a period of more than transitory duration;

(4) to "distribute" means to sell, or to lease, bail, or otherwise transfer, or to offer to sell, lease, bail, or otherwise transfer;

(5) to "commercially exploit" a mask work is to distribute to the public for commercial purposes a semiconductor chip product embodying the mask work; except that such term includes an offer to sell or transfer a semiconductor chip product only when the offer is in writing and occurs after the mask work is fixed in the semiconductor chip product;

(6) the "owner" of a mask work is the person who created the mask work, the legal representative of that person if that person is deceased or under a legal incapacity, or a party to whom all the rights under this chapter of such person or representative are transferred in accordance with section 903(b); except that, in the case of a work made within the scope of a person's employment, the owner is the employer for whom the person created the mask work or a party to whom all the rights under this chapter of the employer are transferred in accordance with section 903(b);

(7) an "innocent purchaser" is a person who purchases a semiconductor chip product in good faith and without having notice of protection with respect to the semiconductor chip product;

(8) having "notice of protection" means having actual knowledge that, or reasonable grounds to believe that, a mask work is protected under this chapter; and

(9) an "infringing semiconductor chip product" is a semiconductor chip product which is made, imported, or distributed in violation of the exclusive rights of the owner of a mask work under this chapter.

(b) For purposes of this chapter, the distribution or importation of a product incorporating a semiconductor chip product as a part thereof is a distribution or importation of that semiconductor chip product.

History of 17 U.S.C. §901: Nov. 8, 1984, P.L. 98-620, §302, 98 Stat. 3347. See also 37 C.F.R. §§211.1-211.7.

ANNOTATIONS

Brooktree Corp. v. Advanced Micro Devices, Inc., 977 F.2d 1555, 1561 (Fed.Cir.1992). "The Semiconductor Chip Protection Act [(SCPA)] of 1984 arose from concerns that existing intellectual property laws did not provide adequate protection of proprietary rights in semiconductor chips that had been designed to perform a particular function. The Act … adopted relevant aspects of existing intellectual property law, but for the most part created a new law, specifically adapted to the protection of design layouts of semiconductor chips. *At 1564:* Although the [SCPA] does not use the word 'copy' to describe infringement, the parallel language reflects the incorporation of the well-explicated copyright principle of substantial similarity into the [SCPA]."

§902. SUBJECT MATTER OF PROTECTION

(a)(1) Subject to the provisions of subsection (b), a mask work fixed in a semiconductor chip product, by or under the authority of the owner of the mask work, is eligible for protection under this chapter if—

(A) on the date on which the mask work is registered under section 908, or is first commercially exploited anywhere in the world, whichever occurs first, the owner of the mask work is (i) a national or domiciliary of the United States, (ii) a national, domiciliary, or sovereign authority of a foreign nation that is a party to a treaty affording protection to mask works to which the United States is also a party, or (iii) a stateless person, wherever that person may be domiciled;

(B) the mask work is first commercially exploited in the United States; or

(C) the mask work comes within the scope of a Presidential proclamation issued under paragraph (2).

(2) Whenever the President finds that a foreign nation extends, to mask works of owners who are nationals or domiciliaries of the United States protection (A) on substantially the same basis as that on which the foreign nation extends protection to mask works of its own nationals and domiciliaries and mask works first commercially exploited in that nation, or (B) on substantially the same basis as provided in this chapter, the President may by proclamation extend protection under this chapter to mask works (i) of owners who are, on the date on which the mask works are registered under section 908, or the date on which the mask works are first commercially exploited anywhere in the world, whichever occurs first, nationals, domiciliaries, or sovereign authorities of that nation, or (ii) which are first commercially exploited in that nation. The President may revise, suspend, or revoke any such proclamation or impose any conditions or limitations on protection extended under any such proclamation.

(b) Protection under this chapter shall not be available for a mask work that—

(1) is not original; or

(2) consists of designs that are staple, commonplace, or familiar in the semiconductor industry, or variations of such designs, combined in a way that, considered as a whole, is not original.

(c) In no case does protection under this chapter for a mask work extend to any idea, procedure, process, system, method of operation, concept, principle, or discovery, regardless of the form in which it is described, explained, illustrated, or embodied in such work.

History of 17 U.S.C. §902: Nov. 8, 1984, P.L. 98-620, §302, 98 Stat. 3348; Nov. 9, 1987, P.L. 100-159, §3, 101 Stat. 900.

See also 37 C.F.R. §§150.1-150.6, 211.1-211.7; NAFTA art. 1710.

ANNOTATIONS

Altera Corp. v. Clear Logic, Inc., 424 F.3d 1079, 1085-86 (9th Cir.2005). "[P] asserts that the placement of groupings of transistors on the chip was copied, and does not specifically address the layout of the transistors within those groupings. [D] argues that the placement of the groupings is a system or an idea and is not entitled to protection under the [Semiconductor Chip Protection Act (SCPA)]. We reject this contention; the boundaries and organization of these groupings are more than conceptual. [T]hese groupings are physically present in the mask work. [¶] Commentators have suggested analyzing the levels of abstraction in the production of a computer program or a mask work to identify the distinction between ideas and expression, and the degree of similarity, in these formats. ... Under this approach, we identify the broad idea behind the design and assess each successive step in the design process, identifying the point at which the idea becomes protectable expression. [¶] In considering the chip design process, we recognize ... that with each step, the ideas become more concrete until they are finally expressed in the layout of the transistors in the mask work. The customer's idea is at the highest level of abstraction, and the schematics and floor plans convey more concrete ideas, designating how the chip may be structured or organized. These drawings are preliminary sketches that would not be protected under traditional copyright principles. It is not until the level of the mask work, the piece of the process that Congress chose to protect, that there is an expression of that idea. Those ideas that are physically expressed in the mask work are subject to protection under the SCPA. [¶] The placement of logic groupings in a mask work is not an abstract concept; it is embodied in the chip and affects the chip's performance and efficiency as well as the chip's timing. [I]t is the province of the jury to determine whether those aspects of the mask work are material, and whether the similarity between the mask works is substantial."

§903. OWNERSHIP, TRANSFER, LICENSING, & RECORDATION

(a) The exclusive rights in a mask work subject to protection under this chapter belong to the owner of the mask work.

(b) The owner of the exclusive rights in a mask work may transfer all of those rights, or license all or less than all of those rights, by any written instrument signed by such owner or a duly authorized agent of the owner. Such rights may be transferred or licensed by operation of law, may be bequeathed by will, and may pass as personal property by the applicable laws of intestate succession.

(c)(1) Any document pertaining to a mask work may be recorded in the Copyright Office if the document filed for recordation bears the actual signature of the person who executed it, or if it is accompanied by a sworn or official certification that it is a true copy of the original, signed document. The Register of Copyrights shall, upon receipt of the document and the fee specified pursuant to section 908(d), record the document and return it with a certificate of recordation. The recordation of any transfer or license under this paragraph gives all persons constructive notice of the facts stated in the recorded document concerning the transfer or license.

(2) In any case in which conflicting transfers of the exclusive rights in a mask work are made, the transfer first executed shall be void as against a subsequent transfer which is made for a valuable consideration and without notice of the first transfer, unless the first transfer is recorded in accordance with paragraph (1) within three months after the date on which it is executed, but in no case later than the day before the date of such subsequent transfer.

(d) Mask works prepared by an officer or employee of the United States Government as part of that person's official duties are not protected under this chapter, but the United States Government is not precluded from receiving and holding exclusive rights in mask works transferred to the Government under subsection (b).

History of 17 U.S.C. §903: Nov. 8, 1984, P.L. 98-620, §302, 98 Stat. 3349. See also NAFTA art. 1710.

§904. DURATION OF PROTECTION

(a) The protection provided for a mask work under this chapter shall commence on the date on which the mask work is registered under section 908, or the date on which the mask work is first commercially exploited anywhere in the world, whichever occurs first.

(b) Subject to subsection (c) and the provisions of this chapter, the protection provided under this chapter to a mask work shall end ten years after the date on which such protection commences under subsection (a).

(c) All terms of protection provided in this section shall run to the end of the calendar year in which they would otherwise expire.

History of 17 U.S.C. §904: Nov. 8, 1984, P.L. 98-620, 98 Stat. 3349.

§905. EXCLUSIVE RIGHTS IN MASK WORKS

The owner of a mask work provided protection under this chapter has the exclusive rights to do and to authorize any of the following:

(1) to reproduce the mask work by optical, electronic, or any other means;

(2) to import or distribute a semiconductor chip product in which the mask work is embodied; and

(3) to induce or knowingly to cause another person to do any of the acts described in paragraphs (1) and (2).

History of 17 U.S.C. §905: Nov. 8, 1984, P.L. 98-620, §302, 98 Stat. 3350. See also NAFTA art. 1710.

ANNOTATIONS

Brooktree Corp. v. Advanced Micro Devices, Inc., 977 F.2d 1555, 1563-64 (Fed.Cir.1992). "The text of the Semiconductor Chip Protection Act [(SCPA)] sets forth the subject matter of protection in terms of certain exclusive rights, including, *inter alia*, the exclusive right to 'reproduce the mask work.' This usage mirrors the words of the Copyright Act, which states the exclusive rights of copyright owners 'to reproduce the copyrighted work.' Although the [SCPA] does not use the word 'copy' to describe infringement, the parallel language reflects the incorporation of the well-explicated copyright principle of substantial similarity into the [SCPA]."

Brooktree Corp. v. Advanced Micro Devices, Inc., 705 F.Supp. 491, 494 (S.D.Cal.1988), *aff'd*, 977 F.2d 1555 (Fed.Cir.1992). The "Mask Work Act does not prohibit independent development of a mask work; an identical but original second mask work is not an infringement of the first."

§906. LIMITATION ON EXCLUSIVE RIGHTS: REVERSE ENGINEERING; FIRST SALE

(a) Notwithstanding the provisions of section 905, it is not an infringement of the exclusive rights of the owner of a mask work for—

(1) a person to reproduce the mask work solely for the purpose of teaching, analyzing, or evaluating the concepts or techniques embodied in the mask work or the circuitry, logic flow, or organization of components used in the mask work; or

(2) a person who performs the analysis or evaluation described in paragraph (1) to incorporate the results of such conduct in an original mask work which is made to be distributed.

(b) Notwithstanding the provisions of section 905(2), the owner of a particular semiconductor chip product made by the owner of the mask work, or by any person authorized by the owner of the mask work, may import, distribute, or otherwise dispose of or use, but not reproduce, that particular semiconductor chip product without the authority of the owner of the mask work.

History of 17 U.S.C. §906: Nov. 8, 1984, P.L. 98-620, §302, 98 Stat. 3350.

ANNOTATIONS

Altera Corp. v. Clear Logic, Inc., 424 F.3d 1079, 1086 (9th Cir.2005). "The second mask work must not be 'substantially identical to the original,' and as long as there is evidence of 'substantial toil and investment' in creating the second mask work, rather than 'mere plagiarism,' the second chip will not 'infringe the original chip, even if the layout of the two chips is, in substantial part, similar.' *At 1088:* The [Semiconductor Chip Protection Act's] reverse engineering provision allows copying the entire mask work. It does not distinguish between the protectable and non-protectable elements of the chip as long as the copying is for the purpose of teaching, evaluating, or analyzing the chip. Although the product created from that analysis must be original, the process of studying the chip is not limited to copying ideas or concepts. The district court's instructions initially define 'legitimate reverse engineering' to allow copying and analyzing only 'non-protectable concepts or techniques.' This is an incorrect statement of the law."

Brooktree Corp. v. Advanced Micro Devices, Inc., 977 F.2d 1555, 1565 (Fed.Cir.1992). "The statute ... provides that one engaged in reverse engineering shall not be liable for infringement when the end product is itself original. In performing reverse engineering a person may disassemble, study, and analyze an existing chip in order to understand it. This knowledge may be used to create an original chip having a different design layout, but which performs the same or equivalent function as the existing chip, without penalty or prohibition. *At 1570:* [Section] 906(a) requires, as an element of the defense of reverse engineering, that the product be original. ... The statute does not reflect an intent to excuse copying, as a matter of law, if the copier had first tried and failed to do the job without copying. The paper trail is evidence of independent effort, but it is not conclusive or incontrovertible proof of either originality or the absence of copying." *See also* ***Sega Enters. v. Accolade, Inc.***, 977 F.2d 1510, 1521 (9th Cir.1992); ***Anadigics, Inc. v. Raytheon Co.***, 37 U.S.P.Q.2d 1666, 1669 (S.D.N.Y.1995).

§907. LIMITATION ON EXCLUSIVE RIGHTS: INNOCENT INFRINGEMENT

(a) Notwithstanding any other provision of this chapter, an innocent purchaser of an infringing semiconductor chip product—

(1) shall incur no liability under this chapter with respect to the importation or distribution of units of the infringing semiconductor chip product that occurs before the innocent purchaser has notice of protection with respect to the mask work embodied in the semiconductor chip product; and

(2) shall be liable only for a reasonable royalty on each unit of the infringing semiconductor chip product that the innocent purchaser imports or distributes after having notice of protection with respect to the mask work embodied in the semiconductor chip product.

(b) The amount of the royalty referred to in subsection (a)(2) shall be determined by the court in a civil action for infringement unless the parties resolve the issue by voluntary negotiation, mediation, or binding arbitration.

(c) The immunity of an innocent purchaser from liability referred to in subsection (a)(1) and the limitation of remedies with respect to an innocent purchaser referred to in subsection (a)(2) shall extend to any person who directly or indirectly purchases an infringing semiconductor chip product from an innocent purchaser.

(d) The provisions of subsections (a), (b), and (c) apply only with respect to those units of an infringing semiconductor chip product that an innocent purchaser purchased before having notice of protection with respect to the mask work embodied in the semiconductor chip product.

History of 17 U.S.C. §907: Nov. 8, 1984, P.L. 98-620, §302, 98 Stat. 3350.

§908. REGISTRATION OF CLAIMS OF PROTECTION

(a) The owner of a mask work may apply to the Register of Copyrights for registration of a claim of protection in a mask work. Protection of a mask work under this chapter shall terminate if application for registration of a claim of protection in the mask work is not made as provided in this chapter within two years after the date on which the mask work is first commercially exploited anywhere in the world.

(b) The Register of Copyrights shall be responsible for all administrative functions and duties under this chapter. Except for section 708, the provisions of chapter 7 of this title relating to the general responsibilities, organization, regulatory authority, actions, records, and publications of the Copyright Office shall apply to this chapter, except that the Register of Copyrights may make such changes as may be necessary in applying those provisions to this chapter.

(c) The application for registration of a mask work shall be made on a form prescribed by the Register of Copyrights. Such form may require any information regarded by the Register as bearing upon the preparation or identification of the mask work, the existence or duration of protection of the mask work under this chapter, or ownership of the mask work. The application shall be accompanied by the fee set pursuant to subsection (d) and the identifying material specified pursuant to such subsection.

(d) The Register of Copyrights shall by regulation set reasonable fees for the filing of applications to register claims of protection in mask works under this chapter, and for other services relating to the administration of this chapter or the rights under this chapter, taking into consideration the cost of providing those services, the benefits of a public record, and statutory fee schedules under this title. The Register shall also specify the identifying material to be deposited in connection with the claim for registration.

(e) If the Register of Copyrights, after examining an application for registration, determines, in accordance with the provisions of this chapter, that the application relates to a mask work which is entitled to protection under this chapter, then the Register shall register the claim of protection and issue to the applicant a certificate of registration of the claim of protection under the seal of the Copyright Office. The effective date of registration of a claim of protection shall be the date on which an application, deposit of identifying material, and fee, which are determined by the Register of Copyrights or by a court of competent jurisdiction to be acceptable for registration of the claim, have all been received in the Copyright Office.

(f) In any action for infringement under this chapter, the certificate of registration of a mask work shall constitute prima facie evidence (1) of the facts stated in the certificate, and (2) that the applicant issued the certificate has met the requirements of this chapter, and the regulations issued under this chapter, with respect to the registration of claims.

(g) Any applicant for registration under this section who is dissatisfied with the refusal of the Register of Copyrights to issue a certificate of registration under this section may seek judicial review of that refusal by bringing an action for such review in an appropriate United States district court not later than sixty days after the refusal. The provisions of chapter 7 of title 5 shall apply to such judicial review. The failure of the Register of Copyrights to issue a certificate of registration within four months after an application for registration is filed shall be deemed to be a refusal to issue a certificate of registration for purposes of this subsection and section 910(b)(2), except that, upon a showing of good cause, the district court may shorten such four-month period.

History of 17 U.S.C. §908: Nov. 8, 1984, P.L. 98-620, §302, 98 Stat. 3351.

§909. MASK WORK NOTICE

(a) The owner of a mask work provided protection under this chapter may affix notice to the mask work, and to masks and semiconductor chip products embodying the mask work, in such manner and location as to give reasonable notice of such protection. The Register of Copyrights shall prescribe by regulation, as examples, specific methods of affixation and positions of notice for purposes of this section, but these specifications shall not be considered exhaustive. The affixation of such notice is not a condition of protection under this chapter, but shall constitute prima facie evidence of notice of protection.

(b) The notice referred to in subsection (a) shall consist of—

(1) the words "mask work," the symbol *M*, or the symbol (M) (the letter M in a circle); and

(2) the name of the owner or owners of the mask work or an abbreviation by which the name is recognized or is generally known.

History of 17 U.S.C. §909: Nov. 8, 1984, P.L. 98-620, §302, 98 Stat. 3352; Nov. 13, 1997, P.L. 105-80, §12(a)(22), 111 Stat. 1535.

§910. ENFORCEMENT OF EXCLUSIVE RIGHTS

(a) Except as otherwise provided in this chapter, any person who violates any of the exclusive rights of the owner of a mask work under this chapter, by conduct in or affecting commerce, shall be liable as an infringer of such rights. As used in this subsection, the term "any person" includes any State, any instrumentality of a State, and any officer or employee of a State or instrumentality of a State acting in his or her official capacity. Any State, and any such instrumentality, officer, or employee, shall be subject to the provisions of this chapter in the same manner and to the same extent as any nongovernmental entity.

(b)(1) The owner of a mask work protected under this chapter, or the exclusive licensee of all rights under this chapter with respect to the mask work, shall, after a certificate of registration of a claim of protection in that mask work has been issued under section 908, be entitled to institute a civil action for any infringement with respect to the mask work which is committed after the commencement of protection of the mask work under section 904(a).

(2) In any case in which an application for registration of a claim of protection in a mask work and the required deposit of identifying material and fee have been received in the Copyright Office in proper form and registration of the mask work has been refused, the applicant is entitled to institute a civil action for infringement under this chapter with respect to the mask work if notice of the action, together with a copy of the complaint, is served on the Register of Copyrights, in accordance with the Federal Rules of Civil Procedure. The Register may, at his or her option, become a party to the action with respect to the issue of whether the claim of protection is eligible for registration by entering an appearance within sixty days after such service, but the failure of the Register to become a party to the action shall not deprive the court of jurisdiction to determine that issue.

(c)(1) The Secretary of the Treasury and the United States Postal Service shall separately or jointly issue regulations for the enforcement of the rights set forth in section 905 with respect to importation. These regulations may require, as a condition for the exclusion of articles from the United States, that the person seeking exclusion take any one or more of the following actions:

(A) Obtain a court order enjoining, or an order of the International Trade Commission under section 1337 of title 19 excluding, importation of the articles.

(B) Furnish proof that the mask work involved is protected under this chapter and that the importation of the articles would infringe the rights in the mask work under this chapter.

(C) Post a surety bond for any injury that may result if the detention or exclusion of the articles proves to be unjustified.

(2) Articles imported in violation of the rights set forth in section 905 are subject to seizure and forfeiture in the same manner as property imported in violation of the customs laws. Any such forfeited articles shall be destroyed as directed by the Secretary of the Treasury or the court, as the case may be, except that the articles may be returned to the country of export whenever it is shown to the satisfaction of the Secretary of the Treasury that the importer had no reasonable grounds for believing that his or her acts constituted a violation of the law.

History of 17 U.S.C. §910: Nov. 8, 1984, P.L. 98-620, §302, 98 Stat. 3352; Nov. 15, 1990, P.L. 101-553, §2(b)(1), 104 Stat. 2750; Nov. 13, 1997, P.L. 105-80, §12(a)(23), 111 Stat. 1535.

§911. CIVIL ACTIONS

(a) Any court having jurisdiction of a civil action arising under this chapter may grant temporary restraining orders, preliminary injunctions, and permanent injunctions on such terms as the court may deem reasonable to prevent or restrain infringement of the exclusive rights in a mask work under this chapter.

(b) Upon finding an infringer liable, to a person entitled under section 910(b)(1) to institute a civil action, for an infringement of any exclusive right under this chapter, the court shall award such person actual damages suffered by the person as a result of the infringement. The court shall also award such person the infringer's profits that are attributable to the infringement and are not taken into account in computing the award of actual damages. In establishing the infringer's profits, such person is required to present proof only of the infringer's gross revenue, and the infringer is required to prove his or her deductible expenses and the elements of profit attributable to factors other than the mask work.

(c) At any time before final judgment is rendered, a person entitled to institute a civil action for infringement may elect, instead of actual damages and profits as provided by subsection (b), an award of statutory damages for all infringements involved in the action, with respect to any one mask work for which any one infringer is liable individually, or for which any two or more infringers are liable jointly and severally, in an amount not more than $250,000 as the court considers just.

(d) An action for infringement under this chapter shall be barred unless the action is commenced within three years after the claim accrues.

(e)(1) At any time while an action for infringement of the exclusive rights in a mask work under this chapter is pending, the court may order the impounding, on such terms as it may deem reasonable, of all semiconductor chip products, and any drawings, tapes, masks, or other products by means of which such products may be reproduced, that are claimed to have been made, imported, or used in violation of those exclusive rights. Insofar as practicable, applications for orders under this paragraph shall be heard and determined in the same manner as an application for a temporary restraining order or preliminary injunction.

(2) As part of a final judgment or decree, the court may order the destruction or other disposition of any infringing semiconductor chip products, and any masks, tapes, or other articles by means of which such products may be reproduced.

(f) In any civil action arising under this chapter, the court in its discretion may allow the recovery of full costs, including reasonable attorneys' fees, to the prevailing party.

(g)(1) Any State, any instrumentality of a State, and any officer or employee of a State or instrumentality of a State acting in his or her official capacity, shall not be immune, under the Eleventh Amendment of the

Constitution of the United States or under any other doctrine of sovereign immunity, from suit in Federal court by any person, including any governmental or nongovernmental entity, for a violation of any of the exclusive rights of the owner of a mask work under this chapter, or for any other violation under this chapter.

(2) In a suit described in paragraph (1) for a violation described in that paragraph, remedies (including remedies both at law and in equity) are available for the violation to the same extent as such remedies are available for such a violation in a suit against any public or private entity other than a State, instrumentality of a State, or officer or employee of a State acting in his or her official capacity. Such remedies include actual damages and profits under subsection (b), statutory damages under subsection (c), impounding and disposition of infringing articles under subsection (e), and costs and attorney's fees under subsection (f).

History of 17 U.S.C. §911: Nov. 8, 1984, P.L. 98-620, §302, 98 Stat. 3353; Nov. 15, 1990, P.L. 101-553, §2(b)(2), 104 Stat. 2750.

ANNOTATIONS

Brooktree Corp. v. Advanced Micro Devices, Inc., 977 F.2d 1555, 1582 (Fed.Cir.1992). "Many aspects of the Semiconductor Chip Protection Act [(SCPA)] are based on copyright concepts. ... In contrast with the attorney fee provision of the patent law, 35 U.S.C. §285, there is no requirement for a threshold finding of 'exceptional case.' However, the award under the [SCPA] continues to be consigned to the court's discretion. We conclude that copyright law principles are more aptly applied to the application of 17 U.S.C. §911(f). *At 1583:* Attorney fee decisions under the Copyright Act are reviewed under the abuse of discretion standard."

§912. RELATION TO OTHER LAWS

(a) Nothing in this chapter shall affect any right or remedy held by any person under chapters 1 through 8 or 10 of this title, or under title 35.

(b) Except as provided in section 908(b) of this title, references to "this title" or "title 17" in chapters 1 through 8 or 10 of this title shall be deemed not to apply to this chapter.

(c) The provisions of this chapter shall preempt the laws of any State to the extent those laws provide any rights or remedies with respect to a mask work which are equivalent to those rights or remedies provided by this chapter, except that such preemption shall be effective only with respect to actions filed on or after January 1, 1986.

(d) Notwithstanding subsection (c), nothing in this chapter shall detract from any rights of a mask work owner, whether under Federal law (exclusive of this chapter) or under the common law or the statutes of a State, heretofore or hereafter declared or enacted, with respect to any mask work first commercially exploited before July 1, 1983.

History of 17 U.S.C. §912: Nov. 8, 1984, P.L. 98-620, §302, 98 Stat. 3354; Nov. 19, 1988, P.L. 100-702, §1020(b), 102 Stat. 4672; Oct. 28, 1992, P.L. 102-563, §3(c), 106 Stat. 4248.

§913. TRANSITIONAL PROVISIONS

(a) No application for registration under section 908 may be filed, and no civil action under section 910 or other enforcement proceeding under this chapter may be instituted, until sixty days after Nov. 8, 1984.

(b) No monetary relief under section 911 may be granted with respect to any conduct that occurred before Nov. 8, 1984, except as provided in subsection (d).

(c) Subject to subsection (a), the provisions of this chapter apply to all mask works that are first commercially exploited or are registered under this chapter, or both, on or after Nov. 8, 1984.

(d)(1) Subject to subsection (a), protection is available under this chapter to any mask work that was first commercially exploited on or after July 1, 1983, and before Nov. 8, 1984, if a claim of protection in the mask work is registered in the Copyright Office before July 1, 1985, under section 908.

(2) In the case of any mask work described in paragraph (1) that is provided protection under this chapter, infringing semiconductor chip product units manufactured before Nov. 8, 1984 may, without liability under sections 910 and 911, be imported into or distributed in the United States, or both, until two years after the date of registration of the mask work under section 908, but only if the importer or distributor, as the case may be, first pays or offers to pay the reasonable royalty referred to in section 907(a)(2) to the mask work owner, on all such units imported or distributed, or both, after Nov. 8, 1984.

(3) In the event that a person imports or distributes infringing semiconductor chip product units described in paragraph (2) of this subsection without first paying or offering to pay the reasonable royalty specified in such paragraph, or if the person refuses or fails to make such payment, the mask work owner shall be entitled to the relief provided in sections 910 and 911.

History of 17 U.S.C. §913: Nov. 8, 1984, P.L. 98-620, §302, 98 Stat. 3354.

§914. INTERNATIONAL TRANSITIONAL PROVISIONS

(a) Notwithstanding the conditions set forth in subparagraphs (A) and (C) of section 902(a)(1) with respect to the availability of protection under this chapter to nationals, domiciliaries, and sovereign authorities of a foreign nation, the Secretary of Commerce may, upon the petition of any person, or upon the Secretary's own motion, issue an order extending protection under this chapter to such foreign nationals, domiciliaries, and sovereign authorities if the Secretary finds—

(1) that the foreign nation is making good faith efforts and reasonable progress toward—

(A) entering into a treaty described in section 902(a)(1)(A); or

(B) enacting or implementing legislation that would be in compliance with subparagraph (A) or (B) of section 902(a)(2); and

(2) that the nationals, domiciliaries, and sovereign authorities of the foreign nation, and persons controlled by them, are not engaged in the misappropriation, or unauthorized distribution or commercial exploitation, of mask works; and

(3) that issuing the order would promote the purposes of this chapter and international comity with respect to the protection of mask works.

(b) While an order under subsection (a) is in effect with respect to a foreign nation, no application for registration of a claim for protection in a mask work under this chapter may be denied solely because the owner of the mask work is a national, domiciliary, or sovereign authority of that foreign nation, or solely because the mask work was first commercially exploited in that foreign nation.

(c) Any order issued by the Secretary of Commerce under subsection (a) shall be effective for such period as the Secretary designates in the order, except that no such order may be effective after the date on which the authority of the Secretary of Commerce terminates under subsection (e). The effective date of any such order shall also be designated in the order. In the case of an order issued upon the petition of a person, such effective date may be no earlier than the date on which the Secretary receives such petition.

(d)(1) Any order issued under this section shall terminate if—

(A) the Secretary of Commerce finds that any of the conditions set forth in paragraphs (1), (2), and (3) of subsection (a) no longer exist; or

(B) mask works of nationals, domiciliaries, and sovereign authorities of that foreign nation or mask works first commercially exploited in that foreign nation become eligible for protection under subparagraph (A) or (C) of section 902(a)(1).

(2) Upon the termination or expiration of an order issued under this section, registrations of claims of protection in mask works made pursuant to that order shall remain valid for the period specified in section 904.

(e) The authority of the Secretary of Commerce under this section shall commence on Nov. 8, 1984, and shall terminate on July 1, 1995.

(f)(1) The Secretary of Commerce shall promptly notify the Register of Copyrights and the Committees on the Judiciary of the Senate and the House of Representatives of the issuance or termination of any order under this section, together with a statement of the reasons for such action. The Secretary shall also publish such notification and statement of reasons in the Federal Register.

(2) Two years after Nov. 8, 1984, the Secretary of Commerce, in consultation with the Register of Copyrights, shall transmit to the Committees on the Judiciary of the Senate and the House of Representatives a report on the actions taken under this section and on the current status of international recognition of mask work protection. The report shall include such recommendations for modifications of the protection accorded under this chapter to mask works owned by nationals, domiciliaries, or sovereign authorities of foreign nations as the Secretary, in consultation with the Register of Copyrights, considers would promote the purposes of this chapter and international comity with respect to mask work protection. Not later than July 1, 1994, the Secretary of Commerce, in consultation with the Register of Copyrights, shall transmit to the Committees on the Judiciary of the Senate and the House of Representatives a report updating the matters contained in the report transmitted under the preceding sentence.

History of 17 U.S.C. §914: Nov. 8, 1984, P.L. 98-620, §302, 98 Stat. 3355; Nov. 9, 1987, P.L. 100-159, §§2, 4, 101 Stat. 899, 900; June 28, 1991, P.L. 102-64, §§3, 4, 105 Stat. 520, 521.

CHAPTER 10. DIGITAL AUDIO RECORDING DEVICES & MEDIA

SUBCHAPTER A. DEFINITIONS

§1001. DEFINITIONS

As used in this chapter, the following terms have the following meanings:

(1) A "digital audio copied recording" is a reproduction in a digital recording format of a digital musical recording, whether that reproduction is made directly from another digital musical recording or indirectly from a transmission.

(2) A "digital audio interface device" is any machine or device that is designed specifically to communicate digital audio information and related interface data to a digital audio recording device through a nonprofessional interface.

(3) A "digital audio recording device" is any machine or device of a type commonly distributed to individuals for use by individuals, whether or not included with or as part of some other machine or device, the digital recording function of which is designed or marketed for the primary purpose of, and that is capable of, making a digital audio copied recording for private use, except for—

(A) professional model products, and

(B) dictation machines, answering machines, and other audio recording equipment that is designed and marketed primarily for the creation of sound recordings resulting from the fixation of nonmusical sounds.

(4)(A) A "digital audio recording medium" is any material object in a form commonly distributed for use by individuals, that is primarily marketed or most commonly used by consumers for the purpose of making digital audio copied recordings by use of a digital audio recording device.

(B) Such term does not include any material object—

(i) that embodies a sound recording at the time it is first distributed by the importer or manufacturer; or

(ii) that is primarily marketed and most commonly used by consumers either for the purpose of making copies of motion pictures or other audiovisual works or for the purpose of making copies of nonmusical literary works, including computer programs or data bases.

(5)(A) A "digital musical recording" is a material object—

(i) in which are fixed, in a digital recording format, only sounds, and material, statements, or instructions incidental to those fixed sounds, if any, and

(ii) from which the sounds and material can be perceived, reproduced, or otherwise communicated, either directly or with the aid of a machine or device.

(B) A "digital musical recording" does not include a material object—

(i) in which the fixed sounds consist entirely of spoken word recordings, or

(ii) in which one or more computer programs are fixed, except that a digital musical recording may contain statements or instructions constituting the fixed sounds and incidental material, and statements or instructions to be used directly or indirectly in order to bring about the perception, reproduction, or communication of the fixed sounds and incidental material.

(C) For purposes of this paragraph—

(i) a "spoken word recording" is a sound recording in which are fixed only a series of spoken words, except that the spoken words may be accompanied by incidental musical or other sounds, and

(ii) the term "incidental" means related to and relatively minor by comparison.

(6) "Distribute" means to sell, lease, or assign a product to consumers in the United States, or to sell, lease, or assign a product in the United States for ultimate transfer to consumers in the United States.

(7) An "interested copyright party" is—

(A) the owner of the exclusive right under section 106(1) of this title to reproduce a sound recording of a musical work that has been embodied in a digital musical recording or analog musical recording lawfully made under this title that has been distributed;

(B) the legal or beneficial owner of, or the person that controls, the right to reproduce in a digital musical recording or analog musical recording a musical work that has been embodied in a digital musical recording or analog musical recording lawfully made under this title that has been distributed;

(C) a featured recording artist who performs on a sound recording that has been distributed; or

(D) any association or other organization—

(i) representing persons specified in subparagraph (A), (B), or (C), or

(ii) engaged in licensing rights in musical works to music users on behalf of writers and publishers.

(8) To "manufacture" means to produce or assemble a product in the United States. A "manufacturer" is a person who manufactures.

(9) A "music publisher" is a person that is authorized to license the reproduction of a particular musical work in a sound recording.

(10) A "professional model product" is an audio recording device that is designed, manufactured, marketed, and intended for use by recording professionals in the ordinary course of a lawful business, in accordance with such requirements as the Secretary of Commerce shall establish by regulation.

(11) The term "serial copying" means the duplication in a digital format of a copyrighted musical work or sound recording from a digital reproduction of a digital musical recording. The term "digital reproduction of a digital musical recording" does not include a digital musical recording as distributed, by authority of the copyright owner, for ultimate sale to consumers.

(12) The "transfer price" of a digital audio recording device or a digital audio recording medium—

(A) is, subject to subparagraph (B)—

(i) in the case of an imported product, the actual entered value at United States Customs (exclusive of any freight, insurance, and applicable duty), and

(ii) in the case of a domestic product, the manufacturer's transfer price (FOB the manufacturer, and exclusive of any direct sales taxes or excise taxes incurred in connection with the sale); and

(B) shall, in a case in which the transferor and transferee are related entities or within a single entity, not be less than a reasonable arms-length price under the principles of the regulations adopted pursuant to section 482 of title 26, or any successor provision to such section.

(13) A "writer" is the composer or lyricist of a particular musical work.

History of 17 U.S.C. §1001: Oct. 28, 1992, P.L. 102-563, §2, 106 Stat. 4237.

ANNOTATIONS

Recording Indus. Ass'n v. Diamond Multimedia Sys., 180 F.3d 1072, 1078 (9th Cir.1999). "Under the plain meaning of the [Audio Home Recording] Act's definition of digital audio recording devices, computers (and their hard drives) are not digital audio recording devices because their 'primary purpose' is not to make digital audio copied recordings. *At 1081:* [A] device falls within the Act's provisions if it can indirectly copy a digital music recording by making a copy from a transmission of that recording. Because [device] cannot make copies from transmissions, but instead, can only make copies from a computer hard drive, it is not a digital audio recording device."

SUBCHAPTER B. COPYING CONTROLS

§1002. INCORPORATION OF COPYING CONTROLS

(a) Prohibition on importation, manufacture, and distribution.—No person shall import, manufacture, or distribute any digital audio recording device or digital audio interface device that does not conform to—

(1) the Serial Copy Management System;

(2) a system that has the same functional characteristics as the Serial Copy Management System and requires that copyright and generation status information be accurately sent, received, and acted upon between devices using the system's method of serial copying regulation and devices using the Serial Copy Management System; or

(3) any other system certified by the Secretary of Commerce as prohibiting unauthorized serial copying.

(b) Development of verification procedure.—The Secretary of Commerce shall establish a procedure to verify, upon the petition of an interested party, that a system meets the standards set forth in subsection (a)(2).

(c) Prohibition on circumvention of the system.—No person shall import, manufacture, or distribute any device, or offer or perform any service, the primary purpose or effect of which is to avoid, bypass, remove, deactivate, or otherwise circumvent any program or circuit which implements, in whole or in part, a system described in subsection (a).

(d) Encoding of information on digital musical recordings—

(1) Prohibition on encoding inaccurate information.—No person shall encode a digital musical recording of a sound recording with inaccurate information relating to the category code, copyright status, or generation status of the source material for the recording.

(2) Encoding of copyright status not required.—Nothing in this chapter requires any person engaged in the importation or manufacture of digital musical recordings to encode any such digital musical recording with respect to its copyright status.

(e) Information accompanying transmissions in digital format.—Any person who transmits or otherwise communicates to the public any sound recording in digital format is not required under this chapter to transmit or otherwise communicate the information relating to the copyright status of the sound recording. Any such person who does transmit or otherwise communicate such copyright status information shall transmit or communicate such information accurately.

History of 17 U.S.C. §1002: Oct. 28, 1992, P.L. 102-563, §2, 106 Stat. 4240.

ANNOTATIONS

Recording Indus. Ass'n v. Diamond Multimedia Sys., 180 F.3d 1072, 1079 (9th Cir.1999). "The term 'transmission' is not defined in [the Audio Home Recording Act of 1992], although the use of the term in the Act implies that a transmission is a communication to the public. In the context of copyright law (from which the term appears to have been taken), to transmit a performance or display is to communicate it by any device or process whereby images or sounds are received beyond the place from which they are sent." (Internal quotes omitted.)

SUBCHAPTER C. ROYALTY PAYMENTS

§1003. OBLIGATION TO MAKE ROYALTY PAYMENTS

(a) Prohibition on importation and manufacture.—No person shall import into and distribute, or manufacture and distribute, any digital audio recording device or digital audio recording medium unless such person records the notice specified by this section and subsequently deposits the statements of account and applicable royalty payments for such device or medium specified in section 1004.

(b) Filing of notice.—The importer or manufacturer of any digital audio recording device or digital audio recording medium, within a product category or utilizing a technology with respect to which such manufacturer or importer has not previously filed a notice under this subsection, shall file with the Register of Copyrights a notice with respect to such device or medium, in such form and content as the Register shall prescribe by regulation.

(c) Filing of quarterly and annual statements of account—

(1) Generally.—Any importer or manufacturer that distributes any digital audio recording device or digital audio recording medium that it manufactured or imported shall file with the Register of Copyrights, in such form and content as the Register shall prescribe by regulation, such quarterly and annual statements of account with respect to such distribution as the Register shall prescribe by regulation.

(2) Certification, verification, and confidentiality.—Each such statement shall be certified as accurate by an authorized officer or principal of the importer or manufacturer. The Register shall issue regulations to provide for the verification and audit of such statements and to protect the confidentiality of the information contained in such statements. Such regulations shall provide for the disclosure, in confidence, of such statements to interested copyright parties.

(3) Royalty payments.—Each such statement shall be accompanied by the royalty payments specified in section 1004.

History of 17 U.S.C. §1003: Oct. 28, 1992, P.L. 102-563, §2, 106 Stat. 4240. See also 37 C.F.R. §§201.27-201.30.

§1004. ROYALTY PAYMENTS

(a) Digital audio recording devices—

(1) Amount of payment.—The royalty payment due under section 1003 for each digital audio recording device imported into and distributed in the United States, or manufactured and distributed in the United States, shall be 2 percent of the transfer price. Only the first person to manufacture and distribute or import and distribute such device shall be required to pay the royalty with respect to such device.

(2) Calculation for devices distributed with other devices.—With respect to a digital audio recording device first distributed in combination with one or more devices, either as a physically integrated unit or as separate components, the royalty payment shall be calculated as follows:

(A) If the digital audio recording device and such other devices are part of a physically integrated unit, the royalty payment shall be based on the transfer price of the unit, but shall be reduced by any royalty payment made on any digital audio recording device included within the unit that was not first distributed in combination with the unit.

(B) If the digital audio recording device is not part of a physically integrated unit and substantially similar devices have been distributed separately at any time during the preceding 4 calendar quarters, the royalty payment shall be based on the average transfer price of such devices during those 4 quarters.

(C) If the digital audio recording device is not part of a physically integrated unit and substantially similar devices have not been distributed separately at any time during the preceding 4 calendar quarters, the royalty payment shall be based on a constructed price reflecting the proportional value of such device to the combination as a whole.

(3) Limits on royalties.—Notwithstanding paragraph (1) or (2), the amount of the royalty payment for each digital audio recording device shall not be less than $1 nor more than the royalty maximum. The royalty maximum shall be $8 per device, except that in the case of a physically integrated unit containing more than 1 digital audio recording device, the royalty maximum for such unit shall be $12. During the 6th year after Oct. 28, 1992, and not more than once each year thereafter, any interested copyright party may petition the Copyright Royalty Judges to increase the royalty maximum and, if more than 20 percent of the royalty payments are at the relevant royalty maximum, the Copyright Royalty Judges shall prospectively increase such royalty maximum with the goal of having no more than 10 percent of such payments at the new royalty maximum; however the amount of any such increase as a percentage of the royalty maximum shall in no event exceed the percentage increase in the Consumer Price Index during the period under review.

(b) Digital audio recording media.—The royalty payment due under section 1003 for each digital audio recording medium imported into and distributed in the United States, or manufactured and distributed in the United States, shall be 3 percent of the transfer price. Only the first person to manufacture and distribute or import and distribute such medium shall be required to pay the royalty with respect to such medium.

History of 17 U.S.C. §1004: Oct. 28, 1992, P.L. 102-563, §2, 106 Stat. 4241; Dec. 17, 1993, P.L. 103-198, §6(b)(1), 107 Stat. 2312; May 30, 2005, P.L. 108-419, §5(i)(1), 118 Stat. 2368.

See also 37 C.F.R. §201.28.

§1005. DEPOSIT OF ROYALTY PAYMENTS & DEDUCTION OF EXPENSES

The Register of Copyrights shall receive all royalty payments deposited under this chapter and, after deducting the reasonable costs incurred by the Copyright Office under this chapter, shall deposit the balance in the Treasury of the United States as offsetting receipts, in such manner as the Secretary of the Treasury directs. All funds held by the Secretary of the Treasury shall be invested in interest-bearing United States securities for later distribution with interest under section 1007. The Register may, in the Register's discretion, 4 years after the close of any calendar year, close out the royalty payments account for that calendar year, and may treat any funds remaining in such account and any subsequent deposits that would otherwise be attributable to that calendar year as attributable to the succeeding calendar year.

History of 17 U.S.C. §1005: Oct. 28, 1992, P.L. 102-563, §2, 106 Stat. 4242; Dec. 17, 1993, P.L. 103-198, §6(b)(2), 107 Stat. 2312.

§1006. ENTITLEMENT TO ROYALTY PAYMENTS

(a) Interested copyright parties.—The royalty payments deposited pursuant to section 1005 shall, in accordance with the procedures specified in section 1007, be distributed to any interested copyright party—

(1) whose musical work or sound recording has been—

(A) embodied in a digital musical recording or an analog musical recording lawfully made under this title that has been distributed, and

(B) distributed in the form of digital musical recordings or analog musical recordings or disseminated to the public in transmissions, during the period to which such payments pertain; and

(2) who has filed a claim under section 1007.

(b) Allocation of royalty payments to groups.—The royalty payments shall be divided into 2 funds as follows:

(1) The sound recordings fund.—66 2/3 percent of the royalty payments shall be allocated to the Sound

Recordings Fund. 2 5/8 percent of the royalty payments allocated to the Sound Recordings Fund shall be placed in an escrow account managed by an independent administrator jointly appointed by the interested copyright parties described in section 1001(7)(A) and the American Federation of Musicians (or any successor entity) to be distributed to nonfeatured musicians (whether or not members of the American Federation of Musicians or any successor entity) who have performed on sound recordings distributed in the United States. 1 3/8 percent of the royalty payments allocated to the Sound Recordings Fund shall be placed in an escrow account managed by an independent administrator jointly appointed by the interested copyright parties described in section 1001(7)(A) and the American Federation of Television and Radio Artists (or any successor entity) to be distributed to nonfeatured vocalists (whether or not members of the American Federation of Television and Radio Artists or any successor entity) who have performed on sound recordings distributed in the United States. 40 percent of the remaining royalty payments in the Sound Recordings Fund shall be distributed to the interested copyright parties described in section 1001(7)(C), and 60 percent of such remaining royalty payments shall be distributed to the interested copyright parties described in section 1001(7)(A).

(2) The musical works fund—

(A) 33 1/3 percent of the royalty payments shall be allocated to the Musical Works Fund for distribution to interested copyright parties described in section 1001(7)(B).

(B)(i) Music publishers shall be entitled to 50 percent of the royalty payments allocated to the Musical Works Fund.

(ii) Writers shall be entitled to the other 50 percent of the royalty payments allocated to the Musical Works Fund.

(c) Allocation of royalty payments within groups.—If all interested copyright parties within a group specified in subsection (b) do not agree on a voluntary proposal for the distribution of the royalty payments within each group, the Copyright Royalty Judges shall, pursuant to the procedures specified under section 1007(c), allocate royalty payments under this section based on the extent to which, during the relevant period—

(1) for the Sound Recordings Fund, each sound recording was distributed in the form of digital musical recordings or analog musical recordings; and

(2) for the Musical Works Fund, each musical work was distributed in the form of digital musical recordings or analog musical recordings or disseminated to the public in transmissions.

History of 17 U.S.C. §1006: Oct. 28, 1992, P.L. 102-563, §2, 106 Stat. 4242; Dec. 17, 1993, P.L. 103-198, §6(b)(3), 107 Stat. 2312; Nov. 13, 1997, P.L. 105-80, §12(a)(24), 111 Stat. 1535; May 30, 2005, P.L. 108-419, §5(i)(2), 118 Stat. 2368.

§1007. PROCEDURES FOR DISTRIBUTING ROYALTY PAYMENTS

(a) Filing of claims and negotiations—

(1) Filing of claims.—During the first 2 months of each calendar year, every interested copyright party seeking to receive royalty payments to which such party is entitled under section 1006 shall file with the Copyright Royalty Judges a claim for payments collected during the preceding year in such form and manner as the Copyright Royalty Judges shall prescribe by regulation.

(2) Negotiations.—Notwithstanding any provision of the antitrust laws, for purposes of this section interested copyright parties within each group specified in section 1006(b) may agree among themselves to the proportionate division of royalty payments, may lump their claims together and file them jointly or as a single claim, or may designate a common agent, including any organization described in section 1001(7)(D), to negotiate or receive payment on their behalf; except that no agreement under this subsection may modify the allocation of royalties specified in section 1006(b).

(b) Distribution of payments in the absence of a dispute.—After the period established for the filing of claims under subsection (a), in each year, the Copyright Royalty Judges shall determine whether there exists a controversy concerning the distribution of royalty payments under section 1006(c). If the Copyright Royalty Judges determine that no such controversy exists, the Copyright Royalty Judges shall, within 30 days after such determination, authorize the distribution of the royalty payments as set forth in the agreements regarding the distribution of royalty payments entered into pursuant to subsection (a). The Librarian of Congress shall, before such royalty payments are distributed, deduct the reasonable administrative costs incurred under this section.

(c) Resolution of disputes.—If the Copyright Royalty Judges find the existence of a controversy, the

Copyright Royalty Judges shall, pursuant to chapter 8 of this title, conduct a proceeding to determine the distribution of royalty payments. During the pendency of such a proceeding, the Copyright Royalty Judges shall withhold from distribution an amount sufficient to satisfy all claims with respect to which a controversy exists, but shall, to the extent feasible, authorize the distribution of any amounts that are not in controversy. The Librarian of Congress shall, before such royalty payments are distributed, deduct the reasonable administrative costs incurred under this section.

History of 17 U.S.C. §1007: Oct. 28, 1992, P.L. 102-563, §2, 106 Stat. 4244; Dec. 17, 1993, P.L. 103-198, §6(b)(4), 107 Stat. 2312; Nov. 13, 1997, P.L. 105-80, §§9, 12(25), 111 Stat. 1534, 1535; May 30, 2005, P.L. 108-419, §5(i)(3), 118 Stat. 2368; May 30, 2005, P.L. 109-303, §4(f), 120 Stat. 1482.

See also 37 C.F.R. §§360.1-360.32.

SUBCHAPTER D. PROHIBITION ON CERTAIN INFRINGEMENT ACTIONS, REMEDIES, & ARBITRATION

§1008. PROHIBITION ON CERTAIN INFRINGEMENT ACTIONS

No action may be brought under this title alleging infringement of copyright based on the manufacture, importation, or distribution of a digital audio recording device, a digital audio recording medium, an analog recording device, or an analog recording medium, or based on the noncommercial use by a consumer of such a device or medium for making digital musical recordings or analog musical recordings.

History of 17 U.S.C. §1008: Oct. 28, 1992, P.L. 102-563, §2, 106 Stat. 4244.

§1009. CIVIL REMEDIES

(a) Civil actions.—Any interested copyright party injured by a violation of section 1002 or 1003 may bring a civil action in an appropriate United States district court against any person for such violation.

(b) Other civil actions.—Any person injured by a violation of this chapter may bring a civil action in an appropriate United States district court for actual damages incurred as a result of such violation.

(c) Powers of the court.—In an action brought under subsection (a), the court—

(1) may grant temporary and permanent injunctions on such terms as it deems reasonable to prevent or restrain such violation;

(2) in the case of a violation of section 1002, or in the case of an injury resulting from a failure to make royalty payments required by section 1003, shall award damages under subsection (d);

(3) in its discretion may allow the recovery of costs by or against any party other than the United States or an officer thereof; and

(4) in its discretion may award a reasonable attorney's fee to the prevailing party.

(d) Award of damages—

(1) Damages for section 1002 or 1003 violations—

(A) Actual damages—

(i) In an action brought under subsection (a), if the court finds that a violation of section 1002 or 1003 has occurred, the court shall award to the complaining party its actual damages if the complaining party elects such damages at any time before final judgment is entered.

(ii) In the case of section 1003, actual damages shall constitute the royalty payments that should have been paid under section 1004 and deposited under section 1005. In such a case, the court, in its discretion, may award an additional amount of not to exceed 50 percent of the actual damages.

(B) Statutory damages for section 1002 violations—

(i) **Device.**—A complaining party may recover an award of statutory damages for each violation of section 1002(a) or (c) in the sum of not more than $2,500 per device involved in such violation or per device on which a service prohibited by section 1002(c) has been performed, as the court considers just.

(ii) **Digital musical recording.**—A complaining party may recover an award of statutory damages for each violation of section 1002(d) in the sum of not more than $25 per digital musical recording involved in such violation, as the court considers just.

(iii) **Transmission.**—A complaining party may recover an award of damages for each transmission or communication that violates section 1002(e) in the sum of not more than $10,000, as the court considers just.

(2) Repeated violations.—In any case in which the court finds that a person has violated section 1002 or 1003 within 3 years after a final judgment against that person for another such violation was entered, the court may increase the award of damages to not more than double the amounts that would otherwise be awarded under paragraph (1), as the court considers just.

(3) Innocent violations of section 1002.—The court in its discretion may reduce the total award of damages against a person violating section 1002 to a sum of not less than $250 in any case in which the court finds that the violator was not aware and had no reason to believe that its acts constituted a violation of section 1002.

(e) Payment of damages.—Any award of damages under subsection (d) shall be deposited with the Register pursuant to section 1005 for distribution to interested copyright parties as though such funds were royalty payments made pursuant to section 1003.

(f) Impounding of articles.—At any time while an action under subsection (a) is pending, the court may order the impounding, on such terms as it deems reasonable, of any digital audio recording device, digital musical recording, or device specified in section 1002(c) that is in the custody or control of the alleged violator and that the court has reasonable cause to believe does not comply with, or was involved in a violation of, section 1002.

(g) Remedial modification and destruction of articles.—In an action brought under subsection (a), the court may, as part of a final judgment or decree finding a violation of section 1002, order the remedial modification or the destruction of any digital audio recording device, digital musical recording, or device specified in section 1002(c) that—

(1) does not comply with, or was involved in a violation of, section 1002, and

(2) is in the custody or control of the violator or has been impounded under subsection (f).

History of 17 U.S.C. §1009: Oct. 28, 1992, P.L. 102-563, §2, 106 Stat. 4245.

§1010. DETERMINATION OF CERTAIN DISPUTES

(a) Scope of determination.—Before the date of first distribution in the United States of a digital audio recording device or a digital audio interface device, any party manufacturing, importing, or distributing such device, and any interested copyright party may mutually agree to petition the Copyright Royalty Judges to determine whether such device is subject to section 1002, or the basis on which royalty payments for such device are to be made under section 1003.

(b) Initiation of proceedings.—The parties under subsection (a) shall file the petition with the Copyright Royalty Judges requesting the commencement of a proceeding. Within 2 weeks after receiving such a petition, the Chief Copyright Royalty Judge shall cause notice to be published in the Federal Register of the initiation of the proceeding.

(c) Stay of judicial proceedings.—Any civil action brought under section 1009 against a party to a proceeding under this section shall, on application of one of the parties to the proceeding, be stayed until completion of the proceeding.

(d) Proceeding.—The Copyright Royalty Judges shall conduct a proceeding with respect to the matter concerned, in accordance with such procedures as the Copyright Royalty Judges may adopt. The Copyright Royalty Judges shall act on the basis of a fully documented written record. Any party to the proceeding may submit relevant information and proposals to the Copyright Royalty Judges. The parties to the proceeding shall each bear their respective costs of participation.

(e) Judicial review.—Any determination of the Copyright Royalty Judges under subsection (d) may be appealed, by a party to the proceeding, in accordance with section 803(d) of this title. The pendency of an appeal under this subsection shall not stay the determination of the Copyright Royalty Judges. If the court modifies the determination of the Copyright Royalty Judges, the court shall have jurisdiction to enter its own decision in accordance with its final judgment. The court may further vacate the determination of the Copyright Royalty Judges and remand the case for proceedings as provided in this section.

History of 17 U.S.C. §1010: Oct. 28, 1992, P.L. 102-563, §2, 106 Stat. 4246; Dec. 17, 1993, P.L. 103-198, §6(b)(5), 107 Stat. 2312; May 30, 2005, P.L. 108-419, §5(i)(4)(A), 118 Stat. 2368.

CHAPTER 11. SOUND RECORDINGS & MUSIC VIDEOS

§1101. UNAUTHORIZED FIXATION & TRAFFICKING IN SOUND RECORDINGS & MUSIC VIDEOS

(a) Unauthorized acts.—Anyone who, without the consent of the performer or performers involved—

(1) fixes the sounds or sounds and images of a live musical performance in a copy or phonorecord, or reproduces copies or phonorecords of such a performance from an unauthorized fixation,

(2) transmits or otherwise communicates to the public the sounds or sounds and images of a live musical performance, or

(3) distributes or offers to distribute, sells or offers to sell, rents or offers to rent, or traffics in any copy or phonorecord fixed as described in paragraph (1), regardless of whether the fixations occurred in the United States,

shall be subject to the remedies provided in sections 502 through 505, to the same extent as an infringer of copyright.

(b) Definition.—In this section, the term "traffic" has the same meaning as in section 2320(e) of title 18.

(c) Applicability.—This section shall apply to any act or acts that occur on or after Dec. 8, 1994.

(d) State law not preempted.—Nothing in this section may be construed to annul or limit any rights or remedies under the common law or statutes of any State.

History of 17 U.S.C. §1101: Dec. 8, 1994, P.L. 103-465, §512(a), 108 Stat. 4974; Mar. 16, 2006, P.L. 109-181, §3(c)(2), 120 Stat. 288.

See also 18 U.S.C. §2319A; NAFTA art. 1706; TRIPs pt. II, §1.

CHAPTER 12. COPYRIGHT PROTECTION & MANAGEMENT SYSTEMS

§1201. CIRCUMVENTION OF COPYRIGHT PROTECTION SYSTEMS

(a) Violations regarding circumvention of technological measures—

(1)(A) No person shall circumvent a technological measure that effectively controls access to a work protected under this title. The prohibition contained in the preceding sentence shall take effect at the end of the 2-year period beginning Oct. 28, 1998.

(B) The prohibition contained in subparagraph (A) shall not apply to persons who are users of a copyrighted work which is in a particular class of works, if such persons are, or are likely to be in the succeeding 3-year period, adversely affected by virtue of such prohibition in their ability to make noninfringing uses of that particular class of works under this title, as determined under subparagraph (C).

(C) During the 2-year period described in subparagraph (A), and during each succeeding 3-year period, the Librarian of Congress, upon the recommendation of the Register of Copyrights, who shall consult with the Assistant Secretary for Communications and Information of the Department of Commerce and report and comment on his or her views in making such recommendation, shall make the determination in a rulemaking proceeding for purposes of subparagraph (B) of whether persons who are users of a copyrighted work are, or are likely to be in the succeeding 3-year period, adversely affected by the prohibition under subparagraph (A) in their ability to make noninfringing uses under this title of a particular class of copyrighted works. In conducting such rulemaking, the Librarian shall examine—

(i) the availability for use of copyrighted works;

(ii) the availability for use of works for nonprofit archival, preservation, and educational purposes;

(iii) the impact that the prohibition on the circumvention of technological measures applied to copyrighted works has on criticism, comment, news reporting, teaching, scholarship, or research;

(iv) the effect of circumvention of technological measures on the market for or value of copyrighted works; and

(v) such other factors as the Librarian considers appropriate.

(D) The Librarian shall publish any class of copyrighted works for which the Librarian has determined, pursuant to the rulemaking conducted under subparagraph (C), that noninfringing uses by persons who are users of a copyrighted work are, or are likely to be, adversely affected, and the prohibition contained in subparagraph (A) shall not apply to such users with respect to such class of works for the ensuing 3-year period.

(E) Neither the exception under subparagraph (B) from the applicability of the prohibition contained in subparagraph (A), nor any determination made in a rulemaking conducted under subparagraph (C), may be used as a defense in any action to enforce any provision of this title other than this paragraph.

(2) No person shall manufacture, import, offer to the public, provide, or otherwise traffic in any technology, product, service, device, component, or part thereof, that—

(A) is primarily designed or produced for the purpose of circumventing a technological measure that effectively controls access to a work protected under this title;

(B) has only limited commercially significant purpose or use other than to circumvent a technological measure that effectively controls access to a work protected under this title; or

(C) is marketed by that person or another acting in concert with that person with that person's knowledge for use in circumventing a technological measure that effectively controls access to a work protected under this title.

(3) As used in this subsection—

(A) to "circumvent a technological measure" means to descramble a scrambled work, to decrypt an encrypted work, or otherwise to avoid, bypass, remove, deactivate, or impair a technological measure, without the authority of the copyright owner; and

(B) a technological measure "effectively controls access to a work" if the measure, in the ordinary course of its operation, requires the application of information, or a process or a treatment, with the authority of the copyright owner, to gain access to the work.

(b) Additional violations—

(1) No person shall manufacture, import, offer to the public, provide, or otherwise traffic in any technology, product, service, device, component, or part thereof, that—

(A) is primarily designed or produced for the purpose of circumventing protection afforded by a technological measure that effectively protects a right of a copyright owner under this title in a work or a portion thereof;

(B) has only limited commercially significant purpose or use other than to circumvent protection afforded by a technological measure that effectively protects a right of a copyright owner under this title in a work or a portion thereof; or

(C) is marketed by that person or another acting in concert with that person with that person's knowledge for use in circumventing protection afforded by a technological measure that effectively protects a right of a copyright owner under this title in a work or a portion thereof.

(2) As used in this subsection—

(A) to "circumvent protection afforded by a technological measure" means avoiding, bypassing, removing, deactivating, or otherwise impairing a technological measure; and

(B) a technological measure "effectively protects a right of a copyright owner under this title" if the measure, in the ordinary course of its operation, prevents, restricts, or otherwise limits the exercise of a right of a copyright owner under this title.

(c) Other rights, etc., not affected—

(1) Nothing in this section shall affect rights, remedies, limitations, or defenses to copyright infringement, including fair use, under this title.

(2) Nothing in this section shall enlarge or diminish vicarious or contributory liability for copyright infringement in connection with any technology, product, service, device, component, or part thereof.

(3) Nothing in this section shall require that the design of, or design and selection of parts and components for, a consumer electronics, telecommunications, or computing product provide for a response to any particular technological measure, so long as such part or component, or the product in which such part or component is integrated, does not otherwise fall within the prohibitions of subsection (a)(2) or (b)(1).

(4) Nothing in this section shall enlarge or diminish any rights of free speech or the press for activities using consumer electronics, telecommunications, or computing products.

(d) Exemption for nonprofit libraries, archives, and educational institutions—

(1) A nonprofit library, archives, or educational institution which gains access to a commercially exploited copyrighted work solely in order to make a good faith determination of whether to acquire a copy of that work for the sole purpose of engaging in conduct permitted under this title shall not be in violation of subsection (a)(1)(A). A copy of a work to which access has been gained under this paragraph—

(A) may not be retained longer than necessary to make such good faith determination; and

(B) may not be used for any other purpose.

(2) The exemption made available under paragraph (1) shall only apply with respect to a work when an identical copy of that work is not reasonably available in another form.

(3) A nonprofit library, archives, or educational institution that willfully for the purpose of commercial advantage or financial gain violates paragraph (1)—

(A) shall, for the first offense, be subject to the civil remedies under section 1203; and

(B) shall, for repeated or subsequent offenses, in addition to the civil remedies under section 1203, forfeit the exemption provided under paragraph (1).

(4) This subsection may not be used as a defense to a claim under subsection (a)(2) or (b), nor may this subsection permit a nonprofit library, archives, or educational institution to manufacture, import, offer to the public, provide, or otherwise traffic in any technology, product, service, component, or part thereof, which circumvents a technological measure.

(5) In order for a library or archives to qualify for the exemption under this subsection, the collections of that library or archives shall be—

(A) open to the public; or

(B) available not only to researchers affiliated with the library or archives or with the institution of which it is a part, but also to other persons doing research in a specialized field.

(e) Law enforcement, intelligence, and other government activities.—This section does not prohibit any lawfully authorized investigative, protective, information security, or intelligence activity of an officer, agent, or employee of the United States, a State, or a political subdivision of a State, or a person acting pursuant to a contract with the United States, a State, or a political subdivision of a State. For purposes of this subsection, the term "information security" means activities carried out in order to identify and address the vulnerabilities of a government computer, computer system, or computer network.

(f) Reverse engineering—

(1) Notwithstanding the provisions of subsection (a)(1)(A), a person who has lawfully obtained the right to use a copy of a computer program may circumvent a technological measure that effectively controls access to a particular portion of that program for the sole purpose of identifying and analyzing those elements of the program that are necessary to achieve interoperability of an independently created computer program with other programs, and that have not previously been readily available to the person engaging in the circumvention, to the extent any such acts of identification and analysis do not constitute infringement under this title.

(2) Notwithstanding the provisions of subsections (a)(2) and (b), a person may develop and employ technological means to circumvent a technological measure, or to circumvent protection afforded by a technological measure, in order to enable the identification and analysis under paragraph (1), or for the purpose of enabling interoperability of an independently created computer program with other programs, if such means are necessary to achieve such interoperability, to the extent that doing so does not constitute infringement under this title.

(3) The information acquired through the acts permitted under paragraph (1), and the means permitted under paragraph (2), may be made available to others if the person referred to in paragraph (1) or (2), as the case may be, provides such information or means solely for the purpose of enabling interoperability of an independently created computer program with other programs, and to the extent that doing so does not constitute infringement under this title or violate applicable law other than this section.

(4) For purposes of this subsection, the term "interoperability" means the ability of computer programs to exchange information, and of such programs mutually to use the information which has been exchanged.

(g) Encryption research—

(1) Definitions.—For purposes of this subsection—

(A) the term "encryption research" means activities necessary to identify and analyze flaws and vulnerabilities of encryption technologies applied to copyrighted works, if these activities are conducted to advance the state of knowledge in the field of encryption technology or to assist in the development of encryption products; and

(B) the term "encryption technology" means the scrambling and descrambling of information using mathematical formulas or algorithms.

(2) Permissible acts of encryption research.—Notwithstanding the provisions of subsection (a)(1)(A), it is not a violation of that subsection for a person to circumvent a technological measure as applied to a copy, phonorecord, performance, or display of a published work in the course of an act of good faith encryption research if—

(A) the person lawfully obtained the encrypted copy, phonorecord, performance, or display of the published work;

(B) such act is necessary to conduct such encryption research;

(C) the person made a good faith effort to obtain authorization before the circumvention; and

(D) such act does not constitute infringement under this title or a violation of applicable law other than this section, including section 1030 of title 18 and those provisions of title 18 amended by the Computer Fraud and Abuse Act of 1986.

(3) Factors in determining exemption.—In determining whether a person qualifies for the exemption under paragraph (2), the factors to be considered shall include—

(A) whether the information derived from the encryption research was disseminated, and if so, whether it was disseminated in a manner reasonably calculated to advance the state of knowledge or development of encryption technology, versus whether it was disseminated in a manner that facilitates infringement under this title or a violation of applicable law other than this section, including a violation of privacy or breach of security;

(B) whether the person is engaged in a legitimate course of study, is employed, or is appropriately trained or experienced, in the field of encryption technology; and

(C) whether the person provides the copyright owner of the work to which the technological measure is applied with notice of the findings and documentation of the research, and the time when such notice is provided.

(4) Use of technological means for research activities.—Notwithstanding the provisions of subsection (a)(2), it is not a violation of that subsection for a person to—

(A) develop and employ technological means to circumvent a technological measure for the sole purpose of that person performing the acts of good faith encryption research described in paragraph (2); and

(B) provide the technological means to another person with whom he or she is working collaboratively for the purpose of conducting the acts of good faith encryption research described in paragraph (2) or for the purpose of having that other person verify his or her acts of good faith encryption research described in paragraph (2).

(5) Report to Congress.—Not later than 1 year after Oct. 28, 1998, the Register of Copyrights and the Assistant Secretary for Communications and Information of the Department of Commerce shall jointly report to the Congress on the effect this subsection has had on—

(A) encryption research and the development of encryption technology;

(B) the adequacy and effectiveness of technological measures designed to protect copyrighted works; and

(C) protection of copyright owners against the unauthorized access to their encrypted copyrighted works.

The report shall include legislative recommendations, if any.

(h) Exceptions regarding minors.—In applying subsection (a) to a component or part, the court may consider the necessity for its intended and actual incorporation in a technology, product, service, or device, which—

(1) does not itself violate the provisions of this title; and

(2) has the sole purpose to prevent the access of minors to material on the Internet.

(i) Protection of personally identifying information—

(1) Circumvention permitted.—Notwithstanding the provisions of subsection (a)(1)(A), it is not a violation of that subsection for a person to circumvent a technological measure that effectively controls access to a work protected under this title, if—

(A) the technological measure, or the work it protects, contains the capability of collecting or disseminating personally identifying information reflecting the online activities of a natural person who seeks to gain access to the work protected;

(B) in the normal course of its operation, the technological measure, or the work it protects, collects or disseminates personally identifying information about the person who seeks to gain access to the work protected, without providing conspicuous notice of such collection or dissemination to such person, and without providing such person with the capability to prevent or restrict such collection or dissemination;

(C) the act of circumvention has the sole effect of identifying and disabling the capability described in subparagraph (A), and has no other effect on the ability of any person to gain access to any work; and

(D) the act of circumvention is carried out solely for the purpose of preventing the collection or dissemination of personally identifying information about a natural person who seeks to gain access to the work protected, and is not in violation of any other law.

(2) Inapplicability to certain technological measures.—This subsection does not apply to a technological measure, or a work it protects, that does not collect or disseminate personally identifying information and that is disclosed to a user as not having or using such capability.

(j) Security testing—

(1) Definition.—For purposes of this subsection, the term "security testing" means accessing a computer, computer system, or computer network, solely for the purpose of good faith testing, investigating, or correcting, a security flaw or vulnerability, with the authorization of the owner or operator of such computer, computer system, or computer network.

(2) Permissible acts of security testing.—Notwithstanding the provisions of subsection (a)(1)(A), it is not a violation of that subsection for a person to engage in an act of security testing, if such act does not constitute infringement under this title or a violation of applicable law other than this section, including section 1030 of title 18 and those provisions of title 18 amended by the Computer Fraud and Abuse Act of 1986.

(3) Factors in determining exemption.—In determining whether a person qualifies for the exemption under paragraph (2), the factors to be considered shall include—

(A) whether the information derived from the security testing was used solely to promote the security of the owner or operator of such computer, computer system or computer network, or shared directly with the developer of such computer, computer system, or computer network; and

(B) whether the information derived from the security testing was used or maintained in a manner that does not facilitate infringement under this title or a violation of applicable law other than this section, including a violation of privacy or breach of security.

(4) Use of technological means for security testing.—Notwithstanding the provisions of subsection (a)(2), it is not a violation of that subsection for a person to develop, produce, distribute or employ technological means for the sole purpose of performing the acts of security testing described in subsection (2),[1] provided such technological means does not otherwise violate section[2] (a)(2).

(k) Certain analog devices and certain technological measures—

(1) Certain analog devices—

(A) Effective 18 months after Oct. 28, 1998, no person shall manufacture, import, offer to the public, provide or otherwise traffic in any—

(i) VHS format analog video cassette recorder unless such recorder conforms to the automatic gain control copy control technology;

(ii) 8mm format analog video cassette camcorder unless such camcorder conforms to the automatic gain control technology;

(iii) Beta format analog video cassette recorder, unless such recorder conforms to the automatic gain control copy control technology, except that this requirement shall not apply until there are 1,000 Beta format analog video cassette recorders sold in the United States in any one calendar year after October 28, 1998;

(iv) 8mm format analog video cassette recorder that is not an analog video cassette camcorder, unless such recorder conforms to the automatic gain control copy control technology, except that this requirement shall not apply until there are 20,000 such recorders sold in the United States in any one calendar year after October 28, 1998; or

(v) analog video cassette recorder that records using an NTSC format video input and that is not otherwise covered under clauses (i) through (iv), unless such device conforms to the automatic gain control copy control technology.

(B) Effective October 28, 1998, no person shall manufacture, import, offer to the public, provide or otherwise traffic in—

(i) any VHS format analog video cassette recorder or any 8mm format analog video cassette recorder if the design of the model of such recorder has been modified after October 28, 1998 so that a model of recorder that previously conformed to the automatic gain control copy control technology no longer conforms to such technology; or

(ii) any VHS format analog video cassette recorder, or any 8mm format analog video cassette recorder that is not an 8mm analog video cassette camcorder, if the design of the model of such recorder has been modified after October 28, 1998 so that a model of recorder that previously conformed to the four-line colorstripe copy control technology no longer conforms to such technology.

Manufacturers that have not previously manufactured or sold a VHS format analog video cassette recorder, or an 8mm format analog cassette recorder, shall be required to conform to the four-line colorstripe copy control technology in the initial model of any such recorder manufactured after October 28, 1998, and thereafter to continue conforming to the four-line colorstripe copy control technology. For purposes of this subparagraph, an analog video cassette recorder "conforms to" the four-line colorstripe copy control technology if it records a signal that, when played back by the playback function of that recorder in the normal viewing mode, exhibits, on a reference display device, a display containing distracting visible lines through portions of the viewable picture.

(2) Certain encoding restrictions.—No person shall apply the automatic gain control copy control technology or colorstripe copy control technology to prevent or limit consumer copying except such copying—

(A) of a single transmission, or specified group of transmissions, of live events or of audiovisual works for which a member of the public has exercised choice in selecting the transmissions, including the content of the transmissions or the time of receipt of such transmissions, or both, and as to which such member is charged a separate fee for each such transmission or specified group of transmissions;

(B) from a copy of a transmission of a live event or an audiovisual work if such transmission is provided by a channel or service where payment is made by a member of the public for such channel or service in the form of a subscription fee that entitles the member of the public to receive all of the programming contained in such channel or service;

(C) from a physical medium containing one or more prerecorded audiovisual works; or

(D) from a copy of a transmission described in subparagraph (A) or from a copy made from a physical medium described in subparagraph (C).

In the event that a transmission meets both the conditions set forth in subparagraph (A) and those set forth in subparagraph (B), the transmission shall be treated as a transmission described in subparagraph (A).

(3) Inapplicability.—This subsection shall not—

(A) require any analog video cassette camcorder to conform to the automatic gain control copy control technology with respect to any video signal received through a camera lens;

(B) apply to the manufacture, importation, offer for sale, provision of, or other trafficking in, any professional analog video cassette recorder; or

(C) apply to the offer for sale or provision of, or other trafficking in, any previously owned analog video cassette recorder, if such recorder was legally manufactured and sold when new and not subsequently modified in violation of paragraph (1)(B).

(4) Definitions.—For purposes of this subsection:

(A) An "analog video cassette recorder" means a device that records, or a device that includes a function that records, on electromagnetic tape in an analog format the electronic impulses produced by the video and audio portions of a television program, motion picture, or other form of audiovisual work.

(B) An "analog video cassette camcorder" means an analog video cassette recorder that contains a recording function that operates through a camera lens and through a video input that may be connected with a television or other video playback device.

(C) An analog video cassette recorder "conforms" to the automatic gain control copy control technology if it—

(i) detects one or more of the elements of such technology and does not record the motion picture or transmission protected by such technology; or

(ii) records a signal that, when played back, exhibits a meaningfully distorted or degraded display.

(D) The term "professional analog video cassette recorder" means an analog video cassette recorder that is designed, manufactured, marketed, and intended for use by a person who regularly employs such a device for a lawful business or industrial use, including making, performing, displaying, distributing, or transmitting copies of motion pictures on a commercial scale.

(E) The terms "VHS format," "8mm format," "Beta format," "automatic gain control copy control technology," "colorstripe copy control technology," "four-line version of the colorstripe copy control technology," and "NTSC" have the meanings that are commonly understood in the consumer electronics and motion picture industries as of Oct. 28, 1998.

(5) Violations.—Any violation of paragraph (1) of this subsection shall be treated as a violation of subsection (b)(1) of this section. Any violation of paragraph (2) of this subsection shall be deemed an "act of circumvention" for the purposes of section 1203(c)(3)(A) of this chapter.

1. **Editor's note:** Probably should be "(a)(2)."

2. **Editor's note:** Probably should be "subsection."

History of 17 U.S.C. §1201: Oct. 28, 1998, P.L. 105-304, §103(a), 112 Stat. 2863; Nov. 29, 1999, P.L. 106-113, §1000(a)(9), 113 Stat. 1536.

See also 37 C.F.R. §201.40; Berne Convention; WIPO Copyright Treaty; WIPO Performances & Phonograms Treaty.

ANNOTATIONS

Causes of Action

Disney Enters. v. VidAngel, Inc., 869 F.3d 848, 864 (9th Cir.2017). "[T]he statute does not provide that a [technological protection measure (TPM)] cannot serve as both an access control and a use control. Its text does not suggest that a defendant could not violate both [17 U.S.C.] §1201(a)(1)(A), by circumventing an access control measure, and [17 U.S.C.] §106, by, for example, reproducing or publicly performing the accessed work. Indeed, this court has acknowledged that a TPM could 'both (1) control[ ] access and (2) protect[ ] against copyright infringement.' [¶] To be sure, 'unlawful circumvention under §1201(a)—descrambling a scrambled work and decrypting an encrypted work—are acts that do not necessarily infringe or facilitate infringement of a copyright.' Thus, a defendant could decrypt the TPMs on the [Ps'] discs on an unlicensed DVD player, but only then 'watch ... without authorization, which is not necessarily an infringement of [Ps'] exclusive rights under §106.' But, when a defendant decrypts the TPMs and then also reproduces that work, it is liable for both circumvention in violation of §1201(a)(1)(A) and copyright infringement in violation of §106(1)."

MDY Indus. v. Blizzard Entm't, Inc., 629 F.3d 928, 943 (9th Cir.2010). "We ... consider whether [software bot] violates DMCA §§1201(a)(2) and (b)(1) by allowing users to circumvent [computer game's secondary software] to access [computer game's] various elements. [I]n our view, an access control measure can both (1) attempt to block initial access and (2) revoke access if a secondary check determines that access was unauthorized. *At 944:* [W]e believe that §1201 is best understood to create two distinct types of claims. First, §1201(a) prohibits the circumvention of any technological measure that effectively controls access to a protected work and grants copyright owners the right to enforce that prohibition. Second, and in contrast to §1201(a), §1201(b)(1) prohibits trafficking in technologies that circumvent technological measures that effectively protect 'a right of a copyright owner.' Section 1201(b)(1)'s prohibition is thus aimed at circumventions of measures that protect the copyright itself: it entitles copyright owners to protect their existing exclusive rights under the Copyright Act. *At 953:* We conclude that [computer game's secondary software] is not an effective access control measure with respect to [computer game's] literal elements [the source code stored on players' hard drives] and individual non-literal elements [the 400,000+ discrete visual and audible components of the game, such as a visual image of a monster or its audible roar], and therefore, that [software-bot creator] does not violate §1201(a)(2) with respect to these elements. [¶] We conclude that [software-bot creator] meets each of the six textual elements for violating §1201(a)(2) with respect to [computer game's] dynamic non-literal elements [the real-time experience of traveling through different worlds, hearing their sounds, viewing their structures, encountering their inhabitants and monsters, and encountering other players]. *At 954 n.16:* A circuit split exists with respect to the meaning of the phrase 'without the authority of the copyright owner' [as used in §1201(a)(3)(A)]. The Federal Circuit has concluded that this definition imposes an additional requirement on a §1201(a)(2) plaintiff: to show that the defendant's circumventing device enables third parties to access the copyrighted work without the copyright owner's authorization. The Second Circuit has adopted a different view, explaining that §1201(a)(3)(A) plainly exempts from §1201(a) liability those whom a copyright owner authorizes to circumvent an access control measure, not those whom a copyright owner authorizes to access the work. [¶] We find the Second Circuit's view to be the sounder construction of the statute's language, and conclude that §1201(a)(2) does not require a plaintiff to show that the accused device enables third parties to access the work without the copyright owner's authorization. Thus, [computer-game licensor] has satisfied the 'circumvention' element of a §1201(a)(2) claim, because [computer-game licensor] has demonstrated that it did not authorize [software-bot creator] to circumvent [computer game's secondary software]. *At 954:* [Computer-game licensor] may prevail under §1201(b)(1) only if [computer game's secondary software] 'effectively protect[s] a right' of [computer-game licensor] under the Copyright Act. [¶] [Computer-game licensor's term of use for] bot prohibition is a license covenant rather than a condition. Thus, a [software-bot] user who violates this covenant does not infringe by continuing to copy code into RAM. Accordingly, [software-bot creator] does not violate §1201(b)(1) by enabling [software-bot] users to avoid [computer game's secondary software's] interruption of their *authorized* copying into RAM." *See also* ***Universal City Studios, Inc. v. Reimerdes***, 111 F.Supp.2d 294, 317 n.137 (S.D.N.Y.2000), *aff'd sub nom.* ***Universal City Studios, Inc. v. Corley***, 273 F.3d 429 (2d Cir.2001).

MGE UPS Sys. v. GE Consumer & Indus., 622 F.3d 361, 366 (5th Cir.2010). "We ... do not construe 'bypass' or 'avoid' [in §1201(a)(3)(A)] to encompass use of a copyrighted work subsequent to a circumvention merely because that use would have been subject to a technological measure that would have controlled access to the work, but for that circumvention. So broad a construction would extend the DMCA beyond its intended purposes to reach extensive conduct already well-regulated by existing copyright laws. [P] did not present any evidence showing that a [D] representative altered the [infringed] software such that a dongle was not required to use the software; rather, employees simply used the software after the alteration was made. As such, the actions by [D] employees did not amount to circumvention. Without proving [D] actually circumvented the technology, [P] does not present a valid DMCA claim."

CoxCom, Inc. v. Chaffee, 536 F.3d 101, 110 (1st Cir.2008). "To establish liability under the DMCA, a plaintiff must establish two elements: '(1) defendant trafficked in a technology; and (2) the technology was primarily designed or produced to circumvent conditional access controls to protected works, or has limited commercially significant use other than such circumvention.'" *See also* ***Storage Tech. v. Custom Hardware Eng'g & Consulting, Inc.***, 421 F.3d 1307, 1318-19 (Fed.Cir.2005).

Davidson & Assocs. v. Jung, 422 F.3d 630, 639-40 (8th Cir.2005). "The DMCA contains three provisions targeted at the circumvention of technological protections. [¶] The first is §1201(a)(1), the anti-circumvention provision. This provision prohibits a person from 'circumvent[ing] a technological measure that effectively controls access to a work protected under [title 17, governing copyright].' ... Section 1201(a)(1) differs from the second and third provisions in that it targets the use of a circumvention technology, not the trafficking in such a technology. [¶] The second and third provisions are §§1201(a)(2) and 1201(b)(1), the 'anti-trafficking provisions.' These sections are similar, except that §1201(a)(2) covers those who traffic in technology that can circumvent 'a technological measure that effectively controls access to a work protected under' Title 17, whereas §1201(b)(1) covers those who traffic in technology that can circumvent 'protection afforded by a technological measure that effectively protects a right of a copyright owner under' Title 17. In other words, although both sections prohibit trafficking in a circumvention technology, the focus of §1201(a)(2) is circumvention of technologies designed to prevent access to a work, and the focus of §1201(b)(1) is circumvention of technologies designed to permit access to a work but prevent copying of the work or some other act that infringes a copyright." *See also* ***Disney Enters. v. VidAngel, Inc.***, 869 F.3d 848, 863-64 (9th Cir.2017); ***Universal City Studios, Inc. v. Corley***, 273 F.3d 429, 441 (2d Cir.2001).

Chamberlain Grp. v. Skylink Techs., 381 F.3d 1178, 1203 (Fed.Cir.2004). "The proper construction of §1201(a)(2) ... makes it clear that [P] cannot prevail. A plaintiff alleging a violation of §1201(a)(2) must prove: (1) ownership of a valid copyright on a work, (2) effectively controlled by a technological measure, which has been circumvented, (3) that third parties can now access (4) without authorization, in a manner that (5) infringes or facilitates infringing a right protected by the Copyright Act, because of a product that (6) the defendant either (i) designed or produced primarily for circumvention; (ii) made available despite only limited commercial significance other than circumvention; or (iii) marketed for use in circumvention of the controlling technological measure. A plaintiff incapable of establishing any one of elements (1) through (5) will have failed to prove a prima facie case. A plaintiff capable of proving elements (1) through (5) need prove only one of (6)(i), (ii), or (iii) to shift the burden back to the defendant. At that point, the various affirmative defenses enumerated throughout §1201 become relevant. *At 1204:* The DMCA does not create a new property right for copyright owners. Nor, for that matter, does it divest the public of the property rights that the Copyright Act has long granted to the public. The anticircumvention and anti-trafficking provisions of the DMCA create new grounds of liability. A copyright owner seeking to impose liability on an accused circumventor must demonstrate a reasonable relationship between the circumvention at issue and a use relating to a property right for which the Copyright Act permits the copyright owner to withhold authorization—as well as notice that authorization was withheld. A copyright owner seeking to impose liability on an accused trafficker must demonstrate that the trafficker's device enables either copyright infringement or a prohibited circumvention." *But see **MDY Indus. v. Blizzard Entm't, Inc.***, 629 F.3d 928, 952 (9th Cir.2010) (anti-circumvention right under §1201(a) does not have infringement-nexus requirement (element 5); authorization must relate to access to a control measure (element 4)).

Defenses

Davidson & Assocs. v. Jung, 422 F.3d 630, 641-42 (8th Cir.2005). "The DMCA contains several exceptions, including one for individuals using circumvention technology 'for the sole purpose' of trying to achieve 'interoperability' of computer programs through reverse engineering.... To successfully prove the interoperability defense under §1201(f), [Ds] must show: (1) they lawfully obtained the right to use a copy of a computer program; (2) the information gathered as a result of the reverse engineering was not previously readily available to the person engaging in the circumvention; (3) the sole purpose of the reverse engineering was to identify and analyze those elements of the program that were necessary to achieve interoperability of an independently created computer program with other programs; and (4) the alleged circumvention did not constitute infringement."

Lexmark Int'l v. Static Control Components, Inc., 387 F.3d 522, 545-46 (6th Cir.2004), *aff'd*, ___ U.S. ___, 134 S.Ct. 1377 (2014). "The statute ... contains three 'reverse engineering' defenses [in §1201(f)(1)-(3)]. ... All three defenses apply only when traditional copyright infringement does not occur and only when the challenged actions (in the case of the third provision) would not violate other 'applicable law[s].' *At 547:* Because [§1201(a)(2)] refers to 'control[ling] access to a work protected under this title,' it does not naturally apply when the 'work protected under this title' is otherwise accessible. *At 551:* [N]othing in [§1201(f)(3)] precludes simultaneous creation of an interoperability device and another computer program; it just must be 'independently' created. [T]he statute is silent about the degree to which the 'technological means' must be necessary, if indeed they must be necessary at all, for interoperability."

Effect on Other Rights

Universal City Studios, Inc. v. Corley, 273 F.3d 429, 443 (2d Cir.2001). Section 1201(c)(1) "simply clarifies that the DMCA targets the circumvention of digital walls guarding copyrighted material (and trafficking in circumvention tools), but does not concern itself with the use of those materials after circumvention has occurred. Subsection 1201(c)(1) ensures that the DMCA is not read to prohibit the 'fair use' of information just because that information was obtained in a manner made illegal by the DMCA. *At 444 n.13:* Congress also sought to implement a balanced approach through statutory provisions that leave limited areas of breathing space for fair use. A good example is §1201(d), which allows a library or educational institution to circumvent a digital wall in order to determine whether it wishes legitimately to obtain the material behind the wall. It would be strange for Congress to open small, carefully limited windows for circumvention to permit fair use in §1201(d) if it then meant to exempt in §1201(c)(1) any circumvention necessary for fair use."

§1202. INTEGRITY OF COPYRIGHT MANAGEMENT INFORMATION

(a) False copyright management information.—No person shall knowingly and with the intent to induce, enable, facilitate, or conceal infringement—

(1) provide copyright management information that is false, or

(2) distribute or import for distribution copyright management information that is false.

(b) Removal or alteration of copyright management information.—No person shall, without the authority of the copyright owner or the law—

(1) intentionally remove or alter any copyright management information,

(2) distribute or import for distribution copyright management information knowing that the copyright management information has been removed or altered without authority of the copyright owner or the law, or

(3) distribute, import for distribution, or publicly perform works, copies of works, or phonorecords, knowing that copyright management information has been removed or altered without authority of the copyright owner or the law,

knowing, or, with respect to civil remedies under section 1203, having reasonable grounds to know, that it will induce, enable, facilitate, or conceal an infringement of any right under this title.

(c) Definition.—As used in this section, the term "copyright management information" means any of the following information conveyed in connection with copies or phonorecords of a work or performances or displays of a work, including in digital form, except that such term does not include any personally identifying information about a user of a work or of a copy, phonorecord, performance, or display of a work:

(1) The title and other information identifying the work, including the information set forth on a notice of copyright.

(2) The name of, and other identifying information about, the author of a work.

(3) The name of, and other identifying information about, the copyright owner of the work, including the information set forth in a notice of copyright.

(4) With the exception of public performances of works by radio and television broadcast stations, the name of, and other identifying information about, a performer whose performance is fixed in a work other than an audiovisual work.

(5) With the exception of public performances of works by radio and television broadcast stations, in the case of an audiovisual work, the name of, and other identifying information about, a writer, performer, or director who is credited in the audiovisual work.

(6) Terms and conditions for use of the work.

(7) Identifying numbers or symbols referring to such information or links to such information.

(8) Such other information as the Register of Copyrights may prescribe by regulation, except that the Register of Copyrights may not require the provision of any information concerning the user of a copyrighted work.

(d) Law enforcement, intelligence, and other government activities.—This section does not prohibit any lawfully authorized investigative, protective, information security, or intelligence activity of an officer, agent, or employee of the United States, a State, or a political subdivision of a State, or a person acting pursuant to a contract with the United States, a State, or a political subdivision of a State. For purposes of this subsection, the term "information security" means activities carried out in order to identify and address the vulnerabilities of a government computer, computer system, or computer network.

(e) Limitations on liability—

(1) Analog transmissions.—In the case of an analog transmission, a person who is making transmissions in its capacity as a broadcast station, or as a cable system, or someone who provides programming to such station or system, shall not be liable for a violation of subsection (b) if—

(A) avoiding the activity that constitutes such violation is not technically feasible or would create an undue financial hardship on such person; and

(B) such person did not intend, by engaging in such activity, to induce, enable, facilitate, or conceal infringement of a right under this title.

(2) Digital transmissions—

(A) If a digital transmission standard for the placement of copyright management information for a category of works is set in a voluntary, consensus standard-setting process involving a representative cross-section of broadcast stations or cable systems and copyright owners of a category of works that are intended for public performance by such stations or systems, a person identified in paragraph (1) shall not be liable for a violation of subsection (b) with respect to the particular copyright management information addressed by such standard if—

(i) the placement of such information by someone other than such person is not in accordance with such standard; and

(ii) the activity that constitutes such violation is not intended to induce, enable, facilitate, or conceal infringement of a right under this title.

(B) Until a digital transmission standard has been set pursuant to subparagraph (A) with respect to the placement of copyright management information for a category of works, a person identified in paragraph (1) shall not be liable for a violation of subsection (b) with respect to such copyright management information, if the activity that constitutes such violation is not intended to induce, enable, facilitate, or conceal infringement of a right under this title, and if—

(i) the transmission of such information by such person would result in a perceptible visual or aural degradation of the digital signal; or

(ii) the transmission of such information by such person would conflict with—

(I) an applicable government regulation relating to transmission of information in a digital signal;

(II) an applicable industry-wide standard relating to the transmission of information in a digital signal that was adopted by a voluntary consensus standards body prior to the effective date of this chapter; or

(III) an applicable industry-wide standard relating to the transmission of information in a digital signal that was adopted in a voluntary, consensus standards-setting process open to participation by a representative cross-section of broadcast stations or cable systems and copyright owners of a category of works that are intended for public performance by such stations or systems.

(3) Definitions.—As used in this subsection—

(A) the term "broadcast station" has the meaning given that term in section 3 of the Communications Act of 1934 (47 U.S.C. 153); and

(B) the term "cable system" has the meaning given that term in section 602 of the Communications Act of 1934 (47 U.S.C. 522).

History of 17 U.S.C. §1202: Oct. 28, 1998, P.L. 105-304, §103(a), 112 Stat. 2872; Aug. 5, 1999, P.L. 106-44, §1(e), 113 Stat. 222.

See also WIPO Copyright Treaty; WIPO Performances & Phonograms Treaty.

ANNOTATIONS

Murphy v. Millennium Radio Grp., 650 F.3d 295, 302 (3d Cir.2011). "Read in isolation, [17 U.S.C.] §1202 simply establishes a cause of action for the removal of (among other things) the name of the author of a work when it has been 'conveyed in connection with copies of' the work. The statute imposes no explicit requirement that such information be part of an 'automated copyright protection or management system,' as [Ds] claim. In fact, it appears to be extremely broad, with no restrictions on the context in which such information must be used in order to qualify as [copyright-management information (CMI)]. If there is a difficulty here, it is a problem of policy, not of logic. Such an interpretation might well provide an additional cause of action under the DMCA in many circumstances in which only an action for copyright infringement could have been brought previously. Whether or not this result is desirable, it is not *absurd*, as might compel us to make a more restrictive reading of §1202's scope. *At 303:* However, nothing in [17 U.S.C.] §1201, the provision regarding circumvention of 'technological measures' ... restricts the meaning of CMI in §1202 to information contained in 'automated copyright protection or management systems.' Section 1201 does not mention '[CMI]'; in fact, it does not refer to §1202 at all. Neither does it contain the phrase 'automated copyright protection or management systems.' Similarly, §1202 does not refer to §1201, and the definition of CMI is located squarely in §1202. *At 305:* [W]e find that CMI, as defined in §1202(c), is *not* restricted to the context of 'automated copyright protection or management systems.' Rather, a cause of action under §1202 of the DMCA potentially lies whenever the types of information listed in §1202(c)(1)-(8) and 'conveyed in connection with copies ... of a work ... including in digital form' is falsified or removed, regardless of the form in which that information is conveyed. In this case, the mere fact that [P's] name appeared in a printed gutter credit near the Image rather than as data in an 'automated copyright protection or management system' does not prevent it from qualifying as CMI or remove it from the protection of §1202." *See also* ***Associated Press v. All Headline News Corp.***, 608 F.Supp.2d 454, 462 (S.D.N.Y.2009).

§1203. CIVIL REMEDIES

(a) Civil actions.—Any person injured by a violation of section 1201 or 1202 may bring a civil action in an appropriate United States district court for such violation.

(b) Powers of the court.—In an action brought under subsection (a), the court—

(1) may grant temporary and permanent injunctions on such terms as it deems reasonable to prevent or restrain a violation, but in no event shall impose a prior restraint on free speech or the press protected under the 1st amendment to the Constitution;

(2) at any time while an action is pending, may order the impounding, on such terms as it deems reasonable, of any device or product that is in the custody or control of the alleged violator and that the court has reasonable cause to believe was involved in a violation;

(3) may award damages under subsection (c);

(4) in its discretion may allow the recovery of costs by or against any party other than the United States or an officer thereof;

(5) in its discretion may award reasonable attorney's fees to the prevailing party; and

(6) may, as part of a final judgment or decree finding a violation, order the remedial modification or the destruction of any device or product involved in the violation that is in the custody or control of the violator or has been impounded under paragraph (2).

(c) Award of damages—

(1) In general.—Except as otherwise provided in this title, a person committing a violation of section 1201 or 1202 is liable for either—

(A) the actual damages and any additional profits of the violator, as provided in paragraph (2), or

(B) statutory damages, as provided in paragraph (3).

(2) Actual damages.—The court shall award to the complaining party the actual damages suffered by the party as a result of the violation, and any profits of the violator that are attributable to the violation and are not taken into account in computing the actual damages, if the complaining party elects such damages at any time before final judgment is entered.

(3) Statutory damages—

(A) At any time before final judgment is entered, a complaining party may elect to recover an award of statutory damages for each violation of section 1201 in the sum of not less than $200 or more than $2,500 per act of circumvention, device, product, component, offer, or performance of service, as the court considers just.

(B) At any time before final judgment is entered, a complaining party may elect to recover an award of statutory damages for each violation of section 1202 in the sum of not less than $2,500 or more than $25,000.

(4) Repeated violations.—In any case in which the injured party sustains the burden of proving, and the court finds, that a person has violated section 1201 or 1202 within 3 years after a final judgment was entered against the person for another such violation, the court may increase the award of damages up to triple the amount that would otherwise be awarded, as the court considers just.

(5) Innocent violations—

(A) In general.—The court in its discretion may reduce or remit the total award of damages in any case in which the violator sustains the burden of proving, and the court finds, that the violator was not aware and had no reason to believe that its acts constituted a violation.

(B) Nonprofit library, archives, educational institutions, or public broadcasting entities—

(i) Definition.—In this subparagraph, the term "public broadcasting entity" has the meaning given such term under section 118(f).

(ii) In general.—In the case of a nonprofit library, archives, educational institution, or public broadcasting entity, the court shall remit damages in any case in which the library, archives, educational institution, or public broadcasting entity sustains the burden of proving, and the court finds, that the library, archives, educational institution, or public broadcasting entity was not aware and had no reason to believe that its acts constituted a violation.

History of 17 U.S.C. §1203: Oct. 28, 1998, P.L. 105-304, §103(a), 112 Stat. 2874; Nov. 29, 1999, P.L. 106-113, §1000(a)(9), 113 Stat. 1536; Dec. 9, 2010, P.L. 111-295, §6(f)(3), 124 Stat. 3181.

See also WIPO Copyright Treaty; WIPO Performances & Phonograms Treaty.

§1204. CRIMINAL OFFENSES & PENALTIES

(a) In general.—Any person who violates section 1201 or 1202 willfully and for purposes of commercial advantage or private financial gain—

(1) shall be fined not more than $500,000 or imprisoned for not more than 5 years, or both, for the first offense; and

(2) shall be fined not more than $1,000,000 or imprisoned for not more than 10 years, or both, for any subsequent offense.

(b) Limitation for nonprofit library, archives, educational institution, or public broadcasting entity.—Subsection (a) shall not apply to a nonprofit library, archives, educational institution, or public broadcasting entity (as defined under section 118(f)).

(c) Statute of limitations.—No criminal proceeding shall be brought under this section unless such proceeding is commenced within 5 years after the cause of action arose.

History of 17 U.S.C. §1204: Oct. 28, 1998, P.L. 105-304, §103(a), 112 Stat. 2876; Nov. 29, 1999, P.L. 106-113, §1000(a)(9), 113 Stat. 1536; Dec. 9, 2010, P.L. 111-295, §6(f)(3), 124 Stat. 3181.

See also WIPO Copyright Treaty; WIPO Performances & Phonograms Treaty.

ANNOTATIONS

U.S. v. Reichert, 747 F.3d 445, 451-52 (6th Cir. 2014). "No court has yet discussed the reach of … §1204(a)'s willfulness requirement, and on this appeal we do not decide its scope. For this appeal, the parties agree that it requires the government to prove that [D] voluntarily and intentionally violated a known legal duty. This is consistent with our typical approach, as generally, in criminal cases, in order to establish a 'willful' violation of a statute, the Government must prove that the defendant acted with knowledge that his conduct was unlawful. It is also ordinarily the case that a defendant need not be aware of the specific provision of law that his conduct violates, as long as he is aware that his act is illegal. [D] also concedes that the DMCA's willfulness requirement may be satisfied by a showing of willful blindness; that is, a defendant's conscious decision to remain ignorant of the illegality of his conduct even when the defendant is aware of a high probability that his conduct is in fact illegal." (Internal quotes omitted.)

U.S. v. Whitehead, 532 F.3d 991, 993 (9th Cir.2008). "[D] argues that his conviction under 17 U.S.C. §1201 must be reversed because the indictment and jury instructions omitted an element of the offense, namely, that the technological measures he circumvented were put in place 'with the authority of the copyright owner.' But the indictment quoted and cited §1201(a)(2)(A), and thereby 'adequately apprised [D] of the charge[ ]'; any mistake here was 'minor or technical' and doesn't require reversal. And the jury instructions defined 'technological measure' using §1201(a)(3)(B)'s exact language. Neither the indictment nor the instructions were erroneous."

§1205. SAVINGS CLAUSE

Nothing in this chapter abrogates, diminishes, or weakens the provisions of, nor provides any defense or element of mitigation in a criminal prosecution or civil action under, any Federal or State law that prevents the violation of the privacy of an individual in connection with the individual's use of the Internet.

History of 17 U.S.C. §1205: Oct. 28, 1998, P.L. 105-304, §103(a), 112 Stat. 2876.

CHAPTER 13. PROTECTION OF ORIGINAL DESIGNS

§1301. DESIGNS PROTECTED

(a) Designs protected—

(1) In general.—The designer or other owner of an original design of a useful article which makes the article attractive or distinctive in appearance to the purchasing or using public may secure the protection provided by this chapter upon complying with and subject to this chapter.

(2) Vessel features.—The design of a vessel hull, deck, or combination of a hull and deck, including a plug or mold, is subject to protection under this chapter, notwithstanding section 1302(4).

(3) Exceptions.—Department of Defense rights in a registered design under this chapter, including the right to build to such registered design, shall be determined solely by operation of section 2320 of title 10 or by the instrument under which the design was developed for the United States Government.

(b) Definitions.—For the purpose of this chapter, the following terms have the following meanings:

(1) A design is "original" if it is the result of the designer's creative endeavor that provides a distinguishable variation over prior work pertaining to similar articles which is more than merely trivial and has not been copied from another source.

(2) A "useful article" is a vessel hull or deck, including a plug or mold, which in normal use has an intrinsic utilitarian function that is not merely to portray the appearance of the article or to convey information. An article which normally is part of a useful article shall be deemed to be a useful article.

(3) A "vessel" is a craft—

(A) that is designed and capable of independently steering a course on or through water through its own means of propulsion; and

(B) that is designed and capable of carrying and transporting one or more passengers.

(4) A "hull" is the exterior frame or body of a vessel, exclusive of the deck, superstructure, masts, sails, yards, rigging, hardware, fixtures, and other attachments.

(5) A "plug" means a device or model used to make a mold for the purpose of exact duplication, regardless of whether the device or model has an intrinsic utilitarian function that is not only to portray the appearance of the product or to convey information.

(6) A "mold" means a matrix or form in which a substance for material is used, regardless of whether the matrix or form has an intrinsic utilitarian function that is not only to portray the appearance of the product or to convey information.

(7) A "deck" is the horizontal surface of a vessel that covers the hull, including exterior cabin and cockpit surfaces, and exclusive of masts, sails, yards, rigging, hardware, fixtures, and other attachments.

History of 17 U.S.C. §1301: Oct. 28, 1998, P.L. 105-304, §502, 112 Stat. 2905; Nov. 29, 1999, P.L. 106-113, §1000(a)(9), 113 Stat. 1536; Oct. 16, 2008, P.L. 110-434, §1(b)-(d), 122 Stat. 4972.

See also 37 C.F.R. §§212.1-212.8; WIPO Copyright Treaty.

§1302. DESIGNS NOT SUBJECT TO PROTECTION

Protection under this chapter shall not be available for a design that is—

(1) not original;

(2) staple or commonplace, such as a standard geometric figure, a familiar symbol, an emblem, or a motif, or another shape, pattern, or configuration which has become standard, common, prevalent, or ordinary;

(3) different from a design excluded by paragraph (2) only in insignificant details or in elements which are variants commonly used in the relevant trades;

(4) dictated solely by a utilitarian function of the article that embodies it; or

(5) embodied in a useful article that was made public by the designer or owner in the United States or a foreign country more than 2 years before the date of the application for registration under this chapter.

History of 17 U.S.C. §1302: Oct. 28, 1998, P.L. 105-304, §502, 112 Stat. 2906; Aug. 5, 1999, P.L. 106-44, §1(f)(1), 113 Stat. 222.

See also 37 C.F.R. §212.3; WIPO Copyright Treaty.

§1303. REVISIONS, ADAPTATIONS, & REARRANGEMENTS

Protection for a design under this chapter shall be available notwithstanding the employment in the design of subject matter excluded from protection under section 1302 if the design is a substantial revision, adaptation, or rearrangement of such subject matter. Such protection shall be independent of any subsisting protection in subject matter employed in the design, and shall not be construed as securing any right to subject matter excluded from protection under this chapter or as extending any subsisting protection under this chapter.

History of 17 U.S.C. §1303: Oct. 28, 1998, P.L. 105-304, §502, 112 Stat. 2906.

ANNOTATIONS

Maverick Boat Co. v. American Mar. Holdings, Inc., 418 F.3d 1186, 1191 (11th Cir.2005). "In order to determine whether [P's] revision was substantial, the district court considered the following factors: (1) the nature of the changes made to the 'original' [hull] design; (2) the similarities between the 'original' design and the 'revised' design; and (3) the lack of evidence of the revision process.... *At 1192:* [T]he correction of an unintended problem does not create a new design, but merely makes the original design what it was always intended to be. Because [P] simply corrected mistakes in its original design, did not inform the public that its corrected version was in fact a revised or improved version, and presented no evidence as to the extent or nature of its corrections, we cannot conclude that its purported revised design constitutes the 'substantial' revision that Congress plainly intended to be protected by ... §1303. Accordingly, we agree with the district court's finding that [P] is not entitled to the protection offered by the [Vessel Hull Design Project Act]."

§1304. COMMENCEMENT OF PROTECTION

The protection provided for a design under this chapter shall commence upon the earlier of the date of publication of the registration under section 1313(a) or the date the design is first made public as defined by section 1310(b).

History of 17 U.S.C. §1304: Oct. 28, 1998, P.L. 105-304, §502, 112 Stat. 2907.

§1305. TERM OF PROTECTION

(a) In general.—Subject to subsection (b), the protection provided under this chapter for a design shall continue for a term of 10 years beginning on the date of the commencement of protection under section 1304.

(b) Expiration.—All terms of protection provided in this section shall run to the end of the calendar year in which they would otherwise expire.

(c) Termination of rights.—Upon expiration or termination of protection in a particular design under this chapter, all rights under this chapter in the design shall terminate, regardless of the number of different articles in which the design may have been used during the term of its protection.

History of 17 U.S.C. §1305: Oct. 28, 1998, P.L. 105-304, §502, 112 Stat. 2907.

§1306. DESIGN NOTICE

(a) Contents of design notice—

(1) Whenever any design for which protection is sought under this chapter is made public under section 1310(b), the owner of the design shall, subject to the provisions of section 1307, mark it or have it marked legibly with a design notice consisting of—

(A) the words "Protected Design," the abbreviation "Prot'd Des.," or the letter "D" with a circle, or the symbol "*D*";

(B) the year of the date on which protection for the design commenced; and

(C) the name of the owner, an abbreviation by which the name can be recognized, or a generally accepted alternative designation of the owner.

Any distinctive identification of the owner may be used for purposes of subparagraph (C) if it has been recorded by the Administrator before the design marked with such identification is registered.

(2) After registration, the registration number may be used instead of the elements specified in subparagraphs (B) and (C) of paragraph (1).

(b) Location of notice.—The design notice shall be so located and applied as to give reasonable notice of design protection while the useful article embodying the design is passing through its normal channels of commerce.

(c) Subsequent removal of notice.—When the owner of a design has complied with the provisions of this section, protection under this chapter shall not be affected by the removal, destruction, or obliteration by others of the design notice on an article.

History of 17 U.S.C. §1306: Oct. 28, 1998, P.L. 105-304, §502, 112 Stat. 2907.

§1307. EFFECT OF OMISSION OF NOTICE

(a) Actions with notice.—Except as provided in subsection (b), the omission of the notice prescribed in section 1306 shall not cause loss of the protection under this chapter or prevent recovery for infringement under this chapter against any person who, after receiving written notice of the design protection, begins an undertaking leading to infringement under this chapter.

(b) Actions without notice.—The omission of the notice prescribed in section 1306 shall prevent any recovery under section 1323 against a person who began an undertaking leading to infringement under this chapter before receiving written notice of the design protection. No injunction shall be issued under this chapter with respect to such undertaking unless the owner of the design reimburses that person for any reasonable expenditure or contractual obligation in connection with such undertaking that was incurred before receiving written notice of the design protection, as the court in its discretion directs. The burden of providing written notice of design protection shall be on the owner of the design.

History of 17 U.S.C. §1307: Oct. 28, 1998, P.L. 105-304, §502, 112 Stat. 2907.

§1308. EXCLUSIVE RIGHTS

The owner of a design protected under this chapter has the exclusive right to—

(1) make, have made, or import, for sale or for use in trade, any useful article embodying that design; and

(2) sell or distribute for sale or for use in trade any useful article embodying that design.

History of 17 U.S.C. §1308: Oct. 28, 1998, P.L. 105-304, §502, 112 Stat. 2908.

§1309. INFRINGEMENT

(a) Acts of infringement.—Except as provided in subsection (b), it shall be infringement of the exclusive rights in a design protected under this chapter for any person, without the consent of the owner of the design, within the United States and during the term of such protection, to—

(1) make, have made, or import, for sale or for use in trade, any infringing article as defined in subsection (e); or

(2) sell or distribute for sale or for use in trade any such infringing article.

(b) Acts of sellers and distributors.—A seller or distributor of an infringing article who did not make or import the article shall be deemed to have infringed on a design protected under this chapter only if that person—

(1) induced or acted in collusion with a manufacturer to make, or an importer to import such article, except that merely purchasing or giving an order to purchase such article in the ordinary course of business shall not of itself constitute such inducement or collusion; or

(2) refused or failed, upon the request of the owner of the design, to make a prompt and full disclosure of that person's source of such article, and that person orders or reorders such article after receiving notice by registered or certified mail of the protection subsisting in the design.

(c) Acts without knowledge.—It shall not be infringement under this section to make, have made, import, sell, or distribute, any article embodying a design which was created without knowledge that a design was protected under this chapter and was copied from such protected design.

(d) Acts in ordinary course of business.—A person who incorporates into that person's product of manufacture an infringing article acquired from others in the ordinary course of business, or who, without knowledge of the protected design embodied in an infringing article, makes or processes the infringing article for the account of another person in the ordinary course of business, shall not be deemed to have infringed the rights in that design under this chapter except under a condition contained in paragraph (1) or (2) of subsection (b). Accepting an order or reorder from the source of the infringing article shall be deemed ordering or reordering within the meaning of subsection (b)(2).

(e) Infringing article defined.—As used in this section, an "infringing article" is any article the design of which has been copied from a design protected under this chapter, without the consent of the owner of the protected design. An infringing article is not an illustration or picture of a protected design in an advertisement, book, periodical, newspaper, photograph, broadcast, motion picture, or similar medium. A design shall not be deemed to have been copied from a protected design if it is original and not substantially similar in appearance to a protected design.

(f) Establishing originality.—The party to any action or proceeding under this chapter who alleges rights under this chapter in a design shall have the burden of establishing the design's originality whenever the opposing party introduces an earlier work which is identical to such design, or so similar as to make prima facie showing that such design was copied from such work.

(g) Reproduction for teaching or analysis.—It is not an infringement of the exclusive rights of a design owner for a person to reproduce the design in a useful article or in any other form solely for the purpose of teaching, analyzing, or evaluating the appearance, concepts, or techniques embodied in the design, or the function of the useful article embodying the design.

History of 17 U.S.C. §1309: Oct. 28, 1998, P.L. 105-304, §502, 112 Stat. 2908.

§1310. APPLICATION FOR REGISTRATION

(a) Time limit for application for registration.—Protection under this chapter shall be lost if application for registration of the design is not made within 2 years after the date on which the design is first made public.

(b) When design is made public.—A design is made public when an existing useful article embodying the design is anywhere publicly exhibited, publicly distributed, or offered for sale or sold to the public by the owner of the design or with the owner's consent.

(c) Application by owner of design.—Application for registration may be made by the owner of the design.

(d) Contents of application.—The application for registration shall be made to the Administrator and shall state—

(1) the name and address of the designer or designers of the design;

(2) the name and address of the owner if different from the designer;

(3) the specific name of the useful article embodying the design;

(4) the date, if any, that the design was first made public, if such date was earlier than the date of the application;

(5) affirmation that the design has been fixed in a useful article; and

(6) such other information as may be required by the Administrator.

The application for registration may include a description setting forth the salient features of the design, but the absence of such a description shall not prevent registration under this chapter.

(e) Sworn statement.—The application for registration shall be accompanied by a statement under oath by the applicant or the applicant's duly authorized agent or representative, setting forth, to the best of the applicant's knowledge and belief—

(1) that the design is original and was created by the designer or designers named in the application;

(2) that the design has not previously been registered on behalf of the applicant or the applicant's predecessor in title; and

(3) that the applicant is the person entitled to protection and to registration under this chapter.

If the design has been made public with the design notice prescribed in section 1306, the statement shall also describe the exact form and position of the design notice.

(f) Effect of errors—

(1) Error in any statement or assertion as to the utility of the useful article named in the application under this section, the design of which is sought to be registered, shall not affect the protection secured under this chapter.

(2) Errors in omitting a joint designer or in naming an alleged joint designer shall not affect the validity of the registration, or the actual ownership or the protection of the design, unless it is shown that the error occurred with deceptive intent.

(g) Design made in scope of employment.—In a case in which the design was made within the regular scope of the designer's employment and individual authorship of the design is difficult or impossible to ascribe and the application so states, the name and address of the employer for whom the design was made may be stated instead of that of the individual designer.

(h) Pictorial representation of design.—The application for registration shall be accompanied by two copies of a drawing or other pictorial representation of the useful article embodying the design, having one or more views, adequate to show the design, in a form and style suitable for reproduction, which shall be deemed a part of the application.

(i) Design in more than one useful article.—If the distinguishing elements of a design are in substantially the same form in different useful articles, the design shall be protected as to all such useful articles when protected as to one of them, but not more than one registration shall be required for the design.

(j) Application for more than one design.—More than one design may be included in the same application under such conditions as may be prescribed by the Administrator. For each design included in an application the fee prescribed for a single design shall be paid.

History of 17 U.S.C. §1310: Oct. 28, 1998, P.L. 105-304, §502, 112 Stat. 2909.

§1311. BENEFIT OF EARLIER FILING DATE IN FOREIGN COUNTRY

An application for registration of a design filed in the United States by any person who has, or whose legal representative or predecessor or successor in title has, previously filed an application for registration of the same design in a foreign country which extends to designs of owners who are citizens of the United States, or to applications filed under this chapter, similar protection to that provided under this chapter shall have that same effect as if filed in the United States on the date on which the application was first filed in such foreign country, if the application in the United States is filed within 6 months after the earliest date on which any such foreign application was filed.

History of 17 U.S.C. §1311: Oct. 28, 1998, P.L. 105-304, §502, 112 Stat. 2910.

§1312. OATHS & ACKNOWLEDGMENTS

(a) In general.—Oaths and acknowledgments required by this chapter—

(1) may be made—

(A) before any person in the United States authorized by law to administer oaths; or

(B) when made in a foreign country, before any diplomatic or consular officer of the United States authorized to administer oaths, or before any official authorized to administer oaths in the foreign country concerned, whose authority shall be proved by a certificate of a diplomatic or consular officer of the United States; and

(2) shall be valid if they comply with the laws of the State or country where made.

(b) Written declaration in lieu of oath—

(1) The Administrator may by rule prescribe that any document which is to be filed under this chapter in the Office of the Administrator and which is required by any law, rule, or other regulation to be under oath, may be subscribed to by a written declaration in such form as the Administrator may prescribe, and such declaration shall be in lieu of the oath otherwise required.

(2) Whenever a written declaration under paragraph (1) is used, the document containing the declaration shall state that willful false statements are punishable by fine or imprisonment, or both, pursuant to

section 1001 of title 18, and may jeopardize the validity of the application or document or a registration resulting therefrom.

History of 17 U.S.C. §1312: Oct. 28, 1998, P.L. 105-304, §502, 112 Stat. 2911.

§1313. EXAMINATION OF APPLICATION & ISSUE OR REFUSAL OF REGISTRATION

(a) Determination of registrability of design; registration.—Upon the filing of an application for registration in proper form under section 1310, and upon payment of the fee prescribed under section 1316, the Administrator shall determine whether or not the application relates to a design which on its face appears to be subject to protection under this chapter, and, if so, the Register shall register the design. Registration under this subsection shall be announced by publication. The date of registration shall be the date of publication.

(b) Refusal to register; reconsideration.—If, in the judgment of the Administrator, the application for registration relates to a design which on its face is not subject to protection under this chapter, the Administrator shall send to the applicant a notice of refusal to register and the grounds for the refusal. Within 3 months after the date on which the notice of refusal is sent, the applicant may, by written request, seek reconsideration of the application. After consideration of such a request, the Administrator shall either register the design or send to the applicant a notice of final refusal to register.

(c) Application to cancel registration.—Any person who believes he or she is or will be damaged by a registration under this chapter may, upon payment of the prescribed fee, apply to the Administrator at any time to cancel the registration on the ground that the design is not subject to protection under this chapter, stating the reasons for the request. Upon receipt of an application for cancellation, the Administrator shall send to the owner of the design, as shown in the records of the Office of the Administrator, a notice of the application, and the owner shall have a period of 3 months after the date on which such notice is mailed in which to present arguments to the Administrator for support of the validity of the registration. The Administrator shall also have the authority to establish, by regulation, conditions under which the opposing parties may appear and be heard in support of their arguments. If, after the periods provided for the presentation of arguments have expired, the Administrator determines that the applicant for cancellation has established that the design is not subject to protection under this chapter, the Administrator shall order the registration stricken from the record. Cancellation under this subsection shall be announced by publication, and notice of the Administrator's final determination with respect to any application for cancellation shall be sent to the applicant and to the owner of record. Costs of the cancellation procedure under this subsection shall be borne by the nonprevailing party or parties, and the Administrator shall have the authority to assess and collect such costs.

History of 17 U.S.C. §1313: Oct. 28, 1998, P.L. 105-304, §502, 112 Stat. 2911; Nov. 29, 1999, P.L. 106-113, §1000(a)(9), 113 Stat. 1536.

§1314. CERTIFICATION OF REGISTRATION

Certificates of registration shall be issued in the name of the United States under the seal of the Office of the Administrator and shall be recorded in the official records of the Office. The certificate shall state the name of the useful article, the date of filing of the application, the date of registration, and the date the design was made public, if earlier than the date of filing of the application, and shall contain a reproduction of the drawing or other pictorial representation of the design. If a description of the salient features of the design appears in the application, the description shall also appear in the certificate. A certificate of registration shall be admitted in any court as prima facie evidence of the facts stated in the certificate.

History of 17 U.S.C. §1314: Oct. 28, 1998, P.L. 105-304, §502, 112 Stat. 2912.

§1315. PUBLICATION OF ANNOUNCEMENTS & INDEXES

(a) Publications of the Administrator.—The Administrator shall publish lists and indexes of registered designs and cancellations of designs and may also publish the drawings or other pictorial representations of registered designs for sale or other distribution.

(b) File of representatives of registered designs.—The Administrator shall establish and maintain a file of the drawings or other pictorial representations of registered designs. The file shall be available for use by the public under such conditions as the Administrator may prescribe.

History of 17 U.S.C. §1315: Oct. 28, 1998, P.L. 105-304, §502, 112 Stat. 2912.

§1316. FEES

The Administrator shall by regulation set reasonable fees for the filing of applications to register designs under this chapter and for other services relating to the administration of this chapter, taking into consideration the cost of providing these services and the benefit of a public record.

History of 17 U.S.C. §1316: Oct. 28, 1998, P.L. 105-304, §502, 112 Stat. 2912.

§1317. REGULATIONS

The Administrator may establish regulations for the administration of this chapter.

History of 17 U.S.C. §1317: Oct. 28, 1998, P.L. 105-304, §502, 112 Stat. 2912.

§1318. COPIES OF RECORDS

Upon payment of the prescribed fee, any person may obtain a certified copy of any official record of the Office of the Administrator that relates to this chapter. That copy shall be admissible in evidence with the same effect as the original.

History of 17 U.S.C. §1318: Oct. 28, 1998, P.L. 105-304, §502, 112 Stat. 2913.

§1319. CORRECTION OF ERRORS IN CERTIFICATES

The Administrator may, by a certificate of correction under seal, correct any error in a registration incurred through the fault of the Office, or, upon payment of the required fee, any error of a clerical or typographical nature occurring in good faith but not through the fault of the Office. Such registration, together with the certificate, shall thereafter have the same effect as if it had been originally issued in such corrected form.

History of 17 U.S.C. §1319: Oct. 28, 1998, P.L. 105-304, §502, 112 Stat. 2913.

§1320. OWNERSHIP & TRANSFER

(a) Property right in design.—The property right in a design subject to protection under this chapter shall vest in the designer, the legal representatives of a deceased designer or of one under legal incapacity, the employer for whom the designer created the design in the case of a design made within the regular scope of the designer's employment, or a person to whom the rights of the designer or of such employer have been transferred. The person in whom the property right is vested shall be considered the owner of the design.

(b) Transfer of property right.—The property right in a registered design, or a design for which an application for registration has been or may be filed, may be assigned, granted, conveyed, or mortgaged by an instrument in writing, signed by the owner, or may be bequeathed by will.

(c) Oath or acknowledgment of transfer.—An oath or acknowledgment under section 1312 shall be prima facie evidence of the execution of an assignment, grant, conveyance, or mortgage under subsection (b).

(d) Recordation of transfer.—An assignment, grant, conveyance, or mortgage under subsection (b) shall be void as against any subsequent purchaser or mortgagee for a valuable consideration, unless it is recorded in the Office of the Administrator within 3 months after its date of execution or before the date of such subsequent purchase or mortgage.

History of 17 U.S.C. §1320: Oct. 28, 1998, P.L. 105-304, §502, 112 Stat. 2913; Aug. 5, 1999, P.L. 106-44, §1(f)(2), 113 Stat. 222.

§1321. REMEDY FOR INFRINGEMENT

(a) In general.—The owner of a design is entitled, after issuance of a certificate of registration of the design under this chapter, to institute an action for any infringement of the design.

(b) Review of refusal to register—

(1) Subject to paragraph (2), the owner of a design may seek judicial review of a final refusal of the Administrator to register the design under this chapter by bringing a civil action, and may in the same action, if the court adjudges the design subject to protection under this chapter, enforce the rights in that design under this chapter.

(2) The owner of a design may seek judicial review under this section if—

(A) the owner has previously duly filed and prosecuted to final refusal an application in proper form for registration of the design;

(B) the owner causes a copy of the complaint in the action to be delivered to the Administrator within 10 days after the commencement of the action; and

(C) the defendant has committed acts in respect to the design which would constitute infringement with respect to a design protected under this chapter.

(c) Administrator as party to action.—The Administrator may, at the Administrator's option, become a party to the action with respect to the issue of registrability of the design claim by entering an appearance within 60 days after being served with the complaint, but the failure of the Administrator to become a party shall not deprive the court of jurisdiction to determine that issue.

(d) Use of arbitration to resolve dispute.—The parties to an infringement dispute under this chapter, within such time as may be specified by the Administrator by regulation, may determine the dispute, or any aspect of the dispute, by arbitration. Arbitration shall be governed by title 9. The parties shall give notice of any arbitration award to the Administrator, and such award shall, as between the parties to the arbitration, be dispositive of the issues to which it relates. The arbitration award shall be unenforceable until such notice is given. Nothing in this subsection shall preclude the Administrator from determining whether a design is subject to registration in a cancellation proceeding under section 1313(c).

History of 17 U.S.C. §1321: Oct. 28, 1998, P.L. 105-304, §502, 112 Stat. 2913.

§1322. INJUNCTIONS

(a) In general.—A court having jurisdiction over actions under this chapter may grant injunctions in accordance with the principles of equity to prevent infringement of a design under this chapter, including, in its discretion, prompt relief by temporary restraining orders and preliminary injunctions.

(b) Damages for injunctive relief wrongfully obtained.—A seller or distributor who suffers damage by reason of injunctive relief wrongfully obtained under this section has a cause of action against the applicant for such injunctive relief and may recover such relief as may be appropriate, including damages for lost profits, cost of materials, loss of good will, and punitive damages in instances where the injunctive relief was sought in bad faith, and, unless the court finds extenuating circumstances, reasonable attorney's fees.

History of 17 U.S.C. §1322: Oct. 28, 1998, P.L. 105-304, §502, 112 Stat. 2914.

§1323. RECOVERY FOR INFRINGEMENT

(a) Damages.—Upon a finding for the claimant in an action for infringement under this chapter, the court shall award the claimant damages adequate to compensate for the infringement. In addition, the court may increase the damages to such amount, not exceeding $50,000 or $1 per copy, whichever is greater, as the court determines to be just. The damages awarded shall constitute compensation and not a penalty. The court may receive expert testimony as an aid to the determination of damages.

(b) Infringer's profits.—As an alternative to the remedies provided in subsection (a), the court may award the claimant the infringer's profits resulting from the sale of the copies if the court finds that the infringer's sales are reasonably related to the use of the claimant's design. In such a case, the claimant shall be required to prove only the amount of the infringer's sales and the infringer shall be required to prove its expenses against such sales.

(c) Statute of limitations.—No recovery under subsection (a) or (b) shall be had for any infringement committed more than 3 years before the date on which the complaint is filed.

(d) Attorney's fees.—In an action for infringement under this chapter, the court may award reasonable attorney's fees to the prevailing party.

(e) Disposition of infringing and other articles.—The court may order that all infringing articles, and any plates, molds, patterns, models, or other means specifically adapted for making the articles, be delivered up for destruction or other disposition as the court may direct.

History of 17 U.S.C. §1323: Oct. 28, 1998, P.L. 105-304, §502, 112 Stat. 2914.

ANNOTATIONS

Maverick Boat Co. v. American Mar. Holdings, Inc., 418 F.3d 1186, 1190 (11th Cir.2005). "We review the district court's decision to award attorneys' fees for abuse of discretion."

§1324. POWER OF COURT OVER REGISTRATION

In any action involving the protection of a design under this chapter, the court, when appropriate, may order registration of a design under this chapter or the cancellation of such a registration. Any such order shall be certified by the court to the Administrator, who shall make an appropriate entry upon the record.

History of 17 U.S.C. §1324: Oct. 28, 1998, P.L. 105-304, §502, 112 Stat. 2915.

§1325. LIABILITY FOR ACTION ON REGISTRATION FRAUDULENTLY OBTAINED

Any person who brings an action for infringement knowing that registration of the design was obtained by a false or fraudulent representation materially affecting the rights under this chapter, shall be liable in the sum of $10,000, or such part of that amount as the court may determine. That amount shall be to compensate the defendant and shall be charged against the plaintiff and paid to the defendant, in addition to such costs and attorney's fees of the defendant as may be assessed by the court.

History of 17 U.S.C. §1325: Oct. 28, 1998, P.L. 105-304, §502, 112 Stat. 2915.

§1326. PENALTY FOR FALSE MARKING

(a) In general.—Whoever, for the purpose of deceiving the public, marks upon, applies to, or uses in advertising in connection with an article made, used, distributed, or sold, a design which is not protected under this chapter, a design notice specified in section 1306, or any other words or symbols importing that the design is protected under this chapter, knowing that the design is not so protected, shall pay a civil fine of not more than $500 for each such offense.

(b) Suit by private persons.—Any person may sue for the penalty established by subsection (a), in which event one-half of the penalty shall be awarded to the person suing and the remainder shall be awarded to the United States.

History of 17 U.S.C. §1326: Oct. 28, 1998, P.L. 105-304, §502, 112 Stat. 2915.

§1327. PENALTY FOR FALSE REPRESENTATION

Whoever knowingly makes a false representation materially affecting the rights obtainable under this chapter for the purpose of obtaining registration of a design under this chapter shall pay a penalty of not less than $500 and not more than $1,000, and any rights or privileges that individual may have in the design under this chapter shall be forfeited.

History of 17 U.S.C. §1327: Oct. 28, 1998, P.L. 105-304, §502, 112 Stat. 2915.

§1328. ENFORCEMENT BY TREASURY & POSTAL SERVICE

(a) Regulations.—The Secretary of the Treasury and the United States Postal Service shall separately or jointly issue regulations for the enforcement of the rights set forth in section 1308 with respect to importation. Such regulations may require, as a condition for the exclusion of articles from the United States, that the person seeking exclusion take any one or more of the following actions:

(1) Obtain a court order enjoining, or an order of the International Trade Commission under section 1337 of title 19 excluding, importation of the articles.

(2) Furnish proof that the design involved is protected under this chapter and that the importation of the articles would infringe the rights in the design under this chapter.

(3) Post a surety bond for any injury that may result if the detention or exclusion of the articles proves to be unjustified.

(b) Seizure and forfeiture.—Articles imported in violation of the rights set forth in section 1308 are subject to seizure and forfeiture in the same manner as property imported in violation of the customs laws. Any such forfeited articles shall be destroyed as directed by the Secretary of the Treasury or the court, as the case may be, except that the articles may be returned to the country of export whenever it is shown to the satisfaction of the Secretary of the Treasury that the importer had no reasonable grounds for believing that his or her acts constituted a violation of the law.

History of 17 U.S.C. §1328: Oct. 28, 1998, P.L. 105-304, §502, 112 Stat. 2916.

§1329. RELATION TO DESIGN PATENT LAW

The issuance of a design patent under title 35, United States Code, for an original design for an article of manufacture shall terminate any protection of the original design under this chapter.

History of 17 U.S.C. §1329: Oct. 28, 1998, P.L. 105-304, §502, 112 Stat. 2916.

§1330. COMMON LAW & OTHER RIGHTS UNAFFECTED

Nothing in this chapter shall annul or limit—

(1) common law or other rights or remedies, if any, available to or held by any person with respect to a design which has not been registered under this chapter; or

(2) any right under the trademark laws or any right protected against unfair competition.

History of 17 U.S.C. §1330: Oct. 28, 1998, P.L. 105-304, §502, 112 Stat. 2916.

§1331. ADMINISTRATOR; OFFICE OF THE ADMINISTRATOR

In this chapter, the "Administrator" is the Register of Copyrights, and the "Office of the Administrator" and the "Office" refer to the Copyright Office of the Library of Congress.

History of 17 U.S.C. §1331: Oct. 28, 1998, P.L. 105-304, §502, 112 Stat. 2916.

§1332. NO RETROACTIVE EFFECT

Protection under this chapter shall not be available for any design that has been made public under section 1310(b) before the effective date of this chapter.

History of 17 U.S.C. §1332: Oct. 28, 1998, P.L. 105-304, §502, 112 Stat. 2916.

DIRECT COPYRIGHT INFRINGEMENT UNDER 17 U.S.C. §501(a)

CHART

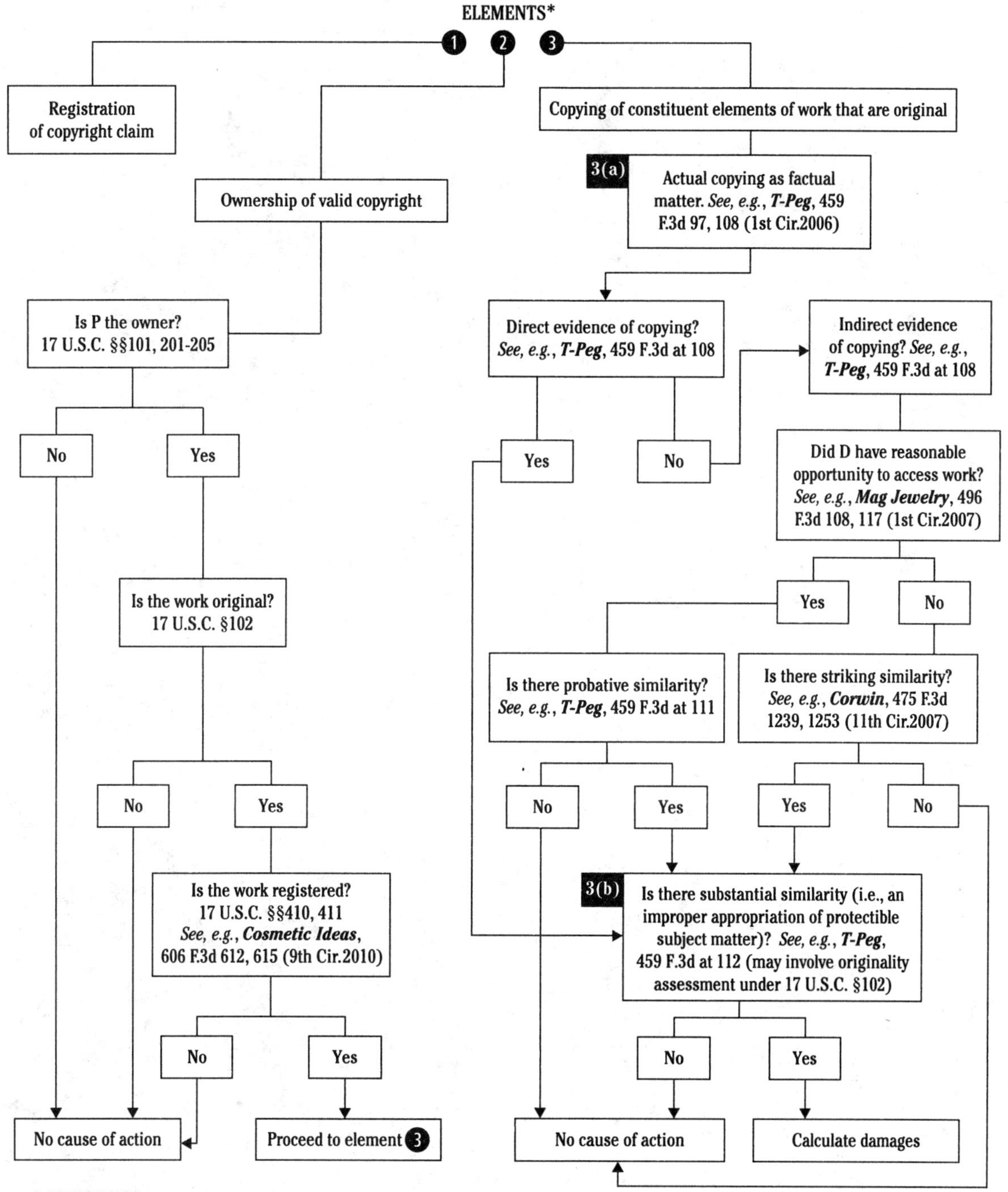

* ELEMENTS

1. ***Reed Elsevier***, 559 U.S. 154, 160-63 (2010); 17 U.S.C. §411(a)
2. ***Feist***, 499 U.S. 340, 361 (1991); 17 U.S.C. §501(a)
3. ***Feist***, 499 U.S. at 361; 17 U.S.C. §501(a)

TABLE OF CONTENTS

COPYRIGHT ACT OF 1909

COPYRIGHT ACT OF 1909

CHAPTER 1. REGISTRATION OF COPYRIGHTS

§1. EXCLUSIVE RIGHTS AS TO COPYRIGHTED WORKS

Any person entitled thereto, upon complying with the provisions of this title, shall have the exclusive right:

(a) To print, reprint, publish, copy, and vend the copyrighted work;

(b) To translate the copyrighted work into other languages or dialects, or make any other version thereof, if it be a literary work; to dramatize it if it be a nondramatic work; to convert it into a novel or other nondramatic work if it be a drama; to arrange or adapt it if it be a musical work; to complete, execute, and finish it if it be a model or design for a work of art;

(c) To deliver, authorize the delivery of, read, or present the copyrighted work in public for profit if it be a lecture, sermon, address or similar production, or other nondramatic literary work; to make or procure the making of any transcription or record thereof by or from which, in whole or in part, it may in any manner or by any method be exhibited, delivered, presented, produced, or reproduced; and to play or perform it in public for profit, and to exhibit, represent, produce, or reproduce it in any manner or by any method whatsoever. The damages for the infringement by broadcast of any work referred to in this subsection shall not exceed the sum of $100 where the infringing broadcaster shows that he was not aware that he was infringing and that such infringement could not have been reasonably foreseen; and

(d) To perform or represent the copyrighted work publicly if it be a drama or, if it be a dramatic work and not reproduced in copies for sale, to vend any manuscript or any record whatsoever thereof; to make or to procure the making of any transcription or record thereof by or from which, in whole or in part, it may in any manner or by any method be exhibited, performed, represented, produced, or reproduced; and to exhibit, perform, represent, produce, or reproduce it in any manner or by any method whatsoever; and

(e) To perform the copyrighted work publicly for profit if it be a musical composition; and for the purpose of public performance for profit, and for the purposes set forth in subsection (a) hereof, to make any arrangement or setting of it or of the melody of it in any system of notation or any form of record in which the thought of an author may be recorded and from which it may be read or reproduced: *Provided*, That the provisions of this title, so far as they secure copyright controlling the parts of instruments serving to reproduce mechanically the musical work, shall include only compositions published and copyrighted after July 1, 1909, and shall not include the works of a foreign author or composer unless the foreign state or nation of which such author or composer is a citizen or subject grants, either by treaty, convention, agreement, or law, to citizens of the United States similar rights. And as a condition of extending the copyrighted control to such mechanical reproductions, that whenever the owner of a musical copyright has used or permitted or knowingly acquiesced in the use of the copyrighted work upon the parts of instruments serving to reproduce mechanically the musical work, any other person may make similar use of the copyrighted work upon the payment to the copyright proprietor of a royalty of 2 cents on each such part manufactured, to be paid by the manufacturer thereof; and the copyright proprietor may require, and if so the manufacturer shall furnish, a report under oath on the 20th day of each month on the number of parts of instruments manufactured during the previous month serving to reproduce mechanically said musical work, and royalties shall be due on the parts manufactured during any month upon the 20th of the next succeeding month. The payment of the royalty provided for by this section shall free the articles or devices for which such royalty has been paid from further contribution to the copyright except in case of public performance for profit. It shall be the duty of the copyright owner, if he uses the musical composition himself for the manufacture of parts of instruments serving to reproduce mechanically the musical work, or licenses others to do so, to file notice thereof, accompanied by a recording fee, in the copyright office, and any failure to file such notice shall be a complete defense to any suit, action, or proceeding for any infringement of such copyright.

In case of failure of such manufacturer to pay to the copyright proprietor within thirty days after demand in writing the full sum of royalties due at said rate at the date of such demand, the court may award taxable costs to the plaintiff and a reasonable counsel fee, and the court may, in its discretion, enter judgment therein for any sum in addition over the amount found to be due as royalty in accordance with the terms of this title, not exceeding three times such amount.

The reproduction or rendition of a musical composition by or upon coin-operated machines shall not be deemed a public performance for profit unless a fee is charged for admission to the place where such reproduction or rendition occurs.

(f) To reproduce and distribute to the public by sale or other transfer of ownership, or by rental, lease, or lending, reproductions of the copyrighted work if it be a sound recording: *Provided*, That the exclusive right of the owner of a copyright in a sound recording to reproduce it is limited to the right to duplicate the sound recording in a tangible form that directly or indirectly recaptures the actual sounds fixed in the recording: *Provided further*, That this right does not extend to the making or duplication of another sound recording that is an independent fixation of other sounds, even though such sounds imitate or simulate those in the copyrighted sound recording; or to reproductions made by transmitting organizations exclusively for their own use.

History of 17 U.S.C. §1 (1909): July 30, 1947, ch. 391, 61 Stat. 652; July 17, 1952, ch. 923, §1, 66 Stat. 752; Oct. 15, 1971, P.L. 92-140, §1(a), 85 Stat. 391.

§2. RIGHTS OF AUTHOR OR PROPRIETOR OF UNPUBLISHED WORK

Nothing in this title shall be construed to annul or limit the right of the author or proprietor of an unpublished work, at common law or in equity, to prevent the copying, publication, or use of such unpublished work without his consent, and to obtain damages therefor.

History of 17 U.S.C. §2 (1909): July 30, 1947, ch. 391, 61 Stat. 654.

§3. PROTECTION OF COMPONENT PARTS OF WORK COPYRIGHTED; COMPOSITE WORKS OR PERIODICALS

The copyright provided by this title shall protect all the copyrightable component parts of the work copyrighted, and all matter therein in which copyright is already subsisting, but without extending the duration or scope of such copyright. The copyright upon composite works or periodicals shall give to the proprietor thereof all the rights in respect thereto which he would have if each part were individually copyrighted under this title.

History of 17 U.S.C. §3 (1909): July 30, 1947, ch. 391, 61 Stat. 654; Oct. 31, 1951, ch. 655, §16(a), 65 Stat. 716.

§4. ALL WRITINGS OF AUTHOR INCLUDED

The works for which copyright may be secured under this title shall include all the writings of an author.

History of 17 U.S.C. §4 (1909): July 30, 1947, ch. 391, 61 Stat. 654.

§5. CLASSIFICATION OF WORKS FOR REGISTRATION

The application for registration shall specify to which of the following classes the work in which copyright is claimed belongs:

(a) Books, including composite and cyclopedic works, directories, gazetteers, and other compilations.

(b) Periodicals, including newspapers.

(c) Lectures, sermons, addresses (prepared for oral delivery).

(d) Dramatic or dramatico-musical compositions.

(e) Musical compositions.

(f) Maps.

(g) Works of art; models or designs for works of art.

(h) Reproductions of a work of art.

(i) Drawings or plastic works of a scientific or technical character.

(j) Photographs.

(k) Prints and pictorial illustrations including prints or labels used for articles of merchandise.

(*l*) Motion-picture photoplays.

(m) Motion pictures other than photoplays.

(n) Sound recordings.

The above specifications shall not be held to limit the subject matter of copyright as defined in section 4 of this title, nor shall any error in classification invalidate or impair the copyright protection secured under this title.

History of 17 U.S.C. §5 (1909): July 30, 1947, ch. 391, 61 Stat. 654; Oct. 15, 1971, P.L. 92-140, §1(b), 85 Stat. 391.

§6. REGISTRATION OF PRINTS & LABELS

Commencing July 1, 1940, the Register of Copyrights is charged with the registration of claims to copyright properly presented, in all prints and labels published in connection with the sale or advertisement of articles of merchandise, including all claims to copyright in prints and labels pending in the Patent Office and uncleared at the close of business June 30, 1940. There shall be paid for registering a claim of copyright in any such print or label not a trade-mark $6, which sum shall cover the expense of furnishing a certificate of such registration, under the seal of the Copyright Office, to the claimant of copyright.

History of 17 U.S.C. §6 (1909): July 30, 1947, ch. 391, 61 Stat. 654.

§7. COPYRIGHT ON COMPILATIONS OF WORKS IN PUBLIC DOMAIN OR OF COPYRIGHTED WORKS; SUBSISTING COPYRIGHTS NOT AFFECTED

Compilations or abridgements, adaptations, arrangements, dramatizations, translations, or other versions of works in the public domain or of copyrighted works when produced with the consent of the proprietor of the copyright in such works, or works republished with new matter, shall be regarded as new works subject to copyright under the provisions of this title; but the publication of any such new works shall not affect the force or validity of any subsisting copyright upon the matter employed or any part thereof, or be construed to imply an exclusive right to such use of the original works, or to secure or extend copyright in such original works.

History of 17 U.S.C. §7 (1909): July 30, 1947, ch. 391, 61 Stat. 655.

§8. COPYRIGHT NOT TO SUBSIST IN WORKS IN PUBLIC DOMAIN, OR PUBLISHED PRIOR TO JULY 1, 1909, & NOT ALREADY COPYRIGHTED, OR GOVERNMENT PUBLICATIONS; PUBLICATION BY GOVERNMENT OF COPYRIGHTED MATERIAL

No copyright shall subsist in the original text of any work which is in the public domain, or in any work which was published in this country or any foreign country prior to July 1, 1909, and has not been already copyrighted in the United States, or in any publication of the United States Government, or any reprint, in whole or in part, thereof, except that the United States Postal Service may secure copyright on behalf of the United States in the whole or any part of the publications authorized by section 405 of title 39.

The publication or republication by the Government, either separately or in a public document, of any material in which copyright is subsisting shall not be taken to cause any abridgment or annulment of the copyright or to authorize any use or appropriation of such copyright material without the consent of the copyright proprietor.

History of 17 U.S.C. §8 (1909): July 30, 1947, ch. 391, 61 Stat. 655; Oct. 31, 1951, ch. 655, §16(b), 65 Stat. 716; Sept. 7, 1962, P.L. 87-646, §21, 76 Stat. 446; Aug. 12, 1970, P.L. 91-375, §6(i), 84 Stat. 777.

§9. AUTHORS OR PROPRIETORS, ENTITLED; ALIENS

The author or proprietor of any work made the subject of copyright by this title, or his executors, administrators, or assigns, shall have copyright for such work under the conditions and for the terms specified in this title: *Provided, however*, That the copyright secured by this title shall extend to the work of an author or proprietor who is a citizen or subject of a foreign state or nation only under the conditions described in subsections (a), (b), or (c) below:

(a) When an alien author or proprietor shall be domiciled within the United States at the time of the first publication of his work; or

(b) When the foreign state or nation of which such author or proprietor is a citizen or subject grants, either by treaty, convention, agreement, or law, to citizens of the United States the benefit of copyright on substantially the same basis as to its own citizens, or copyright protection, substantially equal to the protection secured to such foreign author under this title or by treaty; or when such foreign state or nation is a party to an international agreement which provides for reciprocity in the granting of copyright, by the terms of which agreement the United States may, at its pleasure, become a party thereto.

The existence of the reciprocal conditions aforesaid shall be determined by the President of the United States, by proclamation made from time to time, as the purposes of this title may require: *Provided*, That whenever the President shall find that the authors, copyright owners, or proprietors of works first produced or published abroad and subject to copyright or to renewal of copyright under the laws of the United States, including works subject to ad interim copyright, are or may have been temporarily unable to comply with the conditions and formalities prescribed with respect to such works by the copyright laws of the United States, because of the disruption or suspension of facilities essential for such compliance, he may by proclamation grant such extension of time as he may deem appropriate for the fulfillment of such conditions or formalities by authors, copyright owners, or proprietors who are citizens of the United States or who are nationals of countries which accord substantially equal treatment in this respect to authors, copyright owners, or proprietors who are citizens of the United States: *Provided further*, That no liability shall attach under this title for lawful uses made or acts done prior to the effective date of such proclamation in connection with such works, or in respect to the continuance for one year subsequent to such date of any business undertaking or enterprise lawfully undertaken prior to such date involving expenditure or contractual obligation in connection with the exploitation, production, reproduction, circulation, or performance of any such work.

The President may at any time terminate any proclamation authorized herein or any part thereof or suspend or extend its operation for such period or periods of time as in his judgment the interests of the United States may require.

(c) When the Universal Copyright Convention, signed at Geneva on September 6, 1952, shall be in force between the United States of America and the foreign state or nation of which such author is a citizen or subject, or in which the work was first published. Any work to which copyright is extended pursuant to this subsection shall be exempt from the following provisions of this title: (1) The requirement in section 1(e) that a foreign state or nation must grant to United States citizens mechanical reproduction rights similar to those specified therein; (2) the obligatory deposit requirements of the first sentence of section 13; (3) the provisions of sections 14, 16, 17, and 18; (4) the import prohibitions of section 107, to the extent that they are related to the manufacturing requirements of section 16; and (5) the requirements of sections 19 and 20: *Provided, however*, That such exemptions shall apply only if from the time of first publication all the copies of the work published with the authority of the author or other copyright proprietor shall bear the symbol © accompanied by the name of the copyright proprietor and the year of first publication placed in such manner and location as to give reasonable notice of claim of copyright.

Upon the coming into force of the Universal Copyright Convention in a foreign state or nation as hereinbefore provided, every book or periodical of a citizen or subject thereof in which ad interim copyright was subsisting on the effective date of said coming into force shall have copyright for twenty-eight years from the date of first publication abroad without the necessity of complying with the further formalities specified in section 23 of this title.

The provisions of this subsection shall not be extended to works of an author who is a citizen of, or domiciled in the United States of America regardless of place of first publication, or to works first published in the United States.

History of 17 U.S.C. §9 (1909): July 30, 1947, ch. 391, 61 Stat. 655; Aug. 31, 1954, ch. 1161, §1, 68 Stat. 1030.

§10. PUBLICATION OF WORK WITH NOTICE

Any person entitled thereto by this title may secure copyright for his work by publication thereof with the notice of copyright required by this title; and such notice shall be affixed to each copy thereof published or offered for sale in the United States by authority of the copyright proprietor, except in the case of books seeking ad interim protection under section 22 of this title.

History of 17 U.S.C. §10 (1909): July 30, 1947, ch. 391, 61 Stat. 656.

§11. REGISTRATION OF CLAIM & ISSUANCE OF CERTIFICATE

Such person may obtain registration of his claim to copyright by complying with the provisions of this title, including the deposit of copies, and upon such compliance the Register of Copyrights shall issue to him the certificates provided for in section 209 of this title.

History of 17 U.S.C. §11 (1909): July 30, 1947, ch. 391, 61 Stat. 656.

§12. WORKS NOT REPRODUCED FOR SALE

Copyright may also be had of the works of an author, of which copies are not reproduced for sale, by the deposit, with claim of copyright, of one complete copy of such work if it be a lecture or similar production or a dramatic, musical, or dramatico-musical composition; of a title and description, with one print taken from each scene or act, if the work be a motion-picture photoplay; of a photographic print if the work be a photograph; of a title and description, with not less than two prints taken from different sections of a complete motion picture, if the work be a motion picture other than a photoplay; or of a photograph or other identifying reproduction thereof, if it be a work of art or a plastic work or drawing. But the privilege of registration of copyright secured hereunder shall not exempt the copyright proprietor from the deposit of copies, under sections 13 and 14 of this title, where the work is later reproduced in copies for sale.

History of 17 U.S.C. §12 (1909): July 30, 1947, ch. 391, 61 Stat. 656.

§13. DEPOSIT OF COPIES AFTER PUBLICATION; ACTION OR PROCEEDING FOR INFRINGEMENT

After copyright has been secured by publication of the work with the notice of copyright as provided in section 10 of this title, there shall be promptly deposited in the Copyright Office or in the mail addressed to the Register of Copyrights, Washington, District of Columbia, two complete copies of the best edition thereof then published, or if the work is by an author who is a citizen or subject of a foreign state or nation and has been published in a foreign country, one complete copy of the best edition then published in such foreign country, which copies or copy, if the work be a book or periodical, shall have been produced in accordance with the manufacturing provisions specified in section 16 of this title; or if such work be a contribution to a periodical, for which contribution special registration is requested, one copy of the issue or issues containing such contribution; or if the work belongs to a class specified in subsections (g), (h), (i) or (k) of section 5 of this title, and if the Register of Copyrights determines that it is impracticable to deposit copies because of their size, weight, fragility, or monetary value he may permit the deposit of photographs or other identifying reproductions in lieu of copies of the work as published under such rules and regulations as he may prescribe with the approval of the Librarian of Congress; or if the work is not reproduced in copies for sale there shall be deposited the copy, print, photograph, or other identifying reproduction provided by section 12 of this title, such copies or copy, print, photograph, or other reproduction to be accompanied in each case by a claim of copyright. No action or proceeding shall be maintained for infringement of copyright in any work until the provisions of this title with respect to the deposit of copies and registration of such work shall have been complied with.

History of 17 U.S.C. §13 (1909): July 30, 1947, ch. 391, 61 Stat. 656; Mar. 29, 1956, ch. 109, 70 Stat. 63.

§14. DEPOSIT OF COPIES AFTER PUBLICATION; FAILURE TO DEPOSIT; DEMAND; PENALTY

Should the copies called for by section 13 of this title not be promptly deposited as provided in this title, the Register of Copyrights may at any time after the publication of the work, upon actual notice, require the proprietor of the copyright to deposit them, and after the said demand shall have been made, in default of the deposit of copies of the work within three months from any part of the United States, except an outlying territorial possession of the United States, or within six months from any outlying territorial possession of the United States, or from any foreign country, the proprietor of the copyright shall be liable to a fine of $100 and to pay to the Library of Congress twice the amount of the retail price of the best edition of the work, and the copyright shall become void.

History of 17 U.S.C. §14 (1909): July 30, 1947, ch. 391, 61 Stat. 657.

§15. DEPOSIT OF COPIES AFTER PUBLICATION; POSTMASTER'S RECEIPT; TRANSMISSION BY MAIL WITHOUT COST

The postmaster to whom are delivered the articles deposited as provided in sections 12 and 13 of this title shall, if requested, give a receipt therefor and shall mail them to their destination without cost to the copyright claimant.

History of 17 U.S.C. §15 (1909): July 30, 1947, ch. 391, 61 Stat. 657.

§16. MECHANICAL WORK TO BE DONE IN UNITED STATES

Of the printed book or periodical specified in section 5, subsections (a) and (b), of this title, except the original text of a book or periodical of foreign origin in a language or languages other than English, the text of all copies accorded protection under this title, except as below provided, shall be printed from type set within the limits of the United States, either by hand or by the aid of any kind of typesetting machine, or from plates made within the limits of the United States from type set therein, or, if the text be produced by lithographic process, or photo-engraving process, then by a process wholly performed within the limits of the United States, and the printing of the text and binding of the said book shall be performed within the limits of the United States; which requirements shall extend also to the illustrations within a book consisting of printed text and illustrations produced by lithographic process, or photo-engraving process, and also to separate lithographs or photo-engravings, except where in either case the subjects represented are located in a foreign country and illustrate a scientific work or reproduce a work of art: *Provided, however*, That said requirements shall not apply to works in raised characters for the use of the blind, or to books or periodicals of foreign origin in a language or languages other than English, or to works printed or produced in the United States by any other process than those above specified in this section, or to copies of books or periodicals, first published abroad in the English language, imported into the United States within five years after first publication in a foreign state or nation up to the number of fifteen hundred copies of each such book or periodical if said copies shall contain notice of copyright in accordance with sections 10, 19, and 20 of this title and if ad interim copyright in said work shall have been obtained pursuant to section 22 of this title prior to the importation into the United States of any copy except those permitted by the provisions of section 107 of this title: *Provided further*, That the provisions of this section shall not affect the right of importation under the provisions of section 107 of this title.

History of 17 U.S.C. §16 (1909): July 30, 1947, ch. 391, 61 Stat. 657; June 3, 1949, ch. 171, §1, 63 Stat. 153; Aug. 31, 1954, ch. 1161, §2, 68 Stat. 1031.

§17. AFFIDAVIT TO ACCOMPANY COPIES

In the case of the book the copies so deposited shall be accompanied by an affidavit under the official seal of any officer authorized to administer oaths within the United States, duly made by the person claiming copyright or by his duly authorized agent or representative residing in the United States, or by the printer who has printed the book, setting forth that the copies deposited have been printed from type set within the limits of the United States or from plates made within the limits of the United States from type set therein; or, if the text be produced by lithographic process, or photo-engraving process, that such process was wholly performed within the limits of the United States and that the printing of the text and binding of the said book have also been performed within the limits of the United States. Such affidavit shall state also the place where and the establishment or establishments in which such type was set or plates were made or lithographic process, or photo-engraving process or printing and binding were performed and the date of the completion of the printing of the book or the date of publication.

History of 17 U.S.C. §17 (1909): July 30, 1947, ch. 391, 61 Stat. 657.

§18. MAKING FALSE AFFIDAVIT

Any person who, for the purpose of obtaining registration of a claim to copyright, shall knowingly make a false affidavit as to his having complied with the above conditions shall be deemed guilty of a misdemeanor, and upon conviction thereof shall be punished by a fine of not more than $1,000, and all of his rights and privileges under said copyright shall thereafter be forfeited.

History of 17 U.S.C. §18 (1909): July 30, 1947, ch. 391, 61 Stat. 658.

§19. NOTICE; FORM

The notice of copyright required by section 10 of this title shall consist either of the word "Copyright," the abbreviation "Copr.," or the symbol C, accompanied by the name of the copyright proprietor, and if the work be a printed literary, musical, or dramatic work, the notice shall include also the year in which the copyright was secured by publication. In the case, however, of copies of works specified in subsections (f) to (k), inclusive, of section 5 of this title, the notice may consist of the letter C enclosed within a circle, thus ©, accompanied by the initials, monogram, mark, or symbol of the copyright proprietor: *Provided*, That on some accessible portion of such copies or of the margin, back, permanent base, or pedestal, or of the substance on which such copies shall be mounted, his name shall appear. But in the case of works in which copyright was subsisting on July 1, 1909, the notice of copyright may be either in one of the forms prescribed herein or may consist of the following words: "Entered according to Act of Congress, in the year ____, by A.B., and in the office of the Librarian of Congress, at Washington, D.C.," or, at his option the word "Copyright," together with the year the copyright was entered and the name of the party by whom it was taken out; thus, "Copyright, 19__, by A.B."

In the case of reproductions of works specified in subsection (n) of section 5 of this title, the notice shall consist of the symbol (P) (the letter P in a circle), the year of first publication of the sound recording, and the name of the owner of copyright in the sound recording, or an abbreviation by which the name can be recognized, or a generally known alternative designation of the owner: *Provided*, That if the producer of the sound recording is named on the labels or containers of the reproduction, and if no other name appears in conjunction with the notice, his name shall be considered a part of the notice.

History of 17 U.S.C. §19 (1909): July 30, 1947, ch. 391, 61 Stat. 658; Aug. 31, 1954, ch. 1161, §3, 68 Stat. 1032; Oct. 15, 1971, P.L. 92-140, §1(c), 85 Stat. 391.

§20. NOTICE; PLACE OF APPLICATION OF, ONE NOTICE IN EACH VOLUME OR NUMBER OF NEWSPAPER OR PERIODICAL

The notice of copyright shall be applied, in the case of a book or other printed publication, upon its title page or the page immediately following, or if a periodical either upon the title page or upon the first page of text of each separate number or under the title heading, or if a musical work either upon its title page or the first page of music, or if a sound recording on the surface of reproductions thereof or on the label or container in such manner and location as to give reasonable notice of the claim of copyright. One notice of copyright in each volume or in each number of a newspaper or periodical published shall suffice.

History of 17 U.S.C. §20 (1909): July 30, 1947, ch. 391, 61 Stat. 658; Oct. 15, 1971, P.L. 92-140, §1(d), 85 Stat. 391.

§21. NOTICE; EFFECT OF ACCIDENTAL OMISSION FROM COPY OR COPIES

Where the copyright proprietor has sought to comply with the provisions of this title with respect to notice, the omission by accident or mistake of the prescribed notice from a particular copy or copies shall not invalidate the copyright or prevent recovery for infringement against any person who, after actual notice of the copyright, begins an undertaking to infringe it, but shall prevent the recovery of damages against an innocent infringer who has been misled by the omission of the notice; and in a suit for infringement no permanent injunction shall be had unless the copyright proprietor shall reimburse to the innocent infringer his reasonable outlay innocently incurred if the court, in its discretion, shall so direct.

History of 17 U.S.C. §21 (1909): July 30, 1947, ch. 391, 61 Stat. 658.

§22. AD INTERIM PROTECTION OF BOOK OR PERIODICAL PUBLISHED ABROAD

In the case of a book or periodical first published abroad in the English language the deposit in the Copyright Office, not later than six months after its publication abroad, of one complete copy of the foreign edition, with a request for the reservation of the copyright and a statement of the name and nationality of the author and of the copyright proprietor and of the date of publication of the said book or periodical, shall secure to the author or proprietor an ad interim copyright therein, which shall have all the force and effect given to copyright by this title, and shall endure until the expiration of five years after the date of first publication abroad.

History of 17 U.S.C. §22 (1909): July 30, 1947, ch. 391, 61 Stat. 659; June 3, 1949, ch. 171, §2, 63 Stat. 154.

§23. AD INTERIM PROTECTION OF BOOK OR PERIODICAL PUBLISHED ABROAD; EXTENSION TO FULL TERM

Whenever within the period of such ad interim protection an authorized edition of such books or periodicals shall be published within the United States, in accordance with the manufacturing provisions specified in section 16 of this title, and whenever the provisions of this title as to deposit of copies, registration, filing of affidavits, and the printing of the copyright notice shall have been duly complied with, the copyright shall be extended to endure in such book or periodical for the term provided in this title.

History of 17 U.S.C. §23 (1909): July 30, 1947, ch. 391, 61 Stat. 659; June 3, 1949, ch. 171, §3, 63 Stat. 154.

§24. DURATION, RENEWAL & EXTENSION

The copyright secured by this title shall endure for twenty-eight years from the date of first publication, whether the copyrighted work bears the author's true name or is published anonymously or under an assumed name: *Provided*, That in the case of any posthumous work or of any periodical, cyclopedic, or other composite work upon which the copyright was originally secured by the proprietor thereof, or of any work copyrighted by a corporate body (otherwise than as assignee or licensee of the individual author) or by an employer for whom such work is made for hire, the proprietor of such copyright shall be entitled to a renewal and extension of the copyright in such work for the further term of twenty-eight years when application for such renewal and extension shall have been made to the copyright office and duly registered therein within one year prior to the expiration of the original term of copyright: *And provided further*, That in the case of any other copyrighted work, including a contribution by an individual author to a periodical or to a cyclopedic or other composite work, the author of such work, if still living, or the widow, widower, or children of the author, if the author be not living, or if such author, widow, widower or children be not living, then the author's executors, or in the absence of a will, his next of kin shall be entitled to a renewal and extension of the copyright in such work for a further term of twenty-eight years when application for such renewal and extension shall have been made to the copyright office and duly registered therein within one year prior to the expiration of the original term of copyright: *And provided further*, That in default of the registration of such application for renewal and extension, the copyright in any work shall determine at the expiration of twenty-eight years from first publication.

History of 17 U.S.C. §24 (1909): July 30, 1947, ch. 391, 61 Stat. 659.

§25. RENEWAL OF COPYRIGHTS REGISTERED IN PATENT OFFICE UNDER REPEALED LAW

Subsisting copyrights originally registered in the Patent Office prior to July 1, 1940, under section 3 of the act of June 18, 1874, shall be subject to renewal in behalf of the proprietor upon application made to the Register of Copyrights within one year prior to the expiration of the original term of twenty-eight years.

History of 17 U.S.C. §25 (1909): July 30, 1947, ch. 391, 61 Stat. 659.

§26. TERMS DEFINED

In the interpretation and construction of this title "the date of publication" shall in the case of a work of which copies are reproduced for sale or distribution be held to be the earliest date when copies of the first authorized edition were placed on sale, sold, or publicly distributed by the proprietor of the copyright or under his authority, and the word "author" shall include an employer in the case of works made for hire.

For the purposes of this section and sections 10, 11, 13, 14, 21, 101, 106, 109, 209, 215, but not for any other purpose, a reproduction of a work described in subsection 5(n) shall be considered to be a copy thereof. "Sound recordings" are works that result from the fixation of a series of musical, spoken, or other sounds, but not including the sounds accompanying a motion picture. "Reproductions of sound recordings" are material objects in which sounds other than those accompanying a motion picture are fixed by any method now known or later developed, and from which the sounds can be perceived, reproduced, or otherwise communicated, either directly or with the aid of a machine or device, and include the "parts of instruments serving to reproduce mechanically the musical work," "mechanical reproductions," and "interchangeable parts, such as discs or tapes for use in mechanical music-producing machines" referred to in sections 1(e) and 101(e) of this title.

History of 17 U.S.C. §26 (1909): July 30, 1947, ch. 391, 61 Stat. 659; Oct. 15, 1971, P.L. 92-140, §1(e), 85 Stat. 391.

§27. COPYRIGHT DISTINCT FROM PROPERTY IN OBJECT COPYRIGHTED; EFFECT OF SALE OF OBJECT, & OF ASSIGNMENT OF COPYRIGHT

The copyright is distinct from the property in the material object copyrighted, and the sale or conveyance, by gift or otherwise, of the material object shall not of itself constitute a transfer of the copyright, nor shall the assignment of the copyright constitute a transfer of the title to the material object; but nothing in this title shall be deemed to forbid, prevent, or restrict the transfer of any copy of a copyrighted work the possession of which has been lawfully obtained.

History of 17 U.S.C. §27 (1909): July 30, 1947, ch. 391, 61 Stat. 660.

§28. ASSIGNMENTS & BEQUESTS

Copyright secured under this title or previous copyright laws of the United States may be assigned, granted, or mortgaged by an instrument in writing signed by the proprietor of the copyright, or may be bequeathed by will.

History of 17 U.S.C. §28 (1909): July 30, 1947, ch. 391, 61 Stat. 660.

§29. ASSIGNMENTS & BEQUESTS; EXECUTED IN FOREIGN COUNTRY; ACKNOWLEDGMENT & CERTIFICATE

Every assignment of copyright executed in a foreign country shall be acknowledged by the assignor before a consular officer or secretary of legation of the United States authorized by law to administer oaths or perform notarial acts. The certificate of such acknowledgment under the hand and official seal of such consular officer or secretary of legation shall be prima facie evidence of the execution of the instrument.

History of 17 U.S.C. §29 (1909): July 30, 1947, ch. 391, 61 Stat. 660.

§30. ASSIGNMENTS & BEQUESTS; RECORD

Every assignment of copyright shall be recorded in the copyright office within three calendar months after its execution in the United States or within six calendar months after its execution without the limits of the United States, in default of which it shall be void as against any subsequent purchaser or mortgagee for a valuable consideration, without notice, whose assignment has been duly recorded.

History of 17 U.S.C. §30 (1909): July 30, 1947, ch. 391, 61 Stat. 660.

§31. ASSIGNMENTS & BEQUESTS; CERTIFICATE OF RECORD

The Register of Copyrights shall, upon payment of the prescribed fee, record such assignment, and shall return it to the sender with a certificate of record attached under seal of the copyright office, and upon the payment of the fee prescribed by this title he shall furnish to any person requesting the same a certified copy thereof under the said seal.

History of 17 U.S.C. §31 (1909): July 30, 1947, ch. 391, 61 Stat. 660.

§32. ASSIGNMENTS & BEQUESTS; USE OF NAME OF ASSIGNEE IN NOTICE

When an assignment of the copyright in a specified book or other work has been recorded the assignee may substitute his name for that of the assignor in the statutory notice of copyright prescribed by this title.

History of 17 U.S.C. §32 (1909): July 30, 1947, ch. 391, 61 Stat. 660.

CHAPTER 2. INFRINGEMENT PROCEEDINGS

§101. INFRINGEMENT

If any person shall infringe the copyright in any work protected under the copyright laws of the United States such person shall be liable:

(a) Injunction.—To an injunction restraining such infringement;

(b) Damages and profits; amount; other remedies.—To pay to the copyright proprietor such damages as the copyright proprietor may have suffered due to the infringement, as well as all the profits which the infringer shall have made from such infringement, and in proving profits the plaintiff shall be required to prove sales only, and the defendant shall be required to prove every element of cost which he claims, or in lieu of actual damages and profits, such damages as to the court shall appear to be just, and in assessing such damages the court may, in its discretion, allow the amounts as hereinafter stated, but in case of a newspaper reproduction of a copyrighted photograph, such damages shall not exceed the sum of $200 nor be less than the sum of $50, and in the case of the infringement of an undramatized or nondramatic work by means of motion pictures, where the infringer shall show that he was not aware that he was infringing, and that such infringement could not have been reasonably foreseen, such damages shall not exceed the sum of $100; and in the case of an infringement of a copyrighted dramatic or dramatico-musical work by a maker of motion pictures and his agencies for distribution thereof to exhibitors, where such infringer shows that he was not aware that he was infringing a copyrighted work, and that such infringements could not reasonably have been foreseen, the entire sum of such damages recoverable by the copyright proprietor from such infringing maker and his agencies for the distribution to exhibitors of such infringing motion picture shall not exceed the sum of $5,000 nor be less than $250, and such damages shall in no other case exceed the sum of $5,000 nor be less than the sum of $250, and shall not be regarded as a penalty. But the foregoing exceptions shall not deprive the copyright proprietor of any other remedy given him under this law, nor shall the limitation as to the amount of recovery apply to infringements occurring after the actual notice to a defendant, either by service of process in a suit or other written notice served upon him.

First.—In the case of a painting, statue, or sculpture, $10 for every infringing copy made or sold by or found in the possession of the infringer or his agents or employees;

Second.—In the case of any work enumerated in section 5 of this title, except a painting, statue, or sculpture, $1 for every infringing copy made or sold by or found in the possession of the infringer or his agents or employees;

Third.—In the case of a lecture, sermon, or address, $50 for every infringing delivery;

Fourth.—In the case of a dramatic or dramatico-musical or a choral or orchestral composition, $100 for the first and $50 for every subsequent infringing performance; in the case of other musical compositions $10 for every infringing performance;

(e)[1] Impounding during action.—To deliver up on oath, to be impounded during the pendency of the action, upon such terms and conditions as the court may prescribe, all articles alleged to infringe a copyright;

(d) Destruction of infringing copies and plates.—To deliver up on oath for destruction all the infringing copies or devices, as well as all plates, molds, matrices, or other means for making such infringing copies as the court may order.

(e) Interchangeable parts for use in mechanical music-producing machines.—Interchangeable parts, such as discs or tapes for use in mechanical music-producing machines adapted to reproduce copyrighted musical works, shall be considered copies of the copyrighted musical works which they serve to reproduce mechanically for the purposes of this section 101 and sections 106 and 109 of this title, and the unauthorized manufacture, use, or sale of such interchangeable parts shall constitute an infringement of the copyrighted work rendering the infringer liable in accordance with all provisions of this title dealing with infringements of copyright and, in a case of willful infringement for profit, to criminal prosecution pursuant to section 104 of this title. Whenever any person, in the absence of a license agreement, intends to use a copyrighted musical composition upon the parts of instruments serving to reproduce mechanically the musical work, relying upon the compulsory license provision of this title, he shall serve notice of such intention, by registered mail, upon the copyright proprietor at his last address disclosed by the records of the copyright office, sending to the copyright office a duplicate of such notice.

1. **Editor's note:** Probably should be "(c)."

History of 17 U.S.C. §101 (1909): July 30, 1947, ch. 391, 61 Stat. 661; June 25, 1948, ch. 646, §39, 62 Stat. 992; Oct. 15, 1971, P.L. 92-140, §2, 85 Stat. 392.

§§102, 103. REPEALED

Repealed June 25, 1948, ch. 646, §39, 62 Stat. 992.

§104. WILLFUL INFRINGEMENT FOR PROFIT

(a) Except as provided in subsection (b), any person who willfully and for profit shall infringe any copyright secured by this title, or who shall knowingly and willfully aid or abet such infringement, shall be deemed guilty of a misdemeanor, and upon conviction thereof shall be punished by imprisonment for not exceeding one year or by a fine of not less than $100 nor more than $1,000, or both, in the discretion of the court: *Provided, however*, That nothing in this title shall be so construed as to prevent the performance of religious or secular works such as oratorios, cantatas, masses, or octavo choruses by public schools, church choirs, or vocal societies, rented, borrowed, or obtained from some public library, public school, church choir, school choir, or vocal society, provided the performance is given for charitable or educational purposes and not for profit.

(b) Any person who willfully and for profit shall infringe any copyright provided by section 1(f) of this title, or who should knowingly and willfully aid or abet such infringement, shall be fined not more than $25,000 or imprisoned not more than one year, or both, for the first offense and shall be fined not more than $50,000 or imprisoned not more than two years, or both for any subsequent offense.

History of 17 U.S.C. §104 (1909): July 30, 1947, ch. 391, 61 Stat. 662; Dec. 31, 1974, P.L. 93-573, §102, 88 Stat. 1873.

§105. FRAUDULENT NOTICE OF COPYRIGHT, OR REMOVAL OR ALTERATION OF NOTICE

Any person who, with fraudulent intent, shall insert or impress any notice of copyright required by this title, or words of the same purport, in or upon any uncopyrighted article or with fraudulent intent shall remove or alter the copyright notice upon any article duly copyrighted shall be guilty of a misdemeanor, punishable by a fine of not less than $100 and not more than $1,000. Any person who shall knowingly issue or sell any article bearing a notice of United States copyright which has not been copyrighted in this country, or who shall knowingly import any article bearing such notice or words of the same purport, which has not been copyrighted in this country, shall be liable to a fine of $100.

History of 17 U.S.C. §105 (1909): July 30, 1947, ch. 391, 61 Stat. 662.

§106. IMPORTATION OF ARTICLE BEARING FALSE NOTICE OR PIRATICAL COPIES OF COPYRIGHTED WORK

The importation into the United States of any article bearing a false notice of copyright when there is no existing copyright thereon in the United States, or of any piratical copies of any work copyrighted in the United States, is prohibited.

History of 17 U.S.C. §106 (1909): July 30, 1947, ch. 391, 61 Stat. 663.

§107. IMPORTATION, DURING EXISTENCE OF COPYRIGHT, OF PIRATICAL COPIES, OR OF COPIES NOT PRODUCED IN ACCORDANCE WITH SECTION 16 OF THIS TITLE

During the existence of the American copyright in any book, the importation into the United States of any piratical copies thereof or of any copies thereof (although authorized by the author or proprietor) which have not been produced in accordance with the manufacturing provisions specified in section 16 of this title, or any plates of the same not made from type set within the limits of the United States, or any copies thereof produced by lithographic or photo-engraving process not performed within the limits of the United States, in accordance with the provisions of section 16 of this title, is prohibited: *Provided, however*, That, except as regards piratical copies, such prohibition shall not apply:

(a) To works in raised characters for the use of the blind.

(b) To a foreign newspaper or magazine, although containing matter copyrighted in the United States printed or reprinted by authority of the copyright proprietor, unless such newspaper or magazine contains also copyright matter printed or reprinted without such authorization.

(c) To the authorized edition of a book in a foreign language or languages of which only a translation into English has been copyrighted in this country.

(d) To any book published abroad with the authorization of the author or copyright proprietor when imported under the circumstances stated in one of the four subdivisions following, that is to say:

First. When imported, not more than one copy at one time, for individual use and not for sale; but such privilege of importation shall not extend to a foreign reprint of a book by an American author copyrighted in the United States.

Second. When imported by the authority or for the use of the United States.

Third. When imported, for use and not for sale, not more than one copy of any such book in any one invoice, in good faith by or for any society or institution incorporated for educational, literary, philosophical, scientific, or religious purposes, or for the encouragement of the fine arts, or for any college, academy, school, or seminary of learning, or for any State, school, college, university, or free public library in the United States.

Fourth. When such books form parts of libraries or collections purchased en bloc for the use of societies, institutions, or libraries designated in the foregoing paragraph, or form parts of the libraries or personal baggage belonging to persons or families arriving from foreign countries and are not intended for sale: *Provided*, That copies imported as above may not lawfully be used in any way to violate the rights of the proprietor of the American copyright or annul or limit the copyright protection secured by this title, and such unlawful use shall be deemed an infringement of copyright.

History of 17 U.S.C. §107 (1909): July 30, 1947, ch. 391, 61 Stat. 663.

§108. FORFEITURE & DESTRUCTION OF ARTICLES PROHIBITED IMPORTATION

Any and all articles prohibited importation by this title which are brought into the United States from any foreign country (except in the mails) shall be seized and forfeited by like proceedings as those provided by law for the seizure and condemnation of property imported into the United States in violation of the customs revenue laws. Such articles when forfeited shall be destroyed in such manner as the Secretary of the Treasury or the court, as the case may be, shall direct: *Provided, however*, That all copies of authorized editions of copyright books imported in the mails or otherwise in violation of the provisions of this title may be exported and returned to the country of export whenever it is shown to the satisfaction of the Secretary of the Treasury, in a written application, that such importation does not involve willful negligence or fraud.

History of 17 U.S.C. §108 (1909): July 30, 1947, ch. 391, 61 Stat. 664.

§109. IMPORTATION OF PROHIBITED ARTICLES; REGULATIONS; PROOF OF DEPOSIT OF COPIES BY COMPLAINANTS

The Secretary of the Treasury and the Postmaster General are hereby empowered and required to make and enforce individually or jointly such rules and regulations as shall prevent the importation into the United States of articles prohibited importation by this title, and may require, as conditions precedent to exclusion of any work in which copyright is claimed, the copyright proprietor or any person claiming actual or potential injury by reason of actual or contemplated importations of copies of such work to file with the Post Office Department or the Treasury Department a certificate of the Register of Copyrights that the provisions of section 13 of this title have been fully complied with, and to give notice of such compliance to postmasters or to customs officers at the ports of entry in the United States in such form and accompanied by such exhibits as may be deemed necessary for the practical and efficient administration and enforcement of the provisions of sections 106 and 107 of this title.

History of 17 U.S.C. §109 (1909): July 30, 1947, ch. 391, 61 Stat. 664.

§§110, 111. REPEALED

Repealed June 25, 1948, ch. 646, §39, 62 Stat. 992.

§112. INJUNCTIONS; SERVICE & ENFORCEMENT

Any court mentioned in section 1338 of Title 28 or judge thereof shall have power, upon complaint filed by any party aggrieved, to grant injunctions to prevent and restrain the violation of any right secured by this title, according to the course and principles of courts of equity, on such terms as said court or judge may deem reasonable. Any injunction that may be granted restraining and enjoining the doing of anything forbidden by this title may be served on the part against whom such injunction may be granted anywhere in the United States, and shall be operative throughout the United States and be enforceable by proceedings in contempt or otherwise by any other court or judge possessing jurisdiction of the defendants.

History of 17 U.S.C. §112 (1909): July 30, 1947, ch. 391, 61 Stat. 664; Oct. 31, 1951, ch. 655, §16(c), 65 Stat. 716.

§113. TRANSMISSION OF CERTIFIED COPIES OF PAPERS FOR ENFORCEMENT OF INJUNCTION BY OTHER COURT

The clerk of the court, or judge granting the injunction, shall when required so to.[1] do by the court hearing the application to enforce said injunction, transmit without delay to said court a certified copy of all the papers in said cause that are on file in his office.

1. **Editor's note:** The period probably should not appear.

History of 17 U.S.C. §113 (1909): July 30, 1947, ch. 391, 61 Stat. 664.

§114. REVIEW OF ORDERS, JUDGMENTS, OR DECREES

The orders, judgments, or decrees of any court mentioned in section 1338 of Title 28 arising under the copyright laws of the United States may be reviewed on appeal in the manner and to the extent now provided by law for the review of cases determined in said courts, respectively.

History of 17 U.S.C. §114 (1909): July 30, 1947, ch. 391, 61 Stat. 665; Oct. 31, 1951, ch. 655, §17, 65 Stat. 717.

§115. LIMITATIONS

(a) Criminal proceedings.—No criminal proceedings shall be maintained under the provisions of this title unless the same is commenced within three years after the cause of action arose.

(b) Civil actions.—No civil action shall be maintained under the provisions of this title unless the same is commenced within three years after the claim accrued.

History of 17 U.S.C. §115 (1909): July 30, 1947, ch. 391, 61 Stat. 665; Sept. 7, 1957, P.L. 85-313, §1, 71 Stat. 633.

§116. COSTS; ATTORNEY'S FEES

In all actions, suits, or proceedings under this title, except when brought by or against the United States or any officer thereof, full costs shall be allowed, and the court may award to the prevailing party a reasonable attorney's fee as part of the costs.

History of 17 U.S.C. §116 (1909): July 30, 1947, ch. 391, 61 Stat. 665.

CHAPTER 3. COPYRIGHT OFFICE

§201. COPYRIGHT OFFICE; PRESERVATION OF RECORDS

All records and other things relating to copyrights required by law to be preserved shall be kept and preserved in the copyright office, Library of Congress, District of Columbia, and shall be under the control of the register of copyrights, who shall under the direction and supervision of the Librarian of Congress, perform all the duties relating to the registration of copyrights.

History of 17 U.S.C. §201 (1909): July 30, 1947, ch. 391, 61 Stat. 665.

§202. REGISTER, ASSISTANT REGISTER, & SUBORDINATES

There shall be appointed by the Librarian of Congress a Register of Copyrights, and one Assistant Register of Copyrights, who shall have authority during the absence of the Register of Copyrights to attach the copyright office seal to all papers issued from the said office and to sign such certificates and other papers as may be necessary. There shall also be appointed by the Librarian such subordinate assistants to the register as may from time to time be authorized by law.

History of 17 U.S.C. §202 (1909): July 30, 1947, ch. 391, 61 Stat. 665.

§203. REGISTER, ASSISTANT REGISTER, & SUBORDINATES; DEPOSIT OF MONEYS RECEIVED; REPORTS

The Register of Copyrights shall make daily deposits in some bank in the District of Columbia, designated for this purpose by the Secretary of the Treasury as a national depository, of all moneys received to be applied as copyright fees, and shall make weekly deposits with the Secretary of the Treasury, in such manner as the latter shall direct, of all copyright fees actually applied under the provisions of this title, and annual deposits of sums received which it has not been possible to apply as copyright fees or to return to the remitters, and shall also make monthly reports to the Secretary of the Treasury and to the Librarian of Congress of the applied copyright fees for each calendar month, together with a statement of all remittances received, trust funds on hand, moneys refunded, and unapplied balances.

All moneys deposited with the Secretary of the Treasury under this section shall be credited to the appropriation for necessary expenses of the Copyright Office.

History of 17 U.S.C. §203 (1909): July 30, 1947, ch. 391, 61 Stat. 665; Aug. 5, 1977, P.L. 95-94, §406, 91 Stat. 682.

§204. REPEALED

Repealed June 6, 1972, P.L. 92-310, §205(a), 86 Stat. 203.

§205. REGISTER, ASSISTANT REGISTER, & SUBORDINATES; ANNUAL REPORT

The Register of Copyrights shall make an annual report to the Librarian of Congress, to be printed in the annual report on the Library of Congress, of all copyright business for the previous fiscal year, including the number and kind of works which have been deposited in the copyright office during the fiscal year, under the provisions of this title.

History of 17 U.S.C. §205 (1909): July 30, 1947, ch. 391, 61 Stat. 666.

§206. SEAL OF COPYRIGHT OFFICE

The seal used in the copyright office on July 1, 1909, shall be the seal of the copyright office, and by it all papers issued from the copyright office requiring authentication shall be authenticated.

History of 17 U.S.C. §206 (1909): July 30, 1947, ch. 391, 61 Stat. 666.

§207. RULES FOR REGISTRATION OF CLAIMS

Subject to the approval of the Librarian of Congress, the Register of Copyrights shall be authorized to make rules and regulations for the registration of claims to copyright as provided by this title.

History of 17 U.S.C. §207 (1909): July 30, 1947, ch. 391, 61 Stat. 666.

§208. RECORD BOOKS IN COPYRIGHT OFFICE

The Register of Copyrights shall provide and keep such record books in the copyright office as are required to carry out the provisions of this title, and whenever deposit has been made in the copyright office of a copy of any work under the provisions of this title he shall make entry thereof.

History of 17 U.S.C. §208 (1909): July 30, 1947, ch. 391, 61 Stat. 666.

§209. CERTIFICATE OF REGISTRATION; EFFECT AS EVIDENCE; RECEIPT FOR COPIES DEPOSITED

In the case of each entry the person recorded as the claimant of the copyright shall be entitled to a certificate of registration under seal of the copyright office, to contain the name and address of said claimant, the name of the country of which the author of the work is a citizen or subject, and when an alien author domiciled in the United States at the time of said registration, then a statement of that fact, including his place of domicile, the name of the author (when the records of the copyright office shall show the same), the title of the work which is registered for which copyright is claimed, the date of the deposit of the copies of such work, the date of publication if the work has been reproduced in copies for sale, or publicly distributed, and such marks as to class designation and entry number as shall fully identify the entry. In the case of a book, the certificate shall also state the receipt of the affidavit, as provided by section 17 of this title, and the date of the completion of the printing, or the date of the publication of the book, as stated in the said affidavit. The Register of Copyrights shall prepare a printed form for the said certificate, to be filled out in each case as above provided for in the case of all registrations made after July 1, 1909, and in the case of all previous registrations so far as the copyright office record books shall show such facts, which certificate, sealed with the seal of the copyright office, shall, upon payment of the prescribed fee, be given to any person making application for the same. Said certificate shall be admitted in any court as prima facie evidence of the facts stated therein. In addition to such certificate the register of copyrights shall furnish, upon request, without additional fee, a receipt for the copies of the work deposited to complete the registration.

History of 17 U.S.C. §209 (1909): July 30, 1947, ch. 391, 61 Stat. 666.

§210. CATALOG OF COPYRIGHT ENTRIES; EFFECT AS EVIDENCE

The Register of Copyrights shall fully index all copyright registrations and assignments and shall print at periodic intervals a catalog of the titles of articles deposited and registered for copyright, together with suitable indexes, and at stated intervals shall print complete and indexed catalog for each class of copyright entries, and may thereupon, if expedient, destroy the original manuscript catalog cards containing the titles included in such printed volumes and representing the entries made during such intervals. The current catalog of copyright entries and the index volumes herein provided for shall be admitted in any court as prima facie evidence of the facts stated therein as regards any copyright registration.

History of 17 U.S.C. §210 (1909): July 30, 1947, ch. 391, 61 Stat. 666.

§211. CATALOG OF COPYRIGHT ENTRIES; EFFECT AS EVIDENCE; DISTRIBUTION & SALE; DISPOSAL OF PROCEEDS

The said printed current catalogs as they are issued shall be promptly distributed by the Superintendent of Documents to the collectors of customs of the United States and to the postmasters of all exchange offices of receipt of foreign mails, in accordance with revised list of such collectors of customs and postmasters prepared by the Secretary of the Treasury and the Postmaster General, and they shall also be furnished in whole or in part to all parties desiring them at a price to be determined by the Register of Copyrights for each part of the catalog not exceeding $75 for the complete yearly catalog of copyright entries. The consolidated catalogs and indexes shall also be supplied to all persons ordering them at such prices as may be fixed by the Register of Copyrights, and all subscriptions for the catalogs shall be received by the Superintendent of Documents, who shall forward the said publications; and the moneys thus received shall be paid into the Treasury of the United States and accounted for under such laws and Treasury regulations as shall be in force at the time.

History of 17 U.S.C. §211 (1909): July 30, 1947, ch. 391, 61 Stat. 667; Apr. 27, 1948, ch. 236, §1, 62 Stat. 202; Oct. 27, 1965, P.L. 89-297, §1, 79 Stat. 1072.

§212. RECORDS & WORKS DEPOSITED IN COPYRIGHT OFFICE OPEN TO PUBLIC INSPECTION; TAKING COPIES OF ENTRIES

The record books of the copyright office, together with the indexes to such record books, and all works deposited and retained in the copyright office, shall be open to public inspection; and copies may be taken of the copyright entries actually made in such record books, subject to such safeguards and regulations as shall be prescribed by the Register of Copyrights and approved by the Librarian of Congress.

History of 17 U.S.C. §212 (1909): July 30, 1947, ch. 391, 61 Stat. 667.

§213. DISPOSITION OF ARTICLES DEPOSITED IN OFFICE

Of the articles deposited in the copyright office under the provisions of the copyright laws of the United States, the Librarian of Congress shall determine what books and other articles shall be transferred to the permanent collections of the Library of Congress, including the law library, and what other books or articles shall be placed in the reserve collections of the Library of Congress for sale or exchange, or be transferred to other governmental libraries in the District of Columbia for use therein.

History of 17 U.S.C. §213 (1909): July 30, 1947, ch. 391, 61 Stat. 667.

§214. DESTRUCTION OF ARTICLES DEPOSITED IN OFFICE REMAINING UNDISPOSED OF; REMOVAL OF BY AUTHOR OR PROPRIETOR; MANUSCRIPTS OF UNPUBLISHED WORKS

Of any articles undisposed of as above provided, together with all titles and correspondence relating thereto, the Librarian of Congress and the Register of Copyrights jointly shall, at suitable intervals, determine what of these received during any period of years it is desirable or useful to preserve in the permanent files of the copyright office, and, after due notice as hereinafter provided, may within their discretion cause the remaining articles and other things to be destroyed: *Provided*, That there shall be printed in the Catalog of Copyright Entries from February to November, inclusive, a statement of the years of receipt of such articles and a notice to permit any author, copyright proprietor, or other lawful claimant to claim and remove before the expiration of the month of December of that year anything found which relates to any of his productions deposited or registered for copyright within the period of years stated, not reserved or disposed of as provided for in this title. No manuscript of an unpublished work shall be destroyed during its term of copyright without specific notice to the copyright proprietor of record, permitting him to claim and remove it.

History of 17 U.S.C. §214 (1909): July 30, 1947, ch. 391, 61 Stat. 667.

§215. FEES

The Register of Copyrights shall receive, and the persons to whom the services designated are rendered shall pay, the following fees:

For the registration of a claim to copyright in any work, including a print or label used for articles of merchandise, $6; for the registration of a claim to renewal of copyright, $4; which fees shall include a certificate for each registration: *Provided*, That only one registration fee shall be required in the case of several volumes of the same book published and deposited at the same time: *And provided further*, That with respect to works of foreign origin, in lieu of payment of the copyright fee of $6 together with one copy of the work and application, the foreign author or proprietor may at any time within six months from the date of first publication abroad deposit in the Copyright Office an application for registration and two copies of the work which shall be accompanied by a catalog card in form and content satisfactory to the Register of Copyrights.

For every additional certificate of registration, $2.

For certifying a copy of an application for registration of copyright, and for all other certifications, $3.

For recording every assignment, agreement, power of attorney or other paper not exceeding six pages, $5; for each additional page or less, 50 cents; for each title over one in the paper recorded, 50 cents additional.

For recording a notice of use, or notice of intention to use, $3, for each notice of not more than five titles; and 50 cents for each additional title.

For any requested search of Copyright Office records, works deposited, or other available material, or services rendered in connection therewith, $5, for each hour of time consumed.

History of 17 U.S.C. §215 (1909): July 30, 1947, ch. 391, 61 Stat. 668; Apr. 27, 1948, ch. 236, §2, 62 Stat. 202; June 3, 1949, ch. 171, §4, 63 Stat. 154; Oct. 27, 1965, P.L. 89-297, §2, 79 Stat. 1072.

§216. WHEN THE DAY FOR TAKING ACTION FALLS ON SATURDAY, SUNDAY, OR A HOLIDAY

When the last day for making any deposit or application, or for paying any fee, or for delivering any other material to the Copyright Office falls on Saturday, Sunday, or a holiday within the District of Columbia, such action may be taken on the next succeeding business day.

History of 17 U.S.C. §216 (1909): Apr. 13, 1954, ch. 137, §1, 68 Stat. 52.

Title 35. Patents

Table of Contents

TITLE 35. PATENTS

TABLE OF CONTENTS

PATENTS

TITLE 35. PATENTS

TABLE OF CONTENTS

35 U.S.C. §	AIA § (P.L. 112-29)	Statutes at Large
2	21(a), 25	125 Stat. 335, 337
3	20(i)(1), 21(b)	125 Stat. 334, 336
6	7(a)(1)	125 Stat. 313
32	3(k), 9(a)	125 Stat. 291, 316
41	11(a)-(e)	125 Stat. 320-323
42	22(a)	125 Stat. 336
42(c)	22(a)	125 Stat. 336
100	3(a)	125 Stat. 285
102	3(b)(1)	125 Stat. 285
103	3(c)	125 Stat. 287
104	3(d)	125 Stat. 287
111	3(e)(2), 4(a)(3), (d)	125 Stat. 287, 295, 296
112	4(c)	125 Stat. 296
115	4(a)(1)	125 Stat. 293
116	20(a)	125 Stat. 333
118	4(b)(1)	125 Stat. 296
119	3(g)(6)	125 Stat. 288
119(e)(1)	15(b)	125 Stat. 328
120	3(f), 15(b)	125 Stat. 288, 328
121	4(a)(2)	125 Stat. 295
122	8(a)	125 Stat. 315
123	10(g)	125 Stat. 318
134	3(j)(1), (3), 7(b)	125 Stat. 290, 313
135	3(i)	125 Stat. 289
141	7(c)(1)	125 Stat. 314
143	7(c)(3)	125 Stat. 314
145	3(j)(1), 9(a)	125 Stat. 290, 316
146	3(j)(1), (2)(A), (4), 9(a)	125 Stat. 290, 316
154	3(j)(1), (2)(B)	125 Stat. 290
154(b)(4)(A)	9(a)	125 Stat. 316
155	20(k)	125 Stat. 335
155A	20(k)	125 Stat. 335
156(d)(1)	37(a)	125 Stat. 341
157	3(e)(1)	125 Stat. 287
172	3(g)(1)	125 Stat. 288

35 U.S.C. §	AIA § (P.L. 112-29)	Statutes at Large
184	20(b)	125 Stat. 333
185	20(c)	125 Stat. 333
202	3(g)(7), 20(i)(2)	125 Stat. 288, 334
202(c)(7)(E)(i)	13(a)	125 Stat. 327
209	20(i)(3)	125 Stat. 335
251	4(b)(2), 20(d)	125 Stat. 296, 333
253	20(e)	125 Stat. 334
256	20(f)	125 Stat. 334
257	12(a)	125 Stat. 325
273	5(a)	125 Stat. 297
282	20(g)	125 Stat. 334
282(b)(3)	15(a)	125 Stat. 328
287	3(g)(2), 20(i)(4)	125 Stat. 288, 335
287(a)	16(a)(1)	125 Stat. 328
288	20(h)	125 Stat. 334
291	3(h)(1)	125 Stat. 288
292	16(b)(1)-(3)	125 Stat. 329
293	9(a)	125 Stat. 316
298	17(a)	125 Stat. 329
299	19(d)(1)	125 Stat. 332
301	6(g)(1)	125 Stat. 311
303	6(h)(1)(A)	125 Stat. 312
305	3(j)(1)	125 Stat. 290
306	6(h)(2)(A)	125 Stat. 312
311 (new)	6(a)	125 Stat. 299
312 (old)	6(c)(3)(A)(i)	125 Stat. 305
312 (new)	6(a)	125 Stat. 300
313 (old)	6(c)(3)(A)(ii)	125 Stat. 305
313 (new)	6(a)	125 Stat. 300
314 (new)	6(a)	125 Stat. 300
315 (new)	6(a)	125 Stat. 300
316 (new)	6(a)	125 Stat. 302
317 (new)	6(a)	125 Stat. 303
318 (new)	6(a)	125 Stat. 304
319 (new)	6(a)	125 Stat. 304

35 U.S.C. §	AIA § (P.L. 112-29)	Statutes at Large
321	6(d)	125 Stat. 306
322	6(d)	125 Stat. 306
323	6(d)	125 Stat. 306
324	6(d)	125 Stat. 306
325	6(d)	125 Stat. 307
326	6(d)	125 Stat. 308
327	6(d)	125 Stat. 310
328	6(d)	125 Stat. 310
329	6(d)	125 Stat. 311
363	3(g)(3)	125 Stat. 288
371	20(i)(5)	125 Stat. 335
374	3(g)(4)	125 Stat. 288
375(a)	3(g)(5)	125 Stat. 288

TITLE 35. PATENTS

PART I. UNITED STATES PATENT & TRADEMARK OFFICE

CHAPTER 1. ESTABLISHMENT, OFFICERS & EMPLOYEES, FUNCTIONS

§1. ESTABLISHMENT

(a) Establishment.—The United States Patent and Trademark Office is established as an agency of the United States, within the Department of Commerce. In carrying out its functions, the United States Patent and Trademark Office shall be subject to the policy direction of the Secretary of Commerce, but otherwise shall retain responsibility for decisions regarding the management and administration of its operations and shall exercise independent control of its budget allocations and expenditures, personnel decisions and processes, procurements, and other administrative and management functions in accordance with this title and applicable provisions of law. Those operations designed to grant and issue patents and those operations which are designed to facilitate the registration of trademarks shall be treated as separate operating units within the Office.

(b) Offices.—The United States Patent and Trademark Office shall maintain its principal office in the metropolitan Washington, D.C., area, for the service of process and papers and for the purpose of carrying out its functions. The United States Patent and Trademark Office shall be deemed, for purposes of venue in civil actions, to be a resident of the district in which its principal office is located, except where jurisdiction is otherwise provided by law. The United States Patent and Trademark Office may establish satellite offices in such other places in the United States as it considers necessary and appropriate in the conduct of its business.

(c) Reference.—For purposes of this title, the United States Patent and Trademark Office shall also be referred to as the "Office" and the "Patent and Trademark Office."

History of 35 U.S.C. §1: July 19, 1952, ch. 950, §1, 66 Stat. 792; Jan. 2, 1975, P.L. 93-596, §1, 88 Stat. 1949; Nov. 29, 1999, P.L. 106-113, §1000(a)(9), 113 Stat. 1536.

§2. POWERS & DUTIES

(a) In general.—The United States Patent and Trademark Office, subject to the policy direction of the Secretary of Commerce—

(1) shall be responsible for the granting and issuing of patents and the registration of trademarks; and

(2) shall be responsible for disseminating to the public information with respect to patents and trademarks.

(b) Specific powers.—The Office—

(1) shall adopt and use a seal of the Office, which shall be judicially noticed and with which letters patent, certificates of trademark registrations, and papers issued by the Office shall be authenticated;

(2) may establish regulations, not inconsistent with law, which—

(A) shall govern the conduct of proceedings in the Office;

(B) shall be made in accordance with section 553 of title 5;

(C) shall facilitate and expedite the processing of patent applications, particularly those which can be filed, stored, processed, searched, and retrieved electronically, subject to the provisions of section 122 relating to the confidential status of applications;

(D) may govern the recognition and conduct of agents, attorneys, or other persons representing applicants or other parties before the Office, and may require them, before being recognized as representatives of applicants or other persons, to show that they are of good moral character and reputation and are possessed of the necessary qualifications to render to applicants or other persons valuable service, advice, and assistance in the presentation or prosecution of their applications or other business before the Office;

(E) shall recognize the public interest in continuing to safeguard broad access to the United States patent system through the reduced fee structure for small entities under section 41(h)(1);

(F) provide for the development of a performance-based process that includes quantitative and qualitative measures and standards for evaluating cost-effectiveness and is consistent with the principles of impartiality and competitiveness; and

(G) may, subject to any conditions prescribed by the Director and at the request of the patent applicant, provide for prioritization of examination of applications for products, processes, or technologies that are important to the national economy or national competitiveness without recovering the aggregate extra cost of providing such prioritization, notwithstanding section 41 or any other provision of law;

(3) may acquire, construct, purchase, lease, hold, manage, operate, improve, alter, and renovate any real, personal, or mixed property, or any interest therein, as it considers necessary to carry out its functions;

(4)(A) may make such purchases, contracts for the construction, maintenance, or management and operation of facilities, and contracts for supplies or services, without regard to the provisions of subtitle I and chapter 33 of title 40, division C (except sections 3302, 3501(b), 3509, 3906, 4710, and 4711) of subtitle I of title 41, and the McKinney-Vento Homeless Assistance Act (42 U.S.C. 11301 et seq.); and

(B) may enter into and perform such purchases and contracts for printing services, including the process of composition, platemaking, presswork, silk screen processes, binding, microform, and the products of such processes, as it considers necessary to carry out the functions of the Office, without regard to sections 501 through 517 and 1101 through 1123 of title 44;

(5) may use, with their consent, services, equipment, personnel, and facilities of other departments, agencies, and instrumentalities of the Federal Government, on a reimbursable basis, and cooperate with such other departments, agencies, and instrumentalities in the establishment and use of services, equipment, and facilities of the Office;

(6) may, when the Director determines that it is practicable, efficient, and cost-effective to do so, use, with the consent of the United States and the agency, instrumentality, Patent and Trademark Office, or international organization concerned, the services, records, facilities, or personnel of any State or local government agency or instrumentality or foreign patent and trademark office or international organization to perform functions on its behalf;

(7) may retain and use all of its revenues and receipts, including revenues from the sale, lease, or disposal of any real, personal, or mixed property, or any interest therein, of the Office;

(8) shall advise the President, through the Secretary of Commerce, on national and certain international intellectual property policy issues;

(9) shall advise Federal departments and agencies on matters of intellectual property policy in the United States and intellectual property protection in other countries;

(10) shall provide guidance, as appropriate, with respect to proposals by agencies to assist foreign governments and international intergovernmental organizations on matters of intellectual property protection;

(11) may conduct programs, studies, or exchanges of items or services regarding domestic and international intellectual property law and the effectiveness of intellectual property protection domestically and throughout the world, and the Office is authorized to expend funds to cover the subsistence expenses and travel-related expenses, including per diem, lodging costs, and transportation costs, of persons attending such programs who are not Federal employees;

(12)(A) shall advise the Secretary of Commerce on programs and studies relating to intellectual property policy that are conducted, or authorized to be conducted, cooperatively with foreign intellectual property offices and international intergovernmental organizations; and

(B) may conduct programs and studies described in subparagraph (A); and

(13)(A) in coordination with the Department of State, may conduct programs and studies cooperatively with foreign intellectual property offices and international intergovernmental organizations; and

(B) with the concurrence of the Secretary of State, may authorize the transfer of not to exceed $100,000 in any year to the Department of State for the purpose of making special payments to international intergovernmental organizations for studies and programs for advancing international cooperation concerning patents, trademarks, and other matters.

(c) Clarification of specific powers—

(1) The special payments under subsection (b)(13)(B) shall be in addition to any other payments or contributions to international organizations described in subsection (b)(13)(B) and shall not be subject to any limitations imposed by law on the amounts of such other payments or contributions by the United States Government.

(2) Nothing in subsection (b) shall derogate from the duties of the Secretary of State or from the duties of the United States Trade Representative as set forth in section 141 of the Trade Act of 1974 (19 U.S.C. 2171).

(3) Nothing in subsection (b) shall derogate from the duties and functions of the Register of Copyrights or otherwise alter current authorities relating to copyright matters.

(4) In exercising the Director's powers under paragraphs (3) and (4)(A) of subsection (b), the Director shall consult with the Administrator of General Services.

(5) In exercising the Director's powers and duties under this section, the Director shall consult with the Register of Copyrights on all copyright and related matters.

(d) Construction.—Nothing in this section shall be construed to nullify, void, cancel, or interrupt any pending request-for-proposal let or contract issued by the General Services Administration for the specific purpose of relocating or leasing space to the United States Patent and Trademark Office.

History of 35 U.S.C. §2: July 19, 1952, ch. 950, §1, 66 Stat. 792; Jan. 2, 1975, P.L. 93-596, §1, 88 Stat. 1949; Nov. 29, 1999, P.L. 106-113, §1000(a)(9), 113 Stat. 1536; Nov. 2, 2002, P.L. 107-273, §13206(a)(1), 116 Stat. 1904; Aug. 21, 2002, P.L. 108-178, §4(g), 117 Stat. 2641; Jan. 4, 2011, P.L. 111-350, §5(i)(1), 124 Stat. 3849; Sept. 16, 2011, P.L. 112-29, §§20(j)(1), 21(a), 25, 125 Stat. 335, 337; Jan. 14, 2013, P.L. 112-274, §1(g), 126 Stat. 2456.

See also 5 U.S.C. §553.

ANNOTATIONS

In re Queen's Univ., 820 F.3d 1287, 1298, 118 U.S.P.Q.2d 1221, 1229 (Fed.Cir.2016). "To the extent Congress has authorized non-attorney patent agents to engage in the practice of law before the [PTO], reason and experience compel us to recognize a patent-agent privilege that is coextensive with the rights granted to patent agents by Congress."

In re Lovin, 652 F.3d 1349, 1353-54, 99 U.S.P.Q.2d 1373, 1376-77 (Fed.Cir.2011). "[W]e [have] held that the PTO's interpretation of its own regulations is entitled to 'substantial deference' unless the interpretation is 'plainly erroneous or inconsistent with the regulation.' [¶] Nonetheless, ... the PTO must still follow judicial interpretations of PTO regulations set forth in the decisions of our court. However, the Supreme Court has made clear that this obligation is not absolute. [A] judicial interpretation would trump an agency's construction only if the judicial precedent 'unambiguously foreclose[d] the agency's interpretation, and therefore contain[ed] no gap for the agency to fill.' [W]e are obligated to follow our earlier judicial decisions—in the face of a new agency interpretation—only if we had found that the language in that decision 'unambiguously foreclose[d]' the Board's interpretation."

Cooper Techs. v. Dudas, 536 F.3d 1330, 1335, 87 U.S.P.Q.2d 1705, 1709-11 (Fed.Cir.2008). "To comply with §2(b)(2)(A), a [PTO] rule must be procedural—i.e., it must govern the conduct of proceedings in the [PTO]. *At F.3d 1336:* We have also previously held that ... §2(b)(2) does not authorize the [PTO] to issue substantive rules. A rule is substantive when it effects a change in existing law or policy which affects individual rights and obligations. In contrast, a rule which merely clarifies or explains existing law or regulations is interpretative. *At F.3d 1337:* An agency's interpretive rule of a statute relating to matters of procedure, subject to notice and comment if required, need not be published in the [C.F.R.] to be entitled to deference." (Internal quotes omitted.)

Bender v. Dudas, 490 F.3d 1361, 1368, 83 U.S.P.Q.2d 1065, 1071 (Fed.Cir.2007). "To the extent the phrase 'before the Office' in [35 U.S.C. §§2(b)(2)(D)] and 32 is ambiguous, we defer to the PTO's reasonable interpretation of that phrase as authorizing regulations that govern a patent attorney's communications with and disclosures to a client in connection with the prosecution of applications before the PTO."

Lacavera v. Dudas, 441 F.3d 1380, 1383, 77 U.S.P.Q.2d 1955, 1957 (Fed.Cir.2006). "[P] argues that the PTO exceeded the authority granted to it by 35 U.S.C. §2(b)(2) in promulgating regulations that take into account visa restrictions when determining whether or not to grant full recognition. [¶] It was reasonable for the PTO to interpret legal authority to render service as being a necessary qualification. Accordingly, it was reasonable for the PTO to enact regulations that limit an alien's ability to practice before it to those activities in which the alien may lawfully engage. Therefore, the PTO did not exceed its statutory authority in promulgating the regulations in question."

§3. OFFICERS & EMPLOYEES

(a) Under Secretary and Director—

(1) In general.—The powers and duties of the United States Patent and Trademark Office shall be vested in an Under Secretary of Commerce for Intellectual Property and Director of the United States Patent and Trademark Office (in this title referred to as the "Director"), who shall be a citizen of the United States and who shall be appointed by the President, by and with the advice and consent of the Senate. The Director shall be a person who has a professional background and experience in patent or trademark law.

(2) Duties—

(A) In general.—The Director shall be responsible for providing policy direction and management supervision for the Office and for the issuance of patents and the registration of trademarks. The Director shall perform these duties in a fair, impartial, and equitable manner.

(B) Consulting with the Public Advisory Committees.—The Director shall consult with the Patent Public Advisory Committee established in section 5 on a regular basis on matters relating to the patent operations of the Office, shall consult with the Trademark Public Advisory Committee established in section 5 on a regular basis on matters relating to the trademark operations of the Office, and shall consult with the respective Public Advisory Committee before submitting budgetary proposals to the Office of Management and Budget or changing or proposing to change patent or trademark user fees or patent or trademark regulations which are subject to the requirement to provide notice and opportunity for public comment under section 553 of title 5, as the case may be.

(3) Oath.—The Director shall, before taking office, take an oath to discharge faithfully the duties of the Office.

(4) Removal.—The Director may be removed from office by the President. The President shall provide notification of any such removal to both Houses of Congress.

(b) Officers and employees of the Office—

(1) Deputy Under Secretary and Deputy Director.—The Secretary of Commerce, upon nomination by the Director, shall appoint a Deputy Under Secretary of Commerce for Intellectual Property and Deputy Director of the United States Patent and Trademark Office who shall be vested with the authority to act in the capacity of the Director in the event of the absence or incapacity of the Director. The Deputy Director shall be a citizen of the United States who has a professional background and experience in patent or trademark law.

(2) Commissioners—

(A) Appointment and duties.—The Secretary of Commerce shall appoint a Commissioner for Patents and a Commissioner for Trademarks, without regard to chapter 33, 51, or 53 of title 5. The Commissioner for Patents shall be a citizen of the United States with demonstrated management ability and professional background and experience in patent law and serve for a term of 5 years. The Commissioner for Trademarks shall be a citizen of the United States with demonstrated management ability and professional background and experience in trademark law and serve for a term of 5 years. The Commissioner for Patents and the Commissioner for Trademarks shall serve as the chief operating officers for the operations of the Office relating to patents and trademarks, respectively, and shall be responsible for the management and direction of all aspects of the activities of the Office that affect the administration of patent and trademark operations, respectively. The Secretary may reappoint a Commissioner to subsequent terms of 5 years as long as the performance of the Commissioner as set forth in the performance agreement in subparagraph (B) is satisfactory.

(B) Salary and performance agreement.—The Commissioners shall be paid an annual rate of basic pay not to exceed the maximum rate of basic pay for the Senior Executive Service established under section 5382 of title 5, including any applicable locality-based comparability payment that may be authorized under section 5304(h)(2)(C) of title 5. The compensation of the Commissioners shall be considered, for purposes of section 207(c)(2)(A) of title 18, to be the equivalent of that described under clause (ii) of section 207(c)(2)(A) of title 18. In addition, the Commissioners may receive a bonus in an amount of up to, but not in excess of, 50 percent of the Commissioners' annual rate of basic pay, based upon an evaluation by the Secretary of Commerce, acting through the Director, of the Commissioners' performance as defined in an annual performance agreement between the Commissioners and the Secretary. The annual performance agreements shall incorporate measurable organization and individual goals in key operational areas as delineated in an annual performance plan agreed to by the Commissioners and the Secretary. Payment of a bonus under this subparagraph may be made to the Commissioners only to the extent that such payment does not cause the Commissioners' total aggregate compensation in a calendar year to equal or exceed the amount of the salary of the Vice President under section 104 of title 3.

(C) Removal.—The Commissioners may be removed from office by the Secretary for misconduct or nonsatisfactory performance under the performance agreement described in subparagraph (B), without regard to the provisions of title 5. The Secretary shall provide notification of any such removal to both Houses of Congress.

(3) Other officers and employees.—The Director shall—

(A) appoint such officers, employees (including attorneys), and agents of the Office as the Director considers necessary to carry out the functions of the Office; and

(B) define the title, authority, and duties of such officers and employees and delegate to them such of the powers vested in the Office as the Director may determine.

The Office shall not be subject to any administratively or statutorily imposed limitation on positions or personnel, and no positions or personnel of the Office shall be taken into account for purposes of applying any such limitation.

(4) Training of examiners.—The Office shall submit to the Congress a proposal to provide an incentive program to retain as employees patent and trademark examiners of the primary examiner grade or higher who are eligible for retirement, for the sole purpose of training patent and trademark examiners.

(5) National security positions.—The Director, in consultation with the Director of the Office of Personnel Management, shall maintain a program for identifying national security positions and providing for appropriate security clearances, in order to maintain the secrecy of certain inventions, as described in section 181, and to prevent disclosure of sensitive and strategic information in the interest of national security.

(6) Administrative patent judges and administrative trademark judges.—The Director may fix the rate of basic pay for the administrative patent judges appointed pursuant to section 6 and the administrative trademark judges appointed pursuant to section 17 of the Trademark Act of 1946 (15 U.S.C. 1067) at not greater than the rate of basic pay payable for level III of the Executive Schedule under section 5314 of title 5. The payment of a rate of basic pay under this paragraph shall not be subject to the pay limitation under section 5306(e) or 5373 of title 5.

(c) Continued applicability of title 5.—Officers and employees of the Office shall be subject to the provisions of title 5, relating to Federal employees.

(d) Adoption of existing labor agreements.—The Office shall adopt all labor agreements which are in effect, as of the day before the effective date of the Patent and Trademark Office Efficiency Act, with respect to such Office (as then in effect).

(e) Carryover of personnel—

(1) From PTO.—Effective as of the effective date of the Patent and Trademark Office Efficiency Act, all officers and employees of the Patent and Trademark Office on the day before such effective date shall become officers and employees of the Office, without a break in service.

(2) Other personnel.—Any individual who, on the day before the effective date of the Patent and Trademark Office Efficiency Act, is an officer or employee of the Department of Commerce (other than an officer or employee under paragraph (1)) shall be transferred to the Office, as necessary to carry out the purposes of that Act, if—

(A) such individual serves in a position for which a major function is the performance of work reimbursed by the Patent and Trademark Office, as determined by the Secretary of Commerce;

(B) such individual serves in a position that performed work in support of the Patent and Trademark Office during at least half of the incumbent's work time, as determined by the Secretary of Commerce; or

(C) such transfer would be in the interest of the Office, as determined by the Secretary of Commerce in consultation with the Director.

Any transfer under this paragraph shall be effective as of the same effective date as referred to in paragraph (1), and shall be made without a break in service.

(f) Transition provisions—

(1) Interim appointment of Director.—On or after the effective date of the Patent and Trademark Office Efficiency Act, the President shall appoint an individual to serve as the Director until the date on which a Director qualifies under subsection (a). The President shall not make more than one such appointment under this subsection.

(2) Continuation in office of certain officers—

(A) The individual serving as the Assistant Commissioner for Patents on the day before the effective date of the Patent and Trademark Office Efficiency Act may serve as the Commissioner for Patents until the date on which a Commissioner for Patents is appointed under subsection (b).

(B) The individual serving as the Assistant Commissioner for Trademarks on the day before the effective date of the Patent and Trademark Office Efficiency Act may serve as the Commissioner for Trademarks until the date on which a Commissioner for Trademarks is appointed under subsection (b).

History of 35 U.S.C. §3: July 19, 1952, ch. 950, §1, 66 Stat. 792; Sept. 6, 1958, P.L. 85-933, §1, 72 Stat. 1793; Sept. 23, 1959, P.L. 86-370, §1(a), 73 Stat. 650; Aug. 14, 1964, P.L. 88-426, §305(26), 78 Stat. 425; Jan. 2, 1975, P.L. 93-596, §1, 88 Stat. 1949; Jan. 2, 1975, P.L. 93-601, §1, 88 Stat. 1956; Aug. 27, 1982, P.L. 97-247, §4, 96 Stat. 319; Oct. 15, 1982, P.L. 97-366, §4, 96 Stat. 1760; Nov. 8, 1984, P.L. 98-622, §405, 98 Stat. 3392; Oct. 28, 1998, P.L. 105-304, §401(a)(1), 112 Stat. 2887; Aug. 5, 1999, P.L. 106-44, §2(c), 113 Stat. 223; Nov. 29, 1999, P.L. 106-113, §1000(a)(9), 113 Stat. 1536; Nov. 2, 2002, P.L. 107-273, §13206(a)(2), 116 Stat. 1904; Sept. 16, 2011, P.L. 112-29, §§20(i)(1), 21(b), 125 Stat. 334, 336; Jan. 14, 2013, P.L. 112-274, §1(g), 126 Stat. 2456.

§4. RESTRICTIONS ON OFFICERS & EMPLOYEES AS TO INTEREST IN PATENTS

Officers and employees of the Patent and Trademark Office shall be incapable, during the period of their appointments and for one year thereafter, of applying for a patent and of acquiring, directly or indirectly, except by inheritance or bequest, any patent or any right or interest in any patent, issued or to be issued by the Office. In patents applied for thereafter they shall not be entitled to any priority date earlier than one year after the termination of their appointment.

History of 35 U.S.C. §4: July 19, 1952, ch. 950, §1, 66 Stat. 793; Jan. 2, 1975, P.L. 93-596, §1, 88 Stat. 1949.

§5. PATENT & TRADEMARK OFFICE PUBLIC ADVISORY COMMITTEES

(a) Establishment of Public Advisory Committees—

(1) Appointment.—The United States Patent and Trademark Office shall have a Patent Public Advisory Committee and a Trademark Public Advisory Committee, each of which shall have nine voting members who shall be appointed by the Secretary of Commerce and serve at the pleasure of the Secretary of Commerce. In each year, 3 members shall be appointed to each Advisory Committee for 3-year terms that shall begin on December 1 of that year. Any vacancy on an Advisory Committee shall be filled within 90 days after it occurs. A new member who is appointed to fill a vacancy shall be appointed to serve for the remainder of the predecessor's term.

(2) Chair.—The Secretary of Commerce, in consultation with the Director, shall designate a Chair and Vice Chair of each Advisory Committee from among the members appointed under paragraph (1). If the Chair resigns before the completion of his or her term, or is otherwise unable to exercise the functions of the Chair, the Vice Chair shall exercise the functions of the Chair.

(b) Basis for appointments.—Members of each Advisory Committee—

(1) shall be citizens of the United States who shall be chosen so as to represent the interests of diverse users of the United States Patent and Trademark Office with respect to patents, in the case of the Patent Public Advisory Committee, and with respect to trademarks, in the case of the Trademark Public Advisory Committee;

(2) shall include members who represent small and large entity applicants located in the United States in proportion to the number of applications filed by such applicants, but in no case shall members who represent small entity patent applicants, including small business concerns, independent inventors, and nonprofit organizations, constitute less than 25 percent of the members of the Patent Public Advisory Committee, and such members shall include at least one independent inventor; and

(3) shall include individuals with substantial background and achievement in finance, management, labor relations, science, technology, and office automation.

In addition to the voting members, each Advisory Committee shall include a representative of each labor organization recognized by the United States Patent and Trademark Office. Such representatives shall be nonvoting members of the Advisory Committee to which they are appointed.

(c) Meetings.—Each Advisory Committee shall meet at the call of the chair to consider an agenda set by the chair.

(d) Duties.—Each Advisory Committee shall—

(1) review the policies, goals, performance, budget, and user fees of the United States Patent and Trademark Office with respect to patents, in the case of the Patent Public Advisory Committee, and with respect to Trademarks, in the case of the Trademark Public Advisory Committee, and advise the Director on these matters;

(2) within 60 days after the end of each fiscal year—

(A) prepare an annual report on the matters referred to in paragraph (1);

(B) transmit the report to the Secretary of Commerce, the President, and the Committees on the Judiciary of the Senate and the House of Representatives; and

(C) publish the report in the Official Gazette of the United States Patent and Trademark Office.

(e) Compensation.—Each member of each Advisory Committee shall be compensated for each day (including travel time) during which such member is attending meetings or conferences of that Advisory Committee or otherwise engaged in the business of that Advisory Committee, at the rate which is the daily equivalent of the annual rate of basic pay in effect for level III of the Executive Schedule under section 5314 of title 5. While away from such member's home or regular place of business such member shall be allowed travel expenses, including per diem in lieu of subsistence, as authorized by section 5703 of title 5.

(f) Access to information.—Members of each Advisory Committee shall be provided access to records and information in the United States Patent and Trademark Office, except for personnel or other privileged information and information concerning patent applications required to be kept in confidence by section 122.

(g) Applicability of certain ethics laws.—Members of each Advisory Committee shall be special Government employees within the meaning of section 202 of title 18.

(h) Inapplicability of Federal Advisory Committee Act.—The Federal Advisory Committee Act (5 U.S.C. App.) shall not apply to each Advisory Committee.

(i) Open meetings.—The meetings of each Advisory Committee shall be open to the public, except that each Advisory Committee may by majority vote meet in executive session when considering personnel, privileged, or other confidential information.

(j) Inapplicability of patent prohibition.—Section 4 shall not apply to voting members of the Advisory Committees.

History of 35 U.S.C. §5: Nov. 29, 1999, P.L. 106-113, §1000(a)(9), 113 Stat. 1536; Nov. 2, 2002, P.L. 107-273, §§13203(b), 13206(a)(3), 116 Stat. 1902, 1904; Jan. 14, 2013, P.L. 112-274, §1(*l*)(1), 126 Stat. 2458.

§6. BOARD OF PATENT APPEALS & INTERFERENCES

Section 6 in its present form does not apply to proceedings commenced on or after Sept. 16, 2012, but continues to apply for any inter partes reexaminations requested under §311 before Sept. 16, 2012, and to interference proceedings declared under 35 U.S.C. §135 after Sept. 15, 2012. The Patent Trial & Appeal Board may be deemed the Board of Patent Appeals & Interferences for purposes of such interference proceedings.

(a) Establishment and composition.—There shall be in the United States Patent and Trademark Office a Board of Patent Appeals and Interferences. The Director, the Deputy Director, the Commissioner for Patents, the Commissioner for Trademarks, and the administrative patent judges shall constitute the Board. The administrative patent judges shall be persons of competent legal knowledge and scientific ability who are appointed by the Secretary of Commerce, in consultation with the Director.

(b) Duties.—The Board of Patent Appeals and Interferences shall, on written appeal of an applicant, review adverse decisions of examiners upon applications for patents and shall determine priority and patentability of invention in interferences declared under section 135(a). Each appeal and interference shall be heard by at least three members of the Board, who shall be designated by the Director. Only the Board of Patent Appeals and Interferences may grant rehearings.

(c) Authority of the Secretary.—The Secretary of Commerce may, in his or her discretion, deem the appointment of an administrative patent judge who, before the date of the enactment of this subsection, held office pursuant to an appointment by the Director to take effect on the date on which the Director initially appointed the administrative patent judge.

(d) Defense to challenge of appointment.—It shall be a defense to a challenge to the appointment of an administrative patent judge on the basis of the judge's having been originally appointed by the Director that the administrative patent judge so appointed was acting as a de facto officer.

History of 35 U.S.C. §6: Nov. 29, 1999, P.L. 106-113, §1000(a)(9), 113 Stat. 1536; Nov. 2, 2002, P.L. 107-273, §13203(a)(2), 116 Stat. 1902; Aug. 12, 2008, P.L. 110-313, §1(a), 122 Stat. 3014.

See also 37 C.F.R. pt. 41.

ANNOTATIONS

Capon v. Eshhar, 418 F.3d 1349, 1351, 76 U.S.P.Q.2d 1078, 1079 (Fed.Cir.2005). "During an interference proceeding the Board is authorized to determine not only priority of invention but also to redetermine patentability."

In re Nilsen, 851 F.2d 1401, 1402-03, 7 U.S.P.Q.2d 1500, 1501 (Fed.Cir.1988). "A board member need not possess 'ordinary skill' in a particular art area to be qualified to render a patentability determination on a claimed invention drawn to that art. The correctness of a board's decision depends on whether the decision is supported by the record, not on the technical background of the Examiners-in-Chief who decided the appeal."

§6. PATENT TRIAL & APPEAL BOARD

Section 6 is effective for proceedings that commence on or after Sept. 16, 2012. Inter partes reexaminations requested under §311 before Sept. 16, 2012, are governed by the provisions in effect before that date.

(a) In general.—There shall be in the Office a Patent Trial and Appeal Board. The Director, the Deputy Director, the Commissioner for Patents, the Commissioner for Trademarks, and the administrative patent judges shall constitute the Patent Trial and Appeal Board. The administrative patent judges shall be persons of competent legal knowledge and scientific ability who are appointed by the Secretary, in consultation with the Director. Any reference in any Federal law, Executive order, rule, regulation, or delegation of authority, or any document of or pertaining to the Board of Patent Appeals and Interferences is deemed to refer to the Patent Trial and Appeal Board.

(b) Duties.—The Patent Trial and Appeal Board shall—

(1) on written appeal of an applicant, review adverse decisions of examiners upon applications for patents pursuant to section 134(a);

(2) review appeals of reexaminations pursuant to section 134(b);

(3) conduct derivation proceedings pursuant to section 135; and

(4) conduct inter partes reviews and post-grant reviews pursuant to chapters 31 and 32.

(c) 3-member panels.—Each appeal, derivation proceeding, post-grant review, and inter partes review shall be heard by at least 3 members of the Patent Trial and Appeal Board, who shall be designated by the Director. Only the Patent Trial and Appeal Board may grant rehearings.

(d) Treatment of prior appointments.—The Secretary of Commerce may, in the Secretary's discretion, deem the appointment of an administrative patent judge who, before the date of the enactment of this subsection, held office pursuant to an appointment by the Director to take effect on the date on which the Director initially appointed the administrative patent judge. It shall be a defense to a challenge to the appointment of an administrative patent judge on the basis of the judge's having been originally appointed by the Director that the administrative patent judge so appointed was acting as a de facto officer.

History of 35 U.S.C. §6: Nov. 29, 1999, P.L. 106-113, §1000(a)(9), 113 Stat. 1536; Nov. 2, 2002, P.L. 107-273, §13203(a)(2), 116 Stat. 1902; Aug. 12, 2008, P.L. 110-313, §1(a), 122 Stat. 3014; Sept. 16, 2011, P.L. 112-29, §7(a)(1), 125 Stat. 313.

See also 37 C.F.R. pt. 41.

§7. LIBRARY

The Director shall maintain a library of scientific and other works and periodicals, both foreign and domestic, in the Patent and Trademark Office to aid the officers in the discharge of their duties.

History of 35 U.S.C. §7: July 19, 1952, ch. 950, §1, 66 Stat. 793; Jan. 2, 1975, P.L. 93-596, §1, 88 Stat. 1949; Nov. 29, 1999, P.L. 106-113, §1000(a)(9), 113 Stat. 1536; Nov. 2, 2002, P.L. 107-273, §13206(b)(1)(B), 116 Stat. 1906.

§8. CLASSIFICATION OF PATENTS

The Director may revise and maintain the classification by subject matter of United States letters patent, and such other patents and printed publications as may be necessary or practicable, for the purpose of determining with readiness and accuracy the novelty of inventions for which applications for patent are filed.

History of 35 U.S.C. §8: July 19, 1952, ch. 950, §1, 66 Stat. 794; Nov. 29, 1999, P.L. 106-113, §1000(a)(9), 113 Stat. 1536; Nov. 2, 2002, P.L. 107-273, §13206(b)(1)(B), 116 Stat. 1906.

§9. CERTIFIED COPIES OF RECORDS

The Director may furnish certified copies of specifications and drawings of patents issued by the Patent and Trademark Office, and of other records available either to the public or to the person applying therefor.

History of 35 U.S.C. §9: July 19, 1952, ch. 950, §1, 66 Stat. 794; Jan. 2, 1975, P.L. 93-596, §1, 88 Stat. 1949; Nov. 29, 1999, P.L. 106-113, §1000(a)(9), 113 Stat. 1536; Nov. 2, 2002, P.L. 107-273, §13206(b)(1)(B), 116 Stat. 1906.

See also 28 U.S.C. §1744; 37 C.F.R. §1.13.

§10. PUBLICATIONS

(a) The Director may publish in printed, typewritten, or electronic form, the following:

1. Patents and published applications for patents, including specifications and drawings, together with copies of the same. The Patent and Trademark Office may print the headings of the drawings for patents for the purpose of photolithography.

2. Certificates of trade-mark registrations, including statements and drawings, together with copies of the same.

3. The Official Gazette of the United States Patent and Trademark Office.

4. Annual indexes of patents and patentees, and of trade-marks and registrants.

5. Annual volumes of decisions in patent and trade-mark cases.

6. Pamphlet copies of the patent laws and rules of practice, laws and rules relating to trade-marks, and circulars or other publications relating to the business of the Office.

(b) The Director may exchange any of the publications specified in items 3, 4, 5, and 6 of subsection (a) of this section for publications desirable for the use of the Patent and Trademark Office.

History of 35 U.S.C. §10: July 19, 1952, ch. 950, §1, 66 Stat. 794; Jan. 2, 1975, P.L. 93-596, §1, 88 Stat. 1949; Nov. 29, 1999, P.L. 106-113, §1000(a)(9), 113 Stat. 1536; Nov. 2, 2002, P.L. 107-273, §§13205(2)(A), 13206(b)(1)(B), (3)(A), 116 Stat. 1903, 1906.

See also 37 C.F.R. §§1.211-1.221.

§11. EXCHANGE OF COPIES OF PATENTS & APPLICATIONS WITH FOREIGN COUNTRIES

The Director may exchange copies of specifications and drawings of United States patents and published applications for patents for those of foreign countries. The Director shall not enter into an agreement to provide such copies of specifications and drawings of United States patents and applications to a foreign country, other than a NAFTA country or a WTO member country, without the express authorization of the Secretary of Commerce. For purposes of this section, the terms "NAFTA country" and "WTO member country" have the meanings given those terms in section 104(b).

History of 35 U.S.C. §11: July 19, 1952, ch. 950, §1, 66 Stat. 794; Nov. 29, 1999, P.L. 106-113, §1000(a)(9), 113 Stat. 1536; Nov. 2, 2002, P.L. 107-273, §§13205(2)(B), 13206(b)(1)(B), 116 Stat. 1903, 1906.

§12. COPIES OF PATENTS & APPLICATIONS FOR PUBLIC LIBRARIES

The Director may supply copies of specifications and drawings of patents and published applications for patents in printed or electronic form to public libraries in the United States which shall maintain such copies for the use of the public, at the rate for each year's issue established for this purpose in section 41(d).

History of 35 U.S.C. §12: July 19, 1952, ch. 950, §1, 66 Stat. 794; Aug. 27, 1982, P.L. 97-247, §15, 96 Stat. 321; Nov. 29, 1999, P.L. 106-113, §1000(a)(9), 113 Stat. 1536; Nov. 2, 2002, P.L. 107-273, §§13205(2)(C), 13206(b)(1)(B), (3)(B), 116 Stat. 1903, 1906; Sept. 16, 2011, P.L. 112-29, §20(j)(1), 125 Stat. 335.

§13. ANNUAL REPORT TO CONGRESS

The Director shall report to the Congress, not later than 180 days after the end of each fiscal year, the moneys received and expended by the Office, the purposes for which the moneys were spent, the quality and quantity of the work of the Office, the nature of training provided to examiners, the evaluation of the Commissioner of Patents and the Commissioner of Trademarks by the Secretary of Commerce, the compensation of the Commissioners, and other information relating to the Office.

History of 35 U.S.C. §13: July 19, 1952, ch. 950, §1, 66 Stat. 794; Nov. 29, 1999, P.L. 106-113, §1000(a)(9), 113 Stat. 1536.

CHAPTER 2. PROCEEDINGS IN THE PATENT & TRADEMARK OFFICE

§21. FILING DATE & DAY FOR TAKING ACTION

(a) The Director may by rule prescribe that any paper or fee required to be filed in the Patent and Trademark Office will be considered filed in the Office on the date on which it was deposited with the United States Postal Service or would have been deposited with the United States Postal Service but for postal service interruptions or emergencies designated by the Director.

(b) When the day, or the last day, for taking any action or paying any fee in the United States Patent and

Trademark Office falls on Saturday, Sunday, or a federal holiday within the District of Columbia, the action may be taken, or the fee paid, on the next succeeding secular or business day.

History of 35 U.S.C. §21: July 19, 1952, ch. 950, §1, 66 Stat. 794; Jan. 2, 1975, P.L. 93-596, §1, 88 Stat. 1949; Aug. 27, 1982, P.L. 97-247, §12, 96 Stat. 321; Nov. 29, 1999, P.L. 106-113, §1000(a)(9), 113 Stat. 1536; Nov. 2, 2002, P.L. 107-273, §13206(b)(1)(B), 116 Stat. 1906.

See also 37 C.F.R. §1.7.

§22. PRINTING OF PAPERS FILED

The Director may require papers filed in the Patent and Trademark Office to be printed, typewritten, or on an electronic medium.

History of 35 U.S.C. §22: July 19, 1952, ch. 950, §1, 66 Stat. 795; Jan. 2, 1975, P.L. 93-596, §1, 88 Stat. 1949; Nov. 29, 1999, P.L. 106-113, §1000(a)(9), 113 Stat. 1536; Nov. 2, 2002, P.L. 107-273, §13206(b)(1)(B), 116 Stat. 1906.

§23. TESTIMONY IN PATENT & TRADEMARK OFFICE CASES

The Director may establish rules for taking affidavits and depositions required in cases in the Patent and Trademark Office. Any officer authorized by law to take depositions to be used in the courts of the United States, or of the State where he resides, may take such affidavits and depositions.

History of 35 U.S.C. §23: July 19, 1952, ch. 950, §1, 66 Stat. 795; Jan. 2, 1975, P.L. 93-596, §1, 88 Stat. 1949; Nov. 29, 1999, P.L. 106-113, §1000(a)(9), 113 Stat. 1536; Nov. 2, 2002, P.L. 107-273, §13206(b)(1)(B), 116 Stat. 1906.

See also 37 C.F.R. §§104.21-104.24.

§24. SUBPOENAS, WITNESSES

The clerk of any United States court for the district wherein testimony is to be taken for use in any contested case in the Patent and Trademark Office, shall, upon the application of any party thereto, issue a subpoena for any witness residing or being within such district, commanding him to appear and testify before an officer in such district authorized to take depositions and affidavits, at the time and place stated in the subpoena. The provisions of the Federal Rules of Civil Procedure relating to the attendance of witnesses and to the production of documents and things shall apply to contested cases in the Patent and Trademark Office.

Every witness subpoenaed and in attendance shall be allowed the fees and traveling expenses allowed to witnesses attending the United States district courts.

A judge of a court whose clerk issued a subpoena may enforce obedience to the process or punish disobedience as in other like cases, on proof that a witness, served with such subpoena, neglected or refused to appear or to testify. No witness shall be deemed guilty of contempt for disobeying such subpoena unless his fees and traveling expenses in going to, and returning from, and one day's attendance at the place of examination, are paid or tendered him at the time of the service of the subpoena; nor for refusing to disclose any secret matter except upon appropriate order of the court which issued the subpoena.

History of 35 U.S.C. §24: July 19, 1952, ch. 950, §1, 66 Stat. 795; Jan. 2, 1975, P.L. 93-596, §1, 88 Stat. 1949.

ANNOTATIONS

El Encanto, Inc. v. Hatch Chile Co., 825 F.3d 1161, 1164, 119 U.S.P.Q.2d 1139, 1142 (10th Cir.2016). "[T]he plain language of [35 U.S.C.] §24 doesn't suggest that a reader must look to the [FRCPs] as they were ... when the statute was enacted. *At F.3d 1167, U.S.P.Q.2d 1144:* [C]onsistent with any of the various statutory interpretations and regulations cited to us, a party to a TTAB proceeding can obtain nonparty documents without wasting everyone's time and money with a deposition no one really wants."

Abbott Labs. v. Cordis Corp., 710 F.3d 1318, 1319-20, 106 U.S.P.Q.2d 1227, 1228 (Fed.Cir.2013). "[S]ection 24 only empowers a district court to issue a subpoena for use in a 'contested case,' and ... contested cases are limited to those in which the regulations of the [PTO] authorize the parties to take depositions. Since the PTO does not provide for depositions in inter partes reexamination proceedings, such proceedings are not 'contested cases' within the meaning of §24, and subpoenas under §24 are not available."

§25. DECLARATION IN LIEU OF OATH

(a) The Director may by rule prescribe that any document to be filed in the Patent and Trademark Office and which is required by any law, rule, or other regulation to be under oath may be subscribed to by a written declaration in such form as the Director may prescribe, such declaration to be in lieu of the oath otherwise required.

(b) Whenever such written declaration is used, the document must warn the declarant that willful false statements and the like are punishable by fine or imprisonment, or both (18 U.S.C. 1001).

History of 35 U.S.C. §25: Mar. 26, 1964, P.L. 88-292, §1, 78 Stat. 171; Jan. 2, 1975, P.L. 93-596, §1, 88 Stat. 1949; Nov. 29, 1999, P.L. 106-113, §1000(a)(9), 113 Stat. 1536; Nov. 2, 2002, P.L. 107-273, §13206(b)(1)(B), 116 Stat. 1906.

§26. EFFECT OF DEFECTIVE EXECUTION

Any document to be filed in the Patent and Trademark Office and which is required by any law, rule, or other regulation to be executed in a specified manner may be provisionally accepted by the Director despite a defective execution, provided a properly executed document is submitted within such time as may be prescribed.

History of 35 U.S.C. §26: Mar. 26, 1964, P.L. 88-292, §1, 78 Stat. 171; Jan. 2, 1975, P.L. 93-596, §1, 88 Stat. 1949; Nov. 29, 1999, P.L. 106-113, §1000(a)(9), 113 Stat. 1536; Nov. 2, 2002, P.L. 107-273, §13206(b)(1)(B), 116 Stat. 1906.

§27. REVIVAL OF APPLICATIONS; REINSTATEMENT OF REEXAMINATION PROCEEDINGS

The Director may establish procedures, including the requirement for payment of the fee specified in section 41(a)(7), to revive an unintentionally abandoned application for patent, accept an unintentionally delayed payment of the fee for issuing each patent, or accept an unintentionally delayed response by the patent owner in a reexamination proceeding, upon petition by the applicant for patent or patent owner.

History of 35 U.S.C. §27: Dec. 18, 2013, P.L. 112-211, §201(b)(1), 126 Stat. 1534.

CHAPTER 3. PRACTICE BEFORE PATENT & TRADEMARK OFFICE

§31. REPEALED

Repealed Nov. 29, 1999, P.L. 106-113, §1009(a)(9), 113 Stat. 1536, 1501A-580.

§32. SUSPENSION OR EXCLUSION FROM PRACTICE

The Director may, after notice and opportunity for a hearing, suspend or exclude, either generally or in any particular case, from further practice before the Patent and Trademark Office, any person, agent, or attorney shown to be incompetent or disreputable, or guilty of gross misconduct, or who does not comply with the regulations established under section 2(b)(2)(D), or who shall, by word, circular, letter, or advertising, with intent to defraud in any manner, deceive, mislead, or threaten any applicant or prospective applicant, or other person having immediate or prospective business before the Office. The reasons for any such suspension or exclusion shall be duly recorded. The Director shall have the discretion to designate any attorney who is an officer or employee of the United States Patent and Trademark Office to conduct the hearing required by this section. A proceeding under this section shall be commenced not later than the earlier of either the date that is 10 years after the date on which the misconduct forming the basis for the proceeding occurred, or 1 year after the date on which the misconduct forming the basis for the proceeding is made known to an officer or employee of the Office as prescribed in the regulations established under section 2(b)(2)(D). The United States District Court for the Eastern District of Virginia, under such conditions and upon such proceedings as it by its rules determines, may review the action of the Director upon the petition of the person so refused recognition or so suspended or excluded.

History of 35 U.S.C. §32: July 19, 1952, ch. 950, §1, 66 Stat. 795; Jan. 2, 1975, P.L. 93-596, §1, 88 Stat. 1949; Nov. 29, 1999, P.L. 106-113, §1000(a)(9), 113 Stat. 1536; Nov. 2, 2002, P.L. 107-273, §13206(b)(1)(B), 116 Stat. 1906; Sept. 16, 2011, P.L. 112-29, §§3(k), 9(a), 20(j)(1), 125 Stat. 291, 316, 335.

See also 37 C.F.R. §§11.1-11.11, 11.15.

ANNOTATIONS

Bender v. Dudas, 490 F.3d 1361, 1365-66, 83 U.S.P.Q.2d 1065, 1069 (Fed.Cir.2007). "The disciplinary action taken by the PTO is subject to review by the U.S. District Court for the District of Columbia according to the provisions of the Administrative Procedure Act. Under that Act, the agency's choice of sanction is held unlawful only if it is 'arbitrary, capricious, an abuse of discretion, or otherwise not in accordance with law.' The underlying factual findings used to support such a sanction are reviewed for substantial evidence. We review the district court's decision on summary judgment without deference, reapplying on appeal the same standards applicable to the district court. *At F.3d 1368, U.S.P.Q.2d 1071:* To the extent the phrase 'before the Office' in [35 U.S.C. §§2(b)(2)(D)] and 32 is ambiguous, we defer to the PTO's reasonable interpretation of that phrase as authorizing regulations that govern a patent attorney's communications with and disclosures to a client in connection with the prosecution of applications before the PTO. *At F.3d 1369, U.S.P.Q.2d 1072:* In deciding what sanction to impose, the PTO normally considers '(1) the public interest; (2) the seriousness of the violation of the Disciplinary Rule; (3) the deterrent effects deemed necessary; (4) the integrity of the legal profession; and (5) any extenuating circumstances.'"

Sheinbein v. Dudas, 465 F.3d 493, 495, 80 U.S.P.Q.2d 1537, 1539 (Fed.Cir.2006). "We agree with the government that it properly excluded [attorney] from practice in the USPTO based on his disbarment in the State of Maryland and the District of Columbia. *At F.3d 496:* Based on the plain language of 37 C.F.R. §10.23(c)(5), we agree that a practitioner may be found unfit to practice based solely on his disbarment in another jurisdiction. In such cases, the exclusion is based on the finding of the other jurisdiction regarding the practitioner's conduct, not based on the conduct that resulted in the disbarment. Here, [attorney] was disbarred in the State of Maryland and the District of Columbia on ethical grounds. Those disbarments fall within the strictures of §10.23(a) and (b), and expressly §10.23(c)(5). Because [attorney's] prior disbarments violated §10.23, the USPTO properly excluded [attorney] from practice."

§33. UNAUTHORIZED REPRESENTATION AS PRACTITIONER

Whoever, not being recognized to practice before the Patent and Trademark Office, holds himself out or permits himself to be held out as so recognized, or as being qualified to prepare or prosecute applications for patent, shall be fined not more than $1,000 for each offense.

History of 35 U.S.C. §33: July 19, 1952, ch. 950, §1, 66 Stat. 796; Jan. 2, 1975, P.L. 93-596, §1, 88 Stat. 1949.

CHAPTER 4. PATENT FEES; FUNDING; SEARCH SYSTEMS

§41. PATENT FEES; PATENT & TRADEMARK SEARCH SYSTEMS

(a) General fees.—The Director shall charge the following fees:

(1) Filing and basic national fees—

(A) On filing each application for an original patent, except for design, plant, or provisional applications, $330.

(B) On filing each application for an original design patent, $220.

(C) On filing each application for an original plant patent, $220.

(D) On filing each provisional application for an original patent, $220.

(E) On filing each application for the reissue of a patent, $330.

(F) The basic national fee for each international application filed under the treaty defined in section 351(a) entering the national stage under section 371, $330.

(G) In addition, excluding any sequence listing or computer program listing filed in an electronic medium as prescribed by the Director, for any application the specification and drawings of which exceed 100 sheets of paper (or equivalent as prescribed by the Director if filed in an electronic medium), $270 for each additional 50 sheets of paper (or equivalent as prescribed by the Director if filed in an electronic medium) or fraction thereof.

(2) Excess claims fees—

(A) In general.—In addition to the fee specified in paragraph (1)—

(i) on filing or on presentation at any other time, $220 for each claim in independent form in excess of 3;

(ii) on filing or on presentation at any other time, $52 for each claim (whether dependent or independent) in excess of 20; and

(iii) for each application containing a multiple dependent claim, $390.

(B) Multiple dependent claims.—For the purpose of computing fees under subparagraph (A), a multiple dependent claim referred to in section 112 or any claim depending therefrom shall be considered as separate dependent claims in accordance with the number of claims to which reference is made.

(C) Refunds; errors in payment.—The Director may by regulation provide for a refund of any part of the fee specified in subparagraph (A) for any claim that is canceled before an examination on the merits, as prescribed by the Director, has been made of the application under section 131. Errors in payment of the additional fees under this paragraph may be rectified in accordance with regulations prescribed by the Director.

(3) Examination fees—

(A) In general—

(i) For examination of each application for an original patent, except for design, plant, provisional, or international applications, $220.

(ii) For examination of each application for an original design patent, $140.

(iii) For examination of each application for an original plant patent, $170.

(iv) For examination of the national stage of each international application, $220.

(v) For examination of each application for the reissue of a patent, $650.

(B) Applicability of other fee provisions.—The provisions of paragraphs (3) and (4) of section 111(a) relating to the payment of the fee for filing the application shall apply to the payment of the fee specified in subparagraph (A) with respect to an application filed under section 111(a). The provisions of section 371(d) relating to the payment of the national fee shall apply to the payment of the fee specified in subparagraph (A) with respect to an international application.

(4) Issue fees—

(A) For issuing each original patent, except for design or plant patents, $1,510.

(B) For issuing each original design patent, $860.

(C) For issuing each original plant patent, $1,190.

(D) For issuing each reissue patent, $1,510.

(5) Disclaimer fee.—On filing each disclaimer, $140.

(6) Appeal fees—

(A) On filing an appeal from the examiner to the Patent Trial and Appeal Board, $540.

(B) In addition, on filing a brief in support of the appeal, $540, and on requesting an oral hearing in the appeal before the Patent Trial and Appeal Board, $1,080.

(7) Revival fees.—On filing each petition for the revival of an abandoned application for a patent, for the delayed payment of the fee for issuing each patent, for the delayed response by the patent owner in any reexamination proceeding, for the delayed payment of the fee for maintaining a patent in force, for the delayed submission of a priority or benefit claim, or for the extension of the 12-month period for filing a subsequent application, $1,700.00. The Director may refund any part of the fee specified in this paragraph, in exceptional circumstances as determined by the Director.

(8) Extension fees.—For petitions for 1-month extensions of time to take actions required by the Director in an application—

(A) on filing a first petition, $130;

(B) on filing a second petition, $360; and

(C) on filing a third or subsequent petition, $620.

(b) Maintenance fees—

(1) In general.—The Director shall charge the following fees for maintaining in force all patents based on applications filed on or after December 12, 1980:

(A) Three years and 6 months after grant, $980.

(B) Seven years and 6 months after grant, $2,480.

(C) Eleven years and 6 months after grant, $4,110.

(2) Grace period; surcharge.—Unless payment of the applicable maintenance fee under paragraph (1) is received in the Office on or before the date the fee is due or within a grace period of 6 months thereafter, the patent shall expire as of the end of such grace period. The Director may require the payment of a surcharge as a condition of accepting within such 6-month grace period the payment of an applicable maintenance fee.

(3) No maintenance fee for design or plant patent.—No fee may be established for maintaining a design or plant patent in force.

(c) Delays in payment of maintenance fees—

(1) Acceptance.—The Director may accept the payment of any maintenance fee required by subsection (b) after the 6-month grace period if the delay is shown to the satisfaction of the Director to have been unintentional. The Director may require the payment of the fee specified in subsection (a)(7) as a condition of accepting payment of any maintenance fee after the 6-month grace period. If the Director accepts payment of a maintenance fee after the 6-month grace period, the patent shall be considered as not having expired at the end of the grace period.

(2) Effect on rights of others.—A patent, the term of which has been maintained as a result of the acceptance of a payment of a maintenance fee under this subsection, shall not abridge or affect the right of any person or that person's successors in business who made, purchased, offered to sell, or used anything protected by the patent within the United States, or imported anything protected by the patent into the United States after the 6-month grace period but prior to the acceptance of a maintenance fee under this subsection, to continue the use of, to offer for sale, or to sell to others to be used, offered for sale, or sold, the specific thing so made, purchased, offered for sale, used, or imported. The court before which such matter is in question may provide for the continued manufacture, use, offer for sale, or sale of the thing made, purchased, offered for sale, or used within the United States, or imported into the United States, as specified, or for the manufacture, use, offer for sale, or sale in the United States of which substantial preparation was made after the 6-month grace period but before the acceptance of a maintenance fee under this subsection, and the court may also provide for the continued practice of any process that is practiced, or for the practice of which substantial preparation was made, after the 6-month grace period but before the acceptance of a maintenance fee under this subsection, to the extent and under such terms as the court deems equitable for the protection of investments made or business commenced after the 6-month grace period but before the acceptance of a maintenance fee under this subsection.

(d) Patent search and other fees—

(1) Patent search fees—

(A) In general.—The Director shall charge the fees specified under subparagraph (B) for the search of each application for a patent, except for provisional applications. The Director shall adjust the fees charged under this paragraph to ensure that the fees recover an amount not to exceed the estimated average cost to the Office of searching applications for patent by Office personnel.

(B) Specific fees.—The fees referred to in subparagraph (A) are—

(i) $540 for each application for an original patent, except for design, plant, provisional, or international applications;

(ii) $100 for each application for an original design patent;

(iii) $330 for each application for an original plant patent;

(iv) $540 for the national stage of each international application; and

(v) $540 for each application for the reissue of a patent.

(C) Applicability of other provisions.—The provisions of paragraphs (3) and (4) of section 111(a) relating to the payment of the fee for filing the application shall apply to the payment of the fee specified in this paragraph with respect to an application filed under section 111(a). The provisions of section 371(d) relating to the payment of the national fee shall apply to the payment of the fee specified in this paragraph with respect to an international application.

(D) Refunds.—The Director may by regulation provide for a refund of any part of the fee specified in this paragraph for any applicant who files a written declaration of express abandonment as prescribed by the Director before an examination has been made of the application under section 131.

(2) Other fees—

(A) In general.—The Director shall establish fees for all other processing, services, or materials relating to patents not specified in this section to recover the estimated average cost to the Office of such processing, services, or materials, except that the Director shall charge the following fees for the following services:

(i) For recording a document affecting title, $40 per property.

(ii) For each photocopy, $.25 per page.

(iii) For each black and white copy of a patent, $3.

(B) Copies for libraries.—The yearly fee for providing a library specified in section 12 with uncertified printed copies of the specifications and drawings for all patents in that year shall be $50.

(e) Waiver of fees; copies regarding notice.—The Director may waive the payment of any fee for any service or material related to patents in connection with an occasional or incidental request made by a department or agency of the Government, or any officer thereof. The Director may provide any applicant issued a notice under section 132 with a copy of the specifications and drawings for all patents referred to in that notice without charge.

(f) Adjustment of fees.—The fees established in subsections (a) and (b) of this section may be adjusted by the Director on October 1, 1992, and every year thereafter, to reflect any fluctuations occurring during the previous 12 months in the Consumer Price Index, as determined by the Secretary of Labor. Changes of less than 1 per centum may be ignored.

(g) Repealed Sept. 16, 2011, P.L. 112-29, §11(e)(3), 125 Stat. 323.

(h) Fees for small entities—

(1) Reductions in fees.—Subject to paragraph (3), fees charged under subsections (a), (b), and (d)(1) shall be reduced by 50 percent with respect to their application to any small business concern as defined under section 3 of the Small Business Act, and to any independent inventor or nonprofit organization as defined in regulations issued by the Director.

(2) Surcharges and other fees.—With respect to its application to any entity described in paragraph (1), any surcharge or fee charged under subsection (c) or (d) shall not be higher than the surcharge or fee required of any other entity under the same or substantially similar circumstances.

(3) Reduction for electronic filing.—The fee charged under subsection (a)(1)(A) shall be reduced by 75 percent with respect to its application to any entity to which paragraph (1) applies, if the application is filed by electronic means as prescribed by the Director.

(i) Electronic patent and trademark data—

(1) Maintenance of collections.—The Director shall maintain, for use by the public, paper, microform, or electronic collections of United States patents, foreign patent documents, and United States trademark registrations arranged to permit search for and retrieval of information. The Director may not impose fees directly for the use of such collections, or for the use of the public patent or trademark search rooms or libraries.

(2) Availability of automated search systems.—The Director shall provide for the full deployment of the automated search systems of the Patent and Trademark Office so that such systems are available for use by the public, and shall assure full access by the public to, and dissemination of, patent and trademark information, using a variety of automated methods, including electronic bulletin boards and remote access by users to mass storage and retrieval systems.

(3) Access fees.—The Director may establish reasonable fees for access by the public to the automated search systems of the Patent and Trademark Office. If such fees are established, a limited amount of free access shall be made available to users of the systems for purposes of education and training. The Director may waive the payment by an individual of fees authorized by this subsection upon a showing of need or hardship, and if such a waiver is in the public interest.

(4) Annual report to Congress.—The Director shall submit to the Congress an annual report on the automated search systems of the Patent and Trademark Office and the access by the public to such systems. The Director shall also publish such report in the Federal Register. The Director shall provide an opportunity for the submission of comments by interested persons on each such report.

History of 35 U.S.C. §41: July 19, 1952, ch. 950, §1, 66 Stat. 796; July 24, 1965, P.L. 89-83, §§1, 2, 79 Stat. 259; Jan. 2, 1975, P.L. 93-596, §1, 88 Stat. 1949; Nov. 14, 1975, P.L. 94-131, §3, 89 Stat. 690; Dec. 12, 1980, P.L. 96-517, §2, 94 Stat. 3017; Aug. 27, 1982, P.L. 97-247, §3(a)-(e), 96 Stat. 317; Sept. 8, 1982, P.L. 97-256, §101(1)-(4), 96 Stat. 816; Nov. 8, 1984, P.L. 98-622, §204(a), 98 Stat. 3388; Nov. 6, 1986, P.L. 99-607, §1(b)(2), 100 Stat. 3470; Dec. 10, 1991, P.L. 102-204, §5(a)-(c)(1), (d)(1), (2)(A), 105 Stat. 1637-1639; Oct. 23, 1992, P.L. 102-444, §1, 106 Stat. 2245; Dec. 8, 1994, P.L. 103-465, §§532(b)(2), 533(b)(1), 108 Stat. 4986, 4988; Nov. 10, 1998, P.L. 105-358, §3, 112 Stat. 3272; Nov. 29, 1999, P.L. 106-113, §1000(a)(9), 113 Stat. 1536; Nov. 2, 2002, P.L. 107-273, §13206(b)(1)(B), 116 Stat. 1906; Sept. 16, 2011, P.L. 112-29, §§11(a)-(e), 20(j)(1), 125 Stat. 320-323, 335; Dec. 18, 2013, P.L. 112-211, §202(b)(1), 126 Stat. 1535.

See also 37 C.F.R. §§1.9, 1.16-1.29, 1.362-1.378, 41.20, 102.11, 102.31.

ANNOTATIONS

Burandt v. Dudas, 528 F.3d 1329, 1333, 87 U.S.P.Q.2d 1134, 1137-38 (Fed.Cir.2008). "'[I]n determining whether a delay in paying a maintenance fee was unavoidable [under 35 U.S.C. §41(c)], one looks to whether the party responsible for payment of the maintenance fee exercised the due care of a reasonably prudent person.' Under the PTO regulations [37 C.F.R. §1.378(b)(3)], a patentee can show unavoidable delay by demonstrating that 'reasonable care was taken to ensure that the maintenance fee would be paid timely and that the petition [to accept an unavoidably delayed payment] was filed promptly after the patentee was notified of, or otherwise became aware of, the expiration of the patent.' In addition, '[t]he showing must enumerate the steps taken to ensure timely payment of the maintenance fee, the date and the manner in which patentee became aware of the expiration of the patent, and the steps taken to file the petition promptly.' *At F.3d 1334:* [I]t is the actions of the party responsible for making payments of the maintenance fees, the legal title owner, that must be considered when evaluating unavoidable delay under … §41(c). To the extent that [P] suggests that the Director cannot rely only on a party's representation of ownership when presented with a petition for reinstatement under … §1.378, we find no basis to adopt such a rule. The Director is entitled to rely on the representations of ownership by the parties and need not engage in a separate analysis to determine title ownership."

Cardiac Pacemakers, Inc. v. St. Jude Med., Inc., 381 F.3d 1371, 1386, 72 U.S.P.Q.2d 1333, 1344 (Fed.Cir. 2004). "[D] argues that [35 U.S.C. §41(c)(1)] does not affect the requirement of [35 U.S.C.] §156(a)(1) that the application for extension must be submitted before patent 'expiration,' and that the later revival of an expired patent does not overcome this stricture." Held: Because the PTO accepted late payments for the extension, the patent did not expire. D's argument was incorrect. *See also* ***Group One Ltd. v. Hallmark Cards, Inc.***, 407 F.3d 1297, 1306, 74 U.S.P.Q.2d 1759, 1766 (Fed. Cir.2005).

§42. PATENT & TRADEMARK OFFICE FUNDING

(a) All fees for services performed by or materials furnished by the Patent and Trademark Office will be payable to the Director.

(b) All fees paid to the Director and all appropriations for defraying the costs of the activities of the Patent and Trademark Office will be credited to the Patent and Trademark Office Appropriation Account in the Treasury of the United States.

(c)(1) To the extent and in the amounts provided in advance in appropriations Acts, fees authorized in this title or any other Act to be charged or established by the Director shall be collected by and shall, subject to paragraph (3), be available to the Director to carry out the activities of the Patent and Trademark Office.

(2) There is established in the Treasury a Patent and Trademark Fee Reserve Fund. If fee collections by the Patent and Trademark Office for a fiscal year exceed the amount appropriated to the Office for that fiscal year, fees collected in excess of the appropriated amount shall be deposited in the Patent and Trademark Fee Reserve Fund. To the extent and in the amounts provided in appropriations Acts, amounts in the Fund shall be made available until expended only for obligation and expenditure by the Office in accordance with paragraph (3).

(3)(A) Any fees that are collected under this title, and any surcharges on such fees, may only be used for expenses of the Office relating to the processing of patent applications and for other activities, services, and materials relating to patents and to cover a proportionate share of the administrative costs of the Office.

(B) Any fees that are collected under section 31 of the Trademark Act of 1946, and any surcharges on such fees, may only be used for expenses of the Office relating to the processing of trademark registrations and for other activities, services, and materials relating to trademarks and to cover a proportionate share of the administrative costs of the Office.

(d) The Director may refund any fee paid by mistake or any amount paid in excess of that required.

(e) The Secretary of Commerce shall, on the day each year on which the President submits the annual budget to the Congress, provide to the Committees on the Judiciary of the Senate and the House of Representatives—

(1) a list of patent and trademark fee collections by the Patent and Trademark Office during the preceding fiscal year;

(2) a list of activities of the Patent and Trademark Office during the preceding fiscal year which were supported by patent fee expenditures, trademark fee expenditures, and appropriations;

(3) budget plans for significant programs, projects, and activities of the Office, including out-year funding estimates;

(4) any proposed disposition of surplus fees by the Office; and

(5) such other information as the committees consider necessary.

History of 35 U.S.C. §42: July 19, 1952, ch. 950, §1, 66 Stat. 796; Nov. 14, 1975, P.L. 94-131, §4, 89 Stat. 690; Dec. 12, 1980, P.L. 96-517, §3, 94 Stat. 3018; Aug. 27, 1982, P.L. 97-247, §3(g), 96 Stat. 319; Sept. 13, 1982, P.L. 97-258, §3(i), 96 Stat. 1065; Dec. 10, 1991, P.L. 102-204, §§4, 5(e), 105 Stat. 1637, 1640; Nov. 10, 1998, P.L. 105-358, §4, 112 Stat. 3274; Nov. 29, 1999, P.L. 106-113, §1000(a)(9), 113 Stat. 1536; Nov. 2, 2002, P.L. 107-273, §13206(b)(1)(B), 116 Stat. 1906; Sept. 16, 2011, P.L. 112-29, §22(a), 125 Stat. 336; Jan. 14, 2013, P.L. 112-274, §1(j), 126 Stat. 2457.

PART II. PATENTABILITY OF INVENTIONS & GRANT OF PATENTS

CHAPTER 10. PATENTABILITY OF INVENTIONS

§100. DEFINITIONS

Section 100 in its present form will continue to apply for applications and patents issued thereon that were filed before Mar. 16, 2013. Section 100 in its present form will also continue to apply for patent applications and patents issued thereon if the filing date of the earliest application for which the patent or application is entitled under §119, §365(a), §365(b), §120, §121, or §365(c) falls before Mar. 16, 2013, unless the application or patent has ever contained (1) a claim to a claimed invention where the filing date of the earliest application for which the claimed invention is entitled under §119, §365(a), §365(b), §120, §121, or §365(c) falls on or after Mar. 16, 2013; or (2) a specific reference under §120, §121, or §365(c) to any patent or application that ever contained such a claim. See transition note for amended §100, p. 495.

When used in this title unless the context otherwise indicates—

(a) The term "invention" means invention or discovery.

(b) The term "process" means process, art or method, and includes a new use of a known process, machine, manufacture, composition of matter, or material.

(c) The terms "United States" and "this country" mean the United States of America, its territories and possessions.

(d) The word "patentee" includes not only the patentee to whom the patent was issued but also the successors in title to the patentee.

(e) The term "third-party requester" means a person requesting ex parte reexamination under section 302 or inter partes reexamination under section 311 who is not the patent owner.

History of 35 U.S.C. §100: July 19, 1952, ch. 950, §1, 66 Stat. 797. Amended Nov. 29, 1999, P.L. 106-113, §1000(a)(9), 113 Stat. 1536.

§100. DEFINITIONS

Section 100 is effective for patent applications and patents issued on those applications that have ever contained (1) a claim to a claimed invention where the filing date of the earliest application for which the claimed invention is entitled under §119, §365(a), §365(b), §120, §121, or §365(c) falls on or after Mar. 16, 2013; or (2) a specific reference under §120, §121, or §365(c) to any patent or application that ever contained such a claim. Section 100 is not effective for patent applications filed before Mar. 16, 2013, or patents issued on those applications. The amendment to subsection (h)(i)(1)(B) is effective May 13, 2015.

When used in this title unless the context otherwise indicates—

(a) The term "invention" means invention or discovery.

(b) The term "process" means process, art or method, and includes a new use of a known process, machine, manufacture, composition of matter, or material.

(c) The terms "United States" and "this country" mean the United States of America, its territories and possessions.

(d) The word "patentee" includes not only the patentee to whom the patent was issued but also the successors in title to the patentee.

(e) The term "third-party requester" means a person requesting ex parte reexamination under section 302 who is not the patent owner.

(f) The term "inventor" means the individual or, if a joint invention, the individuals collectively who invented or discovered the subject matter of the invention.

(g) The terms "joint inventor" and "coinventor" mean any 1 of the individuals who invented or discovered the subject matter of a joint invention.

(h) The term "joint research agreement" means a written contract, grant, or cooperative agreement entered into by 2 or more persons or entities for the performance of experimental, developmental, or research work in the field of the claimed invention.

(i)(1) The term "effective filing date" for a claimed invention in a patent or application for patent means—

(A) if subparagraph (B) does not apply, the actual filing date of the patent or the application for the patent containing a claim to the invention; or

(B) the filing date of the earliest application for which the patent or application is entitled, as to such invention, to a right of priority under section 119, 365(a), 365(b), 386(a), or 386(b) or to the benefit of an earlier filing date under section 120, 121, 365(c), or 386(c).

(2) The effective filing date for a claimed invention in an application for reissue or reissued patent shall be determined by deeming the claim to the invention to have been contained in the patent for which reissue was sought.

(j) The term "claimed invention" means the subject matter defined by a claim in a patent or an application for a patent.

History of 35 U.S.C. §100: July 19, 1952, ch. 950, §1, 66 Stat. 797; Nov. 29, 1999, P.L. 106-113, §1000(a)(9), 113 Stat. 1536; Sept. 16, 2011, P.L. 112-29, §3(a), 125 Stat. 285; May 13, 2015, P.L. 112-211, §102(1), 126 Stat. 1531.

ANNOTATIONS

Invention

Pfaff v. Wells Elecs., Inc., 525 U.S. 55, 60-61, 48 U.S.P.Q.2d 1641, 1644 (1998). "The primary meaning of the word 'invention' in the Patent Act unquestionably refers to the inventor's conception rather than to a physical embodiment of that idea. The statute does not contain any express requirement that an invention must be reduced to practice before it can be patented. Neither the statutory definition of the term in [35 U.S.C.] §100 nor the basic conditions for obtaining a patent set forth in [35 U.S.C.] §101 make any mention of 'reduction to practice.' The statute's only specific reference to that term is found in [35 U.S.C.] §102(g), which sets forth the standard for resolving priority contests between two competing claimants to a patent."

McNeil-PPC, Inc. v. L. Perrigo Co., 207 F.Supp.2d 356, 374, 63 U.S.P.Q.2d 1493, 1507 (E.D.Pa.2002), *rev'd in part on other grounds*, 337 F.3d 1362 (Fed.Cir.2003). "[A] discovery is an act of 'gaining knowledge of or ascertaining the existence of something previously unknown or unrecognized.'"

Process

In re Schrader, 22 F.3d 290, 295, 30 U.S.P.Q.2d 1455, 1459 (Fed.Cir.1994). "When Congress approved the addition of the term 'process' to the categories of patentable subject matter in 1952, it incorporated the definition of 'process' that had evolved in the courts. As of 1952, that term included a requirement that there be a transformation or reduction of subject matter."

In re Waldbaum, 457 F.2d 997, 1002-03, 173 U.S.P.Q. 430, 434 (C.C.P.A.1972). "The language pertaining to the new use of known processes, machines, etc. was not placed in [35 U.S.C.] §100(b) to impose special standards for inventions pertaining to such uses, but rather to dispel all doubt that these inventions are patentable and to place them under the 'process' category of 35 [U.S.C.] §101. The word 'new' as used in both §§100(b) and 101 is defined in [35 U.S.C.] §102[,] which sets forth the conditions for novelty. The use of the term 'new' does not add any special novelty requirement to that already found in those conditions."

Caterpillar Inc. v. Detroit Diesel Corp., 961 F.Supp. 1249, 1252, 41 U.S.P.Q.2d 1876, 1879 (N.D.Ind. 1996). "A 'process' is further defined as a 'process, art or method.' Three of the four classes of utility inventions—machines, manufactures, and compositions of matter—may be grouped into 'products,' leaving products and processes as the two general categories of patents."

Bendix Corp. v. U.S., 199 U.S.P.Q. 203, 226 n.21 (Ct.Cl.1978). "Since 'invention' is defined in 35 U.S.C. §100 as either 'invention or discovery,' an invention is 'made' at the time of conception. Actual or constructive 'reduction to practice' is merely the 'carrot' which inspires the 'donkey' in the race for a patent in the event two or more parties invent the same thing at about the same time."

Patentee

Pandrol USA, LP v. Airboss Ry. Prods., 320 F.3d 1354, 1367, 65 U.S.P.Q.2d 1985, 1994 (Fed.Cir.2003). "The word 'patentee' includes 'successors in title to the patentee,' ... and exclusive licensees holding all substantial rights to the patent."

In re Borg, 392 F.2d 642, 644, 157 U.S.P.Q. 359, 361 (C.C.P.A.1968). "[T]he parties authorized by the statute to file the terminal disclaimer are 'any patentee or applicant.' It seems clear that Congress intended that the remedies of [35 U.S.C. §253] were also to be available to assignees in view of the express provision of 35 U.S.C. §100(d)...."

§101. INVENTIONS PATENTABLE

Whoever invents or discovers any new and useful process, machine, manufacture, or composition of matter, or any new and useful improvement thereof, may obtain a patent therefor, subject to the conditions and requirements of this title.

History of 35 U.S.C. §101: July 19, 1952, ch. 950, §1, 66 Stat. 797.

ANNOTATIONS

Generally

Alice Corp. Pty. LTD v. CLS Bank Int'l, ___ U.S. ___, 134 S.Ct. 2347, 2351-52, 110 U.S.P.Q.2d 1976, 1978 (2014). "The patents at issue in this case disclose a computer-implemented scheme for mitigating settlement risk (*i.e.*, the risk that only one party to a financial transaction will pay what it owes) by using a third-party intermediary. The question presented is whether these claims are patent eligible under ... §101, or are instead drawn to a patent-ineligible abstract idea. We hold that the claims at issue are drawn to the abstract idea of intermediated settlement, and that merely requiring generic computer implementation fails to transform that abstract idea into a patent-eligible invention. *At U.S. ___, S.Ct. 2355, U.S.P.Q.2d 1981:* In ***Mayo Collaborative Servs. v. Prometheus Labs.***, 566 U.S. [66] (2012), we set forth a framework for distinguishing patents that claim laws of nature, natural phenomena, and abstract ideas from those that claim patent-eligible applications of those concepts. First, we determine whether the claims at issue are directed to one of those patent-ineligible concepts. If so, we then ask, what else is there in the claims before us? To answer that question, we consider the elements of each claim both individually and as an ordered combination to determine whether the additional elements transform the nature of the claim into a patent-eligible application. We have described step two of this analysis as a search for an inventive concept—*i.e.*, an element or combination of elements that is sufficient to ensure that the patent in practice amounts to significantly more than a patent upon the ineligible concept itself. *At U.S. ___, S.Ct. 2358, U.S.P.Q.2d 1983-84:* [T]he mere recitation of a generic computer cannot transform a patent-ineligible abstract idea into a patent-eligible invention. Stating an abstract idea while adding the words 'apply it' is not enough for patent eligibility. Nor is limiting the use of an abstract idea to a particular technological environment. Stating an abstract idea while adding the words 'apply it with a computer' simply combines those two steps, with the same deficient result. Thus, if a patent's recitation of a computer amounts to a mere instruction to implement an abstract idea on a computer, ... that addition cannot impart patent eligibility. This conclusion accords with the preemption concern that undergirds our §101 jurisprudence. Given the ubiquity of computers, ... wholly generic computer implementation is not generally the sort of additional feature that provides any practical assurance that the process is more than a drafting effort designed to monopolize the abstract idea itself." (Internal quotes omitted.) *See also* ***University of Utah Research Found. v. Ambry Genetics Corp.***, 774 F.3d 755, 763, 113 U.S.P.Q.2d 1241, 1246 (Fed.Cir.2014).

Association for Molecular Pathology v. Myriad Genetics, Inc., 569 U.S. 576, 580, 106 U.S.P.Q.2d 1972, 1974-75 (2013). "This case ... requires us to resolve whether a naturally occurring segment of deoxyribonucleic acid (DNA) is patent eligible under ... §101 by virtue of its isolation from the rest of the human genome. We also address the patent eligibility of synthetically created DNA known as complementary DNA (cDNA), which contains the same protein-coding information found in a segment of natural DNA but omits portions within the DNA segment that do not code for proteins. [W]e hold that a naturally occurring DNA segment is a product of nature and not patent eligible merely because it has been isolated, but that cDNA is patent eligible because it is not naturally occurring."

Mayo Collaborative Servs. v. Prometheus Labs., 566 U.S. 66, 70-71, 101 U.S.P.Q.2d 1961, 1965 (2012). "The Court has long held that [§101] contains an important implicit exception. Laws of nature, natural phenomena, and abstract ideas are not patentable. Thus, the Court has written that a new mineral discovered in the earth or a new plant found in the wild is not patentable subject matter. Likewise, Einstein could not patent his celebrated law that $E=mc^2$; nor could Newton have patented the law of gravity. Such discoveries are manifestations of nature, free to all men and reserved exclusively to none. [¶] The Court has recognized, however, that too broad an interpretation of this exclusionary principle could eviscerate patent law. For all inventions at some level embody, use, reflect, rest upon, or apply laws of nature, natural phenomena, or abstract ideas. Thus, in [***Diamond v.***] ***Diehr***[, 450 U.S. 175 (1981),] the Court pointed out that a process is not unpatentable simply because it contains a law of nature or a mathematical algorithm. It added that an *application* of a law of nature or mathematical formula to a known structure or process may well be deserving of patent protection. *At U.S. 72:* Still, as the Court has also made clear, to transform an unpatentable law of nature into a patent-eligible *application* of such a law, one must do more than simply state the law of nature while adding the words 'apply it.' *At U.S. 77, U.S.P.Q.2d 1968-69:* The question before us is whether the claims do significantly more than simply describe these natural relations. To put the matter more precisely, do the patent claims add *enough* to their statements of the correlations to allow the processes they describe to qualify as patent-eligible processes that *apply* natural laws? We believe that the answer to this question is no. [¶] If a law of nature is not patentable, then neither is a process reciting a law of nature, unless that process has additional features that provide practical assurance that the process is more than a drafting effort designed to monopolize the law of nature itself. *At U.S. 79-80:* [T]he claims inform a relevant audience about certain laws of nature; any additional steps consist of well-understood, routine, conventional activity already engaged in by the scientific community; and those steps, when viewed as a whole, add nothing significant beyond the sum of their parts taken separately. For these reasons we believe that the steps are not sufficient to transform unpatentable natural correlations into patentable applications of those regularities. *At U.S. 87, U.S.P.Q.2d 1971:* We need not, and do not, now decide whether were the steps at issue here less conventional, these features of the claims would prove sufficient to invalidate them. *At U.S. 88, U.S.P.Q.2d 1972:* [I]n stating that the 'machine-or-transformation' test is an *im-*

portant and useful clue to patentability, we have neither said nor implied that the test trumps the 'law of nature' exclusion." (Internal quotes omitted.)

Diamond v. Diehr, 450 U.S. 175, 185, 209 U.S.P.Q. 1, 7 (1981). "'An idea of itself is not patentable'.... 'A principle, in the abstract, is a fundamental truth; an original cause; a motive; these cannot be patented, as no one can claim in either of them an exclusive right.'"

Diamond v. Chakrabarty, 447 U.S. 303, 309, 206 U.S.P.Q. 193, 197 (1980). "Congress intended statutory subject matter to 'include anything under the sun that is made by man.'"

Two-Way Media Ltd. v. Comcast Cable Comms., 874 F.3d 1329, 1338, 124 U.S.P.Q.2d 1521, 1526 (Fed.Cir. 2017). "While ... the specification ... describes a system architecture as a technological innovation, ... the claim does not recite this architecture.... The main problem that [P] cannot overcome is that the *claim*—as opposed to something purportedly described in the specification—is missing an inventive concept." Held: The claim is directed to an abstract idea.

Smart Sys. Innovations, LLC v. Chicago Transit Auth., 873 F.3d 1364, 1372, 124 U.S.P.Q.2d 1441, 1446 (Fed.Cir.2017). "We have determined that claims directed to the collection, storage, and recognition of data are directed to an abstract idea."

Secured Mail Solutions LLC v. Universal Wilde, Inc., 873 F.3d 905, 912, 124 U.S.P.Q.2d 1502, 1507 (Fed. Cir.2017). "[T]his court has determined claims to be patent-ineligible at the motion to dismiss stage based on intrinsic evidence from the specification without need for 'extraneous fact finding outside the record.' *At F.3d 913:* In ruling on [an FRCP] 12(b)(6) motion, a court need not 'accept as true allegations that contradict matters properly subject to judicial notice or by exhibit,' such as the claims and the patent specification."

Cleveland Clinic Found. v. True Health Diagnostics LLC, 859 F.3d 1352, 1361, 123 U.S.P.Q.2d 1081, 1087 (Fed.Cir.2017). "[T]he testing patents purport to detect [enzyme] and other [enzyme]-related products, which are naturally occurring in bodily samples. The method then employs the natural relationship between those [enzyme] values and predetermined or control values to predict a patient's risk of developing or having cardiovascular disease. [T]he method starts and ends with naturally occurring phenomena with no meaningful non-routine steps in between.... The claims are therefore directed to a natural law."

Amdocs (Isr.) Ltd. v. Openet Telecom, Inc., 841 F.3d 1288, 1294, 120 U.S.P.Q.2d 1527, 1531-32 (Fed.Cir. 2016). "Our cases generally follow the step one/step two Supreme Court format [in ***Mayo***], reserving step two for the more comprehensive analysis in search of the 'inventive concept.' Recent cases, however, suggest that there is considerable overlap between step one and step two, and in some situations this analysis could be accomplished without going beyond step one. [¶] Whether the more detailed analysis is undertaken at step one or at step two, the analysis presumably would be based on a generally-accepted and understood *definition* of, or test for, what an 'abstract idea' encompasses. However, a search for a single test or definition in the decided cases concerning §101 from this court, and indeed from the Supreme Court, reveals that at present there is no such single, succinct, usable definition or test. The problem with articulating a single, universal definition of 'abstract idea' is that it is difficult to fashion a workable definition to be applied to as-yet-unknown cases with as-yet-unknown inventions. That is not for want of trying; to the extent the efforts so far have been unsuccessful it is because they often end up using alternative but equally abstract terms or are overly narrow. [¶] Instead of a definition, then, the decisional mechanism courts now apply is to examine earlier cases in which a similar or parallel descriptive nature can be seen—what prior cases were about, and which way they were decided. That is the classic common law methodology for creating law when a single governing definitional context is not available. This more flexible approach is also the approach employed by the Supreme Court. We shall follow that approach here."

FairWarning IP, LLC v. Iatric Sys., 839 F.3d 1089, 1093, 120 U.S.P.Q.2d 1293, 1295 (Fed.Cir.2016). "We have explained that the 'realm of abstract ideas' includes 'collecting information, including when limited to particular content.' We have also 'treated analyzing information by steps people go through in their minds, or by mathematical algorithms, without more, as essentially mental processes within the abstract-idea category.' And we have found that 'merely presenting the results of abstract processes of collecting and analyzing information, without more (such as identifying a particular tool for presentation), is abstract as an ancillary part of such collection and analysis.'"

McRO, Inc. v. Bandai Namco Games Am. Inc., 837 F.3d 1299, 1311-12, 120 U.S.P.Q.2d 1091, 1099-1100 (Fed.Cir.2016). "In ***Alice***, the Court applied a two-step framework for analyzing whether claims are patent eligible. First, we determine whether the claim at issue is directed to a judicial exception, such as an abstract idea. Mathematical formulas are a type of abstract idea. The abstract idea exception prevents patenting a result where it matters not by what process or machinery the result is accomplished. We do not assume that such claims are directed to patent ineligible subject matter because all inventions at some level embody, use, reflect, rest upon, or apply laws of nature, natural phenomena, or abstract ideas. Instead, the claims are considered in their entirety to ascertain whether their character as a whole is directed to excluded subject matter. If the claims are not directed to an abstract idea, the inquiry ends. If the claims are directed to an abstract idea, then the inquiry proceeds to the second step of the ***Alice*** framework. [¶] In step two we consider whether the claims contain an 'inventive concept' sufficient to transform the nature of the claim into a patent-eligible application. To do so we look to both the claim as a whole and the individual claim elements to determine whether the claims contain an element or combination of elements that is sufficient to ensure that the patent in practice amounts to significantly more than a patent upon the ineligible concept itself." (Internal quotes omitted.)

Enfish, LLC v. Microsoft Corp., 822 F.3d 1327, 1335, 118 U.S.P.Q.2d 1684, 1689 (Fed.Cir.2016). "We ... see no reason to conclude that all claims directed to improvements in computer-related technology, including those directed to software, are abstract and necessarily analyzed at the second step of ***Alice***, nor do we believe that ***Alice*** so directs. Therefore, we find it relevant to ask whether the claims are directed to an improvement to computer functionality versus being directed to an abstract idea, even at the first step of the ***Alice*** analysis."

Genetic Techs. v. Merial L.L.C., 818 F.3d 1369, 1373-74, 118 U.S.P.Q.2d 1541, 1544 (Fed.Cir.2016). "We have repeatedly recognized that in many cases it is possible and proper to determine patent eligibility under 35 U.S.C. §101 on [an FRCP] 12(b)(6) motion. In many cases, too, evaluation of a patent claim's subject matter eligibility under §101 can proceed even before a formal claim construction. '[C]laim construction is not an inviolable prerequisite to a validity determination under §101.'"

Mortgage Grader, Inc. v. First Choice Loan Servs., 811 F.3d 1314, 1322, 117 U.S.P.Q.2d 1693, 1698 (Fed.Cir.2016). ***Ultramercial, Inc. v. Hulu, LLC***, 772 F.3d 709 (Fed.Cir.2014), "demonstrates that a §101 defense previously lacking in merit may be meritorious after ***Alice***. This scenario is most likely to occur with respect to patent claims that involve implementations of economic arrangements using generic computer technology, as the claims do here. *At F.3d 1325, U.S.P.Q.2d 1700:* The §101 inquiry '***may*** contain underlying factual issues.' But it is also possible, as numerous cases have recognized, that a §101 analysis may sometimes be undertaken without resolving fact issues. [¶] The mere existence in the record of dueling expert testimony does not necessarily raise a genuine issue of material fact."

Versata Dev. Grp. v. SAP Am., Inc., 793 F.3d 1306, 1330, 115 U.S.P.Q.2d 1681, 1698 (Fed.Cir.2015). "[W]e ... hold that, looking at the entirety of the statutory framework and considering the basic purpose of CBM reviews, the PTAB acted within the scope of its authority delineated by Congress in permitting a [35 U.S.C.] §101 challenge under AIA §18."

Ariosa Diagnostics, Inc. v. Sequenom, Inc., 788 F.3d 1371, 1376, 115 U.S.P.Q.2d 1152, 1156 (Fed.Cir. 2015). "It is undisputed that the existence of cffDNA in maternal blood is a natural phenomenon. *At F.3d 1377, U.S.P.Q.2d 1157:* The method at issue here amounts to a general instruction to doctors to apply routine, conventional techniques when seeking to detect cffDNA. Because the method steps were well-understood, conventional and routine, the method of detecting paternally inherited cffDNA is not new and useful. The only subject matter new and useful as of the date of the application was the discovery of the presence of cffDNA in maternal plasma or serum. *At F.3d 1378:* Where claims of a method patent are directed to an application that starts and ends with a naturally occurring phenomenon, the patent fails to disclose patent eligible subject matter if the methods themselves are conventional, routine and well understood applications in the art. *At F.3d 1380, U.S.P.Q.2d 1159:* We do not disagree that detecting cffDNA in maternal plasma or serum that before was discarded as waste material is a positive and valuable contribution to science. But even such valuable contributions can fall short of statutory patentable subject matter, as it does here."

DDR Holdings, LLC v. Hotels.com, L.P., 773 F.3d 1245, 1258-59, 113 U.S.P.Q.2d 1097, 1106-07 (Fed.Cir. 2014). "[T]he claims at issue here specify how interactions with the Internet are manipulated to yield a desired result—a result that overrides the routine and conventional sequence of events ordinarily triggered by the click of a hyperlink. ... When the limitations of the ... patent's asserted claims are taken together as an ordered combination, the claims recite an invention that is not merely the routine or conventional use of the Internet."

Digitech Image Techs. v. Electronics for Imaging, Inc., 758 F.3d 1344, 1348-49, 111 U.S.P.Q.2d 1717, 1719-20 (Fed.Cir.2014). "For all categories [in §101] except process claims, the eligible subject matter must exist in some physical or tangible form. To qualify as a machine under §101, the claimed invention must be a 'concrete thing, consisting of parts, or of certain devices and combination of devices.' To qualify as a manufacture, the invention must be a tangible article that is given a new form, quality, property, or combination through man-made or artificial means. Likewise, a composition of matter requires the combination of two or more substances and includes all composite articles."

In re Roslin Inst. (Edinburgh), 750 F.3d 1333, 1336, 110 U.S.P.Q.2d 1668, 1671-72 (Fed.Cir.2014). "[D]iscoveries that possess 'markedly different characteristics from any found in nature[]' ... are eligible for patent protection. In contrast, any existing organism or newly discovered plant found in the wild is not patentable. *At F.3d 1337:* While [petitioner] does not dispute that the donor sheep whose genetic material was used to create [cloned sheep] could not be patented, [petitioner] contends that copies (clones) are eligible for protection because they are 'the product of human ingenuity' and 'not nature's handiwork, but [their] own.' [Petitioner] argues that such copies are either compositions of matter or manufactures within the scope of §101. However, [cloned sheep] herself is an exact genetic replica of another sheep and does not possess 'markedly different characteristics from any [farm animals] found in nature.' [Cloned sheep's] genetic identity to her donor parent renders her unpatentable."

In re Bilski, 545 F.3d 943, 950-51, 88 U.S.P.Q.2d 1385, 1388 (Fed.Cir.2008), *aff'd sub nom.* ***Bilski v. Kappos***, 561 U.S. 593 (2010). "Whether a claim is drawn to patent-eligible subject matter under §101 is a threshold inquiry, and any claim of an application failing the requirements of §101 must be rejected even if it meets all of the other legal requirements of patentability."

Amgen Inc. v. Hoechst Marion Roussel, Inc., 314 F.3d 1313, 1329, 65 U.S.P.Q.2d 1385, 1396 (Fed.Cir. 2003). "[P]atentees can use *negative* limitations such as 'non-human' and 'non-natural' to avoid rejection under §101."

Animal Legal Def. Fund v. Quigg, 932 F.2d 920, 929-30, 18 U.S.P.Q.2d 1677, 1685 (Fed.Cir.1991). "[W]hether patents are allowable for animal life forms is not a matter of discretion but of law. ... Either the subject matter falls within §101 or it does not, and that question does not turn on any discretion residing in examiners."

In re Newman, 782 F.2d 971, 973-74, 228 U.S.P.Q. 450, 452 (Fed.Cir.1986). "[T]he PTO is entitled to reject an application for insufficient proof when a device by its nature occasions reasonable skepticism as to its operativeness under §101. We discern no abuse of discretion in the holding of the district court that additional tests of petitioner's device should be conducted."

Double Patenting

For more annotations on this topic, see 35 U.S.C. §103, *Double Patenting*, p. 547.

In re Janssen Biotech, Inc., 880 F.3d 1315, 1322, 125 U.S.P.Q.2d 1525, ___ (Fed.Cir.2018). "[A] patent owner cannot retroactively bring its challenged patent within the scope of the safe-harbor provision by amendment in a reexamination proceeding. *At F.3d 1323:* [I]n order to fall within the scope of the safe harbor, a challenged patent must have 'issue[d] on' a divisional application. The ... patent cannot retroactively become, for the purposes of [35 U.S.C.] §121, a 'patent issued on' a divisional application after it already issued on a [continuation-in-part] application...."

AbbVie Inc. v. Mathilda & Terence Kennedy Inst. of Rheumatology Trust, 764 F.3d 1366, 1372, 112 U.S.P.Q.2d 1001, 1005 (Fed.Cir.2014). "While often described as a court-created doctrine, obviousness-type double patenting is grounded in the text of the Patent Act. ... Thus, §101 forbids an individual from obtaining more than one patent on the same invention, *i.e.*, double patenting. *At F.3d 1373, U.S.P.Q.2d 1006:* [T]he doctrine of obviousness-type double patenting ensures that a particular invention (and obvious variants thereof) does not receive an undue patent term extension. *At F.3d 1374, U.S.P.Q.2d 1007:* We now make explicit what was implicit in ***Gilead***: the doctrine of obviousness-type double patenting continues to apply where two patents that claim the same invention have different expiration dates."

Gilead Sci., Inc. v. Natco Pharma Ltd., 753 F.3d 1208, 1215, 110 U.S.P.Q.2d 1551, 1556 (Fed.Cir.2014). "[F]or double patenting inquiries, looking to patent issue dates had previously served as a reliable stand-in for the date that really mattered—patent expiration. But as this case illustrates, that tool does not necessarily work properly for patents to which the [Uruguay Round Agreements Act] applies, because there are now instances, like here, in which a patent that issues first does not expire first. Therefore, in light of the principles reflected in our prior case law as explained above, it is the comparison of [P's] patent expiration dates that should control, not merely the issuance dates. *At F.3d 1217, U.S.P.Q.2d 1558:* We therefore hold that an earlier-expiring patent can qualify as an obviousness-type double patenting reference for a later-expiring patent under the circumstances here."

Sun Pharm. Indus. v. Eli Lilly & Co., 611 F.3d 1381, 1384-85, 95 U.S.P.Q.2d 1797, 1799 (Fed.Cir.2010). "An obviousness-type double patenting analysis, which 'compares claims in an earlier patent to claims in a later patent or application,' ... consists of two steps.... First, the court 'construes the claim[s] in the earlier patent and the claim[s] in the later patent and determines the differences.' Second, the court 'determines whether those differences render the claims patentably distinct.' 'A later claim that is not patentably distinct from,' i.e., 'is obvious over[ ] or anticipated by,' an earlier claim is invalid for obviousness-type double patenting. *At U.S.P.Q.2d 1800:* Our prior obviousness-type double patenting decisions in ***Geneva*** [***Pharms. v. GlaxoSmithKline PLC***, 349 F.3d 1373 (Fed.Cir.2003)] and ***Pfizer*** [***Inc. v. Teva Pharms. USA, Inc.***, 518 F.3d 1353 (Fed.Cir.2008),] control this case. In both cases, we found claims of a later patent invalid for obviousness-type double patenting where an earlier patent claimed a compound, disclosing its utility in the specification, and a later patent claimed a method of using the compound for a use described in the specification of the earlier patent. We held that a 'claim to a method of using a composition is not patentably distinct from an earlier claim to the identical composition in a patent disclosing the identical use.' *At F.3d 1387, U.S.P.Q.2d 1801:* Thus, the holding of ***Geneva*** and ***Pfizer*** ... extends to any and all such uses disclosed in the specification of the earlier patent. *At F.3d 1388, U.S.P.Q.2d 1802:* [W]here a patent claims a compound, a court performing an obviousness-type double patenting analysis should examine the specification to ascertain the coverage of the claim."

Boehringer Ingelheim Int'l v. Barr Labs., 592 F.3d 1340, 1347, 93 U.S.P.Q.2d 1417, 1422 (Fed.Cir.2010). "We agree with [P] that a patentee may file a disclaimer after issuance of the challenged patent or during litigation, even after a finding that the challenged patent is invalid for obviousness-type double patenting. The question here is whether a *retroactive* terminal disclaimer—i.e., a terminal disclaimer that is filed after the expiration date of an earlier commonly owned patent—is effective to overcome obviousness-type double patenting. *At F.3d 1348, U.S.P.Q.2d 1423:* We ... hold that a terminal disclaimer filed after the expiration of the earlier patent over which claims have been found obvious cannot cure obviousness-type double patenting."

Takeda Pharm. Co. v. Doll, 561 F.3d 1372, 1375, 90 U.S.P.Q.2d 1496, 1498 (Fed.Cir.2009). "[T]he doctrine [of double patenting] bars an applicant from obtaining separate patents with separate terms for both a product and process for making that product, unless the product and process are 'patentably distinct.' [¶] The parties agree that product and process claims are patentably distinct if multiple processes for creating a product exist at the time of the invention. *At U.S.P.Q.2d 1499:* The novel legal question in this case asks if later-developed alternative processes are relevant in the product-process 'patentably distinct' inquiry. *At F.3d 1377, U.S.P.Q.2d 1500:* [T]he relevant time frame for determining whether a product and process are 'patentably distinct' should be at the filing date of the secondary application. ... This approach allows an applicant to rely on some later-developed methods to show that the product and process are 'patentably distinct,' even though the alternative processes for making that product may not have been known at the filing date of the primary application. This rule gives the applicant the benefit of future developments in the art. At the same time, however, it prevents the inequitable situation that arises when an applicant attempts to rely on developments occurring decades after the filing date of the secondary application."

In re Basell Poliolefine Italia S.P.A., 547 F.3d 1371, 1375-76, 89 U.S.P.Q.2d 1030, 1033-34 (Fed.Cir. 2008). "Double patenting is a question of law that we review de novo. [¶] In determining double patenting, a one-way test is normally applied, in which 'the examiner asks whether the application claims are obvious over the patent claims.' In unusual circumstances, where an applicant has been unable to issue its first-filed application, a two-way test may apply, in which 'the examiner also asks whether the patent claims are obvious over the application claims.' [¶] The two-way test is 'a narrow exception to the general rule of the one-way test.' The test arose out of the concern 'to prevent rejections for obviousness-type double patenting when the applicants filed first for a basic invention and later for an improvement, but, through no fault of the applicants, the PTO decided the applications in reverse order of filing, rejecting the basic application although it would have been allowed if the applications had been decided in the order of their filing.'"

In re Metoprolol Succinate Patent Litig., 494 F.3d 1011, 1018, 83 U.S.P.Q.2d 1545, 1550 (Fed.Cir.2007). "[T]his court's 'precedent makes clear that the *disclosure* of a patent cited in support of a double patenting rejection cannot be used as though it were prior art, *even where the disclosure is found in the claims.*' This is true. The disclosure of the claims forming the basis of a double patenting rejection cannot be used as 'prior art' for a rejection under 35 U.S.C. §§102, 103. [H]owever, ... what is *claimed*, as opposed to what is *disclosed* to one skilled in the art, remains critical."

Perricone v. Medicis Pharm., 432 F.3d 1368, 1372-73, 77 U.S.P.Q.2d 1321, 1323 (Fed.Cir.2005). "The proscription against double patenting takes two forms: statutory and non-statutory. Statutory, or 'same invention,' double patenting is based on the language in §101 ... mandating 'a patent' for any new and useful invention. Non-statutory, or 'obviousness-type,' double patenting is a judicially created doctrine adopted to prevent claims in separate applications or patents that do not recite the 'same' invention, but nonetheless claim inventions so alike that granting both exclusive rights would effectively extend the life of patent protection. *At F.3d 1375, U.S.P.Q.2d 1325:* [T]he pre-issuance timing requirement of a terminal disclaimer to overcome a double patenting rejection does not dictate a prohibition on post-issuance terminal disclaimers. A terminal disclaimer can indeed supplant a finding of invalidity for double patenting."

In re Lonardo, 119 F.3d 960, 965, 43 U.S.P.Q.2d 1262, 1266 (Fed.Cir.1997). "The doctrine of double patenting is intended to prevent a patentee from obtaining a time-wise extension of patent for the same invention or an obvious modification thereof. 'Same invention' double patenting is based upon ... §101, which states that an inventor may obtain 'a patent' for an invention. The statute thus permits only one patent to be obtained for a single invention, and the phrase 'same invention' refers to an invention drawn to substantially identical subject matter. Obviousness-type double patenting, on the other hand, is judicially created and prohibits an inventor from obtaining a second patent for claims that are not patentably distinct from the claims of the first patent. With obviousness-type double patenting, however, a terminal disclaimer may overcome that basis for unpatentability, assuming that the first patent has not expired." *See also* ***Eli Lilly & Co. v. Teva Pharms.***, 619 F.3d 1329, 1341-42, 96 U.S.P.Q.2d 1375, 1385 (Fed.Cir. 2010); ***Boehringer Ingelheim Int'l v. Barr Labs.***, 592 F.3d 1340, 1346-50, 93 U.S.P.Q.2d 1417, 1421-24 (Fed. Cir.2010); ***Takeda Pharm. Co. v. Doll***, 561 F.3d 1372, 1375-78, 90 U.S.P.Q.2d 1496, 1498-1500 (Fed.Cir.2009); ***Perricone v. Medicis Pharm.***, 432 F.3d 1368, 1372-73, 77 U.S.P.Q.2d 1321, 1323 (Fed.Cir.2005); ***Amgen Inc. v. Hoechst Marion Roussel, Inc.***, 314 F.3d 1313, 1345, 65 U.S.P.Q.2d 1385, 1409 (Fed.Cir.2003); ***In re Goodman***, 11 F.3d 1046, 1052, 29 U.S.P.Q.2d 2010, 2015-16 (Fed. Cir.1993).

Quad Envtl. Techs. v. Union Sanitary Dist., 946 F.2d 870, 873-74, 20 U.S.P.Q.2d 1392, 1394 (Fed.Cir. 1991). "Only the claims are compared in a rejection for double patenting. Such a rejection by the [PTO] does not mean that the first-filed patent is a prior art reference under [35 U.S.C.] §102 against the later-filed application. Thus the 'obviation' of obvious-type double patenting by filing a terminal disclaimer has no effect on a rejection under [35 U.S.C.] §103 based on the first-filed patent. Such a rejection can not be overcome by a terminal disclaimer. A reference patent that is not of common ownership, or a publication or public use or sale more than one year before the filing date of the later-filed application, can not be removed as prior art by the filing of a terminal disclaimer. [¶] Thus, a terminal disclaimer is of circumscribed availability and effect. It is not an admission of obviousness of the later-filed *claimed* invention in light of the earlier-filed *disclosure*, for that is not the basis of the disclaimer."

In re Van Ornum, 686 F.2d 937, 942-43, 214 U.S.P.Q. 761, 765-66 (C.C.P.A.1982). "[T]his court had decided that 'same invention' meant claims to identical subject matter, i.e., that a claim limitation to halogen was not the same as a claim to chlorine and that meat was not the same as pork, or beef, but that a claim to a yard and a claim to 36 inches or three feet were for the same invention despite their differences in wording. The significance of that was that the court had also decided that ... §101 precluded two patents for the same invention, wherefore a terminal disclaimer could be of no help. On the other hand, numerous cases were considered in which application claims were directed to mere obvious modifications of, or improvements on, inventions defined in the claims of patents already issued to the same inventors, or to common assignees, and it had been decided that they might be allowed to go to patent if the applicants filed terminal disclaimers. We classified these as 'obviousness type double patenting.' This latter classification has, in the course of time, come, somewhat loosely, to indicate any 'double patenting' situation other than one of the 'same invention' type, although it is not altogether appropriate in cases such as this where, as appellants argue with some justification, their present claims bear a genus-species relation to the claims in the two issued patents, the application claims being generic and the patent claims specific."

In re Schneller, 397 F.2d 350, 355-56, 158 U.S.P.Q. 210, 216 (C.C.P.A.1968). Patentee's "first application disclosed ABCXY and other matters. He obtained a patent claiming BCX and ABCX, but *so* claiming these combinations as to cover them *no matter what other feature is incorporated in them*, thus *covering effectively ABCXY*. He now, many years later, seeks more claims directed to ABCY *and ABCXY*. Thus, protection he already had would be extended, albeit in somewhat different form, for several years beyond the expiration of his patent, were we to reverse. ... He was shown no justification for such *extended* protection. He has made no effort not to extend it."

New & Useful

In re Bilski, 545 F.3d 943, 958, 88 U.S.P.Q.2d 1385, 1393 (Fed.Cir.2008), *aff'd sub nom.* ***Bilski v. Kappos***, 561 U.S. 593 (2010). "[W]hether a claimed process is novel or non-obvious is irrelevant to the [35 U.S.C.] §101 analysis. ... Although §101 refers to 'new and useful' processes, it is overall a general statement of the type of subject matter that is eligible for patent protection subject to the conditions and requirements of this title. As the legislative history of §101 indicates, Congress did not intend the 'new and useful' language of §101 to constitute an independent requirement of novelty or non-obviousness distinct from the more specific and detailed requirements of [35 U.S.C.] §§102 and 103, respectively." (Internal quotes omitted.)

Utility

J.E.M. Ag Sup. v. Pioneer Hi-Bred Int'l, 534 U.S. 124, 127, 60 U.S.P.Q.2d 1865, 1867 (2001). "We hold that utility patents may be issued for plants. *At U.S. 131, U.S.P.Q.2d 1868:* To obtain utility patent protection, a plant breeder must show that the plant he has developed is new, useful, and non-obvious. In addition, the plant must meet the specifications of [35 U.S.C.] §112, which require a written description of the plant and a deposit of seed that is publicly accessible. *At U.S. 145, U.S.P.Q.2d 1874:* [W]e hold that newly developed plant breeds fall within the terms of [35 U.S.C.] §101, and that neither the [Plant Patent Act] nor the [Plant Variety Protection Act] limits the scope of §101's coverage."

In re Fisher, 421 F.3d 1365, 1371, 76 U.S.P.Q.2d 1225, 1229 (Fed.Cir.2005). We require "a claimed invention to have a specific and substantial utility to satisfy §101. *At U.S.P.Q.2d 1230:* Courts have used the labels 'practical utility' and 'real world' utility interchangeably in determining whether an invention offers a 'substantial' utility. [A]n application must show that an invention is useful to the public as disclosed in its current form, not that it may prove useful at some future date after further research. Simply put, to satisfy the 'substantial' utility requirement, an asserted use must show that that claimed invention has a significant and presently available benefit to the public. [¶] Turning to the 'specific' utility requirement, an application must disclose a use which is not so vague as to be meaningless. [I]n addition to providing a 'substantial' utility, an asserted use must also show that that claimed invention can be used to provide a well-defined and particular benefit to the public."

In re Swartz, 232 F.3d 862, 863, 56 U.S.P.Q.2d 1703, 1703-04 (Fed.Cir.2000). "The questions of whether a specification provides an enabling disclosure under [35 U.S.C.] §112, ¶1, and whether an application satisfies the utility requirement of [35 U.S.C.] §101 are closely related. ... The utility requirement of §101 mandates that the invention be operable to achieve useful results. Thus, if the claims in an application fail to meet the utility requirement because the invention is inoperative, they also fail to meet the enablement requirement because a person skilled in the art cannot practice the invention. Lack of utility is a question of fact ... and the absence of enablement is a legal conclusion based on underlying factual inquiries.... In appeals from the Board, we review questions of fact for substantial evidence." *See also* ***EMI Grp. v. Cypress Semiconductor Corp.***, 268 F.3d 1342, 1348-49, 60 U.S.P.Q.2d 1423, 1427-28 (Fed.Cir.2001); ***Process Control Corp. v. HydReclaim Corp.***, 190 F.3d 1350, 1358-59, 52 U.S.P.Q.2d 1029, 1035 (Fed.Cir.1999).

Juicy Whip, Inc. v. Orange Bang, Inc., 185 F.3d 1364, 1366, 51 U.S.P.Q.2d 1700, 1702 (Fed.Cir.1999). "An invention is 'useful' under §101 if it is capable of providing some identifiable benefit. *At F.3d 1368, U.S.P.Q.2d 1703:* [W]e find no basis in §101 to hold that inventions can be ruled unpatentable for lack of utility simply because they have the capacity to fool some members of the public."

In re Ziegler, 992 F.2d 1197, 1201, 26 U.S.P.Q.2d 1600, 1603 (Fed.Cir.1993). "In the context of a constructive reduction to practice, practical utility for the invention is determined by reference to, and a factual analysis of, the disclosures of the application. *At F.2d 1203, U.S.P.Q.2d 1605:* The utility of a chemical compound may not reside in its potential role as an object of use-testing. To satisfy 35 U.S.C. §101, to be able to serve as a predicate for a [35 U.S.C.] §119 claim, the disclosure must assert a specific benefit in currently available form." (Internal quotes omitted.)

Stiftung v. Renishaw PLC, 945 F.2d 1173, 1180, 20 U.S.P.Q.2d 1094, 1100 (Fed.Cir.1991). "An invention need not be the best or the only way to accomplish a certain result, and it need only be useful to some extent and in certain applications: '[T]he fact that an invention has only limited utility and is only operable in certain applications is not grounds for finding lack of utility.' Whether an invention claimed in a patent lacks utility is a question of fact, which we therefore review for clear error."

Barmag Barmer Maschinenfabrik AG v. Murata Mach., 731 F.2d 831, 839, 221 U.S.P.Q. 561, 567 (Fed. Cir.1984). "[P] appears to be equating the utility requirement of ... §101 with commercial marketability. [C]ommercial marketability is not a requirement of reduction to practice."

Wilden Pump & Eng'g v. Pressed & Welded Prods., 655 F.2d 984, 988, 213 U.S.P.Q. 282, 285 (9th Cir. 1981). "Generally, '[c]ommercial success is strong evidence of utility and patentability especially in the absence of other competing devices; and where followed by defendants copying the patented device as closely as possible ... is sufficient to establish utility.'"

In re Jolles, 628 F.2d 1322, 1326, 206 U.S.P.Q. 885, 889 (C.C.P.A.1980). "With respect to the Examiner's contention that it has not been demonstrated that the claimed invention is safe, ... claims may satisfy the requirements of ... §101 for utility despite the lack of safety."

Pharmacological Utility

In re '318 Patent Infringement Litig., 583 F.3d 1317, 1324-25, 92 U.S.P.Q.2d 1385, 1389 (Fed.Cir.2009). "[H]uman trials are not required for a therapeutic invention to be patentable. [P]atent applications need not prove that compounds or other materials which the applicant is claiming, and which the applicant has stated are useful for 'pharmaceutical applications' are safe, effective, and reliable for use with humans. [¶] We have held that results from animal tests or in vitro experiments may be sufficient to satisfy the utility requirement." (Internal quotes omitted.)

In re Brana, 51 F.3d 1560, 1568, 34 U.S.P.Q.2d 1436, 1442-43 (Fed.Cir.1995). "FDA approval ... is not a prerequisite for finding a compound useful within the meaning of the patent laws. Usefulness in patent law, and in particular in the context of pharmaceutical inventions, necessarily includes the expectation of further research and development. The stage at which an invention in this field becomes useful is well before it is ready to be administered to humans."

Nelson v. Bowler, 626 F.2d 853, 856, 206 U.S.P.Q. 881, 883 (C.C.P.A.1980). "Knowledge of the pharmacological activity of any compound is obviously beneficial to the public. It is inherently faster and easier to combat illnesses and alleviate symptoms when the medical profession is armed with an arsenal of chemicals having known pharmacological activities. Since it is crucial to provide researchers with an incentive to disclose pharmacological activities in as many compounds as possible, we conclude that adequate proof of any such activity constitutes a showing of practical utility."

Process

Bilski v. Kappos, 561 U.S. 593, 602, 95 U.S.P.Q.2d 1001, 1006 (2010). "The present case involves an invention that is claimed to be a 'process' under [35 U.S.C.] §101. [¶] The Court first considers two proposed categorical limitations on 'process' patents under §101 that would, if adopted, bar petitioners' application in the present case: the machine-or-transformation test and the categorical exclusion of business method patents. *At U.S. 604, U.S.P.Q.2d 1007:* This Court's precedents establish that the machine-or-transformation test is a useful and important clue, an investigative tool, for determining whether some claimed inventions are processes under §101. The machine-or-transformation test is not the sole test for deciding whether an invention is a patent-eligible 'process.' *At U.S. 606, U.S.P.Q.2d 1008:* Section 101 ... precludes the broad contention that the term 'process' categorically excludes business methods. The term 'method,' which is within [35 U.S.C.] §100(b)'s definition of 'process,' at least as a textual matter and before consulting other limitations in the Patent Act and this Court's precedents, may include at least some methods of doing business. The Court is unaware of any argument that the ordinary, contemporary, common meaning ... of 'method' excludes business methods. [¶] [A] business method is simply one kind of 'method' that is, at least in some circumstances, eligible for patenting under §101. *At U.S. 612, U.S.P.Q.2d 1010:* The patent application here can be rejected under our precedents on the unpatentability of abstract ideas. The Court, therefore, need not define further what constitutes a patentable 'process,' beyond pointing to the definition of that term provided in §100(b) and looking to the guideposts in [***Gottschalk v.***] ***Benson***, [409 U.S. 63 (1972), ***Parker v.***] ***Flook***, [437 U.S. 584 (1978),] and [***Diamond v.***] ***Diehr***[, 450 U.S. 175 (1981)]." (Internal quotes omitted.)

Diamond v. Diehr, 450 U.S. 175, 183-84, 209 U.S.P.Q. 1, 6 (1981). "A process is a mode of treatment of certain materials to produce a given result. It is an act, or a series of acts, performed upon the subject-matter to be transformed and reduced to a different state or thing. If new and useful, it is just as patentable as is a piece of machinery. ... The process requires that certain things should be done with certain substances, and in a certain order; but the tools to be used in doing this may be of secondary consequence. *At U.S.P.Q. 7:* Transformation and reduction of an article to a different state or thing is the clue to the patentability of a process claim that does not include particular machines. *At U.S. 188-89, U.S.P.Q. 9:* In determining the eligibility of respondents' claimed process for patent protection under §101, their claims must be considered as a whole. It is inappropriate to dissect the claims into old and new elements and then to ignore the presence of the old elements in the analysis. This is particularly true in a process claim because a new combination of steps in a process may be patentable even though all the constituents of the combination were well known and in common use before the combination was made. The novelty of any element or steps in a process, or even of the process itself, is of no relevance in determining whether the subject matter of a claim falls within the §101 categories of possibly patentable subject matter." (Internal quotes omitted.)

Parker v. Flook, 437 U.S. 584, 594, 198 U.S.P.Q. 193, 199 (1978). "Respondent's process is unpatentable under §101, not because it contains a mathematical algorithm [which is analogous to a law of nature] as one component, but because once that algorithm is assumed to be within the prior art, the application, considered as a whole, contains no patentable invention. Even though a phenomenon of nature or mathematical formula may be well known, an inventive application of the principle may be patented. Conversely, the discovery of such a phenomenon cannot support a patent unless there is some other inventive concept in its application. *At U.S. 595 n.18, U.S.P.Q. 199 n.18:* [O]ur holding today is that a claim for an improved method of calculation, even when tied to a specific end use, is unpatentable subject matter under §101."

Brenner v. Manson, 383 U.S. 519, 534-35, 148 U.S.P.Q. 689, 695 (1966). "[A] process patent in the chemical field, which has not been developed and pointed to the degree of specific utility, creates a monopoly of knowledge which should be granted only if clearly commanded by the statute. Until the process claim has been reduced to production of a product shown to be useful, the metes and bounds of that monopoly are not capable of precise delineation. ... Unless and until a process is refined and developed to this point—where specific benefit exists in currently available form—there is insufficient justification for permitting an applicant to engross what may prove to be a broad field."

Accenture Global Servs. v. Guidewire Software, Inc., 728 F.3d 1336, 1341, 108 U.S.P.Q.2d 1173, 1177 (Fed.Cir.2013). "Although ***CLS Bank [Int'l v. Alice Corp. Pty. Ltd.***, 717 F.3d 1269 (Fed.Cir.2013),] issued as a plurality opinion, in that case a majority of the court held that system claims that closely track method claims and are grounded by the same meaningful limitations will generally rise and fall together."

CyberSource Corp. v. Retail Decisions, Inc., 654 F.3d 1366, 1374-75, 99 U.S.P.Q.2d 1690, 1697 (Fed.Cir. 2011). "Regardless of what statutory category ('process, machine, manufacture, or composition of matter[ ]' ...) a claim's language is crafted to literally invoke, we look to the underlying invention for patent-eligibility purposes. [¶] In the present case, [P] has not met its burden to demonstrate that claim ... is 'truly drawn to a specific' computer readable medium, rather than to the underlying method of credit card fraud detection. ... Thus, despite its ***Beauregard*** claim format [a claim to a computer-readable medium (e.g., a disk, hard drive, or other data-storage device) containing program instructions for a computer to perform a particular process], under [***In re***] ***Abele***, [684 F.2d 902 (C.C.P.A.1982),] we treat claim ... as a process claim for patent-eligibility purposes."

In re Comiskey, 554 F.3d 967, 979, 89 U.S.P.Q.2d 1655, 1663 (Fed.Cir.2009). "[A] claim that involves both a mental process and one of the other categories of statutory subject matter (i.e., a machine, manufacture, or composition) may be patentable under §101. *At F.3d 980, U.S.P.Q.2d 1664:* [Section 101] does not allow patents to be issued on particular business systems—such as a particular type of arbitration—that depend entirely on the use of mental processes. In other words, the patent statute does not allow patents on particular systems that depend for their operation on human intelligence alone, a field of endeavor that both the framers and Congress intended to be beyond the reach of patentable subject matter. Thus, it is established that the application of human intelligence to the solution of practical problems is not in and of itself patentable."

In re Bilski, 545 F.3d 943, 961-62, 88 U.S.P.Q.2d 1385, 1396 (Fed.Cir.2008), *aff'd sub nom.* ***Bilski v. Kappos***, 561 U.S. 593 (2010). "The machine-or-transformation test is a two-branched inquiry; an applicant may show that a process claim satisfies §101 either by showing that his claim is tied to a particular machine, or by showing that his claim transforms an article. Certain considerations are applicable to analysis under either branch. First, ... the use of a specific machine or transformation of an article must impose meaningful limits on the claim's scope to impart patent-eligibility. Second, the involvement of the machine or transformation in the claimed process must not merely be insignificant extra-solution activity. [¶] But the main aspect of the transformation test that requires clarification here is what sorts of things constitute 'articles' such that their transformation is sufficient to impart patent-eligibility under §101. It is virtually self-evident that a process for a chemical or physical transformation of *physical objects or substances* is patent-eligible subject matter. *At F.3d 963, U.S.P.Q.2d 1397:* This court and our predecessor court have frequently stated that adding a data-gathering step to an algorithm is insufficient to convert that algorithm into a patent-eligible process."

Eolas Techs. v. Microsoft Corp., 399 F.3d 1325, 1339, 73 U.S.P.Q.2d 1782, 1793 (Fed.Cir.2005), *overruled on other grounds*, ***Cardiac Pacemakers, Inc. v. St. Jude Med., Inc.***, 576 F.3d 1348, 91 U.S.P.Q.2d 1898 (Fed.Cir.2009). "[S]oftware code alone qualifies as an invention eligible for patenting under [35 U.S.C. §§100 and 101], at least as processes."

Grinnell Corp. v. Virginia Elec. & Power Co., 401 F.2d 451, 453, 159 U.S.P.Q. 9, 10 (4th Cir.1968). "[P] puts heavy emphasis on 35 U.S.C. §100(b) which includes within the term 'process' a new use of a known process or machine. However, a different use of a known machine or process is not a 'new use' if it is merely analogous or cognate to the uses theretofore made. Moreover, 'process' is not the same thing as invention. The definition of process to include a 'new use' does not constitute a new statutory class of patentable subject matter different from those set forth in [35 U.S.C.] §101.... The new use must still meet requisite standards of invention, ... including that it not have been obvious to a person having ordinary skill in the art to which the subject matter pertains. The application of an apparatus to a new use, with no change in the apparatus to adapt it to its new use, and with the apparatus functioning without change in its mode of operation, does not constitute invention." *See also* ***Exer-Genie, Inc. v. McDonald***, 453 F.2d 132, 133 n.1, 171 U.S.P.Q. 277, 278 n.1 (9th Cir.1971).

Machine

In re Nuijten, 500 F.3d 1346, 1355, 84 U.S.P.Q.2d 1495, 1501 (Fed.Cir.2007). "The Supreme Court [in ***Burr v. Duryee***, 68 U.S. (1 Wall.) 531 (1863),] has defined the term 'machine' as 'a concrete thing, consisting of parts, or of certain devices and combination of devices.' This 'includes every mechanical device or combination of mechanical powers and devices to perform some function and produce a certain effect or result.'"

Manufacture

Diamond v. Chakrabarty, 447 U.S. 303, 308, 206 U.S.P.Q. 193, 196-97 (1980). "[T]his Court has read the term 'manufacture' in §101 in accordance with its dictionary definition to mean 'the production of articles for use from raw or prepared materials by giving to these materials new forms, qualities, properties, or combinations, whether by hand-labor or by machinery.'"

In re Nuijten, 500 F.3d 1346, 1356, 84 U.S.P.Q.2d 1495, 1502 (Fed.Cir.2007). "The term ['manufacture'] is used in the statute in its noun form ... and therefore refers to 'articles' resulting from the process of manufacture. The same dictionary the Supreme Court relied on for its definition of 'manufacture' in turn defines 'article' as 'a particular substance or commodity: as, an *article* of merchandise; an *article* of clothing; salt is a necessary *article*.' [¶] These definitions address 'articles' of 'manufacture' as being tangible articles or commodities."

Bayer AG v. Housey Pharms., 340 F.3d 1367, 1373, 68 U.S.P.Q.2d 1001, 1005 (Fed.Cir.2003). "We see nothing in [35 U.S.C.] §101 that suggests that 'made' in [35 U.S.C.] §271(g) should be construed to be broader than 'manufacture.'"

Composition of Matter

Diamond v. Chakrabarty, 447 U.S. 303, 308, 206 U.S.P.Q. 193, 197 (1980). "'[C]omposition of matter' has been construed consistent with its common usage to include 'all compositions of two or more substances and ... all composite articles, whether they be the results of chemical union, or of mechanical mixture, or whether they be gases, fluids, powders or solids.'"

In re Breslow, 616 F.2d 516, 521, 205 U.S.P.Q. 221, 226 (C.C.P.A.1980). "It appears to us that the PTO would read into [35 U.S.C.] §101 a requirement that compositions of matter must be stable—which is a relative term to say the least. We see no good reason to do so. It would appear that many compounds may find their greatest or even their sole utility in the fact that they are not stable. *At F.2d 522, U.S.P.Q. 227:* Considering the origins and history of [35 U.S.C.] §114, we do not believe that it was ever intended to impose any limitations on the scope of §101 or that there is any reason why it should."

Mathematical Formula

In re Alappat, 33 F.3d 1526, 1543, 31 U.S.P.Q.2d 1545, 1557 (Fed.Cir.1994), *overruled on other grounds*, ***In re Bilski***, 545 F.3d 943, 88 U.S.P.Q.2d 1385 (Fed.Cir. 2008). "It is ... not necessary to determine whether a claim contains, as merely a part of the whole, any mathematical subject matter which standing alone would not be entitled to patent protection. Indeed, because the dispositive inquiry is whether the claim *as a whole* is directed to statutory subject matter, it is irrelevant that a claim may contain, as part of the whole, subject matter which would not be patentable by itself."

§102. CONDITIONS FOR PATENTABILITY; NOVELTY & LOSS OF RIGHT TO PATENT

Section 102 in its present form will continue to apply for applications and patents issued thereon that were filed before Mar. 16, 2013. Section 102 in its present form will also continue to apply for patent applications and patents issued thereon if the filing date of the earliest application for which the patent or application is entitled under §119, §365(a), §365(b), §120, §121, or §365(c) falls before Mar. 16, 2013, unless the application or patent has ever contained (1) a claim to a claimed invention that has an "effective filing date," as defined in §100(i), p. 495, on or after Mar. 16, 2013; or (2) a specific reference under §120, §121, or §365(c) to any patent or application that ever contained such a claim. In addition, §102(g) continues to apply in its current form to patent applications and patents issued thereon that have ever contained (1) a claim to a claimed invention that has an "effective filing date," as defined in §100(i), p. 495, before Mar. 16, 2013; or (2) a specific reference under §120, §121, or §365(c) to any patent or application that ever contained such a claim. See transition note for amended §102, p. 531.

A person shall be entitled to a patent unless—

(a) the invention was known or used by others in this country, or patented or described in a printed publication in this or a foreign country, before the invention thereof by the applicant for patent, or

(b) the invention was patented or described in a printed publication in this or a foreign country or in public use or on sale in this country, more than one year prior to the date of the application for patent in the United States, or

(c) he has abandoned the invention, or

(d) the invention was first patented or caused to be patented, or was the subject of an inventor's certificate, by the applicant or his legal representatives or assigns in a foreign country prior to the date of the application for patent in this country on an application for patent or inventor's certificate filed more than twelve months before the filing of the application in the United States, or

(e) the invention was described in (1) an application for patent, published under section 122(b), by another filed in the United States before the invention by the applicant for patent or (2) a patent granted on an application for patent by another filed in the United States before the invention by the applicant for patent, except that an international application filed under the treaty defined in section 351(a) shall have the effects for the purposes of this subsection of an application filed in the United States only if the international application designated the United States and was published under Article 21(2) of such treaty in the English language;[1] or

(f) he did not himself invent the subject matter sought to be patented, or

(g)(1) during the course of an interference conducted under section 135 or section 291, another inventor involved therein establishes, to the extent permitted in section 104, that before such person's invention thereof the invention was made by such other inventor and not abandoned, suppressed, or concealed, or

(2) before such person's invention thereof, the invention was made in this country by another inventor who had not abandoned, suppressed, or concealed it. In determining priority of invention under this subsection, there shall be considered not only the respective dates of conception and reduction to practice of the invention, but also the reasonable diligence of one who was first to conceive and last to reduce to practice, from a time prior to conception by the other.

1. **Editor's note:** The semicolon probably should be a comma.

History of 35 U.S.C. §102: July 19, 1952, ch. 950, §1, 66 Stat. 797; July 28, 1972, P.L. 92-358, §2, 86 Stat. 502; Nov. 14, 1975, P.L. 94-131, §5, 89 Stat. 691; Nov. 29, 1999, P.L. 106-113, §1000(a)(9), 113 Stat. 1536; Nov. 2, 2002, P.L. 107-273, §13205(1), 116 Stat. 1902.

See also Paris Convention arts. 4, 5; Patent Cooperation Treaty.

PRE-AIA §102

CHARTS

See "Public Accessibility of Printed Publication Under 35 U.S.C. §102," p. 772.

ANNOTATIONS

Anticipation—Generally

Eibel Process Co. v. Minnesota & Ont. Paper Co., 261 U.S. 45, 66 (1923). "[A]ccidental results, not intended and not appreciated, do not constitute anticipation."

Ineos USA LLC v. Berry Plastics Corp., 783 F.3d 865, 869, 114 U.S.P.Q.2d 1568, 1571 (Fed.Cir.2015). "When a patent claims a range, ... that range is anticipated by a prior art reference if the reference discloses a point within the range. If the prior art discloses its own range, rather than a specific point, then the prior art is only anticipatory if it describes the claimed range with sufficient specificity such that a reasonable fact finder could conclude that there is no reasonable difference in how the invention operates over the ranges."

In re Gleave, 560 F.3d 1331, 1337-38, 90 U.S.P.Q.2d 1235, 1240 (Fed.Cir.2009). "For the purposes of whether they are anticipatory, lists and genera are often treated differently under our case law. This distinction collapses when the class of compounds that falls within the genus is so limited that a person of ordinary skill in the art can 'at once envisage each member of this limited class.' In that limited circumstance, a reference describing the genus anticipates every species within the genus."

Net MoneyIN, Inc. v. VeriSign, Inc., 545 F.3d 1359, 1371, 88 U.S.P.Q.2d 1751, 1759-60 (Fed.Cir.2008). "[D]ifferences between the prior art reference and a claimed invention, however slight, invoke the question of obviousness, not anticipation. Thus, it is not enough that the prior art reference discloses part of the claimed invention, which an ordinary artisan might supplement to make the whole, or that it includes multiple, distinct teachings that the artisan might somehow combine to achieve the claimed invention."

Cohesive Techs. v. Waters Corp., 543 F.3d 1351, 1363, 88 U.S.P.Q.2d 1903, 1910 (Fed.Cir.2008). "Despite the often quoted maxim that anticipation is the 'epitome of obviousness,' ... novelty under 35 U.S.C. §102 and nonobviousness under 35 U.S.C. §103 are separate conditions of patentability and therefore separate defenses available in an infringement action.

At F.3d 1364-65, U.S.P.Q.2d 1911: The tests for anticipation and obviousness are different. Obviousness can be proven by combining existing prior art references, while anticipation requires all elements of a claim to be disclosed within a single reference. Moreover, obviousness requires analysis of secondary considerations of nonobviousness, while secondary considerations are not an element of a claim of anticipation. And although anticipation can be proven inherently, proof of inherent anticipation is not the same as proof of obviousness. Thus, 'it does not follow that every technically anticipated invention would also have been obvious.' *At U.S.P.Q.2d 1912:* A court cannot refuse to submit the issue of anticipation to the jury simply because the accused infringer has also asserted an obviousness defense. It is for the litigants—not the court—to make the strategic decision as to whether to assert one, both, or neither of these defenses in a jury trial. An accused infringer that introduces a prior art reference and makes a non-frivolous argument that 'each and every limitation of a claim is found, expressly or inherently, in [that] single prior art reference' generally is entitled to have anticipation decided by the finder of fact."

💣 ***Zenith Elecs. Corp. v. PDI Comm. Sys.***, 522 F.3d 1348, 1363, 86 U.S.P.Q.2d 1513, 1524 (Fed.Cir.2008). "Our law requires patent challengers to prove invalidity by clear and convincing evidence. Where an accused infringer is clearly practicing only that which was in the prior art, and nothing more, and the patentee's proffered construction reads on the accused device, meeting this burden of proof should not prove difficult. Nevertheless, accused infringers are not free to flout the requirement of proving invalidity by clear and convincing evidence by asserting a 'practicing prior art' defense to literal infringement under the less stringent preponderance of the evidence standard. Likewise, mere proof that the prior art is identical, in all material respects, to an allegedly infringing product cannot constitute clear and convincing evidence of invalidity. Anticipation requires a showing that each element of the claim at issue, properly construed, is found in a single prior art reference. It is the presence of the prior art and its relationship to the claim language that matters for invalidity." (Internal quotes omitted.)

💣 ***Impax Labs. v. Aventis Pharms.***, 468 F.3d 1366, 1381, 81 U.S.P.Q.2d 1001, 1011-12 (Fed.Cir.2006). "In order to be anticipating, a prior art reference must be enabling so that the claimed subject matter may be made or used by one skilled in the art. Prior art is not enabling so as to be anticipating if it does not enable a person of ordinary skill in the art to carry out the invention. [¶] The enablement requirement for prior art to anticipate under [35 U.S.C.] §102 does not require utility, unlike the enablement requirement for patents under [35 U.S.C.] §112. *At F.3d 1382, U.S.P.Q.2d 1013:* 'Whether a prior art reference is enabling is a question of law based upon underlying factual findings.' ... However, '[i]f a patentee presents evidence of nonenablement that a court finds persuasive, the trial court must then exclude the particular prior art patent in any anticipation inquiry, for then the presumption has been overcome.'" *See also* ***In re NTP, Inc.***, 654 F.3d 1279, 1301, 99 U.S.P.Q.2d 1481, 1496-97 (Fed.Cir.2011).

💣 ***Amgen Inc. v. Hoechst Marion Roussel, Inc.***, 457 F.3d 1293, 1304, 79 U.S.P.Q.2d 1705, 1713 (Fed.Cir. 2006). "Anticipation under ... §102 is a question of fact, which we review for clear error after a bench trial. The district court's factual findings on anticipation are clearly erroneous when although there is evidence to support it, the reviewing court on the entire evidence is left with the definite and firm conviction that a mistake has been committed. *At F.3d 1306-07, U.S.P.Q.2d 1715:* [A] prior art reference is enabled even if some routine experimentation is required in order to practice a claimed invention, but ... such experimentation must not be undue. When considering whether or not a prior art reference requires undue experimentation we look at the reference from the perspective of a person of ordinary skill in the art. [¶] We established in ***Amgen II*** that when a piece of prior art is a patent, ... there is a presumption of enablement. The patentee ... must present persuasive evidence of non-enablement to overcome this presumption." (Internal quotes omitted.)

💣 ***SmithKline Beecham Corp. v. Apotex Corp.***, 439 F.3d 1312, 1318-19, 78 U.S.P.Q.2d 1097, 1102 (Fed.Cir. 2006). "[A]nticipation by an earlier product patent cannot be avoided by claiming the same product more narrowly in a product-process claim. It makes no difference here whether [P's second] patent's product-by-process claims are construed broadly to cover the product made by any process or narrowly to cover only the product made by a dry admixing process. Either way, anticipation by an earlier product disclosure (which disclosed the product itself) cannot be avoided. While the process set forth in the product-by-process claim may be new, that novelty can only be captured by obtaining a process claim. We agree with the district court's conclusion that [P's first] patent disclosure anticipated the identical product claimed by [P's second] patent even though that product was produced by an allegedly novel process."

- ***In re Crish***, 393 F.3d 1253, 1256, 73 U.S.P.Q.2d 1364, 1366-67 (Fed.Cir.2004). "A determination that a claim is anticipated ... involves two analytical steps. First, the [Board of Patent Appeals and Interferences] must interpret the claim language, where necessary. Because the PTO is entitled to give claims their broadest reasonable interpretation, our review of the Board's claim construction is limited to determining whether it was reasonable. Secondly, the Board must compare the construed claim to a prior art reference and make factual findings that 'each and every limitation is found either expressly or inherently in [that] single prior art reference.' We review those factual findings for substantial evidence. Substantial evidence is such relevant evidence as a reasonable mind might accept as adequate to support a conclusion ... and 'the possibility of drawing two inconsistent conclusions from the evidence does not prevent an administrative agency's finding from being supported by substantial evidence....'"

- ***Schering Corp. v. Geneva Pharms.***, 339 F.3d 1373, 1377, 67 U.S.P.Q.2d 1664, 1667 (Fed.Cir.2003). "[R]ecognition by a person of ordinary skill in the art before the critical date of the ... patent is not required to show anticipation by inherency. *At F.3d 1379, U.S.P.Q.2d 1669:* Because inherency places subject matter in the public domain as well as an express disclosure, the inherent disclosure of the entire claimed subject matter anticipates as well as inherent disclosure of a single feature of the claimed subject matter. The extent of the inherent disclosure does not limit its anticipatory effect. In general, a limitation or the entire invention is inherent and in the public domain if it is the 'natural result flowing from' the explicit disclosure of the prior art."

- ***Rosco, Inc. v. Mirror Lite Co.***, 304 F.3d 1373, 1380, 64 U.S.P.Q.2d 1676, 1680 (Fed.Cir.2002). "Under the doctrine of inherency, if an element is not expressly disclosed in a prior art reference, the reference will still be deemed to anticipate a subsequent claim if the missing element is necessarily present in the thing described in the reference, and that it would be so recognized by persons of ordinary skill. Inherent anticipation requires that the missing descriptive material is necessarily present, not merely probably or possibly present, in the prior art." (Internal quotes omitted.) *See also* ***Leggett & Platt, Inc. v. VUTEk, Inc.***, 537 F.3d 1349, 1354, 87 U.S.P.Q.2d 1947, 1951 (Fed.Cir.2008); ***In re Omeprazole Patent Litig.***, 483 F.3d 1364, 1373, 82 U.S.P.Q.2d 1643, 1650 (Fed.Cir.2007); ***Perricone v. Medicis Pharm.***, 432 F.3d 1368, 1375-76, 77 U.S.P.Q.2d 1321, 1325-26 (Fed.Cir.2005).

- ***Bristol-Myers Squibb Co. v. Ben Venue Labs.***, 246 F.3d 1368, 1378, 58 U.S.P.Q.2d 1508, 1515 (Fed.Cir. 2001). "[I]t is axiomatic that that which would infringe if later anticipates if earlier [than the date of invention]. *At F.3d 1379, U.S.P.Q.2d 1516:* Enablement of an anticipatory reference may be demonstrated by a later reference. ... Although anticipation requires a showing of each limitation of a claim in a single reference, we looked to [separate references] only 'to show that the claimed subject matter ... was in the public's possession.' [A]dditional references may be relied on for anticipation under ... §102(b) 'solely as evidence that, more than one year prior to appellant's filing date, a method of preparing the claimed subject matter ... would have been known by, or would have been obvious to, one of ordinary skill in the art.' Furthermore, ... additional references used solely to show enablement of an anticipatory reference need not antedate that reference, but must show that the claimed subject matter was in possession of the public more than one year prior to the applicant's filing date."

- ***Celeritas Techs. v. Rockwell Int'l***, 150 F.3d 1354, 1361, 47 U.S.P.Q.2d 1516, 1522 (Fed.Cir.1998). "A reference is no less anticipatory if, after disclosing the invention, the reference then disparages it. Thus the question whether a reference 'teaches away' from the invention is inapplicable to an anticipation analysis."

- ***Scripps Clinic & Research Found. v. Genentech, Inc.***, 927 F.2d 1565, 1576-77, 18 U.S.P.Q.2d 1001, 1010 (Fed.Cir.1991), *overruled on other grounds*, ***Abbott Labs. v. Sandoz, Inc.***, 566 F.3d 1282, 90 U.S.P.Q.2d 1769 (Fed.Cir.2009). "It is sometimes appropriate to consider extrinsic evidence to explain the disclosure of a reference. Such factual elaboration is necessarily of limited scope and probative value, for a finding of anticipation requires that all aspects of the claimed invention were already described in a single reference: a finding that is not supportable if it is necessary to prove facts beyond those disclosed in the reference in order to meet the claim limitations. The role of extrinsic evidence is to educate the decision-maker to what the reference meant to persons of ordinary skill in the field of the invention, not to fill gaps in the reference. If it is necessary to reach beyond the boundaries of a single reference to provide missing disclosure of the claimed invention, the proper ground is not [35 U.S.C.] §102 anticipation, but [35 U.S.C.] §103 obviousness."

In re Spada, 911 F.2d 705, 708, 15 U.S.P.Q.2d 1655, 1657 (Fed.Cir.1990). "Rejection for anticipation or lack of novelty requires, as the first step in the inquiry, that all the elements of the claimed invention be described in a single reference. Further, the reference must describe the applicant's claimed invention sufficiently to have placed a person of ordinary skill in the field of the invention in possession of it. *At F.2d 709, U.S.P.Q.2d 1658:* [D]iscovery of an unobvious property and use does not overcome the statutory restraint of §102 when the claimed composition is known. ... This burden was not met by simply including the assertedly different properties in the claims. When the claimed compositions are not novel they are not rendered patentable by recitation of properties, whether or not these properties are shown or suggested in the prior art." *See also* ***In re Crish***, 393 F.3d 1253, 1258, 73 U.S.P.Q.2d 1364, 1368 (Fed.Cir.2004).

Anticipation—Design Patents

International Seaway Trading Corp. v. Walgreens Corp., 589 F.3d 1233, 1239-40, 93 U.S.P.Q.2d 1001, 1005 (Fed.Cir.2009). "The ordinary observer test originated in 1871 when the Supreme Court held that if, in the eye of an ordinary observer, giving such attention as a purchaser usually gives, two designs are substantially the same, if the resemblance is such as to deceive such an observer, inducing him to purchase one supposing it to be the other, the first one patented is infringed by the other. In ***Egyptian Goddess***, we also refined the ordinary observer test by characterizing the ordinary observer as being deemed to view the differences between the patented design and the accused product in the context of the prior art. We explained: When the differences between the claimed and accused design are viewed in light of the prior art, the attention of the hypothetical ordinary observer will be drawn to those aspects of the claimed design that differ from the prior art. And when the claimed design is close to the prior art designs, small differences between the accused design and the claimed design are likely to be important to the eye of the hypothetical ordinary observer. [¶] [W]e now conclude that the ordinary observer test must logically be the sole test for anticipation as well." (Internal quotes omitted.)

§102—Corroboration

Washburn & Moen Mfg. v. Beat'Em All Barbed-Wire Co., 143 U.S. 275, 284 (1892). "We have now to deal with certain unpatented devices, claimed to be complete anticipations of this patent, the existence and use of which are proven only by oral testimony. In view of the unsatisfactory character of testimony, arising from the forgetfulness of witnesses, their liability to mistakes, their proneness to recollect things as the party calling them would have them recollect them, aside from the temptation to actual perjury, courts have not only imposed upon defendants the burden of proving such devices, but have required that the proof shall be clear, satisfactory, and beyond a reasonable doubt."

NFC Tech. v. Matal, 871 F.3d 1367, 1371-72, 124 U.S.P.Q.2d 1169, 1172 (Fed.Cir.2017). "Conception is a question of law based on subsidiary factual findings. [¶] An inventor's testimony, standing alone, is insufficient to prove conception—some form of corroboration must be shown. There is no particular formula that an inventor must follow in providing corroboration of his testimony of conception. Instead, corroboration is determined by a 'rule of reason' analysis, in which an evaluation of all pertinent evidence must be made so that a sound determination of the credibility of the inventor's story may be reached. Under the rule of reason, the evidence must be considered as a whole, not individually. Thus, an inventor's conception can be corroborated even though no one piece of evidence in and of itself establishes that fact, ... and even through circumstantial evidence.... At bottom, the goal of the analysis is to determine whether the inventor's story is credible." (Internal quotes omitted.)

EmeraChem Holdings, LLC v. Volkswagen Grp., 859 F.3d 1341, 1347, 123 U.S.P.Q.2d 1146, 1150 (Fed.Cir. 2017). The inventor's declaration "is insufficient to demonstrate that the cited portions of [the patent] are not 'by another.' [Our caselaw] require[s] more than a naked assertion by the inventor. [We have allowed] an attached drawing [or] an additional explanation as to the facts in [a] case. [¶] In certain cases, we have recognized that even non-documentary, circumstantial evidence may sufficiently corroborate."

i4i L.P. v. Microsoft Corp., 598 F.3d 831, 847, 93 U.S.P.Q.2d 1943, 1955 (Fed.Cir.2010), *aff'd*, 564 U.S. 91 (2011). "Anticipation is an affirmative defense. We do not agree that [P] was required to come forward with corroboration to 'rebut' [D's] prima facie case of anticipation. Corroboration is required in certain circumstances. [¶] Though we require corroboration of 'any witness whose testimony alone is asserted to *invalidate* a patent,' ... here the inventor testimony was offered by [P] in *response* to [D's] attack on the validity of the ... patent. It was not offered to meet [D's] burden of proving invalidity by clear and convincing evidence. ... Accordingly, we hold that corroboration was not required in this instance, where the testimony was offered in response to a claim of anticipation and pertained to whether the prior art practiced the claimed invention."

Lacks Indus. v. McKechnie Vehicle Components, 322 F.3d 1335, 1349, 66 U.S.P.Q.2d 1083, 1093 (Fed.Cir. 2003). "The requirement for corroboration of oral testimony occurs most often in the context of priority disputes, wherein we have held an inventor's testimony, standing alone, cannot support a claim of derivation (§102(f)) or priority (§102(g)). Corroboration is also required where ... the testimony is from an accused infringer concerning the sale (or offer to sell) or public use of an invention more than one year before the filing of a patent. Whether the asserted identity of the product with the claimed invention has been sufficiently corroborated, either by documentary or testimonial evidence, is generally measured under a 'rule of reason' standard. Under this analysis, '[a]n evaluation of all pertinent evidence must be made so that a sound determination of the credibility of [evidence] may be reached.' In evaluating such evidence, we use the [following] factors ...: (1) the relationship between the corroborating witness and the alleged prior user, (2) the time period between the event and trial, (3) the interest of the corroborating witness in the subject matter in suit, (4) contradiction or impeachment of the witness' testimony, (5) the extent and details of the corroborating testimony, (6) the witness' familiarity with the subject matter of the patented invention and the prior use, (7) probability that a prior use could occur considering the state of the art at the time, and (8) impact of the invention on the industry, and the commercial value of its practice." *See also* ***Checkpoint Sys. v. All-Tag Sec. S.A.***, 412 F.3d 1331, 1339, 75 U.S.P.Q.2d 1200, 1205-06 (Fed.Cir.2005); ***Juicy Whip, Inc. v. Orange Bang, Inc.***, 292 F.3d 728, 741, 63 U.S.P.Q.2d 1251, 1260 (Fed.Cir.2002); ***Sandt Tech. v. Resco Metal & Plastics Corp.***, 264 F.3d 1344, 1351, 60 U.S.P.Q.2d 1091, 1095 (Fed.Cir.2001); ***Finnigan Corp. v. I.T.C.***, 180 F.3d 1354, 1367, 51 U.S.P.Q.2d 1001, 1010 (Fed.Cir.1999).

Juicy Whip, Inc. v. Orange Bang, Inc., 292 F.3d 728, 740, 63 U.S.P.Q.2d 1251, 1259 (Fed.Cir.2002). "Even if the testimony at trial were sufficient to correlate each element of the alleged anticipatory [prior art] with each claim limitation, this court must still ascertain whether that type of evidence was adequate to support the jury's finding. Historically, courts have looked with disfavor upon finding anticipation with only oral testimony. *At F.3d 743, U.S.P.Q.2d 1261-62:* [W]e conclude that the evidence presented by [D] was insufficient as a matter of law to surmount the clear and convincing evidence hurdle. ... None of the six witnesses can be said to be disinterested. ... The six witnesses are sufficiently inter-connected to consider them 'interested witnesses' in the context of the ***Reuter*** factors. [¶] The one writing proffered to corroborate the oral testimony in this case is inadequate to meet the applicable standard of proof. Reliable evidence of corroboration preferably comes in the form of physical records that were made contemporaneously with the alleged prior invention. Here, the sketches of the 1983 dispenser were not drawn by [witnesses] until their depositions in this case. Thus, they are no more reliable than the oral testimony accompanying the drawings. ... We do not conclude that the witnesses below were not credible. Rather, with the guidance of precedent cautioning against the reliance on oral testimony alone, we hold that the evidence of record did not provide the clear and convincing evidence necessary to invalidate the patent for prior public knowledge. The district court, therefore, erred by denying [P's] motion for JMOL on anticipation."

Finnigan Corp. v. I.T.C., 180 F.3d 1354, 1367, 51 U.S.P.Q.2d 1001, 1010 (Fed.Cir.1999). "While this court has in the past applied the requirement of corroboration more often in the context of priority disputes under ... §102(g), corroboration has been required to prove invalidity under other subsections of §102 as well. In the context of §102(f) (derivation) and §102(g) (priority), we have stated that 'the case law is unequivocal that an inventor's testimony respecting facts surrounding a claim of derivation or priority of invention cannot, standing alone, rise to the level of clear and convincing proof.' No principled reason appears for applying a different rule when other subsections of §102 are implicated: a witness's uncorroborated testimony is equally suspect as clear and convincing evidence if he testifies concerning the use of the invention in public before invention by the patentee (§102(a)), use of the invention in public one year before the patentee filed his patent (§102(b)), or invention before the patentee (§102(g)). *At U.S.P.Q.2d 1011:* Moreover, the need for corroboration exists regardless whether the party testifying concerning the invalidating activity is interested in the outcome of the litigation (*e.g.*, because that party is the accused infringer) or is uninterested but testifying on behalf of an interested party. *At F.3d 1369, U.S.P.Q.2d 1012:* In any event, corroboration is required of any witness whose testimony alone is asserted to invalidate a patent, regardless of his or her level of interest."

§102(a)—Known or Used by Others

Ecolochem, Inc. v. Southern Cal. Edison Co., 227 F.3d 1361, 1369, 56 U.S.P.Q.2d 1065, 1071 (Fed.Cir. 2000). "A presentation indicative of the state of knowledge and use in this country ... qualifies as prior art for anticipation purposes under §102."

Woodland Trust v. Flowertree Nursery, Inc., 148 F.3d 1368, 1370, 47 U.S.P.Q.2d 1363, 1365 (Fed.Cir. 1998). "Section 102(a) establishes that a person can not patent what was already known to others. If the invention was known to or used by others in this country before the date of the patentee's invention, the later inventor has not contributed to the store of knowledge, and has no entitlement to a patent. Accordingly, in order to invalidate a patent based on prior knowledge or use, that knowledge or use must have been available to the public." *See also* ***Minnesota Mining & Mfg. v. Chemque, Inc.***, 303 F.3d 1294, 1301, 64 U.S.P.Q.2d 1270, 1274 (Fed.Cir.2002).

§102(a)—Before the Invention

Mahurkar v. C.R. Bard, Inc., 79 F.3d 1572, 1576, 38 U.S.P.Q.2d 1288, 1290 (Fed.Cir.1996). "In ex parte patent prosecution, an examiner may refer to a document published within one year before the filing date of a patent application as prior art. However, this label only applies until the inventor comes forward with evidence showing an earlier date of invention. Once the inventor shows an earlier date of invention, the document is no longer prior art under §102(a). [¶] Any suggestion that a document is prior art because it appears before the filing date of a patent ignores the requirements of §102(a). Section 102(a) explicitly refers to invention dates, not filing dates. Thus, under §102(a), a document is prior art only when published before the invention date."

§102(b)—Generally

Kewanee Oil Co. v. Bicron Corp., 416 U.S. 470, 484 n.13, 181 U.S.P.Q. 673, 679 n.13 (1974). "An invention may be placed 'in public use or on sale' within the meaning of ... §102(b) without losing its secret character."

Minton v. National Ass'n of Secs. Dealers, Inc., 336 F.3d 1373, 1376, 67 U.S.P.Q.2d 1614, 1616-17 (Fed. Cir.2003). "An assessment of the validity of a patent claim in light of an alleged sale involves, first, determining whether a sale is truly a 'sale' within the meaning of ... §102(b), a question of law based on underlying facts. The next step is claim construction, during which the court determines the scope and meaning of the patent claims.... The final step involves a comparison of the asserted claims with the device or process that was sold. A determination that a claim is invalid as being anticipated requires factual findings that 'each and every limitation is found either expressly or inherently' in the device or process that was sold. Because 'a patent is presumed to be valid ... and this presumption can only be overcome by clear and convincing evidence of facts to the contrary,' ... the facts underlying a conclusion that a claim is unpatentable in light of a sale must be proven with clear and convincing evidence."

Lacks Indus. v. McKechnie Vehicle Components, 322 F.3d 1335, 1346, 66 U.S.P.Q.2d 1083, 1091 (Fed.Cir. 2003). "[A]n inventor's own disclosure 'will not anticipate his later invention unless that prior work is such as to constitute a statutory bar under §102(b).'" *See also* ***Specialty Composites v. Cabot Corp.***, 845 F.2d 981, 990-91 n.9, 6 U.S.P.Q.2d 1601, 1607 n.9 (Fed.Cir. 1988).

Dana Corp. v. American Axle & Mfg., 279 F.3d 1372, 1375, 61 U.S.P.Q.2d 1609, 1611 (Fed.Cir.2002). "When the asserted basis of invalidity is a public use or on-sale bar, the court should determine 'whether the subject of the barring activity met each of the limitations of the claim, and thus was an embodiment of the claimed invention.'"

Woodland Trust v. Flowertree Nursery, Inc., 148 F.3d 1368, 1370, 47 U.S.P.Q.2d 1363, 1365-66 (Fed.Cir. 1998). "[A]n inventor's own prior commercial use, albeit kept secret, may constitute a public use or sale under §102(b), barring him from obtaining a patent. *At F.3d 1371:* However, when an asserted prior use is not that of the applicant, §102(b) is not a bar when that prior use or knowledge is not available to the public."

§102(b)—Critical Date

Scaltech, Inc. v. Retec/Tetra, L.L.C., 269 F.3d 1321, 1327, 60 U.S.P.Q.2d 1687, 1691 (Fed.Cir.2001). "The date exactly one year prior to the date of application for the patent is known as the critical date."

§102(b)—Printed Publication

See also chart, "Public Accessibility of Printed Publication Under 35 U.S.C. §102," p. 772.

Blue Calypso, LLC v. Groupon, Inc., 815 F.3d 1331, 1348, 118 U.S.P.Q.2d 1035, 1048 (Fed.Cir.2016). "The issue of public accessibility has frequently arisen in the context of references stored in libraries. In these cases, we generally inquire whether the reference was sufficiently indexed or cataloged."

Suffolk Techs. v. AOL Inc., 752 F.3d 1358, 1365, 110 U.S.P.Q.2d 2034, 2039 (Fed.Cir.2014). "[A] printed publication need not be easily searchable after publication if it was sufficiently disseminated at the time of its publication."

Cordis Corp. v. Boston Sci. Corp., 561 F.3d 1319, 1333-34, 90 U.S.P.Q.2d 1401, 1412 (Fed.Cir.2009). The question is "whether the distribution to a limited number of entities without a legal obligation of confidentiality renders the monographs printed publications under §102(b). We have held that where a distribution is made to a limited number of entities, a binding agreement of confidentiality may defeat a finding of public accessibility. But we have also held that such a binding legal obligation is not essential. We have noted that where professional and behavioral norms entitle a party to a reasonable expectation that information will not be copied or further distributed, we are more reluctant to find something a 'printed publication.' [¶] The district court properly concluded that [inventor's] distribution of the monographs to his academic and research colleagues did not render the monographs prior art printed publications." (Internal quotes omitted.)

Kyocera Wireless Corp. v. ITC, 545 F.3d 1340, 1350, 89 U.S.P.Q.2d 1057, 1064 (Fed.Cir.2008). "Because there are many ways in which a reference may be disseminated to the interested public, 'public accessibility' has been called the touchstone in determining whether a reference constitutes a 'printed publication' bar under 35 U.S.C. §102(b). A reference is publicly accessible upon a satisfactory showing that such document has been disseminated or otherwise made available to the extent that persons interested and ordinarily skilled in the subject matter or art exercising reasonable diligence, can locate it. This court assesses public accessibility on a case-by-case basis." (Internal quotes omitted.) *See also* **Bruckelmyer v. Ground Heaters, Inc.**, 445 F.3d 1374, 1378, 78 U.S.P.Q.2d 1684, 1687 (Fed. Cir.2006); **In re Klopfenstein**, 380 F.3d 1345, 1350-51, 72 U.S.P.Q.2d 1117, 1120 (Fed.Cir.2004); **In re Cronyn**, 890 F.2d 1158, 1160, 13 U.S.P.Q.2d 1070, 1071-72 (Fed. Cir.1989).

SRI Int'l v. Internet Sec. Sys., 511 F.3d 1186, 1196, 85 U.S.P.Q.2d 1489, 1497 (Fed.Cir.2008). Publication "was placed 'on' the [File Transfer Protocol (FTP)] server. Yet, the FTP server did not contain an index or catalogue or other tools for customary and meaningful research. [¶] The record on summary judgment does not show that an anonymous user skilled in the art in 1997 would have gained access to the FTP server and would have freely navigated through the directory structure to find [publication]. *At F.3d 1197:* Indeed the record does not show that anyone accessed [publication] via the FTP server during the seven days in which it was posted. While actual retrieval of a publication is not a requirement for public accessibility, this record does not evince that [publication] was accessible to anyone other than the peer-review committee, thus further suggesting an absence of actual public accessibility. [¶] Therefore, on summary judgment, this court finds that the prepublication [publication], though on the FTP server, was not catalogued or indexed in a meaningful way and not intended for dissemination to the public." *But see* **Voter Verified, Inc. v. Premier Election Solutions, Inc.**, 698 F.3d 1374, 1380, 104 U.S.P.Q.2d 1553, 1556-57 (Fed.Cir.2012) (while relevant to public accessibility, indexing is not absolute prerequisite to establishing online references as printed publications).

In re Elsner, 381 F.3d 1125, 1128, 72 U.S.P.Q.2d 1038, 1041 (Fed.Cir.2004). "The particular question … before us is whether evidence of the foreign sale of a claimed reproducible plant variety may enable an otherwise non-enabled printed publication disclosing that plant, thereby creating a §102(b) bar. On that issue of first impression, we hold in the affirmative."

Cooper Cameron Corp. v. Kvaerner Oilfield Prods., 291 F.3d 1317, 1321, 62 U.S.P.Q.2d 1846, 1849 (Fed.Cir.2002). "Whether an asserted anticipatory document qualifies as a 'printed publication' under §102 is a legal conclusion based on underlying factual determinations. *At F.3d 1324, U.S.P.Q.2d 1851:* [W]e disagree with the court's conclusion that the 'confidential' label on that report removed it as an available prior art reference. [T]he report contained only a single confidentiality notice relating to financial information.... That notice does not render the entire document inaccessible in light of evidence that the reports were available to participants who were allowed to share confidential data with others." *See also* **Northern Telecom Inc. v. Datapoint Corp.**, 908 F.2d 931, 936, 15 U.S.P.Q.2d 1321, 1324-25 (Fed.Cir.1990).

Advanced Display Sys. v. Kent State Univ., 212 F.3d 1272, 1282, 54 U.S.P.Q.2d 1673, 1679 (Fed.Cir. 2000). "[I]nvalidity by anticipation requires that the four corners of a single, prior art document describe every element of the claimed invention, either expressly or inherently, such that a person of ordinary skill in the art could practice the invention without undue experimentation. Material not explicitly contained in the single, prior art document may still be considered for purposes of anticipation if that material is incorporated by reference into the document. Incorporation by reference provides a method for integrating material from various documents into a host document—a patent or printed publication in an anticipation determination—by citing such material in a manner that makes clear that the material is effectively part of the host document as if it were explicitly contained therein. To incorporate material by reference, the host document must identify with detailed particularity what specific material it incorporates and clearly indicate where that material is found in the various documents." *See also* **Apple Inc. v. International Trade Comm'n**, 725 F.3d 1356, 1362, 107 U.S.P.Q.2d 1864, 1868 (Fed.Cir. 2013); **Commonwealth Sci. & Indus. Research Org. v. Buffalo Tech.**, 542 F.3d 1363, 1371-72, 88 U.S.P.Q.2d 1564, 1570 (Fed.Cir.2008); **Finnigan Corp. v. I.T.C.**, 180 F.3d 1354, 1365, 51 U.S.P.Q.2d 1001, 1009 (Fed.Cir. 1999).

Constant v. Advanced Micro-Devices, Inc., 848 F.2d 1560, 1569, 7 U.S.P.Q.2d 1057, 1062-63 (Fed.Cir. 1988). "Evidence of routine business practice can be sufficient to prove that a reference was made accessible before a critical date. Accessibility goes to the issue of whether interested members of the relevant public could obtain the information if they wanted to. If accessibility is proved, there is no requirement to show that particular members of the public actually received the information."

§102(b)—Public Use

Dey, L.P. v. Sunovion Pharms., 715 F.3d 1351, 1355-56, 106 U.S.P.Q.2d 1916, 1919-20 (Fed.Cir.2013). "Although prior uses are often carried out by or at the direction of the inventor-patentee, we have held that 'third party prior use accessible to the public is a §102(b) bar.' But even in the case of third-party uses, being 'accessible to the public' still requires public availability; secret or confidential third-party uses do not invalidate later-filed patents. For that reason, we have applied §102(b) to invalidate a patent based on third-party use when the third party 'made no attempt to maintain confidentiality or to deliberately evade disclosure,' ... made no 'discernible effort to maintain the [invention] as confidential,' ... or 'made no efforts to conceal the device or keep anything about it secret[ ]'.... [¶] The degree of confidentiality necessary to avoid a finding of public use naturally depends on the circumstances. For example, if there is no confidentiality agreement in place, the skill and knowledge of those observing an invention can shed light on the degree to which it was kept confidential. Even limited disclosure to those who are skilled enough to know, understand, and 'easily demonstrate the invention to others,' may mean that there was no reasonable expectation of secrecy and that the invention was therefore in public use. By contrast, when disclosure is limited to a small number of uninformed observers there may be no reason to believe 'that a viewer ... could thereby learn anything of [the later-patented invention]' and disclose the invention to others. In such cases, a finder of fact might reasonably conclude that the third party's use remained confidential and that the invention was not 'accessible to the public.' *At F.3d 1357, U.S.P.Q.2d 1921:* We have never required a formal confidentiality agreement to show non-public use ...; in the absence of such an agreement, we simply ask whether there were 'circumstances creating a similar expectation of secrecy[ ]'.... *At F.3d 1358:* Many cases concern studies in which investigators sign strict confidentiality agreements but patients do not, and courts have routinely rejected the argument that such an arrangement necessarily strips the trial of confidentiality protection or renders it accessible to the public."

Zenith Elecs. Corp. v. PDI Comm. Sys., 522 F.3d 1348, 1356, 86 U.S.P.Q.2d 1513, 1518 (Fed.Cir.2008). "Determining whether a patent claim is invalid for prior public use under §102(b) requires comparing the claim to the alleged public use. 'Section 102(b) may bar patentability by anticipation if the device used in public includes every limitation of the later claimed invention....' Contrary to [P's] arguments, however, we note that the public use itself need not be enabling. Rather, we must simply determine whether the public use related to a device that embodied the invention."

American Seating Co. v. USSC Grp., 514 F.3d 1262, 1267, 85 U.S.P.Q.2d 1683, 1685-86 (Fed.Cir.2008). "The test for whether an invention is ineligible for a patent due to the §102(b) public use bar 'is whether the purported use: (1) was accessible to the public; or (2) was commercially exploited.' Consideration of public use includes analysis of, *inter alia*, the nature of and public access to activities involving the invention; confidentiality obligations imposed upon observers; commercial exploitation; and the circumstances surrounding testing and experimentation. An invention is in public use if it is shown to or used by an individual other than the inventor under no limitation, restriction, or obligation of confidentiality. *At F.3d 1268:* [T]he fact that the inventors revealed the prototype to a select group of individuals without a written confidentiality agreement is not dispositive. When access to an invention is clearly limited and controlled by the inventor, depending upon the relationships of the observers and the inventor, an understanding of confidentiality can be implied."

Adenta GmbH v. OrthoArm, Inc., 501 F.3d 1364, 1369, 84 U.S.P.Q.2d 1428, 1431 (Fed.Cir.2007). "Whether a patent is invalid for a public use or sale is a question of law, reviewed *de novo*, based on underlying facts, reviewed for substantial evidence following a jury verdict."

Invitrogen Corp. v. Biocrest Mfg., 424 F.3d 1374, 1380, 76 U.S.P.Q.2d 1741, 1744 (Fed.Cir.2005). "[T]he ready for patenting component of ***Pfaff***'s two-part test [is] another necessary requirement of a public use bar." *See also* ***In re Omeprazole Patent Litig.***, 536 F.3d 1361, 1372, 87 U.S.P.Q.2d 1865, 1873 (Fed.Cir.2008).

Eolas Techs. v. Microsoft Corp., 399 F.3d 1325, 1334, 73 U.S.P.Q.2d 1782, 1789 (Fed.Cir.2005), *overruled on other grounds*, ***Cardiac Pacemakers, Inc. v. St. Jude Med., Inc.***, 576 F.3d 1348, 91 U.S.P.Q.2d 1898 (Fed.Cir.2009). "The district court erred in linking its §102(b) public use finding to its §102(g) abandonment finding. A public use under §102(b) cannot be undone by subsequent actions. The inquiry into a §102(b) public use proceeds independent of the inquiry into a §102(g) abandonment. [T]hird party prior use accessible to the public is a §102(b) bar."

Minnesota Mining & Mfg. v. Chemque, Inc., 303 F.3d 1294, 1307, 64 U.S.P.Q.2d 1270, 1278 (Fed.Cir. 2002). "Although 'public use' for purposes of §102(b) is defined differently from 'use' for purposes of §102(a), both require actual use by someone at some point." *See also* ***In re Epstein***, 32 F.3d 1559, 1564, 31 U.S.P.Q.2d 1817, 1820 (Fed.Cir.1994).

Tone Bros. v. Sysco Corp., 28 F.3d 1192, 1197 n.4, 31 U.S.P.Q.2d 1321, 1323 n.4 (Fed.Cir.1994). "The party asserting the public use bar has the initial burden of showing by clear and convincing evidence facts which support the existence of a public use within the meaning of [35 U.S.C.] §102(b). Once the challenger has made out this *prima facie* case of public use, a burden of production is placed upon the patent owner; the patent owner must come forward with convincing evidence to counter the *prima facie* case. At all times, however, because patents are given a presumption of validity under 35 U.S.C. §282, the burden of persuasion remains with the party asserting the bar. *At F.3d 1200 n.8, U.S.P.Q.2d 1326 n.8:* [E]xistence of a confidentiality agreement is not dispositive of the public use issue." *See also* ***Sinskey v. Pharmacia Ophthalmics, Inc.***, 982 F.2d 494, 498, 25 U.S.P.Q.2d 1290, 1293 (Fed.Cir. 1992).

§102(b)—Public Use—Examples

Motionless Keyboard Co. v. Microsoft Corp., 486 F.3d 1376, 1385, 82 U.S.P.Q.2d 1801, 1807 (Fed.Cir. 2007). Held: Inventor's disclosure of an ergonomic keyboard to his business partner, a friend, and potential investors did not constitute public use because the keyboard was not connected to a computer or any other device and thus only provided a visual view of the new keyboard design without any disclosure of the invention's ability to translate finger movements into actuation of keys to transmit data.

Lockwood v. American Airlines, Inc., 107 F.3d 1565, 1570, 41 U.S.P.Q.2d 1961, 1964 (Fed.Cir.1997). "[T]he public was aware that [prior-art system] possessed [a certain capability] and that the public had been using [prior-art system] to make travel reservations from independent travel agencies prior to [P's] date of invention. *At U.S.P.Q.2d 1965:* [D's] public use of the high-level aspects of [prior-art] system was enough to place the *claimed* features of the ... patent in the public's possession." Held: Public use of the high-level aspects of prior-art computer reservation system was "public use" under §102.

Beachcombers, Int'l v. Wildewood Creative Prods., 31 F.3d 1154, 1159-60, 31 U.S.P.Q.2d 1653, 1657 (Fed.Cir.1994). Held: Presentation and display of a prototype of the claimed invention at a party where 20 to 30 guests were present constituted public use. The host personally demonstrated the device to some of the guests for the purpose of getting feedback on the device, and she made no efforts to conceal the device or keep anything about it secret.

Moleculon Research Corp. v. CBS, Inc., 793 F.2d 1261, 1266-67, 229 U.S.P.Q. 805, 808 (Fed.Cir.1986). Held: Inventor's disclosure of his claimed invention—a puzzle—to a few close colleagues did not constitute public use because inventor had not given over the invention for free and unrestricted use by another person, and, based on the personal relationships and surrounding circumstances, inventor at all times retained control over puzzle's use and the distribution of information concerning it.

§102(b)—On Sale

Pfaff v. Wells Elecs., Inc., 525 U.S. 55, 67-68, 48 U.S.P.Q.2d 1641, 1646 (1998). "We conclude ... that the on-sale bar applies when two conditions are satisfied before the critical date. First, the product must be the subject of a commercial offer for sale. *At U.S.P.Q.2d 1647:* Second, the invention must be ready for patenting. That condition may be satisfied in at least two ways: by proof of reduction to practice before the critical date; or by proof that prior to the critical date the inventor had prepared drawings or other descriptions of the invention that were sufficiently specific to enable a person skilled in the art to practice the invention." *See also* ***Honeywell Int'l v. Universal Avionics Sys.***, 488 F.3d 982, 996-97, 82 U.S.P.Q.2d 1886, 1897-98 (Fed.Cir. 2007); ***Robotic Vision Sys. v. View Eng'g***, 249 F.3d 1307, 1313, 58 U.S.P.Q.2d 1723, 1727-28 (Fed.Cir.2001).

Medicines Co. v. Hospira, Inc., 881 F.3d 1347, 1351, 125 U.S.P.Q.2d 1598, ___ (Fed.Cir.2018). "A patent is invalid under the on-sale bar if, before the critical date, (1) the product is the subject of a commercial offer for sale, and (2) the invention is ready for patenting. [There is] a framework for determining whether there is an offer for sale. We apply Federal Circuit law and analyze the issue under the law of contracts as generally understood, focusing on those activities that would be understood to be commercial sales and offers for sale in the commercial community. Although the Uniform Commercial Code ... is not dispositive, it is a useful guide for defining whether a communication or series of communications rises to the level of a commercial offer for sale. A commercial sale is a contract between parties to give and to pass rights of property for consideration which the buyer pays or promises to pay the seller for the thing bought or sold. An offer for sale is one which the other party could make into a binding contract by simple acceptance." (Internal quotes omitted.) *See also* ***Group One, Ltd. v. Hallmark Cards, Inc.***, 254 F.3d 1041, 1047-48, 59 U.S.P.Q.2d 1121, 1125-26 (Fed.Cir.2001); ***Lacks Indus. v. McKechnie Vehicle Components***, 322 F.3d 1335, 1347-48, 66 U.S.P.Q.2d 1083, 1092 (Fed.Cir.2003).

Helsinn Healthcare S.A. v. Teva Pharms. USA, Inc., 855 F.3d 1356, 1365, 123 U.S.P.Q.2d 1045, 1051 (Fed.Cir.2017). "[A]n agreement contracting for the sale of the claimed invention contingent on regulatory approval is still a commercial sale as the commercial community would understand that term. *At F.3d 1370, U.S.P.Q.2d 1054:* Our cases explicitly rejected a requirement that the details of the invention be disclosed in the terms of sale."

Medicines Co. v. Hospira, Inc., 827 F.3d 1363, 1376, 119 U.S.P.Q.2d 1329, 1338 (Fed.Cir.2016). "[W]e have held that the sale of products made using patented methods triggers the on-sale bar, even though title to the claimed method itself did not pass. *At U.S.P.Q.2d 1339:* Like the absence of title transfer, the confidential nature of the transactions is a factor which weighs against the conclusion that the transactions were commercial in nature. Again, this factor is not disqualifying in all instances.... Indeed, we, and our predecessors, have found confidential transactions to be patent invalidating sales under §102(b). *At F.3d 1377:* [W]e find that the mere stockpiling of a patented invention by the purchaser of manufacturing services does not constitute a 'commercial sale' under §102(b). Stockpiling—or building inventory—is, when not accompanied by an actual sale or offer for sale of the invention, mere pre-commercial activity in preparation for future sale. *At F.3d 1380, U.S.P.Q.2d 1341-42:* We still do not recognize a blanket 'supplier exception' to what would otherwise constitute a commercial sale as we have characterized it today. While the fact that a transaction is between a supplier and inventor is an important indicator that the transaction is not a commercial sale, understood as such in the commercial marketplace, it is not alone determinative. Where the supplier has title to the patented product or process, the supplier receives blanket authority to market the product or disclose the process for manufacturing the product to others, or the transaction is a sale of product at full market value, even a transfer of product to the inventor may constitute a commercial sale under §102(b). The focus must be on the commercial character of the transaction, not solely on the identity of the participants."

- ***August Tech. v. Camtek, Ltd.***, 655 F.3d 1278, 1289, 99 U.S.P.Q.2d 1766, 1775 (Fed.Cir.2011). "[W]e conclude that an invention cannot be offered for sale until its conception date. Hence, if an offer for sale is made and retracted prior to conception, there has been no offer for sale of the invention. In contrast, if an offer for sale is extended and remains open, a subsequent conception will cause it to become an offer for sale of the invention as of the conception date. In such a case, the seller is offering to sell *the invention* once he has conceived of it. Before that time, he was merely offering to sell an idea for a product." *See also* ***Sparton Corp. v. U.S.***, 399 F.3d 1321, 1324-25, 73 U.S.P.Q.2d 1919, 1922-23 (Fed.Cir.2005).

- ***In re Cygnus Telecomms. Tech., LLC, Patent Litig.***, 536 F.3d 1343, 1355, 87 U.S.P.Q.2d 1801, 1808 (Fed.Cir.2008). "With respect to the argument that [patentee's system] was not ready for patenting because the ... system would not work on a commercial scale, the district court correctly ruled that the question whether the ... system would work on a commercial scale is distinct from whether the system embodied the claims in the two patents at issue."

- ***Atlanta Attachment Co. v. Leggett & Platt, Inc.***, 516 F.3d 1361, 1365, 85 U.S.P.Q.2d 1995, 1998 (Fed.Cir. 2008). "To meet the first, commercial offer, prong, the offer must be sufficiently definite that another party could make a binding contract by simple acceptance, assuming consideration. In determining such definiteness, we review the language of the proposal in accordance with the principles of general contract law. ... Neither profit, revenue, nor even an actual sale is required for the use to be a commercial offer under §102(b)—an attempt to sell is sufficient if it rises to an offer upon which a contract can be made merely by accepting it. *At F.3d 1366-67, U.S.P.Q.2d 1999-2000:* The first ***Pfaff*** prong is also met, and experimental use negated, because [P] had presented a commercial offer for sale of the invention en masse. [¶] We now turn to the second ***Pfaff*** prong, ready for patenting. [¶] An invention is reduced to practice when it works for its intended purpose. An invention is said to work for its intended purpose when there is a demonstration of its workability or utility. [¶] [A]n invention can be considered reduced to practice 'even though it may later be refined or improved.' ... Consistent with the rule that later refinements do not preclude reduction to practice, it is improper to conclude that an invention is not reduced to practice merely because further testing is being conducted."

- ***Plumtree Software, Inc. v. Datamize, LLC***, 473 F.3d 1152, 1162, 81 U.S.P.Q.2d 1251, 1258 (Fed.Cir. 2006). Petitioner "could meet the first prong of the ***Pfaff*** test [commercial sale or offer for sale] under either of two alternative theories. First, [petitioner] could demonstrate that before the critical date [patent assignor] made a commercial offer to perform the patented method (even if the performance itself occurred after the critical date). Second, [petitioner] could demonstrate that before the critical date [patent assignor] in fact performed the patented method for a promise of future compensation. Under the second theory, [petitioner] would not need to prove that the contract itself required performance of the patented method. [¶] Under [the first theory], it is clear that the offeror must be legally bound to perform the patented method if the offer is accepted. Whether there has been a commercial offer is governed by federal common law." *See also* ***Schumer v. Laboratory Computer Sys.***, 308 F.3d 1304, 1315, 64 U.S.P.Q.2d 1832, 1841 (Fed.Cir.2002).

- ***TorPharm Inc. v. Ranbaxy Pharms.***, 336 F.3d 1322, 1327, 67 U.S.P.Q.2d 1511, 1514 (Fed.Cir.2003). "[I]f [patentee] had, more than one year before the filing of the application for [patent], sold [product] made by the claimed process, then its process claims would be invalid under §102(b)—regardless of whether the process was disclosed to the public or not. In contrast, if the product were sold by one other than the patentee, and the process of making remained unknown, then sale of the product would not pose a statutory bar to a claim on the process."

Minnesota Mining & Mfg. v. Chemque, Inc., 303 F.3d 1294, 1301, 64 U.S.P.Q.2d 1270, 1274 (Fed.Cir. 2002). "In order to invalidate a patent under the on-sale bar of ... §102(b), an accused infringer must demonstrate by clear and convincing evidence that there was a definite sale or offer to sell more than one year before the application for the patent and that the product sold or offered for sale anticipated the claimed invention or rendered it obvious. A determination that a product was placed on sale prior to the critical date is a conclusion of law based on underlying findings of fact. We review the ultimate determination *de novo*."

Netscape Comm. v. Konrad, 295 F.3d 1315, 1324, 63 U.S.P.Q.2d 1580, 1586 (Fed.Cir.2002). "[W]e have held that a sale or offer to sell under §102(b) must be between two separate entities. Where ... both parties to an alleged commercial offer for sale receive research funds from the same entity, it may be more difficult to determine whether the inventor is attempting to commercialize his invention. Accordingly, in such cases whether there is a bar depends on whether the seller so controls the purchaser that the invention remains out of the public's hands." *See also* ***Ferag AG v. Quipp Inc.***, 45 F.3d 1562, 1567, 33 U.S.P.Q.2d 1512, 1515 (Fed.Cir. 1995), *overruled on other grounds*, ***Pfaff v. Wells Elecs., Inc.***, 525 U.S. 55, 48 U.S.P.Q.2d 1641 (1998).

In re Kollar, 286 F.3d 1326, 1329, 62 U.S.P.Q.2d 1425, 1427 (Fed.Cir.2002). "The PTO bears the initial burden of demonstrating that the preponderance of the evidence establishes, *prima facie*, facts supporting the conclusion that the claimed invention was on sale within the meaning of §102(b). Whether an invention is 'on sale' within the meaning of §102(b) is a question of law based on underlying factual findings. We review legal determinations of the Board, including whether an invention was on sale before the critical date, without deference. We review the factual findings underlying that determination for substantial evidence. *At F.3d 1331, U.S.P.Q.2d 1428:* [M]erely granting a license to an invention, without more, does not trigger the on-sale bar of §102(b). *At F.3d 1330-31 n.3, U.S.P.Q.2d 1428 n.3:* We use the term 'license' here to refer to rights under a patent, not to describe a commercial transaction arranged as a 'license' or a 'lease' of a product or a device that may or may not have been patented. In certain situations, a 'license' in the latter sense of the word may be tantamount to a sale (*e.g.*, a standard computer software license), whereupon the bar of §102(b) would be triggered because the product is just as immediately transferred to the 'buyer' as if it were sold. However, ... a 'license' that merely grants rights under a patent cannot *per se* trigger the application of the on-sale bar. *At F.3d 1332, U.S.P.Q.2d 1429:* [T]he offer of a license under a patent and a description of the invention, without more, does not fall within the on-sale bar of §102(b). [¶] A process is ... not sold in the same sense as is a tangible item. 'Know-how' describing what the process consists of and how the process should be carried out may be sold in the sense that the buyer acquires knowledge of the process and obtains the freedom to carry it out pursuant to the terms of the transaction. However, such a transaction is not a 'sale' of the invention within the meaning of §102(b) because the process has not been carried out or performed as a result of the transaction. The same applies to a license to a patent covering a process. *At F.3d 1333, U.S.P.Q.2d 1430:* [T]he issue concerning the on-sale bar is not whether the process is physically represented or enabled by a written description, but whether the process has been commercialized. The transmission of a written description of the process does not meet that test. [¶] We hold only that licensing the invention, under which development of the claimed process would have to occur before the process is successfully commercialized, is not such a sale." (Internal quotes omitted.)

Special Devices, Inc. v. OEA, Inc., 270 F.3d 1353, 1355, 60 U.S.P.Q.2d 1537, 1539 (Fed.Cir.2001). "By phrasing the statutory bar in the passive voice, Congress indicated that it does not matter who places the invention 'on sale'; it only matters that someone—inventor, supplier or other third party—placed it on sale. [¶] [E]ven if a thief 'stole' the claimed invention and passed it on to an innocent buyer, the innocent buyer's subsequent offer to sell still triggered the plain language of the on-sale bar. [P]atentees could still protect themselves in these circumstances by taking 'prompt action' and filing a patent application within the one-year deadline. *At F.3d 1357, U.S.P.Q.2d 1541:* [T]he on-sale bar would apply even if a patentee's commercial activities took place in secret. We see no reason why sales for the purpose of the commercial stockpiling of an invention, even if they took place in secret, should merit different treatment."

Scaltech, Inc. v. Retec/Tetra, L.L.C., 269 F.3d 1321, 1328, 60 U.S.P.Q.2d 1687, 1692 (Fed.Cir.2001). "An offer for sale does not have to be accepted to implicate the on sale bar."

Monon Corp. v. Stoughton Trailers, Inc., 239 F.3d 1253, 1260, 57 U.S.P.Q.2d 1699, 1705 (Fed.Cir.2001). "Whether payment is made for the device is an important factual consideration, but the fact that a company paid for the use of patentee's device is not dispositive."

C.R. Bard, Inc. v. M3 Sys., 157 F.3d 1340, 1356, 48 U.S.P.Q.2d 1225, 1235 (Fed.Cir.1998). "Generally cost defrayal arrangements between collaborators are not deemed to be invalidating sales, nor are payments for use substantially for test purposes. *At F.3d 1357, U.S.P.Q.2d 1236:* To satisfy the on-sale requirement of §102(b) there must be more than an informational exchange of price information, when there is no reasonable contemplation that the quotation will be followed by purchase and sale as a commercial transaction."

Evans Cooling Sys. v. General Motors Corp., 125 F.3d 1448, 1451, 44 U.S.P.Q.2d 1037, 1040 (Fed.Cir. 1997). "[W]here there is a specific and definite offer for sale of a successfully tested device, such as that evidenced by a completed contract for sale, that embodies every limitation of the later patented invention as claimed prior to the critical date and that sale is clearly for commercial purposes, the analysis need not go any further. It is not that the totality of the circumstances test is not to be applied in such a case, but that there are then no circumstances, short of fraud or duress, that could turn such an offer into something other than a barring event. *At F.3d 1452:* [T]he mere fact that the offer for sale was illegal or ineffective does not remove it from the purview of the §102(b) bar. ... Similarly, the fact that the contract was cancelable or changeable under certain circumstances does not mean that it does not evidence a definite offer for sale."

W.L. Gore & Assocs. v. Garlock, Inc., 721 F.2d 1540, 1550, 220 U.S.P.Q. 303, 310 (Fed.Cir.1983), *overruled on other grounds*, ***eBay, Inc. v. MercExchange, L.L.C.***, 547 U.S. 388 (2006). "Assuming ... that [third party] sold tape produced on [a machine using the allegedly anticipating process] and that that tape was made by a process set forth in a claim of [P's] patent, the issue under §102(b) is whether that sale would defeat [P's] right to a patent on the process inventions set forth in the claims. [¶] There is no reason or statutory basis ... on which [third party's] secret commercialization of a process, if established, could be held a bar to the grant of a patent to [P] on that process. [¶] As between a prior inventor who benefits from a process by selling its product but suppresses, conceals, or otherwise keeps the process from the public, and a later inventor who promptly files a patent application from which the public will gain a disclosure of the process, the law favors the latter."

§102(b)—Experimental Use

Clock Spring, L.P. v. Wrapmaster, Inc., 560 F.3d 1317, 1326, 90 U.S.P.Q.2d 1212, 1217-18 (Fed.Cir.2009). "The experimental use exception is not a doctrine separate or apart from the public use bar. Rather, something that would otherwise be a public use may not be invalidating if it qualifies as an experimental use. *At F.3d 1327:* A use may be experimental only if it is designed to (1) test claimed features of the invention or (2) to determine whether an invention will work for its intended purpose—itself a requirement of patentability. In other words, an invention may not be ready for patenting if claimed features or overall workability are being tested. But, there is no experimental use unless claimed features or overall workability are being tested for purposes of the filing of a patent application. Indeed, the experimental use negation of the §102(b) bar only exists to allow an inventor to perfect his discovery through testing without losing his right to obtain a patent for his invention."

In re Omeprazole Patent Litig., 536 F.3d 1361, 1372, 87 U.S.P.Q.2d 1865, 1872 (Fed.Cir.2008). "[E]xperimental use cannot negate a public use when it is shown that the invention was reduced to practice before the experimental use."

Atlanta Attachment Co. v. Leggett & Platt, Inc., 516 F.3d 1361, 1365, 85 U.S.P.Q.2d 1995, 1998 (Fed.Cir. 2008). "The law has long recognized a distinction between experimental usage and commercial exploitation of an invention. While '[a]ny attempt to use [an invention] for profit ... would deprive the inventor of his right to a patent,' an inventor's use 'by way of experiment' does not bar patentability. Therefore, we must consider whether the suspect activities were experiments as opposed to an attempt to profit from the invention, that is, whether the primary purpose of the offers and sales was to conduct experimentation. *At F.3d 1366:* [E]xperimentation conducted to determine whether the invention would suit a particular customer's purposes does not fall within the experimental use exception. *At U.S.P.Q.2d 1999:* Additionally, [D] is correct to emphasize that [P] did not retain control over the prototypes when they were in [potential purchaser's] possession. While we have held that control *may* not be the lodestar test in all cases, we have also said that it is important, and sometimes dispositive. ... The fact that [potential purchaser] experimented with the prototypes is immaterial because the experimental use exception only concerns the actions of the inventors and their agents, and [potential purchaser] was not under the inventors' control." *See also* ***Honeywell Int'l v. Universal Avionics Sys.***, 488 F.3d 982, 998, 82 U.S.P.Q.2d 1886, 1898 (Fed.Cir.2007).

- ***General Motors Corp. v. General Elec. Co.***, 417 F.3d 1203, 1213, 75 U.S.P.Q.2d 1650, 1657 (Fed.Cir. 2005). "[W]e catalogued and consolidated all [the] considerations [of whether a sale or public use was for experimentation] into a list of 13 objective factors: (1) the necessity for public testing; (2) the amount of control over the experiment retained by the inventor; (3) the nature of the invention; (4) the length of the test period; (5) whether payment was made; (6) whether there was a secrecy obligation; (7) whether records of the experiment were kept; (8) who conducted the experiment; (9) the degree of commercial exploitation during testing; (10) whether the invention reasonably requires evaluation under actual conditions of use; (11) whether testing was systematically performed; (12) whether the inventor continually monitored the invention during testing; and (13) the nature of the contacts made with potential customers. This list is not exhaustive, and all of the experimentation factors may not apply in a particular case. They simply represent various kinds of evidence relevant to the question of whether pre-critical date activities involving the patented invention—either public use or sale[—]were primarily experimental and not commercial. *At F.3d 1214-15, U.S.P.Q.2d 1658:* If an inventor fails to communicate to a customer that the sale of the invention was made in pursuit of experimentation, then the customer, as well as the general public, can only view the sale as a normal commercial transaction. [W]e hold not only that customer awareness is among the experimentation factors, but also that it is critical. [¶] [W]e conclude that control and customer awareness ordinarily must be proven if experimentation is to be found."

- ***Netscape Comm. v. Konrad***, 295 F.3d 1315, 1320, 63 U.S.P.Q.2d 1580, 1583 (Fed.Cir.2002). "We look to the totality of the circumstances when evaluating whether there has been a public use within the meaning of §102(b). The totality of the circumstances is considered in conjunction with the policies underlying the public use bar. The circumstances may include: the nature of the activity that occurred in public; the public access to and knowledge of the public use; whether there was any confidentiality obligation imposed on persons who observed the use; whether persons other than the inventor performed the testing; the number of tests; the length of the test period in relation to tests of similar devices; and whether the inventor received payment for the testing. There may be additional factors in a particular case relevant to the public nature of the use or any asserted experimental aspect. *At F.3d 1321-22, U.S.P.Q.2d 1584:* The experimental use negation is unavailable to a patentee when the evidence presented does not establish that he was conducting a bona fide experiment." *See also* ***New Railhead Mfg. v. Vermeer Mfg.***, 298 F.3d 1290, 1297, 63 U.S.P.Q.2d 1843, 1848-49 (Fed.Cir.2002).

- ***Baxter Int'l v. COBE Labs.***, 88 F.3d 1054, 1060-61, 39 U.S.P.Q.2d 1437, 1442 (Fed.Cir.1996). "Further refinement of an invention to test additional uses is not the type of experimental use that will negate a public use. [¶] The inventor's lack of direction or control over [a third party's] use of the invention also supports a conclusion that the use was not experimental.... Accordingly, we hold that public testing before the critical date by a third party for his own unique purposes of an invention previously reduced to practice and obtained from someone other than the patentee, when such testing is independent of and not controlled by the patentee, is an invalidating public use, not an experimental public use."

- ***Allied Colloids Inc. v. American Cyanamid Co.***, 64 F.3d 1570, 1574, 35 U.S.P.Q.2d 1840, 1842-43 (Fed. Cir.1995). "[T]he public use bar of §102(b) requires that (1) the invention was used in public and (2) the use was not primarily experimental in purpose. *At F.3d 1575:* [P]ublic acts may range from experimentation where there are many unknowns, to simply using an already proven product in an unrestricted public location. Commercial purpose underlies virtually every contact between inventor and potential customer. When testing an invention entails customer contact, that does not convert an otherwise experimental purpose into a public use. *At F.3d 1576, U.S.P.Q.2d 1844:* A public use under §102(b) does not start the one-year period until the invention has left the experimental stage.... We have explained that this is a factor to be considered, for the absence of payment supports the inference that the tests were for the benefit of the patentee, and thus contravenes the inference of public use for or by the potential customer."

- ***Paragon Podiatry Lab. v. KLM Labs.***, 984 F.2d 1182, 1185, 25 U.S.P.Q.2d 1561, 1563 (Fed.Cir.1993). "[A] product embodying the patented invention, which is sold or offered for sale more than a year before the application's filing date, may escape the statutory bar where such sale was primarily for a bona fide experimental purpose to perfect the invention, rather than for commercial exploitation. Thus, any sales of the later patented product outside of the grace period must be merely incidental to the primary purpose of experimentation. *At F.2d 1185 n.3, U.S.P.Q.2d 1563 n.3:* There are not ... two separable issues, *i.e.*, Was the invention 'on sale?' and then, Was the sale an experimental use? The correct statement of the sole issue is Was the invention 'on sale' within the meaning of §102(b)? *At F.2d 1186, U.S.P.Q.2d 1564:* The fact that an inventor had an intent to experiment in making the sale need not be overcome or disputed to invoke the statutory bar. Such intent is merely a fact to be taken into account in resolving the ultimate legal question. Moreover, as a factor in the ultimate conclusion, we have held, [t]he expression by an inventor of his subjective intent to experiment, particularly after institution of litigation, is generally of minimal value. Further, we have held that the assertion of experimental sales, *at a minimum*, requires that customers must be made aware of the experimentation. *At F.2d 1188, U.S.P.Q.2d 1565-66:* The limited extent of sales may be relevant to determining whether the scope of the inventor's testing was appropriate but only where other evidence indicates that the sales were restricted and controlled as appropriate for experimental use. ... Even a single sale outside the grace period may be sufficient to invoke §102(b). Clearly, there is no license to test the invention by commercial sales outside the grace period." (Internal quotes omitted.) *See also* ***Allen Eng'g v. Bartell Indus.***, 299 F.3d 1336, 1354, 63 U.S.P.Q.2d 1769, 1779 (Fed.Cir.2002); ***Sinskey v. Pharmacia Ophthalmics, Inc.***, 982 F.2d 494, 498-99, 25 U.S.P.Q.2d 1290, 1294 (Fed.Cir.1992).

§102(d)—Generally

- ***In re Carlson***, 983 F.2d 1032, 1035, 25 U.S.P.Q.2d 1207, 1210 (Fed.Cir.1992). "With respect to design patents ..., Congress has provided that the time bar in §102(d) is six months."

§102(d)—Already Patented

- ***Bayer AG v. Schein Pharms.***, 301 F.3d 1306, 1312, 64 U.S.P.Q.2d 1001, 1005 (Fed.Cir.2002). "Three things must occur for a patent to be invalid under §102(d). First, the applicant must file an application on the invention in another country. Then, more than 12 months later, the applicant must file for a patent on the same invention in this country. Third, the foreign patent must issue before the applicant filed the U.S. patent application. If all three occur, then the U.S. patent is invalid under §102(d)."
- ***In re Kathawala***, 9 F.3d 942, 945, 28 U.S.P.Q.2d 1785, 1787 (Fed.Cir.1993). "When a foreign patent issues with claims directed to the same invention as the U.S. application, the invention is 'patented' within the meaning of §102(d); validity of the foreign claims is irrelevant to the §102(d) inquiry. This is true irrespective of whether the applicant asserts that the claims in the foreign patent are invalid on grounds of non-statutory subject matter or more conventional patentability reasons such as prior art or inadequate disclosure. *At F.3d 946:* [A] foreign patent need not be publicly available to be 'patented' under §102(d). *At U.S.P.Q.2d 1788:* [A]n invention is 'patented' in a foreign country under §102(d) when the patentee's rights under the patent become fixed. *At F.3d 947:* [W]hen an applicant files a foreign application fully disclosing his invention and having the potential to claim his invention in a number of different ways, the reference in §102(d) to 'invention ... patented' necessarily includes all disclosed aspects of the invention. Thus, the §102(d) bar applies regardless whether the foreign patent contains claims to less than all aspects of the invention."

§102(e)

- ***EmeraChem Holdings, LLC v. Volkswagen Grp.***, 859 F.3d 1341, 1345, 123 U.S.P.Q.2d 1146, 1148 (Fed.Cir. 2017). "The statute's reference to 'by another' means that an application issued to the same inventive entity cannot qualify as §102(e) prior art."
- ***Dynamic Drinkware, LLC v. National Graphics, Inc.***, 800 F.3d 1375, 1382, 116 U.S.P.Q.2d 1045, 1050 (Fed.Cir.2015). "A reference patent is only entitled to claim the benefit of the filing date of its provisional ap-

plication if the disclosure of the provisional application provides support for the claims in the reference patent in compliance with [35 U.S.C.] §112, ¶1."

Spansion, Inc. v. International Trade Comm'n, 629 F.3d 1331, 1356, 97 U.S.P.Q.2d 1417, 1434 (Fed.Cir. 2010). "A reference patent anticipates an invention under §102(e) only if the reference patent's effective filing date is before the date of the invention."

In re Giacomini, 612 F.3d 1380, 1383, 95 U.S.P.Q.2d 1698, 1700 (Fed.Cir.2010). "An application that a patent was 'granted on' is the first U.S. application to disclose the invention claimed in the patent. ... Under [35 U.S.C. §111(b)(8)], 'applications for patent' under [35 U.S.C.] §102 includes both provisional and non-provisional patent applications. Therefore, an applicant is not entitled to a patent if another's patent discloses the same invention, which was carried forward from an earlier U.S. provisional application or U.S. non-provisional application. [¶] [35 U.S.C.] §119(e) treats a nonprovisional application as though filed on the date of its corresponding provisional application. [¶] An important limitation is that the provisional application must provide written description support for the claimed invention."

Riverwood Int'l v. R.A. Jones & Co., 324 F.3d 1346, 1355-56, 66 U.S.P.Q.2d 1331, 1338 (Fed.Cir.2003). "[J]ust as a patent issued to the same inventive entity cannot be prior art by admission, an application issued to the same inventive entity cannot be prior art under §102(e)."

Purdue Pharma L.P. v. Boehringer Ingelheim GmbH, 98 F.Supp.2d 362, 380, 55 U.S.P.Q.2d 1168, 1180 (S.D.N.Y.2000), *aff'd*, 237 F.3d 1359, 57 U.S.P.Q.2d 1647 (Fed.Cir.2001). "[W]here the inventive entity listed on a prior art patent overlaps with the inventive entity listed on a later patent, but is not identical to the latter entity, the prior art patent constitutes a patent 'by another' pursuant to §102(e) and therefore is capable of anticipating the later patented invention. *At F.Supp.2d 381, U.S.P.Q.2d 1181:* [However,] if a parent patent fully discloses an invention that in fact is the work of an overlapping inventive entity and that is claimed in a continuing application listing that entity, then the presence of that subject matter in the earlier patent indicates that the present invention was already in existence as of the filing date of the parent application. And on that rationale, the invention disclosed in the earlier patent does not constitute prior art capable of anticipating the present invention."

§102(f)—Derivation

Brand v. Miller, 487 F.3d 862, 869-70, 82 U.S.P.Q.2d 1705, 1710 (Fed.Cir.2007). "A party may ... assert that the patentee did not invent the patented invention by showing derivation. In an interference proceeding, the person challenging the Senior Party's priority date bears the burden of proof on derivation and must make two showings. First, he must 'establish prior conception of the claimed subject matter.' Second, he must prove 'communication of that conception to the patentee that is sufficient to enable [him] to construct and successfully operate the invention.' This court reviews a finding of derivation as a question of fact." *See also* ***Eaton Corp. v. Rockwell Int'l***, 323 F.3d 1332, 1344, 66 U.S.P.Q.2d 1271, 1280 (Fed.Cir.2003); ***Solomon v. Kimberly-Clark Corp.***, 216 F.3d 1372, 1381, 55 U.S.P.Q.2d 1279, 1284-85 (Fed.Cir.2000); ***OddzOn Prods. v. Just Toys, Inc.***, 122 F.3d 1396, 1401-04, 43 U.S.P.Q.2d 1641, 1644-46 (Fed.Cir.1997).

Board of Educ. v. American Bioscience, Inc., 333 F.3d 1330, 1340, 67 U.S.P.Q.2d 1252, 1259 (Fed.Cir. 2003). "Invention requires conception, and 'conception does not occur unless one has a mental picture of the structure of the chemical ... or whatever characteristics sufficiently distinguish it. It is not sufficient to define it solely by its principal biological property....' Moreover, general knowledge regarding the anticipated biological properties of groups of complex chemical compounds is insufficient to confer inventorship status with respect to specifically claimed compounds. ... While we agree with [P] that the law does not usually require actual reduction to practice to establish conception of a chemical compound, ... invention does require conception, and there is no evidence that [P's] inventors conceived any of the claimed compounds. Having in mind specific portions of a claimed compound is not the same as conceiving the compound with all of its components. *At F.3d 1344, U.S.P.Q.2d 1262:* Inventorship is indeed relevant to patentability under ... §102(f), and patents have in the past been held unenforceable for failure to correctly name inventors in cases where the named inventors acted in bad faith or with deceptive intent."

§102(f)—Named Inventor

Pannu v. Iolab Corp., 155 F.3d 1344, 1349-51, 47 U.S.P.Q.2d 1657, 1662-63 (Fed.Cir.1998). 35 U.S.C.

§102(f) "still makes the naming of the correct inventor or inventors a condition of patentability; failure to name them renders a patent invalid. [¶] However, in cases of misjoinder and nonjoinder the operation of §102(f) is ameliorated by [35 U.S.C.] §256. [¶] When a party asserts invalidity under §102(f) due to nonjoinder, a district court should first determine whether there exists clear and convincing proof that the alleged unnamed inventor was in fact a co-inventor. Upon such a finding of incorrect inventorship, a patentee may invoke §256 to save the patent from invalidity. Accordingly, the patentee must then be given an opportunity to correct inventorship pursuant to that section. Nonjoinder may be corrected 'on notice and hearing of all parties concerned' and upon a showing that the error occurred without any deceptive intent on the part of the unnamed inventor. Finally, a patent with improper inventorship does not avoid invalidation simply because it *might* be corrected under §256. Rather, the patentee must claim entitlement to relief under the statute and the court must give the patentee an opportunity to correct the inventorship. If the inventorship is successfully corrected, §102(f) will not render the patent invalid. On the other hand, if the patentee does not claim relief under the statute and a party asserting invalidity proves incorrect inventorship, the court should hold the patent invalid for failure to comply with §102(f)."

§102(g)—Generally

Teva Pharm. Indus. v. AstraZeneca Pharms., 661 F.3d 1378, 1382, 100 U.S.P.Q.2d 1852, 1855 (Fed.Cir. 2011). "It is undisputed that [D] conceived and reduced its drug to practice before [P's] first conception of the claimed subject matter. It is also undisputed that [D] did not understand [a particular property] in its drug prior to [P's] conception, if at all. Therefore, this appeal does not involve a dispute of fact. Thus, this court need only determine, as a matter of law, whether [D] had to understand [the property] in order to win a priority dispute under §102(g)(2). [D] did not. *At F.3d 1384, U.S.P.Q.2d 1856:* To establish prior invention, the party asserting it must prove that it appreciated what it had made. The prior inventor does not need to know everything about how or why its invention worked. Nor must it conceive of its invention using the same words as the patentee would later use to claim it. In this light, it is apparent that the district court correctly entered summary judgment."

Dow Chem. Co. v. Astro-Valcour, Inc., 267 F.3d 1334, 1336, 60 U.S.P.Q.2d 1519, 1519 (Fed.Cir.2001). "This case presents the question of whether, when challenging the validity of a patent under ... §102(g), a prior inventor must have known that he was an inventor. We conclude that such a state of mind is not required. *At F.3d 1339, U.S.P.Q.2d 1522:* [T]he challenger of the validity of a patent must establish prior invention by clear and convincing evidence. If the challenger does so, the burden of production shifts to the patentee to produce evidence sufficient to create a genuine issue of material fact as to whether the prior inventor abandoned, suppressed, or concealed the invention. If the patentee carries this burden of production, the challenger may rebut the evidence of abandonment, suppression, or concealment, with clear and convincing evidence to the contrary. *At F.3d 1341, U.S.P.Q.2d 1523:* Thus, the cases establish that the date of the conception of a prior inventor's invention is the date the inventor first appreciated the fact of what he made. These cases do not establish that an inventor must be the first to appreciate the patentability of the invention, and we hold that he need not be."

Apotex, Inc. v. Merck & Co., 254 F.3d 1031, 1035, 59 U.S.P.Q.2d 1139, 1142 (Fed.Cir.2001). "In addition to governing priority determinations in interference proceedings in the [PTO], §102(g) may be asserted as a basis for invalidating a patent in defense to an infringement suit. ... Therefore, if a patentee's invention has been made by another, prior inventor who has not abandoned, suppressed, or concealed the invention, §102(g) will invalidate that patent."

Eaton v. Evans, 204 F.3d 1094, 1097, 53 U.S.P.Q.2d 1696, 1698 (Fed.Cir.2000). "Priority and its constituent issues of conception and reduction to practice are questions of law predicated on subsidiary factual findings. Accordingly, we review *de novo* the PTO Board's legal conclusions regarding priority, conception, and reduction to practice."

Innovative Scuba Concepts, Inc. v. Feder Indus., 26 F.3d 1112, 1115, 31 U.S.P.Q.2d 1132, 1134 (Fed.Cir. 1994). "In reviewing a judgment based on a conclusion of prior invention under 35 U.S.C. §102(g), we must consider not only whether the underlying findings were clearly erroneous, but also whether there was legal error."

§102(g)—Interference

Singh v. Brake, 317 F.3d 1334, 1343, 65 U.S.P.Q.2d 1641, 1645 (Fed.Cir.2003). "A junior party ... seeking a determination of priority must demonstrate by a preponderance of the evidence either reduction to practice before the senior party's priority date, or prior conception coupled with reasonable diligence in reducing the invention to practice from a time just prior to the senior party's entry into the field to the junior party's own reduction to practice." *See also* **Griffin v. Bertina**, 285 F.3d 1029, 1032, 62 U.S.P.Q.2d 1431, 1433 (Fed.Cir. 2002).

Apotex, Inc. v. Merck & Co., 254 F.3d 1031, 1037, 59 U.S.P.Q.2d 1139, 1143 (Fed.Cir.2001). "[U]nder §102(g) interference law involving co-pending applications, once the first party to invent has established priority of invention, the second party to conceive and reduce the invention to practice has the burden of proving that the first party suppressed or concealed the invention. In such an interference, the first party to invent does not bear any burden of proof regarding suppression or concealment once it has established an earlier date of invention."

Cooper v. Goldfarb, 240 F.3d 1378, 1382, 57 U.S.P.Q.2d 1990, 1992 (Fed.Cir.2001). "When two patent applications are directed to the same invention, the [PTO] declares an 'interference' between the applications to determine which applicant is entitled to priority of invention. The precise scope of the interfering subject matter is defined by the interference 'count.'"

Eaton v. Evans, 204 F.3d 1094, 1097, 53 U.S.P.Q.2d 1696, 1698 (Fed.Cir.2000). "In an interference proceeding, a party seeking to establish an actual reduction to practice must satisfy a two-prong test: (1) the party constructed an embodiment or performed a process that met every element of the interference count, and (2) the embodiment or process operated for its intended purpose. With regard to the first prong, this Court's well-established precedent requires that the constructed embodiment or performed process include the precise elements recited in the count. Thus, for purposes of an interference, there can be no actual reduction to practice if the constructed embodiment or performed process lacks an element recited in the count or uses an equivalent of that element."

Hyatt v. Boone, 146 F.3d 1348, 1351, 47 U.S.P.Q.2d 1128, 1129 (Fed.Cir.1998). "The general rule is that the first person to conceive the invention is the first inventor, ... provided that when the first to conceive the invention is the last to reduce it to practice, the person who was first to conceive must have exercised reasonable diligence to his own actual or constructive reduction to practice, 'from a time prior to conception by the other.' Thus, during an interference proceeding evidence may be presented of conception, reduction to practice, and diligence, as appropriate to the positions of the parties, or a party may rely on the patent document to establish the facts of priority of invention."

§102(g)—Conception

Perfect Surgical Techniques, Inc. v. Olympus Am., Inc., 841 F.3d 1004, 1007, 120 U.S.P.Q.2d 1606, 1607-08 (Fed.Cir.2016). "Pre-AIA §102(g) allows a patent owner to antedate a reference by proving earlier conception and reasonable diligence in reducing to practice. *At F.3d 1009, U.S.P.Q.2d 1609:* A patent owner need not prove the inventor *continuously* exercised reasonable diligence throughout the critical period; it must show there was *reasonably continuous* diligence. Under this standard, an inventor is not required to work on reducing his invention to practice every day during the critical period. And periods of inactivity within the critical period do not automatically vanquish a patent owner's claim of reasonable diligence. ... In determining whether an invention antedates another, the point of the diligence analysis is not to scour the patent owner's corroborating evidence in search of intervals of time where the patent owner has failed to substantiate some sort of activity. It is to assure that, in light of the evidence as a whole, 'the invention was not abandoned or unreasonably delayed.' That an inventor overseeing a study did not record its progress on a daily, weekly, or even monthly basis does not mean the inventor necessarily abandoned his invention or unreasonably delayed it. The same logic applies to the preparation of a patent application: the absence of evidence that an inventor and his attorney revised or discussed the application on a daily basis is alone insufficient to determine that the invention was abandoned or unreasonably delayed. One must weigh the collection of evidence over the entire critical period to make such a determination."

Tyco Healthcare Grp. v. Ethicon Endo-Surgery, Inc., 774 F.3d 968, 975, 112 U.S.P.Q.2d 1979, 1985 (Fed. Cir.2014). "As the district court properly found, ... the [prototype], originated by [third party] and perfected by [D], existed in the form of detailed drawings and physical embodiments in 1996, before [P's] conception date of January 1997. Based on this evidence and corroborating testimony, there was a 'definite and permanent idea' of an ultrasonic surgical device that could cut and coagulate and fit down a five millimeter trocar. This idea persisted despite [D's] limited design changes to only the cam mechanism and blade size, which is not a feature that the 26 anticipated claims recite. [D's] design changes therefore do not preclude the district court's finding of prior conception."

Amkor Tech. v. International Trade Comm'n, 692 F.3d 1250, 1255, 106 U.S.P.Q.2d 1565, 1569 (Fed.Cir. 2012). "'[T]he inventor of an invention of foreign origin may rely on the date that the invention was disclosed in the U.S.[ ] as a conception date for priority purposes.' *At F.3d 1256, U.S.P.Q.2d 1570-71:* While this court's limited precedent on this issue establishes that writings *can* satisfy the full domestic disclosure requirement, the cases do not establish any per se requirement that such disclosure must be in writing. *At F.3d 1257:* The content of the domestic disclosure must be *specific enough* to encompass the 'complete and operative' invention, ... and an inventor's oral testimony to this extent is a question of proof.... [¶] [Complainant] argues that the ***Oka*** rule—*i.e.*, according the last possible conception date to a party who can only provide a range of dates—applies only to the party with the burden of persuasion on the issue of prior invention. *At F.3d 1258:* The ***Oka*** rule does not apply to [third-party inventors of prior art] in validity disputes. This is not an interference, and the standards that apply to interferences do not necessarily apply to disputes over validity. An issued patent is entitled to a presumption of validity under 35 U.S.C. §282, which can be overcome only with clear and convincing evidence. The presumption of validity and the clear and convincing burden associated with it did not apply in the interference in ***Oka***. In ***Oka***, the question of entitlement to priority did not carry any presumption and was determined based on preponderant evidence. In ***Oka***, even under the preponderant evidence standard, the junior party could not prove prior invention by presenting a range of dates that primarily predated but overlapped by one day with the senior party's conception date."

Teva Pharm. Indus. v. AstraZeneca Pharms., 661 F.3d 1378, 1382, 100 U.S.P.Q.2d 1852, 1855 (Fed.Cir. 2011). "[T]his court need only determine, as a matter of law, whether [D] had to understand that crospovidone[, a chemical compound,] stabilized its drug in order to win a priority dispute under §102(g)(2). *At F.3d 1385, U.S.P.Q.2d 1856:* [D] had to appreciate that the compound it asserted as its invention was stable and what the components of this formulation were. There is no question that [D] had this appreciation. However, [D] did not need to appreciate which component was responsible for the stabilization. [P] effectively asks this court to fault [D] for not first conceiving of its drug in the same words in which [P] later chose to claim it. This case therefore falls squarely within the holdings of ***Dow*** [***Chem. Co. v. Astro-Valcour, Inc.***, 267 F.3d 1334 (Fed.Cir.2001),] and ***Silvestri*** [***v. Grant***, 496 F.2d 593 (CCPA 1974)]. Because '[t]he invention is not the language of the [claim] but the subject matter thereby defined,' [P's] argument must fail."

Solvay S.A. v. Honeywell Int'l, 622 F.3d 1367, 1376-78, 96 U.S.P.Q.2d 1870, 1877-78 (Fed.Cir.2010). "We have regularly applied 'the rules governing the determination of priority of invention' in cases involving the question of prior inventorship under §102(g)(2). The question thus becomes whether [D] conceived of the invention at issue and reduced it to practice in the U.S., such that [D] is 'another inventor' of the process claimed in the ... patent under §102(g)(2). [¶] [D] is not 'another inventor' under §102(g)(2). [¶] Conception is 'the formation in the mind of the inventor, of a definite and permanent idea of the complete and operative invention, as it is hereafter to be applied in practice.' The test for conception is whether the inventor had an idea that was definite and permanent enough that one skilled in the art could understand the invention. In this case, [D] did not have, or formulate, a definite and permanent 'idea' of its own capable of being reduced to practice. Rather, it reproduced the invention previously conceived and reduced to practice by [researchers under contract to D] in Russia. Such reproduction cannot be conception because, if it were, the result would be that one who simply followed another inventor's instructions to reproduce that person's prior conceived invention would, by so doing, also become an 'inventor.' Although the district court declined to read the 'originality' requirement of ... §102(f) into §102(g), originality is, nevertheless, inherent to the notion of conception. The definition and test of conception ..., which speaks to the formation of an idea in the mind of the inventor, necessitates that the conception of an invention be an original idea of the inventor.

Since it is undisputed that [D] did not originate the invention, but reproduced it in the U.S. by following [researcher's] instructions, [D] cannot be said to have conceived of the invention and cannot, consequently, be an inventor for purposes of §102(g)(2)."

Invitrogen Corp. v. Clontech Labs., 429 F.3d 1052, 1064, 77 U.S.P.Q.2d 1161, 1168-69 (Fed.Cir.2005). "[U]nder some conditions conception is delayed until a reduction to practice. Such delayed conception is often described by the rule against *nunc pro tunc* conception. That is, a reduction to practice at time A necessarily requires the inventor to possess the knowledge about the invention to show a conception. However, the law will not sanction the inference that reduction to practice at time A implies conception at earlier time B. [¶] With unrecognized accidental duplication, the invention exists but remains unrecognized. The priority determination requires evidence that the inventor actually first made the invention, and that he understood his creation to have the features that, comprise the inventive subject matter at bar. Thus, the court must identify when, during an emerging recognition that a particular invention includes something new, the inventor's understanding reaches the level needed for appreciation. In the appreciation analysis, the relevant uncertainty relates to the emerging recognition of something new. [¶] That analysis requires objective corroboration of the inventor's subjective beliefs. *At F.3d 1065-66:* [I]t is not enough that a party adduce evidence that objective test results comport with an inventor's testimony concerning his state of mind. Rather, there must also be evidence that the junior party timely interpreted or evaluated the results, and understood them to show the existence [of] the invention. *At U.S.P.Q.2d 1170:* [There should be an] objective basis corroborating the inventor's belief to show, consistent with the appropriate burden at trial, that persons skilled in the art at the time of the recognition would have recognized the existence of the relevant inventive features."

Hitzeman v. Rutter, 243 F.3d 1345, 1357, 58 U.S.P.Q.2d 1161, 1169 (Fed.Cir.2001). "When a research plan requires extensive research before the inventor can have a reasonable expectation that the limitations of the count will actually be met, complete conception has not occurred."

Burroughs Wellcome Co. v. Barr Labs., 40 F.3d 1223, 1227-28, 32 U.S.P.Q.2d 1915, 1919 (Fed.Cir.1994). "Conception is the touchstone of inventorship, the completion of the mental part of invention. [¶] [T]he test for conception is whether the inventor had an idea that was definite and permanent enough that one skilled in the art could understand the invention; the inventor must prove his conception by corroborating evidence, preferably by showing a contemporaneous disclosure. An idea is definite and permanent when the inventor has a specific, settled idea, a particular solution to the problem at hand, not just a general goal or research plan he hopes to pursue. The conception analysis necessarily turns on the inventor's ability to describe his invention with particularity. Until he can do so, he cannot prove possession of the complete mental picture of the invention. These rules ensure that patent rights attach only when an idea is so far developed that the inventor can point to a definite, particular invention."

Bosies v. Benedict, 27 F.3d 539, 542, 30 U.S.P.Q.2d 1862, 1864-65 (Fed.Cir.1994). "Conception is a question of law that we review *de novo*. '[I]t is well established in our law that conception of a chemical compound requires that the inventor be able to define it so as to distinguish it from other materials, and to describe how to obtain it.'"

§102(g)—Reasonable Diligence

Fleming v. Escort Inc., 774 F.3d 1371, 1379, 113 U.S.P.Q.2d 1426, 1432-33 (Fed.Cir.2014). "Although [P] has not made an argument based on a pre-1999 priority date, the conclusion [of no suppression, abandonment, or concealment] would not change even if we assumed a May 1998 conception date for [P] (for which there is evidence). On that assumption, the crucial period for the abandonment analysis would be the time between [the] February 1997 bankruptcy [of D's predecessor company] and [D's consultant's] July 1998 employment at [D-company]. But what occurred during that period does not warrant an inference of suppression, concealment, or abandonment. At most, there was a reasonable pause in active work: the rights to the invention were transferred from one owner to a new owner during a period of bankruptcy; the new owner concentrated its initial efforts on products ready for immediate sale; and even during that period, the new owner maintained communication with [D's consultant] and made efforts to bring him to the firm precisely to resume the work needed to perfect the prior invention. The delay of active work in these circumstances was not unreasonable and was consistent with a continuing commitment to pursuing the project to the full extent conditions allowed. In brief, the concepts of abandonment, suppression, and concealment do not fit the facts as reasonably found by the jury."

Brown v. Barbacid, 436 F.3d 1376, 1378, 77 U.S.P.Q.2d 1848, 1850 (Fed.Cir.2006). "The party that is first to conceive the invention in interference, if last to reduce the invention to practice, is entitled to the patent based on prior conception if, as first to conceive, he exercised reasonable diligence from a time before the other party's conception date to his own reduction to practice date. *At F.3d 1379:* The question of reasonable diligence is one of fact. *At F.3d 1380, U.S.P.Q.2d 1851:* [D]iligence and its corroboration may be shown by a variety of activities, as precedent illustrates. ... The basic inquiry is whether, on all of the evidence, there was reasonably continuing activity to reduce the invention to practice. There is no rule requiring a specific kind of activity in determining whether the applicant was reasonably diligent in proceeding toward an actual or constructive reduction to practice. *At F.3d 1382, U.S.P.Q.2d 1853:* The Board is charged with expertise appropriate to the invention under examination, and with understanding that a laboratory notebook recording daily experimentation, reasonably considered from the viewpoint of persons experienced in the field, need not reproduce on each page a statement of the larger research purpose; this purpose may reasonably be shown in the various declarations."

Monsanto Co. v. Mycogen Plant Sci., Inc., 261 F.3d 1356, 1362, 59 U.S.P.Q.2d 1930, 1933-34 (Fed.Cir. 2001). "This court has interpreted §102(g) to provide that 'priority of invention goes to the first party to reduce an invention to practice unless the other party can show that it was the first to conceive the invention and that it exercised reasonable diligence in later reducing that invention to practice.' *At F.3d 1369, U.S.P.Q.2d 1938:* The evidence must show that the alleged earlier inventor was diligent throughout the entire critical period. However, there need not necessarily be evidence of activity on every single day if a satisfactory explanation is evidenced. Additionally, determining whether the required 'reasonable diligence' ... has been satisfied is a case specific inquiry." *See also* ***In re Jolley***, 308 F.3d 1317, 1326, 64 U.S.P.Q.2d 1901, 1908 (Fed.Cir. 2002).

Bey v. Kollonitsch, 806 F.2d 1024, 1027, 231 U.S.P.Q. 967, 969 (Fed.Cir.1986). "[R]easonable diligence can be shown if it is established that the attorney worked reasonably hard on the particular application in question during the continuous critical period. *At F.2d 1028, U.S.P.Q. 970:* [C]ourts have recognized that *reasonable* diligence is all that is required of the attorney.... [¶] Generally, the patent attorney must show that unrelated cases are taken up in chronological order, thus, the attorney has the burden of keeping good records of the dates when cases are docketed as well as the dates when specific work is done on the applications."

§102(g)—Reduction to Practice

Tyco Healthcare Grp. v. Ethicon Endo-Surgery, Inc., 774 F.3d 968, 976, 112 U.S.P.Q.2d 1979, 1986 (Fed. Cir.2014). "[P] asserts that [prototype] cannot serve as prior art under [35 U.S.C.] §102(g) because there was no reduction to practice before [P's] priority date. [P] contends that the absence of prior reduction to practice is dispositive of the issue, but also argues that based on ***In re Clemens***, 622 F.2d 1029 ... (CCPA 1980), §102(g) prior art cannot be prior art under [35 U.S.C.] §103 if it was 'unknown to both the applicant and the art at the time the applicant makes his invention,' because doing so would 'establish a standard for patentability in which an applicant's contribution would be measured against secret prior art.' [¶] The district court erred when it inconsistently applied §102(g) to [prototype] by not requiring prior reduction to practice for anticipation purposes but requiring it for the obviousness analysis. The clear language of §102(g) does not require prior reduction to practice so long as the inventor can prove that he or she conceived of the invention first and was diligent in later reducing it to practice. Here, the district court already determined that [prototype] satisfied this statutory provision when it held that the prototype anticipates the other 26 asserted claims. [W]e [have] held that §102(g) prior art established by prior reduction to practice could constitute prior art under §103. That holding, however, does not preclude an invention from satisfying §102(g) through prior conception and later diligent reduction to practice. ... We therefore hold that neither §102(g) nor §103 make prior reduction to practice the *only* avenue through which §102(g) prior art can constitute prior art under §103. [¶] Furthermore, the clear language of §102(g) and §103 contains no requirement that a prior invention under §102(g) be 'known to the art' or the patentee at the time of invention to constitute prior art under §103. To the extent that our predecessor court inserted such a requirement into §102(g) in ***In re Clemens***, we discontinued that requirement as dictum in ***E.I. du Pont de Nemours & Co. v. Phillips Pet. Co.***, 849 F.2d 1430 ... (Fed.Cir.1988).... *At F.3d 977:* [Section] 103(c) creates an exception (though inapplicable here) for when §102(g) prior art may not qualify as prior art for obviousness purposes. The presence of this exception strongly indicates that the statute itself contemplates that §102(g) prior art may constitute prior art under §103. Thus, absent the application of a statutory exception, §102(g) prior art may serve as prior art under §103. The district court should have therefore considered [prototype] as prior art for obviousness purposes, having already determined that the prototype is prior art under §102(g)."

Solvay S.A. v. Honeywell Int'l, 742 F.3d 998, 999-1000, 109 U.S.P.Q.2d 1609, 1610 (Fed.Cir.2014). "The question at the heart of this appeal is when an invention conceived by a foreign inventor and reduced to practice in the U.S. qualifies as prior art under §102(g)(2). ... A patent is invalid under that section if the claimed invention was made in this country by another inventor before the patent's priority date. Making the invention requires conception and reduction to practice. *At F.3d 1006, U.S.P.Q.2d 1614-15:* [P] argues that (1) the doctrine of inurement, defining when the activities of others inure to the benefit of the inventor, controls the question of whether [D's] work can be attributed to the [foreign engineers in contract with D], and (2) the undisputed facts do not establish inurement because the ... engineers did not expressly ask [D-researchers] to perform the inventive process. [¶] Assuming that the inurement doctrine governs, inurement does not require that the inventor expressly request or direct the non-inventor to perform reductive work. To be sure, no inurement can arise from a third party's 'unwarranted and hostile use' of another's invention, ... but an express request or direction is not required. The request may be 'implicit[].' [¶] [O]ur case law does not support [P's] contention that an inventor must make an express directive or request to benefit from a third party's reduction to practice. Rather, inurement exists if the inventor authorizes another to reduce his invention to practice. Here, the research agreement between the [foreign engineers] and [D] confirms that the [foreign engineers] authorized [D] to practice its invention in the U.S. and contemplated that [D] would do so. *At F.3d 1007-08, U.S.P.Q.2d 1616:* We therefore agree with the district court that the process invented by the ... engineers was made in this country when [D] successfully performed the process because the [engineers] authorized [D] to practice the invention and specifically contemplated that they would do so. We affirm the district court's judgment that the ... patent is invalid under §102(g)(2)."

Medichem, S.A. v. Rolabo, S.L., 437 F.3d 1157, 1169-71, 77 U.S.P.Q.2d 1865, 1873 (Fed.Cir.2006). "In order to establish an actual reduction to practice, [P] must establish three things: (1) construction of an embodiment or performance of a process that met all the limitations of the interference count; (2) determination that the invention would work for its intended purpose; and (3) the existence of sufficient evidence to corroborate inventor testimony regarding these events. [¶] [N]o similar condition of corroboration is imposed on an inventor's notebook, or indeed on any documentary or physical evidence, as a condition for its serving as evidence of reduction to practice. ... Once properly admitted into evidence, documentary and physical evidence is assigned probative value and collectively weighed to determine whether reduction to practice has been achieved. This is what is meant by the maxim that documentary and physical evidence do not require corroboration. *At U.S.P.Q.2d 1874:* Sufficiency of corroboration is determined by using a rule of reason analysis, under which all pertinent evidence is examined when determining the credibility of an inventor's testimony. [¶] The requirement of independent knowledge remains key to the corroboration inquiry. Independent corroboration may consist of testimony of a witness, other than the inventor, to the actual reduction to practice or it may consist of evidence of surrounding facts and circumstances independent of information received from the inventor. One consequence of the independence requirement is that testimony of one co-inventor cannot be used to help corroborate the testimony of another. [¶] Despite the importance of the independence requirement, however, the law does not impose an impossible standard of independence on corroborative evidence by requiring that every point of a reduction to practice be corroborated by evidence having a source totally independent of the inventor. Similarly, it is not necessary to produce an actual over-the-shoulder observer. Rather, sufficient circumstantial evidence of an independent nature can satisfy the corroboration requirement. [¶] When an inventor claims a process for making a chemical compound rather than the compound itself, it is the successful reduction to practice of the process that must be corroborated, and not merely the successful production of the compound *per se*. Thus, spectral evidence that might be sufficient *per se* to corroborate a claim directed to the product will generally not be sufficient to corroborate a claim directed to the process, in the absence of some evidence to corroborate that the product was produced via that process. *At U.S.P.Q.2d 1875:* Whether or not corroboration exists is a question of fact, the district court's determination of which we review for clear error. *At F.3d 1173, U.S.P.Q.2d 1876:* Where a laboratory notebook authored by a non-inventor is offered into evidence pursuant to authentication by an inventor, where the author of the notebook has not testified at trial or otherwise attested to its authenticity, and where the notebook has not been signed or witnessed and has not been maintained in reasonable accordance with good laboratory practices sufficient to reasonably ensure its genuineness under the circumstances, then the corroborative value of the notebook is minimal." (Internal quotes omitted.)

Cooper v. Goldfarb, 240 F.3d 1378, 1382, 57 U.S.P.Q.2d 1990, 1993 (Fed.Cir.2001). "To establish reduction to practice, the inventor must prove that he made an embodiment of the invention that met all of the limitations of the interference count and that he determined that the invention would work for its intended purpose. When testing is necessary to establish that the invention will work for its intended purpose, the embodiment relied upon as evidence of reduction to practice must work for the intended purpose. Moreover, 'the inventor must contemporaneously appreciate that the embodiment worked and that it met all the limitations of the interference count.'"

§102(g)—Abandonment

Checkpoint Sys. v. U.S. Int'l Trade Comm'n, 54 F.3d 756, 761-62, 35 U.S.P.Q.2d 1042, 1046-47 (Fed.Cir. 1995). "One way a prior inventor may avoid the disqualifying effect of §102(g) is by promptly filing a patent application claiming the invention. In the usual context of an interference proceeding, each inventor involved in the proceeding will have filed a patent application, one of which may have matured into a patent. However, §102(g) is applicable in other contexts as well, such as when it is asserted as a basis for invalidating a patent in defense to an infringement suit. In such a case, a first inventor may seek to avoid a determination of abandonment by showing that he or she marketed or sold a commercial embodiment of the invention or described the invention in a publicly disseminated document. If the prior inventor's activities following completion of the invention do not evidence abandonment, suppression, or concealment, §102(g) will bar a later inventor from obtaining a patent. In cases in which an invention is disclosed to the public by commercialization, courts have excused delay upon proof that the first inventor engaged in reasonable efforts to bring the invention to market." *See also* ***Sandt Tech. v. Resco Metal & Plastics Corp.***, 264 F.3d 1344, 1353, 60 U.S.P.Q.2d 1091, 1096 (Fed.Cir.2001).

§102(g)—Suppression or Concealment

Fox Grp. v. Cree, Inc., 700 F.3d 1300, 1306, 105 U.S.P.Q.2d 1097, 1101 (Fed.Cir.2012). "There are numerous ways to support an inference of abandonment, suppression, or concealment, such as '[t]he failure to file a patent application, to describe the invention in a published document, or to use the invention publicly, within a reasonable time after first making the invention....' [¶] Filing a patent application and commercializing a product are only two convenient ways of proving an invention has been disclosed to the public. There are other ways to prove public disclosure including, e.g., the use of a printed publication[] as prior art under ... §102(a), (b). [¶] [P] claims that public use or descriptions in a published document must be enabling, given the policy and purpose of the patent system to enrich the art by disclosing how to make the invention. *At F.3d 1307, U.S.P.Q.2d 1102:* As [P] effectively admits, all of the cases it cites to support its assertion that §102(g) requires an enabling disclosure are process claims. The '130 patent is a patent directed to a product, ... but [P] argues that any distinction between product and process claims is irrelevant. We disagree."

Flex-Rest, LLC v. Steelcase, Inc., 455 F.3d 1351, 1358-59, 80 U.S.P.Q.2d 1620, 1624-25 (Fed.Cir.2006). "Intentional suppression occurs when an inventor 'designedly, and with the view of applying it indefinitely and exclusively for his own profit, withholds his invention from the public.' ... 'Intentional suppression, however, requires more than the passage of time. It requires evidence that the inventor *intentionally delayed filing* in order to prolong the period during which the invention is maintained in secret.' The record demonstrates that after reduction to practice, [D] moved almost immediately towards both filing a patent application and commercially disclosing [invention] at a trade show, actions which indicate an intent to make a public disclosure. Both the patent application and commercialization efforts came to fruition about six and one-half months later. That the device was kept secret during this time is not, by itself, indicative of intentional suppression or concealment. [¶] 'The failure to file a patent application, to describe the invention in a published document, or to use the invention publicly, within a reasonable time after first making the invention may constitute abandonment, suppression, or concealment.' There is no particular length of delay that is *per se* unreasonable, and '[m]ere delay, without more, is not sufficient to establish suppression or concealment.' '[E]ach case involving the issue of suppression or concealment must be considered on its own particular set of facts.'"

- ***Eolas Techs. v. Microsoft Corp.***, 399 F.3d 1325, 1333, 73 U.S.P.Q.2d 1782, 1788-89 (Fed.Cir.2005), *overruled on other grounds*, ***Cardiac Pacemakers, Inc. v. St. Jude Med., Inc.***, 576 F.3d 1348, 91 U.S.P.Q.2d 1848 (Fed.Cir.2009). There are "two types of conduct that invoke the exception within §102(g). The first arises when an inventor actively conceals his invention from the public. Active concealment 'refers to situations in which an inventor designedly, and with the view of applying it indefinitely and exclusively for his own profit, withholds his invention from the public.' The second occurs when 'abandonment, suppression, or concealment may be inferred based upon the prior inventor's unreasonable delay in making the invention publicly known.'"

- ***Apotex, Inc. v. Merck & Co.***, 254 F.3d 1031, 1036, 59 U.S.P.Q.2d 1139, 1142 (Fed.Cir.2001). "Whether suppression or concealment has occurred is a question of law, which we review *de novo*. [¶] [W]e conclude that the language 'in this country' only applies to the country where 'the invention was made,' and that proof negating suppression or concealment is not limited to activities occurring within the U.S. *At F.3d 1037 n.1, U.S.P.Q.2d 1143 n.1:* Generally speaking, the presumption of validity does not apply to patents involved in interference proceedings, and thus the invalidity of a patent involved in an interference under [35 U.S.C.] §102(g) need only be proven by preponderant evidence. However, the presumption may effectively be implicated in the case of a priority contest between an issued patent and an application that was filed after the issuance of the patent. In such a situation, the junior party must establish priority of invention by clear and convincing evidence. *At F.3d 1037, U.S.P.Q.2d 1143-44:* We ... interpret §102(g) as requiring that once a challenger of a patent has proven by clear and convincing evidence that 'the invention was made in this country by another inventor,' ... the burden of production shifts to the patentee to produce evidence sufficient to create a genuine issue of material fact as to whether the prior inventor has suppressed or concealed the invention. However, in accordance with the statutory presumption in 35 U.S.C. §282, the ultimate burden of persuasion remains with the party challenging the validity of the patent. Once the patentee has satisfied its burden of production, the party alleging invalidity under §102(g) must rebut any alleged suppression or concealment with clear and convincing evidence to the contrary. [¶] Although a prior inventor implicated in a §102(g) infringement defense may not have filed a patent application, in contrast to an interference contestant, that party's delay in otherwise bringing the knowledge of the invention to the public may nevertheless raise a similar inference of suppression or concealment. ... Absent a satisfactory explanation for the delay or the presence of other mitigating facts, a prior invention will ... be deemed suppressed or concealed within the meaning of §102(g) 'if, within a reasonable time after completion, no steps are taken to make the invention publicly known.' [¶] [A]lthough §102(g) prior art must be somehow made available to the public in order to defeat another patent, a §102(g) prior inventor is under no obligation to file a patent application. *At F.3d 1039-40, U.S.P.Q.2d 1145:* '[T]he first inventor will not be barred from relying on later, resumed activity antedating an opponent's entry into the field, merely because the work done before the delay was sufficient to amount to a reduction to practice.'"

§102. CONDITIONS FOR PATENTABILITY; NOVELTY

Section 102 is effective for patent applications and patents issued on those applications that have ever contained (1) a claim to a claimed invention that has an "effective filing date," as defined in §100(i), p. 495, on or after Mar. 16, 2013; or (2) a specific reference under §120, §121, or §365(c) to any patent or application that ever contained such a claim. Section 102 is not effective for patent applications filed before Mar. 16, 2013, or patents issued on those applications.

(a) Novelty; prior art.—A person shall be entitled to a patent unless—

(1) the claimed invention was patented, described in a printed publication, or in public use, on sale, or otherwise available to the public before the effective filing date of the claimed invention; or

(2) the claimed invention was described in a patent issued under section 151, or in an application for patent published or deemed published under section 122(b), in which the patent or application, as the case may be, names another inventor and was effectively filed before the effective filing date of the claimed invention.

(b) Exceptions—

(1) Disclosures made 1 year or less before the effective filing date of the claimed invention.—A disclosure made 1 year or less before the effective filing date of a claimed invention shall not be prior art to the claimed invention under subsection (a)(1) if—

(A) the disclosure was made by the inventor or joint inventor or by another who obtained the subject matter disclosed directly or indirectly from the inventor or a joint inventor; or

(B) the subject matter disclosed had, before such disclosure, been publicly disclosed by the inventor or a joint inventor or another who obtained the subject matter disclosed directly or indirectly from the inventor or a joint inventor.

(2) Disclosures appearing in applications and patents.—A disclosure shall not be prior art to a claimed invention under subsection (a)(2) if—

(A) the subject matter disclosed was obtained directly or indirectly from the inventor or a joint inventor;

(B) the subject matter disclosed had, before such subject matter was effectively filed under subsection (a)(2), been publicly disclosed by the inventor or a joint inventor or another who obtained the subject matter disclosed directly or indirectly from the inventor or a joint inventor; or

(C) the subject matter disclosed and the claimed invention, not later than the effective filing date of the claimed invention, were owned by the same person or subject to an obligation of assignment to the same person.

(c) Common ownership under joint research agreements.—Subject matter disclosed and a claimed invention shall be deemed to have been owned by the same person or subject to an obligation of assignment to the same person in applying the provisions of subsection (b)(2)(C) if—

(1) the subject matter disclosed was developed and the claimed invention was made by, or on behalf of, 1 or more parties to a joint research agreement that was in effect on or before the effective filing date of the claimed invention;

(2) the claimed invention was made as a result of activities undertaken within the scope of the joint research agreement; and

(3) the application for patent for the claimed invention discloses or is amended to disclose the names of the parties to the joint research agreement.

(d) Patents and published applications effective as prior art.—For purposes of determining whether a patent or application for patent is prior art to a claimed invention under subsection (a)(2), such patent or application shall be considered to have been effectively filed, with respect to any subject matter described in the patent or application—

(1) if paragraph (2) does not apply, as of the actual filing date of the patent or the application for patent; or

(2) if the patent or application for patent is entitled to claim a right of priority under section 119, 365(a), or 365(b), or to claim a right of priority under section 119, 365(a), 365(b), 386(a), or 386(b), or to claim the benefit of an earlier filing date under section 120, 121, 365(c), or 386(c), based upon 1 or more prior filed applications for patent, as of the filing date of the earliest such application that describes the subject matter.

History of 35 U.S.C. §102: July 19, 1952, ch. 950, §1, 66 Stat. 797; July 28, 1972, P.L. 92-358, §2, 86 Stat. 502; Nov. 14, 1975, P.L. 94-131, §5, 89 Stat. 691; Nov. 29, 1999, P.L. 106-113, §1000(a)(9), 113 Stat. 1536; Nov. 2, 2002, P.L. 107-273, §13205(1), 116 Stat. 1902; Sept. 16, 2011, P.L. 112-29, §3(b)(1), 125 Stat. 285; May 13, 2015, P.L. 112-211, §102(2), 126 Stat. 1531.

See also *Examination Guidelines for Implementing the First Inventor to File Provisions of the Leahy-Smith America Invents Act*, p. 1047.

ANNOTATIONS

Helsinn Healthcare S.A. v. Teva Pharms. USA, Inc., 855 F.3d 1356, 1367, 123 U.S.P.Q.2d 1045, 1052 (Fed.Cir.2017). "We … address whether the AIA changed the meaning of the on-sale bar under 35 U.S.C. §102 so that there was no qualifying sale as to the … patent. *At F.3d 1368, U.S.P.Q.2d 1053:* By enacting the AIA, Congress amended §102 to bar the patentability of an 'invention [that] was patented, described in a printed publication, or in public use, *on sale*, or otherwise available to the public before the effective filing date of the claimed invention.' [¶] [D] assert[s] that by reenacting the existing statutory term, 'on sale,' Congress did not change the meaning of the on-sale bar or disturb settled law. [¶] We decline the invitation by the parties to decide this case more broadly than necessary. At most the [congressional comments] show an intent 'to do away with precedent under current [§102] law[ ]'.... Such precedent had held certain secret uses to be invalidating under the 'public use' prong of §102(b). *At F.3d 1371, U.S.P.Q.2d 1055:* We conclude that, after the AIA, if the existence of the sale is public, the details of the invention need not be publicly disclosed in the terms of sale."

§103. CONDITIONS FOR PATENTABILITY; NON-OBVIOUS SUBJECT MATTER

Section 103 in its present form will continue to apply for applications and patents issued thereon that were filed before Mar. 16, 2013. Section 103 in its present form will also continue to apply for patent applications and patents issued thereon if the filing date of the earliest application for which the patent or application is entitled under §119, §365(a), §365(b), §120, §121, or §365(c) falls before Mar. 16, 2013, unless the application or patent has ever contained (1) a claim to a claimed invention that has an "effective filing date," as defined in §100(i), p. 495, on or after Mar. 16, 2013; or (2) a specific reference under §120, §121, or §365(c) to any patent or application that ever contained such a claim. See transition note for amended §103, p. 549.

(a) A patent may not be obtained though the invention is not identically disclosed or described as set forth in section 102, if the differences between the subject matter sought to be patented and the prior art are such that the subject matter as a whole would have been obvious at the time the invention was made to a person having ordinary skill in the art to which said subject matter pertains. Patentability shall not be negated by the manner in which the invention was made.

(b)(1) Notwithstanding subsection (a), and upon timely election by the applicant for patent to proceed under this subsection, a biotechnological process using or resulting in a composition of matter that is novel under section 102 and nonobvious under subsection (a) of this section shall be considered nonobvious if—

(A) claims to the process and the composition of matter are contained in either the same application for patent or in separate applications having the same effective filing date; and

(B) the composition of matter, and the process at the time it was invented, were owned by the same person or subject to an obligation of assignment to the same person.

(2) A patent issued on a process under paragraph (1)—

(A) shall also contain the claims to the composition of matter used in or made by that process, or

(B) shall, if such composition of matter is claimed in another patent, be set to expire on the same date as such other patent, notwithstanding section 154.

(3) For purposes of paragraph (1), the term "biotechnological process" means—

(A) a process of genetically altering or otherwise inducing a single- or multi-celled organism to—

(i) express an exogenous nucleotide sequence,

(ii) inhibit, eliminate, augment, or alter expression of an endogenous nucleotide sequence, or

(iii) express a specific physiological characteristic not naturally associated with said organism;

(B) cell fusion procedures yielding a cell line that expresses a specific protein, such as a monoclonal antibody; and

(C) a method of using a product produced by a process defined by subparagraph (A) or (B), or a combination of subparagraphs (A) and (B).

(c)(1) Subject matter developed by another person, which qualifies as prior art only under one or more of subsections (e), (f), and (g) of section 102, shall not preclude patentability under this section where the subject matter and the claimed invention were, at the time the claimed invention was made, owned by the same person or subject to an obligation of assignment to the same person.

(2) For purposes of this subsection, subject matter developed by another person and a claimed invention shall be deemed to have been owned by the same person or subject to an obligation of assignment to the same person if—

(A) the claimed invention was made by or on behalf of parties to a joint research agreement that was in effect on or before the date the claimed invention was made;

(B) the claimed invention was made as a result of activities undertaken within the scope of the joint research agreement; and

(C) the application for patent for the claimed invention discloses or is amended to disclose the names of the parties to the joint research agreement.

(3) For purposes of paragraph (2), the term "joint research agreement" means a written contract, grant, or cooperative agreement entered into by two or more persons or entities for the performance of experimental, developmental, or research work in the field of the claimed invention.

History of 35 U.S.C. §103: July 19, 1952, ch. 950, §1, 66 Stat. 798; Nov. 8, 1984, P.L. 98-622, §103, 98 Stat. 3384; Nov. 1, 1995, P.L. 104-41, §1, 109 Stat. 351; Nov. 29, 1999, P.L. 106-113, §1000(a)(9), 113 Stat. 1536; Dec. 10, 2004, P.L. 108-453, §2, 118 Stat. 3596; Sept. 16, 2011, P.L. 112-29, §20(j)(1), 125 Stat. 335.

ANNOTATIONS

Generally

Bonito Boats, Inc. v. Thunder Craft Boats, Inc., 489 U.S. 141, 150, 9 U.S.P.Q.2d 1847, 1852 (1989). "The nonobviousness requirement extends the field of unpatentable material beyond that which is known to the public under [35 U.S.C.] §102, to include that which could readily be deduced from publicly available material by a person of ordinary skill in the pertinent field of endeavor." *See also* ***Sakraida v. AG Pro, Inc.***, 425 U.S. 273, 279, 189 U.S.P.Q. 449, 451-52 (1976).

Graham v. John Deere Co., 383 U.S. 1, 17-18, 148 U.S.P.Q. 459, 467 (1966). "While the ultimate question of patent validity is one of law, ... the §103 condition [of obviousness], which is but one of three conditions [including novelty and utility], each of which must be satisfied, lends itself to several basic factual inquiries. Under §103, the scope and content of the prior art are to be determined; differences between the prior art and the claims at issue are to be ascertained; and the level of ordinary skill in the pertinent art resolved. Against this background, the obviousness or nonobviousness of the subject matter is determined. Such secondary considerations as commercial success, long felt but unsolved needs, failure of others, etc., might be utilized to give light to the circumstances surrounding the origin of the subject matter sought to be patented. As indicia of obviousness or nonobviousness, these inquiries may have relevancy." *See also* ***Iron Grip Barbell Co. v. USA Sports, Inc.***, 392 F.3d 1317, 1323-24, 73 U.S.P.Q.2d 1225, 1229 (Fed.Cir.2004); ***McNeil-PPC, Inc. v. L. Perrigo Co.***, 337 F.3d 1362, 1368, 67 U.S.P.Q.2d 1649, 1653 (Fed.Cir.2003).

Sundance, Inc. v. DeMonte Fabricating Ltd., 550 F.3d 1356, 1363, 89 U.S.P.Q.2d 1535, 1540 (Fed.Cir. 2008). "We hold that it is an abuse of discretion to permit a witness to testify as an expert on the issues of noninfringement or invalidity unless that witness is qualified as an expert in the pertinent art. ... We understand that patent lawyers are often qualified to testify as technical experts, but such a qualification must derive from a lawyer's technical qualifications in the pertinent art. *At F.3d 1364:* With regard to invalidity, ... a witness not qualified in the pertinent art may not testify as an expert as to anticipation, or any of the underlying questions, such as the nature of the claimed invention, what a prior art references discloses, or whether the asserted claims read on the prior art reference. [¶] Nor may a witness not qualified in the pertinent art testify as an expert on obviousness, or any of the underlying technical questions, such as the nature of the claimed invention, the scope and content of prior art, the differences between the claimed invention and the prior art, or the motivation of one of ordinary skill in the art to combine these references to achieve the claimed invention." *See also* ***Outside the Box Innovations, LLC v. Travel Caddy, Inc.***, 695 F.3d 1285, 1297, 104 U.S.P.Q.2d 1890, 1898 (Fed.Cir.2012) (excluding testimony of prior-art expert because he was not patent attorney was abuse of discretion).

Quad Envtl. Techs. v. Union Sanitary Dist., 946 F.2d 870, 875-76, 20 U.S.P.Q.2d 1392, 1395-96 (Fed.Cir. 1991). "In an infringement suit before a district court, the invalidity of a patent under 35 U.S.C. §103 must be decided on the basis of prior art adduced in the proceeding before the court. The issue cannot be decided merely by accepting or rejecting the adequacy of the positions taken by the patentee in order to obtain a Certificate of Reexamination for the patent." *See also* ***In re Braat***, 937 F.2d 589, 592-93, 19 U.S.P.Q.2d 1289, 1291-92 (Fed.Cir.1991).

In re Fine, 837 F.2d 1071, 1076, 5 U.S.P.Q.2d 1596, 1600 (Fed.Cir.1988). "Dependent claims are nonobvious under §103 if the independent claims from which they depend are nonobvious."

Prior Art & Obviousness—Generally

KSR Int'l v. Teleflex Inc., 550 U.S. 398, 407, 82 U.S.P.Q.2d 1385, 1391 (2007). "Seeking to resolve the question of obviousness with more uniformity and consistency, the [Federal Circuit] has employed ... the 'teaching, suggestion, or motivation' test (TSM test), under which a patent claim is only proved obvious if 'some motivation or suggestion to combine the prior art teachings' can be found in the prior art, the nature of the problem, or the knowledge of a person having ordinary skill in the art. *At U.S. 417, U.S.P.Q.2d 1396:* When a work is available in one field of endeavor, design incentives and other market forces can prompt variations of it, either in the same field or a different one. If a person of ordinary skill can implement a predictable variation, §103 likely bars its patentability. For the same reason, if a technique has been used to improve one device, and a person of ordinary skill in the art would recognize that it would improve similar devices in the same way, using the technique is obvious unless its actual application is beyond his or her skill. [A] court must ask whether the improvement is more than the predictable use of prior art elements according to their established functions. *At U.S. 418:* Often, it will be necessary for a court to look to interrelated teachings of multiple patents; the effects of demands known to the design community or present in the marketplace; and the background knowledge possessed by a person having ordinary skill in the art, all in order to determine whether there was an apparent reason to combine the known elements in the fashion claimed by the patent at issue. To facilitate review, this analysis should be made explicit. [T]he analysis need not seek out precise teachings directed to the specific subject matter of the challenged claim, for a court can take account of the inferences and creative steps that a person of ordinary skill in the art would employ. [¶] [A] patent composed of several elements is not proved obvious merely by demonstrating that each of its elements was, independently, known in the prior art. Although common sense directs one to look with care at a patent application that claims as innovation the combination of two known devices according to their established functions, it can be important to identify a reason that would have prompted a person of ordinary skill in the relevant field to combine the elements in the way the claimed new invention does. *At U.S. 419-21:* Helpful insights, however, need not become rigid and mandatory formulas; and when it is so applied, the TSM test is incompatible with our precedents. The obviousness analysis cannot be confined by a formalistic conception of the words teaching, suggestion, and motivation, or by overemphasis on the importance of published articles and the explicit content of issued patents. *At U.S.P.Q.2d 1397:* In determining whether the subject matter of a patent claim is obvious, neither the particular motivation nor the avowed purpose of the patentee controls. What matters is the objective reach of the claim. If the claim extends to what is obvious, it is invalid under §103. One of the ways in which a patent's subject matter can be proved obvious is by noting that there existed at the time of invention a known problem for which there was an obvious solution encompassed by the patent's claims. [¶] The [Court of Appeals erred] by holding that courts and patent examiners should look only to the problem the patentee was trying to solve. The Court of Appeals failed to recognize that the problem motivating the patentee may be only one of many addressed by the patent's subject matter. The question is not whether the combination was obvious to the patentee but whether the combination was obvious to a person with ordinary skill in the art. Under the correct analysis, any need or problem known in the field of endeavor at the time of invention and addressed by the patent can provide a reason for combining the elements in the manner claimed. [¶] The [Court of Appeals erred] in its assumption that a person of ordinary skill attempting to solve a problem will be led only to those elements of prior art designed to solve the same problem. ... Common sense teaches, however, that familiar items may have obvious uses beyond their primary purposes, and in many cases a person of ordinary skill will be able to fit the teachings of multiple patents together like pieces of a puzzle. ... A person of ordinary skill is also a person of ordinary creativity, not an automaton. [¶] The [Court of Appeals erred by holding] that a patent claim cannot be proved obvious merely by showing that the combination of elements was '[o]bvious to try.' When there is a design need or market pressure to solve a problem and there are a finite number of identified, predictable solutions, a person of ordinary skill has good reason to pursue the known options within his or her technical grasp. If this leads to the anticipated success, it is likely the product [is] not of innovation but of ordinary skill and common sense. In that instance the fact that a combination was obvious to try might show that it was obvious under §103. [¶] The [Court of Appeals erred on] the risk of courts and patent examiners falling prey to hindsight bias. A factfinder should be aware, of course, of the distortion caused by hindsight bias and must be cautious of arguments reliant upon *ex post* reasoning. Rigid preventative rules that deny factfinders recourse to common sense, however, are neither necessary under our case law nor consistent with it. *At U.S. 422, U.S.P.Q.2d 1398:* [T]he fundamental misunderstandings identified above led the Court of Appeals in this case to apply a test inconsistent with our patent law decisions."

Hazeltine Research, Inc. v. Brenner, 382 U.S. 252, 252, 147 U.S.P.Q. 429, 430 (1965). "The sole question presented here is whether an application for patent pending in the [PTO] at the time a second application is filed constitutes part of the 'prior art' as that term is used in … §103…. *At U.S. 256, U.S.P.Q. 431:* We see no reason to read into §103 a restricted definition of 'prior art' which would lower standards of patentability to such an extent that there might exist two patents where the Congress has plainly directed that there should be only one."

Exmark Mfg. Co. v. Briggs & Stratton Power Prods. Grp., 879 F.3d 1332, 1341, 125 U.S.P.Q.2d 1421, ___ (Fed.Cir.2018). "The question … presented is whether a reexamination confirming patentability of a claim can form the sole basis for granting summary judgment that a claim is not invalid based on the same prior art. [¶] We hold that a reexamination confirming patentability of a patent claim alone is not determinative of whether a genuine issue of fact precludes summary judgment of no invalidity. Surviving a reexamination does not warrant *ipso facto* summary judgment that a patent is not invalid. Holding otherwise would improperly give complete deference and preclusive effect to the PTO's patentability determination, foreclosing challenges to patent validity in district court based on the same prior art. [¶] Our holding is supported by our prior decisions stating that a district court 'is never bound by an examiner's finding in an ex parte patent application proceeding.' We have said the same regarding an examiner's findings during reissue proceedings. While the PTO's findings during reexamination are 'evidence the court must consider in determining whether the party asserting invalidity has met its statutory burden by clear and convincing evidence,' they are not dispositive. [¶] Instead, the '*deference* [owed] to the decisions of the USPTO takes the form of the *presumption of validity* under 35 U.S.C. §282. That is, by statute a patent is valid upon issuance and included within the presumption of validity is a presumption of non-obviousness.'"

Arendi S.A.R.L. v. Apple Inc., 832 F.3d 1355, 1361, 119 U.S.P.Q.2d 1822, 1825 (Fed.Cir.2016). "[W]e do consider common sense, common wisdom, and common knowledge in analyzing obviousness. [¶] But there are at least three caveats to note in applying 'common sense' in an obviousness analysis. First, common sense is typically invoked to provide a known *motivation to combine*, not to supply a missing claim limitation. *At F.3d 1362, U.S.P.Q.2d 1826:* Second, in … the only case [petitioners identify] in which common sense was invoked to supply a limitation that was admittedly *missing* from the prior art, the limitation in question was unusually simple and the technology particularly straightforward. [¶] Third, our cases repeatedly warn that references to 'common sense'—whether to supply a motivation to combine or a missing limitation—cannot be used as a wholesale substitute for reasoned analysis and evidentiary support, especially when dealing with a limitation missing from the prior art references specified. Indeed, we stated that although there is no problem with using common sense without any specific hint or suggestion in a particular reference, the [PTAB's] utter failure to explain the 'common knowledge and common sense' on which it relied is problematic." (Internal quotes omitted.)

Par Pharm. v. TWi Pharms., 773 F.3d 1186, 1194-95, 112 U.S.P.Q.2d 1945, 1951-52 (Fed.Cir.2014). "'The inherent teaching of a prior art reference' is a 'question of fact.' We have recognized that inherency may supply a missing claim limitation in an obviousness analysis. We have, however, also explained that the use of inherency, a doctrine originally rooted in anticipation, must be carefully circumscribed in the context of obviousness. [I]nherency in an obviousness analysis … 'may not be established by probabilities or possibilities. The mere fact that a certain thing may result from a given set of circumstances is not sufficient. If, however, the disclosure is sufficient to show that *the natural result flowing* from the operation as taught would result in the performance of the questioned function, it seems to be well settled that the disclosure should be regarded as sufficient.' Thus, our early precedent, and that of our predecessor court, established that the concept of inherency must be limited when applied to obviousness, and is present only when the limitation at issue is the 'natural result' of the combination of prior art elements."

In re Antor Media Corp., 689 F.3d 1282, 1289, 103 U.S.P.Q.2d 1555, 1559 (Fed.Cir.2012). "[W]e ... hold that, during patent prosecution, an examiner is entitled to reject claims as anticipated by a prior art publication or patent without conducting an inquiry into whether or not that prior art reference is enabling. As long as an examiner makes a proper prima facie case of anticipation by giving adequate notice under [35 U.S.C.] §132, the burden shifts to the applicant to submit rebuttal evidence of nonenablement."

Star Sci., Inc. v. R.J. Reynolds Tobacco Co., 655 F.3d 1364, 1374, 99 U.S.P.Q.2d 1924, 1931 (Fed.Cir. 2011). "Obviousness is a determination of law based on underlying determinations of fact. These factual determinations include the scope and content of the prior art, the level of ordinary skill in the art, the differences between the claimed invention and the prior art, and secondary considerations of nonobviousness. [¶] Whether prior art invalidates a patent claim as obvious is determined from the perspective of one of ordinary skill in the art."

Perfect Web Techs. v. InfoUSA, Inc., 587 F.3d 1324, 1329, 92 U.S.P.Q.2d 1849, 1854 (Fed.Cir.2009). "We ... hold that while an analysis of obviousness always depends on evidence that supports the required *Graham* factual findings, it also may include recourse to logic, judgment, and common sense available to the person of ordinary skill that do not necessarily require explication in any reference or expert opinion."

Ritchie v. Vast Res., 563 F.3d 1334, 1337, 90 U.S.P.Q.2d 1668, 1669 (Fed.Cir.2009). "Among the inventions that the law deems obvious are those modest, routine, everyday, incremental improvements of an existing product or process that confer commercial value (otherwise they would not be undertaken) but do not involve sufficient inventiveness to merit patent protection. This class of inventions is well illustrated by efforts at routine experimentation with different standard grades of a material used in a product—standard in the sense that their properties, composition, and method of creation are well known, making successful results of experimentation predictable."

In re Kubin, 561 F.3d 1351, 1360, 90 U.S.P.Q.2d 1417, 1424 (Fed.Cir.2009). "This court ... declines to cabin *KSR* to the 'predictable arts' (as opposed to the 'unpredictable art' of biotechnology). In fact, this record shows that one of skill in [biotechnology] would find these claimed 'results' profoundly 'predictable.' [T]his court cannot deem irrelevant the ease and predictability of cloning the gene that codes for that protein. This court cannot, in the face of *KSR*, cling to formalistic rules for obviousness, customize its legal tests for specific scientific fields in ways that deem entire classes of prior art teachings irrelevant, or discount the significant abilities of artisans of ordinary skill in an advanced area of art."

Innogenetics, N.V. v. Abbott Labs., 512 F.3d 1363, 1373-74, 85 U.S.P.Q.2d 1641, 1647-48 (Fed.Cir.2008). "For each of the claims that he analyzes for obviousness, [witness] merely lists a number of prior art references and then concludes with the stock phrase 'to one skilled in the art it would have been obvious to perform the genotyping method in [claims 1-9 and 12-13] of the '704 patent.' ... Nowhere does [witness] state how or why a person ordinarily skilled in the art would have found the claims of the '704 patent obvious in light of some combination of those particular references. ... Such vague testimony would not have been helpful to a lay jury in avoiding the pitfalls of hindsight that belie a determination of obviousness. [¶] We cannot conclude that the district court abused its discretion when it precluded [witness's] vague and conclusory obviousness testimony which did not offer any motivation for one skilled in the art to combine the particular references he cites in order to practice the claimed method."

Leapfrog Enters. v. Fisher-Price, Inc., 485 F.3d 1157, 1161, 82 U.S.P.Q.2d 1687, 1691 (Fed.Cir.2007). "[T]he goal of ... device was to allow a child to press a switch associated with a single letter in a word and hear the sound of the letter as it is used in that word. In this way, the child would both associate the sound of the letter with the letter itself and be able to sound out the word one letter at a time to learn to read phonetically. Accommodating a prior art mechanical device that accomplishes that goal to modern electronics would have been reasonably obvious to one of ordinary skill in designing children's learning devices. Applying modern electronics to older mechanical devices has been commonplace in recent years."

Ormco Corp. v. Align Tech., 463 F.3d 1299, 1311, 79 U.S.P.Q.2d 1931, 1940 (Fed.Cir.2006). "Where a claimed range overlaps with a range disclosed in the prior art, there is a presumption of obviousness. The presumption can be rebutted if it can be shown that the prior art teaches away from the claimed range, or the claimed range produces new and unexpected results."

Knoll Pharm. v. Teva Pharms., 367 F.3d 1381, 1385, 70 U.S.P.Q.2d 1957, 1960 (Fed.Cir.2004). To refute a claim of obviousness, "[e]vidence developed after the patent grant is not excluded from consideration, for understanding of the full range of an invention is not always achieved at the time of filing the patent application. It is not improper to obtain additional support consistent with the patented invention, to respond to litigation attacks on validity. There is no requirement that an invention's properties and advantages were fully known before the patent application was filed, or that the patent application contains all of the work done in studying the invention, in order for that work to be introduced into evidence in response to litigation attack. Nor is it improper to conduct additional experiments and provide later-obtained data in support of patent validity."

TorPharm Inc. v. Ranbaxy Pharms., 336 F.3d 1322, 1326 n.3, 67 U.S.P.Q.2d 1511, 1513 n.3 (Fed.Cir. 2003). "[N]ovelty and nonobviousness are separate concepts that are best kept analytically distinct. *At F.2d 1327, U.S.P.Q.2d 1514:* [T]here are no per se rules relating the patentability of product and process in either direction. A process yielding a novel and nonobvious product may nonetheless be obvious; conversely, a process yielding a well-known product may yet be nonobvious."

Riverwood Int'l v. R.A. Jones & Co., 324 F.3d 1346, 1354, 66 U.S.P.Q.2d 1331, 1337 (Fed.Cir.2003). "The term 'prior art' as used in [35 U.S.C.] §103 refers at least to the statutory material named in 35 U.S.C. §102. However, §102 is not the only source of §103 prior art. Valid prior art may be created by the admissions of the parties. [¶] [Although] a reference can become prior art by admission, that doctrine is inapplicable when the subject matter at issue is the inventor's own work. ... '[A] finding of obviousness should not be based on an implied admission erroneously creating imaginary prior art. That is not the intent of §103.'"

Ruiz v. A.B. Chance Co., 234 F.3d 654, 665, 57 U.S.P.Q.2d 1161, 1167 (Fed.Cir.2000). "Because there is 'a general rule that combination claims can consist of combinations of old elements as well as new elements,' ... '[t]he notion ... that combination claims can be declared invalid merely upon finding similar elements in separate prior patents would necessarily destroy virtually all patents and cannot be the law under ... §103.' The test is not whether one device can be an appropriate substitute for another."

In re Ochiai, 71 F.3d 1565, 1570 n.5, 37 U.S.P.Q.2d 1127, 1132 n.5 (Fed.Cir.1995). "Similarity is ... not necessarily obviousness. *At F.3d 1572, U.S.P.Q.2d 1133:* [O]ur precedents do not establish any *per se* rules of obviousness, just as those precedents themselves expressly declined to create such rules. Any conflicts [in decisions] as may be perceived to exist derive from an impermissible effort to extract *per se* rules from decisions that disavow precisely such extraction."

In re Chu, 66 F.3d 292, 299, 36 U.S.P.Q.2d 1089, 1095 (Fed.Cir.1995). "We have found no cases supporting the position that a patent applicant's evidence and/or arguments traversing a §103 rejection must be contained within the specification. There is no logical support for such a proposition as well, given that obviousness is determined by the totality of the record including ... the evidence and arguments proffered during the give-and-take of ex parte patent prosecution."

Merck & Co. v. Biocraft Labs., 874 F.2d 804, 807, 10 U.S.P.Q.2d 1843, 1846 (Fed.Cir.1989). "[I]n a §103 inquiry, 'the fact that a specific [embodiment] is taught to be preferred is not controlling, since all disclosures of the prior art, including unpreferred embodiments, must be considered.' [¶] [T]he mere absence from the prior art of a teaching or a limitation recited in the patent at issue is insufficient for a conclusion of nonobviousness."

Prior Art & Obviousness—Prima Facie Case

Otsuka Pharm. Co. v. Sandoz, Inc., 678 F.3d 1280, 1291-93, 102 U.S.P.Q.2d 1729, 1737-38 (Fed.Cir.2012). "Our case law demonstrates that whether a new chemical compound would have been *prima facie* obvious over particular prior art compounds ordinarily follows a two-part inquiry. First, the court determines whether a chemist of ordinary skill would have selected the asserted prior art compounds as lead compounds, or starting points, for further development efforts. A lead compound ... is a compound in the prior art that would be most promising to modify in order to improve upon its activity and obtain a compound with better activity. As such, a lead compound is a natural choice for further development efforts. In recent cases involving the alleged obviousness of a new chemical compound, the parties have frequently focused upon the notion that a chemist must select one or more lead compounds. In such cases our analysis focuses on those proposed lead

PRE-AIA §103

compounds that the alleged infringer has attempted to prove, by clear and convincing evidence, that the skilled artisan would have had a reason to select from the panoply of known compounds in the prior art. [¶] In determining whether a chemist would have selected a prior art compound as a lead, the analysis is guided by evidence of the compound's pertinent properties. Such properties may include positive attributes such as activity and potency, ... adverse effects such as toxicity, ... and other relevant characteristics in evidence.... Absent a reason or motivation based on such prior art evidence, mere structural similarity between a prior art compound and the claimed compound does not inform the lead compound selection. Were it otherwise, the analysis would impermissibly rely upon *ex post* reasoning. [¶] The second inquiry in the analysis is whether the prior art would have supplied one of ordinary skill in the art with a reason or motivation to modify a lead compound to make the claimed compound with a reasonable expectation of success. [¶] In keeping with the flexible nature of the obviousness inquiry, the reason or motivation for modifying a lead compound may come from any number of sources and need not necessarily be explicit in the prior art. Again, pertinent properties guide the analysis, for it is the possession of promising useful properties in a lead compound that motivates a chemist to make structurally similar compounds. As we have explained, it is sufficient to show that the claimed and prior art compounds possess a sufficiently close relationship to create an expectation, in light of the totality of the prior art, that the new compound will have similar properties to the old." (Internal quotes omitted.)

- ***Daiichi Sankyo Co. v. Matrix Labs.***, 619 F.3d 1346, 1352, 96 U.S.P.Q.2d 1526, 1531 (Fed.Cir.2010). "When a patent claims a chemical compound, a *prima facie* case of obviousness under the third ***Graham*** factor frequently turns on the structural similarities and differences between the compounds claimed and those in the prior art. Proof of obviousness based on structural similarity requires clear and convincing evidence that a medicinal chemist of ordinary skill would have been motivated to select and then to modify a prior art compound (*e.g.*, a lead compound) to arrive at a claimed compound with a reasonable expectation that the new compound would have similar or improved properties compared with the old. In keeping with the flexible nature of the inquiry after ***KSR*** ..., the motivation to select and modify a lead compound need not be explicit in the art." *See also* ***Unigene Labs. v. Apotex Inc.***, 655 F.3d 1352, 1361-62, 99 U.S.P.Q.2d 1858, 1863-64 (Fed.Cir.2011) (lead compound more appropriately called reference composition).

- ***Aventis Pharma Deutschland GmbH v. Lupin, Ltd.***, 499 F.3d 1293, 1301, 84 U.S.P.Q.2d 1197, 1204 (Fed.Cir.2007). "[A] claimed composition [may be] a purified form of a mixture that existed in the prior art. Such a purified compound is not always prima facie obvious over the mixture; for example, it may not be known that the purified compound is present in or an active ingredient of the mixture, or the state of the art may be such that discovering how to perform the purification is an invention of patentable weight in itself. However, if it is known that some desirable property of a mixture derives in whole or in part from a particular one of its components, or if the prior art would provide a person of ordinary skill in the art with reason to believe that this is so, the purified compound is prima facie obvious over the mixture even without an explicit teaching that the ingredient should be concentrated or purified."

- ***Eli Lilly & Co. v. Zenith Goldline Pharms.***, 471 F.3d 1369, 1377, 81 U.S.P.Q.2d 1324, 1329 (Fed.Cir. 2006). "For a chemical compound, a prima facie case of obviousness requires 'structural similarity between claimed and prior art subject matter ... where the prior art gives reason or motivation to make the claimed compositions.' *At F.3d 1380, U.S.P.Q.2d 1331:* [P] overcame any prima facie case of obviousness. Among other things, [P] proved extensive secondary considerations to rebut obviousness. The trial court found the evidence clearly established four of the five proffered secondary considerations. [P] established (1) a long-felt and unmet need; (2) failure of others; (3) industry acclaim; and (4) unexpected results." *See also* ***Takeda Chem. Indus. v. Alphapharm Pty., Ltd.***, 492 F.3d 1350, 1356-57, 83 U.S.P.Q.2d 1169, 1174 (Fed.Cir.2007).

- ***In re Kumar***, 418 F.3d 1361, 1366, 76 U.S.P.Q.2d 1048, 1050 (Fed.Cir.2005). "During examination, the examiner bears the initial burden of establishing a *prima facie* case of obviousness. The *prima facie* case is a procedural tool, and requires that the examiner initially produce evidence sufficient to support a ruling of obviousness; thereafter the burden shifts to the applicant to come forward with evidence or argument in rebuttal. When rebuttal evidence is provided, the *prima* *facie* case dissolves, and the decision is made on the entirety of the evidence. *At U.S.P.Q.2d 1051:* A *prima facie* case of obviousness may be made when the only difference from the prior art is a difference in the range or value of a particular variable. *At F.3d 1368, U.S.P.Q.2d 1052-53:* An applicant may rebut a *prima facie* case of obviousness by providing a 'showing of facts supporting the opposite conclusion.' Such a showing dissipates the *prima facie* holding and requires the examiner to 'consider all of the evidence anew.' Rebuttal evidence may show, for example, that the claimed invention achieved unexpected results relative to the prior art; that the prior art teaches away from the claimed invention; that objective evidence (*e.g.*, commercial success) supports the conclusion that the invention would not have been obvious to a skilled artisan; or that the prior art did not enable one skilled in the art to produce the now-claimed invention. [¶] Although published subject matter is 'prior art' for all that it discloses, in order to render an invention unpatentable for obviousness, the prior art must enable a person of ordinary skill to make and use the invention. Thus when a *prima facie* case of obviousness is deemed made based on similarity to a known composition or device, rebuttal may take the form of evidence that the prior art does not enable the claimed subject matter. [¶] The applicant has the burden of coming forward with evidence in rebuttal, when the prior art includes a method that appears, on its face, to be capable of producing the claimed composition. This burden may be met by presenting sufficient reason or authority or evidence, on the facts of the case, to show that the prior art method would not produce or would not be expected to produce the claimed subject matter." *See also* ***In re Harris***, 409 F.3d 1339, 1341, 74 U.S.P.Q.2d 1951, 1953-54 (Fed.Cir.2005); ***In re Rouffet***, 149 F.3d 1350, 1355, 47 U.S.P.Q.2d 1453, 1455 (Fed.Cir.1998); ***In re Eli Lilly & Co.***, 902 F.2d 943, 945, 14 U.S.P.Q.2d 1741, 1743 (Fed.Cir.1990).

In re Peterson, 315 F.3d 1325, 1329, 65 U.S.P.Q.2d 1379, 1382-83 (Fed.Cir.2003). "A *prima facie* case of obviousness typically exists when the ranges of a claimed composition overlap the ranges disclosed in the prior art. [¶] We have also held that a *prima facie* case of obviousness exists when the claimed range and the prior art range do not overlap but are close enough such that one skilled in the art would have expected them to have the same properties. *At F.3d 1330:* We therefore conclude that a prior art reference that discloses a range encompassing a somewhat narrower claimed range is sufficient to establish a *prima facie* case of obviousness. That is not to say that the claimed composition having a narrower range is unpatentable. Rather, the existence of overlapping or encompassing ranges shifts the burden to the applicant to show that his invention would not have been obvious.... [¶] [A]n applicant may overcome a *prima facie* case of obviousness by establishing 'that the [claimed] range is critical, generally by showing that the claimed range achieves unexpected results relative to the prior art range.' That same standard applies when ... the applicant seeks to optimize certain variables by selecting narrow ranges from broader ranges disclosed in the prior art. Moreover, the applicant's showing of unexpected results must be commensurate in scope with the claimed range. *At F.3d 1331, U.S.P.Q.2d 1384:* Alternatively, an applicant may rebut a *prima facie* case of obviousness by showing that the prior art teaches away from the claimed invention in any material respect."

Prior Art & Obviousness—Secondary Considerations

Graham v. John Deere Co., 383 U.S. 1, 17-18, 148 U.S.P.Q. 459, 467 (1966). "Such secondary considerations as commercial success, long felt but unsolved needs, failure of others, etc., might be utilized to give light to the circumstances surrounding the origin of the subject matter sought to be patented. As indicia of obviousness or nonobviousness, these inquiries may have relevancy."

Polaris Indus. v. Arctic Cat, Inc., 882 F.3d 1056, 1072, ___ U.S.P.Q.2d ___ (Fed.Cir.2018). "'[O]bjective evidence of non-obviousness must be commensurate in scope with the claims which the evidence is offered to support.' We presume that such a nexus applies for objective indicia when the patentee shows that the asserted objective evidence is tied to a specific product and that product 'embodies the claimed features, and is coextensive with them.' Conversely, '[w]hen the thing that is commercially successful is not coextensive with the patented invention—for example, if the patented invention is only a component of a commercially successful machine or process—the patentee must show prima facie a legally sufficient relationship between that which is patented and that which is sold.'"

In re Cyclobenzaprine Hydrochloride Extended-Release Capsule Patent Litig., 676 F.3d 1063, 1075-76, 102 U.S.P.Q.2d 1760, 1770-71 (Fed.Cir.2012). "In ***Stratoflex, Inc. v. Aeroquip Corp.***, [713 F.2d 1530

(Fed.Cir.1983),] we held that a fact finder in district court litigation may not defer examination of the objective considerations until after the fact finder makes an obviousness finding: It is jurisprudentially inappropriate to disregard any relevant evidence on any issue in any case, patent cases included. Thus evidence rising out of the so-called 'secondary considerations' must always when present be considered en route to a determination of obviousness. Indeed, evidence of secondary considerations may often be the most probative and cogent evidence in the record. It may often establish that an invention appearing to have been obvious in light of the prior art was not. It is to be considered as part of all the evidence, not just when the decision-maker remains in doubt after reviewing the art. Many subsequent cases have expressly followed ***Stratoflex***'s directive that courts consider all objective evidence before reaching an obviousness conclusion. [¶] While many panels of this court have adhered to ***Stratoflex***'s directive, some instead have spoken of the obviousness analysis in terms of a 'prima facie' case which must then be 'rebutted' by the patentee. Under that framework, a court inquires whether the party challenging validity has proven a 'prima facie' case of obviousness, based only on reference to the patent and the proffered prior art, and only then considers objective evidence, asking whether such evidence is sufficient to *overcome* the prima facie case. *At F.3d 1077:* Despite this language, however, those cases should not be interpreted as establishing a formal burden-shifting framework. *At F.3d 1079-80, U.S.P.Q.2d 1774:* In sum, opinions of this court should not be read to require a burden-shifting framework in derogation of ***Stratoflex***'s directive that objective evidence be considered before making an obviousness determination and in disregard of where the burdens of proof and persuasion are properly placed in district court litigation." (Internal quotes omitted.) *See also* ***Transocean Offshore Deepwater Drilling, Inc. v. Maersk Contractors USA, Inc.***, 617 F.3d 1296, 1303, 96 U.S.P.Q.2d 1104, 1107 (Fed.Cir.2010).

Genetics Inst. v. Novartis Vaccines & Diagnostics, Inc., 655 F.3d 1291, 1307, 99 U.S.P.Q.2d 1713, 1726 (Fed.Cir.2011). "[E]very property of a claimed compound need not be fully recognized as of the filing date of the patent application to be relevant to nonobviousness. For those reasons, we have held that evidence of unexpected results may be used to rebut a case of *prima facie* obviousness even if that evidence was obtained after the patent's filing or issue date. [¶] Although the §103 analysis remains properly focused 'at the time the invention was made,' it would be error to prohibit a patent applicant or patentee from presenting relevant indicia of nonobviousness, whether or not this evidence was available or expressly contemplated at the filing of the patent application. Relevant secondary considerations often are not manifest even until well after the issuance of a patent. The dissent would require either an express prediction of unexpected properties in the patent specification or a showing of the inventors' contemporaneous knowledge of such properties before the PTO or any court could consider such probative evidence. Our precedent contains no such requirement."

Geo M. Martin Co. v. Alliance Mach. Sys. Int'l, 618 F.3d 1294, 1305, 96 U.S.P.Q.2d 1212, 1219 (Fed.Cir. 2010). "Industry praise must ... be linked to the patented invention [to prove commercial success]. *At U.S.P.Q.2d 1220:* [P] points to evidence that [D] copied the claimed invention.... This court has noted, however, 'that a showing of copying is only equivocal evidence of non-obviousness in the absence of more compelling objective indicia of other secondary considerations.' [¶] Independently made, simultaneous inventions, made 'within a comparatively short space of time,' are persuasive evidence that the claimed apparatus 'was the product only of ordinary mechanical or engineering skill.'"

Procter & Gamble Co. v. Teva Pharms. USA, Inc., 566 F.3d 989, 998, 90 U.S.P.Q.2d 1947, 1953 (Fed.Cir. 2009). "[D] argues that the long-felt need must be unmet at the time the invention becomes available on the market, when it can actually satisfy that need. ... Under ***Monarch [Knitting Mach. Corp. v. Sulzer Morat GmbH***, 139 F.3d 877 (Fed.Cir.1998)], we look to the filing date of the challenged invention to assess the presence of a long-felt and unmet need."

Ormco Corp. v. Align Tech., 463 F.3d 1299, 1311-12, 79 U.S.P.Q.2d 1931, 1941 (Fed.Cir.2006). "Evidence of commercial success, or other secondary considerations, is only significant if there is a nexus between the claimed invention and the commercial success. '[W]hen a patentee can demonstrate commercial success, usually shown by significant sales in a relevant market, and that the successful product is the invention disclosed and claimed in the patent, it is presumed that the commercial success is due to the patented invention.' Thus, if the commercial success is due to an unclaimed feature of the device, the commercial success is irrelevant. So too if the feature that creates the commercial success was known in the prior art, the success is not pertinent." *See also* ***Syntex L.L.C. v. Apotex, Inc.***, 407 F.3d 1371, 1383, 74 U.S.P.Q.2d 1823, 1832 (Fed.Cir.2005); ***In re GPAC Inc.***, 57 F.3d 1573, 1580, 35 U.S.P.Q.2d 1116, 1121-22 (Fed. Cir.1995).

In re Soni, 54 F.3d 746, 750, 34 U.S.P.Q.2d 1684, 1687 (Fed.Cir.1995). "When a chemical composition is claimed, a *prima facie* case of obviousness under §103 may be established by the PTO's citation of a reference to a similar composition, the presumption being that similar compositions have similar properties. One way for a patent applicant to rebut a *prima facie* case of obviousness is to make a showing of 'unexpected results,' *i.e.*, to show that the claimed invention exhibits some superior property or advantage that a person of ordinary skill in the relevant art would have found surprising or unexpected. The basic principle behind this rule is straightforward—that which would have been surprising to a person of ordinary skill in a particular art would not have been obvious. The principle applies most often to the less predictable fields, such as chemistry, where minor changes in a product or process may yield substantially different results." *See also* ***In re Dillon***, 919 F.2d 688, 692-93, 16 U.S.P.Q.2d 1897, 1901 (Fed.Cir.1990).

Prior Art & Obviousness—Motivation

Intercontinental Great Brands LLC v. Kellogg N. Am. Co., 869 F.3d 1336, 1344, 124 U.S.P.Q.2d 1081, 1087 (Fed.Cir.2017). "The court should consider a range of real-world facts to determine 'whether there was an apparent reason to combine the known elements in the fashion claimed by the patent at issue.'"

Spectrum Pharms. v. Sandoz Inc., 802 F.3d 1326, 1334, 116 U.S.P.Q.2d 1717, 1721 (Fed.Cir.2015). "If it is known that the desired activity all lies in one isomer, surely, it is better, and there is generally motivation, to try to obtain the purest compound possible. A physician would not likely want to administer a contaminant or a less pure material to a patient if one could use a pure material. Thus, there is always in such cases a motivation to aim for obtaining a pure, resolved material. [¶] Conversely, if the pure material is known, no reason has been shown why one would want to have an impure material."

Eisai Co. v. Dr. Reddy's Labs., 533 F.3d 1353, 1356-57, 87 U.S.P.Q.2d 1452, 1455 (Fed.Cir.2008). "Where ... the patent at issue claims a chemical compound, the analysis of the third ***Graham*** factor (the differences between the claimed invention and the prior art) often turns on the structural similarities and differences between the claimed compound and the prior art compounds. Obviousness based on structural similarity thus can be proved by identification of some motivation that would have led one of ordinary skill in the art to select and then modify a known compound (i.e. a lead compound) in a particular way to achieve the claimed compound. In keeping with the flexible nature of the obviousness inquiry, ... the requisite motivation can come from any number of sources and need not necessarily be explicit in the art. Rather it is sufficient to show that the claimed and prior art compounds possess a sufficiently close relationship to create an expectation, in light of the totality of the prior art, that the new compound will have similar properties to the old. *At F.3d 1359, U.S.P.Q.2d 1456-57:* In ***KSR***, the Supreme Court noted that an invention may have been obvious when there was a design need or market pressure to solve a problem and there were ... a finite number of identified predictable solutions. The Supreme Court's analysis in ***KSR*** thus relies on several assumptions about the prior art landscape. First, ***KSR*** assumes a starting reference point or points in the art, prior to the time of invention, from which a skilled artisan might identify a problem and pursue potential solutions. Second, ***KSR*** presupposes that the record up to the time of invention would give some reasons, available within the knowledge of one of skill in the art, to make particular modifications to achieve the claimed compound. Third, the Supreme Court's analysis in ***KSR*** presumes that the record before the time of invention would supply some reasons for narrowing the prior art universe to a finite number of identified, predicable solutions.... To the extent an art is unpredictable, as the chemical arts often are, ***KSR***'s focus on these identified, predictable solutions may present a difficult hurdle because potential solutions are less likely to be genuinely predictable." (Internal quotes omitted.)

DyStar Textilfarben GmbH v. C.H. Patrick Co., 464 F.3d 1356, 1367, 80 U.S.P.Q.2d 1641, 1650 (Fed.Cir. 2006). "Our suggestion test is in actuality quite flexible and not only permits, but *requires*, consideration of common knowledge and common sense. *At F.3d 1368,*

U.S.P.Q.2d 1651: Indeed, we have repeatedly held that an implicit motivation to combine exists not only when a suggestion may be gleaned from the prior art as a whole, but when the 'improvement' is technology-independent and the combination of references results in a product or process that is more desirable, for example because it is stronger, cheaper, cleaner, faster, lighter, smaller, more durable, or more efficient. Because the desire to enhance commercial opportunities by improving a product or process is universal—and even common-sensical—we have held that there exists in these situations a motivation to combine prior art references even absent any hint of suggestion in the references themselves. In such situations, the proper question is whether the ordinary artisan possesses knowledge and skills rendering him *capable* of combining the prior art references. *At F.3d 1370, U.S.P.Q.2d 1653:* Although this court customarily discusses a motivation to combine as part of the first ***Graham*** factor, the scope and content of the prior art, motivation to combine is also inextricably linked to the level of ordinary skill. If, as is usually the case, no prior art reference contains an express suggestion to combine references, then the level of ordinary skill will often predetermine whether an implicit suggestion exists."

In re Johnston, 435 F.3d 1381, 1385, 77 U.S.P.Q.2d 1788, 1790 (Fed.Cir.2006). "An explicit teaching that identifies and selects elements from different sources and states that they should be combined in the same way as the invention at issue, is rarely found in the prior art. As precedent illustrates, many factors are relevant to the motivation-to-combine aspect of the obviousness inquiry, such as the field of the specific invention, the subject matter of the references, the extent to which they are in the same or related fields of technology, the nature of the advance made by the applicant, and the maturity and congestion of the field."

Sibia Neurosciences, Inc. v. Cadus Pharm., 225 F.3d 1349, 1355-56, 55 U.S.P.Q.2d 1927, 1931 (Fed.Cir. 2000). "While the presentation at trial of a reference that was not before the examiner does not change the presumption of validity, the alleged infringer's burden may be more easily carried because of this additional reference. [¶] In appropriate circumstances, a single prior art reference can render a claim obvious. However, there must be a showing of a suggestion or motivation to modify the teachings of that reference to the claimed invention in order to support the obviousness conclusion. This suggestion or motivation may be derived from the prior art reference itself, ... from the knowledge of one of ordinary skill in the art, or from the nature of the problem to be solved. Determining whether there is a suggestion or motivation to modify a prior art reference is one aspect of determining the scope and content of the prior art, a fact question subsidiary to the ultimate conclusion of obviousness."

Prior Art & Obviousness—Teaching Away

Meiresonne v. Google, Inc., 849 F.3d 1379, 1382, 121 U.S.P.Q.2d 1797, 1799 (Fed.Cir.2017). "A reference that 'merely expresses a general preference for an alternative invention but does not criticize, discredit, or otherwise discourage investigation into' the claimed invention does not teach away." *See also* ***Polaris Indus. v. Arctic Cat, Inc.***, 882 F.3d 1056, 1068-70, ___ U.S.P.Q.2d ___ (Fed.Cir.2018).

DePuy Spine, Inc. v. Medtronic Sofamor Danek, Inc., 567 F.3d 1314, 1326, 90 U.S.P.Q.2d 1865, 1873 (Fed. Cir.2009). "An inference of nonobviousness is especially strong where the prior art's teachings undermine the very reason being proffered as to why a person of ordinary skill would have combined the known elements."

Medichem, S.A. v. Rolabo, S.L., 437 F.3d 1157, 1165, 77 U.S.P.Q.2d 1865, 1870 (Fed.Cir.2006). "When a piece of prior art 'suggests that the line of development flowing from the reference's disclosure is unlikely to be productive of the result sought by the applicant' the piece of prior art is said to 'teach away' from the claimed invention. ... Where the prior art contains 'apparently conflicting' teachings (i.e., where some references teach the combination and others teach away from it) each reference must be considered 'for its power to suggest solutions to an artisan of ordinary skill ... consider[ing] the degree to which one reference might accurately discredit another.'"

Syntex L.L.C. v. Apotex, Inc., 407 F.3d 1371, 1378, 74 U.S.P.Q.2d 1823, 1828 (Fed.Cir.2005). "'What the prior art teaches, whether it teaches away from the claimed invention, and whether it motivates a combination of teachings from different references are questions of fact.' *At F.3d 1380, U.S.P.Q.2d 1830:* Under the proper legal standard, a reference will teach away when it suggests that the developments flowing from its disclosures are unlikely to produce the objective of the applicant's invention. A statement that a particular combination is not a preferred embodiment does not teach away absent clear discouragement of that combination."

Prior Art & Obviousness—§102 Prior Art

Geo M. Martin Co. v. Alliance Mach. Sys. Int'l, 618 F.3d 1294, 1302, 96 U.S.P.Q.2d 1212, 1218 (Fed.Cir. 2010). "Under an obviousness analysis, a reference need not work to qualify as prior art; 'it qualifies as prior art, regardless, for whatever is disclosed therein.' 'Even if a reference discloses an inoperative device, it is prior art for all that it teaches.'"

Cohesive Techs. v. Waters Corp., 543 F.3d 1351, 1363, 88 U.S.P.Q.2d 1903, 1910 (Fed.Cir.2008). "Despite the often quoted maxim that anticipation is the 'epitome of obviousness,' ... novelty under 35 U.S.C. §102 and nonobviousness under 35 U.S.C. §103 are separate conditions of patentability and therefore separate defenses available in an infringement action. *At F.3d 1364-65, U.S.P.Q.2d 1911:* While it is commonly understood that prior art references that anticipate a claim will usually render that claim obvious, it is not necessarily true that a verdict of nonobviousness forecloses anticipation. The tests for anticipation and obviousness are different. Obviousness can be proven by combining existing prior art references, while anticipation requires all elements of a claim to be disclosed within a single reference. Moreover, obviousness requires analysis of secondary considerations of nonobviousness, while secondary considerations are not an element of a claim of anticipation. And although anticipation can be proven inherently, proof of inherent anticipation is not the same as proof of obviousness. Thus, 'it does not follow that every technically anticipated invention would also have been obvious.' *At U.S.P.Q.2d 1912:* A court cannot refuse to submit the issue of anticipation to the jury simply because the accused infringer has also asserted an obviousness defense. It is for the litigants—not the court—to make the strategic decision as to whether to assert one, both, or neither of these defenses in a jury trial. An accused infringer that introduces a prior art reference and makes a non-frivolous argument that 'each and every limitation of a claim is found, expressly or inherently, in [that] single prior art reference' generally is entitled to have anticipation decided by the finder of fact."

Ormco Corp. v. Align Tech., 463 F.3d 1299, 1305, 79 U.S.P.Q.2d 1931, 1936 (Fed.Cir.2006). "'Prior art' in the obviousness context includes the material identified in [35 U.S.C.] §102(a). Section 102(a) provides that a person is not entitled to a patent if 'the invention was known or used by others in this country, or patented or described in a printed publication in this or a foreign country, before the invention thereof by the applicant for patent.' Art that is not accessible to the public is generally not recognized as prior art."

TorPharm Inc. v. Ranbaxy Pharms., 336 F.3d 1322, 1327, 67 U.S.P.Q.2d 1511, 1514-15 (Fed.Cir.2003). "'If a device was in public use or on sale before the critical date, then that device becomes a reference under [35 U.S.C.] §103 against the claimed invention.' The analysis is the same whether one regards this principle as an application of the on-sale bar, or an application of the law of nonobviousness, for which reason it has been termed the [35 U.S.C.] '§§102(b)/103' bar to patentability. The court's task upon such a challenge is to determine whether 'the claimed invention would have been obvious from the on-sale [invention] in conjunction with the prior art.' *At F.3d 1329-30, U.S.P.Q.2d 1516:* [W]here the factual bases of an examiner's decision to allow a claim have been undermined—as in other cases where prior art not before the examiner is brought to light during litigation—a court's responsibility is not to speculate what a particular examiner would or would not have done in light of the new information, but rather to assess independently the validity of the claim against the prior art under §102 or §103. Such determination must take into account the statutory presumption of patent validity." *See also* ***Pfaff v. Wells Elecs., Inc.***, 124 F.3d 1429, 1436, 43 U.S.P.Q.2d 1928, 1933-34 (Fed.Cir.1997), *aff'd*, 525 U.S. 55, 119 S.Ct. 304, 48 U.S.P.Q.2d 1641 (1998).

Thomson, S.A. v. Quixote Corp., 166 F.3d 1172, 1175 n.3, 49 U.S.P.Q.2d 1530, 1532 n.3 (Fed.Cir.1999). "[W]e have made clear that art qualifying only under [35 U.S.C. §102(g)] may not be used under [35 U.S.C. §103] to invalidate other patents of fellow employees engaged in team research."

OddzOn Prods. v. Just Toys, Inc., 122 F.3d 1396, 1401, 43 U.S.P.Q.2d 1641, 1644 (Fed.Cir.1997). 35 U.S.C. §102(f) "is a prior art provision for purposes of [35 U.S.C.] §103. *At F.3d 1403-04, U.S.P.Q.2d 1646:* [S]ubject matter derived from another not only is itself unpatentable to the party who derived it under §102(f), but, when combined with other prior art, may make a resulting obvious invention unpatentable to that party under a combination of §§102(f) and 103."

Symbol Techs. v. Opticon, Inc., 935 F.2d 1569, 1578, 19 U.S.P.Q.2d 1241, 1247 (Fed.Cir.1991). "While a reference must enable someone to practice the invention in order to anticipate under [35 U.S.C.] §102(b), a non-enabling reference may qualify as prior art for the purpose of determining obviousness under [35 U.S.C.] §103."

***In re* Bartfeld**, 925 F.2d 1450, 1451 n.4, 17 U.S.P.Q.2d 1885, 1886 n.4 (Fed.Cir.1991). "Though not anticipatory, a reference that would otherwise qualify as prior art under 35 U.S.C. §102(e) may form the basis of an obviousness rejection under 35 U.S.C. §103; hence, '§102(e)/§103' rejections. The effective date of the §102(e) reference is the application filing date, not the patent issuance date. *At F.2d 1451, U.S.P.Q.2d 1886-87:* PTO practice does not permit the use of a terminal disclaimer to overcome §102(e)/§103 rejections."

E.I. Du Pont de Nemours & Co. v. Phillips Pet., 849 F.2d 1430, 1437, 7 U.S.P.Q.2d 1129, 1135 (Fed.Cir. 1988). "[T]he term 'prior art' as it is used in 35 U.S.C. §103 should include all inventions which were made in this country before an applicant or patentee made his invention, regardless of when those inventions are made public or patent applications on them are filed, so long as those inventions are found not to have been abandoned, suppressed, or concealed. [The Supreme Court] does not *require* that a patent application be filed or a patent be issued before [35 U.S.C.] §102(g) prior work can qualify as §103 prior art. [¶] Despite its concern over 'secret prior art,' the [Supreme Court] allowed prior work to be used as prior art in a §103 context so long as it satisfied the requirements of §102(g)." (Internal quotes omitted.)

Prior Art & Obviousness—Analogous Art

***In re* GPAC Inc.**, 57 F.3d 1573, 1577-78, 35 U.S.P.Q.2d 1116, 1120 (Fed.Cir.1995). "We have recognized the scope of the relevant prior art as including that 'reasonably pertinent to the particular problem with which the inventor was involved.' Therefore, the prior art relevant to an obviousness determination necessarily encompasses not only the field of the inventor's endeavor but also any analogous arts. In deciding whether a reference is from a relevant art, we first must determine whether the reference is within the inventor's field of endeavor, and if it is not we next must determine whether the reference is reasonably pertinent to the particular problem confronting the inventor." *See also* **Wang Labs. v. Toshiba Corp.**, 993 F.2d 858, 864, 26 U.S.P.Q.2d 1767, 1773 (Fed.Cir.1993).

Heidelberger Druckmaschinen AG v. Hantscho Commercial Prods., 21 F.3d 1068, 1071, 30 U.S.P.Q.2d 1377, 1379 (Fed.Cir.1994). "The prior art primarily comprises references that are within the field of the inventor's endeavor. References that are not within the field of the inventor's endeavor may also be relied on in patentability determinations, and thus are described as 'analogous art,' when a person of ordinary skill would reasonably have consulted those references and applied their teachings in seeking a solution to the problem that the inventor was attempting to solve. Whether a reference is 'analogous art' is a question of fact ... and is part of the analysis of the scope and content of the prior art." *See also* ***In re* ICON Health & Fitness, Inc.**, 496 F.3d 1374, 1379-80, 83 U.S.P.Q.2d 1746, 1750 (Fed.Cir.2007).

Prior Art & Obviousness—"Obvious to Try"

KSR Int'l v. Teleflex Inc., 550 U.S. 398, 421, 82 U.S.P.Q.2d 1385, 1397 (2007). "[T]he Court of Appeals ... conclude[d], in error, that a patent claim cannot be proved obvious merely by showing that the combination of elements was '[o]bvious to try.' When there is a design need or market pressure to solve a problem and there are a finite number of identified, predictable solutions, a person of ordinary skill has good reason to pursue the known options within his or her technical grasp. If this leads to the anticipated success, it is likely the product [is] not of innovation but of ordinary skill and common sense. In that instance the fact that a combination was obvious to try might show that it was obvious under §103."

Bayer Schering Pharma AG v. Barr Labs., 575 F.3d 1341, 1347, 91 U.S.P.Q.2d 1569, 1572-73 (Fed.Cir. 2009). "[M]ost inventions that are obvious were also obvious to try, but [there are two exceptions]. [¶] First, an invention would not have been obvious to try when the inventor would have had to try all possibilities in a field unreduced by direction of the prior art. When what would have been 'obvious to try' would have been to vary all parameters or try each of numerous possible choices until one possibly arrived at a successful result, where the prior art gave either no indication of which parameters were critical or no direction as to which of many possible choices is likely to be successful[,] an invention would not have been obvious. This is another way to express the ***KSR*** prong requiring the field of search to be among a finite number of identified solutions. It is also consistent with our interpretation that ***KSR*** requires the number of options to be small or easily traversed. [¶] Second, an invention is not obvious to try where vague prior art does not guide an inventor toward a particular solution. A finding of obviousness would not obtain where what was 'obvious to try' was to explore a new technology or general approach that seemed to be a promising field of experimentation, where the prior art gave only general guidance as to the particular form of the claimed invention or how to achieve it. This expresses the same idea as the ***KSR*** requirement that the identified solutions be predictable." (Internal quotes omitted.)

In re Eli Lilly & Co., 902 F.2d 943, 945, 14 U.S.P.Q.2d 1741, 1743 (Fed.Cir.1990). "An 'obvious-to-try' situation exists when a general disclosure may pique the scientist's curiosity, such that further investigation might be done as a result of the disclosure, but the disclosure itself does not contain a sufficient teaching of how to obtain the desired result, or that the claimed result would be obtained if certain directions were pursued."

Person Having Ordinary Skill

Rovalma, S.A. v. Bohler-Edelstahl GmbH & Co. KG, 856 F.3d 1019, 1027, 122 U.S.P.Q.2d 1575, 1581 (Fed.Cir.2017). "Here, the Board resolved an active dispute over claim construction in favor of the patent owner and, using the patent owner's construction, relied on the patent owner's own submissions to determine how a skilled artisan would have read the very prior-art references on which the petitioner's obviousness challenge was based. *At F.3d 1029, U.S.P.Q.2d 1583:* To the extent that the Board did rely on [respondent's] submissions, and drew reasonably disputable inferences from those submissions, [respondent] was entitled to adequate notice of and opportunity to address those inferences."

Innovention Toys, LLC v. MGA Entm't, Inc., 637 F.3d 1314, 1323, 98 U.S.P.Q.2d 1013, 1019-20 (Fed.Cir. 2011). "A determination of obviousness requires a factual finding of the level of ordinary skill in the art. Yet, a district court's failure to make a correct finding on the level of skill constitutes reversible error only where it affects the ultimate conclusion under §103. For example, no reversal is necessary where a district court makes a determination that an invention would have been obvious to one having the lowest level of skill, *i.e.*, a layperson, because what is obvious to a layperson is necessarily obvious to one with a higher level of skill in the field of the invention. Conversely, no reversal is necessary where a district court makes a determination of *non* obviousness based on a finding of the highest possible level of skill in the relevant art, as fewer inventions are obvious to a person with a lower level of skill than to one with a higher level of skill. A less sophisticated level of skill generally favors a determination of nonobviousness, and thus the patentee, while a higher level of skill favors the reverse."

In re Lee, 277 F.3d 1338, 1345, 61 U.S.P.Q.2d 1430, 1435 (Fed.Cir.2002). "The patent examiner and the Board are deemed to have experience in the field of the invention; however, this experience, insofar as applied to the determination of patentability, must be applied from the viewpoint of 'the person having ordinary skill in the art to which said subject matter pertains,' the words of §103. In finding the relevant facts, in assessing the significance of the prior art, and in making the ultimate determination of the issue of obviousness, the examiner and the Board are presumed to act from this viewpoint. Thus when they rely on what they assert to be general knowledge to negate patentability, that knowledge must be articulated and placed on the record. The failure to do so is not consistent with either effective administrative procedure or effective judicial review."

Ruiz v. A.B. Chance Co., 234 F.3d 654, 666-67, 57 U.S.P.Q.2d 1161, 1168-69 (Fed.Cir.2000). "Factors that may be considered in determining the ordinary level of skill in the art include: (1) the types of problems encountered in the art; (2) the prior art solutions to those problems; (3) the rapidity with which innovations are made; (4) the sophistication of the technology; and (5) the educational level of active workers in the field. 'Not all such factors may be present in every case, and one or more of them may predominate.' Some of our cases indicate that the failure to make explicit findings on the level of ordinary skill is not always reversible error. However, … in those cases, 'it was not shown that the failure to make a finding or an incorrect finding on level of skill influenced the ultimate conclusion under §103 and, hence, constituted reversible error.'"

Life Tech. v. Clontech Labs., 224 F.3d 1320, 1326, 56 U.S.P.Q.2d 1186, 1191 (Fed.Cir.2000). "Reasonable expectation of success is assessed from the perspective of the person of ordinary skill in the art. That the inventors were ultimately successful is irrelevant to whether one of ordinary skill in the art, at the time the invention was made, would have reasonably expected success. The court's finding to the contrary represents impermissible use of hindsight—using the inventors' success as evidence that the success would have been expected." *See also* ***In re Oetiker***, 977 F.2d 1443, 1447, 24 U.S.P.Q.2d 1443, 1445-46 (Fed.Cir.1992).

Double Patenting

For more annotations on this topic, see 35 U.S.C. §101, *Double Patenting*, p. 500.

In re Hubbell, 709 F.3d 1140, 1145-46, 106 U.S.P.Q.2d 1032, 1035-36 (Fed.Cir.2013). "[T]he Director argues that: (1) whether the application and patent were ever commonly owned is immaterial to the policy of preventing harassment by multiple assignees; (2) identity of inventors is not required where there is an overlap in the inventors [for an obviousness-type double-patenting rejection]; (3) [P] has not established any grounds upon which he should be allowed to file a terminal disclaimer [where the application and patent were not commonly owned and there was no joint research agreement]; and (4) [P] is not entitled to a two-way obviousness analysis because he admitted that he partially is responsible for the delay that caused the ... patent claims to issue first. [W]e agree with the Director on each point."

Otsuka Pharm. Co. v. Sandoz, Inc., 678 F.3d 1280, 1297, 102 U.S.P.Q.2d 1729, 1741-42 (Fed.Cir.2012). "[P] contends that there is no difference between obviousness under [35 U.S.C.] §103 and obviousness-type double patenting. That is not entirely correct. We have noted that 'a double patenting of the obviousness type rejection is analogous to [a failure to meet] the non-obviousness requirement of 35 U.S.C. §103.' Important differences remain, however. The patent principally underlying the double patenting rejection need not be prior art. Moreover, when analyzing obviousness-type double patenting in cases involving claimed chemical compounds, the issue is not whether a skilled artisan would have selected the earlier compound as a lead compound. That is so because the analysis must necessarily focus on the earlier claimed compound over which double patenting has been alleged, lead compound or not. [¶] [Ds] assert that, unlike an analysis under §103, the test for obviousness-type double patenting never asks whether the prior art would have supplied a motivation to modify the earlier claimed compound. That is also incorrect. Unless the earlier claim anticipates the later claim under [35 U.S.C.] §102, the question whether the two claimed compounds are 'patentably distinct' implicates the question of obviousness under §103, ... which in the chemical context requires identifying some reason that would have led a chemist to modify the earlier compound to make the later compound with a reasonable expectation of success.... *At F.3d 1298:* The court in this case applied the correct test for non-statutory obviousness-type double patenting: In the context of claimed chemical compounds, an analysis of nonstatutory obviousness-type double patenting—like an analysis under §103—entails determining, *inter alia*, whether one of ordinary skill in the art would have had reason or motivation to modify the earlier claimed compound to make the compound of the asserted claim with a reasonable expectation of success. There is no other way to consider the obviousness of compound B over compound A without considering whether one of ordinary skill would have had reason to modify A to make B. That is traditional obviousness analysis."

Prior Art & Obviousness—Design Patent

MRC Innovations, Inc. v. Hunter Mfg., 747 F.3d 1326, 1332, 110 U.S.P.Q.2d 1235, 1240 (Fed.Cir.2014). "[I]t is true that the district court did not expressly undertake to translate the claimed design into a verbal description. However, ***High Point*** makes clear that the purpose of requiring district courts to describe the claimed design in words is so that the parties and appellate courts can discern the trial court's reasoning in identifying a primary reference. It is entirely clear from the district court's opinion what it considered to be the relevant design characteristics of the ... patented design. [¶] Thus, the district court did not err by failing to provide an express verbal description of the claimed design; rather, it described the claimed design in the context of comparing it to the prior art."

High Point Design LLC v. Buyer's Direct, Inc., 730 F.3d 1301, 1311, 108 U.S.P.Q.2d 1183, 1191 (Fed.Cir. 2013). "When assessing the potential obviousness of a design patent, a finder of fact employs two distinct steps: first, one must find a single reference, a something in existence, the design characteristics of which are basically the same as the claimed design; second, once this primary reference is found, other references may be used to modify it to create a design that has the same overall visual appearance as the claimed design.

At F.3d 1312: Under the first step, a court must both (1) discern the correct visual impression created by the patented design as a whole; and (2) determine whether there is a single reference that creates basically the same visual impression. The ultimate inquiry in an obviousness analysis is whether the claimed design would have been obvious to a designer of ordinary skill who designs articles of the type involved. *At F.3d 1313, U.S.P.Q.2d 1192:* The use of an 'ordinary observer' standard to assess the potential obviousness of a design patent runs contrary to the precedent of this court and our predecessor court, under which the obviousness of a design patent must, instead, be assessed from the viewpoint of an ordinary designer. *At U.S.P.Q.2d 1193:* Although obviousness is assessed from the vantage point of an ordinary designer in the art, an expert's opinion on the legal conclusion of obviousness is neither necessary nor controlling. That said, an expert's opinion may be relevant to the factual aspects of the analysis leading to that legal conclusion. *At F.3d 1314:* On remand, the district court should add sufficient detail to its verbal description of the claimed design to evoke a visual image consonant with that design. [¶] As to the second part of the first step[,] the court erred by failing to provide its reasoning, as required under this court's precedent. ... On remand, the district court should do a side-by-side comparison of the two designs to determine if they create the same visual impression." (Internal quotes omitted.)

💣 ***In re Harvey***, 12 F.3d 1061, 1063, 29 U.S.P.Q.2d 1206, 1208 (Fed.Cir.1993). "In ornamental design cases, a proper obviousness rejection based on a combination of references requires that the visual ornamental features (design characteristics) of the claimed design appear in the prior art in a manner which suggests such features as used in the claimed design. If, however, the combined teachings suggest only components of a claimed design, but not its overall appearance, an obviousness rejection is inappropriate."

Standard of Review

💣 ***KSR Int'l v. Teleflex Inc.***, 550 U.S. 398, 427, 82 U.S.P.Q.2d 1385, 1400 (2007). "The ultimate judgment of obviousness is a legal determination. Where, as here, the content of the prior art, the scope of the patent claim, and the level of ordinary skill in the art are not in material dispute, and the obviousness of the claim is apparent in light of these factors, summary judgment is appropriate."

💣 ***Randall Mfg. v. Rea***, 733 F.3d 1355, 1362, 108 U.S.P.Q.2d 1727, 1732 (Fed.Cir.2013). "Whether a claimed invention would have been obvious is a question of law, based on factual determinations regarding the scope and content of the prior art, differences between the prior art and the claims at issue, the level of ordinary skill in the pertinent art, and any objective indicia of non-obviousness. On appeal, we review the Board's compliance with governing legal standards de novo and its underlying factual determinations for substantial evidence."

💣 ***In re Translogic Tech.***, 504 F.3d 1249, 1256, 84 U.S.P.Q.2d 1929, 1934 (Fed.Cir.2007). "'[D]uring examination proceedings, claims are given their broadest reasonable interpretation consistent with the specification.' [¶] 'If the evidence in [the] record will support several reasonable but contradictory conclusions, we will not find the Board's decision unsupported by substantial evidence simply because the Board chose one conclusion over another plausible alternative.'"

💣 ***Oakley, Inc. v. Sunglass Hut Int'l***, 316 F.3d 1331, 1339, 65 U.S.P.Q.2d 1321, 1325 (Fed.Cir.2003). "We review a district court's underlying findings of fact for clear error, while we rule *de novo* on the ultimate issue of obviousness." *See also* ***Duro-Last, Inc. v. Custom Seal, Inc.***, 321 F.3d 1098, 1108, 66 U.S.P.Q.2d 1025, 1030-31 (Fed.Cir.2003).

💣 ***Okajima v. Bourdeau***, 261 F.3d 1350, 1356, 59 U.S.P.Q.2d 1795, 1798 (Fed.Cir.2001). "When it sets forth distinct findings of fact, and particularly when it does so in the manner that a district court must under [FRCP] 52(a), the Board's findings are entitled to broad deference. Indeed, such express findings of fact are the key to meaningful appellate review, and obviate the need for us to remand for further proceedings at great cost and inefficiency to the parties." *See also* ***In re Gartside***, 203 F.3d 1305, 1312, 53 U.S.P.Q.2d 1769, 1774-75 (Fed.Cir.2000).

💣 ***Apple Computer, Inc. v. Articulate Sys.***, 234 F.3d 14, 26, 57 U.S.P.Q.2d 1057, 1066 (Fed.Cir.2000). "A failure to enumerate and analyze the ***Graham*** factors explicitly is not necessarily reversible error, provided the proper factual determinations were made and the court considered them in rendering its conclusion of obviousness."

TEC Air, Inc. v. Denso Mfg., 192 F.3d 1353, 1359, 52 U.S.P.Q.2d 1294, 1298 (Fed.Cir.1999). "In reviewing 'a jury special verdict on patent claim obviousness where the underlying facts have been disputed[,] ... [w]e first presume that the jury resolved the underlying factual disputes in favor of the verdict winner and leave those presumed findings undisturbed if they are supported by substantial evidence. Then we examine the legal conclusion *de novo* to see whether it is correct in light of the presumed jury fact findings.' The same rule also applies to special interrogatories."

Roton Barrier, Inc. v. Stanley Works, 79 F.3d 1112, 1127, 37 U.S.P.Q.2d 1816, 1828 (Fed.Cir.1996). "What a reference teaches is a question of fact reviewed under the clearly erroneous standard."

Schneider AG v. SciMed Life Sys., 39 U.S.P.Q.2d 1596, 1597 (Fed.Cir.1995). "The district court's determination of the hypothetical person of ordinary skill in the relevant art is one such finding of fact subject only to review for clear error."

§103. CONDITIONS FOR PATENTABILITY; NON-OBVIOUS SUBJECT MATTER

Section 103 is effective for patent applications and patents issued on those applications that have ever contained (1) a claim to a claimed invention that has an "effective filing date," as defined in §100(i), p. 495, on or after Mar. 16, 2013; or (2) a specific reference under §120, §121, or §365(c) to any patent or application that ever contained such a claim. Section 103 is not effective for patent applications filed before Mar. 16, 2013, or patents issued on those applications.

A patent for a claimed invention may not be obtained, notwithstanding that the claimed invention is not identically disclosed as set forth in section 102, if the differences between the claimed invention and the prior art are such that the claimed invention as a whole would have been obvious before the effective filing date of the claimed invention to a person having ordinary skill in the art to which the claimed invention pertains. Patentability shall not be negated by the manner in which the invention was made.

History of 35 U.S.C. §103: July 19, 1952, ch. 950, §1, 66 Stat. 798; Nov. 8, 1984, P.L. 98-622, §103, 98 Stat. 3384; Nov. 1, 1995, P.L. 104-41, §1, 109 Stat. 351; Nov. 29, 1999, P.L. 106-113, §1000(a)(9), 113 Stat. 1536; Dec. 10, 2004, P.L. 108-453, §2, 118 Stat. 3596; Sept. 16, 2011, P.L. 112-29, §3(c), 125 Stat. 287.

See also *Examination Guidelines for Implementing the First Inventor to File Provisions of the Leahy-Smith America Invents Act*, p. 1047.

§104. INVENTION MADE ABROAD

Section 104 was repealed effective Mar. 16, 2013. Section 104 will remain effective for patent applications and patents issued on those applications that contain or contained a claim to a claimed invention that has an effective filing date before Mar. 16, 2013, or for any applications or patents that contain or contained a claim to a specific reference under §120, §121, or §365(c) that have an effective filing date before Mar. 16, 2013.

(a) In general—

(1) Proceedings.—In proceedings in the Patent and Trademark Office, in the courts, and before any other competent authority, an applicant for a patent, or a patentee, may not establish a date of invention by reference to knowledge or use thereof, or other activity with respect thereto, in a foreign country other than a NAFTA country or a WTO member country, except as provided in sections 119 and 365.

(2) Rights.—If an invention was made by a person, civil or military—

(A) while domiciled in the United States, and serving in any other country in connection with operations by or on behalf of the United States,

(B) while domiciled in a NAFTA country and serving in another country in connection with operations by or on behalf of that NAFTA country, or

(C) while domiciled in a WTO member country and serving in another country in connection with operations by or on behalf of that WTO member country,

that person shall be entitled to the same rights of priority in the United States with respect to such invention as if such invention had been made in the United States, that NAFTA country, or that WTO member country, as the case may be.

(3) Use of information.—To the extent that any information in a NAFTA country or a WTO member country concerning knowledge, use, or other activity relevant to proving or disproving a date of invention has not been made available for use in a proceeding in the Patent and Trademark Office, a court, or any other competent authority to the same extent as such information could be made available in the United States, the Director, court, or such other authority shall draw appropriate inferences, or take other action permitted by statute, rule, or regulation, in favor of the party that requested the information in the proceeding.

(b) Definitions.—As used in this section—

(1) the term "NAFTA country" has the meaning given that term in section 3301(4) of title 19; and

(2) the term "WTO member country" has the meaning given that term in section 3501(10) of title 19.

History of 35 U.S.C. §104: July 19, 1952, ch. 950, §1, 66 Stat. 798; Jan. 2, 1975, P.L. 93-596, §1, 88 Stat. 1949; Nov. 14, 1975, P.L. 94-131, §6, 89 Stat. 691; Nov. 8, 1984, P.L. 98-622, §403(a), 98 Stat. 3392; Dec. 8, 1993, P.L. 103-182, §331, 107 Stat. 2113; Dec. 8, 1994, P.L. 103-465, §531(a), 108 Stat. 4982; Nov. 29, 1999, P.L. 106-113, §1000(a)(9), 113 Stat. 1536; Nov. 2, 2002, P.L. 107-273, §13206(b)(1)(B), 116 Stat. 1906; Sept. 16, 2011, P.L. 112-29, §§3(d), 20(j)(1), 125 Stat. 287, 335.

See also NAFTA art. 1709; Patent Cooperation Treaty; TRIPs pt. II, §5.

§105. INVENTIONS IN OUTER SPACE

(a) Any invention made, used or sold in outer space on a space object or component thereof under the jurisdiction or control of the United States shall be considered to be made, used or sold within the United States for the purposes of this title, except with respect to any space object or component thereof that is specifically identified and otherwise provided for by an international agreement to which the United States is a party, or with respect to any space object or component thereof that is carried on the registry of a foreign state in accordance with the Convention on Registration of Objects Launched into Outer Space.

(b) Any invention made, used or sold in outer space on a space object or component thereof that is carried on the registry of a foreign state in accordance with the Convention on Registration of Objects Launched into Outer Space, shall be considered to be made, used or sold within the United States for the purposes of this title if specifically so agreed in an international agreement between the United States and the state of registry.

History of 35 U.S.C. §105: Nov. 15, 1990, P.L. 101-580, §1(a), 104 Stat. 2863.

CHAPTER 11. APPLICATION FOR PATENT

§111. APPLICATION

Section 111 is effective for requests for statutory invention registrations filed on or after Mar. 16, 2013.

(a) In general—

(1) Written application.—An application for patent shall be made, or authorized to be made, by the inventor, except as otherwise provided in this title, in writing to the Director.

(2) Contents.—Such application shall include—

(A) a specification as prescribed by section 112;

(B) a drawing as prescribed by section 113; and

(C) an oath or declaration as prescribed by section 115.

(3) Fee, oath or declaration, and claims.—The application shall be accompanied by the fee required by law. The fee, oath or declaration, and 1 or more claims may be submitted after the filing date of the application, within such period and under such conditions, including the payment of a surcharge, as may be prescribed by the Director. Upon failure to submit the fee, oath or declaration, and 1 or more claims within such prescribed period, the application shall be regarded as abandoned.

(4) Filing date.—The filing date of an application shall be the date on which a specification, with or without claims, is received in the United States Patent and Trademark Office.

(b) Provisional application—

(1) Authorization.—A provisional application for patent shall be made or authorized to be made by the inventor, except as otherwise provided in this title, in writing to the Director. Such application shall include—

(A) a specification as prescribed by section 112(a); and

(B) a drawing as prescribed by section 113.

(2) Claim.—A claim, as required by subsections (b) through (e) of section 112, shall not be required in a provisional application.

(3) Fee.—The application shall be accompanied by the fee required by law. The fee may be submitted after the filing date of the application, within such period and under such conditions, including the payment of a surcharge, as may be prescribed by the Director. Upon failure to submit the fee within such prescribed period, the application shall be regarded as abandoned.

(4) Filing date.—The filing date of a provisional application shall be the date on which a specification, with or without claims, is received in the United States Patent and Trademark Office.

(5) Abandonment.—Notwithstanding the absence of a claim, upon timely request and as prescribed by the Director, a provisional application may be treated as an application filed under subsection (a). Subject to section 119(e)(3), if no such request is made, the provisional application shall be regarded as abandoned 12 months after the filing date of such application and shall not be subject to revival after such 12-month period.

(6) Other basis for provisional application.—Subject to all the conditions in this subsection and section 119(e), and as prescribed by the Director, an application for patent filed under subsection (a) may be treated as a provisional application for patent.

(7) No right of priority or benefit of earliest filing date.—A provisional application shall not be entitled to the right of priority of any other application under section 119, 365(a), or 386(a) or to the benefit of an earlier filing date in the United States under section 120, 121, 365(c), or 386(c).

(8) Applicable provisions.—The provisions of this title relating to applications for patent shall apply to provisional applications for patent, except as otherwise provided, and except that provisional applications for patent shall not be subject to sections 131 and 135.

(c) Prior filed application.—Notwithstanding the provisions of subsection (a), the Director may prescribe the conditions, including the payment of a surcharge, under which a reference made upon the filing of an application under subsection (a) to a previously filed application, specifying the previously filed application by application number and the intellectual property authority or country in which the application was filed, shall constitute the specification and any drawings of the subsequent application for purposes of a filing date. A copy of the specification and any drawings of the previously filed application shall be submitted within such period and under such conditions as may be prescribed by the Director. A failure to submit the copy of the specification and any drawings of the previously filed application within the prescribed period shall result in the application being regarded as abandoned. Such application shall be treated as having never been filed, unless—

(1) the application is revived under section 27; and

(2) a copy of the specification and any drawings of the previously filed application are submitted to the Director.

History of 35 U.S.C. §111: July 19, 1952, ch. 950, §1, 66 Stat. 798; Aug. 27, 1982, P.L. 97-247, §5, 96 Stat. 319; Dec. 8, 1994, P.L. 103-465, §532(b)(3), 108 Stat. 4986; Nov. 29, 1999, P.L. 106-113, §1000(a)(9), 113 Stat. 1536; Nov. 2, 2002, P.L. 107-273, §13206(b)(1)(B), 116 Stat. 1906; Sept. 16, 2011, P.L. 112-29, §§3(e)(2), 4(a)(3), (d), 20(j)(1), 125 Stat. 287, 295, 296, 335; Dec. 18, 2013, P.L. 112-211, §201(a), 126 Stat. 1533; May 13, 2015, P.L. 112-211, §102(3), 126 Stat. 1531.

See also 26 U.S.C. §1239; 37 C.F.R. §§1.41, 1.51-1.59, 1.141-1.146, 1.151-1.155, 1.161-1.167, 1.821-1.825; TRIPs pt. II, §5.

§112. SPECIFICATION

Section 112 in its present form will continue to apply for patent applications filed before Sept. 16, 2012. See transition note for amended §112, p. 552. In actions commenced on or after Sept. 16, 2011, failure to meet the best-mode requirement of §112 may not form the basis on which any claim of a patent may be canceled or held invalid or otherwise unenforceable.

The specification shall contain a written description of the invention, and of the manner and process of making and using it, in such full, clear, concise, and exact terms as to enable any person skilled in the art to which it pertains, or with which it is most nearly connected, to make and use the same, and shall set forth the best mode contemplated by the inventor of carrying out his invention.

The specification shall conclude with one or more claims particularly pointing out and distinctly claiming the subject matter which the applicant regards as his invention.

A claim may be written in independent or, if the nature of the case admits, in dependent or multiple dependent form.

Subject to the following paragraph, a claim in dependent form shall contain a reference to a claim previously set forth and then specify a further limitation of the subject matter claimed. A claim in dependent form shall be construed to incorporate by reference all the limitations of the claim to which it refers.

A claim in multiple dependent form shall contain a reference, in the alternative only, to more than one claim previously set forth and then specify a further limitation of the subject matter claimed. A multiple dependent claim shall not serve as a basis for any other multiple dependent claim. A multiple dependent claim shall be construed to incorporate by reference all the limitations of the particular claim in relation to which it is being considered.

An element in a claim for a combination may be expressed as a means or step for performing a specified function without the recital of structure, material, or acts in support thereof, and such claim shall be construed to cover the corresponding structure, material, or acts described in the specification and equivalents thereof.

History of 35 U.S.C. §112: July 19, 1952, ch. 950, §1, 66 Stat. 798. Amended July 24, 1965, P.L. 89-83, §9, 79 Stat. 261; Nov. 14, 1975, P.L. 94-131, §7, 89 Stat. 691.

See also 37 C.F.R. §§1.71-1.79, 1.96, 1.151; Paris Convention art. 4; Patent Cooperation Treaty.

§112. SPECIFICATION

Section 112 is effective for patent applications filed on or after Sept. 16, 2012.

(a) In general.—The specification shall contain a written description of the invention, and of the manner and process of making and using it, in such full, clear, concise, and exact terms as to enable any person skilled in the art to which it pertains, or with which it is most nearly connected, to make and use the same, and shall set forth the best mode contemplated by the inventor or joint inventor of carrying out the invention.

(b) Conclusion.—The specification shall conclude with one or more claims particularly pointing out and distinctly claiming the subject matter which the inventor or a joint inventor regards as the invention.

(c) Form.—A claim may be written in independent or, if the nature of the case admits, in dependent or multiple dependent form.

(d) Reference in dependent forms.—Subject to subsection (e), a claim in dependent form shall contain a reference to a claim previously set forth and then specify a further limitation of the subject matter claimed. A claim in dependent form shall be construed to incorporate by reference all the limitations of the claim to which it refers.

(e) Reference in multiple dependent form.—A claim in multiple dependent form shall contain a reference, in the alternative only, to more than one claim previously set forth and then specify a further limitation of the subject matter claimed. A multiple dependent claim shall not serve as a basis for any other multiple dependent claim. A multiple dependent claim shall be construed to incorporate by reference all the limitations of the particular claim in relation to which it is being considered.

(f) Element in claim for a combination.—An element in a claim for a combination may be expressed as a means or step for performing a specified function without the recital of structure, material, or acts in support thereof, and such claim shall be construed to cover the corresponding structure, material, or acts described in the specification and equivalents thereof.

History of 35 U.S.C. §112: July 19, 1952, ch. 950, §1, 66 Stat. 798; July 24, 1965, P.L. 89-83, §9, 79 Stat. 261; Nov. 14, 1975, P.L. 94-131, §7, 89 Stat. 691; Sept. 16, 2011, P.L. 112-29, §4(c), 125 Stat. 296.

See also 37 C.F.R. §§1.71-1.79, 1.96, 1.151; Paris Convention art. 4; Patent Cooperation Treaty.

ANNOTATIONS

Generally

Markman v. Westview Instrs., Inc., 517 U.S. 370, 373, 38 U.S.P.Q.2d 1461, 1463 (1996). "[A] patent must describe the exact scope of an invention and its manufacture to 'secure to [patentee] all to which he is entitled, [and] to apprise the public of what is still open to them.' Under the modern American system, these objectives are served by two distinct elements of a patent document. First, it contains a specification describing the invention 'in such full, clear, concise, and exact terms as to enable any person skilled in the art ... to make and use the same.' Second, a patent includes one or more 'claims,' which 'particularly poin[t] out and distinctly clai[m] the subject matter which the applicant regards as his invention.'"

Aristocrat Techs. Australia Pty Ltd. v. International Game Tech., 543 F.3d 657, 662, 88 U.S.P.Q.2d 1458, 1461 (Fed.Cir.2008). "[T]he requirements in §112 are not conditions for patentability; they are merely requirements for obtaining a valid patent."

Baldwin Graphic Sys. v. Siebert, Inc., 512 F.3d 1338, 1342-43, 85 U.S.P.Q.2d 1503, 1507 (Fed.Cir.2008). "This court has repeatedly emphasized that an indefinite article 'a' or 'an' in patent parlance carries the meaning of 'one or more' in open-ended claims containing the transitional phrase 'comprising.' That 'a' or 'an' can mean 'one or more' is best described as a rule, rather than merely as a presumption or even a convention. The exceptions to this rule are extremely limited: a patentee must evince a clear intent to limit 'a' or 'an' to 'one.' The subsequent use of definite articles 'the' or 'said' in a claim to refer back to the same claim term does not change the general plural rule, but simply reinvokes that non-singular meaning. An exception to the general rule that 'a' or 'an' means more than one only arises where the language of the claims themselves, the specification, or the prosecution history necessitate a departure from the rule." (Internal quotes omitted.)

§112, ¶1—Best Mode

In actions commenced on or after Sept. 16, 2011, failure to meet the best-mode requirement of §112 may not form the basis on which any claim of a patent may be canceled or held invalid or otherwise unenforceable.

High Concrete Structures, Inc. v. New Enter. Stone & Lime Co., 377 F.3d 1379, 1383, 71 U.S.P.Q.2d 1948, 1951 (Fed.Cir.2004). "The best mode requirement of §112 is not violated by unintentional omission of information that would be readily known to persons in the field of the invention."

Hoffmann-La Roche, Inc. v. Promega Corp., 323 F.3d 1354, 1367, 66 U.S.P.Q.2d 1385, 1394 (Fed.Cir. 2003). "The best mode requirement ... does not entitle the inventor to suggest that the best mode has been performed when it has not, and to report results that have not actually been observed."

Bayer AG v. Schein Pharms., 301 F.3d 1306, 1314-15, 64 U.S.P.Q.2d 1001, 1006-07 (Fed.Cir.2002). "The best mode requirement is 'separate and distinct' from enablement and requires an inventor to disclose the best mode contemplated by him, as of the time he executes the application, of carrying out the invention. Unlike enablement, the existence of a best mode is a purely subjective matter depending upon what the inventor actually believed at the time the application was filed. Because of the subjective nature of the best mode inquiry, the best mode disclosure requirement—unlike enablement—cannot be met by mute reference to the knowledge of one of skill in the art. [B]ecause the existence of a best mode of carrying out the invention is by definition known only to the inventor, §112 demands actual disclosure regardless of whether, as an abstract matter, practicing that mode would be within the knowledge of one of ordinary skill in the art. [¶] [T]he best mode requirement ... does [not] demand disclosure of every preference an inventor possesses as of the filing date. [O]nly preferred ways of 'carrying out [the] invention' need be disclosed. [T]he term 'mode' and the phrase 'carrying out the invention' are not definable with precision. Nonetheless, ... we [have] referred to the best mode 'for making and using' the claimed invention ... thus suggesting that the statute is susceptible [to] interpretation." (Internal quotes omitted.)

Teleflex, Inc. v. Ficosa Corp., 299 F.3d 1313, 1330, 63 U.S.P.Q.2d 1374, 1384-85 (Fed.Cir.2002). "Compliance with the best mode requirement is a question of fact which involves a two-pronged inquiry. The first prong is subjective, focusing on the inventor's state of mind at the time he filed the patent application, and asks whether the inventor considered a particular mode of practicing the invention to be superior to all other modes at the time of filing. The second prong is objective and asks whether the inventor adequately disclosed the mode he considered to be superior. [¶] With respect to both the first and second prongs, '[t]he best mode inquiry is directed to what the applicant regards as the invention, which in turn is measured by the claims.' *At F.3d 1331-32:* The best mode requirement does not extend to 'production details,' including commercial considerations such as equipment on hand, availability of materials, relationships with suppliers, or customer requirements. Further, the best mode requirement does not extend to 'routine details' apparent to one of ordinary skill in the art. Routine details need not be disclosed because one skilled in the art is aware of alternative means for accomplishing the routine detail that would still produce the best mode of the claimed invention." *See also* ***AllVoice Computing PLC v. Nuance Comms.***, 504 F.3d 1236, 1246-47, 84 U.S.P.Q.2d 1886, 1894 (Fed.Cir.2007); ***Liquid Dynamics Corp. v. Vaughan Co.***, 449 F.3d 1209, 1223, 79 U.S.P.Q.2d 1094, 1103-04 (Fed.Cir.2006).

§112, ¶1 (& Amended §112(a))—Enablement

Promega Corp. v. Life Techs., 773 F.3d 1338, 1346, 113 U.S.P.Q.2d 1181, 1186 (Fed.Cir.2014), *rev'd on other grounds*, ___ U.S. ___, 137 S.Ct. 734 (2017). "Whether a claim satisfies the enablement requirement of ... §112, ¶1 is a question of law reviewed *de novo*. Any facts underlying the enablement determination are reviewed for clear error. A party must prove invalidity based on non-enablement by clear and convincing evidence."

Wyeth & Cordis Corp. v. Abbott Labs., 720 F.3d 1380, 1386, 107 U.S.P.Q.2d 1273, 1276-77 (Fed.Cir. 2013). "Here, the specification similarly discloses only a starting point for further iterative research in an unpredictable and poorly understood field. ... We ... hold that there is no genuine dispute that practicing the full scope of the claims, measured at the filing date, required undue experimentation."

Cephalon, Inc. v. Watson Pharms., 707 F.3d 1330, 1338, 105 U.S.P.Q.2d 1817, 1823 (Fed.Cir.2013). "[E]xtensive experimentation does not necessarily render the experiments unduly extensive where the experiments involve repetition of known or commonly used techniques."

In re Antor Media Corp., 689 F.3d 1282, 1289-90, 103 U.S.P.Q.2d 1555, 1560 (Fed.Cir.2012). "[T]he mere use of forward-looking language (such as terms like 'should') does not show one way or another whether a person of ordinary skill in the art would have to engage in undue experimentation to perform the claimed invention. Indeed, undue experimentation is determined based on both the nature of the invention and the state of the art. The word 'should' thus constitutes a disclosure even if it is only precatory and does not necessarily convey the meaning of 'did.' Thus, the verb tense and word choice used in a prior art reference, taken without an understanding of the state of the art and the nature of the invention, shed no light on enablement. That reality is consistent with our precedent holding that the invention in a prior art publication need not have actually been made or performed to satisfy enablement."

MagSil Corp. v. Hitachi Global Storage Techs., 687 F.3d 1377, 1380-81, 103 U.S.P.Q.2d 1769, 1771 (Fed. Cir.2012). "Enablement serves the dual function in the patent system of ensuring adequate disclosure of the claimed invention and of preventing claims broader than the disclosed invention. This important doctrine prevents both inadequate disclosure of an invention and overbroad claiming that might otherwise attempt to cover more than was actually invented. Thus, a patentee chooses broad claim language at the peril of losing any claim that cannot be enabled across its full scope of coverage. 'The scope of the claims must be less than or equal to the scope of the enablement to ensure that the public knowledge is enriched by the patent specification to a degree at least commensurate with the scope of the claims.'"

Streck, Inc. v. Research & Diagnostic Sys., 665 F.3d 1269, 1288, 101 U.S.P.Q.2d 1225, 1237 (Fed.Cir. 2012). "Enablement is a legal determination of whether a patent enables one skilled in the art to make and use the claimed invention. To be enabling, a patent's specification must teach those skilled in the art how to make and use the full scope of the claimed invention without 'undue experimentation.' It is well-established, however, that a specification need not disclose what is well-known in the art. It is true, however, that, the rule that a specification need not disclose what is well known in the art is merely a rule of supplementation, not a substitute for a basic enabling disclosure. [¶] The enablement requirement is met where one skilled in the art, having read the specification, could practice the invention without 'undue experimentation.' Whether undue experimentation is required is not a single, simple factual determination, but rather is a conclusion reached by weighing many factual considerations. In [***In re Wands***, 858 F.2d 731 (Fed.Cir.1988)], this court set forth the following factors to consider when determining whether a disclosure requires undue experimentation: (1) the quantity of experimentation necessary, (2) the amount of direction or guidance presented, (3) the presence or absence of working examples, (4) the nature of the invention, (5) the state of the prior art, (6) the relative skill of those in the art, (7) the predictability or unpredictability of the art, and (8) the breadth of the claims. It is not necessary that a court review all the ***Wands*** factors to find a disclosure enabling. They are illustrative, not mandatory. [¶] Enablement is a matter of law that we review without deference; however, this Court reviews the factual underpinnings of enablement for substantial evidence. Because patents are presumed valid, lack of enablement must be shown by clear and convincing evidence." (Internal quotes omitted.)

Finisar Corp. v. DirecTV Grp., 523 F.3d 1323, 1336, 86 U.S.P.Q.2d 1609, 1619 (Fed.Cir.2008). "[T]his court [has] used general principles of English grammar for the proposition that referential and qualifying words and phrases, *where no contrary intention appears*, refer solely to the last antecedent, which consists of the last word, phrase, or clause that can be made an antecedent without impairing the meaning of the sentence for purposes of statutory construction. Thus, this court has addressed this grammatical guideline referred to as the doctrine of the last antecedent. In ***Anhydrides*** [***& Chems., Inc. v. U.S.***, 130 F.3d 1481 (Fed.Cir.1997)], a case without a contrary intention in the passage at issue, this court construed the qualifying phrase to apply only to the immediately preceding antecedent. [¶] In contrast, when a modifier is set off from a series of antecedents by a comma, the modifier should be read to apply to each of those antecedents. But while the meaning of a statute will typically heed the commands of its punctuation, ... the doctrine of the last antecedent and its corollary, the rule of punctuation, ... are more guidelines than absolute rules. [¶] Of course, ***Anhydrides*** and the other cases discussed above apply the rules of English grammar to statutory construction, whereas the present dispute involves the meaning of a prior art reference. These exercises are not entirely coterminous because the meaning of a prior art reference requires analysis of the understanding of an artisan of ordinary skill. In contrast, statutory construction does not include a skilled artisan component but considers instead the object and policy of the law. Still words, in context, receive their meaning according to their placement in grammatical structure. [¶] Therefore, to avoid slipping into a realm of ambiguity that could render jury verdicts wholly unreviewable, this court imputes an understanding of English grammar and usage to the jury. Moreover this court consults the overall context of the passage [of the prior-art reference]." (Internal quotes omitted.)

Automotive Techs. Int'l v. BMW, 501 F.3d 1274, 1283, 84 U.S.P.Q.2d 1108, 1114-15 (Fed.Cir.2007). "'It is the specification, not the knowledge of one skilled in the art, that must supply the novel aspects of an invention in order to constitute adequate enablement.' Although the knowledge of one skilled in the art is indeed relevant, the novel aspect of an invention must be enabled in the patent." *See also* ***Genentech, Inc. v. Novo Nordisk A/S***, 108 F.3d 1361, 1366, 42 U.S.P.Q.2d 1001, 1005 (Fed.Cir.1997).

AK Steel Corp. v. Sollac & Ugine, 344 F.3d 1234, 1245, 68 U.S.P.Q.2d 1280, 1287 (Fed.Cir.2003). "[W]e dispel the notion that the failure of the PTO to issue an enablement rejection automatically creates an 'especially weighty presumption' of compliance with ... §112." *See also* ***Invitrogen Corp. v. Clontech Labs.***, 429 F.3d 1052, 1070-71, 77 U.S.P.Q.2d 1161, 1173-74 (Fed.Cir.2005).

Plant Genetic Sys. v. Dekalb Genetics Corp., 315 F.3d 1335, 1339, 65 U.S.P.Q.2d 1452, 1455 (Fed.Cir. 2003). "Enablement is determined as of the effective filing date of the patent.... *At F.3d 1344, U.S.P.Q.2d 1459:* 'This court has approved use of later publications as evidence of the state of art existing on the filing date of an application. That approval does not extend, however, to the use of a later ... publication disclosing a later ... existing state of the art in testing an earlier ... application for compliance with §112 [¶1]. The difference may be described as that between the permissible application of later knowledge about art-related facts existing on the filing date and the impermissible application of later knowledge about later art-related facts ... which did not exist on the filing date.'"

Enzo Biochem, Inc. v. Calgene, Inc., 188 F.3d 1362, 1371-72, 52 U.S.P.Q.2d 1129, 1136 (Fed.Cir.1999). "[P] contends that the ***Wands*** factors do not apply ... because in contrast to *ex parte* prosecution, the need for 'prediction' is not present in *inter partes* litigation. ... We disagree.... The ***Wands*** factors, when applied from the proper temporal perspective ..., are a useful methodology for determining enablement in either the *ex parte* prosecution or *inter partes* litigation context."

§112, ¶1 (& Amended §112(a))—Written Description

Amgen Inc. v. Sanofi, 872 F.3d 1367, 1374, 124 U.S.P.Q.2d 1354, 1358 (Fed.Cir.2017). "[P]ost-priority-date evidence of a particular species can reasonably bear on whether a patent fails to disclose a representative number of species falling within the scope of the genus or structural features common to the members of the genus so that one of skill in the art can visualize or recognize the members of the genus." (Internal quotes omitted.)

Yeda Research & Dev. Co. v. Abbott GmbH & Co. KG, 837 F.3d 1341, 1345, 120 U.S.P.Q.2d 1299, 1302 (Fed.Cir.2016). "Under the doctrine of inherent disclosure, when a specification describes an invention that has certain undisclosed yet inherent properties, that specification serves as adequate written description to support a subsequent patent application that explicitly recites the invention's inherent properties."

AbbVie Deutschland GmbH & Co., KG v. Janssen Biotech, Inc., 759 F.3d 1285, 1299-1300, 111 U.S.P.Q.2d 1780, 1789-90 (Fed.Cir.2014). "One particular question regarding the written description requirement has been raised when a genus is claimed but the specification only describes a part of that genus that is insufficient to constitute a description of the genus. ... Whether the written description requirement for a genus is met by a particular disclosure depends upon the facts. This case presents such a question. The jury found that the requirement was not met, and we agree. [¶] For generic claims, we have set forth a number of factors for evaluating the adequacy of the disclosure, including the existing knowledge in the particular field, the extent and content of the prior art, the maturity of the science or technology, and the predictability of the aspect at issue. When a patent claims a genus using functional language to define a desired result, the specification must demonstrate that the applicant has made a generic invention that achieves the claimed result and do so by showing that the applicant has invented species sufficient to support a claim to the functionally-defined genus. We have held that a sufficient description of a genus requires the disclosure of either a representative number of species falling within the scope of the genus or structural features common to the members of the genus so that one of skill in the art can visualize or recognize the members of the genus. [¶] One factor in considering the question is how large a genus is involved and what species of the genus are described in the patent. If the genus is not large or, even if it is, the specification discloses species representing the genus throughout its scope, the requirement may be met. On the other hand, analogizing the genus to a plot of land, if the disclosed species only abide in a corner of the genus, one has not described the genus sufficiently to show that the inventor invented, or had possession of, the genus. He only described a portion of it. That is the case here. [¶] It is important not to take the analogy of a plot of land too far in thinking of written description issues because, even if one builds a house only in one corner of the plot, one may still own the whole plot. One describes a plot of land by its furthest coordinates, in effect drawing a perimeter fence around it. That may be akin to the function of patent claims to particularly point out and distinctly circumscribe the outer boundaries of a claimed invention. With the *written description* of a genus, however, merely drawing a fence around a perceived genus is not a description of the genus. One needs to show that one has truly invented the genus, *i.e.*, that one has conceived and described sufficient representative species encompassing the breadth of the genus. Otherwise, one has only a research plan, leaving it to others to explore the unknown contours of the claimed genus." (Internal quotes omitted.)

Novozymes A/S v. DuPont Nutrition Biosciences APS, 723 F.3d 1336, 1344, 107 U.S.P.Q.2d 1457, 1463 (Fed.Cir.2013). "[C]laims added during prosecution must find support sufficient to satisfy §112 in the written description of the original priority application."

Santarus, Inc. v. Par Pharm., 694 F.3d 1344, 1351, 104 U.S.P.Q.2d 1641, 1647 (Fed.Cir.2012). "Negative claim limitations are adequately supported when the specification describes a reason to exclude the relevant limitation. Such written description support need not rise to the level of disclaimer. In fact, it is possible for the patentee to support both the inclusion and exclusion of the same material." *See also* ***Inphi Corp. v. Netlist, Inc.***, 805 F.3d 1350, 1357, 116 U.S.P.Q.2d 2006, 2011 (Fed.Cir.2015) (***Santarus*** did not create heightened written description standard for negative claim limitations and that properly described, alternative features are sufficient to satisfy written description standard of §112, ¶1 for negative claim limitations).

Ariad Pharms. v. Eli Lilly & Co., 598 F.3d 1336, 1344, 94 U.S.P.Q.2d 1161, 1167 (Fed.Cir.2010). "We … hold that §112, ¶1, contains two separate description requirements: a 'written description (i) of the invention, *and* (ii) of the manner and process of making and using [the invention].'" *See also* ***Capon v. Eshhar***, 418 F.3d 1349, 1357-58, 76 U.S.P.Q.2d 1078, 1084-85 (Fed. Cir.2005).

Carnegie Mellon Univ. v. Hoffman-La Roche Inc., 541 F.3d 1115, 1124, 88 U.S.P.Q.2d 1233, 1239 (Fed. Cir.2008). "[T]o satisfy the written description requirement for a claimed genus, a specification must describe the claimed invention in such a way that a person of skill in the art would understand that the genus that is being claimed has been invented, not just a species of the genus. *At F.3d 1126, U.S.P.Q.2d 1240:* To satisfy the written description requirement in the case of a chemical or biotechnological genus, more than a statement of the genus is normally required. One must show that one has possession, as described in the application, of sufficient species to show that he or she invented and disclosed the totality of the genus."

Hyatt v. Dudas, 492 F.3d 1365, 1369-70, 83 U.S.P.Q.2d 1373, 1376 (Fed.Cir.2007). "In the context of the written description requirement, an adequate prima facie case must … sufficiently explain to the applicant what, in the examiner's view, is missing from the written description. The PTO expressed this requirement in [Manual of Patent Examining Procedure] §2163.04(I)(B). We hold that §2163.04(I)(B) as written is a lawful formulation of the prima facie standard for a lack of written description rejection. [¶] Adequate written description means that, in the specification, the applicant must 'convey with reasonable clarity to those skilled in the art that, as of the filing date sought, he or she was in possession of the [claimed] invention.' When no such description can be found in the specification, the only thing the PTO can reasonably be expected to do is to point out its nonexistence. This is not to say that the PTO can reject a complex claim with numerous limitations by summarily declaring that no written description support exists. Rather, §2163.04(I) expressly instructs the examiner to specify which claim limitation is lacking adequate support in the written description."

Falkner v. Inglis, 448 F.3d 1357, 1366, 79 U.S.P.Q.2d 1001, 1007 (Fed.Cir.2006). "[W]e hold, in accordance with our prior case law, that (1) examples are not necessary to support the adequacy of a written description[;] (2) the written description standard may be met (as it is here) even where actual reduction to practice of an invention is absent; and (3) there is no *per se* rule that an adequate written description of an invention that involves a biological macromolecule must contain a recitation of known structure."

Kao Corp. v. Andrew Jergens Co., 441 F.3d 963, 967, 78 U.S.P.Q.2d 1257, 1260 (Fed.Cir.2006). "Because compliance with the written description requirement is a question of fact, we review the trial court's determination for clear error."

LizardTech, Inc. v. Earth Res. Mapping, Inc., 424 F.3d 1336, 1345, 76 U.S.P.Q.2d 1724, 1732 (Fed.Cir. 2005). The written description and enablement "requirements usually rise and fall together. That is, a recitation of how to make and use the invention across the full breadth of the claim is ordinarily sufficient to demonstrate that the inventor possesses the full scope of the invention, and vice versa. *At F.3d 1346, U.S.P.Q.2d 1733:* [A] patentee cannot always satisfy the requirements of §112, in supporting expansive claim language, merely by clearly describing one embodiment of the thing claimed."

Capon v. Eshhar, 418 F.3d 1349, 1360, 76 U.S.P.Q.2d 1078, 1087 (Fed.Cir.2005). "The predictability or unpredictability of the science is relevant to deciding how much experimental support is required to adequately describe the scope of an invention."

In re Wallach, 378 F.3d 1330, 1335, 71 U.S.P.Q.2d 1939, 1943 (Fed.Cir.2004). "[T]he written description requirement can in some cases be satisfied by functional description. Nonetheless, such functional description can be sufficient only if there is also a structure-function relationship known to those of ordinary skill in the art."

Cordis Corp. v. Medtronic AVE, Inc., 339 F.3d 1352, 1364, 67 U.S.P.Q.2d 1876, 1885 (Fed.Cir.2003). "The [written description] as originally filed does not ... have to provide *in haec verba* support for the claimed subject matter at issue. *At F.3d 1365, U.S.P.Q.2d 1886:* '[A]n applicant is not required to describe in the specification every conceivable and possible future embodiment of his invention.' 'A specification may, within the meaning of 35 U.S.C. §112 ¶1, contain a written description of a broadly claimed invention without describing all species that [the] claim encompasses.'"

Moba, B.V. v. Diamond Automation, Inc., 325 F.3d 1306, 1319, 66 U.S.P.Q.2d 1429, 1437-38 (Fed.Cir. 2003). "Federal Circuit case law reflects two applications of 35 U.S.C. §112, ¶1. First, in 1967, this court's predecessor inaugurated use of §112 to prevent the addition of new matter to claims. As this court's predecessor noted, '[t]he function of the description requirement is to ensure that the inventor had possession, as of the filing date of the application relied on, of the specific subject matter later claimed by him.' Although the statute proscribes addition of new matter to a specification or claims under [35 U.S.C.] §132, the U.S. Court of Customs and Patent Appeals decided to police the addition of new matter to claims separately using §112. This court's predecessor explained that the use of §132 or §112 was synonymous because 'a rejection of an amended claim under §132 is equivalent to a rejection under §112, [¶1].' Since then, this court has continued to use §112 to ensure that a patentee had possession at the time of filing of subject matter subsequently claimed. *At F.3d 1320:* The second application of the written description requirement [requires] a precise definition [of a claimed invention to distinguish it from other materials] in the patent specification. *At U.S.P.Q.2d 1439:* The test for compliance with §112 has always required sufficient information in the original disclosure to show that the inventor possessed the invention at the time of the original filing."

Singh v. Brake, 317 F.3d 1334, 1343, 65 U.S.P.Q.2d 1641, 1647 (Fed.Cir.2003). "Whether a specification supports a claim corresponding to a count, and thus satisfies the written description requirement of ... §112, ¶1, is a question of fact ... and is, in appeals from the [PTO], reviewed under the substantial evidence standard."

Enzo Biochem, Inc. v. Gen-Probe Inc., 323 F.3d 956, 965, 63 U.S.P.Q.2d 1609, 1613 (Fed.Cir.2002). "[W]e hold that reference in the specification to a deposit in a public depository, which makes its contents accessible to the public when it is not otherwise available in written form, constitutes an adequate description of the deposited material sufficient to comply with the written description requirement of §112, ¶1. *At F.3d 969, U.S.P.Q.2d 1617:* [W]e conclude that proof of a reduction to practice, absent an adequate description in the specification of what is reduced to practice, does not serve to describe or identify the invention for purposes of §112, ¶1. As with 'possession,' proof of a reduction to practice may show priority of invention or allow one to antedate a reference, but it does not by itself provide a written description *in the patent specification*." *See also* ***Monsanto Co. v. Scruggs***, 459 F.3d 1328, 1336, 79 U.S.P.Q.2d 1813, 1818 (Fed.Cir.2006).

Cooper Cameron Corp. v. Kvaerner Oilfield Prods., 291 F.3d 1317, 1322, 62 U.S.P.Q.2d 1846, 1850 (Fed.Cir.2002). "Drawings constitute an adequate description if they describe what is claimed and convey to those of skill in the art that the patentee actually invented what is claimed."

Regents of the Univ. of Cal. v. Eli Lilly & Co., 119 F.3d 1559, 1568, 43 U.S.P.Q.2d 1398, 1405 (Fed.Cir. 1997). "A written description of an invention involving a chemical genus, like a description of a chemical species, 'requires a precise definition, such as by structure, formula, [or] chemical name,' of the claimed subject matter sufficient to distinguish it from other materials. *At U.S.P.Q.2d 1406:* A definition by function, as we have previously indicated, does not suffice to define the genus because it is only an indication of what the gene does, rather than what it is. It is only a definition of a useful result rather than a definition of what achieves that result. Many such genes may achieve that result. The description requirement of the patent statute requires a description of an invention, not an indication of a result that one might achieve if one made that invention."

Vas-Cath Inc. v. Mahurkar, 935 F.2d 1555, 1560, 19 U.S.P.Q.2d 1111, 1114 (Fed.Cir.1991). "[T]he 'written description' requirement most often comes into play where claims not presented in the application when filed are presented thereafter. Alternatively, patent applicants often seek the benefit of the filing date of an earlier-filed foreign or U.S. application under 35 U.S.C. §119 or 35 U.S.C. §120, respectively, for claims of a later-filed application. The question raised by these situations is most often phrased as whether the application provides 'adequate support' for the claim(s) at issue; it has also been analyzed in terms of 'new matter' under 35 U.S.C. §132. The 'written description' question similarly arises in the interference context, where the issue is whether the specification of one party to the interference can support the claim corresponding to count(s) at issue, i.e., whether that party 'can make the claim' corresponding to the interference count." *See also* ***Agilent Techs. v. Affymetrix, Inc.***, 567 F.3d 1366, 1379, 91 U.S.P.Q.2d 1161, 1169-70 (Fed. Cir.2009).

§112, ¶2 (& Amended §112(b))

Nautilus, Inc. v. Biosig Instrs., Inc., ___ U.S. ___, 134 S.Ct. 2120, 2124, 110 U.S.P.Q.2d 1688, 1689-90 (2014). "The Patent Act requires that a patent specification conclude with one or more claims *particularly pointing out and distinctly claiming* the subject matter which the applicant regards as the invention. This case ... concerns the proper reading of the statute's clarity and precision demand. According to the Federal Circuit, a patent claim passes the §112, ¶2 threshold so long as the claim is amenable to construction, and the claim, as construed, is not 'insolubly ambiguous.' We conclude that the Federal Circuit's formulation, which tolerates some ambiguous claims but not others, does not satisfy the statute's definiteness requirement. In place of the 'insolubly ambiguous' standard, we hold that a patent is invalid for indefiniteness if its claims, read in light of the specification delineating the patent, and the prosecution history, fail to inform, with reasonable certainty, those skilled in the art about the scope of the invention. *At U.S. ___, S.Ct. 2129, U.S.P.Q.2d 1693:* At the same time, a patent must be precise enough to afford clear notice of what is claimed, thereby apprising the public of what is still open to them. Otherwise there would be a zone of uncertainty which enterprise and experimentation may enter only at the risk of infringement claims. And absent a meaningful definiteness check, we are told, patent applicants face powerful incentives to inject ambiguity into their claims. Eliminating that temptation is in order, and the patent drafter is in the best position to resolve the ambiguity in patent claims." (Internal quotes omitted.)

MasterMine Software, Inc. v. Microsoft Corp., 874 F.3d 1307, 1313, 124 U.S.P.Q.2d 1618, 1622 (Fed.Cir. 2017). "Following ***IPXL Holdings***, we have been called on to review applications of this holding to numerous different claims. [W]hile a claim directed to both a method and an apparatus may be indefinite, 'apparatus claims are not necessarily indefinite for using functional language.'"

Sonix Tech. Co. v. Publications Int'l, 844 F.3d 1370, 1377, 121 U.S.P.Q.2d 1247, 1252 (Fed.Cir.2017). "Because language is limited, we have rejected the proposition that claims involving terms of degree are inherently indefinite. Thus, 'a patentee need not define his invention with mathematical precision in order to comply with the definiteness requirement.' Indeed, '[c]laim language employing terms of degree has long been found definite where it provided enough certainty to one of skill in the art when read in the context of the invention.' [¶] We have found terms of degree indefinite, however, when such guidance is lacking. *At F.3d 1380-81, U.S.P.Q.2d 1254:* Our holding in this case does not mean that the existence of examples in the written description will always render a claim definite, or that listing requirements always provide sufficient certainty. Neither does the fact that an expert has applied a contested claim term without difficulty render a claim immune from an indefiniteness challenge. As always, whether a claim is indefinite must be judged 'in light of the specification and prosecution history' of the patent in which it appears."

Dow Chem. Co. v. Nova Chems. Corp., 803 F.3d 620, 634, 115 U.S.P.Q.2d 2024, 2034 (Fed.Cir.2015). "The question is whether the existence of multiple methods leading to different results without guidance in the patent or the prosecution history as to which method should be used renders the claims indefinite. Before ***Nautilus***, a claim was not indefinite if someone skilled in the art could arrive at a method and practice that method. [¶] Under ***Nautilus*** this is no longer sufficient. '[A] patent is invalid for indefiniteness if its claims, read in light of the specification delineating the patent, and the prosecution history, fail to inform, with reasonable certainty, those skilled in the art about the scope of the invention.'"

Teva Pharms. USA, Inc. v. Sandoz, Inc., 789 F.3d 1335, 1341, 115 U.S.P.Q.2d 1210, 1215 (Fed.Cir.2015). "[W]e look to the patent record—the claims, specification, and prosecution history—to ascertain if they convey to one of skill in the art with reasonable certainty the scope of the invention claimed. We conclude in this case that they do not convey with reasonable certainty the measure of molecular weight to be used. Claim 1 ... recites 'molecular weight' without specifying the meaning of that term. The parties agree that ... each of [the] measures [of molecular weight] is calculated in a different way and would typically yield a different result for a given polymer sample. But the claim on its face offers no guidance on which measure of 'molecular weight' the claims cover." *But see* ***Ethicon Endo-Surgery, Inc. v. Covidien, Inc.***, 796 F.3d 1312, 1319, 115 U.S.P.Q.2d 1880, 1886 (Fed.Cir.2015) (one skilled in the art could rely on basic concepts of physics and mathematics to understand average clamping pressures).

Interval Licensing LLC v. AOL, Inc., 766 F.3d 1364, 1370-71, 112 U.S.P.Q.2d 1188, 1192 (Fed.Cir. 2014). "We do not understand the Supreme Court to have implied in ***Nautilus***, and we do not hold today, that terms of degree are inherently indefinite. Claim language employing terms of degree has long been found definite where it provided enough certainty to one of skill in the art when read in the context of the invention. *At U.S.P.Q.2d 1193:* Although absolute or mathematical precision is not required, it is not enough, as some of the language in our prior cases may have suggested, to identify '*some standard* for measuring the scope of the phrase.' The Supreme Court explained that a patent does not satisfy the definiteness requirement of §112 merely because 'a court can ascribe *some* meaning to a patent's claims.' The claims, when read in light of the specification and the prosecution history, must provide objective boundaries for those of skill in the art."

In re Packard, 751 F.3d 1307, 1311, 110 U.S.P.Q.2d 1785, 1787 (Fed.Cir.2014). "[W]hen the USPTO has initially issued a well-grounded rejection that identifies ways in which language in a claim is ambiguous, vague, incoherent, opaque, or otherwise unclear in describing and defining the claimed invention, and thereafter the applicant fails to provide a satisfactory response, the USPTO can properly reject the claim as failing to meet the statutory requirements of §112(b). The satisfactory response by the applicant can take the form of a modification of the language identified as unclear, a separate definition of the unclear language, or, in an appropriate case, a persuasive explanation for the record of why the language at issue is not actually unclear."

Young v. Lumenis, Inc., 492 F.3d 1336, 1346, 83 U.S.P.Q.2d 1191, 1197 (Fed.Cir.2007), *overruled on other grounds*, ***Nautilus, Inc. v. Biosig Instruments, Inc.***, ___ U.S. ___, 134 S.Ct. 2120 (2014). "Indefiniteness requires a determination whether those skilled in the art would understand what is claimed. To make that determination, we have explained that 'in the face of an allegation of indefiniteness, general principles of claim construction apply.' In that regard, claim construction involves consideration of primarily the intrinsic evidence, *viz.*, the claim language, the specification, and the prosecution history."

Energizer Holdings, Inc. v. ITC, 435 F.3d 1366, 1370-71, 77 U.S.P.Q.2d 1625, 1628 (Fed.Cir.2006), *overruled on other grounds*, ***Nautilus, Inc. v. Biosig Instruments, Inc.***, ___ U.S. ___, 134 S.Ct. 2120 (2014). "When the meaning of the claim would reasonably be understood by persons of ordinary skill when read in light of the specification, the claim is not subject to invalidity upon departure from the protocol of 'antecedent basis.' [¶] The requirement of antecedent basis is a rule of patent drafting, administered during patent examination. The *Manual of Patent Examining Procedure* states that '[o]bviously, however, the failure to provide explicit antecedent basis for terms does not always render a claim indefinite.' [¶] [D]espite the absence of explicit antecedent basis, '[i]f the scope of a claim would be reasonably ascertainable by those skilled in the art, then the claim is not indefinite.'"

IPXL Holdings, L.L.C. v. Amazon.com, Inc., 430 F.3d 1377, 1384, 77 U.S.P.Q.2d 1140, 1145 (Fed.Cir. 2005). "Whether a single claim covering both an apparatus and a method of use of that apparatus is invalid is an issue of first impression in this court. The Board of Patent Appeals and Interferences ('Board') of the PTO, however, has made it clear that reciting both an apparatus and a method of using that apparatus renders a claim indefinite under §112, ¶2. … The Board correctly surmised that, as a result of the combination of two separate statutory classes of invention, a manufacturer or seller of the claimed apparatus would not know from the claim whether it might also be liable for contributory infringement because a buyer or user of the apparatus later performs the claimed method of using the apparatus. Thus, such a claim is not sufficiently precise to provide competitors with an accurate determination of the metes and bounds of protection involved and is ambiguous and properly rejected under §112, ¶2." (Internal quotes omitted.) *See also* ***In re Katz Interactive Call Processing Patent Litig.***, 639 F.3d 1303, 1318, 97 U.S.P.Q.2d 1737, 1748-49 (Fed.Cir.2011).

Default Proof Credit Card Sys. v. Home Depot, Inc., 412 F.3d 1291, 1298, 75 U.S.P.Q.2d 1116, 1121 (Fed. Cir.2005). "'Indefiniteness …, like claim construction, is a question of law that we review de novo. [¶] 'Although expert testimony and declarations are useful to confirm that the construed meaning is consistent with the denotation ascribed by those in the field of the art, such extrinsic evidence cannot be used to vary the plain language of the patent document.' [¶] '[I]f one employs means-plus-function language in a claim, one must set forth in the specification an adequate disclosure showing what is meant by that language. If an applicant fails to set forth an adequate disclosure, the applicant has in effect failed to particularly point out and distinctly claim the invention as required by the second paragraph of §112.'" *See also* ***Eidos Display, LLC v. AU Optronics Corp.***, 779 F.3d 1360, 1364-65, 113 U.S.P.Q.2d 1975, 1978 (Fed.Cir.2015).

Honeywell Int'l v. International Trade Comm., 341 F.3d 1332, 1338-39, 68 U.S.P.Q.2d 1023, 1028 (Fed. Cir.2003), *overruled on other grounds*, ***Nautilus, Inc. v. Biosig Instruments, Inc.***, ___ U.S. ___, 134 S.Ct. 2120 (2014). "The definiteness requirement of §112, ¶2 'focuses on whether the claims, as interpreted in view of the written description, adequately perform their function of notifying the public of the [scope of the] patentee's right to exclude.'" *See also* ***Amgen Inc. v. Hoechst Marion Roussel, Inc.***, 314 F.3d 1313, 1342, 65 U.S.P.Q.2d 1385, 1406 (Fed.Cir.2003), *overruled on other grounds*, ***Nautilus, Inc. v. Biosig Instruments, Inc.***, ___ U.S. ___, 134 S.Ct. 2120 (2014).

Intel Corp. v. VIA Tech., 319 F.3d 1357, 1367, 65 U.S.P.Q.2d 1934, 1941 (Fed.Cir.2003). "[I]f a chair is disclosed in the specification that corresponds to the 'means for seating' limitation in a claim, asserting that there are infinite numbers of structures that could make a chair or there are unlimited types of chairs in the world would not necessarily make the claim indefinite."

Verve, LLC v. Crane Cams, Inc., 311 F.3d 1116, 1120, 65 U.S.P.Q.2d 1051, 1054 (Fed.Cir.2002). "Expressions such as 'substantially' are used in patent documents when warranted by the nature of the invention, in order to accommodate the minor variations that may be appropriate to secure the invention. Such usage may well satisfy the charge to particularly point out and distinctly claim the invention, … and indeed may be necessary in order to provide the inventor with the benefit of his invention. [U]sages such as 'substantially equal' and 'closely approximate' may serve to describe the invention with precision appropriate to the technology and without intruding on the prior art. [L]ike the term 'about,' the term 'substantially' is a descriptive term commonly used in patent claims to avoid a strict numerical boundary to the specified parameter...." (Internal quotes omitted.)

Crown Oper. Int'l v. Solutia Inc., 289 F.3d 1367, 1378 n.5, 62 U.S.P.Q.2d 1917, 1924 n.5 (Fed.Cir.2002). "'[D]efiniteness and enablement are analytically distinct requirements.... The definiteness requirement of ... §112, ¶2 is a legal requirement, based on the court's role as construer of patent claims.... Definiteness requires the language of the claim to set forth clearly the domain over which the applicant seeks exclusive rights....'"

Johnson & Johnston Assocs. v. R.E. Serv. Co., 285 F.3d 1046, 1053, 62 U.S.P.Q.2d 1225, 1229 (Fed.Cir. 2002). "'[T]he claim of a specific device or combination, and an omission to claim other devices or combinations apparent on the face of the patent, are, in law, a dedication to the public of that which is not claimed.' (Quoting ***Miller v. Bridgeport Brass***, 104 U.S. 350 (1881).)"

§112, ¶3 (& Amended §112(c))

Honeywell Int'l v. Hamilton Sundstrand Corp., 370 F.3d 1131, 1134, 71 U.S.P.Q.2d 1065, 1066 (Fed.Cir. 2004). "[W]e hold that the rewriting of dependent claims into independent form coupled with the cancellation of the original independent claims creates a presumption of prosecution history estoppel."

§112, ¶4 (& Amended §112(d))

Monsanto Co. v. Syngenta Seeds, Inc., 503 F.3d 1352, 1357, 84 U.S.P.Q.2d 1705, 1708 (Fed.Cir.2007). "To establish whether a claim is dependent upon another, this court examines if the new claim both refers to an earlier claim and further limits that referent. A claim's status as dependent or independent depends on the substance of the claim in light of the language of §112, ¶4, and not the form alone."

Pfizer, Inc. v. Ranbaxy Labs., 457 F.3d 1284, 1291-92, 79 U.S.P.Q.2d 1583, 1589-90 (Fed.Cir.2006). "[W]e have suggested that a violation of [35 U.S.C.] §112, ¶4 renders a patent invalid just as violations of other paragraphs of §112 would. In ***Curtiss-Wright [Flow Control Corp. v. Velan, Inc.***, 438 F.3d 1374 (Fed.Cir. 2006)], the issue was one of claim differentiation. The court reasoned that 'reading an additional limitation from a dependent claim into an independent claim would not only make that additional limitation superfluous, it might render the dependent claim invalid' for failing to add a limitation to those recited in the independent claim, as required by ... §112, ¶4. Indeed, '[i]nvalidity of the patent or any claim in suit for failure to comply with *any* requirement of [35 U.S.C.] §§112 or 251 ...' is expressly included among the available defenses to an infringement suit. [¶] We recognize that the patentee was attempting to claim what might otherwise have been patentable subject matter. Indeed, claim 6 could have been properly drafted either as dependent from claim 1 or as an independent claim.... But, we 'should not rewrite claims to preserve validity.' [D] correctly argues that claim 6 fails to 'specify a further limitation of the subject matter' of the claim to which it refers because it is completely outside the scope of claim 2. We must therefore reverse the district court with respect to this issue and hold claim 6 invalid for failure to comply with §112, ¶4. [¶] Although the district court was reluctant to find the fourth paragraph of §112 to be an invalidating provision, doing so does not exalt form over substance. Rather, it is consistent with the overall statutory scheme that requires applicants to satisfy certain requirements before obtaining a patent, some of which are more procedural or technical than others."

§112, ¶6 (& Amended §112(f))

Warner-Jenkinson Co. v. Hilton Davis Chem. Co., 520 U.S. 17, 27-28, 41 U.S.P.Q.2d 1865, 1870-71 (1997). "[A]n applicant can describe an element of his invention by the result accomplished or the function served, rather than describing the item or element to be used (*e.g.*, 'a means of connecting Part A to Part B,' rather than 'a two-penny nail'). ... Section 112, ¶6, now expressly allows so-called 'means' claims, with the proviso that application of the broad literal language of such claims must be limited to only those means that are 'equivalen[t]' to the actual means shown in the patent specification. This is an application of the doctrine of equivalents in a restrictive role, narrowing the application of broad literal claim elements. ... The added provision, however, is silent on the doctrine of equivalents as applied where there is no literal infringement."

Williamson v. Citrix Online, LLC, 792 F.3d 1339, 1349, 115 U.S.P.Q.2d 1105, 1111 (Fed.Cir.2015). "Our opinions ... have ... established a heightened bar to overcoming the presumption that a limitation expressed in functional language without using the word 'means' is not subject to §112, ¶6. [¶] Our consideration of this case has led us to conclude that such a heightened burden is unjustified and that we should abandon characterizing as 'strong' the presumption that a limitation lacking the word 'means' is not subject to §112, ¶6. ... Henceforth, we will apply the presumption as we have done prior to ***Lighting World**[, **Inc. v. Birchwood Lighting, Inc.***, 382 F.3d 1354 (Fed.Cir. 2004)], without requiring any heightened evidentiary showing and expressly overrule the characterization of that presumption as 'strong.' We also overrule the strict requirement of a showing that the limitation essentially is devoid of anything that can be construed as structure. [¶] The standard is whether the words of the claim are understood by persons of ordinary skill in the art to have a sufficiently definite meaning as the name for structure. When a claim term lacks the word 'means,' the presumption can be overcome and §112, ¶6 will apply if the challenger demonstrates that the claim term fails to recite sufficiently definite structure or else recites function without reciting sufficient structure for performing that function. The converse presumption remains unaffected: use of the word 'means' creates a presumption that §112, ¶6 applies." (Internal quotes omitted.)

Ibormeith IP, LLC v. Mercedes-Benz USA, LLC, 732 F.3d 1376, 1379, 108 U.S.P.Q.2d 1643, 1645-46 (Fed. Cir.2013). "Section 112(f) allows patentees to put structural details into the specification and build into the literal coverage of the claim a certain scope for equivalents in performing a defined function. The price of using this form of claim, however, is that the claim be tied to a structure defined with sufficient particularity in the specification. For a claim to be definite, a recited algorithm, or other type of structure for a §112(f) claim limitation, need not be so particularized as to eliminate the need for any implementation choices by a skilled artisan; but it must be sufficiently defined to render the bounds of the claim—declared by §112(f) to cover the particular structure and its equivalents—understandable by the implementer."

Noah Sys. v. Intuit Inc., 675 F.3d 1302, 1313, 102 U.S.P.Q.2d 1410, 1417 (Fed.Cir.2012). "Currently, our case law regarding special purpose computer-implemented means-plus-functions claims is divided into two distinct groups: First, cases in which the specification discloses no algorithm; and second, cases in which the specification does disclose an algorithm but a defendant contends that disclosure is inadequate. This distinction is important because we have clarified that, while '[i]t is certainly true that the sufficiency of the disclosure of algorithmic structure must be judged in light of what one of ordinary skill in the art would understand the disclosure to impart,' in a situation in which the specification discloses no algorithm, '[t]hat principle ... has no application....' Where no structure appears, the question 'is not whether the algorithm that was disclosed was described with sufficient specificity, but whether an algorithm was disclosed at all.' When the specification discloses some algorithm, on the other hand, the question is whether the disclosed algorithm, from the viewpoint of a person of ordinary skill, is sufficient to define the structure and make the bounds of the claim understandable. *At F.3d 1318-19, U.S.P.Q.2d 1421:* [W]here a disclosed algorithm supports some, but not all, of the functions associated with a means-plus-function limitation, we treat the specification as if no algorithm has been disclosed at all. In such instances, we are not faced with a disclosure which addresses itself to an identifiable function, but arguably does so inadequately. We are faced with an identifiable function, which all parties concede is claimed, but as to which there is a total absence of structure. We cannot allow disclosure as to one function to fill the gaps in a specification as to a different, albeit related, function. To hold otherwise would allow a patentee to employ generic functional claiming 'unbounded by any reference to structure in the specification.' This outcome is impermissible under the plain terms of §112 ¶6." *See also* ***In re Katz Interactive Call Processing Patent Litig.***, 639 F.3d 1303, 1316, 97 U.S.P.Q.2d 1737, 1747 (Fed.Cir.2011) (for functions that can be achieved by any general-purpose computer without special programming, it was not necessary to disclose more structure than the general-purpose processor that performs those functions); ***Aristocrat Techs. Australia Pty Ltd. v. International Game Tech.***, 521 F.3d 1328, 1337-38, 86 U.S.P.Q.2d 1235, 1243 (Fed.Cir.2008) (special-purpose computer must execute the specific function).

Typhoon Touch Techs. v. Dell, Inc., 659 F.3d 1376, 1384, 100 U.S.P.Q.2d 1690, 1696 (Fed.Cir.2011). "The usage 'algorithm' in computer systems has broad meaning, for it encompasses 'in essence a series of instructions for the computer to follow,' ... whether in mathematical formula, or a word description of the procedure to be implemented by a suitably programmed computer. *At F.3d 1385-86, U.S.P.Q.2d 1697:* [A patentee may] express that procedural algorithm 'in any understandable terms including as a mathematical formula, in prose, or as a flow chart, or in any other manner that provides sufficient structure.' [T]he patent need only disclose sufficient structure for a person of skill in the field to provide an operative software program for the specified function. [¶] For computer-implemented procedures, the computer code is not required to be included in the patent specification. A description of the function in words may 'disclose, at least to the satisfaction of one of ordinary skill in the art, enough of an algorithm to provide the necessary structure under §112, ¶6.'"

Net MoneyIN, Inc. v. VeriSign, Inc., 545 F.3d 1359, 1367, 88 U.S.P.Q.2d 1751, 1756-57 (Fed.Cir.2008). "To avoid purely functional claiming in cases involving computer-implemented inventions, we have consistently required that the structure disclosed in the specification be more than simply a general purpose computer or microprocessor. Because general purpose computers can be programmed to perform very different tasks in very different ways, simply disclosing a computer as the structure designated to perform a particular function does not limit the scope of the claim to the corresponding structure, material, or acts that perform the function, as required by §112 ¶6. Thus, in a means-plus-function claim in which the disclosed structure is a computer, or microprocessor, programmed to carry out an algorithm, the disclosed structure is not the general purpose computer, but rather the special purpose computer programmed to perform the disclosed algorithm. Consequently, a means-plus-function claim element for which the only disclosed structure is a general purpose computer is invalid if the specification fails to disclose an algorithm for performing the claimed function." (Internal quotes omitted.) *See also* ***Blackboard, Inc. v. Desire2Learn, Inc.***, 574 F.3d 1371, 1382-85, 91 U.S.P.Q.2d 1481, 1490-93 (Fed.Cir.2009).

Biomedino, LLC v. Waters Techs., 490 F.3d 946, 948, 83 U.S.P.Q.2d 1118, 1119 (Fed.Cir.2007). Section 112, ¶6 permits "'broad means-plus-function language, but provide[s] a standard to make the broad claim language more definite[:] ... [t]he applicant must describe in the patent specification some structure which performs the specified function.' Thus, in return for generic claiming ability, the applicant must indicate in the specification what structure constitutes the means. 'If the specification is not clear as to the structure that the patentee intends to correspond to the claimed function, then the patentee has not paid the price but is rather attempting to claim in functional terms unbounded by any reference to structure in the specification.' Thus, '[i]f an applicant fails to set forth an adequate disclosure, the applicant has in effect failed to particularly point out and distinctly claim the invention as required by the second paragraph of §112.' *At F.3d 951, U.S.P.Q.2d 1121:* Essentially this case asks the following question: for purposes of §112, ¶6, is sufficient corresponding structure disclosed when the specification simply recites that a claimed function can be performed by known methods or using known equipment where prior art of record and the testimony of experts suggest that known methods and equipment exist? *At F.3d 953, U.S.P.Q.2d 1123:* The inquiry is whether one of skill in the art would understand the specification itself to disclose a structure, not simply whether that person would be capable of implementing a structure. Accordingly, a bare statement that known techniques or methods can be used does not disclose structure. To conclude otherwise would vitiate the language of the statute requiring 'corresponding structure, material, or acts described in the specification.'" *See also* ***Atmel Corp. v. Information Storage Devices, Inc.***, 198 F.3d 1374, 1382, 53 U.S.P.Q.2d 1225, 1230 (Fed.Cir.1999).

Harris Corp. v. Ericsson Inc., 417 F.3d 1241, 1253, 75 U.S.P.Q.2d 1705, 1713-14 (Fed.Cir.2005). "***WMS Gaming*** restricts computer-implemented means-plus-function terms to the algorithm disclosed in the specification. [T]he court in ***WMS Gaming*** rejected the argument that the corresponding structure was merely 'an algorithm executed by a computer,' holding instead that it was limited to the specific algorithm disclosed in the specification. [Patentee] argues that this court's construction in ***WMS Gaming*** was merely a restatement of the function, not a legal holding that means-plus-function claims involving a microprocessor are always limited to the disclosed algorithm. We do not read ***WMS Gaming*** to be so limited. The ***WMS Gaming*** court could have relied on the function to limit the claim, but explicitly based the claim construction portion of its ruling on structure instead. A computer-implemented means-plus-function term is limited to the corresponding structure disclosed in the specification and equivalents thereof, and the corresponding structure is the algorithm."

Frank's Casing Crew & Rental Tools, Inc. v. Weatherford Int'l, 389 F.3d 1370, 1379, 73 U.S.P.Q.2d 1065, 1070 (Fed.Cir.2004). "The primary difference between structural equivalents under §112, ¶6 and the doctrine of equivalents is a question of timing. As this court has explained, '[a] proposed equivalent must have arisen at a definite period in time, i.e., either before or after [patent filing]. If before, a §112, ¶6 structural equivalents analysis applies and any analysis for equivalent structure under the doctrine of equivalents collapses into the §112, ¶6 analysis. If after, a non-textual infringement analysis proceeds under the doctrine of equivalents.'"

Apex Inc. v. Raritan Computer, Inc., 325 F.3d 1364, 1371-72, 66 U.S.P.Q.2d 1444, 1450 (Fed.Cir.2003). "It is well settled that [a] claim limitation that actually uses the word 'means' invokes a rebuttable presumption that §112, ¶6 applies. By contrast, a claim term that does not use 'means' will trigger the rebuttable presumption that §112, ¶6 does not apply. [T]he term 'means' is central to the analysis. [¶] From a procedural standpoint, this presumption 'imposes on [D] the burden of going forward with evidence to rebut ... the presumption, but does not shift to such party the burden of proof in the sense of the risk of nonpersuasion, which remains throughout the trial upon the party on whom it was originally cast.' [D] can rebut this presumption if it demonstrates that the claim term fails to recite sufficiently definite structure or else recites a function without reciting sufficient structure for performing that function. This burden must be met by a preponderance of the evidence. If the party who must bring forth evidence fails to proffer sufficient evidence to meet its burden, the presumption, either for or against the application of §112, ¶6, prevails. *At F.3d 1374, U.S.P.Q.2d 1451:* [E]very use of the term in the asserted claims includes additional adjectival qualifications further identifying sufficient structure to perform the claimed functions to one of ordinary skill in the art. The district court therefore erred in its interpretation of all the limitations as means-plus-function limitations by failing to consider the limitations as a whole." *See also* ***CCS Fitness, Inc. v. Brunswick Corp.***, 288 F.3d 1359, 1368-69, 62 U.S.P.Q.2d 1658, 1664-65 (Fed. Cir.2002).

Northrop Grumman Corp. v. Intel Corp., 325 F.3d 1346, 1352, 66 U.S.P.Q.2d 1341, 1345 (Fed.Cir.2003). "A court may not import into the claim features that are unnecessary to perform the claimed function. Features that do not perform the recited function do not constitute corresponding structure and thus do not serve as claim limitations." *See also* ***Asyst Tech. v. Empak, Inc.***, 268 F.3d 1364, 1369-70, 60 U.S.P.Q.2d 1567, 1571 (Fed.Cir.2001).

Altiris, Inc. v. Symantec Corp., 318 F.3d 1363, 1375, 65 U.S.P.Q.2d 1865, 1874 (Fed.Cir.2003). "Once the court has concluded the claim limitation is a means-plus-function limitation, the court must first identify the function of the limitation. The court next ascertains the corresponding structure in the written description that is necessary to perform that function. Structure disclosed in the specification is corresponding structure only if the specification or prosecution history clearly links or associates that structure to the function recited in the claim." (Internal quotes omitted.) *See also* ***Medical Instr. & Diagnostics Corp. v. Elekta AB***, 344 F.3d 1205, 1219, 68 U.S.P.Q.2d 1263, 1274 (Fed.Cir.2003).

Creo Prods. v. Presstek, Inc., 305 F.3d 1337, 1346, 64 U.S.P.Q.2d 1385, 1391-92 (Fed.Cir.2002). "[P]roper application of §112 ¶6 generally reads the claim element to embrace distinct and alternative described structures for performing the claimed function. Specifically, 'disclosed structure includes that which is described in a patent specification, including any alternative structures identified.'"

Masco Corp. v. U.S., 303 F.3d 1316, 1326, 64 U.S.P.Q.2d 1182, 1188 (Fed.Cir.2002). Section 112, ¶6 "can apply not only to a combination of mechanical elements, but also to 'a combination of ... steps in a process claim.' [T]he use of the term 'steps for' signals the drafter's intent to invoke §112, ¶6. However, even where the drafter employs the 'step for' language, '§112, ¶6 is implicated ... only when steps plus function *without acts* are present.' *At F.3d 1327:* Neither of these claims employs the 'step for' language that signals the drafter's intent to invoke §112, ¶6; rather, the claims employ the term 'steps of.' Thus, there is no presumption that these limitations are in step-plus-function format. *At U.S.P.Q.2d 1189:* We thus hold that where a method claim does not contain the term 'step[s] for,' a limitation of that claim cannot be construed as a step-plus-function limitation without a showing that the limitation contains no act."

Interactive Pictures Corp. v. Infinite Pictures, Inc., 274 F.3d 1371, 1381-82, 61 U.S.P.Q.2d 1152, 1160 (Fed.Cir.2001). "[A] finding that a component of an accused product is not a structure 'equivalent' to the corresponding structure of a means-plus-function limitation for purposes of literal infringement analysis precludes a finding that the same *structure* is equivalent for purposes of the doctrine of equivalents, unless the component constitutes technology arising after the issuance of the patent. However, when a finding of non-infringement under ... §112, ¶6, is premised on an absence of identical *function*, then infringement under the doctrine of equivalents is not thereby automatically precluded. That is because infringement under the doctrine of equivalents may be premised on the accused and the patented component having *substantially* the same function, whereas structure corresponding to the disclosed limitation in a means-plus-function clause must perform the *identical* function."

WMS Gaming, Inc. v. International Game Tech., 184 F.3d 1339, 1348, 51 U.S.P.Q.2d 1385, 1391 (Fed.Cir. 1999). "The structure of a microprocessor programmed to carry out an algorithm is limited by the disclosed algorithm. *At F.3d 1349:* In a means-plus-function claim in which the disclosed structure is a computer, or microprocessor, programmed to carry out an algorithm, the disclosed structure is not the general purpose computer, but rather the special purpose computer programmed to perform the disclosed algorithm."

Chiuminatta Concrete Concepts, Inc. v. Cardinal Indus., 145 F.3d 1303, 1308, 46 U.S.P.Q.2d 1752, 1755-56 (Fed.Cir.1998). "'To determine whether a claim limitation is met literally, where expressed as a means for performing a stated function, the court must compare the accused structure *with the disclosed structure*, and must find equivalent *structure* as well as *identity* of claimed *function* for that structure.' A determination of the claimed function, being a matter of construction of specific terms in the claim, is a question of law, reviewed *de novo*. Likewise, the 'means' term in a means-plus-function limitation is essentially a generic reference for the corresponding structure disclosed in the specification. Accordingly, a determination of corresponding structure is a determination of the meaning of the 'means' term in the claim and is thus also a matter of claim construction. *At F.3d 1309:* '[S]ection 112, ¶6, rules out the possibility that any and every means which performs the function specified in the claim *literally* satisfies that limitation.' The proper test is whether the differences between the structure in the accused device and any disclosed in the specification are insubstantial."

§113. DRAWINGS

The applicant shall furnish a drawing where necessary for the understanding of the subject matter sought to be patented. When the nature of such subject matter admits of illustration by a drawing and the applicant has not furnished such a drawing, the Director may require its submission within a time period of not less than two months from the sending of a notice thereof. Drawings submitted after the filing date of the application may not be used (i) to overcome any insufficiency of the specification due to lack of an enabling disclosure or otherwise inadequate disclosure therein, or (ii) to supplement the original disclosure thereof for the purpose of interpretation of the scope of any claim.

History of 35 U.S.C. §113: July 19, 1952, ch. 950, §1, 66 Stat. 799; Nov. 14, 1975, P.L. 94-131, §8, 89 Stat. 691; Nov. 29, 1999, P.L. 106-113, §1000(a)(9), 113 Stat. 1536; Nov. 2, 2002, P.L. 107-273, §13206(b)(1)(B), 116 Stat. 1906.

See also 37 C.F.R. §§1.81-1.85, 1.96, 1.152; Patent Cooperation Treaty.

§114. MODELS, SPECIMENS

The Director may require the applicant to furnish a model of convenient size to exhibit advantageously the several parts of his invention.

When the invention relates to a composition of matter, the Director may require the applicant to furnish specimens or ingredients for the purpose of inspection or experiment.

History of 35 U.S.C. §114: July 19, 1952, ch. 950, §1, 66 Stat. 799; Nov. 29, 1999, P.L. 106-113, §1000(a)(9), 113 Stat. 1536; Nov. 2, 2002, P.L. 107-273, §13206(b)(1)(B), 116 Stat. 1906.

See also 37 C.F.R. §§1.91-1.95.

§115. OATH OF APPLICANT

Section 115 is effective for patent applications filed before Sept. 16, 2012.

The applicant shall make oath that he believes himself to be the original and first inventor of the process, machine, manufacture, or composition of matter, or improvement thereof, for which he solicits a patent; and shall state of what country he is a citizen. Such oath may be made before any person within the United States authorized by law to administer oaths, or, when, made in a foreign country, before any diplomatic or consular officer of the United States authorized to administer oaths, or before any officer having an official seal and authorized to administer oaths in the foreign country in which the applicant may be, whose authority is proved by certificate of a diplomatic or consular officer of the United States, or apostille of an official designated by a foreign country which, by treaty or convention, accords like effect to apostilles of designated officials in the United States, and such oath shall be valid if it complies with the laws of the state or country where made. When the application is made as provided in this title by a person other than the inventor, the oath may be so varied in form that it can be made by him. For purposes of this section, a consular officer shall include any United States citizen serving overseas, authorized to perform notarial functions pursuant to section 1750 of the Revised Statutes, as amended (22 U.S.C. 4221).

History of 35 U.S.C. §115: July 19, 1952, ch. 950, §1, 66 Stat. 799; Aug. 27, 1982, P.L. 97-247, §14(a), 96 Stat. 321; Oct. 21, 1998, P.L. 105-277, §2222(d), 112 Stat. 2681-818.

See also 37 C.F.R. §§1.63-1.69.

ANNOTATIONS

Weil v. Fritz, 572 F.2d 856, 863, 196 U.S.P.Q. 600, 606 (C.C.P.A.1978). "[T]he applicant's *oath* is not a requirement of [35 U.S.C.] §112, [¶1], but of 35 U.S.C. §115; therefore, the sufficiency of [prior] oath is not material [for securing an earlier filing date] under [35 U.S.C.] §120."

§115. INVENTOR'S OATH OR DECLARATION

Section 115 is effective for patent applications filed on or after Sept. 16, 2012.

(a) Naming the inventor; inventor's oath or declaration.—An application for patent that is filed under section 111(a) or commences the national stage under section 371 shall include, or be amended to include, the name of the inventor for any invention claimed in the application. Except as otherwise provided in this section, each individual who is the inventor or a joint inventor of a claimed invention in an application for patent shall execute an oath or declaration in connection with the application.

(b) Required statements.—An oath or declaration under subsection (a) shall contain statements that—

(1) the application was made or was authorized to be made by the affiant or declarant; and

(2) such individual believes himself or herself to be the original inventor or an original joint inventor of a claimed invention in the application.

(c) Additional requirements.—The Director may specify additional information relating to the inventor and the invention that is required to be included in an oath or declaration under subsection (a).

(d) Substitute statement—

(1) In general.—In lieu of executing an oath or declaration under subsection (a), the applicant for patent may provide a substitute statement under the circumstances described in paragraph (2) and such additional circumstances that the Director may specify by regulation.

(2) Permitted circumstances.—A substitute statement under paragraph (1) is permitted with respect to any individual who—

(A) is unable to file the oath or declaration under subsection (a) because the individual—

(i) is deceased;

(ii) is under legal incapacity; or

(iii) cannot be found or reached after diligent effort; or

(B) is under an obligation to assign the invention but has refused to make the oath or declaration required under subsection (a).

(3) Contents.—A substitute statement under this subsection shall—

(A) identify the individual with respect to whom the statement applies;

(B) set forth the circumstances representing the permitted basis for the filing of the substitute statement in lieu of the oath or declaration under subsection (a); and

(C) contain any additional information, including any showing, required by the Director.

(e) Making required statements in assignment of record.—An individual who is under an obligation of assignment of an application for patent may include the required statements under subsections (b) and (c) in the assignment executed by the individual, in lieu of filing such statements separately.

(f) Time for filing.—The applicant for patent shall provide each required oath or declaration under subsection (a), substitute statement under subsection (d), or recorded assignment meeting the requirements of subsection (e) no later than the date on which the issue fee for the patent is paid.

(g) Earlier-filed application containing required statements or substitute statement—

(1) Exception.—The requirements under this section shall not apply to an individual with respect to an application for patent in which the individual is named as the inventor or a joint inventor and that claims the benefit under section 120, 121, 365(c), or 386(c) of the filing of an earlier-filed application, if—

(A) an oath or declaration meeting the requirements of subsection (a) was executed by the individual and was filed in connection with the earlier-filed application;

(B) a substitute statement meeting the requirements of subsection (d) was filed in connection with the earlier filed application with respect to the individual; or

(C) an assignment meeting the requirements of subsection (e) was executed with respect to the earlier-filed application by the individual and was recorded in connection with the earlier-filed application.

(2) Copies of oaths, declarations, statements, or assignments.—Notwithstanding paragraph (1), the Director may require that a copy of the executed oath or declaration, the substitute statement, or the assignment filed in connection with the earlier-filed application be included in the later-filed application.

(h) Supplemental and corrected statements; filing additional statements—

(1) In general.—Any person making a statement required under this section may withdraw, replace, or otherwise correct the statement at any time. If a change is made in the naming of the inventor requiring the filing of 1 or more additional statements under this section, the Director shall establish regulations under which such additional statements may be filed.

(2) Supplemental statements not required.—If an individual has executed an oath or declaration meeting the requirements of subsection (a) or an assignment meeting the requirements of subsection (e) with respect to an application for patent, the Director may not thereafter require that individual to make any additional oath, declaration, or other statement equivalent to those required by this section in connection with the application for patent or any patent issuing thereon.

(3) Savings clause.—A patent shall not be invalid or unenforceable based upon the failure to comply with a requirement under this section if the failure is remedied as provided under paragraph (1).

(i) Acknowledgment of penalties.—Any declaration or statement filed pursuant to this section shall contain an acknowledgment that any willful false statement made in such declaration or statement is punishable under section 1001 of title 18 by fine or imprisonment of not more than 5 years, or both.

History of 35 U.S.C. §115: July 19, 1952, ch. 950, §1, 66 Stat. 799; Aug. 27, 1982, P.L. 97-247, §14(a), 96 Stat. 321; Oct. 21, 1998, P.L. 105-277, §2222(d), 112 Stat. 2681-818; Sept. 16, 2011, P.L. 112-29, §4(a)(1), 125 Stat. 293; Dec. 18, 2012, P.L. 112-211, §102(4), 126 Stat. 1531; Jan. 14, 2013, P.L. 112-274, §1(f), 126 Stat. 2456.

See also 37 C.F.R. §§1.63-1.69.

§116. INVENTORS

Section 116 in its present form will continue to apply for proceedings instituted before Sept. 16, 2012.

When an invention is made by two or more persons jointly, they shall apply for patent jointly and each make the required oath, except as otherwise provided in this title. Inventors may apply for a patent jointly even though (1) they did not physically work together or at the same time, (2) each did not make the same type or amount of contribution, or (3) each did not make a contribution to the subject matter of every claim of the patent.

If a joint inventor refuses to join in an application for patent or cannot be found or reached after diligent effort, the application may be made by the other inventor on behalf of himself and the omitted inventor. The Director, on proof of the pertinent facts and after such notice to the omitted inventor as he prescribes, may grant a patent to the inventor making the application, subject to the same rights which the omitted inventor would have had if he had been joined. The omitted inventor may subsequently join in the application.

Whenever through error a person is named in an application for patent as the inventor, or through error an inventor is not named in an application, and such error arose without any deceptive intention on his part, the Director may permit the application to be amended accordingly, under such terms as he prescribes.

History of 35 U.S.C. §116: July 19, 1952, ch. 950, §1, 66 Stat. 799. Amended Aug. 27, 1982, P.L. 97-247, §6(a), 96 Stat. 320; Nov. 8, 1984, P.L. 98-622, §104(a), 98 Stat. 3384; Nov. 29, 1999, P.L. 106-113, §1000(a)(9), 113 Stat. 1536; Nov. 2, 2002, P.L. 107-273, §13206(b)(1)(B), 116 Stat. 1906.

See also 28 U.S.C. §1928; 37 C.F.R. §§1.45, 1.48, 1.110.

ANNOTATIONS

Bard Peripheral Vascular, Inc. v. W.L. Gore & Assocs., 776 F.3d 837, 845-46, 113 U.S.P.Q.2d 1380, 1385 (Fed.Cir.2015), *overruled on other grounds*, ***Halo Elecs., Inc. v. Pulse Elecs., Inc.***, ___ U.S. ___, 136 S.Ct. 1923 (2016). "Because conception is the touchstone of inventorship, each joint inventor must generally contribute to the conception of the invention. Con-

PRE-AIA §116

ception is precisely defined as existing when a definite and permanent idea of an operative invention, including every feature of the subject matter sought to be patented, is known. In other words, conception is only complete when the idea is so clearly defined in the inventor's mind that only ordinary skill would be necessary to reduce the invention to practice, without extensive research or experimentation. [¶] As to the required degree of contribution to conception, we have recognized that the determination of whether a person is a joint inventor is fact specific, and no bright-line standard will suffice in every case. The underlying principle from our case law is that a joint inventor's contribution must be not insignificant in quality, when that contribution is measured against the dimension of the full invention. [I]f an individual supplies a component essential to an invention, that is an insufficiently significant contribution if the component and the principles of its use were known in the prior art. Moreover, while joint inventors need not 'physically' work together under §116, the statutory word 'jointly' is not mere surplusage. We require that inventors have some open line of communication during or in temporal proximity to their inventive efforts. Critically, each inventor must contribute to the joint arrival at a definite and permanent idea of the invention as it will be used in practice." (Internal quotes omitted.)

Falana v. Kent State Univ., 669 F.3d 1349, 1358, 101 U.S.P.Q.2d 1414, 1421 (Fed.Cir.2012). "This case is simply the application of the well-known principle that conception of a compound requires knowledge of both the chemical structure of the compound and an operative method of making it. Accordingly, this court holds that a putative inventor who envisioned the structure of a novel genus of chemical compounds and contributes the method of making that genus contributes to the conception of that genus. This holding does not mean that such an inventor necessarily has a right to claim inventorship of all species within that genus which are discovered in the future. Once the method of making the novel genus of compounds becomes public knowledge, it is then assimilated into the storehouse of knowledge that comprises ordinary skill in the art. Additionally, joint inventorship arises only 'when collaboration or concerted effort occurs—that is, when the inventors have some open line of communication during or in temporal proximity to their inventive efforts.'"

HIF Bio, Inc. v. Yung Shin Pharms. Indus. Co., 600 F.3d 1347, 1353, 94 U.S.P.Q.2d 1286, 1291 (Fed.Cir. 2010). "[B]ecause this dispute involves *pending* patent applications, [Ps'] requested relief—a declaration of the 'true' inventor—is tantamount to a request for either a modification of inventorship on pending patent applications or an interference proceeding. *At F.3d 1354:* [W]e expressly hold that [35 U.S.C.] §116 does not provide a private right of action to challenge inventorship of a pending patent application. Once a patent issues, however, 35 U.S.C. §256 provides a private right of action to challenge inventorship, and such a challenge arises under [28 U.S.C.] §1338(a). [¶] Given their proper import, §116 and [35 U.S.C.] §135(a) preclude the district court from granting [Ps'] requested relief.... Accordingly, while the district court has jurisdiction over the cause of action, it should have dismissed the claim under [FRCP] 12(b)(6) because no private right of action exists." *But see* ***Camsoft Data Sys. v. Southern Elecs. Sup.***, 756 F.3d 327, 335-36, 111 U.S.P.Q.2d 1321, 1326-27 (5th Cir.2014) (only PTO Director has jurisdiction to hear arguments regarding inventorship for pending patents).

University of Pittsburgh v. Hedrick, 573 F.3d 1290, 1297-98, 91 U.S.P.Q.2d 1423, 1428 (Fed.Cir.2009). "Inventorship is a question of law that we review *de novo*, based on underlying facts which we review for clear error. A joint invention is the product of collaboration between two or more persons working together to solve the problem addressed. The inventors need not work physically together or contemporaneously to be joint inventors; nor must each inventor contribute equally or to each claim of the patent. The inventors named in an issued patent are presumed correct, and a party alleging misjoinder of inventors must prove its case by clear and convincing evidence. The movants must also show that the persons to be removed did not contribute to the invention of any of the allowed claims. [¶] Conception is the touchstone of inventorship under ... §116. It is the formation in the mind of the inventor, of a definite and permanent idea of the complete and operative invention, as it is hereafter to be applied in practice. The test for conception is whether the inventor had an idea that was definite and permanent enough that one skilled in the art could understand the invention; the inventor must prove his conception by corroborating evidence, preferably by showing contemporaneous disclosures. Such corroborating evidence is taken as a whole; conception of an entire invention need not be reflected in a single source. An inventor need not know that his invention will work for conception to be complete. He need only show that he had the complete mental picture and could describe it with particularity; the discovery that the invention actually works is part of its reduction to practice. In a joint invention, each inventor must contribute to the joint arrival at a definite and permanent idea of the invention as it will be used in practice. *At F.3d 1299, U.S.P.Q.2d 1429-30:* Under the 'rule of reason' standard for corroborating evidence, the trial court must consider corroborating evidence in context, make necessary credibility determinations, and assign appropriate probative weight to the evidence to determine whether clear and convincing evidence supports a claim of co-inventorship. Evidence need not always expressly show possession of the invention to corroborate conception, and a court may properly weigh evidence that a claimed attribute is merely an obvious property of a greater discovery at issue." (Internal quotes omitted.)

Symantec Corp. v. Computer Assocs., 522 F.3d 1279, 1295, 86 U.S.P.Q.2d 1449, 1459 (Fed.Cir.2008). "To show co-inventorship, [D] is required to prove his contribution to the conception of the claims by clear and convincing evidence. An alleged co-inventor's testimony, standing alone, cannot rise to the level of clear and convincing evidence; he must supply evidence to corroborate his testimony. [W]hether the co-inventor's testimony has been sufficiently corroborated is evaluated under a rule of reason analysis, which requires that an evaluation of *all* pertinent evidence must be made so that a sound determination of the credibility of the inventor's story may be reached. Corroborating evidence may be in the form of records made contemporaneously with the inventive process, circumstantial evidence of an independent nature, or oral testimony from someone other than the alleged inventor." (Internal quotes omitted.)

Eli Lilly & Co. v. Aradigm Corp., 376 F.3d 1352, 1358-59, 71 U.S.P.Q.2d 1787, 1791 (Fed.Cir.2004). "[S]ection 116 'sets no explicit lower limit on the quantum or quality of inventive contribution required for a person to qualify as a joint inventor.' However, ... a person is a joint inventor only if he contributes to the conception of the claimed invention. The line between actual contributions to conception and the remaining, more prosaic contributions to the inventive process that do not render the contributor a co-inventor is sometimes a difficult one to draw. Contributions to realizing an invention may not amount to a contribution to conception if they merely explain what was 'then state of the art' if they are too far removed from the real-world realization of an invention, or if they are focused solely on such realization. [¶] Joint inventorship under §116 can only arise when collaboration or concerted effort occurs—that is, when the inventors have some open line of communication during or in temporal proximity to their inventive efforts...."

§116. INVENTORS

Section 116 is effective for proceedings instituted on or after Sept. 16, 2012.

(a) Joint inventions.—When an invention is made by two or more persons jointly, they shall apply for patent jointly and each make the required oath, except as otherwise provided in this title. Inventors may apply for a patent jointly even though (1) they did not physically work together or at the same time, (2) each did not make the same type or amount of contribution, or (3) each did not make a contribution to the subject matter of every claim of the patent.

(b) Omitted inventor.—If a joint inventor refuses to join in an application for patent or cannot be found or reached after diligent effort, the application may be made by the other inventor on behalf of himself and the omitted inventor. The Director, on proof of the pertinent facts and after such notice to the omitted inventor as he prescribes, may grant a patent to the inventor making the application, subject to the same rights which the omitted inventor would have had if he had been joined. The omitted inventor may subsequently join in the application.

(c) Correction of errors in application.—Whenever through error a person is named in an application for patent as the inventor, or through error an inventor is not named in an application, the Director may permit the application to be amended accordingly, under such terms as he prescribes.

History of 35 U.S.C. §116: July 19, 1952, ch. 950, §1, 66 Stat. 799; Aug. 27, 1982, P.L. 97-247, §6(a), 96 Stat. 320; Nov. 8, 1984, P.L. 98-622, §104(a), 98 Stat. 3384; Nov. 29, 1999, P.L. 106-113, §1000(a)(9), 113 Stat. 1536; Nov. 2, 2002, P.L. 107-273, §13206(b)(1)(B), 116 Stat. 1906; Sept. 16, 2011, P.L. 112-29, §20(a), 125 Stat. 333.

See also 28 U.S.C. §1928; 37 C.F.R. §§1.45, 1.48, 1.110.

§117. DEATH OR INCAPACITY OF INVENTOR

Legal representatives of deceased inventors and of those under legal incapacity may make application for patent upon compliance with the requirements and on the same terms and conditions applicable to the inventor.

History of 35 U.S.C. §117: July 19, 1952, ch. 950, §1, 66 Stat. 799.
See also 37 C.F.R. §§1.42, 1.43.

§118. FILING BY OTHER THAN INVENTOR

Section 118 is effective for patent applications filed before Sept. 16, 2012.

Whenever an inventor refuses to execute an application for patent, or cannot be found or reached after diligent effort, a person to whom the inventor has assigned or agreed in writing to assign the invention or who otherwise shows sufficient proprietary interest in the matter justifying such action, may make application for patent on behalf of and as agent for the inventor on proof of the pertinent facts and a showing that such action is necessary to preserve the rights of the parties or to prevent irreparable damage; and the Director may grant a patent to such inventor upon such notice to him as the Director deems sufficient, and on compliance with such regulations as he prescribes.

History of 35 U.S.C. §118: July 19, 1952, ch. 950, §1, 66 Stat. 799; Nov. 29, 1999, P.L. 106-113, §1000(a)(9), 113 Stat. 1536; Nov. 2, 2002, P.L. 107-273, §13206(b)(1)(B), 116 Stat. 1906.
See also 37 C.F.R. §1.46.

§118. FILING BY OTHER THAN INVENTOR

Section 118 is effective for patent applications filed on or after Sept. 16, 2012.

A person to whom the inventor has assigned or is under an obligation to assign the invention may make an application for patent. A person who otherwise shows sufficient proprietary interest in the matter may make an application for patent on behalf of and as agent for the inventor on proof of the pertinent facts and a showing that such action is appropriate to preserve the rights of the parties. If the Director grants a patent on an application filed under this section by a person other than the inventor, the patent shall be granted to the real party in interest and upon such notice to the inventor as the Director considers to be sufficient.

History of 35 U.S.C. §118: July 19, 1952, ch. 950, §1, 66 Stat. 799; Nov. 29, 1999, P.L. 106-113, §1000(a)(9), 113 Stat. 1536; Nov. 2, 2002, P.L. 107-273, §13206(b)(1)(B), 116 Stat. 1906; Sept. 16, 2011, P.L. 112-29, §4(b)(1), 125 Stat. 296.
See also 37 C.F.R. §1.46.

§119. BENEFIT OF EARLIER FILING DATE; RIGHT OF PRIORITY

Section 119(a) in its present form will continue to apply for applications and patents issued thereon that were filed before Mar. 16, 2013. Section 119(a) in its present form will also continue to apply for patent applications and patents issued thereon if the filing date of the earliest application for which the patent or application is entitled under §119, §365(a), §365(b), §120, §121, or §365(c) falls before Mar. 16, 2013, unless the application or patent has ever contained (1) a claim to a claimed invention that has an "effective filing date," as defined in §100(i), p. 495, on or after Mar. 16, 2013; or (2) a specific reference under §120, §121, or §365(c) to any patent or application that ever contained such a claim. See transition note for amended §119, p. 572.

(a) An application for patent for an invention filed in this country by any person who has, or whose legal representatives or assigns have, previously regularly filed an application for a patent for the same invention in a foreign country which affords similar privileges in the case of applications filed in the United States or to citizens of the United States, or in a WTO member country, shall have the same effect as the same application would have if filed in this country on the date on which the application for patent for the same invention was first filed in such foreign country, if the application in this country is filed within 12 months from the earliest date on which such foreign application was filed; but no patent shall be granted on any application for patent for an invention which had been patented or described in a printed publication in any country more than one year before the date of the actual filing of the application in this country, or which had been in public use or on sale in this country more than one year prior to such filing. The Director may prescribe regulations, including the requirement for payment of the fee specified in section 41(a)(7), pursuant to which the 12-month period set forth in this subsection may be extended by an additional 2 months if the delay in filing the application in this country within the 12-month period was unintentional.

(b)(1) No application for patent shall be entitled to this right of priority unless a claim is filed in the

Patent and Trademark Office, identifying the foreign application by specifying the application number on that foreign application, the intellectual property authority or country in or for which the application was filed, and the date of filing the application, at such time during the pendency of the application as required by the Director.

(2) The Director may consider the failure of the applicant to file a timely claim for priority as a waiver of any such claim. The Director may establish procedures, including the requirement for payment of the fee specified in section 41(a)(7), to accept an unintentionally delayed claim under this section.

(3) The Director may require a certified copy of the original foreign application, specification, and drawings upon which it is based, a translation if not in the English language, and such other information as the Director considers necessary. Any such certification shall be made by the foreign intellectual property authority in which the foreign application was filed and show the date of the application and of the filing of the specification and other papers.

(c) In like manner and subject to the same conditions and requirements, the right provided in this section may be based upon a subsequent regularly filed application in the same foreign country instead of the first filed foreign application, provided that any foreign application filed prior to such subsequent application has been withdrawn, abandoned, or otherwise disposed of, without having been laid open to public inspection and without leaving any rights outstanding, and has not served, nor thereafter shall serve, as a basis for claiming a right of priority.

(d) Applications for inventors' certificates filed in a foreign country in which applicants have a right to apply, at their discretion, either for a patent or for an inventor's certificate shall be treated in this country in the same manner and have the same effect for purpose of the right of priority under this section as applications for patents, subject to the same conditions and requirements of this section as apply to applications for patents, provided such applicants are entitled to the benefits of the Stockholm Revision of the Paris Convention at the time of such filing.

(e)(1) An application for patent filed under section 111(a) or section 363 for an invention disclosed in the manner provided by section 112(a) (other than the requirement to disclose the best mode) in a provisional application filed under section 111(b), by an inventor or inventors named in the provisional application, shall have the same effect, as to such invention, as though filed on the date of the provisional application filed under section 111(b), if the application for patent filed under section 111(a) or section 363 is filed not later than 12 months after the date on which the provisional application was filed and if it contains or is amended to contain a specific reference to the provisional application. The Director may prescribe regulations, including the requirement for payment of the fee specified in section 41(a)(7), pursuant to which the 12-month period set forth in this subsection may be extended by an additional 2 months if the delay in filing the application under section 111(a) or section 363 within the 12-month period was unintentional. No application shall be entitled to the benefit of an earlier filed provisional application under this subsection unless an amendment containing the specific reference to the earlier filed provisional application is submitted at such time during the pendency of the application as required by the Director. The Director may consider the failure to submit such an amendment within that time period as a waiver of any benefit under this subsection. The Director may establish procedures, including the payment of the fee specified in section 41(a)(7), to accept an unintentionally delayed submission of an amendment under this subsection.

(2) A provisional application filed under section 111(b) may not be relied upon in any proceeding in the Patent and Trademark Office unless the fee set forth in subparagraph (A) or (C) of section 41(a)(1) has been paid.

(3) If the day that is 12 months after the filing date of a provisional application falls on a Saturday, Sunday, or Federal holiday within the District of Columbia, the period of pendency of the provisional application shall be extended to the next succeeding secular or business day. For an application for patent filed under section 363 in a Receiving Office other than the Patent and Trademark Office, the 12-month and additional 2-month period set forth in this subsection shall be extended as provided under the treaty and Regulations as defined in section 351.

(f) Applications for plant breeder's rights filed in a WTO member country (or in a foreign UPOV Contracting Party) shall have the same effect for the purpose of the right of priority under subsections (a) through (c) of this section as applications for patents, subject to the same conditions and requirements of this section as apply to applications for patents.

(g) As used in this section—

(1) the term "WTO member country" has the same meaning as the term is defined in section 104(b)(2) of this title; and

(2) the term "UPOV Contracting Party" means a member of the International Convention for the Protection of New Varieties of Plants.

History of 35 U.S.C. §119: July 19, 1952, ch. 950, §1, 66 Stat. 800; Oct. 3, 1961, P.L. 87-333, §1, 75 Stat. 748; July 28, 1972, P.L. 92-358, §1, 86 Stat. 501; Jan. 2, 1975, P.L. 93-596, §1, 88 Stat. 1949; Dec. 8, 1994, P.L. 103-465, §532(b)(1), 108 Stat. 4985; Nov. 29, 1999, P.L. 106-113, §1000(a)(9), 113 Stat. 1536; Nov. 2, 2002, P.L. 107-273, §13206(b)(2), 116 Stat. 1906; Dec. 18, 2013, P.L. 112-211, §§201(c)(1), 202(b)(2), 126 Stat. 1534, 1536.

See also 37 C.F.R. §§1.55, 1.109; Paris Convention arts. 4, 5; TRIPs pt. II, §5.

§119. BENEFIT OF EARLIER FILING DATE; RIGHT OF PRIORITY

Section 119 is effective for patent applications and patents issued on those applications that have ever contained (1) a claim to a claimed invention that has an "effective filing date," as defined in §100(i), p. 495, on or after Mar. 16, 2013; or (2) a specific reference under §120, §121, or §365(c) to any patent or application that ever contained such a claim. Section 119 is not effective for patent applications filed before Mar. 16, 2013, or patents issued on those applications.

(a) An application for patent for an invention filed in this country by any person who has, or whose legal representatives or assigns have, previously regularly filed an application for a patent for the same invention in a foreign country which affords similar privileges in the case of applications filed in the United States or to citizens of the United States, or in a WTO member country, shall have the same effect as the same application would have if filed in this country on the date on which the application for patent for the same invention was first filed in such foreign country, if the application in this country is filed within 12 months from the earliest date on which such foreign application was filed. The Director may prescribe regulations, including the requirement for payment of the fee specified in section 41(a)(7), pursuant to which the 12-month period set forth in this subsection may be extended by an additional 2 months if the delay in filing the application in this country within the 12-month period was unintentional.

(b)(1) No application for patent shall be entitled to this right of priority unless a claim is filed in the Patent and Trademark Office, identifying the foreign application by specifying the application number on that foreign application, the intellectual property authority or country in or for which the application was filed, and the date of filing the application, at such time during the pendency of the application as required by the Director.

(2) The Director may consider the failure of the applicant to file a timely claim for priority as a waiver of any such claim. The Director may establish procedures, including the requirement for payment of the fee specified in section 41(a)(7), to accept an unintentionally delayed claim under this section.

(3) The Director may require a certified copy of the original foreign application, specification, and drawings upon which it is based, a translation if not in the English language, and such other information as the Director considers necessary. Any such certification shall be made by the foreign intellectual property authority in which the foreign application was filed and show the date of the application and of the filing of the specification and other papers.

(c) In like manner and subject to the same conditions and requirements, the right provided in this section may be based upon a subsequent regularly filed application in the same foreign country instead of the first filed foreign application, provided that any foreign application filed prior to such subsequent application has been withdrawn, abandoned, or otherwise disposed of, without having been laid open to public inspection and without leaving any rights outstanding, and has not served, nor thereafter shall serve, as a basis for claiming a right of priority.

(d) Applications for inventors' certificates filed in a foreign country in which applicants have a right to apply, at their discretion, either for a patent or for an inventor's certificate shall be treated in this country in the same manner and have the same effect for purpose of the right of priority under this section as applications for patents, subject to the same conditions and requirements of this section as apply to applications for patents, provided such applicants are entitled to the benefits of the Stockholm Revision of the Paris Convention at the time of such filing.

(e)(1) An application for patent filed under section 111(a) or section 363 for an invention disclosed in the manner provided by section 112(a) (other than the requirement to disclose the best mode) in a provisional application filed under section 111(b), by an inventor or inventors named in the provisional application, shall have the same effect, as to such invention, as though filed on the date of the provisional application filed under section 111(b), if the application for patent filed under section 111(a) or section 363 is filed not later than 12 months after the date on which the provisional application was filed and if it contains or is amended to contain a specific reference to the provisional application. The Director may prescribe regulations, including the requirement for payment of the fee specified in section 41(a)(7), pursuant to which the 12-month period set forth in this subsection may be extended by an additional 2 months if the delay in filing the application under section 111(a) or section 363 within the 12-month period was unintentional. No application shall be entitled to the benefit of an earlier filed provisional application under this subsection unless an amendment containing the specific reference to the earlier filed provisional application is submitted at such time during the pendency of the application as required by the Director. The Director may consider the failure to submit such an amendment within that time period as a waiver of any benefit under this subsection. The Director may establish procedures, including the payment of the fee specified in section 41(a)(7), to accept an unintentionally delayed submission of an amendment under this subsection.

(2) A provisional application filed under section 111(b) may not be relied upon in any proceeding in the Patent and Trademark Office unless the fee set forth in subparagraph (A) or (C) of section 41(a)(1) has been paid.

(3) If the day that is 12 months after the filing date of a provisional application falls on a Saturday, Sunday, or Federal holiday within the District of Columbia, the period of pendency of the provisional application shall be extended to the next succeeding secular or business day. For an application for patent filed under section 363 in a Receiving Office other than the Patent and Trademark Office, the 12-month and additional 2-month period set forth in this subsection shall be extended as provided under the treaty and Regulations as defined in section 351.

(f) Applications for plant breeder's rights filed in a WTO member country (or in a foreign UPOV Contracting Party) shall have the same effect for the purpose of the right of priority under subsections (a) through (c) of this section as applications for patents, subject to the same conditions and requirements of this section as apply to applications for patents.

(g) As used in this section—

(1) the term "WTO member country" has the same meaning as the term is defined in section 104(b)(2); and

(2) the term "UPOV Contracting Party" means a member of the International Convention for the Protection of New Varieties of Plants.

History of 35 U.S.C. §119: July 19, 1952, ch. 950, §1, 66 Stat. 800; Oct. 3, 1961, P.L. 87-333, §1, 75 Stat. 748; July 28, 1972, P.L. 92-358, §1, 86 Stat. 501; Jan. 2, 1975, P.L. 93-596, §1, 88 Stat. 1949; Dec. 8, 1994, P.L. 103-465, §532(b)(1), 108 Stat. 4985; Nov. 29, 1999, P.L. 106-113, §1000(a)(9), 113 Stat. 1536; Nov. 2, 2002, P.L. 107-273, §13206(b)(2), 116 Stat. 1906; Sept. 16, 2011, P.L. 112-29, §§3(g)(6), 15(b), 20(j)(1), 125 Stat. 288, 328, 335; Dec. 18, 2013, P.L. 112-211, §§201(c)(1), 202(b)(2), 126 Stat. 1534, 1536.

See also 37 C.F.R. §§1.55, 1.109; Paris Convention arts. 4, 5; TRIPs pt. II, §5.

ANNOTATIONS

Star Sci., Inc. v. R.J. Reynolds Tobacco Co., 655 F.3d 1364, 1371, 99 U.S.P.Q.2d 1924, 1929 (Fed.Cir. 2011). "Claims deserve the provisional application's earlier filing date so long as that application contains adequate written description under 35 U.S.C. §112. Consistent with ... §112 ¶1, the written description of the provisional application must enable one of ordinary skill in the art to practice the invention claimed in the non-provisional application."

E.I. du Pont de Nemours & Co. v. MacDermid Printing Solutions, L.L.C., 525 F.3d 1353, 1358, 86 U.S.P.Q.2d 1732, 1737-38 (Fed.Cir.2008). "Under [35 U.S.C. §119(e)(1)], four requirements must be met for a non-provisional application to claim priority to a provisional application: (1) the provisional must comply with the requirements of [35 U.S.C.] §112, ¶1, and the non-provisional must be for the same invention; (2) the non-provisional must be filed within 12 months of the provisional; (3) there must be an overlap of inventorship; and (4) the non-provisional must include a specific reference to the provisional. *At F.3d 1360-61:* This court has held that 'for [a] non-provisional utility application to be afforded the priority date of the provisional application, the two applications must share at least one common inventor.' *At U.S.P.Q.2d 1739:* Section 119(e)(1) requires, for a claim of priority, that the non-provisional application contain 'a specific reference to the provisional application.' Under [Manual of Patent

POST-AIA §119

Examining Procedure] §201.11, the specific reference can be either in the first sentence of the specification or in the application data sheet. 'If the specific reference is only contained in the application data sheet, then the benefit claim information will be included on the front page of any patent or patent application publication, but will not be included in the first sentence(s) of the specification.'"

Frazer v. Schlegel, 498 F.3d 1283, 1287, 83 U.S.P.Q.2d 1850, 1853 (Fed.Cir.2007). "In accordance with U.S. law, when the priority claim is based on subject matter disclosed in a foreign patent application whose filing date is properly claimed, ... the foreign application has the same effect as if filed in the U.S. The invention must be 'disclosed in the manner provided by the first paragraph of [35 U.S.C.] §112.' [¶] Constructive reduction to practice does not invoke different standards whether the priority document is foreign or domestic. When interference priority is at issue, constructive reduction to practice of a count may be established by disclosure of an embodiment within the count. *At U.S.P.Q.2d 1854:* Although the Board analyzed the Australian application in terms of 'conception,' when reliance is on a patent document already filed, the question is whether the document discloses the invention of the count by meeting the written description and enablement requirements of ... §112 ¶1, for a filed application serves as a constructive reduction to practice of its content."

Boston Sci. Scimed, Inc. v. Medtronic Vascular, Inc., 497 F.3d 1293, 1296-97, 83 U.S.P.Q.2d 1669, 1671 (Fed.Cir.2007). "At issue here is whether ... §119(a) permits an applicant for a U.S. patent to benefit from the priority of a foreign application previously filed by an entity that was not acting on behalf of the U.S. applicant at the time of filing. We hold that it does not."

Bayer AG v. Schein Pharms., 301 F.3d 1306, 1312, 64 U.S.P.Q.2d 1001, 1005 (Fed.Cir.2002). "[W]hether an applicant can claim the benefit of an earlier-filed foreign application under [35 U.S.C.] §119 in order to defeat a [35 U.S.C.] §102(d) bar presents a pure issue of law, which receives plenary review."

New Railhead Mfg. v. Vermeer Mfg., 298 F.3d 1290, 1295-96, 63 U.S.P.Q.2d 1843, 1847 (Fed.Cir.2002). "Although we have recently noted the particular usefulness of the 'possession' inquiry when a patentee claims an earlier filing date under 35 U.S.C. §119, we have at the same time cautioned that the written description requirement [of 35 U.S.C. §112] is not subsumed by the possession inquiry. ... Identity of that which is described, however, is necessary: What is claimed by the patent application must be the same as what is disclosed in the specification...." (Internal quotes omitted.)

In re Ziegler, 992 F.2d 1197, 1200-01, 26 U.S.P.Q.2d 1600, 1603 (Fed.Cir.1993). "A foreign patent application must meet the requirements of 35 U.S.C. §112 [¶1] in order for a later filed U.S. application to be entitled to the benefit of the foreign filing date under 35 U.S.C. §119. The applicant for a U.S. patent bears the burden of establishing its entitlement to the filing date of a previously filed application. [¶] Whether disclosure is enabling is a question of law. The how to use prong of §112 incorporates as a matter of law the requirement of 35 U.S.C. §101 that the specification disclose as a matter of fact a practical utility for the invention. If the application fails as a matter of fact to satisfy 35 U.S.C. §101, then the application also fails as a matter of law to enable one of ordinary skill in the art to use the invention under 35 U.S.C. §112. The benefit of the foreign application's filing date cannot then be obtained under 35 U.S.C. §119. *At F.2d 1203, U.S.P.Q.2d 1605:* To satisfy 35 U.S.C. §101, to be able to serve as a predicate for a §119 claim, the disclosure must assert a 'specific benefit ... in currently available form.'" *See also* ***Transco Prods. v. Performance Contracting, Inc.***, 38 F.3d 551, 558 n.7, 32 U.S.P.Q.2d 1077, 1082 n.7 (Fed.Cir.1994).

In re Gosteli, 872 F.2d 1008, 1010, 10 U.S.P.Q.2d 1614, 1616 (Fed.Cir.1989). "The reference to the 'invention' in §119 clearly refers to what the claims define, not what is disclosed in the foreign application."

Utter v. Hiraga, 845 F.2d 993, 998, 6 U.S.P.Q.2d 1709, 1713 (Fed.Cir.1988). "A party who ... relies on an earlier-filed application under 35 U.S.C. §§119 or 120 has the burden to show that the foreign or parent application supports later-added claims under 35 U.S.C. §112 ¶1, regardless of whether that party is the junior or senior party in an interference."

Stein Assocs. v. Heat & Control, Inc., 748 F.2d 653, 658, 223 U.S.P.Q. 1277, 1280 (Fed.Cir.1984). Section 119 "deals only with an application filed in the PTO and claiming priority based on a foreign application. It has no relation whatever to the determination by a British court under British law on whether [British patent owner] is entitled to claim for its British patents the priority benefit of the U.S. filing date of its patent application."

In re Mulder, 716 F.2d 1542, 1545, 219 U.S.P.Q. 189, 193 (Fed.Cir.1983). Section 119 "entitles appellants to rely on their [foreign-country] filing date for a constructive reduction to practice. Section 119 is a 'patent-saving' provision for the benefit of applicants, and an applicant is entitled to rely on it as a constructive reduction to practice to overcome the date of a reference under [PTO] Rule 131 [for an affidavit of prior invention]. If entitlement to a foreign filing date can completely overcome a reference we see no reason why it cannot partially overcome a reference by providing the constructive reduction to practice element of proof required by Rule 131. It is a *statutory* priority right which cannot be interfered with by a construction placed on a PTO rule."

Vogel v. Jones, 486 F.2d 1068, 1072, 179 U.S.P.Q. 425, 428 (C.C.P.A.1973). "[A]n applicant for a U.S. patent can rely for priority on the 'first filed' application by an assignee on his behalf."

In re Hilmer, 424 F.2d 1108, 1112-13, 165 U.S.P.Q. 255, 258 (C.C.P.A.1970). 35 U.S.C. §119 "does not remove the limitation of [35 U.S.C.] §102(g) found in the phrase 'in this country.' [¶] [S]ection 119 and [35 U.S.C.] §104 relate, respectively, only to what an applicant or patentee may and ... may not do to *protect himself* against patent-defeating events occurring between his invention date and his U.S. filing date." *See also* ***Studiengesellschaft Kohle mbH v. Eastman Kodak Co.***, 616 F.2d 1315, 1337, 206 U.S.P.Q. 577, 597 (5th Cir. 1980).

In re Hilmer, 359 F.2d 859, 862, 149 U.S.P.Q. 480, 482 (C.C.P.A.1966). 35 U.S.C. §119 "only deals with 'right of priority.' The section does not provide for the use of a U.S. patent as an anticipatory reference as of its foreign filing date. *At F.2d 878, U.S.P.Q. 496:* [T]he prohibitions of [35 U.S.C.] §104, the limitations in [35 U.S.C.] §102(a) and 102(g) to 'in this country,' and the specifying in §102(e) of an application filed 'in the U.S.' clearly demonstrate a policy in our patent statutes to the effect that knowledge and acts in a foreign country are not to defeat the rights of applicants for patents, except as applicants may become involved in *priority* disputes. We think it follows that §119 must be interpreted as giving only a positive right or benefit to an applicant who has first filed abroad to *protect him* against possible intervening patent-defeating events in *obtaining* a patent. ... So construed, it has no effect on the effective date of a U.S. patent as a reference under §102(e)." *See also* ***Studiengesellschaft Kohle mbH v. Eastman Kodak Co.***, 616 F.2d 1315, 1337, 206 U.S.P.Q. 577, 597 (5th Cir.1980).

§120. BENEFIT OF EARLIER FILING DATE IN THE UNITED STATES

The amendment to §120 is effective May 13, 2015. Section 120 is effective for patent applications and patents issued on those applications that contain or contained a claim to a claimed invention that has an effective filing date on or after Mar. 16, 2013, or for any applications or patents that contain or contained a claim to a specific reference under §120, §121, or §365(c) that have an effective filing date on or after Mar. 16, 2013.

An application for patent for an invention disclosed in the manner provided by section 112(a) (other than the requirement to disclose the best mode) in an application previously filed in the United States, or as provided by section 363 or 385, which names an inventor or joint inventor in the previously filed application shall have the same effect, as to such invention, as though filed on the date of the prior application, if filed before the patenting or abandonment of or termination of proceedings on the first application or on an application similarly entitled to the benefit of the filing date of the first application and if it contains or is amended to contain a specific reference to the earlier filed application. No application shall be entitled to the benefit of an earlier filed application under this section unless an amendment containing the specific reference to the earlier filed application is submitted at such time during the pendency of the application as required by the Director. The Director may consider the failure to submit such an amendment within that time period as a waiver of any benefit under this section. The Director may establish procedures, including the requirement for payment of the fee specified in section 41(a)(7), to accept an unintentionally delayed submission of an amendment under this section.

History of 35 U.S.C. §120: July 19, 1952, ch. 950, §1, 66 Stat. 800; Nov. 14, 1975, P.L. 94-131, §9, 89 Stat. 691; Nov. 8, 1984, P.L. 98-622, §104(b), 98 Stat. 3385; Nov. 29, 1999, P.L. 106-113, §1000(a)(9), 113 Stat. 1536; Sept. 16, 2011, P.L. 112-29, §§3(f), 15(b), 20(j)(1), 125 Stat. 288, 328, 335; May 13, 2015, P.L. 112-211, §102(5), 126 Stat. 1531; Dec. 18, 2013, P.L. 112-211, §202(b)(3), 126 Stat. 1536.

See also 35 U.S.C. §§363, 385; 37 C.F.R. §§1.78, 1.109; Paris Convention arts. 4, 5; Patent Cooperation Treaty.

ANNOTATIONS

Generally

Encyclopaedia Britannica, Inc. v. Alpine Elecs., 609 F.3d 1345, 1349, 95 U.S.P.Q.2d 1660, 1663 (Fed.Cir. 2010). "The sole issue on appeal, one of first impression for this court, is whether … §120 requires an intermediate application in a priority chain to 'contain a specific reference to the earlier filed application.' *At F.3d 1352, U.S.P.Q.2d 1665:* We conclude that §120 requires each application in the chain of priority to refer to the prior applications."

Technology Licensing Corp. v. Videotek, Inc., 545 F.3d 1316, 1326, 88 U.S.P.Q.2d 1865, 1872 (Fed.Cir. 2008). "[I]n a chain of continuing applications, a claim in a later application receives the benefit of the filing date of an earlier application so long as the disclosure in the earlier application meets the requirements of 35 U.S.C. §112, ¶1, including the written description requirement, with respect to that claim. *At F.3d 1327, U.S.P.Q.2d 1873:* [P], alleging infringement by [D], has the burden of persuasion that [D] infringes, under the usual civil law standard of preponderance of the evidence. *At F.3d 1328, U.S.P.Q.2d 1874:* Assuming then that [P's] evidence and argument in support of the earlier filing date is now before the court, the burden of going forward again shifts to the proponent of the invalidity defense, [D], to convince the court that [P] is not entitled to the benefit of the earlier filing date. 'Convince' is the operative word, because if the court is not persuaded by clear and convincing evidence that [D] is correct, [D] has failed to carry its ultimate burden of persuasion, and its defense of invalidity, based on anticipation …, fails."

Pfizer, Inc. v. Teva Pharms., 518 F.3d 1353, 1359-60, 86 U.S.P.Q.2d 1001, 1005-06 (Fed.Cir.2008). "Although both are types of continuing applications, divisionals and [continuations in part (CIPs)] differ significantly in at least one respect: a divisional application contains an identical disclosure to its parent application, but a CIP introduces new matter. A CIP is 'just what its name implies. It partly continues subject matter disclosed in a prior application, but it adds new subject matter not disclosed in the prior application.' A divisional application is defined as '[a] later application for an independent or distinct invention, carved out of a pending application and disclosing and claiming only subject matter disclosed in the earlier or parent application….' A divisional application 'is often filed as a result of a restriction requirement made by the examiner.'"

Studiengesellschaft Kohle, mbH v. Shell Oil, 112 F.3d 1561, 1564, 42 U.S.P.Q.2d 1674, 1677 (Fed.Cir. 1997). "[A] claim complies with … §120 and acquires an earlier filing date if, and only if, it could have been added to an earlier application without introducing new matter."

Lemelson v. TRW, Inc., 760 F.2d 1254, 1266-67, 225 U.S.P.Q. 697, 706 (Fed.Cir.1985). "In order for [two patents in question] to be entitled under … §120 to the filing date of an earlier application in the chain of applications of which they are part, it must be shown that as to the inventions claimed there has been 'continuing disclosure through the chain of applications, without hiatus.'"

In re Costello, 717 F.2d 1346, 1348-49, 219 U.S.P.Q. 389, 390-91 (Fed.Cir.1983). "This appeal presents the question whether appellants are entitled to rely on an application, abandoned prior to the effective date of a reference, as a constructive reduction to practice to overcome that reference, where appellants later filed a substantially identical application which is not entitled under [35 U.S.C.] §120 to the date of the abandoned application. [¶] Even if an applicant is unable to secure an effective filing date previous to the effective date of a prior art reference under §120, the applicant may overcome a reference by evidence of prior invention. A prior art reference that is not a statutory bar may be overcome by two generally recognized methods. The most common way to 'antedate' a reference is to submit an affidavit satisfying the requirements of [PTO] Rule 131. … An applicant may also overcome a reference by showing that the relevant disclosure is a description of the applicant's own work. The pertinent inquiry is under 35 U.S.C. §102(e). Appellants can overcome a reference by showing that they were in possession of their invention prior to the effective date of the reference. The real issue is whether *all* the evidence, including the references, truly shows knowledge by another *prior to the time appellants made their invention* or whether it shows the contrary. *At F.2d 1350 n.14, U.S.P.Q. 392 n.14:* [R]eviewed as documentary evidence, the original application is not accorded the 'same effect' as if the requirements of §120 had been satisfied. The filing is not relied on as a legally operative reduction to practice, but rather, as evidence. [S]ection 120 governs the receipt of the same benefit as if the second application were filed on the date of the filing of the original application. Thus, no perturbation of §120 results from consideration of the filing of the original application merely as evidence of conception of the invention." (Internal quotes omitted.)

In re Bauman, 683 F.2d 405, 407, 214 U.S.P.Q. 585, 587 (C.C.P.A.1982). "The basic requirements of §120 are copendency, continuity of disclosure and inventorship, and reference to the earlier application."

In re Hogan, 559 F.2d 595, 604, 194 U.S.P.Q. 527, 536 (C.C.P.A.1977). "Nothing in [35 U.S.C.] §120 limits its application to any specific grounds for rejection, or permits the examiner, denied use of references to reject or to require narrowing of a claim under [35 U.S.C.] §102 or §103, to achieve the same result by use of the same references under [35 U.S.C.] §112. Just as justice and reason require application of §112 in the same manner to applicants and examiners, symmetry in the law, and evenness of its application, require that §120 be held applicable to all bases for rejection, that its words 'same effect' be given their full meaning and intent."

§112, ¶1 (& amended §112(a))

For more annotations on this topic, see 35 U.S.C. §112, p. 552.

PowerOasis, Inc. v. T-Mobile USA, Inc., 522 F.3d 1299, 1306, 86 U.S.P.Q.2d 1385, 1389-90 (Fed.Cir.2008). "'[A] patent application is entitled to the benefit of the filing date of an earlier filed application only if the disclosure of the earlier application provides support for the claims of the later application, as required by 35 U.S.C. §112.' [¶] To satisfy the written description requirement the disclosure of the prior application must 'convey with reasonable clarity to those skilled in the art that, as of the filing date sought, [inventor] was in possession *of the invention*.' While a prior application need not contain precisely the same words as are found in the asserted claims, ... the prior application must indicate to a person skilled in the art that the inventor was 'in possession' of the invention as later claimed. 'Entitlement to a filing date does not extend to subject matter which is not disclosed, but would be obvious over what is expressly disclosed.' [¶] [T]o satisfy the written description requirement, 'the missing descriptive matter must necessarily be present in [original] application's specification such that one skilled in the art would recognize such a disclosure.' This requires that the written description actually or inherently disclose the claim element."

Reiffin v. Microsoft Corp., 214 F.3d 1342, 1346, 54 U.S.P.Q.2d 1915, 1918 (Fed.Cir.2000). "Although [35 U.S.C.] §120 incorporates the requirements of [35 U.S.C.] §112 ¶1, these requirements and the statutory mechanism allowing the benefit of an earlier filing date are separate provisions with distinct consequences. In accordance with §120, claims to subject matter in a later-filed application not supported by an ancestor application in terms of §112 ¶1 are not invalidated; they simply do not receive the benefit of the earlier application's filing date."

Tronzo v. Biomet, Inc., 156 F.3d 1154, 1158, 47 U.S.P.Q.2d 1829, 1832 (Fed.Cir.1998). "To meet [the] requirement [of complying with the written-description requirement of 35 U.S.C. §112, ¶1], the disclosure of the earlier application, the parent, must reasonably convey to one of skill in the art that the inventor possessed the later-claimed subject matter at the time the parent application was filed. A disclosure in a parent application that merely renders the later-claimed invention obvious is not sufficient to meet the written description requirement; the disclosure must describe the claimed invention with all its limitations. Because the issue of whether the written description requirement has been satisfied is a question of fact, we must determine whether substantial evidence supports the jury's verdict that the requirement has been met." *See also* ***Tenneco Chems. v. William T. Burnett & Co.***, 691 F.2d 658, 662, 216 U.S.P.Q. 846, 849 (4th Cir.1982).

Baxter Int'l v. McGaw, Inc., 149 F.3d 1321, 1333-34, 47 U.S.P.Q.2d 1225, 1234 (Fed.Cir.1998). "While we agree that the evidence is clear that [P] intended to file claims 60-124, [35 U.S.C.] §120 does not require an intent to file a complete application, it requires a divisional application to be filed in compliance with [35 U.S.C.] §112 before the parent application is abandoned. [¶] In instructing the PTO to ignore claims 1-59 as of the time the application was received at the PTO, [P] has essentially stated that claims 1-59 were never part of the application from the beginning. These claims were not submitted as part of the original application due to the clear instruction of the applicant to cancel these claims upon receipt. ... Because [P] filed an application without any claims, the application failed to meet the statutory requirement that the 'specification shall conclude with one or more claims particularly pointing out and distinctly claiming the subject matter which the applicant regards as his invention.' Therefore, because [P's] submission failed to meet the requirements of §112, it also failed to meet the definition of 'application' in 35 U.S.C. §111 and is not an 'application' entitled to the filing date of [original] application under §120."

In re Daniels, 144 F.3d 1452, 1456, 46 U.S.P.Q.2d 1788, 1790 (Fed.Cir.1998). "[W]hen an issue of priority arises under [35 U.S.C.] §120, one looks to the drawings of the earlier application for disclosure of the subject matter claimed in the later application. The inquiry is simply to determine whether the inventor had possession at the earlier date of what was claimed at the later date. *At F.3d 1457, U.S.P.Q.2d 1791:* The Board was incorrect in holding that any change in the design defeats a priority claim as a matter of law. As for any application asserting a priority claim, §120 requires that the subject matter for which priority is requested must be disclosed in accordance with the requirements of [35 U.S.C.] §112."

Modine Mfg. v. U.S. Int'l Trade Comm'n, 75 F.3d 1545, 1556, 37 U.S.P.Q.2d 1609, 1617 (Fed.Cir.1996). "A later application is entitled to the earlier filing date for all common subject matter that is contained in the earlier application, whether the subject matter appears in the body of the specification or in the claims or drawings."

U.S. Steel Corp. v. Phillips Pet., 865 F.2d 1247, 1251, 9 U.S.P.Q.2d 1461, 1464 (Fed.Cir.1989). "'[A]pplication sufficiency under [35 U.S.C.] §112, [¶1], must be judged as of the filing date.' In the context of [35 U.S.C.] §120, ... focusing on the filing date requires that the claim of [P's patent] be treated as though it were filed in 1953 [because patent was filed as a continuation-in-part of a 1953 application]. Only if that claim would at that time have been correctly rejected for lack of support in the 1953 specification may the patentee be denied use of §120 to predate the intervening reference to [allegedly anticipatory patent]."

Collateral Estoppel

In re Szwarc, 319 F.2d 277, 282, 138 U.S.P.Q. 208, 212 (C.C.P.A.1963). We must "determine, by comparing the appealed claims and the claims rejected in the parent case, whether 'the invention' of the appealed claims is the same or is different from 'the invention' in the prior [claims rejected by the Board of Patent Appeals]. Only after such a comparison can it be decided if estoppel by judgment or collateral estoppel prevents us from making a determination of whether, under ... §120, the appealed claims are entitled to the benefit of the filing date of the earlier filed parent application." *See also* ***Gould v. Mossinghoff***, 711 F.2d 396, 398-99, 219 U.S.P.Q. 393, 395 (D.C.Cir.1983).

Continuation Applications

Immersion Corp. v. HTC Corp., 826 F.3d 1357, 1359, 119 U.S.P.Q.2d 1083, 1084 (Fed.Cir.2016). "This case involves one necessary condition, under ... §120, for treating a patent application, filed as a continuation of an earlier application, as having the earlier application's filing date, not its own filing date. That timing benefit shrinks the universe of 'prior' art for determining validity. The condition at issue ... is that the continuation application be 'filed before the patenting' of the earlier application. The question is whether, for that condition to be met, the continuing application has to be filed at least one *day* before the earlier application is patented, or whether an application may be 'filed before the patenting' of the earlier application when both legal acts, filing and patenting, occur on the same day. [¶] We adopt the latter position."

Hollmer v. Harari, 681 F.3d 1351, 1356, 102 U.S.P.Q.2d 1958, 1962 (Fed.Cir.2012). "[W]e address whether [the] reasonable examiner standard ... applies for determining if the intermediary ... applications sufficiently incorporate the [earlier] application by reference such that they satisfy [35 U.S.C.] §120's continuity requirements. [Respondent] argues that the ***Harari I*** reasonable examiner standard is limited to situations in which an applicant seeks to clarify an ambiguous incorporation statement through an amendment that triggers a potential 35 U.S.C. §132 new matter problem. Where, as here, §120 priority is at issue, [respondent] contends that the incorporation by reference inquiry takes place within the §120 context, applying the person of ordinary skill standard. [¶] [W]e agree with [respondent] that the Board should have applied the person of ordinary skill standard in assessing the disputed language in the [intermediary] applications."

Harari v. Hollmer, 602 F.3d 1348, 1352-53, 94 U.S.P.Q.2d 1380, 1383 (Fed.Cir.2010). "The disputed continuation application is at the initial filing stage, where the examiner is first presented with an original disclosure and a preliminary amendment. The proper standard by which to evaluate the sufficiency of incorporation by reference language, at this stage of the proceedings, is whether the identity of the incorporated reference is clear to a reasonable examiner in light of the documents presented. In other words, the relevant inquiry is whether a reasonable examiner would be so befuddled by the language of the original disclosure, despite the explanation provided in the transmittal and preliminary amendment, that he could not determine what document was intended to be incorporated by reference."

Zenon Envtl., Inc. v. U.S. Filter Corp., 506 F.3d 1370, 1378-79, 85 U.S.P.Q.2d 1118, 1123-24 (Fed.Cir. 2007). "'In order to gain the benefit of the filing date of an earlier application under 35 U.S.C. §120, each application in the chain leading back to the earlier application must comply with the written description requirement of 35 U.S.C. §112.' Thus, in order for [later] patent to be entitled to priority from [earlier] patent, continuity of disclosure must have been maintained throughout a chain of patents from [earlier] patent leading up to [later] patent. [¶] Incorporation by reference 'provides a method for integrating material from various documents into a host document ... by citing such material in a manner that makes clear that the material is effectively part of the host document as if it were explicitly contained therein.' 'To incorporate material by reference, the host document must identify with *detailed particularity* what specific material it incorporates and *clearly indicate where* that material is found in the various documents.' Whether material has been incorporated by reference into a host document, and the extent to which it has been incorporated, is a question of law. In making that determination, 'the standard of one reasonably skilled in the art should be used to determine whether the host document describes the material to be incorporated by reference with sufficient particularity.'"

In re Bauman, 683 F.2d 405, 408, 214 U.S.P.Q. 585, 588 (C.C.P.A.1982). "A continuing application enables an applicant to, *inter alia*, claim inventions disclosed but not previously claimed, to develop objective evidence of unobviousness, or to replace claims rejected for obviousness with narrower claims that can be approved. [¶] [I]t does not follow that the ... parent and continuing applications are considered 'parts of the same transaction, and ... as constituting one continuous application' means that a continuing application must be based on an application upon which a valid patent could have issued. There is no reason that a barrier to the patentability of claims in a parent application that is unrelated to the date of constructive reduction to practice, necessarily, precludes claims in a later application from receiving the benefit of the parent's filing date."

Continuation-in-Part Applications

Litton Sys. v. Whirlpool Corp., 728 F.2d 1423, 1438, 221 U.S.P.Q. 97, 106 (Fed.Cir.1984), *overruled on other grounds*, ***Two Pesos, Inc. v. Taco Cabana, Inc.***, 505 U.S. 763 (1992). "A [continuation-in-part (C-I-P)] application is different from an original patent application ... in that it often generates two effective filing dates applicable to different parts of the same patent. New matter in a C-I-P application has the filing date of *that* C-I-P application. The earlier filing date of the parent application pertains to material in the C-I-P application also disclosed in the prior application. If matter added through amendment to a C-I-P application is deemed inherent in whatever the original parent application discloses, however, that matter also is entitled to the filing date of the original, parent application. Before any factual determination can be made as to whether newly added matter is inherent in the parent application, however, the circumstances surrounding the prosecution of the patent in the PTO must be examined. [¶] [P] voluntarily turned its [PTO] Rule 60 continuation application into a C-I-P application. [¶] The district court ... concluded that [P] did not really add new matter [to the C-I-P]. The court relied on [P's] contentions that the PTO had abandoned its position that the added limitations were new matter. A conclusion, however, whether of fact or law, that [P] did not really add new matter to its C-I-P disclosure cannot retroactively contradict the prosecution history of the '859 patent in which [P], by recasting its Rule 60 continuation application as a C-I-P, implied that it did add new matter. [P's] own actions before the PTO require such a holding. We hold, therefore, that [P] is estopped from arguing that [C-I-P claim limitations are inherent in the parent application]." *See also* ***Pennwalt Corp. v. Akzona Inc.***, 740 F.2d 1573, 1578, 222 U.S.P.Q. 833, 836 (Fed.Cir.1984).

Stearn v. Superior Distrib. Co., 674 F.2d 539, 544-45, 215 U.S.P.Q. 1089, 1093 (6th Cir.1982). "To the extent that a [continuation-in-part (CIP)] application adds new matter, claims that are dependent upon the new matter are entitled to the filing date of the CIP only and not that of the parent application. The inquiry required by §120 demands a comparison of (1) the claims of the parent and the CIP application and (2) any other disclosures made in the applications such as the specification and drawings. *At F.2d 548, U.S.P.Q. 1096:* A generic claim in a CIP cannot have its genesis in a combination claim in the parent application. It necessarily follows that the requirements of §120 have not been met."

Copendency

Antares Pharma, Inc. v. Medac Pharma Inc., 771 F.3d 1354, 1358, 112 U.S.P.Q.2d 1865, 1867-68 (Fed.Cir. 2014). "The filing of continuations and divisionals is limited by the co-pendency requirement of [35 U.S.C.] §120: a continuing application cannot be filed after the original parent application issues. In such circumstances, an applicant can only seek to add claims by filing a reissue application. The delay in seeking to broaden the claims is not without cost. By waiting until after the patent is issued, the applicant becomes subject to two additional requirements relevant here: first, the claims must not violate the recapture rule; second, the claims must satisfy the statutory original patent requirement of 35 U.S.C. §251."

In re Doyle, 293 F.3d 1355, 1363, 63 U.S.P.Q.2d 1161, 1167-68 (Fed.Cir.2002). "The copendency requirement of [35 U.S.C.] §120 refers to the requirement that a patent application filed as a continuation or divisional application upon an originally filed application must be filed 'before the patenting or abandonment of or termination of proceedings on the first application or on an application similarly entitled to the benefit of the filing date of the first application' in order to receive the benefit of the earlier filing date. [¶] The Solicitor's argument [against reissue] presumes a situation in which the claims sought on reissue have been restricted from an application in earlier proceedings.... In that situation, the copendency requirements of [35 U.S.C.] §§120 and 121 are relevant. In this case, the matter sought on reissue could have been presented with the original application, so §§120 and 121 are not implicated."

Baxter Int'l v. McGaw, Inc., 149 F.3d 1321, 1333, 47 U.S.P.Q.2d 1225, 1233 (Fed.Cir.1998). "Section 120 requires that the two applications be co-pendent and that the later-filed application reference the earlier-filed application."

Design Patents

In re Daniels, 144 F.3d 1452, 1456, 46 U.S.P.Q.2d 1788, 1790 (Fed.Cir.1998). "The statutory provision governing the effective filing date of the subject matter of continuing applications, 35 U.S.C. §120, applies to design patents as to utility patents." *See also* ***Racing Strollers, Inc. v. TRI Indus.***, 878 F.2d 1418, 1421, 11 U.S.P.Q.2d 1300, 1302 (Fed.Cir.1989).

KangaROOS, Inc. v. Caldor, Inc., 778 F.2d 1571, 1574, 228 U.S.P.Q. 32, 33-34 (Fed.Cir.1985). "There is no statutory prohibition against an applicant's reliance, in claiming priority under 35 U.S.C. §120, on a disclosure in a design application if the statutory conditions are met. Of particular pertinence is the condition that the disclosure of the design application meet the requirements of the first paragraph of [35 U.S.C.] §112 as applied to one or more claims of the continuation-in-part utility application. The determination of whether any claim of the utility application is adequately supported in the prior design application depends on the facts of each case."

Laches

Webster Elec. Co. v. Splitdorf Elec. Co., 264 U.S. 463, 466 (1924). "The repeated assertion of interferences in narrower terms, resulting in delays incident to their determination, affords no just excuse for the failure to assert the broader claims [of applicant] at an earlier date. The subject matter of these claims is not of such complicated character that it might not have been readily described in the original application or in one of the subsequent applications ... as it was described in 1918; and the long delay of [applicant] and his assignee in coming to the point tends strongly to confirm the view that the final determination to do so was an exigent afterthought, rather than a logical development of the original application. We have no hesitation in saying that the delay was unreasonable, and, under the circumstances shown by the record, constitutes laches, by which the petitioner lost whatever rights it might otherwise have been entitled to." *See also* ***Symbol Techs. v. Lemelson Med.***, 277 F.3d 1361, 1365-66, 61 U.S.P.Q.2d 1515, 1518 (Fed.Cir.2002).

Symbol Techs. v. Lemelson Med., Educ. & Research Found., 422 F.3d 1378, 1384-86, 76 U.S.P.Q.2d 1354, 1359 (Fed.Cir.2005), *amended*, 429 F.3d 1051 (Fed.Cir.2005). "The doctrine of prosecution laches is an equitable defense and we review the judgment of the district court on that issue for an abuse of discretion. [P]rosecution laches may render a patent unenforceable when it has issued only after an unreasonable and unexplained delay in prosecution. *At U.S.P.Q.1360:* [R]efiling an application solely containing previously-allowed claims for the business purpose of delaying their issuance can be considered an abuse of the patent system. In particular, multiple examples of repetitive refilings that demonstrate a pattern of unjustifiably delayed prosecution may be held to constitute laches. Taken singly, the delay in the prosecution on any one particular application will surely not appear to merit relief by the courts in equity. On the other hand, an examination of the totality of the circumstances, including the prosecution history of all of a series of related patents and overall delay in issuing claims, may trigger laches."

Reissue Patents

Johnson & Johnston Assocs. v. R.E. Serv. Co., 285 F.3d 1046, 1055, 62 U.S.P.Q.2d 1225, 1231 (Fed.Cir. 2002). "A patentee who inadvertently fails to claim disclosed subject matter ... is not left without remedy. Within two years from the grant of the original patent, a patentee may file a reissue application and attempt to enlarge the scope of the original claims to include the disclosed but previously unclaimed subject matter. In addition, a patentee can file a separate application claiming the disclosed subject matter under ... §120...."

In re Bauman, 683 F.2d 405, 407, 214 U.S.P.Q. 585, 587 (C.C.P.A.1982). "[R]eissue applications continuing from reissue applications are within the scope of §120. *At F.2d 409, U.S.P.Q. 589:* Reissue patents are issued 'for the unexpired part of the term of the original patent ...,' are subject to the doctrine of intervening rights ..., and will issue only upon surrender of the original patent. [A] patentee can avoid the restrictions applicable to reissue applications by filing a regular application directed to subject matter disclosed but not claimed in his patent within one year of the patent's issue date. Thus, if a patentee desires a reissue application with its earlier effective filing date, he must accept reissue restrictions. If he desires a regular application without such restrictions, he must accept a later filing date. In making this statutory choice, a patentee does not circumvent [§120]. *At F.2d 410, U.S.P.Q. 590:* [A] regular application continuing from a reissue application is not entitled to the filing date of the patent. To hold that it is impossible to obtain the *actual* filing date of the reissue application because its *effective* filing date is the patent filing date would exalt form over substance and serve no useful purpose. Only a reissue application can be entitled to the filing date of a patent in the absence of copendency. The instant application is not a reissue application and, thus, cannot possibly enjoy the earlier date."

Standard of Review

In re Daniels, 144 F.3d 1452, 1455-56, 46 U.S.P.Q.2d 1788, 1790 (Fed.Cir.1998). "Entitlement to priority under §120 is a matter of law, and receives plenary review on appeal. Any disputed factual questions are reviewed on the clearly erroneous standard."

§121. DIVISIONAL APPLICATIONS

If two or more independent and distinct inventions are claimed in one application, the Director may require the application to be restricted to one of the inventions. If the other invention is made the subject of a divisional application which complies with the requirements of section 120 it shall be entitled to the benefit of the filing date of the original application. A patent issuing on an application with respect to which a requirement for restriction under this section has been made, or on an application filed as a result of such a requirement, shall not be used as a reference either in the Patent and Trademark Office or in the courts against a divisional application or against the original application or any patent issued on either of them, if the divisional application is filed before the issuance of the patent on the other application. The validity of a patent shall not be questioned for failure of the Director to require the application to be restricted to one invention.

History of 35 U.S.C. §121: July 19, 1952, ch. 950, §1, 66 Stat. 800; Jan. 2, 1975, P.L. 93-596, §1, 88 Stat. 1949; Nov. 29, 1999, P.L. 106-113, §1000(a)(9), 113 Stat. 1536; Nov. 2, 2002, P.L. 107-273, §13206(b)(1)(B), 116 Stat. 1906; Sept. 16, 2011, P.L. 112-29, §§4(a)(2), 20(j)(1), 125 Stat. 295, 335.

See also 37 C.F.R. §§1.78, 1.109.

ANNOTATIONS

G.D. Searle LLC v. Lupin Pharms., 790 F.3d 1349, 1354, 115 U.S.P.Q.2d 1326, 1330 (Fed.Cir.2015). "The safe harbor provision of §121 protects a patent issuing on an application with respect to which a restriction requirement has been made, or on an application filed as a result of such a restriction requirement. It is undisputed that the reference ... patent issued on a divisional of the original ... application, which was filed as a result of [a] restriction requirement. The challenged ... patent, however, is not entitled to safe harbor protection, because it did not issue on either the [original] application or a divisional of the [original] application."

St. Jude Med., Inc. v. Access Closure, Inc., 729 F.3d 1369, 1376-77, 108 U.S.P.Q.2d 1285, 1290 (Fed.Cir. 2013). "The safe harbor provision arose from difficulties created by restriction requirements imposed by the [PTO] during examination, followed by double patenting challenges in the courts. A restriction requirement arises during examination at the PTO when an applicant pursues what are determined to be *multiple patentably distinct* inventions in the *same application*.... Subsequently, a double patenting challenge may arise when, in an infringement suit, the patentee is charged with having pursued the *same or obviously similar* inventions in *multiple applications*, one or more of which later issued as the patent in suit.... A successful double patenting defense invalidates the offending claims in the patent. [¶] Prior to the 1952 Patent Act, when §121 was enacted, patentees could be faced with a situation in which the PTO and courts caused these two doctrines to collide. To illustrate, assume the PTO imposes a restriction requirement on a patent application because the PTO concludes that the application claims invention A and invention B which are deemed to be *patentably distinct* inventions. The applicant then removes claims to invention B from the restricted application and files those claims in a subsequent application. The restricted application and the subsequent application later issue as patents. [¶] In a later court challenge, a court concludes that invention A and invention B are *not* patentably distinct, and thus the claims in the patent resulting from the subsequent application are invalid for double patenting of the same invention. This conflicting result was recognized as inherently unfair, and the safe harbor was created to preclude it. *At U.S.P.Q.2d 1291:* The judicially-created consonance concept derives from the safe harbor's 'as a result of' requirement and specifies that the line of demarcation between the independent and distinct inventions that prompted the restriction requirement be maintained. An applicant's pursuit of two or more non-elected inventions in the same subsequent application does not *by itself* violate the line of demarcation. However, in ***Gerber*** [***Garment Tech. v. Lectra Sys.***, 916 F.2d 683 (Fed.Cir.1990)], we concluded that plain common sense dictates that a divisional application filed as a result of a restriction requirement may not contain claims drawn to the invention set forth in the claims elected and prosecuted to patent in the parent application. [¶] The requirement for consonance applies to both the patent challenged for double patenting (the challenged patent) and the patent being used as a reference against the challenged patent (the reference patent). Consonance in a case like this requires that the challenged patent, the reference patent, *and* the patent in which the restriction requirement was imposed (the restricted patent) do not claim any of the same inventions identified by the examiner. *At F.3d 1378:* The parties' dispute turns in large measure on the nature and effect of the examiner-imposed election of species. An election of species is similar to a restriction and again is explained best by example. An applicant may file an application containing claims to a generic invention, such as a widget. The application may also include claims to several patentably distinct species of the generic invention, such as the widget + X, the widget + Y, and the widget + Z. [¶] After reviewing the application, the examiner may impose an election of species that requires the applicant to choose one of the species for examination. The election of species, like a typical restriction, helps the examiner to focus the examination process. The applicant typically elects a species (e.g., widget + X), focuses on prosecuting the generic claims to the widget and any claims to the widget + X species, and withdraws the claims to the non-elected species, widget + Y and widget + Z. If the generic claim to the widget is allowed, the applicant may obtain claim coverage on all of the species. If the generic claim is not allowed, the application is restricted." (Internal quotes omitted.)

Boehringer Ingelheim Int'l v. Barr Labs., 592 F.3d 1340, 1350-51, 93 U.S.P.Q.2d 1417, 1424 (Fed.Cir.2010). "'When the PTO requires an applicant to withdraw claims to a patentably distinct invention (a restriction requirement), §121 shields those withdrawn claims in a later divisional application against rejection over a patent that issues from the original application.' *At U.S.P.Q.2d 1425:* The safe harbor is provided to protect an applicant from losing rights when an application is *divided*. The safe harbor of §121 is not lost if an applicant does not file separate divisional applications for every invention or when independent and distinct inventions are prosecuted together. The statute, in referring to 'two *or more* independent and distinct inventions,' recognizes that the safe harbor is not limited to only one divisional application. Thus, where the third sentence of §121 refers to a patent issuing on an application filed as a result of a restriction requirement, it is referring to patents issuing from any number of multiple divisional applications and precludes any one from being used as a reference against any other. *At F.3d 1352, U.S.P.Q.2d 1426:* We see no reason why §121 would not likewise extend to a divisional of a divisional. [¶] We have repeatedly held that the 'as a result of' requirement applies to the challenged patent as well as the reference patent. *At F.3d 1353:* [P] argues that when an examiner issues a restriction requirement identifying more than two independent and distinct inventions, the choice of how to prosecute non-elected inventions is up to the applicant and is constrained neither by the terms of an examiner's restriction requirement nor by the language of §121. According to [P], so long as consonance is met, it makes no difference in terms of compliance with the 'as a result of' requirement whether the applicant responds to the examiner's restriction requirement by filing one or more divisional applications from the original application, or instead files a single divisional application followed by successive additional divisionals. [¶] We agree with [P]."

Amgen Inc. v. F. Hoffman-LA Roche Ltd., 580 F.3d 1340, 1350, 92 U.S.P.Q.2d 1289, 1297 (Fed.Cir.2009). "[T]he third sentence of §121 shields patents that issue on applications filed as a result of a restriction requirement from double patenting invalidation."

Pfizer, Inc. v. Teva Pharms., 518 F.3d 1353, 1359-60, 86 U.S.P.Q.2d 1001, 1005-06 (Fed.Cir.2008). "In addition to the express requirements of §121, we have also construed the statute to require consonance: the applicant must maintain the line of demarcation between the independent and distinct inventions that prompted the restriction requirement. This consonance requirement prevents an applicant from amending the claims in the divisional application in a way that would violate the originally imposed restriction requirement and thereby impermissibly extend the patent term as to that subject matter. [¶] Although both are types of continuing applications, divisionals and [continuations in part (CIPs)] differ significantly in at least one respect: a divisional application contains an identical disclosure to its parent application, but a CIP introduces new matter. A CIP is 'just what its name implies. It partly continues subject matter disclosed in a prior application, but it adds new subject matter not disclosed in the prior application.' A divisional application is defined as '[a] later application for an independent or distinct invention, carved out of a pending application and disclosing and claiming only subject matter disclosed in the earlier or parent application....' A divisional application 'is often filed as a result of a restriction requirement made by the examiner.' *At F.3d 1362, U.S.P.Q.2d 1007-08:* We conclude that the protection afforded by §121 to applications (or patents issued therefrom) filed as a result of a restriction requirement is limited to divisional applications."

Symbol Techs. v. Lemelson Med., Educ. & Research Found., 422 F.3d 1378, 1385, 76 U.S.P.Q.2d 1354, 1360 (Fed.Cir.2005), *amended*, 429 F.3d 1051 (Fed.Cir.2005). "Filing a divisional application in response to a requirement for restriction is [a] legitimate reason for refiling a patent application. Given one's entitlement to claim an invention in various ways, and the PTO's practice of limiting its examination of an application to only one of what it considers to be several inventions, it cannot, without more, be an abuse of the system to file divisional applications on various aspects that the PTO has considered to be separate and distinct from each other. That is so even when one defers the filing of a divisional application until just before the issuance of the parent application. Such action is expressly allowed by statute."

§122. CONFIDENTIAL STATUS OF APPLICATIONS; PUBLICATION OF PATENT APPLICATIONS

(a) Confidentiality.—Except as provided in subsection (b), applications for patents shall be kept in confidence by the Patent and Trademark Office and no information concerning the same given without authority of the applicant or owner unless necessary to carry out the provisions of an Act of Congress or in such special circumstances as may be determined by the Director.

(b) Publication—

(1) In general—

(A) Subject to paragraph (2), each application for a patent shall be published, in accordance with procedures determined by the Director, promptly after the expiration of a period of 18 months from the earliest filing date for which a benefit is sought under this title. At the request of the applicant, an application may be published earlier than the end of such 18-month period.

(B) No information concerning published patent applications shall be made available to the public except as the Director determines.

(C) Notwithstanding any other provision of law, a determination by the Director to release or not to release information concerning a published patent application shall be final and nonreviewable.

(2) Exceptions—

(A) An application shall not be published if that application is—

(i) no longer pending;

(ii) subject to a secrecy order under section 181;

(iii) a provisional application filed under section 111(b); or

(iv) an application for a design patent filed under chapter 16.

(B)(i) If an applicant makes a request upon filing, certifying that the invention disclosed in the application has not and will not be the subject of an application filed in another country, or under a multilateral international agreement, that requires publication of applications 18 months after filing, the application shall not be published as provided in paragraph (1).

(ii) An applicant may rescind a request made under clause (i) at any time.

(iii) An applicant who has made a request under clause (i) but who subsequently files, in a foreign country or under a multilateral international agreement specified in clause (i), an application directed to the invention disclosed in the application filed in the Patent and Trademark Office, shall notify the Director of such filing not later than 45 days after the date of the filing of such foreign or international application. A failure of the applicant to provide such notice within the prescribed period shall result in the application being regarded as abandoned.

(iv) If an applicant rescinds a request made under clause (i) or notifies the Director that an application was filed in a foreign country or under a multilateral international agreement specified in clause (i), the application shall be published in accordance with the provisions of paragraph (1) on or as soon as is practical after the date that is specified in clause (i).

(v) If an applicant has filed applications in one or more foreign countries, directly or through a multilateral international agreement, and such foreign filed applications corresponding to an application filed in the Patent and Trademark Office or the description of the invention in such foreign filed applications is less extensive than the application or description of the invention in the application filed in the Patent and Trademark Office, the applicant may submit a redacted copy of the application filed in the Patent and Trademark Office eliminating any part or description of the invention in such application that is not also contained in any of the corresponding applications filed in a foreign country. The Director may only publish the redacted copy of the application unless the redacted copy of the application is not received within 16 months after the earliest effective filing date for which a benefit is sought under this title. The provisions of section 154(d) shall not apply to a claim if the description of the invention published in the redacted application filed under this clause with respect to the claim does not enable a person skilled in the art to make and use the subject matter of the claim.

(c) Protest and pre-issuance opposition.—The Director shall establish appropriate procedures to ensure that no protest or other form of pre-issuance opposition to the grant of a patent on an application may be initiated after publication of the application without the express written consent of the applicant.

(d) National security.—No application for patent shall be published under subsection (b)(1) if the publication or disclosure of such invention would be detrimental to the national security. The Director shall establish appropriate procedures to ensure that such applications are promptly identified and the secrecy of such inventions is maintained in accordance with chapter 17.

(e) Preissuance submissions by third parties—

(1) In general.—Any third party may submit for consideration and inclusion in the record of a patent application, any patent, published patent application, or other printed publication of potential relevance to the examination of the application, if such submission is made in writing before the earlier of—

(A) the date a notice of allowance under section 151 is given or mailed in the application for patent; or

(B) the later of—

(i) 6 months after the date on which the application for patent is first published under section 122 by the Office, or

(ii) the date of the first rejection under section 132 of any claim by the examiner during the examination of the application for patent.

(2) Other requirements.—Any submission under paragraph (1) shall—

(A) set forth a concise description of the asserted relevance of each submitted document;

(B) be accompanied by such fee as the Director may prescribe; and

(C) include a statement by the person making such submission affirming that the submission was made in compliance with this section.

History of 35 U.S.C. §122: July 19, 1952, ch. 950, §1, 66 Stat. 801; Jan. 2, 1975, P.L. 93-596, §1, 88 Stat. 1949; Nov. 29, 1999, P.L. 106-113, §1000(a)(9), 113 Stat. 1536; Sept. 16, 2011, P.L. 112-29, §§8(a), 20(j)(1), 125 Stat. 315, 335; Dec. 18, 2013, P.L. 112-211, §202(b)(4), 126 Stat. 1536.

See also 37 C.F.R. §1.290.

ANNOTATIONS

Hyatt v. USPTO, 797 F.3d 1374, 1380, 116 U.S.P.Q.2d 1331, 1335 (Fed.Cir.2015). Section 122(a) "lays out only two exceptions to its general bar on disclosure. The first exception permits disclosure only when it is 'necessary to carry out the provisions of an Act of Congress.' Because this exception is limited to disclosures that are 'necessary' to carry out a Congressional mandate, it is narrow and affords no agency discretion. In light of this statutory structure, it would be odd if the second exception was broad, sweeping, or unbounded. The language of the second exception supports our conclusion that the PTO's determination is reviewable. The PTO is not free to disclose confidential information whenever it chooses, or at its discretion; rather, it may disclose confidential information only in 'such special circumstances as may be determined by the Director.' We conclude that the structure and language of this statutory section indicate that Congress intended the exceptions to confidentiality to be narrow and reviewable. *At F.3d 1383, U.S.P.Q.2d 1337-38:* Section 122(a) lays out a general prohibition against disclosure; any determination by the Director that special circumstances exist must be made in light of this bar against disclosure. The special circumstances must justify the otherwise-prohibited disclosure of confidential information. This means that the information that is disclosed must be linked to the 'special circumstances' justifying the disclosure. We review for abuse of discretion the Director's determination that special circumstances exist, and that such special circumstances justify the disclosure of otherwise-confidential information."

§123. MICRO ENTITY DEFINED

(a) In general.—For purposes of this title, the term "micro entity" means an applicant who makes a certification that the applicant—

(1) qualifies as a small entity, as defined in regulations issued by the Director;

(2) has not been named as an inventor on more than 4 previously filed patent applications, other than applications filed in another country, provisional applications under section 111(b), or international applications filed under the treaty defined in section 351(a) for which the basic national fee under section 41(a) was not paid;

(3) did not, in the calendar year preceding the calendar year in which the applicable fee is being paid, have a gross income, as defined in section 61(a) of the Internal Revenue Code of 1986, exceeding 3 times the median household income for that preceding calendar year, as most recently reported by the Bureau of the Census; and

(4) has not assigned, granted, or conveyed, and is not under an obligation by contract or law to assign, grant, or convey, a license or other ownership interest in the application concerned to an entity that, in the calendar year preceding the calendar year in which the applicable fee is being paid, had a gross income, as defined in section 61(a) of the Internal Revenue Code of 1986, exceeding 3 times the median household income for that preceding calendar year, as most recently reported by the Bureau of the Census.

(b) Applications resulting from prior employment.—An applicant is not considered to be named on a previously filed application for purposes of subsection (a)(2) if the applicant has assigned, or is under an obligation by contract or law to assign, all ownership rights in the application as the result of the applicant's previous employment.

(c) Foreign currency exchange rate.—If an applicant's or entity's gross income in the preceding calendar year is not in United States dollars, the average currency exchange rate, as reported by the Internal Revenue Service, during that calendar year shall be used to determine whether the applicant's or entity's gross income exceeds the threshold specified in paragraphs (3) or (4) of subsection (a).

(d) Institutions of higher education.—For purposes of this section, a micro entity shall include an applicant who certifies that—

(1) the applicant's employer, from which the applicant obtains the majority of the applicant's income, is an institution of higher education as defined in section 101(a) of the Higher Education Act of 1965 (20 U.S.C. 1001(a)); or

(2) the applicant has assigned, granted, conveyed, or is under an obligation by contract or law, to assign, grant, or convey, a license or other ownership interest in the particular applications to such an institution of higher education.

(e) Director's authority.—In addition to the limits imposed by this section, the Director may, in the Director's discretion, impose income limits, annual filing limits, or other limits on who may qualify as a micro entity pursuant to this section if the Director determines that such additional limits are reasonably necessary to avoid an undue impact on other patent applicants or owners or are otherwise reasonably necessary and appropriate. At least 3 months before any limits proposed to be imposed pursuant to this subsection take effect, the Director shall inform the Committee on the Judiciary of the House of Representatives and the Committee on the Judiciary of the Senate of any such proposed limits.

History of 35 U.S.C. §123: Sept. 16, 2011, P.L. 112-29, §10(g), 125 Stat. 318; Jan. 14, 2013, P.L. 112-274, §1(m), 126 Stat. 2459.

See also 37 C.F.R. §1.29.

CHAPTER 12. EXAMINATION OF APPLICATION

§131. EXAMINATION OF APPLICATION

The Director shall cause an examination to be made of the application and the alleged new invention; and if on such examination it appears that the applicant is entitled to a patent under the law, the Director shall issue a patent therefor.

History of 35 U.S.C. §131: July 19, 1952, ch. 950, §1, 66 Stat. 801; Nov. 29, 1999, P.L. 106-113, §1000(a)(9), 113 Stat. 1536; Nov. 2, 2002, P.L. 107-273, §13206(b)(1)(B), 116 Stat. 1906.

See also 37 C.F.R. §§1.102-1.105, 1.111-1.114.

ANNOTATIONS

In re Buszard, 504 F.3d 1364, 1366-67, 84 U.S.P.Q.2d 1749, 1750 (Fed.Cir.2007). "During examination, the patent application claims may be given their broadest interpretation consistent with the specification, in order to facilitate sharpening and clarifying the claims at the application stage. Thus the patent examiner and the applicant, in the give and take of rejection and response, work toward defining the metes and bounds of the invention to be patented."

§132. NOTICE OF REJECTION; REEXAMINATION

(a) Whenever, on examination, any claim for a patent is rejected, or any objection or requirement made, the Director shall notify the applicant thereof, stating the reasons for such rejection, or objection or requirement, together with such information and references as may be useful in judging of the propriety of continuing the prosecution of his application; and if after receiving such notice, the applicant persists in his claim for a patent, with or without amendment, the application shall be reexamined. No amendment shall introduce new matter into the disclosure of the invention.

(b) The Director shall prescribe regulations to provide for the continued examination of applications for patent at the request of the applicant. The Director may establish appropriate fees for such continued examination and shall provide a 50 percent reduction in such fees for small entities that qualify for reduced fees under section 41(h)(1).

History of 35 U.S.C. §132: July 19, 1952, ch. 950, §1, 66 Stat. 801; Nov. 29, 1999, P.L. 106-113, §1000(a)(9), 113 Stat. 1536; Nov. 2, 2002, P.L. 107-273, §13206(b)(1)(B), 116 Stat. 1906; Sept. 16, 2011, P.L. 112-29, §20(j)(1), 125 Stat. 335.

See also 37 C.F.R. §§1.113-1.138.

ANNOTATIONS

Festo Corp. v. Shoketsu Kinzoku Kogyo Kabushiki Co., 535 U.S. 722, 733-35, 62 U.S.P.Q.2d 1705, 1710-11 (2002). "A rejection indicates that the patent examiner does not believe the original claim could be patented. While the patentee has the right to appeal, his decision to forgo an appeal and submit an amended claim is taken as a concession that the invention as patented does not reach as far as the original claim."

In re Jung, 637 F.3d 1356, 1362, 98 U.S.P.Q.2d 1174, 1177 (Fed.Cir.2011). Applicant "does not challenge the *substance* of the prima facie rejection, but only the *procedure*. [¶] '[T]he prima facie case is merely a procedural device that enables an appropriate shift of the burden of production.' [T]he PTO carries its procedural burden of establishing a prima facie case when its rejection satisfies 35 U.S.C. §132, in 'notify[ing] the applicant ... [by] stating the reasons for [its] rejection, or objection or requirement, together with such information and references as may be useful in judging of the propriety of continuing the prosecution of [the] application.' That section 'is violated when a rejection is so uninformative that it prevents the applicant from recognizing and seeking to counter the grounds for rejection.' *At F.3d 1363, U.S.P.Q.2d 1178:* [Applicant] contends that establishing a prima facie case requires more than just notice under §132, and that whatever else may be required is part of the examiner's burden in rejecting any claim. According to [applicant], until that burden is met by the examiner, the rejection need not be challenged on the merits by the applicant. This court disagrees and sees no reason to impose a heightened burden on examiners beyond the notice requirement of §132. [¶] There has never been a requirement for an examiner to make an on-the-record claim construction of every term in every rejected claim and to explain every possible difference between the prior art and the claimed invention in order to make out a prima facie rejection. This court declines to create such a burdensome and unnecessary requirement. '[Section 132] does not mandate that in order to establish prima facie anticipation, the PTO must explicitly preempt every possible response to a [35 U.S.C.] §102 rejection. Section 132 merely ensures that an applicant at least be informed of the broad statutory basis for the rejection of his claims, so that he may determine what the issues are on which he can or should produce evidence.'"

Commonwealth Sci. & Indus. Research Org. v. Buffalo Tech., 542 F.3d 1363, 1379, 88 U.S.P.Q.2d 1564, 1575-76 (Fed.Cir.2008). "The question presented by this issue is whether the specification of the original application contained a written description of the invention sufficient to allow persons of ordinary skill in the art to recognize that the inventor invented the subject matter that is claimed in the asserted claims. If it did not, the legal consequences would be that the 1995 amendment would be considered to have added new matter to the application, and the newly added claims would not be supported by the original specification. *At F.3d 1380:* The question whether new matter has been added to an application is a question of fact. [W]e interpret the court's action as constituting a ruling on the §132 issue on both legal and factual grounds, including making findings of fact based on the evidence submitted to the court, as the court was permitted to do by the parties' stipulations. We therefore review the district court's new matter ruling under the clear error standard. [¶] [I]n the context of a validity challenge based on new matter, the fact that the [PTO] has allowed an amendment without objection 'is entitled to an especially weighty presumption of correctness' in a subsequent validity challenge based on the alleged introduction of new matter. [D] therefore not only must overcome the clear error standard, but it must do so in the face of a presumption of validity based on the PTO's issuance of the patent despite the amendments." Held: New matter was not added to second application.

SmithKline Beecham Corp. v. Excel Pharm., 356 F.3d 1357, 1364, 69 U.S.P.Q.2d 1712, 1717 (Fed.Cir. 2004). "[N]ew matter prohibitions are not directly germane to the doctrine of equivalents or the patentee's proof to overcome the ***Festo*** presumption. The new matter doctrine prevents an applicant from adding new subject matter to the claims unless the specification shows that the inventor had support for the addition at the time of the original filing. Thus, the new matter doctrine ensures the temporal integrity of the amendment process in the [PTO] and does not apply to nontextual infringement. In fact, the quintessential example of an enforceable equivalent, after-arising technology, would always be unclaimable new matter. In that sense, the doctrine of equivalents compensates for the patentee's inability to claim unforeseeable new matter." *See also* ***Turbocare v. General Elec. Co.***, 264 F.3d 1111, 1118, 60 U.S.P.Q.2d 1017, 1022 (Fed.Cir. 2001).

Regents of the Univ. of N.M. v. Knight, 321 F.3d 1111, 1122, 66 U.S.P.Q.2d 1001, 1009 (Fed.Cir.2003). "As assignee of the ... inventions, [P] was entitled to prosecute the applications and to make amendments during prosecution. [Inventors] were contractually obligated to assist [P] in the prosecution of any and all patent applications relating to their inventions. Their refusal to do so did not impair [P's] right to continue prosecution. Accordingly, [P] acted reasonably in relying on [other scientists] to verify the accuracy of the descriptions of the inventions as disclosed in the patent applications and amendments. [¶] [P's] subsequent amendments to ... applications, based on [other scientists' work], did not alter the inventorship or ownership rights in those applications and the resulting patents. The amendments did not describe different inventions; they only clarified and corrected the erroneous characterization of the already disclosed inventions. Such amendments do not add to or change the nature of the disclosed inventions. [Amendments] amended the specifications and claims to describe [inventors'] inventions more accurately. Such amendments are not new matter, and the district court did not err in its holding to that effect."

Schering Corp. v. Amgen Inc., 222 F.3d 1347, 1352, 55 U.S.P.Q.2d 1650, 1653-54 (Fed.Cir.2000). "[T]he new matter prohibition is closely related to the adequate disclosure requirements of 35 U.S.C. §112. ... Thus, to avoid the new matter prohibition, an applicant must show that its original application supports the amended matter." *See also* ***Moba, B.V. v. Diamond Automation, Inc.***, 325 F.3d 1306, 1319-21, 66 U.S.P.Q.2d 1429, 1437-39 (Fed.Cir.2003).

In re Lundak, 773 F.2d 1216, 1223, 227 U.S.P.Q. 90, 96 (Fed.Cir.1985). "[T]he insertion of depository data [in the form of biological material] after filing is not new matter under ... §132."

35 U.S.C. §132

§133. TIME FOR PROSECUTING APPLICATION

Upon failure of the applicant to prosecute the application within six months after any action therein, of which notice has been given or mailed to the applicant, or within such shorter time, not less than thirty days, as fixed by the Director in such action, the application shall be regarded as abandoned by the parties thereto.

History of 35 U.S.C. §133: July 19, 1952, ch. 950, §1, 66 Stat. 801; Nov. 29, 1999, P.L. 106-113, §1000(a)(9), 113 Stat. 1536; Nov. 2, 2002, P.L. 107-273, §13206(b)(1)(B), 116 Stat. 1906; Dec. 18, 2013, P.L. 112-211, §202(b)(5), 126 Stat. 1536.

§134. APPEAL TO THE PATENT TRIAL & APPEAL BOARD

The change from "Board of Patent Appeals and Interferences" to "Patent Trial and Appeal Board" is effective for patent applications and patents issued on those applications that contain or contained a claim to a claimed invention that has an effective filing date on or after Mar. 16, 2013, or for any applications or patents that contain or contained a claim to a specific reference under §120, §121, or §365(c) that have an effective filing date on or after Mar. 16, 2013.

(a) Patent applicant.—An applicant for a patent, any of whose claims has been twice rejected, may appeal from the decision of the primary examiner to the Patent Trial and Appeal Board, having once paid the fee for such appeal.

(b) Patent owner.—A patent owner in a reexamination may appeal from the final rejection of any claim by the primary examiner to the Patent Trial and Appeal Board, having once paid the fee for such appeal.

History of 35 U.S.C. §134: July 19, 1952, ch. 950, §1, 66 Stat. 801; Nov. 8, 1984, P.L. 98-622, §204(b)(1), 98 Stat. 3388; Nov. 29, 1999, P.L. 106-113, §1000(a)(9), 113 Stat. 1536; Nov. 2, 2002, P.L. 107-273, §§13106(b), 13202(b)(1), 116 Stat. 1901; Sept. 16, 2011, P.L. 112-29, §§3(j)(1), (3), 7(b), 125 Stat. 290, 313.

See also 37 C.F.R. §§1.191-1.198, pt. 41.

ANNOTATIONS

MaxLinear, Inc. v. CF CRESPE LLC, 880 F.3d 1373, 1377, 125 U.S.P.Q.2d 1577, ___ (Fed.Cir.2018). "We note that the collateral-estoppel effect of an administrative decision of unpatentability generally requires the invalidation of related claims that present identical issues of patentability. In ***Ohio Willow Wood Co. v. Alps [S.], LLC***, 735 F.3d 1333, 1342 (Fed.Cir.2013), we pointed out that 'precedent does not limit collateral estoppel to patent claims that are identical.... If the differences between the unadjudicated patent claims and adjudicated patent claims do not materially alter the question of invalidity, collateral estoppel applies.'"

In re Biedermann, 733 F.3d 329, 336, 108 U.S.P.Q.2d 1623, 1627 (Fed.Cir.2013). "The central question in the present case is whether the Board and the examiner properly relied on the same articulated reasoning and factual underpinnings in rejecting [petitioner's] claims or whether the Board made new findings and adopted different reasons to support a new ground of rejection, thus depriving [petitioner] of both notice and an opportunity to respond. *At F.3d 337, U.S.P.Q.2d 1628:* When considering whether the Board issued a new ground of rejection, the ultimate criterion of whether a rejection is considered new in a decision by the Board is whether applicants have had fair opportunity to react to the thrust of the rejection. While the Board need not recite and agree with the examiner's rejection *in haec verba* to avoid issuing a new ground of rejection, mere reliance on the same statutory basis and the same prior art references, alone, is insufficient to avoid making a new ground of rejection when the Board relies on new facts and rationales not previously raised to the applicant by the examiner. This court's predecessor long acknowledged the right of the Board to make additional findings of fact based upon the

Board's own knowledge and experience to fill in the gaps that might exist in the examiner's evidentiary showing. But the Board's power to do so is construed narrowly and when reliance upon such facts changes the thrust of the rejection, the Board's action does everything but cry out for an opportunity to respond. A new ground of rejection, however, generally will not be found based on the Board further explaining the examiner's rejection or the Board's thoroughness in responding to an applicant's argument." Held: The Board relied on a new ground for rejection. (Internal quotes omitted.)

In re Stepan Co., 660 F.3d 1341, 1343, 100 U.S.P.Q.2d 1489, 1490 (Fed.Cir.2011). "On reexamination, the examiner ruled that all the claims of the ... patent were invalid as anticipated under 35 U.S.C. §102(b) or, in the alternative, obvious under 35 U.S.C. §103(a). On appeal, the Board affirmed the examiner's obviousness rejection. In so ruling, the Board relied upon the identical prior art references that the examiner had cited. ... The difference between the two rejections, however, was that the examiner found the ... patent obvious in light of [reference] as §102(b) prior art, which includes publications or inventions patented 'more than one year prior to the date of the application' of the patent in question, while the Board treated [reference] as prior art under §102(a), which includes publications or inventions patented 'before the invention thereof by the applicant.' [¶] [I]f the appellant has not had a full and fair opportunity to litigate the Board's actual basis of rejection, the administrative validity proceedings before the [PTO] should be allowed to continue. *At F.3d 1344-45, U.S.P.Q.2d 1491:* [T]he Board's failure to identify the new rejection and new rationale as a new ground of rejection, [petitioner] contends, violates its administrative due process rights. [¶] The PTO responds that the Board's decision is not a new ground of rejection because the thrust of the rejection was the same, i.e., obviousness. [¶] [Petitioner] is correct. By making and relying on new fact findings regarding an issue the examiner did not raise, i.e., the sufficiency of [petitioner's] Declaration to swear behind the ... reference as §102(a) prior art, the Board relied on a new ground of rejection. It is crucial that the examiner issue a rejection (even if that rejection is subsequently withdrawn) so the applicant is on notice that it is obligated to respond. Mere reliance by the Board on the same type of rejection or the same prior art references relied upon by the examiner, alone, is insufficient to avoid a new ground of rejection where it propounds new facts and rationales to advance a rejection—none of which were previously raised by the examiner."

In re Trans Tex. Holdings Corp., 498 F.3d 1290, 1296-97, 83 U.S.P.Q.2d 1835, 1839-40 (Fed.Cir.2007). Patent assignee "primarily argues that the Board should have given preclusive effect to the district court's ***Markman*** order.... [¶] Traditionally, issue preclusion, also known as collateral estoppel, applied only where the same parties to an earlier proceeding were involved in later litigation involving the same issue. More modern decisions in some circumstances apply issue preclusion even where the parties to the subsequent suit are not the same. The latter doctrine is known as non-mutual collateral estoppel, and it is this latter doctrine that [reexamination requester] relies on here. [¶] Issue preclusion is not warranted in this case because the PTO was not a party to the earlier litigation. Our case law has identified four prerequisites to the application of issue preclusion: (1) identity of the issues in a prior proceeding; (2) the issues were actually litigated; (3) the determination of the issues was necessary to the resulting judgment; and, (4) *the party defending against preclusion had a full and fair opportunity to litigate the issues.* [¶] The PTO as the party against whom the earlier decision is asserted thus must have been accorded a full and fair opportunity to litigate that issue in the earlier case. However, the PTO was not even a party to the earlier district court litigation and cannot be bound by its outcome." (Internal quotes omitted.)

§135[A*]. INTERFERENCES

Section 135[A] applies to applications and patents issued thereon that were filed before Mar. 16, 2013. Section 135[A*] also applies to patent applications and patents issued thereon if the filing date of the earliest application for which the patent or application is entitled under §119, §365(a), §365(b), §120, §121, or §365(c) is before Mar. 16, 2013, unless the application or patent has ever contained (1) a claim to a claimed invention that has an "effective filing date," as defined in §100(i), p. 495, on or after Mar. 16, 2013; or (2) a specific reference under §120, §121, or §365(c) to any patent or application that ever contained such a claim. In addition, §135[A*] applies to patent applications and patents issued thereon that have ever contained (1) a claim to a* *claimed invention that has an "effective filing date," as defined in §100(i), p. 495, before Mar. 16, 2013; or (2) a specific reference under §120, §121, or §365(c) to any patent or application that ever contained such a claim. See transition note for amended §135[B*], p. 595.*

(a) Whenever an application is made for a patent which, in the opinion of the Director, would interfere with any pending application, or with any unexpired patent, an interference may be declared and the Director shall give notice of such declaration to the applicants, or applicant and patentee, as the case may be. The Board of Patent Appeals and Interferences shall determine questions of priority of the inventions and may determine questions of patentability. Any final decision, if adverse to the claim of an applicant, shall constitute the final refusal by the Patent and Trademark Office of the claims involved, and the Director may issue a patent to the applicant who is adjudged the prior inventor. A final judgment adverse to a patentee from which no appeal or other review has been or can be taken or had shall constitute cancellation of the claims involved in the patent, and notice of such cancellation shall be endorsed on copies of the patent distributed after such cancellation by the Patent and Trademark Office.

(b)(1) A claim which is the same as, or for the same or substantially the same subject matter as, a claim of an issued patent may not be made in any application unless such a claim is made prior to one year from the date on which the patent was granted.

(2) A claim which is the same as, or for the same or substantially the same subject matter as, a claim of an application published under section 122(b) may be made in an application filed after the application is published only if the claim is made before 1 year after the date on which the application is published.

(c) Any agreement or understanding between parties to an interference, including any collateral agreements referred to therein, made in connection with or in contemplation of the termination of the interference, shall be in writing and a true copy thereof filed in the Patent and Trademark Office before the termination of the interference as between the said parties to the agreement or understanding. If any party filing the same so requests, the copy shall be kept separate from the file of the interference, and made available only to Government agencies on written request, or to any person on a showing of good cause. Failure to file the copy of such agreement or understanding shall render permanently unenforceable such agreement or understanding and any patent of such parties involved in the interference or any patent subsequently issued on any application of such parties so involved. The Director may, however, on a showing of good cause for failure to file within the time prescribed, permit the filing of the agreement or understanding during the six-month period subsequent to the termination of the interference as between the parties to the agreement or understanding.

The Director shall give notice to the parties or their attorneys of record, a reasonable time prior to said termination, of the filing requirement of this section. If the Director gives such notice at a later time, irrespective of the right to file such agreement or understanding within the six-month period on a showing of good cause, the parties may file such agreement or understanding within sixty days of the receipt of such notice.

Any discretionary action of the Director under this subsection shall be reviewable under section 10 of the Administrative Procedure Act.

(d) Parties to a patent interference, within such time as may be specified by the Director by regulation, may determine such contest or any aspect thereof by arbitration. Such arbitration shall be governed by the provisions of title 9 to the extent such title is not inconsistent with this section. The parties shall give notice of any arbitration award to the Director, and such award shall, as between the parties to the arbitration, be dispositive of the issues to which it relates. The arbitration award shall be unenforceable until such notice is given. Nothing in this subsection shall preclude the Director from determining patentability of the invention involved in the interference.

History of 35 U.S.C. §135[A*]: July 19, 1952, ch. 950, §1, 66 Stat. 801; Oct. 15, 1962, P.L. 87-831, 76 Stat. 958; Jan. 2, 1975, P.L. 93-596, §1, 88 Stat. 1949; Nov. 8, 1984, P.L. 98-622, §§105, 202, 98 Stat. 3385, 3386; Nov. 29, 1999, P.L. 106-113, §1000(a)(9), 113 Stat. 1536; Nov. 2, 2002, P.L. 107-273, §13206(b)(1)(B), 116 Stat. 1906; Sept. 16, 2011, P.L. 112-29, §20(j)(1), 125 Stat. 335.

See also 37 C.F.R. pt. 41.

ANNOTATIONS

Generally

Rolls-Royce, PLC v. United Techs., 603 F.3d 1325, 1330, 95 U.S.P.Q.2d 1097, 1101 (Fed.Cir.2010). "The purpose of a patent interference proceeding is to determine whether two parties claim the same patentable invention, and if so, who under the law is entitled to priority of invention. An interference-in-fact 'exists if the subject matter of a claim of one party would, if prior art, have anticipated or rendered obvious the subject matter of a claim of the opposing party and vice versa.'"

Henkel Corp. v. Procter & Gamble Co., 485 F.3d 1370, 1375, 82 U.S.P.Q.2d 1784, 1788 (Fed.Cir.2007). "As a matter of law, we do not require that a junior party in an interference demonstrate that it recognized the exact language of the ultimate count—only the subject matter of the invention. *At F.3d 1376:* [A]n inventor can demonstrate appreciation without enunciating the precise language of the interference count. [¶] We have held that because appreciation depends on 'an inventor's subjective beliefs about his invention,' an inventor claiming priority must put forward 'objective evidence to corroborate [his] testimony concerning his understanding of the invention.' In other words, 'it is not enough that a party adduce evidence that objective test results comport with an inventor's testimony concerning his state of mind. Rather, there must also be evidence that the junior party timely interpreted or evaluated the results, and understood them to show the existence [of] the invention.'"

Vas-Cath, Inc. v. University of Mo., 473 F.3d 1376, 1379, 81 U.S.P.Q.2d 1524, 1525 (Fed.Cir.2007). "Occasionally the examiner does not act with respect to interfering applications, and a patent is issued to one applicant while another application on the same invention is still pending. In such event the applicant can request that an interference be conducted between the pending application and the issued patent. Following such proceeding and upon the PTO's determination of priority, the prior inventor is granted a patent and, if the losing party has already obtained a patent, the lost claims of the issued patent will be cancelled by operation of law."

Capon v. Eshhar, 418 F.3d 1349, 1351, 76 U.S.P.Q.2d 1078, 1079 (Fed.Cir.2005). "A patent interference is an administrative proceeding pursuant to 35 U.S.C. §§102(g) and 135(a), conducted for the purpose of determining which of competing applicants is the first inventor of common subject matter. An interference is instituted after the separate patent applications have been examined and found to contain patentable subject matter."

Eli Lilly & Co. v. Aradigm Corp., 376 F.3d 1352, 1365, 71 U.S.P.Q.2d 1787, 1796 (Fed.Cir.2004). "To succeed in an interference proceeding, regardless of whether it is conducted in the PTO or a district court under 35 U.S.C. §291, a party that does not have the earliest effective filing date needs only to demonstrate by a preponderance of the evidence that it was the first to invent if the two patents or applications at issue were co-pending before the PTO."

Slip Track Sys. v. Metal-Lite, Inc., 304 F.3d 1256, 1263, 64 U.S.P.Q.2d 1423, 1427 (Fed.Cir.2002). "Most interferences arise in the PTO, involve an interference between two applications or an application and one or more patents, and begin with the creation of a 'count.' The count defines the interfering subject matter and corresponds to a patentable invention. The count may be identical to a single claim at issue or may be broader than the particular claims at issue."

Minnesota Mining & Mfg. v. Norton Co., 929 F.2d 670, 674, 18 U.S.P.Q.2d 1302, 1306 (Fed.Cir.1991). "Issues of patentability can be considered [in an interference proceeding], but infringement will not be."

§135(a)—Generally

Robertson v. Timmermans, 603 F.3d 1309, 1312, 94 U.S.P.Q.2d 1954, 1956 (Fed.Cir.2010). "When a patent applicant copies claims from another application or patent to provoke an interference, and those claims are the subject of a written description challenge during the interference, which disclosure should be used to construe the claims? Our cases now clearly hold that 'when a party challenges written description support for an interference count or the copied claim in an interference, *the originating disclosure provides the meaning of the pertinent claim language.*' *At U.S.P.Q.2d 1957:* In ***Agilent***, we examined two prior decisions of this court, ***In re Spina***, 975 F.2d 854 (Fed.Cir.1992), and ***Rowe v. Dror***, 112 F.3d 473 (Fed.Cir.1997). ***Spina*** involved an appeal from an examiner's rejection of a claim for lack of written description support. We held that the claim, which had been copied from an issued patent in an attempt to provoke an interference, should be 'viewed in the context of the patent from which it was copied.' ***Rowe*** involved an interference in which claims copied from one party's patent into the other party's application were the subject of a motion for invalidity based on prior art. We held that the ***Spina*** rule did not apply, but instead the claims should be interpreted in light of their host disclosure, just as they would during *ex parte* prosecution. [¶] ***Agilent*** clarified that in interference proceedings, the ***Spina*** rule applies when a claim copied from another party's patent or application is challenged for lack of written description requirement support under [35 U.S.C.]

§112, ¶1, and the ***Rowe*** rule applies when the copied claim's validity under 35 U.S.C. §102 or §103 is challenged. That is, the Board must interpret the copied claim in view of the originating disclosure for a written description challenge, and the Board must interpret the copied claim in view of the host disclosure for a validity challenge based on prior art."

Eli Lilly & Co. v. Board of Regents, 334 F.3d 1264, 1267, 67 U.S.P.Q.2d 1161, 1163 (Fed.Cir.2003). Section 135 creates the two-way test that "governs patent interference proceedings, which are designed to determine whether two patent applications (or a patent application and an issued patent) are drawn to the 'same patentable invention' and, if so, which of the competing parties was first to invent the duplicative subject matter. [T]he declaration of an interference pursuant to §135 [is] discretionary. Section 135(a) states that the Board shall determine questions of priority once an interference proceeding is declared. This authority for the Board to determine questions of priority, however, does not vitiate the Director's discretion to begin or discontinue an interference once declared. Accordingly, the mandatory language only instructs the Board of its jurisdiction over an active interference."

In re Gartside, 203 F.3d 1305, 1316-17, 53 U.S.P.Q.2d 1769, 1776-77 (Fed.Cir.2000). "[U]nder §135(a), the Board *should* decide issues relating to priority and patentability that are fairly raised and fully developed during the interference, despite the permissive language of §135(a) with respect to patentability issues. [T]he permissive language ['may determine issues of patentability'] addresses 'the situation when patentability is not placed at issue during the priority contest, but it would contradict the remedial purpose of the legislation if the Board could refuse to decide questions of patentability for which there had been adduced an appropriate record.'"

Tofe v. Winchell, 645 F.2d 58, 62, 209 U.S.P.Q. 379, 383 (C.C.P.A.1981). "When the issue of whether the best mode requirement has been satisfied by a party is raised in an interference, we hold that the issue must be resolved before the issue of priority is addressed."

Fontijn v. Okamoto, 518 F.2d 610, 617-18, 186 U.S.P.Q. 97, 103 (C.C.P.A.1975). "Either party may seek to benefit from broad construction of [a] count so that different embodiments of the invention defined in the count may be supported by the specification of a previously filed application in the U.S. pursuant to [35 U.S.C.] §120 and/or a previously filed foreign application for the same invention pursuant to [35 U.S.C.] §119. Whether the previously filed application is a foreign application sought to be relied upon pursuant to 35 U.S.C. §119 or a domestically filed application governed by 35 U.S.C. §120, its disclosure must satisfy the requirements of the first paragraph of 35 U.S.C. §112 with regard to the invention relied upon therein." *See also* ***In re Wertheim***, 541 F.2d 257, 262 n.6, 191 U.S.P.Q. 90, 96 n.6 (C.C.P.A.1976).

§135(a)—Patentability

Wu v. Wang, 129 F.3d 1237, 1240, 44 U.S.P.Q.2d 1641, 1644 (Fed.Cir.1997). "When resolving [patentability issues within an interference], the Board 'must separately determine the patentability of each claim in the interference, just as it would in an *ex parte* prosecution.'"

§135(a)—Priority

Frazer v. Schlegel, 498 F.3d 1283, 1287, 83 U.S.P.Q.2d 1850, 1853 (Fed.Cir.2007). "In accordance with U.S. law, when the priority claim is based on subject matter disclosed in a foreign patent application whose filing date is properly claimed, ... the foreign application has the same effect as if filed in the U.S. The invention must be 'disclosed in the manner provided by the first paragraph of [35 U.S.C.] §112.' [¶] Constructive reduction to practice does not invoke different standards whether the priority document is foreign or domestic. When interference priority is at issue, constructive reduction to practice of a count may be established by disclosure of an embodiment within the count. *At U.S.P.Q.2d 1854:* Although the Board analyzed the Australian application in terms of 'conception,' when reliance is on a patent document already filed, the question is whether the document discloses the invention of the count by meeting the written description and enablement requirements of ... §112 ¶1, for a filed application serves as a constructive reduction to practice of its content."

Cooper v. Goldfarb, 240 F.3d 1378, 1382, 57 U.S.P.Q.2d 1990, 1992-93 (Fed.Cir.2001). "Priority is generally awarded to the applicant who was first to reduce the invention to practice; however, an applicant who was first to conceive the invention but last to reduce it to practice will be awarded priority if he demonstrates reasonable diligence in his reduction to practice. 'Conception is the formation, in the mind of the inventor, of a definite and permanent idea of the complete and operative invention, as it is thereafter to be applied in practice.' To establish reduction to practice, the inventor must prove that he made an embodiment of the invention that met all of the limitations of the interference count and that he determined that the invention would work for its intended purpose. When testing is necessary to establish that the invention will work for its intended purpose, the embodiment relied upon as evidence of reduction to practice must work for the intended purpose. Moreover, 'the inventor must contemporaneously appreciate that the embodiment worked and that it met all the limitations of the interference count.'" *See also* ***Hitzeman v. Rutter***, 243 F.3d 1345, 1353, 58 U.S.P.Q.2d 1161, 1166 (Fed.Cir.2001).

Rexam Indus. v. Eastman Kodak Co., 182 F.3d 1366, 1369, 51 U.S.P.Q.2d 1457, 1459 (Fed.Cir.1999). "[P]riority issues that have been fully developed and presented to the Board for decision in interference proceedings should be decided by the Board even if a count is deemed unpatentable to one party."

Beech Aircraft Corp. v. EDO Corp., 990 F.2d 1237, 1249, 26 U.S.P.Q.2d 1572, 1582 (Fed.Cir.1993). "In making ... priority determinations, the Board has no interest whatsoever in who may or may not have ownership rights in the subject matter at issue, and therefore, such information has no bearing on the Board's ultimate decision regarding inventorship and priority."

Woods v. Tsuchiya, 754 F.2d 1571, 1581, 225 U.S.P.Q. 11, 17 (Fed.Cir.1985). "The Board ... has jurisdiction over questions which are 'ancillary to priority.' An issue may be so 'logically related' to priority that an award of priority cannot be decided without first resolving that issue, which is then consequently described as 'ancillary.' This 'may require rulings on matters not *per se priority questions*.'"

§135(b)

Loughlin v. Ling, 684 F.3d 1289, 1291, 103 U.S.P.Q.2d 1413, 1414-15 (Fed.Cir.2012). "[Applicant] asserted that [respondent] was barred by [35 U.S.C.] §135(b)(2) from provoking an interference because [respondent's] application is 'an application filed' after the publication date of [applicant's] application and [respondent] copied [applicant's] claim more than one year after its publication date. [¶] The Board concluded that the bar imposed by §135(b)(2) does not apply to an application filed before a published application. Noting that [applicant's] motion raised the issue whether [respondent's] application is 'an application filed' after the date on which [applicant's] application was published, the Board observed that it has consistently determined that [35 U.S.C.] §120 is applicable when considering whether 'an application filed' is after the date on which another application is published. The Board thus held that, since [respondent] was granted §120 priority benefit of its [a]pplication, then [respondent's] involved ... application, having an effective filing date of 16 January 2004, is not an application filed after [applicant's] Application published on 18 November 2004. *At F.3d 1294, U.S.P.Q.2d 1417:* [T]he Board correctly interpreted 'an application filed' in §135(b)(2) as including the possibility of claiming benefit under §120 to an earlier effective filing date." (Internal quotes omitted.)

Adair v. Carter, 668 F.3d 1334, 1337, 101 U.S.P.Q.2d 1625, 1628 (Fed.Cir.2012). Respondent argues "that the question of '[w]hether there is a sufficient degree of identity between pre- and post-critical date claims for compliance with §135(b) is an inquiry that is distinct and independent' from any comparison with the patent claims copied. According to [respondent], the Board correctly interpreted §135(b)(1) in holding that 'establishing support for post-critical date claims does not entail looking at material limitations of the patented claims.' [¶] This court agrees with [respondent]. ... Notwithstanding the seemingly strict language of the statute, a limited exception to this one year bar exists 'where the copier had already been claiming substantially the same invention as the patentee' during the critical time period. *At F.3d 1339, U.S.P.Q.2d 1629:* [T]his court holds that to overcome a §135(b) bar for a post-critical date claim, an applicant must show that such claim is not materially different from a pre-critical date claim present in the application or any predecessor thereto in order to obtain the benefit of the earlier filing date. Any claims filed within the critical period, whether or not later cancelled, may provide pre-critical date support for the later filed patent claim(s), so long as the pre-critical date claims are not materially different from the later filed claim(s). *At U.S.P.Q.2d 1630:* When an applicant adds limitations in response to an examiner's rejection, and those limitations result in allowance, there exists a well established presumption [from ***Festo***] that those limitations are necessary to patentability and thus material. This presumption applies with equal force in the interference context."

Regents of the Univ. of Cal. v. University of Iowa Research Found., 455 F.3d 1371, 1374, 79 U.S.P.Q.2d 1687, 1689 (Fed.Cir.2006). "[A] party confronted with a §135(b)(1) bar [may] show that claims filed after the critical date find support in claims filed before the critical date. If a party can show such support, §135(b)(1) will not act as a bar. Thus, [senior party's] position that the relationship between the post- and pre-critical date claims is not relevant to §135(b)(1) contravenes the weight of precedent. This court has already explained that such a relationship is not only relevant, but dispositive of the §135(b)(1) question. *At F.3d 1375-76, U.S.P.Q.2d 1690-91:* Section 135(b)(1) does not include any language suggesting that a pre-critical date request for an interference makes any difference. Section 135(b)(1) bars any claim having a degree of identity with a claim in an issued patent unless such a claim is filed before the critical date. Thus, title 35 in this section does not demand notice of an impending interference, but instead prohibits unsupported, post-critical date identity. [Senior party] cannot satisfy §135(b)(1) by supplying notice of an interference. Instead, [senior party] must demonstrate that claims in the '191 application provide pre-critical date support for the post-critical date identity between claim 205 and the '646 patent. That demonstration necessarily entails a comparison between pre- and post-critical date claims. [¶] [T]he statutory term 'such a claim' refers to the claim that the potentially interfering party seeks to add, which is directed to the same or substantially the same subject matter as that claimed in a patent, regardless of whether that party earlier filed a different claim having the required identity with a patented claim. The statute requires 'such a claim' to come before the critical date. Thus, §135(b)(1) does not refer to some unrelated claim made earlier in prosecution even if accompanied by a request for interference. The language of the statute, '[a] claim ... may not be made ... unless such a claim is made prior to ...,' necessarily requires that in the event a party seeks to add any claim sharing identity with a patented claim, 'such a claim' must appear before the critical date. When a party seeks to add a new claim, or to amend an existing claim, beyond the critical date for §135(b)(1), this court applies the material differences test discussed in opinions like *Berger* to determine if 'such a claim' is barred. [Senior party's] position that any claim filed within the critical time period supports, for §135(b)(1) purposes, any later added claims, regardless of the relationship between the pre- and post-critical date claims, is simply not consistent with the language of the statute. [¶] [W]hile an interference based on a post-critical date claim is not desirable, where such an interference is merely belated, meaning the same interference should have been earlier declared by the PTO, the interference should not be barred by operation of §135(b)(1). Thus, the limited exception to the one year bar, provided by the 'such a claim' language in §135(b)(1), allows for belated interferences. Beyond such belated interferences, [senior party's] construction of §135(b)(1) would permit different interferences because that construction removes from §135(b)(1) any requirement for a nexus between the pre- and post-critical date claims."

Berman v. Housey, 291 F.3d 1345, 1352, 63 U.S.P.Q.2d 1023, 1028 (Fed.Cir.2002). "[A] determination that the claims involved in an interference are not barred by [35 U.S.C.] §135(b) is a condition precedent to the declaration of an interference that should be resolved before issues of priority and patentability are addressed, and thus when the board is presented with both a preliminary motion involving a §135(b) issue and a preliminary motion involving a garden-variety patentability issue, it should first address the former. ... However, because §135(b) is a threshold issue in an interference, the discretion normally afforded the Board under [37 C.F.R.] §1.640(b) should be tempered by the importance of addressing that issue at a preliminary stage of an interference...."

In re Berger, 279 F.3d 975, 980, 61 U.S.P.Q.2d 1523, 1526 (Fed.Cir.2002). "We review the Board's construction of ... §135(b) de novo, as statutory interpretation is a question of law. *At F.3d 982-83, U.S.P.Q.2d 1527-28:* [S]ection 135(b) was enacted to codify a legal principle akin to laches.... To further that purpose, a copied claim may be entitled to the earlier effective date of prior claims in an application only if the copied claim does not differ from the prior claims in any material limitation. The analysis focuses on the copied claim to determine whether all material limitations of the copied claim necessarily occur in the prior claims. If all material limitations of the copied claim are present in, or necessarily result from, the limitations of the prior claims, then the copied claim is entitled to the earlier effective filing date of those prior claims for purposes of satisfying ... §135(b). [¶] Inclusion of a limitation in a claim to avoid the prior art provides strong evidence of the materiality of the included limitation. Because the prior art applies in like manner to the claims as copied, the materiality of a limitation in a claim copied to provoke an interference translates to the copying inventor's application for purposes of assessing compliance with ... §135(b). [¶] To establish entitlement to the effective filing date of an earlier claim for compliance with §135(b), a material limitation need not be expressed explicitly, but may also be expressed inherently if the material limitation 'necessarily results' from other limitations in the claim."

Case v. CPC Int'l, 730 F.2d 745, 749-50, 221 U.S.P.Q. 196, 200 (Fed.Cir.1984). "[I]n appropriate circumstances, phantom counts may be used to define the subject matter of an interference, whether it involves two applications or a patent and an application.... Specifically, we reject [patent owner's] contention that an interference could only be declared if [patent applicant] copied his patent claims precisely. The import of ... §135(b) is clearly to the contrary."

Cytologic, Inc. v. Biopheresis GmbH, 682 F.Supp.2d 1, 15 (D.D.C.2010). "Once an interference has been declared, ... the parties disagree as to who bears the burden of showing materiality (or immateriality) when a preliminary §135(b)(1) motion is filed during interference proceedings. *At 17:* [T]he patent examiner must be satisfied that the conditions for an interference have been met before an interference is declared. This in turn requires that the party requesting the interference sufficiently demonstrate that any claims filed after the one year critical date are able to benefit from the earlier filing date of prior claims, such that they are not barred by §135(b)(1)."

§135(c)

In re Lueders, 111 F.3d 1569, 1577, 42 U.S.P.Q.2d 1481, 1486 (Fed.Cir.1997). "[T]he express application of the [Administrative Procedure Act (APA)] to [35 U.S.C. §135(c)] strongly supports the conclusion that the APA should not apply elsewhere in §135 and surely not to other sections in Title 35, like [35 U.S.C.] §141 (Appeal to Court of Appeals for the Federal Circuit)."

CTS Corp. v. Piher Int'l, 727 F.2d 1550, 1555, 221 U.S.P.Q. 11, 14 (Fed.Cir.1984). "As a means to prevent anti-competitive settlements between parties involved in patent interferences, any settlement agreements between parties must be filed with the PTO. *At F.2d 1556, U.S.P.Q. 15:* [P]ursuant to §135(c), there must be a causal relationship between the agreements and the termination of the interference."

U.S. v. FMC Corp., 717 F.2d 775, 776, 219 U.S.P.Q. 761, 762 (3d Cir.1983). "[T]he U.S. claims a right of action to sue to invalidate a patent under ... §135(c). No provision of law expressly sanctions such an action. It is now necessary to decide whether Congress nevertheless impliedly authorized lawsuits by the U.S. to invalidate a patent when the patent holder violates ... §135(c) by not filing with the government the agreements executed to settle a patent interference dispute. We hold that it did not."

§135[B*]. DERIVATION PROCEEDINGS

Section 135[B] is effective for patent applications and patents issued on those applications that have ever contained (1) a claim to a claimed invention that has an "effective filing date," as defined in §100(i), p. 495, on or after Mar. 16, 2013; or (2) a specific reference under §120, §121, or §365(c) to any patent or application that ever contained such a claim. However, §135[B*] will not apply to patent applications and patents issued thereon that have ever contained (1) a claim to a claimed invention that has an "effective filing date," as defined in §100(i), p. 495, before Mar. 16, 2013; or (2) a specific reference under §120, §121, or §365(c) to any patent or application that ever contained such a claim. Section 135[B*] is not effective for patent applications filed before Mar. 16, 2013, or patents issued on those applications.*

(a) Institution of proceeding—

(1) In general.—An applicant for patent may file a petition with respect to an invention to institute a derivation proceeding in the Office. The petition shall set forth with particularity the basis for finding that an individual named in an earlier application as the inventor or a joint inventor derived such invention from an individual named in the petitioner's application as the inventor or a joint inventor and, without authorization, the earlier application claiming such invention was filed. Whenever the Director determines that a petition filed under this subsection demonstrates that the standards for instituting a derivation proceeding are met, the Director may institute a derivation proceeding.

(2) Time for filing.—A petition under this section with respect to an invention that is the same or substantially the same invention as a claim contained in a patent issued on an earlier application, or contained in an earlier application when published or deemed published under section 122(b), may not be filed unless such petition is filed during the 1-year period following the date on which the patent containing such claim was granted or the earlier application containing such claim was published, whichever is earlier.

(3) Earlier application.—For purposes of this section, an application shall not be deemed to be an earlier application with respect to an invention, relative to another application, unless a claim to the invention was or could have been made in such application having an effective filing date that is earlier than the effective filing date of any claim to the invention that was or could have been made in such other application.

(4) No appeal.—A determination by the Director whether to institute a derivation proceeding under paragraph (1) shall be final and not appealable.

(b) Determination by Patent Trial and Appeal Board.—In a derivation proceeding instituted under subsection (a), the Patent Trial and Appeal Board shall determine whether an inventor named in the earlier application derived the claimed invention from an inventor named in the petitioner's application and, without authorization, the earlier application claiming such invention was filed. In appropriate circumstances, the Patent Trial and Appeal Board may correct the naming of the inventor in any application or patent at issue. The Director shall prescribe regulations setting forth standards for the conduct of derivation proceedings, including requiring parties to provide sufficient evidence to prove and rebut a claim of derivation.

(c) Deferral of decision.—The Patent Trial and Appeal Board may defer action on a petition for a derivation proceeding until the expiration of the 3-month period beginning on the date on which the Director issues a patent that includes the claimed invention that is the subject of the petition. The Patent Trial and Appeal Board also may defer action on a petition for a derivation proceeding, or stay the proceeding after it has been instituted, until the termination of a proceeding under chapter 30, 31, or 32 involving the patent of the earlier applicant.

(d) Effect of final decision.—The final decision of the Patent Trial and Appeal Board, if adverse to claims in an application for patent, shall constitute the final refusal by the Office on those claims. The final decision of the Patent Trial and Appeal Board, if adverse to claims in a patent, shall, if no appeal or other review of the decision has been or can be taken or had, constitute cancellation of those claims, and notice of such cancellation shall be endorsed on copies of the patent distributed after such cancellation.

(e) Settlement.—Parties to a proceeding instituted under subsection (a) may terminate the proceeding by filing a written statement reflecting the agreement of the parties as to the correct inventor of the claimed invention in dispute. Unless the Patent Trial and Appeal Board finds the agreement to be inconsistent with the evidence of record, if any, it shall take action consistent with the agreement. Any written settlement or understanding of the parties shall be filed with the Director. At the request of a party to the proceeding, the agreement or understanding shall be treated as business confidential information, shall be kept separate from the file of the involved patents or applications, and shall be made available only to Government agencies on written request, or to any person on a showing of good cause.

(f) Arbitration.—Parties to a proceeding instituted under subsection (a) may, within such time as may be specified by the Director by regulation, determine such contest or any aspect thereof by arbitration. Such arbitration shall be governed by the provisions of title 9, to the extent such title is not inconsistent with this section. The parties shall give notice of any arbitration award to the Director, and such award shall, as between the parties to the arbitration, be dispositive of the issues to which it relates. The arbitration award shall be unenforceable until such notice is given. Nothing in this subsection shall preclude the Director from determining the patentability of the claimed inventions involved in the proceeding.

History of 35 U.S.C. §135[B*]: July 19, 1952, ch. 950, §1, 66 Stat. 801; Oct. 15, 1962, P.L. 87-831, 76 Stat. 958; Jan. 2, 1975, P.L. 93-596, §1, 88 Stat. 1949; Nov. 8, 1984, P.L. 98-622, §§105, 202, 98 Stat. 3385, 3386; Nov. 29, 1999, P.L. 106-113, §1000(a)(9), 113 Stat. 1536; Nov. 2, 2002, P.L. 107-273, §13206(b)(1)(B), 116 Stat. 1906; Sept. 16, 2011, P.L. 112-29, §3(i), 125 Stat. 289; Jan. 14, 2013, P.L. 112-274, §1(e), (k)(1), 126 Stat. 2456, 2457.

See also 37 C.F.R. §§42.1-42.80, 42.400-42.412; Office Patent Trial Practice Guide, p. 1336.

CHAPTER 13. REVIEW OF PATENT & TRADEMARK OFFICE DECISIONS

§141. APPEAL TO COURT OF APPEALS FOR THE FEDERAL CIRCUIT

(a) Examinations.—An applicant who is dissatisfied with the final decision in an appeal to the Patent Trial and Appeal Board under section 134(a) may appeal the Board's decision to the United States Court of Appeals for the Federal Circuit. By filing such an appeal, the applicant waives his or her right to proceed under section 145.

(b) Reexaminations.—A patent owner who is dissatisfied with the final decision in an appeal of a reexamination to the Patent Trial and Appeal Board under section 134(b) may appeal the Board's decision only to the United States Court of Appeals for the Federal Circuit.

(c) Post-grant and inter partes reviews.—A party to an inter partes review or a post-grant review who is dissatisfied with the final written decision of the Patent Trial and Appeal Board under section 318(a) or 328(a) (as the case may be) may appeal the Board's decision only to the United States Court of Appeals for the Federal Circuit.

(d) Derivation proceedings.—A party to a derivation proceeding who is dissatisfied with the final decision of the Patent Trial and Appeal Board in the proceeding may appeal the decision to the United States Court of Appeals for the Federal Circuit, but such appeal shall be dismissed if any adverse party to such derivation proceeding, within 20 days after the appellant has filed notice of appeal in accordance with section 142, files notice with the Director that the party elects to have all further proceedings conducted as provided in section 146. If the appellant does not, within 30 days after the filing of such notice by the adverse party, file a civil action under section 146, the Board's decision shall govern the further proceedings in the case.

History of 35 U.S.C. §141: July 19, 1952, ch. 950, §1, 66 Stat. 802; Apr. 2, 1982, P.L. 97-164, §163(a)(7), (b)(2), 96 Stat. 49, 50; Nov. 8, 1984, P.L. 98-622, §203(a), 98 Stat. 3387; Nov. 29, 1999, P.L. 106-113, §1000(a)(9), 113 Stat. 1536; Nov. 2, 2002, P.L. 107-273, §§13106(c), 13206(b)(1)(B), 116 Stat. 1901, 1906; Sept. 16, 2011, P.L. 112-29, §7(c)(1), 125 Stat. 314.

See also 28 U.S.C. §§1292, 1295; 37 C.F.R. pt. 90.

ANNOTATIONS

Biogen MA, Inc. v. Japanese Found. for Cancer Research, 785 F.3d 648, 653-54, 114 U.S.P.Q.2d 1669, 1673 (Fed.Cir.2015). "[A]n election of [35 U.S.C.] §146 review would foreclose [35 U.S.C.] §141 review in this court and deprive us of jurisdiction. But of course, this is true only if §146 review were available, since, in general, 'an election will be found only if a party has chosen to pursue one position that is inconsistent with another possible position....' [¶] In short, we have jurisdiction under §141 as a result of the transfer if §146 review was unavailable, but we lack jurisdiction if this case was properly brought to the district court under §146. We thus must determine if the district court indeed lacked jurisdiction under §146 in order to determine whether we lack jurisdiction and should retransfer the case. *At U.S.P.Q.2d 1674:* We turn now to the question of whether pre-AIA §146 conferred jurisdiction on the district court in this case. ... Ultimately, we conclude that specific statutory provisions in the AIA as amended govern the availability of §146 review for interferences declared after September 15, 2012, and that for interferences declared after that date, §146 review is not available. *At F.3d 657, U.S.P.Q.2d 1676:* In short, because the AIA and its technical corrections provided that only pre-AIA §141 review in this court would be available for interferences declared after September 15, 2012, and the ... interference here was declared July 16, 2013, the district court properly found that it lacked subject matter jurisdiction. It follows that we have jurisdiction to hear [P's] appeal pursuant to §141."

In re Comiskey, 554 F.3d 967, 974, 89 U.S.P.Q.2d 1655, 1659 (Fed.Cir.2009). "[A] reviewing court can (and should) affirm an agency decision on a legal ground not relied on by the agency if there is no issue of fact, policy, or agency expertise."

Mazzari v. Rogan, 323 F.3d 1000, 1004, 66 U.S.P.Q.2d 1049, 1051-52 (Fed.Cir.2003). "A [35 U.S.C.] §145 review is distinct from a [35 U.S.C.] §141 appeal in that it affords the applicant an opportunity to present additional evidence or argue the previous evidence afresh, either by simply relying upon the record below or by reintroducing the same evidence through alternative means such as live testimony."

§142. NOTICE OF APPEAL

When an appeal is taken to the United States Court of Appeals for the Federal Circuit, the appellant shall file in the Patent and Trademark Office a written notice of appeal directed to the Director, within such time after the date of the decision from which the appeal is taken as the Director prescribes, but in no case less than 60 days after that date.

History of 35 U.S.C. §142: July 19, 1952, ch. 950, §1, 66 Stat. 802; Jan. 2, 1975, P.L. 93-596, §1, 88 Stat. 1949; Apr. 2, 1982, P.L. 97-164, §163(a)(7), 96 Stat. 49; Nov. 8, 1984, P.L. 98-620, §414(a), 98 Stat. 3363; Nov. 29, 1999, P.L. 106-113, §1000(a)(9), 113 Stat. 1536; Nov. 2, 2002, P.L. 107-273, §13206(b)(1)(B), 116 Stat. 1906.

See also 28 U.S.C. §§1292, 1295; 37 C.F.R. §90.2.

ANNOTATIONS

In re McNeil-PPC, Inc., 574 F.3d 1393, 1397, 91 U.S.P.Q.2d 1576, 1579-80 (Fed.Cir.2009). "The crux of the matter is what the phrase 'the date of the decision,' which appears in [§142], means. *At F.3d 1398:* Based on the evidence before us, it appears that only when an opinion is released to the public (or at least the parties) is it truly decided—until then, it is possible for the Board to decide to revise it. [¶] [W]e find that the Board issued its decision on [appellant's] request on [the date opinion was mailed], and that the Board therefore decided this case on [the date opinion was mailed], not [the date printed on opinion]. [Appellant's] appeal is therefore timely."

§143. PROCEEDINGS ON APPEAL

With respect to an appeal described in section 142, the Director shall transmit to the United States Court of Appeals for the Federal Circuit a certified list of the documents comprising the record in the Patent and Trademark Office. The court may request that the Director forward the original or certified copies of such documents during pendency of the appeal. In an ex parte case, the Director shall submit to the court in writing the grounds for the decision of the Patent and Trademark Office, addressing all of the issues raised in the appeal. The Director shall have the right to intervene in an appeal from a decision entered by the Patent Trial and Appeal Board in a derivation proceeding under section 135 or in an inter partes or post-grant review under chapter 31 or 32. The court shall, before hearing an appeal, give notice of the time and place of the hearing to the Director and the parties in the appeal.

History of 35 U.S.C. §143: July 19, 1952, ch. 950, §1, 66 Stat. 802; Jan. 2, 1975, P.L. 93-596, §1, 88 Stat. 1949; Apr. 2, 1982, P.L. 97-164, §163(a)(7), 96 Stat. 49; Nov. 8, 1984, P.L. 98-620, §414(a), 98 Stat. 3363; Nov. 29, 1999, P.L. 106-113, §1000(a)(9), 113 Stat. 1536; Nov. 2, 2002, P.L. 107-273, §§13202(b)(2), 13206(b)(1)(B), 116 Stat. 1901, 1906; Sept. 16, 2011, P.L. 112-29, §§7(c)(3), 20(j)(1), 125 Stat. 314, 335.

§144. DECISION ON APPEAL

The United States Court of Appeals for the Federal Circuit shall review the decision from which an appeal is taken on the record before the Patent and Trademark Office. Upon its determination the court shall issue to the Director its mandate and opinion, which shall be entered of record in the Patent and Trademark Office and shall govern the further proceedings in the case.

History of 35 U.S.C. §144: July 19, 1952, ch. 950, §1, 66 Stat. 802; Jan. 2, 1975, P.L. 93-596, §1, 88 Stat. 1949; Apr. 2, 1982, P.L. 97-164, §163(a)(7) in part, 96 Stat. 49; Nov. 8, 1984, P.L. 98-620, §414(a), 98 Stat. 3363; Nov. 29, 1999, P.L. 106-113, §1000(a)(9), 113 Stat. 1536; Nov. 2, 2002, P.L. 107-273, §13206(b)(1)(B), 116 Stat. 1906.

ANNOTATIONS

Board of Trs. of the Leland Stanford Jr. Univ. v. Chinese Univ. of Hong Kong, 860 F.3d 1367, 1374, 123 U.S.P.Q.2d 1395, 1400 (Fed.Cir.2017). "Our precedent makes clear that our review of a [PTAB] interference decision must be confined to the 'four corners' of the record before the [PTAB]."

Brand v. Miller, 487 F.3d 862, 868, 82 U.S.P.Q.2d 1705, 1709 (Fed.Cir.2007). Section 144 "directs us to review 'on the record' the decisions of the Board. [F]indings of fact by the Board must in all cases be supported by substantial evidence in the record. [¶] Under the substantial evidence standard of review, we search for evidence, clearly set forth in the record below, to justify the conclusions that the Board has drawn. *At F.3d 869, U.S.P.Q.2d 1710:* [I]n the context of a contested case, it is impermissible for the Board to base its factual findings on its expertise, rather than on evidence in the record, although the Board's expertise appropriately plays a role in interpreting record evidence."

§145. CIVIL ACTION TO OBTAIN PATENT

The change from "Board of Patent Appeals and Interferences" to "Patent Trial and Appeal Board" is effective for patent applications and patents issued on those applications that contain or contained a claim to a claimed invention that has an effective filing date on or after Mar. 16, 2013, or for any applications or patents that contain or contained a claim to a specific reference under §120, §121, or §365(c) that have an effective filing date on or after Mar. 16, 2013.

An applicant dissatisfied with the decision of the Patent Trial and Appeal Board in an appeal under section 134(a) may, unless appeal has been taken to the United States Court of Appeals for the Federal Circuit, have remedy by civil action against the Director in the United States District Court for the Eastern District of Virginia if commenced within such time after such decision, not less than sixty days, as the Director appoints. The court may adjudge that such applicant is entitled to receive a patent for his invention, as specified in any of his claims involved in the decision of the Patent Trial and Appeal Board, as the facts in the case may appear and such adjudication shall authorize the Director to issue such patent on compliance with the requirements of law. All the expenses of the proceedings shall be paid by the applicant.

History of 35 U.S.C. §145: July 19, 1952, ch. 950, §1, 66 Stat. 803; Apr. 2, 1982, P.L. 97-164, §163(a)(7) in part, 96 Stat. 49; Nov. 8, 1984, P.L. 98-622, 98 Stat. 3387; Nov. 29, 1999, P.L. 106-113, §1000(a)(9), 113 Stat. 1536; Nov. 2, 2002, P.L. 107-273, §13206(b)(1)(B), 116 Stat. 1906; Sept. 16, 2011, P.L. 112-29, §§3(j)(1), 9(a), 20(j)(1), 125 Stat. 290, 316, 335.

See also 28 U.S.C. §1338; 48 U.S.C. §1405q.

ANNOTATIONS

Kappos v. Hyatt, 566 U.S. 431, 433-34, 102 U.S.P.Q.2d 1337, 1339 (2012). "This case requires us to consider two questions. First, we must decide whether there are any limitations on the applicant's ability to introduce new evidence before the district court. For the reasons set forth below, we conclude that there are no evidentiary restrictions beyond those already imposed by the [FREs] and the [FRCPs]. Second, we must determine what standard of review the district court should apply when considering new evidence. On this question, we hold that the district court must make a *de novo* finding when new evidence is presented on a disputed question of fact."

NantKwest, Inc. v. Matal, 869 F.3d 1327, 1327, 124 U.S.P.Q.2d 1068, 1069 (Fed.Cir.2017). Issue on en banc rehearing: Did the panel in ***NantKwest, Inc. v. Matal***, 860 F.3d 1352 (Fed.Cir.2017), correctly determine that 35 U.S.C. §145's "all the expenses of the proceedings" provision authorizes an award of the PTO's attorney fees?

In re Teles AG Informationstechnologien, 747 F.3d 1357, 1359, 110 U.S.P.Q.2d 1310, 1312 (Fed.Cir. 2014). "The [PTO] conducted an *ex parte* reexamination of the ... patent and rejected claims ... as obvious under 35 U.S.C. §103. The Board of Patent Appeals and Interferences ('Board') affirmed. [Petitioner] brought suit in the [D.C.] U.S. District Court ..., challenging the Board's decision pursuant to 35 U.S.C. §145.... We agree with the district court that it lacked subject matter jurisdiction, and hold that the version of §145 in effect at the time did not authorize a patent owner in an *ex parte* reexamination to bring suit in district court challenging the Board's action. But we hold that the district court erred in dismissing the case and instead should have transferred the case as it attempted to do after the dismissal. We treat the case as having been transferred to this court and consider it as an appeal from the Board's decision."

§146. CIVIL ACTION IN CASE OF DERIVATION PROCEEDING

Any party to a derivation proceeding dissatisfied with the decision of the Patent Trial and Appeal Board on the derivation proceeding, may have remedy by civil action, if commenced within such time after such decision, not less than sixty days, as the Director appoints or as provided in section 141, unless he has appealed to the United States Court of Appeals for the Federal Circuit, and such appeal is pending or has been decided. In such suits the record in the Patent and Trademark Office shall be admitted on motion of either party upon the terms and conditions as to costs, expenses, and the further cross-examination of the witnesses as the court imposes, without prejudice to the right of the parties to take further testimony. The testimony and exhibits of the record in the Patent and Trademark Office when admitted shall have the same effect as if originally taken and produced in the suit.

Such suit may be instituted against the party in interest as shown by the records of the Patent and Trademark Office at the time of the decision complained of, but any party in interest may become a party to the action. If there be adverse parties residing in a plurality of districts not embraced within the same state, or an adverse party residing in a foreign country, the United States District Court for the Eastern District of Virginia shall have jurisdiction and may issue summons against the adverse parties directed to the marshal of any district in which any adverse party resides. Summons against adverse parties residing in foreign countries may be served by publication or otherwise as the court directs. The Director shall not be a necessary party but he shall be notified of the filing of the suit by the clerk of the court in which it is filed and shall have the right to intervene. Judgment of the court in favor of the right of an applicant to a patent shall authorize the Director to issue such patent on the filing in the Patent and Trademark Office of a certified copy of the judgment and on compliance with the requirements of law.

History of 35 U.S.C. §146: July 19, 1952, ch. 950, §1, 66 Stat. 803; Jan. 2, 1975, P.L. 93-596, §1, 88 Stat. 1949; Apr. 2, 1982, P.L. 97-164, §163(a)(7) in part, 96 Stat. 49; Nov. 8, 1984, P.L. 98-622, §203(c), 98 Stat. 3387; Nov. 29, 1999, P.L. 106-113, §1000(a)(9), 113 Stat. 1536; Nov. 2, 2002, P.L. 107-273, §13206(b)(1)(B), 116 Stat. 1906; Sept. 16, 2011, P.L. 112-29, §§3(j)(1), (2)(A), (4), 9(a), 20(j)(1), 125 Stat. 290, 316, 335.

ANNOTATIONS

Generally

Streck, Inc. v. Research & Diagnostic Sys., 659 F.3d 1186, 1188-89, 100 U.S.P.Q.2d 1613, 1615 (Fed.Cir. 2011). A 35 U.S.C. §146 "action requires that there first have been an interference proceeding [now derivation proceeding] in the PTO. The losing party may either appeal directly to the Federal Circuit on the PTO record, in accordance with 35 U.S.C. §141; or may obtain a 'remedy by civil action' in district court as provided by ... §146, followed by appeal to the Federal Circuit. *At F.3d 1191-92, U.S.P.Q.2d 1617:* [T]he district court appropriately considered additional evidence and conducted a *de novo* determination of the issue of priority under §146. [¶] Because ... a §146 action is a new civil proceeding subject to *de novo* determination, the district court properly placed the burden of persuasion on [appellant]. *At U.S.P.Q.2d 1618:* [T]he standard of proof in this §146 proceeding was by a preponderance of the evidence and was ... a lesser burden than was imposed on [appellant] in the infringement proceeding, where invalidity based on [appellant's] asserted prior invention was required to be proved by clear and convincing evidence. [¶] Determination of priority as between competing inventors is guided by rules that have arisen from the activities of technology-based creativity. In priority disputes, including disputes under §146, the questions of conception and reduction to practice are deemed to be matters of law, founded on facts. The district court's determination of priority in a §146 action is reviewed *de novo* on appeal, and the court's factual findings supporting its legal conclusions are reviewed for clear error."

Robertson v. Timmermans, 603 F.3d 1309, 1312, 94 U.S.P.Q.2d 1954, 1956 (Fed.Cir.2010). "When a patent applicant copies claims from another application or patent to provoke an interference [now derivation], and those claims are the subject of a written description challenge during the interference, which disclosure should be used to construe the claims? Our cases now clearly hold that 'when a party challenges written description support for an interference count or the copied claim in an interference, *the originating disclosure provides the meaning of the pertinent claim language.*' *At U.S.P.Q.2d 1957:* In ***Agilent***, we examined two prior decisions of this court, ***In re Spina***, 975 F.2d 854 (Fed.Cir.1992), and ***Rowe v. Dror***, 112 F.3d 473 (Fed.Cir.1997). ***Spina*** involved an appeal from an examiner's rejection of a claim for lack of written description support. We held that the claim, which had been copied from an issued patent in an attempt to provoke an interference, should be 'viewed in the context of the patent from which it was copied.' ***Rowe*** involved an interference in which claims copied from one party's patent into the other party's application were the subject of a motion for invalidity based on prior art. We held that the ***Spina*** rule did not apply, but instead the claims should be interpreted in light of their host disclosure, just as they would during *ex parte* prosecution. [¶] ***Agilent*** clarified that in interference proceedings, the ***Spina*** rule applies when a claim copied from another party's patent or application is challenged for lack of written description requirement support under [35 U.S.C.] §112, ¶1, and the ***Rowe*** rule applies when the copied claim's validity under 35 U.S.C. §102 or §103 is challenged. That is, the Board must interpret the copied claim in view of the originating disclosure for a written description challenge, and the Board must interpret the copied claim in view of the host disclosure for a validity challenge based on prior art." *See also* ***Agilent Techs. v. Affymetrix, Inc.***, 567 F.3d 1366, 1374-75, 91 U.S.P.Q.2d 1161, 1166-67 (Fed.Cir.2009).

Vas-Cath, Inc. v. University of Mo., 473 F.3d 1376, 1383, 81 U.S.P.Q.2d 1524, 1528 (Fed.Cir.2007). "[H]ere [appellee] did not simply procure a patent through the routine of *ex parte* examination, but requested the PTO to conduct litigation-type activity, obtaining a favorable agency ruling for which [§146] authorizes judicial review. *At F.3d 1385, U.S.P.Q.2d 1530:* [Appellee] initiated and participated in the contested PTO interference [now derivation] against [appellant]; we conclude that [appellee] cannot both retain the fruits of that action and bar the losing party from its statutory right of review, even if that review is conducted in federal court. [T]he state's actions with respect to the interference include waiver with respect to the ensuing civil action. Having waived any potential immunity as to the interference contest in the PTO, we conclude that [appellee] waived any Constitution-based objection to [appellant's] statutory right of judicial review. The dismissal of the §146 action is reversed...."

Tibbetts Indus. v. Knowles Elec., Inc., 386 F.2d 209, 212, 156 U.S.P.Q. 65, 67 (7th Cir.1967). "'No violence is done to [35 U.S.C.] §§141 and 146 by reading the word 'decision' to refer to every independent adjudication made by the Board. Nothing in the statute requires a waiver following one decision to reach a second decision in the same interference [now derivation]. The statute speaks solely in terms of 'decisions,' not interferences or proceedings.'"

Burden of Proof

Kirschke v. Lamar, 426 F.2d 870, 873 n.3, 165 U.S.P.Q. 679, 681 n.3 (8th Cir.1970). "With respect to issues presented to the Board and decided by it adversely to appellants, they have the burden of proof in the district court. That burden is onerous, considering the appropriate deference which must be rendered to the considered judgment of the Board in determining who is entitled to priority. The party seeking to overturn that question of fact must establish 'by testimony which in character and amount carries thorough conviction' that the Board's decision was clearly erroneous."

Election of Forum

Winner Int'l Royalty Corp. v. Wang, 202 F.3d 1340, 1343, 53 U.S.P.Q.2d 1580, 1582 (Fed.Cir.2000). "Because [P] filed his appeal first, and responded in timely fashion to [D's] notice of election by filing a [35 U.S.C.] §146 action in the District Court for the District of Columbia, [P's] choice of forum governed. We then dismissed the [35 U.S.C.] §141 appeal as superseded by the §146 action." *See also* ***Wu v. Wang***, 129 F.3d 1237, 1242, 44 U.S.P.Q.2d 1641, 1646 (Fed.Cir.1997).

In re Van Geuns, 946 F.2d 845, 849, 20 U.S.P.Q.2d 1291, 1294 (Fed.Cir.1991). "To promote efficient judicial management and conservation of scarce judicial resources, this court may enjoin parties under its jurisdiction from proceeding with a concurrent action [in district court under §146] involving the same or related issues. In deciding whether to enjoin concurrent litigation, this court must determine whether resolution of this case disposes of the other litigation."

Minnesota Mining & Mfg. v. Norton Co., 929 F.2d 670, 674-75, 18 U.S.P.Q.2d 1302, 1306 (Fed.Cir.1991). "We ... hold that it was an abuse of discretion to have dismissed a declaratory judgment action for non-infringement based on a pending interference proceeding [now derivation proceeding], when the interference cannot decide (or is not likely to moot) the infringement issues raised and when the declaratory judgment plaintiff will likely suffer significant ongoing harm during any delay."

Issue Jurisdiction

Rexam Indus. v. Eastman Kodak Co., 182 F.3d 1366, 1370, 51 U.S.P.Q.2d 1457, 1460 (Fed.Cir.1999). "The fact that the [priority] issue comes before a district court in a §146 proceeding is of no moment, since such an action is derivative of the interference [now derivation] conducted in the PTO. Priority was at issue at the Board level; it can also be at the district court level. Issues properly raised at the Board are fair ground for litigation in the district court."

Standard Oil v. Montedison, S.p.A., 540 F.2d 611, 616, 191 U.S.P.Q. 657, 660-61 (3d Cir.1976). "A civil action brought under ... §146 is essentially a proceeding to review the action of the Board of Patent Interferences [now Patent Trial and Appeal Board] in an interference proceeding [now derivation proceeding] in denying priority of invention to the plaintiff. If the district court decides the question of priority against the plaintiff, the latter has obtained the full remedy which the statute gives him. While in form a trial *de novo*, the review proceeding is ordinarily subject to the general rule of estoppel applicable to proceedings for the review of administrative agency actions that consideration of issues ancillary to priority is limited to those issues which have been raised before the Board in the interference proceeding. Fraud in prosecuting a party's case in an interference proceeding may obviously affect the Board's determination of priority and may, therefore, be raised before the Board. If so raised, it may, of course, also be raised in the §146 suit in the district court. *At F.2d 617:* [I]n appropriate circumstances the district court may, ... in the exercise of a sound discretion, permit an issue of fraud which infected the Board's determination to be raised though it was not raised in the interference proceeding. In determining whether to make in this regard a discretionary exception to the general rule against raising new issues, the district court will consider, *inter alia*, whether there was suppression, bad faith or gross negligence on the part of the plaintiff in failing to raise the issue of fraud before the Board of Patent Interferences or whether, on the other hand, the evidence of such fraud was not then reasonably available to him. Whether the issue has been or may be more conveniently and expeditiously raised in another judicial proceeding has relevance. If after considering all relevant factors the court concludes that manifest injustice to the parties and the public will otherwise result, it should permit the issue to be raised for the first time in the §146 proceeding. [¶] We do not regard the discretionary power of the district court to permit an issue of fraud to be raised for the first time in a §146 action as extending to issues of fraud which are not involved in the interference proceeding itself. For it is only fraud which may have affected the determination by the Board of the factual issue of priority of invention, i.e., the question as to which of the parties involved in the interference actually first used the device or process of the invention, which could have any effect on the determination by the Board of that historical fact. *At F.2d 618, U.S.P.Q. 662:* [A] defendant in a §146 action is entitled to notice in the complaint, or by amendment to it, of an issue of fraud which, in the exercise of the court's discretion, has been permitted for the first time to be litigated in that action."

Montecatini Edison, S.P.A. v. Ziegler, 486 F.2d 1279, 1283, 179 U.S.P.Q. 458, 460 (D.C.Cir.1973). "The counterclaim pleads a common law cause of action sounding in tort and seeks various legal and equitable relief. Such a claim is obviously beyond the jurisdiction of a [PTO] tribunal. It was not presented before the Board of Patent Interferences [now Patent Trial and Appeal Board] because it *could not* be presented there. Under these circumstances, failure to assert the claim is not a waiver and [D] is not estopped from interposing his counterclaim in this action. *At F.2d 1287, U.S.P.Q. 463:* We hold … that a counterclaim, whether permissive or compulsory, may be asserted by a §146 defendant to the same extent as in any other civil action governed by the Federal Rules, subject to the requirements of the doctrine of exhaustion of administrative remedies."

Boyce v. Anderson, 405 F.2d 605, 608, 160 U.S.P.Q. 180, 182 (9th Cir.1968). "[T]he fact that, upon a judicial determination of priority in favor of the challenger the court may inquire further concerning validity issues, such as the 'in public use or on sale' requirement of 35 U.S.C. §102(b), does not mean that the court may, as it did here, bypass the priority issue and proceed directly and exclusively to other validity issues concerning the plaintiff's application for a patent. The result of such a course is to disregard completely the primary purpose of a [35 U.S.C.] §146 proceeding."

Parties

Rexam Indus. v. Eastman Kodak Co., 182 F.3d 1366, 1371, 51 U.S.P.Q.2d 1457, 1461 (Fed.Cir.1999). "[D] won the interference [now derivation] at the Board level and it is entitled to defend itself in a suit that [P] brought against it. [U.S. Const.] art. 3 … limits federal courts to hearing actual 'cases or controversies,' and a 'mere' competitor is not entitled to challenge another's patent absent a threat sufficient to constitute a 'case or controversy.' Here, however, [D] won a properly constituted interference and is now defending the Board's judgment against [P's] challenge. [D] is entitled to defend that judgment when challenged. The matter is therefore not moot. … Thus, even though the patentability of [D's] claims has been decided adversely to [D] in a proceeding with a third party …, [D] is entitled to defend itself in the [35 U.S.C.] §146 proceeding brought by [P]."

Commonwealth of Australia v. Radio Corp., 399 F.2d 807, 809 n.2, 159 U.S.P.Q. 1, 2 n.2 (2d Cir.1968). "The civil suit authorized under 35 U.S.C. §146 need not involve the same parties as did the interference proceedings [now derivation proceedings] in the [PTO]; by the terms of §146 it is permissible for the real parties in interest to be the named parties in the district court action."

Barr Rubber Prods. v. Burlington Mills, Inc., 306 F.2d 268, 269, 133 U.S.P.Q. 617, 618 (D.C.Cir.1962). "[T]he Commissioner [now Director] is not an 'adverse' party for the jurisdictional purposes of the statute…."

Standard of Review & Additional Evidence

Morgan v. Daniels, 153 U.S. 120, 125 (1894). "[I]t must be laid down as a rule that, where the question decided in the [PTO] is one between contesting parties as to priority of invention, the decision there made must be accepted as controlling upon that question of fact in any subsequent suit between the same parties, unless the contrary is established by testimony which in character and amount carries thorough conviction." *See also* ***Rex Chainbelt Inc. v. Borg-Warner Corp.***, 477 F.2d 481, 484, 177 U.S.P.Q. 549, 551 (7th Cir.1973).

Troy v. Samson Mfg., 758 F.3d 1322, 1325, 111 U.S.P.Q.2d 1722, 1724 (Fed.Cir.2014). "We conclude that the Supreme Court's decision in [***Kappos v.***] ***Hyatt***[, 566 U.S. 431 (2012),] permits new evidence to be admitted without regard to whether the issue was raised before the Board. [¶] Based on the Supreme Court's holding in ***Hyatt*** that there are no limits on the admissibility of evidence in such civil actions except those in the [FREs] and [FRCPs], we conclude that new evidence on new issues is admissible in such pro-

35 U.S.C. §146

ceedings. *At F.3d 1326:* We conclude that to the extent that our prior precedent ... held that new evidence on an issue not presented to the Board was generally to be excluded in district court proceedings, it is no longer viable following the Supreme Court's ***Hyatt*** decision. *At F.3d 1327-28, U.S.P.Q.2d 1726:* We ... conclude that the Supreme Court's decision in ***Hyatt*** applies with equal force to both [35 U.S.C.] §145 and §146 actions."

Rolls-Royce, PLC v. United Techs., 603 F.3d 1325, 1330, 95 U.S.P.Q.2d 1097, 1101 (Fed.Cir.2010). "This court gives pending claims in interference proceedings [now derivation proceedings] their broadest reasonable construction in light of the specification. This court will uphold any reasonable interpretation of disputed claim language by the PTO."

Winner Int'l Royalty Corp. v. Wang, 202 F.3d 1340, 1345, 53 U.S.P.Q.2d 1580, 1584 (Fed.Cir.2000). "Because the record before the district court may include the evidence before the Board as well as evidence that was not before the Board, we have often described the district court proceeding as 'a hybrid of an appeal and a trial *de novo*.' *At F.3d 1347, U.S.P.Q.2d 1585-86:* We hold that the admission of live testimony on all matters before the Board in a §146 action ... makes a factfinder of the district court and requires a *de novo* trial. Thus, although the live testimony before the district court might be the same or similar to testimony before the Board in the form of affidavits and deposition transcripts, a district court should still make *de novo* factual findings, while treating the record before the Board when offered by a party 'as if [it was] originally taken and produced' in the district court. *At F.3d 1348:* The ultimate determination of obviousness by a district court is reviewed by this court *de novo* while the underlying factual inquiries are reviewed for clear error. We hold that this is so as much in a §146 action as on review of the judgment in an infringement suit." *See also* ***Genentech, Inc. v. Chiron Corp.***, 220 F.3d 1345, 1351, 55 U.S.P.Q.2d 1636, 1640-41 (Fed.Cir.2000).

Standard Oil v. Montedison, S.p.A., 664 F.2d 356, 362, 212 U.S.P.Q. 327, 332 (3d Cir.1981). "[A] §146 proceeding is governed by the strict rule that the Board's decision on priority, a 'question of fact,' is not to be disturbed 'unless the contrary is established by testimony which in character and amount carries thorough conviction.' *At F.2d 376, U.S.P.Q. 345:* [N]ew expert testimony is clearly admissible in a §146 action without such justification to the extent that it aids the court in understanding issues already presented to the Board." *See also* ***Stamicarbon, N.V. v. Chemical Constr. Corp.***, 544 F.2d 645, 647, 192 U.S.P.Q. 11, 13 (3d Cir. 1976).

Velsicol Chem. v. Monsanto Co., 579 F.2d 1038, 1042, 198 U.S.P.Q. 584, 588 (7th Cir.1978). "The 'thorough conviction' determination [from ***Morgan***] is to be made on the basis of the entire record before the district court, including both the record that was before the Board and any additional evidence admitted by the court. Although a court may end up with a 'thorough conviction' that the Board was mistaken even when there is no new evidence beyond the record before the Board ... this court has recognized that the less 'new' evidence there is before the district court, the more blatant the Board's factual errors must have been before the district court is justified in reversing the Board's award.... *At F.2d 1046, U.S.P.Q. 591-92:* [W]e conclude that absent special circumstances, the proper question for the district court was whether the failure of the proponent of the additional evidence to uncover its existence earlier or to procure it for the interference proceeding occurred in spite of the proponent's diligence in preparing his case before the Board. ... Conversely, a litigant who has been reasonably diligent in identifying and procuring evidence for the interference proceeding [now derivation proceeding] will not be precluded from strengthening his presentation in the district court if new evidence should become available to him in the interim." (Internal quotes omitted.)

CHAPTER 14. ISSUE OF PATENT

§151. ISSUE OF PATENT

(a) In general.—If it appears that an applicant is entitled to a patent under the law, a written notice of allowance of the application shall be given or mailed to the applicant. The notice shall specify a sum, constituting the issue fee and any required publication fee, which shall be paid within 3 months thereafter.

(b) Effect of payment.—Upon payment of this sum the patent may issue, but if payment is not timely made, the application shall be regarded as abandoned.

History of 35 U.S.C. §151: July 19, 1952, ch. 950, §1, 66 Stat. 803; July 24, 1965, P.L. 89-83, §4, 79 Stat. 260; Jan. 2, 1975, P.L. 93-601, §3, 88 Stat. 1956; Nov. 29, 1999, P.L. 106-113, §1000(a)(9), 113 Stat. 1536; Nov. 2, 2002, P.L. 107-273, §13206(b)(1)(B), 116 Stat. 1906; Dec. 18, 2013, P.L. 112-211, §202(b)(6), 126 Stat. 1536.

See also 37 C.F.R. §§1.311-1.316.

ANNOTATIONS

Blacklight Power, Inc. v. Rogan, 295 F.3d 1269, 1273, 63 U.S.P.Q.2d 1534, 1537 (Fed.Cir.2002). Section 151 "does not prohibit withdrawal by the PTO of a patent application after the issue fee has been paid. [¶] The complexity of the examination process, and the potential for error in any human activity, weigh on the side of according the PTO latitude to withdraw an application from issue without a final determination of unpatentability when the exigencies of time do not allow for such determination."

§152. ISSUE OF PATENT TO ASSIGNEE

Patents may be granted to the assignee of the inventor of record in the Patent and Trademark Office, upon the application made and the specification sworn to by the inventor, except as otherwise provided in this title.

History of 35 U.S.C. §152: July 19, 1952, ch. 950, §1, 66 Stat. 804; Jan. 2, 1975, P.L. 93-596, §1, 88 Stat. 1949.

§153. HOW ISSUED

Patents shall be issued in the name of the United States of America, under the seal of the Patent and Trademark Office, and shall be signed by the Director or have his signature placed thereon and shall be recorded in the Patent and Trademark Office.

History of 35 U.S.C. §153: July 19, 1952, ch. 950, §1, 66 Stat. 804; Jan. 2, 1975, P.L. 93-596, §1, 88 Stat. 1949; Nov. 29, 1999, P.L. 106-113, §1000(a)(9), 113 Stat. 1536; Nov. 2, 2002, P.L. 107-273, §§13203(c), 13206(b)(1)(B), 116 Stat. 1902, 1906.

§154. CONTENTS & TERM OF PATENT; PROVISIONAL RIGHTS

(a) In general—

(1) Contents.—Every patent shall contain a short title of the invention and a grant to the patentee, his heirs or assigns, of the right to exclude others from making, using, offering for sale, or selling the invention throughout the United States or importing the invention into the United States, and, if the invention is a process, of the right to exclude others from using, offering for sale or selling throughout the United States, or importing into the United States, products made by that process, referring to the specification for the particulars thereof.

(2) Term.—Subject to the payment of fees under this title, such grant shall be for a term beginning on the date on which the patent issues and ending 20 years from the date on which the application for the patent was filed in the United States or, if the application contains a specific reference to an earlier filed application or applications under section 120, 121, 365(c), or 386(c), from the date on which the earliest such application was filed.

(3) Priority.—Priority under section 119, 365(a), 365(b), 386(a), or 386(b) shall not be taken into account in determining the term of a patent.

(4) Specification and drawing.—A copy of the specification and drawing shall be annexed to the patent and be a part of such patent.

(b) Adjustment of patent term—

(1) Patent term guarantees—

(A) Guarantee of prompt Patent and Trademark Office responses.—Subject to the limitations under paragraph (2), if the issue of an original patent is delayed due to the failure of the Patent and Trademark Office to—

(i) provide at least one of the notifications under section 132 or a notice of allowance under section 151 not later than 14 months after—

(I) the date on which an application was filed under section 111(a); or

(II) the date of commencement of the national stage under section 371 in an international application;

(ii) respond to a reply under section 132, or to an appeal taken under section 134, within 4 months after the date on which the reply was filed or the appeal was taken;

(iii) act on an application within 4 months after the date of a decision by the Patent Trial and Appeal Board under section 134 or 135 or a decision by a Federal court under section 141, 145, or 146 in a case in which allowable claims remain in the application; or

(iv) issue a patent within 4 months after the date on which the issue fee was paid under section 151 and all outstanding requirements were satisfied,

the term of the patent shall be extended 1 day for each day after the end of the period specified in clause (i), (ii), (iii), or (iv), as the case may be, until the action described in such clause is taken.

(B) Guarantee of no more than 3-year application pendency.—Subject to the limitations under paragraph (2), if the issue of an original patent is delayed due to the failure of the United States Patent and Trademark Office to issue a patent within 3 years after the actual filing date of the application under section 111(a) in the United States or, in the case of an international application, the date of commencement of the national stage under section 371 in the international application, not including—

(i) any time consumed by continued examination of the application requested by the applicant under section 132(b);

(ii) any time consumed by a proceeding under section 135(a), any time consumed by the imposition of an order under section 181, or any time consumed by appellate review by the Patent Trial and Appeal Board or by a Federal court; or

(iii) any delay in the processing of the application by the United States Patent and Trademark Office requested by the applicant except as permitted by paragraph (3)(C),

the term of the patent shall be extended 1 day for each day after the end of that 3-year period until the patent is issued.

(C) Guarantee or adjustments for delays due to derivation proceedings, secrecy orders, and appeals.—Subject to the limitations under paragraph (2), if the issue of an original patent is delayed due to—

(i) a proceeding under section 135(a);

(ii) the imposition of an order under section 181; or

(iii) appellate review by the Patent Trial and Appeal Board or by a Federal court in a case in which the patent was issued under a decision in the review reversing an adverse determination of patentability,

the term of the patent shall be extended 1 day for each day of the pendency of the proceeding, order, or review, as the case may be.

(2) Limitations—

(A) In general.—To the extent that periods of delay attributable to grounds specified in paragraph (1) overlap, the period of any adjustment granted under this subsection shall not exceed the actual number of days the issuance of the patent was delayed.

(B) Disclaimed term.—No patent the term of which has been disclaimed beyond a specified date may be adjusted under this section beyond the expiration date specified in the disclaimer.

(C) Reduction of period of adjustment—

(i) The period of adjustment of the term of a patent under paragraph (1) shall be reduced by a period equal to the period of time during which the applicant failed to engage in reasonable efforts to conclude prosecution of the application.

(ii) With respect to adjustments to patent term made under the authority of paragraph (1)(B), an applicant shall be deemed to have failed to engage in reasonable efforts to conclude processing or examination of an application for the cumulative total of any periods of time in excess of 3 months that are taken to respond to a notice from the Office making any rejection, objection, argument, or other request, measuring such 3-month period from the date the notice was given or mailed to the applicant.

(iii) The Director shall prescribe regulations establishing the circumstances that constitute a failure of an applicant to engage in reasonable efforts to conclude processing or examination of an application.

(3) Procedures for patent term adjustment determination—

(A) The Director shall prescribe regulations establishing procedures for the application for and determination of patent term adjustments under this subsection.

(B) Under the procedures established under subparagraph (A), the Director shall—

(i) make a determination of the period of any patent term adjustment under this subsection, and shall transmit a notice of that determination no later than the date of issuance of the patent; and

(ii) provide the applicant one opportunity to request reconsideration of any patent term adjustment determination made by the Director.

(C) The Director shall reinstate all or part of the cumulative period of time of an adjustment under paragraph (2)(C) if the applicant, prior to the issuance of the patent, makes a showing that, in spite of all due care, the applicant was unable to respond within the 3-month period, but in no case shall more than three additional months for each such response beyond the original 3-month period be reinstated.

(D) The Director shall proceed to grant the patent after completion of the Director's determination of a patent term adjustment under the procedures established under this subsection, notwithstanding any appeal taken by the applicant of such determination.

(4) Appeal of patent term adjustment determination—

(A) An applicant dissatisfied with the Director's decision on the applicant's request for reconsideration under paragraph (3)(B)(ii) shall have exclusive remedy by a civil action against the Director filed in the United States District Court for the Eastern District of Virginia within 180 days after the date of the Director's decision on the applicant's request for reconsideration. Chapter 7 of title 5 shall apply to such action. Any final judgment resulting in a change to the period of adjustment of the patent term shall be served on the Director, and the Director shall thereafter alter the term of the patent to reflect such change.

(B) The determination of a patent term adjustment under this subsection shall not be subject to appeal or challenge by a third party prior to the grant of the patent.

(c) Continuation—

(1) Determination.—The term of a patent that is in force on or that results from an application filed before the date that is 6 months after the date of the enactment of the Uruguay Round Agreements Act shall be the greater of the 20-year term as provided in subsection (a), or 17 years from grant, subject to any terminal disclaimers.

(2) Remedies.—The remedies of sections 283, 284, and 285 shall not apply to acts which—

(A) were commenced or for which substantial investment was made before the date that is 6 months after the date of the enactment of the Uruguay Round Agreements Act; and

(B) became infringing by reason of paragraph (1).

(3) Remuneration.—The acts referred to in paragraph (2) may be continued only upon the payment of an equitable remuneration to the patentee that is determined in an action brought under chapter 28 and chapter 29 (other than those provisions excluded by paragraph (2)).

(d) Provisional rights—

(1) In general.—In addition to other rights provided by this section, a patent shall include the right to obtain a reasonable royalty from any person who, during the period beginning on the date of publication of the application for such patent under section 122(b), or in the case of an international application filed under the treaty defined in section 351(a) designating the United States under Article 21(2)(a) of such treaty or an international design application filed under the treaty defined in section 381(a)(1) designating the United States under Article 5 of such treaty, the date of publication of the application, and ending on the date the patent is issued—

(A)(i) makes, uses, offers for sale, or sells in the United States the invention as claimed in the published patent application or imports such an invention into the United States; or

(ii) if the invention as claimed in the published patent application is a process, uses, offers for sale, or sells in the United States or imports into the United States products made by that process as claimed in the published patent application; and

(B) had actual notice of the published patent application and, in a case in which the right arising under this paragraph is based upon an international application designating the United States that is published in a language other than English, had a translation of the international application into the English language.

(2) Right based on substantially identical inventions.—The right under paragraph (1) to obtain a reasonable royalty shall not be available under this subsection unless the invention as claimed in the patent is substantially identical to the invention as claimed in the published patent application.

(3) Time limitation on obtaining a reasonable royalty.—The right under paragraph (1) to obtain a reasonable royalty shall be available only in an action brought not later than 6 years after the patent is issued. The right under paragraph (1) to obtain a reasonable royalty shall not be affected by the duration of the period described in paragraph (1).

(4) Requirements for international applications—

(A) Effective date.—The right under paragraph (1) to obtain a reasonable royalty based upon the publication under the treaty defined in section 351(a) of an international application designating the United States shall commence on the date of publication under the treaty of the international application, or, if the publication under the treaty of the international application is in a language other than English, on the date on which the Patent and Trademark Office receives a translation of the publication in the English language.

(B) Copies.—The Director may require the applicant to provide a copy of the international application and a translation thereof.

History of 35 U.S.C. §154: July 19, 1952, ch. 950, §1, 66 Stat. 804; July 24, 1965, P.L. 89-83, §5, 79 Stat. 261; Dec. 12, 1980, P.L. 96-517, §4, 94 Stat. 3018; Aug. 23, 1988, P.L. 100-418, §9002, 102 Stat. 1563; Dec. 8, 1994, P.L. 103-465, §532(a)(1), 108 Stat. 4983; Oct. 11, 1996, P.L. 104-295, §20(e)(1), 110 Stat. 3529; Nov. 29, 1999, P.L. 106-113, §1000(a)(9), 113 Stat. 1536; Nov. 2, 2002, P.L. 107-273, §§13204, 13206(a)(8), 116 Stat. 1902, 1904; Sept. 16, 2011, P.L. 112-29, §§3(j)(1), (2)(B), 9(a), 20(j)(1), 125 Stat. 290, 316, 335; May 13, 2015, P.L. 112-211, §102(6), 126 Stat. 1531; Jan. 14, 2013, P.L. 112-274, §1(h), 126 Stat. 2457.

See also 28 U.S.C. §1744; 37 C.F.R. §§1.701-1.705; TRIPs pt. II, §5.

ANNOTATIONS

Generally

King Instrs. Corp. v. Perego, 65 F.3d 941, 949, 36 U.S.P.Q.2d 1129, 1134-35 (Fed.Cir.1995). "Inventors possess the natural right to exploit their inventions (subject to the patent rights of others in a dominant patent) apart from any Government grant. Therefore, patent rights do not depend upon the exercise of rights already in the patentee's possession. [A] patent confers the right to exclude others from exploiting an invention. It does not confer the right to exploit the invention already possessed by the inventor."

§154(a)—Generally

Monsanto Co. v. Scruggs, 459 F.3d 1328, 1338, 79 U.S.P.Q.2d 1813, 1819 (Fed.Cir.2006). "Under the patent laws, a patentee has the right to exclude others from making, using, or selling a patented invention. Conduct falling within the scope of protection includes, *inter alia*, limited use licensing and charging of royalties. Field of use licensing restrictions, i.e., permitting the use of inventions in one field and excluding it in others, are also within the scope of the patent grant."

Eli Lilly & Co. v. Barr Labs., 251 F.3d 955, 967-68, 58 U.S.P.Q.2d 1869, 1877-78 (Fed.Cir.2001). "The judicially-created doctrine of obviousness-type double patenting cements [the] legislative limitation [in §154(a)(2)] by prohibiting a party from obtaining an extension of the right to exclude through claims in a later patent that are not patentably distinct from claims in a commonly owned earlier patent. As one of our predecessor courts explained, '[t]he fundamental reason for the rule [of obviousness-type double patenting] is to prevent unjustified timewise extension of the right to exclude granted by a patent no matter how the extension is brought about.'"

Kearns v. Chrysler Corp., 32 F.3d 1541, 1549-50, 31 U.S.P.Q.2d 1746, 1752 (Fed.Cir.1994). "In view of the fact that the principal right afforded by a patent is the 'right to exclude,' we have noted that '[t]he nature of the patent grant ... weighs against holding that monetary damages will always suffice to make the patentee whole.' Indeed, '[w]hile monetary relief is often the sole remedy for past infringement, it does not follow that a monetary award is also the sole remedy against *future* infringement.' However, [injunctive] relief is available only to 'prevent the violations of any right secured by patent.' Thus, when the rights secured by a patent are no longer protectable by virtue of expiration or unenforceability, entitlement to injunctive relief becomes moot because such relief is no longer available."

Mallinckrodt, Inc. v. Medipart, Inc., 976 F.2d 700, 703, 24 U.S.P.Q.2d 1173, 1176 (Fed.Cir.1992). "[T]he right to exclude may be waived in whole or in part. The conditions of such waiver are subject to patent, contract, antitrust, and any other applicable law, as well as equitable considerations such as are reflected in the law of patent misuse. As in other areas of commerce, private parties may contract as they choose, provided that no law is violated thereby...."

Miller Insituform, Inc. v. Insituform, Inc., 830 F.2d 606, 609, 4 U.S.P.Q.2d 1463, 1465 (6th Cir.1987). "A patent holder who lawfully acquires a patent cannot be held liable under [Sherman Antitrust Act] §2 ... for maintaining the monopoly power he lawfully acquired by refusing to license the patent to others. Similarly, we conclude that the holder of a patent retains the power to exclude others from manufacturing, using, and selling his inventions without running afoul of the antitrust laws. Here, by terminating the sublicense agreement with the appellant, appellee merely exercised his power to exclude others from using the [patented] process, as was its right under 35 U.S.C. §154. In so doing, it did not violate §2...." *See also* ***CSU, L.L.C. v. Xerox Corp.***, 203 F.3d 1322, 1327-28, 53 U.S.P.Q.2d 1852, 1855 (Fed.Cir.2000); ***Roberts v. Sears, Roebuck & Co.***, 723 F.2d 1324, 1329 n.5, 221 U.S.P.Q. 504, 510 n.5 (7th Cir. 1983); ***SCM Corp. v. Xerox Corp.***, 645 F.2d 1195, 1203-04, 209 U.S.P.Q. 889, 898-99 (2d Cir.1981).

Paper Converting Mach. v. Magna-Graphics Corp., 745 F.2d 11, 16, 223 U.S.P.Q. 591, 594 (Fed.Cir. 1984). "Congress has never deemed it necessary to define any of this triad of excludable activities, ... leaving instead the meaning of 'make,' 'use,' and 'sell' for judicial interpretation. Nevertheless, by the terms of the patent grant, *no* activity other than the unauthorized making, using, or selling of the claimed invention can constitute direct infringement of a patent, *no matter* how great the adverse impact of that activity on the economic value of a patent."

Johnson & Johnson, Inc. v. Wallace A. Erickson & Co., 627 F.2d 57, 59, 206 U.S.P.Q. 873, 876 (7th Cir. 1980). "The ... exclusion is a right and not a matter of grace or favor. It is a property right ... of which the patentee cannot be deprived without due process of law."

§154(a)—Licenses

For more annotations on this topic, see 35 U.S.C. §261, *Assignment & License*, p. 645.

Monsanto Co. v. Scruggs, 459 F.3d 1328, 1336, 79 U.S.P.Q.2d 1813, 1818 (Fed.Cir.2006). "In order to establish an implied license, the circumstances of the sale must plainly indicate that the grant of a license should be inferred." (Internal quotes omitted.)

Deprenyl Animal Health, Inc. v. University of Toronto Innovations Found., 297 F.3d 1343, 1353-54, 63 U.S.P.Q.2d 1705, 1712 (Fed.Cir.2002). "A patent allows a patentee to exclude others from practicing an invention in the U.S. that they otherwise might be free to practice without providing consideration to anyone. A patentee who grants a license thus contracts for valuable consideration in exchange for surrendering the right to exclude the licensee from practicing the patented invention. Thus, the act of contracting for consideration in exchange for licensing the practice of an invention claimed in a U.S. patent constitutes purposeful availment of the benefits of U.S. patent law." *See also* ***Carborundum Co. v. Molten Metal Equip. Innovations***, 72 F.3d 872, 878, 37 U.S.P.Q.2d 1169, 1172 (Fed. Cir.1995).

Genetic Implant Sys. v. Core-Vent Corp., 123 F.3d 1455, 1458, 43 U.S.P.Q.2d 1786, 1789 (Fed.Cir.1997). "The appointment of a distributor to sell a product covered by a patent is analogous to a grant of a patent license. Such an action conveys an implied license to the distributor, thereby surrendering the patentee's right to exclude the distributor under the patent."

Spindelfabrik Suessen-Schurr Stahlecker & Grill GmbH v. Schubert & Salzer Maschinenfabrik, 829 F.2d 1075, 1081, 4 U.S.P.Q.2d 1044, 1048 (Fed.Cir. 1987). "[A] patent license agreement is in essence nothing more than a promise by the licensor not to sue the licensee. Even if couched in terms of '[l]icensee is given the right to make, use, or sell X,' the agreement cannot convey that absolute right because not even the patentee of X is given that right. His right is merely one to exclude others from making, using or selling X.... Indeed, the patentee of X and his licensee, when making, using, or selling X, can be subject to suit under other patents. In any event, patent license agreements can be written to convey different scopes of promises not to sue, *e.g.*, a promise not to sue under a specific patent or, more broadly, a promise not to sue under any patent the licensor now has or may acquire in the future." *See also* ***Vaupel Textilmaschinen KG v. Meccanica Euro Italia S.P.A.***, 944 F.2d 870, 879 n.4, 20 U.S.P.Q.2d 1045, 1052 n.4 (Fed.Cir.1991).

ProteoTech, Inc. v. Unicity Int'l, 542 F.Supp.2d 1216, 1219 (W.D.Wash.2008). "[T]he Court HOLDS that the type of license, exclusive or non-exclusive, does not affect assignability; in either event, the licensor must consent to, or the license must expressly allow, sublicensing."

§154(a)—Limits of Right to Exclude

Wilbur-Ellis Co. v. Kuther, 377 U.S. 422, 423-24, 141 U.S.P.Q. 703, 704 (1964). "The question ... is whether what was done to these machines, the original manufacture and sale of which had been licensed by the patentee, amounted to 'repair,' in which event there was no infringement, or 'reconstruction,' in which event there was. The idea of 'reconstruction' in this context has the special connotation of those acts which would impinge on the patentee's right '*to exclude others from making*,' ... the article." Held: The modification and cleaning of invention to extend its useful life was not an infringement. *See also* ***Wells Mfg. v. Littelfuse, Inc.***, 547 F.2d 346, 350-51, 192 U.S.P.Q. 256, 260 (7th Cir.1976).

Monsanto Co. v. Scruggs, 459 F.3d 1328, 1339, 79 U.S.P.Q.2d 1813, 1820 (Fed.Cir.2006). "The policy of the patent misuse doctrine is to prevent a patentee from using the patent to obtain market benefit beyond that which inures in the statutory patent right. In order for competitive behavior to amount to patent misuse, one must impermissibly broaden the scope of the patent grant with anticompetitive effect. Thus, in the cases in which the restriction is reasonably within the patent grant, the patent misuse defense can never succeed." (Internal quotes omitted.)

§154(b)

Actelion Pharms. v. Matal, 881 F.3d 1339, 1344, 125 U.S.P.Q.2d 1585, ___ (Fed.Cir.2018). The "A Delay calculation must be based on the date on which the entirety of [35 U.S.C.] §371 has been complied with, including §371(c) as well as §371(b) and §371(f). We conclude that, to commence the national stage early, [P] was required to make an express request pursuant to §371(f) regardless whether the pre- or post-[Technical Corrections Act (TCA)] version of [35 U.S.C.] §154(b)(1)(A)(i)(II) applies to the ... patent. [¶] We agree with the PTO that, under either the pre- or post-TCA version of §154(b)(1)(A)(i)(II), the A Delay calculation must be based on the date on which the entirety of §371 is complied with, including §371(b) and (f). As such, we conclude that under either pre- or post-TCA law, [P] was required to comply with the 'express request' provision of §371(f) if it wished to commence the national stage before the expiration date provided in §371(b)."

Pfizer, Inc. v. Lee, 811 F.3d 466, 471-72, 117 U.S.P.Q.2d 1781, 1785-86 (Fed.Cir.2016). A 35 U.S.C. §154(b)(1)(A) delay "will stop accruing when the PTO 'provide[s] at least one of the notifications under [35 U.S.C.] §132.' Thus, under the statute's plain meaning, the issue of whether the PTO provided a notification under §132 is dispositive of this case. In ***Chester v. Miller***, [906 F.2d 1574 (Fed.Cir.1990),] we held that '§132 is violated when a rejection is so uninformative that it prevents the applicant from recognizing and seeking to counter the grounds for rejection.' ***Chester*** concerned whether an examiner's rejection on the basis of anticipation under [35 U.S.C.] §102 satisfied the notice requirements of §132. We noted that, to make a successful rejection under §132, the PTO does not have to 'explicitly preempt every possible response to a §102 rejection.' Instead, §132 merely requires that an applicant 'at least be informed of the broad statutory basis for [the rejection of] his claims, so that he may determine what the issues are on which he can or should produce evidence.' Applying these principles, we found the examiner's rejection in ***Chester*** sufficient to satisfy the requirements of §132."

Mohsenzadeh v. Lee, 790 F.3d 1377, 1381, 115 U.S.P.Q.2d 1483, 1487 (Fed.Cir.2015). "The language of ... §154(b)(1)(A)[] clearly shows that Congress intended delay in the prosecution of an application to be restored to a single patent, the patent issuing directly from that application. In other words, the term of any patent arising from a continuing application is not restored for delay in the prosecution of the parent patent's application."

Novartis AG v. Lee, 740 F.3d 593, 598-99, 109 U.S.P.Q.2d 1385, 1389-90 (Fed.Cir.2014). "It is undisputed in this court that the 180-day clock [under §154(b)(4)(A)] does not run while the PTO considers a timely request for reconsideration under regulations promulgated pursuant to §[154](b)(3)(B)(ii)'s guarantee of 'one opportunity to request reconsideration of any patent term adjustment determination made by the Director.' [¶] [P] contends, however, that the 180-day period is inapplicable. Subparagraph (b)(4)(A) by its terms applies only to 'a determination made by the Director under paragraph (3)' of subsection (b). [P] asserts that a determination of the final patent term adjustment, announced upon issuance of the patent, is not made under 'paragraph (3),' which, it says, addresses only the provisional adjustment announced upon allowance of claims (when the PTO process is not complete, so that the final adjustment cannot yet be calculated). Therefore, [P] argues that the 180-day period is not applicable to its challenges to the final patent term adjustment determinations because, it says, the Director did not make those determinations under paragraph (b)(3). [P's] contention thus turns on its interpretation of paragraph (b)(3). That interpretation is, ultimately, unreasonable. [¶] The applicable version of paragraph (b)(3)—the whole of which subparagraph (b)(4)(A) refers to—addresses all patent term adjustment determinations, not just some."

Wyeth v. Kappos, 591 F.3d 1364, 1369-70, 93 U.S.P.Q.2d 1257, 1260 (Fed.Cir.2010). "This court detects no ambiguity in the terms 'periods of delay' and 'overlap.' Each term has an evident meaning within the context of §154(b). The limitation in §154(b) only arises when 'periods of delay' resulting from violations of the three guarantees [in subsection (b)(1)] 'overlap.' Significantly, the A and B guarantees [from subsections (b)(1)(A) and (B)] expressly designate when and for what period they each respectively apply. Thus, this court can easily detect any overlap by examining the delay periods covered by the A and B guarantees. [¶] A violation of the A guarantee—delays in meeting examination deadlines—begins with a 'failure of the [PTO]' to meet one of the deadlines specified in subparagraphs (i)-(iv). It ends when 'the action described ... is taken.' The 'period of delay' for purposes of the A clause therefore runs from the date the PTO misses the specified deadline to the date (past the deadline) of response to the underlying action. [¶] Correspondingly, a violation of the B guarantee—the one at the heart of the issue in this case—begins when the PTO fails 'to issue a patent within three years after the actual filing date of the application in the U.S....' It ends when 'the patent is issued.' The 'period of delay' under the express language of the B clause therefore runs from the three-year mark after filing until the application issues. [¶] Reading this framework into §154(b)'s limitation provision makes it clear that no 'overlap' happens unless the violations occur at the same time. Each 'period of delay' has its own discrete time span whose boundaries are defined in §154(b)(1). That is, each has a start and an end. Before the three-year mark, no 'overlap' can transpire between the A delay and the B delay because the B delay has yet to begin or take any effect. If an A delay occurs on one day and a B delay occurs on a different day, those two days do not 'overlap' under §154(b)(2)."

Merck & Co. v. Kessler, 80 F.3d 1543, 1548, 38 U.S.P.Q.2d 1347, 1350 (Fed.Cir.1996). "Congress did not expressly address the question whether a restoration extension under [35 U.S.C.] §156 could be added to the term of a patent which could also invoke the [35 U.S.C.] §154 transition provision. Delineating the combined effects of the [Uruguay Round Agreements Act (URAA)] and the Hatch-Waxman Act for patents issued prior to June 8, 1995, is thus the task before us. *At F.3d 1551, U.S.P.Q.2d 1352:* 35 U.S.C. §154(b)(2) provides for a term extension where issuance of a patent is delayed due to appellate review of an adverse determination of patentability. This new type of extension could be determined and granted post-issuance and would be added to the term *prior* to the addition of a restoration extension which, under §156(a), is added to the end of what otherwise would be the patent term. Thus, the 'original expiration date' of such patent would be its expiration date with the appellate review extension added, *i.e.*, such patent's 'original expiration date' would not be the expiration date at the grant of the patent. Nothing in the amendment effecting appellate review extensions suggests otherwise. Thus, we do not find the argument persuasive that, in all instances, the 'original expiration date' for a pre-URAA patent must be fixed at 17 years from issuance under §156(a). ... Accordingly, we see no impediment to applying the restoration extension to a 20-year from filing term by reason of this statutory language. *At F.3d 1553, U.S.P.Q.2d 1354:* In sum, patents that were in force on June 8, 1995, only because of a Hatch-Waxman extension are not entitled to reapply a restoration extension to a 20-year from filing term. Except for those patents, a patent in force on June 8, 1995, is entitled to have a restoration extension, whenever granted, added to the longer term of either 17 years from issuance or 20 years from filing."

§154(c)

Golan v. Pingel Enter., 310 F.3d 1360, 1364-65 n.1, 64 U.S.P.Q.2d 1911, 1913 n.1 (Fed.Cir.2002). "Effective June 8, 1995, the patent laws were amended to change the term of a patent from 17 years measured from the date the patent issued to 20 years measured from the filing date of the earliest U.S. application for which priority benefit is claimed. Applications that were filed on or after June 8, 1995 have a 20 year term measured from the date of filing. All patents that were in force on June 8, 1995, or that issued on an application that was filed before June 8, 1995, have a term that is the greater of the 20 year term or 17 years from the patent grant." *See also* ***Abbott Labs. v. Novopharm Ltd.***, 104 F.3d 1305, 1308, 41 U.S.P.Q.2d 1535, 1537-38 (Fed.Cir.1997).

Bristol-Myers Squibb Co. v. Royce Labs., 69 F.3d 1130, 1132, 36 U.S.P.Q.2d 1641, 1644 (Fed.Cir.1995). "[T]he [Uruguay Round Agreements Act (URAA)] creates a limited safe harbor for persons who commenced particular acts, or made substantial investment toward commission of those acts before June 8, 1995 (the date six months after the URAA was enacted), which acts became infringing because of the extension of the patent period by the URAA. Under the URAA's safe harbor provision, a patent owner may not assert the traditional remedies of 35 U.S.C. §§283, 284, and 285 for qualifying acts of infringement committed during the period of a patent's extension (the 'Delta' period). The patent owner is entitled to an equitable remuneration, however, for such acts." *See also* ***DuPont Merck Pharm. v. Bristol-Myers Squibb Co.***, 62 F.3d 1397, 1402, 35 U.S.P.Q.2d 1718, 1722 (Fed.Cir.1995).

§154(d)

Rosebud LMS Inc. v. Adobe Sys., 812 F.3d 1070, 1073-74, 117 U.S.P.Q.2d 1717, 1719-20 (Fed.Cir.2016). Section "154(d) provides for damages that take place before a patent issues if the infringer 'had actual notice of the published patent application.' [¶] We agree with [D] and the district court that constructive knowledge would not satisfy the actual notice requirement. We do not, however, agree with [D] that §154(d)'s requirement of actual notice requires an affirmative act by the applicant giving notice of the published patent application to the infringer. Certainly, 'actual notice' includes a party affirmatively acting to provide notice. But the ordinary meaning of 'actual notice' also includes knowledge obtained without an affirmative act of notification. *At F.3d 1075:* [W]e interpret the actual notice requirement of §154(d) as it is clearly written to have its ordinary meaning."

§§155, 155A. REPEALED

Repealed Sept. 16, 2012, P.L. 112-29, §20(k), 125 Stat. 335.

§156. EXTENSION OF PATENT TERM

(a) The term of a patent which claims a product, a method of using a product, or a method of manufacturing a product shall be extended in accordance with this section from the original expiration date of the patent, which shall include any patent term adjustment granted under section 154(b), if—

(1) the term of the patent has not expired before an application is submitted under subsection (d)(1) for its extension;

(2) the term of the patent has never been extended under subsection (e)(1) of this section;

(3) an application for extension is submitted by the owner of record of the patent or its agent and in accordance with the requirements of paragraphs (1) through (4) of subsection (d);

(4) the product has been subject to a regulatory review period before its commercial marketing or use;

(5)(A) except as provided in subparagraph (B) or (C), the permission for the commercial marketing or use of the product after such regulatory review period is the first permitted commercial marketing or use of the product under the provision of law under which such regulatory review period occurred;

(B) in the case of a patent which claims a method of manufacturing the product which primarily uses recombinant DNA technology in the manufacture of the product, the permission for the commercial marketing or use of the product after such regulatory review period is the first permitted commercial marketing or use of a product manufactured under the process claimed in the patent; or

(C) for purposes of subparagraph (A), in the case of a patent which—

(i) claims a new animal drug or a veterinary biological product which (I) is not covered by the claims in any other patent which has been extended, and (II) has received permission for the commercial marketing or use in non-food-producing animals and in food-producing animals, and

(ii) was not extended on the basis of the regulatory review period for use in non-food-producing animals,

the permission for the commercial marketing or use of the drug or product after the regulatory review period for use in food-producing animals is the first permitted commercial marketing or use of the drug or product for administration to a food-producing animal.

The product referred to in paragraphs (4) and (5) is hereinafter in this section referred to as the "approved product."

(b) Except as provided in subsection (d)(5)(F), the rights derived from any patent the term of which is extended under this section shall during the period during which the term of the patent is extended—

(1) in the case of a patent which claims a product, be limited to any use approved for the product—

(A) before the expiration of the term of the patent—

(i) under the provision of law under which the applicable regulatory review occurred, or

(ii) under the provision of law under which any regulatory review described in paragraph (1), (4), or (5) of subsection (g) occurred, and

(B) on or after the expiration of the regulatory review period upon which the extension of the patent was based;

(2) in the case of a patent which claims a method of using a product, be limited to any use claimed by the patent and approved for the product—

(A) before the expiration of the term of the patent—

(i) under any provision of law under which an applicable regulatory review occurred, and

(ii) under the provision of law under which any regulatory review described in paragraph (1), (4), or (5) of subsection (g) occurred, and

(B) on or after the expiration of the regulatory review period upon which the extension of the patent was based; and

(3) in the case of a patent which claims a method of manufacturing a product, be limited to the method of manufacturing as used to make—

(A) the approved product, or

(B) the product if it has been subject to a regulatory review period described in paragraph (1), (4), or (5) of subsection (g).

As used in this subsection, the term "product" includes an approved product.

(c) The term of a patent eligible for extension under subsection (a) shall be extended by the time equal to the regulatory review period for the approved product which period occurs after the date the patent is issued, except that—

(1) each period of the regulatory review period shall be reduced by any period determined under subsection (d)(2)(B) during which the applicant for the patent extension did not act with due diligence during such period of the regulatory review period;

(2) after any reduction required by paragraph (1), the period of extension shall include only one-half of the time remaining in the periods described in paragraphs (1)(B)(i), (2)(B)(i), (3)(B)(i), (4)(B)(i), and (5)(B)(i) of subsection (g);

(3) if the period remaining in the term of a patent after the date of the approval of the approved product under the provision of law under which such regulatory review occurred when added to the regulatory review period as revised under paragraphs (1) and (2) exceeds fourteen years, the period of extension shall be reduced so that the total of both such periods does not exceed fourteen years; and

(4) in no event shall more than one patent be extended under subsection (e)(1) for the same regulatory review period for any product.

(d)(1) To obtain an extension of the term of a patent under this section, the owner of record of the patent or its agent shall submit an application to the Director. Except as provided in paragraph (5), such an application may only be submitted within the sixty-day period beginning on the date the product received permission under the provision of law under which the applicable regulatory review period occurred for commercial marketing or use, or in the case of a drug product described in subsection (i), within the sixty-day period beginning on the covered date (as defined in subsection (i)). The application shall contain—

(A) the identity of the approved product and the Federal statute under which regulatory review occurred;

(B) the identity of the patent for which an extension is being sought and the identity of each claim of such patent which claims the approved product or a method of using or manufacturing the approved product;

(C) information to enable the Director to determine under subsections (a) and (b) the eligibility of a patent for extension and the rights that will be derived from the extension and information to enable the Director and the Secretary of Health and Human Services or the Secretary of Agriculture to determine the period of the extension under subsection (g);

(D) a brief description of the activities undertaken by the applicant during the applicable regulatory review period with respect to the approved product and the significant dates applicable to such activities; and

(E) such patent or other information as the Director may require.

For purposes of determining the date on which a product receives permission under the second sentence of this paragraph, if such permission is transmitted after 4:30 P.M., Eastern Time, on a business day, or is transmitted on a day that is not a business day, the product shall be deemed to receive such permission on the next business day. For purposes of the preceding sentence, the term "business day" means any Monday, Tuesday, Wednesday, Thursday, or Friday, excluding any legal holiday under section 6103 of title 5.

(2)(A) Within 60 days of the submittal of an application for extension of the term of a patent under paragraph (1), the Director shall notify—

(i) the Secretary of Agriculture if the patent claims a drug product or a method of using or manufacturing a drug product and the drug product is subject to the Virus-Serum-Toxin Act, and

(ii) the Secretary of Health and Human Services if the patent claims any other drug product, a medical device, or a food additive or color additive or a method of using or manufacturing such a product, device, or additive and if the product, device, and additive are subject to the Federal Food, Drug, and Cosmetic Act,

of the extension application and shall submit to the Secretary who is so notified a copy of the application. Not later than 30 days after the receipt of an application from the Director, the Secretary receiving the application shall review the dates contained in the application pursuant to paragraph (1)(C) and determine the applicable regulatory review period, shall notify the Director of the determination, and shall publish in the Federal Register a notice of such determination.

(B)(i) If a petition is submitted to the Secretary making the determination under subparagraph (A), not later than 180 days after the publication of the determination under subparagraph (A), upon which it may reasonably be determined that the applicant did not act with due diligence during the applicable regulatory review period, the Secretary making the determination shall, in accordance with regulations promulgated by such Secretary, determine if the applicant acted with due diligence during the applicable regulatory review period. The Secretary making the determination shall make such determination not later than 90 days after the receipt of such a petition. For a drug product, device, or additive subject to the Federal Food, Drug, and Cosmetic Act or the Public Health Service Act, the Secretary may not delegate the authority to make the determination prescribed by this clause to an office below the Office of the Director[1] of Food and Drugs. For a product subject to the Virus-Serum-Toxin Act, the Secretary of Agriculture may not delegate the authority to make the determination prescribed by this clause to an office below the Office of the Assistant Secretary for Marketing and Inspection Services.

(ii) The Secretary making a determination under clause (i) shall notify the Director of the determination and shall publish in the Federal Register a notice of such determination together with the factual and legal basis for such determination. Any interested person may request, within the 60-day period beginning on the publication of a determination, the Secretary making the determination to hold an informal hearing on the determination. If such a request is made within such period, such Secretary shall hold such hearing not later than 30 days after the date of the request, or at the request of the person making the request, not later than 60 days after such date. The Secretary who is holding the hearing shall provide notice of the hearing to the owner of the patent involved and to any interested person and provide the owner and any interested person an opportunity to participate in the hearing. Within 30 days after the completion of the hearing, such Secretary shall affirm or revise the determination which was the subject of the hearing and shall notify the Director of any revision of the determination and shall publish any such revision in the Federal Register.

(3) For the purposes of paragraph (2)(B), the term "due diligence" means that degree of attention, continuous directed effort, and timeliness as may reasonably be expected from, and are ordinarily exercised by, a person during a regulatory review period.

(4) An application for the extension of the term of a patent is subject to the disclosure requirements prescribed by the Director.

(5)(A) If the owner of record of the patent or its agent reasonably expects that the applicable regulatory review period described in paragraph (1)(B)(ii), (2)(B)(ii), (3)(B)(ii), (4)(B)(ii), or (5)(B)(ii) of subsection (g) that began for a product that is the subject of such patent may extend beyond the expiration of the patent term in effect, the owner or its agent may submit an application to the Director for an interim extension during the period beginning 6 months, and ending 15 days, before such term is due to expire. The application shall contain—

(i) the identity of the product subject to regulatory review and the Federal statute under which such review is occurring;

(ii) the identity of the patent for which interim extension is being sought and the identity of each claim of such patent which claims the product under regulatory review or a method of using or manufacturing the product;

(iii) information to enable the Director to determine under subsection (a)(1), (2), and (3) the eligibility of a patent for extension;

(iv) a brief description of the activities undertaken by the applicant during the applicable regulatory review period to date with respect to the product under review and the significant dates applicable to such activities; and

(v) such patent or other information as the Director may require.

(B) If the Director determines that, except for permission to market or use the product commercially, the patent would be eligible for an extension of the patent term under this section, the Director shall publish in the Federal Register a notice of such determination, including the identity of the product under regulatory review, and shall issue to the applicant a certificate of interim extension for a period of not more than 1 year.

(C) The owner of record of a patent, or its agent, for which an interim extension has been granted under subparagraph (B), may apply for not more than 4 subsequent interim extensions under this paragraph, except that, in the case of a patent subject to subsection (g)(6)(C), the owner of record of the patent, or its agent, may apply for only 1 subsequent interim extension under this paragraph. Each such subsequent application shall be made during the period beginning 60 days before, and ending 30 days before, the expiration of the preceding interim extension.

(D) Each certificate of interim extension under this paragraph shall be recorded in the official file of the patent and shall be considered part of the original patent.

(E) Any interim extension granted under this paragraph shall terminate at the end of the 60-day period beginning on the date on which the product involved receives permission for commercial marketing or use, except that, if within that 60-day period the applicant notifies the Director of such permission and submits any additional information under paragraph (1) of this subsection not previously contained in the application for interim extension, the patent shall be further extended, in accordance with the provisions of this section—

(i) for not to exceed 5 years from the date of expiration of the original patent term; or

(ii) if the patent is subject to subsection (g)(6)(C), from the date on which the product involved receives approval for commercial marketing or use.

(F) The rights derived from any patent the term of which is extended under this paragraph shall, during the period of interim extension—

(i) in the case of a patent which claims a product, be limited to any use then under regulatory review;

(ii) in the case of a patent which claims a method of using a product, be limited to any use claimed by the patent then under regulatory review; and

(iii) in the case of a patent which claims a method of manufacturing a product, be limited to the method of manufacturing as used to make the product then under regulatory review.

(e)(1) A determination that a patent is eligible for extension may be made by the Director solely on the basis of the representations contained in the application for the extension. If the Director determines that a patent is eligible for extension under subsection (a) and that the requirements of paragraphs (1) through (4) of subsection (d) have been complied with, the Director shall issue to the applicant for the extension of the term of the patent a certificate of extension, under seal, for the period prescribed by subsection (c). Such certificate shall be recorded in the official file of the patent and shall be considered as part of the original patent.

(2) If the term of a patent for which an application has been submitted under subsection (d)(1) would expire before a certificate of extension is issued or denied under paragraph (1) respecting the application, the Director shall extend, until such determination is made, the term of the patent for periods of up to one year if he determines that the patent is eligible for extension.

(f) For purposes of this section:

(1) The term "product" means:

(A) A drug product.

(B) Any medical device, food additive, or color additive subject to regulation under the Federal Food, Drug, and Cosmetic Act.

(2) The term "drug product" means the active ingredient of—

(A) a new drug, antibiotic drug, or human biological product (as those terms are used in the Federal Food, Drug, and Cosmetic Act and the Public Health Service Act), or

(B) a new animal drug or veterinary biological product (as those terms are used in the Federal Food, Drug, and Cosmetic Act and the Virus-Serum-Toxin Act) which is not primarily manufactured using recombinant DNA, recombinant RNA, hybridoma technology, or other processes involving site specific genetic manipulation techniques,

including any salt or ester of the active ingredient, as a single entity or in combination with another active ingredient.

(3) The term "major health or environmental effects test" means a test which is reasonably related to the evaluation of the health or environmental effects of a product, which requires at least six months to conduct, and the data from which is submitted to receive permission for commercial marketing or use. Periods of analysis or evaluation of test results are not to be included in determining if the conduct of a test required at least six months.

(4)(A) Any reference to section 351 is a reference to section 262 of title 42.

(B) Any reference to section 503, 505, 512, or 515 is a reference to section 353, 355, 360b, or 360e of title 21.

(C) Any reference to the Virus-Serum-Toxin Act is a reference to the Act of March 4, 1913 (21 U.S.C. 151-158).

(5) The term "informal hearing" has the meaning prescribed for such term by section 201(y)[2] of the Federal Food, Drug, and Cosmetic Act.

(6) The term "patent" means a patent issued by the United States Patent and Trademark Office.

(7) The term "date of enactment" as used in this section means September 24, 1984, for a human drug product, a medical device, food additive, or color additive.

(8) The term "date of enactment" as used in this section means the date of enactment of the Generic Animal Drug and Patent Term Restoration Act for an animal drug or a veterinary biological product.

(g) For purposes of this section, the term "regulatory review period" has the following meanings:

(1)(A) In the case of a product which is a new drug, antibiotic drug, or human biological product, the term means the period described in subparagraph (B) to which the limitation described in paragraph (6) applies.

(B) The regulatory review period for a new drug, antibiotic drug, or human biological product is the sum of—

(i) the period beginning on the date an exemption under subsection (i) of section 355 of title 21 or subsection (d) of section 357 of title 21 became effective for the approved product and ending on the date an application was initially submitted for such drug product under section 262 of title 42, section 355 of title 21, or section 357 of title 21, and

(ii) the period beginning on the date the application was initially submitted for the approved product under section 262 of title 42, section 357 of title 21 and ending on the date such application was approved under such section.

(2)(A) In the case of a product which is a food additive or color additive, the term means the period described in subparagraph (B) to which the limitation described in paragraph (6) applies.

(B) The regulatory review period for a food or color additive is the sum of—

(i) the period beginning on the date a major health or environmental effects test on the additive was initiated and ending on the date a petition was initially submitted with respect to the product under the Federal Food, Drug, and Cosmetic Act requesting the issuance of a regulation for use of the product, and

(ii) the period beginning on the date a petition was initially submitted with respect to the product under the Federal Food, Drug, and Cosmetic Act requesting the issuance of a regulation for use of the product, and ending on the date such regulation became effective or, if objections were filed to such regulation, ending on the date such objections were resolved and commercial marketing was permitted or, if commercial marketing was permitted and later revoked pending further proceedings as a result of such objections, ending on the date such proceedings were finally resolved and commercial marketing was permitted.

(3)(A) In the case of a product which is a medical device, the term means the period described in subparagraph (B) to which the limitation described in paragraph (6) applies.

(B) The regulatory review period for a medical device is the sum of—

(i) the period beginning on the date a clinical investigation on humans involving the device was begun and ending on the date an application was initially submitted with respect to the device under section 515, and

(ii) the period beginning on the date an application was initially submitted with respect to the device under section 515 and ending on the date such application was approved under such Act or the period beginning on the date a notice of completion of a product development protocol was initially submitted under section 515(f)(5) and ending on the date the protocol was declared completed under section 515(f)(6).

(4)(A) In the case of a product which is a new animal drug, the term means the period described in subparagraph (B) to which the limitation described in paragraph (6) applies.

(B) The regulatory review period for a new animal drug product is the sum of—

(i) the period beginning on the earlier of the date a major health or environmental effects test on the drug was initiated or the date an exemption under subsection (j) of section 512 became effective for the approved new animal drug product and ending on the date an application was initially submitted for such animal drug product under section 512, and

(ii) the period beginning on the date the application was initially submitted for the approved animal drug product under subsection (b) of section 512 and ending on the date such application was approved under such section.

(5)(A) In the case of a product which is a veterinary biological product, the term means the period described in subparagraph (B) to which the limitation described in paragraph (6) applies.

(B) The regulatory period for a veterinary biological product is the sum of—

(i) the period beginning on the date the authority to prepare an experimental biological product under the Virus-Serum-Toxin Act became effective and ending on the date an application for a license was submitted under the Virus-Serum-Toxin Act, and

(ii) the period beginning on the date an application for a license was initially submitted for approval under the Virus-Serum-Toxin Act and ending on the date such license was issued.

(6) A period determined under any of the preceding paragraphs is subject to the following limitations:

(A) If the patent involved was issued after the date of the enactment of this section, the period of extension determined on the basis of the regulatory review period determined under any such paragraph may not exceed five years.

(B) If the patent involved was issued before Sept. 24, 1984 and—

(i) no request for an exemption described in paragraph (1)(B) or (4)(B) was submitted and no request for the authority described in paragraph (5)(B) was submitted,

(ii) no major health or environmental effects test described in paragraph (2)(B) or (4)(B) was initiated and no petition for a regulation or application for registration described in such paragraph was submitted, or

(iii) no clinical investigation described in paragraph (3) was begun or product development protocol described in such paragraph was submitted,

before such date for the approved product the period of extension determined on the basis of the regulatory review period determined under any such paragraph may not exceed five years.

(C) If the patent involved was issued before Sept. 24, 1984 and if an action described in subparagraph (B) was taken before Sept. 24, 1984 with respect to the approved product and the commercial marketing or use of the product has not been approved before such date, the period of extension determined on the basis of the regulatory review period determined under such paragraph may not exceed two years or in the case of an approved product which is a new animal drug or veterinary biological product (as those terms are used in the Federal Food, Drug, and Cosmetic Act or the Virus-Serum-Toxin Act), three years.

(h) The Director may establish such fees as the Director determines appropriate to cover the costs to the Office of receiving and acting upon applications under this section.

(i)(1) For purposes of this section, if the Secretary of Health and Human Services provides notice to the sponsor of an application or request for approval, conditional approval, or indexing of a drug product for which the Secretary intends to recommend controls under the Controlled Substances Act, beginning on the covered date, the drug product shall be considered to—

(A) have been approved or indexed under the relevant provision of the Public Health Service Act or Federal Food, Drug, and Cosmetic Act; and

(B) have permission for commercial marketing or use.

(2) In this subsection, the term "covered date" means the later of—

(A) the date an application is approved—

(i) under section 351(a)(2)(C) of the Public Health Service Act; or

(ii) under section 505(b) or 512(c) of the Federal Food, Drug, and Cosmetic Act;

(B) the date an application is conditionally approved under section 571(b) of the Federal Food, Drug, and Cosmetic Act;

(C) the date a request for indexing is granted under section 572(d) of the Federal Food, Drug, and Cosmetic Act; or

(D) the date of issuance of the interim final rule controlling the drug under section 201(j) of the Controlled Substances Act.

1. **Editor's note:** Probably should be "Commissioner."

2. **Editor's note:** "Informal hearing" is now defined in 21 U.S.C. §321(x).

History of 35 U.S.C. §156: Sept. 24, 1984, P.L. 98-417, §201(a), 98 Stat. 1598; Nov. 16, 1988, P.L. 100-670, §201(a)-(h), 102 Stat. 3984; Dec. 3, 1993, P.L. 103-179, §§5, 6, 107 Stat. 2040; Dec. 8, 1994, P.L. 103-465, §532(c)(1), 108 Stat. 4987; Nov. 21, 1997, P.L. 105-115, §125(b)(2)(P), 111 Stat. 2326; Nov. 29, 1999, P.L. 106-113, §1000(a)(9), 113 Stat. 1536; Nov. 2, 2002, P.L. 107-273, §13206(a)(9), (b)(1)(B), 116 Stat. 1904, 1906; Sept. 16, 2011, P.L. 112-29, §37(a), 125 Stat. 341; Nov. 25, 2015, P.L. 114-89, §2(c), 129 Stat. 700.

See also 21 U.S.C. §§355, 355a, 360b; 9 C.F.R. pt. 124; 21 C.F.R. pt. 60; 37 C.F.R. §§1.710-1.791.

ANNOTATIONS

Generally

Ortho-McNeil Pharm. v. Lupin Pharms., 603 F.3d 1377, 1382, 95 U.S.P.Q.2d 1246, 1250 (Fed.Cir.2010). "[A]n extended patent term does not apply to unrelated uses of an FDA-approved product."

Merck & Co. v. Kessler, 80 F.3d 1543, 1546, 38 U.S.P.Q.2d 1347, 1348 (Fed.Cir.1996). "The Drug, Price Competition and Patent Term Restoration Act, codified in part at 35 U.S.C. §156, (also known as the Hatch-Waxman Act), provides generally for a limited extension of the term of a patent, *inter alia*, for a drug as to which marketing was held up during the patent term by the process of obtaining [FDA] approval (hereinafter 'restoration extension'). ... The [Uruguay Round Agreements Act (URAA)] provides an alternative calculation of the term for patents in force on June 8, 1995, namely, 20 years from filing of the patent application. For patents that were prosecuted to issuance in less than three years, URAA effects an extension of its term, that is, the difference between 17 years from issuance and 20 years from filing. *At F.3d 1548, U.S.P.Q.2d 1350:* Congress did not expressly address the question whether a restoration extension under §156 could be added to the term of a patent which could also invoke the [35 U.S.C.] §154 transition provision. Delineating the combined effects of the URAA and the Hatch-Waxman Act for patents issued prior to June 8, 1995, is thus the task before us. *At F.3d 1551, U.S.P.Q.2d 1352:* 35 U.S.C. §154(b)(2) provides for a term extension where issuance of a patent is delayed due to appellate review of an adverse determination of patentability. This new type of extension could be determined and granted post-issuance and would be added to the term *prior* to the addition of a restoration extension which, under §156(a), is added to the end of what otherwise would be the patent term. [W]e see no impediment to applying the restoration extension to a 20-year from filing term by reason of [§156(b)(2)]. *At F.3d 1553, U.S.P.Q.2d 1354:* In sum, patents that were in force on June 8, 1995, only because of a Hatch-Waxman extension are not entitled to reapply a restoration extension to a 20-year from filing term. Except for those patents, a patent in force on June 8, 1995, is entitled to have a restoration extension, whenever granted, added to the longer term of either 17 years from issuance or 20 years from filing."

§156(a)

Photocure ASA v. Kappos, 603 F.3d 1372, 1376, 95 U.S.P.Q.2d 1250, 1252 (Fed.Cir.2010). "'[P]roduct' in §156(a) means the product that is present in the drug for which federal approval was obtained."

Merck & Co. v. Hi-Tech Pharmacal Co., 482 F.3d 1317, 1318, 82 U.S.P.Q.2d 1203, 1204 (Fed.Cir.2007). "This case presents the question of whether a patent term extension under the Hatch-Waxman Act, 35 U.S.C. §156, may be applied to a patent subject to a terminal disclaimer under 35 U.S.C. §253, filed to overcome an obviousness-type double-patenting rejection. Because the language of §156 is unambiguous and fulfills a purpose unrelated to and not in conflict with that of §253, we hold that a Hatch-Waxman term extension may be so applied."

Cardiac Pacemakers, Inc. v. St. Jude Med., Inc., 381 F.3d 1371, 1386, 72 U.S.P.Q.2d 1333, 1344 (Fed.Cir. 2004). "[D] argues that [35 U.S.C. §41(c)(1)] does not affect the requirement of [35 U.S.C.] §156(a)(1) that the application for extension must be submitted before patent 'expiration,' and that the later revival of an expired patent does not overcome this stricture." Held: Because the PTO accepted late payments for extension, patent did not expire. D's argument was incorrect.

Baxter Diagnostics Inc. v. AVL Sci. Corp., 798 F.Supp. 612, 620, 25 U.S.P.Q.2d 1428, 1434 (C.D.Cal. 1992). "[S]ince only Class III medical devices must endure the requisite 'regulatory review period' [under 21 U.S.C. §360e,] Congress only intended to provide a patent-term extension for Class III medical devices. Although Class I or Class II devices may be subject to some limited form of premarket notification, they are not subject to the 'regulatory review period' necessary for patent-term extension." *See also* ***Eli Lilly & Co. v. Medtronic, Inc.***, 496 U.S. 661, 663-64, 15 U.S.P.Q.2d 1121, 1124 (1990).

§156(c)

Pfizer, Inc. v. Ranbaxy Labs., 457 F.3d 1284, 1290, 79 U.S.P.Q.2d 1583, 1588 (Fed.Cir.2006). "In applying for a patent extension, the patentee has a duty of candor and good faith towards the PTO and must disclose any 'material information adverse to a determination of entitlement to the extension sought.' The Director of the PTO is charged with deciding whether the patent is entitled to term extension, a decision which is given 'great deference.'"

§156(d)

Unimed, Inc. v. Quigg, 888 F.2d 826, 828, 12 U.S.P.Q.2d 1644, 1646 (Fed.Cir.1989). "[S]ection 156(d)(1) admits of no other meaning than that the 60-day period begins on the FDA approval date [regardless of whether action by another agency is necessary before commercial use of drug]. [¶] [T]he date of marketing approval for all new drugs is the date appearing on its approval letters. [T]he date when a new drug is 'approved' by the FDA is the date of the FDA approval letter, even where the applicant still needs to submit final printed labeling to the FDA."

§156(f)

Pfizer Inc. v. Dr. Reddy's Labs., 359 F.3d 1361, 1366, 69 U.S.P.Q.2d 2016, 2019 (Fed.Cir.2004). Section 156(f) "defines the drug product as including any salt or ester of the active ingredient. The FDA ruled that the term 'active ingredient' as used in the phrase 'active ingredient including any salt or ester of the active ingredient' means active moiety. The FDA has defined active moiety as the molecule or ion, excluding those appended portions of the molecule that cause the drug to be an ester [or salt,] responsible for the physiological or pharmacological action of the drug substance. [¶] [D's] attempt to limit the extension [of patent] to the specific approved salt on the basis of the 'rights derived' provision of §156(b) to the approved product is unsound." (Internal quotes omitted.)

Glaxo Operations Ltd. v. Quigg, 894 F.2d 392, 393, 13 U.S.P.Q.2d 1628, 1629 (Fed.Cir.1990). "The active ingredient of [the] tablets is [the] compound ... that ... becomes therapeutically active and effective when orally administered. *At F.2d 393 n.2, U.S.P.Q.2d 1629 n.2:* An ester is a compound derived from an acid by the exchange of a replaceable hydrogen of the latter for an organic radical, usually using an alcohol or other organic compound rich in OH groups. *At F.2d 393 n.3, U.S.P.Q.2d 1629 n.3:* A salt is a compound formed when the hydrogen of an acid is replaced by a metal or its equivalent."

Fisons plc v. Quigg, 876 F.2d 99, 100, 10 U.S.P.Q.2d 1869, 1870 (Fed.Cir.1989). "Applying the definition of 'product' provided in §156(f) to the extension requirement of §156(a)(5)(A), the PTO and district court interpreted the statute as limiting extensions to the term of the patent on the first permitted marketing or use of a particular *active ingredient*. Under that interpretation, it follows that because [P's] patented new products containing [active ingredient] did not qualify as the *first* permitted commercial marketing or use of the active ingredient ..., extensions of the patent term for the subject patents were not permissible." Held: The PTO and district court were correct.

§156(g)

Wyeth Holdings Corp. v. Sebelius, 603 F.3d 1291, 1297, 95 U.S.P.Q.2d 1233, 1238 (Fed.Cir.2010). "We agree with the district court that the plain language does not clearly indicate when an application is initially submitted under 35 U.S.C. §156(g). *At F.3d 1298, U.S.P.Q.2d 1239:* Because the text of §156(g) is ambiguous with regard to when an application is initially submitted, we must determine whether FDA's interpretation falls within the permissible range of interpretations left open by the statute. *At F.3d 1299-1300, U.S.P.Q.2d 1240:* We conclude that FDA's interpretation is permissible. Section 156(g) created a range of ambiguity by not explicitly defining the term 'application,' leaving that term open to interpretation. FDA's interpretation tracks the requirements of 21 U.S.C. §360b(b). As explained by FDA, the administrative [New Animal Drug Application (NADA)] is the first document containing or referencing all of the parts required by ... §360b(b). Thus, it is permissible to characterize the administrative NADA as the first application submitted for purposes of ... §156(g). Because the administrative NADA is the first application submitted, it is reasonable to interpret the date that it is submitted as the 'initially submitted' date. Prior to the submission of an administrative NADA, no application has been submitted, initially or otherwise. Thus, FDA's interpretation 'reasonably resolves the ambiguity in applying the relevant statutes to a factual situation not fully foreseen or provided for by the Congress when it enacted the statutes or the FDA when it promulgated regulations.' It is permissible to interpret §156(g) to mean that 'an application' is 'initially submitted' when a sponsor submits an administrative NADA in phased review."

Hoechst A.G. v. Quigg, 917 F.2d 522, 524, 16 U.S.P.Q.2d 1549, 1550-51 (Fed.Cir.1990). Section 156(g)(1)(B) "essentially provides that the length of the regulatory review period is the sum of (i) the testing phase period and (ii) the approval phase period for the drug. *At F.2d 527-28, U.S.P.Q.2d 1553:* [W]e conclude that [§156(g)(1)(B)] describes the regulatory review period and [§156(g)(6)] describes the limitation which applies to that regulatory review period.

Thus, the phrase 'to which the limitation described in paragraph (6) applies' [in §156(g)(1)(A)] is not superfluous, but is merely an internal cross-reference. [T]he limitation is applicable to a *previously* established regulatory review period. Thus, we reject the Commissioner's argument that the phrase 'to which the limitation described in paragraph (6) applies' is equivalent to '[a] regulatory review period within the meaning of §156(a)(4) and §156(g)(1) has occurred if the limitation of paragraph (6) applies.'"

§157. STATUTORY INVENTION REGISTRATION

Section 157 was repealed effective Mar. 16, 2013. Section 157 is effective for requests for statutory invention registrations filed before Mar. 16, 2013.

(a) Notwithstanding any other provision, the Director is authorized to publish a statutory invention registration containing the specification and drawings of a regularly filed application for a patent without examination if the applicant—

(1) meets the requirements of section 112;

(2) has complied with the requirements for printing, as set forth in regulations of the Director;

(3) waives the right to receive a patent on the invention within such period as may be prescribed by the Director; and

(4) pays application, publication, and other processing fees established by the Director.

If an interference is declared with respect to such an application, a statutory invention registration may not be published unless the issue of priority of invention is finally determined in favor of the applicant.

(b) The waiver under subsection (a)(3) of this section by an applicant shall take effect upon publication of the statutory invention registration.

(c) A statutory invention registration published pursuant to this section shall have all of the attributes specified for patents in this title except those specified in section 183 and sections 271 through 289. A statutory invention registration shall not have any of the attributes specified for patents in any other provision of law other than this title. A statutory invention registration published pursuant to this section shall give appropriate notice to the public, pursuant to regulations which the Director shall issue, of the preceding provisions of this subsection. The invention with respect to which a statutory invention certificate is published is not a patented invention for purposes of section 292.

(d) The Director shall report to the Congress annually on the use of statutory invention registrations. Such report shall include an assessment of the degree to which agencies of the Federal Government are making use of the statutory invention registration system, the degree to which it aids the management of federally developed technology, and an assessment of the cost savings to the Federal Government of the use of such procedures.

History of 35 U.S.C. §157: Nov. 8, 1984, P.L. 98-622, §102(a), 98 Stat. 3383; Nov. 29, 1999, P.L. 106-113, §1000(a)(9), 113 Stat. 1536; Nov. 2, 2002, P.L. 107-273, §13206(b)(1)(B), 116 Stat. 1906; Sept. 16, 2011, P.L. 112-29, §§3(e)(1), 20(j)(1), 125 Stat. 287, 335.

CHAPTER 15. PLANT PATENTS

§161. PATENTS FOR PLANTS

Whoever invents or discovers and asexually reproduces any distinct and new variety of plant, including cultivated sports, mutants, hybrids, and newly found seedlings, other than a tuber propagated plant or a plant found in an uncultivated state, may obtain a patent therefor, subject to the conditions and requirements of this title.

The provisions of this title relating to patents for inventions shall apply to patents for plants, except as otherwise provided.

History of 35 U.S.C. §161: July 19, 1952, ch. 950, §1, 66 Stat. 804; Sept. 3, 1954, ch. 1259, 68 Stat. 1190.

See also 7 U.S.C. §§2321-2582; 37 C.F.R. §§1.161-1.167.

ANNOTATIONS

In re Beineke, 690 F.3d 1344, 1347, 103 U.S.P.Q.2d 1872, 1874 (Fed.Cir.2012). "[A]n applicant for a patent under §161 must establish that the inventor has 'recognized [the plant's] uniqueness and difference,' ... and has 'take[n] the step of asexual reproduction[]'.... *At F.3d 1352, U.S.P.Q.2d 1877:* [T]he provisions of the original 1930 Act, incorporated in the present plant patent statute, provided patent protection to only those plants (e.g., sports, mutants, and hybrids) that were created as a result of plant breeding or other agricultural and horticultural efforts *and* that were created by the inventor, that is, the one applying for the patent. *At F.3d 1353, U.S.P.Q.2d 1878:* [I]n the 1954 amendments Congress 'added another class of plants, newly found seedlings,' but made them 'subject to the exception that such seedlings found in an uncultivated state cannot be patented.' [¶] Congress sought to extend the statute to provide that 'newly found seedlings' found in a cultivated state by the applicant were patentable. These seedlings did not need to have been created by a plant breeder so long as they were discovered by the applicant on cultivated land (such as [a garden]). The apparent assumption underlying this amendment was that an exception was warranted for newly found seedlings because, the plant having been a seedling at the time of its discovery, it could be assumed that it was cultivated in its inception and that the cultivation of the land by man contributed to its creation."

§162. DESCRIPTION, CLAIM

No plant patent shall be declared invalid for noncompliance with section 112 if the description is as complete as is reasonably possible.

The claim in the specification shall be in formal terms to the plant shown and described.

History of 35 U.S.C. §162: July 19, 1952, ch. 950, §1, 66 Stat. 804; Sept. 16, 2011, P.L. 112-29, §20(j)(1), 125 Stat. 335.

ANNOTATIONS

J.E.M. Ag Sup. v. Pioneer Hi-Bred Int'l, 534 U.S. 124, 142, 60 U.S.P.Q.2d 1865, 1873 (2001). "It is much more difficult to obtain a utility patent for a plant than to obtain a [Plant Variety Protection] certificate because a utility patentable plant must be new, useful, and nonobvious. In addition, to obtain a utility patent, a breeder must describe the plant with sufficient specificity to enable others to 'make and use' the invention after the patent term expires. The disclosure required by the Patent Act is 'the *quid pro quo* of the right to exclude.' The description requirement for plants includes a deposit of biological material, for example seeds, and mandates that such material be accessible to the public."

§163. GRANT

In the case of a plant patent, the grant shall include the right to exclude others from asexually reproducing the plant, and from using, offering for sale, or selling the plant so reproduced, or any of its parts, throughout the United States, or from importing the plant so reproduced, or any parts thereof, into the United States.

History of 35 U.S.C. §163: July 19, 1952, ch. 950, §1, 66 Stat. 804; Oct. 27, 1998, §3(a), 112 Stat. 2781.

§164. ASSISTANCE OF DEPARTMENT OF AGRICULTURE

The President may by Executive order direct the Secretary of Agriculture, in accordance with the requests of the Director, for the purpose of carrying into effect the provisions of this title with respect to plants (1) to furnish available information of the Department of Agriculture, (2) to conduct through the appropriate bureau or division of the Department research upon special problems, or (3) to detail to the Director officers and employees of the Department.

History of 35 U.S.C. §164: July 19, 1952, ch. 950, §1, 66 Stat. 804; Nov. 29, 1999, P.L. 106-113, §1000(a)(9), 113 Stat. 1536; Nov. 2, 2002, P.L. 107-273, §13206(b)(1)(B), 116 Stat. 1906.

CHAPTER 16. DESIGNS

§171. PATENTS FOR DESIGNS

(a) In general.—Whoever invents any new, original and ornamental design for an article of manufacture may obtain a patent therefor, subject to the conditions and requirements of this title.

(b) Applicability of this title.—The provisions of this title relating to patents for inventions shall apply to patents for designs, except as otherwise provided.

(c) Filing date.—The filing date of an application for patent for design shall be the date on which the specification as prescribed by section 112 and any required drawings are filed.

History of 35 U.S.C. §171: July 19, 1952, ch. 950, §1, 66 Stat. 805; Dec. 18, 2013, P.L. 112-211, §202(a), 126 Stat. 1535.

See also 35 U.S.C. §289; 37 C.F.R. §§1.151-1.155, 1.1052.

ANNOTATIONS

Ethicon Endo-Surgery, Inc. v. Covidien, Inc., 796 F.3d 1312, 1328, 115 U.S.P.Q.2d 1880, 1892 (Fed.Cir. 2015). "Design patents enjoy the same presumption of validity as utility patents under 35 U.S.C. §282. Thus, [D] has the burden to prove invalidity of the Design Patents by clear and convincing evidence. We have described as 'stringent' this standard as it applies to invalidating design patents on grounds of functionality. We review the district court's finding that the patented designs are dictated by their function for clear error. [¶] Articles of manufacture necessarily serve a utilitarian purpose, but design patents are directed to ornamental designs of such articles. If a particular design is essential to the use of an article, it cannot be the subject of a design patent. We have found designs to be essential to the use of an article when the claimed design is dictated by the use or purpose of the article. Design patents on such primarily functional rather than ornamental designs are invalid. [¶] In determining whether a claimed design is primarily functional, the function of the article itself must not be confused with 'functionality' of the design of the article. *At F.3d 1329-30, U.S.P.Q.2d 1893:* We have also instructed that the overall appearance of the article—the claimed design viewed in its entirety—is the basis of the relevant inquiry, not the functionality of elements of the claimed design viewed in isolation. ... Nevertheless, we explained that the utility of each of the various elements that comprise the design is not the relevant inquiry with respect to a design patent because whether a design is primarily functional or primarily ornamental requires viewing the claimed design in its entirety. [¶] We have not mandated applying any particular test for determining whether a claimed design is dictated by its function and therefore impermissibly functional. We have often focused, however, on the availability of alternative designs as an important—if not dispositive—factor in evaluating the legal functionality of a claimed design. *At U.S.P.Q.2d 1894:* In our instructions on remand, we explained that where the existence of alternative designs is not dispositive of the invalidity inquiry, the district court may look to several other factors for its analysis: whether the protected design represents the best design; whether alternative designs would adversely affect the utility of the specified article; whether there are any concomitant utility patents; whether the advertising touts particular features of the design as having specific utility; and whether there are any elements in the design or an overall appearance clearly not dictated by function. We explained that evaluating these other considerations might be relevant to assessing whether the overall appearance of a claimed design is dictated by functional considerations. Thus, while the ... factors can provide useful guidance, an inquiry into whether a claimed design is primarily functional should begin with an inquiry into the existence of alternative designs." (Internal quotes omitted.) *See also* ***PHG Techs. v. St. John Cos.***, 469 F.3d 1361, 1366-67, 81 U.S.P.Q.2d 1088, 1091-92 (Fed.Cir. 2006).

§172. RIGHT OF PRIORITY

The right of priority provided for by subsections (a) through (d) of section 119 shall be six months in the case of designs. The right of priority provided for by section 119(e) shall not apply to designs.

History of 35 U.S.C. §172: July 19, 1952, ch. 950, §1, 66 Stat. 805; Dec. 8, 1994, P.L. 103-465, §532(c)(2), 108 Stat. 4987; Sept. 16, 2011, P.L. 112-29, §§3(g)(1), 20(j)(1), 125 Stat. 288, 335.

See also TRIPs pt. II, §5.

§173. TERM OF DESIGN PATENT

Patents for designs shall be granted for the term of 15 years from the date of grant.

History of 35 U.S.C. §173: July 19, 1952, ch. 950, §1, 66 Stat. 805; Aug. 27, 1982, P.L. 97-247, §16, 96 Stat. 321; Dec. 8, 1994, P.L. 103-465, §532(c)(3), 108 Stat. 4987; May 13, 2015, P.L. 112-211, §102(7), 126 Stat. 1532.

See also TRIPs pt. II, §5.

CHAPTER 17. SECRECY OF CERTAIN INVENTIONS & FILING APPLICATIONS IN FOREIGN COUNTRY

§181. SECRECY OF CERTAIN INVENTIONS & WITHHOLDING OF PATENT

Whenever publication or disclosure by the publication of an application or by the grant of a patent on an invention in which the Government has a property interest might, in the opinion of the head of the interested Government agency, be detrimental to the national security, the Commissioner of Patents upon being so notified shall order that the invention be kept secret and shall withhold the publication of the application or the grant of a patent therefor under the conditions set forth hereinafter.

Whenever the publication or disclosure of an invention by the publication of an application or by the granting of a patent, in which the Government does not have a property interest, might, in the opinion of the Commissioner of Patents, be detrimental to the national security, he shall make the application for patent in which such invention is disclosed available for inspection to the Atomic Energy Commission, the Secretary of Defense, and the chief officer of any other department or agency of the Government designated by the President as a defense agency of the United States.

Each individual to whom the application is disclosed shall sign a dated acknowledgment thereof, which acknowledgment shall be entered in the file of the application. If, in the opinion of the Atomic Energy Commission, the Secretary of a Defense Department, or the chief officer of another department or agency so designated, the publication or disclosure of the invention by the publication of an application or by the granting of a patent therefor would be detrimental to the national security, the Atomic Energy Commission, the Secretary of a Defense Department, or such other chief officer shall notify the Commissioner of Patents and the Commissioner of Patents shall order that the invention be kept secret and shall withhold the publication of the application or the grant of a patent for such period as the national interest requires, and notify the applicant thereof. Upon proper showing by the head of the department or agency who caused the secrecy order to be issued that the examination of the application might jeopardize the national interest, the Commissioner of Patents shall thereupon maintain the application in a sealed condition and notify the applicant thereof. The owner of an application which has been placed under a secrecy order shall have a right to appeal from the order to the Secretary of Commerce under rules prescribed by him.

An invention shall not be ordered kept secret and the publication of the application or the grant of a patent withheld for a period of more than one year. The Commissioner of Patents shall renew the order at the end thereof, or at the end of any renewal period, for additional periods of one year upon notification by the head of the department or the chief officer of the agency who caused the order to be issued that an affirmative determination has been made that the national interest continues so to require. An order in effect, or issued, during a time when the United States is at war, shall remain in effect for the duration of hostilities and one year following cessation of hostilities. An order in effect, or issued, during a national emergency declared by the President shall remain in effect for the duration of the national emergency and six months thereafter. The Commissioner of Patents may rescind any order upon notification by the heads of the departments and the chief officers of the agencies who caused the order to be issued that the publication or disclosure of the invention is no longer deemed detrimental to the national security.

History of 35 U.S.C. §181: July 19, 1952, ch. 950, §1, 66 Stat. 805; Nov. 29, 1999, P.L. 106-113, §1000(a)(9), 113 Stat. 1536.

See also 37 C.F.R. pt. 5.

§182. ABANDONMENT OF INVENTION FOR UNAUTHORIZED DISCLOSURE

The invention disclosed in an application for patent subject to an order made pursuant to section 181 may be held abandoned upon its being established by the Commissioner of Patents that in violation of said order the invention has been published or disclosed or that an application for a patent therefor has been filed in a foreign country by the inventor, his successors, assigns, or legal representatives, or anyone in privity with him or them, without the consent of the Commissioner of Patents. The abandonment shall be held to have occurred as of the time of violation. The consent of the Commissioner of Patents shall not be given without the concurrence of the heads of the departments and the chief officers of the agencies who caused the order to be issued. A holding of abandonment shall constitute forfeiture by the applicant, his successors, assigns, or legal representatives, or anyone in privity with him or them, of all claims against the United States based upon such invention.

History of 35 U.S.C. §182: July 19, 1952, ch. 950, §1, 66 Stat. 806; Nov. 29, 1999, P.L. 106-113, §1000(a)(9), 113 Stat. 1536; Sept. 16, 2011, P.L. 112-29, §20(j)(1), 125 Stat. 335.

§183. RIGHT TO COMPENSATION

An applicant, his successors, assigns, or legal representatives, whose patent is withheld as herein provided, shall have the right, beginning at the date the applicant is notified that, except for such order, his application is otherwise in condition for allowance, or February 1, 1952, whichever is later, and ending six years after a patent is issued thereon, to apply to the head of any department or agency who caused the order to be issued for compensation for the damage caused by the order of secrecy and/or for the use of the invention by the Government, resulting from his disclosure. The right to compensation for use shall begin on the date of the first use of the invention by the Government. The head of the department or agency is authorized, upon the presentation of a claim, to enter into an agreement with the applicant, his successors, assigns, or legal representatives, in full settlement for the damage and/or use. This settlement agreement shall be conclusive for all purposes notwithstanding any other provision of law to the contrary. If full settlement of the claim cannot be effected, the head of the department or agency may award and pay to such applicant, his successors, assigns, or legal representatives, a sum not exceeding 75 per centum of the sum which the head of the department or agency considers just compensation for the damage and/or use. A claimant may bring suit against the United States in the United States Court of Federal Claims or in the District Court of the United States for the district in which such claimant is a resident for an amount which when added to the award shall constitute just compensation for the damage and/or use of the invention by the Government. The owner of any patent issued upon an application that was subject to a secrecy order issued pursuant to section 181, who did not apply for compensation as above provided, shall have the right, after the date of issuance of such patent, to bring suit in the United States Court of Federal Claims for just compensation for the damage caused by reason of the order of secrecy and/or use by the Government of the invention resulting from his disclosure. The right to compensation for use shall begin on the date of the first use of the invention by the Government. In a suit under the provisions of this section the United States may avail itself of all defenses it may plead in an action under section 1498 of title 28. This section shall not confer a right of action on anyone or his successors, assigns, or legal representatives who, while in the full-time employment or service of the United States, discovered, invented, or developed the invention on which the claim is based.

History of 35 U.S.C. §183: July 19, 1952, ch. 950, §1, 66 Stat. 806; Apr. 2, 1982, P.L. 97-164, §160(a)(12), 96 Stat. 48; Sept. 16, 2011, P.L. 112-29, §20(j)(1), 125 Stat. 335.

ANNOTATIONS

Hornback v. U.S., 601 F.3d 1382, 1383, 94 U.S.P.Q.2d 1669, 1669 (Fed.Cir.2010). "[T]he Invention Secrecy Act, ... §183, does not provide [P] with a cause of action for the government's use of an invention subject to a secrecy order after the issuance of a patent on that invention.... *At F.3d 1387, U.S.P.Q.2d 1672:* [T]his court holds that 'use of the invention' in ... §183 does not include use of an invention after a patent for the invention has issued. This interpretation is consistent with the reading provided by this court's predecessor, which noted, in dicta, that '§183 provides for damages to be paid to patent holders in two situations: when the Government wrongfully uses the patented device *during the period of secrecy*, and when the secrecy order itself causes damages.'"

Stein v. U.S., 135 F.Supp.2d 265, 271, 64 U.S.P.Q.2d 1017, 1022 (D.Mass.2001). "[F]or suits brought under §183, no presumption of laches should arise because of the unique design of that section. Section 183 explicitly sets out two routes, one administrative and judicial and one purely judicial, by which an inventor can seek compensation for governmental use of her invention.... Under both routes, §183 allows an inventor to bring suit for all of the damages that arose from her application disclosure as late as six years after the issuance of the patent, regardless of when the use by the Government first occurred."

Honeywell Int'l v. U.S., 107 Fed.Cl. 659, 665 (Fed. Cl.2012). "[T]he court construes the text of §183 to require that Government use of a patent application, subject to an Invention Secrecy Act Order, must result from the Government's disclosure of that application, *i.e.*, so that the use is 'wrongful,' before the Government is liable for monetary damages."

§184. FILING OF APPLICATION IN FOREIGN COUNTRY

(a) Filing in foreign country.—Except when authorized by a license obtained from the Commissioner of Patents a person shall not file or cause or authorize to be filed in any foreign country prior to six months after filing in the United States an application for patent or for the registration of a utility model, industrial design, or model in respect of an invention made in this country. A license shall not be granted with respect to an invention subject to an order issued by the Commissioner of Patents pursuant to section 181 without the concurrence of the head of the departments and the chief officers of the agencies who caused the order to be issued. The license may be granted retroactively where an application has been filed abroad through error and the application does not disclose an invention within the scope of section 181.

(b) Application.—The term "application" when used in this chapter includes applications and any modifications, amendments, or supplements thereto, or divisions thereof.

(c) Subsequent modifications, amendments, and supplements.—The scope of a license shall permit subsequent modifications, amendments, and supplements containing additional subject matter if the application upon which the request for the license is based is not, or was not, required to be made available for inspection under section 181 and if such modifications, amendments, and supplements do not change the general nature of the invention in a manner which would require such application to be made available for inspection under such section 181. In any case in which a license is not, or was not, required in order to file an application in any foreign country, such subsequent modifications, amendments, and supplements may be made, without a license, to the application filed in the foreign country if the United States application was not required to be made available for inspection under section 181 and if such modifications, amendments, and supplements do not, or did not, change the general nature of the invention in a manner which would require the United States application to have been made available for inspection under such section 181.

History of 35 U.S.C. §184: July 19, 1952, ch. 950, §1, 66 Stat. 807; Aug. 23, 1988, P.L. 100-418, §9101(b)(1), 102 Stat. 1567; Nov. 29, 1999, P.L. 106-113, §1000(a)(9), 113 Stat. 1536; Sept. 16, 2011, P.L. 112-29, §20(b), (j)(1), 125 Stat. 333, 335.

ANNOTATIONS

Honeywell Int'l v. U.S., 609 F.3d 1292, 1303, 95 U.S.P.Q.2d 1193, 1202 (Fed.Cir.2010). Section 184 "states that the term 'application' when used in this chapter includes applications and any modifications, amendments, or supplements thereto, or divisions thereof. [¶] The '269 application issued, albeit after amendment, as the '914 patent. Section 184 explicitly includes amendments made to an application. [P] owns the '914 patent, this patent issued from the '269 application, this application was subject to a secrecy order. [P] thus has standing to assert a claim for just compensation under the Invention Secrecy Act." (Internal quotes omitted.)

§185. PATENT BARRED FOR FILING WITHOUT LICENSE

Notwithstanding any other provisions of law any person, and his successors, assigns, or legal representatives, shall not receive a United States patent for an invention if that person, or his successors, assigns, or legal representatives shall, without procuring the license prescribed in section 184, have made, or consented to or assisted another's making, application in a foreign country for a patent or for the registration of a utility model, industrial design, or model in respect of the invention. A United States patent issued to such person, his successors, assigns, or legal representatives shall be invalid, unless the failure to procure such license was through error, and the patent does not disclose subject matter within the scope of section 181.

History of 35 U.S.C. §185: July 19, 1952, ch. 950, §1, 66 Stat. 807; Aug. 23, 1988, P.L. 100-418, §9101(b)(2), 102 Stat. 1568; Nov. 2, 2002, P.L. 107-273, §13206(a)(11), 116 Stat. 1904; Sept. 16, 2011, P.L. 112-29, §20(c), (j)(1), 125 Stat. 333, 335.

ANNOTATIONS

Aristocrat Techs. Australia Pty Ltd. v. International Game Tech., 543 F.3d 657, 662, 88 U.S.P.Q.2d 1458, 1462 (Fed.Cir.2008). "35 U.S.C. §185 states that a patent issued to a person who has violated the secrecy provisions of [35 U.S.C.] §184 'shall be invalid,' except under certain circumstances."

§186. PENALTY

Whoever, during the period or periods of time an invention has been ordered to be kept secret and the grant of a patent thereon withheld pursuant to section 181, shall, with knowledge of such order and without due authorization, willfully publish or disclose or authorize or cause to be published or disclosed the invention, or material information with respect thereto, or whoever willfully, in violation of the provisions of section 184, shall file or cause or authorize to be filed in any foreign country an application for patent or for the registration of a utility model, industrial design, or model in respect of any invention made in the United States, shall, upon conviction, be fined not more than $10,000 or imprisoned for not more than two years, or both.

History of 35 U.S.C. §186: July 19, 1952, ch. 950, §1, 66 Stat. 807; Aug. 23, 1988, P.L. 100-418, §9101(b)(3), 102 Stat. 1568; Sept. 16, 2011, P.L. 112-29, §20(j)(1), 125 Stat. 335.

ANNOTATIONS

Damnjanovic v. U.S. Dept. of the Air Force, 135 F.Supp.3d 601, 604 (E.D.Mich.2015). "After the Commissioner orders an invention to be kept secret, §186 ... makes it a criminal offense to disclose the invention, or material information about the invention, without authorization."

§187. NONAPPLICABILITY TO CERTAIN PERSONS

The prohibitions and penalties of this chapter shall not apply to any officer or agent of the United States acting within the scope of his authority, nor to any person acting upon his written instructions or permission.

History of 35 U.S.C. §187: July 19, 1952, ch. 950, §1, 66 Stat. 808.

§188. RULES & REGULATIONS, DELEGATION OF POWER

The Atomic Energy Commission, the Secretary of a defense department, the chief officer of any other department or agency of the Government designated by the President as a defense agency of the United States, and the Secretary of Commerce, may separately issue rules and regulations to enable the respective department or agency to carry out the provisions of this chapter, and may delegate any power conferred by this chapter.

History of 35 U.S.C. §188: July 19, 1952, ch. 950, §1, 66 Stat. 808.

CHAPTER 18. PATENT RIGHTS IN INVENTIONS MADE WITH FEDERAL ASSISTANCE

§200. POLICY & OBJECTIVE

It is the policy and objective of the Congress to use the patent system to promote the utilization of inventions arising from federally supported research or development; to encourage maximum participation of small business firms in federally supported research and development efforts; to promote collaboration between commercial concerns and nonprofit organizations, including universities; to ensure that inventions made by nonprofit organizations and small business firms are used in a manner to promote free competition and enterprise without unduly encumbering future research and discovery; to promote the commercialization and public availability of inventions made in the United States by United States industry and labor; to ensure that the Government obtains sufficient rights in federally supported inventions to meet the needs of the Government and protect the public against nonuse or unreasonable use of inventions; and to minimize the costs of administering policies in this area.

History of 35 U.S.C. §200: Dec. 12, 1980, P.L. 96-517, §6(a), 94 Stat. 3019; Nov. 1, 2000, P.L. 106-404, §5, 114 Stat. 1745.

See also 14 C.F.R. pt. 1245; 45 C.F.R. pt. 650; 48 C.F.R. pt. 2527.

ANNOTATIONS

Campbell Plastics Eng'g v. Brownlee, 389 F.3d 1243, 1247, 73 U.S.P.Q.2d 1357, 1361 (Fed.Cir.2004). The Bayh-Dole Act "allows nonprofit organizations and small business firms to elect to retain title to any invention by the contractor developed pursuant to a government contract."

Hochendoner v. Genzyme Corp., 95 F.Supp.3d 15, 27-28 (D.Mass.2015), *aff'd*, 823 F.3d 724 (1st Cir.2016). "Congress has ... exhibited no intent to create a private remedy for violation of the Bayh-Dole Act."

§201. DEFINITIONS

As used in this chapter—

(a) The term "Federal agency" means any executive agency as defined in section 105 of title 5, and the military departments as defined by section 102 of title 5.

(b) The term "funding agreement" means any contract, grant, or cooperative agreement entered into between any Federal agency, other than the Tennessee Valley Authority, and any contractor for the performance of experimental, developmental, or research work funded in whole or in part by the Federal Government. Such term includes any assignment, substitution of parties, or subcontract of any type entered into for the performance of experimental, developmental, or research work under a funding agreement as herein defined.

(c) The term "contractor" means any person, small business firm, or nonprofit organization that is a party to a funding agreement.

(d) The term "invention" means any invention or discovery which is or may be patentable or otherwise protectable under this title or any novel variety of plant which is or may be protectable under the Plant Variety Protection Act (7 U.S.C. 2321 et seq.).

(e) The term "subject invention" means any invention of the contractor conceived or first actually reduced to practice in the performance of work under a funding agreement: *Provided*, That in the case of a variety of plant, the date of determination (as defined in section 41(d) of the Plant Variety Protection Act (7 U.S.C. 2401(d))) must also occur during the period of contract performance.

(f) The term "practical application" means to manufacture in the case of a composition or product, to practice in the case of a process or method, or to operate in the case of a machine or system; and, in each case, under such conditions as to establish that the invention is being utilized and that its benefits are to the extent permitted by law or Government regulations available to the public on reasonable terms.

(g) The term "made" when used in relation to any invention means the conception or first actual reduction to practice of such invention.

(h) The term "small business firm" means a small business concern as defined at section 2 of Public Law 85-536 (15 U.S.C. 632) and implementing regulations of the Administrator of the Small Business Administration.

(i) The term "nonprofit organization" means universities and other institutions of higher education or an organization of the type described in section 501(c)(3) of the Internal Revenue Code of 1986 (26 U.S.C. 501(c)) and exempt from taxation under section 501(a) of the Internal Revenue Code (26 U.S.C. 501(a)) or any nonprofit scientific or educational organization qualified under a State nonprofit organization statute.

History of 35 U.S.C. §201: Dec. 12, 1980, P.L. 96-517, §6(a), 94 Stat. 3019; Nov. 8, 1984, P.L. 98-620, §501(1), (2), 98 Stat. 3364; Nov. 2, 2002, P.L. 107-273, §13206(a)(12), 116 Stat. 1904.

§202. DISPOSITION OF RIGHTS

(a) Each nonprofit organization or small business firm may, within a reasonable time after disclosure as required by paragraph (c)(1) of this section, elect to retain title to any subject invention: *Provided, however*, That a funding agreement may provide otherwise (i) when the contractor is not located in the United States or does not have a place of business located in the United States or is subject to the control of a foreign government, (ii) in exceptional circumstances when it is determined by the agency that restriction or elimination of the right to retain title to any subject invention will better promote the policy and objectives of this chapter[,] (iii) when it is determined by a Government authority which is authorized by statute or Executive order to conduct foreign intelligence or counter-intelligence activities that the restriction or elimination of the right to retain title to any subject invention is necessary to protect the security of such activities or, (iv) when the funding agreement includes the operation of a Government-owned, contractor-operated facility of the Department of Energy primarily dedicated to that Department's naval nuclear propulsion or weapons related programs and all funding agreement limitations under this subparagraph on the contractor's right to elect title to a subject invention are limited to inventions occurring under the above two programs of the Department of Energy. The rights of the nonprofit organization or small business firm shall be subject to the provisions of paragraph (c) of this section and the other provisions of this chapter.

(b)(1) The rights of the Government under subsection (a) shall not be exercised by a Federal agency unless it first determines that at least one of the conditions identified in clauses (i) through (iv) of subsection (a) exists. Except in the case of subsection (a)(iii), the agency shall file with the Secretary of Commerce, within thirty days after the award of the applicable funding agreement, a copy of such determination. In the case of a determination under subsection (a)(ii), the statement shall include an analysis justifying the determination. In the case of determinations applicable to funding agreements with small business firms, copies shall also be sent to the Chief Counsel for Advocacy of the Small Business Administration. If the Secretary of Commerce believes that any individual determination or pattern of determinations is contrary to the policies and objectives of this chapter or otherwise not in conformance with this chapter, the Secretary shall so advise the head of the agency concerned and the Administrator of the Office of Federal Procurement Policy, and recommend corrective actions.

(2) Whenever the Administrator of the Office of Federal Procurement Policy has determined that one or more Federal agencies are utilizing the authority of clause (i) or (ii) of subsection (a) of this section in a manner that is contrary to the policies and objectives of this chapter, the Administrator is authorized to issue regulations describing classes of situations in which agencies may not exercise the authorities of those clauses.

(3) If the contractor believes that a determination is contrary to the policies and objectives of this chapter or constitutes an abuse of discretion by the agency, the determination shall be subject to section 203(b).

(c) Each funding agreement with a small business firm or nonprofit organization shall contain appropriate provisions to effectuate the following:

(1) That the contractor disclose each subject invention to the Federal agency within a reasonable time after it becomes known to contractor personnel responsible for the administration of patent matters, and that the Federal Government may receive title to any subject invention not disclosed to it within such time.

(2) That the contractor make a written election within two years after disclosure to the Federal agency (or such additional time as may be approved by the Federal agency) whether the contractor will retain title to a subject invention: *Provided*, That in any case where the 1-year period referred to in section 102(b) would end before the end of that 2-year period, the period for election may be shortened by the Federal agency to a date that is not more than sixty days before the end of that 1-year period: And provided further, That the Federal Government may receive title to any subject invention in which the contractor does not elect to retain rights or fails to elect rights within such times.

(3) That a contractor electing rights in a subject invention agrees to file a patent application prior to the expiration of the 1-year period referred to in section 102(b), and shall thereafter file corresponding patent applications in other countries in which it wishes to retain title within reasonable times, and that the Federal Government may receive title to any subject inventions in the United States or other countries in which the contractor has not filed patent applications on the subject invention within such times.

(4) With respect to any invention in which the contractor elects rights, the Federal agency shall have a nonexclusive, nontransferrable, irrevocable, paid-up license to practice or have practiced for or on behalf of the United States any subject invention throughout the world: *Provided*, That the funding agreement may provide for such additional rights, including the right to assign or have assigned foreign patent rights in the subject invention, as are determined by the agency as necessary for meeting the obligations of the United States under any treaty, international agreement, arrangement of cooperation, memorandum of understanding, or similar arrangement, including military agreement relating to weapons development and production.

(5) The right of the Federal agency to require periodic reporting on the utilization or efforts at obtaining utilization that are being made by the contractor or his licensees or assignees: *Provided*, That any such information as well as any information on utilization or efforts at obtaining utilization obtained as part of a proceeding under section 203 of this chapter shall be treated by the Federal agency as commercial and financial information obtained from a person and privileged and confidential and not subject to disclosure under section 552 of title 5.

(6) An obligation on the part of the contractor, in the event a United States patent application is filed by or on its behalf or by any assignee of the contractor, to include within the specification of such application and any patent issuing thereon, a statement specifying that the invention was made with Government support and that the Government has certain rights in the invention.

(7) In the case of a nonprofit organization, (A) a prohibition upon the assignment of rights to a subject invention in the United States without the approval of the Federal agency, except where such assignment is made to an organization which has as one of its primary functions the management of inventions (provided that such assignee shall be subject to the same provisions as the contractor); (B) a requirement that the contractor share royalties with the inventor; (C) except with respect to a funding agreement for the operation of a Government-owned-contractor-operated facility, a requirement that the balance of any royalties or income earned by the contractor with respect to subject inventions, after payment of expenses (including payments to inventors) incidental to the administration of subject inventions, be utilized for the support of scientific research or education; (D) a requirement that, except where it is determined to be infeasible following a reasonable inquiry, a preference in the licensing of subject inventions shall be given to small business firms; and (E) with respect to a funding agreement for the operation of a Government-owned-contractor-operated facility, requirements (i) that after payment of patenting costs, licensing costs, payments to inventors, and other expenses incidental to the administration of subject inventions, 100 percent of the balance of any royalties or income earned and retained by the contractor during any fiscal year up to an amount equal to 5 percent of the annual budget of the facility, shall be used by the contractor for scientific research, development, and education consistent with the research and development mission and objectives of the facility, including activities that increase the licensing potential of other inventions of the facility; provided that if said balance exceeds 5 percent of the annual budget of the facility, that 15 percent of such excess shall be paid to the Treasury of the United States and the remaining 85 percent shall be used for the same purposes described above in this clause; and (ii) that, to the extent it provides the most effective technology transfer, the licensing of subject inventions shall be administered by contractor employees on location at the facility.

(8) The requirements of sections 203 and 204 of this chapter.

(d) If a contractor does not elect to retain title to a subject invention in cases subject to this section, the Federal agency may consider and after consultation with the contractor grant requests for retention of rights by the inventor subject to the provisions of this Act and regulations promulgated hereunder.

(e) In any case when a Federal employee is a coinventor of any invention made with a nonprofit organization, a small business firm, or a non-Federal inventor, the Federal agency employing such coinventor may, for the purpose of consolidating rights in the invention and if it finds that it would expedite the development of the invention—

(1) license or assign whatever rights it may acquire in the subject invention to the nonprofit organization, small business firm, or non-Federal inventor in accordance with the provisions of this chapter; or

(2) acquire any rights in the subject invention from the nonprofit organization, small business firm, or non-Federal inventor, but only to the extent the party from whom the rights are acquired voluntarily enters into the transaction and no other transaction under this chapter is conditioned on such acquisition.

(f)(1) No funding agreement with a small business firm or nonprofit organization shall contain a provision allowing a Federal agency to require the licensing to third parties of inventions owned by the contractor that are not subject inventions unless such provision has been approved by the head of the agency and a written justification has been signed by the head of the agency. Any such provision shall clearly state whether the licensing may be required in connection with the practice of a subject invention, a specifically identified work object, or both. The head of the agency may not delegate the authority to approve provisions or sign justifications required by this paragraph.

(2) A Federal agency shall not require the licensing of third parties under any such provision unless the head of the agency determines that the use of the invention by others is necessary for the practice of a subject invention or for the use of a work object of the funding agreement and that such action is necessary to achieve the practical application of the subject invention or work object. Any such determination shall be on the record after an opportunity for an agency hearing. Any action commenced for judicial review of such determination shall be brought within sixty days after notification of such determination.

History of 35 U.S.C. §202: Dec. 12, 1980, P.L. 96-517, §6(a), 94 Stat. 3020; Nov. 8, 1984, P.L. 98-620, §501(3)-(8), 98 Stat. 3364; Dec. 10, 1991, P.L. 102-204, §10, 105 Stat. 1641; Nov. 29, 1999, P.L. 106-113, §1000(a)(9), 113 Stat. 1536; Nov. 1, 2000, P.L. 106-404, §6(1), 114 Stat. 1745; Nov. 2, 2002, P.L. 107-273, §13206(a)(13), 116 Stat. 1905; Sept. 30, 2009, P.L. 111-8, §1301(h), 123 Stat. 829; Sept. 16, 2011, P.L. 112-29, §§3(g)(7), 13(a), 20(i)(2), 125 Stat. 288, 327, 334.

See also 37 C.F.R. §§401.1-401.17, 404.1-404.14; 48 C.F.R. §§52.227-11 to 52.227-23, 252.227-7038.

ANNOTATIONS

Board of Trs. of Leland Stanford Junior Univ. v. Roche Molecular Sys., 563 U.S. 776, 780, 131 S.Ct. 2188, 2192, 98 U.S.P.Q.2d 1761, 1764 (2011). "Since 1790, the patent law has operated on the premise that rights in an invention belong to the inventor. The question here is whether ... the Bayh-Dole Act ... displaces that norm and automatically vests title to federally funded inventions in federal contractors. We hold that it does not. *At U.S. 789-90, S.Ct. 2197, U.S.P.Q.2d 1768:* The Bayh-Dole Act's provision stating that contractors may 'elect to *retain* title' confirms that the Act does not *vest* title. ... The Bayh-Dole Act does not confer title to federally funded inventions on contractors or authorize contractors to unilaterally take title to those inventions; it simply assures contractors that they may keep title to whatever it is they already have."

Central Admixture Pharm. v. Advanced Cardiac Solutions, P.C., 482 F.3d 1347, 1352-53, 82 U.S.P.Q.2d 1293, 1297 (Fed.Cir.2007). "When a violation [of §202] occurs, the government can choose to take action; thus, title to the patent may be voidable. However, it is not void: title remains with the named inventors or their assignees. Nothing in the statute, regulations, or our caselaw indicates that title is automatically forfeited. The government must take an affirmative action to establish its title and invoke forfeiture."

Campbell Plastics Eng'g v. Brownlee, 389 F.3d 1243, 1247, 73 U.S.P.Q.2d 1357, 1361 (Fed.Cir.2004). "Though the [Bayh-Dole] Act provides nonprofit organizations and small business firms the right to elect title to a subject invention, it also vests in the government the right to a paid-up license to practice the invention when the contractor elects to retain title, and the right to receive title to the invention in the U.S. or any other country in which the contractor has not filed a patent application on the invention prior to any pertinent statutory bar date. The disclosure provisions of [35 U.S.C.] §202(c)(1) thus provide the government adequate means with which to protect these rights. *At F.3d 1248, U.S.P.Q.2d 1362:* A single, written report containing the information required by [Federal Acquisition Regulation] 52.227-11(c)(1) effectively provides such a safeguard." Held: Contractor's piecemeal disclosures were inadequate to retain title in its invention.

§203. MARCH-IN RIGHTS

(a) With respect to any subject invention in which a small business firm or nonprofit organization has acquired title under this chapter, the Federal agency under whose funding agreement the subject invention was made shall have the right, in accordance with such procedures as are provided in regulations promulgated hereunder to require the contractor, an assignee or exclusive licensee of a subject invention to grant a nonexclusive, partially exclusive, or exclusive license in any field of use to a responsible applicant or applicants, upon terms that are reasonable under the circumstances, and if the contractor, assignee, or exclusive licensee refuses such request, to grant such a license itself, if the Federal agency determines that such—

(1) action is necessary because the contractor or assignee has not taken, or is not expected to take within a reasonable time, effective steps to achieve practical application of the subject invention in such field of use;

(2) action is necessary to alleviate health or safety needs which are not reasonably satisfied by the contractor, assignee, or their licensees;

(3) action is necessary to meet requirements for public use specified by Federal regulations and such requirements are not reasonably satisfied by the contractor, assignee, or licensees; or

(4) action is necessary because the agreement required by section 204 has not been obtained or waived or because a licensee of the exclusive right to use or sell any subject invention in the United States is in breach of its agreement obtained pursuant to section 204.

(b) A determination pursuant to this section or section 202(b)(4) shall not be subject to chapter 71 of title 41. An administrative appeals procedure shall be established by regulations promulgated in accordance with section 206. Additionally, any contractor, inventor, assignee, or exclusive licensee adversely affected by a determination under this section may, at any time within sixty days after the determination is issued, file a petition in the United States Court of Federal Claims, which shall have jurisdiction to determine the appeal on the record and to affirm, reverse, remand or modify, as appropriate, the determination of the Federal agency. In cases described in paragraphs (1) and (3) of subsection (a), the agency's determination shall be held in abeyance pending the exhaustion of appeals or petitions filed under the preceding sentence.

History of 35 U.S.C. §203: Dec. 12, 1980, P.L. 96-517, §6(a), 94 Stat. 3022; Nov. 8, 1984, P.L. 98-620, §501(9), 98 Stat. 3367; Nov. 2, 2002, P.L. 107-273, §13206(a)(14), 116 Stat. 1905; Jan. 4, 2011, P.L. 111-350, §5(i)(2), 124 Stat. 3850.

See also 37 C.F.R. §401.6.

§204. PREFERENCE FOR UNITED STATES INDUSTRY

Notwithstanding any other provision of this chapter, no small business firm or nonprofit organization which receives title to any subject invention and no assignee of any such small business firm or nonprofit organization shall grant to any person the exclusive right to use or sell any subject invention in the United States unless such person agrees that any products embodying the subject invention or produced through the use of the subject invention will be manufactured substantially in the United States. However, in individual cases, the requirement for such an agreement may be waived by the Federal agency under whose funding agreement the invention was made upon a showing by the small business firm, nonprofit organization, or assignee that reasonable but unsuccessful efforts have been made to grant licenses on similar terms to potential licensees that would be likely to manufacture substantially in the United States or that under the circumstances domestic manufacture is not commercially feasible.

History of 35 U.S.C. §204: Dec. 12, 1980, P.L. 96-517, §6(a), 94 Stat. 3023.

See also 37 C.F.R. §401.7.

§205. CONFIDENTIALITY

Federal agencies are authorized to withhold from disclosure to the public information disclosing any invention in which the Federal Government owns or may own a right, title, or interest (including a nonexclusive license) for a reasonable time in order for a patent application to be filed. Furthermore, Federal agencies shall not be required to release copies of any document which is part of an application for patent filed with the United States Patent and Trademark Office or with any foreign patent office.

History of 35 U.S.C. §205: Dec. 12, 1980, P.L. 96-517, §6(a), 94 Stat. 3023.

§206. UNIFORM CLAUSES & REGULATIONS

The Secretary of Commerce may issue regulations which may be made applicable to Federal agencies implementing the provisions of sections 202 through 204 of this chapter and shall establish standard funding agreement provisions required under this chapter. The regulations and the standard funding agreement shall be subject to public comment before their issuance.

History of 35 U.S.C. §206: Dec. 12, 1980, P.L. 96-517, §6(a), 94 Stat. 3023; Nov. 8, 1984, P.L. 98-620, §501(10), 98 Stat. 3367.

See also 37 C.F.R. pt. 401.

§207. DOMESTIC & FOREIGN PROTECTION OF FEDERALLY OWNED INVENTIONS

(a) Each Federal agency is authorized to—

(1) apply for, obtain, and maintain patents or other forms of protection in the United States and in foreign countries on inventions in which the Federal Government owns a right, title, or interest;

(2) grant nonexclusive, exclusive, or partially exclusive licenses under federally owned inventions, royalty-free or for royalties or other consideration, and on such terms and conditions, including the grant to the licensee of the right of enforcement pursuant to the provisions of chapter 29 as determined appropriate in the public interest;

(3) undertake all other suitable and necessary steps to protect and administer rights to federally owned inventions on behalf of the Federal Government either directly or through contract, including acquiring rights for and administering royalties to the Federal Government in any invention, but only to the extent the party from whom the rights are acquired voluntarily enters into the transaction, to facilitate the licensing of a federally owned invention; and

(4) transfer custody and administration, in whole or in part, to another Federal agency, of the right, title, or interest in any federally owned invention.

(b) For the purpose of assuring the effective management of Government-owned inventions, the Secretary of Commerce is authorized to—

(1) assist Federal agency efforts to promote the licensing and utilization of Government-owned inventions;

(2) assist Federal agencies in seeking protection and maintaining inventions in foreign countries, including the payment of fees and costs connected therewith; and

(3) consult with and advise Federal agencies as to areas of science and technology research and development with potential for commercial utilization.

History of 35 U.S.C. §207: Dec. 12, 1980, P.L. 96-517, §6(a), 94 Stat. 3023; Nov. 8, 1984, P.L. 98-620, §501(11), 98 Stat. 3367; Nov. 1, 2000, P.L. 106-404, §6(2), 114 Stat. 1745; Sept. 16, 2011, P.L. 112-29, §20(j)(1), 125 Stat. 335.

§208. REGULATIONS GOVERNING FEDERAL LICENSING

The Secretary of Commerce is authorized to promulgate regulations specifying the terms and conditions upon which any federally owned invention, other than inventions owned by the Tennessee Valley Authority, may be licensed on a nonexclusive, partially exclusive, or exclusive basis.

History of 35 U.S.C. §208: Dec. 12, 1980, P.L. 96-517, §6(a), 94 Stat. 3024; Nov. 8, 1984, P.L. 98-620, §501(12), 98 Stat. 3367.

§209. LICENSING FEDERALLY OWNED INVENTIONS

(a) Authority.—A Federal agency may grant an exclusive or partially exclusive license on a federally owned invention under section 207(a)(2) only if—

(1) granting the license is a reasonable and necessary incentive to—

(A) call forth the investment capital and expenditures needed to bring the invention to practical application; or

(B) otherwise promote the invention's utilization by the public;

(2) the Federal agency finds that the public will be served by the granting of the license, as indicated by the applicant's intentions, plans, and ability to bring the invention to practical application or otherwise promote the invention's utilization by the public, and that the proposed scope of exclusivity is not greater than reasonably necessary to provide the incentive for bringing the invention to practical application, as proposed by the applicant, or otherwise to promote the invention's utilization by the public;

(3) the applicant makes a commitment to achieve practical application of the invention within a reasonable time, which time may be extended by the agency upon the applicant's request and the applicant's demonstration that the refusal of such extension would be unreasonable;

(4) granting the license will not tend to substantially lessen competition or create or maintain a violation of the Federal antitrust laws; and

(5) in the case of an invention covered by a foreign patent application or patent, the interests of the Federal

Government or United States industry in foreign commerce will be enhanced.

(b) Manufacture in United States.—A Federal agency shall normally grant a license under section 207(a)(2) to use or sell any federally owned invention in the United States only to a licensee who agrees that any products embodying the invention or produced through the use of the invention will be manufactured substantially in the United States.

(c) Small business.—First preference for the granting of any exclusive or partially exclusive licenses under section 207(a)(2) shall be given to small business firms having equal or greater likelihood as other applicants to bring the invention to practical application within a reasonable time.

(d) Terms and conditions.—Any licenses granted under section 207(a)(2) shall contain such terms and conditions as the granting agency considers appropriate, and shall include provisions—

(1) retaining a nontransferable, irrevocable, paid-up license for any Federal agency to practice the invention or have the invention practiced throughout the world by or on behalf of the Government of the United States;

(2) requiring periodic reporting on utilization of the invention, and utilization efforts, by the licensee, but only to the extent necessary to enable the Federal agency to determine whether the terms of the license are being complied with, except that any such report shall be treated by the Federal agency as commercial and financial information obtained from a person and privileged and confidential and not subject to disclosure under section 552 of title 5; and

(3) empowering the Federal agency to terminate the license in whole or in part if the agency determines that—

(A) the licensee is not executing its commitment to achieve practical application of the invention, including commitments contained in any plan submitted in support of its request for a license, and the licensee cannot otherwise demonstrate to the satisfaction of the Federal agency that it has taken, or can be expected to take within a reasonable time, effective steps to achieve practical application of the invention;

(B) the licensee is in breach of an agreement described in subsection (b);

(C) termination is necessary to meet requirements for public use specified by Federal regulations issued after the date of the license, and such requirements are not reasonably satisfied by the licensee; or

(D) the licensee has been found by a court of competent jurisdiction to have violated the Federal antitrust laws in connection with its performance under the license agreement.

(e) Public notice.—No exclusive or partially exclusive license may be granted under section 207(a)(2) unless public notice of the intention to grant an exclusive or partially exclusive license on a federally owned invention has been provided in an appropriate manner at least 15 days before the license is granted, and the Federal agency has considered all comments received before the end of the comment period in response to that public notice. This subsection shall not apply to the licensing of inventions made under a cooperative research and development agreement entered into under section 12 of the Stevenson-Wydler Technology Innovation Act of 1980 (15 U.S.C. 3710a).

(f) Plan.—No Federal agency shall grant any license under a patent or patent application on a federally owned invention unless the person requesting the license has supplied the agency with a plan for development or marketing of the invention, except that any such plan shall be treated by the Federal agency as commercial and financial information obtained from a person and privileged and confidential and not subject to disclosure under section 552 of title 5.

History of 35 U.S.C. §209: Dec. 12, 1980, P.L. 96-517, §6(a), 94 Stat. 3024; Nov. 1, 2000, P.L. 106-404, §4(a), 114 Stat. 1743; Nov. 2, 2002, P.L. 107-273, §13206(15), 116 Stat. 1905; Sept. 16, 2011, P.L. 112-29, §20(i)(3), 125 Stat. 335. See also 42 U.S.C. §7608.

§210. PRECEDENCE OF CHAPTER

(a) This chapter shall take precedence over any other Act which would require a disposition of rights in subject inventions of small business firms or nonprofit organizations contractors in a manner that is inconsistent with this chapter, including but not necessarily limited to the following:

(1) section 10(a) of the Act of June 29, 1935, as added by title I of the Act of August 14, 1946 (7 U.S.C. 427i(a); 60 Stat. 1085);

(2) section 205(a) of the Act of August 14, 1946 (7 U.S.C. 1624(a); 60 Stat. 1090);

(3) section 501(c) of the Federal Mine Safety and Health Act of 1977 (30 U.S.C. 951(c); 83 Stat. 742);

(4) section 30168(e) of title 49;

(5) section 12 of the National Science Foundation Act of 1950 (42 U.S.C. 1871(a); 82 Stat. 360);

(6) section 152 of the Atomic Energy Act of 1954 (42 U.S.C. 2182; 68 Stat. 943);

(7) section 20135 of title 51;

(8) section 6 of the Coal Research and Development Act of 1960 (30 U.S.C. 666; 74 Stat. 337);

(9) section 4 of the Helium Act Amendments of 1960 (50 U.S.C. 167b; 74 Stat. 920);

(10) section 32 of the Arms Control and Disarmament Act of 1961 (22 U.S.C. 2572; 75 Stat. 634);

(11) section 9 of the Federal Nonnuclear Energy Research and Development Act of 1974 (42 U.S.C. 5908; 88 Stat. 1878);

(12) section 5(d) of the Consumer Product Safety Act (15 U.S.C. 2054(d); 86 Stat. 1211);

(13) section 3 of the Act of April 5, 1944 (30 U.S.C. 323; 58 Stat. 191);

(14) section 8001(c)(3) of the Solid Waste Disposal Act (42 U.S.C. 6981(c); 90 Stat. 2829);

(15) section 219 of the Foreign Assistance Act of 1961 (22 U.S.C. 2179; 83 Stat. 806);

(16) section 427(b) of the Federal Mine Health and Safety Act of 1977 (30 U.S.C. 937(b); 86 Stat. 155);

(17) section 306(d) of the Surface Mining and Reclamation Act of 1977 (30 U.S.C. 1226(d); 91 Stat. 455);

(18) section 21(d) of the Federal Fire Prevention and Control Act of 1974 (15 U.S.C. 2218(d); 88 Stat. 1548);

(19) section 6(b) of the Solar Photovoltaic Energy Research Development and Demonstration Act of 1978 (42 U.S.C. 5585(b); 92 Stat. 2516);

(20) section 12 of the Native Latex Commercialization and Economic Development Act of 1978 (7 U.S.C. 178j; 92 Stat. 2533); and

(21) section 408 of the Water Resources and Development Act of 1978 (42 U.S.C. 7879; 92 Stat. 1360).

The Act creating this chapter shall be construed to take precedence over any future Act unless that Act specifically cites this Act and provides that it shall take precedence over this Act.

(b) Nothing in this chapter is intended to alter the effect of the laws cited in paragraph (a) of this section or any other laws with respect to the disposition of rights in inventions made in the performance of funding agreements with persons other than nonprofit organizations or small business firms.

(c) Nothing in this chapter is intended to limit the authority of agencies to agree to the disposition of rights in inventions made in the performance of work under funding agreements with persons other than nonprofit organizations or small business firms in accordance with the Statement of Government Patent Policy issued on February 18, 1983, agency regulations, or other applicable regulations or to otherwise limit the authority of agencies to allow such persons to retain ownership of inventions except that all funding agreements, including those with other than small business firms and nonprofit organizations, shall include the requirements established in section 202(c)(4) and section 203. Any disposition of rights in inventions made in accordance with the Statement or implementing regulations, including any disposition occurring before enactment of this section, are hereby authorized.

(d) Nothing in this chapter shall be construed to require the disclosure of intelligence sources or methods or to otherwise affect the authority granted to the Director of Central Intelligence by statute or Executive order for the protection of intelligence sources or methods.

(e) The provisions of the Stevenson-Wydler Technology Innovation Act of 1980 shall take precedence over the provisions of this chapter to the extent that they permit or require a disposition of rights in subject inventions which is inconsistent with this chapter.

History of 35 U.S.C. §210: Dec. 12, 1980, P.L. 96-517, §6(a), 94 Stat. 3026; Nov. 8, 1984, P.L. 98-620, §501(13), 98 Stat. 3367; Oct. 20, 1986, P.L. 99-502, §9(c), 100 Stat. 1796; July 5, 1994, P.L. 103-272, §5(j), 108 Stat. 1375; Mar. 7, 1996, P.L. 104-113, §7, 110 Stat. 779; Nov. 13, 1998, P.L. 105-393, §220(c)(2), 112 Stat. 3625; Nov. 2, 2002, P.L. 107-273, §13206(a)(16), 116 Stat. 1905; Aug. 8, 2005, P.L. 109-58, §1009(a)(2), 119 Stat. 934; Dec. 18, 2010, P.L. 111-314, §4(c), 124 Stat. 3440; Sept. 16, 2011, P.L. 112-29, §20(j)(1), 125 Stat. 335.

ANNOTATIONS

Board of Trs. of Leland Stanford Junior Univ. v. Roche Molecular Sys., 563 U.S. 776, 790, 98 U.S.P.Q.2d 1761, 1768 (2011). "[B]ecause the Bayh-Dole Act, including §210(a), applies only to 'subject inventions'—'inventions of the contractor'—it does not displace an inventor's antecedent title to his invention. Only when an invention belongs to the contractor does the Bayh-Dole Act come into play. The Act's disposition of rights—like much of the rest of the Bayh-Dole Act—serves to clarify the order of priority of rights between the Federal Government and a federal contractor in a federally funded invention that already belongs to the contractor. Nothing more."

§211. RELATIONSHIP TO ANTITRUST LAWS

Nothing in this chapter shall be deemed to convey to any person immunity from civil or criminal liability, or to create any defenses to actions, under any antitrust law.

History of 35 U.S.C. §211: Dec. 12, 1980, P.L. 96-517, §6(a), 94 Stat. 3027.

§212. DISPOSITION OF RIGHTS IN EDUCATIONAL AWARDS

No scholarship, fellowship, training grant, or other funding agreement made by a Federal agency primarily to an awardee for educational purposes will contain any provision giving the Federal agency any rights to inventions made by the awardee.

History of 35 U.S.C. §212: Nov. 8, 1984, P.L. 98-620, §501(14), 98 Stat. 3368.

PART III. PATENTS & PROTECTION OF PATENT RIGHTS

CHAPTER 25. AMENDMENT & CORRECTION OF PATENTS

§251. REISSUE OF DEFECTIVE PATENTS

(a) In general.—Whenever any patent is, through error, deemed wholly or partly inoperative or invalid, by reason of a defective specification or drawing, or by reason of the patentee claiming more or less than he had a right to claim in the patent, the Director shall, on the surrender of such patent and the payment of the fee required by law, reissue the patent for the invention disclosed in the original patent, and in accordance with a new and amended application, for the unexpired part of the term of the original patent. No new matter shall be introduced into the application for reissue.

(b) Multiple reissued patents.—The Director may issue several reissued patents for distinct and separate parts of the thing patented, upon demand of the applicant, and upon payment of the required fee for a reissue for each of such reissued patents.

(c) Applicability of this title.—The provisions of this title relating to applications for patent shall be applicable to applications for reissue of a patent, except that application for reissue may be made and sworn to by the assignee of the entire interest if the application does not seek to enlarge the scope of the claims of the original patent or the application for the original patent was filed by the assignee of the entire interest.

(d) Reissue patent enlarging scope of claims.—No reissued patent shall be granted enlarging the scope of the claims of the original patent unless applied for within two years from the grant of the original patent.

History of 35 U.S.C. §251: July 19, 1952, ch. 950, §1, 66 Stat. 808; Nov. 29, 1999, P.L. 106-113, §1000(a)(9), 113 Stat. 1536; Nov. 2, 2002, P.L. 107-273, §13206(b)(1)(B), 116 Stat. 1906; Sept. 16, 2011, P.L. 112-29, §§4(b)(2), 20(d), 125 Stat. 296, 333.

See also 37 C.F.R. §§1.171-1.178.

ANNOTATIONS

Generally

Antares Pharma, Inc. v. Medac Pharma Inc., 771 F.3d 1354, 1358, 112 U.S.P.Q.2d 1865, 1867-69 (Fed.Cir. 2014). "The filing of continuations and divisionals is limited by the co-pendency requirement of [35 U.S.C.] §120: a continuing application cannot be filed after the original parent application issues. In such circumstances, an applicant can only seek to add claims by filing a reissue application. The delay in seeking to broaden the claims is not without cost. By waiting until after the patent is issued, the applicant becomes subject to two additional requirements relevant here: first, the claims must not violate the recapture rule; second, the claims must satisfy the statutory original patent requirement of 35 U.S.C. §251. [¶] The original patent requirement is well-established, being recognized in the reissue statute and long-standing Supreme Court jurisprudence. *At F.3d 1359:* The Supreme Court's definitive explanation of the original patent requirement appears in ***U.S. Indus. Chems., Inc. v. Carbide & Carbon Chems. Corp.***, 315 U.S. 668 ... (1942). ... It explained that a reissue claim is for the 'same invention' if the original patent specification fully describes the claimed inventions, but not if the broader claims 'are [] merely suggested or indicated in the original specification.' '[I]t is not enough that an invention might have been claimed in the original patent because it was suggested or indicated in the specification.' The reissue claims were invalid because, although the original specification hinted at the fact that water might be optional ..., it was nonetheless clear that the invention disclosed in the original patent required the

35 U.S.C. §251

presence of water. That hint, suggestion, or indication that water was optional was not enough to save the reissue claims. Circuit cases immediately following ***Industrial Chemicals*** adopted the same test."

Intel Corp. v. Negotiated Data Solutions, Inc., 703 F.3d 1360, 1367, 105 U.S.P.Q.2d 1157, 1162 (Fed.Cir. 2012). "The [license agreement] does not explicitly discuss reissue patents, but the grant of license under the [patents] is without limitation and without reference to any specific claims. The [license agreement] thus evinces the parties' intent that the license so granted extend not only to the claims then in existence but also to the full scope of any coverage available by way of reissue for the invention disclosed."

In re Yamazaki, 702 F.3d 1327, 1330, 104 U.S.P.Q.2d 2024, 2026 (Fed.Cir.2012). "The question presented in this appeal is whether §251 permits the use of reissue proceedings to withdraw a terminal disclaimer that was in effect upon issuance of the '991 patent. *At F.3d 1331, U.S.P.Q.2d 2027:* We ... conclude that when the '991 patent issued with its terminal disclaimer in effect, that disclaimer became part of the original '991 patent and served to define its term, regardless of any further term that might have been otherwise available in the absence of the disclaimer. *At F.3d 1333, U.S.P.Q.2d 2028:* [Petitioner's] terminal disclaimer eliminated any term from the original '991 patent beyond December 22, 2003. The intended and undisputed language of the terminal disclaimer tied the original term of the '991 patent to that of the commonly owned '476 patent, and there is no question that the '476 patent lawfully expired in 2003."

Revolution Eyewear, Inc. v. Aspex Eyewear, Inc., 563 F.3d 1358, 1366, 90 U.S.P.Q.2d 1733, 1738 (Fed. Cir.2009). "When a patentee seeks reissuance of his patent, he cannot introduce any new matter into the reissue application. Therefore, the new claims or other added material must find support in the original specification. In other words, the original specification must satisfy the written description requirement [under 35 U.S.C. §112, ¶1]."

Forest Labs. v. Ivax Pharms., 501 F.3d 1263, 1270, 84 U.S.P.Q.2d 1099, 1105 (Fed.Cir.2007). "[T]he claims of a reissue patent filed [more than two years after the grant of the original patent] are invalid if they enlarge the scope of the original claims. However, a change in a reissue application that is only clerical does not necessarily broaden the scope of the claims and so does not render the patent invalid. [¶] Comparison of the scope of the reissue claims with the claims of the original patent is a matter of claim construction, and it is performed from the perspective of one having ordinary skill in the art. Whether the claims of a reissue patent violate ... §251 is a question of law that we review *de novo* based on underlying facts reviewed for clear error."

Johnson & Johnston Assocs. v. R.E. Serv. Co., 285 F.3d 1046, 1055, 62 U.S.P.Q.2d 1225, 1231 (Fed.Cir. 2002). "A patentee who inadvertently fails to claim disclosed subject matter ... is not left without remedy. Within two years from the grant of the original patent, a patentee may file a reissue application and attempt to enlarge the scope of the original claims to include the disclosed but previously unclaimed subject matter. In addition, a patentee can file a separate application claiming the disclosed subject matter under 35 U.S.C. §120."

Superior Fireplace Co. v. Majestic Prods., 270 F.3d 1358, 1370-71, 60 U.S.P.Q.2d 1668, 1677 (Fed.Cir. 2001). "Section 251 addresses the correction of an 'error' and it is understood that corrections under §251 can result in the broadening of a claim. The patentee's right to broaden a claim is not absolute, however. First, §251 requires that the broadened claim be supported by the original specification. Second, §251 precludes a patentee from applying for a broadening reissue more than two years after a patent has issued. Third, ... Congress further protected the public by providing intervening rights for the public with respect to claims that were broadened under §251."

Correctable Errors

In re Dinsmore, 757 F.3d 1343, 1346, 111 U.S.P.Q.2d 1229, 1231 (Fed.Cir.2014). "The applicants argue that, because the ... patents are not and never have been commonly owned, the recorded terminal disclaimer was 'an ineffective, invalid terminal disclaimer' and its filing therefore was an 'error' within the meaning of the reissue statute.... *At F.3d 1347-49, U.S.P.Q.2d 1232:* At bottom, therefore, the applicants can only be arguing, more broadly, that the disclaimer was 'ineffective' in the sense that it did not produce a patent they could actually enforce by themselves (without common ownership) and that they erred in producing that result (which they deem to be inoperativeness) by choosing to file the terminal disclaimer in order to include in the ... patent, in their final form, the four claims that led to the obviousness-type double-patenting rejection. This argument, however, is an insufficient basis for reissue, even if the condition of present inability to enforce constitutes inoperativeness within the meaning of §251. It is ultimately no more than a statement of a now-regretted choice, because the applicants identify no cognizable false or deficient understanding of fact or law that underlay the choice. This is not 'error' as required by §251. [¶] Section 251 requires not only that the original patent be 'wholly or partly inoperative or invalid,' and that the inoperativeness or invalidity be by reason of a defective specification or drawing or unduly broad or narrow claiming, but that 'error' be the cause of the infirmity. Section 251 often applies to applicants' choices, *i.e.*, their deliberate decisions about what to say in their patents, not just slips of the pen. But not every choice that produces inoperativeness or invalidity by reason of a specification, drawing, or claiming problem (within the meaning of §251) can qualify. Only choices based on 'error' count."

In re Tanaka, 640 F.3d 1246, 1249, 98 U.S.P.Q.2d 1331, 1333 (Fed.Cir.2011). "As interpreted by this court, the reissue statute imposes two requirements for properly invoking the reissue process. First, the original patent must be 'wholly or partly inoperative or invalid.' Second, 'the defective, inoperative, or invalid patent' must have arisen 'through error without deceptive intent.' There is no dispute in this case that any defect arose without deceptive intent. [¶] Nearly a half century ago, our predecessor court, the [C.C.P.A.], clearly stated that adding dependent claims as a hedge against possible invalidity of original claims 'is a proper reason for asking that a reissue be granted.' The basis for the reissue application in [that case] was nearly identical to that in this case. The patentee had mistakenly failed to include narrow claims that he had a right to claim and later sought reissue to obtain those narrower claims without proposing to cancel any broader claims encompassing the claims sought to be added. The proposed reissue claims differed from the existing claims simply by the inclusion of additional limitations. *At F.3d 1250, U.S.P.Q.2d 1334:* Even though the rule that adding a dependent claim as a hedge against possible invalidity is a proper reason to seek reissue has seemingly never been formally embodied in a holding of this court or its predecessor, articulation of the rule in [that case] was not simply a passing observation—it was a considered explanation of the scope of the reissue authority of the PTO in the context of a detailed explanation of the reissue statute. [¶] This court also rejects the PTO's assertion that the omission of a narrower claim from an original patent does not constitute an error under §251 because the omission of a dependent claim does not render the patent inoperative. *At F.3d 1251:* Finally, this court rejects the Board's conclusion that adding a single dependent claim to the originally issued claims is equivalent to the disallowed practice of filing a 'no defect' reissue."

In re Serenkin, 479 F.3d 1359, 1362, 81 U.S.P.Q.2d 2011, 2013 (Fed.Cir.2007). "[W]e must determine whether the action of [applicant's] attorney, specifically, the act of choosing a later filing date during prosecution of the [Patent Cooperation Treaty] application in exchange for inclusion of missing drawings, constitutes an 'error' that is correctable under §251. We conclude that it does not. *At U.S.P.Q.2d 2014:* [T]he deliberate action of an inventor or attorney during prosecution generally fails to qualify as a correctable error under §251."

Medrad, Inc. v. Tyco Healthcare Grp., 466 F.3d 1047, 1051, 80 U.S.P.Q.2d 1526, 1528 (Fed.Cir.2006). "[T]he issue on appeal [is] whether the [language from §251, ¶1, 'by reason of the patentee claiming more or less than he had a right to claim in the patent,'] requires that the error occur in the actual language of a patent's claims ... or refers broadly to errors that result in patent rights with more or less scope than would have been provided but for the error.... *At F.3d 1052, U.S.P.Q.2d 1529:* [T]he highlighted language in §251 can be read to encompass any error that causes a patentee to claim more or less than he had a right to claim. ... Accordingly, we do not interpret the disputed language in §251 ... to require that the error occur in the actual language of the claims."

Medtronic, Inc. v. Guidant Corp., 465 F.3d 1360, 1372, 80 U.S.P.Q.2d 1558, 1566 (Fed.Cir.2006). "'[A]n attorney's failure to appreciate the full scope of the invention is one of the most common sources of defects in patents,' and is generally sufficient to justify reissuing a patent. It is not necessary that the error be unavoidable or that the error could not have been discovered by the patentee through proper communication with the prosecuting attorney."

Recapture Rule

MBO Labs. v. Becton, Dickinson & Co., 602 F.3d 1306, 1313, 94 U.S.P.Q.2d 1598, 1602-03 (Fed.Cir.2010). "Under the rule against recapture, a patentee's reissue claims are invalid when the patentee broadens the scope of a claim in reissue to cover subject matter that he surrendered during prosecution of the original claims. [¶] This court bars recapture because a patentee is only entitled to a reissue patent for broader claims when the patentee claimed less than he had a right to claim in the patent through error without any deceptive intent, not through deliberate amendments or arguments designed to convince an examiner to allow the claims. Moreover, the court prohibits recapture based on principles of equity. An applicant's surrender of subject matter places competitors and the public on notice and may have caused them to rely on the consequent limitations on claim scope. *At F.3d 1314:* In applying the rule against recapture, we follow a three-step test. First, the court construes the reissued claims to determine whether and in what 'aspect' the reissue claims are broader than the original patent claims. Second, if the reissue claims are broader, the court determines whether the patentee surrendered subject matter and whether the broader aspects of the reissued claim relate to the surrendered subject matter. To determine whether a patentee surrendered subject matter, we ask whether an objective observer viewing the prosecution history would conclude that the purpose of the patentee's amendment or argument was to overcome prior art and secure the patent. If the patentee surrendered by argument, he must clearly and unmistakably argue that his invention does not cover certain subject matter to overcome an examiner's rejection based on prior art. Third, a court must determine whether the reissued claims were materially narrowed in other respects to avoid the recapture rule. *At F.3d 1316, U.S.P.Q.2d 1604-05:* In holding that [P] violated the rule against recapture, we seek to clarify that a patentee may violate the rule against recapture by claiming subject matter in a reissue patent that the patentee surrendered while prosecuting a related patent application. ... We have never limited our review of recapture only to the prosecution history for the patent corrected by reissue. *At F.3d 1318, U.S.P.Q.2d 1606:* Because the rule against recapture and prosecution history estoppel both protect the public's interest in relying on a patent's prosecution history, we think equity requires a review of a patent family's prosecution history to protect against recapture in a reissue patent." (Internal quotes omitted.)

Fontijn v. Okamoto, 518 F.2d 610, 621, 186 U.S.P.Q. 97, 106 (C.C.P.A.1975). "We hold that a reissue application filed for the sole purpose of perfecting a claim to priority does not broaden the scope of the claims of the original patent and is not in contravention of the requirements of §251 even though filed more than two years after the patent grant."

§252. EFFECT OF REISSUE

The surrender of the original patent shall take effect upon the issue of the reissued patent, and every reissued patent shall have the same effect and operation in law, on the trial of actions for causes thereafter arising, as if the same had been originally granted in such amended form, but in so far as the claims of the original and reissued patents are substantially identical, such surrender shall not affect any action then pending nor abate any cause of action then existing, and the reissued patent, to the extent that its claims are substantially identical with the original patent, shall constitute a continuation thereof and have effect continuously from the date of the original patent.

A reissued patent shall not abridge or affect the right of any person or that person's successors in business who, prior to the grant of a reissue, made, purchased, offered to sell, or used within the United States, or imported into the United States, anything patented by the reissued patent, to continue the use of, to offer to sell, or to sell to others to be used, offered for sale, or sold, the specific thing so made, purchased, offered for sale, used, or imported unless the making, using, offering for sale, or selling of such thing infringes a valid claim of the reissued patent which was in the original patent. The court before which such matter is in question may provide for the continued manufacture, use, offer for sale, or sale of the thing made, purchased, offered for sale, used, or imported as specified, or for the manufacture, use, offer for sale, or sale in the United States of which substantial preparation was made before the grant of the reissue, and the court may also provide for the continued practice of any process patented by the reissue that is practiced, or for the practice of which substantial preparation was made, before the grant of the reissue, to the extent and under such terms as the court deems equitable for the protection of investments made or business commenced before the grant of the reissue.

History of 35 U.S.C. §252: July 19, 1952, ch. 950, §1, 66 Stat. 808; Dec. 8, 1994, P.L. 103-465, §533(b)(2), 108 Stat. 4989; Nov. 29, 1999, P.L. 106-113, §1000(a)(9), 113 Stat. 1536.

See also TRIPs pt. II, §5.

ANNOTATIONS

Presidio Components, Inc. v. American Tech. Ceramics Corp., 875 F.3d 1369, 1377-78, 124 U.S.P.Q.2d 1745, 1749-50 (Fed.Cir.2017). "An owner of a patent that survives reexamination is not entitled to infringement damages for the time period between the date of issuance of the original claims and the date of issuance of the reexamined claims if the original and amended claims are not 'substantially identical.' In other words, if an amendment during reexamination makes a substantive change to an original claim, the patentee is only entitled to infringement damages for the changed claim for the period following issuance of the reexamination certificate. [¶] [T]he patentee's intent in making the amendment is not determinative or controlling in determining claim scope. [¶] Instead, the relevant inquiry is whether the scope of the amended claims is actually identical to the scope of the original claims based on normal claim construction analysis, articulated in our en banc ***Phillips*** decision. To determine whether an amended claim is narrower in scope, 'we determine whether there is any product or process that would infringe the original claim, but not infringe the amended claim.' Typically, we need to determine de novo the scope of the original and amended claims."

Technology Licensing Corp. v. Videotek, Inc., 545 F.3d 1316, 1331, 88 U.S.P.Q.2d 1865, 1876 (Fed.Cir. 2008). "The reissuance of the patent occurred after the trial court rendered its final judgment. An appellate court ordinarily declines to consider new evidence or argument not previously presented to the trial forum whose judgment is under review. We think that, in a circumstance such as this, judicial efficiency and the policy of repose counsels against our re-weighing of the evidence to add an additional deference-thumb to the scale, or, even more disruptive, our asking the trial court to reopen the entire invalidity question to reweigh the intangible worth of additional deference. [¶] In some circumstances a party may be able to obtain a stay from the trial court while awaiting the sought-for agency action; absent that, and absent extenuating circumstances not here present, the case must be decided on the record the litigants present for appeal."

Shockley v. Arcan, Inc., 248 F.3d 1349, 1359-60, 58 U.S.P.Q.2d 1692, 1698 (Fed.Cir.2001). "Before addition of the 'offered to sell' language, this court's case law under §252 permitted an accused infringer to continue to use or sell a product that was already made by the issue date of a reissued patent. Absent a clear showing, this court will not assume that the 1994 amendments changed this aspect of §252."

BIC Leisure Prods. v. Windsurfing Int'l, 1 F.3d 1214, 1220-21, 27 U.S.P.Q.2d 1671, 1676 (Fed.Cir.1993). "The second paragraph of §252 provides for two separate and distinct defenses under the doctrine of intervening rights: 'absolute' intervening rights and 'equitable' intervening rights. The paragraph consists of two sentences which address two distinct situations and provide two different types of protection. [¶] The first sentence defines 'absolute' intervening rights. This sentence provides an accused infringer with the absolute right to use or sell a product that was made, used, or purchased before the grant of the reissue patent as long as this activity does not infringe a claim of the reissue patent that was in the original patent. This right is absolute. [¶] This absolute right extends only to anything made, purchased, or used before the grant of the reissue patent. In other words, it covers products already made at the time of reissue. [¶] The second sentence of the second paragraph of §252 defines 'equitable' intervening rights. By its terms, this sentence provides for the court to grant much broader rights than does the first sentence. The second sentence permits the continued manufacture, use, or sale of additional products covered by the reissue patent when the defendant made, purchased, or used identical products, or made substantial preparations to make, use, or sell identical products, before the reissue date. [¶] This equitable right is not absolute. ... Thus, under this language, the trial court may, as dictated by the equities, protect investments made before reissue."

Hewlett-Packard Co. v. Bausch & Lomb Inc., 882 F.2d 1556, 1563, 11 U.S.P.Q.2d 1750, 1756 (Fed.Cir. 1989). "[I]n ***Kingsdown [Med. Consultants, Ltd. v. Hollister, Inc.***, 863 F.2d 867 (Fed.Cir.1988)], we reaffirmed that, when inequitable conduct is found, all claims of the patent are rendered unenforceable, not merely those claims directly affected by the misconduct. We are unpersuaded that a different consequence should follow when the inequitable conduct occurs during reissue proceedings rather than during original prosecution. [¶] In sum, we conclude that, with respect to inequitable conduct, it is appropriate to give the same extent of unenforceability to a reissue patent as to an original patent and that the same level of misconduct is required in both instances."

Seattle Box Co. v. Industrial Crating & Packing, Inc., 731 F.2d 818, 827, 221 U.S.P.Q. 568, 574 (Fed.Cir. 1984). "An original patent cannot be infringed once a reissue patent has issued, for the original patent is surrendered. ... Courts acted, in other words, as if the original patent never was."

§253. DISCLAIMER

(a) In general.—Whenever a claim of a patent is invalid the remaining claims shall not thereby be rendered invalid. A patentee, whether of the whole or any sectional interest therein, may, on payment of the fee required by law, make disclaimer of any complete claim, stating therein the extent of his interest in such patent. Such disclaimer shall be in writing, and recorded in the Patent and Trademark Office; and it shall thereafter be considered as part of the original patent to the extent of the interest possessed by the disclaimant and by those claiming under him.

(b) Additional disclaimer or dedication.—In the manner set forth in subsection (a), any patentee or applicant may disclaim or dedicate to the public the entire term, or any terminal part of the term, of the patent granted or to be granted.

History of 35 U.S.C. §253: July 19, 1952, ch. 950, §1, 66 Stat. 809; Jan. 2, 1975, P.L. 93-596, §1, 88 Stat. 1949; Sept. 16, 2011, P.L. 112-29, §20(e), 125 Stat. 334.

See also 35 U.S.C. §288; 37 C.F.R. §1.321.

ANNOTATIONS

Perricone v. Medicis Pharm., 432 F.3d 1368, 1375, 77 U.S.P.Q.2d 1321, 1325 (Fed.Cir.2005). "[T]he Patent Act and PTO rules support the filing of a terminal disclaimer even after issuance of the second patent. ... Thus, while [patentee] might still file a terminal disclaimer to overcome prospectively the double patenting basis for invalidity, this court makes no determination about the retrospective effect of such a terminal disclaimer."

Vectra Fitness, Inc. v. TNWK Corp., 162 F.3d 1379, 1384-85, 49 U.S.P.Q.2d 1144, 1148 (Fed.Cir.1998). "[A]llowing [patentee] to later recapture some of the subject matter that was explicitly disclaimed would negate the finality and certainty of the disclaimer." Held: Subsequent reissue claims cannot recapture subject matter explicitly disclaimed under §253.

Guinn v. Kopf, 96 F.3d 1419, 1422, 40 U.S.P.Q.2d 1157, 1160 (Fed.Cir.1996). "A statutory disclaimer under ... §253 has the effect of canceling the claims from the patent and the patent is viewed as though the disclaimed claims had never existed in the patent. Therefore, by filing a statutory disclaimer, [patentee] relinquished any right to exclude others from the subject matter of claim 9."

Ortho Pharm. v. Smith, 959 F.2d 936, 942, 22 U.S.P.Q.2d 1119, 1124 (Fed.Cir.1992). "Where obviousness-type double patenting is recognized before issuance of a patent, the price extracted for obtaining the second patent is disclaimer of part of the term of protection for all claims in the patent, *i.e.*, even those claims which standing alone would not run afoul of the rule against double patenting. However, we conclude that this unitary treatment of the claims with respect to their term of protection does not carry over into an obviousness-type double patenting attack on the claims after the patent is issued." *See also* ***Ex parte Kumagai***, 9 U.S.P.Q.2d 1642, 1646 (Bd.Pat.App. & Int.1988).

§254. CERTIFICATE OF CORRECTION OF PATENT & TRADEMARK OFFICE MISTAKE

Whenever a mistake in a patent, incurred through the fault of the Patent and Trademark Office, is clearly disclosed by the records of the Office, the Director may issue a certificate of correction stating the fact and nature of such mistake, under seal, without charge, to be recorded in the records of patents. A printed copy thereof shall be attached to each printed copy of the patent, and such certificate shall be considered as part of the original patent. Every such patent, together with such certificate, shall have the same effect and operation in law on the trial of actions for causes thereafter arising as if the same had been originally issued in such corrected form. The Director may issue a corrected patent without charge in lieu of and with like effect as a certificate of correction.

History of 35 U.S.C. §254: July 19, 1952, ch. 950, §1, 66 Stat. 809; Jan. 2, 1975, P.L. 93-596, §1, 88 Stat. 1949; Nov. 29, 1999, P.L. 106-113, §1000(a)(9), 113 Stat. 1536; Nov. 2, 2002, P.L. 107-273, §13206(b)(1)(B), 116 Stat. 1906.

See also 37 C.F.R. §§1.322, 1.325.

ANNOTATIONS

E.I. du Pont de Nemours & Co. v. MacDermid Printing Solutions, L.L.C., 525 F.3d 1353, 1362, 86 U.S.P.Q.2d 1732, 1740 (Fed.Cir.2008). "[P] could have corrected its published application under 37 C.F.R. §1.221 and [Manual of Patent Examining Procedure] §1130. While failure to make such a correction may have potential consequences, we see no reason why failure to correct a published application should prevent the patentee from later correcting his issued patent under 35 U.S.C. §254."

Group One Ltd. v. Hallmark Cards, Inc., 407 F.3d 1297, 1302-03, 74 U.S.P.Q.2d 1759, 1763 (Fed.Cir.2005). "Even though the PTO has the authority to correct its own errors under §254, we have held that in some circumstances the district court can correct errors retroactively. But the district court can correct an error only if the error is evident from the face of the patent. 'A district court can correct a patent only if (1) the correction is not subject to reasonable debate based on consideration of the claim language and the specification *and* (2) the prosecution history does not suggest a different interpretation of the claims.'"

Hoffer v. Microsoft Corp., 405 F.3d 1326, 1331, 74 U.S.P.Q.2d 1481, 1484 (Fed.Cir.2005). Patentee "obtained a certificate of correction in accordance with 35 U.S.C. §254 after this action was filed, changing the antecedent claim '38' to '21.' The district court declined to accept the correction, deeming it tardily made. [¶] The district court stated that it was powerless to correct the error. We do not agree that such correction exceeds the judicial power. Absent evidence of culpability or intent to deceive by delaying formal correction, a patent should not be invalidated based on an obvious administrative error. [Ds] did not state that they were prejudiced, or even confused, by the error. The district court held that it has no authority to correct or ignore even a typographical error in a patent. That is inaccurate. When a harmless error in a patent is not subject to reasonable debate, it can be corrected by the court, as for other legal documents."

Southwest Software, Inc. v. Harlequin Inc., 226 F.3d 1280, 1295-96, 56 U.S.P.Q.2d 1161, 1172 (Fed.Cir. 2000). "[F]or causes arising after the PTO issues a certificate of correction, the certificate of correction is to be treated as part of the original patent—i.e., as if the certificate had been issued along with the original patent. By necessary implication, for causes arising before its issuance, the certificate of correction is not effective. *At U.S.P.Q.2d 1173:* Until the PTO issues a certificate of correction ..., such a claim would appear invalid to the public, and reasonable competitors would be justified in conducting their affairs accordingly. In such a case, where the claim is invalid on its face without the certificate of correction, it strikes us as an illogical result to allow the patent holder, once the certificate of correction has issued, to sue an alleged infringer for activities that occurred before the issuance of the certificate of correction." *See also* ***Novo Indus. v. Micro Molds Corp.***, 350 F.3d 1348, 1356, 69 U.S.P.Q.2d 1128, 1133 (Fed.Cir.2003); ***Superior Fireplace Co. v. Majestic Prods.***, 270 F.3d 1358, 1380 n.1, 60 U.S.P.Q.2d 1668, 1684 n.2 (Fed.Cir.2001) (Dyk, J., dissenting) (***Southwest*** applies to certificates issued under 35 U.S.C. §255).

§255. CERTIFICATE OF CORRECTION OF APPLICANT'S MISTAKE

Whenever a mistake of a clerical or typographical nature, or of minor character, which was not the fault of the Patent and Trademark Office, appears in a patent and a showing has been made that such mistake occurred in good faith, the Director may, upon payment of the required fee, issue a certificate of correction, if the correction does not involve such changes in the patent as would constitute new matter or would require re-examination. Such patent, together with the certificate, shall have the same effect and operation in law on the trial of actions for causes thereafter arising as if the same had been originally issued in such corrected form.

History of 35 U.S.C. §255: July 19, 1952, ch. 950, §1, 66 Stat. 809; Jan. 2, 1975, P.L. 93-596, §1, 88 Stat. 1949; Nov. 29, 1999, P.L. 106-113, §1000(a)(9), 113 Stat. 1536; Nov. 2, 2002, P.L. 107-273, §13206(b)(1)(B), 116 Stat. 1906.

See also 37 C.F.R. §§1.323, 1.325.

ANNOTATIONS

Generally

Central Admixture Pharm. v. Advanced Cardiac Solutions, P.C., 482 F.3d 1347, 1353, 82 U.S.P.Q.2d 1293, 1297 (Fed.Cir.2007). "Invalidating a certificate of correction for impermissible broadening ... requires proof of two elements: (1) the corrected claims are broader than the original claims; and (2) the presence of the clerical or typographical error, or how to correct that error, is not clearly evident to one of skill in the art. The first element poses a question of law, since the correct scope and meaning of a claim is an issue for the court to decide. To answer the question of whether a claim has been broadened through correction requires interpreting the old and new versions of that claim, and then determining whether the new version covers territory the old one did not. This same inquiry has been treated as a question of law in [35 U.S.C.] §251 reissue cases, and should be treated as such in the [35 U.S.C.] §255 context as well. *At F.3d 1354, U.S.P.Q.2d 1298:* The second element, whether the error and its correction would both be clearly evident to one of skill in the art, has been treated as a factual question." *See also* ***Koito Mfg. Co. v. Turn-Key-Tech, LLC***, 381 F.3d 1142, 1154, 72 U.S.P.Q.2d 1190, 1198-99 (Fed.Cir.2004).

Superior Fireplace Co. v. Majestic Prods., 270 F.3d 1358, 1369-70, 60 U.S.P.Q.2d 1668, 1676 (Fed.Cir. 2001). "The phrase 'clerical or typographical nature' is not explicitly defined in §255, so we first look to the plain meaning and common understanding of the phrase. [C]lerical or typographical mistakes are generally understood to include simple mistakes such as obvious misspellings that are immediately apparent. [¶] The common understanding of a clerical or typographical mistake certainly includes mistakes that, upon correction, would either broaden or narrow a claim. ... Accordingly, we interpret §255 to allow broadening corrections of clerical or typographical mistakes. *At F.3d 1372, U.S.P.Q.2d 1678:* Placing due weight on the public notice function of patent claims suggests that we should interpret §255 to allow a broadening correction of a typographical error only where it is clearly evident from the specification, drawings, and prosecution history how the error should appropriately be corrected. Such an interpretation of §255 insures that the public is provided with notice as to the scope of the claims. *At F.3d 1373, U.S.P.Q.2d 1679:* Accordingly, we interpret §255 to require that a broadening correction of a clerical or typographical error be allowed only where it is clearly evident from the specification, drawings, and prosecution history how the error should appropriately be corrected. *At F.3d 1375, U.S.P.Q.2d 1681:* Regarding corrections of mistakes of 'minor character': [B]ased on the plain meaning of the statutory language, we interpret 'a mistake of ... minor character' to exclude mistakes that broaden a claim." *See also* ***Arthrocare Corp. v. Smith & Nephew, Inc.***, 406 F.3d 1365, 1374-75, 74 U.S.P.Q.2d 1749, 1757 (Fed.Cir.2005).

Fina Tech. v. Ewen, 265 F.3d 1325, 1328, 60 U.S.P.Q.2d 1314, 1317 (Fed.Cir.2001). "Examples of mistakes that fall under §255 typically include correcting a misspelled word or adding a prior art reference that was submitted to and discussed by the examiner but inadvertently omitted by the applicant on PTO Form 1449 for listing references. [T]he order of inventors is not a clerical error contemplated by §255, and cannot be corrected in a judicial proceeding under that provision."

Correction by District Court

I.T.S. Rubber Co. v. Essex Rubber Co., 272 U.S. 429, 442 (1926). "We concur in the finding of the District Judge that the omission of the word 'rear' was through a clerical error due to oversight and that both the counsel for the applicant and the examiner understood that it was contained in claim 8 as well as the others; and we are of opinion that the claim should be construed and have the same effect as if it had been included. This is not in any real sense, a re-making of the claim; but is merely giving to it the meaning which was intended by the applicant and understood by the examiner."

CBT Flint Partners v. Return Path, Inc., 654 F.3d 1353, 1358, 99 U.S.P.Q.2d 1610, 1613-14 (Fed.Cir.2011). "[I]n ***Ultimax Cement Mfg. v. CTS Cement Mfg.***[, 587 F.3d 1339 (Fed.Cir.2009)], we found authority for the district court to correct a claim by adding a comma between the symbols for fluorine and chlorine. We concluded that one of ordinary skill in the art would know that the formula should contain a comma. Thus, we emphasized that in deciding whether it had authority to correct a claim, a district court must consider any proposed correction 'from the point of view of one skilled in the art.'"

Novo Indus. v. Micro Molds Corp., 350 F.3d 1348, 1354, 69 U.S.P.Q.2d 1128, 1132 (Fed.Cir.2003). "This case presents the question whether a district court can act to correct an error in a patent by interpretation of the patent when no certificate of correction has been issued. We hold that a district court can do so only if (1) the correction is not subject to reasonable debate based on consideration of the claim language and specification, and (2) the prosecution history does not suggest a different interpretation of the claims. *At F.3d 1356-57, U.S.P.Q.2d 1134:* [T]he authority of the PTO to make corrections under §255, while limited to review of the intrinsic record, ... is not limited to obvious errors. Rather it extends even to broadening corrections, so long as 'it is clearly evident from the specification, drawings, and prosecution history how the error should appropriately be corrected.'" *See also* ***Mobile Hi-Tech Wheels v. CIA Wheel Grp.***, 514 F.Supp.2d 1172, 1181 (C.D.Cal.2007) (***Novo***'s analysis applies to both utility and design patents).

§256. CORRECTION OF NAMED INVENTOR

(a) Correction.—Whenever through error a person is named in an issued patent as the inventor, or through error an inventor is not named in an issued patent, the Director may, on application of all the parties and assignees, with proof of the facts and such other requirements as may be imposed, issue a certificate correcting such error.

(b) Patent valid if error corrected.—The error of omitting inventors or naming persons who are not inventors shall not invalidate the patent in which such error occurred if it can be corrected as provided in this section. The court before which such matter is called in question may order correction of the patent on notice and hearing of all parties concerned and the Director shall issue a certificate accordingly.

History of 35 U.S.C. §256: July 19, 1952, ch. 950, §1, 66 Stat. 810; Aug. 27, 1982, P.L. 97-247, §6(b), 96 Stat. 320; Nov. 29, 1999, P.L. 106-113, §1000(a)(9), 113 Stat. 1536; Nov. 2, 2002, P.L. 107-273, §13206(b)(1)(B), 116 Stat. 1906; Sept. 16, 2011, P.L. 112-29, §20(f), 125 Stat. 334.

See also 28 U.S.C. §1928; 35 U.S.C. §116; 37 C.F.R. §§1.324, 1.325.

ANNOTATIONS

Vapor Point LLC v. Moorhead, 832 F.3d 1343, 1348-49, 119 U.S.P.Q.2d 1722, 1726 (Fed.Cir.2016). "'A person who alleges that he is a co-inventor of the invention claimed in an issued patent who was not listed as an inventor on the patent may bring a cause of action to correct inventorship in a district court under ... §256.' Inventorship is a question of law entitled to de novo review by this court. [¶] All inventors, even those who contribute to only one claim or one aspect of one claim of a patent, must be listed on that patent. [¶] Co-inventors need not 'physically work together or at the same time,' 'make the same type or amount of contribution,' or 'make a contribution to the subject matter of every claim of the patent.' '[I]nventorship is determined on a claim-by-claim basis.' *At F.3d 1350, U.S.P.Q.2d 1727:* '[I]nventorship is a question of who actually invented the subject matter claimed in a patent. Ownership, however, is a question of who owns legal title to the subject matter claimed in a patent, patents having the attributes of personal property.' The parties agree that ownership is not an affirmative defense to an inventorship claim under §256."

TriReme Med., LLC v. AngioScore, Inc., 812 F.3d 1050, 1053, 117 U.S.P.Q.2d 1568, 1570 (Fed.Cir.2016). "When the owner of a patent assigns away all rights to the patent, neither he nor his later assignee has a 'concrete financial interest in the patent' that would support standing in a correction of inventorship action."

Shukh v. Seagate Tech., 803 F.3d 659, 663, 116 U.S.P.Q.2d 1248, 1252 (Fed.Cir.2015). "[W]e hold that concrete and particularized reputational injury can give rise to Article III standing [for a §256 claim]."

Pei-Herng Hor v. Ching-Wu Chu, 699 F.3d 1331, 1334, 104 U.S.P.Q.2d 1685, 1687 (Fed.Cir.2012). "For inventorship claims under §256, a delay of six years after a claim accrues creates a rebuttable presumption of laches. *At F.3d 1335, U.S.P.Q.2d 1688:* Does the laches period for a §256 claim begin to run before a patent issues when the omitted inventors knew or should have known prior to patent issuance that their names were omitted from the patent application? We conclude that the answer is no. [¶] A §256 claim for correction of inventorship does not accrue until the patent issues."

HIF Bio, Inc. v. Yung Shin Pharms. Indus. Co., 600 F.3d 1347, 1353, 94 U.S.P.Q.2d 1286, 1291 (Fed.Cir. 2010). "[B]ecause this dispute involves *pending* patent applications, [Ps'] requested relief—a declaration of the 'true' inventor—is tantamount to a request for either a modification of inventorship on pending patent applications or an interference proceeding. *At F.3d 1354:* [W]e expressly hold that [35 U.S.C.] §116 does not provide a private right of action to challenge inventorship of a pending patent application. Once a patent issues, however, 35 U.S.C. §256 provides a private right of action to challenge inventorship, and such a challenge arises under [28 U.S.C.] §1338(a)."

Shum v. Intel Corp., 499 F.3d 1272, 1277, 83 U.S.P.Q.2d 1933, 1936-37 (Fed.Cir.2007). "A correction for inventorship claim under §256 creates a cause of action in federal courts that authorizes a district court to resolve inventorship disputes over issued patents. At oral argument, the parties agreed that an action for correction of inventorship under §256, standing alone, is an equitable claim to which no right to a jury trial attaches. *At F.3d 1279, U.S.P.Q.2d 1938:* While [P] would not be entitled to a jury trial on the §256 inventorship claim standing alone, given the co-pendency of the asserted fraud claim [based on named inventor misrepresenting that he is sole inventor], a jury should determine the facts regarding inventorship. Accordingly, the court's decision to try the inventorship claim before a jury trial on the state law claim ran afoul of the Seventh Amendment, and thus was an abuse of discretion."

Gemstar-TV Guide Int'l v. International Trade Comm'n, 383 F.3d 1352, 1381-82, 72 U.S.P.Q.2d 1609, 1630 (Fed.Cir.2004). "Because co-inventors need not contribute to the subject matter of every claim of the patent, inventorship is determined on a claim-by-claim basis. Moreover, the inventorship analysis, like an infringement or invalidity analysis, first requires the construction of each disputed claim to determine the subject matter encompassed thereby. The second step is a comparison of the alleged contributions of each asserted co-inventor with the subject matter of the correctly construed claim to determine whether the correct inventors were named."

Xechem Int'l v. University of Tex., 382 F.3d 1324, 1326, 72 U.S.P.Q.2d 1253, 1254 (Fed.Cir.2004). "The only issue on appeal is whether [governmental unit] is subject to suit in federal court to obtain correction of the inventorship.... *At F.3d 1327-28, U.S.P.Q.2d 1256:* [Governmental unit] is deemed to be an arm of the State of Texas, and [P] does not dispute that [governmental unit] is properly accorded 11th Amendment immunity." Held: Immunity was not waived by governmental unit, and it could not be named party to suit. Correction of inventorship could not be obtained.

Frank's Casing Crew & Rental Tools, Inc. v. PMR Techs., 292 F.3d 1363, 1377, 63 U.S.P.Q.2d 1065, 1075 (Fed.Cir.2002). "Nothing in [§256] prevents a court from correcting the inventorship of an unenforceable patent."

Fina Tech. v. Ewen, 265 F.3d 1325, 1328, 60 U.S.P.Q.2d 1314, 1316-17 (Fed.Cir.2001). Section 256 addresses "two varieties of error in inventorship, misjoinder and nonjoinder. Additionally, ... the standards of both paragraphs of §256 pertain to administrative as well as judicial proceedings, thereby giving courts the power to correct either type of error in inventorship when all parties are given notice and an opportunity to be heard. [T]he language of §256 directs courts to correct inventorship under standards 'provided in this section.' The language of §256 is not broad enough, however, to be read as giving a district court authority to order the Director to change the order of inventors on an issued patent."

Chou v. University of Chi., 254 F.3d 1347, 1358, 59 U.S.P.Q.2d 1257, 1262 (Fed.Cir.2001). "The question [is] whether a putative inventor who is obligated to assign her invention to another is entitled to sue for correction of inventorship under §256. [¶] We conclude that an expectation of ownership of a patent is not a prerequisite for a putative inventor to possess standing to sue to correct inventorship under §256."

Pannu v. Iolab Corp., 155 F.3d 1344, 1350, 47 U.S.P.Q.2d 1657, 1662 (Fed.Cir.1998). "[I]n cases of misjoinder and nonjoinder the operation of [35 U.S.C.] §102(f) is ameliorated by [35 U.S.C.] §256.... If a patentee demonstrates that inventorship can be corrected as provided for in §256, a district court must order correction of the patent, thus saving it from being rendered invalid. When a party asserts invalidity under §102(f) due to non-joinder, a district court should first determine whether there exists clear and convincing proof that the alleged unnamed inventor was in fact a co-inventor. Upon such a finding of incorrect inventorship, a patentee may invoke §256 to save the patent from invalidity. [However,] a patent with improper inventorship does not avoid invalidation simply because it might be corrected under §256. Rather, the patentee must claim entitlement to relief under the statute and the court must give the patentee an opportunity to correct the inventorship. If the inventorship is successfully corrected, §102(f) will not render the patent invalid. On the other hand, if the patentee does not claim relief under the statute and a party asserting invalidity proves incorrect inventorship, the court should hold the patent invalid for failure to comply with §102(f)."

Ethicon, Inc. v. U.S. Surgical Corp., 135 F.3d 1456, 1461, 45 U.S.P.Q.2d 1545, 1548 (Fed.Cir.1998). "'[A]n inventor's testimony respecting the facts surrounding a claim of derivation or priority of invention cannot, standing alone, rise to the level of clear and convincing proof.' The rule is the same for an alleged co-inventor's testimony. Thus, an alleged co-inventor must supply evidence to corroborate his testimony. Whether the inventor's testimony has been sufficiently corroborated is evaluated under a 'rule of reason' analysis. Under this analysis, '[a]n evaluation of *all* pertinent evidence must be made so that a sound determination of the credibility of [alleged] inventor's story may be reached.' Corroborating evidence may take many forms. Often contemporaneous documents prepared by a putative inventor serve to corroborate an inventor's testimony. Circumstantial evidence about the inventive process may also corroborate. Additionally, oral testimony of someone other than the alleged inventor may corroborate." *See also* ***General Elec. Co. v. Wilkins***, 750 F.3d 1324, 1330, 110 U.S.P.Q.2d 1937, 1942 (Fed.Cir.

2014); ***Caterpillar Inc. v. Sturman Indus.***, 387 F.3d 1358, 1377, 73 U.S.P.Q.2d 1609, 1623 (Fed.Cir.2004).

Stark v. Advanced Magnetics, Inc., 119 F.3d 1551, 1555, 43 U.S.P.Q.2d 1321, 1324 (Fed.Cir.1997). "[T]his court construes the term 'error' to extend to mistakes, whether deceptive and 'dishonest' or merely uninformed and 'honest.' Therefore, §256 allows deletion of a misjoined inventor whether that error occurred by deception or by innocent mistake. As well, the section allows addition of an unnamed actual inventor, but this error of nonjoinder cannot betray any deceptive intent by that inventor. In other words, the statute allows correction in all misjoinder cases featuring an error and in those nonjoinder cases where the unnamed inventor is free of deceptive intent."

Stark v. Advanced Magnetics, Inc., 29 F.3d 1570, 1575, 31 U.S.P.Q.2d 1290, 1294 (Fed.Cir.1994). "Neither 35 U.S.C. §256 nor 37 C.F.R. §1.324 requires that an omitted inventor of an issued patent must diligently bring a lawsuit to correct inventorship or be forever barred from doing so. Absent any statutory or regulatory requirement of diligence in bringing legal action to correct inventorship of an issued patent, it was error to hold that [omitted inventor] was barred for lack of diligence as a matter of law. Whether diligent action is required in a particular case must be determined on the facts of that case."

§257. SUPPLEMENTAL EXAMINATIONS TO CONSIDER, RECONSIDER, OR CORRECT INFORMATION

(a) Request for supplemental examination.—A patent owner may request supplemental examination of a patent in the Office to consider, reconsider, or correct information believed to be relevant to the patent, in accordance with such requirements as the Director may establish. Within 3 months after the date a request for supplemental examination meeting the requirements of this section is received, the Director shall conduct the supplemental examination and shall conclude such examination by issuing a certificate indicating whether the information presented in the request raises a substantial new question of patentability.

(b) Reexamination ordered.—If the certificate issued under subsection (a) indicates that a substantial new question of patentability is raised by 1 or more items of information in the request, the Director shall order reexamination of the patent. The reexamination shall be conducted according to procedures established by chapter 30, except that the patent owner shall not have the right to file a statement pursuant to section 304. During the reexamination, the Director shall address each substantial new question of patentability identified during the supplemental examination, notwithstanding the limitations in chapter 30 relating to patents and printed publication or any other provision of such chapter.

(c) Effect—

(1) In general.—A patent shall not be held unenforceable on the basis of conduct relating to information that had not been considered, was inadequately considered, or was incorrect in a prior examination of the patent if the information was considered, reconsidered, or corrected during a supplemental examination of the patent. The making of a request under subsection (a), or the absence thereof, shall not be relevant to enforceability of the patent under section 282.

(2) Exceptions—

(A) Prior allegations.—Paragraph (1) shall not apply to an allegation pled with particularity in a civil action, or set forth with particularity in a notice received by the patent owner under section 505(j)(2)(B)(iv)(II) of the Federal Food, Drug, and Cosmetic Act (21 U.S.C. 355(j)(2)(B)(iv)(II)), before the date of a supplemental examination request under subsection (a) to consider, reconsider, or correct information forming the basis for the allegation.

(B) Patent enforcement actions.—In an action brought under section 337(a) of the Tariff Act of 1930 (19 U.S.C. 1337(a)), or section 281 of this title, paragraph (1) shall not apply to any defense raised in the action that is based upon information that was considered, reconsidered, or corrected pursuant to a supplemental examination request under subsection (a), unless the supplemental examination, and any reexamination ordered pursuant to the request, are concluded before the date on which the action is brought.

(d) Fees and regulations—

(1) Fees.—The Director shall, by regulation, establish fees for the submission of a request for supplemental examination of a patent, and to consider each item of information submitted in the request. If reexamination is ordered under subsection (b), fees established and applicable to ex parte reexamination proceedings under chapter 30 shall be paid, in addition to fees applicable to supplemental examination.

(2) Regulations.—The Director shall issue regulations governing the form, content, and other requirements of requests for supplemental examination, and establishing procedures for reviewing information submitted in such requests.

(e) Fraud.—If the Director becomes aware, during the course of a supplemental examination or reexamination proceeding ordered under this section, that a material fraud on the Office may have been committed in connection with the patent that is the subject of the supplemental examination, then in addition to any other actions the Director is authorized to take, including the cancellation of any claims found to be invalid under section 307 as a result of a reexamination ordered under this section, the Director shall also refer the matter to the Attorney General for such further action as the Attorney General may deem appropriate. Any such referral shall be treated as confidential, shall not be included in the file of the patent, and shall not be disclosed to the public unless the United States charges a person with a criminal offense in connection with such referral.

(f) Rule of construction.—Nothing in this section shall be construed—

(1) to preclude the imposition of sanctions based upon criminal or antitrust laws (including section 1001(a) of title 18, the first section of the Clayton Act, and section 5 of the Federal Trade Commission Act to the extent that section relates to unfair methods of competition);

(2) to limit the authority of the Director to investigate issues of possible misconduct and impose sanctions for misconduct in connection with matters or proceedings before the Office; or

(3) to limit the authority of the Director to issue regulations under chapter 3 relating to sanctions for misconduct by representatives practicing before the Office.

History of 35 U.S.C. §257: Sept. 16, 2011, P.L. 112-29, §12(a), 125 Stat. 325.
See also 37 C.F.R. §§1.601-1.625.

CHAPTER 26. OWNERSHIP & ASSIGNMENT

§261. OWNERSHIP; ASSIGNMENT

Subject to the provisions of this title, patents shall have the attributes of personal property. The Patent and Trademark Office shall maintain a register of interests in patents and applications for patents and shall record any document related thereto upon request, and may require a fee therefor.

Applications for patent, patents, or any interest therein, shall be assignable in law by an instrument in writing. The applicant, patentee, or his assigns or legal representatives may in like manner grant and convey an exclusive right under his application for patent, or patents, to the whole or any specified part of the United States.

A certificate of acknowledgment under the hand and official seal of a person authorized to administer oaths within the United States, or, in a foreign country, of a diplomatic or consular officer of the United States or an officer authorized to administer oaths whose authority is proved by a certificate of a diplomatic or consular officer of the United States, or apostille of an official designated by a foreign country which, by treaty or convention, accords like effect to apostilles of designated officials in the United States, shall be prima facie evidence of the execution of an assignment, grant or conveyance of a patent or application for patent.

An interest that constitutes an assignment, grant or conveyance shall be void as against any subsequent purchaser or mortgagee for a valuable consideration, without notice, unless it is recorded in the Patent and Trademark Office within three months from its date or prior to the date of such subsequent purchase or mortgage.

History of 35 U.S.C. §261: July 19, 1952, ch. 950, §1, 66 Stat. 810; Jan. 2, 1975, P.L. 93-596, §1, 88 Stat. 1949; Aug. 27, 1982, P.L. 97-247, §14(b), 96 Stat. 321; Dec. 18, 2013, P.L. 112-211, §201(d), 126 Stat. 1535.
See also 26 U.S.C. §§1235, 1249; 42 U.S.C. §7608; 37 C.F.R. §1.46, pt. 3.

ANNOTATIONS

Generally

Board of Trs. of Leland Stanford Junior Univ. v. Roche Molecular Sys., 583 F.3d 832, 841, 92 U.S.P.Q.2d 1442, 1448 (Fed.Cir.2009), *aff'd*, 563 U.S. 776, 131 S.Ct. 2188 (2011). "'[T]he question of who owns the patent rights and on what terms typically is a question exclusively for state courts.' However, this rule has exceptions: the question of whether contractual language effects a present assignment of patent rights, or an agreement to assign rights in the future, is resolved by

Federal Circuit law. [¶] We have held that the contract language 'agree to assign' reflects a mere promise to assign rights in the future, not an immediate transfer of expectant interests. ... In contrast ... the [agreement's] language of 'do hereby assign' effected a present assignment of [inventor's] future inventions to [company]." *See also* ***WesternGeco L.L.C. v. ION Geophysical Corp.***, 791 F.3d 1340, 1346, 115 U.S.P.Q.2d 1597, 1602 (Fed.Cir.2015), *vacated*, ___ U.S. ___, 136 S.Ct. 2486 (2016), *reinstated by* 837 F.3d 1358 (Fed.Cir. 2016); ***Abraxis Bioscience, Inc. v. Navinta LLC***, 625 F.3d 1359, 1364-65, 96 U.S.P.Q.2d 1977, 1981-82 (Fed. Cir.2010).

Antitrust

Moraine Prods. v. ICI Am., Inc., 538 F.2d 134, 143, 191 U.S.P.Q. 65, 73 (7th Cir.1976). "Nothing in ... §261 or the decided cases sanctions an arrangement wherein competitors agree with one another that they will not grant further sublicenses. The bare language of §261 does allow a patentee or his assignee to grant an exclusive license to make, use, or sell the patented invention. But the statutory language must be construed in connection with antitrust law."

Miller Insituform, Inc. v. Insituform, Inc., 605 F.Supp. 1125, 1131, 225 U.S.P.Q. 1232, 1235 (M.D.Tenn. 1985), *aff'd*, 830 F.2d 606, 4 U.S.P.Q.2d 1463 (6th Cir.1987). "Pursuant to the 'inherency doctrine,' §261 immunizes from antitrust analysis an allocation of territories created by a patentee's use of exclusive licenses. The immunity also extends to a patent licensee's division of its territory among its various sublicensees. A patentee has a legal monopoly which he may exploit to the bounds of his right, and accordingly, the patentee can convey exclusive rights to another, in whole or in part, and may give a licensee an exclusive right to manufacture, use or sell a patented product, or practice a patent process, in a particular zone or territory."

Assignment & License

Waterman v. Mackenzie, 138 U.S. 252, 255-56 (1891). "The patentee or his assigns may, by instrument in writing, assign, grant, and convey, either (1) the whole patent, comprising the exclusive right to make, use, and vend the invention throughout the U.S.; or, (2) an undivided part or share of that exclusive right; or, (3) the exclusive right under the patent within and throughout a specified part of the U.S. A transfer of either of these three kinds of interests is an assignment, properly speaking, and vests in the assignee a title in so much of the patent itself, with a right to sue infringers. In the second case, jointly with the assignor. In the first and third cases, in the name of the assignee alone. Any assignment or transfer, short of one of these, is a mere license, giving the licensee no title in the patent, and no right to sue at law in his own name for an infringement. In equity, as at law, when the transfer amounts to a license only, the title remains in the owner of the patent; and suit must be brought in his name, and never in the name of the licensee alone unless that it necessary to prevent an absolute failure of justice, as where the patentee is the infringer, and cannot sue himself. Any rights of the licensee must be enforced through or in the name of the owner of the patent, and perhaps, if necessary to protect the rights of all parties, joining the licensee with him as a plaintiff. Whether a transfer of a particular right or interest under a patent is an assignment or a license does not depend upon the name by which it calls itself, but upon the legal effect of its provisions." *See also* ***Aspex Eyewear, Inc. v. Miracle Optics, Inc.***, 434 F.3d 1336, 1341-42, 77 U.S.P.Q.2d 1456, 1460-61 (Fed.Cir.2006); ***In re CFLC, Inc.***, 89 F.3d 673, 676 n.2, 39 U.S.P.Q.2d 1518, 1520-21 n.2 (9th Cir.1996).

Delano Farms Co. v. California Table Grape Comm'n, 655 F.3d 1337, 1342, 99 U.S.P.Q.2d 1827, 1830 (Fed.Cir.2011). "It is well established that a patentee is a necessary party to an action on the patent, whether it be a coercive action or a declaratory judgment suit. If the patentee has transferred all substantial rights in the patent to an exclusive licensee, however, the licensee is treated as the assignee. In that event, the assignor, which is no longer regarded as the owner of the patent, need not be joined in any action brought on the patent. [¶] In determining whether a licensee has obtained all substantial rights in the patent, an important consideration is whether the license grants to the licensee the right to enforce the patent and divests the licensor of that same right. When a licensing agreement restrains or controls the licensee's sublicensing power, the licensor is generally regarded as having retained substantial control over patent enforcement, and the agreement is not treated as having given the licensee all substantial rights in the patent."

Waymark Corp. v. Porta Sys., 334 F.3d 1358, 1364, 67 U.S.P.Q.2d 1303, 1308 (Fed.Cir.2003). "Only assignments need be in writing under ... §261. Licenses may be oral."

Textile Prods. v. Mead Corp., 134 F.3d 1481, 1484, 45 U.S.P.Q.2d 1633, 1635 (Fed.Cir.1998). "Determining whether a licensee is an exclusive licensee or a bare licensee is a question of ascertaining the intent of the parties to the license as manifested by the terms of their agreement and examining the substance of the grant. The use of the word 'exclusive' is not controlling; what matters is the substance of the arrangement."

Enzo APA & Son, Inc. v. Geapag A.G., 134 F.3d 1090, 1093, 45 U.S.P.Q.2d 1368, 1370-71 (Fed.Cir.1998). "While we acknowledge that a license may be written, verbal, or implied, if the license is to be considered a virtual assignment to assert standing, it must be in writing. The limited exception we have provided conferring standing on licensees is restricted to virtual assignees. As such, the licensing arrangement conferring such must, logically, resemble an assignment in both form and substance. [¶] [Nonexclusive licensee] argues that the nunc pro tunc [license] renders it a virtual assignee for the purposes of standing. However, ... nunc pro tunc assignments are not sufficient to confer retroactive standing on the basis that: 'As a general matter, parties should possess rights before seeking to have them vindicated in court. Allowing a subsequent assignment to automatically cure a standing defect would unjustifiably expand the number of people who are statutorily authorized to sue.'" *But see* ***Bard Peripheral Vascular, Inc. v. W.L. Gore & Assocs.***, 776 F.3d 837, 843-44, 113 U.S.P.Q.2d 1380, 1384 (Fed.Cir. 2015), *overruled on other grounds*, ***Halo Elecs., Inc. v. Pulse Elecs., Inc.***, ___ U.S. ___, 136 S.Ct. 1923 (2016) (distinguishing between nunc pro tunc written agreements occurring before suit is filed and after suit is filed).

FilmTec Corp. v. Allied-Signal Inc., 939 F.2d 1568, 1572, 19 U.S.P.Q.2d 1508, 1511 (Fed.Cir.1991). "[A]n application for patent as well as the patent itself may be assigned. Further, it is settled law that between the time of an invention and the issuance of a patent, rights in an invention may be assigned and legal title to the ensuing patent will pass to the assignee upon grant of the patent. [¶] Once the invention is made and an application for patent is filed, ... legal title to the rights accruing thereunder would be in the assignee (subject to the rights of a subsequent purchaser under §261), and the assignor-inventor would have nothing remaining to assign."

Assignor Estoppel & Licensor Estoppel

Husky Injection Molding Sys. v. Athena Automation Ltd., 838 F.3d 1236, 1247, 120 U.S.P.Q.2d 1324, 1331 (Fed.Cir.2016). "[A]ssignor estoppel operates to prevent 'one who has assigned the rights to a patent (or [a] patent application) from later contending that what was assigned' lacks value. It does not foreclose all challenges to a patent's validity from the remainder of the general public. To that end, it does not prevent a tribunal from evaluating the validity of any challenged claims generally, but rather simply limits the parties that may ask the tribunal for such an evaluation. [¶] In that way, assignor estoppel differs from the certain statutory limits placed on the [PTAB's] authority in a CBM review." Held: Federal Circuit lacks jurisdiction to review PTAB decision that assignor estoppel does not bar assignor or privies from petition for *inter partes* review.

Semiconductor Energy Lab. Co. v. Nagata, 706 F.3d 1365, 1367, 105 U.S.P.Q.2d 1778, 1779 (Fed.Cir. 2013). "[T]here is no federal cause of action based on assignor estoppel.... *At F.3d 1370, U.S.P.Q.2d 1781:* [A]ssignor estoppel is a form of estoppel, and with rare exception, estoppel is a shield; it is an affirmative defense, not a claim for relief on its own."

Rates Tech. v. Speakeasy, Inc., 685 F.3d 163, 164, 103 U.S.P.Q.2d 1462, 1463 (2d Cir.2012). "This case requires us to consider whether a clause in a settlement agreement which bars a patent licensee from later challenging the patent's validity is void for public policy reasons under the Supreme Court's decision in ***Lear, Inc. v. Adkins***, 395 U.S. 653 ... (1969), where the parties entered into the agreement after an accusation of infringement by the patent owner but prior to any litigation. We hold that, in these circumstances, such a no-challenge clause is void under ***Lear***."

Dane Indus. v. Ameritek Indus., 154 Fed.Appx. 894, 899 (Fed.Cir.2005). "'[A]n assignor and parties in privity with the assignor are estopped or barred from asserting invalidity defenses.' Mere employment is insufficient to establish privity. However, a company may be in privity with an assignor if the company avails itself of the assignor's knowledge and assistance to conduct the infringement."

Diamond Sci. Co. v. Ambico, Inc., 848 F.2d 1220, 1224, 6 U.S.P.Q.2d 2028, 2030-31 (Fed.Cir.1988). Assignor estoppel "historically has applied to invalidity challenges based on 'novelty, utility, patentable invention, anticipatory matter, and the state of the art.' [¶] The four most frequently mentioned justifications for applying assignor estoppel are the following: '(1) to prevent unfairness and injustice; (2) to prevent one [from] benefiting from his own wrong; (3) by analogy to estoppel by deed in real estate; and (4) by analogy to a landlord-tenant relationship.'" *See also* ***Pandrol USA, LP v. Airboss Ry. Prods.***, 424 F.3d 1161, 1166, 76 U.S.P.Q.2d 1524, 1527 (Fed.Cir.2005).

Bona Fide Purchaser Defense

Board of Trs. of Leland Stanford Junior Univ. v. Roche Molecular Sys., 583 F.3d 832, 843, 92 U.S.P.Q.2d 1442, 1449 (Fed.Cir.2009), *aff'd*, 563 U.S. 776, 131 S.Ct. 2188 (2011). "'Notice' under [the bona fide-purchaser defense] can include constructive or inquiry notice, in addition to actual notice." *See also* ***Katz v. Lear Siegler Inc.***, 29 U.S.P.Q.2d 1450, 1453-54 (Fed.Cir.1993).

Rhone-Poulenc Agro, S.A. v. DeKalb Genetics Corp., 284 F.3d 1323, 1327, 62 U.S.P.Q.2d 1188, 1190 (Fed.Cir.2002). "Under some circumstances the bona fide purchaser defense in patent cases is governed by a federal statute, ... §261. [¶] That statute is by its terms limited to situations in which the patent owner makes inconsistent assignments, grants, or conveyances to two entities, and the question is whether the later assignee should prevail. Section 261 provides that a later bona fide purchaser for value without notice (a later assignee) prevails if the earlier assignment was not timely recorded in the [PTO]. This case, however, involves a different situation—the circumstance in which the interest in the patent held by the grantor is voidable and the question is whether a grantee may retain its interest even if the grantor's interest is voided. Section 261 does not directly govern the resolution of this question. *At F.3d 1328, U.S.P.Q.2d 1191:* [B]ecause of the importance of having a uniform national rule, we hold that the bona fide purchaser defense to patent infringement is a matter of federal law. Because such a federal rule implicates an issue of patent law, the law of this circuit governs the rule. *At F.3d 1333, U.S.P.Q.2d 1195:* Even if the general common law extended the protection of the bona fide purchaser rule to holders of non-exclusive licenses, it would not be appropriate for us to extend such protection to non-exclusive licenses as a matter of federal common law. *At F.3d 1334:* Here the license is non-exclusive, and there is no contention that the license agreement transferred 'all substantial rights.' Thus, an assignment did not occur, and in the absence of an 'assignment, grant or conveyance,' Congress contemplated that there would be no bona fide purchaser defense."

FilmTec Corp. v. Allied-Signal Inc., 939 F.2d 1568, 1574, 19 U.S.P.Q.2d 1508, 1513 (Fed.Cir.1991). "[I]t may be useful for us to clarify what is required before [P] can properly be considered a subsequent purchaser entitled to the protections of §261. In the first place, [P] must be in fact a purchaser for a valuable consideration. [T]he requirement is that the subsequent purchaser, in order to cut off the rights of the prior purchaser, must be more than a donee or other gratuitous transferee. There must be in fact valuable consideration paid so that the subsequent purchaser can, as a matter of law, claim record reliance as a premise upon which the purchase was made. [¶] In addition, the subsequent transferee/assignee ... must be without notice of any such prior assignment."

Patent as Personal Property

Akazawa v. Link New Tech., 520 F.3d 1354, 1356, 86 U.S.P.Q.2d 1279, 1281 (Fed.Cir.2008). "[P]atent ownership may be transferred by assignment, and §261 addresses such a transfer—requiring assignments to be in writing. However, there is nothing that limits assignment as the only means for transferring patent ownership. Indeed, the case law illustrates that ownership of a patent may be changed by operation of law." Held: Foreign laws of intestacy may decide patent ownership and therefore standing to sue for infringement.

Aptix Corp. v. Quickturn Design Sys., 269 F.3d 1369, 1377, 60 U.S.P.Q.2d 1705, 1710 (Fed.Cir.2001). "In the absence of any showing of misconduct before the PTO, [patent] remains a presumptively valid grant of personal property. No case law from the Supreme Court or this court provides a basis for nullifying property rights granted by the U.S. when such property rights did not themselves accrue through inequitable conduct." Held: Patent is not to be declared unenforceable because of misconduct in infringement litigation.

Ethicon, Inc. v. U.S. Surgical Corp., 135 F.3d 1456, 1466, 45 U.S.P.Q.2d 1545, 1552 (Fed.Cir.1998). Section 261 "suggests that property rights, including ownership, attach to patents as a whole, not individual claims."

Recording

In re Cybernetic Servs., 252 F.3d 1039, 1044, 59 U.S.P.Q.2d 1097, 1097 (9th Cir.2001). "The question that we decide today is whether 35 U.S.C. §261 [or]

Uniform Commercial Code (UCC) [art. 9], as adopted in California, requires the holder of a security interest in a patent to record that interest with the federal [PTO] in order to perfect the interest as against a subsequent lien creditor. We answer 'no'; neither [§261] nor Art. 9 so requires. *At F.3d 1059, U.S.P.Q.2d 1109:* Because ... §261 concerns only transactions that effect a transfer of an ownership interest in a patent, [§261] does not preempt Art. 9.... Petitioners perfected their security interest in Debtor's patent by recording it with the California Secretary of State."

CMS Indus. v. L.P.S. Int'l, 643 F.2d 289, 295, 217 U.S.P.Q. 20, 24 (5th Cir.1981). "The unrecorded agreement, by its terms, was an unrecorded attempt to retain in [patent owner] all benefits enjoyable by an assignee of the patents, as if those patents had not been assigned to its subsidiary, ... while, at the same time, [subsidiary] was identified to the public as the owner of the 'entire right, title and interest' in those patents on the [PTO] records. In such a situation, ... §261 operates to protect one who acquires those patents for value without knowledge of the unrecorded agreement, and the district court therefore properly held the unrecorded agreement void against [exclusive licensee's transferee], the creditor in the Chancery proceeding."

Shop Rights

McElmurry v. Arkansas Power & Light Co., 995 F.2d 1576, 1580, 27 U.S.P.Q.2d 1129, 1132-33 (Fed.Cir. 1993). "A 'shop right' is generally accepted as being a right that is created at common law, when the circumstances demand it, under principles of equity and fairness, entitling an employer to use without charge an invention patented by one or more of its employees without liability for infringement. *At F.2d 1581-82, U.S.P.Q.2d 1134:* [T]he proper methodology for determining whether an employer has acquired a 'shop right' in a patented invention is to look to the totality of the circumstances on a case by case basis and determine whether the facts of a particular case demand, under principles of equity and fairness, a finding that a 'shop right' exists. In such an analysis, one should look to such factors as the circumstances surrounding the development of the patented invention and the inventor's activities respecting that invention, once developed, to determine whether equity and fairness demand that the employer be allowed to use that invention in his business."

§262. JOINT OWNERS

In the absence of any agreement to the contrary, each of the joint owners of a patent may make, use, offer to sell, or sell the patented invention within the United States, or import the patented invention into the United States, without the consent of and without accounting to the other owners.

History of 35 U.S.C. §262: July 19, 1952, ch. 950, §1, 66 Stat. 810; Dec. 8, 1994, P.L. 103-465, §533(b)(3), 108 Stat. 4989.

See also FRCP 19; TRIPs pt. II, §5.

ANNOTATIONS

Wisconsin Alumni Research Found. v. Xenon Pharms., 591 F.3d 876, 882, 93 U.S.P.Q.2d 1361, 1366 (7th Cir.2010). "[E]ach co-owner is 'at the mercy' of the other in that the right of each to license independently may, for all practical purposes, destroy the monopoly and so amount to an appropriation of the whole value of the patent. This statutory rule is subject to an important exception, however: Joint patent owners may vary their rights by contract. ... The statutory default rule therefore controls *unless* there is an agreement to the contrary." (Internal quotes omitted.)

Massachusetts Eye & Ear Infirmary v. QLT Phototherapeutics, Inc., 412 F.3d 215, 235, 75 U.S.P.Q.2d 1225, 1237 (1st Cir.2005). "[D] suggests that ['any agreement to the contrary'] only applies where there is a written, legally enforceable contract. But §262 says no such thing. Congress knew how to insist upon a contract, and even how to specify that it must be reduced to writing. However, §262 simply speaks of 'any agreement.'"

International Nutrition Co. v. Horphag Research Ltd., 257 F.3d 1324, 1331, 59 U.S.P.Q.2d 1532, 1537 (Fed.Cir.2001). "While the ownership of the ... patent is properly the subject of French law, the right to bring suit on the U.S. patent in the district court is governed by U.S. patent law, which requires that all co-owners normally must join as plaintiffs in an infringement suit. Even if [entity that ultimately acquired rights of co-owner] does hold the 50% interest in ... patent that formerly belonged to [acquired co-owner, it] would still be barred from bringing suit without the consent of ... co-owner of the patent. A co-owner may waive his right to refuse to join a suit to enforce the patent, in which case his co-owners may subsequently-force him to join in a suit, but [co-owner here] did not waive this right."

Ethicon, Inc. v. U.S. Surgical Corp., 135 F.3d 1456, 1467, 45 U.S.P.Q.2d 1545, 1554 (Fed.Cir.1998). "An action for infringement must join as plaintiffs all co-owners. *At F.3d 1468:* Further, ... all co-owners must ordinarily consent to join as plaintiffs in an infringement suit. Consequently, 'one co-owner has the right to impede the other co-owner's ability to sue infringers by refusing to voluntarily join in such a suit.' *At F.3d 1468 n.9, U.S.P.Q.2d 1554 n.9:* Two established exceptions exist. First, when any patent owner has granted an exclusive license, he stands in a relationship of trust to his licensee and must permit the licensee to sue in his name. Second, the obligation may arise by contract among co-owners. If, by agreement, a co-owner waives his right to refuse to join suit, his co-owners may subsequently force him to join in a suit against infringers. *At F.3d 1468, U.S.P.Q.2d 1554:* This freedom to exploit the patent without a duty to account to other co-owners also allows co-owners to freely license others to exploit the patent without the consent of other co-owners." *See also* ***Schering Corp. v. Roussel-UCLAF SA***, 104 F.3d 341, 345, 41 U.S.P.Q.2d 1359, 1362-63 (Fed.Cir.1997); ***Willingham v. Lawton***, 555 F.2d 1340, 1344-45, 194 U.S.P.Q. 249, 252 (6th Cir.1977).

CHAPTER 27. GOVERNMENT INTERESTS IN PATENTS

§266. REPEALED

Repealed July 24, 1965, P.L. 89-83, §8, 79 Stat. 261.

§267. TIME FOR TAKING ACTION IN GOVERNMENT APPLICATIONS

Notwithstanding the provisions of sections 133 and 151, the Director may extend the time for taking any action to three years, when an application has become the property of the United States and the head of the appropriate department or agency of the Government has certified to the Director that the invention disclosed therein is important to the armament or defense of the United States.

History of 35 U.S.C. §267: July 19, 1952, ch. 950, §1, 66 Stat. 811; Nov. 29, 1999, P.L. 106-113, §1000(a)(9), 113 Stat. 1536; Nov. 2, 2002, P.L. 107-273, §13206(b)(1)(B), 116 Stat. 1906; Sept. 16, 2011, P.L. 112-29, §20(j)(1), 125 Stat. 335.

CHAPTER 28. INFRINGEMENT OF PATENTS

§271. INFRINGEMENT OF PATENT

(a) Except as otherwise provided in this title, whoever without authority makes, uses, offers to sell, or sells any patented invention, within the United States or imports into the United States any patented invention during the term of the patent therefor, infringes the patent.

(b) Whoever actively induces infringement of a patent shall be liable as an infringer.

(c) Whoever offers to sell or sells within the United States or imports into the United States a component of a patented machine, manufacture, combination or composition, or a material or apparatus for use in practicing a patented process, constituting a material part of the invention, knowing the same to be especially made or especially adapted for use in an infringement of such patent, and not a staple article or commodity of commerce suitable for substantial noninfringing use, shall be liable as a contributory infringer.

(d) No patent owner otherwise entitled to relief for infringement or contributory infringement of a patent shall be denied relief or deemed guilty of misuse or illegal extension of the patent right by reason of his having done one or more of the following: (1) derived revenue from acts which if performed by another without his consent would constitute contributory infringement of the patent; (2) licensed or authorized another to perform acts which if performed without his consent would constitute contributory infringement of the patent; (3) sought to enforce his patent rights against infringement or contributory infringement; (4) refused to license or use any rights to the patent; or (5) conditioned the license of any rights to the patent or the sale of the patented product on the acquisition of a license to rights in another patent or purchase of a separate product, unless, in view of the circumstances, the patent owner has market power in the relevant market for the patent or patented product on which the license or sale is conditioned.

(e)(1) It shall not be an act of infringement to make, use, offer to sell, or sell within the United States or import into the United States a patented invention (other than a new animal drug or veterinary biological product (as those terms are used in the Federal Food, Drug, and Cosmetic Act and the Act of March 4, 1913) which is primarily manufactured using recombinant DNA, recombinant RNA, hybridoma technology, or other processes involving site specific genetic manipulation techniques) solely for uses reasonably related to the development and submission of information under a Federal law which regulates the manufacture, use, or sale of drugs or veterinary biological products.

(2) It shall be an act of infringement to submit—

(A) an application under section 355(j) of title 21 or described in section 355(b)(2)of title 21 for a drug claimed in a patent or the use of which is claimed in a patent,

(B) an application under section 360b of title 21 or under the Act of March 4, 1913 (21 U.S.C. 151-158) for a drug or veterinary biological product which is not primarily manufactured using recombinant DNA, recombinant RNA, hybridoma technology, or other processes involving site specific genetic manipulation techniques and which is claimed in a patent or the use of which is claimed in a patent, or

(C)(i) with respect to a patent that is identified in the list of patents described in section 262(*l*)(3) of title 42 (including as provided under section 262(*l*)(7) of title 42), an application seeking approval of a biological product, or

(ii) if the applicant for the application fails to provide the application and information required under section 262(*l*)(2)(A) of title 42, an application seeking approval of a biological product for a patent that could be identified pursuant to section 262(*l*)(3)(A)(i) of title 42,

if the purpose of such submission is to obtain approval under such Act to engage in the commercial manufacture, use, or sale of a drug, veterinary biological product, or biological product claimed in a patent or the use of which is claimed in a patent before the expiration of such patent.

(3) In any action for patent infringement brought under this section, no injunctive or other relief may be granted which would prohibit the making, using, offering to sell, or selling within the United States or importing into the United States of a patented invention under paragraph (1).

(4) For an act of infringement described in paragraph (2)—

(A) the court shall order the effective date of any approval of the drug or veterinary biological product involved in the infringement to be a date which is not earlier than the date of the expiration of the patent which has been infringed,

(B) injunctive relief may be granted against an infringer to prevent the commercial manufacture, use, offer to sell, or sale within the United States or importation into the United States of an approved drug, veterinary biological product, or biological product,

(C) damages or other monetary relief may be awarded against an infringer only if there has been commercial manufacture, use, offer to sell, or sale within the United States or importation into the United States of an approved drug, veterinary biological product, or biological product, and

(D) the court shall order a permanent injunction prohibiting any infringement of the patent by the biological product involved in the infringement until a date which is not earlier than the date of the expiration of the patent that has been infringed under paragraph (2)(C), provided the patent is the subject of a final court decision, as defined in section 262(k)(6) of title 42, in an action for infringement of the patent under section 262(*l*)(6) of title 42, and the biological product has not yet been approved because of section 262(k)(7) of title 42.

The remedies prescribed by subparagraphs (A), (B), (C), and (D) are the only remedies which may be granted by a court for an act of infringement described in paragraph (2), except that a court may award attorney fees under section 285.

(5) Where a person has filed an application described in paragraph (2) that includes a certification under subsection (b)(2)(A)(iv) or (j)(2)(A)(vii)(IV) of section 505 of the Federal Food, Drug, and Cosmetic Act (21 U.S.C. 355), and neither the owner of the patent that is the subject of the certification nor the holder of the approved application under subsection (b) of such section for the drug that is claimed by the patent or a use of which is claimed by the patent brought an action for infringement of such patent before the expiration of 45 days after the date on which the notice given under subsection (b)(3) or (j)(2)(B) of such section was received, the courts of the United States shall, to the extent consistent with the Constitution, have subject matter jurisdiction in any action brought by such person under section 2201 of title 28 for a declaratory judgment that such patent is invalid or not infringed.

(6)(A) Subparagraph (B) applies, in lieu of paragraph (4), in the case of a patent—

(i) that is identified, as applicable, in the list of patents described in section 262(*l*)(4) of title 42 or the lists of patents described in section 262(*l*)(5)(B) of title 42 with respect to a biological product; and

(ii) for which an action for infringement of the patent with respect to the biological product—

(I) was brought after the expiration of the 30-day period described in subparagraph (A) or (B), as applicable, of section 262(*l*)(6) of title 42; or

(II) was brought before the expiration of the 30-day period described in subclause (I), but which was dismissed without prejudice or was not prosecuted to judgment in good faith.

(B) In an action for infringement of a patent described in subparagraph (A), the sole and exclusive remedy that may be granted by a court, upon a finding that the making, using, offering to sell, selling, or importation into the United States of the biological product that is the subject of the action infringed the patent, shall be a reasonable royalty.

(C) The owner of a patent that should have been included in the list described in section 262(*l*)(3)(A) of title 42, including as provided under section 262(*l*)(7) of title 42 for a biological product, but was not timely included in such list, may not bring an action under this section for infringement of the patent with respect to the biological product.

(f)(1) Whoever without authority supplies or causes to be supplied in or from the United States all or a substantial portion of the components of a patented invention, where such components are uncombined in whole or in part, in such manner as to actively induce the combination of such components outside of the United States in a manner that would infringe the patent if such combination occurred within the United States, shall be liable as an infringer.

(2) Whoever without authority supplies or causes to be supplied in or from the United States any component of a patented invention that is especially made or especially adapted for use in the invention and not a staple article or commodity of commerce suitable for substantial noninfringing use, where such component is uncombined in whole or in part, knowing that such component is so made or adapted and intending that such component will be combined outside of the United States in a manner that would infringe the patent if such combination occurred within the United States, shall be liable as an infringer.

(g) Whoever without authority imports into the United States or offers to sell, sells, or uses within the United States a product which is made by a process patented in the United States shall be liable as an infringer, if the importation, offer to sell, sale, or use of the product occurs during the term of such process patent. In an action for infringement of a process patent, no remedy may be granted for infringement on account of the noncommercial use or retail sale of a product unless there is no adequate remedy under this title for infringement on account of the importation or other use, offer to sell, or sale of that product. A product which is made by a patented process will, for purposes of this title, not be considered to be so made after—

(1) it is materially changed by subsequent processes; or

(2) it becomes a trivial and nonessential component of another product.

(h) As used in this section, the term "whoever" includes any State, any instrumentality of a State, and any officer or employee of a State or instrumentality of a State acting in his official capacity. Any State, and any such instrumentality, officer, or employee, shall be subject to the provisions of this title in the same manner and to the same extent as any nongovernmental entity.

(i) As used in this section, an "offer for sale" or an "offer to sell" by a person other than the patentee, or any designee of the patentee, is that in which the sale will occur before the expiration of the term of the patent.

History of 35 U.S.C. §271: July 19, 1952, ch. 950, §1, 66 Stat. 811; Sept. 24, 1984, P.L. 98-417, §202, 98 Stat. 1603; Nov. 8, 1984, P.L. 98-622, §101(a), 98 Stat. 3383; Aug. 23, 1988, P.L. 100-418, §9003, 102 Stat. 1564; Nov. 16, 1988, P.L. 100-670, §201(i), 102 Stat. 3988; Nov. 19, 1988, P.L. 100-703, §201, 102 Stat. 4676; Oct. 28, 1992, P.L. 102-560, §2(a)(1), 106 Stat. 4230; Dec. 8, 1994, P.L. 103-465, §533(a), 108 Stat. 4988; Dec. 8, 2003, P.L. 108-173, §1101(d), 117 Stat. 2457; Mar. 23, 2010, P.L. 111-148, §7002(c)(1), 124 Stat. 815.

See also 19 U.S.C. §1337; 21 U.S.C. §§355, 360b; 22 U.S.C. §2356; 28 U.S.C. §§1292, 1295, 1400, 1498, 1694, 1928; TRIPs pt. II, §5.

ANNOTATIONS

Generally

Technology Licensing Corp. v. Videotek, Inc., 545 F.3d 1316, 1327, 88 U.S.P.Q.2d 1865, 1873 (Fed.Cir. 2008). "[P], alleging infringement by [D], has the burden of persuasion that [D] infringes, under the usual civil law standard of preponderance of the evidence."

Warner-Lambert Co. v. Teva Pharms., 418 F.3d 1326, 1340, 75 U.S.P.Q.2d 1865, 1874 (Fed.Cir.2005). "A determination as to patent infringement is a two-step process. First, the court must construe the claims. Second, the court must compare the accused product or process to the properly construed claims. The first step is a question of law and the second step is a question of fact. Infringement may be found only where the accused product or process contains each limitation of the claim, either literally or under the doctrine of equivalents." *See also* ***JVW Enters. v. Interact Accessories, Inc.***, 424 F.3d 1324, 1329, 76 U.S.P.Q.2d 1641, 1644 (Fed.Cir.2005). *But see* ***Bard Peripheral Vascular, Inc. v. W.L. Gore & Assocs.***, 776 F.3d 837, 843-44, 113 U.S.P.Q.2d 1380, 1384 (Fed.Cir.2015), *overruled on other grounds*, ***Halo Elecs., Inc. v. Pulse Elecs., Inc.***, ___ U.S. ___, 136 S.Ct. 1923 (2016) (distinguishing between nunc pro tunc written agreements occurring before suit is filed and after suit is filed).

Frank's Casing Crew & Rental Tools, Inc. v. Weatherford Int'l, 389 F.3d 1370, 1376, 73 U.S.P.Q.2d 1065, 1068 (Fed.Cir.2004). "Infringement … either literal or by equivalents, is a question of fact."

Declaratory Judgment

MedImmune, Inc. v. Genentech, Inc., 549 U.S. 118, 127, 81 U.S.P.Q.2d 1225, 1229 (2007). For the case-or-controversy requirement, "[o]ur decisions have required that the dispute be 'definite and concrete, touching the legal relations of parties having adverse legal interests'; and that it be 'real and substantial' and 'admi[t] of specific relief through a decree of a conclusive character, as distinguished from an opinion advising what the law would be upon a hypothetical state of facts.' … 'Basically, the question in each case is whether the facts alleged, under all the circumstances, show that there is a substantial controversy, between parties having adverse legal interests, of sufficient immediacy and reality to warrant the issuance of a declaratory judgment.'"

Sandoz Inc. v. Amgen Inc., 773 F.3d 1274, 1277-78, 112 U.S.P.Q.2d 2004, 2006-07 (Fed.Cir.2014). "We have frequently applied ***MedImmune***'s 'all the circumstances' standard to determine, in the patent context, whether a declaratory-judgment plaintiff has presented a case of sufficient 'immediacy and reality.' The immediacy requirement is not concerned in the abstract with the amount of time that will occur between the filing of the declaratory judgment action and the liability-creating event. An event that is several years in the future may be an appropriate subject for a declaratory judgment. The immediacy requirement is concerned with whether there is an immediate impact on the plaintiff and whether the lapse of time creates uncertainty. The two issues—immediacy and reality—are thus related. [¶] We have assessed 'immediacy' by considering how far in the future the potential infringement is, whether the passage of time might eliminate or change any dispute, and how much if any harm the potential infringer is experiencing, at the time of suit, that an adjudication might redress. We have assessed 'reality' by examining any uncertainties about whether the plaintiff will take an action that will expose it to potential infringement liability and, if so, exactly what action. In short, we have focused on related questions of timing and contingency regarding the existence and content of any needed patent adjudication, as well as current concrete harms to the declaratory-judgment plaintiff from delaying an adjudication. [¶] Reflecting ***MedImmune***'s suggestion that justiciability problems can be described in terms of standing and ripeness, … we have said that standing and ripeness, as well as mootness, serve as helpful guides in applying the all-the-circumstances test because satisfying these doctrines represents the absolute constitutional minimum for a justiciable controversy under [U.S. Const. art. 3]. Here, ripeness principles in particular reinforce the importance of contingency in the analysis. A claim is not ripe for adjudication if it rests upon contingent future events that may not occur as anticipated, or indeed may not occur at all. More broadly, a ripeness analysis considers whether further factual development would significantly advance the court's ability to deal with the legal issues presented, … and whether the complained-of conduct has an 'immediate and substantial impact' on the plaintiff…." (Internal quotes omitted.)

Streck, Inc. v. Research & Diagnostic Sys., 665 F.3d 1269, 1282, 101 U.S.P.Q.2d 1225, 1233 (Fed.Cir. 2012). "After ***MedImmune***, courts must look at 'all the circumstances' to determine whether a declaratory judgment plaintiff has shown a case or controversy between the parties. As this court has explained, moreover, although the Supreme Court rejected the reasonable apprehension of suit test as the *sole* test for jurisdiction, 'it did not completely do away with the relevance of a reasonable apprehension of suit.' Instead, in the wake of ***MedImmune***, 'proving a reasonable apprehension of suit is one of multiple ways that a declaratory judgment plaintiff can satisfy the more general all-the-circumstances test' to establish jurisdiction."

Arris Grp. v. British Telecomms., 639 F.3d 1368, 1374-75, 98 U.S.P.Q.2d 1812, 1816-17 (Fed.Cir.2011). "In the absence of a controversy as to a legal right, a mere adverse *economic* interest is insufficient to create declaratory judgment jurisdiction. Although economic injury alone is insufficient to create standing, we nonetheless conclude that [P] has standing based on other well-established standards. [¶] We have recognized that, where a patent holder accuses customers of direct infringement based on the sale or use of a supplier's equipment, the supplier has standing to commence a declaratory judgment action if (a) the supplier is obligated to indemnify its customers from infringement liability, or (b) there is a controversy between the patentee and the supplier as to the supplier's liability for induced or contributory infringement based on the alleged acts of direct infringement by its customers. Though there was no express indemnification agreement here, [P] contends it risks being held liable to [alleged infringer] for indemnification under Georgia's Uniform Commercial Code...."

SanDisk Corp. v. STMicroelectronics, Inc., 480 F.3d 1372, 1381, 82 U.S.P.Q.2d 1173, 1180 (Fed.Cir. 2007). "We hold only that where a patentee asserts rights under a patent based on certain identified ongoing or planned activity of another party, and where that party contends that it has the right to engage in the accused activity without license, [a U.S. Const.] art. 3 case or controversy will arise and the party need not risk a suit for infringement by engaging in the identified activity before seeking a declaration of its legal rights." *See also* ***Revolution Eyewear, Inc. v. Aspex Eyewear, Inc.***, 556 F.3d 1294, 1300, 89 U.S.P.Q.2d 1885, 1888 (Fed.Cir.2009) (covenant not to sue did not divest court of jurisdiction to hear declaratory-judgment claim where covenant only covered previous, not future, conduct). *But see* ***Benitec Australia, Ltd. v. Nucleonics, Inc.***, 495 F.3d 1340, 1345-48, 83 U.S.P.Q.2d 1449, 1453-55 (Fed.Cir.2007) (covenant not to sue and lack of immediate threat of infringement divest court of jurisdiction to hear declaratory-judgment claim).

Schinzing v. Mid-States Stainless, Inc., 415 F.3d 807, 813, 75 U.S.P.Q.2d 1693, 1698 (8th Cir.2005). "A claim for a declaration of non-infringement makes a counterclaim for patent infringement compulsory. A party that does not assert a compulsory counterclaim waives its right to bring the counterclaim and is forever barred from asserting that claim in future litigation. The burden is always on the patent holder to show infringement."

Claim Construction—Generally

Teva Pharms. USA, Inc. v. Sandoz, Inc., ___ U.S. ___, 135 S.Ct. 831, 837, 113 U.S.P.Q.2d 1269, 1273-74 (2015). "Should a jury or a judge construe patent claims? [C]laim construction falls 'exclusively within the province of the court,' not that of the jury. *At U.S. ___, S.Ct. 841, U.S.P.Q2d 1277:* [T]he question we have answered here concerns review of the district court's resolution of a subsidiary factual dispute that helps that court determine the proper interpretation of the written patent claim. The district judge, after deciding the factual dispute, will then interpret the patent claim in light of the facts as he has found them. This ultimate interpretation is a legal conclusion. The appellate court can still review the district court's ultimate construction of the claim *de novo*. But, to overturn the judge's resolution of an underlying factual dispute, the Court of Appeals must find that the judge, in respect to those factual findings, has made a clear error." *See also* ***In re Papst Licensing Digital Camera Patent Litig.***, 778 F.3d 1255, 1261, 113 U.S.P.Q.2d 1533, 1537-38 (Fed.Cir. 2015).

Markman v. Westview Instrs., Inc., 517 U.S. 370, 372, 38 U.S.P.Q.2d 1461, 1463 (1996). "We hold that the construction of a patent, including terms of art within its claim, is exclusively within the province of the court. *At U.S. 374, U.S.P.Q.2d 1464:* Victory in an infringement suit requires a finding that the patent claim 'covers the alleged infringer's product or process,' which in turn necessitates a determination of 'what the words in the claim mean.'"

MasterMine Software, Inc. v. Microsoft Corp., 874 F.3d 1307, 1311 n.2, 124 U.S.P.Q.2d 1618, 1621 n.2 (Fed.Cir.2017). "We have often held that the meaning of claim terms in one patent can be informed by statements made during prosecution of other patents in the same family. We have explained, for example, that 'past and future prosecution of related patents may be relevant to the construction of a given claim term.'"

In re CBS-Sys. Int'l, 832 F.3d 1335, 1341 (Fed.Cir. 2016). "When a patent expires during a reexamination proceeding, the PTO should thereafter apply the ***Phillips*** standard for claim construction."

CardSoft, LLC v. VeriFone, Inc., 807 F.3d 1346, 1350, 117 U.S.P.Q.2d 1354, 1356 (Fed.Cir.2015). "[I]t is not enough that the district court may have heard extrinsic evidence during a claim construction proceeding—rather, the district court must have actually made a factual finding in order to trigger ***Teva***'s deferential review. And even then, we may nevertheless review the district court's constructions de novo if the intrinsic record fully determines the proper scope of the disputed claim terms."

Aventis Pharma S.A. v. Hospira, Inc., 675 F.3d 1324, 1330, 102 U.S.P.Q.2d 1445, 1448 (Fed.Cir.2012). "[W]e explained that we will only interpret a claim term more narrowly than its ordinary meaning under two circumstances: (1) when a patentee sets out a definition and acts as its own lexicographer, or (2) when the patentee disavows the full scope of a claim term either in the specification or during prosecution. [¶] To act as its own lexicographer, a patentee must clearly set forth a definition of the disputed claim term other than its plain and ordinary meaning. In other words, the patentee must clearly express an intent to redefine the term. This clear expression need not be in *haec verba* but may be inferred from clear limiting descriptions of the invention in the specification or prosecution history. Similarly, to disavow claim scope, the patentee may demonstrate intent to deviate from the ordinary and accustomed meaning of a claim term by including in the specification expressions of manifest exclusion or restriction, representing a clear disavowal of claim scope. Moreover, it is not enough that the only embodiments, or all of the embodiments, contain a particular limitation to limit a claim term beyond its ordinary meaning." (Internal quotes omitted.)

ERBE Elektromedizin GmbH v. Canady Tech., 629 F.3d 1278, 1286, 97 U.S.P.Q.2d 1048, 1054-55 (Fed. Cir.2010). "Generally, '[a]ll the limitations of a claim must be considered meaningful.' However, 'no canon of [claim] construction is absolute in its application.' Claim differentiation may be helpful in some cases, but it is just one of many tools used by courts in the analysis of claim terms. Similarly, surplusage may exist in some claims. As we have stated, '[a]ll rules of construction must be understood in terms of the factual situations that produced them, and applied in fidelity to their origins.'"

Abbott Labs. v. Sandoz, Inc., 566 F.3d 1282, 1293, 90 U.S.P.Q.2d 1769, 1777 (Fed.Cir.2009). "[B]ased on Supreme Court precedent and the treatment of product-by-process claims throughout the years by the PTO and other binding court decisions, this court now restates that 'process terms in product-by-process claims serve as limitations in determining infringement.' [T]his holding follows this court's clear statement in ***In re Thorpe***[, 777 F.2d 695 (Fed.Cir.1985),] that 'product by process claims are limited by and defined by the process.'"

ICU Med., Inc. v. Alaris Med. Sys., 558 F.3d 1368, 1375, 90 U.S.P.Q.2d 1072, 1076 (Fed.Cir.2009). "[I]t is 'entirely proper to consider the functions of an invention in seeking to determine the meaning of particular claim language.'"

Abbott Labs. v. Sandoz, Inc., 544 F.3d 1341, 1360, 89 U.S.P.Q.2d 1161, 1177 (Fed.Cir.2008). "[C]laim construction often calls upon words other than those of the patent, lest the claim simply define itself. 'Claim construction' is for the purpose of explaining and defining terms in the claims, and usually requires use of words other than the words that are being defined."

Praxair, Inc. v. ATMI, Inc., 543 F.3d 1306, 1319, 88 U.S.P.Q.2d 1705, 1714 (Fed.Cir.2008). "Indefiniteness is a matter of claim construction, and the same principles that generally govern claim construction are applicable to determining whether allegedly indefinite claim language is subject to construction."

Elbex Video, Ltd. v. Sensormatic Elecs. Corp., 508 F.3d 1366, 1373, 85 U.S.P.Q.2d 1137, 1142 (Fed.Cir. 2007). "For a prosecution statement to prevail over the plain language of the claim, the statement must be clear and unmistakable such that the public should be entitled to rely on any 'definitive statements made during prosecution.'"

In re Translogic Tech., 504 F.3d 1249, 1256, 84 U.S.P.Q.2d 1929, 1934 (Fed.Cir.2007). "'[D]uring examination proceedings, claims are given their broadest reasonable interpretation consistent with the specification.'"

Pfizer, Inc. v. Ranbaxy Labs., 457 F.3d 1284, 1290, 79 U.S.P.Q.2d 1583, 1588 (Fed.Cir.2006). "[W]e agree with the district court's conclusion that the statements made during prosecution of foreign counterparts to ... patent are irrelevant to claim construction because they were made in response to patentability requirements unique to [foreign] law."

On Demand Mach. Corp. v. Ingram Indus., 442 F.3d 1331, 1337-38, 78 U.S.P.Q.2d 1428, 1432 (Fed.Cir. 2006). "This court in ***Phillips*** emphasized that the proper judicial construction of a claim and its terms is from the viewpoint of a person of ordinary skill in the field of the invention; the court must determine how such a person would understand the claim in the context of the particular technology and the description in the specification, with due reference to the prosecution history. Thus the court in ***Phillips***, resolving conflict, stressed the dominance of the specification in understanding the scope and defining the limits of the terms used in the claim. *At F.3d 1340, U.S.P.Q.2d 1434:* [W]hen the scope of the invention is clearly stated in the specification, and is described as the advantage and distinction of the invention, it is not necessary to disavow explicitly a different scope. [¶] In ***Phillips*** the *en banc* court explained that the role of the specification is to describe and enable the invention. In turn, the claims cannot be of broader scope than the invention that is set forth in the specification."

Wilson Sporting Goods Co. v. Hillerich & Bradsby Co., 442 F.3d 1322, 1330-31, 78 U.S.P.Q.2d 1382, 1389 (Fed.Cir.2006). "This court ... repeats its rule 'that claims may not be construed with reference to the accused device.' [T]hat rule posits that a court may not use the accused product or process as a form of extrinsic evidence to supply limitations for patent claim language. Thus, the rule forbids a court from tailoring a claim construction to fit the dimensions of the accused product or process and to reach a preconceived judgment of infringement or noninfringement. In other words, it forbids biasing the claim construction process to exclude or include specific features of the accused product or process. The rule, however, does not forbid awareness of the accused product or process to supply the parameters and scope of the infringement analysis, including its claim construction component. In other words, the 'reference' rule ... does not forbid any glimpse of the accused product or process during or before claim construction. In light of these principles, if the litigants cannot themselves inform a trial court of the specific issues presented by the infringement inquiry—that is, issues of the breadth of the claim construction analysis and the most useful terms to facilitate that defining process—then a trial court may refer to the accused product or process for that context during the process."

Nystrom v. TREX Co., 424 F.3d 1136, 1145, 76 U.S.P.Q.2d 1481, 1488 (Fed.Cir.2005). "What ***Phillips*** now counsels is that in the absence of something in the written description and/or prosecution history to provide explicit or implicit notice to the public—i.e., those of ordinary skill in the art—that the inventor intended a disputed term to cover more than the ordinary and customary meaning revealed by the context of the intrinsic record, it is improper to read the term to encompass a broader definition simply because it may be found in a dictionary, treatise, or other extrinsic source."

Phillips v. AWH Corp., 415 F.3d 1303, 1313, 75 U.S.P.Q.2d 1321, 1326 (Fed.Cir.2005). "[T]he person of ordinary skill in the art is deemed to read the claim term not only in the context of the particular claim in which the disputed term appears, but in the context of the entire patent, including the specification. *At F.3d 1314, U.S.P.Q.2d 1327:* Because the meaning of a claim term as understood by persons of skill in the art is often not immediately apparent, and because patentees frequently use terms idiosyncratically, the court looks to 'those sources available to the public that show what a person of skill in the art would have understood disputed claim language to mean.' Those sources include 'the words of the claims themselves, the remainder of the specification, the prosecution history, and extrinsic evidence concerning relevant scientific principles, the meaning of technical terms, and the state of the art.' [¶] [T]he claims themselves provide substantial guidance as to the meaning of particular claim terms. [¶] To begin with, the context in which a term is used in the asserted claim can be highly instructive. [¶] Other claims of the patent in question, both asserted and unasserted, can also be valuable sources of enlightenment as to the meaning of a claim term. Because claim terms are normally used consistently throughout the patent, the usage of a term in one claim can often illuminate the meaning of the same term in other claims. Differences among claims can also be a useful guide in understanding the meaning of particular claim terms. *At F.3d 1315:* The claims ... are part of 'a fully integrated written instrument,' consisting principally of a specification that concludes with the claims. For that reason, claims 'must be read in view of the specification, of which they are a part.' *At U.S.P.Q.2d 1328:* '[T]he best source for understanding a technical term is the specification from which it arose, informed, as needed, by the prosecution history.' *At F.3d 1316, U.S.P.Q.2d 1329:* [T]he specification may reveal a special definition given to a claim term by the patentee that differs from the meaning it would otherwise possess. In such cases, the inventor's lexicography governs. In other cases, the specification may reveal an intentional disclaimer, or disavowal, of claim scope by the inventor. In that instance as well, the inventor has dictated the correct claim scope, and the inventor's intention, as expressed in the specification, is regarded as dispositive. *At F.3d 1317:* It is therefore entirely appropriate for a court, when conducting claim construction, to rely heavily on the written description for guidance as to the meaning of the claims. [¶] In addition to consulting the specification, we have held that a court 'should also consider the patent's prosecution history, if it is in evidence.' The prosecution history, which we have designated as part of the 'intrinsic evidence,' consists of the complete record of the proceedings before the PTO and includes the prior art cited during the examination of the patent. [B]ecause the prosecution history represents an ongoing negotiation between the PTO and the applicant, rather than the final product of that negotiation, it often lacks the clarity of the specification and thus is less useful for claim construction purposes. Nonetheless, the prosecution history can often inform the meaning of the claim language by demonstrating how the inventor understood the invention and whether the inventor limited the invention in the course of prosecution, making the claim scope narrower than it would otherwise be. [¶] Although we have emphasized the importance of intrinsic evidence in claim construction, we have also authorized district courts to rely on extrinsic evidence, which 'consists of all evidence external to the patent and prosecution history, including expert and inventor testimony, dictionaries, and learned treatises.' *At F.3d 1319, U.S.P.Q.2d 1331:* [E]xtrinsic evidence may be useful to the court, but it is unlikely to result in a reliable interpretation of patent claim scope unless considered in the context of the intrinsic evidence. Nonetheless, because extrinsic evidence can help educate the court regarding the field of the invention and can help the court determine what a person of ordinary skill in the art would understand claim terms to mean, it is permissible for the district court in its sound discretion to admit and use such evidence. In exercising that discretion, and in weighing all the evidence bearing on claim construction, the court should keep in mind the flaws inherent in each type of evidence and assess that evidence accordingly. *At F.3d 1321, U.S.P.Q.2d 1332:* [H]eavy reliance on the dictionary divorced from the intrinsic evidence risks transforming the meaning of the claim term to the artisan into the meaning of the term in the abstract, out of its particular context, which is the specification." *See also* ***Vitronics Corp. v. Conceptronic, Inc.***, 90 F.3d 1576, 1582, 39 U.S.P.Q.2d 1573, 1576 (Fed.Cir.1996).

Irdeto Access, Inc. v. Echostar Satellite Corp., 383 F.3d 1295, 1300, 72 U.S.P.Q.2d 1678, 1682 (Fed.Cir. 2004). "[W]here evidence such as expert testimony or technical dictionaries demonstrates that artisans would attach a special meaning to a claim term or would attach no meaning at all to the claim term independent of the specification 'general-usage dictionaries are rendered irrelevant with respect to that term....' '[A] general-usage dictionary cannot overcome credible art-specific evidence of the meaning or lack of meaning of a claim term.'"

Ex parte Schulhauser, ___ U.S.P.Q.2d ___ (PTAB 2016) (No. 2013-007847; 4-28-16). "The broadest reasonable interpretation of a system claim having structure that performs a function, which only needs to occur if a condition precedent is met, still requires structure for performing the function should the condition occur. This interpretation of the system claim differs from the method claim because the structure (i.e., a processor programmed to perform an algorithm for carrying out the recited function should the recited condition be met) *is present in the system regardless* of whether the condition is met and the function is actually performed."

Claim Construction—Grammar & Syntax

Multilayer Stretch Cling Film Holdings, Inc. v. Berry Plastics Corp., 831 F.3d 1350, 1358, 119 U.S.P.Q.2d 1773, 1780 (Fed.Cir.2016). "'[C]onsisting of,' is a term of art in patent law with a distinct and well-established meaning. Use of the transitional phrase 'consisting of' to set off a patent claim element creates a very strong presumption that that claim element is 'closed' and therefore excludes any elements, steps, or ingredients not specified in the claim. 'Consisting of' is a term of patent convention meaning that the claimed invention contains only what is expressly set forth in the claim. Thus, if a patent claim recites a member selected from the group consisting of A, B, and C, the 'member' is presumed to be closed to alternative ingredients D, E, and F. By contrast, the alternative transitional term 'comprising' creates a presumption that the recited elements are only a part of the device, that the claim does not exclude additional, unrecited elements. *At F.3d 1359:* But to overcome the exceptionally strong presumption that a claim term set off with 'consisting of' is closed to unrecited elements, the specification and prosecution history must unmistakably manifest an alternative meaning." (Internal quotes omitted.)

Harari v. Lee, 656 F.3d 1331, 1341, 100 U.S.P.Q.2d 1052, 1059 (Fed.Cir.2011). "***Baldwin*** [***Graphic Sys. v. Siebert, Inc.***, 512 F.3d 1338 (Fed.Cir.2008),] does not set a hard and fast rule that 'a' always means one or more than one. Instead, we read the limitation in light of the claim and specification to discern its meaning. When the claim language and specification indicate that 'a' means one and only one, it is appropriate to construe it as such even in the context of an open-ended 'comprising' claim."

Baldwin Graphic Sys. v. Siebert, Inc., 512 F.3d 1338, 1342-43, 85 U.S.P.Q.2d 1503, 1507 (Fed.Cir.2008). "This court has repeatedly emphasized that an indefinite article 'a' or 'an' in patent parlance carries the meaning of 'one or more' in open-ended claims containing the transitional phrase 'comprising.' That 'a' or 'an' can mean 'one or more' is best described as a rule, rather than merely as a presumption or even a convention. The exceptions to this rule are extremely limited: a patentee must 'evince[] a clear intent' to limit 'a' or 'an' to 'one.' The subsequent use of definite articles 'the' or 'said' in a claim to refer back to the same claim term does not change the general plural rule, but simply reinvokes that non-singular meaning. An exception to the general rule that 'a' or 'an' means more than one only arises where the language of the claims themselves, the specification, or the prosecution history necessitate a departure from the rule."

Dippin' Dots, Inc. v. Mosey, 476 F.3d 1337, 1343, 81 U.S.P.Q.2d 1633, 1637 (Fed.Cir.2007). "[W]e acknowledge that [claim] term 'comprising' raises a presumption that the list of elements is nonexclusive. However, 'comprising' is not a weasel word with which to abrogate claim limitations. 'Comprising' appears at the beginning of the claim—'comprising the steps of'—and indicates here that an infringing process could practice other steps in addition to the ones mentioned. Those six enumerated steps must, however, all be practiced as recited in the claim for a process to infringe. The presumption raised by the term 'comprising' does not reach into each of the six steps to render every word and phrase therein open-ended—especially where, as here, the patentee has narrowly defined the claim term it now seeks to have broadened." (Internal quotes omitted.) *See also* ***SanDisk Corp. v. Memorex Prods.***, 415 F.3d 1278, 1284, 75 U.S.P.Q.2d 1475, 1480 (Fed.Cir.2005).

Claim Construction—Claim Differentiation

ICU Med., Inc. v. Alaris Med. Sys., 558 F.3d 1368, 1376, 90 U.S.P.Q.2d 1072, 1076 (Fed.Cir.2009). "[C]laim differentiation ... is not a rigid rule but rather is one of several claim construction tools."

Curtiss-Wright Flow Control Corp. v. Velan, Inc., 438 F.3d 1374, 1379-80, 77 U.S.P.Q.2d 1988, 1993-94 (Fed.Cir.2006). "In the most specific sense, 'claim differentiation' refers to the presumption that an independent claim should not be construed as requiring a limitation added by a dependent claim. Thus, the claim differentiation tool works best in the relationship between independent and dependent claims. Indeed [35 U.S.C. §112, ¶4] stresses that a dependent claim must add a limitation to those recited in the independent claim. Thus, reading an additional limitation from a dependent claim into an independent claim would not only make that additional limitation superfluous, it might render the dependent claim invalid. [¶] Beyond the independent/dependent claim scenario, this court has characterized claim differentiation more generally, i.e., as the 'presumption that each claim in a patent has a different scope.' Different claims with different words can, of course, define different subject matter within the ambit of the invention. On the other hand, claim drafters can also use different terms to define the exact same subject matter. Indeed this court has acknowledged that two claims with different terminology can define the exact same subject matter. *At F.3d 1381:* With those precedents in mind, this court observes that two considerations generally govern this claim construction tool when applied to two independent claims: (1) claim differentiation takes on relevance in the context of a claim construction that would render additional, or different, language in another independent claim superfluous; and (2) claim differentiation 'can not broaden claims beyond their correct scope.'"

Claim Construction—Disclaimer

TriVascular, Inc. v. Samuels, 812 F.3d 1056, 1063-64, 117 U.S.P.Q.2d 1802, 1807 (Fed.Cir.2016). "The same general tenets that apply to prosecution history estoppel apply to prosecution history disclaimer. Both doctrines require that the claims of a patent be interpreted in light of the proceedings in the PTO during the application process. As applied to a disclaimer analysis, the prosecution history can often inform the meaning of the claim language by demonstrating how the inventor understood the invention. Any explanation, elaboration, or qualification presented by the inventor during patent examination is relevant, for the role of claim construction is to capture the scope of the actual invention that is disclosed, described, and patented. Accordingly, disclaimer ensures that claims are interpreted by reference to those that have been cancelled or rejected. The party seeking to invoke prosecution history disclaimer bears the burden of proving the existence of a clear and unmistakable disclaimer that would have been evident to one skilled in the art." (Internal quotes omitted.)

Computer Docking Station Corp. v. Dell, Inc., 519 F.3d 1366, 1374-75, 86 U.S.P.Q.2d 1129, 1134 (Fed. Cir.2008). "Statements made during prosecution may also affect the scope of the claims. Specifically, a patentee may limit the meaning of a claim term by making a clear and unmistakable disavowal of scope during prosecution. A patentee could do so, for example, by clearly characterizing the invention in a way to try to overcome rejections based on prior art. The doctrine of prosecution disclaimer protects the public's reliance on definitive statements made during prosecution by precluding patentees from recapturing through claim interpretation specific meanings clearly and unmistakably disclaimed during prosecution. Claims should not be construed one way in order to obtain their allowance and in a different way against accused infringers. [¶] Prosecution disclaimer does not apply to an ambiguous disavowal. Prosecution disclaimer does not apply, for example, if the applicant simply describes features of the prior art and does not distinguish the claimed invention based on those features. And if the specification expressly defines a claim term and remarks made to distinguish claims from the prior art are broader than necessary to distinguish the prior art, the full breadth of the remark is not a clear and unambiguous disavowal of claim scope as required to depart from the meaning of the term provided in the written description." (Internal quotes omitted.)

Ormco Corp. v. Align Tech., 498 F.3d 1307, 1314, 84 U.S.P.Q.2d 1146, 1151 (Fed.Cir.2007). "When the application of prosecution disclaimer involves statements from prosecution of a familial patent relating to the same subject matter as the claim language at issue in the patent being construed, those statements in the familial application are relevant in construing the claims at issue."

MBO Labs. v. Becton, Dickinson & Co., 474 F.3d 1323, 1332 n.3, 81 U.S.P.Q.2d 1661, 1668 n.3 (Fed.Cir. 2007). "[T]he recapture rule may ... properly factor into claim construction. In a case where the available techniques of construction yield two possible interpretations of a reissue claim, only one of which includes previously surrendered matter, it would be correct to resolve the ambiguity by selecting the interpretation not barred by the recapture rule."

Ventana Med. Sys. v. Biogenex Labs., 473 F.3d 1173, 1182, 81 U.S.P.Q.2d 1314, 1320 (Fed.Cir.2006). "[T]he doctrine of prosecution disclaimer generally does not apply when the claim term in the descendant patent uses different language."

Sorensen v. ITC, 427 F.3d 1375, 1378-79, 77 U.S.P.Q.2d 1083, 1085 (Fed.Cir.2005). "During prosecution, a patent applicant may consistently and clearly use a term in a manner either more or less expansive than it is used in the relevant art, thereby expanding or limiting the scope of the term in the context of the patent claims. However, in order to disavow claim scope, a patent applicant must clearly and unambiguously express surrender of subject matter during prosecution."

SanDisk Corp. v. Memorex Prods., 415 F.3d 1278, 1286, 75 U.S.P.Q.2d 1475, 1482 (Fed.Cir.2005). "When the patentee makes clear and unmistakable prosecution arguments limiting the meaning of a claim term in order to overcome a rejection, the courts limit the relevant claim term to exclude the disclaimed matter. *At F.3d 1287:* An ambiguous disclaimer, however, does not advance the patent's notice function or justify public reliance, and the court will not use it to limit a claim term's ordinary meaning. There is no 'clear and unmistakable' disclaimer if a prosecution argument is subject to more than one reasonable interpretation, one of which is consistent with a proffered meaning of the disputed term." *See also* ***Omega Eng'g v. Raytek Corp.***, 334 F.3d 1314, 1324, 67 U.S.P.Q.2d 1321, 1327

(Fed.Cir.2003) (declining to apply doctrine of prosecution disclaimer where alleged disavowal of claim scope was ambiguous).

Claim Construction—§112, ¶6/§112(e) Issues

Williamson v. Citrix Online, LLC, 792 F.3d 1339, 1348, 115 U.S.P.Q.2d 1105, 1110 (Fed.Cir.2015). "To determine whether [35 U.S.C.] §112, ¶6 applies to a claim limitation, our precedent has long recognized the importance of the presence or absence of the word 'means.' [T]he use of the word 'means' in a claim element creates a rebuttable presumption that §112, ¶6 applies. Applying the converse, ... the failure to use the word 'means' also creates a rebuttable presumption—this time that §112, ¶6 does not apply. *At F.3d 1349, U.S.P.Q.2d 1111:* Our consideration of this case has led us to conclude that ... a heightened burden is unjustified and that we should abandon characterizing as 'strong' the presumption that a limitation lacking the word 'means' is not subject to §112, ¶6. [¶] The standard is whether the words of the claim are understood by persons of ordinary skill in the art to have a sufficiently definite meaning as the name for structure. When a claim term lacks the word 'means,' the presumption can be overcome and §112, ¶6 will apply if the challenger demonstrates that the claim term fails to recite sufficiently definite structure or else recites function without reciting sufficient structure for performing that function. The converse presumption remains unaffected: use of the word 'means' creates a presumption that §112, ¶6 applies." (Internal quotes omitted.)

Massachusetts Inst. of Tech. & Elecs. for Imaging, Inc. v. Abacus Software, 462 F.3d 1344, 1354, 80 U.S.P.Q.2d 1225, 1231 (Fed.Cir.2006). "The generic terms 'mechanism,' 'means,' 'element,' and 'device,' typically do not connote sufficiently definite structure. *At F.3d 1356, U.S.P.Q.2d 1233:* [I]n considering whether a claim term recites sufficient structure to avoid application of [35 U.S.C.] §112 ¶6, we have not required the claim term to denote a specific structure. Instead, we have held that it is sufficient if the claim term is used in common parlance or by persons of skill in the pertinent art to designate structure, even if the term covers a broad class of structures and even if the term identifies the structures by their function." (Internal quotes omitted.)

JVW Enters. v. Interact Accessories, Inc., 424 F.3d 1324, 1331, 76 U.S.P.Q.2d 1641, 1646 (Fed.Cir. 2005). "[A] court may not construe a means-plus-function limitation 'by adopting a function different from that explicitly recited in the claim.' *At F.3d 1333, U.S.P.Q.2d 1647:* 'Literal infringement of a [35 U.S.C.] §112, ¶6 limitation requires that the relevant structure in the accused device perform the identical function recited in the claim and be identical or equivalent' to the structure identified in the written description as corresponding to the recited function. For the relevant structure in the accused device to be equivalent to the structure in the written description, differences between the two must be insubstantial. For example, the structure in the accused device must perform the claimed function in substantially the same way to achieve substantially the same result as the structure in the written description."

Harris Corp. v. Ericsson Inc., 417 F.3d 1241, 1253, 75 U.S.P.Q.2d 1705, 1714 (Fed.Cir.2005). "A computer-implemented means-plus-function term is limited to the corresponding structure disclosed in the specification and equivalents thereof, and the corresponding structure is the algorithm. *At F.3d 1254:* [P]recedent establishes that corresponding structure of [term at issue] cannot be merely a 'symbol processor,' as the district court held. The 'symbol processor' construction does not incorporate any disclosed algorithm."

Default Proof Credit Card Sys. v. Home Depot, Inc., 412 F.3d 1291, 1301, 75 U.S.P.Q.2d 1116, 1123 (Fed. Cir.2005). "[M]aterial incorporated by reference cannot provide the corresponding structure necessary to satisfy the definiteness requirement for a means-plus-function clause. The inquiry under [35 U.S.C.] §112, ¶2, does not turn on whether a patentee has 'incorporated by reference' material into the specification relating to structure, but instead asks first 'whether structure is described in the specification, and, if so, whether one skilled in the art would identify the structure from that description.'"

Apex Inc. v. Raritan Computer, Inc., 325 F.3d 1364, 1371-72, 66 U.S.P.Q.2d 1444, 1450 (Fed.Cir.2003). "It is well settled that a claim limitation that actually uses the word 'means' invokes a rebuttable presumption that [35 U.S.C.] §112, ¶6 applies. By contrast, a claim term that does not use 'means' will trigger the rebuttable presumption that §112, ¶6 does not apply. [T]he term 'means' is central to the analysis. [¶] From a procedural standpoint, this presumption imposes on [D] the burden of going forward with evidence to rebut ... the presumption, but does not shift to such party the burden of proof in the sense of the risk of nonpersuasion, which remains throughout the trial upon the party on whom it was originally cast. [D] can rebut this presumption if it demonstrates that the claim term fails to recite sufficiently definite structure or else recites a function without reciting sufficient structure for performing that function. This burden must be met by a preponderance of the evidence. If the party who must bring forth evidence fails to proffer sufficient evidence to meet its burden, the presumption, either for or against the application of §112, ¶6, prevails." (Internal quotes omitted.) *See also* ***CCS Fitness, Inc. v. Brunswick Corp.***, 288 F.3d 1359, 1369, 62 U.S.P.Q.2d 1658, 1664-65 (Fed.Cir.2002).

Northrop Grumman Corp. v. Intel Corp., 325 F.3d 1346, 1352, 66 U.S.P.Q.2d 1341, 1345 (Fed.Cir.2003). "A court may not import into the claim features that are unnecessary to perform the claimed function. Features that do not perform the recited function do not constitute corresponding structure and thus do not serve as claim limitations."

Cardiac Pacemakers, Inc. v. St. Jude Med., Inc., 296 F.3d 1106, 1113-14, 63 U.S.P.Q.2d 1725, 1730 (Fed. Cir.2002). "Construction of a means-plus-function limitation involves two steps. First, the court must identify the claimed function. The court must construe the function of a means-plus-function limitation to include the limitations contained in the claim language, and only those limitations. It is improper to narrow the scope of the function beyond the claim language. It is equally improper to broaden the scope of the claimed function by ignoring clear limitations in the claim language. Ordinary principles of claim construction govern interpretation of the claim language used to describe the function. [¶] After identifying the claimed function, the court must then determine what structure, if any, disclosed in the specification corresponds to the claimed function. In order to qualify as corresponding, the structure must not only perform the claimed function, but the specification must clearly associate the structure with performance of the function. This inquiry is undertaken from the perspective of a person of ordinary skill in the art. Alternative embodiments may disclose different corresponding structure, and the claim is valid even if only one embodiment discloses corresponding structure. If, however, this inquiry reveals that no embodiment discloses corresponding structure, the claim is invalid for failure to satisfy the definiteness requirement of [35 U.S.C.] §112, ¶2." *See also* ***Callicrate v. Wadsworth Mfg.***, 427 F.3d 1361, 1368, 77 U.S.P.Q.2d 1041, 1047 (Fed.Cir. 2005); ***Altiris, Inc. v. Symantec Corp.***, 318 F.3d 1363, 1375, 65 U.S.P.Q.2d 1865, 1874 (Fed.Cir.2003); ***Texas Digital Sys. v. Telegenix, Inc.***, 308 F.3d 1193, 1208, 64 U.S.P.Q.2d 1812, 1822 (Fed.Cir.2002), *overruled on other grounds*, ***Phillips v. AWH Corp.***, 415 F.3d 1303, 75 U.S.P.Q.2d 1321 (Fed.Cir.2005).

Interactive Pictures Corp. v. Infinite Pictures, Inc., 274 F.3d 1371, 1381-82, 61 U.S.P.Q.2d 1152, 1160 (Fed.Cir.2001). "[W]e [have] held that a finding that a component of an accused product is not a structure 'equivalent' to the corresponding structure of a means-plus-function limitation for purposes of literal infringement analysis precludes a finding that the same *structure* is equivalent for purposes of the doctrine of equivalents, unless the component constitutes technology arising after the issuance of the patent. However, when a finding of noninfringement under 35 U.S.C. §112, ¶6, is premised on an absence of identical *function*, then infringement under the doctrine of equivalents is not thereby automatically precluded. That is because infringement under the doctrine of equivalents may be premised on the accused and the patented component having *substantially* the same function, whereas structure corresponding to the disclosed limitation in a means-plus-function clause must perform the *identical* function." *See also* ***Lockheed Martin Corp. v. Space Sys./Loral, Inc.***, 324 F.3d 1308, 1320, 66 U.S.P.Q.2d 1282, 1291 (Fed.Cir.2003).

Chiuminatta Concrete Concepts, Inc. v. Cardinal Indus., 145 F.3d 1303, 1308, 46 U.S.P.Q.2d 1752, 1755-56 (Fed.Cir.1998). "'To determine whether a claim limitation is met literally, where expressed as a means for performing a stated function, the court must compare the accused structure *with the disclosed structure*, and must find equivalent *structure* as well as *identity* of claimed *function* for that structure.' A determination of the claimed function, being a matter of construction of specific terms in the claim, is a question of law, reviewed *de novo*. Likewise, the 'means' term in a means-plus-function limitation is essentially a generic reference for the corresponding structure disclosed in the specification. Accordingly, a determination of corresponding structure is a determination of the meaning of the 'means' term in the claim and is thus also a matter of claim construction. *At F.3d 1309:* '[35 U.S.C.] §112, ¶6, rules out the possibility that any and every means which performs the function specified in the claim *literally* satisfies that limitation.' The proper test is whether the differences between the structure in the accused device and any disclosed in the specification are insubstantial."

Claim Construction—Preamble as a Limitation

Georgetown Rail Equip. Co. v. Holland L.P., 867 F.3d 1229, 1236, 123 U.S.P.Q.2d 1766, 1770 (Fed.Cir. 2017). "'Generally, the preamble does not limit the claims.' [¶] A preamble is not a claim limitation if the claim body 'defines a structurally complete invention ... and uses the preamble only to state a purpose or intended use for the invention.'"

Symantec Corp. v. Computer Assocs., 522 F.3d 1279, 1289, 86 U.S.P.Q.2d 1449, 1454 (Fed.Cir.2008). "Although [D] is correct that when construing terms in the body of a claim, the general assumption is that different terms have different meanings, ... the same generally is not true for terms in the preamble. The use of different language in the preamble than in the body of the claims does not suggest that the preamble imposes a limitation. Rather it is assumed that the preamble language is duplicative of the language found in the body of the claims or merely provides context for the claims, absent any indication to the contrary in the claims, the specification or the prosecution history."

Catalina Mktg. Int'l v. Coolsavings.com, Inc., 289 F.3d 801, 808-09, 62 U.S.P.Q.2d 1781, 1784-85 (Fed. Cir.2002). "In general, a preamble limits the invention if it recites essential structure or steps, or if it is 'necessary to give life, meaning, and vitality' to the claim. Conversely, a preamble is not limiting 'where a patentee defines a structurally complete invention in the claim body and uses the preamble only to state a purpose or intended use for the invention.' [¶] No litmus test defines when a preamble limits claim scope. Some guideposts, however, have emerged from various cases discussing the preamble's effect on claim scope. For example, this court has held that ***Jepson*** claiming generally indicates intent to use the preamble to define the claimed invention, thereby limiting claim scope. Additionally, dependence on a particular disputed preamble phrase for antecedent basis may limit claim scope because it indicates a reliance on both the preamble and claim body to define the claimed invention. Likewise, when the preamble is essential to understand limitations or terms in the claim body, the preamble limits claim scope. [¶] Further, when reciting additional structure or steps underscored as important by the specification, the preamble may operate as a claim limitation. [¶] [C]lear reliance on the preamble during prosecution to distinguish the claimed invention from the prior art transforms the preamble into a claim limitation because such reliance indicates use of the preamble to define, in part, the claimed invention. Without such reliance, however, a preamble generally is not limiting when the claim body describes a structurally complete invention such that deletion of the preamble phrase does not affect the structure or steps of the claimed invention. [¶] [P]reambles describing the use of an invention generally do not limit the claims because the patentability of apparatus or composition claims depends on the claimed structure, not on the use or purpose of that structure. [S]tatements of intended use or asserted benefits in the preamble may, in rare instances, limit apparatus claims, but only if the applicant clearly and unmistakably relied on those uses or benefits to distinguish prior art. Likewise, this principle does not mean that apparatus claims necessarily prevent a subsequent inventor from obtaining a patent on a new method of using the apparatus where that new method is useful and nonobvious."

Infringement—Burden of Proof

Medtronic, Inc. v. Mirowski Family Ventures, LLC, ___ U.S. ___, 134 S.Ct. 843, 846, 109 U.S.P.Q.2d 1341, 1343 (2014). "We hold that, when a licensee seeks a declaratory judgment against a patentee to establish that there is no infringement, the burden of proving infringement remains with the patentee. We reverse the Federal Circuit's determination to the contrary."

Centricut L.L.C. v. Esab Grp., 390 F.3d 1361, 1367, 73 U.S.P.Q.2d 1135, 1139 (Fed.Cir.2004). "The patentee has the burden of proving infringement by a preponderance of the evidence. *At F.3d 1370, U.S.P.Q.2d 1141:* [I]n a case involving complex technology, where the accused infringer offers expert testimony negating infringement, the patentee cannot satisfy its burden of proof by relying only on testimony from those who are admittedly not expert in the field."

Infringement—Standard of Review

Uniloc USA, Inc. v. Microsoft Corp., 632 F.3d 1292, 1301-02, 98 U.S.P.Q.2d 1203, 1211-12 (Fed.Cir. 2011). "[D] argues that because there is no dispute about how the accused products work, infringement should be reviewed de novo. It is well-settled that infringement is a factual issue, reviewed for substantial evidence. The cases cited by [D] involve a procedural posture not present in this case. [T]he infringement issue in ***General Mills*[*, Inc. v. Hunt-Wesson, Inc.*,** 103 F.3d 978 (Fed.Cir.1997),] collapsed into claim construction because 'the parties agreed with each other and the district court about how each of two competing claim constructions would apply to the undisputed structure of the accused invention.' In other words, the parties conceded that under one claim construction there was infringement and under the other there was none, and were arguing only over which claim construction was appropriate. [T]his case presents the opposite procedural posture; the claim construction itself is not contested, but the application of that claim construction to the accused device is. Thus, this court applies the traditional rule for review of jury verdicts of factual issues [for substantial evidence]."

Doctrine of Equivalents—Generally

Warner-Jenkinson Co. v. Hilton Davis Chem. Co., 520 U.S. 17, 21, 41 U.S.P.Q.2d 1865, 1868 (1997). "Under [the doctrine of equivalents], a product or process that does not literally infringe upon the express terms of a patent claim may nonetheless be found to infringe if there is 'equivalence' between the elements of the accused product or process and the claimed elements of the patented invention. *At U.S. 29, U.S.P.Q.2d 1871:* Each element contained in a patent claim is deemed material to defining the scope of the patented invention, and thus the doctrine of equivalents must be applied to individual elements of the claim, not to the invention as a whole. It is important to ensure that the application of the doctrine, even as to an individual element, is not allowed such broad play as to effectively eliminate that element in its entirety. *At U.S. 39, U.S.P.Q.2d 1875-76:* [The] 'triple identity' test [used to determine equivalence focuses] on the *function* served by a particular claim element, the *way* that element serves that function, and the *result* thus obtained by that element.... *At U.S. 40:* [T]he test [must be] probative of the essential inquiry: Does the accused product or process contain elements identical or equivalent to each claimed element of the patented invention? ... An analysis of the role played by each element in the context of the specific patent claim will thus inform the inquiry as to whether a substitute element matches the function, way, and result of the claimed element, or whether the substitute element plays a role substantially different from the claimed element. ... We expect that the Federal Circuit will refine the formulation of the test for equivalence in the orderly course of case-by-case determinations.... [¶] The determination of equivalence should be applied as an objective inquiry on an element-by-element basis." *See also* ***DePuy Spine, Inc. v. Medtronic Sofamor Danek, Inc.***, 469 F.3d 1005, 1016-17, 80 U.S.P.Q.2d 1865, 1872-73 (Fed. Cir.2006).

VirnetX, Inc. v. Cisco Sys., 767 F.3d 1308, 1322-23, 113 U.S.P.Q.2d 1112, 1122-23 (Fed.Cir.2014). "To find infringement under the doctrine of equivalents, any differences between the claimed invention and the accused product must be insubstantial. Insubstantiality may be determined by whether the accused device performs substantially the same function in substantially the same way to obtain substantially the same result as the claim limitation. This is a question of fact. Vitiation is not an exception to the doctrine of equivalents. Rather, it is a legal determination that 'the evidence is such that no reasonable jury could determine two elements to be equivalent.'"

Ring & Pinion Serv. v. ARB Corp., 743 F.3d 831, 834, 109 U.S.P.Q.2d 1779, 1781 (Fed.Cir.2014). "There is not, nor has there ever been, a foreseeability limitation on the application of the doctrine of equivalents. It has long been clear that known interchangeability weighs in favor of finding infringement under the doctrine of equivalents. Excluding equivalents that were foreseeable at the time of patenting would directly conflict with these holdings that 'known interchangeability' supports infringement under the doctrine of equivalents. We conclude that the foreseeability of an equivalent at the time of patenting is not a bar to a finding of infringement under the doctrine of equivalents."

Cohesive Techs. v. Waters Corp., 543 F.3d 1351, 1371, 88 U.S.P.Q.2d 1903, 1916 (Fed.Cir.2008). "We have never held that the doctrine of equivalents is inapplicable to broad claims; to the contrary, we have emphasized that pioneering inventions often, by their very nature, result in broader application of the doctrine of equivalents. [T]he district court's analysis suggests that the doctrine of equivalents cannot be used to broaden a numeric range. But as we have repeatedly held, 'the fact that a claim recites numeric ranges does not, by itself, preclude [reliance] on the doctrine of equivalents.'"

Voda v. Cordis Corp., 536 F.3d 1311, 1326, 87 U.S.P.Q.2d 1742, 1753-54 (Fed.Cir.2008). "This court applies two articulations of the test for equivalence. Under the insubstantial differences test, '[a]n element in the accused device is equivalent to a claim limitation if the only differences between the two are insubstantial.' Alternatively, under the function-way-result test, an element in the accused device is equivalent to a claim limitation if it 'performs substantially the same function in substantially the same way to obtain substantially the same result.'"

Roche Palo Alto LLC v. Apotex, Inc., 531 F.3d 1372, 1377-78, 87 U.S.P.Q.2d 1308, 1311 (Fed.Cir.2008). "The reverse doctrine of equivalents is an equitable doctrine designed 'to prevent unwarranted extension of the claims beyond a fair scope of the patentee's invention.' According to the Supreme Court: '[W]here a device is so far changed in *principle* from a patented article that it performs the same or similar function in a *substantially different way*, but nevertheless falls within the literal words of the claim, [reverse] doctrine of equivalents may be used to restrict the claim and defeat the patentee's action for infringement.' While the patentee bears the burden of proving infringement, if the patentee establishes literal infringement, the burden shifts to the accused infringer to set forth a prima facie case of non-infringement under the reverse doctrine of equivalents. If the accused infringer is successful in making a prima facie case, the patentee must then rebut that prima facie case. The reverse doctrine of equivalents is rarely applied, and this court has never affirmed a finding of non-infringement under the reverse doctrine of equivalents." *See also* ***Graver Tank & Mfg. v. Linde Air Prods.***, 339 U.S. 605, 608-09, 85 U.S.P.Q. 328, 330 (1950); ***Tate Access Floors, Inc. v. Interface Architectural Res.***, 279 F.3d 1357, 1368, 61 U.S.P.Q.2d 1647, 1655 (Fed.Cir.2002).

Paice LLC v. Toyota Motor Corp., 504 F.3d 1293, 1304-05, 85 U.S.P.Q.2d 1001, 1009 (Fed.Cir.2007). "We have stated that 'a patentee must ... provide *particularized testimony and linking argument* ... with respect to the function, way, result test when such evidence is presented to support a finding of infringement under the doctrine of equivalents.' 'Generalized testimony as to the overall similarity between the claims and the accused infringer's product or process will not suffice.'"

Allen Eng'g v. Bartell Indus., 299 F.3d 1336, 1345, 63 U.S.P.Q.2d 1769, 1772-73 (Fed.Cir.2002). "Literal infringement of a claim exists when each of the claim limitations 'reads on,' or in other words is found in, the accused device. Even if one or more of the claim limitations are not literally present in the accused device, thus precluding a finding of literal infringement, the claim may still be held infringed if equivalents of those limitations are present."

Interactive Pictures Corp. v. Infinite Pictures, Inc., 274 F.3d 1371, 1376, 61 U.S.P.Q.2d 1152, 1156 (Fed. Cir.2001). "Whether a patentee can avail itself of the doctrine of equivalents implicates certain questions of law, which we review *de novo*. Determination of infringement by equivalents is an issue of fact, which after a jury trial we review for substantial evidence. We will not disturb a jury finding of infringement by equivalents unless 'the evidence so favors the accused infringer that reasonable jurors could not arrive at a contrary verdict.'"

Doctrine of Equivalents—Limitations

Festo Corp. v. Shoketsu Kinzoku Kogyo Kabushiki Co., 535 U.S. 722, 736, 62 U.S.P.Q.2d 1705, 1711-12 (2002). "[A] narrowing amendment made to satisfy any requirement of the Patent Act may give rise to an estoppel. *At U.S. 737:* Our conclusion that prosecution history estoppel arises when a claim is narrowed to comply with [35 U.S.C.] §112 gives rise to the ... question ... Does the estoppel bar the inventor from asserting infringement against any equivalent to the narrowed element or might some equivalents still infringe? [Held: No, some equivalents might still infringe.] *At U.S. 740-41, U.S.P.Q.2d 1713-14:* [W]hen the court is unable to determine the purpose underlying a narrowing amendment—and hence a rationale for limiting the estoppel to the surrender of particular equivalents—the court should presume that the patentee surrendered all subject matter between the broader and the narrower language. [¶] [W]e hold here that the patentee should bear the burden of showing that the amendment does not surrender the particular equivalent in question. ... A patentee's decision to narrow his claims through amendment may be presumed to be a general disclaimer of the territory between the original claim and the amended claim. There are some cases, however, where the amendment cannot reasonably be viewed as surrendering a particular equivalent. The equivalent may have been unforeseeable at the time of the application; the rationale underlying the amendment may bear no more than a tangential relation to the equivalent in question; or there may be some other reason suggesting that the patentee could not reasonably be expected to have described the insubstantial substitute in question. In those cases the patentee can overcome the presumption that prosecution history estoppel bars a finding of equivalence."

DePuy Spine, Inc. v. Medtronic Sofamor Danek, Inc., 567 F.3d 1314, 1322, 90 U.S.P.Q.2d 1865, 1870 (Fed. Cir.2009). "Ensnarement bars a patentee from asserting a scope of equivalency that would encompass, or 'ensnare,' the prior art. [D] argues that it was entitled to present its defense to a jury rather than to the district court. We ... address the jury issue and hold that ensnarement, like prosecution history estoppel, is a legal limitation on the doctrine of equivalents to be decided by the court, not a jury. *At F.3d 1324, U.S.P.Q.2d 1871:* [E]nsnarement, like prosecution history estoppel, is 'to be determined by the court, either on a pretrial motion for partial summary judgment or on a motion for judgment as a matter of law at the close of the evidence and after the jury verdict.' [¶] For guidance on resolving ensnarement's factual issues, we again draw analogy to prosecution history estoppel, particularly in the context of rebutting the presumption of surrender under the 'foreseeability' criterion. [¶] A helpful first step in an ensnarement analysis is to construct a hypothetical claim that literally covers the accused device. *At F.3d 1325, U.S.P.Q.2d 1872:* Next, the district court must assess the prior art introduced by the accused infringer and determine whether the patentee has carried its burden of persuading the court that the hypothetical claim is patentable over the prior art. Ultimately, '[i]f such a claim would be unpatentable under 35 U.S.C. §§102 or 103, then the patentee has overreached, and the accused device is noninfringing as a matter of law.'"

Honeywell Int'l v. Hamilton Sundstrand Corp., 523 F.3d 1304, 1315-16, 86 U.S.P.Q.2d 1718, 1727 (Fed. Cir.2008). "The tangential relation criterion for overcoming the ***Festo*** presumption is very narrow. As this court provided in its [***Festo Corp. v. Shoketsu Kinzoku Kogyo Kabushiki Co.***, 344 F.3d 1359 (Fed.Cir. 2003) (***Festo IX***),] opinion on remand from the Supreme Court, the tangential relation criterion focuses on the 'patentee's objectively apparent reason for the narrowing amendment.' To rebut the estoppel presumption with tangentiality, a patentee must 'demonstrate that the rationale underlying the amendment bore no more than a tangential relation to the equivalent in question,' or, in other words, that 'the narrowing amendment was peripheral, or not directly relevant, to the alleged equivalent.' Additionally, the reason for the narrowing amendment 'should be discernible from the prosecution history record....' If the prosecution history reveals no reason for the narrowing amendment, the presumption is not rebutted. Silence does not overcome the presumption. [¶] '[W]hether an amendment was merely tangential to an alleged equivalent necessarily requires focus on the context in which the amendment was made....'"

Festo Corp. v. Shoketsu Kinzoku Kogyo Kabushiki Co., 493 F.3d 1368, 1370, 83 U.S.P.Q.2d 1385, 1386 (Fed.Cir.2007). "This case raises the question of whether an equivalent is foreseeable within the meaning of ***Festo Corp. v. Shoketsu Kinzoku Kogyo Kabushiki Co.***, 535 U.S. 722 ... (2002) ("***Festo VIII***"), and subject to surrender under the doctrine of prosecution history estoppel. We conclude that foreseeability does not require the applicant to be aware that a particular equivalent would satisfy the insubstantial differences test or the function/way/result test with respect to the claim as amended. *At F.3d 1377, U.S.P.Q.2d 1391:* The doctrine of prosecution history estoppel acts as a 'legal limitation on the doctrine of equivalents.' '[P]rosecution history estoppel limits the range of equivalents available to a patentee by preventing recapture of subject matter surrendered during prosecution of the patent.' The burden is on the patentee to establish that the reason for the amendment was unrelated to patentability. If the patentee fails to meet this burden, the court must presume that the patentee 'had a substantial reason related to patentability for including the limiting element added by amendment.' If there is a substantial reason related to patentability 'prosecution history estoppel would bar the application of the doctrine of equivalents as to that element.' However, in ***Festo VIII***, ... the Supreme Court held that the patentee may prove that the amendment did not surrender the particular equivalent by demonstrating that one of three exceptions is met. *At F.3d 1378:* [A]n equivalent is foreseeable when the equivalent is known in the pertinent prior art at the time of amendment. *At F.3d 1379, U.S.P.Q.2d 1392:* We disagree that the foreseeability test requires application of the function/way/result or insubstantial differences test. Rather, we find that an alternative is foreseeable if it is disclosed in the pertinent prior art in the field of the invention. In other words, an alternative is foreseeable if it is known in the field of the invention as reflected in the claim scope before amendment. *At F.3d 1381, U.S.P.Q.2d 1394:* The question is not whether *after* the narrowing amendment the alternative was a known equivalent, but rather whether it was a known equivalent *before* the narrowing amendment. [A]n equivalent that is foreseeable as an alternative to the broader claimed feature does not become unforeseeable simply because the claimed feature is narrowed. For example, if a claim before amendment broadly claimed a metal filament for a light bulb but was later amended to avoid prior art and to specify metal A because of its longevity, the equivalent metal B, known in the prior art to function as a bulb filament, is not unforeseeable even though its longevity was unknown at the time of amendment." *See also* ***Honeywell Int'l v. Hamilton Sundstrand Corp.***, 523 F.3d 1304, 1313, 86 U.S.P.Q.2d 1718, 1724 (Fed.Cir.2008).

AquaTex Indus. v. Techniche Solutions, 419 F.3d 1374, 1382, 76 U.S.P.Q.2d 1213, 1219 (Fed.Cir.2005). "[D] does not allege amendment-based estoppel. Instead it asserts argument-based estoppel. To invoke argument-based estoppel, the prosecution history 'must evince a clear and unmistakable surrender of subject matter.' To determine if subject matter has been relinquished, an objective test is applied, inquiring 'whether a competitor would reasonably believe that the applicant had surrendered the relevant subject matter.'"

Seachange Int'l v. C-COR Inc., 413 F.3d 1361, 1378, 75 U.S.P.Q.2d 1385, 1396 (Fed.Cir.2005). "The determination of infringement under the doctrine of equivalents is limited by two primary legal doctrines: (1) prosecution history estoppel and (2) the all elements rule. The application of these doctrines is a question of law. The all elements rule provides that the doctrine of equivalents does not apply if applying the doctrine would vitiate an entire claim limitation." (Internal quotes omitted.)

Willful Infringement

For more annotations on this topic, see 35 U.S.C. §284, *Enhanced Damages*, p. 715.

Exmark Mfg. Co. v. Briggs & Stratton Power Prods. Grp., 879 F.3d 1332, 1353, 125 U.S.P.Q.2d 1421, ___ (Fed.Cir.2018). "The district court must reconsider its decision to exclude evidence of the prior art during the jury trial on willfulness to determine whether [D] had developed any views about the prior art at the time of accused infringement or whether the evidence only relates to [D's] litigation-inspired defenses. Whether there is a genuine issue of material fact about when [D] knew of its prior art defenses, and thus whether a new jury trial is required, we leave to the district court to determine in the first instance."

Presidio Components, Inc. v. American Tech. Ceramics Corp., 875 F.3d 1369, 1382-83, 124 U.S.P.Q.2d 1745, 1753 (Fed.Cir.2017). "[T]he district court is not required to discuss the ***Read*** factors. ... The ***Halo*** test merely requires the district court to consider the particular circumstances of the case to determine whether it is egregious. Here, the district court considered the particular circumstances of the case and determined the situation was not sufficiently egregious to warrant enhanced damages."

WesternGeco L.L.C. v. ION Geophysical Corp., 837 F.3d 1358, 1362, 120 U.S.P.Q.2d 1177, 1180 (Fed.Cir. 2016). "***Halo*** did not disturb the substantive standard for the second prong of ***Seagate***, subjective willfulness. Rather, ***Halo*** emphasized that subjective willfulness alone—i.e., proof that the defendant acted despite a risk of infringement that was either known or so obvious that it should have been known to the accused infringer ... —can support an award of enhanced damages." (Internal quotes omitted.)

§271(a)—Generally

Commil USA, LLC v. Cisco Sys., ___ U.S. ___, 135 S.Ct. 1920, 1926, 114 U.S.P.Q.2d 1577, 1580 (2015). "Under [direct infringement], a defendant's mental state is irrelevant. Direct infringement is a strict-liability offense."

Florida Prepaid Postsecondary Educ. Expense Bd. v. College Sav. Bank, 527 U.S. 627, 645, 51 U.S.P.Q.2d 1081, 1089 (1999). "Actions predicated on direct patent infringement ... do not require any showing of intent to infringe; instead, knowledge and intent are considered only with respect to damages." *See also* ***Intel Corp. v. International Trade Comm'n***, 946 F.2d 821, 832, 20 U.S.P.Q.2d 1161, 1171 (Fed.Cir.1991).

Uniloc USA, Inc. v. Microsoft Corp., 632 F.3d 1292, 1309, 98 U.S.P.Q.2d 1203, 1217 (Fed.Cir.2011). "That other parties are necessary to complete the environment in which the claimed element functions does not necessarily divide the infringement between the necessary parties. For example, a claim that reads 'An algorithm incorporating means for receiving e-mails' may require two parties to function, but could nevertheless be infringed by the single party who uses an algorithm that receives e-mails."

Fujitsu Ltd. v. Netgear Inc., 620 F.3d 1321, 1327-28, 96 U.S.P.Q.2d 1742, 1747 (Fed.Cir.2010). "We hold that a district court may rely on an industry standard in analyzing infringement. If a district court construes the claims and finds that the reach of the claims includes any device that practices a standard, then this can be sufficient for a finding of infringement. We agree that claims should be compared to the accused product to determine infringement. However, if an accused product operates in accordance with a standard, then comparing the claims to that standard is the same as comparing the claims to the accused product. ... An accused infringer is free to either prove that the claims do not cover all implementations of the standard or to prove that it does not practice the standard. [¶] We acknowledge, however, that in many instances, an industry standard does not provide the level of specificity required to establish that practicing that standard would always result in infringement. Or ... the relevant section of the standard is optional, and standards compliance alone would not establish that the accused infringer chooses to implement the optional section. In these instances, it is not sufficient for the patent owner to establish infringement by arguing that the product admittedly practices the standard, therefore it infringes. In these cases, the patent owner must compare the claims to the accused products or, if appropriate, prove that the accused products implement any relevant optional sections of the standard. This should alleviate any concern about the use of standard compliance in assessing patent infringement. Only in the situation where a patent covers every possible implementation of a standard will it be enough to prove infringement by showing standard compliance."

Wordtech Sys. v. Integrated Networks Solutions, Inc., 609 F.3d 1308, 1313, 95 U.S.P.Q.2d 1619, 1624 (Fed.Cir.2010). "According to [employee-Ds], [corporation-D's] corporate veil shielded them from direct infringement liability under ... §271(a) because they acted as company employees, and [corporation-D] was a valid corporation during all periods of alleged infringement. [¶] 'Patent infringement is a tort,' ... and '[i]n general, a corporate officer is personally liable for his tortious acts, just as any individual may be liable for a civil wrong[ ]'.... However, the 'corporate veil' shields a company's officers from personal liability for direct infringement that the officers commit in the name of the corporation, unless the corporation is the officers' 'alter ego.' 'To determine whether corporate officers are personally liable for the direct infringement of the corporation under §271(a) requires invocation of those general principles relating to piercing the corporate veil.' *At F.3d 1314-15, U.S.P.Q.2d 1625:* [F]ailure to instruct the jury [about piercing the corporate veil] was plainly erroneous because '[p]ersonal liability under §271(a) ... requires sufficient evidence to justify piercing the corporate veil.' Because resolution of [corporation-D's] corporate status was a legal prerequisite to finding [employee-Ds] individually liable, the jury omissions were obvious, important, and seriously affected the trial's fairness. [P] needed to prove either that [corporation-D] was not a valid corporation when [employee-Ds] committed infringing acts on its behalf, or that [corporation-D's] corporate veil should be disregarded under state law. We recognize that if 'the error in the jury instruction is harmless, it does not warrant reversal.' In this case, however, we cannot deem the error harmless."

Monsanto Co. v. Syngenta Seeds, Inc., 503 F.3d 1352, 1359, 84 U.S.P.Q.2d 1705, 1710 (Fed.Cir.2007). "In ***Wahpeton*** [***Canvas Co. v. Frontier, Inc.***, 870 F.2d 1546 (Fed.Cir.1989)], this court explained: 'One may infringe an independent claim and not infringe a claim dependent on that claim. The reverse is not true. One who does not infringe an independent claim cannot infringe a claim dependent on (and thus containing all the limitations of) that claim.'"

Liquid Dynamics Corp. v. Vaughan Co., 449 F.3d 1209, 1219, 79 U.S.P.Q.2d 1094, 1101 (Fed.Cir.2006). "A patentee may prove direct infringement or inducement of infringement by either direct or circumstantial evidence. There is no requirement that direct evidence be introduced, nor is a jury's preference for circumstantial evidence over direct evidence unreasonable *per se*."

Applied Med. Res. v. U.S. Surgical Corp., 435 F.3d 1356, 1362, 77 U.S.P.Q.2d 1666, 1671 (Fed.Cir.2006). "[S]imply because the *same* company sold two *different* products which infringed a patent does not prevent the patentee from litigating and collecting *separate* damages for *each* infringement."

Moba, B.V. v. Diamond Automation, Inc., 325 F.3d 1306, 1313, 66 U.S.P.Q.2d 1429, 1433 (Fed.Cir. 2003). "The sale or manufacture of equipment to perform a claimed method is not direct infringement within the meaning of ... §271(a)."

Johns Hopkins Univ. v. CellPro, Inc., 152 F.3d 1342, 1366, 47 U.S.P.Q.2d 1705, 1723 (Fed.Cir.1998). "Mere possession of a product which becomes covered by a subsequently issued patent does not constitute an infringement of that patent until the product is used, sold, or offered for sale in the U.S. during the term of the patent. Likewise, neither export from the U.S. nor use in a foreign country of a product covered by a U.S. patent constitutes infringement [under §271(a)]."

North Am. Philips Corp. v. American Vending Sales, Inc., 35 F.3d 1576, 1579, 32 U.S.P.Q.2d 1203, 1205 (Fed.Cir.1994). "[T]he statute on its face clearly suggests the conception that the 'tort' of patent infringement occurs where the offending act is committed and not where the injury is felt."

SRI Int'l v. Matsushita Elec. Corp., 775 F.2d 1107, 1123, 227 U.S.P.Q. 577, 587 (Fed.Cir.1985). "One who takes a claimed structure and merely uses it in a way that differs from that in which a specification-described embodiment uses it, does not thereby escape infringement."

§271(a)—Divided Infringement

Eli Lilly & Co. v. Teva Parenteral Meds., Inc., 845 F.3d 1357, 1366-67, 121 U.S.P.Q.2d 1277, 1283 (Fed.Cir. 2017). "We ... reject [Ds'] argument that an actor can only condition the performance of a step 'by imposing a legal obligation to do so, by interposing that step as an unavoidable technological prerequisite to participation, or, as in [***Akamai V***], both.'"

Akamai Techs. v. Limelight Networks, Inc., 797 F.3d 1020, 1022-23, 116 U.S.P.Q.2d 1344, 1345-46 (Fed. Cir.2015) (en banc). "Direct infringement under §271(a) occurs where all steps of a claimed method are performed by or attributable to a single entity. Where more than one actor is involved in practicing the steps, a court must determine whether the acts of one are attributable to the other such that a single entity is responsible for the infringement. We will hold an entity responsible for others' performance of method steps in two sets of circumstances: (1) where that entity directs or controls others' performance, and (2) where the actors form a joint enterprise. [¶] To determine if a single entity directs or controls the acts of another, we continue to consider general principles of vicarious liability. In the past, we have held that an actor is liable for infringement under §271(a) if it acts through an agent (applying traditional agency principles) or contracts with another to perform one or more steps of a claimed method. We conclude, on the facts of this case, that liability under §271(a) can also be found when an alleged infringer conditions participation in an activity or receipt of a benefit upon performance of a step or steps of a patented method and establishes the manner or timing of that performance. In those instances, the third party's actions are attributed to the alleged infringer such that the alleged infringer becomes the single actor chargeable with direct infringement. Whether a single actor directed or controlled the acts of one or more third parties is a question of fact, reviewable on appeal for substantial evidence, when tried to a jury. [¶] Alternatively, where two or more actors form a joint enterprise, all can be charged with the acts of the other, rendering each liable for the steps performed by the other as if each is a single actor. A joint enterprise requires proof of four elements: '(1) an agreement, express or implied, among the members of the group; (2) a common purpose to be carried out by the group; (3) a community of pecuniary interest in that purpose, among the members; and (4) an equal right to a voice in the direction of the enterprise, which gives an equal right of control.' As with direction or control, whether actors entered into a joint enterprise is a question of fact, reviewable on appeal for substantial evidence. [¶] Section 271(a) is not limited solely to principal-agent relationships, contractual arrangements, and joint enterprise, as the vacated panel decision held. Rather, to determine direct infringement, we consider whether all method steps can be attributed to a single entity."

§271(a)—Imports

MEMC Elec. Materials, Inc. v. Mitsubishi Materials Silicon Corp., 420 F.3d 1369, 1375, 76 U.S.P.Q.2d 1276, 1281 (Fed.Cir.2005). "[T]he reach of §271(a) is limited to infringing activities that occur within the U.S. *At F.3d 1377, U.S.P.Q.2d 1282:* Mere knowledge that a product sold overseas will ultimately be imported into the U.S. is insufficient to establish liability under §271(a)."

§271(a)—Offers to Sell, or Sells

Halo Elecs., Inc. v. Pulse Elecs., Inc., 831 F.3d 1369, 1376-77, 119 U.S.P.Q.2d 1654, 1660 (Fed.Cir. 2016). "We first consider whether the products that [D] manufactured, shipped, and delivered to buyers abroad were *sold within* the U.S. for purposes of §271(a). [¶] [P]atent infringement occurs where the infringing sales are made. ... The 'selling' of an infringing article has both a physical and a conceptual dimension to it. That is to say, it is possible to define the situs of the tort of infringement-by-sale either in real terms as including the location of the seller and the buyer and perhaps the points along the shipment route in between, or in formal terms as the single point at which some legally operative act took place, such as the place where the sales transaction would be deemed to have occurred as a matter of commercial law. [A] sale may occur at multiple locations, including the location of the buyer, for purposes of personal jurisdiction. [¶] Although the place of contracting may be one of several possible locations of a sale to confer personal jurisdiction, we have not deemed a sale to have occurred within the U.S. for purposes of liability under §271(a) based solely on negotiation and contracting activities in the U.S. when the vast majority of activities underlying the sales transaction occurred wholly outside the U.S. For such a sale, one must examine whether the activities in the U.S. are sufficient to constitute a 'sale' under §271(a), recognizing that a strong policy against extraterritorial liability exists in the patent law. *At F.3d 1378, U.S.P.Q.2d 1661:* [W]e conclude that, when substantial activities of a sales transaction, including the final formation of a contract for sale encompassing all essential terms as well as the delivery and performance under that sales contract, occur entirely outside the U.S., pricing and contracting negotiations in the U.S. alone do not constitute or transform those extraterritorial activities into a sale within the U.S. for purposes of §271(a). [¶] Any doubt as to whether [D's] contracting activities in the U.S. constituted a sale within the U.S. under §271(a) is resolved by the presumption against extraterritorial application of U.S. laws. *At F.3d 1379-80, U.S.P.Q.2d 1662-63:* We next consider whether [D] *offered to sell within* the U.S. those products that [D] manufactured, shipped, and delivered abroad. An 'offer to sell' generally occurs when one communicates a manifestation of willingness to enter into a bargain, so made as to justify another person in understanding that his assent to that bargain is invited and will conclude it. We have held that a description of the allegedly infringing merchandise and the price at which it can be purchased may constitute an offer to sell. [That holding] did not, however, involve international transactions and in that case this court considered the issue of offer to sell in a personal jurisdiction context. [¶] More importantly, we have held that the location of the contemplated sale controls whether there is an offer to sell *within the U.S.* In order for an offer to sell to constitute infringement, the offer must be to sell a patented invention within the U.S. In ***Transocean [Offshore Deepwater Drilling, Inc. v. Maersk Contractors USA, Inc.***, 617 F.3d 1296 (Fed.Cir.2010)], contract negotiations occurred outside the U.S. for delivery and performance in the U.S. This court held that the location of the contemplated sale controlled and that the offer to sell infringed the patent at issue. [¶] [D] did not directly infringe [P's] patents under the 'offer to sell' provision by offering to sell in the U.S. the products at issue, because the locations of the contemplated sales were outside the U.S. [¶] An offer to sell, in order to be an infringement, must be an offer contemplating sale in the U.S. Otherwise, the presumption against extraterritoriality would be breached. If a sale outside the U.S. is not an infringement of a U.S. patent, an offer to sell, even if made in the U.S., when the sale would occur outside the U.S., similarly would not be an infringement of a U.S. patent. We therefore hold that [D] did not offer to sell the products at issue within the U.S. for purposes of §271(a)." (Internal quotes omitted.)

Transocean Offshore Deepwater Drilling, Inc. v. Maersk Contractors USA, Inc., 617 F.3d 1296, 1308, 96 U.S.P.Q.2d 1104, 1111 (Fed.Cir.2010). "An offer to sell is a distinct act of infringement separate from an actual sale. An offer to sell differs from a sale in that an offer to sell need not be accepted to constitute an act of infringement. Moreover, the damages that would flow from an unaccepted offer to sell and an actual sale would likely be quite different. We analyze an offer to sell under §271(a) using traditional contract principles. *At F.3d 1309, U.S.P.Q.2d 1112:* This case presents the question whether an offer which is made in Norway by a U.S. company to a U.S. company to sell a product within the U.S., for delivery and use within the U.S. constitutes an offer to sell within the U.S. under §271(a). We conclude that it does. ... In order for an offer to sell to constitute infringement, the offer must be to sell a patented invention within the U.S. The focus should not be on the location of the offer, but rather the location of the future sale that would occur pursuant to the offer. *At F.3d 1310, U.S.P.Q.2d 1113:* As with the offer to sell, we hold that a contract between two U.S. companies for the sale of the patented invention with delivery and performance in the U.S. constitutes a sale under §271(a) as a matter of law. *At F.3d 1311:* Finally, we reject [D's] claim that the entire apparatus must have been constructed and ready for use in order to have been sold. Our precedent establishes that a contract can constitute a sale to trigger infringement liability. A 'sale' is not limited to the transfer of tangible property; a sale may also be the agreement by which such a transfer takes place."

Ricoh Co. v. Quanta Computer Inc., 550 F.3d 1325, 1335, 89 U.S.P.Q.2d 1577, 1585 (Fed.Cir.2008). "[W]e hold that a party that sells or offers to sell software containing instructions to perform a patented method does not infringe the patent under §271(a)."

NTP, Inc. v. Research In Motion, Ltd., 418 F.3d 1282, 1318, 75 U.S.P.Q.2d 1763, 1791 (Fed.Cir.2005), *abrogated on other grounds*, ***Zoltek Corp. v. U.S.***, 672 F.3d 1309 (Fed.Cir.2012) (en banc). The court analyzes the phrase "offers to sell, or sells." "Because we conclude that [D's] customers could not have infringed the asserted method claims ... under the 'use' prong of §271(a), and thus, could not have provided the necessary predicate for the charges of induced or contributory infringement of those claims, we must consider whether [D] could have directly infringed the method claims under the 'sell' or 'offer to sell' prongs of §271(a). *At F.3d 1320-21, U.S.P.Q.2d 1792:* [W]e conclude that the jury could not have found that [D] infringed the asserted method claims under the 'sells' or 'offers to sell' prongs of §271(a). We need not and do not hold that method claims may not be infringed under the 'sells' and 'offers to sell' prongs of §271(a). Rather, we conclude only that [D's] performance of at least some of the recited steps of the asserted method claims as a service for its customers cannot be considered to be selling or offering to sell the invention covered by the asserted method claims."

Rotec Indus. v. Mitsubishi Corp., 215 F.3d 1246, 1254-55, 55 U.S.P.Q.2d 1001, 1006-07 (Fed.Cir.2000). "[T]he analysis of an 'offer to sell' under [35 U.S.C.] §271(a) is consistent with the Court's analysis in ***Pfaff*** of [35 U.S.C.] §102(b). [We] define §271(a)'s 'offer to sell' liability according to the norms of traditional contractual analysis." *See also* ***Pfaff v. Wells Elecs., Inc.***, 525 U.S. 55, 67-68, 48 U.S.P.Q.2d 1641, 1646-47 (1998).

HollyAnne Corp. v. TFT, Inc., 199 F.3d 1304, 1308, 53 U.S.P.Q.2d 1201, 1205 (Fed.Cir.1999). "[T]his court must ... decide whether an offer to donate is the legal equivalent of an 'offer to sell' for purposes of patent infringement under §271(a).... We hold that it is not."

§271(a)—Uses

Intellectual Ventures I LLC v. Motorola Mobility LLC, 870 F.3d 1320, 1329, 124 U.S.P.Q.2d 1129, 1136 (Fed.Cir.2017). "In an analysis of a system claim under ***Centillion***, proof of an infringing 'use' of the claimed system under §271(a) requires the patentee to demonstrate that the direct infringer obtained 'benefit' from each and every element of the claimed system. In addition, the direct or indirect control required 'is the ability to place the system as a whole into service.'"

Centillion Data Sys. v. Qwest Comms. Int'l, 631 F.3d 1279, 1284, 97 U.S.P.Q.2d 1697, 1701 (Fed.Cir. 2011). "We hold that to 'use' a system for purposes of infringement, a party must put the invention into service, *i.e.*, control the system as a whole and obtain benefit from it. *At F.3d 1285, U.S.P.Q.2d 1702:* We hold that the [customer's] on-demand operation is a 'use' of the system as a matter of law. *At F.3d 1286, U.S.P.Q.2d 1703:* While [D] may make the back-end processing elements, it never 'uses' the entire claimed system because it never puts into service the personal computer data processing means. Supplying the software for the customer to use is not the same as using the system. *At F.3d 1288, U.S.P.Q.2d 1704:* [D's] customers do not act as [D's] agents as a matter of law nor are they contractually obligated by [D] to act."

Silicon Graphics, Inc. v. ATI Techs., 607 F.3d 784, 794, 95 U.S.P.Q.2d 1417, 1426 (Fed.Cir.2010). "The district court erred in assuming that direct infringement requires the performance of all of the elements in these apparatus claims. In addition to the actual use of the product described, infringement of an apparatus claim occurs when the invention is, among other things, made or sold in the U.S. Thus, even absent its use (or performance), this court has held that an apparatus claim directed to a computer that is claimed in functional terms is nonetheless infringed so long as the product is designed 'in such a way as to enable a user of that [product] to utilize the function ... without having to modify [the product].' Where ... a product includes the structural means for performing a claimed function, it can still infringe 'separate and apart' from the operating system that is needed to use the product."

Medical Solutions, Inc. v. C Change Surgical LLC, 541 F.3d 1136, 1140, 88 U.S.P.Q.2d 1275, 1278 (Fed. Cir.2008). "Several courts addressing whether a defendant has 'used' a patented invention have held that 'the mere demonstration or display of an accused product, even in an obviously commercial atmosphere' is not an act of infringement for purposes of §271(a). *At F.3d 1140 n.3, U.S.P.Q.2d 1278 n.3:* A demonstration of an accused device plus the simultaneous solicitation of purchase orders has been held to amount to a sufficient degree of 'selling' activity. However, that holding is inapposite here since [P] hangs its hat on the 'uses' rather than the 'sells' prong of §271(a). *At F.3d 1141:* The inquiry as to what constitutes a 'use' of a patented item is highly case-specific.... [¶] The ordinary meaning of 'use' is 'to put into action or service.' *At F.3d 1141 n.4, U.S.P.Q.2d 1279 n.4:* [W]e do recognize other courts have held that demonstrations of a device are not proper evidence of 'use' because using a device means using it to perform its actual function or service, not using it as a demonstrative display."

NTP, Inc. v. Research In Motion, Ltd., 418 F.3d 1282, 1315, 75 U.S.P.Q.2d 1763, 1788 (Fed.Cir.2005), *abrogated on other grounds*, ***Zoltek Corp. v. U.S.***, 672 F.3d 1309 (Fed.Cir.2012) (en banc). "The question before us is whether the using, offering to sell, or selling of a patented invention is an infringement under §271(a) if a component or step of the patented invention is located or performed abroad. ... The grammatical structure of the statute indicates that 'within the U.S.' is a separate requirement from the infringing acts clause. Thus, it is unclear from the statutory language how the territoriality requirement limits direct infringement where the location of at least a part of the 'patented invention' is not the same as the location of the infringing act. *At F.3d 1317, U.S.P.Q.2d 1789:* [The court analyzes the phrase 'uses ... within the U.S.'] The use of a claimed system under §271(a) is the place at which the system as a whole is put into service, *i.e.*, the place where control of the system is exercised and beneficial use of the system obtained. *At U.S.P.Q.2d 1790-91:* When [D's] U.S. customers send and receive messages by manipulating the handheld devices in their possession in the U.S., the location of the use of the communication system as a whole occurs in the U.S. This satisfactorily establishes that the situs of the 'use' of [D's] system by [D's] U.S. customers for purposes of §271(a) is the U.S. [¶] We reach a different conclusion as to [P's] asserted method claims. *At F.3d 1318:* [A] process cannot be used 'within' the U.S. as required by §271(a) unless each of the steps is performed within this country. [¶] [W]e agree with [D] that a finding of direct infringement by [D's] customers under §271(a) of the method claims reciting an 'interface switch' or an 'interface' is precluded by the location of [D's network component] in Canada."

§271(b)

Commil USA, LLC v. Cisco Sys., ___ U.S. ___, 135 S.Ct. 1920, 1926, 114 U.S.P.Q.2d 1577, 1580 (2015). "In contrast to direct infringement, liability for inducing infringement attaches only if the defendant knew of the patent and that 'the induced acts constitute patent infringement.' *At U.S.P.Q.2d 1581:* This case asks a question of first impression: whether knowledge of, or belief in, a patent's validity is required for induced infringement under §271(b). *At U.S. ___, S.Ct. 1928, U.S.P.Q.2d 1582:* The question the Court confronts today concerns whether a defendant's belief regarding patent validity is a defense to a claim of induced infringement. It is not. The scienter element for induced infringement concerns infringement; that is a different issue than validity. Section 271(b) requires that the defendant 'actively induce[d] infringement.' That language requires intent to 'bring about the desired result,' which is infringement. And because infringement and validity are separate issues under the Act, belief regarding validity cannot negate the scienter required under §271(b). [¶] Were this Court to interpret §271(b) as permitting a defense of belief in invalidity, it would conflate the issues of infringement and validity."

Limelight Networks, Inc. v. Akamai Techs., ___ U.S. ___, 134 S.Ct. 2111, 2115, 110 U.S.P.Q.2d 1681, 1683 (2014). "This case presents the question whether a defendant may be liable for inducing infringement of a patent under ... §271(b) when no one has directly infringed the patent under §271(a) or any other statutory provision. The statutory text and structure and our prior case law require that we answer this question in the negative. *At U.S. ___, S.Ct. 2118:* [I]n this case, performance of all the claimed steps cannot be attributed to a single person, so direct infringement never occurred."

Global-Tech Appliances, Inc. v. SEB S.A., 563 U.S. 754, 757, 131 S.Ct. 2060, 2063, 98 U.S.P.Q.2d 1665, 1667 (2011). "We consider whether a party who 'actively induces infringement of a patent' under ... §271(b) must know that the induced acts constitute patent infringement. *At U.S. 766, S.Ct. 2068, U.S.P.Q.2d 1671:* [W]e now hold that induced infringement under §271(b) requires knowledge that the induced acts constitute patent infringement. [¶] [W]e agree that deliberate indifference to a known risk that a patent exists is not the appropriate standard under §271(b). *At U.S. 768, S.Ct. 2069, U.S.P.Q.2d 1672-73:* Given the long history of willful blindness and its wide acceptance in the Federal Judiciary, we can see no reason why the doctrine should not apply in civil lawsuits for induced patent infringement under ... §271(b). *At U.S. 769-70, S.Ct. 2070-71:* While the Courts of Appeals articulate the doctrine of willful blindness in slightly different ways, all appear to agree on two basic requirements: (1) the defendant must subjectively believe that there is a high probability that a fact exists and (2) the defendant must take deliberate actions to avoid learning of that fact. We think these requirements give willful blindness an appropriately limited scope that surpasses recklessness and negligence. Under this formulation, a willfully blind defendant is one who takes deliberate actions to avoid confirming a high probability of wrongdoing and who can almost be said to have actually known the critical facts. By contrast, a reckless defendant is one who merely knows of a substantial and unjustified risk of such wrongdoing, ... and a negligent defendant is one who should have known of a similar risk but, in fact, did not...."

Sanofi v. Watson Labs., 875 F.3d 636, 644, 124 U.S.P.Q.2d 1601, 1607 (Fed.Cir.2017). "This court has ... explained that, for a court to find induced infringement, '[i]t must be established that the defendant possessed specific intent to encourage another's infringement.' The court has articulated certain necessary conditions: the plaintiff must show 'that the alleged infringer's actions induced infringing acts and that he knew or should have known his actions would induce actual infringements.' And the court has repeatedly explained that, for the finder of fact to find the required intent to encourage, '[w]hile proof of intent is necessary, direct evidence is not required; rather, circumstantial evidence may suffice.' When proof of intent to encourage depends on the label accompanying the marketing of a drug, '[t]he label must encourage, recommend, or promote infringement.' *At F.3d 646, U.S.P.Q.2d 1609:* The content of the label in this case permits the inference of specific intent to encourage the infringing use. '[D]epending on the clarity of the [drug label's] instructions, the decision to continue seeking FDA approval of those instructions may be sufficient evidence of specific intent to induce infringement.' Unlike in ***Takeda [Pharms. U.S.A., Inc. v. West-Ward Pharm.***, 785 F.3d 625 (Fed.Cir.2015)], the inference in the present case is based on interpreting the label's express statement of indications of use and the internally referred-to elaboration of those indications. And this case is not like ***Vita-Mix Corp. v. Basic Holding, Inc.*** [, 581 F.3d 1317 (Fed.Cir.2009)], in which the defendant, in its (non-pharmaceutical) product instructions, encouraged a noninfringing use in a way that showed an intent to discourage infringement. The evidence in this case supports the finding of intentional encouragement of infringing use and, therefore, of inducement."

Static Control Components, Inc. v. Lexmark Int'l, 697 F.3d 387, 415, 104 U.S.P.Q.2d 1352, 1371 (6th Cir.2012), *aff'd*, ___ U.S. ___, 134 S.Ct. 1377 (2014). "To establish a claim for patent inducement under ... §271(b), [P] bore the burden of showing by a preponderance of the evidence that (1) [D's] customers directly infringed [P's] patents; (2) [D] took active steps that induced the customers' infringement; (3) [D] intended the customers to take the infringing acts; and (4) [D] knew or willfully disregarded the risk that those actions by its customers would constitute direct infringement. Patent infringement by a third-party is therefore a necessary predicate to inducement to infringe. [¶] A plaintiff can establish the first element of inducement to infringe either by demonstrating 'specific instances of direct infringement or a finding that the accused products necessarily infringe.' When the plaintiff can show only individual instances of direct infringement, the plaintiff may recover only for the damages from those individual acts. If the plaintiff can show an entire class of customers necessarily infringed, damages can be sought more broadly across the entire class. [¶] Literal infringement alone is not enough to support a claim for inducement, because the predicate to inducement is a violation of ... §271(a), which requires more than that the accused devices literally infringe. For example, a party could not be liable for inducing infringement if an accused device literally infringed a patent claim but the literal infringer had authority to use the patent or a patent had otherwise expired, thereby defeating a determination of direct patent infringement. *At F.3d 416:* An accused device will necessarily infringe, permitting a finding of direct infringement by a class of customers and an inference that the inducer intended the infringement, if the 'customers can only use the [defendant's] products in an infringing way.' When an accused device could be used in either an infringing or a non-infringing way, a claim of direct infringement based on necessary infringement fails and cannot sustain an inducement claim."

Merial Ltd. v. Cipla Ltd., 681 F.3d 1283, 1302-03, 103 U.S.P.Q.2d 1001, 1015 (Fed.Cir.2012). "[W]here a foreign party, with the requisite knowledge and intent, employs extraterritorial means to actively induce acts of direct infringement that occur within the U.S., such conduct is not categorically exempt from redress under §271(b)."

Kinetic Concepts, Inc. v. Blue Sky Med. Grp., 554 F.3d 1010, 1024-25, 89 U.S.P.Q.2d 1801, 1810-11 (Fed. Cir.2009). The Federal Circuit upheld a jury verdict that D did not induce infringement based in part on testimony that D thought it was practicing the prior art. Practicing the prior art can be a defense to inducement of infringement. The patentee "may be correct that 'practicing the prior art' is not a defense to patent infringement. However, it does not follow that a defendant's belief that it can freely practice inventions found in the public domain cannot support a jury's finding that the intent required for induced infringement was lacking."

Warner-Lambert Co. v. Apotex Corp., 316 F.3d 1348, 1365, 65 U.S.P.Q.2d 1481, 1491-92 (Fed.Cir.2003). "[W]here a product has substantial noninfringing uses, intent to induce infringement cannot be inferred even when the defendant has actual knowledge that some users of its product may be infringing the patent. Where there are many uses for a product, ... we are not in a position to infer or not infer intent on the part of [D] without any direct evidence."

National Presto Indus. v. West Bend Co., 76 F.3d 1185, 1195, 37 U.S.P.Q.2d 1685, 1692 (Fed.Cir.1996). "The question ... is whether remedy under §271(b) is available, subject to proof, against persons who deliberately place later-infringing items into the chain of commerce before the patent issues. *At F.3d 1196, U.S.P.Q.2d 1693:* We conclude ... as a matter of law §271(b) does not reach actions taken before issuance of the adverse patent. [¶] The principle of liability for 'aiding and abetting' the wrongful acts of others is not imposed retrospectively, to make illegal an act that was not illegal when it was done."

§271(c)

Commil USA, LLC v. Cisco Sys., ___ U.S. ___, 135 S.Ct. 1920, 1926, 114 U.S.P.Q.2d 1577, 1581 (2015). "Like induced infringement, contributory infringement requires knowledge of the patent in suit and knowledge of patent infringement."

Aro Mfg. Co. v. Convertible Top Replacement Co., 377 U.S. 476, 483, 141 U.S.P.Q. 681, 684-85 (1964). "It is plain that §271(c) ... made no change in the fundamental precept that there can be no contributory infringement in the absence of a direct infringement." (Internal quotes omitted.) *See also* ***Porter v. Farmers Sup. Serv.***, 790 F.2d 882, 884, 229 U.S.P.Q. 814, 815 (Fed.Cir.1986).

Suprema, Inc. v. International Trade Comm'n, 796 F.3d 1338, 1345-46, 116 U.S.P.Q.2d 1177, 1182 (Fed. Cir.2015). "We begin with our standard of review ... owed to the [International Trade] Commission's interpretation of [35 U.S.C.] §337. [W]e review the Commission's interpretation pursuant to ***Chevron U.S.A., Inc. v. Natural Res. Def. Council, Inc.***, 467 U.S. 837 ... (1984). [¶] Section 337 refers not just to infringement, but to '*articles* that infringe.' That phrase does not narrow the provision to exclude inducement of post-importation infringement. *At F.3d 1352-53, U.S.P.Q.2d 1186:* We hold that the Commission's interpretation that the phrase 'articles that infringe' covers goods that were used by an importer to directly infringe post-importation as a result of the seller's inducement is reasonable."

Toshiba Corp. v. Imation Corp., 681 F.3d 1358, 1362, 103 U.S.P.Q.2d 1097, 1099-1100 (Fed.Cir.2012). "To establish contributory infringement liability, the patent owner must show, among other things, that there are no substantial noninfringing uses. '[N]on-infringing uses are substantial when they are not unusual, far-fetched, illusory, impractical, occasional, aberrant, or experimental.' In assessing whether a use is substantial, the fact-finder may consider 'the use's frequency, ... the use's practicality, the invention's intended purpose, and the intended market.'"

35 U.S.C. §271

Arris Grp. v. British Telecomms., 639 F.3d 1368, 1376, 98 U.S.P.Q.2d 1812, 1817-18 (Fed.Cir.2011). "Pursuant to §271(c) ..., an act of contributory infringement may include either the sale of a 'component of a patented machine, manufacture, combination or composition' (including a component used in a claimed system), or the sale of a 'material or apparatus for use in practicing a patented process.' This covers both contributory infringement of system claims and method claims. To hold a component supplier liable for contributory infringement, a patent holder must show, inter alia, that (a) the supplier's product was used to commit acts of direct infringement; (b) the product's use constituted 'a material part of the invention'; (c) the supplier knew its product was 'especially made or especially adapted for use in an infringement' of the patent; and (d) the product is 'not a staple article or commodity of commerce suitable for substantial noninfringing use.'"

Fujitsu Ltd. v. Netgear Inc., 620 F.3d 1321, 1330, 96 U.S.P.Q.2d 1742, 1749 (Fed.Cir.2010). "[W]e disagree with [P's] claim that it need only show that [D] knew of the patent and of the relevant acts, not whether these acts constituted infringement. Our case law is clear that [P] must show that [D] 'knew that the combination for which its components were especially made was both patented and infringing.' [¶] [I]n determining whether there are substantial noninfringing uses, we must only consider the 'particular tool' in question when that tool is 'a separate and distinct feature' of a larger product. [P] argues that the fragmentation software and hardware is a 'separate and distinct' tool and it has no uses other than the infringing method. *At F.3d 1331, U.S.P.Q.2d 1750:* [D] argues that because a user can turn off the infringing features, then there are substantial noninfringing uses. However, it is undisputed that, when activated, the product is infringing. Whether a user activates fragmentation is relevant to the extent of direct infringement, but does not establish substantial noninfringing uses. Therefore, the undisputed facts establish that the fragmentation software does not have substantial noninfringing uses and we cannot affirm summary judgment of noninfringement on this basis."

Ricoh Co. v. Quanta Computer Inc., 550 F.3d 1325, 1337, 89 U.S.P.Q.2d 1577, 1586 (Fed.Cir.2008). "It appears to be undisputed that, assuming direct infringement is found, [D] would be liable under §271(c) if it imported into or sold within the U.S. a bare component (say, a microcontroller containing routines to execute the patented methods) that had no use other than practicing the methods of the '552 and '755 patents. Such a component, specially adapted for use in the patented process and with no substantial noninfringing use, would plainly be 'good for nothing else' but infringement of the patented process. [¶] It thus follows that [D] should not be permitted to escape liability as a contributory infringer merely by embedding that microcontroller in a larger product with some additional, separable feature before importing and selling it. *At F.3d 1338, U.S.P.Q.2d 1587:* [T]he purpose of the 'substantial noninfringing use' exception of §271(c) is to allow determination of instances where the intent to infringe may be presumed based on the distribution of a product that has an unlawful use. When a manufacturer includes in its product a component that can *only* infringe, the inference that infringement is intended is unavoidable. While selling a potentially infringing product where each component part thereof has a substantial lawful use may well be 'equivocal,' ... it is entirely appropriate to presume that one who sells a product containing *a component that has no substantial noninfringing use* in that product does so with the intent that the component will be used to infringe."

PharmaStem Therapeutics, Inc. v. ViaCell, Inc., 491 F.3d 1342, 1357, 83 U.S.P.Q.2d 1289, 1300 (Fed.Cir. 2007). "Under the plain language of the statute, a person who provides a service that assists another in committing patent infringement may be subject to liability under §271(b) for active inducement of infringement, but not under §271(c) for contributory infringement."

Cross Med. Prods. v. Medtronic Sofamor Danek, Inc., 424 F.3d 1293, 1312, 76 U.S.P.Q.2d 1662, 1677 (Fed. Cir.2005). "In order to succeed on a claim of contributory infringement, in addition to proving an act of direct infringement, [P] must show that [D] 'knew that the combination for which its components were especially made was both patented and infringing' and that [D's] components have 'no substantial non-infringing uses.'"

Husky Injection Molding Sys. v. R&D Tool & Eng'g, 291 F.3d 780, 784, 62 U.S.P.Q.2d 1834, 1837 (Fed. Cir.2002). "Both an alleged direct infringer and an alleged contributory infringer benefit from the permissible repair exception."

Joy Tech. v. Flakt, Inc., 6 F.3d 770, 774, 28 U.S.P.Q.2d 1378, 1381 (Fed.Cir.1993). "That the sale of equipment to perform a process is not a direct infringement of the process within the meaning of §271(a) is further highlighted by ... §271(c) ..., which provides in pertinent part that such a sale may be a contributory infringement. To hold that the sale of equipment which performs a patented process is itself a direct infringement would make that portion of §271(c) relating to the sale of an apparatus for use in practicing a patented process meaningless. *At U.S.P.Q.2d 1382:* Although not direct infringement under §271(a), a party's acts in connection with selling equipment may, however, constitute active inducement of infringement or contributory infringement of a method claim under ... §271(b) and (c)."

Hodosh v. Block Drug Co., 833 F.2d 1575, 1577, 4 U.S.P.Q.2d 1935, 1937 (Fed.Cir.1987). "In considering a plaintiff's claim of contributory infringement under §271(c), a court must review the defendant's acts. *At F.2d 1578:* Section 271(c) requires examination of the patented method only in determining whether the material the accused actually sells constitutes a material part of the invention and is known by the accused to be especially made or adapted for use in infringing the patent."

§271(d)

Kimble v. Marvel Entm't, LLC, ___ U.S. ___, 135 S.Ct. 2401, 2405, 114 U.S.P.Q.2d 1941, 1943 (2015). "In ***Brulotte v. Thys Co.***, 379 U.S. 29 ... (1964), this Court held that a patent holder cannot charge royalties for the use of his invention after its patent term has expired. The sole question presented here is whether we should overrule ***Brulotte***. Adhering to principles of *stare decisis*, we decline to do so. Critics of the ***Brulotte*** rule must seek relief not from this Court but from Congress."

Dawson Chem. v. Rohm & Haas Co., 448 U.S. 176, 186 n.6, 206 U.S.P.Q. 385, 392 n.6 (1980). "We [use] the term 'nonstaple' throughout this opinion to refer to a component as defined in ... §271(c), the unlicensed sale of which would constitute contributory infringement. A 'staple' component is one that does not fit this definition. We recognize that the terms 'staple' and 'nonstaple' have not always been defined precisely in this fashion. *At U.S. 186, U.S.P.Q. 392:* [O]ur chief focus of inquiry [is] the scope of the doctrine of patent misuse in light of the limitations placed upon that doctrine by §271(d). *At U.S 201, U.S.P.Q. 398-99:* The limitations on contributory infringement written into §271(c) are counterbalanced by limitations on patent misuse in §271(d). Three species of conduct by patentees are expressly excluded from characterization as misuse. First, the patentee may 'derive revenue' from acts that 'would constitute contributory infringement' if 'performed by another without his consent.' This provision clearly signifies that a patentee may make and sell nonstaple goods used in connection with his invention. Second, the patentee may 'license or authorize another to perform acts' which without such authorization would constitute contributory infringement. This provision's use in the disjunctive of the term 'authorize' suggests that more than explicit licensing agreements is contemplated. Finally, the patentee may 'enforce his patent rights against ... contributory infringement.' This provision plainly means that the patentee may bring suit without fear that his doing so will be regarded as an unlawful attempt to suppress competition. The statute explicitly states that a patentee may do 'one or more' of these permitted acts, and it does not state that he must do any of them. [¶] In our view, the provisions of §271(d) effectively confer upon the patentee, as a lawful adjunct of his patent rights, a limited power to exclude others from competition in nonstaple goods." *See also* ***Hodosh v. Block Drug Co.***, 833 F.2d 1575, 1577-78, 4 U.S.P.Q.2d 1935, 1937 (Fed.Cir.1987).

Princo Corp. v. International Trade Comm'n, 616 F.3d 1318, 1321, 96 U.S.P.Q.2d 1233, 1234 (Fed.Cir. 2010). "This case requires us to consider the scope of the doctrine of patent misuse. Patent misuse developed as a nonstatutory defense to claims of patent infringement. In the licensing context, the doctrine limits a patentee's right to impose conditions on a licensee that exceed the scope of the patent right. Because patent misuse is a judge-made doctrine that is in derogation of statutory patent rights against infringement, this court has not applied the doctrine of patent misuse expansively. *At F.3d 1327, U.S.P.Q.2d 1238:* [T]he Supreme Court established the basic rule of patent misuse: that the patentee may exploit his patent but may not use it to acquire a monopoly not embraced in the patent. As for the most common form of patent misuse—requiring the purchase of an unpatented product as a condition for obtaining a license to the patent, the Court observed, [h]e who uses his patent to obtain protection from competition in the sale of unpatented materials extends by contract his patent monopoly to articles as respects which the law sanctions neither monopolies nor restraints of trade. *At F.3d 1328, U.S.P.Q.2d 1239-40:* [T]he key inquiry under the patent misuse doctrine is whether, by imposing the condition in question, the patentee has impermissibly broadened the physical or temporal scope of the patent grant and has done so in a manner that has anticompetitive effects. Where the patentee has not leveraged its patent beyond the scope of rights granted by the Patent Act, misuse has not been found. *At F.3d 1329-30:* Given that the patent grant entitles the patentee to impose a broad range of conditions in licensing the right to practice the patent, the doctrine of patent misuse has largely been confined to a handful of specific practices by which the patentee seemed to be trying to extend his patent grant beyond its statutory limits. [¶] Recognizing the narrow scope of the doctrine, we have emphasized that the defense of patent misuse is not available to a presumptive infringer simply because a patentee engages in some kind of wrongful commercial conduct, even conduct that may have anticompetitive effects. ... While proof of an antitrust violation shows that the patentee has committed wrongful conduct having anticompetitive effects, that does not establish misuse of the patent in suit unless the conduct in question restricts the use of that patent and does so in one of the specific ways that have been held to be outside the otherwise broad scope of the patent grant. [¶] [S]ection 271(d) ... sets forth five types of conduct that may not provide the basis for finding misuse or illegal extension of the patent right. [¶] Importantly, Congress enacted §271(d) not to broaden the doctrine of patent misuse, but to cabin it. *At F.3d 1331, U.S.P.Q.2d 1241:* Section 271(d) is not directly implicated in this case because the conduct here at issue does not fall within any of the five statutorily defined categories. Nonetheless, the statute is pertinent because ... Congress was concerned about the open-ended scope of the doctrine and sought to confine it to anticompetitive conduct by patentees who leverage their patents to obtain economic advantages outside the legitimate scope of the patent grant. [¶] This case presents a completely different scenario from the cases previously identified by the Supreme Court and by this court as implicating the doctrine of patent misuse. [¶] Reduced to its simplest elements, the question in this case comes down to this: When a patentee offers to license a patent, does the patentee misuse that patent by inducing a third party not to license its separate, competitive technology?" (Internal quotes omitted.) Held: No, the patentee does not misuse the patent.

U.S. Philips Corp. v. ITC, 424 F.3d 1179, 1186, 76 U.S.P.Q.2d 1545, 1549-50 (Fed.Cir.2005). "Because [§271(d)(5)] is phrased in the negative, it does not require that patent misuse be found in the case of all such conditional licenses in which the patent owner has market power; instead, the statute simply excludes such conditional licenses in which the patent owner lacks market power from the category of arrangements that may be found to constitute patent misuse. [¶] [T]he defense of patent misuse differs from traditional antitrust law principles in an important respect, as applied to tying arrangements involving patent rights. In the case of an antitrust claim based on a tying arrangement involving patent rights, this court has held that ownership of a patent on the tying good is presumed to give the patentee monopoly power. Section 271(d)(5) makes clear, however, that such a presumption does not apply in the case of patent misuse. To establish the defense of patent misuse, the accused infringer must show that the patentee has power in the market for the tying product. *At F.3d 1189-90, U.S.P.Q.2d 1552:* In the case of patent-to-product tying, the patent owner uses the market power conferred by the patent to compel customers to purchase a product in a separate market that the customer might otherwise purchase from a competitor. The patent owner is thus able to use the market power conferred by the patent to foreclose competition in the market for the product. [¶] By contrast, a package licensing agreement that includes both essential and nonessential patents does not impose any requirement on the licensee. It does not bar the licensee from using any alternative technology that may be offered by a competitor of the licensor. Nor does it foreclose the competitor from licensing his alternative technology; it merely puts the competitor in the same position he would be in if he were competing with unpatented technology. [¶] A package license is in effect a promise by the patentee not to sue his customer for infringing any patents on whatever technology the customer employs in making commercial use of the licensed patent. *At F.3d 1191-92, U.S.P.Q.2d 1554:* It is entirely rational for a patentee who has a patent that is essential to particular technology, as well as other patents that are not essential, to charge what the market will bear for the essential patent and to offer the others for free. Because a license to the essential patent is, by definition, a prerequisite to practice the technology in question, the patentee can charge whatever maximum amount a willing licensee is able to pay to practice the technology in question. If the patentee allocates royalty fees between its essential and nonessential patents, it runs the risk that licensees will take a license to the essential patent but not to the nonessential patents. The effect of that choice will be that the patentee will not be able to obtain the full royalty value of the essential patent. For the patentee in this situation to offer its nonessential patents as part of a package with the essential patent at no additional charge is no more anticompetitive than if it had surrendered the nonessential patents or had simply announced a policy that it would not enforce them against persons who licensed the essential patent. *At F.3d 1194, U.S.P.Q.2d 1556:* Patents within a patent package can be regarded as 'nonessential' only if there are 'commercially feasible' alternatives to those patents. If there are no commercially practicable alternatives to the allegedly nonessential patents, packaging those patents together with so-called essential patents can have no anticompetitive effect in the marketplace, because no competition for a viable alternative product is foreclosed. In such a case, the only effect of finding per se patent misuse is to give licensees a way of avoiding their obligations under the licensing agreements, with no corresponding benefit to competition in any real-world market."

Virginia Panel Corp. v. MAC Panel Co., 133 F.3d 860, 869, 45 U.S.P.Q.2d 1225, 1232 (Fed.Cir.1997). "The courts have identified certain specific practices as constituting *per se* patent misuse, including so-called 'tying' arrangements in which a patentee conditions a license under the patent on the purchase of a separable, staple good, and arrangements in which a patentee effectively extends the term of its patent by requiring post-expiration royalties[.] Congress, however, has established that other specific practices may not support a finding of patent misuse. A 1988 amendment to §271(d) provides that, *inter alia*, in the absence of market power, even a tying arrangement does not constitute patent misuse. [¶] When a practice alleged to constitute patent misuse is neither *per se* patent misuse nor specifically excluded from a misuse analysis by §271(d), a court must determine if that practice is 'reasonably within the patent grant, *i.e.*, that it relates to subject matter within the scope of the patent claims.' If so, the practice does not have the effect of broadening the scope of the patent claims and thus cannot constitute patent misuse. If, on the other hand, the practice has the effect of extending the patentee's statutory rights and does so with an anti-competitive effect, that practice must then be analyzed in accordance with the 'rule of reason.' Under the rule of reason, 'the finder of fact must decide whether the questioned practice imposes an unreasonable restraint on competition, taking into account a variety of factors, including specific information about the relevant business, its condition before and after the restraint was imposed, and the restraint's history, nature, and effect.'" *See also* ***Mercoid Corp. v. Mid-Continent Inv.***, 320 U.S. 661, 664, 60 U.S.P.Q. 21, 24 (1944); ***B. Braun Med. Inc. v. Abbott Labs.***, 124 F.3d 1419, 1426, 43 U.S.P.Q.2d 1896, 1901-02 (Fed.Cir.1997).

Data Gen. Corp. v. Grumman Sys. Support Corp., 36 F.3d 1147, 1187, 32 U.S.P.Q.2d 1385, 1417 (1st Cir.1994), *overruled on other grounds*, ***Reed Elsevier, Inc. v. Muchnick***, 559 U.S. 154 (2010). "Section 271(d) clearly prevents an infringer from using a patent misuse defense when the patent owner has unilaterally refused a license, and may even herald the prohibition of all antitrust claims and counterclaims premised on a refusal to license a patent."

Windsurfing Int'l v. AMF, Inc., 782 F.2d 995, 1001-02, 228 U.S.P.Q. 562, 566-67 (Fed.Cir.1986). "We have been cited to no authority, and are aware of none, for the proposition that patent misuse may be found on the basis of a patent license agreement provision recognizing and forbidding use of the licensor's validly registered trademarks. [¶] To sustain a misuse defense involving a licensing arrangement not held to have been per se anticompetitive by the Supreme Court, a factual determination must reveal that the overall effect of the license tends to restrain competition unlawfully in an appropriately defined relevant market. A provision in a patent license agreement requiring the licensee to acknowledge the validity of registered trademarks, and to avoid their use, cannot possibly restrain competition unlawfully in an appropriately defined relevant market. ... The assertion of trademark rights can have procompetitive effects, and thus under only the most rare of circumstances could such assertion, separately or as a provision in a patent license agreement, form in itself the basis for a holding of inequitable conduct such as that labeled 'patent misuse.'"

§271(e)(1)

Merck KGaA v. Integra Lifesciences I, Ltd., 545 U.S. 193, 195, 74 U.S.P.Q.2d 1801, 1802 (2005). "This case presents the question whether uses of patented inventions in preclinical research, the results of which are not ultimately included in a submission to the [FDA], are exempted from infringement by ... §271(e)(1). *At U.S. 207-08, U.S.P.Q.2d 1807-08:* Properly construed, §271(e)(1) leaves adequate space for experimentation and failure on the road to regulatory approval: At least where a drugmaker has a reasonable basis for believing that a patented compound may work, through a particular biological process, to produce a particular physiological effect, and uses the compound in research that, if successful, would be appropriate to include in a submission to the FDA, that use is 'reasonably related' to the 'development and submission of information under ... Federal law.' [¶] For similar reasons, the use of a patented compound in experiments that are not themselves included in a 'submission of information' to the FDA does not, standing alone, render the use infringing. [T]he use of patented compounds in preclinical studies is protected under §271(e)(1) as long as there is a reasonable basis for believing that the experiments will produce 'the types of information that are relevant to an [investigational new drug application] or [new drug application].'"

Eli Lilly & Co. v. Medtronic, Inc., 496 U.S. 661, 663-64, 15 U.S.P.Q.2d 1121, 1124 (1990). "This case presents the question whether 35 U.S.C. §271(e)(1) renders activities that would otherwise constitute patent infringement noninfringing if they are undertaken for the purpose of developing and submitting to the [FDA] information necessary to obtain marketing approval for a medical device under ... 21 U.S.C. §360e." Held: Section 271(e)(1) applies to medical devices. *See also* ***AbTox, Inc. v. Exitron Corp.***, 122 F.3d 1019, 1027, 43 U.S.P.Q.2d 1545, 1552-53 (Fed.Cir.1997), *aff'd as modified*, 131 F.3d 1009 (Fed.Cir.1997). *But see* ***Baxter Diagnostics Inc. v. AVL Sci. Corp.***, 798 F.Supp. 612, 619-20, 25 U.S.P.Q.2d 1428, 1434 (C.D.Cal.1992) (§271(e)(1) applies only to Class III medical devices).

Momenta Pharms. v. Amphastar Pharms., 686 F.3d 1348, 1355, 103 U.S.P.Q.2d 1800, 1806-07 (Fed.Cir. 2012). "Unlike the closely related infringement provision, 35 U.S.C. §271(e)(2), Congress did not link the safe harbor to the submission of an application for approval under the Federal Food, Drug, and Cosmetic Act. We cannot change the statutory language. We will not import the limitation of §271(e)(2) into §271(e)(1). ... The statute here applies to *any* use of a patented invention as long as the use is 'reasonably related to the development and submission of information under a Federal law which regulates the manufacture, use, or sale of drugs....' [¶] As long as the allegedly infringing use is 'for uses reasonably related' to the development and submission of that information it is not an act of infringement, regardless of where that requirement resides in the law. *At F.3d 1358, U.S.P.Q.2d 1808:* We, of course, are bound by the ***Classen*** decision unless it is overruled en banc or by the Supreme Court. Accordingly, the scope of the safe harbor provision does not extend to 'information that may be routinely reported to the FDA, long after marketing approval has been obtained.' [¶] This case, however, fits well within ***Classen*** because the information submitted is necessary both to the continued approval of the [abbreviated new drug application] and to the ability to market the generic drug. Here, the submissions are not 'routine submissions' to the FDA, but instead are submissions that are required to maintain FDA approval." Held: The district court's preliminary injunction is vacated.

Classen Immunotherapies, Inc. v. Biogen Idec, 659 F.3d 1057, 1070, 100 U.S.P.Q.2d 1492, 1503 (Fed.Cir. 2011). Section 271(e)(1) "provides an exception to the law of infringement in order to expedite development of information for regulatory approval of generic counterparts of patented products. The statute does not apply to information that may be routinely reported to the FDA, long after marketing approval has been obtained."

Amgen, Inc. v. ITC, 565 F.3d 846, 848, 90 U.S.P.Q.2d 1842, 1845 (Fed.Cir.2009). "[T]he safe harbor provided by [35 U.S.C.] §271(e)(1) applies in proceedings under the Tariff Act [19 U.S.C. §1337] relating to process patents as well as product patents, for imported product that is used for exempt purposes."

Proveris Sci. Corp. v. Innovasystems, Inc., 536 F.3d 1256, 1265, 87 U.S.P.Q.2d 1602, 1608-09 (Fed.Cir. 2008). "[T]he question before us [is] whether §271(e)(1) immunizes the manufacture, marketing, or sale of [P's analytical device], which is used in the development of FDA regulatory submissions, but is not itself subject to the FDA premarket approval process. [W]e hold that the §271(e)(1) safe harbor does not immunize [device] from infringement."

§271(e)(2)

Amgen Inc. v. Apotex Inc., 827 F.3d 1052, 1058, 119 U.S.P.Q.2d 1318, 1322 (Fed.Cir.2016). "The two circumstances [for infringement in 35 U.S.C. §271(e)(2)(C)(i), (ii)] involve, respectively, an applicant that has launched the Biologics Act information-exchange process ... and an applicant that has not. [¶] Specifically, one circumstance is when the patent 'is identified in the list of patents described in' [42 U.S.C. §262(*l*)(3)], 'including as provided under' [§262(*l*)(7)]. Filing the biosimilar application is an act of infringement of patents that the reference product sponsor has listed through the Biologics Act's prescribed processes, which occurs only when the applicant has provided the [§262(*l*)(2)(A)] notice. The other circumstance involves an applicant that 'fails to provide the application and information required' under [§262(*l*)(2)(A)]. In that case, filing the biosimilar application is an act of infringement as to a patent that 'could be identified pursuant to' [§262(*l*)(3)(A)], *i.e.*, a patent that the reference product sponsor could identify as one it believes 'could reasonably be asserted' with respect to the biosimilar product at issue."

Ferring B.V. v. Watson Labs., 764 F.3d 1382, 1387-88, 112 U.S.P.Q.2d 1059, 1063 (Fed.Cir.2014). "***Sunovion*** [***Pharms. v. Teva Pharms. USA, Inc.***, 731 F.3d 1271 (Fed.Cir.2013),] only applies when 'an [abbreviated new drug application (ANDA)] specification defines a compound such that it meets the limitations of an asserted claim.' In ***Sunovion***, that was the case. The ANDA specified an infringing product. The ***Sunovion*** court concluded that a generic drug company could not then avoid infringement by certifying that it would not infringe, overriding the language of its own ANDA. [¶] When an ANDA is silent with respect to infringement, ... the correct analysis is under ***Glaxo, Inc. v. Novopharm, Ltd.***, 110 F.3d 1562, 1570 (Fed.Cir. 1997), not ***Sunovion***. In ***Glaxo***, the patent-holder argued ... that 'the alleged infringer must disprove infringement if the ANDA permits sale of a composition that may include an infringing product.' We disagreed and concluded that '[t]he relevant inquiry is whether the patentee has proven by a preponderance of the evidence that the alleged infringer will likely market an infringing product. What is likely to be sold, or, preferably, what will be sold, will ultimately determine whether infringement exists.' For the patent-holder to prove that a ***Glaxo***-type ANDA is infringing, it must rely on evidence that the ANDA applicant 'would likely sell an infringing composition pursuant to an approved ANDA.'"

Alcon Research Ltd. v. Barr Labs., 745 F.3d 1180, 1186, 110 U.S.P.Q.2d 1008, 1012 (Fed.Cir.2014). "We agree with [D] that [P] failed to present evidence of infringement. Unlike a classic patent infringement case in which infringement exists if at least one claim of an asserted patent reads on a product or process that the accused infringer has introduced into the U.S. marketplace, an infringement inquiry provoked by an [abbreviated new drug application (ANDA)] filing under the Hatch-Waxman system pursuant to ... §271(e)(2)(A) is focused on a comparison of the asserted patent against 'the product that is likely to be sold following ANDA approval.' That determination is based on consideration of all of the relevant evidence and, '[b]ecause drug manufacturers are bound by strict statutory provisions to sell only those products that comport with the ANDA's description of the drug, an ANDA specification defining a proposed generic drug in a manner that directly addresses the issue of infringement will control the infringement inquiry.'"

Takeda Chem. Indus. v. Mylan Labs., 549 F.3d 1381, 1387-88, 89 U.S.P.Q.2d 1218, 1223 (Fed.Cir.2008). "[W]e [have] stated that '[t]he joint operation of [35 U.S.C.] §§271(e) and 285 require[s] the paragraph (2) infringer to display care and regard for the strict standards of the Hatch-Waxman Act when challenging patent validity.... The Hatch-Waxman Act thus imposes a duty of care on an [abbreviated new drug application (ANDA)] certifier.' [An ANDA] filing would amount to litigation misconduct supporting an exceptional case finding if it were 'baseless' and if it 'fail[ed] to present even a prima facie case of invalidity in filing the paragraph IV certification.'"

Caraco Pharm. v. Forest Labs., 527 F.3d 1278, 1283, 86 U.S.P.Q.2d 1289, 1291 (Fed.Cir.2008). "'Section 271(e)(2) is designed to create an *artificial* act of infringement for purposes of establishing jurisdiction in the federal courts.'"

Allergan, Inc. v. Alcon Labs., 324 F.3d 1322, 1326, 66 U.S.P.Q.2d 1225, 1228 (Fed.Cir.2003). "The exemption to infringement under [35 U.S.C.] §271(e)(1) allows a generic drug manufacturer to take the steps needed to bring a generic drug to market without waiting until the patent expires. At the same time, by deeming the filing of an [abbreviated new drug application (ANDA)] to be an act of infringement under

§271(e)(2), the Hatch-Waxman Act allows a brand name drug manufacturer to challenge the ANDA ... and a generic drug manufacturer to challenge the validity and infringement of an asserted patent before the patent expires. *At F.3d 1330-31, U.S.P.Q.2d 1231:* Section 271(e)(2) is not a jurisdictional statute in the strict sense of the word. [S]ection 271(e)(2) 'provides patentees with a defined act of infringement sufficient to create case or controversy jurisdiction to enable a court to promptly resolve any dispute concerning infringement and validity.' Once Congress creates an act of infringement, jurisdiction in the district court is proper under 28 U.S.C. §1338(a). Section 1338(a) states that 'the district courts shall have original jurisdiction of any civil action arising under any Act of Congress relating to patents....' Section 271(e)(2) is an Act of Congress relating to patents. Therefore, §1338(a) provides for jurisdiction in the district court for [P's] suit. [¶] [W]e must determine whether ... §271(e)(2) may serve as an umbrella for a claim of induced infringement for a method of use patent. *At U.S.P.Q.2d 1232:* [S]ection 271(e)(2) may support an action for induced infringement. *At F.3d 1332:* Summary judgment of noninfringement under §271(e)(2) ... is inappropriate where the plaintiff can demonstrate the existence of a genuine issue of material fact with respect to the claim that the ANDA filer will induce infringement of its patent upon approval of the ANDA."

Warner-Lambert Co. v. Apotex Corp., 316 F.3d 1348, 1354-55, 65 U.S.P.Q.2d 1481, 1484 (Fed.Cir.2003). "The central issue in the present case is whether it is an act of infringement under ... §271(e)(2)(A) to submit an [abbreviated new drug application (ANDA)] seeking approval to make, use, or sell a drug for an approved use if any other use of the drug is claimed in a patent, or if it is only an act of infringement to submit an ANDA seeking approval to make, use, or sell a drug if the drug or the use *for which FDA approval is sought* is claimed in a patent. [I]t is not an act of infringement to submit an ANDA for approval to market a drug for a use when neither the drug nor that use is covered by an existing patent, and the patent at issue is for a use not approved under the [new drug application]. *At F.3d 1356, U.S.P.Q.2d 1485:* [T]he statute does not make the filing of an ANDA prior to patent expiration an act of infringement unless the ANDA seeks approval to manufacture, use, or sell the drug prior to expiration of a patent *that would otherwise be infringed* by such manufacture, use, or sale, *apart from* the provisions of §271(e)(2)." *See also* ***Andrx Pharms. v. Biovail Corp.***, 276 F.3d 1368, 1371, 61 U.S.P.Q.2d 1414, 1415-16 (Fed.Cir.2002).

Abbott Labs. v. TorPharm, Inc., 300 F.3d 1367, 1373, 63 U.S.P.Q.2d 1929, 1932 (Fed.Cir.2002). "An infringement inquiry provoked by an [abbreviated new drug application (ANDA)] filing under ... §271(e)(2)(A) is focused on the product that is likely to be sold following FDA approval. This determination is based on consideration of all the relevant evidence, including the ANDA filing, other materials submitted by the accused infringer to the FDA, and other evidence provided by the parties. Because drug manufacturers are bound by strict statutory provisions to sell only those products that comport with the ANDA's description of the drug, an ANDA specification defining a proposed generic drug in a manner that directly addresses the issue of infringement will control the infringement inquiry."

Bayer AG v. Biovail Corp., 279 F.3d 1340, 1350, 61 U.S.P.Q.2d 1675, 1683 (Fed.Cir.2002). "[I]nfringement under §271(e)(2)(A) by submission of an [abbreviated new drug application] is not synonymous with infringement under §271(a) by a commercial product. Evidence of actual infringement (contrasted with evidence of a 'hypothetical' infringement) may differ in substance and may become available only after manufacture of the composition." *See also* ***Novartis Corp. v. Ben Venue Labs.***, 271 F.3d 1043, 1047, 60 U.S.P.Q.2d 1836, 1839 (Fed.Cir.2001); ***Glaxo Grp. v. Ranbaxy Pharms.***, 262 F.3d 1333, 1337-38, 59 U.S.P.Q.2d 1950, 1953-54 (Fed.Cir.2001).

Glaxo, Inc. v. Novopharm, Ltd., 110 F.3d 1562, 1570, 42 U.S.P.Q.2d 1257, 1264 (Fed.Cir.1997). "While ... §271(e)(2) provides the federal courts with jurisdiction to hear infringement cases regarding claims directed to drugs or to methods of using drugs, it does not provide jurisdiction to hear infringement cases regarding claims directed to methods for making drugs."

DuPont Merck Pharm. v. Bristol-Myers Squibb Co., 62 F.3d 1397, 1402, 35 U.S.P.Q.2d 1718, 1722 (Fed. Cir.1995). "[T]he [Uruguay Round Agreements Act (URAA)], by its terms, exempts a qualified infringer from the remedies of [35 U.S.C.] §§283, 284, and 285.... The URAA, however, works no change on the definition of infringement under [35 U.S.C.] §271(e)(2) and has no [effect] on the statutory provisions relating to FDA approval of ANDAs [abbreviated new drug applications] that are triggered by that act of infringement."

§271(e)(4)

Amgen Inc. v. Apotex Inc., 827 F.3d 1052, 1066, 119 U.S.P.Q.2d 1318, 1328 (Fed.Cir.2016). "[A]n applicant must provide a reference product sponsor with 180 days' post-licensure notice before commercial marketing begins, regardless of whether the applicant provided the [42 U.S.C. §262(*l*)(2)(A)] notice of FDA review."

Ferring B.V. v. Watson Labs., 764 F.3d 1382, 1389-90, 112 U.S.P.Q.2d 1059, 1064-65 (Fed.Cir.2014). "[P] objects to the district court's decision to consider the 2014 [abbreviated new drug application (ANDA)], stating that 35 U.S.C. §271(e)(4)(A) requires that once a §271(e)(2) infringement is found based on the ANDA as first submitted, the district court *must* order a change in the effective date of the ANDA. ... Section 271(e)(4)(A) specifies that '[f]or an act of infringement described in [§271(e)(2)] the court *shall* order the effective date of any approval of the drug or veterinary biological product involved in the infringement to be a date which is not earlier than the date of the expiration of the patent which has been infringed.' The district court is not precluded from considering an amended ANDA when deciding the issue of infringement. [¶] Both [21 U.S.C.] §355(j), referred to in §271(e)(2), and the FDA's regulations contemplate that a pending application may be amended for various reasons. For the purposes of §271(e)(2), 'an application' means the ANDA as filed and all amendments to that application that have been allowed by the FDA. There is no support for the proposition that the question of infringement must be addressed solely based on the initial ANDA filing, given that the statute contemplates that the ANDA will be amended as a matter of course. Nor does it appear that [P] contends otherwise. [¶] Indeed, our own precedent conclusively establishes that [ ]§271(e)(2) and (4) require consideration of the amended ANDA."

In re Omeprazole Patent Litig., 536 F.3d 1361, 1367-68, 87 U.S.P.Q.2d 1865, 1869 (Fed.Cir.2008). "If the patent holder proves infringement of a valid patent resulting from the filing of an [abbreviated new drug application (ANDA)], [35 U.S.C.] §271(e)(4) provides three remedies. Subparagraphs (B) and (C) provide the typical remedies for infringement: injunctive relief and damages. Subparagraph (A), however, provides an additional type of relief after a finding of infringement under §271(e)(2) by requiring the district court to 'order the effective date of any approval of the drug or veterinary biological product involved in the infringement to be a date which is not earlier than the date of the expiration of the patent which has been infringed.' If the FDA has not approved the ANDA before the district court determines that the patent has been infringed, the FDA may not approve the ANDA until the effective date specified by the district court under §271(e)(4)(A). If the FDA has already approved the ANDA, the district court's order would alter the effective date of the application, thereby converting a final approval into a tentative approval. [¶] In most circumstances, the effective date in a district court's order under §271(e)(4)(A) will be the date of patent expiration, including any patent extensions. In this case, however, [patent holder] was entitled to an additional six-month period of market exclusivity (sometimes known as a period of 'pediatric exclusivity') under the [FDA] Modernization Act.... A provision of that Act, codified at 21 U.S.C. §355a, authorizes the [FDA] to make a written request to the holder of an approved new drug application ('NDA') for the holder to perform pediatric studies. If the NDA holder agrees to the request and performs the pediatric studies, the period during which the FDA is barred from approving an ANDA filed by competing drug manufacturers is extended by six months."

Glaxo Grp. v. Apotex, Inc., 376 F.3d 1339, 1350-51, 71 U.S.P.Q.2d 1801, 1809 (Fed.Cir.2004). "[W]e now hold that the mere fact that a company has filed an [abbreviated new drug] application or certification cannot support a finding of willful infringement for purposes of awarding attorney's fees pursuant to ... §271(e)(4)."

§271(e)(5)

Dey Pharma, LP v. Sunovion Pharms., 677 F.3d 1158, 1160-61, 102 U.S.P.Q.2d 1710, 1712-13 (Fed.Cir. 2012). "Congress specified that an [abbreviated new drug application (ANDA)] filer who is not sued within 45 days could bring a declaratory judgment action under 28 U.S.C. §2201 against the [new drug application (NDA)] holder, ... and that the federal courts would have declaratory judgment jurisdiction 'to the extent consistent with the Constitution[ ]'.... Under this amended Hatch-Waxman frame-work, if the first ANDA filer 'parked' its 180-day exclusivity under an agreement with the brandname company, a subsequent

ANDA filer could independently trigger the first filer's exclusivity period through a declaratory judgment action leading to a final judgment of invalidity or noninfringement, thereby accelerating the second ANDA filer's ability to market its drug. [¶] This case involves such a declaratory judgment claim by the second ANDA filer [P] against the patent holder and NDA filer [D], designed to trigger the first ANDA filer's ... exclusivity period. *At F.3d 1162:* Whether an 'actual controversy' exists that is sufficient to sustain federal jurisdiction under the Declaratory Judgment Act ... is a question of law that we review de novo. In the Hatch-Waxman context, Congress extended declaratory judgment jurisdiction to ANDA ¶IV disputes ... and has directed federal courts to exercise jurisdiction over these disputes 'to the extent consistent with the Constitution[ ]'.... Under the Supreme Court's decision in ***MedImmune, Inc. v. Genentech, Inc.***, declaratory judgment jurisdiction is created when 'the facts alleged, under all the circumstances, show that there is a substantial controversy[ ] between parties having adverse legal interests[ ] of sufficient immediacy and reality to warrant the issuance of a declaratory judgment.'"

§271(e)(6)

Amgen Inc. v. Apotex Inc., 827 F.3d 1052, 1058, 119 U.S.P.Q.2d 1318, 1323 (Fed.Cir.2016). "35 U.S.C. §271(e)(6) ... limits the ... remedies [in §271(e)(4)] in two ways evidently designed to reinforce the reference product sponsor's incentives to follow the distinctive Biologics Act's patent process where the applicant has launched that process. *First:* If the reference product sponsor is late in bringing the first-stage infringement action under [42 U.S.C.] §262(*l*)'s paragraph (6), *i.e.*, does so more than 30 days after the scope of that litigation has been determined under [§262(*l*)(4) or (5)], the only remedy the reference product sponsor can get in that action is a reasonable royalty. *Second:* If a patent that the reference product sponsor should have included on its [§262(*l*)(3)(A)] list or its [§262(*l*)(7)] supplement 'was not timely included,' then the owner of that patent may not sue for infringement under ... §271 with respect to the biological product at issue."

§271(f)

WesternGeco LLC v. ION Geophysical Corp., 138 S.Ct. 734, 734 (2018). Issue for review: Whether the court of appeals erred in holding that lost profits arising from prohibited combinations occurring outside of the U.S. are categorically unavailable in cases where patent infringement is proven under 35 U.S.C. §271(f).

Life Techs. v. Promega Corp., ___ U.S. ___, 137 S.Ct. 734, 737, 121 U.S.P.Q.2d 1641, 1642 (2017). "This case concerns the intersection of international supply chains and federal patent law. Section 271(f)(1) ... prohibits the supply from the U.S. of 'all or a substantial portion' of the components of a patented invention for combination abroad. We granted certiorari to determine whether a party that supplies a single component of a multicomponent invention for manufacture abroad can be held liable for infringement under §271(f)(1). We hold that a single component does not constitute a substantial portion of the components that can give rise to liability under §271(f)(1). *At U.S. ___, S.Ct. 741, U.S.P.Q.2d 1645:* Having determined that the term 'substantial portion' refers to a quantitative measurement, we must next decide whether, as a matter of law, a single component can ever constitute a 'substantial portion' so as to trigger liability under §271(f)(1). The answer is no."

Microsoft Corp. v. AT&T Corp., 550 U.S. 437, 449, 82 U.S.P.Q.2d 1400, 1406 (2007). "First, when, or in what form, does software become a 'component' under §271(f)? *At U.S.P.Q.2d 1407:* Until it is expressed as a computer-readable 'copy,' e.g., on a CD-ROM, [D's] software—indeed any software detached from an activating medium—remains uncombinable. It cannot be inserted into a CD-ROM drive or downloaded from the Internet; it cannot be installed or executed on a computer. Abstract software code is an idea without physical embodiment, and as such, it does not match §271(f)'s categorization: 'components' amenable to 'combination.' *At U.S. 451-52, U.S.P.Q.2d 1408:* In sum, a copy of [D's software], not [D's software] in the abstract, qualifies as a 'component' under §271(f). [¶] The next question, has [D] 'supplie[d] ... from the U.S.' components of the computers here involved? *At U.S.P.Q.2d 1409:* [T]he copies of [D's software] actually installed on the foreign computers were not themselves supplied from the U.S. ... The absence of anything addressing copying in the statutory text weighs against a judicial determination that replication abroad of a master dispatched from the U.S. 'supplies' the foreign-made copies from the U.S. within the intendment of §271(f)."

Cardiac Pacemakers, Inc. v. St. Jude Med., Inc., 576 F.3d 1348, 1365, 91 U.S.P.Q.2d 1898, 1912 (Fed.Cir. 2009). "Section 271(f) does not apply to method patents."

NTP, Inc. v. Research In Motion, Ltd., 418 F.3d 1282, 1322-23, 75 U.S.P.Q.2d 1763, 1794 (Fed.Cir.2005), *abrogated on other grounds*, ***Zoltek Corp. v. U.S.***, 672 F.3d 1309 (Fed.Cir.2012) (en banc). "While it is difficult to conceive of how one might supply or cause to be supplied all or a substantial portion of the steps of a patented method in the sense contemplated by the phrase 'components of a patented invention' in §271(f), it is clear [D's] supply of ... devices and ... products to its customers in the U.S. is not the statutory 'supply' of any 'component' steps for combination into [P's] patented methods. By merely supplying products to its customers in the U.S., [D] is not supplying or causing to be supplied in this country any steps of a patented process invention for combination outside the U.S. and cannot infringe [P's] asserted method claims under §271(f) as a matter of law."

Pellegrini v. Analog Devices, Inc., 375 F.3d 1113, 1115, 71 U.S.P.Q.2d 1630, 1632 (Fed.Cir.2004). "This case presents the question whether components that are manufactured outside the U.S. and never physically shipped to or from the U.S. may nonetheless be 'supplied or caused to be supplied in or from the U.S.' within the meaning of 35 U.S.C. §271(f)(1) if those components are designed within the U.S. and the instructions for their manufacture and disposition are transmitted from within the U.S." Held: Components such as those in case are not supplied in or from the U.S. Therefore, §271(f) cannot be used to hold D liable as an infringer.

Waymark Corp. v. Porta Sys., 245 F.3d 1364, 1367-68, 58 U.S.P.Q.2d 1456, 1459 (Fed.Cir.2001). "On its face, §271(f)(2) requires that the infringer only intend[] that such component will be combined. At no point does the statutory language require or suggest that the infringer must actually combine or assemble the components. [¶] Also, §271(f)(2) does not incorporate the doctrine of contributory infringement. Section 271(f)(2) states that whoever meets its requirements shall be liable as an infringer. In contrast, §271(c), a contributory infringement subsection, states that whoever meets its requirements shall be liable as a *contributory* infringer, thereby making infringement under §271(c) dependent on an act of direct infringement. *At U.S.P.Q.2d 1460:* [T]he district court erred by holding that §271(f)(2) required an actual combination of shipped components."

§271(g)

Momenta Pharms. v. Teva Pharms. USA, Inc., 809 F.3d 610, 616, 116 U.S.P.Q.2d 1961, 1964 (Fed.Cir. 2015). "[T]he ordinary meaning of 'made' as used in §271(g) means 'manufacture,' and extends to the creation or transformation of a product, such as by synthesizing, combining components, or giving raw materials new properties. However, 'ma[king]' does not extend to testing to determine whether an already-synthesized drug substance possesses existing qualities or properties. *At F.3d 617, U.S.P.Q.2d 1965:* [A] product is not 'made by' a patented process within the meaning of §271(g) if it is used merely to determine whether the intended product of a separate and perhaps separately-patented process has in fact already been manufactured."

Zoltek Corp. v. U.S., 672 F.3d 1309, 1323, 102 U.S.P.Q.2d 1001, 1011 (Fed.Cir.2012). "If a private party had used [P's] patented process to create the resulting product, there would be liability for infringing [P's] patent right under §154(a)(1) and §271(g). We hold that the Government is subject to the same liability in this case, and that precedent and legislative intent dictate that result. *At F.3d 1326, U.S.P.Q.2d 1014:* [W]e hold that for the purposes of §1498, the use or importation 'within the U.S. [of] a product which is made by a process patented in the U.S.' constitutes use of the invention without lawful right because the products embody the invention itself. We add that nothing in this opinion should be construed to affect our Title 35 jurisprudence."

Monsanto Co. v. Syngenta Seeds, Inc., 503 F.3d 1352, 1360, 84 U.S.P.Q.2d 1705, 1710 (Fed.Cir.2007). Section 271(g) "'requires that the patent be issued and in force at the time that the process is practiced and the product is made.' '[B]ecause domestic entities do not infringe a process patent if they practice the process before the beginning of the patent term, even if they sell the products of the process during the term of the patent, parallel treatment of overseas entities indicates that the statute does not reach pre-issuance use of the later-patented process.' Further, ... a method or process claim is directly infringed only when the process is performed. Thus, infringement of a multi-step method claim cannot lie by the performance of a single step after issuance of the patent when the initial steps were performed prior to issuance."

NTP, Inc. v. Research In Motion, Ltd., 418 F.3d 1282, 1323, 75 U.S.P.Q.2d 1763, 1795 (Fed.Cir.2005), *abrogated on other grounds*, ***Zoltek Corp. v. U.S.***, 672 F.3d 1309 (Fed.Cir.2012) (en banc). "Because the 'transmission of information,' like the 'production of information,' does not entail the manufacturing of a physical product, §271(g) does not apply to the asserted method claims in this case…."

Kinik Co. v. ITC, 362 F.3d 1359, 1363, 70 U.S.P.Q.2d 1300, 1303 (Fed.Cir.2004). "We affirm the [International Trade] Commission's ruling that the defenses established in [35 U.S.C.] §271(g) are not available in [19 U.S.C.] §1337(a)(1)(B)(ii) actions."

Bayer AG v. Housey Pharms., 340 F.3d 1367, 1371, 68 U.S.P.Q.2d 1001, 1004 (Fed.Cir.2003). "We are concerned … with the meaning of the phrase 'a product which is made by a patented process.' *At F.3d 1372, U.S.P.Q.2d 1005:* By referring to the party that produces a product as a 'manufacturer' and the maker as a 'person engaged in the manufacture of a product,' the statute clearly contemplates that 'made' means 'manufactured.' *At F.3d 1378, U.S.P.Q.2d 1009:* The pertinent dictionary definitions of 'by' are 'through the means or instrumentality of; … through the direct agency of; … through the medium of; … through the work or operation of.' Thus, the process must be used directly in the manufacture of the product, and not merely as a predicate process to identify the product to be manufactured. A drug product, the characteristics of which were studied using the claimed research processes, therefore, is not a product 'made by' those claimed processes."

Ajinomoto Co. v. Archer-Daniels-Midland Co., 228 F.3d 1338, 1348, 56 U.S.P.Q.2d 1332, 1340 (Fed.Cir. 2000). "Section 271(g) by its terms applies to unauthorized actions within the U.S.; it is irrelevant that the product was authorized to be produced outside of the U.S. When the process used abroad is the same as the process covered by a U.S. patent, liability for infringement arises only upon importation, sale or offers, or use in the U.S. as set forth in §271(g)." *See also* ***Biotec Biologische Naturverpackungen GmbH v. Biocorp, Inc.***, 249 F.3d 1341, 1350, 58 U.S.P.Q.2d 1737, 1743 (Fed. Cir.2001).

Bio-Tech. Gen. Corp. v. Genentech, Inc., 80 F.3d 1553, 1560, 38 U.S.P.Q.2d 1321, 1326 (Fed.Cir.1996), *overruled on other grounds*, ***eBay Inc. v. MercExchange, L.L.C.***, 547 U.S. 388, 78 U.S.P.Q.2d 1577 (2006). "The 'materially changed' exception of §271(g) requires, at a minimum, that there be a real difference between the product imported, offered for sale, sold, or used in the U.S. and the products produced by the patented process. *At F.3d 1561, U.S.P.Q.2d 1327:* The statute does not specify what products will be considered to have been 'made by' the patented process, apparently because Congress wanted the courts to resolve this critical question of proximity to the product of the patented process on a case-by-case basis."

§271(h)

Florida Prepaid Postsecondary Educ. Expense Bd. v. College Sav. Bank, 527 U.S. 627, 647, 51 U.S.P.Q.2d 1081, 1090 (1999). "[T]he Patent Remedy Act [§271(h)] cannot be sustained under §5 of the 14th Amendment."

Pennington Seed, Inc. v. Produce Exch., 457 F.3d 1334, 1341-43, 79 U.S.P.Q.2d 1777, 1781-82 (Fed.Cir. 2006). "[C]ontinuing prospective violations of a federal patent right by state officials may be enjoined by federal courts under the ***Ex parte Young***[, 209 U.S. 123 (1908),] doctrine; however, the 11th Amendment precludes the plaintiff from obtaining monetary damages from individual defendants in their official capacities. Moreover, this procedure cannot be applied to an action against any random state official. As noted in ***Ex parte Young***, there must be a connection between the state officer and the enforcement of the act or else the suit will merely make him a representative of the state and therefore improperly make the state a party to the suit. [¶] Allegations that a state official directs a University's patent policy are insufficient to causally connect that state official to a violation of federal patent law—i.e., patent infringement. A nexus between the violation of federal law and the individual accused of violating that law requires more than simply a broad general obligation to prevent a violation; it requires an actual violation of federal law by that individual. The fact that a University Official has a general, state-law obligation to oversee a University's patent policy does not give rise to a violation of federal patent law."

§272. TEMPORARY PRESENCE IN THE UNITED STATES

The use of any invention in any vessel, aircraft or vehicle of any country which affords similar privileges to vessels, aircraft or vehicles of the United States, entering the United States temporarily or accidentally, shall not constitute infringement of any patent, if the invention is used exclusively for the needs of the vessel, aircraft or vehicle and is not offered for sale or sold in or used for the manufacture of anything to be sold in or exported from the United States.

History of 35 U.S.C. §272: July 19, 1952, ch. 950, §1, 66 Stat. 812; Dec. 8, 1994, P.L. 103-465, §533(b)(4), 108 Stat. 4989.

See also Paris Convention art. 5; TRIPs pt. II, §5.

ANNOTATIONS

National Steel Car, Ltd. v. Canadian Pac. Ry., 357 F.3d 1319, 1328, 69 U.S.P.Q.2d 1641, 1648 (Fed.Cir. 2004). "Although we recognize that in some instances there may be ambiguity between containers that are merely the cargo of a vessel or vehicle, and vessels or vehicles that are themselves aggregated and transported in a collective fashion for greater efficiency, we discern no such ambiguity here.... Congress has provided [in 1 U.S.C. §4] that the word 'vehicle' includes every description of carriage or other artificial contrivance used, or capable of being used, as a means of transportation on land. ... This definition controls our interpretation of 'vehicle' in [35 U.S.C.] §272.... *At F.3d 1331, U.S.P.Q.2d 1650:* [W]e hold that the definition of entering 'temporarily,' as the word is used in §272, is entering for a period of time of finite duration with the sole purpose of engaging in international commerce." (Internal quotes omitted.)

§273. DEFENSE TO INFRINGEMENT BASED ON PRIOR COMMERCIAL USE

(a) In general.—A person shall be entitled to a defense under section 282(b) with respect to subject matter consisting of a process, or consisting of a machine, manufacture, or composition of matter used in a manufacturing or other commercial process, that would otherwise infringe a claimed invention being asserted against the person if—

(1) such person, acting in good faith, commercially used the subject matter in the United States, either in connection with an internal commercial use or an actual arm's length sale or other arm's length commercial transfer of a useful end result of such commercial use; and

(2) such commercial use occurred at least 1 year before the earlier of either—

(A) the effective filing date of the claimed invention; or

(B) the date on which the claimed invention was disclosed to the public in a manner that qualified for the exception from prior art under section 102(b).

(b) Burden of proof.—A person asserting a defense under this section shall have the burden of establishing the defense by clear and convincing evidence.

(c) Additional commercial uses—

(1) Premarketing regulatory review.—Subject matter for which commercial marketing or use is subject to a premarketing regulatory review period during which the safety or efficacy of the subject matter is established, including any period specified in section 156(g), shall be deemed to be commercially used for purposes of subsection (a)(1) during such regulatory review period.

(2) Nonprofit laboratory use.—A use of subject matter by a nonprofit research laboratory or other nonprofit entity, such as a university or hospital, for which the public is the intended beneficiary, shall be deemed to be a commercial use for purposes of subsection (a)(1), except that a defense under this section may be asserted pursuant to this paragraph only for continued and noncommercial use by and in the laboratory or other nonprofit entity.

(d) Exhaustion of rights.—Notwithstanding subsection (e)(1), the sale or other disposition of a useful end result by a person entitled to assert a defense under this section in connection with a patent with respect to that useful end result shall exhaust the patent owner's rights under the patent to the extent that such rights would have been exhausted had such sale or other disposition been made by the patent owner.

(e) Limitations and exceptions—

(1) Personal defense—

(A) In general.—A defense under this section may be asserted only by the person who performed or directed the performance of the commercial use described in subsection (a), or by an entity that controls, is controlled by, or is under common control with such person.

(B) Transfer of right.—Except for any transfer to the patent owner, the right to assert a defense under this section shall not be licensed or assigned or transferred to another person except as an ancillary and subordinate part of a good-faith assignment or transfer for other reasons of the entire enterprise or line of business to which the defense relates.

(C) Restriction on sites.—A defense under this section, when acquired by a person as part of an assignment or transfer described in subparagraph (B), may only be asserted for uses at sites where the subject matter that would otherwise infringe a claimed invention is in use before the later of the effective filing date of the claimed invention or the date of the assignment or transfer of such enterprise or line of business.

(2) Derivation.—A person may not assert a defense under this section if the subject matter on which the defense is based was derived from the patentee or persons in privity with the patentee.

(3) Not a general license.—The defense asserted by a person under this section is not a general license under all claims of the patent at issue, but extends only to the specific subject matter for which it has been established that a commercial use that qualifies under this section occurred, except that the defense shall also extend to variations in the quantity or volume of use of the claimed subject matter, and to improvements in the claimed subject matter that do not infringe additional specifically claimed subject matter of the patent.

(4) Abandonment of use.—A person who has abandoned commercial use (that qualifies under this section) of subject matter may not rely on activities performed before the date of such abandonment in establishing a defense under this section with respect to actions taken on or after the date of such abandonment.

(5) University exception—

(A) In general.—A person commercially using subject matter to which subsection (a) applies may not assert a defense under this section if the claimed invention with respect to which the defense is asserted was, at the time the invention was made, owned or subject to an obligation of assignment to either an institution of higher education (as defined in section 101(a) of the Higher Education Act of 1965 (20 U.S.C. 1001(a)),[1] or a technology transfer organization whose primary purpose is to facilitate the commercialization of technologies developed by one or more such institutions of higher education.

(B) Exception.—Subparagraph (A) shall not apply if any of the activities required to reduce to practice the subject matter of the claimed invention could not have been undertaken using funds provided by the Federal Government.

(f) Unreasonable assertion of defense.—If the defense under this section is pleaded by a person who is found to infringe the patent and who subsequently fails to demonstrate a reasonable basis for asserting the defense, the court shall find the case exceptional for the purpose of awarding attorney fees under section 285.

(g) Invalidity.—A patent shall not be deemed to be invalid under section 102 or 103 solely because a defense is raised or established under this section.

1. **Editor's note:** A third closing parenthesis probably should appear.

History of 35 U.S.C. §273: Nov. 29, 1999, P.L. 106-113, §1000(a)(9), 113 Stat. 1536; Sept. 16, 2011, P.L. 112-29, §5(a), 125 Stat. 297.

CHAPTER 29. REMEDIES FOR INFRINGEMENT OF PATENT, & OTHER ACTIONS

§281. REMEDY FOR INFRINGEMENT OF PATENT

A patentee shall have remedy by civil action for infringement of his patent.

History of 35 U.S.C. §281: July 19, 1952, ch. 950, §1, 66 Stat. 812.
See also FRCP 19.

ANNOTATIONS

Standing

Waterman v. Mackenzie, 138 U.S. 252, 255-56 (1891). "The patentee or his assigns may, by instrument in writing, assign, grant, and convey, either (1) the whole patent, comprising the exclusive right to make, use, and vend the invention throughout the U.S.; or, (2) an undivided part or share of that exclusive right; or, (3) the exclusive right under the patent within and throughout a specified part of the U.S. A transfer of either of these three kinds of interests is an assignment, properly speaking, and vests in the assignee a title in so much of the patent itself, with a right to sue infringers. In the second case, jointly with the assignor. In the first and third cases, in the name of the assignee alone. Any assignment or transfer, short of one of these, is a mere license, giving the licensee no title in the patent, and no right to sue at law in his own name for an infringement. In equity, as at law, when the transfer amounts to a license only, the title remains in the owner of the patent; and suit must be brought in his name, and never in the name of the licensee alone unless that is necessary to prevent an absolute failure of justice, as where the patentee is the infringer, and cannot sue himself. Any rights of the licensee must be enforced through or in the name of the owner of the patent, and perhaps, if necessary to protect the rights of all parties, joining the licensee with him as a plaintiff. Whether a transfer of a particular right or interest under a patent is an assignment or a license does not depend upon the name by which it calls itself, but upon the legal effect of its provisions." *See also* ***Aspex Eyewear, Inc. v. Miracle Optics, Inc.***, 434 F.3d 1336, 1341-42, 77 U.S.P.Q.2d 1456, 1460 (Fed.Cir.2006); ***State Contracting & Eng'g v. Condotte Am., Inc.***, 346 F.3d 1057, 1062-63, 68 U.S.P.Q.2d 1481, 1484 (Fed.Cir.2003); ***Pandrol USA, LP v. Airboss Ry. Prods.***, 320 F.3d 1354, 1367-68, 65 U.S.P.Q.2d 1985, 1994 (Fed.Cir.2003); ***Mentor H/S, Inc. v. Medical Device Alliance, Inc.***, 240 F.3d 1016, 1017, 57 U.S.P.Q.2d 1819, 1820 (Fed.Cir. 2001).

Drone Techs. v. Parrot S.A., 838 F.3d 1283, 1292, 120 U.S.P.Q.2d 1336, 1341 (Fed.Cir.2016). "When multiple inventors are listed on the face of a patent, 'each co-owner presumptively owns a pro rata undivided interest in the entire patent, no matter what their respective contributions.' Consequently, if a co-inventor assigns his or her ownership interest to a third party, the assignee cannot sue infringers '[a]bsent the voluntary joinder of all co-owners.'"

STC.UNM v. Intel Corp., 754 F.3d 940, 941, 111 U.S.P.Q.2d 1033, 1034 (Fed.Cir.2014). "The district court held that [P] could not maintain its suit because non-party ... is a co-owner of the patent, had not voluntarily joined as a co-plaintiff, and could not be involuntarily joined. Because, 'as a matter of substantive patent law, all co-owners must ordinarily consent to join as plaintiffs in an infringement suit,' ... and because [non-party] cannot be involuntarily joined under [FRCP] 19, this court affirms."

WiAV Solutions LLC v. Motorola, Inc., 631 F.3d 1257, 1263, 97 U.S.P.Q.2d 1484, 1488 (Fed.Cir.2010). "The sole issue presented by this appeal is whether [third-party licensee] has constitutional standing to assert the [licensed patents] against [Ds]. *At F.3d 1264-65, U.S.P.Q.2d 1489-90:* The [Patent] Act provides that a 'patentee' has the right to initiate a 'civil action for infringement of [its] patent.' The term 'patentee' encompasses both the owner of the patent and the assignee of all substantial rights in the patent. The Patent Act, however, does not limit the right to sue to only patent owners and assignees. This court has explained that a party has the right to sue for infringement of the patent 'if that party has a legally protected interest in the patent created by the Patent Act, so that it can be said to suffer legal injury from [the] act of infringement.' [¶] Because the legally protected interests in a patent are the exclusionary rights created by the Patent Act, a party holding one or more of those exclusionary rights—such as an exclusive licensee—suffers a legally cognizable injury when an unauthorized party encroaches upon those rights and therefore has standing to sue. By contrast, a so-called 'bare licensee' holds nothing more than a promise from the patentee that the patentee will not sue the licensee for practicing the patented invention. Such a licensee 'suffers no legal injury from infringement and, thus, has no standing to bring suit or even join in a suit with the patentee.' [¶] Thus, the touchstone of constitutional standing in a patent infringement suit is whether a party can establish that it has an exclusionary right in a patent that, if violated by another, would cause the party holding the exclusionary right to suffer legal injury. *At F.3d 1266-67, U.S.P.Q.2d 1491:* Depending on the scope of its exclusionary rights, an exclusive licensee may have standing to sue some parties and not others. For example, an exclusive licensee lacks standing to sue a party for infringement if that party holds a preexisting license under the patent to engage in the allegedly infringing activity. Similarly, an exclusive licensee lacks standing to sue a party who has the ability to obtain such a license from another party with the right to grant it. In both of these scenarios, the exclusive licensee does not have an exclusionary right with respect to the alleged infringer and thus is not injured by that alleged infringer.

But if an exclusive licensee has the right to exclude others from practicing a patent, and a party accused of infringement does not possess, and is incapable of obtaining, a license of those rights from any other party, the exclusive licensee's exclusionary right is violated. [¶] This court therefore holds that an exclusive licensee does not lack constitutional standing to assert its rights under the licensed patent merely because its license is subject not only to rights in existence at the time of the license but also to future licenses that may be granted only to parties other than the accused. If the accused neither possesses nor can obtain such a license, the exclusive licensee's exclusionary rights with respect to that accused party are violated by any acts of infringement that such party is alleged to have committed, and the injury predicate to constitutional standing is met."

Abraxis Bioscience, Inc. v. Navinta LLC, 625 F.3d 1359, 1364, 96 U.S.P.Q.2d 1977, 1982 (Fed.Cir.2010). "[I]n a patent infringement action, 'the plaintiff must demonstrate that it held enforceable title to the patent at the inception of the lawsuit' to assert standing. Thus, 'if the original plaintiff lacked [U.S. Const. art. 3] initial standing, the suit must be dismissed, and the jurisdictional defect cannot be cured' after the inception of the lawsuit. *At F.3d 1367, U.S.P.Q.2d 1984:* A party may sue for past infringement transpiring before it acquired legal title if a written assignment expressly grants the party a right to do so."

Spine Solutions, Inc. v. Medtronic Sofamor Danek USA, Inc., 620 F.3d 1305, 1317, 96 U.S.P.Q.2d 1640, 1649 (Fed.Cir.2010). "To be an exclusive licensee for standing purposes, 'a party must have received, not only the right to practice the invention within a given territory, but also the patentee's express or implied promise that others shall be excluded from practicing the invention within that territory as well.'"

Enovsys LLC v. Nextel Comms., 614 F.3d 1333, 1341, 95 U.S.P.Q.2d 1947, 1952 (Fed.Cir.2010). "When a patent is co-owned, a joint owner must join all other co-owners to establish standing. [¶] In this case, we must decide whether [an assignee] had standing to bring and maintain this suit without joining [the assignor's] ex-wife.... This question turns on whether [ex-wife] had any ownership interest in the asserted patents at the time this suit was filed. *At F.3d 1342:* Who has legal title to a patent is a question of state law."

Alfred E. Mann Found. for Sci. Research v. Cochlear Corp., 604 F.3d 1354, 1360-61, 95 U.S.P.Q.2d 1321, 1325 (Fed.Cir.2010). "A patent 'is, in effect, a bundle of rights which may be divided and assigned, or retained in whole or part.' Thus, although all the various rights available under the patent are initially held by the named inventor or inventors, they may, as a result of licensing agreements and assignments, become separated and be held by multiple individuals. When a sufficiently large portion of this bundle of rights is held by one individual, we refer to that individual as the owner of the patent, and that individual is permitted to sue for infringement in his own name. When a plaintiff lacking a sufficiently large portion of rights brings suit, that plaintiff does not have standing to sue on his own, and the suit must be dismissed, or additional holders of rights under the patent must be joined as parties to the suit, as appropriate given the plaintiff's status as either an exclusive or a nonexclusive licensee. [¶] Our prior decisions have never purported to establish a complete list of the rights whose holders must be examined to determine whether a licensor has transferred away sufficient rights to render an exclusive licensee the owner of a patent. But we have listed at least some of the rights that should be examined. Of course, transfer of the exclusive right to make, use, and sell products or services under the patent is vitally important to an assignment. We have also examined the scope of the licensee's right to sublicense, the nature of license provisions regarding the reversion of rights to the licensor following breaches of the license agreement, the right of the licensor to receive a portion of the recovery in infringement suits brought by the licensee, the duration of the license rights granted to the licensee, the ability of the licensor to supervise and control the licensee's activities, the obligation of the licensor to continue paying patent maintenance fees, and the nature of any limits on the licensee's right to assign its interests in the patent. Frequently, though, the nature and scope of the exclusive licensee's purported right to bring suit, together with the nature and scope of any right to sue purportedly retained by the licensor, is the most important consideration. Where the licensor retains a right to sue accused infringers, that right often precludes a finding that all substantial rights were transferred to the licensee. It does not, however, preclude such a finding if the licensor's right to sue is rendered illusory by the licensee's ability to settle licensor-initiated litigation by granting royalty-free sublicenses to the accused infringers. Under the prior decisions of this court, the nature and scope of the licensor's retained right to sue accused infringers is the most important factor in determining whether an exclusive license transfers sufficient rights to render the licensee the owner of the patent."

International Gamco, Inc. v. Multimedia Games, Inc., 504 F.3d 1273, 1274, 84 U.S.P.Q.2d 2017, 2018 (Fed.Cir.2007). "[T]his court concludes that an exclusive enterprise licensee, like a field of use licensee, does not hold all substantial rights in the licensed patent within the licensed territory.... *At F.3d 1276, U.S.P.Q.2d 2019:* Prudential standing to sue for patent infringement derives from 35 U.S.C. §281.... In turn 'patentee' includes the patentee's successors in title. Transfers of title, otherwise known as assignments, are controlled by 35 U.S.C. §261.... *At F.3d 1278-79, U.S.P.Q.2d 2021:* Allowing a licensee, even one with exclusive rights to the patent for a particular field of use, to sue in its own name alone poses a substantial risk of multiple suits and multiple liabilities against an alleged infringer for a single act of infringement. To alleviate this risk, this court's prudential standing requirement compels an exclusive licensee with less than all substantial rights, such as a field of use licensee, to join the patentee before initiating suit. In contrast, an exclusive territorial license does not involve the same multiplicity risks because a single act of infringement is likely to give rise to only one viable suit for infringement by the exclusive territorial licensee in the jurisdiction where the infringement occurred. In holding that an exclusive field of use licensee does not have standing to sue in its own name without joining the patent owner, this court also honors the mainstay of Supreme Court patent standing jurisprudence in ***Waterman***. *At U.S.P.Q.2d 2022:* The problem of a multiplicity of lawsuits arising from an exclusive field of use license is not cured by adding a geographic restriction." *See also* ***Sicom Sys. v. Agilent Techs.***, 427 F.3d 971, 976, 76 U.S.P.Q.2d 1933, 1936-37 (Fed.Cir.2005); ***Ortho Pharm. v. Genetics Inst.***, 52 F.3d 1026, 1030-32, 34 U.S.P.Q.2d 1444, 1446 (Fed.Cir.1995).

Schreiber Foods, Inc. v. Beatrice Cheese, Inc., 402 F.3d 1198, 1203, 74 U.S.P.Q.2d 1204, 1208 (Fed.Cir. 2005). "In the area of patent infringement, this court has held that if the original plaintiff lacked [U.S. Const.] Art. 3 initial standing, the suit must be dismissed, and the jurisdictional defect cannot be cured by the addition of a party with standing, ... nor by the subsequent purchase of an interest in the patent in suit. *At F.3d 1204:* This court has also held that the temporary loss of standing during patent litigation can be cured before judgment. *At U.S.P.Q.2d 1209:* Here [P] reacquired its stake in the litigation by reacquiring the '860 patent (and causes of action thereunder) before the entry of judgment. The jurisdictional defect that had existed was cured before the entry of judgment and thus the judgment was not void."

Intellectual Prop. Dev., Inc. v. TCI Cablevision, Inc., 248 F.3d 1333, 1346, 58 U.S.P.Q.2d 1681, 1689-90 (Fed.Cir.2001), *overruled on other grounds*, ***MedImmune, Inc. v. Genentech, Inc.***, 549 U.S. 118 (2007). U.S. Const. art. 3 "standing requires a party invoking federal jurisdiction to establish three elements. First, the plaintiff must have suffered an injury in fact—an invasion of a legally protected interest which is (a) concrete and particularized and (b) actual or imminent, not conjectural or hypothetical. Second, there must be a causal connection between the injury and the conduct complained of—the injury has to be fairly ... traceable to the challenged action of the defendant and not ... the result of the independent action of some third party not before the court. Third, it must be likely, as opposed to merely speculative, that the injury will be redressed by a favorable decision." (Internal quotes omitted.) *See also* ***Evident Corp. v. Church & Dwight Co.***, 399 F.3d 1310, 1314, 73 U.S.P.Q.2d 1910, 1912-13 (Fed.Cir.2005).

Textile Prods. v. Mead Corp., 134 F.3d 1481, 1483, 45 U.S.P.Q.2d 1633, 1635 (Fed.Cir.1998). "The question of standing to sue for patent infringement is one which this court reviews *de novo*."

Minco, Inc. v. Combustion Eng'g, 95 F.3d 1109, 1117, 40 U.S.P.Q.2d 1001, 1006 (Fed.Cir.1996). "[T]he right to sue for prior infringement is not transferred unless the assignment agreement manifests an intent to transfer this right. Neither statute nor common law precedent, however, requires a particular formula or set prescription of words to express that conveyance." *See also* ***Duplan Corp. v. Deering Milliken Research Corp.***, 522 F.2d 809, 811 n.2, 186 U.S.P.Q. 369, 370 n.2 (4th Cir.1975).

Ortho Pharm. v. Genetics Inst., 52 F.3d 1026, 1034, 34 U.S.P.Q.2d 1444, 1450 (Fed.Cir.1995). "[A] licensee with sufficient proprietary interest in a patent has standing regardless of whether the licensing agreement so provides. Express covenants may, of course, regulate the duties between the licensor and licensee to implement the rights of the parties. However, a contract cannot change the statutory requirement for suit to be brought by the 'patentee.' By the same token, a right to sue clause cannot negate the requirement that, for co-plaintiff standing, a licensee must have beneficial ownership of some of the patentee's proprietary rights. A patentee may not give a right to sue to a party who has no proprietary interest in the patent. [A] nonexclusive licensee ... has no inherent or implied right to sue which the clause regulates as between the parties. Thus, we conclude the right to sue clause has no effect on [nonexclusive licensee's] standing, one way or the other." *See also* ***Abbott Labs. v. Diamedix Corp.***, 47 F.3d 1128, 1130, 33 U.S.P.Q.2d 1771, 1773-74 (Fed.Cir.1995).

Calgon Corp. v. Nalco Chem., 726 F.Supp. 983, 988, 13 U.S.P.Q.2d 1529, 1533 (D.Del.1989). "The exclusive licensee should, in equity, be able to commence an action for infringement when the patent owner refuses to vindicate his rights. There is an implied obligation on the part of the patent owner to allow his name to be used by the exclusive licensee."

Afros S.P.A. v. Krauss-Maffei Corp., 671 F.Supp. 1402, 1446, 5 U.S.P.Q.2d 1145, 1180 (D.Del.1987), *aff'd*, 848 F.2d 1244 (Fed.Cir.1988) (table case). "Permitting a presently invalid assignment to serve as the basis of a claim under ... §281 on the ground that it later 'became' valid, which ratification transposes itself back in time, will impermissibly expand the class of persons able to sue for infringement. Moreover, permitting a claim where a foreign nation's law provides the basis for avoiding the owner/assignee rule may give foreign U.S. patent owners a distinct advantage over their domestic counterparts by allowing them to manipulate the scope of their liability through a transaction subsequent to the filing of the suit."

Personal Jurisdiction

3D Sys. v. Aarotech Labs., 160 F.3d 1373, 1377, 48 U.S.P.Q.2d 1773, 1775-76 (Fed.Cir.1998), *overruled on other grounds*, ***Pfaff v. Wells Elecs., Inc.***, 525 U.S. 85, 48 U.S.P.Q.2d 1641 (1998). "While we defer to the interpretation of a state's long-arm statute given by that state's highest court, particularly whether or not the statute is intended to reach the limit of federal due process, ... when analyzing personal jurisdiction for purposes of compliance with federal due process, Federal Circuit law, rather than regional circuit law, applies...."

Subject-Matter Jurisdiction

Microsoft Corp. v. DataTern, Inc., 755 F.3d 899, 903, 110 U.S.P.Q.2d 1561, 1565 (Fed.Cir.2014). "In ***Arris*** [***Grp. v. British Telecomms. PLC***, 639 F.3d 1368 (Fed.Cir.2011)], we recognized that 'where a patent holder accuses customers of direct infringement based on the sale or use of a supplier's equipment, the supplier has standing to commence a declaratory judgment action *if* ... there is a controversy between the patentee and the supplier as to the supplier's liability for induced or contributory infringement based on the alleged acts of direct infringement by its customers.' We determined that declaratory judgment jurisdiction existed because the patentee's charges of infringement against the declaratory judgment plaintiffs customers carried an 'implied assertion that [the declaratory judgment plaintiff] was committing contributory infringement, and [the patentee] repeatedly communicated this implicit accusation directly to [the declaratory judgment plaintiff] during the course of a protracted negotiation process.' Notably, ***Arris*** analyzed each element required for contributory infringement under [35 U.S.C.] §271(c) before determining that there was an implied assertion of contributory infringement that supported jurisdiction. *At F.3d 904-05, U.S.P.Q.2d 1566:* To the extent that [Ps] argue that [D's] suits against its customers automatically give rise to a case or controversy regarding induced infringement, we do not agree. To prove inducement of infringement, unlike direct infringement, the patentee must show that the accused inducer took an affirmative act to encourage infringement with the knowledge that the induced acts constitute patent infringement. Absent the knowledge and affirmative act of encouragement, no party could be charged with inducement. Thus, in determining whether there is a case or controversy of sufficient immediacy to establish declaratory judgment jurisdiction we look to the elements of the potential cause of action."

Robert Bosch, LLC v. Pylon Mfg., 719 F.3d 1305, 1308, 107 U.S.P.Q.2d 1113, 1115 (Fed.Cir.2013). "We sua sponte took this case en banc to answer two questions. First, does 28 U.S.C. §1292(c)(2) confer jurisdiction on this court to entertain appeals from patent infringement liability determinations when a trial on damages has not yet occurred? Second, does ... §1292(c)(2) confer jurisdiction on this court to entertain appeals from patent infringement liability determinations when willfulness issues are outstanding and remain undecided? We answer both questions in the affirmative and return the case to the panel for disposition on the merits."

Litecubes, LLC v. Northern Light Prods., 523 F.3d 1353, 1366, 86 U.S.P.Q.2d 1753, 1762 (Fed.Cir.2008). "Congress has not clearly stated that any of the limitations in [35 U.S.C.] §271 are jurisdictional. Accordingly, we hold that whether the allegedly infringing act happened in the U.S. is an element of the claim for patent infringement, not a prerequisite for subject matter jurisdiction. [P], by alleging a violation of §271, has properly invoked federal question jurisdiction under [28 U.S.C.] §1331 and §1338. This jurisdiction does not depend on whether [P] is able to succeed on the merits in proving all of the elements of patent infringement that it alleged in the complaint."

Texas Instrs. v. Tessera, Inc., 231 F.3d 1325, 1330, 56 U.S.P.Q.2d 1674, 1678 (Fed.Cir.2000). "For alleged domestic infringement, a patentee can file an action in a district court. For alleged infringement through importation, a patentee can also file an action in a district court or in the [International Trade Commission (ITC)]. In fact, a patentee can bring suit both in a district court and in the ITC against an alleged infringer who is importing an allegedly infringing product."

Right to Jury Trial

Kennedy v. Lakso Co., 414 F.2d 1249, 1252, 163 U.S.P.Q. 136, 138 (3d Cir.1969). "The use of the term 'civil action' in §281 was taken from the [FRCPs]. [¶] We ... reject [D's] contention that §281 ... expressed an intention to overthrow the well-settled principle that jury trials are available in actions for damages for infringement...."

Claim Preclusion

Senju Pharm. Co. v. Apotex Inc., 746 F.3d 1344, 1348, 110 U.S.P.Q.2d 1261, 1263 (Fed.Cir.2014). "[P's] appeal requires us to decide whether [P's] second action is barred by the judicial doctrine now generally known as claim preclusion, earlier known as res judicata and still referred to by that name. Under the doctrine of res judicata, a judgment on the merits in a prior suit involving the same parties or their privies bars a second suit based on the same cause of action. [¶] The rule provides that when a court of competent jurisdiction has entered a final judgment on the merits of a cause of action, the parties to the suit and their privies are thereafter bound not only as to every matter which was offered and received to sustain or defeat the claim or demand, but as to any other admissible matter which might have been offered for that purpose. [¶] Whether a cause of action is barred by claim preclusion is a question of law that we review without deference. We look to the law of the regional circuit in which the district court sits for guidance regarding the principles of claim preclusion; however, whether a particular cause of action in a patent case is the same as or different from another cause of action has special application to patent cases, and we therefore apply our own law to that issue. *At F.3d 1349, U.S.P.Q.2d 1264:* In applying the policies expressed by the doctrine of claim preclusion, our court has identified certain significant factors to be considered in determining when a cause of action is the same. In ***Acumed*** [***LLC v. Stryker Corp.***, 525 F.3d 1319 (Fed.Cir.2008)], we followed the approach in the Restatement (Second) of Judgments, which states that a cause of action is defined by the transactional facts from which it arises, and the extent of the factual overlap. [¶] One of the areas of factual overlap that we consider in a patent case involving claim preclusion is the overlap of *the product or process* accused in the instant action with *the product or process* accused in the prior action. If the products or processes are essentially the same, then claim preclusion may apply. [¶] We also consider whether the *same patents* are involved in both suits. Ordinarily, each patent asserted raises an independent and distinct cause of action. Claim preclusion will generally apply when a patentee seeks to assert the same patent against the same party and the same subject matter. How this general rule is to be understood is a key issue in this case." (Internal quotes omitted.)

§282. PRESUMPTION OF VALIDITY; DEFENSES

(a) In general.—A patent shall be presumed valid. Each claim of a patent (whether in independent, dependent, or multiple dependent form) shall be presumed valid independently of the validity of other claims; dependent or multiple dependent claims shall be presumed valid even though dependent upon an invalid claim. The burden of establishing invalidity of a patent or any claim thereof shall rest on the party asserting such invalidity.

(b) Defenses.—The following shall be defenses in any action involving the validity or infringement of a patent and shall be pleaded:

(1) Noninfringement, absence of liability for infringement or unenforceability.

(2) Invalidity of the patent or any claim in suit on any ground specified in part II as a condition for patentability.

(3) Invalidity of the patent or any claim in suit for failure to comply with—

(A) any requirement of section 112, except that the failure to disclose the best mode shall not be a basis on which any claim of a patent may be canceled or held invalid or otherwise unenforceable; or

(B) any requirement of section 251.

(4) Any other fact or act made a defense by this title.

(c) Notice of actions; actions during extension of patent term.—In an action involving the validity or infringement of a patent the party asserting invalidity or noninfringement shall give notice in the pleadings or otherwise in writing to the adverse party at least thirty days before the trial, of the country, number, date, and name of the patentee of any patent, the title, date, and page numbers of any publication to be relied upon as anticipation of the patent in suit or, except in actions in the United States Court of Federal Claims, as showing the state of the art, and the name and address of any person who may be relied upon as the prior inventor or as having prior knowledge of or as having previously used or offered for sale the invention of the patent in suit. In the absence of such notice proof of the said matters may not be made at the trial except on such terms as the court requires. Invalidity of the extension of a patent term or any portion thereof under section 154(b) or 156 because of the material failure—

(1) by the applicant for the extension, or

(2) by the Director,

to comply with the requirements of such section shall be a defense in any action involving the infringement of a patent during the period of the extension of its term and shall be pleaded. A due diligence determination under section 156(d)(2) is not subject to review in such an action.

History of 35 U.S.C. §282: July 19, 1952, ch. 950, §1, 66 Stat. 812; July 24, 1965, P.L. 89-83, §10, 79 Stat. 261; Nov. 14, 1975, P.L. 94-131, §10, 89 Stat. 692; Apr. 2, 1982, P.L. 97-164, §161(7), 96 Stat. 49; Sept. 24, 1984, P.L. 98-417, §203, 98 Stat. 1603; Nov. 1, 1995, P.L. 104-41, §2, 109 Stat. 352; Nov. 29, 1999, P.L. 106-113, §1000(a)(9), 113 Stat. 1536; Nov. 2, 2002, P.L. 107-273, §13206(b)(1)(B), (4), 116 Stat. 1906; Sept. 16, 2011, P.L. 112-29, §§15(a), 20(g), (j)(1), 125 Stat. 328, 334, 335.

See also 35 U.S.C. §§102, 103, 112, 271; Patent Cooperation Treaty.

ANNOTATIONS

Generally

Aristocrat Techs. Australia Pty Ltd. v. International Game Tech., 543 F.3d 657, 662, 88 U.S.P.Q.2d 1458, 1461 (Fed.Cir.2008). 35 U.S.C. §282 "itself draws a distinction between invalidity based 'on any ground specified in part II of this title as a condition for patentability,' ... and invalidity 'for failure to comply with any requirement of [35 U.S.C.] §§112 or 251.' ... Section 282(3), relating to invalidity under §112, would be redundant if the requirements in §112 were conditions for patentability because, if so, that defense would fall within the boundaries of §282(2). Section 282(2), by virtue of its applicability to 'condition[s] for patentability,' relates only to defenses of invalidity for lack of utility and eligibility, novelty, and nonobviousness, and does not encompass a defense based upon the alleged improper revival of a patent application." *See also* ***Sextant Avionique, S.A. v. Analog Devices, Inc.***, 172 F.3d 817, 828-29, 49 U.S.P.Q.2d 1865, 1872-73 (Fed.Cir. 1999).

Diversey Lever, Inc. v. Ecolab, Inc., 191 F.3d 1350, 1353, 52 U.S.P.Q.2d 1062, 1064 (Fed.Cir.1999). "[R]egardless of its classification under §282, an affirmative defense must be raised in response to a summary judgment motion, or it is waived."

Quantum Corp. v. Rodime, PLC, 65 F.3d 1577, 1584, 36 U.S.P.Q.2d 1162, 1168 (Fed.Cir.1995). "Section 282 does not state that the list of invalidity defenses contained therein are the only ones available; the statute merely says 'the following shall be defenses.' The express words of §282 therefore allow for the existence of other invalidity defenses."

Presumption of Validity

Microsoft Corp. v. i4i L.P., 564 U.S. 91, 95, 98 U.S.P.Q.2d 1857, 1859 (2011). "We consider whether §282 requires an invalidity defense to be proved by clear and convincing evidence. We hold that it does. *At U.S. 111, U.S.P.Q.2d 1866:* [I]f the PTO did not have all material facts before it, its considered judgment may lose significant force. And, concomitantly, the challenger's burden to persuade the jury of its invalidity defense by clear and convincing evidence may be easier to sustain."

Ethicon Endo-Surgery, Inc. v. Covidien, Inc., 796 F.3d 1312, 1328, 115 U.S.P.Q.2d 1880, 1892 (Fed.Cir. 2015). "Design patents enjoy the same presumption of validity as utility patents under ... §282. Thus, [D] has the burden to prove invalidity of the Design Patents by clear and convincing evidence."

Tokai Corp. v. Easton Enters., 632 F.3d 1358, 1367, 97 U.S.P.Q.2d 1673, 1679 (Fed.Cir.2011). "Under ... §282, each claim of a patent shall be presumed valid; an accused infringer must prove invalidity by clear and convincing evidence. [D] is correct in noting that, although the standard of proof does not depart from that of clear and convincing evidence, a party challenging validity shoulders an enhanced burden if the invalidity argument relies on the same prior art considered during examination by the [PTO]. ... An added burden of deference to the PTO is not required, however, with respect to invalidity arguments based on evidence that the PTO did not consider."

Pfizer, Inc. v. Apotex, Inc., 480 F.3d 1348, 1359-60, 82 U.S.P.Q.2d 1321, 1329-30 (Fed.Cir.2007). "Since we must presume a patent valid, the patent challenger bears the burden of proving the factual elements of invalidity by clear and convincing evidence. That burden of proof never shifts to the patentee to prove validity. 'The presumption [of validity] remains intact and [the burden of proof remains] on the challenger throughout the litigation, and the clear and convincing standard does not change.'"

Superior Fireplace Co. v. Majestic Prods., 270 F.3d 1358, 1367, 60 U.S.P.Q.2d 1668, 1674 (Fed.Cir. 2001). "Challenges to the validity of claims, whether regularly issued, issued after a reexamination pursuant to 35 U.S.C. §§301-307, or issued after a reissue pursuant to 35 U.S.C. §§251-252, must meet the clear and convincing standard of persuasion."

Eli Lilly & Co. v. Barr Labs., 251 F.3d 955, 962, 58 U.S.P.Q.2d 1869, 1874 (Fed.Cir.2001). A party moving for summary judgment "seeking to invalidate a patent ... must submit such clear and convincing evidence of invalidity so that no reasonable jury could find otherwise. Alternatively, a moving party seeking to have a patent held not invalid at summary judgment must show that the nonmoving party, who bears the burden of proof at trial, failed to produce clear and convincing evidence on an essential element of a defense upon which a reasonable jury could invalidate the patent. In determining whether a genuine issue of material fact exists, the court views the evidence in the light most favorable to the nonmoving party and resolves all doubts in its favor." *See also* ***Mas-Hamilton Grp. v. LaGard, Inc.***, 156 F.3d 1206, 1216, 48 U.S.P.Q.2d 1010, 1018 (Fed. Cir.1998).

Helifix, Ltd. v. Blok-Lok, Ltd., 208 F.3d 1339, 1351, 54 U.S.P.Q.2d 1299, 1307 (Fed.Cir.2000). "The presumption of the patent's validity created by ... §282 'does not relieve a patentee who moves for a preliminary injunction from carrying the normal burden of demonstrating that it will likely succeed on all disputed liability issues at trial, even when the issue concerns the patent's validity.' If the alleged infringer raises a substantial question concerning validity, *i.e.*, asserts an invalidity defense that the patentee cannot prove 'lacks substantial merit,' the preliminary injunction should not issue."

In re Morris, 127 F.3d 1048, 1054, 44 U.S.P.Q.2d 1023, 1027-28 (Fed.Cir.1997). "No ... presumption [of validity] attaches before the PTO. It is the PTO's duty to assure that the statutory requirements for patentability are met."

In re Etter, 756 F.2d 852, 857, 225 U.S.P.Q. 1, 4-5 (Fed.Cir.1985). "That one challenging validity in court bears the burden assigned by §282, that the same party may request reexamination upon submission of art not previously cited, and that, if that art raises a substantial new question of patentability, the PTO may during reexamination consider the same and new and amended claims in light of that art free of any presumption, are concepts not in conflict. *At F.2d 858:* [S]ection 282 has no application in reexamination proceedings."

Structural Rubber Prods. v. Park Rubber Co., 749 F.2d 707, 714, 223 U.S.P.Q. 1264, 1269 (Fed.Cir. 1984). "Validity encompasses three 'separate tests of patentability': novelty, utility and nonobviousness. Thus, included within the presumption of validity is a presumption of novelty, a presumption of nonobviousness and a presumption of utility, each of which must be presumed to have been met."

Jervis B. Webb Co. v. Southern Sys., 742 F.2d 1388, 1392, 222 U.S.P.Q. 943, 945 (Fed.Cir.1984). "[T]he district court misapplied the presumption of patent validity as enunciated in ... §282. The district court stated that since '[t]he most relevant prior art ... was not cited by the [PTO] during the prosecution of the application which matured into [P's] patent ... any presumption of validity which [P's] patent may have had is largely, if not wholly, vitiated.' We, however, disagree. Regardless of the prior art introduced by the party asserting invalidity, the presumption remains intact. Rather, the party asserting invalidity, having offered new prior art, would be more likely to carry the burden of persuasion imposed by §282."

SSIH Equip. S.A. v. U.S. Int'l. Trade Comm'n, 718 F.2d 365, 375, 218 U.S.P.Q. 678, 687 (Fed.Cir.1983). "The presumption of validity afforded by … §282 does not have independent evidentiary value. Rather the presumption places the burden of going forward, as well as the burden of persuasion, upon the party asserting invalidity." *See also* ***American Hoist & Derrick Co. v. Sowa & Sons, Inc.***, 725 F.2d 1350, 1358, 220 U.S.P.Q. 763, 769 (Fed.Cir.1984), *overruled on other grounds*, ***Therasense, Inc. v. Becton, Dickinson & Co.***, 649 F.3d 1276 (Fed.Cir.2011).

Each Claim Is Presumed Valid

Dayco Prods. v. Total Containment, Inc., 329 F.3d 1358, 1370-71, 66 U.S.P.Q.2d 1801, 1810 (Fed.Cir.2003). "The burden of proving the invalidity of the claims was on [D]. [I]t is permissible to group claims together for disposition where resolution involves the same issues of validity; however, the justification for such grouping is possible only where those issues are substantially materially identical. Where claims differ in scope in an aspect material to the analysis, those claims must be addressed individually."

Sandt Tech. v. Resco Metal & Plastics Corp., 264 F.3d 1344, 1356, 60 U.S.P.Q.2d 1091, 1098 (Fed.Cir. 2001). "Because dependent claims contain additional limitations, they cannot be presumed to be invalid as obvious just because the independent claims from which they depend have properly been so found."

Enzo Biochem, Inc. v. Calgene, Inc., 188 F.3d 1362, 1379, 52 U.S.P.Q.2d 1129, 1141 (Fed.Cir.1999). "While evidence of invalidity regarding the claims of one patent may certainly apply to those of another, a party may not avoid its burden of proof by making a blanket statement that its proofs with respect to one patent apply to another and not provide a formal analysis as to why that is true."

Miles Labs. v. Shandon Inc., 997 F.2d 870, 878-79, 27 U.S.P.Q.2d 1123, 1129 (Fed.Cir.1993). "Section 282 requires an independent analysis of the validity of each claim. A party challenging the validity of a claim, absent a pretrial agreement or stipulation, must submit evidence supporting a conclusion of invalidity for each contested claim. Where the parties stipulate to 'representative' claims, however, a validity resolution for the representative claims applies to the other claims as well." *See also* ***Ortho Pharm. v. Smith***, 959 F.2d 936, 942, 22 U.S.P.Q.2d 1119, 1124 (Fed.Cir.1992).

§282(b), ¶1—Inequitable Conduct

For more annotations on this topic, see 35 U.S.C. §285, *Inequitable Conduct*, p. 719.

Therasense, Inc. v. Becton, Dickinson & Co., 649 F.3d 1276, 1285, 99 U.S.P.Q.2d 1065, 1069 (Fed.Cir. 2011). "Inequitable conduct is an equitable defense to patent infringement that, if proved, bars enforcement of a patent. *At F.3d 1290-93, U.S.P.Q.2d 1072:* To prevail on a claim of inequitable conduct, the accused infringer must prove that the patentee acted with the specific intent to deceive the PTO. A finding that the misrepresentation or omission amounts to gross negligence or negligence under a 'should have known' standard does not satisfy this intent requirement. 'In a case involving nondisclosure of information, clear and convincing evidence must show that the applicant *made a deliberate decision* to withhold a *known* material reference.' In other words, the accused infringer must prove by clear and convincing evidence that the applicant knew of the reference, knew that it was material, and made a deliberate decision to withhold it. *At U.S.P.Q.2d 1073-74:* Intent and materiality are separate requirements. A district court should not use a 'sliding scale,' where a weak showing of intent may be found sufficient based on a strong showing of materiality, and vice versa. Moreover, a district court may not infer intent solely from materiality. Instead, a court must weigh the evidence of intent to deceive independent of its analysis of materiality. Proving that the applicant knew of a reference, should have known of its materiality, and decided not to submit it to the PTO does not prove specific intent to deceive. [¶] Because direct evidence of deceptive intent is rare, a district court may infer intent from indirect and circumstantial evidence. However, to meet the clear and convincing evidence standard, the specific intent to deceive must be 'the single most reasonable inference able to be drawn from the evidence.' Indeed, the evidence 'must be sufficient to *require* a finding of deceitful intent in the light of all the circumstances.' Hence, when there are multiple reasonable inferences that may be drawn, intent to deceive cannot be found. This court reviews the district court's factual findings regarding what reasonable inferences may be drawn from the evidence for clear error. [¶] Because the party alleging inequitable conduct bears the burden of proof, the 'patentee need not offer any good faith explanation unless the accused infringer first ... prove[s] a threshold level of intent to deceive by clear and convincing evidence.' The absence of a good faith explanation for withholding a material reference does not, by itself, prove intent to deceive. [¶] This court holds that, as a general matter, the materiality required to establish inequitable conduct is but-for materiality. When an applicant fails to disclose prior art to the PTO, that prior art is but-for material if the PTO would not have allowed a claim had it been aware of the undisclosed prior art. Hence, in assessing the materiality of a withheld reference, the court must determine whether the PTO would have allowed the claim if it had been aware of the undisclosed reference. In making this patentability determination, the court should apply the preponderance of the evidence standard and give claims their broadest reasonable construction. Often the patentability of a claim will be congruent with the validity determination—if a claim is properly invalidated in district court based on the deliberately withheld reference, then that reference is necessarily material because a finding of invalidity in a district court requires clear and convincing evidence, a higher evidentiary burden than that used in prosecution at the PTO. However, even if a district court does not invalidate a claim based on a deliberately withheld reference, the reference may be material if it would have blocked patent issuance under the PTO's different evidentiary standards. [¶] Although but-for materiality generally must be proved to satisfy the materiality prong of inequitable conduct, this court recognizes an exception in cases of affirmative egregious misconduct. ... When the patentee has engaged in affirmative acts of egregious misconduct, such as the filing of an unmistakably false affidavit, the misconduct is material. After all, a patentee is unlikely to go to great lengths to deceive the PTO with a falsehood unless it believes that the falsehood will affect issuance of the patent. Because neither mere nondisclosure of prior art references to the PTO nor failure to mention prior art references in an affidavit constitutes affirmative egregious misconduct, claims of inequitable conduct that are based on such omissions require proof of but-for materiality. *At U.S.P.Q.2d 1075:* This court does not adopt the definition of materiality in PTO Rule 56." *See also* ***American Calcar, Inc. v. American Honda Motor Co.***, 768 F.3d 1185, 1190-91, 112 U.S.P.Q.2d 1353, 1357 (Fed.Cir.2014).

Advanced Magnetic Closures, Inc. v. Rome Fastener Corp., 607 F.3d 817, 828, 95 U.S.P.Q.2d 1513, 1519 (Fed.Cir.2010). "We have held that when named inventors deliberately conceal a true inventor's involvement, the applicants have committed inequitable conduct and the patent is unenforceable even as to an innocent co-inventor."

Innogenetics, N.V. v. Abbott Labs., 512 F.3d 1363, 1379, 85 U.S.P.Q.2d 1641, 1652 (Fed.Cir.2008). "In direct contrast to the statement made to the PTO, [patentee's] prosecuting attorney admitted that he did not actually examine the prior art identified, and that his statement that 'the references do not relate to the invention' was the same boilerplate language he used in other prior art statements. [¶] [Patentee's] representation of [prior-art reference submitted to the PTO] amounted to mere attorney argument and our precedent has made clear that an applicant is free to advocate its interpretation of its claims and the teachings of prior art."

Nilssen v. Osram Sylvania, Inc., 504 F.3d 1223, 1230, 84 U.S.P.Q.2d 1811, 1816 (Fed.Cir.2007). "Because inequitable conduct with respect to one or more patents in a family can infect related applications, we find no abuse of discretion in the district court's holding [four patents not in suit] unenforceable prior to determining whether the inequitable conduct related to each of those four patents should render additional related patents unenforceable as well. Trial judges are entitled to arrange the priority of issues in a manner that they consider efficient. *At F.3d 1231, U.S.P.Q.2d 1817:* While a misrepresentation of small entity status is not strictly speaking inequitable conduct in the prosecution of a patent, as the patent has already issued if maintenance fees are payable (excepting an issue fee), it is not beyond the authority of a district court to hold a patent unenforceable for inequitable conduct in misrepresenting one's status as justifying small entity maintenance payments. *At F.3d 1233, U.S.P.Q.2d 1818:* It is not necessary for a holding of inequitable conduct that an examiner rely on a claim for priority or that entitlement to an earlier priority be expressly argued in order to overcome prior art. [¶] A claim for priority is inherently material to patentability because a priority date may determine validity, whether an issue arises in prosecution or later in court challenges to validity. While an active misrepresentation made during prosecution in order to avoid prior art is no doubt 'highly material,' a misrepresentation that would not have immediately affected patentability is still material."

In re Metoprolol Succinate Patent Litig., 494 F.3d 1011, 1020, 83 U.S.P.Q.2d 1545, 1551 (Fed.Cir.2007). "Because '[t]his court has consistently treated inequitable conduct as an equitable defense that may be adjudicated by the trial court without a jury,' a 'patentee has no right to a jury trial respecting the factual element of culpable intent as part of the defense of inequitable conduct.' 'Thus, a disputed finding of intent to mislead or to deceive is one for the judge to resolve, not the jury, *albeit not on summary judgment if there is a genuine dispute*.'" *See also* ***Agfa Corp. v. Creo Prods.***, 451 F.3d 1366, 1375, 79 U.S.P.Q.2d 1385, 1391 (Fed.Cir.2006).

McKesson Info. Solutions, Inc. v. Bridge Med., Inc., 487 F.3d 897, 913, 82 U.S.P.Q.2d 1865, 1876 (Fed. Cir.2007). "'[I]nequitable conduct requires not intent to withhold, but rather intent to deceive. Intent to deceive cannot be inferred simply from the decision to withhold [information] where the reasons given for the withholding are plausible.'"

Ferring B.V. v. Barr Labs., 437 F.3d 1181, 1194-95, 78 U.S.P.Q.2d 1161, 1172 (Fed.Cir.2006). "[W]hen an inventor is asked to provide supportive declarations to the PTO, it may be completely natural for the inventor to recommend, and even contact, his own colleagues or people who are, or who have been, affiliated with his employer and to submit declarations from such people. [W]here the objectivity of the declarant is an issue in the prosecution, the inventor must disclose the known relationships and affiliations of the declarants so that those interests can be considered in weighing the declarations."

Ulead Sys. v. Lex Computer & Mgmt., 351 F.3d 1139, 1144, 69 U.S.P.Q.2d 1097, 1100-01 (Fed.Cir.2003). "Historically issues of unenforceability have arisen in cases involving inequitable conduct occurring in the prosecution of patents. But, we see no reason why the doctrine should not extend into other contexts, like the present one, where the allegation is that inequitable conduct has occurred after the patent has issued and during the course of establishing and paying the appropriate maintenance fee. In this context, it is equally important that the PTO receive accurate information from those who practice before it." *See also* ***Scanner Techs. v. ICOS Vision Sys.***, 528 F.3d 1365, 1375, 87 U.S.P.Q.2d 1225, 1232-33 (Fed.Cir.2008).

Ferguson Beauregard/Logic Controls, Division of Dover Res. v. Mega Sys., 350 F.3d 1327, 1344, 69 U.S.P.Q.2d 1001, 1013 (Fed.Cir.2003). "[I]nequitable conduct, while a broader concept than fraud, must be pled with particularity." *See also* ***Exergen Corp. v. Wal-Mart Stores***, 575 F.3d 1312, 1325-31, 91 U.S.P.Q.2d 1656, 1665-70 (Fed.Cir.2009).

Nobelpharma AB v. Implant Innovations, Inc., 141 F.3d 1059, 1070, 46 U.S.P.Q.2d 1097, 1106 (Fed.Cir. 1998). "Inequitable conduct is ... an equitable defense in a patent infringement action and serves as a shield, while a more serious finding of fraud potentially exposes a patentee to antitrust liability and thus serves as a sword. Antitrust liability can include treble damages. In contrast, the remedies for inequitable conduct, while serious enough, only include unenforceability of the affected patent or patents and possible attorney fees."

§282(b), ¶1—Permissive Repair

Aro Mfg. Co. v. Convertible Top Replacement Co., 365 U.S. 336, 346, 128 U.S.P.Q. 354, 359 (1961). "[M]aintenance of the 'use of the whole' of the patented combination through replacement of a spent, unpatented element does not constitute reconstruction. [¶] The decisions of this Court require the conclusion that reconstruction of a patented entity, comprised of unpatented elements, is limited to such a true reconstruction of the entity as to in fact make a new article, after the entity, viewed as a whole, has become spent. ... Mere replacement of individual unpatented parts, one at a time, whether of the same part repeatedly or different parts successively, is no more than the lawful right of the owner to repair his property."

§282(b), ¶1—Laches & Equitable Defenses

For more annotations on this topic, see 35 U.S.C. §286, *Generally*, p. 722.

SCA Hygiene Prods. A.B. v. First Quality Baby Prods., ___ U.S. ___, 137 S.Ct. 954, 966, 121 U.S.P.Q.2d 1873, 1881 (2017). "After surveying the pre-1952 case law, we are not convinced that Congress, in enacting [35 U.S.C.] §282 ..., departed from the general rule regarding the application of laches to damages suffered within the time for filing suit set out in a statute of limitations. *At U.S. ___, S.Ct. 967:* Laches cannot be interposed as a defense against damages where the infringement occurred within the period prescribed by [35 U.S.C.] §286."

Hynix Semiconductor Inc. v. Rambus Inc., 645 F.3d 1336, 1347-48, 98 U.S.P.Q.2d 1711, 1721 (Fed.Cir. 2011). "A member of an open standard setting organization may be equitably estopped or may have impliedly waived its right to assert infringement claims against standard-compliant products. [¶] To support a finding of implied waiver in the standard setting organization context, the accused must show by clear and convincing evidence that the patentee's conduct was so inconsistent with an intent to enforce its rights as to induce a reasonable belief that such right has been relinquished. Such conduct can be shown where (1) the patentee had a duty of disclosure to the standard setting organization, and (2) the patentee breached that duty. [¶] To support a finding of equitable estoppel, the accused must show that the patentee, through misleading conduct, led the alleged infringer to reasonably infer that the patentee does not intend to enforce its patent against the alleged infringer. 'Conduct' may include specific statements, action, inaction, or silence where there was an obligation to speak. [¶] The two elements of implied waiver must also be shown to prove equitable estoppel, because without a disclosure duty, [D] could not 'reasonably infer' that [P] did not intend to enforce its patents against it, and without a breach of that duty, [P's] nondisclosure could not be 'misleading conduct.'" (Internal quotes omitted.)

Cancer Research Tech. v. Barr Labs., 625 F.3d 724, 728-29, 96 U.S.P.Q.2d 1937, 1940 (Fed.Cir.2010). "Prosecution laches is an equitable defense to a charge of patent infringement. The doctrine 'may render a patent unenforceable when it has issued only after an unreasonable and unexplained delay in prosecution' that constitutes an egregious misuse of the statutory patent system under the totality of the circumstances. We review a district court's determination of prosecution laches for abuse of discretion, ... but we review the legal standard applied by the district court *de novo*.... *At U.S.P.Q.2d 1941:* We agree with [P] that prosecution laches' requirement of an unreasonable and unexplained delay includes a finding of prejudice, as does any laches defense. We also agree and now hold that to establish prejudice an accused infringer must show evidence of intervening rights, *i.e.*, that either the accused infringer or others invested in, worked on, or used the claimed technology during the period of delay." *See also* ***Symbol Techs. v. Lemelson Med., Educ. & Research Found.***, 422 F.3d 1378, 1385, 76 U.S.P.Q.2d 1354, 1359-60 (Fed.Cir.2005), *amended*, 429 F.3d 1051 (Fed.Cir.2005).

Aspex Eyewear Inc. v. Clariti Eyewear, Inc., 605 F.3d 1305, 1310, 94 U.S.P.Q.2d 1856, 1859 (Fed.Cir. 2010). "In the context of patent infringement, the three elements of equitable estoppel that must be established are: (1) the patentee, through misleading conduct, led the alleged infringer to reasonably believe that the patentee did not intend to enforce its patent against the infringer; (2) the alleged infringer relied on that conduct; and (3) due to its reliance, the alleged infringer would be materially prejudiced if the patentee were permitted to proceed with its charge of infringement. Misleading 'conduct' may include specific statements, action, inaction, or silence when there was an obligation to speak. In deciding whether to bar the suit on estoppel grounds, the court must consider all evidence relevant to the equities. *At F.3d 1312, U.S.P.Q.2d 1861:* [D] need not show a total loss of value in order to show material prejudice. Prejudice may be shown by a change of economic position flowing from actions taken or not taken by the patentee."

Qualcomm Inc. v. Broadcom Corp., 548 F.3d 1004, 1022, 89 U.S.P.Q.2d 1321, 1333-34 (Fed.Cir.2008). "'[A] duty to speak can arise from a group relationship in which the working policy of disclosure of related intellectual property rights ... is treated by the group as a whole as imposing an obligation to disclose information in order to support and advance the purposes of the group.' [A]fter participating in [standard-setting body] and shielding the asserted patents from consideration during development of ... standard, [P] filed a patent infringement lawsuit against [D], alleging infringement primarily, if not solely, based on [D's] compliance [with standard]. In these circumstances, we conclude that it was within the district court's authority, sitting as a court of equity, to determine that [P's] misconduct falls within the doctrine of waiver. *At F.3d 1026, U.S.P.Q.2d 1336:* [W]e conclude that a district court may in appropriate circumstances order patents unenforceable as a result of silence in the face of [a standard-setting body] disclosure duty, as long as the scope of the district court's unenforceability remedy is properly limited in relation to the underlying breach."

Symantec Corp. v. Computer Assocs., 522 F.3d 1279, 1294, 86 U.S.P.Q.2d 1449, 1458 (Fed.Cir.2008). "A defendant, in order to invoke the defense of laches, must prove: '(1) [that] the plaintiff delayed filing suit for an unreasonable and inexcusable length of time from the time the plaintiff knew or reasonably should have known of its claim against the defendant, and (2) [that] the delay operated to the prejudice or injury of the defendant.' A presumption of laches arises 'upon proof that the patentee delayed filing suit for more than six years after actual or constructive knowledge of the defendant's alleged infringing activity.'" *See also* ***A.C. Aukerman Co. v. R.L. Chaides Constr. Co.***, 960 F.2d 1020, 1030-31, 22 U.S.P.Q.2d 1321, 1327 (Fed.Cir.1992).

Abbott Labs. v. Andrx Pharms., 473 F.3d 1196, 1203, 81 U.S.P.Q.2d 1289, 1294 (Fed.Cir.2007). ***Blonder-Tongue Labs. v. University of Ill. Found.***, 402 U.S. 313 (1971), "permitted the use of defensive collateral estoppel when the accused infringer shows (1) that a patent was found invalid in a prior case that had proceeded through final judgment and in which all procedural opportunities were available to the patentee; (2) that the issues litigated were identical; and (3) that the party against whom estoppel is applied had a full and fair opportunity to litigate. *At F.3d 1206, U.S.P.Q.2d 1296:* [T]he determinations made in [earlier and separate preliminary-injunction] proceedings ... were not 'full litigation and decision on the merits for purposes of issue preclusion.'"

In re Bogese, 303 F.3d 1362, 1367, 64 U.S.P.Q.2d 1448, 1452 (Fed.Cir.2002). 35 U.S.C. §§120 and 121, "which entitled continuation and divisional applications to the filing dates of their parent applications, did not foreclose the application of prosecution history laches to bar enforcement of a patent claim."

§282(b), ¶1—Experimental Use

Madey v. Duke Univ., 307 F.3d 1351, 1362, 64 U.S.P.Q.2d 1737, 1746 (Fed.Cir.2002). "[R]egardless of whether a particular institution or entity is engaged in an endeavor for commercial gain, so long as the act is in furtherance of the alleged infringer's legitimate business and is not solely for amusement, to satisfy idle curiosity, or for strictly philosophical inquiry, the act does not qualify for the very narrow and strictly limited experimental use defense."

§282(b), ¶1—License, Implied License & Patent Exhaustion

Impression Prods. v. Lexmark Int'l, ___ U.S. ___, 137 S.Ct. 1523, 1529, 122 U.S.P.Q.2d 1605, 1608 (2017). "When a patentee sells one of its products, ... the patentee can no longer control that item through the patent laws—its patent rights are said to 'exhaust.' The purchaser and all subsequent owners are free to use or resell the product just like any other item of personal property, without fear of an infringement lawsuit. [¶] This case presents two questions about the scope of the patent exhaustion doctrine: First, whether a patentee that sells an item under an express restriction on the purchaser's right to reuse or resell the product may enforce that restriction through an infringement lawsuit. And second, whether a patentee exhausts its patent rights by selling its product outside the U.S., where American patent laws do not apply. We conclude that a patentee's decision to sell a product exhausts all of its patent rights in that item, regardless of any restrictions the patentee purports to impose or the location of the sale."

Bowman v. Monsanto Co., 569 U.S. 278, 280, 106 U.S.P.Q.2d 1593, 1594 (2013). "Under the doctrine of patent exhaustion, the authorized sale of a patented article gives the purchaser, or any subsequent owner, a right to use or resell that article. Such a sale, however, does not allow the purchaser to make new copies of the patented invention. The question in this case is whether a farmer who buys patented seeds may reproduce them through planting and harvesting without the patent holder's permission. We hold that he may not. *At U.S. 289, U.S.P.Q.2d 1598:* Our holding today is limited—addressing the situation before us, rather than every one involving a self-replicating product. We recognize that such inventions are becoming ever more prevalent, complex, and diverse. In another case, the article's self-replication might occur outside the purchaser's control. Or it might be a necessary but incidental step in using the item for another purpose."

Quanta Computer, Inc. v. LG Elecs., Inc., 553 U.S. 617, 629, 86 U.S.P.Q.2d 1673, 1679 (2008). "[T]his Court has repeatedly held that method patents were exhausted by the sale of an item that embodied the method. *At U.S. 631, U.S.P.Q.2d 1680:* '[T]he authorized sale of an article which is capable of use only in practicing the patent is a relinquishment of the patent monopoly with respect to the article sold.' *At U.S. 633:* Here, as in [***U.S. v. Univis***, 316 U.S. 241 (1942)], the incomplete article substantially embodies the patent because the only step necessary to practice the patent is the application of common processes or the addition of standard parts. *At U.S. 634, U.S.P.Q.2d 1681:* [Products] embody the essential features of [patents] because they carry out all the inventive processes when combined, according to their design, with standard components. [¶] The sale of a device that practices patent A does not, by virtue of practicing patent A, exhaust patent B. But if the device practices patent A *while substantially embodying* patent B, its relationship to patent A does not prevent exhaustion of patent B. *At U.S. 636:* Exhaustion is triggered only by a sale authorized by the patent holder. *At U.S. 638, U.S.P.Q.2d 1682:* The authorized sale of an article that substantially embodies a patent exhausts the patent holder's rights and prevents the patent holder from invoking patent law to control postsale use of the article." *See also* ***Helferich Patent Licensing, LLC v. New York Times Co.***, 778 F.3d 1293, 1301-02, 113 U.S.P.Q.2d 1705, 1712 (Fed.Cir.2015).

Adams v. Burke, 84 U.S. 453, 456-57 (1873). "[W]hen the patentee, or the person having his rights, sells a machine or instrument whose sole value is in its use, he receives the consideration for its use and he parts with the right to restrict that use. The article, in the language of the court, passes without the limit of the monopoly. [¶] Whatever ... may be the rule when patentees subdivide territorially their patents, as to the exclusive right *to make* or *to sell* within a limited territory, we hold that in the class of machines or implements we have described, when they are once lawfully made and sold, there is no restriction on their *use* to be implied for the benefit of the patentee or his assignees or licensees."

LifeScan Scot., Ltd. v. Shasta Techs., 734 F.3d 1361, 1374, 108 U.S.P.Q.2d 1757, 1766 (Fed.Cir.2013). "[I]n the case of an authorized and unconditional transfer of title, the absence of consideration is no barrier to the application of patent exhaustion principles. *At U.S.P.Q.2d 1767:* Thus, despite frequent references to 'sales' and 'purchasers,' the [Supreme] Court has more fundamentally described exhaustion as occurring when the patented product 'passes to the hands' of a transferee and when he 'legally acquires a title' to it. Similarly, the Court has stated that exhaustion can occur by a transfer 'from any other person ... authorized [by the patentee] to *convey* it.'"

Keurig, Inc. v. Sturm Foods, Inc., 732 F.3d 1370, 1374, 108 U.S.P.Q.2d 1648, 1652 (Fed.Cir.2013). "[P's] argument that patent exhaustion must be adjudicated on a claim-by-claim basis is unavailing. The Court's patent exhaustion jurisprudence has focused on the exhaustion of the patents at issue in their entirety, rather than the exhaustion of the claims at issue on an individual basis."

TransCore, LP v. Electronic Transaction Consultants Corp., 563 F.3d 1271, 1274, 90 U.S.P.Q.2d 1372, 1375 (Fed.Cir.2009). "The question for this court is whether an unconditional covenant not to sue authorizes sales by the covenantee for purposes of patent exhaustion. We hold that it does."

Zenith Elecs. Corp. v. PDI Comm. Sys., 522 F.3d 1348, 1360, 86 U.S.P.Q.2d 1513, 1521 (Fed.Cir.2008). "The implied license defense is typically presented when a patentee or its licensee sells an article and the question is whether the sale carries with it a license to engage in conduct that would infringe the patent owner's rights. In that setting, this court has set forth two requirements for the grant of an implied license. First, the equipment involved must have no noninfringing uses. If there is no noninfringing use, it may be reasonable to infer that there has been a relinquishment of the patent monopoly with respect to the article sold. Second, the circumstances of the sale must plainly indicate that the grant of a license should be inferred." (Internal quotes omitted.)

Met-Coil Sys. v. Korners Unlimited, Inc., 803 F.2d 684, 687, 231 U.S.P.Q. 474, 476 (Fed.Cir.1986). "As the alleged infringer, [D] has the burden of showing the establishment of an implied license." *See also* ***Bandag, Inc. v. Al Bolser's Tire Stores***, 750 F.2d 903, 924-25, 223 U.S.P.Q. 982, 998 (Fed.Cir.1984).

§282(b), ¶2—Anticipation

For annotations on this topic, see 35 U.S.C. §102, p. 508.

§282(b), ¶2—Obviousness

For annotations on this topic, see 35 U.S.C. §103, p. 534.

§282(b), ¶2—On Sale

For annotations on this topic, see 35 U.S.C. §102, *§102(b)—On Sale*, p. 517.

§282(b), ¶3

For more annotations on this topic, see 35 U.S.C. §112, p. 552.

In re Antor Media Corp., 689 F.3d 1282, 1287-88, 103 U.S.P.Q.2d 1555, 1558 (Fed.Cir.2012). "We ... address [petitioner's] argument that the Board erred by holding that prior art publications cited by an examiner are presumptively enabling during prosecution. [B]oth claimed and unclaimed materials disclosed in a patent are presumptively enabling…. [T]hat presumption applies in the district court as well as the PTO, placing the burden on the patentee to show that unclaimed disclosures in a prior art patent are not enabling. [W]e now hold that a prior art printed publication cited by an examiner is presumptively enabling barring any showing to the contrary by a patent applicant or patentee." *See also* ***Amgen Inc. v. Hoechst Marion Roussel, Inc.***, 314 F.3d 1313, 1355, 65 U.S.P.Q.2d 1385, 1416 (Fed.Cir. 2003).

AK Steel Corp. v. Sollac & Ugine, 344 F.3d 1234, 1238-39, 68 U.S.P.Q.2d 1280, 1283 (Fed.Cir.2003). "Whether the subject matter of a patent claim satisfies the enablement requirement of 35 U.S.C. §112, ¶1, is a question of law based on underlying facts, and, because a patent is presumed to be valid, the evidentiary burden to show facts supporting a conclusion of invalidity is one of clear and convincing evidence."

Intellectual Prop. Dev., Inc. v. UA-Columbia Cablevision, Inc., 336 F.3d 1308, 1319, 67 U.S.P.Q.2d 1385, 1393 (Fed.Cir.2003), *overruled on other grounds*, ***MedImmune, Inc. v. Genentech, Inc.***, 549 U.S. 118 (2007). "[A] challenge to a claim containing a means-plus-function limitation as lacking structural support requires a finding, by clear and convincing evidence, that the specification lacks disclosure of structure sufficient to be understood by one skilled in the art as being adequate to perform the recited function."

§282(b), ¶4—Generally

For more annotations on this topic, see 35 U.S.C. §116, p. 567.

Aristocrat Techs. Australia Pty Ltd. v. International Game Tech., 543 F.3d 657, 662-63, 88 U.S.P.Q.2d 1458, 1462 (Fed.Cir.2008). "The salient question … is whether improper revival is 'made a defense' by title 35. We think that it is not. Congress made it clear in various provisions of the statute when it intended to create a defense of invalidity or noninfringement, but indicated no such intention in the statutes pertaining to revival of abandoned applications. … Because the proper revival of an abandoned application is neither a fact or act made a defense by title 35 nor a ground specified in part II of title 35 as a condition for patentability, we hold that improper revival may not be asserted as a defense in an action involving the validity or infringement of a patent."

Trovan, Ltd. v. Sokymat SA, Irori, 299 F.3d 1292, 1301, 63 U.S.P.Q.2d 1865, 1870 (Fed.Cir.2002). "A patent is invalid if more or less than the true inventors are named. However, because a patent is presumed valid, there follows a presumption that the named inventors on a patent are the true and only inventors. Moreover, to the extent that fewer than the true inventors are named on a patent, the patent may be corrected to so reflect as long as the nonjoinder was done without deceptive intent on the part of the person erroneously left off the patent." *See also* ***Acromed Corp. v. Sofamor Danek Grp.***, 253 F.3d 1371, 1379, 59 U.S.P.Q.2d 1130, 1135 (Fed.Cir.2001).

Quantum Corp. v. Rodime, PLC, 65 F.3d 1577, 1583, 36 U.S.P.Q.2d 1162, 1167 (Fed.Cir.1995). "[A] district court could declare that reissued claims are invalid as a matter of law if they were impermissibly broadened in violation of 35 U.S.C. §251, ¶4."

§282(b), ¶4—Misuse

For annotations on this topic, see 35 U.S.C. §271, *§271(d)*, p. 674.

§282(c)

Woods v. DeAngelo Mar. Exhaust, Inc., 692 F.3d 1272, 1278-79, 104 U.S.P.Q.2d 1169, 1173-74 (Fed.Cir. 2012). "[D's] principal argument is that the district court erred by excluding the engineering drawings disclosed … as an untimely interrogatory supplement despite [D's] identification of the drawings immediately upon finding them and on the final day of the scheduled discovery period. [D] points out that it stated in its initial interrogatory response that it had not decided which prior art references it would use and would disclose the references on which it would rely as required by 35 U.S.C. §282. It is undisputed that these drawings were disclosed more than 30 days before trial as specified by §282. *At F.3d 1280, U.S.P.Q.2d 1175:* Section 282 does not eliminate a defendant's obligations under the [FRCPs]. To the contrary, the statute and the rules are intended to coexist. *At F.3d 1282, U.S.P.Q.2d 1177:* Having properly found that [D's] failure to supplement its interrogatory response was a violation of [FRCP] 26(e), the district court was well within its discretion in excluding the drawings under [FRCP] 37(c)."

§283. INJUNCTION

The several courts having jurisdiction of cases under this title may grant injunctions in accordance with the principles of equity to prevent the violation of any right secured by patent, on such terms as the court deems reasonable.

History of 35 U.S.C. §283: July 19, 1952, ch. 950, §1, 66 Stat. 812.
See also FRCP 65.

ANNOTATIONS

Generally

eBay Inc. v. MercExchange, L.L.C., 547 U.S. 388, 391, 78 U.S.P.Q.2d 1577, 1578-79 (2006). "According to well-established principles of equity, a plaintiff seeking a permanent injunction must satisfy a four-factor test before a court may grant such relief. A plaintiff must demonstrate: (1) that it has suffered an irreparable injury; (2) that remedies available at law, such as monetary damages, are inadequate to compensate for that injury; (3) that, considering the balance of hardships between the plaintiff and defendant, a remedy in equity is warranted; and (4) that the public interest would not be disserved by a permanent injunction. [¶] These familiar principles apply with equal force to disputes arising under the Patent Act. *At U.S. 394, U.S.P.Q.2d 1580:* [T]he decision whether to grant or deny injunctive relief rests within the equitable discretion of the district courts, and that such discretion must be exercised consistent with traditional principles of equity, in patent disputes no less than in other cases governed by such standards."

Apple Inc. v. Samsung Elecs. Co., 809 F.3d 633, 639, 117 U.S.P.Q.2d 1469, 1473 (Fed.Cir.2015). "To satisfy the first ***eBay*** factor, the patentee must show that it is irreparably harmed by the infringement. This requires proof that a 'causal nexus relates the alleged harm to the alleged infringement.' *At F.3d 640, U.S.P.Q.2d 1474:* [A] causal nexus linking the harm and the infringing acts must be established regardless of whether the injunction is sought for an entire product or is narrowly limited to particular features. *At F.3d 642, U.S.P.Q.2d 1475:* The district court ... erred when it required [P] to prove that the infringing features were the exclusive or predominant reason why consumers bought [D's] products to find irreparable harm. Instead, the district court should have considered whether there is 'some connection' between the patented features and the demand for [D's] products. That is, the district court should have required [P] to show that the patented features impact consumers' decisions to purchase the accused devices."

ePlus, Inc. v. Lawson Software, Inc., 789 F.3d 1349, 1354, 115 U.S.P.Q.2d 1273, 1277 (Fed.Cir.2015). "The ... question is whether the district court's modified injunction against [D] must be set aside now that the PTO has cancelled the patent claim on which it is based. It is well established that an injunction must be set aside when the legal basis for it has ceased to exist."

Douglas Dynamics, LLC v. Buyers Prods., 717 F.3d 1336, 1345, 107 U.S.P.Q.2d 1024, 1031 (Fed.Cir. 2013). "Where two companies are in competition against one another, the patentee suffers the harm—often irreparable—of being forced to compete against products that incorporate and infringe its own patented inventions."

Innogenetics, N.V. v. Abbott Labs., 512 F.3d 1363, 1380, 85 U.S.P.Q.2d 1641, 1653 (Fed.Cir.2008). "The reasonable royalties awarded to [P] include an upfront entry fee that contemplates or is based upon future sales by [D] in a long term market. When a patentee requests and receives such compensation, it cannot be heard to complain that it will be irreparably harmed by future sales."

International Rectifier Corp. v. IXYS Corp., 383 F.3d 1312, 1317, 72 U.S.P.Q.2d 1571, 1575 (Fed.Cir. 2004). FRCP 65(d) "requires an injunction to prohibit only those acts sought to be restrained, which in this case are infringement of the patent by the devices adjudged to infringe and infringement by devices no more than colorably different therefrom."

Rite-Hite Corp. v. Kelley Co., 56 F.3d 1538, 1547, 35 U.S.P.Q.2d 1065, 1071 (Fed.Cir.1995). "If a patentee's failure to practice a patented invention frustrates an important public need for the invention, a court need not enjoin infringement of the patent. Accordingly, courts have in rare instances exercised their discretion to deny injunctive relief in order to protect the public interest."

Joy Tech. v. Flakt, Inc., 6 F.3d 770, 773, 28 U.S.P.Q.2d 1378, 1380 (Fed.Cir.1993). "An injunction for infringement may not be punitive."

MercExchange, L.L.C. v. eBay, Inc., 500 F.Supp.2d 556, 571, 83 U.S.P.Q.2d 1688, 1699 (E.D.Va.2007). "[I]t is apparent that the Federal Circuit has repeatedly recognized that 'the lack of commercial activity by the patentee is a *significant factor in the calculus*' of whether the patentee will suffer irreparable harm absent an injunction. [P's] lack of commercial activity and pattern of granting licenses to market participants that were knowingly or unwittingly practicing its patents does not *eliminate* [P's] ability to establish irreparable harm, but it weighs against the need for an equitable remedy as it evidences [P's] willingness to forgo its right to exclude in return for money."

Contempt of Injunction

TiVo Inc. v. Echostar Corp., 646 F.3d 869, 881, 98 U.S.P.Q.2d 1413, 1421 (Fed.Cir.2011). "What is required for a district court to hold a contempt proceeding is a detailed accusation from the injured party setting forth the alleged facts constituting the contempt. As with appeals from findings of civil contempt in other areas of law, we will only review whether the injunction at issue is both enforceable and violated, and whether the sanctions imposed were proper. Allegations that contempt proceedings were improper in the first instance do not state a defense to contempt. As to the question whether an injunction against patent infringement has been violated, courts should continue to employ a 'more than colorable differences' standard.... *At F.3d 882-83, U.S.P.Q.2d 1422:* [T]he party seeking to enforce the injunction must prove both that the newly accused product is not more than colorably different from the product found to infringe and that the newly accused product actually infringes. [¶] Instead of focusing solely on infringement, the contempt analysis must focus initially on the differences between the features relied upon to establish infringement and the modified features of the newly accused products. [¶] The primary question on contempt should be whether the newly accused product is so different from the product previously found to infringe that it raises 'a fair ground of doubt as to the wrongfulness of the defendant's conduct.' The analysis must focus not on differences between randomly chosen features of the product found to infringe in the earlier infringement trial and the newly accused product, ... but on those aspects of the accused product that were previously alleged to be, and were a basis for, the prior finding of infringement, and the modified features of the newly accused product. Specifically, one should focus on those elements of the adjudged infringing products that the patentee previously contended, and proved, satisfy specific limitations of the asserted claims. Where one or more of those elements previously found to infringe has been modified, or removed, the court must make an inquiry into whether that modification is significant. If those differences between the old and new elements are significant, the newly accused product as a whole shall be deemed more than colorably different from the adjudged infringing one, and the inquiry into whether the newly accused product actually infringes is irrelevant. Contempt is then inappropriate. [¶] The significance of the differences between the two products is much dependent on the nature of the products at issue. The court must also look to the relevant prior art, if any is available, to determine if the modification merely employs or combines elements already known in the prior art in a manner that would have been obvious to a person of ordinary skill in the art at the time the modification was made. A nonobvious modification may well result in a finding of more than a colorable difference. Where useful, a district court may seek expert testimony in making the determination. The analysis may also take account of the policy that legitimate design-around efforts should always be encouraged as a path to spur further innovation. But an assertion that one has permissibly designed around a patent should not be used to mask continued infringement. Determining the requisite level of difference is a question of fact."

Preliminary Injunction—Factors

Trebro Mfg. v. FireFly Equip., LLC, 748 F.3d 1159, 1166, 110 U.S.P.Q.2d 1429, 1434 (Fed.Cir.2014). "To prove a likelihood of success on the merits, a patentee must prove that success in establishing infringement is 'more likely than not.' *At F.3d 1169, U.S.P.Q.2d 1435-36:* Even if a patentee shows the likelihood of proving infringement, the accused infringer can defeat the likelihood of success on the merits by raising a substantial question as to the validity of the patent in suit."

Titan Tire Corp. v. Case New Holland, Inc., 566 F.3d 1372, 1375-76, 90 U.S.P.Q.2d 1918, 1921 (Fed.Cir. 2009). "The factors the trial court considers when determining whether to grant a preliminary injunction are of longstanding and universal applicability. As the Supreme Court recently reiterated, there are four: '[a] plaintiff seeking a preliminary injunction must establish (1) that he is likely to succeed on the merits, (2) that he is likely to suffer irreparable harm in the absence of preliminary relief, (3) that the balance of equities tips in his favor, and (4) that an injunction is in the public interest.' We note in passing that some cases state the first factor as requiring a 'reasonable' likelihood of success on the merits. It is not clear whether the addition of 'reasonable' adds anything substantive to the test, but in any event, for our purposes the Supreme Court's current statement of the test is the definitive one." *See also* ***Anton/Bauer, Inc. v. PAG, Ltd.***, 329 F.3d 1343, 1348, 66 U.S.P.Q.2d 1675, 1677-78 (Fed.Cir.2003); ***High Tech Med. Instrumentation, Inc. v. New Image Indus.***, 49 F.3d 1551, 1553, 33 U.S.P.Q.2d 2005, 2006-07 (Fed.Cir.1995); ***Illinois Tool Works, Inc. v. Grip-Pak, Inc.***, 906 F.2d 679, 681, 15 U.S.P.Q.2d 1307, 1310 (Fed. Cir.1990) (discussing balance of hardships).

Abbott Labs. v. Sandoz, Inc., 544 F.3d 1341, 1362, 89 U.S.P.Q.2d 1161, 1179 (Fed.Cir.2008). "We agree that the fact that a patentee has licensed others under its patents does not mean that unlicensed infringement must also be permitted while the patents are litigated. Precedent illustrates that when the patentee is simply interested in obtaining licenses, without itself engaging in commerce, equity may add weight to permitting infringing activity to continue during litigation, on the premise that the patentee is readily made whole if infringement is found. *At F.3d 1364, U.S.P.Q.2d 1180-81:* The correct standard [for granting a preliminary injunction] is not whether a substantial question has been raised, but whether the patentee is likely to succeed on the merits, upon application of the standards of proof that will prevail at trial. The question is not whether the patent is vulnerable; the question is who is likely to prevail in the end, considered with equitable factors that relate to whether the status quo should or should not be preserved while the trial is ongoing. The presentation of sufficient evidence to show the likelihood of prevailing on the merits is quite different from the presentation of substantial evidence to show vulnerability. [¶] Thus the evidence that favors the patent must be considered in deciding a motion for a preliminary injunction, as well as the evidence against the patent. The trial court then decides which side is likely ultimately to prevail." *But see* ***Conceal City, L.L.C. v. Looper Law Enforcement, LLC***, No. 3:10-CV-2506-D (N.D.Tex.2011) (memo op.; 11-15-11) (footnote 6; explaining inconsistency in Federal Circuit in applying "substantial question" standard for denying preliminary injunction).

Abbott Labs. v. Andrx Pharms., 452 F.3d 1331, 1335, 79 U.S.P.Q.2d 1321, 1324 (Fed.Cir.2006). "[I]f the defendant raises a substantial question concerning validity, i.e. an invalidity defense that the patentee cannot prove lacks substantial merit then the patentee has not established a likelihood of success on the merits. Furthermore, as this case involves multiple patent claims, the patentee must demonstrate that at least one of the allegedly infringed claims will likely withstand the validity challenges presented by the accused infringer. As to the burden regarding invalidity allegations, validity challenges during preliminary injunction proceedings can be successful, that is, they may raise substantial questions of invalidity, on evidence that would not suffice to support a judgment of invalidity at trial. In resisting a preliminary injunction, however, one need not make out a case of actual invalidity. Vulnerability is the issue at the preliminary injunction stage, while validity is the issue at trial. The showing of a substantial question as to invalidity thus requires less proof than the clear and convincing showing necessary to establish invalidity itself. When moving for the extraordinary relief of a preliminary injunction, a patentee need not establish the validity of a patent beyond question. The patentee must, however, present a clear case supporting the validity of the patent in suit. *At F.3d 1348, U.S.P.Q.2d 1334:* [W]here a patentee has not shown a likelihood of success on the merits, and where the patentee has not clearly established that monetary damages could not suffice but the defendant has not established that monetary damages do suffice, we cannot say that the irreparable harm prong of the analysis favors either party. [¶] Lastly, as to the public interest factor, the district court determined that to the extent that this court has found that the patents in suit are valid, the public interest is best served by enforcing them. Although the public interest inquiry is not necessarily or always bound to the likelihood of success [on] the merits, in this case absent any other relevant concerns, we agree with the district court that the public is best served by enforcing patents that are likely valid and infringed. As [patentee] did not establish a likelihood of success on the merits, we conclude that the public interest is best served by denying the preliminary injunction." (Internal quotes omitted.) *See also* ***Titan Tire Corp. v. Case New Holland, Inc.***, 566 F.3d 1372, 1375-80, 90 U.S.P.Q.2d 1918, 1921-24 (Fed.Cir.2009). *But see* ***MGM Studios, Inc. v. Grokster, Ltd.***, 518 F.Supp.2d 1197, 1212-13 (C.D.Cal.2007) (noting that many courts do not presume irreparable harm after finding likelihood of success on the merits for granting preliminary injunction because of ***eBay***, p. 700).

Jeneric/Pentron, Inc. v. Dillon Co., 205 F.3d 1377, 1380, 54 U.S.P.Q.2d 1086, 1088 (Fed.Cir.2000). "In reviewing a preliminary injunction decision, the likelihood of success factor plays a key role. This showing requires proof on both validity and infringement. To determine the likelihood of success on patent infringement, this court may construe the claim as a matter of law. The court then determines whether the accused product is likely to fall within the properly construed claim. An accused product infringes if it embodies each claim element or its equivalent."

Procedural Issues

TiVo Inc. v. Echostar Corp., 646 F.3d 869, 889, 98 U.S.P.Q.2d 1413, 1427 (Fed.Cir.2011). "The time to appeal the scope of an injunction is when it is handed down, not when a party is later found to be in contempt."

Ortho Pharm. v. Smith, 959 F.2d 936, 945, 22 U.S.P.Q.2d 1119, 1127 (Fed.Cir.1992). "[T]he grant, denial, or modification of an injunction under ... §283 is reviewable under an abuse of discretion standard." *See also* ***Mylan Pharms. v. Thompson***, 268 F.3d 1323, 1329, 60 U.S.P.Q.2d 1576, 1580 (Fed.Cir.2001).

Becton Dickinson & Co. v. Syntron Bioresearch, Inc., 51 U.S.P.Q.2d 1722, 1724-25 n.1 (S.D.Cal.1998). "Federal Circuit law governs the issuance of injunctions pursuant to ... §283. Purely procedural questions involving the issuance of such preliminary injunctions are controlled by the law of the Ninth Circuit." *See also* ***Revision Military, Inc. v. Balboa Mfg.***, 700 F.3d 524, 525-26, 104 U.S.P.Q.2d 1945, 1946 (Fed.Cir.2012).

§284. DAMAGES

Upon finding for the claimant the court shall award the claimant damages adequate to compensate for the infringement, but in no event less than a reasonable royalty for the use made of the invention by the infringer, together with interest and costs as fixed by the court.

When the damages are not found by a jury, the court shall assess them. In either event the court may increase the damages up to three times the amount found or assessed. Increased damages under this paragraph shall not apply to provisional rights under section 154(d).

The court may receive expert testimony as an aid to the determination of damages or of what royalty would be reasonable under the circumstances.

History of 35 U.S.C. §284: July 19, 1952, ch. 950, §1, 66 Stat. 813; Nov. 29, 1999, P.L. 106-113, §1000(a)(9), 113 Stat. 1536; Sept. 16, 2011, P.L. 112-29, §20(j)(1), 125 Stat. 335.

See also 28 U.S.C. §1920.

ANNOTATIONS

Generally

Carnegie Mellon Univ. v. Marvell Tech. Grp., 807 F.3d 1283, 1306, 116 U.S.P.Q.2d 1081, 1098 (Fed.Cir. 2015). "Where a physical product is being employed to measure damages for the infringing use of patented methods, we conclude[ ] territoriality is satisfied when and only when any one of those domestic actions for that unit (*e.g.*, sale) is proved to be present, even if others of the listed activities for that unit (*e.g.*, making, using) take place abroad."

Power Integrations, Inc. v. Fairchild Semiconductor Int'l, 711 F.3d 1348, 1371, 106 U.S.P.Q.2d 1361, 1377-78 (Fed.Cir.2013). "[T]he underlying question [is] whether [P] is entitled to compensatory damages for injury caused by infringing activity that occurred outside the territory of the U.S. The answer is no."

Spectralytics, Inc. v. Cordis Corp., 649 F.3d 1336, 1345, 99 U.S.P.Q.2d 1012, 1019 (Fed.Cir.2011). "[O]n post-trial JMOL motions, district court judges must scrutinize the evidence carefully to ensure that the 'substantial evidence' standard is satisfied, while keeping in mind that a reasonable royalty analysis necessarily involves an element of approximation and uncertainty." (Internal quotes omitted.)

Uniloc USA, Inc. v. Microsoft Corp., 632 F.3d 1292, 1315, 98 U.S.P.Q.2d 1203, 1222 (Fed.Cir.2011). "The patentee bears the burden of proving damages. To properly carry this burden, the patentee must 'sufficiently [tie the expert testimony on damages] to the facts of the case.' If the patentee fails to tie the theory to the facts of the case, the testimony must be excluded."

Minco, Inc. v. Combustion Eng'g, 95 F.3d 1109, 1119, 40 U.S.P.Q.2d 1001, 1008 (Fed.Cir.1996). "The Patent Act permits damages awards to encompass both lost profits and a reasonable royalty on that portion of an infringer's sales not included in the lost profit calculation. A segment of the infringer's sales may not warrant a lost profits award because the patentee cannot establish causation for that segment. For instance, a patent owner may not operate in the specific geographical area covered by the infringer or may not have had the manufacturing or marketing capacity to make the infringer's sales. However, the patentee would still be entitled to a reasonable royalty on each of those sales."

King Instrs. Corp. v. Perego, 65 F.3d 941, 949, 36 U.S.P.Q.2d 1129, 1135 (Fed.Cir.1995). "A patentee qualifies for damages adequate to compensate for infringement without exploiting its patent. [¶] '[D]amages' in §284 encompasses an amount necessary to redress any direct injury from infringement. *At F.3d 952, U.S.P.Q.2d 1137:* To adequately compensate for infringement of the right to exclude, as §284 requires, 'damages' includes lost profits on competing products not covered by the infringed claims."

Lost Profits—Generally

WesternGeco L.L.C. v. ION Geophysical Corp., 791 F.3d 1340, 1351, 115 U.S.P.Q.2d 1597, 1605-06 (Fed. Cir.2015), *vacated*, ___ U.S. ___, 136 S.Ct. 2486 (2016), *reinstated by* 837 F.3d 1358 (Fed.Cir.2016). "[B]y its terms, [35 U.S.C.] §271(f) operates to attach liability to domestic entities who export components they know and intend to be combined in a would-be infringing manner abroad. But the liability attaches in the U.S. It is the act of exporting the components from the U.S. which creates the liability. A construction that would allow recovery of foreign profits would make §271(f), relating to components, broader than §271(a), which covers finished products. In fact, §271(f) was designed to put domestic entities who export components to be assembled into a final product in a similar position to domestic manufacturers who sell the final product domestically or export the final product. Just as the U.S. seller or exporter of a final product cannot be liable for use abroad, so too the U.S. exporter of the component parts cannot be liable for use of the infringing article abroad. [¶] Of course, the fact that [P] is not entitled under U.S. patent law to lost profits from the foreign uses of its patented invention does not mean that it is entitled to no compensation."

DePuy Spine, Inc. v. Medtronic Sofamor Danek, Inc., 567 F.3d 1314, 1330, 90 U.S.P.Q.2d 1865, 1875 (Fed. Cir.2009). Demand for the patented product "does not require any allocation of consumer demand among the various limitations recited in a patent claim. Instead, [this] factor simply asks whether demand existed for the 'patented product,' i.e., a product that is 'covered by the patent in suit' or that 'directly competes with the infringing device.' *At F.3d 1331, U.S.P.Q.2d 1876-77:* [T]he focus on particular features corresponding to individual claim limitations is unnecessary when considering whether demand exists for a patented product under [this] factor. Rather, the elimination or substitution of particular features corresponding to one or more claim limitations goes to the availability of acceptable noninfringing substitutes under the second ... factor...."

Wechsler v. Macke Int'l Trade, Inc., 486 F.3d 1286, 1293, 82 U.S.P.Q.2d 1742, 1746 (Fed.Cir.2007). "[T]he availability of lost profits is a question of law for the court, not the jury. Only after the court has decided, as a matter of law, that lost profits are available does the jury then get to determine the amount of those lost profits. [¶] 'Normally, if the patentee is not selling a product, by definition there can be no lost profits.' The only exception is where the patentee has the ability to manufacture and market a product, but for some legitimate reason does not. Even in these situations, though, 'the burden on a patentee who has not begun to manufacture the patented product is commensurately heavy.'"

Poly-America, L.P. v. GSE Lining Tech., 383 F.3d 1303, 1311, 72 U.S.P.Q.2d 1685, 1690 (Fed.Cir.2004). "While we do not speculate concerning the benefits that the two companies reap from dividing their operations and separating the owner of the patent from the seller of the patented product, [Ps] may not enjoy the advantages of their separate corporate structure and, at the same time, avoid the consequential limitations of that structure—in this case, the inability of the patent holder to claim the lost profits of its non-exclusive licensee."

Juicy Whip, Inc. v. Orange Bang, Inc., 382 F.3d 1367, 1370, 72 U.S.P.Q.2d 1385, 1386 (Fed.Cir.2004). "Whether lost profits are available to a patentee is a question of law that [appellate court reviews] *de novo*. *At F.3d 1371, U.S.P.Q.2d 1387:* [T]he entire market value rule [is] a principle of patent damages that define[] a patentee's ability to recover lost profits on unpatented components typically sold with a patented item. Although the rule traditionally had been applied to permit recovery when both the patented and unpatented items were part of the same machine, ... 'the rule has been extended to allow inclusion of physically separate unpatented components normally sold with the patented components' with the caveat that both were 'considered to be components of a single assembly or parts of a complete machine, or they together constituted a functional unit.'"

Catalina Lighting, Inc. v. Lamps Plus, Inc., 295 F.3d 1277, 1291, 63 U.S.P.Q.2d 1545, 1554 (Fed.Cir. 2002). "When only a design patent is at issue, a patentee may not recover both infringer profits and additional damages under §284."

Amstar Corp. v. Envirotech Corp., 823 F.2d 1538, 1543, 3 U.S.P.Q.2d 1412, 1415 (Fed.Cir.1987). "A patentee may recover lost profits by proving that but for the infringement, the patentee would have made the sales the infringer made, charged higher prices, or incurred lower expenses. Otherwise the patentee may recover only a reasonable royalty. In a market with only two viable competitors, one may infer that the patentee would have made the infringer's sales or charged higher prices but for the infringing competition."

Panduit Corp. v. Stahlin Bros. Fibre Works, Inc., 575 F.2d 1152, 1156, 197 U.S.P.Q. 726, 729-30 (6th Cir. 1978). "To obtain as damages the profits on sales he would have made absent the infringement, i.e., the sales made by the infringer, a patent owner must prove: (1) demand for the patented product, (2) absence of acceptable noninfringing substitutes, (3) his manufacturing and marketing capability to exploit the demand, and (4) the amount of the profit he would have made." *See also* ***Tate Access Floors, Inc. v. Maxcess Techs.***, 222 F.3d 958, 971, 55 U.S.P.Q.2d 1513, 1521 (Fed.Cir. 2000).

Lost Profits—Causation

American Seating Co. v. USSC Grp., 514 F.3d 1262, 1269, 85 U.S.P.Q.2d 1683, 1687-88 (Fed.Cir.2008). "To prove lost profits from lost sales, the patent owner bears the initial burden to show a reasonable probability that 'but for' the infringement, he would have made the sales. Once this reasonable probability is shown, the burden shifts to the infringer to show that the 'but for' causation analysis is unreasonable under the specific circumstances."

Fiskars, Inc. v. Hunt Mfg., 279 F.3d 1378, 1383, 61 U.S.P.Q.2d 1851, 1855 (Fed.Cir.2002). "Although the parties must support their positions with sound economic proof, absolute certainty is not required, for reconstruction of the 'but for' market is 'by definition a hypothetical enterprise' based on the evidence introduced at trial."

Interactive Pictures Corp. v. Infinite Pictures, Inc., 274 F.3d 1371, 1386, 61 U.S.P.Q.2d 1152, 1163 (Fed. Cir.2001). "[A] decrease in a company's stock value is generally too remotely related to patent infringement to be compensable under the patent laws…."

Shockley v. Arcan, Inc., 248 F.3d 1349, 1362, 58 U.S.P.Q.2d 1692, 1700 (Fed.Cir.2001). "To show causation and entitlement to lost profits, a patentee must reconstruct the market to show 'likely outcomes with infringement factored out of the economic picture.'" *See also* ***Ericsson, Inc. v. Harris Corp.***, 352 F.3d 1369, 1377, 69 U.S.P.Q.2d 1109, 1115 (Fed.Cir.2003).

Grain Processing Corp. v. American Maize-Prods., 185 F.3d 1341, 1349, 51 U.S.P.Q.2d 1556, 1562 (Fed.Cir.1999). "The phrase 'damages adequate to compensate' means full compensation for any damages [patent owner] suffered as a result of the infringement. Full compensation includes any foreseeable lost profits the patent owner can prove. *At F.3d 1352-53, U.S.P.Q.2d 1564:* [Section 284] specifically envisions a reasonable royalty as a form of adequate compensation. While damages adequate to compensate means full compensation, full compensation does not entitle [patent assignee] to lost profits in the absence of 'but for' causation." (Internal quotes omitted.)

Minco, Inc. v. Combustion Eng'g, 95 F.3d 1109, 1118, 40 U.S.P.Q.2d 1001, 1008 (Fed.Cir.1996). "The assessment of adequate damages under §284 does not limit the patent holder to the amount of diverted sales of a commercial embodiment of the patented product. Rather, the patent holder may recover for an injury caused by the infringement if it 'was or should have been reasonably foreseeable by an infringing competitor in the relevant market, broadly defined.'"

Rite-Hite Corp. v. Kelley Co., 56 F.3d 1538, 1546, 35 U.S.P.Q.2d 1065, 1069-70 (Fed.Cir.1995). "[T]he 'test' for compensability of damages under §284 is not solely a 'but for' test in the sense that an infringer must compensate a patentee for any and all damages that proceed from the act of patent infringement. [A]long with establishing that a particular injury suffered by a patentee is a 'but for' consequence of infringement, there may also be a background question whether the asserted injury is of the type for which the patentee may be compensated. [¶] We believe that under §284 of the patent statute, the balance between full compensation, which is the meaning that the Supreme Court has attributed to the statute, and the reasonable limits of liability encompassed by general principles of law can best be viewed in terms of reasonable, objective foreseeability. If a particular injury was or should have been reasonably foreseeable by an infringing competitor in the relevant market, broadly defined, that injury is generally compensable absent a persuasive reason to the contrary. … Being responsible for lost sales of a competitive product is surely foreseeable…."

Lost Profits—Collateral Sales

American Seating Co. v. USSC Grp., 514 F.3d 1262, 1268, 85 U.S.P.Q.2d 1683, 1686 (Fed.Cir.2008). "A 'conveyed sale' refers to the relationship between the sale of a patented product and a functionally associated non-patented product. A patentee may recover lost profits on unpatented components sold with a patented item, a convoyed sale, if both the patented and unpatented products 'together were considered to be components of a single assembly or parts of a complete machine, or they together constituted a functional unit.' 'Our precedent has not extended liability to include items that have essentially no functional relationship to the patented invention and that may have been sold with an infringing device only as a matter of convenience or business advantage.' Damages on these items would exceed that which suitably compensates for the infringement. [¶] A functional relationship does not exist when independently operating patented and unpatented products are purchased as a package solely because of customer demand. The fact that customers prefer that passenger seats and tie-down wheelchair restraint systems come from a single supplier for ease of purchase, repair, and uniform design and appearance, does not compel the conclusion that the seats and tie-down system are 'analogous to components of a single assembly or … parts of a complete machine.'" *See also* ***Micro Chem., Inc. v. Lextron, Inc.***, 318 F.3d 1119, 1125-26, 65 U.S.P.Q.2d 1695, 1700 (Fed.Cir.2003).

Rite-Hite Corp. v. Kelley Co., 56 F.3d 1538, 1550, 35 U.S.P.Q.2d 1065, 1073 (Fed.Cir.1995). "[T]he facts of past cases clearly imply a limitation on damages, when recovery is sought on sales of unpatented components sold with patented components, to the effect that the unpatented components must function together with the patented component in some manner so as to produce a desired end product or result. All the components together must be analogous to components of a single assembly or be parts of a complete machine, or they must constitute a functional unit. *At F.3d 1551, U.S.P.Q.2d 1074*: It is a clear purpose of the patent law to redress competitive damages resulting from infringement of the patent, but there is no basis for extending that recovery to include damages for items that are neither competitive with nor function with the patented invention."

Lost Profits—Noninfringing Alternatives

Cohesive Techs. v. Waters Corp., 543 F.3d 1351, 1373, 88 U.S.P.Q.2d 1903, 1917 (Fed.Cir.2008). "[T]he 'acceptable noninfringing substitutes' analysis [is]: '[T]he mere existence of a competing device does not necessarily make that device an acceptable substitute. A product on the market which lacks the advantages of the patented product can hardly be termed a substitute acceptable to the customer who wants those advantages. Accordingly, if purchasers are motivated to purchase because of particular features available only from the patented product, products without such features—even if otherwise competing in the marketplace—would not be acceptable noninfringing substitutes. [¶] Thus, to prove that there are no acceptable noninfringing substitutes, the patent owner must show either that (1) the purchasers in the marketplace generally were willing to buy the patented product for its advantages, or (2) the specific purchasers of the infringing product purchased on that basis.'"

Grain Processing Corp. v. American Maize-Prods., 185 F.3d 1341, 1349, 51 U.S.P.Q.2d 1556, 1562 (Fed.Cir.1999). "[A]n alleged substitute not 'on the market' or 'for sale' during the infringement can figure prominently in determining whether a patentee would have made additional profits 'but for' the infringement. '[T]o be an acceptable non-infringing substitute, the product or process must have been available *or* on the market at the time of infringement.' This statement is an apt summary of this court's precedent, which permits available alternatives—including but not limited to products on the market—to preclude lost profits damages."

Lost Profits—Price Erosion

Power Integrations, Inc. v. Fairchild Semiconductor Int'l, 711 F.3d 1348, 1379-80, 106 U.S.P.Q.2d 1361, 1383-84 (Fed.Cir.2013). "[W]hile the marking statute [35 U.S.C. §287] precludes recovery of damages for pre-notice infringement, we must assess damages for post-notice infringement relative to market conditions at the point in time when infringement began. Even the infringer's pre-notice infringing activity is part of her whole infringement, and it is the whole of her infringement which we must consider in calculating damages for legally compensable post-notice infringement. To the extent an infringer's pre-notice infringement erodes the market price of a patented product, that price erosion is relevant in determining for each post-notice act of infringement what the patentee would have made *but for the infringement*. Accordingly, we hold that a price erosion analysis relating to damages arising from post-notice infringement must measure price changes against *infringement-free* market conditions, and thus the proper starting point of such a price erosion analysis is the date of first infringement."

Crystal Semiconductor Corp. v. TriTech Microelectronics Int'l, 246 F.3d 1336, 1357, 57 U.S.P.Q.2d 1953, 1965 (Fed.Cir.2001). "'Reduction of prices, and consequent loss of profits, enforced by infringing competition, is a proper ground for awarding of damages. The only question is as to the character and sufficiency of the evidence in the particular case.' This court has since explained that 'the question as to the character and sufficiency of the evidence' places the burden on the patentee to show that 'but for' infringement, it would have sold its product at higher prices. Moreover, in a credible economic analysis, the patentee cannot show entitlement to a higher price divorced from the effect of that higher price on demand for the product. In other words, the patentee must also present evidence of the (presumably reduced) amount of product the patentee would have sold at the higher price. Thus ... the patentee's price erosion theory must account for the nature, or definition, of the market, similarities between any benchmark market and the market in which price erosion is alleged, and the effect of the hypothetically increased price on the likely number of sales at that price in that market." *See also* ***Ericsson, Inc. v. Harris Corp.***, 352 F.3d 1369, 1378-79, 69 U.S.P.Q.2d 1109, 1116-17 (Fed.Cir.2003).

Reasonable Royalty—Generally

Finjan, Inc. v. Blue Coat Sys., 879 F.3d 1299, 1309-10, 125 U.S.P.Q.2d 1282, ___ (Fed.Cir.2018). "The only measure of damages at issue in this case is a reasonable royalty.... [¶] [D] argues that, in calculating a royalty base, [P] failed to apportion damages to the infringing functionality. We agree. [¶] When the accused technology does not make up the whole of the accused product, apportionment is required. '[T]he ultimate combination of royalty base and royalty rate must reflect the value attributable to the infringing features of the product, and no more.' In such cases, the patentee must 'give evidence tending to separate or apportion the [infringer]'s profits and the patentee's damages between the patented feature and the unpatented features, and such evidence must be reliable and tangible, and not conjectural or speculative.' [P], as the present patent holder, had the burden of proving damages by a preponderance of the evidence."

Commonwealth Sci. & Indus. Research Org. v. Cisco Sys., 809 F.3d 1295, 1301, 117 U.S.P.Q.2d 1527, 1532 (Fed.Cir.2015). "'[T]he essential requirement' for reliability under ***Daubert*** 'is that the ultimate reasonable royalty award must be based on the incremental value that the patented invention adds to the end product.' *At F.3d 1305, U.S.P.Q.2d 1534:* [A] reasonable royalty calculation under §284 attempts to measure the value of the patented invention. This value—the value of the technology—is distinct from any value that artificially accrues to the patent due to the standard's adoption. Without this rule, patentees would receive all of the benefit created by standardization—benefit that would otherwise flow to consumers and businesses practicing the standard. We therefore reaffirm that reasonable royalties for [standard-essential patents] generally—and not only those subject to a [reasonable and non-discriminatory] commitment—must not include any value flowing to the patent from the standard's adoption."

Ericsson, Inc. v. D-Link Sys., 773 F.3d 1201, 1230, 113 U.S.P.Q.2d 1001, 1022-23 (Fed.Cir.2014). "Although we have never described the ***Georgia-Pacific*** factors as a talisman for royalty rate calculations, district courts regularly turn to this 15-factor list when fashioning their jury instructions. Indeed, courts often parrot all 15 factors to the jury, even if some of those factors clearly are not relevant to the case at hand. [¶] In a case involving [reasonable and nondiscriminatory (RAND)]-encumbered patents, many of the ***Georgia-Pacific*** factors simply are not relevant; many are even contrary to RAND principles. *At F.3d 1231:* Other factors may also need to be adapted on a case-by-case basis depending on the technology at issue. Consequently, the trial court must carefully consider the evidence presented in the case when crafting an appropriate jury instruction. In this case, the district court erred by instructing the jury on multiple ***Georgia-Pacific*** factors that are not relevant, or are misleading, on the record before it, including, at least, factors 4, 5, 8, 9, and 10 of the ***Georgia-Pacific*** factors. *At F.3d 1232:* We believe it unwise to create a new set of ***Georgia-Pacific***-like factors for all cases involving RAND-encumbered patents.

Although we recognize the desire for bright line rules and the need for district courts to start somewhere, courts must consider the facts of record when instructing the jury and should avoid rote reference to any particular damages formula."

Apple Inc. v. Motorola, Inc., 757 F.3d 1286, 1327-28, 110 U.S.P.Q.2d 1695, 1723-24 (Fed.Cir.2014), *overruled on other grounds*, ***Williamson v. Citrix Online, LLC***, 792 F.3d 1339, 115 U.S.P.Q.2d 1105 (Fed.Cir.2015). "If a patentee's evidence fails to support its specific royalty estimate, the fact finder is still required to determine what royalty is supported by the record. Indeed, if the record evidence does not fully support either party's royalty estimate, the fact finder must still determine what constitutes a reasonable royalty from the record evidence. Certainly, if the patentee's proof is weak, the court is free to award a low, perhaps nominal, royalty, as long as that royalty is supported by the record. [¶] Thus, a fact finder may award no damages only when the record supports a zero royalty award. For example, in a case completely lacking any evidence on which to base a damages award, the record may well support a zero royalty award. Also, a record could demonstrate that, at the time of infringement, the defendant considered the patent valueless and the patentee would have accepted no payment for the defendant's infringement. Of course, it seems unlikely that a willing licensor and willing licensee would agree to a zero royalty payment in a hypothetical negotiation, where both infringement and validity are assumed."

Energy Transp. Grp. v. William Demant Holding A/S, 697 F.3d 1342, 1358, 105 U.S.P.Q.2d 1061, 1072 (Fed.Cir.2012). "[T]his court cannot 'correct' a damages figure by extrapolating a royalty rate from the jury's lump sum damages award and multiplying that royalty rate by a revised sales base. 'Except in those cases in which it is apparent as a matter of law that certain identifiable sums included in the verdict should not have been there, the court may not arbitrarily reduce the amount of damages, for to do so would deprive the parties of their constitutional right to a jury.' An 'identifiable sum' typically must be separately listed on the jury verdict form."

Powell v. Home Depot U.S.A., Inc., 663 F.3d 1221, 1238-39, 100 U.S.P.Q.2d 1742, 1753 (Fed.Cir.2011). "[A]n *infringer's* net profit margin is not the ceiling by which a reasonable royalty is capped. It is equally appropriate to impose that rule when … the infringer argues that the *patentee's* profit expectation must be a cap on the reasonable royalty that the patentee may receive. While either the infringer's or the patentee's profit expectation may be considered in the overall reasonable royalty analysis, … neither is an absolute limit to the amount of the reasonable royalty that may be awarded upon a reasoned hypothetical negotiation analysis under the ***Georgia-Pacific*** factors. Indeed, damages to the patent holder cannot simply be calculated in all cases by determining the difference between his pecuniary condition after the infringement, and what his condition would have been if the infringement had not occurred." (Internal quotes omitted.) *See also* ***King Instrs. Corp. v. Perego***, 65 F.3d 941, 947 n.2, 36 U.S.P.Q.2d 1129, 1133 n.2 (Fed.Cir.1995); ***Del Mar Avionics, Inc. v. Quinton Instr. Co.***, 836 F.2d 1320, 1326, 5 U.S.P.Q.2d 1255, 1260 (Fed.Cir.1987).

Uniloc USA, Inc. v. Microsoft Corp., 632 F.3d 1292, 1312, 98 U.S.P.Q.2d 1203, 1220 (Fed.Cir.2011). "The 25% rule of thumb is a tool that has been used to approximate the reasonable royalty rate that the manufacturer of a patented product would be willing to offer to pay to the patentee during a hypothetical negotiation. *At F.3d 1315, U.S.P.Q.2d 1222:* This court now holds as a matter of Federal Circuit law that the 25% rule of thumb is a fundamentally flawed tool for determining a baseline royalty rate in a hypothetical negotiation. Evidence relying on the 25% rule of thumb is thus inadmissible under ***Daubert*** and the [FREs], because it fails to tie a reasonable royalty base to the facts of the case at issue. *At F.3d 1317, U.S.P.Q.2d 1224:* [T]here must be a basis in fact to associate the royalty rates used in prior licenses to the particular hypothetical negotiation at issue in the case. The 25% rule of thumb as an abstract and largely theoretical construct fails to satisfy this fundamental requirement."

Mars, Inc. v. Coin Acceptors, Inc., 527 F.3d 1359, 1374, 87 U.S.P.Q.2d 1076, 1088 (Fed.Cir.2008). "[W]e reject [D's] argument that a reasonable royalty can never result in an infringer operating at a loss. Although an infringer's anticipated profit from use of the patented invention is among the factors to be considered in determining a reasonable royalty, the law does not require that an infringer be permitted to make a profit." (Internal quotes omitted.)

Paice LLC v. Toyota Motor Corp., 504 F.3d 1293, 1314-15, 85 U.S.P.Q.2d 1001, 1016 (Fed.Cir.2007). The issue "is whether an order *permitting* use of a patented invention in exchange for a royalty is properly characterized as *preventing* the violation of the rights secured by the patent. [¶] Under some circumstances, awarding an ongoing royalty for patent infringement in lieu of an injunction may be appropriate. *At U.S.P.Q.2d 1017:* But, awarding an ongoing royalty where 'necessary' to effectuate a remedy, be it for antitrust violations or patent infringement, does not justify the provision of such relief as a matter of course whenever a permanent injunction is not imposed. In most cases, where the district court determines that a permanent injunction is not warranted, the district court may wish to allow the parties to negotiate a license amongst themselves regarding future use of a patented invention before imposing an ongoing royalty. Should the parties fail to come to an agreement, the district court could step in to assess a reasonable royalty in light of the ongoing infringement. [¶] In this case, the district court, after applying the four-factor test for a permanent injunction and declining to issue one, imposed an ongoing royalty sua sponte upon the parties. But, the district court's order provides no reasoning to support the selection of $25 per infringing vehicle as the royalty rate. Thus, this court is unable to determine whether the district court abused its discretion in setting the ongoing royalty rate. Accordingly, we think it prudent to remand the case for the limited purpose of having the district court reevaluate the ongoing royalty rate. Upon remand, the court may take additional evidence if necessary to account for any additional economic factors arising out of the imposition of an ongoing royalty. The district court may determine that $25 is, in fact, an appropriate royalty rate going forward. However, without any indication as to why that rate is appropriate, we are unable to determine whether the district court abused its discretion."

Monsanto Co. v. McFarling, 488 F.3d 973, 978-79, 82 U.S.P.Q.2d 1942, 1945-46 (Fed.Cir.2007). "An established royalty is usually the best measure of a 'reasonable' royalty for a given use of an invention because it removes the need to guess at the terms to which parties would hypothetically agree. When the patentee has consistently licensed others to engage in conduct comparable to the defendant's at a uniform royalty, that royalty is taken as established and indicates the terms upon which the patentee would have licensed the defendant's use of the invention."

Embrex, Inc. v. Service Eng'g, 216 F.3d 1343, 1350, 55 U.S.P.Q.2d 1161, 1165 (Fed.Cir.2000). "Because the only cognizable infringement in this case is the testing and those tests were not shown to cause any loss of profits to [patent licensee], this court vacates the district court's award of $500,000 in direct damages. However, under ... §284, [patent licensee] 'in no event' loses entitlement to a reasonable royalty for [infringer's] infringing tests. Royalties are ordinarily computed based upon the sales of a patented product or process. However, parties may choose other methods to compute the amount that a licensee may pay for the right to use a patented product or process, such as flat fees or milestone payments in the case of pre-commercialization licenses."

Georgia-Pac. Corp. v. U.S. Plywood Corp., 318 F.Supp. 1116, 1120, 166 U.S.P.Q. 235, 238 (S.D.N.Y. 1970), *modified on other grounds*, 446 F.2d 295, 170 U.S.P.Q. 369 (2d Cir.1971). "The following are some of the factors [pertinent to determination of a reasonable royalty]: (1) The royalties received by the patentee for the licensing of the patent in suit, proving or tending to prove an established royalty. (2) The rates paid by the licensee for the use of other patents comparable to the patent in suit. (3) The nature and scope of the license, as exclusive or non-exclusive; or as restricted or non-restricted in terms of territory or with respect to whom the manufactured product may be sold. (4) The licensor's established policy and marketing program to maintain his patent monopoly by not licensing others to use the invention or by granting licenses under special conditions designed to preserve that monopoly. (5) The commercial relationship between the licensor and licensee, such as, whether they are competitors in the same territory in the same line of business; or whether they are inventor and [promoter]. (6) The effect of selling the patented specialty in promoting sales of other products of the licensee; the existing value of the invention to the licensor as a generator of sales of his non-patented items; and the extent of such derivative or convoyed sales. (7) The duration of the patent and the term of the license. (8) The established profitability of the product made under the patent; its commercial success; and its current popularity. (9) The utility and advantages of the patent property over the old modes or devices, if any, that had been used for working out similar results. (10) The nature of the patented invention; the character of the commercial embodiment of it as owned and produced by the licensor; and the benefits to those who have used the invention. (11) The extent to which the infringer has made use of the invention; and any evidence probative of the value of that use. (12) The portion of the profit or of the selling price that may be customary in the particular business or in comparable businesses to allow for the use of the invention or analogous inventions. (13) The portion of the realizable profit that should be credited to the invention as distinguished from non-patented elements, the manufacturing process, business risks, or significant features or improvements added by the infringer. (14) The opinion testimony of qualified experts. (15) The amount that a licensor (such as the patentee) and a licensee (such as the infringer) would have agreed upon (at the time the infringement began) if both had been reasonably and voluntarily trying to reach an agreement; that is, the amount which a prudent licensee—who desired, as a business proposition, to obtain a license to manufacture and sell a particular article embodying the patented invention—would have been willing to pay as a royalty and yet be able to make a reasonable profit and which amount would have been acceptable by a prudent patentee who was willing to grant a license." *See also* ***Lucent Techs. v. Gateway, Inc.***, 580 F.3d 1301, 1325-36, 92 U.S.P.Q.2d 1555, 1571-80 (Fed.Cir.2009).

Reasonable Royalty—Hypothetical Negotiations

Aqua Shield v. Inter Pool Cover Team, 774 F.3d 766, 770-72, 113 U.S.P.Q.2d 1347, 1350-52 (Fed.Cir. 2014). "After making a finding of infringement, the court shall award the claimant damages adequate to compensate for the infringement, but in no event less than a reasonable royalty for the use made of the invention by the infringer. The value of what was taken—the value of the use of the patented technology—measures the royalty. A traditional heuristic for assessing this market value is to posit a hypothetical negotiation between the patentee and adjudicated infringer and to attempt to ascertain the royalty upon which the parties would have agreed had they successfully negotiated an agreement just before infringement began. The inquiry, besides being hypothetical, involves approximation: the hypothetical negotiation tries, as best as possible, to recreate the *ex ante* licensing negotiation scenario and to describe the resulting agreement. [¶] What an infringer's profits actually turned out to have been during the infringement period may be relevant, but only in an indirect and limited way—as some evidence bearing on a directly relevant inquiry into anticipated profits. Thus, when the infringer is a profit-making enterprise, a reasonable royalty is the amount that a person, desiring to manufacture, use, or sell a patented article, as a business proposition, would be willing to pay as a royalty and yet be able to make, use, or sell the patented article, in the market, at a reasonable profit. In hypothetical-negotiation terms, the core economic question is what the infringer, in a hypothetical pre-infringement negotiation under hypothetical conditions, would have *anticipated* the profit-making potential of use of the patented technology to be, compared to using non-infringing alternatives. If a potential user of the patented technology would expect to earn X profits in the future without using the patented technology, and X + Y profits by using the patented technology, it would seem, as a prima facie matter, economically irrational to pay more than Y as a royalty—paying more would produce a loss compared to forgoing use of the patented technology. [¶] The hypothetical negotiation is hypothetical not only because, in the typical case, no successful pre-infringement negotiation ever occurred, but also because the negotiation is constructed on hypothetical assumptions. Most basically, the method assumes infringement and validity of the patents and willingness of the parties to negotiate an agreement. Another hypothetical assumption, bearing particularly on the anticipated-profits inquiry, abstracts away from the particular infringer's degree of efficiency. An especially inefficient infringer—*e.g.*, one operating with needlessly high costs, wasteful practices, or poor management—is not entitled to an especially low royalty rate simply because that is all it can afford to pay without forfeiting or unduly limiting its profit if it uses the patented technology rather than alternatives. Thus, the royalty the particular infringer could profitably pay by going about its business in its particular way does not set the market value that the hypothetical negotiation aims to identify. [¶] Real-world application of this conceptual structure often involves approximation and uncertainty, ... and the ultimate royalty determination must reflect the two-sided nature of the posited negotiation. The inquiry, besides being hypothetical, asks about a comparative business prediction in an uncertain, complex world, and many variables may affect the hypothetical forecast, including costs and availability of non-infringing alternatives, the patented technology's role in the firm's (expected) overall business, and the (expected) actions of competing firms in the market. Moreover, various kinds of evidence, such as licenses, business prognostications, and information about cost savings or value enhancements compared to alternatives, where such evidence is reliable, relevant, and not unduly prejudicial, may be used in the inquiry to determine the economic value of the patented technology in the marketplace at the relevant time. But we do not have before us broad questions about what evidence meets admissibility standards or would support a sustainable royalty award. [¶] We deal here only with a challenge to the soundness of the district court's particular use of [D's] profits in its rationale. For purposes of [P's] challenge, two points are key. First, anticipated incremental profits under the hypothesized conditions are conceptually central to constraining the royalty negotiation.... Second, evidence of the infringer's actual profits generally is admissible as probative of his anticipated profits." (Internal quotes omitted.)

VirnetX, Inc. v. Cisco Sys., 767 F.3d 1308, 1326, 113 U.S.P.Q.2d 1112, 1125 (Fed.Cir.2014). "No matter what the form of the royalty, a patentee must take care to seek only those damages attributable to the infringing features. [¶] Thus, when claims are drawn to an individual component of a multi-component product, it is the exception, not the rule, that damages may be based upon the value of the multi-component product. Indeed, ... '[a] patentee may assess damages based on the entire market value of the accused product *only where* the patented feature creates the basis for customer demand or substantially creates the value of the component parts.'" *See also* ***LaserDynamics, Inc. v. Quanta Computer, Inc.***, 694 F.3d 51, 67-68, 104 U.S.P.Q.2d 1573, 1585 (Fed.Cir.2012) (affirming that in any case involving multi-component products, patentees may not calculate damages based on sales of entire product, as opposed to smallest salable patent-practicing unit, without showing that demand for entire product is attributable to patented feature).

Minks v. Polaris Indus., 546 F.3d 1364, 1373, 89 U.S.P.Q.2d 1102, 1109 (Fed.Cir.2008). "[T]he hypothetical negotiation is deemed to be an arm's length transaction. Courts should not, therefore, accept 'as conclusive the royalty arrangement between the patent owner and the single licensee, a close corporation owned by the inventor's family....'"

Riles v. Shell Expl. & Prod., 298 F.3d 1302, 1311, 63 U.S.P.Q.2d 1819, 1825 (Fed.Cir.2002). "Upon a finding of infringement, ... the statutory measure of 'damages' is 'the difference between [the patent owner's] pecuniary condition after the infringement, and what his condition would have been if the infringement had not occurred.' This formulation requires the patentee to reconstruct the market, by definition a hypothetical enterprise, to project economic results that did not occur. ... The statute guarantees patentees a reasonable royalty even when they are unable to prove entitlement to lost profits or an established royalty rate." *See also* ***Integra LifeSci. I Ltd. v. Merck KGaA***, 331 F.3d 860, 869-70, 66 U.S.P.Q.2d 1865, 1871-72 (Fed.Cir.2003), *vacated & remanded*, 545 U.S. 193 (2005); ***Rite-Hite Corp. v. Kelley Co.***, 56 F.3d 1538, 1554, 35 U.S.P.Q.2d 1065, 1076-77 (Fed.Cir.1995).

Wang Labs. v. Toshiba Corp., 993 F.2d 858, 870, 26 U.S.P.Q.2d 1767, 1778 (Fed.Cir.1993). "In this case, infringing products were being sold on the date of issuance of [P's] patent. Therefore, ... hypothetical royalty negotiations should have been considered to have occurred on the patent issuance date."

Georgia-Pac. Corp. v. U.S. Plywood Corp., 318 F.Supp. 1116, 1121, 166 U.S.P.Q. 235, 239 (S.D.N.Y. 1970), *modified on other grounds*, 446 F.2d 295, 170 U.S.P.Q. 369 (2d Cir.1971). "The parties rely upon the traditional array of facts probative of a reasonable royalty. But, in addition, [patentee] places heavy reliance upon a later formulation called 'the willing buyer and willing seller' rule. [¶] [The rule is] 'what the parties would have agreed upon, if both were reasonably trying to reach an agreement.' [¶] What a willing licensor and a willing licensee would have agreed upon in a suppositious negotiation for a reasonable royalty would entail consideration of ... specific factors ..., to the extent of their relevance. Where a willing licensor and a willing licensee are negotiating for a royalty, the hypothetical negotiations would not occur in a vacuum of pure logic. They would involve a market place confrontation of the parties, the outcome of which would depend upon such factors as their relative bargaining strength; the anticipated amount of profits that the prospective licensor reasonably thinks he would lose as a result of licensing the patent as compared to the anticipated royalty income; the anticipated amount of net profits that the prospective licensee reasonably thinks he will make; the commercial past performance of the invention in terms of public acceptance and profits; the market to be tapped; and any other economic factor that normally prudent businessmen would, under similar circumstances, take into consideration in negotiating the hypothetical license."

Reasonable Royalty—Entire-Market-Value Rule

Commonwealth Sci. & Indus. Research Org. v. Cisco Sys., 809 F.3d 1295, 1302, 117 U.S.P.Q.2d 1527, 1532 (Fed.Cir.2015). "[T]he smallest salable patent-practicing unit principle provides that, where a damages model apportions from a royalty base, the model should use the smallest salable patent-practicing unit as the base."

Ericsson, Inc. v. D-Link Sys., 773 F.3d 1201, 1232-33, 113 U.S.P.Q.2d 1001, 1023 (Fed.Cir.2014). "As with all patents, the royalty rate for [standard essential patents (SEPs)] must be apportioned to the value of the patented invention. When dealing with SEPs, there are two special apportionment issues that arise. First, the patented feature must be apportioned from all of the unpatented features reflected in the standard. Second, the patentee's royalty must be premised on the value of the patented feature, not any value added by the standard's adoption of the patented technology. These steps are necessary to ensure that the royalty award is based on the incremental value that the patented *invention* adds to the product, not any value added by the standardization of that technology. *At U.S.P.Q.2d 1024:* Just as we apportion damages for a patent that covers a small part of a device, we must also apportion damages for SEPs that cover only a small part of a standard. In other words, a royalty award for a SEP must be apportioned to the value of the patented invention (or at least to the approximate value thereof), not the value of the standard as a whole. A jury must be instructed accordingly. [¶] Because SEP holders should only be compensated for the added benefit of their inventions, the jury must be told to differentiate the added benefit from any value the innovation gains because it has become standard essential. Although the jury, as the fact finder, should determine the appropriate value for that added benefit and may do so with some level of imprecision, we conclude that they must be told to consider the difference between the added value of the technological invention and the added value of that invention's standardization."

LaserDynamics, Inc. v. Quanta Computer, Inc., 694 F.3d 51, 67-68, 104 U.S.P.Q.2d 1573, 1585 (Fed.Cir. 2012). "We reaffirm that in any case involving multi-component products, patentees may not calculate damages based on sales of the entire product, as opposed to the smallest salable patent-practicing unit, without showing that the demand for the entire product is attributable to the patented feature. [¶] Regardless of the chosen royalty rate, one way in which the error of an improperly admitted entire market value rule theory manifests itself is in the disclosure of the revenues earned by the accused infringer associated with a complete product rather than the patented component only. In ***Uniloc***, we observed that such disclosure to the jury of the overall product revenues 'cannot help but skew the damages horizon for the jury, regardless of the contribution of the patented component to this revenue.' Admission of such overall revenues, which have no demonstrated correlation to the value of the patented feature alone, only serve to make a patentee's proffered damages amount appear modest by comparison, and to artificially inflate the jury's damages calculation beyond that which is 'adequate to compensate for the infringement.' [¶] [P]roof that consumers would not want a laptop computer without [many] features is not tantamount to proof that any one of those features alone drives the market for laptop computers. Put another way, if given a choice between two otherwise equivalent laptop computers, only one of which practices optical disc discrimination, proof that consumers would choose the laptop computer having the disc discrimination functionality says nothing as to whether the presence of that functionality is what motivates consumers to buy a laptop computer in the first place. It is this latter and higher degree of proof that must exist to support an entire market value rule theory." *See also* ***Uniloc USA, Inc. v. Microsoft Corp.***, 632 F.3d 1292, 1318, 98 U.S.P.Q.2d 1203, 1225 (Fed.Cir.2011).

Minks v. Polaris Indus., 546 F.3d 1364, 1372 n.6, 89 U.S.P.Q.2d 1102, 1109 n.6 (Fed.Cir.2008). "In ***Rite-Hite*** [***Corp. v. Kelley Co.***, 56 F.3d 1538 (Fed.Cir.1995)], this court clarified that 'the relevance of anticipated collateral sales to the determination of a reasonable royalty *rate*' is not to be confused with the application of the entire market value rule to a determination of the royalty base."

Imonex Servs. v. W.H. Munzprufer Dietmar Trenner GmbH, 408 F.3d 1374, 1379, 74 U.S.P.Q.2d 1936, 1940 (Fed.Cir.2005). "The entire market value rule permits recovery of damages based on the value of the entire apparatus containing several features, where the patent related feature is the basis for customer demand. This measure of damages arises where both the patented and unpatented components together are analogous to components of a single assembly, parts of a complete machine, or constitute a functional unit but not where the unpatented components have essentially no functional relationship to the patented invention and … may have been sold with an infringing device only as a matter of convenience or business advantage." (Internal quotes omitted.)

Riles v. Shell Expl. & Prod., 298 F.3d 1302, 1311, 63 U.S.P.Q.2d 1819, 1825 (Fed.Cir.2002). Expert's "model [for royalty damages] was based upon a percentage (2-5%) of the cost of [D's product]. *At F.3d 1312, U.S.P.Q.2d 1826:* [T]his model cannot support the jury verdict. [Expert's] model does not associate his proposed royalty with the value of the patented method at all, but with the unrelated cost of [D's] entire [product], which includes much more than [use of P's invention]. Stated otherwise, in the hypothetical negotiation that characterizes the reasonable royalty calculation, [D] may have had non-infringing alternatives to [using P's invention]. Thus, under the constraints of the hypothetical negotiation, the market could not award [P] a royalty for his method divorced of all relation to a potential non-infringing alternative method. The economic relationship between the patented method and non-infringing alternative methods, of necessity, would limit the hypothetical negotiation. On the other hand, the cost of [D's] entire [product] would have little, if any, relevance in the hypothetical negotiation. [Expert's] model does not account for the actual losses due to infringement of the patented method."

Reasonable Royalty—Lump Sum

Summit 6, LLC v. Samsung Elecs. Co., 802 F.3d 1283, 1300-01, 116 U.S.P.Q.2d 1637, 1649-50 (Fed.Cir. 2015). "This court has not directly addressed whether a jury can award lump-sum damages through the life of the patent. We have, however, permitted such relief. [¶] In this case, the district court properly denied [P's] request for an ongoing royalty because the jury award compensated [P] for both past and future infringement through the life of the patent. [D's] expert … testified that a lump-sum award was appropriate. … When the jury returned its verdict, it indicated on the verdict form that the award was a lump sum by writing 'lump sum' on the verdict form. We see no basis to disturb the district court's determination and hold that the district court did not abuse its discretion in denying [P's] request for an ongoing royalty."

Reasonable Royalty—Past Licenses

LaserDynamics, Inc. v. Quanta Computer, Inc., 694 F.3d 51, 79-80, 104 U.S.P.Q.2d 1573, 1594 (Fed.Cir. 2012). "When relying on licenses to prove a reasonable royalty, alleging a loose or vague comparability between different technologies or licenses does not suffice. [¶] Actual licenses to the patents-in-suit are probative not only of the proper amount of a reasonable royalty, but also of the proper form of the royalty structure."

ResQNet.com, Inc. v. Lansa, Inc., 594 F.3d 860, 872-73, 93 U.S.P.Q.2d 1553, 1562 (Fed.Cir.2010). "This court observes … that the most reliable license in this record arose out of litigation. On other occasions, this court has acknowledged that the hypothetical reasonable royalty calculation occurs before litigation and that litigation itself can skew the results of the hypothetical negotiation. Similarly this court has long recognized that a reasonable royalty can be different than a given royalty when, for example, widespread infringement artificially depressed past licenses. And a reasonable royalty may permissibly reflect '[t]he fact that an infringer had to be ordered by a court to pay damages, rather than agreeing to a reasonable royalty.' [¶] [T]he trial court should not rely on unrelated licenses to increase the reasonable royalty rate above rates more clearly linked to the economic demand for the claimed technology."

Reasonable Royalty—Ongoing Infringement

Mondis Tech. v. Chimei Innolux Corp., 822 F.Supp.2d 639, 646 (E.D.Tex.2011), *aff'd*, 499 Fed.Appx. 971 (Fed.Cir.2013). "[T]he Court will proceed by first determining a post-judgment reasonable (ongoing) royalty rate under ***Georgia-Pacific*** and will use the jury's verdict in this case as a starting point and determine how the circumstances may have changed. Then the Court will consider whether the ongoing infringement will be willful. If so, the Court will consider how much to enhance the damages in light of this willful infringement. [¶] The Court first performs this ***Georgia-Pacific*** analysis assuming that [D's] continued infringement is not willful and thus not considering the changed legal relationship between the parties as a result of [D's] status as an adjudicated infringer. … In light of this assumption of no willful infringement, … the Court holds that the ongoing reasonable royalty rate will be 0.75% for monitors under solely ***Georgia-Pa-***

cific framework. *At 649:* The Court holds that ongoing infringement by [D] is willful. [¶] [T]he Court holds that the earlier calculated reasonable royalty rate of 0.75% should be doubled to account for enhancement due to willfulness."

Paice LLC v. Toyota Motor Corp., 609 F.Supp.2d 620, 623-24, 91 U.S.P.Q.2d 1835, 1837 (E.D.Tex 2009). "The Federal Circuit has made it clear that damages for past infringement are separate and distinct from damages for future acts of infringement and may require different royalty rates given the change in the parties' legal relationship, among other factors. [¶] District courts have frequently looked to ***Georgia-Pacific Corp. v. U.S. Plywood Corp.***, 318 F.Supp. 1116 (S.D. N.Y.1970), for guidance on reasonable royalty damages assessment. [¶] Many of the factors noted by the ***Georgia-Pacific*** Court are also seemingly applicable to an ongoing royalty rate analysis. A post-judgment, ongoing royalty negotiation, however, is logically different from the pre-trial hypothetical negotiation discussed in ***Georgia-Pacific***. In the case of an ongoing royalty, the hypothetical negotiation occurs post-judgment; therefore, the 'willing licensee' in this negotiation is an adjudged infringer, unlike the situation described in ***Georgia-Pacific***. [¶] In many ongoing royalty negotiations, the threat of a permanent injunction serves as a big stick, essentially framing negotiation in terms of how much an adjudged infringer would pay for a license to continue its infringing conduct. However, when an injunction is not proper under ***eBay***[***, Inc. v. MercExchange, L.L.C.***, 547 U.S. 388 (2006)], the question instead becomes: what amount of money would reasonably compensate a patentee for giving up his right to exclude yet allow an ongoing willful infringer to make a reasonable profit? It is under this modified ***Georgia-Pacific*** framework that the Court proceeds."

Indirect Infringement

Glenayre Elecs., Inc. v. Jackson, 443 F.3d 851, 858-59, 78 U.S.P.Q.2d 1641, 1647 (Fed.Cir.2006). "[W]here a patentee alleges that a manufacturer contributes to and induces infringement by its customers simply because it sells infringing products to its customers, damages assessed for indirect infringement normally will be the same as damages that would be assessed had the patentee sued and obtained a judgment against the customers. Indeed, in most cases damages assessed for indirect infringement will be equal to damages assessed for the underlying direct infringement. This case does not fit within one of the exceptions to the basic rule, such as 'when the indirect infringer does not cause the original infringement but merely prolongs an infringing use of a product by providing supplies or spare parts.' *At F.3d 873, U.S.P.Q.2d 1657-58:* [A]n award of damages for particular infringing acts, unlike a comprehensive license, does not automatically entitle the infringer or others to continue infringing conduct in the form of additional sales or uses of infringing products throughout the life of the patent. But in this case, the theory of recovery [D] presented [in its counterclaim] at the first trial was based on a reasonable royalty for past manufacture and sale of infringing products by [P] and, importantly, past benefits derived from use of the same products by [P's] customers. The district court considered that theory and found that that reasonable royalty is, at most, $2.65 million. [D] accepted that award of damages. Therefore, the district court was correct to conclude that, as a matter of law, the damages award, once collected, fully compensated [D] for direct infringement by [P], direct infringement by [P's] customers, and indirect infringement by [P] based on [P's] customers' direct infringement."

Interest

General Motors Corp. v. Devex Corp., 461 U.S. 648, 653, 217 U.S.P.Q. 1185, 1187 (1983). "We have little doubt that §284 does not incorporate the ***Duplate*** [***Corp. v. Triplex Safety Glass Co.***, 298 U.S. 448 (1936),] standard. Under that standard, ... prejudgment interest could not be awarded where damages were unliquidated, absent bad faith or other exceptional circumstances. By contrast, §284 gives a court general authority to fix interest and costs. On the face of §284, a court's authority to award interest is not restricted to exceptional circumstances, and there is no warrant for imposing such a limitation. *At U.S. 656-57, U.S.P.Q. 1189:* We do not construe §284 as requiring the award of prejudgment interest whenever infringement is found. ... We hold only that prejudgment interest should be awarded under §284 absent some justification for withholding such an award."

Group One Ltd. v. Hallmark Cards, Inc., 407 F.3d 1297, 1307-08, 74 U.S.P.Q.2d 1759, 1767 (Fed.Cir.2005). "We review a district court's denial of prejudgment interest for abuse of discretion."

Crystal Semiconductor Corp. v. TriTech Microelectronics Int'l, 246 F.3d 1336, 1361-62, 57 U.S.P.Q.2d 1953, 1968-69 (Fed.Cir.2001). "'[A]bsent prejudice to [Ds], any delay by [patentee] does not support the denial of prejudgment interest.' [¶] [P's] two year delay in initiating the present suit caused the damages owed by [Ds] to escalate. The record contains sufficient evidence for the district court to determine that [P's] delay was self-serving and resulted in prejudice to [Ds]. Thus, the district court acted within its discretion in denying [P] prejudgment interest."

Gyromat Corp. v. Champion Spark Plug Co., 735 F.2d 549, 556, 222 U.S.P.Q. 4, 9 (Fed.Cir.1984). "[T]here is no convincing reason to treat [royalties and lost-profits] damages differently [for the purposes of prejudgment interest]. [¶] [O]rdinarily prejudgment interest should be awarded on both the lost profits and the royalty portions of the damages awarded for patent infringement."

Enhanced Damages

For more annotations on this topic, see 35 U.S.C. §271, *Willful Infringement*, p. 665; 35 U.S.C. §285, *Generally*, p. 717.

Halo Elecs., Inc. v. Pulse Elecs., Inc., ___ U.S. ___, 136 S.Ct. 1923, 1932, 118 U.S.P.Q.2d 1761, 1765 (2016). "Awards of enhanced damages under the Patent Act over the past 180 years establish that they are not to be meted out in a typical infringement case, but are instead designed as a 'punitive' or 'vindictive' sanction for egregious infringement behavior. The sort of conduct warranting enhanced damages has been variously described in our cases as willful, wanton, malicious, bad-faith, deliberate, consciously wrongful, flagrant, or—indeed—characteristic of a pirate. *At U.S. ___, S.Ct. 1933-34, U.S.P.Q.2d 1766-67:* [35 U.S.C.] §284 allows district courts to punish the full range of culpable behavior. Yet none of this is to say that enhanced damages must follow a finding of egregious misconduct. As with any exercise of discretion, courts should continue to take into account the particular circumstances of each case in deciding whether to award damages, and in what amount. Section 284 permits district courts to exercise their discretion in a manner free from the inelastic constraints of the ***Seagate*** test. Consistent with nearly two centuries of enhanced damages under patent law, however, such punishment should generally be reserved for egregious cases typified by willful misconduct. [¶] The ***Seagate*** test is also inconsistent with §284 because it requires clear and convincing evidence to prove recklessness. ... Like [35 U.S.C.] §285, §284 'imposes no specific evidentiary burden, much less such a high one.' And the fact that Congress expressly erected a higher standard of proof elsewhere in the Patent Act, ... but not in §284, is telling. Furthermore, nothing in historical practice supports a heightened standard. As we explained in ***Octane Fitness***, 'patent-infringement litigation has always been governed by a preponderance of the evidence standard.' Enhanced damages are no exception. [¶] [B]ecause we eschew any rigid formula for awarding enhanced damages under §284, we likewise reject the Federal Circuit's tripartite framework for appellate review. In [***Highmark Inc. v. Allcare Health Mgmt. Sys.***, ___ U.S. ___, 134 S.Ct. 1744 (2014)], we built on our ***Octane Fitness*** holding to reject a similar multipart standard of review. *At U.S. ___, S.Ct. 1935, U.S.P.Q.2d 1768:* Section 284 gives district courts the discretion to award enhanced damages against those guilty of patent infringement. In applying this discretion, district courts are 'to be guided by [the] sound legal principles' developed over nearly two centuries of application and interpretation of the Patent Act. Those principles channel the exercise of discretion, limiting the award of enhanced damages to egregious cases of misconduct beyond typical infringement."

In re EchoStar Comms., 448 F.3d 1294, 1298, 78 U.S.P.Q.2d 1676, 1679 (Fed.Cir.2006). "This case involves the extent to which a party waives its attorney-client privilege and work-product immunity when it asserts the advice-of-counsel defense in response to a charge of willful patent infringement. 'Federal Circuit law applies when deciding whether particular written or other materials are discoverable in a patent case, if those materials relate to an issue of substantive patent law.' *At F.3d 1299:* Once a party announces that it will rely on advice of counsel ... in response to an assertion of willful infringement, the attorney-client privilege is waived. 'The widely applied standard for determining the scope of a waiver of attorney-client privilege is that the waiver applies to all other communications relating to the same subject matter.' *At F.3d 1300, U.S.P.Q.2d 1680:* [D] asserts that to apply the broad scope employed by the district court to the waiver of both attorney-client privilege and work-product doctrine was an abuse of discretion. We agree. *At F.3d 1302-03, U.S.P.Q.2d 1682:* [W]e recognize at least three categories of work product that are potentially relevant to the advice-of-counsel defense here. They include: (1) documents that embody a communication between the attorney and client concerning the subject matter of the case, such as a traditional opinion letter; (2) documents analyzing the law, facts, trial strategy, and so forth that reflect the attorney's mental impressions but were not given to the client; and (3) documents that discuss a communication between attorney and client concerning the subject matter of the case but are not themselves communications to or from the client. As to the first category, ... when a party relies on the advice-of-counsel as a defense to willful infringement the party waives its attorney-client privilege for all communications between the attorney and client, including any documentary communications such as opinion letters and memoranda. [W]e conclude that waiver extends to the third category but does not extend so far as the second. *At F.3d 1302 n.3, U.S.P.Q.2d 1682 n.3:* We by no means anticipate that all work product in every case will fit into one of these three categories. *At F.3d 1304, U.S.P.Q.2d 1683:* [W]hen an alleged infringer asserts its advice-of-counsel defense regarding willful infringement of a particular patent, it waives its immunity for any document or opinion that embodies or discusses a communication to or from it concerning whether that patent is valid, enforceable, and infringed by the accused. This waiver of both the attorney-client privilege and the work-product immunity includes not only any letters, memorandum, conversation, or the like between the attorney and his or her client, but also includes, when appropriate, any documents referencing a communication between attorney and client."

Knorr-Bremse Sys. v. Dana Corp., 383 F.3d 1337, 1344, 72 U.S.P.Q.2d 1560, 1565 (Fed.Cir.2004). "When the attorney-client privilege and/or work-product privilege is invoked by a defendant in an infringement suit, is it appropriate for the trier of fact to draw an adverse inference with respect to willful infringement? [¶] The answer is 'no.' *At F.3d 1345, U.S.P.Q.2d 1566:* When the defendant had not obtained legal advice, is it appropriate to draw an adverse inference with respect to willful infringement? [¶] The answer, again, is 'no.' *At F.3d 1347, U.S.P.Q.2d 1567:* Should the existence of a substantial defense to infringement be sufficient to defeat liability for willful infringement even if no legal advice has been secured? [¶] The answer is 'no.' Precedent includes this factor with others to be considered among the totality of circumstances, stressing the 'theme of whether a prudent person would have sound reason to believe that the patent was not infringed or was invalid or unenforceable, and would be so held if litigated[.]'"

Read Corp. v. Portec, Inc., 970 F.2d 816, 826-27, 23 U.S.P.Q.2d 1426, 1435-36 (Fed.Cir.1992). "The paramount determination in deciding to grant enhancement and the amount thereof is the egregiousness of the defendant's conduct based on all the facts and circumstances. The court must consider factors that render defendant's conduct more culpable, as well as factors that are mitigating or ameliorating. [The] factors ... identified for consideration in determining when an infringer 'acted in such bad faith as to merit an increase in damages awarded against him' [are]: (1) whether the infringer deliberately copied the ideas or design of another; (2) whether the infringer, when he knew of the other's patent protection, investigated the scope of the patent and formed a good-faith belief that it was invalid or that it was not infringed; ... (3) the infringer's behavior as a party to the litigation[;] (4) [infringer's] size and financial condition[;] (5) [c]loseness of the case[;] (6) [d]uration of [infringer's] misconduct[;] (7) [r]emedial action by the [infringer;] (8) [infringer's] motivation for harm[;] (9) [w]hether [infringer] attempted to conceal its misconduct." *See also* ***Liquid Dynamics Corp. v. Vaughan Co.***, 449 F.3d 1209, 1225, 79 U.S.P.Q.2d 1094, 1105 (Fed.Cir.2006).

Shiley, Inc. v. Bentley Labs., 794 F.2d 1561, 1568, 230 U.S.P.Q. 112, 115 (Fed.Cir.1986). "The first sentence of §284 deals with actual damages, which, if not found by the jury, must be found by the court. The second sentence deals with increasing damages, which is assigned to the court, whether the facts of willful infringement justifying an increase are found by a jury, or by a court in a non-jury trial. Thus, if a jury finding of willful infringement is not overturned on a motion for JNOV, the court has discretion to award increased damages on the basis of the jury's finding; if the jury finding is that willful infringement did not occur and that finding is not overturned on a motion for JNOV, no basis for assessing increased damages for willful infringement exists; if the jury finding is that willful infringement did not occur, and the court does overturn that finding on a motion for JNOV because no reasonable jury could on all the facts find an absence of willful infringement, the court may increase damages within its discretion under §284."

Dickey-john Corp. v. International Tapetronics Corp., 710 F.2d 329, 349, 219 U.S.P.Q. 402, 418 (7th Cir. 1983). "While there has been a tendency in our cases to lump together the questions of willful and wanton infringement under 35 U.S.C. §284 and bad faith in litigation under 35 U.S.C. §285, the issues are discrete to the extent they are concerned with different time frames, and the fact that defendants may have litigated the case in good faith does not establish their good faith in developing and marketing the infringing device."

Standard of Review

Monsanto Co. v. McFarling, 488 F.3d 973, 981, 82 U.S.P.Q.2d 1942, 1947 (Fed.Cir.2007). "In reviewing damages awards in patent cases, we give broad deference to the conclusions reached by the finder of fact. [A] jury's damages award 'must be upheld unless the amount is grossly excessive or monstrous, clearly not supported by the evidence or based only on speculation or guesswork.'"

Vulcan Eng'g Co. v. Fata Aluminium, Inc., 278 F.3d 1366, 1376, 61 U.S.P.Q.2d 1545, 1551 (Fed.Cir. 2002). "The district court's determination of the amount of damages is a question of fact that is reviewed for clear error, while the method used by a district court in reaching that determination is reviewed for an abuse of discretion. The patentee bears the burden of proving its damages by a preponderance of the evidence." *See also* ***WMS Gaming, Inc. v. International Game Tech.***, 184 F.3d 1339, 1360, 51 U.S.P.Q.2d 1385, 1401 (Fed.Cir.1999).

§285. ATTORNEY FEES

The court in exceptional cases may award reasonable attorney fees to the prevailing party.

History of 35 U.S.C. §285: July 19, 1952, ch. 950, §1, 66 Stat. 813.

ANNOTATIONS

Generally

For more annotations on this topic, see 35 U.S.C. §271, *Willful Infringement*, p. 665; 35 U.S.C. §284, *Enhanced Damages*, p. 715.

Octane Fitness, LLC v. ICON Health & Fitness, Inc., ___ U.S. ___, 134 S.Ct. 1749, 1756-57, 110 U.S.P.Q.2d 1337, 1341 (2014). "The Patent Act does not define 'exceptional,' so we construe it in accordance with its ordinary meaning. [¶] We hold, then, that an 'exceptional' case is simply one that stands out from others with respect to the substantive strength of a party's litigating position (considering both the governing law and the facts of the case) or the unreasonable manner in which the case was litigated. District courts may determine whether a case is 'exceptional' in the case-by-case exercise of their discretion, considering the totality of the circumstances. As in the comparable context of the Copyright Act, there is no precise rule or formula for making these determinations, but instead equitable discretion should be exercised in light of the considerations we have identified. *At U.S.P.Q.2d 1342:* [T]he first category of cases in which the Federal Circuit allows fee awards—those involving litigation misconduct or certain other misconduct—appears to extend largely to independently sanctionable conduct. But sanctionable conduct is not the appropriate benchmark. Under the standard announced today, a district court may award fees in the rare case in which a party's unreasonable conduct—while not necessarily independently sanctionable—is nonetheless so 'exceptional' as to justify an award of fees. [¶] The second category of cases in which the Federal Circuit allows fee awards is also too restrictive. In order for a case to fall within this second category, a district court must determine *both* that the litigation is objectively baseless *and* that the plaintiff brought it in subjective bad faith. But a case presenting either subjective bad faith or exceptionally meritless claims may sufficiently set itself apart from mine-run cases to warrant a fee award. *At U.S. ___, S.Ct. 1758, U.S.P.Q.2d 1343:* Finally, we reject the Federal Circuit's requirement that patent litigants establish their entitlement to fees under §285 by clear and convincing evidence.... We have not interpreted comparable fee-shifting statutes to require proof of entitlement to fees by clear and convincing evidence. And nothing in §285 justifies such a high standard of proof. Section 285 demands a simple discretionary inquiry; it imposes no specific evidentiary burden, much less such a high one. Indeed, patent-infringement litigation has always been governed by a preponderance of the evidence standard, ... and that is the standard generally applicable in civil actions, because it allows both parties to share the risk of error in roughly equal fashion...." (Internal quotes omitted.)

AIA Am., Inc. v. Avid Radiopharmaceuticals, 866 F.3d 1369, 1371, 123 U.S.P.Q.2d 1703, 1704 (Fed.Cir. 2017). "[T]he Seventh Amendment right to a jury trial does not apply to requests for attorney's fees under §285 of the Patent Act...."

Advanced Magnetic Closures, Inc. v. Rome Fastener Corp., 607 F.3d 817, 827, 95 U.S.P.Q.2d 1513, 1518 (Fed.Cir.2010). "This court has held that a district court retains jurisdiction to consider a motion for attorney's fees under 35 U.S.C. §285 and to make findings of inequitable conduct—even after a party has dismissed its counterclaims as to that patent."

Taltech Ltd. v. Esquel Enters., 604 F.3d 1324, 1329, 95 U.S.P.Q.2d 1257, 1260 (Fed.Cir.2010). "'The trial judge's discretion in the award of attorney fees permits the judge to weigh intangible as well as tangible factors: the degree of culpability of the infringer, the closeness of the question, litigation behavior, and any other factors whereby fee shifting may serve as an instrument of justice.'"

Samsung Elecs. Co. v. Rambus, Inc., 523 F.3d 1374, 1379-80, 86 U.S.P.Q.2d 1604, 1607 (Fed.Cir.2008). "The district court harbored the misimpression that 35 U.S.C. §285 authorizes the imposition of two separate sanctions: the finding of exceptionality and the award of attorneys fees. To the contrary, 35 U.S.C. §285 authorizes the award of attorney fees in exceptional cases. Exceptionality is only an element for the award, not a separate sanction. In other words, the trial court did not have independent jurisdiction to assess exceptionality after full completion of the attorney fees litigation. [¶] After [D] offered the entire amount of attorney fees in dispute, the case became moot. The district court had no case or controversy to continue to consider. Thus, the trial court lacked subject matter jurisdiction to perpetuate an attorney fees dispute that was complete."

Digeo, Inc. v. Audible, Inc., 505 F.3d 1362, 1368-69, 85 U.S.P.Q.2d 1246, 1249 (Fed.Cir.2007). "Once a litigant moves based upon non-frivolous allegations for a [FRCP] 11 sanction, the burden of proof *shifts* to the non-movant to show it made a reasonable pre-suit inquiry into its claim. However, the burden of proof for [35 U.S.C.] §285 motions remains with the movant to show by clear and convincing evidence that the case is exceptional. Although a Rule 11 violation can serve as the basis for finding a case exceptional, there was no Rule 11 motion or finding by the district court below upon which to base a finding of exceptionality. *At U.S.P.Q.2d 1250:* Therefore, the burden here is not on [P] to show it conducted a reasonable pre-suit investigation into its infringement claim, namely an investigation of its legal title to [patent], as in a Rule 11 context. Instead, the burden is on [D] to prove by clear and convincing evidence [now a preponderance of evidence] that the case is exceptional by showing that [P] brought a frivolous lawsuit because it knew or should have known that it lacked legal title to [patent]."

Knorr-Bremse Sys. v. Dana Corp., 383 F.3d 1337, 1347, 72 U.S.P.Q.2d 1560, 1567 (Fed.Cir.2004). "That there were not actual damages does not render the award of attorney fees punitive. Attorney fees are compensatory, and may provide a fair remedy in appropriate cases. Upon a finding of willful infringement, the award of attorney fees is within the district court's sound discretion."

Forest Labs. v. Abbott Labs., 339 F.3d 1324, 1329, 67 U.S.P.Q.2d 1682, 1686 (Fed.Cir.2003), *overruled on other grounds*, ***Octane Fitness, LLC v. ICON Health & Fitness, Inc.***, ___ U.S. ___, 134 S.Ct. 1749 (2014). "We have not ... upheld a finding of exceptionality based on a patentee's bad-faith business conduct toward an accused infringer prior to litigation, and we decline to expand the scope of the statutory term 'exceptional' in that manner. Equitable estoppel may be imposed in a patent case when a patentee induces another party to believe that it will not sue that party for infringement."

Gustafson, Inc. v. Intersystems Indus. Prods., 897 F.2d 508, 511, 13 U.S.P.Q.2d 1972, 1974-75 (Fed.Cir. 1990). "Exercising due care, ... a party may continue to manufacture and may present what in good faith it believes to be a legitimate defense without risk of being found on that basis alone a willful infringer. That such a defense proves unsuccessful does not establish that infringement was willful. Presentation in bad faith of a totally unsupportable, frivolous defense may in itself provide a basis for attorney fees under §285 and may, in light of all the circumstances, also constitute some evidence that continued infringement was willful. There is no finding here that [D's] defenses were frivolous. That fact, coupled with [D's] simultaneous receipt of knowledge of the patent and a court summons, precludes a finding of willfulness. [¶] In our patent system, patent applications are secret, and patentees are authorized to sue 'innocent' manufacturers immediately after their patents issue and without warning. To hold such patentees entitled to increased damages or attorney fees on the ground of willful infringement, however, would be to reward use of the patent system as a form of ambush."

Bad Faith

Kilopass Tech. v. Sidense Corp., 738 F.3d 1302, 1310, 109 U.S.P.Q.2d 1085, 1091 (Fed.Cir.2013). "[S]ubjective bad faith only requires proof that the lack of objective foundation for the claim was *either* known *or* so obvious that it should have been known by the party asserting the claim. Thus, actual knowledge of baselessness is not required. Like a plaintiff seeking to recover attorneys' fees under §285 based on alleged willful infringement, a defendant need only prove reckless conduct to satisfy the subjective component of the §285 analysis. *At U.S.P.Q.2d 1092:* Our case law has long held that, in considering a party's subjective state of mind, we are to take into account the totality of the circumstances. *At F.3d 1311-12:* The primacy of objective evidence over assertions of subjective good faith or lack of knowledge is well established in our §285 case law. The totality of the circumstances does include an evaluation of subjective good faith, but mostly as a negative. If a smoking gun is found, revealing that a patentee knew that he had no chance of winning a lawsuit, then subjective bad faith is easily shown. But one's misguided belief, based on zealousness rather than reason, is simply not sufficient by itself to show that a case is not exceptional in light of objective evidence that a patentee has pressed meritless claims. Thus, we have observed that, where the patentee is manifestly unreasonable in assessing infringement, while continuing to assert infringement in court, an inference is proper of bad faith. [¶] Factors such as the failure to conduct an adequate presuit investigation, vexatious or unduly burdensome litigation tactics, misconduct in procuring the patent, or an oppressive purpose are factors which can be indicative of bad faith. The wide variety of ways available to establish bad faith is why our case law has long required a party seeking fees under §285 to prove the other guilty of bad faith litigation by clear and convincing evidence *in light of the totality of the circumstances*." (Internal quotes omitted.)

MarcTec, LLC v. Johnson & Johnson, 664 F.3d 907, 919-20, 101 U.S.P.Q.2d 1177, 1185-87 (Fed.Cir. 2012). "[P's] proposed claim construction was so lacking in any evidentiary support that assertion of this construction was unreasonable and reflects a lack of good faith. And, [P's] decision to continue the litigation after claim construction further supports the district court's finding that this is an exceptional case. [¶] [P] engaged in litigation misconduct when it: (1) misrepresented both the law of claim construction and the constructions ultimately adopted by the court; and (2) introduced and relied on expert testimony that failed to meet even minimal standards of reliability, thereby prolonging the litigation and the expenses attendant thereto. [¶] Although we agree with [P] that exclusion of expert testimony under ***Daubert*** does not automatically trigger a finding of litigation misconduct, and in most cases likely would not do so, we find that the circumstances of this case were sufficiently egregious to support an award of attorney fees."

Inequitable Conduct

For more annotations on this topic, see 35 U.S.C. §282, *§282(b), ¶1—Inequitable Conduct*, p. 693.

Nilssen v. Osram Sylvania, Inc., 528 F.3d 1352, 1358, 87 U.S.P.Q.2d 1161, 1164 (Fed.Cir.2008). "[T]here is no per se rule of exceptionality in cases involving inequitable conduct. ... However, the lack of a per se exceptionality rule in inequitable conduct cases does not mean that inequitable conduct is insufficient for a finding of an exceptional case. We have held that inequitable conduct 'may constitute a basis for an award of attorney fees under ... §285.' In short, our case law provides wide discretion to district courts; courts may award attorney fees in inequitable conduct cases, but are not required to do so."

Monsanto Co. v. Bayer Bioscience N.V., 514 F.3d 1229, 1243, 85 U.S.P.Q.2d 1582, 1593 (Fed.Cir.2008). "The question facing this court is ... whether a district court's jurisdiction under [35 U.S.C.] §285 to determine whether there was inequitable conduct in the prosecution of patents that are otherwise no longer in suit confers on that court the jurisdiction to hold such patents unenforceable for inequitable conduct. We hold that it does. [¶] A district court has no discretion to decide whether a patent is unenforceable once it enters a finding of inequitable conduct. To the contrary, this court has long held that the unenforceability of a patent follows automatically once a patent is found to have been obtained via inequitable conduct. Any distinction between the two findings is merely semantic. As a result, jurisdiction to decide whether a patent was obtained through inequitable conduct necessarily includes the jurisdiction to declare a patent unenforceable as a result of that inequitable conduct."

Enzo Biochem, Inc. v. Calgene, Inc., 188 F.3d 1362, 1380, 52 U.S.P.Q.2d 1129, 1142-43 (Fed.Cir.1999). D contends "that the district court erred by not deciding the issue of inequitable conduct prior to ruling on whether this was an exceptional case under 35 U.S.C. §285. [D] specifically alleges that the district court should have considered evidence that both [inventor and patent assignee] withheld information from the PTO, thus committing 'fraud on the [PTO].' [¶] We agree with [D] that the court erred in not making an inequitable conduct determination prior to ruling on the exceptional case issue."

Litigation Misconduct

Haynes Int'l v. Jessop Steel Co., 8 F.3d 1573, 1579, 28 U.S.P.Q.2d 1652, 1657 (Fed.Cir.1993), *aff'd as modified*, 15 F.3d 1076 (Fed.Cir.1994). "[I]n certain instances, a 'frivolous' case can be 'exceptional' for purposes of 35 U.S.C. §285. A frivolous infringement suit is one which the patentee knew or, on reasonable investigation, should have known, was baseless."

Read Corp. v. Portec, Inc., 970 F.2d 816, 831, 23 U.S.P.Q.2d 1426, 1439 (Fed.Cir.1992). "[W]hen attorney fees under 35 U.S.C. §285 are awarded solely on the basis of litigation misconduct, the amount of the award must bear some relation to the extent of the misconduct."

Measure of Fees

Automated Bus. Cos. v. NEC, Inc., 202 F.3d 1353, 1356, 53 U.S.P.Q.2d 1601, 1603 (Fed.Cir.2000). "In determining the compensatory quantum of an award under §285 in an egregious case, courts should not be, and have not been, limited to reimbursement of only those amounts actually paid by the injured named party. In a case such as this in which a company's closely related, grandparent company assisted in the defense of an infringement action properly deemed exceptional and assumed some of the legal expenses, the company is no less due an award of attorney fees for the total amount it would have paid had it defended against the action on its own. The terms under which [subsidiary corporation] arranged for payment of at least some of its legal fees with [parent corporation] is not relevant in such a case." *See also* ***Junker v. Eddings***, 396 F.3d 1359, 1365-66, 73 U.S.P.Q.2d 1850, 1855-56 (Fed.Cir.2005).

Central Soya Co. v. Geo. A. Hormel & Co., 723 F.2d 1573, 1578, 220 U.S.P.Q. 490, 493 (Fed.Cir.1983). "The purpose of §285 is, in a proper case and in the discretion of the trial judge, to compensate the prevailing party for its monetary outlays in the prosecution or defense of the suit. We interpret attorney fees to include those sums that the prevailing party incurs in the preparation for and performance of legal services related to the suit."

Prevailing Party

SSL Servs. v. Citrix Sys., 769 F.3d 1073, 1086, 112 U.S.P.Q.2d 1464, 1474 (Fed.Cir.2014). "We review the district court's determination of whether a party is the prevailing party under [FRCP] 54(d) and 35 U.S.C. §285 de novo. ... To be the prevailing party, we require: (1) that the party received at least some relief on the merits, and (2) that relief must materially alter the legal relationship between the parties by modifying one party's behavior in a way that directly benefits the opposing party. *At F.3d 1087, U.S.P.Q.2d 1475:* [T]here is a distinction between being *eligible* for fees as the prevailing party and the discretionary decision to award fees. A party prevails when actual relief on the merits of his claim materially alters the legal relationship between the parties in a way that directly benefits the party. For example, the Supreme Court in ***Farrar*** [*v.* ***Hobby***, 506 U.S. 103 (1992),] found that a plaintiff who won nominal damages was still the prevailing party because a judgment for damages in any amount modified the defendant's behavior to the plaintiff's benefit. The Court explained that the degree of the overall success impacts only the reasonableness of the fee award. Therefore, a district court may award minimal or no fees after considering the amount of success to the prevailing party." (Internal quotes omitted.)

RFR Indus. v. Century Steps, Inc., 477 F.3d 1348, 1353, 81 U.S.P.Q.2d 1915, 1918-19 (Fed.Cir.2007). "We hold that a plaintiff's voluntary dismissal without prejudice pursuant to [FRCP] 41(a)(1)(i) does not bestow prevailing party status upon the defendant. In order for a defendant to be said to have prevailed as the result of a Rule 41 dismissal, the dismissal must have sufficient judicial imprimatur to constitute a judicially sanctioned change in the legal relationship of the parties. A plaintiff's voluntary dismissal without prejudice pursuant to Rule 41(a)(1)(i), however, does not constitute a change in the legal relationship of the parties because the plaintiff is free to refile its action." (Internal quotes omitted.)

Highway Equip. Co. v. FECO, Ltd., 469 F.3d 1027, 1035-36, 81 U.S.P.Q.2d 1120, 1126-27 (Fed.Cir.2006). "[A]s a matter of patent law, the dismissal with prejudice, based on the covenant [not to sue for patent infringement] and granted pursuant to the district court's discretion under [FRCP] 41(a)(2), has the necessary judicial imprimatur to constitute a judicially sanctioned change in the legal relationship of the parties, such that the district court properly could entertain [D's] fee claim under 35 U.S.C. §285. [D's] prevailing party status is not predicated on whether [P] filed a Rule 41(a)(2) motion to dismiss with prejudice at the outset but is sufficiently based on its having filed a covenant not to sue with the court to end the litigation, resulting in a dismissal with prejudice."

Exigent Tech. v. Atrana Solutions, Inc., 442 F.3d 1301, 1312, 78 U.S.P.Q.2d 1321, 1328-29 (Fed.Cir.2006). "[P] appeals the district court's award of attorney fees and costs. An award of fees and costs was not proper unless [D] was a prevailing party. [D] cannot be a prevailing party if the case was resolved by settlement (not incorporated by judicial decree) prior to any relief on the merits."

Brooks Furniture Mfg. v. Dutailier Int'l, 393 F.3d 1378, 1381, 73 U.S.P.Q.2d 1457, 1459 (Fed.Cir.2005), *overruled on other grounds*, ***Octane Fitness, LLC v. Icon Health & Fitness, Inc.***, ___ U.S. ___, 134 S.Ct. 1749 (2014). "Determination of the prevailing party is based on the relation of the litigation result to the overall objective of the litigation, and not on a count of the number of claims and defenses." *See also* ***Beckman Instrs., Inc. v. LKB Produkter AB***, 892 F.2d 1547, 1553-54, 13 U.S.P.Q.2d 1301, 1306-07 (Fed.Cir.1989).

Robinson v. Bartlow, No. 3:12-cv-00024 (W.D.Va. 2014) (memo op.; 6-3-14). "Although the Fourth Circuit has not decided whether the *denial* of a preliminary injunction can make a defendant a prevailing party, the U.S. Court of Appeals for the Tenth Circuit has held that '[i]f a plaintiff who is granted a non-merits-based injunction cannot be a prevailing party, it logically ... follows that a defendant who defeats an injunction cannot be a prevailing party if the denial similarly is based on non-merits grounds.' The Tenth Circuit further explained that a non-merits-based injunction is one 'that does not provide a plaintiff with relief on the merits of [his] claim,' and that an injunction issued or denied based on the likelihood of harm and a balancing of harms is not merits-based. Additionally, denial of a preliminary injunction does not materially alter the legal relationship of the parties unless the preliminary injunction is the only relief that the plaintiff seeks. [¶] *[T]he denial* of a preliminary injunction no more confers prevailing party status than does *the grant* of a preliminary injunction.... Although this is an issue of first impression in this circuit, I agree with the [Tenth Circuit] and hold that denying a preliminary injunction under these circumstances does not confer prevailing party status."

Procedural Issues

Highmark Inc. v. Allcare Health Mgmt. Sys., ___ U.S. ___, 134 S.Ct. 1744, 1746-47, 110 U.S.P.Q.2d 1343, 1344-45 (2014). "We granted certiorari to determine whether an appellate court should accord deference to a district court's determination that litigation is 'objectively baseless.' On the basis of our opinion in ***Octane Fitness, LLC v. ICON Health & Fitness, Inc.***, [___ U.S. ___, 134 S.Ct. 1749 (2014)], argued together with this case and also issued today, we hold that an appellate court should review all aspects of a district court's §285 determination for abuse of discretion."

Monsanto Co. v. Bayer Bioscience N.V., 514 F.3d 1229, 1243, 85 U.S.P.Q.2d 1582, 1593 (Fed.Cir.2008). "In ***Nilssen*** [***v. Osram Sylvania, Inc.***, 528 F.3d 1352 (Fed.Cir.2008),] the jurisdiction of the court to reach the inequitable conduct inquiry for the withdrawn patents was itself in question because the district court reached the issue only collaterally to determining whether there was inequitable conduct regarding patents that remained in suit. Here, the outcome is even clearer as there is no dispute that the court had an independent grant of jurisdiction under §285 to consider inequitable conduct relating to the withdrawn patents. The district court, therefore, did not lack jurisdiction to hold [three of D's] patents unenforceable."

In re Omeprazole Patent Litig., 483 F.3d 1364, 1375, 82 U.S.P.Q.2d 1643, 1652 (Fed.Cir.2007). "This court reviews a denial of attorney fees under 35 U.S.C. §285 for an abuse of discretion; however, this court reviews the factual determination of whether a case is exceptional under §285 for clear error."

IPXL Holdings, L.L.C. v. Amazon.com, Inc., 430 F.3d 1377, 1380, 77 U.S.P.Q.2d 1140, 1142 (Fed.Cir. 2005). "[W]e hold that the correct way to perfect a claim to attorney fees under 35 U.S.C. §285 is through compliance with [FRCP] 54. Because [D] did not file a timely request for attorney fees under that rule, the district court erred in granting attorney fees to [D]."

Transclean Corp. v. Bridgewood Servs., 290 F.3d 1364, 1379, 62 U.S.P.Q.2d 1865, 1876 (Fed.Cir.2002). "[T]he district court must normally explain why it decides that a case is not exceptional under 35 U.S.C.

§285 when a factual finding of willful infringement has been established and, if exceptional, why it decides not to award attorney fees. However, we have recognized an exception to that general rule in cases where the record adequately sets forth grounds for affirming the district court's actions. In this case, the court's careful analysis of the ***Read*** factors regarding enhancement of damages suffices as grounds for affirming the court's implicit conclusion that the infringement case was not exceptional within the meaning of 35 U.S.C. §285." *See also* ***Electro Sci. Indus. v. General Scanning Inc.***, 247 F.3d 1341, 1353, 58 U.S.P.Q.2d 1498, 1506 (Fed.Cir. 2001); ***Modine Mfg. v. Allen Grp.***, 917 F.2d 538, 543, 16 U.S.P.Q.2d 1622, 1625-26 (Fed.Cir.1990).

Special Devices, Inc. v. OEA, Inc., 269 F.3d 1340, 1343, 60 U.S.P.Q.2d 1694, 1696 (Fed.Cir.2001). "The issue presented by this case is whether an award of attorney fees in an exceptional case, pursuant to 35 U.S.C. §285, where that award is unquantified, is a final decision within the meaning of 28 U.S.C. §1295(a)(1). We conclude that it is not."

Brasseler, L.P. v. Stryker Sales Corp., 182 F.3d 888, 892, 51 U.S.P.Q.2d 1470, 1474 (Fed.Cir.1999). "[D's] claim for attorney fees under [35 U.S.C.] §285 was never put in issue before the district court: neither party moved for summary judgment on the issue. Furthermore, [D] was not obligated to raise the issue in its motion for summary judgment of invalidity under [35 U.S.C.] §102(b). [A] claim for attorney fees under §285 is a separate claim. ... Until the 'prevailing party' is known, a party that has pled a claim for attorney fees under §285 cannot be expected to bring a motion for such fees. [¶] [W]e hold that the district court erred in concluding that [D] abandoned its claim for attorney fees under §285 by not raising the claim in its motion for summary judgment under §102(b)."

Sun-Tek Indus. v. Kennedy Sky Lites, Inc., 929 F.2d 676, 678-79, 18 U.S.P.Q.2d 1332, 1334 (Fed.Cir. 1991). "Neither [P] nor the district court, *sua sponte*, preserved jurisdiction to permit the court to make a discretionary award of attorney fees under [35 U.S.C.] §285 within the ten-day limit prescribed by [FRCP] 59 [motions for new trial and to amend/alter judgment]. Thus, under our previous holding that attorney fees were improperly awarded, [P] must repay all it collected in the original grant of attorney fees. Since these fees were not timely returned after remand, we also direct the district court to award [D] interest on the amount of attorney fees...."

Types of Cases

Interspiro, Inc. v. Figgie Int'l, 18 F.3d 927, 933, 30 U.S.P.Q.2d 1070, 1074 (Fed.Cir.1994). "[I]n deciding the applicability of §285 fees, we look to the rights at issue and whether they properly invoke the patent laws. It matters not whether those rights arise in a patent suit or in an action to enforce an agreement settling that litigation."

Beckman Instrs., Inc. v. LKB Produkter AB, 892 F.2d 1547, 1552 n.2, 13 U.S.P.Q.2d 1301, 1305 n.2 (Fed. Cir.1989). "[I]n an action having both patent and non-patent claims, recovery may be had under §285 for the non-patent claims if the issues involved therewith are intertwined with the patent issues. *At F.2d 1552, U.S.P.Q.2d 1305-06:* [W]e are aware of few cases in which a patent owner has been granted attorney fees solely on the basis of litigation misconduct, without a concurrent finding of willful infringement."

§286. TIME LIMITATION ON DAMAGES

Except as otherwise provided by law, no recovery shall be had for any infringement committed more than six years prior to the filing of the complaint or counterclaim for infringement in the action.

In the case of claims against the United States Government for use of a patented invention, the period before bringing suit, up to six years, between the date of receipt of a written claim for compensation by the department or agency of the Government having authority to settle such claim, and the date of mailing by the Government of a notice to the claimant that his claim has been denied shall not be counted as part of the period referred to in the preceding paragraph.

History of 35 U.S.C. §286: July 19, 1952, ch. 950, §1, 66 Stat. 813.

ANNOTATIONS

Generally

For more annotations on this topic, see 35 U.S.C. §282, *§282(b), ¶1—Laches & Equitable Defenses*, p. 695.

A. Stucki Co. v. Buckeye Steel Castings Co., 963 F.2d 360, 363, 22 U.S.P.Q.2d 1581, 1583-84 (Fed.Cir. 1992). "[W]here a patentee complained of no acts of contributory infringement within the six years prior to commencement of the action, no recovery could be had against the alleged contributory infringer, regardless of whether others directly infringed within the six-year period."

A.C. Aukerman Co. v. R.L. Chaides Constr. Co., 960 F.2d 1020, 1030, 22 U.S.P.Q.2d 1321, 1326 (Fed.Cir. 1992). 35 U.S.C. §286 "is not a statute of limitations in the sense of barring a suit for infringement. Assuming a finding of liability, the effect of §286 is to limit recovery to damages for infringing acts committed within six years of the date of the filing of the infringement action. One counts backwards from the date of the complaint to limit pre-filing damages arbitrarily. [¶] We are unpersuaded that §286 should be interpreted to preclude the defense of laches and provide, in effect, a guarantee of six years damages regardless of equitable considerations arising from delay in assertion of one's rights. *At U.S.P.Q.2d 1327:* [W]e have no difficulty in reading §286 harmoniously with the recognition under [35 U.S.C.] §282 of the laches defense. By §286, Congress imposed an *arbitrary* limitation on the period for which damages may be awarded on any claim for patent infringement. Laches, on the other hand, invokes the *discretionary* power of the district court to limit the defendant's liability for infringement by reason of the equities between the particular parties. Recognition of laches as a defense, thus, does not affect the general enforceability of the patent against others or the presumption of its validity under §282."

Standard Oil Co. v. Nippon Shokubai Kagaku Kogyo Co., 754 F.2d 345, 348, 224 U.S.P.Q. 863, 865 (Fed.Cir.1985). "Since §286 cannot properly be called a 'statute of limitations' in the sense that it defeats the right to bring suit, it cannot be said that the statute 'begins to run' on some date or other. In the application of §286, one starts from the filing of a complaint or counterclaim and counts *backward* to determine the date before which infringing *acts* cannot give rise to a right to recover damages. *At U.S.P.Q.2d 866:* If [D's] acts ever gave rise to a liability, the liability arose *as of the time the acts were committed*, not at some future date determined by the acts of others. On the record before us, it committed no act within the period of six years preceding the filing of the complaint and therefore no recovery can be had against it for infringement."

Leinoff v. Louis Milona & Sons, Inc., 726 F.2d 734, 741, 220 U.S.P.Q. 845, 850 (Fed.Cir.1984). "This limitation only restricts the extent one can recover *pre-filing* damages. It places no other limitation on the filing of an infringement action during a patent's 17-year [now 20-year] term."

"Limitations" Period

Phonometrics, Inc. v. Northern Telecom Inc., 133 F.3d 1459, 1461-62 n.2, 45 U.S.P.Q.2d 1421, 1423 n.2 (Fed.Cir.1998). "Because the ... patent term expired on October 30, 1990, and civil actions alleging infringement must be filed within six years, the suit [filed July 8, 1993,] only covered allegedly infringing activities that occurred between July 8, 1987, and October 30, 1990."

In re Morgan, 990 F.2d 1230, 1232, 26 U.S.P.Q.2d 1392, 1393 (Fed.Cir.1992). "A patent may be sued on after it expires, but it can no longer be reissued."

Claims Against U.S. Government

Bendix Corp. v. U.S., 209 U.S.P.Q. 778, 782 (Ct.Cl. 1980). "The administrative claim was pending for a total period of 12 years 1 month 14 days (March 15, 1958[,] to April 29, 1970). Since 35 U.S.C. §286 (second sentence) provides that a maximum of 6 years may be added to the normal 6-year period of recovery, allowed in the first sentence of that section, the earliest date for which recovery may be had is March 5, 1959."

Custer v. U.S., 622 F.2d 554, 558, 208 U.S.P.Q. 886, 886 (Ct.Cl.1980) (adopting district court opinion from 203 U.S.P.Q. 784, 787). "In determining the applicability of the tolling provision of 35 U.S.C. §286, ... the decisive question is whether the patent owner's notice to the Government of its claim for infringement is sufficiently detailed to afford the Government a *realistic* opportunity to consider and settle the claim."

General Elec. Co. v. U.S., 206 U.S.P.Q. 260, 267 n.6 (Ct.Cl.1979). "The second paragraph of 35 U.S.C. §286 merely extends the *period* for which *damages* may be calculated beyond that set in the first paragraph of that section. It does not purport to be jurisdictional and, therefore, cannot be read to enlarge the 6-year jurisdictional statute of limitations which appears in 28 U.S.C. §2501."

§287. LIMITATION ON DAMAGES & OTHER REMEDIES; MARKING & NOTICE

(a) Patentees, and persons making, offering for sale, or selling within the United States any patented article for or under them, or importing any patented article into the United States, may give notice to the public that the same is patented, either by fixing thereon the word "patent" or the abbreviation "pat.," together with the number of the patent, or by fixing thereon the word "patent" or the abbreviation "pat." together with an address of a posting on the Internet, accessible to the public without charge for accessing the address, that associates the patented article with the number of the patent, or when, from the character of the article, this can not be done, by fixing to it, or to the package wherein one or more of them is contained, a label containing a like notice. In the event of failure so to mark, no damages shall be recovered by the patentee in any action for infringement, except on proof that the infringer was notified of the infringement and continued to infringe thereafter, in which event damages may be recovered only for infringement occurring after such notice. Filing of an action for infringement shall constitute such notice.

(b)(1) An infringer under section 271(g) shall be subject to all the provisions of this title relating to damages and injunctions except to the extent those remedies are modified by this subsection or section 9006 of the Process Patent Amendments Act of 1988. The modifications of remedies provided in this subsection shall not be available to any person who—

(A) practiced the patented process;

(B) owns or controls, or is owned or controlled by, the person who practiced the patented process; or

(C) had knowledge before the infringement that a patented process was used to make the product the importation, use, offer for sale, or sale of which constitutes the infringement.

(2) No remedies for infringement under section 271(g) shall be available with respect to any product in the possession of, or in transit to, the person subject to liability under such section before that person had notice of infringement with respect to that product. The person subject to liability shall bear the burden of proving any such possession or transit.

(3)(A) In making a determination with respect to the remedy in an action brought for infringement under section 271(g), the court shall consider—

(i) the good faith demonstrated by the defendant with respect to a request for disclosure,

(ii) the good faith demonstrated by the plaintiff with respect to a request for disclosure, and

(iii) the need to restore the exclusive rights secured by the patent.

(B) For purposes of subparagraph (A), the following are evidence of good faith:

(i) a request for disclosure made by the defendant;

(ii) a response within a reasonable time by the person receiving the request for disclosure; and

(iii) the submission of the response by the defendant to the manufacturer, or if the manufacturer is not known, to the supplier, of the product to be purchased by the defendant, together with a request for a written statement that the process claimed in any patent disclosed in the response is not used to produce such product.

The failure to perform any acts described in the preceding sentence is evidence of absence of good faith unless there are mitigating circumstances. Mitigating circumstances include the case in which, due to the nature of the product, the number of sources for the product, or like commercial circumstances, a request for disclosure is not necessary or practicable to avoid infringement.

(4)(A) For purposes of this subsection, a "request for disclosure" means a written request made to a person then engaged in the manufacture of a product to identify all process patents owned by or licensed to that person, as of the time of the request, that the person then reasonably believes could be asserted to be infringed under section 271(g) if that product were imported into, or sold, offered for sale, or used in, the United States by an unauthorized person. A request for disclosure is further limited to a request—

(i) which is made by a person regularly engaged in the United States in the sale of the same type of products as those manufactured by the person to whom the request is directed, or which includes facts showing that the person making the request plans to engage in the sale of such products in the United States;

(ii) which is made by such person before the person's first importation, use, offer for sale, or sale of units of the product produced by an infringing process and before the person had notice of infringement with respect to the product; and

(iii) which includes a representation by the person making the request that such person will promptly submit the patents identified pursuant to the request to the manufacturer, or if the manufacturer is not known, to the supplier, of the product to be purchased by the person making the request, and will request from that manufacturer or supplier a written statement that none of the processes claimed in those patents is used in the manufacture of the product.

(B) In the case of a request for disclosure received by a person to whom a patent is licensed, that person shall either identify the patent or promptly notify the licensor of the request for disclosure.

(C) A person who has marked, in the manner prescribed by subsection (a), the number of the process patent on all products made by the patented process which have been offered for sale or sold by that person in the United States, or imported by the person into the United States, before a request for disclosure is received is not required to respond to the request for disclosure. For purposes of the preceding sentence, the term "all products" does not include products made before the effective date of the Process Patent Amendments Act of 1988.

(5)(A) For purposes of this subsection, notice of infringement means actual knowledge, or receipt by a person of a written notification, or a combination thereof, of information sufficient to persuade a reasonable person that it is likely that a product was made by a process patented in the United States.

(B) A written notification from the patent holder charging a person with infringement shall specify the patented process alleged to have been used and the reasons for a good faith belief that such process was used. The patent holder shall include in the notification such information as is reasonably necessary to explain fairly the patent holder's belief, except that the patent holder is not required to disclose any trade secret information.

(C) A person who receives a written notification described in subparagraph (B) or a written response to a request for disclosure described in paragraph (4) shall be deemed to have notice of infringement with respect to any patent referred to in such written notification or response unless that person, absent mitigating circumstances—

(i) promptly transmits the written notification or response to the manufacturer or, if the manufacturer is not known, to the supplier, of the product purchased or to be purchased by that person; and

(ii) receives a written statement from the manufacturer or supplier which on its face sets forth a well grounded factual basis for a belief that the identified patents are not infringed.

(D) For purposes of this subsection, a person who obtains a product made by a process patented in the United States in a quantity which is abnormally large in relation to the volume of business of such person or an efficient inventory level shall be rebuttably presumed to have actual knowledge that the product was made by such patented process.

(6) A person who receives a response to a request for disclosure under this subsection shall pay to the person to whom the request was made a reasonable fee to cover actual costs incurred in complying with the request, which may not exceed the cost of a commercially available automated patent search of the matter involved, but in no case more than $500.

(c)(1) With respect to a medical practitioner's performance of a medical activity that constitutes an infringement under section 271(a) or (b), the provisions of sections 281, 283, 284, and 285 shall not apply against the medical practitioner or against a related health care entity with respect to such medical activity.

(2) For the purposes of this subsection:

(A) the term "medical activity" means the performance of a medical or surgical procedure on a body, but shall not include (i) the use of a patented machine, manufacture, or composition of matter in violation of such patent, (ii) the practice of a patented use of a composition of matter in violation of such patent, or (iii) the practice of a process in violation of a biotechnology patent.

(B) the term "medical practitioner" means any natural person who is licensed by a State to provide the medical activity described in subsection (c)(1) or who is acting under the direction of such person in the performance of the medical activity.

(C) the term "related health care entity" shall mean an entity with which a medical practitioner has a professional affiliation under which the medical practitioner performs the medical activity, including but not limited to a nursing home, hospital, university, medical school, health maintenance organization, group medical practice, or a medical clinic.

(D) the term "professional affiliation" shall mean staff privileges, medical staff membership, employment or contractual relationship, partnership or ownership interest, academic appointment, or other affiliation under which a medical practitioner provides the medical activity on behalf of, or in association with, the health care entity.

(E) the term "body" shall mean a human body, organ or cadaver, or a nonhuman animal used in medical research or instruction directly relating to the treatment of humans.

(F) the term "patented use of a composition of matter" does not include a claim for a method of performing a medical or surgical procedure on a body that recites the use of a composition of matter where the use of that composition of matter does not directly contribute to achievement of the objective of the claimed method.

(G) the term "State" shall mean any State or territory of the United States, the District of Columbia, and the Commonwealth of Puerto Rico.

(3) This subsection does not apply to the activities of any person, or employee or agent of such person (regardless of whether such person is a tax exempt organization under section 501(c) of title 26), who is engaged in the commercial development, manufacture, sale, importation, or distribution of a machine, manufacture, or composition of matter or the provision of pharmacy or clinical laboratory services (other than clinical laboratory services provided in a physician's office), where such activities are:

(A) directly related to the commercial development, manufacture, sale, importation, or distribution of a machine, manufacture, or composition of matter or the provision of pharmacy or clinical laboratory services (other than clinical laboratory services provided in a physician's office), and

(B) regulated under the Federal Food, Drug, and Cosmetic Act, the Public Health Service Act, or the Clinical Laboratories Improvement Act.

(4) This subsection shall not apply to any patent issued based on an application which has an effective filing date before September 30, 1996.

History of 35 U.S.C. §287: July 19, 1952, ch. 950, §1, 66 Stat. 813; Aug. 23, 1988, P.L. 100-418, §9004(a), 102 Stat. 1564; Dec. 8, 1994, P.L. 103-465, §533(b)(5), 108 Stat. 4989; Sept. 30, 1996, P.L. 104-208, §101(a) [§616], 110 Stat. 3009-67; Nov. 29, 1999, P.L. 106-113, §1000(a)(9), 113 Stat. 1536; Sept. 16, 2011, P.L. 112-29, §§3(g)(2), 16(a)(1), 20(i)(4), (j)(1), 125 Stat. 288, 328, 335.

See also TRIPs pt. II, §5.

ANNOTATIONS

Generally

Monsanto Co. v. Bowman, 657 F.3d 1341, 1348, 100 U.S.P.Q.2d 1224, 1229-30 (Fed.Cir.2011), *aff'd*, 569 U.S. 278 (2013). "[D] argues that, although he did not expressly cite §287(a) at the district court, [P's] failure to provide notice formed one of his primary arguments on summary judgment, and that he should be entitled to leniency as a *pro se* litigant. *At F.3d 1349:* While [D] did not cite §287(a) as the legal basis for this 'lack of notice' contention, this court holds that, as a *pro se* litigant, he alleged facts and proffered argument sufficient to preserve the issue for appeal."

GP Indus. v. Eran Indus., 500 F.3d 1369, 1373-74, 84 U.S.P.Q.2d 1604, 1607 (Fed.Cir.2007). "[W]e wish to note the rarity of an injunction being granted against communicating with others concerning one's patent rights. ... One has a right to inform others of his or her patent rights. Thus, an injunction against communication is strong medicine that must be used with care and only in exceptional circumstances."

Nike, Inc. v. Wal-Mart Stores, 138 F.3d 1437, 1446, 46 U.S.P.Q.2d 1001, 1008 (Fed.Cir.1998). "[T]he marking requirement ... applies to design patents whether remedy for infringement is sought under [35 U.S.C.] §284 or §289."

Goodrich-Gulf Chems. v. Phillips Pet. Co., 376 F.2d 1015, 1019, 153 U.S.P.Q. 436, 438 (6th Cir.1967). "[T]he holder of a patent may institute an action against an alleged infringer without notice and without an allegation that the alleged infringer has made any claim of invalidity as to the patent even though [under §287] only limited relief may be available."

Wokas v. Dresser Indus., 978 F.Supp. 839, 843, 45 U.S.P.Q.2d 1600, 1603 (N.D.Ind.1997). "The marking and notice requirements of §287(a) are not applicable to situations where the patented item is not made or sold by the patentee or persons operating 'for or under' the patentee. Accordingly, 'a patentee with an unutilized patent may do nothing before bringing a suit to collect damages for infringement, while one producing or selling the goods is under an obligation to provide notice before exercising patent rights.'"

Actual Notice

DSW, Inc. v. Shoe Pavilion, Inc., 537 F.3d 1342, 1348, 87 U.S.P.Q.2d 1687, 1692 (Fed.Cir.2008). "[A] patentee may indeed recover damages for infringement that continues after actual notice is provided. Without a doubt, the law offers an infringer no exception to liability for the time it takes to terminate infringing activities, no matter how expeditious and reasonable its efforts."

U.S. Philips Corp. v. Iwasaki Elec. Co., 505 F.3d 1371, 1375, 85 U.S.P.Q.2d 1097, 1100 (Fed.Cir.2007). "'[T]he actual notice requirement of §287(a) demands notice of the patentee's identity as well as notice of infringement,' and that the notice must arise by 'an affirmative act on the part of the patentee which informs the defendant of infringement.' [¶] Although the assignation printed on the face of a patent is not a conclusive indication of the patent's current ownership, we hold that when the information printed on the patent is correct, it is enough to put an accused infringer on notice of the patentee's identity."

SRI Int'l v. Advanced Tech. Labs., 127 F.3d 1462, 1470, 44 U.S.P.Q.2d 1422, 1428 (Fed.Cir.1997). "Although [P's] letter offered a license instead of demanding that [D] 'cease and desist,' a patentee whose goal is licensing does not defeat actual notice by offering a license."

Amsted Indus. v. Buckeye Steel Castings Co., 24 F.3d 178, 187, 30 U.S.P.Q.2d 1462, 1469 (Fed.Cir.1994). "Actual notice requires the affirmative communication of a specific charge of infringement by a specific accused product or device. ... It is irrelevant ... whether [D] knew of the patent or knew of his own infringement. The correct approach to determining notice under §287 must focus on the action of the patentee, not the knowledge or understanding of the infringer. [P's] letter was merely informational, of the kind that companies often send to others without intending to charge infringement. Just as such letters tend not to be threats sufficient to justify a declaratory judgment action, they also are not charges of infringement for 'notice' purposes." *See also* ***Lans v. Digital Equip. Corp.***, 252 F.3d 1320, 1327, 59 U.S.P.Q.2d 1057, 1061 (Fed.Cir.2001).

Adequacy of Mark

Allen Eng'g v. Bartell Indus., 299 F.3d 1336, 1356, 63 U.S.P.Q.2d 1769, 1781 (Fed.Cir.2002). "A manifestly obvious typographical error that does not prevent interested members of the public from discerning the number of a patent alleged to protect an article does not result in a failure to mark."

Nike, Inc. v. Wal-Mart Stores, 138 F.3d 1437, 1446, 46 U.S.P.Q.2d 1001, 1009 (Fed.Cir.1998). "In determining whether the patentee marked its products sufficiently to comply with the constructive notice requirement, the focus is not on what the infringer actually knew, but on whether the patentee's actions were sufficient, in the circumstances, to provide notice *in rem*. [¶] In order to satisfy the constructive notice provision of the marking statute, [P] must have shown that substantially all of [products] being distributed were marked, and that once marking was begun, the marking was substantially consistent and continuous."

Amsted Indus. v. Buckeye Steel Castings Co., 24 F.3d 178, 185, 30 U.S.P.Q.2d 1462, 1467 (Fed.Cir.1994). "The question before us is the scope to be accorded the 'for or under' language of §287(a). ... A licensee who makes or sells a patented article does so 'for or under' the patentee, thereby limiting the patentee's damage recovery when the patented article is not marked. [T]here is no reason why §287 should only apply to express licensees and not to implied licensees."

Constructive Notice

Funai Elec. Co. v. Daewoo Elecs. Corp., 616 F.3d 1357, 1373, 96 U.S.P.Q.2d 1329, 1341 (Fed.Cir.2010). "Satisfaction of the constructive notice requirements of §287(a) is a question of fact, ... and when tried to a jury, is reviewed accordingly."

Sentry Prot. Prods. v. Eagle Mfg., 400 F.3d 910, 918, 73 U.S.P.Q.2d 1929, 1935 (Fed.Cir.2005). "In cases where a patent owner sells a product embodying the invention, a patent owner may seek damages for infringement occurring during a period in which the accused infringer had actual or constructive notice of the asserted patent. ... Constructive notice is provided 'when the patentee consistently mark[s] substantially all of its patented products[.]'"

Bazz, Inc. v. Catalina Lighting, Inc., 49 U.S.P.Q.2d 2009, 2012 (S.D.Fla.1998). "Under the ... scenario [of notice to infringer and infringer's continuing infringement], damages are recoverable only for the infringement that occurred after notice. Whether the plaintiff attempts to prove either actual or constructive notice of infringement, the burden of proving notice lies with the plaintiff. [¶] [M]arking a product 'patent pending' is insufficient constructive notice pursuant to §287(a)."

Licensees

Maxwell v. J. Baker, Inc., 86 F.3d 1098, 1111-12, 39 U.S.P.Q.2d 1001, 1010 (Fed.Cir.1996). "A patentee who makes, uses, or sells its own invention is obligated to comply with the marking provisions to obtain the benefit of constructive notice. The marking provisions also apply to 'persons making or selling any patented article for or under the patentees.' Thus, licensees ... and other authorized parties, such as [licensee's] manufacturers, must also comply. However, with third parties unrelated to the patentee, it is often more difficult for a patentee to ensure compliance with the marking provisions. A 'rule of reason' approach is justified in such a case and substantial compliance may be found to satisfy the statute. Therefore, when third parties are involved, the number of [articles] sold without proper marking is not conclusive of the issue whether the patentee's marking was 'substantially consistent and continuous.' When the failure to mark is caused by someone other than the patentee, the court may consider whether the patentee made reasonable efforts to ensure compliance with the marking requirements."

Limitations on Damages

Rembrandt Wireless Techs. v. Samsung Elecs. Co., 853 F.3d 1370, 1383, 122 U.S.P.Q.2d 1301, 1309 (Fed.Cir.2017). "Marking under the statute is permissive, not mandatory. ... A licensee who makes or sells a patented article does so 'for or under' the patentee, thereby limiting the patentee's damage recovery when the patented article is not marked. *At F.3d 1384, U.S.P.Q.2d 1310:* [W]e hold that disclaimer cannot serve to retroactively dissolve the §287(a) marking requirement for a patentee to collect pre-notice damages." (Internal quotes omitted.)

Texas Digital Sys. v. Telegenix, Inc., 308 F.3d 1193, 1220, 64 U.S.P.Q.2d 1812, 1832 (Fed.Cir.2002), *overruled on other grounds*, ***Phillips v. AWH Corp.***, 415 F.3d 1303, 75 U.S.P.Q.2d 1321 (Fed.Cir.2005). "[S]ection 287 'penalizes the use of unauthorized marks upon manufactured articles' and limits the extent to which damages may be recovered where products covered by a U.S. patent are sold without the notice defined in the statute. The recovery of damages is not limited where there is no failure to mark, i.e., where the proper patent notice appears on products or where there are no products to mark."

Nike, Inc. v. Wal-Mart Stores, 138 F.3d 1437, 1440, 46 U.S.P.Q.2d 1001, 1003 (Fed.Cir.1998). "We conclude that the term 'damages' as it appears in the marking statute [35 U.S.C. §287] is not limited to the recovery at law from which it arose, but includes recovery measured by the infringer's profits, and continues to be so used although such recovery is now limited to design patent infringement. The statutory history establishes that the marking requirement has always applied, and continues to apply, to both recovery of the infringer's profit under [35 U.S.C.] §289, and recovery of damages, however measured, under [35 U.S.C.] §284."

Rite-Hite Corp. v. Kelley Co., 56 F.3d 1538, 1549 n.8, 35 U.S.P.Q.2d 1065, 1072 n.8 (Fed.Cir.1995). "That a patentee cannot recover damages in the absence of actual notice when it has not marked remains the law, but that law does not preclude assessing damages for lost sales of diverted products *after* actual notice of infringement has been given."

American Med. Sys. v. Medical Eng'g, 6 F.3d 1523, 1537, 28 U.S.P.Q.2d 1321, 1331 (Fed.Cir.1993). "[W]e construe §287(a) to preclude recovery of damages only for infringement for any time prior to compliance with the marking or actual notice requirements of the statute. Therefore, a delay between issuance of the patent and compliance with the marking provisions of §287(a) will not prevent recovery of damages after the date that marking has begun. We caution, however, that once marking has begun, it must be substantially consistent and continuous in order for the party to avail itself of the constructive notice provisions of the statute."

Medical Immunity

Lamson v. U.S., 117 F.Cl. 755, 756 (Fed.Cl.2014). "This is a case of first impression in which the court must determine whether the medical immunity provision of 35 U.S.C. §287(c) applies to the U.S. [¶] The government has moved for summary judgment, arguing that because the activities allegedly giving rise to his [28 U.S.C.] §1498(a) claim occurred during medical treatment by or under the direction of licensed medical practitioners at medical treatment facilities operated by the U.S., the government has a complete defense to liability under ... §287(c). *At 757:* [T]he court holds that the defense provided for in §287(c) is available to the U.S. in actions brought under §1498(a)."

Procedural Issues

Arctic Cat Inc. v. Bombardier Recreational Prods., 876 F.3d 1350, 1367, 124 U.S.P.Q.2d 1885, 1895 (Fed.Cir.2017). "There is a split among the district courts regarding which party must initially identify the products which it believes the patentee failed to mark. Some courts require the alleged infringer to initially identify products it believes practice the asserted patents. *At F.3d 1368:* Other courts have required the patentee prove that none of its unmarked goods practice the asserted claims. [¶] We hold an alleged infringer who challenges the patentee's compliance with §287 bears an initial burden of production to articulate the products it believes are unmarked 'patented articles' subject to §287. To be clear, this is a low bar. The alleged infringer need only put the patentee on notice that he or his authorized licensees sold specific unmarked products which the alleged infringer believes practice the patent. The alleged infringer's burden is a burden of production, not one of persuasion or proof."

Gart v. Logitech, Inc., 254 F.3d 1334, 1339, 59 U.S.P.Q.2d 1290, 1293 (Fed.Cir.2001). "Like the determination of infringement, compliance with the marking statute is a question of fact. Thus, this issue is properly decided upon summary judgment when no reasonable jury could find that the patentee either has or has not provided actual notice to the particular defendants by informing them of his patent and of their infringement of it." (Internal quotes omitted.)

Process Patents

State Contracting & Eng'g v. Condotte Am., Inc., 34 F.3d 1057, 1073, 68 U.S.P.Q.2d 1481, 1492 (Fed.Cir. 2003). "'[T]he notice requirement of this statute does not apply where the patent is directed to a process or method.' *At F.3d 1074:* We have not previously held that a patent containing only method claims is examined to see if something could have been marked in order to assess whether [§287(a)] applies, and we decline to do so now." *See also* ***Crown Packaging Tech. v. Rexam Bev. Can Co.***, 559 F.3d 1308, 1316-17, 90 U.S.P.Q.2d 1186, 1192 (Fed.Cir.2009); ***Hanson v. Alpine Valley Ski Area, Inc.***, 718 F.2d 1075, 1082-83, 219 U.S.P.Q. 679, 685 (Fed.Cir.1983); ***Bandag, Inc. v. Gerrard Tire Co.***, 704 F.2d 1578, 1581, 217 U.S.P.Q. 977, 979 (Fed.Cir.1983).

American Med. Sys. v. Medical Eng'g, 6 F.3d 1523, 1538-39, 28 U.S.P.Q.2d 1321, 1332 (Fed.Cir.1993). "Where the patent contains both apparatus and method claims ..., to the extent that there is a tangible item to mark by which notice of the asserted method claims can be given, a party is obliged to do so if it intends to avail itself of the constructive notice provisions of §287(a)."

System Patents

IMX, Inc. v. LendingTree, LLC, 79 U.S.P.Q.2d 1373, 1376 n.4 (D.Del.2005). "There is no meaningful distinction between a patented method that results in a product that can be marked and a patented system that results in a service implemented through an Internet-based website that can be marked." *But see* ***State Contracting & Eng'g v. Condotte Am., Inc.***, this page.

§288. ACTION FOR INFRINGEMENT OF A PATENT CONTAINING AN INVALID CLAIM

Whenever a claim of a patent is invalid, an action may be maintained for the infringement of a claim of the patent which may be valid. The patentee shall recover no costs unless a disclaimer of the invalid claim has been entered at the Patent and Trademark Office before the commencement of the suit.

History of 35 U.S.C. §288: July 19, 1952, ch. 950, §1, 66 Stat. 813; Jan. 2, 1975, P.L. 93-596, §1, 88 Stat. 1949; Sept. 16, 2011, P.L. 112-29, §20(h), 125 Stat. 334.

See also 35 U.S.C. §253.

ANNOTATIONS

Allen Archery, Inc. v. Browning Mfg., 819 F.2d 1087, 1096, 2 U.S.P.Q.2d 1490, 1496 (Fed.Cir.1987). Replacing former 35 U.S.C. §71 with §288 "eliminated the provision in §71 that a patentee could sue for infringement of claims definitely distinguishable from the invalid claims unless 'he has unreasonably neglected or delayed to enter a disclaimer.' Under the new statute, disclaimer was required only before filing suit, and the sanction for failing thus to disclaim was not invalidity of the patent but merely the denial of costs. *At F.2d 1097, U.S.P.Q.2d 1497-98:* We therefore agree with and adopt the Ninth Circuit's conclusions in [***Allen Archery, Inc. v. Jennings Compound Bow, Inc.***, 686 F.2d 780 (9th Cir.1982),] that '[t]he failure of a patentee to disclaim an invalid patent claim does not prevent the patentee from enforcing any remaining claims in the same patent which are otherwise valid.'"

§289. ADDITIONAL REMEDY FOR INFRINGEMENT OF DESIGN PATENT

Whoever during the term of a patent for a design, without license of the owner, (1) applies the patented design, or any colorable imitation thereof, to any article of manufacture for the purpose of sale, or (2) sells or exposes for sale any article of manufacture to which such design or colorable imitation has been applied shall be liable to the owner to the extent of his total profit, but not less than $250, recoverable in any United States district court having jurisdiction of the parties.

Nothing in this section shall prevent, lessen, or impeach any other remedy which an owner of an infringed patent has under the provisions of this title, but he shall not twice recover the profit made from the infringement.

History of 35 U.S.C. §289: July 19, 1952, ch. 950, §1, 66 Stat. 813.

ANNOTATIONS

Damages

Samsung Elecs. Co. v. Apple Inc., ___ U.S. ___, 137 S.Ct. 429, 434, 120 U.S.P.Q.2d 1749, 1752 (2016). "Arriving at a damages award under §289 … involves two steps. First, identify the 'article of manufacture' to which the infringed design has been applied. Second, calculate the infringer's total profit made on that article of manufacture. *At U.S. ___, S.Ct. 436, U.S.P.Q.2d 1753:* [T]he term 'article of manufacture' is broad enough to embrace both a product sold to a consumer and a component of that product, whether sold separately or not. Thus, reading 'article of manufacture' in §289 to cover only an end product sold to a consumer gives too narrow a meaning to the phrase."

Catalina Lighting, Inc. v. Lamps Plus, Inc., 295 F.3d 1277, 1291, 63 U.S.P.Q.2d 1545, 1554-55 (Fed.Cir. 2002). Patentee "is entitled to damages for each infringement, but once it receives profits under §289 for each sale, [patentee] is not entitled to a further recovery from the same sale because the award of infringer profits under §289 also constitutes 'damages adequate to compensate for the infringement, but in no event less than a reasonable royalty for the use made of the invention by the infringer.'"

Nike, Inc. v. Wal-Mart Stores, 138 F.3d 1437, 1448, 46 U.S.P.Q.2d 1001, 1010 (Fed.Cir.1998). Patentee "points out that an award of only the infringers' post-tax profits would leave the appellants in possession of their tax refunds, and that if the appellants still enjoy a profit the award can not be their 'total profits' as mandated by the statute. The district court agreed with that position, as do we. [Section 289] requires the disgorgement of the infringers' profits to the patent holder, such that the infringers retain no profit from their wrong."

Infringement Analysis

Gorham Co. v. White, 81 U.S. 511, 528 (1871). "We hold … that if, in the eye of an ordinary observer, giving such attention as a purchaser usually gives, two designs are substantially the same, if the resemblance is such as to deceive such an observer, inducing him to purchase one supposing it to be the other, the first one patented is infringed by the other." *See also* ***Arminak & Assocs. v. Saint-Gobain Calmar, Inc.***, 501 F.3d 1314, 1320, 84 U.S.P.Q.2d 1258, 1261-62 (Fed.Cir.2007), *overruled on other grounds*, ***Egyptian Goddess, Inc. v. Swisa, Inc.***, 543 F.3d 665 (Fed.Cir.2008); ***Goodyear Tire & Rubber Co. v. Hercules Tire & Rubber Co.***, 162 F.3d 1113, 1117 (Fed.Cir.1998), *overruled on other grounds*, ***Egyptian Goddess, Inc. v. Swisa, Inc.***, 543 F.3d 665 (Fed.Cir.2008).

Pacific Coast Mar. Windshields Ltd. v. Malibu Boats, LLC, 739 F.3d 694, 697, 109 U.S.P.Q.2d 1225, 1227 (Fed.Cir.2014). "We hold that the principles of prosecution history estoppel apply to design patents…."

Crocs, Inc. v. International Trade Comm'n, 598 F.3d 1294, 1302-03, 93 U.S.P.Q.2d 1777, 1782 (Fed.Cir. 2010). "This court has cautioned, and continues to caution, trial courts about excessive reliance on a detailed verbal description in a design infringement case. [¶] Design patents are typically claimed as shown in drawings, and claim construction must be adapted to a pictorial setting. Thus an illustration depicts a design better 'than it could be by any description and a description would probably not be intelligible without the illustration.' '[A]s a rule, the illustration in the drawing views is its own best description.'"

Richardson v. Stanley Works, Inc., 597 F.3d 1288, 1295, 93 U.S.P.Q.2d 1937, 1941 (Fed.Cir.2010). "The ordinary observer test … applies in cases where the patented design incorporates numerous functional elements. In evaluating infringement, we determine whether 'the deception that arises is a result of the similarities in the overall design, not of similarities in ornamental features in isolation.'"

Egyptian Goddess, Inc. v. Swisa, Inc., 543 F.3d 665, 677-78, 88 U.S.P.Q.2d 1658, 1668 (Fed.Cir.2008). "An ordinary observer, comparing the claimed and accused designs in light of the prior art, will attach importance to differences between the claimed design and the prior art depending on the overall effect of those differences on the design. If the claimed design consists of a combination of old features that creates an appearance deceptively similar to the accused design, even to an observer familiar with similar prior art designs, a finding of infringement would be justified. Otherwise, infringement would not be found."

Elmer v. ICC Fabricating, Inc., 67 F.3d 1571, 1577, 36 U.S.P.Q.2d 1417, 1420 (Fed.Cir.1995). "Determining whether a design patent claim has been infringed requires, first, as with utility patents, that the claim be properly construed to determine its meaning and scope. Second, the claim as properly construed must be compared to the accused design to determine whether there has been infringement." *See also* ***Egyptian Goddess, Inc. v. Swisa, Inc.***, 543 F.3d 665, 679, 88 U.S.P.Q.2d 1658, 1669 (Fed.Cir.2008); ***Arminak & Assocs. v. Saint-Gobain Calmar, Inc.***, 501 F.3d 1314, 1319-20, 84 U.S.P.Q.2d 1258, 1261-62 (Fed.Cir.2007), *overruled on other grounds*, ***Egyptian Goddess, Inc. v. Swisa, Inc.***, 543 F.3d 665 (Fed.Cir.2008).

§290. NOTICE OF PATENT SUITS

The clerks of the courts of the United States, within one month after the filing of an action under this title shall give notice thereof in writing to the Director, setting forth so far as known the names and addresses of the parties, name of the inventor, and the designating number of the patent upon which the action has been brought. If any other patent is subsequently included in the action he shall give like notice thereof. Within one month after the decision is rendered or a judgment issued the clerk of the court shall give notice thereof to the Director. The Director shall, on receipt of such notices, enter the same in the file of such patent.

History of 35 U.S.C. §290: July 19, 1952, ch. 950, §1, 66 Stat. 814; Nov. 29, 1999, P.L. 106-113, §1000(a)(9), 113 Stat. 1536; Nov. 2, 2002, P.L. 107-273, §13206(b)(1)(B), 116 Stat. 1906.

§291[A*]. INTERFERING PATENTS

Section 291[A] applies to applications and patents issued thereon that were filed before Mar. 16, 2013. Section 291[A*] also applies to patent applications and patents issued thereon if the filing date of the earliest application for which the patent or application is entitled under §119, §365(a), §365(b), §120, §121, or §365(c) falls before Mar. 16, 2013, unless the application or patent has ever contained (1) a claim to a claimed invention that has an "effective filing date," as defined in §100(i), p. 495, on or after Mar. 16, 2013; or (2) a specific reference under §120, §121, or §365(c) to any patent or application that ever contained such a claim. In addition, §291[A*] applies to patent applications and patents issued thereon that have ever contained (1) a claim to a claimed invention that has an "effective filing date," as defined in §100(i), p. 495, before Mar. 16, 2013; or (2) a specific reference under §120, §121, or §365(c) to any patent or application that ever contained such a claim. See transition note for amended §291[B*], p. 732.*

The owner of an interfering patent may have relief against the owner of another by civil action, and the court may adjudge the question of the validity of any of the interfering patents, in whole or in part. The provisions of the second paragraph of section 146 shall apply to actions brought under this section.

History of 35 U.S.C. §291[A*]: July 19, 1952, ch. 950, §1, 66 Stat. 814; Sept. 16, 2011, P.L. 112-29, §20(j)(1), 125 Stat. 335.

ANNOTATIONS

Genetics Inst. v. Novartis Vaccines & Diagnostics, Inc., 655 F.3d 1291, 1297-98, 99 U.S.P.Q.2d 1713, 1718 (Fed.Cir.2011). "[T]he district court entered final judgment on February 25 ... and the extended term of the ... patent expired three days later, on February 28.... On April 12, [D] filed a motion in this court to dismiss [P's] appeal for lack of subject matter jurisdiction in light of the expiration of the ... patent. In an order dated December 1, ... we denied the motion to dismiss [P's] appeal.... *At F.3d 1299-1300, U.S.P.Q.2d 1720:* We ... note an important distinction between [35 U.S.C.] §291 and the statute governing interferences before the PTO, 35 U.S.C. §135. Whereas an interfering patents action under §291 involves two 'interfering patents' without qualification, a §135 action, in contrast, is declared between one pending application and 'any pending application, or ... any *unexpired* patent.' This meaningful difference in statutory language indicates that §291, unlike §135, is not limited to 'unexpired' patents. [¶] [W]e hold that the expiration of the ... patent following the district court's final decision does not strip our court of jurisdiction over the present appeal."

Medichem, S.A. v. Rolabo, S.L., 437 F.3d 1157, 1161, 77 U.S.P.Q.2d 1865, 1867 (Fed.Cir.2006). "[T]he first step in an interference analysis is for the court to determine whether an interference exists under 35 U.S.C. §291 by asking whether the 'patents ... have the same or substantially the same subject matter in similar form as that required by the PTO pursuant to 35 U.S.C. §135.' In order to make this determination, we use the 'two-way' test which states that two patents interfere only if (1) invention *A* either anticipates or renders obvious invention *B*, where Party *A*'s claimed invention is presumed to be prior art vis-a-vis Party *B* and (2) vice versa. *At F.3d 1164, U.S.P.Q.2d 1869:* In reviewing a district court's finding of an interference-in-fact pursuant to the two-way test, this court reviews, where necessary, both the subsidiary findings of anticipation and/or obviousness as they relate to the application of the test."

Slip Track Sys. v. Metal-Lite, Inc., 304 F.3d 1256, 1263, 64 U.S.P.Q.2d 1423, 1427-28 (Fed.Cir.2002). "Most interferences arise in the PTO, involve an interference between two applications or an application and one or more patents, and begin with the creation of a 'count.' The count defines the interfering subject matter and corresponds to a patentable invention. The count may be identical to a single claim at issue or may be broader than the particular claims at issue. This case, however, is one of a handful where the interference is between issued patents and arises in district court, where PTO procedures do not govern. Nonetheless, in order to provoke an interference in district court under [35 U.S.C.] §291, the interfering patents must have the same or substantially the same subject matter in similar form as that required by the PTO pursuant to 35 U.S.C. §135. *At F.3d 1264:* This court has not yet had occasion to determine whether district courts handling interfering patent suits under §291 must define this interfering subject matter in a way similar to a count. ... While we need not resolve this question in its entirety, it is necessary for us to hold that given interfering patents, a single description of the interfering subject matter is necessary for a determination of priority."

§291[B*]. DERIVED PATENTS

Section 291[B] applies to patent applications and patents issued on those applications that have ever contained (1) a claim to a claimed invention that has an "effective filing date," as defined in §100(i), p. 495, on or after Mar. 16, 2013; or (2) a specific reference under §120, §121, or §365(c) to any patent or application that ever contained such a claim. However, §291[B*] will not apply to patent applications and patents issued thereon that have ever contained (1) a claim to a claimed invention that has an "effective filing date," as defined in §100(i), p. 495, before Mar. 16, 2013; or (2) a specific reference under §120, §121, or §365(c) to any patent or application that ever contained such a claim. Section 291[B*] is not effective for patent applications filed before Mar. 16, 2013, or patents issued on those applications.*

(a) In general.—The owner of a patent may have relief by civil action against the owner of another patent that claims the same invention and has an earlier effective filing date, if the invention claimed in such other patent was derived from the inventor of the invention claimed in the patent owned by the person seeking relief under this section.

(b) Filing limitation.—An action under this section may be filed only before the end of the 1-year period beginning on the date of the issuance of the first patent containing a claim to the allegedly derived invention and naming an individual alleged to have derived such invention as the inventor or joint inventor.

History of 35 U.S.C. §291[B*]: July 19, 1952, ch. 950, §1, 66 Stat. 814; Sept. 16, 2011, P.L. 112-29, §3(h)(1), 125 Stat. 288.

§292. FALSE MARKING

(a) Whoever, without the consent of the patentee, marks upon, or affixes to, or uses in advertising in connection with anything made, used, offered for sale, or sold by such person within the United States, or imported by the person into the United States, the name or any imitation of the name of the patentee, the patent number, or the words "patent," "patentee," or the like, with the intent of counterfeiting or imitating the mark of the patentee, or of deceiving the public and inducing them to believe that the thing was made, offered for sale, sold, or imported into the United States by or with the consent of the patentee; or

Whoever marks upon, or affixes to, or uses in advertising in connection with any unpatented article, the word "patent" or any word or number importing that the same is patented for the purpose of deceiving the public; or

Whoever marks upon, or affixes to, or uses in advertising in connection with any article, the words "patent applied for," "patent pending," or any word importing that an application for patent has been made, when no application for patent has been made, or if made, is not pending, for the purpose of deceiving the public—

Shall be fined not more than $500 for every such offense. Only the United States may sue for the penalty authorized by this subsection.

(b) A person who has suffered a competitive injury as a result of a violation of this section may file a civil action in a district court of the United States for recovery of damages adequate to compensate for the injury.

(c) The marking of a product, in a manner described in subsection (a), with matter relating to a patent that covered that product but has expired is not a violation of this section.

History of 35 U.S.C. §292: July 19, 1952, ch. 950, §1, 66 Stat. 814; Dec. 8, 1994, P.L. 103-465, §533(b)(6), 108 Stat. 4990; Sept. 16, 2011, P.L. 112-29, §16(b)(1)-(3), 125 Stat. 329.

ANNOTATIONS

Sukumar v. Nautilus, Inc., 785 F.3d 1396, 1400, 114 U.S.P.Q.2d 1626, 1628 (Fed.Cir.2015). "This case … presents the question of whether (or to what extent) an entity that has not entered the relevant market can suffer 'competitive injury.' … We hold that a potential competitor may suffer competitive injury if it has attempted to enter the market. An attempt is made up of two components: (1) intent to enter the market with a reasonable possibility of success, and (2) an action to enter the market. *At F.3d 1402, U.S.P.Q.2d 1630:* [W]e conclude that §292(b) extends standing to sue for a violation of §292(a) to some potential competitors. Nevertheless, it is equally clear that the amended statute does not confer standing upon any entity that claims a subjective intent to compete. Rather, §292 limits standing to entities that have 'suffered a competitive injury as a result of a violation of [§292(a)].' A potential competitor can only suffer a *competitive* injury if it engages in competition. Dreaming of an idea but never attempting to put it into practice is insufficient. … Therefore, an injury is only a 'competitive injury' if it results from competition, and a potential competitor is engaged in competition if it has attempted to enter the market, which includes intent to enter the market and action to enter the market. And, for the sake of completeness, an entity has standing under §292(b) if it can demonstrate competitive injury that was caused by the alleged false marking."

Frolow v. Wilson Sporting Goods Co., 710 F.3d 1303, 1308-09, 106 U.S.P.Q.2d 1089, 1093 (Fed.Cir. 2013). "Under the doctrine of 'marking estoppel' recognized in some circuits, 'a party that marks its product with a patent number is estopped from asserting that the product is not covered by the patent.' We note that the Supreme Court has never adopted or approved the doctrine. [P] asks us to adopt this doctrine and to hold that [D] is estopped from arguing that its 14 marked rackets fall outside [P's] patent claims. We decline to create a separate, equitable doctrine unique to patent law, where Congress has spoken and standard evidentiary practices provide adequate remedy. [¶] Although we do not endorse [P's] patent marking doctrine, we do agree that the fact that [D] marked their products with [P's] patent number is a fact which supports his allegation that [D's] products fall within the patent claims. The practice of marking a product with a patent number is a form of extrajudicial admission that the product falls within the patent claims. Extrajudicial admissions of fact are statements made by a party outside the context of the litigation that are introduced into evidence by that party's opponent. Generally, extrajudicial admissions of facts, such as patent marking, are simply evidence that may be countered by the party that made the admission. These admissions are not 'binding,' and 'may be controverted or explained by the party' that made the statement. The doctrine of marking estoppel would conflict with the normal evidentiary treatment of these sorts of admissions. We decline to adopt a special equitable doctrine for the treatment of these 'admissions.' *At F.3d 1310, U.S.P.Q.2d 1094:* Like any other type of extrajudicial admission, evidence of marking is relevant evidence. And such an admission, that the accused product falls within the asserted claims, is certainly relevant on the issue of infringement. Of course, whether a party's marking, in view of the record as a whole, raises a genuine issue of material fact, will depend on the facts of each case."

Juniper Networks, Inc. v. Shipley, 643 F.3d 1346, 1351, 98 U.S.P.Q.2d 1491, 1494 (Fed.Cir.2011). "[P] alleges that the falsely marked unpatented article is 'the Website and any firewall or other security products or services operating thereon, as well as web pages generated by the Website.' [¶] [T]his court holds that websites can qualify as unpatented articles within the scope of §292."

Forest Grp. v. Bon Tool Co., 590 F.3d 1295, 1304, 93 U.S.P.Q.2d 1097, 1103 (Fed.Cir.2009). "We hold that the plain language of … §292 requires courts to impose penalties for false marking on a per article basis."

Clontech Labs. v. Invitrogen Corp., 406 F.3d 1347, 1352-53, 74 U.S.P.Q.2d 1598, 1602-03 (Fed.Cir.2005). "According to [§292], when an unpatented article is marked with the word 'patent' or any word or number that imports that the article is patented, and such marking is for the purpose of deceiving the public, the fine is invoked. When the statute refers to an 'unpatented article' the statute means that the article in question is not covered by at least one claim of each patent with which the article is marked. Thus, in order to determine if an article is 'unpatented' for purposes of §292, it must be first determined whether the claims of a patent cover the article in question. To make that determination, the claim in question must be interpreted to ascertain its correct scope, and then it must be ascertained if the claim reads on the article in question. [¶]

35 U.S.C. §292

Assuming an article is mismarked as 'patented' because the claims of the cited patent do not read on the article, the question arises whether more is required by way of proof to establish that the mismarking is for the purpose of deceiving the public. That is, should the statute be read to cause all actual mismarking to be subject to the civil fine? [¶] Intent to deceive is a state of mind arising when a party acts with sufficient knowledge that what it is saying is not so and consequently that the recipient of its saying will be misled into thinking that the statement is true. Intent to deceive, while subjective in nature, is established in law by objective criteria. Thus, 'objective standards' control and 'the fact of misrepresentation coupled with proof that the party making it had knowledge of its falsity is enough to warrant drawing the inference that there was a fraudulent intent.' Thus, under such circumstances, the mere assertion by a party that it did not intend to deceive will not suffice to escape statutory liability. ... But in order to establish knowledge of falsity the plaintiff must show by a preponderance of the evidence that the party accused of false marking did not have a reasonable belief that the articles were properly marked (i.e., covered by a patent). Absent such proof of lack of reasonable belief, no liability under the statute ensues."

Arcadia Mach. & Tool, Inc. v. Sturm, Ruger & Co., 786 F.2d 1124, 1125, 229 U.S.P.Q. 124, 125 (Fed.Cir. 1986). "[T]he *omission* of 'applicable patents' from a label listing patents purporting to cover the contents of a box of course cannot, in itself, be a violation of the *false* marking statute [35 U.S.C. §292]."

Two Moms & a Toy, LLC v. International Playthings, LLC, 898 F.Supp.2d 1213, 1216 (D.Colo.2012). "[S]ince the passage of the [AIA], ... a plaintiff asserting a false marking claim must also establish 'competitive injury.' *At 1218:* Several district courts ... have required a plaintiff to be a competitor of the defendant in order to show competitive injury."

§293. NONRESIDENT PATENTEE; SERVICE & NOTICE

Every patentee not residing in the United States may file in the Patent and Trademark Office a written designation stating the name and address of a person residing within the United States on whom may be served process or notice of proceedings affecting the patent or rights thereunder. If the person designated cannot be found at the address given in the last designation, or if no person has been designated, the United States District Court for the Eastern District of Virginia shall have jurisdiction and summons shall be served by publication or otherwise as the court directs. The court shall have the same jurisdiction to take any action respecting the patent or rights thereunder that it would have if the patentee were personally within the jurisdiction of the court.

History of 35 U.S.C. §293: July 19, 1952, ch. 950, §1, 66 Stat. 814; Jan. 2, 1975, P.L. 93-596, §1, 88 Stat. 1949; Sept. 16, 2011, P.L. 112-29, §9(a), 125 Stat. 316.

ANNOTATIONS

Avocent Huntsville Corp. v. Aten Int'l, 552 F.3d 1324, 1331-33, 89 U.S.P.Q.2d 1481, 1486-87 (Fed.Cir. 2008). "[W]e have held in the context of patent infringement litigation that an assertion of *general* jurisdiction requires that the defendant have continuous and systematic contacts with the forum state, and that such activity will confer general personal jurisdiction even when the cause of action has no relationship with those contacts. With respect to *specific* jurisdiction, this court employs a three-prong test, in which we determine whether: (1) the defendant purposefully directed its activities at residents of the forum, (2) the claim arises out of or relates to those activities, and (3) assertion of personal jurisdiction is reasonable and fair. With respect to the last prong, the burden of proof is on the defendant, which must present a compelling case that the presence of some other considerations would render jurisdiction unreasonable under the five-factor test articulated by the Supreme Court in ***Burger King***. The first two factors correspond with the 'minimum contacts' prong of the ***International Shoe*** analysis, and the third factor corresponds with the 'fair play and substantial justice' prong of the analysis. We have also applied the stream of commerce theory, although we have not resolved the split in authority reflected in the competing plurality opinions in ***Asahi***. [¶] In the ordinary patent infringement suit, the claim asserted by the patentee plaintiff is that some act of making, using, offering to sell, selling, or importing products or services by the defendant constitutes an infringement of the presumptively valid patent named in suit. Thus, for purposes of specific jurisdiction, the jurisdictional inquiry is relatively easily discerned from the nature and extent of the commercialization of the accused products or services by the defendant in the forum. In such litigation, the claim both 'arises out of' and 'relates to' the defendant's alleged manufacturing, using, or selling of the claimed invention. But in the context of an action for declaratory judgment of non-infringement, invalidity, and/or unenforceability, the patentee is the defendant, and the claim asserted by the plaintiff relates to the wrongful restraint by the patentee on the free exploitation of non-infringing goods such as the threat of an infringement suit. Thus, the nature of the claim in a declaratory judgment action is to clear the air of infringement charges. Such a claim neither directly arises out of nor relates to the making, using, offering to sell, selling, or importing of arguably infringing products in the forum, but instead arises out of or relates to the activities of the defendant patentee in enforcing the patent or patents in suit. The relevant inquiry for specific personal jurisdiction purposes then becomes to what extent has the defendant patentee purposefully directed such enforcement activities at residents of the forum, and the extent to which the declaratory judgment claim arises out of or relates to those activities. This inquiry necessarily places greater focus in a declaratory judgment action on the differences, if any, in the meaning of the 'arises out of' and 'relates to' inquiries for personal jurisdiction. [¶] [W]e have held that, based on policy considerations unique to the patent context, letters threatening suit for patent infringement sent to the alleged infringer *by themselves* do not suffice to create personal jurisdiction. *At F.3d 1336, U.S.P.Q.2d 1489:* [A] defendant patentee's mere acts of making, using, offering to sell, selling, or importing products—whether covered by the relevant patent(s) or not—do not, in the jurisdictional sense, relate in any material way to the patent right that is at the center of any declaratory judgment claim for non-infringement, invalidity, and/or unenforceability. Thus, we hold that such sales do not constitute such 'other activities' as will support a claim of specific personal jurisdiction over a defendant patentee. While such activities may in the aggregate justify the exercise of *general* jurisdiction over the patentee, they do not establish a basis for *specific* jurisdiction in this context. However, based on our precedent, ... if the defendant patentee purposefully directs activities at the forum which relate in some material way to the enforcement or the defense of the patent, those activities may suffice to support specific jurisdiction. For example, when the patentee enters into an exclusive license or other obligation relating to the exploitation of the patent by such licensee or contracting party in the forum, the patentee's contractual undertaking may impose certain obligations to enforce the patent against infringers. By such conduct, the patentee may be said to purposefully avail itself of the forum and to engage in activity that relates to the validity and enforceability of the patent." (Internal quotes omitted.)

Deprenyl Animal Health, Inc. v. University of Toronto Innovations Found., 297 F.3d 1343, 1353, 63 U.S.P.Q.2d 1705, 1711 (Fed.Cir.2002). "Section 293 is a special long-arm statute that requires patentees residing outside the U.S. either to designate an agent residing somewhere within the U.S. for service of process or to submit to jurisdiction in the U.S. District Court for the District of Columbia. Although §293 does not directly authorize the exercise of jurisdiction over [D-Canadian foundation], the statute represents an important Congressional judgment that in exchange for obtaining the benefits of a U.S. patent, it is appropriate to require foreign patentees to submit to broader jurisdiction in U.S. Federal Court than that to which they would otherwise be subject."

§294. VOLUNTARY ARBITRATION

(a) A contract involving a patent or any right under a patent may contain a provision requiring arbitration of any dispute relating to patent validity or infringement arising under the contract. In the absence of such a provision, the parties to an existing patent validity or infringement dispute may agree in writing to settle such dispute by arbitration. Any such provision or agreement shall be valid, irrevocable, and enforceable, except for any grounds that exist at law or in equity for revocation of a contract.

(b) Arbitration of such disputes, awards by arbitrators and confirmation of awards shall be governed by title 9, to the extent such title is not inconsistent with this section. In any such arbitration proceeding, the defenses provided for under section 282 shall be considered by the arbitrator if raised by any party to the proceeding.

(c) An award by an arbitrator shall be final and binding between the parties to the arbitration but shall have no force or effect on any other person. The parties to an arbitration may agree that in the event a patent which is the subject matter of an award is subsequently determined to be invalid or unenforceable in a judgment rendered by a court of competent jurisdiction from which no appeal can or has been taken, such award may be modified by any court of competent jurisdiction upon application by any party to the arbitration. Any such modification shall govern the rights and obligations between such parties from the date of such modification.

(d) When an award is made by an arbitrator, the patentee, his assignee or licensee shall give notice thereof in writing to the Director. There shall be a separate notice prepared for each patent involved in such proceeding. Such notice shall set forth the names and addresses of the parties, the name of the inventor, and the name of the patent owner, shall designate the number of the patent, and shall contain a copy of the award. If an award is modified by a court, the party requesting such modification shall give notice of such modification to the Director. The Director shall, upon receipt of either notice, enter the same in the record of the prosecution of such patent. If the required notice is not filed with the Director, any party to the proceeding may provide such notice to the Director.

(e) The award shall be unenforceable until the notice required by subsection (d) is received by the Director.

History of 35 U.S.C. §294: Aug. 27, 1982, P.L. 97-247, §17(b)(1), 96 Stat. 322; Nov. 29, 1999, P.L. 106-113, §1000(a)(9), 113 Stat. 1536; Nov. 2, 2002, P.L. 107-273, §13206(a)(19), (b)(1)(B), 116 Stat. 1905, 1906; Sept. 16, 2011, P.L. 112-29, §20(j)(1), 125 Stat. 335.

See also 37 C.F.R. §1.335.

ANNOTATIONS

Deprenyl Animal Health, Inc. v. University of Toronto Innovations Found., 297 F.3d 1343, 1357, 63 U.S.P.Q.2d 1705, 1714 (Fed.Cir.2002). "Nothing prevents patent-related disputes ... from being resolved in binding foreign arbitration. As with other property rights, patent-related rights can be contracted away. Parties may agree to arbitrate patent infringement and validity issues, and such agreements bind the parties. Section 294 is not limited to domestic arbitration, nor is there any compelling reason to so interpret its authorization of the arbitration of disputes over patent-related rights."

§295. PRESUMPTION: PRODUCT MADE BY PATENTED PROCESS

In actions alleging infringement of a process patent based on the importation, sale, offer for sale, or use of a product which is made from a process patented in the United States, if the court finds—

(1) that a substantial likelihood exists that the product was made by the patented process, and

(2) that the plaintiff has made a reasonable effort to determine the process actually used in the production of the product and was unable to so determine,

the product shall be presumed to have been so made, and the burden of establishing that the product was not made by the process shall be on the party asserting that it was not so made.

History of 35 U.S.C. §295: Aug. 23, 1988, P.L. 100-418, §9005(a), 102 Stat. 1566; Dec. 8, 1994, P.L. 103-465, §533(b)(7), 108 Stat. 4990.

See also 35 U.S.C. §271(g); TRIPs pt. II, §5.

ANNOTATIONS

Nutrinova Nutrition Specialties & Food Ingredients GmbH v. International Trade Comm'n, 224 F.3d 1356, 1359-60, 55 U.S.P.Q.2d 1951, 1954 (Fed.Cir.2000). 35 U.S.C. §295 "on its face is a burden shifting mechanism. As a general proposition, the law places the burden of proving infringement on the patentee who alleges it. When two conditions are met, the statute shifts that burden and requires the alleged infringer to disprove infringement. The two conditions are that a finding is made by the court that: (1) a substantial likelihood exists that the product was made by the patented process, and (2) the plaintiff has made a reasonable effort to determine the process actually used in the production of the product and was unable so to determine. The statute also has a significant punitive element. It provides the trial court with a potent weapon to use against a non-cooperative defendant. *At F.3d 1359 n.1, U.S.P.Q.2d 1954 n.1:* It is possible that §295 has no application to proceedings before the [International Trade Commission], since the statute on its face applies to courts, not agencies. However, the Commission did not raise that point, and we therefore treat it as waived for purposes of this opinion. *At F.3d 1360, U.S.P.Q.2d 1954:* The specific point during a trial when the trial court should decide a §295 motion raised by the patentee will vary with the facts and circumstances of each case. It would be as arbitrary for this court to identify a specific point at which the [administrative-law judge] must make his §295 decision as it would be for this court to mandate a specific point in a proceeding when a court must enter summary judgment. The patentee has every right to urge the court to apply §295 when circumstances warrant it; likewise, the court has every right to exercise its discretion in determining at what point in the decisional process the statute will be brought into play."

§296. LIABILITY OF STATES, INSTRUMENTALITIES OF STATES, & STATE OFFICIALS FOR INFRINGEMENT OF PATENTS

(a) In general.—Any State, any instrumentality of a State, and any officer or employee of a State or instrumentality of a State acting in his official capacity, shall not be immune, under the eleventh amendment of the Constitution of the United States or under any other doctrine of sovereign immunity, from suit in Federal court by any person, including any governmental or nongovernmental entity, for infringement of a patent under section 271, or for any other violation under this title.

(b) Remedies.—In a suit described in subsection (a) for a violation described in that subsection, remedies (including remedies both at law and in equity) are available for the violation to the same extent as such remedies are available for such a violation in a suit against any private entity. Such remedies include damages, interest, costs, and treble damages under section 284, attorney fees under section 285, and the additional remedy for infringement of design patents under section 289.

History of 35 U.S.C. §296: Oct. 28, 1992, P.L. 102-560, §2(a)(2), 106 Stat. 4230.

ANNOTATIONS

Florida Prepaid Postsecondary Educ. Expense Bd. v. College Sav. Bank, 527 U.S. 627, 647, 51 U.S.P.Q.2d 1081, 1090 (1999). "[T]he Patent Remedy Act [35 U.S.C. §271(h)] cannot be sustained under §5 of the 14th Amendment."

Biomedical Patent Mgmt. v. State of Cal., 505 F.3d 1328, 1339-40, 85 U.S.P.Q.2d 1074, 1081 (Fed.Cir. 2007). "[W]here a waiver of immunity occurs in an earlier action that is dismissed, or an entirely separate action, courts, including our own, have held that the waiver does not extend to the separate lawsuit. *At U.S.P.Q.2d 1082:* [W]e do not mean to draw a bright-line rule whereby a State's waiver of sovereign immunity can never extend to a re-filed or separate lawsuit. We note only that the case law relied upon by [P] does not support its contention that waiver of immunity in one suit should extend to a separate action *simply because* the action involves the same parties and same subject matter. Indeed, two relevant principles we can extract from these cases are that a State's waiver of immunity generally does *not* extend to a separate or re-filed suit, and that ... even a waiver by litigation conduct must nonetheless be 'clear.' These principles, of course, are related, as a waiver that does not 'clearly' extend to a separate lawsuit generally would not preclude a State from asserting immunity in that separate action."

Vas-Cath, Inc. v. University of Mo., 473 F.3d 1376, 1383, 81 U.S.P.Q.2d 1524, 1528 (Fed.Cir.2007). "[H]ere [appellee] did not simply procure a patent through the routine of *ex parte* examination, but requested the PTO to conduct litigation-type activity, obtaining a favorable agency ruling for which [35 U.S.C. §146] authorizes judicial review. *At F.3d 1385, U.S.P.Q.2d 1530:* [Appellee] initiated and participated in the contested PTO interference against [appellant]; we conclude that [appellee] cannot both retain the fruits of that action and bar the losing party from its statutory right of review, even if that review is conducted in federal court. [T]he state's actions with respect to the interference include waiver with respect to the ensuing civil action. Having waived any potential immunity as to the interference contest in the PTO, we conclude that [appellee] waived any Constitution-based objection to [appellant's] statutory right of judicial review. The dismissal of the §146 action is reversed...."

Pennington Seed, Inc. v. Produce Exch., 457 F.3d 1334, 1341-43, 79 U.S.P.Q.2d 1777, 1781-82 (Fed.Cir. 2006). "[C]ontinuing prospective violations of a federal patent right by state officials may be enjoined by federal courts under the ***Ex parte Young***[, 209 U.S. 123 (1908),] doctrine; however, the 11th Amendment precludes the plaintiff from obtaining monetary damages from individual defendants in their official capacities. Moreover, this procedure cannot be applied to an action against any random state official. As noted in ***Ex parte Young***, there must be a connection between the state officer and the enforcement of the act or else the suit will merely make him a representative of the state and therefore improperly make the state a party to the suit. [¶] Allegations that a state official directs a University's patent policy are insufficient to causally connect that state official to a violation of federal patent law—i.e., patent infringement. A nexus between the violation of federal law and the individual accused of violating that law requires more than simply a broad general obligation to prevent a violation; it requires an actual violation of federal law by that individual. The fact that a University Official has a general, state-law obligation to oversee a University's patent policy does not give rise to a violation of federal patent law."

§297. IMPROPER & DECEPTIVE INVENTION PROMOTION

(a) In general.—An invention promoter shall have a duty to disclose the following information to a customer in writing, prior to entering into a contract for invention promotion services:

(1) the total number of inventions evaluated by the invention promoter for commercial potential in the past 5 years, as well as the number of those inventions that received positive evaluations, and the number of those inventions that received negative evaluations;

(2) the total number of customers who have contracted with the invention promoter in the past 5 years, not including customers who have purchased trade show services, research, advertising, or other nonmarketing services from the invention promoter, or who have defaulted in their payment to the invention promoter;

(3) the total number of customers known by the invention promoter to have received a net financial profit as a direct result of the invention promotion services provided by such invention promoter;

(4) the total number of customers known by the invention promoter to have received license agreements for their inventions as a direct result of the invention promotion services provided by such invention promoter; and

(5) the names and addresses of all previous invention promotion companies with which the invention promoter or its officers have collectively or individually been affiliated in the previous 10 years.

(b) Civil action—

(1) Any customer who enters into a contract with an invention promoter and who is found by a court to have been injured by any material false or fraudulent statement or representation, or any omission of material fact, by that invention promoter (or any agent, employee, director, officer, partner, or independent contractor of such invention promoter), or by the failure of that invention promoter to disclose such information as required under subsection (a), may recover in a civil action against the invention promoter (or the officers, directors, or partners of such invention promoter), in addition to reasonable costs and attorneys' fees—

(A) the amount of actual damages incurred by the customer; or

(B) at the election of the customer at any time before final judgment is rendered, statutory damages in a sum of not more than $5,000, as the court considers just.

(2) Notwithstanding paragraph (1), in a case where the customer sustains the burden of proof, and the court finds, that the invention promoter intentionally misrepresented or omitted a material fact to such customer, or willfully failed to disclose such information as required under subsection (a), with the purpose of deceiving that customer, the court may increase damages to not more than three times the amount awarded, taking into account past complaints made against the invention promoter that resulted in regulatory sanctions or other corrective actions based on those records compiled by the Commissioner of Patents under subsection (d).

(c) Definitions.—For purposes of this section—

(1) a "contract for invention promotion services" means a contract by which an invention promoter undertakes invention promotion services for a customer;

(2) a "customer" is any individual who enters into a contract with an invention promoter for invention promotion services;

(3) the term "invention promoter" means any person, firm, partnership, corporation, or other entity who offers to perform or performs invention promotion services for, or on behalf of, a customer, and who holds itself out through advertising in any mass media as providing such services, but does not include—

(A) any department or agency of the Federal Government or of a State or local government;

(B) any nonprofit, charitable, scientific, or educational organization, qualified under applicable State law or described under section 170(b)(1)(A) of title 26;

(C) any person or entity involved in the evaluation to determine commercial potential of, or offering to license or sell, a utility patent or a previously filed nonprovisional utility patent application;

(D) any party participating in a transaction involving the sale of the stock or assets of a business; or

(E) any party who directly engages in the business of retail sales of products or the distribution of products; and

(4) the term "invention promotion services" means the procurement or attempted procurement for a customer of a firm, corporation, or other entity to develop and market products or services that include the invention of the customer.

(d) Records of complaints—

(1) Release of complaints.—The Commissioner of Patents shall make all complaints received by the Patent and Trademark Office involving invention promoters publicly available, together with any response of the invention promoters. The Commissioner of Patents shall notify the invention promoter of a complaint and provide a reasonable opportunity to reply prior to making such complaint publicly available.

(2) Request for complaints.—The Commissioner of Patents may request complaints relating to invention promotion services from any Federal or State agency and include such complaints in the records maintained under paragraph (1), together with any response of the invention promoters.

History of 35 U.S.C. §297: Nov. 29, 1999, P.L. 106-113, §1000(a)(9), 113 Stat. 1536.

See also 37 C.F.R. pt. 4.

§298. ADVICE OF COUNSEL

The failure of an infringer to obtain the advice of counsel with respect to any allegedly infringed patent, or the failure of the infringer to present such advice to the court or jury, may not be used to prove that the accused infringer willfully infringed the patent or that the infringer intended to induce infringement of the patent.

History of 35 U.S.C. §298: Sept. 16, 2011, P.L. 112-29, §17(a), 125 Stat. 329.

§299. JOINDER OF PARTIES

(a) Joinder of accused infringers.—With respect to any civil action arising under any Act of Congress relating to patents, other than an action or trial in which an act of infringement under section 271(e)(2) has been pled, parties that are accused infringers may be joined in one action as defendants or counterclaim defendants, or have their actions consolidated for trial, only if—

(1) any right to relief is asserted against the parties jointly, severally, or in the alternative with respect to or arising out of the same transaction, occurrence, or series of transactions or occurrences relating to the making, using, importing into the United States, offering for sale, or selling of the same accused product or process; and

(2) questions of fact common to all defendants or counterclaim defendants will arise in the action.

(b) Allegations insufficient for joinder.—For purposes of this subsection, accused infringers may not be joined in one action as defendants or counterclaim defendants, or have their actions consolidated for trial, based solely on allegations that they each have infringed the patent or patents in suit.

(c) Waiver.—A party that is an accused infringer may waive the limitations set forth in this section with respect to that party.

History of 35 U.S.C. §299: Sept. 16, 2011, P.L. 112-29, §19(d)(1), 125 Stat. 332; Jan. 14, 2013, P.L. 112-274, §1(c), 126 Stat. 2456.

ANNOTATIONS

Richmond v. Lumisol Elec. Ltd., No. 13-1944 (MLC) (D.N.J.2014) (memo op.; 4-30-14). "The primary issue before the Court is whether competitors can be joined in a patent infringement action under 35 U.S.C. §299 when they are not alleged to have conspired or acted in concert. This is purely an issue of law, and thus the Court's review of the Magistrate Judge's Decision is de novo. [¶] This is an issue of first impression in this district. The prevailing view in other jurisdictions is that §299 does not permit such joinder. The Court agrees with this approach and concludes that direct competitors may not be joined in a patent infringement action pursuant to §299, absent allegations of concerted action. Logically, competitors, absent a conspiracy, are not part of the same transaction. For example, where the same manufacturer sells the same accused product to two importers who then sell to the same retailer, there are multiple streams of commerce and multiple transactions: (1) manufacturer A to importer A to retailer A; and (2) manufacturer A to importer B to retailer A. The two importers—who are competitors—are not part of the 'same transaction,' as demonstrated by this example. [¶] The secondary issue before the Court is whether participants at different levels in the same stream of commerce—e.g., manufacturer A to importer A to retailer A—are part of the same transaction. The Court concludes, consistently with the decisions of other district courts, that these participants may be part of the same transaction under §299. However, satisfaction of the same product and same transaction requirements of §299 is a necessary, but not a sufficient, precondition to joinder in a patent infringement action. Other considerations include judicial economy and fundamental fairness. Also, pursuant to [FRCP] 21, '[o]n motion or on its own, the court may at any time, on just terms, add or drop a party' or 'sever any claim against a party.'"

CHAPTER 30. PRIOR ART CITATIONS TO OFFICE & EX PARTE REEXAMINATION OF PATENTS

§301. CITATION OF PRIOR ART & WRITTEN STATEMENTS

(a) In general.—Any person at any time may cite to the Office in writing—

(1) prior art consisting of patents or printed publications which that person believes to have a bearing on the patentability of any claim of a particular patent; or

(2) statements of the patent owner filed in a proceeding before a Federal court or the Office in which the patent owner took a position on the scope of any claim of a particular patent.

(b) Official file.—If the person citing prior art or written statements pursuant to subsection (a) explains in writing the pertinence and manner of applying the prior art or written statements to at least 1 claim of the patent, the citation of the prior art or written statements and the explanation thereof shall become a part of the official file of the patent.

(c) Additional information.—A party that submits a written statement pursuant to subsection (a)(2) shall include any other documents, pleadings, or evidence from the proceeding in which the statement was filed that addresses the written statement.

(d) Limitations.—A written statement submitted pursuant to subsection (a)(2), and additional information submitted pursuant to subsection (c), shall not be considered by the Office for any purpose other than to determine the proper meaning of a patent claim in a proceeding that is ordered or instituted pursuant to section 304, 314, or 324. If any such written statement or additional information is subject to an applicable protective order, such statement or information shall be redacted to exclude information that is subject to that order.

(e) Confidentiality.—Upon the written request of the person citing prior art or written statements pursuant to subsection (a), that person's identity shall be excluded from the patent file and kept confidential.

History of 35 U.S.C. §301: Dec. 12, 1980, P.L. 96-517, §1, 94 Stat. 3015; Sept. 16, 2011, P.L. 112-29, §6(g)(1), 125 Stat. 311.

See also 37 C.F.R. §§1.501, 1.502.

ANNOTATIONS

Patlex Corp. v. Mossinghoff, 758 F.2d 594, 597, 225 U.S.P.Q. 243, 245 (Fed.Cir.1985), *modified on other grounds*, 771 F.2d 480, 226 U.S.P.Q. 985 (Fed.Cir.1985). "Under 35 U.S.C. §301, any person may call to the PTO's attention prior art that may have a bearing on the patentability of any claim."

§302. REQUEST FOR REEXAMINATION

Any person at any time may file a request for reexamination by the Office of any claim of a patent on the basis of any prior art cited under the provisions of section 301. The request must be in writing and must be accompanied by payment of a reexamination fee established by the Director pursuant to the provisions of section 41. The request must set forth the pertinency and manner of applying cited prior art to every claim for which reexamination is requested. Unless the requesting person is the owner of the patent, the Director promptly will send a copy of the request to the owner of record of the patent.

History of 35 U.S.C. §302: Dec. 12, 1980, P.L. 96-517, §1, 94 Stat. 3015; Nov. 29, 1999, P.L. 106-113, §1000(a)(9), 113 Stat. 1536; Nov. 2, 2002, P.L. 107-273, §13206(b)(1)(B), 116 Stat. 1906; Sept. 16, 2011, P.L. 112-29, §20(j)(1), 125 Stat. 335.

See also 37 C.F.R. §§1.510-1.570.

§303. DETERMINATION OF ISSUE BY DIRECTOR

(a) Within three months following the filing of a request for reexamination under the provisions of section 302, the Director will determine whether a substantial new question of patentability affecting any claim of the patent concerned is raised by the request, with or without consideration of other patents or printed publications. On his own initiative, and any time, the Director may determine whether a substantial new question of patentability is raised by patents and publications discovered by him or cited under the provisions of section 301 or 302. The existence of a substantial new question of patentability is not precluded by the fact that a patent or printed publication was previously cited by or to the Office or considered by the Office.

(b) A record of the Director's determination under subsection (a) of this section will be placed in the official file of the patent, and a copy promptly will be given or mailed to the owner of record of the patent and to the person requesting reexamination, if any.

(c) A determination by the Director pursuant to subsection (a) of this section that no substantial new question of patentability has been raised will be final and nonappealable. Upon such a determination, the Director may refund a portion of the reexamination fee required under section 302.

History of 35 U.S.C. §303: Dec. 12, 1980, P.L. 96-517, §1, 94 Stat. 3015; Nov. 29, 1999, P.L. 106-113, §1000(a)(9), 113 Stat. 1536; Nov. 2, 2002, P.L. 107-273, §§13105(a), 13206(b)(1)(A), (B), 116 Stat. 1900, 1905; Sept. 16, 2011, P.L. 112-29, §§6(h)(1)(A), 20(j)(1), 125 Stat. 312, 335.

See also 37 C.F.R. §§1.515, 1.520.

ANNOTATIONS

In re Baxter Int'l, 678 F.3d 1357, 1364, 102 U.S.P.Q.2d 1925, 1932-33 (Fed.Cir.2012). "[T]he PTO in reexamination proceedings and the court system in patent infringement actions take different approaches in determining validity and on the same evidence could quite correctly come to different conclusions. In particular, a challenger that attacks the validity of patent claims in civil litigation has a statutory burden to prove invalidity by clear and convincing evidence. Should the challenger fail to meet that burden, the court will not find the patent 'valid,' only that the patent challenger did not carry the burden of establishing invalidity in the *particular case* before the court. In contrast, in PTO reexaminations the standard of proof—a preponderance of the evidence—is substantially lower than in a civil case and there is no presumption of validity in reexamination proceedings." (Internal quotes omitted.)

In re Swanson, 540 F.3d 1368, 1376, 88 U.S.P.Q.2d 1196, 1201 (Fed.Cir.2008). "According to the House Report accompanying [amendment to] §303(a), the appropriate test to determine whether a substantial new question of patentability exists should not merely look at the number of references or whether they were previously considered or cited but their combination in the appropriate context of a new light as it bears on the question of the validity of the patent. *At F.3d 1379, U.S.P.Q.2d 1204:* [T]he Board did not err in holding that the prior district court litigation did not prevent the [cited] reference from raising a substantial new question of patentability under §303(a). As properly interpreted a substantial new question of patentability refers to a question which has never been considered by the PTO; thus, a substantial new question can exist even if a federal court previously considered the question. *At F.3d 1380-81:* [U]nder §303(a) as amended, a reference may present a substantial new question even if the examiner considered or cited a reference for one purpose in earlier proceedings. Nothing in the statute creates an exception to this rule for references considered in the context of a rejection of prior claims. *At U.S.P.Q.2d 1205:* As the legislative history clarifies, to decide whether a reference that was previously considered by the PTO creates a substantial new question of patentability, the PTO should evaluate the context in which the reference was previously considered and the scope of the prior consideration and determine whether the reference is now being considered for a substantially different purpose. [¶] Determining the scope of an examiner's previous consideration of a reference will generally require an analysis of the record of the prior proceedings to determine if and how the examiner used the reference in making his initial decisions. As we believe that this inquiry is most accurately viewed as a question of fact, we will review the Board's findings regarding the scope of consideration of a reference during prior examinations for substantial evidence. However, the ultimate question of whether the reexamination is based on a substantial new question of patentability, in light of how a reference was previously considered, remains a question of law, which we review de novo." (Internal quotes omitted.)

In re ICON Health & Fitness, Inc., 496 F.3d 1374, 1379, 83 U.S.P.Q.2d 1746, 1749 (Fed.Cir.2007). "During reexamination, as with original examination, the PTO must give claims their broadest reasonable construction consistent with the specification. Therefore, we look to the specification to see if it provides a definition for claim terms, but otherwise apply a broad interpretation. [T]his methodology produces claims with only justifiable breadth."

§304. REEXAMINATION ORDER BY DIRECTOR

If, in a determination made under the provisions of subsection 303(a), the Director finds that a substantial new question of patentability affecting any claim of a patent is raised, the determination will include an order for reexamination of the patent for resolution of the question. The patent owner will be given a reasonable period, not less than two months from the date a copy of the determination is given or mailed to him, within which he may file a statement on such question, including any amendment to his patent and new claim or claims he may wish to propose, for consideration in the reexamination. If the patent owner files such a statement, he promptly will serve a copy of it on the person who has requested reexamination under the provisions of section 302. Within a period of two months from the date of service, that person may file and have considered in the reexamination a reply to any statement filed by the patent owner. That person promptly will serve on the patent owner a copy of any reply filed.

History of 35 U.S.C. §304: Dec. 12, 1980, P.L. 96-517, §1, 94 Stat. 3016; Nov. 29, 1999, P.L. 106-113, §1000(a)(9), 113 Stat. 1536; Nov. 2, 2002, P.L. 107-273, §13206(b)(1)(B), 116 Stat. 1906; Sept. 16, 2011, P.L. 112-29, §20(j)(1), 125 Stat. 335.

See also 37 C.F.R. §§1.520, 1.525.

§305. CONDUCT OF REEXAMINATION PROCEEDINGS

After the times for filing the statement and reply provided for by section 304 have expired, reexamination will be conducted according to the procedures established for initial examination under the provisions of sections 132 and 133. In any reexamination proceeding under this chapter, the patent owner will be permitted to propose any amendment to his patent and a new claim or claims thereto, in order to distinguish the invention as claimed from the prior art cited under the provisions of section 301, or in response to a decision adverse to the patentability of a claim of a patent. No proposed amended or new claim enlarging the scope of a claim of the patent will be permitted in a reexamination proceeding under this chapter. All reexamination proceedings under this section, including any appeal to the Patent Trial and Appeal Board, will be conducted with special dispatch within the Office.

History of 35 U.S.C. §305: Dec. 12, 1980, P.L. 96-517, §1, 94 Stat. 3016; Nov. 8, 1984, P.L. 98-622, §204(c), 98 Stat. 3388; Sept. 16, 2011, P.L. 112-29, §§3(j)(1), 20(j)(1), 125 Stat. 290, 335.

ANNOTATIONS

In re NTP, Inc., 654 F.3d 1268, 1275-76, 99 U.S.P.Q.2d 1500, 1505 (Fed.Cir.2011). "Reexamination proceedings ... are intended to 'permit any party to petition the [PTO] to review the efficacy of a patent, following its issuance, on the basis of new information about preexisting technology that may have escaped review at the time of the initial examination.' The scope of reexamination proceedings is limited to 'substantial new question[s] of patentability,' ... which are questions that have not previously been considered by the PTO.... These new considerations must be based only on 'prior art consisting of patents or printed publications.' Thus, other challenges to the patentability of original claims—such as qualification as patentable subject matter under [35 U.S.C.] §101 or satisfaction of the written description and enablement requirements of [35 U.S.C.] §112—may not be raised in reexamination proceedings. Moreover, during reexamination, the patent claims no longer carry the statutory presumption of validity. *At F.3d 1277, U.S.P.Q.2d 1506:* [W]hen a patentee argues that its claims are entitled to the priority date of an earlier filed application, the examiner must undertake a priority analysis to determine if the patentee meets the requirements of [35 U.S.C.] §120. There is no statutory limitation during a reexamination proceeding prohibiting the examiner from conducting a priority analysis."

Cordis Corp. v. Medtronic Ave, Inc., 511 F.3d 1157, 1185, 85 U.S.P.Q.2d 1427, 1447 (Fed.Cir.2008). "Section 305 does not require the patent owner to include an express statement that the new claims distinguish the prior art or remarks indicating how the new claims distinguish the prior art references. If the claims fail to distinguish the prior art, the claims will be rejected on the appropriate grounds; for that reason, it may frequently be in the patent owner's interest to include such remarks, but they are not necessary to satisfy §305. For purposes of assessing validity under §305, the [Manual of Patent Examining Procedure] directs the examiner to determine only whether any added claims impermissibly 'enlarge the scope of the original claims.'"

Laitram Corp. v. NEC Corp., 163 F.3d 1342, 1346-47, 49 U.S.P.Q.2d 1199, 1202 (Fed.Cir.1998). "A patentee of a reexamined patent is entitled to infringement damages, inter alia, for the period between the date of issuance of the original claims and the date of issuance of the reexamined claims if the original and reexamined claims are 'identical.' Reexamined claims are 'identical' to their original counterparts if they are 'without substantive change.' Furthermore, in determining whether substantive changes have been made, we must discern whether the scope of the claims are identical, not merely whether different words are used. If substantive changes have been made to the original claims, the patentee is entitled to infringement damages only for the period following the issuance of the reexamination certificate. [¶] 'This court reviews without deference the district court's conclusion that the reexamined claims remained identical in scope.' This rule flows from the general principle that 'the interpretation and construction of patent claims, which define the scope of the patentee's rights under the patent, is a matter of law, exclusively for the court.' *At U.S.P.Q.2d 1203:* In ***Laitram I*** we held that a claim amendment made during reexamination following a prior art rejection is not per se a substantive change. Rather, '[t]o determine whether a claim change is substantive it is necessary to analyze the claims of the original and the reexamined patents in light of the particular facts, including the prior art, the prosecution history, other claims, and any other pertinent information.'"

Quantum Corp. v. Rodime, PLC, 65 F.3d 1577, 1584, 36 U.S.P.Q.2d 1162, 1168 (Fed.Cir.1995). "We conclude that a violation of 35 U.S.C. §305 is an invalidity defense in a patent infringement action...."

In re Freeman, 30 F.3d 1459, 1464, 31 U.S.P.Q.2d 1444, 1447 (Fed.Cir.1994). "Whether amendments enlarge the scope of a claim is a matter of claim construction. Claim construction is a question of law which we review *de novo*. [¶] A claim is enlarged if it includes within its scope any subject matter that would not have infringed the original patent. The test for when a new claim enlarges the scope of an original claim under [35 U.S.C.] §305 is the same as that under the two-year limitation for reissue applications adding enlarging claims under 35 U.S.C. §251, last paragraph. In the reissue context this court has stated that 'a claim of a reissue application is broader in scope than the original claim if it contains within its scope any conceivable apparatus or process which would not have infringed the original patent. ... A claim that is broader in any respect is considered to be broader than the original claims even though it may be narrower in other respects.'" *See also* ***Predicate Logic, Inc. v. Distributive Software, Inc.***, 544 F.3d 1298, 1303, 88 U.S.P.Q.2d 1526, 1529 (Fed.Cir.2008); ***Creo Prods. v. Presstek, Inc.***, 305 F.3d 1337, 1344, 64 U.S.P.Q.2d 1385, 1389 (Fed. Cir.2002).

§306. APPEAL

The patent owner involved in a reexamination proceeding under this chapter may appeal under the provisions of section 134, and may seek court review under the provisions of sections 141 to 144, with respect to any decision adverse to the patentability of any original or proposed amended or new claim of the patent.

History of 35 U.S.C. §306: Dec. 12, 1980, P.L. 96-517, §1, 94 Stat. 3016; Sept. 16, 2011, P.L. 112-29, §§6(h)(2)(A), 20(j)(1), 125 Stat. 312, 335.

ANNOTATIONS

Syntex Inc. v. USPTO, 882 F.2d 1570, 1576, 11 U.S.P.Q.2d 1866, 1871 (Fed.Cir.1989). "Although a third-party requester has some rights vis-à-vis the PTO, from our review of the entirety of the reexamination provisions, we conclude that [a third-party] requester has no right to challenge the validity of the Reexamination Certificate by suit against the PTO. [¶] [Third-party requester's] remedy, if any, must await confrontation with the patent owner."

§307. CERTIFICATE OF PATENTABILITY, UNPATENTABILITY, & CLAIM CANCELLATION

(a) In a reexamination proceeding under this chapter, when the time for appeal has expired or any appeal proceeding has terminated, the Director will issue and publish a certificate canceling any claim of the patent finally determined to be unpatentable, confirming any claim of the patent determined to be patentable, and incorporating in the patent any proposed amended or new claim determined to be patentable.

(b) Any proposed amended or new claim determined to be patentable and incorporated into a patent following a reexamination proceeding will have the same effect as that specified in section 252 for reissued patents on the right of any person who made, purchased, or used within the United States, or imported into the United States, anything patented by such proposed amended or new claim, or who made substantial preparation for the same, prior to issuance of a certificate under the provisions of subsection (a) of this section.

History of 35 U.S.C. §307: Dec. 12, 1980, P.L. 96-517, §1, 94 Stat. 3016; Dec. 8, 1994, P.L. 103-465, §533(b)(8), 108 Stat. 4990; Nov. 29, 1999, P.L. 106-113, §1000(a)(9), 113 Stat. 1536; Nov. 2, 2002, P.L. 107-273, §13206(b)(1)(B), 116 Stat. 1906; Sept. 16, 2011, P.L. 112-29, §20(j)(1), 125 Stat. 335.

ANNOTATIONS

R+L Carriers, Inc. v. Qualcomm, Inc., 801 F.3d 1346, 1349, 116 U.S.P.Q.2d 1150, 1153 (Fed.Cir.2015). "A patentee of a patent that survives reexamination is only entitled to infringement damages for the time period between the date of issuance of the original claims and the date of issuance of the reexamined claims if the original and the reexamined claims are 'substantially identical.' If, on the other hand, a substantive change has been made to the original claims during reexamination, the patentee is entitled to infringement damages only for the time period following issuance of the reexamination certificate. To determine whether substantive changes have been made, we consider 'whether the *scope* of the claims are identical, not merely whether different words are used.' *At F.3d 1350-51, U.S.P.Q.2d 1154:* [W]e must review the district court's subsidiary factual findings on the scope of the reexamined and original claims for clear error, but the ultimate conclusion regarding the scope of the claims de novo. [¶] Under the statute and our prior case law, it is irrelevant *why* an amended claim is narrowed during reexamination, or even whether the patentee intended to narrow the claim in a particular way. If the scope of the amended claim is not 'substantially identical' to the scope of the original claim—based on a normal claim construction analysis—per [35 U.S.C.] §252, that fact affects intervening rights. The fact that the reason for the amendment during reexamination might not have been for the purpose of narrowing the claim in a particular way does not matter. And, the court is not charged with assessing why a claim might have been narrowed as a predicate to determining whether it has been narrowed. Indeed, we explained in the analogous context of considering whether a claim was *broadened* on reexamination that we consider 'whether any conceivable process would infringe the amended claim, but not infringe the original claim.' Similarly, in determining whether an amended claim is *narrower*, we determine whether there is any product or process that would infringe the original claim, but not infringe the amended claim. The purpose of the amendment is irrelevant to this inquiry." *See also* ***Presidio Components, Inc. v. American Tech. Ceramics Corp.***, 875 F.3d 1369, 1377-78, 124 U.S.P.Q.2d 1745, 1749-50 (Fed.Cir. 2017).

Fresenius USA, Inc. v. Baxter Int'l, 721 F.3d 1330, 1336, 107 U.S.P.Q.2d 1365, 1369 (Fed.Cir.2013). "[T]he question in this case is whether, under the reexamination statute [§307], the cancellation of claims by the PTO is binding in pending district court infringement litigation." Held: The cancellation is binding precedent.

Marine Polymer Techs. v. HemCon, Inc., 672 F.3d 1350, 1361-62, 102 U.S.P.Q.2d 1161, 1167 (Fed.Cir. 2012). "The doctrine of intervening rights first developed as courts recognized that permitting substantive changes to the scope of patent claims through post-issuance procedures left 'the door … open for gross injustice' where a third party, having already begun to make, use, or sell a given article, finds its previously lawful activities rendered newly infringing under a modified patent. In such situations, the defendant 'acquired at least a right to continue to use the [articles] as if it held a license therefor under the reissued patent.' With respect to reissued patents, the concept of intervening rights was codified by the Patent Act of 1952, and the statute provides for two types of intervening rights: (1) intervening rights that abrogate liability for infringing claims added to or modified from the original patent if the accused products were made or used before the reissue, often referred to as absolute intervening rights; and (2) intervening rights that apply as a matter of judicial discretion to mitigate liability for infringing such claims even as to products made or used after the reissue if the accused infringer made substantial preparations for the infringing activities prior to reissue, often referred to as equitable intervening rights. Intervening rights do not accrue, however, where the accused product or activity infringes a claim that existed in the original patent and remains 'without substantive change' after reissue. [¶] Although intervening rights originated as a defense against patents modified through reissue procedures, the doctrine has since been extended to the context of patent reexamination. Pursuant to 35 U.S.C. §§307(b) and 316(b), respectively, both *ex parte* and *inter partes* reexaminations can give rise to intervening rights. … Thus, after a patent emerges from reexamination, the statute makes available absolute and equitable intervening rights to the same extent provided in the reissue statute, but only with respect to 'amended or new' claims in the reexamined patent. *At F.3d 1363, U.S.P.Q.2d 1168:* [U]nder §307(b), the first question when assessing whether intervening rights arose from a reexamination is whether the asserted claim is 'amended or new'; if the answer is no, that ends the inquiry. Only if the claim at issue is new or has been amended may the court proceed to the second step in the analysis and assess the substantive effect of any such change pursuant to [35 U.S.C.] §252."

Predicate Logic, Inc. v. Distributive Software, Inc., 544 F.3d 1298, 1304-05, 88 U.S.P.Q.2d 1526, 1531 (Fed.Cir.2008). "Under 35 U.S.C. §307, a claim that is amended in reexamination has the same effect as a claim that is amended in reissue proceedings under 35 U.S.C. §252. Correspondingly, under … §252, a reissued patent is enforceable against infringing activity that occurred after the issuance of the original patent, to the extent that its claims are substantially identical to the claims of the original patent. Thus, unless a claim granted or confirmed upon reexamination is identical to an original claim, the patent can not be enforced against infringing activity that occurred before issuance of the reexamination certificate. Identical does not mean verbatim, but means at most without substantive change. An amendment that clarifies the text of the claim or makes it more definite without affecting its scope is generally viewed as identical." (Internal quotes omitted.)

In re Bass, 314 F.3d 575, 577, 65 U.S.P.Q.2d 1156, 1157 (Fed.Cir.2002). "Until a matter has been completed ... the PTO may reconsider an earlier action. A reexamination is complete upon the statutorily mandated issuance of a reexamination certificate; the [Notice of Intent to Issue Reexamination Certificate (NIRC)] merely notifies the applicant of the PTO's intent to issue a certificate. A NIRC does not wrest jurisdiction from the PTO precluding further review of the matter."

University of Va. Patent Found. v. General Elec. Co., 755 F.Supp.2d 738, 748 (W.D.Va.2011) (memo op.; 2-8-11). "Whether the term 'amended' limits the application of §307(b) to only explicit wording changes, as opposed to changes through other means—such as prosecution disclaimer—appears to be an issue of first impression. [¶] On the particular facts presented in this case, I held that [P's] disclaimer by statements it made in reexamination, together with its cancellation of Claim 4, operated to 'amend' Claim 1 within the meaning of the statute. [¶] [P] has provided no reason to believe that my prior interpretation of §307(b) was in error, so I decline to reverse it. Section 307(b) was intended to reach instances where the patent holder effects a change in claim scope in reexamination to secure its validity over prior art while avoiding an explicit change in wording."

CHAPTER 31[A*]. OPTIONAL INTER PARTES REEXAMINATION PROCEDURES

Chapter 31[A]'s optional inter partes procedures in §§311[A*] through 318[A*] are effective for requests for inter partes reexamination filed before Sept. 16, 2012. After Sept. 16, 2012, inter partes reexamination was replaced by inter partes reviews. See ch. 31[B*], p. 749.*

§311[A*]. REQUEST FOR INTER PARTES REEXAMINATION

(a) In general.—Any third-party requester at any time may file a request for inter partes reexamination by the Office of a patent on the basis of any prior art cited under the provisions of section 301.

(b) Requirements.—The request shall—

(1) be in writing, include the identity of the real party in interest, and be accompanied by payment of an inter partes reexamination fee established by the Director under section 41; and

(2) set forth the pertinency and manner of applying cited prior art to every claim for which reexamination is requested.

(c) Copy.—The Director promptly shall send a copy of the request to the owner of record of the patent.

History of 35 U.S.C. §311[A*]: Nov. 29, 1999, P.L. 106-113, §1000(a)(9), 113 Stat. 1536; Nov. 2, 2002, P.L. 107-273, §13202(a)(1), (c)(1), 116 Stat. 1901, 1902.

See also 37 C.F.R. §§1.902-1.997.

ANNOTATIONS

Cooper Techs. v. Dudas, 536 F.3d 1330, 1331, 87 U.S.P.Q.2d 1705, 1706 (Fed.Cir.2008). "Pursuant to [American Inventors Protection Act (AIPA)] §4608 ..., the inter partes reexamination procedure is available for 'any patent that issues from an *original application* filed in the U.S. on or after' November 29, 1999—the date of the enactment of the AIPA. The [PTO] has interpreted the phrase 'original application' in §4608 'to encompass utility, plant and design applications, including first filed applications, continuations, divisionals, continuations-in-part, continued prosecution applications and the national stage phase of international applications.'"

§312[A*]. DETERMINATION OF ISSUE BY DIRECTOR

Section 312[A] is effective for requests for inter partes reexamination filed on or after Sept. 16, 2011, but before Sept. 16, 2012.*

(a) Reexamination.—Not later than 3 months after the filing of a request for inter partes reexamina-

35 U.S.C. §312[A*]

tion under section 311, the Director shall determine whether the information presented in the request shows that there is a reasonable likelihood that the requester would prevail with respect to at least 1 of the claims challenged in the request, with or without consideration of other patents or printed publications. A showing that there is a reasonable likelihood that the requester would prevail with respect to at least 1 of the claims challenged in the request is not precluded by the fact that a patent or printed publication was previously cited by or to the Office or considered by the Office.

(b) Record.—A record of the Director's determination under subsection (a) shall be placed in the official file of the patent, and a copy shall be promptly given or mailed to the owner of record of the patent and to the third-party requester.

(c) Final decision.—A determination by the Director under subsection (a) shall be final and nonappealable. Upon a determination that the showing required by subsection (a) has not been made, the Director may refund a portion of the inter partes reexamination fee required under section 311.

History of 35 U.S.C. §312[A*]: Nov. 29, 1999, P.L. 106-113, §1000(a)(9), 113 Stat. 1536; Nov. 2, 2002, P.L. 107-273, §§13105(a), 13202(a)(2), (c)(1), 116 Stat. 1900, 1901, 1902; Sept. 16, 2011, P.L. 112-29, §6(c)(3)(A)(i), 125 Stat. 305.

§313[A*]. INTER PARTES REEXAMINATION ORDER BY DIRECTOR

Section 313[A] is effective for requests for inter partes reexamination filed on or after Sept. 16, 2011, but before Sept. 16, 2012.*

If, in a determination made under section 312(a), the Director finds that it has been shown that there is a reasonable likelihood that the requester would prevail with respect to at least 1 of the claims challenged in the request, the determination shall include an order for inter partes reexamination of the patent for resolution of the question. The order may be accompanied by the initial action of the Patent and Trademark Office on the merits of the inter partes reexamination conducted in accordance with section 314.

History of 35 U.S.C. §313[A*]: Nov. 29, 1999, P.L. 106-113, §1000(a)(9), 113 Stat. 1536; Nov. 2, 2002, P.L. 107-273, §13202(c)(1), 116 Stat. 1902; Sept. 16, 2011, P.L. 112-29, §6(c)(3)(A)(ii), 125 Stat. 305.

§314[A*]. CONDUCT OF INTER PARTES REEXAMINATION PROCEEDINGS

(a) In general.—Except as otherwise provided in this section, reexamination shall be conducted according to the procedures established for initial examination under the provisions of sections 132 and 133. In any inter partes reexamination proceeding under this chapter, the patent owner shall be permitted to propose any amendment to the patent and a new claim or claims, except that no proposed amended or new claim enlarging the scope of the claims of the patent shall be permitted.

(b) Response—

(1) With the exception of the inter partes reexamination request, any document filed by either the patent owner or the third-party requester shall be served on the other party. In addition, the Office shall send to the third-party requester a copy of any communication sent by the Office to the patent owner concerning the patent subject to the inter partes reexamination proceeding.

(2) Each time that the patent owner files a response to an action on the merits from the Patent and Trademark Office, the third-party requester shall have one opportunity to file written comments addressing issues raised by the action of the Office or the patent owner's response thereto, if those written comments are received by the Office within 30 days after the date of service of the patent owner's response.

(3) Redesignated.

(c) Special dispatch.—Unless otherwise provided by the Director for good cause, all inter partes reexamination proceedings under this section, including any appeal to the Board of Patent Appeals and Interferences, shall be conducted with special dispatch within the Office.

History of 35 U.S.C. §314[A*]: Nov. 29, 1999, P.L. 106-113, §1000(a)(9), 113 Stat. 1536; Nov. 2, 2002, P.L. 107-273, §13202(a)(3), (c)(1), 116 Stat. 1901, 1902.

ANNOTATIONS

Airbus S.A.S. v. Firepass Corp., 793 F.3d 1376, 1381, 115 U.S.P.Q.2d 1860, 1864 (Fed.Cir.2015). "[O]nce the Director ordered *inter partes* reexamination it was [37 C.F.R.] §1.948(a), not a determination of a substantial new question of patentability, that governed the limitations on [third-party requester's] submission of prior art. Thus, the Examiner erred in evaluating [prior art] for a substantial new question of patentability, when his evaluation should have been conducted under §1.948(a)(2)."

Institut Pasteur v. Focarino, 738 F.3d 1337, 1343, 109 U.S.P.Q.2d 1134, 1140 (Fed.Cir.2013). "Because amending the claim ... substantively altered (narrowed) its scope, the PTO may not issue the amended claim now that the patent has expired, as stated in applicable provisions of a PTO regulation, 37 C.F.R. §1.530(j), (k). That rule follows from the relevant statutory provisions. Looking backward, if the claim were to issue on reexamination, [petitioner] could not enforce it for the period before issuance of the reexamination certificate. That is because, for *inter partes* reexaminations under the pre-2013 version of 35 U.S.C. §316(b) applicable here, as for reissues under 35 U.S.C. §252, when a claim is substantively amended, the analysis of intervening rights after issuance, considering pertinent references and prosecution history, treats the amendment as raising an irrebuttable presumption that the original claim was materially flawed, so there can be no liability for acts of infringement before the amended claim issues."

Sony Computer Entm't Am. Inc. v. Dudas, 85 U.S.P.Q.2d 1594, 1604 (E.D.Va.2006). "[P's] argument that the PTO was required to reexamine all claims of the two patents is unpersuasive; the [American Inventors Protection Act], PTO regulations and the [Manual of Patent Examining Procedure] do not, individually or collectively, compel the conclusion that the PTO is obligated to reexamine every claim under a patent once it determines that a substantial question of validity exists as to any claim. It further follows that the PTO did not abuse its discretion in concluding that there was good cause to suspend reexamination of the litigated claims in light of the more advanced Federal Circuit appeal focusing on the same claims and the operation of the statutory estoppel."

§315[A*]. APPEAL

(a) Patent owner.—The patent owner involved in an inter partes reexamination proceeding under this chapter—

(1) may appeal under the provisions of section 134 and may appeal under the provisions of sections 141 through 144, with respect to any decision adverse to the patentability of any original or proposed amended or new claim of the patent; and

(2) may be a party to any appeal taken by a third-party requester under subsection (b).

(b) Third-party requester.—A third-party requester—

(1) may appeal under the provisions of section 134, and may appeal under the provisions of sections 141 through 144, with respect to any final decision favorable to the patentability of any original or proposed amended or new claim of the patent; and

(2) may, subject to subsection (c), be a party to any appeal taken by the patent owner under the provisions of section 134 or sections 141 through 144.

(c) Civil action.—A third-party requester whose request for an inter partes reexamination results in an order under section 313 is estopped from asserting at a later time, in any civil action arising in whole or in part under section 1338 of title 28, the invalidity of any claim finally determined to be valid and patentable on any ground which the third-party requester raised or could have raised during the inter partes reexamination proceedings. This subsection does not prevent the assertion of invalidity based on newly discovered prior art unavailable to the third-party requester and the Patent and Trademark Office at the time of the inter partes reexamination proceedings.

History of 35 U.S.C. §315[A*]: Nov. 29, 1999, P.L. 106-113, §1000(a)(9), 113 Stat. 1536; Nov. 2, 2002, P.L. 107-273, §§13106(a), 13202(a)(4), (c)(1), 116 Stat. 1900, 1901, 1902.

ANNOTATIONS

Bettcher Indus. v. Bunzl USA, Inc., 661 F.3d 629, 648, 100 U.S.P.Q.2d 1433, 1446 (Fed.Cir.2011). "[W]e hold that the estoppel provision of 35 U.S.C. §315(c) applies only after all appeal rights are exhausted, including appeals to this court."

§316[A*]. CERTIFICATE OF PATENTABILITY, UNPATENTABILITY, & CLAIM CANCELLATION

(a) In general.—In an inter partes reexamination proceeding under this chapter, when the time for appeal has expired or any appeal proceeding has terminated, the Director shall issue and publish a certificate canceling any claim of the patent finally determined to be unpatentable, confirming any claim of the patent determined to be patentable, and incorporating in the patent any proposed amended or new claim determined to be patentable.

(b) Amended or new claim.—Any proposed amended or new claim determined to be patentable and incorporated into a patent following an inter partes reexamination proceeding shall have the same effect as that specified in section 252 for reissued patents on the right of any person who made, purchased, or used within the United States, or imported into the United

States, anything patented by such proposed amended or new claim, or who made substantial preparation therefor, prior to issuance of a certificate under the provisions of subsection (a) of this section.

History of 35 U.S.C. §316[A*]: Nov. 29, 1999, P.L. 106-113, §1000(a)(9), 113 Stat. 1536; Nov. 2, 2002, P.L. 107-273, §13202(c)(1), 116 Stat. 1902; Sept. 16, 2011, P.L. 112-29, §20(j)(1), 125 Stat. 335.

ANNOTATIONS

Bettcher Indus. v. Bunzl USA, Inc., 661 F.3d 629, 644-45, 100 U.S.P.Q.2d 1433, 1444 (Fed.Cir.2011). "According to [D], §316 defines finality as the exhaustion of all appeal rights. This court agrees with [D] that §316 defines a determination of patentability to occur only after all appeals have terminated."

§317[A*]. INTER PARTES REEXAMINATION PROHIBITED

(a) Order for reexamination.—Notwithstanding any provision of this chapter, once an order for inter partes reexamination of a patent has been issued under section 313, neither the third-party requester nor its privies,[1] may file a subsequent request for inter partes reexamination of the patent until an inter partes reexamination certificate is issued and published under section 316, unless authorized by the Director.

(b) Final decision.—Once a final decision has been entered against a party in a civil action arising in whole or in part under section 1338 of title 28,[1] that the party has not sustained its burden of proving the invalidity of any patent claim in suit or if a final decision in an inter partes reexamination proceeding instituted by a third-party requester is favorable to the patentability of any original or proposed amended or new claim of the patent, then neither that party nor its privies may thereafter request an inter partes reexamination of any such patent claim on the basis of issues which that party or its privies raised or could have raised in such civil action or inter partes reexamination proceeding, and an inter partes reexamination requested by that party or its privies on the basis of such issues may not thereafter be maintained by the Office, notwithstanding any other provision of this chapter. This subsection does not prevent the assertion of invalidity based on newly discovered prior art unavailable to the third-party requester and the Patent and Trademark Office at the time of the inter partes reexamination proceedings.

1. **Editor's note:** The comma probably should not appear.

History of 35 U.S.C. §317[A*]: Nov. 29, 1999, P.L. 106-113, §1000(a)(9), 113 Stat. 1536; Nov. 2, 2002, P.L. 107-273, §13202(a)(5), (c)(1), 116 Stat. 1901, 1902.

ANNOTATIONS

In re Affinity Labs, 856 F.3d 883, 892-93, 122 U.S.P.Q.2d 1497, 1504 (Fed.Cir.2017). "Upon review of the text, structure, and history of the *inter partes* reexamination statute, we decline to read §317(b) in an incongruous way that would cause the statutory estoppel provision to apply differently for requesting an *inter partes* reexamination compared to maintenance of a pending *inter partes* reexamination. ... We, therefore, conclude that §317(b) plainly limited the scope of estoppel in all circumstances to only those *claims* actually challenged and for which the requesting party received an adverse final decision in the district court proceeding."

§318[A*]. STAY OF LITIGATION

Once an order for inter partes reexamination of a patent has been issued under section 313, the patent owner may obtain a stay of any pending litigation which involves an issue of patentability of any claims of the patent which are the subject of the inter partes reexamination order, unless the court before which such litigation is pending determines that a stay would not serve the interests of justice.

History of 35 U.S.C. §318[A*]: Nov. 29, 1999, P.L. 106-113, §1000(a)(9), 113 Stat. 1536; Nov. 2, 2002, P.L. 107-273, §13202(c)(1), 116 Stat. 1902.

ANNOTATIONS

Procter & Gamble Co. v. Kraft Foods Global, Inc., 549 F.3d 842, 849, 89 U.S.P.Q.2d 1085, 1089-90 (Fed.Cir.2008). Section 318 "must be read as enabling a patentee to obtain a stay of district court proceedings more readily than it could otherwise when its patent is subjected to inter partes reexamination by the PTO. A holding to the contrary would rest on a conclusion that Congress intended to strip district courts of the full scope of their inherent power with no mention of that effect. Thus, when an order granting inter partes reexamination issues, a patentee may move for a stay under §318, but the defendant may nevertheless seek a stay under the district court's inherent power. [¶] [W]e note that the district court ordinarily should not grant both a preliminary injunction and a stay. A preliminary injunction should not be granted if there is a substantial issue of patent validity. Similarly, a stay should ordinarily not be granted unless there is a substantial patentability issue raised in the inter partes reexamination proceeding. Thus, both a preliminary injunction and a stay ordinarily should not be granted at the same time. A grant of a preliminary injunction followed by a stay of the district court proceedings could subject an accused infringer to unfair and undesirable delay in reaching a final resolution."

CHAPTER 31[B*]. INTER PARTES REVIEW

§311[B*]. INTER PARTES REVIEW

Section 311[B] is effective Sept. 16, 2012, and is effective for patents issued before, on, or after that date.*

(a) In general.—Subject to the provisions of this chapter, a person who is not the owner of a patent may file with the Office a petition to institute an inter partes review of the patent. The Director shall establish, by regulation, fees to be paid by the person requesting the review, in such amounts as the Director determines to be reasonable, considering the aggregate costs of the review.

(b) Scope.—A petitioner in an inter partes review may request to cancel as unpatentable 1 or more claims of a patent only on a ground that could be raised under section 102 or 103 and only on the basis of prior art consisting of patents or printed publications.

(c) Filing deadline.—A petition for inter partes review shall be filed after the later of either—

(1) the date that is 9 months after the grant of a patent; or

(2) if a post-grant review is instituted under chapter 32, the date of the termination of such post-grant review.

History of 35 U.S.C. §311[B*]: Sept. 16, 2011, P.L. 112-29, §6(a), 125 Stat. 299; Jan. 14, 2013, P.L. 112-274, §1(d), 126 Stat. 2456.

See also 37 C.F.R. §§42.1-42.123; Office Patent Trial Practice Guide, p. 1336.

ANNOTATIONS

Oil States Energy Servs. v. Greene's Energy Grp., 137 S.Ct. 2239, 2239 (2017). Issue for review: Whether inter partes review—an adversarial process used by the PTO to analyze the validity of existing patents—violates the Constitution by extinguishing private property rights through a non-Article III forum without a jury.

MPHJ Tech. Invs. v. Ricoh Ams. Corp., 847 F.3d 1363, 1364, 121 U.S.P.Q.2d 1625, 1626 (Fed.Cir.2017). "[W]hen unexpired patents are reviewed by the Board, the claims are given their broadest reasonable interpretation consistent with the specification and the prosecution history, from the viewpoint of persons skilled in the field of the invention."

§312[B*]. PETITIONS

Section 312[B] is effective Sept. 16, 2012, and is effective for patents issued before, on, or after that date.*

(a) Requirements of petition.—A petition filed under section 311 may be considered only if—

(1) the petition is accompanied by payment of the fee established by the Director under section 311;

(2) the petition identifies all real parties in interest;

(3) the petition identifies, in writing and with particularity, each claim challenged, the grounds on which the challenge to each claim is based, and the evidence that supports the grounds for the challenge to each claim, including—

(A) copies of patents and printed publications that the petitioner relies upon in support of the petition; and

(B) affidavits or declarations of supporting evidence and opinions, if the petitioner relies on expert opinions;

(4) the petition provides such other information as the Director may require by regulation; and

(5) the petitioner provides copies of any of the documents required under paragraphs (2), (3), and (4) to the patent owner or, if applicable, the designated representative of the patent owner.

(b) Public availability.—As soon as practicable after the receipt of a petition under section 311, the Director shall make the petition available to the public.

History of 35 U.S.C. §312[B*]: Sept. 16, 2011, P.L. 112-29, §6(a), 125 Stat. 300.

See also 37 C.F.R. §§42.20-42.25, 42.100-42.107; Office Patent Trial Practice Guide, p. 1336.

§313[B*]. PRELIMINARY RESPONSE TO PETITION

Section 313[B] is effective Sept. 16, 2012, and is effective for patents issued before, on, or after that date.*

If an inter partes review petition is filed under section 311, the patent owner shall have the right to file a preliminary response to the petition, within a time period set by the Director, that sets forth reasons why no inter partes review should be instituted based upon the failure of the petition to meet any requirement of this chapter.

History of 35 U.S.C. §313[B*]: Sept. 16, 2011, P.L. 112-29, §6(a), 125 Stat. 300.

See also 37 C.F.R. §§42.20-42.25, 42.100-42.107, 42.120; Office Patent Trial Practice Guide, p. 1336.

§314[B*]. INSTITUTION OF INTER PARTES REVIEW

Section 314[B] is effective Sept. 16, 2012, and is effective for patents issued before, on, or after that date.*

(a) Threshold.—The Director may not authorize an inter partes review to be instituted unless the Director determines that the information presented in the petition filed under section 311 and any response filed under section 313 shows that there is a reasonable likelihood that the petitioner would prevail with respect to at least 1 of the claims challenged in the petition.

(b) Timing.—The Director shall determine whether to institute an inter partes review under this chapter pursuant to a petition filed under section 311 within 3 months after—

(1) receiving a preliminary response to the petition under section 313; or

(2) if no such preliminary response is filed, the last date on which such response may be filed.

(c) Notice.—The Director shall notify the petitioner and patent owner, in writing, of the Director's determination under subsection (a), and shall make such notice available to the public as soon as is practicable. Such notice shall include the date on which the review shall commence.

(d) No appeal.—The determination by the Director whether to institute an inter partes review under this section shall be final and nonappealable.

History of 35 U.S.C. §314[B*]: Sept. 16, 2011, P.L. 112-29, §6(a), 125 Stat. 300.

See also 37 C.F.R. §§42.100-42.123; Office Patent Trial Practice Guide, p. 1336.

ANNOTATIONS

Cuozzo Speed Techs. v. Lee, ___ U.S. ___, 136 S.Ct. 2131, 2136, 119 U.S.P.Q.2d 1065, 1068 (2016). "Does [§314(d)] bar a court from considering whether the [PTO] wrongly 'determin[ed] ... to institute an [IPR]' ... when it did so on grounds not specifically mentioned in a third party's review request? [¶] We conclude that [§314(d)], though it may not bar consideration of a constitutional question, for example, does bar judicial review of the kind of mine-run claim at issue here, involving the [PTO's] decision to institute [IPR]. *At U.S. ___, S.Ct. 2141, U.S.P.Q.2d 1072:* [I]n light of §314(d)'s own text and the presumption favoring review, we emphasize that our interpretation applies where the grounds for attacking the decision to institute [IPR] consist of questions that are closely tied to the application and interpretation of statutes related to the [PTO's] decision to initiate [IPR]. This means that we need not, and do not, decide the precise effect of §314(d) on appeals that implicate constitutional questions, that depend on other less closely related statutes, or that present other questions of interpretation that reach, in terms of scope and impact, well beyond 'this section.'"

Aylus Networks, Inc. v. Apple Inc., 856 F.3d 1353, 1360, 122 U.S.P.Q.2d 1672, 1677 (Fed.Cir.2017). "[W]e should apply the [prosecution-disclaimer] doctrine in IPR proceedings before the PTO. Extending the prosecution disclaimer doctrine to IPR proceedings will ensure that claims are not argued one way in order to maintain their patentability and in a different way against accused infringers. *At F.3d 1361:* Because an IPR proceeding involves reexamination of an earlier administrative grant of a patent, it follows that statements made by a patent owner during an IPR proceeding can be considered during claim construction and relied upon to support a finding of prosecution disclaimer. Of course, to invoke the doctrine of prosecution disclaimer, any such statements must 'be both clear and unmistakable.' *At F.3d 1362, U.S.P.Q.2d 1678:* [W]e hold that statements made by a patent owner during an IPR proceeding, whether before or after an institution decision, can be considered for claim construction and relied upon to support a finding of prosecution disclaimer."

Medtronic, Inc. v. Robert Bosch Healthcare Sys., 839 F.3d 1382, 1384, 120 U.S.P.Q.2d 1484, 1486 (Fed.Cir. 2016). "We conclude that under ***Cuozzo*** a decision whether to institute [IPR] proceedings pursuant to §314(a) (the issue in ***Cuozzo***) and a reconsideration of that decision (the situation here) are both barred from review by §314(d). Interpreting the 'closely related' language in ***Cuozzo***, we recently concluded that questions regarding the application and interpretation of statutes 'closely related' to the decision whether to institute are necessarily, and at least, those that define the metes and bounds of the [IPR] process. It is difficult to conceive of a case more 'closely related' to a decision to institute proceedings than a reconsideration of that very decision." (Internal quotes omitted.)

Husky Injection Molding Sys. v. Athena Automation Ltd., 838 F.3d 1236, 1245, 120 U.S.P.Q.2d 1324, 1329-30 (Fed.Cir.2016). There is "a two-part inquiry for determining whether we may review a particular challenge to the decision whether to institute. First, we must determine whether the challenge at issue is closely tied to the application and interpretation of statutes related to the [PTO's] decision to initiate [IPR], or if it instead implicates constitutional questions, depends on other less closely related statutes, or presents other questions of interpretation that reach, in terms of scope and impact, well beyond this section. If the latter, our authority to review the decision to institute appears unfettered. But if the former, §314(d) forbids our review. One further exception remains, however. At the second step of the inquiry, we must ask if, despite the challenge being grounded in a statute closely related to that decision to institute, ... it is nevertheless directed to the [PTAB's] ultimate invalidation authority with respect to a specific patent.... *At F.3d 1246, U.S.P.Q.2d 1331:* [W]e conclude that the assignor estoppel question is not entitled to review under the three exceptions in ***Cuozzo***...." (Internal quotes omitted.)

In re Magnum Oil Tools Int'l, 829 F.3d 1364, 1381, 119 U.S.P.Q.2d 1541, 1552-53 (Fed.Cir.2016). "[W]e find no support for the PTO's position that the [PTAB] is free to adopt arguments on behalf of petitioners that could have been, but were not, raised by the petitioner during an IPR. Instead, the [PTAB] must base its decision on arguments that were advanced by a party, and to which the opposing party was given a chance to respond. ... Thus, while the PTO has broad authority to establish procedures for revisiting earlier-granted patents in IPRs, that authority is not so broad that it allows the PTO to raise, address, and decide unpatentability theories never presented by the petitioner and not supported by record evidence."

In re Dominion Dealer Solutions, LLC, 749 F.3d 1379, 1381, 110 U.S.P.Q.2d 1780, 1781 (Fed.Cir.2014). Petitioner "has no 'clear and indisputable' right to challenge a non-institution decision directly in this court, including by way of mandamus."

St. Jude Med., Cardiology Div., Inc. v. Volcano Corp., 749 F.3d 1373, 1375-76, 110 U.S.P.Q.2d 1777, 1779 (Fed.Cir.2014). "The statute separates the Director's decision to 'institute' the review, [35 U.S.C.] §314, on one hand, from the [PTAB's] 'conduct' of the review 'instituted' by the Director, [35 U.S.C.] §316(c), and the [PTAB's] subsequent 'written decision,' [35 U.S.C.] §318, on the other. And it applies one standard—based on 'reasonable likelihood' of success—to the Director's decision to institute, §314(a), and another standard—based on 'patentability'—to the [PTAB's] decision on the merits, §318(a). The statute thus establishes a two-step procedure for [IPR]: the Director's decision whether to institute a proceeding, followed (if the proceeding is instituted) by the [PTAB's] conduct of the proceeding and decision with respect to patentability. The statute provides for an appeal to this court only of the [PTAB's] decision at the second step, not the Director's decision at the first step."

§315[B*]. RELATION TO OTHER PROCEEDINGS OR ACTIONS

Section 315[B] is effective Sept. 16, 2012, and is effective for patents issued before, on, or after that date.*

(a) Infringer's civil action—

(1) Inter partes review barred by civil action.—An inter partes review may not be instituted if, before the date on which the petition for such a review is filed, the petitioner or real party in interest filed a civil action challenging the validity of a claim of the patent.

(2) Stay of civil action.—If the petitioner or real party in interest files a civil action challenging the validity of a claim of the patent on or after the date on which the petitioner files a petition for inter partes review of the patent, that civil action shall be automatically stayed until either—

(A) the patent owner moves the court to lift the stay;

(B) the patent owner files a civil action or counterclaim alleging that the petitioner or real party in interest has infringed the patent; or

(C) the petitioner or real party in interest moves the court to dismiss the civil action.

(3) Treatment of counterclaim.—A counterclaim challenging the validity of a claim of a patent does not constitute a civil action challenging the validity of a claim of a patent for purposes of this subsection.

(b) Patent owner's action.—An inter partes review may not be instituted if the petition requesting the proceeding is filed more than 1 year after the date on which the petitioner, real party in interest, or privy of the petitioner is served with a complaint alleging infringement of the patent. The time limitation set forth in the preceding sentence shall not apply to a request for joinder under subsection (c).

(c) Joinder.—If the Director institutes an inter partes review, the Director, in his or her discretion, may join as a party to that inter partes review any person who properly files a petition under section 311 that the Director, after receiving a preliminary response under section 313 or the expiration of the time for filing such a response, determines warrants the institution of an inter partes review under section 314.

(d) Multiple proceedings.—Notwithstanding sections 135(a), 251, and 252, and chapter 30, during the pendency of an inter partes review, if another proceeding or matter involving the patent is before the Office, the Director may determine the manner in which the inter partes review or other proceeding or matter may proceed, including providing for stay, transfer, consolidation, or termination of any such matter or proceeding.

(e) Estoppel—

(1) Proceedings before the office.—The petitioner in an inter partes review of a claim in a patent under this chapter that results in a final written decision under section 318(a), or the real party in interest or privy of the petitioner, may not request or maintain a proceeding before the Office with respect to that claim on any ground that the petitioner raised or reasonably could have raised during that inter partes review.

(2) Civil actions and other proceedings.—The petitioner in an inter partes review of a claim in a patent under this chapter that results in a final written decision under section 318(a), or the real party in interest or privy of the petitioner, may not assert either in a civil action arising in whole or in part under section 1338 of title 28 or in a proceeding before the International Trade Commission under section 337 of the Tariff Act of 1930 that the claim is invalid on any ground that the petitioner raised or reasonably could have raised during that inter partes review.

History of 35 U.S.C. §315[B*]: Sept. 16, 2011, P.L. 112-29, §6(a), 125 Stat. 300.

See also 37 C.F.R. §§42.101, 42.122; Office Patent Trial Practice Guide, p. 1336.

ANNOTATIONS

Wi-Fi One, LLC v. Broadcom Corp., 878 F.3d 1364, 1367, 125 U.S.P.Q.2d 1269, 1270 (Fed.Cir.2018). "Congress has prohibited the Director of the [PTO] from instituting [IPR] if the petition requesting that review is filed more than one year after the petitioner, real party in interest, or privy of the petitioner is served with a complaint for patent infringement. Congress also provided that the Director's determination 'whether to institute an [IPR] under this section shall be final and nonappealable.' The question before us is whether the bar on judicial review of institution decisions in [35 U.S.C.] §314(d) applies to time-bar determinations made under [35 U.S.C.] §315(b). [¶] We recognize the strong presumption in favor of judicial review of agency actions. To overcome this presumption, Congress must clearly and convincingly indicate its intent to prohibit judicial review. We find no clear and convincing indication of such congressional intent. We therefore hold that the time-bar determinations under §315(b) are appealable…."

Bosch Auto. Serv. Solutions, LLC v. Matal, 878 F.3d 1027, 1040, 125 U.S.P.Q.2d 1130, 1140 (Fed.Cir. 2017). "[T]he petitioner bears the burden of proving that the proposed amended claims are unpatentable 'by a preponderance of the evidence.' This burden of proof allocation applies for questions of indefiniteness, as with other questions of unpatentability."

Aqua Prods. v. Matal, 872 F.3d 1290, 1310-11, 124 U.S.P.Q.2d 1257, 1268 (Fed.Cir.2017). Section 315 "is only consistent with the remainder of the AIA if the petitioner bears the burden to prove all propositions of unpatentability. Where the petitioner bears the burden, it is logical to estop the petitioner from raising that ground in the future, whether related to originally challenged claims or entered amended claims. If the patent owner were to bear the burden to demonstrate the patentability of proposed amended claims and to do so by reference to prior art not addressed in the IPR, it would be illogical to say that the *petitioner* is thereafter estopped from anything as to those claims."

MCM Portfolio LLC v. Hewlett-Packard Co., 812 F.3d 1284, 1285, 117 U.S.P.Q.2d 1284, 1285 (Fed.Cir. 2015). "We hold that we lack jurisdiction to review the [PTAB's] decision that the institution of [IPR] was not barred by … §315(b)…."

§316[B*]. CONDUCT OF INTER PARTES REVIEW

Section 316[B] is effective Sept. 16, 2012, and is effective for patents issued before, on, or after that date.*

(a) Regulations.—The Director shall prescribe regulations—

(1) providing that the file of any proceeding under this chapter shall be made available to the public, except that any petition or document filed with the intent that it be sealed shall, if accompanied by a motion to seal, be treated as sealed pending the outcome of the ruling on the motion;

(2) setting forth the standards for the showing of sufficient grounds to institute a review under section 314(a);

(3) establishing procedures for the submission of supplemental information after the petition is filed;

(4) establishing and governing inter partes review under this chapter and the relationship of such review to other proceedings under this title;

(5) setting forth standards and procedures for discovery of relevant evidence, including that such discovery shall be limited to—

(A) the deposition of witnesses submitting affidavits or declarations; and

(B) what is otherwise necessary in the interest of justice;

(6) prescribing sanctions for abuse of discovery, abuse of process, or any other improper use of the proceeding, such as to harass or to cause unnecessary delay or an unnecessary increase in the cost of the proceeding;

(7) providing for protective orders governing the exchange and submission of confidential information;

(8) providing for the filing by the patent owner of a response to the petition under section 313 after an inter partes review has been instituted, and requiring that the patent owner file with such response, through affidavits or declarations, any additional factual evidence and expert opinions on which the patent owner relies in support of the response;

(9) setting forth standards and procedures for allowing the patent owner to move to amend the patent under subsection (d) to cancel a challenged claim or propose a reasonable number of substitute claims, and ensuring that any information submitted by the patent owner in support of any amendment entered under subsection (d) is made available to the public as part of the prosecution history of the patent;

(10) providing either party with the right to an oral hearing as part of the proceeding;

(11) requiring that the final determination in an inter partes review be issued not later than 1 year after the date on which the Director notices the institution of a review under this chapter, except that the Director may, for good cause shown, extend the 1-year period by not more than 6 months, and may adjust the time periods in this paragraph in the case of joinder under section 315(c);

(12) setting a time period for requesting joinder under section 315(c); and

(13) providing the petitioner with at least 1 opportunity to file written comments within a time period established by the Director.

(b) Considerations.—In prescribing regulations under this section, the Director shall consider the effect of any such regulation on the economy, the integrity of the patent system, the efficient administration of the Office, and the ability of the Office to timely complete proceedings instituted under this chapter.

(c) Patent trial and appeal board.—The Patent Trial and Appeal Board shall, in accordance with section 6, conduct each inter partes review instituted under this chapter.

(d) Amendment of the patent—

(1) In general.—During an inter partes review instituted under this chapter, the patent owner may file 1 motion to amend the patent in 1 or more of the following ways:

(A) Cancel any challenged patent claim.

(B) For each challenged claim, propose a reasonable number of substitute claims.

(2) Additional motions.—Additional motions to amend may be permitted upon the joint request of the petitioner and the patent owner to materially advance the settlement of a proceeding under section 317, or as permitted by regulations prescribed by the Director.

(3) Scope of claims.—An amendment under this subsection may not enlarge the scope of the claims of the patent or introduce new matter.

(e) Evidentiary standards.—In an inter partes review instituted under this chapter, the petitioner shall have the burden of proving a proposition of unpatentability by a preponderance of the evidence.

History of 35 U.S.C. §316[B*]: Sept. 16, 2011, P.L. 112-29, §6(a), 125 Stat. 302.

See also 37 C.F.R. §§42.100-42.123; Office Patent Trial Practice Guide, p. 1336.

ANNOTATIONS

Cuozzo Speed Techs. v. Lee, ___ U.S. ___, 136 S.Ct. 2131, 2136, 119 U.S.P.Q.2d 1065, 1068 (2016). "Does [35 U.S.C. §316(a)(4)] authorize the [PTO] to issue a regulation stating that the agency, in [IPR], 'shall [construe a patent claim according to] its broadest reasonable construction in light of the specification of the patent in which it appears'? [¶] We ... conclude that [§316(a)(4)] authorizes the [PTO] to issue [37 C.F.R. §42.100(b)]. *At U.S. ___, S.Ct. 2146, U.S.P.Q.2d 1075:* A district court may find a patent claim to be valid, and the agency may later cancel that claim in its own review. ... This possibility, however, has long been present in our patent system, which provides different tracks—one in the [PTO] and one in the courts—for the review and adjudication of patent claims."

Aqua Prods. v. Matal, 872 F.3d 1290, 1295-96, 124 U.S.P.Q.2d 1257, 1258 (Fed.Cir.2017). "[W]e consider the proper allocation of the burden of proof when amended claims are proffered during [IPRs]. Specifically, we consider how the AIA's statutory language in 35 U.S.C. §316(e), which places 'the burden of proving a proposition of unpatentability by a preponderance of the evidence' onto the petitioner in an IPR, applies to claim amendments authorized by ... §316(d), and whether the [PTAB's] current practices with respect to amendments accord with that application. [¶] [W]e believe that §316(e) unambiguously requires the petitioner to prove all propositions of unpatentability, including for amended claims. ... Because a majority of the judges participating in this en banc proceeding believe the statute is ambiguous on this point, we conclude in the alternative that there is no interpretation of the statute by the Director of the [PTO] to which this court must defer under ***Chevron, U.S.A. Inc. v. [Natural Res. Def. Council, Inc.]***, 467 U.S. 837 ... (1984). And we believe that, in the absence of any required deference, the most reasonable reading of the AIA is one that places the burden of persuasion with respect to the patentability of amended claims on the petitioner. [¶] Because the participating judges have different views—both as to the judgment we should reach and as to the rationale we should employ in support of that judgment, ... today's judgment is narrow. The final written decision of the [PTAB] in this case is vacated insofar as it denied the patent owner's motion to amend the patent. The matter is remanded for the [PTAB] to issue a final decision under [35 U.S.C.] §318(a) assessing the patentability of the proposed substitute claims without placing the burden of persuasion on the patent owner."

In re Smith Int'l, 871 F.3d 1375, 1382-83, 124 U.S.P.Q.2d 1210, 1215 (Fed.Cir.2017). "'[T]he protocol of giving claims their broadest reasonable interpretation ... does not include giving claims a legally incorrect interpretation' 'divorced from the specification and the record evidence.' [¶] The correct inquiry in giving a claim term its broadest reasonable interpretation in light of the specification is not whether the specification proscribes or precludes some broad reading of the claim term adopted by the examiner. And it is not simply an interpretation that is not inconsistent with the specification. It is an interpretation that corresponds with what and how the inventor describes his invention in the specification, *i.e.*, an interpretation that is 'consistent with the specification.'"

Ethicon Endo-Surgery, Inc. v. Covidien LP, 812 F.3d 1023, 1028, 117 U.S.P.Q.2d 1639, 1642 (Fed.Cir. 2016). Appellant "challenges the final decision of the [PTAB], arguing that the final decision should be set aside because it was made by the same panel that made the decision to institute [IPR]. *At F.3d 1029, U.S.P.Q.2d 1643:* [W]here ... there are no other separate procedural-fairness infirmities alleged, the PTO's assignment of the institution and final decisions to one panel of the [PTAB] does not violate due process under governing Supreme Court precedent. *At F.3d 1033, U.S.P.Q.2d 1646:* [B]oth as a matter of inherent authority and general rulemaking authority, the Director had authority to delegate the institution decision to the [PTAB]. There is nothing in the Constitution or the statute that precludes the same [PTAB] panel from making the decision to institute and then rendering the final decision."

Abbott Labs. v. Cordis Corp., 710 F.3d 1318, 1326, 106 U.S.P.Q.2d 1227, 1233 (Fed.Cir.2013). "Congress replaced inter partes reexamination with a new proceeding called [IPR]. The purpose of this reform was to 'convert[] inter partes reexamination from an examinational to an adjudicative proceeding,' and one of its touted 'improvements' over the former proceeding is to allow the limited use of depositions. In particular, Congress provided for depositions of affiants in the proceeding, and also authorized parties to 'seek such discovery as the Patent Office determines is otherwise necessary in the interest of justice.' In the course of implementing these mandates, the PTO has recognized that the AIA authorizes parties to seek [35 U.S.C.] §24 subpoenas in the new proceedings."

§317[B*]. SETTLEMENT

Section 317[B] is effective Sept. 16, 2012, and is effective for patents issued before, on, or after that date.*

(a) In general.—An inter partes review instituted under this chapter shall be terminated with respect to any petitioner upon the joint request of the petitioner and the patent owner, unless the Office has decided the merits of the proceeding before the request for termination is filed. If the inter partes review is terminated with respect to a petitioner under this section, no estoppel under section 315(e) shall attach to the petitioner, or to the real party in interest or privy of the petitioner, on the basis of that petitioner's institution of that inter partes review. If no petitioner remains in the inter partes review, the Office may terminate the review or proceed to a final written decision under section 318(a).

(b) Agreements in writing.—Any agreement or understanding between the patent owner and a petitioner, including any collateral agreements referred to in such agreement or understanding, made in connection with, or in contemplation of, the termination of an inter partes review under this section shall be in writing and a true copy of such agreement or understanding shall be filed in the Office before the termination of the inter partes review as between the parties. At the request of a party to the proceeding, the agreement or understanding shall be treated as business confidential information, shall be kept separate from the file of the involved patents, and shall be made available only to Federal Government agencies on written request, or to any person on a showing of good cause.

History of 35 U.S.C. §317[B*]: Sept. 16, 2011, P.L. 112-29, §6(a), 125 Stat. 303.

See also 37 C.F.R. §42.74; Office Patent Trial Practice Guide, p. 1336.

ANNOTATIONS

Aqua Prods. v. Matal, 872 F.3d 1290, 1311, 124 U.S.P.Q.2d 1257, 1268 (Fed.Cir.2017). "[A] petitioner in an IPR may decline to maintain a challenge to a narrower amended claim if the patent owner agrees not to seek to enforce any claim scope broader than the scope of the proposed amendment. The first sentence of [35 U.S.C.] §317(a) states that the PTO *must* terminate the participation of a particular petitioner, in a particular IPR, based on the filing of a joint motion and settlement by that petitioner and the patent owner. At that point, either (1) the patent owner is the only party remaining in the IPR, and the PTO can terminate the review or proceed to a final written decision as described in [35 U.S.C.] §318(a); or (2) other petitioners are still participating in the IPR, and the IPR moves forward as usual. [¶] If a settlement occurs and the IPR is terminated, no certificate incorporating the amendment into the patent ever issues. [¶] The final sentence of §317(a) gives the [PTAB] the option to proceed to final judgment in any proceeding where the original petitioners choose not to continue their challenge. The [PTAB] might do this for any number of reasons. For example, the [PTAB] may decide that the showing of unpatentability with respect to the challenged claims is so strong that the public is better served by a cancellation of those claims; it may decide that even the narrower, amended claims are unpatentable in the face of the prior art on which the IPR was predicated and that confirmation of that fact is important; or it may decide that the amended claims are patentable in the face of the prior art challenges precisely because they are narrower than the original claims, and that it is important for the patent to be amended to reflect that fact so the public can benefit from that narrowing."

§318[B*]. DECISION OF THE BOARD

Section 318[B] is effective Sept. 16, 2012, and is effective for patents issued before, on, or after that date.*

(a) Final written decision.—If an inter partes review is instituted and not dismissed under this chapter, the Patent Trial and Appeal Board shall issue a final written decision with respect to the patentability of any patent claim challenged by the petitioner and any new claim added under section 316(d).

(b) Certificate.—If the Patent Trial and Appeal Board issues a final written decision under subsection (a) and the time for appeal has expired or any appeal has terminated, the Director shall issue and publish a certificate canceling any claim of the patent finally determined to be unpatentable, confirming any claim of the patent determined to be patentable, and incorporating in the patent by operation of the certificate any new or amended claim determined to be patentable.

(c) Intervening rights.—Any proposed amended or new claim determined to be patentable and incorporated into a patent following an inter partes review under this chapter shall have the same effect as that specified in section 252 for reissued patents on the right of any person who made, purchased, or used within the United States, or imported into the United States, anything patented by such proposed amended or new claim, or who made substantial preparation therefor, before the issuance of a certificate under subsection (b).

(d) Data on length of review.—The Office shall make available to the public data describing the length of time between the institution of, and the issuance of a final written decision under subsection (a) for, each inter partes review.

History of 35 U.S.C. §318[B*]: Sept. 16, 2011, P.L. 112-29, §6(a), 125 Stat. 304.

See also 37 C.F.R. pt. 42; Office Patent Trial Practice Guide, p. 1336.

ANNOTATIONS

SAS Inst. v. Lee, 137 S.Ct. 2160, 2160 (2017). Issue for review: Whether 35 U.S.C. §318(a), which provides that the PTAB in an IPR shall issue a final written decision with respect to the patentability of any patent claim challenged by the petitioner, requires that the PTAB issue a final written decision as to every claim challenged by the petitioner, or whether it allows that Board to issue a final written decision with respect to the patentability of only some of the patent claims challenged by the petitioner, as the U.S. Court of Appeals for the Federal Circuit held.

Aqua Prods. v. Matal, 872 F.3d 1290, 1296, 124 U.S.P.Q.2d 1257, 1258 (Fed.Cir.2017). "[W]e believe that the [PTAB] must consider the entirety of the record before it when assessing the patentability of amended claims under §318(a) and must justify any conclusions of unpatentability with respect to amended claims based on that record. [¶] Because the participating judges have different views—both as to the judgment we should reach and as to the rationale we should employ in support of that judgment ... today's judgment is narrow. *At F.3d 1311, U.S.P.Q.2d 1268:* Should the [PTAB] elect to continue to a final written decision in this scenario, §318(a) requires the [PTAB] to undertake a patentability analysis on all original and amended claims in the proceeding. Thus, it is *at that point*, and not earlier, that the statute contemplates consideration of an amended claim's patentability."

Synopsys, Inc. v. Mentor Graphics Corp., 814 F.3d 1309, 1316-17, 117 U.S.P.Q.2d 1753, 1760 (Fed.Cir. 2016), *overruled on other grounds*, ***Aqua Prods. v. Matal***, 872 F.3d 1290 (Fed.Cir.2017). "[W]e find no statutory requirement that the [PTAB's] final decision address every claim raised in a petition for [IPR]. Section 318(a) only requires the [PTAB] to address claims as to which review was granted."

§319[B*]. APPEAL

Section 319[B] is effective Sept. 16, 2012, and is effective for patents issued before, on, or after that date.*

A party dissatisfied with the final written decision of the Patent Trial and Appeal Board under section 318(a) may appeal the decision pursuant to sections 141 through 144. Any party to the inter partes review shall have the right to be a party to the appeal.

History of 35 U.S.C. §319[B*]: Sept. 16, 2011, P.L. 112-29, §6(a), 125 Stat. 304.

See also Office Patent Trial Practice Guide, p. 1336.

ANNOTATIONS

Arthrex, Inc. v. Smith & Nephew, Inc., 880 F.3d 1345, 1349, 125 U.S.P.Q.2d 1532, ___ (Fed.Cir.2018). "Because [35 U.S.C.] §319 does not on its face provide the exclusive means for appeal over IPR decisions not subject to the appeal bar, and [28 U.S.C.] §1295(a)(4)(A) on its face provides a right to appeal, we conclude that a final decision that disposes of an IPR proceeding in the form of an adverse judgment is a 'decision' from the [PTAB] with respect to IPRs under title 35 and that §1295 provides a right to appeal a final adverse judgment. This is also not a situation in which §319 impliedly precludes review under §1295."

Synopsys, Inc. v. Mentor Graphics Corp., 814 F.3d 1309, 1314, 117 U.S.P.Q.2d 1753, 1758 (Fed.Cir. 2016), *overruled on other grounds*, ***Aqua Prods. v. Matal***, 872 F.3d 1290 (Fed.Cir.2017). "The decision of the [PTAB] to institute [IPR] cannot be appealed. The PTO argues that the 'logical import' of [appellant's] challenge is a challenge to the decision to institute. However, [appellant] does not challenge the decision to institute but rather the scope of the final decision itself. Because [appellant] challenges the final decision, we can hear this appeal. The statute allows '[a] party dissatisfied with the final written decision of the [PTAB]' to 'appeal the decision.' *At F.3d 1314 n.4, U.S.P.Q.2d 1758 n.4:* We note that an issue relating to institution does not become appealable simply because the [PTAB] mentions that issue in its final decision."

CHAPTER 32. POST-GRANT REVIEW

Chapter 32 is effective Sept. 16, 2012. Generally, chapter 32 is effective for patent applications and patents issued on those applications that contain or contained a claim to a claimed invention that has an effective filing date on or after Mar. 16, 2013, or for any applications or patents that contain or contained a claim to a specific reference under §120, §121, or §365(c) that have an effective filing date on or after Mar. 16, 2013. For purposes of an interference that is commenced before Sept. 16, 2012, the Director may deem the Patent Trial and Appeal Board to be the Board of Patent Appeals and Interferences, and may allow the Patent Trial and Appeal Board to conduct any further proceedings in that interference. The authorization to appeal or have remedy from derivation proceedings in §§141(d) and 146, and the jurisdiction to entertain appeals from derivation proceedings in 28 U.S.C. §1295(a)(4)(A), extends to any final decision in an interference that is commenced before Sept. 16, 2012, and that is not dismissed.

There is also a transitional post-grant review for covered business-method (CBM) patents under chapter 32. This transitional post-grant review is Sept. 16, 2012, and applies to any CBM patent issued before, on, or after that date, unless the patent is eligible for post-grant review. The effectiveness is subject to several exceptions: (1) A person may not file a petition for a transitional proceeding with respect to a CBM patent unless the person or the person's real party in interest or privy has been sued for infringement of the patent or has been charged with infringement under that patent. (2) A petitioner in a transitional proceeding who challenges the validity of one or more claims in a CBM patent on a ground raised under §102 or §103 in effect before Mar. 16, 2013, may support the ground only on the basis of (A) prior art that is described by §102(a) in effect before Mar. 16, 2013, or (B) prior art that discloses the invention more than one year before the date of the application for patent in the U.S. and would be described by §102(a) in effect before Mar. 16, 2013, if the disclosure had been made by another before the invention by the applicant for patent. (3) A petitioner (or the real party in interest) in a transitional proceeding that results in a final written decision under §328(a) with respect to a claim in a CBM patent may not assert, either in a civil action arising in whole or in part under 28 U.S.C. §1338 or in a proceeding before the International Trade Commission under 19 U.S.C. §1337, that the claim is invalid on any ground that the petitioner raised during that transitional proceeding. (4) The Director of the USPTO may institute a transitional proceeding only for a patent that is a CBM patent.

§321. POST-GRANT REVIEW

Subsection (c) does not apply to a transitional post-grant review proceeding for business-method patents.

(a) In general.—Subject to the provisions of this chapter, a person who is not the owner of a patent may file with the Office a petition to institute a post-grant review of the patent. The Director shall establish, by regulation, fees to be paid by the person requesting the review, in such amounts as the Director determines to be reasonable, considering the aggregate costs of the post-grant review.

(b) Scope.—A petitioner in a post-grant review may request to cancel as unpatentable 1 or more claims of a patent on any ground that could be raised under paragraph (2) or (3) of section 282(b) (relating to invalidity of the patent or any claim).

(c) Filing deadline.—A petition for a post-grant review may only be filed not later than the date that is 9 months after the date of the grant of the patent or of the issuance of a reissue patent (as the case may be).

History of 35 U.S.C. §321: Sept. 16, 2011, P.L. 112-29, §6(d), 125 Stat. 306.

See also 37 C.F.R. §§42.1-42.80, 42.200-42.304; Office Patent Trial Practice Guide, p. 1336.

ANNOTATIONS

Secure Axcess, LLC v. PNC Bank, 848 F.3d 1370, 1380-81, 121 U.S.P.Q.2d 1647, 1653 (Fed.Cir.2017). "In the case before us, the [PTAB,] as part of its broader discussion of what is a 'financial product or service,' concluded that '[t]he method and apparatus claimed by the ... patent perform operations used in the practice, administration, or management of a financial product or service *and are incidental to a financial activity*.' Consistent with ***Unwired Planet***, we hold that the emphasized phrase is not a part of the statutory definition of what is a CBM patent, and, as we did in ***Unwired Planet***, we conclude that such a definition of a CBM patent is beyond the scope of the statutory standard and thus 'not in accordance with law.' *At F.3d 1382, U.S.P.Q.2d 1654:* Like the lightbulb example in ***Unwired Planet***, just because an invention could be used by various institutions that include a financial institution, among others, does not mean a patent on the invention qualifies under the proper definition of a CBM patent."

Unwired Planet, LLC v. Google Inc., 841 F.3d 1376, 1382, 120 U.S.P.Q.2d 1679, 1683-84 (Fed.Cir. 2016). "The [PTAB's] application of the 'incidental to' and 'complementary to' language from the PTO policy statement instead of the statutory definition renders superfluous the limits Congress placed on the definition of a CBM patent. CBM patents are limited to those with claims that are directed to methods and apparatuses of particular types and with particular uses 'in the practice, administration, or management of a financial product or service.' The patent for a novel lightbulb that is found to work particularly well in bank vaults does not become a CBM patent because of its incidental or complementary use in banks. Likewise, it cannot be the case that a patent covering a method and corresponding apparatuses becomes a CBM patent because its practice could involve a potential sale of a good or service."

Intellectual Ventures II LLC v. JPMorgan Chase & Co., 781 F.3d 1372, 1379, 114 U.S.P.Q.2d 1387, 1392 (Fed.Cir.2015). "[W]e do not have jurisdiction under §18(b)(2) of the AIA to consider an interlocutory appeal from a decision on a motion to stay until the PTAB institutes a [CBM review] proceeding."

§322. PETITIONS

(a) Requirements of petition.—A petition filed under section 321 may be considered only if—

(1) the petition is accompanied by payment of the fee established by the Director under section 321;

(2) the petition identifies all real parties in interest;

(3) the petition identifies, in writing and with particularity, each claim challenged, the grounds on which the challenge to each claim is based, and the evidence that supports the grounds for the challenge to each claim, including—

(A) copies of patents and printed publications that the petitioner relies upon in support of the petition; and

(B) affidavits or declarations of supporting evidence and opinions, if the petitioner relies on other factual evidence or on expert opinions;

(4) the petition provides such other information as the Director may require by regulation; and

(5) the petitioner provides copies of any of the documents required under paragraphs (2), (3), and (4) to the patent owner or, if applicable, the designated representative of the patent owner.

(b) Public availability.—As soon as practicable after the receipt of a petition under section 321, the Director shall make the petition available to the public.

History of 35 U.S.C. §322: Sept. 16, 2011, P.L. 112-29, §6(d), 125 Stat. 306.

See also 37 C.F.R. §§42.204-42.207, 42.304; Office Patent Trial Practice Guide, p. 1336.

§323. PRELIMINARY RESPONSE TO PETITION

If a post-grant review petition is filed under section 321, the patent owner shall have the right to file a preliminary response to the petition, within a time period set by the Director, that sets forth reasons why no post-grant review should be instituted based upon the failure of the petition to meet any requirement of this chapter.

History of 35 U.S.C. §323: Sept. 16, 2011, P.L. 112-29, §6(d), 125 Stat. 306.

See also 37 C.F.R. §42.207; Office Patent Trial Practice Guide, p. 1336.

§324. INSTITUTION OF POST-GRANT REVIEW

(a) Threshold.—The Director may not authorize a post-grant review to be instituted unless the Director determines that the information presented in the petition filed under section 321, if such information is not rebutted, would demonstrate that it is more likely than not that at least 1 of the claims challenged in the petition is unpatentable.

(b) Additional grounds.—The determination required under subsection (a) may also be satisfied by a showing that the petition raises a novel or unsettled legal question that is important to other patents or patent applications.

(c) Timing.—The Director shall determine whether to institute a post-grant review under this chapter pursuant to a petition filed under section 321 within 3 months after—

(1) receiving a preliminary response to the petition under section 323; or

(2) if no such preliminary response is filed, the last date on which such response may be filed.

(d) Notice.—The Director shall notify the petitioner and patent owner, in writing, of the Director's determination under subsection (a) or (b), and shall make such notice available to the public as soon as is practicable. Such notice shall include the date on which the review shall commence.

(e) No appeal.—The determination by the Director whether to institute a post-grant review under this section shall be final and nonappealable.

History of 35 U.S.C. §324: Sept. 16, 2011, P.L. 112-29, §6(d), 125 Stat. 306.

See also 37 C.F.R. §§42.208, 42.302, 42.303; Office Patent Trial Practice Guide, p. 1336.

ANNOTATIONS

Return Mail, Inc. v. U.S. Postal Serv., 868 F.3d 1350, 1359, 123 U.S.P.Q.2d 1813, 1819 (Fed.Cir.2017). "[W]e hold that [35 U.S.C.] §324(e) does not bar judicial review of the [PTAB's] decision that a party satisfies [AIA] §18(a)(1)(B)'s requirements to petition for CBM review."

SightSound Techs. v. Apple Inc., 809 F.3d 1307, 1313-14, 117 U.S.P.Q.2d 1341, 1345 (Fed.Cir.2015). Appellant "argues that the [PTAB] erred in considering obviousness because [appellee] failed to include such argument in its petitions. As in [***In re Cuozzo Speed Techs.***, 793 F.3d 1268 (Fed.Cir.2015),] the statute does not limit the [PTAB's] authority at the final decision stage to grounds alleged in the CBM petitions. The reasoning of ***Cuozzo*** and ***Achates*** [***Reference Publ'g v. Apple Inc.***, 803 F.3d 652 (Fed.Cir.2015),] applies not only to [35 U.S.C.] §314(d), involved in ***Cuozzo*** and ***Achates***, but also to [35 U.S.C.] §324(e), the identical provision applicable to CBM review. [Appellant] argues that the 'under this section' language in §324(e) only bars review of challenges to institution decisions based on the grounds specified in §324(a) and (b). We reject this argument. Section 324(e) bars review of any institution decision. ***Cuozzo*** and ***Achates*** control, and the challenge is therefore barred by §324. We also see no basis for mandamus relief on the [PTAB's] initiation decision, because 'the situation here is far from satisfying the clear-and-indisputable requirement for mandamus.'"

Editor's note: The holding of ***SightSound*** is in doubt after the Federal Circuit's en banc decision in ***Wi-Fi One, LLC v. Broadcom Corp.***, 878 F.3d 1364, 1375 (Fed.Cir.2018), overruling the holding in ***Achates***.

Versata Dev. Grp. v. SAP Am., Inc., 793 F.3d 1306, 1320, 115 U.S.P.Q.2d 1681, 1690-91 (Fed.Cir.2015). "[W]hen doubt about congressional intent exists, the general presumption favoring judicial review of rights-changing administrative action is controlling. [A]n agency seeking to overcome this strong presumption faces a 'heavy burden' and must do so by 'clear and convincing' evidence. [¶] [N]othing in [35 U.S.C.] §324(e) meets the high standard for precluding review of whether the PTAB has violated a limit on its invalidation authority under §18 [of the AIA]."

VirtualAgility Inc. v. Salesforce.com, Inc., 759 F.3d 1307, 1313, 111 U.S.P.Q.2d 1763, 1768-69 (Fed.Cir. 2014). "Congress made post-grant review more difficult to obtain than reexamination by raising the standard from 'a substantial new question of patentability[ ]' ... to 'more likely than not ... unpatentable[ ]'.... Congress clearly did not intend district courts to hold mini-trials reviewing the PTAB's decision on the merits of the [covered-business-method (CBM)] review. To do so would overwhelm and dramatically expand the nature of the stay determination. If the district court were required to 'review' the merits of the PTAB's decision to institute a CBM proceeding as part of its stay determination, it would undermine the purpose of the stay. When the stay decision is then appealed to this court, we would be required to likewise review the PTAB's decision to institute a CBM proceeding. This is clearly not how or when Congress intended review of the PTAB's CBM determinations to take place. The stay determination is not the time or the place to review the PTAB's decisions to institute a CBM proceeding."

§325. RELATION TO OTHER PROCEEDINGS OR ACTIONS

Subsections (b), (e)(2), and (f) do not apply to a transitional post-grant review proceeding for business-method patents.

(a) Infringer's civil action—

(1) Post-grant review barred by civil action.—A post-grant review may not be instituted under this chapter if, before the date on which the petition for such a review is filed, the petitioner or real party in interest filed a civil action challenging the validity of a claim of the patent.

(2) Stay of civil action.—If the petitioner or real party in interest files a civil action challenging the validity of a claim of the patent on or after the date on which the petitioner files a petition for post-grant review of the patent, that civil action shall be automatically stayed until either—

(A) the patent owner moves the court to lift the stay;

(B) the patent owner files a civil action or counterclaim alleging that the petitioner or real party in interest has infringed the patent; or

(C) the petitioner or real party in interest moves the court to dismiss the civil action.

(3) Treatment of counterclaim.—A counterclaim challenging the validity of a claim of a patent does not constitute a civil action challenging the validity of a claim of a patent for purposes of this subsection.

(b) Preliminary injunctions.—If a civil action alleging infringement of a patent is filed within 3 months after the date on which the patent is granted, the court may not stay its consideration of the patent owner's motion for a preliminary injunction against infringement of the patent on the basis that a petition for post-grant review has been filed under this chapter or that such a post-grant review has been instituted under this chapter.

(c) Joinder.—If more than 1 petition for a post-grant review under this chapter is properly filed against the same patent and the Director determines that more than 1 of these petitions warrants the institution of a post-grant review under section 324, the Director may consolidate such reviews into a single post-grant review.

(d) Multiple proceedings.—Notwithstanding sections 135(a), 251, and 252, and chapter 30, during the pendency of any post-grant review under this chapter, if another proceeding or matter involving the patent is before the Office, the Director may determine the manner in which the post-grant review or other proceeding or matter may proceed, including providing for the stay, transfer, consolidation, or termination of any such matter or proceeding. In determining whether to institute or order a proceeding under this chapter, chapter 30, or chapter 31, the Director may take into account whether, and reject the petition or request because, the same or substantially the same prior art or arguments previously were presented to the Office.

(e) Estoppel—

(1) Proceedings before the office.—The petitioner in a post-grant review of a claim in a patent under this chapter that results in a final written decision under section 328(a), or the real party in interest or privy of the petitioner, may not request or maintain a proceeding before the Office with respect to that claim on any ground that the petitioner raised or reasonably could have raised during that post-grant review.

(2) Civil actions and other proceedings.—The petitioner in a post-grant review of a claim in a patent under this chapter that results in a final written decision under section 328(a), or the real party in interest or privy of the petitioner, may not assert either in a civil action arising in whole or in part under section 1338 of title 28 or in a proceeding before the International Trade Commission under section 337 of the Tariff Act of 1930 that the claim is invalid on any ground that the petitioner raised or reasonably could have raised during that post-grant review.

(f) Reissue patents.—A post-grant review may not be instituted under this chapter if the petition requests cancellation of a claim in a reissue patent that is identical to or narrower than a claim in the original patent from which the reissue patent was issued, and the time limitations in section 321(c) would bar filing a petition for a post-grant review for such original patent.

History of 35 U.S.C. §325: Sept. 16, 2011, P.L. 112-29, §6(d), 125 Stat. 307.
See also Office Patent Trial Practice Guide, p. 1336.

ANNOTATIONS

Credit Acceptance Corp. v. Westlake Servs., 859 F.3d 1044, 1049, 123 U.S.P.Q.2d 1100, 1104 (Fed.Cir. 2017). Petitioner "argue[s] that a determination by the [PTAB] on 35 U.S.C. §325(e)(1) is nonappealable, and therefore, this court has no jurisdiction to review the [PTAB's] estoppel determination. We disagree. *At F.3d 1051, U.S.P.Q.2d 1105:* [T]he estoppel dispute in this case is neither a challenge to the [PTAB's] institution decision, nor is it 'closely tied' to any 'statute[] related to the [PTO's] decision to initiate [CBM] review.' *At F.3d 1052, U.S.P.Q.2d 1106-07:* We conclude that we have jurisdiction to review the [respondent's] estoppel argument regarding 35 U.S.C. §325(e)(1). [¶] Because a final written decision does not determine the patentability of non-instituted claims, it follows that estoppel does not apply to those non-instituted claims in future proceedings before the PTO. On its face, the relevant IPR estoppel statute, [35 U.S.C.] §315(e)(1) (similar to the [post-grant review] estoppel statute, §325(e)(1)) applies on a claim-by-claim basis. It provides, '[t]he petitioner in an [IPR] *of a claim* in a patent ... that results in a final written decision under [35 U.S.C.] §318(a) ... may not request or maintain a proceeding before the [PTO] *with respect to that claim*....' There is no IPR estoppel with respect to a claim as to which no final written decision results. *At F.3d 1053:* We conclude that 35 U.S.C. §325(e)(1) does not apply in a subsequent proceeding to claims upon which the [PTAB] declined to institute review."

§326. CONDUCT OF POST-GRANT REVIEW

(a) Regulations.—The Director shall prescribe regulations—

(1) providing that the file of any proceeding under this chapter shall be made available to the public, except that any petition or document filed with the intent that it be sealed shall, if accompanied by a motion to seal, be treated as sealed pending the outcome of the ruling on the motion;

(2) setting forth the standards for the showing of sufficient grounds to institute a review under subsections (a) and (b) of section 324;

(3) establishing procedures for the submission of supplemental information after the petition is filed;

(4) establishing and governing a post-grant review under this chapter and the relationship of such review to other proceedings under this title;

(5) setting forth standards and procedures for discovery of relevant evidence, including that such discovery shall be limited to evidence directly related to factual assertions advanced by either party in the proceeding;

(6) prescribing sanctions for abuse of discovery, abuse of process, or any other improper use of the proceeding, such as to harass or to cause unnecessary delay or an unnecessary increase in the cost of the proceeding;

(7) providing for protective orders governing the exchange and submission of confidential information;

(8) providing for the filing by the patent owner of a response to the petition under section 323 after a post-grant review has been instituted, and requiring that the patent owner file with such response, through affidavits or declarations, any additional factual evidence and expert opinions on which the patent owner relies in support of the response;

(9) setting forth standards and procedures for allowing the patent owner to move to amend the patent under subsection (d) to cancel a challenged claim or propose a reasonable number of substitute claims, and ensuring that any information submitted by the patent owner in support of any amendment entered under subsection (d) is made available to the public as part of the prosecution history of the patent;

(10) providing either party with the right to an oral hearing as part of the proceeding;

(11) requiring that the final determination in any post-grant review be issued not later than 1 year after the date on which the Director notices the institution of a proceeding under this chapter, except that the Director may, for good cause shown, extend the 1-year period by not more than 6 months, and may adjust the time periods in this paragraph in the case of joinder under section 325(c); and

(12) providing the petitioner with at least 1 opportunity to file written comments within a time period established by the Director.

(b) Considerations.—In prescribing regulations under this section, the Director shall consider the effect of any such regulation on the economy, the integrity of the patent system, the efficient administration of the Office, and the ability of the Office to timely complete proceedings instituted under this chapter.

(c) Patent Trial and Appeal Board.—The Patent Trial and Appeal Board shall, in accordance with section 6, conduct each post-grant review instituted under this chapter.

(d) Amendment of the patent—

(1) In general.—During a post-grant review instituted under this chapter, the patent owner may file 1 motion to amend the patent in 1 or more of the following ways:

(A) Cancel any challenged patent claim.

(B) For each challenged claim, propose a reasonable number of substitute claims.

(2) Additional motions.—Additional motions to amend may be permitted upon the joint request of the petitioner and the patent owner to materially advance the settlement of a proceeding under section 327, or upon the request of the patent owner for good cause shown.

(3) Scope of claims.—An amendment under this subsection may not enlarge the scope of the claims of the patent or introduce new matter.

(e) Evidentiary standards.—In a post-grant review instituted under this chapter, the petitioner shall have the burden of proving a proposition of unpatentability by a preponderance of the evidence.

History of 35 U.S.C. §326: Sept. 16, 2011, P.L. 112-29, §6(d), 125 Stat. 308.

See also 37 C.F.R. §§42.220-42.224; Office Patent Trial Practice Guide, p. 1336.

§327. SETTLEMENT

(a) In general.—A post-grant review instituted under this chapter shall be terminated with respect to any petitioner upon the joint request of the petitioner and the patent owner, unless the Office has decided the merits of the proceeding before the request for termination is filed. If the post-grant review is terminated with respect to a petitioner under this section, no estoppel under section 325(e) shall attach to the petitioner, or to the real party in interest or privy of the petitioner, on the basis of that petitioner's institution of that post-grant review. If no petitioner remains in the post-grant review, the Office may terminate the post-grant review or proceed to a final written decision under section 328(a).

(b) Agreements in writing.—Any agreement or understanding between the patent owner and a petitioner, including any collateral agreements referred to in such agreement or understanding, made in connection with, or in contemplation of, the termination of a post-grant review under this section shall be in writing, and a true copy of such agreement or understanding shall be filed in the Office before the termination of the post-grant review as between the parties. At the request of a party to the proceeding, the agreement or understanding shall be treated as business confidential information, shall be kept separate from the file of the involved patents, and shall be made available only to Federal Government agencies on written request, or to any person on a showing of good cause.

History of 35 U.S.C. §327: Sept. 16, 2011, P.L. 112-29, §6(d), 125 Stat. 310.

See also Office Patent Trial Practice Guide, p. 1336.

§328. DECISION OF THE BOARD

(a) Final written decision.—If a post-grant review is instituted and not dismissed under this chapter, the Patent Trial and Appeal Board shall issue a final written decision with respect to the patentability of any patent claim challenged by the petitioner and any new claim added under section 326(d).

(b) Certificate.—If the Patent Trial and Appeal Board issues a final written decision under subsection (a) and the time for appeal has expired or any appeal has terminated, the Director shall issue and publish a certificate canceling any claim of the patent finally determined to be unpatentable, confirming any claim of the patent determined to be patentable, and incorporating in the patent by operation of the certificate any new or amended claim determined to be patentable.

(c) Intervening rights.—Any proposed amended or new claim determined to be patentable and incorporated into a patent following a post-grant review under this chapter shall have the same effect as that specified in section 252 for reissued patents on the right of any person who made, purchased, or used within the United States, or imported into the United States, anything patented by such proposed amended or new claim, or who made substantial preparation therefor, before the issuance of a certificate under subsection (b).

(d) Data on length of review.—The Office shall make available to the public data describing the length of time between the institution of, and the issuance of a final written decision under subsection (a) for, each post-grant review.

History of 35 U.S.C. §328: Sept. 16, 2011, P.L. 112-29, §§6(d), 20(j)(1), 125 Stat. 310, 335.

See also Office Patent Trial Practice Guide, p. 1336.

§329. APPEAL

A party dissatisfied with the final written decision of the Patent Trial and Appeal Board under section 328(a) may appeal the decision pursuant to sections 141 through 144. Any party to the post-grant review shall have the right to be a party to the appeal.

History of 35 U.S.C. §329: Sept. 16, 2011, P.L. 112-29, §6(d), 125 Stat. 311.

See also Office Patent Trial Practice Guide, p. 1336.

ANNOTATIONS

Personal Audio, LLC v. Electronic Frontier Found., 867 F.3d 1246, 1249, 123 U.S.P.Q.2d 1592, 1594 (Fed.Cir.2017). "We asked the parties to brief the question of whether [petitioner] has standing to participate in this appeal, in view of the court's holding in ***Consumer Watchdog v. Wisconsin Alumni Research [Found.]***, 753 F.3d 1258 (Fed.Cir.2014), that a PTAB petitioner that does not meet the [U.S. Const.] Art. 3 case-or-controversy requirement does not have standing to invoke judicial power, and thus does not have standing to appeal to this court from a PTAB decision on *inter partes* reexamination. *At U.S.P.Q.2d 1595:* 35 U.S.C. §141(c) provides the right of appeal to the Federal Circuit for '[a] party to an inter partes review or a post-grant review who is dissatisfied with the final written decision of the [PTAB].' *At F.3d 1250, U.S.P.Q.2d ___:* With Art. 3 satisfied as to the appellant, [petitioner] is not constitutionally excluded from appearing in court to defend the PTAB decision in its favor."

Phigenix, Inc. v. ImmunoGen, Inc., 845 F.3d 1168, 1171-72, 121 U.S.P.Q.2d 1242, 1244 (Fed.Cir.2017).

35 U.S.C. §327

"'[A]lthough [U.S. Const.] Art. 3 standing is not necessarily a requirement to appear before an administrative agency,' ... an appellant must nevertheless supply the requisite proof of an injury in fact when it seeks review of an agency's final action in a federal court...."

Blue Calypso, LLC v. Groupon, Inc., 815 F.3d 1331, 1338, 118 U.S.P.Q.2d 1035, 1040 (Fed.Cir.2016). "Although the [PTAB's] decision to institute a CBM review is, per the AIA, 'final and nonappealable,' ... we have held that the question of whether a challenged patent claim is a CBM relates to the [PTAB's] authority to issue a final decision in a CBM review. Thus, because we have jurisdiction to review the [PTAB's] final decisions in CBM reviews, ... the AIA does not preclude us from reviewing the [PTAB's] conclusion that the challenged patent claims are '[CBMs]' that lack any 'technological invention[]'...."

GTNX, Inc. v. INTTRA, Inc., 789 F.3d 1309, 1310, 115 U.S.P.Q.2d 1178, 1179 (Fed.Cir.2015). "At the request of [petitioner], the [PTAB] instituted '[CBM] patent' review proceedings.... A few months later, the [PTAB] reconsidered its institution decisions, determined that institution of proceedings in these matters violated a statutory proscription, vacated the institution decisions, and terminated the proceedings. [Petitioner] appeals, and [respondent] moves to dismiss the appeal. We grant the motion. In addition, treating the appeal in the alternative as a mandamus petition, we deny mandamus relief. *At F.3d 1311, U.S.P.Q.2d 1180:* By its terms, [35 U.S.C.] §329 authorizes appeal, under [35 U.S.C.] §141(c), only from a 'final written decision of the [PTAB] under [35 U.S.C.] §328(a).' Similarly, §141(c), as relevant here, authorizes appeal only from a 'final written decision of the [PTAB] under [§328(a)].' In turn, §328(a) refers only to 'a final written decision *with respect to the patentability of any patent claim challenged by the petitioner and any new claim added under [35 U.S.C.] §326(d).*' Here, the [PTAB] made no decision 'with respect to the patentability' of any claim. The [PTAB] decision at issue, therefore, is outside §328(a) and, hence, outside §§141(c) and 329. *At F.3d 1312:* The [PTAB] decision [petitioner] is seeking to appeal was not reached after conduct of the review and did not make a determination with respect to patentability. The decision is therefore outside ... §§141(c), 328(a), 329 and, in turn, outside 28 U.S.C. §1295(a)(4)(A)."

PART IV. PATENT COOPERATION TREATY

CHAPTER 35. DEFINITIONS

§351. DEFINITIONS

When used in this part unless the context otherwise indicates—

(a) The term "treaty" means the Patent Cooperation Treaty done at Washington, on June 19, 1970.

(b) The term "Regulations," when capitalized, means the Regulations under the treaty, done at Washington on the same date as the treaty. The term "regulations," when not capitalized, means the regulations established by the Director under this title.

(c) The term "international application" means an application filed under the treaty.

(d) The term "international application originating in the United States" means an international application filed in the Patent and Trademark Office when it is acting as a Receiving Office under the treaty, irrespective of whether or not the United States has been designated in that international application.

(e) The term "international application designating the United States" means an international application specifying the United States as a country in which a patent is sought, regardless where such international application is filed.

(f) The term "Receiving Office" means a national patent office or intergovernmental organization which receives and processes international applications as prescribed by the treaty and the Regulations.

(g) The terms "International Searching Authority" and "International Preliminary Examining Authority" mean a national patent office or intergovernmental organization as appointed under the treaty which processes international applications as prescribed by the treaty and the Regulations.

(h) The term "International Bureau" means the international intergovernmental organization which is recognized as the coordinating body under the treaty and the Regulations.

(i) Terms and expressions not defined in this part are to be taken in the sense indicated by the treaty and the Regulations.

History of 35 U.S.C. §351: Nov. 14, 1975, P.L. 94-131, §1, 89 Stat. 685; Nov. 8, 1984, P.L. 98-622, §403(a) in part, 98 Stat. 3392; Nov. 6, 1986, P.L. 99-616, §2(a)-(c), 100 Stat. 3485; Nov. 29, 1999, P.L. 106-113, §1000(a)(9), 113 Stat. 1536; Nov. 2, 2002, P.L. 107-273, §13206(b)(1)(B), 116 Stat. 1906.

See also 37 C.F.R. §1.401; Patent Cooperation Treaty.

CHAPTER 36. INTERNATIONAL STAGE

§361. RECEIVING OFFICE

(a) The Patent and Trademark Office shall act as a Receiving Office for international applications filed by nationals or residents of the United States. In accordance with any agreement made between the United States and another country, the Patent and Trademark Office may also act as a Receiving Office for international applications filed by residents or nationals of such country who are entitled to file international applications.

(b) The Patent and Trademark Office shall perform all acts connected with the discharge of duties required of a Receiving Office, including the collection of international fees and their transmittal to the International Bureau.

(c) International applications filed in the Patent and Trademark Office shall be filed in the English language, or an English translation shall be filed within such later time as may be fixed by the Director.

(d) The international fee, and the transmittal and search fees prescribed under section 376(a) of this part, shall either be paid on filing of an international application or within such later time as may be fixed by the Director.

History of 35 U.S.C. §361: Nov. 14, 1975, P.L. 94-131, §1, 89 Stat. 686; Nov. 8, 1984, P.L. 98-622, §§401(a), 403(a) in part, 98 Stat. 3391, 3392; Nov. 6, 1986, P.L. 99-616, §2(d), 100 Stat. 3485; Nov. 29, 1999, P.L. 106-113, §1000(a)(9), 113 Stat. 1536; Nov. 2, 2002, P.L. 107-273, §13206(b)(1)(B), 116 Stat. 1906; Dec. 18, 2013, P.L. 112-211, §202(b)(7), 126 Stat. 1536.

See also 37 C.F.R. §§1.412-1.499; Patent Cooperation Treaty.

§362. INTERNATIONAL SEARCHING AUTHORITY & INTERNATIONAL PRELIMINARY EXAMINING AUTHORITY

(a) The Patent and Trademark Office may act as an International Searching Authority and International Preliminary Examining Authority with respect to international applications in accordance with the terms and conditions of an agreement which may be concluded with the International Bureau, and may discharge all duties required of such Authorities, including the collection of handling fees and their transmittal to the International Bureau.

(b) The handling fee, preliminary examination fee, and any additional fees due for international preliminary examination shall be paid within such time as may be fixed by the Director.

History of 35 U.S.C. §362: Nov. 14, 1975, P.L. 94-131, §1, 89 Stat. 686; Nov. 8, 1984, P.L. 98-622, §403(a) in part, 98 Stat. 3392; Nov. 6, 1986, P.L. 99-616, §4, 100 Stat. 3485; Nov. 29, 1999, P.L. 106-113, §1000(a)(9), 113 Stat. 1536; Nov. 2, 2002, P.L. 107-273, §13206(b)(1)(B), 116 Stat. 1906.

§363. INTERNATIONAL APPLICATION DESIGNATING THE UNITED STATES: EFFECT

An international application designating the United States shall have the effect, from its international filing date under article 11 of the treaty, of a national application for patent regularly filed in the Patent and Trademark Office.

History of 35 U.S.C. §363: Nov. 14, 1975, P.L. 94-131, §1, 89 Stat. 686; Nov. 8, 1984, P.L. 98-622, §403(a), 98 Stat. 3392; Sept. 16, 2011, P.L. 112-29, §3(g)(3), 125 Stat. 288.

ANNOTATIONS

Broadcast Innovation, L.L.C. v. Charter Comms., 420 F.3d 1364, 1368, 76 U.S.P.Q.2d 1220, 1222 (Fed.Cir.2005). "[T]he international filing date of a [Patent Cooperation Treaty] application is also the U.S. filing date for the corresponding national stage application."

§364. INTERNATIONAL STAGE: PROCEDURE

(a) International applications shall be processed by the Patent and Trademark Office when acting as a Receiving Office, International Searching Authority, or International Preliminary Examining Authority, in accordance with the applicable provisions of the treaty, the Regulations, and this title.

(b) An applicant's failure to act within prescribed time limits in connection with requirements pertaining to an international application may be excused as provided in the treaty and the Regulations.

History of 35 U.S.C. §364: Nov. 14, 1975, P.L. 94-131, §1, 89 Stat. 686; Nov. 8, 1984, P.L. 98-622, §403(a) in part, 98 Stat. 3392; Nov. 6, 1986, P.L. 99-616, §5, 100 Stat. 3485; Nov. 29, 1999, P.L. 106-113, §1000(a)(9), 113 Stat. 1536; Nov. 2, 2002, P.L. 107-273, §13206(b)(1)(B), 116 Stat. 1906; Dec. 18, 2013, P.L. 112-211, §202(b)(8), 126 Stat. 1536.

ANNOTATIONS

Helfgott & Karas, P.C. v. Dickinson, 209 F.3d 1328, 1334, 54 U.S.P.Q.2d 1425, 1429 (Fed.Cir.2000). "[T]he actions of the PTO in complying with the dictates of 35 U.S.C. §364 clearly raise substantial questions under the patent laws. We thus hold that the question of whether the Commissioner has violated the [Administrative Procedure Act] in applying the [Patent Cooperation Treaty] rules and regulations, as well as its own regulations, raises a substantial question under the patent laws sufficient to vest jurisdiction with the district court based in part upon 28 U.S.C. §1338(a). Therefore, the sole avenue of appeal for these claims is to [the Federal Circuit]."

§365. RIGHT OF PRIORITY; BENEFIT OF THE FILING DATE OF A PRIOR APPLICATION

(a) In accordance with the conditions and requirements of subsections (a) through (d) of section 119, a national application shall be entitled to the right of priority based on a prior filed international application which designated at least one country other than the United States.

(b) In accordance with the conditions and requirement of section 119(a) and the treaty and the Regulations, an international application designating the United States shall be entitled to the right of priority based on a prior foreign application, or a prior international application designating at least one country other than the United States. The Director may establish procedures, including the requirement for payment of the fee specified in section 41(a)(7), to accept an unintentionally delayed claim for priority under the treaty and the Regulations, and to accept a priority claim that pertains to an application that was not filed within the priority period specified in the treaty and Regulations, but was filed within the additional 2-month period specified under section 119(a) or the treaty and Regulations.

(c) In accordance with the conditions and requirements of section 120, an international application designating the United States shall be entitled to the benefit of the filing date of a prior national application, a prior international application designating the United States, or a prior international design application as defined in section 381(a)(6) designating the United States, and a national application shall be entitled to the benefit of the filing date of a prior international application designating the United States. If any claim for the benefit of an earlier filing date is based on a prior international application which designated but did not originate in the United States or a prior international design application as defined in section 381(a)(6) which designated but did not originate in the United States, the Director may require the filing in the Patent and Trademark Office of a certified copy of such application together with a translation thereof into the English language, if it was filed in another language.

History of 35 U.S.C. §365: Nov. 14, 1975, P.L. 94-131, §1, 89 Stat. 686; Nov. 8, 1984, P.L. 98-622, §403(a) in part, 98 Stat. 3392; Dec. 8, 1994, P.L. 103-465, §532(c)(4), 108 Stat. 4987; Nov. 29, 1999, P.L. 106-113, §1000(a)(9), 113 Stat. 1536; Nov. 2, 2002, P.L. 107-273, §13206(b)(1)(B), 116 Stat. 1906; Sept. 16, 2011, P.L. 112-29, §20(j)(1), 125 Stat. 335; May 13, 2015, P.L. 112-211, §102(8), 126 Stat. 1532; Dec. 18, 2013, P.L. 112-211, §201(c)(2), 126 Stat. 1535.

See also 37 C.F.R. §§1.78, 1.109.

§366. WITHDRAWN INTERNATIONAL APPLICATION

Subject to section 367 of this part, if an international application designating the United States is withdrawn or considered withdrawn, either generally or as to the United States, under the conditions of the treaty and the Regulations, before the applicant has complied with the applicable requirements prescribed by section 371(c) of this part, the designation of the United States shall have no effect after the date of withdrawal, and shall be considered as not having been made, unless a claim for benefit of a prior filing date under section 365(c) of this section was made in a national application, or an international application designating the United States, or a claim for benefit under section 386(c) was made in an international design application designating the United States, filed before the date of such withdrawal. However, such withdrawn international application may serve as the basis for a claim of priority under section 365(a) and (b), or under section 386(a) or (b), if it designated a country other than the United States.

History of 35 U.S.C. §366: Nov. 14, 1975, P.L. 94-131, §1, 89 Stat. 687; Nov. 8, 1984, P.L. 98-622, §401(b), 98 Stat. 3391; May 13, 2015, P.L. 112-211, §102(9), 126 Stat. 1532.

§367. ACTIONS OF OTHER AUTHORITIES: REVIEW

(a) Where a Receiving Office other than the Patent and Trademark Office has refused to accord an international filing date to an international application designating the United States or where it has held such application to be withdrawn either generally or as to the United States, the applicant may request review of the matter by the Director, on compliance with the requirements of and within the time limits specified by the treaty and the Regulations. Such review may result in a determination that such application be considered as pending in the national stage.

(b) The review under subsection (a) of this section, subject to the same requirements and conditions, may also be requested in those instances where an international application designating the United States is considered withdrawn due to a finding by the International Bureau under article 12(3) of the treaty.

History of 35 U.S.C. §367: Nov. 14, 1975, P.L. 94-131, §1, 89 Stat. 687; Nov. 8, 1984, P.L. 98-622, §403(a) in part, 98 Stat. 3392; Nov. 29, 1999, P.L. 106-113, §1000(a)(9), 113 Stat. 1536; Nov. 2, 2002, P.L. 107-273, §13206(b)(1)(B), 116 Stat. 1906.

§368. SECRECY OF CERTAIN INVENTIONS; FILING INTERNATIONAL APPLICATIONS IN FOREIGN COUNTRIES

(a) International applications filed in the Patent and Trademark Office shall be subject to the provisions of chapter 17.

(b) In accordance with article 27(8) of the treaty, the filing of an international application in a country other than the United States on the invention made in this country shall be considered to constitute the filing of an application in a foreign country within the meaning of chapter 17, whether or not the United States is designated in that international application.

(c) If a license to file in a foreign country is refused or if an international application is ordered to be kept secret and a permit refused, the Patent and Trademark Office when acting as a Receiving Office, International Searching Authority, or International Preliminary Examining Authority, may not disclose the contents of such application to anyone not authorized to receive such disclosure.

History of 35 U.S.C. §368: Nov. 14, 1975, P.L. 94-131, §1, 89 Stat. 687; Nov. 8, 1984, P.L. 98-622, §403(a) in part, 98 Stat. 3392; Nov. 6, 1986, P.L. 99-616, §6, 100 Stat. 3486; Sept. 16, 2011, P.L. 112-29, §20(j)(1), 125 Stat. 335.

CHAPTER 37. NATIONAL STAGE

§371. NATIONAL STAGE: COMMENCEMENT

(a) Receipt from the International Bureau of copies of international applications with any amendments to the claims, international search reports, and international preliminary examination reports including any annexes thereto may be required in the case of international applications designating or electing the United States.

(b) Subject to subsection (f) of this section, the national stage shall commence with the expiration of the applicable time limit under article 22(1) or (2), or under article 39(1)(a) of the treaty.

(c) The applicant shall file in the Patent and Trademark Office—

(1) the national fee provided in section 41(a);

(2) a copy of the international application, unless not required under subsection (a) of this section or already communicated by the International Bureau, and a translation into the English language of the international application, if it was filed in another language;

(3) amendments, if any, to the claims in the international application, made under article 19 of the treaty, unless such amendments have been communicated to the Patent and Trademark Office by the International Bureau, and a translation into the English language if such amendments were made in another language;

(4) an oath or declaration of the inventor (or other person authorized under chapter 11) complying with the requirements of section 115 and with regulations prescribed for oaths or declarations of applicants;

(5) a translation into the English language of any annexes to the international preliminary examination report, if such annexes were made in another language.

(d) The requirements with respect to the national fee referred to in subsection (c)(1), the translation referred to in subsection (c)(2), and the oath or declaration referred to in subsection (c)(4) of this section shall be complied with by the date of the commencement of the national stage or by such later time as may be fixed by the Director. The copy of the international application referred to in subsection (c)(2) shall be submitted by the date of the commencement of the national stage. Failure to comply with these requirements shall be regarded as abandonment of the application by the parties thereof. The payment of a surcharge may be required as a condition of accepting the national fee referred to in subsection (c)(1) or the oath or declaration referred to in subsection (c)(4) of this section if these requirements are not met by the date of the commencement of the national stage. The requirements of subsection (c)(3) of this section shall be complied with by the date of the commencement of the national stage, and failure to do so shall be regarded as a cancellation of the amendments to the claims in the international application made under article 19 of the treaty. The requirement of subsection (c)(5) shall be complied with at such time as may be fixed by the Director and failure to do so shall be regarded as cancellation of the amendments made under article 34(2)(b) of the treaty.

(e) After an international application has entered the national stage, no patent may be granted or refused thereon before the expiration of the applicable time limit under article 28 or article 41 of the treaty, except with the express consent of the applicant. The applicant may present amendments to the specification, claims and drawings of the application after the national stage has commenced.

(f) At the express request of the applicant, the national stage of processing may be commenced at any time at which the application is in order for such purpose and the applicable requirements of subsection (c) of this section have been complied with.

History of 35 U.S.C. §371: Nov. 14, 1975, P.L. 94-131, §1, 89 Stat. 688; Nov. 8, 1984, P.L. 98-622, §§402(a)-(d), 403(a) in part, 98 Stat. 3391, 3392; Nov. 6, 1986, P.L. 99-616, §7, 100 Stat. 3486; Dec. 10, 1991, P.L. 102-204, §5(g)(2), 105 Stat. 1641; Nov. 29, 1999, P.L. 106-113, §1000(a)(9), 113 Stat. 1536; Nov. 2, 2002, P.L. 107-273, §13206(a)(20), (b)(1)(B), 116 Stat. 1905, 1906; Sept. 16, 2011, P.L. 112-29, §20(i)(5), (j)(1), 125 Stat. 335; Dec. 18, 2013, P.L. 112-211, §202(b)(9), 126 Stat. 1536.

See also 37 C.F.R. §§1.491-1.499; Patent Cooperation Treaty.

ANNOTATIONS

Actelion Pharms. v. Matal, 881 F.3d 1339, 1344, 125 U.S.P.Q.2d 1585, ___ (Fed.Cir.2018). The "A Delay calculation must be based on the date on which the entirety of [35 U.S.C.] §371 has been complied with, including §371(c) as well as §371(b) and §371(f). We conclude that, to commence the national stage early, [P] was required to make an express request pursuant to §371(f) regardless whether the pre- or post-[Technical Corrections Act (TCA)] version of [35 U.S.C.] §154(b)(1)(A)(i)(II) applies to the ... patent. [¶] We agree with the PTO that, under either the pre- or post-TCA version of §154(b)(1)(A)(i)(II), the A Delay calculation must be based on the date on which the entirety of §371 is complied with, including §371(b) and (f). As such, we conclude that under either pre- or post-TCA law, [P] was required to comply with the 'express request' provision of §371(f) if it wished to commence the national stage before the expiration date provided in §371(b)."

Exela Pharma Sci., LLC v. Lee, 781 F.3d 1349, 1350, 114 U.S.P.Q.2d 1328, 1329 (Fed.Cir.2015). "This appeal presents the question of whether a third party has the right to challenge, by way of the Administrative Procedure Act (APA), a ruling of the [PTO] reviving a patent application that had become abandoned by failure to meet a filing schedule established by the Patent Cooperation Treaty and its implementing statute. *At F.3d 1352, U.S.P.Q.2d 1330:* We conclude that Congress did not intend to permit judicial review for challenges such as the one brought here."

§372. NATIONAL STAGE: REQUIREMENTS & PROCEDURE

(a) All questions of substance and, within the scope of the requirements of the treaty and Regulations, procedure in an international application designating the United States shall be determined as in the case of national applications regularly filed in the Patent and Trademark Office.

(b) In case of international applications designating but not originating in, the United States—

(1) the Director may cause to be reexamined questions relating to form and contents of the application in accordance with the requirements of the treaty and the Regulations;

(2) the Director may cause the question of unity of invention to be reexamined under section 121, within the scope of the requirements of the treaty and the Regulations; and

(3) the Director may require a verification of the translation of the international application or any other document pertaining to the application if the application or other document was filed in a language other than English.

History of 35 U.S.C. §372: Nov. 14, 1975, P.L. 94-131, §1, 89 Stat. 689; Nov. 8, 1984, P.L. 98-622, §§402(e), (f), 403(a) in part, 98 Stat. 3392; Nov. 29, 1999, P.L. 106-113, §1000(a)(9), 113 Stat. 1536; Nov. 2, 2002, P.L. 107-273, §13206(b)(1)(B), 116 Stat. 1906; Sept. 16, 2011, P.L. 112-29, §20(j)(1), 125 Stat. 335.

ANNOTATIONS

Stevens v. Tamai, 366 F.3d 1325, 1333, 70 U.S.P.Q.2d 1765, 1771 (Fed.Cir.2004). "[T]he [PTO] is not required to accept an applicant's transmittal letter requesting entry into the national stage as conclusive proof that a foreign language application contains a particular disclosure."

§373. REPEALED

Repealed Jan. 14, 2013, P.L. 112-274, §1(i), 126 Stat. 2457.

§374. PUBLICATION OF INTERNATIONAL APPLICATION

The publication under the treaty defined in section 351(a), of an international application designating the United States shall be deemed a publication under section 122(b), except as provided in section 154(d).

History of 35 U.S.C. §374: Nov. 14, 1975, P.L. 94-131, §1, 89 Stat. 689; Nov. 29, 1999, P.L. 106-113, §1000(a)(9), 113 Stat. 1536; Nov. 2, 2002, P.L. 107-273, §13205(2)(E), 116 Stat. 1903; Sept. 16, 2011, P.L. 112-29, §§3(g)(4), 20(j)(1), 125 Stat. 288, 335.

§375. PATENT ISSUED ON INTERNATIONAL APPLICATION: EFFECT

(a) A patent may be issued by the Director based on an international application designating the United States, in accordance with the provisions of this title. Such patent shall have the force and effect of a patent issued on a national application filed under the provisions of chapter 11.

(b) Where due to an incorrect translation the scope of a patent granted on an international application designating the United States, which was not originally filed in the English language, exceeds the scope of the international application in its original language, a court of competent jurisdiction may retroactively limit the scope of the patent, by declaring it unenforceable to the extent that it exceeds the scope of the international application in its original language.

History of 35 U.S.C. §375: Nov. 14, 1975, P.L. 94-131, §1, 89 Stat. 689; Nov. 29, 1999, P.L. 106-113, §1000(a)(9), 113 Stat. 1536; Nov. 2, 2002, P.L. 107-273, §13206(b)(1)(B), 116 Stat. 1906; Sept. 16, 2011, P.L. 112-29, §§3(g)(5), 20(j)(1), 125 Stat. 288, 335.

§376. FEES

(a) The required payment of the international fee and the handling fee, which amounts are specified in the Regulations, shall be paid in United States currency. The Patent and Trademark Office shall charge a national fee as provided in section 41(a), and may also charge the following fees:

(1) A transmittal fee (see section 361(d)).

(2) A search fee (see section 361(d)).

(3) A supplemental search fee (to be paid when required).

(4) A preliminary examination fee and any additional fees (see section 362(b)).

(5) Such other fees as established by the Director.

(b) The amounts of fees specified in subsection (a) of this section, except the international fee and the handling fee, shall be prescribed by the Director. He may refund any sum paid by mistake or in excess of the fees so specified, or if required under the treaty and the Regulations. The Director may also refund any part of the search fee, the national fee, the preliminary examination fee, and any additional fees, where he determines such refund to be warranted.

History of 35 U.S.C. §376: Nov. 14, 1975, P.L. 94-131, §1, 89 Stat. 690; Nov. 8, 1984, P.L. 98-622, §§402(g), 403(a) in part, 98 Stat. 3392; Nov. 6, 1986, P.L. 99-616, §8, 100 Stat. 3486; Dec. 10, 1991, P.L. 102-204, §5(g)(1), 105 Stat. 1640; Nov. 29, 1999, P.L. 106-113, §1000(a)(9), 113 Stat. 1536; Nov. 2, 2002, P.L. 107-273, §13206(a)(21), (b)(1)(B), 116 Stat. 1905, 1906.

See also 37 C.F.R. §§1.445, 1.446.

PART V. THE HAGUE AGREEMENT CONCERNING INTERNATIONAL REGISTRATION OF INDUSTRIAL DESIGNS

CHAPTER 38. INTERNATIONAL DESIGN APPLICATIONS

§381. DEFINITIONS

(a) In general.—When used in this part, unless the context otherwise indicates—

(1) the term "treaty" means the Geneva Act of the Hague Agreement Concerning the International Registration of Industrial Designs adopted at Geneva on July 2, 1999;

(2) the term "regulations"—

(A) when capitalized, means the Common Regulations under the treaty; and

(B) when not capitalized, means the regulations established by the Director under this title;

(3) the terms "designation," "designating," and "designate" refer to a request that an international registration have effect in a Contracting Party to the treaty;

(4) the term "International Bureau" means the international intergovernmental organization that is recognized as the coordinating body under the treaty and the Regulations;

(5) the term "effective registration date" means the date of international registration determined by the International Bureau under the treaty;

(6) the term "international design application" means an application for international registration; and

(7) the term "international registration" means the international registration of an industrial design filed under the treaty.

(b) Rule of construction.—Terms and expressions not defined in this part are to be taken in the sense indicated by the treaty and the Regulations.

History of 35 U.S.C. §381: Effective May 13, 2015, P.L. 112-211, §101(a), 126 Stat. 1535.

See also 37 C.F.R. §§1.1001-1.1071.

§382. FILING INTERNATIONAL DESIGN APPLICATIONS

(a) In general.—Any person who is a national of the United States, or has a domicile, a habitual residence, or a real and effective industrial or commercial establishment in the United States, may file an international design application by submitting to the Patent and Trademark Office an application in such form, together with such fees, as may be prescribed by the Director.

(b) Required action.—The Patent and Trademark Office shall perform all acts connected with the discharge of its duties under the treaty, including the collection of international fees and transmittal thereof to the International Bureau. Subject to chapter 17, international design applications shall be forwarded by the Patent and Trademark Office to the International Bureau, upon payment of a transmittal fee.

(c) Applicability of chapter 16.—Except as otherwise provided in this chapter, the provisions of chapter 16 shall apply.

(d) Application filed in another country.—An international design application on an industrial design made in this country shall be considered to constitute the filing of an application in a foreign country within the meaning of chapter 17 if the international design application is filed—

(1) in a country other than the United States;

(2) at the International Bureau; or

(3) with an intergovernmental organization.

History of 35 U.S.C. §382: Effective May 13, 2015, P.L. 112-211, §101(a), 126 Stat. 1536.

See also 37 C.F.R. §§1.1001-1.1071.

§383. INTERNATIONAL DESIGN APPLICATION

In addition to any requirements pursuant to chapter 16, the international design application shall contain—

(1) a request for international registration under the treaty;

(2) an indication of the designated Contracting Parties;

(3) data concerning the applicant as prescribed in the treaty and the Regulations;

(4) copies of a reproduction or, at the choice of the applicant, of several different reproductions of the industrial design that is the subject of the international design application, presented in the number and manner prescribed in the treaty and the Regulations;

(5) an indication of the product or products that constitute the industrial design or in relation to which the industrial design is to be used, as prescribed in the treaty and the Regulations;

(6) the fees prescribed in the treaty and the Regulations; and

(7) any other particulars prescribed in the Regulations.

History of 35 U.S.C. §383: Effective May 13, 2015, P.L. 112-211, §101(a), 126 Stat. 1536.

See also 37 C.F.R. §§1.1001-1.1071.

§384. FILING DATE

(a) In general.—Subject to subsection (b), the filing date of an international design application in the United States shall be the effective registration date. Notwithstanding the provisions of this part, any international design application designating the United States that otherwise meets the requirements of chapter 16 may be treated as a design application under chapter 16.

(b) Review.—An applicant may request review by the Director of the filing date of the international design application in the United States. The Director may determine that the filing date of the international design application in the United States is a date other than the effective registration date. The Director may establish procedures, including the payment of a surcharge, to review the filing date under this section. Such review may result in a determination that the application has a filing date in the United States other than the effective registration date.

History of 35 U.S.C. §384: Effective May 13, 2015, P.L. 112-211, §101(a), 126 Stat. 1537.

See also 37 C.F.R. §§1.1001-1.1071.

§385. EFFECT OF INTERNATIONAL DESIGN APPLICATION

An international design application designating the United States shall have the effect, for all purposes, from its filing date determined in accordance with section 384, of an application for patent filed in the Patent and Trademark Office pursuant to chapter 16.

History of 35 U.S.C. §385: Effective May 13, 2015, P.L. 112-211, §101(a), 126 Stat. 1537.

See also 37 C.F.R. §§1.1001-1.1071.

§386. RIGHT OF PRIORITY

(a) National application.—In accordance with the conditions and requirements of subsections (a) through (d) of section 119 and section 172, a national application shall be entitled to the right of priority based on a prior international design application that designated at least 1 country other than the United States.

(b) Prior foreign application.—In accordance with the conditions and requirements of subsections (a) through (d) of section 119 and section 172 and the treaty and the Regulations, an international design application designating the United States shall be entitled to the right of priority based on a prior foreign application, a prior international application as defined in section 351(c) designating at least 1 country other than the United States, or a prior international design application designating at least 1 country other than the United States.

(c) Prior national application.—In accordance with the conditions and requirements of section 120, an international design application designating the United States shall be entitled to the benefit of the filing date of a prior national application, a prior international application as defined in section 351(c) designating the United States, or a prior international design application designating the United States, and a national application shall be entitled to the benefit of the filing date of a prior international design application designating the United States. If any claim for the benefit of an earlier filing date is based on a prior international application as defined in section 351(c) which designated but did not originate in the United States or a prior international design application which designated but did not originate in the United States, the Director may require the filing in the Patent and Trademark Office of a certified copy of such application together with a translation thereof into the English language, if it was filed in another language.

History of 35 U.S.C. §386: Effective May 13, 2015, P.L. 112-211, §101(a), 126 Stat. 1537.

See also 37 C.F.R. §§1.1001-1.1071.

§387. RELIEF FROM PRESCRIBED TIME LIMITS

An applicant's failure to act within prescribed time limits in connection with requirements pertaining to an international design application may be excused as to the United States upon a showing satisfactory to the Director of unintentional delay and under such conditions, including a requirement for payment of the fee specified in section 41(a)(7), as may be prescribed by the Director.

History of 35 U.S.C. §387: Effective May 13, 2015, P.L. 112-211, §101(a), 126 Stat. 1538.

See also 37 C.F.R. §§1.1001-1.1071.

§388. WITHDRAWN OR ABANDONED INTERNATIONAL DESIGN APPLICATION

Subject to sections 384 and 387, if an international design application designating the United States is withdrawn, renounced or canceled or considered withdrawn or abandoned, either generally or as to the United States, under the conditions of the treaty and the Regulations, the designation of the United States shall have no effect after the date of withdrawal, renunciation, cancellation, or abandonment and shall be considered as not having been made, unless a claim for benefit of a prior filing date under section 386(c) was made in a national application, or an international design application designating the United States, or a claim for benefit under section 365(c) was made in an international application designating the United States, filed before the date of such withdrawal, renunciation, cancellation, or abandonment. However, such withdrawn, renounced, canceled, or abandoned international design application may serve as the basis for a claim of priority under subsections (a) and (b) of section 386, or under subsection (a) or (b) of section 365, if it designated a country other than the United States.

History of 35 U.S.C. §388: Effective May 13, 2015, P.L. 112-211, §101(a), 126 Stat. 1538.

See also 37 C.F.R. §§1.1001-1.1071.

§389. EXAMINATION OF INTERNATIONAL DESIGN APPLICATION

(a) In general.—The Director shall cause an examination to be made pursuant to this title of an international design application designating the United States.

(b) Applicability of chapter 16.—All questions of substance and, unless otherwise required by the treaty and Regulations, procedures regarding an international design application designating the United States shall be determined as in the case of applications filed under chapter 16.

(c) Fees.—The Director may prescribe fees for filing international design applications, for designating the United States, and for any other processing, services, or materials relating to international design applications, and may provide for later payment of such fees, including surcharges for later submission of fees.

(d) Issuance of patent.—The Director may issue a patent based on an international design application designating the United States, in accordance with the provisions of this title. Such patent shall have the force and effect of a patent issued on an application filed under chapter 16.

History of 35 U.S.C. §389: Effective May 13, 2015, P.L. 112-211, §101(a), 126 Stat. 1538.

See also 37 C.F.R. §§1.1001-1.1071.

§390. PUBLICATION OF INTERNATIONAL DESIGN APPLICATION

The publication under the treaty of an international design application designating the United States shall be deemed a publication under section 122(b).

History of 35 U.S.C. §390: Effective May 13, 2015, P.L. 112-211, §101(a), 126 Stat. 1539.

See also 37 C.F.R. §§1.1001-1.1071.

PUBLIC ACCESSIBILITY OF PRINTED PUBLICATION UNDER 35 U.S.C. §102

CHART

Prior art	Publicly accessible?	Reason	Case
Abstract available only at request of author	No	Insufficient evidence that abstract had been disseminated at convention, even though author attended and it was customary practice to disseminate abstracts	***Norian Corp.***, 363 F.3d 1321, 1330, 70 U.S.P.Q.2d 1508, 1515 (Fed.Cir.2004)
Copyrighted manuscript	No	Insufficient evidence to show manuscript was accessible in commercial databases prior to critical date	***In re Lister***, 583 F.3d 1307, 1317, 92 U.S.P.Q.2d 1225, 1230-32 (Fed.Cir.2009)
Documents housed in corporation's library where access was restricted to persons authorized by corporation	No	A person could not have access to documents even using reasonable diligence	***Northern Telecom, Inc.***, 908 F.2d 931, 937, 15 U.S.P.Q.2d 1321, 1325 (Fed.Cir.1990)
Monographs distributed to commercial entities without guarantee of confidentiality	No	There was a reasonable expectation of confidentiality and no evidence the monographs were distributed	***Cordis Corp.***, 561 F.3d 1319, 1335, 90 U.S.P.Q.2d 1401, 1412-13 (Fed.Cir.2009)
Online article	Yes	Although not indexed, article was accessible using expected search terms and was on website well known to the interested community	***Voter Verified, Inc.***, 698 F.3d 1374, 1380, 104 U.S.P.Q.2d 1553, 1556-57 (Fed.Cir.2012)
Online article	No	Article was not indexed nor available to anyone other than those with access to restricted FTP website	***SRI Int'l***, 511 F.3d 1186, 1196-97 (Fed.Cir.2008)
Patent application—Australian patent application that was laid out at the Australian Patent Office and five suboffices	Yes	Sufficiently accessible to the public and to persons skilled in the pertinent art	***In re Wyer***, 655 F.2d 221, 227, 210 U.S.P.Q. 790, 795 (C.C.P.A.1981)
Patent application—figures in issued Canadian patent application	Yes	Although figures did not appear in the issued patent, a person skilled in the art could have found the figures in the patent application	***Bruckelmyer***, 445 F.3d 1374, 1380, 78 U.S.P.Q.2d 1684, 1687 (Fed.Cir.2006)
Promotional catalog	Yes	Available to those interested before the critical date	***Orion IP***, 605 F.3d 967, 974-75, 95 U.S.P.Q.2d 1297, 1301-02 (Fed.Cir.2010)
Separate standards listed in a printed publication	Yes	25,000 copies of the standards were printed, clearly making them publicly accessible	***Kyocera Wireless Corp.***, 545 F.3d 1340, 1353, 89 U.S.P.Q.2d 1057, 1064-65 (Fed.Cir.2008)
Set of volumes describing mobile data networks	Yes	The sets, introduced by third-party-reexamination requester, were both authentic and accessible even though located in university library in Norway	***In re NTP***, 654 F.3d 1279, 1294-97, 99 U.S.P.Q.2d 1481, 1491-93 (Fed.Cir.2011)
Slide presentation with 14 slides	Yes	Slides were on display for three days to persons likely to have ordinary skill in the art, and no protective measures were taken to prevent copying of material	***In re Klopfenstein***, 380 F.3d 1345, 1352, 72 U.S.P.Q.2d 1117, 1120-21 (Fed.Cir.2004)
Thesis—indexed, catalogued, and shelved German doctoral thesis	Yes	Affidavits of general library procedure for indexing, cataloguing, and shelving were sufficient to show accessibility date of more than one year	***In re Hall***, 781 F.2d 897, 900, 228 U.S.P.Q. 453, 455-56 (Fed.Cir.1986)
Thesis—three student theses, indexed with no reference to subject matter	No	Theses had not been catalogued or indexed in a meaningful way	***In re Cronyn***, 890 F.2d 1158, 1161, 13 U.S.P.Q.2d 1070, 1072 (Fed.Cir.1989)

Prior art	Publicly accessible?	Reason	Case
Thesis—uncatalogued and unshelved thesis	No	Only graduate committee had knowledge of subject matter of thesis	***Application of Bayer***, 568 F.2d 1357, 1362, 196 U.S.P.Q. 670, 674-75 (C.C.P.A.1978)
User manuals	No	One manual was unpublished and considered a trade secret. Also, both manuals were included in Information Disclosure Statement during reexamination of different patent. IDS disclosures are not admissions that manuals are prior art.	***ResQNet.com, Inc.***, 594 F.3d 860, 865-66, 93 U.S.P.Q.2d 1553, 1557 (Fed.Cir.2010)

Uniform Trade Secrets Act
with 1985 Amendments

UTSA

Uniform Trade Secrets Act

Uniform Trade Secrets Act with 1985 Amendments*

§1. Definitions

As used in this [Act], unless the context requires otherwise:

(1) "Improper means" includes theft, bribery, misrepresentation, breach or inducement of a breach of a duty to maintain secrecy, or espionage through electronic or other means;

(2) "Misappropriation" means:

(i) acquisition of a trade secret of another by a person who knows or has reason to know that the trade secret was acquired by improper means; or

(ii) disclosure or use of a trade secret of another without express or implied consent by a person who

(A) used improper means to acquire knowledge of the trade secret; or

(B) at the time of disclosure or use, knew or had reason to know that his knowledge of the trade secret was

(I) derived from or through a person who had utilized improper means to acquire it;

(II) acquired under circumstances giving rise to a duty to maintain its secrecy or limit its use; or

(III) derived from or through a person who owed a duty to the person seeking relief to maintain its secrecy or limit its use; or

(C) before a material change of his [or her] position, knew or had reason to know that it was a trade secret and that knowledge of it had been acquired by accident or mistake.

(3) "Person" means a natural person, corporation, business trust, estate, trust, partnership, association, joint venture, government, governmental subdivision or agency, or any other legal or commercial entity.

(4) "Trade secret" means information, including a formula, pattern, compilation, program, device, method, technique, or process, that:

(i) derives independent economic value, actual or potential, from not being generally known to, and not being readily ascertainable by proper means by, other persons who can obtain economic value from its disclosure or use, and

(ii) is the subject of efforts that are reasonable under the circumstances to maintain its secrecy.

See also NAFTA art. 1711; Restatement of Unfair Competition (3d) §39 (Definition of Trade Secret), §40 (Appropriation of Trade Secrets), §41 (Duty of Confidence), §42 (Breach of Confidence by Employees), §43 (Improper Acquisition of Trade Secrets).

Official Comment

One of the broadly stated policies behind trade secret law is "the maintenance of standards of commercial ethics." *Kewanee Oil Co. v. Bicron Corp.*, 416 U.S. 470 (1974). The Restatement of Torts, Section 757, Official Comment (f), notes: "A complete catalogue of improper means is not possible," but Section 1(1) includes a partial listing.

Proper means include:

1. Discovery by independent invention;

2. Discovery by "reverse engineering," that is, by starting with the known product and working backward to find the method by which it was developed. The acquisition of the known product must, of course, also be by a fair and honest means, such as purchase of the item on the open market for reverse engineering to be lawful;

3. Discovery under a license from the owner of the trade secret;

4. Observation of the item in public use or on public display;

5. Obtaining the trade secret from published literature.

Improper means could include otherwise lawful conduct which is improper under the circumstances; *e.g.*, an airplane overflight used as aerial reconnaissance to determine the competitor's plant layout during construction of the plant. *E. I. du Pont de Nemours & Co., Inc. v. Christopher*, 431 F.2d 1012 (CA5, 1970), cert. den. 400 U.S. 1024 (1970). Because the trade secret can be destroyed through public knowledge, the unauthorized disclosure of a trade secret is also a misappropriation.

The type of accident or mistake that can result in a misappropriation under Section 1(2)(ii)(C) involves conduct by a person seeking relief that does not constitute a failure of efforts that are reasonable under the circumstances to maintain its secrecy under Section 1(4)(ii).

The definition of "trade secret" contains a reasonable departure from the Restatement of Torts (First) definition which required that a trade secret be "continuously used in one's business." The broader definition in the proposed Act extends protection to a plaintiff who has not yet had an opportunity or acquired the means to put a trade secret to use. The definition includes information that has commercial value from a negative viewpoint, for example the results of lengthy and expensive research which proves that a certain process will not work could be of great value to a competitor.

Cf. Telex Corp. v. IBM Corp., 510 F.2d 894 (CA10, 1975) per curiam, cert. dismissed 423 U.S. 802 (1975) (liability imposed for developmental cost savings with respect to product not marketed). Because a trade secret need not be exclusive to confer a competitive advantage, different independent developers can acquire rights in the same trade secret.

The words "method, technique" are intended to include the concept of "know-how."

The language "not being generally known to and not being readily ascertainable by proper means by other persons" does not require that information be generally known to the public for trade secret rights to be lost. If the principal persons who can obtain economic benefit from information are aware of it, there is no trade secret. A method of casting metal, for example, may be unknown to the general public but readily known within the foundry industry.

Information is readily ascertainable if it is available in trade journals, reference books, or published materials. Often, the nature of a product lends itself to being readily copied as soon as it is available on the market. On the other hand, if reverse engineering is lengthy and expensive, a person who discovers the trade secret through reverse engineering can have a trade secret in the information obtained from reverse engineering.

Finally, reasonable efforts to maintain secrecy have been held to include advising employees of the existence of a trade secret, limiting access to a trade secret on "need to know basis," and controlling plant access. On the other hand, public disclosure of information through display, trade journal publications, advertising, or other carelessness can preclude protection.

The efforts required to maintain secrecy are those "reasonable under the circumstances." The courts do not require that extreme and unduly expensive procedures be taken to protect trade secrets against flagrant industrial espionage. *See E. I. du Pont de Nemours & Co., Inc. v. Christopher*, supra. It follows that reasonable use of a trade secret including controlled disclosure to employees and licensees is consistent with the requirement of relative secrecy.

ANNOTATIONS

Misappropriation

USA Power, LLC v. PacifiCorp, 235 P.3d 749, 758 (Utah 2010). "To establish a claim for misappropriation of trade secrets, [P] must show '(1) the existence of a trade secret, (2) communication of the trade secret to [D] under an express or implied agreement limiting disclosure of the secret, and (3) [D's] use of the secret that injures [P].' *At 761:* [W]e hold that a jury can infer misappropriation under the Utah [TSA] if presented with circumstantial evidence that shows access to information similar to the trade secret at issue." *See also* ***StorageCraft Tech. v. Kirby***, 744 F.3d 1183, 1187-88 & n.1 (10th Cir.2014) (interpreting Utah UTSA; D's disclosure of trade secret can satisfy common-law requirement that D "use" secret); ***Collelo v. Geographic Servs.***, 727 S.E.2d 55, 61 (Va.2012) (P does not have to show D used trade secret to compete with P).

Lydall, Inc. v. Ruschmeyer, 919 A.2d 421, 437-38 (Conn.2007). "In a publicly traded corporation, the persons entitled to profit from their investments in the corporation are its shareholders. An employee who plans to purchase a publicly traded corporation from its shareholders is not *competing* with the shareholders and does not seek to deprive them wrongfully of their right to profit from their investment. Rather, he seeks to offer them a fair return on their investment. In such circumstances, therefore, the employee does not undermine the primary purposes of [the UTSA]. [¶] We recognize that, as [P] claims, the purchasing employee may reap the reward of any 'hidden value' in the corporation. Contrary to [P's] contention, however, any such profit will not be had at the expense of the corporation's shareholders because the employee, in a voluntary transaction, will have *purchased* the right to reap that profit rather than have acquired it free of cost. We do not believe that [the UTSA] was intended to prohibit this type of activity, which, as [D] observes, promotes corporate efficiency and is 'a familiar feature of the American business landscape.' Accordingly, we conclude that the trial court's finding that [D] had used or disclosed the strategic plan [for growth] as a whole was not supported by the evidence and, therefore, was clearly erroneous."

Reeves v. Hanlon, 95 P.3d 513, 522 (Cal.2004). "[A]lthough an individual may violate the UTSA by using a former employer's confidential client list to *solicit* clients, the UTSA does not forbid an individual from announcing a change of employment, even to clients on a protected trade secret client list. As one decision explains, merely announcing a new business affiliation, without more, is not prohibited by the UTSA definition of misappropriation because such conduct is 'basic to an individual's right to engage in fair competition.'"

Microstrategy Inc. v. Li, 601 S.E.2d 580, 589 (Va. 2004). "[T]he issue whether a trade secret has been misappropriated generally presents a question of fact."

Northwest Bec-Corp v. Home Living Serv., 41 P.3d 263, 268 (Idaho 2002). "In order to prevail on a misappropriation claim, the claimant must prove that the adverse party acquired, disclosed, or used the claimant's trade secrets. ... An employee will naturally take with her to a new company the skills, training, and knowledge she has acquired from her time with her previous employer. This basic transfer of information cannot be stopped, unless an employee is not allowed to pursue her livelihood by changing employers. [D's] training on maintaining good customer relationships, developing new clients, and serving current clients is not a trade secret, but rather job skills she developed over time while employed with [P]." *See also* ***Saunders v. Florence Enameling Co.***, 540 So.2d 651, 654-55 (Ala.1988).

Frantz v. Johnson, 999 P.2d 351, 358 (Nev.2000). "The elements of a misappropriation of trade secrets claim include: (1) a valuable trade secret; (2) misappropriation of the trade secret through use, disclosure, or nondisclosure of use of the trade secret; and (3) the requirement that the misappropriation be wrongful because it was made in breach of an express or implied contract or by a party with a duty not to disclose."

Weins v. Sporleder, 569 N.W.2d 16, 24 (S.D.1997). "[Ps] have the burden of proving [Ds] misappropriated the trade secret…."

Minuteman, Inc. v. Alexander, 434 N.W.2d 773, 774 (Wis.1989). "What remedy, if any, is available if a trade secret is improperly acquired, but not subsequently used, by a wrongful taker? We conclude that under [Wisconsin TSA] §134.90(2)(a) [(UTSA §1(2)(i))], an improper acquisition is enough to constitute a misappropriation of a trade secret, and therefore, all remedies in [the UTSA] are available."

Marsteller v. ECS Fed., Inc., No. 1:13cv593 (JCC/JFA) (E.D.Va.2013) (memo op.; 9-5-13). "The Court concludes that [D] validly pleads the element of misappropriation. [P] argues that [D's] Counterclaim fails to adequately allege 'disclosure or use' of a trade secret. [P] ignores, however, the question of improper acquisition of a trade secret. Under the [Virginia UTSA], improper acquisition of a trade secret, even in the absence of allegations of use or disclosure, is sufficient to state a claim."

Sufficiency of Pleading a Claim

TE Connectivity Networks, Inc. v. All Sys. Broadband, Inc., No. 13-1356 ADM/FLN (D.Minn. 2013) (memo op.; 12-26-13). "In the context of pleading a claim for the misappropriation of trade secrets, a plaintiff is understandably hesitant to reveal the exact parameters of the trade secrets it believes have been misappropriated because a trade secret made public is not a secret. However, a plaintiff cannot rely on conclusory statements that simply repeat the elements of its claim; the plaintiff must disclose sufficient information to infer more than a mere possibility of misconduct. [This] court [has considered an allegation] that an executive had 'access to and knowledge of [P's] trade secrets and confidential information.' The court found it could not 'reasonably infer the existence of trade secrets' because [P] did not 'set forth facts showing that the information had independent economic value due to its secrecy, was not readily ascertainable by others and that [P] took efforts to maintain its secrecy.' The court thus found the pleadings conclusory as to the [Minnesota UTSA] claim."

Trade Secret

First Express Servs. Grp. v. Easter, 286 Neb. 912, 925 (Neb.2013). "Although the [Nebraska] Act is based on the [UTSA], the Act's definition of a trade secret differs significantly from the uniform act. Under the uniform act, a trade secret is something that derives independent economic value from not being generally known to, and not being readily ascertainable by proper means by, other persons. The Legislature, however, deleted the qualifiers generally and readily from the statutory definition. And as one commentator noted, Nebraska's statute greatly narrows the definition of a trade secret: Under the literal terms of the language, if an alleged trade secret is *ascertainable at all* by any means that are not 'improper,' the would-be secret is peremptorily excluded from coverage under the Act. The question, then, is whether the information on the list here was ascertainable by proper means." (Internal quotes omitted.)

Iowa Film Prod. v. Iowa Dept. of Econ. Dev., 818 N.W.2d 207, 220 (Iowa 2012). "The definition of a trade secret under [Iowa TSA] §550.2(4) is a mixed question of law and fact. The first part of the definition—information, including but not limited to a formula, pattern, compilation, program, device, method, technique, or process—is the legal question. The two elements—subsections (a) and (b) of §550.2(4)—present questions of fact. [¶] There is virtually no category of information that cannot, as long as the information is protected from disclosure to the public, constitute a trade secret. Business information may fall within the definition of a trade secret, including such matters as maintenance of data on customer lists and needs, source of supplies, *confidential costs*, price data and figures. Trade secrets can range from customer information, to *financial information*, to information about manufacturing processes, to the composition of products. *At 222-23:* The economic value inquiry requires us to consider whether the information at issue protects the owner's competitive edge or advantage. Information kept secret that would be useful to a competitor and require cost, time and effort to duplicate is of economic value. Additionally, the owner must demonstrate the information was unknown to, and not readily ascertainable by, a person who would profit from its disclosure or use. *At 224:* [Ps] have not shown that the information was the subject of reasonable efforts under the circumstances to maintain its secrecy. The key to this test here is found in the statutory phrase 'reasonable under the circumstances.'" (Internal quotes omitted.)

Gognat v. Ellsworth, 259 P.3d 497, 503-04 (Colo. 2011). "We cannot find that the words of the [Colorado TSA] admit of a construction requiring, by reason of the confidential relationship alone, the designation of all proprietary information disclosed by the same plaintiff to the same defendant as one trade secret. Nevertheless, circumstances surrounding the acquisition or disclosure of proprietary information, like the nature, timing, and reasons for the disclosure, clearly permit reasonable inferences about the unity or relatedness of the information disclosed. In the absence of any contention that the disclosure was made, for instance, to someone in the business of buying and selling trade secrets of various kinds, or that different parts of the secret information or process were discovered or developed at distinctly different times, for distinctly different purposes, and using distinctly different experiments or analyses, the fact that a body of secret information was disclosed to the same individual, at the same time, normally provides a powerful reason for treating it as a single trade secret. And the disclosure of a body of proprietary information in exchange for an agreement to embark on a joint commercial venture to profit from the development or application of that information offers perhaps the strongest or most natural reason for treating all of the subject information as the same trade secret for purposes of the statutory limitations period. [¶] But both the specific provisions and overall structure of the Act militate against dividing into multiple trade secrets a single body of proprietary information disclosed to the same person, at substantially the same time, and in furtherance of the same commercial venture."

Wesco Autobody Sup. v. Ernest, 243 P.3d 1069, 1085-86 (Idaho 2010). "In order to prevail in a misappropriation action under the Idaho [TSA], the plaintiff must show that a trade secret actually existed. [T]his Court look[s] to the Restatement [of Torts §757] for six factors that can be used to show that given information is a trade secret: '(1) the extent to which the information is known outside [the plaintiff's] business; (2) the extent to which it is known by employees and others involved in the business; (3) the extent of measures taken by him to guard the secrecy of the information; (4) the value of the information to him and his competitors; (5) the amount of effort or money expended by him in developing the information; and (6) the ease or difficulty with which the information could be properly acquired or duplicated by others.' All of these factors address the issue of whether the information in question is generally known or readily ascertainable." *See also* ***USA Power, LLC v. PacifiCorp***, 235 P.3d 749, 759-60 (Utah 2010) (same as annotation); ***Ohio v. Cincinnati Pub. Sch.***, 916 N.E.2d 1049, 1053 (Ohio 2009) (same as annotation); ***Cemen Tech, Inc. v. Three D Indus.***, 753 N.W.2d 1, 7 (Iowa 2008) (same as annotation); ***Tyson Foods, Inc. v. ConAgra, Inc.***, 79 S.W.3d 326, 331 (Ark.2002) (same as annotation); ***Frantz v. Johnson***, 999 P.2d 351, 358-59 (Nev.2000) (factors specific to customer lists and pricing lists).

USA Power, LLC v. PacifiCorp, 235 P.3d 749, 759-60 (Utah 2010). "We must ... address whether an alchemy of information may constitute a trade secret when its separate parts are each generally known and readily ascertainable, but, when analyzed together such parts derive independent economic value. [¶] '[A] unique combination of generally known elements or steps can qualify as a trade secret, if it represents a valuable contribution attributable to the independent efforts of the one claiming to have conceived it.' '[A] trade secret may include a grouping in which the components are in the public domain but there has been accomplished an effective, successful and valuable integration of those public elements such that the owner derives a competitive advantage from it.' [¶] The compilation of information already within the public domain, however, must not itself be generally known or readily ascertainable. The 'generally known or readily ascertainable' standard 'cannot be viewed as whether the information is generally known and readily ascertainable to the general public, but, based on the defendant['s] knowledge and experience, whether the information was known or ascertainable to [the defendant].' 'It is not enough to point to broad areas of technology and assert that something there must have been secret and misappropriated.' [¶] We hold that a compilation of information within the public domain may constitute a trade secret. To determine whether the product, design, or vision constitutes a trade secret is an intensely factual inquiry to be conducted by the trial court." *See also* ***Lydall, Inc. v. Ruschmeyer***, 919 A.2d 421, 440-41 (Conn.2007); ***Essex Grp. v. Southwire Co.***, 501 S.E.2d 501, 503 (Ga.1998); ***AvidAir Helicopter Sup. v. Rolls-Royce Corp.***, 663 F.3d 966, 972 (8th Cir.2011) (interpreting Indiana and Missouri UTSAs).

Ohio v. Cincinnati Pub. Sch., 916 N.E.2d 1049, 1053 (Ohio 2009). "'An entity claiming trade secret status bears the burden to identify and demonstrate that the material is included in categories of protected information under the statute and additionally must take some active steps to maintain its secrecy.' *At 1054:* [P]ublic entities [can] possess trade secrets." Held: School semester exams are trade secrets.

Cemen Tech, Inc. v. Three D Indus., 753 N.W.2d 1, 7-8 (Iowa 2008). "A trade secret need not be in writing; any secret acquired through an employee's job may be the subject of trade-secret protection. During employment, an employee may acquire two classes of information. First, an employee may obtain information of a general nature simply by being on the job. An employer would have no reasonable expectation that such information would be treated as a trade secret. An employee is free to use or disclose this type of general information. The second class of information is that which the employer intends to keep secret by, for example, physically hiding it from view or ... by requiring confidentiality. While the first class of information is not entitled to trade-secret protection, the second class may be entitled to it. [¶] Whether an employee is subject to a covenant not to compete is not determinative of whether the information gathered through employment constitutes a trade secret. As a general rule, an employee who has not signed an agreement not to compete is free, upon leaving employment, to engage in competitive employment. In so doing, the former employee may freely use general knowledge, skills, and experience acquired under his or her former employer. However, the former employee, even in the absence of an enforceable covenant not to compete, remains under a duty not to use or disclose, to the detriment of the former employer, trade secrets acquired in the course of previous employment. Where the former employee seeks to use the trade secrets of the former employer in order to obtain a competitive advantage, then competitive activity can be enjoined or result in an award of damages. [¶] Additionally, nondisclosure and confidentiality agreements are relevant to determine whether information constitutes a trade secret. [¶] It is not only the nature of the information itself that is significant; the manner of its acquisition is also significant in determining whether information constitutes a trade secret. The subject matter of a trade secret must be secret. Matters of public knowledge or of general knowledge in an industry cannot be appropriated by one as his secret. *However, the interest protected by this branch of the law is not secrecy as such. The protection is merely against breach of faith and reprehensible means of learning another's secret.* Accordingly, a substantial element of secrecy must exist, so that, except by the use of improper means, there would be difficulty in acquiring the information. *At 9:* [T]he fact that information may be obtained by lawful means, including reverse engineering, is not necessarily dispositive of the trade-secret issue." (Internal quotes omitted.)

Pincheira v. Allstate Ins., 190 P.3d 322, 334 (N.M. 2008). "Economic value is one of the defining characteristics of a trade secret. Placing a value on trade secrets is a difficult task, even after the information has been misappropriated and used by a competitor. Uncertainty about the *computation* of value, however, does not mean there must be uncertainty as to the *fact* of value. [¶] In determining whether a trade secret exists, we are concerned only with the fact of the information's value, not the computation of that value. The value does not need to be large, only 'more than trivial,' and it can be shown by circumstantial evidence such as the amount of resources invested in development of the information, efforts to protect its secrecy, and its use in the business. *At 335:* [A]ge alone can never destroy a trade secret. Information remains a trade secret so long as it is kept secret and retains value to both the holder and its competitors. When the information 'encompasses strategies, techniques, goals and plans' that may change over time, the information remains valuable to the extent that it 'still reflects current thinking.' Even if the information no longer reflects current thinking, a competitor could, for example, use old business data to extrapolate a business's current strategy. Age therefore indicates a need for greater scrutiny, but otherwise does not limit information's status as a trade secret. [¶] Information that is publicly available cannot, by definition, be a trade secret. As we have already noted, however, a collection of pages or documents may comprise a trade secret, even though the individual pages or documents, by themselves, are not trade secrets. This may be true even if the individual pages are publicly available."

Ex parte W.L. Halsey Grocery Co., 897 So.2d 1028, 1034 (Ala.2004). "The consumer price volume report and [P's] financial statements, tax returns, and sales evaluations are all created by assembling information from different sources and combining them into one document—be it a report, a statement, or a tax return. This appears to meet the definition of a 'compilation' and to fulfill the second element of a trade secret under the [Alabama TSA]."

Microstrategy Inc. v. Li, 601 S.E.2d 580, 588 (Va. 2004). "Absolute secrecy is not required to establish the existence of a trade secret. Thus, the owner of a trade secret will not lose protection of the law by disclosing the secret to a licensee, an employee, or others, provided that the disclosure is made in express or implied confidence. [¶] '[T]he owner of a trade secret is not entitled to prevent others from using public information to replicate his product, nor may the owner prevent others from making similar products which are not derived from the trade secret.' [¶] In order for a plaintiff to establish ... a trade secret violation, two statutory elements must be proved, namely, the existence of a 'trade secret' and its 'misappropriation' by the defendant. Thus, if a plaintiff fails to prove either required element, the plaintiff is not entitled to relief under the [Virginia TSA]." *See also* ***Boeing Co. v. Sierracin Corp.***, 738 P.2d 665, 674-75 (Wash.1987).

Ex parte Ocwen Fed. Bank, 872 So.2d 810, 816 (Ala.2003). "The mere recitation ... that certain information is a trade secret does not automatically bestow immunity from disclosure. '[T]o receive protection under the [Alabama TSA]' the person or entity attempting to exercise the privilege must show that the information sought to be protected satisfies the definition of a trade secret."

Elm City Cheese Co. v. Federico, 752 A.2d 1037, 1049 (Conn.1999). "[R]easonable efforts to maintain secrecy 'often include some of the following techniques: requiring employees to sign confidentiality agreements or otherwise advising them of the confidential nature of the process; posting of warning or cautionary signs, or placing legends on documents; taking precautions regarding visitors, by requiring them to sign confidentiality agreements, having them sign in, and shielding the process from their view; segregating information, so that no one person or written source discloses the entire manufacturing process; and using unnamed or coded ingredients.' *At 1050:* It is important to note ... that the measures cited ... are merely examples of the types of actions that may be considered, under the appropriate circumstances, to be reasonable efforts to maintain secrecy. [¶] The question of whether, in a specific case, a party has made reasonable efforts to maintain the secrecy of a purported trade secret is by nature a highly fact-specific inquiry."

Spottiswoode v. Levine, 730 A.2d 166, 175 n.7 (Me. 1999). "Some factors a court may examine to determine whether the information '[i]s the subject of efforts that are reasonable under the circumstances to maintain its secrecy' include: (1) the extent to which the information is known outside the plaintiff's business; (2) the extent to which employees and others involved in the plaintiff's business know the information; (3) the nature and extent of measures the plaintiff took to guard the secrecy of the information; (4) the existence or absence of an express agreement restricting disclosure; and (5) the circumstances under which the information was disclosed to any employee, to the extent that the circumstances give rise to a reasonable inference that further disclosure without the plaintiff's consent is prohibited." *See also* ***Dicks v. Jensen***, 768 A.2d 1279, 1284-85 (Vt.2001); ***Minuteman, Inc. v. Alexander***, 434 N.W.2d 773, 777 (Wis.1989).

Paint Brush Corp. v. Neu, 599 N.W.2d 384, 389 (S.D.1999). "The existence of a trade secret is a mixed question of law and fact. 'The legal part of the question is whether the information in question could constitute a trade secret under the first part of the definition of trade secret.' ... The factual part of the question is determined ... from a review of the remaining statutory provisions found in the subdivisions of [South Dakota Statutes] 37-29-1(4) [(UTSA §1(4))]." *See also* ***Home Pride Foods, Inc. v. Johnson***, 634 N.W.2d 774, 781 (Neb.2001).

Ed Nowogroski Ins. v. Rucker, 971 P.2d 936, 942 (Wash.1999). "In determining whether information has 'independent economic value' under the [UTSA], one of the key factors used by the courts is the effort and expense that was expended on developing the information. *At 944:* Trade secret protection will not generally attach to customer lists where the information is readily ascertainable. If information is readily ascertainable from public sources such as trade directories or phone books, then customer lists will not be considered a trade secret and a prior employee, not subject to a noncompetition agreement, would be free to solicit business after leaving employment. [¶] Briefly expressed, whether a customer list is protected as a trade secret depends on three factual inquiries: (1) whether the list is a compilation of information; (2) whether it is valuable because [it is] unknown to others; and (3) whether the owner has made reasonable attempts to keep the information secret. [¶] The question before us is whether the fact that the customer information was in one of the employee's memory allows him to use with impunity the information which was otherwise a trade secret under our statute. *At 948:* [W]e conclude that trade secret protection does not depend on whether the list is taken in written form or memorized." *See also* ***Home Pride Foods, Inc. v. Johnson***, 634 N.W.2d 774, 781 (Neb.2001); ***Public Sys. v. Towry***, 587 So.2d 969, 972-73 (Ala.1991).

Weins v. Sporleder, 569 N.W.2d 16, 20 (S.D.1997). "The burden is upon [P] to show the existence of a trade secret. *At 21:* [Subsection (i)] states there must be economic value which is not readily ascertainable by other means. [T]his requirement precludes trade secret protection for information generally known within an industry even if not to the public at large. [¶] [I]f the information can be readily duplicated without involving considerable time, effort or expense, then it is not secret. [¶] The ease with which one can develop a similar product is examined by focusing on the time and expense involved. *At 22-23:* Secrecy is fundamental to the existence of a trade secret. Although the secrecy is not required to be absolute, reasonable precautions must be taken. [¶] [P] fails to demonstrate active measures were taken to maintain his product's secrecy. ... A few instances of nondisclosure of the alleged secret do not amount to 'reasonable efforts' to maintain secrecy. Furthermore, although confidentiality agreements are not always necessary, there must be other precautions." (Internal quotes omitted.) *See also* ***Centrol, Inc. v. Morrow***, 489 N.W.2d 890, 894-95 (S.D. 1992).

Amoco Prod. v. Laird, 622 N.E.2d 912, 919 (Ind. 1993). "The requirement that there be some measure of time, effort, and funding expended in the duplication or acquisition of information appears calculated to assure not 'that trade secrets be unascertainable at all by proper means, but only that they not be *readily* or *quickly* ascertainable by such means.' [¶] Although the standard ... varies, we find no case holding that 'not being readily ascertainable' adheres when measures required to duplicate or acquire information are so prohibitively burdensome as to be 'economically infeasible.' [¶] We thus find that, consistent with the interpretation of the UTSA in other jurisdictions, where the duplication or acquisition of alleged trade secret information requires a substantial investment of time, expense, or effort, such information may be found 'not being readily ascertainable'...."

§2. INJUNCTIVE RELIEF

(a) Actual or threatened misappropriation may be enjoined. Upon application to the court, an injunction shall be terminated when the trade secret has ceased to exist, but the injunction may be continued for an additional reasonable period of time in order to eliminate commercial advantage that otherwise would be derived from the misappropriation.

(b) In exceptional circumstances, an injunction may condition future use upon payment of a reasonable royalty for no longer than the period of time for which use could have been prohibited. Exceptional circumstances include, but are not limited to, a material and prejudicial change of position prior to acquiring knowledge or reason to know of misappropriation that renders a prohibitive injunction inequitable.

(c) In appropriate circumstances, affirmative acts to protect a trade secret may be compelled by court order.

See also NAFTA art. 1711; Restatement of Unfair Competition (3d) §44 (Injunctions: Appropriation of Trade Secrets).

Official Comment

Injunctions restraining future use and disclosure of misappropriated trade secrets frequently are sought. Although punitive perpetual injunctions have been granted, *e.g.*, *Elcor Chemical Corp. v. Agri-Sul, Inc.*, 494 S.W.2d 204 (Tex.Civ.App.1973), Section 2(a) of this Act adopts the position of the trend of authority limiting the duration of injunctive relief to the extent of the temporal advantage over good faith competitors gained by a misappropriator. *See, e.g.*, *K-2 Ski Co. v. Head Ski Co., Inc.*, 506 F.2d 471 (CA9, 1974) (maximum appropriate duration of both temporary and permanent injunctive relief is period of time it would have taken defendant to discover trade secrets lawfully through either independent development or reverse engineering of plaintiff's products).

The general principle of Section 2(a) and (b) is that an injunction should last for as long as is necessary, but no longer than is necessary, to eliminate the commercial advantage or "lead time" with respect to good faith competitors that a person has obtained through misappropriation. Subject to any additional period of restraint necessary to negate lead time, an injunction accordingly should terminate when a former trade secret becomes either generally known to good faith competitors or generally knowable to them because of the lawful availability of products that can be reverse engineered to reveal a trade secret.

For example, assume that A has a valuable trade secret of which B and C, the other industry members, are originally unaware. If B subsequently misappropriates the trade secret and is enjoined from use, but C later lawfully reverse engineers the trade secret, the injunction restraining B is subject to termination as soon as B's lead time has been dissipated. All of the persons who could derive economic value from use of the information are now aware of it, and there is no longer a trade secret under Section 1(4). It would be anti-competitive to continue to restrain B after any lead time that B had derived from misappropriation had been removed.

If a misappropriator either has not taken advantage of lead time or good faith competitors already have caught up with a misappropriator at the time that a case is decided, future disclosure and use of a former trade secret by a misappropriator will not damage a trade secret owner and no injunctive restraint of future disclosure and use is appropriate. *See, e.g., Northern Petrochemical Co. v. Tomlinson*, 484 F.2d 1057 (CA7, 1973) (affirming trial court's denial of preliminary injunction in part because an explosion at its plant prevented an alleged misappropriator from taking advantage of lead time); *Kubik, Inc. v. Hull*, 185 U.S.P.Q. 391 (Mich.App.1974) (discoverability of trade secret by lawful reverse engineering made by injunctive relief punitive rather than compensatory).

Section 2(b) deals with the special situation in which future use by a misappropriator will damage a trade secret owner but an injunction against future use nevertheless is inappropriate due to exceptional circumstances. Exceptional circumstances include the existence of an overriding public interest which requires the denial of a prohibitory injunction against future damaging use and a person's reasonable reliance upon acquisition of a misappropriated trade secret in good faith and without reason to know of its prior misappropriation that would be prejudiced by a prohibitory injunction against future damaging use. *Republic Aviation Corp. v. Schenk*, 152 U.S.P.Q. 830 (N.Y.Sup.Ct.1967) illustrates the public interest justification for withholding prohibitory injunctive relief. The court considered that enjoining a misappropriator from supplying the U.S. with an aircraft weapons control system would have endangered military personnel in Viet Nam. The prejudice to a good faith third party justification for withholding prohibitory injunctive relief can arise upon a trade secret owner's notification to a good faith third party that the third party has knowledge of a trade secret as a result of misappropriation by another. This notice suffices to make the third party a misappropriator thereafter under Section 1(2)(ii)(B)(I). In weighing an aggrieved person's interests and the interests of a third party who has relied in good faith upon his or her ability to utilize information, a court may conclude that restraining future use of the information by the third party is unwarranted. With respect to innocent acquirers of misappropriated trade secrets, Section 2(b) is consistent with the principle of 4 Restatement Torts (First) §758(b) (1939), but rejects the Restatement's literal conferral of absolute immunity upon all third parties who have paid value in good faith for a trade secret misappropriated by another. The position taken by the Uniform Act is supported by *Forest Laboratories, Inc. v. Pillsbury Co.*, 452 F.2d 621 (CA7, 1971) in which a defendant's purchase of assets of a corporation to which a trade secret had been disclosed in confidence was not considered to confer immunity upon the defendant.

When Section 2(b) applies, a court has discretion to substitute an injunction conditioning future use upon payment of a reasonable royalty for an injunction prohibiting future use. Like all injunctive relief for misappropriation, a royalty order injunction is appropriate only if a misappropriator has obtained a competitive advantage through misappropriation and only for the duration of that competitive advantage. In some situations, typically those involving good faith acquirers of trade secrets misappropriated by others, a court may conclude that the same considerations that render a prohibitory injunction against future use inappropriate also render a royalty order injunction inappropriate. *See generally, Prince Manufacturing, Inc. v. Automatic Partner, Inc.*, 198 U.S.P.Q. 618 (N.J.Super.Ct.1976) (purchaser of misappropriator's assets from receiver after trade secret disclosed to public through sale of product not subject to liability for misappropriation).

A royalty order injunction under Section 2(b) should be distinguished from a reasonable royalty alternative measure of damages under Section 3(a). See the Official Comment to Section 3 for discussion of the differences in the remedies.

Section 2(c) authorizes mandatory injunctions requiring that a misappropriator return the fruits of misappropriation to an aggrieved person, *e.g.*, the return of stolen blueprints or the surrender of surreptitious photographs or recordings.

Where more than one person is entitled to trade secret protection with respect to the same information, only that one from whom misappropriation occurred is entitled to a remedy.

ANNOTATIONS

Lejeune v. Coin Acceptors, Inc., 849 A.2d 451, 465-66 (Md.2004). "A court ... can issue an injunction to prevent either of the following: (1) the actual or threatened acquisition of a trade secret by improper means or (2) the actual or threatened disclosure of a trade secret. *At 470:* No court interpreting the provisions of [the Maryland UTSA (MUTSA)] has applied the theory of 'inevitable disclosure.' [I]ncluding those [courts] interpreting other versions of the [UTSA], the theory remains the subject of considerable disagreement. *At 471:* [W]e conclude that the theory of 'inevitable disclosure' cannot serve as a basis for granting a plaintiff injunctive relief under MUTSA." *See also* ***Holton v. Physician Oncology Servs.***, 742 S.E.2d 702, 706 (Ga.2013) (inevitable discovery is not independent claim under which trial court may enjoin employee from working for employer or disclosing trade secrets). *But see* ***Bendinger v. Marshalltown Trowell Co.***, p. 783.

Georgia Dept. of Nat. Res. v. Theragenics Corp., 545 S.E.2d 904, 906 (Ga.2001). "A business entity does not lose the right to assert that material is a trade secret unless it does not make reasonable efforts to prevent disclosure to those to whom it is not otherwise legally required to divulge the information. Thus, so long as [P] has attempted to prevent its competitors or the public at large from obtaining its proprietary material, [D] cannot contend that the compelled governmental disclosure without an initial claim of confidentiality authorizes it to make a future disclosure of that which [P] has at all times in the past tried to protect. There is no contention that any of the material on file with [D] that [P] originally or subsequently designated as trade secrets lost its confidentiality by disclosure other than to [D]. Accordingly, the Court of Appeals correctly reversed the trial court's denial of [P's] application for a preliminary injunction against [D's] unauthorized disclosure of proprietary material."

Motion Control Sys. v. East, 546 S.E.2d 424, 426 (Va.2001). "Mere knowledge of trade secrets is insufficient to support an injunction under the terms of [Virginia] Code §59.1-337 [(UTSA §2)]."

Bendinger v. Marshalltown Trowell Co., 994 S.W.2d 468, 474 (Ark.1999). "[T]his court adopted the inevitable-disclosure rule.... [W]e recognized that a number of federal cases dealing with trade secrets have held that a plaintiff may prove a claim of trade-secrets misappropriation by demonstrating that a defendant's new employment will inevitably lead him to rely on the plaintiff's trade secrets. *At 475:* While [D] has assumed a position with a competitor of [P's], that position is managerial in nature and does not require him to use his engineering expertise. So, [D] has not even assumed a *similar position* which would render the disclosure of [P's] trade secrets inevitable. ... Because [D] is only using his *general* knowledge gained through his education and his 27 years of experience in [industry], he poses no threat to [P's] trade secrets." *But see* ***Lejeune v. Coin Acceptors, Inc.***, p. 782.

Minuteman, Inc. v. Alexander, 434 N.W.2d 773, 774 (Wis.1989). "What effect, if any, does the possibility of reverse engineering the chemical formula of a trade secret have on remedies available under [the UTSA]? We hold the possibility of reverse engineering is not enough to prevent a temporary injunction from being issued, but rather should be considered when determining the length of the temporary injunction."

§3. DAMAGES

(a) Except to the extent that a material and prejudicial change of position prior to acquiring knowledge or reason to know of misappropriation renders a monetary recovery inequitable, a complainant is entitled to recover damages for misappropriation. Damages can include both the actual loss caused by misappropriation and the unjust enrichment caused by misappropriation that is not taken into account in computing actual loss. In lieu of damages measured by any other methods, the damages caused by misappropriation may be measured by imposition of liability for a reasonable royalty for a misappropriator's unauthorized disclosure or use of a trade secret.

(b) If willful and malicious misappropriation exists, the court may award exemplary damages in an amount not exceeding twice any award made under subsection (a).

See also Restatement of Unfair Competition (3d) §45 (Monetary Relief: Appropriation of Trade Secrets).

Official Comment

Like injunctive relief, a monetary recovery for trade secret misappropriation is appropriate only for the period in which information is entitled to protection as a trade secret, plus the additional period, if any, in which a misappropriator retains an advantage over good faith competitors because of misappropriation. Actual damage to a complainant and unjust benefit to a misappropriator are caused by misappropriation during this time alone. See *Conmar Products Corp. v. Universal Slide Fastener Co.*, 172 F.2d 150 (CA2, 1949) (no remedy for period subsequent to disclosure of trade secret by issued patent); *Carboline Co. v. Jarboe*, 454 S.W.2d 540 (Mo.1970) (recoverable monetary relief limited to period that it would have taken misappropriator to discover trade secret without misappropriation). A claim for actual damages and net profits can be combined with a claim for injunctive relief, but, if both claims are granted, the injunctive relief ordinarily will preclude a monetary award for a period in which the injunction is effective.

As long as there is no double counting, Section 3(a) adopts the principle of the recent cases allowing recovery of both a complainant's actual losses and a misappropriator's unjust benefit that are caused by misappropriation. *E.g.*, *Tri-Tron International v. Velto*, 525 F.2d 432 (CA9, 1975) (complainant's loss and misappropriator's benefit can be combined). Because certain cases may have sanctioned double counting in a combined award of losses and unjust benefit, *e.g.*, *Telex Corp. v. IBM Corp.*, 510 F.2d 894 (CA10, 1975) (per curiam), cert. dismissed, 423 U.S. 802 (1975) (IBM recovered rentals lost due to displacement by misappropriator's products without deduction for expenses saved by displacement; as a result of rough approximations adopted by the trial judge, IBM also may have recovered developmental costs saved by misappropriator through misappropriation with respect to the same customers), the Act adopts an express prohibition upon the counting of the same item as both a loss to a complainant and an unjust benefit to a misappropriator.

As an alternative to all other methods of measuring damages caused by a misappropriator's past conduct, a complainant can request that damages be based upon a demonstrably reasonable royalty for a misappropriator's unauthorized disclosure or use of a trade secret. In order to justify this alternative measure of damages, there must be competent evidence of the amount of a reasonable royalty.

The reasonable royalty alternative measure of damages for a misappropriator's past conduct under Section 3(a) is readily distinguishable from a Section 2(b) royalty order injunction, which conditions a misappropriator's future ability to use a trade secret upon payment of a reasonable royalty. A Section 2(b) royalty order injunction is appropriate only in exceptional circumstances; whereas a reasonable royalty measure of damages is a general option. Because Section 3(a) damages are awarded for a misappropriator's past conduct and a Section 2(b) royalty order injunction regulates a misappropriator's future conduct, both remedies cannot be awarded for the same conduct. If a royalty order injunction is appropriate because of a person's material and prejudicial change of position prior to having reason to know that a trade secret has been acquired from a misappropriator, damages, moreover, should not be awarded for past conduct that occurred prior to notice that a misappropriated trade secret has been acquired.

Monetary relief can be appropriate whether or not injunctive relief is granted under Section 2. If a person charged with misappropriation has materially and prejudicially changed position in reliance upon knowledge of a trade secret acquired in good faith and without reason to know of its misappropriation by another, however, the same considerations that can justify denial of all injunctive relief also can justify denial of all monetary relief. See *Conmar Products Corp. v. Universal Slide Fastener Co.*, 172 F.2d 1950 (CA2, 1949) (no relief against new employer of employee subject to contractual obligation not to disclose former employer's trade secrets where new employer innocently had committed $40,000 to develop the trade secrets prior to notice of misappropriation).

If willful and malicious misappropriation is found to exist, Section 3(b) authorizes the court to award a complainant exemplary damages in addition to the actual recovery under Section 3(a) an amount not exceeding twice that recovery. This provision follows federal patent law in leaving discretionary trebling to the judge even though there may be a jury, *compare* 35 U.S.C. Section 284 (1976).

Whenever more than one person is entitled to trade secret protection with respect to the same information, only that one from whom misappropriation occurred is entitled to a remedy.

ANNOTATIONS

Pro-Comp Mgmt. v. R.K. Enters., 237 S.W.3d 20, 23 (Ark.2006). "[A]ctual loss noted in the statute is calculated as the plaintiff's lost profits or the defendant's gain, whichever affords the greater recovery." (Internal quotes omitted.)

World Wide Prosthetic Sup. v. Mikulsky, 640 N.W.2d 764, 770 (Wis.2002). "[W]e determine that 'actual loss' as used in [Wisconsin TSA] §134.90(4)(a) [(UTSA §3(a))] may include lost profits resulting from [D's] manufacture and distribution of a defective product incorporating [P's] trade secret."

Home Pride Foods, Inc. v. Johnson, 634 N.W.2d 774, 784 (Neb.2001). "Courts in other jurisdictions have held that it is impermissible double recovery for a court to award damages for future use and, at the same time, issue a permanent injunction barring such use. [¶] The court's award for the value of future sales is inconsistent with the issuance of a permanent injunction. [P] requested, and was given, a permanent injunction. The court's award of $10,000 for future sales was an impermissible double recovery and is reversed."

McFarland v. Brier, 769 A.2d 605, 611 (R.I.2001). "[W]e are satisfied that in the case of a violation of the [UTSA], punitive damages are available for conduct that is willful and malicious and need not rise to the level of criminality."

Ed Nowogroski Ins. v. Rucker, 971 P.2d 936, 942 (Wash.1999). "A plaintiff seeking damages for misappropriation of a trade secret under the [UTSA] has the burden of proving that legally protectable secrets exist."

Olson v. Nieman's, Ltd., 579 N.W.2d 299, 310 (Iowa 1998). "Determining a reasonable royalty is analogous to a jury's determination of a proper amount of damages for pain and suffering in a personal injury suit. Like reasonable royalties, pain and suffering cannot be measured by any exact mathematical formula. *At 311:* Such flexibility in determining a reasonable royalty is imperative in cases involving business torts such as misappropriation of trade secrets. ... This is especially important where (1) a defendant has destroyed the value of [a] plaintiff's secret through publication and has not enjoyed any profits and (2) the plaintiff is hard-pressed to show any loss. [¶] [Expert's] calculation of damages not only assumes a market for [P's] device but also a profitable one. [Expert's] assumptions are reasonable because they are based on (1) [another expert's] testimony that the device was patentable and (2) statements [D's] competitors made that there would be a demand for the device."

Lemmon v. Hendrickson, 559 N.W.2d 278, 279 (Iowa 1997). "There are three recognized prerequisites for relief based on the appropriation of a trade secret: (1) existence of a trade secret, (2) acquisition of the secret as a result of a confidential relationship, and (3) unauthorized use of the secret. [P] has the burden to establish each of these elements by a preponderance of the evidence."

§4. ATTORNEY'S FEES

If (i) a claim of misappropriation is made in bad faith, (ii) a motion to terminate an injunction is made or resisted in bad faith, or (iii) willful and malicious misappropriation exists, the court may award reasonable attorney's fees to the prevailing party.

Official Comment

Section 4 allows a court to award reasonable attorney fees to a prevailing party in specified circumstances as a deterrent to specious claims of misappropriation, to specious efforts by a misappropriator to terminate injunctive relief, and to willful and malicious misappropriation. In the latter situation, the court should take into consideration the extent to which a complainant will recover exemplary damages in determining whether additional attorney's fees should be awarded. Again, patent law is followed in allowing the judge to determine whether attorney's fees should be awarded even if there is a jury, *compare* 35 U.S.C. Section 285 (1976).

ANNOTATIONS

Halifax-Am. Energy Co. v. Provider Power, LLC, ___ A.3d ___ (N.H.2018) (No. 2016-0241; 2-9-18). "[T]he trial court used a totality of the circumstances test to determine whether to award attorney's fees to the plaintiffs under the NHUTSA. The court considered the fact that the jury did not award [Ps] damages for their misappropriation claim, but concluded that the extent of [Ds'] malice and willfulness outweighed that fact. The court also observed that awarding fees in this case furthered the goals of the NHUTSA to maintain standards of commercial ethics and deter intentional misappropriation of trade secrets. [¶] [W]e conclude that the trial court did not unsustainably exercise its discretion when it awarded [Ps] their attorney's fees under the NHUTSA."

Tradesman Int'l v. Black, 724 F.3d 1004, 1016 (7th Cir.2013). "[W]e conclude that 'made in bad faith' is correctly interpreted as either bringing or maintaining a suit in bad faith. [¶] A claim is made in bad faith when it is initiated in bad faith, maintained in bad faith, or both." (Interpreting Illinois UTSA.)

§5. PRESERVATION OF SECRECY

In an action under this [Act], a court shall preserve the secrecy of an alleged trade secret by reasonable means, which may include granting protective orders in connection with discovery proceedings, holding in-camera hearings, sealing the records of the action, and ordering any person involved in the litigation not to disclose an alleged trade secret without prior court approval.

Official Comment

If reasonable assurances of maintenance of secrecy could not be given, meritorious trade secret litigation would be chilled. In fashioning safeguards of confidentiality, a court must ensure that a respondent is provided sufficient information to present a defense and a trier of fact sufficient information to resolve the merits. In addition to the illustrative techniques specified in the statute, courts have protected secrecy in these cases by restricting disclosures to a party's counsel and his or her assistants and by appointing a disinterested expert as a special master to hear secret information and report conclusions to the court.

ANNOTATIONS

Sioux Pharm, Inc. v. Eagle Labs., 865 N.W.2d 528, 536 (Iowa 2015). "[T]he nature of disclosure in a trade-secret case is singularly within the discretion of the district court, ... and ... the unique character of the discovery process requires that the trial court have substantial latitude to fashion protective orders.... *At 537:* There is no true privilege against discovery of trade secrets or other confidential information. Yet, once a trade secret is disclosed to a competitor and litigation adversary, it may be too late to grant an adequate remedy to the holder of the secret—the disclosure destroys the value of the secret data. [A] trade secret must and should be disclosed if the disclosure is relevant and necessary to the proper presentation of a plaintiff's or defendant's case. [¶] Once a district court has found information sought in discovery is a trade secret, it must determine whether good cause exists for a protective order. The court should employ three criteria: The harm posed by dissemination must be substantial and serious; the restraining order must be narrowly drawn and precise; and there must be no alternative means of protecting the public interest which intrudes less directly on expression. The district court is to strike a balance between the policy favoring discovery and free expression on one side and a party's interest in avoiding commercial damage and preventing an abuse of discovery on the other. After the court has weighed the harm from disclosure against the need for the information, the court must issue an appropriate protective order to safeguard the rights of the parties. *At 539:* The caselaw uniformly and sensibly holds, all other things being equal, that the risk of harm from disclosure to a competitor is generally greater than the risk of harm related to disclosure to a noncompetitor. [¶] On the other hand, the opposing party seeking disclosure, even if a competitor, may claim that disclosure of documents to its decision-makers is necessary to allow it to litigate effectively. ... A naked contention, however, that access will affect the ability of the defendant to defend its case, without more, is not sufficient. In order to evaluate the asserted need for further disclosure, the court must have a thorough understanding of the contested issues in the case, how the documents relate to the contested issues, and how the fact-finding process would be aided by disclosure of the documents to the persons seeking to view the documents. [¶] There appears to be a prevailing view among courts addressing the issue that competitive decision-makers of direct competitors should be denied access to trade secrets in litigation." (Internal quotes omitted.)

Laffitte v. Bridgestone Corp., 674 S.E.2d 154, 162 (S.C.2009). The South Carolina TSA, unlike the UTSA, "clearly indicates that trade secrets may be protected during discovery not only in misappropriation cases, but in 'any civil action' where trade secrets are sought during discovery. [¶] [The court adopts the Indiana Supreme Court's balancing test from ***Bridgestone Americas Holding, Inc. v. Mayberry***, 878 N.E.2d 189 (Ind.2007).] *At 163:* Regarding the requirement that the trade secret information must be 'relevant,' we hold that the information must be relevant not only to the general subject matter of the litigation, but also relevant specifically to the issues involved in the litigation. For the trade secret information to be deemed 'necessary,' we hold that the party seeking the information 'cannot merely assert unfairness but must demonstrate with specificity exactly how the lack of the information will impair the presentation of the case on the merits to the point that an unjust result is a real, rather than a merely possible, threat.' 'Implicit in this is the notion that suitable substitutes must be completely lacking.' In other words, the trial court must evaluate whether there are reasonable alternatives available to the party seeking the discovery of the information, and ultimately, the trial court must require the discovery of a trade secret only when 'the issues cannot be fairly adjudicated unless the information is available.'"

Bridgestone Americas Holding, Inc. v. Mayberry, 878 N.E.2d 189, 193 (Ind.2007). "[F]ederal courts have consistently applied a three-part balancing test when a party seeks an order protecting trade secrets from discovery. First, the party opposing discovery must show that the information sought is a 'trade secret or other confidential research, development, or commercial information' and that disclosure would be harmful. Then the burden shifts to the party seeking discovery to show that the information is relevant and necessary to bring the matter to trial. If both parties satisfy their burden, the court must weigh the potential harm of disclosure against the need for the information in reaching a decision. *At 194:* [W]e adopt the three-part balancing test as the proper analysis for whether 'good cause' has been shown and whether a protective order should be issued for a trade secret during discovery. *At 196:* [I]t is clear from the case law that establishing necessity is the heart of this three-part analysis. When necessity is established, courts frequently hold that the trade secret must be disclosed, albeit with some protection. [¶] 'Necessity' means that without discovery of the particular trade secret, the discovering party would be unable to present its case 'to the point that an unjust result is a real, rather than a merely possible, threat.' Implicit in this is the notion that suitable substitutes must be completely lacking."

DVD Copy Control Ass'n v. Bunner, 75 P.3d 1, 14 (Cal.2003). "The First Amendment does not prohibit courts from incidentally enjoining speech in order to protect a legitimate property right. And the mere fact that [D] claims an expressive purpose does not give him a First Amendment right to appropriate ... the harvest of those who have sown. Indeed, the protection of trade secrets and the benefits to research and development derived from the government's recognition of this property right *depend* on the judiciary's power to enjoin disclosures by those who know or have reason to know of their misappropriation. [W]e can think of[ ] no less restrictive way of protecting an owner's constitutionally recognized property interest in its trade secrets. Thus, the preliminary injunction burdens no more speech than necessary to serve the government's interest in encouraging innovation and development." (Internal quotes omitted.) *But see* ***State ex rel. Sports Mgmt. News, Inc. v. Nachtigal***, this page.

State ex rel. Sports Mgmt. News, Inc. v. Nachtigal, 921 P.2d 1304, 1309 (Or.1996). Oregon TSA 646.469 "authorizes a court to compel silence from one who desires to speak. And that statute authorizes the judicial prohibition based on the subject or content of the desired speech. The nondisclosure provision of the statute is invalid as violative of [Oregon Const.] Art. I, §8...." *But see* ***DVD Copy Control Ass'n v. Bunner***, this page.

Boeing Co. v. Sierracin Corp., 738 P.2d 665, 676 (Wash.1987). "[P] did not lose its trade secrets through publication of exhibits at trial. Prior to trial [P] moved to exclude the general public from the courtroom during presentation of certain testimony and evidence. [¶] Furthermore, the trial court was justified in sealing the record. [Washington TSA] 19.108.050 [(UTSA §5)] allows for this procedure as it is obvious that otherwise trade secrets holders would be prevented from defending their rights in court. The same reasoning applies to use of exhibits at trial. As a trade secrets holder who in good faith sought legal remedy to protect its rights, [P] did not thereby 'publish' and lose its secrets at trial."

§6. STATUTE OF LIMITATIONS

An action for misappropriation must be brought within 3 years after the misappropriation is discovered or by the exercise of reasonable diligence should have been discovered. For the purposes of this section, a continuing misappropriation constitutes a single claim.

Official Comment

There presently is a conflict of authority as to whether trade secret misappropriation is a continuing wrong. *Compare Monolith Portland Midwest Co. v. Kaiser Aluminum & Chemical Corp.*, 407 F.2d 288 (CA9, 1969) (not a continuing wrong under California law—limitation period upon all recovery begins upon initial misappropriation) with *Underwater Storage, Inc. v. U. S. Rubber Co.*, 371 F.2d 950 (CADC, 1966), cert. den., 386 U.S. 911 (1967) (continuing wrong under general principles—limitation period with respect to a specific act of misappropriation begins at the time that the act of misappropriation occurs).

This Act rejects a continuing wrong approach to the statute of limitations but delays the commencement of the limitation period until an aggrieved person discovers or reasonably should have discovered the existence of misappropriation. If objectively reasonable notice of misappropriation exists, three years is sufficient time to vindicate one's legal rights.

ANNOTATIONS

Gognat v. Ellsworth, 259 P.3d 497, 501 (Colo. 2011). "[T]he legislative decision to measure the limitations period for continuing misappropriations from the initial discovery of a single act of misappropriation has the clear effect of precluding an injured party from delaying until the misuse of his trade secret has become sufficiently profitable to make his resort to legal action economically worthwhile. Despite this clear statutory design, however, the question remains, with regard to the facts and circumstances of each individual claim, whether any specific act of misappropriation constitutes a continuing misappropriation of the same trade secret or the separate and distinct misappropriation of a different trade secret. *At 503:* Consistent with the statutory language, ... multiple acts of misappropriation constitute a 'continuing misappropriation,' and consequently a single claim within the meaning of the statute, only to the extent that the processes, procedures, or other pieces of information used in each separate act of misappropriation are related to each other as portions or phases of a single trade secret—not merely as related trade secrets. [¶] The difference between 'related trade secrets' and related designs, processes, procedures, formulas, and improvements themselves, however, may be largely a matter of terminology. In either case, avoiding arbitrariness in differentiating one from another requires a rational[ ] basis or controlling principle consistent with the purposes of the statutory accrual rule. While the actual language of the statute may not classify a subsequent misappropriation of related trade secrets as a single claim, the distinction between related trade secrets and the related pieces of proprietary information forming a single trade secret would appear to be subtle at best."

Pincheira v. Allstate Ins., 190 P.3d 322, 335 (N.M. 2008). "[W]e note that the three-year statute of limitations ... has nothing to do with whether information has lost its trade secret status because of its age. Information can remain a trade secret for much longer than three years. The purpose of the statute of limitations is not to set a maximum age on a trade secret, but to 'compel the exercise of a right of action within a reasonable time so that the party against whom the action is brought will have a fair opportunity to defend.'"

Cadence Design Sys. v. Avant! Corp., 57 P.3d 647, 651 (Cal.2002). Continuing misappropriation "is the continuing use or disclosure of a trade secret after that secret was acquired by improper means or as otherwise specified [under the UTSA]. Thus, for statute of limitations purposes, a continuing misappropriation is viewed as a single claim. The drafters of the UTSA explicitly affirmed [this view]. [¶] [A] distinction between a 'misappropriation' and a 'claim' emerges. A *misappropriation* within the meaning of the UTSA occurs not only at the time of the initial acquisition of the trade secret by wrongful means, but also with each misuse or wrongful disclosure of the secret. But a *claim* for misappropriation of a trade secret arises for a given plaintiff against a given defendant only once, at the time of the initial misappropriation.... Each new misuse or wrongful disclosure is viewed as augmenting a single claim of continuing misappropriation rather than as giving rise to a separate claim."

Ordnance Techs. (N. Am.) Inc. v. Raytheon Co., No. CV 12-386-TUC-CKJ (D.Ariz.2014) (order; 2-26-14). "[T]he three year limitations period starts when the misappropriation is discovered (or by reasonable diligence should have been discovered) and a continuing misappropriation is only one claim. Although jurisdictions treat continuing violations differently, ... Arizona's statute is not ambiguous. In other words, once the misappropriation is discovered, it does not matter if it is ongoing, the period begins to run when it is discovered." (Interpreting Arizona UTSA.)

§7. EFFECT ON OTHER LAW

(a) Except as provided in subsection (b), this [Act] displaces conflicting tort, restitutionary, and other law of this State providing civil remedies for misappropriation of a trade secret.

(b) This [Act] does not affect:

(1) contractual remedies, whether or not based upon misappropriation of a trade secret;

(2) other civil remedies that are not based upon misappropriation of a trade secret; or

(3) criminal remedies, whether or not based upon misappropriation of a trade secret.

See also NAFTA art. 1711.

Official Comment

This Act does not deal with criminal remedies for trade secret misappropriation and is not a comprehensive statement of civil remedies. It applies to a duty to protect competitively significant secret information that is imposed by law. It does not apply to a duty voluntarily assumed through an express or an implied-in-fact contract. The enforceability of covenants not to disclose trade secrets and covenants not to compete that are intended to protect trade secrets, for example, is governed by other law. The Act also does not apply to a duty imposed by law that is not dependent upon the existence of competitively significant secret information, like an agent's duty of loyalty to his or her principal.

ANNOTATIONS

CaremarkPCS Health, LLC v. New Hampshire Dept. of Admin. Servs., 116 A.3d 1054, 1059 (N.H. 2015). "[W]e hold that a 'misappropriation' of a trade secret is 'prohibited' by the UTSA. Accordingly, because disclosure of the designated information by [respondent] would be a misappropriation of [petitioner's] trade secrets under the UTSA, we conclude that disclosure of that information is 'prohibited by statute' under RSA 91-A:4, I, [the New Hampshire Right-to-Know Law] and, therefore, we hold that the designated information is exempt from disclosure under RSA 91-A:4, I. [¶] We note that our holding is in accord with cases in other jurisdictions, in which courts have held that, if the disclosure of trade secrets would constitute a misappropriation, such information is exempt from disclosure under public record laws." *See also* ***Pfizer Inc. v. Oregon Dept. of Justice***, 294 P.3d 496, 510 (Or.Ct.App. 2012); ***American Family Mut. Ins. v. Missouri Dept. of Ins.***, 169 S.W.3d 905, 913-14 (Mo.Ct.App.2005); ***State v. Ohio State Univ.***, 721 N.E.2d 1044, 1049 (Ohio 2000); ***Progressive Animal Welfare Soc'y v. University of Wash.***, 884 P.2d 592, 603 (Wash.1994).

Orca Comms. Unlimited, LLC v. Noder, 337 P.3d 545, 546 (Ariz.2014). "We hold that [the Arizona UTSA] does not displace common-law claims based on alleged misappropriation of confidential information that is not a trade secret. *At 548:* Because [the] displacement provision [§7] is expressly limited to claims 'providing civil remedies for misappropriation of a trade secret,' ... and because [P's] unfair-competition claim ... is not limited to trade secrets, the superior court erred in dismissing that claim on preemption grounds. [¶] We acknowledge ... the split of authority on whether the Uniform Act displaces all common-law tort claims based on misappropriation of confidential information, whether or not the information constitutes a statutorily defined trade secret."

Robbins v. Supermarket Equip. Sales, LLC, 722 S.E.2d 55, 58 (Ga.2012). "The [Georgia TSA] supersedes all conflicting laws providing restitution or civil remedies for the misappropriation of trade secrets. For the GTSA to maintain its exclusiveness, a plaintiff cannot be allowed to plead a lesser and alternate theory of restitution simply because the information does not qualify as a trade secret under the act. [T]he 'GTSA preempts claims [that] rely on the same allegations as those underlying the plaintiff's claim for misappropriation of a trade secret.' [¶] The fact that the [purported trade secrets] were not ultimately found to be trade secrets under the act did not make the preemption clause inapplicable. Rather the key inquiry is whether the same factual allegations of misappropriation are being used to obtain relief outside the GTSA."

BlueEarth Biofuels, LLC v. Hawaiian Elec. Co., 235 P.3d 310, 328 (Haw.2010). "[W]e answer the certified questions as follows. [¶] (1) When are 'tort, restitutionary, and other law[s] of this state' displaced because they 'conflict' with [Hawaiian UTSA (HUTSA)] §482B-8 [(UTSA §7)]? [¶] 'Tort, restitutionary, and other law[s] of this state' [that] conflict with the HUTSA, are ... displaced[ ] to the extent that they are based upon misappropriation of a trade secret. That is, 'if proof of a [non-HUTSA] claim would also simultaneously establish a claim for misappropriation of trade secrets, it is preempted irrespective of whatever surplus elements or proof were necessary to establish it.' [¶] (2) When a claim is found to 'conflict' with HUTSA, what is the scope of preemption, or displacement, of that claim under ... §482B-8 [(UTSA §7)]? [¶] For those claims found to conflict with the HUTSA, the scope of displacement is complete. However, a claim may survive to the extent it alleges wrongful conduct independent of the misappropriation of trade secrets. *At 329:* (3) May a claim that is found not to 'conflict' with HUTSA still be preempted, or displaced, under ... §482B-8 [(UTSA §7)]? [¶] Only claims that are found to conflict with the HUTSA are preempted. [¶] (4) Does HUTSA also preempt, or displace, claims based upon the alleged misuse of 'confidential information,' which is determined, before or during trial, not to meet the definition of 'trade secret' under … §482B-8 [(UTSA §7)]? [¶] The HUTSA displaces non-contract civil claims based upon the alleged acquisition, disclosure, or use of confidential information that does not rise to the level of a statutorily-defined trade secret. Accordingly, it is unnecessary to determine whether or not the information at issue meets the definition of a trade secret before addressing displacement under the HUTSA." *See also* ***HDNET, LLC v. North Am. Boxing Council***, 972 N.E.2d 920, 924-25 (Ind.Ct.App.2012).

Mortgage Specialists, Inc. v. Davey, 904 A.2d 652, 664 (N.H.2006). Section 7 "provides that the [UTSA] preempts claims that are based upon the unauthorized use of information, regardless of whether that information meets the statutory definition of a trade secret. Thus, except as otherwise provided in [§7(b)], the [UTSA] essentially creates a system in which information is classified only as either a protected trade secret or unprotected general knowledge. [¶] [W]e agree with the trial court's conclusion that the preemption provision did not require that it make a determination of whether the information at issue constituted a trade secret under the [New Hampshire UTSA (NHUTSA)] prior to determining whether any of [P's] common law or [Consumer Protection Act] claims [were] preempted by the NHUTSA. *At 665:* In determining whether a claim conflicts with the UTSA, we agree with the majority of courts, which have looked to the facts alleged or proved in support of the claim and have found that the claim is preempted when it is based solely on, or to the extent that it is based on, the allegations or the factual showings of unauthorized use of information or misappropriation of a trade secret. We also agree with courts that have concluded that a claim is not preempted where the elements of the claim require some allegation or factual showing in addition to that which forms the basis for a claim of misappropriation of a trade secret. *At 666:* We conclude that, to determine whether [P's] claims are preempted by the NHUTSA, a court must examine the facts alleged in support of each claim to determine the extent to which the claim is based upon the misappropriation of trade secrets or other information." (Internal quotes omitted.) *But see* ***Burbank Grease Servs. v. Sokolowski***, this page.

Burbank Grease Servs. v. Sokolowski, 717 N.W.2d 781, 785 (Wis.2006). "This case requires us to determine whether the trade secret statute … precludes all civil law remedies based on the misappropriation of confidential information that falls outside of the statutory definition of a trade secret. … We conclude that [UTSA §7(a)] does not preclude all other civil remedies based on the misappropriation of confidential information, if the information does not meet the statutory definition of a trade secret under [UTSA §1(4)]. Accordingly, in the case before us, [UTSA §7(b)(2)] permits civil tort remedies based on the misappropriation of confidential information." *But see* ***Mortgage Specialists, Inc. v. Davey***, this page.

Frantz v. Johnson, 999 P.2d 351, 357-58 (Nev. 2000). "[T]he district court erred in relying on numerous tort and restitutionary causes of action that were explicitly excluded by statute, as they all related to a misappropriation of a trade secret. Specifically, the district court erred in awarding damages based on the following causes of action: (1) misappropriation of confidential information, (2) breach of fiduciary duty, (3) intentional interference with contractual relations, (4) intentional interference with prospective advantage, (5) the tort of breach of the covenant of good faith and fair dealing, (6) civil conspiracy, and (7) unjust enrichment. These causes of action would normally be precluded by [Nevada TSA] 600A.090 [(UTSA §7)] because they arose from a single factual episode, namely misappropriation of bidding and pricing information."

Weins v. Sporleder, 605 N.W.2d 488, 491-92 (S.D. 2000). "South Dakota's adoption of the [UTSA] prevents a plaintiff from merely restating their trade secret claims as separate tort claims. In analyzing claims for the purpose of applying the displacement provision, the issue is not what label the plaintiff puts on their claims. Rather, the court is to look beyond the label to the facts being asserted in support of the claims. A plaintiff 'may not rely on acts that constitute trade secret misappropriation to support other causes of action.' [¶] In examining a plaintiff's claims to determine if claims are related, numerous courts have specifically found that tort claims such as fraud, unfair competition, and breach of fiduciary duty are preempted by the [UTSA]."

Angelica Textile Servs. v. Park (4th Dist.2013) 220 Cal.App.4th 495, 505, *modified*, No. D062405 (4th Dist.2013) (order; 11-7-13). "[T]he determination of whether a claim is based on trade secret misappropriation is largely factual. *At 506:* In considering whether a particular claim has been displaced, we must recognize a prime purpose of the law was to sweep away the adopting states' bewildering web of rules and rationales and replace it with a uniform set of principles for determining when one is—and is not—liable for acquiring, disclosing, or using information of value. In general, the acquisition, disclosure or transfer of information that does not fit UTSA's definition of a trade secret does not give rise to any liability, even when that liability is couched in terms of a separate tort or statutory violation. [¶] However, … UTSA by its terms does not displace a contract claim, even if it is based on the misappropriation of a trade secret. Moreover, UTSA does not displace noncontract claims that, although related to a trade secret misappropriation, are independent and based on facts distinct from the facts that support the misappropriation claim. *At 507:* Our review of the record shows that none of the non-UTSA claims asserted [by P] were displaced. [P's] claims for breach of contract, breach of fiduciary duty, unfair competition, interference with business relations and conversion each have a basis independent of any misappropriation of a trade secret." (Internal quotes omitted.)

§8. UNIFORMITY OF APPLICATION & CONSTRUCTION

This [Act] shall be applied and construed to effectuate its general purpose to make uniform the law with respect to the subject of this [Act] among states enacting it.

ANNOTATIONS

Orca Comms. Unlimited, LLC v. Noder, 337 P.3d 545, 549 (Ariz.2014). The Arizona UTSA (AUTSA) "does not contain the Uniform Act's [§8]. Because other statutes derived from uniform acts include similar language, … its absence from AUTSA suggests that the legislature intentionally omitted it."

§9. SHORT TITLE

This [Act] may be cited as the Uniform Trade Secrets Act.

§10. SEVERABILITY

If any provision of this [Act] or its application to any person or circumstances is held invalid, the invalidity does not affect other provisions or applications of the [Act] which can be given effect without the invalid provision or application, and to this end the provisions of this [Act] are severable.

§11. TIME OF TAKING EFFECT

This [Act] takes effect on ________________, and does not apply to misappropriation occurring prior to the effective date. With respect to a continuing misappropriation that began prior to the effective date, the [Act] also does not apply to the continuing misappropriation that occurs after the effective date.

Official Comment

The Act applies exclusively to misappropriation that begins after its effective date. Neither misappropriation that began and ended before the effective date nor misappropriation that began before the effective date and continued thereafter is subject to the Act.

§12. REPEAL[1]

The following Acts and parts of Acts are repealed:

(1)

(2)

(3)

1. Editor's note: Section 12 was proposed by the NCCUSL to allow states to explicitly repeal conflicting trade-secret laws in their enactments of the UTSA.

UTSA Chart

Differences from State Enactments

Uniform Trade Secrets Act vs. State Enactments

This chart highlights the substantive differences between the Uniform Trade Secrets Act (UTSA) sections and the corresponding sections in a particular state's enactment of the UTSA. (Not all states have enacted the UTSA.) Although UTSA §10 ("Severability") may have no corresponding state enactment, many states have a general statute or case law governing severability.

UTSA	State Act	Difference
		Alabama
§1	8-27-2	Slightly different definitions of "trade secret" and "improper means"; definition of "misappropriation" converted into cause of action in 8-27-3
§§2-4	8-27-4	Combines injunction, damages, and attorney-fees provisions into one section (8-27-4); remedies and conditions for remedies are altered
§5	None	No corresponding section
§6	8-27-5	Two-year statute of limitations
§7	8-27-6	More succinct statement of UTSA's effect on other law
§8	None	No corresponding section (uniformity and construction)
§9	8-27-1	None
§10	None	No corresponding section (severability)
§11	None	No corresponding section (effective date)
§12	None	No corresponding section (repealer)
		Alaska
§1	45.50.940	No definition of "person"
§2	45.50.910(b)	Unreasonable prohibition rather than "exceptional circumstances" for court to allow future use of trade secret
§3	45.50.915(a)	No prohibition of inequitable monetary recovery; no measurement for misappropriation damages
§4	None	No corresponding section
§5	45.50.920	None
§6	45.50.925	None
§7	45.50.930	None
None	45.50.930(c)	State law does not apply to certain investigations by Attorney General
§8	45.50.935	None
§9	45.50.945	None
§10	None	No corresponding section (severability)
§11	None	No corresponding section (effective date)
§12	None	No corresponding section (repealer)
		Arizona
§1	44-401	None
§2	44-402	None
§3	44-403	None
§4	44-404	None

UTSA	STATE ACT	DIFFERENCE
Arizona (continued)		
§5	44-405	None
§6	44-406	None
§7	44-407	None
§8	None	No corresponding section (uniformity and construction)
§9	None	No corresponding section (short title)
§10	None	No corresponding section (severability)
§11	None	No corresponding section (effective date)
§12	None	No corresponding section (repealer)
Arkansas		
§1	4-75-601	None
§2	4-75-604(c)	Unreasonable prohibition rather than "exceptional circumstances" for court to allow future use of trade secret
§3	4-75-606	No prohibition of inequitable monetary recovery; no measurement for misappropriation damages; no exemplary damages
§4	4-75-607	None
§5	4-75-605	None
§6	4-75-603	None
§7	4-75-602	None
§8	None	No corresponding section (uniformity and construction)
§9	None	No corresponding section (short title)
§10	None	No corresponding section (severability)
§11	None	No corresponding section (effective date)
§12	None	No corresponding section (repealer)
California		
§1	3426.1(a)	Reverse engineering and independent derivation alone are not "improper means"
§1	3426.1(c)	"Person" includes limited-liability company
§1	3426.1(d)(1)	No requirement that trade secret not be readily ascertainable by proper means
§2	3426.2(a)	No "reasonable" requirement for additional time for injunction
§2	3426.2(b)	Unreasonable prohibition rather than "exceptional circumstances" for court to allow future use of trade secret
§3(a)	3426.3(a)	No prohibition of inequitable monetary recovery
§3(a)	3426.3(b)	Different calculation for unprovable damages
§4	3426.4	None
§5	3426.5	None
§6	3426.6	None
§7	3426.7(a)	Exceptions must be expressly provided (refers only to state statutes)

UTSA Chart
Differences from State Enactments

UTSA	State Act	Difference
California (continued)		
§7	3426.7(c)	Does not affect disclosures under California Public Records Act
§8	3426.8	None
§9	3426	None
§10	3426.9	None
§11	3426.10	None
§12	None	No corresponding section (repealer)
None	3426.11	Privacy statement about disclosures in judicial and legislative proceedings, reservation of personal rights, and reporting improper government activity
Colorado		
§1	7-74-102(4)	Broader definition of "trade secret"; no "economic value" language; no requirement that information not be readily ascertainable by proper means
§1	None	No definition of "person"
§2(a)	7-74-103	No termination or continuation language, only a requirement of "reasonable terms"
§2(b), (c)	7-74-103	No "future use" or "affirmative acts" language
§3(b)	7-74-104(2)	Exemplary damages awarded if misappropriation is accompanied by fraud, malice, or willful or wanton behavior; exemplary damages may be awarded by court or jury; no doubling of exemplary damages
§4	7-74-105	None
§5	7-74-106	None
§6	7-74-107	None
§7	7-74-108	None
§8	7-74-109	None
§9	7-74-101	None
§10	7-74-110	None
§11	None	No corresponding section (effective date)
§12	None	No corresponding section (repealer)
Connecticut		
§1	35-51(a)	"Improper means" includes searching through trash
§1	35-51(b)	"Misappropriation" applies to public records, inspection, and toxic-substances statute
§1	35-51(c)	"Person" includes limited-liability company
§1	35-51(d)	"Trade secret" includes public records, inspection, and toxic-substances statute
§2	35-52	Unreasonable prohibition rather than "exceptional circumstances" for court to allow future use of trade secret
§3	35-53	No measurement for misappropriation damages
§4	35-54	None
§5	35-55	None
§6	35-56	None

UTSA	STATE ACT	DIFFERENCE
		Connecticut (continued)
§7	35-57(a)	Parties can agree if Act supersedes conflicting law
§7	35-57(b)	Exceptions for certain disclosures (public records, inspection, and toxic-substances statute)
§8	35-58	None
§9	35-50	None
§10	None	No corresponding section (severability)
§11	None	No corresponding section (effective date)
§12	None	No corresponding section (repealer)
		Delaware
	6 Del.C. 2001-2009	No substantive changes
		Florida
	688.001-688.009	No substantive changes
		Georgia
§1	10-1-761(1)	Broader definition of "improper means"; reverse engineering and independent derivation are not "improper means"
§1	10-1-761(4)	Broader definition of "trade secret"
§2	10-1-762(a)	Injunction continued for "appropriate circumstances," including improper means
§2	10-1-762(b)	Unreasonable prohibition and "exceptional circumstances" for court to allow future use of trade secret
None	10-1-762(d)	Contract is not required to obtain injunctive relief
§3(a)	10-1-763(a)	Reasonable royalty applies when no preponderance of evidence shows damages or unjust enrichment
None	10-1-763(c)	Contract is not required to recover damages
§4	10-1-764	None
§5	10-1-765	None
§6	10-1-766	Five-year statute of limitations; misappropriation and receiving misappropriated trade secret are separate claims
§7	10-1-767	Contractual duty to maintain or limit use of trade secret not void or unenforceable for lack of durational or geographic limitation
§8	None	No corresponding section (uniformity and construction)
§9	10-1-760	None
§10	None	No corresponding section (severability)
§11	None	No corresponding section (effective date)
§12	None	No corresponding section (repealer)
		Hawaii
§1	482B-2	None
§2	482B-3(b)	Wrongful user bears burden of proof of exceptional circumstances
§3	482B-4	None
§4	482B-5	None

UTSA Chart
Differences from State Enactments

UTSA	State Act	Difference
		Hawaii (continued)
§5	482B-6	None
§6	482B-7	None
§7	482B-8	None
§8	None	No corresponding section (uniformity and construction)
§9	482B-1	None
§10	482B-9	None
§11	None	No corresponding section (effective date)
§12	None	No corresponding section (repealer)
		Idaho
§1	48-801(4)	Includes definition of "computer program"
§1	48-801(5)(b)	Trade secrets are subject to certain disclosures by public agencies
§2	48-802	None
§3	48-803	None
§4	None	No corresponding section (attorney fees)
§5	48-804	None
§6	48-805	None
§7	48-806	None
§8	None	No corresponding section (uniformity and construction)
§9	48-807	None
§10	None	No corresponding section (severability)
§11	None	No corresponding section (effective date)
§12	None	No corresponding section (repealer)
		Illinois
§1	765 ILCS 1065/2(a)	Reverse engineering and independent derivation are not "improper means"
§1	765 ILCS 1065/2(c)	"Person" includes for-profit and nonprofit legal entities
§2	765 ILCS 1065/3(b)	Injunction continuation available for "overriding public interest"
§2	765 ILCS 1065/3(b)	Unreasonable prohibition rather than "exceptional circumstances" for court to allow future use of trade secret
§3(a)	765 ILCS 1065/4(a)	No prohibition of inequitable monetary recovery; reasonable royalty applies when no preponderance of evidence shows damages or unjust enrichment
§4	765 ILCS 1065/5	None
§5	765 ILCS 1065/6	None
§6	765 ILCS 1065/7	Five-year statute of limitations
§7	765 ILCS 1065/8	Intended to replace conflicting unfair-competition law; contractual duty to maintain or limit use of trade secret not void or unenforceable for lack of durational or geographic limitation; Act does not affect definitions of "trade secret" in other acts
§8	None	No corresponding section (uniformity and construction)

UTSA	State Act	Difference
		Illinois (continued)
§9	765 ILCS 1065/1	None
§10	None	No corresponding section (severability)
§11	765 ILCS 1065/9	No mention of continuing misappropriation
§12	None	No corresponding section (repealer)
		Indiana
§1	24-2-3-2	"Person" includes limited-liability company
§2	24-2-3-3	Unreasonable prohibition and "exceptional circumstances" for court to allow future use of trade secret; no definition of "exceptional circumstances"
§3(a)	24-2-3-4	No prohibition of inequitable monetary recovery; different calculation for unprovable damages
§4	24-2-3-5	None
§5	24-2-3-6	None
§6	24-2-3-7	None
§7	24-2-3-1(c)	None
§8	24-2-3-1(b)	None
§9	24-2-3-1(a)	None
§10	None	No corresponding section (severability)
§11	24-2-3-8	Applies to part of continuing misappropriation that occurs after effective date
§12	None	No corresponding section (repealer)
		Iowa
§1	550.2	Includes definition of "knows/knowledge"; no definition of "person"
§2	550.3	Only owner of trade secret can petition district court for injunction or recover for misappropriation
§3	550.4	None
None	550.5	Implied or express consent of owner is defense against injunction or damages
§4	550.6	None
§5	550.7	None
§6	550.8	None
§7	None	No corresponding section (effect on other laws)
§8	None	No corresponding section (uniformity and construction)
§9	550.1	None
§10	None	No corresponding section (severability)
§11	None	No corresponding section (effective date)
§12	None	No corresponding section (repealer)
		Kansas
	60-3320–60-3330	No substantive changes

UTSA	STATE ACT	DIFFERENCE
		Kentucky
§1	365.880(4)	Broader definition of "trade secret"
§§2-11	365.882-365.900	None
§12	None	No corresponding section (repealer)
		Louisiana
§1	51:1431	None
§2	51:1432	Unreasonable prohibition rather than "exceptional circumstances" for court to allow future use of trade secret
§3	51:1433	No prohibition of inequitable monetary recovery; no measurement for misappropriation damages; no exemplary-damages language
§4	51:1434	None
§5	51:1435	None
§6	51:1436	None
§7	51:1437	None
§8	51:1438	None
§9	51:1439	None
§10	None	No corresponding section (severability)
§11	None	No corresponding section (effective date)
§12	None	No corresponding section (repealer)
		Maine
§1	10 M.R.S.A. 1542	None
§2	10 M.R.S.A. 1543.4	Applies to all forms of injunctive relief
§3	10 M.R.S.A. 1544	None
§4	10 M.R.S.A. 1545	None
§5	10 M.R.S.A. 1546	None
§6	10 M.R.S.A. 1547	Four-year statute of limitations
§7	10 M.R.S.A. 1548	Act has no effect on duty to disclose when required by law or on Maine Tort Claims Act
§8	None	No corresponding section (uniformity and construction)
§9	10 M.R.S.A. 1541	None
§10	None	No corresponding section (severability)
§11	None	No corresponding section (effective date)
§12	None	No corresponding section (repealer)
		Maryland
§1	11-1201	"Person" includes statutory trust
§2	11-1202	None
§3	11-1203	None
§4	11-1204	None

UTSA	STATE ACT	DIFFERENCE
		Maryland (continued)
§5	11-1205	None
§6	11-1206	None
§7	11-1207(2)	Act does not waive defenses or immunity of state personnel
§8	11-1208	None
§9	11-1209	None
§10	None	No corresponding section (severability)
§11	None	No corresponding section (effective date)
§12	None	No corresponding section (repealer)
		Massachusetts
		Restatement state. See Restatement of Unfair Competition (3d) §§39-45.
		Michigan
§1	445.1902	None
§2	445.1903(2)	Unreasonable prohibition rather than "exceptional circumstances" for court to allow future use of trade secret
§3(b)	445.1904	No exemplary-damages language
§4	445.1905	None
§5	445.1906	None
§6	445.1907	None
§7	445.1908	None
§8	445.1909	None
§9	445.1901	None
§10	None	No corresponding section (severability)
§11	445.1910	None
§12	None	No corresponding section (repealer)
		Minnesota
§1	325C.01(5)(ii)	Trade secret is not negated when person acquires trade secret without notice of its status as a trade secret, if person knew or had reason to know owner intended or expected secrecy to be maintained
§2	325C.02	None
§3	325C.03	None
§4	325C.04	None
§5	325C.05	None
§6	325C.06	None
§7	325C.07	None
§8	None	No corresponding section (uniformity and construction)
§9	325C.08	None
§10	None	No corresponding section (severability)

UTSA	STATE ACT	DIFFERENCE
Minnesota (continued)		
§11	None	No corresponding section (effective date)
§12	None	No corresponding section (repealer)
Mississippi		
§1	75-26-3	None
§2	75-26-5	None
§3(b)	75-26-7	Exemplary damages are not doubled
§4	75-26-9	None
§5	75-26-11	None
§6	75-26-13	None
§7	75-26-15	None
§8	75-26-17	None
§9	75-26-1	None
§10	75-26-19	None
§11	None	No corresponding section (effective date)
§12	None	No corresponding section (repealer)
Missouri		
§1	417.453(3)	"Person" includes for-profit and nonprofit entities
§1	417.453(4)	Broader definition of "trade secret"
§2	417.455	None
§3	417.457.2	Punitive damages for "evil motive" or "reckless indifference" rather than "willful and malicious conduct"
§4	None	No corresponding section (attorney fees)
§5	417.459	None
§6	417.461	Five-year statute of limitations
§7	417.463.2(4)	Act does not apply to matters discoverable in nonmisappropriation litigation
§8	417.465	None
§9	417.450	None
§10	None	No corresponding section (severability)
§11	417.467	None
§12	None	No corresponding section (repealer)
Montana		
§1	30-14-402(4)	"Trade secret" includes computer software
§2	30-14-403	None
§3	30-14-404	Exemplary damages are not doubled
§4	30-14-405	Court may award costs

UTSA	State Act	Difference
		Montana (continued)
§5	30-14-406	None
§6	30-14-407	None
§7	30-14-408	None
§8	30-14-409	None
§9	30-14-401	None
§10	None	No corresponding section (severability)
§11	None	No corresponding section (effective date)
§12	None	No corresponding section (repealer)
		Nebraska
§1	87-502(3)	"Person" includes limited-liability company
§2	87-503	None
§3(b)	87-504	No exemplary-damages language
§4	None	No corresponding section (attorney fees)
§5	87-505	Different examples of preserving secrecy during court proceedings; disclosure in court proceedings is not abandonment
§6	87-506	Four-year statute of limitations
§7	None	No corresponding section (effect on other law)
§8	None	No corresponding section (uniformity and construction)
§9	87-501	None
§10	None	No corresponding section (severability)
§11	87-507	None
§12	None	No corresponding section (repealer)
		Nevada
§1	600A.030	Includes definition of "owner"; "improper means" not limited to examples and includes willful breach and willful inducement of duty; broader definition of "trade secret"
None	600A.032	Rebuttable presumption of reasonable efforts to maintain secrecy
None	600A.035	Criminal-penalty statute
§2	600A.040.1	Injunction can be issued to prevent any advantage
§2	600A.040.3	Includes definition of "affirmative acts"
§3(b)	600A.050	Exemplary damages for wanton or reckless misappropriation
None	600A.055	Preservation of information posted or disseminated on Internet
§4	600A.060	None
§5	600A.070	Broader range of examples of preserving secrecy during court proceedings
§6	600A.080	None
§7	600A.090	None
§8	None	No corresponding section (uniformity and construction)

UTSA	State Act	Difference
		Nevada (continued)
§9	600A.010	None
§10	None	No corresponding section (severability)
§11	600A.100	None
§12	None	No corresponding section (repealer)
		New Hampshire
	350-B:1–350-B:9	No substantive changes
		New Jersey
§1	56:15-2	Expands definition of "improper means" and the disclosure method of "misappropriation"; includes definitions of "proper means" and "reverse engineering"; includes more examples of what a "trade secret" is
§2	56:15-3	None
§3	56:15-4	Provides broader scope of recovery for damages than just "material and prejudicial change"
None	56:15-5	Proper means to acquire trade secret is no defense
§4	56:15-6	Includes definition of "bad faith"
§5	56:15-7	Preservation of trade secret must be consistent with New Jersey Rules of Court
§6	56:15-8	None
§7	56:15-9	New Jersey Tort Claims Act supersedes conflicting provisions of New Jersey Trade Secrets Act
§8	None	No corresponding section (uniformity and construction)
§9	56:15-1	None
§10	None	No corresponding section (severability)
§11	None	No corresponding section (effective date)
§12	None	No corresponding section (repealer)
		New Mexico
§1	57-3A-2	None
§2	57-3A-3	None
§3	57-3A-4	None
§4	57-3A-5	None
§5	57-3A-6	None
§6	57-3A-7	None
§7	None	No corresponding section (effect on other law)
§8	None	No corresponding section (uniformity and construction)
§9	57-3A-1	None
§10	None	No corresponding section (severability)
§11	None	No corresponding section (effective date)
§12	None	No corresponding section (repealer)

UTSA CHART

DIFFERENCES FROM STATE ENACTMENTS

UTSA	STATE ACT	DIFFERENCE
		New York
		Restatement state. See Restatement of Unfair Competition (3d) §§39-45.
		North Carolina
		State has not adopted the UTSA, but its Trade Secrets Protection Act is similar. *See* N.C. Gen. Stat. §§66-152 to 66-157.
		North Dakota
§1	47-25.1-01.3	"Person" includes limited-liability company
§2	47-25.1-02	None
§3	47-25.1-03	None
§4	47-25.1-04	None
§5	47-25.1-05	None
§6	47-25.1-06	None
§7	47-25.1-07	None
§8	None	No corresponding section (uniformity and construction)
§9	47-25.1-08	None
§10	None	No corresponding section (severability)
§11	None	No corresponding section (effective date)
§12	None	No corresponding section (repealer)
		Ohio
§1	1333.61	Definition of "person" refers to another section in Ohio Revised Code; broader definition of "trade secret"
§2	1333.62(A)	Continuation of injunction is mandatory after finding that misappropriation is likely to provide commercial advantage
§3(a)	1333.63(A)	Royalty given in lieu of damages should be equitable under circumstances
§3(b)	1333.63(B)	Punitive damages or exemplary damages may be three times award
§4	1333.64	None
§5	1333.65	None
§6	1333.66	Four-year statute of limitations
§7	1333.67	None
§8	1333.68	None
§9	1333.69	None
§10	None	No corresponding section (severability)
§11	None	No corresponding section (effective date)
§12	None	No corresponding section (repealer)
		Oklahoma
	78-86–78-94	No substantive changes

UTSA	STATE ACT	DIFFERENCE
		Oregon
§1	646.461(1)	Reverse engineering and independent development alone are not "improper means"
§2	646.463	None
§3(a)	646.465(1)	Damages should be adequate to compensate for misappropriation
§3(a)	646.465(2)	Damages should not be less than reasonable royalty would have been
§3(b)	646.465(3)	Punitive damages for willful or malicious misappropriation
§4	646.467	Attorney fees if willful or malicious misappropriation found by court or jury
§5	646.469	None
§6	646.471	None
§7	646.473(3)	Act does not waive defenses or immunity of state or state personnel
§8	646.475(1)	None
§9	646.475(2)	None
§10	646.475(3)	None
§11	None	No corresponding section (effective date)
§12	None	No corresponding section (repealer)
		Pennsylvania
§1	12 §5302	Includes definition of "willful and malicious"; broader definition of "trade secret"
§2	12 §5303	None
§3	12 §5304	None
§4	12 §5305	Prevailing party may get expenses and costs
§5	12 §5306	None
§6	12 §5307	None
§7	12 §5308	None
§8	None	No corresponding section (uniformity and construction)
§9	12 §5301	None
§10	None	No corresponding section (severability)
§11	None	No corresponding section (effective date)
§12	None	No corresponding section (repealer)
		Rhode Island
	6-41-1–6-41-11	No substantive changes
		South Carolina
§1	39-8-20	Includes definition of "owner"; broader definitions of "improper means," "misappropriation," and "trade secret"
None	39-8-30	Includes employee's obligations to refrain from disclosing trade secret
§2	39-8-50	Reasonable time for injunction should consider average rate of business growth
§3(c)	39-8-40	Exemplary damages for wanton or reckless disregard of rights

UTSA	State Act	Difference
		South Carolina (continued)
§4	39-8-80	None
§5	39-8-60	Expanded requirements regarding discovery of trade-secret information and preservation of secrecy in court proceedings
§6	39-8-70	None
None	39-8-90	Criminal-penalty statute
None	39-8-100	Criminal proceedings and protective orders
§7	39-8-110(B)(2)	Does not apply to South Carolina Tort Claims Act
§8	None	No corresponding section (uniformity and construction)
§9	39-8-10	None
§10	39-8-120	None
§11	39-8-130	None
§12	None	No corresponding section (repealer)
		South Dakota
§1	37-29-1(3)	"Person" includes limited-liability company
§2	37-29-2	None
§3	37-29-3	None
§4	37-29-4	None
§5	37-29-5	None
§6	37-29-6	None
§7	37-29-7	None
§8	37-29-8	None
§9	37-29-9	None
§10	None	No corresponding section (severability)
§11	37-29-11	None
§12	None	No corresponding section (repealer)
		Tennessee
§1	47-25-1702	Broader definition of "trade secret"
§2	47-25-1703(a)	Nonexclusive list of reasons for injunction continuance
§3	47-25-1704	None
§4	47-25-1705	None
§5	47-25-1706	None
§6	47-25-1707	Misappropriation and receiving misappropriated trade secret are separate claims
§7	47-25-1708	Written contract not required to recover; contractual duty to maintain or limit use is not void or unenforceable for lack of durational or geographic limitation on the duty
§8	47-25-1709	None
§9	47-25-1701	None

UTSA	STATE ACT	DIFFERENCE
Tennessee (continued)		
§10	None	No corresponding section (severability)
§11	None	No corresponding section (effective date)
§12	None	No corresponding section (repealer)
Texas		
§1	§134A.002	Includes definitions of "claimaint," "proper means," and "reverse engineering"; no definition of "person"
§2	§134A.003	None
§3	§134A.004	Requires clear and convincing evidence for exemplary damages
§4	§134A.005	None
§5	§134A.006	Includes a presumption of granting a protective order
§6	None	No corresponding section (statute of limitations)
§7	§134A.007	Chapter 134A controls over the Texas Rules of Civil Procedure; chapter 134A does not affect required disclosures of public information under Tex. Gov't Code ch. 552
§8	§134A.008	None
§9	§134A.001	None
§10	None	No corresponding section (severability)
§11	None	No corresponding section (effective date)
§12	None	No corresponding section (repealer)
Utah		
	13-24-1–13-24-9	No substantive changes
Vermont		
§1	9 V.S.A. 4601	No definition of "person"
§2	9 V.S.A. 4602	None
§3	9 V.S.A. 4603	Punitive damages for malicious misappropriation; no limitation on punitive-damages amount
§4	None	No corresponding section (attorney fees)
§5	9 V.S.A. 4605	None
§6	None	No corresponding section (statute of limitations)
§7	9 V.S.A. 4607	None
§8	9 V.S.A. 4608	None
§9	None	No corresponding section (short title)
§10	None	No corresponding section (severability)
§11	9 V.S.A. 4609	None
§12	None	No corresponding section (repealer)

UTSA	STATE ACT	DIFFERENCE
Virginia		
§1	59.1-336	"Misappropriation" includes acquisition by accident or mistake without a requirement of material change; broader definitions of "improper means" and "trade secret"
§2	59.1-337	None
§3(a)	59.1-338(A)	Complainant may receive the greater of actual damages or a reasonable royalty
§3(b)	59.1-338(B)	Punitive damages may not exceed two times award or $350,000, whichever is less
§4	59.1-338.1	Court determines whether attorney fees are awarded
§5	59.1-339	None
§6	59.1-340	None
§7	59.1-341	None
§8	None	No corresponding section (uniformity and construction)
§9	59.1-336	None
§10	None	No corresponding section (severability)
§11	59.1-343	None
§12	None	No corresponding section (repealer)
Washington		
§1	19.108.010	None
§2	19.108.020	Unreasonable prohibition rather than "exceptional circumstances" for court to allow future use of trade secret
§3(a)	19.108.030	No prohibition of inequitable monetary recovery; no reasonable royalty in lieu of other damages
§4	19.108.040	None
§5	19.108.050	None
§6	19.108.060	None
§7	19.108.900	None
§8	19.108.910	None
§9	19.108.920	None
§10	19.108.940	None
§11	19.108.930	None
§12	None	No corresponding section (repealer)
Washington, D.C.		
	36-401–36-409	No substantive changes
None	36-410	Disclosure of information to enforce the Occupational Safety and Health Act of 1988 and Pesticide Operations Act of 1978
West Virginia		
	47-22-1–47-22-10	No substantive changes

UTSA	STATE ACT	DIFFERENCE
Wisconsin		
§1	134.90(1)	Includes definition of "readily ascertainable"; definition of "improper means" does not list espionage
§1	134.90(2)	State may not misappropriate; "misappropriation" includes acquisition by accident or mistake without a requirement of material change
§2	134.90(3)(a)1	Injunction may be granted ex parte; application must include description of each alleged trade secret or disclosure of secret; application for injunction must be served on party when injunction is made or restraining order is served, whichever is earlier
§3	134.90(4)(a)	Complainant may receive greater of actual damages or reasonable royalty
§4	134.90(4)(c)	None
§5	134.90(5)	None
§6	None	No corresponding section (statute of limitations)
§7	134.90(6)	None
§8	134.90(7)	None
§9	None	No corresponding section (short title)
§10	None	No corresponding section (severability)
§11	None	No corresponding section (effective date)
§12	None	No corresponding section (repealer)
Wyoming		
§1	40-24-101	None
§2	40-24-102	None
§3	40-24-103	None
§4	40-24-104	None
§5	40-24-105	None
§6	40-24-106	Four-year statute of limitations
§7	40-24-107	None
§8	40-24-108	None
§9	40-24-109	None
§10	None	No corresponding section (severability)
§11	40-24-110	None
§12	None	No corresponding section (repealer)

TABLE OF CONTENTS

UNITED STATES CODE

PLUS CODES—SELECTED PROVISIONS
TABLE OF CONTENTS

United States Code
Plus Codes—Selected Provisions
Table of Contents

TITLE 2. THE CONGRESS

CHAPTER 5. LIBRARY OF CONGRESS

§170. AMERICAN TELEVISION & RADIO ARCHIVES

(a) Establishment and maintenance in Library of Congress; purpose; determination of composition, cataloging, indexing and availability by Librarian.—The Librarian of Congress (hereinafter referred to as the "Librarian") shall establish and maintain in the Library of Congress a library to be known as the American Television and Radio Archives (hereinafter referred to as the "Archives"). The purpose of the Archives shall be to preserve a permanent record of the television and radio programs which are the heritage of the people of the United States and to provide access to such programs to historians and scholars without encouraging or causing copyright infringement.

(1) The Librarian, after consultation with interested organizations and individuals, shall determine and place in the Archives such copies and phonorecords of television and radio programs transmitted to the public in the United States and in other countries which are of present or potential public or cultural interest, historical significance, cognitive value, or otherwise worthy of preservation, including copies and phonorecords of published and unpublished transmission programs—

(A) acquired in accordance with sections 407 and 408 of Title 17; and

(B) transferred from the existing collections of the Library of Congress; and

(C) given to or exchanged with the Archives by other libraries, archives, organizations, and individuals; and

(D) purchased from the owner thereof.

(2) The Librarian shall maintain and publish appropriate catalogs and indexes of the collections of the Archives, and shall make such collections available for study and research under the conditions prescribed under this section.

(b) Reproduction, compilation, and distribution for research of regularly scheduled newscasts or on-the-spot coverage of news events by Librarian; promulgation of regulations.—Notwithstanding the provisions of section 106 of Title 17, the Librarian is authorized with respect to a transmission program which consists of a regularly scheduled newscast or on-the-spot coverage of news events and, under standards and conditions that the Librarian shall prescribe by regulation—

(1) to reproduce a fixation of such a program, in the same or another tangible form, for the purposes of preservation or security or for distribution under the conditions of clause (3) of this subsection;

(2) to compile, without abridgment or any other editing, portions of such fixations according to subject matter, and to reproduce such compilations for the purpose of clause (1) of this subsection; and

(3) to distribute a reproduction made under clause (1) or (2) of this subsection—

(A) by loan to a person engaged in research; and

(B) for deposit in a library or archives which meets the requirements of section 108(a) of Title 17,

in either case for use only in research and not for further reproduction or performance.

(c) Liability for copyright infringement by Librarian or any employee of Librarian.—The Librarian or any employee of the Library who is acting under the authority of this section shall not be liable in any action for copyright infringement committed by any other person unless the Librarian or such employee knowingly participated in the act of infringement committed by such person. Nothing in this section shall be construed to excuse or limit liability under Title 17 for any act not authorized by that title or this section, or for any act performed by a person not authorized to act under that title or this section.

(d) Short title.—This section may be cited as the "American Television and Radio Archives Act."

History of 2 U.S.C. §170: Oct. 19, 1976, P.L. 94-553, §113, 90 Stat. 2601.

CHAPTER 27. SOUND RECORDING PRESERVATION BY THE LIBRARY OF CONGRESS

SUBCHAPTER I. NATIONAL RECORDING REGISTRY

§1703. SEAL OF THE NATIONAL RECORDING REGISTRY

(a) In general.—The Librarian shall provide a seal to indicate that a sound recording has been included in the National Recording Registry and is the Registry version of that recording.

(b) Use of seal.—The Librarian shall establish guidelines for approval of the use of the seal provided under subsection (a) of this section, and shall include in the guidelines the following:

(1) The seal may only be used on recording copies of the Registry version of a sound recording.

(2) The seal may be used only after the Librarian has given approval to those persons seeking to apply the seal in accordance with the guidelines.

(3) In the case of copyrighted mass distributed, broadcast, or published works, only the copyright legal owner or an authorized licensee of that copyright owner may place or authorize the placement of the seal on any recording copy of the Registry version of any sound recording that is maintained in the National Recording Registry Collection in the Library of Congress.

(4) Anyone authorized to place the seal on any recording copy of any Registry version of a sound recording may accompany such seal with the following language: "This sound recording is selected for inclusion in the National Recording Registry by the Librarian of Congress in consultation with the National Recording Preservation Board of the Library of Congress because of its cultural, historical, or aesthetic significance."

(c) Effective date of the seal.—The use of the seal provided under subsection (a) of this section with respect to a sound recording shall be effective beginning on the date the Librarian publishes in the Federal Register (in accordance with section 1702(b) of this title) the name of the recording, as selected for inclusion in the National Recording Registry.

(d) Prohibited uses of the seal—

(1) Prohibition on distribution and exhibition.—No person may knowingly distribute or exhibit to the public a version of a sound recording or any copy of a sound recording which bears the seal described in subsection (a) of this section if such recording—

(A) is not included in the National Recording Registry; or

(B) is included in the National Recording Registry but has not been approved for use of the seal by the Librarian pursuant to the guidelines established under subsection (b) of this section.

(2) Prohibition on promotion.—No person may knowingly use the seal described in subsection (a) of this section to promote any version of a sound recording or recording copy other than a Registry version.

(e) Remedies for violations—

(1) Jurisdiction.—The several district courts of the United States shall have jurisdiction, for cause shown, to prevent and restrain violations of subsection (d) of this section.

(2) Relief—

(A) Removal of seal.—Except as provided in subparagraph (B), relief for violation of subsection (d) of this section shall be limited to the removal of the seal from the sound recording involved in the violation.

(B) Fine and injunctive relief.—In the case of a pattern or practice of the willful violation of subsection (d) of this section, the court may order a civil fine of not more than $10,000 and appropriate injunctive relief.

(3) Limitation of remedies.—The remedies provided in this subsection shall be the exclusive remedies under this chapter, or any other Federal or State law, regarding the use of the seal described in subsection (a) of this section.

History of 2 U.S.C. §1703: Nov. 9, 2000, P.L. 106-474, §103, 114 Stat. 2086.

TITLE 7. AGRICULTURE

CHAPTER 57. PLANT VARIETY PROTECTION

SUBCHAPTER I. PLANT VARIETY PROTECTION OFFICE

PART A. ORGANIZATION & PUBLICATIONS

§2321. ESTABLISHMENT

There is hereby established in the Department of Agriculture an office to be known as the Plant Variety Protection Office, which shall have the functions set forth in this chapter.

History of 7 U.S.C. §2321: Dec. 24, 1970, P.L. 91-577, §1, 84 Stat. 1542; Dec. 22, 1980, P.L. 96-574, §1, 94 Stat. 3350.

§2322. SEAL

The Plant Variety Protection Office shall have a seal with which documents and certificates evidencing plant variety protection shall be authenticated.

History of 7 U.S.C. §2322: Dec. 24, 1970, P.L. 91-577, §2, 84 Stat. 1542.

§2323. ORGANIZATION

The organization of the Plant Variety Protection Office shall, except as provided herein, be determined by the Secretary of Agriculture (hereinafter called the Secretary). The office shall devote itself substantially exclusively to the administration of this chapter.

History of 7 U.S.C. §2323: Dec. 24, 1970, P.L. 91-577, §3, 84 Stat. 1542.

§2324. RESTRICTIONS ON EMPLOYEES AS TO INTEREST IN PLANT VARIETY PROTECTION

Employees of the Plant Variety Protection Office shall be ineligible during the periods of their employment, to apply for plant variety protection and to acquire directly or indirectly, except by inheritance or bequest, any right or interest in any matters before that office. This section shall not apply to members of the Plant Variety Protection Board who are not otherwise employees of the Plant Variety Protection Office.

History of 7 U.S.C. §2324: Dec. 24, 1970, P.L. 91-577, §4, 84 Stat. 1542.

§2325. REPEALED

Repealed Dec. 22, 1980, P.L. 96-574, §2, 94 Stat. 3350.

§2326. REGULATIONS

The Secretary may establish regulations, not inconsistent with law, for the conduct of proceedings in the Plant Variety Protection Office after consultations with the Plant Variety Protection Board.

History of 7 U.S.C. §2326: Dec. 24, 1970, P.L. 91-577, §6, 84 Stat. 1542.

§2327. PLANT VARIETY PROTECTION BOARD

(a) Appointment.—The Secretary shall appoint a Plant Variety Protection Board. The Board shall consist of individuals who are experts in various areas of varietal development covered by this chapter. Membership of the Board shall include farmer representation and shall be drawn approximately equally from the private or seed industry sector and from the sector of government or the public. The Secretary or the designee of the Secretary shall act as chairperson of the Board without voting rights except in the case of ties.

(b) Functions of Board.—The functions of the Plant Variety Protection Board shall include:

(1) Advising the Secretary concerning the adoption of Rules and Regulations to facilitate the proper administration of this chapter;

(2) Making advisory decisions on all appeals from the examiner. The Board shall determine whether to act as a full Board or by panels it selects; and whether to review advisory decisions made by a panel. For service on such appeals, the Board may select, as temporary members, experts in the area to which the particular appeal relates; and

(3) Advising the Secretary on all questions under section 2404 of this title.

(c) Compensation of Board.—The members of the Plant Variety Protection Board shall serve without compensation except for standard government reimbursable expenses.

History of 7 U.S.C. §2327: Dec. 24, 1970, P.L. 91-577, §7, 84 Stat. 1543; Oct. 6, 1994, P.L. 103-349, §13(a), 108 Stat. 3142.

§2328. LIBRARY

The Secretary shall maintain a library of scientific and other works and periodicals, both foreign and domestic, in the Plant Variety Protection Office to aid the examiners in the discharge of their duties.

History of 7 U.S.C. §2328: Dec. 24, 1970, P.L. 91-577, §8, 84 Stat. 1543; Dec. 22, 1980, P.L. 96-574, §3, 94 Stat. 3350.

§2329. REGISTER OF PROTECTED PLANT VARIETIES

The Secretary shall maintain a register of descriptions of United States protected plant varieties.

History of 7 U.S.C. §2329: Dec. 24, 1970, P.L. 91-577, §9, 84 Stat. 1543; Dec. 22, 1980, P.L. 96-574, §4, 94 Stat. 3350.

§2330. PUBLICATIONS

(a) The Secretary may publish, or cause to be published, in such format as the Secretary shall determine to be suitable, the following:

(1) The descriptions of plant varieties protected including drawings and photographs.

(2) The Official Journal of the Plant Variety Protection Office, including annual indices.

(3) Pamphlet copies of the plant variety protection laws and rules of practice and circulars or other publications relating to the business of the Office.

(b) The Secretary may (1) establish public facilities for the searching of plant variety protection records and materials, and (2) from time to time, as through an information service, disseminate to the public those portions of the technological and other public information available to or within the Plant Variety Protection Office to encourage innovation and promote the progress of plant breeding.

(c) The Secretary may exchange any of the publications specified for publications desirable for the use of the Plant Variety Protection Office. The Secretary may exchange copies of descriptions, drawings, and photographs of United States protected plant varieties for copies of descriptions, drawings, and photographs of applications and protected plant varieties of foreign countries.

History of 7 U.S.C. §2330: Dec. 24, 1970, P.L. 91-577, §10, 84 Stat. 1543; Dec. 22, 1980, P.L. 96-574, §§5-8, 94 Stat. 3350; Oct. 6, 1994, P.L. 103-349, §13(b), 108 Stat. 3143.

§2331. COPIES FOR PUBLIC LIBRARIES

The Secretary may supply printed copies of descriptions, drawings, and photographs of protected plant varieties to public libraries in the United States which shall maintain such copies for the use of the public.

History of 7 U.S.C. §2331: Dec. 24, 1970, P.L. 91-577, §11, 84 Stat. 1544; Dec. 22, 1980, P.L. 96-574, §9, 94 Stat. 3350.

PART B. LEGAL PROVISIONS AS TO THE PLANT VARIETY PROTECTION OFFICE

§2351. DAY FOR TAKING ACTION FALLING ON SATURDAY, SUNDAY, OR HOLIDAY

When the day, or the last day, for taking any action or paying any fee in the United States Plant Variety Protection Office falls on Saturday, Sunday, a holiday within the District of Columbia, or on any other day the Plant Variety Protection Office is closed for the receipt of papers, the action may be taken or the fee paid, on the next succeeding business day.

History of 7 U.S.C. §2351: Dec. 24, 1970, P.L. 91-577, §21, 84 Stat. 1544.

§2352. FORM OF PAPERS FILED

The Secretary may by regulations prescribe the form of papers to be filed in the Plant Variety Protection Office.

History of 7 U.S.C. §2352: Dec. 24, 1970, P.L. 91-577, §22, 84 Stat. 1544.

§2353. TESTIMONY IN PLANT VARIETY PROTECTION OFFICE CASES

The Secretary may establish regulations for taking affidavits, depositions, and other evidence required in cases before the Plant Variety Protection Office. Any officer authorized by law to take depositions to be used in the courts of the United States, or of the State where the officer resides, may take such affidavits and depositions, and swear the witnesses. If any person acts as a hearing officer by authority of the Secretary, the person shall have like power.

History of 7 U.S.C. §2353: Dec. 24, 1970, P.L. 91-577, §23, 84 Stat. 1544; Oct. 6, 1994, P.L. 103-349, §13(c), 108 Stat. 3143.

§2354. SUBPOENAS; WITNESSES

(a) The clerk of any United States court for the district wherein testimony is to be taken in accordance with regulations established by the Secretary for use in any contested case in the Plant Variety Protection Office shall, upon the application of any party thereof, issue a subpoena for any witness residing or being within such district or within one hundred miles of the stated place in such district, commanding the witness to appear and testify before an officer in such district authorized to take depositions and affidavits, at the time and place stated in the subpoena. The provisions of the Federal Rules of Civil Procedure relating to the attendance of witnesses and the production of documents and things shall apply to contested cases in the Plant Variety Protection Office insofar as consistent with such regulations.

(b) Every witness subpoenaed or testifying shall be allowed the fees and traveling expenses allowed to witnesses attending the United States district courts.

(c) A judge of a court whose clerk issued a subpoena may enforce obedience to the process or punish disobedience as in other like cases, on proof that a witness, served with such subpoena, neglected or refused to appear or to testify. No witness shall be deemed guilty of contempt for disobeying such subpoena unless the fees and traveling expenses of the witness in going to, and returning from, one day's attendance at the place of examination, are paid or tendered the witness at the time of the service of the subpoena; nor for refusing to disclose any secret matter except upon appropriate order of the court which issued the subpoena or of the Secretary.

History of 7 U.S.C. §2354: Dec. 24, 1970, P.L. 91-577, §24, 84 Stat. 1544; Oct. 6, 1994, P.L. 103-349, §13(d), 108 Stat. 3143.

§2355. EFFECT OF DEFECTIVE EXECUTION

Any document to be filed in the Plant Variety Protection Office and which is required by any law or regulation to be executed in a specified manner may be provisionally accepted by the Secretary despite a defective execution, provided a properly executed document is submitted within such time as may be prescribed.

History of 7 U.S.C. §2355: Dec. 24, 1970, P.L. 91-577, §25, 84 Stat. 1545.

§2356. REGULATIONS FOR PRACTICE BEFORE THE OFFICE

The Secretary shall prescribe regulations governing the admission to practice and conduct of persons representing applicants or other parties before the Plant Variety Protection Office. The Secretary may, after notice and opportunity for a hearing, suspend or exclude, either generally or in any particular case, from further practice before the Office of Plant Variety Protection any person shown to be incompetent or disreputable or guilty of gross misconduct.

History of 7 U.S.C. §2356: Dec. 24, 1970, P.L. 91-577, §26, 84 Stat. 1545.

§2357. UNAUTHORIZED PRACTICE

Anyone who in the United States engages in direct or indirect practice before the Office of Plant Variety Protection while suspended or excluded under section 2356 of this title, or without being admitted to practice before the Office, shall be liable in a civil action for the return of all money received, and for compensation for damage done by such person and also may be enjoined from such practice. However, there shall be no liability for damage if such person establishes that the work was done competently and without negligence. This section does not apply to anyone who, without a claim of self-sufficiency, works under the supervision of another who stands admitted and is the responsible party; or to anyone who establishes that the person acted only on behalf of any employer by whom the person was regularly employed.

History of 7 U.S.C. §2357: Dec. 24, 1970, P.L. 91-577, §27, 84 Stat. 1545; Oct. 6, 1994, P.L. 103-349, §13(e), 108 Stat. 3143.

PART C. PLANT VARIETY PROTECTION FEES

§2371. PLANT VARIETY PROTECTION FEES

(a) In general.—The Secretary shall, under such regulations as the Secretary may prescribe, charge and collect reasonable fees for services performed under this chapter.

(b) Late payment penalty.—On failure to pay such fees, the Secretary shall assess a late payment penalty. Such overdue fees shall accrue interest as required by section 3717 of Title 31.

(c) Disposition of funds.—Such fees, late payment penalties, and accrued interest collected shall be credited to the account that incurs the cost and shall remain available without fiscal year limitation to pay the expenses incurred by the Secretary in carrying out this chapter. Such funds collected (including late payment penalties and any interest earned) may be invested by the Secretary in insured or fully collateralized, interest-bearing accounts or, at the discretion of the Secretary, by the Secretary of the Treasury in United States Government debt instruments.

(d) Actions for nonpayment.—The Attorney General may bring an action for the recovery of charges that have not been paid in accordance with this chapter against any person obligated for payment of such charges under this chapter in any United States district court or other United States court for any territory or possession in any jurisdiction in which the person is found, resides, or transacts business. The court shall have jurisdiction to hear and decide the action.

(e) Authorization of appropriations.—There are authorized to be appropriated such sums as are necessary to carry out this chapter.

History of 7 U.S.C. §2371: Dec. 24, 1970, P.L. 91-577, §31, 84 Stat. 1545; Dec. 22, 1980, P.L. 96-574, §10, 94 Stat. 3350; Dec. 22, 1987, P.L. 100-203, §1505, 101 Stat. 1330-28.

§2372. PAYMENT OF PLANT VARIETY PROTECTION FEES; RETURN OF EXCESS AMOUNTS

All fees shall be paid to the Secretary, and the Secretary may refund any sum paid by mistake or in excess of the fee required.

History of 7 U.S.C. §2372: Dec. 24, 1970, P.L. 91-577, §32, 84 Stat. 1545.

SUBCHAPTER II. PROTECTABILITY OF PLANT VARIETIES & CERTIFICATES OF PROTECTION

PART D. PROTECTABILITY OF PLANT VARIETIES

§2401. DEFINITIONS & RULES OF CONSTRUCTION

(a) Definitions.—As used in this chapter:

(1) Basic seed.—The term "basic seed" means the seed planted to produce certified or commercial seed.

(2) Breeder.—The term "breeder" means the person who directs the final breeding creating a variety or who discovers and develops a variety. If the actions are conducted by an agent on behalf of a principal, the principal, rather than the agent, shall be considered the breeder. The term does not include a person who redevelops or rediscovers a variety the existence of which is publicly known or a matter of common knowledge.

(3) Essentially derived variety—

(A) In general.—The term "essentially derived variety" means a variety that—

(i) is predominantly derived from another variety (referred to in this paragraph as the "initial variety") or from a variety that is predominantly derived from the initial variety, while retaining the expression of the essential characteristics that result from the genotype or combination of genotypes of the initial variety;

(ii) is clearly distinguishable from the initial variety; and

(iii) except for differences that result from the act of derivation, conforms to the initial variety in the expression of the essential characteristics that result from the genotype or combination of genotypes of the initial variety.

(B) Methods.—An essentially derived variety may be obtained by the selection of a natural or induced mutant or of a somaclonal variant, the selection of a variant individual from plants of the initial variety, backcrossing, transformation by genetic engineering, or other method.

(4) Kind.—The term "kind" means one or more related species or subspecies singly or collectively known by one common name, such as soybean, flax, or radish.

(5) Seed.—The term "seed," with respect to a tuber propagated variety, means the tuber or the part of the tuber used for propagation.

(6) Sexually reproduced.—The term "sexually reproduced" includes any production of a variety by seed, but does not include the production of a variety by tuber propagation.

(7) Tuber propagated.—The term "tuber propagated" means propagated by a tuber or a part of a tuber.

(8) United States.—The terms "United States" and "this country" mean the United States, the territories and possessions of the United States, and the Commonwealth of Puerto Rico.

(9) Variety.—The term "variety" means a plant grouping within a single botanical taxon of the lowest known rank, that, without regard to whether the conditions for plant variety protection are fully met, can be defined by the expression of the characteristics resulting from a given genotype or combination of genotypes, distinguished from any other plant grouping by the expression of at least one characteristic and considered as a unit with regard to the suitability of the plant grouping for being propagated unchanged. A variety may be represented by seed, transplants, plants, tubers, tissue culture plantlets, and other matter.

(b) Rules of construction.—For the purposes of this chapter:

(1) Sale or disposition for nonreproductive purposes.—The sale or disposition, for other than reproductive purposes, of harvested material produced as a result of experimentation or testing of a variety to ascertain the characteristics of the variety, or as a by-product of increasing a variety, shall not be considered to be a sale or disposition for purposes of exploitation of the variety.

(2) Sale or disposition for reproductive purposes.—The sale or disposition of a variety for reproductive purposes shall not be considered to be a sale or disposition for the purposes of exploitation of the variety if the sale or disposition is done as an integral part of a program of experimentation or testing to ascertain the characteristics of the variety, or to increase the variety on behalf of the breeder or the successor in interest of the breeder.

(3) Sale or disposition of hybrid seed.—The sale or disposition of hybrid seed shall be considered to be a sale or disposition of harvested material of the varieties from which the seed was produced.

(4) Application for protection or entering into a register of varieties.—The filing of an application for the protection or for the entering of a variety in an official register of varieties, in any country, shall be considered to render the variety a matter of common knowledge from the date of the application, if the application leads to the granting of protection or to the entering of the variety in the official register of varieties, as the case may be.

(5) Distinctness.—The distinctness of one variety from another may be based on one or more identifiable morphological, physiological, or other characteristics (including any characteristics evidenced by processing or product characteristics, such as milling and baking characteristics in the case of wheat) with respect to which a difference in genealogy may contribute evidence.

(6) Publicly known varieties—

(A) In general.—A variety that is adequately described by a publication reasonably considered to be a part of the public technical knowledge in the United States shall be considered to be publicly known and a matter of common knowledge.

(B) Description.—A description that meets the requirements of subparagraph (A) shall include a disclosure of the principal characteristics by which a variety is distinguished.

(C) Other means.—A variety may become publicly known and a matter of common knowledge by other means.

History of 7 U.S.C. §2401: Dec. 24, 1970, P.L. 91-577, §41, 84 Stat. 1546; Oct. 6, 1994, P.L. 103-349, §2, 108 Stat. 3136.

§2402. RIGHT TO PLANT VARIETY PROTECTION; PLANT VARIETIES PROTECTABLE

(a) In general.—The breeder of any sexually reproduced or tuber propagated plant variety (other than fungi or bacteria) who has so reproduced the variety, or the successor in interest of the breeder, shall be entitled to plant variety protection for the variety, subject to the conditions and requirements of this chapter, if the variety is—

(1) new, in the sense that, on the date of filing of the application for plant variety protection, propagating or harvested material of the variety has not been sold or otherwise disposed of to other persons, by or with the consent of the breeder, or the successor in interest of the breeder, for purposes of exploitation of the variety—

(A) in the United States, more than 1 year prior to the date of filing; or

(B) in any area outside of the United States—

(i) more than 4 years prior to the date of filing, except that in the case of a tuber propagated plant variety the Secretary may waive the 4-year limitation for a period ending 1 year after April 4, 1996; or

(ii) in the case of a tree or vine, more than 6 years prior to the date of filing;

(2) distinct, in the sense that the variety is clearly distinguishable from any other variety the existence of which is publicly known or a matter of common knowledge at the time of the filing of the application;

(3) uniform, in the sense that any variations are describable, predictable, and commercially acceptable; and

(4) stable, in the sense that the variety, when reproduced, will remain unchanged with regard to the essential and distinctive characteristics of the variety with a reasonable degree of reliability commensurate with that of varieties of the same category in which the same breeding method is employed.

(b) Multiple applicants—

(1) In general.—If 2 or more applicants submit applications on the same effective filing date for varieties that cannot be clearly distinguished from one another, but that fulfill all other requirements of subsection (a) of this section, the applicant who first complies with all requirements of this chapter shall be entitled to a certificate of plant variety protection, to the exclusion of any other applicant.

(2) Requirements completed on same date—

(A) In general.—Except as provided in subparagraph (B), if 2 or more applicants comply with all requirements for protection on the same date, a certificate shall be issued for each variety.

(B) Varieties indistinguishable.—If the varieties that are the subject of the applications cannot be distinguished in any manner, a single certificate shall be issued jointly to the applicants.

History of 7 U.S.C. §2402: Dec. 24, 1970, P.L. 91-577, §42, 84 Stat. 1547; Oct. 6, 1994, P.L. 103-349, §3, 108 Stat. 3138; Apr. 4, 1996, P.L. 104-127, §913(a), 110 Stat. 1186.

§2403. RECIPROCITY LIMITS

Protection under this chapter may, by regulation, be limited to nationals of the United States, except where this limitation would violate a treaty and except that nationals of a foreign state in which they are domiciled shall be entitled to so much of the protection here afforded as is afforded by said foreign state to nationals of the United States for the same genus and species.

History of 7 U.S.C. §2403: Dec. 24, 1970, P.L. 91-577, §43, 84 Stat. 1547.

§2404. PUBLIC INTEREST IN WIDE USAGE

The Secretary may declare a protected variety open to use on a basis of equitable remuneration to the owner, not less than a reasonable royalty, when the Secretary determines that such declaration is necessary in order to insure an adequate supply of fiber, food, or feed in this country and that the owner is unwilling or unable to supply the public needs for the variety at a price which may reasonably be deemed fair. Such declaration may be, with or without limitation, with or without designation of what the remuneration is to be; and shall be subject to review as under section 2461 or 2462 of this title (any finding that the price is not reasonable being reviewable), and shall remain in effect not more than two years. In the event litigation is required to collect such remuneration, a higher rate may be allowed by the court.

History of 7 U.S.C. §2404: Dec. 24, 1970, P.L. 91-577, §44, 84 Stat. 1547; Oct. 6, 1994, P.L. 103-349, §13(f), 108 Stat. 3143.

PART E. APPLICATIONS; FORM; WHO MAY FILE; RELATING BACK; CONFIDENTIALITY

§2421. APPLICATION FOR RECOGNITION OF PLANT VARIETY RIGHTS

(a) An application for a certificate of Plant Variety Protection may be filed by the owner of the variety sought to be protected. The application shall be made in writing to the Secretary, shall be signed by or on behalf of the applicant, and shall be accompanied by the prescribed fee.

(b) An error as to the naming of the breeder, without deceptive intent, may be corrected at any time, in accordance with regulations established by the Secretary.

History of 7 U.S.C. §2421: Dec. 24, 1970, P.L. 91-577, §51, 84 Stat. 1548.

§2422. CONTENT OF APPLICATION

An application for a certificate recognizing plant variety rights shall contain:

(1) The name of the variety except that a temporary designation will suffice until the certificate is to be issued. The variety shall be named in accordance with regulations issued by the Secretary.

(2) A description of the variety setting forth its distinctiveness, uniformity, and stability and a description of the genealogy and breeding procedure, when known. The Secretary may require amplification, including the submission of adequate photographs or drawings or plant specimens, if the description is not adequate or as complete as is reasonably possible, and submission of records or proof of ownership or of allegations made in the application. An applicant may add to or correct the description at any time, before the certificate is issued, upon a showing acceptable to the Secretary that the revised description is retroactively accurate. Courts shall protect others from any injustice which would result. The Secretary may accept records of the breeder and of any official seed certifying agency in this country as evidence of stability where applicable.

(3) A statement of the basis of the claim of the applicant that the variety is new.

(4) A declaration that a viable sample of basic seed (including any propagating material) necessary for propagation of the variety will be deposited and replenished periodically in a public repository in accordance with regulations to be established hereunder.

(5) A statement of the basis of applicant's ownership.

History of 7 U.S.C. §2422: Dec. 24, 1970, P.L. 91-577, §52, 84 Stat. 1548; Dec. 22, 1980, P.L. 96-574, §11, 94 Stat. 3350; Oct. 6, 1994, P.L. 103-349, §4, 108 Stat. 3139.

§2423. JOINT BREEDERS

(a) When two or more persons are the breeders, one person (or the successor of the person) may apply, naming the others.

(b) The Secretary, after such notice as the Secretary may prescribe, may issue a certificate of plant variety protection to the applicant and such of the other breeders (or their successors in interest) as may have subsequently joined in the application.

History of 7 U.S.C. §2423: Dec. 24, 1970, P.L. 91-577, §53, 84 Stat. 1548; Oct. 6, 1994, P.L. 103-349, §13(g), 108 Stat. 3143.

§2424. DEATH OR INCAPACITY OF BREEDER

Legal representatives of deceased breeders and of those under legal incapacity may make application for plant variety protection upon compliance with the requirements and on the same terms and conditions applicable to the breeder or the successor in interest of the breeder.

History of 7 U.S.C. §2424: Dec. 24, 1970, P.L. 91-577, §54, 84 Stat. 1548; Oct. 6, 1994, P.L. 103-349, §13(h), 108 Stat. 3143.

§2425. BENEFIT OF EARLIER FILING DATE

(a)(1) An application for a certificate of plant variety protection filed in this country based on the same variety, and on rights derived from the same breeder, on which there has previously been filed an application for plant variety protection in a foreign country which affords similar privileges in the case of applications filed in the United States by nationals of the United States, shall have the same effect as the same application would have if filed in the United States on the date on which the application for plant variety protection for the same variety was first filed in such foreign country, if the application in this country is filed within twelve months from the earliest date on which such foreign application was filed, not including the date on which the application is filed in the foreign country.

(2) No application shall be entitled to a right of priority under this section, unless the applicant designates the foreign application in the application filed in the United States or by amendment thereto and, if required by the Secretary, furnishes such copy, translation or both, as the Secretary may specify.

(3)(A) An applicant entitled to a right of priority under this subsection shall be allowed to furnish any necessary information, document, or material required for the purpose of the examination of the application during—

(i) the 2-year period beginning on the date of the expiration of the period of priority; or

(ii) if the first application is rejected or withdrawn, an appropriate period after the rejection or withdrawal, to be determined by the Secretary.

(B) An event occurring within the period of priority (such as the filing of another application or use of the variety that is the subject of the first application) shall not constitute a ground for rejecting the application or give rise to any third party right.

(b) An application for a certificate of plant variety protection for the same variety as was the subject of an application previously filed in the United States by or on behalf of the same person, or by the predecessor in title of the person, shall have the same effect as to such variety as though filed on the date of the prior application if filed before the issuance of the certificate or other termination of proceedings on the first application or on an application similarly entitled to the benefit of the filing date of the first application and if it contains or is amended to contain a specific reference to the earlier filed application.

(c) A later application shall not by itself establish that a characteristic newly described was in the variety at the time of the earlier application.

History of 7 U.S.C. §2425: Dec. 24, 1970, P.L. 91-577, §55, 84 Stat. 1548; Oct. 6, 1994, P.L. 103-349, §§5, 13(i), 108 Stat. 3139, 3143.

§2426. CONFIDENTIAL STATUS OF APPLICATION

Applications for plant variety protection and their contents shall be kept in confidence by the Plant Variety Protection Office, by the Board, and by the offices in the Department of Agriculture to which access may be given under regulations. No information concerning the same shall be given without the authority of the owner, unless necessary under special circumstances as may be determined by the Secretary, except that the Secretary may publish the variety names designated in applications, stating the kind to which each applies, the name of the applicant, and whether the applicant specified that the variety is to be sold by variety name only as a class of certified seed.

History of 7 U.S.C. §2426: Dec. 24, 1970, P.L. 91-577, §56, 84 Stat. 1549; Dec. 22, 1980, P.L. 96-574, §12, 94 Stat. 3350.

§2427. PUBLICATION

The Secretary may establish regulations for the publication of information regarding any pending application when publication is requested by the owner.

History of 7 U.S.C. §2427: Dec. 24, 1970, P.L. 91-577, §57, 84 Stat. 1549; Dec. 22, 1980, P.L. 96-574, §13, 94 Stat. 3350.

PART F. EXAMINATION; RESPONSE TIME; INITIAL APPEALS

§2441. EXAMINATION OF APPLICATION

The Secretary shall cause an examination to be made of the application and if on such examination it is determined that the applicant is entitled to plant variety protection under the law, the Secretary shall issue a notice of allowance of plant variety protection therefor as hereinafter provided.

History of 7 U.S.C. §2441: Dec. 24, 1970, P.L. 91-577, §61, 84 Stat. 1549.

§2442. NOTICE OF REFUSAL; RECONSIDERATION

(a) Whenever an application is refused, or any objection or requirement made by the examiner, the Secretary shall notify the applicant thereof, stating the reasons therefor, together with such information and references as may be useful in judging the propriety of continuing the prosecution of the application; and if after receiving such notice the applicant requests reconsideration, with or without amendment, the application shall be reconsidered.

(b) For taking appropriate action after the mailing to an applicant of an action other than allowance, the applicant shall be allowed at least 30 days, and not more than 180 days, or such other time as the Secretary shall set in the refusal, or such time as the Secretary may allow as an extension. Without such extension, action may be taken up to three months late by paying an additional fee to be prescribed by the Secretary.

History of 7 U.S.C. §2442: Dec. 24, 1970, P.L. 91-577, §62, 84 Stat. 1549; Oct. 6, 1994, P.L. 103-349, §§6, 13(j), 108 Stat. 3140, 3143.

§2443. INITIAL APPEAL

When an application for plant variety protection has been refused by the Plant Variety Protection Office, the applicant may appeal to the Secretary. The Secretary shall seek the advice of the Plant Variety Protection Board on all appeals, before deciding the appeal.

History of 7 U.S.C. §2443: Dec. 24, 1970, P.L. 91-577, §63, 84 Stat. 1550.

PART G. APPEALS TO COURTS & OTHER REVIEW

§2461. APPEALS

From the decisions made under sections 2404, 2443, 2501, and 2568 of this title appeal may, within sixty days or such further times as the Secretary allows, be taken under the Federal Rules of Appellate Procedure. The United States Court of Appeals for the Federal Circuit shall have jurisdiction of any such appeal.

History of 7 U.S.C. §2461: Dec. 24, 1970, P.L. 91-577, §71, 84 Stat. 1550; Apr. 2, 1982, P.L. 97-164, §145, 96 Stat. 45; Oct. 6, 1994, P.L. 103-349, §8(d)(1), 108 Stat. 3141.

§2462. CIVIL ACTION AGAINST SECRETARY

An applicant dissatisfied with a decision under section 2443 or 2501 of this title, may, as an alternative to appeal, have remedy by civil action against the Secretary in the United States District Court for the District of Columbia. Such action shall be commenced within sixty days after such decision or within such further time as the Secretary allows. The court may, in the case of review of a decision by the Secretary refusing plant variety protection, adjudge that such applicant is entitled to receive a certificate of plant variety protection for the variety as specified in the application as the facts of the case may appear, on compliance with the requirements of this chapter.

History of 7 U.S.C. §2462: Dec. 24, 1970, P.L. 91-577, §72, 84 Stat. 1550; Oct. 6, 1994, P.L. 103-349, §13(k), 108 Stat. 3143.

§2463. REPEALED

Repealed Oct. 6, 1994, P.L. 103-349, §8(c)(2), 108 Stat. 3141.

PART H. CERTIFICATES OF PLANT VARIETY PROTECTION

§2481. PLANT VARIETY PROTECTION

(a) If it appears that a certificate of plant variety protection should be issued on an application, a written notice of allowance shall be given or mailed to the owner. The notice shall specify the sum, constituting the issue fee, which shall be paid within one month thereafter.

(b) Upon timely payment of this sum, and provided that deposit of seed has been made in accordance with section 2422(3) of this title, the certificate of plant variety protection shall issue.

(c) If any payment required by this section is not timely made, but is submitted with an additional fee prescribed by the Secretary within nine months after the due date or within such further time as the Secretary may allow, it shall be accepted.

History of 7 U.S.C. §2481: Dec. 24, 1970, P.L. 91-577, §81, 84 Stat. 1551.

§2482. HOW ISSUED

A certificate of plant variety protection shall be issued in the name of the United States of America under the seal of the Plant Variety Protection Office, and shall be signed by the Secretary or have the signature of the Secretary placed thereon, and shall be recorded in the Plant Variety Protection Office.

History of 7 U.S.C. §2482: Dec. 24, 1970, P.L. 91-577, §82, 84 Stat. 1551; Oct. 6, 1994, P.L. 103-349, §13(*l*), 108 Stat. 3143.

§2483. CONTENTS & TERM OF PLANT VARIETY PROTECTION

(a) Certificate—

(1) Every certificate of plant variety protection shall certify that the breeder (or the successor in interest of the breeder),[1] has the right, during the term of the plant variety protection, to exclude others from selling the variety, or offering it for sale, or reproducing it, or importing it, or exporting it, or using it in producing (as distinguished from developing) a hybrid or different variety therefrom, to the extent provided by this chapter.

(2) If the owner so elects, the certificate shall—

(A) specify that seed of the variety shall be sold in the United States only as a class of certified seed; and

(B) if so specified, conform to the number of generations designated by the owner.

(3) An owner may waive a right provided under this subsection, other than a right that is elected by the owner under paragraph (2)(A).

(4) The Secretary may at the discretion of the Secretary permit such election or waiver to be made after certificating and amend the certificate accordingly, without retroactive effect.

(b) Term—

(1) In general.—Except as provided in paragraph (2), the term of plant variety protection shall expire 20 years from the date of issue of the certificate in the United States, except that—

(A) in the case of a tuber propagated plant variety subject to a waiver granted under section 2402(a)(1)(B)(i) of this title, the term of the plant variety protection shall expire 20 years after the date of the original grant of the plant breeder's rights to the variety outside the United States; and

(B) in the case of a tree or vine, the term of the plant variety protection shall expire 25 years from the date of issue of the certificate.

(2) Exceptions.—If the certificate is not issued within three years from the effective filing date, the Secretary may shorten the term by the amount of delay in the prosecution of the application attributed by the Secretary to the applicant.

(c) Expiration upon failure to comply with regulations; notice—

The term of plant variety protection shall also expire if the owner fails to comply with regulations, in force at the time of certificating, relating to replenishing seed in a public repository, or requiring the submission of a different name for the variety, except that this expiration shall not occur unless notice is mailed to the last owner recorded as provided in section 2531(d) of this title and the last owner fails, within the time allowed thereafter, not less than three months, to comply with said regulations, paying an additional fee to be prescribed by the Secretary.

1. **Editor's note:** The comma probably should not appear.

History of 7 U.S.C. §2483: Dec. 24, 1970, P.L. 91-577, §83, 84 Stat. 1551; Dec. 22, 1980, P.L. 96-574, §14, 94 Stat. 3350; Oct. 6, 1994, P.L. 103-349, §§7, 13(m), 108 Stat. 3140, 3143; Apr. 4, 1996, P.L. 104-127, §913(b), 110 Stat. 1186.

§2484. CORRECTION OF PLANT VARIETY PROTECTION OFFICE MISTAKE

Whenever a mistake in a certificate of plant variety protection incurred through the fault of the Plant Variety Protection Office is clearly disclosed by the records of the Office, the Secretary may issue, without charge, a corrected certificate of plant variety protection, stating the fact and nature of such mistake. Such certificate of plant variety protection shall have the same effect and operation in law as if the same had been originally issued in such corrected form.

History of 7 U.S.C. §2484: Dec. 24, 1970, P.L. 91-577, §84, 84 Stat. 1552; Dec. 22, 1980, P.L. 96-574, §15, 94 Stat. 3350.

§2485. CORRECTION OF APPLICANT'S MISTAKE

Whenever a mistake of a clerical or typographical nature, or of minor character, or in the description of the variety, which was not the fault of the Plant Variety Protection Office, appears in a certificate of plant variety protection and a showing has been made that such mistake occurred in good faith, the Secretary may, upon payment of the required fee, issue a corrected certificate if the correction could have been made before the certificate issued. Such certificate of plant variety protection shall have the same effect and operation in law as if the same had been originally issued in such corrected form.

History of 7 U.S.C. §2485: Dec. 24, 1970, P.L. 91-577, §85, 84 Stat. 1552; Dec. 22, 1980, P.L. 96-574, §16, 94 Stat. 3351.

§2486. CORRECTION OF NAMED BREEDER

An error as to the naming of a breeder in the application, without deceptive intent, shall not affect validity of plant variety protection and may be corrected at any time by the Secretary in accordance with regulations established by the Secretary or upon order of a federal court before which the matter is called in question. Upon such correction the Secretary shall issue a certificate accordingly. Such correction shall not deprive any person of any rights the person otherwise would have had.

History of 7 U.S.C. §2486: Dec. 24, 1970, P.L. 91-577, §86, 84 Stat. 1552; Oct. 6, 1994, P.L. 103-349, §13(n), 108 Stat. 3143.

PART I. REEXAMINATION AFTER ISSUE, & CONTESTED PROCEEDINGS

§2501. REEXAMINATION AFTER ISSUE

(a) Any person may, within five years after the issuance of a certificate of plant variety protection, notify the Secretary in writing of facts which may have a bearing on the protectability of the variety, and the Secretary may cause such plant variety protection to be reexamined in the light thereof.

(b) Reexamination of plant variety protection under this section and appeals shall be pursuant to the same procedures and with the same rights as for original examinations. Abandonment of the procedure while subject to a ruling against the retention of the certificate shall result in cancellation of the plant variety certificate thereon and notice thereof shall be endorsed on copies of the description of the protected plant variety thereafter distributed by the Plant Variety Protection Office.

(c) If a person acting under subsection (a) of this section makes a prima facie showing of facts needing proof, the Secretary may direct that the reexamination include such interparty proceedings as the Secretary shall establish.

History of 7 U.S.C. §2501: Dec. 24, 1970, P.L. 91-577, §91, 84 Stat. 1552; Dec. 22, 1980, P.L. 96-574, §17, 94 Stat. 3351; Oct. 6, 1994, P.L. 103-349, §13(o), 108 Stat. 3144.

§§2502, 2503. REPEALED

Repealed Oct. 6, 1994, P.L. 103-349, §8(a), 108 Stat. 3140.

§2504. INTERFERING PLANT VARIETY PROTECTION

(a) The owner of a certificate of plant variety protection may have relief against another owner of a certificate of the same variety by civil action, and the court may adjudge the question of validity of the respective certificates, or the ownership of the certificate.

(b) Such suit may be instituted against the party in interest as shown by the record of the Plant Variety Protection Office at the time of the decision complained of, but any party in interest may become a party to the action. If there be adverse parties residing in a plurality of districts not embraced within the same State, or an adverse party residing in a foreign country, the United States District Court for the District of Columbia, or any United States district court to which it may transfer the case, shall have jurisdiction and may issue summons against the adverse parties directed to the marshall of any district in which any adverse party resides. Summons against adverse parties residing in foreign countries may be served by publication or otherwise as the court directs. The Secretary shall not be made a party but the Secretary shall have the right to intervene. Judgment of the court in favor of the right of an applicant to plant variety protection shall authorize the Secretary to issue a certificate of plant variety protection on the filing in the Plant Variety Protection Office of a certified copy of the judgment and on compliance with the requirements of this chapter.

History of 7 U.S.C. §2504: Dec. 24, 1970, P.L. 91-577, §92, formerly §94, 84 Stat. 1553. Redesignated as §92 and amended Oct. 6, 1994, P.L. 103-349, §§8(b), (c)(1), 13(p), 108 Stat. 3140, 3144.

SUBCHAPTER III. PLANT VARIETY PROTECTION & RIGHTS

PART J. OWNERSHIP & ASSIGNMENT

§2531. OWNERSHIP & ASSIGNMENT

(a) Subject to the provisions of this subchapter, plant variety protection shall have the attributes of personal property.

(b) Applications for certificates of plant variety protection, or any interest in a variety, shall be assignable by an instrument in writing. The owner may in like manner license or grant and convey an exclusive right to use of the variety in the whole or any specified part of the United States.

(c) A certificate of acknowledgment under the hand and official seal of a person authorized to administer oaths within the United States, or in a foreign country, of a diplomatic or consular officer of the United States or an officer authorized to administer oaths whose authority is proved by a certificate of a diplomatic or consular officer of the United States, shall be prima facie evidence of the execution of an assignment, grant, license, or conveyance of plant variety protection or application for plant variety protection.

(d) An assignment, grant, conveyance or license shall be void as against any subsequent purchaser or mortgagee for a valuable consideration, without notice, unless it, or an acknowledgment thereof by the person giving such encumbrance that there is such encumbrance, is filed for recording in the Plant Variety Protection Office within one month from its date or at least one month prior to the date of such subsequent purchase or mortgage.

History of 7 U.S.C. §2531: Dec. 24, 1970, P.L. 91-577, §101, 84 Stat. 1554.

§2532. OWNERSHIP DURING TESTING

An owner who, with notice that release is for testing only, releases possession of seed or other sexually reproducible or tuber propagable plant material for testing retains ownership with respect thereto; and any diversion from authorized testing, or any unauthorized retention, of such material by anyone who has knowledge that it is under such notice, or who is chargeable with notice, is prohibited, and violates the property rights of the owner. Anyone receiving the material tagged or labeled with the notice is chargeable with the notice. The owner is entitled to remedy and redress in a civil action hereunder. No remedy available by State or local law is hereby excluded. No such notice shall be used, or if used be effective, when the owner has made identical sexually reproducible or tuber propagable plant material available to the public, as by sale thereof.

History of 7 U.S.C. §2532: Dec. 24, 1970, P.L. 91-577, §102, 84 Stat. 1554; Oct. 6, 1994, P.L. 103-349, §8(d)(2), 108 Stat. 3141.

PART K. INFRINGEMENT OF PLANT VARIETY PROTECTION

§2541. INFRINGEMENT OF PLANT VARIETY PROTECTION

(a) Acts constituting infringement.—Except as otherwise provided in this subchapter, it shall be an infringement of the rights of the owner of a protected variety to perform without authority, any of the following acts in the United States, or in commerce which can be regulated by Congress or affecting such commerce, prior to expiration of the right to plant variety protection but after either the issue of the certificate or the distribution of a protected plant variety with the notice under section 2567 of this title:

(1) sell or market the protected variety, or offer it or expose it for sale, deliver it, ship it, consign it, exchange it, or solicit an offer to buy it, or any other transfer of title or possession of it;

(2) import the variety into, or export it from, the United States;

(3) sexually multiply, or propagate by a tuber or a part of a tuber, the variety as a step in marketing (for growing purposes) the variety;

(4) use the variety in producing (as distinguished from developing) a hybrid or different variety therefrom;

(5) use seed which had been marked "Unauthorized Propagation Prohibited" or "Unauthorized Seed Multiplication Prohibited" or progeny thereof to propagate the variety;

(6) dispense the variety to another, in a form which can be propagated, without notice as to being a protected variety under which it was received;

(7) condition the variety for the purpose of propagation, except to the extent that the conditioning is related to the activities permitted under section 2543 of this title;

(8) stock the variety for any of the purposes referred to in paragraphs (1) through (7);

(9) perform any of the foregoing acts even in instances in which the variety is multiplied other than sexually, except in pursuance of a valid United States plant patent; or

(10) instigate or actively induce performance of any of the foregoing acts.

(b) Uses authorized by owner—

(1) Subject to paragraph (2), the owner of a protected variety may authorize the use of the variety under this section subject to conditions and limitations specified by the owner.

(2) In the case of a contract between a seed producer and the owner of a protected variety of lawn, turf, or forage grass seed, or alfalfa or clover seed for the production of seed of the protected variety, the producer shall be deemed to be authorized by the owner to sell such seed and to use the variety if—

(A) the producer has fulfilled the terms of the contract;

(B) the owner refuses to take delivery of the seed or refuses to pay any amounts due under the contract within 30 days of the payment date specified in the contract; and

(C) after the expiration of the period specified in subparagraph (B), the producer notifies the owner of the producer's intent to sell the seed and unless the owner fails to pay the amounts due under the contract and take delivery of the seed within 30 days of such notification. For the purposes of this paragraph, the term "owner" shall include any licensee of the owner.

(3) Paragraph (2) shall apply to contracts entered into with respect to plant varieties protected under this chapter as in effect on the day before the effective date of this provision as well as plant varieties protected under this chapter as amended by the Plant Variety Protection Act Amendments of 1994.

(4) Nothing in this subsection shall affect any other rights or remedies of producers or owners that may exist under other Federal or State laws.

(c) Applicability to certain plant varieties.— This section shall apply equally to—

(1) any variety that is essentially derived from a protected variety, unless the protected variety is an essentially derived variety;

(2) any variety that is not clearly distinguishable from a protected variety;

(3) any variety whose production requires the repeated use of a protected variety; and

(4) harvested material (including entire plants and parts of plants) obtained through the unauthorized use of propagating material of a protected variety, unless the owner of the variety has had a reasonable opportunity to exercise the rights provided under this chapter with respect to the propagating material.

(d) Acts not considered infringing.—It shall not be an infringement of the rights of the owner of a variety to perform any act concerning propagating material of any kind, or harvested material, including entire plants and parts of plants, of a protected variety that is sold or otherwise marketed with the consent of the owner in the United States, unless the act involves further propagation of the variety or involves an export of material of the variety, that enables the propagation of the variety, into a country that does not protect varieties of the plant genus or species to which the variety belongs, unless the exported material is for final consumption purposes.

(e) Private noncommercial uses.—It shall not be an infringement of the rights of the owner of a variety to perform any act done privately and for noncommercial purposes.

(f) "Perform without authority" defined.—As used in this section, the term "perform without authority" includes performance without authority by any State, any instrumentality of a State, and any officer or employee of a State or instrumentality of a State acting in the official capacity of the officer or employee. Any State, and any such instrumentality, officer, or employee, shall be subject to the provisions of this chapter in the same manner and to the same extent as any nongovernmental entity.

History of 7 U.S.C. §2541: Dec. 24, 1970, P.L. 91-577, §111, 84 Stat. 1554; Dec. 22, 1980, P.L. 96-574, §19(a), 94 Stat. 3351; Oct. 28, 1992, P.L. 102-560, §3(a), 106 Stat. 4231; Oct. 6, 1994, P.L. 103-349, §§9, 13(q), 108 Stat. 3141, 3144.

§2542. GRANDFATHER CLAUSE

Nothing in this chapter shall abridge the right of any person, or the successor in interest of the person, to reproduce or sell a variety developed and produced by such person more than one year prior to the effective filing date of an adverse application for a certificate of plant variety protection.

History of 7 U.S.C. §2542: Dec. 24, 1970, P.L. 91-577, §112, 84 Stat. 1555; Oct. 6, 1994, P.L. 103-349, §13(r), 108 Stat. 3144.

§2543. RIGHT TO SAVE SEED; CROP EXEMPTION

Except to the extent that such action may constitute an infringement under subsections (3) and (4) of section 2541 of this title, it shall not infringe any right hereunder for a person to save seed produced by the person from seed obtained, or descended from seed obtained, by authority of the owner of the variety for seeding purposes and use such saved seed in the production of a crop for use on the farm of the person, or for sale as provided in this section. A bona fide sale for other than reproductive purposes, made in channels usual for such other purposes, of seed produced on a farm either from seed obtained by authority of the owner for seeding purposes or from seed produced by descent on such farm from seed obtained by authority of the owner for seeding purposes shall not constitute an infringement. A purchaser who diverts seed from such channels to seeding purposes shall be deemed to have notice under section 2567 of this title that the actions of the purchaser constitute an infringement.

History of 7 U.S.C. §2543: Dec. 24, 1970, P.L. 91-577, §113, 84 Stat. 1555; Oct. 6, 1994, P.L. 103-349, §§10, 13(s), 108 Stat. 3142, 3144.

§2544. RESEARCH EXEMPTION

The use and reproduction of a protected variety for plant breeding or other bona fide research shall not constitute an infringement of the protection provided under this chapter.

History of 7 U.S.C. §2544: Dec. 24, 1970, P.L. 91-577, §114, 84 Stat. 1555.

§2545. INTERMEDIARY EXEMPTION

Transportation or delivery by a carrier in the ordinary course of its business as a carrier, or advertising by a person in the advertising business in the ordinary course of that business, shall not constitute an infringement of the protection provided under this chapter.

History of 7 U.S.C. §2545: Dec. 24, 1970, P.L. 91-577, §115, 84 Stat. 1555.

PART L. REMEDIES FOR INFRINGEMENT OF PLANT VARIETY PROTECTION, & OTHER ACTIONS

§2561. REMEDY FOR INFRINGEMENT OF PLANT VARIETY PROTECTION

An owner shall have remedy by civil action for infringement of plant variety protection under section 2541 of this title. If a variety is sold under the name of a variety shown in a certificate, there is a prima facie presumption that it is the same variety.

History of 7 U.S.C. §2561: Dec. 24, 1970, P.L. 91-577, §121, 84 Stat. 1556; Oct. 6, 1994, P.L. 103-349, §13(t), 108 Stat. 3144.

§2562. PRESUMPTION OF VALIDITY; DEFENSES

(a) Certificates of plant variety protection shall be presumed valid. The burden of establishing invalidity of a plant variety protection shall rest on the party asserting invalidity.

(b) The following shall be defenses in any action charging infringement and shall be pleaded: (1) noninfringement, absence of liability for infringement, or unenforceability; (2) invalidity of the plant variety protection in suit on any ground specified in section 2402 of this title as a condition for protectability; (3) invalidity of the plant variety protection in suit for failure to comply with any requirement of section 2422 of this title; (4) that the asserted infringement was performed under an existing certificate adverse to that asserted and prior to notice of the infringement; and (5) any other fact or act made a defense by this chapter.

History of 7 U.S.C. §2562: Dec. 24, 1970, P.L. 91-577, §122, 84 Stat. 1556.

§2563. INJUNCTION

The several courts having jurisdiction of cases under this subchapter may grant injunctions in accordance with the principles of equity to prevent the violation of any right hereunder on such terms as the court deems reasonable.

History of 7 U.S.C. §2563: Dec. 24, 1970, P.L. 91-577, §123, 84 Stat. 1556.

§2564. DAMAGES

(a) Upon finding an infringement the court shall award damages adequate to compensate for the infringement but in no event less than a reasonable royalty for the use made of the variety by the infringer, together with interest and costs as fixed by the court.

(b) When the damages are not determined by the jury, the court shall determine them. In either event the court may increase the damages up to three times the amount determined.

(c) The court may receive expert testimony as an aid to the determination of damages or of what royalty would be reasonable under the circumstances.

(d) As to infringement prior to, or resulting from a planting prior to, issuance of a certificate for the infringed variety, a court finding the infringer to have established innocent intentions, shall have discretion as to awarding damages.

History of 7 U.S.C. §2564: Dec. 24, 1970, P.L. 91-577, §124, 84 Stat. 1556.

§2565. ATTORNEY FEES

The court in exceptional cases may award reasonable attorney fees to the prevailing party.

History of 7 U.S.C. §2565: Dec. 24, 1970, P.L. 91-577, §125, 84 Stat. 1556.

§2566. TIME LIMITATION ON DAMAGES

(a) No recovery shall be had for that part of any infringement committed more than six years (or known to the owner more than one year) prior to the filing of the complaint or counterclaim for infringement in the action.

(b) In the case of claims against the United States Government for unauthorized use of a protected variety, the period between the date of receipt of written claim for compensation by the department or agency of the Government having authority to settle such claim, and the date of mailing by the Government of a notice to the claimant that the claim has been denied shall not be counted as part of the period referred to in the preceding paragraph.

History of 7 U.S.C. §2566: Dec. 24, 1970, P.L. 91-577, §126, 84 Stat. 1556; Oct. 6, 1994, P.L. 103-349, §13(u), 108 Stat. 3144.

§2567. LIMITATION OF DAMAGES; MARKING & NOTICE

Owners may give notice to the public by physically associating with or affixing to the container of seed of a variety or by fixing to the variety, a label containing either the words "Unauthorized Propagation Prohibited" or the words "Unauthorized Seed Multiplication Prohibited" and after the certificate issues, such additional words as "U.S. Protected Variety." In the event the variety is distributed by authorization of the owner and is received by the infringer without such marking, no damages shall be recovered against such infringer by the owner in any action for infringement, unless the infringer has actual notice or knowledge that propagation is prohibited or that the variety is a protected variety, in which event damages may be recovered only for infringement occurring after such notice. As to both damages and injunction, a court shall have discretion to be lenient as to disposal of materials acquired in good faith by acts prior to such notice.

History of 7 U.S.C. §2567: Dec. 24, 1970, P.L. 91-577, §127, 84 Stat. 1557; Dec. 22, 1980, P.L. 96-574, §19(b), 94 Stat. 3351; Oct. 6, 1994, P.L. 103-349, §11, 108 Stat. 3142.

§2568. FALSE MARKING; CEASE & DESIST ORDERS

(a) Each of the following acts, if performed in connection with the sale, offering for sale, or advertising of sexually reproducible plant material or tubers or parts of tubers, is prohibited, and the Secretary may, if the Secretary determines after an opportunity for hearing that the act is being so performed, issue an order to cease and desist, said order being binding unless appealed under section 2461 of this title:

(1) Use of the words "U.S. Protected Variety" or any word or number importing that the material is a variety protected under certificate, when it is not.

(2) Use of any wording importing that the material is a variety for which an application for plant variety protection is pending, when it is not.

(3) Use of either the phrase "Unauthorized Propagation Prohibited" or "Unauthorized Seed Multiplication Prohibited" or similar phrase without reasonable basis. Any reasonable basis expires one year after the first sale of the variety except as justified thereafter by a pending application or a certificate still in force.

(4) Failure to use the name of a variety for which a certificate of protection has been issued under this chapter, even after the expiration of the certificate, except that lawn, turf, or forage grass seed, or alfalfa or clover seed may be sold without a variety name unless use of the name of a variety for which a certificate of protection has been issued under this chapter is required under State law.

(b) Anyone convicted of violating a binding cease and desist order, or of performing any act prohibited in subsection (a) of this section for the purpose of deceiving the public, shall be fined not more than $10,000 and not less than $500.

(c) Anyone whose business is damaged or is likely to be damaged by an act prohibited in subsection (a) of this section, or is subjected to competition in connection with which such act is performed, may have remedy by civil action.

History of 7 U.S.C. §2568: Dec. 24, 1970, P.L. 91-577, §128, 84 Stat. 1557; Dec. 22, 1980, P.L. 96-574, §19(c), 94 Stat. 3352; Oct. 6, 1994, P.L. 103-349, §§12, 13(v), 108 Stat. 3142, 3144.

§2569. NONRESIDENT PROPRIETORS; SERVICE & NOTICE

Every owner not residing in the United States may file in the Plant Variety Protection Office a written designation stating the name and address of a person residing within the United States on whom may be served process or notice of proceedings affecting the plant variety protection or rights thereunder. If the person designated cannot be found at the address given in the last designation, or if no person has been designated, the United States District Court for the District of Columbia shall have jurisdiction and summons shall be served by publication or otherwise as the court directs. The court shall have the same jurisdiction to take any action respecting the plant variety protection, or rights thereunder that it would have if the owner were personally within the jurisdiction of the court.

History of 7 U.S.C. §2569: Dec. 24, 1970, P.L. 91-577, §129, 84 Stat. 1557.

§2570. LIABILITY OF STATES, INSTRUMENTALITIES OF STATES, & STATE OFFICIALS FOR INFRINGEMENT OF PLANT VARIETY PROTECTION

(a) Any State, any instrumentality of a State, and any officer or employee of a State or instrumentality of a State acting in the official capacity of the officer or employee, shall not be immune, under the eleventh amendment of the Constitution of the United States or under any other doctrine of sovereign immunity, from suit in Federal court by any person, including any governmental or nongovernmental entity, for infringement of plant variety protection under section 2541 of this title, or for any other violation under this subchapter.

(b) In a suit described in subsection (a) of this section for a violation described in that subsection, remedies (including remedies both at law and in equity) are available for the violation to the same extent as such remedies are available for such a violation in a suit against any private entity. Such remedies include damages, interest, costs, and treble damages under section 2564 of this title, and attorney fees under section 2565 of this title.

History of 7 U.S.C. §2570: Oct. 28, 1992, P.L. 91-577, §130, as added Oct. 28, 1992, P.L. 102-560, §3(b), 106 Stat. 4231; Oct. 6, 1994, P.L. 103-349, §13(w), 108 Stat. 3144.

PART M. INTENT & SEVERABILITY

§2581. INTENT

It is the intent of Congress to provide the indicated protection for new varieties by exercise of any constitutional power needed for that end, so as to afford adequate encouragement for research, and for marketing when appropriate, to yield for the public the benefits of new varieties. Constitutional clauses 3 and 8 of article I, section 8 are both relied upon.

History of 7 U.S.C. §2581: Dec. 24, 1970, P.L. 91-577, §131, 84 Stat. 1558.

§2582. SEVERABILITY

If this chapter is held unconstitutional as to some provisions or circumstances, it shall remain in force as to the remaining provisions and other circumstances.

History of 7 U.S.C. §2582: Dec. 24, 1970, P.L. 91-577, §132, 84 Stat. 1558.

§2583. REPEALED

Repealed Dec. 22, 1980, P.L. 96-574, §20, 94 Stat. 3352.

TITLE 10. ARMED FORCES

SUBTITLE A. GENERAL MILITARY LAW

PART IV. SERVICE, SUPPLY, & PROCUREMENT

CHAPTER 134. MISCELLANEOUS ADMINISTRATIVE PROVISIONS

SUBCHAPTER II. MISCELLANEOUS ADMINISTRATIVE AUTHORITY

§2260. LICENSING OF INTELLECTUAL PROPERTY: RETENTION OF FEES

(a) **Authority.**—Under regulations prescribed by the Secretary of Defense or the Secretary of Homeland Security, the Secretary concerned may license trademarks, service marks, certification marks, and collective marks owned or controlled by the Secretary concerned and may retain and expend fees received from such licensing in accordance with this section.

(b) **Designated marks.**—The Secretary concerned shall designate the trademarks, service marks, certification marks, and collective marks regarding which the Secretary will exercise the authority to retain licensing fees under this section.

(c) **Licenses for qualifying companies**—

(1) The Secretary concerned may license trademarks, service marks, certification marks, and collec-

tive marks owned or controlled by the Secretary relating to military designations and likenesses of military weapons systems to any qualifying company upon receipt of a request from the company.

(2) For purposes of paragraph (1), a qualifying company is any United States company that—

(A) is a toy or hobby manufacturer; and

(B) is determined by the Secretary concerned to be qualified in accordance with such criteria as determined appropriate by the Secretary of Defense.

(3) The fee for a license under this subsection shall not exceed by more than a nominal amount the amount needed to recover all costs of the Department of Defense in processing the request for the license and supplying the license.

(4) A license to a qualifying company under this subsection shall provide that the license may not be transferred, sold, or relicensed by the qualifying company.

(5) A license under this subsection shall not be an exclusive license.

(d) Use of fees.—The Secretary concerned shall use fees retained under this section for the following purposes:

(1) For payment of the following costs incurred by the Secretary:

(A) Costs of securing trademark registrations.

(B) Costs of operating the licensing program under this section.

(2) For morale, welfare, and recreation activities under the jurisdiction of the Secretary, to the extent (if any) that the total amount of the licensing fees available under this section for a fiscal year exceed the total amount needed for such fiscal year under paragraph (1).

(e) Availability.—Fees received in a fiscal year and retained under this section shall be available for obligation in such fiscal year and the following two fiscal years.

(f) Definitions.—In this section:

(1) The terms "trademark," "service mark," "certification mark," and "collective mark" have the meanings given such terms in section 45 of the Act of July 5, 1946 (commonly referred to as the Trademark Act of 1946; 15 U.S.C. 1127).

(2) The term "Secretary concerned" has the meaning provided in section 101(a)(9) of this title and also includes—

(A) the Secretary of Defense, with respect to matters concerning the Defense Agencies and Department of Defense Field Activities; and

(B) the Secretary of Homeland Security, with respect to matters concerning the Coast Guard when it is not operating as a service in the Department of the Navy.

History of 10 U.S.C. §2260: Oct. 28, 2004, P.L. 108-375, §1004(a), 118 Stat. 2035; Jan. 28, 2008, P.L. 110-181, §882(a), 122 Stat. 263; Oct. 14, 2008, P.L. 110-417, §881, 122 Stat. 4559.

TITLE 11. BANKRUPTCY

CHAPTER 3. CASE ADMINISTRATION

SUBCHAPTER IV. ADMINISTRATIVE POWERS

§365. EXECUTORY CONTRACTS & UNEXPIRED LEASES

(a) Except as provided in sections 765 and 766 of this title and in subsections (b), (c), and (d) of this section, the trustee, subject to the court's approval, may assume or reject any executory contract or unexpired lease of the debtor.

(b)(1) If there has been a default in an executory contract or unexpired lease of the debtor, the trustee may not assume such contract or lease unless, at the time of assumption of such contract or lease, the trustee—

(A) cures, or provides adequate assurance that the trustee will promptly cure, such default other than a default that is a breach of a provision relating to the satisfaction of any provision (other than a penalty rate or penalty provision) relating to a default arising from any failure to perform nonmonetary obligations under an unexpired lease of real property, if it is impossible for the trustee to cure such default by performing nonmonetary acts at and after the time of assumption, except that if such default arises from a failure to operate in accordance with a nonresidential real property lease, then such default shall be cured by performance at and after the time of assumption in accordance with such lease, and pecuniary losses resulting from such default shall be compensated in accordance with the provisions of this paragraph;

(B) compensates, or provides adequate assurance that the trustee will promptly compensate, a party other than the debtor to such contract or lease, for any actual pecuniary loss to such party resulting from such default; and

(C) provides adequate assurance of future performance under such contract or lease.

(2) Paragraph (1) of this subsection does not apply to a default that is a breach of a provision relating to—

(A) the insolvency or financial condition of the debtor at any time before the closing of the case;

(B) the commencement of a case under this title;

(C) the appointment of or taking possession by a trustee in a case under this title or a custodian before such commencement; or

(D) the satisfaction of any penalty rate or penalty provision relating to a default arising from any failure by the debtor to perform nonmonetary obligations under the executory contract or unexpired lease.

(3) For the purposes of paragraph (1) of this subsection and paragraph (2)(B) of subsection (f), adequate assurance of future performance of a lease of real property in a shopping center includes adequate assurance—

(A) of the source of rent and other consideration due under such lease, and in the case of an assignment, that the financial condition and operating performance of the proposed assignee and its guarantors, if any, shall be similar to the financial condition and operating performance of the debtor and its guarantors, if any, as of the time the debtor became the lessee under the lease;

(B) that any percentage rent due under such lease will not decline substantially;

(C) that assumption or assignment of such lease is subject to all the provisions thereof, including (but not limited to) provisions such as a radius, location, use, or exclusivity provision, and will not breach any such provision contained in any other lease, financing agreement, or master agreement relating to such shopping center; and

(D) that assumption or assignment of such lease will not disrupt any tenant mix or balance in such shopping center.

(4) Notwithstanding any other provision of this section, if there has been a default in an unexpired lease of the debtor, other than a default of a kind specified in paragraph (2) of this subsection, the trustee may not require a lessor to provide services or supplies incidental to such lease before assumption of such lease unless the lessor is compensated under the terms of such lease for any services and supplies provided under such lease before assumption of such lease.

(c) The trustee may not assume or assign any executory contract or unexpired lease of the debtor, whether or not such contract or lease prohibits or restricts assignment of rights or delegation of duties, if—

(1)(A) applicable law excuses a party, other than the debtor, to such contract or lease from accepting performance from or rendering performance to an entity other than the debtor or the debtor in possession, whether or not such contract or lease prohibits or restricts assignment of rights or delegation of duties; and

(B) such party does not consent to such assumption or assignment; or

(2) such contract is a contract to make a loan, or extend other debt financing or financial accommodations, to or for the benefit of the debtor, or to issue a security of the debtor; or

(3) such lease is of nonresidential real property and has been terminated under applicable nonbankruptcy law prior to the order for relief.

(4) Repealed Apr. 20, 2005, P.L. 109-8, §328(a)(2)(C), 119 Stat. 100.

(d)(1) In a case under chapter 7 of this title, if the trustee does not assume or reject an executory contract or unexpired lease of residential real property or of personal property of the debtor within 60 days after the order for relief, or within such additional time as the court, for cause, within such 60-day period, fixes, then such contract or lease is deemed rejected.

(2) In a case under chapter 9, 11, 12, or 13 of this title, the trustee may assume or reject an executory contract or unexpired lease of residential real property or of personal property of the debtor at any time before the confirmation of a plan but the court, on the request of any party to such contract or lease, may order the trustee to determine within a specified period of time whether to assume or reject such contract or lease.

(3) The trustee shall timely perform all the obligations of the debtor, except those specified in section 365(b)(2), arising from and after the order for relief under any unexpired lease of nonresidential real property, until such lease is assumed or rejected, notwithstanding section 503(b)(1) of this title. The court may extend, for cause, the time for performance of any such

obligation that arises within 60 days after the date of the order for relief, but the time for performance shall not be extended beyond such 60-day period. This subsection shall not be deemed to affect the trustee's obligations under the provisions of subsection (b) or (f) of this section. Acceptance of any such performance does not constitute waiver or relinquishment of the lessor's rights under such lease or under this title.

(4)(A) Subject to subparagraph (B), an unexpired lease of nonresidential real property under which the debtor is the lessee shall be deemed rejected, and the trustee shall immediately surrender that nonresidential real property to the lessor, if the trustee does not assume or reject the unexpired lease by the earlier of—

(i) the date that is 120 days after the date of the order for relief; or

(ii) the date of the entry of an order confirming a plan.

(B)(i) The court may extend the period determined under subparagraph (A), prior to the expiration of the 120-day period, for 90 days on the motion of the trustee or lessor for cause.

(ii) If the court grants an extension under clause (i), the court may grant a subsequent extension only upon prior written consent of the lessor in each instance.

(5) The trustee shall timely perform all of the obligations of the debtor, except those specified in section 365(b)(2), first arising from or after 60 days after the order for relief in a case under chapter 11 of this title under an unexpired lease of personal property (other than personal property leased to an individual primarily for personal, family, or household purposes), until such lease is assumed or rejected notwithstanding section 503(b)(1) of this title, unless the court, after notice and a hearing and based on the equities of the case, orders otherwise with respect to the obligations or timely performance thereof. This subsection shall not be deemed to affect the trustee's obligations under the provisions of subsection (b) or (f). Acceptance of any such performance does not constitute waiver or relinquishment of the lessor's rights under such lease or under this title.

(e)(1) Notwithstanding a provision in an executory contract or unexpired lease, or in applicable law, an executory contract or unexpired lease of the debtor may not be terminated or modified, and any right or obligation under such contract or lease may not be terminated or modified, at any time after the commencement of the case solely because of a provision in such contract or lease that is conditioned on—

(A) the insolvency or financial condition of the debtor at any time before the closing of the case;

(B) the commencement of a case under this title; or

(C) the appointment of or taking possession by a trustee in a case under this title or a custodian before such commencement.

(2) Paragraph (1) of this subsection does not apply to an executory contract or unexpired lease of the debtor, whether or not such contract or lease prohibits or restricts assignment of rights or delegation of duties, if—

(A)(i) applicable law excuses a party, other than the debtor, to such contract or lease from accepting performance from or rendering performance to the trustee or to an assignee of such contract or lease, whether or not such contract or lease prohibits or restricts assignment of rights or delegation of duties; and

(ii) such party does not consent to such assumption or assignment; or

(B) such contract is a contract to make a loan, or extend other debt financing or financial accommodations, to or for the benefit of the debtor, or to issue a security of the debtor.

(f)(1) Except as provided in subsections (b) and (c) of this section, notwithstanding a provision in an executory contract or unexpired lease of the debtor, or in applicable law, that prohibits, restricts, or conditions the assignment of such contract or lease, the trustee may assign such contract or lease under paragraph (2) of this subsection.

(2) The trustee may assign an executory contract or unexpired lease of the debtor only if—

(A) the trustee assumes such contract or lease in accordance with the provisions of this section; and

(B) adequate assurance of future performance by the assignee of such contract or lease is provided, whether or not there has been a default in such contract or lease.

(3) Notwithstanding a provision in an executory contract or unexpired lease of the debtor, or in applicable law that terminates or modifies, or permits a party other than the debtor to terminate or modify, such contract or lease or a right or obligation under such contract or lease on account of an assignment of such contract or lease, such contract, lease, right, or obligation may not be terminated or modified under such provision because of the assumption or assignment of such contract or lease by the trustee.

(g) Except as provided in subsections (h)(2) and (i)(2) of this section, the rejection of an executory contract or unexpired lease of the debtor constitutes a breach of such contract or lease—

(1) if such contract or lease has not been assumed under this section or under a plan confirmed under chapter 9, 11, 12, or 13 of this title, immediately before the date of the filing of the petition; or

(2) if such contract or lease has been assumed under this section or under a plan confirmed under chapter 9, 11, 12, or 13 of this title—

(A) if before such rejection the case has not been converted under section 1112, 1208, or 1307 of this title, at the time of such rejection; or

(B) if before such rejection the case has been converted under section 1112, 1208, or 1307 of this title—

(i) immediately before the date of such conversion, if such contract or lease was assumed before such conversion; or

(ii) at the time of such rejection, if such contract or lease was assumed after such conversion.

(h)(1)(A) If the trustee rejects an unexpired lease of real property under which the debtor is the lessor and—

(i) if the rejection by the trustee amounts to such a breach as would entitle the lessee to treat such lease as terminated by virtue of its terms, applicable nonbankruptcy law, or any agreement made by the lessee, then the lessee under such lease may treat such lease as terminated by the rejection; or

(ii) if the term of such lease has commenced, the lessee may retain its rights under such lease (including rights such as those relating to the amount and timing of payment of rent and other amounts payable by the lessee and any right of use, possession, quiet enjoyment, subletting, assignment, or hypothecation) that are in or appurtenant to the real property for the balance of the term of such lease and for any renewal or extension of such rights to the extent that such rights are enforceable under applicable nonbankruptcy law.

(B) If the lessee retains its rights under subparagraph (A)(ii), the lessee may offset against the rent reserved under such lease for the balance of the term after the date of the rejection of such lease and for the term of any renewal or extension of such lease, the value of any damage caused by the nonperformance after the date of such rejection, of any obligation of the debtor under such lease, but the lessee shall not have any other right against the estate or the debtor on account of any damage occurring after such date caused by such nonperformance.

(C) The rejection of a lease of real property in a shopping center with respect to which the lessee elects to retain its rights under subparagraph (A)(ii) does not affect the enforceability under applicable nonbankruptcy law of any provision in the lease pertaining to radius, location, use, exclusivity, or tenant mix or balance.

(D) In this paragraph, "lessee" includes any successor, assign, or mortgagee permitted under the terms of such lease.

(2)(A) If the trustee rejects a timeshare interest under a timeshare plan under which the debtor is the timeshare interest seller and—

(i) if the rejection amounts to such a breach as would entitle the timeshare interest purchaser to treat the timeshare plan as terminated under its terms, applicable nonbankruptcy law, or any agreement made by timeshare interest purchaser, the timeshare interest purchaser under the timeshare plan may treat the timeshare plan as terminated by such rejection; or

(ii) if the term of such timeshare interest has commenced, then the timeshare interest purchaser may retain its rights in such timeshare interest for the balance of such term and for any term of renewal or extension of such timeshare interest to the extent that such rights are enforceable under applicable nonbankruptcy law.

(B) If the timeshare interest purchaser retains its rights under subparagraph (A), such timeshare interest purchaser may offset against the moneys due for such timeshare interest for the balance of the term after the date of the rejection of such timeshare interest, and the term of any renewal or extension of such timeshare interest, the value of any damage caused by the nonperformance after the date of such rejection, of any obligation of the debtor under such timeshare plan, but the timeshare interest purchaser shall not have any right against the estate or the debtor on account of any damage occurring after such date caused by such nonperformance.

(i)(1) If the trustee rejects an executory contract of the debtor for the sale of real property or for the sale of a timeshare interest under a timeshare plan, under which the purchaser is in possession, such purchaser may treat such contract as terminated, or, in the alternative, may remain in possession of such real property or timeshare interest.

(2) If such purchaser remains in possession—

(A) such purchaser shall continue to make all payments due under such contract, but may,[1] offset against such payments any damages occurring after the date of the rejection of such contract caused by the nonperformance of any obligation of the debtor after such date, but such purchaser does not have any rights against the estate on account of any damages arising after such date from such rejection, other than such offset; and

(B) the trustee shall deliver title to such purchaser in accordance with the provisions of such contract, but is relieved of all other obligations to perform under such contract.

(j) A purchaser that treats an executory contract as terminated under subsection (i) of this section, or a party whose executory contract to purchase real property from the debtor is rejected and under which such party is not in possession, has a lien on the interest of the debtor in such property for the recovery of any portion of the purchase price that such purchaser or party has paid.

(k) Assignment by the trustee to an entity of a contract or lease assumed under this section relieves the trustee and the estate from any liability for any breach of such contract or lease occurring after such assignment.

(*l*) If an unexpired lease under which the debtor is the lessee is assigned pursuant to this section, the lessor of the property may require a deposit or other security for the performance of the debtor's obligations under the lease substantially the same as would have been required by the landlord upon the initial leasing to a similar tenant.

(m) For purposes of this section 365 and sections 541(b)(2) and 362(b)(10), leases of real property shall include any rental agreement to use real property.

(n)(1) If the trustee rejects an executory contract under which the debtor is a licensor of a right to intellectual property, the licensee under such contract may elect—

(A) to treat such contract as terminated by such rejection if such rejection by the trustee amounts to such a breach as would entitle the licensee to treat such contract as terminated by virtue of its own terms, applicable nonbankruptcy law, or an agreement made by the licensee with another entity; or

(B) to retain its rights (including a right to enforce any exclusivity provision of such contract, but excluding any other right under applicable nonbankruptcy law to specific performance of such contract) under such contract and under any agreement supplementary to such contract, to such intellectual property (including any embodiment of such intellectual property to the extent protected by applicable nonbankruptcy law), as such rights existed immediately before the case commenced, for—

(i) the duration of such contract; and

(ii) any period for which such contract may be extended by the licensee as of right under applicable nonbankruptcy law.

(2) If the licensee elects to retain its rights, as described in paragraph (1)(B) of this subsection, under such contract—

(A) the trustee shall allow the licensee to exercise such rights;

(B) the licensee shall make all royalty payments due under such contract for the duration of such contract and for any period described in paragraph (1)(B) of this subsection for which the licensee extends such contract; and

(C) the licensee shall be deemed to waive—

(i) any right of setoff it may have with respect to such contract under this title or applicable nonbankruptcy law; and

(ii) any claim allowable under section 503(b) of this title arising from the performance of such contract.

(3) If the licensee elects to retain its rights, as described in paragraph (1)(B) of this subsection, then on the written request of the licensee the trustee shall—

(A) to the extent provided in such contract, or any agreement supplementary to such contract, provide to the licensee any intellectual property (including such embodiment) held by the trustee; and

(B) not interfere with the rights of the licensee as provided in such contract, or any agreement supplementary to such contract, to such intellectual property (including such embodiment) including any right to obtain such intellectual property (or such embodiment) from another entity.

(4) Unless and until the trustee rejects such contract, on the written request of the licensee the trustee shall—

(A) to the extent provided in such contract or any agreement supplementary to such contract—

(i) perform such contract; or

(ii) provide to the licensee such intellectual property (including any embodiment of such intellectual property to the extent protected by applicable nonbankruptcy law) held by the trustee; and

(B) not interfere with the rights of the licensee as provided in such contract, or any agreement supplementary to such contract, to such intellectual property (including such embodiment), including any right to obtain such intellectual property (or such embodiment) from another entity.

(o) In a case under chapter 11 of this title, the trustee shall be deemed to have assumed (consistent with the debtor's other obligations under section 507), and shall immediately cure any deficit under, any commitment by the debtor to a Federal depository institutions regulatory agency (or predecessor to such agency) to maintain the capital of an insured depository institution, and any claim for a subsequent breach of the obligations thereunder shall be entitled to priority under section 507. This subsection shall not extend any commitment that would otherwise be terminated by any act of such an agency.

(p)(1) If a lease of personal property is rejected or not timely assumed by the trustee under subsection (d), the leased property is no longer property of the estate and the stay under section 362(a) is automatically terminated.

(2)(A) If the debtor in a case under chapter 7 is an individual, the debtor may notify the creditor in writing that the debtor desires to assume the lease. Upon being so notified, the creditor may, at its option, notify the debtor that it is willing to have the lease assumed by the debtor and may condition such assumption on cure of any outstanding default on terms set by the contract.

(B) If, not later than 30 days after notice is provided under subparagraph (A), the debtor notifies the lessor in writing that the lease is assumed, the liability under the lease will be assumed by the debtor and not by the estate.

(C) The stay under section 362 and the injunction under section 524(a)(2) shall not be violated by notification of the debtor and negotiation of cure under this subsection.

(3) In a case under chapter 11 in which the debtor is an individual and in a case under chapter 13, if the debtor is the lessee with respect to personal property and the lease is not assumed in the plan confirmed by the court, the lease is deemed rejected as of the conclusion of the hearing on confirmation. If the lease is rejected, the stay under section 362 and any stay under section 1301 is automatically terminated with respect to the property subject to the lease.

1. **Editor's note:** The comma probably should not appear.

History of 11 U.S.C. §365: Nov. 6, 1978, P.L. 95-598, 92 Stat. 2574; July 10, 1984, P.L. 98-353, §§362, 402-404, 98 Stat. 361, 367; Oct. 27, 1986, P.L. 99-554, §§257(j), (m), 283(e), 100 Stat. 3115, 3117; Oct. 18, 1988, P.L. 100-506, §1(b), 102 Stat. 2538; Nov. 29, 1990, P.L. 101-647, §2522(c), 104 Stat. 4866; Sept. 3, 1992, P.L. 102-365, §19(b)-(e), 106 Stat. 982-984; Oct. 22, 1994, P.L. 103-394, §§205(a), 219(a), (b), 501(d)(10), 108 Stat. 4122, 4128, 4145; Oct. 31, 1994, P.L. 103-429, §1, 108 Stat. 4377; Apr. 20, 2005, P.L. 109-8, §§309(b), 328(a), 404, 119 Stat. 82, 100, 404.

See also 11 U.S.C. §101(35A) (definition of "intellectual property").

TITLE 15. COMMERCE & TRADE

CHAPTER 2. FEDERAL TRADE COMMISSION; PROMOTION OF EXPORT TRADE & PREVENTION OF UNFAIR METHODS OF COMPETITION

SUBCHAPTER V. TEXTILE FIBER PRODUCTS IDENTIFICATION

§70b. MISBRANDED & FALSELY ADVERTISED TEXTILE FIBER PRODUCTS

(a) False or deceptive identification.—Except as otherwise provided in this subchapter, a textile fiber product shall be misbranded if it is falsely or deceptively stamped, tagged, labeled, invoiced, advertised, or otherwise identified as to the name or amount of constituent fibers contained therein.

(b) Stamp, tag, label or other means of identification; contents.—Except as otherwise provided in this subchapter, a textile fiber product shall be misbranded if a stamp, tag, label, or other means of identification, or substitute therefor authorized by section 70c of this title, is not on or affixed to the product showing in words and figures plainly legible, the following:

(1) The constituent fiber or combination of fibers in the textile fiber product, designating with equal prominence each natural or manufactured fiber in the textile fiber product by its generic name in the order of predominance by the weight thereof if the weight of such fiber is 5 per centum or more of the total fiber weight of the product, but nothing in this section shall be construed as prohibiting the use of a nondeceptive trademark in conjunction with a designated generic name: *Provided*, That exclusive of permissible ornamentation, any fiber or group of fibers present in an amount of 5 per centum or less by weight of the total fiber content shall not be designated by the generic name or the trademark of such fiber or fibers, but shall be designated only as "other fiber" or "other fibers" as the case may be but nothing in this section shall be construed as prohibiting the disclosure of any fiber present in a textile fiber product, which has a clearly established and definite functional significance where present in the amount contained in such product.

(2) The percentage of each fiber present, by weight, in the total fiber content of the textile fiber product, exclusive of ornamentation not exceeding 5 per centum by weight of the total fiber content: *Provided*, That, exclusive of permissible ornamentation, any fiber or group of fibers present in an amount of 5 per centum or less by weight of the total fiber content shall not be designated by the generic name or trademark of such fiber or fibers, but shall be designated only as "other fiber" or "other fibers" as the case may be, but nothing in this section shall be construed as prohibiting the disclosure of any fiber present in a textile fiber product which has a clearly established and definite functional significance where present in the amount stated: *Provided further*, That in the case of a textile fiber product which contains more than one kind of fiber, deviation in the fiber content of any fiber in such product from the amount stated on the stamp, tag, label, or other identification shall not be a misbranding under this section unless such deviation is in excess of reasonable tolerances which shall be established by the Commission: *And provided further*, That any such deviation which exceeds said tolerances shall not be a misbranding if the person charged proves that the deviation resulted from unavoidable variations in manufacture and despite due care to make accurate the statements on the tag, stamp, label, or other identification.

(3) The name, or other identification issued and registered by the Commission, of the manufacturer of the product or one or more persons subject to section 70a of this title with respect to such product.

(4) If it is an imported textile fiber product the name of the country where processed or manufactured.

(5) If it is a textile fiber product processed or manufactured in the United States, it be so identified.

(c) False or deceptive advertisement.—For the purposes of this subchapter, a textile fiber product shall be considered to be falsely or deceptively advertised if any disclosure or implication of fiber content is made in any written advertisement which is used to aid, promote, or assist directly or indirectly in the sale or offering for sale of such textile fiber product, unless the same information as that required to be shown on the stamp, tag, label, or other identification under subsection (b)(1) and (2) of this section is contained in the heading, body, or other part of such written advertisement, except that the percentages of the fiber present in the textile fiber product need not be stated.

(d) Additional information allowed.—In addition to the information required in this section, the stamp, tag, label, or other means of identification, or advertisement may contain other information not violating the provisions of this subchapter.

(e) Labelling of packages.—For purposes of this subchapter, in addition to the textile fiber products contained therein, a package of textile fiber products intended for sale to the ultimate consumer shall be misbranded unless such package has affixed to it a stamp, tag, label, or other means of identification bearing the information required by subsection (b) of this section, with respect to such contained textile fiber products, or is transparent to the extent it allows for the clear reading of the stamp, tag, label, or other means of identification on the textile fiber product, or in the case of hosiery items, this section shall not be construed as requiring the affixing of a stamp, tag, label, or other means of identification to each hosiery product contained in a package if (1) such hosiery products are intended for sale to the ultimate consumer in such package, (2) such package has affixed to it a stamp, tag, label, or other means of identification bearing, with respect to the hosiery products contained therein, the information required by subsection (b) of this section, and (3) the information on the stamp, tag, label, or other means of identification affixed to such package is equally applicable with respect to each textile fiber product contained therein.

(f) Fabric severed from bolts, pieces or rolls of fabric.—This section shall not be construed as requiring designation of the fiber content of any portion of fabric, when sold at retail, which is severed from bolts, pieces, or rolls of fabric labeled in accordance with the provisions of this section at the time of such sale: *Provided*, That if any portion of fabric severed from a bolt, piece, or roll of fabric is in any manner represented as containing percentages of natural or manufactured fibers, other than that which is set forth on the labeled bolt, piece, or roll, this section shall be applicable thereto, and the information required shall be separately set forth and segregated as required by this section.

(g) Advertisement of textile product by use of name or symbol of fur-bearing animal.—For the purposes of this subchapter, a textile fiber product shall be considered to be falsely or deceptively advertised if the name or symbol of any fur-bearing animal is used in the advertisement of such product unless such product, or the part thereof in connection with which the name or symbol of a fur-bearing animal is used, is a fur or fur product within the meaning of the Fur Products Labeling Act [15 U.S.C. §69 et seq.]: *Provided, however*, That where a textile fiber product contains the hair or fiber of a fur-bearing animal, the name of such animal, in conjunction with the word "fiber," "hair," or "blend," may be used.

(h) Reused stuffing.—For the purposes of this subchapter, a textile fiber product shall be misbranded if it is used as stuffing in any upholstered product, mattress, or cushion after having been previously used as stuffing in any other upholstered product, mattress, or cushion, unless the upholstered product, mattress, or cushion containing such textile fiber product bears a stamp, tag, or label approved by the Commission indicating in words plainly legible that it contains reused stuffing.

(i) Mail order catalog or promotional material.—For the purposes of this subchapter, a textile fiber product shall be considered to be falsely or deceptively advertised in any mail order catalog or mail order promotional material which is used in the direct sale or direct offering for sale of such textile fiber product, unless such textile fiber product description states in a clear and conspicuous manner that such textile fiber product is processed or manufactured in the United States of America, or imported, or both.

(j) Location of stamp, tag, label, or other identification.—For purposes of this subchapter, any textile fiber product shall be misbranded if a stamp, tag, label, or other identification conforming to the requirements of this section is not on or affixed to the inside center of the neck midway between the shoulder seams or, if such product does not contain a neck, in the most conspicuous place on the inner side of such product, unless it is on or affixed on the outer side of such product, or in the case of hosiery items on the outer side of such product or package.

(k) Marking of certain sock products—

(1) Notwithstanding any other provision of law, socks provided for in subheading 6115.92.90, 6115.93.90, 6115.99.18, 6111.20.60, 6111.30.50, or 6111.90.50 of the Harmonized Tariff Schedule of the United States, as in effect on September 1, 2003, shall be marked as legibly, indelibly, and permanently as the nature of the article or package will permit in such a manner as to indicate to the ultimate consumer in the United States the English name of the country of origin of the article. The marking required by this subsection shall be on the front of the package, adjacent to the size designation of the product, and shall be set forth in such a manner as to be clearly legible, conspicuous, and readily accessible to the ultimate consumer.

(2) Exceptions.—Any package that contains several different types of goods and includes socks classified under subheading 6115.92.90, 6115.93.90, 6115.99.18, 6111.20.60, 6111.30.50, or 6111.90.50 of the Harmonized Tariff Schedule of the United States, as in effect on September 1, 2003, shall not be subject to the requirements of paragraph (1).

History of 15 U.S.C. §70b: Sept. 2, 1958, P.L. 85-897, §4, 72 Stat. 1719; June 5, 1965, P.L. 89-35, §§1, 2, 79 Stat. 124; Sept. 24, 1984, P.L. 98-417, §§301-303, 98 Stat. 1603, 1604; Dec. 3, 2004, P.L. 108-429, §4002(h)(1), (2), 118 Stat. 2594.

CHAPTER 8. FALSELY STAMPED GOLD OR SILVER OR GOODS MANUFACTURED THEREFROM

§297. STAMPING PLATED ARTICLES

(a) Words "sterling" or "coin" forbidden.—In the case of articles of merchandise made in whole or in part of an inferior metal, having deposited or plated thereon or brazed or otherwise affixed thereto a plating, covering, or sheet composed of gold or silver, or of an alloy of either of said metals, and known in the market as rolled gold plate, gold plate, gold filled, silver plate, or gold or silver electroplate, or by any similar designation, so imported into or exported from the United States, or so deposited in the United States mails for transmission, or so delivered to any common carrier, or so transported or caused to be transported as specified in section 294 of this title, no such article, nor any tag, card, or label attached thereto, nor any box, package, cover, or wrapper in which such article is encased or inclosed, shall be stamped, branded, engraved, or imprinted with any word or mark usually employed to indicate the fineness of gold, unless such word or mark be accompanied by other words, plainly indicating that such article or part thereof is made of rolled gold plate, gold plate, or gold electroplate, or is gold filled, as the case may be, and no such article, nor any tag, card, or label attached thereto, nor any box, package, cover, or wrapper in which such article is incased or inclosed, shall be stamped, branded, engraved, or imprinted with the word "sterling" or the word "coin," either alone or in conjunction with other words or marks.

(b) Identifying trademark.—Whenever any person, firm, corporation, or association, being a manufacturer or dealer subject to section 294 of this title—

(1) applies or causes to be applied to any article of merchandise intended for sale or customarily sold as a complete product to consumers in any State, by stamping, branding, engraving, or otherwise, any quality mark or stamp indicating or purporting to indicate that such article is made in whole or in part of gold or silver or of an alloy of either such metal; or

(2) imports into any State any such article of merchandise bearing any such quality mark or stamp which indicates or purports to indicate that such article is made in whole or in part of gold or silver or of an alloy of either such metal,

such person, firm, corporation, or association, before depositing any such article manufactured or imported after six months after the effective date of this Act in the United States mails, or causing such article to be so deposited, for transmission thereby, or delivering such article or causing such article to be delivered to any common carrier for transportation from one State to any other State, or transporting such article or causing such article to be transported from one State to any other State, shall—

(A) apply or cause to be applied to that article a trademark of such persons, which has been duly registered or applied for registration under the laws of the United States within thirty days after an article bearing the trademark is placed in commerce or imported into the United States, or the name of such person; and

(B) if such article of merchandise is composed of two or more parts which are complete in themselves but which are not identical in quality, and any one of such parts bears such a quality mark or stamp, apply or cause to be applied to each other part of that article of merchandise a quality mark or stamp of like pattern and size disclosing the quality of that other part.

Each identifying trademark or name applied to any article of merchandise in compliance with clause (A) of this subsection shall be applied to that article by the same means as that used in applying the quality mark or stamp appearing thereon, in type or lettering at least as large as that used in such quality mark or stamp, and in a position as close as possible to that quality mark or stamp. For the purposes of this subsection, the term "State" includes the Commonwealth of Puerto Rico, the Virgin Islands, Guam, American Samoa, and the District of Columbia.

History of 15 U.S.C. §297: June 13, 1906, ch. 3289, §4, 34 Stat. 261; Oct. 4, 1961, P.L. 87-354, §1, 75 Stat. 775; July 31, 1970, P.L. 91-366, §1(e), 84 Stat. 691.

CHAPTER 61. SOFT DRINK INTERBRAND COMPETITION

§3501. EXCLUSIVE TERRITORIAL LICENSES TO MANUFACTURE, DISTRIBUTE, & SELL TRADEMARKED SOFT DRINK PRODUCTS; ULTIMATE RESALE TO CONSUMERS; SUBSTANTIAL & EFFECTIVE COMPETITION

Nothing contained in any antitrust law shall render unlawful the inclusion and enforcement in any trademark licensing contract or agreement, pursuant to which the licensee engages in the manufacture (including manufacture by a sublicensee, agent, or subcontractor), distribution, and sale of a trademarked soft drink product, of provisions granting the licensee the sole and exclusive right to manufacture, distribute, and sell such product in a defined geographic area or limiting the licensee, directly or indirectly, to the manufacture, distribution, and sale of such product only for ultimate resale to consumers within a defined geographic area: *Provided*, That such product is in substantial and effective competition with other products of the same general class in the relevant market or markets.

History of 15 U.S.C. §3501: July 9, 1980, P.L. 96-308, §2, 94 Stat. 939.

CHAPTER 63. TECHNOLOGY INNOVATION

§3701. FINDINGS

The Congress finds and declares that:

(1) Technology and industrial innovation are central to the economic, environmental, and social well-being of citizens of the United States.

(2) Technology and industrial innovation offer an improved standard of living, increased public and private sector productivity, creation of new industries and employment opportunities, improved public services and enhanced competitiveness of United States products in world markets.

(3) Many new discoveries and advances in science occur in universities and Federal laboratories, while the application of this new knowledge to commercial and useful public purposes depends largely upon actions by business and labor. Cooperation among academia, Federal laboratories, labor, and industry, in such forms as technology transfer, personnel exchange, joint research projects, and others, should be renewed, expanded, and strengthened.

(4) Small businesses have performed an important role in advancing industrial and technological innovation.

(5) Industrial and technological innovation in the United States may be lagging when compared to historical patterns and other industrialized nations.

(6) Increased industrial and technological innovation would reduce trade deficits, stabilize the dollar, increase productivity gains, increase employment, and stabilize prices.

(7) Government antitrust, economic, trade, patent, procurement, regulatory, research and development, and tax policies have significant impacts upon industrial innovation and development of technology, but there is insufficient knowledge of their effects in particular sectors of the economy.

(8) No comprehensive national policy exists to enhance technological innovation for commercial and public purposes. There is a need for such a policy, including a strong national policy supporting domestic technology transfer and utilization of the science and technology resources of the Federal Government.

(9) It is in the national interest to promote the adaptation of technological innovations to State and local government uses. Technological innovations can improve services, reduce their costs, and increase productivity in State and local governments.

(10) The Federal laboratories and other performers of federally funded research and development frequently provide scientific and technological developments of potential use to State and local governments and private industry. These developments, which include inventions, computer software, and training technologies, should be made accessible to those governments and industry. There is a need to provide means of access and to give adequate personnel and funding support to these means.

(11) The Nation should give fuller recognition to individuals and companies which have made outstanding contributions to the promotion of technology or technological manpower for the improvement of the economic, environmental, or social well-being of the United States.

History of 15 U.S.C. §3701: Oct. 21, 1980, P.L. 96-480, §2, 94 Stat. 2311; Oct. 20, 1986, P.L. 99-502, §9(f)(1), 100 Stat. 1797.

§3702. PURPOSE

It is the purpose of this chapter to improve the economic, environmental, and social well-being of the United States by—

(1) establishing organizations in the executive branch to study and stimulate technology;

(2) promoting technology development through the establishment of cooperative research centers;

(3) stimulating improved utilization of federally funded technology developments, including inventions, software, and training technologies, by State and local governments and the private sector;

(4) providing encouragement for the development of technology through the recognition of individuals and companies which have made outstanding contributions in technology; and

(5) encouraging the exchange of scientific and technical personnel among academia, industry, and Federal laboratories.

History of 15 U.S.C. §3702: Oct. 21, 1980, P.L. 96-480, §3, 94 Stat. 2312; Oct. 20, 1986, P.L. 99-502, §9(b)(1), (f)(2), 100 Stat. 1795, 1797.

§3703. DEFINITIONS

As used in this chapter, unless the context otherwise requires, the term—

(1) "Secretary" means the Secretary of Commerce.

(2) "Centers" means the Cooperative Research Centers established under section 3705 or 3707 of this title.

(3) "Nonprofit institution" means an organization owned and operated exclusively for scientific or educational purposes, no part of the net earnings of which inures to the benefit of any private shareholder or individual.

(4) "Federal laboratory" means any laboratory, any federally funded research and development center, or any center established under section 3705 or 3707 of this title that is owned, leased, or otherwise used by a

Federal agency and funded by the Federal Government, whether operated by the Government or by a contractor.

(5) "Supporting agency" means either the Department of Commerce or the National Science Foundation, as appropriate.

(6) "Federal agency" means any executive agency as defined in section 105 of Title 5 and the military departments as defined in section 102 of such title, as well as any agency of the legislative branch of the Federal Government.

(7) "Invention" means any invention or discovery which is or may be patentable or otherwise protected under Title 35 or any novel variety of plant which is or may be protectable under the Plant Variety Protection Act (7 U.S.C. 2321 et seq.).

(8) "Made" when used in conjunction with any invention means the conception or first actual reduction to practice of such invention.

(9) "Small business firm" means a small business concern as defined in section 632 of this title and implementing regulations of the Administrator of the Small Business Administration.

(10) "Training technology" means computer software and related materials which are developed by a Federal agency to train employees of such agency, including but not limited to software for computer-based instructional systems and for interactive video disc systems.

(11) "Clearinghouse" means the Clearinghouse for State and Local Initiatives on Productivity, Technology, and Innovation established by section 3704a of this title.

History of 15 U.S.C. §3703: Oct. 21, 1980, P.L. 96-480, §4, 94 Stat. 2312; Oct. 20, 1986, P.L. 99-502, §9(b)(2), (d), 100 Stat. 1795, 1796; Aug. 23, 1988, P.L. 100-418, §5122(b), 102 Stat. 1439; Oct. 24, 1988, P.L. 100-519, §201(d)(1), 102 Stat. 2594; Feb. 14, 1992, P.L. 102-245, §304, 106 Stat. 20; Nov. 1, 2000, P.L. 106-404, §7(1), (2), 114 Stat. 1745; Aug. 9, 2007, P.L. 110-69, §3002(c)(3), 121 Stat. 586.

§3704. EXPERIMENTAL PROGRAM TO STIMULATE COMPETITIVE TECHNOLOGY

(a) Program establishment—

(1) In general.—Beginning in fiscal year 1999, the Secretary shall establish a program to be known as the Experimental Program to Stimulate Competitive Technology (referred to in this subsection as the "program"). The purpose of the program shall be to strengthen the technological competitiveness of those States that have historically received less Federal research and development funds than those received by a majority of the States.

(2) Arrangements.—In carrying out the program, the Secretary shall—

(A) enter into such arrangements as may be necessary to provide for the coordination of the program through the State committees established under the Experimental Program to Stimulate Competitive Research of the National Science Foundation; and

(B) cooperate with—

(i) any State science and technology council established under the program under subparagraph (A); and

(ii) representatives of small business firms and other appropriate technology-based businesses.

(3) Grants and cooperative agreements.—In carrying out the program, the Secretary may make grants or enter into cooperative agreements to provide for—

(A) technology research and development;

(B) technology transfer from university research;

(C) technology deployment and diffusion; and

(D) the strengthening of technological capabilities through consortia comprised of—

(i) technology-based small business firms;

(ii) industries and emerging companies;

(iii) universities; and

(iv) State and local development agencies and entities.

(4) Requirements for making awards—

(A) In general.—In making awards under this subsection, the Secretary shall ensure that the awards are awarded on a competitive basis that includes a review of the merits of the activities that are the subject of the award.

(B) Matching requirement.—The non-Federal share of the activities (other than planning activities) carried out under an award under this subsection shall be not less than 25 percent of the cost of those activities.

(5) Criteria for States.—The Secretary shall establish criteria for achievement by each State that participates in the program. Upon the achievement of all such criteria, a State shall cease to be eligible to participate in the program.

(b) Coordination.—To the extent practicable, in carrying out subsection (a) of this section, the Secretary shall coordinate the program with other programs of the Department of Commerce.

(c) Minority Serving Institution Digital and Wireless Technology Opportunity Program—

(1) In general.—The Secretary shall establish a Minority Serving Institution Digital and Wireless Technology Opportunity Program that awards grants, cooperative agreements, and contracts to eligible institutions to enable the eligible institutions in acquiring, and augmenting the institutions' use of, digital and wireless networking technologies to improve the quality and delivery of educational services at eligible institutions.

(2) Application and review procedures—

(A) In general.—To be eligible to receive a grant, cooperative agreement, or contract under this subsection, an eligible institution shall submit an application to the Secretary at such time, in such manner, and containing such information as the Secretary may require. Such application, at a minimum, shall include a description of how the funds will be used, including a description of any digital and wireless networking technology to be acquired, and a description of how the institution will ensure that digital and wireless networking technology will be made accessible to, and employed by, students, faculty, and administrators. The Secretary, consistent with subparagraph (C) and in consultation with the advisory council established under subparagraph (B), shall establish procedures to review such applications. The Secretary shall publish the application requirements and review criteria in the Federal Register, along with a statement describing the availability of funds.

(B) Advisory council.—The Secretary shall establish an advisory council to advise the Secretary on the best approaches to encourage maximum participation by eligible institutions in the program established under paragraph (1), and on the procedures to review applications submitted to the program. In selecting the members of the advisory council, the Secretary shall consult with representatives of appropriate organizations, including representatives of eligible institutions, to ensure that the membership of the advisory council includes representatives of minority businesses and eligible institution communities. The Secretary shall also consult with experts in digital and wireless networking technology to ensure that such expertise is represented on the advisory council.

(C) Review panels.—Each application submitted under this subsection by an eligible institution shall be reviewed by a panel of individuals selected by the Secretary to judge the quality and merit of the proposal, including the extent to which the eligible institution can effectively and successfully utilize the proposed grant, cooperative agreement, or contract to carry out the program described in paragraph (1). The Secretary shall ensure that the review panels include representatives of minority serving institutions and others who are knowledgeable about eligible institutions and technology issues. The Secretary shall ensure that no individual assigned under this subsection to review any application has a conflict of interest with regard to that application. The Secretary shall take into consideration the recommendations of the review panel in determining whether to award a grant, cooperative agreement, or contract to an eligible institution.

(3) Awards—

(A) Limitation.—An eligible institution that receives a grant, cooperative agreement, or contract under this subsection that exceeds $2,500,000 shall not be eligible to receive another grant, cooperative agreement, or contract under this subsection.

(B) Consortia.—Grants, cooperative agreements, and contracts may only be awarded to eligible institutions. Eligible institutions may seek funding under this subsection for consortia, which may include other eligible institutions, a State or a State educational agency, local educational agencies, institutions of higher education, community-based organizations, national nonprofit organizations, or businesses, including minority businesses.

(C) Planning grants.—The Secretary may provide funds to develop strategic plans to implement grants, cooperative agreements, or contracts awarded under this subsection.

(D) Institutional diversity.—In awarding grants, cooperative agreements, and contracts to eligible institutions, the Secretary shall ensure, to the extent practicable, that awards are made to all types of institutions eligible for assistance under this subsection.

(E) Need.—In awarding funds under this subsection, the Secretary shall give priority to the eligible institution with the greatest demonstrated need for assistance.

(4) Authorized activities.—An eligible institution may use a grant, cooperative agreement, or contract awarded under this subsection—

(A) to acquire equipment, instrumentation, networking capability, hardware and software, digital network technology, wireless technology, and infrastructure to further the objective of the program described in paragraph (1);

(B) to develop and provide training, education, and professional development programs, including faculty development, to increase the use of, and usefulness of, digital and wireless networking technology;

(C) to provide teacher education, including the provision of preservice teacher training and in-service professional development at eligible institutions, library and media specialist training, and preschool and teacher aid certification to individuals who seek to acquire or enhance technology skills in order to use digital and wireless networking technology in the classroom or instructional process, including instruction in science, mathematics, engineering, and technology subjects;

(D) to obtain capacity-building technical assistance, including through remote technical support, technical assistance workshops, and distance learning services; or

(E) to foster the use of digital and wireless networking technology to improve research and education, including scientific, mathematics, engineering, and technology instruction.

(5) Information dissemination.—The Secretary shall convene an annual meeting of eligible institutions receiving grants, cooperative agreements, or contracts under this subsection to foster collaboration and capacity-building activities among eligible institutions.

(6) Matching requirement.—The Secretary may not award a grant, cooperative agreement, or contract to an eligible institution under this subsection unless such institution agrees that, with respect to the costs incurred by the institution in carrying out the program for which the grant, cooperative agreement, or contract was awarded, such institution shall make available, directly, or through donations from public or private entities, non-Federal contributions in an amount equal to 25 percent of the grant, cooperative agreement, or contract awarded by the Secretary, or $500,000, whichever is the lesser amount. The Secretary shall waive the matching requirement for any institution or consortium with no endowment, or an endowment that has a current dollar value lower than $50,000,000.

(7) Annual report and assessments—

(A) Annual report required from recipients.—Each eligible institution that receives a grant, cooperative agreement, or contract awarded under this subsection shall provide an annual report to the Secretary on its use of the grant, cooperative agreement, or contract.

(B) Independent assessments—

(i) Contract to conduct assessments.—Not later than 6 months after August 14, 2008, the Secretary shall enter into a contract with the National Academy of Public Administration to conduct periodic assessments of the program established under paragraph (1). The assessments shall be conducted once every 3 years during the 10-year period following August 14, 2008.

(ii) Evaluations and recommendations.—The assessments described in clause (i) shall include—

(I) an evaluation of the effectiveness of the program established under paragraph (1) in improving the education and training of students, faculty, and staff at eligible institutions that have been awarded grants, cooperative agreements, or contracts under the program;

(II) an evaluation of the effectiveness of the program in improving access to, and familiarity with, digital and wireless networking technology for students, faculty, and staff at all eligible institutions;

(III) an evaluation of the procedures established under paragraph (2)(A); and

(IV) recommendations for improving the program, including recommendations concerning the continuing need for Federal support.

(iii) Review of reports.—In carrying out the assessments under this subparagraph, the National Academy of Public Administration shall review the reports submitted to the Secretary under subparagraph (A).

(iv) Report to Congress.—Upon completion of each assessment under this subparagraph, the Secretary shall transmit the assessment to Congress along with a summary of the Secretary's plans, if any, to implement the recommendations of the National Academy of Public Administration.

(8) Definitions.—In this subsection:

(A) Digital and wireless networking technology.—The term "digital and wireless networking technology" means computer and communications equipment and software that facilitates the transmission of information in a digital format.

(B) Eligible institution.—The term "eligible institution" means an institution that is—

(i) a part B institution, as defined in section 1061(2) of Title 20, an institution identified in subparagraph (A), (B), or (C) of section 1063b(e)(1) of Title 20, or a consortium of institutions described in this clause;

(ii) a Hispanic-serving institution, as defined in section 1101a(a)(5) of Title 20;

(iii) a Tribal College or University, as defined in section 1059c(b)(3) of Title 20;

(iv) an Alaska Native-serving institution, as defined in section 1059d(b) of Title 20;

(v) a Native Hawaiian-serving institution, as defined in section 1059d(b) of Title 20;

(vi) a Predominately Black Institution, as defined in section 1059e of Title 20;

(vii) a Native American-serving, nontribal institution, as defined in section 1059f of Title 20;

(viii) an Asian American and Native American Pacific Islander-serving institution, as defined in section 1059g of Title 20; or

(ix) a minority institution, as defined in section 1067k of Title 20, with an enrollment of needy students, as defined in section 1058(d) of Title 20.

(C) **Institution of higher education.**—The term "institution of higher education" has the meaning given the term in section 1001 of Title 20.

(D) **Local educational agency.**—The term "local educational agency" has the meaning given the term in section 7801 of title 20.

(E) **Minority business.**—The term "minority business" includes HUBZone small business concerns (as defined in section 632(p) of this title).

(F) **Minority individual.**—The term "minority individual" means an American Indian, Alaskan Native, Black (not of Hispanic origin), Hispanic (including persons of Mexican, Puerto Rican, Cuban, and Central or South American origin), or Pacific Islander individual.

(G) **State.**—The term "State" has the meaning given the term in section 7801 of title 20.

(H) **State educational agency.**—The term "State educational agency" has the meaning given the term in section 7801 of title 20.

History of 15 U.S.C. §3704: Oct. 21, 1980, P.L. 96-480, §5, 94 Stat. 2312; Aug. 14, 1986, P.L. 99-382, §2, 100 Stat. 811; Oct. 20, 1986, P.L. 99-502, §9(b)(3)-(5), (e)(2)(A), 100 Stat. 1795, 1797; Oct. 24, 1988, P.L. 100-519, §201(a)-(c), (d)(2), 102 Stat. 2593, 2594; Feb. 14, 1992, P.L. 102-245, §306, 106 Stat. 20; Oct. 30, 1998, P.L. 105-309, §9, 112 Stat. 2938; Nov. 1, 2000, P.L. 106-404, §7(3), 114 Stat. 1745; Aug. 9, 2007, P.L. 110-69, §3002(a), 121 Stat. 586; Aug. 14, 2008, P.L. 110-315, §971, 122 Stat. 3473; Dec. 10, 2015, P.L. 114-95, §9215(sss), 129 Stat. 2190.

§3704a. CLEARINGHOUSE FOR STATE & LOCAL INITIATIVES ON PRODUCTIVITY, TECHNOLOGY, & INNOVATION

(a) **Establishment.**—There is established within the Office of Productivity, Technology, and Innovation a Clearinghouse for State and Local Initiatives on Productivity, Technology, and Innovation. The Clearinghouse shall serve as a central repository of information on initiatives by State and local governments to enhance the competitiveness of American business through the stimulation of productivity, technology, and innovation and Federal efforts to assist State and local governments to enhance competitiveness.

(b) **Responsibilities.**—The Clearinghouse may—

(1) establish relationships with State and local governments, and regional and multistate organizations of such governments, which carry out such initiatives;

(2) collect information on the nature, extent, and effects of such initiatives, particularly information useful to the Congress, Federal agencies, State and local governments, regional and multistate organizations of such governments, businesses, and the public throughout the United States;

(3) disseminate information collected under paragraph (2) through reports, directories, handbooks, conferences, and seminars;

(4) provide technical assistance and advice to such governments with respect to such initiatives, including assistance in determining sources of assistance from Federal agencies which may be available to support such initiatives;

(5) study ways in which Federal agencies, including Federal laboratories, are able to use their existing policies and programs to assist State and local governments, and regional and multistate organizations of such governments, to enhance the competitiveness of American business;

(6) make periodic recommendations to the Secretary, and to other Federal agencies upon their request, concerning modifications in Federal policies and programs which would improve Federal assistance to State and local technology and business assistance programs;

(7) develop methodologies to evaluate State and local programs, and, when requested, advise State and lo-

cal governments, and regional and multistate organizations of such governments, as to which programs are most effective in enhancing the competitiveness of American business through the stimulation of productivity, technology, and innovation; and

(8) make use of, and disseminate, the nationwide study of State industrial extension programs conducted by the Secretary.

(c) Contracts.—In carrying out subsection (b) of this section, the Secretary may enter into contracts for the purpose of collecting information on the nature, extent, and effects of initiatives.

History of 15 U.S.C. §3704a: Aug. 23, 1988, P.L. 100-418, §5122(a)(2), 102 Stat. 1438.

§3704b. NATIONAL TECHNICAL INFORMATION SERVICE

(a) Powers—

(1) The Secretary of Commerce, acting through the Director of the National Technical Information Service (hereafter in this section referred to as the "Director") is authorized to do the following:

(A) Enter into such contracts, cooperative agreements, joint ventures, and other transactions, in accordance with all relevant provisions of Federal law applicable to such contracts and agreements, and under reasonable terms and conditions, as may be necessary in the conduct of the business of the National Technical Information Service (hereafter in this section referred to as the "Service").

(B) In addition to the authority regarding fees contained in section 2 of the Act entitled "An Act to provide for the dissemination of technological, scientific, and engineering information to American business and industry, and for other purposes" enacted September 9, 1950 (15 U.S.C. 1152), retain and, subject to appropriations Acts, utilize its net revenues to the extent necessary to implement the plan submitted under subsection (f)(3)(D) of this section.

(C) Enter into contracts for the performance of part or all of the functions performed by the Promotion Division of the Service prior to October 24, 1988. The details of any such contract, and a statement of its effect on the operations and personnel of the Service, shall be provided to the appropriate committees of the Congress 30 days in advance of the execution of such contract.

(D) Employ such personnel as may be necessary to conduct the business of the Service.

(E) For the period of October 1, 1991 through September 30, 1992, only, retain and use all earned and unearned monies heretofore or hereafter received, including receipts, revenues, and advanced payments and deposits, to fund all obligations and expenses, including inventories and capital equipment.

An increase or decrease in the personnel of the Service shall not affect or be affected by any ceilings on the number or grade of personnel.

(2) The functions and activities of the Service specified in subsection (e)(1) through (6) of this section are permanent Federal functions to be carried out by the Secretary through the Service and its employees, and shall not be transferred from the Service, by contract or otherwise, to the private sector on a permanent or temporary basis without express approval of the Congress. Functions or activities—

(A) for the procurement of supplies, materials, and equipment by the Service;

(B) referred to in paragraph (1)(C); or

(C) to be performed through joint ventures or cooperative agreements which do not result in a reduction in the Federal workforce of the affected programs of the service,[1]

shall not be considered functions or activities for purposes of this paragraph.

(3) For the purposes of this subsection, the term "net revenues" means the excess of revenues and receipts from any source, other than royalties and other income described in section 3710c(a)(4) of this title, over operating expenses.

(4) Omitted.

(b) Director of the Service.—The management of the Service shall be vested in a Director who shall report to the Director of the National Institute of Standards and Technology and the Secretary of Commerce.

(c) Advisory Board—

(1) There is established the Advisory Board of the National Technical Information Service, which shall be composed of a chairman and four other members appointed by the Secretary.

(2) In appointing members of the Advisory Board the Secretary shall solicit recommendations from the major users and beneficiaries of the Service's activities and shall select individuals experienced in providing or utilizing technical information.

(3) The Advisory Board shall review the general policies and operations of the Service, including policies in connection with fees and charges for its services, and shall advise the Secretary and the Director with respect thereto.

(4) The Advisory Board shall meet at the call of the Secretary, but not less often than once each six months.

(d) Audits.—The Secretary of Commerce shall provide for annual independent audits of the Service's financial statements beginning with fiscal year 1988, to be conducted in accordance with generally accepted accounting principles.

(e) Functions.—The Secretary of Commerce, acting through the Service, shall—

(1) establish and maintain a permanent repository of nonclassified scientific, technical, and engineering information;

(2) cooperate and coordinate its operations with other Government scientific, technical, and engineering information programs;

(3) make selected bibliographic information products available in a timely manner to depository libraries as part of the Depository Library Program of the Government Publishing Office;

(4) in conjunction with the private sector as appropriate, collect, translate into English, and disseminate unclassified foreign scientific, technical, and engineering information;

(5) implement new methods or media for the dissemination of scientific, technical, and engineering information, including producing and disseminating information products in electronic format; and

(6) carry out the functions and activities of the Secretary under the Act entitled "An Act to provide for the dissemination of technological, scientific, and engineering information to American business and industry, and for other purposes" enacted September 9, 1950 [15 U.S.C. §1151 et seq.], and the functions and activities of the Secretary performed through the National Technical Information Service as of October 24, 1988, under this chapter.

(f) Notification of Congress—

(1) The Secretary of Commerce and the Director shall keep the appropriate committees of Congress fully and currently informed about all activities related to the carrying out of the functions of the Service, including changes in fee policies.

(2) Within 90 days after October 24, 1988, the Secretary of Commerce shall submit to the Congress a report on the current fee structure of the Service, including an explanation of the basis for the fees, taking into consideration all applicable costs, and the adequacy of the fees, along with reasons for the declining sales at the Service of scientific, technical, and engineering publications. Such report shall explain any actions planned or taken to increase such sales at reasonable fees.

(3) The Secretary shall submit an annual report to the Congress which shall—

(A) summarize the operations of the Service during the preceding year, including financial details and staff levels broken down by major activities;

(B) detail the operating plan of the Service, including specific expense and staff needs, for the upcoming year;

(C) set forth details of modernization progress made in the preceding year;

(D) describe the long-term modernization plans of the Service; and

(E) include the results of the most recent annual audit carried out under subsection (d) of this section.

(4) The Secretary shall also give the Congress detailed advance notice of not less than 30 calendar days of—

(A) any proposed reduction-in-force;

(B) any joint venture or cooperative agreement which involves a financial incentive to the joint venturer or contractor; and

(C) any change in the operating plan submitted under paragraph (3)(B) which would result in a variation from such plan with respect to expense levels of more than 10 percent.

1. **Editor's note:** The word "service" probably should be capitalized.

History of 15 U.S.C. §3704b: Oct. 24, 1988, P.L. 100-519, §212, 102 Stat. 2594; Oct. 28, 1991, P.L. 102-140, 105 Stat. 804; Feb. 14, 1992, P.L. 102-245, §506(c), 106 Stat. 27; Dec. 26, 2007, P.L. 110-161, §109, 121 Stat. 1893; Dec. 16, 2014, P.L. 113-235, §1301(b), 128 Stat. 2537.

§3704b-1. RECOVERY OF OPERATING COSTS THROUGH FEE COLLECTIONS

Operating costs for the National Technical Information Service associated with the acquisition, processing, storage, bibliographic control, and archiving of information and documents shall be recovered primarily through the collection of fees.

History of 15 U.S.C. §3704b-1: Feb. 14, 1992, P.L. 102-245, §103(c), 106 Stat. 8.

§3704b-2. TRANSFER OF FEDERAL SCIENTIFIC & TECHNICAL INFORMATION

(a) Transfer.—The head of each Federal executive department or agency shall transfer in a timely manner to the National Technical Information Service unclassified scientific, technical, and engineering information which results from federally funded research and development activities for dissemination to the private sector, academia, State and local governments, and Federal agencies. Only information which would otherwise be available for public dissemination shall be transferred under this subsection. Such information shall include technical reports and information, computer software, application assessments generated pursuant to section 3710(c) of this title, and information regarding training technology and other federally owned or originated technologies. The Secretary shall issue regulations within one year after February 14, 1992, outlining procedures for the ongoing transfer of such information to the National Technical Information Service.

(b) Annual report to Congress.—As part of the annual report required under section 3704b(f)(3) of this title, the Secretary shall report to Congress on the status of efforts under this section to ensure access to Federal scientific and technical information by the public. Such report shall include—

(1) an evaluation of the comprehensiveness of transfers of information by each Federal executive department or agency under subsection (a) of this section;

(2) a description of the use of Federal scientific and technical information;

(3) plans for improving public access to Federal scientific and technical information; and

(4) recommendations for legislation necessary to improve public access to Federal scientific and technical information.

History of 15 U.S.C. §3704b-2: Feb. 14, 1992, P.L. 102-245, §108, 106 Stat. 13.

§3705. COOPERATIVE RESEARCH CENTERS

(a) Establishment.—The Secretary shall provide assistance for the establishment of Cooperative Research Centers. Such Centers shall be affiliated with any university, or other nonprofit institution, or group thereof, that applies for and is awarded a grant or enters into a cooperative agreement under this section. The objective of the Centers is to enhance technological innovation through—

(1) the participation of individuals from industry and universities in cooperative technological innovation activities;

(2) the development of the generic research base, important for technological advance and innovative activity, in which individual firms have little incentive to invest, but which may have significant economic or strategic importance, such as manufacturing technology;

(3) the education and training of individuals in the technological innovation process;

(4) the improvement of mechanisms for the dissemination of scientific, engineering, and technical information among universities and industry;

(5) the utilization of the capability and expertise, where appropriate, that exists in Federal laboratories; and

(6) the development of continuing financial support from other mission agencies, from State and local government, and from industry and universities through, among other means, fees, licenses, and royalties.

(b) Activities.—The activities of the Centers shall include, but need not be limited to—

(1) research supportive of technological and industrial innovation including cooperative industry-university research;

(2) assistance to individuals and small businesses in the generation, evaluation, and development of technological ideas supportive of industrial innovation and new business ventures;

(3) technical assistance and advisory services to industry, particularly small businesses; and

(4) curriculum development, training, and instruction in invention, entrepreneurship, and industrial innovation.

Each Center need not undertake all of the activities under this subsection.

(c) Requirements.—Prior to establishing a Center, the Secretary shall find that—

(1) consideration has been given to the potential contribution of the activities proposed under the Center to productivity, employment, and economic competitiveness of the United States;

(2) a high likelihood exists of continuing participation, advice, financial support, and other contributions from the private sector;

(3) the host university or other nonprofit institution has a plan for the management and evaluation of the activities proposed within the particular Center, including:

(A) the agreement between the parties as to the allocation of patent rights on a nonexclusive, partially exclusive, or exclusive license basis to and inventions conceived or made under the auspices of the Center; and

(B) the consideration of means to place the Center, to the maximum extent feasible, on a self-sustaining basis;

(4) suitable consideration has been given to the university's or other nonprofit institution's capabilities and geographical location; and

(5) consideration has been given to any effects upon competition of the activities proposed under the Center.

(d) Planning grants.—The Secretary is authorized to make available nonrenewable planning grants to universities or nonprofit institutions for the purpose of developing a plan required under subsection (c)(3) of this section.

(e) Research and development utilization.—In the promotion of technology from research and development efforts by Centers under this section, chapter 18 of Title 35 shall apply to the extent not inconsistent with this section.

History of 15 U.S.C. §3705: Oct. 21, 1980, P.L. 96-480, §6, 94 Stat. 2313; Oct. 20, 1986, P.L. 99-502, §9(b)(6)-(10), 100 Stat. 1796; Aug. 23, 1988, P.L. 100-418, §5122(a)(1), 102 Stat. 1438.

§3706. GRANTS & COOPERATIVE AGREEMENTS

(a) In general.—The Secretary may make grants and enter into cooperative agreements according to the provisions of this section in order to assist any activity consistent with this chapter, including activities performed by individuals.

(b) Eligibility and procedure.—Any person or institution may apply to the Secretary for a grant or cooperative agreement available under this section. Application shall be made in such form and manner, and with such content and other submissions, as the Assistant Secretary shall prescribe. The Secretary shall act upon each such application within 90 days after the date on which all required information is received.

(c) Terms and conditions—

(1) Any grant made, or cooperative agreement entered into, under this section shall be subject to the limitations and provisions set forth in paragraph (2) of this subsection, and to such other terms, conditions, and requirements as the Secretary deems necessary or appropriate.

(2) Any person who receives or utilizes any proceeds of any grant made or cooperative agreement entered into under this section shall keep such records as the Secretary shall by regulation prescribe as being necessary and appropriate to facilitate effective audit and evaluation, including records which fully disclose the amount and disposition by such recipient of such proceeds, the total cost of the program or project in connection with which such proceeds were used, and the amount, if any, of such costs which was provided through other sources.

History of 15 U.S.C. §3706: Oct. 21, 1980, P.L. 96-480, §7, 94 Stat. 2315; Aug. 23, 1988, P.L. 100-418, §§5115(b)(1), 5122(a)(1), 102 Stat. 1433, 1438; Jan. 6, 2017, P.L. 114-329, §203, 130 Stat. 2988.

§3707. NATIONAL SCIENCE FOUNDATION COOPERATIVE RESEARCH CENTERS

(a) Establishment and provisions.—The National Science Foundation shall provide assistance for the establishment of Cooperative Research Centers. Such Centers shall be affiliated with a university, or other nonprofit institution, or a group thereof. The objective of the Centers is to enhance technological innovation as provided in section 3705(a) of this title through the conduct of activities as provided in section 3705(b) of this title.

(b) Planning grants.—The National Science Foundation is authorized to make available nonrenewable planning grants to universities or nonprofit institutions for the purpose of developing the plan, as described under section 3705(c)(3) of this title.

(c) Terms and conditions.—Grants, contracts, and cooperative agreements entered into by the National Science Foundation in execution of the powers and duties of the National Science Foundation under this chapter shall be governed by the National Science Foundation Act of 1950 [42 U.S.C. §1861 et seq.] and other pertinent Acts.

History of 15 U.S.C. §3707: Oct. 21, 1980, P.L. 96-480, §8, 94 Stat. 2316; Oct. 20, 1986, P.L. 99-502, §9(b)(11), (12), (e)(2)(B), 100 Stat. 1796, 1797; Aug. 23, 1988, P.L. 100-418, §5122(a)(1), 102 Stat. 1438; Nov. 1, 2000, P.L. 106-404, §7(4), 114 Stat. 1745.

§3708. ADMINISTRATIVE ARRANGEMENTS

(a) Coordination.—The Secretary and the National Science Foundation shall, on a continuing basis, obtain the advice and cooperation of departments and agencies whose missions contribute to or are affected by the programs established under this chapter, including the development of an agenda for research and policy experimentation. These departments and agencies shall include but not be limited to the Departments of Defense, Energy, Education, Health and Human Services, Housing and Urban Development, the Environmental Protection Agency, National Aeronautics and Space Administration, Small Business Administration, Council of Economic Advisers, Council on Environmental Quality, and Office of Science and Technology Policy.

(b) Cooperation.—It is the sense of the Congress that departments and agencies, including the Federal laboratories, whose missions are affected by, or could contribute to, the programs established under this chapter, should, within the limits of budgetary authorizations and appropriations, support or participate in activities or projects authorized by this chapter.

(c) Administrative authorization—

(1) Departments and agencies described in subsection (b) of this section are authorized to participate in, contribute to, and serve as resources for the Centers and for any other activities authorized under this chapter.

(2) The Secretary and the National Science Foundation are authorized to receive moneys and to receive other forms of assistance from other departments or agencies to support activities of the Centers and any other activities authorized under this chapter.

(d) Cooperative efforts.—The Secretary and the National Science Foundation shall, on a continuing basis, provide each other the opportunity to comment on any proposed program of activity under section 3705, 3707, 3710, 3710d, 3711a, or 3712 of this title before funds are committed to such program in order to mount complementary efforts and avoid duplication.

History of 15 U.S.C. §3708: Oct. 21, 1980, P.L. 96-480, §9, 94 Stat. 2316; Oct. 20, 1986, P.L. 99-502, §9(e)(2)(C), 100 Stat. 1797; Aug. 20, 1987, P.L. 100-107, §3(b), 101 Stat. 727; Aug. 23, 1988, P.L. 100-418, §5122(a)(1), (c), 102 Stat. 1438, 1439; Dec. 18, 1991, P.L. 102-240, §6019, 105 Stat. 2183.

§3709. REPEALED

Repealed Oct. 20, 1986, P.L. 99-502, §9(a), 100 Stat. 1795.

§3710. UTILIZATION OF FEDERAL TECHNOLOGY

(a) Policy—

(1) It is the continuing responsibility of the Federal Government to ensure the full use of the results of the Nation's Federal investment in research and development. To this end the Federal Government shall strive where appropriate to transfer federally owned or originated technology to State and local governments and to the private sector.

(2) Technology transfer, consistent with mission responsibilities, is a responsibility of each laboratory science and engineering professional.

(3) Each laboratory director shall ensure that efforts to transfer technology are considered positively in laboratory job descriptions, employee promotion policies, and evaluation of the job performance of scientists and engineers in the laboratory.

(b) Establishment of Research and Technology Applications Offices.—Each Federal laboratory shall establish an Office of Research and Technology Applications. Laboratories having existing organizational structures which perform the functions of this section may elect to combine the Office of Research and Technology Applications within the existing organization. The staffing and funding levels for these offices shall be determined between each Federal laboratory and the Federal agency operating or directing the laboratory, except that (1) each laboratory having 200 or more full-time equivalent scientific, engineering, and related technical positions shall provide one or more full-time equivalent positions as staff for its Office of Research and Technology Applications, and (2) each Federal agency which operates or directs one or more Federal laboratories shall make available sufficient funding, either as a separate line item or from the agency's research and development budget, to support the technology transfer function at the agency and at its laboratories, including support of the Offices of Research and Technology Applications.

Furthermore, individuals filling positions in an Office of Research and Technology Applications shall be included in the overall laboratory/agency management development program so as to ensure that highly competent technical managers are full participants in the technology transfer process.

(c) Functions of Research and Technology Applications Offices.—It shall be the function of each Office of Research and Technology Applications—

(1) to prepare application assessments for selected research and development projects in which that laboratory is engaged and which in the opinion of the laboratory may have potential commercial applications;

(2) to provide and disseminate information on federally owned or originated products, processes, and services having potential application to State and local governments and to private industry;

(3) to cooperate with and assist the National Technical Information Service, the Federal Laboratory Consortium for Technology Transfer, and other organizations which link the research and development resources of that laboratory and the Federal Government as a whole to potential users in State and local government and private industry;

(4) to provide technical assistance to State and local government officials; and

(5) to participate, where feasible, in regional, State, and local programs designed to facilitate or stimulate the transfer of technology for the benefit of the region, State, or local jurisdiction in which the Federal laboratory is located.

Agencies which have established organizational structures outside their Federal laboratories which have as their principal purpose the transfer of federally owned or originated technology to State and local government and to the private sector may elect to perform the functions of this subsection in such organizational structures. No Office of Research and Technology Applications or other organizational structures performing the functions of this subsection shall substantially compete with similar services available in the private sector.

(d) Dissemination of technical information.—The National Technical Information Service shall—

(1) serve as a central clearinghouse for the collection, dissemination and transfer of information on federally owned or originated technologies having potential application to State and local governments and to private industry;

(2) utilize the expertise and services of the National Science Foundation and the Federal Laboratory Consortium for Technology Transfer; particularly in dealing with State and local governments;

(3) receive requests for technical assistance from State and local governments, respond to such requests with published information available to the Service, and refer such requests to the Federal Laboratory Consortium for Technology Transfer to the extent that such requests require a response involving more than the published information available to the Service;

(4) provide funding, at the discretion of the Secretary, for Federal laboratories to provide the assistance specified in subsection (c)(3) of this section;

(5) use appropriate technology transfer mechanisms such as personnel exchanges and computer-based systems; and

(6) maintain a permanent archival repository and clearinghouse for the collection and dissemination of nonclassified scientific, technical, and engineering information.

(e) Establishment of Federal Laboratory Consortium for Technology Transfer—

(1) There is hereby established the Federal Laboratory Consortium for Technology Transfer (hereinafter referred to as the "Consortium") which, in cooperation with Federal laboratories and the private sector, shall—

(A) develop and (with the consent of the Federal laboratory concerned) administer techniques, training courses, and materials concerning technology transfer to increase the awareness of Federal laboratory employees regarding the commercial potential of laboratory technology and innovations;

(B) furnish advice and assistance requested by Federal agencies and laboratories for use in their technology transfer programs (including the planning of seminars for small business and other industry);

(C) provide a clearinghouse for requests, received at the laboratory level, for technical assistance from States and units of local governments, businesses, industrial development organizations, not-for-profit organizations including universities, Federal agencies and laboratories, and other persons, and—

(i) to the extent that such requests can be responded to with published information available to the National Technical Information Service, refer such requests to that Service, and

(ii) otherwise refer these requests to the appropriate Federal laboratories and agencies;

(D) facilitate communication and coordination between Offices of Research and Technology Applications of Federal laboratories;

(E) utilize (with the consent of the agency involved) the expertise and services of the National Science Foundation, the Department of Commerce, the National Aeronautics and Space Administration, and other Federal agencies, as necessary;

(F) with the consent of any Federal laboratory, facilitate the use by such laboratory of appropriate technology transfer mechanisms such as personnel exchanges and computer-based systems;

(G) with the consent of any Federal laboratory, assist such laboratory to establish programs using technical volunteers to provide technical assistance to communities related to such laboratory;

(H) facilitate communication and cooperation between Offices of Research and Technology Applications of Federal laboratories and regional, State, and local technology transfer organizations;

(I) when requested, assist colleges or universities, businesses, nonprofit organizations, State or local governments, or regional organizations to establish programs to stimulate research and to encourage technology transfer in such areas as technology program development, curriculum design, long-term research planning, personnel needs projections, and productivity assessments;

(J) seek advice in each Federal laboratory consortium region from representatives of State and local governments, large and small business, universities, and other appropriate persons on the effectiveness of the program (and any such advice shall be provided at no expense to the Government); and

(K) work with the Director of the National Institute on Disability and Rehabilitation Research to compile a compendium of current and projected Federal Laboratory technologies and projects that have or will have an intended or recognized impact on the available range of assistive technology for individuals with disabilities (as defined in section 3002 of Title 29), including technologies and projects that incorporate the principles of universal design (as defined in section 3002 of Title 29), as appropriate.

(2) The membership of the Consortium shall consist of the Federal laboratories described in clause (1) of subsection (b) of this section and such other laboratories as may choose to join the Consortium. The representatives to the Consortium shall include a senior staff member of each Federal laboratory which is a member of the Consortium and a senior representative appointed from each Federal agency with one or more member laboratories.

(3) The representatives to the Consortium shall elect a Chairman of the Consortium.

(4) The Director of the National Institute of Standards and Technology shall provide the Consortium, on a reimbursable basis, with administrative services, such as office space, personnel, and support services of the Institute, as requested by the Consortium and approved by such Director.

(5) Each Federal laboratory or agency shall transfer technology directly to users or representatives of users, and shall not transfer technology directly to the Consortium. Each Federal laboratory shall conduct and transfer technology only in accordance with the practices and policies of the Federal agency which owns, leases, or otherwise uses such Federal laboratory.

(6) Not later than one year after October 20, 1986, and every year thereafter, the Chairman of the Consortium shall submit a report to the President, to the appropriate authorization and appropriation committees of both Houses of the Congress, and to each agency with respect to which a transfer of funding is made (for the fiscal year or years involved) under paragraph (7), concerning the activities of the Consortium and the expenditures made by it under this subsection during the year for which the report is made. Such report shall include an annual independent audit of the financial statements of the Consortium, conducted in accordance with generally accepted accounting principles.

(7)(A) Subject to subparagraph (B), an amount equal to 0.008 percent of the budget of each Federal agency from any Federal source, including related overhead, that is to be utilized by or on behalf of the laboratories of such agency for a fiscal year referred to in subparagraph (B)(ii)[1] shall be transferred by such agency to the National Institute of Standards and Technology at the beginning of the fiscal year involved. Amounts so transferred shall be provided by the Institute to the Consortium for the purpose of carrying out activities of the Consortium under this subsection.

(B) A transfer shall be made by any Federal agency under subparagraph (A), for any fiscal year, only if the amount so transferred by that agency (as determined under such subparagraph) would exceed $10,000.

(C) The heads of Federal agencies and their designees, and the directors of Federal laboratories, may provide such additional support for operations of the Consortium as they deem appropriate.

(f) Agency reports on utilization—

(1) In general.—Each Federal agency which operates or directs one or more Federal laboratories or which conducts activities under sections 207 and 209 of Title 35 shall report annually to the Office of Management and Budget, as part of the agency's annual budget submission, on the activities performed by that agency and its Federal laboratories under the provisions of this section and of sections 207 and 209 of Title 35.

(2) Contents.—The report shall include—

(A) an explanation of the agency's technology transfer program for the preceding fiscal year and the agency's plans for conducting its technology transfer function, including its plans for securing intellectual property rights in laboratory innovations with commercial promise and plans for managing its intellectual property so as to advance the agency's mission and benefit the competitiveness of United States industry; and

(B) information on technology transfer activities for the preceding fiscal year, including—

(i) the number of patent applications filed;

(ii) the number of patents received;

(iii) the number of fully-executed licenses which received royalty income in the preceding fiscal year, categorized by whether they are exclusive, partially-exclusive, or non-exclusive, and the time elapsed from the date on which the license was requested by the licensee in writing to the date the license was executed;

(iv) the total earned royalty income including such statistical information as the total earned royalty income, of the top 1 percent, 5 percent, and 20 percent of the licenses, the range of royalty income, and the median, except where disclosure of such information would reveal the amount of royalty income associated with an individual license or licensee;

(v) what disposition was made of the income described in clause (iv);

(vi) the number of licenses terminated for cause; and

(vii) any other parameters or discussion that the agency deems relevant or unique to its practice of technology transfer.

(3) Copy to Secretary; Attorney General; Congress.—The agency shall transmit a copy of the report to the Secretary of Commerce and the Attorney General for inclusion in the annual report to Congress and the President required by subsection (g)(2) of this section.

(4) Public availability.—Each Federal agency reporting under this subsection is also strongly encouraged to make the information contained in such report available to the public through Internet sites or other electronic means.

(g) Functions of Secretary—

(1) The Secretary, in consultation with other Federal agencies, may—

(A) make available to interested agencies the expertise of the Department of Commerce regarding the commercial potential of inventions and methods and options for commercialization which are available to the Federal laboratories, including research and development limited partnerships;

(B) develop and disseminate to appropriate agency and laboratory personnel model provisions for use on a voluntary basis in cooperative research and development arrangements; and

(C) furnish advice and assistance, upon request, to Federal agencies concerning their cooperative research and development programs and projects.

(2) Reports—

(A) Annual report required.—The Secretary, in consultation with the Attorney General and the Commissioner of Patents and Trademarks, shall submit each fiscal year, beginning 1 year after November 1, 2000, a summary report to the President, the United States Trade Representative, and the Congress on the use by Federal agencies and the Secretary of the technology transfer authorities specified in this chapter and in sections 207 and 209 of Title 35.

(B) Content.—The report shall—

(i) draw upon the reports prepared by the agencies under subsection (f) of this section;

(ii) discuss technology transfer best practices and effective approaches in the licensing and transfer of technology in the context of the agencies' missions; and

(iii) discuss the progress made toward development of additional useful measures of the outcomes of technology transfer programs of Federal agencies.

(C) Public availability.—The Secretary shall make the report available to the public through Internet sites or other electronic means.

(3) Not later than one year after October 20, 1986, the Secretary shall submit to the President and the Congress a report regarding—

(A) any copyright provisions or other types of barriers which tend to restrict or limit the transfer of federally funded computer software to the private sector and to State and local governments, and agencies of such State and local governments; and

(B) the feasibility and cost of compiling and maintaining a current and comprehensive inventory of all federally funded training software.

(h) Duplication of reporting.—The reporting obligations imposed by this section—

(1) are not intended to impose requirements that duplicate requirements imposed by the Government Performance and Results Act of 1993 (31 U.S.C. 1101 note);

(2) are to be implemented in coordination with the implementation of that Act; and

(3) are satisfied if an agency provided the information concerning technology transfer activities described in this section in its annual submission under the Government Performance and Results Act of 1993 (31 U.S.C. 1101 note).

(i) Research equipment.—The Director of a laboratory, or the head of any Federal agency or department, may loan, lease, or give research equipment that is excess to the needs of the laboratory, agency, or department to an educational institution or nonprofit organization for the conduct of technical and scientific education and research activities. Title of ownership shall transfer with a gift under this section.

1. **Editor's note:** Subsection (B)(ii) was deleted by P.L. 104-113, §3, Mar. 7, 1996, 110 Stat. 775.

History of 15 U.S.C. §3710: Oct. 21, 1980, P.L. 96-480, §11, 94 Stat. 2318; Oct. 20, 1986, P.L. 99-502, §§3-5, 9(e)(1), 100 Stat. 1787, 1789, 1791, 1797; Aug. 23, 1988, P.L. 100-418, §§5115(b)(2), 5122(a)(1), 5162(b), 5163(c)(1), (3), 102 Stat. 1433, 1438, 1450, 1451; Oct. 24, 1988, P.L. 100-519, §§201(d)(3), 212(a)(4), 102 Stat. 2594, 2595; Nov. 29, 1989, P.L. 101-189, §3133(e), 103 Stat. 1679; Feb. 14, 1992, P.L. 102-245, §§301, 303, 106 Stat. 19, 20; Dec. 21, 1995, P.L. 104-66, §3001(f), 109 Stat. 734; Mar. 7, 1996, P.L. 104-113, §§3, 9, 110 Stat. 775, 779; Nov. 13, 1998, P.L. 105-394, §212(d), 112 Stat. 3655; Nov. 1, 2000, P.L. 106-404, §§7(5), (6), 10(a), 114 Stat. 1745-1747; Aug. 9, 2007, P.L. 110-69, §3002(c)(4), 121 Stat. 586.

§3710a. COOPERATIVE RESEARCH & DEVELOPMENT AGREEMENTS

(a) General authority.—Each Federal agency may permit the director of any of its Government-operated Federal laboratories, and, to the extent provided in an agency-approved joint work statement or, if permitted by the agency, in an agency-approved annual strategic plan, the director of any of its Government-owned, contractor-operated laboratories—

(1) to enter into cooperative research and development agreements on behalf of such agency (subject to subsection (c) of this section) with other Federal agencies; units of State or local government; industrial organizations (including corporations, partnerships, and limited partnerships, and industrial development organizations); public and private foundations; nonprofit organizations (including universities); or other persons (including licensees of inventions owned by the Federal agency); and

(2) to negotiate licensing agreements under section 207 of Title 35, or under other authorities (in the case of a Government-owned, contractor-operated laboratory, subject to subsection (c) of this section) for inventions made or other intellectual property developed at the laboratory and other inventions or other intellectual property that may be voluntarily assigned to the Government.

(b) Enumerated authority—

(1) Under an agreement entered into pursuant to subsection (a)(1) of this section, the laboratory may grant, or agree to grant in advance, to a collaborating party patent licenses or assignments, or options thereto, in any invention made in whole or in part by a laboratory employee under the agreement, or, subject to section 209 of Title 35, may grant a license to an invention which is federally owned, for which a patent application was filed before the signing of the agreement, and directly within the scope of the work under the agreement, for reasonable compensation when appropriate. The laboratory shall ensure, through such agreement, that the collaborating party has the option to choose an exclusive license for a pre-negotiated field of use for any such invention under the agreement or, if there is more than one collaborating party, that the collaborating parties are offered the option to hold licensing rights that collectively encompass the rights that would be held under such an exclusive license by one party. In consideration for the Government's contribution under the agreement, grants under this paragraph shall be subject to the following explicit conditions:

(A) A nonexclusive, nontransferable, irrevocable, paid-up license from the collaborating party to the laboratory to practice the invention or have the invention practiced throughout the world by or on behalf of the Government. In the exercise of such license, the Government shall not publicly disclose trade secrets or commercial or financial information that is privileged or confidential within the meaning of section 552(b)(4) of

Title 5 or which would be considered as such if it had been obtained from a non-Federal party.

(B) If a laboratory assigns title or grants an exclusive license to such an invention, the Government shall retain the right—

(i) to require the collaborating party to grant to a responsible applicant a nonexclusive, partially exclusive, or exclusive license to use the invention in the applicant's licensed field of use, on terms that are reasonable under the circumstances; or

(ii) if the collaborating party fails to grant such a license, to grant the license itself.

(C) The Government may exercise its right retained under subparagraph (B) only in exceptional circumstances and only if the Government determines that—

(i) the action is necessary to meet health or safety needs that are not reasonably satisfied by the collaborating party;

(ii) the action is necessary to meet requirements for public use specified by Federal regulations, and such requirements are not reasonably satisfied by the collaborating party; or

(iii) the collaborating party has failed to comply with an agreement containing provisions described in subsection (c)(4)(B) of this section.

This determination is subject to administrative appeal and judicial review under section 203(2) of Title 35.

(2) Under agreements entered into pursuant to subsection (a)(1) of this section, the laboratory shall ensure that a collaborating party may retain title to any invention made solely by its employee in exchange for normally granting the Government a nonexclusive, nontransferable, irrevocable, paid-up license to practice the invention or have the invention practiced throughout the world by or on behalf of the Government for research or other Government purposes.

(3) Under an agreement entered into pursuant to subsection (a)(1) of this section, a laboratory may—

(A) accept, retain, and use funds, personnel, services, and property from a collaborating party and provide personnel, services, and property to a collaborating party;

(B) use funds received from a collaborating party in accordance with subparagraph (A) to hire personnel to carry out the agreement who will not be subject to full-time-equivalent restrictions of the agency;

(C) to the extent consistent with any applicable agency requirements or standards of conduct, permit an employee or former employee of the laboratory to participate in an effort to commercialize an invention made by the employee or former employee while in the employment or service of the Government; and

(D) waive, subject to reservation by the Government of a nonexclusive, irrevocable, paid-up license to practice the invention or have the invention practiced throughout the world by or on behalf of the Government, in advance, in whole or in part, any right of ownership which the Federal Government may have to any subject invention made under the agreement by a collaborating party or employee of a collaborating party.

(4) A collaborating party in an exclusive license in any invention made under an agreement entered into pursuant to subsection (a)(1) of this section shall have the right of enforcement under chapter 29 of Title 35.

(5) A Government-owned, contractor-operated laboratory that enters into a cooperative research and development agreement pursuant to subsection (a)(1) of this section may use or obligate royalties or other income accruing to the laboratory under such agreement with respect to any invention only—

(A) for payments to inventors;

(B) for purposes described in clauses (i), (ii), (iii), and (iv) of section 3710c(a)(1)(B) of this title; and

(C) for scientific research and development consistent with the research and development missions and objectives of the laboratory.

(6)(A) In the case of a laboratory that is part of the National Nuclear Security Administration, a designated official of that Administration may waive any license retained by the Government under paragraph (1)(A), (2), or (3)(D), in whole or in part and according to negotiated terms and conditions, if the designated official finds that the retention of the license by the Government would substantially inhibit the commercialization of an invention that would otherwise serve an important national security mission.

(B) The authority to grant a waiver under subparagraph (A) shall expire on the date that is five years after October 30, 2000. The expiration under the preceding sentence of authority to grant a waiver under subparagraph (A) shall not affect any waiver granted under that subparagraph before the expiration of such authority.

(C) Not later than February 15 of each year, the Administrator for Nuclear Security shall submit to Congress a report on any waivers granted under this paragraph during the preceding year.

(c) Contract considerations—

(1) A Federal agency may issue regulations on suitable procedures for implementing the provisions of this section; however, implementation of this section shall not be delayed until issuance of such regulations.

(2) The agency in permitting a Federal laboratory to enter into agreements under this section shall be guided by the purposes of this chapter.

(3)(A) Any agency using the authority given it under subsection (a) of this section shall review standards of conduct for its employees for resolving potential conflicts of interest to make sure they adequately establish guidelines for situations likely to arise through the use of this authority, including but not limited to cases where present or former employees or their partners negotiate licenses or assignments of titles to inventions or negotiate cooperative research and development agreements with Federal agencies (including the agency with which the employee involved is or was formerly employed).

(B) If, in implementing subparagraph (A), an agency is unable to resolve potential conflicts of interest within its current statutory framework, it shall propose necessary statutory changes to be forwarded to its authorizing committees in Congress.

(4) The laboratory director in deciding what cooperative research and development agreements to enter into shall—

(A) give special consideration to small business firms, and consortia involving small business firms; and

(B) give preference to business units located in the United States which agree that products embodying inventions made under the cooperative research and development agreement or produced through the use of such inventions will be manufactured substantially in the United States and, in the case of any industrial organization or other person subject to the control of a foreign company or government, as appropriate, take into consideration whether or not such foreign government permits United States agencies, organizations, or other persons to enter into cooperative research and development agreements and licensing agreements.

(5)(A) If the head of the agency or his designee desires an opportunity to disapprove or require the modification of any such agreement presented by the director of a Government-operated laboratory, the agreement shall provide a 30-day period within which such action must be taken beginning on the date the agreement is presented to him or her by the head of the laboratory concerned.

(B) In any case in which the head of an agency or his designee disapproves or requires the modification of an agreement presented by the director of a Government-operated laboratory under this section, the head of the agency or such designee shall transmit a written explanation of such disapproval or modification to the head of the laboratory concerned.

(C)(i) Any non-Federal entity that operates a laboratory pursuant to a contract with a Federal agency shall submit to the agency any cooperative research and development agreement that the entity proposes to enter into and the joint work statement if required with respect to that agreement.

(ii) A Federal agency that receives a proposed agreement and joint work statement under clause (i) shall review and approve, request specific modifications to, or disapprove the proposed agreement and joint work statement within 30 days after such submission. No agreement may be entered into by a Government-owned, contractor-operated laboratory under this section before both approval of the agreement and approval of a joint work statement under this clause.

(iii) In any case in which an agency which has contracted with an entity referred to in clause (i) disapproves or requests the modification of a cooperative research and development agreement or joint work statement submitted under that clause, the agency shall transmit a written explanation of such disapproval or modification to the head of the laboratory concerned.

(iv) Any agency that has contracted with a non-Federal entity to operate a laboratory may develop and provide to such laboratory one or more model cooperative research and development agreements for purposes of standardizing practices and procedures, resolving common legal issues, and enabling review of cooperative research and development agreements to be carried out in a routine and prompt manner.

(v) A Federal agency may waive the requirements of clause (i) or (ii) under such circumstances as the agency considers appropriate.

(6) Each agency shall maintain a record of all agreements entered into under this section.

(7)(A) No trade secrets or commercial or financial information that is privileged or confidential, under the meaning of section 552(b)(4) of Title 5, which is obtained in the conduct of research or as a result of activities under this chapter from a non-Federal party participating in a cooperative research and development agreement shall be disclosed.

(B) The director, or in the case of a contractor-operated laboratory, the agency, for a period of up to 5 years after development of information that results from research and development activities conducted under this chapter and that would be a trade secret or commercial or financial information that is privileged or confidential if the information had been obtained from a non-Federal party participating in a cooperative research and development agreement, may provide appropriate protections against the dissemination of such information, including exemption from subchapter II of chapter 5 of Title 5.

(d) Definitions.—As used in this section—

(1) the term "cooperative research and development agreement" means any agreement between one or more Federal laboratories and one or more non-Federal parties under which the Government, through its laboratories, provides personnel, services, facilities, equipment, intellectual property, or other resources with or without reimbursement (but not funds to non-Federal parties) and the non-Federal parties provide funds, personnel, services, facilities, equipment, intellectual property, or other resources toward the conduct of specified research or development efforts which are consistent with the missions of the laboratory; except that such term does not include a procurement contract or cooperative agreement as those terms are used in sections 6303, 6304, and 6305 of Title 31;

(2) the term "laboratory" means—

(A) a facility or group of facilities owned, leased, or otherwise used by a Federal agency, a substantial purpose of which is the performance of research, development, or engineering by employees of the Federal Government;

(B) a group of Government-owned, contractor-operated facilities (including a weapon production facility of the Department of Energy) under a common contract, when a substantial purpose of the contract is the performance of research and development, or the production, maintenance, testing, or dismantlement of a nuclear weapon or its components, for the Federal Government; and

(C) a Government-owned, contractor-operated facility (including a weapon production facility of the Department of Energy) that is not under a common contract described in subparagraph (B), and the primary purpose of which is the performance of research and development, or the production, maintenance, testing, or dismantlement of a nuclear weapon or its components, for the Federal Government,

but such term does not include any facility covered by Executive Order No. 12344, dated February 1, 1982, pertaining to the naval nuclear propulsion program;

(3) the term "joint work statement" means a proposal prepared for a Federal agency by the director of a Government-owned, contractor-operated laboratory describing the purpose and scope of a proposed cooperative research and development agreement, and assigning rights and responsibilities among the agency, the laboratory, and any other party or parties to the proposed agreement; and

(4) the term "weapon production facility of the Department of Energy" means a facility under the control or jurisdiction of the Secretary of Energy that is operated for national security purposes and is engaged in the production, maintenance, testing, or dismantlement of a nuclear weapon or its components.

(e) Determination of laboratory missions.—For purposes of this section, an agency shall make separate determinations of the mission or missions of each of its laboratories.

(f) Relationship to other laws.—Nothing in this section is intended to limit or diminish existing authorities of any agency.

(g) Principles.—In implementing this section, each agency which has contracted with a non-Federal entity to operate a laboratory shall be guided by the following principles:

(1) The implementation shall advance program missions at the laboratory, including any national security mission.

(2) Classified information and unclassified sensitive information protected by law, regulation, or Executive order shall be appropriately safeguarded.

History of 15 U.S.C. §3710a: Oct. 20, 1986, P.L. 99-502, §§2, 9(e)(1), 100 Stat. 1785, 1797; Aug. 23, 1988, P.L. 100-418, §5122(a)(1), 102 Stat. 1438; Oct. 24, 1988, P.L. 100-519, §301, 102 Stat. 2597; Nov. 29, 1989, P.L. 101-189, §3133(a), (b), 103 Stat. 1675-1677; Apr. 6, 1991, P.L. 102-25, §705(g), 105 Stat. 121; Feb. 14, 1992, P.L. 102-245, §302(a), 106 Stat. 20; Oct. 23, 1992, P.L.

102-484, §3135(a), 106 Stat. 2640; Nov. 30, 1993, P.L. 103-160, §3160, 107 Stat. 1957; Mar. 7, 1996, P.L. 104-113, §4, 110 Stat. 775; Oct. 30, 2000, P.L. 106-398, §1, 114 Stat. 1654, 1654A-481; Nov. 1, 2000, P.L. 106-404, §3, 114 Stat. 1742.

§3710b. REWARDS FOR SCIENTIFIC, ENGINEERING & TECHNICAL PERSONNEL OF FEDERAL AGENCIES

The head of each Federal agency that is making expenditures at a rate of more than $50,000,000 per fiscal year for research and development in its Government-operated laboratories shall use the appropriate statutory authority to develop and implement a cash awards program to reward its scientific, engineering, and technical personnel for—

(1) inventions, innovations, computer software, or other outstanding scientific or technological contributions of value to the United States due to commercial application or due to contributions to missions of the Federal agency or the Federal government,[1] or

(2) exemplary activities that promote the domestic transfer of science and technology development within the Federal Government and result in utilization of such science and technology by American industry or business, universities, State or local governments, or other non-Federal parties.

1. **Editor's note:** The word "government" probably should be capitalized.

History of 15 U.S.C. §3710b: Oct. 20, 1986, P.L. 99-502, §§6, 9(e)(1), 100 Stat. 1792, 1797; Aug. 23, 1988, P.L. 100-418, §5122(a)(1), 102 Stat. 1438; Oct. 24, 1988, P.L. 100-519, §302, 102 Stat. 2597.

§3710c. DISTRIBUTION OF ROYALTIES RECEIVED BY FEDERAL AGENCIES

(a) In general—

(1) Except as provided in paragraphs (2) and (4), any royalties or other payments received by a Federal agency from the licensing and assignment of inventions under agreements entered into by Federal laboratories under section 3710a of this title, and from the licensing of inventions of Federal laboratories under section 207 of Title 35 or under any other provision of law, shall be retained by the laboratory which produced the invention and shall be disposed of as follows:

(A)(i) The head of the agency or laboratory, or such individual's designee, shall pay each year the first $2,000, and thereafter at least 15 percent, of the royalties or other payments, other than payments of patent costs as delineated by a license or assignment agreement, to the inventor or coinventors, if the inventor's or coinventor's rights are assigned to the United States.

(ii) An agency or laboratory may provide appropriate incentives, from royalties, or other payments, to laboratory employees who are not an inventor of such inventions but who substantially increased the technical value of such inventions.

(iii) The agency or laboratory shall retain the royalties and other payments received from an invention until the agency or laboratory makes payments to employees of a laboratory under clause (i) or (ii).

(B) The balance of the royalties or other payments shall be transferred by the agency to its laboratories, with the majority share of the royalties or other payments from any invention going to the laboratory where the invention occurred. The royalties or other payments so transferred to any laboratory may be used or obligated by that laboratory during the fiscal year in which they are received or during the 2 succeeding fiscal years—

(i) to reward scientific, engineering, and technical employees of the laboratory, including developers of sensitive or classified technology, regardless of whether the technology has commercial applications;

(ii) to further scientific exchange among the laboratories of the agency;

(iii) for education and training of employees consistent with the research and development missions and objectives of the agency or laboratory, and for other activities that increase the potential for transfer of the technology of the laboratories of the agency;

(iv) for payment of expenses incidental to the administration and licensing of intellectual property by the agency or laboratory with respect to inventions made at that laboratory, including the fees or other costs for the services of other agencies, persons, or organizations for intellectual property management and licensing services; or

(v) for scientific research and development consistent with the research and development missions and objectives of the laboratory.

(C) All royalties or other payments retained by the agency or laboratory after payments have been made pursuant to subparagraphs (A) and (B) that is unobligated and unexpended at the end of the second fiscal year succeeding the fiscal year in which the royalties and other payments were received shall be paid into the Treasury.

(2) If, after payments to inventors under paragraph (1), the royalties or other payments received by an agency in any fiscal year exceed 5 percent of the budget of the agency for that year, 75 percent of such excess shall be paid to the Treasury of the United States and the remaining 25 percent may be used or obligated under paragraph (1)(B). Any funds not so used or obligated shall be paid into the Treasury of the United States.

(3) Any payment made to an employee under this section shall be in addition to the regular pay of the employee and to any other awards made to the employee, and shall not affect the entitlement of the employee to any regular pay, annuity, or award to which he is otherwise entitled or for which he is otherwise eligible or limit the amount thereof. Any payment made to an inventor as such shall continue after the inventor leaves the laboratory or agency. Payments made under this section shall not exceed $150,000 per year to any one person, unless the President approves a larger award (with the excess over $150,000 being treated as a Presidential award under section 4504 of Title 5).

(4) A Federal agency receiving royalties or other payments as a result of invention management services performed for another Federal agency or laboratory under section 207 of Title 35, may retain such royalties or payments to the extent required to offset payments to inventors under clause (i) of paragraph (1)(A), costs and expenses incurred under clause (iv) of paragraph (1)(B), and the cost of foreign patenting and maintenance for any invention of the other agency. All royalties and other payments remaining after offsetting the payments to inventors, costs, and expenses described in the preceding sentence shall be transferred to the agency for which the services were performed, for distribution in accordance with paragraph (1)(B).

(b) Certain assignments.—If the invention involved was one assigned to the Federal agency—

(1) by a contractor, grantee, or participant, or an employee of a contractor, grantee, or participant, in an agreement or other arrangement with the agency, or

(2) by an employee of the agency who was not working in the laboratory at the time the invention was made,

the agency unit that was involved in such assignment shall be considered to be a laboratory for purposes of this section.

(c) Reports.—The Comptroller General shall transmit a report to the appropriate committees of the Senate and House of Representatives on the effectiveness of Federal technology transfer programs, including findings, conclusions, and recommendations for improvements in such programs. The report shall be integrated with, and submitted at the same time as, the report required by section 202(b)(3) of Title 35.

History of 15 U.S.C. §3710c: Oct. 20, 1986, P.L. 99-502, §§7, 9(e)(1), (3), 100 Stat. 1792, 1797; Aug. 23, 1988, P.L. 100-418, §§5122(a)(1), 5162(a), 102 Stat. 1438, 1450; Oct. 24, 1988, P.L. 100-519, §303(a), 102 Stat. 2597; Nov. 29, 1989, P.L. 101-189, §3133(c), 103 Stat. 1677; Mar. 7, 1996, P.L. 104-113, §5, 110 Stat. 777; Nov. 1, 2000, P.L. 106-404, §§7(7), 10(b), 114 Stat. 1746, 1749.

§3710d. EMPLOYEE ACTIVITIES

(a) In general.—If a Federal agency which has ownership of or the right of ownership to an invention made by a Federal employee does not intend to file for a patent application or otherwise to promote commercialization of such invention, the agency shall allow the inventor, if the inventor is a Government employee or former employee who made the invention during the course of employment with the Government, to obtain or retain title to the invention (subject to reservation by the Government of a nonexclusive, nontransferrable,[1] irrevocable, paid-up license to practice the invention or have the invention practiced throughout the world by or on behalf of the Government). In addition, the agency may condition the inventor's right to title on the timely filing of a patent application in cases when the Government determines that it has or may have a need to practice the invention.

(b) "Special Government employees" defined.—For purposes of this section, Federal employees include "special Government employees" as defined in section 202 of Title 18.

(c) Relationship to other laws.—Nothing in this section is intended to limit or diminish existing authorities of any agency.

1. Editor's note: Probably should be "nontransferable."

History of 15 U.S.C. §3710d: Oct. 20, 1986, P.L. 99-502, §§8, 9(e)(1), 100 Stat. 1794, 1797; Aug. 23, 1988, P.L. 100-418, §5122(a)(1), 102 Stat. 1438; Mar. 7, 1996, P.L. 104-113, §6, 110 Stat. 779.

Sections 3711 & 3711a omitted by editor

§3711b. CONFERENCE ON ADVANCED AUTOMOTIVE TECHNOLOGIES

Not later than 180 days after December 18, 1991, the Secretary of Commerce, through the Under Secretary of Commerce for Technology, in consultation with other appropriate officials, shall convene a conference of domestic motor vehicle manufacturers, parts suppliers, Federal laboratories, and motor vehicle users to explore ways in which cooperatively they can improve the competitiveness of the United States motor vehicle industry by developing new technologies which will enhance the safety and energy savings, and lessen the environmental impact of domestic motor vehicles, and the results of such conference shall be published and then submitted to the President and to the Committees on Science, Space, and Technology and Public Works and Transportation of the House of Representatives and the Committee on Commerce, Science, and Transportation of the Senate.

History of 15 U.S.C. §3711b: Dec. 18, 1991, P.L. 102-240, §6019, 105 Stat. 2183.

Section 3711c omitted by editor

§3712. PERSONNEL EXCHANGES

The Secretary, the Secretary of Energy, and the Director of the National Science Foundation, jointly, shall establish a program to foster the exchange of scientific and technical personnel among academia, industry, and Federal laboratories. Such program shall include both (1) federally supported exchanges and (2) efforts to stimulate exchanges without Federal funding.

History of 15 U.S.C. §3712: Oct. 21, 1980, P.L. 96-480, §13, 94 Stat. 2320; Oct. 20, 1986, P.L. 99-502, §§2, 9(e)(1), 100 Stat. 1785, 1797; Aug. 20, 1987, P.L. 100-107, §3(a), 101 Stat. 725; Aug. 23, 1988, P.L. 100-418, §5122(a)(1), 102 Stat. 1438; Dec. 18, 1991, P.L. 102-240, §6019, 105 Stat. 2183; Aug. 8, 2005, P.L. 109-58, §1009(c), 119 Stat. 936.

Section 3713 omitted by editor

§3714. SPENDING AUTHORITY

No payments shall be made or contracts shall be entered into pursuant to the provisions of this chapter (other than sections 3710a, 3710b, and 3710c of this title) except to such extent or in such amounts as are provided in advance in appropriation Acts.

History of 15 U.S.C. §3714: Oct. 21, 1980, P.L. 96-480, §15, 94 Stat. 2320; Oct. 20, 1986, P.L. 99-502, §§2, 9(b)(13), (e)(1), (4), 100 Stat. 1785, 1796, 1797; Aug. 20, 1987, P.L. 100-107, §3(a), 101 Stat. 725; Aug. 23, 1988, P.L. 100-418, §5122(a)(1), 102 Stat. 1438; Dec. 18, 1991, P.L. 102-240, §6019, 105 Stat. 2183; Nov. 1, 2000, P.L. 106-404, §7(8), 114 Stat. 1746.

§3715. USE OF PARTNERSHIP INTERMEDIARIES

(a) Authority.—Subject to the approval of the Secretary or head of the affected department or agency, the Director of a Federal laboratory, or in the case of a federally funded research and development center that is not a laboratory (as defined in section 3710a(d)(2) of this title), the Federal employee who is the contract officer, may—

(1) enter into a contract or memorandum of understanding with a partnership intermediary that provides for the partnership intermediary to perform services for the Federal laboratory that increase the likelihood of success in the conduct of cooperative or joint activities of such Federal laboratory with small business firms, institutions of higher education as defined in section 1141(a) of Title 20, or educational institutions within the meaning of section 2194 of Title 10; and

(2) pay the Federal costs of such contract or memorandum of understanding out of funds available for the support of the technology transfer function pursuant to section 3710(b) of this title.

(b) *Omitted by editor.*

(c) "Partnership intermediary" defined.—For purposes of this section, the term "partnership intermediary" means an agency of a State or local government, or a nonprofit entity owned in whole or in part by, chartered by, funded in whole or in part by, or operated in whole or in part by or on behalf of a State or local government, that assists, counsels, advises, evaluates, or otherwise cooperates with small business firms, institutions of higher education as defined in section 1141(a) of Title 20, or educational institutions within the meaning of section 2194 of Title 10, that need or can make demonstrably productive use of technology-related assistance from a Federal laboratory, including State programs receiving funds under cooperative agreements entered into under section 5121(b) of the Omnibus Trade and Competitiveness Act of 1988 (15 U.S.C. 278*l* note).

History of 15 U.S.C. §3715: Nov. 5, 1990, P.L. 101-510, §827(a), 104 Stat. 1606; Dec. 5, 1991, P.L. 102-190, §836, 105 Stat. 1448; Dec. 18, 1991, P.L. 102-240, §6019, 105 Stat. 2183; Nov. 1, 2000, P.L. 106-404, §9, 114 Stat. 1747.

§3716. CRITICAL INDUSTRIES

(a) Identification of industries and development of plan.—The Secretary shall—

(1) identify those civilian industries in the United States that are necessary to support a robust manufacturing infrastructure and critical to the economic security of the United States; and

(2) list the major research and development initiatives being undertaken, and the substantial investments being made, by the Federal Government, including its research laboratories, in each of the critical industries identified under paragraph (1).

(b) Initial report.—The Secretary shall submit a report to the Congress within 1 year after February 14, 1992, on the actions taken under subsection (a) of this section.

History of 15 U.S.C. §3716: Feb. 14, 1992, P.L. 102-245, §504, 106 Stat. 24.

§3717. NATIONAL QUALITY COUNCIL

(a) Establishment and functions.—There is established a National Quality Council (hereafter in this section referred to as the "Council"). The functions of the Council shall be—

(1) to establish national goals and priorities for Quality performance in business, education, government, and all other sectors of the Nation;

(2) to encourage and support the voluntary adoption of these goals and priorities by companies, unions, professional and business associations, coalition groups, and units of government, as well as private and nonprofit organizations;

(3) to arouse and maintain the interest of the people of the United States in Quality performance, and to encourage the adoption and institution of Quality performance methods by all corporations, government agencies, and other organizations; and

(4) to conduct a White House Conference on Quality Performance in the American Workplace that would bring together in a single forum national leaders in business, labor, education, professional societies, the media, government, and politics to address Quality performance as a means of improving United States competitiveness.

(b) Membership.—The Council shall consist of not less than 17 or more than 20 members, appointed by the Secretary. Members shall include—

(1) at least 2 but not more than 3 representatives from manufacturing industry;

(2) at least 2 but not more than 3 representatives from service industry;

(3) at least 2 but not more than 3 representatives from national Quality not-for-profit organizations;

(4) two representatives from education, one with expertise in elementary and secondary education, and one with expertise in post-secondary education;

(5) one representative from labor;

(6) one representative from professional societies;

(7) one representative each from local and State government;

(8) one representative from the Federal Quality Institute;

(9) one representative from the National Institute of Standards and Technology;

(10) one representative from the Department of Defense;

(11) one representative from a civilian Federal agency not otherwise represented on the Council, to be rotated among such agencies every 2 years; and

(12) one representative from the Foundation for the Malcolm Baldrige National Quality Award.

(c) Terms.—The term of office of each member of the Council appointed under paragraphs (1) through (7) of subsection (b) of this section shall be 2 years, except that when making the initial appointments under such paragraphs; the Secretary shall appoint not more than 50 percent of the members to 1 year terms. No member appointed under such paragraphs shall serve on the Council for more than 2 consecutive terms.

(d) Chairman and Vice Chairman.—The Secretary shall designate one of the members initially appointed to the Council as Chairman. Thereafter, the members of the Council shall annually elect one of their number as Chairman. The members of the Council shall also annually elect one of their members as Vice Chairman. No individual shall serve as Chairman or Vice Chairman for more than 2 consecutive years.

(e) Executive Director and employees.—The Council shall appoint and fix the compensation of an Executive Director, who shall hire and fix the compensation of such additional employees as may be necessary to assist the Council in carrying out its functions. In hiring such additional employees, the Executive Director shall ensure that no individual hired has a conflict of interest with the responsibilities of the Council.

(f) Funding.—There is established in the Treasury of the United States a National Quality Performance Trust Fund, into which all funds received by the Council, through private donations or otherwise, shall be deposited. Amounts in such Trust Fund shall be available to the Council, to the extent provided in advance in appropriations Acts, for the purpose of carrying out the functions of the Council under this Act.

(g) Contributions.—The Council may not accept private donations from a single source in excess of $25,000 per year. Private donations from a single source in excess of $10,000 per year may be accepted by the Council only on approval of two-thirds of the Council.

(h) Annual report.—The Council shall annually submit to the President and the Congress a comprehensive and detailed report on—

(1) the progress in meeting the goals and priorities established by the Council;

(2) the Council's operations, activities, and financial condition;

(3) contributions to the Council from non-Federal sources;

(4) plans for the Council's operations and activities for the future; and

(5) any other information or recommendations the Council considers appropriate.

History of 15 U.S.C. §3717: Feb. 14, 1992, P.L. 102-245, §507, 106 Stat. 27.

§3718. PRESIDENT'S COUNCIL ON INNOVATION & COMPETITIVENESS

(a) In general.—The President shall establish a President's Council on Innovation and Competitiveness.

(b) Duties.—The duties of the Council shall include—

(1) monitoring implementation of public laws and initiatives for promoting innovation, including policies related to research funding, taxation, immigration, trade, and education that are proposed in this Act or in any other Act;

(2) providing advice to the President with respect to global trends in competitiveness and innovation and allocation of Federal resources in education, job training, and technology research and development considering such global trends in competitiveness and innovation;

(3) in consultation with the Director of the Office of Management and Budget, developing a process for using metrics to assess the impact of existing and proposed policies and rules that affect innovation capabilities in the United States;

(4) identifying opportunities and making recommendations for the heads of executive agencies to improve innovation, monitoring, and reporting on the implementation of such recommendations;

(5) developing metrics for measuring the progress of the Federal Government with respect to improving conditions for innovation, including through talent development, investment, and infrastructure improvements; and

(6) submitting to the President and Congress an annual report on such progress.

(c) Membership and coordination—

(1) Membership.—The Council shall be composed of the Secretary or head of each of the following:

(A) The Department of Commerce.

(B) The Department of Defense.

(C) The Department of Education.

(D) The Department of Energy.

(E) The Department of Health and Human Services.

(F) The Department of Homeland Security.

(G) The Department of Labor.

(H) The Department of the Treasury.

(I) The National Aeronautics and Space Administration.

(J) The Securities and Exchange Commission.

(K) The National Science Foundation.

(L) The Office of the United States Trade Representative.

(M) The Office of Management and Budget.

(N) The Office of Science and Technology Policy.

(O) The Environmental Protection Agency.

(P) The Small Business Administration.

(Q) Any other department or agency designated by the President.

(2) Chairperson.—The Secretary of Commerce shall serve as Chairperson of the Council.

(3) Coordination.—The Chairperson of the Council shall ensure appropriate coordination between the Council and the National Economic Council, the National Security Council, and the National Science and Technology Council.

(4) Meetings.—The Council shall meet on a semi-annual basis at the call of the Chairperson and the initial meeting of the Council shall occur not later than 6 months after August 9, 2007.

(d) Development of innovation agenda—

(1) In general.—The Council shall develop a comprehensive agenda for strengthening the innovation and competitiveness capabilities of the Federal Government, State governments, academia, and the private sector in the United States.

(2) Contents.—The comprehensive agenda required by paragraph (1) shall include the following:

(A) An assessment of current strengths and weaknesses of the United States investment in research and development.

(B) Recommendations for addressing weaknesses and maintaining the United States as a world leader in research and development and technological innovation, including strategies for increasing the participation of individuals identified in section 1885a or 1885b of Title 42 in science, technology, engineering, and mathematics fields.

(C) Recommendations for strengthening the innovation and competitiveness capabilities of the Federal Government, State governments, academia, and the private sector in the United States.

(3) Advisors—

(A) Recommendation.—Not later than 30 days after August 9, 2007, the National Academy of Sciences, in consultation with the National Academy of Engineering, the Institute of Medicine, and the National Research Council, shall develop and submit to the President a list of 50 individuals that are recommended to serve as advisors to the Council during the development of the comprehensive agenda required by paragraph (1). The list of advisors shall include appropriate representatives from the following:

(i) The private sector of the economy.

(ii) Labor.

(iii) Various fields including information technology, energy, engineering, high-technology manufacturing, health care, and education.

(iv) Scientific organizations.

(v) Academic organizations and other nongovernmental organizations working in the area of science or technology.

(vi) Nongovernmental organizations, such as professional organizations, that represent individuals identified in section 1885a or 1885b of Title 42 in the areas of science, engineering, technology, and mathematics.

(B) Designation.—Not later than 30 days after the date that the National Academy of Sciences submits the list of recommended individuals to serve as advisors, the President shall designate 50 individuals to serve as advisors to the Council.

(C) Requirement to consult.—The Council shall develop the comprehensive agenda required by paragraph (1) in consultation with the advisors.

(4) Initial submission and updates—

(A) Initial submission.—Not later than 1 year after August 9, 2007, the Council shall submit to Congress and the President the comprehensive agenda required by paragraph (1).

(B) Updates.—At least once every 2 years, the Council shall update the comprehensive agenda required by paragraph (1) and submit each such update to Congress and the President.

(e) Optional assignment.—Notwithstanding subsection (a) of this section and paragraphs (1) and (2) of subsection (c) of this section, the President may designate an existing council to carry out the requirements of this section.

History of 15 U.S.C. §3718: Aug. 9, 2007, P.L. 110-69, §1006, 121 Stat. 578.

§3719. PRIZE COMPETITIONS

(a) Definitions.—In this section:

(1) Agency.—The term "agency" means a Federal agency.

(2) Director.—The term "Director" means the Director of the Office of Science and Technology Policy.

(3) Federal agency.—The term "Federal agency" has the meaning given under section 3703 of this title, except that term shall not include any agency of the legislative branch of the Federal Government.

(4) Head of an agency.—The term "head of an agency" means the head of a Federal agency.

(b) In general.—Each head of an agency, or the heads of multiple agencies in cooperation, may carry out a program to award prizes competitively to stimulate innovation that has the potential to advance the mission of the respective agency.

(c) Prize competitions.—For purposes of this section, a prize competition may be 1 or more of the following types of activities:

(1) A point solution prize that rewards and spurs the development of solutions for a particular, well-defined problem.

(2) An exposition prize competition that helps identify and promote a broad range of ideas and practices that may not otherwise attract attention, facilitating further development of the idea or practice by third parties.

(3) Participation prize competitions that create value during and after the competition by encouraging contestants to change their behavior or develop new skills that may have beneficial effects during and after the competition.

(4) Such other types of prize competitions as each head of an agency considers appropriate to stimulate innovation that has the potential to advance the mission of the respective agency.

(d) Topics.—In selecting topics for prize competitions, the head of an agency shall consult widely both within and outside the Federal Government, and may empanel advisory committees.

(e) Advertising.—The head of an agency shall widely advertise each prize competition to encourage broad participation.

(f) Requirements and registration.—For each prize competition, the head of an agency shall publish a notice on a publicly accessible Government website, such as www.challenge.gov, announcing—

(1) the subject of the prize competition;

(2) the rules for being eligible to participate in the prize competition;

(3) the process for participants to register for the prize competition;

(4) the amount of the cash prize purse or non-cash prize award; and

(5) the basis on which a winner will be selected.

(g) Eligibility.—To be eligible to win a cash prize purse under this section, an individual or entity—

(1) shall have registered to participate in the prize competition under any rules promulgated by the head of an agency under subsection (f);

(2) shall have complied with all the requirements under this section;

(3) in the case of a private entity, shall be incorporated in and maintain a primary place of business in the United States, and in the case of an individual, whether participating singly or in a group, shall be a citizen or permanent resident of the United States; and

(4) may not be a Federal entity or Federal employee acting within the scope of their employment.

(h) Consultation with Federal employees.—An individual or entity shall not be deemed ineligible under subsection (g) because the individual or entity used Federal facilities or consulted with Federal employees during a prize competition if the facilities and employees are made available to all individuals and entities participating in the prize competition on an equitable basis.

(i) Liability—

(1) In general—

(A) Definition.—In this paragraph, the term "related entity" means a contractor or subcontractor at any tier, and a supplier, user, customer, cooperating party, grantee, investigator, or detailee.

(B) Liability.—Registered participants shall be required to agree to assume any and all risks and waive claims against the Federal Government and its related entities, except in the case of willful misconduct, for any injury, death, damage, or loss of property, revenue, or profits, whether direct, indirect, or consequential, arising from their participation in a prize competition, whether the injury, death, damage, or loss arises through negligence or otherwise.

(2) Insurance.—Participants shall be required to obtain liability insurance or demonstrate financial responsibility, in amounts determined by the head of an agency, for claims by—

(A) a third party for death, bodily injury, or property damage, or loss resulting from an activity carried out in connection with participation in a prize competition, with the Federal Government named as an additional insured under the registered participant's insurance policy and registered participants agreeing to indemnify the Federal Government against third party claims for damages arising from or related to prize competition activities; and

(B) the Federal Government for damage or loss to Government property resulting from such an activity.

(3) Waivers—

(A) In general.—An agency may waive the requirement under paragraph (2).

(B) List.—The Director shall include a list of all of the waivers granted under this paragraph during the preceding fiscal year, including a detailed explanation of the reason for granting the waiver.

(4) Exception.—The head of an agency may not require a participant to waive claims against the administering entity arising out of the unauthorized use or disclosure by the agency of the intellectual property, trade secrets, or confidential business information of the participant.

(j) Intellectual property—

(1) Prohibition on the government acquiring intellectual property rights.—The Federal Government may not gain an interest in intellectual property developed by a participant in a prize competition without the written consent of the participant.

(2) Licenses.—As appropriate and to further the goals of a prize competition, the Federal Government may negotiate a license for the use of intellectual property developed by a registered participant in a prize competition.

(k) Judges—

(1) In general.—For each prize competition, the head of an agency, either directly or through an agreement under subsection (*l*), shall appoint one or more qualified judges to select the winner or winners of the prize competition on the basis described under subsection (f). Judges for each prize competition may include individuals from outside the agency, including from the private sector.

(2) Restrictions.—A judge may not—

(A) have personal or financial interests in, or be an employee, officer, director, or agent of any entity that is a registered participant in a prize competition; or

(B) have a familial or financial relationship with an individual who is a registered participant.

(3) Guidelines.—The heads of agencies who carry out prize competitions under this section shall develop guidelines to ensure that the judges appointed for such prize competitions are fairly balanced and operate in a transparent manner.

(4) Exemption from FACA.—The Federal Advisory Committee Act (5 U.S.C. App.) shall not apply to any committee, board, commission, panel, task force, or similar entity, created solely for the purpose of judging prize competitions under this section.

(*l*) Administering the competition.—The head of an agency may enter into a grant, contract, cooperative agreement, or other agreement with a private sector for-profit or nonprofit entity or State or local government agency to administer the prize competition, subject to the provisions of this section.

(m) Funding—

(1) In general.—Support for a prize competition under this section, including financial support for the design and administration of a prize competition or funds for a cash prize purse, may consist of Federal appropriated funds and funds provided by private sector for-profit and nonprofit entities. The head of an agency may request and accept funds from other Federal agencies, State, United States territory, local, or tribal government agencies, private sector for-profit entities, and nonprofit entities, to be available to the extent provided by appropriations Acts, to support such prize competitions. The head of an agency may not give any special consideration to any agency or entity in return for a donation.

(2) Availability of funds.—Notwithstanding any other provision of law, funds appropriated for cash prize purses or non-cash prize awards under this section shall remain available until expended. No provision in this section permits obligation or payment of funds in violation of section 1341 of Title 31.

(3) Amount of prize—

(A) Announcement.—No prize competition may be announced under subsection (f) until all the funds needed to pay out the announced amount of the cash prize purse have been appropriated or committed in writing by a private or State, United States territory, local, or tribal government source.

(B) Increase in amount.—The head of an agency may increase the amount of a cash prize purse or non-cash prize award after an initial announcement is made under subsection (f) only if—

(i) notice of the increase is provided in the same manner as the initial notice of the prize competition; and

(ii) the funds needed to pay out the announced amount of the increase have been appropriated or committed in writing by a private or State, United States territory, local, or tribal government source.

(4) Limitation on amount—

(A) Notice to Congress.—No prize competition under this section may offer a cash prize purse or a non-cash prize award in an amount greater than $50,000,000 unless 30 days have elapsed after written notice has been transmitted to the Committee on Commerce, Science, and Transportation of the Senate and the Committee on Science, Space, and Technology of the House of Representatives.

(B) Approval of head of agency.—No prize competition under this section may result in the award of more than $1,000,000 in cash prize purses or non-cash prize awards without the approval of the head of an agency.

(n) General Services Administration assistance.—Not later than 180 days after January 6, 2017, the General Services Administration shall provide government wide services to share best practices and assist agencies in developing guidelines for issuing prize competitions. The General Services Administration shall develop a contract vehicle for both for-profit and nonprofit entities and State, United States territory, local, and tribal government entities, to provide agencies access to relevant products and services, including technical assistance in structuring and conducting prize competitions to take maximum benefit of the marketplace as they identify and pursue prize competitions to further the policy objectives of the Federal Government.

(o) Compliance with existing law—

(1) In general.—The Federal Government shall not, by virtue of offering a prize competition or providing a cash prize purse or non-cash prize award under this section, be responsible for compliance by registered participants in a prize competition with Federal law, including licensing, export control, and nonproliferation laws, and related regulations.

(2) Other prize authority.—Nothing in this section affects the prize authority authorized by any other provision of law.

(p) Biennial report—

(1) In general.—Not later than March 1 of every other year, the Director shall submit to the Committee on Commerce, Science, and Transportation of the Senate and the Committee on Science, Space, and Technology of the House of Representatives a report on the activities carried out during the preceding 2 fiscal years under the authority in subsection (b).

(2) Information included.—A report under this subsection shall include, for each prize competition under subsection (b), the following:

(A) Proposed goals.—A description of the proposed goals of each prize competition.

(B) Preferable method.—An analysis of why the utilization of the authority in subsection (b) was the preferable method of achieving the goals described in subparagraph (A) as opposed to other authorities available to the agency, such as contracts, grants, and cooperative agreements.

(C) Amount of cash prize purses or non-cash prize awards.—The total amount of cash prize purses or non-cash prize awards awarded for each prize competition, including a description of amount of private funds contributed to the program, the sources of such funds, and the manner in which the amounts of cash prize purses or non-cash prize awards awarded and claimed were allocated among the accounts of the agency for recording as obligations and expenditures.

(D) Solicitations and evaluation of submissions.—The methods used for the solicitation and evaluation of submissions under each prize competition, together with an assessment of the effectiveness of such methods and lessons learned for future prize competitions.

(E) Resources.—A description of the resources, including personnel and funding, used in the execution of each prize competition together with a detailed description of the activities for which such resources were used and an accounting of how funding for execution was allocated among the accounts of the agency for recording as obligations and expenditures.

(F) Results.—A description of how each prize competition advanced the mission of the agency concerned.

(G) Plan.—A description of crosscutting topical areas and agency-specific mission needs that may be the strongest opportunities for prize competitions during the upcoming 2 fiscal years.

History of 15 U.S.C. §3719: Jan. 4, 2011, P.L. 111-358, §105(a), 124 Stat. 3989; Jan. 6, 2017, P.L. 114-329, §401(b), 130 Stat. 3016.

§3720. OFFICE OF INNOVATION & ENTREPRENEURSHIP

(a) In general.—The Secretary shall establish an Office of Innovation and Entrepreneurship to foster innovation and the commercialization of new technologies, products, processes, and services with the goal of promoting productivity and economic growth in the United States.

(b) Duties.—The Office of Innovation and Entrepreneurship shall be responsible for—

(1) developing policies to accelerate innovation and advance the commercialization of research and development, including federally funded research and development;

(2) identifying existing barriers to innovation and commercialization, including access to capital and other resources, and ways to overcome those barriers, particularly in States participating in the Experimental Program to Stimulate Competitive Research;

(3) providing access to relevant data, research, and technical assistance on innovation and commercialization;

(4) strengthening collaboration on and coordination of policies relating to innovation and commercialization, including those focused on the needs of small businesses and rural communities, within the Department of Commerce, between the Department of Commerce and other Federal agencies, and between the Department of Commerce and appropriate State government agencies and institutions, as appropriate; and

(5) any other duties as determined by the Secretary.

(c) Advisory committee.—The Secretary shall establish an Advisory Council on Innovation and Entrepreneurship to provide advice to the Secretary on carrying out subsection (b).

History of 15 U.S.C. §3720: Jan. 4, 2011, P.L. 111-358, §601, 124 Stat. 4026.

§3721. Federal Loan Guarantees for Innovative Technologies in Manufacturing

(a) Establishment.—The Secretary shall establish a program to provide loan guarantees for obligations to small- or medium-sized manufacturers for the use or production of innovative technologies.

(b) Eligible projects.—A loan guarantee may be made under the program only for a project that re-equips, expands, or establishes a manufacturing facility in the United States—

(1) to use an innovative technology or an innovative process in manufacturing;

(2) to manufacture an innovative technology product or an integral component of such a product; or

(3) to commercialize an innovative product, process, or idea that was developed by research funded in whole or in part by a grant from the Federal government.

(c) Eligible borrower.—A loan guarantee may be made under the program only for a borrower who is a small- or medium-sized manufacturer, as determined by the Secretary under the criteria established pursuant to subsection (*l*).

(d) Limitation on amount.—A loan guarantee shall not exceed an amount equal to 80 percent of the obligation, as estimated at the time at which the loan guarantee is issued.

(e) Limitations on loan guarantee.—No loan guarantee shall be made unless the Secretary determines that—

(1) there is a reasonable prospect of repayment of the principal and interest on the obligation by the borrower;

(2) the amount of the obligation (when combined with amounts available to the borrower from other sources) is sufficient to carry out the project;

(3) the obligation is not subordinate to other financing;

(4) the obligation bears interest at a rate that does not exceed a level that the Secretary determines appropriate, taking into account the prevailing rate of interest in the private sector for similar loans and risks; and

(5) the term of an obligation requires full repayment over a period not to exceed the lesser of—

(A) 30 years; or

(B) 90 percent of the projected useful life, as determined by the Secretary, of the physical asset to be financed by the obligation.

(f) Defaults—

(1) Payment by Secretary—

(A) In general.—If a borrower defaults (as defined in regulations promulgated by the Secretary and specified in the loan guarantee) on the obligation, the holder of the loan guarantee shall have the right to demand payment of the unpaid amount from the Secretary.

(B) Payment required.—Within such period as may be specified in the loan guarantee or related agreements, the Secretary shall pay to the holder of the loan guarantee the unpaid interest on and unpaid principal of the obligation as to which the borrower has defaulted, unless the Secretary finds that there was no default by the borrower in the payment of interest or principal or that the default has been remedied.

(C) Forbearance.—Nothing in this subsection precludes any forbearance by the holder of the obligation for the benefit of the borrower which may be agreed upon by the parties to the obligation and approved by the Secretary.

(2) Subrogation—

(A) In general.—If the Secretary makes a payment under paragraph (1), the Secretary shall be subrogated to the rights, as specified in the loan guarantee, of the recipient of the payment or related agreements including, if appropriate, the authority (notwithstanding any other provision of law)—

(i) to complete, maintain, operate, lease, or otherwise dispose of any property acquired pursuant to such loan guarantee or related agreement; or

(ii) to permit the borrower, pursuant to an agreement with the Secretary, to continue to pursue the purposes of the project if the Secretary determines that such an agreement is in the public interest.

(B) Superiority of rights.—The rights of the Secretary, with respect to any property acquired pursuant to a loan guarantee or related agreements, shall be superior to the rights of any other person with respect to the property.

(3) Notification.—If the borrower defaults on an obligation, the Secretary shall notify the Attorney General of the default.

(g) Terms and conditions.—A loan guarantee under this section shall include such detailed terms and conditions as the Secretary determines appropriate—

(1) to protect the interests of the United States in the case of default; and

(2) to have available all the patents and technology necessary for any person selected, including the Secretary, to complete and operate the project.

(h) Consultation.—In establishing the terms and conditions of a loan guarantee under this section, the Secretary shall consult with the Secretary of the Treasury.

(i) Fees—

(1) In general.—The Secretary shall charge and collect fees for loan guarantees in amounts the Secretary determines are sufficient to cover applicable administrative expenses.

(2) Availability.—Fees collected under this subsection shall—

(A) be deposited by the Secretary into the Treasury of the United States; and

(B) remain available until expended, subject to such other conditions as are contained in annual appropriations Acts.

(3) Limitation.—In charging and collecting fees under paragraph (1), the Secretary shall take into consideration the amount of the obligation.

(j) Records—

(1) In general.—With respect to a loan guarantee under this section, the borrower, the lender, and any other appropriate party shall keep such records and other pertinent documents as the Secretary shall prescribe by regulation, including such records as the Secretary may require to facilitate an effective audit.

(2) Access.—The Secretary and the Comptroller General of the United States, or their duly authorized representatives, shall have access to records and other pertinent documents for the purpose of conducting an audit.

(k) Full faith and credit.—The full faith and credit of the United States is pledged to the payment of all loan guarantees issued under this section with respect to principal and interest.

(*l*) Regulations.—The Secretary shall issue final regulations before making any loan guarantees under the program. The regulations shall include—

(1) criteria that the Secretary shall use to determine eligibility for loan guarantees under this section, including—

(A) whether a borrower is a small- or medium-sized manufacturer; and

(B) whether a borrower demonstrates that a market exists for the innovative technology product, or the integral component of such a product, to be manufactured, as evidenced by written statements of interest from potential purchasers;

(2) criteria that the Secretary shall use to determine the amount of any fees charged under subsection (i), including criteria related to the amount of the obligation;

(3) policies and procedures for selecting and monitoring lenders and loan performance; and

(4) any other policies, procedures, or information necessary to implement this section.

(m) Audit—

(1) Annual independent audits.—The Secretary shall enter into an arrangement with an independent auditor for annual evaluations of the program under this section.

(2) Comptroller General review.—The Comptroller General of the United States shall conduct a biennial review of the Secretary's execution of the program under this section.

(3) Report.—The results of the independent audit under paragraph (1) and the Comptroller General's review under paragraph (2) shall be provided directly to the Committee on Science and Technology of the House of Representatives and the Committee on Commerce, Science, and Transportation of the Senate.

(n) Report to Congress.—Concurrent with the submission to Congress of the President's annual budget request in each year after January 4, 2011, the Secretary shall transmit to the Committee on Science and

Technology of the House of Representatives and the Committee on Commerce, Science, and Transportation of the Senate a report containing a summary of all activities carried out under this section.

(o) Coordination and nonduplication.—To the maximum extent practicable, the Secretary shall ensure that the activities carried out under this section are coordinated with, and do not duplicate the efforts of, other loan guarantee programs within the Federal Government.

(p) MEP centers.—The Secretary may use centers established under section 278k of this title to provide information about the program established under this section and to conduct outreach to potential borrowers, as appropriate.

(q) Minimizing risk.—The Secretary shall promulgate regulations and policies to carry out this section in accordance with Office of Management and Budget Circular No. A-129, entitled "Policies for Federal Credit Programs and Non-Tax Receivables," as in effect on January 4, 2011.

(r) Sense of Congress.—It is the sense of Congress that no loan guarantee shall be made under this section unless the borrower agrees to use a federally-approved electronic employment eligibility verification system to verify the employment eligibility of—

(1) all persons hired during the contract term by the borrower to perform employment duties within the United States; and

(2) all persons assigned by the borrower to perform work within the United States on the project.

(s) Definitions.—In this section:

(1) Cost.—The term "cost" has the meaning given such term under section 661a of Title 2.

(2) Innovative process.—The term "innovative process" means a process that is significantly improved as compared to the process in general use in the commercial marketplace in the United States at the time the loan guarantee is issued.

(3) Innovative technology.—The term "innovative technology" means a technology that is significantly improved as compared to the technology in general use in the commercial marketplace in the United States at the time the loan guarantee is issued.

(4) Loan guarantee.—The term "loan guarantee" has the meaning given such term in section 661a of Title 2. The term includes a loan guarantee commitment (as defined in section 661a of Title 2).

(5) Obligation.—The term "obligation" means the loan or other debt obligation that is guaranteed under this section.

(6) Program.—The term "program" means the loan guarantee program established in subsection (a).

(t) Authorization of appropriations.—There are authorized to be appropriated $20,000,000 for each of fiscal years 2011 through 2013 to provide the cost of loan guarantees under this section.

History of 15 U.S.C. §3721: Jan. 4, 2011, P.L. 111-358, §602, 124 Stat. 4026.

§3722. REGIONAL INNOVATION PROGRAM

(a) Establishment.—The Secretary shall establish a regional innovation program to encourage and support the development of regional innovation strategies, including regional innovation clusters.

(b) Cluster grants—

(1) In general.—As part of the program established under subsection (a), the Secretary may award grants on a competitive basis to eligible recipients for activities relating to the formation and development of regional innovation clusters.

(2) Permissible activities.—Grants awarded under this subsection may be used for activities determined appropriate by the Secretary, including the following:

(A) Feasibility studies.

(B) Planning activities.

(C) Technical assistance.

(D) Developing or strengthening communication and collaboration between and among participants of a regional innovation cluster.

(E) Attracting additional participants to a regional innovation cluster.

(F) Facilitating market development of products and services developed by a regional innovation cluster, including through demonstration, deployment, technology transfer, and commercialization activities.

(G) Developing relationships between a regional innovation cluster and entities or clusters in other regions.

(H) Interacting with the public and State and local governments to meet the goals of the cluster.

(3) Eligible recipient defined.—In this subsection, the term "eligible recipient" means—

(A) a State;

(B) an Indian tribe;

(C) a city or other political subdivision of a State;

(D) an entity that—

(i) is a nonprofit organization, an institution of higher education, a public-private partnership, a science or research park, a Federal laboratory, or an economic development organization or similar entity; and

(ii) has an application that is supported by a State or a political subdivision of a State;

(E) a consortium of any of the entities described in subparagraphs (A) through (D).

(4) Application—

(A) In general.—An eligible recipient shall submit an application to the Secretary at such time, in such manner, and containing such information and assurances as the Secretary may require.

(B) Components.—The application shall include, at a minimum, a description of the regional innovation cluster supported by the proposed activity, including a description of—

(i) whether the regional innovation cluster is supported by the private sector, State and local governments, and other relevant stakeholders;

(ii) how the existing participants in the regional innovation cluster will encourage and solicit participation by all types of entities that might benefit from participation, including newly formed entities and those rival existing participants;

(iii) the extent to which the regional innovation cluster is likely to stimulate innovation and have a positive impact on regional economic growth and development;

(iv) whether the participants in the regional innovation cluster have access to, or contribute to, a well-trained workforce;

(v) whether the participants in the regional innovation cluster are capable of attracting additional funds from non-Federal sources; and

(vi) the likelihood that the participants in the regional innovation cluster will be able to sustain activities once grant funds under this subsection have been expended.

(C) Special consideration.—The Secretary shall give special consideration to applications from regions that contain communities negatively impacted by trade.

(5) Special consideration.—The Secretary shall give special consideration to an eligible recipient who agrees to collaborate with local workforce investment area boards.

(6) Cost share.—The Secretary may not provide more than 50 percent of the total cost of any activity funded under this subsection.

(7) Outreach to rural communities.—The Secretary shall conduct outreach to public and private sector entities in rural communities to encourage those entities to participate in regional innovation cluster activities under this subsection.

(8) Funding.—The Secretary may accept funds from other Federal agencies to support grants and activities under this subsection.

(c) Regional innovation research and information program—

(1) In general.—As part of the program established under subsection (a), the Secretary shall establish a regional innovation research and information program—

(A) to gather, analyze, and disseminate information on best practices for regional innovation strategies (including regional innovation clusters), including information relating to how innovation, productivity, and economic development can be maximized through such strategies;

(B) to provide technical assistance, including through the development of technical assistance guides, for the development and implementation of regional innovation strategies (including regional innovation clusters);

(C) to support the development of relevant metrics and measurement standards to evaluate regional innovation strategies (including regional innovation clusters), including the extent to which such strategies stimulate innovation, productivity, and economic development; and

(D) to collect and make available data on regional innovation cluster activity in the United States, including data on—

(i) the size, specialization, and competitiveness of regional innovation clusters;

(ii) the regional domestic product contribution, total jobs and earnings by key occupations, establishment size, nature of specialization, patents, Federal research and development spending, and other relevant information for regional innovation clusters; and

(iii) supply chain product and service flows within and between regional innovation clusters.

(2) Research grants.—The Secretary may award research grants on a competitive basis to support and further the goals of the program established under this subsection.

(3) Dissemination of information.—Data and analysis compiled by the Secretary under the program established in this subsection shall be made available to other Federal agencies, State and local governments, and nonprofit and for-profit entities.

(4) Regional innovation grant program.—The Secretary shall incorporate data and analysis relating to any grant under subsection (b) into the program established under this subsection.

(d) Interagency coordination—

(1) In general.—To the maximum extent practicable, the Secretary shall ensure that the activities carried out under this section are coordinated with, and do not duplicate the efforts of, other programs at the Department of Commerce or other Federal agencies.

(2) Collaboration—

(A) In general.—The Secretary shall explore and pursue collaboration with other Federal agencies, including through multiagency funding opportunities, on regional innovation strategies.

(B) Small businesses.—The Secretary shall ensure that such collaboration with Federal agencies prioritizes the needs and challenges of small businesses.

(e) Evaluation—

(1) In general.—Not later than 3 years after December 16, the Secretary shall enter into a contract with an independent entity, such as the National Academy of Sciences, to conduct an evaluation of the program established under subsection (a).

(2) Requirements.—The evaluation shall include—

(A) whether the program is achieving its goals;

(B) any recommendations for how the program may be improved; and

(C) a recommendation as to whether the program should be continued or terminated.

(f) Definitions.—In this section:

(1) Regional innovation cluster.—The term "regional innovation cluster" means a geographically bounded network of similar, synergistic, or complementary entities that—

(A) are engaged in or with a particular industry sector and its related sectors;

(B) have active channels for business transactions and communication;

(C) share specialized infrastructure, labor markets, and services; and

(D) leverage the region's unique competitive strengths to stimulate innovation and create jobs.

(2) State.—The term "State" means one of the several States, the District of Columbia, the Commonwealth of Puerto Rico, the Virgin Islands, Guam, American Samoa, the Commonwealth of the Northern Mariana Islands, or any other territory or possession of the United States.

(g) Funding—

(1) General rule.—Except as provided in paragraph (2), no funds are authorized to be appropriated by the Revitalize American Manufacturing and Innovation Act of 2014 for carrying out this section.

(2) Authority.—To the extent provided for in advance by appropriations Acts, the Secretary may use not to exceed $10,000,000 for each of the fiscal years 2015 through 2019 to carry out this section from amounts appropriated for economic development assistance programs.

History of 15 U.S.C. §3722: Jan. 4, 2011, P.L. 111-358, §603, 124 Stat. 4030; Dec. 16, 2014, P.L. 113-235, §705, 128 Stat. 2230.

CHAPTER 107. PROTECTION OF INTELLECTUAL PROPERTY RIGHTS

SUBCHAPTER II. CYBERSQUATTING PROTECTION

§8131. CYBERPIRACY PROTECTIONS FOR INDIVIDUALS

(1) In general—

(A) Civil liability.—Any person who registers a domain name that consists of the name of another living person, or a name substantially and confusingly similar thereto, without that person's consent, with the specific intent to profit from such name by selling the domain name for financial gain to that person or any third party, shall be liable in a civil action by such person.

(B) Exception.—A person who in good faith registers a domain name consisting of the name of another living person, or a name substantially and confusingly similar thereto, shall not be liable under this paragraph if such name is used in, affiliated with, or related to a work of authorship protected under title 17, including a work made for hire as defined in section 101 of title 17, and if the person registering the domain name is the copyright owner or licensee of the work, the person intends to sell the domain name in conjunction with the lawful exploitation of the work, and such registration is not prohibited by a contract between the registrant and the named person. The exception under this subparagraph shall apply only to a civil action brought under paragraph (1) and shall in no manner limit the protections afforded under the Trademark Act of 1946 (15 U.S.C. §1051 et seq.) or other provision of Federal or State law.

(2) Remedies.—In any civil action brought under paragraph (1), a court may award injunctive relief, including the forfeiture or cancellation of the domain name or the transfer of the domain name to the plaintiff. The court may also, in its discretion, award costs and attorneys fees to the prevailing party.

(3) Definition.—In this section, the term "domain name" has the meaning given that term in section 45 of the Trademark Act of 1946 (15 U.S.C. §1127).

(4) Effective date.—This section shall apply to domain names registered on or after November 29, 1999.

History of 15 U.S.C. §8131: Nov. 29, 1999, P.L. 106-113, §3002(b), 113 Stat. 1536. Transferred from 15 U.S.C. §1129.

TITLE 18. CRIMES & CRIMINAL PROCEDURE

PART I. CRIMES

CHAPTER 90. PROTECTION OF TRADE SECRETS

§1831. ECONOMIC ESPIONAGE

(a) In general.—Whoever, intending or knowing that the offense will benefit any foreign government, foreign instrumentality, or foreign agent, knowingly—

(1) steals, or without authorization appropriates, takes, carries away, or conceals, or by fraud, artifice, or deception obtains a trade secret;

(2) without authorization copies, duplicates, sketches, draws, photographs, downloads, uploads, alters, destroys, photocopies, replicates, transmits, delivers, sends, mails, communicates, or conveys a trade secret;

(3) receives, buys, or possesses a trade secret, knowing the same to have been stolen or appropriated, obtained, or converted without authorization;

(4) attempts to commit any offense described in any of paragraphs (1) through (3); or

(5) conspires with one or more other persons to commit any offense described in any of paragraphs (1) through (3), and one or more of such persons do any act to effect the object of the conspiracy,

shall, except as provided in subsection (b), be fined not more than $5,000,000 or imprisoned not more than 15 years, or both.

(b) Organizations.—Any organization that commits any offense described in subsection (a) shall be fined not more than the greater of $10,000,000 or 3 times the value of the stolen trade secret to the organization, including expenses for research and design and other costs of reproducing the trade secret that the organization has thereby avoided.

History of 18 U.S.C. §1831: Oct. 11, 1996, P.L. 104-294, §101(a), 110 Stat. 3488; Jan. 14, 2013, P.L. 112-269, §2, 126 Stat. 2442.

§1832. THEFT OF TRADE SECRETS

(a) Whoever, with intent to convert a trade secret, that is related to a product or service used in or intended for use in interstate or foreign commerce, to the economic benefit of anyone other than the owner thereof, and intending or knowing that the offense will, injure any owner of that trade secret, knowingly—

(1) steals, or without authorization appropriates, takes, carries away, or conceals, or by fraud, artifice, or deception obtains such information;

(2) without authorization copies, duplicates, sketches, draws, photographs, downloads, uploads, alters, destroys, photocopies, replicates, transmits, delivers, sends, mails, communicates, or conveys such information;

(3) receives, buys, or possesses such information, knowing the same to have been stolen or appropriated, obtained, or converted without authorization;

(4) attempts to commit any offense described in paragraphs (1) through (3); or

(5) conspires with one or more other persons to commit any offense described in paragraphs (1) through (3), and one or more of such persons do any act to effect the object of the conspiracy,

shall, except as provided in subsection (b), be fined under this title or imprisoned not more than 10 years, or both.

(b) Any organization that commits any offense described in subsection (a) shall be fined not more than the greater of $5,000,000 or 3 times the value of the stolen trade secret to the organization, including expenses for research and design and other costs of reproducing the trade secret that the organization has thereby avoided.

History of 18 U.S.C. §1832: Oct. 11, 1996, P.L. 104-294, §101(a), 110 Stat. 3489; Dec. 28, 2012, P.L. 112-236, §2, 126 Stat. 1627; May 11, 2016, P.L. 114-153, §3(a)(1), 130 Stat. 382.

§1833. EXCEPTIONS TO PROHIBITIONS

(a) In general.—This chapter does not prohibit or create a private right of action for—

(1) any otherwise lawful activity conducted by a governmental entity of the United States, a State, or a political subdivision of a State; or

(2) the disclosure of a trade secret in accordance with subsection (b).

(b) Immunity from liability for confidential disclosure of a trade secret to the Government or in a court filing—

(1) Immunity.—An individual shall not be held criminally or civilly liable under any Federal or State trade secret law for the disclosure of a trade secret that—

(A) is made—

(i) in confidence to a Federal, State, or local government official, either directly or indirectly, or to an attorney; and

(ii) solely for the purpose of reporting or investigating a suspected violation of law; or

(B) is made in a complaint or other document filed in a lawsuit or other proceeding, if such filing is made under seal.

(2) Use of trade secret information in anti-retaliation lawsuit.—An individual who files a lawsuit for retaliation by an employer for reporting a suspected violation of law may disclose the trade secret to the attorney of the individual and use the trade secret information in the court proceeding, if the individual—

(A) files any document containing the trade secret under seal; and

(B) does not disclose the trade secret, except pursuant to court order.

(3) Notice—

(A) In general.—An employer shall provide notice of the immunity set forth in this subsection in any contract or agreement with an employee that governs the use of a trade secret or other confidential information.

(B) Policy document.—An employer shall be considered to be in compliance with the notice requirement in subparagraph (A) if the employer provides a cross-reference to a policy document provided to the employee that sets forth the employer's reporting policy for a suspected violation of law.

(C) Non-compliance.—If an employer does not comply with the notice requirement in subparagraph (A), the employer may not be awarded exemplary damages or attorney fees under subparagraph (C) or (D) of section 1836(b)(3) in an action against an employee to whom notice was not provided.

(D) Applicability.—This paragraph shall apply to contracts and agreements that are entered into or updated after the date of enactment of this subsection.

(4) Employee defined.—For purposes of this subsection, the term "employee" includes any individual performing work as a contractor or consultant for an employer.

(5) Rule of construction.—Except as expressly provided for under this subsection, nothing in this subsection shall be construed to authorize, or limit liability for, an act that is otherwise prohibited by law, such as the unlawful access of material by unauthorized means.

History of 18 U.S.C. §1833: Oct. 11, 1996, P.L. 104-294, §101(a), 110 Stat. 3489; May 11, 2016, P.L. 114-153, §§2(c), 7(a), 130 Stat. 381, 384.

§1834. CRIMINAL FORFEITURE

Forfeiture, destruction, and restitution relating to this chapter shall be subject to section 2323, to the extent provided in that section, in addition to any other similar remedies provided by law.

History of 18 U.S.C. §1834: Oct. 11, 1996, P.L. 104-294, §101(a), 110 Stat. 3489; Oct. 13, 2008, P.L. 110-403, §207, 122 Stat. 4263.

§1835. ORDERS TO PRESERVE CONFIDENTIALITY

(a) In general.—In any prosecution or other proceeding under this chapter, the court shall enter such orders and take such other action as may be necessary and appropriate to preserve the confidentiality of trade secrets, consistent with the requirements of the Federal Rules of Criminal and Civil Procedure, the Federal Rules of Evidence, and all other applicable laws. An interlocutory appeal by the United States shall lie from a decision or order of a district court authorizing or directing the disclosure of any trade secret.

(b) Rights of trade secret owners.—The court may not authorize or direct the disclosure of any information the owner asserts to be a trade secret unless the court allows the owner the opportunity to file a submission under seal that describes the interest of the owner in keeping the information confidential. No submission under seal made under this subsection may be used in a prosecution under this chapter for any purpose other than those set forth in this section, or otherwise required by law. The provision of information relating to a trade secret to the United States or the court in connection with a prosecution under this chapter shall not constitute a waiver of trade secret protection, and the disclosure of information relating to a trade secret in connection with a prosecution under this chapter shall not constitute a waiver of trade secret protection unless the trade secret owner expressly consents to such waiver.

History of 18 U.S.C. §1835: Oct. 11, 1996, P.L. 104-294, §101(a), 110 Stat. 3490; May 11, 2016, P.L. 114-153, §3(a)(2), 130 Stat. 382.

§1836. CIVIL PROCEEDINGS

(a) The Attorney General may, in a civil action, obtain appropriate injunctive relief against any violation of this chapter.

(b) Private civil actions—

(1) In general.—An owner of a trade secret that is misappropriated may bring a civil action under this subsection if the trade secret is related to a product or service used in, or intended for use in, interstate or foreign commerce.

(2) Civil seizure—

(A) In general—

(i) Application.—Based on an affidavit or verified complaint satisfying the requirements of this paragraph, the court may, upon ex parte application but only in extraordinary circumstances, issue an order providing for the seizure of property necessary to prevent the propagation or dissemination of the trade secret that is the subject of the action.

(ii) Requirements for issuing order.—The court may not grant an application under clause (i) unless the court finds that it clearly appears from specific facts that—

(I) an order issued pursuant to Rule 65 of the Federal Rules of Civil Procedure or another form of equitable relief would be inadequate to achieve the purpose of this paragraph because the party to which the order would be issued would evade, avoid, or otherwise not comply with such an order;

(II) an immediate and irreparable injury will occur if such seizure is not ordered;

(III) the harm to the applicant of denying the application outweighs the harm to the legitimate interests of the person against whom seizure would be ordered of granting the application and substantially outweighs the harm to any third parties who may be harmed by such seizure;

(IV) the applicant is likely to succeed in showing that—

(aa) the information is a trade secret; and

(bb) the person against whom seizure would be ordered—

(AA) misappropriated the trade secret of the applicant by improper means; or

(BB) conspired to use improper means to misappropriate the trade secret of the applicant;

(V) the person against whom seizure would be ordered has actual possession of—

(aa) the trade secret; and

(bb) any property to be seized;

(VI) the application describes with reasonable particularity the matter to be seized and, to the extent reasonable under the circumstances, identifies the location where the matter is to be seized;

(VII) the person against whom seizure would be ordered, or persons acting in concert with such person, would destroy, move, hide, or otherwise make such matter inaccessible to the court, if the applicant were to proceed on notice to such person; and

(VIII) the applicant has not publicized the requested seizure.

(B) Elements of order.—If an order is issued under subparagraph (A), it shall—

(i) set forth findings of fact and conclusions of law required for the order;

(ii) provide for the narrowest seizure of property necessary to achieve the purpose of this paragraph and direct that the seizure be conducted in a manner that minimizes any interruption of the business operations of third parties and, to the extent possible, does not interrupt the legitimate business operations of the person accused of misappropriating the trade secret;

(iii)(I) be accompanied by an order protecting the seized property from disclosure by prohibiting access by the applicant or the person against whom the order is directed, and prohibiting any copies, in whole or in part, of the seized property, to prevent undue damage to the party against whom the order has issued or others, until such parties have an opportunity to be heard in court; and

(II) provide that if access is granted by the court to the applicant or the person against whom the order is directed, the access shall be consistent with subparagraph (D);

(iv) provide guidance to the law enforcement officials executing the seizure that clearly delineates the scope of the authority of the officials, including—

(I) the hours during which the seizure may be executed; and

(II) whether force may be used to access locked areas;

(v) set a date for a hearing described in subparagraph (F) at the earliest possible time, and not later than 7 days after the order has issued, unless the party against whom the order is directed and others harmed by the order consent to another date for the hearing, except that a party against whom the order has issued or any person harmed by the order may move the court at any time to dissolve or modify the order after giving notice to the applicant who obtained the order; and

(vi) require the person obtaining the order to provide the security determined adequate by the court for the payment of the damages that any person may be entitled to recover as a result of a wrongful or excessive seizure or wrongful or excessive attempted seizure under this paragraph.

(C) Protection from publicity.—The court shall take appropriate action to protect the person against whom an order under this paragraph is directed from publicity, by or at the behest of the person obtaining the order, about such order and any seizure under such order.

(D) Materials in custody of court—

(i) In general.—Any materials seized under this paragraph shall be taken into the custody of the court. The court shall secure the seized material from physical and electronic access during the seizure and while in the custody of the court.

(ii) Storage medium.—If the seized material includes a storage medium, or if the seized material is stored on a storage medium, the court shall prohibit the medium from being connected to a network or the Internet without the consent of both parties, until the hearing required under subparagraph (B)(v) and described in subparagraph (F).

(iii) Protection of confidentiality.—The court shall take appropriate measures to protect the confidentiality of seized materials that are unrelated to the trade secret information ordered seized pursuant to this paragraph unless the person against whom the order is entered consents to disclosure of the material.

(iv) Appointment of special master.—The court may appoint a special master to locate and isolate all misappropriated trade secret information and to facilitate the return of unrelated property and data to the person from whom the property was seized. The special master appointed by the court shall agree to be bound by a non-disclosure agreement approved by the court.

(E) Service of order.—The court shall order that service of a copy of the order under this paragraph, and the submissions of the applicant to obtain the order, shall be made by a Federal law enforcement officer who, upon making service, shall carry out the seizure under the order. The court may allow State or local law enforcement officials to participate, but may not permit the applicant or any agent of the applicant to participate in the seizure. At the request of law enforcement officials, the court may allow a technical expert who is unaffiliated with the applicant and who is bound by a court-approved non-disclosure agreement to participate in the seizure if the court determines that the participation of the expert will aid the efficient execution of and minimize the burden of the seizure.

(F) Seizure hearing—

(i) Date.—A court that issues a seizure order shall hold a hearing on the date set by the court under subparagraph (B)(v).

(ii) Burden of proof.—At a hearing held under this subparagraph, the party who obtained the order under subparagraph (A) shall have the burden to prove the facts supporting the findings of fact and conclusions of law necessary to support the order. If the party fails to meet that burden, the seizure order shall be dissolved or modified appropriately.

(iii) Dissolution or modification of order.—A party against whom the order has been issued or any person harmed by the order may move the court at any time to dissolve or modify the order after giving notice to the party who obtained the order.

(iv) Discovery time limits.—The court may make such orders modifying the time limits for discovery under the Federal Rules of Civil Procedure as may be necessary to prevent the frustration of the purposes of a hearing under this subparagraph.

(G) Action for damage caused by wrongful seizure.—A person who suffers damage by reason of a wrongful or excessive seizure under this paragraph has a cause of action against the applicant for the order under which such seizure was made, and shall be entitled to the same relief as is provided under section 34(d)(11) of the Trademark Act of 1946 (15 U.S.C. 1116(d)(11)). The security posted with the court under subparagraph (B)(vi) shall not limit the recovery of third parties for damages.

(H) Motion for encryption.—A party or a person who claims to have an interest in the subject matter seized may make a motion at any time, which may be heard ex parte, to encrypt any material seized or to be seized under this paragraph that is stored on a storage medium. The motion shall include, when possible, the desired encryption method.

(3) Remedies.—In a civil action brought under this subsection with respect to the misappropriation of a trade secret, a court may—

(A) grant an injunction—

(i) to prevent any actual or threatened misappropriation described in paragraph (1) on such terms as the court deems reasonable, provided the order does not—

(I) prevent a person from entering into an employment relationship, and that conditions placed on such employment shall be based on evidence of threatened misappropriation and not merely on the information the person knows; or

(II) otherwise conflict with an applicable State law prohibiting restraints on the practice of a lawful profession, trade, or business;

(ii) if determined appropriate by the court, requiring affirmative actions to be taken to protect the trade secret; and

(iii) in exceptional circumstances that render an injunction inequitable, that conditions future use of the trade secret upon payment of a reasonable royalty for no longer than the period of time for which such use could have been prohibited;

(B) award—

(i)(I) damages for actual loss caused by the misappropriation of the trade secret; and

(II) damages for any unjust enrichment caused by the misappropriation of the trade secret that is not addressed in computing damages for actual loss; or

(ii) in lieu of damages measured by any other methods, the damages caused by the misappropriation measured by imposition of liability for a reasonable royalty for the misappropriator's unauthorized disclosure or use of the trade secret;

(C) if the trade secret is willfully and maliciously misappropriated, award exemplary damages in an amount not more than 2 times the amount of the damages awarded under subparagraph (B); and

(D) if a claim of the misappropriation is made in bad faith, which may be established by circumstantial evidence, a motion to terminate an injunction is made or opposed in bad faith, or the trade secret was willfully and maliciously misappropriated, award reasonable attorney's fees to the prevailing party.

(c) Jurisdiction.—The district courts of the United States shall have original jurisdiction of civil actions brought under this section.

(d) Period of limitations.—A civil action under subsection (b) may not be commenced later than 3 years after the date on which the misappropriation with respect to which the action would relate is discovered or by the exercise of reasonable diligence should have been discovered. For purposes of this subsection, a continuing misappropriation constitutes a single claim of misappropriation.

History of 18 U.S.C. §1836: Oct. 11, 1996, P.L. 104-294, §101(a), 110 Stat. 3490; Nov. 2, 2002, P.L. 107-273, §4002(e)(9), 116 Stat. 1810; May 11, 2016, P.L. 114-153, §2(a), (d)(1), 130 Stat. 376, 381.

§1837. APPLICABILITY TO CONDUCT OUTSIDE THE UNITED STATES

This chapter also applies to conduct occurring outside the United States if—

(1) the offender is a natural person who is a citizen or permanent resident alien of the United States, or an organization organized under the laws of the United States or a State or political subdivision thereof; or

(2) an act in furtherance of the offense was committed in the United States.

History of 18 U.S.C. §1837: Oct. 11, 1996, P.L. 104-294, §101(a), 110 Stat. 3490.

§1838. CONSTRUCTION WITH OTHER LAWS

Except as provided in section 1833(b), this chapter shall not be construed to preempt or displace any other remedies, whether civil or criminal, provided by United

States Federal, State, commonwealth, possession, or territory law for the misappropriation of a trade secret, or to affect the otherwise lawful disclosure of information by any Government employee under section 552 of title 5 (commonly known as the Freedom of Information Act).

History of 18 U.S.C. §1838: Oct. 11, 1996, P.L. 104-294, §101(a), 110 Stat. 3490; May 11, 2016, P.L. 114-153, §7(b), 130 Stat. 385.

§1839. DEFINITIONS

As used in this chapter—

(1) the term "foreign instrumentality" means any agency, bureau, ministry, component, institution, association, or any legal, commercial, or business organization, corporation, firm, or entity that is substantially owned, controlled, sponsored, commanded, managed, or dominated by a foreign government;

(2) the term "foreign agent" means any officer, employee, proxy, servant, delegate, or representative of a foreign government;

(3) the term "trade secret" means all forms and types of financial, business, scientific, technical, economic, or engineering information, including patterns, plans, compilations, program devices, formulas, designs, prototypes, methods, techniques, processes, procedures, programs, or codes, whether tangible or intangible, and whether or how stored, compiled, or memorialized physically, electronically, graphically, photographically, or in writing if—

(A) the owner thereof has taken reasonable measures to keep such information secret; and

(B) the information derives independent economic value, actual or potential, from not being generally known to, and not being readily ascertainable through proper means by, another person who can obtain economic value from the disclosure or use of the information;

(4) the term "owner," with respect to a trade secret, means the person or entity in whom or in which rightful legal or equitable title to, or license in, the trade secret is reposed;

(5) the term "misappropriation" means—

(A) acquisition of a trade secret of another by a person who knows or has reason to know that the trade secret was acquired by improper means; or

(B) disclosure or use of a trade secret of another without express or implied consent by a person who—

(i) used improper means to acquire knowledge of the trade secret;

(ii) at the time of disclosure or use, knew or had reason to know that the knowledge of the trade secret was—

(I) derived from or through a person who had used improper means to acquire the trade secret;

(II) acquired under circumstances giving rise to a duty to maintain the secrecy of the trade secret or limit the use of the trade secret; or

(III) derived from or through a person who owed a duty to the person seeking relief to maintain the secrecy of the trade secret or limit the use of the trade secret; or

(iii) before a material change of the position of the person, knew or had reason to know that—

(I) the trade secret was a trade secret; and

(II) knowledge of the trade secret had been acquired by accident or mistake;

(6) the term "improper means"—

(A) includes theft, bribery, misrepresentation, breach or inducement of a breach of a duty to maintain secrecy, or espionage through electronic or other means; and

(B) does not include reverse engineering, independent derivation, or any other lawful means of acquisition; and

(7) the term "Trademark Act of 1946" means the Act entitled "An Act to provide for the registration and protection of trademarks used in commerce, to carry out the provisions of certain international conventions, and for other purposes, approved July 5, 1946 (15 U.S.C. 1051 et seq.) (commonly referred to as the 'Trademark Act of 1946' or the 'Lanham Act')".[1]

1. **Editor's note:** The closing quotation marks probably should follow "purposes" instead of "'Lanham Act')."

History of 18 U.S.C. §1839: Oct. 11, 1996, P.L. 104-294, §101(a), 110 Stat. 3490; May 11, 2016, P.L. 114-153, §2(b), 130 Stat. 380.

CHAPTER 113. STOLEN PROPERTY

§2318. TRAFFICKING IN COUNTERFEIT LABELS, ILLICIT LABELS, OR COUNTERFEIT DOCUMENTATION OR PACKAGING

(a)(1)[1] Whoever, in any of the circumstances described in subsection (c), knowingly traffics in—

(A) a counterfeit label or illicit label affixed to, enclosing, or accompanying, or designed to be affixed to, enclose, or accompany—

(i) a phonorecord;

(ii) a copy of a computer program;

(iii) a copy of a motion picture or other audiovisual work;

(iv) a copy of a literary work;

(v) a copy of a pictorial, graphic, or sculptural work;

(vi) a work of visual art; or

(vii) documentation or packaging; or

(B) counterfeit documentation or packaging,

shall be fined under this title or imprisoned for not more than 5 years, or both.

(b) As used in this section—

(1) the term "counterfeit label" means an identifying label or container that appears to be genuine, but is not;

(2) the term "traffic" has the same meaning as in section 2320(f) of this title;

(3) the terms "copy," "phonorecord," "motion picture," "computer program," "audiovisual work," "literary work," "pictorial, graphic, or sculptural work," "sound recording," "work of visual art," and "copyright owner" have, respectively, the meanings given those terms in section 101 (relating to definitions) of title 17;

(4) the term "illicit label" means a genuine certificate, licensing document, registration card, or similar labeling component—

(A) that is used by the copyright owner to verify that a phonorecord, a copy of a computer program, a copy of a motion picture or other audiovisual work, a copy of a literary work, a copy of a pictorial, graphic, or sculptural work, a work of visual art, or documentation or packaging is not counterfeit or infringing of any copyright; and

(B) that is, without the authorization of the copyright owner—

(i) distributed or intended for distribution not in connection with the copy, phonorecord, or work of visual art to which such labeling component was intended to be affixed by the respective copyright owner; or

(ii) in connection with a genuine certificate or licensing document, knowingly falsified in order to designate a higher number of licensed users or copies than authorized by the copyright owner, unless that certificate or document is used by the copyright owner solely for the purpose of monitoring or tracking the copyright owner's distribution channel and not for the purpose of verifying that a copy or phonorecord is noninfringing;

(5) the term "documentation or packaging" means documentation or packaging, in physical form, for a phonorecord, copy of a computer program, copy of a motion picture or other audiovisual work, copy of a literary work, copy of a pictorial, graphic, or sculptural work, or work of visual art; and

(6) the term "counterfeit documentation or packaging" means documentation or packaging that appears to be genuine, but is not.

(c) The circumstances referred to in subsection (a) of this section are—

(1) the offense is committed within the special maritime and territorial jurisdiction of the United States; or within the special aircraft jurisdiction of the United States (as defined in section 46501 of title 49);

(2) the mail or a facility of interstate or foreign commerce is used or intended to be used in the commission of the offense;

(3) the counterfeit label or illicit label is affixed to, encloses, or accompanies, or is designed to be affixed to, enclose, or accompany—

(A) a phonorecord of a copyrighted sound recording or copyrighted musical work;

(B) a copy of a copyrighted computer program;

(C) a copy of a copyrighted motion picture or other audiovisual work;

(D) a copy of a literary work;

(E) a copy of a pictorial, graphic, or sculptural work;

(F) a work of visual art; or

(G) copyrighted documentation or packaging; or

(4) the counterfeited documentation or packaging is copyrighted.

(d) Forfeiture and destruction of property; restitution.—Forfeiture, destruction, and restitution relating to this section shall be subject to section 2323, to the extent provided in that section, in addition to any other similar remedies provided by law.

(e) Civil remedies—

(1) In general.—Any copyright owner who is injured, or is threatened with injury, by a violation of subsection (a) may bring a civil action in an appropriate United States district court.

(2) Discretion of court.—In any action brought under paragraph (1), the court—

(A) may grant 1 or more temporary or permanent injunctions on such terms as the court determines to be reasonable to prevent or restrain a violation of subsection (a);

(B) at any time while the action is pending, may order the impounding, on such terms as the court determines to be reasonable, of any article that is in the custody or control of the alleged violator and that the court has reasonable cause to believe was involved in a violation of subsection (a); and

(C) may award to the injured party—

(i) reasonable attorney fees and costs; and

(ii)(I) actual damages and any additional profits of the violator, as provided in paragraph (3); or

(II) statutory damages, as provided in paragraph (4).

(3) Actual damages and profits—

(A) In general.—The injured party is entitled to recover—

(i) the actual damages suffered by the injured party as a result of a violation of subsection (a), as provided in subparagraph (B) of this paragraph; and

(ii) any profits of the violator that are attributable to a violation of subsection (a) and are not taken into account in computing the actual damages.

(B) Calculation of damages.—The court shall calculate actual damages by multiplying—

(i) the value of the phonorecords, copies, or works of visual art which are, or are intended to be, affixed with, enclosed in, or accompanied by any counterfeit labels, illicit labels, or counterfeit documentation or packaging, by

(ii) the number of phonorecords, copies, or works of visual art which are, or are intended to be, affixed with, enclosed in, or accompanied by any counterfeit labels, illicit labels, or counterfeit documentation or packaging.

(C) Definition.—For purposes of this paragraph, the "value" of a phonorecord, copy, or work of visual art is—

(i) in the case of a copyrighted sound recording or copyrighted musical work, the retail value of an authorized phonorecord of that sound recording or musical work;

(ii) in the case of a copyrighted computer program, the retail value of an authorized copy of that computer program;

(iii) in the case of a copyrighted motion picture or other audiovisual work, the retail value of an authorized copy of that motion picture or audiovisual work;

(iv) in the case of a copyrighted literary work, the retail value of an authorized copy of that literary work;

(v) in the case of a pictorial, graphic, or sculptural work, the retail value of an authorized copy of that work; and

(vi) in the case of a work of visual art, the retail value of that work.

(4) Statutory damages.—The injured party may elect, at any time before final judgment is rendered, to recover, instead of actual damages and profits, an award of statutory damages for each violation of subsection (a) in a sum of not less than $2,500 or more than $25,000, as the court considers appropriate.

(5) Subsequent violation.—The court may increase an award of damages under this subsection by 3 times the amount that would otherwise be awarded, as the court considers appropriate, if the court finds that a person has subsequently violated subsection (a) within 3 years after a final judgment was entered against that person for a violation of that subsection.

(6) Limitation on actions.—A civil action may not be commenced under this subsection unless it is commenced within 3 years after the date on which the claimant discovers the violation of subsection (a).

1. **Editor's note:** So in original. No par. (2) has been enacted.

History of 18 U.S.C. §2318: Oct. 9, 1962, P.L. 87-773, §1, 76 Stat. 775; Dec. 31, 1974, P.L. 93-573, §103, 88 Stat. 1873; Oct. 19, 1976, P.L. 94-553, §111, 90 Stat. 2600; May 24, 1982, P.L. 97-180, §2, 96 Stat. 91; Nov. 29, 1990, P.L. 101-647, §3567, 104 Stat. 4928; July 5, 1994, P.L. 103-272, §5(e)(10), 108 Stat. 1374; Sept. 13, 1994, P.L. 103-322, §330016(1)(U), 108 Stat. 2148; July 2, 1996, P.L. 104-153, §4(a), (b)(1), 110 Stat. 1386, 1387; Dec. 23, 2004, P.L. 108-482, §102(a), (b), 118 Stat. 3912, 3914; Mar. 16, 2006, P.L. 109-181, §3(c)(2), 120 Stat. 288; Oct. 13, 2008, P.L. 110-403, §202, 122 Stat. 4260; Dec. 9, 2010, P.L. 111-295, §6(e), 124 Stat. 3182; May 16, 2016, P.L. 114-154, §3(1), 130 Stat. 387.

§2319. CRIMINAL INFRINGEMENT OF A COPYRIGHT

(a) Any person who violates section 506(a) (relating to criminal offenses) of title 17 shall be punished as provided in subsections (b), (c), and (d) and such penalties shall be in addition to any other provisions of title 17 or any other law.

(b) Any person who commits an offense under section 506(a)(1)(A) of title 17—

(1) shall be imprisoned not more than 5 years, or fined in the amount set forth in this title, or both, if the offense consists of the reproduction or distribution, including by electronic means, during any 180-day period, of at least 10 copies or phonorecords, of 1 or more copyrighted works, which have a total retail value of more than $2,500;

(2) shall be imprisoned not more than 10 years, or fined in the amount set forth in this title, or both, if the offense is a felony and is a second or subsequent offense under subsection (a); and

(3) shall be imprisoned not more than 1 year, or fined in the amount set forth in this title, or both, in any other case.

(c) Any person who commits an offense under section 506(a)(1)(B) of title 17—

(1) shall be imprisoned not more than 3 years, or fined in the amount set forth in this title, or both, if the offense consists of the reproduction or distribution of 10 or more copies or phonorecords of 1 or more copyrighted works, which have a total retail value of $2,500 or more;

(2) shall be imprisoned not more than 6 years, or fined in the amount set forth in this title, or both, if the offense is a felony and is a second or subsequent offense under subsection (a); and

(3) shall be imprisoned not more than 1 year, or fined in the amount set forth in this title, or both, if the offense consists of the reproduction or distribution of 1 or more copies or phonorecords of 1 or more copyrighted works, which have a total retail value of more than $1,000.

(d) Any person who commits an offense under section 506(a)(1)(C) of title 17—

(1) shall be imprisoned not more than 3 years, fined under this title, or both;

(2) shall be imprisoned not more than 5 years, fined under this title, or both, if the offense was committed for purposes of commercial advantage or private financial gain;

(3) shall be imprisoned not more than 6 years, fined under this title, or both, if the offense is a felony and is a second or subsequent offense under subsection (a); and

(4) shall be imprisoned not more than 10 years, fined under this title, or both, if the offense is a felony and is a second or subsequent offense under paragraph (2).

(e)(1) During preparation of the presentence report pursuant to Rule 32(c) of the Federal Rules of Criminal Procedure, victims of the offense shall be permitted to submit, and the probation officer shall receive, a victim impact statement that identifies the victim of the offense and the extent and scope of the injury and loss suffered by the victim, including the estimated economic impact of the offense on that victim.

(2) Persons permitted to submit victim impact statements shall include—

(A) producers and sellers of legitimate works affected by conduct involved in the offense;

(B) holders of intellectual property rights in such works; and

(C) the legal representatives of such producers, sellers, and holders.

(f) As used in this section—

(1) the terms "phonorecord" and "copies" have, respectively, the meanings set forth in section 101 (relating to definitions) of title 17;

(2) the terms "reproduction" and "distribution" refer to the exclusive rights of a copyright owner under clauses (1) and (3) respectively of section 106 (relating to exclusive rights in copyrighted works), as limited by sections 107 through 122, of title 17;

(3) the term "financial gain" has the meaning given the term in section 101 of title 17; and

(4) the term "work being prepared for commercial distribution" has the meaning given the term in section 506(a) of title 17.

History of 18 U.S.C. §2319: May 24, 1982, P.L. 97-180, §3, 96 Stat. 92; Oct. 28, 1992, P.L. 102-561, 106 Stat. 4233; Nov. 13, 1997, P.L. 105-80, §12(b)(2), 111 Stat. 1536; Dec. 16, 1997, P.L. 105-147, §2(d), 111 Stat. 2678; Nov. 2, 2002, P.L. 107-273, §13211(a), 116 Stat. 1910; Apr. 27, 2005, P.L. 109-9, §103(b), 119 Stat. 220; Oct. 13, 2008, P.L. 110-403, §208, 122 Stat. 4263.

§2319A. UNAUTHORIZED FIXATION OF & TRAFFICKING IN SOUND RECORDINGS & MUSIC VIDEOS OF LIVE MUSICAL PERFORMANCES

(a) Offense.—Whoever, without the consent of the performer or performers involved, knowingly and for purposes of commercial advantage or private financial gain—

(1) fixes the sounds or sounds and images of a live musical performance in a copy or phonorecord, or reproduces copies or phonorecords of such a performance from an unauthorized fixation;

(2) transmits or otherwise communicates to the public the sounds or sounds and images of a live musical performance; or

(3) distributes or offers to distribute, sells or offers to sell, rents or offers to rent, or traffics in any copy or phonorecord fixed as described in paragraph (1), regardless of whether the fixations occurred in the United States;

shall be imprisoned for not more than 5 years or fined in the amount set forth in this title, or both, or if the offense is a second or subsequent offense, shall be imprisoned for not more than 10 years or fined in the amount set forth in this title, or both.

(b) Forfeiture and destruction of property; restitution.—Forfeiture, destruction, and restitution relating to this section shall be subject to section 2323, to the extent provided in that section, in addition to any other similar remedies provided by law.

(c) Seizure and forfeiture.—If copies or phonorecords of sounds or sounds and images of a live musical performance are fixed outside of the United States without the consent of the performer or performers involved, such copies or phonorecords are subject to seizure and forfeiture in the United States in the same manner as property imported in violation of the customs laws. The Secretary of Homeland Security shall issue regulations by which any performer may, upon payment of a specified fee, be entitled to notification by United States Customs and Border Protection of the importation of copies or phonorecords that appear to consist of unauthorized fixations of the sounds or sounds and images of a live musical performance.

(d) Victim impact statement—

(1) During preparation of the presentence report pursuant to Rule 32(c) of the Federal Rules of Criminal Procedure, victims of the offense shall be permitted to submit, and the probation officer shall receive, a victim impact statement that identifies the victim of the offense and the extent and scope of the injury and loss suffered by the victim, including the estimated economic impact of the offense on that victim.

(2) Persons permitted to submit victim impact statements shall include—

(A) producers and sellers of legitimate works affected by conduct involved in the offense;

(B) holders of intellectual property rights in such works; and

(C) the legal representatives of such producers, sellers, and holders.

(e) Definitions.—As used in this section—

(1) the terms "copy," "fixed," "musical work," "phonorecord," "reproduce," "sound recordings," and "transmit" mean those terms within the meaning of title 17; and

(2) the term "traffic" has the same meaning as in section 2320(e) of this title.

(f) Applicability.—This section shall apply to any Act or Acts that occur on or after the date of the enactment of the Uruguay Round Agreements Act.

History of 18 U.S.C. §2319A: Dec. 8, 1994, P.L. 103-465, §513(a), 108 Stat. 4974; Dec. 16, 1997, P.L. 105-147, §2(e), 111 Stat. 2679; Mar. 16, 2006, P.L. 109-181, §2(c)(1), 120 Stat. 288; Oct. 13, 2008, P.L. 110-403, §203, 122 Stat. 4261.

§2319B. UNAUTHORIZED RECORDING OF MOTION PICTURES IN A MOTION PICTURE EXHIBITION FACILITY

(a) Offense.—Any person who, without the authorization of the copyright owner, knowingly uses or attempts to use an audiovisual recording device to transmit or make a copy of a motion picture or other audiovisual work protected under title 17, or any part thereof, from a performance of such work in a motion picture exhibition facility, shall—

(1) be imprisoned for not more than 3 years, fined under this title, or both; or

(2) if the offense is a second or subsequent offense, be imprisoned for no more than 6 years, fined under this title, or both.

The possession by a person of an audiovisual recording device in a motion picture exhibition facility may be considered as evidence in any proceeding to determine whether that person committed an offense under this subsection, but shall not, by itself, be sufficient to support a conviction of that person for such offense.

(b) Forfeiture and destruction of property; restitution.—Forfeiture, destruction, and restitution relating to this section shall be subject to section 2323, to the extent provided in that section, in addition to any other similar remedies provided by law.

(c) Authorized activities.—This section does not prevent any lawfully authorized investigative, protective, or intelligence activity by an officer, agent, or employee of the United States, a State, or a political subdivision of a State, or by a person acting under a contract with the United States, a State, or a political subdivision of a State.

(d) Immunity for theaters.—With reasonable cause, the owner or lessee of a motion picture exhibition facility where a motion picture or other audiovisual work is being exhibited, the authorized agent or employee of such owner or lessee, the licensor of the motion picture or other audiovisual work being exhibited, or the agent or employee of such licensor—

(1) may detain, in a reasonable manner and for a reasonable time, any person suspected of a violation of this section with respect to that motion picture or audiovisual work for the purpose of questioning or summoning a law enforcement officer; and

(2) shall not be held liable in any civil or criminal action arising out of a detention under paragraph (1).

(e) Victim impact statement—

(1) In general.—During the preparation of the presentence report under rule 32(c) of the Federal Rules of Criminal Procedure, victims of an offense under this section shall be permitted to submit to the probation officer a victim impact statement that identifies the victim of the offense and the extent and scope of the injury and loss suffered by the victim, including the estimated economic impact of the offense on that victim.

(2) Contents.—A victim impact statement submitted under this subsection shall include—

(A) producers and sellers of legitimate works affected by conduct involved in the offense;

(B) holders of intellectual property rights in the works described in subparagraph (A); and

(C) the legal representatives of such producers, sellers, and holders.

(f) State law not preempted.—Nothing in this section may be construed to annul or limit any rights or remedies under the laws of any State.

(g) Definitions.—In this section, the following definitions shall apply:

(1) Title 17 definitions.—The terms "audiovisual work," "copy," "copyright owner," "motion picture," "motion picture exhibition facility," and "transmit" have, respectively, the meanings given those terms in section 101 of title 17.

(2) Audiovisual recording device.—The term "audiovisual recording device" means a digital or analog photographic or video camera, or any other technology or device capable of enabling the recording or transmission of a copyrighted motion picture or other audiovisual work, or any part thereof, regardless of whether audiovisual recording is the sole or primary purpose of the device.

History of 18 U.S.C. §2319B: Apr. 27, 2005, P.L. 109-9, §102(a), 119 Stat. 218; Oct. 13, 2008, P.L. 110-403, §204, 122 Stat. 4261.

§2320. TRAFFICKING IN COUNTERFEIT GOODS OR SERVICES

(a) Offenses.—Whoever intentionally—

(1) traffics in goods or services and knowingly uses a counterfeit mark on or in connection with such goods or services,

(2) traffics in labels, patches, stickers, wrappers, badges, emblems, medallions, charms, boxes, containers, cans, cases, hangtags, documentation, or packaging of any type or nature, knowing that a counterfeit mark has been applied thereto, the use of which is likely to cause confusion, to cause mistake, or to deceive,

(3) traffics in goods or services knowing that such good or service is a counterfeit military good or service the use, malfunction, or failure of which is likely to cause serious bodily injury or death, the disclosure of classified information, impairment of combat operations, or other significant harm to a combat operation, a member of the Armed Forces, or to national security, or

(4) traffics in a drug and knowingly uses a counterfeit mark on or in connection with such drug,

or attempts or conspires to violate any of paragraphs (1) through (4) shall be punished as provided in subsection (b).

(b) Penalties—

(1) In general.—Whoever commits an offense under subsection (a)—

(A) if an individual, shall be fined not more than $2,000,000 or imprisoned not more than 10 years, or both, and, if a person other than an individual, shall be fined not more than $5,000,000; and

(B) for a second or subsequent offense under subsection (a), if an individual, shall be fined not more than $5,000,000 or imprisoned not more than 20 years, or both, and if other than an individual, shall be fined not more than $15,000,000.

(2) Serious bodily injury or death—

(A) Serious bodily injury.—Whoever knowingly or recklessly causes or attempts to cause serious bodily injury from conduct in violation of subsection (a), if an individual, shall be fined not more than $5,000,000 or imprisoned for not more than 20 years, or both, and if other than an individual, shall be fined not more than $15,000,000.

(B) Death.—Whoever knowingly or recklessly causes or attempts to cause death from conduct in violation of subsection (a), if an individual, shall be fined not more than $5,000,000 or imprisoned for any term of years or for life, or both, and if other than an individual, shall be fined not more than $15,000,000.

(3) Counterfeit military goods or services and counterfeit drugs.—Whoever commits an offense under subsection (a) involving a counterfeit military good or service or drug that uses a counterfeit mark on or in connection with the drug—

(A) if an individual, shall be fined not more than $5,000,000, imprisoned not more than 20 years, or both, and if other than an individual, be fined not more than $15,000,000; and

(B) for a second or subsequent offense, if an individual, shall be fined not more than $15,000,000, imprisoned not more than 30 years, or both, and if other than an individual, shall be fined not more than $30,000,000.

(c) Forfeiture and destruction of property; restitution.—Forfeiture, destruction, and restitution relating to this section shall be subject to section 2323, to the extent provided in that section, in addition to any other similar remedies provided by law.

(d) Defenses.—All defenses, affirmative defenses, and limitations on remedies that would be applicable in an action under the Lanham Act shall be applicable in a prosecution under this section. In a prosecution under this section, the defendant shall have the burden of proof, by a preponderance of the evidence, of any such affirmative defense.

(e) Presentence report—

(1) During preparation of the presentence report pursuant to Rule 32(c) of the Federal Rules of Criminal Procedure, victims of the offense shall be permitted to submit, and the probation officer shall receive, a victim impact statement that identifies the victim of the offense and the extent and scope of the injury and loss suffered by the victim, including the estimated economic impact of the offense on that victim.

(2) Persons permitted to submit victim impact statements shall include—

(A) producers and sellers of legitimate goods or services affected by conduct involved in the offense;

(B) holders of intellectual property rights in such goods or services; and

(C) the legal representatives of such producers, sellers, and holders.

(f) Definitions.—For the purposes of this section—

(1) the term "counterfeit mark" means—

(A) a spurious mark—

(i) that is used in connection with trafficking in any goods, services, labels, patches, stickers, wrappers, badges, emblems, medallions, charms, boxes, containers, cans, cases, hangtags, documentation, or packaging of any type or nature;

(ii) that is identical with, or substantially indistinguishable from, a mark registered on the principal register in the United States Patent and Trademark Office and in use, whether or not the defendant knew such mark was so registered;

(iii) that is applied to or used in connection with the goods or services for which the mark is registered with the United States Patent and Trademark Office, or is applied to or consists of a label, patch, sticker, wrapper, badge, emblem, medallion, charm, box, container, can, case, hangtag, documentation, or packaging of any type or nature that is designed, marketed, or otherwise intended to be used on or in connection with the goods or services for which the mark is registered in the United States Patent and Trademark Office; and

(iv) the use of which is likely to cause confusion, to cause mistake, or to deceive; or

(B) a spurious designation that is identical with, or substantially indistinguishable from, a designation as to which the remedies of the Lanham Act are made available by reason of section 220506 of title 36;

but such term does not include any mark or designation used in connection with goods or services, or a mark or designation applied to labels, patches, stickers, wrappers, badges, emblems, medallions, charms, boxes, containers, cans, cases, hangtags, documentation, or packaging of any type or nature used in connection with such goods or services, of which the manufacturer or producer was, at the time of the manufacture or production in question, authorized to use the mark or designation for the type of goods or services so manufactured or produced, by the holder of the right to use such mark or designation;

(2) the term "financial gain" includes the receipt, or expected receipt, of anything of value;

(3) the term "Lanham Act" means the Act entitled "An Act to provide for the registration and protection of trademarks used in commerce, to carry out the provisions of certain international conventions, and for other purposes", approved July 5, 1946 (15 U.S.C. 1051 et seq.);

(4) the term "counterfeit military good or service" means a good or service that uses a counterfeit mark on or in connection with such good or service and that—

(A) is falsely identified or labeled as meeting military specifications, or

(B) is intended for use in a military or national security application;

(5) the term "traffic" means to transport, transfer, or otherwise dispose of, to another, for purposes of commercial advantage or private financial gain, or to make, import, export, obtain control of, or possess, with intent to so transport, transfer, or otherwise dispose of; and

(6) the term "drug" means a drug, as defined in section 201 of the Federal Food, Drug, and Cosmetic Act (21 U.S.C. 321).

(g) Limitation on cause of action.—Nothing in this section shall entitle the United States to bring a criminal cause of action under this section for the repackaging of genuine goods or services not intended to deceive or confuse.

(h) Report to Congress—

(1) Beginning with the first year after the date of enactment of this subsection, the Attorney General shall include in the report of the Attorney General to Congress on the business of the Department of Justice prepared pursuant to section 522 of title 28, an accounting, on a district by district basis, of the following with respect to all actions taken by the Department of Justice that involve trafficking in counterfeit labels for phonorecords, copies of computer programs or computer program documentation or packaging, copies of motion pictures or other audiovisual works (as defined in section 2318 of this title), criminal infringement of copyrights (as defined in section 2319 of this title), unauthorized fixation of and trafficking in sound recordings and music videos of live musical performances (as defined in section 2319A of this title), or trafficking in goods or services bearing counterfeit marks (as defined in section 2320 of this title):

(A) The number of open investigations.

(B) The number of cases referred by the United States Customs Service.

(C) The number of cases referred by other agencies or sources.

(D) The number and outcome, including settlements, sentences, recoveries, and penalties, of all prosecutions brought under sections 2318, 2319, 2319A, and 2320 of title 18.

(2)(A) The report under paragraph (1), with respect to criminal infringement of copyright, shall include the following:

(i) The number of infringement cases in these categories: audiovisual (videos and films); audio (sound recordings); literary works (books and musical compositions); computer programs; video games; and, others.

(ii) The number of online infringement cases.

(iii) The number and dollar amounts of fines assessed in specific categories of dollar amounts. These categories shall be: no fines ordered; fines under $500; fines from $500 to $1,000; fines from $1,000 to $5,000; fines from $5,000 to $10,000; and fines over $10,000.

(iv) The total amount of restitution ordered in all copyright infringement cases.

(B) In this paragraph, the term "online infringement cases" as used in paragraph (2) means those cases where the infringer—

(i) advertised or publicized the infringing work on the Internet; or

(ii) made the infringing work available on the Internet for download, reproduction, performance, or distribution by other persons.

(C) The information required under subparagraph (A) shall be submitted in the report required in fiscal year 2005 and thereafter.

(i) Transshipment and exportation.—No goods or services, the trafficking in of which is prohibited by this section, shall be transshipped through or exported from the United States. Any such transshipment or exportation shall be deemed a violation of section 42 of an Act to provide for the registration of trademarks used in commerce, to carry out the provisions of certain international conventions, and for other purposes, approved July 5, 1946 (commonly referred to as the "Trademark Act of 1946" or the "Lanham Act").

History of 18 U.S.C. §2320: Oct. 12, 1984, P.L. 98-473, §1502(a), 98 Stat. 2178; Sept. 13, 1994, P.L. 103-322, §§320104(a), 330016(1)(U), 108 Stat. 2110, 2148; July 2, 1996, P.L. 104-153, §5, 110 Stat. 1387; Dec. 16, 1997, P.L. 105-147, §2(f), 111 Stat. 2679; Aug. 12, 1998, P.L. 105-225, §4(b), 112 Stat. 1499; Nov. 3, 1998, P.L. 105-354, §2(c), 112 Stat. 3244; Feb. 8, 2002, P.L. 107-140, §1, 116 Stat. 12; Nov. 2, 2002, P.L. 107-273, §205(e), 116 Stat. 1778; Mar. 16, 2006, P.L. 109-181,

§§1(b), 2(b), 120 Stat. 285, 288; Oct. 13, 2008, P.L. 110-403, §205, 122 Stat. 4261; Dec. 31, 2011, P.L. 112-81, §818(h), 125 Stat. 1497; July 9, 2012, P.L. 112-144, §717(a)(1)-(3), 126 Stat. 1076; May 16, 2016, P.L. 114-154, §3(2), 130 Stat. 387.

§2323. FORFEITURE, DESTRUCTION & RESTITUTION

(a) Civil forfeiture—

(1) Property subject to forfeiture.—The following property is subject to forfeiture to the United States Government:

(A) Any article, the making or trafficking of which is, prohibited under section 506 of title 17, or section 2318, 2319, 2319A, 2319B, or 2320, or chapter 90, of this title.

(B) Any property used, or intended to be used, in any manner or part to commit or facilitate the commission of an offense referred to in subparagraph (A).

(C) Any property constituting or derived from any proceeds obtained directly or indirectly as a result of the commission of an offense referred to in subparagraph (A).

(2) Procedures.—The provisions of chapter 46 relating to civil forfeitures shall extend to any seizure or civil forfeiture under this section. For seizures made under this section, the court shall enter an appropriate protective order with respect to discovery and use of any records or information that has been seized. The protective order shall provide for appropriate procedures to ensure that confidential, private, proprietary, or privileged information contained in such records is not improperly disclosed or used. At the conclusion of the forfeiture proceedings, unless otherwise requested by an agency of the United States, the court shall order that any property forfeited under paragraph (1) be destroyed, or otherwise disposed of according to law.

(b) Criminal forfeiture—

(1) Property subject to forfeiture.—The court, in imposing sentence on a person convicted of an offense under section 506 of title 17, or section 2318, 2319, 2319A, 2319B, or 2320, or chapter 90, of this title, shall order, in addition to any other sentence imposed, that the person forfeit to the United States Government any property subject to forfeiture under subsection (a) for that offense.

(2) Procedures—

(A) In general.—The forfeiture of property under paragraph (1), including any seizure and disposition of the property and any related judicial or administrative proceeding, shall be governed by the procedures set forth in section 413 of the Comprehensive Drug Abuse Prevention and Control Act of 1970 (21 U.S.C. §853), other than subsection (d) of that section.

(B) Destruction.—At the conclusion of the forfeiture proceedings, the court, unless otherwise requested by an agency of the United States shall order that any—

(i) forfeited article or component of an article bearing or consisting of a counterfeit mark be destroyed or otherwise disposed of according to law; and

(ii) infringing items or other property described in subsection (a)(1)(A) and forfeited under paragraph (1) of this subsection be destroyed or otherwise disposed of according to law.

(c) Restitution.—When a person is convicted of an offense under section 506 of title 17 or section 2318, 2319, 2319A, 2319B, or 2320, or chapter 90, of this title, the court, pursuant to sections 3556, 3663A, and 3664 of this title, shall order the person to pay restitution to any victim of the offense as an offense against property referred to in section 3663A(c)(1)(A)(ii) of this title.

History of 18 U.S.C. §2323: Oct. 13, 2008, P.L. 110-403, §206(a), 122 Stat. 4261.

TITLE 19. CUSTOMS DUTIES

CHAPTER 4. TARIFF ACT OF 1930

SUBTITLE II. SPECIAL PROVISIONS

PART II. UNITED STATES INTERNATIONAL TRADE COMMISSION

§1337. UNFAIR PRACTICES IN IMPORT TRADE

(a) Unlawful activities; covered industries; definitions—

(1) Subject to paragraph (2), the following are unlawful, and when found by the Commission to exist shall be dealt with, in addition to any other provision of law, as provided in this section:

(A) Unfair methods of competition and unfair acts in the importation of articles (other than articles provided for in subparagraphs (B), (C), (D), and (E)) into the United States, or in the sale of such articles by the owner, importer, or consignee, the threat or effect of which is—

(i) to destroy or substantially injure an industry in the United States;

(ii) to prevent the establishment of such an industry; or

(iii) to restrain or monopolize trade and commerce in the United States.

(B) The importation into the United States, the sale for importation, or the sale within the United States after importation by the owner, importer, or consignee, of articles that—

(i) infringe a valid and enforceable United States patent or a valid and enforceable United States copyright registered under Title 17; or

(ii) are made, produced, processed, or mined under, or by means of, a process covered by the claims of a valid and enforceable United States patent.

(C) The importation into the United States, the sale for importation, or the sale within the United States after importation by the owner, importer, or consignee, of articles that infringe a valid and enforceable United States trademark registered under the Trademark Act of 1946 [15 U.S.C. §1051 et seq.].

(D) The importation into the United States, the sale for importation, or the sale within the United States after importation by the owner, importer, or consignee, of a semiconductor chip product in a manner that constitutes infringement of a mask work registered under chapter 9 of Title 17.

(E) The importation into the United States, the sale for importation, or the sale within the United States after importation by the owner, importer, or consigner, of an article that constitutes infringement of the exclusive rights in a design protected under chapter 13 of Title 17 [17 U.S.C. §1301 et seq.].

(2) Subparagraphs (B), (C), (D), and (E) of paragraph (1) apply only if an industry in the United States, relating to the articles protected by the patent, copyright, trademark, mask work, or design concerned, exists or is in the process of being established.

(3) For purposes of paragraph (2), an industry in the United States shall be considered to exist if there is in the United States, with respect to the articles protected by the patent, copyright, trademark, mask work, or design concerned—

(A) significant investment in plant and equipment;

(B) significant employment of labor or capital; or

(C) substantial investment in its exploitation, including engineering, research and development, or licensing.

(4) For the purposes of this section, the phrase "owner, importer, or consignee" includes any agent of the owner, importer, or consignee.

(b) Investigation of violations by Commission—

(1) The Commission shall investigate any alleged violation of this section on complaint under oath or upon its initiative. Upon commencing any such investigation, the Commission shall publish notice thereof in the Federal Register. The Commission shall conclude any such investigation and make its determination under this section at the earliest practicable time after the date of publication of notice of such investigation. To promote expeditious adjudication, the Commission shall, within 45 days after an investigation is initiated, establish a target date for its final determination.

(2) During the course of each investigation under this section, the Commission shall consult with, and seek advice and information from, the Department of Health and Human Services, the Department of Justice, the Federal Trade Commission, and such other departments and agencies as it considers appropriate.

(3) Whenever, in the course of an investigation under this section, the Commission has reason to believe, based on information before it, that a matter, in whole or in part, may come within the purview of part II of subtitle IV of this chapter, it shall promptly notify the Secretary of Commerce so that such action may be taken as is otherwise authorized by such part II. If the Commission has reason to believe that the matter before it (A) is based solely on alleged acts and effects which are within the purview of section 1671 or 1673 of this title, or (B) relates to an alleged copyright infringement with respect to which action is prohibited by section 1008 of Title 17, the Commission shall terminate, or not institute, any investigation into the matter. If the Commission has reason to believe the matter before it is based in part on alleged acts and effects which are within the purview of section 1671 or 1673 of this title, and in part on alleged acts and effects which may, independently from or in conjunction with those within the purview of such section, establish a basis for relief under this section, then it may institute or continue an investigation into the matter. If the Commission notifies the Secretary or the administering authority (as defined in section 1677(1) of this title) with respect to a matter under this paragraph, the Commission may suspend its investigation during the time the matter is before the Secretary or administering authority for final decision. Any final decision by the administering authority under section 1671 or 1673 of this title with respect to the matter within such section 1671 or 1673 of this title of which the Commission has notified the Secretary or administering authority shall be conclusive upon the Commission with respect to the issue of less-than-fair-value sales or subsidization and the matters necessary for such decision.

(c) Determinations; review.—The Commission shall determine, with respect to each investigation conducted by it under this section, whether or not there is a violation of this section, except that the Commission may, by issuing a consent order or on the basis of an agreement between the private parties to the investigation, including an agreement to present the matter for arbitration, terminate any such investigation, in whole or in part, without making such a determination. Each determination under subsection (d) or (e) of this section shall be made on the record after notice and opportunity for a hearing in conformity with the provisions of subchapter II of chapter 5 of Title 5. All legal and equitable defenses may be presented in all cases. A respondent may raise any counterclaim in a manner prescribed by the Commission. Immediately after a counterclaim is received by the Commission, the respondent raising such counterclaim shall file a notice of removal with a United States district court in which venue for any of the counterclaims raised by the party would exist under section 1391 of Title 28. Any counterclaim raised pursuant to this section shall relate back to the date of the original complaint in the proceeding before the Commission. Action on such counterclaim shall not delay or affect the proceeding under this section, including the legal and equitable defenses that may be raised under this subsection. Any person adversely affected by a final determination of the Commission under subsection (d), (e), (f), or (g) of this section may appeal such determination, within 60 days after the determination becomes final, to the United States Court of Appeals for the Federal Circuit for review in accordance with chapter 7 of Title 5. Notwithstanding the foregoing provisions of this subsection, Commission determinations under subsections (d), (e), (f), and (g) of this section with respect to its findings on the public health and welfare, competitive conditions in the United States economy, the production of like or directly competitive articles in the United States, and United States consumers, the amount and nature of bond, or the appropriate remedy shall be reviewable in accordance with section 706 of Title 5. Determinations by the Commission under subsections (e), (f), and (j) of this section with respect to forfeiture of bonds and under subsection (h) of this section with respect to the imposition of sanctions for abuse of discovery or abuse of process shall also be reviewable in accordance with section 706 of Title 5.

(d) Exclusion of articles from entry—

(1) If the Commission determines, as a result of an investigation under this section, that there is a violation of this section, it shall direct that the articles concerned, imported by any person violating the provision of this section, be excluded from entry into the United States, unless, after considering the effect of such exclusion upon the public health and welfare, competitive conditions in the United States economy, the production of like or directly competitive articles in the United States, and United States consumers, it finds that such articles should not be excluded from entry. The Commission shall notify the Secretary of the Treasury of its action under this subsection directing such exclusion from entry, and upon receipt of such notice, the Secretary shall, through the proper officers, refuse such entry.

(2) The authority of the Commission to order an exclusion from entry of articles shall be limited to persons determined by the Commission to be violating this section unless the Commission determines that—

(A) a general exclusion from entry of articles is necessary to prevent circumvention of an exclusion order limited to products of named persons; or

(B) there is a pattern of violation of this section and it is difficult to identify the source of infringing products.

(e) Exclusion of articles from entry during investigation except under bond; procedures applicable; preliminary relief—

(1) If, during the course of an investigation under this section, the Commission determines that there is reason to believe that there is a violation of this section, it may direct that the articles concerned, imported by any person with respect to whom there is reason to believe that such person is violating this section, be excluded from entry into the United States, unless, after considering the effect of such exclusion upon the public health and welfare, competitive conditions in the United States economy, the production of like or directly competitive articles in the United States, and United States consumers, it finds that such articles should not be excluded from entry. The Commission shall notify the Secretary of the Treasury of its action under this subsection directing such exclusion from entry, and upon receipt of such notice, the Secretary shall, through the proper officers, refuse such entry, except that such articles shall be entitled to entry under bond prescribed by the Secretary in an amount determined by the Commission to be sufficient to protect the complainant from any injury. If the Commission later determines that the respondent has violated the provisions of this section, the bond may be forfeited to the complainant.

(2) A complainant may petition the Commission for the issuance of an order under this subsection. The Commission shall make a determination with regard to such petition by no later than the 90th day after the date on which the Commission's notice of investigation is published in the Federal Register. The Commission may extend the 90-day period for an additional 60 days in a case it designates as a more complicated case. The Commission shall publish in the Federal Register its reasons why it designated the case as being more complicated. The Commission may require the complainant to post a bond as a prerequisite to the issuance of an order under this subsection. If the Commission later determines that the respondent has not violated the provisions of this section, the bond may be forfeited to the respondent.

(3) The Commission may grant preliminary relief under this subsection or subsection (f) of this section to the same extent as preliminary injunctions and temporary restraining orders may be granted under the Federal Rules of Civil Procedure.

(4) The Commission shall prescribe the terms and conditions under which bonds may be forfeited under paragraphs (1) and (2).

(f) Cease and desist orders; civil penalty for violation of orders—

(1) In addition to, or in lieu of, taking action under subsection (d) or (e) of this section, the Commission may issue and cause to be served on any person violating this section, or believed to be violating this section, as the case may be, an order directing such person to cease and desist from engaging in the unfair methods or acts involved, unless after considering the effect of such order upon the public health and welfare, competitive conditions in the United States economy, the production of like or directly competitive articles in the United States, and United States consumers, it finds that such order should not be issued. The Commission may at any time, upon such notice and in such manner as it deems proper, modify or revoke any such order, and, in the case of a revocation, may take action under subsection (d) or (e) of this section, as the case may be. If a temporary cease and desist order is issued in addition to, or in lieu of, an exclusion order under subsection (e) of this section, the Commission may require the complainant to post a bond, in an amount determined by the Commission to be sufficient to protect the respondent from any injury, as a prerequisite to the issuance of an order under this subsection. If the Commission later determines that the respondent has not violated the provisions of this section, the bond may be forfeited to the respondent. The Commission shall prescribe the terms and conditions under which the bonds may be forfeited under this paragraph.

(2) Any person who violates an order issued by the Commission under paragraph (1) after it has become final shall forfeit and pay to the United States a civil penalty for each day on which an importation of articles, or their sale, occurs in violation of the order of not more than the greater of $100,000 or twice the domestic value of the articles entered or sold on such day in violation of the order. Such penalty shall accrue to the United States and may be recovered for the United States in a civil action brought by the Commission in the Federal District Court for the District of Columbia or for the district in which the violation occurs. In such actions, the United States district courts may issue mandatory injunctions incorporating the relief sought by the Commission as they deem appropriate in the enforcement of such final orders of the Commission.

(g) Exclusion from entry or cease and desist order; conditions and procedures applicable—

(1) If—

(A) a complaint is filed against a person under this section;

(B) the complaint and a notice of investigation are served on the person;

(C) the person fails to respond to the complaint and notice or otherwise fails to appear to answer the complaint and notice;

(D) the person fails to show good cause why the person should not be found in default; and

(E) the complainant seeks relief limited solely to that person;

the Commission shall presume the facts alleged in the complaint to be true and shall, upon request, issue an exclusion from entry or a cease and desist order, or both, limited to that person unless, after considering the effect of such exclusion or order upon the public health and welfare, competitive conditions in the United States economy, the production of like or directly competitive articles in the United States, and United States consumers, the Commission finds that such exclusion or order should not be issued.

(2) In addition to the authority of the Commission to issue a general exclusion from entry of articles when a respondent appears to contest an investigation concerning a violation of the provisions of this section, a general exclusion from entry of articles, regardless of the source or importer of the articles, may be issued if—

(A) no person appears to contest an investigation concerning a violation of the provisions of this section,

(B) such a violation is established by substantial, reliable, and probative evidence, and

(C) the requirements of subsection (d)(2) of this section are met.

(h) Sanctions for abuse of discovery and abuse of process.—The Commission may by rule prescribe sanctions for abuse of discovery and abuse of process to the extent authorized by Rule 11 and Rule 37 of the Federal Rules of Civil Procedure.

(i) Forfeiture—

(1) In addition to taking action under subsection (d) of this section, the Commission may issue an order providing that any article imported in violation of the provisions of this section be seized and forfeited to the United States if—

(A) the owner, importer, or consignee of the article previously attempted to import the article into the United States;

(B) the article was previously denied entry into the United States by reason of an order issued under subsection (d) of this section; and

(C) upon such previous denial of entry, the Secretary of the Treasury provided the owner, importer, or consignee of the article written notice of—

(i) such order, and

(ii) the seizure and forfeiture that would result from any further attempt to import the article into the United States.

(2) The Commission shall notify the Secretary of the Treasury of any order issued under this subsection and, upon receipt of such notice, the Secretary of the Treasury shall enforce such order in accordance with the provisions of this section.

(3) Upon the attempted entry of articles subject to an order issued under this subsection, the Secretary of the Treasury shall immediately notify all ports of entry of the attempted importation and shall identify the persons notified under paragraph (1)(C).

(4) The Secretary of the Treasury shall provide—

(A) the written notice described in paragraph (1)(C) to the owner, importer, or consignee of any article that is denied entry into the United States by reason of an order issued under subsection (d) of this section; and

(B) a copy of such written notice to the Commission.

(j) Referral to President—

(1) If the Commission determines that there is a violation of this section, or that, for purposes of subsection (e) of this section, there is reason to believe that there is such a violation, it shall—

(A) publish such determination in the Federal Register, and

(B) transmit to the President a copy of such determination and the action taken under subsection (d), (e), (f), (g), or (i) of this section, with respect thereto, together with the record upon which such determination is based.

(2) If, before the close of the 60-day period beginning on the day after the day on which he receives a copy of such determination, the President, for policy reasons, disapproves such determination and notifies the Commission of his disapproval, then, effective on the date of such notice, such determination and the action taken under subsection (d), (e), (f), (g), or (i) of this section with respect thereto shall have no force or effect.

(3) Subject to the provisions of paragraph (2), such determination shall, except for purposes of subsection (c) of this section, be effective upon publication thereof in the Federal Register, and the action taken under subsection (d), (e), (f), (g), or (i) of this section, with respect thereto shall be effective as provided in such subsections, except that articles directed to be excluded from entry under subsection (d) of this section or subject to a cease and desist order under subsection (f) of this section shall, until such determination becomes final, be entitled to entry under bond prescribed by the Secretary in an amount determined by the Commission to be sufficient to protect the complainant from any injury. If the determination becomes final, the bond may be forfeited to the complainant. The Commission shall prescribe the terms and conditions under which bonds may be forfeited under this paragraph.

(4) If the President does not disapprove such determination within such 60-day period, or if he notifies the Commission before the close of such period that he approves such determination, then, for purposes of paragraph (3) and subsection (c) of this section such determination shall become final on the day after the close of such period or the day on which the President notifies the Commission of his approval, as the case may be.

(k) Period of effectiveness; termination of violation or modification or rescission of exclusion or order—

(1) Except as provided in subsections (f) and (j) of this section, any exclusion from entry or order under this section shall continue in effect until the Commission finds, and in the case of exclusion from entry notifies the Secretary of the Treasury, that the conditions which led to such exclusion from entry or order no longer exist.

(2) If any person who has previously been found by the Commission to be in violation of this section petitions the Commission for a determination that the petitioner is no longer in violation of this section or for a modification or rescission of an exclusion from entry or order under subsection (d), (e), (f), (g), or (i) of this section—

(A) the burden of proof in any proceeding before the Commission regarding such petition shall be on the petitioner; and

(B) relief may be granted by the Commission with respect to such petition—

(i) on the basis of new evidence or evidence that could not have been presented at the prior proceeding, or

(ii) on grounds which would permit relief from a judgment or order under the Federal Rules of Civil Procedure.

(*l*) Importation by or for United States.—Any exclusion from entry or order under subsection (d), (e), (f), (g), or (i) of this section, in cases based on a proceeding involving a patent, copyright, mask work, or design under subsection (a)(1) of this section, shall not apply to any articles imported by and for the use of the United States, or imported for, and to be used for, the United States with the authorization or consent of the Government. Whenever any article would have been excluded from entry or would not have been entered pursuant to the provisions of such subsections but for the operation of this subsection, an owner of the patent, copyright, mask work, or design adversely affected shall be entitled to reasonable and entire compensation in an action before the United States Court of Federal Claims pursuant to the procedures of section 1498 of Title 28.

(m) "United States" defined.—For purposes of this section and sections 1338 and 1340 of this title, the term "United States" means the customs territory of the United States as defined in general note 2 of the Harmonized Tariff Schedule of the United States.

(n) Disclosure of confidential information—

(1) Information submitted to the Commission or exchanged among the parties in connection with proceedings under this section which is properly designated as confidential pursuant to Commission rules may not be disclosed (except under a protective order issued under regulations of the Commission which authorizes limited disclosure of such information) to any person (other than a person described in paragraph (2)) without the consent of the person submitting it.

(2) Notwithstanding the prohibition contained in paragraph (1), information referred to in that paragraph may be disclosed to—

(A) an officer or employee of the Commission who is directly concerned with—

(i) carrying out the investigation or related proceeding in connection with which the information is submitted,

(ii) the administration of a bond posted pursuant to subsection (e), (f), or (j) of this section,

(iii) the administration or enforcement of an exclusion order issued pursuant to subsection (d), (e), or (g) of this section, a cease and desist order issued pursuant to subsection (f) of this section, or a consent order issued pursuant to subsection (c) of this section,

(iv) proceedings for the modification or rescission of a temporary or permanent order issued under subsection (d), (e), (f), (g), or (i) of this section, or a consent order issued under this section, or

(v) maintaining the administrative record of the investigation or related proceeding,

(B) an officer or employee of the United States Government who is directly involved in the review under subsection (j) of this section, or

(C) an officer or employee of the United States Customs Service who is directly involved in administering an exclusion from entry under subsection (d), (e), or (g) of this section resulting from the investigation or related proceeding in connection with which the information is submitted.

History of 19 U.S.C. §1337: June 17, 1930, ch. 497, §337, 46 Stat. 703; July 4, 1946, Proc. No. 2695, 11 F.R. 7517, 60 Stat. 1352; Aug. 20, 1958, P.L. 85-686, §9(c)(1), 72 Stat. 679; Jan. 3, 1975, P.L. 93-618, §341(a), 88 Stat. 2053; July 26, 1979, P.L. 96-39, §§106(b)(1), 1105, 93 Stat. 193, 310; Oct. 10, 1980, P.L. 96-417, §604, 94 Stat. 1744; Apr. 2, 1982, P.L. 97-164, §§160(a)(5), 163(a)(4), 96 Stat. 48, 49; Nov. 8, 1984, P.L. 98-620, §413, 98 Stat. 3362; Aug. 23, 1988, P.L. 100-418, §§1214(h)(3), 1342(a), (b), 102 Stat. 1157, 1212, 1215; Nov. 10, 1988, P.L. 100-647, §9001(a)(7), (12), 102 Stat. 3807; Oct. 28, 1992, P.L. 102-563, §3(d), 106 Stat. 4248; Dec. 8, 1994, P.L. 103-465, §§261(d)(1)(B)(ii), 321(a), 108 Stat. 4909, 4943; Oct. 11, 1996, P.L. 104-295, §20(b)(11), (12), (c)(2), 110 Stat. 3527, 3528; Nov. 29, 1999, P.L. 106-113, §1000(a)(9) [§5005(b)], 113 Stat. 1536, 1501A-594; Dec. 3, 2004, P.L. 108-429, §2004(d)(5), 118 Stat. 2592.

SUBTITLE III. ADMINISTRATIVE PROVISIONS

PART III. ASCERTAINMENT, COLLECTION, & RECOVERY OF DUTIES

§1526. MERCHANDISE BEARING AMERICAN TRADE-MARK

(a) Importation prohibited.—Except as provided in subsection (d) of this section, it shall be unlawful to import into the United States any merchandise of foreign manufacture if such merchandise, or the label, sign, print, package, wrapper, or receptacle, bears a trademark owned by a citizen of, or by a corporation or association created or organized within, the United States, and registered in the Patent and Trademark Office by a person domiciled in the United States, under the provisions of sections 81 to 109 of Title 15, and if a copy of the certificate of registration of such trademark is filed with the Secretary of the Treasury, in the manner provided in section 106 of said Title 15, unless written consent of the owner of such trademark is produced at the time of making entry.

(b) Seizure and forfeiture.—Any such merchandise imported into the United States in violation of the provisions of this section shall be subject to seizure and forfeiture for violation of the customs laws.

(c) Injunction and damages.—Any person dealing in any such merchandise may be enjoined from dealing therein within the United States or may be required to export or destroy such merchandise or to remove or obliterate such trademark and shall be liable for the same damages and profits provided for wrongful use of a trademark, under the provisions of sections 81 to 109 of Title 15.

(d) Exemptions; publication in Federal Register; forfeitures; rules and regulations—

(1) The trademark provisions of this section and section 1124 of Title 15, do not apply to the importation of articles accompanying any person arriving in the United States when such articles are for his personal use and not for sale if (A) such articles are within the limits of types and quantities determined by the Secretary pursuant to paragraph (2) of this subsection, and (B) such person has not been granted an exemption under this subsection within thirty days immediately preceding his arrival.

(2) The Secretary shall determine and publish in the Federal Register lists of the types of articles and the quantities of each which shall be entitled to the exemption provided by this subsection. In determining such quantities of particular types of trade-marked articles, the Secretary shall give such consideration as he deems necessary to the numbers of such articles usually purchased at retail for personal use.

(3) If any article which has been exempted from the restrictions on importation of the trade-mark laws under this subsection is sold within one year after the date of importation, such article, or its value (to be recovered from the importer), is subject to forfeiture. A sale pursuant to a judicial order or in liquidation of the estate of a decedent is not subject to the provisions of this paragraph.

(4) The Secretary may prescribe such rules and regulations as may be necessary to carry out the provisions of this subsection.

(e) Merchandise bearing counterfeit mark; seizure and forfeiture; disposition of seized goods.—Any such merchandise bearing a counterfeit mark (within the meaning of section 1127 of Title 15) imported into the United States in violation of the provisions of section 1124 of Title 15, shall be seized and, in the absence of the written consent of the trademark owner, forfeited for violations of the customs laws. Upon seizure of such merchandise, the Secretary shall notify the owner of the trademark, and shall, after forfeiture, destroy the merchandise. Alternatively, if the merchandise is not unsafe or a hazard to health, and the Secretary has the consent of the trademark owner, the Secretary may obliterate the trademark where feasible and dispose of the goods seized—

(1) by delivery to such Federal, State, and local government agencies as in the opinion of the Secretary have a need for such merchandise,

(2) by gift to such eleemosynary institutions as in the opinion of the Secretary have a need for such merchandise, or

(3) more than 90 days after the date of forfeiture, by sale by the Customs Service at public auction under such regulations as the Secretary prescribes, except that before making any such sale the Secretary shall determine that no Federal, State, or local government agency or eleemosynary institution has established a need for such merchandise under paragraph (1) or (2).

(f) Civil penalties—

(1) Any person who directs, assists financially or otherwise, or aids and abets the importation of merchandise for sale or public distribution that is seized under subsection (e) of this section shall be subject to a civil fine.

(2) For the first such seizure, the fine shall be not more than the value that the merchandise would have had if it were genuine, according to the manufacturer's suggested retail price, determined under regulations promulgated by the Secretary.

(3) For the second seizure and thereafter, the fine shall be not more than twice the value that the merchandise would have had if it were genuine, as determined under regulations promulgated by the Secretary.

(4) The imposition of a fine under this subsection shall be within the discretion of the Customs Service, and shall be in addition to any other civil or criminal penalty or other remedy authorized by law.

History of 19 U.S.C. §1526: June 17, 1930, ch. 497, §526, 46 Stat. 741; Jan. 2, 1975, P.L. 93-596, §3, 88 Stat. 1949; Oct. 3, 1978, P.L. 95-410, §211(a), (c), 92 Stat. 903; Dec. 8, 1993, P.L. 103-182, §663, 107 Stat. 2214; July 2, 1996, P.L. 104-153, §§9, 10, 110 Stat. 1388.

PART V. ENFORCEMENT PROVISIONS

§1595a. FORFEITURES & OTHER PENALTIES

(a) Importation, removal, etc. contrary to laws of United States.—Except as specified in subsection (b) or (c) of section 1594 of this title, every vessel, vehicle, animal, aircraft, or other thing used in, to aid in, or to facilitate, by obtaining information or in any other way, the importation, bringing in, unlading, landing, removal, concealing, harboring, or subsequent transportation of any article which is being or has been introduced, or attempted to be introduced, into the United States contrary to law, whether upon such vessel, vehicle, animal, aircraft, or other thing or otherwise, may be seized and forfeited together with its tackle, apparel, furniture, harness, or equipment.

(b) Penalty for aiding unlawful importation.—Every person who directs, assists financially or otherwise, or is in any way concerned in any unlawful activity mentioned in the preceding subsection shall be liable to a penalty equal to the value of the article or articles introduced or attempted to be introduced.

(c) Merchandise introduced contrary to law.—Merchandise which is introduced or attempted to be introduced into the United States contrary to law shall be treated as follows:

(1) The merchandise shall be seized and forfeited if it—

(A) is stolen, smuggled, or clandestinely imported or introduced;

(B) is a controlled substance, as defined in the Controlled Substances Act (21 U.S.C. §801 et seq.), and is not imported in accordance with applicable law;

(C) is a contraband article, as defined in section 80302 of Title 49; or

(D) is a plastic explosive, as defined in section 841(q) of Title 18, which does not contain a detection agent, as defined in section 841(p) of such title.

(2) The merchandise may be seized and forfeited if—

(A) its importation or entry is subject to any restriction or prohibition which is imposed by law relating to health, safety, or conservation and the merchandise is not in compliance with the applicable rule, regulation, or statute;

(B) its importation or entry requires a license, permit or other authorization of an agency of the United States Government and the merchandise is not accompanied by such license, permit, or authorization;

(C) it is merchandise or packaging in which copyright, trademark, or trade name protection violations are involved (including, but not limited to, violations of section 1124, 1125, or 1127 of Title 15, section 506 of Title 17, or section 2318 or 2320 of Title 18);

(D) it is trade dress merchandise involved in the violation of a court order citing section 1125 of Title 15;

(E) it is merchandise which is marked intentionally in violation of section 1304 of this title;

(F) it is merchandise for which the importer has received written notices that previous importations of identical merchandise from the same supplier were found to have been marked in violation of section 1304 of this title; or

(G) U.S. Customs and Border Protection determines it is a technology, product, service, device, component, or part thereof the importation of which is prohibited under subsection (a)(2) or (b)(1) of section 1201 of Title 17.

(3) If the importation or entry of the merchandise is subject to quantitative restrictions requiring a visa, permit, license, or other similar document, or stamp from the United States Government or from a foreign government or issuing authority pursuant to a bilateral or multilateral agreement, the merchandise shall be subject to detention in accordance with section 1499 of this title unless the appropriate visa, license, permit, or similar document or stamp is presented to the Customs Service; but if the visa, permit, license, or similar document or stamp which is presented in connection with the importation or entry of the merchandise is counterfeit, the merchandise may be seized and forfeited.

(4) If the merchandise is imported or introduced contrary to a provision of law which governs the classification or value of merchandise and there are no issues as to the admissibility of the merchandise into the United States, it shall not be seized except in accordance with section 1592 of this title.

(5) In any case where the seizure and forfeiture of merchandise are required or authorized by this section, the Secretary may—

(A) remit the forfeiture under section 1618 of this title, or

(B) permit the exportation of the merchandise, unless its release would adversely affect health, safety, or conservation or be in contravention of a bilateral or multilateral agreement or treaty.

(d) Merchandise exported contrary to law.—Merchandise exported or sent from the United States or attempted to be exported or sent from the United States contrary to law, or the proceeds or value thereof, and property used to facilitate the exporting or sending of such merchandise, the attempted exporting or sending of such merchandise, or the receipt, purchase, transportation, concealment, or sale of such merchandise prior to exportation shall be seized and forfeited to the United States.

History of 19 U.S.C. §1595a: June 17, 1930, ch. 497, §596, as added Sept. 1, 1954, ch. 1213, §502, 68 Stat. 1140; Oct. 27, 1986, P.L. 99-570, §3123, 100 Stat. 3207-87; Dec. 8, 1993, P.L. 103-182, §624, 107 Stat. 2187; Apr. 24, 1996, P.L. 104-132, §606, 110 Stat. 1290; Mar. 9, 2006, P.L. 109-177, §311(d), 120 Stat. 242; Oct. 13, 2008, P.L. 110-403, §209(b), 122 Stat. 4264; Feb. 24, 2016, P.L. 114-125, §303(a), 130 Stat. 150.

TITLE 21. FOOD & DRUGS

CHAPTER 9. FEDERAL FOOD, DRUG, & COSMETIC ACT

SUBCHAPTER V. DRUGS & DEVICES

PART A. DRUGS & DEVICES

A §355. NEW DRUGS

(a) Necessity of effective approval of application.—No person shall introduce or deliver for introduction into interstate commerce any new drug, unless an approval of an application filed pursuant to subsection (b) or (j) of this section is effective with respect to such drug.

(b) Filing application; contents—

(1) Any person may file with the Secretary an application with respect to any drug subject to the provisions of subsection (a) of this section. Such person shall submit to the Secretary as a part of the application (A) full reports of investigations which have been made to show whether or not such drug is safe for use and whether such drug is effective in use; (B) a full list of the articles used as components of such drug; (C) a full statement of the composition of such drug; (D) a full description of the methods used in, and the facilities and controls used for, the manufacture, processing, and packing of such drug; (E) such samples of such drug and of the articles used as components thereof as the Secretary may require; (F) specimens of the labeling proposed to be used for such drug, and (G) any assessments required under section 355c of this title. The applicant shall file with the application the patent number and the expiration date of any patent which claims the drug for which the applicant submitted the application or which claims a method of using such drug and with respect to which a claim of patent infringement could reasonably be asserted if a person not licensed by the owner engaged in the manufacture, use, or sale of the drug. If an application is filed under this subsection for a drug and a patent which claims such drug or a method of using such drug is issued after the filing date but before approval of the application, the applicant shall amend the application to include the information required by the preceding sentence. Upon approval of the application, the Secretary shall publish information submitted under the two preceding sentences. The Secretary shall, in consultation with the Director of the National Institutes of Health and with representatives of the drug manufacturing industry, review and develop guidance, as appropriate, on the inclusion of women and minorities in clinical trials required by clause (A).

(2) An application submitted under paragraph (1) for a drug for which the investigations described in clause (A) of such paragraph and relied upon by the applicant for approval of the application were not conducted by or for the applicant and for which the applicant has not obtained a right of reference or use from the person by or for whom the investigations were conducted shall also include—

(A) a certification, in the opinion of the applicant and to the best of his knowledge, with respect to each patent which claims the drug for which such investigations were conducted or which claims a use for such drug for which the applicant is seeking approval under this subsection and for which information is required to be filed under paragraph (1) or subsection (c) of this section—

(i) that such patent information has not been filed,

(ii) that such patent has expired,

(iii) of the date on which such patent will expire, or

(iv) that such patent is invalid or will not be infringed by the manufacture, use, or sale of the new drug for which the application is submitted; and

(B) if with respect to the drug for which investigations described in paragraph (1)(A) were conducted information was filed under paragraph (1) or subsection (c) of this section for a method of use patent which does not claim a use for which the applicant is seeking approval under this subsection, a statement that the method of use patent does not claim such a use.

(3) Notice of opinion that patent is invalid or will not be infringed—

(A) Agreement to give notice.—An applicant that makes a certification described in paragraph (2)(A)(iv) shall include in the application a statement that the applicant will give notice as required by this paragraph.

(B) Timing of notice.—An applicant that makes a certification described in paragraph (2)(A)(iv) shall give notice as required under this paragraph—

(i) if the certification is in the application, not later than 20 days after the date of the postmark on the notice with which the Secretary informs the applicant that the application has been filed; or

(ii) if the certification is in an amendment or supplement to the application, at the time at which the applicant submits the amendment or supplement, regardless of whether the applicant has already given notice with respect to another such certification contained in the application or in an amendment or supplement to the application.

(C) Recipients of notice.—An applicant required under this paragraph to give notice shall give notice to—

(i) each owner of the patent that is the subject of the certification (or a representative of the owner designated to receive such a notice); and

(ii) the holder of the approved application under this subsection for the drug that is claimed by the patent or a use of which is claimed by the patent (or a representative of the holder designated to receive such a notice).

(D) Contents of notice.—A notice required under this paragraph shall—

(i) state that an application that contains data from bioavailability or bioequivalence studies has been submitted under this subsection for the drug with respect to which the certification is made to obtain approval to engage in the commercial manufacture, use, or sale of the drug before the expiration of the patent referred to in the certification; and

(ii) include a detailed statement of the factual and legal basis of the opinion of the applicant that the patent is invalid or will not be infringed.

(4)(A) An applicant may not amend or supplement an application referred to in paragraph (2) to seek approval of a drug that is a different drug than the drug identified in the application as submitted to the Secretary.

(B) With respect to the drug for which such an application is submitted, nothing in this subsection or subsection (c)(3) prohibits an applicant from amending or supplementing the application to seek approval of a different strength.

(5)(A) The Secretary shall issue guidance for the individuals who review applications submitted under paragraph (1) or under section 262 of title 42, which shall relate to promptness in conducting the review, technical excellence, lack of bias and conflict of interest, and knowledge of regulatory and scientific standards, and which shall apply equally to all individuals who review such applications.

(B) The Secretary shall meet with a sponsor of an investigation or an applicant for approval for a drug under this subsection or section 262 of title 42 if the sponsor or applicant makes a reasonable written request for a meeting for the purpose of reaching agreement on the design and size—

(i)(I) of clinical trials intended to form the primary basis of an effectiveness claim; or

(II) in the case where human efficacy studies are not ethical or feasible, of animal and any associated clinical trials which, in combination, are intended to form the primary basis of an effectiveness claim; or

(ii) with respect to an application for approval of a biological product under section 262(k) of Title 42, of any necessary clinical study or studies.

The sponsor or applicant shall provide information necessary for discussion and agreement on the design and size of the clinical trials. Minutes of any such meeting shall be prepared by the Secretary and made available to the sponsor or applicant upon request.

(C) Any agreement regarding the parameters of the design and size of clinical trials of a new drug under this paragraph that is reached between the Secretary and a sponsor or applicant shall be reduced to writing and made part of the administrative record by the Secretary. Such agreement shall not be changed after the testing begins, except—

(i) with the written agreement of the sponsor or applicant; or

(ii) pursuant to a decision, made in accordance with subparagraph (D) by the director of the reviewing division, that a substantial scientific issue essential to determining the safety or effectiveness of the drug has been identified after the testing has begun.

(D) A decision under subparagraph (C)(ii) by the director shall be in writing and the Secretary shall provide to the sponsor or applicant an opportunity for a meeting at which the director and the sponsor or applicant will be present and at which the director will document the scientific issue involved.

(E) The written decisions of the reviewing division shall be binding upon, and may not directly or indirectly be changed by, the field or compliance division personnel unless such field or compliance division personnel demonstrate to the reviewing division why such decision should be modified.

(F) No action by the reviewing division may be delayed because of the unavailability of information from or action by field personnel unless the reviewing division determines that a delay is necessary to assure the marketing of a safe and effective drug.

(G) For purposes of this paragraph, the reviewing division is the division responsible for the review of an application for approval of a drug under this subsection or section 262 of title 42 (including all scientific and medical matters, chemistry, manufacturing, and controls).

(6) An application submitted under this subsection shall be accompanied by the certification required under section 282(j)(5)(B) of title 42. Such certification shall not be considered an element of such application.

(c) Period for approval of application; period for, notice, and expedition of hearing; period for issuance of order—

(1) Within one hundred and eighty days after the filing of an application under subsection (b) of this section, or such additional period as may be agreed upon by the Secretary and the applicant, the Secretary shall either—

(A) approve the application if he then finds that none of the grounds for denying approval specified in subsection (d) of this section applies, or

(B) give the applicant notice of an opportunity for a hearing before the Secretary under subsection (d) of this section on the question whether such application is approvable. If the applicant elects to accept the opportunity for hearing by written request within thirty days after such notice, such hearing shall commence not more than ninety days after the expiration of such thirty days unless the Secretary and the applicant otherwise agree. Any such hearing shall thereafter be conducted on an expedited basis and the Secretary's order thereon shall be issued within ninety days after the date fixed by the Secretary for filing final briefs.

(2) If the patent information described in subsection (b) of this section could not be filed with the submission of an application under subsection (b) of this section because the application was filed before the patent information was required under subsection (b) of this section or a patent was issued after the application was approved under such subsection, the holder of an approved application shall file with the Secretary the patent number and the expiration date of any patent which claims the drug for which the application was submitted or which claims a method of using such drug and with respect to which a claim of patent infringement could reasonably be asserted if a person not licensed by the owner engaged in the manufacture, use, or sale of the drug. If the holder of an approved application could not file patent information under subsection (b) of this section because it was not required at the time the application was approved, the holder shall file such information under this subsection not later than thirty days after September 24, 1984, and if the holder of an approved application could not file patent information under subsection (b) of this section because no patent had been issued when an application was filed or approved, the holder shall file such information under this subsection not later than thirty days after the date the patent involved is issued. Upon the submission of patent information under this subsection, the Secretary shall publish it.

(3) The approval of an application filed under subsection (b) of this section which contains a certification required by paragraph (2) of such subsection shall be made effective on the last applicable date determined by applying the following to each certification made under subsection (b)(2)(A) of this section:

(A) If the applicant only made a certification described in clause (i) or (ii) of subsection (b)(2)(A) of this section or in both such clauses, the approval may be made effective immediately.

(B) If the applicant made a certification described in clause (iii) of subsection (b)(2)(A) of this section, the approval may be made effective on the date certified under clause (iii).

(C) If the applicant made a certification described in clause (iv) of subsection (b)(2)(A) of this section, the approval shall be made effective immediately unless, before the expiration of 45 days after the date on which the notice described in subsection (b)(3) is received, an action is brought for infringement of the patent that is the subject of the certification and for which information was submitted to the Secretary under paragraph (2) or subsection (b)(1) before the date on which the application (excluding an amendment or supplement to the application) was submitted. If such an action is brought before the expiration of such days, the approval may be made effective upon the expiration of the thirty-month period beginning on the date of the receipt of the notice provided under subsection (b)(3) or such shorter or longer period as the court may order because either party to the action failed to reasonably cooperate in expediting the action, except that—

(i) if before the expiration of such period the district court decides that the patent is invalid or not infringed (including any substantive determination that there is no cause of action for patent infringement or invalidity), the approval shall be made effective on—

(I) the date on which the court enters judgment reflecting the decision; or

(II) the date of a settlement order or consent decree signed and entered by the court stating that the patent that is the subject of the certification is invalid or not infringed;

(ii) if before the expiration of such period the district court decides that the patent has been infringed—

(I) if the judgment of the district court is appealed, the approval shall be made effective on—

(aa) the date on which the court of appeals decides that the patent is invalid or not infringed (including any substantive determination that there is no cause of action for patent infringement or invalidity); or

(bb) the date of a settlement order or consent decree signed and entered by the court of appeals stating that the patent that is the subject of the certification is invalid or not infringed; or

(II) if the judgment of the district court is not appealed or is affirmed, the approval shall be made effective on the date specified by the district court in a court order under section 271(e)(4)(A) of title 35;

(iii) if before the expiration of such period the court grants a preliminary injunction prohibiting the applicant from engaging in the commercial manufacture or sale of the drug until the court decides the issues of patent validity and infringement and if the court decides that such patent is invalid or not infringed, the approval shall be made effective as provided in clause (i); or

(iv) if before the expiration of such period the court grants a preliminary injunction prohibiting the applicant from engaging in the commercial manufacture or sale of the drug until the court decides the issues of patent validity and infringement and if the court decides that such patent has been infringed, the approval shall be made effective as provided in clause (ii).

In such an action, each of the parties shall reasonably cooperate in expediting the action.

(D) Civil action to obtain patent certainty—

(i) Declaratory judgment absent infringement action—

(I) In general.—No action may be brought under section 2201 of title 28, by an applicant referred to in subsection (b)(2) for a declaratory judgment with respect to a patent which is the subject of the certification referred to in subparagraph (C) unless—

(aa) the 45-day period referred to in such subparagraph has expired;

(bb) neither the owner of such patent nor the holder of the approved application under subsection (b) for the drug that is claimed by the patent or a use of which is claimed by the patent brought a civil action against the applicant for infringement of the patent before the expiration of such period; and

(cc) in any case in which the notice provided under paragraph (2)(B) relates to noninfringement, the notice was accompanied by a document described in subclause (III).

(II) Filing of civil action.—If the conditions described in items (aa), (bb), and as applicable, (cc) of subclause (I) have been met, the applicant referred to in such subclause may, in accordance with section 2201 of title 28, bring a civil action under such section against the owner or holder referred to in such subclause (but not against any owner or holder that has brought such a civil action against the applicant, unless that civil action was dismissed without prejudice) for a declaratory judgment that the patent is invalid or will not be infringed by the drug for which the applicant seeks approval, except that such civil action may be brought for a declaratory judgment that the patent will not be infringed only in a case in which the condition described in subclause (I)(cc) is applicable. A civil action referred to in this subclause shall be brought in the judicial district where the defendant has its principal place of business or a regular and established place of business.

(III) Offer of confidential access to application.—For purposes of subclause (I)(cc), the document described in this subclause is a document providing an offer of confidential access to the application that is in the custody of the applicant referred to in subsection (b)(2) for the purpose of determining whether an action referred to in subparagraph (C) should be brought. The document providing the offer of confidential access shall contain such restrictions as to persons entitled to access, and on the use and disposition of any information accessed, as would apply had a protective order been entered for the purpose of protecting trade secrets and other confidential business information. A request for access to an application under an offer of confidential access shall be considered acceptance of the offer of confidential access with the restrictions as to persons entitled to access, and on the use and disposition of any information accessed, contained in the offer of confidential access, and those restrictions and other terms of the offer of confidential access shall be considered terms of an enforceable contract. Any person provided an offer of confidential access shall review the application for the sole and limited purpose of evaluating possible infringement of the patent that is the subject of the certification under subsection (b)(2)(A)(iv) and for no other purpose, and may not disclose information of no relevance to any issue of patent infringement to any person other than a person provided an offer of confidential access. Further, the application may be redacted by the applicant to remove any information of no relevance to any issue of patent infringement.

(ii) Counterclaim to infringement action—

(I) In general.—If an owner of the patent or the holder of the approved application under subsection (b) for the drug that is claimed by the patent or a use of which is claimed by the patent brings a patent infringement action against the applicant, the applicant may assert a counterclaim seeking an order requiring the holder to correct or delete the patent information submitted by the holder under subsection (b) or this subsection on the ground that the patent does not claim either—

(aa) the drug for which the application was approved; or

(bb) an approved method of using the drug.

(II) No independent cause of action.—Subclause (I) does not authorize the assertion of a claim described in subclause (I) in any civil action or proceeding other than a counterclaim described in subclause (I).

(iii) No damages.—An applicant shall not be entitled to damages in a civil action under clause (i) or a counterclaim under clause (ii).

(E)(i) If an application (other than an abbreviated new drug application) submitted under subsection (b) of this section for a drug, no active ingredient (including any ester or salt of the active ingredient) of which has been approved in any other application under subsection (b) of this section, was approved during the period beginning January 1, 1982, and ending on September 24, 1984, the Secretary may not make the approval of another application for a drug for which the investigations described in clause (A) of subsection (b)(1) of this section and relied upon by the applicant for approval of the application were not conducted by or for the applicant and for which the applicant has not obtained a right of reference or use from the person by or for whom the investigations were conducted effective before the expiration of ten years from the date of the approval of the application previously approved under subsection (b) of this section.

(ii) If an application submitted under subsection (b) of this section for a drug, no active ingredient (including any ester or salt of the active ingredient) of which has been approved in any other application under subsection (b) of this section, is approved after September 24, 1984, no application which refers to the drug for which the subsection (b) application was submitted and for which the investigations described in clause (A) of subsection (b)(1) of this section and relied upon by the applicant for approval of the application were not conducted by or for the applicant and for which the applicant has not obtained a right of reference or use from the person by or for whom the investigations were conducted may be submitted under subsection (b) of this section before the expiration of five years from the date of the approval of the application under subsection (b) of this section, except that such an application may be submitted under subsection (b) of this section after the expiration of four years from the date of the approval of the subsection (b) application if it contains a certification of patent invalidity or noninfringement described in clause (iv) of subsection (b)(2)(A) of this section. The approval of such an application shall be made effective in accordance with this paragraph except that, if an action for patent infringement is commenced during the one-year period beginning forty-eight months after the date of the approval of the subsection (b) application, the thirty-month period referred to in subparagraph (C) shall be extended by such amount of time (if any) which is required for seven and one-half years to have elapsed from the date of approval of the subsection (b) application.

(iii) If an application submitted under subsection (b) of this section for a drug, which includes an active ingredient (including any ester or salt of the active ingredient) that has been approved in another application approved under subsection (b) of this section, is approved after September 24, 1984, and if such application contains reports of new clinical investigations (other than bioavailability studies) essential to the approval of the application and conducted or sponsored by the applicant, the Secretary may not make the approval of an application submitted under subsection (b) of this section for the conditions of approval of such drug in the approved subsection (b) application effective before the expiration of three years from the date of the approval of the application under subsection (b) of this section if the investigations described in clause (A) of subsection (b)(1) of this section and relied upon by the applicant for approval of the application were not conducted by or for the applicant and if the applicant has not obtained a right of reference or use from the person by or for whom the investigations were conducted.

(iv) If a supplement to an application approved under subsection (b) of this section is approved after September 24, 1984, and the supplement contains reports of new clinical investigations (other than bio-availability[1] studies) essential to the approval of the supplement and conducted or sponsored by the person submitting the supplement, the Secretary may not make the approval of an application submitted under subsection (b) of this section for a change approved in the supplement effective before the expiration of three years from the date of the approval of the supplement under subsection (b) of this section if the investigations described in clause (A) of subsection (b)(1) of this section and relied upon by the applicant for approval of the application were not conducted by or for the applicant and if the applicant has not obtained a right of reference or use from the person by or for whom the investigations were conducted.

(v) If an application (or supplement to an application) submitted under subsection (b) of this section for a drug, which includes an active ingredient (including any ester or salt of the active ingredient) that has been approved in another application under subsection (b) of this section, was approved during the period beginning January 1, 1982, and ending on September 24, 1984, the Secretary may not make the approval of an application submitted under this subsection and for which the investigations described in clause (A) of subsection (b)(1) of this section and relied upon by the applicant for approval of the application were not conducted by or for the applicant and for which the applicant has not obtained a right of reference or use from the person by or for whom the investigations were conducted and which refers to the drug for which the subsection (b) application was submitted effective before the expiration of two years from September 24, 1984.

(4) A drug manufactured in a pilot or other small facility may be used to demonstrate the safety and effectiveness of the drug and to obtain approval for the drug prior to manufacture of the drug in a larger facility, unless the Secretary makes a determination that a full scale production facility is necessary to ensure the safety or effectiveness of the drug.

(5)(A) The Secretary may rely upon qualified data summaries to support the approval of a supplemental application, with respect to a qualified indication for a drug, submitted under subsection (b), if such supplemental application complies with subparagraph (B).

(B) A supplemental application is eligible for review as described in subparagraph (A) only if—

(i) there is existing data available and acceptable to the Secretary demonstrating the safety of the drug; and

(ii) all data used to develop the qualified data summaries are submitted to the Secretary as part of the supplemental application.

(C) The Secretary shall post on the Internet website of the Food and Drug Administration and update annually—

(i) the number of applications reviewed solely under subparagraph (A) or section 262(a)(2)(E) of Title 42;

(ii) the average time for completion of review under subparagraph (A) or section 262(a)(2)(E) of Title 42;

(iii) the average time for review of supplemental applications where the Secretary did not use review flexibility under subparagraph (A) or section 262(a)(2)(E) of Title 42; and

(iv) the number of applications reviewed under subparagraph (A) or section 262(a)(2)(E) of Title 42 for which the Secretary made use of full data sets in addition to the qualified data summary.

(D) In this paragraph—

(i) the term "qualified indication" means an indication for a drug that the Secretary determines to be appropriate for summary level review under this paragraph; and

(ii) the term "qualified data summary" means a summary of clinical data that demonstrates the safety and effectiveness of a drug with respect to a qualified indication.

(d) Grounds for refusing application; approval of application; "substantial evidence" defined.—If the Secretary finds, after due notice to the applicant in accordance with subsection (c) of this section and giving him an opportunity for a hearing, in accordance with said subsection, that (1) the investigations, reports of which are required to be submitted to the Secretary pursuant to subsection (b) of this section, do not include adequate tests by all methods reasonably applicable to show whether or not such drug is safe for use under the conditions prescribed, recommended, or suggested in the proposed labeling thereof; (2) the results of such tests show that such drug is unsafe for use under such conditions or do not show that such drug is safe for use under such conditions; (3) the methods used in, and the facilities and controls used for, the manufacture, processing, and packing of such drug are inadequate to preserve its identity, strength, quality, and purity; (4) upon the basis of the information submitted to him as part of the application, or upon the basis of any other information before him with respect to such drug, he has insufficient information to determine whether such drug is safe for use under such conditions; or (5) evaluated on the basis of the information submitted to him as part of the application and any other information before him with respect to such drug, there is a lack of substantial evidence that the drug will have the effect it purports or is represented to have under the conditions of use prescribed, recommended, or suggested in the proposed labeling thereof; or (6) the application failed to contain the patent information prescribed by subsection (b) of this section; or (7) based on a fair evaluation of all material facts, such labeling is false or misleading in any particular; he shall issue an order refusing to approve the application. If, after such notice and opportunity for hearing, the Secretary finds that clauses (1) through

(6) do not apply, he shall issue an order approving the application. As used in this subsection and subsection (e) of this section, the term "substantial evidence" means evidence consisting of adequate and well-controlled investigations, including clinical investigations, by experts qualified by scientific training and experience to evaluate the effectiveness of the drug involved, on the basis of which it could fairly and responsibly be concluded by such experts that the drug will have the effect it purports or is represented to have under the conditions of use prescribed, recommended, or suggested in the labeling or proposed labeling thereof. If the Secretary determines, based on relevant science, that data from one adequate and well-controlled clinical investigation and confirmatory evidence (obtained prior to or after such investigation) are sufficient to establish effectiveness, the Secretary may consider such data and evidence to constitute substantial evidence for purposes of the preceding sentence. The Secretary shall implement a structured risk-benefit assessment framework in the new drug approval process to facilitate the balanced consideration of benefits and risks, a consistent and systematic approach to the discussion and regulatory decision-making, and the communication of the benefits and risks of new drugs. Nothing in the preceding sentence shall alter the criteria for evaluating an application for marketing approval of a drug.

(e) Withdrawal of approval; grounds; immediate suspension upon finding imminent hazard to public health.—The Secretary shall, after due notice and opportunity for hearing to the applicant, withdraw approval of an application with respect to any drug under this section if the Secretary finds (1) that clinical or other experience, tests, or other scientific data show that such drug is unsafe for use under the conditions of use upon the basis of which the application was approved; (2) that new evidence of clinical experience, not contained in such application or not available to the Secretary until after such application was approved, or tests by new methods, or tests by methods not deemed reasonably applicable when such application was approved, evaluated together with the evidence available to the Secretary when the application was approved, shows that such drug is not shown to be safe for use under the conditions of use upon the basis of which the application was approved; or (3) on the basis of new information before him with respect to such drug, evaluated together with the evidence available to him when the application was approved, that there is a lack of substantial evidence that the drug will have the effect it purports or is represented to have under the conditions of use prescribed, recommended, or suggested in the labeling thereof; or (4) the patent information prescribed by subsection (c) of this section was not filed within thirty days after the receipt of written notice from the Secretary specifying the failure to file such information; or (5) that the application contains any untrue statement of a material fact: *Provided*, That if the Secretary (or in his absence the officer acting as Secretary) finds that there is an imminent hazard to the public health, he may suspend the approval of such application immediately, and give the applicant prompt notice of his action and afford the applicant the opportunity for an expedited hearing under this subsection; but the authority conferred by this proviso to suspend the approval of an application shall not be delegated. The Secretary may also, after due notice and opportunity for hearing to the applicant, withdraw the approval of an application submitted under subsection (b) or (j) of this section with respect to any drug under this section if the Secretary finds (1) that the applicant has failed to establish a system for maintaining required records, or has repeatedly or deliberately failed to maintain such records or to make required reports, in accordance with a regulation or order under subsection (k) of this section or to comply with the notice requirements of section 360(k)(2) of this title, or the applicant has refused to permit access to, or copying or verification of, such records as required by paragraph (2) of such subsection; or (2) that on the basis of new information before him, evaluated together with the evidence before him when the application was approved, the methods used in, or the facilities and controls used for, the manufacture, processing, and packing of such drug are inadequate to assure and preserve its identity, strength, quality, and purity and were not made adequate within a reasonable time after receipt of written notice from the Secretary specifying the matter complained of; or (3) that on the basis of new information before him, evaluated together with the evidence before him when the application was approved, the labeling of such drug, based on a fair evaluation of all material facts, is false or misleading in any particular and was not corrected within a reasonable time after receipt of written notice from the Secretary specifying the matter complained of.

Any order under this subsection shall state the findings upon which it is based. The Secretary may withdraw the approval of an application submitted under this section, or suspend the approval of such an application, as provided under this subsection, without first ordering the applicant to submit an assessment of the approved risk evaluation and mitigation strategy for the drug under section 355-1(g)(2)(D) of this title.

(f) Revocation of order refusing, withdrawing or suspending approval of application.—Whenever the Secretary finds that the facts so require, he shall revoke any previous order under subsection (d) or (e) of this section refusing, withdrawing, or suspending approval of an application and shall approve such application or reinstate such approval, as may be appropriate.

(g) Service of orders.—Orders of the Secretary issued under this section shall be served (1) in person by any officer or employee of the department designated by the Secretary or (2) by mailing the order by registered mail or by certified mail addressed to the applicant or respondent at his last-known address in the records of the Secretary.

(h) Appeal from order.—An appeal may be taken by the applicant from an order of the Secretary refusing or withdrawing approval of an application under this section. Such appeal shall be taken by filing in the United States court of appeals for the circuit wherein such applicant resides or has his principal place of business, or in the United States Court of Appeals for the District of Columbia Circuit, within sixty days after the entry of such order, a written petition praying that the order of the Secretary be set aside. A copy of such petition shall be forthwith transmitted by the clerk of the court to the Secretary, or any officer designated by him for that purpose, and thereupon the Secretary shall certify and file in the court the record upon which the order complained of was entered, as provided in section 2112 of title 28. Upon the filing of such petition such court shall have exclusive jurisdiction to affirm or set aside such order, except that until the filing of the record the Secretary may modify or set aside his order. No objection to the order of the Secretary shall be considered by the court unless such objection shall have been urged before the Secretary or unless there were reasonable grounds for failure so to do. The finding of the Secretary as to the facts, if supported by substantial evidence, shall be conclusive. If any person shall apply to the court for leave to adduce additional evidence, and shall show to the satisfaction of the court that such additional evidence is material and that there were reasonable grounds for failure to adduce such evidence in the proceeding before the Secretary, the court may order such additional evidence to be taken before the Secretary and to be adduced upon the hearing in such manner and upon such terms and conditions as to the court may seem proper. The Secretary may modify his findings as to the facts by reason of the additional evidence so taken, and he shall file with the court such modified findings which, if supported by substantial evidence, shall be conclusive, and his recommendation, if any, for the setting aside of the original order. The judgment of the court affirming or setting aside any such order of the Secretary shall be final, subject to review by the Supreme Court of the United States upon certiorari or certification as provided in section 1254 of title 28. The commencement of proceedings under this subsection shall not, unless specifically ordered by the court to the contrary, operate as a stay of the Secretary's order.

(i) Exemptions of drugs for research; discretionary and mandatory conditions; direct reports to Secretary—

(1) The Secretary shall promulgate regulations for exempting from the operation of the foregoing subsections of this section drugs intended solely for investigational use by experts qualified by scientific training and experience to investigate the safety and effectiveness of drugs. Such regulations may, within the discretion of the Secretary, among other conditions relating to the protection of the public health, provide for conditioning such exemption upon—

(A) the submission to the Secretary, before any clinical testing of a new drug is undertaken, of reports, by the manufacturer or the sponsor of the investigation of such drug, of preclinical tests (including tests on animals) of such drug adequate to justify the proposed clinical testing;

(B) the manufacturer or the sponsor of the investigation of a new drug proposed to be distributed to investigators for clinical testing obtaining a signed agreement from each of such investigators that patients to whom the drug is administered will be under his personal supervision, or under the supervision of investigators responsible to him, and that he will not supply such drug to any other investigator, or to clinics, for administration to human beings;

(C) the establishment and maintenance of such records, and the making of such reports to the Secretary, by the manufacturer or the sponsor of the investigation of such drug, of data (including but not limited to analytical reports by investigators) obtained as the result of such investigational use of such drug, as the Secretary finds will enable him to evaluate the safety and effectiveness of such drug in the event of the filing of an application pursuant to subsection (b) of this section; and

(D) the submission to the Secretary by the manufacturer or the sponsor of the investigation of a new drug of a statement of intent regarding whether the manufacturer or sponsor has plans for assessing pediatric safety and efficacy.

(2) Subject to paragraph (3), a clinical investigation of a new drug may begin 30 days after the Secretary has received from the manufacturer or sponsor of the investigation a submission containing such information about the drug and the clinical investigation, including—

(A) information on design of the investigation and adequate reports of basic information, certified by the applicant to be accurate reports, necessary to assess the safety of the drug for use in clinical investigation; and

(B) adequate information on the chemistry and manufacturing of the drug, controls available for the drug, and primary data tabulations from animal or human studies.

(3)(A) At any time, the Secretary may prohibit the sponsor of an investigation from conducting the investigation (referred to in this paragraph as a "clinical hold") if the Secretary makes a determination described in subparagraph (B). The Secretary shall specify the basis for the clinical hold, including the specific information available to the Secretary which served as the basis for such clinical hold, and confirm such determination in writing.

(B) For purposes of subparagraph (A), a determination described in this subparagraph with respect to a clinical hold is that—

(i) the drug involved represents an unreasonable risk to the safety of the persons who are the subjects of the clinical investigation, taking into account the qualifications of the clinical investigators, information about the drug, the design of the clinical investigation, the condition for which the drug is to be investigated, and the health status of the subjects involved; or

(ii) the clinical hold should be issued for such other reasons as the Secretary may by regulation establish (including reasons established by regulation before November 21, 1997).

(C) Any written request to the Secretary from the sponsor of an investigation that a clinical hold be removed shall receive a decision, in writing and specifying the reasons therefor, within 30 days after receipt of such request. Any such request shall include sufficient information to support the removal of such clinical hold.

(4) Regulations under paragraph (1) shall provide that such exemption shall be conditioned upon the manufacturer, or the sponsor of the investigation, requiring that experts using such drugs for investigational purposes certify to such manufacturer or sponsor that they will inform any human beings to whom such drugs, or any controls used in connection therewith, are being administered, or their representatives, that such drugs are being used for investigational purposes and will obtain the consent of such human beings or their representatives, except where it is not feasible, it is contrary to the best interests of such human beings, or the proposed clinical testing poses no more than minimal risk to such human beings and includes appropriate safeguards as prescribed to protect the rights, safety, and welfare of such human beings. Nothing in this subsection shall be construed to require any clinical investigator to submit directly to the Secretary reports on the investigational use of drugs. The Secretary shall update such regulations to require inclusion in the informed consent documents and process a statement that clinical trial information for such clinical investigation has been or will be submitted for inclusion in the registry data bank pursuant to subsection (j) of section 282 of title 42.

(j) Abbreviated new drug applications—

(1) Any person may file with the Secretary an abbreviated application for the approval of a new drug.

(2)(A) An abbreviated application for a new drug shall contain—

(i) information to show that the conditions of use prescribed, recommended, or suggested in the labeling proposed for the new drug have been previously approved for a drug listed under paragraph (7) (hereinafter in this subsection referred to as a "listed drug");

(ii)(I) if the listed drug referred to in clause (i) has only one active ingredient, information to show that the active ingredient of the new drug is the same as that of the listed drug;

(II) if the listed drug referred to in clause (i) has more than one active ingredient, information to show that the active ingredients of the new drug are the same as those of the listed drug, or

(III) if the listed drug referred to in clause (i) has more than one active ingredient and if one of the active ingredients of the new drug is different and the application is filed pursuant to the approval of a petition filed under subparagraph (C), information to show that the other active ingredients of the new drug are the same as the active ingredients of the listed drug, information to show that the different active ingredient is an active ingredient of a listed drug or of a drug which does not meet the requirements of section 321(p) of this title, and such other information respecting the different active ingredient with respect to which the petition was filed as the Secretary may require;

(iii) information to show that the route of administration, the dosage form, and the strength of the new drug are the same as those of the listed drug referred to in clause (i) or, if the route of administration, the dosage form, or the strength of the new drug is different and the application is filed pursuant to the approval of a petition filed under subparagraph (C), such information respecting the route of administration, dosage form, or strength with respect to which the petition was filed as the Secretary may require;

(iv) information to show that the new drug is bioequivalent to the listed drug referred to in clause (i), except that if the application is filed pursuant to the approval of a petition filed under subparagraph (C), information to show that the active ingredients of the new drug are of the same pharmacological or therapeutic class as those of the listed drug referred to in clause (i) and the new drug can be expected to have the same therapeutic effect as the listed drug when administered to patients for a condition of use referred to in clause (i);

(v) information to show that the labeling proposed for the new drug is the same as the labeling approved for the listed drug referred to in clause (i) except for changes required because of differences approved under a petition filed under subparagraph (C) or because the new drug and the listed drug are produced or distributed by different manufacturers;

(vi) the items specified in clauses (B) through (F) of subsection (b)(1) of this section;

(vii) a certification, in the opinion of the applicant and to the best of his knowledge, with respect to each patent which claims the listed drug referred to in clause (i) or which claims a use for such listed drug for which the applicant is seeking approval under this subsection and for which information is required to be filed under subsection (b) or (c) of this section—

(I) that such patent information has not been filed,

(II) that such patent has expired,

(III) of the date on which such patent will expire, or

(IV) that such patent is invalid or will not be infringed by the manufacture, use, or sale of the new drug for which the application is submitted; and

(viii) if with respect to the listed drug referred to in clause (i) information was filed under subsection (b) or (c) of this section for a method of use patent which does not claim a use for which the applicant is seeking approval under this subsection, a statement that the method of use patent does not claim such a use.

The Secretary may not require that an abbreviated application contain information in addition to that required by clauses (i) through (viii).

(B) Notice of opinion that patent is invalid or will not be infringed—

(i) Agreement to give notice.—An applicant that makes a certification described in subparagraph (A)(vii)(IV) shall include in the application a statement that the applicant will give notice as required by this subparagraph.

(ii) Timing of notice.—An applicant that makes a certification described in subparagraph (A)(vii)(IV) shall give notice as required under this subparagraph—

(I) if the certification is in the application, not later than 20 days after the date of the postmark on the notice with which the Secretary informs the applicant that the application has been filed; or

(II) if the certification is in an amendment or supplement to the application, at the time at which the applicant submits the amendment or supplement, regardless of whether the applicant has already given notice with respect to another such certification contained in the application or in an amendment or supplement to the application.

(iii) Recipients of notice.—An applicant required under this subparagraph to give notice shall give notice to—

(I) each owner of the patent that is the subject of the certification (or a representative of the owner designated to receive such a notice); and

(II) the holder of the approved application under subsection (b) for the drug that is claimed by the patent or a use of which is claimed by the patent (or a representative of the holder designated to receive such a notice).

(iv) Contents of notice.—A notice required under this subparagraph shall—

(I) state that an application that contains data from bioavailability or bioequivalence studies has been submitted under this subsection for the drug with respect to which the certification is made to obtain approval to engage in the commercial manufacture, use, or sale of the drug before the expiration of the patent referred to in the certification; and

(II) include a detailed statement of the factual and legal basis of the opinion of the applicant that the patent is invalid or will not be infringed.

(C) If a person wants to submit an abbreviated application for a new drug which has a different active ingredient or whose route of administration, dosage form, or strength differ from that of a listed drug, such person shall submit a petition to the Secretary seeking permission to file such an application. The Secretary shall approve or disapprove a petition submitted under this subparagraph within ninety days of the date the petition is submitted. The Secretary shall approve such a petition unless the Secretary finds—

(i) that investigations must be conducted to show the safety and effectiveness of the drug or of any of its active ingredients, the route of administration, the dosage form, or strength which differ from the listed drug; or

(ii) that any drug with a different active ingredient may not be adequately evaluated for approval as safe and effective on the basis of the information required to be submitted in an abbreviated application.

(D)(i) An applicant may not amend or supplement an application to seek approval of a drug referring to a different listed drug from the listed drug identified in the application as submitted to the Secretary.

(ii) With respect to the drug for which an application is submitted, nothing in this subsection prohibits an applicant from amending or supplementing the application to seek approval of a different strength.

(iii) Within 60 days after December 8, 2003, the Secretary shall issue guidance defining the term "listed drug" for purposes of this subparagraph.

(3)(A) The Secretary shall issue guidance for the individuals who review applications submitted under paragraph (1), which shall relate to promptness in conducting the review, technical excellence, lack of bias and conflict of interest, and knowledge of regulatory and scientific standards, and which shall apply equally to all individuals who review such applications.

(B) The Secretary shall meet with a sponsor of an investigation or an applicant for approval for a drug under this subsection if the sponsor or applicant makes a reasonable written request for a meeting for the purpose of reaching agreement on the design and size of bioavailability and bioequivalence studies needed for approval of such application. The sponsor or applicant shall provide information necessary for discussion and agreement on the design and size of such studies. Minutes of any such meeting shall be prepared by the Secretary and made available to the sponsor or applicant.

(C) Any agreement regarding the parameters of design and size of bioavailability and bioequivalence studies of a drug under this paragraph that is reached between the Secretary and a sponsor or applicant shall be reduced to writing and made part of the administrative record by the Secretary. Such agreement shall not be changed after the testing begins, except—

(i) with the written agreement of the sponsor or applicant; or

(ii) pursuant to a decision, made in accordance with subparagraph (D) by the director of the reviewing division, that a substantial scientific issue essential to determining the safety or effectiveness of the drug has been identified after the testing has begun.

(D) A decision under subparagraph (C)(ii) by the director shall be in writing and the Secretary shall provide to the sponsor or applicant an opportunity for a meeting at which the director and the sponsor or applicant will be present and at which the director will document the scientific issue involved.

(E) The written decisions of the reviewing division shall be binding upon, and may not directly or indirectly be changed by, the field or compliance office personnel unless such field or compliance office personnel demonstrate to the reviewing division why such decision should be modified.

(F) No action by the reviewing division may be delayed because of the unavailability of information from or action by field personnel unless the reviewing division determines that a delay is necessary to assure the marketing of a safe and effective drug.

(G) For purposes of this paragraph, the reviewing division is the division responsible for the review of an application for approval of a drug under this subsection (including scientific matters, chemistry, manufacturing, and controls).

(4) Subject to paragraph (5), the Secretary shall approve an application for a drug unless the Secretary finds—

(A) the methods used in, or the facilities and controls used for, the manufacture, processing, and packing of the drug are inadequate to assure and preserve its identity, strength, quality, and purity;

(B) information submitted with the application is insufficient to show that each of the proposed conditions of use have been previously approved for the listed drug referred to in the application;

(C)(i) if the listed drug has only one active ingredient, information submitted with the application is insufficient to show that the active ingredient is the same as that of the listed drug;

(ii) if the listed drug has more than one active ingredient, information submitted with the application is insufficient to show that the active ingredients are the same as the active ingredients of the listed drug, or

(iii) if the listed drug has more than one active ingredient and if the application is for a drug which has an active ingredient different from the listed drug, information submitted with the application is insufficient to show—

(I) that the other active ingredients are the same as the active ingredients of the listed drug, or

(II) that the different active ingredient is an active ingredient of a listed drug or a drug which does not meet the requirements of section 321(p) of this title, or no petition to file an application for the drug with the different ingredient was approved under paragraph (2)(C);

(D)(i) if the application is for a drug whose route of administration, dosage form, or strength of the drug is the same as the route of administration, dosage form, or strength of the listed drug referred to in the application, information submitted in the application is insufficient to show that the route of administration, dosage form, or strength is the same as that of the listed drug, or

(ii) if the application is for a drug whose route of administration, dosage form, or strength of the drug is different from that of the listed drug referred to in the application, no petition to file an application for the drug with the different route of administration, dosage form, or strength was approved under paragraph (2)(C);

(E) if the application was filed pursuant to the approval of a petition under paragraph (2)(C), the application did not contain the information required by the Secretary respecting the active ingredient, route of administration, dosage form, or strength which is not the same;

(F) information submitted in the application is insufficient to show that the drug is bioequivalent to the listed drug referred to in the application or, if the application was filed pursuant to a petition approved under paragraph (2)(C), information submitted in the application is insufficient to show that the active ingredients of the new drug are of the same pharmacological or therapeutic class as those of the listed drug referred to in paragraph (2)(A)(i) and that the new drug can be expected to have the same therapeutic effect as the listed drug when administered to patients for a condition of use referred to in such paragraph;

(G) information submitted in the application is insufficient to show that the labeling proposed for the drug is the same as the labeling approved for the listed drug referred to in the application except for changes required because of differences approved under a petition filed under paragraph (2)(C) or because the drug and the listed drug are produced or distributed by different manufacturers;

(H) information submitted in the application or any other information available to the Secretary shows that (i) the inactive ingredients of the drug are unsafe for use under the conditions prescribed, recommended, or suggested in the labeling proposed for the drug, or (ii) the composition of the drug is unsafe under such conditions because of the type or quantity of inactive ingredients included or the manner in which the inactive ingredients are included;

(I) the approval under subsection (c) of this section of the listed drug referred to in the application under this subsection has been withdrawn or suspended for grounds described in the first sentence of subsection (e) of this section, the Secretary has published a notice of opportunity for hearing to withdraw approval of the listed drug under subsection (c) of this section for grounds described in the first sentence of subsection (e) of this section, the approval under this subsection of the listed drug referred to in the application under this subsection has been withdrawn or suspended under paragraph (6), or the Secretary has determined that the listed drug has been withdrawn from sale for safety or effectiveness reasons;

(J) the application does not meet any other requirement of paragraph (2)(A); or

(K) the application contains an untrue statement of material fact.

(5)(A) Within one hundred and eighty days of the initial receipt of an application under paragraph (2) or within such additional period as may be agreed upon by the Secretary and the applicant, the Secretary shall approve or disapprove the application.

(B) The approval of an application submitted under paragraph (2) shall be made effective on the last applicable date determined by applying the following to each certification made under paragraph (2)(A)(vii):

(i) If the applicant only made a certification described in subclause (I) or (II) of paragraph (2)(A)(vii) or in both such subclauses, the approval may be made effective immediately.

(ii) If the applicant made a certification described in subclause (III) of paragraph (2)(A)(vii), the approval may be made effective on the date certified under subclause (III).

(iii) If the applicant made a certification described in subclause (IV) of paragraph (2)(A)(vii), the approval shall be made effective immediately unless, before the expiration of 45 days after the date on which the notice described in paragraph (2)(B) is received, an action is brought for infringement of the patent that is the subject of the certification and for which information was submitted to the Secretary under subsection (b)(1) or (c)(2) before the date on which the application (excluding an amendment or supplement to the application), which the Secretary later determines to be substantially complete, was submitted. If such an action is brought before the expiration of such days, the approval shall be made effective upon the expiration of the thirty-month period beginning on the date of the receipt of the notice provided under paragraph (2)(B)(i) or such shorter or longer period as the court may order because either party to the action failed to reasonably cooperate in expediting the action, except that—

(I) if before the expiration of such period the district court decides that the patent is invalid or not infringed (including any substantive determination that there is no cause of action for patent infringement or invalidity), the approval shall be made effective on—

(aa) the date on which the court enters judgment reflecting the decision; or

(bb) the date of a settlement order or consent decree signed and entered by the court stating that the patent that is the subject of the certification is invalid or not infringed;

(II) if before the expiration of such period the district court decides that the patent has been infringed—

(aa) if the judgment of the district court is appealed, the approval shall be made effective on—

(AA) the date on which the court of appeals decides that the patent is invalid or not infringed (including any substantive determination that there is no cause of action for patent infringement or invalidity); or

(BB) the date of a settlement order or consent decree signed and entered by the court of appeals stating that the patent that is the subject of the certification is invalid or not infringed; or

(bb) if the judgment of the district court is not appealed or is affirmed, the approval shall be made effective on the date specified by the district court in a court order under section 271(e)(4)(A) of title 35;

(III) if before the expiration of such period the court grants a preliminary injunction prohibiting the applicant from engaging in the commercial manufacture or sale of the drug until the court decides the issues of patent validity and infringement and if the court decides that such patent is invalid or not infringed, the approval shall be made effective as provided in subclause (I); or

(IV) if before the expiration of such period the court grants a preliminary injunction prohibiting the applicant from engaging in the commercial manufacture or sale of the drug until the court decides the issues of patent validity and infringement and if the court decides that such patent has been infringed, the approval shall be made effective as provided in subclause (II).

In such an action, each of the parties shall reasonably cooperate in expediting the action.

(iv) 180-day exclusivity period—

(I) Effectiveness of application.—Subject to subparagraph (D), if the application contains a certification described in paragraph (2)(A)(vii)(IV) and is for a drug for which a first applicant has submitted an application containing such a certification, the application shall be made effective on the date that is 180 days after the date of the first commercial marketing of the drug (including the commercial marketing of the listed drug) by any first applicant.

(II) Definitions.—In this paragraph:

(aa) 180-day exclusivity period.—The term "180-day exclusivity period" means the 180-day period ending on the day before the date on which an application submitted by an applicant other than a first applicant could become effective under this clause.

(bb) First applicant.—As used in this subsection, the term "first applicant" means an applicant that, on the first day on which a substantially complete application containing a certification described in paragraph (2)(A)(vii)(IV) is submitted for approval of a drug, submits a substantially complete application that contains and lawfully maintains a certification described in paragraph (2)(A)(vii)(IV) for the drug.

(cc) Substantially complete application.—As used in this subsection, the term "substantially complete application" means an application under this subsection that on its face is sufficiently complete to permit a substantive review and contains all the information required by paragraph (2)(A).

(dd) Tentative approval—

(AA) In general.—The term "tentative approval" means notification to an applicant by the Secretary that an application under this subsection meets the requirements of paragraph (2)(A), but cannot receive effective approval because the application does not meet the requirements of this subparagraph, there is a period of exclusivity for the listed drug under subparagraph (F) or section 355a of this title, or there is a 7-year period of exclusivity for the listed drug under section 360cc of this title.

(BB) Limitation.—A drug that is granted tentative approval by the Secretary is not an approved drug and shall not have an effective approval until the Secretary issues an approval after any necessary additional review of the application.

(v) 180-day exclusivity period for competitive generic therapies—

(I) Effectiveness of application.—Subject to subparagraph (D)(iv), if the application is for a drug that is the same as a competitive generic therapy for which any first approved applicant has commenced commercial marketing, the application shall be made effective on the date that is 180 days after the date of the first commercial marketing of the competitive generic therapy (including the commercial marketing of the listed drug) by any first approved applicant.

(II) Limitation.—The exclusivity period under subclause (I) shall not apply with respect to a competitive generic therapy that has previously received an exclusivity period under subclause (I).

(III) Definitions.—In this clause and subparagraph (D)(iv):

(aa) The term "competitive generic therapy" means a drug—

(AA) that is designated as a competitive generic therapy under section 356h of this title; and

(BB) for which there are no unexpired patents or exclusivities on the list of products described in section 355(j)(7)(A) of this title at the time of submission.

(bb) The term "first approved applicant" means any applicant that has submitted an application that—

(AA) is for a competitive generic therapy that is approved on the first day on which any application for such competitive generic therapy is approved;

(BB) is not eligible for a 180-day exclusivity period under clause (iv) for the drug that is the subject of the application for the competitive generic therapy; and

(CC) is not for a drug for which all drug versions have forfeited eligibility for a 180-day exclusivity period under clause (iv) pursuant to subparagraph (D).

(C) Civil action to obtain patent certainty—

(i) Declaratory judgment absent infringement action—

(I) In general.—No action may be brought under section 2201 of title 28, by an applicant under paragraph (2) for a declaratory judgment with respect to a patent which is the subject of the certification referred to in subparagraph (B)(iii) unless—

(aa) the 45-day period referred to in such subparagraph has expired;

(bb) neither the owner of such patent nor the holder of the approved application under subsection (b) for the drug that is claimed by the patent or a use of which is claimed by the patent brought a civil action against the applicant for infringement of the patent before the expiration of such period; and

(cc) in any case in which the notice provided under paragraph (2)(B) relates to noninfringement, the notice was accompanied by a document described in subclause (III).

(II) Filing of civil action.—If the conditions described in items (aa), (bb), and as applicable, (cc) of subclause (I) have been met, the applicant referred to in such subclause may, in accordance with section 2201 of title 28, bring a civil action under such section against the owner or holder referred to in such subclause (but not against any owner or holder that has brought such a civil action against the applicant, unless that civil action was dismissed without prejudice) for a declaratory judgment that the patent is invalid or will not be infringed by the drug for which the applicant seeks approval, except that such civil action may be brought for a declaratory judgment that the patent will not be infringed only in a case in which the condition described in subclause (I)(cc) is applicable. A civil action referred to in this subclause shall be brought in the judicial district where the defendant has its principal place of business or a regular and established place of business.

(III) Offer of confidential access to application.—For purposes of subclause (I)(cc), the document described in this subclause is a document providing an offer of confidential access to the application that is in the custody of the applicant under paragraph (2) for the purpose of determining whether an action referred to in subparagraph (B)(iii) should be brought. The document providing the offer of confidential access shall contain such restrictions as to persons entitled to access, and on the use and disposition of any information accessed, as would apply had a protective order been entered for the purpose of protecting trade secrets and other confidential business information. A request for access to an application under an offer of confidential access shall be considered acceptance of the offer of confidential access with the restrictions as to persons entitled to access, and on the use and disposition of any information accessed, contained in the offer of confidential access, and those restrictions and other terms of the offer of confidential access shall be considered terms of an enforceable contract. Any person provided an offer of confidential access shall review the application for the sole and limited purpose of evaluating possible infringement of the patent that is the subject of the certification under paragraph (2)(A)(vii)(IV) and for no other purpose, and may not disclose information of no relevance to any issue of patent infringement to any person other than a person provided an offer of confidential access. Further, the application may be redacted by the applicant to remove any information of no relevance to any issue of patent infringement.

(ii) Counterclaim to infringement action—

(I) In general.—If an owner of the patent or the holder of the approved application under subsection (b) for the drug that is claimed by the patent or a use of which is claimed by the patent brings a patent infringement action against the applicant, the applicant may assert a counterclaim seeking an order requiring the holder to correct or delete the patent information submitted by the holder under subsection (b) or (c) on the ground that the patent does not claim either—

(aa) the drug for which the application was approved; or

(bb) an approved method of using the drug.

(II) No independent cause of action.—Subclause (I) does not authorize the assertion of a claim described in subclause (I) in any civil action or proceeding other than a counterclaim described in subclause (I).

(iii) No damages.—An applicant shall not be entitled to damages in a civil action under clause (i) or a counterclaim under clause (ii).

(D) Forfeiture of 180-day exclusivity period—

(i) Definition of forfeiture event.—In this subparagraph, the term "forfeiture event," with respect to an application under this subsection, means the occurrence of any of the following:

(I) Failure to market.—The first applicant fails to market the drug by the later of—

(aa) the earlier of the date that is—

(AA) 75 days after the date on which the approval of the application of the first applicant is made effective under subparagraph (B)(iii); or

(BB) 30 months after the date of submission of the application of the first applicant; or

(bb) with respect to the first applicant or any other applicant (which other applicant has received tentative approval), the date that is 75 days after the date as of which, as to each of the patents with respect to which the first applicant submitted and lawfully maintained a certification qualifying the first applicant for the 180-day exclusivity period under subparagraph (B)(iv), at least 1 of the following has occurred:

(AA) In an infringement action brought against that applicant with respect to the patent or in a declaratory judgment action brought by that applicant with respect to the patent, a court enters a final decision from which no appeal (other than a petition to the Supreme Court for a writ of certiorari) has been or can be taken that the patent is invalid or not infringed.

(BB) In an infringement action or a declaratory judgment action described in subitem (AA), a court signs a settlement order or consent decree that enters a final judgment that includes a finding that the patent is invalid or not infringed.

(CC) The patent information submitted under subsection (b) or (c) is withdrawn by the holder of the application approved under subsection (b) of this section.

(II) Withdrawal of application.—The first applicant withdraws the application or the Secretary considers the application to have been withdrawn as a result of a determination by the Secretary that the application does not meet the requirements for approval under paragraph (4).

(III) Amendment of certification.—The first applicant amends or withdraws the certification for all of the patents with respect to which that applicant submitted a certification qualifying the applicant for the 180-day exclusivity period.

(IV) Failure to obtain tentative approval.—The first applicant fails to obtain tentative approval of the application within 30 months after the date on which the application is filed, unless the failure is caused by a change in or a review of the requirements for approval of the application imposed after the date on which the application is filed.

(V) Agreement with another applicant, the listed drug application holder, or a patent owner.—The first applicant enters into an agreement with another applicant under this subsection for the drug, the holder of the application for the listed drug, or an owner of the patent that is the subject of the certification under paragraph (2)(A)(vii)(IV), the Federal Trade Commission or the Attorney General files a complaint, and there is a final decision of the Federal Trade Commission or the court with regard to the complaint from which no appeal (other than a petition to the Supreme Court for a writ of certiorari) has been or can be taken that the agreement has violated the antitrust laws (as defined in section 12 of title 15, except that the term includes section 45 of title 15 to the extent that that section applies to unfair methods of competition).

(VI) Expiration of all patents.—All of the patents as to which the applicant submitted a certification qualifying it for the 180-day exclusivity period have expired.

(ii) Forfeiture.—The 180-day exclusivity period described in subparagraph (B)(iv) shall be forfeited by a first applicant if a forfeiture event occurs with respect to that first applicant.

(iii) Subsequent applicant.—If all first applicants forfeit the 180-day exclusivity period under clause (ii)—

(I) approval of any application containing a certification described in paragraph (2)(A)(vii)(IV) shall be made effective in accordance with subparagraph (B)(iii); and

(II) no applicant shall be eligible for a 180-day exclusivity period.

(iv) Special forfeiture rule for competitive generic therapy.—The 180-day exclusivity period described in subparagraph (B)(v) shall be forfeited by a first approved applicant if the applicant fails to market the competitive generic therapy within 75 days after the date on which the approval of the first approved applicant's application for the competitive generic therapy is made effective.

(E) If the Secretary decides to disapprove an application, the Secretary shall give the applicant notice of an opportunity for a hearing before the Secretary on the question of whether such application is approvable. If the applicant elects to accept the opportunity for hearing by written request within thirty days after such notice, such hearing shall commence not more than ninety days after the expiration of such thirty days unless the Secretary and the applicant otherwise agree. Any such hearing shall thereafter be conducted on an expedited basis and the Secretary's order thereon shall be issued within ninety days after the date fixed by the Secretary for filing final briefs.

(F)(i) If an application (other than an abbreviated new drug application) submitted under subsection (b) of this section for a drug, no active ingredient (including any ester or salt of the active ingredient) of which has been approved in any other application under subsection (b) of this section, was approved during the period beginning January 1, 1982, and ending on September 24, 1984, the Secretary may not make the approval of an application submitted under this subsection which refers to the drug for which the subsection (b) application was submitted effective before the expiration of ten years from the date of the approval of the application under subsection (b) of this section.

(ii) If an application submitted under subsection (b) of this section for a drug, no active ingredient (including any ester or salt of the active ingredient) of which has been approved in any other application under subsection (b) of this section, is approved after September 24, 1984, no application may be submitted under this subsection which refers to the drug for which the subsection (b) application was submitted before the expiration of five years from the date of the approval of the application under subsection (b) of this section, except that such an application may be submitted under this subsection after the expiration of four years from the date of the approval of the subsection (b) application if it contains a certification of patent invalidity or noninfringement described in subclause (IV) of paragraph (2)(A)(vii). The approval of such an application shall be made effective in accordance with subparagraph (B) except that, if an action for patent infringement is commenced during the one-year period beginning forty-eight months after the date of the approval of the subsection (b) application, the thirty-month period referred to in subparagraph (B)(iii) shall be extended by such amount of time (if any) which is required for seven and one-half years to have elapsed from the date of approval of the subsection (b) application.

(iii) If an application submitted under subsection (b) of this section for a drug, which includes an active ingredient (including any ester or salt of the active ingredient) that has been approved in another application approved under subsection (b) of this section, is approved after September 24, 1984, and if such application contains reports of new clinical investigations (other than bioavailability studies) essential to the approval of the application and conducted or sponsored by the applicant, the Secretary may not make the approval of an application submitted under this subsection for the conditions of approval of such drug in the subsection (b) application effective before the expiration of three years from the date of the approval of the application under subsection (b) of this section for such drug.

(iv) If a supplement to an application approved under subsection (b) of this section is approved after September 24, 1984, and the supplement contains reports of new clinical investigations (other than bioavailability studies) essential to the approval of the supplement and conducted or sponsored by the person submitting the supplement, the Secretary may not make the approval of an application submitted under this subsection for a change approved in the supplement effective before the expiration of three years from the date of the approval of the supplement under subsection (b) of this section.

(v) If an application (or supplement to an application) submitted under subsection (b) of this section for a drug, which includes an active ingredient (including any ester or salt of the active ingredient) that has been approved in another application under subsection (b) of this section, was approved during the period beginning January 1, 1982, and ending on September 24, 1984, the Secretary may not make the approval of an application submitted under this subsection which refers to the drug for which the subsection (b) application was submitted or which refers to a change approved in a supplement to the subsection (b) application effective before the expiration of two years from September 24, 1984.

(6) If a drug approved under this subsection refers in its approved application to a drug the approval of which was withdrawn or suspended for grounds described in the first sentence of subsection (e) of this section or was withdrawn or suspended under this paragraph or which, as determined by the Secretary, has been withdrawn from sale for safety or effectiveness reasons, the approval of the drug under this subsection shall be withdrawn or suspended—

(A) for the same period as the withdrawal or suspension under subsection (e) of this section or this paragraph, or

(B) if the listed drug has been withdrawn from sale, for the period of withdrawal from sale or, if earlier, the period ending on the date the Secretary determines that the withdrawal from sale is not for safety or effectiveness reasons.

(7)(A)(i) Within sixty days of September 24, 1984, the Secretary shall publish and make available to the public—

(I) a list in alphabetical order of the official and proprietary name of each drug which has been approved for safety and effectiveness under subsection (c) of this section before September 24, 1984;

(II) the date of approval if the drug is approved after 1981 and the number of the application which was approved; and

(III) whether in vitro or in vivo bioequivalence studies, or both such studies, are required for applications filed under this subsection which will refer to the drug published.

(ii) Every thirty days after the publication of the first list under clause (i) the Secretary shall revise the list to include each drug which has been approved for safety and effectiveness under subsection (c) of this section or approved under this subsection during the thirty-day period.

(iii) When patent information submitted under subsection (b) or (c) of this section respecting a drug included on the list is to be published by the Secretary, the Secretary shall, in revisions made under clause (ii), include such information for such drug.

(B) A drug approved for safety and effectiveness under subsection (c) of this section or approved under this subsection shall, for purposes of this subsection, be considered to have been published under subparagraph (A) on the date of its approval or September 24, 1984, whichever is later.

(C) If the approval of a drug was withdrawn or suspended for grounds described in the first sentence of subsection (e) of this section or was withdrawn or suspended under paragraph (6) or if the Secretary determines that a drug has been withdrawn from sale for safety or effectiveness reasons, it may not be published in the list under subparagraph (A) or, if the withdrawal or suspension occurred after its publication in such list, it shall be immediately removed from such list—

(i) for the same period as the withdrawal or suspension under subsection (e) of this section or paragraph (6), or

(ii) if the listed drug has been withdrawn from sale, for the period of withdrawal from sale or, if earlier, the period ending on the date the Secretary determines that the withdrawal from sale is not for safety or effectiveness reasons.

A notice of the removal shall be published in the Federal Register.

(8) For purposes of this subsection:

(A)(i) The term "bioavailability" means the rate and extent to which the active ingredient or therapeutic ingredient is absorbed from a drug and becomes available at the site of drug action.

(ii) For a drug that is not intended to be absorbed into the bloodstream, the Secretary may assess bioavailability by scientifically valid measurements intended to reflect the rate and extent to which the active ingredient or therapeutic ingredient becomes available at the site of drug action.

(B) A drug shall be considered to be bioequivalent to a listed drug if—

(i) the rate and extent of absorption of the drug do not show a significant difference from the rate and extent of absorption of the listed drug when administered at the same molar dose of the therapeutic ingredient under similar experimental conditions in either a single dose or multiple doses; or

(ii) the extent of absorption of the drug does not show a significant difference from the extent of absorption of the listed drug when administered at the same molar dose of the therapeutic ingredient under similar experimental conditions in either a single dose or multiple doses and the difference from the listed drug in the rate of absorption of the drug is intentional, is reflected in its proposed labeling, is not essential to the attainment of effective body drug concentrations on chronic use, and is considered medically insignificant for the drug.

(C) For a drug that is not intended to be absorbed into the bloodstream, the Secretary may establish alternative, scientifically valid methods to show bioequivalence if the alternative methods are expected to detect a significant difference between the drug and the listed drug in safety and therapeutic effect.

(9) The Secretary shall, with respect to each application submitted under this subsection, maintain a record of—

(A) the name of the applicant,

(B) the name of the drug covered by the application,

(C) the name of each person to whom the review of the chemistry of the application was assigned and the date of such assignment, and

(D) the name of each person to whom the bioequivalence review for such application was assigned and the date of such assignment.

The information the Secretary is required to maintain under this paragraph with respect to an application submitted under this subsection shall be made available to the public after the approval of such application.

(10)(A) If the proposed labeling of a drug that is the subject of an application under this subsection differs from the listed drug due to a labeling revision described under clause (i), the drug that is the subject of such application shall, notwithstanding any other provision of this chapter, be eligible for approval and shall not be considered misbranded under section 352 of this title if—

(i) the application is otherwise eligible for approval under this subsection but for expiration of patent, an exclusivity period, or of a delay in approval described in paragraph (5)(B)(iii), and a revision to the labeling of the listed drug has been approved by the Secretary within 60 days of such expiration;

(ii) the labeling revision described under clause (i) does not include a change to the "Warnings" section of the labeling;

(iii) the sponsor of the application under this subsection agrees to submit revised labeling of the drug that is the subject of such application not later than 60 days after the notification of any changes to such labeling required by the Secretary; and

(iv) such application otherwise meets the applicable requirements for approval under this subsection.

(B) If, after a labeling revision described in subparagraph (A)(i), the Secretary determines that the continued presence in interstate commerce of the labeling of the listed drug (as in effect before the revision described in subparagraph (A)(i)) adversely impacts the safe use of the drug, no application under this subsection shall be eligible for approval with such labeling.

(11)(A) Subject to subparagraph (B), the Secretary shall prioritize the review of, and act within 8 months of the date of the submission of, an original abbreviated new drug application submitted for review under this subsection that is for a drug—

(i) for which there are not more than 3 approved drug products listed under paragraph (7) and for which there are no blocking patents and exclusivities; or

(ii) that has been included on the list under section 356e of this title.

(B) To qualify for priority review under this paragraph, not later than 60 days prior to the submission of an application described in subparagraph (A) or that the Secretary may prioritize pursuant to subparagraph (D), the applicant shall provide complete, accurate information regarding facilities involved in manufacturing processes and testing of the drug that is the subject of the application, including facilities in corresponding Type II active pharmaceutical ingredients drug master files referenced in an application and sites or organizations involved in bioequivalence and clinical studies used to support the application, to enable the Secretary to make a determination regarding whether an inspection of a facility is necessary. Such information shall include the relevant (as determined by the Secretary) sections of such application, which shall be unchanged relative to the date of the submission of such application, except to the extent that a change is made to such information to exclude a facility that was not used to generate data to meet any application requirements for such submission and that is not the only facility intended to conduct one or more unit operations in commercial production. Information provided by an applicant under this subparagraph shall not be considered the submission of an application under this subsection.

(C) The Secretary may expedite an inspection or reinspection under section 374 of this title of an establishment that proposes to manufacture a drug described in subparagraph (A).

(D) Nothing in this paragraph shall prevent the Secretary from prioritizing the review of other applications as the Secretary determines appropriate.

(12) The Secretary shall publish on the internet website of the Food and Drug Administration, and update at least once every 6 months, a list of all drugs approved under subsection (c) for which all patents and periods of exclusivity under this chapter have expired and for which no application has been approved under this subsection.

(13) Upon the request of an applicant regarding one or more specified pending applications under this subsection, the Secretary shall, as appropriate, provide review status updates indicating the categorical status of the applications by each relevant review discipline.

(k) Records and reports; required information; regulations and orders; access to records—

(1) In the case of any drug for which an approval of an application filed under subsection (b) or (j) of this section is in effect, the applicant shall establish and maintain such records, and make such reports to the Secretary, of data relating to clinical experience and other data or information, received or otherwise obtained by such applicant with respect to such drug, as the Secretary may by general regulation, or by order with respect to such application, prescribe on the basis of a finding that such records and reports are necessary in order to enable the Secretary to determine, or facilitate a determination, whether there is or may be ground for invoking subsection (e) of this section. Regulations and orders issued under this subsection and under subsection (i) of this section shall have due regard for the professional ethics of the medical profession and the interests of patients and shall provide, where the Secretary deems it to be appropriate, for the examination, upon request, by the persons to whom such regulations or orders are applicable, of similar information received or otherwise obtained by the Secretary.

(2) Every person required under this section to maintain records, and every person in charge or custody thereof, shall, upon request of an officer or employee designated by the Secretary, permit such officer or employee at all reasonable times to have access to and copy and verify such records.

(3) Active postmarket risk identification—

(A) Definition.—In this paragraph, the term "data" refers to information with respect to a drug approved under this section or under section 262 of title 42, including claims data, patient survey data, standardized analytic files that allow for the pooling and analysis of data from disparate data environments, and any other data deemed appropriate by the Secretary.

(B) Development of postmarket risk identification and analysis methods.—The Secretary shall, not later than 2 years after September 27, 2007, in collaboration with public, academic, and private entities—

(i) develop methods to obtain access to disparate data sources including the data sources specified in subparagraph (C);

(ii) develop validated methods for the establishment of a postmarket risk identification and analysis system to link and analyze safety data from multiple sources, with the goals of including, in aggregate—

(I) at least 25,000,000 patients by July 1, 2010; and

(II) at least 100,000,000 patients by July 1, 2012; and

(iii) convene a committee of experts, including individuals who are recognized in the field of protecting data privacy and security, to make recommendations to the Secretary on the development of tools and methods for the ethical and scientific uses for, and communication of, postmarketing data specified under subparagraph (C), including recommendations on the development of effective research methods for the study of drug safety questions.

(C) Establishment of the postmarket risk identification and analysis system—

(i) In general.—The Secretary shall, not later than 1 year after the development of the risk identification and analysis methods under subparagraph (B), establish and maintain procedures—

(I) for risk identification and analysis based on electronic health data, in compliance with the regulations promulgated under section 264(c) of the Health Insurance Portability and Accountability Act of 1996, and in a manner that does not disclose individually identifiable health information in violation of paragraph (4)(B);

(II) for the reporting (in a standardized form) of data on all serious adverse drug experiences (as defined in section 355-1(b) of this title) submitted to the Secretary under paragraph (1), and those adverse events submitted by patients, providers, and drug sponsors, when appropriate;

(III) to provide for active adverse event surveillance using the following data sources, as available:

(aa) Federal health-related electronic data (such as data from the Medicare program and the health systems of the Department of Veterans Affairs);

(bb) private sector health-related electronic data (such as pharmaceutical purchase data and health insurance claims data); and

(cc) other data as the Secretary deems necessary to create a robust system to identify adverse events and potential drug safety signals;

(IV) to identify certain trends and patterns with respect to data accessed by the system;

(V) to provide regular reports to the Secretary concerning adverse event trends, adverse event patterns, incidence and prevalence of adverse events, and other information the Secretary determines appropriate, which may include data on comparative national adverse event trends; and

(VI) to enable the program to export data in a form appropriate for further aggregation, statistical analysis, and reporting.

(ii) Timeliness of reporting.—The procedures established under clause (i) shall ensure that such data are accessed, analyzed, and reported in a timely, routine, and systematic manner, taking into consideration the need for data completeness, coding, cleansing, and standardized analysis and transmission.

(iii) Private sector resources.—To ensure the establishment of the active postmarket risk identification and analysis system under this subsection not later than 1 year after the development of the risk identification and analysis methods under subparagraph (B), as required under clause (i), the Secretary may, on a temporary or permanent basis, implement systems or products developed by private entities.

(iv) Complementary approaches.—To the extent the active postmarket risk identification and analysis system under this subsection is not sufficient to gather data and information relevant to a priority drug safety question, the Secretary shall develop, support, and participate in complementary approaches to gather and analyze such data and information, including—

(I) approaches that are complementary with respect to assessing the safety of use of a drug in domestic populations not included, or underrepresented, in the trials used to approve the drug (such as older people, people with comorbidities, pregnant women, or children); and

(II) existing approaches such as the Vaccine Adverse Event Reporting System and the Vaccine Safety Datalink or successor databases.

(v) Authority for contracts.—The Secretary may enter into contracts with public and private entities to fulfill the requirements of this subparagraph.

(4) Advanced analysis of drug safety data—

(A) Purpose.—The Secretary shall establish collaborations with public, academic, and private entities, which may include the Centers for Education and Research on Therapeutics under section 299b-1 of title 42, to provide for advanced analysis of drug safety data described in paragraph (3)(C) and other information that is publicly available or is provided by the Secretary, in order to—

(i) improve the quality and efficiency of postmarket drug safety risk-benefit analysis;

(ii) provide the Secretary with routine access to outside expertise to study advanced drug safety questions; and

(iii) enhance the ability of the Secretary to make timely assessments based on drug safety data.

(B) Privacy.—Such analysis shall not disclose individually identifiable health information when presenting such drug safety signals and trends or when responding to inquiries regarding such drug safety signals and trends.

(C) Public process for priority questions.—At least biannually, the Secretary shall seek recommendations from the Drug Safety and Risk Management Advisory Committee (or any successor committee) and from other advisory committees, as appropriate, to the Food and Drug Administration on—

(i) priority drug safety questions; and

(ii) mechanisms for answering such questions, including through—

(I) active risk identification under paragraph (3); and

(II) when such risk identification is not sufficient, postapproval studies and clinical trials under subsection (o)(3).

(D) Procedures for the development of drug safety collaborations—

(i) In general.—Not later than 180 days after the date of the establishment of the active postmarket risk identification and analysis system under this subsection, the Secretary shall establish and implement procedures under which the Secretary may routinely contract with one or more qualified entities to—

(I) classify, analyze, or aggregate data described in paragraph (3)(C) and information that is publicly available or is provided by the Secretary;

(II) allow for prompt investigation of priority drug safety questions, including—

(aa) unresolved safety questions for drugs or classes of drugs; and

(bb) for a newly-approved drugs,[2] safety signals from clinical trials used to approve the drug and other preapproval trials; rare, serious drug side effects; and the safety of use in domestic populations not included, or underrepresented, in the trials used to approve the drug (such as older people, people with comorbidities, pregnant women, or children);

(III) perform advanced research and analysis on identified drug safety risks;

(IV) focus postapproval studies and clinical trials under subsection (o)(3) more effectively on cases for which reports under paragraph (1) and other safety signal detection is not sufficient to resolve whether there is an elevated risk of a serious adverse event associated with the use of a drug; and

(V) carry out other activities as the Secretary deems necessary to carry out the purposes of this paragraph.

(ii) Request for specific methodology.—The procedures described in clause (i) shall permit the Secretary to request that a specific methodology be used by the qualified entity. The qualified entity shall work with the Secretary to finalize the methodology to be used.

(E) Use of analyses.—The Secretary shall provide the analyses described in this paragraph, including the methods and results of such analyses, about a drug to the sponsor or sponsors of such drug.

(F) Qualified entities—

(i) In general.—The Secretary shall enter into contracts with a sufficient number of qualified entities to develop and provide information to the Secretary in a timely manner.

(ii) Qualification.—The Secretary shall enter into a contract with an entity under clause (i) only if the Secretary determines that the entity has a significant presence in the United States and has one or more of the following qualifications:

(I) The research, statistical, epidemiologic, or clinical capability and expertise to conduct and complete the activities under this paragraph, including the capability and expertise to provide the Secretary de-identified data consistent with the requirements of this subsection.

(II) An information technology infrastructure in place to support electronic data and operational standards to provide security for such data.

(III) Experience with, and expertise on, the development of drug safety and effectiveness research using electronic population data.

(IV) An understanding of drug development or risk/benefit balancing in a clinical setting.

(V) Other expertise which the Secretary deems necessary to fulfill the activities under this paragraph.

(G) Contract requirements.—Each contract with a qualified entity under subparagraph (F)(i) shall contain the following requirements:

(i) Ensuring privacy.—The qualified entity shall ensure that the entity will not use data under this subsection in a manner that—

(I) violates the regulations promulgated under section 264(c) of the Health Insurance Portability and Accountability Act of 1996;

(II) violates sections 552 or 552a of title 5 with regard to the privacy of individually-identifiable beneficiary health information; or

(III) discloses individually identifiable health information when presenting drug safety signals and trends or when responding to inquiries regarding drug safety signals and trends.

Nothing in this clause prohibits lawful disclosure for other purposes.

(ii) Component of another organization.—If a qualified entity is a component of another organization—

(I) the qualified entity shall establish appropriate security measures to maintain the confidentiality and privacy of such data; and

(II) the entity shall not make an unauthorized disclosure of such data to the other components of the organization in breach of such confidentiality and privacy requirement.

(iii) Termination or nonrenewal.—If a contract with a qualified entity under this subparagraph is terminated or not renewed, the following requirements shall apply:

(I) Confidentiality and privacy protections.—The entity shall continue to comply with the confidentiality and privacy requirements under this paragraph with respect to all data disclosed to the entity.

(II) Disposition of data.—The entity shall return any data disclosed to such entity under this subsection to which it would not otherwise have access or, if returning the data is not practicable, destroy the data.

(H) Competitive procedures.—The Secretary shall use competitive procedures (as defined in section 132 of Title 41) to enter into contracts under subparagraph (G).

(I) Review of contract in the event of a merger or acquisition.—The Secretary shall review the contract with a qualified entity under this paragraph in the event of a merger or acquisition of the entity in order to ensure that the requirements under this paragraph will continue to be met.

(J) Coordination.—In carrying out this paragraph, the Secretary shall provide for appropriate communications to the public, scientific, public health, and medical communities, and other key stakeholders, and to the extent practicable shall coordinate with the activities of private entities, professional associations, or other entities that may have sources of drug safety data.

(5) The Secretary shall—

(A) conduct regular screenings of the Adverse Event Reporting System database and post a quarterly report on the Adverse Event Reporting System Web site of any new safety information or potential signal of a serious risk identified by Adverse[3] Event Reporting System within the last quarter; and[4]

(B) on an annual basis, review the entire backlog of postmarket safety commitments to determine which commitments require revision or should be eliminated, report to the Congress on these determinations, and assign start dates and estimated completion dates for such commitments; and

(C) make available on the Internet website of the Food and Drug Administration—

(i) guidelines, developed with input from experts qualified by scientific training and experience to evaluate the safety and effectiveness of drugs, that detail best practices for drug safety surveillance using the Adverse Event Reporting System; and

(ii) criteria for public posting of adverse event signals.

(*l*)(1) Public disclosure of safety and effectiveness data and action package.—Safety and effectiveness data and information which has been submitted in an application under subsection (b) of this section for a drug and which has not previously been disclosed to the public shall be made available to the public, upon request, unless extraordinary circumstances are shown—

(A) if no work is being or will be undertaken to have the application approved,

(B) if the Secretary has determined that the application is not approvable and all legal appeals have been exhausted,

(C) if approval of the application under subsection (c) of this section is withdrawn and all legal appeals have been exhausted,

(D) if the Secretary has determined that such drug is not a new drug, or

(E) upon the effective date of the approval of the first application under subsection (j) of this section which refers to such drug or upon the date upon which the approval of an application under subsection (j) of this section which refers to such drug could be made effective if such an application had been submitted.

(2) Action package for approval—

(A) Action package.—The Secretary shall publish the action package for approval of an application under subsection (b) or section 262 of title 42 on the Internet Web site of the Food and Drug Administration—

(i) not later than 30 days after the date of approval of such application for a drug no active ingredient (including any ester or salt of the active ingredient) of which has been approved in any other application under this section or section 262 of title 42; and

(ii) not later than 30 days after the third request for such action package for approval received under section 552 of title 5 for any other drug.

(B) Immediate publication of summary review.—Notwithstanding subparagraph (A), the Secretary shall publish, on the Internet Web site of the Food and Drug Administration, the materials described in subparagraph (C)(iv) not later than 48 hours after the date of approval of the drug, except where such materials require redaction by the Secretary.

(C) Contents.—An action package for approval of an application under subparagraph (A) shall be dated and shall include the following:

(i) Documents generated by the Food and Drug Administration related to review of the application.

(ii) Documents pertaining to the format and content of the application generated during drug development.

(iii) Labeling submitted by the applicant.

(iv) A summary review that documents conclusions from all reviewing disciplines about the drug, noting any critical issues and disagreements with the applicant and within the review team and how they were resolved, recommendations for action, and an explanation of any nonconcurrence with review conclusions.

(v) The Division Director and Office Director's decision document which includes—

(I) a brief statement of concurrence with the summary review;

(II) a separate review or addendum to the review if disagreeing with the summary review; and

(III) a separate review or addendum to the review to add further analysis.

(vi) Identification by name of each officer or employee of the Food and Drug Administration who—

(I) participated in the decision to approve the application; and

(II) consents to have his or her name included in the package.

(D) Review.—A scientific review of an application is considered the work of the reviewer and shall not be altered by management or the reviewer once final.

(E) Confidential information.—This paragraph does not authorize the disclosure of any trade secret, confidential commercial or financial information, or other matter listed in section 552(b) of title 5.

(m) "Patent" defined.—For purposes of this section, the term "patent" means a patent issued by the United States Patent and Trademark Office.

(n) Scientific advisory panels—

(1) For the purpose of providing expert scientific advice and recommendations to the Secretary regarding a clinical investigation of a drug or the approval for marketing of a drug under this section or section 262 of title 42, the Secretary shall establish panels of experts or use panels of experts established before November 21, 1997, or both.

(2) The Secretary may delegate the appointment and oversight authority granted under section 394 of this title to a director of a center or successor entity within the Food and Drug Administration.

(3) The Secretary shall make appointments to each panel established under paragraph (1) so that each panel shall consist of—

(A) members who are qualified by training and experience to evaluate the safety and effectiveness of the drugs to be referred to the panel and who, to the extent feasible, possess skill and experience in the development, manufacture, or utilization of such drugs;

(B) members with diverse expertise in such fields as clinical and administrative medicine, pharmacy, pharmacology, pharmacoeconomics, biological and physical sciences, and other related professions;

(C) a representative of consumer interests, and a representative of interests of the drug manufacturing industry not directly affected by the matter to be brought before the panel; and

(D) two or more members who are specialists or have other expertise in the particular disease or condition for which the drug under review is proposed to be indicated.

Scientific, trade, and consumer organizations shall be afforded an opportunity to nominate individuals for appointment to the panels. No individual who is in the regular full-time employ of the United States and engaged in the administration of this chapter may be a voting member of any panel. The Secretary shall designate one of the members of each panel to serve as chairman thereof.

(4) The Secretary shall, as appropriate, provide education and training to each new panel member before such member participates in a panel's activities, including education regarding requirements under this chapter and related regulations of the Secretary, and the administrative processes and procedures related to panel meetings.

(5) Panel members (other than officers or employees of the United States), while attending meetings or conferences of a panel or otherwise engaged in its business, shall be entitled to receive compensation for each day so engaged, including travel time, at rates to be fixed by the Secretary, but not to exceed the daily equivalent of the rate in effect for positions classified above grade GS-15 of the General Schedule. While serving away from their homes or regular places of business, panel members may be allowed travel expenses (including per diem in lieu of subsistence) as authorized by section 5703 of title 5, for persons in the Government service employed intermittently.

(6) The Secretary shall ensure that scientific advisory panels meet regularly and at appropriate intervals so that any matter to be reviewed by such a panel can be presented to the panel not more than 60 days after the matter is ready for such review. Meetings of the panel may be held using electronic communication to convene the meetings.

(7) Within 90 days after a scientific advisory panel makes recommendations on any matter under its review, the Food and Drug Administration official responsible for the matter shall review the conclusions and recommendations of the panel, and notify the affected persons of the final decision on the matter, or of the reasons that no such decision has been reached. Each such final decision shall be documented including the rationale for the decision.

(o) Postmarket studies and clinical trials; labeling—

(1) In general.—A responsible person may not introduce or deliver for introduction into interstate commerce the new drug involved if the person is in violation of a requirement established under paragraph (3) or (4) with respect to the drug.

(2) Definitions.—For purposes of this subsection:

(A) Responsible person.—The term "responsible person" means a person who—

(i) has submitted to the Secretary a covered application that is pending; or

(ii) is the holder of an approved covered application.

(B) Covered application.—The term "covered application" means—

(i) an application under subsection (b) for a drug that is subject to section 353(b) of title 21; and

(ii) an application under section 262 of title 42.

(C) New safety information; serious risk.—The terms "new safety information," "serious risk," and "signal of a serious risk" have the meanings given such terms in section 355-1(b) of title 21.

(3) Studies and clinical trials—

(A) In general.—For any or all of the purposes specified in subparagraph (B), the Secretary may, subject to subparagraph (D), require a responsible person for a drug to conduct a postapproval study or studies of the drug, or a postapproval clinical trial or trials of the drug, on the basis of scientific data deemed appropriate by the Secretary, including information regarding chemically-related or pharmacologically-related drugs.

(B) Purposes of study or clinical trial.—The purposes referred to in this subparagraph with respect to a postapproval study or postapproval clinical trial are the following:

(i) To assess a known serious risk related to the use of the drug involved.

(ii) To assess signals of serious risk related to the use of the drug.

(iii) To identify an unexpected serious risk when available data indicates the potential for a serious risk.

(C) Establishment of requirement after approval of covered application.—The Secretary may require a postapproval study or studies or postapproval clinical trial or trials for a drug for which an approved covered application is in effect as of the date on which the Secretary seeks to establish such requirement only if the Secretary becomes aware of new safety information.

(D) Determination by Secretary—

(i) Postapproval studies.—The Secretary may not require the responsible person to conduct a study under this paragraph, unless the Secretary makes a determination that the reports under subsection (k)(1) and the active postmarket risk identification and analysis system as available under subsection (k)(3) will not be sufficient to meet the purposes set forth in subparagraph (B).

(ii) Postapproval clinical trials.—The Secretary may not require the responsible person to conduct a clinical trial under this paragraph, unless the Secretary makes a determination that a postapproval study or studies will not be sufficient to meet the purposes set forth in subparagraph (B).

(E) Notification; timetables; periodic reports—

(i) Notification.—The Secretary shall notify the responsible person regarding a requirement under this paragraph to conduct a postapproval study or clinical trial by the target dates for communication of feedback from the review team to the responsible person regarding proposed labeling and postmarketing study commitments as set forth in the letters described in section 101(c) of the Food and Drug Administration Amendments Act of 2007.

(ii) Timetable; periodic reports.—For each study or clinical trial required to be conducted under this paragraph, the Secretary shall require that the responsible person submit a timetable for completion of the study or clinical trial. With respect to each study required to be conducted under this paragraph or otherwise undertaken by the responsible person to investigate a safety issue, the Secretary shall require the responsible person to periodically report to the Secretary on the status of such study including whether any difficulties in completing the study have been encountered. With respect to each clinical trial required to be conducted under this paragraph or otherwise undertaken by the responsible person to investigate a safety issue, the Secretary shall require the responsible person to periodically report to the Secretary on the status of such clinical trial including whether enrollment has begun, the number of participants enrolled, the expected completion date, whether any difficulties completing the clinical trial have been encountered, and registration information with respect to the requirements under section 282(j) of title 42. If the responsible person fails to comply with such timetable or violates any other requirement of this subparagraph, the responsible person shall be considered in violation of this subsection, unless the responsible person demonstrates good cause for such noncompliance or such other violation. The Secretary shall determine what constitutes good cause under the preceding sentence.

(F) Dispute resolution.—The responsible person may appeal a requirement to conduct a study or clinical trial under this paragraph using dispute resolution procedures established by the Secretary in regulation and guidance.

(4) Safety labeling changes requested by Secretary—

(A) New safety information.—If the Secretary becomes aware of new safety information that the Secretary believes should be included in the labeling of the drug, the Secretary shall promptly notify the responsible person or, if the same drug approved under subsection (b) is not currently marketed, the holder of an approved application under subsection (j).

(B) Response to notification.—Following notification pursuant to subparagraph (A), the responsible person or the holder of the approved application under subsection (j) shall within 30 days—

(i) submit a supplement proposing changes to the approved labeling to reflect the new safety information, including changes to boxed warnings, contraindications, warnings, precautions, or adverse reactions; or

(ii) notify the Secretary that the responsible person or the holder of the approved application under subsection (j) does not believe a labeling change is warranted and submit a statement detailing the reasons why such a change is not warranted.

(C) Review.—Upon receipt of such supplement, the Secretary shall promptly review and act upon such supplement. If the Secretary disagrees with the proposed changes in the supplement or with the statement setting forth the reasons why no labeling change is necessary, the Secretary shall initiate discussions to reach agreement on whether the labeling for the drug should be modified to reflect the new safety information, and if so, the contents of such labeling changes.

(D) Discussions.—Such discussions shall not extend for more than 30 days after the response to the notification under subparagraph (B), unless the Secretary determines an extension of such discussion period is warranted.

(E) Order.—Within 15 days of the conclusion of the discussions under subparagraph (D), the Secretary may issue an order directing the responsible person or the holder of the approved application under subsection (j) to make such a labeling change as the Secretary deems appropriate to address the new safety information. Within 15 days of such an order, the responsible person or the holder of the approved application under subsection (j) shall submit a supplement containing the labeling change.

(F) Dispute resolution.—Within 5 days of receiving an order under subparagraph (E), the responsible person or the holder of the approved application under subsection (j) may appeal using dispute resolution procedures established by the Secretary in regulation and guidance.

(G) Violation.—If the responsible person or the holder of the approved application under subsection (j) has not submitted a supplement within 15 days of the date of such order under subparagraph (E), and there is no appeal or dispute resolution proceeding pending, the responsible person or holder shall be considered to be in violation of this subsection. If at the conclusion of any dispute resolution procedures the Secretary determines that a supplement must be submitted and such a supplement is not submitted within 15 days of the date of that determination, the responsible person or holder shall be in violation of this subsection.

(H) Public health threat.—Notwithstanding subparagraphs (A) through (F), if the Secretary concludes that such a labeling change is necessary to protect the public health, the Secretary may accelerate the timelines in such subparagraphs.

(I) Rule of construction.—This paragraph shall not be construed to affect the responsibility of the responsible person or the holder of the approved application under subsection (j) to maintain its label in accordance with existing requirements, including subpart B of part 201 and sections 314.70 and 601.12 of title 21,

Code of Federal Regulations (or any successor regulations).

(5) Non-delegation.—Determinations by the Secretary under this subsection for a drug shall be made by individuals at or above the level of individuals empowered to approve a drug (such as division directors within the Center for Drug Evaluation and Research).

(p) Risk evaluation and mitigation strategy—

(1) In general.—A person may not introduce or deliver for introduction into interstate commerce a new drug if—

(A)(i) the application for such drug is approved under subsection (b) or (j) and is subject to section 353(b) of title 21; or

(ii) the application for such drug is approved under section 262 of title 42; and

(B) a risk evaluation and mitigation strategy is required under section 355-1 of title 21 with respect to the drug and the person fails to maintain compliance with the requirements of the approved strategy or with other requirements under section 355-1 of title 21, including requirements regarding assessments of approved strategies.

(2) Certain postmarket studies.—The failure to conduct a postmarket study under section 356 of title 21, subpart H of part 314, or subpart E of part 601 of title 21, Code of Federal Regulations (or any successor regulations), is deemed to be a violation of paragraph (1).

(q) Petitions and civil actions regarding approval of certain applications—

(1) In general—

(A) Determination.—The Secretary shall not delay approval of a pending application submitted under subsection (b)(2) or (j) of this section or section 262(k) of Title 42 because of any request to take any form of action relating to the application, either before or during consideration of the request, unless—

(i) the request is in writing and is a petition submitted to the Secretary pursuant to section 10.30 or 10.35 of title 21, Code of Federal Regulations (or any successor regulations); and

(ii) the Secretary determines, upon reviewing the petition, that a delay is necessary to protect the public health.

Consideration of the petition shall be separate and apart from review and approval of any application.

(B) Notification.—If the Secretary determines under subparagraph (A) that a delay is necessary with respect to an application, the Secretary shall provide to the applicant, not later than 30 days after making such determination, the following information:

(i) Notification of the fact that a determination under subparagraph (A) has been made.

(ii) If applicable, any clarification or additional data that the applicant should submit to the docket on the petition to allow the Secretary to review the petition promptly.

(iii) A brief summary of the specific substantive issues raised in the petition which form the basis of the determination.

(C) Format.—The information described in subparagraph (B) shall be conveyed via either, at the discretion of the Secretary—

(i) a document; or

(ii) a meeting with the applicant involved.

(D) Public disclosure.—Any information conveyed by the Secretary under subparagraph (C) shall be considered part of the application and shall be subject to the disclosure requirements applicable to information in such application.

(E) Denial based on intent to delay.—If the Secretary determines that a petition or a supplement to the petition was submitted with the primary purpose of delaying the approval of an application and the petition does not on its face raise valid scientific or regulatory issues, the Secretary may deny the petition at any point based on such determination. The Secretary may issue guidance to describe the factors that will be used to determine under this subparagraph whether a petition is submitted with the primary purpose of delaying the approval of an application.

(F) Final agency action.—The Secretary shall take final agency action on a petition not later than 150 days after the date on which the petition is submitted. The Secretary shall not extend such period for any reason, including—

(i) any determination made under subparagraph (A);

(ii) the submission of comments relating to the petition or supplemental information supplied by the petitioner; or

(iii) the consent of the petitioner.

(G) Extension of 30-month period.—If the filing of an application resulted in first-applicant status under subsection (j)(5)(D)(i)(IV) and approval of the application was delayed because of a petition, the 30-month period under such subsection is deemed to be extended by a period of time equal to the period beginning on the date on which the Secretary received the petition and ending on the date of final agency action on the petition (inclusive of such beginning and ending dates), without regard to whether the Secretary grants, in whole or in part, or denies, in whole or in part, the petition.

(H) Certification.—The Secretary shall not consider a petition for review unless the party submitting such petition does so in written form and the subject document is signed and contains the following certification: "I certify that, to my best knowledge and belief: (a) this petition includes all information and views upon which the petition relies; (b) this petition includes representative data and/or information known to the petitioner which are unfavorable to the petition; and (c) I have taken reasonable steps to ensure that any representative data and/or information which are unfavorable to the petition were disclosed to me. I further certify that the information upon which I have based the action requested herein first became known to the party on whose behalf this petition is submitted on or about the following date: XXXXXXXXXX. If I received or expect to receive payments, including cash and other forms of consideration, to file this information or its contents, I received or expect to receive those payments from the following persons or organizations: XXXXXXXXXXXXX. I verify under penalty of perjury that the foregoing is true and correct as of the date of the submission of this petition.", with the date on which such information first became known to such party and the names of such persons or organizations inserted in the first and second blank space, respectively.

(I) Verification.—The Secretary shall not accept for review any supplemental information or comments on a petition unless the party submitting such information or comments does so in written form and the subject document is signed and contains the following verification: "I certify that, to my best knowledge and belief: (a) I have not intentionally delayed submission of this document or its contents; and (b) the information upon which I have based the action requested herein first became known to me on or about XXXXXXXXXX. If I received or expect to receive payments, including cash and other forms of consideration, to file this information or its contents, I received or expect to receive those payments from the following persons or organizations: XXXXX. I verify under penalty of perjury that the foregoing is true and correct as of the date of the submission of this petition.", with the date on which such information first became known to the party and the names of such persons or organizations inserted in the first and second blank space, respectively.

(2) Exhaustion of administrative remedies—

(A) Final agency action within 150 days.—The Secretary shall be considered to have taken final agency action on a petition if—

(i) during the 150-day period referred to in paragraph (1)(F), the Secretary makes a final decision within the meaning of section 10.45(d) of title 21, Code of Federal Regulations (or any successor regulation); or

(ii) such period expires without the Secretary having made such a final decision.

(B) Dismissal of certain civil actions.—If a civil action is filed against the Secretary with respect to any issue raised in the petition before the Secretary has taken final agency action on the petition within the meaning of subparagraph (A), the court shall dismiss without prejudice the action for failure to exhaust administrative remedies.

(C) Administrative record.—For purposes of judicial review related to the approval of an application for which a petition under paragraph (1) was submitted, the administrative record regarding any issue raised by the petition shall include—

(i) the petition filed under paragraph (1) and any supplements and comments thereto;

(ii) the Secretary's response to such petition, if issued; and

(iii) other information, as designated by the Secretary, related to the Secretary's determinations regarding the issues raised in such petition, as long as the information was considered by the agency no later than the date of final agency action as defined under subparagraph (2)(A), and regardless of whether the Secretary responded to the petition at or before the approval of the application at issue in the petition.

(3) Annual report on delays in approvals per petitions.—The Secretary shall annually submit to the Congress a report that specifies—

(A) the number of applications that were approved during the preceding 12-month period;

(B) the number of such applications whose effective dates were delayed by petitions referred to in paragraph (1) during such period;

(C) the number of days by which such applications were so delayed; and

(D) the number of such petitions that were submitted during such period.

(4) Exceptions—

(A) This subsection does not apply to—

(i) a petition that relates solely to the timing of the approval of an application pursuant to subsection (j)(5)(B)(iv); or

(ii) a petition that is made by the sponsor of an application and that seeks only to have the Secretary take or refrain from taking any form of action with respect to that application.

(B) Paragraph (2) does not apply to a petition addressing issues concerning an application submitted pursuant to section 262(k) of Title 42.

(5) Definitions—

(A) Application.—For purposes of this subsection, the term "application" means an application submitted under subsection (b)(2) or (j) of this section or section 262(k) of Title 42.

(B) Petition.—For purposes of this subsection, other than paragraph (1)(A)(i), the term "petition" means a request described in paragraph (1)(A)(i).

(r) Postmarket drug safety information for patients and providers—

(1) Establishment.—Not later than 1 year after September 27, 2007, the Secretary shall improve the transparency of information about drugs and allow patients and health care providers better access to information about drugs by developing and maintaining an Internet Web site that—

(A) provides links to drug safety information listed in paragraph (2) for prescription drugs that are approved under this section or licensed under section 262 of title 42; and

(B) improves communication of drug safety information to patients and providers.

(2) Internet Web site.—The Secretary shall carry out paragraph (1) by—

(A) developing and maintaining an accessible, consolidated Internet Web site with easily searchable drug safety information, including the information found on United States Government Internet Web sites, such as the United States National Library of Medicine's Daily Med and Medline Plus Web sites, in addition to other such Web sites maintained by the Secretary;

(B) ensuring that the information provided on the Internet Web site is comprehensive and includes, when available and appropriate—

(i) patient labeling and patient packaging inserts;

(ii) a link to a list of each drug, whether approved under this section or licensed under such section 262, for which a Medication Guide, as provided for under part 208 of title 21, Code of Federal Regulations (or any successor regulations), is required;

(iii) a link to the registry and results data bank provided for under subsections (i) and (j) of section 282 of title 42;

(iv) the most recent safety information and alerts issued by the Food and Drug Administration for drugs approved by the Secretary under this section, such as product recalls, warning letters, and import alerts;

(v) publicly available information about implemented RiskMAPs and risk evaluation and mitigation strategies under subsection (o);

(vi) guidance documents and regulations related to drug safety; and

(vii) other material determined appropriate by the Secretary;

(C) providing access to summaries of the assessed and aggregated data collected from the active surveillance infrastructure under subsection (k)(3) to provide information of known and serious side-effects for drugs approved under this section or licensed under such section 262 of title 42;

(D) preparing and making publicly available on the Internet website established under paragraph (1) best practices for drug safety surveillance activities for drugs approved under this section or section 262 of Title 42;

(E) enabling patients, providers, and drug sponsors to submit adverse event reports through the Internet Web site;

(F) providing educational materials for patients and providers about the appropriate means of disposing of expired, damaged, or unusable medications; and

(G) supporting initiatives that the Secretary determines to be useful to fulfill the purposes of the Internet Web site.

(3) Posting of drug labeling.—The Secretary shall post on the Internet Web site established under paragraph (1) the approved professional labeling and any required patient labeling of a drug approved under this section or licensed under such section 262 of title 42 not later than 21 days after the date the drug is approved or licensed, including in a supplemental application with respect to a labeling change.

(4) Private sector resources.—To ensure development of the Internet Web site by the date described in paragraph (1), the Secretary may, on a temporary or permanent basis, implement systems or products developed by private entities.

(5) Authority for contracts.—The Secretary may enter into contracts with public and private entities to fulfill the requirements of this subsection.

(6) Review.—The Advisory Committee on Risk Communication under section 360bbb-6 of title 21 shall, on a regular basis, perform a comprehensive review and evaluation of the types of risk communication information provided on the Internet Web site established under paragraph (1) and, through other means, shall identify, clarify, and define the purposes and types of information available to facilitate the efficient flow of information to patients and providers, and shall recommend ways for the Food and Drug Administration to work with outside entities to help facilitate the dispensing of risk communication information to patients and providers.

(s) Referral to advisory committee.—Prior to the approval of a drug no active ingredient (including any ester or salt of the active ingredient) of which has been approved in any other application under this section or section 262 of title 42, the Secretary shall—

(1) refer such drug to a Food and Drug Administration advisory committee for review at a meeting of such advisory committee; or

(2) if the Secretary does not refer such a drug to a Food and Drug Administration advisory committee prior to the approval of the drug, provide in the action letter on the application for the drug a summary of the reasons why the Secretary did not refer the drug to an advisory committee prior to approval.

(t) Database for authorized generic drugs—

(1) In general—

(A) Publication.—The Commissioner shall—

(i) not later than 9 months after September 27, 2007, publish a complete list on the Internet Web site of the Food and Drug Administration of all authorized generic drugs (including drug trade name, brand company manufacturer, and the date the authorized generic drug entered the market); and

(ii) update the list quarterly to include each authorized generic drug included in an annual report submitted to the Secretary by the sponsor of a listed drug during the preceding 3-month period.

(B) Notification.—The Commissioner shall notify relevant Federal agencies, including the Centers for Medicare & Medicaid Services and the Federal Trade Commission, when the Commissioner first publishes the information described in subparagraph (A) that the information has been published and that the information will be updated quarterly.

(2) Inclusion.—The Commissioner shall include in the list described in paragraph (1) each authorized generic drug included in an annual report submitted to the Secretary by the sponsor of a listed drug after January 1, 1999.

(3) Authorized generic drug.—In this section, the term "authorized generic drug" means a listed drug (as that term is used in subsection (j)) that—

(A) has been approved under subsection (c); and

(B) is marketed, sold, or distributed directly or indirectly to retail class of trade under a different labeling, packaging (other than repackaging as the listed drug in blister packs, unit doses, or similar packaging for use in institutions), product code, labeler code, trade name, or trade mark than the listed drug.

(u) Certain drugs containing single enantiomers—

(1) In general.—For purposes of subsections (c)(3)(E)(ii) and (j)(5)(F)(ii), if an application is submitted under subsection (b) for a non-racemic drug containing as an active ingredient (including any ester or salt of the active ingredient) a single enantiomer that is contained in a racemic drug approved in another application under subsection (b), the applicant may, in the application for such non-racemic drug, elect to have the single enantiomer not be considered the same active ingredient as that contained in the approved racemic drug, if—

(A)(i) the single enantiomer has not been previously approved except in the approved racemic drug; and

(ii) the application submitted under subsection (b) for such non-racemic drug—

(I) includes full reports of new clinical investigations (other than bioavailability studies)—

(aa) necessary for the approval of the application under subsections (c) and (d); and

(bb) conducted or sponsored by the applicant; and

(II) does not rely on any clinical investigations that are part of an application submitted under subsection (b) for approval of the approved racemic drug; and

(B) the application submitted under subsection (b) for such non-racemic drug is not submitted for approval of a condition of use—

(i) in a therapeutic category in which the approved racemic drug has been approved; or

(ii) for which any other enantiomer of the racemic drug has been approved.

(2) Limitation—

(A) No approval in certain therapeutic categories.—Until the date that is 10 years after the date of approval of a non-racemic drug described in paragraph (1) and with respect to which the applicant has made the election provided for by such paragraph, the Secretary shall not approve such non-racemic drug for any condition of use in the therapeutic category in which the racemic drug has been approved.

(B) Labeling.—If applicable, the labeling of a non-racemic drug described in paragraph (1) and with respect to which the applicant has made the election provided for by such paragraph shall include a statement that the non-racemic drug is not approved, and has not been shown to be safe and effective, for any condition of use of the racemic drug.

(3) Definition—

(A) In general.—For purposes of this subsection, the term "therapeutic category" means a therapeutic category identified in the list developed by the United States Pharmacopeia pursuant to section 1395w-104(b)(3)(C)(ii) of title 42 and as in effect on September 27, 2007.

(B) Publication by Secretary.—The Secretary shall publish the list described in subparagraph (A) and may amend such list by regulation.

(4) Availability.—The election referred to in paragraph (1) may be made only in an application that is submitted to the Secretary after September 27, 2007, and before October 1, 2022.

(v) Antibiotic drugs submitted before November 21, 1997—

(1) Antibiotic drugs approved before November 21, 1997—

(A) In general.—Notwithstanding any provision of the Food and Drug Administration Modernization Act of 1997 or any other provision of law, a sponsor of a drug that is the subject of an application described in subparagraph (B)(i) shall be eligible for, with respect to the drug, the 3-year exclusivity period referred to under clauses (iii) and (iv) of subsection (c)(3)(E) and under clauses (iii) and (iv) of subsection (j)(5)(F), subject to the requirements of such clauses, as applicable.

(B) Application; antibiotic drug described—

(i) Application.—An application described in this clause is an application for marketing submitted under this section after October 8, 2008 in which the drug that is the subject of the application contains an antibiotic drug described in clause (ii).

(ii) Antibiotic drug.—An antibiotic drug described in this clause is an antibiotic drug that was the subject of an application approved by the Secretary under section 357 of this title (as in effect before November 21, 1997).

(2) Antibiotic drugs submitted before November 21, 1997, but not approved—

(A) In general.—Notwithstanding any provision of the Food and Drug Administration Modernization Act of 1997 or any other provision of law, a sponsor of a drug that is the subject of an application described in subparagraph (B)(i) may elect to be eligible for, with respect to the drug—

(i)(I) the 3-year exclusivity period referred to under clauses (iii) and (iv) of subsection (c)(3)(E) and under clauses (iii) and (iv) of subsection (j)(5)(F), subject to the requirements of such clauses, as applicable; and

(II) the 5-year exclusivity period referred to under clause (ii) of subsection (c)(3)(E) and under clause (ii) of subsection (j)(5)(F), subject to the requirements of such clauses, as applicable; or

(ii) a patent term extension under section 156 of Title 35, subject to the requirements of such section.

(B) Application; antibiotic drug described—

(i) Application.—An application described in this clause is an application for marketing submitted under this section after October 8, 2008 in which the drug that is the subject of the application contains an antibiotic drug described in clause (ii).

(ii) Antibiotic drug.—An antibiotic drug described in this clause is an antibiotic drug that was the subject of 1 or more applications received by the Secretary under section 357 of this title (as in effect before November 21, 1997), none of which was approved by the Secretary under such section.

(3) Limitations—

(A) Exclusivities and extensions.—Paragraphs (1)(A) and (2)(A) shall not be construed to entitle a drug that is the subject of an approved application described in subparagraphs[5] (1)(B)(i) or (2)(B)(i), as applicable, to any market exclusivities or patent extensions other than those exclusivities or extensions described in paragraph (1)(A) or (2)(A).

(B) Conditions of use.—Paragraphs (1)(A) and (2)(A)(i) shall not apply to any condition of use for which the drug referred to in subparagraph (1)(B)(i) or (2)(B)(i), as applicable, was approved before October 8, 2008.

(4) Application of certain provisions.—Notwithstanding section 125, or any other provision, of the Food and Drug Administration Modernization Act of 1997, or any other provision of law, and subject to the limitations in paragraphs (1), (2), and (3), the provisions of the Drug Price Competition and Patent Term Restoration Act of 1984 shall apply to any drug subject to paragraph (1) or any drug with respect to which an election is made under paragraph (2)(A).

(w) Deadline for determination on certain petitions.—The Secretary shall issue a final, substantive determination on a petition submitted pursuant to subsection (b) of section 314.161 of title 21, Code of Federal Regulations (or any successor regulations), no later than 270 days after the date the petition is submitted.

(x) Date of approval in the case of recommended controls under the CSA—

(1) In general.—In the case of an application under subsection (b) with respect to a drug for which the Secretary provides notice to the sponsor that the Secretary intends to issue a scientific and medical evaluation and recommend controls under the Controlled Substances Act, approval of such application shall not take effect until the interim final rule controlling the drug is issued in accordance with section 201(j) of the Controlled Substances Act.

(2) Date of approval.—For purposes of this section, with respect to an application described in paragraph (1), the term "date of approval" shall mean the later of—

(A) the date an application under subsection (b) is approved under subsection (c); or

(B) the date of issuance of the interim final rule controlling the drug.

(y) Contrast agents intended for use with applicable medical imaging devices—

(1) In general.—The sponsor of a contrast agent for which an application has been approved under this section may submit a supplement to the application seeking approval for a new use following the authorization of a premarket submission for an applicable medical imaging device for that use with the contrast agent pursuant to section 360j(p)(1) of this title.

(2) Review of supplement.—In reviewing a supplement submitted under this subsection, the agency center charged with the premarket review of drugs may—

(A) consult with the center charged with the premarket review of devices; and

(B) review information and data submitted to the Secretary by the sponsor of an applicable medical imaging device pursuant to section 360e, 360(k), or 360c(f)(2) of this title so long as the sponsor of such applicable medical imaging device has provided to the sponsor of the contrast agent a right of reference.

(3) Definitions.—For purposes of this subsection—

(A) the term "new use" means a use of a contrast agent that is described in the approved labeling of an applicable medical imaging device described in section 360j(p) of this title, but that is not described in the approved labeling of the contrast agent; and

(B) the terms "applicable medical imaging device" and "contrast agent" have the meanings given such terms in section 360j(p) of this title.

1. **Editor's note:** Probably should be "bioavailability."
2. **Editor's note:** Probably should be "drug."
3. **Editor's note:** Probably should be preceded by "the."
4. **Editor's note:** The word "and" probably should not appear.
5. **Editor's note:** Probably should be "subparagraph."

History of 21 U.S.C. §355: June 25, 1938, ch. 675, §505, 52 Stat. 1052; June 11, 1960, P.L. 86-507, §1(18), 74 Stat. 201; Oct. 10, 1962, P.L. 87-781, §§102(b)-(d), 103(a), (b), 104(a)-(d)(2), 76 Stat. 781-785; Aug. 16, 1972, P.L. 92-387, §4(d), 86 Stat. 562; Sept. 24, 1984, P.L. 98-417, §§101, 102(a)-(b)(5), 103, 104, 98 Stat. 1585, 1592, 1593, 1597; May 13, 1992, P.L. 102-282, §5, 106 Stat. 161; Aug. 13, 1993, P.L. 103-80, §3(n), 107 Stat. 777; Nov. 21, 1997, P.L. 105-115,

§§115, 117, 119, 120, 124(a), 111 Stat. 2313, 2315, 2316, 2318, 2324; Nov. 29, 1999, P.L. 106-113, §1000(a)(9) [§4732(b)(11)], 113 Stat. 1536, 1501A-584; Jan. 4, 2002, P.L. 107-109, §15(c)(1), 115 Stat. 1420; Dec. 3, 2003, P.L. 108-155, §2(b)(1), 117 Stat. 1941; Dec. 8, 2003, P.L. 108-173, §§1101(a), (b), 1102(a), 1103(a), 117 Stat. 2448, 2452, 2457, 2460; Oct. 1, 2007, P.L. 110-85, §§701(b), 801(b)(3)(A), (B), 901(a), 903, 905(a), 914(a), 915, 916, 918, 920, 921, 1113, 121 Stat. 903, 921, 922, 943, 944, 953, 957, 958, 960-962, 976; Aug. 14, 2008, P.L. 110-316, §301, 122 Stat. 3524; Oct. 8, 2008, P.L. 110-379, §4, 122 Stat. 4076; June 22, 2009, P.L. 111-31, §101(e), 123 Stat. 1837; Mar. 23, 2010, P.L. 111-148, §§7002(d), 10609, 124 Stat. 816, 1014; July 9, 2012, P.L. 112-144, §§905, 1101, 1134(a), 1135, 126 Stat. 1092, 1108, 1123; Mar. 13, 2013, P.L. 113-5, §301, 127 Stat. 179; Nov. 25, 2015, P.L. 114-89, §2(a)(1), 129 Stat. 698; Dec. 13, 2016, P.L. 114-255, §§3024(b), 3031(a), 3075(a), (b), 3101(a)(2)(B), 3102(1), 130 Stat. 1099, 1138, 1152, 1156; Aug. 18, 2017, P.L. 115-52, §§601, 706(b), 801, 802, 808, 901(a), 131 Stat. 1048, 1059, 1068, 1069, 1074, 1076.

A §355a. PEDIATRIC STUDIES OF DRUGS

(a) Definitions.—As used in this section, the term "pediatric studies" or "studies" means at least one clinical investigation (that, at the Secretary's discretion, may include pharmacokinetic studies) in pediatric age groups (including neonates in appropriate cases) in which a drug is anticipated to be used, and, at the discretion of the Secretary, may include preclinical studies.

(b) Market exclusivity for new drugs—

(1) In general.—Except as provided in paragraph (2), if, prior to approval of an application that is submitted under section 355(b)(1) of title 21, the Secretary determines that information relating to the use of a new drug in the pediatric population may produce health benefits in that population, the Secretary makes a written request for pediatric studies (which shall include a timeframe for completing such studies), the applicant agrees to the request, such studies are completed using appropriate formulations for each age group for which the study is requested within any such timeframe, and the reports thereof are submitted and accepted in accordance with subsection (d)(4)—

(A)(i)(I) the period referred to in subsection (c)(3)(E)(ii) of section 355 of title 21, and in subsection (j)(5)(F)(ii) of such section, is deemed to be five years and six months rather than five years, and the references in subsections (c)(3)(E)(ii) and (j)(5)(F)(ii) of such section to four years, to forty-eight months, and to seven and one-half years are deemed to be four and one-half years, fifty-four months, and eight years, respectively; or

(II) the period referred to in clauses (iii) and (iv) of subsection (c)(3)(E) of such section, and in clauses (iii) and (iv) of subsection (j)(5)(F) of such section, is deemed to be three years and six months rather than three years; and

(ii) if the drug is designated under section 360bb of title 21 for a rare disease or condition, the period referred to in section 360cc(a) of title 21 is deemed to be seven years and six months rather than seven years; and

(B)(i) if the drug is the subject of—

(I) a listed patent for which a certification has been submitted under subsection (b)(2)(A)(ii) or (j)(2)(A)(vii)(II) of section 355 of title 21 and for which pediatric studies were submitted prior to the expiration of the patent (including any patent extensions); or

(II) a listed patent for which a certification has been submitted under subsections (b)(2)(A)(iii) or (j)(2)(A)(vii)(III) of section 355 of title 21,

the period during which an application may not be approved under section 355(c)(3) of title 21 or section 355(j)(5)(B) of title 21 shall be extended by a period of six months after the date the patent expires (including any patent extensions); or

(ii) if the drug is the subject of a listed patent for which a certification has been submitted under subsection (b)(2)(A)(iv) or (j)(2)(A)(vii)(IV) of section 355 of title 21, and in the patent infringement litigation resulting from the certification the court determines that the patent is valid and would be infringed, the period during which an application may not be approved under section 355(c)(3) or section 355(j)(5)(B) of title 21 shall be extended by a period of six months after the date the patent expires (including any patent extensions).

(2) Exception.—The Secretary shall not extend the period referred to in paragraph (1)(A) or (1)(B) if the determination made under subsection (d)(4) is made later than 9 months prior to the expiration of such period.

(c) Market exclusivity for already-marketed drugs—

(1) In general.—Except as provided in paragraph (2), if the Secretary determines that information relating to the use of an approved drug in the pediatric population may produce health benefits in that population and makes a written request to the holder of an approved application under section 355(b)(1) of title 21 for pediatric studies (which shall include a timeframe for completing such studies), the holder agrees to the request, such studies are completed using appropriate formulations for each age group for which the study is requested within any such timeframe, and the reports thereof are submitted and accepted in accordance with subsection (d)(4)—

(A)(i)(I) the period referred to in subsection (c)(3)(E)(ii) of section 355 of title 21, and in subsection (j)(5)(F)(ii) of such section, is deemed to be five years and six months rather than five years, and the references in subsections (c)(3)(E)(ii) and (j)(5)(F)(ii) of such section to four years, to forty-eight months, and to seven and one-half years are deemed to be four and one-half years, fifty-four months, and eight years, respectively; or

(II) the period referred to in clauses (iii) and (iv) of subsection (c)(3)(D) of such section, and in clauses (iii) and (iv) of subsection (j)(5)(F) of such section, is deemed to be three years and six months rather than three years; and

(ii) if the drug is designated under section 360bb of title 21 for a rare disease or condition, the period referred to in section 360cc(a) of title 21 is deemed to be seven years and six months rather than seven years; and

(B)(i) if the drug is the subject of—

(I) a listed patent for which a certification has been submitted under subsection (b)(2)(A)(ii) or (j)(2)(A)(vii)(II) of section 355 of title 21 and for which pediatric studies were submitted prior to the expiration of the patent (including any patent extensions); or

(II) a listed patent for which a certification has been submitted under subsection (b)(2)(A)(iii) or (j)(2)(A)(vii)(III) of section 355 of title 21,

the period during which an application may not be approved under section 355(c)(3) of title 21 or section 355(j)(5)(B)(ii) of title 21 shall be extended by a period of six months after the date the patent expires (including any patent extensions); or

(ii) if the drug is the subject of a listed patent for which a certification has been submitted under subsection (b)(2)(A)(iv) or (j)(2)(A)(vii)(IV) of section 355 of title 21, and in the patent infringement litigation resulting from the certification the court determines that the patent is valid and would be infringed, the period during which an application may not be approved under section 355(c)(3) of title 21 or section 355(j)(5)(B) of title 21 shall be extended by a period of six months after the date the patent expires (including any patent extensions).

(2) Exception.—The Secretary shall not extend the period referred to in paragraph (1)(A) or (1)(B) if the determination made under subsection (d)(4) is made later than 9 months prior to the expiration of such period.

(d) Conduct of pediatric studies—

(1) Request for studies—

(A) In general.—The Secretary may, after consultation with the sponsor of an application for an investigational new drug under section 355(i) of title 21, the sponsor of an application for a new drug under section 355(b)(1) of title 21, or the holder of an approved application for a drug under section 355(b)(1) of title 21, issue to the sponsor or holder a written request for the conduct of pediatric studies for such drug. In issuing such request, the Secretary shall take into account adequate representation of children of ethnic and racial minorities. Such request to conduct pediatric studies shall be in writing and shall include a timeframe for such studies and a request to the sponsor or holder to propose pediatric labeling resulting from such studies. If a request under this subparagraph does not request studies in neonates, such request shall include a statement describing the rationale for not requesting studies in neonates.

(B) Single written request.—A single written request—

(i) may relate to more than one use of a drug; and

(ii) may include uses that are both approved and unapproved.

(2) Written request for pediatric studies—

(A) Request and response—

(i) In general.—If the Secretary makes a written request for pediatric studies (including neonates, as appropriate) under subsection (b) or (c), the applicant or holder, not later than 180 days after receiving the written request, shall respond to the Secretary as to the intention of the applicant or holder to act on the request by—

(I) indicating when the pediatric studies will be initiated, if the applicant or holder agrees to the request; or

(II) indicating that the applicant or holder does not agree to the request and stating the reasons for declining the request.

(ii) Disagree with request.—If, on or after September 27, 2007, the applicant or holder does not agree to the request on the grounds that it is not possible to develop the appropriate pediatric formulation, the applicant or holder shall submit to the Secretary the reasons such pediatric formulation cannot be developed.

(B) Adverse event reports.—An applicant or holder that, on or after September 27, 2007, agrees to the request for such studies shall provide the Secretary, at the same time as the submission of the reports of such studies, with all postmarket adverse event reports regarding the drug that is the subject of such studies and are available prior to submission of such reports.

(3) Action on submissions.—The Secretary shall review and act upon a submission by a sponsor or holder of a proposed pediatric study request or a proposed amendment to a written request for pediatric studies within 120 calendar days of the submission.

(4) Meeting the studies requirement.—Not later than 180 days after the submission of the reports of the studies, the Secretary shall accept or reject such reports and so notify the sponsor or holder. The Secretary's only responsibility in accepting or rejecting the reports shall be to determine, within the 180-day period, whether the studies fairly respond to the written request, have been conducted in accordance with commonly accepted scientific principles and protocols, and have been reported in accordance with the requirements of the Secretary for filing.

(5) Effect of subsection.—Nothing in this subsection alters or amends section 331(j) of title 21 this Act or section 552 of title 5 or section 1905 of title 18.

(6) Consultation.—With respect to a drug that is a qualified countermeasure (as defined in section 247d-6a of Title 42), a security countermeasure (as defined in section 247d-6b of Title 42), or a qualified pandemic or epidemic product (as defined in section 247d-6d of Title 42), the Secretary shall solicit input from the Assistant Secretary for Preparedness and Response regarding the need for and, from the Director of the Biomedical Advanced Research and Development Authority regarding the conduct of, pediatric studies under this section.

(e) Notice of determinations on studies requirement—

(1) In general.—The Secretary shall publish a notice of any determination, made on or after September 27, 2007, that the requirements of subsection (d) have been met and that submissions and approvals under subsection (b)(2) or (j) of section 355 of title 21 for a drug will be subject to the provisions of this section. Such notice shall be published not later than 30 days after the date of the Secretary's determination regarding market exclusivity and shall include a copy of the written request made under subsection (b) or (c).

(2) Identification of certain drugs.—The Secretary shall publish a notice identifying any drug for which, on or after September 27, 2007, a pediatric formulation was developed, studied, and found to be safe and effective in the pediatric population (or specified subpopulation) if the pediatric formulation for such drug is not introduced onto the market within one year after the date that the Secretary publishes the notice described in paragraph (1). Such notice identifying such drug shall be published not later than 30 days after the date of the expiration of such one year period.

(f) Internal review of written requests and pediatric studies—

(1) Internal review.—The Secretary shall utilize the internal review committee established under section 355d of title 21 to review all written requests issued on or after September 27, 2007, in accordance with paragraph (2).

(2) Review of written requests.—The committee referred to in paragraph (1) shall review all written requests issued pursuant to this section prior to being issued.

(3) Review of pediatric studies.—The committee referred to in paragraph (1) may review studies conducted pursuant to this section to make a recommendation to the Secretary whether to accept or reject such reports under subsection (d)(4).

(4) Activity by committee.—The committee referred to in paragraph (1) may operate using appropriate members of such committee and need not convene all members of the committee.

(5) Documentation of committee action.—For each drug, the committee referred to in paragraph (1) shall document, for each activity described in paragraph (2) or (3), which members of the committee participated in such activity.

(6) Tracking pediatric studies and labeling changes.—The Secretary, in consultation with the committee referred to in paragraph (1), shall track and make available to the public, in an easily accessible manner, including through posting on the Web site of the Food and Drug Administration—

(A) the number of studies conducted under this section and under section 284m of title 42;

(B) the specific drugs and drug uses, including labeled and off-labeled indications, studied under such sections;

(C) the types of studies conducted under such sections, including trial design, the number of pediatric patients studied, and the number of centers and countries involved;

(D) the number of pediatric formulations developed and the number of pediatric formulations not developed and the reasons such formulations were not developed;

(E) the labeling changes made as a result of studies conducted under such sections;

(F) an annual summary of labeling changes made as a result of studies conducted under such sections for distribution pursuant to subsection (k)(2); and

(G) information regarding reports submitted on or after September 27, 2007.

(7) Informing internal review committee.—The Secretary shall provide to the committee referred to in paragraph (1) any response issued to an applicant or holder with respect to a proposed pediatric study request.

(g) Limitations.—Notwithstanding subsection (c)(2), a drug to which the six-month period under subsection (b) or (c) has already been applied—

(1) may receive an additional six-month period under subsection (c)(1)(A)(i)(II) for a supplemental application if all other requirements under this section are satisfied, except that such drug may not receive any additional such period under subsection (c)(1)(B); and

(2) may not receive any additional such period under subsection (c)(1)(A)(ii).

(h) Relationship to pediatric research requirements.—Exclusivity under this section shall only be granted for the completion of a study or studies that are the subject of a written request and for which reports are submitted and accepted in accordance with subsection (d)(4). Written requests under this section may consist of a study or studies required under section 355c of this title.

(i) Labeling changes—

(1) Priority status for pediatric applications and supplements.—Any application or supplement to an application under section 355 of this title proposing a labeling change as a result of any pediatric study conducted pursuant to this section—

(A) shall be considered to be a priority application or supplement; and

(B) shall be subject to the performance goals established by the Commissioner for priority drugs.

(2) Dispute resolution—

(A) Request for labeling change and failure to agree.—If, on or after September 27, 2007, the Commissioner determines that the sponsor and the Commissioner have been unable to reach agreement on appropriate changes to the labeling for the drug that is the subject of the application, not later than 180 days after the date of submission of the application—

(i) the Commissioner shall request that the sponsor of the application make any labeling change that the Commissioner determines to be appropriate; and

(ii) if the sponsor of the application does not agree within 30 days after the Commissioner's request to make a labeling change requested by the Commissioner, the Commissioner shall refer the matter to the Pediatric Advisory Committee.

(B) Action by the Pediatric Advisory Committee.—Not later than 90 days after receiving a referral under subparagraph (A)(ii), the Pediatric Advisory Committee shall—

(i) review the pediatric study reports; and

(ii) make a recommendation to the Commissioner concerning appropriate labeling changes, if any.

(C) Consideration of recommendations.—The Commissioner shall consider the recommendations of the Pediatric Advisory Committee and, if appropriate, not later than 30 days after receiving the recommendation, make a request to the sponsor of the application to make any labeling change that the Commissioner determines to be appropriate.

(D) Misbranding.—If the sponsor of the application, within 30 days after receiving a request under subparagraph (C), does not agree to make a labeling change requested by the Commissioner, the Commissioner may deem the drug that is the subject of the application to be misbranded.

(E) No effect on authority.—Nothing in this subsection limits the authority of the United States to bring an enforcement action under this chapter when a drug lacks appropriate pediatric labeling. Neither course of action (the Pediatric Advisory Committee process or an enforcement action referred to in the preceding sentence) shall preclude, delay, or serve as the basis to stay the other course of action.

(j) Other labeling changes.—If, on or after September 27, 2007, the Secretary determines that a pediatric study conducted under this section does or does not demonstrate that the drug that is the subject of the study is safe and effective, including whether such study results are inconclusive, in pediatric populations or subpopulations, the Secretary shall order the labeling of such product to include information about the results of the study and a statement of the Secretary's determination.

(k) Dissemination of pediatric information—

(1) In general.—Not later than 210 days after the date of submission of a report on a pediatric study under this section, the Secretary shall make available to the public the medical, statistical, and clinical pharmacology reviews of pediatric studies conducted under subsection (b) or (c).

(2) Dissemination of information regarding labeling changes.—Beginning on September 27, 2007, the Secretary shall include as a requirement of a written request that the sponsors of the studies that result in labeling changes that are reflected in the annual summary developed pursuant to subsection (f)(6)(F) distribute, at least annually (or more frequently if the Secretary determines that it would be beneficial to the public health), such information to physicians and other health care providers.

(3) Effect of subsection.—Nothing in this subsection alters or amends section 331(j) of title 21 or section 552 of title 5 or section 1905 of title 18.

(*l*) Adverse event reporting—

(1) Reporting in first 18-month period.—Beginning on September 27, 2007, during the 18-month period beginning on the date a labeling change is approved pursuant to subsection (i), the Secretary shall ensure that all adverse event reports that have been received for such drug (regardless of when such report was received) are referred to the Office of Pediatric Therapeutics established under section 393a of title 21. In considering the reports, the Director of such Office shall provide for the review of the reports by the Pediatric Advisory Committee, including obtaining any recommendations of such Committee regarding whether the Secretary should take action under this chapter in response to such reports.

(2) Reporting in subsequent periods.—Following the 18-month period described in paragraph (1), the Secretary shall, as appropriate, refer to the Office of Pediatric Therapeutics all pediatric adverse event reports for a drug for which a pediatric study was conducted under this section. In considering such reports, the Director of such Office may provide for the review of such reports by the Pediatric Advisory Committee, including obtaining any recommendation of such Committee regarding whether the Secretary should take action in response to such reports.

(3) Preservation of authority.—Nothing in this subsection shall prohibit the Office of Pediatric Therapeutics from providing for the review of adverse event reports by the Pediatric Advisory Committee prior to the 18-month period referred to in paragraph (1), if such review is necessary to ensure safe use of a drug in a pediatric population.

(4) Effect.—The requirements of this subsection shall supplement, not supplant, other review of such adverse event reports by the Secretary.

(m) Clarification of interaction of market exclusivity under this section and market exclusivity awarded to an applicant for approval of a drug under section 355(j).—If a 180-day period under section 355(j)(5)(B)(iv) of title 21 overlaps with a 6-month exclusivity period under this section, so that the applicant for approval of a drug under section 355(j) of title 21 entitled to the 180-day period under that section loses a portion of the 180-day period to which the applicant is entitled for the drug, the 180-day period shall be extended from—

(1) the date on which the 180-day period would have expired by the number of days of the overlap, if the 180-day period would, but for the application of this subsection, expire after the 6-month exclusivity period; or

(2) the date on which the 6-month exclusivity period expires, by the number of days of the overlap if the 180-day period would, but for the application of this subsection, expire during the six-month exclusivity period.

(n) Referral if pediatric studies not submitted—

(1) In general.—Beginning on September 27, 2007, if pediatric studies of a drug have not been submitted by the date specified in the written request issued or if the applicant or holder does not agree to the request under subsection (d) and if the Secretary, through the committee established under section 355d of title 21, determines that there is a continuing need for information relating to the use of the drug in the pediatric population (including neonates, as appropriate), the Secretary shall carry out the following:

(A) For a drug for which a listed patent has not expired, or for which a period of exclusivity eligible for extension under subsection (b)(1) or (c)(1) of this section or under subsection (m)(2) or (m)(3) of section 262 of Title 42 has not ended, make a determination regarding whether an assessment shall be required to be submitted under section 355c(b) of title 21.

(B) For a drug that has no unexpired listed patents and for which no unexpired periods of exclusivity eligible for extension under subsection (b)(1) or (c)(1) of this section or under subsection (m)(2) or (m)(3) of section 262 of Title 42 apply, the Secretary shall refer the drug for inclusion on the list established under section 284m of title 42 for the conduct of studies.

(C) For a drug that is a qualified countermeasure (as defined in section 247d-6a of Title 42), a security countermeasure (as defined in section 247d-6b of Title 42), or a qualified pandemic or epidemic product (as defined in section 247d-6d of Title 42), in addition to any action with respect to such drug under subparagraph (A) or (B), the Secretary shall notify the Assistant Secretary for Preparedness and Response and the Director of the Biomedical Advanced Research and Development Authority of all pediatric studies in the written request issued by the Commissioner of Food and Drugs.

(2) Public notice.—The Secretary shall give the public notice of a decision under paragraph (1)(A) not to require an assessment under section 355c of title 21 and the basis for such decision.

(3) Effect of subsection.—Nothing in this subsection alters or amends section 331(j) of title 21 or section 552 of title 5 or section 1905 of title 18.

(o) Prompt approval of drugs when pediatric information is added to labeling—

(1) General rule.—A drug for which an application has been submitted or approved under subsection (b)(2) or (j) of 355 of title 21 shall not be considered ineligible for approval under that section or misbranded under section 352 of title 21 on the basis that the labeling of the drug omits a pediatric indication or any other aspect of labeling pertaining to pediatric use when the omitted indication or other aspect is protected by patent, or by exclusivity under clause (iii) or (iv) of section 355(j)(5)(F), clause (iii) or (iv) of section 355(c)(3)(E), or section 360cc(a), or by an extension of such exclusivity under this section or section 355f of title 21.

(2) Labeling.—Notwithstanding clauses (iii) and (iv) of section 355(j)(5)(F), clauses (iii) and (iv) of section 355(c)(3)(E), or section 360cc of title 21, the Secretary may require that the labeling of a drug approved pursuant to an application submitted under subsection (b)(2) or (j) of section 355 of title 21 that omits a pediatric indication or other aspect of labeling as described in paragraph (1) include—

(A) a statement that, because of marketing exclusivity for a manufacturer—

(i) the drug is not labeled for pediatric use; or

(ii) in the case of a drug for which there is an additional pediatric use not referred to in paragraph (1), the drug is not labeled for the pediatric use under paragraph (1); and

(B) a statement of any appropriate pediatric contraindications, warnings, precautions, or other information that the Secretary considers necessary to assure safe use.

(3) Preservation of pediatric exclusivity and extensions.—This subsection does not affect—

(A) the availability or scope of exclusivity under—

(i) this section;

(ii) section 355 for pediatric formulations; or

(iii) section 360cc;

(B) the availability or scope of an extension to any such exclusivity, including an extension under this section or section 355f;

(C) the question of the eligibility for approval under section 355 of any application described in subsection (b)(2) or (j) of such section that omits any other aspect of labeling protected by exclusivity under—

(i) clause (iii) or (iv) of section 355(j)(5)(F);

(ii) clause (iii) or (iv) of section 355(c)(3)(E); or

(iii) section 360cc(a); or

(D) except as expressly provided in paragraphs (1) and (2), the operation of section 355 or section 360cc.

History of 21 U.S.C. §355a: June 25, 1938, ch. 675, §505A; Nov. 21, 1997, P.L. 105-115, §111, 111 Stat. 2305; Jan. 4, 2002, P.L. 107-109, §§2, 4, 5(b)(2), 7-11(a), 18(a), 19, 115 Stat. 1408, 1411, 1413-1415, 1423, 1424; Dec. 3, 2003, P.L. 108-155, §§2(b)(2), 3(a), (b)(1), 117 Stat. 1941; Dec. 8, 2003, P.L. 108-173, §1104, 117 Stat. 2461; Oct. 1, 2007, P.L. 110-85, §502(a)(1), 121 Stat. 876; Mar. 23, 2010, P.L. 111-148, §7002(g)(2)(B), 124 Stat. 820; July 9, 2012, P.L. 112-144, §§501(a), 502(a)(1), (b), 509, 126 Stat. 1039, 1040, 1047, 1048; Mar. 13, 2013, P.L. 113-5, §307(a), 127 Stat. 191; Dec. 13, 2016, P.L. 114-255, §3102(2), 130 Stat. 1156; Aug. 18, 2017, P.L. 115-52, §§505(a), (b)(1), (2)(A), 608, 131 Stat. 1046, 1050.

§360b. NEW ANIMAL DRUGS

(a) Unsafe new animal drugs and animal feed containing such drugs; conditions of safety; exemption of drugs for research; import tolerances—

(1) A new animal drug shall, with respect to any particular use or intended use of such drug, be deemed unsafe for purposes of section 351(a)(5) of this title and section 342(a)(2)(C)(ii) of this title unless—

(A) there is in effect an approval of an application filed pursuant to subsection (b) of this section with respect to such use or intended use of such drug, and such drug, its labeling, and such use conform to such approved application;

(B) there is in effect a conditional approval of an application filed pursuant to section 360ccc of this title with respect to such use or intended use of such drug, and such drug, its labeling, and such use conform to such conditionally approved application;

(C) there is in effect an index listing pursuant to section 360ccc-1 of this title with respect to such use or intended use of such drug in a minor species, and such drug, its labeling, and such use conform to such index listing; or

(D) there is in effect an authorization pursuant to section 360bbb-3 of this title with respect to such use or intended use of such drug, and such drug, its labeling, and such use conform to any conditions of such authorization.

A new animal drug shall also be deemed unsafe for such purposes in the event of removal from the establishment of a manufacturer, packer, or distributor of such drug for use in the manufacture of animal feed in any State unless at the time of such removal such manufacturer, packer, or distributor has an unrevoked written statement from the consignee of such drug, or notice from the Secretary, to the effect that, with respect to the use of such drug in animal feed, such consignee (i) holds a license issued under subsection (m) of this section and has in its possession current approved labeling for such drug in animal feed; or (ii) will, if the consignee is not a user of the drug, ship such drug only to a holder of a license issued under subsection (m) of this section.

(2) An animal feed bearing or containing a new animal drug shall, with respect to any particular use or intended use of such animal feed be deemed unsafe for purposes of section 351(a)(6) of this title unless—

(A) there is in effect—

(i) an approval of an application filed pursuant to subsection (b) of this section with respect to such drug, as used in such animal feed, and such animal feed and its labeling, distribution, holding, and use conform to such approved application;

(ii) a conditional approval of an application filed pursuant to section 360ccc of this title with respect to such drug, as used in such animal feed, and such animal feed and its labeling, distribution, holding, and use conform to such conditionally approved application; or

(iii) an index listing pursuant to section 360ccc-1 of this title with respect to such drug, as used in such animal feed, and such animal feed and its labeling, distribution, holding, and use conform to such index listing; and

(B) such animal feed is manufactured at a site for which there is in effect a license issued pursuant to subsection (m)(1) of this section to manufacture such animal feed.

(3) A new animal drug or an animal feed bearing or containing a new animal drug shall not be deemed unsafe for the purposes of section 351(a)(5) or (6) of this title if such article is for investigational use and conforms to the terms of an exemption in effect with respect thereto under subsection (j) of this section.

(4)(A) Except as provided in subparagraph (B), if an approval of an application filed under subsection (b) of this section is in effect with respect to a particular use or intended use of a new animal drug, the drug shall not be deemed unsafe for the purposes of paragraph (1) and shall be exempt from the requirements of section 352(f) of this title with respect to a different use or intended use of the drug, other than a use in or on animal feed, if such use or intended use—

(i) is by or on the lawful written or oral order of a licensed veterinarian within the context of a veterinarian-client-patient relationship, as defined by the Secretary; and

(ii) is in compliance with regulations promulgated by the Secretary that establish the conditions for such different use or intended use.

The regulations promulgated by the Secretary under clause (ii) may prohibit particular uses of an animal drug and shall not permit such different use of an animal drug if the labeling of another animal drug that contains the same active ingredient and which is in the same dosage form and concentration provides for such different use.

(B) If the Secretary finds that there is a reasonable probability that a use of an animal drug authorized under subparagraph (A) may present a risk to the public health, the Secretary may—

(i) establish a safe level for a residue of an animal drug when it is used for such different use authorized by subparagraph (A); and

(ii) require the development of a practical, analytical method for the detection of residues of such drug above the safe level established under clause (i).

The use of an animal drug that results in residues exceeding a safe level established under clause (i) shall be considered an unsafe use of such drug under paragraph (1). Safe levels may be established under clause (i) either by regulation or order.

(C) The Secretary may by general regulation provide access to the records of veterinarians to ascertain any use or intended use authorized under subparagraph (A) that the Secretary has determined may present a risk to the public health.

(D) If the Secretary finds, after affording an opportunity for public comment, that a use of an animal drug authorized under subparagraph (A) presents a risk to the public health or that an analytical method required under subparagraph (B) has not been developed and submitted to the Secretary, the Secretary may, by order, prohibit any such use.

(5) If the approval of an application filed under section 355 of this title is in effect, the drug under such application shall not be deemed unsafe for purposes of paragraph (1) and shall be exempt from the requirements of section 352(f) of this title with respect to a use or intended use of the drug in animals if such use or intended use—

(A) is by or on the lawful written or oral order of a licensed veterinarian within the context of a veterinarian-client-patient relationship, as defined by the Secretary; and

(B) is in compliance with regulations promulgated by the Secretary that establish the conditions for the use or intended use of the drug in animals.

(6) For purposes of section 342(a)(2)(D) of this title, a use or intended use of a new animal drug shall not be deemed unsafe under this section if the Secretary establishes a tolerance for such drug and any edible portion of any animal imported into the United States does not contain residues exceeding such tolerance. In establishing such tolerance, the Secretary shall rely on data sufficient to demonstrate that a proposed tolerance is safe based on similar food safety criteria used by the Secretary to establish tolerances for applications for new animal drugs filed under subsection (b)(1) of this section. The Secretary may consider and rely on data submitted by the drug manufacturer, including data submitted to appropriate regulatory authorities in any country where the new animal drug is lawfully used or data available from a relevant international organization, to the extent such data are not inconsistent with the criteria used by the Secretary to establish a tolerance for applications for new animal drugs filed under subsection (b)(1) of this section. For purposes of this paragraph, "relevant international organization" means the Codex Alimenterius Commission or other international organization deemed appropriate by the Secretary. The Secretary may, under procedures specified by regulation, revoke a tolerance established under this paragraph if information demonstrates that the use of the new animal drug under actual use conditions results in food being imported into the United States with residues exceeding the tolerance or if scientific evidence shows the tolerance to be unsafe.

(b) Filing application for uses of new animal drug; contents; patent information; abbreviated application; presubmission conference—

(1) Any person may file with the Secretary an application with respect to any intended use or uses of a new animal drug. Such person shall submit to the Secretary as a part of the application (A) full reports of investigations which have been made to show whether or not such drug is safe and effective for use; (B) a full list of the articles used as components of such drug; (C) a full statement of the composition of such drug; (D) a full description of the methods used in, and the facilities and controls used for, the manufacture, processing, and packing of such drug; (E) such samples of such drug and of the articles used as components thereof, of any animal feed for use in or on which such drug is intended, and of the edible portions or products (before or after slaughter) of animals to which such drug (directly or in or on animal feed) is intended to be administered, as the Secretary may require; (F) specimens of the labeling proposed to be used for such drug, or in case such drug is intended for use in animal feed, proposed labeling appropriate for such use, and specimens of the labeling for the drug to be manufactured, packed, or distributed by the applicant; (G) a description of practicable methods for determining the quantity, if any, of such drug in or on food, and any substance formed in or on food, because of its use; and (H) the proposed tolerance or withdrawal period or other use restrictions for such drug if any tolerance or withdrawal period or other use restrictions are required in order to assure that the proposed use of such drug will be safe. The applicant shall file with the application the patent number and the expiration date of any patent which claims the new animal drug for which the applicant filed the application or which claims a method of using such drug and with respect to which a claim of patent infringement could reasonably be asserted if a person not licensed by the owner engaged in the manufacture, use, or sale of the drug. If an application is filed under this subsection for a drug and a patent which claims such drug or a method of using such drug is issued after the filing date but before approval of the application, the applicant shall amend the application to include the information required by the preceding sentence. Upon approval of the application, the Secretary shall publish information submitted under the two preceding sentences.

(2) Any person may file with the Secretary an abbreviated application for the approval of a new animal drug. An abbreviated application shall contain the information required by subsection (n) of this section.

(3) Any person intending to file an application under paragraph (1), section 360ccc of this title, or a request for an investigational exemption under subsection (j) of this section shall be entitled to one or more conferences prior to such submission to reach an agreement acceptable to the Secretary establishing a submission or an investigational requirement, which may include a requirement for a field investigation. A decision establishing a submission or an investigational requirement shall bind the Secretary and the applicant or requestor unless (A) the Secretary and the applicant or requestor mutually agree to modify the requirement, or (B) the Secretary by written order determines that a substantiated scientific requirement essential to the determination of safety or effectiveness of the animal drug involved has appeared after the conference. No later than 25 calendar days after each such conference, the Secretary shall provide a written order setting forth a scientific justification specific to the animal drug and intended uses under consideration if the agreement referred to in the first sentence requires more than one field investigation as being essential to provide substantial evidence of effectiveness for the intended uses of the drug. Nothing in this paragraph shall be construed as compelling the Secretary to require a field investigation.

(c) Period for submission and approval of application; period for notice, and expedition of hearing; period for issuance of order; abbreviated applications; withdrawal periods; effective date of approval; relationship to other applications; withdrawal or suspension of approval; bioequivalence; filing of additional patent information—

(1) Within one hundred and eighty days after the filing of an application pursuant to subsection (b) of this section, or such additional period as may be agreed upon by the Secretary and the applicant, the Secretary shall either (A) issue an order approving the application if he then finds that none of the grounds for denying approval specified in subsection (d) of this section applies, or (B) give the applicant notice of an opportunity for a hearing before the Secretary under subsection (d) of this section on the question whether such application is approvable. If the applicant elects to accept the opportunity for a hearing by written request within thirty days after such notice, such hearing shall commence not more than ninety days after the expiration of such thirty days unless the Secretary and the applicant otherwise agree. Any such hearing shall thereafter be conducted on an expedited basis and the Secretary's order thereon shall be issued within ninety days after the date fixed by the Secretary for filing final briefs.

(2)(A) Subject to subparagraph (C), the Secretary shall approve an abbreviated application for a drug unless the Secretary finds—

(i) the methods used in, or the facilities and controls used for, the manufacture, processing, and packing of the drug are inadequate to assure and preserve its identity, strength, quality, and purity;

(ii) the conditions of use prescribed, recommended, or suggested in the proposed labeling are not reasonably certain to be followed in practice or, except as provided in subparagraph (B), information submitted with the application is insufficient to show that each of the proposed conditions of use or similar limitations (whether in the labeling or published pursuant to subsection (i) of this section) have been previously approved for the approved new animal drug referred to in the application;

(iii) information submitted with the application is insufficient to show that the active ingredients are the same as those of the approved new animal drug referred to in the application;

(iv)(I) if the application is for a drug whose active ingredients, route of administration, dosage form, strength, or use with other animal drugs in animal feed is the same as the active ingredients, route of administration, dosage form, strength, or use with other animal drugs in animal feed of the approved new animal drug referred to in the application, information submitted in the application is insufficient to show that the active ingredients, route of administration, dosage form, strength, or use with other animal drugs in animal feed is the same as that of the approved new animal drug, or

(II) if the application is for a drug whose active ingredients, route of administration, dosage form, strength, or use with other animal drugs in animal feed is different from that of the approved new animal drug referred to in the application, no petition to file an application for the drug with the different active ingredients, route of administration, dosage form, strength, or use with other animal drugs in animal feed was approved under subsection (n)(3) of this section;

(v) if the application was filed pursuant to the approval of a petition under subsection (n)(3) of this section, the application did not contain the information required by the Secretary respecting the active ingredients, route of administration, dosage form, strength, or use with other animal drugs in animal feed which is not the same;

(vi) information submitted in the application is insufficient to show that the drug is bioequivalent to the approved new animal drug referred to in the application, or if the application is filed under a petition approved pursuant to subsection (n)(3) of this section, information submitted in the application is insufficient to show that the active ingredients of the new animal drug are of the same pharmacological or therapeutic class as the pharmacological or therapeutic class of the approved new animal drug and that the new animal drug can be expected to have the same therapeutic effect as the approved new animal drug when used in accordance with the labeling;

(vii) information submitted in the application is insufficient to show that the labeling proposed for the drug is the same as the labeling approved for the approved new animal drug referred to in the application except for changes required because of differences approved under a petition filed under subsection (n)(3) of this section, because of a different withdrawal period, or because the drug and the approved new animal drug are produced or distributed by different manufacturers;

(viii) information submitted in the application or any other information available to the Secretary shows that (I) the inactive ingredients of the drug are unsafe for use under the conditions prescribed, recommended, or suggested in the labeling proposed for the drug, (II) the composition of the drug is unsafe under such conditions because of the type or quantity of inactive ingredients included or the manner in which the inactive ingredients are included, or (III) in the case of a drug for food producing animals, the inactive ingredients of the drug or its composition may be unsafe with respect to human food safety;

(ix) the approval under subsection (b)(1) of this section of the approved new animal drug referred to in the application filed under subsection (b)(2) of this section has been withdrawn or suspended for grounds described in paragraph (1) of subsection (e) of this section, the Secretary has published a notice of a hearing to withdraw approval of the approved new animal drug for such grounds, the approval under this paragraph of the new animal drug for which the application under subsection (b)(2) of this section was filed has been withdrawn or suspended under subparagraph (G) for such grounds, or the Secretary has determined that the approved new animal drug has been withdrawn from sale for safety or effectiveness reasons;

(x) the application does not meet any other requirement of subsection (n) of this section; or

(xi) the application contains an untrue statement of material fact.

(B) If the Secretary finds that a new animal drug for which an application is submitted under subsection (b)(2) of this section is bioequivalent to the approved new animal drug referred to in such application and that residues of the new animal drug are consistent with the tolerances established for such approved new animal drug but at a withdrawal period which is different than the withdrawal period approved for such approved new animal drug, the Secretary may establish, on the basis of information submitted, such different withdrawal period as the withdrawal period for the new animal drug for purposes of the approval of such application for such drug.

(C) Within 180 days of the initial receipt of an application under subsection (b)(2) of this section or within such additional period as may be agreed upon by the Secretary and the applicant, the Secretary shall approve or disapprove the application.

(D) The approval of an application filed under subsection (b)(2) of this section shall be made effective on the last applicable date determined under the following:

(i) If the applicant only made a certification described in clause (i) or (ii) of subsection (n)(1)(G) of this section or in both such clauses, the approval may be made effective immediately.

(ii) If the applicant made a certification described in clause (iii) of subsection (n)(1)(G) of this section, the approval may be made effective on the date certified under clause (iii).

(iii) If the applicant made a certification described in clause (iv) of subsection (n)(1)(G) of this section, the approval shall be made effective immediately unless an action is brought for infringement of a patent which is the subject of the certification before the expiration of 45 days from the date the notice provided under subsection (n)(2)(B)(i) of this section is received. If such an action is brought before the expiration of such days, the approval shall be made effective upon the expiration of the 30 month period beginning on the date of the receipt of the notice provided under subsection (n)(2)(B) of this section or such shorter or longer period as the court may order because either party to the action failed to reasonably cooperate in expediting the action, except that if before the expiration of such period—

(I) the court decides that such patent is invalid or not infringed, the approval shall be made effective on the date of the court decision,

(II) the court decides that such patent has been infringed, the approval shall be made effective on such date as the court orders under section 271(e)(4)(A) of Title 35, or

(III) the court grants a preliminary injunction prohibiting the applicant from engaging in the commercial manufacture or sale of the drug until the court decides the issues of patent validity and infringement and if the court decides that such patent is invalid or not infringed, the approval shall be made effective on the date of such court decision.

In such an action, each of the parties shall reasonably cooperate in expediting the action. Until the expiration of 45 days from the date the notice made under subsection (n)(2)(B) of this section is received, no action may be brought under section 2201 of Title 28 for a declaratory judgment with respect to the patent. Any action brought under section 2201 of Title 28 shall be brought in the judicial district where the defendant has its principal place of business or a regular and established place of business.

(iv) If the application contains a certification described in clause (iv) of subsection (n)(1)(G) of this section and is for a drug for which a previous application has been filed under this subsection containing such a certification, the application shall be made effective not earlier than 180 days after—

(I) the date the Secretary receives notice from the applicant under the previous application of the first commercial marketing of the drug under the previous application, or

(II) the date of a decision of a court in an action described in subclause (III)[1] holding the patent which is the subject of the certification to be invalid or not infringed,

whichever is earlier.

(E) If the Secretary decides to disapprove an application, the Secretary shall give the applicant notice of an opportunity for a hearing before the Secretary on the question of whether such application is approvable. If the applicant elects to accept the opportunity for hearing by written request within 30 days after such notice, such hearing shall commence not more than 90 days after the expiration of such 30 days unless the Secretary and the applicant otherwise agree. Any such hearing shall thereafter be conducted on an expedited basis and the Secretary's order thereon shall be issued within 90 days after the date fixed by the Secretary for filing final briefs.

(F)(i) If an application submitted under subsection (b)(1) of this section for a drug, no active ingredient (including any ester or salt of the active ingredient) of which has been approved in any other application under subsection (b)(1) of this section, is approved after November 16, 1988, no application may be submitted under subsection (b)(2) of this section which refers to the drug for which the subsection (b)(1) application was submitted before the expiration of 5 years from the date of the approval of the application under subsection (b)(1) of this section, except that such an application may be submitted under subsection (b)(2) of this section after the expiration of 4 years from the date of the approval of the subsection (b)(1) application if it contains a certification of patent invalidity or noninfringement described in clause (iv) of subsection (n)(1)(G) of this section. The approval of such an application shall be made effective in accordance with subparagraph (B) except that, if an action for patent infringement is commenced during the one-year period beginning 48 months after the date of the approval of the subsection (b) application, the 30 month period referred to in subparagraph (D)(iii) shall be extended by such amount of time (if any) which is required for seven and one-half years to have elapsed from the date of approval of the subsection (b) application.

(ii) If an application submitted under subsection (b)(1) of this section for a drug, which includes an active ingredient (including any ester or salt of the active ingredient) that has been approved in another application approved under such subsection, is approved after November 16, 1988, and if such application contains substantial evidence of the effectiveness of the drug involved, any studies of animal safety, or, in the case of food producing animals, human food safety studies (other than bioequivalence studies or residue depletion studies, except residue depletion studies for minor uses or minor species) required for the approval of the application and conducted or sponsored by the applicant, the Secretary may not make the approval of an application submitted under subsection (b)(2) of this section for the conditions of approval of such drug in the subsection (b)(1) application effective before the expiration of 3 years from the date of the approval of the application under subsection (b)(1) of this section for such drug.

(iii) If a supplement to an application approved under subsection (b)(1) of this section is approved after November 16, 1988, and the supplement contains substantial evidence of the effectiveness of the drug involved, any studies of animal safety, or, in the case of food producing animals, human food safety studies (other than bioequivalence studies or residue depletion studies, except residue depletion studies for minor uses or minor species) required for the approval of the supplement and conducted or sponsored by the person submitting the supplement, the Secretary may not make the approval of an application submitted under subsection (b)(2) of this section for a change approved in the supplement effective before the expiration of 3 years from the date of the approval of the supplement.

(iv) An applicant under subsection (b)(1) of this section who comes within the provisions of clause (i) of this subparagraph as a result of an application which seeks approval for a use solely in non-food producing animals, may elect, within 10 days of receiving such approval, to waive clause (i) of this subparagraph, in which event the limitation on approval of applications submitted under subsection (b)(2) of this section set forth in clause (ii) of this subparagraph shall be applicable to the subsection (b)(1) application.

(v) If an application (including any supplement to a new animal drug application) submitted under subsection (b)(1) of this section for a new animal drug for a food-producing animal use, which includes an active ingredient (including any ester or salt of the active ingredient) which has been the subject of a waiver under clause (iv) is approved after November 16, 1988, and if the application contains substantial evidence of the effectiveness of the drug involved, any studies of animal safety, or human food safety studies (other than bioequivalence studies or residue depletion studies, except residue depletion studies for minor uses or minor species) required for the new approval of the application and conducted or sponsored by the applicant, the Secretary may not make the approval of an application (including any supplement to such application) submitted under subsection (b)(2) of this section for the new conditions of approval of such drug in the subsection (b)(1) application effective before the expiration of five years from the date of approval of the application under subsection (b)(1) of this section for such drug. The provisions of this paragraph shall apply only to the first approval for a food-producing animal use for the same applicant after the waiver under clause (iv).

(G) If an approved application submitted under subsection (b)(2) of this section for a new animal drug refers to a drug the approval of which was withdrawn or suspended for grounds described in paragraph (1) or (2) of subsection (e) of this section or was withdrawn or suspended under this subparagraph or which, as determined by the Secretary, has been withdrawn from sale for safety or effectiveness reasons, the approval of the drug under this paragraph shall be withdrawn or suspended—

(i) for the same period as the withdrawal or suspension under subsection (e) of this section or this subparagraph, or

(ii) if the approved new animal drug has been withdrawn from sale, for the period of withdrawal from sale or, if earlier, the period ending on the date the Secretary determines that the withdrawal from sale is not for safety or effectiveness reasons.

(H) For purposes of this paragraph:

(i) The term "bioequivalence" means the rate and extent to which the active ingredient or therapeutic ingredient is absorbed from a new animal drug and becomes available at the site of drug action.

(ii) A new animal drug shall be considered to be bioequivalent to the approved new animal drug referred to in its application under subsection (n) of this section if—

(I) the rate and extent of absorption of the drug do not show a significant difference from the rate and extent of absorption of the approved new animal drug referred to in the application when administered at the same dose of the active ingredient under similar experimental conditions in either a single dose or multiple doses;

(II) the extent of absorption of the drug does not show a significant difference from the extent of absorption of the approved new animal drug referred to in the application when administered at the same dose of the active ingredient under similar experimental conditions in either a single dose or multiple doses and the difference from the approved new animal drug in the rate of absorption of the drug is intentional, is reflected in its proposed labeling, is not essential to the attainment of effective drug concentrations in use, and is considered scientifically insignificant for the drug in attaining the intended purposes of its use and preserving human food safety; or

(III) in any case in which the Secretary determines that the measurement of the rate and extent of absorption or excretion of the new animal drug in biological fluids is inappropriate or impractical, an appropriate acute pharmacological effects test or other test of the new animal drug and, when deemed scientifically necessary, of the approved new animal drug referred to in the application in the species to be tested or in an appropriate animal model does not show a significant difference between the new animal drug and such approved new animal drug when administered at the same dose under similar experimental conditions.

If the approved new animal drug referred to in the application for a new animal drug under subsection (n) of this section is approved for use in more than one animal species, the bioequivalency information described in subclauses (I), (II), and (III) shall be obtained for one species, or if the Secretary deems appropriate based on scientific principles, shall be obtained for more than one species. The Secretary may prescribe the dose to be used in determining bioequivalency under subclause (I), (II), or (III). To assure that the residues of the new animal drug will be consistent with the established tolerances for the approved new animal drug referred to in the application under subsection (b)(2) of this section upon the expiration of the withdrawal period contained in the application for the new animal drug, the Secretary shall require bioequivalency data or residue depletion studies of the new animal drug or such other data or studies as the Secretary considers appropriate based on scientific principles. If the Secretary requires one or more residue studies under the preceding sentence, the Secretary may not require that the assay methodology used to determine the withdrawal period of the new animal drug be more rigorous than the methodology used to determine the withdrawal period for the approved new animal drug referred to in the application. If such studies are required and if the approved new animal drug, referred to in the application for the new animal drug for which such studies are required, is approved for use in more than one animal species, such studies shall be conducted for one species, or if the Secretary deems appropriate based on scientific principles, shall be conducted for more than one species.

(3) If the patent information described in subsection (b)(1) of this section could not be filed with the submission of an application under subsection (b)(1) of this section because the application was filed before the patent information was required under subsection (b)(1) of this section or a patent was issued after the application was approved under such subsection, the holder of an approved application shall file with the Secretary the patent number and the expiration date of any patent which claims the new animal drug for which the application was filed or which claims a method of using such drug and with respect to which a claim of patent infringement could reasonably be asserted if a person not licensed by the owner engaged in the manufacture, use, or sale of the drug. If the holder of an approved application could not file patent information under subsection (b)(1) of this section because it was not required at the time the application was approved, the holder shall file such information under this subsection not later than 30 days after November 16, 1988, and if the holder of an approved application could not file patent information under subsection (b)(1) of this section because no patent had been issued when an application was filed or approved, the holder shall file such information under this subsection not later than 30 days after the date the patent involved is issued. Upon the submission of patent information under this subsection, the Secretary shall publish it.

(4) A drug manufactured in a pilot or other small facility may be used to demonstrate the safety and effectiveness of the drug and to obtain approval for the drug prior to manufacture of the drug in a larger facility, unless the Secretary makes a determination that a full scale production facility is necessary to ensure the safety or effectiveness of the drug.

(d) Grounds for refusing application; approval of application; factors; "substantial evidence" defined; combination drugs—

(1) If the Secretary finds, after due notice to the applicant in accordance with subsection (c) of this section and giving him an opportunity for a hearing, in accordance with said subsection, that—

(A) the investigations, reports of which are required to be submitted to the Secretary pursuant to subsection (b) of this section, do not include adequate tests by all methods reasonably applicable to show whether or not such drug is safe for use under the conditions prescribed, recommended, or suggested in the proposed labeling thereof;

(B) the results of such tests show that such drug is unsafe for use under such conditions or do not show that such drug is safe for use under such conditions;

(C) the methods used in, and the facilities and controls used for, the manufacture, processing, and packing of such drug are inadequate to preserve its identity, strength, quality, and purity;

(D) upon the basis of the information submitted to him as part of the application, or upon the basis of any other information before him with respect to such drug, he has insufficient information to determine whether such drug is safe for use under such conditions;

(E) evaluated on the basis of the information submitted to him as part of the application and any other information before him with respect to such drug, there is a lack of substantial evidence that the drug will have the effect it purports or is represented to have under the conditions of use prescribed, recommended, or suggested in the proposed labeling thereof;

(F) upon the basis of information submitted to the Secretary as part of the application or any other information before the Secretary with respect to such drug, any use prescribed, recommended, or suggested in labeling proposed for such drug will result in a residue of such drug in excess of a tolerance found by the Secretary to be safe for such drug;

(G) the application failed to contain the patent information prescribed by subsection (b)(1) of this section;

(H) based on a fair evaluation of all material facts, such labeling is false or misleading in any particular; or

(I) such drug induces cancer when ingested by man or animal or, after tests which are appropriate for the evaluation of the safety of such drug, induces cancer in man or animal, except that the foregoing provisions of this subparagraph shall not apply with respect to such drug if the Secretary finds that, under the conditions of use specified in proposed labeling and reasonably certain to be followed in practice (i) such drug will not adversely affect the animals for which it is intended, and (ii) no residue of such drug will be found (by methods of examination prescribed or approved by the Secretary by regulations, which regulations shall not be subject to subsections (c), (d), and (h) of this section), in any edible portion of such animals after slaughter or in any food yielded by or derived from the living animals;

he shall issue an order refusing to approve the application. If, after such notice and opportunity for hearing, the Secretary finds that subparagraphs (A) through (I) do not apply, he shall issue an order approving the application.

(2) In determining whether such drug is safe for use under the conditions prescribed, recommended, or suggested in the proposed labeling thereof, the Secretary shall consider, among other relevant factors, (A) the probable consumption of such drug and of any substance formed in or on food because of the use of such drug, (B) the cumulative effect on man or animal of such drug, taking into account any chemically or pharmacologically related substance, (C) safety factors which in the opinion of experts, qualified by scientific training and experience to evaluate the safety of such drugs, are appropriate for the use of animal experimentation data, and (D) whether the conditions of use prescribed, recommended, or suggested in the proposed labeling are reasonably certain to be followed in practice. Any order issued under this subsection refusing to approve an application shall state the findings upon which it is based.

(3) As used in this section, the term "substantial evidence" means evidence consisting of one or more adequate and well controlled investigations, such as—

(A) a study in a target species;

(B) a study in laboratory animals;

(C) any field investigation that may be required under this section and that meets the requirements of subsection (b)(3) of this section if a presubmission conference is requested by the applicant;

(D) a bioequivalence study; or

(E) an in vitro study;

by experts qualified by scientific training and experience to evaluate the effectiveness of the drug involved, on the basis of which it could fairly and reasonably be concluded by such experts that the drug will have the effect it purports or is represented to have under the conditions of use prescribed, recommended, or suggested in the labeling or proposed labeling thereof.

(4) In a case in which an animal drug contains more than one active ingredient, or the labeling of the drug prescribes, recommends, or suggests use of the drug in combination with one or more other animal drugs, and the active ingredients or drugs intended for use in the combination have previously been separately approved pursuant to an application submitted under section 360b(b)(1) of this title for particular uses and conditions of use for which they are intended for use in the combination—

(A) the Secretary shall not issue an order under paragraph (1)(A), (1)(B), or (1)(D) refusing to approve the application for such combination on human food safety grounds unless the Secretary finds that the application fails to establish that—

(i) none of the active ingredients or drugs intended for use in the combination, respectively, at the longest withdrawal time of any of the active ingredients or drugs in the combination, respectively, exceeds its established tolerance; or

(ii) none of the active ingredients or drugs in the combination interferes with the methods of analysis for another of the active ingredients or drugs in the combination, respectively;

(B) the Secretary shall not issue an order under paragraph (1)(A), (1)(B), or (1)(D) refusing to approve the application for such combination on target animal safety grounds unless the Secretary finds that—

(i)(I) there is a substantiated scientific issue, specific to one or more of the active ingredients or animal drugs in the combination, that cannot adequately be evaluated based on information contained in the application for the combination (including any investigations, studies, or tests for which the applicant has a right of reference or use from the person by or for whom the investigations, studies, or tests were conducted); or

(II) there is a scientific issue raised by target animal observations contained in studies submitted to the Secretary as part of the application; and

(ii) based on the Secretary's evaluation of the information contained in the application with respect to the issues identified in clauses (i)(I) and (II), paragraph (1)(A), (B), or (D) apply;

(C) except in the case of a combination that contains a nontopical antibacterial ingredient or animal drug, the Secretary shall not issue an order under paragraph (1)(E) refusing to approve an application for a combination animal drug intended for use other than in animal feed or drinking water unless the Secretary finds that the application fails to demonstrate that—

(i) there is substantial evidence that any active ingredient or animal drug intended only for the same use as another active ingredient or animal drug in the combination makes a contribution to labeled effectiveness;

(ii) each active ingredient or animal drug intended for at least one use that is different from all other active ingredients or animal drugs used in the combination provides appropriate concurrent use for the intended target population; or

(iii) where based on scientific information the Secretary has reason to believe the active ingredients or animal drugs may be physically incompatible or have disparate dosing regimens, such active ingredients or animal drugs are physically compatible or do not have disparate dosing regimens; and

(D) the Secretary shall not issue an order under paragraph (1)(E) refusing to approve an application for a combination animal drug intended for use in animal feed or drinking water unless the Secretary finds that the application fails to demonstrate that—

(i) there is substantial evidence that any active ingredient or animal drug intended only for the same use as another active ingredient or animal drug in the combination makes a contribution to the labeled effectiveness;

(ii) each of the active ingredients or animal drugs intended for at least one use that is different from all other active ingredients or animal drugs used in the combination provides appropriate concurrent use for the intended target population;

(iii) where a combination contains more than one nontopical antibacterial ingredient or animal drug, there is substantial evidence that each of the nontopical antibacterial ingredients or animal drugs makes a contribution to the labeled effectiveness, except that for purposes of this clause, antibacterial ingredient or animal drug does not include the ionophore or arsenical classes of animal drugs; or

(iv) where based on scientific information the Secretary has reason to believe the active ingredients or animal drugs intended for use in drinking water may be physically incompatible, such active ingredients or animal drugs intended for use in drinking water are physically compatible.

(5) In reviewing an application that proposes a change to add an intended use for a minor use or a minor species to an approved new animal drug application, the Secretary shall reevaluate only the relevant information in the approved application to determine whether the application for the minor use or minor species can be approved. A decision to approve the application for the minor use or minor species is not, implicitly or explicitly, a reaffirmation of the approval of the original application.

(e) Withdrawal of approval; grounds; immediate suspension upon finding imminent hazard to health of man or animals—

(1) The Secretary shall, after due notice and opportunity for hearing to the applicant, issue an order withdrawing approval of an application filed pursuant to subsection (b) of this section with respect to any new animal drug if the Secretary finds—

(A) that experience or scientific data show that such drug is unsafe for use under the conditions of use upon the basis of which the application was approved or the condition of use authorized under subsection (a)(4)(A) of this section;

(B) that new evidence not contained in such application or not available to the Secretary until after such application was approved, or tests by new methods, or tests by methods not deemed reasonably applicable when such application was approved, evaluated together with the evidence available to the Secretary when the application was approved, shows that such drug is not shown to be safe for use under the conditions of use upon the basis of which the application was approved or that subparagraph (I) of paragraph (1) of subsection (d) of this section applies to such drug;

(C) on the basis of new information before him with respect to such drug, evaluated together with the evidence available to him when the application was approved, that there is a lack of substantial evidence that such drug will have the effect it purports or is represented to have under the conditions of use prescribed, recommended, or suggested in the labeling thereof;

(D) the patent information prescribed by subsection (c)(3) of this section was not filed within 30 days after the receipt of written notice from the Secretary specifying the failure to file such information;

(E) that the application contains any untrue statement of a material fact; or

(F) that the applicant has made any changes from the standpoint of safety or effectiveness beyond the variations provided for in the application unless he has supplemented the application by filing with the Secretary adequate information respecting all such changes and unless there is in effect an approval of the supplemental application. The supplemental application shall be treated in the same manner as the original application.

If the Secretary (or in his absence the officer acting as Secretary) finds that there is an imminent hazard to the health of man or of the animals for which such drug is intended, he may suspend the approval of such application immediately, and give the applicant prompt notice of his action and afford the applicant the opportunity for an expedited hearing under this subsection; but the authority conferred by this sentence to suspend the approval of an application shall not be delegated.

(2) The Secretary may also, after due notice and opportunity for hearing to the applicant, issue an order withdrawing the approval of an application with respect to any new animal drug under this section if the Secretary finds—

(A) that the applicant has failed to establish a system for maintaining required records, or has repeatedly or deliberately failed to maintain such records or to make required reports in accordance with a regulation or order under subsection (l) of this section, or the applicant has refused to permit access to, or copying or verification of, such records as required by paragraph (2) of such subsection;

(B) that on the basis of new information before him, evaluated together with the evidence before him when the application was approved, the methods used in, or the facilities and controls used for, the manufacture, processing, and packing of such drug are inadequate to assure and preserve its identity, strength, quality, and purity and were not made adequate within a reasonable time after receipt of written notice from the Secretary specifying the matter complained of; or

(C) that on the basis of new information before him, evaluated together with the evidence before him when the application was approved, the labeling of such drug, based on a fair evaluation of all material facts, is false or misleading in any particular and was not corrected within a reasonable time after receipt of written notice from the Secretary specifying the matter complained of.

(3) Any order under this subsection shall state the findings upon which it is based.

(f) Revocation of order refusing, withdrawing or suspending approval of application—

Whenever the Secretary finds that the facts so require, he shall revoke any previous order under subsection (d), (e), or (m) of this section, or section 360ccc(c), (d), or (e) of this title refusing, withdrawing, or suspending approval of an application and shall approve such application or reinstate such approval, as may be appropriate.

(g) Service of orders.—Orders of the Secretary issued under this section, or section 360ccc of this title (other than orders issuing, amending, or repealing regulations) shall be served (1) in person by any officer or employee of the department designated by the Secretary or (2) by mailing the order by registered mail or by certified mail addressed to the applicant or respondent at his last known address in the records of the Secretary.

(h) Appeal from order.—An appeal may be taken by the applicant from an order of the Secretary refusing or withdrawing approval of an application filed under subsection (b) or (m) of this section. The provisions of subsection (h) of section 355 of this title shall govern any such appeal.

(i) Publication in Federal Register; effective date and revocation or suspension of regulation.—When a new animal drug application filed pursuant to subsection (b) of this section or section 360ccc of this title is approved, the Secretary shall by notice, which upon publication shall be effective as a regulation, publish in the Federal Register the name and address of the applicant and the conditions and indications of use of the new animal drug covered by such application, including any tolerance and withdrawal period or other use restrictions and, if such new animal drug is intended for use in animal feed, appropriate purposes and conditions of use (including special labeling requirements and any requirement that an animal feed bearing or containing the new animal drug be limited to use under the professional supervision of a licensed veterinarian) applicable to any animal feed for use in which such drug is approved, and such other information, upon the basis of which such application was approved, as the Secretary deems necessary to assure the safe and effective use of such drug. Upon withdrawal of approval of such new animal drug application or upon its suspension or upon failure to renew a conditional approval under section 360ccc of this title, the Secretary shall forthwith revoke or suspend, as the case may be, the regulation published pursuant to this subsection (i) insofar as it is based on the approval of such application.

(j) Exemption of drugs for research; discretionary and mandatory conditions.—To the extent consistent with the public health, the Secretary shall promulgate regulations for exempting from the operation of this section new animal drugs, and animal feeds bearing or containing new animal drugs, intended solely for investigational use by experts qualified by scientific training and experience to investigate the safety and effectiveness of animal drugs. Such regulations may, in the discretion of the Secretary, among other conditions relating to the protection of the public health, provide for conditioning such exemption upon the establishment and maintenance of such records, and the making of such reports to the Secretary, by the manufacturer or the sponsor of the investigation of such article, of data (including but not limited to analytical reports by investigators) obtained as a result of such investigational use of such article, as the Secretary finds will enable him to evaluate the safety and effectiveness of such article in the event of the filing of an application pursuant to this section. Such regulations, among other things, shall set forth the conditions (if any) upon which animals treated with such articles, and any products of such animals (before or after slaughter), may be marketed for food use.

(k) Food containing new animal drug considered unadulterated while approval of application for such drug is effective.—While approval of an application for a new animal drug is effective, a food shall not, by reason of bearing or containing such drug or any substance formed in or on the food because of its use in accordance with such application (including the conditions and indications of use prescribed pursuant to subsection (i) of this section), be considered adulterated within the meaning of clause (1) of section 342(a) of this title.

(*l*) Records and reports; required information; regulations and orders; examination of data; access to records—

(1) In the case of any new animal drug for which an approval of an application filed pursuant to subsection (b) of this section or section 360ccc of this title is in effect, the applicant shall establish and maintain such records, and make such reports to the Secretary, of data relating to experience, including experience with uses authorized under subsection (a)(4)(A) of this section, and other data or information, received or otherwise obtained by such applicant with respect to such drug, or with respect to animal feeds bearing or containing such drug, as the Secretary may by general regulation, or by order with respect to such application, prescribe on the basis of a finding that such records and reports are necessary in order to enable the Secretary to determine, or facilitate a determination, whether there is or may be ground for invoking subsection (e) or subsection (m)(4) of this section. Such regulation or order shall provide, where the Secretary deems it to be appropriate, for the examination, upon request, by the persons to whom such regulation or order is applicable, of similar information received or otherwise obtained by the Secretary.

(2) Every person required under this subsection to maintain records, and every person in charge or custody thereof, shall, upon request of an officer or employee designated by the Secretary, permit such officer or employee at all reasonable times to have access to and copy and verify such records.

(3)(A) In the case of each new animal drug described in paragraph (1) that contains an antimicrobial active ingredient, the sponsor of the drug shall submit an annual report to the Secretary on the amount of each antimicrobial active ingredient in the drug that is sold or distributed for use in food-producing animals, including information on any distributor-labeled product.

(B) Each report under this paragraph shall specify the amount of each antimicrobial active ingredient—

(i) by container size, strength, and dosage form;

(ii) by quantities distributed domestically and quantities exported; and

(iii) by dosage form, including, for each such dosage form, a listing of the target animals, indications, and production classes that are specified on the approved label of the product.

(C) Each report under this paragraph shall—

(i) be submitted not later than March 31 each year;

(ii) cover the period of the preceding calendar year; and

(iii) include separate information for each month of such calendar year.

(D) The Secretary may share information reported under this paragraph with the Antimicrobial Resistance Task Force established under section 247d-5 of Title 42.

(E) The Secretary shall make summaries of the information reported under this paragraph publicly available, except that—

(i) the summary data shall be reported by antimicrobial class, and no class with fewer than 3 distinct sponsors of approved applications shall be independently reported; and

(ii) the data shall be reported in a manner consistent with protecting both national security and confidential business information.

(m) Feed mill licenses—

(1) Any person may file with the Secretary an application for a license to manufacture animal feeds bearing or containing new animal drugs. Such person shall submit to the Secretary as part of the application (A) a full statement of the business name and address of the specific facility at which the manufacturing is to take place and the facility's registration number, (B) the name and signature of the responsible individual or individuals for that facility, (C) a certification that the animal feeds bearing or containing new animal drugs are manufactured and labeled in accordance with the applicable regulations published pursuant to subsection (i) of this section or for indexed new animal drugs in accordance with the index listing published pursuant to section 360ccc-1(e)(2) of this title and the labeling requirements set forth in section 360ccc-1(h) of this title, and (D) a certification that the methods used in, and the facilities and controls used for, manufacturing, processing, packaging, and holding such animal feeds are in conformity with current good manufacturing practice as described in section 351(a)(2)(B) of this title.

(2) Within 90 days after the filing of an application pursuant to paragraph (1), or such additional period as may be agreed upon by the Secretary and the applicant, the Secretary shall (A) issue an order approving the application if the Secretary then finds that none of the grounds for denying approval specified in paragraph (3) applies, or (B) give the applicant notice of an opportunity for a hearing before the Secretary under paragraph (3) on the question whether such application is approvable. The procedure governing such a hearing shall be the procedure set forth in the last two sentences of subsection (c)(1) of this section.

(3) If the Secretary, after due notice to the applicant in accordance with paragraph (2) and giving the applicant an opportunity for a hearing in accordance with such paragraph, finds, on the basis of information submitted to the Secretary as part of the application, on the basis of a preapproval inspection, or on the basis of any other information before the Secretary—

(A) that the application is incomplete, false, or misleading in any particular;

(B) that the methods used in, and the facilities and controls used for, the manufacture, processing, and packing of such animal feed are inadequate to preserve the identity, strength, quality, and purity of the new animal drug therein; or

(C) that the facility manufactures animal feeds bearing or containing new animal drugs in a manner that does not accord with the specifications for manufacture or labels animal feeds bearing or containing new animal drugs in a manner that does not accord with the conditions or indications of use that are published pursuant to subsection (i) of this section or an index listing pursuant to section 360ccc-1(e) of this title,

the Secretary shall issue an order refusing to approve the application. If, after such notice and opportunity for hearing, the Secretary finds that subparagraphs (A) through (C) do not apply, the Secretary shall issue an order approving the application. An order under this subsection approving an application for a license to manufacture animal feeds bearing or containing new animal drugs shall permit a facility to manufacture only those animal feeds bearing or containing new animal drugs for which there are in effect regulations pursuant to subsection (i) of this section or an index listing pursuant to section 360ccc-1(e) of this title relating to the use of such drugs in or on such animal feed.

(4)(A) The Secretary shall, after due notice and opportunity for hearing to the applicant, revoke a license to manufacture animal feeds bearing or containing new animal drugs under this subsection if the Secretary finds—

(i) that the application for such license contains any untrue statement of a material fact; or

(ii) that the applicant has made changes that would cause the application to contain any untrue statements of material fact or that would affect the safety or effectiveness of the animal feeds manufactured at the facility unless the applicant has supplemented the application by filing with the Secretary adequate information respecting all such changes and unless there is in effect an approval of the supplemental application.

If the Secretary (or in the Secretary's absence the officer acting as the Secretary) finds that there is an imminent hazard to the health of humans or of the animals for which such animal feed is intended, the Secretary may suspend the license immediately, and give the applicant prompt notice of the action and afford the applicant the opportunity for an expedited hearing under this subsection; but the authority conferred by this sentence shall not be delegated.

(B) The Secretary may also, after due notice and opportunity for hearing to the applicant, revoke a license to manufacture animal feed under this subsection if the Secretary finds—

(i) that the applicant has failed to establish a system for maintaining required records, or has repeatedly or deliberately failed to maintain such records or to make required reports in accordance with a regulation or order under paragraph (5)(A) of this subsection or section 354(a)(3)(A) of this title, or the applicant has refused to permit access to, or copying or verification of, such records as required by subparagraph (B) of such paragraph or section 354(a)(3)(B) of this title;

(ii) that on the basis of new information before the Secretary, evaluated together with the evidence before the Secretary when such license was issued, the methods used in, or the facilities and controls used for, the manufacture, processing, packing, and holding of such animal feed are inadequate to assure and preserve the identity, strength, quality, and purity of the new animal drug therein, and were not made adequate within a reasonable time after receipt of written notice from the Secretary, specifying the matter complained of;

(iii) that on the basis of new information before the Secretary, evaluated together with the evidence before the Secretary when such license was issued, the labeling of any animal feeds, based on a fair evaluation of all material facts, is false or misleading in any particular and was not corrected within a reasonable time after receipt of written notice from the Secretary specifying the matter complained of; or

(iv) that on the basis of new information before the Secretary, evaluated together with the evidence before the Secretary when such license was issued, the facility has manufactured, processed, packed, or held animal feed bearing or containing a new animal drug adulterated under section 351(a)(6) of this title and the facility did not discontinue the manufacture, processing, packing, or holding of such animal feed within a reasonable time after receipt of written notice from the Secretary specifying the matter complained of.

(C) The Secretary may also revoke a license to manufacture animal feeds under this subsection if an applicant gives notice to the Secretary of intention to discontinue the manufacture of all animal feed covered under this subsection and waives an opportunity for a hearing on the matter.

(D) Any order under this paragraph shall state the findings upon which it is based.

(5) When a license to manufacture animal feeds bearing or containing new animal drugs has been issued—

(A) the applicant shall establish and maintain such records, and make such reports to the Secretary, or (at the option of the Secretary) to the appropriate person or persons holding an approved application filed under subsection (b) of this section, as the Secretary may by general regulation, or by order with respect to such application, prescribe on the basis of a finding that such records and reports are necessary in order to enable the Secretary to determine, or facilitate a determination, whether there is or may be ground for invoking subsection (e) of this section or paragraph (4); and

(B) every person required under this subsection to maintain records, and every person in charge or custody thereof, shall, upon request of an officer or employee designated by the Secretary, permit such officer or employee at all reasonable times to have access to and copy and verify such records.

(6) To the extent consistent with the public health, the Secretary may promulgate regulations for exempting from the operation of this subsection facilities that manufacture, process, pack, or hold animal feeds bearing or containing new animal drugs.

(n) Abbreviated applications for new animal drugs; contents, filing, etc.; lists of approved drugs—

(1) An abbreviated application for a new animal drug shall contain—

(A)(i) except as provided in clause (ii), information to show that the conditions of use or similar limitations (whether in the labeling or published pursuant to subsection (i) of this section) prescribed, recommended, or suggested in the labeling proposed for the new animal drug have been previously approved for a new animal drug listed under paragraph (4) (hereinafter in this subsection referred to as an "approved new animal drug"), and

(ii) information to show that the withdrawal period at which residues of the new animal drug will be consistent with the tolerances established for the approved new animal drug is the same as the withdrawal period previously established for the approved new animal drug or, if the withdrawal period is proposed to be different, information showing that the residues of the new animal drug at the proposed different withdrawal period will be consistent with the tolerances established for the approved new animal drug;

(B)(i) information to show that the active ingredients of the new animal drug are the same as those of the approved new animal drug, and

(ii) if the approved new animal drug has more than one active ingredient, and if one of the active ingredients of the new animal drug is different from one of the active ingredients of the approved new animal drug and the application is filed pursuant to the approval of a petition filed under paragraph (3)—

(I) information to show that the other active ingredients of the new animal drug are the same as the active ingredients of the approved new animal drug,

(II) information to show either that the different active ingredient is an active ingredient of another approved new animal drug or of an animal drug which does not meet the requirements of section 321(v) of this title, and

(III) such other information respecting the different active ingredients as the Secretary may require;

(C)(i) if the approved new animal drug is permitted to be used with one or more animal drugs in animal feed, information to show that the proposed uses of the new animal drug with other animal drugs in animal feed are the same as the uses of the approved new animal drug, and

(ii) if the approved new animal drug is permitted to be used with one or more other animal drugs in animal feed, and one of the other animal drugs proposed for use with the new animal drug in animal feed is different from one of the other animal drugs permitted to be used in animal feed with the approved new animal drug, and the application is filed pursuant to the approval of a petition filed under paragraph (3)—

(I) information to show either that the different animal drug proposed for use with the approved new animal drug in animal feed is an approved new animal drug permitted to be used in animal feed or does not meet the requirements of section 321(v) of this title when used with another animal drug in animal feed,

(II) information to show that other animal drugs proposed for use with the new animal drug in animal feed are the same as the other animal drugs permitted to be used with the approved new animal drug, and

(III) such other information respecting the different animal drug or combination with respect to which the petition was filed as the Secretary may require,

(D) information to show that the route of administration, the dosage form, and the strength of the new animal drug are the same as those of the approved new animal drug or, if the route of administration, the dosage form, or the strength of the new animal drug is different and the application is filed pursuant to the approval of a petition filed under paragraph (3), such information respecting the route of administration, dosage form, or strength with respect to which the petition was filed as the Secretary may require;

(E) information to show that the new animal drug is bioequivalent to the approved new animal drug, except that if the application is filed pursuant to the approval of a petition filed under paragraph (3) for the purposes described in subparagraph (B) or (C), information to show that the active ingredients of the new animal drug are of the same pharmacological or therapeutic class as the pharmacological or therapeutic class of the approved new animal drug and that the new animal drug can be expected to have the same therapeutic effect as the approved new animal drug when used in accordance with the labeling;

(F) information to show that the labeling proposed for the new animal drug is the same as the labeling approved for the approved new animal drug except for changes required because of differences approved under a petition filed under paragraph (3), because of a different withdrawal period, or because the new animal drug and the approved new animal drug are produced or distributed by different manufacturers;

(G) the items specified in clauses (B) through (F) of subsection (b)(1) of this section;

(H) a certification, in the opinion of the applicant and to the best of his knowledge, with respect to each patent which claims the approved new animal drug or which claims a use for such approved new animal drug for which the applicant is seeking approval under this subsection and for which information is required to be filed under subsection (b)(1) or (c)(3) of this section

(i) that such patent information has not been filed,

(ii) that such patent has expired,

(iii) of the date on which such patent will expire, or

(iv) that such patent is invalid or will not be infringed by the manufacture, use, or sale of the new animal drug for which the application is filed; and

(I) if with respect to the approved new animal drug information was filed under subsection (b)(1) or (c)(3) of this section for a method of use patent which does not claim a use for which the applicant is seeking approval of an application under subsection (c)(2) of this section, a statement that the method of use patent does not claim such a use.

The Secretary may not require that an abbreviated application contain information in addition to that required by subparagraphs (A) through (I).

(2)(A) An applicant who makes a certification described in paragraph (1)(G)(iv) shall include in the application a statement that the applicant will give the notice required by subparagraph (B) to—

(i) each owner of the patent which is the subject of the certification or the representative of such owner designated to receive such notice, and

(ii) the holder of the approved application under subsection (c)(1) of this section for the drug which is claimed by the patent or a use of which is claimed by the patent or the representative of such holder designated to receive such notice.

(B) The notice referred to in subparagraph (A) shall state that an application, which contains data from bioequivalence studies, has been filed under this subsection for the drug with respect to which the certification is made to obtain approval to engage in the commercial manufacture, use, or sale of such drug before the expiration of the patent referred to in the certification. Such notice shall include a detailed statement of the factual and legal basis of the applicant's opinion that the patent is not valid or will not be infringed.

(C) If an application is amended to include a certification described in paragraph (1)(G)(iv), the notice required by subparagraph (B) shall be given when the amended application is filed.

(3) If a person wants to submit an abbreviated application for a new animal drug—

(A) whose active ingredients, route of administration, dosage form, or strength differ from that of an approved new animal drug, or

(B) whose use with other animal drugs in animal feed differs from that of an approved new animal drug,

such person shall submit a petition to the Secretary seeking permission to file such an application. The Secretary shall approve a petition for a new animal drug unless the Secretary finds that—

(C) investigations must be conducted to show the safety and effectiveness, in animals to be treated with the drug, of the active ingredients, route of administration, dosage form, strength, or use with other animal drugs in animal feed which differ from the approved new animal drug, or

(D) investigations must be conducted to show the safety for human consumption of any residues in food resulting from the proposed active ingredients, route of administration, dosage form, strength, or use with other animal drugs in animal feed for the new animal drug which is different from the active ingredients, route of administration, dosage form, strength, or use with other animal drugs in animal feed of the approved new animal drug.

The Secretary shall approve or disapprove a petition submitted under this paragraph within 90 days of the date the petition is submitted.

(4)(A)(i) Within 60 days of November 16, 1988, the Secretary shall publish and make available to the public a list in alphabetical order of the official and proprietary name of each new animal drug which has been approved for safety and effectiveness before November 16, 1988.

(ii) Every 30 days after the publication of the first list under clause (i) the Secretary shall revise the list to include each new animal drug which has been approved for safety and effectiveness under subsection (c) of this section during the 30 day period.

(iii) When patent information submitted under subsection (b)(1) or (c)(3) of this section respecting a new animal drug included on the list is to be published by the Secretary, the Secretary shall, in revisions made under clause (ii), include such information for such drug.

(B) A new animal drug approved for safety and effectiveness before November 16, 1988, or approved for safety and effectiveness under subsection (c) of this section shall, for purposes of this subsection, be considered to have been published under subparagraph (A) on the date of its approval or November 16, 1988, whichever is later.

(C) If the approval of a new animal drug was withdrawn or suspended under subsection (c)(2)(G) of this section or for grounds described in subsection (e) of this section or if the Secretary determines that a drug has been withdrawn from sale for safety or effectiveness reasons, it may not be published in the list under subparagraph (A) or, if the withdrawal or suspension occurred after its publication in such list, it shall be immediately removed from such list—

(i) for the same period as the withdrawal or suspension under subsection (c)(2)(G) or (e) of this section, or

(ii) if the listed drug has been withdrawn from sale, for the period of withdrawal from sale or, if earlier, the period ending on the date the Secretary determines that the withdrawal from sale is not for safety or effectiveness reasons.

A notice of the removal shall be published in the Federal Register.

(5) If an application contains the information required by clauses (A), (G), and (H) of subsection (b)(1) of this section and such information—

(A) is relied on by the applicant for the approval of the application, and

(B) is not information derived either from investigations, studies, or tests conducted by or for the applicant or for which the applicant had obtained a right of reference or use from the person by or for whom the investigations, studies, or tests were conducted,

such application shall be considered to be an application filed under subsection (b)(2) of this section.

(o) "Patent" defined.—For purposes of this section, the term "patent" means a patent issued by the United States Patent and Trademark Office.

(p) Safety and effectiveness data—

(1) Safety and effectiveness data and information which has been submitted in an application filed under subsection (b)(1) of this section or section 360ccc(a) of this title for a drug and which has not previously been disclosed to the public shall be made available to the public, upon request, unless extraordinary circumstances are shown—

(A) if no work is being or will be undertaken to have the application approved,

(B) if the Secretary has determined that the application is not approvable and all legal appeals have been exhausted,

(C) if approval of the application under subsection (c) of this section is withdrawn and all legal appeals have been exhausted,

(D) if the Secretary has determined that such drug is not a new drug, or

(E) upon the effective date of the approval of the first application filed under subsection (b)(2) of this section which refers to such drug or upon the date upon which the approval of an application filed under subsection (b)(2) of this section which refers to such drug could be made effective if such an application had been filed.

(2) Any request for data and information pursuant to paragraph (1) shall include a verified statement by the person making the request that any data or information received under such paragraph shall not be disclosed by such person to any other person—

(A) for the purpose of, or as part of a plan, scheme, or device for, obtaining the right to make, use, or market, or making, using, or marketing, outside the United States, the drug identified in the application filed under subsection (b)(1) of this section or section 360ccc(a) of this title, and

(B) without obtaining from any person to whom the data and information are disclosed an identical verified statement, a copy of which is to be provided by such person to the Secretary, which meets the requirements of this paragraph.

(q) Date of approval in the case of recommended controls under the CSA—

(1) In general.—In the case of an application under subsection (b) with respect to a drug for which the Secretary provides notice to the sponsor that the Secretary intends to issue a scientific and medical evaluation and recommend controls under the Controlled Substances Act, approval of such application shall not take effect until the interim final rule controlling the drug is issued in accordance with section 201(j) of the Controlled Substances Act.

(2) Date of approval.—For purposes of this section, with respect to an application described in paragraph (1), the term "date of approval" shall mean the later of—

(A) the date an application under subsection (b) is approved under subsection (c); or

(B) the date of issuance of the interim final rule controlling the drug.

1. **Editor's note:** Probably should be "clause (iii)(III)."

History of 21 U.S.C. §360b: June 25, 1938, ch. 675, §512; July 13, 1968, P.L. 90-399, §101(b), 82 Stat. 343; Nov. 16, 1988, P.L. 100-670, §§101, 102, 104, 107(a)(2), 102 Stat. 3971, 3981, 3982, 3984; Aug. 17, 1991, P.L. 102-108, §2(e), 105 Stat. 550; Aug. 13, 1993, P.L. 103-80, §3(r), 107 Stat. 777; Oct. 22, 1994, P.L. 103-396, §2(a), (b)(2), (3), 108 Stat. 4153, 4154; Oct. 9, 1996, P.L. 104-250, §§2(a)-(d), 3, 4, 5(c), 6(a), (b), 110 Stat. 3151-3153, 3155-3157; Nov. 21, 1997, P.L. 105-115, §124(b), 111 Stat. 2325; Oct. 21, 1998, P.L. 105-277, §101(a) [§737], 112 Stat. 2681-30; Nov. 29, 1999, P.L. 106-113, §1000(a)(9) [§4732(b)(11)], 113 Stat. 1536, 1501A-584; Aug. 2, 2004, P.L. 108-282, §102(b)(2), (3), (5)(I)-(S), 118 Stat. 892, 903, 904; Aug. 14, 2008, P.L. 110-316, §105(a), 122 Stat. 3514; Nov. 25, 2015, P.L. 114-89, §2(a)(3)(A), 129 Stat. 699; Dec. 13, 2016, P.L. 114-255, §3088(b), 130 Stat. 1149.

TITLE 22. FOREIGN RELATIONS & INTERCOURSE

CHAPTER 32. FOREIGN ASSISTANCE

SUBCHAPTER III. GENERAL & ADMINISTRATIVE PROVISIONS

PART I. GENERAL PROVISIONS

§2356. PATENTS & TECHNICAL INFORMATION

(a) Practice of invention or disclosure of information; suits against United States for reasonable compensation; jurisdiction; limitation of action; defenses.—Whenever, in connection with the furnishing of assistance under this chapter—

(1) an invention or discovery covered by a patent issued by the United States Government is practiced within the United States without the authorization of the owner, or

(2) information, which is (A) protected by law, and (B) held by the United States Government subject to restrictions imposed by the owner, is disclosed by the United States Government or any of its officers, employees, or agents in violation of such restrictions,

the exclusive remedy of the owner, except as provided in subsection (b) of this section, is to sue the United States Government for reasonable and entire compensation for such practice or disclosure in the district court of the United States for the district in which such owner is a resident, or in the United States Court of Federal Claims, within six years after the cause of action arises. Any period during which the United States Government is in possession of a written claim under subsection (b) of this section before mailing a notice of denial of that claim does not count in computing the six years. In any such suit, the United States Government may plead any defense that may be pleaded by a private person in such an action. The last paragraph of section 1498(a) of Title 28 shall apply to inventions and information covered by this section.

(b) Settlement of claims.—Before suit against the United States Government has been instituted, the head of the agency of the United States Government concerned may settle and pay any claim arising under the circumstances described in subsection (a) of this section. No claim may be paid under this subsection unless the amount tendered is accepted by the claimant in full satisfaction.

(c) Drug products manufactured outside the United States.—Funds appropriated pursuant to this chapter shall not be expended by the United States Government for the acquisition of any drug product or pharmaceutical product manufactured outside the United States if the manufacture of such drug product or pharmaceutical product in the United States would involve the use of, or be covered by, an unexpired patent of the United States which has not previously been held invalid by an unappealed or unappealable judgment or decree of a court of competent jurisdiction, unless such manufacture is expressly authorized by the owner of such patent.

History of 22 U.S.C. §2356: Sept. 4, 1961, P.L. 87-195, §606, 75 Stat. 440; Apr. 2, 1982, P.L. 97-164, §160(a)(6), 96 Stat. 48; Oct. 29, 1992, P.L. 102-572, §902(b)(1), 106 Stat. 4516.

TITLE 26. INTERNAL REVENUE CODE

SUBTITLE A. INCOME TAXES

CHAPTER 1. NORMAL TAXES & SURTAXES

SUBCHAPTER P. CAPITAL GAINS & LOSSES

PART IV. SPECIAL RULES FOR DETERMINING CAPITAL GAINS & LOSSES

§1235. SALE OR EXCHANGE OF PATENTS

(a) General.—A transfer (other than by gift, inheritance, or devise) of property consisting of all substantial rights to a patent, or an undivided interest therein which includes a part of all such rights, by any holder shall be considered the sale or exchange of a capital asset held for more than 1 year, regardless of whether or not payments in consideration of such transfer are—

(1) payable periodically over a period generally coterminous with the transferee's use of the patent, or

(2) contingent on the productivity, use, or disposition of the property transferred.

(b) "Holder" defined.—For purposes of this section, the term "holder" means—

(1) any individual whose efforts created such property, or

(2) any other individual who has acquired his interest in such property in exchange for consideration in money or money's worth paid to such creator prior to actual reduction to practice of the invention covered by the patent, if such individual is neither—

(A) the employer of such creator, nor

(B) related to such creator (within the meaning of subsection (c)).

(c) Related persons.—Subsection (a) shall not apply to any transfer, directly or indirectly, between persons specified within any one of the paragraphs of section 267(b) or persons described in section 707(b); except that, in applying section 267(b) and (c) and section 707(b) for purposes of this section—

(1) the phrase "25 percent or more" shall be substituted for the phrase "more than 50 percent" each place it appears in section 267(b) or 707(b), and

(2) paragraph (4) of section 267(c) shall be treated as providing that the family of an individual shall include only his spouse, ancestors, and lineal descendants.

(d) Cross reference.—For special rule relating to nonresident aliens, see section 871(a).

History of 26 U.S.C. §1235: Aug. 16, 1954, ch. 736, 68A Stat. 329; Sept. 2, 1958, P.L. 85-866, §54(a), 72 Stat. 1644; Oct. 4, 1976, P.L. 94-455, §1402(b)(1)(V), (2), 90 Stat. 1732; July 18, 1984, P.L. 98-369, §§174(b)(5)(C), 1001(b)(19), (e), 98 Stat. 707, 1012; July 22, 1998, P.L. 105-206, §§5001(a)(5), 6005(d)(4), 112 Stat. 788, 805; Dec. 19, 2014, P.L. 113-295, §221(a)(82), 128 Stat. 4049.

§1239. GAIN FROM SALE OF DEPRECIABLE PROPERTY BETWEEN CERTAIN RELATED TAXPAYERS

(a) Treatment of gain as ordinary income.—In the case of a sale or exchange of property, directly or indirectly, between related persons, any gain recognized to the transferor shall be treated as ordinary income if such property is, in the hands of the transferee, of a character which is subject to the allowance for depreciation provided in section 167.

(b) Related persons.—For purposes of subsection (a), the term "related persons" means—

(1) a person and all entities which are controlled entities with respect to such person,

(2) a taxpayer and any trust in which such taxpayer (or his spouse) is a beneficiary, unless such beneficiary's interest in the trust is a remote contingent interest (within the meaning of section 318(a)(3)(B)(i)), and

(3) except in the case of a sale or exchange in satisfaction of a pecuniary bequest, an executor of an estate and a beneficiary of such estate.

(c) Controlled entity defined—

(1) General rule.—For purposes of this section, the term "controlled entity" means, with respect to any person—

(A) a corporation more than 50 percent of the value of the outstanding stock of which is owned (directly or indirectly) by or for such person,

(B) a partnership more than 50 percent of the capital interest or profits interest in which is owned (directly or indirectly) by or for such person, and

(C) any entity which is a related person to such person under paragraph (3), (10), (11), or (12) of section 267(b).

(2) Constructive ownership.—For purposes of this section, ownership shall be determined in accordance with rules similar to the rules under section 267(c) (other than paragraph (3) thereof).

(d) Employer and related employee association.—For purposes of subsection (a), the term "related person" also includes—

(1) an employer and any person related to the employer (within the meaning of subsection (b)), and

(2) a welfare benefit fund (within the meaning of section 419(e)) which is controlled directly or indirectly by persons referred to in paragraph (1).

(e) Patent applications treated as depreciable property.—For purposes of this section, a patent application shall be treated as property which, in the hands of the transferee, is of a character which is subject to the allowance for depreciation provided in section 167.

History of 26 U.S.C. §1239: Aug. 16, 1954, ch. 736, 68A Stat. 332; Sept. 2, 1958, P.L. 85-866, §56, 72 Stat. 1645; Oct. 4, 1976, P.L. 94-455, §2129(a), 90 Stat. 1922; Nov. 6, 1978, P.L. 95-600, §701(v)(1), 92 Stat. 2920; Oct. 19, 1980, P.L. 96-471, §5, 94 Stat. 2255; Jan. 12, 1983, P.L. 97-448, §301, 96 Stat. 2397; July 18, 1984, P.L. 98-369, §§175(a), (b), 421(b)(6), 557(a), 98 Stat. 708, 794, 898; Oct. 22, 1986, P.L. 99-514, §642(a)(1)(A)-(C), 100 Stat. 2283, 2284; Aug. 5, 1997, P.L. 105-34, §1308(b), 111 Stat. 1041.

§1249. GAIN FROM CERTAIN SALES OR EXCHANGES OF PATENTS, ETC., TO FOREIGN CORPORATIONS

(a) General rule.—Gain from the sale or exchange of a patent, an invention, model, or design (whether or not patented), a copyright, a secret formula or process, or any other similar property right to any foreign corporation by any United States person (as defined in section 7701(a)(30)) which controls such foreign corporation shall, if such gain would (but for the provisions of this subsection) be gain from the sale or exchange of a capital asset or of property described in section 1231, be considered as ordinary income.

(b) Control.—For purposes of subsection (a), control means, with respect to any foreign corporation, the ownership, directly or indirectly, of stock possessing more than 50 percent of the total combined voting power of all classes of stock entitled to vote. For purposes of this subsection, the rules for determining ownership of stock prescribed by section 958 shall apply.

History of 26 U.S.C. §1249: Oct. 16, 1962, P.L. 87-834, §16(a), 76 Stat. 1045; Nov. 13, 1966, P.L. 89-809, §104(m)(3), 80 Stat. 1563; Oct. 4, 1976, P.L. 94-455, §1901(b)(3)(K), 90 Stat. 1793; Dec. 19, 2014, P.L. 113-295, §221(a)(84), 128 Stat. 4049.

§1253. TRANSFERS OF FRANCHISES, TRADEMARKS, & TRADE NAMES

(a) General rule.—A transfer of a franchise, trademark, or trade name shall not be treated as a sale or exchange of a capital asset if the transferor retains any significant power, right, or continuing interest with respect to the subject matter of the franchise, trademark, or trade name.

(b) Definitions.—For purposes of this section—

(1) Franchise.—The term "franchise" includes an agreement which gives one of the parties to the agreement the right to distribute, sell, or provide goods, services, or facilities, within a specified area.

(2) Significant power, right, or continuing interest.—The term "significant power, right, or continuing interest" includes, but is not limited to, the following rights with respect to the interest transferred:

(A) A right to disapprove any assignment of such interest, or any part thereof.

(B) A right to terminate at will.

(C) A right to prescribe the standards of quality of products used or sold, or of services furnished, and of the equipment and facilities used to promote such products or services.

(D) A right to require that the transferee sell or advertise only products or services of the transferor.

(E) A right to require that the transferee purchase substantially all of his supplies and equipment from the transferor.

(F) A right to payments contingent on the productivity, use, or disposition of the subject matter of the interest transferred, if such payments constitute a substantial element under the transfer agreement.

(3) Transfer.—The term "transfer" includes the renewal of a franchise, trademark, or trade name.

(c) Treatment of contingent payments by transferor.—Amounts received or accrued on account of a transfer, sale, or other disposition of a franchise, trademark, or trade name which are contingent on the productivity, use, or disposition of the franchise, trademark, or trade name transferred shall be treated as amounts received or accrued from the sale or other disposition of property which is not a capital asset.

(d) Treatment of payments by transferee—

(1) Contingent serial payments—

(A) In general.—Any amount described in subparagraph (B) which is paid or incurred during the taxable year on account of a transfer, sale, or other disposition of a franchise, trademark, or trade name shall be allowed as a deduction under section 162(a) (relating to trade or business expenses).

(B) Amounts to which paragraph applies.—An amount is described in this subparagraph if it—

(i) is contingent on the productivity, use, or disposition of the franchise, trademark, or trade name, and

(ii) is paid as part of a series of payments—

(I) which are payable not less frequently than annually throughout the entire term of the transfer agreement, and

(II) which are substantially equal in amount (or payable under a fixed formula).

(2) Other payments.—Any amount paid or incurred on account of a transfer, sale, or other disposition of a franchise, trademark, or trade name to which paragraph (1) does not apply shall be treated as an amount chargeable to capital account.

(3) Renewals, etc.—For purposes of determining the term of a transfer agreement under this section, there shall be taken into account all renewal options (and any other period for which the parties reasonably expect the agreement to be renewed).

(e) Repealed Oct. 22, 2004, P.L. 108-357, §886(b)(3), 118 Stat. 1641.

History of 26 U.S.C. §1253: Dec. 30, 1969, P.L. 91-172, §516(c)(1), 83 Stat. 647; Oct. 4, 1976, P.L. 94-455, §1906(b)(13)(A), 90 Stat. 1834; Dec. 19, 1989, P.L. 101-239, §7622(a)-(c), 103 Stat. 2377; Nov. 5, 1990, P.L. 101-508, §11701(i), 104 Stat. 1388-508; Aug. 10, 1993, P.L. 103-66, §13261(c), 107 Stat. 539; Oct. 22, 2004, P.L. 108-357, §886(b)(3), 118 Stat. 1641.

TITLE 27. INTOXICATING LIQUORS

CHAPTER 8. FEDERAL ALCOHOL ADMINISTRATION ACT

SUBCHAPTER I. FEDERAL ALCOHOL ADMINISTRATION

§205. UNFAIR COMPETITION & UNLAWFUL PRACTICES

It shall be unlawful for any person engaged in business as a distiller, brewer, rectifier, blender, or other producer, or as an importer or wholesaler, of distilled spirits, wine, or malt beverages, or as a bottler, or warehouseman and bottler, of distilled spirits, directly or indirectly or through an affiliate:

(a) Exclusive outlet.—To require, by agreement or otherwise, that any retailer engaged in the sale of distilled spirits, wine, or malt beverages, purchase any such products from such person to the exclusion in whole or in part of distilled spirits, wine, or malt beverages sold or offered for sale by other persons in interstate or foreign commerce, if such requirement is made in the course of interstate or foreign commerce, or if such person engages in such practice to such an extent as substantially to restrain or prevent transactions in interstate or foreign commerce in any such products, or if the direct effect of such requirement is to prevent, deter, hinder, or restrict other persons from selling or offering for sale any such products to such retailer in interstate or foreign commerce; or

(b) "Tied house."—To induce through any of the following means, any retailer, engaged in the sale of distilled spirits, wine, or malt beverages, to purchase any such products from such person to the exclusion in whole or in part of distilled spirits, wine, or malt beverages sold or offered for sale by other persons in interstate or foreign commerce, if such inducement is made in the course of interstate or foreign commerce, or if such person engages in the practice of using such means, or any of them, to such an extent as substantially to restrain or prevent transactions in interstate or foreign commerce in any such products, or if the direct effect of such inducement is to prevent, deter, hinder, or restrict other persons from selling or offering for sale any such products to such retailer in interstate or foreign commerce: (1) By acquiring or holding (after the expiration of any existing license) any interest in any license with respect to the premises of the retailer; or (2) by acquiring any interest in real or personal property owned, occupied, or used by the retailer in the conduct of his business; or (3) by furnishing, giving, renting, lending, or selling to the retailer, any equipment, fixtures, signs, supplies, money, services, or other thing of value, subject to such exceptions as the Secretary of the Treasury shall by regulation prescribe, having due regard for public health, the quantity and value of articles involved, established trade customs not contrary to the public interest and the purposes of this subsection; or (4) by paying or crediting the retailer for any advertising, display, or distribution service; or (5) by guaranteeing any loan or the repayment of any financial obligation of the retailer; or (6) by extending to the retailer credit for a period in excess of the credit period usual and customary to the industry for the particular class of transactions, as ascertained by the Secretary of the Treasury and prescribed by regulations by him; or (7) by requiring the retailer to take and dispose of a certain quota of any of such products; or

(c) Commercial bribery.—To induce through any of the following means, any trade buyer engaged in the sale of distilled spirits, wine, or malt beverages, to purchase any such products from such person to the exclusion in whole or in part of distilled spirits, wine, or malt beverages sold or offered for sale by other persons in interstate or foreign commerce, if such inducement is made in the course of interstate or foreign commerce, or if such person engages in the practice of using such means, or any of them, to such an extent as substantially to restrain or prevent transactions in interstate or foreign commerce in any such products, or if the direct effect of such inducement is to prevent, deter, hinder, or restrict other persons from selling or offering for sale any such products to such trade buyer in interstate or foreign commerce: (1) By commercial bribery; or (2) by offering or giving any bonus, premium, or compensation to any officer, or employee, or representative of the trade buyer; or

(d) Consignment sales.—To sell, offer for sale, or contract to sell to any trade buyer engaged in the sale of distilled spirits, wine, or malt beverages, or for any such trade buyer to purchase, offer to purchase, or contract to purchase, any such products on consignment or under conditional sale or with the privilege of return or on any basis otherwise than a bona fide sale, or where any part of such transaction involves, directly or indirectly, the acquisition by such person from the trade buyer or his agreement to acquire from the trade buyer other distilled spirits, wine, or malt beverages—if such sale, purchase, offer, or contract is made in the course of interstate or foreign commerce, or if such person or trade buyer engages in such practice to such an extent as substantially to restrain or prevent transactions in interstate or foreign commerce in any such products or if the direct effect of such sale, purchase, offer, or contract is to prevent, deter, hinder, or restrict other persons from selling or offering for sale any such products to such trade buyer in interstate or foreign commerce: *Provided*, That this subsection shall not apply to transactions involving solely the bona fide return of merchandise for ordinary and usual commercial reasons arising after the merchandise has been sold; or

(e) Labeling.—To sell or ship or deliver for sale or shipment, or otherwise introduce in interstate or foreign commerce, or to receive therein, or to remove from customs custody for consumption, any distilled spirits, wine, or malt beverages in bottles, unless such products are bottled, packaged, and labeled in conformity with such regulations, to be prescribed by the Secretary of the Treasury, with respect to packaging, marking, branding, and labeling and size and fill of container (1) as will prohibit deception of the consumer with respect to such products or the quantity thereof and as will prohibit, irrespective of falsity, such statements relating to age, manufacturing processes, analyses, guarantees, and scientific or irrelevant matters as the Secretary of the Treasury finds to be likely to mislead the consumer; (2) as will provide the consumer with adequate information as to the identity and quality of the products, the alcoholic content thereof (except that statements of, or statements likely to be considered as statements of, alcoholic content of malt beverages are prohibited unless required by State law and except that, in case of wines, statements of alcoholic content shall be required only for wines containing more than 14 per centum of alcohol by volume), the net contents of the package, and the manufacturer or bottler or importer of the product; (3) as will require an accurate statement, in the case of distilled spirits (other than cordials, liqueurs, and specialties) produced by blending or rectification, if neutral spirits have been used in the production thereof, informing the consumer of the percentage of neutral spirits so used and of the name of the commodity from which such neutral spirits have been distilled, or in case of neutral spirits or of gin produced by a process of continuous distillation, the name of the commodity from which distilled; (4) as will prohibit statements on the label that are disparaging of a competitor's products or are false, misleading, obscene, or indecent; and (5) as will prevent deception of the consumer by use of a trade or brand name that is the name of any living individual of public prominence, or existing private or public organization, or is a name that is in simulation or is an abbreviation thereof, and as will prevent the use of a graphic, pictorial, or emblematic representation of any such individual or organization, if the use of such name or representation is likely falsely to lead the consumer to believe that the product has been indorsed, made, or used by, or produced for, or under the supervision of, or in accordance with the specifications of, such individual or organization: *Provided*, That this clause shall not apply to the use of the name of any person engaged in business as a distiller, brewer, rectifier, blender, or other producer, or as an importer, wholesaler, retailer, bottler, or warehouseman, of distilled spirits, wine, or malt beverages, nor to the use by any person of a trade or brand name used by him or his predecessor in interest prior to August 19, 1935; including regulations requiring, at time of release from customs custody, certificates issued by foreign governments covering origin, age, and identity of imported products: *Provided further*, That nothing herein nor any decision, ruling, or regulation of any Department of the Government shall deny the right of any person to use any trade name or brand of foreign origin not presently effectively registered in the United States Patent and Trademark Office which has been used by such person or predecessors in the United States for a period of at least five years last past, if the use of such name or brand is qualified by the name of the locality in the United States in which the product is produced, and, in the case of the use of such name or brand on any label or in any advertisement, if such qualification is as conspicuous as such name or brand.

It shall be unlawful for any person to alter, mutilate, destroy, obliterate, or remove any mark, brand, or label upon distilled spirits, wine, or malt beverages held for sale in interstate or foreign commerce or after shipment therein, except as authorized by Federal law or except pursuant to regulations of the Secretary of the Treasury authorizing relabeling for purposes of compliance with the requirements of this subsection or of State law.

In order to prevent the sale or shipment or other introduction of distilled spirits, wine, or malt beverages in interstate or foreign commerce, if bottled, packaged, or labeled in violation of the requirements of this subsection, (1) no bottler of distilled spirits, no producer, blender, or wholesaler of wine, or proprietor of a bonded wine storeroom, and no brewer or wholesaler of malt beverages shall bottle, and (2) no person shall remove from customs custody, in bottles, for sale or any other commercial purpose, distilled spirits, wine, or malt beverages, respectively, after such date as the Secretary of the Treasury fixes as the earliest practicable date for the application of the provisions of this subsection to any class of such persons (but not later than August 15, 1936, in the case of distilled spirits, and December 15, 1936, in the case of wine and malt beverages, and only after thirty days' public notice), unless, upon application to the Secretary of the Treasury, he has obtained and has in his possession a certificate of label approval covering the distilled spirits, wine, or malt beverages, issued by the Secretary in such manner and form as he shall by regulations prescribe: *Provided*, That any such bottler of distilled spirits, or producer, blender, or wholesaler of wine, or proprietor of a bonded wine storeroom, or brewer or wholesaler of malt beverages shall be exempt from the requirements of this subsection if, upon application to the Secretary, he shows to the satisfaction of the Secretary that the distilled spirits, wine, or malt beverages to be bottled by the applicant are not to be sold, or offered for sale, or shipped or delivered for shipment, or otherwise introduced, in interstate or foreign commerce. Officers of internal revenue are authorized and directed to withhold the release of distilled spirits from the bottling plant unless such certificates have been obtained, or unless the application of the bottler for exemption has been granted by the Secretary; and customs officers are authorized and directed to withhold the release from customs custody of distilled spirits, wine, and malt beverages, unless such certificates have been obtained. The District Courts of the United States, and the United States court for any Territory shall have jurisdiction of suits to enjoin, annul, or suspend in whole or in part any final action by the Secretary upon any application under this subsection; or

(f) Advertising.—To publish or disseminate or cause to be published or disseminated by radio broadcast, or in any newspaper, periodical or other publication or by any sign or outdoor advertisement or any other printed or graphic matter, any advertisement of distilled spirits, wine, or malt beverages, if such advertisement is in, or is calculated to induce sales in, interstate or foreign commerce, or is disseminated by mail, unless such advertisement is in conformity with such regulations, to be prescribed by the Secretary of the Treasury, (1) as will prevent deception of the consumer with respect to the products advertised and as will prohibit, irrespective of falsity, such statements relating to age, manufacturing processes, analyses, guaranties, and scientific or irrelevant matters as the Secretary of the Treasury finds to be likely to mislead the consumer; (2) as will provide the consumer with adequate information as to the identity and quality of the products advertised, the alcoholic content thereof (except the statements of, or statements likely to be considered as statements of, alcoholic content of malt beverages and wines are prohibited), and the person responsible for the advertisement; (3) as will require an accurate statement, in the case of distilled spirits (other than cordials, liqueurs, and specialties) produced by blending or rectification, if neutral spirits have been used in the production thereof, informing the consumer of the percentage of neutral spirits so used and of the name of the commodity from which such neutral spirits have been distilled, or in case of neutral spirits or of gin produced by a process of continuous distillation, the name of the commodity from which distilled; (4) as will prohibit statements that are disparaging of a competitor's products or are false, misleading, obscene, or indecent; (5) as will prevent statements inconsistent with any statement on the labeling of the products advertised. This subsection shall not apply to outdoor advertising in place on June 18, 1935, but shall apply upon replacement, restoration, or renovation of any such advertising. The prohibitions of this subsection and regulations thereunder shall not apply to the publisher of any newspaper, periodical, or other publication, or radio broadcaster, unless such publisher or radio broadcaster is engaged in business as a distiller, brewer, rectifier, or other producer, or as an importer or wholesaler, of distilled spirits, wine, or malt beverages, or as a bottler, or warehouseman and bottler, of distilled spirits, directly or indirectly or through an affiliate.

The provisions of subsections (a), (b), and (c) of this section shall not apply to any act done by an agency of a State or political subdivision thereof, or by any officer or employee of such agency.

In the case of malt beverages, the provisions of subsections (a), (b), (c), and (d) of this section shall apply to transactions between a retailer or trade buyer in any

State and a brewer, importer, or wholesaler of malt beverages outside such State only to the extent that the law of such State imposes similar requirements with respect to similar transactions between a retailer or trade buyer in such State and a brewer, importer, or wholesaler of malt beverages in such State, as the case may be. In the case of malt beverages, the provisions of this subsection and subsection (e) of this section shall apply to the labeling of malt beverages sold or shipped or delivered for shipment or otherwise introduced into or received in any State from any place outside thereof, or the advertising of malt beverages intended to be sold or shipped or delivered for shipment or otherwise introduced into or received in any State from any place outside thereof, only to the extent that the law of such State imposes similar requirements with respect to the labeling or advertising, as the case may be, of malt beverages not sold or shipped or delivered for shipment or otherwise introduced into or received in such State from any place outside thereof.

The Secretary of the Treasury shall give reasonable public notice, and afford to interested parties opportunity for hearing, prior to prescribing regulations to carry out the provisions of this section.

History of 27 U.S.C. §205: Aug. 29, 1935, ch. 814, §5 [§105], 49 Stat. 981; Feb. 29, 1936, ch. 105, §2, 49 Stat. 1152; June 25, 1936, ch. 804, 49 Stat. 1921; June 26, 1936, ch. 830, §§505, 506, 49 Stat. 1965, 1966; 1940 Reorg. Plan No. III, §2, eff. June 30, 1940, 5 F.R. 2108, 54 Stat. 1232; Apr. 20, 1942, ch. 244, §1(h), 56 Stat. 219; June 25, 1948, ch. 646, §32(b), 62 Stat. 991; May 24, 1949, ch. 139, §127, 63 Stat. 107; Jan. 2, 1975, P.L. 93-596, §3, 88 Stat. 1949. Renumbered Nov. 18, 1988, P.L. 100-690, §8001(a)(2), 102 Stat. 4517; Nov. 18, 1988, P.L. 100-690, §8001(b)(2), 102 Stat. 4521; Nov. 29, 1999, P.L. 106-113, §1000(a)(9) [§4732(b)(13)], 113 Stat. 1536, 1501A-584.

TITLE 28. JUDICIARY & JUDICIAL PROCEDURE

CHAPTER 83. COURTS OF APPEALS

§1292. INTERLOCUTORY DECISIONS

(a) Except as provided in subsections (c) and (d) of this section, the courts of appeals shall have jurisdiction of appeals from:

(1) Interlocutory orders of the district courts of the United States, the United States District Court for the District of the Canal Zone, the District Court of Guam, and the District Court of the Virgin Islands, or of the judges thereof, granting, continuing, modifying, refusing or dissolving injunctions, or refusing to dissolve or modify injunctions, except where a direct review may be had in the Supreme Court;

(2) Interlocutory orders appointing receivers, or refusing orders to wind up receiverships or to take steps to accomplish the purposes thereof, such as directing sales or other disposals of property;

(3) Interlocutory decrees of such district courts or the judges thereof determining the rights and liabilities of the parties to admiralty cases in which appeals from final decrees are allowed.

(b) When a district judge, in making in a civil action an order not otherwise appealable under this section, shall be of the opinion that such order involves a controlling question of law as to which there is substantial ground for difference of opinion and that an immediate appeal from the order may materially advance the ultimate termination of the litigation, he shall so state in writing in such order. The Court of Appeals which would have jurisdiction of an appeal of such action may thereupon, in its discretion, permit an appeal to be taken from such order, if application is made to it within ten days after the entry of the order: *Provided, however*, That application for an appeal hereunder shall not stay proceedings in the district court unless the district judge or the Court of Appeals or a judge thereof shall so order.

(c) The United States Court of Appeals for the Federal Circuit shall have exclusive jurisdiction—

(1) of an appeal from an interlocutory order or decree described in subsection (a) or (b) of this section in any case over which the court would have jurisdiction of an appeal under section 1295 of this title; and

(2) of an appeal from a judgment in a civil action for patent infringement which would otherwise be appealable to the United States Court of Appeals for the Federal Circuit and is final except for an accounting.

(d)(1) When the chief judge of the Court of International Trade issues an order under the provisions of section 256(b) of this title, or when any judge of the Court of International Trade, in issuing any other interlocutory order, includes in the order a statement that a controlling question of law is involved with respect to which there is a substantial ground for difference of opinion and that an immediate appeal from that order may materially advance the ultimate termination of the litigation, the United States Court of Appeals for the Federal Circuit may, in its discretion, permit an appeal to be taken from such order, if application is made to that Court within ten days after the entry of such order.

(2) When the chief judge of the United States Court of Federal Claims issues an order under section 798(b) of this title, or when any judge of the United

States Court of Federal Claims, in issuing an interlocutory order, includes in the order a statement that a controlling question of law is involved with respect to which there is a substantial ground for difference of opinion and that an immediate appeal from that order may materially advance the ultimate termination of the litigation, the United States Court of Appeals for the Federal Circuit may, in its discretion, permit an appeal to be taken from such order, if application is made to that Court within ten days after the entry of such order.

(3) Neither the application for nor the granting of an appeal under this subsection shall stay proceedings in the Court of International Trade or in the Court of Federal Claims, as the case may be, unless a stay is ordered by a judge of the Court of International Trade or of the Court of Federal Claims or by the United States Court of Appeals for the Federal Circuit or a judge of that court.

(4)(A) The United States Court of Appeals for the Federal Circuit shall have exclusive jurisdiction of an appeal from an interlocutory order of a district court of the United States, the District Court of Guam, the District Court of the Virgin Islands, or the District Court for the Northern Mariana Islands, granting or denying, in whole or in part, a motion to transfer an action to the United States Court of Federal Claims under section 1631 of this title.

(B) When a motion to transfer an action to the Court of Federal Claims is filed in a district court, no further proceedings shall be taken in the district court until 60 days after the court has ruled upon the motion. If an appeal is taken from the district court's grant or denial of the motion, proceedings shall be further stayed until the appeal has been decided by the Court of Appeals for the Federal Circuit. The stay of proceedings in the district court shall not bar the granting of preliminary or injunctive relief, where appropriate and where expedition is reasonably necessary. However, during the period in which proceedings are stayed as provided in this subparagraph, no transfer to the Court of Federal Claims pursuant to the motion shall be carried out.

(e) The Supreme Court may prescribe rules, in accordance with section 2072 of this title, to provide for an appeal of an interlocutory decision to the courts of appeals that is not otherwise provided for under subsection (a), (b), (c), or (d).

History of 28 U.S.C. §1292: June 25, 1948, ch. 646, 62 Stat. 929; Oct. 31, 1951, ch. 655, §49, 65 Stat. 726; July 7, 1958, P.L. 85-508, §12(e), 72 Stat. 348; Sept. 2, 1958, P.L. 85-919, 72 Stat. 1770; Apr. 2, 1982, P.L. 97-164, §125, 96 Stat. 36; Nov. 8, 1984, P.L. 98-620, §412, 98 Stat. 3362; Nov. 19, 1988, P.L. 100-702, §501, 102 Stat. 4652; Oct. 29, 1992, P.L. 102-572, §§101, 902(b), 906(c), 106 Stat. 4506, 4516, 4518.

§1295. JURISDICTION OF THE UNITED STATES COURT OF APPEALS FOR THE FEDERAL CIRCUIT

(a) The United States Court of Appeals for the Federal Circuit shall have exclusive jurisdiction—

(1) of an appeal from a final decision of a district court of the United States, the District Court of Guam, the District Court of the Virgin Islands, or the District Court of the Northern Mariana Islands, in any civil action arising under, or in any civil action in which a party has asserted a compulsory counterclaim arising under, any Act of Congress relating to patents or plant variety protection;

(2) of an appeal from a final decision of a district court of the United States, the United States District Court for the District of the Canal Zone, the District Court of Guam, the District Court of the Virgin Islands, or the District Court for the Northern Mariana Islands, if the jurisdiction of that court was based, in whole or in part, on section 1346 of this title, except that jurisdiction of an appeal in a case brought in a district court under section 1346(a)(1), 1346(b), 1346(e), or 1346(f) of this title or under section 1346(a)(2) when the claim is founded upon an Act of Congress or a regulation of an executive department providing for internal revenue shall be governed by sections 1291, 1292, and 1294 of this title;

(3) of an appeal from a final decision of the United States Court of Federal Claims;

(4) of an appeal from a decision of—

(A) the Patent Trial and Appeal Board of the United States Patent and Trademark Office with respect to a patent application, derivation proceeding, reexamination, post-grant review, or inter partes review under title 35, at the instance of a party who exercised that party's right to participate in the applicable proceeding before or appeal to the Board, except that an applicant or a party to a derivation proceeding may also have remedy by civil action pursuant to section 145 or 146 of title 35; an appeal under this subparagraph of a decision of the Board with respect to an application or derivation proceeding shall waive the right of such applicant or party to proceed under section 145 or 146 of title 35;

(B) the Under Secretary of Commerce for Intellectual Property and Director of the United States Patent and Trademark Office or the Trademark Trial and Appeal Board with respect to applications for registration of marks and other proceedings as provided in section 21 of the Trademark Act of 1946 (15 U.S.C. 1071); or

(C) a district court to which a case was directed pursuant to section 145, 146, or 154(b) of title 35;

(5) of an appeal from a final decision of the United States Court of International Trade;

(6) to review the final determinations of the United States International Trade Commission relating to unfair practices in import trade, made under section 337 of the Tariff Act of 1930 (19 U.S.C. 1337);

(7) to review, by appeal on questions of law only, findings of the Secretary of Commerce under U.S. note 6 to subchapter X of chapter 98 of the Harmonized Tariff Schedule of the United States (relating to importation of instruments or apparatus);

(8) of an appeal under section 71 of the Plant Variety Protection Act (7 U.S.C. 2461);

(9) of an appeal from a final order or final decision of the Merit Systems Protection Board, pursuant to sections 7703(b)(1) and 7703(d) of title 5;

(10) of an appeal from a final decision of an agency board of contract appeals pursuant to section 7107(a)(1) of title 41;

(11) of an appeal under section 211 of the Economic Stabilization Act of 1970;

(12) of an appeal under section 5 of the Emergency Petroleum Allocation Act of 1973 [15 U.S.C. 754];

(13) of an appeal under section 506(c) of the Natural Gas Policy Act of 1978 [15 U.S.C. 3146(c)]; and

(14) of an appeal under section 523 of the Energy Policy and Conservation Act [42 U.S.C. 6393].

(b) The head of any executive department or agency may, with the approval of the Attorney General, refer to the Court of Appeals for the Federal Circuit for judicial review any final decision rendered by a board of contract appeals pursuant to the terms of any contract with the United States awarded by that department or agency which the head of such department or agency has concluded is not entitled to finality pursuant to the review standards specified in section 7107(b) of title 41. The head of each executive department or agency shall make any referral under this section within one hundred and twenty days after the receipt of a copy of the final appeal decision.

(c) The Court of Appeals for the Federal Circuit shall review the matter referred in accordance with the standards specified in section 7107(b) of title 41. The court shall proceed with judicial review on the administrative record made before the board of contract appeals on matters so referred as in other cases pending in such court, shall determine the issue of finality of the appeal decision, and shall, if appropriate, render judgment thereon, or remand the matter to any administrative or executive body or official with such direction as it may deem proper and just.

History of 28 U.S.C. §1295: Apr. 2, 1982, P.L. 97-164, §127(a), 96 Stat. 37; Nov. 8, 1984, P.L. 98-622, §205(a), 98 Stat. 3388; Aug. 23, 1988, P.L. 100-418, §1214(a)(3), 102 Stat. 1156; Nov. 19, 1988, P.L. 100-702, §1020(a)(3), 102 Stat. 4671; Oct. 29, 1992, P.L. 102-572, §§102(c), 902(b)(1), 106 Stat. 4507, 4516; Nov. 29, 1999, P.L. 106-113-Appx. I, §§4402(b)(2), 4732(b)(14), 113 Stat. 1501A-560, 1501A-584; Jan. 4, 2011, P.L. 111-350, §5(g)(5), 124 Stat. 3848; Sept. 16, 2011, P.L. 112-29, §§7(c)(2), 19(b), 125 Stat. 314, 331.

CHAPTER 85. DISTRICT COURTS; JURISDICTION

§1338. PATENTS, PLANT VARIETY PROTECTION, COPYRIGHTS, MASK WORKS, DESIGNS, TRADEMARKS, & UNFAIR COMPETITION

(a) The district courts shall have original jurisdiction of any civil action arising under any Act of Congress relating to patents, plant variety protection, copyrights and trademarks. No State court shall have jurisdiction over any claim for relief arising under any Act of Congress relating to patents, plant variety protection, or copyrights. For purposes of this subsection, the term "State" includes any State of the United States, the District of Columbia, the Commonwealth of Puerto Rico, the United States Virgin Islands, American Samoa, Guam, and the Northern Mariana Islands.

(b) The district courts shall have original jurisdiction of any civil action asserting a claim of unfair competition when joined with a substantial and related claim under the copyright, patent, plant variety protection or trademark laws.

(c) Subsections (a) and (b) apply to exclusive rights in mask works under chapter 9 of title 17, and to exclusive rights in designs under chapter 13 of title 17, to the same extent as such subsections apply to copyrights.

History of 28 U.S.C. §1338: June 25, 1948, ch. 646, 62 Stat. 931; Dec. 24, 1970, P.L. 91-577, §143(b), 84 Stat. 1559; Nov. 19, 1988, P.L. 100-702, §1020(a)(4), 102 Stat. 4671; Oct. 28, 1998, P.L. 105-304, §503(b)(1), 2(A), 112 Stat. 2917; Nov. 29, 1999, P.L. 106-113-Appx. I, §3009, 113 Stat. 1501A-551; Sept. 16, 2011, P.L. 112-29, §19(a), 125 Stat. 331.

CHAPTER 87. DISTRICT COURTS; VENUE

§1400. PATENTS & COPYRIGHTS, MASK WORKS, & DESIGNS

(a) Civil actions, suits, or proceedings arising under any Act of Congress relating to copyrights or exclusive rights in mask works or designs may be instituted in the district in which the defendant or his agent resides or may be found.

(b) Any civil action for patent infringement may be brought in the judicial district where the defendant resides, or where the defendant has committed acts of infringement and has a regular and established place of business.

History of 28 U.S.C. §1400: June 25, 1948, ch. 646, 62 Stat. 936; Nov. 19, 1988, P.L. 100-702, §1020(a)(5), 102 Stat. 4671; Oct. 28, 1998, P.L. 105-304, §503(b)(2)(B), 112 Stat. 2917; Aug. 5, 1999, P.L. 106-44, §2(a), 113 Stat. 223.

CHAPTER 89. DISTRICT COURTS; REMOVAL OF CASES FROM STATE COURTS

§1454. PATENT, PLANT VARIETY PROTECTION, & COPYRIGHT CASES

(a) In general. A civil action in which any party asserts a claim for relief arising under any Act of Congress relating to patents, plant variety protection, or copyrights may be removed to the district court of the United States for the district and division embracing the place where the action is pending.

(b) Special rules. The removal of an action under this section shall be made in accordance with section 1446, except that if the removal is based solely on this section—

(1) the action may be removed by any party; and

(2) the time limitations contained in section 1446(b) may be extended at any time for cause shown.

(c) Clarification of jurisdiction in certain cases. The court to which a civil action is removed under this section is not precluded from hearing and determining any claim in the civil action because the State court from which the civil action is removed did not have jurisdiction over that claim.

(d) Remand. If a civil action is removed solely under this section, the district court—

(1) shall remand all claims that are neither a basis for removal under subsection (a) nor within the original or supplemental jurisdiction of the district court under any Act of Congress; and

(2) may, under the circumstances specified in section 1367(c), remand any claims within the supplemental jurisdiction of the district court under section 1367.

History of 28 U.S.C. §1454: Sept. 16, 2011, P.L. 112-29, §19(c)(1), 125 Stat. 332.

CHAPTER 91. UNITED STATES COURT OF FEDERAL CLAIMS

§1498. PATENT & COPYRIGHT CASES

(a) Whenever an invention described in and covered by a patent of the United States is used or manufactured by or for the United States without license of the owner thereof or lawful right to use or manufacture the same, the owner's remedy shall be by action against the United States in the United States Court of Federal Claims for the recovery of his reasonable and entire compensation for such use and manufacture. Reasonable and entire compensation shall include the owner's reasonable costs, including reasonable fees for expert witnesses and attorneys, in pursuing the action if the owner is an independent inventor, a nonprofit organization, or an entity that had no more than 500 employees at any time during the 5-year period preceding the use or manufacture of the patented invention by or for the United States. Notwithstanding the preceding sentences, unless the action has been pending for more than 10 years from the time of filing to the time that the owner applies for such costs and fees, reasonable and entire compensation shall not include such costs and fees if the court finds that the position of the United States was substantially justified or that special circumstances make an award unjust.

For the purposes of this section, the use or manufacture of an invention described in and covered by a patent of the United States by a contractor, a subcontractor, or any person, firm, or corporation for the Government and with the authorization or consent of the Government, shall be construed as use or manufacture for the United States.

The court shall not award compensation under this section if the claim is based on the use or manufacture by or for the United States of any article owned, leased, used by, or in the possession of the United States prior to July 1, 1918.

A Government employee shall have the right to bring suit against the Government under this section except where he was in a position to order, influence, or induce use of the invention by the Government. This section shall not confer a right of action on any patentee or any assignee of such patentee with respect to any invention discovered or invented by a person while in the employment or service of the United States, where the invention was related to the official functions of the employee, in cases in which such functions included research and development, or in the making of which Government time, materials or facilities were used.

(b) Hereafter, whenever the copyright in any work protected under the copyright laws of the United States shall be infringed by the United States, by a corporation owned or controlled by the United States, or by a contractor, subcontractor, or any person, firm, or corporation acting for the Government and with the authorization or consent of the Government, the exclusive action which may be brought for such infringement shall be an action by the copyright owner against the United States in the Court of Federal Claims for the recovery of his reasonable and entire compensation as damages for such infringement, including the minimum statutory damages as set forth in section 504(c) of title 17, United States Code: *Provided*, That a Government employee shall have a right of action against the Government under this subsection except where he was in a position to order, influence, or induce use of the copyrighted work by the Government: *Provided, however*, That this subsection shall not confer a right of action on any copyright owner or any assignee of such owner with respect to any copyrighted work prepared by a person while in the employment or service of the United States, where the copyrighted work was prepared as a part of the official functions of the employee, or in the preparation of which Government time, material, or facilities were used: *And provided further*, That before such action against the United States has been instituted the appropriate corporation owned or controlled by the United States or the head of the appropriate department or agency of the Government, as the case may be, is authorized to enter into an agreement with the copyright owner in full settlement and compromise for the damages accruing to him by reason of such infringement and to settle the claim administratively out of available appropriations.

Except as otherwise provided by law, no recovery shall be had for any infringement of a copyright covered by this subsection committed more than three years prior to the filing of the complaint or counterclaim for infringement in the action, except that the period between the date of receipt of a written claim for compensation by the Department or agency of the Government or corporation owned or controlled by the United States, as the case may be, having authority to settle such claim and the date of mailing by the Government of a notice to the claimant that his claim has been denied shall not be counted as a part of the three years, unless suit is brought before the last-mentioned date.

(c) The provisions of this section shall not apply to any claim arising in a foreign country.

(d) Hereafter, whenever a plant variety protected by a certificate of plant variety protection under the laws of the United States shall be infringed by the United States, by a corporation owned or controlled by the United States, or by a contractor, subcontractor, or any person, firm, or corporation acting for the Government, and with the authorization and consent of the Government, the exclusive remedy of the owner of such certificate shall be by action against the United States in the Court of Federal Claims for the recovery of his reasonable and entire compensation as damages for such infringement: *Provided*, That a Government employee shall have a right of action against the Government under this subsection except where he was in a position to order, influence, or induce use of the protected plant variety by the Government: *Provided, however*, That this subsection shall not confer a right of action on any certificate owner or any assignee of such owner with respect to any protected plant variety made by a person while in the employment or service of the United States, where such variety was prepared as a part of the official functions of the employee, or in the preparation of which Government time, material, or facilities were used: And provided further, That before such action against the United States has been instituted, the appropriate corporation owned or controlled by the United States or the head of the appropriate agency of the Government, as the case may be, is authorized to enter into an agreement with the certificate owner in full settlement and compromise, for the damages accrued to him by reason of such infringement and to settle the claim administratively out of available appropriations.

(e) Subsections (b) and (c) of this section apply to exclusive rights in mask works under chapter 9 of title 17, and to exclusive rights in designs under chapter 13 of title 17, to the same extent as such subsections apply to copyrights.

History of 28 U.S.C. §1498: June 25, 1948, ch. 646, 62 Stat. 941; May 24, 1949, ch. 139, §87, 63 Stat. 102; Oct. 31, 1951, ch. 655, §50(c), 65 Stat. 727; July 17, 1952, ch. 930, 66 Stat. 757; Sept. 8, 1960, P.L. 86-726, §§1, 4, 74 Stat. 855, 856; Dec. 24, 1970, P.L. 91-577, §143(d), 84 Stat. 1559; Oct. 19, 1976, P.L. 94-553, §105(c), 90 Stat. 2599; Apr. 2, 1982, P.L. 97-164, §133(d), 96 Stat. 40; Nov. 19, 1988, P.L. 100-702, §1020(a)(6), 102 Stat. 4671; Oct. 29, 1992, P.L. 102-572, §902(a), 106 Stat. 4516; Oct. 19, 1996, P.L. 104-308, §1, 110 Stat. 3814; Dec. 16, 1997, P.L. 105-147, §3, 111 Stat. 2680; Oct. 28, 1998, P.L. 105-304, §503(d), 112 Stat. 2917.

CHAPTER 113. PROCESS

§1694. PATENT INFRINGEMENT ACTION

In a patent infringement action commenced in a district where the defendant is not a resident but has a regular and established place of business, service of process, summons or subpoena upon such defendant may be made upon his agent or agents conducting such business.

History of 28 U.S.C. §1694: June 25, 1948, ch. 646, 62 Stat. 945.

CHAPTER 115. EVIDENCE; DOCUMENTARY

§1744. COPIES OF UNITED STATES PATENT & TRADEMARK OFFICE DOCUMENTS, GENERALLY

Copies of letters patent or of any records, books, papers, or drawings belonging to the United States Patent and Trademark Office and relating to patents, authenticated under the seal of the United States Patent and Trademark Office and certified by the Under Secretary of Commerce for Intellectual Property and Director of the United States Patent and Trademark Office, or by another officer of the United States Patent and Trademark Office authorized to do so by the Director, shall be admissible in evidence with the same effect as the originals.

Any person making application and paying the required fee may obtain such certified copies.

History of 28 U.S.C. §1744: June 25, 1948, ch. 646, 62 Stat. 948; May 24, 1949, ch. 139, §92(c), 63 Stat. 103; Nov. 29, 1999, P.L. 106-113-Appx. I, §4732(b)(15), 113 Stat. 1501A-584.

§1745. COPIES OF FOREIGN PATENT DOCUMENTS

Copies of the specifications and drawings of foreign letters patent, or applications for foreign letters patent, and copies of excerpts of the official journals and other official publications of foreign patent offices belonging to the United States Patent and Trademark Office, certified in the manner provided by section 1744 of this title are prima facie evidence of their contents and of the dates indicated on their face.

History of 28 U.S.C. §1745: June 25, 1948, ch. 646, 62 Stat. 948, §1746. Renumbered May 24, 1949, ch. 139, §92(e), 63 Stat. 103; Oct. 3, 1964, P.L. 88-619, §7(a), 78 Stat. 996; Nov. 29, 1999, P.L. 106-113-Appx. I, §4732(b)(16), 113 Stat. 1501A-585.

CHAPTER 123. FEES & COSTS

§1928. PATENT INFRINGEMENT ACTION; DISCLAIMER NOT FILED

Whenever a judgment is rendered for the plaintiff in any patent infringement action involving a part of a patent and it appears that the patentee, in his specifications, claimed to be, but was not, the original and first inventor or discoverer of any material or substantial part of the thing patented, no costs shall be included in such judgment, unless the proper disclaimer has been filed in the United States Patent and Trademark Office prior to the commencement of the action.

History of 28 U.S.C. §1928: June 25, 1948, ch. 646, 62 Stat. 957; Nov. 29, 1999, P.L. 106-113-Appx. I, §4732(b)(17), 113 Stat. 1501A-585.

CHAPTER 180. ASSUMPTION OF CERTAIN CONTRACTUAL OBLIGATIONS

§4001. ASSUMPTION OF CONTRACTUAL OBLIGATIONS RELATED TO TRANSFERS OF RIGHTS IN MOTION PICTURES

(a) Assumption of obligations—

(1) In the case of a transfer of copyright ownership under United States law in a motion picture (as the terms "transfer of copyright ownership" and "motion picture" are defined in section 101 of title 17) that is produced subject to 1 or more collective bargaining agreements negotiated under the laws of the United States, if the transfer is executed on or after the effective date of this chapter and is not limited to public performance rights, the transfer instrument shall be deemed to incorporate the assumption agreements applicable to the copyright ownership being transferred that are required by the applicable collective bargaining agreement, and the transferee shall be subject to the obligations under each such assumption agreement to make residual payments and provide related notices, accruing after the effective date of the transfer and applicable to the exploitation of the rights transferred, and any remedies under each such assumption agreement for breach of those obligations, as those obligations and remedies are set forth in the applicable collective bargaining agreement, if—

(A) the transferee knows or has reason to know at the time of the transfer that such collective bargaining agreement was or will be applicable to the motion picture; or

(B) in the event of a court order confirming an arbitration award against the transferor under the collective bargaining agreement, the transferor does not have the financial ability to satisfy the award within 90 days after the order is issued.

(2) For purposes of paragraph (1)(A), "knows or has reason to know" means any of the following:

(A) Actual knowledge that the collective bargaining agreement was or will be applicable to the motion picture.

(B)(i) Constructive knowledge that the collective bargaining agreement was or will be applicable to the motion picture, arising from recordation of a document pertaining to copyright in the motion picture under section 205 of title 17 or from publication, at a site available to the public on-line that is operated by the relevant union, of information that identifies the motion picture as subject to a collective bargaining agreement with that union, if the site permits commercially reasonable verification of the date on which the information was available for access.

(ii) Clause (i) applies only if the transfer referred to in subsection (a)(1) occurs—

(I) after the motion picture is completed, or

(II) before the motion picture is completed and—

(aa) within 18 months before the filing of an application for copyright registration for the motion picture under section 408 of title 17, or

(bb) if no such application is filed, within 18 months before the first publication of the motion picture in the United States.

(C) Awareness of other facts and circumstances pertaining to a particular transfer from which it is apparent that the collective bargaining agreement was or will be applicable to the motion picture.

(b) Scope of exclusion of transfers of public performance rights.—For purposes of this section, the exclusion under subsection (a) of transfers of copyright ownership in a motion picture that are limited to public performance rights includes transfers to a terrestrial broadcast station, cable system, or programmer to the extent that the station, system, or programmer is functioning as an exhibitor of the motion picture, either by exhibiting the motion picture on its own network, system, service, or station, or by initiating the transmission of an exhibition that is carried on another network, system, service, or station. When a terrestrial broadcast station, cable system, or programmer, or other transferee, is also functioning otherwise as a distributor or as a producer of the motion picture, the public performance exclusion does not affect any obligations imposed on the transferee to the extent that it is engaging in such functions.

(c) Exclusion for grants of security interests.—Subsection (a) shall not apply to—

(1) a transfer of copyright ownership consisting solely of a mortgage, hypothecation, or other security interest; or

(2) a subsequent transfer of the copyright ownership secured by the security interest described in paragraph (1) by or under the authority of the secured party, including a transfer through the exercise of the secured party's rights or remedies as a secured party, or by a subsequent transferee.

The exclusion under this subsection shall not affect any rights or remedies under law or contract.

(d) Deferral pending resolution of bona fide dispute.—A transferee on which obligations are imposed under subsection (a) by virtue of paragraph (1) of that subsection may elect to defer performance of such obligations that are subject to a bona fide dispute between a union and a prior transferor until that dispute is resolved, except that such deferral shall not stay accrual of any union claims due under an applicable collective bargaining agreement.

(e) Scope of obligations determined by private agreement.—Nothing in this section shall expand or diminish the rights, obligations, or remedies of any person under the collective bargaining agreements or assumption agreements referred to in this section.

(f) Failure to notify.—If the transferor under subsection (a) fails to notify the transferee under subsection (a) of applicable collective bargaining obligations before the execution of the transfer instrument, and subsection (a) is made applicable to the transferee solely by virtue of subsection (a)(1)(B), the transferor shall be liable to the transferee for any damages suffered by the transferee as a result of the failure to notify.

(g) Determination of disputes and claims.—Any dispute concerning the application of subsections (a) through (f) shall be determined by an action in United States district court, and the court in its discretion may allow the recovery of full costs by or against any party and may also award a reasonable attorney's fee to the prevailing party as part of the costs.

(h) Study.—The Comptroller General, in consultation with the Register of Copyrights, shall conduct a study of the conditions in the motion picture industry that gave rise to this section, and the impact of this section on the motion picture industry. The Comptroller General shall report the findings of the study to the Congress within 2 years after the effective date of this chapter.

History of 28 U.S.C. §4001: Oct. 28, 1998, P.L. 105-304, §406, 112 Stat. 2902.

TITLE 42. THE PUBLIC HEALTH & WELFARE

CHAPTER 85. AIR POLLUTION PREVENTION & CONTROL

SUBCHAPTER III. GENERAL PROVISIONS

§7608. MANDATORY LICENSING

Whenever the Attorney General determines, upon application of the Administrator—

(1) that—

(A) in the implementation of the requirements of section 7411, 7412, or 7521 of this title, a right under any United States letters patent, which is being used or intended for public or commercial use and not otherwise reasonably available, is necessary to enable any person required to comply with such limitation to so comply, and

(B) there are no reasonable alternative methods to accomplish such purpose, and

(2) that the unavailability of such right may result in a substantial lessening of competition or tendency to create a monopoly in any line of commerce in any section of the country,

the Attorney General may so certify to a district court of the United States, which may issue an order requiring the person who owns such patent to license it on such reasonable terms and conditions as the court, after hearing, may determine. Such certification may be made to the district court for the district in which the person owning the patent resides, does business, or is found.

History of 42 U.S.C. §7608: July 14, 1955, ch. 360, §308; Dec. 31, 1970, P.L. 91-604, §12(a), 84 Stat. 1708.

TITLE 44. PUBLIC PRINTING & DOCUMENTS

CHAPTER 21. NATIONAL ARCHIVES & RECORDS ADMINISTRATION

§2117. LIMITATION ON LIABILITY

When letters and other intellectual productions (exclusive of patented material, published works under copyright protection, and unpublished works for which copyright registration has been made) come into the custody or possession of the Archivist, the United States or its agents are not liable for infringement of copyright or analogous rights arising out of use of the materials for display, inspection, research, reproduction, or other purposes.

History of 44 U.S.C. §2117: Oct. 22, 1968, P.L. 90-620, §2113, 82 Stat. 1291; Oct. 19, 1976, P.L. 94-553, §105(b), 90 Stat. 2599. Renumbered from §2113 and amended Oct. 19, 1984, P.L. 98-497, §§102(a)(1), 107(a)(7), 98 Stat. 2280, 2286.

TITLE 48. TERRITORIES & INSULAR POSSESSIONS

CHAPTER 7. THE VIRGIN ISLANDS

SUBCHAPTER II. CIVIL GOVERNMENT

§1405q. LAWS CONTINUED IN FORCE UNTIL MODIFIED; PATENT, TRADE MARK, & COPYRIGHT LAWS EXTENDED TO VIRGIN ISLANDS; JURISDICTION OF DISTRICT COURT

The laws of the United States applicable to the Virgin Islands on June 22, 1936, and all local laws and ordinances in force on such date in the Virgin Islands, not inconsistent with this subchapter, shall continue in force and effect: *Provided*, That the Municipal Council of Saint Croix and the Municipal Council of Saint Thomas and Saint John, and the legislative assembly, shall have power, when not inconsistent with this subchapter and within their respective jurisdictions, to amend, alter, modify, or repeal any law of the United States of local application only, or any ordinance, public or private, civil or criminal, continued in force and effect by this subchapter, except as herein otherwise provided, and to enact new laws and ordinances not inconsistent with this subchapter and not inconsistent with the laws of the United States hereafter made applicable to the Virgin Islands or any part thereof, subject to the power of the Congress to annul the same. The laws of the United States relating to patents, trade marks, and copyrights, and to the enforcement of rights arising thereunder, shall have the same force and effect in the Virgin Islands as in the continental United States, and the District Court of the Virgin Islands shall have the same jurisdiction in causes arising under such laws as is exercised by United States district courts.

History of 48 U.S.C. §1405q: June 22, 1936, ch. 699, §18, 49 Stat. 1811.

CHAPTER 8A. GUAM

SUBCHAPTER I. GENERAL PROVISIONS

§1421n. APPLICABILITY OF FEDERAL COPYRIGHT LAWS

The laws of the United States relating to copyrights, and to the enforcement of rights arising thereunder, shall have the same force and effect in Guam as in the continental United States.

History of 48 U.S.C. §1421n: Aug. 1, 1956, ch. 852, §24, 70 Stat. 911.

CHAPTER 12. THE VIRGIN ISLANDS

SUBCHAPTER VII. FISCAL PROVISIONS

§1643. IMPORT PROVISIONS WITH RESPECT TO TRADE-MARKS

Section 1124 of Title 15, and section 1526 of Title 19, shall not apply to importations into the Virgin Islands of genuine foreign merchandise bearing a genuine foreign trade-mark, but shall remain applicable to importations of such merchandise from the Virgin Islands into the United States or its possessions; and the dealing in or possession of any such merchandise in the Virgin Islands shall not constitute a violation of any registrant's right under the Trade Mark Act [15 U.S.C. §1051 et seq.].

History of 48 U.S.C. §1643: July 22, 1954, ch. 558, §28(c), 68 Stat. 509.

UNIFORM DOMAIN NAME DISPUTE RESOLUTION POLICY

(As Approved by ICANN on October 24, 1999)

1. **Purpose.** This Uniform Domain Name Dispute Resolution Policy (the "Policy") has been adopted by the Internet Corporation for Assigned Names and Numbers ("ICANN"), is incorporated by reference into your Registration Agreement, and sets forth the terms and conditions in connection with a dispute between you and any party other than us (the registrar) over the registration and use of an Internet domain name registered by you. Proceedings under Paragraph 4 of this Policy will be conducted according to the Rules for Uniform Domain Name Dispute Resolution Policy (the "Rules of Procedure"), which are available at www.icann.org/udrp/udrp-rules-24oct99.htm, and the selected administrative-dispute-resolution service provider's supplemental rules.

2. **Your Representations.** By applying to register a domain name, or by asking us to maintain or renew a domain name registration, you hereby represent and warrant to us that (a) the statements that you made in your Registration Agreement are complete and accurate; (b) to your knowledge, the registration of the domain name will not infringe upon or otherwise violate the rights of any third party; (c) you are not registering the domain name for an unlawful purpose; and (d) you will not knowingly use the domain name in violation of any applicable laws or regulations. It is your responsibility to determine whether your domain name registration infringes or violates someone else's rights.

3. **Cancellations, Transfers, and Changes.** We will cancel, transfer or otherwise make changes to domain name registrations under the following circumstances:

a. subject to the provisions of Paragraph 8, our receipt of written or appropriate electronic instructions from you or your authorized agent to take such action;

b. our receipt of an order from a court or arbitral tribunal, in each case of competent jurisdiction, requiring such action; and/or

c. our receipt of a decision of an Administrative Panel requiring such action in any administrative proceeding to which you were a party and which was conducted under this Policy or a later version of this Policy adopted by ICANN. (See Paragraph 4(i) and (k) below.)

We may also cancel, transfer or otherwise make changes to a domain name registration in accordance with the terms of your Registration Agreement or other legal requirements.

4. **Mandatory Administrative Proceeding.** This Paragraph sets forth the type of disputes for which you are required to submit to a mandatory administrative proceeding. These proceedings will be conducted before one of the administrative-dispute-resolution service providers listed at www.icann.org/udrp/approved-providers.htm (each, a "Provider").

a. **Applicable Disputes.** You are required to submit to a mandatory administrative proceeding in the event that a third party (a "complainant") asserts to the applicable Provider, in compliance with the Rules of Procedure, that

(i) your domain name is identical or confusingly similar to a trademark or service mark in which the complainant has rights; and

(ii) you have no rights or legitimate interests in respect of the domain name; and

(iii) your domain name has been registered and is being used in bad faith.

In the administrative proceeding, the complainant must prove that each of these three elements are present.

b. **Evidence of Registration and Use in Bad Faith.** For the purposes of Paragraph 4(a)(iii), the following circumstances, in particular but without limitation, if found by the Panel to be present, shall be evidence of the registration and use of a domain name in bad faith:

(i) circumstances indicating that you have registered or you have acquired the domain name primarily for the purpose of selling, renting, or otherwise transferring the domain name registration to the complainant who is the owner of the trademark or service mark or to a competitor of that complainant, for valuable consideration in excess of your documented out-of-pocket costs directly related to the domain name; or

(ii) you have registered the domain name in order to prevent the owner of the trademark or service mark from reflecting the mark in a corresponding domain name, provided that you have engaged in a pattern of such conduct; or

(iii) you have registered the domain name primarily for the purpose of disrupting the business of a competitor; or

(iv) by using the domain name, you have intentionally attempted to attract, for commercial gain, Internet users to your web site or other on-line location, by creating a likelihood of confusion with the complainant's mark as to the source, sponsorship, affiliation, or endorsement of your web site or location or of a product or service on your web site or location.

c. How to Demonstrate Your Rights to and Legitimate Interests in the Domain Name in Responding to a Complaint. When you receive a complaint, you should refer to Paragraph 5 of the Rules of Procedure in determining how your response should be prepared. Any of the following circumstances, in particular but without limitation, if found by the Panel to be proved based on its evaluation of all evidence presented, shall demonstrate your rights or legitimate interests to the domain name for purposes of Paragraph 4(a)(ii):

(i) before any notice to you of the dispute, your use of, or demonstrable preparations to use, the domain name or a name corresponding to the domain name in connection with a bona fide offering of goods or services; or

(ii) you (as an individual, business, or other organization) have been commonly known by the domain name, even if you have acquired no trademark or service mark rights; or

(iii) you are making a legitimate noncommercial or fair use of the domain name, without intent for commercial gain to misleadingly divert consumers or to tarnish the trademark or service mark at issue.

d. Selection of Provider. The complainant shall select the Provider from among those approved by ICANN by submitting the complaint to that Provider. The selected Provider will administer the proceeding, except in cases of consolidation as described in Paragraph 4(f).

e. Initiation of Proceeding and Process and Appointment of Administrative Panel. The Rules of Procedure state the process for initiating and conducting a proceeding and for appointing the panel that will decide the dispute (the "Administrative Panel").

f. Consolidation. In the event of multiple disputes between you and a complainant, either you or the complainant may petition to consolidate the disputes before a single Administrative Panel. This petition shall be made to the first Administrative Panel appointed to hear a pending dispute between the parties. This Administrative Panel may consolidate before it any or all such disputes in its sole discretion, provided that the disputes being consolidated are governed by this Policy or a later version of this Policy adopted by ICANN.

g. Fees. All fees charged by a Provider in connection with any dispute before an Administrative Panel pursuant to this Policy shall be paid by the complainant, except in cases where you elect to expand the Administrative Panel from one to three panelists as provided in Paragraph 5(b)(iv) of the Rules of Procedure, in which case all fees will be split evenly by you and the complainant.

h. Our Involvement in Administrative Proceedings. We do not, and will not, participate in the administration or conduct of any proceeding before an Administrative Panel. In addition, we will not be liable as a result of any decisions rendered by the Administrative Panel.

i. Remedies. The remedies available to a complainant pursuant to any proceeding before an Administrative Panel shall be limited to requiring the cancellation of your domain name or the transfer of your domain name registration to the complainant.

j. Notification and Publication. The Provider shall notify us of any decision made by an Administrative Panel with respect to a domain name you have registered with us. All decisions under this Policy will be published in full over the Internet, except when an Administrative Panel determines in an exceptional case to redact portions of its decision.

k. Availability of Court Proceedings. The mandatory administrative proceeding requirements set forth in Paragraph 4 shall not prevent either you or the complainant from submitting the dispute to a court of competent jurisdiction for independent resolution before such mandatory administrative proceeding is commenced or after such proceeding is concluded. If an Administrative Panel decides that your domain name registration should be canceled or transferred, we will wait ten (10) business days (as observed in the location of our principal office) after we are informed by the applicable Provider of the Administrative Panel's decision before implementing that decision. We will then implement the decision unless we have received from you during that ten (10) business day period official documentation (such as a copy of a complaint, file-stamped by the clerk of the court) that you have commenced a lawsuit against the complainant in a jurisdiction to which the complainant has submitted under Paragraph 3(b)(xiii) of the Rules of Procedure. (In general, that jurisdiction is either the location of our principal office or of your address as shown in our Whois database. See Paragraphs 1 and 3(b)(xiii) of the Rules of Procedure for details.) If we receive such documentation within the ten (10) business day period, we will not implement the Administrative Panel's decision, and we will take no further action, until we receive (i) evidence satisfactory to us of a resolution between the parties; (ii) evidence satisfactory to us that your lawsuit has been dismissed or withdrawn; or (iii) a copy of an order from such court dismissing your lawsuit or ordering that you do not have the right to continue to use your domain name.

5. All Other Disputes and Litigation. All other disputes between you and any party other than us regarding your domain name registration that are not brought pursuant to the mandatory administrative proceeding provisions of Paragraph 4 shall be resolved between you and such other party through any court, arbitration or other proceeding that may be available.

6. Our Involvement in Disputes. We will not participate in any way in any dispute between you and any party other than us regarding the registration and use of your domain name. You shall not name us as a party or otherwise include us in any such proceeding. In the event that we are named as a party in any such proceeding, we reserve the right to raise any and all defenses deemed appropriate, and to take any other action necessary to defend ourselves.

7. Maintaining the Status Quo. We will not cancel, transfer, activate, deactivate, or otherwise change the status of any domain name registration under this Policy except as provided in Paragraph 3 above.

8. Transfers During a Dispute.

a. Transfers of a Domain Name to a New Holder. You may not transfer your domain name registration to another holder (i) during a pending administrative proceeding brought pursuant to Paragraph 4 or for a period of fifteen (15) business days (as observed in the location of our principal place of business) after such proceeding is concluded; or (ii) during a pending court proceeding or arbitration commenced regarding your domain name unless the party to whom the domain name registration is being transferred agrees, in writing, to be bound by the decision of the court or arbitrator. We reserve the right to cancel any transfer of a domain name registration to another holder that is made in violation of this subparagraph.

b. Changing Registrars. You may not transfer your domain name registration to another registrar during a pending administrative proceeding brought pursuant to Paragraph 4 or for a period of fifteen (15) business days (as observed in the location of our principal place of business) after such proceeding is concluded. You may transfer administration of your domain name registration to another registrar during a pending court action or arbitration, provided that the domain name you have registered with us shall continue to be subject to the proceedings commenced against you in accordance with the terms of this Policy. In the event that you transfer a domain name registration to us during the pendency of a court action or arbitration, such dispute shall remain subject to the domain name dispute policy of the registrar from which the domain name registration was transferred.

9. Policy Modifications. We reserve the right to modify this Policy at any time with the permission of ICANN. We will post our revised Policy at least thirty (30) calendar days before it becomes effective. Unless this Policy has already been invoked by the submission of a complaint to a Provider, in which event the version of the Policy in effect at the time it was invoked will apply to you until the dispute is over, all such changes will be binding upon you with respect to any domain name registration dispute, whether the dispute arose before, on or after the effective date of our change. In the event that you object to a change in this Policy, your sole remedy is to cancel your domain name registration with us, provided that you will not be entitled to a refund of any fees you paid to us. The revised Policy will apply to you until you cancel your domain name registration.

TITLE 37. CODE OF FEDERAL REGULATIONS

TABLE OF CONTENTS

The following regulations are not the official version of Code of Federal Regulations title 37. The official version is on file with the National Archives & Records Administration, Office of the Federal Register, 8601 Adelphi Road, College Park, MD 20740-6001; 1-866-272-6272; www.archives.gov/federal-register. Updates to title 37 can be found in the Federal Register or at www.regulations.gov.

CFR

TITLE 37. PATENTS, TRADEMARKS, & COPYRIGHTS

TABLE OF CONTENTS

Title 37. Code of Federal Regulations

Table of Contents

TABLE OF CONTENTS

TABLE OF CONTENTS

TABLE OF CONTENTS

CFR

TABLE OF CONTENTS

TABLE OF CONTENTS

TABLE OF CONTENTS

TABLE OF CONTENTS

TABLE OF CONTENTS

TABLE OF CONTENTS

CFR

TABLE OF CONTENTS

TABLE OF CONTENTS

TABLE OF CONTENTS

TABLE OF CONTENTS

TABLE OF CONTENTS

TITLE 37. PATENTS, TRADEMARKS, & COPYRIGHTS

CHAPTER I. UNITED STATES PATENT & TRADEMARK OFFICE, DEPARTMENT OF COMMERCE

SUBCHAPTER A. GENERAL

PART 1. RULES OF PRACTICE IN PATENT CASES

SUBPART A. GENERAL PROVISIONS

GENERAL INFORMATION & CORRESPONDENCE

§1.1. ADDRESSES FOR NON-TRADEMARK CORRESPONDENCE WITH THE UNITED STATES PATENT & TRADEMARK OFFICE

(a) In general. Except as provided in paragraphs (a)(3)(i), (a)(3)(ii), and (d)(1) of this section, all correspondence intended for the United States Patent and Trademark Office must be addressed to either "Director of the United States Patent and Trademark Office, P.O. Box 1450, Alexandria, Virginia 22313-1450" or to specific areas within the Office as set out in paragraphs (a)(1), and (a)(3)(iii) of this section. When appropriate, correspondence should also be marked for the attention of a particular office or individual.

(1) Patent correspondence.

(i) In general. All correspondence concerning patent matters processed by organizations reporting to the Commissioner for Patents should be addressed to: Commissioner for Patents, PO Box 1450, Alexandria, Virginia 22313-1450.

(ii) Patent Trial and Appeal Board. See §41.10 or §42.6 of this title. Notices of appeal, appeal briefs, reply briefs, requests for oral hearing, as well as all other correspondence in an application or a patent involved in an appeal to the Board for which an address is not otherwise specified, should be addressed as set out in paragraph (a)(1)(i) of this section.

(2) [Reserved]

(3) Office of General Counsel correspondence—

(i) Litigation and service. Correspondence relating to pending litigation or otherwise within the scope of part 104 of this title shall be addressed as provided in §104.2.

(ii) Disciplinary proceedings. Correspondence to counsel for the Director of the Office of Enrollment and Discipline relating to disciplinary proceedings pending before a Hearing Officer or the Director shall be mailed to: Mail Stop 8, Office of the Solicitor, United States Patent and Trademark Office, P.O. Box 1450, Alexandria, Virginia 22313-1450.

(iii) Solicitor, in general. Correspondence to the Office of the Solicitor not otherwise provided for shall be addressed to: Mail Stop 8, Office of the Solicitor, United States Patent and Trademark Office, P.O. Box 1450, Alexandria, Virginia 22313-1450.

(iv) General Counsel. Correspondence to the Office of the General Counsel not otherwise provided for, including correspondence to the General Counsel relating to disciplinary proceedings, shall be addressed to: General Counsel, United States Patent and Trademark Office, PO Box 1450, Alexandria, Virginia 22313-1450.

(v) Improper correspondence. Correspondence improperly addressed to a Post Office Box specified in paragraphs (a)(3)(i) and (a)(3)(ii) of this section will not be filed elsewhere in the United States Patent and Trademark Office, and may be returned.

(4) Office of Public Records correspondence.

(i) Assignments. All patent-related documents submitted by mail to be recorded by Assignment Services Division, except for documents filed together with a new application, should be addressed to: Mail Stop Assignment Recordation Services, Director of the United States Patent and Trademark Office, P.O. Box 1450, Alexandria, Virginia 22313-1450. See §3.27.

(ii) Documents. All requests for certified or uncertified copies of patent documents should be addressed to: Mail Stop Document Services, Director of the United States Patent and Trademark Office, P.O. Box 1450, Alexandria, Virginia 22313-1450.

(5) Office of Enrollment and Discipline correspondence. All correspondence directed to the Office of Enrollment and Discipline concerning enrollment, registration, and investigation matters should be addressed to Mail Stop OED, Director of the United States Patent and Trademark Office, P.O. Box 1450, Alexandria, Virginia 22313-1450.

(b) Patent Cooperation Treaty. Letters and other communications relating to international applications during the international stage and prior to the assignment of a national serial number should be additionally marked "Mail Stop PCT."

(c) For reexamination or supplemental examination proceedings.

(1) All correspondence concerning ex parte reexamination, other than correspondence to the Office of the General Counsel pursuant to §1.1(a)(3) and §102.4 of this chapter, should be additionally marked "Mail Stop Ex Parte Reexam."

(2) All correspondence concerning inter partes reexamination, other than correspondence to the Office of the General Counsel pursuant to §1.1(a)(3) and §102.4 of this chapter, should be additionally marked "Mail Stop Inter Partes Reexam."

(3) Requests for supplemental examination (original and corrected request papers) and any other paper filed in a supplemental examination proceeding, should be additionally marked "Mail Stop Supplemental Examination."

(4) All correspondence concerning a reexamination proceeding ordered as a result of a supplemental reexamination proceeding, other than correspondence to the Office of the General Counsel pursuant to §1.1(a)(3) and §102.4 of this chapter should be additionally marked "Mail Stop Ex Parte Reexam."

(d) Payments of maintenance fees in patents not submitted electronically over the Internet, and correspondence related to maintenance fees may be addressed to: Director of the United States Patent and Trademark Office, Attn: Maintenance Fee, 2051 Jamieson Avenue, Suite 300, Alexandria, Virginia 22314.

(e) Patent term extension. All applications for extension of patent term under 35 U.S.C. 156 and any communications relating thereto intended for the United States Patent and Trademark Office should be additionally marked "Mail Stop Hatch-Waxman PTE." When appropriate, the communication should also be marked to the attention of a particular individual, as where a decision has been rendered.

(f) [Reserved]

History of 37 C.F.R. §1.1: 46 FR 29181, May 29, 1981; 49 FR 34724, Aug. 31, 1984; 49 FR 48451, Dec. 12, 1984; 52 FR 9394, Mar. 24, 1987; 53 FR 16413, May 9, 1988; 54 FR 37588, Sept. 11, 1989; 60 FR 20220, Apr. 25, 1995; 61 FR 56446, Nov. 1, 1996; 64 FR 48917, Sept. 8, 1999; 66 FR 39448, July 31, 2001; 68 FR 14335, Mar. 25, 2003; 68 FR 19371, Apr. 21, 2003; 68 FR 48287, Aug. 13, 2003; 68 FR 71006, Dec. 22, 2003; 69 FR 29877, May 26, 2004; 69 FR 35451, June 24, 2004; 69 FR 49997, Aug. 12, 2004; 72 FR 18904, May 16, 2007; 73 FR 47540, Oct. 2, 2008; 75 FR 36295, June 25, 2010; 77 FR 46624, Sept. 16, 2012; 77 FR 48811, Sept. 16, 2012; 78 FR 62393, Dec. 18, 2013.

Source of 37 C.F.R. Part 1A: 24 FR 10332, Dec. 22, 1959; 60 FR 14518, Mar. 17, 1995; 65 FR 14871, Mar. 20, 2000; 65 FR 33455, May 24, 2000; 65 FR 50103, Aug. 16, 2000; 65 FR 56793, Sept. 20, 2000; 65 FR 70490, Nov. 24, 2000, unless otherwise noted.

§1.2. BUSINESS TO BE TRANSACTED IN WRITING

All business with the Patent and Trademark Office should be transacted in writing. The personal attendance of applicants or their attorneys or agents at the Patent and Trademark Office is unnecessary. The action of the Patent and Trademark Office will be based exclusively on the written record in the Office. No attention will be paid to any alleged oral promise, stipulation, or understanding in relation to which there is disagreement or doubt.

§1.3. BUSINESS TO BE CONDUCTED WITH DECORUM & COURTESY

Applicants and their attorneys or agents are required to conduct their business with the United States Patent and Trademark Office with decorum and courtesy. Papers presented in violation of this requirement will be submitted to the Director and will not be entered. A notice of the non-entry of the paper will be provided. Complaints against examiners and other employees must be made in correspondence separate from other papers.

History of 37 C.F.R. §1.3: 61 FR 56446, Nov. 1, 1996; 68 FR 38624, June 30, 2003.

§1.4. NATURE OF CORRESPONDENCE & SIGNATURE REQUIREMENTS

(a) Correspondence with the Patent and Trademark Office comprises:

(1) Correspondence relating to services and facilities of the Office, such as general inquiries, requests for publications supplied by the Office, orders for printed copies of patents, orders for copies of records, transmission of assignments for recording, and the like, and

(2) Correspondence in and relating to a particular application or other proceeding in the Office. See particularly the rules relating to the filing, processing, or other proceedings of national applications in subpart B of this part; of international applications in subpart C of this part; of ex parte reexaminations of patents in subpart D of this part; of supplemental examination of patents in subpart E of this part; of extension of patent term in subpart F of this part; of inter partes reexaminations of patents in subpart H of this part; of international design applications in subpart I of this part; and of the Patent Trial and Appeal Board in parts 41 and 42 of this chapter.

(b) Since each file must be complete in itself, a separate copy of every paper to be filed in a patent application, patent file, or other proceeding must be furnished for each file to which the paper pertains, even though the contents of the papers filed in two or more files may be identical. The filing of duplicate copies of correspondence in the file of an application, patent, or other proceeding should be avoided, except in situations in which the Office requires the filing of duplicate copies. The Office may dispose of duplicate copies of correspondence in the file of an application, patent, or other proceeding.

(c) Since different matters may be considered by different branches or sections of the Office, each distinct subject, inquiry, or order must be contained in a separate paper to avoid confusion and delay in answering papers dealing with different subjects. Subjects provided for on a single Office or World Intellectual Property Organization form may be contained in a single paper.

(d)(1) Handwritten signature. Each piece of correspondence, except as provided in paragraphs (d)(2), (d)(3), (d)(4), (e), and (f) of this section, filed in an application, patent file, or other proceeding in the Office which requires a person's signature, must:

(i) Be an original, that is, have an original handwritten signature personally signed, in permanent dark ink or its equivalent, by that person; or

(ii) Be a direct or indirect copy, such as a photocopy or facsimile transmission (§1.6(d)), of an original. In the event that a copy of the original is filed, the original should be retained as evidence of authenticity. If a question of authenticity arises, the Office may require submission of the original.

(2) S-signature. An S-signature is a signature inserted between forward slash marks, but not a handwritten signature as defined by paragraph (d)(1) of this section. An S-signature includes any signature made by electronic or mechanical means, and any other mode of making or applying a signature other than a handwritten signature as provided for in paragraph (d)(1) of this section. Correspondence being filed in the Office in paper, by facsimile transmission as provided in §1.6(d), or via the Office electronic filing system as an attachment as provided in §1.6(a)(4), for a patent application, patent, or a reexamination or supplemental examination proceeding may be S-signature signed instead of being personally signed (i.e., with a handwritten signature) as provided for in paragraph (d)(1) of this section. The requirements for an S-signature under this paragraph (d)(2) of this section are as follows.

(i) The S-signature must consist only of letters, or Arabic numerals, or both, with appropriate spaces and commas, periods, apostrophes, or hyphens for punctuation, and the person signing the correspondence must insert his or her own S-signature with a first single forward slash mark before, and a second single forward slash mark after, the S-signature (e.g., /Dr. James T. Jones, Jr./); and

(ii) A patent practitioner (§1.32(a)(1)), signing pursuant to §§1.33(b)(1) or 1.33(b)(2), must supply his/her registration number either as part of the S-signature, or immediately below or adjacent to the S-signature. The number (#) character may be used only as part of the S-signature when appearing before a practitioner's registration number; otherwise the number character may not be used in an S-signature.

(iii) The signer's name must be:

(A) Presented in printed or typed form preferably immediately below or adjacent the S-signature, and

(B) Reasonably specific enough so that the identity of the signer can be readily recognized.

(3) Electronically submitted correspondence. Correspondence permitted via the Office electronic filing system may be signed by a graphic representation of a handwritten signature as provided for in paragraph (d)(1) of this section or a graphic representation of an S-signature as provided for in paragraph (d)(2) of this section when it is submitted via the Office electronic filing system.

(4) Certifications—

(i) Certification as to the paper presented. The presentation to the Office (whether by signing, filing, submitting, or later advocating) of any paper by a party, whether a practitioner or non-practitioner, constitutes a certification under §11.18(b) of this subchapter. Violations of §11.18(b)(2) of this subchapter by a party, whether a practitioner or non-practitioner, may result in the imposition of sanctions under §11.18(c) of this subchapter. Any practitioner violating §11.18(b) of this subchapter may also be subject to disciplinary action. See §11.18(d) of this subchapter.

(ii) Certification as to the signature. The person inserting a signature under paragraph (d)(2) or (d)(3) of this section in a document submitted to the Office certifies that the inserted signature appearing in the document is his or her own signature. A person submitting a document signed by another under paragraph (d)(2) or (d)(3) of this section is obligated to have a reasonable basis to believe that the person whose signature is present on the document was actually inserted by that person, and should retain evidence of authenticity of the signature. Violations of the certification as to the signature of another or a person's own signature as set forth in this paragraph may result in the imposition of sanctions under §11.18(c) and (d) of this chapter.

(5) Forms. The Office provides forms for the public to use in certain situations to assist in the filing of correspondence for a certain purpose and to meet certain requirements for patent applications and proceedings. Use of the forms for purposes for which they were not designed is prohibited. No changes to certification statements on the Office forms (e.g., oath or declaration forms, terminal disclaimer forms, petition forms, and nonpublication request forms) may be made. The existing text of a form, other than a certification statement, may be modified, deleted, or added to, if all text identifying the form as an Office form is removed. The presentation to the Office (whether by signing, filing, submitting, or later advocating) of any Office form with text identifying the form as an Office form by a party, whether a practitioner or non-practitioner, constitutes a certification under §11.18(b) of this chapter that the existing text and any certification statements on the form have not been altered other than permitted by EFS-Web customization.

(e) The following correspondence must be submitted with an original handwritten signature personally signed in permanent dark ink or its equivalent:

(1) Correspondence requiring a person's signature and relating to registration to practice before the Patent and Trademark Office in patent cases, enrollment and disciplinary investigations, or disciplinary proceedings; and

(2) Payments by credit cards where the payment is not being made via the Office's electronic filing systems.

(f) When a document that is required by statute to be certified must be filed, a copy, including a photocopy or facsimile transmission, of the certification is not acceptable.

(g) An applicant who has not made of record a registered attorney or agent may be required to state whether assistance was received in the preparation or prosecution of the patent application, for which any compensation or consideration was given or charged, and if so, to disclose the name or names of the person or persons providing such assistance. Assistance includes the preparation for the applicant of the specification and amendments or other papers to be filed in the Patent and Trademark Office, as well as other assistance in such matters, but does not include merely making drawings by draftsmen or stenographic services in typing papers.

(h) Ratification/confirmation/evidence of authenticity: The Office may require ratification, confirmation (which includes submission of a duplicate document but with a proper signature), or evidence of authenticity of a signature, such as when the Office has reasonable doubt as to the authenticity (veracity) of the signature, e.g., where there are variations of a signature, or where the signature and the typed or printed name, do not clearly identify the person signing.

History of 37 C.F.R. §1.4: 24 FR 10332, Dec. 22, 1959; 43 FR 20461, May 11, 1978; 48 FR 2707, Jan. 20, 1983; 49 FR 48451, Dec. 12, 1984; 53 FR 47807, Nov. 28, 1988; 58 FR 54501, Oct. 22, 1993; 62 FR 53180, Oct. 10, 1997; 64 FR 48917, Sept. 8, 1999; 65 FR 54656, Sept. 8, 2000; 65 FR 76772, Dec. 7, 2000; 67 FR 79522, Dec. 30, 2002; 68 FR 48287, Aug. 13, 2003; 69 FR 49997, Aug. 12, 2004; 69 FR 56535, Sept. 21, 2004; 70 FR 56126, Sept. 26, 2005; 72 FR 2775, Jan. 23, 2007; 73 FR 47684, Sept. 15, 2008; 77 FR 46624, Sept. 16, 2012; 77 FR 48811, Sept. 16, 2012; 78 FR 20196, Apr. 3, 2013; 78 FR 62393, Dec. 18, 2013; 80 FR 17952, May 13, 2015.

§1.5. IDENTIFICATION OF PATENT, PATENT APPLICATION, OR PATENT-RELATED PROCEEDING

(a) No correspondence relating to an application should be filed prior to receipt of the assigned application number (i.e., U.S. application number, international application number, or international registration number as appropriate). When correspondence directed to the Patent and Trademark Office concerns a previously filed application for a patent, it must identify on the top page in a conspicuous location, the application number (consisting of the series code and the serial number; e.g., 07/123,456), or the serial number and filing date assigned to that application by the Patent and Trademark Office, or the international application number of the international application, or the international registration number of an international design application. Any correspondence not containing such identification will be returned to the sender where a return address is available. The returned correspondence will be accompanied with a cover letter, which will indicate to the sender that if the returned correspondence is resubmitted to the Patent and Trademark Office within two weeks of the mail date on the cover letter, the original date of receipt of the correspondence will be considered by the Patent and Trademark Office as the date of receipt of the correspondence. Applicants may use either the Certificate of Mailing or Transmission procedure under §1.8 or the Priority Mail Express® procedure under §1.10 for resubmissions of returned correspondence if they desire to have the benefit of the date of deposit in the United States Postal Service. If the returned correspondence is not resubmitted within the two-week period, the date of receipt of the resubmission will be considered to be the date of receipt of the correspondence. The two-week period to resubmit the returned correspondence will not be extended. In addition to the application number, all correspondence directed to the Patent and Trademark Office concerning applications for patent should also state the name of the first listed inventor, the title of the invention, the date of filing the same, and if known, the group art unit or other unit within the Patent and Trademark Office responsible for considering the correspondence and the name of the examiner or other person to which it has been assigned.

(b) When the letter concerns a patent other than for purposes of paying a maintenance fee, it should state the number and date of issue of the patent, the name of the patentee, and the title of the invention. For letters concerning payment of a maintenance fee in a patent, see the provisions of §1.366(c).

(c) Correspondence relating to a trial proceeding before the Patent Trial and Appeal Board (part 42 of this title) are governed by §42.6 of this title.

(d) A letter relating to a reexamination or supplemental examination proceeding should identify it as such by the number of the patent undergoing reexamination or supplemental examination, the request control number assigned to such proceeding, and, if known, the group art unit and name of the examiner to which it been[1] assigned.

(e) [Reserved]

(f) When a paper concerns a provisional application, it should identify the application as such and include the application number.

1. **Editor's note:** Probably should be "has been."

History of 37 C.F.R. §1.5: 24 FR 10332, Dec. 22, 1959; 34 FR 18857, Nov. 26, 1969; 43 FR 20461, May 11, 1978; 46 FR 29181, May 29, 1981; 49 FR 552, Jan. 4, 1984; 49 FR 48451, Dec. 12, 1984; 53 FR 47807, Nov. 28, 1988; 58 FR 54501, Oct. 22, 1993; 61 FR 42802, Aug. 19, 1996; 61 FR 56446, Nov. 1, 1996; 64 FR 48917, Sept. 8, 1999; 68 FR 48288, Aug. 13, 2003; 69 FR 49997, Aug. 12, 2004; 77 FR 46624, Sept. 16, 2012; 77 FR 48812, Sept. 16, 2012; 78 FR 62394, Dec. 18, 2013; 79 FR 63039, Oct. 22, 2014; 80 FR 17952, May 13, 2015.

§1.6. RECEIPT OF CORRESPONDENCE

(a) Date of receipt and Priority Mail Express® date of deposit. Correspondence received in the Patent and Trademark Office is stamped with the date of receipt except as follows:

(1) The Patent and Trademark Office is not open for the filing of correspondence on any day that is a Saturday, Sunday, or Federal holiday within the District of Columbia. Except for correspondence transmitted by facsimile under paragraph (a)(3) of this section, or filed electronically under paragraph (a)(4) of this section, no correspondence is received in the Office on Saturdays, Sundays, or Federal holidays within the District of Columbia.

(2) Correspondence filed in accordance with §1.10 will be stamped with the date of deposit as Priority Mail Express® with the United States Postal Service.

(3) Correspondence transmitted by facsimile to the Patent and Trademark Office will be stamped with the date on which the complete transmission is received in the Patent and Trademark Office unless that date is a Saturday, Sunday, or Federal holiday within the District of Columbia, in which case the date stamped will be the next succeeding day which is not a Saturday, Sunday, or Federal holiday within the District of Columbia.

(4) Correspondence may be submitted using the Office electronic filing system only in accordance with the Office electronic filing system requirements. Correspondence submitted to the Office by way of the Office electronic filing system will be accorded a receipt date, which is the date the correspondence is received at the correspondence address for the Office set forth in §1.1 when it was officially submitted.

(b) [Reserved]

(c) Correspondence delivered by hand. In addition to being mailed, correspondence may be delivered by hand during hours the Office is open to receive correspondence.

(d) Facsimile transmission. Except in the cases enumerated below, correspondence, including authorizations to charge a deposit account, may be transmitted by facsimile. The receipt date accorded to the correspondence will be the date on which the complete transmission is received in the United States Patent and Trademark Office, unless that date is a Saturday, Sunday, or Federal holiday within the District of Columbia. See paragraph (a)(3) of this section. To facilitate proper processing, each transmission session should be limited to correspondence to be filed in a single application or other proceeding before the United States Patent and Trademark Office. The application number of a patent application, the control number of a reexamination or supplemental examination proceeding, the interference number of an interference proceeding, the trial number of a trial proceeding before the Board, or the patent number of a patent should be entered as a part of the sender's identification on a facsimile cover sheet. Facsimile transmissions are not permitted and, if submitted, will not be accorded a date of receipt in the following situations:

(1) Correspondence as specified in §1.4(e), requiring an original signature;

(2) Certified documents as specified in §1.4(f);

(3) Correspondence that cannot receive the benefit of the certificate of mailing or transmission as specified in §1.8(a)(2)(i)(A) through (D), (F), (I), and (K) and §1.8(a)(2)(iii)(A), except that a continued prosecution application under §1.53(d) may be transmitted to the Office by facsimile;

(4) Color drawings submitted under §§1.81, 1.83 through 1.85, 1.152, 1.165, 1.173, 1.437, or 1.1026;

(5) A request for reexamination under §1.510 or §1.913, or a request for supplemental examination under §1.610;

(6) Correspondence to be filed in an application subject to a secrecy order under §§5.1 through 5.5 of this chapter and directly related to the secrecy order content of the application;

(7) In contested cases and trials before the Patent Trial and Appeal Board, except as the Board may expressly authorize.

(e) [Reserved]

(f) Facsimile transmission of a patent application under §1.53(d). In the event that the Office has no evidence of receipt of an application under §1.53(d) (a continued prosecution application) transmitted to the Office by facsimile transmission, the party who transmitted the application under §1.53(d) may petition the Director to accord the application under §1.53(d) a filing date as of the date the application under §1.53(d) is shown to have been transmitted to and received in the Office,

(1) Provided that the party who transmitted such application under §1.53(d):

(i) Informs the Office of the previous transmission of the application under §1.53(d) promptly after becoming aware that the Office has no evidence of receipt of the application under §1.53(d);

(ii) Supplies an additional copy of the previously transmitted application under §1.53(d); and

(iii) Includes a statement which attests on a personal knowledge basis or to the satisfaction of the Director to the previous transmission of the application under §1.53(d) and is accompanied by a copy of the sending unit's report confirming transmission of the application under §1.53(d) or evidence that came into being after the complete transmission and within one business day of the complete transmission of the application under §1.53(d).

(2) The Office may require additional evidence to determine if the application under §1.53(d) was transmitted to and received in the Office on the date in question.

(g) Submission of the national stage correspondence required by §1.495 via the Office electronic filing system. In the event that the Office has no evidence of receipt of the national stage correspondence required by §1.495, which was submitted to the Office by the Office electronic filing system, the party who submitted the correspondence may petition the Director to accord the national stage correspondence a receipt date as of the date the correspondence is shown to have been officially submitted to the Office.

(1) The petition of this paragraph (g) requires that the party who submitted such national stage correspondence:

(i) Informs the Office of the previous submission of the correspondence promptly after becoming aware that the Office has no evidence of receipt of the correspondence under §1.495;

(ii) Supplies an additional copy of the previously submitted correspondence;

(iii) Includes a statement that attests on a personal knowledge basis, or to the satisfaction of the Director, that the correspondence was previously officially submitted; and

(iv) Supplies a copy of an acknowledgment receipt generated by the Office electronic filing system, or equivalent evidence, confirming the submission to support the statement of paragraph (g)(1)(iii) of this section.

(2) The Office may require additional evidence to determine if the national stage correspondence was submitted to the Office on the date in question.

History of 37 C.F.R. §1.6: 24 FR 10332, Dec. 22, 1959; 34 FR 18857, Nov. 26, 1969; 48 FR 2707, Jan. 20, 1983; 48 FR 4285, Jan. 31, 1983; 49 FR 552, Jan. 4, 1984; 58 FR 54501, Oct. 22, 1993; 58 FR 64154, Dec. 6, 1993; 61 FR 56447, Nov. 1, 1996; 62 FR 53180, Oct. 10, 1997; 64 FR 48917, Sept. 8, 1999; 65 FR 54657, Sept. 8, 2000; 65 FR 76772, Dec. 7, 2000; 68 FR 14336, Mar. 25, 2003; 68 FR 48288, Aug. 13, 2003; 69 FR 49997, Aug. 12, 2004; 69 FR 56536, Sept. 21, 2004; 72 FR 2775, Jan. 23, 2007; 77 FR 42173, Sept. 16, 2012; 77 FR 46624, Sept. 16, 2012; 78 FR 62394, Dec. 18, 2013; 79 FR 63039, Oct. 22, 2014; 80 FR 17952, May 13, 2015.

§1.7. TIMES FOR TAKING ACTION; EXPIRATION ON SATURDAY, SUNDAY OR FEDERAL HOLIDAY

(a) Whenever periods of time are specified in this part in days, calendar days are intended. When the day, or the last day fixed by statute or by or under this part for taking any action or paying any fee in the United States Patent and Trademark Office falls on Saturday, Sunday, or on a Federal holiday within the District of Columbia, the action may be taken, or the fee paid, on the next succeeding business day which is not a Saturday, Sunday, or a Federal holiday. See §90.3 of this chapter for time for appeal or for commencing civil action.

(b) If the day that is twelve months after the filing date of a provisional application under 35 U.S.C. 111(b) and §1.53(c) falls on Saturday, Sunday, or on a Federal holiday within the District of Columbia, the period of pendency shall be extended to the next succeeding secular or business day which is not a Saturday, Sunday, or a Federal holiday.

History of 37 C.F.R. §1.7: 24 FR 10332, Dec. 22, 1959; 48 FR 2707, Jan. 20, 1983; 48 FR 4285, Jan. 31, 1983; 65 FR 14871, Mar. 20, 2000; 65 FR 50103, Aug. 16, 2000; 78 FR 62395, Dec. 18, 2013.

§1.8. CERTIFICATE OF MAILING OR TRANSMISSION

(a) Except in the situations enumerated in paragraph (a)(2) of this section or as otherwise expressly excluded in this chapter, correspondence required to be filed in the U.S. Patent and Trademark Office within a set period of time will be considered as being timely filed if the procedure described in this section is followed. The actual date of receipt will be used for all other purposes.

(1) Correspondence will be considered as being timely filed if:

(i) The correspondence is mailed or transmitted prior to expiration of the set period of time by being:

(A) Addressed as set out in §1.1(a) and deposited with the U.S. Postal Service with sufficient postage as first class mail;

(B) Transmitted by facsimile to the Patent and Trademark Office in accordance with §1.6(d); or

(C) Transmitted via the Office electronic filing system in accordance with §1.6(a)(4); and

(ii) The correspondence includes a certificate for each piece of correspondence stating the date of deposit or transmission. The person signing the certificate should have reasonable basis to expect that the correspondence would be mailed or transmitted on or before the date indicated.

(2) The procedure described in paragraph (a)(1) of this section does not apply to, and no benefit will be given to a Certificate of Mailing or Transmission on the following:

(i) Relative to Patents and Patent Applications—

(A) The filing of a national patent application specification and drawing or other correspondence for the purpose of obtaining an application filing date, including a request for a continued prosecution application under §1.53(d);

(B) Papers filed in trials before the Patent Trial and Appeal Board, which are governed by §42.6(b) of this title;

(C) Papers filed in contested cases before the Patent Trial and Appeal Board, which are governed by §41.106(f) of this title;

(D) The filing of an international application for patent;

(E) The filing of correspondence in an international application before the U.S. Receiving Office, the U.S. International Searching Authority, or the U.S. International Preliminary Examining Authority;

(F) The filing of a copy of the international application and the basic national fee necessary to enter the national stage, as specified in §1.495(b).

(G) The filing of a written declaration of abandonment under §1.138;

(H) The filing of a submission under §1.217 for publication of a redacted copy of an application;

(I) The filing of a third-party submission under §1.290;

(J) The calculation of any period of adjustment, as specified in §1.703(f); and

(K) The filing of an international design application.

(ii) [Reserved]

(iii) Relative to Disciplinary Proceedings—

(A) Correspondence filed in connection with a disciplinary proceeding under part 11 of this chapter.

(B) [Reserved]

(b) In the event that correspondence is considered timely filed by being mailed or transmitted in accordance with paragraph (a) of this section, but not received in the U.S. Patent and Trademark Office after a reasonable amount of time has elapsed from the time of mailing or transmitting of the correspondence, or after the application is held to be abandoned, or after the proceeding is dismissed or decided with prejudice, or the prosecution of a reexamination proceeding is terminated pursuant to §1.550(d) or §1.957(b) or limited pursuant to §1.957(c), or a requester paper is refused consideration pursuant to §1.957(a), the correspondence will be considered timely if the party who forwarded such correspondence:

(1) Informs the Office of the previous mailing or transmission of the correspondence promptly after becoming aware that the Office has no evidence of receipt of the correspondence;

(2) Supplies an additional copy of the previously mailed or transmitted correspondence and certificate; and

(3) Includes a statement that attests on a personal knowledge basis or to the satisfaction of the Director to the previous timely mailing, transmission or submission. If the correspondence was sent by facsimile transmission, a copy of the sending unit's report confirming transmission may be used to support this statement. If the correspondence was transmitted via the Office electronic filing system, a copy of an acknowledgment receipt generated by the Office electronic filing system confirming submission may be used to support this statement.

(c) The Office may require additional evidence to determine if the correspondence was timely filed.

History of 37 C.F.R. §1.8: 41 FR 43721, Oct. 4, 1976; 43 FR 20461, May 11, 1978; 47 FR 47381, Oct. 26, 1982; 48 FR 2708, Jan. 20, 1983; 49 FR 48451, Dec. 12, 1984; 50 FR 5171, Feb. 6, 1985; 50 FR 23123, May 31, 1985; 52 FR 20046, May 28, 1987; 54 FR 37588, Sept. 11, 1989; 56 FR 14648, Apr. 11, 1991; 58 FR 54502, Oct. 22, 1993; 58 FR 64154, Dec. 6, 1993; 61 FR 56447, Nov. 1, 1996; 62 FR 53181, Oct. 10, 1997; 67 FR 523, Jan. 4, 2002; 68 FR 48288, Aug. 13, 2003; 69 FR 49997, Aug. 12, 2004; 69 FR 56536, Sept. 21, 2004; 72 FR 2775, Jan. 23, 2007; 72 FR 18904, May 16, 2007; 73 FR 47684, Sept. 15, 2008; 77 FR 42173, Sept. 16, 2012; 80 FR 17953, May 13, 2015.

§1.9. DEFINITIONS

(a)(1) A national application as used in this chapter means either a U.S. application for patent which was filed in the Office under 35 U.S.C. 111, an international application filed under the Patent Cooperation Treaty in which the basic national fee under 35 U.S.C. 41(a)(1)(F) has been paid, or an international design application filed under the Hague Agreement in which the Office has received a copy of the international registration pursuant to Hague Agreement Article 10.

(2) A provisional application as used in this chapter means a U.S. national application for patent filed in the Office under 35 U.S.C. 111(b).

(3) A nonprovisional application as used in this chapter means either a U.S. national application for patent which was filed in the Office under 35 U.S.C. 111(a), an international application filed under the Patent Cooperation Treaty in which the basic national fee under 35 U.S.C. 41(a)(1)(F) has been paid, or an international design application filed under the Hague Agreement in which the Office has received a copy of the international registration pursuant to Hague Agreement Article 10.

(b) An international application as used in this chapter means an international application for patent filed under the Patent Cooperation Treaty prior to entering national processing at the Designated Office stage.

(c) A published application as used in this chapter means an application for patent which has been published under 35 U.S.C. 122(b).

(d)(1) The term inventor or inventorship as used in this chapter means the individual or, if a joint invention, the individuals collectively who invented or discovered the subject matter of the invention.

(2) The term joint inventor or coinventor as used in this chapter means any one of the individuals who invented or discovered the subject matter of a joint invention.

(e) The term joint research agreement as used in this chapter means a written contract, grant, or cooperative agreement entered into by two or more persons or entities for the performance of experimental, developmental, or research work in the field of the claimed invention.

(f) The term claimed invention as used in this chapter means the subject matter defined by a claim in a patent or an application for a patent.

(g) For definitions in Patent Trial and Appeal Board proceedings, see parts 41 and 42 of this title.

(h) A Federal holiday within the District of Columbia as used in this chapter means any day, except Saturdays and Sundays, when the Patent and Trademark Office is officially closed for business for the entire day.

(i) National security classified as used in this chapter means specifically authorized under criteria established by an Act of Congress or Executive Order to be kept secret in the interest of national defense or foreign policy and, in fact, properly classified pursuant to such Act of Congress or Executive Order.

(j) Director as used in this chapter, except for part 11 of this chapter, means the Under Secretary of Commerce for Intellectual Property and Director of the United States Patent and Trademark Office.

(k) Paper as used in this chapter means a document that may exist in electronic form, or in physical form, and therefore does not necessarily imply physical sheets of paper.

(*l*) Hague Agreement as used in this chapter means the Geneva Act of the Hague Agreement Concerning the International Registration of Industrial Designs adopted at Geneva, Switzerland, on July 2, 1999, and Hague Agreement Article as used in this chapter means an Article under the Hague Agreement.

(m) Hague Agreement Regulations as used in this chapter means the Common Regulations Under the 1999 Act and the 1960 Act of the Hague Agreement, and Hague Agreement Rule as used in this chapter means one of the Hague Agreement Regulations.

(n) An international design application as used in this chapter means an application for international registration of a design filed under the Hague Agreement. Unless otherwise clear from the wording, reference to "design application" or "application for a design patent" in this chapter includes an international design application that designates the United States.

History of 37 C.F.R. §1.9: 43 FR 20461, May 11, 1978; 47 FR 40139, Sept. 10, 1982; 47 FR 43275, Sept. 30, 1982; 49 FR 34724, Aug. 31, 1984; 49 FR 48451, Dec. 12, 1984; 58 FR 54508, Oct. 22, 1993; 60 FR 20220, Apr. 25, 1995; 61 FR 56447, Nov. 1, 1996; 62 FR 53181, Oct. 10, 1997; 65 FR 54657, Sept. 8, 2000; 65 FR 57051, Sept. 20, 2000; 68 FR 14336, Mar. 25, 2003; 68 FR 38624, June 30, 2003; 69 FR 49997, Aug. 12, 2004; 73 FR 47685, Sept. 15, 2008; 77 FR 46624, Sept. 16, 2012; 77 FR 48812, Sept. 16, 2012; 78 FR 11052, Mar. 16, 2013; 80 FR 17953, May 13, 2015.

§1.10. FILING OF CORRESPONDENCE BY PRIORITY MAIL EXPRESS®

(a)(1) Any correspondence received by the U.S. Patent and Trademark Office (USPTO) that was delivered by the Priority Mail Express® Post Office to Addressee service of the United States Postal Service (USPS) will be considered filed with the USPTO on the date of deposit with the USPS.

(2) The date of deposit with USPS is shown by the "date accepted" on the Priority Mail Express® label or other official USPS notation. If the USPS deposit date cannot be determined, the correspondence will be accorded the USPTO receipt date as the filing date. See §1.6(a).

(b) Correspondence should be deposited directly with an employee of the USPS to ensure that the person depositing the correspondence receives a legible copy of the Priority Mail Express® mailing label with the "date accepted" clearly marked. Persons dealing indirectly with the employees of the USPS (such as by deposit in a Priority Mail Express® drop box) do so at the risk of not receiving a copy of the Priority Mail Express® mailing label with the desired "date accepted" clearly marked. The paper(s) or fee(s) that constitute the correspondence should also include the Priority Mail Express® mailing label number thereon. See paragraphs (c), (d) and (e) of this section.

(c) Any person filing correspondence under this section that was received by the Office and delivered by the Priority Mail Express® Post Office to Addressee service of the USPS, who can show that there is a discrepancy between the filing date accorded by the Office to the correspondence and the date of deposit as shown by the "date accepted" on the Priority Mail Express® mailing label or other official USPS notation, may petition the Director to accord the correspondence a filing date as of the "date accepted" on the Priority Mail Express® mailing label or other official USPS notation, provided that:

(1) The petition is filed promptly after the person becomes aware that the Office has accorded, or will accord, a filing date other than the USPS deposit date;

(2) The number of the Priority Mail Express® mailing label was placed on the paper(s) or fee(s) that constitute the correspondence prior to the original mailing by Priority Mail Express®; and

(3) The petition includes a true copy of the Priority Mail Express® mailing label showing the "date accepted," and of any other official notation by the USPS relied upon to show the date of deposit.

(d) Any person filing correspondence under this section that was received by the Office and delivered by the Priority Mail Express® Post Office to Addressee service of the USPS, who can show that the "date accepted" on the Priority Mail Express® mailing label or other official notation entered by the USPS was incorrectly entered or omitted by the USPS, may petition the Director to accord the correspondence a filing date as of the date the correspondence is shown to have been deposited with the USPS, provided that:

(1) The petition is filed promptly after the person becomes aware that the Office has accorded, or will accord, a filing date based upon an incorrect entry by the USPS;

(2) The number of the Priority Mail Express® mailing label was placed on the paper(s) or fee(s) that constitute the correspondence prior to the original mailing by Priority Mail Express®; and

(3) The petition includes a showing which establishes, to the satisfaction of the Director, that the requested filing date was the date the correspondence was deposited in the Priority Mail Express® Post Office to Addressee service prior to the last scheduled pickup for that day. Any showing pursuant to this paragraph must be corroborated by evidence from the USPS or that came into being after deposit and within one business day of the deposit of the correspondence in the Priority Mail Express® Post Office to Addressee service of the USPS.

(e) Any person mailing correspondence addressed as set out in §1.1(a) to the Office with sufficient postage utilizing the Priority Mail Express® Post Office to Addressee service of the USPS but not received by the Office, may petition the Director to consider such correspondence filed in the Office on the USPS deposit date, provided that:

(1) The petition is filed promptly after the person becomes aware that the Office has no evidence of receipt of the correspondence;

(2) The number of the Priority Mail Express® mailing label was placed on the paper(s) or fee(s) that constitute the correspondence prior to the original mailing by Priority Mail Express®;

(3) The petition includes a copy of the originally deposited paper(s) or fee(s) that constitute the correspondence showing the number of the Priority Mail Express® mailing label thereon, a copy of any returned postcard receipt, a copy of the Priority Mail Express® mailing label showing the "date accepted," a copy of any other official notation by the USPS relied upon to show the date of deposit, and, if the requested filing date is a date other than the "date accepted" on the Priority Mail Express® mailing label or other official notation entered by the USPS, a showing pursuant to paragraph (d)(3) of this section that the requested filing date was the date the correspondence was deposited in the Priority Mail Express® Post Office to Addressee service prior to the last scheduled pickup for that day; and

(4) The petition includes a statement which establishes, to the satisfaction of the Director, the original deposit of the correspondence and that the copies of the correspondence, the copy of the Priority Mail Express® mailing label, the copy of any returned postcard receipt, and any official notation entered by the USPS are true copies of the originally mailed correspondence, original Priority Mail Express® mailing label, returned postcard receipt, and official notation entered by the USPS.

(f) The Office may require additional evidence to determine if the correspondence was deposited as Priority Mail Express® with the USPS on the date in question.

(g) Any person who mails correspondence addressed as set out in §1.1(a) to the Office with sufficient postage utilizing the Priority Mail Express® Post Office to Addressee service of the USPS, but has the correspondence returned by the USPS due to an interruption or emergency in Priority Mail Express® service, may petition the Director to consider such correspondence as filed on a particular date in the Office, provided that:

(1) The petition is filed promptly after the person becomes aware of the return of the correspondence;

(2) The number of the Priority Mail Express® mailing label was placed on the paper(s) or fee(s) that constitute the correspondence prior to the original mailing by Priority Mail Express®;

(3) The petition includes the original correspondence or a copy of the original correspondence showing the number of the Priority Mail Express® mailing label thereon and a copy of the Priority Mail Express® mailing label showing the "date accepted"; and

(4) The petition includes a statement which establishes, to the satisfaction of the Director, the original deposit of the correspondence and that the correspondence or copy of the correspondence is the original correspondence or a true copy of the correspondence originally deposited with the USPS on the requested filing date. The Office may require additional evidence to determine if the correspondence was returned by the USPS due to an interruption or emergency in Priority Mail Express® service.

(h) Any person who attempts to mail correspondence addressed as set out in §1.1(a) to the Office with sufficient postage utilizing the Priority Mail Express® Post Office to Addressee service of the USPS, but has the correspondence refused by an employee of the USPS due to an interruption or emergency in Priority Mail Express® service, may petition the Director to consider such correspondence as filed on a particular date in the Office, provided that:

(1) The petition is filed promptly after the person becomes aware of the refusal of the correspondence;

(2) The number of the Priority Mail Express® mailing label was placed on the paper(s) or fee(s) that constitute the correspondence prior to the attempted mailing by Priority Mail Express®;

(3) The petition includes the original correspondence or a copy of the original correspondence showing the number of the Priority Mail Express® mailing label thereon; and

(4) The petition includes a statement by the person who originally attempted to deposit the correspondence with the USPS which establishes, to the satisfaction of the Director, the original attempt to deposit the correspondence and that the correspondence or copy of the correspondence is the original correspondence or a true copy of the correspondence originally attempted to be deposited with the USPS on the requested filing date. The Office may require additional evidence to determine if the correspondence was refused by an employee of the USPS due to an interruption or emergency in Priority Mail Express® service.

(i) Any person attempting to file correspondence under this section that was unable to be deposited with the USPS due to an interruption or emergency in Priority Mail Express® service which has been so designated by the Director, may petition the Director to consider such correspondence as filed on a particular date in the Office, provided that:

(1) The petition is filed in a manner designated by the Director promptly after the person becomes aware of the designated interruption or emergency in Priority Mail Express® service;

(2) The petition includes the original correspondence or a copy of the original correspondence; and

(3) The petition includes a statement which establishes, to the satisfaction of the Director, that the correspondence would have been deposited with the USPS but for the designated interruption or emergency in Priority Mail Express® service, and that the correspondence or copy of the correspondence is the original correspondence or a true copy of the correspondence originally attempted to be deposited with the USPS on the requested filing date.

History of 37 C.F.R. §1.10: 48 FR 2708, Jan. 20, 1983; 48 FR 4285, Jan. 31, 1983; 49 FR 552, Jan. 4, 1984; 61 FR 56447, Nov. 1, 1996; 62 FR 53181, Oct. 10, 1997; 67 FR 36101, May 23, 2002; 68 FR 48288, Aug. 13, 2003; 69 FR 56536, Sept. 21, 2004; 79 FR 63039, Oct. 22, 2014.

RECORDS & FILES OF THE PATENT & TRADEMARK OFFICE

§1.11. FILES OPEN TO THE PUBLIC

(a) The specification, drawings, and all papers relating to the file of: A published application; a patent; or a statutory invention registration are open to inspection by the public, and copies may be obtained upon the payment of the fee set forth in §1.19(b)(2). If an application was published in redacted form pursuant to §1.217, the complete file wrapper and contents of the patent application will not be available if: The requirements of paragraphs (d)(1), (d)(2), and (d)(3) of §1.217 have been met in the application; and the application is still pending. See §2.27 of this title for trademark files.

(b) All reissue applications, all applications in which the Office has accepted a request to open the complete application to inspection by the public, and related papers in the application file, are open to inspection by the public, and copies may be furnished upon paying the fee therefor. The filing of reissue applications, other than continued prosecution applications under §1.53(d) of reissue applications, will be announced in the Official Gazette. The announcement shall include at least the filing date, reissue application and original patent numbers, title, class and subclass, name of the inventor, name of the owner of record, name of the attorney or agent of record, and examining group to which the reissue application is assigned.

(c) All requests for reexamination for which all the requirements of §1.510 or §1.915 have been satisfied will be announced in the Official Gazette. Any reexaminations at the initiative of the Director pursuant to §1.520 will also be announced in the Official Gazette. The announcement shall include at least the date of the request, if any, the reexamination request control number or the Director initiated order control number, patent number, title, class and subclass, name of the inventor, name of the patent owner of record, and the examining group to which the reexamination is assigned.

(d) All papers or copies thereof relating to a reexamination proceeding which have been entered of record in the patent or reexamination file are open to inspection by the general public, and copies may be furnished upon paying the fee therefor.

(e) Except as prohibited in §41.6(b), §42.14 or §42.410(b), the file of any interference or trial before the Patent Trial and Appeal Board is open to public inspection and copies of the file may be obtained upon payment of the fee therefor.

History of 37 C.F.R. §1.11: 42 FR 5593, Jan. 28, 1977; 43 FR 28477, June 30, 1978; 46 FR 29181, May 29, 1981; 47 FR 41272, Sept. 17, 1982; 49 FR 48451, Dec. 12, 1984; 50 FR 9378, Mar. 7, 1985; 60 FR 14518, Mar. 17, 1995; 62 FR 53181, Oct. 10, 1997; 65 FR 57051, Sept. 20, 2000; 69 FR 49997, Aug. 12, 2004; 70 FR 56126, Sept. 26, 2005; 71 FR 44223, Aug. 4, 2006; 77 FR 46624, Sept. 16, 2012.

§1.12. ASSIGNMENT RECORDS OPEN TO PUBLIC INSPECTION

(a)(1) Separate assignment records are maintained in the United States Patent and Trademark Office for patents and trademarks. The assignment records, relating to original or reissue patents, including digests and indexes (for assignments recorded on or after May 1, 1957), and published patent applications, are open to public inspection at the United States Patent and Trademark Office, and copies of patent assignment records may be obtained upon request and payment of the fee set forth in §1.19 of this chapter. See §2.200 of this chapter regarding trademark assignment records.

(2) All records of assignments of patents recorded before May 1, 1957, are maintained by the National Archives and Records Administration (NARA). The records are open to public inspection. Certified and uncertified copies of those assignment records are provided by NARA upon request and payment of the fees required by NARA.

(b) Assignment records, digests, and indexes relating to any pending or abandoned patent application, which is open to the public pursuant to §1.11 or for which copies or access may be supplied pursuant to §1.14, are available to the public. Copies of any assignment records, digests, and indexes that are not available to the public shall be obtainable only upon written authority of an inventor, the applicant, the assignee or an assignee of an undivided part interest, or a patent practitioner of record, or upon a showing that the person seeking such information is a bona fide prospective or actual purchaser, mortgagee, or licensee of such application, unless it shall be necessary to the proper conduct of business before the Office or as provided in this part.

(c) Any request by a member of the public seeking copies of any assignment records of any pending or abandoned patent application preserved in confidence under §1.14, or any information with respect thereto, must:

(1) Be in the form of a petition including the fee set forth in §1.17(g); or

(2) Include written authority granting access to the member of the public to the particular assignment records from an inventor, the applicant, the assignee or an assignee of an undivided part interest, or a patent practitioner of record.

(d) An order for a copy of an assignment or other document should identify the reel and frame number where the assignment or document is recorded. If a document is identified without specifying its correct reel and frame, an extra charge as set forth in §1.21(j) will be made for the time consumed in making a search for such assignment.

History of 37 C.F.R. §1.12: 43 FR 20461, May 11, 1978; 47 FR 41272, Sept. 17, 1982; 54 FR 6900, Feb. 15, 1989; 56 FR 65151, Dec. 13, 1991; 56 FR 66670, Dec. 24, 1991; 57 FR 29641, July 6, 1992; 60 FR 20221, Apr. 25, 1995; 61 FR 42802, Aug. 19, 1996; 65 FR 54657, Sept. 8, 2000; 65 FR 57051, Sept. 20, 2000; 68 FR 48288, Aug. 13, 2003; 69 FR 29877, May 26, 2004; 69 FR 56536, Sept. 21, 2004; 77 FR 48812, Sept. 16, 2012.

§1.13. COPIES & CERTIFIED COPIES

(a) Non-certified copies of patents, and patent application publications and of any records, books, papers, or drawings within the jurisdiction of the United States Patent and Trademark Office and open to the public, will be furnished by the United States Patent and Trademark Office to any person, and copies of other records or papers will be furnished to persons entitled thereto, upon payment of the appropriate fee. See §2.201 of this chapter regarding copies of trademark records.

(b) Certified copies of patents, patent application publications, and trademark registrations and of any records, books, papers, or drawings within the jurisdiction of the United States Patent and Trademark Office and open to the public or persons entitled thereto will be authenticated by the seal of the United States Patent and Trademark Office and certified by the Director, or in his or her name, upon payment of the fee for the certified copy.

History of 37 C.F.R. §1.13: 56 FR 65151, Dec. 13, 1991; 58 FR 54508, Oct. 22, 1993; 65 FR 57051, Sept. 20, 2000; 68 FR 48288, Aug. 13, 2003; 68 FR 71006, Dec. 22, 2003.

§1.14. PATENT APPLICATIONS PRESERVED IN CONFIDENCE

(a) Confidentiality of patent application information. Patent applications that have not been published under 35 U.S.C. 122(b) are generally preserved in confidence pursuant to 35 U.S.C. 122(a). Information concerning the filing, pendency, or subject matter of an application for patent, including status information, and access to the application, will only be given to the public as set forth in §1.11 or in this section.

(1) Records associated with patent applications (see paragraph (g) of this section for international applications and paragraph (j) of this section for international design applications) may be available in the following situations:

(i) Patented applications and statutory invention registrations. The file of an application that has issued as a patent or published as a statutory invention registration is available to the public as set forth in §1.11(a). A copy of the patent application-as-filed, the file contents of the application, or a specific document in the file of such an application may be provided upon request and payment of the appropriate fee set forth in §1.19(b).

(ii) Published abandoned applications. The file of an abandoned published application is available to the public as set forth in §1.11(a). A copy of the application-as-filed, the file contents of the published application, or a specific document in the file of the published application may be provided to any person upon request and payment of the appropriate fee set forth in §1.19(b).

(iii) Published pending applications. A copy of the application-as-filed, the file contents of the application, or a specific document in the file of a pending published application may be provided to any person upon request and payment of the appropriate fee set forth in §1.19(b). If a redacted copy of the application was used for the patent application publication, the copy of the specification, drawings, and papers may be limited to a redacted copy. The Office will not provide access to the paper file of a pending application that has been published, except as provided in paragraph (c) or (i) of this section.

(iv) Unpublished abandoned applications (including provisional applications) that are identified or relied upon. The file contents of an unpublished, abandoned application may be made available to the public if the application is identified in a U.S. patent, a statutory invention registration, a U.S. patent application publication, an international publication of an international application under PCT Article 21(2), or a publication of an international registration under Hague Agreement Article 10(3) of an international design application designating the United States. An application is considered to have been identified in a document, such as a patent, when the application number or serial number and filing date, first named inventor, title, and filing date or other application specific information are provided in the text of the patent, but not when the same identification is made in a paper in the file contents of the patent and is not included in the printed patent. Also, the file contents may be made available to the public, upon a written request, if benefit of the abandoned application is claimed under 35 U.S.C. 119(e), 120, 121, 365(c), or 386(c) in an application that has issued as a U.S. patent, or has published as a statutory invention registration, a U.S. patent application publication, an international publication of an international application under PCT Article 21(2), or a publication of an international registration under Hague Agreement Article 10(3). A copy of the application-as-filed, the file contents of the application, or a specific document in the file of the application may be provided to any person upon written request and payment of the appropriate fee (§1.19(b)).

(v) Unpublished pending applications (including provisional applications) whose benefit is claimed. A copy of the file contents of an unpublished pending application may be provided to any person, upon written request and payment of the appropriate fee (§1.19(b)), if the benefit of the application is claimed under 35 U.S.C. 119(e), 120, 121, 365(c), or 386(c) in an application that has issued as a U.S. patent, or in an application that has published as a statutory invention registration, a U.S. patent application publication, an international publication of an international application under PCT Article 21(2), or a publication of an international registration under Hague Agreement Article 10(3). A copy of the application-as-filed or a specific document in the file of the pending application may also be provided to any person upon written request and payment of the appropriate fee (§1.19(b)). The Office will not provide access to the paper file of a pending application, except as provided in paragraph (c) or (i) of this section.

(vi) Unpublished pending applications (including provisional applications) that are incorporated by reference or otherwise identified. A copy of the application as originally filed of an unpublished pending application may be provided to any person, upon written request and payment of the appropriate fee (§1.19(b)), if the application is incorporated by reference or otherwise identified in a U.S. patent, a statutory invention registration, a U.S. patent application publication, an international publication of an international application under PCT Article 21(2), or a publication of an international registration under Hague Agreement Article 10(3) of an international design application designating the United States. The Office will not provide access to the paper file of a pending application, except as provided in paragraph (c) or (i) of this section.

(vii) When a petition for access or a power to inspect is required. Applications that were not published or patented, that are not the subject of a benefit claim under 35 U.S.C. 119(e), 120, 121, 365(c), or 386(c) in an application that has issued as a U.S. patent, an application that has published as a statutory invention registration, a U.S. patent application publication, an international publication of an international application under PCT Article 21(2), or a publication of an international registration under Hague Agreement Article 10(3), or are not identified in a U.S. patent, a statutory invention registration, a U.S. patent application publication, an international publication of an international application under PCT Article 21(2), or a publication of an international registration under Hague Agreement Article 10(3) of an international design application designating the United States, are not available to the public. If an application is identified in the file contents of another application, but not the published patent application or patent itself, a granted petition for access (see paragraph (i)) or a power to inspect (see paragraph (c) of this section) is necessary to obtain the application, or a copy of the application.

(2) Information concerning a patent application may be communicated to the public if the patent application is identified in a published patent document or in an application as set forth in paragraphs (a)(1)(i) through (a)(1)(vi) of this section. The information that may be communicated to the public (i.e., status information) includes:

(i) Whether the application is pending, abandoned, or patented;

(ii) Whether the application has been published under 35 U.S.C. 122(b);

(iii) The application "numerical identifier" which may be:

(A) The eight-digit application number (the two-digit series code plus the six-digit serial number); or

(B) The six-digit serial number plus any one of the filing date of the national application, the international filing date, or date of entry into the national stage; and

(iv) Whether another application claims the benefit of the application (i.e., whether there are any applications that claim the benefit of the filing date under 35 U.S.C. 119(e), 120, 121, 365, or 386 of the application), and if there are any such applications, the numerical identifier of the application, the specified relationship between the applications (e.g., continuation), whether the application is pending, abandoned or patented, and whether the application has been published under 35 U.S.C. 122(b).

(b) Electronic access to an application. Where a copy of the application file or access to the application may be made available pursuant to this section, the Office may at its discretion provide access to only an electronic copy of the specification, drawings, and file contents of the application.

(c) Power to inspect a pending or abandoned application. Access to an application may be provided to any person if the application file is available, and the application contains written authority (e.g., a power to inspect) granting access to such person. The written authority must be signed by:

(1) The applicant;

(2) A patent practitioner of record;

(3) The assignee or an assignee of an undivided part interest;

(4) The inventor or a joint inventor; or

(5) A registered attorney or agent named in the papers accompanying the application papers filed under §1.53 or the national stage documents filed under §1.495, if a power of attorney has not been appointed under §1.32.

(d) Applications reported to Department of Energy. Applications for patents which appear to disclose, purport to disclose or do disclose inventions or discoveries relating to atomic energy are reported to the Department of Energy, which Department will be given access to the applications. Such reporting does not constitute a determination that the subject matter of each application so reported is in fact useful or is an invention or discovery, or that such application in fact discloses subject matter in categories specified by 42 U.S.C. 2181(c) and (d).

(e) Decisions by the Director. Any decision by the Director that would not otherwise be open to public inspection may be published or made available for public inspection if:

(1) The Director believes the decision involves an interpretation of patent laws or regulations that would be of precedential value; and

(2) The applicant is given notice and an opportunity to object in writing within two months on the ground that the decision discloses a trade secret or other confidential information. Any objection must identify the deletions in the text of the decision considered necessary to protect the information, or explain why the entire decision must be withheld from the public to protect such information. An applicant or party will be given time, not less than twenty days, to request reconsideration and seek court review before any portions of a decision are made public under this paragraph over his or her objection.

(f) Notice to inventor of the filing of an application. The Office may publish notice in the Official Gazette as to the filing of an application on behalf of an inventor by a person who otherwise shows sufficient proprietary interest in the matter.

(g) International applications.

(1) Copies of international application files for international applications which designate the U.S. and which have been published in accordance with PCT Article 21(2), or copies of a document in such application files, will be furnished in accordance with PCT Articles 30 and 38 and PCT Rules 94.2 and 94.3, upon written request including a showing that the publication of the application has occurred and that the U.S. was designated, and upon payment of the appropriate fee (see §1.19(b)), if:

(i) With respect to the Home Copy (the copy of the international application kept by the Office in its capacity as the Receiving Office, see PCT Article 12(1)), the international application was filed with the U.S. Receiving Office;

(ii) With respect to the Search Copy (the copy of an international application kept by the Office in its capacity as the International Searching Authority, see PCT Article 12(1)), the U.S. acted as the International Searching Authority, except for the written opinion of the International Searching Authority which shall not be available until the expiration of thirty months from the priority date; or

(iii) With respect to the Examination Copy (the copy of an international application kept by the Office in its capacity as the International Preliminary Examining Authority), the

United States acted as the International Preliminary Examining Authority, an International Preliminary Examination Report has issued, and the United States was elected.

(2) A copy of an English language translation of a publication of an international application which has been filed in the United States Patent and Trademark Office pursuant to 35 U.S.C. 154(d)(4) will be furnished upon written request including a showing that the publication of the application in accordance with PCT Article 21(2) has occurred and that the U.S. was designated, and upon payment of the appropriate fee (§1.19(b)(4)).

(3) Access to international application files for international applications which designate the U.S. and which have been published in accordance with PCT Article 21(2), or copies of a document in such application files, will be permitted in accordance with PCT Articles 30 and 38 and PCT Rules 44*ter*.1, 94.2 and 94.3, upon written request including a showing that the publication of the application has occurred and that the U.S. was designated.

(4) In accordance with PCT Article 30, copies of an international application-as-filed under paragraph (a) of this section will not be provided prior to the international publication of the application pursuant to PCT Article 21(2).

(5) Access to international application files under paragraphs (a)(1)(i) through (a)(1)(vi) and (g)(3) of this section will not be permitted with respect to the Examination Copy in accordance with PCT Article 38.

(h) Access by a Foreign Intellectual Property Office.

(1) Access to an application-as-filed may be provided to any foreign intellectual property office participating with the Office in a bilateral or multilateral priority document exchange agreement (participating foreign intellectual property office), if the application contains written authority granting such access. Written authority provided under this paragraph (h)(1) will be treated as authorizing the Office to provide the following to all participating foreign intellectual property offices in accordance with their respective agreements with the Office:

(i) A copy of the application-as-filed and its related bibliographic data;

(ii) A copy of the application-as-filed of any application the filing date of which is claimed by the application in which written authority under this paragraph (h)(1) is filed and its related bibliographic data; and

(iii) The date of filing of the written authorization under this paragraph (h)(1).

(2) Access to the file contents of an application may be provided to a foreign intellectual property office that has imposed a requirement for information on a counterpart application filed with the foreign intellectual property office where the foreign intellectual property office is a party to a bilateral or multilateral agreement with the Office to provide the required information from the application filed with the Office and the application contains written authority granting such access. Written authority provided under this paragraph (h)(2) will be treated as authorizing the Office to provide the following to all foreign intellectual property offices in accordance with their respective agreements with the Office:

(i) Bibliographic data related to the application; and

(ii) Any content of the application file necessary to satisfy the foreign intellectual property office requirement for information imposed on the counterpart application as indicated in the respective agreement.

(3) Written authority provided under paragraphs (h)(1) and (h)(2) of this section must include the title of the invention (§1.72(a)), comply with the requirements of paragraph (c) of this section, and be submitted on an application data sheet (§1.76) or on a separate document (§1.4(c)). The written authority provided under these paragraphs should be submitted before filing any subsequent foreign application in which priority is claimed to the application.

(i) Access or copies in other circumstances. The Office, either sua sponte or on petition, may also provide access or copies of all or part of an application if necessary to carry out an Act of Congress or if warranted by other special circumstances. Any petition by a member of the public seeking access to, or copies of, all or part of any pending or abandoned application preserved in confidence pursuant to paragraph (a) of this section, or any related papers, must include:

(1) The fee set forth in §1.17(g); and

(2) A showing that access to the application is necessary to carry out an Act of Congress or that special circumstances exist which warrant petitioner being granted access to all or part of the application.

(j) International design applications.

(1) With respect to an international design application maintained by the Office in its capacity as a designated office (§1.1003) for national processing, the records associated with the international design application may be made available as provided under paragraphs (a) through (i) of this section.

(2) With respect to an international design application maintained by the Office in its capacity as an office of indirect filing (§1.1002), the records of the international design application may be made available under paragraph (j)(1) of this section where contained in the file of the international design application maintained by the Office for national processing. Also, if benefit of the international design application is claimed under 35 U.S.C. 386(c) in a U.S. patent or published application, the file contents of the application may be made available to the public, or the file contents of the application, a copy of the application-as-filed, or a specific document in the file of the application may be provided to any person upon written request and payment of the appropriate fee (§1.19(b)).

History of 37 C.F.R. §1.14: 24 FR 10332, Dec. 22, 1959; 42 FR 5593, Jan. 28, 1977; 43 FR 20462, May 11, 1978; 47 FR 41273, Sept. 17, 1982; 49 FR 552, Jan. 4, 1984; 49 FR 48451, Dec. 12, 1984; 50 FR 9378, Mar. 7, 1985; 53 FR 23733, June

23, 1988; 54 FR 6900, Feb. 15, 1989; 56 FR 55461, Oct. 28, 1991; 58 FR 54509, Oct. 22, 1993; 60 FR 20221, Apr. 25, 1995; 61 FR 42802, Aug. 19, 1996; 62 FR 53182, Oct. 10, 1997; 63 FR 29617, June 1, 1998; 63 FR 66041, Dec. 1, 1998; 65 FR 54657, Sept. 8, 2000; 65 FR 57051, Sept. 20, 2000; 65 FR 78959, Dec. 18, 2000; 66 FR 67094, Dec. 28, 2001; 67 FR 523, Jan. 4, 2002; 68 FR 38624, June 30, 2003; 68 FR 59886, Oct. 20, 2003; 68 FR 67805, Dec. 4, 2003; 68 FR 71006, Dec. 22, 2003; 69 FR 49997, Aug. 12, 2004; 69 FR 56536, Sept. 21, 2004; 79 FR 1667, Jan. 16, 2007; 77 FR 48812, Sept. 16, 2012; 78 FR 11052, Mar. 16, 2013; 80 FR 17953, May 13, 2015; 80 FR 65655, Nov. 30, 2015.

§1.15. RESERVED

History of 37 C.F.R. §1.15: 68 FR 14336, Mar. 25, 2003.

FEES & PAYMENT OF MONEY

Authority: Sections 1.16 through 1.22 also issued under 35 U.S.C. 41, 111, 119, 120, 132(b), 156, 157, 255, 302, and 311, Public Laws 103-465, 106-113, and 112-29.

A §1.16. NATIONAL APPLICATION FILING, SEARCH, & EXAMINATION FEES

(a) Basic fee for filing each application under 35 U.S.C. 111 for an original patent, except design, plant, or provisional applications:

By a micro entity (§1.29)—$75.00

By a small entity (§1.27(a))—$150.00

By a small entity (§1.27(a)) if the application is submitted in compliance with the Office electronic filing system (§1.27(b)(2))—$75.00

By other than a small or micro entity—$300.00

(b) Basic fee for filing each application under 35 U.S.C. 111 for an original design patent:

By a micro entity (§1.29)—$50.00

By a small entity (§1.27(a))—$100.00

By other than a small or micro entity—$200.00

(c) Basic fee for filing each application for an original plant patent:

By a micro entity (§1.29)—$50.00

By a small entity (§1.27(a))—$100.00

By other than a small or micro entity—$200.00

(d) Basic fee for filing each provisional application:

By a micro entity (§1.29)—$70.00

By a small entity (§1.27(a))—$140.00

By other than a small or micro entity—$280.00

(e) Basic fee for filing each application for the reissue of a patent:

By a micro entity (§1.29)—$75.00

By a small entity (§1.27(a))—$150.00

By other than a small or micro entity—$300.00

(f) Surcharge for filing the basic filing fee, search fee, examination fee, or the inventor's oath or declaration on a date later than the filing date of the application, an application that does not contain at least one claim on the filing date of the application, or an application filed by reference to a previously filed application under §1.57(a), except provisional applications:

By a micro entity (§1.29)—$40.00

By a small entity (§1.27(a))—$80.00

By other than a small or micro entity—$160.00

(g) Surcharge for filing the basic filing fee or cover sheet (§1.51(c)(1)) on a date later than the filing date of the provisional application:

By a micro entity (§1.29)—$15.00

By a small entity (§1.27(a))—$30.00

By other than a small or micro entity—$60.00

(h) In addition to the basic filing fee in an application, other than a provisional application, for filing or later presentation at any other time of each claim in independent form in excess of 3:

By a micro entity (§1.29)—$115.00

By a small entity (§1.27(a))—$230.00

By other than a small or micro entity—$460.00

(i) In addition to the basic filing fee in an application, other than a provisional application, for filing or later presentation at any other time of each claim (whether dependent or independent) in excess of 20 (note that §1.75(c) indicates how multiple dependent claims are considered for fee calculation purposes):

By a micro entity (§1.29)—$25.00

By a small entity (§1.27(a))—$50.00

By other than a small or micro entity—$100.00

(j) In addition to the basic filing fee in an application, other than a provisional application, that contains, or is amended to contain, a multiple dependent claim, per application:

By a micro entity (§1.29)—$205.00

By a small entity (§1.27(a))—$410.00

By other than a small or micro entity—$820.00

(k) Search fee for each application filed under 35 U.S.C. 111 for an original patent, except design, plant, or provisional applications:

By a micro entity (§1.29)—$165.00

By a small entity (§1.27(a))—$330.00

By other than a small or micro entity—$660.00

(l) Search fee for each application under 35 U.S.C. 111 for an original design patent:

By a micro entity (§1.29)—$40.00

By a small entity (§1.27(a))—$80.00

By other than a small or micro entity—$160.00

(m) Search fee for each application for an original plant patent:

By a micro entity (§1.29)—$105.00

By a small entity (§1.27(a))—$210.00

By other than a small or micro entity—$420.00

(n) Search fee for each application for the reissue of a patent:

By a micro entity (§1.29)—$165.00

By a small entity (§1.27(a))—$330.00

By other than a small or micro entity—$660.00

(o) Examination fee for each application filed under 35 U.S.C. 111 for an original patent, except design, plant, or provisional applications:

By a micro entity (§1.29)—$190.00

By a small entity (§1.27(a))—$380.00

By other than a small or micro entity—$760.00

(p) Examination fee for each application under 35 U.S.C. 111 for an original design patent:

By a micro entity (§1.29)—$150.00

By a small entity (§1.27(a))—$300.00

By other than a small or micro entity—$600.00

(q) Examination fee for each application for an original plant patent:

By a micro entity (§1.29)—$155.00

By a small entity (§1.27(a))—$310.00

By other than a small or micro entity—$620.00

(r) Examination fee for each application for the reissue of a patent:

By a micro entity (§1.29)—$550.00

By a small entity (§1.27(a))—$1,100.00

By other than a small or micro entity—$2,200.00

(s) Application size fee for any application filed under 35 U.S.C. 111 for the specification and drawings which exceed 100 sheets of paper, for each additional 50 sheets or fraction thereof:

By a micro entity (§1.29)—$100.00

By a small entity (§1.27(a))—$200.00

By other than a small or micro entity—$400.00

(t) Non-electronic filing fee for any application under 35 U.S.C. 111(a) that is filed on or after November 15, 2011, other than by the Office electronic filing system, except for a reissue, design, or plant application:

By a small entity (§1.27(a))—$200.00

By other than a small entity—$400.00

Note to §1.16: See §§1.445, 1.482 and 1.492 for international application filing and processing fees.

History of 37 C.F.R. §1.16: 47 FR 41273, Sept. 17, 1982; 50 FR 31824, Aug. 6, 1985; 50 FR 32410, Aug. 12, 1985; 54 FR 6900, Feb. 15, 1989; 55 FR 49041, Nov. 26, 1990; 56 FR 65151, Dec. 13, 1991; 57 FR 38194, Aug. 21, 1992; 59 FR 43740, Aug. 25, 1994; 60 FR 20221, Apr. 25, 1995; 60 FR 41022, Aug. 11, 1995; 61 FR 39587, July 30, 1996; 61 FR 43400, Aug. 22, 1996; 62 FR 40452, July 29, 1997; 62 FR 53182, Oct. 10, 1997; 63 FR 39733, July 24, 1998; 63 FR 52610, Oct. 1, 1998; 63 FR 67579, Dec. 8, 1998; 64 FR 67777, Dec. 3, 1999; 65 FR 49195, Aug. 11, 2000; 65 FR 78959, Dec. 18, 2000; 66 FR 39449, July 31, 2001; 67 FR 70849, Nov. 27, 2002; 68 FR 41534, July 14, 2003; 69 FR 52605, Aug. 27, 2004; 70 FR 3887, Jan. 27, 2005; 70 FR 30365, May 26, 2005; 72 FR 46901, Sept. 30, 2007; 73 FR 46540, Oct. 2, 2008; 76 FR 70653, Nov. 15, 2011; 77 FR 48812, Sept. 16, 2012; 77 FR 54365, Oct. 5, 2012; 78 FR 4284, Mar. 19, 2013; 78 FR 62395, Dec. 18, 2013; 80 FR 17954, May 13, 2015; 82 FR 52813, Jan. 16, 2018.

A §1.17. PATENT APPLICATION & REEXAMINATION PROCESSING FEES

(a) Extension fees pursuant to §1.136(a):

(1) For reply within first month:

By a micro entity (§1.29)—$50.00

By a small entity (§1.27(a))—$100.00

By other than a small or micro entity—$200.00

(2) For reply within second month:

By a micro entity (§1.29)—$150.00

By a small entity (§1.27(a))—$300.00

By other than a small or micro entity—$600.00

(3) For reply within third month:

By a micro entity (§1.29)—$350.00

By a small entity (§1.27(a))—$700.00

By other than a small or micro entity—$1,400.00

(4) For reply within fourth month:

By a micro entity (§1.29)—$550.00

By a small entity (§1.27(a))—$1,100.00

By other than a small or micro entity—$2,200.00

(5) For reply within fifth month:

By a micro entity (§1.29)—$750.00

By a small entity (§1.27(a))—$1,500.00

By other than a small or micro entity—$3,000.00

(b) For fees in proceedings before the Patent Trial and Appeal Board, see §41.20 and §42.15 of this title.

(c) For filing a request for prioritized examination under §1.102(e):

By a micro entity (§1.29)—$1,000.00

By a small entity (§1.27(a))—$2,000.00

By other than a small or micro entity—$4,000.00

(d) For correction of inventorship in an application after the first action on the merits:

By a micro entity (§1.29)—$150.00

By a small entity (§1.27(a))—$300.00

By other than a small or micro entity—$600.00

(e) To request continued examination pursuant to §1.114:

(1) For filing a first request for continued examination pursuant to §1.114 in an application:

By a micro entity (§1.29)—$325.00

By a small entity (§1.27(a))—$650.00

By other than a small or micro entity—$1,300.00

(2) For filing a second or subsequent request for continued examination pursuant to §1.114 in an application:

By a micro entity (§1.29)—$475.00

By a small entity (§1.27(a))—$950.00

By other than a small or micro entity—$1,900.00

(f) For filing a petition under one of the following sections which refers to this paragraph:

By a micro entity (§1.29)—$100.00

By a small entity (§1.27(a))—$200.00

By other than a small or micro entity—$400.00

§1.36(a)—for revocation of a power of attorney by fewer than all of the applicants.

§1.53(e)—to accord a filing date.

§1.182—for decision on a question not specifically provided for in an application for patent.

§1.183—to suspend the rules in an application for patent.

§1.741(b)—to accord a filing date to an application under §1.740 for extension of a patent term.

§1.1023—to review the filing date of an international design application.

(g) For filing a petition under one of the following sections which refers to this paragraph:

By a micro entity (§1.29)—$50.00

By a small entity (§1.27(a))—$100.00

By other than a small or micro entity—$200.00

§1.12—for access to an assignment record.

§1.14—for access to an application.

§1.46—for filing an application on behalf of an inventor by a person who otherwise shows sufficient proprietary interest in the matter.

§1.55(f)—for filing a belated certified copy of a foreign application.

§1.55(g)—for filing a belated certified copy of a foreign application.

§1.57(a)—for filing a belated certified copy of a foreign application.

§1.59—for expungement of information.

§1.103(a)—to suspend action in an application.

§1.136(b)—for review of a request for extension of time when the provisions of §1.136(a) are not available.

§1.377—for review of decision refusing to accept and record payment of a maintenance fee filed prior to expiration of a patent.

§1.550(c)—for patent owner requests for extension of time in ex parte reexamination proceedings.

§1.956—for patent owner requests for extension of time in inter partes reexamination proceedings.

§5.12—for expedited handling of a foreign filing license.

§5.15—for changing the scope of a license.

§5.25—for retroactive license.

(h) For filing a petition under one of the following sections which refers to this paragraph (h):

By a micro entity (§1.29)—$35.00

By a small entity (§1.27(a))—$70.00

By other than a small or micro entity—$140.00

§1.84—for accepting color drawings or photographs.

§1.91—for entry of a model or exhibit.

§1.102(d)—to make an application special.

§1.138(c)—to expressly abandon an application to avoid publication.

§1.313—to withdraw an application from issue.

§1.314—to defer issuance of a patent.

(i) Processing fees.

(1) For taking action under one of the following sections which refers to this paragraph:

By a micro entity (§1.29)—$35.00

By a small entity (§1.27(a))—$70.00

By other than a small or micro entity—$140.00

§1.28(c)(3)—for processing a non-itemized fee deficiency based on an error in small entity status.

§1.29(k)(3)—for processing a non-itemized fee deficiency based on an error in micro entity status.

§1.41(b)—for supplying the name or names of the inventor or joint inventors in an application without either an application data sheet or the inventor's oath or declaration, except in provisional applications.

§1.48—for correcting inventorship, except in provisional applications.

§1.52(d)—for processing a nonprovisional application filed with a specification in a language other than English.

§1.53(c)(3)—t[1] convert a provisional application filed under §1.53(c) into a nonprovisional application under §1.53(b).

§1.71(g)(2)—for processing a belated amendment under §1.71(g).

§1.102(e)—for requesting prioritized examination of an application.

§1.103(b)—for requesting limited suspension of action, continued prosecution application for a design patent (§1.53(d)).

§1.103(c)—for requesting limited suspension of action, request for continued examination (§1.114).

§1.103(d)—for requesting deferred examination of an application.

§1.291(c)(5)—for processing a second or subsequent protest by the same real party in interest.

§3.81—for a patent to issue to assignee, assignment submitted after payment of the issue fee.

(j) [Reserved]

(k) For filing a request for expedited examination under §1.155(a):

By a micro entity (§1.29)—$225.00

By a small entity (§1.27(a))—$450.00

By other than a small or micro entity—$900.00

(*l*) [Reserved]

(m) For filing a petition for the revival of an abandoned application for a patent, for the delayed payment of the fee for issuing each patent, for the delayed response by the patent owner in any reexamination proceeding, for the delayed payment of the fee for maintaining a patent in force, for the delayed submission of a priority or benefit claim, for the extension of the twelve-month (six-month for designs) period for filing a subsequent application (§§1.55(c) and (e), 1.78(b), (c), and (e), 1.137, 1.378, and 1.452), or for filing a petition to excuse applicant's failure to act within prescribed time limits in an international design application (§1.1051):

By a micro entity (§1.29)—$500.00

By a small entity (§1.27(a))—$1,000.00

By other than a small or micro entity—$2,000.00

(n) [Reserved]

(o) For every ten items or fraction thereof in a third-party submission under §1.290:

By a small entity (§1.27(a)) or micro entity (§1.29)—$90.00

By other than a small entity—$180.00

(p) For an information disclosure statement under §1.97(c) or (d):

By a micro entity (§1.29)—$60.00

By a small entity (§1.27(a))—$120.00

By other than a small or micro entity—$240.00

(q) Processing fee for taking action under one of the following sections which refers to this paragraph—$50.00.

§1.41—to supply the name or names of the inventor or inventors after the filing date without a cover sheet as prescribed by §1.51(c)(1) in a provisional application.

§1.48—for correction of inventorship in a provisional application.

§1.53(c)(2)—to convert a nonprovisional application filed under §1.53(b) to a provisional application under §1.53(c).

(r) For entry of a submission after final rejection under §1.129(a):

By a micro entity (§1.29)—$210.00

By a small entity (§1.27(a))—$420.00

By other than a small or micro entity—$840.00

(s) For each additional invention requested to be examined under §1.129(b):

By a micro entity (§1.29)—$210.00

By a small entity (§1.27(a))—$420.00

By other than a small or micro entity—$840.00

(t) For filing a petition to convert an international design application to a design application under 35 U.S.C. chapter 16 (§1.1052):

By a micro entity (§1.29)—$45.00

By a small entity (§1.27(a))—$90.00

By other than a small or micro entity—$180.00

1. **Editor's note:** Probably should be "to."

History of 37 C.F.R. §1.17: 47 FR 41273, Sept. 17, 1982; 48 FR 2708, Jan. 20, 1983; 49 FR 13461, Apr. 4, 1984; 49 FR 34724, Aug. 31, 1984; 49 FR 48451, Dec. 12, 1984; 50 FR 9379, Mar. 7, 1985; 50 FR 31824, Aug. 6, 1985; 54 FR 6901, Feb. 15, 1989; 54 FR 9431, Mar. 7, 1989; 54 FR 47518, Nov. 15, 1989; 55 FR 49041, Nov. 26, 1990; 56 FR 65152, Dec. 13, 1991; 57 FR 2033, Jan. 17, 1992; 57 FR 29642, July 6, 1992; 57 FR 32439, July 22, 1992; 57 FR 38194, Aug. 21, 1992; 58 FR 38723, July 20, 1993; 58 FR 45841, Aug. 31, 1993; 59 FR 43740, Aug. 25, 1994; 60 FR 20221, Apr. 25, 1995; 60 FR 41022, Aug. 11, 1995; 61 FR 39587, July 30, 1996; 62 FR 40452, July 29, 1997; 62 FR 53182, Oct. 10, 1997; 62 FR 61235, Nov. 17, 1997; 63 FR 39733, July 24, 1998; 63 FR 52610, Oct. 1, 1998; 63 FR 67580, Dec. 8, 1998; 64 FR 67777, Dec. 3, 1999; 65 FR 14871, Mar. 20, 2000; 65 FR 49195, Aug. 11, 2000; 65 FR 50103, Aug. 16, 2000; 65 FR 54658, Sept. 8, 2000; 65 FR 57052, Sept. 20, 2000; 65 FR 78959, Dec. 18, 2000; 66 FR 39449, July 31, 2001; 66 FR 47389, Sept. 12, 2001; 67 FR 70849, Nov. 27, 2002; 68 FR 38626, June 30, 2003; 68 FR 41534, July 14, 2003; 69 FR 49997, Aug. 12, 2004; 69 FR 52605, Aug. 27, 2004; 69 FR 56536, Sept. 21, 2004; 70 FR 3888, Jan. 27, 2005; 70 FR 54265, Sept. 14, 2005; 70 FR 56126, Sept. 26, 2005; 72 FR 18904, May 16, 2007; 72 FR 46902, Sept. 30, 2007; 73 FR 47540, Oct. 2, 2008; 74 FR 52688, Oct. 14, 2009; 76 FR 18407, Apr. 4, 2011; 76 FR 23876, Apr. 29, 2011; 76 FR 59054, Sept. 23, 2011; 77 FR 42173, Sept. 16, 2012; 77 FR 46624, Sept. 16, 2012; 77 FR 48812, Sept. 16, 2012; 77 FR 54365, Oct. 5, 2012; 78 FR 4285, Mar. 19, 2013; 78 FR 11052, Mar. 16, 2013; 78 FR 17105, Mar. 20, 2013; 78 FR 62395, Dec. 18, 2013; 78 FR 75252, Dec. 18, 2013; 80 FR 17954, May 13, 2015; 82 FR 52814, Jan. 16, 2018.

A §1.18. PATENT POST ALLOWANCE (INCLUDING ISSUE) FEES

(a)(1) Issue fee for issuing each original patent, except a design or plant patent, or for issuing each reissue patent:

By a micro entity (§1.29)—$250.00

By a small entity (§1.27(a))—$500.00

By other than a small or micro entity—$1,000.00

(2) [Reserved]

(b)(1) Issue fee for issuing an original design patent:

By a micro entity (§1.29)—$175.00

By a small entity (§1.27(a))—$350.00

By other than a small or micro entity—$700.00

(2) [Reserved]

(3) Issue fee for issuing an international design application designating the United States, where the issue fee is paid through the International Bureau (Hague Agreement Rule 12(3)(c)) as an alternative to paying the issue fee under paragraph (b)(1) of this section: The amount established in Swiss currency pursuant to Hague Agreement Rule 28 as of the date of mailing of the notice of allowance (§1.311).

(c)(1) Issue fee for issuing an original plant patent:

By a micro entity (§1.29)—$200.00

By a small entity (§1.27(a))—$400.00

By other than a small or micro entity—$800.00

(2) [Reserved]

(d)(1) Publication fee on or after January 1, 2014—$0.00

(2) Publication fee before January 1, 2014—$300.00

(3) Republication fee (§1.221(a))—$300.00

(e) For filing an application for patent term adjustment under §1.705: $200.00.

(f) For filing a request for reinstatement of all or part of the term reduced pursuant to §1.704(b) in an application for patent term adjustment under §1.705: $400.00.

History of 37 C.F.R. §1.18: 47 FR 41273, Sept. 17, 1982; 50 FR 31825, Aug. 6, 1985; 54 FR 6901, Feb. 15, 1989; 55 FR 49041, Nov. 26, 1990; 56 FR 65152, Dec. 13, 1991; 57 FR 38195, Aug. 21, 1992; 59 FR 43741, Aug. 25, 1994; 60 FR 41022,

Aug. 11, 1995; 61 FR 39588, July 30, 1996; 62 FR 40452, July 29, 1997; 63 FR 39733, July 24, 1998; 63 FR 52610, Oct. 1, 1998; 63 FR 67580, Dec. 8, 1998; 65 FR 49195, Aug. 11, 2000; 65 FR 56391, Sept. 18, 2000; 65 FR 57053, Sept. 20, 2000; 65 FR 78959, Dec. 18, 2000; 66 FR 39449, July 31, 2001; 67 FR 70849, Nov. 27, 2002; 68 FR 41534, July 14, 2003; 69 FR 52606, Aug. 27, 2004; 70 FR 3888, Jan. 27, 2005; 72 FR 46902, Sept. 30, 2007; 72 FR 55055, Sept. 30, 2007; 72 FR 51563, Nov. 9, 2007; 72 FR 57864, Nov. 9, 2007; 73 FR 47541, Oct. 2, 2008; 77 FR 54366, Oct. 5, 2012; 78 FR 4286, Mar. 19, 2013; 80 FR 17955, May 13, 2015; 82 FR 52814, Jan. 16, 2018.

A §1.19. DOCUMENT SUPPLY FEES

The United States Patent and Trademark Office will supply copies of the following patent-related documents upon payment of the fees indicated. Paper copies will be in black and white unless the original document is in color, a color copy is requested and the fee for a color copy is paid.

(a) Uncertified copies of patent application publications and patents:

(1) Printed copy of the paper portion of a patent application publication or patent including a design patent, statutory invention registration, or defensive publication document. Service includes preparation of copies by the Office within two to three business days and delivery by United States Postal Service; and preparation of copies by the Office within one business day of receipt and delivery to an Office Box or by electronic means (e.g., facsimile, electronic mail): $3.00.

(2) Printed copy of a plant patent in color: $15.00.

(3) Color copy of a patent (other than a plant patent) or statutory invention registration containing a color drawing: $25.00.

(b) Copies of Office documents to be provided in paper, or in electronic form, as determined by the Director (for other patent-related materials see §1.21(k)):

(1) Copy of a patent application as filed, or a patent-related file wrapper and contents, stored in paper in a paper file wrapper, in an image format in an image file wrapper, or if color documents, stored in paper in an Artifact Folder:

(i) If provided on paper:

(A) Application as filed: $35.00.

(B) File wrapper and contents: $280.00.

(C) [Reserved]

(D) Individual application documents, other than application as filed, per document: $25.00.

(ii) If provided on compact disc or other physical electronic medium in single order or if provided electronically (e.g., by electronic transmission) other than on a physical electronic medium:

(A) Application as filed: $35.00.

(B) File wrapper and contents: $55.00.

(C) [Reserved]

(iii) [Reserved]

(iv) If provided to a foreign intellectual property office pursuant to a bilateral or multilateral agreement (see §1.14(h)): $0.00.

(2) [Reserved]

(3) Copy of Office records, except copies available under paragraph (b)(1) or (2) of this section: $25.00.

(4) For assignment records, abstract of title and certification, per patent: $35.00.

(c) Library service (35 U.S.C. 13): For providing to libraries copies of all patents issued annually, per annum: $50.00.

(d) [Reserved]

(e) [Reserved]

(f) Uncertified copy of a non-United States patent document, per document: $25.00.

(g) [Reserved]

(h) Copy of Patent Grant Single-Page TIFF Images (52 week subscription): $10,400.00.

(i) Copy of Patent Grant Full-Text W/Embedded Images, Patent Application Publication Single-Page TIFF Images, or Patent Application Publication Full-Text W/Embedded Images (52 week subscription): $5,200.00.

(j) Copy of Patent Technology Monitoring Team (PTMT) Patent Bibliographic Extract and Other DVD (Optical Disc) Products: $50.00.

(k) Copy of U.S. Patent Custom Data Extracts: $100.00.

(*l*) Copy of Selected Technology Reports, Miscellaneous Technology Areas: $30.00.

History of 37 C.F.R. §1.19: 47 FR 41273, Sept. 17, 1982; 49 FR 552, Jan. 4, 1984; 49 FR 34724, Aug. 31, 1984; 50 FR 9379, Mar. 7, 1985; 50 FR 31825, Aug. 6, 1985; 54 FR 6901, Feb. 15, 1989; 54 FR 9432, Mar. 7, 1989; 56 FR 65152, Dec. 13, 1991; 57 FR 38195, Aug. 21, 1992; 58 FR 38723, July 20, 1993; 60 FR 41022, Aug. 11, 1995; 62 FR 40452, July 29, 1997; 64 FR 67486, Dec. 2, 1999; 65 FR 54658, Sept. 8, 2000; 65 FR 57053, Sept. 20, 2000; 67 FR 70849, Nov. 27, 2002; 69 FR 56537, Sept. 21, 2004; 72 FR 1668, Jan. 16, 2007; 78 FR 4287, Mar. 19, 2013; 80 FR 65655, Nov. 30, 2015; 82 FR 52814, Jan. 16, 2018.

A §1.20. POST ISSUANCE FEES

(a) For providing a certificate of correction for applicant's mistake (§1.323)—$150.00.

(b) Processing fee for correcting inventorship in a patent (§1.324)—$150.00.

(c) In reexamination proceedings:

(1)(i) For filing a request for ex parte reexamination (§1.510(a)) having:

(A) Forty (40) or fewer pages;

(B) Lines that are double-spaced or one-and-a-half spaced;

(C) Text written in a non-script type font such as Arial, Times New Roman, or Courier;

(D) A font size no smaller than 12 point;

(E) Margins which conform to the requirements of §1.52(a)(1)(ii); and

(F) Sufficient clarity and contrast to permit direct reproduction and electronic capture by use of digital imaging and optical character recognition.

By a micro entity (§1.29)—$1,500.00

By a small entity (§1.27(a))—$3,000.00

By other than a small or micro entity—$6,000.00

(ii) The following parts of an ex parte reexamination request are excluded from paragraphs (c)(1)(i)(A) through (F) of this section:

(A) The copies of every patent or printed publication relied upon in the request pursuant to §1.510(b)(3);

(B) The copy of the entire patent for which reexamination is requested pursuant to §1.510(b)(4); and

(C) The certifications required pursuant to §1.510(b)(5) and (6).

(2) For filing a request for ex parte reexamination (§1.510(b)) which has sufficient clarity and contrast to permit direct reproduction and electronic capture by use of digital imaging and optical character recognition, and which otherwise does not comply with the provisions of paragraph (c)(1) of this section:

By a micro entity (§1.29)—$3,000.00

By a small entity (§1.27(a))—$6,000.00

By other than a small or micro entity—$12,000.00

(3) For filing with a request for reexamination or later presentation at any other time of each claim in independent form in excess of three and also in excess of the number of claims in independent form in the patent under reexamination:

By a micro entity (§1.29)—$115.00

By a small entity (§1.27(a))—$230.00

By other than a small or micro entity—$460.00

(4) For filing with a request for reexamination or later presentation at any other time of each claim (whether dependent or independent) in excess of 20 and also in excess of the number of claims in the patent under reexamination (note that §1.75(c) indicates how multiple dependent claims are considered for fee calculation purposes):

By a micro entity (§1.29)—$25.00

By a small entity (§1.27(a))—$50.00

By other than a small or micro entity—$100.00

(d) For filing each statutory disclaimer (§1.321)—$160.00

(e) For maintaining an original or any reissue patent, except a design or plant patent, based on an application filed on or after December 12, 1980, in force beyond four years, the fee being due by three years and six months after the original grant:

By a micro entity (§1.29)—$400.00

By a small entity (§1.27(a))—$800.00

By other than a small or micro entity—$1,600.00

(f) For maintaining an original or any reissue patent, except a design or plant patent, based on an application filed on or after December 12, 1980, in force beyond eight years, the fee being due by seven years and six months after the original grant:

By a micro entity (§1.29)—$900.00

By a small entity (§1.27(a))—$1,800.00

By other than a small or micro entity—$3,600.00

(g) For maintaining an original or any reissue patent, except a design or plant patent, based on an application filed on or after December 12, 1980, in force beyond twelve years, the fee being due by eleven years and six months after the original grant:

By a micro entity (§1.29)—$1,850.00

By a small entity (§1.27(a))—$3,700.00

By other than a small or micro entity—$7,400.00

(h) Surcharge for paying a maintenance fee during the six-month grace period following the expiration of three years and six months, seven years and six months, and eleven years and six months after the date of the original grant of a patent based on an application filed on or after December 12, 1980:

(1) By a micro entity (§1.29)—$40.00

(2) By a small entity (§1.27(a))—$80.00

(3) By other than a small or micro entity—$160.00

(i) [Reserved]

(j) For filing an application for extension of the term of a patent

Application for extension under §1.740—$1,120.00.

Initial application for interim extension under §1.790—$420.00.

Subsequent application for interim extension under §1.790—$220.00.

(k) In supplemental examination proceedings:

(1) For processing and treating a request for supplemental examination:

By a micro entity (§1.29)—$1,100.00

By a small entity (§1.27(a))—$2,200.00

By other than a small or micro entity—$4,400.00

(2) For ex parte reexamination ordered as a result of a supplemental examination proceeding:

By a micro entity (§1.29)—$3,025.00

By a small entity (§1.27(a))—$6,050.00

By other than a small or micro entity—$12,100.00

(3) For processing and treating, in a supplemental examination proceeding, a non-patent document over 20 sheets in length, per document:

(i) Between 21 and 50 sheets:

By a micro entity (§1.29)—$45.00

By a small entity (§1.27(a))—$90.00

By other than a small or micro entity—$180.00

(ii) For each additional 50 sheets or a fraction thereof:
By a micro entity (§1.29)—$70.00
By a small entity (§1.27(a))—$140.00
By other than a small or micro entity—$280.00

History of 37 C.F.R. §1.20: 47 FR 41274, Sept. 17, 1982; 49 FR 34724, Aug. 31, 1984; 50 FR 9379, Mar. 7, 1985; 50 FR 31825, Aug. 6, 1985; 52 FR 9394, Mar. 24, 1987; 54 FR 6902, Feb. 15, 1989; 54 FR 8053, Feb. 24, 1989; 55 FR 49042, Nov. 26, 1990; 56 FR 65153, Dec. 13, 1991; 57 FR 38195, Aug. 21, 1992; 57 FR 56450, Nov. 30, 1992; 58 FR 44280, Aug. 20, 1993; 59 FR 43741, Aug. 25, 1994; 60 FR 25618, May 12, 1995; 60 FR 41022, Aug. 11, 1995; 61 FR 39588, July 30, 1996; 62 FR 40453, July 29, 1997; 63 FR 39733, July 24, 1998; 63 FR 52610, Oct. 1, 1998; 63 FR 67580, Dec. 8, 1998; 64 FR 67777, Dec. 3, 1999; 65 FR 49195, Aug. 11, 2000; 65 FR 76772, Dec. 7, 2000; 65 FR 78960, Dec. 18, 2000; 65 FR 80755, Dec. 22, 2000; 66 FR 39449, July 31, 2001; 67 FR 70849, Nov. 27, 2002; 68 FR 41534, July 14, 2003; 69 FR 52606, Aug. 27, 2004; 70 FR 3888, Jan. 27, 2005; 72 FR 46902, Sept. 30, 2007; 73 FR 47541, Oct. 2, 2008; 77 FR 48851, Sept. 16, 2012; 77 FR 54366, Oct. 5, 2012; 78 FR 4287, Mar. 19, 2013; 78 FR 17106, Mar. 20, 2013; 78 FR 62395, Dec. 18, 2013; 82 FR 52815, Jan. 16, 2018.

A §1.21. MISCELLANEOUS FEES & CHARGES

The Patent and Trademark Office has established the following fees for the services indicated:

(a) Registration of attorneys and agents:

(1) For admission to examination for registration to practice:

(i) Application Fee (non-refundable): $100.00.

(ii) Registration examination fee.

(A) For test administration by commercial entity: $200.00.

(B) For test administration by the USPTO: $450.00.

(iii) For USPTO-administered review of registration examination: $450.00.

(2) On registration to practice or grant of limited recognition:

(i) On registration to practice under §11.6 of this chapter: $200.00.

(ii) On grant of limited recognition under §11.9(b) of this chapter: $200.00.

(iii) On change of registration from agent to attorney: $100.00.

(3) [Reserved]

(4) For certificate of good standing as an attorney or agent:

(i) Standard: $40.00.

(ii) Suitable for framing: $50.00.

(5) For review of decision:

(i) By the Director of Enrollment and Discipline under §11.2(c) of this chapter: $400.00.

(ii) Of the Director of Enrollment and Discipline under §11.2(d) of this chapter: $400.00.

(6) Recovery/Retrieval of OED Information System Customer Interface account by USPTO:

(i) For USPTO-assisted recovery of ID or reset of password: $70.00.

(ii) For USPTO-assisted change of address: $70.00.

(7) [Reserved]

(8) [Reserved]

(9)(i) Delinquency fee: $50.00.

(ii) Administrative reinstatement fee: $200.00.

(10) On application by a person for recognition or registration after disbarment or suspension on ethical grounds, or resignation pending disciplinary proceedings in any other jurisdiction; on application by a person for recognition or registration who is asserting rehabilitation from prior conduct that resulted in an adverse decision in the Office regarding the person's moral character; and on application by a person for recognition or registration after being convicted of a felony or crime involving moral turpitude or breach of fiduciary duty; on petition for reinstatement by a person excluded or suspended on ethical grounds, or excluded on consent from practice before the Office: $1,600.00.

(b) Deposit accounts:

(1) [Reserved]

(2) Service charge for each month when the balance at the end of the month is below $1,000: $25.00.

(3) Service charge for each month when the balance at the end of the month is below $300 for restricted subscription deposit accounts used exclusively for subscription order of patent copies as issued: $25.00.

(c) [Reserved]

(d) [Reserved]

(e) International type search reports: For preparing an international type search report of an international type search made at the time of the first action on the merits in a national patent application: $40.00.

(f) [Reserved]

(g) [Reserved]

(h) For recording each assignment, agreement, or other paper relating to the property in a patent or application, per property:

(1) If submitted electronically, on or after January 1, 2014: $0.00.

(2) If not submitted electronically: $50.00.

(i) Publication in Official Gazette: For publication in the Official Gazette of a notice of the availability of an application or a patent for licensing or sale: Each application or patent: $25.00.

(j) [Reserved]

(k) [Reserved]

(*l*) [Reserved]

(m) For processing each payment refused (including a check returned "unpaid") or charged back by a financial institution: $50.00.

(n) For handling an application in which proceedings are terminated pursuant to §1.53(e): $130.00.

(o) The submission of very lengthy sequence listings (mega-sequence listings) are subject to the following fees:

(1) Submission of sequence listings in electronic form ranging in size from 300 MB to 800 MB:

By a micro entity (§1.29)—$250.00

By a small entity (§1.27(a))—$500.00

By other than a small or micro entity—$1,000.00

(2) Submission of sequence listings in electronic form exceeding 800 MB in size:

By a micro entity (§1.29)—$2,500.00

By a small entity (§1.27(a))—$5,000.00

By other than a small or micro entity—$10,000.00

(p) Additional Fee for Overnight Delivery: $40.00.

(q) Additional Fee for Expedited Service: $160.00.

History of 37 C.F.R. §1.21: 24 FR 10332, Dec. 22, 1959; 25 FR 4679, May 27, 1960; 30 FR 6391, May 7, 1965; 30 FR 12844, Oct. 8, 1965; 31 FR 7284, May 19, 1966; 34 FR 2207, Feb. 14, 1969; 36 FR 12617, July 2, 1971; 40 FR 57358, Dec. 9, 1975; 43 FR 20462, May 11, 1978; 46 FR 2612, Jan. 12, 1981; 46 FR 24179, Apr. 30, 1981; 47 FR 41274, Sept. 17, 1982; 49 FR 553, Jan. 4, 1984; 50 FR 5171, Feb. 6, 1985; 50 FR 31825, Aug. 6, 1985; 50 FR 32410, Aug. 6, 1985; 54 FR 6902, Feb. 15, 1989; 54 FR 8053, Feb. 24, 1989; 54 FR 9432, Mar. 7, 1989; 54 FR 34282, Aug. 18, 1989; 54 FR 47518, Nov. 15, 1989; 54 FR 50949, Dec. 11, 1989; 54 FR 51550, Dec. 15, 1989; 56 FR 65153, Dec. 13, 1991; 57 FR 38195, Aug. 21, 1992; 57 FR 40493, Sept. 3, 1992; 59 FR 43741, Aug. 25, 1994; 60 FR 20222, Apr. 25, 1995; 60 FR 41022, Aug. 11, 1995; 61 FR 39588, July 30, 1996; 61 FR 43400, Aug. 22, 1996; 62 FR 40453, July 29, 1997; 62 FR 53183, Oct. 10, 1997; 63 FR 39734, July 24, 1998; 63 FR 52610, Oct. 1, 1998; 63 FR 67580, Dec. 8, 1998; 65 FR 33455, May 24, 2000; 65 FR 49195, Aug. 11, 2000; 66 FR 39450, July 31, 2001; 69 FR 35451, June 24, 2004; 70 FR 30365, May 26, 2005; 71 FR 64639, Nov. 3, 2006; 73 FR 67756, Dec. 17, 2008; 78 FR 4288, Mar. 19, 2013; 78 FR 20196, Apr. 3, 2013; 82 FR 52815, Jan. 16, 2018.

§1.22. FEES PAYABLE IN ADVANCE

(a) Patent fees and charges payable to the United States Patent and Trademark Office are required to be paid in advance; that is, at the time of requesting any action by the Office for which a fee or charge is payable, with the exception that under §1.53 applications for patent may be assigned a filing date without payment of the basic filing fee.

(b) All fees paid to the United States Patent and Trademark Office must be itemized in each individual application, patent, or other proceeding in such a manner that it is clear for which purpose the fees are paid. The Office may return fees that are not itemized as required by this paragraph. The provisions of §1.5(a) do not apply to the resubmission of fees returned pursuant to this paragraph.

History of 37 C.F.R. §1.22: 24 FR 10332, Dec. 22, 1959; 48 FR 2708, Jan. 20, 1983; 65 FR 54659, Sept. 8, 2000; 68 FR 48288, Aug. 13, 2003.

§1.23. METHODS OF PAYMENT

(a) All payments of money required for United States Patent and Trademark Office fees, including fees for the processing of international applications (§1.445), shall be made in U.S. dollars and in the form of a cashier's or certified check, Treasury note, national bank notes, or United States Postal Service money order. If sent in any other form, the Office may delay or cancel the credit until collection is made. Checks and money orders must be made payable to the Director of the United States Patent and Trademark Office. (Checks made payable to the Commissioner of Patents and Trademarks will continue to be accepted.) Payments from foreign countries must be payable and immediately negotiable in the United States for the full amount of the fee required. Money sent to the Office by mail will be at the risk of the sender, and letters containing money should be registered with the United States Postal Service.

(b) Payments of money required for United States Patent and Trademark Office fees may also be made by credit card, except for replenishing a deposit account. Payment of a fee by credit card must specify the amount to be charged to the credit card and such other information as is necessary to process the charge, and is subject to collection of the fee. The Office will not accept a general authorization to charge fees to a credit card. If credit card information is provided on a form or document other than a form provided by the Office for the payment of fees by credit card, the Office will not be liable if the credit card number becomes public knowledge.

(c) A fee transmittal letter may be signed by a juristic applicant or patent owner.

History of 37 C.F.R. §1.23: 43 FR 20462, May 11, 1978; 64 FR 48917, Sept. 8, 1999; 65 FR 33455, May 24, 2000; 69 FR 43752, July 22, 2004; 78 FR 62395, Dec. 18, 2013.

§1.24. RESERVED

History of 37 C.F.R. §1.24: 65 FR 57053, Sept. 20, 2000.

§1.25. DEPOSIT ACCOUNTS

(a) For the convenience of attorneys, and the general public in paying any fees due, in ordering services offered by the Office, copies of records, etc., deposit accounts may be established in the Patent and Trademark Office upon payment of the fee for establishing a deposit account (§1.21(b)(1)). A minimum deposit of $1,000 is required for paying any fees due or in ordering any services offered by the Office. However, a minimum deposit of $300 may be paid to establish a restricted subscription deposit account used exclusively for subscription order of patent copies as issued. At the end of each month, a deposit account statement will be rendered. A remittance must be made promptly upon receipt of the statement to cover the value of items or services charged to the account and thus restore the account to its established normal deposit. An amount sufficient to cover all fees, services, copies, etc., requested must always be on deposit. Charges to accounts with insufficient funds will not be accepted. A service charge (§1.21(b)(2)) will be assessed for each month that the balance at the end of the month is below $1,000. For restricted subscription deposit accounts, a service charge (§1.21(b)(3)) will be assessed for each month that the balance at the end of the month is below $300.

(b) Filing, issue, appeal, international-type search report, international application processing, international design application fees, petition, and post-issuance fees may be charged against these accounts if sufficient funds are on deposit to cover such fees. A general authorization to charge all fees, or only certain fees, set forth in §§1.16 through 1.18 to a deposit account containing sufficient funds may be filed in an individual application, either for the entire pendency of the application or with a particular paper filed. A general authorization to charge fees in an international design application set forth in §1.1031 will only be effective for the transmittal fee (§1.1031(a)). An authorization to charge fees under §1.16 in an international application entering the national stage under 35 U.S.C. 371 will be treated as an authorization to charge fees under §1.492. An authorization to charge fees set forth in §1.18 to a deposit account is subject to the provisions of §1.311(b). An authorization to charge to a deposit account the fee for a request for reexamination pursuant to §1.510 or 1.913 and any other fees required in a reexamination proceeding in a patent may also be filed with the request for reexamination, and an authorization to charge to a deposit account the fee for a request for supplemental examination pursuant to §1.610 and any other fees required in a supplemental examination proceeding in a patent may also be filed with the request for supplemental examination. An authorization to charge a fee to a deposit account will not be considered payment of the fee on the date the authorization to charge the fee is effective unless sufficient funds are present in the account to cover the fee.

(c) A deposit account holder may replenish the deposit account by submitting a payment to the United States Patent and Trademark Office. A payment to replenish a deposit account must be submitted by one of the methods set forth in paragraphs (c)(1), (c)(2), (c)(3), or (c)(4) of this section.

(1) A payment to replenish a deposit account may be submitted by electronic funds transfer through the Federal Reserve Fedwire System, which requires that the following information be provided to the deposit account holder's bank or financial institution:

(i) Name of the Bank, which is Treas NYC (Treasury New York City);

(ii) Bank Routing Code, which is 021030004;

(iii) United States Patent and Trademark Office account number with the Department of the Treasury, which is 13100001; and

(iv) The deposit account holder's company name and deposit account number.

(2) A payment to replenish a deposit account may be submitted by electronic funds transfer over the Office's Internet Web site (www.uspto.gov).

(3) A payment to replenish a deposit account may be addressed to: Director of the United States Patent and Trademark Office, Attn: Deposit Accounts, 2051 Jamieson Avenue, Suite 300, Alexandria, Virginia 22314.

History of 37 C.F.R. §1.25: 40 FR 57359, Dec. 9, 1975; 43 FR 20462, May 11, 1978; 47 FR 41274, Sept. 17, 1982; 49 FR 553, Jan. 4, 1984; 50 FR 31826, Aug. 6, 1985; 65 FR 54659, Sept. 8, 2000; 65 FR 76772, Dec. 7, 2000; 67 FR 523, Jan. 4, 2002; 68 FR 14336, Mar. 25, 2003; 69 FR 43752, July 22, 2004; 70 FR 56127, Sept. 26, 2005; 73 FR 47541, Oct. 2, 2008; 78 FR 62395, Dec. 18, 2013; 80 FR 17955, May 13, 2015.

§1.26. REFUNDS

(a) The Director may refund any fee paid by mistake or in excess of that required. A change of purpose after the payment of a fee, such as when a party desires to withdraw a patent filing for which the fee was paid, including an application, an appeal, or a request for an oral hearing, will not entitle a party to a refund of such fee. The Office will not refund amounts of twenty-five dollars or less unless a refund is specifically requested, and will not notify the payor of such amounts. If a party paying a fee or requesting a refund does not provide the banking information necessary for making refunds by electronic funds transfer (31 U.S.C. 3332 and 31 CFR part 208), or instruct the Office that refunds are to be credited to a deposit account, the Director may require such information, or use the banking information on the payment instrument to make a refund. Any refund of a fee paid by credit card will be by a credit to the credit card account to which the fee was charged.

(b) Any request for refund must be filed within two years from the date the fee was paid, except as otherwise provided in this paragraph or in §1.28(a). If the Office charges a deposit account by an amount other than an amount specifically indicated in an authorization (§1.25(b)), any request for refund based upon such charge must be filed within two years from the date of the deposit account statement indicating such charge, and include a copy of that deposit account statement. The time periods set forth in this paragraph are not extendable.

(c) If the Director decides not to institute a reexamination proceeding in response to a request for reexamination or supplemental examination, fees paid with the request for reexamination or supplemental examination will be refunded or returned in accordance with paragraphs (c)(1) through (c)(3) of this section. The reexamination requester or the patent owner who requested a supplemental examination proceeding, as appropriate, should indicate the form in which any refund should be made (e.g., by check, electronic funds transfer, credit to a deposit account). Generally, refunds will be issued in the form that the original payment was provided.

(1) For an ex parte reexamination request, the ex parte reexamination filing fee paid by the reexamination requester, less the fee set forth in §1.20(c)(7), will be refunded to the requester if the Director decides not to institute an ex parte reexamination proceeding.

(2) For an inter partes reexamination request, a refund of $7,970 will be made to the reexamination requester if the Director decides not to institute an inter partes reexamination proceeding.

(3) For a supplemental examination request, the fee for reexamination ordered as a result of supplemental examination, as set forth in §1.20(k)(2), will be returned to the patent owner who requested the supplemental examination proceeding if the Director decides not to institute a reexamination proceeding.

History of 37 C.F.R. §1.26: 46 FR 24179, Apr. 30, 1981; 47 FR 41274, Sept. 17, 1982; 50 FR 31826, Aug. 6, 1985; 54 FR 6902, Feb. 15, 1989; 56 FR 65153, Dec. 13, 1991; 57 FR 38195, Aug. 21, 1992; 62 FR 53183, Oct. 10, 1997; 65 FR 54659, Sept. 8, 2000; 65 FR 76773, Dec. 7, 2000; 68 FR 48289, Aug. 13, 2003; 74 FR 52688, Oct. 14, 2009; 77 FR 48851, Sept. 16, 2012.

§1.27. DEFINITION OF SMALL ENTITIES & ESTABLISHING STATUS AS A SMALL ENTITY TO PERMIT PAYMENT OF SMALL ENTITY FEES; WHEN A DETERMINATION OF ENTITLEMENT TO SMALL ENTITY STATUS & NOTIFICATION OF LOSS OF ENTITLEMENT TO SMALL ENTITY STATUS ARE REQUIRED; FRAUD ON THE OFFICE

(a) Definition of small entities. A small entity as used in this chapter means any party (person, small business concern, or nonprofit organization) under paragraphs (a)(1) through (a)(3) of this section.

(1) Person. A person, as used in paragraph (c) of this section, means any inventor or other individual (*e.g.*, an individual to whom an inventor has transferred some rights in the invention) who has not assigned, granted, conveyed, or licensed, and is under no obligation under contract or law to assign, grant, convey, or license, any rights in the invention. An inventor or other individual who has transferred some rights in the invention to one or more parties, or is under an obligation to transfer some rights in the invention to one or more parties, can also qualify for small entity status if all the parties who have had rights in the invention transferred to them also qualify for small entity status either as a person, small business concern, or nonprofit organization under this section.

(2) Small business concern. A small business concern, as used in paragraph (c) of this section, means any business concern that:

(i) Has not assigned, granted, conveyed, or licensed, and is under no obligation under contract or law to assign, grant, convey, or license, any rights in the invention to any person, concern, or organization which would not qualify for small entity status as a person, small business concern, or nonprofit organization; and

(ii) Meets the size standards set forth in 13 CFR 121.801 through 121.805 to be eligible for reduced patent fees. Questions related to standards for a small business concern may be directed to: Small Business Administration, Size Standards Staff, 409 Third Street, SW., Washington, DC 20416.

(3) Nonprofit Organization. A nonprofit organization, as used in paragraph (c) of this section, means any nonprofit organization that:

(i) Has not assigned, granted, conveyed, or licensed, and is under no obligation under contract or law to assign, grant, convey, or license, any rights in the invention to any person, concern, or organization which would not qualify as a person, small business concern, or a nonprofit organization; and

(ii) Is either:

(A) A university or other institution of higher education located in any country;

(B) An organization of the type described in section 501(c)(3) of the Internal Revenue Code of 1986 (26 U.S.C. 501(c)(3)) and exempt from taxation under section 501(a) of the Internal Revenue Code (26 U.S.C. 501(a));

(C) Any nonprofit scientific or educational organization qualified under a nonprofit organization statute of a state of this country (35 U.S.C. 201(i)); or

(D) Any nonprofit organization located in a foreign country which would qualify as a nonprofit organization under paragraphs (a)(3)(ii)(B) of this section or (a)(3)(ii)(C) of this section if it were located in this country.

(4) License to a Federal agency.

(i) For persons under paragraph (a)(1) of this section, a license to the Government resulting from a rights determination under Executive Order 10096 does not constitute a license so as to prohibit claiming small entity status.

(ii) For small business concerns and nonprofit organizations under paragraphs (a)(2) and (a)(3) of this section, a license to a Federal agency resulting from a funding agreement with that agency pursuant to 35 U.S.C. 202(c)(4) does not constitute a license for the purposes of paragraphs (a)(2)(i) and (a)(3)(i) of this section.

(5) Security Interest. A security interest does not involve an obligation to transfer rights in the invention for the purposes of paragraphs (a)(1) through (a)(3) of this section unless the security interest is defaulted upon.

(b) Establishment of small entity status permits payment of reduced fees.

(1) A small entity, as defined in paragraph (a) of this section, who has properly asserted entitlement to small entity status pursuant to paragraph (c) of this section will be accorded small entity status by the Office in the particular application or patent in which entitlement to small entity status was asserted. Establishment of small entity status allows the payment of certain reduced patent fees pursuant to 35 U.S.C. 41(h)(1).

(2) Submission of an original utility application in compliance with the Office electronic filing system by an applicant who has properly asserted entitlement to small entity status pursuant to paragraph (c) of this section in that application allows the payment of a reduced filing fee pursuant to 35 U.S.C. 41(h)(3).

(c) Assertion of small entity status. Any party (person, small business concern or nonprofit organization) should make a determination, pursuant to paragraph (f) of this section, of entitlement to be accorded small entity status based on the definitions set forth in paragraph (a) of this section, and must, in order to establish small entity status for the purpose of paying small entity fees, actually make an assertion of entitlement to small entity status, in the manner set forth in paragraphs (c)(1) or (c)(3) of this section, in the application or patent in which such small entity fees are to be paid.

(1) Assertion by writing. Small entity status may be established by a written assertion of entitlement to small entity status. A written assertion must:

(i) Be clearly identifiable;

(ii) Be signed (see paragraph (c)(2) of this section); and

(iii) Convey the concept of entitlement to small entity status, such as by stating that applicant is a small entity, or that small entity status is entitled to be asserted for the application or patent. While no specific words or wording are required to assert small entity status, the intent to assert small entity status must be clearly indicated in order to comply with the assertion requirement.

(2) Parties who can sign the written assertion. The written assertion can be signed by:

(i) The applicant (§1.42 or §1.421);

(ii) A patent practitioner of record or a practitioner acting in a representative capacity under §1.34;

(iii) The inventor or a joint inventor, if the inventor is the applicant; or

(iv) The assignee.

(3) Assertion by payment of the small entity basic filing, basic transmittal, basic national fee, international search fee, or individual designation fee in an international design application. The payment, by any party, of the exact amount of one of the small entity basic filing fees set forth in §1.16(a), (b), (c), (d), or (e), the small entity transmittal fee set forth in §1.445(a)(1), the small entity international search fee set forth in §1.445(a)(2) to a Receiving Office other than the United States Receiving Office in the exact amount established for that Receiving Office pursuant to PCT Rule 16, or the small entity basic national fee set forth in §1.492(a), will be treated as a written assertion of entitlement to small entity status even if the type of basic filing, basic transmittal, or basic national fee is inadvertently selected in error. The payment, by any party, of the small entity first part of the individual designation fee for the United States to the International Bureau (§1.1031) will be treated as a written assertion of entitlement to small entity status.

(i) If the Office accords small entity status based on payment of a small entity basic filing or basic national fee under paragraph (c)(3) of this section that is not applicable to that application, any balance of the small entity fee that is applicable to that application will be due along with the appropriate surcharge set forth in §1.16(f), or §1.16(g).

(ii) The payment of any small entity fee other than those set forth in paragraph (c)(3) of this section (whether in the exact fee amount or not) will not be treated as a written assertion of entitlement to small entity status and will not be sufficient to establish small entity status in an application or a patent.

(4) Assertion required in related, continuing, and reissue applications. Status as a small entity must be specifically established by an assertion in each related, continuing and reissue application in which status is appropriate and desired. Status as a small entity in one application or patent does not affect the status of any other application or patent, regardless of the relationship of the applications or patents. The refiling of an application under §1.53 as a continuation, divisional, or continuation-in-part application (including a continued prosecution application under §1.53(d)), or the filing of a reissue application, requires a new assertion as to continued entitlement to small entity status for the continuing or reissue application.

(d) When small entity fees can be paid. Any fee, other than the small entity basic filing fees and the small entity national fees of paragraph (c)(3) of this section, can be paid in the small entity amount only if it is submitted with, or subsequent to, the submission of a written assertion of entitlement to small entity status, except when refunds are permitted by §1.28(a).

(e) Only one assertion required.

(1) An assertion of small entity status need only be filed once in an application or patent. Small entity status, once established, remains in effect until changed pursuant to paragraph (g)(1) of this section. Where an assignment of rights or an obligation to assign rights to other parties who are small entities occurs subsequent to an assertion of small entity status, a second assertion is not required.

(2) Once small entity status is withdrawn pursuant to paragraph (g)(2) of this section, a new written assertion is required to again obtain small entity status.

(f) Assertion requires a determination of entitlement to pay small entity fees. Prior to submitting an assertion of entitlement to small entity status in an application, including a related, continuing, or reissue application, a determination of such entitlement should be made pursuant to the requirements of paragraph (a) of this section. It should be determined that all parties holding rights in the invention qualify for small entity status. The Office will generally not question any assertion of small entity status that is made in accordance with the requirements of this section, but note paragraph (h) of this section.

(g)(1) New determination of entitlement to small entity status is needed when issue and maintenance fees are due. Once status as a small entity has been established in an application or patent, fees as a small entity may thereafter be paid in that application or patent without regard to a change in status until the issue fee is due or any maintenance fee is due.

(2) Notification of loss of entitlement to small entity status is required when issue and maintenance fees are due. Notification of a loss of entitlement to small entity status must be filed in the application or patent prior to paying, or at the time of paying, the earliest of the issue fee or any maintenance fee due after the date on which status as a small entity as defined in paragraph (a) of this section is no longer appropriate. The notification that small entity status is no longer appropriate must be signed by a party identified in §1.33(b). Payment of a fee in other than the small entity amount is not sufficient notification that small entity status is no longer appropriate.

(h) Fraud attempted or practiced on the Office.

(1) Any attempt to fraudulently establish status as a small entity, or pay fees as a small entity, shall be considered as a fraud practiced or attempted on the Office.

(2) Improperly, and with intent to deceive, establishing status as a small entity, or paying fees as a small entity, shall be considered as a fraud practiced or attempted on the Office.

History of 37 C.F.R. §1.27: 47 FR 40139, Sept. 10, 1982; 47 FR 43276, Sept. 30, 1982; 49 FR 553, Jan. 4, 1984; 62 FR 53183, Oct. 10, 1997; 65 FR 54659, Sept. 8, 2000; 69 FR 56538, Sept. 21, 2004; 70 FR 3889, Jan. 27, 2005; 77 FR 48813, Sept. 16, 2012; 78 FR 4289, Mar. 19, 2013; 80 FR 17955, May 13, 2015.

§1.28. REFUNDS WHEN SMALL ENTITY STATUS IS LATER ESTABLISHED; HOW ERRORS IN SMALL ENTITY STATUS ARE EXCUSED

(a) Refunds based on later establishment of small entity status. A refund pursuant to §1.26, based on establishment of small entity status, of a portion of fees timely paid in full prior to establishing status as a small entity may only be obtained if an assertion under §1.27(c) and a request for a refund of the excess amount are filed within three months of the date of the timely payment of the full fee. The three-month time period is not extendable under §1.136. Status as a small entity is waived for any fee by the failure to establish the status prior to paying, at the time of paying, or within three months of the date of payment of, the full fee.

(b) Date of payment.

(1) The three-month period for requesting a refund, pursuant to paragraph (a) of this section, starts on the date that a full fee has been paid;

(2) The date when a deficiency payment is paid in full determines the amount of deficiency that is due, pursuant to paragraph (c) of this section.

(c) How errors in small entity status are excused. If status as a small entity is established in good faith, and fees as a small entity are paid in good faith, in any application or patent, and it is later discovered that such status as a small entity was established in error, or that through error the Office was not notified of a loss of entitlement to small entity status as required by §1.27(g)(2), the error will be excused upon: compliance with the separate submission and itemization requirements of paragraphs (c)(1) and (c)(2) of this section, and the deficiency payment requirement of paragraph (c)(2) of this section:

(1) Separate submission required for each application or patent. Any paper submitted under this paragraph must be limited to the deficiency payment (all fees paid in error), required by paragraph (c)(2) of this section, for one application or one patent. Where more than one application or patent is involved, separate submissions of deficiency payments (*e.g.*, checks) and itemizations are required for each application or patent. See §1.4(b).

(2) Payment of deficiency owed. The deficiency owed, resulting from the previous erroneous payment of small entity fees, must be paid.

(i) Calculation of the deficiency owed. The deficiency owed for each previous fee erroneously paid as a small entity is the difference between the current fee amount (for other than a small entity) on the date the deficiency is paid in full and the amount of the previous erroneous (small entity) fee payment. The total deficiency payment owed is the sum of the individual deficiency owed amounts for each fee amount previously erroneously paid as a small entity. Where a fee paid in error as a small entity was subject to a fee decrease between the time the fee was paid in error and the time the deficiency is paid in full, the deficiency owed is equal to the amount (previously) paid in error;

(ii) Itemization of the deficiency payment. An itemization of the total deficiency payment is required. The itemization must include the following information:

(A) Each particular type of fee that was erroneously paid as a small entity, (*e.g.*, basic statutory filing fee, two-month extension of time fee) along with the current fee amount for a non-small entity;

(B) The small entity fee actually paid, and when. This will permit the Office to differentiate, for example, between two one-month extension of time fees erroneously paid as a small entity but on different dates;

(C) The deficiency owed amount (for each fee erroneously paid); and

(D) The total deficiency payment owed, which is the sum or total of the individual deficiency owed amounts set forth in paragraph (c)(2)(ii)(C) of this section.

(3) Failure to comply with requirements. If the requirements of paragraphs (c)(1) and (c)(2) of this section are not complied with, such failure will either: be treated as an authorization for the Office to process the deficiency payment and charge the processing fee set forth in §1.17(i), or result in a requirement for compliance within a one-month non-extendable time period under §1.136(a) to avoid the return of the fee deficiency paper, at the option of the Office.

(d) Payment of deficiency operates as notification of loss of status. Any deficiency payment (based on a previous erroneous payment of a small entity fee) submitted under paragraph (c) of this section will be treated under §1.27(g)(2) as a notification of a loss of entitlement to small entity status.

History of 37 C.F.R. §1.28: 47 FR 40140, Sept. 10, 1982; 49 FR 553, Jan. 4, 1984; 57 FR 2033, Jan. 17, 1992; 58 FR 54509, Oct. 22, 1993; 60 FR 20222, Apr. 25, 1995; 62 FR 53183, Oct. 10, 1997; 65 FR 54661, Sept. 8, 2000.

§1.29. MICRO ENTITY STATUS

(a) To establish micro entity status under this paragraph, the applicant must certify that:

(1) The applicant qualifies as a small entity as defined in §1.27;

(2) Neither the applicant nor the inventor nor a joint inventor has been named as the inventor or a joint inventor on more than four previously filed patent applications, other than applications filed in another country, provisional applications under 35 U.S.C. 111(b), or international applications for which the basic national fee under 35 U.S.C. 41(a) was not paid;

(3) Neither the applicant nor the inventor nor a joint inventor, in the calendar year preceding the calendar year in which the applicable fee is being paid, had a gross income, as defined in section 61(a) of the Internal Revenue Code of 1986 (26 U.S.C. 61(a)), exceeding three times the median household income for that preceding calendar year, as most recently reported by the Bureau of the Census; and

(4) Neither the applicant nor the inventor nor a joint inventor has assigned, granted, or conveyed, nor is under an obligation by contract or law to assign, grant, or convey, a license or other ownership interest in the application concerned to an entity that, in the calendar year preceding the calendar year in which the applicable fee is being paid, had a gross income, as defined in section 61(a) of the Internal Revenue Code of 1986, exceeding three times the median household income for that preceding calendar year, as most recently reported by the Bureau of the Census.

(b) An applicant, inventor, or joint inventor is not considered to be named on a previously filed application for purposes of paragraph (a)(2) of this section if the applicant, inventor, or joint inventor has assigned, or is under an obligation by contract or law to assign, all ownership rights in the application as the result of the applicant's, inventor's, or joint inventor's previous employment.

(c) If an applicant's, inventor's, joint inventor's, or entity's gross income in the preceding calendar year is not in United States dollars, the average currency exchange rate, as reported by the Internal Revenue Service, during that calendar year shall be used to determine whether the applicant's, inventor's, joint inventor's, or entity's gross income exceeds the threshold specified in paragraph (a)(3) or (4) of this section.

(d) To establish micro entity status under this paragraph, the applicant must certify that:

(1) The applicant qualifies as a small entity as defined in §1.27; and

(2)(i) The applicant's employer, from which the applicant obtains the majority of the applicant's income, is an institution of higher education as defined in section 101(a) of the Higher Education Act of 1965 (20 U.S.C. 1001(a)); or

(ii) The applicant has assigned, granted, conveyed, or is under an obligation by contract or law, to assign, grant, or convey, a license or other ownership interest in the particular application to such an institution of higher education.

(e) Micro entity status is established in an application by filing a micro entity certification in writing complying with the requirements of either paragraph (a) or (d) of this section and signed either in compliance with §1.33(b), in an international application filed in a Receiving Office other than the United States Receiving Office by a person authorized to represent the applicant under §1.455, or in an international design application by a person authorized to represent the applicant under §1.1041 before the International Bureau where the micro entity certification is filed with the International Bureau. Status as a micro entity must be specifically established in each related, continuing and reissue application in which status is appropriate and desired. Status as a micro entity in one application or patent does not affect the status of any other application or patent, regardless of the relationship of the applications or patents. The refiling of an application under §1.53 as a continuation, divisional, or continuation-in-part application (including a continued prosecution application under §1.53(d)), or the filing of a reissue application, requires a new certification of entitlement to micro entity status for the continuing or reissue application.

(f) A fee may be paid in the micro entity amount only if it is submitted with, or subsequent to, the submission of a certification of entitlement to micro entity status.

(g) A certification of entitlement to micro entity status need only be filed once in an application or patent. Micro entity status, once established, remains in effect until changed pursuant to paragraph (i) of this section. However, a fee may be paid in the micro entity amount only if status as a micro entity as defined in paragraph (a) or (d) of this section is appropriate on the date the fee is being paid. Where an assignment of rights or an obligation to assign rights to other parties who are micro entities occurs subsequent to the filing of a certification of entitlement to micro entity status, a second certification of entitlement to micro entity status is not required.

(h) Prior to submitting a certification of entitlement to micro entity status in an application, including a related, continuing, or reissue application, a determination of such entitlement should be made pursuant to the requirements of this section. It should be determined that each applicant qualifies for micro entity status under paragraph (a) or (d) of this section, and that any other party holding rights in the invention qualifies for small entity status under §1.27. The Office will generally not question certification of entitlement to micro entity status that is made in accordance with the requirements of this section.

(i) Notification of a loss of entitlement to micro entity status must be filed in the application or patent prior to paying, or at the time of paying, any fee after the date on which status as a micro entity as defined in paragraph (a) or (d) of this section is no longer appropriate. The notification that micro entity status is no longer appropriate must be signed by a party identified in §1.33(b). Payment of a fee in other than the micro entity amount is not sufficient notification that micro entity status is no longer appropriate. A notification that micro entity status is no longer appropriate will not be treated as a notification that small entity status is also no longer appropriate unless it also contains a notification of loss of entitlement to small entity status under §1.27(f)(2). Once a notification of a loss of entitlement to micro entity status is filed in the application or patent, a new certification of entitlement to micro entity status is required to again obtain micro entity status.

(j) Any attempt to fraudulently establish status as a micro entity, or pay fees as a micro entity, shall be considered as a fraud practiced or attempted on the Office. Improperly, and with intent to deceive, establishing status as a micro entity, or paying fees as a micro entity, shall be considered as a fraud practiced or attempted on the Office.

(k) If status as a micro entity is established in good faith in an application or patent, and fees as a micro entity are paid in good faith in the application or patent, and it is later discovered that such micro entity status either was established in error, or that the Office was not notified of a loss of entitlement to micro entity status as required by paragraph (i) of this section through error, the error will be excused upon compliance with the separate submission and itemization requirements of paragraph (k)(1) of this section and the deficiency payment requirement of paragraph (k)(2) of this section.

(1) Any paper submitted under this paragraph must be limited to the deficiency payment (all fees paid in error) required for a single application or patent. Where more than one application or patent is involved, separate submissions of deficiency payments are required for each application or patent (see §1.4(b)). The paper must contain an itemization of the total deficiency payment for the single application or patent and include the following information:

(i) Each particular type of fee that was erroneously paid as a micro entity, (e.g., basic statutory filing fee, two-month extension of time fee) along with the current fee amount for a small or non-small entity, as applicable;

(ii) The micro entity fee actually paid, and the date on which it was paid;

(iii) The deficiency owed amount (for each fee erroneously paid); and

(iv) The total deficiency payment owed, which is the sum or total of the individual deficiency owed amounts as set forth in paragraph (k)(2) of this section.

(2) The deficiency owed, resulting from the previous erroneous payment of micro entity fees, must be paid. The deficiency owed for each previous fee erroneously paid as a micro entity is the difference between the current fee amount for a small entity or non-small entity, as applicable, on the date the deficiency is paid in full and the amount of the previous erroneous micro entity fee payment. The total deficiency payment owed is the sum of the individual deficiency owed amounts for each fee amount previously and erroneously paid as a micro entity.

(3) If the requirements of paragraphs (k)(1) and (2) of this section are not complied with, such failure will either be treated at the option of the Office as an authorization for the Office to process the deficiency payment and charge the processing fee set forth in §1.17(i), or result in a requirement for compliance within a one-month time period that is not extendable under §1.136(a) to avoid the return of the fee deficiency payment.

(4) Any deficiency payment (based on a previous erroneous payment of a micro entity fee) submitted under this paragraph will be treated as a notification of a loss of entitlement to micro entity status under paragraph (i) of this section.

History of 37 C.F.R. §1.29: 77 FR 75033, Mar. 19, 2013; 78 FR 62396, Dec. 18, 2013; 80 FR 17955, May 13, 2015.

SUBPART B. NATIONAL PROCESSING PROVISIONS

PROSECUTION OF APPLICATION & APPOINTMENT OF ATTORNEY OR AGENT

§1.31. APPLICANT MAY BE REPRESENTED BY ONE OR MORE PATENT PRACTITIONERS OR JOINT INVENTORS

An applicant for patent may file and prosecute the applicant's own case, or the applicant may give power of attorney so as to be represented by one or more patent practitioners or joint inventors, except that a juristic entity (e.g., organizational assignee) must be represented by a patent practitioner even if the juristic entity is the applicant. The Office cannot aid in the selection of a patent practitioner.

History of 37 C.F.R. §1.31: 50 FR 5171, Feb. 6, 1985; 69 FR 29877, May 26, 2004; 69 FR 35452, June 24, 2004; 70 FR 56127, Sept. 26, 2005; 77 FR 48813, Sept. 16, 2012.

Source of 37 C.F.R. Part 1B: 24 FR 10332, Dec. 22, 1959; 60 FR 14518, Mar. 17, 1995; 65 FR 14871, Mar. 20, 2000; 65 FR 33455, May 24, 2000; 65 FR 50103, Aug. 16, 2000; 65 FR 56793, Sept. 20, 2000; 65 FR 70490, Nov. 24, 2000, unless otherwise noted.

§1.32. POWER OF ATTORNEY

(a) Definitions.

(1) Patent practitioner means a registered patent attorney or registered patent agent under §11.6.

(2) Power of attorney means a written document by which a principal authorizes one or more patent practitioners or joint inventors to act on the principal's behalf.

(3) Principal means the applicant (§1.42) for an application for patent and the patent owner for a patent, including a patent in a supplemental examination or reexamination proceeding. The principal executes a power of attorney designating one or more patent practitioners or joint inventors to act on the principal's behalf.

(4) Revocation means the cancellation by the principal of the authority previously given to a patent practitioner or joint inventor to act on the principal's behalf.

(5) Customer Number means a number that may be used to:

(i) Designate the correspondence address of a patent application or patent such that the correspondence address for the patent application, patent or other patent proceeding would be the address associated with the Customer Number;

(ii) Designate the fee address (§1.363) of a patent such that the fee address for the patent would be the address associated with the Customer Number; and

(iii) Submit a list of patent practitioners such that those patent practitioners associated with the Customer Number would have power of attorney.

(6) Patent practitioner of record means a patent practitioner who has been granted a power of attorney in an application, patent, or other proceeding in compliance with paragraph (b) of this section. The phrases practitioner of record and attorney or agent of record also mean a patent practitioner who has been granted a power of attorney in an application, patent, or other proceeding in compliance with paragraph (b) of this section.

(b) A power of attorney must:

(1) Be in writing;

(2) Name one or more representatives in compliance with paragraph (c) of this section;

(3) Give the representative power to act on behalf of the principal; and

(4) Be signed by the applicant for patent (§1.42) or the patent owner. A patent owner who was not the applicant under §1.46 must appoint any power of attorney in compliance with §§3.71 and 3.73 of this chapter.

(c) A power of attorney may only name as representative:

(1) One or more joint inventors (§1.45);

(2) Those registered patent practitioners associated with a Customer Number;

(3) Ten or fewer patent practitioners, stating the name and registration number of each patent practitioner. Except as provided in paragraph (c)(1) or (c)(2) of this section, the Office will not recognize more than ten patent practitioners as being of record in an application or patent. If a power of attorney names more than ten patent practitioners, such power of attorney must be accompanied by a separate paper indicating which ten patent practitioners named in the power of attorney are to be recognized by the Office as being of record in the application or patent to which the power of attorney is directed.

(d) A power of attorney from a prior national application for which benefit is claimed under 35 U.S.C. 120, 121, 365(c), or 386(c) in a continuing application may have effect in the continuing application if a copy of the power of attorney from the prior application is filed in the continuing application unless:

(1) The power of attorney was granted by the inventor; and

(2) The continuing application names an inventor who was not named as an inventor in the prior application.

(e) If the power of attorney was granted by the originally named inventive entity, and an added inventor pursuant to §1.48 does not provide a power of attorney consistent with the power of attorney granted by the originally named inventive entity, the addition of the inventor results in the loss of that power of attorney upon grant of the §1.48 request. This provision does not preclude a practitioner from acting pursuant to §1.34, if applicable.

History of 37 C.F.R. §1.32: 57 FR 29642, July 6, 1992; 69 FR 29877, May 26, 2004; 70 FR 56127, Sept. 26, 2005; 77 FR 48813, Sept. 16, 2012; 80 FR 17956, May 13, 2015.

§1.33. CORRESPONDENCE RESPECTING PATENT APPLICATIONS, PATENT REEXAMINATION PROCEEDINGS, & OTHER PROCEEDINGS

(a) Correspondence address and daytime telephone number. When filing an application, a correspondence address must be set forth in either an application data sheet (§1.76), or elsewhere, in a clearly identifiable manner, in any paper submitted with an application filing. If no correspondence address is specified, the Office may treat the mailing address of the first named inventor (if provided, see §§1.76(b)(1) and 1.63(b)(2)) as the correspondence address. The Office will direct, or otherwise make available, all notices, official letters, and other communications relating to the application to the person associated with the correspondence address. For correspondence submitted via the Office's electronic filing system, however, an electronic acknowledgment receipt will be sent to the submitter. The Office will generally not engage in double correspondence with an applicant and a patent practitioner, or with more than one patent practitioner except as deemed necessary by the Director. If more than one correspondence address is specified, the Office will select one of the specified addresses for use as the correspondence address and, if given, may select the address associated with a Customer Number over a typed correspondence address. For the party to whom correspondence is to be addressed, a daytime telephone number should be supplied in a clearly identifiable manner and may be changed by any party who may change the correspondence address. The correspondence address may be changed by the parties set forth in paragraph (b)(1) or (b)(3) of this section. Prior to the appointment of any power of attorney under §1.32(b), the correspondence address may also be changed by any patent practitioner named in the application transmittal papers who acts in a representative capacity under the provisions of §1.34.

(b) Amendments and other papers. Amendments and other papers, except for written assertions pursuant to §1.27(c)(2)(iii) or (c)(2)(iv), filed in the application must be signed by:

(1) A patent practitioner of record;

(2) A patent practitioner not of record who acts in a representative capacity under the provisions of §1.34; or

(3) The applicant (§1.42). Unless otherwise specified, all papers submitted on behalf of a juristic entity must be signed by a patent practitioner.

(c) All notices, official letters, and other communications for the patent owner or owners in a reexamination or supplemental examination proceeding will be directed to the correspondence address in the patent file. Amendments filed in a reexamination proceeding, and other papers filed in a reexamination or supplemental examination proceeding, on behalf of the patent owner must be signed by the patent owner, or if there is more than one owner by all the owners, or by an attorney or agent of record in the patent file, or by a registered attorney or agent not of record who acts in a representative capacity under the provisions of §1.34. Double correspondence with the patent owner or owners and the patent owner's attorney or agent, or with more than one attorney or agent, will not be undertaken.

(d) A "correspondence address" or change thereto may be filed with the Patent and Trademark Office during the enforceable life of the patent. The "correspondence address" will be used in any correspondence relating to maintenance fees unless a separate "fee address" has been specified. See §1.363 for "fee address" used solely for maintenance fee purposes.

(e) A change of address filed in a patent application or patent does not change the address for a patent practitioner in the roster of patent attorneys and agents. See §11.11 of this title.

(f) Where application papers from a prior application are used in a continuing application and the correspondence address was changed during the prosecution of the prior application, an application data sheet or separate paper identifying the correspondence address to be used for the continuing application must be submitted. Otherwise, the Office may not recognize the change of correspondence address effected during the prosecution of the prior application.

(g) A patent practitioner acting in a representative capacity whose correspondence address is the correspondence address of record in an application may change the correspondence address after the patent has issued, provided that the change of correspondence address is accompanied by a statement that notice has been given to the patentee or owner.

History of 37 C.F.R. §1.33: 36 FR 12617, July 2, 1971; 46 FR 29181, May 29, 1981; 49 FR 34724, Aug. 31, 1984; 50 FR 5171, Feb. 6, 1985; 62 FR 53184, Oct. 10, 1997; 65 FR 54661, Sept. 8, 2000; 69 FR 29877, May 26, 2004; 69 FR 35452, June 24, 2004; 70 FR 3889, Jan. 27, 2005; 70 FR 56127, Sept. 26, 2005; 72 FR 2776, Jan. 23, 2007; 72 FR 18904, May 16, 2007; 77 FR 48814, Sept. 16, 2012; 78 FR 62396, Dec. 18, 2013.

§1.34. ACTING IN A REPRESENTATIVE CAPACITY

When a patent practitioner acting in a representative capacity appears in person or signs a paper in practice before the United States Patent and Trademark Office in a patent case, his or her personal appearance or signature shall constitute a representation to the United States Patent and Trademark Office that under the provisions of this subchapter and the law, he or she is authorized to represent the particular party on whose behalf he or she acts. In filing such a paper, the patent practitioner must set forth his or her registration number, his or her name and signature. Further proof of authority to act in a representative capacity may be required.

History of 37 C.F.R. §1.34: 46 FR 29181, May 29, 1981; 50 FR 5171, Feb. 6, 1985; 65 FR 54662, Sept. 8, 2000; 69 FR 29878, May 26, 2004; 70 FR 56127, Sept. 26, 2005.

§1.36. REVOCATION OF POWER OF ATTORNEY; WITHDRAWAL OF PATENT ATTORNEY OR AGENT

(a) A power of attorney, pursuant to §1.32(b), may be revoked at any stage in the proceedings of a case by the applicant or patent owner. A power of attorney to the patent practitioners associated with a Customer Number will be treated as a request to revoke any powers of attorney previously given. Fewer than all of the applicants (or fewer than all patent owners in a supplemental examination or reexamination proceeding) may revoke the power of attorney only upon a showing of sufficient cause, and payment of the petition fee set forth in §1.17(f). A patent practitioner will be notified of the revocation of the power of attorney. Where power of attorney is given to the patent practitioners associated with a Customer Number (§1.32(c)(2)), the practitioners so appointed will also be notified of the revocation of the power of attorney when the power of attorney to all of the practitioners associated with the Customer Number is revoked. The notice of revocation will be mailed to the correspondence address for the application (§1.33) in effect before the revocation. An assignment will not of itself operate as a revocation of a power previously given, but the assignee may become the applicant under §1.46(c) and revoke any previous power of attorney and grant a power of attorney as provided in §1.32(b).

(b) A registered patent attorney or patent agent who has been given a power of attorney pursuant to §1.32(b) may withdraw as attorney or agent of record upon application to and approval by the Director. The applicant or patent owner will be notified of the withdrawal of the registered patent attorney or patent agent. Where power of attorney is given to the patent practitioners associated with a Customer Number, a request to delete all of the patent practitioners associated with the Customer Number may not be granted if an applicant has given power of attorney to the patent practitioners associated with the Customer Number in an application that has an Office action to which a reply is due, but insufficient time remains for the applicant to file a reply. See §41.5 of this title for withdrawal during proceedings before the Patent Trial and Appeal Board.

History of 37 C.F.R. §1.36: 46 FR 29182, May 29, 1981; 49 FR 48452, Dec. 12, 1984; 65 FR 54662, Sept. 8, 2000; 69 FR 29878, May 26, 2004; 69 FR 49997, Aug. 12, 2004; 70 FR 56128, Sept. 26, 2005; 77 FR 46624, Sept. 16, 2012; 77 FR 48814, Sept. 16, 2012.

WHO MAY APPLY FOR A PATENT

§1.41. INVENTORSHIP

(a) An application must include, or be amended to include, the name of the inventor for any invention claimed in the application.

(b) The inventorship of a nonprovisional application under 35 U.S.C. 111(a) is the inventor or joint inventors set forth in the application data sheet in accordance with §1.76 filed before or concurrently with the inventor's oath or declaration. If an application data sheet is not filed before or concurrently with the inventor's oath or declaration, the inventorship is the inventor or joint inventors set forth in the inventor's oath or declaration, except as provided for in §§1.53(d)(4) and 1.63(d). Once an application data sheet or the inventor's oath or declaration is filed in a nonprovisional application, any correction of inventorship must be pursuant to §1.48. If neither an application data sheet nor the inventor's oath or declaration is filed during the pendency of a nonprovisional application, the inventorship is the inventor or joint inventors set forth in the application papers filed pursuant to §1.53(b), unless the applicant files a paper, including the processing fee set forth in §1.17(i), supplying the name or names of the inventor or joint inventors.

(c) The inventorship of a provisional application is the inventor or joint inventors set forth in the cover sheet as prescribed by §1.51(c)(1). Once a cover sheet as prescribed by §1.51(c)(1) is filed in a provisional application, any correction of inventorship must be pursuant to §1.48. If a cover sheet as prescribed by §1.51(c)(1) is not filed during the pendency of a provisional application, the inventorship is the inventor or joint inventors set forth in the application papers filed pursuant to §1.53(c), unless applicant files a paper including the processing fee set forth in §1.17(q), supplying the name or names of the inventor or joint inventors.

(d) In a nonprovisional application under 35 U.S.C. 111(a) filed without an application data sheet or the inventor's oath or declaration, or in a provisional application filed without a cover sheet as prescribed by §1.51(c)(1), the name and residence of each person believed to be an actual inventor should be provided when the application papers pursuant to §1.53(b) or §1.53(c) are filed.

(e) The inventorship of an international application entering the national stage under 35 U.S.C. 371 is the inventor or joint inventors set forth in the application data sheet in accordance with §1.76 filed with the initial submission under 35 U.S.C. 371. Unless the initial submission under 35 U.S.C. 371 is accompanied by an application data sheet in accordance with §1.76 setting forth the inventor or joint inventors, the inventorship is the inventor or joint inventors set forth in the international application, which includes any change effected under PCT Rule 92*bis*.

(f) The inventorship of an international design application designating the United States is the creator or creators set forth in the publication of the international registration under Hague Agreement Article 10(3). Any correction of inventorship must be pursuant to §1.48.

History of 37 C.F.R. §1.41: 24 FR 10332, Dec. 22, 1959; 36 FR 12690, July 3, 1971; 48 FR 2708, Jan. 20, 1983; 48 FR 4285, Jan. 31, 1983; 62 FR 53184, Oct. 10, 1997; 65 FR 54662, Sept. 8, 2000; 67 FR 523, Jan. 4, 2002; 77 FR 48814, Sept. 16, 2012; 80 FR 17956, May 13, 2015.

§1.42. APPLICANT FOR PATENT

(a) The word "applicant" when used in this title refers to the inventor or all of the joint inventors, or to the person applying for a patent as provided in §§1.43, 1.45, or 1.46.

(b) If a person is applying for a patent as provided in §1.46, the word "applicant" refers to the assignee, the person to whom the inventor is under an obligation to assign the invention, or the person who otherwise shows sufficient proprietary interest in the matter, who is applying for a patent under §1.46 and not the inventor.

(c) If fewer than all joint inventors are applying for a patent as provided in §1.45, the phrase "the applicant" means the joint inventors who are applying for the patent without the omitted inventor(s).

(d) Any person having authority may deliver an application and fees to the Office on behalf of the applicant. However, an oath or declaration, or substitute statement in lieu of an oath or declaration, may be executed only in accordance with §1.63 or 1.64, a correspondence address may be provided only in accordance with §1.33(a), and amendments and other papers must be signed in accordance with §1.33(b).

(e) The Office may require additional information where there is a question concerning ownership or interest in an application, and a showing may be required from the person filing the application that the filing was authorized where such authorization comes into question.

History of 37 C.F.R. §1.42: 24 FR 10332, Dec. 22, 1959; 29 FR 18503, Dec. 29, 1964; 48 FR 2709, Jan. 20, 1983; 77 FR 48815, Sept. 16, 2012.

§1.43. APPLICATION FOR PATENT BY A LEGAL REPRESENTATIVE OF A DECEASED OR LEGALLY INCAPACITATED INVENTOR

If an inventor is deceased or under legal incapacity, the legal representative of the inventor may make an application for patent on behalf of the inventor. If an inventor dies during the time intervening between the filing of the application and the granting of a patent thereon, the letters patent may be issued to the legal representative upon proper intervention. See §1.64 concerning the execution of a substitute statement by a legal representative in lieu of an oath or declaration.

History of 37 C.F.R. §1.43: 24 FR 10332, Dec. 22, 1959; 29 FR 18503, Dec. 29, 1964; 48 FR 2709, Jan. 20, 1983; 77 FR 48815, Sept. 16, 2012.

§1.44. RESERVED

History of 37 C.F.R. §1.44: 65 FR 54662, Sept. 8, 2000.

§1.45. APPLICATION FOR PATENT BY JOINT INVENTORS

(a) Joint inventors must apply for a patent jointly, and each must make an inventor's oath or declaration as required by §1.63, except as provided for in §1.64. If a joint inventor refuses to join in an application for patent or cannot be found or reached after diligent effort, the other joint inventor or inventors may make the application for patent on behalf of themselves and the omitted inventor. See §1.64 concerning the execution of a substitute statement by the other joint inventor or inventors in lieu of an oath or declaration.

(b) Inventors may apply for a patent jointly even though:

(1) They did not physically work together or at the same time;

(2) Each inventor did not make the same type or amount of contribution; or

(3) Each inventor did not make a contribution to the subject matter of every claim of the application.

(c) If multiple inventors are named in a nonprovisional application, each named inventor must have made a contribution, individually or jointly, to the subject matter of at least one claim of the application and the application will be considered to be a joint application under 35 U.S.C. 116. If multiple inventors are named in a provisional application, each named inventor must have made a contribution, individually or jointly, to the subject matter disclosed in the provisional application and the provisional application will be considered to be a joint application under 35 U.S.C. 116.

History of 37 C.F.R. §1.45: 24 FR 10332, Dec. 22, 1959; 29 FR 18503, Dec. 29, 1964; 48 FR 2709, Jan. 20, 1983; 50 FR 9379, Mar. 7, 1985; 60 FR 20222, Apr. 25, 1995; 77 FR 48815, Sept. 16, 2012.

§1.46. APPLICATION FOR PATENT BY AN ASSIGNEE, OBLIGATED ASSIGNEE, OR A PERSON WHO OTHERWISE SHOWS SUFFICIENT PROPRIETARY INTEREST IN THE MATTER

(a) A person to whom the inventor has assigned or is under an obligation to assign the invention may make an application for patent. A person who otherwise shows sufficient proprietary interest in the matter may make an application for patent on behalf of and as agent for the inventor on proof of the pertinent facts and a showing that such action is appropriate to preserve the rights of the parties.

(b) If an application under 35 U.S.C. 111 is made by a person other than the inventor under paragraph (a) of this section, the application must contain an application data sheet under §1.76 specifying in the applicant information section (§1.76(b)(7)) the assignee, person to whom the inventor is under an obligation to assign the invention, or person who otherwise shows sufficient proprietary interest in the matter. If an application entering the national stage under 35 U.S.C. 371, or a nonprovisional international design application, is applied for by a person other than the inventor under paragraph (a) of this section, the assignee, person to whom the inventor is under an obligation to assign the invention, or person who otherwise shows sufficient proprietary interest in the matter must have been identified as the applicant for the United States in the international stage of the international application or as the applicant in the publication of the international registration under Hague Agreement Article 10(3).

(1) If the applicant is the assignee or a person to whom the inventor is under an obligation to assign the invention, documentary evidence of ownership (e.g., assignment for an assignee, employment agreement for a person to whom the inventor is under an obligation to assign the invention) should be recorded as provided for in part 3 of this chapter no later than the date the issue fee is paid in the application.

(2) If the applicant is a person who otherwise shows sufficient proprietary interest in the matter, such applicant must submit a petition including:

(i) The fee set forth in §1.17(g);

(ii) A showing that such person has sufficient proprietary interest in the matter; and

(iii) A statement that making the application for patent by a person who otherwise shows sufficient proprietary interest in the matter on behalf of and as agent for the inventor is appropriate to preserve the rights of the parties.

(c)(1) Correction or update in the name of the applicant. Any request to correct or update the name of the applicant under this section must include an application data sheet under §1.76 specifying the correct or updated name of the applicant in the applicant information section (§1.76(b)(7)) in accordance with §1.76(c)(2). A change in the name of the applicant recorded pursuant to Hague Agreement Article 16(1)(ii) will be effective to change the name of the applicant in a nonprovisional international design application.

(2) Change in the applicant. Any request to change the applicant under this section after an original applicant has been specified must include an application data sheet under §1.76 specifying the applicant in the applicant information section (§1.76(b)(7)) in accordance with §1.76(c)(2) and comply with §§3.71 and 3.73 of this title.

(d) Even if the whole or a part interest in the invention or in the patent to be issued is assigned or obligated to be assigned, an oath or declaration must be executed by the actual inventor or each actual joint inventor, except as provided for in §1.64. See §1.64 concerning the execution of a substitute statement by an assignee, person to whom the inventor is under an obligation to assign the invention, or a person who otherwise shows sufficient proprietary interest in the matter.

(e) If a patent is granted on an application filed under this section by a person other than the inventor, the patent shall be granted to the real party in interest. Otherwise, the patent may be issued to the assignee or jointly to the inventor and the assignee as provided in §3.81. Where a real party in interest has filed an application under §1.46, the applicant shall notify the Office of any change in the real party in interest no later than payment of the issue fee. The Office will treat the absence of such a notice as an indication that there has been no change in the real party in interest.

(f) The Office may publish notice of the filing of the application by a person who otherwise shows sufficient proprietary interest in the Official Gazette.

History of 37 C.F.R. §1.46: 24 FR 10332, Dec. 22, 1959; 48 FR 2709, Jan. 20, 1983; 57 FR 29642, July 6, 1992; 77 FR 48815, Sept. 16, 2012; 80 FR 17956, May 13, 2015.

§1.47. REMOVED & RESERVED

History of 37 C.F.R. §1.47: 77 FR 48816, Sept. 16, 2012.

§1.48. CORRECTION OF INVENTORSHIP PURSUANT TO 35 U.S.C. 116 OR CORRECTION OF THE NAME OR ORDER OF NAMES IN A PATENT APPLICATION, OTHER THAN A REISSUE APPLICATION

(a) Nonprovisional application: Any request to correct or change the inventorship once the inventorship has been established under §1.41 must include:

(1) An application data sheet in accordance with §1.76 that identifies each inventor by his or her legal name; and

(2) The processing fee set forth in §1.17(i).

(b) Inventor's oath or declaration for added inventor: An oath or declaration as required by §1.63, or a substitute statement in compliance with §1.64, will be required for any actual inventor who has not yet executed such an oath or declaration.

(c) Any request to correct or change the inventorship under paragraph (a) of this section filed after the Office action on the merits has been given or mailed in the application must also be accompanied by the fee set forth in §1.17(d), unless the request is accompanied by a statement that the request to correct or change the inventorship is due solely to the cancelation of claims in the application.

(d) Provisional application. Once a cover sheet as prescribed by §1.51(c)(1) is filed in a provisional application, any request to correct or change the inventorship must include:

(1) A request, signed by a party set forth in §1.33(b), to correct the inventorship that identifies each inventor by his or her legal name; and

(2) The processing fee set forth in §1.17(q).

(e) Additional information may be required. The Office may require such other information as may be deemed appropriate under the particular circumstances surrounding the correction of inventorship.

(f) Correcting or updating the name of an inventor: Any request to correct or update the name of the inventor or a joint inventor, or the order of the names of joint inventors, in a nonprovisional application must include:

(1) An application data sheet in accordance with §1.76 that identifies each inventor by his or her legal name in the desired order; and

(2) The processing fee set forth in §1.17(i).

(g) Reissue applications not covered. The provisions of this section do not apply to reissue applications. See §§1.171 and 1.175 for correction of inventorship in a patent via a reissue application.

(h) Correction of inventorship in patent. See §1.324 for correction of inventorship in a patent.

(i) Correction of inventorship in an interference or contested case before the Patent Trial and Appeal Board. In an interference under part 41, subpart D, of this title, a request for correction of inventorship in an application must be in the form of a motion under §41.121(a)(2) of this title. In a contested case under part 42, subpart D, of this title, a request for correction of inventorship in an application must be in the form of a motion under §42.22 of this title. The motion under §41.121(a)(2) or 42.22 of this title must comply with the requirements of paragraph (a) of this section.

History of 37 C.F.R. §1.48: 48 FR 2709, Jan. 20, 1983; 49 FR 48452, Dec. 12, 1984; 50 FR 9379, Mar. 7, 1985; 57 FR 56447, Nov. 30, 1992; 60 FR 20222, Apr. 25, 1995; 62 FR 53185, Oct. 10, 1997; 65 FR 54663, Sept. 8, 2000; 67 FR 523, Jan. 4, 2002; 69 FR 49998, Aug. 12, 2004; 77 FR 48816, Sept. 16, 2012; 78 FR 4289, Mar. 19, 2013.

THE APPLICATION

§1.51. GENERAL REQUISITES OF AN APPLICATION

(a) Applications for patents must be made to the Director of the United States Patent and Trademark Office. An application transmittal letter limited to the transmittal of the documents and fees comprising a patent application under this section may be signed by a juristic applicant or patent owner.

(b) A complete application filed under §1.53(b) or §1.53(d) comprises:

(1) A specification as prescribed by 35 U.S.C. 112, including a claim or claims, see §§1.71 to 1.77;

(2) The inventor's oath or declaration, see §§1.63 and 1.64;

(3) Drawings, when necessary, see §§1.81 to 1.85; and

(4) The prescribed filing fee, search fee, examination fee, and application size fee, see §1.16.

(c) A complete provisional application filed under §1.53(c) comprises:

(1) A cover sheet identifying:

(i) The application as a provisional application,

(ii) The name or names of the inventor or inventors, (see §1.41(a)(2)),

(iii) The residence of each named inventor,

(iv) The title of the invention,

(v) The name and registration number of the attorney or agent (if applicable),

(vi) The docket number used by the person filing the application to identify the application (if applicable),

(vii) The correspondence address, and

(viii) The name of the U.S. Government agency and Government contract number (if the invention was made by an agency of the U.S. Government or under a contract with an agency of the U.S. Government);

(2) A specification as prescribed by 35 U.S.C. 112(a), see §1.71;

(3) Drawings, when necessary, see §§1.81 to 1.85; and

(4) The prescribed filing fee and application size fee, see §1.16.

(d) Applicants are encouraged to file an information disclosure statement in nonprovisional applications. See §1.97 and §1.98. No information disclosure statement may be filed in a provisional application.

History of 37 C.F.R. §1.51: 42 FR 5593, Jan. 28, 1977; 47 FR 41275, Sept. 17, 1982; 48 FR 2709, Jan. 20, 1983; 57 FR 2033, Jan. 17, 1992; 60 FR 20222, Apr. 25, 1995; 62 FR 53185, Oct. 10, 1997; 65 FR 54664, Sept. 8, 2000; 68 FR 14336, Mar. 25, 2003; 70 FR 3889, Jan. 27, 2005; 77 FR 46624, Sept. 16, 2012; 77 FR 48816, Sept. 16, 2012; 78 FR 62396, Dec. 18, 2013.

§1.52. LANGUAGE, PAPER, WRITING, MARGINS, COMPACT DISC SPECIFICATIONS

(a) Papers that are to become a part of the permanent United States Patent and Trademark Office records in the file of a patent application, or a reexamination or supplemental examination proceeding.

(1) All papers, other than drawings, that are submitted on paper or by facsimile transmission, and are to become a part of the permanent United States Patent and Trademark Office records in the file of a patent application or reexamination or supplemental examination proceeding, must be on sheets of paper that are the same size, not permanently bound together, and:

(i) Flexible, strong, smooth, non-shiny, durable, and white;

(ii) Either 21.0 cm by 29.7 cm (DIN size A4) or 21.6 cm by 27.9 cm (8½ by 11 inches), with each sheet including a top margin of at least 2.0 cm (¾ inch), a left side margin of at least 2.5 cm (1 inch), a right side margin of at least 2.0 cm (¾ inch), and a bottom margin of at least 2.0 cm (¾ inch);

(iii) Written on only one side in portrait orientation;

(iv) Plainly and legibly written either by a typewriter or machine printer in permanent dark ink or its equivalent; and

(v) Presented in a form having sufficient clarity and contrast between the paper and the writing thereon to permit the direct reproduction of readily legible copies in any number by use of photographic, electrostatic, photo-offset, and microfilming processes and electronic capture by use of digital imaging and optical character recognition.

(2) All papers that are submitted on paper or by facsimile transmission and are to become a part of the permanent records of the United States Patent and Trademark Office should have no holes in the sheets as submitted.

(3) The provisions of this paragraph and paragraph (b) of this section do not apply to the pre-printed information on paper forms provided by the Office, or to the copy of the patent submitted on paper in double column format as the specification in a reissue application or request for reexamination.

(4) See §1.58 for chemical and mathematical formulae and tables, and §1.84 for drawings.

(5) Papers that are submitted electronically to the Office must be formatted and transmitted in compliance with the Office's electronic filing system requirements.

(b) The application (specification, including the claims, drawings, and the inventor's oath or declaration) or reexamination or supplemental examination proceeding, any amendments to the application or reexamination proceeding, or any corrections to the application, or reexamination or supplemental examination proceeding.

(1) The application or proceeding and any amendments or corrections to the application (including any translation submitted pursuant to paragraph (d) of this section) or proceeding, except as provided for in §1.69 and paragraph (d) of this section, must:

(i) Comply with the requirements of paragraph (a) of this section; and

(ii) Be in the English language or be accompanied by a translation of the application and a translation of any corrections or amendments into the English language together with a statement that the translation is accurate.

(2) The specification (including the abstract and claims) for other than reissue applications and reexamination or supplemental examination proceedings, and any amendments for applications (including reissue applications) and reexamination proceedings to the specification, except as provided for in §§1.821 through 1.825, must have:

(i) Lines that are 1½ or double spaced;

(ii) Text written in a nonscript type font (e.g., Arial, Times Roman, or Courier, preferably a font size of 12) lettering style having capital letters which should be at least 0.3175 cm. (0.125 inch) high, but may be no smaller than 0.21 cm. (0.08 inch) high (e.g., a font size of 6); and

(iii) Only a single column of text.

(3) The claim or claims must commence on a separate physical sheet or electronic page (§1.75(h)).

(4) The abstract must commence on a separate physical sheet or electronic page or be submitted as the first page of

the patent in a reissue application or reexamination or supplemental examination proceeding (§1.72(b)).

(5) Other than in a reissue application or a reexamination or supplemental examination proceeding, the pages of the specification including claims and abstract must be numbered consecutively, starting with 1, the numbers being centrally located above or preferably, below, the text.

(6) Other than in a reissue application or reexamination or supplemental examination proceeding, the paragraphs of the specification, other than in the claims or abstract, may be numbered at the time the application is filed, and should be individually and consecutively numbered using Arabic numerals, so as to unambiguously identify each paragraph. The number should consist of at least four numerals enclosed in square brackets, including leading zeros (e.g., [0001]). The numbers and enclosing brackets should appear to the right of the left margin as the first item in each paragraph, before the first word of the paragraph, and should be highlighted in bold. A gap, equivalent to approximately four spaces, should follow the number. Nontext elements (e.g., tables, mathematical or chemical formulae, chemical structures, and sequence data) are considered part of the numbered paragraph around or above the elements, and should not be independently numbered. If a nontext element extends to the left margin, it should not be numbered as a separate and independent paragraph. A list is also treated as part of the paragraph around or above the list, and should not be independently numbered. Paragraph or section headers (titles), whether abutting the left margin or centered on the page, are not considered paragraphs and should not be numbered.

(c) Interlineation, erasure, cancellation, or other alteration of the application papers may be made before or after the signing of the inventor's oath or declaration referring to those application papers, provided that the statements in the inventor's oath or declaration pursuant to §1.63 remain applicable to those application papers. A substitute specification (§1.125) may be required if the application papers do not comply with paragraphs (a) and (b) of this section.

(d) A nonprovisional or provisional application under 35 U.S.C. 111 may be in a language other than English.

(1) Nonprovisional application. If a nonprovisional application under 35 U.S.C. 111(a) is filed in a language other than English, an English language translation of the non-English language application, a statement that the translation is accurate, and the processing fee set forth in §1.17(i) are required. If these items are not filed with the application, the applicant will be notified and given a period of time within which they must be filed in order to avoid abandonment.

(2) Provisional application. If a provisional application under 35 U.S.C. 111(b) is filed in a language other than English, an English language translation of the non-English language provisional application will not be required in the provisional application. See §1.78(a) for the requirements for claiming the benefit of such provisional application in a nonprovisional application.

(e) Electronic documents that are to become part of the permanent United States Patent and Trademark Office records in the file of a patent application, or reexamination or supplemental examination proceeding.

(1) The following documents may be submitted to the Office on a compact disc in compliance with this paragraph:

(i) A computer program listing (see §1.96);

(ii) A "Sequence Listing" (submitted under §1.821(c)); or

(iii) Any individual table (see §1.58) if the table is more than 50 pages in length, or if the total number of pages of all the tables in an application exceeds 100 pages in length, where a table page is a page printed on paper in conformance with paragraph (b) of this section and §1.58(c).

(2) A compact disc as used in this part means a Compact Disc-Read Only Memory (CD-ROM) or a Compact Disc-Recordable (CD-R) in compliance with this paragraph. A CD-ROM is a "read-only" medium on which the data is pressed into the disc so that it cannot be changed or erased. A CD-R is a "write once" medium on which once the data is recorded, it is permanent and cannot be changed or erased.

(3)(i) Each compact disc must conform to the International Organization for Standardization (ISO) 9660 standard, and the contents of each compact disc must be in compliance with the American Standard Code for Information Interchange (ASCII).

(ii) Each compact disc must be enclosed in a hard compact disc case within an unsealed padded and protective mailing envelope and accompanied by a transmittal letter on paper in accordance with paragraph (a) of this section. The transmittal letter must list for each compact disc the machine format (e.g., IBM-PC, Macintosh), the operating system compatibility (e.g., MS-DOS, MS-Windows, Macintosh, Unix), a list of files contained on the compact disc including their names, sizes in bytes, and dates of creation, plus any other special information that is necessary to identify, maintain, and interpret (e.g., tables in landscape orientation should be identified as landscape orientation or be identified when inquired about) the information on the compact disc. Compact discs submitted to the Office will not be returned to the applicant.

(4) Any compact disc must be submitted in duplicate unless it contains only the "Sequence Listing" in computer readable form required by §1.821(e). The compact disc and duplicate copy must be labeled "Copy 1" and "Copy 2," respectively. The transmittal letter which accompanies the compact disc must include a statement that the two compact discs are identical. In the event that the two compact discs are not identical, the Office will use the compact disc labeled "Copy 1" for further processing. Any amendment to the information on a compact disc must be by way of a replacement compact disc in compliance with this paragraph containing the substitute information, and must be accompanied by a statement that the replacement compact disc contains no new matter. The compact disc and copy must be labeled "COPY 1 REPLACEMENT MM/DD/YYYY" (with the month, day and year of creation indicated), and "COPY 2 REPLACEMENT MM/DD/YYYY," respectively.

(5) The specification must contain an incorporation-by-reference of the material on the compact disc in a separate paragraph (§1.77(b)(5)), identifying each compact disc by the names of the files contained on each of the compact discs, their date of creation and their sizes in bytes. The Office may require applicant to amend the specification to include in the paper portion any part of the specification previously submitted on compact disc.

(6) A compact disc must also be labeled with the following information:

(i) The name of each inventor (if known);

(ii) Title of the invention;

(iii) The docket number, or application number if known, used by the person filing the application to identify the application;

(iv) A creation date of the compact disc;

(v) If multiple compact discs are submitted, the label shall indicate their order (e.g., "1 of X"); and

(vi) An indication that the disc is "Copy 1" or "Copy 2" of the submission. See paragraph (b)(4) of this section.

(7) If a file is unreadable on both copies of the disc, the unreadable file will be treated as not having been submitted. A file is unreadable if, for example, it is of a format that does not comply with the requirements of paragraph (e)(3) of this section, it is corrupted by a computer virus, or it is written onto a defective compact disc.

(f)(1) Any sequence listing in an electronic medium in compliance with §§1.52(e) and 1.821(c) or (e), and any computer program listing filed in an electronic medium in compliance with §§1.52(e) and 1.96, will be excluded when determining the application size fee required by §1.16(s) or §1.492(j). For purposes of determining the application size fee required by §1.16(s) or §1.492(j), for an application the specification and drawings of which, excluding any sequence listing in compliance with §1.821(c) or (e), and any computer program listing filed in an electronic medium in compliance with §§1.52(e) and 1.96, are submitted in whole or in part on an electronic medium other than the Office electronic filing system, each three kilobytes of content submitted on an electronic medium shall be counted as a sheet of paper.

(2) Except as otherwise provided in this paragraph, the paper size equivalent of the specification and drawings of an application submitted via the Office electronic filing system will be considered to be seventy-five percent of the number of sheets of paper present in the specification and drawings of the application when entered into the Office file wrapper after being rendered by the Office electronic filing system for purposes of determining the application size fee required by §1.16(s). Any sequence listing in compliance with §1.821(c) or (e), and any computer program listing in compliance with §1.96, submitted via the Office electronic filing system will be excluded when determining the application size fee required by §1.16(s) if the listing is submitted in ASCII text as part of an associated file.

History of 37 C.F.R. §1.52: 37 FR 21994, Oct. 18, 1972; 43 FR 20462, May 11, 1978; 47 FR 41275, Sept. 17, 1982; 48 FR 2709, Jan. 20, 1983; 49 FR 554, Jan. 4, 1984; 57 FR 2033, Jan. 17, 1992; 61 FR 42803, Aug. 19, 1996; 62 FR 53186, Oct. 10, 1997; 65 FR 54664, Sept. 8, 2000; 65 FR 57053, Sept. 20, 2000; 65 FR 78958, Dec. 18, 2000; 68 FR 38627, June 30, 2003; 69 FR 56538, Sept. 21, 2004; 70 FR 3889, Jan. 27, 2005; 70 FR 30365, May 26, 2005; 70 FR 54266, Sept. 14, 2005; 70 FR 56128, Sept. 26, 2005; 74 FR 52688, Oct. 14, 2009; 77 FR 48816, Sept. 16, 2012; 78 FR 62396, Dec. 18, 2013.

§1.53. APPLICATION NUMBER, FILING DATE, & COMPLETION OF APPLICATION

(a) Application number. Any papers received in the Patent and Trademark Office which purport to be an application for a patent will be assigned an application number for identification purposes.

(b) Application filing requirements—Nonprovisional application. The filing date of an application for patent filed under this section, other than an application for a design patent or a provisional application under paragraph (c) of this section, is the date on which a specification, with or without claims, is received in the Office. The filing date of an application for a design patent filed under this section, except for a continued prosecution application under paragraph (d) of this section, is the date on which the specification as prescribed by 35 U.S.C. 112, including at least one claim, and any required drawings are received in the Office. No new matter may be introduced into an application after its filing date. A continuing application, which may be a continuation, divisional, or continuation-in-part application, may be filed under the conditions specified in 35 U.S.C. 120, 121, 365(c), or 386(c) and §1.78.

(1) A continuation or divisional application that names as inventors the same or fewer than all of the inventors named in the prior application may be filed under this paragraph or paragraph (d) of this section.

(2) A continuation-in-part application (which may disclose and claim subject matter not disclosed in the prior application) or a continuation or divisional application naming an inventor not named in the prior application must be filed under this paragraph.

(c) Application filing requirements—Provisional application. The filing date of a provisional application is the date on which a specification, with or without claims, is received in the Office. No amendment, other than to make the provisional application comply with the patent statute and all applicable regulations, may be made to the provisional application after the filing date of the provisional application.

(1) A provisional application must also include the cover sheet required by §1.51(c)(1), which may be an application data sheet (§1.76), or a cover letter identifying the application as a provisional application. Otherwise, the application will be treated as an application filed under paragraph (b) of this section.

(2) An application for patent filed under paragraph (b) of this section may be converted to a provisional application and be accorded the original filing date of the application filed under paragraph (b) of this section. The grant of such a request for conversion will not entitle applicant to a refund of the fees that were properly paid in the application filed under paragraph (b) of this section. Such a request for conversion must be accompanied by the processing fee set forth in §1.17(q) and be filed prior to the earliest of:

(i) Abandonment of the application filed under paragraph (b) of this section;

(ii) Payment of the issue fee on the application filed under paragraph (b) of this section; or

(iii) Expiration of twelve months after the filing date of the application filed under paragraph (b) of this section.

(3) A provisional application filed under paragraph (c) of this section may be converted to a nonprovisional application filed under paragraph (b) of this section and accorded the original filing date of the provisional application. The conversion of a provisional application to a nonprovisional application will not result in either the refund of any fee properly paid in the provisional application or the application of any such fee to the filing fee, or any other fee, for the nonprovisional application. Conversion of a provisional application to a nonprovisional application under this paragraph will result in the term of any patent to issue from the application being measured from at least the filing date of the provisional application for which conversion is requested. Thus, applicants should consider avoiding this adverse patent term impact by filing a nonprovisional application claiming the benefit of the provisional application under 35 U.S.C. 119(e), rather than converting the provisional application into a nonprovisional application pursuant to this paragraph. A request to convert a provisional application to a nonprovisional application must be accompanied by the fee set forth in §1.17(i) and an amendment including at least one claim as prescribed by 35 U.S.C. 112(b), unless the provisional application under paragraph (c) of this section otherwise contains at least one claim as prescribed by 35 U.S.C. 112(b). The nonprovisional application resulting from conversion of a provisional application must also include the filing fee, search fee, and examination fee for a nonprovisional application, and the surcharge required by §1.16(f) if either the basic filing fee for a nonprovisional application or the inventor's oath or declaration was not present on the filing date accorded the resulting nonprovisional application (i.e., the filing date of the original provisional application). A request to convert a provisional application to a nonprovisional application must also be filed prior to the earliest of:

(i) Abandonment of the provisional application filed under paragraph (c) of this section; or

(ii) Expiration of twelve months after the filing date of the provisional application filed under paragraph (c) of this section.

(4) A provisional application is not entitled to the right of priority under 35 U.S.C. 119, 365(a), or 386(a) or §1.55, or to the benefit of an earlier filing date under 35 U.S.C. 120, 121, 365(c), or 386(c) or §1.78 of any other application. No claim for priority under 35 U.S.C. 119(e) or §1.78(a) may be made in a design application based on a provisional application. The requirements of §§1.821 through 1.825 regarding application disclosures containing nucleotide and/or amino acid sequences are not mandatory for provisional applications.

(d) Application filing requirements—Continued prosecution (nonprovisional) application.

(1) A continuation or divisional application (but not a continuation-in-part) of a prior nonprovisional application may be filed as a continued prosecution application under this paragraph, provided that:

(i) The application is for a design patent;

(ii) The prior nonprovisional application is a design application, but not an international design application, that is complete as defined by §1.51(b), except for the inventor's oath or declaration if the application is filed on or after September 16, 2012, and the prior nonprovisional application contains an application data sheet meeting the conditions specified in §1.53(f)(3)(i); and

(iii) The application under this paragraph is filed before the earliest of:

(A) Payment of the issue fee on the prior application, unless a petition under §1.313(c) is granted in the prior application;

(B) Abandonment of the prior application; or

(C) Termination of proceedings on the prior application.

(2) The filing date of a continued prosecution application is the date on which a request on a separate paper for an application under this paragraph is filed. An application filed under this paragraph:

(i) Must identify the prior application;

(ii) Discloses and claims only subject matter disclosed in the prior application;

(iii) Names as inventors the same inventors named in the prior application on the date the application under this paragraph was filed, except as provided in paragraph (d)(4) of this section;

(iv) Includes the request for an application under this paragraph, will utilize the file jacket and contents of the prior application, including the specification, drawings and the inventor's oath or declaration from the prior application, to constitute the new application, and will be assigned the application number of the prior application for identification purposes; and

(v) Is a request to expressly abandon the prior application as of the filing date of the request for an application under this paragraph.

(3) The filing fee, search fee, and examination fee for a continued prosecution application filed under this paragraph are the basic filing fee as set forth in §1.16(b), the search fee as set forth in §1.16(*l*), and the examination fee as set forth in §1.16(p).

(4) An application filed under this paragraph may be filed by fewer than all the inventors named in the prior application, provided that the request for an application under this paragraph when filed is accompanied by a statement requesting deletion of the name or names of the person or persons who are not inventors of the invention being claimed in the new application. No person may be named as an inventor in an application filed under this paragraph who was not named as an inventor in the prior application on the date the application under this paragraph was filed, except by way of correction of inventorship under §1.48.

(5) Any new change must be made in the form of an amendment to the prior application as it existed prior to the filing of an application under this paragraph. No amendment in an application under this paragraph (a continued prosecution application) may introduce new matter or matter that would have been new matter in the prior application. Any new specification filed with the request for an application under this paragraph will not be considered part of the original application papers, but will be treated as a substitute specification in accordance with §1.125.

(6) The filing of a continued prosecution application under this paragraph will be construed to include a waiver of confidentiality by the applicant under 35 U.S.C. 122 to the extent that any member of the public, who is entitled under the provisions of §1.14 to access to, copies of, or information concerning either the prior application or any continuing application filed under the provisions of this paragraph, may be given similar access to, copies of, or similar information concerning the other application or applications in the file jacket.

(7) A request for an application under this paragraph is the specific reference required by 35 U.S.C. 120 to every application assigned the application number identified in such request. No amendment in an application under this paragraph may delete this specific reference to any prior application.

(8) In addition to identifying the application number of the prior application, applicant should furnish in the request for an application under this paragraph the following information relating to the prior application to the best of his or her ability:

(i) Title of invention;

(ii) Name of applicant(s); and

(iii) Correspondence address.

(9) See §1.103(b) for requesting a limited suspension of action in an application filed under this paragraph.

(e) Failure to meet filing date requirements.

(1) If an application deposited under paragraph (b), (c), or (d) of this section does not meet the requirements of such paragraph to be entitled to a filing date, applicant will be so notified, if a correspondence address has been provided, and given a period of time within which to correct the filing error. If, however, a request for an application under paragraph (d) of this section does not meet the requirements of that paragraph because the application in which the request was filed is not a design application, and if the application in which the request was filed was itself filed on or after June 8, 1995, the request for an application under paragraph (d) of this section will be treated as a request for continued examination under §1.114.

(2) Any request for review of a notification pursuant to paragraph (e)(1) of this section, or a notification that the original application papers lack a portion of the specification or drawing(s), must be by way of a petition pursuant to this paragraph accompanied by the fee set forth in §1.17(f). In the absence of a timely (§1.181(f)) petition pursuant to this paragraph, the filing date of an application in which the applicant was notified of a filing error pursuant to paragraph (e)(1) of this section will be the date the filing error is corrected.

(3) If an applicant is notified of a filing error pursuant to paragraph (e)(1) of this section, but fails to correct the filing error within the given time period or otherwise timely (§1.181(f)) take action pursuant to this paragraph, proceedings in the application will be considered terminated. Where proceedings in an application are terminated pursuant to this paragraph, the application may be disposed of, and any filing fees, less the handling fee set forth in §1.21(n), will be refunded.

(f) Completion of application subsequent to filing—Nonprovisional (including continued prosecution or reissue) application.

(1) If an application which has been accorded a filing date pursuant to paragraph (b) or (d) of this section does not include the basic filing fee, search fee, or examination fee, or if an application which has been accorded a filing date pursuant to paragraph (b) of this section does not include at least one claim or the inventor's oath or declaration (§§1.63, 1.64, 1.162, or 1.175), and the applicant has provided a correspondence address (§1.33(a)), the applicant will be notified and given a period of time within which to file a claim or claims, pay the basic filing fee, search fee, and examination fee, and pay the surcharge if required by §1.16(f), to avoid abandonment.

(2) If an application which has been accorded a filing date pursuant to paragraph (b) of this section does not include the basic filing fee, search fee, examination fee, at least one claim, or the inventor's oath or declaration, and the applicant has not provided a correspondence address (§1.33(a)), the applicant has three months from the filing date of the application within which to file a claim or claims, pay the basic filing fee, search fee, and examination fee, and pay the surcharge required by §1.16(f), to avoid abandonment.

(3) The inventor's oath or declaration in an application under §1.53(b) must also be filed within the period specified in paragraph (f)(1) or (f)(2) of this section, except that the filing of the inventor's oath or declaration may be postponed until the application is otherwise in condition for allowance under the conditions specified in paragraphs (f)(3)(i) and (f)(3)(ii) of this section.

(i) The application must be an original (non-reissue) application that contains an application data sheet in accordance with §1.76 identifying:

(A) Each inventor by his or her legal name;

(B) A mailing address where the inventor customarily receives mail, and residence, if an inventor lives at a location which is different from where the inventor customarily receives mail, for each inventor.

(ii) The applicant must file each required oath or declaration in compliance with §1.63, or substitute statement in compliance with §1.64, no later than the date on which the issue fee for the patent is paid. If the applicant is notified in a notice of allowability that an oath or declaration in compliance with §1.63, or substitute statement in compliance with §1.64, executed by or with respect to each named inventor has not been filed, the applicant must file each required oath or declaration in compliance with §1.63, or substitute statement in compliance with §1.64, no later than the date on which the issue fee is paid to avoid abandonment. This time period is not extendable under §1.136 (see §1.136(c)). The Office may dispense with the notice provided for in paragraph (f)(1) of this section if each required oath or declaration in compliance with §1.63, or substitute statement in compliance with §1.64, has been filed before the application is in condition for allowance.

(4) If the excess claims fees required by §1.16(h) and (i) and multiple dependent claim fee required by §1.16(j) are not paid on filing or on later presentation of the claims for which the excess claims or multiple dependent claim fees are due, the fees required by §1.16(h), (i), and (j) must be paid or the claims canceled by amendment prior to the expiration of the time period set for reply by the Office in any notice of fee deficiency. If the application size fee required by §1.16(s) (if any) is not paid on filing or on later presentation of the amendment necessitating a fee or additional fee under §1.16(s), the fee required by §1.16(s) must be paid prior to the expiration of the time period set for reply by the Office in any notice of fee deficiency in order to avoid abandonment.

(5) This paragraph applies to continuation or divisional applications under paragraphs (b) or (d) of this section and to continuation-in-part applications under paragraph (b) of this section. See §1.63(d) concerning the submission of a copy of the inventor's oath or declaration from the prior application for a continuing application under paragraph (b) of this section.

(6) If applicant does not pay the basic filing fee during the pendency of the application, the Office may dispose of the application.

(g) Completion of application subsequent to filing—Provisional application.

(1) If a provisional application which has been accorded a filing date pursuant to paragraph (c) of this section does not include the cover sheet required by §1.51(c)(1) or the basic filing fee (§1.16(d)), and applicant has provided a correspondence address (§1.33(a)), applicant will be notified and given a period of time within which to pay the basic filing fee, file a cover sheet (§1.51(c)(1)), and pay the surcharge required by §1.16(g) to avoid abandonment.

(2) If a provisional application which has been accorded a filing date pursuant to paragraph (c) of this section does not include the cover sheet required by §1.51(c)(1) or the basic filing fee (§1.16(d)), and applicant has not provided a correspondence address (§1.33(a)), applicant has two months from the filing date of the application within which to pay the basic filing fee, file a cover sheet (§1.51(c)(1)), and pay the surcharge required by §1.16(g) to avoid abandonment.

(3) If the application size fee required by §1.16(s) (if any) is not paid on filing, the fee required by §1.16(s) must be paid prior to the expiration of the time period set for reply by the Office in any notice of fee deficiency in order to avoid abandonment.

(4) If applicant does not pay the basic filing fee during the pendency of the application, the Office may dispose of the application.

(h) Subsequent treatment of application—Nonprovisional (including continued prosecution) application. An application for a patent filed under paragraphs (b) or (d) of this section will not be placed on the files for examination until all its required parts, complying with the rules relating thereto, are received, except that the inventor's oath or declaration may be filed when the application is otherwise in condition for allowance pursuant to paragraph (f)(3) of this section and minor informalities may be waived subject to subsequent correction whenever required.

(i) Subsequent treatment of application—Provisional application. A provisional application for a patent filed under paragraph (c) of this section will not be placed on the files for examination and will become abandoned no later than twelve months after its filing date pursuant to 35 U.S.C. 111(b)(1).

History of 37 C.F.R. §1.53: 24 FR 10332, Dec. 22, 1959; 48 FR 2709, Jan. 20, 1983; 49 FR 554, Jan. 4, 1984; 50 FR 31826, Aug. 6, 1985; 53 FR 47808, Nov. 28, 1988; 54 FR 47518, Nov. 15, 1989; 60 FR 20223, Apr. 25, 1995; 62 FR 53186, Oct. 10, 1997; 63 FR 5734, Feb. 4, 1998; 63 FR 36185, July 2, 1998; 65 FR 14871, Mar. 20, 2000; 65 FR 50103, Aug. 16, 2000; 65 FR 50104, Aug. 16, 2000; 65 FR 54665,

Sept. 8, 2000; 65 FR 78960, Dec. 18, 2000; 68 FR 14336, Mar. 25, 2003; 68 FR 32380, May 30, 2003; 69 FR 29878, May 26, 2004; 69 FR 56539, Sept. 21, 2004; 70 FR 3890, Jan. 27, 2005; 70 FR 30365, May 26, 2005; 74 FR 52688, Oct. 14, 2009; 77 FR 48817, Sept. 16, 2012; 78 FR 11053, Mar. 16, 2013; 78 FR 62398, Dec. 18, 2013; 79 FR 12386, Mar. 5, 2014; 79 FR 68121, Nov. 14, 2014; 80 FR 17956, May 13, 2015.

§1.54. PARTS OF APPLICATION TO BE FILED TOGETHER; FILING RECEIPT

(a) It is desirable that all parts of the complete application be deposited in the Office together; otherwise, a letter must accompany each part, accurately and clearly connecting it with the other parts of the application. See §1.53(f) and (g) with regard to completion of an application.

(b) Applicant will be informed of the application number and filing date by a filing receipt, unless the application is an application filed under §1.53(d). A letter limited to a request for a filing receipt may be signed by a juristic applicant or patent owner.

History of 37 C.F.R. §1.54: 24 FR 10332, Dec. 22, 1959; 48 FR 2710, Jan. 20, 1983; 61 FR 42803, Aug. 19, 1996; 62 FR 53188, Oct. 10, 1997; 78 FR 62399, Dec. 18, 2013.

§1.55. CLAIM FOR FOREIGN PRIORITY

(a) In general. An applicant in a nonprovisional application may claim priority to one or more prior foreign applications under the conditions specified in 35 U.S.C. 119(a) through (d) and (f), 172, 365(a) and (b), and 386(a) and (b) and this section.

(b) Time for filing subsequent application. The nonprovisional application must be:

(1) Filed not later than twelve months (six months in the case of a design application) after the date on which the foreign application was filed, subject to paragraph (c) of this section (a subsequent application); or

(2) Entitled to claim the benefit under 35 U.S.C. 120, 121, 365(c), or 386(c) of a subsequent application that was filed within the period set forth in paragraph (b)(1) of this section.

(c) Delayed filing of subsequent application. If the subsequent application has a filing date which is after the expiration of the period set forth in paragraph (b)(1) of this section, but within two months from the expiration of the period set forth in paragraph (b)(1) of this section, the right of priority in the subsequent application may be restored under PCT Rule 26*bis*.3 for an international application, or upon petition pursuant to this paragraph, if the delay in filing the subsequent application within the period set forth in paragraph (b)(1) of this section was unintentional. A petition to restore the right of priority under this paragraph filed on or after May 13, 2015, must be filed in the subsequent application, or in the earliest nonprovisional application claiming benefit under 35 U.S.C. 120, 121, 365(c), or 386(c) to the subsequent application, if such subsequent application is not a nonprovisional application. Any petition to restore the right of priority under this paragraph must include:

(1) The priority claim under 35 U.S.C. 119(a) through (d) or (f), 365(a) or (b), or 386(a) or (b) in an application data sheet (§1.76(b)(6)), identifying the foreign application to which priority is claimed, by specifying the application number, country (or intellectual property authority), day, month, and year of its filing, unless previously submitted;

(2) The petition fee as set forth in §1.17(m); and

(3) A statement that the delay in filing the subsequent application within the period set forth in paragraph (b)(1) of this section was unintentional. The Director may require additional information where there is a question whether the delay was unintentional.

(d) Time for filing priority claim—

(1) Application under 35 U.S.C. 111(a). The claim for priority must be filed within the later of four months from the actual filing date of the application or sixteen months from the filing date of the prior foreign application in an original application filed under 35 U.S.C. 111(a), except as provided in paragraph (e) of this section. The claim for priority must be presented in an application data sheet (§1.76(b)(6)) and must identify the foreign application to which priority is claimed by specifying the application number, country (or intellectual property authority), day, month, and year of its filing. The time periods in this paragraph do not apply if the later-filed application is:

(i) An application for a design patent; or

(ii) An application filed under 35 U.S.C. 111(a) before November 29, 2000.

(2) Application under 35 U.S.C. 371. The claim for priority must be made within the time limit set forth in the PCT and the Regulations under the PCT in an international application entering the national stage under 35 U.S.C. 371, except as provided in paragraph (e) of this section.

(e) Delayed priority claim. Unless such claim is accepted in accordance with the provisions of this paragraph, any claim for priority under 35 U.S.C. 119(a) through (d) or (f), 365(a) or (b), or 386(a) or 386(b) not presented in the manner required by paragraph (d) or (m) of this section during pendency and within the time period provided by paragraph (d) of this section (if applicable) is considered to have been waived. If a claim for priority is considered to have been waived under this section, the claim may be accepted if the priority claim was unintentionally delayed. A petition to accept a delayed claim for priority under 35 U.S.C. 119(a) through (d) or (f), 365(a) or (b), or 386(a) or 386(b) must be accompanied by:

(1) The priority claim under 35 U.S.C. 119(a) through (d) or (f), 365(a) or (b), or 386(a) or 386(b) in an application data sheet (§1.76(b)(6)), identifying the foreign application to which priority is claimed, by specifying the application number, country (or intellectual property authority), day, month, and year of its filing, unless previously submitted;

(2) A certified copy of the foreign application, unless previously submitted or an exception in paragraph (h), (i), or (j) of this section applies;

(3) The petition fee as set forth in §1.17(m); and

(4) A statement that the entire delay between the date the priority claim was due under this section and the date the priority claim was filed was unintentional. The Director may require additional information where there is a question whether the delay was unintentional.

(f) Time for filing certified copy of foreign application—

(1) Application under 35 U.S.C. 111(a). A certified copy of the foreign application must be filed within the later of four months from the actual filing date of the application, or sixteen months from the filing date of the prior foreign application, in an original application under 35 U.S.C. 111(a) filed on or after March 16, 2013, except as provided in paragraphs (h), (i), and (j) of this section. The time period in this paragraph does not apply in a design application.

(2) Application under 35 U.S.C. 371. A certified copy of the foreign application must be filed within the time limit set forth in the PCT and the Regulations under the PCT in an international application entering the national stage under 35 U.S.C. 371. If a certified copy of the foreign application is not filed during the international stage in an international application in which the national stage commenced on or after December 18, 2013, a certified copy of the foreign application must be filed within the later of four months from the date on which the national stage commenced under 35 U.S.C. 371(b) or (f) (§1.491(a)), four months from the date of the initial submission under 35 U.S.C. 371 to enter the national stage, or sixteen months from the filing date of the prior foreign application, except as provided in paragraphs (h), (i), and (j) of this section.

(3) If a certified copy of the foreign application is not filed within the time period specified[1] paragraph (f)(1) of this section in an application under 35 U.S.C. 111(a) or within the period specified in paragraph (f)(2) of this section in an international application entering the national stage under 35 U.S.C. 371, and an exception in paragraph (h), (i), or (j) of this section is not applicable, the certified copy of the foreign application must be accompanied by a petition including a showing of good and sufficient cause for the delay and the petition fee set forth in §1.17(g).

(g) Requirement for filing priority claim, certified copy of foreign application, and translation in any application.

(1) The claim for priority and the certified copy of the foreign application specified in 35 U.S.C. 119(b) or PCT Rule 17 must, in any event, be filed within the pendency of the application, unless filed with a petition under paragraph (e) or (f) of this section, or with a petition accompanied by the fee set forth in §1.17(g) which includes a showing of good and sufficient cause for the delay in filing the certified copy of the foreign application in a design application. If the claim for priority or the certified copy of the foreign application is filed after the date the issue fee is paid, the patent will not include the priority claim unless corrected by a certificate of correction under 35 U.S.C. 255 and §1.323.

(2) The Office may require that the claim for priority and the certified copy of the foreign application be filed earlier than otherwise provided in this section:

(i) When the application is involved in an interference (see §41.202 of this chapter) or derivation (see part 42 of this chapter) proceeding;

(ii) When necessary to overcome the date of a reference relied upon by the examiner; or

(iii) When deemed necessary by the examiner.

(3) An English language translation of a non-English language foreign application is not required except:

(i) When the application is involved in an interference (see §41.202 of this chapter) or derivation (see part 42 of this chapter) proceeding;

(ii) When necessary to overcome the date of a reference relied upon by the examiner; or

(iii) When specifically required by the examiner.

(4) If an English language translation of a non-English language foreign application is required, it must be filed together with a statement that the translation of the certified copy is accurate.

(h) Certified copy in another U.S. patent or application. The requirement in paragraphs (f) and (g) of this section for a certified copy of the foreign application will be considered satisfied in a reissue application if the patent for which reissue is sought satisfies the requirement of this section for a certified copy of the foreign application and such patent is identified as containing a certified copy of the foreign application. The requirement in paragraphs (f) and (g) of this section for a certified copy of the foreign application will also be considered satisfied in an application if a prior-filed nonprovisional application for which a benefit is claimed under 35 U.S.C. 120, 121, 365(c), or 386(c) contains a certified copy of the foreign application and such prior-filed nonprovisional application is identified as containing a certified copy of the foreign application.

(i) Foreign intellectual property office participating in a priority document exchange agreement. The requirement in paragraphs (f) and (g) of this section for a certified copy of the foreign application to be filed within the time limit set forth therein will be considered satisfied if:

(1) The foreign application was filed in a foreign intellectual property office participating with the Office in a bilateral or multilateral priority document exchange agreement (participating foreign intellectual property office), or a copy of the foreign application was filed in an application subsequently filed in a participating foreign intellectual property office that permits the Office to obtain such a copy;

(2) The claim for priority is presented in an application data sheet (§1.76(b)(6)), identifying the foreign application for which priority is claimed, by specifying the application number, country (or intellectual property authority), day, month, and year of its filing, and the applicant provides the information necessary for the participating foreign intellectual property office to provide the Office with access to the foreign application;

(3) The copy of the foreign application is received by the Office from the participating foreign intellectual property office, or a certified copy of the foreign application is filed, within the period specified in paragraph (g)(1) of this section; and

(4) The applicant files in a separate document a request that the Office obtain a copy of the foreign application from a participating intellectual property office that permits the Office to obtain such a copy where, although the foreign application was not filed in a participating foreign intellectual property office, a copy of the foreign application was filed in an application subsequently filed in a participating foreign intellectual property office that permits the Office to obtain such a copy. The request must identify the participating intellectual property office and the subsequent application by the application number, day, month, and year of its filing in which a copy of the foreign application was filed. The request must be filed within the later of sixteen months from the filing date of the prior foreign application, four months from the actual filing date of an application under 35 U.S.C. 111(a), four months from the date on which the national stage commenced under 35 U.S.C. 371(b) or (f) (§1.491(a)), or four months from the date of the initial submission under 35 U.S.C. 371 to enter the national stage, or the request must be accompanied by a petition under paragraph (e) or (f) of this section.

(j) Interim copy. The requirement in paragraph (f) of this section for a certified copy of the foreign application to be filed within the time limit set forth therein will be considered satisfied if:

(1) A copy of the original foreign application clearly labeled as "Interim Copy," including the specification, and any drawings or claims upon which it is based, is filed in the Office together with a separate cover sheet identifying the foreign application by specifying the application number, country (or intellectual property authority), day, month, and year of its filing, and stating that the copy filed in the Office is a true copy of the original application as filed in the foreign country (or intellectual property authority);

(2) The copy of the foreign application and separate cover sheet are filed within the later of sixteen months from the filing date of the prior foreign application, four months from the actual filing date of an application under 35 U.S.C. 111(a), four months from the date on which the national stage commenced under 35 U.S.C. 371(b) or (f) (§1.491(a)), four months from the date of the initial submission under 35 U.S.C. 371 to enter the national stage, or with a petition under paragraph (e) or (f) of this section; and

(3) A certified copy of the foreign application is filed within the period specified in paragraph (g)(1) of this section.

(k) Requirements for certain applications filed on or after March 16, 2013. If a nonprovisional application filed on or after March 16, 2013, other than a nonprovisional international design application, claims priority to a foreign application filed prior to March 16, 2013, and also contains, or contained at any time, a claim to a claimed invention that has an effective filing date as defined in §1.109 that is on or after March 16, 2013, the applicant must provide a statement to that effect within the later of four months from the actual filing date of the nonprovisional application, four months from the date of entry into the national stage as set forth in §1.491 in an international application, sixteen months from the filing date of the prior foreign application, or the date that a first claim to a claimed invention that has an effective filing date on or after March 16, 2013, is presented in the nonprovisional application. An applicant is not required to provide such a statement if the applicant reasonably believes on the basis of information already known to the individuals designated in §1.56(c) that the nonprovisional application does not, and did not at any time, contain a claim to a claimed invention that has an effective filing date on or after March 16, 2013.

(*l*) Inventor's certificates. An applicant in a nonprovisional application may under certain circumstances claim priority on the basis of one or more applications for an inventor's certificate in a country granting both inventor's certificates and patents. To claim the right of priority on the basis of an application for an inventor's certificate in such a country under 35 U.S.C. 119(d), the applicant, when submitting a claim for such right as specified in this section, must include an affidavit or declaration. The affidavit or declaration must include a specific statement that, upon an investigation, he or she is satisfied that to the best of his or her knowledge, the applicant, when filing the application for the inventor's certificate, had the option to file an application for either a patent or an inventor's certificate as to the subject matter of the identified claim or claims forming the basis for the claim of priority.

(m) Time for filing priority claim and certified copy of foreign application in an international design application designating the United States. In an international design application designating the United States, the claim for priority may be made in accordance with the Hague Agreement and the Hague Agreement Regulations. In a nonprovisional international design application, the priority claim, unless made in accordance with the Hague Agreement and the Hague Agreement Regulations, must be presented in an application data sheet (§1.76(b)(6)), identifying the foreign application for which priority is claimed, by specifying the application number, country (or intellectual property authority), day, month, and year of its filing. In a nonprovisional international design application, the priority claim and certified copy must be furnished in accordance with the time period and other conditions set forth in paragraph (g) of this section.

(n) Applications filed before September 16, 2012. Notwithstanding the requirement in paragraphs (d)(1), (e)(1), and (i)(2) of this section that any priority claim be presented in an application data sheet (§1.76), this requirement in paragraphs (d)(1), (e)(1), and (i)(2) of this section will be satisfied by the presentation of such priority claim in the oath or declaration under §1.63 in a nonprovisional application filed under 35 U.S.C. 111(a) before September 16, 2012, or resulting from an international application filed under 35 U.S.C. 363 before September 16, 2012. The provisions of this paragraph do not apply to any priority claim submitted for a petition under paragraph (c) of this section to restore the right of priority to a foreign application.

(o) Priority under 35 U.S.C. 386(a) or (b). The right of priority under 35 U.S.C. 386(a) or (b) with respect to an international design application is applicable only to nonprovisional applications, international applications, and international design applications filed on or after May 13, 2015, and patents issuing thereon.

(p) Time periods in this section. The time periods set forth in this section are not extendable, but are subject to 35 U.S.C. 21(b) (and §1.7(a)), PCT Rule 80.5, and Hague Agreement Rule 4(4).

1. **Editor's note:** Probably should be "specified in."

History of 37 C.F.R. §1.55: 24 FR 10332, Dec. 22, 1959; 34 FR 12629, Aug. 2, 1969; 34 FR 18857, Nov. 26, 1969; 38 FR 9297, Apr. 13, 1973; 43 FR 20463, May 11, 1978; 48 FR 2710, Jan. 20, 1983; 49 FR 554, Jan. 4, 1984; 49 FR 48452, Dec. 12, 1984; 54 FR 6902, Feb. 15, 1989; 54 FR 9432, Mar. 7, 1989; 54 FR 47518, Nov. 15, 1989; 58 FR 54509, Oct. 22, 1993; 60 FR 20224, Apr. 25, 1995; 62 FR 53188, Oct. 10, 1997; 65 FR 54666, Sept. 8, 2000; 65 FR 57053, Sept. 20, 2000; 65 FR 66502, Nov. 6, 2000; 66 FR 67094, Dec. 28, 2001; 69 FR 49998, Aug. 12, 2004; 72 FR 1668, Jan. 16, 2007; 77 FR 48818, Sept. 16, 2012; 78 FR 11053, Mar. 16, 2013; 78 FR 16182, Mar. 16, 2013; 78 FR 62399, Dec. 18, 2013; 80 FR 17956, May 13, 2015.

§1.56. DUTY TO DISCLOSE INFORMATION MATERIAL TO PATENTABILITY

(a) A patent by its very nature is affected with a public interest. The public interest is best served, and the most effective patent examination occurs when, at the time an application is being examined, the Office is aware of and evaluates the teachings of all information material to patentability. Each individual associated with the filing and prosecution of a patent application has a duty of candor and good faith in dealing with the Office, which includes a duty to disclose to the Office all information known to that individual to be material to patentability as defined in this section. The duty to disclose information exists with respect to each pending claim until the claim is cancelled or withdrawn from consideration, or the application becomes abandoned. Information material to the patentability of a claim that is cancelled or withdrawn from consideration need not be submitted if the information is not material to the patentability of any claim remaining under consideration in the application. There is no duty to submit information which is not material to the patentability of any existing claim. The duty to disclose all information known to be material to patentability is deemed to be satisfied if all information known to be material to patentability of any claim issued in a patent was cited by the Office or submitted to the Office in the manner prescribed by §§1.97(b)-(d) and 1.98. However, no patent will be granted on an application in connection with which fraud on the Office was practiced or attempted or the duty of disclosure was violated through bad faith or intentional misconduct. The Office encourages applicants to carefully examine:

(1) Prior art cited in search reports of a foreign patent office in a counterpart application, and

(2) The closest information over which individuals associated with the filing or prosecution of a patent application believe any pending claim patentably defines, to make sure that any material information contained therein is disclosed to the Office.

(b) Under this section, information is material to patentability when it is not cumulative to information already of record or being made of record in the application, and

(1) It establishes, by itself or in combination with other information, a prima facie case of unpatentability of a claim; or

(2) It refutes, or is inconsistent with, a position the applicant takes in:

(i) Opposing an argument of unpatentability relied on by the Office, or

(ii) Asserting an argument of patentability.

A prima facie case of unpatentability is established when the information compels a conclusion that a claim is unpatentable under the preponderance of evidence, burden-of-proof standard, giving each term in the claim its broadest reasonable construction consistent with the specification, and before any consideration is given to evidence which may be submitted in an attempt to establish a contrary conclusion of patentability.

(c) Individuals associated with the filing or prosecution of a patent application within the meaning of this section are:

(1) Each inventor named in the application;

(2) Each attorney or agent who prepares or prosecutes the application; and

(3) Every other person who is substantively involved in the preparation or prosecution of the application and who is associated with the inventor, the applicant, an assignee, or anyone to whom there is an obligation to assign the application.

(d) Individuals other than the attorney, agent or inventor may comply with this section by disclosing information to the attorney, agent, or inventor.

(e) In any continuation-in-part application, the duty under this section includes the duty to disclose to the Office all information known to the person to be material to patentability, as defined in paragraph (b) of this section, which became available between the filing date of the prior application and the national or PCT international filing date of the continuation-in-part application.

History of 37 C.F.R. §1.56: 42 FR 5593, Jan. 28, 1977; 47 FR 21751, May 19, 1982; 48 FR 2710, Jan. 20, 1983; 49 FR 554, Jan. 4, 1984; 50 FR 5171, Feb. 6, 1985; 53 FR 47808, Nov. 28, 1988; 57 FR 2034, Jan. 17, 1992; 65 FR 54666, Sept. 8, 2000; 77 FR 48818, Sept. 16, 2012.

§1.57. INCORPORATION BY REFERENCE

(a) Subject to the conditions and requirements of this paragraph, a reference made in the English language in an application data sheet in accordance with §1.76 upon the filing of an application under 35 U.S.C. 111(a) to a previously filed application, indicating that the specification and any drawings of the application under 35 U.S.C. 111(a) are replaced by the reference to the previously filed application, and specifying the previously filed application by application number, filing date, and the intellectual property authority or country in which the previously filed application was filed, shall constitute the specification and any drawings of the application under 35 U.S.C. 111(a) for purposes of a filing date under §1.53(b).

(1) If the applicant has provided a correspondence address (§1.33(a)), the applicant will be notified and given a period of time within which to file a copy of the specification and drawings from the previously filed application, an English language translation of the previously filed application, and the fee required by §1.17(i) if it is in a language other than English, and pay the surcharge required by §1.16(f), to avoid abandonment. Such a notice may be combined with a notice under §1.53(f).

(2) If the applicant has not provided a correspondence address (§1.33(a)), the applicant has three months from the filing date of the application to file a copy of the specification and drawings from the previously filed application, an English language translation of the previously filed application, and the fee required by §1.17(i) if it is in a language other than English, and pay the surcharge required by §1.16(f), to avoid abandonment.

(3) An application abandoned under paragraph (a)(1) or (a)(2) of this section shall be treated as having never been filed, unless:

(i) The application is revived under §1.137; and

(ii) A copy of the specification and any drawings of the previously filed application are filed in the Office.

(4) A certified copy of the previously filed application must be filed in the Office, unless the previously filed application is an application filed under 35 U.S.C. 111 or 363, or the previously filed application is a foreign priority application and the conditions set forth in §1.55(i) are satisfied with respect to such foreign priority application. The certified copy of the previously filed application, if required by this paragraph, must be filed within the later of four months from the filing date of the application or sixteen months from the filing date of the previously filed application, or be accompanied by a petition including a showing of good and sufficient cause for the delay and the petition fee set forth in §1.17(g).

(b) Subject to the conditions and requirements of this paragraph, if all or a portion of the specification or drawing(s) is inadvertently omitted from an application, but the application contains a claim under §1.55 for priority of a prior-filed foreign application or a claim under §1.78 for the benefit of a prior-filed provisional, nonprovisional, international application, or international design application, that was present on the filing date of the application, and the inadvertently omitted portion of the specification or drawing(s) is completely contained in the prior-filed application, the claim under §1.55 or 1.78 shall also be considered an incorporation by reference of the prior-filed application as to the inadvertently omitted portion of the specification or drawing(s).

(1) The application must be amended to include the inadvertently omitted portion of the specification or drawing(s) within any time period set by the Office, but in no case later than the close of prosecution as defined by §1.114(b), or abandonment of the application, whichever occurs earlier. The applicant is also required to:

(i) Supply a copy of the prior-filed application, except where the prior-filed application is an application filed under 35 U.S.C. 111;

(ii) Supply an English language translation of any prior-filed application that is in a language other than English; and

(iii) Identify where the inadvertently omitted portion of the specification or drawings can be found in the prior-filed application.

(2) Any amendment to an international application pursuant to paragraph (b)(1) of this section shall be effective only as to the United States, and shall have no effect on the international filing date of the application. In addition, no request under this section to add the inadvertently omitted portion of the specification or drawings in an international application designating the United States will be acted upon by the Office prior to the entry and commencement of the national stage (§1.491) or the filing of an application under 35 U.S.C. 111(a) which claims benefit of the international application. Any omitted portion of the international application which applicant desires to be effective as to all designated States, subject to PCT Rule 20.8(b), must be submitted in accordance with PCT Rule 20.

(3) If an application is not otherwise entitled to a filing date under §1.53(b), the amendment must be by way of a petition pursuant to §1.53(e) accompanied by the fee set forth in §1.17(f).

(4) Any amendment to an international design application pursuant to paragraph (b)(1) of this section shall be effective only as to the United States and shall have no effect on the filing date of the application. In addition, no request under this section to add the inadvertently omitted portion of the specification or drawings in an international design application will be acted upon by the Office prior to the international design application becoming a nonprovisional application.

(c) Except as provided in paragraph (a) or (b) of this section, an incorporation by reference must be set forth in the specification and must:

(1) Express a clear intent to incorporate by reference by using the root words "incorporat(e)" and "reference" (e.g., "incorporate by reference"); and

(2) Clearly identify the referenced patent, application, or publication.

(d) "Essential material" may be incorporated by reference, but only by way of an incorporation by reference to a U.S. patent or U.S. patent application publication, which patent or patent application publication does not itself incorporate such essential material by reference. "Essential material" is material that is necessary to:

(1) Provide a written description of the claimed invention, and of the manner and process of making and using it, in such full, clear, concise, and exact terms as to enable any person skilled in the art to which it pertains, or with which it is most nearly connected, to make and use the same, and set forth the best mode contemplated by the inventor of carrying out the invention as required by 35 U.S.C. 112(a);

(2) Describe the claimed invention in terms that particularly point out and distinctly claim the invention as required by 35 U.S.C. 112(b); or

(3) Describe the structure, material, or acts that correspond to a claimed means or step for performing a specified function as required by 35 U.S.C. 112(f).

(e) Other material ("Nonessential material") may be incorporated by reference to U.S. patents, U.S. patent application publications, foreign patents, foreign published applications, prior and concurrently filed commonly owned U.S. applications, or non-patent publications. An incorporation by reference by hyperlink or other form of browser executable code is not permitted.

(f) The examiner may require the applicant to supply a copy of the material incorporated by reference. If the Office requires the applicant to supply a copy of material incorporated by reference, the material must be accompanied by a statement that the copy supplied consists of the same material incorporated by reference in the referencing application.

(g) Any insertion of material incorporated by reference into the specification or drawings of an application must be by way of an amendment to the specification or drawings. Such an amendment must be accompanied by a statement that the material being inserted is the material previously incorporated by reference and that the amendment contains no new matter.

(h) An incorporation of material by reference that does not comply with paragraphs (c), (d), or (e) of this section is not effective to incorporate such material unless corrected within any time period set by the Office, but in no case later than the close of prosecution as defined by §1.114(b), or abandonment of the application, whichever occurs earlier. In addition:

(1) A correction to comply with paragraph (c)(1) of this section is permitted only if the application as filed clearly conveys an intent to incorporate the material by reference. A mere reference to material does not convey an intent to incorporate the material by reference.

(2) A correction to comply with paragraph (c)(2) of this section is only permitted for material that was sufficiently described to uniquely identify the document.

(i) An application transmittal letter limited to the transmittal of a copy of the specification and drawings from a previously filed application submitted under paragraph (a) or (b) of this section may be signed by a juristic applicant or patent owner.

History of 37 C.F.R. §1.57: 69 FR 56539, Sept. 21, 2004; 72 FR 51563, Sept. 10, 2007; 77 FR 46624, Sept. 16, 2012; 78 FR 62400, Dec. 18, 2013; 80 FR 17959, May 13, 2015.

§1.58. CHEMICAL & MATHEMATICAL FORMULAE & TABLES

(a) The specification, including the claims, may contain chemical and mathematical formulae, but shall not contain drawings or flow diagrams. The description portion of the specification may contain tables, but the same tables should not be included in both the drawings and description portion of the specification. Claims may contain tables either if necessary to conform to 35 U.S.C. 112 or if otherwise found to be desirable.

(b) Tables that are submitted in electronic form (§§1.96(c) and 1.821(c)) must maintain the spatial relationships (e.g., alignment of columns and rows) of the table elements when displayed so as to visually preserve the relational information they convey. Chemical and mathematical formulae must be encoded to maintain the proper positioning of their characters when displayed in order to preserve their intended meaning.

(c) Chemical and mathematical formulae and tables must be presented in compliance with §1.52(a) and (b), except that chemical and mathematical formulae or tables may be placed in a landscape orientation if they cannot be presented satisfactorily in a portrait orientation. Typewritten characters used in such formulae and tables must be chosen from a block (nonscript) type font or lettering style having capital letters which should be at least 0.422 cm. (0.166 inch) high (*e.g.*, preferably Arial, Times Roman, or Courier with a font size of 12), but may be no smaller than 0.21 cm. (0.08 inch) high (*e.g.*, a font size of 6). A space at least 0.64 cm. (¼ inch) high should be provided between complex formulae and tables and the text. Tables should have the lines and columns of data closely spaced to conserve space, consistent with a high degree of legibility.

History of 37 C.F.R. §1.58: 43 FR 20463, May 11, 1978; 61 FR 42803, Aug. 19, 1996; 65 FR 54667, Sept. 8, 2000; 69 FR 56540, Sept. 21, 2004; 78 FR 62401, Dec. 18, 2013.

§1.59. EXPUNGEMENT OF INFORMATION OR COPY OF PAPERS IN APPLICATION FILE

(a)(1) Information in an application will not be expunged, except as provided in paragraph (b) of this section or §41.7(a) or §42.7(a) of this title.

(2) Information forming part of the original disclosure (i.e., written specification including the claims, drawings, and any preliminary amendment present on the filing date of the application) will not be expunged from the application file.

(b) An applicant may request that the Office expunge information, other than what is excluded by paragraph (a)(2) of this section, by filing a petition under this paragraph. Any petition to expunge information from an application must include the fee set forth in §1.17(g) and establish to the satisfaction of the Director that the expungement of the information is appropriate in which case a notice granting the petition for expungement will be provided.

(c) Upon request by an applicant and payment of the fee specified in §1.19(b), the Office will furnish copies of an application, unless the application has been disposed of (see §§1.53(e), (f) and (g)). The Office cannot provide or certify copies of an application that has been disposed of.

History of 37 C.F.R. §1.59: 36 FR 9775, May 28, 1971; 48 FR 2710, Jan. 20, 1983; 49 FR 554, Jan. 4, 1984; 49 FR 48452, Dec. 12, 1984; 50 FR 23123, May 31, 1985; 60 FR 20224, Apr. 25, 1995; 62 FR 53188, Oct. 10, 1997; 65 FR 54667, Sept. 8, 2000; 68 FR 38628, June 30, 2003; 69 FR 49999, Aug. 12, 2004; 69 FR 56540, Sept. 21, 2004; 77 FR 46624, Sept. 16, 2012; 77 FR 48818, Sept. 16, 2012.

§§1.60 TO 1.62. RESERVED

OATH OR DECLARATION

§1.63. INVENTOR'S OATH OR DECLARATION

(a) The inventor, or each individual who is a joint inventor of a claimed invention, in an application for patent must execute an oath or declaration directed to the application, except as provided for in §1.64. An oath or declaration under this section must:

(1) Identify the inventor or joint inventor executing the oath or declaration by his or her legal name;

(2) Identify the application to which it is directed;

(3) Include a statement that the person executing the oath or declaration believes the named inventor or joint inventor to be the original inventor or an original joint inventor of a claimed invention in the application for which the oath or declaration is being submitted; and

(4) State that the application was made or was authorized to be made by the person executing the oath or declaration.

(b) Unless the following information is supplied in an application data sheet in accordance with §1.76, the oath or declaration must also identify:

(1) Each inventor by his or her legal name; and

(2) A mailing address where the inventor customarily receives mail, and residence, if an inventor lives at a location which is different from where the inventor customarily receives mail, for each inventor.

(c) A person may not execute an oath or declaration for an application unless that person has reviewed and understands the contents of the application, including the claims, and is aware of the duty to disclose to the Office all information known to the person to be material to patentability as defined in §1.56. There is no minimum age for a person to be qualified to execute an oath or declaration, but the person must be competent to execute, i.e., understand, the document that the person is executing.

(d)(1) A newly executed oath or declaration under §1.63, or substitute statement under §1.64, is not required under §§1.51(b)(2) and 1.53(f), or under §§1.497 and 1.1021(d), for an inventor in a continuing application that claims the benefit under 35 U.S.C. 120, 121, 365(c), or 386(c) in compliance with §1.78 of an earlier-filed application, provided that an oath or declaration in compliance with this section, or substitute statement under §1.64, was executed by or with respect to such inventor and was filed in the earlier-filed application, and a copy of such oath, declaration, or substitute statement showing the signature or an indication thereon that it was executed, is submitted in the continuing application.

(2) The inventorship of a continuing application filed under 35 U.S.C. 111(a) is the inventor or joint inventors specified in the application data sheet filed before or concurrently with the copy of the inventor's oath or declaration from the earlier-filed application. If an application data sheet is not filed before or concurrently with the copy of the inventor's oath or declaration from the earlier-filed application, the inventorship is the inventorship set forth in the copy of the inventor's oath or declaration from the earlier-filed application, unless it is accompanied by a statement signed pursuant to §1.33(b) stating the name of each inventor in the continuing application.

(3) Any new joint inventor named in the continuing application must provide an oath or declaration in compliance with this section, except as provided for in §1.64.

(e)(1) An assignment may also serve as an oath or declaration required by this section if the assignment as executed:

(i) Includes the information and statements required under paragraphs (a) and (b) of this section; and

(ii) A copy of the assignment is recorded as provided for in part 3 of this chapter.

(2) Any reference to an oath or declaration under this section includes an assignment as provided for in this paragraph.

(f) With respect to an application naming only one inventor, any reference to the inventor's oath or declaration in this chapter includes a substitute statement executed under §1.64. With respect to an application naming more than one inventor, any reference to the inventor's oath or declaration in this chapter means the oaths, declarations, or substitute statements that have been collectively executed by or with respect to all of the joint inventors, unless otherwise clear from the context.

(g) An oath or declaration under this section, including the statement provided for in paragraph (e) of this section, must be executed (i.e., signed) in accordance either with §1.66 or with an acknowledgment that any willful false statement made in such declaration or statement is punishable under 18 U.S.C. 1001 by fine or imprisonment of not more than five (5) years, or both.

(h) An oath or declaration filed at any time pursuant to 35 U.S.C. 115(h)(1) will be placed in the file record of the application or patent, but may not necessarily be reviewed by the Office. Any request for correction of the named inventorship must comply with §1.48 in an application and §1.324 in a patent.

History of 37 C.F.R. §1.63: 48 FR 2711, Jan. 20, 1983; 48 FR 4285, Jan. 31, 1983; 57 FR 2034, Jan. 17, 1992; 60 FR 20225, Apr. 25, 1995; 62 FR 53188, Oct. 10, 1997; 65 FR 54667, Sept. 8, 2000; 69 FR 56540, Sept. 21, 2004; 77 FR 48818, Sept. 16, 2012; 80 FR 17959, May 13, 2015.

§1.64. SUBSTITUTE STATEMENT IN LIEU OF AN OATH OR DECLARATION

(a) An applicant under §1.43, 1.45 or 1.46 may execute a substitute statement in lieu of an oath or declaration under §1.63 if the inventor is deceased, is under a legal incapacity, has refused to execute the oath or declaration under §1.63, or cannot be found or reached after diligent effort.

(b) A substitute statement under this section must:

(1) Comply with the requirements of §1.63(a), identifying the inventor or joint inventor with respect to whom a substitute statement in lieu of an oath or declaration is executed, and stating upon information and belief the facts which such inventor is required to state;

(2) Identify the person executing the substitute statement and the relationship of such person to the inventor or joint inventor with respect to whom the substitute statement is executed, and unless such information is supplied in an application data sheet in accordance with §1.76, the residence and mailing address of the person signing the substitute statement;

(3) Identify the circumstances permitting the person to execute the substitute statement in lieu of an oath or declaration under §1.63, namely whether the inventor is deceased, is under a legal incapacity, cannot be found or reached after a diligent effort was made, or has refused to execute the oath or declaration under §1.63; and

(4) Unless the following information is supplied in an application data sheet in accordance with §1.76, also identify:

(i) Each inventor by his or her legal name; and

(ii) The last known mailing address where the inventor customarily receives mail, and last known residence, if an inventor lives at a location which is different from where the inventor customarily receives mail, for each inventor who is not deceased or under a legal incapacity.

(c) A person may not execute a substitute statement provided for in this section for an application unless that person has reviewed and understands the contents of the application, including the claims, and is aware of the duty to disclose to the Office all information known to the person to be material to patentability as defined in §1.56.

(d) Any reference to an inventor's oath or declaration includes a substitute statement provided for in this section.

(e) A substitute statement under this section must contain an acknowledgment that any willful false statement made in such statement is punishable under section 1001 of title 18 by fine or imprisonment of not more than 5 years, or both.

(f) A nonsigning inventor or legal representative may subsequently join in the application by submitting an oath or declaration under §1.63. The submission of an oath or declaration by a nonsigning inventor or legal representative in an application filed under §1.43, 1.45 or 1.46 will not permit the nonsigning inventor or legal representative to revoke or grant a power of attorney.

History of 37 C.F.R. §1.64: 48 FR 2711, Jan. 20, 1983; 65 FR 54667, Sept. 8, 2000; 77 FR 48819, Sept. 16, 2012.

§1.65. RESERVED

§1.66. STATEMENTS UNDER OATH

An oath or affirmation may be made before any person within the United States authorized by law to administer oaths. An oath made in a foreign country may be made before any diplomatic or consular officer of the United States authorized to administer oaths, or before any officer having an official seal and authorized to administer oaths in the foreign country in which the applicant may be, whose authority shall be proved by a certificate of a diplomatic or consular officer of the United States, or by an apostille of an official designated by a foreign country which, by treaty or convention, accords like effect to apostilles of designated officials in the United States. The oath shall be attested in all cases in this and other countries, by the proper official seal of the officer before whom the oath or affirmation is made. Such oath or affirmation shall be valid as to execution if it complies with the laws of the State or country where made. When the person before whom the oath or affirmation is made in this country is not provided with a seal, his official character shall be established by competent evidence, as by a certificate from a clerk of a court of record or other proper officer having a seal.

History of 37 C.F.R. §1.66: 24 FR 10332, Dec. 22, 1959; 47 FR 41275, Sept. 17, 1982; 77 FR 48819, Sept. 16, 2012.

§1.67. SUPPLEMENTAL OATH OR DECLARATION

(a) The applicant may submit an inventor's oath or declaration meeting the requirements of §1.63, §1.64, or §1.162 to correct any deficiencies or inaccuracies present in an earlier-filed inventor's oath or declaration. Deficiencies or inaccuracies due to the failure to meet the requirements of §1.63(b) in an oath or declaration may be corrected with an application data sheet in accordance with §1.76, except that any correction of inventorship must be pursuant to §1.48.

(b) A supplemental inventor's oath or declaration under this section must be executed by the person whose inventor's oath or declaration is being withdrawn, replaced, or otherwise corrected.

(c) The Office will not require a person who has executed an oath or declaration in compliance with 35 U.S.C. 115 and §1.63 or 1.162 for an application to provide an additional inventor's oath or declaration for the application.

(d) No new matter may be introduced into a nonprovisional application after its filing date even if an inventor's oath or declaration is filed to correct deficiencies or inaccuracies present in the earlier-filed inventor's oath or declaration.

History of 37 C.F.R. §1.67: 24 FR 10332, Dec. 22, 1959; 29 FR 18503, Dec. 29, 1964; 40 FR 6339, Feb. 11, 1975; 48 FR 2711, Jan. 20, 1983; 57 FR 2034, Jan. 17, 1992; 60 FR 20225, Apr. 25, 1995; 62 FR 53189, Oct. 10, 1997; 65 FR 54667, Sept. 8, 2000; 77 FR 48819, Sept. 16, 2012.

§1.68. DECLARATION IN LIEU OF OATH

Any document to be filed in the Patent and Trademark Office and which is required by any law, rule, or other regulation to be under oath may be subscribed to by a written declaration. Such declaration may be used in lieu of the oath otherwise required, if, and only if, the declarant is on the same document, warned that willful false statements and the like are punishable by fine or imprisonment, or both (18 U.S.C. 1001) and may jeopardize the validity of the application or any patent issuing thereon. The declarant must set forth in the body of the declaration that all statements made of the declarant's own knowledge are true and that all statements made on information and belief are believed to be true.

History of 37 C.F.R. §1.68: 34 FR 14430, Sept. 16, 1969; 49 FR 48452, Dec. 12, 1984.

§1.69. FOREIGN LANGUAGE OATHS & DECLARATIONS

(a) Whenever an individual making an oath or declaration cannot understand English, the oath or declaration must be in a language that such individual can understand and shall state that such individual understands the content of any documents to which the oath or declaration relates.

(b) Unless the text of any oath or declaration in a language other than English is in a form provided by the Patent and Trademark Office or in accordance with PCT Rule 4.17(iv), it must be accompanied by an English translation together with a statement that the translation is accurate, except that in the case of an oath or declaration filed under §1.63, the translation may be filed in the Office no later than two months from the date applicant is notified to file the translation.

History of 37 C.F.R. §1.69: 42 FR 5594, Jan. 28, 1977; 48 FR 2711, Jan. 20, 1983; 62 FR 53189, Oct. 10, 1997; 69 FR 56540, Sept. 21, 2004; 70 FR 3890, Jan. 27, 2005.

§1.70. RESERVED

THE SPECIFICATION

§1.71. DETAILED DESCRIPTION & SPECIFICATION OF THE INVENTION

(a) The specification must include a written description of the invention or discovery and of the manner and process of making and using the same, and is required to be in such full, clear, concise, and exact terms as to enable any person skilled in the art or science to which the invention or discovery appertains, or with which it is most nearly connected, to make and use the same.

(b) The specification must set forth the precise invention for which a patent is solicited, in such manner as to distinguish it from other inventions and from what is old. It must describe completely a specific embodiment of the process, machine, manufacture, composition of matter or improvement invented, and must explain the mode of operation or principle whenever applicable. The best mode contemplated by the inventor of carrying out his invention must be set forth.

(c) In the case of an improvement, the specification must particularly point out the part or parts of the process, machine, manufacture, or composition of matter to which the improvement relates, and the description should be confined to the specific improvement and to such parts as necessarily cooperate with it or as may be necessary to a complete understanding or description of it.

(d) A copyright or mask work notice may be placed in a design or utility patent application adjacent to copyright and mask work material contained therein. The notice may appear at any appropriate portion of the patent application disclosure. For notices in drawings, see §1.84(s). The content of the notice must be limited to only those elements provided for by law. For example, "© 1983 John Doe" (17 U.S.C. 401) and "*M* John Doe" (17 U.S.C. 909) would be properly limited and, under current statutes, legally sufficient notices of copyright and mask work, respectively. Inclusion of a copyright or mask work notice will be permitted only if the authorization language set forth in paragraph (e) of this section is included at the beginning (preferably as the first paragraph) of the specification.

(e) The authorization shall read as follows:

A portion of the disclosure of this patent document contains material which is subject to (copyright or mask work) protection. The (copyright or mask work) owner has no objection to the facsimile reproduction by anyone of the patent document or the patent disclosure, as it appears in the Patent and Trademark Office patent file or records, but otherwise reserves all (copyright or mask work) rights whatsoever.

(f) The specification must commence on a separate sheet. Each sheet including part of the specification may not include other parts of the application or other information. The claim(s), abstract and sequence listing (if any) should not be included on a sheet including any other part of the application.

(g)(1) The specification may disclose or be amended to disclose the names of the parties to a joint research agreement as defined in §1.9(e).

(2) An amendment under paragraph (g)(1) of this section must be accompanied by the processing fee set forth in §1.17(i) if not filed within one of the following time periods:

(i) Within three months of the filing date of a national application;

(ii) Within three months of the date of entry of the national stage as set forth in §1.491 in an international application;

(iii) Before the mailing of a first Office action on the merits; or

(iv) Before the mailing of a first Office action after the filing of a request for continued examination under §1.114.

(3) If an amendment under paragraph (g)(1) of this section is filed after the date the issue fee is paid, the patent as issued may not necessarily include the names of the parties to the joint research agreement. If the patent as issued does not include the names of the parties to the joint research agreement, the patent must be corrected to include the names of the parties to the joint research agreement by a certificate of correction under 35 U.S.C. 255 and §1.323 for the amendment to be effective.

History of 37 C.F.R. §1.71: 53 FR 47808, Nov. 28, 1988; 58 FR 38723, July 20, 1993; 68 FR 38628, June 30, 2003; 70 FR 1823, Jan. 11, 2005; 70 FR 54266, Sept. 14, 2005; 78 FR 11055, Mar. 16, 2013.

§1.72. TITLE & ABSTRACT

(a) The title of the invention may not exceed 500 characters in length and must be as short and specific as possible. Characters that cannot be captured and recorded in the Office's automated information systems may not be reflected in the Office's records in such systems or in documents created by the Office. Unless the title is supplied in an application data sheet (§1.76), the title of the invention should appear as a heading on the first page of the specification.

(b) A brief abstract of the technical disclosure in the specification must commence on a separate sheet, preferably following the claims, under the heading "Abstract" or "Abstract of the Disclosure." The sheet or sheets presenting the abstract may not include other parts of the application or other material. The abstract must be as concise as the disclosure permits, preferably not exceeding 150 words in length. The purpose of the abstract is to enable the Office and the public generally to determine quickly from a cursory inspection the nature and gist of the technical disclosure.

History of 37 C.F.R. §1.72: 31 FR 12922, Oct. 4, 1966; 43 FR 20464, May 11, 1978; 61 FR 42803, Aug. 19, 1996; 65 FR 54667, Sept. 8, 2000; 65 FR 57054, Sept. 20, 2000; 68 FR 38628, June 30, 2003; 78 FR 62402, Dec. 18, 2013.

§1.73. SUMMARY OF THE INVENTION

A brief summary of the invention indicating its nature and substance, which may include a statement of the object of the invention, should precede the detailed description. Such summary should, when set forth, be commensurate with the invention as claimed and any object recited should be that of the invention as claimed.

§1.74. REFERENCE TO DRAWINGS

When there are drawings, there shall be a brief description of the several views of the drawings and the detailed description of the invention shall refer to the different views by specifying the numbers of the figures and to the different parts by use of reference letters or numerals (preferably the latter).

§1.75. CLAIM(S)

(a) The specification must conclude with a claim particularly pointing out and distinctly claiming the subject matter which the applicant regards as his invention or discovery.

(b) More than one claim may be presented provided they differ substantially from each other and are not unduly multiplied.

(c) One or more claims may be presented in dependent form, referring back to and further limiting another claim or claims in the same application. Any dependent claim which refers to more than one other claim ("multiple dependent claim") shall refer to such other claims in the alternative only. A multiple dependent claim shall not serve as a basis for any other multiple dependent claim. For fee calculation purposes under §1.16, a multiple dependent claim will be considered to be that number of claims to which direct reference is made therein. For fee calculation purposes also, any claim depending from a multiple dependent claim will be considered to be that number of claims to which direct reference is made in that multiple dependent claim. In addition to the other filing fees, any original application which is filed with, or is amended to include, multiple dependent claims must have paid therein the fee set forth in §1.16(j). Claims in dependent form shall be construed to include all the limitations of the claim incorporated by reference into the dependent claim. A multiple dependent claim shall be construed to incorporate by reference all the limitations of each of the particular claims in relation to which it is being considered.

(d)(1) The claim or claims must conform to the invention as set forth in the remainder of the specification and the terms and phrases used in the claims must find clear support or antecedent basis in the description so that the meaning of the terms in the claims may be ascertainable by reference to the description. (See §1.58(a).)

(2) See §§1.141 to 1.146 as to claiming different inventions in one application.

(e) Where the nature of the case admits, as in the case of an improvement, any independent claim should contain in the following order: (1) a preamble comprising a general description of all the elements or steps of the claimed combination which are conventional or known, (2) a phrase such as "wherein the improvement comprises," and (3) those elements, steps and/or relationships which constitute that portion of the claimed combination which the applicant considers as the new or improved portion.

(f) If there are several claims, they shall be numbered consecutively in Arabic numerals.

(g) The least restrictive claim should be presented as claim number 1, and all dependent claims should be grouped together with the claim or claims to which they refer to the extent practicable.

(h) The claim or claims must commence on a separate physical sheet or electronic page. Any sheet including a claim or portion of a claim may not contain any other parts of the application or other material.

(i) Where a claim sets forth a plurality of elements or steps, each element or step of the claim should be separated by a line indentation.

History of 37 C.F.R. §1.75: 31 FR 12922, Oct. 4, 1966; 36 FR 12690, July 3, 1971; 37 FR 21995, Oct. 18, 1972; 43 FR 4015, Jan. 31, 1978; 47 FR 41276, Sept. 17, 1982; 61 FR 42803, Aug. 19, 1996; 68 FR 38628, June 30, 2003; 70 FR 3891, Jan. 27, 2005; 74 FR 52688, Oct. 14, 2009.

§1.76. APPLICATION DATA SHEET

(a) Application data sheet. An application data sheet is a sheet or sheets that may be submitted in a provisional application under 35 U.S.C. 111(b), a nonprovisional application under 35 U.S.C. 111(a), a nonprovisional international design application, or a national stage application under 35 U.S.C. 371 and must be submitted when required by §1.55 or 1.78 to claim priority to or the benefit of a prior-filed application under 35 U.S.C. 119, 120, 121, 365, or 386. An application data sheet must be titled "Application Data Sheet." An application data sheet must contain all of the section headings listed in paragraph (b) of this section, except as provided in paragraph (c)(2) of this section, with any appropriate data for each section heading. If an application data sheet is provided, the application data sheet is part of the application for which it has been submitted.

(b) Bibliographic data. Bibliographic data as used in paragraph (a) of this section includes:

(1) Inventor information. This information includes the legal name, residence, and mailing address of the inventor or each joint inventor.

(2) Correspondence information. This information includes the correspondence address, which may be indicated by reference to a customer number, to which correspondence is to be directed (see §1.33(a)).

(3) Application information. This information includes the title of the invention, the total number of drawing sheets, a suggested drawing figure for publication (in a nonprovisional application), any docket number assigned to the application, the type of application (e.g., utility, plant, design, reissue, provisional), whether the application discloses any significant part of the subject matter of an application under a secrecy order pursuant to §5.2 of this chapter (see §5.2(c)), and, for plant applications, the Latin name of the genus and species of the plant claimed, as well as the variety denomination. When information concerning the previously filed application is required under §1.57(a), application information also includes the reference to the previously filed application, indicating that the specification and any drawings of the application are replaced by the reference to the previously filed application, and specifying the previously filed application by application number, filing date, and the intellectual property authority or country in which the previously filed application was filed.

(4) Representative information. This information includes the registration number of each practitioner having a power of attorney in the application (preferably by reference to a customer number). Providing this information in the application data sheet does not constitute a power of attorney in the application (see §1.32).

(5) Domestic benefit information. This information includes the application number, the filing date, the status (including patent number if available), and relationship of each application for which a benefit is claimed under 35 U.S.C. 119(e), 120, 121, 365(c), or 386(c). Providing this information in the application data sheet constitutes the specific reference required by 35 U.S.C. 119(e) or 120 and §1.78.

(6) Foreign priority information. This information includes the application number, country (or intellectual property authority), and filing date of each foreign application for which priority is claimed. Providing this information in the application data sheet constitutes the claim for priority as required by 35 U.S.C. 119(b) and §1.55.

(7) Applicant information: This information includes the name (either natural person or juristic entity) and address of the legal representative, assignee, person to whom the inventor is under an obligation to assign the invention, or person who otherwise shows sufficient proprietary interest in the matter who is the applicant under §1.43 or §1.46. Providing assignment information in the application data sheet does not substitute for compliance with any requirement of part 3 of this chapter to have an assignment recorded by the Office.

(c) Correcting and updating an application data sheet. **(1)** Information in a previously submitted application data sheet, inventor's oath or declaration under §1.63, §1.64 or §1.67, or otherwise of record, may be corrected or updated until payment of the issue fee by a new application data sheet providing corrected or updated information, except that inventorship changes must comply with the requirements of §1.48, foreign priority and domestic benefit information changes must comply with §§1.55 and 1.78, and correspondence address changes are governed by §1.33(a).

(2) An application data sheet providing corrected or updated information may include all of the sections listed in paragraph (b) of this section or only those sections containing changed or updated information. The application data sheet must include the section headings listed in paragraph (b) of this section for each section included in the application data sheet, and must identify the information that is being changed, with underlining for insertions, and strike-through or brackets for text removed, except that identification of information being changed is not required for an application data sheet included with an initial submission under 35 U.S.C. 371.

(d) Inconsistencies between application data sheet and other documents. For inconsistencies between information that is supplied by both an application data sheet under this section and other documents:

(1) The most recent submission will govern with respect to inconsistencies as between the information provided in an application data sheet, a designation of a correspondence address, or by the inventor's oath or declaration, except that:

(i) The most recent application data sheet will govern with respect to foreign priority (§1.55) or domestic benefit (§1.78) claims; and

(ii) The naming of the inventorship is governed by §1.41 and changes to inventorship or the names of the inventors is governed by §1.48.

(2) The information in the application data sheet will govern when inconsistent with the information supplied at the same time by a designation of correspondence address or the inventor's oath or declaration. The information in the application data sheet will govern when inconsistent with the information supplied at any time in a Patent Cooperation Treaty Request Form, Patent Law Treaty Model International Request Form, Patent Law Treaty Model International Request for Recordation of Change in Name or Address Form, or Patent Law Treaty Model International Request for Recordation of Change in Applicant or Owner Form.

(3) The Office will capture bibliographic information from the application data sheet. The Office will generally not review the inventor's oath or declaration to determine if the bibliographic information contained therein is consistent with the bibliographic information provided in an application data sheet. Incorrect bibliographic information contained in an application data sheet may be corrected as provided in paragraph (c)(1) of this section.

(e) Signature requirement. An application data sheet must be signed in compliance with §1.33(b). An unsigned application data sheet will be treated only as a transmittal letter.

(f) Patent Law Treaty Model International Forms. The requirement in §1.55 or §1.78 for the presentation of a priority or benefit claim under 35 U.S.C. 119, 120, 121, or 365 in an application data sheet will be satisfied by the presentation of such priority or benefit claim in the Patent Law Treaty Model International Request Form, and the requirement in §1.57(a) for a reference to the previously filed application in an application data sheet will be satisfied by the presentation of such reference to the previously filed application in the Patent Law Treaty Model International Request Form. The requirement in §1.46 for the presentation of the name of the applicant under 35 U.S.C. 118 in an application data sheet will be satisfied by the presentation of the name of the applicant in the Patent Law Treaty Model International Request Form, Patent Law Treaty Model International Request for Recordation of Change in Name or Address Form, or Patent Law Treaty Model International Request for Recordation of Change in Applicant or Owner Form, as applicable.

(g) Patent Cooperation Treaty Request Form. The requirement in §1.78 for the presentation of a benefit claim under 35 U.S.C. 119, 120, 121, or 365 in an application data sheet will be satisfied in a national stage application under 35 U.S.C. 371 by the presentation of such benefit claim in the Patent Cooperation Treaty Request Form contained in the international application or the presence of such benefit claim on the front page of the publication of the international application under PCT Article 21(2). The requirement in §1.55 or §1.78 for the presentation of a priority or benefit claim under 35 U.S.C. 119, 120, 121, or 365 in an application data sheet and the requirement in §1.46 for the presentation of the name of the applicant under 35 U.S.C. 118 in an application data sheet will be satisfied in an application under 35 U.S.C. 111 by the presentation of such priority or benefit claim and presentation of the name of the applicant in a Patent Cooperation Treaty Request Form. If a Patent Cooperation Treaty Request Form is submitted in an application under 35 U.S.C. 111, the Patent Cooperation Treaty Request Form must be accompanied by a clear indication that treatment of the application as an application under 35 U.S.C. 111 is desired.

History of 37 C.F.R. §1.76: 65 FR 54668, Sept. 8, 2000; 65 FR 57054, Sept. 20, 2000; 69 FR 56540, Sept. 21, 2004; 70 FR 54266, Sept. 14, 2005; 74 FR 52689, Oct. 14, 2009; 77 FR 48820, Sept. 16, 2012; 78 FR 11055, Mar. 16, 2013; 78 FR 62402, Dec. 18, 2013; 80 FR 17959, May 13, 2015.

§1.77. ARRANGEMENT OF APPLICATION ELEMENTS

(a) The elements of the application, if applicable, should appear in the following order:

(1) Utility application transmittal form.

(2) Fee transmittal form.

(3) Application data sheet (see §1.76).

(4) Specification.

(5) Drawings.

(6) The inventor's oath or declaration.

(b) The specification should include the following sections in order:

(1) Title of the invention, which may be accompanied by an introductory portion stating the name, citizenship, and residence of the applicant (unless included in the application data sheet).

(2) Cross-reference to related applications.

(3) Statement regarding federally sponsored research or development.

(4) The names of the parties to a joint research agreement.

(5) Reference to a "Sequence Listing," a table, or a computer program listing appendix submitted on a compact disc and an incorporation-by-reference of the material on the compact disc (see §1.52(e)(5)). The total number of compact discs including duplicates and the files on each compact disc shall be specified.

(6) Statement regarding prior disclosures by the inventor or a joint inventor.

(7) Background of the invention.

(8) Brief summary of the invention.

(9) Brief description of the several views of the drawing.

(10) Detailed description of the invention.

(11) A claim or claims.

(12) Abstract of the disclosure.

(13) "Sequence Listing," if on paper (see §§1.821 through 1.825).

(c) The text of the specification sections defined in paragraphs (b)(1) through (b)(12) of this section, if applicable, should be preceded by a section heading in uppercase and without underlining or bold type.

History of 37 C.F.R. §1.77: 43 FR 20464, May 11, 1978; 46 FR 2612, Jan. 12, 1981; 48 FR 2712, Jan. 20, 1983; 61 FR 42803, Aug. 19, 1996; 65 FR 54668, Sept. 8, 2000; 70 FR 1823, Jan. 11, 2005; 77 FR 48820, Sept. 16, 2012; 78 FR 11055, Mar. 16, 2013.

§1.78. CLAIMING BENEFIT OF EARLIER FILING DATE & CROSS-REFERENCES TO OTHER APPLICATIONS

(a) Claims under 35 U.S.C. 119(e) for the benefit of a prior-filed provisional application. An applicant in a nonprovisional application, other than for a design patent, or an international application designating the United States may claim the benefit of one or more prior-filed provisional applications under the conditions set forth in 35 U.S.C. 119(e) and this section.

(1) The nonprovisional application or international application designating the United States must be:

(i) Filed not later than twelve months after the date on which the provisional application was filed, subject to paragraph (b) of this section (a subsequent application); or

(ii) Entitled to claim the benefit under 35 U.S.C. 120, 121, or 365(c) of a subsequent application that was filed within the period set forth in paragraph (a)(1)(i) of this section.

(2) Each prior-filed provisional application must name the inventor or a joint inventor named in the later-filed application as the inventor or a joint inventor. In addition, each prior-filed provisional application must be entitled to a filing date as set forth in §1.53(c), and the basic filing fee set forth in §1.16(d) must have been paid for such provisional application within the time period set forth in §1.53(g).

(3) Any nonprovisional application or international application designating the United States that claims the benefit of one or more prior-filed provisional applications must contain, or be amended to contain, a reference to each such prior-filed provisional application, identifying it by the provisional application number (consisting of series code and serial number). If the later-filed application is a nonprovisional application, the reference required by this paragraph must be included in an application data sheet (§1.76(b)(5)).

(4) The reference required by paragraph (a)(3) of this section must be submitted during the pendency of the later-filed application. If the later-filed application is an application filed under 35 U.S.C. 111(a), this reference must also be submitted within the later of four months from the actual filing date of the later-filed application or sixteen months from the filing date of the prior-filed provisional application. If the later-filed application is a nonprovisional application entering the national stage from an international application under 35 U.S.C. 371, this reference must also be submitted within the later of four months from the date on which the national stage commenced under 35 U.S.C. 371(b) or (f) (§1.491(a)), four months from the date of the initial submission under 35 U.S.C. 371 to enter the national stage, or sixteen months from the filing date of the prior-filed provisional application. Except as provided in paragraph (c) of this section, failure to timely submit the reference is considered a waiver of any benefit under 35 U.S.C. 119(e) of the prior-filed provisional application. The time periods in this paragraph do not apply if the later-filed application is:

(i) An application filed under 35 U.S.C. 111(a) before November 29, 2000; or

(ii) An international application filed under 35 U.S.C. 363 before November 29, 2000.

(5) If the prior-filed provisional application was filed in a language other than English and both an English-language translation of the prior-filed provisional application and a statement that the translation is accurate were not previously filed in the prior-filed provisional application, the applicant will be notified and given a period of time within which to file, in the prior-filed provisional application, the translation and the statement. If the notice is mailed in a pending nonprovisional application, a timely reply to such a notice must include the filing in the nonprovisional application of either a confirmation that the translation and statement were filed in the provisional application, or an application data sheet (§1.76(b)(5)) eliminating the reference under paragraph (a)(3) of this section to the prior-filed provisional application, or the nonprovisional application will be abandoned. The translation and statement may be filed in the provisional application, even if the provisional application has become abandoned.

(6) If a nonprovisional application filed on or after March 16, 2013, claims the benefit of the filing date of a provisional application filed prior to March 16, 2013, and also contains, or contained at any time, a claim to a claimed invention that has an effective filing date as defined in §1.109 that is on or after March 16, 2013, the applicant must provide a statement to that effect within the later of four months from the actual filing date of the nonprovisional application, four months from the date of entry into the national stage as set forth in §1.491 in an international application, sixteen months from the filing date of the prior-filed provisional application, or the date that a first claim to a claimed invention that has an effective filing date on or after March 16, 2013, is presented in the nonprovisional application. An applicant is not required to provide such a statement if the applicant reasonably believes on the basis of information already known to the individuals designated in §1.56(c) that the nonprovisional application does not, and did not at any time, contain a claim to a claimed invention that has an effective filing date on or after March 16, 2013.

(b) Delayed filing of the subsequent nonprovisional application or international application designating the United States. If the subsequent nonprovisional application or international application designating the United States has a filing date which is after the expiration of the twelve-month period set forth in paragraph (a)(1)(i) of this section but within two months from the expiration of the period set forth in paragraph (a)(1)(i) of this section, the benefit of the provisional application may be restored under PCT Rule 26*bis*.3 for an international application, or upon petition pursuant to this paragraph, if the delay in filing the subsequent nonprovisional application or international application designating the United States within the period set forth in paragraph (a)(1)(i) of this section was unintentional.

(1) A petition to restore the benefit of a provisional application under this paragraph filed on or after May 13, 2015, must be filed in the subsequent application, and any petition to restore the benefit of a provisional application under this paragraph must include:

(i) The reference required by 35 U.S.C. 119(e) to the prior-filed provisional application in an application data sheet (§1.76(b)(5)) identifying it by provisional application number (consisting of series code and serial number), unless previously submitted;

(ii) The petition fee as set forth in §1.17(m); and

(iii) A statement that the delay in filing the subsequent nonprovisional application or international application designating the United States within the twelve-month period set forth in paragraph (a)(1)(i) of this section was unintentional. The Director may require additional information where there is a question whether the delay was unintentional.

(2) The restoration of the right of priority under PCT Rule 26*bis*.3 to a provisional application does not affect the requirement to include the reference required by paragraph (a)(3) of this section to the provisional application in a national stage application under 35 U.S.C. 371 within the time period provided by paragraph (a)(4) of this section to avoid the benefit claim being considered waived.

(c) Delayed claims under 35 U.S.C. 119(e) for the benefit of a prior-filed provisional application. If the reference required by 35 U.S.C. 119(e) and paragraph (a)(3) of this section is presented in an application after the time period provided by paragraph (a)(4) of this section, the claim under 35 U.S.C. 119(e) for the benefit of a prior-filed provisional application may be accepted if the reference identifying the prior-filed application by provisional application number was unintentionally delayed. A petition to accept an unintentionally delayed claim under 35 U.S.C. 119(e) for the benefit of a prior-filed provisional application must be accompanied by:

(1) The reference required by 35 U.S.C. 119(e) and paragraph (a)(3) of this section to the prior-filed provisional application, unless previously submitted;

(2) The petition fee as set forth in §1.17(m); and

(3) A statement that the entire delay between the date the benefit claim was due under paragraph (a)(4) of this section and the date the benefit claim was filed was unintentional. The Director may require additional information where there is a question whether the delay was unintentional.

(d) Claims under 35 U.S.C. 120, 121, 365(c), or 386(c) for the benefit of a prior-filed nonprovisional application, international application, or international design application. An applicant in a nonprovisional application (including a nonprovisional application resulting from an international application or international design application), an international application designating the United States, or an international design application designating the United States may claim the benefit of one or more prior-filed copending nonprovisional applications, international applications designating the United States, or international design applications designating the United States under the conditions set forth in 35 U.S.C. 120, 121, 365(c), or 386(c) and this section.

(1) Each prior-filed application must name the inventor or a joint inventor named in the later-filed application as the inventor or a joint inventor. In addition, each prior-filed application must either be:

(i) An international application entitled to a filing date in accordance with PCT Article 11 and designating the United States;

(ii) An international design application entitled to a filing date in accordance with §1.1023 and designating the United States; or

(iii) A nonprovisional application under 35 U.S.C. 111(a) that is entitled to a filing date as set forth in §1.53(b) or (d) for which the basic filing fee set forth in §1.16 has been paid within the pendency of the application.

(2) Except for a continued prosecution application filed under §1.53(d), any nonprovisional application, international application designating the United States, or international design application designating the United States that claims the benefit of one or more prior-filed nonprovisional applications, international applications designating the United States, or international design applications designating the United States must contain or be amended to contain a reference to each such prior-filed application, identifying it by application number (consisting of the series code and serial number), international application number and international filing date, or international registration number and filing date under §1.1023. If the later-filed application is a nonprovisional application, the reference required by this paragraph must be included in an application data sheet (§1.76(b)(5)). The reference also must identify the relationship of the applications, namely, whether the later-filed application is a continuation, divisional, or continuation-in-part of the prior-filed nonprovisional application, international application, or international design application.

(3)(i) The reference required by 35 U.S.C. 120 and paragraph (d)(2) of this section must be submitted during the pendency of the later-filed application.

(ii) If the later-filed application is an application filed under 35 U.S.C. 111(a), this reference must also be submitted within the later of four months from the actual filing date of the later-filed application or sixteen months from the filing date of the prior-filed application. If the later-filed application is a nonprovisional application entering the national stage from an international application under 35 U.S.C. 371, this reference must also be submitted within the later of four months from the date on which the national stage commenced under 35 U.S.C. 371(b) or (f) (§1.491(a)), four months from the date of the initial submission under 35 U.S.C. 371 to enter the national stage, or sixteen months from the filing date of the prior-filed application. The time periods in this paragraph do not apply if the later-filed application is:

(A) An application for a design patent;

(B) An application filed under 35 U.S.C. 111(a) before November 29, 2000; or

(C) An international application filed under 35 U.S.C. 363 before November 29, 2000.

(iii) Except as provided in paragraph (e) of this section, failure to timely submit the reference required by 35 U.S.C. 120 and paragraph (d)(2) of this section is considered a waiver of any benefit under 35 U.S.C. 120, 121, 365(c), or 386(c) to the prior-filed application.

(4) The request for a continued prosecution application under §1.53(d) is the specific reference required by 35 U.S.C. 120 to the prior-filed application. The identification of an application by application number under this section is the identification of every application assigned that application number necessary for a specific reference required by 35 U.S.C. 120 to every such application assigned that application number.

(5) Cross-references to other related applications may be made when appropriate (see §1.14), but cross-references to applications for which a benefit is not claimed under title 35, United States Code, must not be included in an application data sheet (§1.76(b)(5)).

(6) If a nonprovisional application filed on or after March 16, 2013, other than a nonprovisional international design application, claims the benefit of the filing date of a nonprovisional application or an international application designating the United States filed prior to March 16, 2013, and also contains, or contained at any time, a claim to a claimed invention that has an effective filing date as defined in §1.109 that is on or after March 16, 2013, the applicant must provide a statement to that effect within the later of four months from the actual filing date of the later-filed application, four months from the date of entry into the national stage as set forth in §1.491 in an international application, sixteen months from the filing date of the prior-filed application, or the date that a first claim to a claimed invention that has an effective filing date on or after March 16, 2013, is presented in the later-filed application. An applicant is not required to provide such a statement if either:

(i) The application claims the benefit of a nonprovisional application in which a statement under §1.55(k), paragraph (a)(6) of this section, or this paragraph that the application contains, or contained at any time, a claim to a claimed invention that has an effective filing date on or after March 16, 2013 has been filed; or

(ii) The applicant reasonably believes on the basis of information already known to the individuals designated in §1.56(c) that the later filed application does not, and did not at any time, contain a claim to a claimed invention that has an effective filing date on or after March 16, 2013.

(7) Where benefit is claimed under 35 U.S.C. 120, 121, 365(c), or 386(c) to an international application or an international design application which designates but did not originate in the United States, the Office may require a certified copy of such application together with an English translation thereof if filed in another language.

(e) Delayed claims under 35 U.S.C. 120, 121, 365(c), or 386(c) for the benefit of a prior-filed nonprovisional application, international application, or international design application. If the reference required by 35 U.S.C. 120 and paragraph (d)(2) of this section is presented after the time period provided by paragraph (d)(3) of this section, the claim under 35 U.S.C. 120, 121, 365(c), or 386(c) for the benefit of a prior-filed copending nonprovisional application, international application designating the United States, or international design application designating the United States may be accepted if the reference required by paragraph (d)(2) of this section was unintentionally delayed. A petition to accept an unintentionally delayed claim under 35 U.S.C. 120, 121, 365(c), or 386(c) for the benefit of a prior-filed application must be accompanied by:

(1) The reference required by 35 U.S.C. 120 and paragraph (d)(2) of this section to the prior-filed application, unless previously submitted;

(2) The petition fee as set forth in §1.17(m); and

(3) A statement that the entire delay between the date the benefit claim was due under paragraph (d)(3) of this section and the date the benefit claim was filed was unintentional. The Director may require additional information where there is a question whether the delay was unintentional.

(f) Applications containing patentably indistinct claims. Where two or more applications filed by the same applicant or assignee contain patentably indistinct claims, elimination of such claims from all but one application may be required in the absence of good and sufficient reason for their retention during pendency in more than one application.

(g) Applications or patents under reexamination naming different inventors and containing patentably indistinct claims. If an application or a patent under reexamination and at least one other application naming different inventors are owned by the same person and contain patentably indistinct claims, and there is no statement of record indicating that the claimed inventions were commonly owned or subject to an obligation of assignment to the same person on the effective filing date (as defined in §1.109), or on the date of the invention, as applicable, of the later claimed invention, the Office may require the applicant or assignee to state whether the claimed inventions were commonly owned or subject to an obligation of assignment to the same person on such date, and if not, indicate which named inventor is the prior inventor, as applicable. Even if the claimed inventions were commonly owned, or subject to an obligation of assignment to the same person on the effective filing date (as defined in §1.109), or on the date of the invention, as applicable, of the later claimed invention, the patentably indistinct claims may be rejected under the doctrine of double patenting in view of such commonly owned or assigned applications or patents under reexamination.

(h) Applications filed before September 16, 2012. Notwithstanding the requirement in paragraphs (a)(3) and (d)(2) of this section that any specific reference to a prior-filed application be presented in an application data sheet (§1.76), this requirement in paragraph (a)(3) and (d)(2) of this section will be satisfied by the presentation of such specific reference in the first sentence(s) of the specification following the title in a nonprovisional application filed under 35 U.S.C. 111(a) before September 16, 2012, or resulting from an international application filed under 35 U.S.C. 363 before September 16, 2012. The provisions of this paragraph do not apply to any specific reference submitted for a petition under paragraph (b) of this section to restore the benefit of a provisional application.

(i) Petitions required in international applications. If a petition under paragraph (b), (c), or (e) of this section is required in an international application that was not filed with the United States Receiving Office and is not a nonprovisional application, then such petition may be filed in the earliest nonprovisional application that claims benefit under 35 U.S.C. 120, 121, 365(c), or 386(c) to the international application and will be treated as having been filed in the international application.

(j) Benefit under 35 U.S.C. 386(c). Benefit under 35 U.S.C. 386(c) with respect to an international design application is applicable only to nonprovisional applications, international applications, and international design applications filed on or after May 13, 2015, and patents issuing thereon.

(k) Time periods in this section. The time periods set forth in this section are not extendable, but are subject to 35 U.S.C. 21(b) (and §1.7(a)), PCT Rule 80.5, and Hague Agreement Rule 4(4).

History of 37 C.F.R. §1.78: 31 FR 12922, Oct. 4, 1966; 36 FR 7312, Apr. 17, 1971; 43 FR 20464, May 11, 1978; 49 FR 555, Jan. 4, 1984; 50 FR 9380, Mar. 7, 1985; 50 FR 11366, Mar. 21, 1985; 58 FR 54509, Oct. 22, 1993; 60 FR 20225, Apr. 25, 1995; 61 FR 42804, Aug. 19, 1996; 62 FR 53189, Oct. 10, 1997; 65 FR 14872, Mar. 20, 2000; 65 FR 50103, Aug. 16, 2000; 65 FR 54669, Sept. 8, 2000; 65 FR 57054, Sept. 20, 2000; 66 FR 67095, Dec. 28, 2001; 68 FR 71006, Dec. 22, 2003; 69 FR 56541, Sept. 21, 2004; 70 FR 3891, Jan. 27, 2005; 70 FR 30365, May 26, 2005; 70 FR 56128, Sept. 26, 2005; 74 FR 52689, Oct. 14, 2009; 77 FR 46625, Sept. 16, 2012; 77 FR 48820, Sept. 16, 2012; 78 FR 11055, Mar. 16, 2013; 78 FR 62402, Dec. 18, 2013; 80 FR 17959, May 13, 2015.

§1.79. RESERVATION CLAUSES NOT PERMITTED

A reservation for a future application of subject matter disclosed but not claimed in a pending application will not be permitted in the pending application, but an application disclosing unclaimed subject matter may contain a reference to a later filed application of the same applicant or owned by a common assignee disclosing and claiming that subject matter.

THE DRAWINGS

§1.81. DRAWINGS REQUIRED IN PATENT APPLICATION

(a) The applicant for a patent is required to furnish a drawing of the invention where necessary for the understanding of the subject matter sought to be patented. Since corrections are the responsibility of the applicant, the original drawing(s) should be retained by the applicant for any necessary future correction.

(b) Drawings may include illustrations which facilitate an understanding of the invention (for example, flow sheets in cases of processes, and diagrammatic views).

(c) Whenever the nature of the subject matter sought to be patented admits of illustration by a drawing without its being necessary for the understanding of the subject matter and the applicant has not furnished such a drawing, the examiner will require its submission within a time period of not less than two months from the date of the sending of a notice thereof.

(d) Drawings submitted after the filing date of the application may not be used to overcome any insufficiency of the specification due to lack of an enabling disclosure or otherwise inadequate disclosure therein, or to supplement the original disclosure thereof for the purpose of interpretation of the scope of any claim.

History of 37 C.F.R. §1.81: 43 FR 4015, Jan. 31, 1978; 53 FR 47808, Nov. 28, 1988; 77 FR 48821, Sept. 16, 2012; 78 FR 62404, Dec. 18, 2013.

§1.83. CONTENT OF DRAWING

(a) The drawing in a nonprovisional application must show every feature of the invention specified in the claims. However, conventional features disclosed in the description and claims, where their detailed illustration is not essential for a proper understanding of the invention, should be illustrated in the drawing in the form of a graphical drawing symbol or a labeled representation (e.g., a labeled rectangular box). In addition, tables that are included in the specification and sequences that are included in sequence listings should not be duplicated in the drawings.

(b) When the invention consists of an improvement on an old machine the drawing must when possible exhibit, in one or more views, the improved portion itself, disconnected from the old structure, and also in another view, so much only of the old structure as will suffice to show the connection of the invention therewith.

(c) Where the drawings in a nonprovisional application do not comply with the requirements of paragraphs (a) and (b) of this section, the examiner shall require such additional illustration within a time period of not less than two months from the date of the sending of a notice thereof. Such corrections are subject to the requirements of §1.81(d).

History of 37 C.F.R. §1.83: 31 FR 12923, Oct. 4, 1966; 43 FR 4015, Jan. 31, 1978; 60 FR 20226, Apr. 25, 1995; 69 FR 56541, Sept. 21, 2004; 78 FR 62405, Dec. 18, 2013.

§1.84. STANDARDS FOR DRAWINGS

(a) Drawings. There are two acceptable categories for presenting drawings in utility and design patent applications.

(1) Black ink. Black and white drawings are normally required. India ink, or its equivalent that secures solid black lines, must be used for drawings; or

(2) Color. Color drawings are permitted in design applications. Where a design application contains color drawings, the application must include the number of sets of color drawings required by paragraph (a)(2)(ii) of this section and the specification must contain the reference required by paragraph (a)(2)(iii) of this section. On rare occasions, color drawings may be necessary as the only practical medium by which to disclose the subject matter sought to be patented in a utility patent application. The color drawings must be of sufficient quality such that all details in the drawings are reproducible in black and white in the printed patent. Color drawings are not permitted in international applications (see PCT Rule 11.13). The Office will accept color drawings in utility patent applications only after granting a petition filed under this paragraph explaining why the color drawings are necessary. Any such petition must include the following:

(i) The fee set forth in §1.17(h);

(ii) One (1) set of color drawings if submitted via the Office electronic filing system or three (3) sets of color drawings if not submitted via the Office electronic filing system; and

(iii) An amendment to the specification to insert (unless the specification contains or has been previously amended to contain) the following language as the first paragraph of the brief description of the drawings:

The patent or application file contains at least one drawing executed in color. Copies of this patent or patent application publication with color drawing(s) will be provided by the Office upon request and payment of the necessary fee.

(b) Photographs—

(1) Black and white. Photographs, including photocopies of photographs, are not ordinarily permitted in utility and design patent applications. The Office will accept photographs in utility and design patent applications, however, if photographs are the only practicable medium for illustrating the claimed invention. For example, photographs or photomicrographs of: electrophoresis gels, blots (*e.g.*, immunological, western, Southern, and northern), autoradiographs, cell cultures (stained and unstained), histological tissue cross sections (stained and unstained), animals, plants, in vivo imaging, thin layer chromatography plates, crystalline structures, and, in a design patent application, ornamental effects, are acceptable. If the subject matter of the application admits of illustration by a drawing, the examiner may require a drawing in place of the photograph. The photographs must be of sufficient quality so that all details in the photographs are reproducible in the printed patent.

(2) Color photographs. Color photographs will be accepted in utility and design patent applications if the conditions for accepting color drawings and black and white photographs have been satisfied. See paragraphs (a)(2) and (b)(1) of this section.

(c) Identification of drawings. Identifying indicia should be provided, and if provided, should include the title of the invention, inventor's name, and application number, or docket number (if any) if an application number has not been assigned to the application. If this information is provided, it must be placed on the front of each sheet within the top margin. Each drawing sheet submitted after the filing date of an application must be identified as either "Replacement Sheet" or "New Sheet" pursuant to §1.121(d). If a marked-up copy of any amended drawing figure including annotations indicating the changes made is filed, such marked-up copy must be clearly labeled as "Annotated Sheet" pursuant to §1.121(d)(1).

(d) Graphic forms in drawings. Chemical or mathematical formulae, tables, and waveforms may be submitted as drawings, and are subject to the same requirements as drawings. Each chemical or mathematical formula must be labeled as a separate figure, using brackets when necessary, to show that information is properly integrated. Each group of waveforms must be presented as a single figure, using a common vertical axis with time extending along the horizontal axis. Each individual waveform discussed in the specification must be identified with a separate letter designation adjacent to the vertical axis.

(e) Type of paper. Drawings submitted to the Office must be made on paper which is flexible, strong, white, smooth, non-shiny, and durable. All sheets must be reasonably free from cracks, creases, and folds. Only one side of the sheet may be used for the drawing. Each sheet must be reasonably free from erasures and must be free from alterations, overwritings, and interlineations. Photographs must be developed on paper meeting the sheet-size requirements of paragraph (f) of this section and the margin requirements of paragraph (g) of this section. See paragraph (b) of this section for other requirements for photographs.

(f) Size of paper. All drawing sheets in an application must be the same size. One of the shorter sides of the sheet is regarded as its top. The size of the sheets on which drawings are made must be:

(1) 21.0 cm. by 29.7 cm. (DIN size A4), or

(2) 21.6 cm. by 27.9 cm. (8½ by 11 inches).

(g) Margins. The sheets must not contain frames around the sight (*i.e.*, the usable surface), but should have scan target points (*i.e.*, cross-hairs) printed on two catercorner margin corners. Each sheet must include a top margin of at least 2.5 cm. (1 inch), a left side margin of at least 2.5 cm. (1 inch), a right side margin of at least 1.5 cm. (5/8 inch), and a bottom margin of at least 1.0 cm. (3/8 inch), thereby leaving a sight no greater than 17.0 cm. by 26.2 cm. on 21.0 cm. by 29.7 cm. (DIN size A4) drawing sheets, and a sight no greater than 17.6 cm. by 24.4 cm. (6 15/16 by 9 5/8 inches) on 21.6 cm. by 27.9 cm. (8½ by 11 inch) drawing sheets.

(h) Views. The drawing must contain as many views as necessary to show the invention. The views may be plan, elevation, section, or perspective views. Detail views of portions of elements, on a larger scale if necessary, may also be used. All views of the drawing must be grouped together and arranged on the sheet(s) without wasting space, preferably in an upright position, clearly separated from one another, and must not be included in the sheets containing the specifications, claims, or abstract. Views must not be connected by projection lines and must not contain center lines. Waveforms of electrical signals may be connected by dashed lines to show the relative timing of the waveforms.

(1) Exploded views. Exploded views, with the separated parts embraced by a bracket, to show the relationship or order of assembly of various parts are permissible. When an exploded view is shown in a figure which is on the same sheet as another figure, the exploded view should be placed in brackets.

(2) Partial views. When necessary, a view of a large machine or device in its entirety may be broken into partial views on a single sheet, or extended over several sheets if there is no loss in facility of understanding the view. Partial views drawn on separate sheets must always be capable of being linked edge to edge so that no partial view contains parts of another partial view. A smaller scale view should be included showing the whole formed by the partial views and indicating the positions of the parts shown. When a portion of a view is enlarged for magnification purposes, the view and the enlarged view must each be labeled as separate views.

(i) Where views on two or more sheets form, in effect, a single complete view, the views on the several sheets must be so arranged that the complete figure can be assembled without concealing any part of any of the views appearing on the various sheets.

(ii) A very long view may be divided into several parts placed one above the other on a single sheet. However, the relationship between the different parts must be clear and unambiguous.

(3) Sectional views. The plane upon which a sectional view is taken should be indicated on the view from which the section is cut by a broken line. The ends of the broken line should be designated by Arabic or Roman numerals corresponding to the view number of the sectional view, and should have arrows to indicate the direction of sight. Hatching must be used to indicate section portions of an object, and must be made by regularly spaced oblique parallel lines spaced sufficiently apart to enable the lines to be distinguished without difficulty. Hatching should not impede the clear reading of the reference characters and lead lines. If it is not possible to place reference characters outside the hatched area, the hatching may be broken off wherever reference characters are inserted. Hatching must be at a substantial angle to the surrounding axes or principal lines, preferably 45 degrees. A cross section must be set out and drawn to show all of the materials as they are shown in the view from which the cross section was taken. The parts in cross section must show proper material(s) by hatching with regularly spaced parallel oblique strokes, the space between strokes being chosen on the basis of the total area to be hatched. The various parts of a cross section of the same item should be hatched in the same manner and should accurately and graphically indicate the nature of the material(s) that is illustrated in cross section. The hatching of juxtaposed different elements must be angled in a different way. In the case of large areas, hatching may be confined to an edging drawn around the entire inside of the outline of the area to be hatched. Different types of hatching should have different conventional meanings as regards the nature of a material seen in cross section.

(4) Alternate position. A moved position may be shown by a broken line superimposed upon a suitable view if this can be done without crowding; otherwise, a separate view must be used for this purpose.

(5) Modified forms. Modified forms of construction must be shown in separate views.

(i) Arrangement of views. One view must not be placed upon another or within the outline of another. All views on the same sheet should stand in the same direction and, if possible, stand so that they can be read with the sheet held in an upright position. If views wider than the width of the sheet are necessary for the clearest illustration of the invention, the sheet may be turned on its side so that the top of the sheet, with the appropriate top margin to be used as the heading space, is on the right-hand side. Words must appear in a horizontal, left-to-right fashion when the page is either upright or turned so that the top becomes the right side, except for graphs utilizing standard scientific convention to denote the axis of abscissas (of X) and the axis of ordinates (of Y).

(j) Front page view. The drawing must contain as many views as necessary to show the invention. One of the views should be suitable for inclusion on the front page of the patent application publication and patent as the illustration of the invention. Views must not be connected by projection lines and must not contain center lines. Applicant may suggest a single view (by figure number) for inclusion on the front page of the patent application publication and patent.

(k) Scale. The scale to which a drawing is made must be large enough to show the mechanism without crowding when the drawing is reduced in size to two-thirds in reproduction. Indications such as "actual size" or "scale ½" on the drawings are not permitted since these lose their meaning with reproduction in a different format.

(l) Character of lines, numbers, and letters. All drawings must be made by a process which will give them satisfactory reproduction characteristics. Every line, number, and letter must be durable, clean, black (except for color drawings), sufficiently dense and dark, and uniformly thick and well-defined. The weight of all lines and letters must be heavy enough to permit adequate reproduction. This requirement applies to all lines however fine, to shading, and to lines representing cut surfaces in sectional views. Lines and strokes of different thicknesses may be used in the same drawing where different thicknesses have a different meaning.

(m) Shading. The use of shading in views is encouraged if it aids in understanding the invention and if it does not reduce legibility. Shading is used to indicate the surface or shape of spherical, cylindrical, and conical elements of an object. Flat parts may also be lightly shaded. Such shading is preferred in the case of parts shown in perspective, but not for cross sections. See paragraph (h)(3) of this section. Spaced lines for shading are preferred. These lines must be thin, as few in number as practicable, and they must contrast with the rest of the drawings. As a substitute for shading, heavy lines on the shade side of objects can be used except where they superimpose on each other or obscure reference characters. Light should come from the upper left corner at an angle of 45 degrees. Surface delineations should preferably be shown by proper shading. Solid black shading areas are not permitted, except when used to represent bar graphs or color.

(n) Symbols. Graphical drawing symbols may be used for conventional elements when appropriate. The elements for which such symbols and labeled representations are used must be adequately identified in the specification. Known devices should be illustrated by symbols which have a universally recognized conventional meaning and are generally accepted in the art. Other symbols which are not universally recognized may be used, subject to approval by the Office, if they are not likely to be confused with existing conventional symbols, and if they are readily identifiable.

(o) Legends. Suitable descriptive legends may be used subject to approval by the Office, or may be required by the examiner where necessary for understanding of the drawing. They should contain as few words as possible.

(p) Numbers, letters, and reference characters.

(1) Reference characters (numerals are preferred), sheet numbers, and view numbers must be plain and legible, and must not be used in association with brackets or inverted commas, or enclosed within outlines, *e.g.*, encircled. They must be oriented in the same direction as the view so as to avoid having to rotate the sheet. Reference characters should be arranged to follow the profile of the object depicted.

(2) The English alphabet must be used for letters, except where another alphabet is customarily used, such as the Greek alphabet to indicate angles, wavelengths, and mathematical formulas.

(3) Numbers, letters, and reference characters must measure at least .32 cm. (1/8 inch) in height. They should not be placed in the drawing so as to interfere with its comprehension. Therefore, they should not cross or mingle with the lines. They should not be placed upon hatched or shaded surfaces. When necessary, such as indicating a surface or cross section, a reference character may be underlined and a blank space may be left in the hatching or shading where the character occurs so that it appears distinct.

(4) The same part of an invention appearing in more than one view of the drawing must always be designated by the same reference character, and the same reference character must never be used to designate different parts.

(5) Reference characters not mentioned in the description shall not appear in the drawings. Reference characters mentioned in the description must appear in the drawings.

(q) Lead lines. Lead lines are those lines between the reference characters and the details referred to. Such lines may be straight or curved and should be as short as possible. They must originate in the immediate proximity of the reference character and extend to the feature indicated. Lead lines must not cross each other. Lead lines are required for each reference character except for those which indicate the surface or cross section on which they are placed. Such a reference character must be underlined to make it clear that a lead line has not been left out by mistake. Lead lines must be executed in the same way as lines in the drawing. See paragraph (1) of this section.

(r) Arrows. Arrows may be used at the ends of the lines, provided that their meaning is clear, as follows:

(1) On a lead line, a freestanding arrow to indicate the entire section towards which it points;

(2) On a lead line, an arrow touching a line to indicate the surface shown by the line looking along the direction of the arrow; or

(3) To show the direction of movement.

(s) Copyright or Mask Work Notice. A copyright or mask work notice may appear in the drawing, but must be placed within the sight of the drawing immediately below the figure representing the copyright or mask work material and be limited to letters having a print size of .32 cm. to .64 cm. (1/8 to ¼ inches) high. The content of the notice must be limited to only those elements provided for by law. For example, "© 1983 John Doe" (17 U.S.C. 401) and "*M* John Doe" (17 U.S.C. 909) would be properly limited and, under current statutes, legally sufficient notices of copyright and mask work, respectively. Inclusion of a copyright or mask work notice will be permitted only if the authorization language set forth in §1.71(e) is included at the beginning (preferably as the first paragraph) of the specification.

(t) Numbering of sheets of drawings. The sheets of drawings should be numbered in consecutive Arabic numerals, starting with 1, within the sight as defined in paragraph (g) of this section. These numbers, if present, must be placed in the middle of the top of the sheet, but not in the margin. The numbers can be placed on the right-hand side if the drawing extends too close to the middle of the top edge of the usable surface. The drawing sheet numbering must be clear and larger than the numbers used as reference characters to avoid confusion. The number of each sheet should be shown by two Arabic numerals placed on either side of an oblique line, with the first being the sheet number, and the second being the total number of sheets of drawings, with no other marking.

(u) Numbering of views.

(1) The different views must be numbered in consecutive Arabic numerals, starting with 1, independent of the numbering of the sheets and, if possible, in the order in which they appear on the drawing sheet(s). Partial views intended to form one complete view, on one or several sheets, must be identified by the same number followed by a capital letter. View numbers must be preceded by the abbreviation "FIG." Where only a single view is used in an application to illustrate the claimed invention, it must not be numbered and the abbreviation "FIG." must not appear.

(2) Numbers and letters identifying the views must be simple and clear and must not be used in association with brackets, circles, or inverted commas. The view numbers must be larger than the numbers used for reference characters.

(v) Security markings. Authorized security markings may be placed on the drawings provided they are outside the sight, preferably centered in the top margin.

(w) Corrections. Any corrections on drawings submitted to the Office must be durable and permanent.

(x) Holes. No holes should be made by applicant in the drawing sheets.

(y) Types of drawings. See §1.152 for design drawings, §1.1026 for international design reproductions, §1.165 for plant drawings, and §1.173(a)(2) for reissue drawings.

History of 37 C.F.R. §1.84: 24 FR 10332, Dec. 22, 1959; 31 FR 12923, Oct. 4, 1966; 36 FR 9775, May 28, 1971; 43 FR 20464, May 11, 1978; 45 FR 73657, Nov. 6, 1980; 53 FR 47809, Nov. 28, 1988; 58 FR 38723, July 20, 1993; 58 FR 45841, Aug. 31, 1993; 58 FR 45842, Aug. 31, 1993; 61 FR 42804, Aug. 19, 1996; 62 FR 53190, Oct. 10, 1997; 65 FR 54669, Sept. 8, 2000; 65 FR 57055, Sept. 20, 2000; 69 FR 56541, Sept. 21, 2004; 70 FR 3891, Jan. 27, 2005; 78 FR 11057, Mar. 16, 2013; 80 FR 17962, May 13, 2015.

§1.85. CORRECTIONS TO DRAWINGS

(a) A utility or plant application will not be placed on the files for examination until objections to the drawings have been corrected. Except as provided in §1.215(c), any patent application publication will not include drawings filed after the application has been placed on the files for examination. Unless applicant is otherwise notified in an Office action, objections to the drawings in a utility or plant application will not be held in abeyance, and a request to hold objections to the drawings in abeyance will not be considered a bona fide attempt to advance the application to final action (§1.135(c)). If a drawing in a design application meets the requirements of §1.84(e), (f), and (g) and is suitable for reproduction, but is not otherwise in compliance with §1.84, the drawing may be admitted for examination.

(b) The Office will not release drawings for purposes of correction. If corrections are necessary, new corrected drawings must be submitted within the time set by the Office.

(c) If a corrected drawing is required or if a drawing does not comply with §1.84 or an amended drawing submitted under §1.121(d) in a nonprovisional international design application does not comply with§1.1026 at the time an application is allowed, the Office may notify the applicant in a notice of allowability and set a three-month period of time from the mail date of the notice of allowability within which the applicant must file a corrected drawing in compliance with §1.84 or 1.1026, as applicable, to avoid abandonment. This time period is not extendable under §1.136 (see §1.136(c)).

History of 37 C.F.R. §1.85: 36 FR 9775, May 28, 1971; 47 FR 41276, Sept. 17, 1982; 53 FR 47810, Nov. 28, 1988; 65 FR 54670, Sept. 8, 2000; 65 FR 57055, Sept. 20, 2000; 69 FR 56541, Sept. 21, 2004; 78 FR 62405, Dec. 18, 2013; 80 FR 17962, May 13, 2015.

§1.88. RESERVED

History of 37 C.F.R. §1.88: 58 FR 38726, July 20, 1993.

MODELS, EXHIBITS, SPECIMENS

§1.91. MODELS OR EXHIBITS NOT GENERALLY ADMITTED AS PART OF APPLICATION OR PATENT

(a) A model or exhibit will not be admitted as part of the record of an application unless it:

(1) Substantially conforms to the requirements of §1.52 or §1.84;

(2) Is specifically required by the Office; or

(3) Is filed with a petition under this section including:

(i) The fee set forth in §1.17(h); and

(ii) An explanation of why entry of the model or exhibit in the file record is necessary to demonstrate patentability.

(b) Notwithstanding the provisions of paragraph (a) of this section, a model, working model, or other physical exhibit may be required by the Office if deemed necessary for any purpose in examination of the application.

(c) Unless the model or exhibit substantially conforms to the requirements of §1.52 or §1.84 under paragraph (a)(1) of this section, it must be accompanied by photographs that show multiple views of the material features of the model or exhibit and that substantially conform to the requirements of §1.84.

History of 37 C.F.R. §1.91: 62 FR 53190, Oct. 10, 1997; 65 FR 54670, Sept. 8, 2000; 69 FR 56541, Sept. 21, 2004.

§1.92. RESERVED

History of 37 C.F.R. §1.92: 62 FR 53190, Oct. 10, 1997.

§1.93. SPECIMENS

When the invention relates to a composition of matter, the applicant may be required to furnish specimens of the composition, or of its ingredients or intermediates, for the purpose of inspection or experiment.

§1.94. RETURN OF MODELS, EXHIBITS OR SPECIMENS

(a) Models, exhibits, or specimens may be returned to the applicant if no longer necessary for the conduct of business before the Office. When applicant is notified that a model, exhibit, or specimen is no longer necessary for the conduct of business before the Office and will be returned, applicant must arrange for the return of the model, exhibit, or specimen at the applicant's expense. The Office will dispose of perishables without notice to applicant unless applicant notifies the Office upon submission of the model, exhibit or specimen that a return is desired and makes arrangements for its return promptly upon notification by the Office that the model, exhibit or specimen is no longer necessary for the conduct of business before the Office.

(b) Applicant is responsible for retaining the actual model, exhibit, or specimen for the enforceable life of any patent resulting from the application. The provisions of this paragraph do not apply to a model or exhibit that substantially conforms to the requirements of §1.52 or §1.84, where the model or exhibit has been described by photographs that substantially conform to §1.84, or where the model, exhibit or specimen is perishable.

(c) Where applicant is notified, pursuant to paragraph (a) of this section, of the need to arrange for return of a model, exhibit or specimen, applicant must arrange for the return within the period set in such notice, to avoid disposal of the model, exhibit or specimen by the Office. Extensions of time are available under §1.136, except in the case of perishables. Failure to establish that the return of the item has been arranged for within the period set or failure to have the item removed from Office storage within a reasonable amount of time notwithstanding any arrangement for return, will permit the Office to dispose of the model, exhibit or specimen.

History of 37 C.F.R. §1.94: 69 FR 56542, Sept. 21, 2004.

§1.95. COPIES OF EXHIBITS

Copies of models or other physical exhibits will not ordinarily be furnished by the Office, and any model or exhibit in an application or patent shall not be taken from the Office except in the custody of an employee of the Office specially authorized by the Director.

§1.96. SUBMISSION OF COMPUTER PROGRAM LISTINGS

(a) General. Descriptions of the operation and general content of computer program listings should appear in the description portion of the specification. A computer program listing for the purpose of this section is defined as a printout that lists in appropriate sequence the instructions, routines, and other contents of a program for a computer. The program listing may be either in machine or machine-independent (object or source) language which will cause a computer to perform a desired procedure or task such as solve a problem, regulate the flow of work in a computer, or control or monitor events. Computer program listings may be submitted in patent applications as set forth in paragraphs (b) and (c) of this section.

(b) Material which will be printed in the patent: If the computer program listing is contained in 300 lines or fewer, with each line of 72 characters or fewer, it may be submitted either as drawings or as part of the specification.

(1) Drawings. If the listing is submitted as drawings, it must be submitted in the manner and complying with the requirements for drawings as provided in §1.84. At least one figure numeral is required on each sheet of drawing.

(2) Specification.

(i) If the listing is submitted as part of the specification, it must be submitted in accordance with the provisions of §1.52.

(ii) Any listing having more than 60 lines of code that is submitted as part of the specification must be positioned at the end of the description but before the claims. Any amendment must be made by way of submission of a substitute sheet.

(c) As an appendix which will not be printed: Any computer program listing may, and any computer program listing having over 300 lines (up to 72 characters per line) must, be submitted on a compact disc in compliance with §1.52(e). A compact disc containing such a computer program listing is to be referred to as a "computer program listing appendix." The "computer program listing appendix" will not be part of the printed patent. The specification must include a reference to the "computer program listing appendix" at the location indicated in §1.77(b)(5).

(1) Multiple computer program listings for a single application may be placed on a single compact disc. Multiple compact discs may be submitted for a single application if necessary. A separate compact disc is required for each application containing a computer program listing that must be submitted on a "computer program listing appendix."

(2) The "computer program listing appendix" must be submitted on a compact disc that complies with §1.52(e) and the following specifications (no other format shall be allowed):

(i) Computer Compatibility: IBM PC/XT/AT, or compatibles, or Apple Macintosh;

(ii) Operating System Compatibility: MS-DOS, MS-Windows, Unix, or Macintosh;

(iii) Line Terminator: ASCII Carriage Return plus ASCII Line Feed;

(iv) Control Codes: the data must not be dependent on control characters or codes which are not defined in the ASCII character set; and

(v) Compression: uncompressed data.

History of 37 C.F.R. §1.96: 46 FR 2612, Jan. 12, 1981; 54 FR 47519, Nov. 15, 1989; 61 FR 42804, Aug. 19, 1996; 65 FR 54670, Sept. 8, 2000; 65 FR 78958, Dec. 18, 2000; 70 FR 54266, Sept. 14, 2005.

INFORMATION DISCLOSURE STATEMENT

§1.97. FILING OF INFORMATION DISCLOSURE STATEMENT

(a) In order for an applicant for a patent or for a reissue of a patent to have an information disclosure statement in compliance with §1.98 considered by the Office during the pendency of the application, the information disclosure statement must satisfy one of paragraphs (b), (c), or (d) of this section.

(b) An information disclosure statement shall be considered by the Office if filed by the applicant within any one of the following time periods:

(1) Within three months of the filing date of a national application other than a continued prosecution application under §1.53(d);

(2) Within three months of the date of entry of the national stage as set forth in §1.491 in an international application;

(3) Before the mailing of a first Office action on the merits;

(4) Before the mailing of a first Office action after the filing of a request for continued examination under §1.114; or

(5) Within three months of the date of publication of the international registration under Hague Agreement Article 10(3) in an international design application.

(c) An information disclosure statement shall be considered by the Office if filed after the period specified in paragraph (b) of this section, provided that the information disclosure statement is filed before the mailing date of any of a final action under §1.113, a notice of allowance under §1.311, or an action that otherwise closes prosecution in the application, and it is accompanied by one of:

(1) The statement specified in paragraph (e) of this section; or

(2) The fee set forth in §1.17(p).

(d) An information disclosure statement shall be considered by the Office if filed by the applicant after the period specified in paragraph (c) of this section, provided that the information disclosure statement is filed on or before payment of the issue fee and is accompanied by:

(1) The statement specified in paragraph (e) of this section; and

(2) The fee set forth in §1.17(p).

(e) A statement under this section must state either:

(1) That each item of information contained in the information disclosure statement was first cited in any communication from a foreign patent office in a counterpart foreign application not more than three months prior to the filing of the information disclosure statement; or

(2) That no item of information contained in the information disclosure statement was cited in a communication from a foreign patent office in a counterpart foreign application, and, to the knowledge of the person signing the certification after making reasonable inquiry, no item of information contained in the information disclosure statement was known to any individual designated in §1.56(c) more than three months prior to the filing of the information disclosure statement.

(f) No extensions of time for filing an information disclosure statement are permitted under §1.136. If a bona fide attempt is made to comply with §1.98, but part of the required content is inadvertently omitted, additional time may be given to enable full compliance.

(g) An information disclosure statement filed in accordance with this section shall not be construed as a representation that a search has been made.

(h) The filing of an information disclosure statement shall not be construed to be an admission that the information cited in the statement is, or is considered to be, material to patentability as defined in §1.56(b).

(i) If an information disclosure statement does not comply with either this section or §1.98, it will be placed in the file but will not be considered by the Office.

History of 37 C.F.R. §1.97: 42 FR 5594, Jan. 28, 1977; 48 FR 2712, Jan. 20, 1983; 57 FR 2034, Jan. 17, 1992; 59 FR 32658, June 24, 1994; 60 FR 20226, Apr. 25, 1995; 61 FR 42805, Aug. 19, 1996; 62 FR 53190, Oct. 10, 1997; 65 FR 14872, Mar. 20, 2000; 65 FR 50103, Aug. 16, 2000; 65 FR 54670, Sept. 8, 2000; 80 FR 17963, May 13, 2015.

§1.98. CONTENT OF INFORMATION DISCLOSURE STATEMENT

(a) Any information disclosure statement filed under §1.97 shall include the items listed in paragraphs (a)(1), (a)(2) and (a)(3) of this section.

(1) A list of all patents, publications, applications, or other information submitted for consideration by the Office. U.S. patents and U.S. patent application publications must be listed in a section separately from citations of other documents. Each page of the list must include:

(i) The application number of the application in which the information disclosure statement is being submitted;

(ii) A column that provides a space, next to each document to be considered, for the examiner's initials; and

(iii) A heading that clearly indicates that the list is an information disclosure statement.

(2) A legible copy of:

(i) Each foreign patent;

(ii) Each publication or that portion which caused it to be listed, other than U.S. patents and U.S. patent application publications unless required by the Office;

(iii) For each cited pending unpublished U.S. application, the application specification including the claims, and any drawing of the application, or that portion of the application which caused it to be listed including any claims directed to that portion; and

(iv) All other information or that portion which caused it to be listed.

(3)(i) A concise explanation of the relevance, as it is presently understood by the individual designated in §1.56(c) most knowledgeable about the content of the information, of each patent, publication, or other information listed that is not in the English language. The concise explanation may be either separate from applicant's specification or incorporated therein.

(ii) A copy of the translation if a written English-language translation of a non-English-language document, or portion thereof, is within the possession, custody, or control of, or is readily available to any individual designated in §1.56(c).

(b)(1) Each U.S. patent listed in an information disclosure statement must be identified by inventor, patent number, and issue date.

(2) Each U.S. patent application publication listed in an information disclosure statement shall be identified by applicant, patent application publication number, and publication date.

(3) Each U.S. application listed in an information disclosure statement must be identified by the inventor, application number, and filing date.

(4) Each foreign patent or published foreign patent application listed in an information disclosure statement must be identified by the country or patent office which issued the patent or published the application, an appropriate document number, and the publication date indicated on the patent or published application.

(5) Each publication listed in an information disclosure statement must be identified by publisher, author (if any), title, relevant pages of the publication, date, and place of publication.

(c) When the disclosures of two or more patents or publications listed in an information disclosure statement are substantively cumulative, a copy of one of the patents or publications as specified in paragraph (a) of this section may be submitted without copies of the other patents or publications, provided that it is stated that these other patents or publications are cumulative.

(d) A copy of any patent, publication, pending U.S. application or other information, as specified in paragraph (a) of this section, listed in an information disclosure statement is required to be provided, even if the patent, publication, pending U.S. application or other information was previously submitted to, or cited by, the Office in an earlier application, unless:

(1) The earlier application is properly identified in the information disclosure statement and is relied on for an earlier effective filing date under 35 U.S.C. 120; and

(2) The information disclosure statement submitted in the earlier application complies with paragraphs (a) through (c) of this section.

History of 37 C.F.R. §1.98: 42 FR 5594, Jan. 28, 1977; 48 FR 2712, Jan. 20, 1983; 57 FR 2035, Jan. 17, 1992; 65 FR 54671, Sept. 8, 2000; 65 FR 57055, Sept. 20, 2000; 68 FR 38628, June 30, 2003; 69 FR 56542, Sept. 21, 2004.

§1.99. REMOVED & RESERVED

History of 37 C.F.R. §1.99: 77 FR 42173, Sept. 16, 2012.

EXAMINATION OF APPLICATIONS

§1.101. RESERVED

History of 37 C.F.R. §1.101: 62 FR 53190, Oct. 10, 1997.

§1.102. ADVANCEMENT OF EXAMINATION

(a) Applications will not be advanced out of turn for examination or for further action except as provided by this part, or upon order of the Director to expedite the business of the Office, or upon filing of a request under paragraph (b) or (e) of this section or upon filing a petition or request under paragraph (c) or (d) of this section with a showing which, in the opinion of the Director, will justify so advancing it.

(b) Applications wherein the inventions are deemed of peculiar importance to some branch of the public service and the head of some department of the Government requests immediate action for that reason, may be advanced for examination.

(c) A petition to make an application special may be filed without a fee if the basis for the petition is:

(1) The applicant's age or health; or

(2) That the invention will materially:

(i) Enhance the quality of the environment;

(ii) Contribute to the development or conservation of energy resources; or

(iii) Contribute to countering terrorism.

(d) A petition to make an application special on grounds other than those referred to in paragraph (c) of this section must be accompanied by the fee set forth in §1.17(h).

(e) A request for prioritized examination under this paragraph must comply with the requirements of this paragraph and be accompanied by the prioritized examination fee set forth in §1.17(c), the processing fee set forth in §1.17(i), and if not already paid, the publication fee set forth in §1.18(d). An application for which prioritized examination has been requested may not contain or be amended to contain more than four independent claims, more than thirty total claims, or any multiple dependent claim. Prioritized examination under this paragraph will not be accorded to international applications that have not entered the national stage under 35 U.S.C. 371, design applications, reissue applications, provisional applications, or reexamination proceedings. A request for prioritized examination must also comply with the requirements of paragraph (e)(1) or paragraph (e)(2) of this section.

(1) A request for prioritized examination may be filed with an original utility or plant nonprovisional application under 35 U.S.C. 111(a). The application must include a specification as prescribed by 35 U.S.C. 112 including at least one claim, a drawing when necessary, and the inventor's oath or declaration on filing, except that the filing of an inventor's oath or declaration may be postponed in accordance with §1.53(f)(3) if an application data sheet meeting the conditions specified in §1.53(f)(3)(i) is present upon filing. If the application is a utility application, it must be filed via the Office's electronic filing system and include the filing fee under §1.16(a), search fee under §1.16(k), and examination fee under §1.16(o) upon filing. If the application is a plant application, it must include the filing fee under §1.16(c), search fee under §1.16(m), and examination fee under §1.16(q) upon filing. The request for prioritized examination in compliance with this paragraph must be present upon filing of the application, except that the applicant may file an amendment to cancel any independent claims in excess of four, any total claims in excess of thirty, and any multiple dependent claim not later than one month from a first decision on the request for prioritized examination. This one-month time period is not extendable.

(2) A request for prioritized examination may be filed with or after a request for continued examination in compliance with §1.114. If the application is a utility application, the request must be filed via the Office's electronic filing system. The request must be filed before the mailing of the first Office action after the filing of the request for continued examination under §1.114. Only a single such request for prioritized examination under this paragraph may be granted in an application.

History of 37 C.F.R. §1.102: 24 FR 10332, Dec. 22, 1959; 47 FR 41276, Sept. 17, 1982; 54 FR 6903, Feb. 15, 1989; 60 FR 20226, Apr. 25, 1995; 62 FR 53190, Oct. 10, 1997; 65 FR 54671, Sept. 8, 2000; 69 FR 56542, Sept. 21, 2004; 76 FR 18407, Apr. 4, 2011; 76 FR 23876, Apr. 29, 2011; 76 FR 59054, Sept. 23, 2011; 76 FR 78569, Dec. 19, 2011; 79 FR 12390, Mar. 5, 2014; 79 FR 68124, Nov. 14, 2014.

§1.103. SUSPENSION OF ACTION BY THE OFFICE

(a) Suspension for cause. On request of the applicant, the Office may grant a suspension of action by the Office under this paragraph for good and sufficient cause. The Office will not suspend action if a reply by applicant to an Office action is outstanding. Any petition for suspension of action under this paragraph must specify a period of suspension not exceeding six months. Any petition for suspension of action under this paragraph must also include:

(1) A showing of good and sufficient cause for suspension of action; and

(2) The fee set forth in §1.17(g), unless such cause is the fault of the Office.

(b) Limited suspension of action in a continued prosecution application (CPA) filed under §1.53(d). On request of the applicant, the Office may grant a suspension of action by the Office under this paragraph in a continued prosecution application filed under §1.53(d) for a period not exceeding three months. Any request for suspension of action under this paragraph must be filed with the request for an application filed under §1.53(d), specify the period of suspension, and include the processing fee set forth in §1.17(i).

(c) Limited suspension of action after a request for continued examination (RCE) under §1.114. On request of the applicant, the Office may grant a suspension of action by the Office under this paragraph after the filing of a request for continued examination in compliance with §1.114 for a period not exceeding three months. Any request for suspension of action under this paragraph must be filed with the request for continued examination under §1.114, specify the period of suspension, and include the processing fee set forth in §1.17(i).

(d) Deferral of examination. On request of the applicant, the Office may grant a deferral of examination under the conditions specified in this paragraph for a period not extending beyond three years from the earliest filing date for which a benefit is claimed under title 35, United States Code. A request for deferral of examination under this paragraph must include the publication fee set forth in §1.18(d) and the processing fee set forth in §1.17(i). A request for deferral of examination under this paragraph will not be granted unless:

(1) The application is an original utility or plant application filed under §1.53(b) or resulting from entry of an international application into the national stage after compliance with §1.495;

(2) The applicant has not filed a nonpublication request under §1.213(a), or has filed a request under §1.213(b) to rescind a previously filed nonpublication request;

(3) The application is in condition for publication as provided in §1.211(c); and

(4) The Office has not issued either an Office action under 35 U.S.C. 132 or a notice of allowance under 35 U.S.C. 151.

(e) Notice of suspension on initiative of the Office. The Office will notify applicant if the Office suspends action by the Office on an application on its own initiative.

(f) Suspension of action for public safety or defense. The Office may suspend action by the Office by order of the Director if the following conditions are met:

(1) The application is owned by the United States;

(2) Publication of the invention may be detrimental to the public safety or defense; and

(3) The appropriate department or agency requests such suspension.

History of 37 C.F.R. §1.103: 24 FR 10332, Dec. 22, 1959; 33 FR 5624, Apr. 11, 1968; 47 FR 41276, Sept. 17, 1982; 49 FR 48452, Dec. 12, 1984; 50 FR 9381, Mar. 7, 1985; 54 FR 6903, Feb. 15, 1989; 60 FR 20226, Apr. 25, 1995; 62 FR 53191, Oct. 10, 1997; 65 FR 50104, Aug. 16, 2000; 65 FR 57056, Sept. 20, 2000; 67 FR 523, Jan. 4, 2002; 69 FR 49999, Aug. 12, 2004; 69 FR 56542, Sept. 21, 2004; 78 FR 11057, Mar. 16, 2013.

§1.104. NATURE OF EXAMINATION

(a) Examiner's action.

(1) On taking up an application for examination or a patent in a reexamination proceeding, the examiner shall make a thorough study thereof and shall make a thorough investigation of the available prior art relating to the subject matter of the claimed invention. The examination shall be complete with respect both to compliance of the application or patent under reexamination with the applicable statutes and rules and to the patentability of the invention as claimed, as well as with respect to matters of form, unless otherwise indicated.

(2) The applicant, or in the case of a reexamination proceeding, both the patent owner and the requester, will be notified of the examiner's action. The reasons for any adverse action or any objection or requirement will be stated in an Office action and such information or references will be given as may be useful in aiding the applicant, or in the case of a reexamination proceeding the patent owner, to judge the propriety of continuing the prosecution.

(3) An international-type search will be made in all national applications filed on and after June 1, 1978.

(4) Any national application may also have an international-type search report prepared thereon at the time of the national examination on the merits, upon specific written request therefor and payment of the international-type search report fee set forth in §1.21(e). The Patent and Trademark Office does not require that a formal report of an international-type search be prepared in order to obtain a search fee refund in a later filed international application.

(b) Completeness of examiner's action. The examiner's action will be complete as to all matters, except that in appropriate circumstances, such as misjoinder of invention, fundamental defects in the application, and the like, the action of the examiner may be limited to such matters before further action is made. However, matters of form need not be raised by the examiner until a claim is found allowable.

(c) Rejection of claims.

(1) If the invention is not considered patentable, or not considered patentable as claimed, the claims, or those considered unpatentable will be rejected.

(2) In rejecting claims for want of novelty or for obviousness, the examiner must cite the best references at his or her command. When a reference is complex or shows or describes inventions other than that claimed by the applicant, the particular part relied on must be designated as nearly as practicable. The pertinence of each reference, if not apparent, must be clearly explained and each rejected claim specified.

(3) In rejecting claims the examiner may rely upon admissions by the applicant, or the patent owner in a reexamination proceeding, as to any matter affecting patentability and, insofar as rejections in applications are concerned, may also rely upon facts within his or her knowledge pursuant to paragraph (d)(2) of this section.

(4)(i) Subject matter which would otherwise qualify as prior art under 35 U.S.C. 102(a)(2) and a claimed invention will be treated as commonly owned for purposes of 35 U.S.C. 102(b)(2)(C) if the applicant or patent owner provides a statement to the effect that the subject matter and the claimed invention, not later than the effective filing date of the claimed invention, were owned by the same person or subject to an obligation of assignment to the same person.

(ii) Subject matter which would otherwise qualify as prior art under 35 U.S.C. 102(a)(2) and a claimed invention will be treated as commonly owned for purposes of 35 U.S.C. 102(b)(2)(C) on the basis of a joint research agreement under 35 U.S.C. 102(c) if:

(A) The applicant or patent owner provides a statement to the effect that the subject matter was developed and the claimed invention was made by or on behalf of one or more parties to a joint research agreement, within the meaning of 35 U.S.C. 100(h) and §1.9(e), that was in effect on or before the effective filing date of the claimed invention, and the claimed invention was made as a result of activities undertaken within the scope of the joint research agreement; and

(B) The application for patent for the claimed invention discloses or is amended to disclose the names of the parties to the joint research agreement.

(5)(i) Subject matter which qualifies as prior art under 35 U.S.C. 102(e), (f), or (g) in effect prior to March 16, 2013, and a claimed invention in an application filed on or after November 29, 1999, or any patent issuing thereon, in an application filed before November 29, 1999, but pending on December 10, 2004, or any patent issuing thereon, or in any patent granted on or after December 10, 2004, will be treated as commonly owned for purposes of 35 U.S.C. 103(c) in effect prior to March 16, 2013, if the applicant or patent owner provides a statement to the effect that the subject matter and the claimed invention, at the time the claimed invention was made, were owned by the same person or subject to an obligation of assignment to the same person.

(ii) Subject matter which qualifies as prior art under 35 U.S.C. 102(e), (f), or (g) in effect prior to March 16, 2013, and a claimed invention in an application pending on or after December 10, 2004, or in any patent granted on or after December 10, 2004, will be treated as commonly owned for purposes of 35 U.S.C. 103(c) in effect prior to March 16, 2013, on the basis of a joint research agreement under 35 U.S.C. 103(c)(2) in effect prior to March 16, 2013, if:

(A) The applicant or patent owner provides a statement to the effect that the subject matter and the claimed invention were made by or on behalf of the parties to a joint research agreement, within the meaning of 35 U.S.C. 100(h) and §1.9(e), which was in effect on or before the date the claimed invention was made, and that the claimed invention was made as a result of activities undertaken within the scope of the joint research agreement; and

(B) The application for patent for the claimed invention discloses or is amended to disclose the names of the parties to the joint research agreement.

(6) Patents issued prior to December 10, 2004, from applications filed prior to November 29, 1999, are subject to 35 U.S.C. 103(c) in effect on November 28, 1999.

(d) Citation of references.

(1) If domestic patents are cited by the examiner, their numbers and dates, and the names of the patentees will be stated. If domestic patent application publications are cited by the examiner, their publication number, publication date, and the names of the applicants will be stated. If foreign published applications or patents are cited, their nationality or country, numbers and dates, and the names of the patentees will be stated, and such other data will be furnished as may be necessary to enable the applicant, or in the case of a reexamination proceeding, the patent owner, to identify the published applications or patents cited. In citing foreign published applications or patents, in case only a part of the document is involved, the particular pages and sheets containing the parts relied upon will be identified. If printed publications are cited, the author (if any), title, date, pages or plates, and place of publication, or place where a copy can be found, will be given.

(2) When a rejection in an application is based on facts within the personal knowledge of an employee of the Office, the data shall be as specific as possible, and the reference must be supported, when called for by the applicant, by the affidavit of such employee, and such affidavit shall be subject to contradiction or explanation by the affidavits of the applicant and other persons.

(e) Reasons for allowance. If the examiner believes that the record of the prosecution as a whole does not make clear his or her reasons for allowing a claim or claims, the examiner may set forth such reasoning. The reasons shall be incorporated into an Office action rejecting other claims of the application or patent under reexamination or be the subject of a separate communication to the applicant or patent owner. The applicant or patent owner may file a statement commenting on the reasons for allowance within such time as may be specified by the examiner. Failure by the examiner to respond to any statement commenting on reasons for allowance does not give rise to any implication.

History of 37 C.F.R. §1.104: 24 FR 10332, Dec. 22, 1959; 43 FR 20465, May 11, 1978; 46 FR 29182, May 29, 1981; 47 FR 41276, Sept. 17, 1982; 50 FR 9381, Mar. 7, 1985; 57 FR 29642, July 6, 1992; 62 FR 53191, Oct. 10, 1997; 65 FR 14872, Mar. 20, 2000; 65 FR 50103, Aug. 16, 2000; 65 FR 54671, Sept. 8, 2000; 65 FR 57056, Sept. 20, 2000; 70 FR 1823, Jan. 11, 2005; 70 FR 54266, Sept. 14, 2005; 74 FR 52690, Oct. 14, 2009; 78 FR 11057, Mar. 16, 2013.

§1.105. REQUIREMENTS FOR INFORMATION

(a)(1) In the course of examining or treating a matter in a pending or abandoned application, in a patent, or in a reexamination proceeding, including a reexamination proceeding ordered as a result of a supplemental examination proceeding, the examiner or other Office employee may require the submission, from individuals identified under §1.56(c), or any assignee, of such information as may be reasonably necessary to properly examine or treat the matter, for example:

(i) Commercial databases: The existence of any particularly relevant commercial database known to any of the inventors that could be searched for a particular aspect of the invention.

(ii) Search: Whether a search of the prior art was made, and if so, what was searched.

(iii) Related information: A copy of any non-patent literature, published application, or patent (U.S. or foreign), by any of the inventors, that relates to the claimed invention.

(iv) Information used to draft application: A copy of any non-patent literature, published application, or patent (U.S. or foreign) that was used to draft the application.

(v) Information used in invention process: A copy of any non-patent literature, published application, or patent (U.S. or foreign) that was used in the invention process, such as by designing around or providing a solution to accomplish an invention result.

(vi) Improvements: Where the claimed invention is an improvement, identification of what is being improved.

(vii) In use: Identification of any use of the claimed invention known to any of the inventors at the time the application was filed notwithstanding the date of the use.

(viii) Technical information known to applicant. Technical information known to applicant concerning the related art, the disclosure, the claimed subject matter, other factual information pertinent to patentability, or concerning the accuracy of the examiner's stated interpretation of such items.

(2) Requirements for factual information known to applicant may be presented in any appropriate manner, for example:

(i) A requirement for factual information;

(ii) Interrogatories in the form of specific questions seeking applicant's factual knowledge; or

(iii) Stipulations as to facts with which the applicant may agree or disagree.

(3) Any reply to a requirement for information pursuant to this section that states either that the information required to be submitted is unknown to or is not readily available to the party or parties from which it was requested may be accepted as a complete reply.

(b) The requirement for information of paragraph (a)(1) of this section may be included in an Office action, or sent separately.

(c) A reply, or a failure to reply, to a requirement for information under this section will be governed by §§1.135 and 1.136.

History of 37 C.F.R. §1.105: 65 FR 54671, Sept. 8, 2000; 69 FR 56542, Sept. 21, 2004; 74 FR 52690, Oct. 14, 2009; 77 FR 48821, Sept. 16, 2012; 80 FR 17963, May 13, 2015.

§§1.106 TO 1.108. RESERVED

History of 37 C.F.R. §§1.106-1.108: 62 FR 53192, Oct. 10, 1997.

§1.109. EFFECTIVE FILING DATE OF A CLAIMED INVENTION UNDER THE LEAHY-SMITH AMERICA INVENTS ACT

(a) The effective filing date for a claimed invention in a patent or application for patent, other than in a reissue application or reissued patent, is the earliest of:

(1) The actual filing date of the patent or the application for the patent containing a claim to the invention; or

(2) The filing date of the earliest application for which the patent or application is entitled, as to such invention, to a right of priority or the benefit of an earlier filing date under 35 U.S.C. 119, 120, 121, 365, or 386.

(b) The effective filing date for a claimed invention in a reissue application or a reissued patent is determined by deeming the claim to the invention to have been contained in the patent for which reissue was sought.

History of 37 C.F.R. §1.109: 78 FR 11057, Mar. 16, 2013; 80 FR 17963, May 13, 2015.

§1.110. INVENTORSHIP & OWNERSHIP OF THE SUBJECT MATTER OF INDIVIDUAL CLAIMS

When one or more joint inventors are named in an application or patent, the Office may require an applicant or patentee to identify the inventorship and ownership or obligation to assign ownership, of each claimed invention on its effective filing date (as defined in §1.109) or on its date of invention, as applicable, when necessary for purposes of an Office proceeding. The Office may also require an applicant or patentee to identify the invention dates of the subject matter of each claim when necessary for purposes of an Office proceeding.

History of 37 C.F.R. §1.110: 50 FR 9381, Mar. 7, 1985; 61 FR 42805, Aug. 19, 1996; 74 FR 52690, Oct. 14, 2009; 78 FR 11058, Mar. 16, 2013.

EXAMINATION GUIDELINES FOR IMPLEMENTING THE FIRST INVENTOR TO FILE PROVISIONS OF THE LEAHY-SMITH AMERICA INVENTS ACT

Table of Contents

Examination Guidelines for 35 U.S.C. 102 and 103 as Amended by the First Inventor To File Provisions of the Leahy-Smith America Invents Act

Examination Guidelines for 35 U.S.C. 102 and 103 as Amended by the First Inventor To File Provisions of the Leahy-Smith America Invents Act

I. Overview of the Changes to 35 U.S.C. 102 and 103 in the AIA

The AIA continues to employ 35 U.S.C. 102 to set forth the scope of prior art that will preclude the grant of a patent on a claimed invention, but adjusts what qualifies as such prior art. Specifically, the AIA sets forth what qualifies as prior art in two paragraphs of 35 U.S.C. 102(a). AIA 35 U.S.C. 102(a)(1) provides that a person is not entitled to a patent if the claimed invention was patented, described in a printed publication, or in public use, on sale, or otherwise available to the public before the effective filing date of the claimed invention. AIA 35 U.S.C. 102(a)(2) provides that a person is not entitled to a patent if the claimed invention was described in a patent issued under 35 U.S.C. 151, or in an application for patent published or deemed published under 35 U.S.C. 122(b), in which the patent or application, as the case may be, names another inventor, and was effectively filed before the effective filing date of the claimed invention. AIA 35 U.S.C. 102(b) sets forth exceptions to prior art established in AIA 35 U.S.C. 102(a). Specifically, AIA 35 U.S.C. 102(b)(1) sets forth exceptions to prior art established in AIA 35 U.S.C. 102(a)(1), and AIA 35 U.S.C. 102(b)(2) sets forth exceptions to prior art established in AIA 35 U.S.C. 102(a)(2).

The AIA also provides definitions in 35 U.S.C. 100 of the meaning of the terms "claimed invention," "effective filing date," "the inventor," and "joint inventor" (or "coinventor"). The AIA defines the term "claimed invention" in 35 U.S.C. 100(j) as the subject matter defined by a claim in a patent or an application for a patent. The AIA defines the term "effective filing date" for a claimed invention in a patent or application for patent (other than a reissue application or reissued patent) in 35 U.S.C. 100(i)(1) as meaning the earliest of: (1) The actual filing date of the patent or the application for the patent containing the claimed invention; or (2) the filing date of the earliest provisional, nonprovisional, international (PCT), or foreign patent application to which the patent or application is entitled to benefit or priority as to such claimed invention. The AIA defines the term "the inventor" as the individual or if a joint invention, the individuals collectively who invented or discovered the subject matter of the invention in 35 U.S.C. 100(f), and defines the term "joint inventor" and "co-inventor" to mean any one of the individuals who invented or discovered the subject matter of a joint invention in 35 U.S.C. 100(g).

As discussed previously, AIA 35 U.S.C. 102(a)(1) provides that a person is not entitled to a patent if the claimed invention was patented, described in a printed publication, or in public use, on sale, or otherwise available to the public before the effective filing date of the claimed invention. Under pre-AIA 35 U.S.C. 102(a) and (b), knowledge or use of the invention (pre-AIA 35 U.S.C. 102(a)), or public use or sale of the invention (pre-AIA 35 U.S.C. 102(b)), was required to be in the United States to qualify as a prior art activity. Under the AIA, a prior public use, sale activity, or other disclosure has no geographic requirement (i.e., need not be in the United States) to qualify as prior art.

AIA 35 U.S.C. 102(b)(1) provides that a disclosure made one year or less before the effective filing date of a claimed invention shall not be prior art under 35 U.S.C. 102(a)(1) with respect to the claimed invention if: (1) The disclosure was made by the inventor or joint inventor or by another who obtained the subject matter disclosed directly or indirectly from the inventor or a joint inventor; or (2) the subject matter disclosed had, before such disclosure, been publicly disclosed by the inventor or a joint inventor or by another who obtained the subject matter disclosed directly or indirectly from the inventor or a joint inventor. Thus, AIA 35 U.S.C. 102(b)(1) provides a one-year grace period (grace period) after a first disclosure of an invention within which the inventor, assignee, obligated assignee, or other party having sufficient interest may file a patent application. The one-year grace period in AIA 35 U.S.C. 102(b)(1) is measured from the filing date of the earliest U.S. or foreign patent application to which a proper benefit or priority claim as to such invention has been asserted in the patent or application. Notably, the one-year grace period in pre-AIA 35 U.S.C. 102(b) is measured from only the filing date of the earliest application filed in the United States (directly or through the PCT).

The date of invention is not relevant under AIA 35 U.S.C. 102. Thus, a prior art disclosure could not be disqualified or antedated by showing that the inventor invented the claimed invention prior to the effective date of the prior art disclosure of the subject matter (e.g., under the provisions of 37 CFR 1.131).

As discussed previously, AIA 35 U.S.C. 102(a)(2) provides that a person is not entitled to a patent if the claimed invention was described in a U.S. patent, a U.S. patent application publication, or an application for patent deemed published under 35 U.S.C. 122(b), that names another inventor and was effectively filed before the effective filing date of the claimed invention. Under 35 U.S.C. 374, a World Intellectual Property Organization (WIPO) publication of a Patent Cooperation Treaty (PCT) international application that designates the United States is an application for patent deemed published under 35 U.S.C. 122(b) for purposes of AIA 35 U.S.C. 102(a)(2). Thus, under the AIA, WIPO publications of PCT applications that designate the United States are treated as U.S. patent application publications for prior art purposes, regardless of the international filing date, whether they are published in English, or whether the PCT international application enters the national stage in the United States. Accordingly, a U.S. patent, a U.S. patent application publication, or a WIPO publication of a PCT application (WIPO published application) that designates the United States, that names another inventor and was effectively filed before the effective filing date of the claimed invention, is prior art under AIA 35 U.S.C. 102(a)(2). Under pre-AIA 35 U.S.C. 102(e), a WIPO published application designating the United States is treated as a U.S. patent application publication only if the PCT application was filed on or after November 29, 2000, and published under PCT Article 21(2) in the English language.[47]

AIA 35 U.S.C. 102(d) defines "effectively filed" for the purpose of determining whether a U.S. patent, U.S. patent application publication, or WIPO published application is prior art under AIA 35 U.S.C. 102(a)(2) to a claimed invention. A U.S. patent, U.S. patent application publication, or WIPO published application is considered to have been effectively filed for purposes of its prior art effect under 35 U.S.C. 102(a)(2) with respect to any subject matter it describes on the earliest of: (1) The actual filing date of the patent or the application for patent; or (2) if the patent or application for patent is entitled to claim the benefit of, or priority to, the filing date of an earlier U.S. provisional, U.S. nonprovisional, international (PCT), or foreign patent application, the filing date of the earliest such application that describes the subject matter of the claimed invention. Thus, a U.S. patent, a U.S. patent application publication, or WIPO published application is effective as prior art as of the filing date of the earliest application to which benefit or priority is claimed and which describes the subject matter relied upon, regardless of whether the earliest such application is a U.S. provisional or nonprovisional application, an international (PCT) application, or a foreign patent application.

AIA 35 U.S.C. 102(b)(2)(A) and (B) provide that a disclosure shall not be prior art to a claimed invention under 35 U.S.C. 102(a)(2) if: (1) The subject matter disclosed was obtained directly or indirectly from the inventor or a joint inventor; or (2) the subject matter disclosed had, before such subject matter was effectively filed under 35 U.S.C. 102(a)(2), been publicly disclosed by the inventor or a joint inventor or another who obtained the subject matter disclosed directly or indirectly from the inventor or a joint inventor. Thus, under the AIA, a U.S. patent, U.S. patent application publication, or WIPO published application that was not issued or published more than one year before the effective filing date of the claimed invention is not prior art to the claimed invention if: (1) The U.S. patent, U.S. patent application publication, or WIPO published application was by another who obtained the subject matter disclosed from the inventor or a joint inventor; or (2) the inventor or a joint inventor, or another who obtained the subject matter disclosed from an inventor or joint inventor, had publicly disclosed the subject matter before the effective filing date of the U.S. patent, U.S. patent application publication, or WIPO published application.

Additionally, AIA 35 U.S.C. 102(b)(2)(C) provides that a disclosure made in a U.S. patent, U.S. patent application publication, or WIPO published application shall not be prior art to a claimed invention under 35 U.S.C. 102(a)(2) if, not later than the effective filing date of the claimed invention, the subject matter disclosed and the claimed invention were owned by the same person or subject to an obligation of assignment to the same person. This provision replaces the exception in pre-AIA 35 U.S.C. 103(c) that applied only in the context of an obviousness analysis under 35 U.S.C. 103 to prior art that was commonly owned at the time the claimed invention was made, and which qualified as prior art only under pre-AIA 35 U.S.C. 102(e), (f), and/or (g). Thus, the AIA provides that certain prior patents and published patent applications of co-workers and collaborators are not prior art either for purposes of determining novelty (35 U.S.C. 102) or nonobviousness (35 U.S.C. 103). This exception, however, applies only to prior art under AIA 35 U.S.C. 102(a)(2), namely, U.S. patents, U.S. patent application publications, or WIPO published applications effectively filed, but not published, before the effective filing date of the claimed invention. This exception does not apply to prior art that is available under 35 U.S.C. 102(a)(1), that is, patents, printed publications, public uses, sale activities, or other publicly available disclosures published or occurring before the effective filing date of the claimed invention. A prior disclosure, as defined in AIA 35 U.S.C. 102(a)(1), by a co-worker or collaborator is prior art under AIA 35 U.S.C. 102(a)(1) unless it falls within an exception under AIA 35 U.S.C. 102(b)(1), regardless of whether the subject matter of the prior disclosure and the claimed invention was commonly owned not later than the effective filing date of the claimed invention.

The AIA eliminates the provisions in pre-AIA 35 U.S.C. 102(c) (abandonment of the invention), 102(d) (premature foreign patenting), 102(f) (derivation), and 102(g) (prior invention by another). Under the AIA, abandonment of the invention or premature foreign patenting is not relevant to patentability. Prior invention by another is likewise not relevant to patentability under the AIA unless there is a prior disclosure or filing of an application by another. The situation in which an application names a person who is not the actual inventor as the inventor (pre-AIA 35 U.S.C. 102(f)) will be handled in a derivation proceeding under 35 U.S.C. 135, by a correction of inventorship under 37 CFR 1.48 to name the actual inventor, or through a rejection under 35 U.S.C. 101[48] and 35 U.S.C. 115.[49]

AIA 35 U.S.C. 102(c) provides for common ownership of subject matter made pursuant to joint research agreements. Under 35 U.S.C. 100(h), the term "joint research agreement" as used in AIA 35 U.S.C. 102(c) is defined as a written contract, grant, or cooperative agreement entered into by two or more persons or entities for the performance of experimental, developmental, or research work in the field of the claimed invention. AIA 35 U.S.C. 102(c) specifically provides that subject matter disclosed and a claimed invention shall be deemed to have been owned by the same person or subject to an obligation of assignment to the same person in applying the provisions of AIA 35 U.S.C. 102(b)(2)(C) if: (1) The subject matter disclosed was developed and the claimed invention was made by, or on behalf of, one or more parties to a joint research agreement that was in effect on or before the effective filing date of the claimed invention; (2) the claimed invention was made as a result of activities undertaken within the scope of the joint research agreement; and (3) the application for patent for the claimed invention discloses or is amended to disclose the names of the parties to the joint research agreement.

AIA 35 U.S.C. 103 provides that a patent for a claimed invention may not be obtained, notwithstanding that the claimed invention is not identically disclosed as set forth in 35 U.S.C. 102, if the differences between the claimed invention and the prior art are such that the claimed invention as a whole would have been obvious before the effective filing date of the claimed invention to a person having ordinary skill in the art to which the claimed invention pertains. In addition, AIA 35 U.S.C. 103 provides that patentability shall not be negated by the manner in which the invention was made. This provision tracks pre-AIA 35 U.S.C. 103(a), except that the temporal focus for the obviousness inquiry is before the effective filing date of the claimed invention, rather than at the time of the invention. The provisions of pre-AIA 35 U.S.C. 103(c) have been replaced with AIA 35 U.S.C. 102(b)(2)(C) and (c), and the provisions of pre-AIA 35 U.S.C. 103(b) pertaining to biotechnological processes have been eliminated.

AIA 35 U.S.C. 102 and 103 take effect on March 16, 2013. These new provisions apply to any patent application that contains or contained at any time: (1) A claim to a claimed invention that has an effective filing date that is on or after March 16, 2013; or (2) a designation as a continuation, divisional, or continuation-in-part of an application that contains or contained at any time a claim to a claimed invention that has an effective filing date that is on or after March 16, 2013.[50] AIA 35 U.S.C. 102 and 103 also apply to any patent resulting from an application to which AIA 35 U.S.C. 102 and 103 were applied.[51]

The AIA provides that the provisions of pre-AIA 35 U.S.C. 102(g)[52] apply to each claim of an application for patent if the patent application: (1) Contains or contained at any time a claim to a claimed invention having an effective filing date that occurs before March 16, 2013; or (2) is ever designated as a continuation, divisional, or continuation-in-part of an application that contains or contained at any time a claim to a claimed invention that has an effective filing date before March 16, 2013.[53] Pre-AIA 35 U.S.C. 102(g) also applies to any patent resulting from an application to which pre-AIA 35 U.S.C. 102(g) applied.[54]

If an application (1) contains or contained at any time a claimed invention having an effective filing date that is before March 16, 2013, or ever claimed a right of priority or the benefit of an earlier filing date under 35 U.S.C. 119, 120, 121, or 365 based upon an earlier application that ever contained a claimed invention having an effective filing date that is before March 16, 2013, and (2) also contains or contained at any time any claimed invention having an effective filing date that is on or after March 16, 2013, or ever claimed a right of priority or the benefit of an earlier filing date under 35 U.S.C. 119, 120, 121, or 365 based upon an earlier application that ever contained a claimed invention having an effective filing date that is on or after March 16, 2013, then AIA 35 U.S.C. 102 and 103 apply to the application, and each claimed invention in the application is also subject to pre-AIA 35 U.S.C. 102(g).

II. Detailed Discussion of AIA 35 U.S.C. 102(a) and (b)

AIA 35 U.S.C. 102(a) defines the prior art that will preclude the grant of a patent on a claimed invention unless an exception in AIA 35 U.S.C. 102(b) is applicable. Specifically, AIA 35 U.S.C. 102(a) provides that:

[a] person shall be entitled to a patent unless—

(1) the claimed invention was patented, described in a printed publication, or in public use, on sale, or otherwise available to the public before the effective filing date of the claimed invention; or

(2) the claimed invention was described in a patent issued under section 151, or in an application for patent published or deemed published under section 122(b), in which the patent or application, as the case may be, names another inventor and was effectively filed before the effective filing date of the claimed invention.[55]

As an initial matter, Office personnel should note that the introductory phrase "[a] person shall be entitled to a patent unless" remains unchanged from the pre-AIA version of 35 U.S.C. 102. Thus, 35 U.S.C. 102 continues to provide that the Office bears the initial burden of explaining why the applicable statutory or regulatory requirements have not been met if a claim in an application is to be rejected. The AIA also does not change the requirement that whenever a claim for a patent is rejected or an objection or requirement is made, the Office shall notify the applicant thereof and state the reasons for such rejection, objection, or requirement, and provide such information and references as may be useful to the applicant in judging of the propriety of continuing the prosecution of the application.[56]

The categories of prior art documents and activities are set forth in AIA 35 U.S.C. 102(a)(1) and (a)(2). These documents and activities are used to determine whether a claimed invention is novel or nonobvious. The documents upon which a prior art rejection may be based are an issued patent, a published application, and a non-patent printed publication. Evidence that the claimed invention was in public use, on sale, or otherwise available to the public may also be used as the basis for a prior art rejection. Note that a printed publication that does not have a sufficiently early publication date to itself qualify as prior art under AIA 35 U.S.C. 102(a)(1) may be competent evidence of a previous public use, sale activity, or other availability of a claimed invention to the public where the public use, sale activity, or other public availability does have a sufficiently early date to qualify as prior art under AIA 35 U.S.C. 102(a)(1).[57]

AIA 35 U.S.C. 102(b) sets out exceptions to AIA 35 U.S.C. 102(a), in that prior art that otherwise would be included in AIA 35 U.S.C. 102(a) shall not be prior art if it falls within an exception in AIA 35 U.S.C. 102(b).

Exceptions to the categories of prior art defined in AIA 35 U.S.C. 102(a)(1) are provided in AIA 35 U.S.C. 102(b)(1). Specifically, AIA 35 U.S.C. 102(b)(1) states that a disclosure made one year or less before the effective filing date of a claimed invention shall not be prior art to the claimed invention under subsection (a)(1) if—

- The disclosure was made by the inventor or a joint inventor or by another who obtained the subject matter disclosed directly or indirectly from the inventor or a joint inventor; or
- The subject matter disclosed had, before such disclosure, been publicly disclosed by the inventor or a joint inventor or another who obtained the subject matter disclosed directly or indirectly from the inventor or a joint inventor.[58]

Exceptions to the categories of prior art defined in AIA 35 U.S.C. 102(a)(2) are provided in AIA 35 U.S.C. 102(b)(2). Specifically, AIA 35 U.S.C. 102(b)(2) states that a disclosure shall not be prior art to a claimed invention under subsection (a)(2) if—

- The subject matter disclosed was obtained directly or indirectly from the inventor or a joint inventor;
- The subject matter disclosed had, before such subject matter was effectively filed under subsection (a)(2), been publicly disclosed by the inventor or a joint inventor or another who obtained the subject matter disclosed directly or indirectly from the inventor or a joint inventor; or
- The subject matter disclosed and the claimed invention, not later than the effective filing date of the claimed

invention, were owned by the same person or subject to an obligation of assignment to the same person.[59]

Although some of the prior art provisions of AIA 35 U.S.C. 102(a) and (b) will seem familiar, especially in comparison to pre-AIA 35 U.S.C. 102(a), (b), and (e), the AIA has introduced a number of important changes with respect to prior art documents and activities (collectively, "disclosures"). First, the availability of a disclosure as prior art is measured from the effective filing date of the claimed invention no matter where that filing occurred. Second, the AIA adopts a global view of prior art disclosures and thus does not require that a public use or sale activity be "in this country" to be a prior art activity. Finally, a catch-all "otherwise available to the public" category of prior art is added.

A. Effective Filing Date of the Claimed Invention

Pre-AIA 35 U.S.C. 102(a) and (e) reference patent-defeating activities occurring before the applicant invented the claimed invention. AIA 35 U.S.C. 102(a)(1) and (a)(2) make no mention of the date of the invention, but instead concern documents that existed or activities that occurred "before the effective filing date of the claimed invention." As a result, it is no longer possible to antedate or "swear behind" certain prior art disclosures by making a showing under 37 CFR 1.131 that the applicant invented the claimed subject matter prior to the effective date of the prior art disclosure.

The AIA defines the term "effective filing date" for a claimed invention in a patent or application for patent (other than a reissue application or reissued patent) as the earliest of: (1) The actual filing date of the patent or the application for the patent containing the claimed invention; or (2) the filing date of the earliest application for which the patent or application is entitled, as to such invention, to a right of priority or the benefit of an earlier filing date under 35 U.S.C. 119, 120, 121, or 365.[60] Thus, the one-year grace period in AIA 35 U.S.C. 102(b)(1) is measured from the filing date of any U.S. or foreign patent application to which the patent or application is entitled to benefit or priority as to such invention, whereas the one-year grace period in pre-AIA 35 U.S.C. 102(b) is measured from only the filing date of the earliest application filed in the United States (directly or through the PCT).

As under pre-AIA law, the effective filing date of a claimed invention is determined on a claim-by-claim basis and not an application-by-application basis. That is, the principle that different claims in the same application may be entitled to different effective filing dates vis-à-vis the prior art remains unchanged by the AIA.[61] However, it is important to note that although prior art is applied on a claim-by-claim basis, the determination of whether pre-AIA 35 U.S.C. 102 and 103 or AIA 35 U.S.C. 102 and 103 apply is made on an application-by-application basis. Section VI discusses the applicability date provisions of section 3 of the AIA.

Finally, the AIA provides that the "effective filing date" for a claimed invention in a reissued patent or application for a reissue patent shall be determined by deeming the claim to the claimed invention to have been contained in the patent for which reissue was sought.[62]

B. Provisions Pertaining to Disclosures Before the Effective Filing Date of the Claimed Invention

1. Prior Art Under AIA 35 U.S.C. 102(a)(1) (Patented, Described in a Printed Publication, or in Public Use, on Sale, or Otherwise Available to the Public)

Prior art documents and activities which may preclude patentability are set forth in AIA 35 U.S.C. 102(a)(1). Such documents and activities include prior patenting of the claimed invention, descriptions of the claimed invention in a printed publication, public use of the claimed invention, placing the claimed invention on sale, and otherwise making the claimed invention available to the public. These examination guidelines will discuss each prior art document and activity that might preclude patentability under AIA 35 U.S.C. 102(a)(1) in turn.

a. Patented. AIA 35 U.S.C. 102(a)(1) indicates that prior patenting of a claimed invention precludes the grant of a patent on the claimed invention. This means that if a claimed invention was patented in this or a foreign country before the effective filing date of the claimed invention, AIA 35 U.S.C. 102(a)(1) precludes the grant of a patent on the claimed invention. The effective date of the patent for purposes of determining whether the patent qualifies as prior art under AIA 35 U.S.C. 102(a)(1) is the grant date of the patent. There is an exception to this rule if the patent is secret as of the date the rights are awarded.[63] In such situations, the patent is available as prior art as of the date the patent was made available to the public by being laid open for public inspection or disseminated in printed form.[64] The phrase "patented" in AIA 35 U.S.C. 102(a)(1) has the same meaning as "patented" in pre-AIA 35 U.S.C. 102(a) and (b). For a discussion of "patented" as used in pre-AIA 35 U.S.C. 102(a) and (b), see generally MPEP §2126.

Although an invention may be described in a patent and not claimed therein, the grant date would also be the applicable prior art date for purposes of relying on the subject matter disclosed therein as "described in a printed publication," provided that the patent was made available to the public on its grant date. It is helpful to note that a U.S. patent that issues after the effective filing date of a claimed invention under examination is not available as prior art against that invention under AIA 35 U.S.C. 102(a)(1), but could be available as prior art under AIA 35 U.S.C. 102(a)(2).

b. Described in a printed publication. If a claimed invention is described in a patent, published patent application, or printed publication, such a document may be available as prior art under AIA 35 U.S.C. 102(a)(1). Both pre-AIA 35 U.S.C. 102(a) and (b) and AIA 35 U.S.C. 102(a)(1) use the term "described" with respect to an invention in a prior art printed publication. Likewise, AIA 35 U.S.C. 102(a)(2) uses that term with respect to U.S. patents, U.S. patent application publications, and WIPO published applications. Thus, the Office does not view the AIA as changing the extent to which a claimed invention must be described for a prior art document to anticipate the claimed invention under 35 U.S.C. 102.

While the conditions for patentability of AIA 35 U.S.C. 112(a) require a written description of the claimed invention that would have enabled a person skilled in the art to make as well as use the invention, the prior art provisions of AIA 35 U.S.C. 102(a)(1) and (a)(2) require only that the claimed invention be "described"[65] in a prior art document (patent, published patent application, or printed publication). The two basic requirements that must be met by a prior art document in order to describe a claimed invention such that it is anticipated under AIA 35 U.S.C. 102 are the same as those under pre-AIA 35 U.S.C. 102. First, "each and every element of the claimed invention" must be disclosed either explicitly or inherently, and the elements must be "arranged or combined in the same way as in the claim."[66] Second, a person of ordinary skill in the art must have been enabled to make the invention without undue experimentation.[67] Thus, in order for a prior art document to describe a claimed invention such that it is anticipated under AIA 35 U.S.C. 102(a)(1) or (a)(2), it must disclose all elements of the claimed invention arranged as they are in the claim, and also provide sufficient guidance to enable a person skilled in the art to make the claimed invention. There is, however, no requirement that a prior art document meet the "how to use" requirement of 35 U.S.C. 112(a) in order to qualify as prior art.[68] Furthermore, compliance with the "how to make" requirement is judged from the viewpoint of a person of ordinary skill in the art, and thus does not require that the prior art document explicitly disclose information within the knowledge of such a person.[69]

There is an additional important distinction between the written description that is necessary to support a claim under 35 U.S.C. 112(a) and the description sufficient to anticipate the subject matter of the claim under AIA 35 U.S.C. 102(a)(1) or (a)(2).[70] To provide support for a claim under 35 U.S.C. 112(a), it is necessary that the specification describe and enable the entire scope of the claimed invention. However, in order for a prior art document to describe a claimed invention under AIA 35 U.S.C. 102(a)(1) or (a)(2), the prior art document need only describe and enable one skilled in the art to make a single species or embodiment of the claimed invention.[71]

An anticipatory description is not required in order for a disclosure to qualify as prior art, unless the disclosure is being used as the basis for an anticipation rejection. In accordance with pre-AIA case law concerning obviousness, a disclosure may be cited for all that it would reasonably have made known to a person of ordinary skill in the art. Thus, the description requirement of AIA 35 U.S.C. 102(a)(1) and (a)(2) does not preclude an examiner from applying a disclosure in an obviousness rejection under AIA 35 U.S.C. 103 simply because the disclosure is not adequate to anticipate the claimed invention under AIA 35 U.S.C. 102(a)(1) or (a)(2).

c. In public use. Under pre-AIA 35 U.S.C. 102(b), that an invention was "in public use" precluded the grant of a patent only if such public use occurred "in this country."

Under AIA 35 U.S.C. 102(a)(1), there is no geographic limitation on where prior public use or public availability occurs. Furthermore, a public use would need to occur before the effective filing date of the claimed invention to constitute prior art under AIA 35 U.S.C. 102(a)(1).

The pre-AIA case law also indicates that a public use will bar patentability if the public use occurs before the critical date[72] and the invention is ready for patenting.[73] Under pre-AIA 35 U.S.C. 102(b), the uses of an invention before the patent's critical date that constitute a "public use" fall into two categories: The use either "(1) was accessible to the public; or (2) was commercially exploited."[74] Whether a use is a pre-AIA 35 U.S.C. 102(b) public use also depends on who is making the use of the invention. "[W]hen an asserted prior use is not that of the applicant, [pre-AIA 35 U.S.C.] 102(b) is not a bar when that prior use or knowledge is not available to the public."[75] In other words, a use by a third party who did not obtain the invention from the inventor named in the application or patent is an invalidating use under pre-AIA 35 U.S.C. 102(b) only if it falls into the first category: That the use was accessible to the public. On the other hand, "an inventor's own prior commercial use, albeit kept secret, may constitute a public use or sale under [pre-AIA 35 U.S.C.] 102(b), barring him from obtaining a patent."[76] Also, an inventor creates a public use bar under pre-AIA 35 U.S.C. 102(b) when the inventor shows the invention to, or allows it to be used by, another person who is "under no limitation, restriction, or obligation of confidentiality" to the inventor.[77]

Further, under pre-AIA 35 U.S.C. 102(a), "in order to invalidate a patent based on prior knowledge or use" by another in this country prior to the patent's priority date, "that knowledge or use must have been available to the public."[78] Patent-defeating "use," under pre-AIA 35 U.S.C. 102(a), includes only that "use which is accessible to the public."[79]

As discussed previously, public use under AIA 35 U.S.C. 102(a)(1) is limited to those uses that are available to the public. The public use provision of AIA 35 U.S.C. 102(a)(1) thus has the same substantive scope, with respect to uses by either the inventor or a third party, as public uses under pre-AIA 35 U.S.C. 102(b) by unrelated third parties or uses by others under pre-AIA 35 U.S.C. 102(a).

As also discussed previously, once an examiner becomes aware that a claimed invention has been the subject of a potentially public use, the examiner may require the applicant to provide information showing that the use did not make the claimed process accessible to the public.

d. On sale. The pre-AIA case law indicates that on sale activity will bar patentability if the claimed invention was: (1) The subject of a commercial sale or offer for sale, not primarily for experimental purposes; and (2) ready for patenting.[80] Contract law principles apply in order to determine whether a commercial sale or offer for sale occurred. In addition, the enablement inquiry is not applicable to the question of whether a claimed invention is "on sale" under pre-AIA 35 U.S.C. 102(b).[81] The phrase "on sale" in AIA 35 U.S.C. 102(a)(1) is treated as having the same meaning as "on sale" in pre-AIA 35 U.S.C. 102(b), except that the sale must make the invention available to the public. For a discussion of "on sale" as used in pre-AIA 35 U.S.C. 102(b), see generally MPEP §2133.03(b) et seq.

Under pre-AIA 35 U.S.C. 102(b), if an invention was "on sale," patentability was precluded only if the invention was on sale "in this country." Under AIA 35 U.S.C. 102(a)(1), there is no geographic limitation on where the sale or offer for sale may occur. When formulating a rejection, Office personnel should consider evidence of sales activity, regardless of where the sale activity took place.

The pre-AIA 35 U.S.C. 102(b) "on sale" provision has been interpreted as including commercial activity even if the activity is secret. AIA 35 U.S.C. 102(a)(1) uses the same "on sale" term as pre-AIA 35 U.S.C. 102(b). The "or otherwise available to the public" residual clause of AIA 35 U.S.C. 102(a)(1), however, indicates that AIA 35 U.S.C. 102(a)(1) does not cover secret sales or offers for sale. For example, an activity (such as a sale, offer for sale, or other commercial activity) is secret (non-public) if it is among individuals having an obligation of confidentiality to the inventor.[82]

e. Otherwise available to the public. AIA 35 U.S.C. 102(a)(1) provides a "catch-all" provision, which defines a new additional category of potential prior art not provided for in pre-AIA 35 U.S.C. 102. Specifically, a claimed invention may not be patented if it was "otherwise available to the public" before its effective filing date. This "catch-all" provision permits decision makers to focus on whether the disclosure was "available to the public," rather than on the means by which the claimed invention became available to the public or on whether a disclosure constitutes a "printed publication" or falls within another category of prior art as defined in AIA 35 U.S.C. 102(a)(1). The availability of the subject matter to the public may arise in situations such as a student thesis in a university library,[83] a poster display or other information disseminated at a scientific meeting,[84] subject matter in a laid-open patent application,[85] a document electronically posted on the Internet,[86] or a commercial transaction that does not constitute a sale under the Uniform Commercial Code.[87] Even if a document or other disclosure is not a printed publication, or a transaction is not a sale, either may be prior art under the "otherwise available to the public" provision of AIA 35 U.S.C. 102(a)(1), provided that the claimed invention is made sufficiently available to the public.

f. No requirement of "by others." A key difference between pre-AIA 35 U.S.C. 102(a) and AIA 35 U.S.C. 102(a)(1) is the requirement in pre-AIA 35 U.S.C. 102(a) that the prior art relied on was "by others." Under AIA 35 U.S.C. 102(a)(1), there is no requirement that the prior art relied upon be by others. Thus, any prior art which falls under AIA 35 U.S.C. 102(a)(1) need not be by another to constitute potentially available prior art. However, disclosures of the subject matter made one year or less before the effective filing date of the claimed invention by the inventor or a joint inventor or another who obtained the subject matter directly or indirectly from the inventor or a joint inventor may fall within an exception under AIA 35 U.S.C. 102(b)(1) to AIA 35 U.S.C. 102(a)(1).

g. Admissions. The Office will continue to treat admissions by the applicant as prior art under the AIA. A statement by an applicant in the specification or made during prosecution identifying the work of another as "prior art" is an admission which can be relied upon for both anticipation and obviousness determinations, regardless of whether the admitted prior art would otherwise qualify as prior art under AIA 35 U.S.C. 102.[88] For a discussion of admissions as prior art, see generally MPEP §2129.

h. The meaning of "disclosure." The AIA does not define the term "disclosure," and AIA 35 U.S.C. 102(a) does not use the term "disclosure." AIA 35 U.S.C. 102(b)(1) and (b)(2), however, each state conditions under which a "disclosure" that otherwise falls within AIA 35 U.S.C. 102(a)(1) or 102(a)(2) is not prior art under AIA 35 U.S.C. 102(a)(1) or 102(a)(2).[89] Thus, the Office is treating the term "disclosure" as a generic expression intended to encompass the documents and activities enumerated in AIA 35 U.S.C. 102(a) (i.e., being patented, described in a printed publication, in public use, on sale, or otherwise available to the public, or being described in a U.S. patent, U.S. patent application publication, or WIPO published application).

2. Prior Art Exceptions Under 35 U.S.C. 102(b)(1) to AIA 35 U.S.C. 102(a)(1)

a. Prior art exception under AIA 35 U.S.C. 102(b)(1)(A) to AIA 35 U.S.C. 102(a)(1) (grace period inventor or inventor-originated disclosure exception). AIA 35 U.S.C. 102(b)(1)(A) provides exceptions to the prior art provisions of AIA 35 U.S.C. 102(a)(1). These exceptions limit the use of an inventor's own work as prior art, when the inventor's own work has been publicly disclosed by the inventor, a joint inventor, or another who obtained the subject matter directly or indirectly from the inventor or joint inventor. AIA 35 U.S.C. 102(b)(1)(A) provides that a disclosure which would otherwise qualify as prior art under AIA 35 U.S.C. 102(a)(1) is not prior art if the disclosure was made: (1) One year or less before the effective filing date of the claimed invention; and (2) by the inventor or a joint inventor, or by another who obtained the subject matter directly or indirectly from the inventor or joint inventor. These guidelines will first discuss issues pertaining to disclosures within the grace period by the inventor or a joint inventor ("grace period inventor disclosures") and then subsequently discuss issues pertaining to disclosures within the grace period by another who obtained the subject matter directly or indirectly from the inventor or joint inventor ("grace period inventor-originated disclosures"). Section II.A. of these examination guidelines discusses the "effective filing date" of a claimed invention.

i. Grace period inventor disclosure exception. AIA 35 U.S.C. 102(b)(1)(A) first provides that a disclosure which would otherwise qualify as prior art under AIA 35 U.S.C. 102(a)(1) may be disqualified as prior art if the disclosure is made: (1) One year or less before the effective filing date of the claimed invention; and (2) by the inventor or a joint inventor. Thus, a disclosure that would otherwise qualify as prior art under AIA 35 U.S.C. 102(a)(1) will not be treated as prior art by Office personnel if the disclosure is made one year or less before the effective filing date of the claimed invention, and the evidence shows that the disclosure is by the inventor or a joint inventor. What evidence is necessary to show that the disclosure is by the inventor or a joint inventor requires case-by-case treatment, depending upon whether it is apparent from the disclosure itself or the patent application specification that the disclosure is by the inventor or a joint inventor.

Office personnel will not apply a disclosure as prior art under AIA 35 U.S.C. 102(a)(1) if it is apparent from the disclosure itself that it is by the inventor or a joint inventor. Specifically, Office personnel will not apply a disclosure as prior art under AIA 35 U.S.C. 102(a)(1) if the disclosure: (1) Was made one year or less before the effective filing date of the claimed invention; (2) names the inventor or a joint inventor as an author or an inventor; and (3) does not name additional persons as authors on a printed publication or inventors on a patent. This means that in circumstances where an application names additional persons as inventors relative to the persons named as authors in the publication (e.g., the application names as inventors A, B, and C, and the publication names as authors A and B), and the publication is one year or less before the effective filing date, it is apparent that the disclosure is a grace period inventor disclosure, and the publication would not be treated as prior art under AIA 35 U.S.C. 102(a)(1). If, however, the application names fewer inventors than a publication (e.g., the application names as inventors A and B, and the publication names as authors A, B and C), it would not be readily apparent from the publication that it is by the inventor or a joint inventor and the publication would be treated as prior art under AIA 35 U.S.C. 102(a)(1).

The Office is also revising the rules of practice in a separate action (RIN 0651-AC77) to provide that applicants can include a statement of any grace period inventor disclosures in the specification (37 CFR 1.77(b)(6)). An applicant is not required to use the format specified in 37 CFR 1.77 or identify any prior disclosures by the inventor or a joint inventor (unless necessary to overcome a rejection), but identifying any prior disclosures by the inventor or a joint inventor may expedite examination of the application and save applicants (and the Office) the costs related to an Office action and reply. If the patent application specification contains a specific reference to a grace period inventor disclosure, the Office will consider it apparent from the specification that the disclosure is by the inventor or a joint inventor, provided that the disclosure does not name additional authors or inventors and there is no other evidence to the contrary. The applicant may also provide a copy of the disclosure (e.g., copy of a printed publication).

The Office is also revising the rules of practice in a separate action (RIN 0651-AC77) to provide a mechanism for filing an affidavit or declaration (under 37 CFR 1.130) to establish that a disclosure is not prior art under AIA 35 U.S.C. 102(a) due to an exception in AIA 35 U.S.C. 102(b). In the situations in which it is not apparent from the disclosure or the patent application specification that the disclosure is by the inventor or a joint inventor, the applicant may establish by way of an affidavit or declaration that a grace period disclosure is not prior art under AIA 35 U.S.C. 102(a)(1) because the disclosure was by the inventor or a joint inventor. Section II.D.1. of these examination guidelines discusses the use of affidavits or declarations to show that the disclosure was made by the inventor or a joint inventor under the exception of AIA 35 U.S.C. 102(b)(1)(A) for a grace period inventor disclosure.

ii. Grace period inventor-originated disclosure exception. AIA 35 U.S.C. 102(b)(1)(A) also provides that a disclosure which would otherwise qualify as prior art under AIA 35 U.S.C. 102(a)(1) may be disqualified as prior art if the disclosure was made: (1) One year or less before the effective filing date of the claimed invention; and (2) by another who obtained the subject matter directly or indirectly from the inventor or a joint inventor. Thus, if a disclosure upon which the rejection is based is by someone who obtained the subject matter from the inventor or a joint inventor, and was made one year or less before the effective filing date of the claimed invention, the applicant may establish by way of an affidavit or declaration that the disclosure is not prior art under AIA 35 U.S.C. 102(a)(1) because the disclosure was by another who obtained the subject matter directly or indirectly from the inventor or a joint inventor. Section II.D.3. of these examination guidelines discusses the use of affidavits or declarations to show that a disclosure was by another who obtained the subject matter disclosed directly or indirectly from the inventor or a joint inventor under the exception of AIA 35 U.S.C. 102(b)(1)(A) for a grace period inventor-originated disclosure.

b. Prior art exception under AIA 35 U.S.C. 102(b)(1)(B) to AIA 35 U.S.C. 102(a)(1) (inventor or inventor-originated prior public disclosure exception). AIA 35 U.S.C. 102(b)(1)(B) provides additional exceptions to the prior art provisions of AIA 35 U.S.C. 102(a)(1). These exceptions disqualify a disclosure of subject matter that occurs after the subject matter had been publicly disclosed by the inventor, a joint inventor, or another who obtained the subject matter directly or indirectly from the inventor or joint inventor. Specifically, AIA 35 U.S.C. 102(b)(1)(B) provides that a disclosure which would otherwise qualify as prior art under AIA 35 U.S.C. 102(a)(1) (patent, printed publication, public use, sale, or other means of public availability) may be disqualified as prior art if: (1) The disclosure was made one year or less before the effective filing date of the claimed invention; and (2) the subject matter disclosed had been previously publicly disclosed by the inventor, a joint inventor, or another who obtained the subject matter directly or indirectly from the inventor or joint inventor. The previous public disclosure of the subject matter by the inventor, a joint inventor, or another who obtained the subject matter directly or indirectly from the inventor or joint inventor must itself be a disclosure within the one-year grace period (i.e., be either a grace period inventor disclosure by the inventor or a joint inventor or be a grace period inventor-originated disclosure by another who obtained the subject matter directly or indirectly from the inventor or joint inventor). Otherwise, the previous public disclosure of the subject matter would qualify as prior art under AIA 35 U.S.C. 102(a)(1) that could not be disqualified under AIA 35 U.S.C. 102(b)(1). Section II.A. of these examination guidelines discusses the "effective filing date" of a claimed invention. Section II.D.2. of these examination guidelines discusses the use of affidavits or declarations to show that the subject matter disclosed had, before such disclosure, been publicly disclosed by the inventor or a joint inventor, and section II.D.3. of these examination guidelines discusses the use of affidavits or declarations to show that another obtained the subject matter disclosed directly or indirectly from the inventor or a joint inventor.

The exception in AIA 35 U.S.C. 102(b)(1)(B) applies if the "subject matter disclosed [in the intervening disclosure] had, before such [intervening] disclosure, been publicly disclosed by the inventor or a joint inventor * * *."[90] The exception in AIA 35 U.S.C. 102(b)(1)(B) focuses on the "subject matter" that had been publicly disclosed by the inventor or a joint inventor. There is no requirement under AIA 35 U.S.C. 102(b)(1)(B) that the mode of disclosure by the inventor or a joint inventor (e.g., patenting, publication, public use, sale activity) be the same as the mode of disclosure of the intervening grace period disclosure. There is also no requirement that the disclosure by the inventor or a joint inventor be a verbatim or ipsissimis verbis disclosure of the intervening grace period disclosure.[91] What is required for subject matter in an intervening grace period disclosure to be excepted under AIA 35 U.S.C. 102(b)(1)(B) is that the subject matter of the disclosure to be disqualified as prior art must have been previously publicly disclosed by the inventor or a joint inventor.

The exception in AIA 35 U.S.C. 102(b)(1)(B) applies to the subject matter in the disclosure being relied upon as prior art for a rejection under AIA 35 U.S.C. 102(a)(1) (an intervening disclosure) that was also publicly disclosed by the inventor or a joint inventor before such intervening disclosure. The subject matter of an intervening grace period disclosure that was not previously publicly disclosed by the inventor or a joint inventor is available as prior art under AIA 35 U.S.C. 102(a)(1). For example, the inventor or a joint inventor had publicly disclosed elements A, B, and C, and a subsequent intervening grace period disclosure discloses elements A, B, C, and D, then only element D of the intervening grace period disclosure is available as prior art under AIA 35 U.S.C. 102(a)(1).

In addition, if subject matter of an intervening grace period disclosure is simply a more general description of the subject matter previously publicly disclosed by the inventor or a joint inventor, the exception in AIA 35 U.S.C. 102(b)(1)(B) applies to such subject matter of the intervening grace period disclosure. For example, if the inventor or a joint inventor had publicly disclosed a species, and a subsequent intervening grace period disclosure discloses a genus (i.e., provides a more generic disclosure of the species), the intervening grace period disclosure of the genus is not available as prior art under AIA 35 U.S.C. 102(a)(1). Conversely, if the inventor or a joint inventor had publicly disclosed a genus, and a subsequent intervening grace period disclosure discloses a species, the intervening grace period disclosure of the species would be available as prior art under AIA 35 U.S.C. 102(a)(1). Likewise, if the inventor or a joint inventor had publicly disclosed a species, and a subsequent intervening grace period disclosure discloses an alternative species not also disclosed by the inventor or a joint inventor, the intervening grace period disclosure of the alternative species would be available as prior art under AIA 35 U.S.C. 102(a)(1).

Finally, AIA 35 U.S.C. 102(b)(1)(B) does not discuss "the claimed invention" with respect to either the subject matter disclosed by the inventor or a joint inventor, or the subject matter of the subsequent intervening grace period disclosure. Any inquiry with respect to the claimed invention is whether or not the subject matter in the prior art disclosure being relied upon anticipates or renders obvious the claimed invention. A determination of whether the exception in AIA 35 U.S.C. 102(b)(1)(B) is applicable to subject matter in an intervening grace period disclosure does not involve a comparison of the subject matter of the claimed invention to either the subject matter disclosed by the inventor or a joint inventor, or to the subject matter of the subsequent intervening grace period disclosure.

C. Provisions Pertaining to Subject Matter in a U.S. Patent or Application for a U.S. Patent Effectively Filed Before the Effective Filing Date of the Claimed Invention

1. Prior Art Under AIA 35 U.S.C. 102(a)(2) (U.S. Patents, U.S. Patent Application Publications, and World Intellectual Property Organization (WIPO) Publications of International Applications (WIPO Published Applications))

AIA 35 U.S.C. 102(a)(2) sets forth three types of patent documents that are available as prior art as of the date they were effectively filed with respect to the subject matter relied upon in the document if they name another inventor: (1) U.S. patents; (2) U.S. patent application publications; and (3) WIPO published applications. These documents may have different prior art effects under pre-AIA 35 U.S.C. 102(e) than under AIA 35 U.S.C. 102(a)(2).

a. WIPO published applications. AIA 35 U.S.C. 102(a)(2) explicitly references U.S. patents and U.S. patent application publications. Moreover, the WIPO publication of a PCT international application that designates the United States is an application for patent deemed published under 35 U.S.C. 122(b) for purposes of AIA 35 U.S.C. 102(a)(2) under 35 U.S.C. 374. Thus, under the AIA, WIPO publications of PCT applications that designate the United States are treated as U.S. patent application publications for prior art purposes, regardless of the international filing date, whether they are published in English, or whether the PCT international application enters the national stage in the United States. Accordingly, a U.S. patent, a U.S. patent application publication, or a WIPO published application that names another inventor and was effectively filed before the effective filing date of the claimed invention, is prior art under AIA 35 U.S.C. 102(a)(2). This differs from the treatment of a WIPO published application under pre-AIA 35 U.S.C. 102(e), where a WIPO published application is treated as a U.S. patent application publication only if the PCT application was filed on or after November 29, 2000, and published under PCT Article 21(2) in the English language.

A U.S. patent, U.S. patent application publication, or WIPO published application is prior art under AIA 35 U.S.C. 102(a)(1) if its issue or publication date is before the effective filing date of the claimed invention in question. If the issue date of the U.S. patent or publication date of the U.S. patent application publication or WIPO published application is not before the effective filing date of the claimed invention, it may still be applicable as prior art under AIA 35 U.S.C. 102(a)(2) if it was "effectively filed" before the effective filing date of the claimed invention in question with respect to the subject matter relied upon to reject the claim. Section II.A. of these examination guidelines discusses the "effective filing date" of a claimed invention. AIA 35 U.S.C. 102(d) sets forth the criteria to determine when subject matter described in a U.S. patent, U.S. patent application publication, or WIPO published application was "effectively filed" for purposes of AIA 35 U.S.C. 102(a)(2).

b. Determining when subject matter was effectively filed under AIA 35 U.S.C. 102(d). AIA 35 U.S.C. 102(d) provides that a U.S. patent, U.S. patent application publication, or WIPO published application is prior art under AIA 35 U.S.C. 102(a)(2) with respect to any subject matter described in the patent or published application as of either its actual filing date (AIA 35 U.S.C. 102(d)(1)), or the filing date of a prior application to which there is a priority or benefit claim (AIA 35 U.S.C. 102(d)(2)). A U.S. patent, U.S. patent application publication, or WIPO published application "is entitled to claim" priority to, or the benefit of, a prior-filed application if it fulfills the ministerial requirements of: (1) Containing a priority or benefit claim to the prior-filed application; (2) being filed within the applicable filing period requirement (copending with or within twelve months of the earlier filing, as applicable); and (3) having a common inventor or being by the same applicant.[92]

The AIA draws a distinction between actually being entitled to priority to, or the benefit of, a prior-filed application in the definition of effective filing date of a claimed invention in AIA 35 U.S.C. 100(i)(1)(B), and merely being entitled to claim priority to, or the benefit of, a prior-filed application in the definition of effectively filed in AIA 35 U.S.C. 102(d).[93] As a result of this distinction, the question of whether a patent or published application is actually entitled to priority or benefit with respect to any of its claims is not at issue in determining the date the patent or published application was "effectively filed" for prior art purposes.[94] Thus, as was the case even prior to the AIA,[95] there is no need to evaluate whether any claim of a U.S. patent, U.S. patent application publication, or WIPO published application is actually entitled to priority or benefit under 35 U.S.C. 119, 120, 121, or 365 when applying such a document as prior art.

AIA 35 U.S.C. 102(d) requires that a prior-filed application to which a priority or benefit claim is made must describe the subject matter from the U.S. patent, U.S. patent application publication, or WIPO published application relied upon in a rejection. However, AIA 35 U.S.C. 102(d) does not require that this description meet the requirements of 35 U.S.C. 112(a). As discussed previously with respect to AIA 35 U.S.C. 102(a)(1), the Office does not view the AIA as changing the extent to which a claimed invention must be described for a prior art document to anticipate the claimed invention under AIA 35 U.S.C. 102.

The AIA also eliminates the so-called *Hilmer* doctrine.[96] Under the *Hilmer* doctrine, pre-AIA 35 U.S.C. 102(e) limited the effective filing date for U.S. patents (and published applications) as prior art to their earliest U.S. filing date. In contrast, AIA 35 U.S.C. 102(d) provides that if the U.S. patent, U.S. patent application publication, or WIPO published application claims priority to one or more prior-filed foreign or international applications under 35 U.S.C. 119 or 365, the patent or published application was effectively filed on the filing date of the earliest such application that describes the subject matter.[97] Therefore, if the subject matter relied upon is described in the application to which there is a priority or benefit claim, a U.S. patent, a U.S. patent application publication, or WIPO published application is effective as prior art as of the filing date of the earliest such application, regardless of where filed.

c. Requirement of "names another inventor." To qualify as prior art under AIA 35 U.S.C. 102(a)(2), the prior art U.S. patent, U.S. patent application publication, or WIPO published application must "name[s] another inventor." This means that if there is any difference in inventive entity between the prior art U.S. patent, U.S. patent application publication, or WIPO published application and the application under examination or patent under reexamination, the U.S. patent, U.S. patent application publication, or WIPO published application satisfies the "names another inventor" requirement of AIA 35 U.S.C. 102(a)(2). Thus, in the case of joint inventors, only one inventor needs to be different for the inventive entities to be different. Even if there are some inventors in common in a U.S. patent, a U.S. patent application publication, or WIPO published application and in a later-filed application under examination or patent under reexamination, the U.S. patent, a U.S. patent application publication, or WIPO published application qualifies as prior art under AIA 35 U.S.C. 102(a)(2) unless an exception in AIA 35 U.S.C. 102(b)(2) is applicable.

2. Prior Art Exceptions Under 35 U.S.C. 102(b)(2) to AIA 35 U.S.C. 102(a)(2)

a. Prior art exception under AIA 35 U.S.C. 102(b)(2)(A) to AIA 35 U.S.C. 102(a)(2) (inventor-originated disclosure exception). AIA 35 U.S.C. 102(b)(2)(A) provides an exception to the prior art provisions of AIA 35 U.S.C. 102(a)(2). This exception limits the use of an inventor's own work as prior art, when the inventor's own work is disclosed in a U.S. patent, U.S. patent application publication, or WIPO published application by another who obtained the subject matter directly or indirectly from the inventor or joint inventor.

Specifically, AIA 35 U.S.C. 102(b)(2)(A) provides that a disclosure which would otherwise qualify as prior art under AIA 35 U.S.C. 102(a)(2) may be disqualified as prior art if the subject matter disclosed was obtained directly or indirectly from the inventor or a joint inventor. Thus, if the subject matter in a U.S. patent, U.S. patent application publication, or WIPO published application upon which the rejection is based is by another who obtained the subject matter from the inventor or a joint inventor, the applicant may establish by way of an affidavit or declaration that a disclosure is not prior art under AIA 35 U.S.C. 102(a)(2). Section II.D.3. of these examination guidelines discusses the use of affidavits or declarations to show that the disclosure was by another who obtained the subject matter disclosed directly or indirectly from the inventor or a joint inventor under the exception of AIA 35 U.S.C. 102(b)(2)(A) for an inventor-originated disclosure.

b. Prior art exception under AIA 35 U.S.C. 102(b)(2)(B) to AIA 35 U.S.C. 102(a)(2) (inventor or inventor-originated prior public disclosure exception). AIA 35 U.S.C. 102(b)(2)(B) provides additional exceptions to the prior art provisions of AIA 35 U.S.C. 102(a)(2). These exceptions disqualify subject matter that was effectively filed by another after the subject matter had been publicly disclosed by the inventor, a joint inventor, or another who obtained the subject matter directly or indirectly from the inventor or joint inventor.

Specifically, AIA 35 U.S.C. 102(b)(2)(B) provides that a disclosure which would otherwise qualify as prior art under AIA 35 U.S.C. 102(a)(2) (a U.S. patent, U.S. patent application publication, or WIPO published application) may be disqualified as prior art if the subject matter disclosed had been previously publicly disclosed by the inventor, a joint inventor, or another who obtained the subject matter directly or indirectly from the inventor or joint inventor. The previous public disclosure of the subject matter by the inventor, a joint inventor, or another who obtained the subject matter directly or indirectly from the inventor or joint inventor must itself be a public disclosure (i.e., be either an inventor disclosure by the inventor or a joint inventor or be an inventor-originated disclosure by another who obtained the subject matter directly or indirectly from the inventor or joint inventor). If a previous public disclosure by the inventor or which originated with the inventor is not within the grace period of AIA 35 U.S.C. 102(b)(1), it would qualify as prior art under AIA 35 U.S.C. 102(a)(1), and could not be disqualified under AIA 35 U.S.C. 102(b)(1). Section II.D.2. of these examination guidelines discusses the use of affidavits or declarations to show that the subject matter disclosed had, before such disclosure, been publicly disclosed by the inventor or a joint inventor, and section II.D.3. of these examination guidelines discusses the use of affidavits or declarations to show that another who obtained the subject matter disclosed directly or indirectly from the inventor or a joint inventor.

Similar to the previous discussion of AIA 35 U.S.C. 102(b)(1)(B), the exception in AIA 35 U.S.C. 102(b)(2)(B) applies if the "subject matter disclosed [in the intervening disclosure] had, before such [intervening] disclosure [was effectively filed], been publicly disclosed by the inventor or a joint inventor * * *."[98] The exception in AIA 35 U.S.C. 102(b)(2)(B) focuses on the "subject matter" that had been publicly disclosed by the inventor or a joint inventor. There is no requirement under 35 U.S.C. 102(b)(2)(B) that the mode of disclosure by the inventor or a joint inventor (e.g., patenting, publication, public use, sale activity) be the same as the mode of disclosure of the intervening U.S. patent, U.S. patent application publication, or WIPO published application. There is also no requirement that the disclosure by the inventor or a joint inventor be a verbatim or ipsissimis verbis disclosure of the intervening U.S. patent, U.S. patent application publication, or WIPO published application. What is required for subject matter in the intervening U.S. patent, U.S. patent application publication, or WIPO published application to be excepted under AIA 35 U.S.C. 102(b)(2)(B) is that the subject matter must have been previously publicly disclosed by the inventor or a joint inventor or must have originated with the inventor.

The exception in AIA 35 U.S.C. 102(b)(2)(B) applies to the subject matter in the intervening U.S. patent, U.S. patent application publication, or WIPO published application being relied upon for a rejection under AIA 35 U.S.C. 102(a)(2) that was also publicly disclosed by the inventor or a joint inventor (or have originated with the inventor) before the date the subject matter relied upon was effectively filed. The subject matter of an intervening U.S. patent, U.S. patent application publication, or WIPO published application that was not previously publicly disclosed by the inventor or a joint inventor (or by another who obtained the subject matter from the inventor or joint inventor) is available as prior art under AIA 35

U.S.C. 102(a)(2). For example, if the inventor or a joint inventor had publicly disclosed elements A, B, and C, and a subsequent intervening U.S. patent, U.S. patent application publication, or WIPO published application discloses elements A, B, C, and D, then only element D of the intervening U.S. patent, U.S. patent application publication, or WIPO published application is available as prior art under AIA 35 U.S.C. 102(a)(2).

In addition, if subject matter of an intervening U.S. patent, U.S. patent application publication, or WIPO published application is simply a more general description of the subject matter previously publicly disclosed by the inventor or a joint inventor, the exception in AIA 35 U.S.C. 102(b)(1)(B) applies to such subject matter of the intervening U.S. patent, U.S. patent application publication, or WIPO published application disclosure. For example, if the inventor or a joint inventor had publicly disclosed a species, and a subsequent intervening U.S. patent, U.S. patent application publication, or WIPO published application discloses a genus (i.e., provides a more generic disclosure of the species), the disclosure of the genus in the intervening U.S. patent, U.S. patent application publication, or WIPO published application is not available as prior art under AIA 35 U.S.C. 102(a)(2). Conversely, if the inventor or a joint inventor had publicly disclosed a genus, and a subsequent intervening U.S. patent, U.S. patent application publication, or WIPO published application discloses a species, the disclosure of the species in the subsequent intervening U.S. patent, U.S. patent application publication, or WIPO published application would be available as prior art under AIA 35 U.S.C. 102(a)(2). Likewise, if the inventor or a joint inventor had publicly disclosed a species, and a subsequent intervening U.S. patent, U.S. patent application publication, or WIPO published application discloses an alternative species not also disclosed by the inventor or a joint inventor, the disclosure of the alternative species in the intervening U.S. patent, U.S. patent application publication, or WIPO published application would be available as prior art under AIA 35 U.S.C. 102(a)(2).

Finally, AIA 35 U.S.C. 102(b)(2)(B) does not discuss "the claimed invention" with respect to either the subject matter disclosed by the inventor or a joint inventor, or the subject matter of the subsequent intervening U.S. patent, U.S. patent application publication, or WIPO published application. Any inquiry with respect to the claimed invention is whether or not the subject matter in the prior art disclosure being relied upon anticipates or renders obvious the claimed invention. A determination of whether the exception in AIA 35 U.S.C. 102(b)(2)(B) is applicable to subject matter in an intervening U.S. patent, U.S. patent application publication, or WIPO published application does not involve a comparison of the subject matter of the claimed invention to either the subject matter disclosed by the inventor or a joint inventor, or to the subject matter of the subsequent intervening U.S. patent, U.S. patent application publication, or WIPO published application.

c. Prior art exception under AIA 35 U.S.C. 102(b)(2)(C) to AIA 35 U.S.C. 102(a)(2) (common ownership or obligation of assignment). AIA 35 U.S.C. 102(b)(2)(C) provides an additional exception to the prior art provisions of AIA 35 U.S.C. 102(a)(2). The exception of AIA 35 U.S.C. 102(b)(2)(C) disqualifies subject matter disclosed in a U.S. patent, U.S. patent application publication, or WIPO published application from constituting prior art under AIA 35 U.S.C. 102(a)(2) if the subject matter disclosed and the claimed invention, not later than the effective filing date of the claimed invention, "were owned by the same person or subject to an obligation of assignment to the same person." AIA 35 U.S.C. 102(b)(2)(C) resembles pre-AIA 35 U.S.C. 103(c) in that both concern common ownership, and both offer an avenue by which an applicant may avoid certain prior art. However, there are significant differences between AIA 35 U.S.C. 102(b)(2)(C) and pre-AIA 35 U.S.C. 103(c).

If the provisions of AIA 35 U.S.C. 102(b)(2)(C) are met, a U.S. patent, U.S. patent application publication, or WIPO published application that might otherwise qualify as prior art under AIA 35 U.S.C. 102(a)(2) is not available as prior art under either AIA 35 U.S.C. 102 or 103. Under pre-AIA 35 U.S.C. 103(c), such prior art could preclude patentability under pre-AIA 35 U.S.C. 102, even if the conditions of pre-AIA 35 U.S.C. 103(c) were met. The consequence of this distinction is that a published application or an issued patent that falls under the common ownership exception of AIA 35 U.S.C. 102(b)(2)(C) may not be applied in either an anticipation or an obviousness rejection.

It is important to note the circumstances in which the AIA 35 U.S.C. 102(b)(2)(C) exception does not remove U.S. patents, U.S. patent application publications, or WIPO published applications as a basis for any rejection. Even if the U.S. patent or U.S. published application is not prior art under AIA 35 U.S.C. 102 or 103 as a result of AIA 35 U.S.C. 102(b)(2)(C), a double patenting rejection (either statutory under 35 U.S.C. 101 or non-statutory, sometimes called obviousness-type) may still be made on the basis of the U.S. patent or U.S. patent application publication. Furthermore, the U.S. patent, U.S. patent application publication, or WIPO published application that does not qualify as prior art as a result of AIA 35 U.S.C. 102(b)(2)(C) may be cited, in appropriate situations, to indicate the state of the art when making a lack of enablement rejection under 35 U.S.C. 112(a). A document need not qualify as prior art to be applied in the context of double patenting[99] or enablement.[100] Also, the AIA 35 U.S.C. 102(b)(2)(C) exception does not apply to a disclosure that qualifies as prior art under AIA 35 U.S.C. 102(a)(1) (disclosures made before the effective filing date of the claimed invention). Thus, if the issue date of a U.S. patent or publication date of a U.S. patent application publication or WIPO published application is before the effective filing date of the claimed invention, it may be prior art under AIA 35 U.S.C. 102(a)(1), regardless of common ownership or the existence of an obligation to assign.

The Office is also revising the rules of practice in a separate action (RIN 0651-AC77) to include provisions that pertain to commonly owned or joint research agreement subject matter (37 CFR 1.104(c)(4) and (c)(5)). 37 CFR 1.104(c)(4) applies to an application that is subject to AIA 35 U.S.C. 102 and 103, and 37 CFR 1.104(c)(5) applies to an application that is subject to pre-AIA 35 U.S.C. 102 and 103. Commonly owned subject matter under AIA 35 U.S.C. 102 and 103 is treated under 37 CFR 1.104(c)(4)(i), and commonly owned subject matter under pre-AIA 35 U.S.C. 102 and 103 is treated under 37 CFR 1.104(c)(5)(i).

A clear and conspicuous statement by the applicant (or the applicant's representative of record) that the claimed invention of the application under examination and the subject matter disclosed in the U.S. patent, U.S. patent application publication, or WIPO published application (prior art) to be excluded under AIA 35 U.S.C. 102(b)(2)(C) were owned by the same person or subject to an obligation of assignment to the same person not later than the effective filing date of the claimed invention will be sufficient to establish that the AIA 35 U.S.C. 102(b)(2)(C) exception applies. When relying on the provisions of pre-AIA 35 U.S.C. 103(c), the applicant (or the applicant's representative) could provide a similar statement required to disqualify the cited prior art. The applicant may present supporting evidence such as copies of assignment documents, but is not required to do so. Furthermore, the Office will not request corroborating evidence in the absence of independent evidence which raises doubt as to the veracity of such a statement. The statement under AIA 35 U.S.C. 102(b)(2)(C) will generally be treated by Office personnel analogously to statements made under pre-AIA 35 U.S.C. 103(c).[101]

D. Use of Affidavits or Declarations Under 37 CFR 1.130 To Overcome Prior Art Rejections

The Office is also revising the rules of practice in a separate action (RIN 0651-AC77) to provide a mechanism in 37 CFR 1.130 for filing an affidavit or declaration to establish that a disclosure that was not made more than one year before the effective filing date of the claimed invention is not prior art under AIA 35 U.S.C. 102(a) due to an exception in AIA 35 U.S.C. 102(b). Under 37 CFR 1.130(a), an affidavit or declaration of attribution may be submitted to disqualify a disclosure as prior art because it was made by the inventor or a joint inventor, or by one who obtained the subject matter disclosed directly or indirectly from the inventor or a joint inventor. Under 37 CFR 1.130(b), an affidavit or declaration of prior public disclosure may be submitted to disqualify an intervening disclosure as prior art if: (1) The subject matter disclosed had been publicly disclosed by the inventor or a joint inventor before the disclosure of the subject matter on which the rejection is based; or (2) the subject matter disclosed had been publicly disclosed by the inventor or a joint inventor before the date the subject matter in the U.S. patent, U.S. patent application publication, or WIPO published application on which the rejection is based was effectively filed.

1. Showing That the Disclosure Was Made by the Inventor or a Joint Inventor

AIA 35 U.S.C. 102(b)(1)(A) provides that a grace period disclosure shall not be prior art to a claimed invention under AIA 35 U.S.C. 102(a)(1) if the disclosure was made by the inventor or a joint inventor. An applicant may show that a disclosure was made by the inventor or a joint inventor by way of an affidavit or declaration under 37 CFR 1.130(a) (an affidavit or declaration of attribution).[102] Where the authorship of the prior art disclosure includes the inventor or a joint inventor named in the application, an "unequivocal" statement from the inventor or a joint inventor that he/she (or some specific combination of named inventors) invented the subject matter of the disclosure, accompanied by a reasonable explanation of the presence of additional authors, may be acceptable in the absence of evidence to the contrary.[103] However, a mere statement from the inventor or a joint inventor without any accompanying reasonable explanation may not be sufficient where there is evidence to the contrary.[104] This is similar to the current process for disqualifying a publication as not being by "others" discussed in MPEP §2132.01, except that AIA 35 U.S.C. 102(b)(1)(A) requires only that the disclosure be by the inventor or a joint inventor.

2. Showing That the Subject Matter Disclosed Had Been Previously Publicly Disclosed by the Inventor or a Joint Inventor

AIA 35 U.S.C. 102(b)(1)(B) provides that a grace period disclosure shall not be prior art to a claimed invention under AIA 35 U.S.C. 102(a)(1) if subject matter disclosed had, before such disclosure, been publicly disclosed by the inventor or a joint inventor. Similarly, AIA 35 U.S.C. 102(b)(2)(B) provides that a disclosure shall not be prior art to a claimed invention under AIA 35 U.S.C. 102(a)(2) if the subject matter disclosed had, before such subject matter was effectively filed under AIA 35 U.S.C. 102(a)(2), been publicly disclosed by the inventor or a joint inventor. An applicant may show that the subject matter disclosed had been publicly disclosed by the inventor or a joint inventor before the disclosure or effective filing date of the subject matter on which the rejection was based by way of an affidavit or declaration under 37 CFR 1.130(b) (an affidavit or declaration of prior public disclosure). Specifically, the affidavit or declaration must identify the subject matter publicly disclosed and establish the date and content of their earlier public disclosure. If the earlier public disclosure was a printed publication, the affidavit or declaration must be accompanied by a copy of the printed publication in accordance with 37 CFR 1.130(b)(1). If the earlier disclosure was not a printed publication, the affidavit or declaration must describe the earlier disclosure with sufficient detail and particularity to determine that the earlier disclosure is a public disclosure of the subject matter, as required by 37 CFR 1.130(b)(2).

The manner of disclosure of subject matter referenced in an affidavit or declaration under 37 CFR 1.130(b) is not critical. Just as the prior art provision of AIA 35 U.S.C. 102(a)(1)

encompasses any disclosure that renders a claimed invention "available to the public," any manner of disclosure may be evidenced in an affidavit or declaration under 37 CFR 1.130(b). That is, when using an affidavit or declaration under 37 CFR 1.130(b) to disqualify an intervening disclosure as prior art based on a prior public disclosure by an inventor or a joint inventor, it is not necessary for the subject matter to have been disclosed in the same manner or using the same words. For example, the inventor or a joint inventor may have publicly disclosed the subject matter in question via a slide presentation at a scientific meeting, while the intervening disclosure of the subject matter may have been made in a journal article. This difference in the manner of disclosure or differences in the words used to describe the subject matter will not preclude the inventor from submitting an affidavit or declaration under 37 CFR 1.130(b) to disqualify the intervening disclosure (e.g., a journal article) as prior art.

3. Showing That the Disclosure was Made, or That Subject Matter had Been Previously Publicly Disclosed, by Another Who Obtained the Subject Matter Disclosed Directly or Indirectly From the Inventor or a Joint Inventor

AIA 35 U.S.C. 102(b)(1)(A), 102(b)(1)(B), 102(b)(2)(A), and 102(b)(2)(B) each provide similar treatment for disclosures of subject matter by another who obtained the subject matter disclosed directly or indirectly from the inventor or a joint inventor. Specifically, AIA 35 U.S.C. 102(b)(1)(A) provides that a grace period disclosure shall not be prior art to a claimed invention under AIA 35 U.S.C. 102(a)(1) if the disclosure was made by another who obtained the subject matter disclosed directly or indirectly from the inventor or a joint inventor, and AIA 35 U.S.C. 102(b)(2)(A) provides that a disclosure shall not be prior art to a claimed invention under AIA 35 U.S.C. 102(a)(2) if the subject matter disclosed was obtained directly or indirectly from the inventor or a joint inventor. In addition, AIA 35 U.S.C. 102(b)(1)(B) and 102(b)(2)(B) provide that a grace period disclosure shall not be prior art to a claimed invention under AIA 35 U.S.C. 102(a)(1), and that a disclosure shall not be prior art to a claimed invention under AIA 35 U.S.C. 102(a)(2), if the subject matter disclosed had, before such disclosure, been publicly disclosed by another who obtained the subject matter disclosed directly or indirectly from the inventor or a joint inventor. An applicant may also show that another obtained the subject matter disclosed directly or indirectly from the inventor or a joint inventor in an affidavit or declaration under 37 CFR 1.130(a) or (b). Thus, an applicant may make use of a prior public disclosure by another during the grace period if the applicant can establish that subject matter disclosed originated with the inventor or a joint inventor and that the subject matter was communicated by the inventor or a joint inventor, directly or indirectly. Any documentation which provides evidence of the communication of the subject matter by the inventor or a joint inventor to the entity that made the disclosure of the subject matter should accompany the affidavit or declaration.

4. Enablement

An affidavit or declaration under 37 CFR 1.130(a) or (b) need not demonstrate that the disclosure by the inventor, a joint inventor, or another who obtained the subject matter disclosed directly or indirectly from an inventor or a joint inventor was an "enabling" disclosure of the subject matter within the meaning of 35 U.S.C. 112(a). Rather, an affidavit or declaration under 37 CFR 1.130 must show that: (1) The disclosure in question was made by the inventor or a joint inventor, or the subject matter disclosed was obtained directly or indirectly from the inventor or a joint inventor (37 CFR 1.130(a));[105] or (2) the subject matter disclosed had, before such disclosure was made or before such subject matter was effectively filed, been publicly disclosed by the inventor or a joint inventor or another who obtained the subject matter disclosed directly or indirectly from the inventor or a joint inventor (37 CFR 1.130(b)).[106]

5. Who may File an Affidavit or Declaration Under 37 CFR 1.130

In accordance with 37 CFR 1.130, the applicant or patent owner may submit an affidavit or declaration. When an assignee, obligated assignee, or person showing sufficient proprietary interest is the applicant under 35 U.S.C. 118 rather than the inventor, the inventor may sign an affidavit or declaration under 37 CFR 1.130 to disqualify a disclosure of the invention as prior art, but the declaration must be filed by a party having authority to take action in the application. Authority to file papers in an application generally does not lie with the inventor if the inventor is not the applicant.

6. Situations in Which an Affidavit or Declaration Is Not Available

The provisions of 37 CFR 1.130 are not available if the rejection is based upon a disclosure made more than one year before the effective filing date of the claimed invention. The AIA retains the principle of the one-year statutory time bar of pre-AIA 35 U.S.C. 102(b) in that a disclosure more than one year before the effective filing date of a claimed invention is prior art under the AIA's 35 U.S.C. 102(a)(1) that cannot be disqualified under 35 U.S.C. 102(b)(1).

Additionally, the provisions of 37 CFR 1.130 may not be available if the rejection is based upon a U.S. patent or U.S. patent application publication of a patented or pending application naming another inventor if: (1) The patent or pending application claims an invention that is the same or substantially the same as the applicant's or patent owner's claimed invention; and (2) the affidavit or declaration contends that an inventor named in the U.S. patent or U.S. patent application publication derived the claimed invention from the inventor or a joint inventor named in the application or patent. The provisions of 37 CFR 1.130 are not available if it would result in the Office issuing or confirming two patents containing patentably indistinct claims to two different parties.[107] In this situation, an applicant or patent owner may file a petition for a derivation proceeding pursuant to 37 CFR 42.401 et seq. (37 CFR 1.130(c)).

III. Joint Research Agreements

AIA 35 U.S.C. 102(c) provides three conditions that must be satisfied in order for subject matter disclosed which might otherwise qualify as prior art, and a claimed invention, to be treated as having been owned by the same person or subject to an obligation of assignment to the same person in applying the joint research agreement provisions of AIA 35 U.S.C. 102(b)(2)(C). First, the subject matter disclosed must have been developed and the claimed invention must have been made by, or on behalf of, one or more parties to a joint research agreement that was in effect on or before the effective filing date of the claimed invention.[108] The AIA defines the term "joint research agreement" as a written contract, grant, or cooperative agreement entered into by two or more persons or entities for the performance of experimental, developmental, or research work in the field of the claimed invention.[109] Second, the claimed invention must have been made as a result of activities undertaken within the scope of the joint research agreement.[110] Third, the application for patent for the claimed invention must disclose, or be amended to disclose, the names of the parties to the joint research agreement.[111] Joint research agreement subject matter under AIA 35 U.S.C. 102 and 103 is treated under 37 CFR 1.104(c)(4)(ii), joint research agreement subject matter under pre-AIA 35 U.S.C. 102 and 103 is treated under 37 CFR 1.104(c)(5)(ii). If these conditions are met, the joint research agreement prior art is not available as prior art under AIA 35 U.S.C. 102(a)(2).

The provisions of AIA 35 U.S.C. 102(c) generally track those of the Cooperative Research and Technology Enhancement Act of 2004 (CREATE Act).[112] The major differences between AIA 35 U.S.C. 102(c) and the CREATE Act are that: (1) The new provision is keyed to the effective filing date of the claimed invention, while the CREATE Act focused on the date that the claimed invention was made; and (2) the CREATE Act provisions only applied to obviousness rejections and not to anticipation rejections.

In order to invoke a joint research agreement to disqualify a disclosure as prior art, the applicant (or the applicant's representative of record) must provide a statement that the disclosure of the subject matter on which the rejection is based and the claimed invention were made by or on behalf of parties to a joint research agreement under AIA 35 U.S.C. 102(c). The statement must also assert that the agreement was in effect on or before the effective filing date of the claimed invention, and that the claimed invention was made as a result of activities undertaken within the scope of the joint research agreement. When relying on the provisions of pre-AIA 35 U.S.C. 103(c), the applicant or his attorney or agent of record could provide a similar statement to disqualify the cited prior art as to the issue of obviousness. If the names of the parties to the joint research agreement are not already stated in the application, it is necessary to amend the application to include the names of the parties to the joint research agreement in accordance with 37 CFR 1.71(g).

As is the case with establishing common ownership, the applicant may, but is not required to, present evidence supporting the existence of the joint research agreement. Furthermore, the Office will not request corroborating evidence in the absence of independent evidence which raises doubt as to the existence of the joint research agreement.

As discussed previously, the AIA 35 U.S.C. 102(b)(2)(C) exception does not apply to a disclosure that qualifies as prior art under AIA 35 U.S.C. 102(a)(1) (disclosures made before the effective filing date of the claimed invention). Thus, if the issue date of a U.S. patent or publication date of a U.S. patent application publication or WIPO published application is before the effective filing date of the claimed invention, it may be prior art under AIA 35 U.S.C. 102(a)(1), regardless of the fact that the subject matter disclosed and the claimed invention resulted from a joint research agreement.

IV. Improper Naming of Inventors

Although the AIA eliminated pre-AIA 35 U.S.C. 102(f), the patent laws still require the naming of the actual inventor or joint inventors of the claimed subject matter.[113] The Office presumes that the named inventor or joint inventors in the application are the actual inventor or joint inventors be named on the patent.[114] Where an application names an incorrect inventorship, the applicant should submit a request to correct inventorship under 37 CFR 1.48. In the rare situation where it is clear that the application does not name the correct inventorship and the applicant has not filed a request to correct inventorship under 37 CFR 1.48, Office personnel should reject the claims under 35 U.S.C. 101 and 35 U.S.C. 115.[115]

V. AIA 35 U.S.C. 103

AIA 35 U.S.C. 103 continues to set forth the nonobviousness requirement for patentability.[116] There are, however, some important changes from pre-AIA 35 U.S.C. 103.

The most significant difference between the AIA 35 U.S.C. 103 and pre-AIA 35 U.S.C. 103(a) is that AIA 35 U.S.C. 103 determines obviousness as of the effective filing date of the claimed invention, rather than as of the time that the claimed invention was made. Under pre-AIA examination practice, the Office uses the effective filing date as a proxy for the invention date, unless there is evidence of record to establish an earlier date of invention. Thus, as a practical matter during examination, this distinction between the AIA 35 U.S.C. 103 and pre-AIA 35 U.S.C. 103 will result in a difference in practice only when the case under examination is subject to pre-AIA 35 U.S.C. 103, and there is evidence in the case concerning a date of invention prior to the effective filing date. Such evidence is ordinarily presented by way of an affidavit or declaration under 37 CFR 1.131.

Next, AIA 35 U.S.C. 103 differs from that of pre-AIA 35 U.S.C. 103 in that AIA 35 U.S.C. 103 requires consideration of "the differences between the claimed invention and the prior art," while pre-AIA 35 U.S.C. 103 refers to "the differences between the subject matter sought to be patented and the prior art." This difference in terminology does not indicate the need for any difference in approach to the question of obviousness.[117]

Further, AIA 35 U.S.C. 103 does not contain any provision similar to pre-AIA 35 U.S.C. 103(b). Pre-AIA 35 U.S.C. 103(b) is narrowly drawn, applying only to nonobviousness of biotechnological inventions, and even then, only when specifically invoked by the patent applicant. Pre-AIA 35 U.S.C. 103(b) provides that under certain conditions, "a biotechnological process using or resulting in a composition of matter that is novel under section 102 and nonobvious under subsection [103(a)] of this section shall be considered nonobvious." In view of the case law since 1995,[118] the need to invoke pre-AIA 35 U.S.C. 103(b) has been rare.

Finally, AIA 35 U.S.C. 103 eliminates pre-AIA 35 U.S.C. 103(c), but corresponding provisions have been introduced in AIA 35 U.S.C. 102(b)(2)(C) and 102(c). Pre-AIA 35 U.S.C. 103(c) applied if subject matter qualified as prior art only under pre-AIA 35 U.S.C. 102(e), (f), and/or (g), and only in the context of obviousness under pre-AIA 35 U.S.C. 103(a). If subject matter developed by another person was commonly owned with the claimed invention, or if the subject matter was subject to an obligation of assignment to the same person, at the time the claimed invention was made, then pre-AIA 35 U.S.C. 103(a) did not preclude patentability. Furthermore, under the pre-AIA 35 U.S.C. 103(c), if a joint research agreement was in place on or before the date that the claimed invention was made, the claimed invention was made as a result of activities undertaken within the scope of the joint research agreement, and the application for patent was amended to disclose the names of the parties to the joint research agreement, common ownership or an obligation to assign was deemed to exist. As discussed previously, AIA 35 U.S.C. 102(b)(2)(C) and 102(c) expand on this concept. Under the AIA, the common ownership, the obligation to assign, or the joint research agreement must exist on or before the effective filing date of the claimed invention, rather than on or before the date the invention was made. If the provisions of AIA 35 U.S.C. 102(b)(2)(C) are met, a disclosure is not prior art at all, whereas under pre-AIA 35 U.S.C. 103(c), certain prior art merely was defined as not precluding patentability. Finally, disclosures disqualified as prior art under AIA 35 U.S.C. 102(b)(2)(C) and 102(c) may not be applied in either an anticipation or an obviousness rejection. However, such disclosures could be the basis for statutory double patenting or non-statutory (sometimes referred to as obviousness-type) double patenting rejections.

Generally speaking, and with the exceptions noted herein, pre-AIA notions of obviousness will continue to apply under the AIA. AIA 35 U.S.C. 102(a) defines what is prior art both for purposes of novelty under AIA 35 U.S.C. 102 as well as for purposes of obviousness under AIA 35 U.S.C. 103.[119] Thus, if a document qualifies as prior art under AIA 35 U.S.C. 102(a)(1) or (a)(2), and is not subject to an exception under AIA 35 U.S.C. 102(b), it may be applied for what it describes or teaches to those skilled in the art in a rejection under AIA 35 U.S.C. 103.[120] Office personnel should continue to follow guidance for formulating an appropriate rationale to support any conclusion of obviousness. See MPEP §2141 et seq. and the guidance documents available at http://www.uspto.gov/patents/law/exam/ksr_training_materials.jsp.

VI. Applicability Date Provisions and Determining Whether an Application Is Subject to the First Inventor To File Provisions of the AIA

Because the changes to 35 U.S.C. 102 and 103 in the AIA apply only to specific applications filed on or after March 16, 2013, determining the effective filing date of a claimed invention for purposes of applying AIA 35 U.S.C. 102 and 103 provisions or pre-AIA 35 U.S.C. 102 and 103 provisions is critical.

A. Applications Filed Before March 16, 2013

The changes to 35 U.S.C. 102 and 103 in the AIA do not apply to any application filed before March 16, 2013. Thus, any application filed before March 16, 2013, is governed by pre-AIA 35 U.S.C. 102 and 103 (i.e., the application is a pre-AIA application). Note that neither the filing of a request for continued examination, nor entry into the national stage under 35 U.S.C. 371, constitutes the filing of a new application. Accordingly, even if a request for continued examination under 37 CFR 1.114 is filed after March 16, 2013, in an application that was filed before March 16, 2013, the application remains subject to pre-AIA 35 U.S.C. 102 and 103. Similarly, a PCT application filed under 35 U.S.C. 363 before March 16, 2013, is subject to pre-AIA 35 U.S.C. 102 and 103, regardless of whether the application enters the national stage under 35 U.S.C. 371 before or after March 16, 2013.

B. Applications Filed on or After March 16, 2013

AIA 35 U.S.C. 102 and 103 take effect on March 16, 2013. AIA 35 U.S.C. 102 and 103 apply to any patent application that contains or contained at any time a claim to a claimed invention that has an effective filing date that is on or after March 16, 2013. If a patent application contains or contained at any time a claim to a claimed invention having an effective filing date on or after March 16, 2013, AIA 35 U.S.C. 102 and 103 apply to the application (i.e., the application is an AIA application). If there is ever even a single claim to a claimed invention in the application having an effective filing date on or after March 16, 2013, AIA 35 U.S.C. 102 and 103 apply in determining the patentability of every claimed invention in the application. This is the situation even if the remaining claimed inventions all have an effective filing date before March 16, 2013, and even if the claim to a claimed invention having an effective filing date on or after March 16, 2013, is canceled.

If an application filed on or after March 16, 2013, that did not previously contain any claim to a claimed invention having an effective filing date on or after March 16, 2013, (a pre-AIA application) is amended to contain a claim to a claimed invention having an effective filing date on or after March 16, 2013, the application becomes an AIA application (AIA 35

U.S.C. 102 and 103 apply to the application), provided that the newly added claimed invention has support under 35 U.S.C. 112(a) in the application filed on or after March 16, 2013. The application also remains subject to AIA 35 U.S.C. 102 and 103 even if the claim to a claimed invention having an effective filing date on or after March 16, 2013, is subsequently canceled. If an amendment after an Office action causes the application to change from being governed by pre-AIA 35 U.S.C. 102 and 103 (from being a pre-AIA application) to being governed by AIA 35 U.S.C. 102 and 103 (to being a AIA application), any new ground of rejection necessitated by the change in applicable law would be considered a new ground of rejection necessitated by an amendment for purposes of determining whether the next Office action may be made final.[121]

As 35 U.S.C. 132(a)[122] prohibits the introduction of new matter into the disclosure, an application may not contain a claim to a claimed invention that does not have support under 35 U.S.C. 112(a) in the application (that is directed to new matter). Thus, an application cannot "contain" a claim to a claimed invention that is directed to new matter for purposes of determining whether the application ever contained a claim to a claimed invention having an effective filing date on or after March 16, 2013.[123] Therefore, an amendment (other than a preliminary amendment filed on the same day as such application) seeking to add a claim to a claimed invention that is directed to new matter in an application filed on or after March 16, 2013, that, as originally filed, discloses and claims only subject matter also disclosed in a previously filed pre-AIA application to which the application filed on or after March 16, 2013, is entitled to priority or benefit under 35 U.S.C. 119, 120, 121, or 365, would not change the application from a pre-AIA application into an AIA application.

C. Applications Subject to the AIA but Also Containing a Claimed Invention Having an Effective Filing Date Before March 16, 2013

Even if AIA 35 U.S.C. 102 and 103 apply to a patent application, pre-AIA 35 U.S.C. 102(g) also applies to every claim in the application if it: (1) contains or contained at any time a claimed invention having an effective filing date that occurs before March 16, 2013; or (2) is ever designated as a continuation, divisional, or continuation-in-part of an application that contains or contained at any time a claimed invention that has an effective filing date that occurs before March 16, 2013. Pre-AIA 35 U.S.C. 102(g) also applies to any patent resulting from an application to which pre-AIA 35 U.S.C. 102(g) applied.

Thus, if an application contains, or contained at any time, any claimed invention having an effective filing date that occurs before March 16, 2013, and also contains, or contained at any time, any claimed invention having an effective filing date that is on or after March 16, 2013, each claim must be patentable under AIA 35 U.S.C. 102 and 103, as well as pre-AIA 35 U.S.C. 102(g), for the applicant to be entitled to a patent. However, an application will not otherwise be concurrently subject to both pre-AIA 35 U.S.C. 102 and 103 and AIA 35 U.S.C. 102 and 103.

For these reasons, when subject matter is claimed in an application having priority to or the benefit of a prior-filed application (e.g., under 35 U.S.C. 120, 121, or 365(c)), care must be taken to accurately determine whether AIA or pre-AIA 35 U.S.C. 102 and 103 applies to the application.

D. Applicant Statement in Transition Applications Containing a Claimed Invention Having an Effective Filing Date on or After March 16, 2013

The Office is revising 37 CFR 1.55 and 1.78 in a separate action (RIN 0651-AC77) to require that if a nonprovisional application filed on or after March 16, 2013, claims the benefit of or priority to the filing date of a foreign, U.S. provisional, U.S. nonprovisional, or international application that was filed prior to March 16, 2013, and also contains or contained at any time a claimed invention having an effective filing date on or after March 16, 2013, the applicant must provide a statement to that effect. This information will assist the Office in determining whether the application is subject to AIA 35 U.S.C. 102 and 103 or pre-AIA 35 U.S.C. 102 and 103.

[47] Under 35 U.S.C. 102(e) as amended by the American Inventors Protection Act of 1999 (AIPA) (Pub. L. 106-113, 113 Stat. 1501 (1999) and the Intellectual Property and High Technology Technical Amendments Act of 2002 (Pub. L. 107-273), the international filing date of a PCT application is a U.S. filing date for prior art purposes under 35 U.S.C. 102(e) if the international application: (1) Has an international filing date on or after November 29, 2000; (2) designated the United States; and (3) was published under PCT Article 21(2) in English. *See* MPEP §706.02(f)(1). The AIA amends 35 U.S.C. 102, 363, and 374 to provide simply that the publication under the PCT of an international application designating the United States shall be deemed a publication under 35 U.S.C. 122(b).

[48] *See* 35 U.S.C. 101 ("[w]hoever invents or discovers * * *, may obtain a patent therefor, subject to the conditions and requirements of this title"); *see also* P.J. Federico, *Commentary on the New Patent Act*, 75 J. Pat. & Trademark Off. Soc'y 161, 179 (1993) (noting that pre-AIA 35 U.S.C. 102(f) is perhaps unnecessary since 35 U.S.C. 101 provides that ("[w]hoever invents or discovers * * *, may obtain a patent therefor, subject to the conditions and requirements of this title").

[49] *See* 35 U.S.C. 115 ("An application for patent that is filed under section 111(a) or commences the national stage under section 371 shall include, or be amended to include, the name of the inventor for any invention claimed in the application.")

[50] *See* Pub. L. 112-29, §3(n)(1), 125 Stat. at 293.

[51] *See* Pub. L. 112-29, §3(n)(1), 125 Stat. at 293.

[52] 35 U.S.C. 102(g) precludes the grant of a patent if: (1) During the course of an interference conducted under 35 U.S.C. 135 or 291, another inventor involved therein establishes, to the extent permitted in 35 U.S.C. 104, that before such person's invention thereof the invention was made by such other inventor and not abandoned, suppressed, or concealed, or (2) before such person's invention thereof, the invention was made in this country by another inventor who had not abandoned, suppressed, or concealed it.

[53] *See* Pub. L. 112-29, §3(n)(2), 125 Stat. at 293.

[54] *See* Pub. L. 112-29, §3(n)(2), 125 Stat. at 293.

[55] *See* 35 U.S.C. 102(a).

[56] *See* 35 U.S.C. 132(a).

[57] *See In re Epstein*, 32 F.3d 1559 (Fed. Cir. 1994).

[58] *See* 35 U.S.C. 102(b)(1).

[59] *See* 35 U.S.C. 102(b)(2).

[60] *See* 35 U.S.C. 100(i)(1).

[61] *See* MPEP §706.02(VI).

[62] *See* 35 U.S.C. 100(i)(2).

[63] *See In re Ekenstam*, 256 F.2d 321, 323 (CCPA 1958); *see also* MPEP §2126.01.

[64] *See In re Carlson*, 983 F.2d 1032, 1037 (Fed. Cir. 1992); *see also* MPEP §2126.

[65] *See Novo Nordisk Pharma., Inc. v. Bio-Tech. Gen. Corp.*, 424 F.3d 1347, 1355 (Fed. Cir. 2005) (discussing pre-AIA 35 U.S.C. 112, first paragraph, and pre-AIA 35 U.S.C. 102).

[66] *See In re Gleave*, 560 F.3d 1331, 1334 (Fed. Cir. 2009), citing *Eli Lilly & Co. v. Zenith Goldline Pharms., Inc.*, 471 F.3d 1369, 1375 (Fed. Cir. 2006); *Net MoneyIN, Inc. v. VeriSign, Inc.*, 545 F.3d 1359, 1370 (Fed. Cir. 2008); *In re Bond*, 910 F.2d 831, 832-33 (Fed. Cir. 1990).

[67] *See In re Gleave*, 560 F.3d 1331, 1334 (Fed. Cir. 2009) (citing *Impax Labs., Inc. v. Aventis Pharms. Inc.*, 545 F.3d 1312, 1314 (Fed. Cir. 2008), and *In re LeGrice*, 301 F.2d 929, 940-44 (CCPA 1962)).

[68] *See In re Gleave*, 560 F.3d 1331, 1334 (Fed. Cir. 2009); *see also In re Schoenwald*, 964 F.2d 1122, 1124 (Fed. Cir. 1992) (holding that a claimed compound was anticipated even though the prior art reference did not disclose a use for the compound); *Schering Corp. v. Geneva Pharms., Inc.*, 339 F.3d 1373, 1380-81 (Fed. Cir. 2003) (pointing out that actually reducing the invention to practice is not necessary in order for a prior art reference to anticipate); *Impax Labs. Inc. v. Aventis Pharm. Inc.*, 468 F.3d 1366, 1382 (Fed. Cir. 2006) (stating that "proof of efficacy is not required for a prior art reference to be enabling for purposes of anticipation").

[69] *See In re Donohue*, 766 F.2d 531, 533 (Fed. Cir. 1985).

[70] *See Rasmussen v. SmithKline Beecham Corp.*, 413 F.3d 1318 (Fed. Cir. 2005).

[71] *See Vas-Cath Inc. v. Mahurkar*, 935 F.2d 1555, 1562 (Fed. Cir. 1991) ("As the court pointed out, 'the description of a single embodiment of broadly claimed subject matter constitutes a description of the invention for anticipation purposes * * *, whereas the same information in a specification might not alone be enough to provide a description of that invention for purposes of adequate disclosure.'") (quoting *In re Lukach*, 442 F.2d 967 (CCPA 1971)); *see also In re Van Langenhoven*, 458 F.2d 132 (CCPA 1972), and *In re Ruscetta*, 255 F.2d 687 (CCPA 1958).

[72] Under pre-AIA 35 U.S.C. 102(b), the critical date is the date that is one year prior to the date of application for patent in the United States.

[73] *See Invitrogen Corp. v. Biocrest Mfg. L.P.*, 424 F.3d 1374, 1379-80 (Fed. Cir. 2005).

[74] *See American Seating Co. v. USSC Group, Inc.*, 514 F.3d 1262, 1267 (Fed. Cir. 2008).

[75] *See Woodland Trust v. Flowertree Nursery, Inc.*, 148 F.3d 1368, 1371 (Fed. Cir. 1998).

[76] *See Woodland Trust v. Flowertree Nursery, Inc.*, 148 F.3d 1368, 1370 (Fed. Cir. 1998).

[77] *See American Seating Co. v. USSC Group, Inc.*, 514 F.3d 1262, 1267 (Fed. Cir. 2008).

[78] *See Woodland Trust v. Flowertree Nursery, Inc.*, 148 F.3d 1368, 1370 (Fed. Cir. 1998).

[79] *See Woodland Trust v. Flowertree Nursery, Inc.*, 148 F.3d 1368, 1370 (Fed. Cir. 1998) (quoting *Carella v. Starlight Archery*, 804 F.2d 135, 139 (Fed. Cir. 1986)).

[80] *See Pfaff v. Wells Elecs., Inc.*, 525 U.S. 55, 67 (1998).

[81] *See In re Epstein*, 32 F.3d 1559, 1568 (Fed. Cir. 1994).

[82] *Cf. Clock Spring, L.P. v. Wrapmaster, Inc.*, 560 F.3d 1317, 1325 (Fed. Cir. 2009) (an invention is in public use if it is shown to or used by an individual other than the inventor under no limitation, restriction, or obligation of confidentiality to the inventor).

[83] *See, e.g., In re Cronyn*, 890 F.2d 1158 (Fed. Cir. 1989); *In re Hall*, 781 F.2d 897 (Fed. Cir. 1986); *In re Bayer*, 568 F.2d 1357 (CCPA 1978).

[84] *See, e.g., In re Klopfenstein*, 380 F.3d 1345 (Fed. Cir. 2004), *Massachusetts Institute of Technology v. AB Fortia*, 774 F.2d 1104 (Fed. Cir. 1985).

[85] *See, e.g., In re Wyer*, 655 F.2d 221 (CCPA 1981); *see also Bruckelmyer v. Ground Heaters, Inc.*, 445 F.3d 1374 (Fed. Cir. 2006).

[86] *See, e.g., Voter Verified, Inc. v. Premier Election Solutions, Inc.*, 687 F.3d 1380-81 (Fed. Cir. 2012), *In re Lister*, 583 F.3d 1307 (Fed. Cir. 2009), and *SRI Int'l, Inc. v. Internet Sec. Sys., Inc.*, 511 F.3d 1186 (Fed. Cir. 2008).

[87] *See, e.g., Group One, Ltd. v. Hallmark Cards, Inc.*, 254 F.3d 1041 (Fed. Cir. 2001).

[88] *See Riverwood Int'l Corp. v. R.A. Jones & Co.*, 324 F.3d 1346, 1354 (Fed. Cir. 2003); *Constant v. Advanced Micro-Devices Inc.*, 848 F.2d 1560, 1570 (Fed. Cir. 1988).

[89] *See* 35 U.S.C. 102(b)(1) ("[a] disclosure made one year or less before the effective filing date of a claimed invention shall not be prior art to the claimed invention under [35 U.S.C. 102](a)(1)") and 102(b)(2) ("[a] disclosure shall not be prior art to a claimed invention under [35 U.S.C. 102](a)(2)"); *see also* H.R. Rep. No. 112-98 at 43 (2011) (indicating that the grace period provision of 35 U.S.C. 102(b) would apply to all patent applicant actions during the grace period that would create prior art under 35 U.S.C. 102(a)).

[90] *See* 35 U.S.C. 102(b)(1)(B).

[91] *See In re Kao*, 639 F.3d 1057, 1066 (Fed. Cir. 2011) (subject matter does not change as a function of how one chooses to describe it).

[92] *See* 157 Cong. Rec. 1370 (Mar. 8, 2011) (distinguishing between the core requirement that the prior-filed application include an enabling disclosure and the ministerial requirements that the applications be copendent and specifically referenced); *see also* MPEP §201.08 (permitting a claim to the benefit of a prior-filed application in a continuation-in-part application provided that the continuation-in-part application has a common inventor, has copendency with the prior-filed application, and includes a specific reference to the prior-filed application, regardless of whether the prior-filed application contains support under 35 U.S.C. 112 for any claim in the continuation-in-part application).

[93] The legislative history of the AIA discusses an important distinction between ministerial entitlement to make a priority or benefit claim, and actual legal entitlement to the priority or benefit. In section 100(i), which defines the effective filing date of the patent under review, the patent must be entitled to the priority or benefit itself under the relevant sections. In section 102(d), however, the application need only be entitled to claim the benefit or priority under those sections. This difference in language distinguishes between the core requirement of section 120 et al.—that the application include an enabling disclosure—and the ministerial requirements of that section—that the application be copendent and specifically referenced. In effect, an application that meets the ministerial requirements of copendency and specific reference is entitled to claim the benefit or priority, but only an application that also offers an enabling disclosure is actually entitled to the benefit or priority itself. See 157 Cong. Rec. 1370 (Mar. 8, 2011).

[94] *See In re Wertheim*, 646 F.2d 527 (CCPA 1981), which relies upon *Alexander Milburn Co. v. Davis-Bournonville*, 270 U.S. 390 (1926), for its conclusion that the patent must actually be entitled to the benefit of the prior-application for any subject matter in the patent to have a prior art date under 35 U.S.C. 102(e) as of the filing date of the prior application. The legislative history of the AIA indicates that paragraph (2) of AIA 102(d) is intended to overrule what remained of *In re Wertheim*, 646 F.2d 527 (CCPA 1981), which appeared to hold that only an application that could have become a patent on the day that it was filed can constitute prior art against another application or patent. *See* 157 Cong. Rec. 1369-70 (Mar. 8, 2011). The Office has previously indicated that the reasoning of *In re Wertheim*, 646 F.2d 527 (CCPA 1981), did not survive the amendment to 35 U.S.C. 102(e) in the American Inventor's Protection Act. *See, e.g., Ex parte Yamaguchi*, 88 U.S.P.Q.2d 1606, 1610-12 (Bd. Pat. App. & Interf. 2008). In *In re Giacomini*, 612 F.3d 1380 (Fed. Cir. 2010), the Federal Circuit held that a patent was effective as prior art as of the filing date of a provisional application claimed under 35 U.S.C. 119(e), so long as the subject matter upon which the rejection was based was described in the provisional application filing.

[95] *See* MPEP §2136.03 IV ("In other words, the subject matter used in the rejection must be disclosed in the earlier-filed application in compliance with 35 U.S.C. 112, first paragraph, in order for that subject matter to be entitled to the earlier filing date under 35 U.S.C. 102(e)."); *see also Ex parte Yamaguchi*, 88 U.S.P.Q.2d 1606, 1610-12 (Bd. Pat. App. & Interf. 2008) (discussing the legislative displacement of *In re Wertheim*, 646 F.2d 527 (CCPA 1981), prior to enactment of the AIA by the provisional application provisions of the Uruguay Round Agreements Act (URAA) (Pub. L. 103-465, 108 Stat. 4809 (1994)), and the eighteen-month publication provisions of the American Inventor's Protection Act of 1999 (AIPA)).

[96] As discussed previously, in *In re Hilmer*, 359 F.2d 859 (CCPA 1966), the CCPA held that reliance on the foreign priority date of a reference applied in a rejection under pre-AIA 35 U.S.C. 102(e) was improper.

[97] When examining an application to which the changes in 35 U.S.C. 102 and 103 do not apply, Office personnel will continue to apply the *Hilmer* doc-

trine, and foreign priority dates may not be used in determining 35 U.S.C. 102(e) prior art dates. Note that the international filing date of a published PCT application may be the 35 U.S.C. 102(e) prior art date under pre-AIA law under certain circumstances. *See* MPEP §706.02(f).

98 *See* 35 U.S.C. 102(b)(2)(B).

99 *See* MPEP §804.03 (prior art disqualified under the CREATE Act may be the basis for a double patenting rejection).

100 *See* MPEP §2124 (publications after the critical date may be used to show factual evidence that, as of an application's filing date, undue experimentation would have been required to make or use the invention, that a parameter absent from the claims was or was not critical, that a statement in the specification was inaccurate, that the invention was inoperative or lacked utility, that a claim was indefinite, or that characteristics of prior art products were known).

101 *See* MPEP §706.02(*l*)(2)(II).

102 *See In re Katz*, 687 F.2d 450, 455 (CCPA 1982).

103 *See In re DeBaun*, 687 F.2d 459, 463 (CCPA 1982).

104 *See Ex parte Kroger*, 219 USPQ 370 (Bd. App. 1982) (affirming rejection notwithstanding declarations by the alleged actual inventors as to their inventorship in view of a nonapplicant author submitting a letter declaring the non-applicant author's inventorship).

105 *See* 35 U.S.C. 102(b)(1)(A) or 102(b)(2)(A).

106 *See* 35 U.S.C. 102(b)(1)(B) or 102(b)(2)(B).

107 *See In re Deckler*, 977 F.2d 1449, 1451-52 (Fed. Cir. 1992) (35 U.S.C. 102, 103, and 135 "clearly contemplate—where different inventive entities are concerned—only one patent should issue for inventions which are either identical to or not patentably distinct from each other") (quoting *Aelony v. Arni*, 547 F.2d 566, 570 (CCPA 1977)).

108 *See* 35 U.S.C. 102(c)(1).

109 *See* 35 U.S.C. 100(h).

110 *See* 35 U.S.C. 102(c)(2).

111 *See* 35 U.S.C. 102(c)(3).

112 *See* Public Law 108-453, 118 Stat. 3596 (2004), which was an amendment to pre-AIA 35 U.S.C. 103(c). Congress has made it clear that the intent of AIA 35 U.S.C. 102(c) is to continue the promotion of joint research activities that was begun under the CREATE Act, stating in section 3(b) of the AIA that "[t]he United States Patent and Trademark Office shall administer section 102(c) of title 35, United States Code, in a manner consistent with the legislative history of the CREATE Act that was relevant to its administration by the United States Patent and Trademark Office." *See* 125 Stat. at 287.

113 *See* 35 U.S.C. 115(a) ("[a]n application for patent that is filed under [35 U.S.C.] 111(a) or commences the national stage under [35 U.S.C.] 371 shall include, or be amended to include, the name of the inventor for any invention claimed in the application").

114 *See* MPEP §2137.01.

115 As discussed previously, 35 U.S.C. 101 provides that "[w]hoever invents or discovers * * *, may obtain a patent therefor, subject to the conditions and requirements of this title," while 35 U.S.C. 115 requires that "[a]n application for patent that is filed under section 111(a) or commences the national stage under section 371 shall include, or be amended to include, the name of the inventor for any invention claimed in the application."

116 AIA 35 U.S.C. 103 provides: "A patent for a claimed invention may not be obtained, notwithstanding that the claimed invention is not identically disclosed as set forth in section 102, if the differences between the claimed invention and the prior art are such that the claimed invention as a whole would have been obvious before the effective filing date of the claimed invention to a person having ordinary skill in the art to which the claimed invention pertains. Patentability shall not be negated by the manner in which the invention was made."

117 As pointed out by the Federal Circuit, "[t]he term 'claims' has been used in patent legislation since the Patent Act of 1836 to define the invention that an applicant believes is patentable." *Hoechst-Roussel Pharms., Inc. v. Lehman*, 109 F.3d 756, 758 (Fed. Cir. 1997) (citing Act of July 4, 1836, ch. 357, §6, 5 Stat. 117). Furthermore, in *Graham v. John Deere*, 383 U.S. 1 (1966), the second of the Supreme Court's factual inquiries (the "*Graham* factors") is that the "differences between the prior art and the claims at issue are to be ascertained." *Graham*, 383 U.S. at 17. Thus, in interpreting 35 U.S.C. 103 as enacted in the 1952 Patent Act—language that remained unchanged until enactment of the AIA—the Court equated "the subject matter sought to be patented" with the claims.

118 As stated in MPEP §706.02(n), in view of the Federal Circuit's decisions in *In re Ochiai*, 71 F.3d 1565 (Fed. Cir. 1995) and *In re Brouwer*, 77 F.3d 422 (Fed. Cir. 1996), the need to invoke pre-AIA 35 U.S.C. 103(b) rarely arose. Those cases continue to retain their validity under the AIA.

119 *See Hazeltine Res., Inc. v. Brenner*, 382 U.S. 252, 256 (1965) (a previously filed patent application to another pending in the Office, but not patented or published, at the time an application is filed constitutes part of the "prior art" within the meaning of 35 U.S.C. 103).

120 This is in accordance with pre-AIA case law indicating that in making determinations under 35 U.S.C. 103, "it must be known whether a patent or publication is in the prior art under 35 U.S.C. 102." *Panduit Corp. v. Dennison Mfg. Co.*, 810 F.2d 1561, 1568 (Fed. Cir. 1987). However, while a disclosure must enable those skilled in the art to make the invention in order to anticipate under 35 U.S.C. 102, a non-enabling disclosure is prior art for all it teaches for purposes of determining obviousness under 35 U.S.C. 103. *Symbol Techs. Inc. v. Opticon Inc.*, 935 F.2d 1569, 1578 (Fed. Cir. 1991); *Beckman Instruments v. LKB Produkter AB*, 892 F.2d 1547, 1551 (Fed. Cir. 1989) ("Even if a reference discloses an inoperative device, it is prior art for all that it teaches.").

121 *See* MPEP §706.07(a).

122 35 U.S.C. 132(a) provides that "[n]o amendment shall introduce new matter into the disclosure of the invention."

123 The MPEP set forth the following process for treating amendments that are believed to contain new matter: (1) A new drawing should not be entered if the examiner discovers that the drawing contains new matter (MPEP §608.02); and (2) amendments to the written description or claims involving new matter are ordinarily entered, but the new matter is required to be canceled from the written description and the claims directed to the new matter are rejected under 35 U.S.C. 112(a) (MPEP §608.04). This process for treating amendments containing new matter is purely an administrative process for handling an amendment seeking to introduce new matter into the disclosure of the invention in violation of 35 U.S.C. 132(a), and for resolving disputes between the applicant and an examiner as to whether a new drawing or amendment to the written description or claims would actually introduce new matter into the disclosure of the invention.

ACTION BY APPLICANT & FURTHER CONSIDERATION

§1.111. REPLY BY APPLICANT OR PATENT OWNER TO A NON-FINAL OFFICE ACTION

(a)(1) If the Office action after the first examination (§1.104) is adverse in any respect, the applicant or patent owner, if he or she persists in his or her application for a patent or reexamination proceeding, must reply and request reconsideration or further examination, with or without amendment. See §§1.135 and 1.136 for time for reply to avoid abandonment.

(2) Supplemental replies.

(i) A reply that is supplemental to a reply that is in compliance with §1.111(b) will not be entered as a matter of right except as provided in paragraph (a)(2)(ii) of this section. The Office may enter a supplemental reply if the supplemental reply is clearly limited to:

(A) Cancellation of a claim(s);

(B) Adoption of the examiner suggestion(s);

(C) Placement of the application in condition for allowance;

(D) Reply to an Office requirement made after the first reply was filed;

(E) Correction of informalities (*e.g.*, typographical errors); or

(F) Simplification of issues for appeal.

(ii) A supplemental reply will be entered if the supplemental reply is filed within the period during which action by the Office is suspended under §1.103(a) or (c).

(b) In order to be entitled to reconsideration or further examination, the applicant or patent owner must reply to the Office action. The reply by the applicant or patent owner must be reduced to a writing which distinctly and specifically points out the supposed errors in the examiner's action and must reply to every ground of objection and rejection in the prior Office action. The reply must present arguments pointing out the specific distinctions believed to render the claims, including any newly presented claims, patentable over any applied references. If the reply is with respect to an application, a request may be made that objections or requirements as to form not necessary to further consideration of the claims be held in abeyance until allowable subject matter is indicated. The applicant's or patent owner's reply must appear throughout to be a bona fide attempt to advance the application or the reexamination proceeding to final action. A general allegation that the claims define a patentable invention without specifically pointing out how the language of the claims patentably distinguishes them from the references does not comply with the requirements of this section.

(c) In amending in reply to a rejection of claims in an application or patent under reexamination, the applicant or patent owner must clearly point out the patentable novelty which he or she thinks the claims present in view of the state of the art disclosed by the references cited or the objections made. The applicant or patent owner must also show how the amendments avoid such references or objections.

History of 37 C.F.R. §1.111: 46 FR 29182, May 29, 1981; 62 FR 53192, Oct. 10, 1997; 65 FR 54672, Sept. 8, 2000; 69 FR 56542, Sept. 21, 2004; 70 FR 3891, Jan. 27, 2005.

§1.112. RECONSIDERATION BEFORE FINAL ACTION

After reply by applicant or patent owner (§1.111 or §1.945) to a non-final action and any comments by an inter partes reexamination requester (§1.947), the application or the patent under reexamination will be reconsidered and again examined. The applicant, or in the case of a reexamination proceeding the patent owner and any third party requester, will be notified if claims are rejected, objections or requirements made, or decisions favorable to patentability are made, in the same manner as after the first examination (§1.104). Applicant or patent owner may reply to such Office action in the same manner provided in §1.111 or §1.945, with or without amendment, unless such Office action indicates that it is made final (§1.113) or an appeal (§41.31 of this title) has been taken (§1.116), or in an inter partes reexamination, that it is an action closing prosecution (§1.949) or a right of appeal notice (§1.953).

History of 37 C.F.R. §1.112: 46 FR 29182, May 29, 1981; 62 FR 53192, Oct. 10, 1997; 65 FR 54672, Sept. 8, 2000; 65 FR 76773, Dec. 7, 2000; 69 FR 49999, Aug. 12, 2004.

§1.113. FINAL REJECTION OR ACTION

(a) On the second or any subsequent examination or consideration by the examiner the rejection or other action may be made final, whereupon applicant's, or for ex parte reexaminations filed under §1.510, patent owner's reply is limited to appeal in the case of rejection of any claim (§41.31 of this title), or to amendment as specified in §1.114 or §1.116. Petition may be taken to the Director in the case of objections or requirements not involved in the rejection of any claim (§1.181). Reply to a final rejection or action must comply with §1.114 or paragraph (c) of this section. For final actions in an inter partes reexamination filed under §1.913, see §1.953.

(b) In making such final rejection, the examiner shall repeat or state all grounds of rejection then considered applicable to the claims in the application, clearly stating the reasons in support thereof.

(c) Reply to a final rejection or action must include cancellation of, or appeal from the rejection of, each rejected claim. If any claim stands allowed, the reply to a final rejection or action must comply with any requirements or objections as to form.

History of 37 C.F.R. §1.113: 24 FR 10332, Dec. 22, 1959; 46 FR 29182, May 29, 1981; 62 FR 53192, Oct. 10, 1997; 65 FR 14872, Mar. 20, 2000; 65 FR 50103, Aug. 16, 2000; 65 FR 76773, Dec. 7, 2000; 69 FR 49999, Aug. 12, 2004.

§1.114. REQUEST FOR CONTINUED EXAMINATION

(a) If prosecution in an application is closed, an applicant may request continued examination of the application by filing a submission and the fee set forth in §1.17(e) prior to the earliest of:

(1) Payment of the issue fee, unless a petition under §1.313 is granted;

(2) Abandonment of the application; or

(3) The filing of a notice of appeal to the U.S. Court of Appeals for the Federal Circuit under 35 U.S.C. 141, or the commencement of a civil action under 35 U.S.C. 145 or 146, unless the appeal or civil action is terminated.

(b) Prosecution in an application is closed as used in this section means that the application is under appeal, or that the last Office action is a final action (§1.113), a notice of allowance (§1.311), or an action that otherwise closes prosecution in the application.

(c) A submission as used in this section includes, but is not limited to, an information disclosure statement, an amendment to the written description, claims, or drawings, new arguments, or new evidence in support of patentability. If reply to an Office action under 35 U.S.C. 132 is outstanding, the submission must meet the reply requirements of §1.111.

(d) If an applicant timely files a submission and fee set forth in §1.17(e), the Office will withdraw the finality of any

Office action and the submission will be entered and considered. If an applicant files a request for continued examination under this section after appeal, but prior to a decision on the appeal, it will be treated as a request to withdraw the appeal and to reopen prosecution of the application before the examiner. An appeal brief (§41.37 of this title) or a reply brief (§41.41 of this title), or related papers, will not be considered a submission under this section.

(e) The provisions of this section do not apply to:

(1) A provisional application;

(2) An application for a utility or plant patent filed under 35 U.S.C. 111(a) before June 8, 1995;

(3) An international application filed under 35 U.S.C. 363 before June 8, 1995, or an international application that does not comply with 35 U.S.C. 371;

(4) An application for a design patent;

(5) An international design application; or

(6) A patent under reexamination.

History of 37 C.F.R. §1.114: 65 FR 14872, Mar. 20, 2000; 65 FR 50103, Aug. 16, 2000; 65 FR 50104, Aug. 16, 2000; 69 FR 49999, Aug. 12, 2004; 74 FR 52691, Oct. 14, 2009; 80 FR 17963, May 13, 2015.

AMENDMENTS

§1.115. PRELIMINARY AMENDMENTS

(a) A preliminary amendment is an amendment that is received in the Office (§1.6) on or before the mail date of the first Office action under §1.104. The patent application publication may include preliminary amendments (§1.215(a)).

(1) A preliminary amendment that is present on the filing date of an application is part of the original disclosure of the application.

(2) A preliminary amendment filed after the filing date of the application is not part of the original disclosure of the application.

(b) A preliminary amendment in compliance with §1.121 will be entered unless disapproved by the Director.

(1) A preliminary amendment seeking cancellation of all the claims without presenting any new or substitute claims will be disapproved.

(2) A preliminary amendment may be disapproved if the preliminary amendment unduly interferes with the preparation of a first Office action in an application. Factors that will be considered in disapproving a preliminary amendment include:

(i) The state of preparation of a first Office action as of the date of receipt (§1.6) of the preliminary amendment by the Office; and

(ii) The nature of any changes to the specification or claims that would result from entry of the preliminary amendment.

(3) A preliminary amendment will not be disapproved under (b)(2) of this section if it is filed no later than:

(i) Three months from the filing date of an application under §1.53(b);

(ii) The filing date of a continued prosecution application under §1.53(d); or

(iii) Three months from the date the national stage is entered as set forth in §1.491 in an international application.

(4) The time periods specified in paragraph (b)(3) of this section are not extendable.

History of 37 C.F.R. §1.115: 65 FR 54672, Sept. 8, 2000; 69 FR 56543, Sept. 21, 2004.

§1.116. AMENDMENTS & AFFIDAVITS OR OTHER EVIDENCE AFTER FINAL ACTION & PRIOR TO APPEAL

(a) An amendment after final action must comply with §1.114 or this section.

(b) After a final rejection or other final action (§1.113) in an application or in an ex parte reexamination filed under §1.510, or an action closing prosecution (§1.949) in an inter partes reexamination filed under §1.913, but before or on the same date of filing an appeal (§41.31 or §41.61 of this title):

(1) An amendment may be made canceling claims or complying with any requirement of form expressly set forth in a previous Office action;

(2) An amendment presenting rejected claims in better form for consideration on appeal may be admitted; or

(3) An amendment touching the merits of the application or patent under reexamination may be admitted upon a showing of good and sufficient reasons why the amendment is necessary and was not earlier presented.

(c) The admission of, or refusal to admit, any amendment after a final rejection, a final action, an action closing prosecution, or any related proceedings will not operate to relieve the application or reexamination proceeding from its condition as subject to appeal or to save the application from abandonment under §1.135, or the reexamination prosecution from termination under §1.550(d) or §1.957(b) or limitation of further prosecution under §1.957(c).

(d)(1) Notwithstanding the provisions of paragraph (b) of this section, no amendment other than canceling claims, where such cancellation does not affect the scope of any other pending claim in the proceeding, can be made in an inter partes reexamination proceeding after the right of appeal notice under §1.953 except as provided in §1.981 or as permitted by §41.77(b)(1) of this title.

(2) Notwithstanding the provisions of paragraph (b) of this section, an amendment made after a final rejection or other final action (§1.113) in an ex parte reexamination filed under §1.510, or an action closing prosecution (§1.949) in an inter partes reexamination filed under §1.913 may not cancel claims where such cancellation affects the scope of any other pending claim in the reexamination proceeding except as provided in §1.981 or as permitted by §41.77(b)(1) of this title.

(e) An affidavit or other evidence submitted after a final rejection or other final action (§1.113) in an application or in an ex parte reexamination filed under §1.510, or an action closing prosecution (§1.949) in an inter partes reexamination filed under §1.913 but before or on the same date of filing an appeal (§41.31 or §41.61 of this title), may be admitted upon a showing of good and sufficient reasons why the affidavit or other evidence is necessary and was not earlier presented.

(f) Notwithstanding the provisions of paragraph (e) of this section, no affidavit or other evidence can be made in an inter partes reexamination proceeding after the right of appeal notice under §1.953 except as provided in §1.981 or as permitted by §41.77(b)(1) of this title.

(g) After decision on appeal, amendments, affidavits and other evidence can only be made as provided in §§1.198 and 1.981, or to carry into effect a recommendation under §41.50(c) of this title.

History of 37 C.F.R. §1.116: 24 FR 10332, Dec. 22, 1959; 46 FR 29183, May 29, 1981; 62 FR 53192, Oct. 10, 1997; 65 FR 14873, Mar. 20, 2000; 65 FR 50103, Aug. 16, 2000; 65 FR 76773, Dec. 7, 2000; 69 FR 49999, Aug. 12, 2004.

§1.117. RESERVED

History of 37 C.F.R. §1.117: 74 FR 52691, Oct. 14, 2009.

§§1.118, 1.119. RESERVED

History of 37 C.F.R. §§1.118, 1.119: 62 FR 53192, Oct. 10, 1997.

§1.121. MANNER OF MAKING AMENDMENTS IN APPLICATIONS

(a) Amendments in applications, other than reissue applications. Amendments in applications, other than reissue applications, are made by filing a paper, in compliance with §1.52, directing that specified amendments be made.

(b) Specification. Amendments to the specification, other than the claims, computer listings (§1.96) and sequence listings (§1.825), must be made by adding, deleting or replacing a paragraph, by replacing a section, or by a substitute specification, in the manner specified in this section.

(1) Amendment to delete, replace, or add a paragraph. Amendments to the specification, including amendment to a section heading or the title of the invention which are considered for amendment purposes to be an amendment of a paragraph, must be made by submitting:

(i) An instruction, which unambiguously identifies the location, to delete one or more paragraphs of the specification, replace a paragraph with one or more replacement paragraphs, or add one or more paragraphs;

(ii) The full text of any replacement paragraph with markings to show all the changes relative to the previous version of the paragraph. The text of any added subject matter must be shown by underlining the added text. The text of any deleted matter must be shown by strike-through except that double brackets placed before and after the deleted characters may be used to show deletion of five or fewer consecutive characters. The text of any deleted subject matter must be shown by being placed within double brackets if strike-through cannot be easily perceived;

(iii) The full text of any added paragraphs without any underlining; and

(iv) The text of a paragraph to be deleted must not be presented with strike-through or placed within double brackets. The instruction to delete may identify a paragraph by its paragraph number or include a few words from the beginning, and end, of the paragraph, if needed for paragraph identification purposes.

(2) Amendment by replacement section. If the sections of the specification contain section headings as provided in §1.77(b), §1.154(b), or §1.163(c), amendments to the specification, other than the claims, may be made by submitting:

(i) A reference to the section heading along with an instruction, which unambiguously identifies the location, to delete that section of the specification and to replace such deleted section with a replacement section; and

(ii) A replacement section with markings to show all changes relative to the previous version of the section. The text of any added subject matter must be shown by underlining the added text. The text of any deleted matter must be shown by strike-through except that double brackets placed before and after the deleted characters may be used to show deletion of five or fewer consecutive characters. The text of any deleted subject matter must be shown by being placed within double brackets if strike-through cannot be easily perceived.

(3) Amendment by substitute specification. The specification, other than the claims, may also be amended by submitting:

(i) An instruction to replace the specification; and

(ii) A substitute specification in compliance with §§1.125(b) and (c).

(4) Reinstatement of previously deleted paragraph or section. A previously deleted paragraph or section may be reinstated only by a subsequent amendment adding the previously deleted paragraph or section.

(5) Presentation in subsequent amendment document. Once a paragraph or section is amended in a first amendment document, the paragraph or section shall not be re-presented in a subsequent amendment document unless it is amended again or a substitute specification is provided.

(c) Claims. Amendments to a claim must be made by rewriting the entire claim with all changes (*e.g.*, additions and deletions) as indicated in this subsection, except when the claim is being canceled. Each amendment document that includes a change to an existing claim, cancellation of an existing claim or addition of a new claim, must include a complete listing of all claims ever presented, including the text of all pending and withdrawn claims, in the application. The claim listing, including the text of the claims, in the amendment document will serve to replace all prior versions of the claims, in the application. In the claim listing, the status of every claim must be indicated after its claim number by using one of the following identifiers in a parenthetical expression: (Original), (Currently amended), (Canceled), (Withdrawn), (Previously presented), (New), and (Not entered).

(1) Claim listing. All of the claims presented in a claim listing shall be presented in ascending numerical order. Consecutive claims having the same status of "canceled" or "not entered" may be aggregated into one statement (*e.g.*, Claims 1-5 (canceled)). The claim listing shall commence on a separate sheet of the amendment document and the sheet(s) that contain the text of any part of the claims shall not contain any other part of the amendment.

(2) When claim text with markings is required. All claims being currently amended in an amendment paper shall be presented in the claim listing, indicate a status of "currently amended," and be submitted with markings to indicate the changes that have been made relative to the immediate prior version of the claims. The text of any added subject matter must be shown by underlining the added text. The text of any deleted matter must be shown by strike-through except that double brackets placed before and after the deleted characters may be used to show deletion of five or fewer consecutive characters. The text of any deleted subject matter must be shown by being placed within double brackets if strike-through cannot be easily perceived. Only claims having the status of "currently amended," or "withdrawn" if also being amended, shall include markings. If a withdrawn claim is currently amended, its status in the claim listing may be identified as "withdrawn—currently amended."

(3) When claim text in clean version is required. The text of all pending claims not being currently amended shall be presented in the claim listing in clean version, *i.e.*, without any markings in the presentation of text. The presentation of a clean version of any claim having the status of "original," "withdrawn" or "previously presented" will constitute an assertion that it has not been changed relative to the immediate prior version, except to omit markings that may have been present in the immediate prior version of the claims of the status of "withdrawn" or "previously presented." Any claim added by amendment must be indicated with the status of "new" and presented in clean version, *i.e.*, without any underlining.

(4) When claim text shall not be presented; canceling a claim.

(i) No claim text shall be presented for any claim in the claim listing with the status of "canceled" or "not entered."

(ii) Cancellation of a claim shall be effected by an instruction to cancel a particular claim number. Identifying the status of a claim in the claim listing as "canceled" will constitute an instruction to cancel the claim.

(5) Reinstatement of previously canceled claim. A claim which was previously canceled may be reinstated only by adding the claim as a "new" claim with a new claim number.

(d) Drawings. One or more application drawings shall be amended in the following manner: Any changes to an application drawing must be in compliance with §1.84 or, for a nonprovisional international design application, in compliance with §§1.84(c) and 1.1026 and must be submitted on a replacement sheet of drawings which shall be an attachment to the amendment document and, in the top margin, labeled "Replacement Sheet." Any replacement sheet of drawings shall include all of the figures appearing on the immediate prior version of the sheet, even if only one figure is amended. Any new sheet of drawings containing an additional figure must be labeled in the top margin as "New Sheet." All changes to the drawings shall be explained, in detail, in either the drawing amendment or remarks section of the amendment paper.

(1) A marked-up copy of any amended drawing figure, including annotations indicating the changes made, may be included. The marked-up copy must be clearly labeled as "Annotated Sheet" and must be presented in the amendment or remarks section that explains the change to the drawings.

(2) A marked-up copy of any amended drawing figure, including annotations indicating the changes made, must be provided when required by the examiner.

(e) Disclosure consistency. The disclosure must be amended, when required by the Office, to correct inaccuracies of description and definition, and to secure substantial correspondence between the claims, the remainder of the specification, and the drawings.

(f) No new matter. No amendment may introduce new matter into the disclosure of an application.

(g) Exception for examiner's amendments. Changes to the specification, including the claims, of an application made by the Office in an examiner's amendment may be made by specific instructions to insert or delete subject matter set forth in the examiner's amendment by identifying the precise point in the specification or the claim(s) where the insertion or deletion is to be made. Compliance with paragraphs (b)(1), (b)(2), or (c) of this section is not required.

(h) Amendment sections. Each section of an amendment document (*e.g.*, amendment to the claims, amendment to the specification, replacement drawings, and remarks) must begin on a separate sheet.

(i) Amendments in reissue applications. Any amendment to the description and claims in reissue applications must be made in accordance with §1.173.

(j) Amendments in reexamination proceedings. Any proposed amendment to the description and claims in patents involved in reexamination proceedings must be made in accordance with §1.530.

(k) Amendments in provisional applications. Amendments in provisional applications are not usually made. If an amendment is made to a provisional application, however, it must comply with the provisions of this section. Any amendments to a provisional application shall be placed in the provisional application file but may not be entered.

History of 37 C.F.R. §1.121: 32 FR 13583, Sept. 28, 1967; 46 FR 29183, May 29, 1981; 49 FR 555, Jan. 4, 1984; 62 FR 53192, Oct. 10, 1997; 62 FR 61235, Nov. 17, 1997; 65 FR 54672, Sept. 8, 2000; 65 FR 76773, Dec. 7, 2000; 68 FR 38628, June 30, 2003; 69 FR 56543, Sept. 21, 2004; 80 FR 17963, May 13, 2015.

§§1.122 TO 1.124. RESERVED

History of 37 C.F.R. §§1.122-1.124: 62 FR 53193, Oct. 10, 1997.

§1.125. SUBSTITUTE SPECIFICATION

(a) If the number or nature of the amendments or the legibility of the application papers renders it difficult to consider the application, or to arrange the papers for printing or copying, the Office may require the entire specification, including the claims, or any part thereof, be rewritten.

(b) Subject to §1.312, a substitute specification, excluding the claims, may be filed at any point up to payment of the issue fee if it is accompanied by a statement that the substitute specification includes no new matter.

(c) A substitute specification submitted under this section must be submitted with markings showing all the changes relative to the immediate prior version of the specification of record. The text of any added subject matter must be shown by underlining the added text. The text of any deleted matter must be shown by strike-through except that double brackets placed before and after the deleted characters may be used to show deletion of five or fewer consecutive characters. The text of any deleted subject matter must be shown by being placed within double brackets if strike-through cannot be easily perceived. An accompanying clean version (without markings) must also be supplied. Numbering the paragraphs of the specification of record is not considered a change that must be shown pursuant to this paragraph.

(d) A substitute specification under this section is not permitted in a reissue application or in a reexamination proceeding.

History of 37 C.F.R. §1.125: 24 FR 10332, Dec. 22, 1959; 48 FR 2712, Jan. 20, 1983; 62 FR 53193, Oct. 10, 1997; 65 FR 54673, Sept. 8, 2000; 68 FR 38630, June 30, 2003.

§1.126. NUMBERING OF CLAIMS

The original numbering of the claims must be preserved throughout the prosecution. When claims are canceled the remaining claims must not be renumbered. When claims are added, they must be numbered by the applicant consecutively beginning with the number next following the highest numbered claim previously presented (whether entered or not). When the application is ready for allowance, the examiner, if necessary, will renumber the claims consecutively in the order in which they appear or in such order as may have been requested by applicant.

History of 37 C.F.R. §1.126: 32 FR 13583, Sept. 28, 1967; 62 FR 53194, Oct. 10, 1997.

§1.127. PETITION FROM REFUSAL TO ADMIT AMENDMENT

From the refusal of the primary examiner to admit an amendment, in whole or in part, a petition will lie to the Director under §1.181.

TRANSITIONAL PROVISIONS

§1.129. TRANSITIONAL PROCEDURES FOR LIMITED EXAMINATION AFTER FINAL REJECTION & RESTRICTION PRACTICE

(a) An applicant in an application, other than for reissue or a design patent, that has been pending for at least two years as of June 8, 1995, taking into account any reference made in such application to any earlier filed application under 35 U.S.C. 120, 121 and 365(c), is entitled to have a first submission entered and considered on the merits after final rejection under the following circumstances: The Office will consider such a submission, if the first submission and the fee set forth in §1.17(r) are filed prior to the filing of an appeal brief and prior to abandonment of the application. The finality of the final rejection is automatically withdrawn upon the timely filing of the submission and payment of the fee set forth in §1.17(r). If a subsequent final rejection is made in the application, applicant is entitled to have a second submission entered and considered on the merits after the subsequent final rejection under the following circumstances: The Office will consider such a submission, if the second submission and a second fee set forth in §1.17(r) are filed prior to the filing of an appeal brief and prior to abandonment of the application. The finality of the subsequent final rejection is automatically withdrawn upon the timely filing of the submission and payment of the second fee set forth in §1.17(r). Any submission filed after a final rejection made in an application subsequent to the fee set forth in §1.17(r) having been twice paid will be treated as set forth in §1.116. A submission as used in this paragraph includes, but is not limited to, an information disclosure statement, an amendment to the written description, claims or drawings and a new substantive argument or new evidence in support of patentability.

(b)(1) In an application, other than for reissue or a design patent, that has been pending for at least three years as of June 8, 1995; taking into account any reference made in the application to any earlier filed application under 35 U.S.C. 120, 121, and 365(c), no requirement for restriction or for the filing of divisional applications shall be made or maintained in the application after June 8, 1995, except where:

(i) The requirement was first made in the application or any earlier filed application under 35 U.S.C. 120, 121 and 365(c) prior to April 8, 1995;

(ii) The examiner has not made a requirement for restriction in the present or parent application prior to April 8, 1995, due to actions by the applicant; or

(iii) The required fee for examination of each additional invention was not paid.

(2) If the application contains more than one independent and distinct invention and a requirement for restriction or for the filing of divisional applications cannot be made or maintained pursuant to this paragraph, applicant will be so notified and given a time period to:

(i) Elect the invention or inventions to be searched and examined, if no election has been made prior to the notice, and pay the fee set forth in §1.17(s) for each independent and distinct invention claimed in the application in excess of one which applicant elects;

(ii) Confirm an election made prior to the notice and pay the fee set forth in §1.17(s) for each independent and distinct invention claimed in the application in addition to the one invention which applicant previously elected; or

(iii) File a petition under this section traversing the requirement. If the required petition is filed in a timely manner, the original time period for electing and paying the fee set forth in §1.17(s) will be deferred and any decision on the petition affirming or modifying the requirement will set a new time period to elect the invention or inventions to be searched and examined and to pay the fee set forth in §1.17(s) for each independent and distinct invention claimed in the application in excess of one which applicant elects.

(3) The additional inventions for which the required fee has not been paid will be withdrawn from consideration under §1.142(b). An applicant who desires examination of an invention so withdrawn from consideration can file a divisional application under 35 U.S.C. 121.

(c) The provisions of this section shall not be applicable to any application filed after June 8, 1995.

History of 37 C.F.R. §1.129: 60 FR 20226, Apr. 25, 1995.

AFFIDAVITS OVERCOMING REJECTIONS

§1.130. AFFIDAVIT OR DECLARATION OF ATTRIBUTION OR PRIOR PUBLIC DISCLOSURE UNDER THE LEAHY-SMITH AMERICA INVENTS ACT

(a) Affidavit or declaration of attribution. When any claim of an application or a patent under reexamination is rejected, the applicant or patent owner may submit an appropriate affidavit or declaration to disqualify a disclosure as prior art by establishing that the disclosure was made by the inventor or a joint inventor, or the subject matter disclosed was obtained directly or indirectly from the inventor or a joint inventor.

(b) Affidavit or declaration of prior public disclosure. When any claim of an application or a patent under reexamination is rejected, the applicant or patent owner may submit an appropriate affidavit or declaration to disqualify a disclosure as prior art by establishing that the subject matter disclosed had, before such disclosure was made or before such subject matter was effectively filed, been publicly disclosed by the inventor or a joint inventor or another who obtained the subject matter disclosed directly or indirectly from the inventor or a joint inventor. An affidavit or declaration under this paragraph must identify the subject matter publicly disclosed and provide the date such subject matter was publicly disclosed by the inventor or a joint inventor or another who obtained the subject matter disclosed directly or indirectly from the inventor or a joint inventor.

(1) If the subject matter publicly disclosed on that date was in a printed publication, the affidavit or declaration must be accompanied by a copy of the printed publication.

(2) If the subject matter publicly disclosed on that date was not in a printed publication, the affidavit or declaration must describe the subject matter with sufficient detail and particularity to determine what subject matter had been publicly disclosed on that date by the inventor or a joint inventor or another who obtained the subject matter disclosed directly or indirectly from the inventor or a joint inventor.

(c) When this section is not available. The provisions of this section are not available if the rejection is based upon a disclosure made more than one year before the effective filing date of the claimed invention. The provisions of this section may not be available if the rejection is based upon a U.S. patent or U.S. patent application publication of a patented or pending application naming another inventor, the patent or pending application claims an invention that is the same or substantially the same as the applicant's or patent owner's claimed invention, and the affidavit or declaration contends that an inventor named in the U.S. patent or U.S. patent application publication derived the claimed invention from the inventor or a joint inventor named in the application or patent, in which case an applicant or a patent owner may file a petition for a derivation proceeding pursuant to §42.401 et seq. of this title.

(d) Applications and patents to which this section is applicable. The provisions of this section apply to any application for patent, and to any patent issuing thereon, that contains, or contained at any time:

(1) A claim to a claimed invention that has an effective filing date as defined in §1.109 that is on or after March 16, 2013; or

(2) A specific reference under 35 U.S.C. 120, 121, 365(c), or 386(c) to any patent or application that contains, or contained at any time, a claim to a claimed invention that has an effective filing date as defined in §1.109 that is on or after March 16, 2013.

History of 37 C.F.R. §1.130: 61 FR 42805, Aug. 19, 1996; 65 FR 57056, Sept. 20, 2000; 70 FR 1824, Jan. 11, 2005; 78 FR 11058, Mar. 16, 2013; 80 FR 17963, May 13, 2015.

§1.131. AFFIDAVIT OR DECLARATION OF PRIOR INVENTION OR TO DISQUALIFY COMMONLY OWNED PATENT OR PUBLISHED APPLICATION AS PRIOR ART

(a) When any claim of an application or a patent under reexamination is rejected, the applicant or patent owner may submit an appropriate oath or declaration to establish invention of the subject matter of the rejected claim prior to the effective date of the reference or activity on which the rejection is based. The effective date of a U.S. patent, U.S. patent application publication, or international application publication under PCT Article 21(2) is the earlier of its publication date or the date that it is effective as a reference under 35 U.S.C. 102(e) as in effect on March 15, 2013. Prior invention may not be established under this section in any country other than the United States, a NAFTA country, or a WTO member country. Prior invention may not be established under this section before December 8, 1993, in a NAFTA country other than the United States, or before January 1, 1996, in a WTO member country other than a NAFTA country. Prior invention may not be established under this section if either:

(1) The rejection is based upon a U.S. patent or U.S. patent application publication of a pending or patented application naming another inventor which claims interfering subject matter as defined in §41.203(a) of this chapter, in which case an applicant may suggest an interference pursuant to §41.202(a) of this chapter; or

(2) The rejection is based upon a statutory bar.

(b) The showing of facts for an oath or declaration under paragraph (a) of this section shall be such, in character and weight, as to establish reduction to practice prior to the effective date of the reference, or conception of the invention prior to the effective date of the reference coupled with due diligence from prior to said date to a subsequent reduction to practice or to the filing of the application. Original exhibits of drawings or records, or photocopies thereof, must accompany and form part of the affidavit or declaration or their absence must be satisfactorily explained.

(c) When any claim of an application or a patent under reexamination is rejected under 35 U.S.C. 103 as in effect on March 15, 2013, on a U.S. patent or U.S. patent application publication which is not prior art under 35 U.S.C. 102(b) as in effect on March 15, 2013, and the inventions defined by the claims in the application or patent under reexamination and by the claims in the patent or published application are not identical but are not patentably distinct, and the inventions are owned by the same party, the applicant or owner of the patent under reexamination may disqualify the patent or patent application publication as prior art. The patent or patent application publication can be disqualified as prior art by submission of:

(1) A terminal disclaimer in accordance with §1.321(c); and

(2) An oath or declaration stating that the application or patent under reexamination and patent or published application are currently owned by the same party, and that the inventor named in the application or patent under reexamination is the prior inventor under 35 U.S.C. 104 as in effect on March 15, 2013.

(d) The provisions of this section apply to any application for patent and to any patent issuing thereon, that contains, or contained at any time:

(1) A claim to an invention that has an effective filing date as defined in §1.109 that is before March 16, 2013; or

(2) A specific reference under 35 U.S.C. 120, 121, 365(c), or 386(c) to any patent or application that contains, or contained at any time, a claim to an invention that has an effective filing date as defined in §1.109 that is before March 16, 2013.

(e) In an application for patent to which the provisions of §1.130 apply, and to any patent issuing thereon, the provisions of this section are applicable only with respect to a rejection under 35 U.S.C. 102(g) as in effect on March 15, 2013.

History of 37 C.F.R. §1.131: 24 FR 10332, Dec. 22, 1959; 34 FR 18857, Nov. 26, 1969; 48 FR 2713, Jan. 20, 1983; 50 FR 9381, Mar. 7, 1985; 50 FR 11366, Mar. 21, 1985; 53 FR 23734, June 23, 1988; 60 FR 21044, May 1, 1995; 61 FR 42806, Aug. 19, 1996; 65 FR 54673, Sept. 8, 2000; 65 FR 57057, Sept. 20, 2000; 69 FR 49999, Aug. 12, 2004; 69 FR 56543, Sept. 21, 2004; 77 FR 48821, Sept. 16, 2012; 78 FR 11058, Mar. 16, 2013; 78 FR 62405, Dec. 18, 2013; 80 FR 17963, May 13, 2015.

§1.132. AFFIDAVITS OR DECLARATIONS TRAVERSING REJECTIONS OR OBJECTIONS

When any claim of an application or a patent under reexamination is rejected or objected to, any evidence submitted to traverse the rejection or objection on a basis not otherwise provided for must be by way of an oath or declaration under this section.

History of 37 C.F.R. §1.132: 24 FR 10332, Dec. 22, 1959; 34 FR 18857, Nov. 26, 1969; 48 FR 2713, Jan. 20, 1983; 61 FR 42806, Aug. 19, 1996; 65 FR 54673, Sept. 8, 2000; 65 FR 57057, Sept. 20, 2000.

INTERVIEWS

§1.133. INTERVIEWS

(a)(1) Interviews with examiners concerning applications and other matters pending before the Office must be conducted on Office premises and within Office hours, as the respective examiners may designate. Interviews will not be permitted at any other time or place without the authority of the Director.

(2) An interview for the discussion of the patentability of a pending application will not occur before the first Office action, unless the application is a continuing or substitute application or the examiner determines that such an interview would advance prosecution of the application.

(3) The examiner may require that an interview be scheduled in advance.

(b) In every instance where reconsideration is requested in view of an interview with an examiner, a complete written statement of the reasons presented at the interview as warranting favorable action must be filed by the applicant. An interview does not remove the necessity for reply to Office actions as specified in §§1.111 and 1.135.

History of 37 C.F.R. §1.133: 62 FR 53194, Oct. 10, 1997; 65 FR 54674, Sept. 8, 2000; 70 FR 56128, Sept. 26, 2005.

TIME FOR REPLY BY APPLICANT; ABANDONMENT OF APPLICATION

§1.134. TIME PERIOD FOR REPLY TO AN OFFICE ACTION

An Office action will notify the applicant of any non-statutory or shortened statutory time period set for reply to an Office action. Unless the applicant is notified in writing that a reply is required in less than six months, a maximum period of six months is allowed.

History of 37 C.F.R. §1.134: 62 FR 53194, Oct. 10, 1997.

§1.135. ABANDONMENT FOR FAILURE TO REPLY WITHIN TIME PERIOD

(a) If an applicant of a patent application fails to reply within the time period provided under §1.134 and §1.136, the application will become abandoned unless an Office action indicates otherwise.

(b) Prosecution of an application to save it from abandonment pursuant to paragraph (a) of this section must include such complete and proper reply as the condition of the application may require. The admission of, or refusal to admit, any amendment after final rejection or any amendment not responsive to the last action, or any related proceedings, will not operate to save the application from abandonment.

(c) When reply by the applicant is a bona fide attempt to advance the application to final action, and is substantially a complete reply to the non-final Office action, but consideration of some matter or compliance with some requirement has been inadvertently omitted, applicant may be given a new time period for reply under §1.134 to supply the omission.

History of 37 C.F.R. §1.135: 62 FR 53194, Oct. 10, 1997.

§1.136. EXTENSIONS OF TIME

(a)(1) If an applicant is required to reply within a nonstatutory or shortened statutory time period, applicant may extend the time period for reply up to the earlier of the expiration of any maximum period set by statute or five months after the time period set for reply, if a petition for an extension of time and the fee set in §1.17(a) are filed, unless:

(i) Applicant is notified otherwise in an Office action;

(ii) The reply is a reply brief submitted pursuant to §41.41 of this title;

(iii) The reply is a request for an oral hearing submitted pursuant to §41.47(a) of this title;

(iv) The reply is to a decision by the Patent Trial and Appeal Board pursuant to §41.50 or §41.52 of this chapter or to §90.3 of this chapter; or

(v) The application is involved in a contested case (§41.101(a) of this title) or a derivation proceeding (§42.4(b) of this title).

(2) The date on which the petition and the fee have been filed is the date for purposes of determining the period of extension and the corresponding amount of the fee. The expiration of the time period is determined by the amount of the fee paid. A reply must be filed prior to the expiration of the period of extension to avoid abandonment of the application (§1.135), but in no situation may an applicant reply later than the maximum time period set by statute, or be granted an extension of time under paragraph (b) of this section when the provisions of paragraph (a) of this section are available.

(3) A written request may be submitted in an application that is an authorization to treat any concurrent or future reply, requiring a petition for an extension of time under this paragraph for its timely submission, as incorporating a petition for extension of time for the appropriate length of time. An authorization to charge all required fees, fees under §1.17, or all required extension of time fees will be treated as a constructive petition for an extension of time in any concurrent or future reply requiring a petition for an extension of time under this paragraph for its timely submission. Submission of the fee set forth in §1.17(a) will also be treated as a constructive petition for an extension of time in any concurrent reply requiring a petition for an extension of time under this paragraph for its timely submission.

(b) When a reply cannot be filed within the time period set for such reply and the provisions of paragraph (a) of this section are not available, the period for reply will be extended only for sufficient cause and for a reasonable time specified. Any request for an extension of time under this paragraph must be filed on or before the day on which such reply is due, but the mere filing of such a request will not effect any extension under this paragraph. In no situation can any extension carry the date on which reply is due beyond the maximum time period set by statute. Any request under this paragraph must be accompanied by the petition fee set forth in §1.17(g).

(c) If an applicant is notified in a "Notice of Allowability" that an application is otherwise in condition for allowance, the following time periods are not extendable if set in the "Notice of Allowability" or in an Office action having a mail date on or after the mail date of the "Notice of Allowability":

(1) The period for submitting the inventor's oath or declaration;

(2) The period for submitting formal drawings set under §1.85(c); and

(3) The period for making a deposit set under §1.809(c).

(d) See §1.550(c) for extensions of time in ex parte reexamination proceedings, §1.956 for extensions of time in inter partes reexamination proceedings; §§41.4(a) and 41.121(a)(3) of this chapter for extensions of time in contested cases before the Patent Trial and Appeal Board; §42.5(c) of this chapter for extensions of time in trials before the Patent Trial and Appeal Board; and §90.3 of this chapter for extensions of time to appeal to the U.S. Court of Appeals for the Federal Circuit or to commence a civil action.

History of 37 C.F.R. §1.136: 62 FR 53194, Oct. 10, 1997; 65 FR 54674, Sept. 8, 2000; 65 FR 76773, Dec. 7, 2000; 66 FR 21092, Apr. 27, 2001; 69 FR 50000, Aug. 12, 2004; 69 FR 56543, Sept. 21, 2004; 70 FR 3891, Jan. 27, 2005; 74 FR 52691, Oct. 14, 2009; 77 FR 46625, Sept. 16, 2012; 77 FR 48821, Sept. 16, 2012; 78 FR 62405, Dec. 18, 2013.

§1.137. REVIVAL OF ABANDONED APPLICATION, OR TERMINATED OR LIMITED REEXAMINATION PROSECUTION

(a) Revival on the basis of unintentional delay. If the delay in reply by applicant or patent owner was unintentional, a petition may be filed pursuant to this section to revive an abandoned application or a reexamination prosecution terminated under §1.550(d) or §1.957(b) or limited under §1.957(c).

(b) Petition requirements. A grantable petition pursuant to this section must be accompanied by:

(1) The reply required to the outstanding Office action or notice, unless previously filed;

(2) The petition fee as set forth in §1.17(m);

(3) Any terminal disclaimer (and fee as set forth in §1.20(d)) required pursuant to paragraph (d) of this section; and

(4) A statement that the entire delay in filing the required reply from the due date for the reply until the filing of a grantable petition pursuant to this section was unintentional. The Director may require additional information where there is a question whether the delay was unintentional.

(c) Reply. In an application abandoned under §1.57(a), the reply must include a copy of the specification and any drawings of the previously filed application. In an application or patent abandoned for failure to pay the issue fee or any portion thereof, the required reply must include payment of the issue fee or any outstanding balance. In an application abandoned for failure to pay the publication fee, the required reply must include payment of the publication fee. In a nonprovisional application abandoned for failure to prosecute, the required reply may be met by the filing of a continuing application. In a nonprovisional utility or plant application filed on or after June 8, 1995, abandoned after the close of prosecution as defined in §1.114(b), the required reply may also be met by the filing of a request for continued examination in compliance with §1.114.

(d) Terminal disclaimer.

(1) Any petition to revive pursuant to this section in a design application must be accompanied by a terminal disclaimer and fee as set forth in §1.321 dedicating to the public a terminal part of the term of any patent granted thereon equivalent to the period of abandonment of the application. Any petition to revive pursuant to this section in either a utility or plant application filed before June 8, 1995, must be accompanied by a terminal disclaimer and fee as set forth in §1.321 dedicating to the public a terminal part of the term of any patent granted thereon equivalent to the lesser of:

(i) The period of abandonment of the application; or

(ii) The period extending beyond twenty years from the date on which the application for the patent was filed in the United States or, if the application contains a specific reference to an earlier filed application(s) under 35 U.S.C. 120, 121, 365(c), or 386(c) from the date on which the earliest such application was filed.

(2) Any terminal disclaimer pursuant to paragraph (d)(1) of this section must also apply to any patent granted on a continuing utility or plant application filed before June 8, 1995, or a continuing design application, that contains a specific reference under 35 U.S.C. 120, 121, 365(c), or 386(c) to the application for which revival is sought.

(3) The provisions of paragraph (d)(1) of this section do not apply to applications for which revival is sought solely for purposes of copendency with a utility or plant application filed on or after June 8, 1995, to reissue applications, or to reexamination proceedings.

(e) Request for reconsideration. Any request for reconsideration or review of a decision refusing to revive an abandoned application, or a terminated or limited reexamination prosecution, upon petition filed pursuant to this section, to be considered timely, must be filed within two months of the decision refusing to revive or within such time as set in the decision. Unless a decision indicates otherwise, this time period may be extended under:

(1) The provisions of §1.136 for an abandoned application;

(2) The provisions of §1.550(c) for a terminated ex parte reexamination prosecution, where the ex parte reexamination was filed under §1.510; or

(3) The provisions of §1.956 for a terminated inter partes reexamination prosecution or an inter partes reexamination limited as to further prosecution, where the inter partes reexamination was filed under §1.913.

(f) Abandonment for failure to notify the Office of a foreign filing. A nonprovisional application abandoned pursuant to 35 U.S.C. 122(b)(2)(B)(iii) for failure to timely notify the Office of the filing of an application in a foreign country or under a multinational treaty that requires publication of applications eighteen months after filing, may be revived pursuant to this section. The reply requirement of paragraph (c) of this section is met by the notification of such filing in a foreign country or under a multinational treaty, but the filing of a petition under this section will not operate to stay any period for reply that may be running against the application.

(g) Provisional applications. A provisional application, abandoned for failure to timely respond to an Office requirement, may be revived pursuant to this section. Subject to the provisions of 35 U.S.C. 119(e)(3) and §1.7(b), a provisional application will not be regarded as pending after twelve months from its filing date under any circumstances.

History of 37 C.F.R. §1.137: 62 FR 53194, Oct. 10, 1997; 65 FR 54674, Sept. 8, 2000; 65 FR 57057, Sept. 20, 2000; 69 FR 56543, Sept. 21, 2004; 72 FR 18904, May 16, 2007; 78 FR 62405, Dec. 18, 2013; 80 FR 17963, May 13, 2015.

§1.138. EXPRESS ABANDONMENT

(a) An application may be expressly abandoned by filing a written declaration of abandonment identifying the application in the United States Patent and Trademark Office. Express abandonment of the application may not be recognized by the Office before the date of issue or publication unless it is actually received by appropriate officials in time to act.

(b) A written declaration of abandonment must be signed by a party authorized under §1.33(b)(1) or (b)(3) to sign a paper in the application, except as otherwise provided in this paragraph. A registered attorney or agent, not of record, who acts in a representative capacity under the provisions of §1.34 when filing a continuing application, may expressly abandon the prior application as of the filing date granted to the continuing application.

(c) An applicant seeking to abandon an application to avoid publication of the application (see §1.211(a)(1)) must submit a declaration of express abandonment by way of a petition under this paragraph including the fee set forth in §1.17(h) in sufficient time to permit the appropriate officials to recognize the abandonment and remove the application from the publication process. Applicants should expect that the petition will not be granted and the application will be published in regular course unless such declaration of express abandonment and petition are received by the appropriate officials more than four weeks prior to the projected date of publication.

(d) An applicant seeking to abandon an application filed under 35 U.S.C. 111(a) and §1.53(b) on or after December 8, 2004, to obtain a refund of the search fee and excess claims fee paid in the application, must submit a declaration of express abandonment by way of a petition under this paragraph before an examination has been made of the application. The date indicated on any certificate of mailing or transmission under §1.8 will not be taken into account in determining whether a petition under §1.138(d) was filed before an examination has been made of the application. If a request for refund of the search fee and excess claims fee paid in the application is not filed with the declaration of express abandonment under this paragraph or within two months from the date on which the declaration of express abandonment under this paragraph was filed, the Office may retain the entire search fee and excess claims fee paid in the application. This two-month period is not extendable. If a petition and declaration of express abandonment under this paragraph are not filed before an examination has been made of the application, the Office will not refund any part of the search fee and excess claims fee paid in the application except as provided in §1.26.

History of 37 C.F.R. §1.138: 34 FR 18857, Nov. 26, 1969; 47 FR 47244, Oct. 25, 1982; 49 FR 48452, Dec. 12, 1984; 65 FR 54674, Sept. 8, 2000; 65 FR 57058, Sept. 20, 2000; 71 FR 12284, Mar. 10, 2006; 78 FR 62406, Dec. 18, 2013.

§1.139. RESERVED

History of 37 C.F.R. §1.139: 62 FR 53194, Oct. 10, 1997.

JOINDER OF INVENTIONS IN ONE APPLICATION; RESTRICTION

§1.141. DIFFERENT INVENTIONS IN ONE NATIONAL APPLICATION

(a) Two or more independent and distinct inventions may not be claimed in one national application, except that more than one species of an invention, not to exceed a reasonable number, may be specifically claimed in different claims in one national application, provided the application also includes an allowable claim generic to all the claimed species and all the claims to species in excess of one are written in dependent form (§1.75) or otherwise include all the limitations of the generic claim.

(b) Where claims to all three categories, product, process of making, and process of use, are included in a national application, a three way requirement for restriction can only be made where the process of making is distinct from the product. If the process of making and the product are not distinct, the process of using may be joined with the claims directed to the product and the process of making the product even though a showing of distinctness between the product and process of using the product can be made.

History of 37 C.F.R. §1.141: 43 FR 20465, May 11, 1978; 52 FR 20046, May 28, 1987.

§1.142. REQUIREMENT FOR RESTRICTION

(a) If two or more independent and distinct inventions are claimed in a single application, the examiner in an Office action will require the applicant in the reply to that action to elect an invention to which the claims will be restricted, this official action being called a requirement for restriction (also known as a requirement for division). Such requirement will normally be made before any action on the merits; however, it may be made at any time before final action.

(b) Claims to the invention or inventions not elected, if not canceled, are nevertheless withdrawn from further consideration by the examiner by the election, subject however to reinstatement in the event the requirement for restriction is withdrawn or overruled.

History of 37 C.F.R. §1.142: 62 FR 53195, Oct. 10, 1997; 74 FR 52691, Oct. 14, 2009.

§1.143. RECONSIDERATION OF REQUIREMENT

If the applicant disagrees with the requirement for restriction, he may request reconsideration and withdrawal or modification of the requirement, giving the reasons therefor. (See §1.111.) In requesting reconsideration the applicant must indicate a provisional election of one invention for prosecution, which invention shall be the one elected in the event the requirement becomes final The requirement for restriction will be reconsidered on such a request. If the requirement is repeated and made final the examiner will at the same time act on the claims to the invention elected.

§1.144. PETITION FROM REQUIREMENT FOR RESTRICTION

After a final requirement for restriction, the applicant, in addition to making any reply due on the remainder of the action, may petition the Director to review the requirement. Petition may be deferred until after final action on or allowance of claims to the invention elected, but must be filed not later than appeal. A petition will not be considered if reconsideration of the requirement was not requested (see §1.181).

History of 37 C.F.R. §1.144: 62 FR 53195, Oct. 10, 1997.

§1.145. SUBSEQUENT PRESENTATION OF CLAIMS FOR DIFFERENT INVENTION

If, after an Office action on an application, the applicant presents claims directed to an invention distinct from and independent of the invention previously claimed, the applicant will be required to restrict the claims to the invention previously claimed if the amendment is entered, subject to reconsideration and review as provided in §§1.143 and 1.144.

History of 37 C.F.R. §1.145: 74 FR 52691, Oct. 14, 2009.

§1.146. ELECTION OF SPECIES

In the first action on an application containing a generic claim to a generic invention (genus) and claims to more than one patentably distinct species embraced thereby, the examiner may require the applicant in the reply to that action to elect a species of his or her invention to which his or her claim will be restricted if no claim to the genus is found to be allowable. However, if such application contains claims directed to more than a reasonable number of species, the examiner may require restriction of the claims to not more than a reasonable number of species before taking further action in the application.

History of 37 C.F.R. §1.146: 43 FR 20465, May 11, 1978; 62 FR 53195, Oct. 10, 1997.

DESIGN PATENTS

§1.151. RULES APPLICABLE

The rules relating to applications for patents for other inventions or discoveries are also applicable to applications for patents for designs except as otherwise provided.

§1.152. DESIGN DRAWINGS

The design must be represented by a drawing that complies with the requirements of §1.84 and must contain a sufficient number of views to constitute a complete disclosure of the appearance of the design. Appropriate and adequate surface shading should be used to show the character or contour of the surfaces represented. Solid black surface shading is not permitted except when used to represent the color black as well as color contrast. Broken lines may be used to show visible environmental structure, but may not be used to show hidden planes and surfaces that cannot be seen through opaque materials. Alternate positions of a design component, illustrated by full and broken lines in the same view are not permitted in a design drawing. Photographs and ink drawings are not permitted to be combined as formal drawings in one application. Photographs submitted in lieu of ink drawings in design patent applications must not disclose environmental structure but must be limited to the design claimed for the article.

History of 37 C.F.R. §1.152: 53 FR 47810, Nov. 28, 1988; 58 FR 38726, July 20, 1993; 62 FR 53195, Oct. 10, 1997; 65 FR 54674, Sept. 8, 2000.

§1.153. TITLE, DESCRIPTION & CLAIM, OATH OR DECLARATION

(a) The title of the design must designate the particular article. No description, other than a reference to the drawing, is ordinarily required. The claim shall be in formal terms to the ornamental design for the article (specifying name) as shown, or as shown and described. More than one claim is neither required nor permitted.

(b) The inventor's oath or declaration must comply with the requirements of §1.63, or comply with the requirements of §1.64 for a substitute statement.

History of 37 C.F.R. §1.153: 24 FR 10332, Dec. 22, 1959; 29 FR 18503, Dec. 29, 1964; 48 FR 2712, Jan. 20, 1983; 77 FR 48821, Sept. 16, 2012.

§1.154. ARRANGEMENT OF APPLICATION ELEMENTS IN A DESIGN APPLICATION

(a) The elements of the design application, if applicable, should appear in the following order:

(1) Design application transmittal form.

(2) Fee transmittal form.

(3) Application data sheet (see §1.76).

(4) Specification.

(5) Drawings or photographs.

(6) The inventor's oath or declaration (see §1.153(b)).

(b) The specification should include the following sections in order:

(1) Preamble, stating the name of the applicant, title of the design, and a brief description of the nature and intended use of the article in which the design is embodied.

(2) Cross-reference to related applications (unless included in the application data sheet).

(3) Statement regarding federally sponsored research or development.

(4) Description of the figure or figures of the drawing.

(5) Feature description.

(6) A single claim.

(c) The text of the specification sections defined in paragraph (b) of this section, if applicable, should be preceded by a section heading in uppercase letters without underlining or bold type.

History of 37 C.F.R. §1.154: 24 FR 10332, Dec. 22, 1959; 48 FR 2713, Jan. 20, 1983; 61 FR 42806, Aug. 19, 1996; 62 FR 53196, Oct. 10, 1997; 65 FR 54674, Sept. 8, 2000; 77 FR 48821, Sept. 16, 2012.

§1.155. EXPEDITED EXAMINATION OF DESIGN APPLICATIONS

(a) The applicant may request that the Office expedite the examination of a design application. To qualify for expedited examination:

(1) The application must include drawings in compliance with §1.84, or for an international design application that designates the United States, must have been published pursuant to Hague Agreement Article 10(3);

(2) The applicant must have conducted a preexamination search; and

(3) The applicant must file a request for expedited examination including:

(i) The fee set forth in §1.17(k); and

(ii) A statement that a preexamination search was conducted. The statement must also indicate the field of search and include an information disclosure statement in compliance with §1.98.

(b) The Office will not examine an application that is not in condition for examination (*e.g.*, missing basic filing fee) even if the applicant files a request for expedited examination under this section.

History of 37 C.F.R. §1.155: 40 FR 44813, Sept. 30, 1975; 47 FR 41277, Sept. 17, 1982; 58 FR 44280, Aug. 20, 1993; 62 FR 53196, Oct. 10, 1997; 65 FR 54674, Sept. 8, 2000; 80 FR 17963, May 13, 2015.

PLANT PATENTS

§1.161. RULES APPLICABLE

The rules relating to applications for patent for other inventions or discoveries are also applicable to applications for patents for plants except as otherwise provided.

§1.162. APPLICANT, OATH OR DECLARATION

The inventor named for a plant patent application must be the person who has invented or discovered and asexually reproduced the new and distinct variety of plant for which a patent is sought. The inventor's oath or declaration, in addition to the averments required by §1.63 or §1.64, must state that the inventor has asexually reproduced the plant. Where the plant is a newly found plant, the inventor's oath or declaration must also state that it was found in a cultivated area.

History of 37 C.F.R. §1.162: 24 FR 10332, Dec. 22, 1959; 29 FR 18503, Dec. 29, 1964; 48 FR 2713, Jan. 20, 1983; 77 FR 48821, Sept. 16, 2012.

§1.163. SPECIFICATION & ARRANGEMENT OF APPLICATION ELEMENTS IN A PLANT APPLICATION

(a) The specification must contain as full and complete a disclosure as possible of the plant and the characteristics thereof that distinguish the same over related known varieties, and its antecedents, and must particularly point out where and in what manner the variety of plant has been asexually reproduced. For a newly found plant, the specification must particularly point out the location and character of the area where the plant was discovered.

(b) The elements of the plant application, if applicable, should appear in the following order:

(1) Plant application transmittal form.

(2) Fee transmittal form.

(3) Application data sheet (see §1.76).

(4) Specification.

(5) Drawings (in duplicate).

(6) The inventor's oath or declaration (§1.162).

(c) The specification should include the following sections in order:

(1) Title of the invention, which may include an introductory portion stating the name, citizenship, and residence of the applicant.

(2) Cross-reference to related applications (unless included in the application data sheet).

(3) Statement regarding federally sponsored research or development.

(4) Latin name of the genus and species of the plant claimed.

(5) Variety denomination.

(6) Background of the invention.

(7) Brief summary of the invention.

(8) Brief description of the drawing.

(9) Detailed botanical description.

(10) A single claim.

(11) Abstract of the disclosure.

(d) The text of the specification or sections defined in paragraph (c) of this section, if applicable, should be preceded by a section heading in upper case, without underlining or bold type.

History of 37 C.F.R. §1.163: 24 FR 10332, Dec. 22, 1959; 48 FR 2713, Jan. 20, 1983; 61 FR 42806, Aug. 19, 1996; 62 FR 53196, Oct. 10, 1997; 65 FR 54675, Sept. 8, 2000; 77 FR 48821, Sept. 16, 2012.

§1.164. CLAIM

The claim shall be in formal terms to the new and distinct variety of the specified plant as described and illustrated, and may also recite the principal distinguishing characteristics. More than one claim is not permitted.

§1.165. PLANT DRAWINGS

(a) Plant patent drawings should be artistically and competently executed and must comply with the requirements of §1.84. View numbers and reference characters need not be employed unless required by the examiner. The drawing must disclose all the distinctive characteristics of the plant capable of visual representation.

(b) The drawings may be in color. The drawing must be in color if color is a distinguishing characteristic of the new variety. Two copies of color drawings or photographs must be submitted.

History of 37 C.F.R. §1.165: 24 FR 10332, Dec. 22, 1959; 40 FR 57359, Dec. 9, 1975; 47 FR 41277, Sept. 17, 1982; 58 FR 38726, July 20, 1993; 65 FR 57058, Sept. 20, 2000; 69 FR 56543, Sept. 21, 2004.

§1.166. SPECIMENS

The applicant may be required to furnish specimens of the plant, or its flower or fruit, in a quantity and at a time in its stage of growth as may be designated, for study and inspection. Such specimens, properly packed, must be forwarded in conformity with instructions furnished to the applicant. When it is not possible to forward such specimens, plants must be made available for official inspection where grown.

§1.167. EXAMINATION

Applications may be submitted by the Patent and Trademark Office to the Department of Agriculture for study and report.

History of 37 C.F.R. §1.167: 24 FR 10332, Dec. 22, 1959; 34 FR 18857, Nov. 26, 1969; 62 FR 53196, Oct. 10, 1997.

REISSUES

§1.171. APPLICATION FOR REISSUE

An application for reissue must contain the same parts required for an application for an original patent, complying with all the rules relating thereto except as otherwise provided, and in addition, must comply with the requirements of the rules relating to reissue applications.

History of 37 C.F.R. §1.171: 24 FR 10332, Dec. 22, 1959; 47 FR 41278, Sept. 17, 1982; 54 FR 6903, Feb. 15, 1989; 54 FR 9432, Mar. 7, 1989; 56 FR 65153, Dec. 13, 1991; 62 FR 53196, Oct. 10, 1997.

§1.172. REISSUE APPLICANT

(a) The reissue applicant is the original patentee, or the current patent owner if there has been an assignment. A reissue application must be accompanied by the written consent of all assignees, if any, currently owning an undivided interest in the patent. All assignees consenting to the reissue must establish their ownership in the patent by filing in the reissue application a submission in accordance with the provisions of §3.73(c) of this chapter.

(b) A reissue will be granted to the original patentee, his legal representatives or assigns as the interest may appear.

History of 37 C.F.R. §1.172: 24 FR 10332, Dec. 22, 1959; 29 FR 10853, Dec. 29, 1964; 48 FR 2713, Jan. 20, 1983; 62 FR 53196, Oct. 10, 1997; 77 FR 48821, Sept. 16, 2012.

§1.173. REISSUE SPECIFICATION, DRAWINGS, & AMENDMENTS

(a) Contents of a reissue application. An application for reissue must contain the entire specification, including the claims, and the drawings of the patent. No new matter shall be introduced into the application. No reissue patent shall be granted enlarging the scope of the claims of the original patent unless applied for within two years from the grant of the original patent, pursuant to 35 U.S.C. 251.

(1) Specification, including claims. The entire specification, including the claims, of the patent for which reissue is requested must be furnished in the form of a copy of the printed patent, in double column format, each page on only one side of a single sheet of paper. If an amendment of the reissue application is to be included, it must be made pursuant to paragraph (b) of this section. The formal requirements for papers making up the reissue application other than those set forth in this section are set out in §1.52. Additionally, a copy of any disclaimer (§1.321), certificate of correction (§§1.322 through 1.324), or reexamination certificate (§1.570) issued in the patent must be included. (See also §1.178.)

(2) Drawings. Applicant must submit a clean copy of each drawing sheet of the printed patent at the time the reissue application is filed. If such copy complies with §1.84, no further drawings will be required. Where a drawing of the reissue application is to include any changes relative to the patent being reissued, the changes to the drawing must be made in accordance with paragraph (b)(3) of this section. The Office will not transfer the drawings from the patent file to the reissue application.

(b) Making amendments in a reissue application. An amendment in a reissue application is made either by physically incorporating the changes into the specification when the application is filed, or by a separate amendment paper. If amendment is made by incorporation, markings pursuant to paragraph (d) of this section must be used. If amendment is made by an amendment paper, the paper must direct that specified changes be made, as follows:

(1) Specification other than the claims. Changes to the specification, other than to the claims, must be made by submission of the entire text of an added or rewritten paragraph, including markings pursuant to paragraph (d) of this section, except that an entire paragraph may be deleted by a statement deleting the paragraph without presentation of the text of the paragraph. The precise point in the specification must be identified where any added or rewritten paragraph is located. This paragraph applies whether the amendment is submitted on paper or compact disc (see §§1.52(e)(1) and 1.821(c), but not for discs submitted under §1.821(e)).

(2) Claims. An amendment paper must include the entire text of each claim being changed by such amendment paper and of each claim being added by such amendment paper. For any claim changed by the amendment paper, a parenthetical expression "amended," "twice amended," etc., should follow the claim number. Each changed patent claim and each added claim must include markings pursuant to paragraph (d) of this section, except that a patent claim or added claim should be canceled by a statement canceling the claim without presentation of the text of the claim.

(3) Drawings. One or more patent drawings shall be amended in the following manner: Any changes to a patent drawing must be submitted as a replacement sheet of drawings which shall be an attachment to the amendment document. Any replacement sheet of drawings must be in compliance with §1.84 and shall include all of the figures appearing on the original version of the sheet, even if only one figure is amended. Amended figures must be identified as "Amended," and any added figure must be identified as "New." In the event that a figure is canceled, the figure must be surrounded by brackets and identified as "Canceled." All changes to the drawing(s) shall be explained, in detail, beginning on a separate sheet accompanying the papers including the amendment to the drawings.

(i) A marked-up copy of any amended drawing figure, including annotations indicating the changes made, may be included. The marked-up copy must be clearly labeled as "Annotated Marked-up Drawings" and must be presented in the amendment or remarks section that explains the change to the drawings.

(ii) A marked-up copy of any amended drawing figure, including annotations indicating the changes made, must be provided when required by the examiner.

(c) Status of claims and support for claim changes. Whenever there is an amendment to the claims pursuant to paragraph (b) of this section, there must also be supplied, on pages separate from the pages containing the changes, the status (*i.e.*, pending or canceled), as of the date of the amendment, of all patent claims and of all added claims, and an explanation of the support in the disclosure of the patent for the changes made to the claims.

(d) Changes shown by markings. Any changes relative to the patent being reissued which are made to the specification, including the claims, upon filing, or by an amendment paper in the reissue application, must include the following markings:

(1) The matter to be omitted by reissue must be enclosed in brackets; and

(2) The matter to be added by reissue must be underlined, except for amendments submitted on compact discs (§§1.96 and 1.821(c)). Matter added by reissue on compact discs must be preceded with "<U>" and end with "</U>" to properly identify the material being added.

(e) Numbering of patent claims preserved. Patent claims may not be renumbered. The numbering of any claim added in the reissue application must follow the number of the highest numbered patent claim.

(f) Amendment of disclosure may be required. The disclosure must be amended, when required by the Office, to correct inaccuracies of description and definition, and to secure substantial correspondence between the claims, the remainder of the specification, and the drawings.

(g) Amendments made relative to the patent. All amendments must be made relative to the patent specification, including the claims, and drawings, which are in effect as of the date of filing of the reissue application.

History of 37 C.F.R. §1.173: 65 FR 54675, Sept. 8, 2000; 68 FR 38630, June 30, 2003; 69 FR 56543, Sept. 21, 2004.

§1.174. RESERVED

History of 37 C.F.R. §1.174: 65 FR 54676, Sept. 8, 2000.

§1.175. INVENTOR'S OATH OR DECLARATION FOR A REISSUE APPLICATION

(a) The inventor's oath or declaration for a reissue application, in addition to complying with the requirements of §1.63, §1.64, or §1.67, must also specifically identify at least one error pursuant to 35 U.S.C. 251 being relied upon as the basis for reissue and state that the applicant believes the original patent to be wholly or partly inoperative or invalid by reason of a defective specification or drawing, or by reason of the patentee claiming more or less than the patentee had the right to claim in the patent.

(b) If the reissue application seeks to enlarge the scope of the claims of the patent (a basis for the reissue is the patentee claiming less than the patentee had the right to claim in the patent), the inventor's oath or declaration for a reissue application must identify a claim that the application seeks to broaden. A claim is a broadened claim if the claim is broadened in any respect.

(c) The inventor, or each individual who is a joint inventor of a claimed invention, in a reissue application must execute an oath or declaration for the reissue application, except as provided for in §1.64, and except that the inventor's oath or declaration for a reissue application may be signed by the assignee of the entire interest if:

(1) The application does not seek to enlarge the scope of the claims of the original patent; or

(2) The application for the original patent was filed under §1.46 by the assignee of the entire interest.

(d) If errors previously identified in the inventor's oath or declaration for a reissue application pursuant to paragraph (a) of this section are no longer being relied upon as the basis for reissue, the applicant must identify an error being relied upon as the basis for reissue.

(e) The inventor's oath or declaration for a reissue application required by paragraph (a) of this section may be submitted under the provisions of §1.53(f), except that the provisions of §1.53(f)(3) do not apply to a reissue application.

(f)(1) The requirement for the inventor's oath or declaration for a continuing reissue application that claims the benefit under 35 U.S.C. 120, 121, 365(c), or 386(c) in compliance with §1.78 of an earlier-filed reissue application may be satisfied by a copy of the inventor's oath or declaration from the earlier-filed reissue application, provided that:

(i) The inventor, or each individual who is a joint inventor of a claimed invention, in the reissue application executed an inventor's oath or declaration for the earlier-filed reissue application, except as provided for in §1.64;

(ii) The continuing reissue application does not seek to enlarge the scope of the claims of the original patent; or

(iii) The application for the original patent was filed under §1.46 by the assignee of the entire interest.

(2) If all errors identified in the inventor's oath or declaration from the earlier-filed reissue application are no longer being relied upon as the basis for reissue, the applicant must identify an error being relied upon as the basis for reissue.

(g) An oath or declaration filed at any time pursuant to 35 U.S.C. 115(h)(1), will be placed in the file record of the reissue application, but may not necessarily be reviewed by the Office.

History of 37 C.F.R. §1.175: 24 FR 10332, Dec. 22, 1959; 29 FR 18503, Dec. 29, 1964; 34 FR 18857, Nov. 26, 1969; 42 FR 5594, Jan. 28, 1977; 47 FR 21752, May 19, 1982; 48 FR 2713, Jan. 20, 1983; 57 FR 2035, Jan. 17, 1992; 59 FR 18300, Apr. 18, 1994; 62 FR 53196, Oct. 10, 1997; 69 FR 56544, Sept. 21, 2004; 77 FR 48821, Sept. 16, 2012; 80 FR 17964, May 13, 2015.

§1.176. Examination of Reissue

(a) A reissue application will be examined in the same manner as a non-reissue, non-provisional application, and will be subject to all the requirements of the rules related to non-reissue applications. Applications for reissue will be acted on by the examiner in advance of other applications.

(b) Restriction between subject matter of the original patent claims and previously unclaimed subject matter may be required (restriction involving only subject matter of the original patent claims will not be required). If restriction is required, the subject matter of the original patent claims will be held to be constructively elected unless a disclaimer of all the patent claims is filed in the reissue application, which disclaimer cannot be withdrawn by applicant.

History of 37 C.F.R. §1.176: 42 FR 5595, Jan. 28, 1977; 65 FR 54676, Sept. 8, 2000.

§1.177. Issuance of Multiple Reissue Patents

(a) The Office may reissue a patent as multiple reissue patents. If applicant files more than one application for the reissue of a single patent, each such application must contain or be amended to contain in the first sentence of the specification a notice stating that more than one reissue application has been filed and identifying each of the reissue applications by relationship, application number and filing date. The Office may correct by certificate of correction under §1.322 any reissue patent resulting from an application to which this paragraph applies that does not contain the required notice.

(b) If applicant files more than one application for the reissue of a single patent, each claim of the patent being reissued must be presented in each of the reissue applications as an amended, unamended, or canceled (shown in brackets) claim, with each such claim bearing the same number as in the patent being reissued. The same claim of the patent being reissued may not be presented in its original unamended form for examination in more than one of such multiple reissue applications. The numbering of any added claims in any of the multiple reissue applications must follow the number of the highest numbered original patent claim.

(c) If any one of the several reissue applications by itself fails to correct an error in the original patent as required by 35 U.S.C. 251 but is otherwise in condition for allowance, the Office may suspend action in the allowable application until all issues are resolved as to at least one of the remaining reissue applications. The Office may also merge two or more of the multiple reissue applications into a single reissue application. No reissue application containing only unamended patent claims and not correcting an error in the original patent will be passed to issue by itself.

History of 37 C.F.R. §1.177: 24 FR 10332, Dec. 22, 1959; 47 FR 41278, Sept. 17, 1982; 54 FR 6903, Feb. 15, 1989; 54 FR 9432, Mar. 7, 1989; 60 FR 20227, Apr. 25, 1995; 65 FR 54676, Sept. 8, 2000.

§1.178. Original Patent; Continuing Duty of Applicant

(a) The application for reissue of a patent shall constitute an offer to surrender that patent, and the surrender shall take effect upon reissue of the patent. Until a reissue application is granted, the original patent shall remain in effect.

(b) In any reissue application before the Office, the applicant must call to the attention of the Office any prior or concurrent proceedings in which the patent (for which reissue is requested) is or was involved, such as interferences or trials before the Patent Trial and Appeal Board, reissues, reexaminations, or litigations and the results of such proceedings (see also §1.173(a)(1)).

History of 37 C.F.R. §1.178: 24 FR 10332, Dec. 22, 1959; 34 FR 18857, Nov. 26, 1969; 65 FR 54676, Sept. 8, 2000; 69 FR 56544, Sept. 21, 2004; 77 FR 46625, Sept. 16, 2012.

§1.179. Reserved

History of 37 C.F.R. §1.179: 69 FR 56544, Sept. 21, 2004.

Petitions & Action by the Director

§1.181. Petition to the Director

(a) Petition may be taken to the Director:

(1) From any action or requirement of any examiner in the ex parte prosecution of an application, or in ex parte or inter partes prosecution of a reexamination proceeding which is not subject to appeal to the Patent Trial and Appeal Board or to the court;

(2) In cases in which a statute or the rules specify that the matter is to be determined directly by or reviewed by the Director; and

(3) To invoke the supervisory authority of the Director in appropriate circumstances. For petitions involving action of the Patent Trial and Appeal Board, see §41.3 of this title.

(b) Any such petition must contain a statement of the facts involved and the point or points to be reviewed and the action requested. Briefs or memoranda, if any, in support thereof should accompany or be embodied in the petition; and where facts are to be proven, the proof in the form of affidavits or declarations (and exhibits, if any) must accompany the petition.

(c) When a petition is taken from an action or requirement of an examiner in the ex parte prosecution of an application, or in the ex parte or inter partes prosecution of a reexamination proceeding, it may be required that there have been a proper request for reconsideration (§1.111) and a repeated action by the examiner. The examiner may be directed by the Director to furnish a written statement, within a specified time, setting forth the reasons for his or her decision upon the matters averred in the petition, supplying a copy to the petitioner.

(d) Where a fee is required for a petition to the Director the appropriate section of this part will so indicate. If any required fee does not accompany the petition, the petition will be dismissed.

(e) Oral hearing will not be granted except when considered necessary by the Director.

(f) The mere filing of a petition will not stay any period for reply that may be running against the application, nor act as a stay of other proceedings. Any petition under this part not filed within two months of the mailing date of the action or notice from which relief is requested may be dismissed as untimely, except as otherwise provided. This two-month period is not extendable.

(g) The Director may delegate to appropriate Patent and Trademark Office officials the determination of petitions.

History of 37 C.F.R. §1.181: 24 FR 10332, Dec. 22, 1959; 34 FR 18857, Nov. 26, 1969; 35 FR 4260, Mar. 7, 1970; 47 FR 41278, Sept. 17, 1982; 49 FR 48452, Dec. 12, 1984; 65 FR 54676, Sept. 8, 2000; 65 FR 76774, Dec. 7, 2000; 69 FR 50000, Aug. 12, 2004; 77 FR 46625, Sept. 16, 2012.

§1.182. QUESTIONS NOT SPECIFICALLY PROVIDED FOR

All situations not specifically provided for in the regulations of this part will be decided in accordance with the merits of each situation by or under the authority of the Director, subject to such other requirements as may be imposed, and such decision will be communicated to the interested parties in writing. Any petition seeking a decision under this section must be accompanied by the petition fee set forth in §1.17(f).

History of 37 C.F.R. §1.182: 24 FR 10332, Dec. 22, 1959; 47 FR 41278, Sept. 17, 1982; 62 FR 53196, Oct. 10, 1997; 69 FR 56544, Sept. 21, 2004.

§1.183. SUSPENSION OF RULES

In an extraordinary situation, when justice requires, any requirement of the regulations in this part which is not a requirement of the statutes may be suspended or waived by the Director or the Director's designee, sua sponte, or on petition of the interested party, subject to such other requirements as may be imposed. Any petition under this section must be accompanied by the petition fee set forth in §1.17(f).

History of 37 C.F.R. §1.183: 24 FR 10332, Dec. 22, 1959; 47 FR 41278, Sept. 17, 1982; 69 FR 56544, Sept. 21, 2004.

§1.184. RESERVED

History of 37 C.F.R. §1.184: 62 FR 53196, Oct. 10, 1997.

APPEAL TO THE PATENT TRIAL & APPEAL BOARD

§1.191. APPEAL TO PATENT TRIAL & APPEAL BOARD

Appeals to the Patent Trial and Appeal Board under 35 U.S.C. 134(a) and (b) are conducted according to part 41 of this title.

History of 37 C.F.R. §1.191: 46 FR 29183, May 29, 1981; 47 FR 41278, Sept. 17, 1982; 49 FR 555, Jan. 4, 1984; 49 FR 48453, Dec. 12, 1984; 54 FR 29552, July 13, 1989; 58 FR 54510, Oct. 22, 1993; 62 FR 53196, Oct. 10, 1997; 65 FR 76774, Dec. 7, 2000; 68 FR 71006, Dec. 22, 2003; 69 FR 50000, Aug. 12, 2004; 77 FR 46625, Sept. 16, 2012.

§§1.192 TO 1.196. RESERVED

History of 37 C.F.R. §§1.192-1.196: 69 FR 50000, Aug. 12, 2004.

§1.197. TERMINATION OF PROCEEDINGS

(a) Proceedings on an application are considered terminated by the dismissal of an appeal or the failure to timely file an appeal to the court or a civil action except:

(1) Where claims stand allowed in an application; or

(2) Where the nature of the decision requires further action by the examiner.

(b) The date of termination of proceedings on an application is the date on which the appeal is dismissed or the date on which the time for appeal to the U.S. Court of Appeals for the Federal Circuit or review by civil action (§90.3 of this chapter) expires in the absence of further appeal or review. If an appeal to the U.S. Court of Appeals for the Federal Circuit or a civil action has been filed, proceedings on an application are considered terminated when the appeal or civil action is terminated. A civil action is terminated when the time to appeal the judgment expires. An appeal to the U.S. Court of Appeals for the Federal Circuit, whether from a decision of the Board or a judgment in a civil action, is terminated when the mandate is issued by the Court.

History of 37 C.F.R. §1.197: 41 FR 757, Jan. 5, 1976; 46 FR 29184, May 29, 1981; 47 FR 41278, Sept. 17, 1982; 49 FR 556, Jan. 4, 1984; 49 FR 48453, Dec. 12, 1984; 54 FR 29552, July 13, 1989; 58 FR 54510, Oct. 22, 1993; 62 FR 53198, Oct. 10, 1997; 68 FR 71006, Dec. 22, 2003; 69 FR 50000, Aug. 12, 2004; 76 FR 72296, Nov. 22, 2011; 78 FR 62406, Dec. 18, 2013; 78 FR 75252, Dec. 18, 2013.

§1.198. REOPENING AFTER A FINAL DECISION OF THE PATENT TRIAL & APPEAL BOARD

When a decision by the Patent Trial and Appeal Board on appeal has become final for judicial review, prosecution of the proceeding before the primary examiner will not be reopened or reconsidered by the primary examiner except under the provisions of §1.114 or §41.50 of this title without the written authority of the Director, and then only for the consideration of matters not already adjudicated, sufficient cause being shown.

History of 37 C.F.R. §1.198: 49 FR 48453, Dec. 12, 1984; 65 FR 14873, Mar. 20, 2000; 65 FR 50103, Aug. 16, 2000; 69 FR 50000, Aug. 12, 2004; 77 FR 46625, Sept. 16, 2012.

PUBLICATION OF APPLICATIONS

§1.211. PUBLICATION OF APPLICATIONS

(a) Each U.S. national application for patent filed in the Office under 35 U.S.C. 111(a) and each international application in compliance with 35 U.S.C. 371 will be published promptly after the expiration of a period of eighteen months from the earliest filing date for which a benefit is sought under title 35, United States Code, unless:

(1) The application is recognized by the Office as no longer pending;

(2) The application is national security classified (see §5.2(c)), subject to a secrecy order under 35 U.S.C. 181, or under national security review;

(3) The application has issued as a patent in sufficient time to be removed from the publication process; or

(4) The application was filed with a nonpublication request in compliance with §1.213(a).

(b) Provisional applications under 35 U.S.C. 111(b) shall not be published, and design applications under 35 U.S.C. chapter 16, international design applications under 35 U.S.C. chapter 38, and reissue applications under 35 U.S.C. chapter 25 shall not be published under this section.

(c) An application filed under 35 U.S.C. 111(a) will not be published until it includes the basic filing fee (§1.16(a) or §1.16(c)) and any English translation required by §1.52(d). The Office may delay publishing any application until it includes any application size fee required by the Office under §1.16(s) or §1.492(j), a specification having papers in compliance with §1.52 and an abstract (§1.72(b)), drawings in compliance with §1.84, a sequence listing in compliance with §§1.821 through 1.825 (if applicable), and the inventor's oath or declaration or application data sheet containing the information specified in §1.63(b).

(d) The Office may refuse to publish an application, or to include a portion of an application in the patent application publication (§1.215), if publication of the application or portion thereof would violate Federal or state law, or if the application or portion thereof contains offensive or disparaging material.

(e) The publication fee set forth in §1.18(d) must be paid in each application published under this section before the patent will be granted. If an application is subject to publication under this section, the sum specified in the notice of allowance under §1.311 will also include the publication fee which must be paid within three months from the date of mailing of the notice of allowance to avoid abandonment of the application. This three-month period is not extendable. If the application is not published under this section, the publication fee (if paid) will be refunded.

History of 37 C.F.R. §1.211: 65 FR 57058, Sept. 20, 2000; 70 FR 3891, Jan. 27, 2005; 77 FR 48822, Sept. 16, 2012; 80 FR 17964, May 13, 2015.

§1.213. NONPUBLICATION REQUEST

(a) If the invention disclosed in an application has not been and will not be the subject of an application filed in another country, or under a multilateral international agreement, that requires publication of applications eighteen months after filing, the application will not be published under 35 U.S.C. 122(b) and §1.211 provided:

(1) A request (nonpublication request) is submitted with the application upon filing;

(2) The request states in a conspicuous manner that the application is not to be published under 35 U.S.C. 122(b);

(3) The request contains a certification that the invention disclosed in the application has not been and will not be the subject of an application filed in another country, or under a multilateral international agreement, that requires publication at eighteen months after filing; and

(4) The request is signed in compliance with §1.33(b).

(b) The applicant may rescind a nonpublication request at any time. A request to rescind a nonpublication request under paragraph (a) of this section must:

(1) Identify the application to which it is directed;

(2) State in a conspicuous manner that the request that the application is not to be published under 35 U.S.C. 122(b) is rescinded; and

(3) Be signed in compliance with §1.33(b).

(c) If an applicant who has submitted a nonpublication request under paragraph (a) of this section subsequently files an application directed to the invention disclosed in the application in which the nonpublication request was submitted in another country, or under a multilateral international agreement, that requires publication of applications eighteen months after filing, the applicant must notify the Office of such filing within forty-five days after the date of the filing of such foreign or international application. The failure to timely notify the Office of the filing of such foreign or international application shall result in abandonment of the application in which the nonpublication request was submitted (35 U.S.C. 122(b)(2)(B)(iii)).

History of 37 C.F.R. §1.213: 65 FR 57058, Sept. 20, 2000.

§1.215. PATENT APPLICATION PUBLICATION

(a) The publication of an application under 35 U.S.C. 122(b) shall include a patent application publication. The date of publication shall be indicated on the patent application publication. The patent application publication will be based upon the specification and drawings deposited on the filing date of the application, as well as the application data sheet and/or the inventor's oath or declaration. The patent application publication may also be based upon amendments to the specification (other than the abstract or the claims) that are reflected in a substitute specification under §1.125(b), amendments to the abstract under §1.121(b), amendments to the claims that are reflected in a complete claim listing under §1.121(c), and amendments to the drawings under §1.121(d), provided that such substitute specification or amendment is submitted in sufficient time to be entered into the Office file wrapper of the application before technical preparations for publication of the application have begun. Technical preparations for publication of an application generally begin four months prior to the projected date of publication. The patent application publication of an application that has entered the national stage under 35 U.S.C. 371 may also include amendments made during the international stage. See paragraph (c) of this section for publication of an application based upon a copy of the application submitted via the Office electronic filing system.

(b) The patent application publication will include the name of the assignee, person to whom the inventor is under an obligation to assign the invention, or person who otherwise shows sufficient proprietary interest in the matter if that information is provided in the application data sheet in an application filed under §1.46. Assignee information may be included on the patent application publication in other applications if the assignee information is provided in an application data sheet submitted in sufficient time to be entered into the Office file wrapper of the application before technical preparations for publication of the application have begun. Providing assignee information in the application data sheet does not substitute for compliance with any requirement of part 3 of this chapter to have an assignment recorded by the Office.

(c) At applicant's option, the patent application publication will be based upon the copy of the application (specification, drawings, and the application data sheet and/or the inventor's oath or declaration) as amended, provided that applicant supplies such a copy in compliance with the Office electronic filing system requirements within one month of the mailing date of the first Office communication that includes a confirmation number for the application, or fourteen months of the earliest filing date for which a benefit is sought under title 35, United States Code, whichever is later.

(d) If the copy of the application submitted pursuant to paragraph (c) of this section does not comply with the Office electronic filing system requirements, the Office will publish the application as provided in paragraph (a) of this section. If, however, the Office has not started the publication process, the Office may use an untimely filed copy of the application supplied by the applicant under paragraph (c) of this section in creating the patent application publication.

History of 37 C.F.R. §1.215: 65 FR 57058, Sept. 20, 2000; 69 FR 56544, Sept. 21, 2004; 77 FR 48822, Sept. 16, 2012.

§1.217. PUBLICATION OF A REDACTED COPY OF AN APPLICATION

(a) If an applicant has filed applications in one or more foreign countries, directly or through a multilateral international agreement, and such foreign-filed applications or the description of the invention in such foreign-filed applications is less extensive than the application or description of the invention in the application filed in the Office, the applicant may submit a redacted copy of the application filed in the Office for publication, eliminating any part or description of the invention that is not also contained in any of the corresponding applications filed in a foreign country. The Office will publish the application as provided in §1.215(a) unless the applicant files a redacted copy of the application in compliance with this section within sixteen months after the earliest filing date for which a benefit is sought under title 35, United States Code.

(b) The redacted copy of the application must be submitted in compliance with the Office electronic filing system requirements. The title of the invention in the redacted copy of the application must correspond to the title of the application at the time the redacted copy of the application is submitted to the Office. If the redacted copy of the application does not comply with the Office electronic filing system requirements, the Office will publish the application as provided in §1.215(a).

(c) The applicant must also concurrently submit in paper (§1.52(a)) to be filed in the application:

(1) A certified copy of each foreign-filed application that corresponds to the application for which a redacted copy is submitted;

(2) A translation of each such foreign-filed application that is in a language other than English, and a statement that the translation is accurate;

(3) A marked-up copy of the application showing the redactions in brackets; and

(4) A certification that the redacted copy of the application eliminates only the part or description of the invention that is not contained in any application filed in a foreign country, directly or through a multilateral international agreement, that corresponds to the application filed in the Office.

(d) The Office will provide a copy of the complete file wrapper and contents of an application for which a redacted copy was submitted under this section to any person upon written request pursuant to §1.14(c)(2), unless applicant complies with the requirements of paragraphs (d)(1), (d)(2), and (d)(3) of this section.

(1) Applicant must accompany the submission required by paragraph (c) of this section with the following:

(i) A copy of any Office correspondence previously received by applicant including any desired redactions, and a second copy of all Office correspondence previously received by applicant showing the redacted material in brackets; and

(ii) A copy of each submission previously filed by the applicant including any desired redactions, and a second copy of each submission previously filed by the applicant showing the redacted material in brackets.

(2) In addition to providing the submission required by paragraphs (c) and (d)(1) of this section, applicant must:

(i) Within one month of the date of mailing of any correspondence from the Office, file a copy of such Office correspondence including any desired redactions, and a second copy of such Office correspondence showing the redacted material in brackets; and

(ii) With each submission by the applicant, include a copy of such submission including any desired redactions, and a second copy of such submission showing the redacted material in brackets.

(3) Each submission under paragraph (d)(1) or (d)(2) of this paragraph must also be accompanied by the processing fee set forth in §1.17(i) and a certification that the redactions are limited to the elimination of material that is relevant only to the part or description of the invention that was not contained in the redacted copy of the application submitted for publication.

(e) The provisions of §1.8 do not apply to the time periods set forth in this section.

History of 37 C.F.R. §1.217: 65 FR 57058, Sept. 20, 2000.

§1.219. EARLY PUBLICATION

(a)[1] Applications that will be published under §1.211 may be published earlier than as set forth in §1.211(a) at the request of the applicant. Any request for early publication must be accompanied by the publication fee set forth in §1.18(d). If the applicant does not submit a copy of the application in compliance with the Office electronic filing system requirements pursuant to §1.215(c), the Office will publish the application as provided in §1.215(a). No consideration will be given to requests for publication on a certain date, and such requests will be treated as a request for publication as soon as possible.

1. **Editor's note:** Enacted without a subsection (b).

History of 37 C.F.R. §1.219: 65 FR 57058, Sept. 20, 2000.

§1.221. VOLUNTARY PUBLICATION OR REPUBLICATION OF PATENT APPLICATION PUBLICATION

(a) Any request for publication of an application filed before, but pending on, November 29, 2000, and any request for republication of an application previously published under §1.211, must include a copy of the application in compliance with the Office electronic filing system requirements and be accompanied by the publication fee set forth in §1.18(d) and the processing fee set forth in §1.17(i). If the request does not comply with the requirements of this paragraph or the copy of the application does not comply with the Office electronic filing system requirements, the Office will not publish the application and will refund the publication fee.

(b) The Office will grant a request for a corrected or revised patent application publication other than as provided in paragraph (a) of this section only when the Office makes a material mistake which is apparent from Office records. Any request for a corrected or revised patent application publication other than as provided in paragraph (a) of this section must be filed within two months from the date of the patent application publication. This period is not extendable.

History of 37 C.F.R. §1.221: 65 FR 57058, Sept. 20, 2000; 65 FR 57060, Sept. 20, 2000.

MISCELLANEOUS PROVISIONS

§1.248. SERVICE OF PAPERS; MANNER OF SERVICE; PROOF OF SERVICE IN CASES OTHER THAN INTERFERENCES & TRIALS

(a) Service of papers must be on the attorney or agent of the party if there be such or on the party if there is no attorney or agent, and may be made in any of the following ways:

(1) By delivering a copy of the paper to the person served;

(2) By leaving a copy at the usual place of business of the person served with someone in his employment;

(3) When the person served has no usual place of business, by leaving a copy at the person's residence, with some person of suitable age and discretion who resides there;

(4) Transmission by first class mail. When service is by mail the date of mailing will be regarded as the date of service;

(5) Whenever it shall be satisfactorily shown to the Director that none of the above modes of obtaining or serving the paper is practicable, service may be by notice published in the Official Gazette.

(b) Papers filed in the Patent and Trademark Office which are required to be served shall contain proof of service. Proof of service may appear on or be affixed to papers filed. Proof of service shall include the date and manner of service. In the case of personal service, proof of service shall also include the name of any person served, certified by the person who made service. Proof of service may be made by: (1) an acknowledgement of service by or on behalf of the person served or (2) a statement signed by the attorney or agent containing the information required by this section.

(c) See §41.106(e) or §42.6(e) of this title for service of papers in contested cases or trials before the Patent Trial and Appeal Board.

History of 37 C.F.R. §1.248: 46 FR 29184, May 29, 1981; 49 FR 48454, Dec. 12, 1984; 69 FR 50000, Aug. 12, 2004; 69 FR 58260, Sept. 30, 2004; 77 FR 46626, Sept. 16, 2012.

§1.251. UNLOCATABLE FILE

(a) In the event that the Office cannot locate the file of an application, patent, or other patent-related proceeding after a reasonable search, the Office will notify the applicant or patentee and set a time period within which the applicant or patentee must comply with the notice in accordance with one of paragraphs (a)(1), (a)(2), or (a)(3) of this section.

(1) Applicant or patentee may comply with a notice under this section by providing:

(i) A copy of the applicant's or patentee's record (if any) of all of the correspondence between the Office and the applicant or patentee for such application, patent, or other proceeding (except for U.S. patent documents);

(ii) A list of such correspondence; and

(iii) A statement that the copy is a complete and accurate copy of the applicant's or patentee's record of all of the correspondence between the Office and the applicant or patentee for such application, patent, or other proceeding (except for U.S. patent documents), and whether applicant or patentee is aware of any correspondence between the Office and the applicant or patentee for such application, patent, or other proceeding that is not among applicant's or patentee's records.

(2) Applicant or patentee may comply with a notice under this section by:

(i) Producing the applicant's or patentee's record (if any) of all of the correspondence between the Office and the applicant or patentee for such application, patent, or other proceeding for the Office to copy (except for U.S. patent documents); and

(ii) Providing a statement that the papers produced by applicant or patentee are applicant's or patentee's complete record of all of the correspondence between the Office and the applicant or patentee for such application, patent, or other proceeding (except for U.S. patent documents), and whether applicant or patentee is aware of any correspondence between the Office and the applicant or patentee for such application, patent, or other proceeding that is not among applicant's or patentee's records.

(3) If applicant or patentee does not possess any record of the correspondence between the Office and the applicant or patentee for such application, patent, or other proceeding, applicant or patentee must comply with a notice under this section by providing a statement that applicant or patentee does not possess any record of the correspondence between the Office and the applicant or patentee for such application, patent, or other proceeding.

(b) With regard to a pending application, failure to comply with one of paragraphs (a)(1), (a)(2), or (a)(3) of this section within the time period set in the notice will result in abandonment of the application.

History of 37 C.F.R. §1.251: 65 FR 69451, Nov. 17, 2000.

PREISSUANCE SUBMISSIONS & PROTESTS BY THIRD PARTIES

§1.290. SUBMISSIONS BY THIRD PARTIES IN APPLICATIONS

(a) A third party may submit, for consideration and entry in the record of a patent application, any patents, published patent applications, or other printed publications of potential relevance to the examination of the application if the submission is made in accordance with 35 U.S.C. 122(e) and this section. A third-party submission may not be entered or considered by the Office if any part of the submission is not in compliance with 35 U.S.C. 122(e) and this section.

(b) Any third-party submission under this section must be filed prior to the earlier of:

(1) The date a notice of allowance under §1.311 is given or mailed in the application; or

(2) The later of:

(i) Six months after the date on which the application is first published by the Office under 35 U.S.C. 122(b) and §1.211, or

(ii) The date the first rejection under §1.104 of any claim by the examiner is given or mailed during the examination of the application.

(c) Any third-party submission under this section must be made in writing.

(d) Any third-party submission under this section must include:

(1) A document list identifying the documents, or portions of documents, being submitted in accordance with paragraph (e) of this section;

(2) A concise description of the asserted relevance of each item identified in the document list;

(3) A legible copy of each item identified in the document list, other than U.S. patents and U.S. patent application publications;

(4) An English language translation of any non-English language item identified in the document list; and

(5) A statement by the party making the submission that:

(i) The party is not an individual who has a duty to disclose information with respect to the application under §1.56; and

(ii) The submission complies with the requirements of 35 U.S.C. 122(e) and this section.

(e) The document list required by paragraph (d)(1) of this section must include a heading that identifies the list as a third-party submission under §1.290, identify on each page of the list the application number of the application in which the submission is being filed, list U.S. patents and U.S. patent application publications in a separate section from other items, and identify each:

(1) U.S. patent by patent number, first named inventor, and issue date;

(2) U.S. patent application publication by patent application publication number, first named inventor, and publication date;

(3) Foreign patent or published foreign patent application by the country or patent office that issued the patent or published the application; the applicant, patentee, or first named inventor; an appropriate document number; and the publication date indicated on the patent or published application; and

(4) Non-patent publication by author (if any), title, pages being submitted, publication date, and, where available, publisher and place of publication. If no publication date is known, the third party must provide evidence of publication.

(f) Any third-party submission under this section must be accompanied by the fee set forth in §1.17(o) for every ten items or fraction thereof identified in the document list.

(g) The fee otherwise required by paragraph (f) of this section is not required for a submission listing three or fewer total items that is accompanied by a statement by the party making the submission that, to the knowledge of the person signing the statement after making reasonable inquiry, the submission is the first and only submission under 35 U.S.C. 122(e) filed in the application by the party or a party in privity with the party.

(h) In the absence of a request by the Office, an applicant need not reply to a submission under this section.

(i) The provisions of §1.8 do not apply to the time periods set forth in this section.

History of 37 C.F.R. §1.290: 77 FR 42173, Sept. 16, 2012; 78 FR 62406, Dec. 18, 2013.

§1.291. PROTESTS BY THE PUBLIC AGAINST PENDING APPLICATIONS

(a) A protest may be filed by a member of the public against a pending application, and it will be matched with the application file if it adequately identifies the patent application. A protest submitted within the time frame of paragraph (b) of this section, which is not matched, or not matched in a timely manner to permit review by the examiner during prosecution, due to inadequate identification, may not be entered and may be returned to the protestor where practical, or, if return is not practical, discarded.

(b) The protest will be entered into the record of the application if, in addition to complying with paragraph (c) of this section, the protest has been served upon the applicant in accordance with §1.248, or filed with the Office in duplicate in the event service is not possible; and, except for paragraph (b)(1) of this section, the protest was filed prior to the date the application was published under §1.211, or the date a notice of allowance under §1.311 was given or mailed, whichever occurs first:

(1) If a protest is accompanied by the written consent of the applicant, the protest will be considered if the protest is filed prior to the date a notice of allowance under §1.311 is given or mailed in the application.

(2) A statement must accompany a protest that it is the first protest submitted in the application by the real party in interest who is submitting the protest; or the protest must comply with paragraph (c)(5) of this section. This section does not apply to the first protest filed in an application.

(c) In addition to compliance with paragraphs (a) and (b) of this section, a protest must include:

(1) An information list of the documents, portions of documents, or other information being submitted, where each:

(i) U.S. patent is identified by patent number, first named inventor, and issue date;

(ii) U.S. patent application publication is identified by patent application publication number, first named inventor, and publication date;

(iii) Foreign patent or published foreign patent application is identified by the country or patent office that issued the patent or published the application; an appropriate document number; the applicant, patentee, or first named inventor; and the publication date indicated on the patent or published application;

(iv) Non-patent publication is identified by author (if any), title, pages being submitted, publication date, and, where available, publisher and place of publication; and

(v) Item of other information is identified by date, if known.

(2) A concise explanation of the relevance of each item identified in the information list pursuant to paragraph (c)(1) of this section;

(3) A legible copy of each item identified in the information list, other than U.S. patents and U.S. patent application publications;

(4) An English language translation of any non-English language item identified in the information list; and

(5) If it is a second or subsequent protest by the same real party in interest, an explanation as to why the issue(s) raised in the second or subsequent protest are significantly different than those raised earlier and why the significantly different issue(s) were not presented earlier, and a processing fee under §1.17(i) must be submitted.

(d) A member of the public filing a protest in an application under this section will not receive any communication from the Office relating to the protest, other than the return of a self-addressed postcard which the member of the public may include with the protest in order to receive an acknowledgment by the Office that the protest has been received. The limited involvement of the member of the public filing a protest pursuant to this section ends with the filing of the protest, and no further submission on behalf of the protestor will be considered, unless the submission is made pursuant to paragraph (c)(5) of this section.

(e) Where a protest raising inequitable conduct issues satisfies the provisions of this section for entry, it will be entered into the application file, generally without comment on the inequitable conduct issues raised in it.

(f) In the absence of a request by the Office, an applicant need not reply to a protest.

(g) Protests that fail to comply with paragraphs (b) or (c) of this section may not be entered, and if not entered, will be returned to the protestor, or discarded, at the option of the Office.

History of 37 C.F.R. §1.291: 42 FR 5595, Jan. 28, 1977; 46 FR 29184, May 29, 1981; 47 FR 21752, May 19, 1982; 57 FR 2035, Jan. 17, 1992; 61 FR 42806, Aug. 19, 1996; 62 FR 53198, Oct. 10, 1997; 65 FR 57060, Sept. 20, 2000; 69 FR 56544, Sept. 21, 2004; 77 FR 42173, Sept. 16, 2012.

§1.292. REMOVED & RESERVED

History of 37 C.F.R. §1.292: 77 FR 42174, Sept. 16, 2012.

§§1.293 TO 1.297. REMOVED & RESERVED

History of 37 C.F.R. §§1.293-1.297: 78 FR 11059, Mar. 16, 2013.

REVIEW OF PATENT & TRADEMARK OFFICE DECISIONS BY COURT

§§1.301 TO 1.304. REMOVED & RESERVED

History of 37 C.F.R. §§1.301-1.304: 77 FR 48669, Sept. 16, 2012.

ALLOWANCE & ISSUE OF PATENT

§1.311. NOTICE OF ALLOWANCE

(a) If, on examination, it appears that the applicant is entitled to a patent under the law, a notice of allowance will be sent to the applicant at the correspondence address indicated in §1.33. The notice of allowance shall specify a sum constituting the issue fee and any required publication fee (§1.211(e)), which issue fee and any required publication fee must both be paid within three months from the date of mailing of the notice of allowance to avoid abandonment of the application. This three-month period is not extendable.

(b) An authorization to charge the issue fee or other post-allowance fees set forth in §1.18 to a deposit account may be filed in an individual application only after mailing of the notice of allowance. The submission of either of the following after the mailing of a notice of allowance will operate as a request to charge the correct issue fee or any publication fee due to any deposit account identified in a previously filed authorization to charge such fees:

(1) An incorrect issue fee or publication fee; or

(2) A fee transmittal form (or letter) for payment of issue fee or publication fee.

History of 37 C.F.R. §1.311: 30 FR 12844, Oct. 8, 1965; 47 FR 41279, Sept. 17, 1982; 65 FR 54676, Sept. 8, 2000; 65 FR 57060, Sept. 20, 2000; 66 FR 67096, Dec. 28, 2001; 69 FR 56545, Sept. 21, 2004; 78 FR 62406, Dec. 18, 2013.

§1.312. AMENDMENTS AFTER ALLOWANCE

No amendment may be made as a matter of right in an application after the mailing of the notice of allowance. Any amendment filed pursuant to this section must be filed before or with the payment of the issue fee, and may be entered on the recommendation of the primary examiner, approved by the Director, without withdrawing the application from issue.

History of 37 C.F.R. §1.312: 34 FR 6844, Apr. 24, 1969; 47 FR 41280, Sept. 17, 1982; 58 FR 54510, Oct. 22, 1993; 60 FR 20227, Apr. 25, 1995; 62 FR 53198, Oct. 10, 1997; 65 FR 14873, Mar. 20, 2000; 65 FR 50103, Aug. 16, 2000.

§1.313. WITHDRAWAL FROM ISSUE

(a) Applications may be withdrawn from issue for further action at the initiative of the Office or upon petition by the applicant. To request that the Office withdraw an application from issue, applicant must file a petition under this section including the fee set forth in §1.17(h) and a showing of good and sufficient reasons why withdrawal of the application from issue is necessary. A petition under this section is not required if a request for continued examination under §1.114 is filed prior to payment of the issue fee. If the Office withdraws the application from issue, the Office will issue a new notice of allowance if the Office again allows the application.

(b) Once the issue fee has been paid, the Office will not withdraw the application from issue at its own initiative for any reason except:

(1) A mistake on the part of the Office;

(2) A violation of §1.56 or illegality in the application;

(3) Unpatentability of one or more claims; or

(4) For an interference or derivation proceeding.

(c) Once the issue fee has been paid, the application will not be withdrawn from issue upon petition by the applicant for any reason except:

(1) Unpatentability of one of more claims, which petition must be accompanied by an unequivocal statement that one or more claims are unpatentable, an amendment to such claim or claims, and an explanation as to how the amendment causes such claim or claims to be patentable;

(2) Consideration of a request for continued examination in compliance with §1.114; or

(3) Express abandonment of the application. Such express abandonment may be in favor of a continuing application.

(d) A petition under this section will not be effective to withdraw the application from issue unless it is actually received and granted by the appropriate officials before the date of issue. Withdrawal of an application from issue after payment of the issue fee may not be effective to avoid publication of application information.

History of 37 C.F.R. §1.313: 30 FR 12844, Oct. 8, 1965; 34 FR 18858, Nov. 26, 1969; 47 FR 41280, Sept. 17, 1982; 54 FR 6903, Feb. 15, 1989; 54 FR 9432, Mar. 7, 1989; 57 FR 2035, Jan. 17, 1992; 60 FR 20227, Apr. 25, 1995; 65 FR 14873, Mar. 20, 2000; 65 FR 50103, Aug. 16, 2000; 65 FR 50105, Aug. 16, 2000; 77 FR 46626, Sept. 16, 2012.

§1.314. ISSUANCE OF PATENT

If applicant timely pays the issue fee, the Office will issue the patent in regular course unless the application is withdrawn from issue (§1.313) or the Office defers issuance of the patent. To request that the Office defer issuance of a patent, applicant must file a petition under this section including the fee set forth in §1.17(h) and a showing of good and sufficient reasons why it is necessary to defer issuance of the patent.

History of 37 C.F.R. §1.314: 30 FR 12844, Oct. 8, 1965; 47 FR 41280, Sept. 17, 1982; 54 FR 6903, Feb. 15, 1989; 60 FR 20227, Apr. 25, 1995; 65 FR 54677, Sept. 8, 2000.

§1.315. DELIVERY OF PATENT

The patent will be delivered or mailed upon issuance to the correspondence address of record. See §1.33(a).

History of 37 C.F.R. §1.315: 61 FR 42807, Aug. 19, 1996.

§1.316. APPLICATION ABANDONED FOR FAILURE TO PAY ISSUE FEE

If the issue fee is not paid within three months from the date of the notice of allowance, the application will be regarded as abandoned. Such an abandoned application will not be considered as pending before the Patent and Trademark Office.

History of 37 C.F.R. §1.316: 30 FR 12844, Oct. 8, 1965; 40 FR 44814, Sept. 30, 1975; 47 FR 41280, Sept. 17, 1982; 58 FR 44281, Aug. 20, 1993; 60 FR 20228, Apr. 25, 1995; 62 FR 53198, Oct. 10, 1997.

§1.317. RESERVED

History of 37 C.F.R. §1.317: 78 FR 62406, Dec. 18, 2013.

§1.318. RESERVED

History of 37 C.F.R. §1.318: 62 FR 53198, Oct. 10, 1997.

DISCLAIMER

§1.321. STATUTORY DISCLAIMERS, INCLUDING TERMINAL DISCLAIMERS

(a) A patentee owning the whole or any sectional interest in a patent may disclaim any complete claim or claims in a patent. In like manner any patentee may disclaim or dedicate to the public the entire term, or any terminal part of the term, of the patent granted. Such disclaimer is binding upon the grantee and its successors or assigns. A notice of the disclaimer is published in the Official Gazette and attached to the printed copies of the specification. The disclaimer, to be recorded in the Patent and Trademark Office, must:

(1) Be signed by the patentee, or an attorney or agent of record;

(2) Identify the patent and complete claim or claims, or term being disclaimed. A disclaimer which is not a disclaimer of a complete claim or claims, or term will be refused recordation;

(3) State the present extent of patentee's ownership interest in the patent; and

(4) Be accompanied by the fee set forth in §1.20(d).

(b) An applicant may disclaim or dedicate to the public the entire term, or any terminal part of the term, of a patent to be granted. Such terminal disclaimer is binding upon the grantee and its successors or assigns. The terminal disclaimer, to be recorded in the Patent and Trademark Office, must:

(1) Be signed by the applicant or an attorney or agent of record;

(2) Specify the portion of the term of the patent being disclaimed;

(3) State the present extent of applicant's ownership interest in the patent to be granted; and

(4) Be accompanied by the fee set forth in §1.20(d).

(c) A terminal disclaimer, when filed to obviate judicially created double patenting in a patent application or in a reexamination proceeding except as provided for in paragraph (d) of this section, must:

(1) Comply with the provisions of paragraphs (b)(2) through (b)(4) of this section;

(2) Be signed in accordance with paragraph (b)(1) of this section if filed in a patent application or in accordance with paragraph (a)(1) of this section if filed in a reexamination proceeding; and

(3) Include a provision that any patent granted on that application or any patent subject to the reexamination proceeding shall be enforceable only for and during such period that said patent is commonly owned with the application or patent which formed the basis for the judicially created double patenting.

(d) A terminal disclaimer, when filed in a patent application or in a reexamination proceeding to obviate double patenting based upon a patent or application that is not commonly owned but was disqualified as prior art as set forth in either §1.104(c)(4)(ii) or (c)(5)(ii) as the result of activities undertaken within the scope of a joint research agreement, must:

(1) Comply with the provisions of paragraphs (b)(2) through (b)(4) of this section;

(2) Be signed in accordance with paragraph (b)(1) of this section if filed in a patent application or be signed in accordance with paragraph (a)(1) of this section if filed in a reexamination proceeding; and

(3) Include a provision waiving the right to separately enforce any patent granted on that application or any patent subject to the reexamination proceeding and the patent or any patent granted on the application which formed the basis for the double patenting, and that any patent granted on that application or any patent subject to the reexamination proceeding shall be enforceable only for and during such period that said patent and the patent, or any patent granted on the application, which formed the basis for the double patenting are not separately enforced.

History of 37 C.F.R. §1.321: 36 FR 7312, Apr. 17, 1971; 47 FR 41281, Sept. 17, 1982; 58 FR 54510, Oct. 22, 1993; 61 FR 42807, Aug. 19, 1996; 70 FR 1824, Jan. 11, 2005; 70 FR 54266, Sept. 14, 2005; 77 FR 48822, Sept. 16, 2012; 78 FR 11059, Mar. 16, 2013.

CORRECTION OF ERRORS IN PATENT

§1.322. CERTIFICATE OF CORRECTION OF OFFICE MISTAKE

(a)(1) The Director may issue a certificate of correction pursuant to 35 U.S.C. 254 to correct a mistake in a patent, incurred through the fault of the Office, which mistake is clearly disclosed in the records of the Office:

(i) At the request of the patentee or the patentee's assignee;

(ii) Acting sua sponte for mistakes that the Office discovers; or

(iii) Acting on information about a mistake supplied by a third party.

(2)(i) There is no obligation on the Office to act on or respond to a submission of information or request to issue a certificate of correction by a third party under paragraph (a)(1)(iii) of this section.

(ii) Papers submitted by a third party under this section will not be made of record in the file that they relate to nor be retained by the Office.

(3) If the request relates to a patent involved in an interference or trial before the Patent Trial and Appeal Board, the request must comply with the requirements of this section and be accompanied by a motion under §41.121(a)(2), §41.121(a)(3), or §42.20 of this title.

(4) The Office will not issue a certificate of correction under this section without first notifying the patentee (including any assignee of record) at the correspondence address of record as specified in §1.33(a) and affording the patentee or an assignee an opportunity to be heard.

(b) If the nature of the mistake on the part of the Office is such that a certificate of correction is deemed inappropriate in form, the Director may issue a corrected patent in lieu thereof as a more appropriate form for certificate of correction, without expense to the patentee.

History of 37 C.F.R. §1.322: 24 FR 10332, Dec. 22, 1959; 34 FR 5550, Mar. 22, 1969; 49 FR 48454, Dec. 12, 1984; 65 FR 54677, Sept. 8, 2000; 69 FR 50001, Aug. 12, 2004; 77 FR 46626, Sept. 16, 2012.

§1.323. CERTIFICATE OF CORRECTION OF APPLICANT'S MISTAKE

The Office may issue a certificate of correction under the conditions specified in 35 U.S.C. 255 at the request of the patentee or the patentee's assignee, upon payment of the fee set forth in §1.20(a). If the request relates to a patent involved in an interference or trial before the Patent Trial and Appeal Board, the request must comply with the requirements of this section and be accompanied by a motion under §41.121(a)(2), §41.121(a)(3) or §42.20 of this title.

History of 37 C.F.R. §1.323: 34 FR 5550, Mar. 22, 1969; 49 FR 48454, Dec. 12, 1984; 65 FR 54677, Sept. 8, 2000; 69 FR 50001, Aug. 12, 2004; 77 FR 46626, Sept. 16, 2012.

§1.324. CORRECTION OF INVENTORSHIP IN PATENT, PURSUANT TO 35 U.S.C. 256

(a) Whenever through error a person is named in an issued patent as the inventor, or an inventor is not named in an issued patent, the Director, pursuant to 35 U.S.C. 256, may, on application of all the parties and assignees, or on order of a court before which such matter is called in question, issue a certificate naming only the actual inventor or inventors.

(b) Any request to correct inventorship of a patent pursuant to paragraph (a) of this section must be accompanied by:

(1) A statement from each person who is being added as an inventor and each person who is currently named as an inventor either agreeing to the change of inventorship or stating that he or she has no disagreement in regard to the requested change;

(2) A statement from all assignees of the parties submitting a statement under paragraph (b)(1) of this section agreeing to the change of inventorship in the patent, which statement must comply with the requirements of §3.73(c) of this chapter; and

(3) The fee set forth in §1.20(b).

(c) For correction of inventorship in an application, see §1.48.

(d) In an interference under part 41, subpart D, of this title, a request for correction of inventorship in a patent must be in the form of a motion under §41.121(a)(2) of this title. In a contested case under part 42, subpart D, of this title, a request for correction of inventorship in a patent must be in the form of a motion under §42.22 of this title. The motion under §41.121(a)(2) or §42.22 of this title must comply with the requirements of this section.

History of 37 C.F.R. §1.324: 24 FR 10332, Dec. 22, 1959; 48 FR 2713, Jan. 20, 1983; 49 FR 48454, Dec. 12, 1984; 50 FR 23123, May 31, 1985; 62 FR 53199, Oct. 10, 1997; 65 FR 54677, Sept. 8, 2000; 69 FR 50001, Aug. 12, 2004; 69 FR 56545, Sept. 21, 2004; 70 FR 3891, Jan. 27, 2005; 77 FR 48822, Sept. 16, 2012.

§1.325. OTHER MISTAKES NOT CORRECTED

Mistakes other than those provided for in §§1.322, 1.323, 1.324, and not affording legal grounds for reissue or for reexamination, will not be corrected after the date of the patent.

History of 37 C.F.R. §1.325: 24 FR 10332, Dec. 22, 1959; 48 FR 2714, Jan. 20, 1983.

ARBITRATION AWARDS

§§1.331 TO 1.334. RESERVED

History of 37 C.F.R. §§1.331-1.334: 57 FR 29642, July 6, 1992.

§1.335. FILING OF NOTICE OF ARBITRATION AWARDS

(a) Written notice of any award by an arbitrator pursuant to 35 U.S.C. 294 must be filed in the Patent and Trademark Office by the patentee, or the patentee's assignee or licensee. If the award involves more than one patent a separate notice must be filed for placement in the file of each patent. The notice must set forth the patent number, the names of the inventor and patent owner, and the names and addresses of the parties to the arbitration. The notice must also include a copy of the award.

(b) If an award by an arbitrator pursuant to 35 U.S.C. 294 is modified by a court, the party requesting the modification must file in the Patent and Trademark Office, a notice of the modification for placement in the file of each patent to which the modification applies. The notice must set forth the patent number, the names of the inventor and patent owner, and the names and addresses of the parties to the arbitration. The notice must also include a copy of the court's order modifying the award.

(c) Any award by an arbitrator pursuant to 35 U.S.C. 294 shall be unenforceable until any notices required by paragraph (a) or (b) of this section are filed in the Patent and Trademark Office. If any required notice is not filed by the party designated in paragraph (a) or (b) of this section, any party to the arbitration proceeding may file such a notice.

History of 37 C.F.R. §1.335: 48 FR 2714, Jan. 20, 1983.

AMENDMENT OF RULES

§1.351. AMENDMENTS TO RULES WILL BE PUBLISHED

All amendments to the regulations in this part will be published in the Official Gazette and in the Federal Register.

§1.352. RESERVED

History of 37 C.F.R. §1.352: 62 FR 53199, Oct. 10, 1997.

MAINTENANCE FEES

A §1.362. TIME FOR PAYMENT OF MAINTENANCE FEES

(a) Maintenance fees as set forth in §§1.20(e) through (g) are required to be paid in all patents based on applications filed on or after December 12, 1980, except as noted in paragraph (b) of this section, to maintain a patent in force beyond 4, 8 and 12 years after the date of grant.

(b) Maintenance fees are not required for any plant patents or for any design patents.

(c) The application filing dates for purposes of payment of maintenance fees are as follows:

(1) For an application not claiming benefit of an earlier application, the actual United States filing date of the application.

(2) For an application claiming benefit of an earlier foreign application under 35 U.S.C. 119, the United States filing date of the application.

(3) For a continuing (continuation, division, continuation-in-part) application claiming the benefit of a prior patent application under 35 U.S.C. 120, the actual United States filing date of the continuing application.

(4) For a reissue application, including a continuing reissue application claiming the benefit of a reissue application under 35 U.S.C. 120, United States filing date of the original non-reissue application on which the patent reissued is based.

(5) For an international application which has entered the United States as a Designated Office under 35 U.S.C. 371, the international filing date granted under Article 11(1) of the Patent Cooperation Treaty which is considered to be the United States filing date under 35 U.S.C. 363.

(d) Maintenance fees may be paid in patents without surcharge during the periods extending respectively from:

(1) 3 years through 3 years and 6 months after grant for the first maintenance fee,

(2) 7 years through 7 years and 6 months after grant for the second maintenance fee, and

(3) 11 years through 11 years and 6 months after grant for the third maintenance fee.

(e) Maintenance fees may be paid with the surcharge set forth in §1.20(h) during the respective grace periods after:

(1) 3 years and 6 months and through the day of the 4th anniversary of the grant for the first maintenance fee.

(2) 7 years and 6 months and through the day of the 8th anniversary of the grant for the second maintenance fee, and

(3) 11 years and 6 months and through the day of the 12th anniversary of the grant for the third maintenance fee.

(f) If the last day for paying a maintenance fee without surcharge set forth in paragraph (d) of this section, or the last day for paying a maintenance fee with surcharge set forth in paragraph (e) of this section, falls on a Saturday, Sunday, or a federal holiday within the District of Columbia, the maintenance fee and any necessary surcharge may be paid under paragraph (d) or paragraph (e) respectively on the next succeeding day which is not a Saturday, Sunday, or federal holiday.

(g) Unless the maintenance fee and any applicable surcharge is paid within the time periods set forth in paragraphs (d), (e) or (f) of this section, the patent will expire as of the end of the grace period set forth in paragraph (e) of this section. A patent which expires for the failure to pay the maintenance fee will expire at the end of the same date (anniversary date) the patent was granted in the 4th, 8th, or 12th year after grant.

(h) The periods specified in §§1.362(d) and (e) with respect to a reissue application, including a continuing reissue application thereof, are counted from the date of grant of the original non-reissue application on which the reissued patent is based.

History of 37 C.F.R. §1.362: 49 FR 34724, Aug. 31, 1984; 56 FR 65154, Dec. 13, 1991; 58 FR 54511, Oct. 22, 1993; 82 FR 52816, Jan. 16, 2018.

§1.363. FEE ADDRESS FOR MAINTENANCE FEE PURPOSES

(a) All notices, receipts, refunds, and other communications relating to payment or refund of maintenance fees will be directed to the correspondence address used during prosecution of the application as indicated in §1.33(a) unless:

(1) A "fee address" for purposes of payment of maintenance fees is set forth when submitting the issue fee, or

(2) A change in the correspondence address for all purposes is filed after payment of the issue fee, or

(3) A "fee address" or a change in the "fee address" is filed for purposes of receiving notices, receipts and other correspondence relating to the payment of maintenance fees after the payment of the issue fee, in which instance, the latest such address will be used.

(b) An assignment of a patent application or patent does not result in a change of the "correspondence address" or "fee address" for maintenance fee purposes.

(c) A fee address must be an address associated with a Customer Number.

History of 37 C.F.R. §1.363: 49 FR 34725, Aug. 31, 1984; 69 FR 29878, May 26, 2004.

§1.366. SUBMISSION OF MAINTENANCE FEES

(a) The patentee may pay maintenance fees and any necessary surcharges, or any person or organization may pay maintenance fees and any necessary surcharges on behalf of a patentee. A maintenance fee transmittal letter may be signed by a juristic applicant or patent owner. A patentee need not file authorization to enable any person or organization to pay maintenance fees and any necessary surcharges on behalf of the patentee.

(b) A maintenance fee and any necessary surcharge submitted for a patent must be submitted in the amount due on the date the maintenance fee and any necessary surcharge are paid. A maintenance fee or surcharge may be paid in the manner set forth in §1.23 or by an authorization to charge a deposit account established pursuant to §1.25. Payment of a maintenance fee and any necessary surcharge or the authorization to charge a deposit account must be submitted within the periods set forth in §1.362(d), (e), or (f). Any payment or authorization of maintenance fees and surcharges filed at any other time will not be accepted and will not serve as a payment of the maintenance fee except insofar as a delayed payment of the maintenance fee is accepted by the Director in an expired patent pursuant to a petition filed under §1.378. Any authorization to charge a deposit account must authorize the immediate charging of the maintenance fee and any necessary surcharge to the deposit account. Payment of less than the required amount, payment in a manner other than that set forth in §1.23, or in the filing of an authorization to charge a deposit account having insufficient funds will not constitute payment of a maintenance fee or surcharge on a patent. The procedures set forth in §1.8 or §1.10 may be utilized in paying maintenance fees and any necessary surcharges.

(c) In submitting maintenance fees and any necessary surcharges, identification of the patents for which maintenance fees are being paid must include the patent number, and the application number of the United States application for the patent on which the maintenance fee is being paid. If the payment includes identification of only the patent number (*i.e.*, does not identify the application number of the United States application for the patent on which the maintenance fee is being paid), the Office may apply the payment to the patent identified by patent number in the payment or may return the payment.

(d) Payment of maintenance fees and any surcharges should identify the fee being paid for each patent as to whether it is the 3½-, 7½-, or 11½-year fee, whether small entity status is being changed or claimed, the amount of the maintenance fee and any surcharge being paid, and any assigned customer number. If the maintenance fee and any necessary surcharge is being paid on a reissue patent, the payment must identify the reissue patent by reissue patent number and reissue application number as required by paragraph (c) of this section and should also include the original patent number.

(e) Maintenance fee payments and surcharge payments relating thereto must be submitted separate from any other payments for fees or charges, whether submitted in the manner set forth in §1.23 or by an authorization to charge a deposit account. If maintenance fee and surcharge payments for more than one patent are submitted together, they should be submitted on as few sheets as possible with the patent numbers listed in increasing patent number order. If the payment submitted is insufficient to cover the maintenance fees and surcharges for all the listed patents, the payment will be applied in the order the patents are listed, beginning at the top of the listing.

(f) Notification of any change in status resulting in loss of entitlement to small entity status must be filed in a patent prior to paying, or at the time of paying, the earliest maintenance fee due after the date on which status as a small entity is no longer appropriate. See §1.27(g).

(g) Maintenance fees and surcharges relating thereto will not be refunded except in accordance with §§1.26 and 1.28(a).

History of 37 C.F.R. §1.366: 49 FR 34725, Aug. 31, 1984; 58 FR 54503, Oct. 22, 1993; 62 FR 53199, Oct. 10, 1997; 65 FR 54677, Sept. 8, 2000; 65 FR 78958, Dec. 18, 2000; 78 FR 62406, Dec. 18, 2013.

§1.377. REVIEW OF DECISION REFUSING TO ACCEPT & RECORD PAYMENT OF A MAINTENANCE FEE FILED PRIOR TO EXPIRATION OF PATENT

(a) Any patentee who is dissatisfied with the refusal of the Patent and Trademark Office to accept and record a maintenance fee which was filed prior to the expiration of the patent may petition the Director to accept and record the maintenance fee.

(b) Any petition under this section must be filed within two months of the action complained of, or within such other time as may be set in the action complained of, and must be accompanied by the fee set forth in §1.17(g). The petition may include a request that the petition fee be refunded if the refusal to accept and record the maintenance fee is determined to result from an error by the Patent and Trademark Office.

(c) Any petition filed under this section must comply with the requirements of §1.181(b) and must be signed by an attorney or agent registered to practice before the Patent and Trademark Office, or by the patentee, the assignee, or other party in interest.

History of 37 C.F.R. §1.377: 49 FR 34725, Aug. 31, 1984; 62 FR 53199, Oct. 10, 1997; 69 FR 56545, Sept. 21, 2004.

§1.378. ACCEPTANCE OF DELAYED PAYMENT OF MAINTENANCE FEE IN EXPIRED PATENT TO REINSTATE PATENT

(a) The Director may accept the payment of any maintenance fee due on a patent after expiration of the patent if, upon petition, the delay in payment of the maintenance fee is shown to the satisfaction of the Director to have been unintentional. If the Director accepts payment of the maintenance fee upon petition, the patent shall be considered as not having expired, but will be subject to the conditions set forth in 35 U.S.C. 41(c)(2).

(b) Any petition to accept an unintentionally delayed payment of a maintenance fee must include:

(1) The required maintenance fee set forth in §1.20(e) through (g);

(2) The petition fee as set forth in §1.17(m); and

(3) A statement that the delay in payment of the maintenance fee was unintentional. The Director may require additional information where there is a question whether the delay was unintentional.

(c) Any petition under this section must be signed in compliance with §1.33(b).

(d) Reconsideration of a decision refusing to accept a delayed maintenance fee may be obtained by filing a petition for reconsideration within two months of the decision, or such other time as set in the decision refusing to accept the delayed payment of the maintenance fee.

(e) If the delayed payment of the maintenance fee is not accepted, the maintenance fee will be refunded following the decision on the petition for reconsideration, or after the expiration of the time for filing such a petition for reconsideration, if none is filed.

History of 37 C.F.R. §1.378: 49 FR 34726, Aug. 31, 1984; 50 FR 9383, Mar. 7, 1985; 53 FR 47810, Nov. 28, 1988; 56 FR 65154, Dec. 13, 1991; 57 FR 56450, Nov. 30, 1992; 58 FR 44282, Aug. 20, 1993; 62 FR 53199, Oct. 10, 1997; 69 FR 56545, Sept. 21, 2004; 78 FR 62407, Dec. 18, 2013.

SUBPART C. INTERNATIONAL PROCESSING PROVISIONS

GENERAL INFORMATION

§1.401. DEFINITIONS OF TERMS UNDER THE PATENT COOPERATION TREATY

(a) The abbreviation "PCT" and the term "Treaty" mean the Patent Cooperation Treaty.

(b) "International Bureau" means the World Intellectual Property Organization located in Geneva, Switzerland.

(c) "Administrative Instructions" means that body of instructions for operating under the Patent Cooperation Treaty referred to in PCT Rule 89.

(d) "Request," when capitalized, means that element of the international application described in PCT Rules 3 and 4.

(e) "International application," as used in this subchapter is defined in §1.9(b).

(f) "Priority date" for the purpose of computing time limits under the Patent Cooperation Treaty is defined in PCT Art. 2(xi). Note also §1.465.

(g) "Demand," when capitalized, means that document filed with the International Preliminary Examining Authority which requests an international preliminary examination.

(h) "Annexes" means amendments made to the claims, description or the drawings before the International Preliminary Examining Authority.

(i) Other terms and expressions in this Subpart C not defined in this section are to be taken in the sense indicated in PCT Art. 2 and 35 U.S.C. 351.

History of 37 C.F.R. §1.401: 52 FR 20047, May 28, 1987.

Source of 37 C.F.R. Part 1C: 24 FR 10332, Dec. 22, 1959; 43 FR 20466, May 11, 1978; 52 FR 20047, May 28, 1987; 60 FR 14518, Mar. 17, 1995; 65 FR 14871, Mar. 20, 2000; 65 FR 33455, May 24, 2000; 65 FR 50103, Aug. 16, 2000; 65 FR 56793, Sept. 20, 2000; 65 FR 70490, Nov. 24, 2000, unless otherwise noted.

§1.412. THE UNITED STATES RECEIVING OFFICE

(a) The United States Patent and Trademark Office is a Receiving Office only for applicants who are residents or nationals of the United States of America.

(b) The Patent and Trademark Office, when acting as a Receiving Office, will be identified by the full title "United States Receiving Office" or by the abbreviation "RO/US."

(c) The major functions of the Receiving Office include:

(1) According of international filing dates to international applications meeting the requirements of PCT Art. 11(1), and PCT Rule 20;

(2) Assuring that international applications meet the standards for format and content of PCT Art. 14(1), PCT Rule 9, 26, 29.1, 37, 38, 91, and portions of PCT Rules 3 through 11;

(3) Collecting and, when required, transmitting fees due for processing international applications (PCT Rule 14, 15, 16);

(4) Transmitting the record and search copies to the International Bureau and International Searching Authority, respectively (PCT Rules 22 and 23); and

(5) Determining compliance with applicable requirements of Part 5 of this chapter.

(6) Reviewing and, unless prescriptions concerning national security prevent the application from being so transmitted (PCT Rule 19.4), transmitting the international application to the International Bureau for processing in its capacity as a Receiving Office:

(i) Where the United States Receiving Office is not the competent Receiving Office under PCT Rule 19.1 or 19.2 and §1.421(a); or

(ii) Where the international application is not in English but is in a language accepted under PCT Rule 12.1(a) by the International Bureau as a Receiving Office; or

(iii) Where there is agreement and authorization in accordance with PCT Rule 19.4(a)(iii).

History of 37 C.F.R. §1.412: 60 FR 21439, May 2, 1995; 63 FR 29617, June 1, 1998; 63 FR 66041, Dec. 1, 1998.

§1.413. THE UNITED STATES INTERNATIONAL SEARCHING AUTHORITY

(a) Pursuant to appointment by the Assembly, the United States Patent and Trademark Office will act as an International Searching Authority for international applications filed in the United States Receiving Office and in other Receiving Offices as may be agreed upon by the Director, in accordance with the agreement between the Patent and Trademark Office and the International Bureau (PCT Art. 16(3)(b)).

(b) The Patent and Trademark Office, when acting as an International Searching Authority, will be identified by the full title "United States International Searching Authority" or by the abbreviation "ISA/US."

(c) The major functions of the International Searching Authority include:

(1) Approving or establishing the title and abstract;

(2) Considering the matter of unity of invention;

(3) Conducting international and international-type searches and preparing international and international-type search reports (PCT Art. 15, 17 and 18, and PCT Rules 25, 33 to 45 and 47), and issuing declarations that no international search report will be established (PCT Article 17(2)(a));

(4) Preparing written opinions of the International Searching Authority in accordance with PCT Rule 43*bis* (when necessary); and

(5) Transmitting the international search report and the written opinion of the International Searching Authority to the applicant and the International Bureau.

History of 37 C.F.R. §1.413: 68 FR 59886, Oct. 20, 2003.

§1.414. THE UNITED STATES PATENT & TRADEMARK OFFICE AS A DESIGNATED OFFICE OR ELECTED OFFICE

(a) The United States Patent and Trademark Office will act as a Designated Office or Elected Office for international applications in which the United States of America has been designated or elected as a State in which patent protection is desired.

(b) The United States Patent and Trademark Office, when acting as a Designated Office or Elected Office during international processing will be identified by the full title "United States Designated Office" or by the abbreviation "DO/US" or by the full title "United States Elected Office" or by the abbreviation "EO/US."

(c) The major functions of the United States Designated Office or Elected Office in respect to international applications in which the United States of America has been designated or elected, include:

(1) Receiving various notifications throughout the international stage and

(2) National stage processing for international applications entering the national stage under 35 U.S.C. 371.

History of 37 C.F.R. §1.414: 52 FR 20047, May 28, 1987; 77 FR 48823, Sept. 16, 2012.

§1.415. THE INTERNATIONAL BUREAU

(a) The International Bureau is the World Intellectual Property Organization located at Geneva, Switzerland. It is the international intergovernmental organization which acts as the coordinating body under the Treaty and the Regulations (PCT Art. 2(xix) and 35 U.S.C. 351(h)).

(b) The major functions of the International Bureau include:

(1) Publishing of international applications and the International Gazette;

(2) Transmitting copies of international applications to Designated Offices;

(3) Storing and maintaining record copies; and

(4) Transmitting information to authorities pertinent to the processing of specific international applications.

§1.416. THE UNITED STATES INTERNATIONAL PRELIMINARY EXAMINING AUTHORITY

(a) Pursuant to appointment by the Assembly, the United States Patent and Trademark Office will act as an International Preliminary Examining Authority for international applications filed in the United States Receiving Office and in other Receiving Offices as may be agreed upon by the Director, in accordance with agreement between the Patent and Trademark Office and the International Bureau.

(b) The United States Patent and Trademark Office, when acting as an International Preliminary Examining Authority, will be identified by the full title "United States International Preliminary Examining Authority" or by the abbreviation "IPEA/US."

(c) The major functions of the International Preliminary Examining Authority include:

(1) Receiving and checking for defects in the Demand;

(2) Forwarding Demands in accordance with PCT Rule 59.3;

(3) Collecting the handling fee for the International Bureau and the preliminary examination fee for the United States International Preliminary Examining Authority;

(4) Informing applicant of receipt of the Demand;

(5) Considering the matter of unity of invention;

(6) Providing an international preliminary examination report which is a non-binding opinion on the questions of whether the claimed invention appears: to be novel, to involve an inventive step (to be nonobvious), and to be industrially applicable; and

(7) Transmitting the international preliminary examination report to applicant and the International Bureau.

History of 37 C.F.R. §1.416: 52 FR 20047, May 28, 1987; 63 FR 29617, June 1, 1998; 63 FR 66041, Dec. 1, 1998.

§1.417. SUBMISSION OF TRANSLATION OF INTERNATIONAL PUBLICATION

The submission of an English language translation of the publication of an international application pursuant to 35 U.S.C. 154(d)(4) must clearly identify the international application to which it pertains (§1.5(a)) and be clearly identified as a submission pursuant to 35 U.S.C. 154(d)(4). Otherwise, the submission will be treated as a filing under 35 U.S.C. 111(a). Such submissions should be marked "Mail Stop PCT."

History of 37 C.F.R. §1.417: 68 FR 14337, Mar. 25, 2003; 68 FR 71007, Dec. 22, 2003.

§1.419. DISPLAY OF CURRENTLY VALID CONTROL NUMBER UNDER THE PAPERWORK REDUCTION ACT

(a) Pursuant to the Paperwork Reduction Act of 1995 (44 U.S.C. 3501 et seq.), the collection of information in this subpart has been reviewed and approved by the Office of Management and Budget under control number 0651-0021.

(b) Notwithstanding any other provision of law, no person is required to respond to nor shall a person be subject to a penalty for failure to comply with a collection of information subject to the requirements of the Paperwork Reduction Act unless that collection of information displays a currently valid Office of Management and Budget control number. This section constitutes the display required by 44 U.S.C. 3512(a) and 5 CFR 1320.5(b)(2)(i) for the collection of information under Office of Management and Budget control number 0651-0021 (see 5 CFR 1320.5(b)(2)(ii)(D)).

History of 37 C.F.R. §1.419: 63 FR 29617, June 1, 1998; 63 FR 66041, Dec. 1, 1998.

WHO MAY FILE AN INTERNATIONAL APPLICATION

§1.421. APPLICANT FOR INTERNATIONAL APPLICATION

(a) Only residents or nationals of the United States of America may file international applications in the United States Receiving Office. If an international application does not include an applicant who is indicated as being a resident or national of the United States of America, and at least one applicant:

(1) Has indicated a residence or nationality in a PCT Contracting State, or

(2) Has no residence or nationality indicated, applicant will be so notified and, if the international application includes a fee amount equivalent to that required by §1.445(a)(4), the international application will be forwarded for processing to the International Bureau acting as a Receiving Office (see also §1.412(c)(6)).

(b) Although the United States Receiving Office will accept international applications filed by any applicant who is a resident or national of the United States of America for international processing, for the purposes of the designation of the United States, an international application will be accepted by the Patent and Trademark Office for the national stage only if the applicant is the inventor or other person as provided in §1.422 or §1.424. Joint inventors must jointly apply for an international application.

(c) A registered attorney or agent of the applicant may sign the international application Request and file the international application for the applicant. A separate power of attorney from each applicant may be required.

(d) Any indication of different applicants for the purpose of different Designated Offices must be shown on the Request portion of the international application.

(e) Requests for changes in the indications concerning the applicant, agent, or common representative of an international application shall be made in accordance with PCT Rule 92*bis* and may be required to be signed by all applicants.

(f) Requests for withdrawals of the international application, designations, priority claims, the Demand, or elections shall be made in accordance with PCT Rule 90*bis* and must be signed by all applicants. A separate power of attorney from the applicants will be required for the purposes of any request for a withdrawal in accordance with PCT Rule 90*bis* which is not signed by all applicants.

History of 37 C.F.R. §1.421: 53 FR 47810, Nov. 28, 1988; 60 FR 21440, May 2, 1995; 68 FR 59887, Oct. 20, 2003; 68 FR 67805, Dec. 4, 2003; 77 FR 48823, Sept. 16, 2012.

§1.422. LEGAL REPRESENTATIVE AS APPLICANT IN AN INTERNATIONAL APPLICATION

If an inventor is deceased or under legal incapacity, the legal representative of the inventor may be an applicant in an international application which designates the United States of America.

History of 37 C.F.R. §1.422: 77 FR 48823, Sept. 16, 2012.

§1.423. REMOVED & RESERVED

History of 37 C.F.R. §1.423: 77 FR 48823, Sept. 16, 2012.

§1.424. ASSIGNEE, OBLIGATED ASSIGNEE, OR PERSON HAVING SUFFICIENT PROPRIETARY INTEREST AS APPLICANT IN AN INTERNATIONAL APPLICATION

(a) A person to whom the inventor has assigned or is under an obligation to assign the invention may be an applicant in an international application which designates the

United States of America. A person who otherwise shows sufficient proprietary interest in the matter may be an applicant in an international application which designates the United States of America on proof of the pertinent facts and a showing that such action is appropriate to preserve the rights of the parties.

(b) Neither any showing required under paragraph (a) of this section nor documentary evidence of ownership or proprietary interest will be required or considered by the Office in the international stage, but will be required in the national stage in accordance with the conditions and requirements of §1.46.

History of 37 C.F.R. §1.424: 77 FR 48823, Sept. 16, 2012.

§1.425. RESERVED

History of 37 C.F.R. §1.425: 68 FR 59887, Oct. 20, 2003.

THE INTERNATIONAL APPLICATION

§1.431. INTERNATIONAL APPLICATION REQUIREMENTS

(a) An international application shall contain, as specified in the Treaty and the Regulations, a Request, a description, one or more claims, an abstract, and one or more drawings (where required). (PCT Art. 3(2) and Section 207 of the Administrative Instructions.)

(b) An international filing date will be accorded by the United States Receiving Office, at the time to receipt of the international application, provided that:

(1) At least one applicant (§1.421) is a United States resident or national and the papers filed at the time of receipt of the international application so indicate (35 U.S.C. 361(a), PCT Art. 11(1)(i)).

(2) The international application is in the English language (35 U.S.C. 361(c), PCT Art. 11(1)(ii)).

(3) The international application contains at least the following elements (PCT Art. 11(1)(iii)):

(i) An indication that it is intended as an international application (PCT Rule 4.2);

(ii) The designation of at least one Contracting State of the International Patent Cooperation Union (§1.432);

(iii) The name of the applicant, as prescribed (note §§1.421, 1.422, and 1.424);

(iv) A part which on the face of it appears to be a description; and

(v) A part which on the face of it appears to be a claim.

(c) Payment of the international filing fee (PCT Rule 15.2) and the transmittal and search fees (§1.445) may be made in full at the time the international application papers required by paragraph (b) of this section are deposited or within one month thereafter. The international filing, transmittal, and search fee payable is the international filing, transmittal, and search fee in effect on the receipt date of the international application.

(1) If the international filing, transmittal and search fees are not paid within one month from the date of receipt of the international application and prior to the sending of a notice of deficiency which imposes a late payment fee, applicant will be notified and given one month within which to pay the deficient fees plus the late payment fee. Subject to paragraph (c)(2) of this section, the late payment fee will be equal to the greater of:

(i) Fifty percent of the amount of the deficient fees; or

(ii) An amount equal to the transmittal fee;

(2) The late payment fee shall not exceed an amount equal to fifty percent of the international filing fee not taking into account any fee for each sheet of the international application in excess of thirty sheets (PCT Rule 16*bis*).

(3) The one-month time limit set pursuant to paragraph (c) of this section to pay deficient fees may not be extended.

(d) If the payment needed to cover the transmittal fee, the international filing fee, the search fee, and the late payment fee pursuant to paragraph (c) of this section is not timely made in accordance with PCT Rule 16*bis*.1(e), the Receiving Office will declare the international application withdrawn under PCT Article 14(3)(a).

History of 37 C.F.R. §1.431: 50 FR 9383, Mar. 7, 1985; 52 FR 20047, May 28, 1987; 58 FR 4344, Jan. 14, 1993; 63 FR 29618, June 1, 1998; 63 FR 66041, Dec. 1, 1998; 68 FR 59887, Oct. 20, 2003; 68 FR 67805, Dec. 4, 2003; 77 FR 48823, Sept. 16, 2012.

§1.432. DESIGNATION OF STATES BY FILING AN INTERNATIONAL APPLICATION

The filing of an international application request shall constitute:

(a) The designation of all Contracting States that are bound by the Treaty on the international filing date;

(b) An indication that the international application is, in respect of each designated State to which PCT Article 43 or 44 applies, for the grant of every kind of protection which is available by way of the designation of that State; and

(c) An indication that the international application is, in respect of each designated State to which PCT Article 45(1) applies, for the grant of a regional patent and also, unless PCT Article 45(2) applies, a national patent.

History of 37 C.F.R. §1.432: 52 FR 20047, May 28, 1987; 58 FR 4344, Jan. 14, 1993; 63 FR 29618, June 1, 1998; 63 FR 66041, Dec. 1, 1998; 68 FR 59887, Oct. 20, 2003.

§1.433. PHYSICAL REQUIREMENTS OF INTERNATIONAL APPLICATION

(a) The international application and each of the documents that may be referred to in the check list of the Request (PCT Rule 3.3(a)(ii)) shall be filed in one copy only.

(b) All sheets of the international application must be on A4 size paper (21.0 x 29.7 cm.).

(c) Other physical requirements for international applications are set forth in PCT Rule 11 and Sections 201-207 of the Administrative Instructions.

§1.434. THE REQUEST

(a) The request shall be made on a standardized form (PCT Rules 3 and 4). Copies of printed Request forms are available from the United States Patent and Trademark Office. Letters requesting printed forms should be marked "Mail Stop PCT."

(b) The Check List portion of the Request form should indicate each document accompanying the international application on filing.

(c) All information, for example, addresses, names of States and dates, shall be indicated in the Request as required by PCT Rule 4 and Administrative Instructions 110 and 201.

(d) For the purposes of the designation of the United States of America, an international application shall include:

(1) The name of the inventor; and

(2) A reference to any prior-filed national application or international application designating the United States of America, if the benefit of the filing date for the prior-filed application is to be claimed.

(e) An international application may also include in the Request a declaration of the inventors as provided for in PCT Rule 4.17(iv).

History of 37 C.F.R. §1.434: 58 FR 4345, Jan. 14, 1993; 66 FR 16006, Mar. 22, 2001; 66 FR 67096, Dec. 28, 2001; 68 FR 14337, Mar. 25, 2003; 68 FR 59887, Oct. 20, 2003.

§1.435. THE DESCRIPTION

(a) The application must meet the requirements as to the content and form of the description set forth in PCT Rules 5, 9, 10, and 11 and sections 204 and 208 of the Administrative Instructions.

(b) In international applications designating the United States the description must contain upon filing an indication of the best mode contemplated by the inventor for carrying out the claimed invention.

History of 37 C.F.R. §1.435: 63 FR 29618, June 1, 1998; 63 FR 66041, Dec. 1, 1998.

§1.436. THE CLAIMS

The requirements as to the content and format of claims are set forth in PCT Art. 6 and PCT Rules 6, 9, 10 and 11 and shall be adhered to. The number of the claims shall be reasonable, considering the nature of the invention claimed.

§1.437. THE DRAWINGS

(a) Drawings are required when they are necessary for the understanding of the invention (PCT Art. 7).

(b) The physical requirements for drawings are set forth in PCT Rule 11 and shall be adhered to.

History of 37 C.F.R. §1.437: 72 FR 51536, Sept. 10, 2007.

§1.438. THE ABSTRACT

(a) Requirements as to the content and form of the abstract are set forth in PCT Rule 8, and shall be adhered to.

(b) Lack of an abstract upon filing of an international application will not affect the granting of a filing date. However, failure to furnish an abstract within one month from the date of the notification by the Receiving Office will result in the international application being declared withdrawn.

FEES

Ⓐ §1.445. INTERNATIONAL APPLICATION FILING, PROCESSING & SEARCH FEES

(a) The following fees and charges for international applications are established by law or by the Director under the authority of 35 U.S.C. 376:

(1) A transmittal fee (see 35 U.S.C. 361(d) and PCT Rule 14) consisting of:

(i) A basic portion:

(A) For an international application having a receipt date that is on or after January 1, 2014:

By a micro entity (§1.29)—$60.00

By a small entity (§1.27(a))—$120.00

By other than a small or micro entity—$240.00

(B) For an international application having a receipt date that is before January 1, 2014—$240.00.

(ii) A non-electronic filing fee portion for any international application designating the United States of America that is filed on or after November 15, 2011, other than by the Office electronic filing system, except for a plant application:

By a small entity (§1.27(a))—$200.00

By other than a small entity—$400.00

(2) A search fee (see 35 U.S.C. 361(d) and PCT Rule 16):

(i) For an international application having a receipt date that is on or after January 1, 2014:

By a micro entity (§1.29)—$520.00

By a small entity (§1.27(a))—$1,040.00

By other than a small or micro entity—$2,080.00

(ii) For an international application having a receipt date that is before January 1, 2014—$2,080.00.

(3) A supplemental search fee when required, per additional invention:

(i) For an international application having a receipt date that is on or after January 1, 2014:

By a micro entity (§1.29)—$520.00

By a small entity (§1.27(a))—$1,040.00

By other than a small or micro entity—$2,080.00

(ii) For an international application having a receipt date that is before January 1, 2014—$2,080.00.

(4) A fee equivalent to the transmittal fee in paragraph (a)(1) of this section that would apply if the USPTO was the Receiving Office for transmittal of an international application to the International Bureau for processing in its capacity as a Receiving Office (PCT Rule 19.4).

(5) Late furnishing fee for providing a sequence listing in response to an invitation under PCT Rule 13*ter*:

By a micro entity (§1.29)—$75.00

By a small entity (§1.27(a))—$150.00

By other than a small or micro entity—$300.00

(b) The international filing fee shall be as prescribed in PCT Rule 15.

History of 37 C.F.R. §1.445: 43 FR 20466, May 11, 1978; 47 FR 41282, Sept. 17, 1982; 50 FR 9384, Mar. 7, 1985; 50 FR 31826, Aug. 6, 1985; 52 FR 20047, May 28, 1987; 54 FR 6903, Feb. 15, 1989; 54 FR 9432, Mar. 7, 1989; 56 FR 65154, Dec. 13, 1991; 57 FR 38195, Aug. 21, 1992; 57 FR 40493, Sept. 3, 1992; 58 FR 4345, Jan. 14, 1993; 59 FR 43741, Aug. 25, 1994; 60 FR 21440, May 2, 1995; 60 FR 41023, Aug. 11, 1995; 61 FR 39588, July 30, 1996; 62 FR 40453, July 29, 1997; 63 FR 29618, June 1, 1998; 63 FR 66041, Dec. 1, 1998; 68 FR 59888, Oct. 20, 2003; 70 FR 3891, Jan. 27, 2005; 72 FR 51563, Sept. 10, 2007; 73 FR 66759, Jan. 12, 2009; 76 FR 70653, Nov. 15, 2011; 78 FR 4289, Mar. 19, 2013; 78 FR 17107, Mar. 20, 2013; 82 FR 52816, Jan. 16, 2018.

§1.446. REFUND OF INTERNATIONAL APPLICATION FILING & PROCESSING FEES

(a) Money paid for international application fees, where paid by actual mistake or in excess, such as a payment not required by law or treaty and its regulations, may be refunded. A mere change of purpose after the payment of a fee will not entitle a party to a refund of such fee. The Office will not refund amounts of twenty-five dollars or less unless a refund is specifically requested and will not notify the payor of such amounts. If the payor or party requesting a refund does not provide the banking information necessary for making refunds by electronic funds transfer, the Office may use the banking information provided on the payment instrument to make any refund by electronic funds transfer.

(b) Any request for refund under paragraph (a) of this section must be filed within two years from the date the fee was paid. If the Office charges a deposit account by an amount other than an amount specifically indicated in an authorization under §1.25(b), any request for refund based upon such charge must be filed within two years from the date of the deposit account statement indicating such charge and include a copy of that deposit account statement. The time periods set forth in this paragraph are not extendable.

(c) Refund of the supplemental search fees will be made if such refund is determined to be warranted by the Director or the Director's designee acting under PCT Rule 40.2(c).

(d) The international and search fees will be refunded if no international filing date is accorded or if the application is withdrawn before transmittal of the record copy to the International Bureau (PCT Rules 15.6 and 16.2). The search fee will be refunded if the application is withdrawn before transmittal of the search copy to the International Searching Authority. The transmittal fee will not be refunded.

(e) The handling fee (§1.482(b)) will be refunded (PCT Rule 57.6) only if:

(1) The Demand is withdrawn before the Demand has been sent by the International Preliminary Examining Authority to the International Bureau, or

(2) The Demand is considered not to have been submitted (PCT Rule 54.4(a)).

History of 37 C.F.R. §1.446: 43 FR 20466, May 11, 1978; 47 FR 41282, Sept. 17, 1982; 50 FR 9384, Mar. 7, 1985; 50 FR 31826, Aug. 6, 1985; 58 FR 4345, Jan. 14, 1993; 65 FR 54677, Sept. 8, 2000.

PRIORITY

§1.451. THE PRIORITY CLAIM & PRIORITY DOCUMENT IN AN INTERNATIONAL APPLICATION

(a) The claim for priority must, subject to paragraph (d) of this section, be made on the Request (PCT Rule 4.10) in a manner complying with sections 110 and 115 of the Administrative Instructions.

(b) Whenever the priority of an earlier United States national application or international application filed with the United States Receiving Office is claimed in an international application, the applicant may request in the Request or in a letter of transmittal accompanying the international application upon filing with the United States Receiving Office or in a separate letter filed in the United States Receiving Office not later than 16 months after the priority date, that the United States Patent and Trademark Office prepare a certified copy of the prior application for transmittal to the International Bureau (PCT Article 8 and PCT Rule 17). The fee for preparing a certified copy is set forth in §1.19(b)(1).

(c) If a certified copy of the priority document is not submitted together with the international application on filing, or, if the priority application was filed in the United States and a request and appropriate payment for preparation of such a certified copy do not accompany the international application on filing or are not filed within 16 months of the priority date, the certified copy of the priority document must be furnished by the applicant to the International Bureau or to the United States Receiving Office within the time limit specified in PCT Rule 17.1(a).

(d) The applicant may correct or add a priority claim in accordance with PCT Rule 26*bis*.1.

History of 37 C.F.R. §1.451: 43 FR 20466, May 11, 1978; 47 FR 41282, Sept. 17, 1982; 50 FR 9384, Mar. 7, 1985; 50 FR 11366, Mar. 21, 1985; 54 FR 6903, Feb. 15, 1989; 58 FR 4345, Jan. 14, 1993; 63 FR 29619, June 1, 1998; 63 FR 66041, Dec. 1, 1998; 66 FR 16006, Mar. 22, 2001.

§1.452. RESTORATION OF RIGHT OF PRIORITY

(a) If the international application has an international filing date which is later than the expiration of the priority period as defined by PCT Rule 2.4 but within two months from the expiration of the priority period, the right of priority in the international application may be restored upon request if the delay in filing the international application within the priority period was unintentional.

(b) A request to restore the right of priority in an international application under paragraph (a) of this section must be filed not later than two months from the expiration of the priority period and must include:

(1) A notice under PCT Rule 26*bis*.1(a) adding the priority claim, if the priority claim in respect of the earlier application is not contained in the international application;

(2) The petition fee as set forth in §1.17(m); and

(3) A statement that the delay in filing the international application within the priority period was unintentional. The Director may require additional information where there is a question whether the delay was unintentional.

(c) If the applicant makes a request for early publication under PCT Article 21(2)(b), any requirement under paragraph (b) of this section filed after the technical preparations for international publication have been completed by the International Bureau shall be considered as not having been submitted in time.

History of 37 C.F.R. §1.452: 72 FR 51563, Nov. 9, 2007; 78 FR 62407, Dec. 18, 2013.

E §1.453. TRANSMITTAL OF DOCUMENTS RELATING TO EARLIER SEARCH OR CLASSIFICATION

(a) Subject to paragraph (c) of this section, where an applicant has requested in an international application filed with the United States Receiving Office pursuant to PCT Rule 4.12 that an International Searching Authority take into account the results of an earlier search, the United States Receiving Office shall prepare and transmit to the International Searching Authority, as applicable, a copy of the results of the earlier search and any earlier classification as provided under PCT Rule 23*bis*.1.

(b) Subject to paragraph (c) of this section, where an international application filed with the United States Receiving Office claims the priority of an earlier application filed with the USPTO in which the USPTO has carried out an earlier search or has classified such earlier application, the United States Receiving Office shall prepare and transmit to the International Searching Authority a copy of the results of any such earlier search and earlier classification as provided under PCT Rule 23*bis*.2.

(c) The United States Receiving Office will not prepare a copy of the results of an earlier search or earlier classification referred to in paragraphs (a) and (b) of this section for transmittal to an International Searching Authority from an application preserved in confidence (§1.14) unless the international application contains written authority granting the International Searching Authority access to such results. Written authority provided under this paragraph must be signed by:

(1) An applicant in the international application who is also an applicant in the application preserved in confidence; or

(2) A person set forth in §1.14(c) permitted to grant access to the application preserved in confidence.

History of 37 C.F.R. §1.453: 82 FR 24252, July 1, 2017.

REPRESENTATION

§1.455. REPRESENTATION IN INTERNATIONAL APPLICATIONS

(a) Applicants of international applications may be represented by attorneys or agents registered to practice before the United States Patent and Trademark Office or by an applicant appointed as a common representative (PCT Art. 49, Rules 4.8 and 90 and §11.9). If applicants have not appointed an attorney or agent or one of the applicants to represent them, and there is more than one applicant, the applicant first named in the request and who is entitled to file in the U.S. Receiving Office shall be considered to be the common representative of all the applicants. An attorney or agent having the right to practice before a national office with which an international application is filed and for which the United States is an International Searching Authority or International Preliminary Examining Authority may be appointed to represent the applicants in the international application before that authority. An attorney or agent may appoint an associate attorney or agent who shall also then be of record (PCT Rule 90.1(d)). The appointment of an attorney or agent, or of a common representative, revokes any earlier appointment unless otherwise indicated (PCT Rule 90.6(b) and (c)).

(b) Appointment of an agent, attorney or common representative (PCT Rule 4.8) must be effected either in the Request form, signed by applicant, in the Demand form, signed by applicant, or in a separate power of attorney submitted either to the United States Receiving Office or to the International Bureau.

(c) Powers of attorney and revocations thereof should be submitted to the United States Receiving Office until the issuance of the international search report.

(d) The addressee for correspondence will be as indicated in Section 108 of the Administrative Instructions.

History of 37 C.F.R. §1.455: 50 FR 5171, Feb. 6, 1985; 58 FR 4345, Jan. 14, 1993; 68 FR 59888, Oct. 20, 2003; 69 FR 35452, June 24, 2004.

TRANSMITTAL OF RECORD COPY

§1.461. PROCEDURES FOR TRANSMITTAL OF RECORD COPY TO THE INTERNATIONAL BUREAU

(a) Transmittal of the record copy of the international application to the International Bureau shall be made by the United States Receiving Office or as provided by PCT Rule 19.4.

(b) [Reserved]

(c) No copy of an international application may be transmitted to the International Bureau, a foreign Designated Office, or other foreign authority by the United States Receiving Office or the applicant, unless the applicable requirements of Part 5 of this chapter have been satisfied.

History of 37 C.F.R. §1.461: 50 FR 9384, Mar. 7, 1985; 63 FR 29619, June 1, 1998; 63 FR 66041, Dec. 1, 1998.

TIMING

§1.465. TIMING OF APPLICATION PROCESSING BASED ON THE PRIORITY DATE

(a) For the purpose of computing time limits under the Treaty, the priority date shall be defined as in PCT Art. 2(xi).

(b) When a claimed priority date is corrected under PCT Rule 26*bis*.1(a), or a priority claim is added under PCT Rule 26*bis*.1(a), withdrawn under PCT Rule 90*bis*.3, or considered not to have been made under PCT Rule 26*bis*.2, the priority date for the purposes of computing any non-expired time limits will be the filing date of the earliest remaining priority claim under PCT Article 8 of the international application, or if none, the international filing date.

(c) When corrections under PCT Art. 11(2), Art. 14(2) or PCT Rule 20.2(a)(i) or (iii) are timely submitted, and the date of receipt of such corrections falls later than one year from the claimed priority date or dates, the Receiving Office shall proceed under PCT Rule 26*bis*.2.

History of 37 C.F.R. §1.465: 63 FR 29619, June 1, 1998; 63 FR 66041, Dec. 1, 1998; 72 FR 51564, Sept. 10, 2007.

§1.468. DELAYS IN MEETING TIME LIMITS

Delays in meeting time limits during international processing of international applications may only be excused as provided in PCT Rule 82. For delays in meeting time limits in a national application, see §1.137.

AMENDMENTS

§1.471. CORRECTIONS & AMENDMENTS DURING INTERNATIONAL PROCESSING

(a) Except as otherwise provided in this paragraph, all corrections submitted to the United States Receiving Office or United States International Searching Authority must be in English, in the form of replacement sheets in compliance with PCT Rules 10 and 11, and accompanied by a letter that draws attention to the differences between the replaced sheets and the replacement sheets. Replacement sheets are not required for the deletion of lines of text, the correction of simple typographical errors, and one addition or change of not more than five words per sheet. These changes may be stated in a letter and, if appropriate, the United States Receiving Office will make the deletion or transfer the correction to the international application, provided that such corrections do not adversely affect the clarity and direct reproducibility of the application (PCT Rule 26.4). Amendments that do not comply with PCT Rules 10 and 11.1 to 11.13 may not be entered.

(b) Amendments of claims submitted to the International Bureau shall be as prescribed by PCT Rule 46.

(c) Corrections or additions to the Request of any declarations under PCT Rule 4.17 should be submitted to the International Bureau as prescribed by PCT Rule 26*ter*.

History of 37 C.F.R. §1.471: 63 FR 29619, June 1, 1998; 63 FR 66041, Dec. 1, 1998; 66 FR 16006, Mar. 22, 2001.

§1.472. CHANGES IN PERSON, NAME, OR ADDRESS OF APPLICANTS & INVENTORS

All requests for a change in person, name or address of applicants and inventor be sent to the United States Receiving Office until the time of issuance of the international search report. Thereafter requests for such changes should be submitted to the International Bureau.

History of 37 C.F.R. §1.472: 52 FR 20047, May 28, 1987.

UNITY OF INVENTION

§1.475. UNITY OF INVENTION BEFORE THE INTERNATIONAL SEARCHING AUTHORITY, THE INTERNATIONAL PRELIMINARY EXAMINING AUTHORITY & DURING THE NATIONAL STAGE

(a) An international and a national stage application shall relate to one invention only or to a group of inventions so linked as to form a single general inventive concept ("requirement of unity of invention"). Where a group of inventions is claimed in an application, the requirement of unity of invention shall be fulfilled only when there is a technical relationship among those inventions involving one or more of the same or corresponding special technical features. The expression "special technical features" shall mean those technical features that define a contribution which each of the claimed inventions, considered as a whole, makes over the prior art.

(b) An international or a national stage application containing claims to different categories of invention will be considered to have unity of invention if the claims are drawn only to one of the following combinations of categories:

(1) A product and a process specially adapted for the manufacture of said product; or

(2) A product and a process of use of said product; or

(3) A product, a process specially adapted for the manufacture of the said product, and a use of the said product; or

(4) A process and an apparatus or means specifically designed for carrying out the said process; or

(5) A product, a process specially adapted for the manufacture of the said product, and an apparatus or means specifically designed for carrying out the said process.

(c) If an application contains claims to more or less than one of the combinations of categories of invention set forth in paragraph (b) of this section, unity of invention might not be present.

(d) If multiple products, processes of manufacture or uses are claimed, the first invention of the category first mentioned in the claims of the application and the first recited invention of each of the other categories related thereto will be considered as the main invention in the claims, see PCT Article 17(3)(a) and §1.476(c).

(e) The determination whether a group of inventions is so linked as to form a single general inventive concept shall be made without regard to whether the inventions are claimed in separate claims or as alternatives within a single claim.

History of 37 C.F.R. §1.475: 52 FR 20047, May 28, 1987; 58 FR 4345, Jan. 14, 1993.

§1.476. DETERMINATION OF UNITY OF INVENTION BEFORE THE INTERNATIONAL SEARCHING AUTHORITY

(a) Before establishing the international search report, the International Searching Authority will determine whether the international application complies with the requirement of unity of invention as set forth in §1.475.

(b) If the International Searching Authority considers that the international application does not comply with the requirement of unity of invention, it shall inform the applicant accordingly and invite the payment of additional fees (note §1.445 and PCT Art. 17(3)(a) and PCT Rule 40). The applicant will be given a time period in accordance with PCT Rule 40.3 to pay the additional fees due.

(c) In the case of non-compliance with unity of invention and where no additional fees are paid, the international search will be performed on the invention first mentioned ("main invention") in the claims.

(d) Lack of unity of invention may be directly evident before considering the claims in relation to any prior art, or after taking the prior art into consideration, as where a document discovered during the search shows the invention claimed in a generic or linking claim lacks novelty or is clearly obvious, leaving two or more claims joined thereby without a common inventive concept. In such a case the International Searching Authority may raise the objection of lack of unity of invention.

History of 37 C.F.R. §1.476: 52 FR 20048, May 28, 1987; 58 FR 4346, Jan. 14, 1993.

§1.477. PROTEST TO LACK OF UNITY OF INVENTION BEFORE THE INTERNATIONAL SEARCHING AUTHORITY

(a) If the applicant disagrees with the holding of lack of unity of invention by the International Searching Authority, additional fees may be paid under protest, accompanied by a request for refund and a statement setting forth reasons for disagreement or why the required additional fees are considered excessive, or both (PCT Rule 40.2(c)).

(b) Protest under paragraph (a) of this section will be examined by the Director or the Director's designee. In the event that the applicant's protest is determined to be justified, the additional fees or a portion thereof will be refunded.

(c) An applicant who desires that a copy of the protest and the decision thereon accompany the international search report when forwarded to the Designated Offices, may notify the International Searching Authority to that effect any time prior to the issuance of the international search report. Thereafter, such notification should be directed to the International Bureau (PCT Rule 40.2(c)).

History of 37 C.F.R. §1.477: 52 FR 20048, May 28, 1987.

INTERNATIONAL PRELIMINARY EXAMINATION

§1.480. DEMAND FOR INTERNATIONAL PRELIMINARY EXAMINATION

(a) On the filing of a proper Demand in an application for which the United States International Preliminary Examining Authority is competent and for which the fees have been paid, the international application shall be the subject of an international preliminary examination. The preliminary examination fee (§1.482(a)(1)) and the handling fee (§1.482(b)) shall be due within the applicable time limit set forth in PCT Rule 57.3.

(b) The Demand shall be made on a standardized form (PCT Rule 53). Copies of the printed Demand forms are available from the United States Patent and Trademark Office. Letters requesting printed Demand forms should be marked "Mail Stop PCT."

(c) Withdrawal of a proper Demand prior to the start of the international preliminary examination will entitle applicant to a refund of the preliminary examination fee minus the amount of the transmittal fee set forth in §1.445(a)(1).

(d) The filing of a Demand shall constitute the election of all Contracting States which are designated and are bound by Chapter II of the Treaty on the international filing date (PCT Rule 53.7).

(e) Any Demand filed after the expiration of the applicable time limit set forth in PCT Rule 54*bis*.1(a) shall be considered as if it had not been submitted (PCT Rule 54*bis*.1(b)).

History of 37 C.F.R. §1.480: 52 FR 20048, May 28, 1987; 53 FR 47810, Nov. 28, 1988; 58 FR 4346, Jan. 14, 1993; 63 FR 29619, June 1, 1998; 63 FR 66041, Dec. 1, 1998; 67 FR 523, Jan. 4, 2002; 68 FR 14337, Mar. 25, 2003; 68 FR 59888, Oct. 20, 2003.

§1.481. PAYMENT OF INTERNATIONAL PRELIMINARY EXAMINATION FEES

(a) The handling and preliminary examination fees shall be paid within the time period set in PCT Rule 57.3. The handling fee or preliminary examination fee payable is the handling fee or preliminary examination fee in effect on the date of payment.

(1) If the handling and preliminary examination fees are not paid within the time period set in PCT Rule 57.3, applicant will be notified and given one month within which to pay the deficient fees plus a late payment fee equal to the greater of:

(i) Fifty percent of the amount of the deficient fees, but not exceeding an amount equal to double the handling fee; or

(ii) An amount equal to the handling fee (PCT Rule 58*bis*.2).

(2) The one-month time limit set in this paragraph to pay deficient fees may not be extended.

(b) If the payment needed to cover the handling and preliminary examination fees, pursuant to paragraph (a) of this section, is not timely made in accordance with PCT Rule 58*bis*.1(d), the United States International Preliminary Examination Authority will declare the Demand to be considered as if it had not been submitted.

History of 37 C.F.R. §1.481: 63 FR 29619, June 1, 1998; 63 FR 66041, Dec. 1, 1998; 68 FR 59888, Oct. 20, 2003.

A §1.482. INTERNATIONAL PRELIMINARY EXAMINATION & PROCESSING FEES

(a) The following fees and charges for international preliminary examination are established by the Director under the authority of 35 U.S.C. 376:

(1) The following preliminary examination fee is due on filing the Demand:

(i) If an international search fee as set forth in §1.445(a)(2) has been paid on the international application to the United States Patent and Trademark Office as an International Searching Authority:

(A) For an international preliminary examination fee paid on or after January 1, 2014:

By a micro entity (§1.29)—$150.00

By a small entity (§1.27(a))—$300.00

By other than a small or micro entity—$600.00

(B) For an international preliminary examination fee paid before January 1, 2014—$600.00.

(ii) If the International Searching Authority for the international application was an authority other than the United States Patent and Trademark Office:

(A) For an international preliminary examination fee paid on or after January 1, 2014:

By a micro entity (§1.29)—$190.00

By a small entity (§1.27(a))—$380.00

By other than a small or micro entity—$760.00

(B) For an international preliminary examination fee paid before January 1, 2014—$750.00.

(2) An additional preliminary examination fee when required, per additional invention:

(i) If the international preliminary examination fee set forth in paragraph (a)(1) of this section was paid on or after January 1, 2014:

By a micro entity (§1.29)—$150.00

By a small entity (§1.27(a))—$300.00

By other than a small or micro entity—$600.00

(ii) If the international preliminary examination fee set forth in paragraph (a)(1) of this section was paid before January 1, 2014—$600.00.

(b) The handling fee is due on filing the Demand and shall be prescribed in PCT Rule 57.

(c) Late furnishing fee for providing a sequence listing in response to an invitation under PCT Rule 13*ter*:

By a micro entity (§1.29)—$75.00

By a small entity (§1.27(a))—$150.00

By other than a small or micro entity—$300.00

History of 37 C.F.R. §1.482: 52 FR 20048, May 28, 1987; 54 FR 6904, Feb. 15, 1989; 56 FR 65154, Dec. 13, 1991; 57 FR 38196, Aug. 21, 1992; 58 FR 4346, Jan. 14, 1993; 59 FR 43741, Aug. 25, 1994; 60 FR 41023, Aug. 11, 1995; 61 FR 39588, July 30, 1996; 62 FR 40453, July 29, 1997; 68 FR 59888, Oct. 20, 2003; 78 FR 4289, Mar. 19, 2013; 78 FR 17107, Mar. 20, 2013; 82 FR 52816, Jan. 16, 2018.

§1.484. CONDUCT OF INTERNATIONAL PRELIMINARY EXAMINATION

(a) An international preliminary examination will be conducted to formulate a non-binding opinion as to whether the claimed invention has novelty, involves an inventive step (is non-obvious) and is industrially applicable.

(b) International preliminary examination will begin in accordance with PCT Rule 69.1.

(c) No international preliminary examination will be conducted on inventions not previously searched by an International Searching Authority.

(d) The International Preliminary Examining Authority will establish a written opinion if any defect exists or if the claimed invention lacks novelty, inventive step or industrial applicability and will set a non-extendable time limit in the written opinion for the applicant to reply.

(e) The written opinion established by the International Searching Authority under PCT Rule 43*bis*.1 shall be considered to be a written opinion of the United States International Preliminary Examining Authority for the purposes of paragraph (d) of this section.

(f) The International Preliminary Examining Authority may establish further written opinions under paragraph (d) of this section.

(g) If no written opinion under paragraph (d) of this section is necessary, or if no further written opinion under paragraph (f) of this section is to be established, or after any written opinion and the reply thereto or the expiration of the time limit for reply to such written opinion, an international preliminary examination report will be established by the International Preliminary Examining Authority. One copy will be submitted to the International Bureau and one copy will be submitted to the applicant.

(h) An applicant will be permitted a personal or telephone interview with the examiner, which may be requested after the filing of a Demand, and must be conducted during the period between the establishment of the written opinion and the establishment of the international preliminary examination report. Additional interviews may be conducted where the examiner determines that such additional interviews may be helpful to advancing the international preliminary examination procedure. A summary of any such personal or telephone interview must be filed by the applicant or, if not filed by applicant be made of record in the file by the examiner.

(i) If the application whose priority is claimed in the international application is in a language other than English, the United States International Preliminary Examining Authority may, where the validity of the priority claim is relevant for the formulation of the opinion referred to in Article 33(1), invite the applicant to furnish an English translation of the priority document within two months from the date of the invitation. If the translation is not furnished within that time limit, the international preliminary report may be established as if the priority had not been claimed.

History of 37 C.F.R. §1.484: 52 FR 20049, May 28, 1987; 58 FR 4346, Jan. 14, 1993; 62 FR 53199, Oct. 10, 1997; 63 FR 29619, June 1, 1998; 63 FR 66041, Dec. 1, 1998; 66 FR 16006, Mar. 22, 2001; 68 FR 59888, Oct. 20, 2003.

§1.485. AMENDMENTS BY APPLICANT DURING INTERNATIONAL PRELIMINARY EXAMINATION

The applicant may make amendments at the time of filing the Demand. The applicant may also make amendments within the time limit set by the International Preliminary Examining Authority for reply to any notification under §1.484(b) or to any written opinion. Any such amendments must be made in accordance with PCT Rule 66.8.

History of 37 C.F.R. §1.485: 52 FR 20049, May 28, 1987; 58 FR 4346, Jan. 14, 1993; 62 FR 53200, Oct. 10, 1997; 63 FR 29620, June 1, 1998; 63 FR 66041, Dec. 1, 1998; 74 FR 31373, July 1, 2009.

§1.487. RESERVED

History of 37 C.F.R. §1.487: 58 FR 4346, Jan. 14, 1993.

§1.488. DETERMINATION OF UNITY OF INVENTION BEFORE THE INTERNATIONAL PRELIMINARY EXAMINING AUTHORITY

(a) Before establishing any written opinion or the international preliminary examination report, the International Preliminary Examining Authority will determine whether the international application complies with the requirement of unity of invention as set forth in §1.475.

(b) If the International Preliminary Examining Authority considers that the international application does not comply with the requirement of unity of invention, it may:

(1) Issue a written opinion and/or an international preliminary examination report, in respect of the entire international application and indicate that unity of invention is lacking and specify the reasons therefor without extending an invitation to restrict or pay additional fees. No international preliminary examination will be conducted on inventions not previously searched by an International Searching Authority.

(2) Invite the applicant to restrict the claims or pay additional fees, pointing out the categories of invention found, within a set time limit which will not be extended. No international preliminary examination will be conducted on inventions not previously searched by an International Searching Authority, or

(3) If applicant fails to restrict the claims or pay additional fees within the time limit set for reply, the International Preliminary Examining Authority will issue a written opinion and/or establish an international preliminary examination report on the main invention and shall indicate the relevant facts in the said report. In case of any doubt as to which invention is the main invention, the invention first mentioned in the claims and previously searched by an International Searching Authority shall be considered the main invention.

(c) Lack of unity of invention may be directly evident before considering the claims in relation to any prior art, or after taking the prior art into consideration, as where a document discovered during the search shows the invention claimed in a generic or linking claim lacks novelty or is clearly obvious, leaving two or more claims joined thereby without a common inventive concept. In such a case the International Preliminary Examining Authority may raise the objection of lack of unity of invention.

History of 37 C.F.R. §1.488: 52 FR 20049, May 28, 1987; 58 FR 4346, Jan. 14, 1993; 62 FR 53200, Oct. 10, 1997.

§1.489. PROTEST TO LACK OF UNITY OF INVENTION BEFORE THE INTERNATIONAL PRELIMINARY EXAMINING AUTHORITY

(a) If the applicant disagrees with the holding of lack of unity of invention by the International Preliminary Examining Authority, additional fees may be paid under protest, accompanied by a request for refund and a statement setting forth reasons for disagreement or why the required additional fees are considered excessive, or both.

(b) Protest under paragraph (a) of this section will be examined by the Director or the Director's designee. In the event that the applicant's protest is determined to be justified, the additional fees or a portion thereof will be refunded.

(c) An applicant who desires that a copy of the protest and the decision thereon accompany the international preliminary examination report when forwarded to the Elected Offices, may notify the International Preliminary Examining Authority to that effect any time prior to the issuance of the international preliminary examination report. Thereafter, such notification should be directed to the International Bureau.

History of 37 C.F.R. §1.489: 52 FR 20050, May 28, 1987.

NATIONAL STAGE

§1.491. NATIONAL STAGE COMMENCEMENT, ENTRY, & FULFILLMENT

(a) Subject to 35 U.S.C. 371(f), the national stage shall commence with the expiration of the applicable time limit under PCT Article 22(1) or (2), or under PCT Article 39(1)(a).

(b) An international application enters the national stage when the applicant has filed the documents and fees required by 35 U.S.C. 371(c)(1) and (c)(2) within the period set in §1.495.

(c) An international application fulfills the requirements of 35 U.S.C. 371 when the national stage has commenced under 35 U.S.C. 371(b) or (f) and all applicable requirements of 35 U.S.C. 371 have been satisfied.

History of 37 C.F.R. §1.491: 52 FR 20050, May 28, 1987; 66 FR 45777, Aug. 30, 2001; 67 FR 523, Jan. 4, 2002; 77 FR 48823, Sept. 16, 2012.

A §1.492. NATIONAL STAGE FEES

The following fees and charges are established for international applications entering the national stage under 35 U.S.C. 371:

(a) The basic national fee for an international application entering the national stage under 35 U.S.C. 371:

By a micro entity (§1.29)—$75.00

By a small entity (§1.27(a))—$150.00

By other than a small or micro entity—$300.00

(b) Search fee for an international application entering the national stage under 35 U.S.C. 371:

(1) If an international preliminary examination report on the international application prepared by the United States International Preliminary Examining Authority or a written opinion on the international application prepared by the United States International Searching Authority states that the criteria of novelty, inventive step (non-obviousness), and industrial applicability, as defined in PCT Article 33(1) to (4) have been satisfied for all of the claims presented in the application entering the national stage:

By a micro entity (§1.29)—$0.00

By a small entity (§1.27(a))—$0.00

By other than a small or micro entity—$0.00

(2) If the search fee as set forth in §1.445(a)(2) has been paid on the international application to the United States Patent and Trademark Office as an International Searching Authority:

By a micro entity (§1.29)—$35.00

By a small entity (§1.27(a))—$70.00

By other than a small or micro entity—$140.00

(3) If an international search report on the international application has been prepared by an International Searching Authority other than the United States International Searching Authority and is provided, or has been previously communicated by the International Bureau, to the Office:

By a micro entity (§1.29)—$130.00

By a small entity (§1.27(a))—$260.00

By other than a small or micro entity—$520.00

(4) In all situations not provided for in paragraph (b)(1), (2), or (3) of this section:

By a micro entity (§1.29)—$165.00

By a small entity (§1.27(a))—$330.00

By other than a small or micro entity—$660.00

(c) The examination fee for an international application entering the national stage under 35 U.S.C. 371:

(1) If an international preliminary examination report on the international application prepared by the United States International Preliminary Examining Authority or a written opinion on the international application prepared by the United States International Searching Authority states that the criteria of novelty, inventive step (non-obviousness), and industrial applicability, as defined in PCT Article 33(1) to (4) have been satisfied for all of the claims presented in the application entering the national stage:

By a micro entity (§1.29)—$0.00

By a small entity (§1.27(a))—$0.00

By other than a small or micro entity—$0.00

(2) In all situations not provided for in paragraph (c)(1) of this section:

By a micro entity (§1.29)—$190.00

By a small entity (§1.27(a))—$380.00

By other than a small or micro entity—$760.00

(d) In addition to the basic national fee, for filing or on later presentation at any other time of each claim in independent form in excess of 3:

By a micro entity (§1.29)—$115.00

By a small entity (§1.27(a))—$230.00

By other than a small or micro entity—$460.00

(e) In addition to the basic national fee, for filing or on later presentation at any other time of each claim (whether dependent or independent) in excess of 20 (note that §1.75(c) indicates how multiple dependent claims are considered for fee calculation purposes):

By a micro entity (§1.29)—$25.00

By a small entity (§1.27(a))—$50.00

By other than a small or micro entity—$100.00

(f) In addition to the basic national fee, if the application contains, or is amended to contain, a multiple dependent claim, per application:

By a micro entity (§1.29)—$205.00

By a small entity (§1.27(a))—$410.00

By other than a small or micro entity—$820.00

(g) If the excess claims fees required by paragraphs (d) and (e) of this section and multiple dependent claim fee required by paragraph (f) of this section are not paid with the basic national fee or on later presentation of the claims for which excess claims or multiple dependent claim fees are due, the fees required by paragraphs (d), (e), and (f) of this section must be paid or the claims canceled by amendment prior to the expiration of the time period set for reply by the Office in any notice of fee deficiency in order to avoid abandonment.

(h) Surcharge for filing any of the search fee, the examination fee, or the oath or declaration after the date of the commencement of the national stage (§1.491(a)) pursuant to §1.495(c):

By a micro entity (§1.29)—$35.00

By a small entity (§1.27(a))—$70.00

By other than a small or micro entity—$140.00

(i) For filing an English translation of an international application or any annexes to an international preliminary examination report later than thirty months after the priority date (§1.495(c) and (e)):

By a micro entity (§1.29)—$35.00

By a small entity (§1.27(a))—$70.00

By other than a small or micro entity—$140.00

(j) Application size fee for any international application, the specification and drawings of which exceed 100 sheets of paper, for each additional 50 sheets or fraction thereof:

By a micro entity (§1.29)—$100.00

By a small entity (§1.27(a))—$200.00

By other than a small or micro entity—$400.00

History of 37 C.F.R. §1.492: 52 FR 20050, May 28, 1987; 54 FR 6903, Feb. 15, 1989; 56 FR 65154, Dec. 13, 1991; 57 FR 38196, Aug. 21, 1992; 58 FR 4346, Jan. 14, 1993; 59 FR 43742, Aug. 25, 1994; 59 FR 47082, Sept. 14, 1994; 60 FR 41023, Aug. 11, 1995; 61 FR 39588, July 30, 1996; 62 FR 40453, July 29, 1997; 62 FR 53200, Oct. 10, 1997; 63 FR 39734, July 24, 1998; 63 FR 46892, Sept. 3, 1998; 63 FR 52610, Oct. 1, 1998; 63 FR 67580, Dec. 8, 1998; 64 FR 67777, Dec. 3, 1999; 65 FR 49195, Aug. 11, 2000; 65 FR 78960, Dec. 18, 2000; 66 FR 39450, July 31, 2001; 67 FR 523, Jan. 4, 2002; 67 FR 70850, Nov. 27, 2002; 68 FR 41535, July 14, 2003; 69 FR 52606, Aug. 27, 2004; 70 FR 3892, Jan. 27, 2005; 70 FR 5054, Feb. 1, 2005; 70 FR 30365, May 26, 2005; 70 FR 35378, June 20, 2005; 72 FR 46902, Sept. 30, 2007; 72 FR 55055, Sept. 30, 2007; 73 FR 47541, Oct. 2, 2008; 77 FR 48823, Sept. 16, 2012; 77 FR 54366, Oct. 5, 2012; 78 FR 4290, Mar. 19, 2013; 82 FR 52816, Jan. 16, 2018.

§1.494. RESERVED

History of 37 C.F.R. §1.494: 67 FR 523, Jan. 4, 2002.

§1.495. ENTERING THE NATIONAL STAGE IN THE UNITED STATES OF AMERICA

(a) The applicant in an international application must fulfill the requirements of 35 U.S.C. 371 within the time periods set forth in paragraphs (b) and (c) of this section in order to prevent the abandonment of the international application as to the United States of America. The thirty-month time period set forth in paragraphs (b), (c), (d), (e) and (h) of this section may not be extended.

(b) To avoid abandonment of the application, the applicant shall furnish to the United States Patent and Trademark Office not later than the expiration of thirty months from the priority date:

(1) A copy of the international application, unless it has been previously communicated by the International Bureau or unless it was originally filed in the United States Patent and Trademark Office; and

(2) The basic national fee (see §1.492(a)).

(c)(1) If applicant complies with paragraph (b) of this section before expiration of thirty months from the priority date, the Office will notify the applicant if he or she has omitted any of:

(i) A translation of the international application, as filed, into the English language, if it was originally filed in another language and if any English language translation of the publication of the international application previously submitted under 35 U.S.C. 154(d) (§1.417) is not also a translation of the international application as filed (35 U.S.C. 371(c)(2));

(ii) The inventor's oath or declaration (35 U.S.C. 371(c)(4) and §1.497), if a declaration of inventorship in compliance with §1.63 has not been previously submitted in the international application under PCT Rule 4.17(iv) within the time limits provided for in PCT Rule 26*ter*.1;

(iii) The search fee set forth in §1.492(b);

(iv) The examination fee set forth in §1.492(c); and

(v) Any application size fee required by §1.492(j).

(2) A notice under paragraph (c)(1) of this section will set a time period within which applicant must provide any omitted translation, search fee set forth in §1.492(b), examination fee set forth in §1.492(c), and any application size fee required by §1.492(j) in order to avoid abandonment of the application.

(3) The inventor's oath or declaration must also be filed within the period specified in paragraph (c)(2) of this section, except that the filing of the inventor's oath or declaration may be postponed until the application is otherwise in condition for allowance under the conditions specified in paragraphs (c)(3)(i) through (c)(3)(iii) of this section.

(i) The application contains an application data sheet in accordance with §1.76 filed prior to the expiration of the time period set in any notice under paragraph (c)(1) identifying:

(A) Each inventor by his or her legal name;

(B) A mailing address where the inventor customarily receives mail, and residence, if an inventor lives at a location which is different from where the inventor customarily receives mail, for each inventor.

(ii) The applicant must file each required oath or declaration in compliance with §1.63, or substitute statement in compliance with §1.64, no later than the date on which the issue fee for the patent is paid. If the applicant is notified in a notice of allowability that an oath or declaration in compliance with §1.63, or substitute statement in compliance with §1.64, executed by or with respect to each named inventor has not been filed, the applicant must file each required oath or declaration in compliance with §1.63, or substitute statement in compliance with §1.64, no later than the date on which the issue fee is paid to avoid abandonment. This time period is not extendable under §1.136 (see §1.136(c)). The

Office may dispense with the notice provided for in paragraph (c)(1) of this section if each required oath or declaration in compliance with §1.63, or substitute statement in compliance with §1.64, has been filed before the application is in condition for allowance.

(iii) An international application in which the basic national fee under 35 U.S.C. 41(a)(1)(F) has been paid and for which an application data sheet in accordance with §1.76 has been filed may be treated as complying with 35 U.S.C. 371 for purposes of eighteen-month publication under 35 U.S.C. 122(b) and §1.211 et seq.

(4) The payment of the processing fee set forth in §1.492(i) is required for acceptance of an English translation later than the expiration of thirty months after the priority date. The payment of the surcharge set forth in §1.492(h) is required for acceptance of any of the search fee, the examination fee, or the inventor's oath or declaration after the date of the commencement of the national stage (§1.491(a)).

(5) A "Sequence Listing" need not be translated if the "Sequence Listing" complies with PCT Rule 12.1(d) and the description complies with PCT Rule 5.2(b).

(d) A copy of any amendments to the claims made under PCT Article 19, and a translation of those amendments into English, if they were made in another language, must be furnished not later than the expiration of thirty months from the priority date. Amendments under PCT Article 19 which are not received by the expiration of thirty months from the priority date will be considered to be canceled.

(e) A translation into English of any annexes to an international preliminary examination report (if applicable), if the annexes were made in another language, must be furnished not later than the expiration of thirty months from the priority date. Translations of the annexes which are not received by the expiration of thirty months from the priority date may be submitted within any period set pursuant to paragraph (c) of this section accompanied by the processing fee set forth in §1.492(f). Annexes for which translations are not timely received will be considered canceled.

(f) Verification of the translation of the international application or any other document pertaining to an international application may be required where it is considered necessary, if the international application or other document was filed in a language other than English.

(g) The documents and fees submitted under paragraphs (b) and (c) of this section must be identified as a submission to enter the national stage under 35 U.S.C. 371. If the documents and fees contain conflicting indications as between an application under 35 U.S.C. 111 and a submission to enter the national stage under 35 U.S.C. 371, the documents and fees will be treated as a submission to enter the national stage under 35 U.S.C. 371.

(h) An international application becomes abandoned as to the United States thirty months from the priority date if the requirements of paragraph (b) of this section have not been complied with within thirty months from the priority date.

History of 37 C.F.R. §1.495: 52 FR 20051, May 28, 1987; 58 FR 4347, Jan. 14, 1993; 62 FR 53200, Oct. 10, 1997; 63 FR 29620, June 1, 1998; 63 FR 66041, Dec. 1, 1998; 65 FR 57060, Sept. 20, 2000; 66 FR 16006, Mar. 22, 2001; 66 FR 28054, May 22, 2001; 67 FR 523, Jan. 4, 2002; 68 FR 71007, Dec. 22, 2003; 70 FR 3892, Jan. 27, 2005; 70 FR 30365, May 26, 2005; 74 FR 52691, Oct. 14, 2009; 77 FR 48824, Sept. 16, 2012; 78 FR 62407, Dec. 18, 2013.

§1.496. EXAMINATION OF INTERNATIONAL APPLICATIONS IN THE NATIONAL STAGE

National stage applications having paid therein the search fee as set forth in §1.492(b)(1) and examination fee as set forth in §1.492(c)(1) may be amended subsequent to the date of commencement of national stage processing only to the extent necessary to eliminate objections as to form or to cancel rejected claims. Such national stage applications will be advanced out of turn for examination.

History of 37 C.F.R. §1.496: 52 FR 20051, May 28, 1987; 70 FR 5055, Feb. 1, 2005; 70 FR 35378, June 20, 2005; 77 FR 48824, Sept. 16, 2012.

§1.497. INVENTOR'S OATH OR DECLARATION UNDER 35 U.S.C. 371(c)(4)

(a) When an applicant of an international application desires to enter the national stage under 35 U.S.C. 371 pursuant to §1.495, and a declaration in compliance with §1.63 has not been previously submitted in the international application under PCT Rule 4.17(iv) within the time limits provided for in PCT Rule 26*ter*.1, the applicant must file the inventor's oath or declaration. The inventor, or each individual who is a joint inventor of a claimed invention, in an application for patent must execute an oath or declaration in accordance with the conditions and requirements of §1.63, except as provided for in §1.64.

(b) An oath or declaration under §1.63 will be accepted as complying with 35 U.S.C. 371(c)(4) if it complies with the requirements of §§1.63(a), (c) and (g). A substitute statement under §1.64 will be accepted as complying with 35 U.S.C. 371(c)(4) if it complies with the requirements of §§1.64(b)(1), (c) and (e) and identifies the person executing the substitute statement. If a newly executed inventor's oath or declaration under §1.63 or substitute statement under §1.64 is not required pursuant to §1.63(d), submission of the copy of the previously executed oath, declaration, or substitute statement under §1.63(d)(1) is required to comply with 35 U.S.C. 371(c)(4).

(c) If an oath or declaration under §1.63, or substitute statement under §1.64, meeting the requirements of §1.497(b) does not also meet the requirements of §1.63 or §1.64, an oath, declaration, substitute statement, or application data sheet in accordance with §1.76 to comply with §1.63 or §1.64 will be required.

History of 37 C.F.R. §1.497: 52 FR 20052, May 28, 1987; 61 FR 42807, Aug. 19, 1996; 65 FR 54677, Sept. 8, 2000; 66 FR 16006, Mar. 22, 2001; 66 FR 28054, May 22, 2001; 67 FR 524, Jan. 4, 2002; 67 FR 6075, Feb. 8, 2002; 77 FR 48824, Sept. 16, 2012.

§1.499. UNITY OF INVENTION DURING THE NATIONAL STAGE

If the examiner finds that a national stage application lacks unity of invention under §1.475, the examiner may in an Office action require the applicant in the response to that action to elect the invention to which the claims shall be restricted. Such requirement may be made before any action on the merits but may be made at any time before the final action at the discretion of the examiner. Review of any such requirement is provided under §§1.143 and 1.144.

History of 37 C.F.R. §1.499: 52 FR 20052, May 28, 1987; 58 FR 4347, Jan. 14, 1993.

SUBPART D. EX PARTE REEXAMINATION OF PATENTS

CITATION OF PRIOR ART & WRITTEN STATEMENTS

§1.501. CITATION OF PRIOR ART & WRITTEN STATEMENTS IN PATENT FILES

(a) Information content of submission: At any time during the period of enforceability of a patent, any person may file a written submission with the Office under this section, which is directed to the following information:

(1) Prior art consisting of patents or printed publications which the person making the submission believes to have a bearing on the patentability of any claim of the patent; or

(2) Statements of the patent owner filed by the patent owner in a proceeding before a Federal court or the Office in which the patent owner took a position on the scope of any claim of the patent. Any statement submitted under this paragraph must be accompanied by any other documents, pleadings, or evidence from the proceeding in which the statement was filed that address the written statement, and such statement and accompanying information under this paragraph must be submitted in redacted form to exclude information subject to an applicable protective order.

(3) Submissions under paragraph (a)(2) of this section must identify:

(i) The forum and proceeding in which patent owner filed each statement;

(ii) The specific papers and portions of the papers submitted that contain the statements; and

(iii) How each statement submitted is a statement in which patent owner took a position on the scope of any claim in the patent.

(b) Explanation: A submission pursuant to paragraph (a) of this section:

(1) Must include an explanation in writing of the pertinence and manner of applying any prior art submitted under paragraph (a)(1) of this section and any written statement and accompanying information submitted under paragraph (a)(2) of this section to at least one claim of the patent, in order for the submission to become a part of the official file of the patent; and

(2) May, if the submission is made by the patent owner, include an explanation of how the claims differ from any prior art submitted under paragraph (a)(1) of this section or any written statements and accompanying information submitted under paragraph (a)(2) of this section.

(c) Reexamination pending: If a reexamination proceeding has been requested and is pending for the patent in which the submission is filed, entry of the submission into the official file of the patent is subject to the provisions of §§1.502 and 1.902.

(d) Identity: If the person making the submission wishes his or her identity to be excluded from the patent file and kept confidential, the submission papers must be submitted anonymously without any identification of the person making the submission.

(e) Certificate of Service: A submission under this section by a person other than the patent owner must include a certification that a copy of the submission was served in its entirety upon patent owner at the address as provided for in §1.33(c). A submission by a person other than the patent owner that fails to include proper proof of service as required by §1.248(b) will not be entered into the patent file.

History of 37 C.F.R. §1.501: 65 FR 76774, Dec. 7, 2000; 77 FR 46626, Sept. 16, 2012.

Source of 37 C.F.R. Part 1D: 24 FR 10332, Dec. 22, 1959; 60 FR 14518, Mar. 17, 1995; 65 FR 14871, Mar. 20, 2000; 65 FR 33455, May 24, 2000; 65 FR 50103, Aug. 16, 2000; 65 FR 56793, Sept. 20, 2000; 65 FR 70490, Nov. 24, 2000; 65 FR 76774, Dec. 7, 2000, unless otherwise noted.

§1.502. PROCESSING OF PRIOR ART CITATIONS DURING AN EX PARTE REEXAMINATION PROCEEDING

Citations by the patent owner under §1.555 and by an ex parte reexamination requester under either §1.510 or §1.535 will be entered in the reexamination file during a reexamination proceeding. The entry in the patent file of citations submitted after the date of an order to reexamine pursuant to §1.525 by persons other than the patent owner, or an ex parte reexamination requester under either §1.510 or §1.535, will be delayed until the reexamination proceeding has been concluded by the issuance and publication of a reexamination certificate. See §1.902 for processing of prior art citations in patent and reexamination files during an inter partes reexamination proceeding filed under §1.913.

History of 37 C.F.R. §1.502: 65 FR 76775, Dec. 7, 2000; 72 FR 18905, May 16, 2007.

REQUEST FOR EX PARTE REEXAMINATION

§1.510. REQUEST FOR EX PARTE REEXAMINATION

(a) Any person may, at any time during the period of enforceability of a patent, file a request for an ex parte reexamination by the Office of any claim of the patent on the basis of prior art patents or printed publications cited under §1.501, unless prohibited by 35 U.S.C. 315(e)(1) or 35 U.S.C.

325(e)(1). The request must be accompanied by the fee for requesting reexamination set in §1.20(c)(1).

(b) Any request for reexamination must include the following parts:

(1) A statement pointing out each substantial new question of patentability based on prior patents and printed publications.

(2) An identification of every claim for which reexamination is requested, and a detailed explanation of the pertinency and manner of applying the cited prior art to every claim for which reexamination is requested. For each statement of the patent owner and accompanying information submitted pursuant to §1.501(a)(2) which is relied upon in the detailed explanation, the request must explain how that statement is being used to determine the proper meaning of a patent claim in connection with the prior art applied to that claim and how each relevant claim is being interpreted. If appropriate, the party requesting reexamination may also point out how claims distinguish over cited prior art.

(3) A copy of every patent or printed publication relied upon or referred to in paragraph (b)(1) and (2) of this section accompanied by an English language translation of all the necessary and pertinent parts of any non-English language patent or printed publication.

(4) A copy of the entire patent including the front face, drawings, and specification/claims (in double column format) for which reexamination is requested, and a copy of any disclaimer, certificate of correction, or reexamination certificate issued in the patent. All copies must have each page plainly written on only one side of a sheet of paper.

(5) A certification that a copy of the request filed by a person other than the patent owner has been served in its entirety on the patent owner at the address as provided for in §1.33(c). The name and address of the party served must be indicated. If service was not possible, a duplicate copy must be supplied to the Office.

(6) A certification by the third party requester that the statutory estoppel provisions of 35 U.S.C. 315(e)(1) or 35 U.S.C. 325(e)(1) do not prohibit the requester from filing the ex parte reexamination request.

(c) If the request does not include the fee for requesting ex parte reexamination required by paragraph (a) of this section and meet all the requirements by paragraph (b) of this section, then the person identified as requesting reexamination will be so notified and will generally be given an opportunity to complete the request within a specified time. Failure to comply with the notice will result in the ex parte reexamination request not being granted a filing date, and will result in placement of the request in the patent file as a citation if it complies with the requirements of §1.501.

(d) The filing date of the request for ex parte reexamination is the date on which the request satisfies all the requirements of this section.

(e) A request filed by the patent owner may include a proposed amendment in accordance with §1.530.

(f) If a request is filed by an attorney or agent identifying another party on whose behalf the request is being filed, the attorney or agent must have a power of attorney from that party or be acting in a representative capacity pursuant to §1.34.

History of 37 C.F.R. §1.510: 46 FR 29185, May 29, 1981; 47 FR 41282, Sept. 17, 1982; 62 FR 53200, Oct. 10, 1997; 65 FR 54678, Sept. 8, 2000; 65 FR 76775, Dec. 7, 2000; 71 FR 9262, Feb. 23, 2006; 71 FR 44223, Aug. 4, 2006; 72 FR 18905, May 16, 2007; 77 FR 46626, Sept. 16, 2012.

§1.515. DETERMINATION OF THE REQUEST FOR EX PARTE REEXAMINATION

(a) Within three months following the filing date of a request for an ex parte reexamination, an examiner will consider the request and determine whether or not a substantial new question of patentability affecting any claim of the patent is raised by the request and the prior art cited therein, with or without consideration of other patents or printed publications. A statement and any accompanying information submitted pursuant to §1.501(a)(2) will not be considered by the examiner when making a determination on the request. The examiner's determination will be based on the claims in effect at the time of the determination, will become a part of the official file of the patent, and will be given or mailed to the patent owner at the address provided for in §1.33(c) and to the person requesting reexamination.

(b) Where no substantial new question of patentability has been found, a refund of a portion of the fee for requesting ex parte reexamination will be made to the requester in accordance with §1.26(c).

(c) The requester may seek review by a petition to the Director under §1.181 within one month of the mailing date of the examiner's determination refusing ex parte reexamination. Any such petition must comply with §1.181(b). If no petition is timely filed or if the decision on petition affirms that no substantial new question of patentability has been raised, the determination shall be final and nonappealable.

History of 37 C.F.R. §1.515: 65 FR 76775, Dec. 7, 2000; 77 FR 46626, Sept. 16, 2012.

§1.520. EX PARTE REEXAMINATION AT THE INITIATIVE OF THE DIRECTOR

The Director, at any time during the period of enforceability of a patent, may determine whether or not a substantial new question of patentability is raised by patents or printed publications which have been discovered by the Director or which have been brought to the Director's attention, even though no request for reexamination has been filed in accordance with §1.510 or §1.913. The Director may initiate ex parte reexamination without a request for reexamination pursuant to §1.510 or §1.913. Normally requests from outside the Office that the Director undertake reexamination on his own initiative will not be considered. Any determination to initiate ex parte reexamination under this section will become a part of the official file of the patent and will be mailed to the patent owner at the address as provided for in §1.33(c).

History of 37 C.F.R. §1.520: 65 FR 76775, Dec. 7, 2000.

EX PARTE REEXAMINATION

§1.525. ORDER FOR EX PARTE REEXAMINATION

(a) If a substantial new question of patentability is found pursuant to §1.515 or §1.520, the determination will include an order for ex parte reexamination of the patent for resolution of the question. If the order for ex parte reexamination resulted from a petition pursuant to §1.515(c), the ex parte reexamination will ordinarily be conducted by an examiner other than the examiner responsible for the initial determination under §1.515(a).

(b) The notice published in the Official Gazette under §1.11(c) will be considered to be constructive notice and ex parte reexamination will proceed.

History of 37 C.F.R. §1.525: 65 FR 76775, Dec. 7, 2000.

§1.530. STATEMENT BY PATENT OWNER IN EX PARTE REEXAMINATION; AMENDMENT BY PATENT OWNER IN EX PARTE OR INTER PARTES REEXAMINATION; INVENTORSHIP CHANGE IN EX PARTE OR INTER PARTES REEXAMINATION

(a) Except as provided in §1.510(e), no statement or other response by the patent owner in an ex parte reexamination proceeding shall be filed prior to the determinations made in accordance with §1.515 or §1.520. If a premature statement or other response is filed by the patent owner, it will not be acknowledged or considered in making the determination, and it will be returned or discarded (at the Office's option).

(b) The order for ex parte reexamination will set a period of not less than two months from the date of the order within which the patent owner may file a statement on the new question of patentability, including any proposed amendments the patent owner wishes to make.

(c) Any statement filed by the patent owner shall clearly point out why the subject matter as claimed is not anticipated or rendered obvious by the prior art patents or printed publications, either alone or in any reasonable combinations. Where the reexamination request was filed by a third party requester, any statement filed by the patent owner must be served upon the ex parte reexamination requester in accordance with §1.248.

(d) Making amendments in a reexamination proceeding. A proposed amendment in an ex parte or an inter partes reexamination proceeding is made by filing a paper directing that proposed specified changes be made to the patent specification, including the claims, or to the drawings. An amendment paper directing that proposed specified changes be made in a reexamination proceeding may be submitted as an accompaniment to a request filed by the patent owner in accordance with §1.510(e), as part of a patent owner statement in accordance with paragraph (b) of this section, or, where permitted, during the prosecution of the reexamination proceeding pursuant to §1.550(a) or §1.937.

(1) Specification other than the claims. Changes to the specification, other than to the claims, must be made by submission of the entire text of an added or rewritten paragraph including markings pursuant to paragraph (f) of this section, except that an entire paragraph may be deleted by a statement deleting the paragraph, without presentation of the text of the paragraph. The precise point in the specification must be identified where any added or rewritten paragraph is located. This paragraph applies whether the amendment is submitted on paper or compact disc (see §§1.96 and 1.825).

(2) Claims. An amendment paper must include the entire text of each patent claim which is being proposed to be changed by such amendment paper and of each new claim being proposed to be added by such amendment paper. For any claim changed by the amendment paper, a parenthetical expression "amended," "twice amended," etc., should follow the claim number. Each patent claim proposed to be changed and each proposed added claim must include markings pursuant to paragraph (f) of this section, except that a patent claim or proposed added claim should be canceled by a statement canceling the claim, without presentation of the text of the claim.

(3) Drawings. Any change to the patent drawings must be submitted as a sketch on a separate paper showing the proposed changes in red for approval by the examiner. Upon approval of the changes by the examiner, only new sheets of drawings including the changes and in compliance with §1.84 must be filed. Amended figures must be identified as "Amended," and any added figure must be identified as "New." In the event a figure is canceled, the figure must be surrounded by brackets and identified as "Canceled."

(4) The formal requirements for papers making up the reexamination proceeding other than those set forth in this section are set out in §1.52.

(e) Status of claims and support for claim changes. Whenever there is an amendment to the claims pursuant to paragraph (d) of this section, there must also be supplied, on pages separate from the pages containing the changes, the status (*i.e.*, pending or canceled), as of the date of the amendment, of all patent claims and of all added claims, and an explanation of the support in the disclosure of the patent for the changes to the claims made by the amendment paper.

(f) Changes shown by markings. Any changes relative to the patent being reexamined which are made to the specification, including the claims, must include the following markings:

(1) The matter to be omitted by the reexamination proceeding must be enclosed in brackets; and

(2) The matter to be added by the reexamination proceeding must be underlined.

(g) Numbering of patent claims preserved. Patent claims may not be renumbered. The numbering of any claims added in the reexamination proceeding must follow the number of the highest numbered patent claim.

(h) Amendment of disclosure may be required. The disclosure must be amended, when required by the Office, to correct inaccuracies of description and definition, and to secure substantial correspondence between the claims, the remainder of the specification, and the drawings.

(i) Amendments made relative to patent. All amendments must be made relative to the patent specification, including the claims, and drawings, which are in effect as of the date of filing the request for reexamination.

(j) No enlargement of claim scope. No amendment may enlarge the scope of the claims of the patent or introduce new matter. No amendment may be proposed for entry in an expired patent. Moreover, no amendment, other than the cancellation of claims, will be incorporated into the patent by a certificate issued after the expiration of the patent.

(k) Amendments not effective until certificate. Although the Office actions will treat proposed amendments as though they have been entered, the proposed amendments will not be effective until the reexamination certificate is issued and published.

(*l*) Correction of inventorship in an ex parte or inter partes reexamination proceeding.

(1) When it appears in a patent being reexamined that the correct inventor or inventors were not named, the Director may, on petition of all the parties set forth in §1.324(b)(1) and (b)(2), including the assignees, and satisfactory proof of the facts and payment of the fee set forth in §1.20(b), or on order of a court before which such matter is called in question, include in the reexamination certificate to be issued under §1.570 or §1.997 an amendment naming only the actual inventor or inventors. The petition must be submitted as part of the reexamination proceeding and must satisfy the requirements of §1.324.

(2) Notwithstanding paragraph (*l*)(1) of this section, if a petition to correct inventorship satisfying the requirements of §1.324 is filed in a reexamination proceeding, and the reexamination proceeding is concluded other than by a reexamination certificate under §1.570 or §1.997, a certificate of correction indicating the change of inventorship stated in the petition will be issued upon request by the patentee.

History of 37 C.F.R. §1.530: 62 FR 53200, Oct. 10, 1997; 65 FR 54678, Sept. 8, 2000; 65 FR 76775, Dec. 7, 2000; 72 FR 18905, May 16, 2007; 77 FR 48825, Sept. 16, 2012.

§1.535. REPLY BY THIRD PARTY REQUESTER IN EX PARTE REEXAMINATION

A reply to the patent owner's statement under §1.530 may be filed by the ex parte reexamination requester within two months from the date of service of the patent owner's statement. Any reply by the ex parte requester must be served upon the patent owner in accordance with §1.248. If the patent owner does not file a statement under §1.530, no reply or other submission from the ex parte reexamination requester will be considered.

History of 37 C.F.R. §1.535: 65 FR 76776, Dec. 7, 2000.

§1.540. CONSIDERATION OF RESPONSES IN EX PARTE REEXAMINATION

The failure to timely file or serve the documents set forth in §1.530 or in §1.535 may result in their being refused consideration. No submissions other than the statement pursuant to §1.530 and the reply by the ex parte reexamination requester pursuant to §1.535 will be considered prior to examination.

History of 37 C.F.R. §1.540: 65 FR 76776, Dec. 7, 2000.

§1.550. CONDUCT OF EX PARTE REEXAMINATION PROCEEDINGS

(a) All ex parte reexamination proceedings, including any appeals to the Board of Patent Appeals and Interferences, will be conducted with special dispatch within the Office. After issuance of the ex parte reexamination order and expiration of the time for submitting any responses, the examination will be conducted in accordance with §§1.104 through 1.116 and will result in the issuance of an ex parte reexamination certificate under §1.570.

(b) The patent owner in an ex parte reexamination proceeding will be given at least thirty days to respond to any Office action. In response to any rejection, such response may include further statements and/or proposed amendments or new claims to place the patent in a condition where all claims, if amended as proposed, would be patentable.

(c) The time for taking any action by a patent owner in an ex parte reexamination proceeding may be extended as provided in this paragraph.

(1) Any request for such an extension must specify the requested period of extension and be accompanied by the petition fee set forth in §1.17(g).

(2) Any request for an extension in a third party requested ex parte reexamination must be filed on or before the day on which action by the patent owner is due, and the mere filing of such a request for extension will not effect the extension. A request for an extension in a third party requested ex parte reexamination will not be granted in the absence of sufficient cause or for more than a reasonable time.

(3) Any request for an extension in a patent owner requested or Director ordered ex parte reexamination for up to two months from the time period set in the Office action must be filed no later than two months from the expiration of the time period set in the Office action. A request for an extension in a patent owner requested or Director ordered ex parte reexamination for more than two months from the time period set in the Office action must be filed on or before the day on which action by the patent owner is due, and the mere filing of a request for an extension for more than two months from the time period set in the Office action will not effect the extension. The time for taking action in a patent owner requested or Director ordered ex parte reexamination will not be extended for more than two months from the time period set in the Office action in the absence of sufficient cause or for more than a reasonable time.

(4) The reply or other action must in any event be filed prior to the expiration of the period of extension, but in no situation may a reply or other action be filed later than the maximum time period set by statute.

(5) See §90.3(c) of this title for extensions of time for filing a notice of appeal to the U.S. Court of Appeals for the Federal Circuit or for commencing a civil action.

(d) If the patent owner fails to file a timely and appropriate response to any Office action or any written statement of an interview required under §1.560(b), the prosecution in the ex parte reexamination proceeding will be a terminated prosecution, and the Director will proceed to issue and publish a certificate concluding the reexamination proceeding under §1.570 in accordance with the last action of the Office.

(e) If a response by the patent owner is not timely filed in the Office, a petition may be filed pursuant to §1.137 to revive a reexamination prosecution terminated under paragraph (d) of this section if the delay in response was unintentional.

(f) The reexamination requester will be sent copies of Office actions issued during the ex parte reexamination proceeding. After filing of a request for ex parte reexamination by a third party requester, any document filed by either the patent owner or the third party requester must be served on the other party in the reexamination proceeding in the manner provided by §1.248. The document must reflect service or the document may be refused consideration by the Office.

(g) The active participation of the ex parte reexamination requester ends with the reply pursuant to §1.535, and no further submissions on behalf of the reexamination requester will be acknowledged or considered. Further, no submissions on behalf of any third parties will be acknowledged or considered unless such submissions are:

(1) in accordance with §1.510 or §1.535; or

(2) entered in the patent file prior to the date of the order for ex parte reexamination pursuant to §1.525.

(h) Submissions by third parties, filed after the date of the order for ex parte reexamination pursuant to §1.525, must meet the requirements of and will be treated in accordance with §1.501(a).

(i) A petition in an ex parte reexamination proceeding must be accompanied by the fee set forth in §1.20(c)(6), except for petitions under paragraph (c) of this section to extend the period for response by a patent owner, petitions under paragraph (e) of this section to accept a delayed response by a patent owner, petitions under §1.78 to accept an unintentionally delayed benefit claim, and petitions under §1.530(*l*) for correction of inventorship in a reexamination proceeding.

History of 37 C.F.R. §1.550: 49 FR 556, Jan. 4, 1984; 49 FR 48455, Dec. 12, 1984; 54 FR 29553, July 13, 1989; 62 FR 53201, Oct. 10, 1997; 65 FR 54678, Sept. 8, 2000; 65 FR 76776, Dec. 7, 2000; 69 FR 56545, Sept. 21, 2004; 72 FR 18905, May 16, 2007; 77 FR 48851, Sept. 16, 2012; 78 FR 62407, Dec. 18, 2013.

§1.552. SCOPE OF REEXAMINATION IN EX PARTE REEXAMINATION PROCEEDINGS

(a) Claims in an ex parte reexamination proceeding will be examined on the basis of patents or printed publications and, with respect to subject matter added or deleted in the reexamination proceeding, on the basis of the requirements of 35 U.S.C. 112.

(b) Claims in an ex parte reexamination proceeding will not be permitted to enlarge the scope of the claims of the patent.

(c) Issues other than those indicated in paragraphs (a) and (b) of this section will not be resolved in a reexamination proceeding. If such issues are raised by the patent owner or third party requester during a reexamination proceeding, the existence of such issues will be noted by the examiner in the next Office action, in which case the patent owner may consider the advisability of filing a reissue application to have such issues considered and resolved.

(d) Any statement of the patent owner and any accompanying information submitted pursuant to §1.501(a)(2) which is of record in the patent being reexamined (which includes any reexamination files for the patent) may be used after a reexamination proceeding has been ordered to determine the proper meaning of a patent claim when applying patents or printed publications.

History of 37 C.F.R. §1.552: 65 FR 76776, Dec. 7, 2000; 77 FR 46627, Sept. 16, 2012.

§1.555. INFORMATION MATERIAL TO PATENTABILITY IN EX PARTE REEXAMINATION & INTER PARTES REEXAMINATION PROCEEDINGS

(a) A patent by its very nature is affected with a public interest. The public interest is best served, and the most effective reexamination occurs when, at the time a reexamination proceeding is being conducted, the Office is aware of and evaluates the teachings of all information material to patentability in a reexamination proceeding. Each individual associated with the patent owner in a reexamination proceeding has a duty of candor and good faith in dealing with the Office, which includes a duty to disclose to the Office all information known to that individual to be material to patentability in a reexamination proceeding. The individuals who have a duty to disclose to the Office all information known to them to be material to patentability in a reexamination proceeding are the patent owner, each attorney or agent who represents the patent owner, and every other individual who is substantively involved on behalf of the patent owner in a reexamination proceeding. The duty to disclose the information exists with respect to each claim pending in the reexamination proceeding until the claim is cancelled. Information material to the patentability of a cancelled claim need not be submitted if the information is not material to patentability of any claim remaining under consideration in the reexamination proceeding. The duty to disclose all information known to be material to patentability in a reexamination proceeding is deemed to be satisfied if all information known to be material to patentability of any claim in the patent after issuance of the reexamination certificate was cited by the Office or submitted to the Office in an information disclosure statement. However, the duties of candor, good faith, and disclosure have not been complied with if any fraud on the Office was practiced or attempted or the duty of disclosure was violated through bad faith or intentional misconduct by, or on behalf of, the patent owner in the reexamination proceeding. Any information disclosure statement must be filed with the items listed in §1.98(a) as applied to individuals associated with the patent owner in a reexamination proceeding, and should be filed within two months of the date of the order for reexamination, or as soon thereafter as possible.

(b) Under this section, information is material to patentability in a reexamination proceeding when it is not cumulative to information of record or being made of record in the reexamination proceeding, and

(1) It is a patent or printed publication that establishes, by itself or in combination with other patents or printed publications, a prima facie case of unpatentability of a claim; or

(2) It refutes, or is inconsistent with, a position the patent owner takes in:

(i) Opposing an argument of unpatentability relied on by the Office, or

(ii) Asserting an argument of patentability.

A prima facie case of unpatentability of a claim pending in a reexamination proceeding is established when the information compels a conclusion that a claim is unpatentable under the preponderance of evidence, burden-of-proof standard, giving each term in the claim its broadest reasonable construction consistent with the specification, and before any consideration is given to evidence which may be submitted in an attempt to establish a contrary conclusion of patentability.

(c) The responsibility for compliance with this section rests upon the individuals designated in paragraph (a) of this section and no evaluation will be made by the Office in the reexamination proceeding as to compliance with this section. If questions of compliance with this section are raised by the patent owner or the third party requester during a reexamination proceeding, they will be noted as unresolved questions in accordance with §1.552(c).

History of 37 C.F.R. §1.555: 47 FR 21752, May 19, 1982; 49 FR 556, Jan. 4, 1984; 57 FR 2036, Jan. 17, 1992; 65 FR 76776, Dec. 7, 2000.

§1.560. INTERVIEWS IN EX PARTE REEXAMINATION PROCEEDINGS

(a) Interviews in ex parte reexamination proceedings pending before the Office between examiners and the owners of such patents or their attorneys or agents of record must be conducted in the Office at such times, within Office hours, as the respective examiners may designate. Interviews will not be permitted at any other time or place without the authority of the Director. Interviews for the discussion of the patentability of claims in patents involved in ex parte reexamination proceedings will not be conducted prior to the first official action. Interviews should be arranged in advance. Requests that reexamination requesters participate in interviews with examiners will not be granted.

(b) In every instance of an interview with an examiner in an ex parte reexamination proceeding, a complete written statement of the reasons presented at the interview as warranting favorable action must be filed by the patent owner. An interview does not remove the necessity for response to Office actions as specified in §1.111. Patent owner's response to an outstanding Office action after the interview does not remove the necessity for filing the written statement. The written statement must be filed as a separate part of a response to an Office action outstanding at the time of the interview, or as a separate paper within one month from the date of the interview, whichever is later.

History of 37 C.F.R. §1.560: 65 FR 76776, Dec. 7, 2000.

§1.565. CONCURRENT OFFICE PROCEEDINGS WHICH INCLUDE AN EX PARTE REEXAMINATION PROCEEDING

(a) In an ex parte reexamination proceeding before the Office, the patent owner must inform the Office of any prior or concurrent proceedings in which the patent is or was involved such as interferences, reissues, ex parte reexaminations, inter partes reexaminations, or litigation and the results of such proceedings. See §1.985 for notification of prior or concurrent proceedings in an inter partes reexamination proceeding.

(b) If a patent in the process of ex parte reexamination is or becomes involved in litigation, the Director shall determine whether or not to suspend the reexamination. See §1.987 for inter partes reexamination proceedings.

(c) If ex parte reexamination is ordered while a prior ex parte reexamination proceeding is pending and prosecution in the prior ex parte reexamination proceeding has not been terminated, the ex parte reexamination proceedings will usually be merged and result in the issuance and publication of a single certificate under §1.570. For merger of inter partes reexamination proceedings, see §1.989(a). For merger of ex parte reexamination and inter partes reexamination proceedings, see §1.989(b).

(d) If a reissue application and an ex parte reexamination proceeding on which an order pursuant to §1.525 has been mailed are pending concurrently on a patent, a decision will usually be made to merge the two proceedings or to suspend one of the two proceedings. Where merger of a reissue application and an ex parte reexamination proceeding is ordered, the merged examination will be conducted in accordance with §§1.171 through 1.179, and the patent owner will be required to place and maintain the same claims in the reissue application and the ex parte reexamination proceeding during the pendency of the merged proceeding. The examiner's actions and responses by the patent owner in a merged proceeding will apply to both the reissue application and the ex parte reexamination proceeding and will be physically entered into both files. Any ex parte reexamination proceeding merged with a reissue application shall be concluded by the grant of the reissued patent. For merger of a reissue application and an inter partes reexamination, see §1.991.

(e) If a patent in the process of ex parte reexamination is or becomes involved in an interference, the Director may suspend the reexamination or the interference. The Director will not consider a request to suspend an interference unless a motion (§41.121(a)(3) of this title) to suspend the interference has been presented to, and denied by, an administrative patent judge, and the request is filed within ten (10) days of a decision by an administrative patent judge denying the motion for suspension or such other time as the administrative patent judge may set. For concurrent inter partes reexamination and interference of a patent, see §1.993.

History of 37 C.F.R. §1.565: 46 FR 29185, May 29, 1981; 47 FR 21753, May 19, 1982; 49 FR 48455, Dec. 12, 1984; 50 FR 23123, May 31, 1985; 65 FR 54679, Sept. 8, 2000; 65 FR 76777, Dec. 7, 2000; 69 FR 50001, Aug. 12, 2004; 72 FR 18905, May 16, 2007.

EX PARTE REEXAMINATION CERTIFICATE

§1.570. ISSUANCE & PUBLICATION OF EX PARTE REEXAMINATION CERTIFICATE CONCLUDES EX PARTE REEXAMINATION PROCEEDING

(a) To conclude an ex parte reexamination proceeding, the Director will issue and publish an ex parte reexamination certificate in accordance with 35 U.S.C. 307 setting forth the results of the ex parte reexamination proceeding and the content of the patent following the ex parte reexamination proceeding.

(b) An ex parte reexamination certificate will be issued and published in each patent in which an ex parte reexamination proceeding has been ordered under §1.525 and has not been merged with any inter partes reexamination proceeding pursuant to §1.989(a). Any statutory disclaimer filed by the patent owner will be made part of the ex parte reexamination certificate.

(c) The ex parte reexamination certificate will be mailed on the day of its date to the patent owner at the address as provided for in §1.33(c). A copy of the ex parte reexamination certificate will also be mailed to the requester of the ex parte reexamination proceeding.

(d) If an ex parte reexamination certificate has been issued and published which cancels all of the claims of the patent, no further Office proceedings will be conducted with that patent or any reissue applications or any reexamination requests relating thereto.

(e) If the ex parte reexamination proceeding is terminated by the grant of a reissued patent as provided in §1.565(d), the reissued patent will constitute the ex parte reexamination certificate required by this section and 35 U.S.C. 307.

(f) A notice of the issuance of each ex parte reexamination certificate under this section will be published in the Official Gazette on its date of issuance.

History of 37 C.F.R. §1.570: 46 FR 29185, May 29, 1981; 47 FR 21753, May 19, 1982; 65 FR 76777, Dec. 7, 2000; 72 FR 18906, May 16, 2007.

SUBPART E. SUPPLEMENTAL EXAMINATION OF PATENTS

§1.601. FILING OF PAPERS IN SUPPLEMENTAL EXAMINATION

(a) A request for supplemental examination of a patent must be filed by the owner(s) of the entire right, title, and interest in the patent.

(b) Any party other than the patent owner (i.e., any third party) is prohibited from filing papers or otherwise participating in any manner in a supplemental examination proceeding.

(c) A request for supplemental examination of a patent may be filed at any time during the period of enforceability of the patent.

History of 37 C.F.R. §1.601: 77 FR 48852, Sept. 16, 2012.

§1.605. ITEMS OF INFORMATION

(a) Each request for supplemental examination may include no more than twelve items of information believed to be relevant to the patent. More than one request for supplemental examination of the same patent may be filed at any time during the period of enforceability of the patent.

(b) An item of information includes a document submitted as part of the request that contains information, believed to be relevant to the patent, that the patent owner requests the Office to consider, reconsider, or correct. If the information to be considered, reconsidered, or corrected is not, at least in part, contained within or based on any document submitted as part of the request, the discussion within the body of the request relative to the information will be considered as an item of information.

(c) An item of information must be in writing in accordance with §1.2. To be considered, any audio or video recording must be submitted in the form of a written transcript.

(d) If one item of information is combined in the request with one or more additional items of information, each item of information of the combination may be separately counted. Exceptions include the combination of a non-English language document and its translation, and the combination of a document that is over 50 pages in length and its summary pursuant to §1.610(b)(8).

History of 37 C.F.R. §1.605: 77 FR 48852, Sept. 16, 2012.

§1.610. CONTENT OF REQUEST FOR SUPPLEMENTAL EXAMINATION

(a) A request for supplemental examination must be accompanied by the fee for filing a request for supplemental examination as set forth in §1.20(k)(1), the fee for reexamination ordered as a result of a supplemental examination proceeding as set forth in §1.20(k)(2), and any applicable document size fees as set forth in §1.20(k)(3).

(b) A request for supplemental examination must include:

(1) An identification of the number of the patent for which supplemental examination is requested.

(2) A list of the items of information that are requested to be considered, reconsidered, or corrected. Where appropriate, the list must meet the requirements of §1.98(b).

(3) A list identifying any other prior or concurrent post-patent Office proceedings involving the patent for which supplemental examination is being requested, including an identification of the type of proceeding, the identifying number of any such proceeding (e.g., a control number or reissue application number), and the filing date of any such proceeding.

(4) An identification of each claim of the patent for which supplemental examination is requested.

(5) A separate, detailed explanation of the relevance and manner of applying each item of information to each claim of the patent for which supplemental examination is requested.

(6) A copy of the patent for which supplemental examination is requested and a copy of any disclaimer or certificate issued for the patent.

(7) A copy of each item of information listed in paragraph (b)(2) of this section, accompanied by a written English translation of all of the necessary and pertinent parts of any non-English language item of information. The patent owner is not required to submit copies of items of information that form part of the discussion within the body of the request as specified in §1.605(b), or copies of U.S. patents and U.S. patent application publications.

(8) A summary of the relevant portions of any submitted document, other than the request, that is over 50 pages in length. The summary must include citations to the particular pages containing the relevant portions.

(9) An identification of the owner(s) of the entire right, title, and interest in the patent requested to be examined, and a submission by the patent owner in compliance with §3.73(c) of this chapter establishing the entirety of the ownership in the patent requested to be examined.

(c) The request may also include:

(1) A cover sheet itemizing each component submitted as part of the request;

(2) A table of contents for the request;

(3) An explanation of how the claims patentably distinguish over the items of information; and

(4) An explanation of why each item of information submitted with the request does or does not raise a substantial new question of patentability.

(d) The filing date of a request for supplemental examination will not be granted if the request is not in compliance with §§1.605, 1.615, and this section, subject to the discretion of the Office. If the Office determines that the request, as originally submitted, is not entitled to a filing date, the patent owner will be so notified and will be given an opportunity to complete the request within a specified time. If the patent owner does not timely comply with the notice, the request for supplemental examination will not be granted a filing date and the fee for reexamination as set forth in §1.20(k)(2) will be refunded. If the patent owner timely files a corrected request in response to the notice that properly addresses all of the defects set forth in the notice and that otherwise complies with all of the requirements of §§1.605, 1.615, and this section, the filing date of the supplemental examination request will be the receipt date of the corrected request.

History of 37 C.F.R. §1.610: 77 FR 48852, Sept. 16, 2012.

§1.615. FORMAT OF PAPERS FILED IN A SUPPLEMENTAL EXAMINATION PROCEEDING

(a) All papers submitted in a supplemental examination proceeding must be formatted in accordance with §1.52.

(b) Court documents and non-patent literature may be redacted, but must otherwise be identical both in content and in format to the original documents, and, if a court document, to the document submitted in court, and must not otherwise be reduced in size or modified, particularly in terms of font type, font size, line spacing, and margins. Patents, patent application publications, and third-party-generated affidavits or declarations must not be reduced in size or otherwise modified in the manner described in this paragraph.

History of 37 C.F.R. §1.615: 77 FR 48852, Sept. 16, 2012.

§1.620. CONDUCT OF SUPPLEMENTAL EXAMINATION PROCEEDING

(a) Within three months after the filing date of a request for supplemental examination, the Office will determine whether a substantial new question of patentability affecting any claim of the patent is raised by any of the items of information presented in the request. The determination will generally be limited to a review of the item(s) of information identified in the request as applied to the identified claim(s) of the patent. The determination will be based on the claims in effect at the time of the determination and will become a part of the official record of the patent.

(b) The Office may hold in abeyance action on any petition or other paper filed in a supplemental examination proceeding until after the proceeding is concluded by the electronic issuance of the supplemental examination certificate as set forth in §1.625.

(c) If an unauthorized or otherwise improper paper is filed in a supplemental examination proceeding, it will not be entered into the official file or considered, or if inadvertently entered, it will be expunged.

(d) The patent owner must, as soon as possible upon the discovery of any other prior or concurrent post-patent Office proceeding involving the patent for which the current supplemental examination is requested, file a paper limited to notifying the Office of the post-patent Office proceeding, if such notice has not been previously provided with the request. The notice shall be limited to an identification of the post-patent Office proceeding, including the type of proceeding, the identifying number of any such proceeding (e.g., a control number or reissue application number), and the filing date of any such proceeding, without any discussion of the issues of the current supplemental examination proceeding or of the identified post-patent Office proceeding(s).

(e) Interviews are prohibited in a supplemental examination proceeding.

(f) No amendment may be filed in a supplemental examination proceeding.

(g) If the Office becomes aware, during the course of supplemental examination or of any reexamination ordered under 35 U.S.C. 257 as a result of the supplemental examination proceeding, that a material fraud on the Office may have been committed in connection with the patent requested to be examined, the supplemental examination proceeding or any reexamination proceeding ordered under 35 U.S.C. 257 will continue, and the matter will be referred to the U.S. Attorney General in accordance with 35 U.S.C. 257(e).

History of 37 C.F.R. §1.620: 77 FR 48852, Sept. 16, 2012.

§1.625. CONCLUSION OF SUPPLEMENTAL EXAMINATION; PUBLICATION OF SUPPLEMENTAL EXAMINATION CERTIFICATE; PROCEDURE AFTER CONCLUSION

(a) A supplemental examination proceeding will conclude with the electronic issuance of a supplemental examination certificate. The supplemental examination certificate will indicate the result of the determination whether any of the items of information presented in the request raised a substantial new question of patentability.

(b) If the supplemental examination certificate states that a substantial new question of patentability is raised by one or more items of information in the request, ex parte reexamination of the patent will be ordered under 35 U.S.C. 257. Upon the conclusion of the ex parte reexamination proceeding, an ex parte reexamination certificate, which will include a statement specifying that ex parte reexamination was ordered under 35 U.S.C. 257, will be published. The electronically issued supplemental examination certificate will remain as part of the public record of the patent.

(c) If the supplemental examination certificate indicates that no substantial new question of patentability is raised by any of the items of information in the request, and ex parte reexamination is not ordered under 35 U.S.C. 257, the electronically issued supplemental examination certificate will be published in due course. The fee for reexamination ordered as a result of supplemental examination, as set forth in §1.20(k)(2), will be refunded in accordance with §1.26(c).

(d) Any ex parte reexamination ordered under 35 U.S.C. 257 will be conducted in accordance with §§1.530 through 1.570, which govern ex parte reexamination, except that:

(1) The patent owner will not have the right to file a statement pursuant to §1.530, and the order will not set a time period within which to file such a statement;

(2) Reexamination of any claim of the patent may be conducted on the basis of any item of information as set forth in §1.605, and is not limited to patents and printed publications or to subject matter that has been added or deleted during the reexamination proceeding, notwithstanding §1.552(a);

(3) Issues in addition to those raised by patents and printed publications, and by subject matter added or deleted during a reexamination proceeding, may be considered and resolved, notwithstanding §1.552(c); and

(4) Information material to patentability will be defined by §1.56(b), notwithstanding §1.555(b).

History of 37 C.F.R. §1.625: 77 FR 48853, Sept. 16, 2012.

SUBPART F. ADJUSTMENT & EXTENSION OF PATENT TERM

ADJUSTMENT OF PATENT TERM DUE TO EXAMINATION DELAY

§1.701. EXTENSION OF PATENT TERM DUE TO EXAMINATION DELAY UNDER THE URUGUAY ROUND AGREEMENTS ACT (ORIGINAL APPLICATIONS, OTHER THAN DESIGNS, FILED ON OR AFTER JUNE 8, 1995, & BEFORE MAY 29, 2000)

(a) A patent, other than for designs, issued on an application filed on or after June 8, 1995, is entitled to extension of the patent term if the issuance of the patent was delayed due to:

(1) Interference or derivation proceedings under 35 U.S.C. 135(a); and/or

(2) The application being placed under a secrecy order under 35 U.S.C. 181; and/or

(3) Appellate review by the Patent Trial and Appeal Board or by a Federal court under 35 U.S.C. 141 or 145, if the patent was issued pursuant to a decision in the review reversing an adverse determination of patentability and if the patent is not subject to a terminal disclaimer due to the issuance of another patent claiming subject matter that is not patentably distinct from that under appellate review. If an application is remanded by a panel of the Patent Trial and Appeal Board and the remand is the last action by a panel of the Patent Trial and Appeal Board prior to the mailing of a notice of allowance under 35 U.S.C. 151 in the application, the remand shall be considered a decision in the review reversing an adverse determination of patentability as that phrase is used in 35 U.S.C. 154(b)(2) as amended by section 532(a) of the Uruguay Round Agreements Act, Public Law 103-465, 108 Stat. 4809, 4983-85 (1994), and a final decision in favor of the applicant under paragraph (c)(3) of this section. A remand by a panel of the Patent Trial and Appeal Board shall not be considered a decision in the review reversing an adverse determination of patentability as provided in this paragraph if there is filed a request for continued examination under 35 U.S.C. 132(b) that was not first preceded by the mailing, after such remand, of at least one of an action under 35 U.S.C. 132 or a notice of allowance under 35 U.S.C. 151.

(b) The term of a patent entitled to extension under paragraph (a) of this section shall be extended for the sum of the periods of delay calculated under paragraphs (c)(1), (c)(2), (c)(3) and (d) of this section, to the extent that these periods are not overlapping, up to a maximum of five years. The extension will run from the expiration date of the patent.

(c)(1) The period of delay under paragraph (a)(1) of this section for an application is the sum of the following periods, to the extent that the periods are not overlapping:

(i) With respect to each interference or derivation proceeding in which the application was involved, the number of days, if any, in the period beginning on the date the interference or derivation proceeding was instituted to involve the application in the interference or derivation proceeding and ending on the date that the interference or derivation proceeding was terminated with respect to the application; and

(ii) The number of days, if any, in the period beginning on the date prosecution in the application was suspended by the Patent and Trademark Office due to interference or derivation proceedings under 35 U.S.C. 135(a) not involving the application and ending on the date of the termination of the suspension.

(2) The period of delay under paragraph (a)(2) of this section for an application is the sum of the following periods, to the extent that the periods are not overlapping:

(i) The number of days, if any, the application was maintained in a sealed condition under 35 U.S.C. 181;

(ii) The number of days, if any, in the period beginning on the date of mailing of an examiner's answer under §41.39 of this title in the application under secrecy order and ending on the date the secrecy order and any renewal thereof was removed;

(iii) The number of days, if any, in the period beginning on the date applicant was notified that an interference or derivation proceeding would be instituted but for the secrecy order and ending on the date the secrecy order and any renewal thereof was removed; and

(iv) The number of days, if any, in the period beginning on the date of notification under §5.3(c) and ending on the date of mailing of the notice of allowance under §1.311.

(3) The period of delay under paragraph (a)(3) of this section is the sum of the number of days, if any, in the period beginning on the date on which an appeal to the Patent Trial and Appeal Board was filed under 35 U.S.C. 134 and ending on the date of a final decision in favor of the applicant by the Patent Trial and Appeal Board or by a Federal court in an appeal under 35 U.S.C. 141 or a civil action under 35 U.S.C. 145.

(d) The period of delay set forth in paragraph (c)(3) shall be reduced by:

(1) Any time during the period of appellate review that occurred before three years from the filing date of the first national application for patent presented for examination; and

(2) Any time during the period of appellate review, as determined by the Director, during which the applicant for patent did not act with due diligence. In determining the due diligence of an applicant, the Director may examine the facts and circumstances of the applicant's actions during the period of appellate review to determine whether the applicant exhibited that degree of timeliness as may reasonably be expected from, and which is ordinarily exercised by, a person during a period of appellate review.

(e) The provisions of this section apply only to original patents, except for design patents, issued on applications filed on or after June 8, 1995, and before May 29, 2000.

History of 37 C.F.R. §1.701: 60 FR 20228, Apr. 25, 1995; 65 FR 56391, Sept. 18, 2000; 69 FR 21710, Apr. 22, 2004; 69 FR 50001, Aug. 12, 2004; 77 FR 46627, Sept. 16, 2012.

Source of 37 C.F.R. Part 1F: 52 FR 9394, Mar. 24, 1987; 65 FR 56391, Sept. 18, 2000, unless otherwise noted.

§1.702. GROUNDS FOR ADJUSTMENT OF PATENT TERM DUE TO EXAMINATION DELAY UNDER THE PATENT TERM GUARANTEE ACT OF 1999 (ORIGINAL APPLICATIONS, OTHER THAN DESIGNS, FILED ON OR AFTER MAY 29, 2000)

(a) Failure to take certain actions within specified time frames. Subject to the provisions of 35 U.S.C. 154(b) and this subpart, the term of an original patent shall be adjusted if the issuance of the patent was delayed due to the failure of the Office to:

(1) Mail at least one of a notification under 35 U.S.C. 132 or a notice of allowance under 35 U.S.C. 151 not later than fourteen months after the date on which the application was filed under 35 U.S.C. 111(a) or the date the national stage commenced under 35 U.S.C. 371(b) or (f) in an international application;

(2) Respond to a reply under 35 U.S.C. 132 or to an appeal taken under 35 U.S.C. 134 not later than four months after the date on which the reply was filed or the appeal was taken;

(3) Act on an application not later than four months after the date of a decision by the Patent Trial and Appeal Board under 35 U.S.C. 134 or 135 or a decision by a Federal court under 35 U.S.C. 141, 145, or 146 where at least one allowable claim remains in the application; or

(4) Issue a patent not later than four months after the date on which the issue fee was paid under 35 U.S.C. 151 and all outstanding requirements were satisfied.

(b) Three-year pendency. Subject to the provisions of 35 U.S.C. 154(b) and this subpart, the term of an original patent shall be adjusted if the issuance of the patent was delayed due to the failure of the Office to issue a patent within three years after the date on which the application was filed under 35 U.S.C. 111(a) or the national stage commenced under 35 U.S.C. 371(b) or (f) in an international application, but not including:

(1) Any time consumed by continued examination of the application under 35 U.S.C. 132(b);

(2) Any time consumed by an interference or derivation proceeding under 35 U.S.C. 135(a);

(3) Any time consumed by the imposition of a secrecy order under 35 U.S.C. 181;

(4) Any time consumed by review by the Patent Trial and Appeal Board or a Federal court; or

(5) Any delay in the processing of the application by the Office that was requested by the applicant.

(c) Delays caused by interference and derivation proceedings. Subject to the provisions of 35 U.S.C. 154(b) and this subpart, the term of an original patent shall be adjusted if the issuance of the patent was delayed due to interference or derivation proceedings under 35 U.S.C. 135(a).

(d) Delays caused by secrecy order. Subject to the provisions of 35 U.S.C. 154(b) and this subpart, the term of an original patent shall be adjusted if the issuance of the patent was delayed due to the application being placed under a secrecy order under 35 U.S.C. 181.

(e) Delays caused by successful appellate review. Subject to the provisions of 35 U.S.C. 154(b) and this subpart, the term of an original patent shall be adjusted if the issuance of the patent was delayed due to review by the Patent Trial and Appeal Board under 35 U.S.C. 134 or by a Federal court under 35 U.S.C. 141 or 145, if the patent was issued under a decision in the review reversing an adverse determination of patentability. If an application is remanded by a panel of the Patent Trial and Appeal Board and the remand is the last action by a panel of the Patent Trial and Appeal Board prior to the mailing of a notice of allowance under 35 U.S.C. 151 in the application, the remand shall be considered a decision by the Patent Trial and Appeal Board as that phrase is used in 35 U.S.C. 154(b)(1)(A)(iii), a decision in the review reversing an adverse determination of patentability as that phrase is used in 35 U.S.C. 154(b)(1)(C)(iii), and a final decision in favor of the applicant under §1.703(e). A remand by a panel of the Patent Trial and Appeal Board shall not be considered a decision in the review reversing an adverse determination of patentability as provided in this paragraph if there is filed a request for continued examination under 35 U.S.C. 132(b) that was not first preceded by the mailing, after such remand, of at least one of an action under 35 U.S.C. 132 or a notice of allowance under 35 U.S.C. 151.

(f) The provisions of this section and §§1.703 through 1.705 apply only to original applications, except applications for a design patent, filed on or after May 29, 2000, and patents issued on such applications.

History of 37 C.F.R. §1.702: 65 FR 56391, Sept. 18, 2000; 69 FR 21711, Apr. 22, 2004; 77 FR 46627, Sept. 16, 2012; 78 FR 19420, Apr. 1, 2013; 79 FR 27755, May 15, 2014.

§1.703. PERIOD OF ADJUSTMENT OF PATENT TERM DUE TO EXAMINATION DELAY

(a) The period of adjustment under §1.702(a) is the sum of the following periods:

(1) The number of days, if any, in the period beginning on the day after the date that is fourteen months after the date on which the application was filed under 35 U.S.C. 111(a) or the date the national stage commenced under 35 U.S.C. 371(b) or (f) in an international application and ending on the date of mailing of either an action under 35 U.S.C. 132, or a notice of allowance under 35 U.S.C. 151, whichever occurs first;

(2) The number of days, if any, in the period beginning on the day after the date that is four months after the date a reply under §1.111 was filed and ending on the date of mailing of either an action under 35 U.S.C. 132, or a notice of allowance under 35 U.S.C. 151, whichever occurs first;

(3) The number of days, if any, in the period beginning on the day after the date that is four months after the date a reply in compliance with §1.113(c) was filed and ending on the date of mailing of either an action under 35 U.S.C. 132, or a notice of allowance under 35 U.S.C. 151, whichever occurs first;

(4) The number of days, if any, in the period beginning on the day after the date that is four months after the date an appeal brief in compliance with §41.37 of this title was filed and ending on the date of mailing of any of an examiner's answer under §41.39 of this title, an action under 35 U.S.C. 132, or a notice of allowance under 35 U.S.C. 151, whichever occurs first;

(5) The number of days, if any, in the period beginning on the day after the date that is four months after the date of a final decision by the Patent Trial and Appeal Board or by a Federal court in an appeal under 35 U.S.C. 141 or a civil action un-

der 35 U.S.C. 145 or 146 where at least one allowable claim remains in the application and ending on the date of mailing of either an action under 35 U.S.C. 132 or a notice of allowance under 35 U.S.C. 151, whichever occurs first; and

(6) The number of days, if any, in the period beginning on the day after the date that is four months after the date the issue fee was paid and all outstanding requirements were satisfied and ending on the date a patent was issued.

(b) The period of adjustment under §1.702(b) is the number of days, if any, in the period beginning on the day after the date that is three years after the date on which the application was filed under 35 U.S.C. 111(a) or the national stage commenced under 35 U.S.C. 371(b) or (f) in an international application and ending on the date a patent was issued, but not including the sum of the following periods:

(1) The number of days, if any, in the period beginning on the date on which any request for continued examination of the application under 35 U.S.C. 132(b) was filed and ending on the date of mailing of the notice of allowance under 35 U.S.C. 151;

(2)(i) The number of days, if any, in the period beginning on the date an interference or derivation proceeding was instituted to involve the application in the interference or derivation proceeding under 35 U.S.C. 135(a) and ending on the date that the interference or derivation proceeding was terminated with respect to the application; and

(ii) The number of days, if any, in the period beginning on the date prosecution in the application was suspended by the Office due to interference or derivation proceedings under 35 U.S.C. 135(a) not involving the application and ending on the date of the termination of the suspension;

(3)(i) The number of days, if any, the application was maintained in a sealed condition under 35 U.S.C. 181;

(ii) The number of days, if any, in the period beginning on the date of mailing of an examiner's answer under §41.39 of this title in the application under secrecy order and ending on the date the secrecy order was removed;

(iii) The number of days, if any, in the period beginning on the date applicant was notified that an interference or derivation proceeding under 35 U.S.C. 135(a) would be instituted but for the secrecy order and ending on the date the secrecy order was removed; and

(iv) The number of days, if any, in the period beginning on the date of notification under §5.3(c) of this chapter and ending on the date of mailing of the notice of allowance under 35 U.S.C. 151; and,

(4) The number of days, if any, in the period beginning on the date on which jurisdiction over the application passes to the Patent Trial and Appeal Board under §41.35(a) of this chapter and ending on the date that jurisdiction by the Patent Trial and Appeal Board ends under §41.35(b) of this chapter or the date of the last decision by a Federal court in an appeal under 35 U.S.C. 141 or a civil action under 35 U.S.C. 145, whichever is later.

(c) The period of adjustment under §1.702(c) is the sum of the following periods, to the extent that the periods are not overlapping:

(1) The number of days, if any, in the period beginning on the date an interference or derivation proceeding was instituted to involve the application in the interference or derivation proceeding under 35 U.S.C. 135(a) and ending on the date that the interference or derivation proceeding was terminated with respect to the application; and

(2) The number of days, if any, in the period beginning on the date prosecution in the application was suspended by the Office due to interference or derivation proceedings under 35 U.S.C. 135(a) not involving the application and ending on the date of the termination of the suspension.

(d) The period of adjustment under §1.702(d) is the sum of the following periods, to the extent that the periods are not overlapping:

(1) The number of days, if any, the application was maintained in a sealed condition under 35 U.S.C. 181;

(2) The number of days, if any, in the period beginning on the date of mailing of an examiner's answer under §41.39 of this title in the application under secrecy order and ending on the date the secrecy order was removed;

(3) The number of days, if any, in the period beginning on the date applicant was notified that an interference or derivation proceeding under 35 U.S.C. 135(a) would be instituted but for the secrecy order and ending on the date the secrecy order was removed; and

(4) The number of days, if any, in the period beginning on the date of notification under §5.3(c) of this chapter and ending on the date of mailing of the notice of allowance under 35 U.S.C. 151.

(e) The period of adjustment under §1.702(e) is the sum of the number of days, if any, in the period beginning on the date on which jurisdiction over the application passes to the Patent Trial and Appeal Board under §41.35(a) of this chapter and ending on the date of a final decision in favor of the applicant by the Patent Trial and Appeal Board or by a Federal court in an appeal under 35 U.S.C. 141 or a civil action under 35 U.S.C. 145.

(f) The adjustment will run from the expiration date of the patent as set forth in 35 U.S.C. 154(a)(2). To the extent that periods of delay attributable to the grounds specified in §1.702 overlap, the period of adjustment granted under this section shall not exceed the actual number of days the issuance of the patent was delayed. The term of a patent entitled to adjustment under §1.702 and this section shall be adjusted for the sum of the periods calculated under paragraphs (a) through (e) of this section, to the extent that such periods are not overlapping, less the sum of the periods calculated under

§1.704. The date indicated on any certificate of mailing or transmission under §1.8 shall not be taken into account in this calculation.

(g) No patent, the term of which has been disclaimed beyond a specified date, shall be adjusted under §1.702 and this section beyond the expiration date specified in the disclaimer.

History of 37 C.F.R. §1.703: 65 FR 56391, Sept. 18, 2000; 69 FR 21711, Apr. 22, 2004; 69 FR 50001, Aug. 12, 2004; 77 FR 46628, Sept. 16, 2012; 77 FR 49360, Sept. 17, 2012; 78 FR 19420, Apr. 1, 2013; 79 FR 27755, May 15, 2014; 80 FR 1356, Jan. 9, 2015.

§1.704. REDUCTION OF PERIOD OF ADJUSTMENT OF PATENT TERM

(a) The period of adjustment of the term of a patent under §§1.703(a) through (e) shall be reduced by a period equal to the period of time during which the applicant failed to engage in reasonable efforts to conclude prosecution (processing or examination) of the application.

(b) With respect to the grounds for adjustment set forth in §§1.702(a) through (e), and in particular the ground of adjustment set forth in §1.702(b), an applicant shall be deemed to have failed to engage in reasonable efforts to conclude processing or examination of an application for the cumulative total of any periods of time in excess of three months that are taken to reply to any notice or action by the Office making any rejection, objection, argument, or other request, measuring such three-month period from the date the notice or action was mailed or given to the applicant, in which case the period of adjustment set forth in §1.703 shall be reduced by the number of days, if any, beginning on the day after the date that is three months after the date of mailing or transmission of the Office communication notifying the applicant of the rejection, objection, argument, or other request and ending on the date the reply was filed. The period, or shortened statutory period, for reply that is set in the Office action or notice has no effect on the three-month period set forth in this paragraph.

(c) Circumstances that constitute a failure of the applicant to engage in reasonable efforts to conclude processing or examination of an application also include the following circumstances, which will result in the following reduction of the period of adjustment set forth in §1.703 to the extent that the periods are not overlapping:

(1) Suspension of action under §1.103 at the applicant's request, in which case the period of adjustment set forth in §1.703 shall be reduced by the number of days, if any, beginning on the date a request for suspension of action under §1.103 was filed and ending on the date of the termination of the suspension;

(2) Deferral of issuance of a patent under §1.314, in which case the period of adjustment set forth in §1.703 shall be reduced by the number of days, if any, beginning on the date a request for deferral of issuance of a patent under §1.314 was filed and ending on the date the patent was issued;

(3) Abandonment of the application or late payment of the issue fee, in which case the period of adjustment set forth in §1.703 shall be reduced by the number of days, if any, beginning on the date of abandonment or the date after the date the issue fee was due and ending on the earlier of:

(i) The date of mailing of the decision reviving the application or accepting late payment of the issue fee; or

(ii) The date that is four months after the date the grantable petition to revive the application or accept late payment of the issue fee was filed;

(4) Failure to file a petition to withdraw the holding of abandonment or to revive an application within two months from the mailing date of a notice of abandonment, in which case the period of adjustment set forth in §1.703 shall be reduced by the number of days, if any, beginning on the day after the date two months from the mailing date of a notice of abandonment and ending on the date a petition to withdraw the holding of abandonment or to revive the application was filed;

(5) Conversion of a provisional application under 35 U.S.C. 111(b) to a nonprovisional application under 35 U.S.C. 111(a) pursuant to 35 U.S.C. 111(b)(5), in which case the period of adjustment set forth in §1.703 shall be reduced by the number of days, if any, beginning on the date the application was filed under 35 U.S.C. 111(b) and ending on the date a request in compliance with §1.53(c)(3) to convert the provisional application into a nonprovisional application was filed;

(6) Submission of a preliminary amendment or other preliminary paper less than one month before the mailing of an Office action under 35 U.S.C. 132 or notice of allowance under 35 U.S.C. 151 that requires the mailing of a supplemental Office action or notice of allowance, in which case the period of adjustment set forth in §1.703 shall be reduced by the lesser of:

(i) The number of days, if any, beginning on the day after the mailing date of the original Office action or notice of allowance and ending on the date of mailing of the supplemental Office action or notice of allowance; or

(ii) Four months;

(7) Submission of a reply having an omission (§1.135(c)), in which case the period of adjustment set forth in §1.703 shall be reduced by the number of days, if any, beginning on the day after the date the reply having an omission was filed and ending on the date that the reply or other paper correcting the omission was filed;

(8) Submission of a supplemental reply or other paper, other than a supplemental reply or other paper expressly requested by the examiner, after a reply has been filed, in which case the period of adjustment set forth in §1.703 shall be reduced by the number of days, if any, beginning on the day after the date the initial reply was filed and ending on the date that the supplemental reply or other such paper was filed;

(9) Submission of an amendment or other paper after a decision by the Patent Trial and Appeal Board, other than a decision designated as containing a new ground of rejection under §41.50(b) of this title or statement under §41.50(c) of this title, or a decision by a Federal court, less than one month before the mailing of an Office action under 35 U.S.C. 132 or notice of allowance under 35 U.S.C. 151 that requires the mailing of a supplemental Office action or supplemental notice of allowance, in which case the period of adjustment set forth in §1.703 shall be reduced by the lesser of:

(i) The number of days, if any, beginning on the day after the mailing date of the original Office action or notice of allowance and ending on the mailing date of the supplemental Office action or notice of allowance; or

(ii) Four months;

(10) Submission of an amendment under §1.312 or other paper, other than a request for continued examination in compliance with §1.114, after a notice of allowance has been given or mailed, in which case the period of adjustment set forth in §1.703 shall be reduced by the lesser of:

(i) The number of days, if any, beginning on the date the amendment under §1.312 or other paper was filed and ending on the mailing date of the Office action or notice in response to the amendment under §1.312 or such other paper; or

(ii) Four months;

(11) Failure to file an appeal brief in compliance with §41.37 of this chapter within three months from the date on which a notice of appeal to the Patent Trial and Appeal Board was filed under 35 U.S.C. 134 and §41.31 of this chapter, in which case the period of adjustment set forth in §1.703 shall be reduced by the number of days, if any, beginning on the day after the date three months from the date on which a notice of appeal to the Patent Trial and Appeal Board was filed under 35 U.S.C. 134 and §41.31 of this chapter, and ending on the date an appeal brief in compliance with §41.37 of this chapter or a request for continued examination in compliance with §1.114 was filed;

(12) Submission of a request for continued examination under 35 U.S.C. 132(b) after any notice of allowance under 35 U.S.C. 151 has been mailed, in which case the period of adjustment set forth in §1.703 shall be reduced by the number of days, if any, beginning on the day after the date of mailing of the notice of allowance under 35 U.S.C. 151 and ending on the date the request for continued examination under 35 U.S.C. 132(b) was filed;

(13) Failure to provide an application in condition for examination as defined in paragraph (f) of this section within eight months from either the date on which the application was filed under 35 U.S.C. 111(a) or the date of commencement of the national stage under 35 U.S.C. 371(b) or (f) in an international application, in which case the period of adjustment set forth in §1.703 shall be reduced by the number of days, if any, beginning on the day after the date that is eight months from either the date on which the application was filed under 35 U.S.C. 111(a) or the date of commencement of the national stage under 35 U.S.C. 371(b) or (f) in an international application and ending on the date the application is in condition for examination as defined in paragraph (f) of this section; and

(14) Further prosecution via a continuing application, in which case the period of adjustment set forth in §1.703 shall not include any period that is prior to the actual filing date of the application that resulted in the patent.

(d)(1) A paper containing only an information disclosure statement in compliance with §§1.97 and 1.98 will not be considered a failure to engage in reasonable efforts to conclude prosecution (processing or examination) of the application under paragraphs (c)(6), (c)(8), (c)(9), or (c)(10) of this section, and a request for continued examination in compliance with §1.114 with no submission other than an information disclosure statement in compliance with §§1.97 and 1.98 will not be considered a failure to engage in reasonable efforts to conclude prosecution (processing or examination) of the application under paragraph (c)(12) of this section, if the paper or request for continued examination is accompanied by a statement that each item of information contained in the information disclosure statement:

(i) Was first cited in any communication from a patent office in a counterpart foreign or international application or from the Office, and this communication was not received by any individual designated in §1.56(c) more than thirty days prior to the filing of the information disclosure statement; or

(ii) Is a communication that was issued by a patent office in a counterpart foreign or international application or by the Office, and this communication was not received by any individual designated in §1.56(c) more than thirty days prior to the filing of the information disclosure statement.

(2) The thirty-day period set forth in paragraph (d)(1) of this section is not extendable.

(e) The submission of a request under §1.705(c) for reinstatement of reduced patent term adjustment will not be considered a failure to engage in reasonable efforts to conclude prosecution (processing or examination) of the application under paragraph (c)(10) of this section.

(f) An application filed under 35 U.S.C. 111(a) is in condition for examination when the application includes a specification, including at least one claim and an abstract (§1.72(b)), and has papers in compliance with §1.52, drawings (if any) in compliance with §1.84, any English translation required by §1.52(d) or §1.57(a), a sequence listing in compliance with §1.821 through §1.825 (if applicable), the inventor's oath or declaration or an application data sheet containing the information specified in §1.63(b), the basic filing fee (§1.16(a) or §1.16(c)), the search fee (§1.16(k) or §1.16(m)), the examination fee (§1.16(o) or §1.16(q)), any certified copy of the previously filed application required by

§1.57(a), and any application size fee required by the Office under §1.16(s). An international application is in condition for examination when the application has entered the national stage as defined in §1.491(b), and includes a specification, including at least one claim and an abstract (§1.72(b)), and has papers in compliance with §1.52, drawings (if any) in compliance with §1.84, a sequence listing in compliance with §1.821 through §1.825 (if applicable), the inventor's oath or declaration or an application data sheet containing the information specified in §1.63(b), the search fee (§1.492(b)), the examination fee (§1.492(c)), and any application size fee required by the Office under §1.492(j). An application shall be considered as having papers in compliance with §1.52, drawings (if any) in compliance with §1.84, and a sequence listing in compliance with §1.821 through §1.825 (if applicable) for purposes of this paragraph on the filing date of the latest reply (if any) correcting the papers, drawings, or sequence listing that is prior to the date of mailing of either an action under 35 U.S.C. 132 or a notice of allowance under 35 U.S.C. 151, whichever occurs first.

History of 37 C.F.R. §1.704: 65 FR 56391, Sept. 18, 2000; 65 FR 56393, Sept. 18, 2000; 69 FR 21711, Apr. 22, 2004; 69 FR 50002, Aug. 12, 2004; 74 FR 52691, Oct. 14, 2009; 76 FR 74702, Dec. 1, 2011; 77 FR 46628, Sept. 16, 2012; 77 FR 49360, Sept. 17, 2012; 78 FR 19420, Apr. 1, 2013; 78 FR 62408, Dec. 18, 2013; 79 FR 27755, May 15, 2014; 80 FR 1356, Jan. 9, 2015.

§1.705. PATENT TERM ADJUSTMENT DETERMINATION

(a) The patent will include notification of any patent term adjustment under 35 U.S.C. 154(b).

(b) Any request for reconsideration of the patent term adjustment indicated on the patent must be by way of an application for patent term adjustment filed no later than two months from the date the patent was granted. This two-month time period may be extended under the provisions of §1.136(a). An application for patent term adjustment under this section must be accompanied by:

(1) The fee set forth in §1.18(e); and

(2) A statement of the facts involved, specifying:

(i) The correct patent term adjustment and the basis or bases under §1.702 for the adjustment;

(ii) The relevant dates as specified in §§1.703(a) through (e) for which an adjustment is sought and the adjustment as specified in §1.703(f) to which the patent is entitled;

(iii) Whether the patent is subject to a terminal disclaimer and any expiration date specified in the terminal disclaimer; and

(iv)(A) Any circumstances during the prosecution of the application resulting in the patent that constitute a failure to engage in reasonable efforts to conclude processing or examination of such application as set forth in §1.704; or

(B) That there were no circumstances constituting a failure to engage in reasonable efforts to conclude processing or examination of such application as set forth in §1.704.

(c) Any request for reinstatement of all or part of the period of adjustment reduced pursuant to §1.704(b) for failing to reply to a rejection, objection, argument, or other request within three months of the date of mailing of the Office communication notifying the applicant of the rejection, objection, argument, or other request must be filed prior to the issuance of the patent. This time period is not extendable. Any request for reinstatement of all or part of the period of adjustment reduced pursuant to §1.704(b) under this paragraph must also be accompanied by:

(1) The fee set forth in §1.18(f); and

(2) A showing to the satisfaction of the Director that, in spite of all due care, the applicant was unable to reply to the rejection, objection, argument, or other request within three months of the date of mailing of the Office communication notifying the applicant of the rejection, objection, argument, or other request. The Office shall not grant any request for reinstatement for more than three additional months for each reply beyond three months from the date of mailing of the Office communication notifying the applicant of the rejection, objection, argument, or other request.

(d) No submission or petition on behalf of a third party concerning patent term adjustment under 35 U.S.C. 154(b) will be considered by the Office. Any such submission or petition will be returned to the third party, or otherwise disposed of, at the convenience of the Office.

History of 37 C.F.R. §1.705: 65 FR 56391, Sept. 18, 2000; 65 FR 56394, Sept. 18, 2000; 69 FR 21711, Apr. 22, 2004; 78 FR 19420, Apr. 1, 2013; 79 FR 27755, May 15, 2014.

EXTENSION OF PATENT TERM DUE TO REGULATORY REVIEW

§1.710. PATENTS SUBJECT TO EXTENSION OF THE PATENT TERM

(a) A patent is eligible for extension of the patent term if the patent claims a product as defined in paragraph (b) of this section, either alone or in combination with other ingredients that read on a composition that received permission for commercial marketing or use, or a method of using such a product, or a method of manufacturing such a product, and meets all other conditions and requirements of this subpart.

(b) The term "product" referred to in paragraph (a) of this section means—

(1) The active ingredient of a new human drug, antibiotic drug, or human biological product (as those terms are used in the Federal Food, Drug, and Cosmetic Act and the Public Health Service Act) including any salt or ester of the active ingredient, as a single entity or in combination with another active ingredient; or

(2) The active ingredient of a new animal drug or veterinary biological product (as those terms are used in the Federal Food, Drug, and Cosmetic Act and the Virus-Serum-Toxin Act) that is not primarily manufactured using recombinant DNA, recombinant RNA, hybridoma technology, or other processes including site specific genetic manipulation techniques, including any salt or ester of the active ingredient, as a single entity or in combination with another active ingredient; or

(3) Any medical device, food additive, or color additive subject to regulation under the Federal Food, Drug, and Cosmetic Act.

History of 37 C.F.R. §1.710: 54 FR 30379, July 20, 1989.

§1.720. CONDITIONS FOR EXTENSION OF PATENT TERM

The term of a patent may be extended if:

(a) The patent claims a product or a method of using or manufacturing a product as defined in §1.710;

(b) The term of the patent has never been previously extended, except for extensions issued pursuant to §§1.701, 1.760, or §1.790;

(c) An application for extension is submitted in compliance with §1.740;

(d) The product has been subject to a regulatory review period as defined in 35 U.S.C. 156(g) before its commercial marketing or use;

(e) The product has received permission for commercial marketing or use and—

(1) The permission for the commercial marketing or use of the product is the first received permission for commercial marketing or use under the provision of law under which the applicable regulatory review occurred, or

(2) In the case of a patent other than one directed to subject matter within §1.710(b)(2) claiming a method of manufacturing the product that primarily uses recombinant DNA technology in the manufacture of the product, the permission for the commercial marketing or use is the first received permission for the commercial marketing or use of a product manufactured under the process claimed in the patent, or

(3) In the case of a patent claiming a new animal drug or a veterinary biological product that is not covered by the claims in any other patent that has been extended, and has received permission for the commercial marketing or use in non-food-producing animals and in food-producing animals, and was not extended on the basis of the regulatory review period for use in non-food-producing animals, the permission for the commercial marketing or use of the drug or product after the regulatory review period for use in food-producing animals is the first permitted commercial marketing or use of the drug or product for administration to a food-producing animal.

(f) The application is submitted within the sixty-day period beginning on the date the product first received permission for commercial marketing or use under the provisions of law under which the applicable regulatory review period occurred; or in the case of a patent claiming a method of manufacturing the product which primarily uses recombinant DNA technology in the manufacture of the product, the application for extension is submitted within the sixty-day period beginning on the date of the first permitted commercial marketing or use of a product manufactured under the process claimed in the patent; or in the case of a patent that claims a new animal drug or a veterinary biological product that is not covered by the claims in any other patent that has been extended, and said drug or product has received permission for the commercial marketing or use in non-food-producing animals, the application for extension is submitted within the sixty-day period beginning on the date of the first permitted commercial marketing or use of the drug or product for administration to a food-producing animal;

(g) The term of the patent, including any interim extension issued pursuant to §1.790, has not expired before the submission of an application in compliance with §1.741; and

(h) No other patent term has been extended for the same regulatory review period for the product.

History of 37 C.F.R. §1.720: 54 FR 30380, July 20, 1989; 65 FR 54679, Sept. 8, 2000.

§1.730. APPLICANT FOR EXTENSION OF PATENT TERM; SIGNATURE REQUIREMENTS

(a) Any application for extension of a patent term must be submitted by the owner of record of the patent or its agent and must comply with the requirements of §1.740.

(b) If the application is submitted by the patent owner, the application must be signed either by:

(1) The patent owner in compliance with §3.73(c) of this chapter; or

(2) A registered practitioner on behalf of the patent owner.

(c) If the application is submitted on behalf of the patent owner by an agent of the patent owner (*e.g.*, a licensee of the patent owner), the application must be signed by a registered practitioner on behalf of the agent. The Office may require proof that the agent is authorized to act on behalf of the patent owner.

(d) If the application is signed by a registered practitioner, the Office may require proof that the practitioner is authorized to act on behalf of the patent owner or agent of the patent owner.

History of 37 C.F.R. §1.730: 65 FR 54679, Sept. 8, 2000; 77 FR 48825, Sept. 16, 2012.

§1.740. FORMAL REQUIREMENTS FOR APPLICATION FOR EXTENSION OF PATENT TERM; CORRECTION OF INFORMALITIES

(a) An application for extension of patent term must be made in writing to the Director. A formal application for the extension of patent term must include:

(1) A complete identification of the approved product as by appropriate chemical and generic name, physical structure or characteristics;

(2) A complete identification of the Federal statute including the applicable provision of law under which the regulatory review occurred;

(3) An identification of the date on which the product received permission for commercial marketing or use under the provision of law under which the applicable regulatory review period occurred;

(4) In the case of a drug product, an identification of each active ingredient in the product and as to each active ingredient, a statement that it has not been previously approved for commercial marketing or use under the Federal Food, Drug, and Cosmetic Act, the Public Health Service Act, or the Virus-Serum-Toxin Act, or a statement of when the active ingredient was approved for commercial marketing or use (either alone or in combination with other active ingredients), the use for which it was approved, and the provision of law under which it was approved.

(5) A statement that the application is being submitted within the sixty day period permitted for submission pursuant to §1.720(f) and an identification of the date of the last day on which the application could be submitted;

(6) A complete identification of the patent for which an extension is being sought by the name of the inventor, the patent number, the date of issue, and the date of expiration;

(7) A copy of the patent for which an extension is being sought, including the entire specification (including claims) and drawings;

(8) A copy of any disclaimer, certificate of correction, receipt of maintenance fee payment, or reexamination certificate issued in the patent;

(9) A statement that the patent claims the approved product, or a method of using or manufacturing the approved product, and a showing which lists each applicable patent claim and demonstrates the manner in which at least one such patent claim reads on:

(i) The approved product, if the listed claims include any claim to the approved product;

(ii) The method of using the approved product, if the listed claims include any claim to the method of using the approved product; and

(iii) The method of manufacturing the approved product, if the listed claims include any claim to the method of manufacturing the approved product;

(10) A statement beginning on a new page of the relevant dates and information pursuant to 35 U.S.C. 156(g) in order to enable the Secretary of Health and Human Services or the Secretary of Agriculture, as appropriate, to determine the applicable regulatory review period as follows:

(i) For a patent claiming a human drug, antibiotic, or human biological product:

(A) The effective date of the investigational new drug (IND) application and the IND number;

(B) The date on which a new drug application (NDA) or a Product License Application (PLA) was initially submitted and the NDA or PLA number; and

(C) The date on which the NDA was approved or the Product License issued;

(ii) For a patent claiming a new animal drug:

(A) The date a major health or environmental effects test on the drug was initiated, and any available substantiation of that date, or the date of an exemption under subsection (j) of Section 512 of the Federal Food, Drug, and Cosmetic Act became effective for such animal drug;

(B) The date on which a new animal drug application (NADA) was initially submitted and the NADA number; and

(C) The date on which the NADA was approved;

(iii) For a patent claiming a veterinary biological product:

(A) The date the authority to prepare an experimental biological product under the Virus-Serum-Toxin Act became effective;

(B) The date an application for a license was submitted under the Virus-Serum-Toxin Act; and

(C) The date the license issued;

(iv) For a patent claiming a food or color additive:

(A) The date a major health or environmental effects test on the additive was initiated and any available substantiation of that date;

(B) The date on which a petition for product approval under the Federal Food, Drug and Cosmetic Act was initially submitted and the petition number; and

(C) The date on which the FDA published a Federal Register notice listing the additive for use;

(v) For a patent claiming a medical device:

(A) The effective date of the investigational device exemption (IDE) and the IDE number, if applicable, or the date on which the applicant began the first clinical investigation involving the device, if no IDE was submitted, and any available substantiation of that date;

(B) The date on which the application for product approval or notice of completion of a product development protocol under Section 515 of the Federal Food, Drug and Cosmetic Act was initially submitted and the number of the application; and

(C) The date on which the application was approved or the protocol declared to be completed;

(11) A brief description beginning on a new page of the significant activities undertaken by the marketing applicant during the applicable regulatory review period with respect to the approved product and the significant dates applicable to such activities;

(12) A statement beginning on a new page that in the opinion of the applicant the patent is eligible for the extension and a statement as to the length of extension claimed, including how the length of extension was determined;

(13) A statement that applicant acknowledges a duty to disclose to the Director of the United States Patent and Trademark Office and the Secretary of Health and Human Services or the Secretary of Agriculture any information which is material to the determination of entitlement to the extension sought (see §1.765);

(14) The prescribed fee for receiving and acting upon the application for extension (see §1.20(j)); and

(15) The name, address, and telephone number of the person to whom inquiries and correspondence relating to the application for patent term extension are to be directed.

(b) The application under this section must be accompanied by two additional copies of such application (for a total of three copies).

(c) If an application for extension of patent term is informal under this section, the Office will so notify the applicant. The applicant has two months from the mail date of the notice, or such time as is set in the notice, within which to correct the informality. Unless the notice indicates otherwise, this time period may be extended under the provisions of §1.136.

History of 37 C.F.R. §1.740: 54 FR 30380, July 20, 1989; 56 FR 65155, Dec. 13, 1991; 65 FR 54679, Sept. 8, 2000; 68 FR 14337, Mar. 25, 2003.

§1.741. COMPLETE APPLICATION GIVEN A FILING DATE; PETITION PROCEDURE

(a) The filing date of an application for extension of a patent term is the date on which a complete application is received in the Office or filed pursuant to the procedures set forth in §1.8 or §1.10. A complete application must include:

(1) An identification of the approved product;

(2) An identification of each Federal statute under which regulatory review occurred;

(3) An identification of the patent for which an extension is being sought;

(4) An identification of each claim of the patent which claims the approved product or a method of using or manufacturing the approved product;

(5) Sufficient information to enable the Director to determine under subsections (a) and (b) of 35 U.S.C. 156 the eligibility of a patent for extension, and the rights that will be derived from the extension, and information to enable the Director and the Secretary of Health and Human Services or the Secretary of Agriculture to determine the length of the regulatory review period; and

(6) A brief description of the activities undertaken by the marketing applicant during the applicable regulatory review period with respect to the approved product and the significant dates applicable to such activities.

(b) If an application for extension of patent term is incomplete under this section, the Office will so notify the applicant. If applicant requests review of a notice that an application is incomplete, or review of the filing date accorded an application under this section, applicant must file a petition pursuant to this paragraph accompanied by the fee set forth in §1.17(f) within two months of the mail date of the notice that the application is incomplete, or the notice according the filing date complained of. Unless the notice indicates otherwise, this time period may be extended under the provisions of §1.136.

History of 37 C.F.R. §1.741: 54 FR 30380, July 20, 1989; 58 FR 54503, Oct. 22, 1993; 61 FR 64028, Dec. 3, 1996; 65 FR 54680, Sept. 8, 2000; 69 FR 56546, Sept. 21, 2004.

§1.750. DETERMINATION OF ELIGIBILITY FOR EXTENSION OF PATENT TERM

A determination as to whether a patent is eligible for extension may be made by the Director solely on the basis of the representations contained in the application for extension filed in compliance with §1.740 or §1.790. This determination may be delegated to appropriate Patent and Trademark Office officials and may be made at any time before the certificate of extension is issued. The Director or other appropriate officials may require from applicant further information or make such independent inquiries as desired before a final determination is made on whether a patent is eligible for extension. In an application for extension filed in compliance with §1.740, a notice will be mailed to applicant containing the determination as to the eligibility of the patent for extension and the period of time of the extension, if any. This notice shall constitute the final determination as to the eligibility and any period of extension of the patent. A single request for reconsideration of a final determination may be made if filed by the applicant within such time as may be set in the notice of final determination or, if no time is set, within one month from the date of the final determination. The time periods set forth herein are subject to the provisions of §1.136.

History of 37 C.F.R. §1.750: 60 FR 25618, May 12, 1995.

§1.760. INTERIM EXTENSION OF PATENT TERM UNDER 35 U.S.C. 156(e)(2)

An applicant who has filed a formal application for extension in compliance with §1.740 may request one or more interim extensions for periods of up to one year each pending a final determination on the application pursuant to §1.750. Any such request should be filed at least three months prior to the expiration date of the patent. The Director may issue interim extensions, without a request by the applicant, for periods of up to one year each until a final determination is made. The patent owner or agent will be notified when an interim extension is granted and notice of the extension will be published in the Official Gazette of the United States Patent and Trademark Office. The notice will be recorded in the official file of the patent and will be considered as part of the original patent. In no event will the interim extensions granted under this section be longer than the maximum period for extension to which the applicant would be eligible.

History of 37 C.F.R. §1.760: 60 FR 25618, May 12, 1995; 65 FR 54680, Sept. 8, 2000.

§1.765. DUTY OF DISCLOSURE IN PATENT TERM EXTENSION PROCEEDINGS

(a) A duty of candor and good faith toward the Patent and Trademark Office and the Secretary of Health and Human Services or the Secretary of Agriculture rests on the patent owner or its agent, on each attorney or agent who represents the patent owner and on every other individual who is substantively involved on behalf of the patent owner in a patent term extension proceeding. All such individuals who are aware, or become aware, of material information adverse to a determination of entitlement to the extension sought, which has not been previously made of record in the patent term extension proceeding must bring such information to the attention of the Office or the Secretary, as appropriate, in accordance with paragraph (b) of this section, as soon as it is practical to do so after the individual becomes aware of the information. Information is material where there is a substantial likelihood that the Office or the Secretary would consider it important in determinations to be made in the patent term extension proceeding.

(b) Disclosures pursuant to this section must be accompanied by a copy of each written document which is being disclosed. The disclosure must be made to the Office or the Secretary, as appropriate, unless the disclosure is material to determinations to be made by both the Office and the Secretary, in which case duplicate copies, certified as such, must be filed in the Office and with the Secretary. Disclosures pursuant to this section may be made to the Office or the Secretary, as appropriate, through an attorney or agent having responsibility on behalf of the patent owner or its agent for the patent term extension proceeding or through a patent owner acting on his or her own behalf. Disclosure to such an attorney, agent or patent owner shall satisfy the duty of any other individual. Such an attorney, agent or patent owner has no duty to transmit information which is not material to the determination of entitlement to the extension sought.

(c) No patent will be determined eligible for extension and no extension will be issued if it is determined that fraud on the Office or the Secretary was practiced or attempted or the duty of disclosure was violated through bad faith or gross negligence in connection with the patent term extension proceeding. If it is established by clear and convincing evidence that any fraud was practiced or attempted on the Office or the Secretary in connection with the patent term extension proceeding or that there was any violation of the duty of disclosure through bad faith or gross negligence in connection with the patent term extension proceeding, a final determination will be made pursuant to §1.750 that the patent is not eligible for extension.

(d) The duty of disclosure pursuant to this section rests on the individuals identified in paragraph (a) of this section and no submission on behalf of third parties, in the form of protests or otherwise, will be considered by the Office. Any such submissions by third parties to the Office will be returned to the party making the submission, or otherwise disposed of, without consideration by the Office.

History of 37 C.F.R. §1.765: 54 FR 30381, July 20, 1989; 60 FR 25618, May 12, 1995.

§1.770. EXPRESS WITHDRAWAL OF APPLICATION FOR EXTENSION OF PATENT TERM

An application for extension of patent term may be expressly withdrawn before a determination is made pursuant to §1.750 by filing in the Office, in duplicate, a written declaration of withdrawal signed by the owner of record of the patent or its agent. An application may not be expressly withdrawn after the date permitted for reply to the final determination on the application. An express withdrawal pursuant to this section is effective when acknowledged in writing by the Office. The filing of an express withdrawal pursuant to this section and its acceptance by the Office does not entitle applicant to a refund of the filing fee (§1.20(j)) or any portion thereof.

History of 37 C.F.R. §1.770: 56 FR 65155, Dec. 13, 1991; 62 FR 53201, Oct. 10, 1997.

§1.775. CALCULATION OF PATENT TERM EXTENSION FOR A HUMAN DRUG, ANTIBIOTIC DRUG OR HUMAN BIOLOGICAL PRODUCT

(a) If a determination is made pursuant to §1.750 that a patent for a human drug, antibiotic drug or human biological product is eligible for extension, the term shall be extended by the time as calculated in days in the manner indicated by this section. The patent term extension will run from the original expiration date of the patent or any earlier date set by terminal disclaimer (§1.321).

(b) The term of the patent for a human drug, antibiotic drug or human biological product will be extended by the length of the regulatory review period for the product as determined by the Secretary of Health and Human Services, reduced as appropriate pursuant to paragraphs (d)(1) through (d)(6) of this section.

(c) The length of the regulatory review period for a human drug, antibiotic drug or human biological product will be determined by the Secretary of Health and Human Services. Under 35 U.S.C. 156(g)(1)(B), it is the sum of—

(1) The number of days in the period beginning on the date an exemption under subsection (i) of section 505 or subsection (d) of section 507 of the Federal Food, Drug, and Cosmetic Act became effective for the approved product and ending on the date the application was initially submitted for such product under those sections or under section 351 of the Public Health Service Act; and

(2) The number of days in the period beginning on the date the application was initially submitted for the approved product under section 351 of the Public Health Service Act, subsection (b) of section 505 or section 507 of the Federal Food, Drug, and Cosmetic Act and ending on the date such application was approved under such section.

(d) The term of the patent as extended for a human drug, antibiotic drug or human biological product will be determined by—

(1) Subtracting from the number of days determined by the Secretary of Health and Human Services to be in the regulatory review period:

(i) The number of days in the periods of paragraphs (c)(1) and (c)(2) of this section which were on and before the date on which the patent issued;

(ii) The number of days in the periods of paragraphs (c)(1) and (c)(2) of this section during which it is determined under 35 U.S.C. 156(d)(2)(B) by the Secretary of Health and Human Services that applicant did not act with due diligence;

(iii) One-half the number of days remaining in the period defined by paragraph (c)(1) of this section after that period is reduced in accordance with paragraphs (d)(1)(i) and (ii) of this section; half days will be ignored for purposes of subtraction;

(2) By adding the number of days determined in paragraph (d)(1) of this section to the original term of the patent as shortened by any terminal disclaimer;

(3) By adding 14 years to the date of approval of the application under section 351 of the Public Health Service Act, or subsection (b) of section 505 or section 507 of the Federal Food, Drug, and Cosmetic Act;

(4) By comparing the dates for the ends of the periods obtained pursuant to paragraphs (d)(2) and (d)(3) of this section with each other and selecting the earlier date;

(5) If the original patent was issued after September 24, 1984,

(i) By adding 5 years to the original expiration date of the patent or any earlier date set by terminal disclaimer; and

(ii) By comparing the dates obtained pursuant to paragraphs (d)(4) and (d)(5)(i) of this section with each other and selecting the earlier date;

(6) If the original patent was issued before September 24, 1984, and

(i) If no request was submitted for an exemption under subsection (i) of section 505 or subsection (d) of section 507 of the Federal Food, Drug, and Cosmetic Act before September 24, 1984, by—

(A) Adding 5 years to the original expiration date of the patent or earlier date set by terminal disclaimer; and

(B) By comparing the dates obtained pursuant to paragraphs (d)(4) and (d)(6)(i)(A) of this section with each other and selecting the earlier date; or

(ii) If a request was submitted for an exemption under subsection (i) of section 505 or subsection (d) of section 507 of the Federal Food, Drug, or Cosmetic Act before September 24, 1984 and the commercial marketing or use of the product was not approved before September 24, 1984, by—

(A) Adding 2 years to the original expiration date of the patent or earlier date set by terminal disclaimer, and

(B) By comparing the dates obtained pursuant to paragraphs (d)(4) and (d)(6)(ii)(A) of this section with each other and selecting the earlier date.

History of 37 C.F.R. §1.775: 54 FR 30381, July 20, 1989.

§1.776. CALCULATION OF PATENT TERM EXTENSION FOR A FOOD ADDITIVE OR COLOR ADDITIVE

(a) If a determination is made pursuant to §1.750 that a patent for a food additive or color additive is eligible for extension, the term shall be extended by the time as calculated in days in the manner indicated by this section. The patent term extension will run from the original expiration date of the patent or earlier date set by terminal disclaimer (§1.321).

(b) The term of the patent for a food additive or color additive will be extended by the length of the regulatory review period for the product as determined by the Secretary of Health and Human Services, reduced as appropriate pursuant to paragraphs (d)(1) through (d)(6) of this section.

(c) The length of the regulatory review period for a food additive or color additive will be determined by the Secretary of Health and Human Services. Under 35 U.S.C. 156(g)(2)(B), it is the sum of—

(1) The number of days in the period beginning on the date a major health or environmental effects test on the additive was initiated and ending on the date a petition was initially submitted with respect to the approved product under the Federal Food, Drug, and Cosmetic Act requesting the issuance of a regulation for use of the product; and

(2) The number of days in the period beginning on the date a petition was initially submitted with respect to the approved product under the Federal Food, Drug, and Cosmetic Act requesting the issuance of a regulation for use of the product, and ending on the date such regulation became effective or, if objections were filed to such regulation, ending on the date such objections were resolved and commercial marketing was permitted or, if commercial marketing was permitted and later revoked pending further proceedings as a result of such objections, ending on the date such proceedings were finally resolved and commercial marketing was permitted.

(d) The term of the patent as extended for a food additive or color additive will be determined by

(1) Subtracting from the number of days determined by the Secretary of Health and Human Services to be in the regulatory review period:

(i) The number of days in the periods of paragraphs (c)(1) and (c)(2) of this section which were on and before the date on which the patent issued;

(ii) The number of days in the periods of paragraphs (c)(1) and (c)(2) of this section during which it is determined under 35 U.S.C. 156(d)(2)(B) by the Secretary of Health and Human Services that applicant did not act with due diligence;

(iii) The number of days equal to one-half the number of days remaining in the period defined by paragraph (c)(1) of this section after that period is reduced in accordance with paragraphs (d)(1) (i) and (ii) of this section; half days will be ignored for purposes of subtraction;

(2) By adding the number of days determined in paragraph (d)(1) of this section to the original term of the patent as shortened by any terminal disclaimer;

(3) By adding 14 years to the date a regulation for use of the product became effective or, if objections were filed to such regulation, to the date such objections were resolved and commercial marketing was permitted or, if commercial marketing was permitted and later revoked pending further proceedings as a result of such objections, to the date such proceedings were finally resolved and commercial marketing was permitted;

(4) By comparing the dates for the ends of the periods obtained pursuant to paragraphs (d)(2) and (d)(3) of this section with each other and selecting the earlier date;

(5) If the original patent was issued after September 24, 1984,

(i) By adding 5 years to the original expiration date of the patent or earlier date set by terminal disclaimer; and

(ii) By comparing the dates obtained pursuant to paragraphs (d)(4) and (d)(5)(i) of this section with each other and selecting the earlier date;

(6) If the original patent was issued before September 24, 1984, and

(i) If no major health or environmental effects test was initiated and no petition for a regulation or application for registration was submitted before September 24, 1984, by

(A) Adding 5 years to the original expiration date of the patent or earlier date set by terminal disclaimer, and

(B) By comparing the dates obtained pursuant to paragraphs (d)(4) and (d)(6)(i)(A) of this section with each other and selecting the earlier date; or

(ii) If a major health or environmental effects test was initiated or a petition for a regulation or application for registration was submitted by September 24, 1984, and the commercial marketing or use of the product was not approved before September 24, 1984, by—

(A) Adding 2 years to the original expiration date of the patent or earlier date set by terminal disclaimer, and

(B) By comparing the dates obtained pursuant to paragraphs (d)(4) and (d)(6)(ii)(A) of this section with each other and selecting the earlier date.

§1.777. CALCULATION OF PATENT TERM EXTENSION FOR A MEDICAL DEVICE

(a) If a determination is made pursuant to §1.750 that a patent for a medical device is eligible for extension, the term shall be extended by the time as calculated in days in the manner indicated by this section. The patent term extension will run from the original expiration date of the patent or earlier date as set by terminal disclaimer (§1.321).

(b) The term of the patent for a medical device will be extended by the length of the regulatory review period for the product as determined by the Secretary of Health and Human Services, reduced as appropriate pursuant to paragraphs (d)(1) through (d)(6) of this section.

(c) The length of the regulatory review period for a medical device will be determined by the Secretary of Health and Human Services. Under 35 U.S.C. 156(g)(3)(B), it is the sum of

(1) The number of days in the period beginning on the date a clinical investigation on humans involving the device was begun and ending on the date an application was initially submitted with respect to the device under section 515 of the Federal Food, Drug, and Cosmetic Act; and

(2) The number of days in the period beginning on the date the application was initially submitted with respect to the device under section 515 of the Federal Food, Drug, and Cosmetic Act, and ending on the date such application was approved under such Act or the period beginning on the date a notice of completion of a product development protocol was initially submitted under section 515(f)(5) of the Act and ending on the date the protocol was declared completed under section 515(f)(6) of the Act.

(d) The term of the patent as extended for a medical device will be determined by—

(1) Subtracting from the number of days determined by the Secretary of Health and Human Services to be in the regulatory review period pursuant to paragraph (c) of this section:

(i) The number of days in the periods of paragraphs (c)(1) and (c)(2) of this section which were on and before the date on which the patent issued;

(ii) The number of days in the periods of paragraphs (c)(1) and (c)(2) of this section during which it is determined under 35 U.S.C. 156(d)(2)(B) by the Secretary of Health and Human Services that applicant did not act with due diligence;

(iii) One-half the number of days remaining in the period defined by paragraph (c)(1) of this section after that period is reduced in accordance with paragraphs (d)(1)(i) and (ii) of this section; half days will be ignored for purposes of subtraction;

(2) By adding the number of days determined in paragraph (d)(1) of this section to the original term of the patent as shortened by any terminal disclaimer;

(3) By adding 14 years to the date of approval of the application under section 515 of the Federal Food, Drug, and Cosmetic Act or the date a product development protocol was declared completed under section 515(f)(6) of the Act;

(4) By comparing the dates for the ends of the periods obtained pursuant to paragraphs (d)(2) and (d)(3) of this section with each other and selecting the earlier date;

(5) If the original patent was issued after September 24, 1984,

(i) By adding 5 years to the original expiration date of the patent or earlier date set by terminal disclaimer; and

(ii) By comparing the dates obtained pursuant to paragraphs (d)(4) and (d)(5)(i) of this section with each other and selecting the earlier date;

(6) If the original patent was issued before September 24, 1984, and

(i) If no clinical investigation on humans involving the device was begun or no product development protocol was submitted under section 515(f)(5) of the Federal Food, Drug, and Cosmetic Act before September 24, 1984, by—

(A) Adding 5 years to the original expiration date of the patent or earlier date set by terminal disclaimer and

(B) By comparing the dates obtained pursuant to paragraphs (d)(4) and (d)(6)(i)(A) of this section with each other and selecting the earlier date; or

(ii) If a clinical investigation on humans involving the device was begun or a product development protocol was submitted under section 515(f)(5) of the Federal Food, Drug, and Cosmetic Act before September 24, 1984 and the commercial marketing or use of the product was not approved before September 24, 1984, by

(A) Adding 2 years to the original expiration date of the patent or earlier date set by terminal disclaimer, and

(B) By comparing the dates obtained pursuant to paragraphs (d)(4) and (d)(6)(ii)(A) of this section with each other and selecting the earlier date.

§1.778. CALCULATION OF PATENT TERM EXTENSION FOR AN ANIMAL DRUG PRODUCT

(a) If a determination is made pursuant to §1.750 that a patent for an animal drug is eligible for extension, the term shall be extended by the time as calculated in days in the manner indicated by this section. The patent term extension will run from the original expiration date of the patent or any earlier date set by terminal disclaimer (§1.321).

(b) The term of the patent for an animal drug will be extended by the length of the regulatory review period for the drug as determined by the Secretary of Health and Human Services, reduced as appropriate pursuant to paragraphs (d)(1) through (d)(6) of this section.

(c) The length of the regulatory review period for an animal drug will be determined by the Secretary of Health and Human Services. Under 35 U.S.C. 156(g)(4)(B), it is the sum of—

(1) The number of days in the period beginning on the earlier of the date a major health or environmental effects test on the drug was initiated or the date an exemption under subsection (j) of section 512 of the Federal Food, Drug, and Cosmetic Act became effective for the approved animal drug and ending on the date an application was initially submitted for such animal drug under section 512 of the Federal Food, Drug, and Cosmetic Act; and

(2) The number of days in the period beginning on the date the application was initially submitted for the approved animal drug under subsection (b) of section 512 of the Federal Food, Drug, and Cosmetic Act and ending on the date such application was approved under such section.

(d) The term of the patent as extended for an animal drug will be determined by—

(1) Subtracting from the number of days determined by the Secretary of Health and Human Services to be in the regulatory review period:

(i) The number of days in the periods of paragraphs (c)(1) and (c)(2) of this section that were on and before the date on which the patent issued;

(ii) The number of days in the periods of paragraphs (c)(1) and (c)(2) of this section during which it is determined under 35 U.S.C. 156(d)(2)(B) by the Secretary of Health and Human Services that applicant did not act with due diligence;

(iii) One-half the number of days remaining in the period defined by paragraph (c)(1) of this section after that period is reduced in accordance with paragraphs (d)(1)(i) and (ii) of this section; half days will be ignored for purposes of subtraction;

(2) By adding the number of days determined in paragraph (d)(1) of this section to the original term of the patent as shortened by any terminal disclaimer;

(3) By adding 14 years to the date of approval of the application under section 512 of the Federal Food, Drug, and Cosmetic Act;

(4) By comparing the dates for the ends of the periods obtained pursuant to paragraphs (d)(2) and (d)(3) of this section with each other and selecting the earlier date;

(5) If the original patent was issued after November 16, 1988, by—

(i) Adding 5 years to the original expiration date of the patent or any earlier date set by terminal disclaimer; and

(ii) Comparing the dates obtained pursuant to paragraphs (d)(4) and (d)(5)(i) of this section with each other and selecting the earlier date;

(6) If the original patent was issued before November 16, 1988, and

(i) If no major health or environmental effects test on the drug was initiated and no request was submitted for an exemption under subsection (j) of section 512 of the Federal Food, Drug, and Cosmetic Act before November 16, 1988, by—

(A) Adding 5 years to the original expiration date of the patent or earlier date set by terminal disclaimer; and

(B) Comparing the dates obtained pursuant to paragraphs (d)(4) and (d)(6)(i)(A) of this section with each other and selecting the earlier date; or

(ii) If a major health or environmental effects test was initiated or a request for an exemption under subsection (j) of section 512 of the Federal Food, Drug, and Cosmetic Act was submitted before November 16, 1988, and the application for commercial marketing or use of the animal drug was not approved before November 16, 1988, by—

(A) Adding 3 years to the original expiration date of the patent or earlier date set by terminal disclaimer, and

(B) Comparing the dates obtained pursuant to paragraphs (d)(4) and (d)(6)(ii)(A) of this section with each other and selecting the earlier date.

History of 37 C.F.R. §1.778: 54 FR 30381, July 20, 1989.

§1.779. CALCULATION OF PATENT TERM EXTENSION FOR A VETERINARY BIOLOGICAL PRODUCT

(a) If a determination is made pursuant to §1.750 that a patent for a veterinary biological product is eligible for extension, the term shall be extended by the time as calculated in days in the manner indicated by this section. The patent term extension will run from the original expiration date of the patent or any earlier date set by terminal disclaimer (§1.321).

(b) The term of the patent for a veterinary biological product will be extended by the length of the regulatory review period for the product as determined by the Secretary of Agriculture, reduced as appropriate pursuant to paragraphs (d)(1) through (d)(6) of this section.

(c) The length of the regulatory review period for a veterinary biological product will be determined by the Secretary of Agriculture. Under 35 U.S.C. 156(g)(5)(B), it is the sum of—

(1) The number of days in the period beginning on the date the authority to prepare an experimental biological product under the Virus-Serum-Toxin Act became effective and ending on the date an application for a license was submitted under the Virus-Serum-Toxin Act; and

(2) The number of days in the period beginning on the date an application for a license was initially submitted for approval under the Virus-Serum-Toxin Act and ending on the date such license was issued.

(d) The term of the patent as extended for a veterinary biological product will be determined by—

(1) Subtracting from the number of days determined by the Secretary of Agriculture to be in the regulatory review period:

(i) The number of days in the periods of paragraphs (c)(1) and (c)(2) of this section that were on and before the date on which the patent issued;

(ii) The number of days in the periods of paragraphs (c)(1) and (c)(2) of this section during which it is determined under 35 U.S.C. 156(d)(2)(B) by the Secretary of Agriculture that applicant did not act with due diligence;

(iii) One-half the number of days remaining in the period defined by paragraph (c)(1) of this section after that period is reduced in accordance with paragraphs (d)(1)(i) and (ii) of this section; half days will be ignored for purposes of subtraction;

(2) By adding the number of days determined in paragraph (d)(1) of this section to the original term of the patent as shortened by any terminal disclaimer;

(3) By adding 14 years to the date of the issuance of a license under the Virus-Serum-Toxin Act;

(4) By comparing the dates for the ends of the periods obtained pursuant to paragraphs (d)(2) and (d)(3) of this section with each other and selecting the earlier date;

(5) If the original patent was issued after November 16, 1988, by—

(i) Adding 5 years to the original expiration date of the patent or any earlier date set by terminal disclaimer; and

(ii) Comparing the dates obtained pursuant to paragraphs (d)(4) and (d)(5)(i) of this section with each other and selecting the earlier date;

(6) If the original patent was issued before November 16, 1988, and

(i) If no request for the authority to prepare an experimental biological product under the Virus-Serum-Toxin Act was submitted before November 16, 1988, by—

(A) Adding 5 years to the original expiration date of the patent or earlier date set by terminal disclaimer; and

(B) Comparing the dates obtained pursuant to paragraphs (d)(4) and (d)(6)(i)(A) of this section with each other and selecting the earlier date; or

(ii) If a request for the authority to prepare an experimental biological product under the Virus-Serum-Toxin Act was submitted before November 16, 1988, and the commercial marketing or use of the product was not approved before November 16, 1988, by—

(A) Adding 3 years to the original expiration date of the patent or earlier date set by terminal disclaimer; and

(B) Comparing the dates obtained pursuant to paragraphs (d)(4) and (d)(6)(ii)(A) of this section with each other and selecting the earlier date.

History of 37 C.F.R. §1.779: 54 FR 30382, July 20, 1989.

§1.780. CERTIFICATE OR ORDER OF EXTENSION OF PATENT TERM

If a determination is made pursuant to §1.750 that a patent is eligible for extension and that the term of the patent is to be extended, a certificate of extension, under seal, or an order granting interim extension under 35 U.S.C. 156(d)(5), will be issued to the applicant for the extension of the patent term. Such certificate or order will be recorded in the official file of the patent and will be considered as part of the original patent. Notification of the issuance of the certificate or order of extension will be published in the Official Gazette of the United States Patent and Trademark Office. Notification of the issuance of the order granting an interim extension under 35 U.S.C. 156(d)(5), including the identity of the product currently under regulatory review, will be published in the Official Gazette of the United States Patent and Trademark Office and in the Federal Register. No certificate of, or order granting, an extension will be issued if the term of the patent cannot be extended, even though the patent is otherwise determined to be eligible for extension. In such situations, the final determination made pursuant to §1.750 will indicate that no certificate or order will issue.

History of 37 C.F.R. §1.780: 60 FR 25618, May 12, 1995; 65 FR 54680, Sept. 8, 2000.

§1.785. MULTIPLE APPLICATIONS FOR EXTENSION OF TERM OF THE SAME PATENT OR OF DIFFERENT PATENTS FOR THE SAME REGULATORY REVIEW PERIOD FOR A PRODUCT

(a) Only one patent may be extended for a regulatory review period for any product (§1.720(h)). If more than one application for extension of the same patent is filed, the certificate of extension of patent term, if appropriate, will be issued based upon the first filed application for extension.

(b) If more than one application for extension is filed by a single applicant which seeks the extension of the term of two or more patents based upon the same regulatory review period, and the patents are otherwise eligible for extension pursuant to the requirements of this subpart, in the absence of an election by the applicant, the certificate of extension of patent term, if appropriate, will be issued upon the application for extension of the patent term having the earliest date of issuance of those patents for which extension is sought.

(c) If an application for extension is filed which seeks the extension of the term of a patent based upon the same regulatory review period as that relied upon in one or more applications for extension pursuant to the requirements of this subpart, the certificate of extension of patent term will be issued on the application only if the patent owner or its agent is the holder of the regulatory approval granted with respect to the regulatory review period.

(d) An application for extension shall be considered complete and formal regardless of whether it contains the identification of the holder of the regulatory approval granted with respect to the regulatory review period. When an application contains such information, or is amended to contain such information, it will be considered in determining whether an application is eligible for an extension under this section. A request may be made of any applicant to supply such information within a non-extendable period of not less than one month whenever multiple applications for extension of more than one patent are received and rely upon the same regulatory review period. Failure to provide such information within the period for reply set shall be regarded as conclusively establishing that the applicant is not the holder of the regulatory approval.

(e) Determinations made under this section shall be included in the notice of final determination of eligibility for extension of the patent term pursuant to §1.750 and shall be regarded as part of that determination.

History of 37 C.F.R. §1.785: 54 FR 30382, July 20, 1989; 60 FR 25618, May 12, 1995; 62 FR 53201, Oct. 10, 1997.

§1.790. INTERIM EXTENSION OF PATENT TERM UNDER 35 U.S.C. 156(d)(5)

(a) An owner of record of a patent or its agent who reasonably expects that the applicable regulatory review period described in paragraph (1)(B)(ii), (2)(B)(ii), (3)(B)(ii), (4)(B)(ii), or (5)(B)(ii) of subsection (g) that began for a product that is the subject of such patent may extend beyond the expiration of the patent term in effect may submit one or more applications for interim extensions for periods of up to one year each. The initial application for interim extension must be filed during the period beginning 6 months and ending 15 days before the patent term is due to expire. Each subsequent application for interim extension must be filed during the period beginning 60 days before and ending 30 days before the expiration of the preceding interim extension. In no event will the interim extensions granted under this section be longer than the maximum period of extension to which the applicant would be entitled under 35 U.S.C. 156(c).

(b) A complete application for interim extension under this section shall include all of the information required for a formal application under §1.740 and a complete application under §1.741. Sections (a)(1), (a)(2), (a)(4), and (a)(6)-(a)(17) of §1.740 and §1.741 shall be read in the context of a product currently undergoing regulatory review. Sections (a)(3) and (a)(5) of §1.740 are not applicable to an application for interim extension under this section.

(c) The content of each subsequent interim extension application may be limited to a request for a subsequent interim extension along with a statement that the regulatory review period has not been completed along with any materials or information required under §1.740 and §1.741 that are not present in the preceding interim extension application.

History of 37 C.F.R. §1.790: 60 FR 25619, May 12, 1995.

§1.791. TERMINATION OF INTERIM EXTENSION GRANTED PRIOR TO REGULATORY APPROVAL OF A PRODUCT FOR COMMERCIAL MARKETING OR USE

Any interim extension granted under 35 U.S.C. 156(d)(5) terminates at the end of the 60-day period beginning on the date on which the product involved receives permission for commercial marketing or use. If within that 60-day period the patent owner or its agent files an application for extension under §1.740 and §1.741 including any additional information required under 35 U.S.C. 156(d)(1) not contained in the application for interim extension, the patent shall be further extended in accordance with the provisions of 35 U.S.C. 156.

History of 37 C.F.R. §1.791: 60 FR 25619, May 12, 1995.

SUBPART G. BIOTECHNOLOGY INVENTION DISCLOSURES

DEPOSIT OF BIOLOGICAL MATERIAL

§1.801. BIOLOGICAL MATERIAL

For the purposes of these regulations pertaining to the deposit of biological material for purposes of patents for inventions under 35 U.S.C. 101, the term biological material shall include material that is capable of self-replication either directly or indirectly. Representative examples include bacteria, fungi including yeast, algae, protozoa, eukaryotic cells, cell lines, hybridomas, plasmids, viruses, plant tissue cells, lichens and seeds. Viruses, vectors, cell organelles and other non-living material existing in and reproducible from a living cell may be deposited by deposit of the host cell capable of reproducing the non-living material.

Source of 37 C.F.R. Part 1G: 54 FR 34880, Aug. 22, 1989, unless otherwise noted.

§1.802. NEED OR OPPORTUNITY TO MAKE A DEPOSIT

(a) Where an invention is, or relies on, a biological material, the disclosure may include reference to a deposit of such biological material.

(b) Biological material need not be deposited unless access to such material is necessary for the satisfaction of the statutory requirements for patentability under 35 U.S.C. 112. If a deposit is necessary, it shall be acceptable if made in accordance with these regulations. Biological material need not be deposited, inter alia, if it is known and readily available to the public or can be made or isolated without undue experimentation. Once deposited in a depository complying with these regulations, a biological material will be considered to be readily available even though some requirement of law or regulation of the United States or of the country in which the depository institution is located permits access to the material only under conditions imposed for safety, public health or similar reasons.

(c) The reference to a biological material in a specification disclosure or the actual deposit of such material by an applicant or patent owner does not create any presumption that such material is necessary to satisfy 35 U.S.C. 112 or that deposit in accordance with these regulations is or was required.

§1.803. ACCEPTABLE DEPOSITORY

(a) A deposit shall be recognized for the purposes of these regulations if made in

(1) Any International Depositary Authority (IDA) as established under the Budapest Treaty on the International Recognition of the Deposit of Microorganisms for the Purposes of Patent Procedure, or

(2) Any other depository recognized to be suitable by the Office. Suitability will be determined by the Director on the basis of the administrative and technical competence, and agreement of the depository to comply with the terms and conditions applicable to deposits for patent purposes. The Director may seek the advice of impartial consultants on the suitability of a depository. The depository must:

(i) Have a continuous existence;

(ii) Exist independent of the control of the depositor;

(iii) Possess the staff and facilities sufficient to examine the viability of a deposit and store the deposit in a manner which ensures that it is kept viable and uncontaminated;

(iv) Provide for sufficient safety measures to minimize the risk of losing biological material deposited with it;

(v) Be impartial and objective;

(vi) Furnish samples of the deposited material in an expeditious and proper manner; and

(vii) Promptly notify depositors of its inability to furnish samples, and the reasons why.

(b) A depository seeking status under paragraph (a)(2) of this section must direct a communication to the Director which shall:

(1) Indicate the name and address of the depository to which the communication relates;

(2) Contain detailed information as to the capacity of the depository to comply with the requirements of paragraph (a)(2) of this section, including information on its legal status, scientific standing, staff and facilities;

(3) Indicate that the depository intends to be available, for the purposes of deposit, to any depositor under these same conditions;

(4) Where the depository intends to accept for deposit only certain kinds of biological material, specify such kinds;

(5) Indicate the amount of any fees that the depository will, upon acquiring the status of suitable depository under paragraph (a)(2) of this section, charge for storage, viability statements and furnishings of samples of the deposit.

(c) A depository having status under paragraph (a)(2) of this section limited to certain kinds of biological material may extend such status to additional kinds of biological material by directing a communication to the Director in accordance with paragraph (b) of this section. If a previous communication under paragraph (b) of this section is of record, items in common with the previous communication may be incorporated by reference.

(d) Once a depository is recognized to be suitable by the Director or has defaulted or discontinued its performance under this section, notice thereof will be published in the Office Gazette of the Patent and Trademark Office.

§1.804. TIME OF MAKING AN ORIGINAL DEPOSIT

(a) Whenever a biological material is specifically identified in an application for patent as filed, an original deposit thereof may be made at any time before filing the application for patent or, subject to §1.809, during pendency of the application for patent.

(b) When the original deposit is made after the effective filing date of an application for patent, the applicant must promptly submit a statement from a person in a position to corroborate the fact, stating that the biological material which is deposited is a biological material specifically identified in the application as filed.

History of 37 C.F.R. §1.804: 62 FR 53202, Oct. 10, 1997.

§1.805. REPLACEMENT OR SUPPLEMENT OF DEPOSIT

(a) A depositor, after receiving notice during the pendency of an application for patent, application for reissue patent or reexamination proceeding, that the depository possessing a deposit either cannot furnish samples thereof or can furnish samples thereof but the deposit has become contaminated or has lost its capability to function as described in the specification, shall notify the Office in writing, in each application for patent or patent affected. In such a case, or where the Office otherwise learns, during the pendency of an application for patent, application for reissue patent or reexamination proceeding, that the depository possessing a deposit either cannot furnish samples thereof or can furnish samples thereof but the deposit has become contaminated or has lost its capability to function as described in the specification, the need for making a replacement or supplemental deposit will be governed by the same considerations governing the need for making an original deposit under the provisions set forth in §1.802(b). A replacement or supplemental deposit made during the pendency of an application for patent shall not be accepted unless it meets the requirements for making an original deposit under these regulations, including the requirement set forth under §1.804(b). A replacement or supplemental deposit made in connection with a patent, whether or not made during the pendency of an application for reissue patent or a reexamination proceeding or both, shall not be accepted unless a certificate of correction under §1.323 is requested by the patent owner which meets the terms of paragraphs (b) and (c) of this section.

(b) A request for certificate of correction under this section shall not be granted unless the certificate identifies:

(1) The accession number for the replacement or supplemental deposit;

(2) The date of the deposit; and

(3) The name and address of the depository.

(c) A request for a certificate of correction under this section shall not be granted unless the request is made promptly after the replacement or supplemental deposit has been made and the request:

(1) Includes a statement of the reason for making the replacement or supplemental deposit;

(2) Includes a statement from a person in a position to corroborate the fact, and stating that the replacement or supplemental deposit is of a biological material which is identical to that originally deposited;

(3) Includes a showing that the patent owner acted diligently—

(i) In the case of a replacement deposit, in making the deposit after receiving notice that samples could no longer be furnished from an earlier deposit; or

(ii) In the case of a supplemental deposit, in making the deposit after receiving notice that the earlier deposit had become contaminated or had lost its capability to function as described in the specification;

(4) Includes a statement that the term of the replacement or supplemental deposit expires no earlier than the term of the deposit being replaced or supplemented; and

(5) Otherwise establishes compliance with these regulations.

(d) A depositor's failure to replace a deposit, or in the case of a patent, to diligently replace a deposit and promptly thereafter request a certificate of correction which meets the terms of paragraphs (b) and (c) of this section, after being notified that the depository possessing the deposit cannot furnish samples thereof, shall cause the application or patent involved to be treated in any Office proceeding as if no deposit were made.

(e) In the event a deposit is replaced according to these regulations, the Office will apply a rebuttable presumption of identity between the original and the replacement deposit where a patent making reference to the deposit is relied upon during any Office proceeding.

(f) A replacement or supplement deposit made during the pendency of an application for patent may be made for any reason.

(g) In no case is a replacement or supplemental deposit of a biological material necessary where the biological material, in accordance with §1.802(b), need not be deposited.

(h) No replacement deposit of a biological material is necessary where a depository can furnish samples thereof but the depository for national security, health or environmental safety reasons is unable to provide samples to requesters outside of the jurisdiction where the depository is located.

(i) The Office will not recognize in any Office proceeding a replacement deposit of a biological material made by a patent owner where the depository could furnish samples of the deposit being replaced.

History of 37 C.F.R. §1.805: 62 FR 53202, Oct. 10, 1997.

§1.806. TERM OF DEPOSIT

A deposit made before or during pendency of an application for patent shall be made for a term of at least thirty (30) years and at least five (5) years after the most recent request for the furnishing of a sample of the deposit was received by the depository. In any case, samples must be stored under agreements that would make them available beyond the enforceable life of the patent for which the deposit was made.

§1.807. VIABILITY OF DEPOSIT

(a) A deposit of biological material that is capable of self-replication either directly or indirectly must be viable at the time of deposit and during the term of deposit. Viability may be tested by the depository. The test must conclude only that the deposited material is capable of reproduction. No evidence is necessarily required regarding the ability of the deposited material to perform any function described in the patent application.

(b) A viability statement for each deposit of a biological material defined in paragraph (a) of this section not made under the Budapest Treaty on the International Recognition of the Deposit of Microorganisms for the Purposes of Patent Procedure must be filed in the application and must contain:

(1) The name and address of the depository;

(2) The name and address of the depositor;

(3) The date of deposit;

(4) The identity of the deposit and the accession number given by the depository;

(5) The date of the viability test;

(6) The procedures used to obtain a sample if the test is not done by the depository; and

(7) A statement that the deposit is capable of reproduction.

(c) If a viability test indicates that the deposit is not viable upon receipt, or the examiner cannot, for scientific or other valid reasons, accept the statement of viability received from the applicant, the examiner shall proceed as if no deposit has been made. The examiner will accept the conclusion set forth in a viability statement issued by a depository recognized under §1.803(a).

§1.808. FURNISHING OF SAMPLES

(a) A deposit must be made under conditions that assure that:

(1) Access to the deposit will be available during pendency of the patent application making reference to the deposit to one determined by the Director to be entitled thereto under §1.14 and 35 U.S.C. 122, and

(2) Subject to paragraph (b) of this section, all restrictions imposed by the depositor on the availability to the public of the deposited material will be irrevocably removed upon the granting of the patent.

(b) The depositor may contract with the depository to require that samples of a deposited biological material shall be furnished only if a request for a sample, during the term of the patent:

(1) Is in writing or other tangible form and dated;

(2) Contains the name and address of the requesting party and the accession number of the deposit; and

(3) Is communicated in writing by the depository to the depositor along with the date on which the sample was furnished and the name and address of the party to whom the sample was furnished.

(c) Upon request made to the Office, the Office will certify whether a deposit has been stated to have been made under conditions which make it available to the public as of the issue date of the patent grant provided the request contains:

(1) The name and address of the depository;

(2) The accession number given to the deposit;

(3) The patent number and issue date of the patent referring to the deposit; and

(4) The name and address of the requesting party.

§1.809. EXAMINATION PROCEDURES

(a) The examiner shall determine pursuant to §1.104 in each application for patent, application for reissue patent or reexamination proceeding if a deposit is needed, and if needed, if a deposit actually made is acceptable for patent purposes. If a deposit is needed and has not been made or replaced or supplemented in accordance with these regulations, the examiner, where appropriate, shall reject the affected claims under the appropriate provision of 35 U.S.C. 112, explaining why a deposit is needed and/or why a deposit actually made cannot be accepted.

(b) The applicant for patent or patent owner shall reply to a rejection under paragraph (a) of this section by—

(1) In the case of an applicant for patent, either making an acceptable original, replacement, or supplemental deposit, or assuring the Office in writing that an acceptable deposit will be made; or, in the case of a patent owner, requesting a certificate of correction of the patent which meets the terms of paragraphs (b) and (c) of §1.805, or

(2) Arguing why a deposit is not needed under the circumstances of the application or patent considered and/or why a deposit actually made should be accepted. Other replies to the examiner's action shall be considered nonresponsive. The rejection will be repeated until either paragraph (b)(1) of this section is satisfied or the examiner is convinced that a deposit is not needed.

(c) If an application for patent is otherwise in condition for allowance except for a needed deposit and the Office has received a written assurance that an acceptable deposit will be made, the Office may notify the applicant in a notice of allowability and set a three-month period of time from the mailing date of the notice of allowability within which the deposit must be made in order to avoid abandonment. This time period is not extendable under §1.136 (see §1.136(c)).

(d) For each deposit made pursuant to these regulations, the specification shall contain:

(1) The accession number for the deposit;

(2) The date of the deposit;

(3) A description of the deposited biological material sufficient to specifically identify it and to permit examination; and

(4) The name and address of the depository.

(e) Any amendment required by paragraphs (d)(1), (d)(2) or (d)(4) of this section must be filed before or with the payment of the issue fee (see §1.312).

History of 37 C.F.R. §1.809: 66 FR 21092, Apr. 27, 2001; 78 FR 62408, Dec. 18, 2013.

APPLICATION DISCLOSURES CONTAINING NUCLEOTIDE &/OR AMINO ACID SEQUENCES

§1.821. NUCLEOTIDE &/OR AMINO ACID SEQUENCE DISCLOSURES IN PATENT APPLICATIONS

(a) Nucleotide and/or amino acid sequences as used in §§1.821 through 1.825 are interpreted to mean an unbranched sequence of four or more amino acids or an unbranched sequence of ten or more nucleotides. Branched sequences are specifically excluded from this definition. Sequences with fewer than four specifically defined nucleotides or amino acids are specifically excluded from this section. "Specifically defined" means those amino acids other than "Xaa" and those nucleotide bases other than "n" defined in accordance with the World Intellectual Property Organization (WIPO) Handbook on Industrial Property Information and Documentation, Standard ST.25: Standard for the Presentation of Nucleotide and Amino Acid Sequence Listings in Patent Applications (1998), including Tables 1 through 6 in Appendix 2, herein incorporated by reference. (Hereinafter "WIPO Standard ST.25 (1998)"). This incorporation by reference was approved by the Director of the Federal Register in accordance with 5 U.S.C. 552(a) and 1 CFR part 51. Copies of WIPO Standard ST.25 (1998) may be obtained from the World Intellectual Property Organization; 34 chemin des Colombettes; 1211 Geneva 20 Switzerland. Copies may also be inspected at the National Archives and Records Administration (NARA). For information on the availability of this material at NARA, call 202-741-6030, or go to: http://www.archives.gov/federal_register/code_of_federal_regulations/ibr_locations.html. Nucleotides and amino acids are further defined as follows:

(1) Nucleotides: Nucleotides are intended to embrace only those nucleotides that can be represented using the symbols set forth in WIPO Standard ST.25 (1998), Appendix 2, Table 1. Modifications, *e.g.*, methylated bases, may be described as set forth in WIPO Standard ST.25 (1998), Appendix 2, Table 2, but shall not be shown explicitly in the nucleotide sequence.

(2) Amino acids: Amino acids are those L-amino acids commonly found in naturally occurring proteins and are listed in WIPO Standard ST.25 (1998), Appendix 2, Table 3. Those amino acid sequences containing D-amino acids are not intended to be embraced by this definition. Any amino acid sequence that contains post-translationally modified amino acids may be described as the amino acid sequence that is initially translated using the symbols shown in WIPO Standard ST.25 (1998), Appendix 2, Table 3 with the modified positions; *e.g.*, hydroxylations or glycosylations, being described as set forth in WIPO Standard ST.25 (1998), Appendix 2, Table 4, but these modifications shall not be shown explicitly in the amino acid sequence. Any peptide or protein that can be expressed as a sequence using the symbols in WIPO Standard ST.25 (1998), Appendix 2, Table 3 in conjunction with a description in the Feature section to describe, for example, modified linkages, cross links and end caps, non-peptidyl bonds, etc., is embraced by this definition.

(b) Patent applications which contain disclosures of nucleotide and/or amino acid sequences, in accordance with the definition in paragraph (a) of this section, shall, with regard to the manner in which the nucleotide and/or amino acid sequences are presented and described, conform exclusively to the requirements of §§1.821 through 1.825.

(c) Patent applications which contain disclosures of nucleotide and/or amino acid sequences must contain, as a separate part of the disclosure, a paper or compact disc copy (see §1.52(e)) disclosing the nucleotide and/or amino acid sequences and associated information using the symbols and format in accordance with the requirements of §§1.822 and 1.823. This paper or compact disc copy is referred to elsewhere in this subpart as the "Sequence Listing." Each sequence disclosed must appear separately in the "Sequence Listing." Each sequence set forth in the "Sequence Listing" must be assigned a separate sequence identifier. The sequence identifiers must begin with 1 and increase sequentially by integers. If no sequence is present for a sequence identifier, the code "000" must be used in place of the sequence. The response for the numeric identifier <160> must include the total number of SEQ ID NOs, whether followed by a sequence or by the code "000."

(d) Where the description or claims of a patent application discuss a sequence that is set forth in the "Sequence Listing" in accordance with paragraph (c) of this section, reference must be made to the sequence by use of the sequence identifier, preceded by "SEQ ID NO:" in the text of the description or claims, even if the sequence is also embedded in the text of the description or claims of the patent application.

(e) A copy of the "Sequence Listing" referred to in paragraph (c) of this section must also be submitted in computer readable form (CRF) in accordance with the requirements of §1.824. The computer readable form must be a copy of the "Sequence Listing" and may not be retained as a part of the patent application file. If the computer readable form of a new application is to be identical with the computer readable form of another application of the applicant on file in the Office, reference may be made to the other application and computer readable form in lieu of filing a duplicate computer readable form in the new application if the computer readable form in the other application was compliant with all of the requirements of this subpart. The new application must be accompanied by a letter making such reference to the other application and computer readable form, both of which shall be completely identified. In the new application, applicant must also request the use of the compliant computer readable "Sequence Listing" that is already on file for the other application and must state that the paper or compact disc copy of the "Sequence Listing" in the new application is identical to the computer readable copy filed for the other application.

(f) In addition to the paper or compact disc copy required by paragraph (c) of this section and the computer readable form required by paragraph (e) of this section, a statement that the "Sequence Listing" content of the paper or compact disc copy and the computer readable copy are the same must be submitted with the computer readable form, *e.g.*, a statement that "the sequence listing information recorded in computer readable form is identical to the written (on paper or compact disc) sequence listing."

(g) If any of the requirements of paragraphs (b) through (f) of this section are not satisfied at the time of filing under 35 U.S.C. 111(a) or at the time of entering the national stage under 35 U.S.C. 371, applicant will be notified and given a period of time within which to comply with such requirements in order to prevent abandonment of the application. Any submission in reply to a requirement under this paragraph must be accompanied by a statement that the submission includes no new matter.

(h) If any of the requirements of paragraphs (b) through (f) of this section are not satisfied at the time of filing an international application under the Patent Cooperation Treaty (PCT), which application is to be searched by the United States International Searching Authority or examined by the United States International Preliminary Examining Authority, applicant will be sent a notice necessitating compliance with the requirements within a prescribed time period. Any submission in reply to a requirement under this paragraph must be accompanied by a statement that the submission does not include matter which goes beyond the disclosure in the international application as filed. If applicant fails to timely provide the required computer readable form, the United States International Searching Authority shall search only to the extent that a meaningful search can be performed without the computer readable form and the United States International Preliminary Examining Authority shall examine only to the extent that a meaningful examination can be performed without the computer readable form.

History of 37 C.F.R. §1.821: 55 FR 18245, May 1, 1990; 58 FR 4348, Jan. 14, 1993; 63 FR 29634, June 1, 1998; 65 FR 54680, Sept. 8, 2000; 65 FR 78958, Dec. 18, 2000; 70 FR 10489, Mar. 4, 2005.

§1.822. SYMBOLS & FORMAT TO BE USED FOR NUCLEOTIDE &/OR AMINO ACID SEQUENCE DATA

(a) The symbols and format to be used for nucleotide and/or amino acid sequence data shall conform to the requirements of paragraphs (b) through (e) of this section.

(b) The code for representing the nucleotide and/or amino acid sequence characters shall conform to the code set forth in the tables in WIPO Standard ST.25 (1998), Appendix 2, Tables 1 and 3. This incorporation by reference was approved by the Director of the Federal Register in accordance with 5 U.S.C. 552(a) and 1 CFR part 51. Copies of ST.25 may be obtained from the World Intellectual Property Organization; 34 chemin des Colombettes; 1211 Geneva 20 Switzerland. Copies may also be inspected at the National Archives and Records Administration (NARA). For information on the availability of this material at NARA, call 202-741-6030, or go to: http://www.archives.gov/federal_register/code_of_federal_regulations/ibr_locations.html. No code other than that specified in these sections shall be used in nucleotide and amino acid sequences. A modified base or modified or unusual amino acid may be presented in a given sequence as the corresponding unmodified base or amino acid if the modified base or modified or unusual amino acid is one of those listed in WIPO Standard ST.25 (1998), Appendix 2, Tables 2 and 4, and the modification is also set forth in the Feature section. Otherwise, each occurrence of a base or amino acid not appearing in WIPO Standard ST.25 (1998), Appendix 2, Tables 1 and 3, shall be listed in a given sequence as "n" or "Xaa," respectively, with further information, as appropriate, given in the Feature section, preferably by including one or more feature keys listed in WIPO Standard ST.25 (1998), Appendix 2, Tables 5 and 6.

(c) Format representation of nucleotides.

(1) A nucleotide sequence shall be listed using the lowercase letter for representing the one-letter code for the nucleotide bases set forth in WIPO Standard ST.25 (1998), Appendix 2, Table 1.

(2) The bases in a nucleotide sequence (including introns) shall be listed in groups of 10 bases except in the coding parts of the sequence. Leftover bases, fewer than 10 in number, at the end of noncoding parts of a sequence shall be grouped together and separated from adjacent groups of 10 or 3 bases by a space.

(3) The bases in the coding parts of a nucleotide sequence shall be listed as triplets (codons). The amino acids corresponding to the codons in the coding parts of a nucleotide sequence shall be typed immediately below the corresponding codons. Where a codon spans an intron, the amino acid symbol shall be typed below the portion of the codon containing two nucleotides.

(4) A nucleotide sequence shall be listed with a maximum of 16 codons or 60 bases per line, with a space provided between each codon or group of 10 bases.

(5) A nucleotide sequence shall be presented, only by a single strand, in the 5 to 3 direction, from left to right.

(6) The enumeration of nucleotide bases shall start at the first base of the sequence with number 1. The enumeration shall be continuous through the whole sequence in the direction 5 to 3. The enumeration shall be marked in the right margin, next to the line containing the one-letter codes for the bases, and giving the number of the last base of that line.

(7) For those nucleotide sequences that are circular in configuration, the enumeration method set forth in paragraph (c)(6) of this section remains applicable with the exception that the designation of the first base of the nucleotide sequence may be made at the option of the applicant.

(d) Representation of amino acids.

(1) The amino acids in a protein or peptide sequence shall be listed using the three-letter abbreviation with the first letter as an upper case character, as in WIPO Standard ST.25 (1998), Appendix 2, Table 3.

(2) A protein or peptide sequence shall be listed with a maximum of 16 amino acids per line, with a space provided between each amino acid.

(3) An amino acid sequence shall be presented in the amino to carboxy direction, from left to right, and the amino and carboxy groups shall not be presented in the sequence.

(4) The enumeration of amino acids may start at the first amino acid of the first mature protein, with the number 1. When presented, the amino acids preceding the mature protein, *e.g.*, pre-sequences, pro-sequences, pre-pro-sequences and signal sequences, shall have negative numbers, counting backwards starting with the amino acid next to number 1. Otherwise, the enumeration of amino acids shall start at the first amino acid at the amino terminal as number 1. It shall be marked below the sequence every 5 amino acids. The enumeration method for amino acid sequences that is set forth in this section remains applicable for amino acid sequences that are circular in configuration, with the exception that the designation of the first amino acid of the sequence may be made at the option of the applicant.

(5) An amino acid sequence that contains internal terminator symbols (*e.g.*, "Ter", "*", or ".", etc.) may not be represented as a single amino acid sequence, but shall be presented as separate amino acid sequences.

(e) A sequence with a gap or gaps shall be presented as a plurality of separate sequences, with separate sequence identifiers, with the number of separate sequences being equal in number to the number of continuous strings of sequence data. A sequence that is made up of one or more noncontiguous segments of a larger sequence or segments from different sequences shall be presented as a separate sequence.

History of 37 C.F.R. §1.822: 55 FR 18246, May 1, 1990; 63 FR 29635, June 1, 1998; 70 FR 10489, Mar. 4, 2005.

§1.823. REQUIREMENTS FOR NUCLEOTIDE &/OR AMINO ACID SEQUENCES AS PART OF THE APPLICATION

(a)(1) If the "Sequence Listing" required by §1.821(c) is submitted on paper: The "Sequence Listing," setting forth the nucleotide and/or amino acid sequence and associated information in accordance with paragraph (b) of this section, must begin on a new page and must be titled "Sequence Listing." The pages of the "Sequence Listing" preferably should be numbered independently of the numbering of the remainder of the application. Each page of the "Sequence Listing" shall contain no more than 66 lines and each line shall contain no more than 72 characters. The sheet or sheets presenting a sequence listing may not include material other than part of the sequence listing. A fixed-width font should be used exclusively throughout the "Sequence Listing."

(2) If the "Sequence Listing" required by §1.821(c) is submitted on compact disc: The "Sequence Listing" must be submitted on a compact disc in compliance with §1.52(e). The compact disc may also contain table information if the application contains table information that may be submitted on a compact disc (§1.52(e)(1)(iii)). The specification must contain an incorporation-by-reference of the Sequence Listing as required by §1.52(e)(5). The presentation of the "Sequence Listing" and other materials on compact disc under §1.821(c) does not substitute for the Computer Readable Form that must be submitted on disk, compact disc, or tape in accordance with §1.824.

(b) The "Sequence Listing" shall, except as otherwise indicated, include the actual nucleotide and/or amino acid sequence, the numeric identifiers and their accompanying information as shown in the following table. The numeric identifier shall be used only in the "Sequence Listing." The order and presentation of the items of information in the "Sequence Listing" shall conform to the arrangement given below. Each item of information shall begin on a new line and shall begin with the numeric identifier enclosed in angle brackets as shown. The submission of those items of information designated with an "M" is mandatory. The submission of those items of information designated with an "O" is optional. Numeric identifiers <110> through <170> shall only be set forth at the beginning of the "Sequence Listing." The following table illustrates the numeric identifiers:

NUMERIC IDENTIFIER	DEFINITION	COMMENTS & FORMAT	MANDATORY (M) OR OPTIONAL (O)
<110>	Applicant	Preferably max. of 10 names; one name per line; preferable format: Surname, Other Names and/or Initials.	M.
<120>	Title of Invention		M.
<130>	File Reference	Personal file reference.	M, when filed prior to assignment of appl. number.
<140>	Current Application Number	Specify as: US 07/999,999 or PCT/US96/ 99999.	M, if available.
<141>	Current Filing Date	Specify as: yyyy-mm-dd.	M, if available.
<150>	Prior Application Number	Specify as: US 07/999,999 or PCT/US96/ 99999.	M, if applicable include priority documents under 35 USC 119 and 120.
<151>	Prior Application Filing Date	Specify as: yyyy-mm-dd.	M, if applicable.
<160>	Number of SEQ ID NOs	Count includes total number of SEQ ID NOs.	M.
<170>	Software	Name of software used to create the Sequence Listing.	O.
<210>	SEQ ID NO: #	Response shall be an integer representing the SEQ ID NO shown.	M.
<211>	Length	Respond with an integer expressing the number of bases or amino acid residues.	M.
<212>	Type	Whether presented sequence molecule is DNA, RNA, or PRT (protein). If a nucleotide sequence contains both DNA and RNA fragments, the type shall be "DNA." In addition, the combined molecule shall be further described in the <220> to <223> feature section.	M.
<213>	Organism	Scientific name, i.e. Genus/species, Unknown or Artificial Sequence. In addition, the "Unknown" or "Artificial Sequence" organisms shall be further described in the <220> to <223> feature section.	M.
<220>	Feature	Leave blank after <220>. <221-223> provide for a description of points of biological significance in the sequence.	M, under the following conditions: if "n," "Xaa," or a modified or unusual L-amino acid or modified base was used in a sequence; if ORGANISM is "Artificial Sequence" or "Unknown"; if molecule is combined DNA/RNA.
<221>	Name/Key	Provide appropriate identifier for feature, preferably from WIPO Standard ST.25 (1998), Appendix 2, Tables 5 and 6.	M, under the following conditions: if "n," or "Xaa," or a modified or unusual L-amino acid or modified base was used in a sequence.
<222>	Location	Specify location within sequence; where appropriate state number of first and last bases/amino acids in feature.	M, under the following conditions: if "n," or "Xaa," or a modified or unusual L-amino acid or modified base was used in a sequence.

NUMERIC IDENTIFIER	DEFINITION	COMMENTS & FORMAT	MANDATORY (M) OR OPTIONAL (O)
<223>	Other Information	Other relevant information; 4 lines maximum.	M, under the following conditions: if "n," "Xaa," or a modified or unusual L-amino acid or modified base was used in a sequence; if ORGANISM is "Artificial Sequence" or "Unknown"; if molecule is combined DNA/RNA.
<300>	Publication	Leave blank after <300>.	O.
<301>	Authors	Preferably max. of 10 named authors of publication; specify one name per line; preferable format: Surname, Other Names and/or Initials.	O.
<302>	Title		O.
<303>	Journal		O.
<304>	Volume		O.
<305>	Issue		O.
<306>	Pages		O.
<307>	Date	Journal date on which data published; specify as yyyy-mm-dd, MMM-yyyy or Season-yyyy.	O.
<308>	Database Accession Number	Accession number assigned by database including database name.	O.
<309>	Database Entry Date	Date of entry in database; specify as yyyy-mm-dd or MMM-yyyy.	O.
<310>	Patent Document Number	Document number; for patent-type citations only. Specify as, for example, US 07/999,999.	O.
<311>	Patent Filing Date	Document filing date, for patent-type citations only; specify as yyyy-mm-dd.	O.
<312>	Publication Date	Document publication date, for patent-type citations only; specify as yyyy-mm-dd.	O.
<313>	Relevant Residues	FROM (position) TO (position).	O.
<400>	Sequence	SEQ ID NO should follow the numeric identifier and should appear on the line preceding the actual sequence.	M.

History of 37 C.F.R. §1.823: 55 FR 18248, May 1, 1990; 63 FR 29636, June 1, 1998; 65 FR 54681, Sept. 8, 2000; 65 FR 78958, Dec. 18, 2000; 68 FR 38630, June 30, 2003.

§1.824. FORM & FORMAT FOR NUCLEOTIDE &/OR AMINO ACID SEQUENCE SUBMISSIONS IN COMPUTER READABLE FORM

(a) The computer readable form required by §1.821(e) shall meet the following requirements:

(1) The computer readable form shall contain a single "Sequence Listing" as either a diskette, series of diskettes, or other permissible media outlined in paragraph (c) of this section.

(2) The "Sequence Listing" in paragraph (a)(1) of this section shall be submitted in American Standard Code for Information Interchange (ASCII) text. No other formats shall be allowed.

(3) The computer readable form may be created by any means, such as word processors, nucleotide/amino acid sequence editors' or other custom computer programs; however, it shall conform to all requirements detailed in this section.

(4) File compression is acceptable when using diskette media, so long as the compressed file is in a self-extracting format that will decompress on one of the systems described in paragraph (b) of this section.

(5) Page numbering must not appear within the computer readable form version of the "Sequence Listing" file.

(6) All computer readable forms must have a label permanently affixed thereto on which has been hand-printed or typed: the name of the applicant, the title of the invention, the date on which the data were recorded on the computer readable form, the operating system used, a reference number, and an application number and filing date, if known. If multiple diskettes are submitted, the diskette labels must indicate their order (*e.g.*, "1 of X").

(b) Computer readable form submissions must meet these format requirements:

(1) Computer Compatibility: IBM PC/XT/AT or Apple Macintosh;

(2) Operating System Compatibility: MS-DOS, MS-Windows, Unix or Macintosh;

(3) Line Terminator: ASCII Carriage Return plus ASCII Line Feed; and

(4) Pagination: Continuous file (no "hard page break" codes permitted).

(c) Computer readable form files submitted may be in any of the following media:

(1) Diskette: 3.50 inch, 1.44 Mb storage; 3.50 inch, 720 Kb storage; 5.25 inch, 1.2 Mb storage; 5.25 inch, 360 Kb storage.

(2) Magnetic tape: 0.5 inch, up to 24000 feet; Density: 1600 or 6250 bits per inch, 9 track; Format: Unix tar command; specify blocking factor (not "block size"); Line Terminator: ASCII Carriage Return plus ASCII Line Feed.

(3) 8mm Data Cartridge: Format: Unix tar command; specify blocking factor (not "block size"); Line Terminator: ASCII Carriage Return plus ASCII Line Feed.

(4) Compact disc: Format: ISO 9660 or High Sierra Format.

(5) Magneto Optical Disk: Size/Storage Specifications: 5.25 inch, 640 Mb.

(d) Computer readable forms that are submitted to the Office will not be returned to the applicant.

History of 37 C.F.R. §1.824: 55 FR 18249, May 1, 1990; 63 FR 29637, June 1, 1998; 65 FR 54681, Sept. 8, 2000; 65 FR 78958, Dec. 18, 2000.

§1.825. AMENDMENTS TO OR REPLACEMENT OF SEQUENCE LISTING & COMPUTER READABLE COPY THEREOF

(a) Any amendment to a paper copy of the "Sequence Listing" (§1.821(c)) must be made by the submission of substitute sheets and include a statement that the substitute sheets include no new matter. Any amendment to a compact disc copy of the "Sequence Listing" (§1.821(c)) must be made by the submission of a replacement compact disc (2 copies) in compliance with §1.52(e). Amendments must also be accompanied by a statement that indicates support for the amendment in the application, as filed, and a statement that the replacement compact disc includes no new matter.

(b) Any amendment to the paper or compact disc copy of the "Sequence Listing," in accordance with paragraph (a) of this section, must be accompanied by a substitute copy of the computer readable form (§1.821(e)) including all previously submitted data with the amendment incorporated therein, accompanied by a statement that the copy in computer readable form is the same as the substitute copy of the "Sequence Listing."

(c) Any appropriate amendments to the "Sequence Listing" in a patent; *e.g.*, by reason of reissue or certificate of correction, must comply with the requirements of paragraphs (a) and (b) of this section.

(d) If, upon receipt, the computer readable form is found to be damaged or unreadable, applicant must provide, within such time as set by the Director, a substitute copy of the data in computer readable form accompanied by a statement that the substitute data is identical to that originally filed.

History of 37 C.F.R. §1.825: 55 FR 18250, May 1, 1990; 63 FR 29638, June 1, 1998; 65 FR 54681, Sept. 8, 2000; 65 FR 78958, Dec. 18, 2000.

APPENDIX A TO SUBPART G—SAMPLE SEQUENCE LISTING

<110> Smith, John
Smith, Jane

<120> Example of a Sequence Listing

<130> 01-00001

<140> US 08/999,999

<141> 1998-02-28

<150> EP 91000000

<151> 1997-12-31

<160> 2
<170> PatentIn ver. 2.0
<210> 1
<211> 403
<212> DNA
<213> Paramecium aurelia
<220>
<221> CDS
<222> 341...394
<300>
<301> Doe, Richard
<302> Isolation and Characterization of a Gene Encoding a Protease from Paramecium sp.
<303> Journal of Fictional Genes
<304> 1
<305> 4
<306> 1 – 7
<307> 1998-06-20
<400> 1
ctactctact ctactctcat ctactatctt ctttggatct ctgagtctgc ctgagtggta 60
ctcttgagtc ctggagatct ctcctctcac atgtgatcgt cgagactgac gatagatcg 120
ctgactgact ctgagatagt cgagcccgta cgagacccgt cgagggtgac agagagtggg 180
cgcgtgcgcg cagagcgccg cgccggtgcg cgcgcgagtg cgcggtgggc cgcgcgaggg 240
ctttcgcggc agcggcggcg ctttccggcg cgcgcccgtc cgcccctaga cctgagaggt 300
cttctcttcc ctcctcttca ctagagaggt ctatatatac atg gtt tca atg ttc 355
Met Val Ser Met Phe
1 5
agc ttg tct tth aaa tgg cct gga ttt tgt ttg ttt gtt tgtttgctc 403
Ser Leu Ser Phe Lys Trp Pro Gly Phe Cys Leu Phe Val
10 15
<210> 2
<211> 18
<212> PRT
<213> Paramecium aurelia
<400> 2
Met Val Ser Met Phe Ser Leu Ser Phe Lys Trp Pro Gly
1 5 10
Phe Cys Leu
15
Phe Val

History of 37 C.F.R. Part 1G, App. A: 24 FR 10332, Dec. 22, 1959; 54 FR 34880, Aug. 22, 1989; 55 FR 18245, May 1, 1990; 63 FR 29620, June 1, 1998; 63 FR 29638, June 1, 1998.

SUBPART H. INTER PARTES REEXAMINATION OF PATENTS THAT ISSUED FROM AN ORIGINAL APPLICATION FILED IN THE UNITED STATES ON OR AFTER NOVEMBER 29, 1999

PRIOR ART CITATIONS

§1.902. PROCESSING OF PRIOR ART CITATIONS DURING AN INTER PARTES REEXAMINATION PROCEEDING

Citations by the patent owner in accordance with §1.933 and by an inter partes reexamination third party requester under §1.915 or §1.948 will be entered in the inter partes reexamination file. The entry in the patent file of other citations submitted after the date of an order for reexamination pursuant to §1.931 by persons other than the patent owner, or the third party requester under either §1.913 or §1.948, will be delayed until the inter partes reexamination proceeding has been concluded by the issuance and publication of a reexamination certificate. See §1.502 for processing of prior art citations in patent and reexamination files during an ex parte reexamination proceeding filed under §1.510.

History of 37 C.F.R. §1.902: 72 FR 18906, May 16, 2007.

Source of 37 C.F.R. Part 1H: 65 FR 76777, Dec. 7, 2000, unless otherwise noted.

REQUIREMENTS FOR INTER PARTES REEXAMINATION PROCEEDINGS

§1.903. SERVICE OF PAPERS ON PARTIES IN INTER PARTES REEXAMINATION

The patent owner and the third party requester will be sent copies of Office actions issued during the inter partes reexamination proceeding. After filing of a request for inter partes reexamination by a third party requester, any document filed by either the patent owner or the third party requester must be served on every other party in the reexamination proceeding in the manner provided in §1.248. Any document must reflect service or the document may be refused consideration by the Office. The failure of the patent owner or the third party requester to serve documents may result in their being refused consideration.

§1.904. NOTICE OF INTER PARTES REEXAMINATION IN OFFICIAL GAZETTE

A notice of the filing of an inter partes reexamination request will be published in the Official Gazette. The notice published in the Official Gazette under §1.11(c) will be considered to be constructive notice of the inter partes reexamination proceeding and inter partes reexamination will proceed.

§1.905. SUBMISSION OF PAPERS BY THE PUBLIC IN INTER PARTES REEXAMINATION

Unless specifically provided for, no submissions on behalf of any third parties other than third party requesters as defined in 35 U.S.C. 100(e) will be considered unless such submissions are in accordance with §1.915 or entered in the patent file prior to the date of the order for reexamination pursuant to §1.931. Submissions by third parties, other than third party requesters, filed after the date of the order for reexamination pursuant to §1.931, must meet the requirements of §1.501 and will be treated in accordance with §1.902. Submissions which do not meet the requirements of §1.501 will be returned.

§1.906. SCOPE OF REEXAMINATION IN INTER PARTES REEXAMINATION PROCEEDING

(a) Claims in an inter partes reexamination proceeding will be examined on the basis of patents or printed publications and, with respect to subject matter added or deleted in the reexamination proceeding, on the basis of the requirements of 35 U.S.C. 112.

(b) Claims in an inter partes reexamination proceeding will not be permitted to enlarge the scope of the claims of the patent.

(c) Issues other than those indicated in paragraphs (a) and (b) of this section will not be resolved in an inter partes reexamination proceeding. If such issues are raised by the patent owner or the third party requester during a reexamination proceeding, the existence of such issues will be noted by the examiner in the next Office action, in which case the patent owner may desire to consider the advisability of filing a reissue application to have such issues considered and resolved.

§1.907. INTER PARTES REEXAMINATION PROHIBITED

(a) Once an order to reexamine has been issued under §1.931, neither the third party requester, nor its privies, may file a subsequent request for inter partes reexamination of the patent until an inter partes reexamination certificate is issued under §1.997, unless authorized by the Director.

(b) Once a final decision has been entered against a party in a civil action arising in whole or in part under 28 U.S.C. 1338 that the party has not sustained its burden of proving invalidity of any patent claim-in-suit, then neither that party nor its privies may thereafter request inter partes reexamination of any such patent claim on the basis of issues which that party, or its privies, raised or could have raised in such civil action, and an inter partes reexamination requested by that party, or its privies, on the basis of such issues may not thereafter be maintained by the Office.

(c) If a final decision in an inter partes reexamination proceeding instituted by a third party requester is favorable to patentability of any original, proposed amended, or new claims of the patent, then neither that party nor its privies may thereafter request inter partes reexamination of any such patent claims on the basis of issues which that party, or its privies, raised or could have raised in such inter partes reexamination proceeding.

§1.913. PERSONS ELIGIBLE TO FILE, & TIME FOR FILING, A REQUEST FOR INTER PARTES REEXAMINATION

(a) Except as provided for in §1.907 and in paragraph (b) of this section, any person other than the patent owner or its privies may, at any time during the period of enforceability of a patent which issued from an original application filed in the United States on or after November 29, 1999, file a request for inter partes reexamination by the Office of any claim of the patent on the basis of prior art patents or printed publications cited under §1.501.

(b) Any request for an inter partes reexamination submitted on or after September 16, 2012, will not be accorded a filing date, and any such request will not be granted.

History of 37 C.F.R. §1.913: 68 FR 71007, Dec. 22, 2003; 76 FR 59057, Sept. 23, 2011.

§1.915. CONTENT OF REQUEST FOR INTER PARTES REEXAMINATION

(a) The request must be accompanied by the fee for requesting inter partes reexamination set forth in §1.20(c)(2).

(b) A request for inter partes reexamination must include the following parts:

(1) An identification of the patent by patent number and every claim for which reexamination is requested.

(2) A citation of the patents and printed publications which are presented to provide a showing that there is a reasonable likelihood that the requester will prevail with respect to at least one of the claims challenged in the request.

(3) A statement pointing out, based on the cited patents and printed publications, each showing of a reasonable likelihood that the requester will prevail with respect to at least one of the claims challenged in the request, and a detailed explanation of the pertinency and manner of applying the patents and printed publications to every claim for which reexamination is requested.

(4) A copy of every patent or printed publication relied upon or referred to in paragraphs (b)(1) through (3) of this section, accompanied by an English language translation of all the necessary and pertinent parts of any non-English language document.

(5) A copy of the entire patent including the front face, drawings, and specification/claims (in double column format) for which reexamination is requested, and a copy of any disclaimer, certificate of correction, or reexamination certificate issued in the patent. All copies must have each page plainly written on only one side of a sheet of paper.

(6) A certification by the third party requester that a copy of the request has been served in its entirety on the patent owner at the address provided for in §1.33(c). The name and address of the party served must be indicated. If service was not possible, a duplicate copy of the request must be supplied to the Office.

(7) A certification by the third party requester that the estoppel provisions of §1.907 do not prohibit the inter partes reexamination.

(8) A statement identifying the real party in interest to the extent necessary for a subsequent person filing an inter partes reexamination request to determine whether that person is a privy.

(c) If an inter partes request is filed by an attorney or agent identifying another party on whose behalf the request is being filed, the attorney or agent must have a power of attorney from that party or be acting in a representative capacity pursuant to §1.34.

(d) If the inter partes request does not include the fee for requesting inter partes reexamination required by paragraph (a) of this section and meet all the requirements of paragraph (b) of this section, then the person identified as requesting inter partes reexamination will be so notified and will generally be given an opportunity to complete the request within a specified time. Failure to comply with the notice will result in the inter partes reexamination request not being granted a filing date, and will result in placement of the request in the patent file as a citation if it complies with the requirements of §1.501.

History of 37 C.F.R. §1.915: 71 FR 9262, Feb. 23, 2006; 71 FR 44223, Aug. 4, 2006; 72 FR 18906, May 16, 2007; 76 FR 59058, Sept. 23, 2011.

§1.919. FILING DATE OF REQUEST FOR INTER PARTES REEXAMINATION

(a) The filing date of a request for inter partes reexamination is the date on which the request satisfies all the requirements for the request set forth in §1.915.

(b) If the request is not granted a filing date, the request will be placed in the patent file as a citation of prior art if it complies with the requirements of §1.501.

History of 37 C.F.R. §1.919: 71 FR 9262, Feb. 23, 2006.

§1.923. EXAMINER'S DETERMINATION ON THE REQUEST FOR INTER PARTES REEXAMINATION

Within three months following the filing date of a request for inter partes reexamination under §1.915, the examiner will consider the request and determine whether or not the request and the prior art establish a reasonable likelihood that the requester will prevail with respect to at least one of the claims challenged in the request. The examiner's determination will be based on the claims in effect at the time of the determination, will become a part of the official file of the patent, and will be mailed to the patent owner at the address as provided for in §1.33(c) and to the third party requester. If the examiner determines that the request has not established a reasonable likelihood that the requester will prevail with respect to at least one of the challenged claims, the examiner shall refuse the request and shall not order inter partes reexamination.

History of 37 C.F.R. §1.923: 72 FR 18906, May 16, 2007; 76 FR 59058, Sept. 23, 2011.

§1.925. PARTIAL REFUND IF REQUEST FOR INTER PARTES REEXAMINATION IS NOT ORDERED

Where inter partes reexamination is not ordered, a refund of a portion of the fee for requesting inter partes reexamination will be made to the requester in accordance with §1.26(c).

§1.927. PETITION TO REVIEW REFUSAL TO ORDER INTER PARTES REEXAMINATION

The third party requester may seek review by a petition to the Director under §1.181 within one month of the mailing date of the examiner's determination refusing to order inter partes reexamination. Any such petition must comply with §1.181(b). If no petition is timely filed or if the decision on petition affirms that a reasonable likelihood that the requester will prevail with respect to at least one of the claims challenged in the request has not been established, the determination shall be final and nonappealable.

History of 37 C.F.R. §1.927: 76 FR 59058, Sept. 23, 2011.

INTER PARTES REEXAMINATION OF PATENTS

§1.931. ORDER FOR INTER PARTES REEXAMINATION

(a) If it is found that there is a reasonable likelihood that the requester will prevail with respect to at least one of the claims challenged in the request, the determination will include an order for inter partes reexamination of the patent for resolution of the question of whether the requester will prevail.

(b) If the order for inter partes reexamination resulted from a petition pursuant to §1.927, the inter partes reexamination will ordinarily be conducted by an examiner other than the examiner responsible for the initial determination under §1.923.

History of 37 C.F.R. §1.931: 76 FR 59058, Sept. 23, 2011.

INFORMATION DISCLOSURE IN INTER PARTES REEXAMINATION

§1.933. PATENT OWNER DUTY OF DISCLOSURE IN INTER PARTES REEXAMINATION PROCEEDINGS

(a) Each individual associated with the patent owner in an inter partes reexamination proceeding has a duty of candor and good faith in dealing with the Office, which includes a duty to disclose to the Office all information known to that individual to be material to patentability in a reexamination proceeding as set forth in §1.555(a) and (b). The duty to disclose all information known to be material to patentability in an inter partes reexamination proceeding is deemed to be satisfied by filing a paper in compliance with the requirements set forth in §1.555(a) and (b).

(b) The responsibility for compliance with this section rests upon the individuals designated in paragraph (a) of this section, and no evaluation will be made by the Office in the reexamination proceeding as to compliance with this section. If questions of compliance with this section are raised by the patent owner or the third party requester during a reexamination proceeding, they will be noted as unresolved questions in accordance with §1.906(c).

OFFICE ACTIONS & RESPONSES (BEFORE THE EXAMINER) IN INTER PARTES REEXAMINATION

§1.935. INITIAL OFFICE ACTION USUALLY ACCOMPANIES ORDER FOR INTER PARTES REEXAMINATION

The order for inter partes reexamination will usually be accompanied by the initial Office action on the merits of the reexamination.

§1.937. CONDUCT OF INTER PARTES REEXAMINATION

(a) All inter partes reexamination proceedings, including any appeals to the Patent Trial and Appeal Board, will be conducted with special dispatch within the Office, unless the Director makes a determination that there is good cause for suspending the reexamination proceeding.

(b) The inter partes reexamination proceeding will be conducted in accordance with §§1.104 through 1.116, the sections governing the application examination process, and will result in the issuance of an inter partes reexamination certificate under §1.997, except as otherwise provided.

(c) All communications between the Office and the parties to the inter partes reexamination which are directed to the merits of the proceeding must be in writing and filed with the Office for entry into the record of the proceeding.

(d) A petition in an inter partes reexamination proceeding must be accompanied by the fee set forth in §1.20(c)(6), except for petitions under §1.956 to extend the period for response by a patent owner, petitions under §1.958 to accept a delayed response by a patent owner, petitions under §1.78 to accept an unintentionally delayed benefit claim, and petitions under §1.530(*l*) for correction of inventorship in a reexamination proceeding.

History of 37 C.F.R. §1.937: 65 FR 76777, as amended at 77 FR 46628, Aug. 6, 2012; 77 FR 48853, Aug. 14, 2012.

§1.939. UNAUTHORIZED PAPERS IN INTER PARTES REEXAMINATION

(a) If an unauthorized paper is filed by any party at any time during the inter partes reexamination proceeding it will not be considered and may be returned.

(b) Unless otherwise authorized, no paper shall be filed prior to the initial Office action on the merits of the inter partes reexamination.

§1.941. AMENDMENTS BY PATENT OWNER IN INTER PARTES REEXAMINATION

Amendments by patent owner in inter partes reexamination proceedings are made by filing a paper in compliance with §§1.530(d)-(k) and 1.943.

§1.943. REQUIREMENTS OF RESPONSES, WRITTEN COMMENTS, & BRIEFS IN INTER PARTES REEXAMINATION

(a) The form of responses, written comments, briefs, appendices, and other papers must be in accordance with the requirements of §1.52.

(b) Responses by the patent owner and written comments by the third party requester shall not exceed 50 pages in length, excluding amendments, appendices of claims, and reference materials such as prior art references.

(c) Appellant's briefs filed by the patent owner and the third party requester shall not exceed thirty pages or 14,000 words in length, excluding appendices of claims and reference materials such as prior art references. All other briefs filed by any party shall not exceed fifteen pages in length or 7,000 words. If the page limit for any brief is exceeded, a certificate is required stating the number of words contained in the brief.

§1.945. RESPONSE TO OFFICE ACTION BY PATENT OWNER IN INTER PARTES REEXAMINATION

(a) The patent owner will be given at least thirty days to file a response to any Office action on the merits of the inter partes reexamination.

(b) Any supplemental response to the Office action will be entered only where the supplemental response is accompanied by a showing of sufficient cause why the supplemental response should be entered. The showing of sufficient cause must include:

(1) An explanation of how the requirements of §1.111(a)(2)(i) are satisfied;

(2) An explanation of why the supplemental response was not presented together with the original response to the Office action; and

(3) A compelling reason to enter the supplemental response.

History of 37 C.F.R. §1.945: 72 FR 18906, May 16, 2007.

§1.947. COMMENTS BY THIRD PARTY REQUESTER TO PATENT OWNER'S RESPONSE IN INTER PARTES REEXAMINATION

Each time the patent owner files a response to an Office action on the merits pursuant to §1.945, a third party requester may once file written comments within a period of 30 days from the date of service of the patent owner's response. These comments shall be limited to issues raised by the Office action or the patent owner's response. The time for submitting comments by the third party requester may not be extended. For the purpose of filing the written comments by the third party requester, the comments will be considered as having been received in the Office as of the date of deposit specified in the certificate under §1.8.

§1.948. LIMITATIONS ON SUBMISSION OF PRIOR ART BY THIRD PARTY REQUESTER FOLLOWING THE ORDER FOR INTER PARTES REEXAMINATION

(a) After the inter partes reexamination order, the third party requester may only cite additional prior art as defined under §1.501 if it is filed as part of a comments submission under §1.947 or §1.951(b) and is limited to prior art:

(1) Which is necessary to rebut a finding of fact by the examiner;

(2) Which is necessary to rebut a response of the patent owner; or

(3) Which for the first time became known or available to the third party requester after the filing of the request for inter partes reexamination proceeding. Prior art submitted under paragraph (a)(3) of this section must be accompanied by a statement as to when the prior art first became known or available to the third party requester and must include a discussion of the pertinency of each reference to the patentability of at least one claim.

(b) [Reserved]

§1.949. EXAMINER'S OFFICE ACTION CLOSING PROSECUTION IN INTER PARTES REEXAMINATION

Upon consideration of the issues a second or subsequent time, or upon a determination of patentability of all claims, the examiner shall issue an Office action treating all claims present in the inter partes reexamination, which may be an action closing prosecution. The Office action shall set forth all rejections and determinations not to make a proposed rejection, and the grounds therefor. An Office action will not usually close prosecution if it includes a new ground of rejection which was not previously addressed by the patent owner, unless the new ground was necessitated by an amendment.

§1.951. OPTIONS AFTER OFFICE ACTION CLOSING PROSECUTION IN INTER PARTES REEXAMINATION

(a) After an Office action closing prosecution in an inter partes reexamination, the patent owner may once file comments limited to the issues raised in the Office action closing prosecution. The comments can include a proposed amendment to the claims, which amendment will be subject to the criteria of §1.116 as to whether or not it shall be admitted. The comments must be filed within the time set for response in the Office action closing prosecution.

(b) When the patent owner does file comments, a third party requester may once file comments responsive to the patent owner's comments within 30 days from the date of service of patent owner's comments on the third party requester.

§1.953. EXAMINER'S RIGHT OF APPEAL NOTICE IN INTER PARTES REEXAMINATION

(a) Upon considering the comments of the patent owner and the third party requester subsequent to the Office action closing prosecution in an inter partes reexamination, or upon expiration of the time for submitting such comments, the examiner shall issue a Right of Appeal Notice, unless the examiner reopens prosecution and issues another Office action on the merits.

(b) Expedited Right of Appeal Notice: At any time after the patent owner's response to the initial Office action on the merits in an inter partes reexamination, the patent owner and all third party requesters may stipulate that the issues are appropriate for a final action, which would include a final rejection and/or a final determination favorable to patentability, and may request the issuance of a Right of Appeal Notice. The request must have the concurrence of the patent owner and all third party requesters present in the proceeding and must identify all of the appealable issues and the positions of the patent owner and all third party requesters on those issues. If the examiner determines that no other issues are present or should be raised, a Right of Appeal Notice limited to the identified issues shall be issued.

(c) The Right of Appeal Notice shall be a final action, which comprises a final rejection setting forth each ground of rejection and/or final decision favorable to patentability including each determination not to make a proposed rejection, an identification of the status of each claim, and the reasons for decisions favorable to patentability and/or the grounds of rejection for each claim. No amendment can be made in response to the Right of Appeal Notice. The Right of Appeal Notice shall set a one-month time period for either party to appeal. If no notice of appeal is filed, prosecution in the inter partes reexamination proceeding will be terminated, and the Director will proceed to issue and publish a certificate under §1.997 in accordance with the Right of Appeal Notice.

History of 37 C.F.R. §1.953: 72 FR 18906, May 16, 2007.

INTERVIEWS PROHIBITED IN INTER PARTES REEXAMINATION

§1.955. INTERVIEWS PROHIBITED IN INTER PARTES REEXAMINATION PROCEEDINGS

There will be no interviews in an inter partes reexamination proceeding which discuss the merits of the proceeding.

EXTENSIONS OF TIME, TERMINATING OF REEXAMINATION PROSECUTION, & PETITIONS TO REVIVE IN INTER PARTES REEXAMINATION

§1.956. PATENT OWNER EXTENSIONS OF TIME IN INTER PARTES REEXAMINATION

The time for taking any action by a patent owner in an inter partes reexamination proceeding will be extended only for sufficient cause and for a reasonable time specified. Any request for such extension must be filed on or before the day on which action by the patent owner is due, but in no case will the mere filing of a request effect any extension. Any request for such extension must be accompanied by the petition fee set forth in §1.17(g). See §1.304(a) for extensions of time for filing a notice of appeal to the U.S. Court of Appeals for the Federal Circuit.

History of 37 C.F.R. §1.956: 69 FR 56546, Sept. 21, 2004.

§1.957. FAILURE TO FILE A TIMELY, APPROPRIATE OR COMPLETE RESPONSE OR COMMENT IN INTER PARTES REEXAMINATION

(a) If the third party requester files an untimely or inappropriate comment, notice of appeal or brief in an inter partes reexamination, the paper will be refused consideration.

(b) If no claims are found patentable, and the patent owner fails to file a timely and appropriate response in an inter partes reexamination proceeding, the prosecution in the reexamination proceeding will be a terminated prosecution and the Director will proceed to issue and publish a certificate concluding the reexamination proceeding under §1.997 in accordance with the last action of the Office.

(c) If claims are found patentable and the patent owner fails to file a timely and appropriate response to any Office action in an inter partes reexamination proceeding, further prosecution will be limited to the claims found patentable at the time of the failure to respond, and to any claims added thereafter which do not expand the scope of the claims which were found patentable at that time.

(d) When action by the patent owner is a bona fide attempt to respond and to advance the prosecution and is substantially a complete response to the Office action, but consideration of some matter or compliance with some requirement has been inadvertently omitted, an opportunity to explain and supply the omission may be given.

History of 37 C.F.R. §1.957: 72 FR 18906, May 16, 2007.

§1.958. PETITION TO REVIVE INTER PARTES REEXAMINATION PROSECUTION TERMINATED FOR LACK OF PATENT OWNER RESPONSE

If a response by the patent owner is not timely filed in the Office, a petition may be filed pursuant to §1.137 to revive a reexamination prosecution terminated under §1.957(b) or limited under §1.957(c) if the delay in response was unintentional.

History of 37 C.F.R. §1.958: 72 FR 18906, May 16, 2007; 78 FR 62408, Dec. 18, 2013.

APPEAL TO THE PATENT TRIAL & APPEAL BOARD IN INTER PARTES REEXAMINATION

§1.959. APPEAL IN INTER PARTES REEXAMINATION

Appeals to the Patent Trial and Appeal Board under 35 U.S.C. 134(c) are conducted according to part 41 of this title.

History of 37 C.F.R. §1.959: 68 FR 71007, Dec. 22, 2003; 69 FR 50002, Aug. 12, 2004; 77 FR 46628, Sept. 16, 2012.

§§1.961 TO 1.977. RESERVED

History of 37 C.F.R. §§1.961-1.977: 69 FR 50002, Aug. 12, 2004.

§1.979. RETURN OF JURISDICTION FROM THE PATENT TRIAL & APPEAL BOARD; TERMINATION OF APPEAL PROCEEDINGS

(a) Jurisdiction over an inter partes reexamination proceeding passes to the examiner after a decision by the Patent Trial and Appeal Board upon transmittal of the file to the examiner, subject to each appellant's right of appeal or other review, for such further action as the condition of the inter partes reexamination proceeding may require, to carry into effect the decision of the Patent Trial and Appeal Board.

(b) Upon judgment in the appeal before the Patent Trial and Appeal Board, if no further appeal has been taken (§1.983), the prosecution in the inter partes reexamination proceeding will be terminated and the Director will issue and publish a certificate under §1.997 concluding the proceeding. If an appeal to the U.S. Court of Appeals for the Federal Circuit has been filed, that appeal is considered terminated when the mandate is issued by the Court.

History of 37 C.F.R. §1.979: 68 FR 71008, Dec. 22, 2003; 69 FR 50002, Aug. 12, 2004; 72 FR 18907, May 16, 2007; 77 FR 46628, Sept. 16, 2012.

§1.981. REOPENING AFTER A FINAL DECISION OF THE PATENT TRIAL & APPEAL BOARD

When a decision by the Patent Trial and Appeal Board on appeal has become final for judicial review, prosecution of the inter partes reexamination proceeding will not be reopened or reconsidered by the primary examiner except under the provisions of §41.77 of this title without the written authority of the Director, and then only for the consideration of matters not already adjudicated, sufficient cause being shown.

History of 37 C.F.R. §1.981: 69 FR 50002, Aug. 12, 2004; 77 FR 46628, Sept. 16, 2012.

APPEAL TO THE UNITED STATES COURT OF APPEALS FOR THE FEDERAL CIRCUIT IN INTER PARTES REEXAMINATION

§1.983. APPEAL TO THE UNITED STATES COURT OF APPEALS FOR THE FEDERAL CIRCUIT IN INTER PARTES REEXAMINATION

(a) The patent owner or third party requester in an inter partes reexamination proceeding who is a party to an appeal to the Patent Trial and Appeal Board and who is dissatisfied with the decision of the Patent Trial and Appeal Board may, subject to §41.81, appeal to the U.S. Court of Appeals for the Federal Circuit and may be a party to any appeal thereto taken from a reexamination decision of the Patent Trial and Appeal Board.

(b) The appellant must take the following steps in such an appeal:

(1) In the U.S. Patent and Trademark Office, timely file a written notice of appeal directed to the Director in accordance with §§1.302 and 1.304;

(2) In the U.S. Court of Appeals for the Federal Circuit, file a copy of the notice of appeal and pay the fee, as provided for in the rules of the U.S. Court of Appeals for the Federal Circuit; and

(3) Serve a copy of the notice of appeal on every other party in the reexamination proceeding in the manner provided in §1.248.

(c) If the patent owner has filed a notice of appeal to the U.S. Court of Appeals for the Federal Circuit, the third party requester may cross appeal to the U.S. Court of Appeals for the Federal Circuit if also dissatisfied with the decision of the Patent Trial and Appeal Board.

(d) If the third party requester has filed a notice of appeal to the U.S. Court of Appeals for the Federal Circuit, the patent owner may cross appeal to the U.S. Court of Appeals for the Federal Circuit if also dissatisfied with the decision of the Patent Trial and Appeal Board.

(e) A party electing to participate in an appellant's appeal must, within fourteen days of service of the appellant's notice of appeal under paragraph (b) of this section, or notice of cross appeal under paragraphs (c) or (d) of this section, take the following steps:

(1) In the U.S. Patent and Trademark Office, timely file a written notice directed to the Director electing to participate in the appellant's appeal to the U.S. Court of Appeals for the Federal Circuit by mail to, or hand service on, the General Counsel as provided in §104.2;

(2) In the U.S. Court of Appeals for the Federal Circuit, file a copy of the notice electing to participate in accordance with the rules of the U.S. Court of Appeals for the Federal Circuit; and

(3) Serve a copy of the notice electing to participate on every other party in the reexamination proceeding in the manner provided in §1.248.

(f) Notwithstanding any provision of the rules, in any reexamination proceeding commenced prior to November 2, 2002, the third party requester is precluded from appealing and cross appealing any decision of the Patent Trial and Appeal Board to the U.S. Court of Appeals for the Federal Circuit, and the third party requester is precluded from participating in any appeal taken by the patent owner to the U.S. Court of Appeals for the Federal Circuit.

History of 37 C.F.R. §1.983: 72 FR 18907, May 16, 2007; 77 FR 46628, Sept. 16, 2012.

CONCURRENT PROCEEDINGS INVOLVING SAME PATENT IN INTER PARTES REEXAMINATION

§1.985. NOTIFICATION OF PRIOR OR CONCURRENT PROCEEDINGS IN INTER PARTES REEXAMINATION

(a) In any inter partes reexamination proceeding, the patent owner shall call the attention of the Office to any prior or concurrent proceedings in which the patent is or was involved, including but not limited to interference or trial before the Patent Trial and Appeal Board, reissue, reexamination, or litigation and the results of such proceedings.

(b) Notwithstanding any provision of the rules, any person at any time may file a paper in an inter partes reexamination proceeding notifying the Office of a prior or concurrent proceeding in which the same patent is or was involved, including but not limited to interference or trial before the Patent Trial and Appeal Board, reissue, reexamination, or litigation and the results of such proceedings. Such paper must be limited to merely providing notice of the other proceeding without discussion of issues of the current inter partes reexamination proceeding.

History of 37 C.F.R. §1.985: 77 FR 46629, Sept. 16, 2012.

§1.987. SUSPENSION OF INTER PARTES REEXAMINATION PROCEEDING DUE TO LITIGATION

If a patent in the process of inter partes reexamination is or becomes involved in litigation, the Director shall determine whether or not to suspend the inter partes reexamination proceeding.

§1.989. MERGER OF CONCURRENT REEXAMINATION PROCEEDINGS

(a) If any reexamination is ordered while a prior inter partes reexamination proceeding is pending for the same patent and prosecution in the prior inter partes reexamination proceeding has not been terminated, a decision may be made to merge the two proceedings or to suspend one of the two proceedings. Where merger is ordered, the merged examination will normally result in the issuance and publication of a single reexamination certificate under §1.997.

(b) An inter partes reexamination proceeding filed under §1.913 which is merged with an ex parte reexamination proceeding filed under §1.510 will result in the merged proceeding being governed by §§1.902 through 1.997, except that the rights of any third party requester of the ex parte reexamination shall be governed by §§1.510 through 1.560.

History of 37 C.F.R. §1.989: 72 FR 18907, May 16, 2007.

§1.991. MERGER OF CONCURRENT REISSUE APPLICATION & INTER PARTES REEXAMINATION PROCEEDING

If a reissue application and an inter partes reexamination proceeding on which an order pursuant to §1.931 has been mailed are pending concurrently on a patent, a decision may be made to merge the two proceedings or to suspend one of the two proceedings. Where merger of a reissue application and an inter partes reexamination proceeding is ordered, the merged proceeding will be conducted in accordance with §§1.171 through 1.179, and the patent owner will be required to place and maintain the same claims in the reissue application and the inter partes reexamination proceeding during the pendency of the merged proceeding. In a merged proceeding the third party requester may participate to the extent provided under §§1.902 through 1.997 and 41.60 through 41.81, except that such participation shall be limited to issues within the scope of inter partes reexamination. The examiner's actions and any responses by the patent owner or third party requester in a merged proceeding will apply to both the reissue application and the inter partes reexamination proceeding and be physically entered into both files. Any inter partes reexamination proceeding merged with a reissue application shall be concluded by the grant of the reissued patent.

History of 37 C.F.R. §1.991: 72 FR 18907, May 16, 2007.

§1.993. SUSPENSION OF CONCURRENT INTERFERENCE & INTER PARTES REEXAMINATION PROCEEDING

If a patent in the process of inter partes reexamination is or becomes involved in an interference or trial before the Patent Trial and Appeal Board, the Director may suspend the inter partes reexamination, interference, or trial. The Director will not consider a request to suspend an interference or trial unless a motion under §41.121(a)(3) of this title to suspend the interference or trial has been presented to, and denied by, an administrative patent judge and the request is filed within ten (10) days of a decision by an administrative patent judge denying the motion for suspension or such other time as the administrative patent judge may set.

History of 37 C.F.R. §1.993: 69 FR 50002, Aug. 12, 2004; 77 FR 46629, Sept. 16, 2012.

§1.995. THIRD PARTY REQUESTER'S PARTICIPATION RIGHTS PRESERVED IN MERGED PROCEEDING

When a third party requester is involved in one or more proceedings, including an inter partes reexamination proceeding, the merger of such proceedings will be accomplished so as to preserve the third party requester's right to participate to the extent specifically provided for in these regulations. In merged proceedings involving different requesters, any paper filed by one party in the merged proceeding shall be served on all other parties of the merged proceeding.

REEXAMINATION CERTIFICATE IN INTER PARTES REEXAMINATION

§1.997. ISSUANCE & PUBLICATION OF INTER PARTES REEXAMINATION CERTIFICATE CONCLUDES INTER PARTES REEXAMINATION PROCEEDING

(a) To conclude an inter partes reexamination proceeding, the Director will issue and publish an inter partes reexamination certificate in accordance with 35 U.S.C. 316 setting forth the results of the inter partes reexamination proceeding and the content of the patent following the inter partes reexamination proceeding.

(b) A certificate will be issued and published in each patent in which an inter partes reexamination proceeding has been ordered under §1.931. Any statutory disclaimer filed by the patent owner will be made part of the certificate.

(c) The certificate will be sent to the patent owner at the address as provided for in §1.33(c). A copy of the certificate will also be sent to the third party requester of the inter partes reexamination proceeding.

(d) If a certificate has been issued and published which cancels all of the claims of the patent, no further Office proceedings will be conducted with that patent or any reissue applications or any reexamination requests relating thereto.

(e) If the inter partes reexamination proceeding is terminated by the grant of a reissued patent as provided in §1.991, the reissued patent will constitute the reexamination certificate required by this section and 35 U.S.C. 316.

(f) A notice of the issuance of each certificate under this section will be published in the Official Gazette.

History of 37 C.F.R. §1.997: 72 FR 18907, May 16, 2007.

SUBPART I. INTERNATIONAL DESIGN APPLICATION

GENERAL INFORMATION

§1.1001. DEFINITIONS RELATED TO INTERNATIONAL DESIGN APPLICATIONS

(a) Article as used in this subpart means an article of the Hague Agreement;

(b) Regulations as used in this subpart, when capitalized, means the "Common Regulations Under the 1999 Act and the 1960 Act of the Hague Agreement";

(c) Rule as used in this subpart, when capitalized, means one of the Regulations;

(d) Administrative Instructions as used in this subpart means the Administrative Instructions referred to in Rule 34;

(e) 1960 Act as used in this subpart means the Act signed at the Hague on November 28, 1960, of the Hague Agreement;

(f) Other terms and expressions in subpart I not defined in this section are as defined in Article 1, Rule 1, and 35 U.S.C. 381.

History of 37 C.F.R. §1.1001: 80 FR 17964, May 13, 2015.

§1.1002. THE UNITED STATES PATENT & TRADEMARK OFFICE AS AN OFFICE OF INDIRECT FILING

(a) The United States Patent and Trademark Office, as an office of indirect filing, shall accept international design applications where the applicant's Contracting Party is the United States.

(b) The major functions of the United States Patent and Trademark Office as an office of indirect filing include:

(1) Receiving and according a receipt date to international design applications;

(2) Collecting and, when required, transmitting fees due for processing international design applications;

(3) Determining compliance with applicable requirements of part 5 of this chapter; and

(4) Transmitting an international design application to the International Bureau, unless prescriptions concerning national security prevent the application from being transmitted.

History of 37 C.F.R. §1.1002: 80 FR 17964, May 13, 2015.

§1.1003. THE UNITED STATES PATENT & TRADEMARK OFFICE AS A DESIGNATED OFFICE

(a) The United States Patent and Trademark Office will act as a designated office ("United States Designated Office") for international design applications in which the United States has been designated as a Contracting Party in which protection is sought.

(b) The major functions of the United States Designated Office include:

(1) Accepting for national examination international design applications which satisfy the requirements of the Hague Agreement, the Regulations, and the regulations;

(2) Performing an examination of the international design application in accordance with 35 U.S.C. chapter 16; and

(3) Communicating the results of examination to the International Bureau.

History of 37 C.F.R. §1.1003: 80 FR 17964, May 13, 2015.

§1.1004. THE INTERNATIONAL BUREAU

(a) The International Bureau is the World Intellectual Property Organization located at Geneva, Switzerland. It is the international intergovernmental organization which acts as the coordinating body under the Hague Agreement and the Regulations.

(b) The major functions of the International Bureau include:

(1) Receiving international design applications directly from applicants and indirectly from an office of indirect filing;

(2) Collecting required fees and crediting designation fees to the accounts of the Contracting Parties concerned;

(3) Reviewing international design applications for compliance with prescribed formal requirements;

(4) Translating international design applications into the required languages for recordation and publication;

(5) Registering international designs in the International Register where the international design application complies with the applicable requirements;

(6) Publishing international registrations in the International Designs Bulletin; and

(7) Sending copies of the publication of the international registration to each designated office.

History of 37 C.F.R. §1.1004: 80 FR 17964, May 13, 2015.

§1.1005. DISPLAY OF CURRENTLY VALID CONTROL NUMBER UNDER THE PAPERWORK REDUCTION ACT

(a) Pursuant to the Paperwork Reduction Act of 1995 (44 U.S.C. 3501 et seq.), the collection of information in this subpart has been reviewed and approved by the Office of Management and Budget under control number 0651-0075.

(b) Notwithstanding any other provision of law, no person is required to respond to nor shall a person be subject to a penalty for failure to comply with a collection of information subject to the requirements of the Paperwork Reduction Act unless that collection of information displays a currently valid Office of Management and Budget control number. This section constitutes the display required by 44 U.S.C. 3512(a) and 5 CFR 1320.5(b)(2)(i) for the collection of information under Office of Management and Budget control number 0651-0075 (see 5 CFR 1320.5(b)(2)(ii)(D)).

History of 37 C.F.R. §1.1005: 80 FR 17965, May 13, 2015.

WHO MAY FILE AN INTERNATIONAL DESIGN APPLICATION

§1.1011. APPLICANT FOR INTERNATIONAL DESIGN APPLICATION

(a) Only persons who are nationals of the United States or who have a domicile, a habitual residence, or a real and effective industrial or commercial establishment in the territory of the United States may file international design applications through the United States Patent and Trademark Office.

(b) Although the United States Patent and Trademark Office will accept international design applications filed by any person referred to in paragraph (a) of this section, an international design application designating the United States may be refused by the Office as a designated office if the applicant is not a person qualified under 35 U.S.C. chapter 11 to be an applicant.

History of 37 C.F.R. §1.1011: 80 FR 17965, May 13, 2015.

§1.1012. APPLICANT'S CONTRACTING PARTY

In order to file an international design application through the United States Patent and Trademark Office as an office of indirect filing, the United States must be applicant's Contracting Party (Articles 4 and 1(xiv)).

History of 37 C.F.R. §1.1012: 80 FR 17965, May 13, 2015.

THE INTERNATIONAL DESIGN APPLICATION

§1.1021. CONTENTS OF THE INTERNATIONAL DESIGN APPLICATION

(a) Mandatory contents. The international design application shall be in English, French, or Spanish (Rule 6(1)) and shall contain or be accompanied by:

(1) A request for international registration under the Hague Agreement (Article 5(1)(i));

(2) The prescribed data concerning the applicant (Article 5(1)(ii) and Rule 7(3)(i) and (ii));

(3) The prescribed number of copies of a reproduction or, at the choice of the applicant, of several different reproductions of the industrial design that is the subject of the international design application, presented in the prescribed manner; however, where the industrial design is two-dimensional and a request for deferment of publication is made in accordance with Article 5(5), the international design application may, instead of containing reproductions, be accompanied by the prescribed number of specimens of the industrial design (Article 5(1)(iii));

(4) An indication of the product or products that constitute the industrial design or in relation to which the industrial design is to be used, as prescribed (Article 5(1)(iv) and Rule 7(3)(iv));

(5) An indication of the designated Contracting Parties (Article 5(1)(v));

(6) The prescribed fees (Article 5(1)(vi) and Rule 12(1));

(7) The Contracting Party or Parties in respect of which the applicant fulfills the conditions to be the holder of an international registration (Rule 7(3)(iii));

(8) The number of industrial designs included in the international design application, which may not exceed 100, and the number of reproductions or specimens of the industrial designs accompanying the international design application (Rule 7(3)(v));

(9) The amount of the fees being paid and the method of payment, or instructions to debit the required amount of fees to an account opened with the International Bureau, and the identification of the party effecting the payment or giving the instructions (Rule 7(3)(vii)); and

(10) An indication of applicant's Contracting Party as required under Rule 7(4)(a).

(b) Additional mandatory contents required by certain Contracting Parties.

(1) Where the international design application contains the designation of a Contracting Party that requires, pursuant to Article 5(2), any of the following elements, then the international design application shall contain such required element(s):

(i) Indications concerning the identity of the creator of the industrial design that is the subject of that application (Rule 11(1));

(ii) A brief description of the reproduction or of the characteristic features of the industrial design that is the subject of that application (Rule 11(2));

(iii) A claim (Rule 11(3)).

(2) Where the international design application contains the designation of a Contracting Party that has made a declaration under Rule 8(1), then the international application shall contain the statement, document, oath or declaration specified in that declaration (Rule 7(4)(c)).

(c) Optional contents. The international design application may contain:

(1) Two or more industrial designs, subject to the prescribed conditions (Article 5(4) and Rule 7(7));

(2) A request for deferment of publication (Article 5(5) and Rule 7(5)(e)) or a request for immediate publication (Rule 17);

(3) An element referred to in item (i) or (ii) of Article 5(2)(b) of the Hague Agreement or in Article 8(4)(a) of the 1960 Act even where that element is not required in consequence of a notification in accordance with Article 5(2)(a) of the Hague Agreement or in consequence of a requirement under Article 8(4)(a) of the 1960 Act (Rule 7(5)(a));

(4) The name and address of applicant's representative, as prescribed (Rule 7(5)(b));

(5) A claim of priority of one or more earlier filed applications in accordance with Article 6 and Rule 7(5)(c);

(6) A declaration, for purposes of Article 11 of the Paris Convention, that the product or products which constitute the industrial design or in which the industrial design is incorporated have been shown at an official or officially recognized international exhibition, together with the place where the exhibition was held and the date on which the product or products were first exhibited there and, where less than all the industrial designs contained in the international design application are concerned, the indication of those industrial designs to which the declaration relates or does not relate (Rule 7(5)(d));

(7) Any declaration, statement or other relevant indication as may be specified in the Administrative Instructions (Rule 7(5)(f));

(8) A statement that identifies information known by the applicant to be material to the eligibility for protection of the industrial design concerned (Rule 7(5)(g));

(9) A proposed translation of any text matter contained in the international design application for purposes of recording and publication (Rule 6(4)).

(d) Required contents where the United States is designated. In addition to the mandatory requirements set forth in paragraph (a) of this section, an international design application that designates the United States shall contain or be accompanied by:

(1) A claim (§§1.1021(b)(1)(iii) and 1.1025);

(2) Indications concerning the identity of the creator (i.e., the inventor, see §1.9(d)) in accordance with Rule 11(1); and

(3) The inventor's oath or declaration (§§1.63 and 1.64). The requirements in §§1.63(b) and 1.64(b)(4) to identify each inventor by his or her legal name, mailing address, and residence, if an inventor lives at a location which is different from the mailing address, and the requirement in §1.64(b)(2) to identify the residence and mailing address of the person signing the substitute statement will be considered satisfied by the presentation of such information in the international design application prior to international registration.

History of 37 C.F.R. §1.1021: 80 FR 17965, May 13, 2015.

§1.1022. FORM & SIGNATURE

(a) The international design application shall be presented on the official form (Rules 7(1) and 1(vi)).

(b) The international design application shall be signed by the applicant.

History of 37 C.F.R. §1.1022: 80 FR 17966, May 13, 2015.

§1.1023. FILING DATE OF AN INTERNATIONAL DESIGN APPLICATION IN THE UNITED STATES

(a) Subject to paragraph (b) of this section, the filing date of an international design application in the United States is the date of international registration determined by the International Bureau under the Hague Agreement (35 U.S.C. 384 and 381(a)(5)).

(b) Where the applicant believes the international design application is entitled under the Hague Agreement to a filing date in the United States other than the date of international registration, the applicant may petition the Director under this paragraph to accord the international design application a filing date in the United States other than the date of international registration. Such petition must be accompanied by the fee set forth in §1.17(f) and include a showing to the satisfaction of the Director that the international design application is entitled to such filing date.

History of 37 C.F.R. §1.1023: 80 FR 17966, May 13, 2015.

§1.1024. THE DESCRIPTION

An international design application designating the United States must include a specification as prescribed by 35 U.S.C. 112 and preferably include a brief description of the reproduction pursuant to Rule 7(5)(a) describing the view or views of the reproductions.

History of 37 C.F.R. §1.1024: 80 FR 17966, May 13, 2015.

§1.1025. THE CLAIM

The specific wording of the claim in an international design application designating the United States shall be in formal terms to the ornamental design for the article (specifying name of article) as shown, or as shown and described. More than one claim is neither required nor permitted for purposes of the United States.

History of 37 C.F.R. §1.1025: 80 FR 17966, May 13, 2015.

§1.1026. REPRODUCTIONS

Reproductions shall comply with the requirements of Rule 9 and Part Four of the Administrative Instructions.

History of 37 C.F.R. §1.1026: 80 FR 17966, May 13, 2015.

§1.1027. SPECIMENS

Where a request for deferment of publication has been filed in respect of a two-dimensional industrial design, the international design application may include specimens of the design in accordance with Rule 10 and Part Four of the Administrative Instructions. Specimens are not permitted in an international design application that designates the United States or any other Contracting Party which does not permit deferment of publication.

History of 37 C.F.R. §1.1027: 80 FR 17966, May 13, 2015.

§1.1028. DEFERMENT OF PUBLICATION

The international design application may contain a request for deferment of publication, provided the application does not designate the United States or any other Contracting Party which does not permit deferment of publication.

History of 37 C.F.R. §1.1028: 80 FR 17966, May 13, 2015.

FEES

A §1.1031. INTERNATIONAL DESIGN APPLICATION FEES

(a) International design applications filed through the Office as an office of indirect filing are subject to payment of a transmittal fee (35 U.S.C. 382(b) and Article 4(2)) in the amount of:

By a micro entity (§1.29)—$30.00

By a small entity (§1.27(a))—$60.00

By other than a small or micro entity—$120.00

(b) The Schedule of Fees annexed to the Regulations (Rule 27(1)), a list of individual designation fee amounts, and a fee calculator may be viewed on the Web site of the World Intellectual Property Organization, currently available at http://www.wipo.int/hague.

(c) The following fees required by the International Bureau may be paid either directly to the International Bureau or through the Office as an office of indirect filing in the amounts specified on the World Intellectual Property Organization Web site described in paragraph (b) of this section:

(1) International application fees (Rule 12(1)); and

(2) Fee for descriptions exceeding 100 words (Rule 11(2)).

(d) The fees referred to in paragraph (c) of this section may be paid as follows:

(1) Directly to the International Bureau in Swiss currency (see Administrative Instruction 801); or

(2) Through the Office as an office of indirect filing, provided such fees are paid no later than the date of payment of the transmittal fee required under paragraph (a) of this section. Any payment through the Office must be in U.S. dollars. Applicants paying the fees in paragraph (c) of this section through the Office may be subject to a requirement by the International Bureau to pay additional amounts where the conversion from U.S. dollars to Swiss currency results in the International Bureau receiving less than the prescribed amounts.

(e) Payment of the fees referred to in Article 17 and Rule 24 for renewing an international registration ("renewal fees") is not required to maintain a U.S. patent issuing on an international design application in force. Renewal fees, if required, must be submitted directly to the International Bureau. Any renewal fee submitted to the Office will not be transmitted to the International Bureau.

(f) The designation fee for the United States shall consist of:

(1) A first part established in Swiss currency pursuant to Hague Rule 28 based on the combined amounts of the basic filing fee (§1.16(b)), search fee (§1.16(*l*)), and examination fee (§1.16(p)) for a design application. The first part is payable at the time of filing the international design application; and

(2) A second part (issue fee) as provided in §1.18(b). The second part is payable within the period specified in a notice of allowance (§1.311).

History of 37 C.F.R. §1.1031: 80 FR 17966, May 13, 2015; 82 FR 52816, Jan. 16, 2018.

REPRESENTATION

§1.1041. REPRESENTATION IN AN INTERNATIONAL DESIGN APPLICATION

(a) The applicant may appoint a representative before the International Bureau in accordance with Rule 3.

(b) Applicants of international design applications may be represented before the Office as an office of indirect filing by a practitioner registered (§11.6) or granted limited recognition (§11.9(a) or (b)) to practice before the Office in patent matters. Such practitioner may act pursuant to §1.34 or pursuant to appointment by the applicant. The appointment must be in writing signed by the applicant, must give the practitioner power to act on behalf of the applicant, and must specify the name and registration number or limited recognition number of each practitioner. An appointment of a representative made in the international design application pursuant to Rule 3(2) that complies with the requirements of this paragraph will be effective as an appointment before the Office as an office of indirect filing.

History of 37 C.F.R. §1.1041: 80 FR 17966, May 13, 2015.

§1.1042. CORRESPONDENCE RESPECTING INTERNATIONAL DESIGN APPLICATIONS FILED WITH THE OFFICE AS AN OFFICE OF INDIRECT FILING

The applicant may specify a correspondence address for correspondence sent by the Office as an office of indirect filing. Where no such address has been specified, the Office will use as the correspondence address the address of applicant's appointed representative (§1.1041) or, where no representative is appointed, the address as specified in Administrative Instruction 302.

History of 37 C.F.R. §1.1042: 80 FR 17967, May 13, 2015.

TRANSMITTAL OF INTERNATIONAL DESIGN APPLICATION TO THE INTERNATIONAL BUREAU

§1.1045. PROCEDURES FOR TRANSMITTAL OF INTERNATIONAL DESIGN APPLICATION TO THE INTERNATIONAL BUREAU

(a) Subject to paragraph (b) of this section and payment of the transmittal fee set forth in §1.1031(a), transmittal of the international design application to the International Bureau shall be made by the Office as provided by Rule 13(1). At the same time as it transmits the international design application to the International Bureau, the Office shall notify the International Bureau of the date on which it received the application. The Office shall also notify the applicant of the date on which it received the application and of the transmittal of the international design application to the International Bureau.

(b) No copy of an international design application may be transmitted to the International Bureau, a foreign designated office, or other foreign authority by the Office or the applicant, unless the applicable requirements of part 5 of this chapter have been satisfied.

(c) Once transmittal of the international design application has been effected under paragraph (a) of this section, except for matters properly before the United States Patent and Trademark Office as an office of indirect filing or as a designated office, all further correspondence concerning the application should be sent directly to the International Bureau. The United States Patent and Trademark Office will generally not forward communications to the International Bureau received after transmittal of the application to the International Bureau. Any reply to an invitation sent to the applicant by the International Bureau must be filed directly with the International Bureau, and not with the Office, to avoid abandonment or other loss of rights under Article 8.

History of 37 C.F.R. §1.1045: 80 FR 17967, May 13, 2015.

RELIEF FROM PRESCRIBED TIME LIMITS; CONVERSION TO A DESIGN APPLICATION UNDER 35 U.S.C. CHAPTER 16

§1.1051. RELIEF FROM PRESCRIBED TIME LIMITS

(a) If the delay in an applicant's failure to act within prescribed time limits under the Hague Agreement in connection with requirements pertaining to an international design application was unintentional, a petition may be filed pursuant to this section to excuse the failure to act as to the United States. A grantable petition pursuant to this section must be accompanied by:

(1) A copy of any invitation sent from the International Bureau setting a prescribed time limit for which applicant failed to timely act;

(2) The reply required under paragraph (c) of this section, unless previously filed;

(3) The fee as set forth in §1.17(m);

(4) A certified copy of the originally filed international design application, unless a copy of the international design application was previously communicated to the Office from the International Bureau or the international design application was filed with the Office as an office of indirect filing, and a translation thereof into the English language if it was filed in another language;

(5) A statement that the entire delay in filing the required reply from the due date for the reply until the filing of a grantable petition pursuant to this paragraph was unintentional. The Director may require additional information where there is a question whether the delay was unintentional; and

(6) A terminal disclaimer (and fee as set forth in §1.20(d)) required pursuant to paragraph (d) of this section.

(b) Any request for reconsideration or review of a decision refusing to excuse the applicant's failure to act within prescribed time limits in connection with requirements pertaining to an international design application upon petition filed pursuant to this section, to be considered timely, must be filed within two months of the decision refusing to excuse or within such time as set in the decision. Unless a decision indicates otherwise, this time period may be extended under the provisions of §1.136.

(c) Reply. The reply required may be:

(1) The filing of a continuing application. If the international design application has not been subject to international registration, the reply must also include a grantable petition under §1.1023(b) to accord the international design application a filing date; or

(2) A grantable petition under §1.1052, where the international design application was filed with the Office as an office of indirect filing.

(d) Terminal disclaimer. Any petition pursuant to this section must be accompanied by a terminal disclaimer and fee as set forth in §1.321 dedicating to the public a terminal part of the term of any patent granted thereon equivalent to the period beginning on the due date for the reply for which applicant failed to timely act and ending on the date of filing of the reply required under paragraph (c) of this section and must also apply to any patent granted on a continuing design application that contains a specific reference under 35 U.S.C. 120, 121, 365(c) or 386(c) to the application for which relief under this section is sought.

History of 37 C.F.R. §1.1051: 80 FR 17967, May 13, 2015.

§1.1052. CONVERSION TO A DESIGN APPLICATION UNDER 35 U.S.C. CHAPTER 16

(a) An international design application designating the United States filed with the Office as an office of indirect filing and meeting the requirements under §1.53(b) for a filing date for an application for a design patent may, on petition under this section, be converted to an application for a design patent under §1.53(b) and accorded a filing date as provided therein. A petition under this section must be accompanied by the fee set forth in §1.17(t) and be filed prior to publication of the international registration under Article 10(3). The conversion of an international design application to an application for a design patent under §1.53(b) will not entitle applicant to a refund of the transmittal fee or any fee forwarded to the International Bureau, or the application of any such fee toward the filing fee, or any other fee, for the application for a design patent under §1.53(b). The application for a design patent resulting from conversion of an international design application must also include the basic filing fee (§1.16(b)), the search fee (§1.16(*l*)), the examination fee (§1.16(p)), the inventor's oath or declaration (§1.63 or 1.64), and a surcharge if required by §1.16(f).

(b) An international design application will be converted to an application for a design patent under §1.53(b) if a decision on petition under this section is granted prior to transmittal of the international design application to the International Bureau pursuant to §1.1045. Otherwise, a decision granting a petition under this section will be effective to convert the international design application to an application for a design patent under §1.53(b) only for purposes of the designation of the United States.

(c) A petition under this section will not be granted in an abandoned international design application absent a grantable petition under §1.1051.

(d) An international design application converted under this section is subject to the regulations applicable to a design application filed under 35 U.S.C. chapter 16.

History of 37 C.F.R. §1.1052: 80 FR 17967, May 13, 2015.

NATIONAL PROCESSING OF INTERNATIONAL DESIGN APPLICATIONS

§1.1061. RULES APPLICABLE

(a) The rules relating to applications for patents for other inventions or discoveries are also applicable to international design applications designating the United States, except as otherwise provided in this chapter or required by the Articles or Regulations.

(b) The provisions of §1.74, §1.84, except for §1.84(c), and §§1.152 through 1.154 shall not apply to international design applications.

History of 37 C.F.R. §1.1061: 80 FR 17968, May 13, 2015.

§1.1062. EXAMINATION

(a) Examination. The Office shall make an examination pursuant to title 35, United States Code, of an international design application designating the United States.

(b) Timing. For each international design application to be examined under paragraph (a) of this section, the Office shall, subject to Rule 18(1)(c)(ii), send to the International Bureau within 12 months from the publication of the international registration under Rule 26(3) a notification of refusal (§1.1063) where it appears that the applicant is not entitled to a patent under the law with respect to any industrial design that is the subject of the international registration.

History of 37 C.F.R. §1.1062: 80 FR 17968, May 13, 2015.

§1.1063. NOTIFICATION OF REFUSAL

(a) A notification of refusal shall contain or indicate:

(1) The number of the international registration;

(2) The grounds on which the refusal is based;

(3) A copy of a reproduction of the earlier industrial design and information concerning the earlier industrial design, where the grounds of refusal refer to similarity with an industrial design that is the subject of an earlier application or registration;

(4) Where the refusal does not relate to all the industrial designs that are the subject of the international registration, those to which it relates or does not relate; and

(5) A time period for reply under §§1.134 and 1.136, where a reply to the notification of refusal is required.

(b) Any reply to the notification of refusal must be filed directly with the Office and not through the International Bureau. The requirements of §1.111 shall apply to a reply to a notification of refusal.

History of 37 C.F.R. §1.1063: 80 FR 17968, May 13, 2015.

§1.1064. ONE INDEPENDENT & DISTINCT DESIGN

(a) Only one independent and distinct design may be claimed in a nonprovisional international design application.

(b) If the requirements under paragraph (a) of this section are not satisfied, the examiner shall in the notification of refusal or other Office action require the applicant in the reply to that action to elect one independent and distinct design for which prosecution on the merits shall be restricted. Such requirement will normally be made before any action on the merits but may be made at any time before the final action. Review of any such requirement is provided under §§1.143 and 1.144.

History of 37 C.F.R. §1.1064: 80 FR 17968, May 13, 2015.

§1.1065. CORRECTIONS & OTHER CHANGES IN THE INTERNATIONAL REGISTER

(a) The effects of any correction in the International Register by the International Bureau pursuant to Rule 22 in a pending nonprovisional international design application shall be decided by the Office in accordance with the merits of each situation, subject to such other requirements as may be imposed. A patent issuing from an international design application may only be corrected in accordance with the provisions of title 35, United States Code, for correcting patents. Any correction under Rule 22 recorded by the International Bureau with respect to an abandoned nonprovisional international design application will generally not be acted upon by the Office and shall not be given effect unless otherwise indicated by the Office.

(b) A recording of a partial change in ownership in the International Register pursuant to Rule 21(7) concerning a transfer of less than all designs shall not have effect in the United States.

History of 37 C.F.R. §1.1065: 80 FR 17968, May 13, 2015.

§1.1066. CORRESPONDENCE ADDRESS FOR A NONPROVISIONAL INTERNATIONAL DESIGN APPLICATION

(a) Unless the correspondence address is changed in accordance with §1.33(a), the Office will use as the correspondence address in a nonprovisional international design application the address according to the following order:

(1) The correspondence address under §1.1042;

(2) The address of applicant's representative identified in the publication of the international registration; and

(3) The address of the applicant identified in the publication of the international registration.

(b) Reference in the rules to the correspondence address set forth in §1.33(a) shall be construed to include a reference to this section for a nonprovisional international design application.

History of 37 C.F.R. §1.1066: 80 FR 17968, May 13, 2015.

§1.1067. TITLE, DESCRIPTION, & INVENTOR'S OATH OR DECLARATION

(a) The title of the design must designate the particular article. Where a nonprovisional international design application does not contain a title of the design, the Office may establish a title. No description, other than a reference to the drawing, is ordinarily required in a nonprovisional international design application.

(b) An international design application designating the United States must include the inventor's oath or declaration. See §1.1021(d). If the applicant is notified in a notice of allowability that an oath or declaration in compliance with §1.63, or substitute statement in compliance with §1.64, executed by or with respect to each named inventor has not been filed, the applicant must file each required oath or declaration in compliance with §1.63, or substitute statement in compliance with §1.64, no later than the date on which the issue fee is paid to avoid abandonment. This time period is not extendable under §1.136 (see §1.136(c)).

History of 37 C.F.R. §1.1067: 80 FR 17968, May 13, 2015.

§1.1068. STATEMENT OF GRANT OF PROTECTION

Upon issuance of a patent on an international design application designating the United States, the Office may send to the International Bureau a statement to the effect that protection is granted in the United States to those industrial design or designs that are the subject of the international registration and covered by the patent.

History of 37 C.F.R. §1.1068: 80 FR 17968, May 13, 2015.

§1.1070. NOTIFICATION OF INVALIDATION

(a) Where a design patent that was granted from an international design application is invalidated in the United States, and the invalidation is no longer subject to any review or appeal, the patentee shall inform the Office.

(b) After receiving a notification of invalidation under paragraph (a) of this section or through other means, the Office will notify the International Bureau in accordance with Hague Rule 20.

History of 37 C.F.R. §1.1070: 80 FR 17968, May 13, 2015.

§1.1071. GRANT OF PROTECTION FOR AN INDUSTRIAL DESIGN ONLY UPON ISSUANCE OF A PATENT

A grant of protection for an industrial design that is the subject of an international registration shall only arise in the United States through the issuance of a patent pursuant to 35 U.S.C. 389(d) or 171, and in accordance with 35 U.S.C. 153.

History of 37 C.F.R. §1.1071: 80 FR 17969, May 13, 2015.

PART 2. RULES OF PRACTICE IN TRADEMARK CASES

§2.1. RESERVED

History of 37 C.F.R. §2.1: 43 FR 35483, Aug. 10, 1978; 51 FR 28709, Aug. 11, 1986; 64 FR 48917, Sept. 8, 1999; 68 FR 48289, Aug. 13, 2003.

§2.2. DEFINITIONS

(a) The Act as used in this part means the Trademark Act of 1946, 60 Stat. 427, as amended, codified in 15 U.S.C. 1051 et seq.

(b) Entity as used in this part includes both natural and juristic persons.

(c) Director as used in this chapter, except for part 11, means the Under Secretary of Commerce for Intellectual Property and Director of the United States Patent and Trademark Office.

(d) Federal holiday within the District of Columbia means any day, except Saturdays and Sundays, when the United States Patent and Trademark Office is officially closed for business for the entire day.

(e) The term Office means the United States Patent and Trademark Office.

(f) The acronym TEAS means the Trademark Electronic Application System, available at http://www.uspto.gov.

(g) The acronym ESTTA means the Electronic System for Trademark Trials and Appeals, available at www.uspto.gov.

(h) The term international application as used in this part means, in addition to the definition in section 60 of the Act, an application seeking an extension of protection of an international registration in an initial designation filed under the Protocol Relating to the Madrid Agreement Concerning the International Registration of Marks.

(i) The term subsequent designation as used in this part means a request for extension of protection of an international registration made after the International Bureau registers the mark on the International Register.

(j) The term holder as used in this part means, in addition to the definition of a "holder of an international registration" in section 60 of the Act, the natural or juristic person in whose name an international registration seeking an extension of protection to the United States is recorded on the International Register.

(k) The term use in commerce or use of the mark in commerce as used in this part means, in addition to the definition of "use in commerce" in section 45 of the Act:

(1) For a trademark or service mark, use of the mark in commerce by an applicant, owner, or holder on or in connection with the goods or services specified in a U.S. application, amendment to allege use, statement of use, or affidavit or declaration of use or excusable nonuse;

(2) For a collective trademark or collective service mark, use of the mark in commerce by members on or in connection with the goods or services specified in a U.S. application, amendment to allege use, statement of use, or affidavit or declaration of use or excusable nonuse;

(3) For a collective membership mark, use of the mark in commerce by members to indicate membership in the collective organization as specified in a U.S. application, amendment to allege use, statement of use, or affidavit or declaration of use or excusable nonuse; and

(4) For a certification mark, use of the mark in commerce by authorized users on or in connection with the goods or services specified in a U.S. application, amendment to allege use, statement of use, or affidavit or declaration of use or excusable nonuse.

(*l*) The term bona fide intention to use the mark in commerce as used in this part means, for a trademark or service mark, that an applicant or holder has a bona fide intention to use the mark in commerce on or in connection with the goods or services specified in a U.S. application or international application/subsequent designation.

(m) The term bona fide intention, and is entitled, to exercise legitimate control over the use of the mark in commerce as used in this part means:

(1) For a collective trademark or collective service mark, that an applicant or holder has a bona fide intention, and is entitled, to exercise legitimate control over the use of the mark in commerce by members on or in connection with the goods or services specified in a U.S. application or international application/subsequent designation;

(2) For a collective membership mark, that an applicant or holder has a bona fide intention, and is entitled, to exercise legitimate control over the use of the mark in commerce by members to indicate membership in the collective organization as specified in a U.S. application or international application/subsequent designation; and

(3) For a certification mark, that an applicant or holder has a bona fide intention, and is entitled, to exercise legitimate control over the use of the mark in commerce by authorized users on or in connection with the goods or services specified in a U.S. application or international application/subsequent designation.

(n) The term verified statement, and the terms verify, verified, or verification as used in this part refers to a statement that is sworn to, made under oath or in an affidavit, or supported by a declaration under §2.20 or 28 U.S.C. 1746, and signed in accordance with the requirements of §2.193.

History of 37 C.F.R. §2.2: 54 FR 37588, Sept. 11, 1989; 68 FR 48289, Aug. 13, 2003; 68 FR 55762, Sept. 26, 2003; 73 FR 47685, Sept. 15, 2008; 78 FR 20197, Apr. 3, 2013; 80 FR 33178, July 11, 2015.

Source of 37 C.F.R. Part 2: 30 FR 13193, Oct. 16, 1965; 51 FR 28057, Aug. 4, 1986; 51 FR 28709, Aug. 11, 1986; 68 FR 14337, Mar. 25, 2003; 68 FR 48289, Aug. 13, 2003, unless otherwise noted.

§2.6. TRADEMARK FEES

(a) Trademark process fees.

(1) Application filing fees.

(i) For filing an application on paper, per class: $600.00.

(ii) For filing an application through TEAS, per class: $400.00.

(iii) For filing a TEAS Reduced Fee (RF) application through TEAS under §2.23, per class: $275.00.

(iv) For filing a TEAS Plus application through TEAS under §2.22, per class: $225.00.

(v) Additional processing fee under §§2.22(c) or 2.23(c), per class: $125.00.

(2) Amendment to allege use.

(i) For filing an amendment to allege use under section 1(c) of the Act on paper, per class: $200.00.

(ii) For filing an amendment to allege use under section 1(c) of the Act through TEAS, per class: $100.00.

(3) Statement of use.

(i) For filing a statement of use under section 1(d)(1) of the Act on paper, per class: $200.00.

(ii) For filing a statement of use under section 1(d)(1) of the Act through TEAS, per class: $100.00.

(4) Extension of time for filing statement of use.

(i) For filing a request under section 1(d)(2) of the Act for a six-month extension of time for filing a statement of use under section 1(d)(1) of the Act on paper, per class: $225.00.

(ii) For filing a request under section 1(d)(2) of the Act for a six-month extension of time for filing a statement of use under section 1(d)(1) of the Act through TEAS, per class: $125.00.

(5) Application for renewal of a registration fees.

(i) For filing an application for renewal of a registration on paper, per class: $500.00.

(ii) For filing an application for renewal of a registration through TEAS, per class: $300.00.

(6) Renewal during grace period.

(i) Additional fee for filing a renewal application during the grace period on paper, per class: $200.00.

(ii) Additional fee for filing a renewal application during the grace period through TEAS, per class: $100.00.

(7) Publishing mark under section 12(c).

(i) For filing to publish a mark under section 12(c) on paper, per class: $200.00.

(ii) For filing to publish a mark under section 12(c) through TEAS, per class: $100.00.

(8) New certificate of registration.

(i) For issuing a new certificate of registration upon request of registrant, request filed on paper: $200.00.

(ii) For issuing a new certificate of registration upon request of registrant, request filed through TEAS: $100.00.

(9) Certificate of correction of registrant's error.

(i) For a certificate of correction of registrant's error, request filed on paper: $200.00.

(ii) For a certificate of correction of registrant's error, request filed through TEAS: $100.00.

(10) Disclaimer to a registration.

(i) For filing a disclaimer to a registration, on paper: $200.00.

(ii) For filing a disclaimer to a registration, through TEAS or ESTTA: $100.00.

(11) Amendment of registration.

(i) For filing an amendment to a registration, on paper: $200.00.

(ii) For filing an amendment to a registration, through TEAS or ESTTA: $100.00.

(12) Affidavit under section 8.

(i) For filing an affidavit under section 8 of the Act on paper, per class: $225.00.

(ii) For filing an affidavit under section 8 of the Act through TEAS, per class: $125.00.

(13) Affidavit under section 15.

(i) For filing an affidavit under section 15 of the Act on paper, per class: $300.00.

(ii) For filing an affidavit under section 15 of the Act through TEAS, per class: $200.00.

(14) Filing section 8 affidavit during grace period.

(i) Additional fee for filing a section 8 affidavit during the grace period on paper, per class: $200.00.

(ii) Additional fee for filing a section 8 affidavit during the grace period through TEAS, per class: $100.00.

(15) Petitions to the Director.

(i) For petitions to the Director filed on paper: $200.00.

(ii) For petitions to the Director filed through TEAS: $100.00.

(16) Petition to cancel.

(i) For filing a petition to cancel on paper, per class: $500.00.

(ii) For filing a petition to cancel through ESTTA, per class: $400.00.

(17) Notice of opposition.

(i) For filing a notice of opposition on paper, per class: $500.00.

(ii) For filing a notice of opposition through ESTTA, per class: $400.00.

(18) Ex parte appeal.

(i) For ex parte appeal to the Trademark Trial and Appeal Board filed on paper, per class: $300.00.

(ii) For ex parte appeal to the Trademark Trial and Appeal Board filed through ESTTA, per class: $200.00.

(19) Dividing an application.

(i) Request to divide an application filed on paper, per new application created: $200.00.

(ii) Request to divide an application filed through TEAS, per new application created: $100.00.

(20) Correcting deficiency in section 8 affidavit.

(i) For correcting a deficiency in a section 8 affidavit via paper filing: $200.00.

(ii) For correcting a deficiency in a section 8 affidavit via TEAS filing: $100.00.

(21) Correcting deficiency in renewal application.

(i) For correcting a deficiency in a renewal application via paper filing: $200.00.

(ii) For correcting a deficiency in a renewal application via TEAS filing: $100.00.

(22) Extension of time for filing notice of opposition under §2.102(c)(1)(ii) or (c)(2).

(i) For filing a request for an extension of time to file a notice of opposition under §2.102(c)(1)(ii) or (c)(2) on paper: $200.00.

(ii) For filing a request for an extension of time to file a notice of opposition under §2.102(c)(1)(ii) or (c)(2) through ESTTA: $100.00.

(23) Extension of time for filing notice of opposition under §2.102(c)(3).

(i) For filing a request for an extension of time to file a notice of opposition under §2.102(c)(3) on paper: $300.00.

(ii) For filing a request for an extension of time to file a notice of opposition under §2.102(c)(3) through ESTTA: $200.00.

(b) Trademark service fees.

(1) For printed copy of registered mark, copy only. Service includes preparation of copies by the Office within two to three business days and delivery by United States Postal Service; and preparation of copies by the Office within one business day of receipt and delivery to an Office Box or by electronic means (e.g., facsimile, electronic mail): $3.00.

(2) Certified or uncertified copy of trademark application as filed processed within seven calendar days: $15.00.

(3) Certified or uncertified copy of a trademark-related official record: $50.00.

(4) Certified copy of a registered mark, showing title and/or status:

(i) Regular service: $15.00.

(ii) Expedited local service: $30.00.

(5) Certified or uncertified copy of trademark records, per document except as otherwise provided in this section: $25.00.

(6) For recording each trademark assignment, agreement or other document relating to the property in a registration or application.

(i) First property in a document: $40.00.

(ii) For each additional property in the same document: $25.00.

(7) For assignment records, abstract of title and certification, per registration: $25.00.

(8) Additional Fee for Overnight Delivery: $40.00.

(9) Additional Fee for Expedited Service: $160.00.

(10) For processing each payment refused (including a check returned "unpaid") or charged back by a financial institution: $50.00.

(11) Deposit account service charge for each month when the balance at the end of the month is below $1,000: $25.00.

History of 37 C.F.R. §2.6: 30 FR 13193, Oct. 16, 1965; 31 FR 5261, Apr. 1, 1966; 40 FR 57359, Dec. 9, 1975; 43 FR 35483, Aug. 10, 1978; 47 FR 41282, Sept. 17, 1982; 51 FR 28057, Aug. 4, 1986; 51 FR 28556, Aug. 8, 1986; 54 FR 6904, Feb. 15, 1989; 54 FR 37588, Sept. 11, 1989; 54 FR 50949, Dec. 11, 1989; 55 FR 37468, Sept. 12, 1990; 56 FR 65155, Dec. 13, 1991; 56 FR 66670, Dec. 24, 1991; 57 FR 38196, Aug. 21, 1992; 59 FR 257, Jan. 4, 1994; 60 FR 41023, Aug. 11, 1995; 62 FR 40453, July 29, 1997; 64 FR 48917, Sept. 8, 1999; 64 FR 67486, Dec. 2, 1999; 64 FR 67777, Dec. 3, 1999; 67 FR 70850, Nov. 27, 2002; 67 FR 79522, Dec. 30, 2002; 68 FR 48289, Aug. 13, 2003; 70 FR 2953, Jan. 19, 2005; 70 FR 38773, July 6, 2005; 73 FR 67767, Jan. 16, 2009; 79 FR 74638, Dec. 16, 2014; 81 FR 72706, Jan. 14, 2017.

§2.7. FASTENER RECORDAL FEES

(a) Application fee for recordal of insignia: $20.00.

(b) Renewal of insignia recordal: $20.00.

(c) Surcharge for late renewal of insignia recordal: $20.00.

History of 37 C.F.R. §2.7: 61 FR 55223, Oct. 25, 1996.

REPRESENTATION BY ATTORNEYS OR OTHER AUTHORIZED PERSONS

§2.11. APPLICANTS MAY BE REPRESENTED BY AN ATTORNEY

Representation before the Office is governed by §11.14 of this chapter. The Office cannot aid in the selection of an attorney.

History of 37 C.F.R. §2.11: 41 FR 758, Jan. 5, 1976; 50 FR 5171, Feb. 6, 1985; 68 FR 55762, Sept. 26, 2003; 73 FR 47685, Sept. 15, 2008.

§§2.12 TO 2.16. RESERVED

§2.17. RECOGNITION FOR REPRESENTATION

(a) Authority to practice in trademark cases. Only an individual qualified to practice under §11.14 of this chapter may represent an applicant, registrant, or party to a proceeding before the Office in a trademark case.

(b)(1) Recognition of practitioner as representative. To be recognized as a representative in a trademark case, a practitioner qualified under §11.14 of this chapter may:

(i) File a power of attorney that meets the requirements of paragraph (c) of this section;

(ii) Sign a document on behalf of an applicant, registrant, or party to a proceeding who is not already represented by a practitioner qualified under §11.14 of this chapter from a different firm; or

(iii) Appear in person on behalf of an applicant, registrant, or party to a proceeding who is not already represented by a practitioner qualified under §11.14 of this chapter from a different firm.

(2) Signature as certificate of authorization to represent. When a practitioner qualified under §11.14 of this chapter appears in person or signs a document pursuant to paragraph (b) of this section, his or her personal appearance or signature shall constitute a representation to the Office that he or she is authorized to represent the person or entity on whose behalf he or she acts. The Office may require further proof of authority to act in a representative capacity.

(c) Requirements for power of attorney. A power of attorney must:

(1) Designate by name at least one practitioner meeting the requirements of §11.14 of this chapter; and

(2) Be signed by the individual applicant, registrant, or party to a proceeding pending before the Office, or by someone with legal authority to bind the applicant, registrant, or party (e.g., a corporate officer or general partner of a partnership). In the case of joint applicants or joint registrants, all must sign. Once the applicant, registrant, or party has designated a practitioner(s) qualified to practice under §11.14 of this chapter, that practitioner may sign an associate power of attorney appointing another qualified practitioner(s) as an additional person(s) authorized to represent the applicant, registrant, or party. If the applicant, registrant, or party revokes the original power of attorney (§2.19(a)), the revocation discharges any associate power signed by the practitioner whose power has been revoked. If the practitioner who signed an associate power withdraws (§2.19(b)), the withdrawal discharges any associate power signed by the withdrawing practitioner upon acceptance of the request for withdrawal by the Office.

(d) Power of attorney relating to multiple applications or registrations. **(1)** The owner of an application or registration may appoint a practitioner(s) qualified to practice under §11.14 of this chapter to represent the owner for all existing applications or registrations that have the identical owner name and attorney through TEAS.

(2) The owner of an application or registration may file a power of attorney that relates to more than one trademark application or registration, or to all existing and future applications and registrations of that owner, on paper. A person relying on such a power of attorney must:

(i) Include a copy of the previously filed power of attorney; or

(ii) Refer to the power of attorney, specifying the filing date of the previously filed power of attorney; the application serial number (if known), registration number, or inter partes proceeding number for which the original power of attorney was filed; and the name of the person who signed the power of attorney; or, if the application serial number is not known, submit a copy of the application or a copy of the mark, and specify the filing date.

(e) Canadian attorneys and agents. **(1)** A Canadian patent agent who is registered and in good standing as a patent agent under §11.6(c) may represent parties located in Canada before the Office in trademark matters.

(2) A Canadian attorney or agent who is registered or in good standing with the Canadian Intellectual Property Office, but not registered as a patent agent under §11.6(c), may represent parties located in Canada if he or she has been authorized to do so by the Director of the Office of Enrollment and Discipline, pursuant to §11.14(f) of this chapter.

(f) Non-lawyers. A non-lawyer may not act as a representative except in the limited circumstances set forth in §11.14(b) of this chapter. Before any non-lawyer who meets the requirements of §11.14(b) of this chapter may take action of any kind with respect to an application, registration or proceeding, a written authorization must be filed, signed by the applicant, registrant, or party to the proceeding, or by someone with legal authority to bind the applicant, registrant, or party (e.g., a corporate officer or general partner of a partnership).

(g) Duration of power of attorney. **(1)** For purposes of recognition as a representative, the Office considers a power of attorney filed while an application is pending to end when the mark registers, when ownership changes, or when the application is abandoned.

(2) The Office considers a power of attorney filed after registration to end when the mark is cancelled or expired, or when ownership changes. If the power was filed in connection with an affidavit under section 8, 12(c), 15 or 71 of the Trademark Act, renewal application under section 9 of the Act, or request for amendment or correction under section 7 of the Act, the power is deemed to end upon acceptance or final rejection of the filing.

History of 37 C.F.R. §2.17: 50 FR 5171, Feb. 6, 1985; 64 FR 48918, Sept. 8, 1999; 68 FR 55762, Sept. 26, 2003; 73 FR 47685, Sept. 15, 2008; 74 FR 54906, Dec. 28, 2009; 80 FR 2310, Jan. 16, 2015.

§2.18. CORRESPONDENCE, WITH WHOM HELD

(a) Establishing the correspondence address. **(1)** If a written power of attorney that meets the requirements of §2.17 is filed, the Office will send correspondence to the practitioner designated in the power.

(2) If a practitioner qualified under §11.14 of this chapter transmits a document(s) on behalf of an applicant, registrant, or party to a proceeding who is not already represented by another qualified practitioner from a different firm, the Office will send correspondence to the practitioner transmitting the documents.

(3) If an application, registration or proceeding is not being prosecuted by a practitioner qualified under §11.14 of this chapter and the applicant, registrant, or party to the proceeding designates a correspondence address in writing, the Office will send correspondence to the designated address if appropriate.

(4) If an application, registration or proceeding is not being prosecuted by a practitioner qualified under §11.14 of this chapter and the applicant, registrant, or party to the proceeding has not designated a correspondence address in writing, but a domestic representative has been appointed, the Office will send correspondence to the domestic representative if appropriate.

(5) If the application, registration or proceeding is not being prosecuted by a practitioner qualified under §11.14 of this chapter, the applicant, registrant, or party to the proceeding has not designated a correspondence address, and no domestic representative has been appointed, the Office will send correspondence directly to the applicant, registrant, or party to the proceeding.

(6) The Office will send correspondence to only one address in an ex parte matter.

(7) Once the Office has recognized a practitioner qualified under §11.14 of this chapter as the representative of an applicant or registrant, the Office will communicate and conduct business only with that practitioner, or with another qualified practitioner from the same firm. The Office will not conduct business directly with the applicant or registrant, or with another practitioner from a different firm, unless the applicant or registrant files a revocation of the power of attorney under §2.19(a), and/or a new power of attorney that meets the requirements of §2.17(c). A written request to change the correspondence address does not revoke a power of attorney.

(b) Changing the correspondence address. **(1)** If a physical or e-mail correspondence address changes, the applicant, registrant, or party to a proceeding must file a written request to change the correspondence address. The request should be promptly filed.

(2) A request to change the correspondence address must be made in writing, signed by the applicant, registrant, or party to a proceeding, someone with legal authority to bind the applicant, registrant, or party (e.g., a corporate officer or general partner of a partnership), or a practitioner qualified to practice under §11.14 of this chapter, in accordance with §2.193(e)(9).

(3) If an applicant or registrant files a new power of attorney that meets the requirements of §2.17(c), the Office will change the correspondence address to that of the practitioner named in the power.

(4) If a practitioner qualified under §11.14 of this chapter transmits a document(s) on behalf of an applicant, registrant, or party to a proceeding who is not already represented by another qualified practitioner, the Office will construe this as including a request to change the correspondence address to that of the practitioner, and will send correspondence to the practitioner.

(c) Post registration filings under sections 7, 8, 9, 12(c), 15, and 71. **(1)** Even if there is no new power of attorney or written request to change the correspondence address, the Office will change the correspondence address upon the examination of an affidavit under section 8, 12(c), 15 or 71 of the Trademark Act, renewal application under section 9 of the Act, or request for amendment or correction under section 7 of the Act. If a practitioner qualified under §11.14 of this chapter transmits the affidavit, renewal application, or section 7 request, the Office will send correspondence to the practitioner. If the owner of the registration is not represented by a qualified practitioner, the Office will send correspondence directly to the owner, or to the domestic representative if appropriate, in accordance with paragraph (a).

(2) Once the Office establishes a correspondence address upon examination of an affidavit, renewal application, or section 7 request, a written request to change the address in accordance with the requirements of paragraph (b)(2) of this section is required to change the address during the pendency of that filing.

History of 37 C.F.R. §2.18: 41 FR 758, Jan. 5, 1976; 54 FR 37588, Sept. 11, 1989; 67 FR 79522, Dec. 30, 2002; 68 FR 55762, Sept. 26, 2003; 73 FR 47685, Sept. 15, 2008; 74 FR 54906, Dec. 28, 2009.

§2.19. REVOCATION OR WITHDRAWAL OF ATTORNEY

(a) Revocation. **(1)** Authority to represent an applicant, registrant or party to a proceeding before the Office may be revoked at any stage in the proceedings of a trademark case, upon written notification signed by the applicant, registrant, or party to the proceeding, or by someone with legal authority to bind the applicant, registrant, or party (e.g., a corporate officer or general partner of a partnership). In the case of joint applicants or joint registrants, all must sign.

(2) When a power of attorney is revoked, the Office will communicate directly with the applicant, registrant, or party to the proceeding, or with the new attorney or domestic representative if appropriate.

(3) A request to change the correspondence address does not revoke a power of attorney.

(4) A new power of attorney that meets the requirements of §2.17(c) will be treated as a revocation of the previous power.

(b) Withdrawal of attorney. If the requirements of §11.116 of this chapter are met, a practitioner authorized to represent an applicant, registrant, or party to a proceeding in a trademark case may withdraw upon application to and approval by the Director or, when applicable, upon motion granted by the Trademark Trial and Appeal Board. The practitioner should file the request to withdraw soon after the practitioner notifies the client of his/her intent to withdraw. The request must include the following:

(1) The application serial number, registration number, or proceeding number;

(2) A statement of the reason(s) for the request to withdraw; and

(3) Either

(i) A statement that the practitioner has given notice to the client that the practitioner is withdrawing from employment and will be filing the necessary documents with the Office; that the client was given notice of the withdrawal at least two months before the expiration of the response period, if applicable; that the practitioner has delivered to the client all documents and property in the practitioner's file concerning the application, registration or proceeding to which the client is entitled; and that the practitioner has notified the client of any responses that may be due, and of the deadline for response; or

(ii) If more than one qualified practitioner is of record, a statement that representation by co-counsel is ongoing.

History of 37 C.F.R. §2.19: 41 FR 758, Jan. 5, 1976; 50 FR 5171, Feb. 6, 1985; 68 FR 55762, Sept. 26, 2003; 73 FR 47685, Sept. 15, 2008; 74 FR 54907, Dec. 28, 2009; 80 FR 2310, Jan. 16, 2015.

DECLARATIONS

§2.20. DECLARATIONS IN LIEU OF OATHS

Instead of an oath, affidavit, or sworn statement, the language of 28 U.S.C. 1746, or the following declaration language, may be used:

The signatory being warned that willful false statements and the like are punishable by fine or imprisonment, or both, under 18 U.S.C. 1001, and that such willful false statements and the like may jeopardize the validity of the application or submission or any registration resulting therefrom, declares that all statements made of his/her own knowledge are true and all statements made on information and belief are believed to be true.

History of 37 C.F.R. §2.20: 31 FR 5261, Apr. 1, 1966; 64 FR 48918, Sept. 8, 1999; 80 FR 33178, July 11, 2015.

APPLICATION FOR REGISTRATION

§2.21. REQUIREMENTS FOR RECEIVING A FILING DATE

(a) The Office will grant a filing date to an application under section 1 or section 44 of the Act that is in the English language and contains all of the following:

(1) The name of the applicant;

(2) A name and address for correspondence;

(3) A clear drawing of the mark;

(4) A listing of the goods or services; and

(5) The filing fee for at least one class of goods or services, required by §2.6.

(b) If the applicant does not submit all the elements required in paragraph (a) of this section, the Office will deny a filing date and issue a notice explaining why the filing date was denied.

History of 37 C.F.R. §2.21: 37 FR 931, Jan. 21, 1972; 47 FR 38695, Sept. 2, 1982; 51 FR 29921, Aug. 21, 1986; 54 FR 37588, Sept. 11, 1989; 64 FR 48918, Sept. 8, 1999; 68 FR 55762, Sept. 26, 2003; 73 FR 67767, Jan. 16, 2009.

§2.22. REQUIREMENTS FOR A TEAS PLUS APPLICATION

(a) A trademark/service mark application for registration on the Principal Register under section 1 and/or section 44 of the Act will be entitled to a reduced filing fee under §2.6(a)(1)(iv) if it is filed through TEAS and includes:

(1) The applicant's name and address;

(2) The applicant's legal entity;

(3) The citizenship of an individual applicant, or the state or country of incorporation or organization of a juristic applicant;

(4) If the applicant is a partnership, the names and citizenship of the applicant's general partners;

(5) A name and address for correspondence;

(6) An e-mail address for correspondence, and an authorization for the Office to send correspondence concerning the application to the applicant or applicant's attorney by e-mail;

(7) One or more bases for filing that satisfy all the requirements of §2.34. If more than one basis is set forth, the applicant must comply with the requirements of §2.34 for each asserted basis;

(8) Correctly classified goods and/or services, with an identification of goods and/or services from the Office's Acceptable Identification of Goods and Services Manual, available through the TEAS Plus form. In an application based on section 44 of the Act, the scope of the goods and/or services covered by the section 44 basis may not exceed the scope of the goods and/or services in the foreign application or registration;

(9) If the application contains goods and/or services in more than one class, compliance with §2.86;

(10) A filing fee for each class of goods and/or services, as required by §2.6(a)(1)(iii);

(11) A verified statement that meets the requirements of §2.33, dated and signed by a person properly authorized to sign on behalf of the owner pursuant to §2.193(e)(1);

(12) A clear drawing of the mark. If the applicant does not claim standard characters, the applicant must attach a digitized image of the mark in .jpg format. If the mark includes color, the drawing must show the mark in color;

(13) If the mark is in standard characters, a mark comprised of only characters in the Office's standard character set, currently available at http://www.uspto.gov, typed in the appropriate field of the TEAS Plus form;

(14) If the mark includes color, a statement naming the color(s) and describing where the color(s) appears on the mark, and a claim that the color(s) is a feature of the mark;

(15) If the mark is not in standard characters, a description of the mark;

(16) If the mark includes non-English wording, an English translation of that wording;

(17) If the mark includes non-Latin characters, a transliteration of those characters;

(18) If the mark includes an individual's name or portrait, either (i) a statement that identifies the living individual whose name or likeness the mark comprises and written consent of the individual, or (ii) a statement that the name or portrait does not identify a living individual (see section 2(c) of the Act);

(19) If the applicant owns one or more registrations for the same mark, and the owner(s) last listed in Office records of the prior registration(s) for the same mark differs from the owner(s) listed in the application, a claim of ownership of the registration(s) identified by the registration number(s), pursuant to §2.36; and

(20) If the application is a concurrent use application, compliance with §2.42.

(b) In addition to the filing requirements under paragraph (a) of this section, the applicant must:

(1) File the following communications through TEAS:

(i) Responses to Office actions (except notices of appeal under section 20 of the Trademark Act);

(ii) Requests to change the correspondence address and owner's address;

(iii) Appointments and/or revocations of power of attorney;

(iv) Appointments and/or revocations of domestic representative;

(v) Voluntary amendments;

(vi) Amendments to allege use under section 1(c) of the Act or statements of use under section 1(d) of the Act;

(vii) Requests for extensions of time to file a statement of use under section 1(d) of the Act; and

(viii) Requests to delete a section 1(b) basis.

(2) Maintain a valid email correspondence address and continue to receive communications from the Office by email.

(c) If an application does not fulfill the requirements of paragraphs (a) and (b) of this section, the applicant must pay the processing fee required by §2.6(a)(1)(v). The application will retain its original filing date, provided that when filed, the application met the filing date requirements of §2.21.

(d) The following types of applications cannot be filed as TEAS Plus applications:

(1) Applications for certification marks (see §2.45);

(2) Applications for collective trademarks and service marks (see §2.44);

(3) Applications for collective membership marks (see §2.44); and

(4) Applications for registration on the Supplemental Register (see §2.47).

History of 37 C.F.R. §2.22: 70 FR 38773, July 6, 2005; 74 FR 54907, Dec. 28, 2009; 79 FR 74638, Dec. 16, 2014; 80 FR 2310, Jan. 16, 2015; 80 FR 33178, July 11, 2015.

§2.23. REQUIREMENTS FOR A TEAS RF APPLICATION

(a) A trademark, service mark, certification mark, collective membership mark, or collective trademark application for registration on the Principal or Supplemental Register under section 1 and/or section 44 of the Act will be entitled to a reduced filing fee under §2.6(a)(1)(iii) if it is filed through TEAS and includes:

(1) An email address for correspondence; and

(2) An authorization for the Office to send correspondence concerning the application to the applicant or applicant's attorney by email.

(b) In addition to the filing requirements under paragraph (a) of this section, the applicant must:

(1) File the following communications through TEAS:

(i) Responses to Office actions (except notices of appeal under section 20 of the Trademark Act);

(ii) Requests to change the correspondence address and owner's address;

(iii) Appointments and/or revocations of power of attorney;

(iv) Appointments and/or revocations of domestic representative;

(v) Voluntary amendments;

(vi) Amendments to allege use under section 1(c) of the Act or statements of use under section 1(d) of the Act;

(vii) Requests for extensions of time to file a statement of use under section 1(d) of the Act; and

(viii) Requests to delete a section 1(b) basis.

(2) Maintain a valid email correspondence address, and continue to receive communications from the Office by email.

(c) If an application does not meet the requirements of paragraphs (a) and (b) of this section, the applicant must pay the processing fee required by §2.6(a)(1)(v). The application will retain its original filing date, provided that when filed, the application met the filing date requirements of §2.21.

History of 37 C.F.R. §2.23: 37 FR 931, Jan. 21, 1972; 70 FR 38773, July 6, 2005; 73 FR 67768, Jan. 16, 2009; 79 FR 74639, Dec. 16, 2014.

§2.24. DESIGNATION & REVOCATION OF DOMESTIC REPRESENTATIVE BY FOREIGN APPLICANT

(a)(1) If an applicant is not domiciled in the United States, the applicant may designate a domestic representative (i.e., a person residing in the United States on whom notices or process in proceedings affecting the mark may be served) by either:

(i) Setting forth the name and address of the domestic representative in the initial application; or

(ii) Filing a separate designation setting forth the name and address of the domestic representative, signed by the applicant, someone with legal authority to bind the applicant (e.g., a corporate officer or general partner of a partnership), or a practitioner qualified to practice under §11.14 of this chapter.

(2) If the applicant does not file a document designating the name and address of a person residing in the United States on whom notices or process in proceedings affecting the mark may be served, or if the last person designated cannot be found at the address given in the designation, then notices or process in proceedings affecting the mark may be served on the Director.

(3) The mere designation of a domestic representative does not authorize the person designated to represent the applicant unless qualified under §11.14 of this chapter.

(b) A request to change or revoke a designation of domestic representative must be signed by the applicant, someone with legal authority to bind the applicant (e.g., a corporate officer or general partner of a partnership), or a practitioner qualified to practice under §11.14 of this chapter.

History of 37 C.F.R. §2.24: 54 FR 37588, Sept. 11, 1989; 67 FR 79522, Dec. 30, 2002; 73 FR 47685, Sept. 15, 2008; 74 FR 54907, Dec. 28, 2009.

§2.25. DOCUMENTS NOT RETURNABLE

Except as provided in §2.27(e), documents filed in the Office by the applicant or registrant become part of the official record and will not be returned or removed.

History of 37 C.F.R. §2.25: 73 FR 67768, Jan. 16, 2009.

§2.27. PENDING TRADEMARK APPLICATION INDEX; ACCESS TO APPLICATIONS

(a) An index of pending applications including the name and address of the applicant, a reproduction or description of the mark, the goods or services with which the mark is used, the class number, the dates of use, and the serial number and filing date of the application will be available for public inspection as soon as practicable after filing.

(b) Except as provided in paragraph (e) of this section, access to the file of a particular pending application will be permitted prior to publication under §2.80 upon written request.

(c) Decisions of the Director and the Trademark Trial and Appeal Board in applications and proceedings relating thereto are published or available for inspection or publication.

(d) Except as provided in paragraph (e) of this section, the official records of applications and all proceedings relating thereto are available for public inspection and copies of the documents may be furnished upon payment of the fee required by §2.6.

(e) Anything ordered to be filed under seal pursuant to a protective order issued or made by any court or by the Trademark Trial and Appeal Board in any proceeding involving an application or a registration shall be kept confidential and shall not be made available for public inspection or copying unless otherwise ordered by the court or the Board, or unless the party protected by the order voluntarily discloses the matter subject thereto. When possible, only confidential portions of filings with the Board shall be filed under seal.

History of 37 C.F.R. §2.27: 36 FR 25406, Dec. 31, 1971; 37 FR 2880, Feb. 9, 1972; 48 FR 23134, May 23, 1983; 48 FR 27225, June 14, 1983; 73 FR 67768, Jan. 16, 2009.

THE WRITTEN APPLICATION

§2.31. RESERVED

History of 37 C.F.R. §2.31: 64 FR 48918, Sept. 8, 1999.

§2.32. REQUIREMENTS FOR A COMPLETE TRADEMARK OR SERVICE MARK APPLICATION

(a) The application must be in English and include the following:

(1) A request for registration;

(2) The name of the applicant(s);

(3)(i) The citizenship of the applicant(s); or

(ii) If the applicant is a corporation, association, partnership or other juristic person, the jurisdiction (usually state or nation) under the laws of which the applicant is organized; and

(iii) If the applicant is a domestic partnership, the names and citizenship of the general partners; or

(iv) If the applicant is a domestic joint venture, the names and citizenship of the active members of the joint venture;

(4) The address of the applicant;

(5) One or more bases, as required by §2.34(a);

(6) A list of the particular goods or services on or in connection with which the applicant uses or intends to use the mark. In a U.S. application filed under section 44 of the Act, the scope of the goods or services covered by the section 44 basis may not exceed the scope of the goods or services in the foreign application or registration;

(7) The international class of goods or services, if known. See §6.1 of this chapter for a list of the international classes of goods and services.

(8) If the mark is not in standard characters, a description of the mark;

(9) If the mark includes non-English wording, an English translation of that wording; and

(10) If the mark includes non-Latin characters, a transliteration of those characters, and either a translation of the transliterated term in English, or a statement that the transliterated term has no meaning in English.

(b) The application must include a verified statement that meets the requirements of §2.33.

(c) The application must include a drawing that meets the requirements of §2.51 and §2.52.

(d) The application must include fee required by §2.6 for each class of goods or services.

(e) For the requirements of a multiple-class application, see §2.86.

(f) For the requirements of all collective mark applications, see §2.44.

(g) For the requirements of a certification mark application, see §2.45.

History of 37 C.F.R. §2.32: 64 FR 48918, Sept. 8, 1999; 73 FR 13784, May 13, 2008; 73 FR 67768, Jan. 16, 2009; 80 FR 33178, July 11, 2015.

§2.33. VERIFIED STATEMENT FOR A TRADEMARK OR SERVICE MARK

(a) The application must include a verified statement.

(b)(1) In an application under section 1(a) of the Act, the verified statement must allege:

That the applicant believes the applicant is the owner of the mark; that the mark is in use in commerce; that to the best of the signatory's knowledge and belief, no other person has the right to use the mark in commerce, either in the identical form or in such near resemblance as to be likely, when applied to the goods or services of such other person, to cause confusion or mistake, or to deceive; that the specimen shows the mark as used on or in connection with the goods or services; and that the facts set forth in the application are true.

(2) In an application under section 1(b) or 44 of the Act, the verified statement must allege:

That the applicant has a bona fide intention to use the mark in commerce; that the applicant believes the applicant is entitled to use the mark in commerce on or in connection with the goods or services specified in the application; that to the best of the signatory's knowledge and belief, no other person has the right to use the mark in commerce, either in the identical form or in such near resemblance as to be likely, when applied to the goods or services of such other person, to cause confusion or mistake, or to deceive; and that the facts set forth in the application are true.

(c) If the verified statement in paragraph (b)(1) or (2) of this section is not filed within a reasonable time after it is signed, the Office may require the applicant to submit a substitute verified statement attesting that the mark was in use in commerce as of the application filing date, or the applicant had a bona fide intention to use the mark in commerce as of the application filing date.

(d) [Reserved]

(e) In an application under section 66(a) of the Act, the verified statement, which is part of the international registration on file with the International Bureau, must allege that:

(1) The applicant/holder has a bona fide intention to use the mark in commerce that the U.S. Congress can regulate on or in connection with the goods or services specified in the international application/subsequent designation;

(2) The signatory is properly authorized to execute the declaration on behalf of the applicant/holder;

(3) The signatory believes the applicant/holder to be entitled to use the mark in commerce that the U.S. Congress can regulate on or in connection with the goods or services specified in the international application/subsequent designation; and

(4) To the best of his/her knowledge and belief, no other person, firm, corporation, association, or other legal entity has the right to use the mark in commerce that the U.S. Congress can regulate either in the identical form thereof or in such near resemblance thereto as to be likely, when used on or in connection with the goods or services of such other person, firm, corporation, association, or other legal entity, to cause confusion, or to cause mistake, or to deceive.

(f) In an application for concurrent use under §2.42, the verified statement in paragraph (b)(1) of this section must be modified to indicate that no other person except as specified in the application has the right to use the mark in commerce.

History of 37 C.F.R. §2.33: 54 FR 37589, Sept. 11, 1989; 54 FR 46231, Nov. 2, 1989; 64 FR 48918, Sept. 8, 1999; 67 FR 79522, Dec. 30, 2002; 68 FR 55762, Sept. 26, 2003; 73 FR 47685, Sept. 15, 2008; 73 FR 67768, Jan. 16, 2009; 74 FR 54908, Dec. 28, 2009; 80 FR 33178, July 11, 2015.

§2.34. BASES FOR FILING A TRADEMARK OR SERVICE MARK APPLICATION

(a) An application for a trademark or service mark must include one or more of the following five filing bases:

(1) Use in commerce under section 1(a) of the Act. The requirements for an application under section 1(a) of the Act are:

(i) The applicant's verified statement that the mark is in use in commerce. If the verified statement is not filed with the initial application, the verified statement must also allege that the mark was in use in commerce as of the application filing date;

(ii) The date of the applicant's first use of the mark anywhere on or in connection with the goods or services;

(iii) The date of the applicant's first use of the mark in commerce;

(iv) One specimen showing how the applicant uses the mark in commerce; and

(v) If the application specifies more than one item of goods or services in a class, the dates of use in paragraphs (a)(1)(ii) and (iii) of this section are required for only one item of goods or services specified in that class.

(2) Intent-to-use under section 1(b) of the Act. In an application under section 1(b) of the Act, the applicant must verify that the applicant has a bona fide intention to use the mark in commerce. If the verified statement is not filed with the initial application, the verified statement must also allege that the applicant had a bona fide intention to use the mark in commerce as of the application filing date.

(3) Registration of a mark in a foreign applicant's country of origin under section 44(e) of the Act. The requirements for an application under section 44(e) of the Act are:

(i) The applicant's verified statement that the applicant has a bona fide intention to use the mark in commerce. If the verified statement is not filed with the initial application, the Office will require submission of the verified statement, which must also allege that the applicant had a bona fide intention to use the mark in commerce as of the application filing date.

(ii) A true copy, a photocopy, a certification, or a certified copy of a registration in the applicant's country of origin showing that the mark has been registered in that country, and that the registration is in full force and effect. The certification or copy of the foreign registration must show the name of the owner, the mark, and the goods or services for which the mark is registered. If the foreign registration is not in the English language, the applicant must submit a translation.

(iii) If the record indicates that the foreign registration will expire before the U.S. registration will issue, the applicant must submit a true copy, a photocopy, a certification, or a certified copy of a proof of renewal from the applicant's country of origin to establish that the foreign registration has been renewed and will be in full force and effect at the time the U.S. registration will issue. If the proof of renewal is not in the English language, the applicant must submit a translation.

(4) Claim of priority, based upon an earlier-filed foreign application, under section 44(d) of the Act. The requirements for an application under section 44(d) of the Act are:

(i) A claim of priority, filed within six months of the filing date of the foreign application. Before publication or registration on the Supplemental Register, the applicant must either:

(A) Specify the filing date, serial number and country of the first regularly filed foreign application; or

(B) State that the application is based upon a subsequent regularly filed application in the same foreign country, and that any prior-filed application has been withdrawn, abandoned, or otherwise disposed of, without having been laid open to public inspection and without having any rights outstanding, and has not served as a basis for claiming a right of priority.

(ii) The applicant's verified statement that the applicant has a bona fide intention to use the mark in commerce. If the verified statement is not filed with the initial application, the Office will require submission of the verified statement, which must also allege that the applicant had a bona fide intention to use the mark in commerce as of the application filing date.

(iii) Before the application can be approved for publication, or for registration on the Supplemental Register, the applicant must establish a basis under section 1 or 44 of the Act.

(5) Extension of protection of an international registration under section 66(a) of the Act. In an application under section 66(a) of the Act, the international application/subsequent designation must contain a signed declaration that meets the requirements of §2.33(a), (e).

(b) More than one basis. In an application under section 1 or 44 of the Act, an applicant may claim more than one basis, provided the applicant satisfies all requirements for the bases claimed. In such case, the applicant must specify each basis and the goods or services to which that basis applies. An applicant must specify the goods or services covered by more than one basis. Section 1(a) and 1(b) of the Act may not both be claimed for identical goods or services in the same application. A basis under section 66(a) of the Act may not be combined with another basis.

History of 37 C.F.R. §2.34: 64 FR 48919, Sept. 8, 1999; 67 FR 79522, Dec. 30, 2002; 68 FR 55763, Sept. 26, 2003; 73 FR 67768, Jan. 16, 2009; 77 FR 30207, June 21, 2012; 80 FR 33179, July 11, 2015.

§2.35. ADDING, DELETING, OR SUBSTITUTING BASES

(a) In an application under section 66(a) of the Act, an applicant may not add, substitute or delete a basis, unless the applicant meets the requirements for transformation under section 70(c) of the Act and §7.31 of this chapter.

(b) In an application under section 1 or section 44 of the Act:

(1) Before publication for opposition, an applicant may add or substitute a basis, if the applicant meets all requirements for the new basis, as stated in §2.34, §2.44, or §2.45. The applicant may delete a basis at any time.

(2) After publication, an applicant may add or substitute a basis in an application that is not the subject of an inter partes proceeding before the Trademark Trial and Appeal Board, but only with the express permission of the Director, after consideration on petition. Republication will be required. The amendment of an application that is the subject of an inter partes proceeding before the Board is governed by §2.133(a).

(3) When an applicant substitutes one basis for another, the Office will presume that there was a continuing valid basis, unless there is contradictory evidence in the record, and the application will retain the original filing date, including a priority filing date under section 44(d), if appropriate.

(4) If an applicant properly claims a section 44(d) basis in addition to another basis, the applicant will retain the priority filing date under section 44(d) no matter which basis the applicant perfects.

(5) The applicant may add or substitute a section 44(d) basis only within the six-month priority period following the filing date of the foreign application.

(6) When the applicant adds or substitutes a basis, the applicant must list each basis and specify the goods, services, or collective membership organization to which that basis applies.

(7) When the applicant deletes a basis, the applicant must also delete any goods, services, or collective membership organization covered solely by the deleted basis.

(8) Once an applicant claims a section 1(b) basis as to any or all of the goods or services, or a collective membership organization, the applicant may not amend the application to seek registration under section 1(a) of the Act for identical goods or services or the same collective membership organization, unless the applicant files an allegation of use under section 1(c) or section 1(d) of the Act.

History of 37 C.F.R. §2.35: 64 FR 48920, Sept. 8, 1999; 68 FR 55763, Sept. 26, 2003; 80 FR 33180, July 11, 2015.

§2.36. IDENTIFICATION OF PRIOR REGISTRATIONS

Prior registrations of the same or similar marks owned by the applicant should be identified in the application if the owner(s) last listed in Office records of the prior registrations differs from the owner(s) listed in the application.

History of 37 C.F.R. §2.36: 80 FR 2310, Jan. 16, 2015.

§2.37. DESCRIPTION OF MARK

A description of the mark must be included if the mark is not in standard characters. In an application where the mark is in standard characters, a description may be included and must be included if required by the trademark examining attorney.

History of 37 C.F.R. §2.37: 64 FR 48920, Sept. 8, 1999; 68 FR 55763, Sept. 26, 2003; 73 FR 13784, May 13, 2008.

§2.38. USE BY PREDECESSOR OR BY RELATED COMPANIES

(a) If the first use of the mark was by a predecessor in title or by a related company (sections 5 and 45 of the Act), and the use inures to the benefit of the applicant, the dates of first use (§§2.34(a)(1)(ii) and (iii)) may be asserted with a statement that first use was by the predecessor in title or by the related company, as appropriate.

(b) The Office may require such details concerning the nature of the relationship and such proofs as may be necessary and appropriate for the purpose of showing that the use by related companies inures to the benefit of the applicant and does not affect the validity of the mark.

History of 37 C.F.R. §2.38: 54 FR 37589, Sept. 11, 1989; 64 FR 48920, Sept. 8, 1999; 80 FR 2310, Jan. 16, 2015.

§2.39. RESERVED

History of 37 C.F.R. §2.39: 64 FR 48920, Sept. 8, 1999.

§2.41. PROOF OF DISTINCTIVENESS UNDER SECTION 2(f)

(a) For a trademark or service mark—

(1) Ownership of prior registration(s). In appropriate cases, ownership of one or more active prior registrations on the Principal Register or under the Trademark Act of 1905 of the same mark may be accepted as prima facie evidence of distinctiveness if the goods or services are sufficiently similar to the goods or services in the application; however, further evidence may be required.

(2) Five years substantially exclusive and continuous use in commerce. In appropriate cases, if a trademark or service mark is said to have become distinctive of the applicant's goods or services by reason of the applicant's substantially exclusive and continuous use of the mark in commerce for the five years before the date on which the claim of distinctiveness is made, a showing by way of verified statements in the application may be accepted as prima facie evidence of distinctiveness; however, further evidence may be required.

(3) Other evidence. In appropriate cases, where the applicant claims that a mark has become distinctive in commerce of the applicant's goods or services, the applicant may, in support of registrability, submit with the application, or in response to a request for evidence or to a refusal to register, verified statements, depositions, or other appropriate evidence showing duration, extent, and nature of the use in commerce and advertising expenditures in connection therewith (identifying types of media and attaching typical advertisements), and verified statements, letters or statements from the trade or public, or both, or other appropriate evidence of distinctiveness.

(b) For a collective trademark or collective service mark—

(1) Ownership of prior registration(s). See the requirements of paragraph (a)(1) of this section.

(2) Five years substantially exclusive and continuous use in commerce. In appropriate cases, if a collective trademark or collective service mark is said to have become distinctive of the members' goods or services by reason of the members' substantially exclusive and continuous use of the mark in commerce for the five years before the date on which the claim of distinctiveness is made, a showing by way of verified statements in the application may be accepted as prima facie evidence of distinctiveness; however, further evidence may be required.

(3) Other evidence. In appropriate cases, where the applicant claims that a mark has become distinctive in commerce of the members' goods or services, the applicant may, in support of registrability, submit with the application, or in response to a request for evidence or to a refusal to register, verified statements, depositions, or other appropriate evidence showing duration, extent, and nature of the use in commerce, and advertising expenditures in connection therewith (identifying types of media and attaching typical advertisements), and verified statements, letters or statements from the trade or public, or both, or other appropriate evidence of distinctiveness.

(c) For a collective membership mark—

(1) Ownership of prior registration(s). In appropriate cases, ownership of one or more active prior registrations on the Principal Register or under the Act of 1905 of the same mark may be accepted as prima facie evidence of distinctiveness if the goods, services, or nature of the collective membership organization are sufficiently similar to the collective membership organization in the application; however, further evidence may be required.

(2) Five years substantially exclusive and continuous use in commerce. In appropriate cases, if a collective membership mark is said to have become distinctive of indicating membership in the applicant's collective membership organization by reason of the members' substantially exclusive and continuous use of the mark in commerce for the five years before the date on which the claim of distinctiveness is made, a showing by way of verified statements in the application may be accepted as prima facie evidence of distinctiveness; however, further evidence may be required.

(3) Other evidence. In appropriate cases, where the applicant claims that a mark has become distinctive in commerce of indicating membership in the applicant's collective membership organization, the applicant may, in support of registrability, submit with the application, or in response to a request for evidence or to a refusal to register, verified statements, depositions, or other appropriate evidence showing duration, extent, and nature of the members' use in commerce, and advertising expenditures in connection therewith (identifying types of media and attaching typical advertisements), and verified statements, letters or statements from the trade or public, or both, or other appropriate evidence of distinctiveness.

(d) For a certification mark—

(1) Ownership of prior certification mark registration(s). In appropriate cases, ownership of one or more active prior certification mark registrations on the Principal Register or under the Act of 1905 of the same mark may be accepted as prima facie evidence of distinctiveness if the authorized users' goods or services are sufficiently similar to the goods or services certified in the application, subject to the limitations of the statement set forth in §2.45(a)(4)(i)(C); however, further evidence may be required.

(2) Five years substantially exclusive and continuous use in commerce. In appropriate cases, if a certification mark is said to have become distinctive of the certified goods or services by reason of the authorized users' substantially exclusive and continuous use of the mark in commerce for the five years before the date on which the claim of distinctiveness is made, a showing by way of verified statements in the application may be accepted as prima facie evidence of distinctiveness; however, further evidence may be required.

(3) Other evidence. In appropriate cases, where the applicant claims that a mark has become distinctive of the certified goods or services program, the applicant may, in support of registrability, submit with the application, or in response to a request for evidence or to a refusal to register, verified statements, depositions, or other appropriate evidence showing duration, extent, and nature of the authorized users' use in commerce and advertising expenditures in connection therewith (identifying types of media and attaching typical advertisements), and verified statements, letters or statements from the trade or public, or both, or other appropriate evidence of distinctiveness.

(e) Certification marks with geographical matter. Paragraph (d) of this section does not apply to geographical matter in a certification mark certifying regional origin because section 2(e)(2) of the Act does not apply to certification marks that are indications of regional origin.

History of 37 C.F.R. §2.41: 54 FR 37590, Sept. 11, 1989; 73 FR 67768, Jan. 16, 2009; 80 FR 33180, July 11, 2015.

§2.42. CONCURRENT USE

(a) Prior to seeking concurrent use, an application for registration on the Principal Register under the Act must assert use in commerce and include all the application elements required by the preceding sections, in addition to §2.44 or §2.45, if applicable.

(b) The applicant must also include a verified statement that indicates the following, to the extent of the applicant's knowledge:

(1) For a trademark or service mark, the geographic area in which the applicant is using the mark in commerce; for a collective mark or certification mark, the geographic area in which the applicant's members or authorized users are using the mark in commerce;

(2) For a trademark or service mark, the applicant's goods or services; for a collective trademark, collective service mark, or certification mark, the applicant's members' or authorized users' goods or services; for a collective membership mark, the nature of the applicant's collective membership organization;

(3) The mode of use for which the applicant seeks registration;

(4) The concurrent users' names and addresses;

(5) The registrations issued to or applications filed by such concurrent users, if any;

(6) For a trademark or service mark, the geographic areas in which the concurrent user is using the mark in commerce; for a collective mark or certification mark, the geographic areas in which the concurrent user's members or authorized users are using the mark in commerce;

(7) For a trademark or service mark, the concurrent user's goods or services; for a collective trademark, collective service mark, or certification mark, the concurrent user's members' or authorized users' goods or services; for a collective membership mark, the nature of the concurrent user's collective membership organization;

(8) The mode of use by the concurrent users or the concurrent users' members or authorized users; and

(9) The time periods of such use by the concurrent users or the concurrent users' members or authorized users.

(c) For the requirements to amend an application to concurrent use, see §2.73.

(d) For the requirements of a concurrent use proceeding, see §2.99.

History of 37 C.F.R. §2.42: 54 FR 34897, Aug. 22, 1989; 80 FR 33181, July 11, 2015.

§2.43. SERVICE MARK

In an application to register a service mark, the application shall specify and contain all the elements required by the preceding sections for trademarks, but shall be modified to relate to services instead of to goods wherever necessary.

§2.44. REQUIREMENTS FOR A COMPLETE COLLECTIVE MARK APPLICATION

(a) A complete application to register a collective trademark, collective service mark, or collective membership mark must include the following:

(1) The requirements specified in §2.32(a) introductory text through (a)(4), (a)(8) through (10), (c), and (d);

(2)(i) For a collective trademark or collective service mark, a list of the particular goods or services on or in connection with which the applicant's members use or intend to use the mark; or

(ii) For a collective membership mark, a description of the nature of the membership organization such as by type, purpose, or area of activity of the members; and

(iii) In a U.S. application filed under section 44 of the Act, the scope of the goods or services or the nature of the membership organization covered by the section 44 basis may not exceed the scope of the goods or services or nature of the membership organization in the foreign application or registration.

(3)(i) For a collective trademark or collective service mark application, the international class of goods or services, if known. See §6.1 of this chapter for a list of the international classes of goods and services; or

(ii) For a collective membership mark application filed under sections 1 or 44 of the Act, classification in U.S. Class 200; and for a collective membership mark application filed under section 66(a) of the Act, the international class(es) assigned by the International Bureau in the corresponding international registration.

(4) One or more of the following five filing bases:

(i) Use in commerce under section 1(a) of the Act. The requirements for an application under section 1(a) of the Act are:

(A) A statement specifying the nature of the applicant's control over the use of the mark by the members;

(B) For a collective trademark or collective service mark, the date of the applicant's member's first use of the mark anywhere on or in connection with the goods or services and the date of the applicant's member's first use of the mark in commerce; or for a collective membership mark, the date of the applicant's member's first use anywhere to indicate membership in the collective organization and the date of the applicant's member's first use in commerce. If the application specifies more than one item of goods or services in a class, the dates of use are required for only one item of goods or services specified in that class;

(C) One specimen showing how a member uses the mark in commerce; and

(D) A verified statement alleging:

That the applicant believes the applicant is the owner of the mark; that the mark is in use in commerce; that the applicant is exercising legitimate control over the use of the mark in commerce; that to the best of the signatory's knowledge and belief, no other persons except members have the right to use the mark in commerce, either in the identical form or in such near resemblance as to be likely, when used on or in connection with the goods, services, or collective membership organization of such other persons to cause confusion or mistake, or to deceive; that the specimen shows the mark as used in commerce by the applicant's members; and that the facts set forth in the application are true.

(ii) Intent-to-use under section 1(b) of the Act. The requirement for an application based on section 1(b) of the Act is a verified statement alleging:

That the applicant has a bona fide intention, and is entitled, to exercise legitimate control over the use of the mark in commerce; that to the best of the signatory's knowledge and belief, no other persons, except members, have the right to use the mark in commerce, either in the identical form or in such near resemblance as to be likely, when used on or in connection with the goods, services, or collective membership organization of such other persons, to cause confusion or mistake, or to deceive; and that the facts set forth in the application are true.

(iii) Registration of a mark in a foreign applicant's country of origin under section 44(e) of the Act. The requirements for an application under section 44(e) of the Act are:

(A) The requirements of §2.34(a)(3)(ii) and (iii); and

(B) A verified statement in accordance with paragraph (a)(4)(ii) of this section.

(iv) Claim of priority, based upon an earlier-filed foreign application, under section 44(d) of the Act. The requirements for an application under section 44(d) of the Act are:

(A) The requirements of §2.34(a)(4)(i) and (iii); and

(B) A verified statement in accordance with paragraph (a)(4)(ii) of this section.

(v) Extension of protection of an international registration under section 66(a) of the Act. The requirement for an application under section 66(a) of the Act is a verified statement alleging that the applicant/holder has a bona fide intention, and is entitled, to exercise legitimate control over the use of the mark in commerce that the U.S. Congress can regulate on or in connection with the goods or services specified in the international application/subsequent designation; that the signatory is properly authorized to execute the declaration on behalf of the applicant/holder; and that to the best of his/her knowledge and belief, no other person, firm, corporation, association, or other legal entity, except members, has the right to use the mark in commerce that the U.S. Congress can regulate either in the identical form thereof or in such near resemblance thereto as to be likely, when used on or in connection with the goods, services, or collective membership organization of such other person, firm, corporation, association, or other legal entity, to cause confusion, or to cause mistake, or to deceive.

(b) Verification not filed within reasonable time or omitted.

(1) If the verified statement in paragraph (a)(4)(i)(D), (a)(4)(ii), (a)(4)(iii)(B), or (a)(4)(iv)(B) of this section is not filed within a reasonable time after it is signed, the Office may require the applicant to submit a substitute verified statement attesting that, as of the application filing date, the mark was in use in commerce and the applicant was exercising legitimate control over the use of the mark in commerce; or, as of the application filing date, the applicant had a bona fide intention, and was entitled, to exercise legitimate control over the use of the mark in commerce; or

(2) If the verified statement in paragraph (a)(4)(i)(D), (a)(4)(ii), (a)(4)(iii)(B), (a)(4)(iv)(B), or (a)(4)(v) of this section is not filed with the initial application, the verified statement must also allege that, as of the application filing date, the mark was in use in commerce and the applicant was exercising legitimate control over the use of the mark in commerce; or, as of the application filing date, the applicant had a bona fide intention, and was entitled, to exercise legitimate control over the use of the mark in commerce.

(c) More than one basis. In an application under section 1 or 44 of the Act, an applicant may claim more than one basis, provided the applicant satisfies all requirements for the bases claimed. In such case, the applicant must specify each basis, followed by the goods, services, or collective membership organization to which that basis applies. An applicant must specify the goods, services, or collective membership organization covered by more than one basis. Section 1(a) and 1(b) of the Act may not both be claimed for identical goods, or services, or the same collective membership organization in one application. A basis under section 66(a) of the Act may not be combined with another basis.

(d) In an application for concurrent use under §2.42, the verified statement in paragraph (a)(4)(i)(D) of this section must be modified to indicate that no other persons except members and the concurrent users as specified in the application have the right to use the mark in commerce.

(e) Multiple-class applications. For the requirements of a multiple-class application, see §2.86.

History of 37 C.F.R. §2.44: 54 FR 37590, Sept. 11, 1989; 73 FR 67769, Jan. 16, 2009; 80 FR 33181, July 11, 2015.

§2.45. REQUIREMENTS FOR A COMPLETE CERTIFICATION MARK APPLICATION; RESTRICTION ON CERTIFICATION MARK APPLICATION

(a) A complete application to register a certification mark must include the following:

(1) The requirements specified in §2.32(a) introductory text through (a)(4), (a)(8) through (10), (c), and (d);

(2) A list of the particular goods or services on or in connection with which the applicant's authorized users use or intend to use the mark. In an application filed under section 44 of the Act, the scope of the goods or services covered by the section 44 basis may not exceed the scope of the goods or services in the foreign application or registration;

(3) For applications filed under section 1 or 44 of the Act, classification in U.S. Class A for an application certifying goods and U.S. Class B for an application certifying services. For applications filed under section 66(a) of the Act, the international class(es) of goods or services assigned by the International Bureau in the corresponding international registration;

(4) One or more of the following five filing bases:

(i) Use in commerce under section 1(a) of the Act. The requirements for an application under section 1(a) of the Act are:

(A) A statement specifying what the applicant is certifying about the goods or services in the application;

(B) A copy of the certification standards governing use of the certification mark on or in connection with the goods or services specified in the application;

(C) A statement that the applicant is not engaged in the production or marketing of the goods or services to which the mark is applied, except to advertise or promote recognition of the certification program or of the goods or services that meet the certification standards of the applicant;

(D) The date of the applicant's authorized user's first use of the mark anywhere on or in connection with the goods or services and the date of the applicant's authorized user's first use of the mark in commerce. If the application specifies more than one item of goods or services in a class, the dates of use are required for only one item of goods or services specified in that class;

(E) One specimen showing how an authorized user uses the mark in commerce; and

(F) A verified statement alleging:

That the applicant believes the applicant is the owner of the mark; that the mark is in use in commerce; that the applicant is exercising legitimate control over the use of the mark in commerce; that to the best of the signatory's knowledge and belief, no other persons except authorized users have the right to use the mark in commerce, either in the identical form or in such near resemblance as to be likely, when used on or in connection with the goods or services of such other persons, to cause confusion or mistake, or to deceive; that the specimen shows the mark as used in commerce by the applicant's authorized users; and that the facts set forth in the application are true.

(ii) Intent-to-use under section 1(b) of the Act. The requirements for an application based on section 1(b) of the Act are:

(A) A statement specifying what the applicant will be certifying about the goods or services in the application;

(B) A statement that the applicant will not engage in the production or marketing of the goods or services to which the mark is applied, except to advertise or promote recognition of the certification program or of the goods or services that meet the certification standards of the applicant; and

(C) A verified statement alleging:

That the applicant has a bona fide intention, and is entitled, to exercise legitimate control over the use of the mark in commerce; that to the best of the signatory's knowledge and belief, no other persons, except authorized users, have the right to use the mark in commerce, either in the identical form or in such near resemblance as to be likely, when used on or in connection with the goods or services of such other persons, to cause confusion or mistake, or to deceive; and that the facts set forth in the application are true.

(iii) Registration of a mark in a foreign applicant's country of origin under section 44(e) of the Act. The requirements for an application under section 44(e) of the Act are:

(A) The requirements of §2.34(a)(3)(ii) and (iii);

(B) The requirements in paragraphs (a)(4)(ii)(A) and (B) of this section; and

(C) A verified statement in accordance with paragraph (a)(4)(ii)(C) of this section.

(iv) Claim of priority, based upon an earlier-filed foreign application, under section 44(d) of the Act. The requirements for an application under section 44(d) of the Act are:

(A) The requirements of §2.34(a)(4)(i) and (iii);

(B) The requirements in paragraphs (a)(4)(ii)(A) and (B) of this section; and

(C) A verified statement in accordance with paragraph (a)(4)(ii)(C) of this section.

(v) Extension of protection of an international registration under section 66(a) of the Act. The requirements for an application under section 66(a) of the Act are:

(A) The requirements of paragraphs (a)(4)(ii)(A) and (B) of this section; and

(B) A verified statement alleging that the applicant/holder has a bona fide intention, and is entitled, to exercise legitimate control over the use of the mark in commerce that the U.S. Congress can regulate on or in connection with the goods or services specified in the international application/subsequent designation; that the signatory is properly authorized to execute the declaration on behalf of the applicant/holder; and that to the best of his/her knowledge and belief, no other person, firm, corporation, association, or other legal entity, except authorized users, has the right to use the mark in commerce that the U.S. Congress can regulate either in the identical form thereof or in such near resemblance thereto as to be likely, when used on or in connection with the goods or services of such other person, firm, corporation, association, or other legal entity, to cause confusion, or to cause mistake, or to deceive.

(b) Verification not filed within reasonable time or omitted.

(1) If the verified statement in paragraph (a)(4)(i)(F), (a)(4)(ii)(C), (a)(4)(iii)(C), or (a)(4)(iv)(C) of this section is not filed within a reasonable time after it is signed, the Office may require the applicant to submit a substitute verified statement attesting that, as of the application filing date, the mark was in use in commerce and the applicant was exercising legitimate control over the use of the mark in commerce; or, as of the application filing date, the applicant had a bona fide intention, and was entitled, to exercise legitimate control over the use of the mark in commerce; or

(2) If the verified statement in paragraph (a)(4)(i)(F), (a)(4)(ii)(C), (a)(4)(iii)(C), (a)(4)(iv)(C), or (a)(4)(v)(B) of this section is not filed with the initial application, the verified statement must also allege that, as of the application filing date, the mark was in use in commerce and the applicant was exercising legitimate control over the use of the mark in commerce; or, as of the application filing date, the applicant had a bona fide intention, and was entitled, to exercise legitimate control over the use of the mark in commerce.

(c) More than one basis. In an application under section 1 or 44 of the Act, an applicant may claim more than one basis, provided the applicant satisfies all requirements for the bases claimed. In such case, the applicant must specify each basis, followed by the goods or services to which that basis applies. An applicant must specify the goods or services covered by more than one basis. Section 1(a) and 1(b) of the Act may not both be claimed for identical goods or services in the same application. A basis under section 66(a) of the Act may not be combined with another basis.

(d) Concurrent use. In an application for concurrent use under §2.42, the verified statement in paragraph (a)(4)(i)(F) of this section must be modified to indicate that no other persons except authorized users and concurrent users as specified in the application have the right to use the mark in commerce.

(e) Multiple-class applications. For the requirements of a multiple-class application, see §2.86.

(f) Restriction on certification mark application. A single application may not include a certification mark and another type of mark. The same mark for the same goods or services is not registrable as both a certification mark and another type of mark. See sections 4 and 14(5)(B) of the Act.

History of 37 C.F.R. §2.45: 54 FR 37590, Sept. 11, 1989; 64 FR 48920, Sept. 8, 1999; 73 FR 67769, Jan. 16, 2009; 80 FR 33182, July 11, 2015.

§2.46. PRINCIPAL REGISTER

All applications will be treated as seeking registration on the Principal Register unless otherwise stated in the application. Service marks, collective marks, and certification marks, registrable in accordance with the applicable provisions of section 2 of the Act, are registered on the Principal Register.

§2.47. SUPPLEMENTAL REGISTER

(a) In an application to register on the Supplemental Register under section 23 of the Act, the application shall so indicate and shall specify that the mark has been in use in commerce.

(b) In an application to register on the Supplemental Register under section 44 of the Act, the application shall so indicate. The statement of lawful use in commerce may be omitted.

(c) An application under section 66(a) of the Act is not eligible for registration on the Supplemental Register.

(d) A mark in an application to register on the Principal Register under section 1(b) of the Act is eligible for registration on the Supplemental Register only after an acceptable amendment to allege use under §2.76 or statement of use under §2.88 has been timely filed.

(e) An application for registration on the Supplemental Register must conform to the requirements for registration on the Principal Register under section 1(a) of the Act, so far as applicable.

History of 37 C.F.R. §2.47: 38 FR 18876, July 16, 1973; 54 FR 37590, Sept. 11, 1989; 68 FR 55763, Sept. 26, 2003; 73 FR 67769, Jan. 16, 2009.

§2.48. OFFICE DOES NOT ISSUE DUPLICATE REGISTRATIONS

If two applications on the same register would result in registrations that are exact duplicates, the Office will permit only one application to mature into registration, and will refuse registration in the other application.

History of 37 C.F.R. §2.48: 73 FR 67769, Jan. 16, 2009.

DRAWING

§2.51. DRAWING REQUIRED

(a) In an application under section 1(a) of the Act, the drawing of the mark must be a substantially exact representation of the mark as used on or in connection with the goods and/or services.

(b) In an application under section 1(b) of the Act, the drawing of the mark must be a substantially exact representation of the mark as intended to be used on or in connection with the goods and/or services specified in the application, and once an amendment to allege use under §2.76 or a statement of use under §2.88 has been filed, the drawing of the mark must be a substantially exact representation of the mark as used on or in connection with the goods and/or services.

(c) In an application under section 44 of the Act, the drawing of the mark must be a substantially exact representation of the mark as it appears in the drawing in the registration certificate of a mark duly registered in the applicant's country of origin.

(d) In an application under section 66(a) of the Act, the drawing of the mark must be a substantially exact representation of the mark as it appears in the international registration.

History of 37 C.F.R. §2.51: 54 FR 37590, Sept. 11, 1989; 64 FR 48920, Sept. 8, 1999; 68 FR 55763, Sept. 26, 2003.

§2.52. TYPES OF DRAWINGS & FORMAT FOR DRAWINGS

A drawing depicts the mark sought to be registered. The drawing must show only one mark. The applicant must include a clear drawing of the mark when the application is filed. There are two types of drawings:

(a) Standard character (typed) drawing. Applicants who seek to register words, letters, numbers, or any combination thereof without claim to any particular font style, size, or color must submit a standard character drawing that shows the mark in black on a white background. An applicant may submit a standard character drawing if:

(1) The application includes a statement that the mark is in standard characters and no claim is made to any particular font style, size, or color;

(2) The mark does not include a design element;

(3) All letters and words in the mark are depicted in Latin characters;

(4) All numerals in the mark are depicted in Roman or Arabic numerals; and

(5) The mark includes only common punctuation or diacritical marks.

(b) Special form drawing. Applicants who seek to register a mark that includes a two or three-dimensional design; color; and/or words, letters, or numbers or the combination thereof in a particular font style or size must submit a special form drawing. The drawing should show the mark in black on a white background, unless the mark includes color.

(1) Marks that include color. If the mark includes color, the drawing must show the mark in color, and the applicant must name the color(s), describe where the color(s) appear on the mark, and submit a claim that the color(s) is a feature of the mark.

(2) Three dimensional marks. If the mark has three-dimensional features, the drawing must depict a single rendition of the mark, and the applicant must indicate that the mark is three-dimensional.

(3) Motion marks. If the mark has motion, the drawing may depict a single point in the movement, or the drawing may depict up to five freeze frames showing various points in the movement, whichever best depicts the commercial impression of the mark. The applicant must also describe the mark.

(4) Broken lines to show placement. If necessary to adequately depict the commercial impression of the mark, the applicant may be required to submit a drawing that shows the placement of the mark by surrounding the mark with a proportionately accurate broken-line representation of the particular goods, packaging, or advertising on which the mark appears. The applicant must also use broken lines to show any other matter not claimed as part of the mark. For any drawing using broken lines to indicate placement of the mark, or matter not claimed as part of the mark, the applicant must describe the mark and explain the purpose of the broken lines.

(5) Description of mark. A description of the mark must be included.

(c) TEAS drawings. A drawing filed through TEAS must meet the requirements of §2.53.

(d) Paper drawings. A paper drawing must meet the requirements of §2.54.

(e) Sound, scent, and non-visual marks. An applicant is not required to submit a drawing if the mark consists only of a sound, a scent, or other completely non-visual matter. For these types of marks, the applicant must submit a detailed description of the mark.

History of 37 C.F.R. §2.52: 30 FR 13193, Oct. 16, 1965; 39 FR 12247, Apr. 4, 1974; 47 FR 38695, Sept. 2, 1982; 51 FR 29921, Aug. 21, 1986; 54 FR 37591, Sept. 11, 1989; 54 FR 46231, Nov. 2, 1989; 64 FR 48920, Sept. 8, 1999; 68 FR 55763, Sept. 26, 2003; 73 FR 13784, May 13, 2008; 73 FR 67769, Jan. 16, 2009.

§2.53. REQUIREMENTS FOR DRAWINGS FILED THROUGH THE TEAS

The drawing must meet the requirements of §2.52. In addition, in a TEAS submission, the drawing must meet the following requirements:

(a) Standard character drawings. If an applicant seeks registration of a standard character mark, the applicant must enter the mark in the appropriate field on the TEAS form, and check the box to claim that the mark consists of standard characters.

(b) Special form drawings: If an applicant is filing a special form drawing, the applicant must attach a digitized image of the mark to the TEAS submission that meets the requirements of paragraph (c) of this section.

(c) Requirements for digitized image: The image must be in .jpg format and scanned at no less than 300 dots per inch and no more than 350 dots per inch with a length and width of no less than 250 pixels and no more than 944 pixels. All lines must be clean, sharp and solid, not fine or crowded, and produce a high quality image when copied.

History of 37 C.F.R. §2.53: 68 FR 55764, Sept. 26, 2003; 70 FR 38774, July 6, 2005; 73 FR 67769, Jan. 16, 2009.

§2.54. REQUIREMENTS FOR DRAWINGS SUBMITTED ON PAPER

The drawing must meet the requirements of §2.52. In addition, in a paper submission, the drawing should:

(a) Be on non-shiny white paper that is separate from the application;

(b) Be on paper that is 8 to 8.5 inches (20.3 to 21.6 cm.) wide and 11 to 11.69 inches (27.9 to 29.7 cm.) long. One of the shorter sides of the sheet should be regarded as its top edge. The image must be no larger than 3.15 inches (8 cm) high by 3.15 inches (8 cm) wide;

(c) Include the caption "DRAWING PAGE" at the top of the drawing beginning one inch (2.5 cm.) from the top edge; and

(d) Depict the mark in black ink, or in color if color is claimed as a feature of the mark.

(e) Drawings must be typed or made with a pen or by a process that will provide high definition when copied. A photolithographic, printer's proof copy, or other high quality reproduction of the mark may be used. All lines must be clean, sharp and solid, and must not be fine or crowded.

History of 37 C.F.R. §2.54: 68 FR 55764, Sept. 26, 2003.

SPECIMENS

§2.56. SPECIMENS

(a) An application under section 1(a) of the Act, an amendment to allege use under §2.76, and a statement of use under §2.88 must each include one specimen per class showing the mark as used on or in connection with the goods or services. When requested by the Office as reasonably necessary to proper examination, additional specimens must be provided.

(b)(1) A trademark specimen is a label, tag, or container for the goods, or a display associated with the goods. The Office may accept another document related to the goods or the sale of the goods when it is impracticable to place the mark on the goods, packaging for the goods, or displays associated with the goods.

(2) A service mark specimen must show the mark as used in the sale or advertising of the services.

(3) A collective trademark or collective service mark specimen must show how a member uses the mark on the member's goods or in the sale or advertising of the member's services.

(4) A collective membership mark specimen must show use by members to indicate membership in the collective organization.

(5) A certification mark specimen must show how a person other than the owner uses the mark to reflect certification of regional or other origin, material, mode of manufacture, quality, accuracy, or other characteristics of that person's goods or services; or that members of a union or other organization performed the work or labor on the goods or services.

(c) A photocopy or other reproduction of a specimen of the mark as used on or in connection with the goods, or in the sale or advertising of the services, is acceptable. However, a photocopy of the drawing required by §2.51 is not a proper specimen.

(d)(1) The specimen should be flat, and not larger than 8½ inches (21.6 cm.) wide by 11.69 inches (29.7 cm.) long. If a specimen of this size is not available, the applicant may substitute a suitable photograph or other facsimile.

(2) If the applicant files a specimen exceeding these size requirements (a "bulky specimen"), the Office will create a digital facsimile of the specimen that meets the requirements of the rule (*i.e.*, is flat and no larger than 8½ inches (21.6 cm.) wide by 11.69 inches (29.7 cm.) long) and put it in the record. The Office may destroy the original bulky specimen.

(3) In the absence of non-bulky alternatives, a specimen of use in another appropriate medium may be designated as acceptable by the Office.

(4) For a TEAS submission, the specimen must be a digitized image in .jpg or .pdf format.

History of 37 C.F.R. §2.56: 39 FR 12248, Apr. 4, 1974; 54 FR 37591, Sept. 11, 1989; 64 FR 48921, Sept. 8, 1999; 68 FR 55764, Sept. 26, 2003; 73 FR 67769, Jan. 16, 2009; 77 FR 30207, June 21, 2012; 80 FR 33183, July 11, 2015.

§§2.57, 2.58. RESERVED

History of 37 C.F.R. §§2.57, 2.58: 64 FR 48921, Sept. 8, 1999.

§2.59. FILING SUBSTITUTE SPECIMEN(S)

(a) In an application under section 1(a) of the Act, the applicant may submit substitute specimens of the mark as used on or in connection with the goods or in the sale or advertising of the services, or as used to indicate membership in the collective organization. The applicant must submit a verified statement that the substitute specimen was in use in commerce at least as early as the filing date of the application. The verified statement is not required if the specimen is a duplicate or facsimile of a specimen already of record in the application.

(b) In an application under section 1(b) of the Act, after filing either an amendment to allege use under §2.76 or a statement of use under §2.88, the applicant may submit substitute specimens of the mark as used on or in connection with the goods or in the sale or advertising of the services, or as used to indicate membership in the collective organization. If the applicant submits substitute specimen(s), the applicant must:

(1) For an amendment to allege use under §2.76, submit a verified statement that the substitute specimen(s) was in use in commerce prior to filing the amendment to allege use.

(2) For a statement of use under §2.88, submit a verified statement that the substitute specimen(s) was in use in commerce either prior to filing the statement of use or prior to the expiration of the deadline for filing the statement of use.

History of 37 C.F.R. §2.59: 54 FR 37591, Sept. 11, 1989; 64 FR 48921, Sept. 8, 1999; 80 FR 33183, July 11, 2015.

EXAMINATION OF APPLICATION & ACTION BY APPLICANTS

§2.61. ACTION BY EXAMINER

(a) Applications for registration, including amendments to allege use under section 1(c) of the Act, and statements of use under section 1(d) of the Act, will be examined and, if the applicant is found not entitled to registration for any reason, applicant will be notified and advised of the reasons therefor and of any formal requirements or objections.

(b) The Office may require the applicant to furnish such information, exhibits, affidavits or declarations, and such additional specimens as may be reasonably necessary to the proper examination of the application.

(c) Whenever it shall be found that two or more parties whose interests are in conflict are represented by the same attorney, each party and also the attorney shall be notified of this fact.

History of 37 C.F.R. §2.61: 30 FR 13193, Oct. 16, 1965; 37 FR 2880, Feb. 9, 1972; 54 FR 37592, Sept. 11, 1989; 77 FR 30207, June 21, 2012.

§2.62. PROCEDURE FOR FILING RESPONSE

(a) Deadline. The applicant's response to an Office action must be received within six months from the date of issuance.

(b) Signature. The response must be signed by the applicant, someone with legal authority to bind the applicant (e.g., a corporate officer or general partner of a partnership), or a practitioner qualified to practice under §11.14 of this chapter, in accordance with the requirements of §2.193(e)(2).

(c) Form. Responses must be filed through TEAS, transmitted by facsimile, mailed, or delivered by hand, as set out in §2.190(a). Responses sent via email will not be accorded a date of receipt.

History of 37 C.F.R. §2.62: 73 FR 67769, Jan. 16, 2009; 74 FR 54908, Dec. 28, 2009; 80 FR 2310, Jan. 16, 2015.

§2.63. ACTION AFTER RESPONSE

(a) Repeated non-final refusal or requirement. After response by the applicant, the examining attorney will review all statutory refusals and/or requirement(s) in light of the response.

(1) If, after review of the applicant's response, the examining attorney issues a non-final action that maintains any previously issued substantive refusal(s) to register or repeats any requirement(s), the applicant may submit a timely response to the action under §2.62(a).

(2) If, after review of the applicant's response, the examining attorney issues a non-final action that contains no substantive refusals to register, but maintains any requirement(s), the applicant may respond to such repeated requirement(s) by filing a timely petition to the Director for relief from the repeated requirement(s) if the subject matter of the repeated requirement(s) is appropriate for petition to the Director (see §2.146(b)).

(b) Final refusal or requirement. Upon review of a response, the examining attorney may state that the refusal(s) to register, or the requirement(s), is final.

(1) If the examining attorney issues a final action that maintains any substantive refusal(s) to register, the applicant may respond by timely filing:

(i) A request for reconsideration under paragraph (b)(3) of this section that seeks to overcome any substantive refusal(s) to register, and comply with any outstanding requirement(s), maintained in the final action; or

(ii) An appeal to the Trademark Trial and Appeal Board under §§2.141 and 2.142.

(2) If the examining attorney issues a final action that contains no substantive refusals to register, but maintains any requirement(s), the applicant may respond by timely filing:

(i) A request for reconsideration under paragraph (b)(3) of this section that seeks to comply with any outstanding requirement(s) maintained in the final action;

(ii) An appeal of the requirement(s) to the Trademark Trial and Appeal Board under §§2.141 and 2.142; or

(iii) A petition to the Director under §2.146 to review the requirement(s), if the subject matter of the requirement(s) is procedural, and therefore appropriate for petition.

(3) Prior to the expiration of the time for filing an appeal or a petition, the applicant may file a request for reconsideration of the final action that seeks to overcome any substantive refusal(s) and/or comply with any outstanding requirement(s). Filing a request for reconsideration does not stay or extend the time for filing an appeal or petition. The Office will enter amendments accompanying requests for reconsideration after final action if the amendments comply with the rules of practice in trademark cases and the Act.

(4) Filing a request for reconsideration that does not result in the withdrawal of all refusals and requirements, without the filing of a timely appeal or petition, will result in abandonment of the application for incomplete response, pursuant to §2.65(a).

(c) If a petition to the Director under §2.146 is denied, the applicant will have six months from the date of issuance of the Office action that repeated the requirement(s), or made it final, or thirty days from the date of the decision on the petition, whichever date is later, to comply with the requirement(s). A requirement that is the subject of a petition decided by the Director subsequently may not be the subject of an appeal to the Trademark Trial and Appeal Board.

(d) If an applicant in an application under section 1(b) of the Act files an amendment to allege use under §2.76 during the six-month response period after issuance of a final action, the examining attorney will examine the amendment. The filing of such an amendment does not stay or extend the time for filing an appeal or petition.

History of 37 C.F.R. §2.63: 30 FR 13193, Oct. 16, 1965; 48 FR 23134, May 23, 1983; 80 FR 2310, Jan. 16, 2015.

E §2.64. REINSTATEMENT OF APPLICATIONS & REGISTRATIONS ABANDONED, CANCELLED, OR EXPIRED DUE TO OFFICE ERROR

(a) Request for Reinstatement of an Abandoned Application. The applicant may file a written request to reinstate an application abandoned due to Office error. There is no fee for a request for reinstatement.

(1) Deadline. The applicant must file the request by not later than:

(i) Two months after the issue date of the notice of abandonment; or

(ii) Two months after the date of actual knowledge of the abandonment and not later than six months after the date the trademark electronic records system indicates that the application is abandoned, where the applicant declares under §2.20 or 28 U.S.C. 1746 that it did not receive the notice of abandonment.

(2) Requirements. A request to reinstate an application abandoned due to Office error must include:

(i) Proof that a response to an Office action, a statement of use, or a request for extension of time to file a statement of use was timely filed and a copy of the relevant document;

(ii) Proof of actual receipt by the Office of a response to an Office action, a statement of use, or a request for extension of time to file a statement of use and a copy of the relevant document;

(iii) Proof that the Office processed a fee in connection with the filing at issue and a copy of the relevant document;

(iv) Proof that the Office sent the Office action or notice of allowance to an address that is not the designated correspondence address; or

(v) Other evidence, or factual information supported by a declaration under §2.20 or 28 U.S.C. 1746, demonstrating Office error in abandoning the application.

(b) Request for Reinstatement of Cancelled or Expired Registration. The registrant may file a written request to reinstate a registration cancelled or expired due to Office error. There is no fee for the request for reinstatement.

(1) Deadline. The registrant must file the request by not later than:

(i) Two months after the issue date of the notice of cancellation/expiration; or

(ii) Where the registrant has timely filed an affidavit of use or excusable non-use under section 8 or 71 of the Act, or a renewal application under section 9 of the Act, two months after the date of actual knowledge of the cancellation/expiration and not later than six months after the date the trademark electronic records system indicates that the registration is cancelled/expired, where the registrant declares under §2.20 or 28 U.S.C. 1746 that it did not receive the notice of cancellation/expiration or where the Office did not issue a notice.

(2) Requirements. A request to reinstate a registration cancelled/expired due to Office error must include:

(i) Proof that an affidavit or declaration of use or excusable nonuse, a renewal application, or a response to an Office action was timely filed and a copy of the relevant document;

(ii) Proof of actual receipt by the Office of an affidavit or declaration of use or excusable nonuse, a renewal application, or a response to an Office action and a copy of the relevant document;

(iii) Proof that the Office processed a fee in connection with the filing at issue and a copy of the relevant document;

(iv) Proof that the Office sent the Office action to an address that is not the designated correspondence address; or

(v) Other evidence, or factual information supported by a declaration under §2.20 or 28 U.S.C. 1746, demonstrating Office error in cancelling/expiring the registration.

(c) Request for Reinstatement May be Construed as Petition. If an applicant or registrant is not entitled to reinstatement, a request for reinstatement may be construed as a petition to the Director under §2.146 or a petition to revive under §2.66, if appropriate. If the applicant or registrant is unable to meet the timeliness requirement under paragraphs (a)(1) or (b)(1) of this section for filing the request, the applicant or registrant may submit a petition to the Director under §2.146(a)(5) to request a waiver of the rule.

History of 37 C.F.R. §2.64: 82 FR 29407, July 8, 2017.

§2.65. Abandonment

(a) An application will be abandoned if an applicant fails to respond to an Office action, or to respond completely, within six months from the date of issuance. A timely petition to the Director pursuant to §§2.63(a) and (b) and 2.146 or notice of appeal to the Trademark Trial and Appeal Board pursuant to §2.142, if appropriate, is a response that avoids abandonment (see §2.63(b)(4)).

(1) If all refusals and/or requirements are expressly limited to certain goods and/or services, the application will be abandoned only as to those goods and/or services.

(2) When a timely response by the applicant is a bona fide attempt to advance the examination of the application and is a substantially complete response to the examining attorney's action, but consideration of some matter or compliance with a requirement has been omitted, the examining attorney may grant the applicant thirty days, or to the end of the response period set forth in the action to which the substantially complete response was submitted, whichever is longer, to explain and supply the omission before the examining attorney considers the question of abandonment.

(b) An application will be abandoned if an applicant expressly abandons the application pursuant to §2.68.

(c) An application will be abandoned if an applicant in an application under section 1(b) of the Act fails to timely file either a statement of use under §2.88 or a request for an extension of time for filing a statement of use under §2.89.

History of 37 C.F.R. §2.65: 30 FR 13193, Oct. 16, 1965; 48 FR 23134, May 23, 1983; 54 FR 37592, Sept. 11, 1989; 68 FR 55764, Sept. 26, 2003; 73 FR 67769, Jan. 16, 2009; 80 FR 2311, Jan. 16, 2015.

A §2.66. Revival of Applications Abandoned in Full or in Part Due to Unintentional Delay

(a) Deadline. The applicant may file a petition to revive an application abandoned in full or in part because the applicant did not timely respond to an Office action or notice of allowance, if the delay was unintentional. The applicant must file the petition by not later than:

(1) Two months after the issue date of the notice of abandonment in full or in part; or

(2) Two months after the date of actual knowledge of the abandonment and not later than six months after the date the trademark electronic records system indicates that the application is abandoned in full or in part, where the applicant declares under §2.20 or 28 U.S.C. 1746 that it did not receive the notice of abandonment.

(b) Petition To Revive Application Abandoned in Full or in Part for Failure To Respond to an Office Action. A petition to revive an application abandoned in full or in part because the applicant did not timely respond to an Office action must include:

(1) The petition fee required by §2.6;

(2) A statement, signed by someone with firsthand knowledge of the facts, that the delay in filing the response on or before the due date was unintentional; and

(3) A response to the Office action, signed pursuant to §2.193(e)(2), or a statement that the applicant did not receive the Office action or the notification that an Office action issued. If the applicant asserts that the unintentional delay is based on non-receipt of an Office action or notification, the applicant may not assert non-receipt of the same Office action or notification in a subsequent petition. When the abandonment is after a final Office action, the response is treated as a request for reconsideration under §2.63(b)(3) and the applicant must also file:

(i) A notice of appeal to the Trademark Trial and Appeal Board under §2.141 or a petition to the Director under §2.146, if permitted by §2.63(b)(2)(iii); or

(ii) A statement that no appeal or petition is being filed from the final refusal(s) or requirement(s).

(c) Petition To Revive Application Abandoned for Failure To Respond to a Notice of Allowance. A petition to revive an application abandoned because the applicant did not timely respond to a notice of allowance must include:

(1) The petition fee required by §2.6;

(2) A statement, signed by someone with firsthand knowledge of the facts, that the delay in filing the statement of use (or request for extension of time to file a statement of use) on or before the due date was unintentional; and one of the following:

(i) A statement of use under §2.88, signed pursuant to §2.193(e)(1), and the required fees for the number of requests for extensions of time to file a statement of use that the applicant should have filed under §2.89 if the application had never been abandoned;

(ii) A request for an extension of time to file a statement of use under §2.89, signed pursuant to §2.193(e)(1), and the required fees for the number of requests for extensions of time to file a statement of use that the applicant should have filed under §2.89 if the application had never been abandoned;

(iii) A statement that the applicant did not receive the notice of allowance and a request to cancel said notice and issue a new notice. If the applicant asserts that the unintentional delay in responding is based on non-receipt of the notice of allowance, the applicant may not assert non-receipt of the notice of allowance in a subsequent petition; or

(iv) In a multiple-basis application, an amendment, signed pursuant to §2.193(e)(2), deleting the section 1(b) basis and seeking registration based on section 1(a) and/or section 44(e) of the Act.

(3) The applicant must file any further requests for extensions of time to file a statement of use under §2.89 that become due while the petition is pending, or file a statement of use under §2.88.

(d) Statement of Use or Petition To Substitute a Basis May Not Be Filed More Than 36 Months After Issuance of the Notice of Allowance. In an application under section 1(b) of the Act, the Director will not grant a petition under this section if doing so would permit an applicant to file a statement of use, or a petition under §2.35(b) to substitute a basis, more than 36 months after the issue date of the notice of allowance under section 13(b)(2) of the Act.

(e) Request for Reconsideration. If the Director denies a petition to revive under this section, the applicant may request reconsideration, if:

(1) The applicant files the request by not later than:

(i) Two months after the issue date of the decision denying the petition; or

(ii) Two months after the date of actual knowledge of the decision denying the petition and not later than six months after the issue date of the decision where the applicant declares under §2.20 or 28 U.S.C. 1746 that it did not receive the decision; and

(2) The applicant pays a second petition fee under §2.6.

History of 37 C.F.R. §2.66: 31 FR 5261, Apr. 1, 1966; 54 FR 37592, Sept. 11, 1989; 64 FR 48921, Sept. 8, 1999; 68 FR 55764, Sept. 26, 2003; 73 FR 67769, Jan. 16, 2009; 82 FR 29408, July 8, 2017.

§2.67. SUSPENSION OF ACTION BY THE PATENT & TRADEMARK OFFICE

Action by the Patent and Trademark Office may be suspended for a reasonable time for good and sufficient cause. The fact that a proceeding is pending before the Patent and Trademark Office or a court which is relevant to the issue of registrability of the applicant's mark, or the fact that the basis for registration is, under the provisions of section 44(e) of the Act, registration of the mark in a foreign country and the foreign application is still pending, will be considered prima facie good and sufficient cause. An applicant's request for a suspension of action under this section filed within the 6-month response period (see §2.62) may be considered responsive to the previous Office action. The first suspension is within the discretion of the Examiner of Trademarks and any subsequent suspension must be approved by the Director.

History of 37 C.F.R. §2.67: 37 FR 3898, Feb. 24, 1972.

§2.68. EXPRESS ABANDONMENT (WITHDRAWAL) OF APPLICATION

(a) Written document required. An applicant may expressly abandon an application by filing a written request for abandonment or withdrawal of the application, signed by the applicant, someone with legal authority to bind the applicant (e.g., a corporate officer or general partner of a partnership), or a practitioner qualified to practice under §11.14 of this chapter, in accordance with the requirements of §2.193(e)(2). A request for abandonment or withdrawal may not subsequently be withdrawn.

(b) Rights in the mark not affected. Except as provided in §2.135, the fact that an application has been expressly abandoned shall not affect any rights that the applicant may have in the mark set forth in the abandoned application in any proceeding before the Office.

History of 37 C.F.R. §2.68: 38 FR 7985, Mar. 27, 1973; 54 FR 34897, Aug. 22, 1989; 74 FR 54908, Dec. 28, 2009; 80 FR 2311, Jan. 16, 2015.

§2.69. COMPLIANCE WITH OTHER LAWS

When the sale or transportation of any product for which registration of a trademark is sought is regulated under an Act of Congress, the Patent and Trademark Office may make appropriate inquiry as to compliance with such Act for the sole purpose of determining lawfulness of the commerce recited in the application.

History of 37 C.F.R. §2.69: 54 FR 37592, Sept. 11, 1989.

AMENDMENT OF APPLICATION

§2.71. AMENDMENTS TO CORRECT INFORMALITIES

The applicant may amend the application during the course of examination, when required by the Office or for other reasons.

(a) The applicant may amend the application to clarify or limit, but not to broaden, the identification of goods and/or services or the description of the nature of the collective membership organization.

(b)(1) If the verified statement in an application under §2.33 is unsigned or signed by the wrong party, the applicant may submit a substitute verification.

(2) If the verified statement in a statement of use under §2.88, or a request for extension of time to file a statement of use under §2.89, is unsigned or signed by the wrong party, the applicant must submit a substitute verification before the expiration of the statutory deadline for filing the statement of use.

(c) The applicant may amend the dates of use, provided that the amendment is verified, except that the following amendments are not permitted:

(1) In an application under section 1(a) of the Act, the applicant may not amend the application to specify a date of use that is subsequent to the filing date of the application;

(2) In an application under section 1(b) of the Act, after filing a statement of use under §2.88, the applicant may not amend the statement of use to specify a date of use that is subsequent to the expiration of the deadline for filing the statement of use.

(d) The applicant may amend the application to correct the name of the applicant, if there is a mistake in the manner in which the name of the applicant is set out in the application. The amendment must be verified. However, the application cannot be amended to set forth a different entity as the applicant. An application filed in the name of an entity that did not own the mark as of the filing date of the application is void.

(e) An amendment that would materially alter the certification statement specified in §2.45(a)(4)(i)(A) or (a)(4)(ii)(A) will not be permitted.

History of 37 C.F.R. §2.71: 54 FR 37592, Sept. 11, 1989; 64 FR 48922, Sept. 8, 1999; 80 FR 33184, July 11, 2015.

§2.72. AMENDMENTS TO DESCRIPTION OR DRAWING OF THE MARK

(a) In an application based on use in commerce under section 1(a) of the Act, the applicant may amend the description or drawing of the mark only if:

(1) The specimens originally filed, or substitute specimens filed under §2.59(a), support the proposed amendment; and

(2) The proposed amendment does not materially alter the mark. The Office will determine whether a proposed amendment materially alters a mark by comparing the proposed amendment with the description or drawing of the mark filed with the original application.

(b) In an application based on a bona fide intention to use a mark in commerce under section 1(b) of the Act, the applicant may amend the description or drawing of the mark only if:

(1) The specimens filed with an amendment to allege use or statement of use, or substitute specimens filed under §2.59(b), support the proposed amendment; and

(2) The proposed amendment does not materially alter the mark. The Office will determine whether a proposed amendment materially alters a mark by comparing the proposed amendment with the description or drawing of the mark filed with the original application.

(c) In an application based on a claim of priority under section 44(d) of the Act, or on a mark duly registered in the country of origin of the foreign applicant under section 44(e) of the Act, the applicant may amend the description or drawing of the mark only if:

(1) The description or drawing of the mark in the foreign registration certificate supports the amendment; and

(2) The proposed amendment does not materially alter the mark. The Office will determine whether a proposed amendment materially alters a mark by comparing the proposed amendment with the description or drawing of the mark filed with the original application.

History of 37 C.F.R. §2.72: 30 FR 13193, Oct. 16, 1965; 48 FR 23134, May 23, 1983; 54 FR 37593, Sept. 11, 1989; 64 FR 48922, Sept. 8, 1999.

§2.73. AMENDMENT TO RECITE CONCURRENT USE

An application that includes section 1(a) of the Trademark Act as a filing basis, or for which an acceptable allegation of use under §2.76 or §2.88 has been filed, may be amended to an application for concurrent use registration, provided that the application as amended meets the requirements of §2.42. The trademark examining attorney will determine whether the application, as amended, is acceptable.

History of 37 C.F.R. §2.73: 54 FR 37593, Sept. 11, 1989; 68 FR 55764, Sept. 26, 2003; 73 FR 67770, Jan. 16, 2009.

§2.74. FORM & SIGNATURE OF AMENDMENT

(a) Form of Amendment. Amendments should be set forth clearly and completely. Applicant should either set forth the entire wording, including the proposed changes, or, if it would be more efficient, indicate which words should be added and which words should be deleted. The examining attorney may require the applicant to rewrite the entire amendment, if necessary for clarification of the record.

(b) Signature. A request for amendment of an application must be signed by the applicant, someone with legal authority to bind the applicant (e.g., a corporate officer or general partner of a partnership), or a practitioner qualified to practice under §11.14 of this chapter, in accordance with the requirements of §2.193(e)(2). If the amendment requires verification, see §2.2(n).

History of 37 C.F.R. §2.74: 73 FR 67770, Jan. 16, 2009; 74 FR 54908, Dec. 28, 2009; 80 FR 33184, July 11, 2015.

§2.75. AMENDMENT TO CHANGE APPLICATION TO DIFFERENT REGISTER

(a) An application for registration on the Principal Register under section 1(a) or 44 of the Act may be changed to an application for registration on the Supplemental Register and vice versa by amending the application to comply with the rules relating to the appropriate register, as the case may be.

(b) An application under section 1(b) of the Act may be amended to change the application to a different register only after submission of an acceptable amendment to allege use under §2.76 or statement of use under §2.88. When such an application is changed from the Principal Register to the Supplemental Register, the effective filing date of the application is the date of the filing of the allegation of use under section 1(c) or 1(d) of the Act.

(c) In an application under section 66(a) of the Act, the applicant may not amend the application to the Supplemental Register.

History of 37 C.F.R. §2.75: 41 FR 758, Jan. 5, 1976; 54 FR 37593, Sept. 11, 1989; 68 FR 55765, Sept. 26, 2003.

§2.76. AMENDMENT TO ALLEGE USE

(a) When to file an amendment to allege use.

(1) An application under section 1(b) of the Act may be amended to allege use of the mark in commerce under section 1(c) of the Act at any time between the filing of the application and the date the examiner approves the mark for publication. Thereafter, an allegation of use may be submitted only as a statement of use under §2.88 after the issuance of a notice of allowance under section 13(b)(2) of the Act. An amendment to allege use filed outside the time period specified in this paragraph will not be reviewed.

(2)(i) For a trademark, service mark, collective trademark, collective service mark, and certification mark, an amendment to allege use may be filed only when the mark has been in use in commerce on or in connection with all the goods or services specified in the application for which the applicant will seek registration. For a collective membership mark, an amendment to allege use may be filed only when the mark has been in use in commerce to indicate membership in the collective organization specified in the application for which the applicant will seek registration.

(ii) An amendment to allege use may be accompanied by a request in accordance with §2.87 to divide out from the application the goods, services, or classes not yet in use in commerce.

(b) A complete amendment to allege use. A complete amendment to allege use must include the following:

(1) A verified statement alleging:

(i) The applicant believes the applicant is the owner of the mark;

(ii) The mark is in use in commerce;

(iii) The date of first use of the mark anywhere on or in connection with the goods or services, and/or to indicate membership in the collective organization specified in the application, and the date of first use of the mark in commerce. If the amendment to allege use specifies more than one item of goods or services in a class, the dates of use are required for only one item of goods or services specified in that class;

(iv) The goods, services, and/or nature of the collective membership organization specified in the application; and

(v) For a collective mark and certification mark, the applicant is exercising legitimate control over the use in commerce of the mark.

(2) One specimen showing how the applicant, member, or authorized user uses the mark in commerce. See §2.56 for the requirements for specimens;

(3) The fee per class required by §2.6;

(4) For a collective mark, the requirements of §2.44(a)(4)(i)(A);

(5) For a certification mark, the requirements of §2.45(a)(4)(i)(A)-(C); and

(6) The title "Amendment to Allege Use" should appear at the top of the first page of the document, if not filed through TEAS.

(c) Minimum filing requirements for a timely filed amendment to allege use. The Office will review a timely filed amendment to allege use to determine whether it meets the following minimum requirements:

(1) The fee required by §2.6 for at least one class;

(2) One specimen of the mark as used in commerce; and

(3) The verified statement in paragraph (b)(1)(ii) of this section.

(d) Deficiency notification. If the amendment to allege use is filed within the permitted time period but does not meet the minimum requirements specified in paragraph (c) of this section, the Office will notify the applicant of the deficiency. The deficiency may be corrected provided the mark has not been approved for publication. If an acceptable amendment to correct the deficiency is not filed prior to approval of the mark for publication, the amendment will not be examined, and the applicant must instead file a statement of use after the notice of allowance issues.

(e) Notification of refusals and requirements. A timely filed amendment to allege use that meets the minimum requirements specified in paragraph (c) of this section will be examined in accordance with §§2.61 through 2.69. If, as a result of the examination of the amendment to allege use, the applicant is found not entitled to registration for any reason not previously stated, the applicant will be notified and advised of the reasons and of any formal requirements or refusals. The notification shall restate or incorporate by reference all unresolved refusals or requirements previously stated. The amendment to allege use may be amended in accordance with §§2.59 and 2.71 through 2.75.

(f) Withdrawal. An amendment to allege use may be withdrawn for any reason prior to approval of a mark for publication.

(g) Verification not filed within reasonable time. If the verified statements in paragraphs (b)(1)(ii) and, if applicable, (b)(1)(v) of this section are not filed within a reasonable time after they are signed, the Office may require the applicant to submit substitute verified statements attesting that the mark is in use in commerce, and, if applicable, the applicant is exercising legitimate control over the use of the mark in commerce.

(h) An amendment to allege use is not a response but may include amendments. The filing of an amendment to allege use does not constitute a response to any outstanding action by the examiner. See §2.62. The amendment to allege use may include amendments in accordance with §§2.59 and 2.71 through 2.75.

(i) If the application is amended to concurrent use under §2.73, the amendment to allege use must include a verified statement modified in accordance with §2.33(f), §2.44(d), or §2.45(d).

(j) Multiple-class application. For the requirements of a multiple-class application, see §2.86.

History of 37 C.F.R. §2.76: 54 FR 37593, Sept. 11, 1989; 63 FR 48097, Sept. 9, 1998; 64 FR 48922, Sept. 8, 1999; 64 FR 51245, Sept. 22, 1999; 73 FR 67770, Jan. 16, 2009; 74 FR 54908, Dec. 28, 2009; 77 FR 30207, June 21, 2012; 80 FR 33184, July 11, 2015.

§2.77. AMENDMENTS BETWEEN NOTICE OF ALLOWANCE & STATEMENT OF USE

(a) The only amendments that may be entered in an application between the issuance of the notice of allowance and the submission of a statement of use are:

(1) The deletion of specified goods or services, or the entire description of the nature of the collective membership organization, from the identification;

(2) The deletion of a basis in a multiple-basis application; and

(3) A change of attorney or change of address.

(b) Other amendments may be entered during this period only with the express permission of the Director, after consideration on petition under §2.146. If the Director determines that the amendment requires review by the examining attorney, the petition will be denied and the amendment may be resubmitted with the statement of use in order for the applicant to preserve its right to review.

History of 37 C.F.R. §2.77: 54 FR 37594, Sept. 11, 1989; 73 FR 67770, Jan. 16, 2009; 80 FR 2311, Jan. 16, 2015; 80 FR 33185, July 11, 2015.

PUBLICATION & POST PUBLICATION

§2.80. PUBLICATION FOR OPPOSITION

If, on examination or reexamination of an application for registration on the Principal Register, it appears that the applicant is entitled to have his mark registered, the mark will be published in the Official Gazette for opposition. The mark will also be published in the case of an application to be placed in interference or concurrent use proceedings, if otherwise registrable.

History of 37 C.F.R. §2.80: 41 FR 758, Jan. 5, 1976.

§2.81. POST PUBLICATION

(a) Except in an application under section 1(b) of the Act for which no amendment to allege use under §2.76 has been submitted and accepted, if no opposition is filed within the time permitted or all oppositions filed are dismissed, and if no interference is declared and no concurrent use proceeding is instituted, the application will be prepared for issuance of the certificate of registration as provided in §2.151.

(b) In an application under section 1(b) of the Act for which no amendment to allege use under §2.76 has been submitted and accepted, if no opposition is filed within the time permitted or all oppositions filed are dismissed, and if no interference is declared, a notice of allowance will issue. Thereafter, the applicant must submit a statement of use as provided in §2.88.

History of 37 C.F.R. §2.81: 31 FR 5555, Apr. 8, 1966. Redesignated at 37 FR 2880, Feb. 9, 1972. Amended at 48 FR 23135, May 23, 1983; 54 FR 37594, Sept. 11, 1989; 73 FR 67770, Jan. 16, 2009; 80 FR 2311, Jan. 16, 2015.

§2.82. MARKS ON SUPPLEMENTAL REGISTER PUBLISHED ONLY UPON REGISTRATION

In the case of an application for registration on the Supplemental Register the mark will not be published for opposition but if it appears, after examination or reexamination, that the applicant is entitled to have the mark registered, a certificate of registration will issue as provided in §2.151. The mark will be published in the "Official Gazette" when registered.

History of 37 C.F.R. §2.82: 30 FR 13193, Oct. 16, 1965. Redesignated at 37 FR 2880, Feb. 9, 1972. Amended at 54 FR 37594, Sept. 11, 1989.

§2.83. CONFLICTING MARKS

(a) Whenever an application is made for registration of a mark which so resembles another mark or marks pending registration as to be likely to cause confusion or mistake or to deceive, the mark with the earliest effective filing date will be published in the "Official Gazette" for opposition if eligible for the Principal Register, or issued a certificate of registration if eligible for the Supplemental Register.

(b) In situations in which conflicting applications have the same effective filing date, the application with the earliest date of execution will be published in the "Official Gazette" for opposition or issued on the Supplemental Register.

(c) Action on the conflicting application which is not published in the Official Gazette for opposition or not issued on the Supplemental Register will be suspended by the Examiner of Trademarks until the published or issued application is registered or abandoned.

History of 37 C.F.R. §2.83: 37 FR 2880, Feb. 9, 1972; 54 FR 37594, Sept. 11, 1989.

§2.84. JURISDICTION OVER PUBLISHED APPLICATIONS

(a) The trademark examining attorney may exercise jurisdiction over an application up to the date the mark is published in the Official Gazette. After publication of an application under section 1(a), 44 or 66(a) of the Act, the trademark examining attorney may, with the permission of the Director, exercise jurisdiction over the application. After publication of an application under section 1(b) of the Act, the trademark examining attorney may exercise jurisdiction over the application after the issuance of the notice of allowance under section 13(b)(2) of the Act. After publication, and prior to issuance of a notice of allowance in an application under section 1(b), the trademark examining attorney may, with the permission of the Director, exercise jurisdiction over the application.

(b) After publication, but before the certificate of registration is issued in an application under section 1(a), 44, or 66(a) of the Act, or before the notice of allowance is issued in an application under section 1(b) of the Act, an application that is not the subject of an inter partes proceeding before the Trademark Trial and Appeal Board may be amended if the amendment meets the requirements of §§2.71, 2.72, and 2.74. Otherwise, an amendment to such an application may be submitted only upon petition to the Director to restore jurisdiction over the application to the examining attorney for consideration of the amendment and further examination. The amendment of an application that is the subject of an inter partes proceeding before the Trademark Trial and Appeal Board is governed by §2.133.

History of 37 C.F.R. §2.84: 54 FR 37594, Sept. 11, 1989; 68 FR 55765, Sept. 26, 2003; 73 FR 67770, Jan. 16, 2009; 80 FR 2311, Jan. 16, 2015.

CLASSIFICATION

§2.85. CLASSIFICATION SCHEDULES

(a) International classification system. Section 6.1 of this chapter sets forth the international system of classification for goods and services, which applies for all statutory purposes to:

(1) Applications filed in the Office on or after September 1, 1973, and resulting registrations; and

(2) Registrations resulting from applications filed on or before August 31, 1973, that have been amended to adopt international classification pursuant to §2.85(e)(3).

(b) Prior United States classification system. Section 6.2 of this chapter sets forth the prior United States system of classification for goods and services, which applies for all statutory purposes to registrations resulting from applications filed on or before August 31, 1973, unless:

(1) The registration has been amended to adopt international classification pursuant to §2.85(e)(3); or

(2) The registration was issued under a classification system prior to that set forth in §6.2.

(c) Certification marks and collective membership marks. Sections 6.3 and 6.4 specify the system of classification which applies to certification marks and collective membership marks in applications based on sections 1 and 44 of the Act, and to registrations resulting from applications based on sections 1 and 44. These sections do not apply to applications under section 66(a) or to registered extensions of protection.

(d) Section 66(a) applications and registered extensions of protection. In an application under section 66(a) of the Act or registered extension of protection, the classification cannot be changed from the classification assigned by the International Bureau of the World Intellectual Property Organization, unless the International Bureau corrects the classification. Classes cannot be added, and goods or services cannot be transferred from one class to another in a multiple-class application.

(e) Changes to Nice Agreement. The international classification system changes periodically, pursuant to the Nice Agreement Concerning the International Classification of Goods and Services for the Purposes of the Registration of Marks. These changes are listed in the International Classification of Goods and Services for the Purposes of the Registration of Marks, which is published by the World Intellectual Property Organization.

(1) If international classification changes pursuant to the Nice Agreement, the new classification applies only to applications filed on or after the effective date of the change.

(2) In a section 1 or section 44 application filed before the effective date of a change to the Nice Agreement, the applicant may amend the application to comply with the requirements of the current edition. The applicant must comply with the current edition for all goods or services identified in the application. The applicant must pay the fees for any added class(es).

(3) In a registration resulting from a section 1 or section 44 application that was filed before the effective date of a change to the Nice Agreement, the owner may amend the registration to comply with the requirements of the current edition. The owner must reclassify all goods or services identified in the registration to the current edition. The owner must pay the fee required by §2.6 for amendments under section 7 of the Act. The owner may reclassify registrations from multiple United States classes (§2.85(b)) into a single international classification, where appropriate.

(f) Classification schedules shall not limit or extend the applicant's rights, except that in a section 66(a) application, the scope of the identification of goods or services for purposes of permissible amendments (see §2.71(a)) is limited by the class, pursuant to §2.85(d).

History of 37 C.F.R. §2.85: 38 FR 14681, June 4, 1973; 39 FR 16885, May 10, 1974; 41 FR 758, Jan. 5, 1976; 47 FR 41282, Sept. 17, 1982; 63 FR 48097, Sept. 9, 1998; 73 FR 67770, Jan. 16, 2009.

§2.86. MULTIPLE-CLASS APPLICATIONS

(a) In a single application for a trademark, service mark, and/or collective mark, an applicant may apply to register the same mark for goods, services, and/or a collective membership organization in multiple classes. In a multiple-class application, the applicant must satisfy the following, in addition to the application requirements of §2.32 for a trademark or service mark, and §2.44 for collective marks:

(1) For an application filed under section 1 or 44 of the Act, identify the goods or services in each international class and/or the nature of the collective membership organization in U.S. Class 200; for applications filed under section 66(a) of the Act, identify the goods, services, and/or the nature of the collective membership organization in each international class assigned by the International Bureau in the corresponding international registration;

(2) Submit the application filing fee required by §2.6 for each class; and

(3) Include either dates of use and one specimen for each class based on section 1(a) of the Act; or a statement that the applicant has a bona fide intention to use the mark in commerce, for a trademark or service mark, or a statement that the applicant has a bona fide intention, and is entitled, to exercise legitimate control over the use of the mark in commerce, for collective marks, for each class based on section 1(b), 44, or 66(a) of the Act. When requested by the Office, additional specimens must be provided.

(b) In a single application for a certification mark, an applicant may apply to register the same certification mark for goods and services. In such case, the applicant must satisfy the following, in addition to the application requirements of §2.45:

(1) For an application filed under section 1 or 44 of the Act, identify the goods in U.S. Class A and the services in U.S. Class B; for applications filed under section 66(a) of the Act, identify the goods and services in each international class assigned by the International Bureau in the corresponding international registration;

(2) Submit the application filing fee required by §2.6 for both classes; and

(3) Include either dates of use and one specimen for each class based on section 1(a) of the Act; or a statement that the applicant has a bona fide intention, and is entitled, to exercise legitimate control over the use of the mark in commerce for each class based on section 1(b), 44, or 66(a) of the Act. When requested by the Office, additional specimens must be provided.

(c) In a single application, both section 1(a) and 1(b) of the Act may not be claimed for identical goods or services.

(d) In a single application based on section 1 or 44 of the Act, goods or services in U.S. Classes A and/or B may not be combined with either goods or services in any international class or with a collective membership organization in U.S. Class 200; and in a single application based on section 66(a) of the Act, a certification mark application may not be combined with goods, services, or a collective membership organization in any international class. See §2.45(f).

(e) An amendment to allege use under §2.76 or a statement of use under §2.88 for multiple classes must include, for each class, the required fee, dates of use, and one specimen. When requested by the Office, additional specimens must be provided. The applicant may not file an amendment to allege use or a statement of use until the applicant has used the mark on or in connection with all the goods, services, or classes, unless the applicant also files a request to divide under §2.87.

(f) The Office will issue a single certificate of registration for the mark, unless the applicant files a request to divide under §2.87.

History of 37 C.F.R. §2.86: 54 FR 37594, Sept. 11, 1989; 64 FR 48923, Sept. 8, 1999; 70 FR 2953, Jan. 19, 2005; 73 FR 67771, Jan. 16, 2009; 77 FR 30207, June 21, 2012; 80 FR 33185, July 11, 2015.

§2.87. DIVIDING AN APPLICATION

(a) Application may be divided. An application may be divided into two or more separate applications upon the payment of a fee for each new application created and submission by the applicant of a request in accordance with paragraph (d) of this section.

(b) Fee. In the case of a request to divide out one or more entire classes from an application, only the fee for dividing an application as set forth in §2.6(a)(19) will be required. However, in the case of a request to divide out some, but not all, of the goods or services in a class, the applicant must submit the application filing fee as set forth in §2.6(a)(1) for each new separate application to be created by the division, in addition to the fee for dividing an application.

(c) Time for filing. **(1)** A request to divide an application may be filed at any time between the application filing date and the date on which the trademark examining attorney approves the mark for publication; or during an opposition, concurrent use, or interference proceeding, upon motion granted by the Trademark Trial and Appeal Board.

(2) In an application under section 1(b) of the Act, a request to divide may also be filed with a statement of use under §2.88 or at any time between the filing of a statement of use and the date on which the trademark examining attorney approves the mark for registration.

(3) In a multiple-basis application, a request to divide out goods or services having a particular basis may also be filed during the period between the issuance of the notice of allowance under section 13(b)(2) of the Act and the filing of a statement of use under §2.88.

(d) Form. A request to divide an application should be made in a separate document from any other amendment or response in the application. The title "Request to Divide Application" should appear at the top of the first page of the document.

(e) Outstanding time periods apply to newly created applications. Any time period for action by the applicant which is outstanding in the original application at the time of the division will apply to each separate new application created by the division, except as follows:

(1) If an Office action pertaining to less than all the classes in a multiple-class application is outstanding, and the applicant files a request to divide out the goods, services, and/or class(es) to which the Office action does not pertain before the response deadline, a response to the Office action is not due in the new (child) application(s) created by the division of the application;

(2) If an Office action pertaining to less than all the bases in a multiple-basis application is outstanding, and the applicant files a request to divide out the goods/services having the basis or bases to which the Office action does not pertain before the response deadline, a response to the Office action is not due in the new (child) application(s) created by the division of the application; or

(3) In a multiple-basis application in which a notice of allowance has issued, if the applicant files a request to divide out the goods/services having the basis or bases to which the notice of allowance does not pertain before the deadline for filing the statement of use, the new (child) applications created by the division are not affected by the notice of allowance.

(f) Signature. The request to divide must be signed by the applicant, someone with legal authority to bind the applicant (e.g., a corporate officer or general partner of a partnership), or a practitioner who meets the requirements of §11.14, in accordance with the requirements of §2.193(e)(2).

(g) Section 66(a) applications—change of ownership with respect to some but not all of the goods or services. **(1)** When the International Bureau of the World Intellectual Property Organization notifies the Office that an international registration has been divided as the result of a change of ownership with respect to some but not all of the goods or services, the Office will construe the International Bureau's notice as a request to divide. The Office will record the partial change of ownership in the Assignment Services Branch, and divide out the assigned goods/services from the original (parent) application. The Office will create a new (child) application serial number, and enter the information about the new application in its automated records.

(2) To obtain a certificate of registration in the name of the new owner for the goods/services that have been divided out, the new owner must pay the fee(s) for the request to divide, as required by §2.6 and paragraph (b) of this section. The examining attorney will issue an Office action in the child application requiring the new owner to pay the required fee(s). If the owner of the child application fails to respond, the child application will be abandoned. It is not necessary for the new owner to file a separate request to divide.

(3) The Office will not divide a section 66(a) application based upon a change of ownership unless the International Bureau notifies the Office that the international registration has been divided.

History of 37 C.F.R. §2.87: 37 FR 3898, Feb. 24, 1972; 54 FR 37595, Sept. 11, 1989; 57 FR 38196, Aug. 21, 1992; 57 FR 40493, Sept. 3, 1992; 63 FR 48097, Sept. 9, 1998; 70 FR 2953, Jan. 19, 2005; 73 FR 67771, Jan. 16, 2009; 74 FR 54908, Dec. 28, 2009.

POST NOTICE OF ALLOWANCE

§2.88. STATEMENT OF USE AFTER NOTICE OF ALLOWANCE

(a) When to file a statement of use.

(1) In an application under section 1(b) of the Act, a statement of use, required under section 1(d) of the Act, must be filed within six months after issuance of a notice of allowance under section 13(b)(2) of the Act, or within an extension of time granted under §2.89. A statement of use filed prior to issuance of a notice of allowance is premature and will not be reviewed.

(2)(i) For a trademark, service mark, collective trademark, collective service mark, and certification mark, a statement of use may be filed only when the mark has been in use in commerce on or in connection with all the goods or services specified in the notice of allowance for which the applicant will seek registration in that application. For a collective membership mark, a statement of use may be filed only when the mark has been in use in commerce to indicate membership in the collective membership organization specified in the notice of allowance for which the applicant will seek registration in that application.

(ii) A statement of use may be accompanied by a request in accordance with §2.87 to divide out from the application the goods, services, or classes not yet in use in commerce.

(b) A complete statement of use. A complete statement of use must include the following:

(1) A verified statement alleging:

(i) The applicant believes the applicant is the owner of the mark;

(ii) The mark is in use in commerce;

(iii) The date of first use of the mark anywhere on or in connection with the goods, services, and/or to indicate membership in the collective organization specified in the application, and the date of first use of the mark in commerce. If the statement of use specifies more than one item of goods or services in a class, the dates of use are required for only one item of goods or services specified in that class;

(iv) The goods, services, and/or nature of the collective membership organization specified in the notice of allowance. The goods or services specified in a statement of use must conform to those goods or services specified in the notice of allowance for trademark, service mark, collective trademark, collective service mark, or certification mark applications. Any goods or services specified in the notice of allowance that are omitted from the identification of goods or services in the statement of use will be presumed to be deleted and the deleted goods or services may not be reinserted in the application. For collective membership mark applications, the description of the nature of the collective membership organization in the statement of use must conform to that specified in the notice of allowance; and

(v) For a collective mark and certification mark, the applicant is exercising legitimate control over the use in commerce of the mark;

(2) One specimen showing how the applicant, member, or authorized user uses the mark in commerce. See §2.56 for the requirements for specimens;

(3) Fee(s). The fee required by §2.6 per class. The applicant must pay a filing fee sufficient to cover at least one class within the statutory time for filing the statement of use, or the application will be abandoned. If the applicant submits a fee insufficient to cover all the classes in a multiple-class application, the applicant should specify the classes to be abandoned. If the applicant timely submits a fee sufficient to pay for at least one class, but insufficient to cover all the classes, and the applicant has not specified the class(es) to be abandoned, the Office will issue a notice granting the applicant additional time to submit the fee(s) for the remaining class(es) or to specify the class(es) to be abandoned. If the applicant does not submit the required fee(s) or specify the class(es) to be abandoned within the set time period, the Office will apply the fees paid, beginning with the lowest numbered class, in ascending order. The Office will delete the class(es) not covered by the fees submitted;

(4) For a collective mark, the requirements of §2.44(a)(4)(i)(A);

(5) For a certification mark, the requirements of §2.45(a)(4)(i)(A) through (C); and

(6) The title "Statement of Use" should appear at the top of the first page of the document, if not filed through TEAS.

(c) Minimum filing requirements for a timely filed statement of use. The Office will review a timely filed statement of use to determine whether it meets the following minimum requirements:

(1) The fee required by §2.6 for at least one class;

(2) One specimen of the mark as used in commerce; and

(3) The verified statement in paragraph (b)(1)(ii) of this section. If this verified statement is unsigned or signed by the wrong party, the applicant must submit a substitute verified statement on or before the statutory deadline for filing the statement of use.

(d) Deficiency notification. If the statement of use is filed within the permitted time period but does not meet the minimum requirements specified in paragraph (c) of this section, the Office will notify the applicant of the deficiency. If the time permitted for the applicant to file a statement of use has not expired, the applicant may correct the deficiency.

(e) Notification of refusals and requirements. A timely filed statement of use that meets the minimum requirements specified in paragraph (c) of this section will be examined in accordance with §§2.61 through 2.69. If, as a result of the examination of the statement of use, the applicant is found not entitled to registration, the applicant will be notified and advised of the reasons and of any formal requirements or refusals. The statement of use may be amended in accordance with §§2.59 and 2.71 through 2.75.

(f) Statement of use may not be withdrawn. The applicant may not withdraw a timely filed statement of use to return to the previous status of awaiting submission of a statement of use, regardless of whether it is in compliance with paragraph (c) of this section.

(g) Verification not filed within reasonable time. If the verified statements in paragraphs (b)(1)(ii) and, if applicable, (b)(1)(v) of this section are not filed within a reasonable time after they are signed, the Office may require the applicant to submit substitute verified statements attesting that the mark is in use in commerce, and, if applicable, the applicant is exercising legitimate control over the use of the mark in commerce.

(h) Amending the application. The statement of use may include amendments in accordance with §§2.51, 2.59, and 2.71 through 2.75.

(i) Concurrent use. If the application is amended to concurrent use under §2.73, the statement of use must include a verified statement modified in accordance with §2.33(f), §2.44(d), or §2.45(d).

(j) Multiple-class application. For the requirements of a multiple-class application, see §2.86.

(k) Abandonment. The failure to timely file a statement of use which meets the minimum requirements specified in paragraph (c) of this section shall result in the abandonment of the application.

History of 37 C.F.R. §2.88: 64 FR 48923, Sept. 8, 1999; 64 FR 51245, Sept. 22, 1999; 68 FR 55765, Sept. 26, 2003; 73 FR 67771, Jan. 16, 2009; 74 FR 54908, Dec. 28, 2009; 77 FR 30207, June 21, 2012; 80 FR 33185, July 11, 2015.

§2.89. EXTENSIONS OF TIME FOR FILING A STATEMENT OF USE

(a) First extension request after issuance of notice of allowance. The applicant may request a six-month extension of time to file the statement of use required by §2.88. The extension request must be filed within six months of the date of issuance of the notice of allowance under section 13(b)(2) of the Act and must include the following:

(1) A written request for an extension of time to file the statement of use;

(2) The fee required by §2.6 per class. The applicant must pay a filing fee sufficient to cover at least one class within the statutory time for filing the extension request, or the request will be denied. If the applicant submits a fee insufficient to cover all the classes in a multiple-class application, the applicant should specify the classes to be abandoned. If the applicant timely submits a fee sufficient to pay for at least one class, but insufficient to cover all the classes, and the applicant has not specified the class(es) to be abandoned, the Office will issue a notice granting the applicant additional time to submit the fee(s) for the remaining classes, or specify the class(es) to be abandoned. If the applicant does not submit the required fee(s) or specify the class(es) to be abandoned within the set time period, the Office will apply the fees paid, beginning with the lowest numbered class, in ascending order. The Office will delete the class(es) not covered by the fees submitted; and

(3) A verified statement that the applicant has a continued bona fide intention to use the mark in commerce, specifying the relevant goods or services, for trademarks or service marks; or that the applicant has a continued bona fide intention, and is entitled, to exercise legitimate control over the use of the mark in commerce, specifying the relevant goods, services, or collective membership organization, for collective marks or certification marks. If this verified statement is unsigned or signed by the wrong party, the applicant must submit a substitute verified statement within six months of the date of issuance of the notice of allowance.

(b) Subsequent extension requests. Before the expiration of the previously granted extension of time, the applicant may request further six-month extensions of time to file the statement of use by submitting the following:

(1) A written request for an extension of time to file the statement of use;

(2) The requirements of paragraph (a)(2) of this section for a fee;

(3) A verified statement that the applicant has a continued bona fide intention to use the mark in commerce, specifying the relevant goods or services, for trademarks or service marks; or that the applicant has a continued bona fide intention, and is entitled, to exercise legitimate control over the use of the mark in commerce, specifying the relevant goods, services, or collective membership organization, for collective marks or certification marks. If this verified statement is unsigned or signed by the wrong party, the applicant must submit a substitute verified statement before the expiration of the previously granted extension; and

(4) A showing of good cause, as specified in paragraph (d) of this section.

(c) Four subsequent extension requests permitted. Extension requests specified in paragraph (b) of this section will be granted only in six-month increments and may not aggregate more than 24 months total.

(d) Good cause. A showing of good cause must include:

(1) For a trademark or service mark, a statement of the applicant's ongoing efforts to make use of the mark in commerce on or in connection with each of the relevant goods or services. Those efforts may include product or service research or development, market research, manufacturing activities, promotional activities, steps to acquire distributors, steps to obtain governmental approval, or other similar activities. In the alternative, the applicant must submit a satisfactory explanation for the failure to make efforts to use the mark in commerce.

(2) For a collective mark, a statement of ongoing efforts to make use of the mark in commerce by members on or in connection with each of the relevant goods or services or in connection with the applicant's collective membership organization. Those efforts may include the development of standards, the steps taken to acquire members such as marketing and promotional activities targeted to potential members, training members regarding the standards, or other similar activities. In the alternative, the applicant must submit a satisfactory explanation for the failure to make efforts for applicant's members to use the mark in commerce.

(3) For a certification mark, a statement of ongoing efforts to make use of the mark in commerce by authorized users on or in connection with each of the relevant goods or services. Those efforts may include the development of certification standards, steps taken to obtain governmental approval or acquire authorized users, marketing and promoting the recognition of the certification program or of the goods or services that meet the certification standards of the applicant, training authorized users regarding the standards, or other similar activities. In the alternative, the applicant must submit a satisfactory explanation for the failure to make efforts for applicant's authorized users to use the mark in commerce.

(e) Extension request filed in conjunction with or after a statement of use.

(1) An applicant may file one request for a six-month extension of time for filing a statement of use when filing a statement of use or after filing a statement of use if time remains in the existing six-month period in which the statement of use was filed, provided that the time requested would not extend beyond 36 months from the date of issuance of the notice of allowance. Thereafter, applicant may not request any further extensions of time.

(2) A request for an extension of time that is filed under paragraph (e)(1) of this section, must comply with all the requirements of paragraph (a) of this section, if it is an applicant's first extension request, or paragraph (b) of this section, if it is a second or subsequent extension request. However, in a request under paragraph (b) of this section, an applicant may satisfy the requirement for a showing of good cause by asserting the applicant believes the applicant has made valid use of the mark in commerce, as evidenced by the submitted statement of use, but that if the statement of use is found by the Office to be fatally defective, the applicant will need additional time in which to file a new statement of use.

(f) Goods or services. For trademark, service mark, collective trademark, collective service mark, or certification mark applications, the goods or services specified in a request for an extension of time for filing a statement of use must conform to those goods or services specified in the notice of allowance. Any goods or services specified in the notice of allowance that are omitted from the identification of goods or services in the request for extension of time will be presumed to be deleted and the deleted goods or services may not thereafter be reinserted in the application. For collective membership mark applications, the description of the nature of the collective membership organization in the request for extension of time must conform to that set forth in the notice of allowance.

(g) Notice of grant or denial. The applicant will be notified of the grant or denial of a request for an extension of time, and of the reasons for a denial. Failure to notify the applicant of the grant or denial of the request prior to the expiration of the existing period or requested extension does not relieve the applicant of the responsibility of timely filing a statement of use under §2.88. If, after denial of an extension request, there is time remaining in the existing six-month period for filing a statement of use, applicant may submit a substitute request for extension of time to correct the defects of the prior request. Otherwise, the only recourse available after denial of a request for an extension of time is to file a petition to the Director in accordance with §2.66 or §2.146. A petition from the denial of an extension request must be filed within two months of the date of issuance of the denial of the request. If the petition is granted, the term of the requested six-month extension that was the subject of the petition will run from the date of expiration of the previously existing six-month period for filing a statement of use.

(h) Verification not filed within reasonable time. If the verified statement in paragraph (a)(3) or (b)(3) of this section is not filed within a reasonable time after it is signed, the Office may require the applicant to submit a substitute verified statement attesting that the applicant has a continued bona fide intention to use the mark in commerce, for trademarks or service marks; or that the applicant has a continued bona fide intention, and is entitled, to exercise legitimate control over the use of the mark in commerce, for collective marks or certification marks.

History of 37 C.F.R. §2.89: 64 FR 48923, Sept. 8, 1999; 64 FR 51245, Sept. 22, 1999; 65 FR 36633, June 9, 2000; 73 FR 67772, Jan. 16, 2009; 74 FR 54908, Dec. 28, 2009; 80 FR 33186, July 11, 2015.

INTERFERENCES & CONCURRENT USE PROCEEDINGS

§2.91. DECLARATION OF INTERFERENCE

(a) An interference will not be declared between two applications or between an application and a registration except upon petition to the Director. Interferences will be declared by the Director only upon a showing of extraordinary circumstances which would result in a party being unduly prejudiced without an interference. In ordinary circumstances, the availability of an opposition or cancellation proceeding to the party will be deemed to remove any undue prejudice.

(b) Registrations and applications to register on the Supplemental Register, registrations under the Act of 1920, and registrations of marks the right to use of which has become incontestable are not subject to interference.

History of 37 C.F.R. §2.91: 37 FR 2881, Feb. 9, 1972; 54 FR 34897, Aug. 22, 1989.

§2.92. PRELIMINARY TO INTERFERENCE

An interference which has been declared by the Director will not be instituted by the Trademark Trial and Appeal Board until the examining attorney has determined that the marks which are to form the subject matter of the controversy are registrable, and all of the marks have been published in the Official Gazette for opposition.

History of 37 C.F.R. §2.92: 37 FR 2881, Feb. 9, 1972; 54 FR 34897, Aug. 22, 1989; 81 FR 69971, Jan. 14, 2017.

§2.93. INSTITUTION OF INTERFERENCE

An interference is instituted by the issuance of a notice of interference to the parties. The notice shall be sent to each applicant, in care of the applicant's attorney or other representative of record, if any, and if one of the parties is a registrant, the notice shall be sent to the registrant or the registrant's assignee of record. The notice shall give the name and address of every adverse party and of the adverse party's attorney or other authorized representative, if any, together with the serial number and date of filing and publication of each of the applications, or the registration number and date of issuance of each of the registrations, involved.

History of 37 C.F.R. §2.93: 41 FR 759, Jan. 5, 1976; 54 FR 34897, Aug. 22, 1989; 73 FR 67772, Jan. 16, 2009.

§§2.94, 2.95. RESERVED

§2.96. ISSUE; BURDEN OF PROOF

The issue in an interference between applications is normally priority of use, but the rights of the parties to registration may also be determined. The party whose application involved in the interference has the latest filing date is the junior party and has the burden of proof. When there are more than two parties to an interference, a party shall be a junior party to and shall have the burden of proof as against every other party whose application involved in the interference has an earlier filing date. If the involved applications of any parties have the same filing date, the application with the latest date of execution will be deemed to have the latest filing date and that applicant will be the junior party. The issue in an interference between an application and a registration shall be the same, but in the event the final decision is adverse to the registrant, a registration to the applicant will not be authorized so long as the interfering registration remains on the register.

History of 37 C.F.R. §2.96: 30 FR 13193, Oct. 16, 1965; 48 FR 23135, May 23, 1983; 48 FR 27225, June 14, 1983.

§2.97. RESERVED

§2.98. ADDING PARTY TO INTERFERENCE

A party may be added to an interference only upon petition to the Director by that party. If an application which is or might be the subject of a petition for addition to an interference is not added, the examining attorney may suspend action on the application pending termination of the interference proceeding.

History of 37 C.F.R. §2.98: 37 FR 2881, Feb. 9, 1972; 48 FR 23135, May 23, 1983; 81 FR 69971, Jan. 14, 2017.

§2.99. APPLICATION TO REGISTER AS CONCURRENT USER

(a) An application for registration as a lawful concurrent user will be examined in the same manner as other applications for registration.

(b) If it appears that the applicant is entitled to have the mark registered, subject to a concurrent use proceeding, the mark will be published in the Official Gazette as provided by §2.80.

(c) If no opposition is filed, or if all oppositions that are filed are dismissed or withdrawn, the Trademark Trial and Appeal Board will send a notice of institution to the applicant for concurrent use registration (plaintiff) and to each applicant, registrant or user specified as a concurrent user in the application (defendants). The notice for each defendant shall state the name and address of the plaintiff and of the plaintiff's attorney or other authorized representative, if any, together with the serial number and filing date of the application. If a party has provided the Office with an email address, the notice may be transmitted via email.

(d)(1) The Board's notice of institution will include a web link or web address to access the concurrent use application proceeding contained in Office records.

(2) An answer to the notice is not required in the case of an applicant or registrant whose application or registration is acknowledged by the concurrent use applicant in the concurrent use application, but a statement, if desired, may be filed within forty days after the issuance of the notice; in the case of any other party specified as a concurrent user in the application, an answer must be filed within forty days after the issuance of the notice.

(3) If an answer, when required, is not filed, judgment will be entered precluding the defaulting user from claiming any right more extensive than that acknowledged in the application(s) for concurrent use registration, but the burden of proving entitlement to registration(s) will remain with the concurrent use applicant(s).

(e) The applicant for a concurrent use registration has the burden of proving entitlement thereto. If there are two or more applications for concurrent use registration involved in a proceeding, the party whose application has the latest filing date is the junior party. A party whose application has a filing date between the filing dates of the earliest involved application and the latest involved application is a junior party to every party whose involved application has an earlier filing date. If any applications have the same filing date, the application with the latest date of execution will be deemed to have the latest filing date and that applicant will be the junior party. A person specified as an excepted user in a concurrent use application but who has not filed an application shall be considered a party senior to every party that has an application involved in the proceeding.

(f) When a concurrent use registration is sought on the basis that a court of competent jurisdiction has finally determined that the parties are entitled to use the same or similar marks in commerce, a concurrent use registration proceeding will not be instituted if all of the following conditions are fulfilled:

(1) The applicant is entitled to registration subject only to the concurrent lawful use of a party to the court proceeding; and

(2) The court decree specifies the rights of the parties; and

(3) A true copy of the court decree is submitted to the examining attorney; and

(4) The concurrent use application complies fully and exactly with the court decree; and

(5) The excepted use specified in the concurrent use application does not involve a registration, or any involved registration has been restricted by the Director in accordance with the court decree.

If any of the conditions specified in this paragraph is not satisfied, a concurrent use registration proceeding shall be prepared and instituted as provided in paragraphs (a) through (e) of this section.

(g) Registrations and applications to register on the Supplemental Register and registrations under the Act of 1920 are not subject to concurrent use registration proceedings. Applications under section 1(b) of the Act of 1946 are subject to concurrent use registration proceedings only after the applicant files an acceptable allegation of use under §2.76 or §2.88. Applications based solely on section 44 or section 66(a) of the Act are not subject to concurrent use registration proceedings.

(h) The Trademark Trial and Appeal Board will consider and determine concurrent use rights only in the context of a concurrent use registration proceeding.

History of 37 C.F.R. §2.99: 30 FR 13193, Oct. 16, 1965; 37 FR 7606, Apr. 18, 1972; 41 FR 759, Jan. 5, 1976; 48 FR 23135, May 23, 1983; 48 FR 27225, June 14, 1983; 54 FR 37596, Sept. 11, 1989; 72 FR 42258, Nov. 1, 2007; 73 FR 67772, Jan. 16, 2009; 81 FR 69971, Jan. 14, 2017.

OPPOSITION

§2.101. FILING AN OPPOSITION

(a) An opposition proceeding is commenced by filing in the Office a timely notice of opposition with the required fee.

(b) Any person who believes that he, she or it would be damaged by the registration of a mark on the Principal Register may file an opposition addressed to the Trademark Trial and Appeal Board. The opposition need not be verified, but must be signed by the opposer or the opposer's attorney, as specified in §11.1 of this chapter, or other authorized representative, as specified in §11.14(b) of this chapter. Electronic signatures pursuant to §2.193(c) are required for oppositions filed through ESTTA under paragraph (b)(1) or (2) of this section.

(1) An opposition to an application must be filed by the due date set forth in paragraph (c) of this section through ESTTA.

(2) In the event that ESTTA is unavailable due to technical problems, or when extraordinary circumstances are present, an opposition against an application based on Section 1 or 44 of the Act may be filed in paper form. A paper opposition to an application based on Section 1 or 44 of the Act must be filed by the due date set forth in paragraph (c) of this section and be accompanied by a Petition to the Director under §2.146, with the fees therefor and the showing required under this paragraph. Timeliness of the paper submission will be determined in accordance with §§2.195 through 2.198.

(3) An opposition to an application based on Section 66(a) of the Act must be filed through ESTTA and may not under any circumstances be filed in paper form.

(c) The opposition must be filed within thirty days after publication (§2.80) of the application being opposed or within an extension of time (§2.102) for filing an opposition. The opposition must be accompanied by the required fee for each party joined as opposer for each class in the application for which registration is opposed (see §2.6).

(d) An otherwise timely opposition cannot be filed via ESTTA unless the opposition is accompanied by a fee that is sufficient to pay in full for each named party opposer to oppose the registration of a mark in each class specified in the opposition. A paper opposition that is not accompanied by the required fee sufficient to pay in full for each named party opposer for each class in the application for which registration is opposed may not be instituted. If time remains in the opposition period as originally set or as extended by the Board, the potential opposer may resubmit the opposition with the required fee.

(e) The filing date of an opposition is the date of electronic receipt in the Office of the notice of opposition, and required fee. In the rare instances that filing by paper is permitted under these rules, the filing date will be determined in accordance with §§2.195 through 2.198.

History of 37 C.F.R. §2.101: 41 FR 759, Jan. 5, 1976; 43 FR 35483, Aug. 10, 1978; 48 FR 3976, Jan. 28, 1983; 51 FR 28709, Aug. 11, 1986; 54 FR 37596, Sept. 11, 1989; 63 FR 48097, Sept. 9, 1998; 64 FR 48924, Sept. 8, 1999; 68 FR 55765, Sept. 26, 2003; 72 FR 42258, Nov. 1, 2007; 73 FR 47685, Sept. 15, 2008; 74 FR 54909, Dec. 28, 2009; 81 FR 69971, Jan. 14, 2017.

§2.102. EXTENSION OF TIME FOR FILING AN OPPOSITION

(a) Any person who believes that he, she or it would be damaged by the registration of a mark on the Principal Register may file a request with the Trademark Trial and Appeal Board to extend the time for filing an opposition. The request need not be verified, but must be signed by the potential opposer or by the potential opposer's attorney, as specified in §11.1 of this chapter, or authorized representative, as specified in §11.14(b) of this chapter. Electronic signatures pursuant to §2.193(c) are required for electronically filed extension requests.

(1) A request to extend the time for filing an opposition to an application must be filed through ESTTA by the opposition due date set forth in §2.101(c). In the event that ESTTA is unavailable due to technical problems, or when extraordinary circumstances are present, a request to extend the opposition period for an application based on Section 1 or 44 of the Act may be filed in paper form by the opposition due date set forth in §2.101(c). A request to extend the opposition period for an application based on Section 66(a) of the Act must be filed through ESTTA and may not under any circumstances be filed in paper form.

(2) A paper request to extend the opposition period for an application based on Section 1 or 44 of the Act must be filed by the due date set forth in §2.101(c) and be accompanied by a Petition to the Director under §2.146, with the fees therefor and the showing required under paragraph (a)(1) of this section. Timeliness of the paper submission will be determined in accordance with §§2.195 through 2.198.

(b) A request to extend the time for filing an opposition must identify the potential opposer with reasonable certainty. Any opposition filed during an extension of time must be in the name of the person to whom the extension was granted, except that an opposition may be accepted if the person in whose name the extension was requested was misidentified through mistake or if the opposition is filed in the name of a person in privity with the person who requested and was granted the extension of time.

(c) The time for filing an opposition shall not be extended beyond 180 days from the date of publication. Any request to extend the time for filing an opposition must be filed before thirty days have expired from the date of publication or before the expiration of a previously granted extension of time, as appropriate. Requests to extend the time for filing an opposition must be filed as follows:

(1) A person may file a first request for:

(i) Either a thirty-day extension of time, which will be granted upon request; or

(ii) A ninety-day extension of time, which will be granted only for good cause shown. A sixty-day extension is not available as a first extension of time to oppose.

(2) If a person was granted an initial thirty-day extension of time, that person may file a request for an additional sixty-day extension of time, which will be granted only for good cause shown.

(3) After receiving one or two extensions of time totaling ninety days, a person may file one final request for an extension of time for an additional sixty days. No other time period will be allowed for a final extension of the opposition period. The Board will grant this request only upon written consent or stipulation signed by the applicant or its authorized representative, or a written request by the potential opposer or its authorized representative stating that the applicant or its authorized representative has consented to the request, or a showing of extraordinary circumstances. No further extensions of time to file an opposition will be granted under any circumstances.

(d) The filing date of a request to extend the time for filing an opposition is the date of electronic receipt in the Office of the request. In the rare instance that filing by paper is permitted under these rules, the filing date will be determined in accordance with §§2.195 through 2.198.

(e) [Reserved]

History of 37 C.F.R. §2.102: 41 FR 759, Jan. 5, 1976; 48 FR 3976, Jan. 28, 1983; 61 FR 36825, July 15, 1996; 63 FR 48097, Sept. 9, 1998; 68 FR 55765, Sept. 26, 2003; 73 FR 47685, Sept. 15, 2008; 74 FR 54909, Dec. 28, 2009; 81 FR 69972, Jan. 14, 2017.

§2.103. [ADDED & RESERVED]

§2.104. CONTENTS OF OPPOSITION

(a) The opposition must set forth a short and plain statement showing why the opposer believes he, she or it would be damaged by the registration of the opposed mark and state the grounds for opposition. ESTTA requires the opposer to select relevant grounds for opposition. The required accompanying statement supports and explains the grounds.

(b) Oppositions to different applications owned by the same party may be joined in a consolidated opposition when appropriate, but the required fee must be included for each party joined as opposer for each class in which registration is opposed in each application against which the opposition is filed.

(c) Oppositions to applications filed under Section 66(a) of the Act are limited to the goods, services and grounds set forth in the ESTTA cover sheet.

History of 37 C.F.R. §2.104: 37 FR 7606, Apr. 18, 1972; 48 FR 23135, May 23, 1983; 51 FR 28709, Aug. 11, 1986; 54 FR 34897, Aug. 22, 1989; 68 FR 55766, Sept. 26, 2003; 81 FR 69972, Jan. 14, 2017.

§2.105. NOTIFICATION TO PARTIES OF OPPOSITION PROCEEDING(S)

(a) When an opposition in proper form (see §§2.101 and 2.104) has been filed with the correct fee(s), and the opposition has been determined to be timely and complete, the Trademark Trial and Appeal Board shall prepare a notice of institution, which shall identify the proceeding as an opposition, number of the proceeding, and the application(s) involved; and the notice shall designate a time, not less than thirty days from the mailing date of the notice, within which an answer must be filed. The notice, which will include a Web link or Web address to access the electronic proceeding record, constitutes service of the notice of opposition to the applicant.

(b) The Board shall forward a copy of the notice to opposer, as follows:

(1) If the opposition is transmitted by an attorney, or a written power of attorney is filed, the Board will send the notice to the attorney transmitting the opposition or to the attorney designated in the power of attorney, provided that the person is an "attorney" as defined in §11.1 of this chapter, at the email or correspondence address for the attorney.

(2) If opposer is not represented by an attorney in the opposition, but opposer has appointed a domestic representative, the Board will send the notice to the domestic representative, at the email or correspondence address of record for the domestic representative, unless opposer designates in writing another correspondence address.

(3) If opposer is not represented by an attorney in the opposition, and no domestic representative has been appointed, the Board will send the notice directly to opposer at the email or correspondence address of record for opposer, unless opposer designates in writing another correspondence address.

(c) The Board shall forward a copy of the notice to applicant, as follows:

(1) If the opposed application contains a clear indication that the application is being prosecuted by an attorney, as defined in §11.1 of this chapter, the Board shall send the notice described in this section to applicant's attorney at the email or correspondence address of record for the attorney.

(2) If the opposed application is not being prosecuted by an attorney but a domestic representative has been appointed, the Board will send the notice described in this section to the domestic representative, at the email or correspondence address of record for the domestic representative, unless applicant designates in writing another correspondence address.

(3) If the opposed application is not being prosecuted by an attorney, and no domestic representative has been appointed, the Board will send the notice described in this section directly to applicant, at the email or correspondence address of record for the applicant, unless applicant designates in writing another correspondence address.

History of 37 C.F.R. §2.105: 41 FR 759, Jan. 5, 1976; 48 FR 23136, May 23, 1983; 68 FR 55766, Sept. 26, 2003; 72 FR 42258, Aug. 31, 2007; 73 FR 47685, Sept. 15, 2008; 81 FR 69972, Jan. 14, 2017.

§2.106. ANSWER

(a) If no answer is filed within the time initially set, or as may later be reset by the Board, the opposition may be decided as in case of default. The failure to file a timely answer tolls all deadlines, including the discovery conference, until the issue of default is resolved.

(b)(1) An answer must be filed through ESTTA. In the event that ESTTA is unavailable due to technical problems, or when extraordinary circumstances are present, an answer may be filed in paper form. An answer filed in paper form must be accompanied by a Petition to the Director under §2.146, with the fees therefor and the showing required under this paragraph (b).

(2) An answer shall state in short and plain terms the applicant's defenses to each claim asserted and shall admit or deny the averments upon which the opposer relies. If the applicant is without knowledge or information sufficient to form a belief as to the truth of an averment, applicant shall so state and this will have the effect of a denial. Denials may take any of the forms specified in Rule 8(b) of the Federal Rules of Civil Procedure. An answer may contain any defense, including the affirmative defenses of unclean hands, laches, estoppel, acquiescence, fraud, mistake, prior judgment, or any other matter constituting an avoidance or affirmative defense. When pleading special matters, the Federal Rules of Civil Procedure shall be followed. A reply to an affirmative defense shall not be filed. When a defense attacks the validity of a registration pleaded in the opposition, paragraph (b)(3) of this section shall govern. A pleaded registration is a registration identified by number by the party in the position of plaintiff in an original notice of opposition or in any amendment thereto made under Rule 15 of the Federal Rules of Civil Procedure.

(3)(i) A defense attacking the validity of any one or more of the registrations pleaded in the opposition shall be a compulsory counterclaim if grounds for such counterclaim exist at the time when the answer is filed. If grounds for a counterclaim are known to the applicant when the answer to the opposition is filed, the counterclaim shall be pleaded with or as part of the answer. If grounds for a counterclaim are learned during the course of the opposition proceeding, the counterclaim shall be pleaded promptly after the grounds therefor are learned. A counterclaim need not be filed if the claim is the subject of another proceeding between the same parties or anyone in privity therewith; but the applicant must promptly inform the Board, in the context of the opposition proceeding, of the filing of the other proceeding.

(ii) An attack on the validity of a registration pleaded by an opposer will not be heard unless a counterclaim or separate petition is filed to seek the cancellation of such registration.

(iii) The provisions of §§2.111 through 2.115, inclusive, shall be applicable to counterclaims. A time, not less than thirty days, will be designated by the Board within which an answer to the counterclaim must be filed.

(iv) The times for pleading, discovery, testimony, briefs or oral argument may be reset or extended when necessary, upon motion by a party, or as the Board may deem necessary, to enable a party fully to present or meet a counterclaim or separate petition for cancellation of a registration.

(c) The opposition may be withdrawn without prejudice before the answer is filed. After the answer is filed, the opposition may not be withdrawn without prejudice except with the written consent of the applicant or the applicant's attorney or other authorized representative.

History of 37 C.F.R. §2.106: 30 FR 13193, Oct. 16, 1965; 46 FR 6940, Jan. 22, 1981; 48 FR 23136, May 23, 1983; 54 FR 34897, Aug. 22, 1989; 81 FR 69973, Jan. 14, 2017.

§2.107. AMENDMENT OF PLEADINGS IN AN OPPOSITION PROCEEDING

(a) Pleadings in an opposition proceeding against an application filed under section 1 or 44 of the Act may be amended in the same manner and to the same extent as in a civil action in a United States district court, except that, after the close of the time period for filing an opposition including any extension of time for filing an opposition, an opposition may not be amended to add to the goods or services opposed, or to add a joint opposer.

(b) Pleadings in an opposition proceeding against an application filed under section 66(a) of the Act may be amended in the same manner and to the same extent as in a civil action in a United States district court, except that, once filed, the opposition may not be amended to add grounds for opposition or goods or services beyond those identified in the notice of opposition, or to add a joint opposer. The grounds for opposition, the goods or services opposed, and the named opposers are limited to those identified in the ESTTA cover sheet regardless of what is contained in any attached statement.

History of 37 C.F.R. §2.107: 30 FR 13193, Oct. 16, 1965; 48 FR 23136, May 23, 1983; 68 FR 55766, Sept. 26, 2003; 81 FR 69973, Jan. 14, 2017.

CANCELLATION

§2.111. FILING PETITION FOR CANCELLATION

(a) A cancellation proceeding is commenced by filing in the Office a timely petition for cancellation with the required fee.

(b) Any person who believes that he, she or it is or will be damaged by a registration may file a petition, addressed to the Trademark Trial and Appeal Board, for cancellation of the registration in whole or in part. The petition for cancellation need not be verified, but must be signed by the petitioner or the petitioner's attorney, as specified in §11.1 of this chapter, or other authorized representative, as specified in §11.14(b) of this chapter. Electronic signatures pursuant to §2.193(c) are required for petitions submitted electronically via ESTTA. The petition for cancellation may be filed at any time in the case of registrations on the Supplemental Register or under the Act of 1920, or registrations under the Act of 1881 or the Act of 1905 which have not been published under section 12(c) of the Act, or on any ground specified in section 14(3) or (5) of the Act. In all other cases, the petition for cancellation and the required fee must be filed within five years from the date of registration of the mark under the Act or from the date of publication under section 12(c) of the Act.

(c)(1) A petition to cancel a registration must be filed through ESTTA.

(2) In the event that ESTTA is unavailable due to technical problems, or when extraordinary circumstances are present, a petition to cancel may be filed in paper form. A paper petition to cancel a registration must be accompanied by a Petition to the Director under §2.146, with the fees therefor and the showing required under this paragraph (c). Timeliness of the paper submission, if relevant to a ground asserted in the petition to cancel, will be determined in accordance with §§2.195 through 2.198.

(d) The petition for cancellation must be accompanied by the required fee for each party joined as petitioner for each class in the registration(s) for which cancellation is sought (see §2.6). A petition cannot be filed via ESTTA unless the petition is accompanied by a fee that is sufficient to pay in full for each named petitioner to seek cancellation of the registration(s) in each class specified in the petition. A petition filed in paper form that is not accompanied by a fee sufficient to pay in full for each named petitioner for each class in the registration(s) for which cancellation is sought may not be instituted.

(e) The filing date of a petition for cancellation is the date of electronic receipt in the Office of the petition and required fee. In the rare instances that filing by paper is permitted under these rules, the filing date of a petition for cancellation will be determined in accordance with §§2.195 through 2.198.

History of 37 C.F.R. §2.111: 41 FR 759, Jan. 5, 1976; 48 FR 3976, Jan. 28, 1983; 54 FR 37596, Sept. 11, 1989; 63 FR 48097, Sept. 9, 1998; 64 FR 48924, Sept. 8, 1999; 68 FR 55766, Sept. 26, 2003; 72 FR 42258, Aug. 31, 2007; 73 FR 47686, Sept. 15, 2008; 74 FR 54909, Dec. 28, 2009; 81 FR 69973, Jan. 14, 2017.

§2.112. CONTENTS OF PETITION FOR CANCELLATION

(a) The petition for cancellation must set forth a short and plain statement showing why the petitioner believes he, she or it is or will be damaged by the registration, state the ground for cancellation, and indicate, to the best of petitioner's knowledge, the name and address, and a current email address(es), of the current owner of the registration. ESTTA requires the petitioner to select relevant grounds for petition to cancel. The required accompanying statement supports and explains the grounds.

(b) When appropriate, petitions for cancellation of different registrations owned by the same party may be joined in a consolidated petition for cancellation. The required fee must be included for each party joined as a petitioner for each class sought to be cancelled in each registration against which the petition for cancellation has been filed.

History of 37 C.F.R. §2.112: 41 FR 759, Jan. 5, 1976; 48 FR 3977, Jan. 28, 1983; 51 FR 28710, Aug. 11, 1986; 54 FR 34897, Aug. 22, 1989; 68 FR 55767, Sept. 26, 2003; 81 FR 69974, Jan. 14, 2017.

§2.113. NOTIFICATION OF CANCELLATION PROCEEDING

(a) When a petition for cancellation in proper form (see §§2.111 and 2.112) has been filed and the correct fee has been submitted, the Trademark Trial and Appeal Board shall prepare a notice of institution which shall identify the proceeding as a cancellation, number of the proceeding and the registration(s) involved; and shall designate a time, not less than thirty days from the mailing date of the notice, within which an answer must be filed. The notice, which will include a Web link or Web address to access the electronic proceeding record, constitutes service to the registrant of the petition to cancel.

(b) The Board shall forward a copy of the notice to petitioner, as follows:

(1) If the petition for cancellation is transmitted by an attorney, or a written power of attorney is filed, the Board will send the notice to the attorney transmitting the petition for cancellation or to the attorney designated in the power of attorney, provided that person is an "attorney" as defined in §11.1 of this chapter, to the attorney's email or correspondence address of record for the attorney.

(2) If petitioner is not represented by an attorney in the cancellation proceeding, but petitioner has appointed a domestic representative, the Board will send the notice to the domestic representative, at the email or correspondence address of record for the domestic representative, unless petitioner designates in writing another correspondence address.

(3) If petitioner is not represented by an attorney in the cancellation proceeding, and no domestic representative has been appointed, the Board will send the notice directly to petitioner, at the email or correspondence address of record for petitioner, unless petitioner designates in writing another correspondence address.

(c)(1) The Board shall forward a copy of the notice to the party shown by the records of the Office to be the current owner of the registration(s) sought to be cancelled at the email or address of record for the current owner, except that the Board, in its discretion, may join or substitute as respondent a party who makes a showing of a current ownership interest in such registration(s).

(2) If the respondent has appointed a domestic representative, and such appointment is reflected in the Office's records, the Board will send the notice only to the domestic representative at the email or correspondence address of record for the domestic representative.

(d) When the party alleged by the petitioner, pursuant to §2.112(a), as the current owner of the registration(s) is not the record owner, a courtesy copy of the notice with a Web link or Web address to access the electronic proceeding record shall be forwarded to the alleged current owner. The alleged current owner may file a motion to be joined or substituted as respondent.

History of 37 C.F.R. §2.113: 30 FR 13193, Oct. 16, 1965; 41 FR 760, Jan. 5, 1976; 48 FR 23136, May 23, 1983; 48 FR 27226, June 14, 1983; 54 FR 34897, Aug. 22, 1989; 54 FR 38041, Sept. 14, 1989; 68 FR 55767, Sept. 26, 2003; 72 FR 42259, Aug. 31, 2007; 73 FR 47686, Sept. 15, 2008; 81 FR 69974, Jan. 14, 2017.

§2.114. ANSWER

(a) If no answer is filed within the time initially set, or as may later be reset by the Board, the petition may be decided as in case of default. The failure to file a timely answer tolls all deadlines, including the discovery conference, until the issue of default is resolved.

(b)(1) An answer must be filed through ESTTA. In the event that ESTTA is unavailable due to technical problems, or when extraordinary circumstances are present, an answer may be filed in paper form. An answer filed in paper form must be accompanied by a Petition to the Director under §2.146, with the fees therefor and the showing required under this paragraph (b).

(2) An answer shall state in short and plain terms the respondent's defenses to each claim asserted and shall admit or deny the averments upon which the petitioner relies. If the respondent is without knowledge or information sufficient to form a belief as to the truth of an averment, respondent shall so state and this will have the effect of a denial. Denials may take any of the forms specified in Rule 8(b) of the Federal Rules of Civil Procedure. An answer may contain any defense, including the affirmative defenses of unclean hands, laches, estoppel, acquiescence, fraud, mistake, prior judgment, or any other matter constituting an avoidance or affirmative defense. When pleading special matters, the Federal Rules of Civil Procedure shall be followed. A reply to an affirmative defense shall not be filed. When a defense attacks the validity of a registration pleaded in the petition, paragraph (b)(3) of this section shall govern. A pleaded registration is a registration identified by number by the party in position of plaintiff in an original petition for cancellation, or a counterclaim petition for cancellation, or in any amendment thereto made under Rule 15 of the Federal Rules of Civil Procedure.

(3)(i) A defense attacking the validity of any one or more of the registrations pleaded in the petition shall be a compulsory counterclaim if grounds for such counterclaim exist at the time when the answer is filed. If grounds for a counterclaim are known to respondent when the answer to the petition is filed, the counterclaim shall be pleaded with or as part of the answer. If grounds for a counterclaim are learned during the course of the cancellation proceeding, the counterclaim shall be pleaded promptly after the grounds therefor are learned. A counterclaim need not be filed if the claim is the subject of another proceeding between the same parties or anyone in privity therewith; but the party in position of respondent and counterclaim plaintiff must promptly inform the Board, in the context of the primary cancellation proceeding, of the filing of the other proceeding.

(ii) An attack on the validity of a registration pleaded by a petitioner for cancellation will not be heard unless a counterclaim or separate petition is filed to seek the cancellation of such registration.

(iii) The provisions of §§2.111 through 2.115, inclusive, shall be applicable to counterclaims. A time, not less than thirty days, will be designated by the Board within which an answer to the counterclaim must be filed. Such response period may be reset as necessary by the Board, for a time period to be determined by the Board.

(iv) The times for pleading, discovery, testimony, briefs, or oral argument may be reset or extended when necessary, upon motion by a party, or as the Board may deem necessary, to enable a party fully to present or meet a counterclaim or separate petition for cancellation of a registration.

(c) The petition for cancellation or counterclaim petition for cancellation may be withdrawn without prejudice before the answer is filed. After the answer is filed, such petition or counterclaim petition may not be withdrawn without prejudice except with the written consent of the registrant or the registrant's attorney or other authorized representative.

History of 37 C.F.R. §2.114: 30 FR 13193, Oct. 16, 1965; 46 FR 6940, Jan. 22, 1981; 46 FR 11548, Feb. 9, 1981; 51 FR 28710, Aug. 11, 1986; 54 FR 34898, Aug. 22, 1989; 81 FR 69974, Jan. 14, 2017.

§2.115. AMENDMENT OF PLEADINGS IN A CANCELLATION PROCEEDING

Pleadings in a cancellation proceeding may be amended in the same manner and to the same extent as in a civil action in a United States district court.

History of 37 C.F.R. §2.115: 30 FR 13193, Oct. 16, 1965; 48 FR 23136, May 23, 1983.

PROCEDURE IN INTER PARTES PROCEEDINGS

§2.116. FEDERAL RULES OF CIVIL PROCEDURE

(a) Except as otherwise provided, and wherever applicable and appropriate, procedure and practice in inter partes proceedings shall be governed by the Federal Rules of Civil Procedure.

(b) The opposer in an opposition proceeding or the petitioner in a cancellation proceeding shall be in the position of plaintiff, and the applicant in an opposition proceeding or the respondent in a cancellation proceeding shall be in the position of defendant. A party that is a junior party in an interference proceeding or in a concurrent use registration proceeding shall be in the position of plaintiff against every party that is senior, and the party that is a senior party in an interference proceeding or in a concurrent use registration proceeding shall be a defendant against every party that is junior.

(c) The notice of opposition or the petition for cancellation and the answer correspond to the complaint and answer in a court proceeding.

(d) The assignment of testimony periods corresponds to setting a case for trial in court proceedings.

(e) The submission of notices of reliance, declarations and affidavits, as well as the taking of depositions, during the assigned testimony periods correspond to the trial in court proceedings.

(f) Oral hearing, if requested, of arguments on the record and merits corresponds to oral summation in court proceedings.

(g) The Trademark Trial and Appeal Board's standard protective order is automatically imposed in all inter partes proceedings unless the parties, by stipulation approved by the Board, agree to an alternative order, or a motion by a party to use an alternative order is granted by the Board. The standard protective order is available at the Office's Web site. No material disclosed or produced by a party, presented at trial, or filed with the Board, including motions or briefs which discuss such material, shall be treated as confidential or shielded from public view unless designated as protected under the Board's standard protective order, or under an alternative order stipulated to by the parties and approved by the Board, or under an order submitted by motion of a party granted by the Board. The Board may treat as not confidential that material which cannot reasonably be considered confidential, notwithstanding a designation as such by a party.

History of 37 C.F.R. §2.116: 30 FR 13193, Oct. 16, 1965. Redesignated and amended at 37 FR 7606, Apr. 18, 1972. Amended at 48 FR 23136, May 23, 1983; 72 FR 42259, Aug. 31, 2007; 81 FR 69975, Jan. 14, 2017.

§2.117. SUSPENSION OF PROCEEDINGS

(a) Whenever it shall come to the attention of the Trademark Trial and Appeal Board that a party or parties to a pending case are engaged in a civil action or another Board proceeding which may have a bearing on the case, proceedings before the Board may be suspended until termination of the civil action or the other Board proceeding.

(b) Whenever there is pending before the Board both a motion to suspend and a motion which is potentially dispositive of the case, the potentially dispositive motion may be decided before the question of suspension is considered regardless of the order in which the motions were filed.

(c) Proceedings may also be suspended sua sponte by the Board, or, for good cause, upon motion or a stipulation of the parties approved by the Board. Many consented or stipulated motions to suspend are suitable for automatic approval by ESTTA, but the Board retains discretion to condition approval on the party or parties providing necessary information about the status of settlement talks, discovery activities, or trial activities, as may be appropriate.

History of 37 C.F.R. §2.117: 37 FR 7606, Apr. 18, 1972; 48 FR 23136, May 23, 1983; 63 FR 48097, Sept. 9, 1998; 81 FR 69975, Jan. 14, 2017.

§2.118. UNDELIVERED OFFICE NOTICES

When a notice sent by the Office to any registrant or applicant is returned to the Office undelivered, including notification to the Office of non-delivery in paper or electronic form, additional notice may be given by publication in the Official Gazette.

History of 37 C.F.R. §2.118: 68 FR 55767, Sept. 26, 2003; 72 FR 42259, Aug. 31, 2007; 81 FR 69975, Jan. 14, 2017.

§2.119. SERVICE & SIGNING

(a) Except for the notice of opposition or the petition to cancel, every submission filed in the Office in inter partes cases, including notices of appeal to the courts, must be served upon the other party or parties. Proof of such service must be made before the submission will be considered by the Office. A statement signed by the attorney or other authorized representative, attached to or appearing on the original submission when filed, clearly stating the date and manner in which service was made will be accepted as prima facie proof of service.

(b) Service of submissions filed with the Board and any other papers served on a party not required to be filed with the Board, must be on the attorney or other authorized representative of the party if there be such or on the party if there is no attorney or other authorized representative, and must be made by email, unless otherwise stipulated, or if the serving party can show by written explanation accompanying the submission or paper, or in a subsequent amended certificate of service, that service by email was attempted but could not be made due to technical problems or extraordinary circumstances, then service may be made in any of the following ways:

(1) By delivering a copy of the submission or paper to the person served;

(2) By leaving a copy at the usual place of business of the person served, with someone in the person's employment;

(3) When the person served has no usual place of business, by leaving a copy at the person's residence, with some person of suitable age and discretion who resides there;

(4) Transmission by the Priority Mail Express® Post Office to Addressee service of the United States Postal Service or by first-class mail, which may also be certified or registered;

(5) Transmission by overnight courier; or

(6) Other forms of electronic transmission.

(c) When service is made by first-class mail, Priority Mail Express®, or overnight courier, the date of mailing or of delivery to the overnight courier will be considered the date of service.

(d) If a party to an inter partes proceeding is not domiciled in the United States and is not represented by an attorney or other authorized representative located in the United States, none of the parties to the proceeding is eligible to use the service option under paragraph (b)(4) of this section. The party not domiciled in the United States may designate by submission filed in the Office the name and address of a person residing in the United States on whom may be served notices or process in the proceeding. If the party has appointed a domestic representative, official communications of the Office will be addressed to the domestic representative unless the proceeding is being prosecuted by an attorney at law or other qualified person duly authorized under §11.14(c) of this chapter. If the party has not appointed a domestic representative and the proceeding is not being prosecuted by an attorney at law or other qualified person, the Office will send correspondence directly to the party, unless the party designates in writing another address to which correspondence is to be sent. The mere designation of a domestic representative does not authorize the person designated to prosecute the proceeding unless qualified under §11.14(a) of this chapter, or qualified under §11.14(b) of this chapter and authorized under §2.17(f).

(e) Every submission filed in an inter partes proceeding, and every request for an extension of time to file an opposition, must be signed by the party filing it, or by the party's attorney or other authorized representative, but an unsigned submission will not be refused consideration if a signed copy is submitted to the Office within the time limit set in the notification of this defect by the Office.

History of 37 C.F.R. §2.119: 37 FR 7606, Apr. 18, 1972; 41 FR 760, Jan. 5, 1976; 54 FR 34898, Aug. 22, 1989; 54 FR 38041, Sept. 14, 1989; 63 FR 48097, Sept. 9, 1998; 67 FR 79523, Dec. 30, 2002; 72 FR 42259, Aug. 31, 2007; 73 FR 47686, Sept. 15, 2008; 74 FR 54909, Dec. 28, 2009; 79 FR 63041, Oct. 22, 2014; 81 FR 69975, Jan. 14, 2017.

A §2.120. DISCOVERY

(a) In general. (1) Except as otherwise provided in this section, and wherever appropriate, the provisions of the Federal Rules of Civil Procedure relating to disclosure and discovery shall apply in opposition, cancellation, interference and concurrent use registration proceedings. The provisions of Rule 26 of the Federal Rules of Civil Procedure relating to required disclosures, the conference of the parties to discuss settlement and to develop a disclosure and discovery plan, the scope, proportionality, timing and sequence of discovery, protective orders, signing of disclosures and discovery responses, and supplementation of disclosures and discovery responses, are applicable to Board proceedings in modified form, as noted in these rules and as may be detailed in any order instituting an inter partes proceeding or subsequent scheduling order. The Board will specify the deadline for a discovery conference, the opening and closing dates for the taking of discovery, and the deadlines within the discovery period for making initial disclosures and expert disclosure. The trial order setting these deadlines and dates will be included within the notice of institution of the proceeding.

(2)(i) The discovery conference shall occur no later than the opening of the discovery period, and the parties must discuss the subjects set forth in Rule 26(f) of the Federal Rules of Civil Procedure and any subjects set forth in the Board's institution order. A Board Interlocutory Attorney or Administrative Trademark Judge will participate in the conference upon request of any party made after answer but no later than ten days prior to the deadline for the conference, or when the Board deems it useful for the parties to have Board involvement. The participating attorney or judge may expand or reduce the number or nature of subjects to be discussed in the conference as may be deemed appropriate. The discovery period will be set for a period of 180 days.

(ii) Initial disclosures must be made no later than thirty days after the opening of the discovery period.

(iii) Disclosure of expert testimony must occur in the manner and sequence provided in Rule 26(a)(2) of the Federal Rules of Civil Procedure, unless alternate directions have been provided by the Board in an institution order or any subsequent order resetting disclosure, discovery or trial dates. If the expert is retained after the deadline for disclosure of expert testimony, the party must promptly file a motion for leave to use expert testimony. Upon disclosure by any party of plans to use expert testimony, whether before or after the deadline for disclosing expert testimony, the Board, either on its own initiative or on notice from either party of the disclosure of expert testimony, may issue an order regarding expert discovery and/or set a deadline for any other party to disclose plans to use a rebuttal expert.

(iv) The parties may stipulate to a shortening of the discovery period, that there will be no discovery, that the number of discovery requests or depositions be limited, or that reciprocal disclosures be used in place of discovery. Limited extensions of the discovery period may be granted upon stipulation of the parties approved by the Board, or upon motion granted by the Board, or by order of the Board. If a motion for an extension is denied, the discovery period may remain as originally set or as reset. Disclosure deadlines and obligations may be modified upon written stipulation of the parties approved by the Board, or upon motion granted by the Board, or by order of the Board, but the expert disclosure deadline must always be scheduled prior to the close of discovery. If a stipulation or motion for modification is denied, discovery disclosure deadlines may remain as originally set or reset and obligations may remain unaltered.

(v) The parties are not required to prepare or transmit to the Board a written report outlining their discovery conference discussions, unless the parties have agreed to alter disclosure or discovery obligations set forth by these rules or applicable Federal Rules of Civil Procedure, or unless directed to file such a report by a participating Board Interlocutory Attorney or Administrative Trademark Judge.

(3) A party must make its initial disclosures prior to seeking discovery, absent modification of this requirement by a stipulation of the parties approved by the Board, or a motion granted by the Board, or by order of the Board. Discovery depositions must be properly noticed and taken during the discovery period. Interrogatories, requests for production of documents and things, and requests for admission must be served early enough in the discovery period, as originally set or as may have been reset by the Board, so that responses will be due no later than the close of discovery. Responses to interrogatories, requests for production of documents and things, and requests for admission must be served within thirty days from the date of service of such discovery requests. The time to respond may be extended upon stipulation of the parties, or upon motion granted by the Board, or by order of the Board, but the response may not be due later than the close of discovery. The resetting of a party's time to respond to an outstanding request for discovery will not result in the automatic rescheduling of the discovery and/or testimony periods; such dates will be rescheduled only upon stipulation of the parties approved by the Board, or upon motion granted by the Board, or by order of the Board.

(b) Discovery deposition within the United States. The deposition of a natural person shall be taken in the Federal judicial district where the person resides or is regularly employed or at any place on which the parties agree in writing. The responsibility rests wholly with the party taking discovery to secure the attendance of a proposed deponent other than a party or anyone who, at the time set for the taking of the deposition, is an officer, director, or managing agent of a party, or a person designated under Rule 30(b)(6) or Rule 31(a) of the Federal Rules of Civil Procedure. (See 35 U.S.C. 24.)

(c) Discovery deposition in foreign countries; or of foreign party within jurisdiction of the United States. **(1)** The discovery deposition of a natural person residing in a foreign country who is a party or who, at the time set for the taking of the deposition, is an officer, director, or managing agent of a party, or a person designated under Rule 30(b)(6) or Rule 31(a) of the Federal Rules of Civil Procedure, shall, if taken in a foreign country, be taken in the manner prescribed by §2.124 unless the Trademark Trial and Appeal Board, upon motion for good cause, orders that the deposition be taken by oral examination, or the parties so stipulate.

(2) Whenever a foreign party is or will be, during a time set for discovery, present within the United States or any territory which is under the control and jurisdiction of the United States, such party may be deposed by oral examination upon notice by the party seeking discovery. Whenever a foreign party has or will have, during a time set for discovery, an officer, director, managing agent, or other person who consents to testify on its behalf, present within the United States or any territory which is under the control and jurisdiction of the United States, such officer, director, managing agent, or other person who consents to testify in its behalf may be deposed by oral examination upon notice by the party seeking discovery. The party seeking discovery may have one or more officers, directors, managing agents, or other persons who consent to testify on behalf of the adverse party, designated under Rule 30(b)(6) of the Federal Rules of Civil Procedure. The deposition of a person under this paragraph shall be taken in the Federal judicial district where the witness resides or is regularly employed, or, if the witness neither resides nor is regularly employed in a Federal judicial district, where the witness is at the time of the deposition. This paragraph (c)(2) does not preclude the taking of a discovery deposition of a foreign party by any other procedure provided by paragraph (c)(1) of this section.

(d) Interrogatories. The total number of written interrogatories which a party may serve upon another party pursuant to Rule 33 of the Federal Rules of Civil Procedure, in a proceeding, shall not exceed seventy-five, counting subparts, except that the Trademark Trial and Appeal Board, in its discretion, may allow additional interrogatories upon motion therefor showing good cause, or upon stipulation of the parties, approved by the Board. A motion for leave to serve additional interrogatories must be filed and granted prior to the service of the proposed additional interrogatories and must be accompanied by a copy of the interrogatories, if any, which have already been served by the moving party, and by a copy of the interrogatories proposed to be served. If a party upon which interrogatories have been served believes that the number of interrogatories exceeds the limitation specified in this paragraph (d), and is not willing to waive this basis for objection, the party shall, within the time for (and instead of) serving answers and specific objections to the interrogatories, serve a general objection on the ground of their excessive number. If the inquiring party, in turn, files a motion to compel discovery, the motion must be accompanied by a copy of the set(s) of the interrogatories which together are said to exceed the limitation, and must otherwise comply with the requirements of paragraph (f) of this section.

(e) Requests for production. The total number of requests for production which a party may serve upon another party pursuant to Rule 34 of the Federal Rules of Civil Procedure, in a proceeding, shall not exceed seventy-five, counting subparts, except that the Trademark Trial and Appeal Board, in its discretion, may allow additional requests upon motion therefor showing good cause, or upon stipulation of the parties, approved by the Board. A motion for leave to serve additional requests must be filed and granted prior to the service of the proposed additional requests and must be accompanied by a copy of the requests, if any, which have already been served by the moving party, and by a copy of the requests proposed to be served. If a party upon which requests have been served believes that the number of requests exceeds the limitation specified in this paragraph, and is not willing to waive this basis for objection, the party shall, within the time for (and instead of) serving responses and specific objections to the requests, serve a general objection on the ground of their excessive number. If the inquiring party, in turn, files a motion to compel discovery, the motion must be accompanied by a copy of the set(s) of the requests which together are said to exceed the limitation, and must otherwise comply with the requirements of paragraph (f) of this section. The time, place, and manner for production of documents, electronically stored information, and tangible things shall comport with the provisions of Rule 34 of the Federal Rules of Civil Procedure, or be made pursuant to agreement of the parties, or where and in the manner which the Trademark Trial and Appeal Board, upon motion, orders.

(f) Motion for an order to compel disclosure or discovery. **(1)** If a party fails to make required initial disclosures or expert testimony disclosure, or fails to designate a person pursuant to Rule 30(b)(6) or Rule 31(a) of the Federal Rules of Civil Procedure, or if a party, or such designated person, or an officer, director or managing agent of a party fails to attend a deposition or fails to answer any question propounded in a discovery deposition, or any interrogatory, or fails to produce and permit the inspection and copying of any document, electronically stored information, or tangible thing, the party entitled to disclosure or seeking discovery may file a motion to compel disclosure, a designation, or attendance at a deposition, or an answer, or production and an opportunity to inspect and copy. A motion to compel initial disclosures must be filed within thirty days after the deadline therefor and include a copy of the disclosure(s), if any, and a motion to compel an expert testimony disclosure must be filed prior to the close of the discovery period. A motion to compel discovery must be filed before the day of the deadline for pretrial disclosures for the first testimony period as originally set or as reset. A motion to compel discovery shall include a copy of the request for designation of a witness or of the relevant portion of the discovery deposition; or a copy of the interrogatory with any answer or objection that was made; or a copy of the request for production, any proffer of production or objection to production in response to the request, and a list and brief description of the documents, electronically stored information, or tangible things that were not produced for inspection and copying. A motion to compel initial disclosures, expert testimony disclosure, or discovery must be supported by a showing from the moving party that such party or the attorney therefor has made a good faith effort, by conference or correspondence, to resolve with the other party or the attorney therefor the issues presented in the motion but the parties were unable to resolve their differences. If issues raised in the motion are subsequently resolved by agreement of the parties, the moving party should inform the Board in writing of the issues in the motion which no longer require adjudication.

(2) When a party files a motion for an order to compel initial disclosures, expert testimony disclosure, or discovery, the case will be suspended by the Board with respect to all matters not germane to the motion. After the motion to compel is filed and served, no party should file any paper that is not germane to the motion, except as otherwise specified in the Board's suspension order. Nor may any party serve any additional discovery until the period of suspension is lifted or expires by or under order of the Board. The filing of a motion to compel any disclosure or discovery shall not toll the time for a party to comply with any disclosure requirement or to respond to any outstanding discovery requests or to appear for any noticed discovery deposition. If discovery has closed, however, the parties need not make pretrial disclosures until directed to do so by the Board.

(g) Motion for a protective order. Upon motion by a party obligated to make initial disclosures or expert testimony disclosure or from whom discovery is sought, and for good cause, the Trademark Trial and Appeal Board may make any order which justice requires to protect a party from annoyance, embarrassment, oppression, or undue burden or expense, including one or more of the types of orders provided by clauses (A) through (H), inclusive, of Rule 26(c)(1) of the Federal Rules of Civil Procedure. If the motion for a protective order is denied in whole or in part, the Board may, on such conditions (other than an award of expenses to the party prevailing on the motion) as are just, order that any party comply with disclosure obligations or provide or permit discovery.

(h) Sanctions. **(1)** If a party fails to participate in the required discovery conference, or if a party fails to comply with an order of the Trademark Trial and Appeal Board relating to disclosure or discovery, including a protective order, the Board may make any appropriate order, including those provided in Rule 37(b)(2) of the Federal Rules of Civil Procedure, except that the Board will not hold any person in contempt or award expenses to any party. The Board may impose against a party any of the sanctions provided in Rule 37(b)(2) in the event that said party or any attorney, agent, or designated witness of that party fails to comply with a protective order made pursuant to Rule 26(c) of the Federal Rules of Civil Procedure. A motion for sanctions against a party for its failure to participate in the required discovery conference must be filed prior to the deadline for any party to make initial disclosures.

(2) If a party fails to make required initial disclosures or expert testimony disclosure, and such party or the party's attorney or other authorized representative informs the party or parties entitled to receive disclosures that required disclosures will not be made, the Board may make any appropriate order, as specified in paragraph (h)(1) of this section. If a party, or an officer, director, or managing agent of a party, or a person designated under Rule 30(b)(6) or 31(a) of the Federal Rules of Civil Procedure to testify on behalf of a party, fails to attend the party's or person's discovery deposition, after being served with proper notice, or fails to provide any response to a set of interrogatories or to a set of requests for production of documents and things, and such party or the party's attorney or other authorized representative informs the party seeking discovery that no response will be made thereto, the Board may make any appropriate order, as specified in paragraph (h)(1) of this section.

(i) Requests for admission. The total number of requests for admission which a party may serve upon another party pursuant to Rule 36 of the Federal Rules of Civil Procedure, in a proceeding, shall not exceed seventy-five, counting subparts, except that the Trademark Trial and Appeal Board, in its discretion, may allow additional requests upon motion therefor showing good cause, or upon stipulation of the parties, approved by the Board. A motion for leave to serve additional requests must be filed and granted prior to the service of the proposed additional requests and must be accompanied by a copy of the requests, if any, which have already been served by the moving party, and by a copy of the requests proposed to be served. If a party upon which requests for admission have been served believes that the number of requests for admission exceeds the limitation specified in this paragraph, and is not willing to waive this basis for objection, the party shall, within the time for (and instead of) serving answers and specific objections to the requests for admission, serve a general objection on the ground of their excessive number. However, independent of this limit, a party may make one comprehensive request for admission of any adverse party that has produced documents for an admission authenticating specific documents, or specifying which of those documents cannot be authenticated.

(1) Any motion by a party to determine the sufficiency of an answer or objection, including testing the sufficiency of a general objection on the ground of excessive number, to a request made by that party for an admission must be filed before the day of the deadline for pretrial disclosures for the first testimony period, as originally set or as reset. The motion shall include a copy of the request for admission and any exhibits thereto and of the answer or objection. The motion must be supported by a written statement from the moving party showing that such party or the attorney therefor has made a good faith effort, by conference or correspondence, to resolve with the other party or the attorney therefor the issues presented in the motion and has been unable to reach agreement. If issues raised in the motion are subsequently resolved by agreement of the parties, the moving party should inform the Board in writing of the issues in the motion which no longer require adjudication.

(2) When a party files a motion to determine the sufficiency of an answer or objection to a request for an admission, the case will be suspended by the Board with respect to all matters not germane to the motion. After the motion is filed and served, no party should file any paper that is not germane to the motion, except as otherwise specified in the Board's suspension order. Nor may any party serve any additional discovery until the period of suspension is lifted or expires by or under order of the Board. The filing of a motion to determine the sufficiency of an answer or objection to a request for admission shall not toll the time for a party to comply with any disclosure requirement or to respond to any outstanding discovery requests or to appear for any noticed discovery deposition. If discovery has closed, however, the parties need not make pretrial disclosures until directed to do so by the Board.

(j) Telephone and pretrial conferences. **(1)** Whenever it appears to the Trademark Trial and Appeal Board that a stipulation or motion filed in an inter partes proceeding is of such nature that a telephone conference would be beneficial, the Board may, upon its own initiative or upon request made by one or both of the parties, schedule a telephone conference.

(2) Whenever it appears to the Trademark Trial and Appeal Board that questions or issues arising during the interlocutory phase of an inter partes proceeding have become so complex that their resolution by correspondence or telephone conference is not practical and that resolution would likely be facilitated by a conference in person of the parties or their attorneys with an Administrative Trademark Judge or an Interlocutory Attorney of the Board, the Board may, upon its own initiative, direct that the parties and/or their attorneys meet with the Board for a disclosure, discovery or pretrial conference on such terms as the Board may order.

(3) Parties may not make a recording of the conferences referenced in paragraphs (j)(1) and (2) of this section.

(k) Use of discovery deposition, answer to interrogatory, admission or written disclosure. **(1)** The discovery deposition of a party or of anyone who at the time of taking the deposition was an officer, director or managing agent of a party, or a person designated by a party pursuant to Rule 30(b)(6) or Rule 31(a) of the Federal Rules of Civil Procedure, may be offered in evidence by an adverse party.

(2) Except as provided in paragraph (k)(1) of this section, the discovery deposition of a witness, whether or not a party, shall not be offered in evidence unless the person whose deposition was taken is, during the testimony period of the party offering the deposition, dead; or out of the United States (unless it appears that the absence of the witness was procured by the party offering the deposition); or unable to testify because of age, illness, infirmity, or imprisonment; or cannot be served with a subpoena to compel attendance at a testimonial deposition; or there is a stipulation by the parties; or upon a showing that such exceptional circumstances exist as to make it desirable, in the interest of justice, to allow the deposition to be used. The use of a discovery deposition by any party under this paragraph will be allowed only by stipulation of the parties approved by the Trademark Trial and Appeal Board, or by order of the Board on motion, which shall be filed when the party makes its pretrial disclosures, unless the motion is based upon a claim that such exceptional circumstances exist as to make it desirable, in the interest of justice, to allow the deposition to be used, even though such deadline has passed, in which case the motion shall be filed promptly after the circumstances claimed to justify use of the deposition became known.

(3)(i) A discovery deposition, an answer to an interrogatory, an admission to a request for admission, or a written initial disclosure, which may be offered in evidence under the provisions of paragraph (k) of this section, may be made of record in the case by filing the deposition or any part thereof with any exhibit to the part that is filed, or a copy of the interrogatory and answer thereto with any exhibit made part of the answer, or a copy of the request for admission and any exhibit thereto and the admission (or a statement that the party from which an admission was requested failed to respond thereto), or a copy of the written initial disclosure, together with a notice of reliance in accordance with §2.122(g). The notice of reliance and the material submitted thereunder should be filed during the testimony period of the party that files the notice of reliance. An objection made at a discovery deposition by a party answering a question subject to the objection will be considered at final hearing.

(ii) A party that has obtained documents from another party through disclosure or under Rule 34 of the Federal Rules of Civil Procedure may not make the documents of record by notice of reliance alone, except to the extent that they are admissible by notice of reliance under the provisions of §2.122(e), or the party has obtained an admission or stipulation from the producing party that authenticates the documents.

(4) If only part of a discovery deposition is submitted and made part of the record by a party, an adverse party may introduce under a notice of reliance any other part of the deposition which should in fairness be considered so as to make not misleading what was offered by the submitting party. A notice of reliance filed by an adverse party must be supported by a written statement explaining why the adverse party needs to rely upon each additional part listed in the adverse party's notice, failing which the Board, in its discretion, may refuse to consider the additional parts.

(5) Written disclosures, an answer to an interrogatory, or an admission to a request for admission, may be submitted and made part of the record only by the receiving or inquiring party except that, if fewer than all of the written disclosures, answers to interrogatories, or fewer than all of the admissions, are offered in evidence by the receiving or inquiring party, the disclosing or responding party may introduce under a notice of reliance any other written disclosures, answers to interrogatories, or any other admissions, which should in fairness be considered so as to make not misleading what was offered by the receiving or inquiring party. The notice of reliance filed by the disclosing or responding party must be supported by a written statement explaining why the disclosing or responding party needs to rely upon each of the additional written disclosures or discovery responses listed in the disclosing or responding party's notice, and absent such statement, the Board, in its discretion, may refuse to consider the additional written disclosures or responses.

(6) Paragraph (k) of this section will not be interpreted to preclude reading or use of written disclosures or documents, a discovery deposition, or answer to an interrogatory, or admission as part of the examination or cross-examination of any witness during the testimony period of any party.

(7) When a written disclosure, a discovery deposition, or a part thereof, or an answer to an interrogatory, or an admission, or an authenticated produced document has been made of record by one party in accordance with the provisions of paragraph (k)(3) of this section, it may be referred to by any party for any purpose permitted by the Federal Rules of Evidence.

(8) Written disclosures or disclosed documents, requests for discovery, responses thereto, and materials or depositions obtained through the disclosure or discovery process should not be filed with the Board, except when submitted with a motion relating to disclosure or discovery, or in support of or in response to a motion for summary judgment, or under a notice of reliance, when permitted, during a party's testimony period.

History of 37 C.F.R. §2.120: 37 FR 7606, Apr. 18, 1972; 41 FR 760, Jan. 5, 1976; 48 FR 23136, May 23, 1983; 54 FR 34898, Aug. 22, 1989; 54 FR 38041, Sept. 14, 1989; 56 FR 46379, Sept. 12, 1991; 56 FR 54917, Oct. 23, 1991; 63 FR 48098, Sept. 9, 1998; 63 FR 52158, Sept. 30, 1998; 72 FR 42259, Aug. 31, 2007; 81 FR 69976, Jan. 14, 2017; 82 FR 33805, July 21, 2017.

§2.121. ASSIGNMENT OF TIMES FOR TAKING TESTIMONY & PRESENTING EVIDENCE

(a) The Trademark Trial and Appeal Board will issue a trial order setting a deadline for each party's required pretrial disclosures and assigning to each party its time for taking testimony and presenting evidence ("testimony period"). No testimony shall be taken or evidence presented except during the times assigned, unless by stipulation of the parties approved by the Board, or upon motion granted by the Board, or by order of the Board. The deadlines for pretrial disclosures and the testimony periods may be rescheduled by stipulation of the parties approved by the Board, or upon motion granted by the Board, or by order of the Board. If a motion to reschedule any pretrial disclosure deadline and/or testimony period is denied, the pretrial disclosure deadline or testimony period and any subsequent remaining periods may remain as set. The resetting of the closing date for discovery will result in the rescheduling of pretrial disclosure deadlines and testimony periods without action by any party. The resetting of a party's testimony period will result in the rescheduling of the remaining pretrial disclosure deadlines without action by any party.

(b)(1) The Trademark Trial and Appeal Board will schedule a testimony period for the plaintiff to present its case in chief, a testimony period for the defendant to present its case and to meet the case of the plaintiff, and a testimony period for the plaintiff to present evidence in rebuttal.

(2) When there is a counterclaim, or when proceedings have been consolidated and one party is in the position of plaintiff in one of the involved proceedings and in the position of defendant in another of the involved proceedings, or when there is an interference or a concurrent use registration proceeding involving more than two parties, the Board will schedule testimony periods so that each party in the position of plaintiff will have a period for presenting its case in chief against each party in the position of defendant, each party in the position of defendant will have a period for presenting its case and meeting the case of each plaintiff, and each party in the position of plaintiff will have a period for presenting evidence in rebuttal.

(c) A testimony period which is solely for rebuttal will be set for fifteen days. All other testimony periods will be set for thirty days. The periods may be shortened or extended by stipulation of the parties approved by the Trademark Trial and Appeal Board, or may be extended upon motion granted by the Board, or by order of the Board. If a motion for an extension is denied, the testimony periods and their associated pretrial disclosure deadlines may remain as set.

(d) When parties stipulate to the rescheduling of a deadline for pretrial disclosures and subsequent testimony periods or to the rescheduling of the closing date for discovery and the rescheduling of subsequent deadlines for pretrial disclosures and testimony periods, a stipulation presented in the form used in a trial order, signed by the parties, or a motion in said form signed by one party and including a statement that every other party has agreed thereto, shall be submitted to the Board through ESTTA, with the relevant dates set forth and an express statement that all parties agree to the new dates.

(e) A party need not disclose, prior to its testimony period, any notices of reliance it intends to file during its testimony period. However, no later than fifteen days prior to the opening of each testimony period, or on such alternate schedule as may be provided by order of the Board, the party scheduled to present evidence must disclose the name and, if not previously provided, the telephone number and address of each witness from whom it intends to take testimony, or may take testimony if the need arises, general identifying information about the witness, such as relationship to any party, including job title if employed by a party, or, if neither a party nor related to a party, occupation and job title, a general summary or list of subjects on which the witness is expected to testify, and a general summary or list of the types of documents and things which may be introduced as exhibits during the testimony of the witness. The testimony of a witness may be taken upon oral examination and transcribed, or presented in the form of an affidavit or declaration, as provided in §2.123. Pretrial disclosure of a witness under this paragraph (e) does not substitute for issuance of a proper notice of examination under §2.123(c) or §2.124(b). If a party does not plan to take testimony from any witnesses, it must so state in its pretrial disclosure. When a party fails to make required pretrial disclosures, any adverse party or parties may have remedy by way of a motion to the Board to delay or reset any subsequent pretrial disclosure deadlines and/or testimony periods. A party may move to quash a noticed testimony deposition of a witness not identified or improperly identified in pretrial disclosures before the deposition. When testimony has been presented by affidavit or declaration, but was not covered by an earlier pretrial disclosure, the remedy for any adverse party is the prompt filing of a motion to strike, as provided in §§2.123 and 2.124.

History of 37 C.F.R. §2.121: 30 FR 13193, Oct. 16, 1965; 48 FR 23138, May 23, 1983; 48 FR 27226, June 14, 1983; 54 FR 34899, Aug. 22, 1989; 63 FR 48099, Sept. 9, 1998; 68 FR 55767, Sept. 26, 2003; 72 FR 42262, Nov. 1, 2007; 81 FR 69979, Jan. 14, 2017.

§2.122. MATTERS IN EVIDENCE

(a) Applicable rules. Unless the parties otherwise stipulate, the rules of evidence for proceedings before the Trademark Trial and Appeal Board are the Federal Rules of Evidence, the relevant provisions of the Federal Rules of Civil Procedure, the relevant provisions of Title 28 of the United States Code, and the provisions of this part. When evidence has been made of record by one party in accordance with these rules, it may be referred to by any party for any purpose permitted by the Federal Rules of Evidence.

(b) Application and registration files. **(1)** The file of each application or registration specified in a notice of interference, of each application or registration specified in the notice of a concurrent use registration proceeding, of the application against which a notice of opposition is filed, or of each registration against which a petition or counterclaim for cancellation is filed forms part of the record of the proceeding without any action by the parties and reference may be made to the file for any relevant and competent purpose in accordance with paragraph (b)(2) of this section.

(2) The allegation in an application for registration, or in a registration, of a date of use is not evidence on behalf of the applicant or registrant; a date of use of a mark must be established by competent evidence. Specimens in the file of an application for registration, or in the file of a registration, are not evidence on behalf of the applicant or registrant unless identified and introduced in evidence as exhibits during the period for the taking of testimony. Statements made in an affidavit or declaration in the file of an application for registration, or in the file of a registration, are not testimony on behalf of the applicant or registrant. Establishing the truth of these or any other matters asserted in the files of these applications and registrations shall be governed by the Federal Rules of Evidence, the relevant provisions of the Federal Rules of Civil Procedure, the relevant provisions of Title 28 of the United States Code, and the provisions of this part.

(c) Exhibits to pleadings. Except as provided in paragraph (d)(1) of this section, an exhibit attached to a pleading is not evidence on behalf of the party to whose pleading the exhibit is attached, and must be identified and introduced in evidence as an exhibit during the period for the taking of testimony.

(d) Registrations. **(1)** A registration of the opposer or petitioner pleaded in an opposition or petition to cancel will be received in evidence and made part of the record if the opposition or petition is accompanied by an original or photocopy of the registration prepared and issued by the Office showing both the current status of and current title to the registration, or by a current copy of information from the electronic database records of the Office showing the current status and title of the registration. For the cost of a copy of a registration showing status and title, see §2.6(b)(4).

(2) A registration owned by any party to a proceeding may be made of record in the proceeding by that party by appropriate identification and introduction during the taking of testimony or by filing a notice of reliance in accordance with paragraph (g) of this section, which shall be accompanied by a copy (original or photocopy) of the registration prepared and issued by the Office showing both the current status of and current title to the registration, or by a current copy of information from the electronic database records of the Office showing the current status and title of the registration. The notice of reliance shall be filed during the testimony period of the party that files the notice.

(e) Printed publications and official records. **(1)** Printed publications, such as books and periodicals, available to the general public in libraries or of general circulation among members of the public or that segment of the public which is relevant in a particular proceeding, and official records, if the publication or official record is competent evidence and relevant to an issue, may be introduced in evidence by filing a notice of reliance on the material being offered in accordance with paragraph (g) of this section. The notice of reliance shall specify the printed publication (including information sufficient to identify the source and the date of the publication) or the official record and the pages to be read; and be accompanied by the official record or a copy thereof whose authenticity is established under the Federal Rules of Evidence, or by the printed publication or a copy of the relevant portion thereof. A copy of an official record of the Office need not be certified to be offered in evidence.

(2) Internet materials may be admitted into evidence under a notice of reliance in accordance with paragraph (g) of this section, in the same manner as a printed publication in general circulation, so long as the date the internet materials were accessed and their source (e.g., URL) are provided.

(f) Testimony from other proceedings. By order of the Trademark Trial and Appeal Board, on motion, testimony taken in another proceeding, or testimony taken in a suit or action in a court, between the same parties or those in privity may be used in a proceeding, so far as relevant and material, subject, however, to the right of any adverse party to recall or demand the recall for examination or cross-examination of any witness whose prior testimony has been offered and to rebut the testimony.

(g) Notices of reliance. The types of evidence admissible by notice of reliance are identified in paragraphs (d)(2) and (e)(1) and (2) of this section and §2.120(k). A notice of reliance shall be filed during the testimony period of the party that files the notice. For all evidence offered by notice of reliance, the notice must indicate generally the relevance of the evidence and associate it with one or more issues in the proceeding. Failure to identify the relevance of the evidence, or associate it with issues in the proceeding, with sufficient specificity is a procedural defect that can be cured by the offering party within the time set by Board order.

History of 37 C.F.R. §2.122: 30 FR 13193, Oct. 16, 1965; 37 FR 7607, Apr. 18, 1972; 48 FR 23138, May 23, 1983; 54 FR 34899, Aug. 22, 1989; 54 FR 38041, Sept. 14, 1989; 63 FR 48099, Sept. 9, 1998; 72 FR 42262, Aug. 31, 2007; 81 FR 69980, Jan. 14, 2017.

§2.123. TRIAL TESTIMONY IN INTER PARTES CASES

(a)(1) The testimony of witnesses in inter partes cases may be submitted in the form of an affidavit or a declaration pursuant to §2.20 and in conformance with the Federal Rules of Evidence, filed during the proffering party's testimony period, subject to the right of any adverse party to elect to take and bear the expense of oral cross-examination of that witness as provided under paragraph (c) of this section if such witness is within the jurisdiction of the United States, or conduct cross-examination by written questions as provided in §2.124 if such witness is outside the jurisdiction of the United States, and the offering party must make that witness available; or taken by deposition upon oral examination as provided by this section; or by deposition upon written questions as provided by §2.124.

(2) Testimony taken in a foreign country shall be taken: by deposition upon written questions as provided by §2.124, unless the Board, upon motion for good cause, orders that the deposition be taken by oral examination, or the parties so stipulate; or by affidavit or declaration, subject to the right of any adverse party to elect to take and bear the expense of cross-examination by written questions of that witness. If a party serves notice of the taking of a testimonial deposition upon written questions of a witness who is, or will be at the time of the deposition, present within the United States or any territory which is under the control and jurisdiction of the United States, any adverse party may, within twenty days from the date of service of the notice, file a motion with the Trademark Trial and Appeal Board, for good cause, for an order that the deposition be taken by oral examination.

(b) Stipulations. If the parties so stipulate in writing, depositions may be taken before any person authorized to administer oaths, at any place, upon any notice, and in any manner, and when so taken may be used like other depositions. The parties may stipulate in writing what a particular witness would testify to if called; or any relevant facts in the case may be stipulated in writing.

(c) Notice of examination of witnesses. Before the oral depositions of witnesses shall be taken by a party, due notice in writing shall be given to the adverse party or parties, as provided in §2.119(b), of the time when and place where the depositions will be taken, of the cause or matter in which they are to be used, and the name and address of each witness to be examined. Depositions may be noticed for any reasonable time and place in the United States. A deposition may not be noticed for a place in a foreign country except as provided in paragraph (a)(2) of this section. No party shall take depositions in more than one place at the same time, nor so nearly at the same time that reasonable opportunity for travel from one place of examination to the other is not available. When a party elects to take oral cross-examination of an affiant or declarant, the notice of such election must be served on the adverse party and a copy filed with the Board within 20 days from the date of service of the affidavit or declaration and completed within 30 days from the date of service of the notice of election. Upon motion for good cause by any party, or upon its own initiative, the Board may extend the periods for electing and taking oral cross-examination. When such election has been made but cannot be completed within that testimony period, the Board, after the close of that testimony period, shall suspend or reschedule other proceedings in the matter to allow for the orderly completion of the oral cross-examination(s).

(d) Persons before whom depositions may be taken. Depositions may be taken before persons designated by Rule 28 of the Federal Rules of Civil Procedure.

(e) Examination of witnesses. **(1)** Each witness before providing oral testimony shall be duly sworn according to law by the officer before whom the deposition is to be taken. Where oral depositions are taken, every adverse party shall have a full opportunity to cross-examine each witness. When testimony is proffered by affidavit or declaration, every adverse party will have the right to elect oral cross-examination of any witness within the jurisdiction of the United States. For examination of witnesses outside the jurisdiction of the United States, see §2.124.

(2) The deposition shall be taken in answer to questions, with the questions and answers recorded in their regular order by the officer, or by some other person (who shall be subject to the provisions of Rule 28 of the Federal Rules of Civil Procedure) in the presence of the officer except when the officer's presence is waived on the record by agreement of the parties. The testimony shall be recorded and transcribed, unless the parties present agree otherwise. Exhibits which are marked and identified at the deposition will be deemed to have been offered into evidence, without any formal offer thereof, unless the intention of the party marking the exhibits is clearly expressed to the contrary.

(3) If pretrial disclosures or the notice of examination of witnesses served pursuant to paragraph (c) of this section are improper or inadequate with respect to any witness, an adverse party may cross-examine that witness under protest while reserving the right to object to the receipt of the testimony in evidence. Promptly after the testimony is completed, the adverse party, to preserve the objection, shall move to strike the testimony from the record, which motion will be decided on the basis of all the relevant circumstances.

(i) A motion to strike the testimony of a witness for lack of proper or adequate pretrial disclosure may seek exclusion of the entire testimony, when there was no pretrial disclosure, or may seek exclusion of that portion of the testimony that was not adequately disclosed in accordance with §2.121(e).

(ii) A motion to strike the testimony of a witness for lack of proper or adequate notice of examination must request the exclusion of the entire testimony of that witness and not only a part of that testimony.

(4) All objections made at the time of an oral examination to the qualifications of the officer taking the deposition, or to the manner of taking it, or to the evidence presented, or to the conduct of any party, and any other objection to the proceedings, shall be noted by the officer upon the deposition. Evidence objected to shall be taken subject to the objections.

(5) When the oral deposition has been transcribed, the deposition transcript shall be carefully read over by the witness or by the officer to the witness, and shall then be signed by the witness in the presence of any officer authorized to administer oaths unless the reading and the signature be waived on the record by agreement of all parties.

(f) Certification and filing of deposition. **(1)** The officer shall annex to the deposition his or her certificate showing:

(i) Due administration of the oath by the officer to the witness before the commencement of his or her deposition;

(ii) The name of the person by whom the deposition was taken down, and whether, if not taken down by the officer, it was taken down in his or her presence;

(iii) The presence or absence of the adverse party;

(iv) The place, day, and hour of commencing and taking the deposition;

(v) The fact that the officer was not disqualified as specified in Rule 28 of the Federal Rules of Civil Procedure.

(2) If any of the foregoing requirements in paragraph (f)(1) of this section are waived, the certificate shall so state. The officer shall sign the certificate and affix thereto his or her seal of office, if he or she has such a seal. The party taking the deposition, or its attorney or other authorized representative, shall then promptly file the transcript and exhibits in electronic form using ESTTA. If the nature of an exhibit precludes electronic transmission via ESTTA, it shall be submitted by mail by the party taking the deposition, or its attorney or other authorized representative.

(g) Form of deposition. **(1)** The pages of each deposition must be numbered consecutively, and the name of the witness plainly and conspicuously written at the top of each page. A deposition must be in written form. The questions propounded to each witness must be consecutively numbered unless the pages have numbered lines. Each question must be followed by its answer. The deposition transcript must be submitted in full-sized format (one page per sheet), not condensed (multiple pages per sheet).

(2) Exhibits must be numbered or lettered consecutively and each must be marked with the number and title of the case and the name of the party offering the exhibit. Entry and consideration may be refused to improperly marked exhibits.

(3) Each deposition must contain a word index and an index of the names of the witnesses, giving the pages where the words appear in the deposition and where witness examination and cross-examination begin, and an index of the exhibits, briefly describing their nature and giving the pages at which they are introduced and offered in evidence.

(h) Depositions must be filed. All depositions which are taken must be duly filed in the Office. On refusal to file, the Office at its discretion will not further hear or consider the contestant with whom the refusal lies; and the Office may, at its discretion, receive and consider a copy of the withheld deposition, attested by such evidence as is procurable.

(i) Effect of errors and irregularities in depositions. Rule 32(d)(1), (2), and (3)(A) and (B) of the Federal Rules of Civil Procedure shall apply to errors and irregularities in depositions. Notice will not be taken of merely formal or technical objections which shall not appear to have wrought a substantial injury to the party raising them; and in case of such injury it must be made to appear that the objection was raised at the time specified in said rule.

(j) Objections to admissibility. Subject to the provisions of paragraph (i) of this section, objection may be made to receiving in evidence any declaration, affidavit, or deposition, or part thereof, or any other evidence, for any reason which would require the exclusion of the evidence from consideration. Objections to the competency of a witness or to the competency, relevancy, or materiality of testimony must be raised at the time specified in Rule 32(d)(3)(A) of the Federal Rules of Civil Procedure. Such objections may not be considered until final hearing.

(k) Evidence not considered. Evidence not obtained and filed in compliance with these sections will not be considered.

History of 37 C.F.R. §2.123: 37 FR 7607, Apr. 18, 1972; 41 FR 760, Jan. 5, 1976; 48 FR 23139, May 23, 1983; 54 FR 34899, Aug. 22, 1989; 54 FR 38041, Sept. 14, 1989; 63 FR 48099, Sept. 9, 1998; 68 FR 14337, Mar. 25, 2003; 68 FR 48289, Aug. 13, 2003; 68 FR 55767, Sept. 26, 2003; 72 FR 42262, Nov. 1, 2007; 81 FR 69981, Jan. 14, 2017; 81 FR 89383, Jan. 14, 2017.

§2.124. DEPOSITIONS UPON WRITTEN QUESTIONS

(a) A deposition upon written questions may be taken before any person before whom depositions may be taken as provided by Rule 28 of the Federal Rules of Civil Procedure.

(b)(1) A party desiring to take a testimonial deposition upon written questions shall serve notice thereof upon each adverse party within ten days from the opening date of the testimony period of the party who serves the notice. The notice shall state the name and address of the witness. A copy of the notice, but not copies of the questions, shall be filed with the Trademark Trial and Appeal Board.

(2) A party desiring to take a discovery deposition upon written questions shall serve notice thereof upon each adverse party and shall file a copy of the notice, but not copies of the questions, with the Board. The notice shall state the name and address, if known, of the person whose deposition is to be taken. If the name of the person is not known, a general description sufficient to identify the witness or the particular class or group to which he or she belongs shall be stated in the notice, and the party from whom the discovery deposition is to be taken shall designate one or more persons to be deposed in the same manner as is provided by Rule 30(b)(6) of the Federal Rules of Civil Procedure.

(3) A party desiring to take cross-examination, by written questions, of a witness who has provided testimony by affidavit or declaration shall serve notice thereof upon each adverse party and shall file a copy of the notice, but not copies of the questions, with the Board.

(c) Every notice given under the provisions of paragraph (b) of this section shall be accompanied by the name or descriptive title of the officer before whom the deposition is to be taken.

(d)(1) Every notice served on any adverse party under the provisions of paragraphs (b)(1) and (2) of this section, for the taking of direct examination, shall be accompanied by the written questions to be propounded on behalf of the party who proposes to take the deposition. Every notice served on any adverse party under the provisions of paragraph (b)(3) of this section, for the taking of cross-examination, shall be accompanied by the written questions to be propounded on behalf of the party who proposes to take the cross-examination. Within twenty days from the date of service of the notice of taking direct examination, or service of a testimony affidavit or declaration, any adverse party may serve cross questions upon the party who proposes to take the deposition. Any party who serves cross questions, whether in response to direct examination questions or under paragraph (b)(3) of this section, shall also serve every other adverse party. Within ten days from the date of service of the cross questions, the party who proposes to take the deposition, or who earlier offered testimony of the witness by affidavit or declaration, may serve redirect questions on every adverse party. Within ten days from the date of service of the redirect questions, any party who served cross questions may serve recross questions upon the party who proposes to take the deposition or who earlier offered testimony of the witness by affidavit or declaration; any party who serves recross questions shall also serve every other adverse party. Written objections to questions may be served on a party propounding questions; any party who objects shall serve a copy of the objections on every other adverse party. In response to objections, substitute questions may be served on the objecting party within ten days of the date of service of the objections; substitute questions shall be served on every other adverse party.

(2) Upon motion for good cause by any party, or upon its own initiative, the Trademark Trial and Appeal Board may extend any of the time periods provided by paragraph (d)(1) of this section. Upon receipt of written notice that one or more testimonial depositions are to be taken upon written questions, the Trademark Trial and Appeal Board shall suspend or reschedule other proceedings in the matter to allow for the orderly completion of the depositions upon written questions.

(3) Service of written questions, responses, and cross-examination questions shall be in accordance with §2.119(b).

(e) Within ten days after the last date when questions, objections, or substitute questions may be served, the party who proposes to take the deposition shall mail a copy of the notice and copies of all the questions to the officer designated in the notice; a copy of the notice and of all the questions mailed to the officer shall be served on every adverse party. The officer designated in the notice shall take the testimony of the witness in response to the questions and shall record each answer immediately after the corresponding question. The officer shall then certify the transcript and mail the transcript and exhibits to the party who took the deposition.

(f) The party who took the deposition shall promptly serve a copy of the transcript, copies of documentary exhibits, and duplicates or photographs of physical exhibits on every adverse party. It is the responsibility of the party who takes the deposition to assure that the transcript is correct (see §2.125(c)). If the deposition is a discovery deposition, it may be made of record as provided by §2.120(k). If the deposition is a testimonial deposition, the original, together with copies of documentary exhibits and duplicates or photographs of physical exhibits, shall be filed promptly with the Trademark Trial and Appeal Board.

(g) Objections to questions and answers in depositions upon written questions may be considered at final hearing.

History of 37 C.F.R. §2.124: 30 FR 13193, Oct. 16, 1965; 37 FR 7608, Apr. 18, 1972; 48 FR 23139, May 23, 1983; 81 FR 69982, Jan. 14, 2017; 81 FR 89383, Jan. 14, 2017.

§2.125. FILING & SERVICE OF TESTIMONY

(a) One copy of the declaration or affidavit prepared in accordance with §2.123, together with copies of documentary exhibits and duplicates or photographs of physical exhibits, shall be served on each adverse party at the time the declaration or affidavit is submitted to the Trademark Trial and Appeal Board during the assigned testimony period.

(b) One copy of the transcript of each testimony deposition taken in accordance with §2.123 or §2.124, together with copies of documentary exhibits and duplicates or photographs of physical exhibits, shall be served on each adverse party within thirty days after completion of the taking of that testimony. If the transcript with exhibits is not served on each adverse party within thirty days or within an extension of time for the purpose, any adverse party which was not served may have remedy by way of a motion to the Trademark Trial and Appeal Board to reset such adverse party's testimony and/or briefing periods, as may be appropriate. If the deposing party fails to serve a copy of the transcript with exhibits on an adverse party after having been ordered to do so by the Board, the Board, in its discretion, may strike the deposition, or enter judgment as by default against the deposing party, or take any such other action as may be deemed appropriate.

(c) The party who takes testimony is responsible for having all typographical errors in the transcript and all errors of arrangement, indexing and form of the transcript corrected, on notice to each adverse party, prior to the filing of one certified transcript with the Trademark Trial and Appeal Board. The party who takes testimony is responsible for serving on each adverse party one copy of the corrected transcript or, if reasonably feasible, corrected pages to be inserted into the transcript previously served.

(d) One certified transcript and exhibits shall be filed with the Trademark Trial and Appeal Board. Notice of such filing shall be served on each adverse party and a copy of each notice shall be filed with the Board.

(e) Each transcript shall comply with §2.123(g) with respect to arrangement, indexing and form.

(f) Upon motion by any party, for good cause, the Trademark Trial and Appeal Board may order that any part of an affidavit or declaration or a deposition transcript or any exhibits that directly disclose any trade secret or other confidential research, development, or commercial information may be filed under seal and kept confidential under the provisions of §2.27(e). If any party or any attorney or agent of a party fails to comply with an order made under this paragraph, the Board may impose any of the sanctions authorized by §2.120(h).

History of 37 C.F.R. §2.125: 37 FR 7608, Apr. 18, 1972; 48 FR 23140, May 23, 1983; 54 FR 34900, Aug. 22, 1989; 63 FR 48099, Sept. 9, 1998; 81 FR 69983, Jan. 14, 2017.

§2.126. FORM OF SUBMISSIONS TO THE TRADEMARK TRIAL & APPEAL BOARD

(a) Submissions must be made to the Trademark Trial and Appeal Board via ESTTA.

(1) Text in an electronic submission must be filed in at least 11-point type and double-spaced.

(2) Exhibits pertaining to an electronic submission must be made electronically as an attachment to the submission and must be clear and legible.

(b) In the event that ESTTA is unavailable due to technical problems, or when extraordinary circumstances are present, submissions may be filed in paper form. All submissions in paper form, except the extensions of time to file a notice of opposition, the notice of opposition, the petition to cancel, or answers thereto (see §§2.101(b)(2), 2.102(a)(2), 2.106(b)(1), 2.111(c)(2), and 2.114(b)(1)), must include a written explanation of such technical problems or extraordinary circumstances. Paper submissions that do not meet the showing required under this paragraph (b) will not be considered. A paper submission, including exhibits and depositions, must meet the following requirements:

(1) A paper submission must be printed in at least 11-point type and double-spaced, with text on one side only of each sheet;

(2) A paper submission must be 8 to 8.5 inches (20.3 to 21.6 cm.) wide and 11 to 11.69 inches (27.9 to 29.7 cm.) long, and contain no tabs or other such devices extending beyond the edges of the paper;

(3) If a paper submission contains dividers, the dividers must not have any extruding tabs or other devices, and must be on the same size and weight paper as the submission;

(4) A paper submission must not be stapled or bound;

(5) All pages of a paper submission must be numbered and exhibits shall be identified in the manner prescribed in §2.123(g)(2);

(6) Exhibits pertaining to a paper submission must be filed on paper and comply with the requirements for a paper submission.

(c) To be handled as confidential, submissions to the Trademark Trial and Appeal Board that are confidential in whole or part pursuant to §2.125(f) must be submitted using the "Confidential" selection available in ESTTA or, where appropriate, under a separate paper cover. Both the submission and its cover must be marked confidential and must identify the case number and the parties. A copy of the submission for public viewing with the confidential portions redacted must be submitted concurrently.

History of 37 C.F.R. §2.126: 68 FR 55767, Sept. 26, 2003; 72 FR 42262, Nov. 1, 2007; 81 FR 69983, Jan. 14, 2017; 81 FR 89383, Jan. 14, 2017.

A §2.127. MOTIONS

(a) Every motion must be submitted in written form and must meet the requirements prescribed in §2.126. It shall contain a full statement of the grounds, and shall embody or be accompanied by a brief. Except as provided in paragraph (e)(1) of this section, a brief in response to a motion shall be filed within twenty days from the date of service of the motion unless another time is specified by the Trademark Trial and Appeal Board, or the time is extended by stipulation of the parties approved by the Board, or upon motion granted by the Board, or upon order of the Board. If a motion for an extension is denied, the time for responding to the motion remains as specified under this section, unless otherwise ordered. Except as provided in paragraph (e)(1) of this section, a reply brief, if filed, shall be filed within twenty days from the date of service of the brief in response to the motion. The time for filing a reply brief will not be extended or reopened. The Board will consider no further papers in support of or in opposition to a motion. Neither the brief in support of a motion nor the brief in response to a motion shall exceed twenty-five pages in length in its entirety, including table of contents, index of cases, description of the record, statement of the issues, recitation of the facts, argument, and summary. A reply brief shall not exceed ten pages in length in its entirety. Exhibits submitted in support of or in opposition to a motion are not considered part of the brief for purposes of determining the length of the brief. When a party fails to file a brief in response to a motion, the Board may treat the motion as conceded. An oral hearing will not be held on a motion except on order by the Board.

(b) Any request for reconsideration or modification of an order or decision issued on a motion must be filed within one month from the date thereof. A brief in response must be filed within twenty days from the date of service of the request.

(c) Interlocutory motions, requests, conceded matters, and other matters not actually or potentially dispositive of a proceeding may be acted upon by a single Administrative Trademark Judge of the Trademark Trial and Appeal Board, or by an Interlocutory Attorney or Paralegal of the Board to whom authority to act has been delegated, or by ESTTA. Motions disposed of by orders entitled "By the Trademark Trial and Appeal Board" have the same legal effect as orders by a panel of three Administrative Trademark Judges of the Board.

(d) When any party timely files a potentially dispositive motion, including, but not limited to, a motion to dismiss, a motion for judgment on the pleadings, or a motion for summary judgment, the case is suspended by the Trademark Trial and Appeal Board with respect to all matters not germane to the motion and no party should file any paper which is not germane to the motion except as otherwise may be specified in a Board order. If the case is not disposed of as a result of the motion, proceedings will be resumed pursuant to an order of the Board when the motion is decided.

(e)(1) A party may not file a motion for summary judgment until the party has made its initial disclosures, except for a motion asserting claim or issue preclusion or lack of jurisdiction by the Trademark Trial and Appeal Board. A motion for summary judgment must be filed before the day of the deadline for pretrial disclosures for the first testimony period, as originally set or as reset. A motion under Rule 56(d) of the Federal Rules of Civil Procedure, if filed in response to a motion for summary judgment, shall be filed within thirty days from the date of service of the summary judgment motion. The time for filing a motion under Rule 56(d) will not be extended or reopened. If no motion under Rule 56(d) is filed, a brief in response to the motion for summary judgment shall be filed within thirty days from the date of service of the motion unless the time is extended by stipulation of the parties approved by the Board, or upon motion granted by the Board, or upon order of the Board. If a motion for an extension is denied, the time for responding to the motion for summary judgment may remain as specified under this section. A reply brief, if filed, shall be filed within twenty days from the date of service of the brief in response to the motion. The time for filing a reply brief will not be extended or reopened. The Board will consider no further papers in support of or in opposition to a motion for summary judgment.

(2) For purposes of summary judgment only, the Board will consider any of the following, if a copy is provided with the party's brief on the summary judgment motion: Written disclosures or disclosed documents, a discovery deposition or any part thereof with any exhibit to the part that is filed, an interrogatory and answer thereto with any exhibit made part of the answer, a request for production and the documents or things produced in response thereto, or a request for admission and any exhibit thereto and the admission (or a statement that the party from which an admission was requested failed to respond thereto). If any motion for summary judgment is denied, the parties may stipulate that the materials submitted with briefs on the motion be considered at trial as trial evidence, which may be supplemented by additional evidence during trial.

(f) The Board will not hold any person in contempt, or award attorneys' fees or other expenses to any party.

History of 37 C.F.R. §2.127: 30 FR 13193, Oct. 16, 1965; 37 FR 7608, Apr. 18, 1972; 41 FR 760, Jan. 5, 1976; 48 FR 23140, May 23, 1983; 54 FR 34900, Aug. 22, 1989; 63 FR 48099, Sept. 9, 1998; 63 FR 52159, Sept. 30, 1998; 68 FR 55768, Sept. 26, 2003; 72 FR 42262, Aug. 31, 2007; 81 FR 69983, Jan. 14, 2017; 82 FR 33806, July 21, 2017.

§2.128. BRIEFS AT FINAL HEARING

(a)(1) The brief of the party in the position of plaintiff shall be due not later than sixty days after the date set for the close of rebuttal testimony. The brief of the party in the position of defendant, if filed, shall be due not later than thirty days after the due date of the first brief. A reply brief by the party in the position of plaintiff, if filed, shall be due not later than fifteen days after the due date of the defendant's brief.

(2) When there is a counterclaim, or when proceedings have been consolidated and one party is in the position of plaintiff in one of the involved proceedings and in the position of defendant in another of the involved proceedings, or when there is an interference or a concurrent use registration proceeding involving more than two parties, the Trademark Trial and Appeal Board will set the due dates for the filing of the main brief, and the answering brief, and the rebuttal brief by the parties.

(3) When a party in the position of plaintiff fails to file a main brief, an order may be issued allowing plaintiff until a set time, not less than fifteen days, in which to show cause why the Board should not treat such failure as a concession of the case. If plaintiff fails to file a response to the order, or files a response indicating that plaintiff has lost interest in the case, judgment may be entered against plaintiff. If a plaintiff files a response to the order showing good cause, but does not have any evidence of record and does not move to reopen its testimony period and make a showing of excusable neglect sufficient to support such reopening, judgment may be entered against plaintiff for failure to take testimony or submit any other evidence.

(b) Briefs must be submitted in written form and must meet the requirements prescribed in §2.126. Each brief shall contain an alphabetical index of cited cases. Without prior leave of the Trademark Trial and Appeal Board, a main brief on the case shall not exceed fifty-five pages in length in its entirety, including the table of contents, index of cases, description of the record, statement of the issues, recitation of the facts, argument, and summary; and a reply brief shall not exceed twenty-five pages in its entirety. Evidentiary objections that may properly be raised in a party's brief on the case may instead be raised in an appendix or by way of a separate statement of objections. The appendix or separate statement is not included within the page limit. Any brief beyond the page limits and any brief with attachments outside the stated requirements may not be considered by the Board.

History of 37 C.F.R. §2.128: 30 FR 13193, Oct. 16, 1965; 37 FR 7608, Apr. 18, 1972; 48 FR 23140, May 23, 1983; 48 FR 27226, June 14, 1983; 54 FR 34900, Aug. 22, 1989; 68 FR 55768, Sept. 26, 2003; 81 FR 69984, Jan. 14, 2017.

§2.129. ORAL ARGUMENT; RECONSIDERATION

(a) If a party desires to have an oral argument at final hearing, the party shall request such argument by a separate notice filed not later than ten days after the due date for the filing of the last reply brief in the proceeding. Oral arguments will be heard by at least three Administrative Trademark Judges or other statutory members of the Trademark Trial and Appeal Board at the time specified in the notice of hearing. If any party appears at the specified time, that party will be heard. Parties and members of the Board may attend in person or, at the discretion of the Board, remotely. If the Board is prevented from hearing the case at the specified time, a new hearing date will be set. Unless otherwise permitted, oral arguments in an inter partes case will be limited to thirty minutes for each party. A party in the position of plaintiff may reserve part of the time allowed for oral argument to present a rebuttal argument.

(b) The date or time of a hearing may be reset, so far as is convenient and proper, to meet the wishes of the parties and their attorneys or other authorized representatives. The Board may, however, deny a request to reset a hearing date for lack of good cause or if multiple requests for rescheduling have been filed.

(c) Any request for rehearing or reconsideration or modification of a decision issued after final hearing must be filed within one month from the date of the decision. A brief in response must be filed within twenty days from the date of service of the request. The times specified may be extended by order of the Trademark Trial and Appeal Board on motion for good cause.

(d) When a party to an inter partes proceeding before the Trademark Trial and Appeal Board cannot prevail without establishing constructive use pursuant to section 7(c) of the Act in an application under section 1(b) of the Act, the Trademark Trial and Appeal Board will enter a judgment in favor of that party, subject to the party's establishment of constructive use. The time for filing an appeal or for commencing a civil action under section 21 of the Act shall run from the date of the entry of the judgment.

History of 37 C.F.R. §2.129: 30 FR 13193, Oct. 16, 1965; 37 FR 7608, Apr. 18, 1972; 41 FR 760, Jan. 5, 1976; 48 FR 23141, May 23, 1983; 54 FR 29544, July 13, 1989; 54 FR 34900, Aug. 22, 1989; 54 FR 37597, Sept. 11, 1989; 72 FR 42263, Aug. 31, 2007; 81 FR 69984, Jan. 14, 2017.

§2.130. NEW MATTER SUGGESTED BY THE TRADEMARK EXAMINING ATTORNEY

If, while an inter partes proceeding involving an application under section 1 or 44 of the Act is pending, facts appear which, in the opinion of the examining attorney, render the mark in the application unregistrable, the examining attorney should request that the Board remand the application. The Board may suspend the proceeding and remand the application to the trademark examining attorney for an ex parte determination of the question of registrability. A copy of the trademark examining attorney's final action will be furnished to the parties to the inter partes proceeding following the final determination of registrability by the trademark examining attorney or the Board on appeal. The Board will consider the application for such further inter partes action as may be appropriate.

History of 37 C.F.R. §2.130: 68 FR 55768, Sept. 26, 2003; 81 FR 69985, Jan. 14, 2017.

§2.131. REMAND AFTER DECISION IN INTER PARTES PROCEEDING

If, during an inter partes proceeding involving an application under section 1 or 44 of the Act, facts are disclosed which appear to render the mark unregistrable, but such matter has not been tried under the pleadings as filed by the parties or as they might be deemed to be amended under Rule 15(b) of the Federal Rules of Civil Procedure to conform to the evidence, the Trademark Trial and Appeal Board, in lieu of determining the matter in the decision on the proceeding, may remand the application to the trademark examining attorney for reexamination in the event the applicant ultimately prevails in the inter partes proceeding. Upon remand, the trademark examining attorney shall reexamine the application in light of the matter referenced by the Board. If, upon reexamination, the trademark examining attorney finally refuses registration to the applicant, an appeal may be taken as provided by §§2.141 and 2.142.

History of 37 C.F.R. §2.131: 30 FR 13193, Oct. 16, 1965; 48 FR 23141, May 23, 1983; 68 FR 55768, Sept. 26, 2003; 81 FR 69985, Jan. 14, 2017.

§2.132. INVOLUNTARY DISMISSAL FOR FAILURE TO TAKE TESTIMONY

(a) If the time for taking testimony by any party in the position of plaintiff has expired and it is clear to the Board from the proceeding record that such party has not taken testimony or offered any other evidence, the Board may grant judgment for the defendant. Also, any party in the position of defendant may, without waiving the right to offer evidence in the event the motion is denied, move for dismissal on the ground of the failure of the plaintiff to prosecute. The party in the position of plaintiff shall have twenty days from the date of service of the motion to show cause why judgment should not be rendered dismissing the case. In the absence of a showing of excusable neglect, judgment may be rendered against the party in the position of plaintiff. If the motion is denied, testimony periods will be reset for the party in the position of defendant and for rebuttal.

(b) If no evidence other than Office records showing the current status and title of plaintiff's pleaded registration(s) is offered by any party in the position of plaintiff, any party in the position of defendant may, without waiving the right to offer evidence in the event the motion is denied, move for dismissal on the ground that upon the law and the facts the party in the position of plaintiff has shown no right to relief. The party in the position of plaintiff shall have twenty days from the date of service of the motion to file a brief in response to the motion. The Trademark Trial and Appeal Board may render judgment against the party in the position of plaintiff, or the Board may decline to render judgment until all testimony periods have passed. If judgment is not rendered on the motion to dismiss, testimony periods will be reset for the party in the position of defendant and for rebuttal.

(c) A motion filed under paragraph (a) or (b) of this section must be filed before the opening of the testimony period of the moving party, except that the Trademark Trial and Appeal Board may in its discretion grant a motion under paragraph (a) even if the motion was filed after the opening of the testimony period of the moving party.

History of 37 C.F.R. §2.132: 30 FR 13193, Oct. 16, 1965; 48 FR 23141, May 23, 1983; 51 FR 28710, Aug. 11, 1986; 81 FR 69985, Jan. 14, 2017.

§2.133. AMENDMENT OF APPLICATION OR REGISTRATION DURING PROCEEDINGS

(a) An application subject to an opposition may not be amended in substance nor may a registration subject to a cancellation be amended or disclaimed in part, except with the consent of the other party or parties and the approval of the Trademark Trial and Appeal Board, or upon motion granted by the Board.

(b) If, in an inter partes proceeding, the Trademark Trial and Appeal Board finds that a party whose application or registration is the subject of the proceeding is not entitled to registration in the absence of a specified restriction to the application or registration, the Board will allow the party time in which to file a motion that the application or registration be amended to conform to the findings of the Board, failing which judgment will be entered against the party.

(c) Geographic limitations will be considered and determined by the Trademark Trial and Appeal Board only in the context of a concurrent use registration proceeding.

(d) A plaintiff's pleaded registration will not be restricted in the absence of a counterclaim to cancel the registration in whole or in part, except that a counterclaim need not be filed if the registration is the subject of another proceeding between the same parties or anyone in privity therewith.

History of 37 C.F.R. §2.133: 54 FR 37597, Sept. 11, 1989; 72 FR 42263, Aug. 31, 2007.

§2.134. SURRENDER OR VOLUNTARY CANCELLATION OF REGISTRATION

(a) After the commencement of a cancellation proceeding, if the respondent applies for cancellation of the involved registration under section 7(e) of the Act of 1946 without the written consent of every adverse party to the proceeding, judgment shall be entered against the respondent. The written consent of an adverse party may be signed by the adverse party or by the adverse party's attorney or other authorized representative.

(b) After the commencement of a cancellation proceeding, if it comes to the attention of the Trademark Trial and Appeal Board that the respondent has permitted its involved registration to be cancelled under section 8 or section 71 of the Act of 1946, or has failed to renew its involved registration under section 9 of the Act of 1946, or has allowed its registered extension of protection to expire under section 70(b) of the Act of 1946, an order may be issued allowing respondent until a set time, not less than fifteen days, in which to show cause why such cancellation, failure to renew, or expiration should not be deemed to be the equivalent of a cancellation by request of respondent without the consent of the adverse party and should not result in entry of judgment against respondent as provided by paragraph (a) of this section. In the absence of a showing of good and sufficient cause, judgment may be entered against respondent as provided by paragraph (a) of this section.

History of 37 C.F.R. §2.134: 30 FR 13193, Oct. 16, 1965; 48 FR 23141, May 23, 1983; 54 FR 34900, Aug. 22, 1989; 63 FR 48100, Sept. 9, 1998; 81 FR 69985, Jan. 14, 2017.

§2.135. ABANDONMENT OF APPLICATION OR MARK

After the commencement of an opposition, concurrent use, or interference proceeding, if the applicant files a written abandonment of the application or of the mark without the written consent of every adverse party to the proceeding, judgment shall be entered against the applicant. The written consent of an adverse party may be signed by the adverse party or by the adverse party's attorney or other authorized representative.

History of 37 C.F.R. §2.135: 30 FR 13193, Oct. 16, 1965; 48 FR 23141, May 23, 1983; 54 FR 34900, Aug. 22, 1989.

§2.136. STATUS OF APPLICATION OR REGISTRATION ON TERMINATION OF PROCEEDING

After the Board has issued its decision in an opposition, cancellation or concurrent use proceeding, and after the time for filing any appeal of the decision has expired, or any appeal that was filed has been decided and the Board's decision affirmed, the proceeding will be terminated by the Board. On termination of an opposition, cancellation or concurrent use proceeding, if the judgment is not adverse to the applicant or registrant, the subject application returns to the status it had before the institution of the proceeding and the otherwise appropriate status of the subject registration is unaffected by the proceeding. If the judgment is adverse to the applicant or registrant, the application stands refused or the registration will be cancelled in whole or in part without further action and all proceedings thereon are considered terminated.

History of 37 C.F.R. §2.136: 81 FR 69985, Jan. 14, 2017.

APPEALS

§2.141. EX PARTE APPEALS FROM ACTION OF TRADEMARK EXAMINING ATTORNEY

(a) An applicant may, upon final refusal by the trademark examining attorney, appeal to the Trademark Trial and Appeal Board upon payment of the prescribed fee for each class in the application for which an appeal is taken, within six months of the date of issuance of the final action. A second refusal on the same grounds may be considered as final by the applicant for purpose of appeal.

(b) The applicant must pay an appeal fee for each class from which the appeal is taken. If the applicant does not pay an appeal fee for at least one class of goods or services before expiration of the six-month statutory filing period, the application will be abandoned. In a multiple-class application, if an appeal fee is submitted for fewer than all classes, the applicant must specify the class(es) in which the appeal is taken. If the applicant timely submits a fee sufficient to pay for an appeal in at least one class, but insufficient to cover all the classes, and the applicant has not specified the class(es) to which the fee applies, the Board will issue a written notice setting a time limit in which the applicant may either pay the additional fees or specify the class(es) being appealed. If the applicant does not submit the required fee or specify the class(es) being appealed within the set time period, the Board will apply the fee(s) to the class(es) in ascending order, beginning with the lowest numbered class.

History of 37 C.F.R. §2.141: 41 FR 760, Jan. 5, 1976; 73 FR 67772, Jan. 16, 2009.

§2.142. TIME & MANNER OF EX PARTE APPEALS

(a) Any appeal filed under the provisions of §2.141 must be filed within six months from the date of the final refusal or the date of the action from which the appeal is taken. An appeal is taken by filing a notice of appeal in written form, as prescribed in §2.126, and paying the appeal fee.

(b)(1) The brief of appellant shall be filed within sixty days from the date of appeal. If the brief is not filed within the time allowed, the appeal may be dismissed. The examining attorney shall, within sixty days after the brief of appellant is sent to the examining attorney, file with the Trademark Trial and Appeal Board a written brief answering the brief of appellant and shall email or mail a copy of the brief to the appellant. The appellant may file a reply brief within twenty days from the date of mailing of the brief of the examining attorney.

(2) Briefs must meet the requirements prescribed in §2.126, except examining attorney submissions need not be filed through ESTTA. Without prior leave of the Trademark Trial and Appeal Board, a brief shall not exceed twenty-five pages in length in its entirety, including the table of contents, index of cases, description of the record, statement of the issues, recitation of the facts, argument, and summary. A reply brief from the appellant, if any, shall not exceed ten pages in length in its entirety. Unless authorized by the Board, no further briefs are permitted.

(3) Citation to evidence in briefs should be to the documents in the electronic application record by date, the name of the paper under which the evidence was submitted, and the page number in the electronic record.

(c) All requirements made by the examining attorney and not the subject of appeal shall be complied with prior to the filing of an appeal, and the statement of issues in the brief should note such compliance.

(d) The record in the application should be complete prior to the filing of an appeal. Evidence should not be filed with the Board after the filing of a notice of appeal. If the appellant or the examining attorney desires to introduce additional evidence after an appeal is filed, the appellant or the examining attorney should submit a request to the Board to suspend the appeal and to remand the application for further examination.

(e)(1) If the appellant desires an oral hearing, a request should be made by a separate notice filed not later than ten days after the due date for a reply brief. Oral argument will be heard by at least three Administrative Trademark Judges or other statutory members of the Trademark Trial and Appeal Board at the time specified in the notice of hearing, which may be reset if the Board is prevented from hearing the argument at the specified time or, so far as is convenient and proper, to meet the wish of the appellant or the appellant's attorney or other authorized representative. Appellants, examining attorneys, and members of the Board may attend in person or, at the discretion of the Board, remotely.

(2) If the appellant requests an oral argument, the examining attorney who issued the refusal of registration or the requirement from which the appeal is taken, or in lieu thereof another examining attorney as designated by a supervisory or managing attorney, shall present an oral argument. If no request for an oral hearing is made by the appellant, the appeal will be decided on the record and briefs.

(3) Oral argument will be limited to twenty minutes by the appellant and ten minutes by the examining attorney. The appellant may reserve part of the time allowed for oral argument to present a rebuttal argument.

(f)(1) If, during an appeal from a refusal of registration, it appears to the Trademark Trial and Appeal Board that an issue not previously raised may render the mark of the appellant unregistrable, the Board may suspend the appeal and remand the application to the examining attorney for further examination to be completed within the time set by the Board.

(2) If the further examination does not result in an additional ground for refusal of registration, the examining attorney shall promptly return the application to the Board, for resumption of the appeal, with a written statement that further examination did not result in an additional ground for refusal of registration.

(3) If the further examination does result in an additional ground for refusal of registration, the examining attorney and appellant shall proceed as provided by §§2.61, 2.62, and 2.63. If the ground for refusal is made final, the examining attorney shall return the application to the Board, which shall thereupon issue an order allowing the appellant sixty days from the date of the order to file a supplemental brief limited to the additional ground for the refusal of registration. If the supplemental brief is not filed by the appellant within the time allowed, the appeal may be dismissed.

(4) If the supplemental brief of the appellant is filed, the examining attorney shall, within sixty days after the supplemental brief of the appellant is sent to the examining attorney, file with the Board a written brief answering the supplemental brief of appellant and shall email or mail a copy of the brief to the appellant. The appellant may file a reply brief within twenty days from the date of mailing of the brief of the examining attorney.

(5) If an oral hearing on the appeal had been requested prior to the remand of the application but not yet held, an oral hearing will be set and heard as provided in paragraph (e) of this section. If an oral hearing had been held prior to the remand or had not been previously requested by the appellant, an oral hearing may be requested by the appellant by a separate notice filed not later than ten days after the due date for a reply brief on the additional ground for refusal of registration. If the appellant files a request for an oral hearing, one will be set and heard as provided in paragraph (e) of this section.

(6) If, during an appeal from a refusal of registration, it appears to the examining attorney that an issue not involved in the appeal may render the mark of the appellant unregistrable, the examining attorney may, by written request, ask the Board to suspend the appeal and to remand the application to the examining attorney for further examination. If the request is granted, the examining attorney and appellant shall proceed as provided by §§2.61, 2.62, and 2.63. After the additional ground for refusal of registration has been withdrawn or made final, the examining attorney shall return the application to the Board, which shall resume proceedings in the appeal and take further appropriate action with respect thereto.

(g) An application which has been considered and decided on appeal will not be reopened except for the entry of a disclaimer under section 6 of the Act of 1946 or upon order of the Director, but a petition to the Director to reopen an application will be considered only upon a showing of sufficient cause for consideration of any matter not already adjudicated.

History of 37 C.F.R. §2.142: 30 FR 13193, Oct. 16, 1965; 48 FR 23141, May 23, 1983; 54 FR 34901, Aug. 22, 1989; 68 FR 55768, Sept. 26, 2003; 72 FR 42263, Aug. 31, 2007; 80 FR 2312, Jan. 16, 2015; 81 FR 69985, Jan. 14, 2017.

§2.143. [ADDED & RESERVED]

§2.144. RECONSIDERATION OF DECISION ON EX PARTE APPEAL

Any request for rehearing or reconsideration, or modification of the decision, must be filed within one month from the date of the decision. Such time may be extended by the Trademark Trial and Appeal Board upon a showing of sufficient cause.

History of 37 C.F.R. §2.144: 41 FR 760, Jan. 5, 1976; 54 FR 29544, July 13, 1989.

§2.145. APPEAL TO COURT & CIVIL ACTION

(a) For an Appeal to the United States Court of Appeals for the Federal Circuit under section 21(a) of the Act. **(1)** An applicant for registration, or any party to an interference, opposition, or cancellation proceeding or any party to an application to register as a concurrent user, hereinafter referred to as inter partes proceedings, who is dissatisfied with the decision of the Trademark Trial and Appeal Board, and any registrant who has filed an affidavit or declaration under section 8 or section 71 of the Act or who has filed an application for renewal and is dissatisfied with the decision of the Director (§§2.165, 2.184), may appeal to the United States Court of Appeals for the Federal Circuit. It is unnecessary to request reconsideration by the Board before filing any such appeal; however, a party requesting reconsideration must do so before filing a notice of appeal.

(2) In all appeals under section 21(a), the appellant must take the following steps:

(i) File the notice of appeal with the Director, addressed to the Office of the General Counsel, as provided in §104.2 of this chapter;

(ii) File a copy of the notice of appeal with the Trademark Trial and Appeal Board via ESTTA; and

(iii) Comply with the requirements of the Federal Rules of Appellate Procedure and Rules for the United States Court of Appeals for the Federal Circuit, including serving the requisite number of copies on the Court and paying the requisite fee for the appeal.

(3) Additional requirements. **(i)** The notice of appeal shall specify the party or parties taking the appeal and shall designate the decision or part thereof appealed from.

(ii) In inter partes proceedings, the notice of appeal must be served as provided in §2.119.

(b) For a notice of election under section 21(a)(1) to proceed under section 21(b) of the Act. **(1)** Any applicant or registrant in an ex parte case who takes an appeal to the United States Court of Appeals for the Federal Circuit waives any right to proceed under section 21(b) of the Act.

(2) If an adverse party to an appeal taken to the United States Court of Appeals for the Federal Circuit by a defeated party in an inter partes proceeding elects to have all further review proceedings conducted under section 21(b) of the Act, that party must take the following steps:

(i) File a notice of election with the Director, addressed to the Office of the General Counsel, as provided in §104.2 of this chapter;

(ii) File a copy of the notice of election with the Trademark Trial and Appeal Board via ESTTA; and

(iii) Serve the notice of election as provided in §2.119.

(c) For a civil action under section 21(b) of the Act. **(1)** Any person who may appeal to the United States Court of Appeals for the Federal Circuit (paragraph (a) of this section), may have remedy by civil action under section 21(b) of the Act. It is unnecessary to request reconsideration by the Board before filing any such civil action; however, a party requesting reconsideration must do so before filing a civil action.

(2) Any applicant or registrant in an ex parte case who seeks remedy by civil action under section 21(b) of the Act must serve the summons and complaint pursuant to Rule 4(i) of the Federal Rules of Civil Procedure with the copy to the Director addressed to the Office of the General Counsel as provided in §104.2 of this chapter. A copy of the complaint must also be filed with the Trademark Trial and Appeal Board via ESTTA.

(3) The party initiating an action for review of a Board decision in an inter partes case under section 21(b) of the Act must file notice thereof with the Trademark Trial and Appeal Board via ESTTA no later than five business days after filing the complaint in the district court. The notice must identify the civil action with particularity by providing the case name, case number, and court in which it was filed. A copy of the complaint may be filed with the notice. Failure to file the required notice can result in termination of the Board proceeding and further action within the United States Patent and Trademark Office consistent with the final Board decision.

(d) Time for appeal or civil action—**(1)** For an appeal under section 21(a). The notice of appeal filed pursuant to section 21(a) of the Act must be filed with the Director no later than sixty-three (63) days from the date of the final decision of the Trademark Trial and Appeal Board or the Director. In inter partes cases, the time for filing a notice of cross-appeal expires 14 days after service of the notice of appeal or 63 days from the date of the decision of the Trademark Trial and Appeal Board or the Director, whichever is later.

(2) For a notice of election under 21(a)(1) and a civil action pursuant to such notice of election. The times for filing a notice of election under section 21(a)(1) and for commencing a civil action pursuant to a notice of election are governed by section 21(a)(1) of the Act.

(3) For a civil action under section 21(b). A civil action must be commenced no later than sixty-three (63) days after the date of the final decision of the Trademark Trial and Appeal Board or Director. In inter partes cases, the time for filing a cross-action expires 14 days after service of the summons and complaint or 63 days from the date of the decision of the Trademark Trial and Appeal Board or the Director, whichever is later.

(4) Time computation. **(i)** If a request for rehearing or reconsideration or modification of the Board decision is filed within the time specified in §2.127(b), §2.129(c), or §2.144, or within any extension of time granted thereunder, the time for filing an appeal or commencing a civil action shall expire no later than sixty-three (63) days after action on the request.

(ii) Holidays. The times specified in this section in days are calendar days. If the last day of time specified for an appeal, notice of election, or commencing a civil action falls on a Saturday, Sunday or Federal holiday in the District of Columbia, the time is extended to the next day which is neither a Saturday, Sunday nor a Federal holiday in the District of Columbia pursuant to §2.196.

(e) Extension of time. **(1)** The Director, or the Director's designee, may extend the time for filing an appeal, or commencing a civil action, upon written request if:

(i) Requested before the expiration of the period for filing an appeal or commencing a civil action, and upon a showing of good cause; or

(ii) Requested after the expiration of the period for filing an appeal or commencing a civil action, and upon a showing that the failure to act was the result of excusable neglect.

(2) The request must be filed as provided in §104.2 of this chapter and addressed to the attention of the Office of the Solicitor. A copy of the request should also be filed with the Trademark Trial and Appeal Board via ESTTA.

History of 37 C.F.R. §2.145: 37 FR 9476, May 11, 1972; 41 FR 761, Jan. 5, 1976; 41 FR 16147, Apr. 16, 1976; 47 FR 47382, Oct. 26, 1982; 51 FR 28710, Aug. 11, 1986; 53 FR 16414, May 9, 1988; 54 FR 29554, July 13, 1989; 54 FR 34901, Aug. 22, 1989; 58 FR 54503, Oct. 22, 1993; 68 FR 14337, Mar. 25, 2003; 68 FR 55769, Sept. 26, 2003; 80 FR 2312, Jan. 16, 2015; 81 FR 69986, Jan. 14, 2017; 81 FR 89383, Jan. 14, 2017.

PETITIONS & ACTION BY THE DIRECTOR

A §2.146. PETITIONS TO THE DIRECTOR

(a) Petition may be taken to the Director:

(1) From any repeated or final formal requirement of the examiner in the ex parte prosecution of an application if permitted by §2.63(a) and (b);

(2) In any case for which the Act of 1946, or Title 35 of the United States Code, or this Part of Title 37 of the Code of Federal Regulations specifies that the matter is to be determined directly or reviewed by the Director;

(3) To invoke the supervisory authority of the Director in appropriate circumstances;

(4) In any case not specifically defined and provided for by this Part of Title 37 of the Code of Federal Regulations; or

(5) In an extraordinary situation, when justice requires and no other party is injured thereby, to request a suspension or waiver of any requirement of the rules not being a requirement of the Act of 1946.

(b) Questions of substance arising during the ex parte prosecution of applications, including, but not limited to, questions arising under sections 2, 3, 4, 5, 6, and 23 of the Act of 1946, are not appropriate subject matter for petitions to the Director.

(c) Every petition to the Director shall include a statement of the facts relevant to the petition, the points to be reviewed, the action or relief requested, and the fee required by §2.6. Any brief in support of the petition shall be embodied in or accompany the petition. The petition must be signed by the petitioner, someone with legal authority to bind the petitioner (e.g., a corporate officer or general partner of a partnership), or a practitioner qualified to practice under §11.14 of this chapter, in accordance with the requirements of §2.193(e)(5). When facts are to be proved on petition, the petitioner must submit proof in the form of verified statements signed by someone with firsthand knowledge of the facts to be proved, and any exhibits.

(d) Unless a different deadline is specified elsewhere in this chapter, a petition under this section must be filed by not later than:

(1) Two months after the issue date of the action, or date of receipt of the filing, from which relief is requested; or

(2) Where the applicant or registrant declares under §2.20 or 28 U.S.C. 1746 that it did not receive the action, or where no action was issued, the petition must be filed by not later than:

(i) Two months of actual knowledge of the abandonment of an application and not later than six months after the date the trademark electronic records system indicates that the application is abandoned in full or in part;

(ii) Where the registrant has timely filed an affidavit of use or excusable non-use under Section 8 or 71 of the Act, or a renewal application under Section 9 of the Act, two months after the date of actual knowledge of the cancellation/expiration of a registration and not later than six months after the date the trademark electronic records system indicates that the registration is cancelled/expired; or

(iii) Two months after the date of actual knowledge of the denial of certification of an international application under §7.13(b) and not later than six months after the trademark electronic records system indicates that certification is denied.

(e)(1) A petition from the grant or denial of a request for an extension of time to file a notice of opposition must be filed by not later than fifteen days after the issue date of the grant or denial of the request. A petition from the grant of a request must be served on the attorney or other authorized representative of the potential opposer, if any, or on the potential opposer. A petition from the denial of a request must be served on the attorney or other authorized representative of the applicant, if any, or on the applicant. Proof of service of the petition must be made as provided by §2.119. The potential opposer or the applicant, as the case may be, may file a response by not later than fifteen days after the date of service of the petition and must serve a copy of the response on the petitioner, with proof of service as provided by §2.119. No further document relating to the petition may be filed.

(2) A petition from an interlocutory order of the Trademark Trial and Appeal Board must be filed by not later than thirty days after the issue date of the order from which relief is requested. Any brief in response to the petition must be filed, with any supporting exhibits, by not later than fifteen days after the date of service of the petition. Petitions and responses to petitions, and any documents accompanying a petition or response under this subsection, must be served on every adverse party pursuant to §2.119.

(f) An oral hearing will not be held on a petition except when considered necessary by the Director.

(g) The mere filing of a petition to the Director will not act as a stay in any appeal or inter partes proceeding that is pending before the Trademark Trial and Appeal Board, nor stay the period for replying to an Office action in an application, except when a stay is specifically requested and is granted or when §§2.63(a) and (b) and 2.65(a) are applicable to an ex parte application.

(h) Authority to act on petitions, or on any petition, may be delegated by the Director.

(i) If the Director denies a petition, the petitioner may request reconsideration, if:

(1) The petitioner files the request by not later than:

(i) Two months after the issue date of the decision denying the petition; or

(ii) Two months after the date of actual knowledge of the decision denying the petition and not later than six months after the issue date of the decision where the petitioner declares under §2.20 or 28 U.S.C. 1746 that it did not receive the decision; and

(2) The petitioner pays a second petition fee under §2.6.

History of 37 C.F.R. §2.146: 30 FR 13193, Oct. 16, 1965; 48 FR 23142, May 23, 1983; 48 FR 27226, June 14, 1983; 63 FR 48100, Sept. 9, 1998; 64 FR 48924, Sept. 8, 1999; 68 FR 55769, Sept. 26, 2003; 73 FR 67773, Jan. 16, 2009; 74 FR 54909, Dec. 28, 2009; 80 FR 2312, Jan. 16, 2015; 80 FR 33188, July 11, 2015; 82 FR 29409, July 8, 2017.

§2.147. RESERVED

§2.148. DIRECTOR MAY SUSPEND CERTAIN RULES

In an extraordinary situation, when justice requires and no other party is injured thereby, any requirement of the rules in this part not being a requirement of the statute may be suspended or waived by the Director.

CERTIFICATE

§2.151. CERTIFICATE

When the Office determines that a mark is registrable, the Office will issue a certificate stating that the applicant is entitled to registration on the Principal Register or on the Supplemental Register. The certificate will state the application filing date, the act under which the mark is registered, the date of issue, and the number of the registration. A reproduction of the mark and pertinent data from the application will be sent with the certificate. A notice of the requirements of sections 8 and 71 of the Act will accompany the certificate.

History of 37 C.F.R. §2.151: 64 FR 48924, Sept. 8, 1999; 68 FR 55769, Sept. 26, 2003.

PUBLICATION OF MARKS REGISTERED UNDER 1905 ACT

§2.153. PUBLICATION REQUIREMENTS

The owner of a mark registered under the provisions of the Trademark Act of 1881 or 1905 may at any time prior to the expiration of the period for which the registration was issued or renewed, upon the payment of the prescribed fee, file an affidavit or declaration in accordance with §2.20 setting forth those goods or services in the registration on or in connection with which said mark is in use in commerce, and stating that the owner claims the benefits of the Act of 1946. The affidavit or declaration must be signed by a person properly authorized to sign on behalf of the owner under §2.193(e)(1).

History of 37 C.F.R. §2.153: 31 FR 5262, Apr. 1, 1966; 73 FR 67773, Jan. 16, 2009; 74 FR 54909, Dec. 28, 2009.

§2.154. PUBLICATION IN OFFICIAL GAZETTE

A notice of the claim of benefits under the Act of 1946 and a reproduction of the mark will then be published in the Official Gazette as soon as practicable. The published mark will retain its original registration number.

§2.155. NOTICE OF PUBLICATION

The Office will send the registrant a notice of publication of the mark and of the requirement for filing the affidavit or declaration required by section 8 of the Act.

History of 37 C.F.R. §2.155: 64 FR 48924, Sept. 8, 1999.

§2.156. NOT SUBJECT TO OPPOSITION; SUBJECT TO CANCELLATION

The published mark is not subject to opposition, but is subject to petitions to cancel as specified in §2.111 and to cancellation for failure to file the affidavit or declaration required by section 8 of the Act.

History of 37 C.F.R. §2.156: 64 FR 48924, Sept. 8, 1999.

REREGISTRATION OF MARKS REGISTERED UNDER PRIOR ACTS

§2.158. REREGISTRATION OF MARKS REGISTERED UNDER ACTS OF 1881, 1905, & 1920

Trademarks registered under the Act of 1881, the Act of 1905 or the Act of 1920 may be reregistered under the Act of 1946, either on the Principal Register, if eligible, or on the Supplemental Register, but a new complete application for registration must be filed complying with the rules relating thereto, and such application will be subject to examination and other proceedings in the same manner as other applications filed under the Act of 1946. See §2.26 for use of old drawing.

CANCELLATION FOR FAILURE TO FILE AFFIDAVIT OR DECLARATION

§2.160. AFFIDAVIT OR DECLARATION OF CONTINUED USE OR EXCUSABLE NONUSE REQUIRED TO AVOID CANCELLATION OF REGISTRATION

(a) During the following time periods, the owner of the registration must file an affidavit or declaration of continued use or excusable nonuse, or the registration will be cancelled:

(1)(i) For registrations issued under the Trademark Act of 1946, on or after the fifth anniversary and no later than the sixth anniversary after the date of registration; or

(ii) For registrations issued under prior Acts, on or after the fifth anniversary and no later than the sixth anniversary after the date of publication under section 12(c) of the Act; and

(2) For all registrations, within the year before the end of every ten-year period after the date of registration.

(3) The affidavit or declaration may be filed within a grace period of six months after the end of the deadline set forth in paragraphs (a)(1) and (a)(2) of this section, with payment of the grace period surcharge per class required by section 8(a)(3) of the Act and §2.6.

(b) For the requirements for the affidavit or declaration, see §2.161.

History of 37 C.F.R. §2.160: 64 FR 48924, Sept. 8, 1999; 73 FR 67773, Jan. 16, 2009; 75 FR 35976, June 24, 2010.

§2.161. REQUIREMENTS FOR A COMPLETE AFFIDAVIT OR DECLARATION OF CONTINUED USE OR EXCUSABLE NONUSE

A complete affidavit or declaration under section 8 of the Act must:

(a) Be filed by the owner within the period set forth in §2.160(a);

(b) Include a verified statement attesting to the use in commerce or excusable nonuse of the mark within the period set forth in section 8 of the Act. This verified statement must be executed on or after the beginning of the filing period specified in §2.160(a);

(c) Include the U.S. registration number;

(d)(1) Include the fee required by §2.6 for each class that the affidavit or declaration covers;

(2) If the affidavit or declaration is filed during the grace period under section 8(a)(3) of the Act, include the grace period surcharge per class required by §2.6;

(3) If at least one fee is submitted for a multiple-class registration, but the fee is insufficient to cover all the classes, and the class(es) to which the fee(s) should be applied are not specified, the Office will issue a notice requiring either submission of the additional fee(s) or specification of the class(es) to which the initial fee(s) should be applied. Additional fee(s) may be submitted if the requirements of §2.164 are met. If the additional fee(s) are not submitted within the time period set out in the Office action and the class(es) to which the original fee(s) should be applied are not specified, the Office will presume that the fee(s) cover the classes in ascending order, beginning with the lowest numbered class;

(e)(1) Specify the goods, services, or nature of the collective membership organization for which the mark is in use in commerce, and/or the goods, services, or nature of the collective membership organization for which excusable nonuse is claimed under paragraph (f)(2) of this section; and

(2) Specify the goods, services, or classes being deleted from the registration, if the affidavit or declaration covers fewer than all the goods, services, or classes in the registration;

(f)(1) State that the registered mark is in use in commerce; or

(2) If the registered mark is not in use in commerce on or in connection with all the goods, services, or classes specified in the registration, set forth the date when such use of the mark in commerce stopped and the approximate date when such use is expected to resume; and recite facts to show that nonuse as to those goods, services, or classes is due to special circumstances that excuse the nonuse and is not due to an intention to abandon the mark; and

(g) Include one specimen showing how the mark is in use in commerce for each class in the registration, unless excusable nonuse is claimed under paragraph (f)(2) of this section. When requested by the Office, additional specimens must be provided. The specimen must meet the requirements of §2.56.

(h) The Office may require the owner to furnish such information, exhibits, affidavits or declarations, and such additional specimens as may be reasonably necessary to the proper examination of the affidavit or declaration under section 8 of the Act or for the Office to assess and promote the accuracy and integrity of the register.

(i) Additional requirements for a collective mark: In addition to the above requirements, a complete affidavit or declaration pertaining to a collective mark must:

(1) State that the owner is exercising legitimate control over the use of the mark in commerce; and

(2) If the registration issued from an application based solely on section 44 of the Act, state the nature of the owner's control over the use of the mark by the members in the first affidavit or declaration filed under paragraph (a) of this section.

(j) Additional requirements for a certification mark: In addition to the above requirements, a complete affidavit or declaration pertaining to a certification mark must:

(1) Include a copy of the certification standards specified in §2.45(a)(4)(i)(B);

(i) Submitting certification standards for the first time. If the registration issued from an application based solely on section 44 of the Act, include a copy of the certification standards in the first affidavit or declaration filed under paragraph (a) of this section; or

(ii) Certification standards submitted in prior filing. If the certification standards in use at the time of filing the affidavit or declaration have not changed since the date they were previously submitted to the Office, include a statement to that effect; if the certification standards in use at the time of filing the affidavit or declaration have changed since the date they were previously submitted to the Office, include a copy of the revised certification standards;

(2) State that the owner is exercising legitimate control over the use of the mark in commerce; and

(3) Satisfy the requirements of §2.45(a)(4)(i)(A) and (C).

(k) For requirements of a complete affidavit or declaration of use in commerce or excusable nonuse for a registration that issued from a section 66(a) basis application, see §7.37.

History of 37 C.F.R. §2.161: 41 FR 761, Jan. 5, 1976; 48 FR 3977, Jan. 28, 1983; 54 FR 37597, Sept. 11, 1989; 64 FR 48924, Sept. 8, 1999; 67 FR 79523, Dec. 30, 2002; 68 FR 55769, Sept. 26, 2003; 73 FR 47686, Sept. 15, 2008; 73 FR 67773, Jan. 16, 2009; 74 FR 54910, Dec. 28, 2009; 75 FR 35976, June 24, 2010; 77 FR 30207, June 21, 2012; 80 FR 33188, July 11, 2015; 82 FR 6265, Feb. 17, 2017; 82 FR 10273, Mar. 21, 2017.

§2.162. NOTICE TO REGISTRANT

When a certificate of registration is originally issued, the Office includes a notice of the requirement for filing the affidavit or declaration of use or excusable nonuse under section 8 of the Act. However the affidavit or declaration must be filed within the time period required by section 8 of the Act even if this notice is not received.

History of 37 C.F.R. §2.162: 41 FR 761, Jan. 5, 1976; 43 FR 35483, Aug. 10, 1978; 47 FR 41282, Sept. 17, 1982; 48 FR 3977, Jan. 28, 1983; 54 FR 37597, Sept. 11, 1989; 64 FR 48925, Sept. 8, 1999.

§2.163. ACKNOWLEDGMENT OF RECEIPT OF AFFIDAVIT OR DECLARATION

The Office will issue a notice as to whether an affidavit or declaration is acceptable, or the reasons for refusal.

(a) If the affidavit or declaration is filed within the time periods set forth in section 8 of the Act, deficiencies may be corrected after notification from the Office if the requirements of §2.164 are met.

(b) A response to the refusal must be filed within six months of the date of issuance of the Office action, or before the end of the filing period set forth in section 8(a) of the Act, whichever is later. The response must be signed by the owner, someone with legal authority to bind the owner (e.g., a corporate officer or general partner of a partnership), or a practitioner qualified to practice under §11.14 of this chapter, in accordance with the requirements of §2.193(e)(2).

(c) If no response is filed within this time period, the registration will be cancelled, unless time remains in the grace period under section 8(a)(3) of the Act. If time remains in the grace period, the owner may file a complete, new affidavit.

History of 37 C.F.R. §2.163: 64 FR 48925, Sept. 8, 1999; 73 FR 67773, Jan. 16, 2009; 74 FR 54910, Dec. 28, 2009; 75 FR 35976, June 24, 2010; 76 FR 69133, Nov. 8, 2011.

§2.164. CORRECTING DEFICIENCIES IN AFFIDAVIT OR DECLARATION

(a) If the affidavit or declaration is filed within the time periods set forth in section 8 of the Act, deficiencies may be corrected after notification from the Office, as follows:

(1) Correcting deficiencies in affidavits or declarations timely filed within the periods set forth in sections 8(a)(1) and 8(a)(2) of the Act. If the affidavit or declaration is timely filed within the relevant filing period set forth in section 8(a)(1) or section 8(a)(2) of the Act, deficiencies may be corrected before the end of this filing period without paying a deficiency surcharge. Deficiencies may be corrected after the end of this filing period with payment of the deficiency surcharge required by section 8(c) of the Act and §2.6.

(2) Correcting deficiencies in affidavits or declarations filed during the grace period. If the affidavit or declaration is filed during the six-month grace period provided by section 8(a)(3) of the Act, deficiencies may be corrected before the expiration of the grace period without paying a deficiency surcharge. Deficiencies may be corrected after the expiration of the grace period with payment of the deficiency surcharge required by section 8(c) of the Act and §2.6.

(b) If the affidavit or declaration is not filed within the time periods set forth in section 8 of the Act, the registration will be cancelled.

History of 37 C.F.R. §2.164: 64 FR 48925, Sept. 8, 1999; 75 FR 35976, June 24, 2010; 76 FR 69133, Nov. 8, 2011.

§2.165. PETITION TO DIRECTOR TO REVIEW REFUSAL

(a) A response to the examiner's initial refusal to accept an affidavit or declaration is required before filing a petition to the Director, unless the examiner directs otherwise. See §2.163(b) for the deadline for responding to an examiner's Office action.

(b) If the examiner maintains the refusal of the affidavit or declaration, the owner may file a petition to the Director to review the action. The petition must be filed within six months of the date of issuance of the action maintaining the refusal, or the Office will cancel the registration and issue a notice of the cancellation.

(c) A decision by the Director is necessary before filing an appeal or commencing a civil action in any court.

History of 37 C.F.R. §2.165: 30 FR 13193, Oct. 16, 1965; 48 FR 23143, May 23, 1983; 58 FR 54503, Oct. 22, 1993; 61 FR 56448, Nov. 1, 1996; 64 FR 48925, Sept. 8, 1999; 73 FR 67773, Jan. 16, 2009.

§2.166. AFFIDAVIT OF CONTINUED USE OR EXCUSABLE NONUSE COMBINED WITH RENEWAL APPLICATION

An affidavit or declaration under section 8 of the Act and a renewal application under section 9 of the Act may be combined into a single document, provided that the document meets the requirements of both sections 8 and 9 of the Act.

History of 37 C.F.R. §2.166: 64 FR 48925, Sept. 8, 1999.

AFFIDAVIT OR DECLARATION UNDER SECTION 15

§2.167. AFFIDAVIT OR DECLARATION UNDER SECTION 15

The affidavit or declaration in accordance with §2.20 provided by section 15 of the Act for acquiring incontestability for a mark registered on the Principal Register or a mark registered under the Trademark Act of 1881 or 1905 and published under section 12(c) of the Act (see §2.153) must:

(a) Be verified;

(b) Identify the certificate of registration by the certificate number and date of registration;

(c) For a trademark, service mark, collective trademark, collective service mark, and certification mark, recite the goods or services stated in the registration on or in connection with which the mark has been in continuous use in commerce for a period of five years after the date of registration or date of publication under section 12(c) of the Act, and is still in use in commerce; for a collective membership mark, describe the nature of the owner's collective membership organization specified in the registration in connection with which the mark has been in continuous use in commerce for a period of five years after the date of registration or date of publication under section 12(c) of the Act, and is still in use in commerce;

(d) Specify that there has been no final decision adverse to the owner's claim of ownership of such mark for such goods, services, or collective membership organization, or to the owner's right to register the same or to keep the same on the register;

(e) Specify that there is no proceeding involving said rights pending in the Office or in a court and not finally disposed of;

(f) Be filed within one year after the expiration of any five-year period of continuous use following registration or publication under section 12(c) of the Act; and

(g) Include the fee required by §2.6 for each class to which the affidavit or declaration pertains in the registration. If no fee, or a fee insufficient to cover at least one class, is filed at an appropriate time, the affidavit or declaration will not be refused if the required fee(s) (see §2.6) is filed in the Office within the time limit set forth in the notification of this defect by the Office. If the submitted fees are insufficient to cover all classes in the registration, the particular class or classes to which the affidavit or declaration pertains should be specified.

(h) If the affidavit or declaration fails to satisfy any of the requirements in paragraphs (a) through (g) of this section, the owner will be notified in an Office action that the affidavit or declaration cannot be acknowledged. If a response is not received within the time period provided or does not satisfy the requirements of the Office action, the affidavit or declaration will be abandoned.

(i) If the affidavit or declaration satisfies paragraphs (a) through (g) of this section, the Office will issue a notice of acknowledgement.

(j) An affidavit or declaration may be abandoned by the owner upon petition to the Director under §2.146 either before or after the notice of acknowledgement has issued.

(k) If an affidavit or declaration is abandoned, the owner may file a new affidavit or declaration with a new filing fee.

History of 37 C.F.R. §2.167: 30 FR 13193, Oct. 16, 1965; 47 FR 41282, Sept. 17, 1982; 64 FR 48925, Sept. 8, 1999; 73 FR 67773, Jan. 16, 2009; 74 FR 54910, Dec. 28, 2009; 80 FR 33188, July 11, 2015.

§2.168. AFFIDAVIT OR DECLARATION UNDER SECTION 15 COMBINED WITH AFFIDAVIT OR DECLARATION UNDER SECTIONS 8 OR 71, OR WITH RENEWAL APPLICATION

(a) The affidavit or declaration filed under section 15 of the Act may also be used as the affidavit or declaration required by section 8, if the affidavit or declaration meets the requirements of both sections 8 and 15. The affidavit or declaration filed under section 15 of the Act may also be used as the affidavit or declaration required by section 71, if the affidavit or declaration meets the requirements of both sections 71 and 15.

(b) The affidavit or declaration filed under section 15 of the Act may be combined with an application for renewal of a registration under section 9 of the Act, if the requirements of both sections 9 and 15 are met.

History of 37 C.F.R. §2.168: 64 FR 48925, Sept. 8, 1999; 75 FR 35976, June 24, 2010.

CORRECTION, DISCLAIMER, SURRENDER, ETC.

§2.171. NEW CERTIFICATE ON CHANGE OF OWNERSHIP

(a) Full change of ownership. If the ownership of a registered mark changes, the new owner may request that a new certificate of registration be issued in the name of the new owner. The assignment or other document changing title must be recorded in the Office. The request for the new certificate must include the fee required by §2.6(a)(8) and be signed by the owner of the registration, someone with legal authority to bind the owner (e.g., a corporate officer or general partner of a partnership), or a practitioner qualified to practice under §11.14 of this chapter. In a registered extension of protection, the assignment must be recorded with the International Bureau of the World Intellectual Property Organization before it can be recorded in the Office (see §7.22).

(b) Partial change of ownership. **(1)** In a registration resulting from an application based on section 1 or section 44 of the Act, if ownership of a registration has changed with respect to some but not all of the goods and/or services, the owner(s) may file a request that the registration be divided into two or more separate registrations. The assignment or other document changing title must be recorded in the Office. The request to divide must include the fee required by §2.6(a)(8) for each new registration created by the division, and be signed by the owner of the registration, someone with legal authority to bind the owner (e.g., a corporate officer or general partner of a partnership), or a practitioner qualified to practice under §11.14 of this chapter, in accordance with §2.193(e)(2) of this chapter.

(2)(i) When the International Bureau of the World Intellectual Property Organization notifies the Office that an international registration has been divided as the result of a change of ownership with respect to some but not all of the goods and/or services, the Office will construe the International Bureau's notice as a request to divide. The Office will update Office records to reflect the change in ownership, divide out the assigned goods and/or services from the registered extension of protection (parent registration), and publish notice of the parent registration in the Official Gazette.

(ii) The Office will create a new registration number for the child registration, and enter the information about the new registration in its automated records. The Office will notify the new owner that the new owner must pay the fee required by §2.6 to obtain a new registration certificate for the child registration. It is not necessary for the new owner to file a separate request to divide.

(iii) The Office will not divide a registered extension of protection unless the International Bureau notifies the Office that the international registration has been divided.

History of 37 C.F.R. §2.171: 31 FR 5262, Apr. 1, 1966; 68 FR 55769, Sept. 26, 2003; 73 FR 67774, Jan. 16, 2009; 74 FR 54910, Dec. 28, 2009; 80 FR 2312, Jan. 16, 2015.

§2.172. SURRENDER FOR CANCELLATION

Upon application by the owner, the Director may permit any registration to be surrendered for cancellation. The application for surrender must be signed by the owner of the registration, someone with legal authority to bind the owner (e.g., a corporate officer or general partner of a partnership), or a practitioner qualified to practice under §11.14 of this chapter. When a registration has more than one class, one or more entire class(es) but fewer than the total number of classes may be surrendered. Deletion of fewer than all the goods or services in a single class constitutes amendment of the registration as to that class (see §2.173), rather than surrender. A surrender for cancellation may not subsequently be withdrawn.

History of 37 C.F.R. §2.172: 41 FR 761, Jan. 5, 1976; 69 FR 51364, Aug. 19, 2004; 74 FR 54910, Dec. 28, 2009; 80 FR 2312, Jan. 16, 2015.

§2.173. AMENDMENT OF REGISTRATION

(a) Form of amendment. The owner of a registration may apply to amend a registration or to disclaim part of the mark in the registration. The owner must submit a written request specifying the amendment or disclaimer. If the registration is involved in an inter partes proceeding before the Trademark Trial and Appeal Board, the request must be filed by appropriate motion to the Board.

(b) Requirements for request. A request for amendment or disclaimer must:

(1) Include the fee required by §2.6;

(2) Be verified and signed in accordance with §2.193(e)(6); and

(3) If the amendment involves a change in the mark: one new specimen per class showing the mark as used on or in connection with the goods, services, or collective membership organization; a verified statement that the specimen was in use in commerce at least as early as the filing date of the amendment; and a new drawing of the amended mark. When requested by the Office, additional specimens must be provided.

(4) The Office may require the owner to furnish such specimens, information, exhibits, and affidavits or declarations as may be reasonably necessary to the proper examination of the amendment.

(c) Registration must still contain registrable matter. The registration as amended must still contain registrable matter, and the mark as amended must be registrable as a whole.

(d) Amendment may not materially alter the mark. An amendment or disclaimer that materially alters the character of the mark will not be permitted, in accordance with section 7(e) of the Act.

(e) Amendment of identification of goods, services, or collective membership organization. No amendment in the identification of goods or services, or description of the nature of the collective membership organization, in a registration will be permitted except to restrict the identification or to change it in ways that would not require republication of the mark.

(f) Amendment of certification statement for certification marks. An amendment of the certification statement specified in §2.45(a)(4)(i)(A) or (a)(4)(ii)(A) that would materially alter the certification statement will not be permitted, in accordance with section 7(e) of the Act.

(g) Conforming amendments may be required. If the registration includes a disclaimer, description of the mark, or other miscellaneous statement, any request to amend the registration must include a request to make any necessary conforming amendments to the disclaimer, description, or other statement.

(h) Elimination of disclaimer. No amendment seeking the elimination of a disclaimer will be permitted, unless deletion of the disclaimed portion of the mark is also sought.

(i) No amendment to add or delete section 2(f) claim of acquired distinctiveness. An amendment seeking the addition or deletion of a claim of acquired distinctiveness will not be permitted.

History of 37 C.F.R. §2.173: 30 FR 13193, Oct. 16, 1965; 31 FR 5262, Apr. 1, 1966; 48 FR 23143, May 23, 1983; 64 FR 48926, Sept. 8, 1999; 69 FR 51364, Aug. 19, 2004; 72 FR 42263, Aug. 31, 2007; 73 FR 67774, Jan. 16, 2009; 77 FR 30207, June 21, 2012; 80 FR 33189, July 11, 2015.

§2.174. CORRECTION OF OFFICE MISTAKE

Whenever Office records clearly disclose a material mistake in a registration, incurred through the fault of the Office, the Office will issue a certificate of correction stating the fact and nature of the mistake, signed by the Director or by an employee designated by the Director, without charge. Thereafter, the corrected certificate shall have the same effect as if it had been originally issued in the corrected form. In the discretion of the Director, the Office may issue a new certificate of registration without charge.

History of 37 C.F.R. §2.174: 69 FR 51364, Aug. 19, 2004; 73 FR 67774, Jan. 16, 2009.

§2.175. CORRECTION OF MISTAKE BY OWNER

(a) Whenever a mistake has been made in a registration and a showing has been made that the mistake occurred in good faith through the fault of the owner, the Director may issue a certificate of correction. In the discretion of the Director, the Office may issue a new certificate upon payment of the required fee, provided that the correction does not involve such changes in the registration as to require republication of the mark.

(b) An application for such action must:

(1) Include the following:

(i) Specification of the mistake for which correction is sought;

(ii) Description of the manner in which it arose; and

(iii) A showing that it occurred in good faith;

(2) Be verified; and

(3) Be accompanied by the required fee.

History of 37 C.F.R. §2.175: 30 FR 13193, Oct. 16, 1965; 31 FR 5262, Apr. 1, 1966; 69 FR 51364, Aug. 19, 2004; 73 FR 67774, Jan. 16, 2009; 80 FR 33189, July 11, 2015.

§2.176. CONSIDERATION OF ABOVE MATTERS

The matters in §§2.171 to 2.175 will be considered in the first instance by the Post Registration examiners, except for requests to amend registrations involved in inter partes proceedings before the Trademark Trial and Appeal Board, as specified in §2.173(a), which shall be considered by the Board. If an action of the examiner is adverse, the owner of the registration may petition the Director to review the action under §2.146. If the owner does not respond to an adverse action of the examiner within six months of the date of issuance, the matter will be considered abandoned.

History of 37 C.F.R. §2.176: 69 FR 51364, Aug. 19, 2004; 72 FR 42263, Aug. 31, 2007; 73 FR 67774, Jan. 16, 2009.

TERM & RENEWAL

§2.181. TERM OF ORIGINAL REGISTRATIONS & RENEWALS

(a)(1) Subject to the provisions of section 8 of the Act requiring an affidavit or declaration of continued use or excusable nonuse, registrations issued or renewed prior to November 16, 1989, whether on the Principal Register or on the Supplemental Register, remain in force for twenty years from their date of issue or the date of renewal, and may be further renewed for periods of ten years, unless previously cancelled or surrendered.

(2) Subject to the provisions of section 8 of the Act requiring an affidavit or declaration of continued use or excusable nonuse, registrations issued or renewed on or after November 16, 1989, whether on the Principal Register or on the Supplemental Register, remain in force for ten years from their date of issue or the date of renewal, and may be further renewed for periods of ten years, unless previously cancelled or surrendered.

(b) Registrations issued under the Acts of 1905 and 1881 remain in force for their unexpired terms and may be renewed in the same manner as registrations under the Act of 1946.

(c) Registrations issued under the Act of 1920 cannot be renewed unless renewal is required to support foreign registrations and in such case may be renewed on the Supplemental Register in the same manner as registrations under the Act of 1946.

History of 37 C.F.R. §2.181: 54 FR 37597, Sept. 11, 1989; 64 FR 48926, Sept. 8, 1999.

§2.182. TIME FOR FILING RENEWAL APPLICATION

An application for renewal must be filed within one year before the expiration date of the registration, or within the six-month grace period after the expiration date of the registration. If no renewal application is filed within this period, the registration will expire.

History of 37 C.F.R. §2.182: 64 FR 48926, Sept. 8, 1999.

§2.183. REQUIREMENTS FOR A COMPLETE RENEWAL APPLICATION

A complete renewal application must include:

(a) A request for renewal of the registration, signed by the registrant or the registrant's representative;

(b) The fee required by §2.6 for each class;

(c) The additional fee required by §2.6 for each class if the renewal application is filed during the six-month grace period set forth in section 9(a) of the Act;

(d) If the renewal application covers less than all the goods, services, or classes in the registration, then a list specifying the particular goods, services, or classes to be renewed.

(e) If at least one fee is submitted for a multiple-class registration, but the fee is insufficient to cover all the classes and the class(es) to which the fee(s) should be applied are not specified, the Office will issue a notice requiring either the submission of additional fee(s) or an indication of the class(es) to which the original fee(s) should be applied. Additional fee(s) may be submitted if the requirements of §2.185 are met. If the required fee(s) are not submitted and the class(es) to which the original fee(s) should be applied are not specified, the Office will presume that the fee(s) cover the classes in ascending order, beginning with the lowest numbered class.

(f) Renewals of registrations issued under a prior classification system will be processed on the basis of that system, unless the registration has been amended to adopt international classification pursuant to §2.85(e)(3).

History of 37 C.F.R. §2.183: 30 FR 13193, Oct. 16, 1965; 31 FR 5262, Apr. 1, 1966; 41 FR 761, Jan. 5, 1976; 64 FR 48926, Sept. 8, 1999; 67 FR 79523, Dec. 30, 2002; 73 FR 67775, Jan. 16, 2009; 80 FR 33189, July 11, 2015.

§2.184. REFUSAL OF RENEWAL

(a) If the renewal application is not acceptable, the Office will issue a notice stating the reason(s) for refusal.

(b)(1) The registrant must file a response to the refusal of renewal within six months of the date of issuance of the Office action, or before the expiration date of the registration, whichever is later. If no response is filed within this time period, the registration will expire, unless time remains in the grace period under section 9(a) of the Act. If time remains in the grace period, the registrant may file a complete new renewal application.

(2) The response must be signed by the registrant, someone with legal authority to bind the registrant (e.g., a corporate officer or general partner of a partnership), or a practitioner who meets the requirements of §11.14 of this chapter, in accordance with the requirements of §2.193(e)(2).

(c) If the renewal application is not filed within the time periods set forth in section 9(a) of the Act, the registration will expire.

History of 37 C.F.R. §2.184: 30 FR 13193, Oct. 16, 1965; 48 FR 23143, May 23, 1983; 64 FR 48926, Sept. 8, 1999; 73 FR 67775, Jan. 16, 2009; 74 FR 54910, Dec. 28, 2009.

§2.185. CORRECTING DEFICIENCIES IN RENEWAL APPLICATION

(a) If the renewal application is filed within the time periods set forth in section 9(a) of the Act, deficiencies may be corrected after notification from the Office, as follows:

(1) Correcting deficiencies in renewal applications filed within one year before the expiration date of the registration. If the renewal application is filed within one year before the expiration date of the registration, deficiencies may be corrected before the expiration date of the registration without paying a deficiency surcharge. Deficiencies may be corrected after the expiration date of the registration with payment of the deficiency surcharge required by section 9(a) of the Act and §2.6.

(2) Correcting deficiencies in renewal applications filed during the grace period. If the renewal application is filed during the six-month grace period, deficiencies may be corrected before the expiration of the grace period without paying a deficiency surcharge. Deficiencies may be corrected after the expiration of the grace period with payment of the deficiency surcharge required by section 9(a) of the Act and §2.6.

(b) If the renewal application is not filed within the time periods set forth in section 9(a) of the Act, the registration will expire. This deficiency cannot be cured.

History of 37 C.F.R. §2.185: 64 FR 48926, Sept. 8, 1999; 80 FR 2312, Jan. 16, 2015.

§2.186. PETITION TO DIRECTOR TO REVIEW REFUSAL OF RENEWAL

(a) A response to the examiner's initial refusal of the renewal application is required before filing a petition to the Director, unless the examiner directs otherwise. See §2.184(b) for the deadline for responding to an examiner's Office action.

(b) If the examiner maintains the refusal of the renewal application, a petition to the Director to review the refusal may be filed. The petition must be filed within six months of the date of issuance of the Office action maintaining the refusal, or the renewal application will be abandoned and the registration will expire.

(c) A decision by the Director is necessary before filing an appeal or commencing a civil action in any court.

History of 37 C.F.R. §2.186: 64 FR 48926, Sept. 8, 1999; 73 FR 67775, Jan. 16, 2009.

GENERAL INFORMATION & CORRESPONDENCE IN TRADEMARK CASES

§§2.187 TO 2.189. RESERVED

History of 37 C.F.R. §§2.187-2.189: 57 FR 29642, July 6, 1992.

§2.190. ADDRESSES FOR TRADEMARK CORRESPONDENCE WITH THE UNITED STATES PATENT & TRADEMARK OFFICE

(a) Trademark correspondence—in general. All trademark-related documents filed on paper, except documents sent to the Assignment Recordation Branch for recordation; requests for copies of trademark documents; and certain documents filed under the Madrid Protocol as specified in paragraph (e) of this section, should be addressed to: Commissioner for Trademarks, P.O. Box 1451, Alexandria, VA 22313-1451. All trademark-related documents may be delivered by hand, during the hours the Office is open to receive correspondence, to the Trademark Assistance Center, James Madison Building—East Wing, Concourse Level, 600 Dulany Street, Alexandria, Virginia 22314.

(b) Electronic trademark documents. An applicant may transmit a trademark document through TEAS, at http://www.uspto.gov. Documents that relate to proceedings before the Trademark Trial and Appeal Board shall be filed directly with the Board electronically through ESTTA, at http://estta.uspto.gov.

(c) Trademark assignments. Requests to record documents in the Assignment Recordation Branch may be filed through the Office's Web site, at http://www.uspto.gov. Paper documents and cover sheets to be recorded in the Assignment Recordation Branch should be addressed to: Mail Stop Assignment Recordation Branch, Director of the United States Patent and Trademark Office, P.O. Box 1450, Alexandria, Virginia 22313-1450. See §3.27 of this chapter.

(d) Requests for copies of trademark documents. Copies of trademark documents can be ordered through the Office's web site at www.uspto.gov. Paper requests for certified or uncertified copies of trademark documents should be addressed to: Mail Stop Document Services, Director of the United States Patent and Trademark Office, P.O. Box 1450, Alexandria, Virginia 22313-1450.

(e) Certain Documents Relating to International Applications and Registrations. International applications under §7.11, subsequent designations under §7.21, responses to notices of irregularity under §7.14, requests to record changes in the International Register under §7.23 and §7.24, requests to note replacements under §7.28, requests for transformation under §7.31, and petitions to the Director to review an action of the Office's Madrid Processing Unit, when filed by mail, must be mailed to: Madrid Processing Unit, 600 Dulany Street, MDE-7B87, Alexandria, VA 22314-5793.

History of 37 C.F.R. §2.190: 69 FR 57184, Sept. 24, 2004; 69 FR 63321, Nov. 1, 2004; 72 FR 18908, Apr. 16, 2007; 81 FR 69987, Jan. 14, 2017.

§2.191. BUSINESS TO BE TRANSACTED IN WRITING

All business with the Office should be transacted in writing. The personal appearance of applicants or their representatives at the Office is unnecessary. The action of the Office will be based exclusively on the written record. No attention will be paid to any alleged oral promise, stipulation, or understanding in relation to which there is disagreement or doubt. The Office encourages parties to file documents through TEAS wherever possible, and mandates that documents in proceedings before the Trademark Trial and Appeal Board be filed through ESTTA.

History of 37 C.F.R. §2.191: 81 FR 69987, Jan. 14, 2017.

§2.192. BUSINESS TO BE CONDUCTED WITH DECORUM & COURTESY

Trademark applicants, registrants, and parties to proceedings before the Trademark Trial and Appeal Board and their attorneys or agents are required to conduct their business with decorum and courtesy. Documents presented in violation of this requirement will be submitted to the Director and will be returned by the Director's direct order. Complaints against trademark examining attorneys and other employees must be made in correspondence separate from other documents.

A §2.193. TRADEMARK CORRESPONDENCE & SIGNATURE REQUIREMENTS

(a) Signature required. Each piece of correspondence that requires a signature must bear:

(1) A handwritten signature personally signed in permanent ink by the person named as the signatory, or a true copy thereof; or

(2) An electronic signature that meets the requirements of paragraph (c) of this section, personally entered by the person named as the signatory. The Office will accept an electronic signature that meets the requirements of paragraph (c) of this section on correspondence filed on paper, by facsimile transmission (§2.195(c)), or through TEAS or ESTTA.

(b) Copy of original signature. If a copy, such as a photocopy or facsimile copy of an original signature is filed, the filer should retain the original as evidence of authenticity. If a question of authenticity arises, the Office may require submission of the original.

(c) Requirements for electronic signature. A person signing a document electronically must:

(1) Personally enter any combination of letters, numbers, spaces and/or punctuation marks that he or she has adopted as a signature, placed between two forward slash ("/") symbols in the signature block on the electronic submission; or

(2) Sign the document using some other form of electronic signature specified by the Director.

(d) Signatory must be identified. The name of the person who signs a document in connection with a trademark application, registration, or proceeding before the Trademark Trial and Appeal Board must be set forth in printed or typed form immediately below or adjacent to the signature, or identified elsewhere in the filing (e.g., in a cover letter or other document that accompanies the filing).

(e) Proper person to sign. Documents filed in connection with a trademark application or registration must be signed by a proper person. Unless otherwise specified by law, the following requirements apply:

(1) Verified statement of facts. A verified statement in support of an application for registration, amendment to an application for registration, allegation of use under §2.76 or §2.88, request for extension of time to file a statement of use under §2.89, or an affidavit under section 8, 12(c), 15, or 71 of the Act must satisfy the requirements of §2.2(n), and be signed by the owner or a person properly authorized to sign on behalf of the owner. A person who is properly authorized to verify facts on behalf of an owner is:

(i) A person with legal authority to bind the owner (e.g., a corporate officer or general partner of a partnership);

(ii) A person with firsthand knowledge of the facts and actual or implied authority to act on behalf of the owner; or

(iii) An attorney as defined in §11.1 of this chapter who has an actual written or verbal power of attorney or an implied power of attorney from the owner.

(2) Responses, amendments to applications, requests for express abandonment, requests for reconsideration of final actions, and requests to divide. Responses to Office actions, amendments to applications, requests for express abandonment, requests for reconsideration of final actions, and requests to divide must be signed by the owner of the application or registration, someone with legal authority to bind the owner (e.g., a corporate officer or general partner of a partnership), or a practitioner qualified to practice under §11.14 of this chapter, in accordance with the following guidelines:

(i) If the owner is represented by a practitioner qualified to practice before the Office under §11.14 of this chapter, the practitioner must sign, except where the owner is required to sign the correspondence; or

(ii) If the owner is not represented by a practitioner qualified to practice under §11.14 of this chapter, the individual owner or someone with legal authority to bind the owner (e.g., a corporate officer or general partner of a partnership) must sign. In the case of joint owners who are not represented by a qualified practitioner, all must sign.

(3) Powers of attorney and revocations of powers of attorney. Powers of attorney and revocations of powers of attorney must be signed by the individual applicant, registrant or party to a proceeding pending before the Office, or by someone with legal authority to bind the applicant, registrant, or party (e.g., a corporate officer or general partner of a partnership). In the case of joint applicants, registrants, or parties, all must sign. Once the applicant, registrant or party has designated a qualified practitioner(s), the named practitioner may sign an associate power of attorney appointing another qualified practitioner(s) as an additional person(s) authorized to prosecute the application or registration. If the applicant, registrant, or party revokes the original power of attorney, the revocation discharges any associate power signed by the practitioner whose power has been revoked. If the practitioner who signed an associate power withdraws, the withdrawal discharges any associate power signed by the withdrawing practitioner upon acceptance of the request for withdrawal by the Office.

(4) Petitions to revive under §2.66. A petition to revive under §2.66 must be signed by someone with firsthand knowledge of the facts regarding unintentional delay.

(5) Petitions to Director under §2.146. A petition to the Director under §2.146 must be signed by the petitioner, someone with legal authority to bind the petitioner (e.g., a corporate officer or general partner of a partnership), or a practitioner qualified to practice under §11.14 of this chapter, in accordance with the following guidelines:

(i) If the petitioner is represented by a practitioner qualified to practice before the Office under §11.14 of this chapter, the practitioner must sign; or

(ii) If the petitioner is not represented by a practitioner authorized to practice before the Office under §11.14 of this chapter, the individual petitioner or someone with legal authority to bind the petitioner (e.g., a corporate officer or general partner of a partnership) must sign. In the case of joint petitioners, all must sign.

(6) Requests for correction, amendment or surrender of registrations. A request for correction, amendment or surrender of a registration must be signed by the owner of the registration, someone with legal authority to bind the owner (e.g., a corporate officer or general partner of a partnership), or a practitioner qualified to practice before the Office under §11.14 of this chapter. In the case of joint owners who are not represented by a qualified practitioner, all must sign.

(7) Renewal applications. A renewal application must be signed by the registrant or the registrant's representative.

(8) Designations and revocations of domestic representative. A designation or revocation of a domestic representative must be signed by the applicant or registrant, someone with legal authority to bind the applicant or registrant (e.g., a corporate officer or general partner of a partnership), or a practitioner qualified to practice under §11.14 of this chapter. In the case of joint applicants or registrants, all must sign.

(9) Requests to change correspondence address in an application or registration. A notice of change of correspondence address in an application or registration must be signed by the applicant or registrant, someone with legal authority to bind the applicant or registrant (e.g., a corporate officer or general partner of a partnership), or a practitioner qualified to practice under §11.14 of this chapter, in accordance with the following guidelines:

(i) If the applicant or registrant is represented by a practitioner qualified to practice before the Office under §11.14 of this chapter, the practitioner must sign; or

(ii) If the applicant or registrant is not represented by a practitioner qualified to practice before the Office under §11.14, the individual applicant or registrant or someone with legal authority to bind the applicant or registrant (e.g., a corporate officer or general partner of a partnership) must sign. In the case of joint applicants or joint registrants, all must sign.

(10) Cover letters. A person transmitting paper documents to the Office may sign a cover letter or transmittal letter. The Office neither requires cover letters nor questions the authority of a person who signs a communication that merely transmits paper documents.

(f) Signature as certification. The presentation to the Office (whether by signing, filing, submitting, or later advocating) of any document by any person, whether a practitioner or non-practitioner, constitutes a certification under §11.18(b) of this chapter. Violations of §11.18(b) of this chapter may jeopardize the validity of the application or registration, and may result in the imposition of sanctions under §11.18(c) of this chapter. Any practitioner violating §11.18(b) of this chapter may also be subject to disciplinary action. See §11.18(d) and §11.804 of this chapter.

(g) Separate copies for separate files. **(1)** Since each file must be complete in itself, a separate copy of every document to be filed in connection with a trademark application, registration, or inter partes proceeding must be furnished for each file to which the document pertains, even though the contents of the documents filed in multiple files may be identical.

(2) Parties should not file duplicate copies of correspondence in a single application, registration, or proceeding file, unless the Office requires the filing of duplicate copies. The Office may dispose of duplicate copies of correspondence.

(h) Separate documents for separate branches of the Office. Since different branches or sections of the Office may consider different matters, each distinct subject, inquiry or order must be contained in a separate document to avoid confusion and delay in answering correspondence.

(i) Certified documents required by statute. When a statute requires that a document be certified, a copy or facsimile transmission of the certification is not acceptable.

History of 37 C.F.R. §2.193: 73 FR 47686, Sept. 15, 2008; 74 FR 54910, Dec. 28, 2009; 80 FR 33189, July 11, 2015; 83 FR 1559, Jan. 12, 2018.

§2.194. IDENTIFICATION OF TRADEMARK APPLICATION OR REGISTRATION

(a) No correspondence relating to a trademark application should be filed prior to receipt of the application serial number.

(b)(1) A letter about a trademark application should identify the serial number, the name of the applicant, and the mark.

(2) A letter about a registered trademark should identify the registration number, the name of the registrant, and the mark.

§2.195. RECEIPT OF TRADEMARK CORRESPONDENCE

(a) Date of receipt and Priority Mail Express® date of deposit. Trademark correspondence received in the Office is given a filing date as of the date of receipt except as follows:

(1) The Office is not open for the filing of correspondence on any day that is a Saturday, Sunday, or Federal holiday within the District of Columbia. Except for correspondence transmitted electronically under paragraph (a)(2) of this section or transmitted by facsimile under paragraph (a)(3) of this section, no correspondence is received in the Office on Saturdays, Sundays, or Federal holidays within the District of Columbia.

(2) Trademark-related correspondence transmitted electronically will be given a filing date as of the date on which the Office receives the transmission.

(3) Correspondence transmitted by facsimile will be given a filing date as of the date on which the complete transmission is received in the Office unless that date is a Saturday, Sunday, or Federal holiday within the District of Columbia, in which case the filing date will be the next succeeding day that is not a Saturday, Sunday, or Federal holiday within the District of Columbia.

(4) Correspondence filed in accordance with §2.198 will be given a filing date as of the date of deposit as Priority Mail Express® with the United States Postal Service.

(b) Correspondence delivered by hand. Correspondence may be delivered by hand during hours the Office is open to receive correspondence.

(c) Facsimile transmission. Except in the cases enumerated in paragraph (d) of this section, correspondence, including authorizations to charge a deposit account, may be transmitted by facsimile. The receipt date accorded to the correspondence will be the date on which the complete transmission is received in the Office, unless that date is a Saturday,

Sunday, or Federal holiday within the District of Columbia. See §2.196. To facilitate proper processing, each transmission session should be limited to correspondence to be filed in a single application, registration or proceeding before the Office. The application serial number, registration number, or proceeding number should be entered as a part of the sender's identification on a facsimile cover sheet.

(d) Facsimile transmissions are not permitted and if submitted, will not be accorded a date of receipt, in the following situations:

(1) Applications for registration of marks;

(2) Drawings submitted under §2.51, §2.52, §2.72, or §2.173;

(3) Correspondence to be filed with the Trademark Trial and Appeal Board;

(4) Requests for cancellation or amendment of a registration under section 7(e) of the Trademark Act; and certificates of registration surrendered for cancellation or amendment under section 7(e) of the Trademark Act; and

(5) Madrid-related correspondence submitted under §7.11, §7.21, §7.14, §7.23, §7.24, or §7.31.

(e) Interruptions in U.S. Postal Service. **(1)** If the Director designates a postal service interruption or emergency within the meaning of 35 U.S.C. 21(a), any person attempting to file correspondence by Priority Mail Express® Post Office to Addressee service who was unable to deposit the correspondence with the United States Postal Service due to the interruption or emergency may petition the Director to consider such correspondence as filed on a particular date in the Office.

(2) The petition must:

(i) Be filed promptly after the ending of the designated interruption or emergency;

(ii) Include the original correspondence or a copy of the original correspondence; and

(iii) Include a statement that the correspondence would have been deposited with the United States Postal Service on the requested filing date but for the designated interruption or emergency in Priority Mail Express® service; and that the correspondence attached to the petition is the original correspondence or a true copy of the correspondence originally attempted to be deposited as Priority Mail Express® on the requested filing date.

(3) Paragraphs (e)(1) and (e)(2) of this section do not apply to correspondence that is excluded from the Priority Mail Express® procedure pursuant to §2.198(a)(1).

History of 37 C.F.R. §2.195: 69 FR 57185, Sept. 24, 2004; 73 FR 67775, Jan. 16, 2009; 79 FR 63041, Oct. 22, 2014; 81 FR 69988, Jan. 14, 2017.

§2.196. TIMES FOR TAKING ACTION: EXPIRATION ON SATURDAY, SUNDAY OR FEDERAL HOLIDAY

Whenever periods of time are specified in this part in days, calendar days are intended. When the day, or the last day fixed by statute or by regulation under this part for taking any action or paying any fee in the Office falls on a Saturday, Sunday, or Federal holiday within the District of Columbia, the action may be taken, or the fee paid, on the next succeeding day that is not a Saturday, Sunday, or a Federal holiday.

§2.197. CERTIFICATE OF MAILING OR TRANSMISSION

(a) Except in the cases enumerated in paragraph (a)(2) of this section, correspondence required to be filed in the Office within a set period of time will be considered as being timely filed if the procedure described in this section is followed. The actual date of receipt will be used for all other purposes.

(1) Correspondence will be considered as being timely filed if:

(i) The correspondence is mailed or transmitted prior to expiration of the set period of time by being:

(A) Addressed as set out in §2.190 and deposited with the U.S. Postal Service with sufficient postage as first class mail; or

(B) Transmitted by facsimile to the Office in accordance with §2.195(c); and

(ii) The correspondence includes a certificate for each piece of correspondence stating the date of deposit or transmission. The person signing the certificate should have a reasonable basis to expect that the correspondence would be mailed or transmitted on or before the date indicated.

(2) The procedure described in paragraph (a)(1) of this section does not apply to:

(i) Applications for the registration of marks under 15 U.S.C. 1051 or 1126; and

(ii) Madrid-related correspondence filed under §7.11, §7.21, §7.14, §7.23, §7.24 or §7.31 of this title.

(b) In the event that correspondence is considered timely filed by being mailed or transmitted in accordance with paragraph (a) of this section, but not received in the Office, and an application is abandoned, a registration is cancelled or expired, or a proceeding is dismissed, terminated, or decided with prejudice, the correspondence will be considered timely if the party who forwarded such correspondence:

(1) Informs the Office of the previous mailing or transmission of the correspondence within two months after becoming aware that the Office has no evidence of receipt of the correspondence;

(2) Supplies an additional copy of the previously mailed or transmitted correspondence and certificate; and

(3) Includes a statement that attests on a personal knowledge basis or to the satisfaction of the Director to the previous timely mailing or transmission. If the correspondence was sent by facsimile transmission, a copy of the sending unit's report confirming transmission may be used to support this statement.

(c) The Office may require additional evidence to determine whether the correspondence was timely filed.

History of 37 C.F.R. §2.197: 69 FR 57185, Sept. 24, 2004.

§2.198. FILING OF CORRESPONDENCE BY PRIORITY MAIL EXPRESS®

(a)(1) Except for documents listed in paragraphs (a)(1)(i) through (vii) of this section, any correspondence received by the Office that was delivered by the Priority Mail Express® Post Office to Addressee service of the United States Postal Service (USPS) will be considered filed with the Office on the date of deposit with the USPS. The Priority Mail Express® procedure does not apply to:

(i) Applications for registration of marks;

(ii) Amendments to allege use under section 1(c) of the Act;

(iii) Statements of use under section 1(d) of the Act;

(iv) Requests for extension of time to file a statement of use under section 1(d) of the Act;

(v) Affidavits of continued use under section 8 of the Act;

(vi) Renewal requests under section 9 of the Act;

(vii) Requests to change or correct addresses; and

(viii) Affidavits of use under section 71 of the Act.

(2) The date of deposit with USPS is shown by the "date accepted" on the Priority Mail Express® label or other official USPS notation. If the USPS deposit date cannot be determined, the correspondence will be accorded the date of receipt in the Office as the filing date.

(b) Correspondence should be deposited directly with an employee of the USPS to ensure that the person depositing the correspondence receives a legible copy of the Priority Mail Express® mailing label with the "date accepted" clearly marked. Persons dealing indirectly with the employees of the USPS (such as by deposit in a Priority Mail Express® drop box) do so at the risk of not receiving a copy of the Priority Mail Express® mailing label with the desired "date accepted" clearly marked. The paper(s) or fee(s) that constitute the correspondence should also include the Priority Mail Express® mailing label number thereon. See paragraphs (c), (d) and (e) of this section.

(c) Any person filing correspondence under this section that was received by the Office and delivered by the Priority Mail Express® Post Office to Addressee service of the USPS, who can show that there is a discrepancy between the filing date accorded by the Office to the correspondence and the date of deposit as shown by the "date accepted" on the Priority Mail Express® mailing label or other official USPS notation, may petition the Director to accord the correspondence a filing date as of the "date accepted" on the Priority Mail Express® mailing label or other official USPS notation, provided that:

(1) The petition is filed within two months after the person becomes aware that the Office has accorded, or will accord, a filing date other than the USPS deposit date;

(2) The number of the Priority Mail Express® mailing label was placed on the paper(s) or fee(s) that constitute the correspondence prior to the original mailing; and

(3) The petition includes a true copy of the Priority Mail Express® mailing label showing the "date accepted," and of any other official notation by the USPS relied upon to show the date of deposit.

(d) Any person filing correspondence under this section that was received by the Office and delivered by the Priority Mail Express® Post Office to Addressee service of the USPS, who can show that the "date accepted" on the Priority Mail Express® mailing label or other official notation entered by the USPS was incorrectly entered or omitted by the USPS, may petition the Director to accord the correspondence a filing date as of the date the correspondence is shown to have been deposited with the USPS, provided that:

(1) The petition is filed within two months after the person becomes aware that the Office has accorded, or will accord, a filing date based upon an incorrect entry by the USPS;

(2) The number of the Priority Mail Express® mailing label was placed on the paper(s) or fee(s) prior to the original mailing; and

(3) The petition includes a showing that establishes, to the satisfaction of the Director, that the correspondence was deposited in the Priority Mail Express® Post Office to Addressee service prior to the last scheduled pickup on the requested filing date. Any showing pursuant to this paragraph must be corroborated by evidence from the USPS or evidence that came into being within one business day after the deposit of the correspondence in the Priority Mail Express® Post Office to Addressee service of the USPS.

(e) If correspondence is properly addressed to the Office pursuant to §2.190 and deposited with sufficient postage in the Priority Mail Express® Post Office to Addressee service of the USPS, but not received by the Office, the party who mailed the correspondence may petition the Director to consider such correspondence filed in the Office on the USPS deposit date, provided that:

(1) The petition is filed within two months after the person becomes aware that the Office has no evidence of receipt of the correspondence;

(2) The number of the Priority Mail Express® mailing label was placed on the paper(s) or fee(s) prior to the original mailing;

(3) The petition includes a copy of the originally deposited paper(s) or fee(s) showing the number of the Priority Mail Express® mailing label thereon, a copy of any returned postcard receipt, a copy of the Priority Mail Express® mailing label showing the "date accepted," a copy of any other official notation by the USPS relied upon to show the date of deposit, and, if the requested filing date is a date other than the "date accepted" on the Priority Mail Express® mailing label or other official notation entered by the USPS, a showing pursuant to paragraph (d)(3) of this section that the correspondence was deposited in the Priority Mail Express® Post Office to Addressee service prior to the last scheduled pickup on the requested filing date; and

(4) The petition includes a statement that establishes, to the satisfaction of the Director, the original deposit of the correspondence and that the copies of the correspondence, the copy of the Priority Mail Express® mailing label, the copy of any returned postcard receipt, and any official notation entered by the USPS are true copies of the originally mailed correspondence, original Priority Mail Express® mailing label, returned postcard receipt, and official notation entered by the USPS.

(f) The Office may require additional evidence to determine whether the correspondence was deposited as Priority Mail Express® with the USPS on the date in question.

History of 37 C.F.R. §2.198: 68 FR 56557, Oct. 1, 2003; 79 FR 63041, Oct. 22, 2014; 80 FR 2312, Jan. 16, 2015.

TRADEMARK RECORDS & FILES OF THE PATENT & TRADEMARK OFFICE

§2.200. ASSIGNMENT RECORDS OPEN TO PUBLIC INSPECTION

(a)(1) Separate assignment records are maintained in the Office for patents and trademarks. The assignment records relating to trademark applications and registrations (for assignments recorded on or after January 1, 1955) are open to public inspection at the Office, and copies of those assignment records may be obtained upon request and payment of the fee set forth in §2.6 of this chapter.

(2) All records of trademark assignments recorded before January 1, 1955, are maintained by the National Archives and Records Administration (NARA). The records are open to public inspection. Certified and uncertified copies of those assignment records are provided by NARA upon request and payment of the fees required by NARA.

(b) An order for a copy of an assignment or other document should identify the reel and frame number where the assignment or document is recorded.

History of 37 C.F.R. §2.200: 81 FR 72707, Jan. 14, 2017.

§2.201. COPIES & CERTIFIED COPIES

(a) Non-certified copies of trademark registrations and of any trademark records or trademark documents within the jurisdiction of the Office and open to the public, will be furnished by the Office to any person entitled thereto, upon payment of the appropriate fee required by §2.6.

(b) Certified copies of trademark registrations and of any trademark records or trademark documents within the jurisdiction of the Office and open to the public will be authenticated by the seal of the Office and certified by the Director, or in his or her name attested by an officer of the Office authorized by the Director, upon payment of the fee required by §2.6.

FEES & PAYMENT OF MONEY IN TRADEMARK CASES

§2.206. TRADEMARK FEES PAYABLE IN ADVANCE

(a) Trademark fees and charges payable to the Office are required to be paid in advance; that is, at the time of requesting any action by the Office for which a fee or charge is payable.

(b) All fees paid to the Office must be itemized in each individual trademark application or registration file, or trademark proceeding, so that the purpose for which the fees are paid is clear. The Office may return fees that are not itemized as required by this paragraph.

§2.207. METHODS OF PAYMENT

(a) All payments of money required in trademark cases, including fees for the processing of international trademark applications and registrations that are paid through the Office, shall be made in U.S. dollars and in the form of a cashier's or certified check, Treasury note, national bank note, or United States Postal Service money order. If sent in any other form, the Office may delay or cancel the credit until collection is made. Checks and money orders must be made payable to the Director of the United States Patent and Trademark Office. (Checks made payable to the Commissioner of Patents and Trademarks will continue to be accepted.) Payments from foreign countries must be payable and immediately negotiable in the United States for the full amount of the fee required. Money sent to the Office by mail will be at the risk of the sender, and letters containing money should be registered with the United States Postal Service.

(b) Payments of money required for trademark fees may also be made by credit card, except for replenishing a deposit account. Payment of a fee by credit card must specify the amount to be charged to the credit card and such other information as is necessary to process the charge, and is subject to collection of the fee. The Office will not accept a general authorization to charge fees to a credit card. If credit card information is provided on a form or document other than a form provided by the Office for the payment of fees by credit card, the Office will not be liable if the credit card number becomes public knowledge.

History of 37 C.F.R. §2.207: 69 FR 43752, July 22, 2004.

§2.208. DEPOSIT ACCOUNTS

(a) For the convenience of attorneys, and the general public in paying any fees due, in ordering copies of records, or services offered by the Office, deposit accounts may be established in the Office. A minimum deposit of $1,000 is required for paying any fees due or in ordering any services offered by the Office. The Office will issue a deposit account statement at the end of each month. A remittance must be made promptly upon receipt of the statement to cover the value of items or services charged to the account and thus restore the account to its established normal deposit. An amount sufficient to cover all fees, copies, or services requested must always be on deposit. Charges to accounts with insufficient funds will not be accepted. A service charge (§2.6(b)(11)) will be assessed for each month that the balance at the end of the month is below $1,000.

(b) A general authorization to charge all fees, or only certain fees to a deposit account containing sufficient funds may be filed in an individual application, either for the entire pendency of the application or with respect to a particular document filed. An authorization to charge a fee to a deposit account will not be considered payment of the fee on the date the authorization to charge the fee is effective as to the particular fee to be charged unless sufficient funds are present in the account to cover the fee.

(c) A deposit account holder may replenish the deposit account by submitting a payment to the Office. A payment to replenish a deposit account must be submitted by one of the methods set forth in paragraphs (c)(1), (c)(2), (c)(3), or (c)(4) of this section.

(1) A payment to replenish a deposit account may be submitted by electronic funds transfer through the Federal Reserve Fedwire System, which requires that the following information be provided to the deposit account holder's bank or financial institution:

(i) Name of the Bank, which is Treas NYC (Treasury New York City);

(ii) Bank Routing Code, which is 021030004;

(iii) United States Patent and Trademark Office account number with the Department of the Treasury, which is 13100001; and

(iv) The deposit account holder's company name and deposit account number.

(2) A payment to replenish a deposit account may be submitted by electronic funds transfer over the Office's Internet Web site (www.uspto.gov).

(3) A payment to replenish a deposit account may be addressed to: Director of the United States Patent and Trademark Office, Attn: Deposit Accounts, 2051 Jamieson Avenue, Suite 300, Alexandria, Virginia 22314.

History of 37 C.F.R. §2.208: 69 FR 43752, July 22, 2004; 70 FR 56128, Sept. 26, 2005; 73 FR 67775, Jan. 16, 2009; 81 FR 72707, Jan. 14, 2017.

§2.209. REFUNDS

(a) The Director may refund any fee paid by mistake or in excess of that required. A change of purpose after the payment of a fee, such as when a party desires to withdraw a trademark application, appeal or other trademark filing for which a fee was paid, will not entitle a party to a refund of such fee. The Office will not refund amounts of twenty-five dollars or less unless a refund is specifically requested, and will not notify the payor of such amounts. If a party paying a fee or requesting a refund does not provide the banking information necessary for making refunds by electronic funds transfer (31 U.S.C. 3332 and 31 CFR part 208), or instruct the Office that refunds are to be credited to a deposit account, the Director may require such information, or use the banking information on the payment instrument to make a refund. Any refund of a fee paid by credit card will be by a credit to the credit card account to which the fee was charged.

(b) Any request for refund must be filed within two years from the date the fee was paid, except as otherwise provided in this paragraph. If the Office charges a deposit account by an amount other than an amount specifically indicated in an authorization (§2.208(b)), any request for refund based upon such charge must be filed within two years from the date of the deposit account statement indicating such charge, and include a copy of that deposit account statement. The time periods set forth in this paragraph are not extendable.

PART 3. ASSIGNMENT, RECORDING & RIGHTS OF ASSIGNEE

§3.1. DEFINITIONS

For purposes of this part, the following definitions shall apply:

Application means a national application for patent, an international patent application that designates the United States of America, an international design application that designates the United States of America, or an application to register a trademark under section 1 or 44 of the Trademark Act, 15 U.S.C. 1051, or 15 U.S.C. 1126, unless otherwise indicated.

Assignment means a transfer by a party of all or part of its right, title and interest in a patent, patent application, registered mark or a mark for which an application to register has been filed.

Document means a document which a party requests to be recorded in the Office pursuant to §3.11 and which affects some interest in an application, patent, or registration.

Office means the United States Patent and Trademark Office.

Recorded document means a document which has been recorded in the Office pursuant to §3.11.

Registration means a trademark registration issued by the Office.

History of 37 C.F.R. §3.1: 69 FR 29878, May 26, 2004; 80 FR 17969, May 13, 2015.

Source of 37 C.F.R. Part 3: 57 FR 29642, July 6, 1992; 65 FR 54681, Sept. 8, 2000, unless otherwise noted.

DOCUMENTS ELIGIBLE FOR RECORDING

§3.11. DOCUMENTS WHICH WILL BE RECORDED

(a) Assignments of applications, patents, and registrations, and other documents relating to interests in patent applications and patents, accompanied by completed cover sheets as specified in §3.28 and §3.31, will be recorded in the Office. Other documents, accompanied by completed cover sheets as specified in §3.28 and §3.31, affecting title to applications, patents, or registrations, will be recorded as provided in this part or at the discretion of the Director.

(b) Executive Order 9424 of February 18, 1944 (9 FR 1959, 3 CFR 1943-1948 Comp., p. 303) requires the several departments and other executive agencies of the Government, including Government-owned or Government-controlled corporations, to forward promptly to the Director for recording all licenses, assignments, or other interests of the Government in or under patents or patent applications. Assignments and other documents affecting title to patents or patent applications and documents not affecting title to patents or patent applications required by Executive Order 9424 to be filed will be recorded as provided in this part.

(c) A joint research agreement or an excerpt of a joint research agreement will also be recorded as provided in this part.

History of 37 C.F.R. §3.11: 62 FR 53202, Oct. 10, 1997; 70 FR 1824, Jan. 11, 2005; 70 FR 54267, Sept. 14, 2005; 78 FR 62408, Dec. 18, 2013.

§3.16. ASSIGNABILITY OF TRADEMARKS PRIOR TO FILING OF AN ALLEGATION OF USE

Before an allegation of use under either 15 U.S.C. 1051(c) or 15 U.S.C. 1051(d) is filed, an applicant may only assign an application to register a mark under 15 U.S.C. 1051(b) to a successor to the applicant's business, or portion of the business to which the mark pertains, if that business is ongoing and existing.

History of 37 C.F.R. §3.16: 64 FR 48926, Sept. 8, 1999.

REQUIREMENTS FOR RECORDING

§3.21. IDENTIFICATION OF PATENTS & PATENT APPLICATIONS

An assignment relating to a patent must identify the patent by the patent number. An assignment relating to a national patent application must identify the national patent application by the application number (consisting of the series code and the serial number; e.g., 07/123,456). An assignment relating to an international patent application which designates the United States of America must identify the international application by the international application number; e.g., PCT/US2012/012345. An assignment relating to an international design application which designates the United States of America must identify the international design application by the international registration number or by the U.S. application number assigned to the international design application. If an assignment of a patent application filed under §1.53(b) of this chapter is executed concurrently with, or subsequent to, the execution of the patent application, but before the patent application is filed, it must identify the patent application by the name of each inventor and the title of the invention so that there can be no mistake as to the patent application intended. If an assignment of a provisional application under §1.53(c) of this chapter is executed before the provisional application is filed, it must identify the provisional application by the name of each inventor and the title of the invention so that there can be no mistake as to the provisional application intended.

History of 37 C.F.R. §3.21: 60 FR 20228, Apr. 25, 1995; 62 FR 53202, Oct. 10, 1997; 69 FR 29878, May 26, 2004; 80 FR 17969, May 13, 2015.

§3.24. REQUIREMENTS FOR DOCUMENTS & COVER SHEETS RELATING TO PATENTS & PATENT APPLICATIONS

(a) For electronic submissions: Either a copy of the original document or an extract of the original document may be submitted for recording. All documents must be submitted as digitized images in Tagged Image File Format (TIFF) or another form as prescribed by the Director. When printed to a paper size of either 21.6 by 27.9 cm (8½ by 11 inches) or 21.0 by 29.7 cm (DIN size A4), the document must be legible and a 2.5 cm (one-inch) margin must be present on all sides.

(b) For paper or facsimile submissions: Either a copy of the original document or an extract of the original document must be submitted for recording. Only one side of each page may be used. The paper size must be either 21.6 by 27.9 cm (8½ by 11 inches) or 21.0 by 29.7 cm (DIN size A4), and in either case, a 2.5 cm (one-inch) margin must be present on all sides. For paper submissions, the paper used should be flexible, strong white, non-shiny, and durable. The Office will not return recorded documents, so original documents must not be submitted for recording.

History of 37 C.F.R. §3.24: 64 FR 48927, Sept. 8, 1999; 69 FR 29879, May 26, 2004.

§3.25. RECORDING REQUIREMENTS FOR TRADEMARK APPLICATIONS & REGISTRATIONS

(a) Documents affecting title. To record documents affecting title to a trademark application or registration, a legible cover sheet (see §3.31) and one of the following must be submitted:

(1) A copy of the original document;

(2) A copy of an extract from the document evidencing the effect on title; or

(3) A statement signed by both the party conveying the interest and the party receiving the interest explaining how the conveyance affects title.

(b) Name changes. Only a legible cover sheet is required (See §3.31).

(c) All documents.

(1) For electronic submissions: All documents must be submitted as digitized images in Tagged Image File Format (TIFF) or another form as prescribed by the Director. When printed to a paper size of either 21.6 by 27.9 cm (8½ by 11 inches) or 21.0 by 29.7 cm (DIN size A4), a 2.5 cm (one-inch) margin must be present on all sides.

(2) For paper or facsimile submissions: All documents should be submitted on white and non-shiny paper that is either 8½ by 11 inches (21.6 by 27.9 cm) or DIN size A4 (21.0 by 29.7 cm) with a one-inch (2.5 cm) margin on all sides in either case. Only one side of each page may be used. The Office will not return recorded documents, so original documents should not be submitted for recording.

History of 37 C.F.R. §3.25: 64 FR 48927, Sept. 8, 1999; 69 FR 29879, May 26, 2004.

§3.26. ENGLISH LANGUAGE REQUIREMENT

The Office will accept and record non-English language documents only if accompanied by an English translation signed by the individual making the translation.

History of 37 C.F.R. §3.26: 62 FR 53202, Oct. 10, 1997.

§3.27. MAILING ADDRESS FOR SUBMITTING DOCUMENTS TO BE RECORDED

Documents and cover sheets submitted by mail for recordation should be addressed to Mail Stop Assignment Recordation Services, Director of the United States Patent and Trademark Office, P.O. Box 1450, Alexandria, Virginia 22313-1450, unless they are filed together with new applications.

History of 37 C.F.R. §3.27: 62 FR 53202, Oct. 10, 1997; 65 FR 54681, Sept. 8, 2000; 68 FR 14337, Mar. 25, 2003; 69 FR 29879, May 26, 2004.

§3.28. REQUESTS FOR RECORDING

Each document submitted to the Office for recording must include a single cover sheet (as specified in §3.31) referring either to those patent applications and patents, or to those trademark applications and registrations, against which the document is to be recorded. If a document to be recorded includes interests in, or transactions involving, both patents and trademarks, then separate patent and trademark cover sheets, each accompanied by a copy of the document to be recorded, must be submitted. If a document to be recorded is not accompanied by a completed cover sheet, the document and the incomplete cover sheet will be returned pursuant to §3.51 for proper completion, in which case the document and a completed cover sheet should be resubmitted.

History of 37 C.F.R. §3.28: 64 FR 48927, Sept. 8, 1999; 70 FR 56128, Sept. 26, 2005.

COVER SHEET REQUIREMENTS

§3.31. COVER SHEET CONTENT

(a) Each patent or trademark cover sheet required by §3.28 must contain:

(1) The name of the party conveying the interest;

(2) The name and address of the party receiving the interest;

(3) A description of the interest conveyed or transaction to be recorded;

(4) Identification of the interests involved:

(i) For trademark assignments and trademark name changes: Each trademark registration number and each trademark application number, if known, against which the Office is to record the document. If the trademark application number is not known, a copy of the application or a reproduction of the trademark must be submitted, along with an estimate of the date that the Office received the application; or

(ii) For any other document affecting title to a trademark or patent application, registration or patent: Each trademark or patent application number or each trademark registration number or patent against which the document is to be recorded, or an indication that the document is filed together with a patent application;

(5) The name and address of the party to whom correspondence concerning the request to record the document should be mailed;

(6) The date the document was executed;

(7) The signature of the party submitting the document. For an assignment document or name change filed electronically, the person who signs the cover sheet must either:

(i) Place a symbol comprised of letters, numbers, and/or punctuation marks between forward slash marks (*e.g.*, /Thomas O'Malley III/) in the signature block on the electronic submission; or

(ii) Sign the cover sheet using some other form of electronic signature specified by the Director.

(8) For trademark assignments, the entity and citizenship of the party receiving the interest. In addition, if the party receiving the interest is a domestic partnership or domestic joint venture, the cover sheet must set forth the names, legal entities, and national citizenship (or the state or country of organization) of all general partners or active members that compose the partnership or joint venture.

(b) A cover sheet should not refer to both patents and trademarks, since any information, including information about pending patent applications, submitted with a request for recordation of a document against a trademark application or trademark registration will become public record upon recordation.

(c) Each patent cover sheet required by §3.28 seeking to record a governmental interest as provided by §3.11(b) must:

(1) Indicate that the document relates to a Government interest; and

(2) Indicate, if applicable, that the document to be recorded is not a document affecting title (see §3.41(b)).

(d) Each trademark cover sheet required by §3.28 seeking to record a document against a trademark application or registration should include, in addition to the serial number or registration number of the trademark, identification of the trademark or a description of the trademark, against which the Office is to record the document.

(e) Each patent or trademark cover sheet required by §3.28 should contain the number of applications, patents or registrations identified in the cover sheet and the total fee.

(f) Each trademark cover sheet should include the citizenship of the party conveying the interest.

(g) The cover sheet required by §3.28 seeking to record a joint research agreement or an excerpt of a joint research agreement as provided by §3.11(c) must:

(1) Identify the document as a "joint research agreement" (in the space provided for the description of the interest conveyed or transaction to be recorded if using an Office-provided form);

(2) Indicate the name of the owner of the application or patent (in the space provided for the name and address of the party receiving the interest if using an Office-provided form);

(3) Indicate the name of each other party to the joint research agreement party (in the space provided for the name of the party conveying the interest if using an Office-provided form); and

(4) Indicate the date the joint research agreement was executed.

(h) The assignment cover sheet required by §3.28 for a patent application or patent will be satisfied by the Patent Law Treaty Model International Request for Recordation of Change in Applicant or Owner Form, Patent Law Treaty Model International Request for Recordation of a License/Cancellation of the Recordation of a License Form, Patent Law Treaty Model Certificate of Transfer Form or Patent Law Treaty Model International Request for Recordation of a Security Interest/Cancellation of the Recordation of a Security Interest Form, as applicable, except where the assignment is also an oath or declaration under §1.63 of this chapter. An assignment cover sheet required by §3.28 must contain a conspicuous indication of an intent to utilize the assignment as an oath or declaration under §1.63 of this chapter.

History of 37 C.F.R. §3.31: 62 FR 53202, Oct. 10, 1997; 64 FR 48927, Sept. 8, 1999; 67 FR 79523, Dec. 30, 2002; 69 FR 29879, May 26, 2004; 70 FR 1824, Jan. 11, 2005; 70 FR 56128, Sept. 26, 2005; 73 FR 67775, Jan. 16, 2009; 77 FR 48825, Sept. 16, 2012; 78 FR 62408, Dec. 18, 2013.

§3.34. CORRECTION OF COVER SHEET ERRORS

(a) An error in a cover sheet recorded pursuant to §3.11 will be corrected only if:

(1) The error is apparent when the cover sheet is compared with the recorded document to which it pertains, and

(2) A corrected cover sheet is filed for recordation.

(b) The corrected cover sheet must be accompanied by a copy of the document originally submitted for recording and by the recording fee as set forth in §3.41.

History of 37 C.F.R. §3.34: 69 FR 29879, May 26, 2004.

FEES

§3.41. RECORDING FEES

(a) All requests to record documents must be accompanied by the appropriate fee. Except as provided in paragraph (b) of this section, a fee is required for each application, patent and registration against which the document is recorded as identified in the cover sheet. The recording fee is set in §1.21(h) of this chapter for patents and in §2.6(b)(6) of this chapter for trademarks.

(b) No fee is required for each patent application and patent against which a document required by Executive Order 9424 is to be filed if:

(1) The document does not affect title and is so identified in the cover sheet (see §3.31(c)(2)); and

(2) The document and cover sheet are either: Faxed or electronically submitted as prescribed by the Director, or mailed to the Office in compliance with §3.27.

History of 37 C.F.R. §3.41: 62 FR 53202, Oct. 10, 1997; 63 FR 48100, Sept. 9, 1998; 63 FR 52159, Sept. 30, 1998; 69 FR 29879, May 26, 2004.

DATE & EFFECT OF RECORDING

§3.51. RECORDING DATE

The date of recording of a document is the date the document meeting the requirements for recording set forth in this part is filed in the Office. A document which does not comply with the identification requirements of §3.21 will not be recorded. Documents not meeting the other requirements for recording, for example, a document submitted without a completed cover sheet or without the required fee, will be returned for correction to the sender where a correspondence address is available. The returned papers, stamped with the original date of receipt by the Office, will be accompanied by a letter which will indicate that if the returned papers are corrected and resubmitted to the Office within the time specified in the letter, the Office will consider the original date of filing of the papers as the date of recording of the document. The procedure set forth in §1.8 or §1.10 of this chapter may be used for resubmissions of returned papers to have the benefit of the date of deposit in the United States Postal Service. If the returned papers are not corrected and resubmitted within the specified period, the date of filing of the corrected papers will be considered to be the date of recording of the document. The specified period to resubmit the returned papers will not be extended.

History of 37 C.F.R. §3.51: 62 FR 53203, Oct. 10, 1997.

§3.54. EFFECT OF RECORDING

The recording of a document pursuant to §3.11 is not a determination by the Office of the validity of the document or the effect that document has on the title to an application, a patent, or a registration. When necessary, the Office will determine what effect a document has, including whether a party has the authority to take an action in a matter pending before the Office.

§3.56. CONDITIONAL ASSIGNMENTS

Assignments which are made conditional on the performance of certain acts or events, such as the payment of money or other condition subsequent, if recorded in the Office, are regarded as absolute assignments for Office purposes until cancelled with the written consent of all parties or by the decree of a court of competent jurisdiction. The Office does not determine whether such conditions have been fulfilled.

§3.58. GOVERNMENTAL REGISTERS

(a) The Office will maintain a Departmental Register to record governmental interests required to be recorded by Executive Order 9424. This Departmental Register will not be open to public inspection but will be available for examination and inspection by duly authorized representatives of the Government. Governmental interests recorded on the Departmental Register will be available for public inspection as provided in §1.12.

(b) The Office will maintain a Secret Register to record governmental interests required to be recorded by Executive Order 9424. Any instrument to be recorded will be placed on this Secret Register at the request of the department or agency submitting the same. No information will be given concerning any instrument in such record or register, and no examination or inspection thereof or of the index thereto will be permitted, except on the written authority of the head of the department or agency which submitted the instrument and requested secrecy, and the approval of such authority by the Director. No instrument or record other than the one specified may be examined, and the examination must take place in the presence of a designated official of the Patent and Trademark Office. When the department or agency which submitted an instrument no longer requires secrecy with respect to that instrument, it must be recorded anew in the Departmental Register.

History of 37 C.F.R. §3.58: 62 FR 53203, Oct. 10, 1997.

ACTION TAKEN BY ASSIGNEE

§3.61. DOMESTIC REPRESENTATIVE

If the assignee of a patent, patent application, trademark application or trademark registration is not domiciled in the United States, the assignee may designate a domestic representative in a document filed in the United States Patent and Trademark Office. The designation should state the name and address of a person residing within the United States on whom may be served process or notice of proceedings affecting the application, patent or registration or rights thereunder.

History of 37 C.F.R. §3.61: 67 FR 79523, Dec. 30, 2002.

PROSECUTION BY ASSIGNEE

§3.71. PROSECUTION BY ASSIGNEE

(a) Patents—conducting of prosecution. One or more assignees as defined in paragraph (b) of this section may conduct prosecution of a national patent application as the applicant under §1.46 of this title, or conduct prosecution of a supplemental examination or reexamination proceeding, to the exclusion of the inventor or previous applicant or patent owner. Conflicts between purported assignees are handled in accordance with §3.73(c)(3).

(b) Patents—assignee(s) who can prosecute. The assignee(s) who may conduct either the prosecution of a national application for patent as the applicant under §1.46 of this title or a supplemental examination or reexamination proceeding are:

(1) A single assignee. An assignee of the entire right, title and interest in the application or patent, or

(2) Partial assignee(s) together or with inventor(s). All partial assignees, or all partial assignees and inventors who have not assigned their right, title and interest in the application or patent, who together own the entire right, title and interest in the application or patent. A partial assignee is any assignee having less than the entire right, title and interest in the application or patent. The word "assignee" as used in this chapter means with respect to patent matters the single assignee of the entire right, title and interest in the application or patent if there is such a single assignee, or all of the partial assignees, or all of the partial assignee and inventors who have not assigned their interest in the application or patent, who together own the entire right, title and interest in the application or patent.

(c) Patents—Becoming of record. An assignee becomes of record as the applicant in a national patent application under §1.46 of this title, and in a supplemental examination or reexamination proceeding, by filing a statement in compliance with §3.73(c) that is signed by a party who is authorized to act on behalf of the assignee.

(d) Trademarks. The assignee of a trademark application or registration may prosecute a trademark application, submit documents to maintain a trademark registration, or file papers against a third party in reliance on the assignee's trademark application or registration, to the exclusion of the original applicant or previous assignee. The assignee must establish ownership in compliance with §3.73(b).

History of 37 C.F.R. §3.71: 65 FR 54682, Sept. 8, 2000; 77 FR 48825, Sept. 16, 2012.

§3.73. ESTABLISHING RIGHT OF ASSIGNEE TO TAKE ACTION

(a) The original applicant is presumed to be the owner of an application for an original patent, and any patent that may issue therefrom, unless there is an assignment. The original applicant is presumed to be the owner of a trademark application or registration, unless there is an assignment.

(b) In order to request or take action in a trademark matter, the assignee must establish its ownership of the trademark property of paragraph (a) of this section to the satisfaction of the Director. The establishment of ownership by the assignee may be combined with the paper that requests or takes the action. Ownership is established by submitting to the Office a signed statement identifying the assignee, accompanied by either:

(1) Documentary evidence of a chain of title from the original owner to the assignee (e.g., copy of an executed assignment). The documents submitted to establish ownership may be required to be recorded pursuant to §3.11 in the assignment records of the Office as a condition to permitting the assignee to take action in a matter pending before the Office; or

(2) A statement specifying where documentary evidence of a chain of title from the original owner to the assignee is recorded in the assignment records of the Office (e.g., reel and frame number).

(c)(1) In order to request or take action in a patent matter, an assignee who is not the original applicant must establish its ownership of the patent property of paragraph (a) of this section to the satisfaction of the Director. The establishment of ownership by the assignee may be combined with the paper that requests or takes the action. Ownership is established by submitting to the Office a signed statement identifying the assignee, accompanied by either:

(i) Documentary evidence of a chain of title from the original owner to the assignee (e.g., copy of an executed assignment). The submission of the documentary evidence must be accompanied by a statement affirming that the documentary evidence of the chain of title from the original owner to the assignee was or concurrently is being submitted for recordation pursuant to §3.11; or

(ii) A statement specifying where documentary evidence of a chain of title from the original owner to the assignee is recorded in the assignment records of the Office (e.g., reel and frame number).

(2) If the submission is by an assignee of less than the entire right, title and interest (e.g., more than one assignee exists) the Office may refuse to accept the submission as an establishment of ownership unless:

(i) Each assignee establishes the extent (by percentage) of its ownership interest, so as to account for the entire right, title and interest in the application or patent by all parties including inventors; or

(ii) Each assignee submits a statement identifying the parties including inventors who together own the entire right, title and interest and stating that all the identified parties own the entire right, title and interest.

(3) If two or more purported assignees file conflicting statements under paragraph (c)(1) of this section, the Director will determine which, if any, purported assignee will be permitted to control prosecution of the application.

(d) The submission establishing ownership under paragraph (b) or (c) of this section must show that the person signing the submission is a person authorized to act on behalf of the assignee by:

(1) Including a statement that the person signing the submission is authorized to act on behalf of the assignee;

(2) Being signed by a person having apparent authority to sign on behalf of the assignee; or

(3) For patent matters only, being signed by a practitioner of record.

History of 37 C.F.R. §3.73: 62 FR 53203, Oct. 10, 1997; 65 FR 54682, Sept. 8, 2000; 70 FR 56128, Sept. 26, 2005; 77 FR 48825, Sept. 16, 2012.

ISSUANCE TO ASSIGNEE

§3.81. ISSUE OF PATENT TO ASSIGNEE

(a) With payment of the issue fee: An application may issue in the name of the assignee consistent with the application's assignment where a request for such issuance is submitted with payment of the issue fee, provided the assignment has been previously recorded in the Office. If the assignment has not been previously recorded, the request must state that the document has been filed for recordation as set forth in §3.11.

(b) After payment of the issue fee: Any request for issuance of an application in the name of the assignee submitted after the date of payment of the issue fee, and any request for a patent to be corrected to state the name of the assignee, must state that the assignment was submitted for recordation as set forth in §3.11 before issuance of the patent, and must include a request for a certificate of correction under §1.323 of this chapter (accompanied by the fee set forth in §1.20(a)) and the processing fee set forth in §1.17(i) of this chapter.

(c) Partial assignees.

(1) If one or more assignee, together with one or more inventor, holds the entire right, title, and interest in the application, the patent may issue in the names of the assignee and the inventor.

(2) If multiple assignees hold the entire right, title, and interest to the exclusion of all the inventors, the patent may issue in the names of the multiple assignees.

History of 37 C.F.R. §3.81: 60 FR 20229, Apr. 25, 1995; 65 FR 54682, Sept. 8, 2000; 69 FR 29879, May 26, 2004.

§3.85. ISSUE OF REGISTRATION TO ASSIGNEE

The certificate of registration may be issued to the assignee of the applicant, or in a new name of the applicant, provided that the party files a written request in the trademark application by the time the application is being prepared for issuance of the certificate of registration, and the appropriate document is recorded in the Office. If the assignment or name change document has not been recorded in the Office, then the written request must state that the document has been filed for recordation. The address of the assignee must be made of record in the application file.

PART 4. COMPLAINTS REGARDING INVENTION PROMOTERS

§4.1. COMPLAINTS REGARDING INVENTION PROMOTERS

These regulations govern the Patent and Trademark Office's (Office) responsibilities under the Inventors' Rights Act of 1999, which can be found in the U.S. Code at 35 U.S.C. 297.

The Act requires the Office to provide a forum for the publication of complaints concerning invention promoters. The Office will not conduct any independent investigation of the invention promoter. Although the Act provides additional civil remedies for persons injured by invention promoters, those remedies must be pursued by the injured party without the involvement of the Office.

Source of 37 C.F.R. Part 4: 65 FR 3129, Jan. 20, 2000; 68 FR 14338, Mar. 25, 2003, unless otherwise noted.

§4.2. DEFINITIONS

(a) Invention Promoter means any person, firm, partnership, corporation, or other entity who offers to perform or performs invention promotion services for, or on behalf of, a customer, and who holds itself out through advertising in any mass media as providing such services, but does not include—

(1) Any department or agency of the Federal Government or of a State or local government;

(2) Any nonprofit, charitable, scientific, or educational organization qualified under applicable State law or described under section 170(b)(1)(A) of the Internal Revenue Code of 1986;

(3) Any person or entity involved in the evaluation to determine commercial potential of, or offering to license or sell, a utility patent or a previously filed nonprovisional utility patent application;

(4) Any party participating in a transaction involving the sale of the stock or assets of a business; or

(5) Any party who directly engages in the business of retail sales of products or the distribution of products.

(b) Customer means any individual who enters into a contract with an invention promoter for invention promotion services.

(c) Contract for Invention Promotion Services means a contract by which an invention promoter undertakes invention promotion services for a customer.

(d) Invention Promotion Services means the procurement or attempted procurement for a customer of a firm, corporation, or other entity to develop and market products or services that include the invention of the customer.

§4.3. SUBMITTING COMPLAINTS

(a) A person may submit a complaint concerning an invention promoter with the Office. A person submitting a complaint should understand that the complaint may be forwarded to the invention promoter and may become publicly available. The Office will not accept any complaint that requests that it be kept confidential.

(b) A complaint must be clearly marked, or otherwise identified, as a complaint under these rules. The complaint must include:

(1) The name and address of the complainant;

(2) The name and address of the invention promoter;

(3) The name of the customer;

(4) The invention promotion services offered or performed by the invention promoter;

(5) The name of the mass media in which the invention promoter advertised providing such services;

(6) An explanation of the relationship between the customer and the invention promoter; and

(7) A signature of the complainant.

(c) The complaint should fairly summarize the action of the invention promoter about which the person complains. Additionally, the complaint should include names and addresses of persons believed to be associated with the invention promoter. Complaints, and any replies, must be addressed to: Mail Stop 24, Commissioner for Patents, P.O. Box 1450, Alexandria, Virginia 22313-1450.

(d) Complaints that do not provide the information requested in paragraphs (b) and (c) of this section will be returned. If complainant's address is not provided, the complaint will be destroyed.

(e) No originals of documents should be included with the complaint.

(f) A complaint can be withdrawn by the complainant or the named customer at any time prior to its publication.

History of 37 C.F.R. §4.3: 68 FR 14338, Mar. 25, 2003.

§4.4. INVENTION PROMOTER REPLY

(a) If a submission appears to meet the requirements of a complaint, the invention promoter named in the complaint will be notified of the complaint and given 30 days to respond. The invention promoter's response will be made available to the public along with the complaint. If the invention promoter fails to reply within the 30-day time period set by the Office, the complaint will be made available to the public. Replies sent after the complaint is made available to the public will also be published.

(b) A response must be clearly marked, or otherwise identified, as a response by an invention promoter. The response must contain:

(1) The name and address of the invention promoter;

(2) A reference to a complaint forwarded to the invention promoter or a complaint previously published;

(3) The name of the individual signing the response; and

(4) The title or authority of the individual signing the response.

§4.5. NOTICE BY PUBLICATION

If the copy of the complaint that is mailed to the invention promoter is returned undelivered, then the USPTO will primarily publish a Notice of Complaint Received on the USPTO's Internet home page at http://www.uspto.gov. Only where the USPTO's Web site is unavailable for publication will the

USPTO publish the Notice of Complaint in the Official Gazette and/or the Federal Register. The invention promoter will be given 30 days from such notice to submit a reply to the Notice of Complaint. If the USPTO does not receive a reply from the invention promoter within 30 days, the complaint alone will become publicly available.

History of 37 C.F.R. §4.5: 68 FR 9553, Feb. 28, 2003.

§4.6. ATTORNEYS & AGENTS

Complaints against registered patent attorneys and agents will not be treated under this section, unless a complaint fairly demonstrates that invention promotion services are involved. Persons having complaints about registered patent attorneys or agents should contact the Office of Enrollment and Discipline at Mail Stop OED, Director of the United States Patent and Trademark Office, PO Box 1450, Alexandria, Virginia 22313-1450, and the attorney discipline section of the attorney's state licensing bar if an attorney is involved.

History of 37 C.F.R. §4.6: 68 FR 14338, Mar. 25, 2003.

PART 5. SECRECY OF CERTAIN INVENTIONS & LICENSES TO EXPORT & FILE APPLICATIONS IN FOREIGN COUNTRIES

SECRECY ORDERS

§5.1. APPLICATIONS & CORRESPONDENCE INVOLVING NATIONAL SECURITY

(a) All correspondence in connection with this part, including petitions, should be addressed to: Mail Stop L & R, Commissioner for Patents, P.O. Box 1450, Alexandria, Virginia 22313-1450.

(b) Definitions.

(1) Application as used in this part includes provisional applications (§1.9(a)(2) of this chapter), nonprovisional applications (§1.9(a)(3)), international applications (§1.9(b)), or international design applications (§1.9(n)).

(2) Foreign application as used in this part includes, for filing in a foreign country, foreign patent office, foreign patent agency, or international agency (other than the United States Patent and Trademark Office acting as a Receiving Office for international applications (35 U.S.C. 361, §1.412) or as an office of indirect filing for international design applications (35 U.S.C. 382, §1.1002)) any of the following: An application for patent, international application, international design application, or application for the registration of a utility model, industrial design, or model.

(c) Patent applications and documents relating thereto that are national security classified (see §1.9(i) of this chapter) and contain authorized national security markings (*e.g.*, "Confidential," "Secret" or "Top Secret") are accepted by the Office. National security classified documents filed in the Office must be either hand-carried to Licensing and Review or mailed to the Office in compliance with paragraph (a) of this section.

(d) The applicant in a national security classified patent application must obtain a secrecy order pursuant to §5.2(a). If a national security classified patent application is filed without a notification pursuant to §5.2(a), the Office will set a time period within which either the application must be declassified, or the application must be placed under a secrecy order pursuant to §5.2(a), or the applicant must submit evidence of a good faith effort to obtain a secrecy order pursuant to §5.2(a) from the relevant department or agency in order to prevent abandonment of the application. If evidence of a good faith effort to obtain a secrecy order pursuant to §5.2(a) from the relevant department or agency is submitted by the applicant within the time period set by the Office, but the application has not been declassified or placed under a secrecy order pursuant to §5.2(a), the Office will again set a time period within which either the application must be declassified, or the application must be placed under a secrecy order pursuant to §5.2(a), or the applicant must submit evidence of a good faith effort to again obtain a secrecy order pursuant to §5.2(a) from the relevant department or agency in order to prevent abandonment of the application.

(e) An application will not be published under §1.211 of this chapter or allowed under §1.311 of this chapter if publication or disclosure of the application would be detrimental to national security. An application under national security review will not be published at least until six months from its filing date or three months from the date the application was referred to a defense agency, whichever is later. A national security classified patent application will not be published under §1.211 of this chapter or allowed under §1.311 of this chapter until the application is declassified and any secrecy order under §5.2(a) has been rescinded.

(f) Applications on inventions made outside the United States and on inventions in which a U.S. Government defense agency has a property interest will not be made available to defense agencies.

History of 37 C.F.R. §5.1: 43 FR 20470, May 11, 1978; 62 FR 53203, Oct. 10, 1997; 65 FR 54682, Sept. 8, 2000; 65 FR 57060, Sept. 20, 2000; 68 FR 14338, Mar. 25, 2003; 69 FR 29880, May 26, 2004; 80 FR 17969, May 13, 2015.

Source of 37 C.F.R. Part 5: 24 FR 10381, Dec. 22, 1959; 53 FR 23735, June 23, 1988; 56 FR 1928, Jan. 18, 1991; 65 FR 54682, Sept. 8, 2000; 65 FR 57060, Sept. 20, 2000; 68 FR 14338, Mar. 25, 2003; 70 FR 56129, Sept. 26, 2005, unless otherwise noted.

§5.2. SECRECY ORDER

(a) When notified by the chief officer of a defense agency that publication or disclosure of the invention by the granting of a patent would be detrimental to the national security, an order that the invention be kept secret will be issued by the Commissioner for Patents.

(b) Any request for compensation as provided in 35 U.S.C. 183 must not be made to the Patent and Trademark Office, but directly to the department or agency which caused the secrecy order to be issued.

(c) An application disclosing any significant part of the subject matter of an application under a secrecy order pursuant to paragraph (a) of this section also falls within the scope of such secrecy order. Any such application that is pending before the Office must be promptly brought to the attention of Licensing and Review, unless such application is itself under a secrecy order pursuant to paragraph (a) of this section. Any subsequently filed application containing any significant part of the subject matter of an application under a secrecy order pursuant to paragraph (a) of this section must either be hand-carried to Licensing and Review or mailed to the Office in compliance with §5.1(a).

History of 37 C.F.R. §5.2: 62 FR 53203, Oct. 10, 1997; 65 FR 54683, Sept. 8, 2000.

§5.3. PROSECUTION OF APPLICATION UNDER SECRECY ORDERS; WITHHOLDING PATENT

Unless specifically ordered otherwise, action on the application by the Office and prosecution by the applicant will proceed during the time an application is under secrecy order to the point indicated in this section:

(a) National applications under secrecy order which come to a final rejection must be appealed or otherwise prosecuted to avoid abandonment. Appeals in such cases must be completed by the applicant but unless otherwise specifically ordered by the Commissioner for Patents will not be set for hearing until the secrecy order is removed.

(b) An interference or derivation will not be instituted involving a national application under secrecy order. An applicant whose application is under secrecy order may suggest an interference (§41.202(a) of this title), but the Office will not act on the request while the application remains under a secrecy order.

(c) When the national application is found to be in condition for allowance except for the secrecy order the applicant and the agency which caused the secrecy order to be issued will be notified. This notice (which is not a notice of allowance under §1.311 of this chapter) does not require reply by the applicant and places the national application in a condition of suspension until the secrecy order is removed. When the secrecy order is removed the Patent and Trademark Office will issue a notice of allowance under §1.311 of this chapter, or take such other action as may then be warranted.

(d) International applications and international design applications under secrecy order will not be mailed, delivered, or otherwise transmitted to the international authorities or the applicant. International applications under secrecy order will be processed up to the point where, if it were not for the secrecy order, record and search copies would be transmitted to the international authorities or the applicant.

History of 37 C.F.R. §5.3: 43 FR 20470, May 11, 1978; 43 FR 28479, June 30, 1978; 53 FR 23736, June 23, 1988; 62 FR 53203, Oct. 10, 1997; 69 FR 50002, Aug. 12, 2004; 77 FR 46629, Sept. 16, 2012; 80 FR 17969, May 13, 2015.

§5.4. PETITION FOR RESCISSION OF SECRECY ORDER

(a) A petition for rescission or removal of a secrecy order may be filed by, or on behalf of, any principal affected thereby. Such petition may be in letter form, and it must be in duplicate.

(b) The petition must recite any and all facts that purport to render the order ineffectual or futile if this is the basis of the petition. When prior publications or patents are alleged the petition must give complete data as to such publications or patents and should be accompanied by copies thereof.

(c) The petition must identify any contract between the Government and any of the principals, under which the subject matter of the application or any significant part thereof was developed, or to which the subject matter is otherwise related. If there is no such contract, the petition must so state.

(d) Appeal to the Secretary of Commerce, as provided by 35 U.S.C. 181, from a secrecy order cannot be taken until after a petition for rescission of the secrecy order has been made and denied. Appeal must be taken within sixty days from the date of the denial, and the party appealing, as well as the department or agency which caused the order to be issued, will be notified of the time and place of hearing.

History of 37 C.F.R. §5.4: 62 FR 53204, Oct. 10, 1997.

§5.5. PERMIT TO DISCLOSE OR MODIFICATION OF SECRECY ORDER

(a) Consent to disclosure, or to the filing of an application abroad, as provided in 35 U.S.C. 182, shall be made by a "permit" or "modification" of the secrecy order.

(b) Petitions for a permit or modification must fully recite the reason or purpose for the proposed disclosure. Where any proposed disclosee is known to be cleared by a defense agency to receive classified information, adequate explanation of such clearance should be made in the petition including the name of the agency or department granting the clearance and the date and degree thereof. The petition must be filed in duplicate.

(c) In a petition for modification of a secrecy order to permit filing abroad, all countries in which it is proposed to file must be made known, as well as all attorneys, agents and others to whom the material will be consigned prior to being lodged in the foreign patent office. The petition should include a statement vouching for the loyalty and integrity of the proposed disclosees and where their clearance status in this or the foreign country is known all details should be given.

(d) Consent to the disclosure of subject matter from one application under secrecy order may be deemed to be consent to the disclosure of common subject matter in other applications under secrecy order so long as not taken out of context in a manner disclosing material beyond the modification granted in the first application.

(e) Organizations requiring consent for disclosure of applications under secrecy order to persons or organizations in connection with repeated routine operation may petition for such consent in the form of a general permit. To be successful such petitions must ordinarily recite the security clearance status of the disclosees as sufficient for the highest classification of material that may be involved.

History of 37 C.F.R. §5.5: 62 FR 53204, Oct. 10, 1997.

§5.6. RESERVED

History of 37 C.F.R. §5.6: 62 FR 53204, Oct. 10, 1997.

§§5.7, 5.8. RESERVED

LICENSES FOR FOREIGN EXPORTING & FILING

§5.11. LICENSE FOR FILING IN, OR EXPORTING TO, A FOREIGN COUNTRY AN APPLICATION ON AN INVENTION MADE IN THE UNITED STATES OR TECHNICAL DATA RELATING THERETO

(a) A license from the Commissioner for Patents under 35 U.S.C. 184 is required before filing any application for patent including any modifications, amendments, or supplements thereto or divisions thereof or for the registration of a utility model, industrial design, or model, in a foreign country, foreign patent office, foreign patent agency, or any international agency (other than the United States Patent and Trademark Office acting as a Receiving Office for international applications (35 U.S.C. 361, §1.412) or as an office of indirect filing for international design applications (35 U.S.C. 382, §1.1002)), if the invention was made in the United States, and:

(1) An application on the invention has been filed in the United States less than six months prior to the date on which the application is to be filed; or

(2) No application on the invention has been filed in the United States.

(b) The license from the Commissioner for Patents referred to in paragraph (a) of this section would also authorize the export of technical data abroad for purposes relating to the preparation, filing or possible filing and prosecution of a foreign application without separately complying with the regulations contained in 22 CFR parts 120 through 130 (International Traffic in Arms Regulations of the Department of State), 15 CFR parts 730 through 774 (Export Administration Regulations of the Bureau of Industry and Security, Department of Commerce), and 10 CFR part 810 (Assistance to Foreign Atomic Energy Activities Regulations of the Department of Energy).

(c) Where technical data in the form of a patent application, or in any form, are being exported for purposes related to the preparation, filing or possible filing and prosecution of a foreign application, without the license from the Commissioner for Patents referred to in paragraphs (a) or (b) of this section, or on an invention not made in the United States, the export regulations contained in 22 CFR parts 120 through 130 (International Traffic in Arms Regulations of the Department of State), 15 CFR parts 730 through 774 (Export Administration Regulations of the Bureau of Industry and Security, Department of Commerce), and 10 CFR part 810 (Assistance to Foreign Atomic Energy Activities Regulations of the Department of Energy) must be complied with unless a license is not required because a United States application was on file at the time of export for at least six months without a secrecy order under §5.2 being placed thereon. The term "exported" means export as it is defined in 22 CFR part 120, 15 CFR part 734, and activities covered by 10 CFR part 810.

(d) If a secrecy order has been issued under §5.2, an application cannot be exported to, or filed in, a foreign country (including an international agency in a foreign country), except in accordance with §5.5.

(e) No license pursuant to paragraph (a) of this section is required:

(1) If the invention was not made in the United States, or

(2) If the corresponding United States application is not subject to a secrecy order under §5.2, and was filed at least six months prior to the date on which the application is filed in a foreign country, or

(3) For subsequent modifications, amendments and supplements containing additional subject matter to, or divisions of, a foreign patent application if:

(i) A license is not, or was not, required under paragraph (e)(2) of this section for the foreign application;

(ii) The corresponding United States application was not required to be made available for inspection under 35 U.S.C. 181; and

(iii) Such modifications, amendments, and supplements do not, or did not, change the general nature of the invention in a manner which would require any corresponding United States application to be or have been available for inspection under 35 U.S.C. 181.

(f) A license pursuant to paragraph (a) of this section can be revoked at any time upon written notification by the United States Patent and Trademark Office. An authorization to file a foreign application resulting from the passage of six months from the date of filing of a United States patent application may be revoked by the imposition of a secrecy order.

History of 37 C.F.R. §5.11: 43 FR 20471, May 11, 1978; 49 FR 13461, Apr. 4, 1984; 56 FR 1928, Jan. 18, 1991; 62 FR 53204, Oct. 10, 1997; 70 FR 56129, Sept. 26, 2005; 80 FR 17969, May 13, 2015.

§5.12. PETITION FOR LICENSE

(a) Filing of an application on an invention made in the United States will be considered to include a petition for license under 35 U.S.C. 184 for the subject matter of the application. The filing receipt or other official notice will indicate if a license is granted. If the initial automatic petition is not granted, a subsequent petition may be filed under paragraph (b) of this section.

(b) A petition for license must include the fee set forth in §1.17(g) of this chapter, the petitioner's address, and full instructions for delivery of the requested license when it is to be delivered to other than the petitioner. The petition should be presented in letter form.

History of 37 C.F.R. §5.12: 24 FR 10381, Dec. 22, 1959; 48 FR 2714, Jan. 20, 1983; 49 FR 13462, Apr. 4, 1984; 62 FR 53204, Oct. 10, 1997; 65 FR 54683, Sept. 8, 2000; 69 FR 56546, Sept. 21, 2004; 80 FR 17970, May 13, 2015.

§5.13. PETITION FOR LICENSE; NO CORRESPONDING APPLICATION

If no corresponding national, international design, or international application has been filed in the United States, the petition for license under §5.12(b) must also be accompanied by a legible copy of the material upon which a license is desired. This copy will be retained as a measure of the license granted.

History of 37 C.F.R. §5.13: 43 FR 20471, May 11, 1978; 49 FR 13462, Apr. 4, 1984; 62 FR 53204, Oct. 10, 1997; 80 FR 17970, May 13, 2015.

§5.14. PETITION FOR LICENSE; CORRESPONDING U.S. APPLICATION

(a) When there is a corresponding United States application on file, a petition for license under §5.12(b) must also identify this application by application number, filing date, inventor, and title, but a copy of the material upon which the license is desired is not required. The subject matter licensed will be measured by the disclosure of the United States application.

(b) Two or more United States applications should not be referred to in the same petition for license unless they are to be combined in the foreign or international application, in which event the petition should so state and the identification of each United States application should be in separate paragraphs.

(c) Where the application to be filed or exported abroad contains matter not disclosed in the United States application or applications, including the case where the combining of two or more United States applications introduces subject matter not disclosed in any of them, a copy of the application as it is to be filed or exported abroad, must be furnished with the petition. If, however, all new matter in the application to be filed or exported is readily identifiable, the new matter may be submitted in detail and the remainder by reference to the pertinent United States application or applications.

History of 37 C.F.R. §5.14: 24 FR 10381, Dec. 22, 1959; 43 FR 20471, May 11, 1978; 49 FR 13462, Apr. 16, 1984; 62 FR 53204, Oct. 10, 1997; 80 FR 17970, May 13, 2015.

§5.15. SCOPE OF LICENSE

(a) Applications or other materials reviewed pursuant to §§5.12 through 5.14, which were not required to be made available for inspection by defense agencies under 35 U.S.C. 181, will be eligible for a license of the scope provided in this paragraph. This license permits subsequent modifications, amendments, and supplements containing additional subject matter to, or divisions of, a foreign application, if such changes to the application do not alter the general nature of the invention in a manner that would require the United States application to have been made available for inspection under 35 U.S.C. 181. Grant of this license authorizes the export and filing of an application in a foreign country or to any foreign patent agency or international patent agency when the subject matter of the foreign application corresponds to that of the domestic application. This license includes authority:

(1) To export and file all duplicate and formal application papers in foreign countries or with international agencies;

(2) To make amendments, modifications, and supplements, including divisions, changes or supporting matter consisting of the illustration, exemplification, comparison, or explanation of subject matter disclosed in the application; and

(3) To take any action in the prosecution of the foreign application provided that the adding of subject matter or taking of any action under paragraph (a)(1) or (2) of this section does not change the general nature of the invention disclosed in the application in a manner that would require such application to have been made available for inspection under 35 U.S.C. 181 by including technical data pertaining to:

(i) Defense services or articles designated in the United States Munitions List applicable at the time of foreign filing, the unlicensed exportation of which is prohibited pursuant to the Arms Export Control Act, as amended, and 22 CFR parts 120 through 130; or

(ii) Restricted Data, sensitive nuclear technology or technology useful in the production or utilization of special nuclear material or atomic energy, dissemination of which is subject to restrictions of the Atomic Energy Act of 1954, as amended, and the Nuclear Non-Proliferation Act of 1978, as implemented by the regulations for Assistance to Foreign Atomic Energy Activities, 10 CFR part 810, in effect at the time of foreign filing.

(b) Applications or other materials which were required to be made available for inspection under 35 U.S.C. 181 will be eligible for a license of the scope provided in this paragraph. Grant of this license authorizes the export and filing of an application in a foreign country or to any foreign patent agency or international patent agency. Further, this license includes authority to export and file all duplicate and formal papers in foreign countries or with foreign and international patent agencies and to make amendments, modifications, and supplements to, file divisions of, and take any action in the prosecution of the foreign application, provided subject matter additional to that covered by the license is not involved.

(c) A license granted under §5.12(b) pursuant to §5.13 or §5.14 shall have the scope indicated in paragraph (a) of this section, if it is so specified in the license. A petition, accompanied by the required fee (§1.17(g) of this chapter), may also be filed to change a license having the scope indicated in paragraph (b) of this section to a license having the scope indicated in paragraph (a) of this section. No such petition will be granted if the copy of the material filed pursuant to §5.13 or any corresponding United States application was required to be made available for inspection under 35 U.S.C. 181. The change in the scope of a license will be effective as of the date of the grant of the petition.

(d) In those cases in which no license is required to file or export the foreign application, no license is required to file papers in connection with the prosecution of the foreign application not involving the disclosure of additional subject matter.

(e) Any paper filed abroad or transmitted to an international patent agency following the filing of a foreign application that changes the general nature of the subject matter disclosed at the time of filing in a manner that would require such application to have been made available for inspection under 35 U.S.C. 181 or that involves the disclosure of subject matter listed in paragraph (a)(3)(i) or (ii) of this section must be separately licensed in the same manner as a foreign application. Further, if no license has been granted under §5.12(a) on filing the corresponding United States application, any paper filed abroad or with an international patent agency that involves the disclosure of additional subject matter must be licensed in the same manner as a foreign application.

(f) Licenses separately granted in connection with two or more United States applications may be exercised by combining or dividing the disclosures, as desired, provided:

(1) Subject matter which changes the general nature of the subject matter disclosed at the time of filing or which involves subject matter listed in paragraph (a)(3)(i) or (ii) of this section is not introduced, and

(2) In the case where at least one of the licenses was obtained under §5.12(b), additional subject matter is not introduced.

(g) A license does not apply to acts done before the license was granted. See §5.25 for petitions for retroactive licenses.

History of 37 C.F.R. §5.15: 24 FR 10381, Dec. 22, 1959; 43 FR 20471, May 11, 1978; 49 FR 13462, Apr. 4, 1984; 56 FR 1928, Jan. 18, 1991; 62 FR 53204, Oct. 10, 1997; 69 FR 56546, Sept. 21, 2004; 80 FR 17970, May 13, 2015.

§§5.16, 5.17. RESERVED

History of 37 C.F.R. §§5.16, 5.17: 62 FR 53205, Oct. 10, 1997.

§5.18. ARMS, AMMUNITION, & IMPLEMENTS OF WAR

(a) The exportation of technical data relating to arms, ammunition, and implements of war generally is subject to the International Traffic in Arms Regulations of the Department of State (22 CFR parts 120 through 130); the articles designated as arms, ammunitions, and implements of war are enumerated in the U.S. Munitions List (22 CFR part 121). However, if a patent applicant complies with regulations issued by the Commissioner for Patents under 35 U.S.C. 184, no separate approval from the Department of State is required unless the applicant seeks to export technical data exceeding that used to support a patent application in a foreign country. This exemption from Department of State regulations is applicable regardless of whether a license from the Commissioner for Patents is required by the provisions of §§5.11 and 5.12 (22 CFR part 125).

(b) When a patent application containing subject matter on the Munitions List (22 CFR part 121) is subject to a secrecy order under §5.2 and a petition is made under §5.5 for a modification of the secrecy order to permit filing abroad, a separate request to the Department of State for authority to export classified information is not required (22 CFR part 125).

History of 37 C.F.R. §5.18: 35 FR 6430, Apr. 22, 1970; 62 FR 53205, Oct. 10, 1997.

§5.19. EXPORT OF TECHNICAL DATA

(a) Under regulations (15 CFR 734.3(b)(1)(v)) established by the Department of Commerce, a license is not required in any case to file a patent application or part thereof in a foreign country if the foreign filing is in accordance with the regulations (§§5.11 through 5.25) of the U.S. Patent and Trademark Office.

(b) An export license is not required for data contained in a patent application prepared wholly from foreign-origin technical data where such application is being sent to the foreign inventor to be executed and returned to the United States for subsequent filing in the U.S. Patent and Trademark Office (15 CFR 734.10(a)).

History of 37 C.F.R. §5.19: 45 FR 72654, Nov. 3, 1980; 58 FR 54511, Oct. 22, 1993; 62 FR 53205, Oct. 10, 1997; 70 FR 56129, Sept. 26, 2005.

§5.20. EXPORT OF TECHNICAL DATA RELATING TO SENSITIVE NUCLEAR TECHNOLOGY

Under regulations (10 CFR 810.7) established by the United States Department of Energy, an application filed in accordance with the regulations (§§5.11 through 5.25) of the Patent and Trademark Office and eligible for foreign filing under 35 U.S.C. 184, is considered to be information available to the public in published form and a generally authorized activity for the purposes of the Department of Energy regulations.

History of 37 C.F.R. §5.20: 49 FR 13463, Apr. 4, 1984; 62 FR 53205, Oct. 10, 1997.

§5.25. PETITION FOR RETROACTIVE LICENSE

(a) A petition for a retroactive license under 35 U.S.C. 184 shall be presented in accordance with §5.13 or §5.14(a), and shall include:

(1) A listing of each of the foreign countries in which the unlicensed patent application material was filed,

(2) The dates on which the material was filed in each country,

(3) A verified statement (oath or declaration) containing:

(i) An averment that the subject matter in question was not under a secrecy order at the time it was filed aboard, and that it is not currently under a secrecy order,

(ii) A showing that the license has been diligently sought after discovery of the proscribed foreign filing, and

(iii) An explanation of why the material was filed abroad through error without the required license under §5.11 first having been obtained, and

(4) The required fee (§1.17(g) of this chapter).

(b) The explanation in paragraph (a) of this section must include a showing of facts rather than a mere allegation of action through error. The showing of facts as to the nature of the error should include statements by those persons having personal knowledge of the acts regarding filing in a foreign country and should be accompanied by copies of any necessary supporting documents such as letters of transmittal or instructions for filing. The acts which are alleged to constitute error should cover the period leading up to and including each of the proscribed foreign filings.

(c) If a petition for a retroactive license is denied, a time period of not less than thirty days shall be set, during which the petition may be renewed. Failure to renew the petition within the set time period will result in a final denial of the petition. A final denial of a petition stands unless a petition is filed under §1.181 within two months of the date of the denial. If the petition for a retroactive license is denied with respect to the invention of a pending application and no petition under §1.181 has been filed, a final rejection of the application under 35 U.S.C. 185 will be made.

History of 37 C.F.R. §5.25: 49 FR 13463, Apr. 4, 1984; 56 FR 1929, Jan. 18, 1991; 62 FR 53206, Oct. 10, 1997; 69 FR 56546, Sept. 21, 2004; 77 FR 48826, Sept. 16, 2012.

GENERAL

§§5.31 TO 5.33. RESERVED

History of 37 C.F.R. §§5.31-5.33: 62 FR 53206, Oct. 10, 1997.

PART 6. CLASSIFICATION OF GOODS & SERVICES UNDER THE TRADEMARK ACT

Ⓐ §6.1. INTERNATIONAL SCHEDULE OF CLASSES OF GOODS & SERVICES

Class	Type of Goods or Services
	Goods
1	Chemicals for use in industry, science and photography, as well as in agriculture, horticulture and forestry; unprocessed artificial resins, unprocessed plastics; fire extinguishing and fire prevention compositions; tempering and soldering preparations; substances for tanning animal skins and hides; adhesives for use in industry; putties and other paste fillers; compost, manures, fertilizers; biological preparations for use in industry and science.
2	Paints, varnishes, lacquers; preservatives against rust and against deterioration of wood; colorants, dyes; inks for printing, marking and engraving; raw natural resins; metals in foil and powder form for use in painting, decorating, printing and art.
3	Non-medicated cosmetics and toiletry preparations; non-medicated dentifrices; perfumery, essential oils; bleaching preparations and other substances for laundry use; cleaning, polishing, scouring and abrasive preparations.
4	Industrial oils and greases, wax; lubricants; dust absorbing, wetting and binding compositions; fuels and illuminants; candles and wicks for lighting.
5	Pharmaceuticals, medical and veterinary preparations; sanitary preparations for medical purposes; dietetic food and substances adapted for medical use or veterinary use, food for babies; dietary supplements for humans and animals; plasters, materials for dressings; material for stopping teeth, dental wax; disinfectants; preparations for destroying vermin; fungicides, herbicides.
6	Common metals and their alloys, ores; metal materials for building and construction; transportable buildings of metal; non-electric cables and wires of common metal; small items of metal hardware; metal containers for storage or transport; safes.
7	Machines, machine tools, power-operated tools; motors and engines, except for land vehicles; machine coupling and transmission components, except for land vehicles; agricultural implements, other than hand-operated hand tools; incubators for eggs; automatic vending machines.
8	Hand tools and implements, hand-operated; cutlery; side arms, except firearms; razors.
9	Scientific, nautical, surveying, photographic, cinematographic, optical, weighing, measuring, signalling, checking (supervision), life-saving and teaching apparatus and instruments; apparatus and instruments for conducting, switching, transforming, accumulating, regulating or controlling electricity; apparatus for recording, transmission or reproduction of sound or images; magnetic data carriers, recording discs; compact discs, DVDs and other digital recording media; mechanisms for coin-operated apparatus; cash registers, calculating machines, data processing equipment, computers; computer software; fire-extinguishing apparatus.
10	Surgical, medical, dental and veterinary apparatus and instruments; artificial limbs, eyes and teeth; orthopaedic articles; suture materials; therapeutic and assistive devices adapted for the disabled; massage apparatus; apparatus, devices and articles for nursing infants; sexual activity apparatus, devices and articles.
11	Apparatus for lighting, heating, steam generating, cooking, refrigerating, drying, ventilating, water supply and sanitary purposes.
12	Vehicles; apparatus for locomotion by land, air or water.
13	Firearms; ammunition and projectiles; explosives; fireworks.
14	Precious metals and their alloys; jewellery, precious and semi-precious stones; horological and chronometric instruments.
15	Musical instruments.

Class	Type of Goods or Services
	Goods (continued)
16	Paper and cardboard; printed matter; bookbinding material; photographs; stationery and office requisites, except furniture; adhesives for stationery or household purposes; drawing materials and materials for artists; paintbrushes; instructional and teaching materials; plastic sheets, films and bags for wrapping and packaging; printers' type, printing blocks.
17	Unprocessed and semi-processed rubber, gutta-percha, gum, asbestos, mica and substitutes for all these materials; plastics and resins in extruded form for use in manufacture; packing, stopping and insulating materials; flexible pipes, tubes and hoses, not of metal.
18	Leather and imitations of leather; animal skins and hides; luggage and carrying bags; umbrellas and parasols; walking sticks; whips, harness and saddlery; collars, leashes and clothing for animals.
19	Building materials (non-metallic); non-metallic rigid pipes for building; asphalt, pitch and bitumen; non-metallic transportable buildings; monuments, not of metal.
20	Furniture, mirrors, picture frames; containers, not of metal, for storage or transport; unworked or semi-worked bone, horn, whalebone or mother-of-pearl; shells; meerschaum; yellow amber.
21	Household or kitchen utensils and containers; cookware and tableware, except forks, knives and spoons; combs and sponges; brushes, except paintbrushes; brush-making materials; articles for cleaning purposes; unworked or semi-worked glass, except building glass; glassware, porcelain and earthenware.
22	Ropes and string; nets; tents and tarpaulins; awnings of textile or synthetic materials; sails; sacks for the transport and storage of materials in bulk; padding, cushioning and stuffing materials, except of paper, cardboard, rubber or plastics; raw fibrous textile materials and substitutes therefor.
23	Yarns and threads, for textile use.
24	Textiles and substitutes for textiles; household linen; curtains of textile or plastic.
25	Clothing, footwear, headgear.
26	Lace and embroidery, ribbons and braid; buttons, hooks and eyes, pins and needles; artificial flowers; hair decorations; false hair.
27	Carpets, rugs, mats and matting, linoleum and other materials for covering existing floors; wall hangings (non-textile).
28	Games, toys and playthings; video game apparatus; gymnastic and sporting articles; decorations for Christmas trees.
29	Meat, fish, poultry and game; meat extracts; preserved, frozen, dried and cooked fruits and vegetables; jellies, jams, compotes; eggs; milk and milk products; oils and fats for food.
30	Coffee, tea, cocoa and artificial coffee; rice; tapioca and sago; flour and preparations made from cereals; bread, pastries and confectionery; edible ices; sugar, honey, treacle; yeast, baking-powder; salt; mustard; vinegar, sauces (condiments); spices; ice (frozen water).
31	Raw and unprocessed agricultural, aquacultural, horticultural and forestry products; raw and unprocessed grains and seeds; fresh fruits and vegetables, fresh herbs; natural plants and flowers; bulbs, seedlings and seeds for planting; live animals; foodstuffs and beverages for animals; malt.
32	Beers; mineral and aerated waters and other non-alcoholic beverages; fruit beverages and fruit juices; syrups and other preparations for making beverages.
33	Alcoholic beverages (except beers).
34	Tobacco; smokers' articles; matches.
	Services
35	Advertising; business management; business administration; office functions.
36	Insurance; financial affairs; monetary affairs; real estate affairs.
37	Building construction; repair; installation services.
38	Telecommunications.
39	Transport; packaging and storage of goods; travel arrangement.
40	Treatment of materials.
41	Education; providing of training; entertainment; sporting and cultural activities.

Class	Type of Goods or Services
	Services (continued)
42	Scientific and technological services and research and design relating thereto; industrial analysis and research services; design and development of computer hardware and software.
43	Services for providing food and drink; temporary accommodation.
44	Medical services; veterinary services; hygienic and beauty care for human beings or animals; agriculture, horticulture and forestry services.
45	Legal services; security services for the physical protection of tangible property and individuals; personal and social services rendered by others to meet the needs of individuals.

History of 37 C.F.R. §6.1: 38 FR 14681, June 4, 1973; 64 FR 48927, Sept. 8, 1999; 66 FR 48339, Sept. 20, 2001; 72 FR 28611, May 22, 2007; 77 FR 47529, Aug. 9, 2012; 80 FR 2312, Jan. 16, 2015; 80 FR 80268, Jan. 1, 2016; 81 FR 76869, Jan. 1, 2017; 82 FR 56889, Jan. 1, 2018.

Source of 37 C.F.R. Part 6: 24 FR 10383, Dec. 22, 1959, unless otherwise noted.

§6.2. PRIOR U.S. SCHEDULE OF CLASSES OF GOODS & SERVICES

Class	Type of Goods or Services
	Goods
1	Raw or partly prepared materials.
2	Receptacles.
3	Baggage, animal equipments, portfolios, and pocket books.
4	Abrasives and polishing materials.
5	Adhesives.
6	Chemicals and chemical compositions.
7	Cordage.
8	Smokers' articles, not including tobacco products.
9	Explosives, firearms, equipments, and projectiles.
10	Fertilizers.
11	Inks and inking materials.
12	Construction materials.
13	Hardware and plumbing and steamfitting supplies.
14	Metals and metal castings and forgings.
15	Oils and greases.
16	Protective and decorative coatings.
17	Tobacco products.
18	Medicines and pharmaceutical preparations.
19	Vehicles.
20	Linoleum and oiled cloth.
21	Electrical apparatus, machines, and supplies.
22	Games, toys, and sporting goods.
23	Cutlery, machinery, and tools, and parts thereof.
24	Laundry appliances and machines.

Class	Type of Goods or Services
	Goods (continued)
25	Locks and safes.
26	Measuring and scientific appliances.
27	Horological instruments.
28	Jewelry and precious-metal ware.
29	Brooms, brushes, and dusters.
30	Crockery, earthenware, and porcelain.
31	Filters and refrigerators.
32	Furniture and upholstery.
33	Glassware.
34	Heating, lighting, and ventilating apparatus.
35	Belting, hose, machinery packing, and nonmetallic tires.
36	Musical instruments and supplies.
37	Paper and stationery.
38	Prints and publications.
39	Clothing.
40	Fancy goods, furnishings, and notions.
41	Canes, parasols, and umbrellas.
42	Knitted, netted, and textile fabrics, and substitutes therefor.
43	Thread and yarn.
44	Dental, medical, and surgical appliances.
45	Soft drinks and carbonated waters.
46	Foods and ingredients of foods.
47	Wines.
48	Malt beverages and liquors.
49	Distilled alcoholic liquors.

Class	Type of Goods or Services
	Goods (continued)
50	Merchandise not otherwise classified.
51	Cosmetics and toilet preparations.
52	Detergents and soaps.
	Services
100	Miscellaneous.
101	Advertising and business.
102	Insurance and financial.
103	Construction and repair.
104	Communication.
105	Transportation and storage.
106	Material treatment.
107	Education and entertainment.

History of 37 C.F.R. §6.2: 24 FR 10383, Dec. 22, 1959. Redesignated at 38 FR 14681, June 4, 1973.

§6.3. SCHEDULE FOR CERTIFICATION MARKS

In applications for registration of certification marks based on sections 1 and 44 of the Trademark Act and registrations resulting from such applications, goods and services are classified in two classes as follows:

A. Goods.

B. Services.

History of 37 C.F.R. §6.3: 24 FR 10383, Dec. 22, 1959. Redesignated at 38 FR 14681, June 4, 1973. Amended at 73 FR 67775, Jan. 16, 2009.

§6.4. SCHEDULE FOR COLLECTIVE MEMBERSHIP MARKS

All collective membership marks in applications based on sections 1 and 44 of the Trademark Act and registrations resulting from such applications are classified as follows:

Class	Title
200	Collective Membership

History of 37 C.F.R. §6.4: 24 FR 10383, Dec. 22, 1959. Redesignated at 38 FR 14681, June 4, 1973. Amended at 73 FR 67775, Jan. 16, 2009.

PART 7. RULES OF PRACTICE IN FILINGS PURSUANT TO THE PROTOCOL RELATING TO THE MADRID AGREEMENT CONCERNING THE INTERNATIONAL REGISTRATION OF MARKS

SUBPART A. GENERAL INFORMATION

§7.1. DEFINITIONS OF TERMS AS USED IN THIS PART

(a) the Act means the Trademark Act of 1946, 60 Stat. 427, as amended, codified in 15 U.S.C. 1051 et seq.

(b) Subsequent designation means a request for extension of protection of an international registration to a Contracting Party made after the International Bureau registers the mark.

(c) The acronym TEAS means the Trademark Electronic Application System, available at http://www.uspto.gov.

(d) The term Office means the United States Patent and Trademark Office.

(e) All references to sections in this part refer to 37 Code of Federal Regulations, except as otherwise stated.

(f) The definitions specified in §2.2(k) and (n) of this chapter apply to this part.

History of 37 C.F.R. §7.1: 80 FR 33190, July 11, 2015.

Source of 37 C.F.R. Part 7A: 68 FR 55769, Sept. 26, 2003, unless otherwise noted.

§7.2. RESERVED

§7.3. CORRESPONDENCE MUST BE IN ENGLISH

International applications and registrations, requests for extension of protection and all other related correspondence with the Office must be in English. The Office will not process correspondence that is in a language other than English.

§7.4. RECEIPT OF CORRESPONDENCE

(a) Correspondence Filed Through TEAS. Correspondence relating to international applications and registrations and requests for extension of protection submitted through TEAS will be accorded the date and time on which the complete transmission is received in the Office based on Eastern Time. Eastern Time means eastern standard time or eastern daylight time, as appropriate.

(b) Correspondence Filed By Mail. International applications under §7.11, subsequent designations under §7.21, responses to notices of irregularity under §7.14, requests to record changes in the International Register under §7.23 and §7.24, requests to note replacement under §7.28, requests for transformation under §7.31, and petitions to the Director to review an action of the Office's Madrid Processing Unit, when filed by mail, must be addressed to: Madrid Processing Unit, 600 Dulany Street, MDE-7B87, Alexandria, VA 22314-5793.

(1) International applications under §7.11, subsequent designations under §7.21, requests to record changes in the International Register under §7.23 and §7.24, and petitions to the Director to review an action of the Office's Madrid Processing Unit, when filed by mail, will be accorded the date of receipt in the Office, unless they are sent by Priority Mail Express® pursuant to §2.198, in which case they will be accorded the date of deposit with the United States Postal Service.

(2) Responses to notices of irregularity under §7.14, requests to note replacement under §7.28, and requests for transformation under §7.31, when filed by mail, will be accorded the date of receipt in the Office.

(c) Hand-Delivered Correspondence. International applications under §7.11, subsequent designations under §7.21, responses to notices of irregularity under §7.14, requests to record changes in the International Register under §7.23 and

§7.24, requests to note replacement under §7.28, requests for transformation under §7.31, and petitions to the Director to review an action of the Office's Madrid Processing Unit, may be delivered by hand during the hours the Office is open to receive correspondence. Madrid-related hand-delivered correspondence must be delivered to the Trademark Assistance Center, James Madison Building—East Wing, Concourse Level, 600 Dulany Street, Alexandria, VA 22314, Attention: MPU.

(d) Facsimile Transmission Not Permitted. The following documents may not be sent by facsimile transmission, and will not be accorded a date of receipt if sent by facsimile transmission:

(1) International applications under §7.11;

(2) Subsequent designations under §7.21;

(3) Responses to notices of irregularity under §7.14;

(4) Requests to record changes of ownership under §7.23;

(5) Requests to record restrictions of the holder's right of disposal, or the release of such restrictions, under §7.24; and

(6) Requests for transformation under §7.31.

(e) Certificate of Mailing or Transmission Procedure Does Not Apply. The certificate of mailing or transmission procedure provided in §2.197 does not apply to the documents specified in paragraph (d) of this section.

History of 37 C.F.R. §7.4: 69 FR 57185, Sept. 24, 2004; 69 FR 63321, Nov. 1, 2004; 72 FR 18908, Apr. 16, 2007; 79 FR 63042, Oct. 22, 2014.

§7.5. RESERVED

§7.6. SCHEDULE OF U.S. PROCESS FEES

(a) The Office requires the following process fees:

(1) Certification of international application based on single application or registration.

(i) For certifying an international application based on a single basic application or registration, filed on paper, per class: $200.00.

(ii) For certifying an international application based on a single basic application or registration, filed through TEAS, per class: $100.00.

(2) Certification of international application based on more than one application or registration.

(i) For certifying an international application based on more than one basic application or registration filed on paper, per class: $250.00.

(ii) For certifying an international application based on more than one basic application or registration filed through TEAS, per class: $150.00.

(3) Transmission of subsequent designation.

(i) For transmitting a subsequent designation under §7.21, filed on paper: $200.00.

(ii) For transmitting a subsequent designation under §7.21, filed through TEAS: $100.00.

(4) Transmission of request to record an assignment or restriction.

(i) For transmitting a request to record an assignment or restriction, or release of a restriction, under §7.23 or §7.24 filed on paper: $200.00.

(ii) For transmitting a request to record an assignment or restriction, or release of a restriction, under §7.23 or §7.24 filed through TEAS: $100.00.

(5) Notice of replacement.

(i) For filing a notice of replacement under §7.28 on paper, per class: $200.00.

(ii) For filing a notice of replacement under §7.28 through TEAS, per class: $100.00.

(6) Affidavit under section 71.

(i) For filing an affidavit under section 71 of the Act on paper, per class: $225.00.

(ii) For filing an affidavit under section 71 of the Act through TEAS, per class: $125.00.

(7) Filing affidavit under section 71 during grace period.

(i) Surcharge for filing an affidavit under section 71 of the Act during the grace period on paper, per class: $200.00.

(ii) Surcharge for filing an affidavit under section 71 of the Act during the grace period through TEAS, per class: $100.00.

(8) Correcting deficiency in section 71 affidavit.

(i) For correcting a deficiency in a section 71 affidavit filed on paper: $200.00.

(ii) For correcting a deficiency in a section 71 affidavit filed through TEAS: $100.00.

(b) The fees required in paragraph (a) of this section must be paid in U.S. dollars at the time of submission of the requested action. See §2.207 of this chapter for acceptable forms of payment and §2.208 of this chapter for payments using a deposit account established in the Office.

History of 37 C.F.R. §7.6: 75 FR 35977, June 24, 2010; 81 FR 72708, Jan. 14, 2017.

§7.7. PAYMENTS OF FEES TO INTERNATIONAL BUREAU

(a) For documents filed through TEAS, the following fees may be paid either directly to the International Bureau or through the Office:

(1) International application fees;

(2) Subsequent designation fees; and

(3) Recording fee for an assignment of an international registration under §7.23.

(b) The fees in paragraph (a) of this section may be paid as follows:

(1)(i) Directly to the International Bureau by debit to a current account with the International Bureau. In this case, an applicant or holder's submission to the Office must include the International Bureau account number; or

(ii) Directly to the International Bureau using any other acceptable method of payment. In this case, an applicant or holder's submission to the Office must include the International Bureau receipt number for payment of the fees; or

(2) Through the Office. Fees paid through the Office must be paid in U.S. dollars at the time of submission. See §2.207 of this chapter for acceptable forms of payment and §2.208 of this chapter for payments using a deposit account established in the Office.

(c) All fees for paper filings must be paid directly to the International Bureau.

(d) The International Bureau fee calculator may be viewed on the web site of the World Intellectual Property Organization, currently available at: http://www.wipo.int/madrid/en/.

History of 37 C.F.R. §7.7: 69 FR 57185, Sept. 24, 2004.

SUBPART B. INTERNATIONAL APPLICATION ORIGINATING FROM THE UNITED STATES

§7.11. REQUIREMENTS FOR INTERNATIONAL APPLICATION ORIGINATING FROM THE UNITED STATES

(a) The Office will grant a date of receipt to an international application That is either filed through TEAS, or typed on the official paper form issued by the International Bureau. The international application must include all of the following:

(1) The filing date and serial number of the basic application and/or the registration date and registration number of the basic registration;

(2) The name and entity of the international applicant that is identical to the name and entity of the applicant or registrant in the basic application or basic registration, and the applicant's current address;

(3) A reproduction of the mark that is the same as the mark in the basic application and/or registration and that meets the requirements of §2.52 of this title.

(i) If the mark in the basic application and/or registration is depicted in black and white and the basic application or registration does not include a color claim, the reproduction of the mark in the international application must be black and white.

(ii) If the mark in the basic application or registration is depicted in black and white and includes a color claim, the international application must include both a black and white reproduction of the mark and a color reproduction of the mark.

(iii) If the mark in the basic application and/or registration is depicted in color, the reproduction of the mark in the international application must be in color.

(iv) If the international application is filed on paper, the mark must be no more than 3.15 inches (8 cm) high by 3.15 inches (8 cm) wide, and must appear in the box designated by the International Bureau on the International Bureau's official form;

(4) A color claim as set out in §7.12, if appropriate;

(5) A description of the mark that is the same as the description of the mark in the basic application or registration, as appropriate;

(6) An indication of the type of mark if the mark in the basic application and/or registration is a three-dimensional mark, a sound mark, a collective mark or a certification mark;

(7) A list of the goods and/or services that is identical to or narrower than the list of goods and/or services in each claimed basic application or registration and classified according to the Nice Agreement Concerning the International Classification of Goods and Services for the Purposes of the Registration of Marks;

(8) A list of the designated Contracting Parties. If the goods and/or services in the international application are not the same for each designated Contracting Party, the application must list the goods and/or services in the international application that pertain to each designated Contracting Party;

(9) The certification fee required by §7.6;

(10) If the application is filed through TEAS, the international application fees for all classes, and the fees for all designated Contracting Parties identified in the international application (see §7.7);

(11) A statement that the applicant is entitled to file an international application in the Office, specifying that applicant: is a national of the United States; has a domicile in the United States; or has a real and effective industrial or commercial establishment in the United States. Where an applicant's address is not in the United States, the applicant must provide the address of its U.S. domicile or establishment; and

(12) If the international application is filed through TEAS, an e-mail address for receipt of correspondence from the Office.

(b) For requirements for certification, see §7.13.

History of 37 C.F.R. §7.11: 69 FR 57185, Sept. 24, 2004; 73 FR 67775, Jan. 16, 2009.

Source of 37 C.F.R. Part 7B: 68 FR 55769, Sept. 26, 2003, unless otherwise noted.

§7.12. CLAIM OF COLOR

(a) If color is claimed as a feature of the mark in the basic application and/or registration, the international application must include a statement that color is claimed as a feature of the mark and set forth the same name(s) of the color(s) claimed in the basic application and/or registration.

(b) If color is not claimed as a feature of the mark in the basic application and/or registration, color may not be claimed as a feature of the mark in the international application.

§7.13. CERTIFICATION OF INTERNATIONAL APPLICATION

(a) When an international application contains all the elements set forth in §7.11(a), the Office will certify to the International Bureau that the information contained in the international application corresponds to the information contained in the basic application(s) and/or basic registration(s) at the time of certification, and will then forward the international application to the International Bureau.

(b) When an international application does not meet the requirements of §7.11(a), the Office will not certify or forward the international application. If the international applicant paid the international application fees (see §7.7) through the Office, the Office will refund the international fees. The Office will not refund the certification fee.

§7.14. CORRECTING IRREGULARITIES IN INTERNATIONAL APPLICATION

(a) Response period. Upon receipt of a notice of irregularities in an international application from the International Bureau, the applicant must respond to the International Bureau within the period set forth in the notice.

(b) Classification and Identification of Goods and Services. Responses to International Bureau notices of irregularities in the classification or identification of goods or services in an international application must be submitted through the Office for forwarding to the International Bureau. The Office will review an applicant's response to a notice of irregularities in the identification of goods or services to ensure that the response does not identify goods or services that are broader than the scope of the goods or services in the basic application or registration.

(c) Fees. If the International Bureau notice of irregularities requires the payment of fees, the fees for correcting irregularities in the international application must be paid directly to the International Bureau.

(d) Other Irregularities Requiring Response from Applicant. Except for responses to irregularities mentioned in paragraph (b) of this section and payment of fees for correcting irregularities mentioned in paragraph (c) of this section, all other responses may be submitted through the Office in accordance with §7.14(e), or filed directly at the International Bureau. The Office will forward timely responses to the International Bureau, but will not review the responses or respond to any irregularities on behalf of the international applicant.

(e) Procedure for response. To be considered timely, a response must be received by the International Bureau before the end of the response period set forth in the International Bureau's notice. Receipt in the Office does not fulfill this requirement. Any response submitted through the Office for forwarding to the International Bureau should be submitted as soon as possible, but at least one month before the end of the response period in the International Bureau's notice. The Office will not process any response received in the Office after the International Bureau's response deadline.

History of 37 C.F.R. §7.14: 69 FR 57186, Sept. 24, 2004; 73 FR 67776, Jan. 16, 2009.

SUBPART C. SUBSEQUENT DESIGNATION SUBMITTED THROUGH THE OFFICE

§7.21. SUBSEQUENT DESIGNATION

(a) A subsequent designation may be filed directly with the International Bureau, or, if it meets the requirements of paragraph (b) of this section, submitted through the Office.

(b) The Office will grant a date of receipt to a subsequent designation that is either filed through TEAS, or typed on the official paper form issued by the International Bureau. The subsequent designation must contain all of the following:

(1) The international registration number;

(2) The serial number of the U.S. application or registration number of the U.S. registration that formed the basis of the international registration;

(3) The name and address of the holder of the international registration;

(4) A statement that the holder is entitled to file a subsequent designation in the Office, specifying that holder: Is a national of the United States; has a domicile in the United States; or has a real and effective industrial or commercial establishment in the United States. Where a holder's address is not in the United States, the holder must provide the address of its U.S. domicile or establishment;

(5) A list of goods and/or services that is identical to or narrower than the list of goods and/or services in the international registration;

(6) A list of the designated Contracting Parties. If the goods and/or services in the subsequent designation are not the same for each designated Contracting Party, the holder must list the goods and/or services covered by the subsequent designation that pertain to each designated Contracting Party;

(7) The U.S. transmittal fee required by §7.6;

(8) If the subsequent designation is filed through TEAS, the subsequent designation fees (see §7.7); and

(9) If the subsequent designation is filed through TEAS, an e-mail address for receipt of correspondence from the Office.

(c) If the subsequent designation is accorded a date of receipt, the Office will then forward the subsequent designation to the International Bureau.

(d) If the subsequent designation fails to contain all the elements set forth in paragraph (b) of this section, the Office will not forward the subsequent designation to the International Bureau. The Office will notify the holder of the reason(s). If the holder paid the subsequent designation fees (see §7.7) through the Office, the Office will refund the subsequent designation fees. The Office will not refund the transmittal fee.

(e) Correspondence to correct any irregularities in a subsequent designation must be made directly with the International Bureau.

History of 37 C.F.R. §7.21: 69 FR 57186, Sept. 24, 2004.

Source of 37 C.F.R. Part 7C: 68 FR 55769, Sept. 26, 2003, unless otherwise noted.

SUBPART D. RECORDING CHANGES TO INTERNATIONAL REGISTRATION

§7.22. RECORDING CHANGES TO INTERNATIONAL REGISTRATION

Except as provided in §§7.23 and 7.24, requests to record changes to an international registration must be filed with the International Bureau. If a request to record an assignment or restriction of a holder's right of disposal of an international registration or the release of such a restriction meets the requirements of §§7.23 or 7.24, the Office will forward the request to the International Bureau. Section 10 of the Act and part 3 of this chapter are not applicable to assignments or restrictions of international registrations.

Source of 37 C.F.R. Part 7D: 68 FR 55769, Sept. 26, 2003, unless otherwise noted.

§7.23. REQUESTS FOR RECORDING ASSIGNMENTS AT THE INTERNATIONAL BUREAU

A request to record an assignment of an international registration may be submitted through the Office for forwarding to the International Bureau only if the assignee cannot obtain the assignor's signature for the request to record the assignment.

(a) A request to record an assignment submitted through the Office must include all of the following:

(1) The international registration number;

(2) The name and address of the holder of the international registration;

(3) The name and address of the assignee of the international registration;

(4) A statement that the assignee: Is a national of the United States; has a domicile in the United States; or has a real and effective industrial or commercial establishment in the United States. Where an assignee's address is not in the United States, the assignee must provide the address of its U.S. domicile or establishment;

(5) A statement, signed and verified (sworn to) or supported by a declaration under §2.20 of this chapter, that, for the request to record the assignment, either the assignee could not obtain the assignor's signature because the holder no longer exists, or, after a good-faith effort, the assignee could not obtain the assignor's signature;

(6) An indication that the assignment applies to the designation to the United States or an international registration that is based on a U.S. application or registration;

(7) A statement that the assignment applies to all the goods and/or services in the international registration, or if less, a list of the goods and/or services in the international registration that have been assigned that pertain to the designation to the United States; and

(8) The U.S. transmittal fee required by §7.6.

(b) If a request to record an assignment contains all the elements set forth in paragraph (a) of this section, the Office will forward the request to the International Bureau. Forwarding the request to the International Bureau is not a determination by the Office of the validity of the assignment or the effect that the assignment has on the title of the international registration.

(c) If the request fails to contain all the elements set forth in paragraph (a) of this section, the Office will not forward the request to the International Bureau. The Office will notify the assignee(s) of the reason(s). If the assignee paid the fees to record the assignment (see §7.7) through the Office, the Office will refund the recording fee. The Office will not refund the transmittal fee.

(d) Correspondence to correct any irregularities in a request to record an assignment must be made directly with the International Bureau.

History of 37 C.F.R. §7.23: 69 FR 57186, Sept. 24, 2004; 80 FR 2313, Jan. 16, 2015.

§7.24. REQUESTS TO RECORD SECURITY INTEREST OR OTHER RESTRICTION OF HOLDER'S RIGHTS OF DISPOSAL OR RELEASE OF SUCH RESTRICTION SUBMITTED THROUGH THE OFFICE

(a) A party who obtained a security interest or other restriction of a holder's right to dispose of an international registration, or the release of such a restriction, may submit a request to record the restriction or release through the Office for forwarding to the International Bureau only if:

(1) The restriction or release:

(i) Is the result of a court order; or

(ii) Is the result of an agreement between the holder of the international registration and the party restricting the holder's right of disposal, and the signature of the holder cannot be obtained for the request to record the restriction or release;

(2) The party who obtained the restriction is a national of, is domiciled in, or has a real and effective industrial or commercial establishment in the United States; and

(3) The restriction or release applies to the holder's right to dispose of the international registration in the United States.

(b) A request to record a restriction or the release of a restriction must be submitted by the party who obtained the restriction of the holder's right of disposal and include all the following:

(1) The international registration number;

(2) The name and address of the holder of the international registration;

(3) The name and address of the party who obtained the restriction;

(4) A statement that the party who submitted the request: Is a national of the United States; has a domicile in the United States; or has a real and effective industrial or commercial establishment in the United States. Where a party's address is not in the United States, the party must provide the address of its U.S. domicile or establishment;

(5)(i) A statement that the restriction is the result of a court order, or

(ii) Where the restriction is the result of an agreement between the holder of the international registration and the party restricting the holder's right of disposal, a statement, signed and verified (sworn to) or supported by a declaration under §2.20 of this chapter, that, for the request to record the restriction, or release of the restriction, either the holder of the international registration could not obtain the signature of the party restricting the holder's right of disposal because the party restricting the holder's right of disposal no longer exists, or, after a good-faith effort, the holder of the international registration could not obtain the signature of the party restricting the holder's right of disposal;

(6) A summary of the main facts concerning the restriction;

(7) An indication that the restriction, or the release of the restriction, of the holder's right of disposal of the international registration applies to the designation to the United States or an international registration that is based on a U.S. application or registration; and

(8) The U.S. transmittal fee required by §7.6.

(c) If a request to record a restriction, or the release of a restriction, contains all the elements set forth in paragraph (b) of this section, the Office will forward the request to the International Bureau. Forwarding the request to the International Bureau is not a determination by the Office of the validity of the restriction, or its release, or the effect that the restriction has on the holder's right to dispose of the international registration.

(d) If the request fails to contain all the elements set forth in paragraph (b) of this section, the Office will not forward the request. The Office will notify the party who submitted the request of the reason(s). The Office will not refund the transmittal fee.

(e) Correspondence to correct any irregularities in a request to record a restriction of a holder's right to dispose of an international registration or the release of such a restriction must be made directly with the International Bureau.

History of 37 C.F.R. §7.24: 80 FR 2313, Jan. 16, 2015.

SUBPART E. EXTENSION OF PROTECTION TO THE UNITED STATES

§7.25. SECTIONS OF PART 2 APPLICABLE TO EXTENSION OF PROTECTION

(a) Except for §§2.21 through 2.23, 2.76, 2.88, 2.89, 2.130, 2.131, 2.160 through 2.166, 2.168, 2.173, 2.175, 2.181 through 2.186, and 2.197, all sections in parts 2 and 11 of this chapter shall apply to an extension of protection of an international registration to the United States, including sections related to proceedings before the Trademark Trial and Appeal Board, unless otherwise stated.

(b) The Office will refer to a request for an extension of protection to the United States as an application under section 66(a) of the Act, and references to applications and registrations in part 2 of this chapter include extensions of protection to the United States.

(c) Upon registration in the United States under section 69 of the Act, an extension of protection to the United States is referred to as a registration, a registered extension of protection, or a section 66(a) registration.

History of 37 C.F.R. §7.25: 69 FR 57186, Sept. 24, 2004; 70 FR 38774, July 6, 2005; 73 FR 47686, Sept. 15, 2008; 73 FR 67776, Jan. 16, 2009; 75 FR 35977, June 24, 2010; 78 FR 20197, Apr. 3, 2013; 80 FR 2313, Jan. 16, 2015.

Source of 37 C.F.R. Part 7E: 68 FR 55769, Sept. 26, 2003, unless otherwise noted.

§7.26. FILING DATE OF EXTENSION OF PROTECTION FOR PURPOSES OF EXAMINATION IN THE OFFICE

(a) If a request for extension of protection of an international registration to the United States is made in an international application and the request includes a declaration of a bona fide intention to use the mark in commerce as set out in §2.33(e) of this chapter, the filing date of the extension of protection to the United States is the international registration date.

(b) If a request for extension of protection of an international registration to the United States is made in a subsequent designation and the request includes a declaration of a bona fide intention to use the mark in commerce as set out in §2.33(e), the filing date of the extension of protection to the United States is the date that the International Bureau records the subsequent designation.

§7.27. PRIORITY CLAIM OF EXTENSION OF PROTECTION FOR PURPOSES OF EXAMINATION IN THE OFFICE

An extension of protection of an international registration to the United States is entitled to a claim of priority under section 67 of the Act if:

(a) The request for extension of protection contains a claim of priority;

(b) The request for extension of protection specifies the filing date, serial number and the country of the application that forms the basis for the claim of priority; and

(c) The date of the international registration or the date of recording of the subsequent designation at the International Bureau of the request for extension of protection to the United States is not later than six months after the filing date of the application that forms the basis for the claim of priority.

§7.28. REPLACEMENT OF U.S. REGISTRATION BY REGISTERED EXTENSION OF PROTECTION

(a) A registered extension of protection affords the same rights as those afforded to a previously issued U.S. registration if:

(1) Both registrations are owned by the same person and identify the same mark; and

(2) All the goods and/or services listed in the U.S. registration are also listed in the registered extension of protection.

(b) The holder of an international registration with a registered extension of protection to the United States that meets the requirements of paragraph (a) of this section may file a request to note replacement of the U.S. registration with the extension of protection. If the request contains all of the following, the Office will take note of the replacement in its automated records:

(1) The serial number or registration number of the extension of protection;

(2) The registration number of the replaced U.S. registration; and

(3) The fee required by §7.6.

(c) If the request to note replacement is denied, the Office will notify the holder of the reason(s) for refusal.

§7.29. EFFECT OF REPLACEMENT ON U.S. REGISTRATION

A U.S. registration that has been replaced by a registered extension of protection under section 74 of the Act and §7.28 will remain in force, unless cancelled, expired or surrendered, as long as:

(a) The owner of the replaced U.S. registration continues to file affidavits or declarations of use in commerce or excusable nonuse under section 8 of the Act; and

(b) The replaced U.S. registration is renewed under section 9 of the Act.

§7.30. EFFECT OF CANCELLATION OR EXPIRATION OF INTERNATIONAL REGISTRATION

When the International Bureau notifies the Office of the cancellation or expiration of an international registration, in whole or in part, the Office shall cancel, in whole or in part, the corresponding pending or registered extension of protection to the United States. The date of cancellation of an extension of protection or relevant part shall be the date of cancellation or expiration of the corresponding international registration or relevant part.

§7.31. REQUIREMENTS FOR TRANSFORMATION OF AN EXTENSION OF PROTECTION TO THE UNITED STATES INTO A U.S. APPLICATION

If the International Bureau cancels an international registration in whole or in part, under Article 6(4) of the Madrid Protocol, the holder of that international registration may file a request to transform the goods and/or services to which the cancellation applies in the corresponding pending or registered extension of protection to the United States into an application under section 1 or 44 of the Act.

(a) The holder of the international registration must file a request for transformation within three months of the date of cancellation of the international registration and include:

(1) The serial number or registration number of the extension of protection to the United States;

(2) The name and address of the holder of the international registration;

(3) Identify the goods and/or services to be transformed, if other than all the goods and/or services that have been cancelled;

(4) The application filing fee for at least one class of goods or services required by §2.6(a)(1) of this chapter; and

(5) An email address for receipt of correspondence from the Office.

(b) If the request for transformation contains all the elements set forth in paragraph (a) of this section, the extension of protection shall be transformed into an application under section 1 and/or 44 of the Act and accorded the same filing date and the same priority that was accorded to the extension of protection.

(c) The application under section 1 and/or 44 of the Act that results from a transformed extension of protection will be examined under part 2 of this chapter.

(d) A request for transformation that fails to contain all the elements set forth in paragraph (a) of this section will not be accepted.

History of 37 C.F.R. §7.31: 69 FR 57186, Sept. 24, 2004; 80 FR 2313, Jan. 16, 2015.

SUBPART F. AFFIDAVIT UNDER SECTION 71 OF THE ACT FOR EXTENSION OF PROTECTION TO THE UNITED STATES

§7.36. AFFIDAVIT OR DECLARATION OF USE IN COMMERCE OR EXCUSABLE NONUSE REQUIRED TO AVOID CANCELLATION OF AN EXTENSION OF PROTECTION TO THE UNITED STATES

(a) Subject to the provisions of section 71 of the Act, a registered extension of protection shall remain in force for the term of the international registration upon which it is based unless the international registration expires or is cancelled under section 70 of the Act due to cancellation of the international registration by the International Bureau.

(b) During the following time periods, the holder of an international registration must file an affidavit or declaration of use or excusable nonuse, or the registered extension of protection will be cancelled under section 71 of the Act:

(1) On or after the fifth anniversary and no later than the sixth anniversary after the date of registration in the United States; and

(2) Within the year before the end of every ten-year period after the date of registration in the United States.

(3) The affidavit or declaration may be filed within a grace period of six months after the end of the deadline set forth in paragraphs (b)(1) and (b)(2) of this section, with payment of the grace period surcharge per class required by section 71(a)(3) of the Act and §7.6.

(c) For the requirements for the affidavit or declaration, see §7.37.

History of 37 C.F.R. §7.36: 75 FR 35977, June 24, 2010.

Source of 37 C.F.R. Part 7F: 68 FR 55769, Sept. 26, 2003, unless otherwise noted.

§7.37. REQUIREMENTS FOR A COMPLETE AFFIDAVIT OR DECLARATION OF USE IN COMMERCE OR EXCUSABLE NONUSE

A complete affidavit or declaration under section 71 of the Act must:

(a) Be filed by the holder of the international registration within the period set forth in §7.36(b);

(b) Include a verified statement attesting to the use in commerce or excusable nonuse of the mark within the period set forth in section 71 of the Act. The verified statement must be executed on or after the beginning of the filing period specified in §7.36(b). A person who is properly authorized to sign on behalf of the holder is:

(1) A person with legal authority to bind the holder;

(2) A person with firsthand knowledge of the facts and actual or implied authority to act on behalf of the holder; or

(3) An attorney as defined in §11.1 of this chapter who has an actual written or verbal power of attorney or an implied power of attorney from the holder.

(c) Include the U.S. registration number;

(d)(1) Include the fee required by §7.6 for each class that the affidavit or declaration covers;

(2) If the affidavit or declaration is filed during the grace period under section 71(a)(3) of the Act, include the grace period surcharge per class required by §7.6;

(3) If at least one fee is submitted for a multiple-class registration, but the fee is insufficient to cover all the classes and the class(es) to which the fee(s) should be applied are not specified, the Office will issue a notice requiring either submission of the additional fee(s) or specification of the class(es) to which the initial fee(s) should be applied. Additional fees may be submitted if the requirements of §7.39 are met. If the additional fee(s) are not submitted within the time period set out in the Office action and the class(es) to which the original fee(s) should be applied are not specified, the Office will presume that the fee(s) cover the classes in ascending order, beginning with the lowest numbered class;

(e)(1) Specify the goods, services, or nature of the collective membership organization for which the mark is in use in commerce, and/or the goods, services, or nature of the collective membership organization for which excusable nonuse is claimed under paragraph (f)(2) of this section; and

(2) Specify the goods, services, or classes being deleted from the registration, if the affidavit or declaration covers fewer than all the goods, services, or classes in the registration;

(f)(1) State that the registered mark is in use in commerce; or

(2) If the registered mark is not in use in commerce on or in connection with all the goods, services, or classes specified in the registration, set forth the date when such use of the mark in commerce stopped and the approximate date when such use is expected to resume; and recite facts to show that nonuse as to those goods, services, or classes is due to special circumstances that excuse the nonuse and is not due to an intention to abandon the mark; and

(g) Include one specimen showing how the mark is in use in commerce for each class in the registration, unless excusable nonuse is claimed under paragraph (f)(2) of this section. When requested by the Office, additional specimens must be provided. The specimen must meet the requirements of §2.56 of this chapter.

(h) The Office may require the holder to furnish such information, exhibits, affidavits or declarations, and such additional specimens as may be reasonably necessary to the proper examination of the affidavit or declaration under section 71 of the Act or for the Office to assess and promote the accuracy and integrity of the register.

(i) Additional requirements for a collective mark: In addition to the above requirements, a complete affidavit or declaration pertaining to a collective mark must:

(1) State that the holder is exercising legitimate control over the use of the mark in commerce; and

(2) State the nature of the holder's control over the use of the mark by the members in the first affidavit or declaration filed under paragraph (a) of this section.

(j) Additional requirements for a certification mark: In addition to the above requirements, a complete affidavit or declaration pertaining to a certification mark must:

(1) Include a copy of the certification standards specified in §2.45(a)(4)(i)(B) of this chapter;

(i) Submitting certification standards for the first time. In the first affidavit or declaration filed under paragraph (a) of this section, include a copy of the certification standards; or

(ii) Certification standards submitted in prior filing. If the certification standards in use at the time of filing the affidavit or declaration have not changed since the date they were previously submitted to the Office, include a statement to that effect; if the certification standards in use at the time of filing the affidavit or declaration have changed since the date they were previously submitted to the Office, include a copy of the revised certification standards;

(2) State that the holder is exercising legitimate control over the use of the mark in commerce; and

(3) Satisfy the requirements of §2.45(a)(4)(i)(A) and (C) of this chapter.

History of 37 C.F.R. §7.37: 73 FR 47686, Sept. 15, 2008; 75 FR 35977, June 24, 2010; 77 FR 30208, June 21, 2012; 80 FR 33190, July 11, 2015; 82 FR 6265, Feb. 17, 2017; 82 FR 10273, Mar. 21, 2017.

§7.38. NOTICE TO HOLDER OF EXTENSION OF PROTECTION

The registration certificate for an extension of protection to the United States includes a notice of the requirement for filing the affidavit or declaration of use or excusable nonuse under section 71 of the Act. However, the affidavit or declaration must be filed within the time period required by section 71 of the Act regardless of whether this notice is received.

§7.39. ACKNOWLEDGMENT OF RECEIPT OF & CORRECTING DEFICIENCIES IN AFFIDAVIT OR DECLARATION OF USE IN COMMERCE OR EXCUSABLE NONUSE

The Office will issue a notice as to whether an affidavit or declaration is acceptable, or the reasons for refusal.

(a) A response to the refusal must be filed within six months of the date of issuance of the Office action, or before the end of the filing period set forth in section 71(a) of the Act, whichever is later. The response must be signed by the holder, someone with legal authority to bind the holder (e.g., a corporate officer or general partner of a partnership), or a practitioner qualified to practice under §11.14 of this chapter, in accordance with the requirements of §2.193(e)(2).

(b) If no response is filed within this time period, the extension of protection will be cancelled, unless time remains in the grace period under section 71(a)(3) of the Act. If time remains in the grace period, the holder may file a complete, new affidavit.

(c) If the affidavit or declaration is filed within the time periods set forth in section 71 of the Act, deficiencies may be corrected after notification from the Office, as follows:

(1) Correcting deficiencies in affidavits or declarations timely filed within the periods set forth in sections 71(a)(1) and 71(a)(2) of the Act. If the affidavit or declaration is timely filed within the relevant filing period set forth in section 71(a)(1) or section 71(a)(2) of the Act, deficiencies may be corrected before the end of this filing period without paying a deficiency surcharge. Deficiencies may be corrected after the end of this filing period with payment of the deficiency surcharge required by section 71(c) of the Act and §7.6.

(2) Correcting deficiencies in affidavits or declarations filed during the grace period. If the affidavit or declaration is filed during the six-month grace period provided by section 71(a)(3) of the Act, deficiencies may be corrected before the expiration of the grace period without paying a deficiency surcharge. Deficiencies may be corrected after the expiration of the grace period with payment of the deficiency surcharge required by section 71(c) of the Act and §7.6.

(d) If the affidavit or declaration is not filed within the time periods set forth in section 71 of the Act, the registration will be cancelled.

History of 37 C.F.R. §7.39: 73 FR 67776, Jan. 16, 2009; 75 FR 35977, June 24, 2010; 76 FR 69133, Nov. 8, 2011.

§7.40. PETITION TO DIRECTOR TO REVIEW REFUSAL

(a) A response to the examiner's initial refusal to accept an affidavit or declaration is required before filing a petition to the Director, unless the examiner directs otherwise. See §7.39(b) for the deadline for responding to an examiner's Office action.

(b) If the examiner maintains the refusal of the affidavit or declaration, the holder may file a petition to the Director to review the examiner's action. The petition must be filed within six months of the date of issuance of the action maintaining the refusal, or the Office will cancel the registration.

(c) A decision by the Director is necessary before filing an appeal or commencing a civil action in any court.

History of 37 C.F.R. §7.40: 73 FR 67776, Jan. 16, 2009.

SUBPART G. RENEWAL OF INTERNATIONAL REGISTRATION & EXTENSION OF PROTECTION

§7.41. RENEWAL OF INTERNATIONAL REGISTRATION & EXTENSION OF PROTECTION

(a) Any request to renew an international registration and its extension of protection to the United States must be made at the International Bureau in accordance with Article 7 of the Madrid Protocol.

(b) A request to renew an international registration or extension of protection to the United States submitted through the Office will not be processed.

Source of 37 C.F.R. Part 7G: 68 FR 55769, Sept. 26, 2003, unless otherwise noted.

PART 10. REMOVED & RESERVED

PART 11. REPRESENTATION OF OTHERS BEFORE THE UNITED STATES PATENT & TRADEMARK OFFICE

SUBPART A. GENERAL PROVISIONS

GENERAL INFORMATION

§11.1. DEFINITIONS

This part governs solely the practice of patent, trademark, and other law before the United States Patent and Trademark Office. Nothing in this part shall be construed to preempt the authority of each State to regulate the practice of law, except to the extent necessary for the United States Patent and Trademark Office to accomplish its Federal objectives. Unless otherwise clear from the context, the following definitions apply to this part:

Attorney or lawyer means an individual who is an active member in good standing of the bar of the highest court of any State. A non-lawyer means a person who is not an attorney or lawyer.

Belief or believes means that the person involved actually supposed the fact in question to be true. A person's belief may be inferred from circumstances.

Confirmed in writing, when used in reference to the informed consent of a person, means informed consent that is given in writing by the person or a writing that a practitioner promptly transmits to the person confirming an oral informed consent. If it is not feasible to obtain or transmit the writing at the time the person gives informed consent, then the practitioner must obtain or transmit it within a reasonable time thereafter.

Conviction or convicted means any confession to a crime; a verdict or judgment finding a person guilty of a crime; any entered plea, including nolo contendre[1] or Alford plea, to a crime; or receipt of deferred adjudication (whether judgment or sentence has been entered or not) for an accused or pled crime.

Crime means any offense declared to be a felony or misdemeanor by Federal or State law in the jurisdiction where the act occurs.

Data sheet means a form used to collect the name, address, and telephone information from individuals recognized to practice before the Office in patent matters.

Disqualified means any action that prohibits a practitioner from participating in or appearing before the program or agency, regardless of how long the prohibition lasts or the specific terminology used.

Federal agency means any authority of the executive branch of the Government of the United States.

Federal program means any program established by an Act of Congress or administered by a Federal agency.

Firm or law firm means a practitioner or practitioners in a law partnership, professional corporation, sole proprietorship or other association authorized to practice law; or practitioners employed in a legal services organization or the legal department of a corporation or other organization.

Fiscal year means the time period from October 1st through the ensuing September 30th.

Fraud or fraudulent means conduct that involves a misrepresentation of material fact made with intent to deceive or a state of mind so reckless respecting consequences as to be the equivalent of intent, where there is justifiable reliance on the misrepresentation by the party deceived, inducing the party to act thereon, and where there is injury to the party deceived resulting from reliance on the misrepresentation. Fraud also may be established by a purposeful omission or failure to state a material fact, which omission or failure to state makes other statements misleading, and where the other elements of justifiable reliance and injury are established.

Good moral character and reputation means the possession of honesty and truthfulness, trustworthiness and reliability, and a professional commitment to the legal process and the administration of justice, as well as the condition of being regarded as possessing such qualities.

Grievance means a written submission from any source received by the OED Director that presents possible grounds for discipline of a specified practitioner.

Informed consent means the agreement by a person to a proposed course of conduct after the practitioner has communicated adequate information and explanation about the material risks of and reasonably available alternatives to the proposed course of conduct.

Knowingly, known, or knows means actual knowledge of the fact in question. A person's knowledge may be inferred from circumstances.

Law-related services means services that might reasonably be performed in conjunction with and in substance are related to the provision of legal services, and that are not prohibited as unauthorized practice of law when provided by a non-lawyer.

OED means the Office of Enrollment and Discipline.

OED Director means the Director of the Office of Enrollment and Discipline.

OED Director's representatives means attorneys within the USPTO Office of General Counsel who act as representatives of the OED Director.

Office means the United States Patent and Trademark Office.

Partner means a member of a partnership, a shareholder in a law firm organized as a professional corporation, or a member of an association authorized to practice law.

Person means an individual, a corporation, an association, a trust, a partnership, and any other organization or legal entity.

Practitioner means:

(1) An attorney or agent registered to practice before the Office in patent matters;

(2) An individual authorized under 5 U.S.C. 500(b), or otherwise as provided by §11.14(a), (b), and (c), to practice before the Office in trademark matters or other non-patent matters;

(3) An individual authorized to practice before the Office in a patent case or matters under §11.9(a) or (b); or

(4) An individual authorized to practice before the Office under §11.16(d).

Proceeding before the Office means an application for patent, an application for reissue, a reexamination, a protest, a public use matter, an inter partes patent matter, correction of a patent, correction of inventorship, an application to register a trademark, an inter partes trademark matter, an appeal, a petition, and any other matter that is pending before the Office.

Reasonable or reasonably when used in relation to conduct by a practitioner means the conduct of a reasonably prudent and competent practitioner.

Reasonable belief or reasonably believes when used in reference to a practitioner means that the practitioner believes the matter in question and that the circumstances are such that the belief is reasonable.

Reasonably should know when used in reference to a practitioner means that a practitioner of reasonable prudence and competence would ascertain the matter in question.

Registration means registration to practice before the Office in patent proceedings.

Roster means a list of individuals who have been registered as either a patent attorney or patent agent.

Screened means the isolation of a practitioner from any participation in a matter through the timely imposition of procedures within a firm that are reasonably adequate under the circumstances to protect information that the isolated practitioner is obligated to protect under these USPTO Rules of Professional Conduct or other law.

Serious crime means:

(1) Any criminal offense classified as a felony under the laws of the United States, any state or any foreign country where the crime occurred; or

(2) Any crime a necessary element of which, as determined by the statutory or common law definition of such crime in the jurisdiction where the crime occurred, includes interference with the administration of justice, false swearing, misrepresentation, fraud, willful failure to file income tax returns, deceit, bribery, extortion, misappropriation, theft, or an attempt or a conspiracy or solicitation of another to commit a "serious crime."

Significant evidence of rehabilitation means satisfactory evidence that is significantly more probable than not that there will be no recurrence in the foreseeable future of the practitioner's prior disability or addiction.

State means any of the 50 states of the United States of America, the District of Columbia, and any Commonwealth or territory of the United States of America.

Substantial when used in reference to degree or extent means a material matter of clear and weighty importance.

Suspend or suspension means a temporary debarring from practice before the Office or other jurisdiction.

Tribunal means the Office, a court, an arbitrator in a binding arbitration proceeding or a legislative body, administrative agency or other body acting in an adjudicative capacity. A legislative body, administrative agency or other body acts in an adjudicative capacity when a neutral official, after the presentation of evidence or legal argument by a party or parties, will render a binding legal judgment directly affecting a party's interests in a particular matter.

United States means the United States of America, and the territories and possessions the United States of America.

USPTO Director means the Director of the United States Patent and Trademark Office, or an employee of the Office delegated authority to act for the Director of the United States Patent and Trademark Office in matters arising under this part.

Writing or written means a tangible or electronic record of a communication or representation, including handwriting, typewriting, printing, photostating, photography, audio or video recording and electronic communications. A "signed" writing includes an electronic sound, symbol or process attached to or logically associated with a writing and executed or adopted by a person with the intent to sign the writing.

1. **Editor's note:** Probably should be "nolo contendere."

History of 37 C.F.R. §11.1: 73 FR 47687, Sept. 15, 2008; 77 FR 45251, Aug. 30, 2012; 78 FR 20197, Apr. 3, 2013; 81 FR 33596, June 27, 2016.

Source of 37 C.F.R. Part 11A: 69 FR 35452, June 24, 2004, unless otherwise noted.

§11.2. DIRECTOR OF THE OFFICE OF ENROLLMENT & DISCIPLINE

(a) Appointment. The USPTO Director shall appoint a Director of the Office of Enrollment and Discipline (OED Director). In the event of a vacancy in the office of the OED Director, the USPTO Director may designate an employee of the Office to serve as acting OED Director. The OED Director shall be an active member in good standing of the bar of the highest court of a State.

(b) Duties. The OED Director shall:

(1) Supervise staff as may be necessary for the performance of the OED Director's duties.

(2) Receive and act upon applications for registration, prepare and grade the examination provided for in §11.7(b), maintain the register provided for in §11.5, and perform such other duties in connection with enrollment and recognition of attorneys and agents as may be necessary.

(3) Conduct investigations into the moral character and reputation of any individual seeking to be registered as an attorney or agent, or of any individual seeking limited recognition, deny registration or recognition of individuals failing to demonstrate possession of good moral character and reputation, and perform such other duties in connection with enrollment matters and investigations as may be necessary.

(4) Conduct investigations of matters involving possible grounds for discipline of practitioners coming to the attention of the OED Director. Except in matters meriting summary dismissal, no disposition under §11.22(h) shall be recommended or undertaken by the OED Director until the accused practitioner shall have been afforded an opportunity to respond to a reasonable inquiry by the OED Director.

(5) With the consent of a panel of three members of the Committee on Discipline, initiate disciplinary proceedings under §11.32 and perform such other duties in connection with investigations and disciplinary proceedings as may be necessary.

(6) Oversee the preliminary screening of information and close investigations as provided for in §11.22.

(c) Petition to OED Director regarding enrollment or recognition. Any petition from any action or requirement of the staff of OED reporting to the OED Director shall be taken to the OED Director accompanied by payment of the fee set forth in §1.21(a)(5)(i) of this chapter. Any such petition not filed within sixty days from the mailing date of the action or notice from which relief is requested will be dismissed as untimely. The filing of a petition will neither stay the period for taking other action which may be running, nor stay other proceedings. The petitioner may file a single request for reconsideration of a decision within thirty days of the date of the decision. Filing a request for reconsideration stays the period for seeking review of the OED Director's decision until a final decision on the request for reconsideration is issued.

(d) Review of OED Director's decision regarding enrollment or recognition. A party dissatisfied with a final decision of the OED Director regarding enrollment or recognition shall seek review of the decision upon petition to the USPTO Director accompanied by payment of the fee set forth in §1.21(a)(5)(ii) of this chapter. By filing such petition to the USPTO Director, the party waives any right to seek reconsideration from the OED Director. Any petition not filed within thirty days after the final decision of the OED Director may be dismissed as untimely. Briefs or memoranda, if any, in support of the petition shall accompany the petition. The petition will be decided on the basis of the record made before the OED Director. The USPTO Director in deciding the petition will consider no new evidence. Copies of documents already of record before the OED Director shall not be submitted with the petition. An oral hearing will not be granted except when considered necessary by the USPTO Director. Any request for reconsideration of the decision of the USPTO Director may be dismissed as untimely if not filed within thirty days after the date of said decision. Only a decision of the USPTO Director regarding denial of a petition constitutes a final decision for the purpose of judicial review.

(e) Petition to USPTO Director in disciplinary matters. A party dissatisfied with any action or notice of any employee of the Office of Enrollment and Discipline during or at the conclusion of a disciplinary investigation shall seek review of the action or notice upon petition to the OED Director. A petition from any action or notice of the staff reporting to the OED Director shall be taken to the OED Director. A party dissatisfied with the OED Director's final decision shall seek review of the final decision upon petition to the USPTO Director to invoke the supervisory authority of the USPTO Director in appropriate circumstances in disciplinary matters. Any petition under this paragraph must contain a statement of the facts involved and the point or points to be reviewed and the action requested. Briefs or memoranda, if any, in support of the petition must accompany the petition. Where facts are to be proven, the proof in the form of affidavits or declarations (and exhibits, if any) must accompany the petition. The OED Director may be directed by the USPTO Director to file a reply to the petition to the USPTO Director, supplying a copy to the petitioner. An oral hearing on petition taken to the USPTO Director will not be granted except when considered necessary by the USPTO Director. The filing of a petition under this paragraph will not stay an investigation, disciplinary proceeding, or other proceedings. Any petition under this part not filed within thirty days of the mailing date of the action or notice from which relief is requested may be dismissed as untimely. Any request for reconsideration of the decision of the OED Director or the USPTO Director may be dismissed as untimely if not filed within thirty days after the date of said decision. Only a decision of the USPTO Director regarding denial of a petition constitutes a final decision for the purpose of judicial review.

History of 37 C.F.R. §11.2: 73 FR 47687, Sept. 15, 2008; 78 FR 20198, Apr. 3, 2013.

§11.3. SUSPENSION OF RULES

(a) In an extraordinary situation, when justice requires, any requirement of the regulations of this Part which is not a requirement of statute may be suspended or waived by the USPTO Director or the designee of the USPTO Director, sua sponte, or on petition by any party, including the OED Director or the OED Director's representative, subject to such other requirements as may be imposed.

(b) No petition under this section shall stay a disciplinary proceeding unless ordered by the USPTO Director or a hearing officer.

History of 37 C.F.R. §11.3: 73 FR 47688, Sept. 15, 2008.

SUBPART B. RECOGNITION TO PRACTICE BEFORE THE USPTO

PATENTS, TRADEMARKS, & OTHER NON-PATENT LAW

§11.4. RESERVED

§11.5. REGISTER OF ATTORNEYS & AGENTS IN PATENT MATTERS; PRACTICE BEFORE THE OFFICE

(a) A register of attorneys and agents is kept in the Office on which are entered the names of all individuals recognized as entitled to represent applicants having prospective or immediate business before the Office in the preparation and prosecution of patent applications. Registration in the Office under the provisions of this part shall entitle the individuals so registered to practice before the Office only in patent matters.

(b) Practice before the Office. Practice before the Office includes, but is not limited to, law-related service that comprehends any matter connected with the presentation to the Office or any of its officers or employees relating to a client's rights, privileges, duties, or responsibilities under the laws or regulations administered by the Office for the grant of a patent or registration of a trademark, or for enrollment or disciplinary matters. Such presentations include preparing necessary documents in contemplation of filing the documents with the Office, corresponding and communicating with the Office, and representing a client through documents or at interviews, hearings, and meetings, as well as communicating with and advising a client concerning matters pending or contemplated to be presented before the Office. Nothing in this section proscribes a practitioner from employing or retaining non-practitioner assistants under the supervision of the practitioner to assist the practitioner in matters pending or contemplated to be presented before the Office.

(1) Practice before the Office in patent matters. Practice before the Office in patent matters includes, but is not limited to, preparing and prosecuting any patent application, consulting with or giving advice to a client in contemplation of filing a patent application or other document with the Office, drafting the specification or claims of a patent application; drafting an amendment or reply to a communication from the Office that may require written argument to establish the patentability of a claimed invention; drafting a reply to a communication from the Office regarding a patent application; and drafting a communication for a public use, interference, reexamination proceeding, petition, appeal to or any other proceeding before the Patent Trial and Appeal Board, or other proceeding. Registration to practice before the Office in patent cases sanctions the performance of those services which are reasonably necessary and incident to the preparation and prosecution of patent applications or other proceeding before the Office involving a patent application or patent in which the practitioner is authorized to participate. The services include:

(i) Considering the advisability of relying upon alternative forms of protection which may be available under state law, and

(ii) Drafting an assignment or causing an assignment to be executed for the patent owner in contemplation of filing or prosecution of a patent application for the patent owner, where the practitioner represents the patent owner after a patent issues in a proceeding before the Office, and when drafting the assignment the practitioner does no more than replicate the terms of a previously existing oral or written obligation of assignment from one person or party to another person or party.

(2) Practice before the Office in trademark matters. Practice before the Office in trademark matters includes, but is not limited to, consulting with or giving advice to a client in contemplation of filing a trademark application or other document with the Office; preparing and prosecuting an application for trademark registration; preparing an amendment which may require written argument to establish the registrability of the mark; and conducting an opposition, cancellation, or concurrent use proceeding; or conducting an appeal to the Trademark Trial and Appeal Board.

History of 37 C.F.R. §11.5: 73 FR 47688, Sept. 15, 2008; 77 FR 46629, Sept. 16, 2012.

Source of 37 C.F.R. Part 11B: 69 FR 35452, June 24, 2004, unless otherwise noted.

§11.6. REGISTRATION OF ATTORNEYS & AGENTS

(a) Attorneys. Any citizen of the United States who is an attorney and who fulfills the requirements of this part may be registered as a patent attorney to practice before the Office. When appropriate, any alien who is an attorney, who lawfully resides in the United States, and who fulfills the requirements of this part may be registered as a patent attorney to practice before the Office, provided that such registration is not inconsistent with the terms upon which the alien was admitted to, and resides in, the United States and further provided that the alien may remain registered only:

(1) If the alien continues to lawfully reside in the United States and registration does not become inconsistent with the terms upon which the alien continues to lawfully reside in the United States, or

(2) If the alien ceases to reside in the United States, the alien is qualified to be registered under paragraph (c) of this section. See also §11.9(b).

(b) Agents. Any citizen of the United States who is not an attorney, and who fulfills the requirements of this part may be registered as a patent agent to practice before the Office. When appropriate, any alien who is not an attorney, who lawfully resides in the United States, and who fulfills the requirements of this part may be registered as a patent agent to practice before the Office, provided that such registration is not inconsistent with the terms upon which the alien was admitted to, and resides in, the United States, and further provided that the alien may remain registered only:

(1) If the alien continues to lawfully reside in the United States and registration does not become inconsistent with the terms upon which the alien continues to lawfully reside in the United States or

(2) If the alien ceases to reside in the United States, the alien is qualified to be registered under paragraph (c) of this section. See also §11.9(b).

(c) Foreigners. Any foreigner not a resident of the United States who shall file proof to the satisfaction of the OED Director that he or she is registered and in good standing before the patent office of the country in which he or she resides and practices, and who is possessed of the qualifications stated in §11.7, may be registered as a patent agent to practice before the Office for the limited purpose of presenting and prosecuting patent applications of applicants located in such country, provided that the patent office of such country allows substantially reciprocal privileges to those admitted to practice before the Office. Registration as a patent agent under this paragraph shall continue only during the period that the conditions specified in this paragraph obtain. Upon notice by the patent office of such country that a patent agent registered under this section is no longer registered or no longer in good standing before the patent office of such country, and absent a showing of cause why his or her name should not be removed from the register, the OED Director shall promptly remove the name of the patent agent from the register and publish the fact of removal. Upon ceasing to reside in such country, the patent agent registered under this section is no longer qualified to be registered under this section, and the OED Director shall promptly remove the name of the patent agent from the register and publish the fact of removal.

(d) Patent Trial and Appeal Board matters. For action by a person who is not registered in a proceeding before the Patent Trial and Appeal Board, see §41.5(a) or §42.10(c) of this title.

History of 37 C.F.R. §11.6: 69 FR 50003, Aug. 12, 2004; 77 FR 46629, Sept. 16, 2012.

§11.7. REQUIREMENTS FOR REGISTRATION

(a) No individual will be registered to practice before the Office unless he or she has:

(1) Applied to the USPTO Director in writing by completing an application for registration form supplied by the OED Director and furnishing all requested information and material; and

(2) Established to the satisfaction of the OED Director that he or she:

(i) Possesses good moral character and reputation;

(ii) Possesses the legal, scientific, and technical qualifications necessary for him or her to render applicants valuable service; and

(iii) Is competent to advise and assist patent applicants in the presentation and prosecution of their applications before the Office.

(b)(1) To enable the OED Director to determine whether an individual has the qualifications specified in paragraph (a)(2) of this section, the individual shall:

(i) File a complete application for registration each time admission to the registration examination is requested. A complete application for registration includes:

(A) An application for registration form supplied by the OED Director wherein all requested information and supporting documents are furnished,

(B) Payment of the fees required by §1.21(a)(1) of this subchapter,

(C) Satisfactory proof of scientific and technical qualifications, and

(D) For aliens, provide proof that recognition is not inconsistent with the terms of their visa or entry into the United States;

(ii) Pass the registration examination, unless the taking and passing of the examination is waived as provided in paragraph (d) of this section. Unless examination is waived pursuant to paragraph (d) of this section, each individual seeking registration must take and pass the registration examination to enable the OED Director to determine whether the individual possesses the legal and competence qualifications specified in paragraphs (a)(2)(ii) and (a)(2)(iii) of this section. An individual failing the examination may, upon receipt of notice of failure from OED, reapply for admission to the examination. An individual failing the examination must wait thirty days after the date the individual last took the examination before retaking the examination. An individual reapplying shall:

(A) File a completed application for registration form wherein all requested information and supporting documents are furnished,

(B) Pay the fees required by §1.21(a)(1) of this subchapter, and

(C) For aliens, provide proof that recognition is not inconsistent with the terms of their visa or entry into the United States; and

(iii) Provide satisfactory proof of possession of good moral character and reputation.

(2) An individual failing to file a complete application for registration will not be admitted to the examination and will be notified of the incompleteness. Applications for registration that are incomplete as originally submitted will be considered only when they have been completed and received by OED, provided that this occurs within sixty days of the mailing date of the notice of incompleteness. Thereafter, a new and complete application for registration must be filed. Only an individual approved as satisfying the requirements of paragraphs (b)(1)(i)(A), (b)(1)(i)(B), (b)(1)(i)(C) and (b)(1)(i)(D) of this section may be admitted to the examination.

(3) If an individual does not reapply until more than one year after the mailing date of a notice of failure, that individual must again comply with paragraph (b)(1)(i) of this section.

(c) Each individual seeking registration is responsible for updating all information and answers submitted in or with the application for registration based upon anything occurring between the date the application for registration is signed by the individual, and the date he or she is registered or recognized to practice before the Office in patent matters. The update shall be filed within thirty days after the date of the occasion that necessitates the update.

(d) Waiver of the Registration Examination for Former Office Employees.

(1) Former patent examiners who by July 26, 2004, had not actively served four years in the patent examining corps, and were serving in the corps at the time of their separation. The OED Director may waive the taking of a registration examination in the case of any individual meeting the requirements of paragraph (b)(1)(i)(C) of this section who is a former patent examiner but by July 26, 2004, had not served four years in the patent examining corps, if the individual demonstrates that he or she:

(i) Actively served in the patent examining corps of the Office and was serving in the corps at the time of separation from the Office;

(ii) Received a certificate of legal competency and negotiation authority;

(iii) After receiving the certificate of legal competency and negotiation authority, was rated at least fully successful in each quality performance element of his or her performance plan for the last two complete fiscal years as a patent examiner; and

(iv) Was not under an oral or written warning regarding the quality performance elements at the time of separation from the patent examining corps.

(2) Former patent examiners who on July 26, 2004, had actively served four years in the patent examining corps, and were serving in the corps at the time of their separation. The OED Director may waive the taking of a registration examination in the case of any individual meeting the requirements of paragraph (b)(1)(i)(C) of this section who is a former patent examiner and by July 26, 2004, had served four years in the patent examining corps, if the individual demonstrates that he or she:

(i) Actively served for at least four years in the patent examining corps of the Office by July 26, 2004, and was serving in the corps at the time of separation from the Office;

(ii) Was rated at least fully successful in each quality performance element of his or her performance plan for the last two complete fiscal years as a patent examiner in the Office; and

(iii) Was not under an oral or written warning regarding the quality performance elements at the time of separation from the patent examining corps.

(3) Certain former Office employees who were not serving in the patent examining corps upon their separation from the Office. The OED Director may waive the taking of a registration examination in the case of a former Office employee meeting the requirements of paragraph (b)(1)(i)(C) of this section who by petition demonstrates possession of the necessary legal qualifications to render to patent applicants and others valuable service and assistance in the preparation and prosecution of their applications or other business before the Office by showing that he or she has:

(i) Exhibited comprehensive knowledge of patent law equivalent to that shown by passing the registration examination as a result of having been in a position of responsibility in the Office in which he or she:

(A) Provided substantial guidance on patent examination policy, including the development of rule or procedure changes, patent examination guidelines, changes to the Manual of Patent Examining Procedure, development of training or testing materials for the patent examining corps, or development of materials for the registration examination or continuing legal education; or

(B) Represented the Office in patent cases before Federal courts; and

(ii) Was rated at least fully successful in each quality performance element of his or her performance plan for said position for the last two complete rating periods in the Office, and was not under an oral or written warning regarding such performance elements at the time of separation from the Office.

(4) To be eligible for consideration for waiver, an individual formerly employed by the Office within the scope of one of paragraphs (d)(1), (d)(2) or (d)(3) of this section must file a complete application for registration and pay the fee required by §1.21(a)(1)(i) of this subchapter within two years of the individual's date of separation from the Office. All other individuals formerly employed by the Office, including former examiners, filing an application for registration or fee more than two years after separation from the Office, are required to take and pass the registration examination. The individual or former examiner must pay the examination fee required by §1.21(a)(1)(ii) of this subchapter within thirty days after notice of non-waiver.

(e) Examination results. Notification of the examination results is final. Within sixty days of the mailing date of a notice of failure, the individual is entitled to inspect, but not copy, the questions and answers he or she incorrectly answered. Review will be under supervision. No notes may be taken during such review. Substantive review of the answers or questions may not be pursued by petition for regrade. An individual who failed the examination has the right to retake the examination an unlimited number of times upon payment of the fees required by §1.21(a)(1)(i) and (ii) of this subchapter, and a fee charged by a commercial entity administering the examination.

(f) Application for reciprocal recognition. An individual seeking reciprocal recognition under §11.6(c), in addition to satisfying the provisions of paragraphs (a) and (b) of this section, and the provisions of §11.8(c), shall pay the application fee required by §1.21(a)(1)(i) of this subchapter upon filing an application for registration.

(g) Investigation of good moral character and reputation.

(1) Every individual seeking recognition shall answer all questions in the application for registration and request(s) for comments issued by OED; disclose all relevant facts, dates and information; and provide verified copies of documents relevant to his or her good moral character and reputation. An individual who is an attorney shall submit a certified copy of each of his or her State bar applications and moral character determinations, if available.

(2)(i) If the OED Director receives information from any source that reflects adversely on the good moral character or reputation of an individual seeking registration or recognition, the OED Director shall conduct an investigation into the good moral character and reputation of that individual. The investigation will be conducted after the individual has passed the registration examination, or after the registration examination has been waived for the individual, as applicable. An individual failing to timely answer questions or respond to an inquiry by OED shall be deemed to have withdrawn his or her application, and shall be required to reapply, pass the examination, and otherwise satisfy all the requirements of this section. No individual shall be certified for registration or recognition by the OED Director until, to the satisfaction of the OED Director, the individual demonstrates his or her possession of good moral character and reputation.

(ii) The OED Director, in considering an application for registration by an attorney, may accept a State bar's character determination as meeting the requirements set forth in paragraph (g) of this section if, after review, the Office finds no substantial discrepancy between the information provided with his or her application for registration and the State bar application and moral character determination, provided that acceptance is not inconsistent with other rules and the requirements of 35 U.S.C. 2(b)(2)(D).

(h) Good moral character and reputation. Evidence showing lack of good moral character and reputation may include, but is not limited to, conviction of a felony or a misdemeanor identified in paragraph (h)(1) of this section, drug or alcohol abuse; lack of candor; suspension or disbarment on ethical grounds from a State bar; and resignation from a State bar while under investigation.

(1) Conviction of felony or misdemeanor. An individual who has been convicted of a felony or a misdemeanor involving moral turpitude, breach of trust, interference with the administration of justice, false swearing, misrepresentation, fraud, deceit, bribery, extortion, misappropriation, theft, or conspiracy to commit any felony or misdemeanor, is presumed not to be of good moral character and reputation in the absence of a pardon or a satisfactory showing of reform and rehabilitation, and shall file with his or her application for registration the fees required by §1.21(a)(1)(ii) and (a)(10) of this subchapter. The OED Director shall determine whether individuals convicted of said felony or misdemeanor provided satisfactory proof of reform and rehabilitation.

(i) An individual who has been convicted of a felony or a misdemeanor identified in paragraph (h)(1) of this section shall not be eligible to apply for registration during the time of any sentence (including confinement or commitment to imprisonment), deferred adjudication, and period of probation or parole as a result of the conviction, and for a period of two years after the date of completion of the sentence, deferred adjudication, and period of probation or parole, whichever is later.

(ii) The following presumptions apply to the determination of good moral character and reputation of an individual convicted of said felony or misdemeanor:

(A) The court record or docket entry of conviction is conclusive evidence of guilt in the absence of a pardon or a satisfactory showing of reform or rehabilitation; and

(B) An individual convicted of a felony or any misdemeanor identified in paragraph (h)(1) of this section is conclusively deemed not to have good moral character and reputation, and shall not be eligible to apply for registration for a period of two years after completion of the sentence, deferred adjudication, and period of probation or parole, whichever is later.

(iii) The individual, upon applying for registration, shall provide satisfactory evidence that he or she is of good moral character and reputation.

(iv) Upon proof that a conviction has been set aside or reversed, the individual shall be eligible to file a complete application for registration and the fee required by §1.21(a)(1)(ii) of this subchapter and, upon passing the registration examination, have the OED Director determine, in accordance with paragraph (h)(1) of this section, whether, absent the conviction, the individual possesses good moral character and reputation.

(2) Good moral character and reputation involving drug or alcohol abuse. An individual's record is reviewed as a whole to see if there is a drug or alcohol abuse issue. An individual appearing to abuse drugs or alcohol may be asked to undergo an evaluation, at the individual's expense, by a qualified professional approved by the OED Director. In instances where, before an investigation commences, there is evidence of a present abuse or an individual has not established a record of recovery, the OED Director may request the individual to withdraw his or her application, and require the individual to satisfactorily demonstrate that he or she is complying with treatment and undergoing recovery.

(3) Moral character and reputation involving lack of candor. An individual's lack of candor in disclosing facts bearing on or relevant to issues concerning good moral character and reputation when completing the application or any time thereafter may be found to be cause to deny registration on moral character and reputation grounds.

(4) Moral character and reputation involving suspension, disbarment, or resignation from a profession.

(i) An individual who has been disbarred or suspended from practice of law or other profession, or has resigned in lieu of a disciplinary proceeding (excluded or disbarred on consent) shall be ineligible to apply for registration as follows:

(A) An individual who has been disbarred from practice of law or other profession, or has resigned in lieu of a disciplinary proceeding (excluded or disbarred on consent) shall be ineligible to apply for registration for a period of five years from the date of disbarment or resignation.

(B) An individual who has been suspended on ethical grounds from the practice of law or other profession shall be ineligible to apply for registration until expiration of the period of suspension.

(C) An individual who was not only disbarred, suspended or resigned in lieu of a disciplinary proceeding, but also convicted in a court of a felony, or of a crime involving moral turpitude or breach of trust, shall be ineligible to apply for registration until the conditions in paragraphs (h)(1) and (h)(4) of this section are fully satisfied.

(ii) An individual who has been disbarred or suspended, or who resigned in lieu of a disciplinary proceeding shall file an application for registration and the fees required by §1.21(a)(1)(ii) and (a)(10) of this subchapter; provide a full and complete copy of the proceedings that led to the disbarment, suspension, or resignation; and provide satisfactory proof that he or she possesses good moral character and reputation. The following presumptions shall govern the determination of good moral character and reputation of an individual who has been licensed to practice law or other profession in any jurisdiction and has been disbarred, suspended on ethical grounds, or allowed to resign in lieu of discipline, in that jurisdiction:

(A) A copy of the record resulting in disbarment, suspension or resignation is prima facie evidence of the matters contained in the record, and the imposition of disbarment or suspension, or the acceptance of the resignation of the individual shall be deemed conclusive that the individual has committed professional misconduct.

(B) The individual is ineligible for registration and is deemed not to have good moral character and reputation during the period of the imposed discipline.

(iii) The only defenses available with regard to an underlying disciplinary matter resulting in disbarment, suspension on ethical grounds, or resignation in lieu of a disciplinary proceeding are set out below, and must be shown to the satisfaction of the OED Director:

(A) The procedure in the disciplinary court was so lacking in notice or opportunity to be heard as to constitute a deprivation of due process;

(B) There was such infirmity of proof establishing the misconduct as to give rise to the clear conviction that the Office could not, consistently with its duty, accept as final the conclusion on that subject; or

(C) The finding of lack of good moral character and reputation by the Office would result in grave injustice.

(i) Factors that may be taken into consideration when evaluating rehabilitation of an individual seeking a moral character and reputation determination. The factors enumerated below are guidelines to assist the OED Director in determining whether an individual has demonstrated rehabilitation from an act of misconduct or moral turpitude. The factors include:

(1) The nature of the act of misconduct, including whether it involved moral turpitude, whether there were aggravating or mitigating circumstances, and whether the activity was an isolated event or part of a pattern;

(2) The age and education of the individual at the time of the misconduct and the age and education of the individual at the present time;

(3) The length of time that has passed between the misconduct and the present, absent any involvement in any further acts of moral turpitude, the amount of time and the extent of rehabilitation being dependent upon the nature and seriousness of the act of misconduct under consideration;

(4) Restitution by the individual to any person who suffered monetary losses through acts or omissions of the individual;

(5) Expungement of a conviction;

(6) Successful completion or early discharge from probation or parole;

(7) Abstinence from the use of controlled substances or alcohol for not less than two years if the specific misconduct was attributable in part to the use of a controlled substance or alcohol, where abstinence may be demonstrated by, but is not necessarily limited to, enrolling in and complying with a self-help or professional treatment program;

(8) If the specific misconduct was attributable in part to a medically recognized mental disease, disorder or illness, proof that the individual sought professional assistance, and complied with the treatment program prescribed by the professional, and submitted letters from the treating psychiatrist/psychologist verifying that the medically recognized mental disease, disorder or illness will not impede the individual's ability to competently practice before the Office;

(9) Payment of the fine imposed in connection with any criminal conviction;

(10) Correction of behavior responsible in some degree for the misconduct;

(11) Significant and conscientious involvement in programs designed to provide social benefits or to ameliorate social problems; and

(12) Change in attitude from that which existed at the time of the act of misconduct in question as evidenced by any or all of the following:

(i) Statements of the individual;

(ii) Statements from persons familiar with the individual's previous misconduct and with subsequent attitudes and behavioral patterns;

(iii) Statements from probation or parole officers or law enforcement officials as to the individual's social adjustments; and

(iv) Statements from persons competent to testify with regard to neuropsychiatry or emotional disturbances.

(j) Notice to Show Cause. The OED Director shall inquire into the good moral character and reputation of an individual seeking registration, providing the individual with the opportunity to create a record on which a decision is made. If, following inquiry and consideration of the record, the OED Director is of the opinion that the individual seeking registration has not satisfactorily established that he or she possesses good moral character and reputation, the OED Director shall issue to the individual a notice to show cause why the individual's application for registration should not be denied.

(1) The individual shall be given no less than ten days from the date of the notice to reply. The notice shall be given by certified mail at the address appearing on the application if the address is in the United States, and by any other reasonable means if the address is outside the United States.

(2) Following receipt of the individual's response, or in the absence of a response, the OED Director shall consider the individual's response, if any, and the record, and determine whether, in the OED Director's opinion, the individual has sustained his or her burden of satisfactorily demonstrating that he or she possesses good moral character and reputation.

(k) Reapplication for registration. An individual who has been refused registration for lack of good moral character or reputation may reapply for registration two years after the date of the decision, unless a shorter period is otherwise ordered by the USPTO Director. An individual, who has been notified that he or she is under investigation for good moral character and reputation may elect to withdraw his or her application for registration, and may reapply for registration two years after the date of withdrawal. Upon reapplication for registration, the individual shall pay the fees required by §1.21(a)(1)(ii) and (a)(10) of this subchapter, and has the burden of showing to the satisfaction of the OED Director his or her possession of good moral character and reputation as prescribed in paragraph (b) of this section. Upon reapplication for registration, the individual also shall complete successfully the examination prescribed in paragraph (b) of this section, even though the individual has previously passed a registration examination.

§11.8. OATH & REGISTRATION FEE

(a) After an individual passes the examination, or the examination is waived, the OED Director shall promptly publish a solicitation for information concerning the individual's good moral character and reputation. The solicitation shall include the individual's name, and business or communication postal address.

(b) An individual shall not be registered as an attorney under §11.6(a), registered as an agent under §11.6(b) or (c), or granted limited recognition under §11.9(b) unless within two years of the mailing date of a notice of passing registration examination or of waiver of the examination the individual files with the OED Director a completed Data Sheet, an oath or declaration prescribed by the USPTO Director, and the registration fee set forth in §1.21(a)(2) of this subchapter. An individual seeking registration as an attorney under §11.6(a) must provide a certificate of good standing of the bar of the highest court of a State that is no more than six months old.

(c) An individual who does not comply with the requirements of paragraph (b) of this section within the two-year period will be required to retake the registration examination.

(d) [Reserved]

History of 37 C.F.R. §11.8: 73 FR 67757, Dec. 17, 2008; 78 FR 20198, Apr. 3, 2013.

§11.9. LIMITED RECOGNITION IN PATENT MATTERS

(a) Any individual not registered under §11.6 may, upon a showing of circumstances which render it necessary or justifiable, and that the individual is of good moral character and reputation, be given limited recognition by the OED Director to prosecute as attorney or agent a specified patent application or specified patent applications. Limited recognition under this paragraph shall not extend further than the application or applications specified. Limited recognition shall not be granted while individuals who have passed the examination or for whom the examination has been waived are awaiting registration to practice before the Office in patent matters.

(b) A nonimmigrant alien residing in the United States and fulfilling the provisions of §11.7(a) and (b) may be granted limited recognition if the nonimmigrant alien is authorized by the United States Government to be employed or trained in the United States in the capacity of representing a patent applicant by presenting or prosecuting a patent application. Limited recognition shall be granted for a period consistent with the terms of authorized employment or training. Limited recognition shall not be granted or extended to a non-United States citizen residing abroad. If granted, limited recognition shall automatically expire upon the nonimmigrant alien's departure from the United States.

(c) An individual not registered under §11.6 may, if appointed by an applicant, prosecute an international patent application only before the United States International Searching Authority and the United States International Preliminary Examining Authority, provided that the individual has the right to practice before the national office with which the international application is filed as provided in PCT Art. 49, Rule 90 and §1.455 of this subchapter, or before the International Bureau when the USPTO is acting as Receiving Office pursuant to PCT Rules 83.1 *bis* and 90.1.

History of 37 C.F.R. §11.9: 78 FR 20198, Apr. 3, 2013.

§11.10. RESTRICTIONS ON PRACTICE IN PATENT MATTERS

(a) Only practitioners who are registered under §11.6 or individuals given limited recognition under §11.9(a) or (b) are permitted to prosecute patent applications of others before the Office; or represent others in any proceedings before the Office.

(b) Post employment agreement of former Office employee. No individual who has served in the patent examining corps or elsewhere in the Office may practice before the Office after termination of his or her service, unless he or she signs a written undertaking agreeing:

(1) To not knowingly act as agent or attorney for, or otherwise represent, or assist in any manner the representation of, any other person:

(i) Before the Office,

(ii) In connection with any particular patent or patent application,

(iii) In which said employee participated personally and substantially as an employee of the Office; and

(2) To not knowingly act within two years after terminating employment by the Office as agent or attorney for, or otherwise represent, or assist in any manner the representation of any other person:

(i) Before the Office,

(ii) In connection with any particular patent or patent application,

(iii) If such patent or patent application was pending under the employee's official responsibility as an officer or employee within a period of one year prior to the termination of such responsibility.

(3) The words and phrases in paragraphs (b)(1) and (b)(2) of this section are construed as follows:

(i) Represent and representation mean acting as patent attorney or patent agent or other representative in any appearance before the Office, or communicating with an employee of the Office with intent to influence.

(ii) Assist in any manner means aid or help another person on a particular patent or patent application involving representation.

(iii) Particular patent or patent application means any patent or patent application, including, but not limited to, a provisional, substitute, international, international design, continuation, divisional, continuation-in-part, or reissue patent application, as well as any protest, reexamination, petition, appeal, interference, or trial proceeding based on the patent or patent application.

(iv) Participate personally and substantially.

(A) Basic requirements. The restrictions of §11.10(a)(1) apply only to those patents and patent applications in which a former Office employee had "personal and substantial participation," exercised "through decision, approval, disapproval, recommendation, the rendering of advice, investigation or otherwise." To participate personally means directly, and includes the participation of a subordinate when actually directed by the former Office employee in the patent or patent application. Substantially means that the employee's involvement must be of significance to the matter, or form a basis for a reasonable appearance of such significance. It requires more than official responsibility, knowledge, perfunctory involvement, or involvement on an administrative or peripheral issue. A finding of substantiality should be based not only on the effort devoted to a patent or patent application, but also on the importance of the effort. While a series of peripheral involvements may be insubstantial, the single act of approving or participation in a critical step may be substantial. It is essential that the participation be related to a "particular patent or patent application." (See paragraph (b)(3)(iii) of this section.)

(B) Participation on ancillary matters. An Office employee's participation on subjects not directly involving the substantive merits of a patent or patent application may not be "substantial," even if it is time-consuming. An employee whose official responsibility is the review of a patent or patent application solely for compliance with administrative control or budgetary considerations and who reviews a particular patent or patent application for such a purpose should not be regarded as having participated substantially in the patent or patent application, except when such considerations also are the subject of the employee's proposed representation.

(C) Role of official responsibility in determining substantial participation. Official responsibility is defined in paragraph (b)(3)(v) of this section. "Personal and substantial participation" is different from "official responsibility." One's responsibility may, however, play a role in determining the "substantiality" of an Office employee's participation.

(v) Official responsibility means the direct administrative or operating authority, whether intermediate or final, and either exercisable alone or with others, and either personally or through subordinates, to approve, disapprove, or otherwise direct Government actions.

(A) Determining official responsibility. Ordinarily, those areas assigned by statute, regulation, Executive Order, job description, or delegation of authority determine the scope of an employee's "official responsibility." All particular matters under consideration in the Office are under the "official responsibility" of the Director of the Office, and each is under that of any intermediate supervisor having responsibility for an employee who actually participates in the patent or patent application within the scope of his or her duties. A patent examiner would have "official responsibility" for the patent applications assigned to him or her.

(B) Ancillary matters and official responsibility. Administrative authority as used in paragraph (v) of this section means authority for planning, organizing and controlling a patent or patent application rather than authority to review or make decisions on ancillary aspects of a patent or patent application such as the regularity of budgeting procedures, public or community relations aspects, or equal employment opportunity considerations. Responsibility for such an ancillary consideration does not constitute official responsibility for the particular patent or patent application, except when such a consideration is also the subject of the employee's proposed representation.

(C) Duty to inquire. In order for a former employee, *e.g.*, former patent examiner, to be barred from representing or assisting in representing another as to a particular patent or patent application, he or she need not have known, while employed by the Office, that the patent or patent application was pending under his or her official responsibility. The former employee has a reasonable duty of inquiry to learn whether the patent or patent application had been under his or her official responsibility. Ordinarily, a former employee who is asked to represent another on a patent or patent application will become aware of facts sufficient to suggest the relationship of the prior matter to his or her former office, *e.g.*, technology center, group or art unit. If so, he or she is under a duty to make further inquiry. It would be prudent for an employee to maintain a record of only patent application numbers of the applications actually acted upon by decision or recommendation, as well as those applications under the employee's official responsibility which he or she has not acted upon.

(D) Self-disqualification. A former employee, *e.g.*, former patent examiner, cannot avoid the restrictions of this section through self-disqualification with respect to a patent or patent application for which he or she otherwise had official responsibility. However, an employee who through self-disqualification does not participate personally and substantially in a particular patent or patent application is not subject to the lifetime restriction of paragraph (b)(1) of this section.

(vi) Pending means that the matter was in fact referred to or under consideration by persons within the employee's area of official responsibility.

(4) Measurement of the two-year restriction period. The two-year period under paragraph (b)(2) of this section is measured from the date when the employee's official responsibility in a particular area ends, not from the termination of service in the Office, unless the two occur simultaneously. The prohibition applies to all particular patents or patent applications subject to such official responsibility in the one-year period before termination of such responsibility.

(c) Former employees of the Office. This section imposes restrictions generally parallel to those imposed in 18 U.S.C. 207(a) and (b)(1). This section, however, does not interpret these statutory provisions or any other post-employment restrictions that may apply to former Office employees, and such former employees should not assume that conduct not prohibited by this section is otherwise permissible. Former employees of the Office, whether or not they are practitioners, are encouraged to contact the Department of Commerce for information concerning applicable post-employment restrictions.

(d) An employee of the Office may not prosecute or aid in any manner in the prosecution of any patent application before the Office.

(e) Practice before the Office by Government employees is subject to any applicable conflict of interest laws, regulations or codes of professional responsibility.

History of 37 C.F.R. §11.10: 69 FR 35452, June 24, 2004, as amended at 77 FR 46630, Aug. 6, 2012; 80 FR 17971, May 13, 2015.

§11.11. ADMINISTRATIVE SUSPENSION, INACTIVATION, RESIGNATION, & READMISSION

(a) Contact information. (1) A registered practitioner must notify the OED Director of his or her postal address for his or her office, up to three email addresses where he or she receives email, and a business telephone number, as well as every change to any of said addresses or telephone number within thirty days of the date of the change. A registered practitioner shall, in addition to any notice of change of address and telephone number filed in individual patent applications, separately file written notice of the change of address or telephone number to the OED Director. A registered practitioner who is an attorney in good standing with the bar of the highest court of one or more States shall provide the OED Director with the State bar identification number associated with each membership. The OED Director shall publish from the roster a list containing the name, postal business addresses, business telephone number, registration number, and registration status as an attorney or agent of each registered practitioner recognized to practice before the Office in patent cases.

(2) A letter may be addressed to any registered practitioner, at the address of which separate notice was last received by the OED Director, for the purpose of ascertaining whether such practitioner desires to remain on the register. Any registered practitioner failing to reply and give any information requested by the OED Director within a time limit specified will be subject to administrative suspension under paragraph (b) of this section.

(b) Administrative suspension. (1) Whenever it appears that a registered practitioner or a person granted limited recognition under §11.9(b) has failed to comply with §11.8(d) or paragraph (a)(2) of this section, the OED Director shall publish and send a notice to the registered practitioner or person granted limited recognition advising of the noncompliance, the consequence of being administratively suspended under paragraph (b)(5) of this section if noncompliance is not timely remedied, and the requirements for reinstatement under paragraph (f) of this section. The notice shall be published and sent to the registered practitioner or person granted limited recognition by mail to the last postal address furnished under paragraph (a) of this section or by email addressed to the last email addresses furnished under paragraph (a) of this section. The notice shall demand compliance and payment of a delinquency fee set forth in §1.21(a)(9)(i) of this subchapter within sixty days after the date of such notice.

(2) In the event a registered practitioner or person granted limited recognition fails to comply with the notice of paragraph (b)(1) of this section within the time allowed, the OED Director shall publish and send in the manner provided for in paragraph (b)(1) of this section to the registered practitioner or person granted limited recognition a Rule to Show Cause why his or her registration or recognition should not be administratively suspended, and he or she no longer be permitted to practice before the Office in patent matters or in any way hold himself or herself out as being registered or authorized to practice before the Office in patent matters. The OED Director shall file a copy of the Rule to Show Cause with the USPTO Director.

(3) Within 30 days of the OED Director's sending the Rule to Show Cause identified in paragraph (b)(2) of this section, the registered practitioner or person granted limited recognition may file a response to the Rule to Show Cause with the USPTO Director. The response must set forth the factual and legal bases why the person should not be administratively suspended. The registered practitioner or person granted limited recognition shall serve the OED Director with a copy of the response at the time it is filed with the USPTO Director. Within ten days of receiving a copy of the response, the OED Director may file a reply with the USPTO Director that includes documents demonstrating that the notice identified in paragraph (b)(1) of this section was published and sent to the practitioner in accordance with paragraph (b)(1) of this section. A copy of the reply by the OED Director shall be served on the registered practitioner or person granted limited recognition. When acting on the Rule to Show Cause, if the USPTO Director determines that there are no genuine issues of material fact regarding the Office's compliance with the notice requirements under this section or the failure of the person to pay the requisite fees, the USPTO Director shall enter an order administratively suspending the registered practitioner or person granted limited recognition. Otherwise, the USPTO Director shall enter an appropriate order dismissing the Rule to Show Cause. Nothing herein shall permit an administratively suspended registered practitioner or person granted limited recognition to seek a stay of the administrative suspension during the pendency of any review of the USPTO Director's final decision.

(4) [Reserved]

(5) An administratively suspended registered practitioner or person granted limited recognition is subject to investigation and discipline for his or her conduct prior to, during, or after the period he or she was administratively suspended.

(6) An administratively suspended registered practitioner or person granted limited recognition is prohibited from practicing before the Office in patent cases while administratively suspended. A registered practitioner or person granted limited recognition who knows he or she has been administratively suspended under this section will be subject to discipline for failing to comply with the provisions of this paragraph (b).

(c) Administrative inactivation. **(1)** Any registered practitioner who shall become employed by the Office shall comply with §11.116 for withdrawal from the applications, patents, and trademark matters wherein he or she represents an applicant or other person, and notify the OED Director in writing of said employment on the first day of said employment. The name of any registered practitioner employed by the Office shall be endorsed on the roster as administratively inactive. Upon separation from the Office, the administratively inactive practitioner may request reactivation by completing and filing an application, Data Sheet, signing a written undertaking required by §11.10, and paying the fee set forth in §1.21(a)(1)(i) of this subchapter. An administratively inactive practitioner remains subject to the provisions of the USPTO Rules of Professional Conduct and to proceedings and sanctions under §§11.19 through 11.58 for conduct that violates a provision of the USPTO Rules of Professional Conduct prior to or during employment at the Office. If, within 30 days after separation from the Office, the registered practitioner does not request active status or another status, the registered practitioner will be endorsed on the roster as voluntarily inactive and be subject to the provisions of paragraph (d) of this section.

(2) Any registered practitioner who is a judge of a court of record, full-time court commissioner, U.S. bankruptcy judge, U.S. magistrate judge, or a retired judge who is eligible for temporary judicial assignment and is not engaged in the practice of law may request, in writing, that his or her name be endorsed on the roster as administratively inactive. Upon acceptance of the request, the OED Director shall endorse the name of the practitioner as administratively inactive. Following separation from the bench, the practitioner may request restoration to active status by completing and filing an application, Data Sheet, and signing a written undertaking required by §11.10.

(d) Voluntary Inactivation. **(1)** Except as provided in paragraph (d)(4) of this section, any registered practitioner may voluntarily enter inactive status by filing a request, in writing, that his or her name be endorsed on the roster as voluntarily inactive. Upon acceptance of the request, the OED Director shall endorse the name as voluntarily inactive.

(2) [Reserved]

(3) A registered practitioner who seeks or enters into voluntary inactive status is subject to investigation and discipline for his or her conduct prior to, during, or after the period of his or her inactivation.

(4) [Reserved]

(5) A registered practitioner in voluntary inactive status is prohibited from practicing before the Office in patent cases while in voluntary inactive status. A registered practitioner in voluntary inactive status will be subject to discipline for failing to comply with the provisions of this paragraph. Upon acceptance of the request for voluntary inactive status, the practitioner must comply with the provisions of §11.116.

(6) Any registered practitioner whose name has been endorsed as voluntarily inactive pursuant to paragraph (d)(1) of this section and is not under investigation and not subject to a disciplinary proceeding may be restored to active status on the register as may be appropriate provided that the practitioner files a written request for restoration, a completed application for registration on a form supplied by the OED Director furnishing all requested information and material, including information and material pertaining to the practitioner's moral character and reputation under §11.7(a)(2)(i) during the period of inactivation, a declaration or affidavit attesting to the fact that the practitioner has read the most recent revisions of the patent laws and the rules of practice before the Office, and pays the fees set forth in §1.21(a)(7)(iii) and (iv) of this subchapter.

(e) Resignation. A registered practitioner or a practitioner recognized under §11.14(c), who is not under investigation under §11.22 for a possible violation of the USPTO Rules of Professional Conduct, subject to discipline under §§11.24 or 11.25, or a practitioner against whom probable cause has been found by a panel of the Committee on Discipline under §11.23(b), may resign by notifying the OED Director in writing that he or she desires to resign. Upon acceptance in writing by the OED Director of such notice, that registered practitioner or practitioner under §11.14 shall no longer be eligible to practice before the Office in patent matters but shall continue to file a change of address for five years thereafter in order that he or she may be located in the event information regarding the practitioner's conduct comes to the attention of the OED Director or any grievance is made about his or her conduct while he or she engaged in practice before the Office. The name of any registered practitioner whose resignation is accepted shall be removed from the register, endorsed as resigned, and notice thereof published in the Official Gazette. Upon acceptance of the resignation by the OED Director, the registered practitioner must comply with the provisions of §11.116.

(f) Administrative reinstatement. **(1)** Any registered practitioner who has been administratively suspended pursuant to paragraph (b) of this section, or who has resigned pursuant to paragraph (e) of this section, may be reinstated on the register provided the practitioner has applied for reinstatement on an application form supplied by the OED Director, demonstrated compliance with the provisions of §11.7(a)(2)(i) and (iii), and paid the fees set forth in §1.21(a)(9)(i) and (a)(9)(ii) of this subchapter. Any person granted limited recognition who has been administratively suspended pursuant to paragraph (b) of this section may have their recognition reactivated provided the practitioner has applied for reinstatement on an application form supplied by the OED Director, demonstrated compliance with the provisions of §11.7(a)(2)(i) and (iii), and paid the fees set forth in §1.21(a)(9)(i) and (a)(9)(ii) of this subchapter. A practitioner who has resigned or was administratively suspended for two or more years before the date the Office receives a completed application from the person who resigned or was administratively suspended must also pass the registration examination under §11.7(b)(1)(ii). Any reinstated practitioner is subject to investigation and discipline for his or her conduct that occurred prior to, during, or after the period of his or her administrative suspension or resignation.

(2) Any registered practitioner whose registration has been administratively inactivated pursuant to paragraph (c) of this section may be reinstated to the register as may be appropriate provided within two years after his or her employment with the Office ceases or within two years after his or her employment in a judicial capacity ceases the following is filed with the OED Director: a request for reinstatement, a completed application for registration on a form supplied by the OED Director furnishing all requested information and material, and the fee set forth in §1.21(a)(9)(ii) of this subchapter. Any registered practitioner inactivated or reinstated is subject to investigation and discipline for his or her conduct before, during, or after the period of his or her inactivation.

History of 37 C.F.R. §11.11: 73 FR 67757, Dec. 17, 2008; 78 FR 20198, Apr. 3, 2013.

§§11.12, 11.13. RESERVED

§11.14. INDIVIDUALS WHO MAY PRACTICE BEFORE THE OFFICE IN TRADEMARK & OTHER NON-PATENT MATTERS

(a) Attorneys. Any individual who is an attorney as defined in §11.1 may represent others before the Office in trademark and other non-patent matters. An attorney is not required to apply for registration or recognition to practice before the Office in trademark and other non-patent matters. Registration as a patent practitioner does not itself entitle an individual to practice before the Office in trademark matters.

(b) Non-lawyers. Individuals who are not attorneys are not recognized to practice before the Office in trademark and other non-patent matters, except that individuals not attorneys who were recognized to practice before the Office in trademark matters under this chapter prior to January 1, 1957, will be recognized as agents to continue practice before the Office in trademark matters. Except as provided in the preceding sentence, registration as a patent agent does not itself entitle an individual to practice before the Office in trademark matters.

(c) Foreigners. Any foreign attorney or agent not a resident of the United States who shall file a written application for reciprocal recognition under paragraph (f) of this section and prove to the satisfaction of the OED Director that he or she is registered or in good standing before the patent or trademark office of the country in which he or she resides and practices and is possessed of good moral character and reputation, may be recognized for the limited purpose of representing parties located in such country before the Office in the presentation and prosecution of trademark matters, provided: the patent or trademark office of such country allows substantially reciprocal privileges to those permitted to practice in trademark matters before the Office. Recognition under this paragraph shall continue only during the period that the conditions specified in this paragraph obtain.

(d) Recognition of any individual under this section shall not be construed as sanctioning or authorizing the performance of any act regarded in the jurisdiction where performed as the unauthorized practice of law.

(e) No individual other than those specified in paragraphs (a), (b), and (c) of this section will be permitted to practice before the Office in trademark matters on behalf of a client. Any individual may appear in a trademark or other non-patent matter in his or her own behalf. Any individual may appear in a trademark matter for:

(1) A firm of which he or she is a member,

(2) A partnership of which he or she is a partner, or

(3) A corporation or association of which he or she is an officer and which he or she is authorized to represent, if such firm, partnership, corporation, or association is a party to a trademark proceeding pending before the Office.

(f) Application for reciprocal recognition. An individual seeking reciprocal recognition under paragraph (c) of this section, in addition to providing evidence satisfying the provisions of paragraph (c) of this section, shall apply in writing to the OED Director for reciprocal recognition, and shall pay the application fee required by §1.21(a)(1)(i) of this subchapter.

History of 37 C.F.R. §11.14: 73 FR 47688, Sept. 15, 2008.

§11.15. REFUSAL TO RECOGNIZE A PRACTITIONER

Any practitioner authorized to appear before the Office may be suspended, excluded, or reprimanded in accordance with the provisions of this Part. Any practitioner who is suspended or excluded under this Part shall not be entitled to practice before the Office in patent, trademark, or other non-patent matters while suspended or excluded.

History of 37 C.F.R. §11.15: 73 FR 47688, Sept. 15, 2008.

§11.16. REQUIREMENTS FOR ADMISSION TO THE USPTO LAW SCHOOL CLINIC CERTIFICATION PROGRAM

(a) The USPTO Law School Clinic Certification Program allows students enrolled in a participating law school's clinic to practice before the Office in patent or trademark matters by drafting, filing, and prosecuting patent or trademark applications on a pro bono basis for clients that qualify for assistance from the law school's clinic. All law schools accredited by the American Bar Association are eligible for participation in the program, and shall be examined for acceptance using identical criteria.

(b) Application for admission and renewal—**(1)** Application for admission. Non-participating law schools seeking admission to the USPTO Law School Clinic Certification Program, and participating law schools seeking to add a practice area, shall submit an application for admission for such practice area to OED in accordance with criteria and time periods set forth by the OED Director.

(2) Renewal application. Each participating law school desiring to continue in the USPTO Law School Clinic Certification Program shall, biennially from a date assigned to the law school by the OED Director, submit a renewal application to OED in accordance with criteria set forth by the OED Director.

(3) The OED Director may refuse admission or renewal of a law school to the USPTO Law School Clinic Certification Program if the OED Director determines that admission, or renewal, of the law school would fail to provide significant benefit to the public or the law students participating in the law school's clinic.

(c) Faculty Clinic Supervisor. Any law school seeking admission to or participating in the USPTO Law School Clinic Certification Program must have at least one Faculty Clinic Supervisor for the patent practice area, if the clinic includes patent practice; and at least one Faculty Clinic Supervisor for the trademark practice area, if the clinic includes trademark practice.

(1) Patent Faculty Clinic Supervisor. A Faculty Clinic Supervisor for a law school clinic's patent practice must:

(i) Be a registered patent practitioner in active status and good standing with OED;

(ii) Demonstrate at least 3 years experience in prosecuting patent applications before the Office within the 5 years immediately prior to the request for approval as a Faculty Clinic Supervisor;

(iii) Assume full responsibility for the instruction and guidance of law students participating in the law school clinic's patent practice;

(iv) Assume full responsibility for all patent applications and legal services, including filings with the Office, produced by the clinic; and

(v) Comply with all additional criteria established by the OED Director.

(2) Trademark Faculty Clinic Supervisor. A Faculty Clinic Supervisor for a law school clinic's trademark practice must:

(i) Be an attorney as defined in §11.1;

(ii) Demonstrate at least 3 years experience in prosecuting trademark applications before the Office within the

5 years immediately prior to the date of the request for approval as a Faculty Clinic Supervisor;

(iii) Assume full responsibility for the instruction, guidance, and supervision of law students participating in the law school clinic's trademark practice;

(iv) Assume full responsibility for all trademark applications and legal services, including filings with the Office, produced by the clinic; and

(v) Comply with all additional criteria established by the OED Director.

(3) A Faculty Clinic Supervisor under paragraph (c) of this section must submit a statement:

(i) Assuming responsibility for performing conflicts checks for each law student and client in the relevant clinic practice area;

(ii) Assuming responsibility for student instruction and work, including instructing, mentoring, overseeing, and supervising all participating law school students in the clinic's relevant practice area;

(iii) Assuming responsibility for content and timeliness of all applications and documents submitted to the Office through the relevant practice area of the clinic;

(iv) Assuming responsibility for all communications by clinic students to clinic clients in the relevant clinic practice area;

(v) Assuming responsibility for ensuring that there is no gap in representation of clinic clients in the relevant practice area during student turnover, school schedule variations, inter-semester transitions, or other disruptions;

(vi) Attesting to meeting the criteria of paragraph (c)(1) or (2) of this section based on relevant practice area of the clinic; and

(vii) Attesting to all other criteria as established by the OED Director.

(d) Limited recognition for law students participating in the USPTO Law School Clinic Certification Program. **(1)** The OED Director may grant limited recognition to practice before the Office in patent or trademark matters, or both, to law school students enrolled in a clinic of a law school that is participating in the USPTO Law School Clinic Certification Program upon submission and approval of an application by a law student to OED in accordance with criteria established by the OED Director.

(2) In order to be granted limited recognition to practice before the Office in patent matters under the USPTO Law School Clinic Certification Program, a law student must:

(i) Be enrolled in a law school that is an active participant in the USPTO Law School Clinic Certification Program;

(ii) Be enrolled in the patent practice area of a clinic of the participating law school;

(iii) Have successfully completed at least one year of law school or the equivalent;

(iv) Have read the USPTO Rules of Professional Conduct and the relevant rules of practice and procedure for patent matters;

(v) Be supervised by an approved Faculty Clinic Supervisor pursuant to paragraph (c)(1) of this section;

(vi) Be certified by the dean of the participating law school, or one authorized to act for the dean, as: Having completed the first year of law school or the equivalent, being in compliance with the law school's ethics code, and being of good moral character and reputation;

(vii) Neither ask for nor receive any fee or compensation of any kind for legal services from a clinic client on whose behalf service is rendered;

(viii) Have proved to the satisfaction of the OED Director that he or she possesses the scientific and technical qualifications necessary for him or her to render patent applicants valuable service; and

(ix) Comply with all additional criteria established by the OED Director.

(3) In order to be granted limited recognition to practice before the Office in trademark matters under the USPTO Law School Clinic Certification Program, a law student must:

(i) Be enrolled in a law school that is an active participant in the USPTO Law School Clinic Certification Program;

(ii) Be enrolled in the trademark practice area of a clinic of the participating law school;

(iii) Have successfully completed at least one year of law school or the equivalent;

(iv) Have read the USPTO Rules of Professional Conduct and the relevant USPTO rules of practice and procedure for trademark matters;

(v) Be supervised by an approved Faculty Clinic Supervisor pursuant to paragraph (c)(2) of this section;

(vi) Be certified by the dean of the participating law school, or one authorized to act for the dean, as: Having completed the first year of law school or the equivalent, being in compliance with the law school's ethics code, and being of good moral character and reputation;

(vii) Neither ask for nor receive any fee or compensation of any kind for legal services from a clinic client on whose behalf service is rendered; and

(viii) Comply with all additional criteria established by the OED Director.

(4) Students registered to practice before the Office in patent matters as a patent agent, or authorized to practice before the Office in trademark matters under §11.14, must complete and submit a student application pursuant to paragraph (d)(1) of this section and meet the criteria of paragraph (d)(2) or (3) of this section, as applicable, in order to participate in the program.

History of 37 C.F.R. §11.16: 81 FR 33596, June 27, 2016.

§11.17. REQUIREMENTS FOR PARTICIPATION IN THE USPTO LAW SCHOOL CLINIC CERTIFICATION PROGRAM

(a) Each law school participating in the USPTO Law School Clinic Certification Program must provide its patent and/or trademark services on a pro bono basis.

(b) Each law school participating in the USPTO Law School Clinic Certification Program shall, on a semi-annual basis, provide OED with a report regarding its clinic activity during the reporting period, which shall include:

(1) The number of law students participating in each of the patent and trademark practice areas of the school's clinic;

(2) The number of faculty participating in each of the patent and trademark practice areas of the school's clinic;

(3) The number of persons to whom the school's clinic provided assistance in any given patent or trademark matter but with whom no practitioner-client relationship had formed;

(4) The number of client representations undertaken for each of the patent and trademark practice areas of the school's clinic;

(5) The identity and number of applications and responses filed in each of the patent and/or trademark practice areas of the school's clinic;

(6) The number of patents issued, or trademarks registered, to clients of the clinic; and

(7) All other information specified by the OED Director.

(c) Inactivation of law schools participating in the USPTO Law School Certification Program. **(1)** The OED Director may inactivate a patent and/or trademark practice area of a participating law school:

(i) If the participating law school does not have an approved Faculty Clinic Supervisor for the relevant practice area, as described in §11.16(c);

(ii) If the participating law school does not meet each of the requirements and criteria for participation in the USPTO Law School Clinic Certification Program as set forth in §11.16, this section, or as otherwise established by the OED Director; or

(iii) For other good cause as determined by the OED Director.

(2) In the event that a practice area of a participating school is inactivated, the participating law school students must:

(i) Immediately cease all student practice before the Office in the relevant practice area and notify each client of such; and

(ii) Disassociate themselves from all client matters relating to practice before the Office in the relevant practice area, including complying with Office and State rules for withdrawal from representation.

(3) A patent or trademark practice area of a law school clinic that has been inactivated may be restored to active status, upon application to and approval by the OED Director.

(d) Removal of law schools participating in the USPTO Law School Clinic Certification Program. **(1)** The OED Director may remove a patent and/or trademark practice area of the clinic of a law school participating in the USPTO Law School Clinic Certification Program:

(i) Upon request from the law school;

(ii) If the participating law school does not meet each of the requirements and criteria for participation in the USPTO Law School Clinic Certification Program as set forth in §11.16, this section, or as otherwise established by the OED Director; or

(iii) For other good cause as determined by the OED Director.

(2) In the event that a practice area of a participating school is removed by the OED Director, the participating law school students must:

(i) Immediately cease all student practice before the Office in the relevant practice area and notify each client of such; and

(ii) Disassociate themselves from all client matters relating to practice before the Office in the relevant practice area, including complying with Office and State rules for withdrawal from representation.

(3) A school that has been removed from participation in the USPTO Law School Clinic Certification Program under this section may reapply to the program in compliance with §11.16.

History of 37 C.F.R. §11.17: 81 FR 33597, June 27, 2016.

§11.18. SIGNATURE & CERTIFICATE FOR CORRESPONDENCE FILED IN THE OFFICE

(a) For all documents filed in the Office in patent, trademark, and other non-patent matters, and all documents filed with a hearing officer in a disciplinary proceeding, except for correspondence that is required to be signed by the applicant or party, each piece of correspondence filed by a practitioner in the Office must bear a signature, personally signed or inserted by such practitioner, in compliance with §1.4(d) or §2.193(a) of this chapter.

(b) By presenting to the Office or hearing officer in a disciplinary proceeding (whether by signing, filing, submitting, or later advocating) any paper, the party presenting such paper, whether a practitioner or non-practitioner, is certifying that—

(1) All statements made therein of the party's own knowledge are true, all statements made therein on information and belief are believed to be true, and all statements made therein are made with the knowledge that whoever, in any matter within the jurisdiction of the Office, knowingly and willfully falsifies, conceals, or covers up by any trick, scheme, or device a material fact, or knowingly and willfully makes any false, fictitious, or fraudulent statements or representations, or knowingly and willfully makes or uses any false writing or document knowing the same to contain any false, fictitious, or fraudulent statement or entry, shall be subject to the penalties set forth under 18 U.S.C. 1001 and any other applicable criminal statute, and violations of the provisions of this section may jeopardize the probative value of the paper; and

(2) To the best of the party's knowledge, information and belief, formed after an inquiry reasonable under the circumstances,

(i) The paper is not being presented for any improper purpose, such as to harass someone or to cause unnecessary delay or needless increase in the cost of any proceeding before the Office;

(ii) The other legal contentions therein are warranted by existing law or by a nonfrivolous argument for the extension, modification, or reversal of existing law or the establishment of new law;

(iii) The allegations and other factual contentions have evidentiary support or, if specifically so identified, are likely to have evidentiary support after a reasonable opportunity for further investigation or discovery; and

(iv) The denials of factual contentions are warranted on the evidence, or if specifically so identified, are reasonably based on a lack of information or belief.

(c) Violations of any of paragraphs (b)(2)(i) through (iv) of this section are, after notice and reasonable opportunity to respond, subject to such sanctions or actions as deemed appropriate by the USPTO Director, which may include, but are not limited to, any combination of—

(1) Striking the offending paper;

(2) Referring a practitioner's conduct to the Director of Enrollment and Discipline for appropriate action;

(3) Precluding a party or practitioner from submitting a paper, or presenting or contesting an issue;

(4) Affecting the weight given to the offending paper; or

(5) Terminating the proceedings in the Office.

(d) Any practitioner violating the provisions of this section may also be subject to disciplinary action.

History of 37 C.F.R. §11.18: 73 FR 47689, Sept. 15, 2008; 74 FR 54912, Dec. 28, 2009; 78 FR 62409, Dec. 18, 2013.

SUBPART C. INVESTIGATIONS & DISCIPLINARY PROCEEDINGS; JURISDICTION, SANCTIONS, INVESTIGATIONS, & PROCEEDINGS

§11.19. DISCIPLINARY JURISDICTION; JURISDICTION TO TRANSFER TO DISABILITY INACTIVE STATUS

(a) All practitioners engaged in practice before the Office; all practitioners administratively suspended; all practitioners registered to practice before the Office in patent cases; all practitioners inactivated; all practitioners authorized under §11.6(d) to take testimony; and all practitioners transferred to disability inactive status, reprimanded, suspended, or excluded from the practice of law by a duly constituted authority, including by the USPTO Director, are subject to the disciplinary jurisdiction of the Office. Practitioners who have resigned shall also be subject to such jurisdiction with respect to conduct undertaken prior to the resignation and conduct in regard to any practice before the Office following the resignation. A person not registered or recognized to practice before the Office is also subject to the disciplinary authority of the Office if the person provides or offers to provide any legal services before the Office.

(b) Grounds for discipline; Grounds for transfer to disability inactive status. The following, whether done individually by a practitioner or in concert with any other person or persons and whether or not done in the course of providing legal services to a client, or in a matter pending before the Office, constitute grounds for discipline or grounds for transfer to disability inactive status.

(1) Grounds for discipline include:

(i) Conviction of a serious crime;

(ii) Discipline on ethical grounds imposed in another jurisdiction or disciplinary disqualification from participating in or appearing before any Federal program or agency;

(iii) Failure to comply with any order of a Court disciplining a practitioner, or any final decision of the USPTO Director in a disciplinary matter;

(iv) Violation of any USPTO Rule of Professional Conduct; or

(v) Violation of the oath or declaration taken by the practitioner. See §11.8.

(2) Grounds for transfer to disability inactive status include:

(i) Being transferred to disability inactive status in another jurisdiction;

(ii) Being judicially declared incompetent, being judicially ordered to be involuntarily committed after a hearing on the grounds of insanity, incompetency or disability, or being placed by court order under guardianship or conservatorship; or

(iii) Filing a motion requesting a disciplinary proceeding be held in abeyance because the practitioner is suffering from a disability or addiction that makes it impossible for the practitioner to adequately defend the charges in the disciplinary proceeding.

(c) Petitions to disqualify a practitioner in *ex parte* or *inter partes* matters in the Office are not governed by §§11.19 through 11.60 and will be handled on a case-by-case basis under such conditions as the USPTO Director deems appropriate.

(d) The OED Director may refer the existence of circumstances suggesting unauthorized practice of law to the authorities in the appropriate jurisdiction(s).

History of 37 C.F.R. §11.19: 73 FR 47689, Sept. 15, 2008; 78 FR 20200, Apr. 3, 2013.

§11.20. DISCIPLINARY SANCTIONS; TRANSFER TO DISABILITY INACTIVE STATUS

(a) Types of discipline. The USPTO Director, after notice and opportunity for a hearing, and where grounds for discipline exist, may impose on a practitioner the following types of discipline:

(1) Exclusion from practice before the Office;

(2) Suspension from practice before the Office for an appropriate period of time;

(3) Reprimand or censure; or

(4) Probation. Probation may be imposed in lieu of or in addition to any other disciplinary sanction. Any conditions of probation shall be stated in writing in the order imposing probation. The order shall also state whether, and to what extent, the practitioner shall be required to notify clients of the probation. Violation of any condition of probation shall be cause for imposition of the disciplinary sanction. Imposition of the disciplinary sanction predicated upon violation of probation shall occur only after an order to show cause why the disciplinary sanction should not be imposed is resolved adversely to the practitioner.

(b) Conditions imposed with discipline. When imposing discipline, the USPTO Director may condition reinstatement upon the practitioner making restitution, successfully completing a professional responsibility course or examination, or any other condition deemed appropriate under the circumstances.

(c) Transfer to disability inactive status. The USPTO Director, after notice and opportunity for a hearing may, and where grounds exist to believe a practitioner has been transferred to disability inactive status in another jurisdiction, or has been judicially declared incompetent; judicially ordered to be involuntarily committed after a hearing on the grounds of incompetency or disability, or placed by court order under guardianship or conservatorship, transfer the practitioner to disability inactive status.

History of 37 C.F.R. §11.20: 73 FR 47689, Sept. 15, 2008; 78 FR 20200, Apr. 3, 2013.

§11.21. WARNINGS

A warning is neither public nor a disciplinary sanction. The OED Director may conclude an investigation with the issuance of a warning. The warning shall contain a brief statement of facts and USPTO Rules of Professional Conduct relevant to the facts.

History of 37 C.F.R. §11.21: 73 FR 47689, Sept. 15, 2008; 78 FR 20200, Apr. 3, 2013.

§11.22. DISCIPLINARY INVESTIGATIONS

(a) The OED Director is authorized to investigate possible grounds for discipline. An investigation may be initiated when the OED Director receives a grievance, information or evidence from any source suggesting possible grounds for discipline. Neither unwillingness nor neglect by a grievant to prosecute a charge, nor settlement, compromise, or restitution with the grievant, shall in itself justify abatement of an investigation.

(b) Any person possessing information or evidence concerning possible grounds for discipline of a practitioner may report the information or evidence to the OED Director. The OED Director may request that the report be presented in the form of an affidavit or declaration.

(c) [Reserved]

(d) Preliminary screening of information or evidence. The OED Director shall examine all information or evidence concerning possible grounds for discipline of a practitioner.

(e) Notification of investigation. The OED Director shall notify the practitioner in writing of the initiation of an investigation into whether a practitioner has engaged in conduct constituting possible grounds for discipline.

(f) Request for information and evidence by OED Director.

(1) In the course of the investigation, the OED Director may request information and evidence regarding possible grounds for discipline of a practitioner from:

(i) The grievant,

(ii) The practitioner, or

(iii) Any person who may reasonably be expected to provide information and evidence needed in connection with the grievance or investigation.

(2) The OED Director may request information and evidence regarding possible grounds for discipline of a practitioner from a non-grieving client either after obtaining the consent of the practitioner or upon a finding by a Contact Member of the Committee on Discipline, appointed in accordance with §11.23(d), that good cause exists to believe that the possible ground for discipline alleged has occurred with respect to non-grieving clients. Neither a request for, nor disclosure of, such information shall constitute a violation of any USPTO Rules of Professional Conduct.

(g) Where the OED Director makes a request under paragraph (f)(2) of this section to a Contact Member of the Committee on Discipline, such Contact Member shall not, with respect to the practitioner connected to the OED Director's request, participate in the Committee on Discipline panel that renders a probable cause determination under paragraph (b)(1) of this section concerning such practitioner, and that forwards the probable cause finding and recommendation to the OED Director under paragraph (b)(2) of this section.

(h) Disposition of investigation. Upon the conclusion of an investigation, the OED Director may:

(1) Close the investigation without issuing a warning, or taking disciplinary action;

(2) Issue a warning to the practitioner;

(3) Institute formal charges upon the approval of the Committee on Discipline; or

(4) Enter into a settlement agreement with the practitioner and submit the same for approval of the USPTO Director.

(i) Closing investigation. The OED Director shall terminate an investigation and decline to refer a matter to the Committee on Discipline if the OED Director determines that:

(1) The information or evidence is unfounded;

(2) The information or evidence relates to matters not within the jurisdiction of the Office;

(3) As a matter of law, the conduct about which information or evidence has been obtained does not constitute grounds for discipline, even if the conduct may involve a legal dispute; or

(4) The available evidence is insufficient to conclude that there is probable cause to believe that grounds exist for discipline.

History of 37 C.F.R. §11.22: 73 FR 47689, Sept. 15, 2008; 77 FR 45251, Aug. 30, 2012; 78 FR 20200, Apr. 3, 2013.

§11.23. COMMITTEE ON DISCIPLINE

(a) The USPTO Director shall appoint a Committee on Discipline. The Committee on Discipline shall consist of at least three employees of the Office. None of the Committee members shall report directly or indirectly to the OED Director or any employee designated by the USPTO Director to decide disciplinary matters. Each Committee member shall be a member in good standing of the bar of the highest court of a State. The Committee members shall select a Chairperson from among themselves. Three Committee members will constitute a panel of the Committee.

(b) Powers and duties of the Committee on Discipline. The Committee shall have the power and duty to:

(1) Meet in panels at the request of the OED Director and, after reviewing evidence presented by the OED Director, by majority vote of the panel, determine whether there is probable cause to bring charges under §11.32 against a practitioner; and

(2) Prepare and forward its own probable cause findings and recommendations to the OED Director.

(c) No discovery shall be authorized of, and no member of the Committee on Discipline shall be required to testify about deliberations of, the Committee on Discipline or of any panel.

(d) The Chairperson shall appoint the members of the panels and a Contact Member of the Committee on Discipline.

History of 37 C.F.R. §11.23: 73 FR 47689, Sept. 15, 2008.

§11.24. RECIPROCAL DISCIPLINE

(a) Notification of OED Director. Within thirty days of being publicly censured, publicly reprimanded, subjected to probation, disbarred or suspended by another jurisdiction, or being disciplinarily disqualified from participating in or appearing before any Federal program or agency, a practitioner subject to the disciplinary jurisdiction of the Office shall notify the OED Director in writing of the same. A practitioner is deemed to be disbarred if he or she is disbarred, excluded on consent, or has resigned in lieu of a disciplinary proceeding. Upon receiving notification from any source or otherwise learning that a practitioner subject to the disciplinary jurisdiction of the Office has been so publicly censured, publicly reprimanded, subjected to probation, disbarred, suspended or disciplinarily disqualified, the OED Director shall obtain a certified copy of the record or order regarding the public censure, public reprimand, probation, disbarment, suspension or disciplinary disqualification and file the same with the USPTO Director. The OED Director shall, in addition, without Committee on Discipline authorization, file with the USPTO Director a complaint complying with §11.34 against the practitioner predicated upon the public censure, public reprimand, probation, disbarment, suspension or disciplinary disqualification. The OED Director shall request the USPTO Director to issue a notice and order as set forth in paragraph (b) of this section.

(b) Notification served on practitioner. Upon receipt of a certified copy of the record or order regarding the practitioner being so publicly censured, publicly reprimanded, subjected to probation, disbarred, suspended or disciplinarily disqualified together with the complaint, the USPTO Director shall issue a notice directed to the practitioner in accordance with §11.35 and to the OED Director containing:

(1) A copy of the record or order regarding the public censure, public reprimand, probation, disbarment, suspension or disciplinary disqualification;

(2) A copy of the complaint; and

(3) An order directing the practitioner to file a response with the USPTO Director and the OED Director, within forty days of the date of the notice establishing a genuine issue of material fact predicated upon the grounds set forth in paragraphs (d)(1)(i) through (d)(1)(iv) of this section that the imposition of the identical public censure, public reprimand, probation, disbarment, suspension or disciplinary disqualification would be unwarranted and the reasons for that claim.

(c) Effect of stay in another jurisdiction. In the event the public censure, public reprimand, probation, disbarment, suspension imposed by another jurisdiction or disciplinary disqualification imposed in the Federal program or agency has been stayed, any reciprocal discipline imposed by the USPTO may be deferred until the stay expires.

(d) Hearing and discipline to be imposed. **(1)** The USPTO Director shall hear the matter on the documentary record unless the USPTO Director determines that an oral hearing is necessary. After expiration of the forty days from the date of the notice pursuant to provisions of paragraph (b) of this section, the USPTO Director shall consider any timely filed response and shall impose the identical public censure, public reprimand, probation, disbarment, suspension or disciplinary disqualification unless the practitioner clearly and convincingly demonstrates, and the USPTO Director finds there is a genuine issue of material fact that:

(i) The procedure elsewhere was so lacking in notice or opportunity to be heard as to constitute a deprivation of due process;

(ii) There was such infirmity of proof establishing the conduct as to give rise to the clear conviction that the Office could not, consistently with its duty, accept as final the conclusion on that subject;

(iii) The imposition of the same public censure, public reprimand, probation, disbarment, suspension or disciplinary disqualification by the Office would result in grave injustice; or

(iv) Any argument that the practitioner was not publicly censured, publicly reprimanded, placed on probation, disbarred, suspended or disciplinarily disqualified.

(2) If the USPTO Director determines that there is no genuine issue of material fact, the USPTO Director shall enter an appropriate final order. If the USPTO Director is unable to make such determination because there is a genuine issue of material fact, the USPTO Director shall enter an appropriate order:

(i) Referring the complaint to a hearing officer for a formal hearing and entry of an initial decision in accordance with the other rules in this part, and

(ii) Directing the practitioner to file an answer to the complaint in accordance with §11.36.

(e) Adjudication in another jurisdiction or Federal agency or program. In all other respects, a final adjudication in another jurisdiction or Federal agency or program that a practitioner, whether or not admitted in that jurisdiction, has been guilty of misconduct shall establish a prima facie case by clear and convincing evidence that the practitioner has engaged in misconduct under §11.804.

(f) Reciprocal discipline—action where practice has ceased. Upon request by the practitioner, reciprocal discipline may be imposed nunc pro tunc only if the practitioner promptly notified the OED Director of his or her censure, public reprimand, probation, disbarment, suspension or disciplinary disqualification in another jurisdiction, and establishes by clear and convincing evidence that the practitioner voluntarily ceased all activities related to practice before the Office and complied with all provisions of §11.58. The effective date of any public censure, public reprimand, probation, suspension, disbarment or disciplinary disqualification imposed nunc pro tunc shall be the date the practitioner voluntarily ceased all activities related to practice before the Office and complied with all provisions of §11.58.

(g) Reinstatement following reciprocal discipline proceeding. A practitioner may petition for reinstatement under conditions set forth in §11.60 no sooner than completion of the period of reciprocal discipline imposed, and compliance with all provisions of §11.58.

History of 37 C.F.R. §11.24: 73 FR 47689, Sept. 15, 2008; 78 FR 20200, Apr. 3, 2013.

§11.25. INTERIM SUSPENSION & DISCIPLINE BASED UPON CONVICTION OF COMMITTING A SERIOUS CRIME

(a) Notification of OED Director. Upon being convicted of a crime in a court of the United States, any State, or a foreign country, a practitioner subject to the disciplinary jurisdiction of the Office shall notify the OED Director in writing of the same within thirty days from the date of such conviction. Upon being advised or learning that a practitioner subject to the disciplinary jurisdiction of the Office has been convicted of a crime, the OED Director shall make a preliminary determination whether the crime constitutes a serious crime warranting interim suspension. If the crime is a serious crime, the OED Director shall file with the USPTO Director proof of the conviction and request the USPTO Director to issue a notice and order set forth in paragraph (b)(2) of this section. The OED Director shall in addition, without Committee on Discipline authorization, file with the USPTO Director a complaint against the practitioner complying with §11.34 predicated upon the conviction of a serious crime. If the crime is not a serious crime, the OED Director shall process the matter in the same manner as any other information or evidence of a possible violation of any USPTO Rule of Professional Conduct coming to the attention of the OED Director.

(b) Interim suspension and referral for disciplinary proceeding. All proceedings under this section shall be handled as expeditiously as possible.

(1) The USPTO Director has authority to place a practitioner on interim suspension after hearing the request for interim suspension on the documentary record.

(2) Notification served on practitioner. Upon receipt of a certified copy of the court record, docket entry or judgment demonstrating that the practitioner has been so convicted together with the complaint, the USPTO Director shall forthwith issue a notice directed to the practitioner in accordance with §§11.35(a), (b) or (c), and to the OED Director, containing:

(i) A copy of the court record, docket entry, or judgment of conviction;

(ii) A copy of the complaint; and

(iii) An order directing the practitioner to file a response with the USPTO Director and the OED Director, within forty days of the date of the notice, establishing that there is a genuine issue of material fact that the crime did not constitute a serious crime, the practitioner is not the individual found guilty of the crime, or that the conviction was so lacking in notice or opportunity to be heard as to constitute a deprivation of due process.

(3) Hearing and final order on request for interim suspension. The request for interim suspension shall be heard by the USPTO Director on the documentary record unless the USPTO Director determines that the practitioner's response establishes a genuine issue of material fact that: The crime did not constitute a serious crime, the practitioner is not the person who committed the crime, or that the conviction was so lacking in notice or opportunity to be heard as to constitute a deprivation of due process. If the USPTO Director determines that there is no genuine issue of material fact regarding the defenses set forth in the preceding sentence, the USPTO Director shall enter an appropriate final order regarding the OED Director's request for interim suspension regardless of the pendency of any criminal appeal. If the USPTO Director is unable to make such determination because there is a genuine issue of material fact, the USPTO Director shall enter a final order dismissing the request and enter a further order referring the complaint to a hearing officer for a hearing and entry of an initial decision in accordance with the other rules in this part and directing the practitioner to file an answer to the complaint in accordance with §11.36.

(4) Termination. The USPTO Director has authority to terminate an interim suspension. In the interest of justice, the USPTO Director may terminate an interim suspension at any time upon a showing of extraordinary circumstances, after affording the OED Director an opportunity to respond to the request to terminate interim suspension.

(5) Referral for disciplinary proceeding. Upon entering a final order imposing interim suspension, the USPTO Director shall refer the complaint to a hearing officer to conduct a formal disciplinary proceeding. The formal disciplinary proceeding, however, shall be stayed by the hearing officer until all direct appeals from the conviction are concluded. Review of the initial decision of the hearing officer shall be pursuant to §11.55.

(c) Proof of conviction and guilt—(1) Conviction in the United States. For purposes of a hearing for interim suspension and a hearing on the formal charges in a complaint filed as a consequence of the conviction, a certified copy of the court record, docket entry, or judgment of conviction in a court of the United States or any State shall establish a prima facie case by clear and convincing evidence that the practitioner was convicted of a serious crime and that the conviction was not lacking in notice or opportunity to be heard as to constitute a deprivation of due process.

(2) Conviction in a foreign country. For purposes of a hearing for interim suspension and on the formal charges filed as a result of a finding of guilt, a certified copy of the court record, docket entry, or judgment of conviction in a court of a foreign country shall establish a prima facie case by clear and convincing evidence that the practitioner was convicted of a serious crime and that the conviction was not lacking in notice or opportunity to be heard as to constitute a deprivation of due process. However, nothing in this paragraph shall preclude the practitioner from demonstrating by clear and convincing evidence in any hearing on a request for interim suspension there is a genuine issue of material fact to be considered when determining if the elements of a serious crime were committed in violating the criminal law of the foreign country and whether a disciplinary sanction should be entered.

(d) Crime determined not to be serious crime. If the USPTO Director determines that the crime is not a serious crime, the complaint shall be referred to the OED Director for investigation under §11.22 and processing as is appropriate.

(e) Reinstatement—(1) Upon reversal or setting aside a finding of guilt or a conviction. If a practitioner suspended solely under the provisions of paragraph (b) of this section demonstrates that the underlying finding of guilt or conviction of serious crimes has been reversed or vacated, the order for interim suspension shall be vacated and the practitioner shall be placed on active status unless the finding of guilt was reversed or the conviction was set aside with respect to less than all serious crimes for which the practitioner was found guilty or convicted. The vacating of the interim suspension will not terminate any other disciplinary proceeding then pending against the practitioner, the disposition of which shall be determined by the hearing officer before whom the matter is pending, on the basis of all available evidence other than the finding of guilt or conviction.

(2) Following conviction of a serious crime. Any practitioner convicted of a serious crime and disciplined in whole or in part in regard to that conviction, may petition for reinstatement under conditions set forth in §11.60 no sooner than five years after being discharged following completion of service of his or her sentence, or after completion of service under probation or parole, whichever is later.

(f) Notice to clients and others of interim suspension. An interim suspension under this section shall constitute a suspension of the practitioner for the purpose of §11.58.

History of 37 C.F.R. §11.25: 73 FR 47689, Sept. 15, 2008; 78 FR 20200, Apr. 3, 2013.

§11.26. SETTLEMENT

Before or after a complaint under §11.34 is filed, a settlement conference may occur between the OED Director and the practitioner. Any offers of compromise and any statements made during the course of settlement discussions shall not be admissible in subsequent proceedings. The OED Director may recommend to the USPTO Director any settlement terms deemed appropriate, including steps taken to correct or mitigate the matter forming the basis of the action, or to prevent recurrence of the same or similar conduct. A settlement agreement shall be effective only upon entry of a final decision by the USPTO Director.

History of 37 C.F.R. §11.26: 73 FR 47689, Sept. 15, 2008.

§11.27. EXCLUSION ON CONSENT

(a) Required affidavit. The OED Director may confer with a practitioner concerning possible violations by the practitioner of the Rules of Professional Conduct whether or not a disciplinary proceeding has been instituted. A practitioner who is the subject of an investigation or a pending disciplinary proceeding based on allegations of grounds for discipline, and who desires to resign, may only do so by consenting to exclusion and delivering to the OED Director an affidavit declaring the consent of the practitioner to exclusion and stating:

(1) That the practitioner's consent is freely and voluntarily rendered, that the practitioner is not being subjected to coercion or duress, and that the practitioner is fully aware of the implications of consenting to exclusion;

(2) That the practitioner is aware that there is currently pending an investigation into, or a proceeding involving allegations of misconduct, the nature of which shall be specifically set forth in the affidavit to the satisfaction of the OED Director;

(3) That the practitioner acknowledges that, if and when he or she applies for reinstatement under §11.60, the OED Director will conclusively presume, for the limited purpose of determining the application for reinstatement, that:

(i) The facts upon which the investigation or complaint is based are true, and

(ii) The practitioner could not have successfully defended himself or herself against the allegations in the investigation or charges in the complaint.

(b) Action by the USPTO Director. Upon receipt of the required affidavit, the OED Director shall file the affidavit and any related papers with the USPTO Director for review and approval. Upon such approval, the USPTO Director will enter an order excluding the practitioner on consent and providing other appropriate actions. Upon entry of the order, the excluded practitioner shall comply with the requirements set forth in §11.58.

(c) When an affidavit under paragraph (a) of this section is received after a complaint under §11.34 has been filed, the OED Director shall notify the hearing officer. The hearing officer shall enter an order transferring the disciplinary proceeding to the USPTO Director, who may enter an order excluding the practitioner on consent.

(d) Reinstatement. Any practitioner excluded on consent under this section may not petition for reinstatement for five years. A practitioner excluded on consent who intends to reapply for admission to practice before the Office must comply with the provisions of §11.58, and apply for reinstatement in accordance with §11.60. Failure to comply with the provisions of §11.58 constitutes grounds for denying an application for reinstatement.

History of 37 C.F.R. §11.27: 73 FR 47689, Sept. 15, 2008.

§11.28. INCAPACITATED PRACTITIONERS IN A DISCIPLINARY PROCEEDING

(a) Holding in abeyance a disciplinary proceeding because of incapacitation due to a current disability or addiction—**(1)** Practitioner's motion. In the course of a disciplinary proceeding under §11.32, but before the date set by the hearing officer for a hearing, the practitioner may file a motion requesting the hearing officer to enter an order holding such proceeding in abeyance based on the contention that the practitioner is suffering from a disability or addiction that makes it impossible for the practitioner to adequately defend the charges in the disciplinary proceeding.

(i) Content of practitioner's motion. The practitioner's motion shall, in addition to any other requirement of §11.43, include or have attached thereto:

(A) A brief statement of all material facts;

(B) Affidavits, medical reports, official records, or other documents and the opinion of at least one medical expert setting forth and establishing any of the material facts on which the practitioner is relying;

(C) A statement that the practitioner acknowledges the alleged incapacity by reason of disability or addiction;

(D) Written consent that the practitioner be transferred to disability inactive status if the motion is granted; and

(E) A written agreement by the practitioner to not practice before the Office in patent, trademark or other non-patent cases while on disability inactive status.

(ii) Response. The OED Director's response to any motion hereunder shall be served and filed within thirty days after service of the practitioner's motion unless such time is shortened or enlarged by the hearing officer for good cause shown, and shall set forth the following:

(A) All objections, if any, to the actions requested in the motion;

(B) An admission, denial or allegation of lack of knowledge with respect to each of the material facts in the practitioner's motion and accompanying documents; and

(C) Affidavits, medical reports, official records, or other documents setting forth facts on which the OED Director intends to rely for purposes of disputing or denying any material fact set forth in the practitioner's papers.

(2) Disposition of practitioner's motion. The hearing officer shall decide the motion and any response thereto. The motion shall be granted upon a showing of good cause to believe the practitioner to be incapacitated as alleged. If the required showing is made, the hearing officer shall enter an order holding the disciplinary proceeding in abeyance. In the case of addiction to drugs or intoxicants, the order may provide that the practitioner will not be returned to active status absent satisfaction of specified conditions. Upon receipt of the order, the OED Director shall transfer the practitioner to disability inactive status, give notice to the practitioner, cause notice to be published, and give notice to appropriate authorities in the Office that the practitioner has been placed on disability inactive status. The practitioner shall comply with the provisions of §11.58, and shall not engage in practice before the Office in patent, trademark and other non-patent law until a determination is made of the practitioner's capability to resume practice before the Office in a proceeding under paragraph (c) or paragraph (d) of this section. A practitioner on disability inactive status must seek permission from the OED Director to engage in an activity authorized under §11.58(e). Permission will be granted only if the practitioner has complied with all the conditions of §§11.58(a) through 11.58(d) applicable to disability inactive status. In the event that permission is granted, the practitioner shall fully comply with the provisions of §11.58(e).

(b) Motion for reactivation. Any practitioner transferred to disability inactive status in a disciplinary proceeding may file with the hearing officer a motion for reactivation once a year beginning at any time not less than one year after the initial effective date of inactivation, or once during any shorter interval provided by the order issued pursuant to paragraph (a)(2) of this section or any modification thereof. If the motion is granted, the disciplinary proceeding shall resume under such schedule as may be established by the hearing officer.

(c) Contents of motion for reactivation. A motion by the practitioner for reactivation alleging that a practitioner has recovered from a prior disability or addiction shall be accompanied by all available medical reports or similar documents relating thereto. The hearing officer may require the practitioner to present such other information as is necessary.

(d) OED Director's motion to resume disciplinary proceeding held in abeyance. **(1)** The OED Director, having good cause to believe a practitioner is no longer incapacitated, may file a motion requesting the hearing officer to terminate a prior order holding in abeyance any pending proceeding because of the practitioner's disability or addiction. The hearing officer shall decide the matter presented by the OED Director's motion hereunder based on the affidavits and other admissible evidence attached to the OED Director's motion and the practitioner's response. The OED Director bears the burden of showing by clear and convincing evidence that the practitioner is able to defend himself or herself. If there is any genuine issue as to one or more material facts, the hearing officer will hold an evidentiary hearing.

(2) The hearing officer, upon receipt of the OED Director's motion under paragraph (d)(1) of this section, may direct the practitioner to file a response. If the hearing officer requires the practitioner to file a response, the practitioner must present clear and convincing evidence that the prior self-alleged disability or addiction continues to make it impossible for the practitioner to defend himself or herself in the underlying proceeding being held in abeyance.

(e) Action by the hearing officer. If, in deciding a motion under paragraph (b) or (d) of this section, the hearing officer determines that there is good cause to believe the practitioner is not incapacitated from defending himself or herself, or is not incapacitated from practicing before the Office, the hearing officer shall take such action as is deemed appropriate, including the entry of an order directing the reactivation of the practitioner and resumption of the disciplinary proceeding.

History of 37 C.F.R. §11.28: 73 FR 47689, Sept. 15, 2008.

§11.29. RECIPROCAL TRANSFER OR INITIAL TRANSFER TO DISABILITY INACTIVE STATUS

(a) Notification of OED Director. **(1)** Transfer to disability inactive status in another jurisdiction as grounds for reciprocal transfer by the Office. Within thirty days of being transferred to disability inactive status in another jurisdiction, a practitioner subject to the disciplinary jurisdiction of the Office shall notify the OED Director in writing of the transfer. Upon notification from any source that a practitioner subject to the disciplinary jurisdiction of the Office has been transferred to disability inactive status in another jurisdiction, the OED Director shall obtain a certified copy of the order. The OED Director shall file with the USPTO Director:

(i) The order;

(ii) A request that the practitioner be transferred to disability inactive status, including the specific grounds therefor; and

(iii) A request that the USPTO Director issue a notice and order as set forth in paragraph (b) of this section.

(2) Involuntary commitment, adjudication of incompetency or court ordered placement under guardianship or conservatorship as grounds for initial transfer to disability inactive status. Within thirty days of being judicially declared incompetent, being judicially ordered to be involuntarily committed after a hearing on the grounds of incompetency or disability, or being placed by court order under guardianship or conservatorship in another jurisdiction, a practitioner subject to the disciplinary jurisdiction of the Office shall notify the OED Director in writing of such judicial action. Upon notification from any source that a practitioner subject to the disciplinary jurisdiction of the Office has been subject to such judicial action, the OED Director shall obtain a certified copy of the order. The OED Director shall file with the USPTO Director:

(i) The order;

(ii) A request that the practitioner be transferred to disability inactive status, including the specific grounds therefor; and

(iii) A request that the USPTO Director issue a notice and order as set forth in paragraph (b) of this section.

(b) Notice served on practitioner. Upon receipt of a certified copy of an order or declaration issued by another jurisdiction demonstrating that a practitioner subject to the disciplinary jurisdiction of the Office has been transferred to disability inactive status, judicially declared incompetent, judicially ordered to be involuntarily committed after a judicial hearing on the grounds of incompetency or disability, or placed by court order under guardianship or conservatorship, together with the OED Director's request, the USPTO Director shall issue a notice, comporting with §11.35, directed to the practitioner containing:

(1) A copy of the order or declaration from the other jurisdiction,

(2) A copy of the OED Director's request; and

(3) An order directing the practitioner to file a response with the USPTO Director and the OED Director, within 30 days from the date of the notice, establishing a genuine issue of material fact supported by an affidavit and predicated upon the grounds set forth in §11.29(d)(1) through (4) that a transfer to disability inactive status would be unwarranted and the reasons therefor.

(c) Effect of stay of transfer, judicially declared incompetence, judicially ordered involuntarily commitment on the grounds of incompetency or disability, or court-ordered placement under guardianship or conservatorship. In the event the transfer, judicially declared incompetence, judicially ordered involuntary commitment on the grounds of incompetency or disability, or court-ordered placement under guardianship or conservatorship in the other jurisdiction has been stayed there, any reciprocal transfer or transfer by the Office may be deferred until the stay expires.

(d) Hearing and transfer to disability inactive status. The request for transfer to disability inactive status shall be heard by the USPTO Director on the documentary record unless the USPTO Director determines that there is a genuine issue of material fact, in which case the USPTO Director may deny the request. Upon the expiration of 30 days from the date of the notice pursuant to the provisions of paragraph (b) of this section, the USPTO Director shall consider any timely filed response and impose the identical transfer to disability inactive status based on the practitioner's transfer to disability status in another jurisdiction, or shall transfer the practitioner to disability inactive status based on judicially declared incompetence, judicially ordered involuntary commitment on the grounds of incompetency or disability, or court-ordered placement under guardianship or conservatorship, unless the practitioner demonstrates by clear and convincing evidence, or the USPTO Director finds there is a genuine issue of material fact by clear and convincing evidence that:

(1) The procedure was so lacking in notice or opportunity to be heard as to constitute a deprivation of due process;

(2) There was such infirmity of proof establishing the transfer to disability status, judicial declaration of incompetence, judicial order for involuntary commitment on the grounds of incompetency or disability, or placement by court order under guardianship or conservatorship that the USPTO Director could not, consistent with Office's duty, accept as final the conclusion on that subject;

(3) The imposition of the same disability status or transfer to disability status by the USPTO Director would result in grave injustice; or

(4) The practitioner is not the individual transferred to disability status, judicially declared incompetent, judicially ordered for involuntary commitment on the grounds of incompetency or disability, or placed by court order under guardianship or conservatorship.

(5) If the USPTO Director determines that there is no genuine issue of material fact with regard to any of the elements of paragraphs (d)(1) through (4) of this section, the USPTO Director shall enter an appropriate final order. If the USPTO Director is unable to make that determination because there is a genuine issue of material fact, the USPTO Director shall enter an appropriate order dismissing the OED Director's request for such reason.

(e) Adjudication in other jurisdiction. In all other aspects, a final adjudication in another jurisdiction that a practitioner be transferred to disability inactive status, is judicially declared incompetent, is judicially ordered to be involuntarily committed on the grounds of incompetency or disability, or is placed by court order under guardianship or conservatorship shall establish the disability for purposes of a reciprocal transfer to or transfer to disability status before the Office.

(f) A practitioner who is transferred to disability inactive status under this section shall be deemed to have been refused recognition to practice before the Office for purposes of 35 U.S.C. 32.

(g) Order imposing reciprocal transfer to disability inactive status or order imposing initial transfer to disability inactive status. An order by the USPTO Director imposing reciprocal transfer to disability inactive status, or transferring a practitioner to disability inactive status shall be effective immediately, and shall be for an indefinite period until further order of the USPTO Director. A copy of the order transferring a practitioner to disability inactive status shall be served upon the practitioner, the practitioner's guardian, and/or the director of the institution to which the practitioner has been committed in the manner the USPTO Director may direct. A practitioner reciprocally transferred or transferred to disability inactive status shall comply with the provisions of §11.58, and shall not engage in practice before the Office in patent, trademark and other non-patent law unless and until reinstated to active status.

(h) Confidentiality of proceeding; Orders to be public— **(1)** Confidentiality of proceeding. All proceedings under this section involving allegations of disability of a practitioner shall be kept confidential until and unless the USPTO Director enters an order reciprocally transferring or transferring the practitioner to disability inactive status.

(2) Orders to be public. The OED Director shall publicize any reciprocal transfer to disability inactive status or transfer to disability inactive status in the same manner as for the imposition of public discipline.

(i) Employment of practitioners on disability inactive status. A practitioner on disability inactive status must seek permission from the OED Director to engage in an activity authorized under §11.58(e). Permission will be granted only if the practitioner has complied with all the conditions of §§11.58(a) through 11.58(d) applicable to disability inactive status. In the event that permission is granted, the practitioner shall fully comply with the provisions of §11.58(e).

(j) Reinstatement from disability inactive status. (1) Generally. No practitioner reciprocally transferred or transferred to disability inactive status under this section may resume active status except by order of the OED Director.

(2) Petition. A practitioner reciprocally transferred or transferred to disability inactive status shall be entitled to petition the OED Director for transfer to active status once a year, or at whatever shorter intervals the USPTO Director may direct in the order transferring or reciprocally transferring the practitioner to disability inactive status or any modification thereof.

(3) Examination. Upon the filing of a petition for transfer to active status, the OED Director may take or direct whatever action is deemed necessary or proper to determine whether the incapacity has been removed, including a direction for an examination of the practitioner by qualified medical or psychological experts designated by the OED Director. The expense of the examination shall be paid and borne by the practitioner.

(4) Required disclosure, waiver of privilege. With the filing of a petition for reinstatement to active status, the practitioner shall be required to disclose the name of each psychiatrist, psychologist, physician and hospital or other institution by whom or in which the practitioner has been examined or treated for the disability since the transfer to disability inactive status. The practitioner shall furnish to the OED Director written consent to the release of information and records relating to the incapacity if requested by the OED Director.

(5) Learning in the law, examination. The OED Director may direct that the practitioner establish proof of competence and learning in law, which proof may include passing the registration examination.

(6) Granting of petition for transfer to active status. The OED Director shall grant the petition for transfer to active status upon a showing by clear and convincing evidence that the incapacity has been removed.

(7) Reinstatement in other jurisdiction. If a practitioner is reciprocally transferred to disability inactive status on the basis of a transfer to disability inactive status in another jurisdiction, the OED Director may dispense with further evidence that the disability has been removed and may immediately direct reinstatement to active status upon such terms as are deemed proper and advisable.

(8) Judicial declaration of competency. If a practitioner is transferred to disability inactive status on the basis of a judicially declared incompetence, judicially ordered involuntary commitment on the grounds of incompetency or disability, or court-ordered placement under guardianship or conservatorship has been declared to be competent, the OED Director may dispense with further evidence that the incapacity to practice law has been removed and may immediately direct reinstatement to active status.

History of 37 C.F.R. §11.29: 73 FR 47689, Sept. 15, 2008.

§§11.30, 11.31. RESERVED

§11.32. INSTITUTING A DISCIPLINARY PROCEEDING

If after conducting an investigation under §11.22(a), the OED Director is of the opinion that grounds exist for discipline under §11.19(b), the OED Director, after complying where necessary with the provisions of 5 U.S.C. 558(c), may convene a meeting of a panel of the Committee on Discipline. If convened, the panel of the Committee on Discipline shall then determine as specified in §11.23(b) whether there is probable cause to bring disciplinary charges. If the panel of the Committee on Discipline determines that probable cause exists to bring charges, the OED Director may institute a disciplinary proceeding by filing a complaint under §11.34.

History of 37 C.F.R. §11.32: 73 FR 47689, Sept. 15, 2008; 78 FR 20201, Apr. 3, 2013.

§11.33. RESERVED

§11.34. COMPLAINT

(a) A complaint instituting a disciplinary proceeding shall:

(1) Name the person who is the subject of the complaint who may then be referred to as the "respondent";

(2) Give a plain and concise description of the respondent's alleged grounds for discipline;

(3) State the place and time, not less than thirty days from the date the complaint is filed, for filing an answer by the respondent;

(4) State that a decision by default may be entered if an answer is not timely filed by the respondent; and

(5) Be signed by the OED Director.

(b) A complaint will be deemed sufficient if it fairly informs the respondent of any grounds for discipline, and where applicable, the USPTO Rules of Professional Conduct that form the basis for the disciplinary proceeding so that the respondent is able to adequately prepare a defense.

(c) The complaint shall be filed in the manner prescribed by the USPTO Director.

(d) Time for filing a complaint. A complaint shall be filed within one year after the date on which the OED Director receives a grievance forming the basis of the complaint. No complaint shall be filed more than ten years after the date on which the misconduct forming the basis for the proceeding occurred.

(e) Tolling agreements. The one-year period for filing a complaint under paragraph (d) of this section shall be tolled if the involved practitioner and the OED Director agree in writing to such tolling.

History of 37 C.F.R. §11.34: 73 FR 47689, Sept. 15, 2008; 77 FR 45251, Aug. 30, 2012; 78 FR 20201, Apr. 3, 2013.

§11.35. SERVICE OF COMPLAINT

(a) A complaint may be served on a respondent in any of the following methods:

(1) By delivering a copy of the complaint personally to the respondent, in which case the individual who gives the complaint to the respondent shall file an affidavit with the OED Director indicating the time and place the complaint was delivered to the respondent.

(2) By mailing a copy of the complaint by Priority Mail Express®, first-class mail, or any delivery service that provides ability to confirm delivery or attempted delivery to:

(i) A respondent who is a registered practitioner at the address provided to OED pursuant to §11.11, or

(ii) A respondent who is not registered at the last address for the respondent known to the OED Director.

(3) By any method mutually agreeable to the OED Director and the respondent.

(4) In the case of a respondent who resides outside the United States, by sending a copy of the complaint by any delivery service that provides ability to confirm delivery or attempted delivery, to:

(i) A respondent who is a registered practitioner at the address provided to OED pursuant to §11.11; or

(ii) A respondent who is not registered at the last address for the respondent known to the OED Director.

(b) If a copy of the complaint cannot be delivered to the respondent through any one of the procedures in paragraph (a) of this section, the OED Director shall serve the respondent by causing an appropriate notice to be published in the Official Gazette for two consecutive weeks, in which case, the time for filing an answer shall be thirty days from the second publication of the notice. Failure to timely file an answer will constitute an admission of the allegations in the complaint in accordance with paragraph (d) of §11.36, and the hearing officer may enter an initial decision on default.

(c) If the respondent is known to the OED Director to be represented by an attorney under §11.40(a), a copy of the complaint shall be served on the attorney in lieu of service on the respondent in the manner provided for in paragraph (a) or (b) of this section.

History of 37 C.F.R. §11.35: 73 FR 47689, Sept. 15, 2008; 78 FR 20201, Apr. 3, 2013; 79 FR 63042, Oct. 22, 2014.

§11.36. ANSWER TO COMPLAINT

(a) Time for answer. An answer to a complaint shall be filed within the time set in the complaint but in no event shall that time be less than thirty days from the date the complaint is filed.

(b) With whom filed. The answer shall be filed in writing with the hearing officer at the address specified in the complaint. The hearing officer may extend the time for filing an answer once for a period of no more than thirty days upon a showing of good cause, provided a motion requesting an extension of time is filed within thirty days after the date the complaint is served on respondent. A copy of the answer, and any exhibits or attachments thereto, shall be served on the OED Director.

(c) Content. The respondent shall include in the answer a statement of the facts that constitute the grounds of defense and shall specifically admit or deny each allegation set forth in the complaint. The respondent shall not deny a material allegation in the complaint that the respondent knows to be true or state that respondent is without sufficient information to form a belief as to the truth of an allegation, when in fact the respondent possesses that information. The respondent shall also state affirmatively in the answer special matters of defense and any intent to raise a disability as a mitigating factor. If respondent intends to raise a special matter of defense or disability, the answer shall specify the defense or disability, its nexus to the misconduct, and the reason it provides a defense or mitigation. A respondent who fails to do so cannot rely on a special matter of defense or disability. The hearing officer may, for good cause, allow the respondent to file the statement late, grant additional hearing preparation time, or make other appropriate orders.

(d) Failure to deny allegations in complaint. Every allegation in the complaint that is not denied by a respondent in the answer shall be deemed to be admitted and may be considered proven. The hearing officer at any hearing need receive no further evidence with respect to that allegation.

(e) Default judgment. Failure to timely file an answer will constitute an admission of the allegations in the complaint and may result in entry of default judgment.

History of 37 C.F.R. §11.36: 73 FR 47689, Sept. 15, 2008.

§11.37. RESERVED

§11.38. CONTESTED CASE

Upon the filing of an answer by the respondent, a disciplinary proceeding shall be regarded as a contested case within the meaning of 35 U.S.C. 24. Evidence obtained by a subpoena issued under 35 U.S.C. 24 shall not be admitted into the record or considered unless leave to proceed under 35 U.S.C. 24 was previously authorized by the hearing officer.

History of 37 C.F.R. §11.38: 73 FR 47689, Sept. 15, 2008.

§11.39. HEARING OFFICER; APPOINTMENT; RESPONSIBILITIES; REVIEW OF INTERLOCUTORY ORDERS; STAYS

(a) Appointment. A hearing officer, appointed by the USPTO Director under 5 U.S.C. 3105 or 35 U.S.C. 32, shall conduct disciplinary proceedings as provided by this Part.

(b) Independence of the Hearing Officer. **(1)** A hearing officer appointed in accordance with paragraph (a) of this section shall not be subject to first level or second level supervision by either the USPTO Director or OED Director, or his or her designee.

(2) A hearing officer appointed in accordance with paragraph (a) of this section shall not be subject to supervision of the person(s) investigating or prosecuting the case.

(3) A hearing officer appointed in accordance with paragraph (a) of this section shall be impartial, shall not be an individual who has participated in any manner in the decision to initiate the proceedings, and shall not have been employed under the immediate supervision of the practitioner.

(4) A hearing officer appointed in accordance with paragraph (a) of this section shall be admitted to practice law and have suitable experience and training conducting hearings, reaching a determination, and rendering an initial decision in an equitable manner.

(c) Responsibilities. The hearing officer shall have authority, consistent with specific provisions of these regulations, to:

(1) Administer oaths and affirmations;

(2) Make rulings upon motions and other requests;

(3) Rule upon offers of proof, receive relevant evidence, and examine witnesses;

(4) Authorize the taking of a deposition of a witness in lieu of personal appearance of the witness before the hearing officer;

(5) Determine the time and place of any hearing and regulate its course and conduct;

(6) Hold or provide for the holding of conferences to settle or simplify the issues;

(7) Receive and consider oral or written arguments on facts or law;

(8) Adopt procedures and modify procedures for the orderly disposition of proceedings;

(9) Make initial decisions under §§11.25 and 11.54; and

(10) Perform acts and take measures as necessary to promote the efficient, timely, and impartial conduct of any disciplinary proceeding.

(d) Time for making initial decision. The hearing officer shall set times and exercise control over a disciplinary proceeding such that an initial decision under §11.54 is normally issued within nine months of the date a complaint is filed. The hearing officer may, however, issue an initial decision more than nine months after a complaint is filed if there exist circumstances, in his or her opinion, that preclude issuance of an initial decision within nine months of the filing of the complaint.

(e) Review of interlocutory orders. The USPTO Director will not review an interlocutory order of a hearing officer except:

(1) When the hearing officer shall be of the opinion:

(i) That the interlocutory order involves a controlling question of procedure or law as to which there is a substantial ground for a difference of opinion, and

(ii) That an immediate decision by the USPTO Director may materially advance the ultimate termination of the disciplinary proceeding, or

(2) In an extraordinary situation where the USPTO Director deems that justice requires review.

(f) Stays pending review of interlocutory order. If the OED Director or a respondent seeks review of an interlocutory order of a hearing officer under paragraph (b)(2) of this section, any time period set by the hearing officer for taking action shall not be stayed unless ordered by the USPTO Director or the hearing officer.

(g) The hearing officer shall engage in no ex parte discussions with any party on the merits of the complaint, beginning with appointment and ending when the final agency decision is issued.

History of 37 C.F.R. §11.39: 73 FR 47689, Sept. 15, 2008.

§11.40. REPRESENTATIVE FOR OED DIRECTOR OR RESPONDENT

(a) A respondent may represent himself or herself, or be represented by an attorney before the Office in connection with an investigation or disciplinary proceeding. The attorney shall file a written declaration that he or she is an attorney within the meaning of §11.1 and shall state:

(1) The address to which the attorney wants correspondence related to the investigation or disciplinary proceeding sent, and

(2) A telephone number where the attorney may be reached during normal business hours.

(b) The Deputy General Counsel for Intellectual Property and Solicitor, and attorneys in the Office of the Solicitor shall represent the OED Director. The attorneys representing the OED Director in disciplinary proceedings shall not consult with the USPTO Director, the General Counsel, the Deputy General Counsel for General Law, or an individual designated by the USPTO Director to decide disciplinary matters regarding the proceeding. The General Counsel and the Deputy General Counsel for General Law shall remain screened from the investigation and prosecution of all disciplinary proceedings in order that they shall be available as counsel to the USPTO Director in deciding disciplinary proceedings unless access is appropriate to perform their duties. After a final decision is entered in a disciplinary proceeding, the OED Director and attorneys representing the OED Director shall be available to counsel the USPTO Director, the General Counsel, and the Deputy General Counsel for General Law in any further proceedings.

History of 37 C.F.R. §11.40: 73 FR 47689, Sept. 15, 2008.

§11.41. FILING OF PAPERS

(a) The provisions of §§1.8 and 2.197 of this subchapter do not apply to disciplinary proceedings. All papers filed after the complaint and prior to entry of an initial decision by the hearing officer shall be filed with the hearing officer at an address or place designated by the hearing officer.

(b) All papers filed after entry of an initial decision by the hearing officer shall be filed with the USPTO Director. A copy of the paper shall be served on the OED Director. The hearing officer or the OED Director may provide for filing papers and other matters by hand, by Priority Mail Express®, or by other means.

History of 37 C.F.R. §11.41: 73 FR 47689, Sept. 15, 2008; 79 FR 63042, Oct. 22, 2014.

§11.42. SERVICE OF PAPERS

(a) All papers other than a complaint shall be served on a respondent who is represented by an attorney by:

(1) Delivering a copy of the paper to the office of the attorney; or

(2) Mailing a copy of the paper by first-class mail, Priority Mail Express®, or other delivery service to the attorney at the address provided by the attorney under §11.40(a)(1); or

(3) Any other method mutually agreeable to the attorney and a representative for the OED Director.

(b) All papers other than a complaint shall be served on a respondent who is not represented by an attorney by:

(1) Delivering a copy of the paper to the respondent; or

(2) Mailing a copy of the paper by first-class mail, Priority Mail Express®, or other delivery service to the respondent at the address to which a complaint may be served or such other address as may be designated in writing by the respondent; or

(3) Any other method mutually agreeable to the respondent and a representative for the OED Director.

(c) A respondent shall serve on the representative for the OED Director one copy of each paper filed with the hearing officer or the OED Director. A paper may be served on the representative for the OED Director by:

(1) Delivering a copy of the paper to the representative; or

(2) Mailing a copy of the paper by first-class mail, Priority Mail Express®, or other delivery service to an address designated in writing by the representative; or

(3) Any other method mutually agreeable to the respondent and the representative.

(d) Each paper filed in a disciplinary proceeding shall contain therein a certificate of service indicating:

(1) The date on which service was made; and

(2) The method by which service was made.

(e) The hearing officer or the USPTO Director may require that a paper be served by hand or by Priority Mail Express®.

(f) Service by mail is completed when the paper mailed in the United States is placed into the custody of the U.S. Postal Service.

History of 37 C.F.R. §11.42: 73 FR 47689, Sept. 15, 2008; 79 FR 63043, Oct. 22, 2014.

§11.43. MOTIONS

Motions, including all prehearing motions commonly filed under the Federal Rules of Civil Procedure, shall be filed with the hearing officer. The hearing officer will determine whether replies to responses will be authorized and the time period for filing such a response. No motion shall be filed with the hearing officer unless such motion is supported by a written statement by the moving party that the moving party or attorney for the moving party has conferred with the opposing party or attorney for the opposing party in an effort in good faith to resolve by agreement the issues raised by the motion and has been unable to reach agreement. If, prior to a decision on the motion, the parties resolve issues raised by a motion presented to the hearing officer, the parties shall promptly notify the hearing officer.

History of 37 C.F.R. §11.43: 73 FR 47689, Sept. 15, 2008.

§11.44. HEARINGS

(a) The hearing officer shall preside over hearings in disciplinary proceedings. The hearing officer shall set the time and place for the hearing. In cases involving an incarcerated respondent, any necessary oral hearing may be held at the location of incarceration. Oral hearings will be stenographically recorded and transcribed, and the testimony of witnesses will be received under oath or affirmation. The hearing officer shall conduct the hearing as if the proceeding were subject to 5 U.S.C. 556. A copy of the transcript of the hearing shall become part of the record. A copy of the transcript shall be provided to the OED Director and the respondent at the expense of the Office.

(b) If the respondent to a disciplinary proceeding fails to appear at the hearing after a notice of hearing has been given by the hearing officer, the hearing officer may deem the respondent to have waived the right to a hearing and may proceed with the hearing in the absence of the respondent.

(c) A hearing under this section will not be open to the public except that the hearing officer may grant a request by a respondent to open his or her hearing to the public and make the record of the disciplinary proceeding available for public inspection, provided, a protective order is entered to exclude from public disclosure information which is privileged or confidential under applicable laws or regulations.

History of 37 C.F.R. §11.44: 73 FR 47689, Sept. 15, 2008.

§11.45. AMENDMENT OF PLEADINGS

The OED Director may, without Committee on Discipline authorization, but with the authorization of the hearing officer, amend the complaint to include additional charges based upon conduct committed before or after the complaint was filed. If amendment of the complaint is authorized, the hearing officer shall authorize amendment of the answer. Any party who would otherwise be prejudiced by the amendment will be given reasonable opportunity to meet the allegations in the complaint or answer as amended, and the hearing officer shall make findings on any issue presented by the complaint or answer as amended.

History of 37 C.F.R. §11.45: 73 FR 47689, Sept. 15, 2008.

§§11.46 TO 11.48. RESERVED

§11.49. BURDEN OF PROOF

In a disciplinary proceeding, the OED Director shall have the burden of proving the violation by clear and convincing evidence and a respondent shall have the burden of proving any affirmative defense by clear and convincing evidence.

History of 37 C.F.R. §11.49: 73 FR 47689, Sept. 15, 2008.

§11.50. EVIDENCE

(a) Rules of evidence. The rules of evidence prevailing in courts of law and equity are not controlling in hearings in disciplinary proceedings. However, the hearing officer shall exclude evidence that is irrelevant, immaterial, or unduly repetitious.

(b) Depositions. Depositions of witnesses taken pursuant to §11.51 may be admitted as evidence.

(c) Government documents. Official documents, records, and papers of the Office, including, but not limited to, all papers in the file of a disciplinary investigation, are admissible without extrinsic evidence of authenticity. These documents, records, and papers may be evidenced by a copy certified as correct by an employee of the Office.

(d) Exhibits. If any document, record, or other paper is introduced in evidence as an exhibit, the hearing officer may authorize the withdrawal of the exhibit subject to any conditions the hearing officer deems appropriate.

(e) Objections. Objections to evidence will be in short form, stating the grounds of objection. Objections and rulings on objections will be a part of the record. No exception to the ruling is necessary to preserve the rights of the parties.

History of 37 C.F.R. §11.50: 73 FR 47689, Sept. 15, 2008.

§11.51. DEPOSITIONS

(a) Depositions for use at the hearing in lieu of personal appearance of a witness before the hearing officer may be taken by respondent or the OED Director upon a showing of good cause and with the approval of, and under such conditions as may be deemed appropriate by, the hearing officer. Depositions may be taken upon oral or written questions, upon not less than ten days' written notice to the other party, before any officer authorized to administer an oath or affirmation in the place where the deposition is to be taken. The parties may waive the requirement of ten days' notice and depositions may then be taken of a witness at a time and place mutually agreed to by the parties. When a deposition is taken upon written questions, copies of the written questions will be served upon the other party with the notice, and copies of any written cross-questions will be served by hand or Priority Mail Express® not less than five days before the date of the taking of the deposition unless the parties mutually agree otherwise. A party on whose behalf a deposition is taken shall file a copy of a transcript of the deposition signed by a court reporter with the hearing officer and shall serve one copy upon the opposing party. Expenses for a court reporter and preparing, serving, and filing depositions shall be borne by the party at whose instance the deposition is taken. Depositions may not be taken to obtain discovery, except as provided for in paragraph (b) of this section.

(b) When the OED Director and the respondent agree in writing, a deposition of any witness who will appear voluntarily may be taken under such terms and conditions as may be mutually agreeable to the OED Director and the respondent. The deposition shall not be filed with the hearing officer and may not be admitted in evidence before the hearing officer unless he or she orders the deposition admitted in evidence. The admissibility of the deposition shall lie within the discretion of the hearing officer who may reject the deposition on any reasonable basis including the fact that demeanor is involved and that the witness should have been called to appear personally before the hearing officer.

History of 37 C.F.R. §11.51: 73 FR 47689, Sept. 15, 2008; 79 FR 63043, Oct. 22, 2014.

§11.52. DISCOVERY

Discovery shall not be authorized except as follows:

(a) After an answer is filed under §11.36 and when a party establishes that discovery is reasonable and relevant, the hearing officer, under such conditions as he or she deems appropriate, may order an opposing party to:

(1) Answer a reasonable number of written requests for admission or interrogatories;

(2) Produce for inspection and copying a reasonable number of documents; and

(3) Produce for inspection a reasonable number of things other than documents.

(b) Discovery shall not be authorized under paragraph (a) of this section of any matter which:

(1) Will be used by another party solely for impeachment;

(2) Is not available to the party under 35 U.S.C. 122;

(3) Relates to any other disciplinary proceeding;

(4) Relates to experts except as the hearing officer may require under paragraph (e) of this section;

(5) Is privileged; or

(6) Relates to mental impressions, conclusions, opinions, or legal theories of any attorney or other representative of a party.

(c) The hearing officer may deny discovery requested under paragraph (a) of this section if the discovery sought:

(1) Will unduly delay the disciplinary proceeding;

(2) Will place an undue burden on the party required to produce the discovery sought; or

(3) Consists of information that is available:

(i) Generally to the public;

(ii) Equally to the parties; or

(iii) To the party seeking the discovery through another source.

(d) Prior to authorizing discovery under paragraph (a) of this section, the hearing officer shall require the party seeking discovery to file a motion (§11.43) and explain in detail, for each request made, how the discovery sought is reasonable and relevant to an issue actually raised in the complaint or the answer.

(e) The hearing officer may require parties to file and serve, prior to any hearing, a pre-hearing statement that contains:

(1) A list (together with a copy) of all proposed exhibits to be used in connection with a party's case-in-chief;

(2) A list of proposed witnesses;

(3) As to each proposed expert witness:

(i) An identification of the field in which the individual will be qualified as an expert;

(ii) A statement as to the subject matter on which the expert is expected to testify; and

(iii) A statement of the substance of the facts and opinions to which the expert is expected to testify;

(4) Copies of memoranda reflecting respondent's own statements to administrative representatives.

History of 37 C.F.R. §11.52: 73 FR 47689, Sept. 15, 2008.

§11.53. PROPOSED FINDINGS & CONCLUSIONS; POST-HEARING MEMORANDUM

Except in cases in which the respondent has failed to answer the complaint or amended complaint, the hearing officer, prior to making an initial decision, shall afford the parties a reasonable opportunity to submit proposed findings and conclusions and a post-hearing memorandum in support of the proposed findings and conclusions.

History of 37 C.F.R. §11.53: 73 FR 47689, Sept. 15, 2008.

§11.54. INITIAL DECISION OF HEARING OFFICER

(a) The hearing officer shall make an initial decision in the case. The decision will include:

(1) A statement of findings of fact and conclusions of law, as well as the reasons or bases for those findings and conclusions with appropriate references to the record, upon all the material issues of fact, law, or discretion presented on the record, and

(2) An order of default judgment, of suspension or exclusion from practice, of reprimand, of probation or an order dismissing the complaint. The order also may impose any conditions deemed appropriate under the circumstances. The hearing officer shall transmit a copy of the decision to the OED Director and to the respondent. After issuing the decision, the hearing officer shall transmit the entire record to the OED Director. In the absence of an appeal to the USPTO Director, the decision of the hearing officer, including a default judgment, will, without further proceedings, become the decision of the USPTO Director thirty days from the date of the decision of the hearing officer.

(b) The initial decision of the hearing officer shall explain the reason for any default judgment, reprimand, suspension, exclusion, or probation, and shall explain any conditions imposed with discipline. In determining any sanction, the following four factors must be considered if they are applicable:

(1) Whether the practitioner has violated a duty owed to a client, to the public, to the legal system, or to the profession;

(2) Whether the practitioner acted intentionally, knowingly, or negligently;

(3) The amount of the actual or potential injury caused by the practitioner's misconduct; and

(4) The existence of any aggravating or mitigating factors.

History of 37 C.F.R. §11.54: 73 FR 47689, Sept. 15, 2008; 78 FR 20201, Apr. 3, 2013.

§11.55. APPEAL TO THE USPTO DIRECTOR

(a) Within thirty days after the date of the initial decision of the hearing officer under §11.25 or §11.54, either party may appeal to the USPTO Director. The appeal shall include the appellant's brief. If more than one appeal is filed, the party who files the appeal first is the appellant for purpose of this rule. If appeals are filed on the same day, the respondent is the appellant. If an appeal is filed, then the OED Director shall transmit the entire record to the USPTO Director. Any cross-appeal shall be filed within fourteen days after the date of service of the appeal pursuant to §11.42, or thirty days after the date of the initial decision of the hearing officer, whichever is later. The cross-appeal shall include the cross-appellant's brief. Any appellee or cross-appellee brief must be filed within thirty days after the date of service pursuant to

§11.42 of an appeal or cross-appeal. Any reply brief must be filed within fourteen days after the date of service of any appellee or cross-appellee brief.

(b) An appeal or cross-appeal must include exceptions to the decisions of the hearing officer and supporting reasons for those exceptions. Any exception not raised will be deemed to have been waived and will be disregarded by the USPTO Director in reviewing the initial decision.

(c) All briefs shall:

(1) Be filed with the USPTO Director at the address set forth in §1.1(a)(3)(ii) of this subchapter and served on the opposing party;

(2) Include separate sections containing a concise statement of the disputed facts and disputed points of law; and

(3) Be typed on 8½ by 11-inch paper, and comply with Rule 32(a)(4)-(6) of the Federal Rules of Appellate Procedure.

(d) An appellant's, cross-appellant's, appellee's, and cross-appellee's brief shall be no more than thirty pages in length, and comply with Rule 28(a)(2), (3), and (5) through (10) of the Federal Rules of Appellate Procedure. Any reply brief shall be no more than fifteen pages in length, and shall comply with Rule 28(a)(2), (3), (8), and (9) of the Federal Rules of Appellate Procedure.

(e) The USPTO Director may refuse entry of a nonconforming brief.

(f) The USPTO Director will decide the appeal on the record made before the hearing officer.

(g) Unless the USPTO Director permits, no further briefs or motions shall be filed.

(h) The USPTO Director may order reopening of a disciplinary proceeding in accordance with the principles that govern the granting of new trials. Any request to reopen a disciplinary proceeding on the basis of newly discovered evidence must demonstrate that the newly discovered evidence could not have been discovered by due diligence.

(i) In the absence of an appeal by the OED Director, failure by the respondent to appeal under the provisions of this section shall result in the initial decision being final and effective thirty days from the date of the initial decision of the hearing officer.

History of 37 C.F.R. §11.55: 73 FR 47689, Sept. 15, 2008.

§11.56. DECISION OF THE USPTO DIRECTOR

(a) The USPTO Director shall decide an appeal from an initial decision of the hearing officer. On appeal from the initial decision, the USPTO Director has authority to conduct a de novo review of the factual record. The USPTO Director may affirm, reverse, or modify the initial decision or remand the matter to the hearing officer for such further proceedings as the USPTO Director may deem appropriate. In making a final decision, the USPTO Director shall review the record or the portions of the record designated by the parties. The USPTO Director shall transmit a copy of the final decision to the OED Director and to the respondent.

(b) A final decision of the USPTO Director may dismiss a disciplinary proceeding, reverse or modify the initial decision, reprimand a practitioner, or may suspend or exclude the practitioner from practice before the Office. A final decision suspending or excluding a practitioner shall require compliance with the provisions of §11.58. The final decision may also condition the reinstatement of the practitioner upon a showing that the practitioner has taken steps to correct or mitigate the matter forming the basis of the action, or to prevent recurrence of the same or similar conduct.

(c) The respondent or the OED Director may make a single request for reconsideration or modification of the decision by the USPTO Director if filed within twenty days from the date of entry of the decision. No request for reconsideration or modification shall be granted unless the request is based on newly discovered evidence or error of law or fact, and the requestor must demonstrate that any newly discovered evidence could not have been discovered any earlier by due diligence. Such a request shall have the effect of staying the effective date of the order of discipline in the final decision. The decision by the USPTO Director is effective on its date of entry.

History of 37 C.F.R. §11.56: 73 FR 47689, Sept. 15, 2008.

§11.57. REVIEW OF FINAL DECISION OF THE USPTO DIRECTOR

(a) Review of the final decision by the USPTO Director in a disciplinary case may be had, subject to §11.55(d), by a petition filed in accordance with 35 U.S.C. 32. The Respondent must serve the USPTO Director with the petition. Respondent must serve the petition in accordance with Rule 4 of the Federal Rules of Civil Procedure and §104.2 of this Title.

(b) Except as provided for in §11.56(c), an order for discipline in a final decision will not be stayed except on proof of exceptional circumstances.

History of 37 C.F.R. §11.57: 73 FR 47689, Sept. 15, 2008.

§11.58. DUTIES OF DISCIPLINED OR RESIGNED PRACTITIONER, OR PRACTITIONER ON DISABILITY INACTIVE STATUS

(a) An excluded, suspended or resigned practitioner, or practitioner transferred to disability inactive status shall not engage in any practice of patent, trademark and other non-patent law before the Office. An excluded, suspended or resigned practitioner will not be automatically reinstated at the end of his or her period of exclusion or suspension. An excluded, suspended or resigned practitioner, or practitioner transferred to disability inactive status must comply with the provisions of this section and §11.60 to be reinstated. Failure to comply with the provisions of this section may constitute both grounds for denying reinstatement or readmission; and cause for further action, including seeking further exclusion, suspension, and for revocation of any pending probation.

(b) Unless otherwise ordered by the USPTO Director, any excluded, suspended or resigned practitioner, or practitioner transferred to disability inactive status shall:

(1) Within thirty days after the date of entry of the order of exclusion, suspension, acceptance of resignation, or transfer to disability inactive status:

(i) File a notice of withdrawal as of the effective date of the exclusion, suspension, acceptance of resignation, or transfer to disability inactive status in each pending patent and trademark application, each pending reexamination and interference or trial proceeding, and every other matter pending in the Office, together with a copy of the notices sent pursuant to paragraphs (b) and (c) of this section;

(ii) Provide notice to all State and Federal jurisdictions and administrative agencies to which the practitioner is admitted to practice and all clients the practitioner represents having immediate or prospective business before the Office in patent, trademark and other non-patent matters of the order of exclusion, suspension, acceptance of resignation, or transferred to disability inactive status and of the practitioner's consequent inability to act as a practitioner after the effective date of the order; and that, if not represented by another practitioner, the client should act promptly to substitute another practitioner, or to seek legal advice elsewhere, calling attention to any urgency arising from the circumstances of the case;

(iii) Provide notice to the practitioner(s) for all opposing parties (or, to the parties in the absence of a practitioner representing the parties) in matters pending before the Office of the practitioner's exclusion, suspension, resignation, or transfer to disability inactive status and, that as a consequence, the practitioner is disqualified from acting as a practitioner regarding matters before the Office after the effective date of the suspension, exclusion, resignation or transfer to disability inactive status, and state in the notice the mailing address of each client of the excluded, suspended or resigned practitioner, or practitioner transferred to disability inactive status who is a party in the pending matter;

(iv) Deliver to all clients having immediate or prospective business before the Office in patent, trademark or other non-patent matters any papers or other property to which the clients are entitled, or shall notify the clients and any co-practitioner of a suitable time and place where the papers and other property may be obtained, calling attention to any urgency for obtaining the papers or other property;

(v) Relinquish to the client, or other practitioner designated by the client, all funds for practice before the Office, including any legal fees paid in advance that have not been earned and any advanced costs not expended;

(vi) Take any necessary and appropriate steps to remove from any telephone, legal, or other directory any advertisement, statement, or representation which would reasonably suggest that the practitioner is authorized to practice patent, trademark, or other non-patent law before the Office; and

(vii) Serve all notices required by paragraphs (b)(1)(ii) and (b)(1)(iii) of this section by certified mail, return receipt requested, unless mailed abroad. If mailed abroad, all notices shall be served with a receipt to be signed and returned to the practitioner.

(2) Within forty-five days after entry of the order of suspension, exclusion, or of acceptance of resignation, the practitioner shall file with the OED Director an affidavit of compliance certifying that the practitioner has fully complied with the provisions of the order, this section, and with §11.116 for withdrawal from representation. Appended to the affidavit of compliance shall be:

(i) A copy of each form of notice, the names and addresses of the clients, practitioners, courts, and agencies to which notices were sent, and all return receipts or returned mail received up to the date of the affidavit. Supplemental affidavits shall be filed covering subsequent return receipts and returned mail. Such names and addresses of clients shall remain confidential unless otherwise ordered by the USPTO Director;

(ii) A schedule showing the location, title and account number of every bank account designated as a client or trust account, deposit account in the Office, or other fiduciary account, and of every account in which the practitioner holds or held as of the entry date of the order any client, trust, or fiduciary funds for practice before the Office;

(iii) A schedule describing the practitioner's disposition of all client and fiduciary funds for practice before the Office in the practitioner's possession, custody or control as of the date of the order or thereafter;

(iv) Such proof of the proper distribution of said funds and the closing of such accounts as has been requested by the OED Director, including copies of checks and other instruments;

(v) A list of all other State, Federal, and administrative jurisdictions to which the practitioner is admitted to practice; and

(vi) An affidavit describing the precise nature of the steps taken to remove from any telephone, legal, or other directory any advertisement, statement, or representation which would reasonably suggest that the practitioner is authorized to practice patent, trademark, or other non-patent law before the Office. The affidavit shall also state the residence or other address of the practitioner to which communications may thereafter be directed, and list all State and Federal jurisdictions, and administrative agencies to which the practitioner is admitted to practice. The OED Director may require such additional proof as is deemed necessary. In addition, for the period of discipline, an excluded or suspended practitioner, or a practitioner transferred to disability inactive status shall continue to file a statement in accordance with §11.11, regarding any change of residence or other address to which communications may thereafter be directed, so that the excluded or suspended practitioner, or practitioner transferred to disability inactive status may be located if a grievance is received regarding any conduct occurring before or after the exclusion or suspension. The practitioner shall retain copies of all notices sent and shall maintain complete records of the steps taken to comply with the notice requirements.

(3) Not hold himself or herself out as authorized to practice law before the Office.

(4) Not advertise the practitioner's availability or ability to perform or render legal services for any person having immediate or prospective business before the Office as to that business.

(5) Not render legal advice or services to any person having immediate or prospective business before the Office as to that business.

(6) Promptly take steps to change any sign identifying the practitioner's or the practitioner's firm's office and the practitioner's or the practitioner's firm's stationery to delete therefrom any advertisement, statement, or representation which would reasonably suggest that the practitioner is authorized to practice law before the Office.

(c) An excluded, suspended or resigned practitioner, or practitioner transferred to disability inactive status after entry of the order of exclusion or suspension, acceptance of resignation, or transfer to disability inactive status shall not accept any new retainer regarding immediate or prospective business before the Office, or engage as a practitioner for another in any new case or legal matter regarding practice before the Office. The excluded, suspended or resigned practitioner, or practitioner transferred to disability inactive status shall be granted limited recognition for a period of thirty days. During the thirty-day period of limited recognition, the excluded, suspended or resigned practitioner, or practitioner transferred to disability inactive status shall conclude work on behalf of a client on any matters that were pending before the Office on the date of entry of the order of exclusion or suspension, or acceptance of resignation. If such work cannot be concluded, the excluded, suspended or resigned practitioner, or practitioner transferred to disability inactive status shall so advise the client so that the client may make other arrangements.

(d) Required records. An excluded, suspended or resigned practitioner, or practitioner transferred to disability inactive status shall keep and maintain records of the various steps taken under this section, so that in any subsequent proceeding proof of compliance with this section and with the exclusion or suspension order will be available. The OED Director will require the practitioner to submit such proof as a condition precedent to the granting of any petition for reinstatement.

(e) An excluded, suspended or resigned practitioner, or practitioner on disability inactive status who aids another practitioner in any way in the other practitioner's practice of law before the Office, may, under the direct supervision of the other practitioner, act as a paralegal for the other practitioner or perform other services for the other practitioner which are normally performed by laypersons, provided:

(1) The excluded, suspended or resigned practitioner, or practitioner transferred to disability inactive status is a salaried employee of:

(i) The other practitioner;

(ii) The other practitioner's law firm; or

(iii) A client-employer who employs the other practitioner as a salaried employee;

(2) The other practitioner assumes full professional responsibility to any client and the Office for any work performed by the excluded, suspended or resigned practitioner for the other practitioner;

(3) The excluded, suspended or resigned practitioner, or practitioner transferred to disability inactive status does not:

(i) Communicate directly in writing, orally, or otherwise with a client of the other practitioner in regard to any immediate or prospective business before the Office;

(ii) Render any legal advice or any legal services to a client of the other practitioner in regard to any immediate or prospective business before the Office; or

(iii) Meet in person or in the presence of the other practitioner in regard to any immediate or prospective business before the Office, with:

(A) Any Office employee in connection with the prosecution of any patent, trademark, or other case;

(B) Any client of the other practitioner, the other practitioner's law firm, or the client-employer of the other practitioner; or

(C) Any witness or potential witness whom the other practitioner, the other practitioner's law firm, or the other practitioner's client-employer may or intends to call as a witness in any proceeding before the Office. The term "witness" includes individuals who will testify orally in a proceeding before, or sign an affidavit or any other document to be filed in, the Office.

(f) When an excluded, suspended or resigned practitioner, or practitioner transferred to disability inactive status acts as a paralegal or performs services under paragraph (e) of this section, the practitioner shall not thereafter be reinstated to practice before the Office unless:

(1) The practitioner shall have filed with the OED Director an affidavit which:

(i) Explains in detail the precise nature of all paralegal or other services performed by the excluded, suspended or resigned practitioner, or practitioner transferred to disability inactive status, and

(ii) Shows by clear and convincing evidence that the excluded, suspended or resigned practitioner, or practitioner transferred to disability inactive status has complied with the provisions of this section and all USPTO Rules of Professional Conduct; and

(2) The other practitioner shall have filed with the OED Director a written statement which:

(i) Shows that the other practitioner has read the affidavit required by paragraph (d)(1) of this section and that the other practitioner believes every statement in the affidavit to be true, and

(ii) States why the other practitioner believes that the excluded, suspended or resigned practitioner, or practitioner transferred to disability inactive status has complied with paragraph (c) of this section.

History of 37 C.F.R. §11.58: 73 FR 47689, Sept. 15, 2008; 77 FR 46630, Sept. 16, 2012; 78 FR 20201, Apr. 3, 2013.

§11.59. DISSEMINATION OF DISCIPLINARY & OTHER INFORMATION

(a) The OED Director shall inform the public of the disposition of each matter in which public discipline has been imposed, and of any other changes in a practitioner's registration status. Public discipline includes exclusion, as well as exclusion on consent; suspension; and public reprimand. Unless otherwise ordered by the USPTO Director, the OED Director shall give notice of public discipline and the reasons for the discipline to disciplinary enforcement agencies in the State where the practitioner is admitted to practice, to courts where the practitioner is known to be admitted, and the public. If public discipline is imposed, the OED Director shall cause a final decision of the USPTO Director to be published. Final decisions of the USPTO Director include default judgments. See §11.54(a)(2). If a private reprimand is imposed, the OED Director shall cause a redacted version of the final decision to be published.

(b) Records available to the public. Unless the USPTO Director orders that the proceeding or a portion of the record be kept confidential, the OED Director's records of every disciplinary proceeding where a practitioner is reprimanded, suspended, or excluded, including when said sanction is imposed by default judgment, shall be made available to the public upon written request, except that information may be withheld as necessary to protect the privacy of third parties or as directed in a protective order issued pursuant to §11.44(c). The record of a proceeding that results in a practitioner's transfer to disability inactive status shall not be available to the public.

(c) Access to records of exclusion by consent. Unless the USPTO Director orders that the proceeding or a portion of the record be kept confidential, an order excluding a practitioner on consent under §11.27 and the affidavit required under paragraph (a) of §11.27 shall be available to the public, except that information in the order or affidavit may be withheld as necessary to protect the privacy of third parties or as directed in a protective order under §11.44(c). The affidavit required under paragraph (a) of §11.27 shall not be used in any other proceeding except by order of the USPTO Director or upon written consent of the practitioner.

History of 37 C.F.R. §11.59: 73 FR 47689, Sept. 15, 2008.

§11.60. PETITION FOR REINSTATEMENT

(a) Restrictions on reinstatement. An excluded, suspended or resigned practitioner shall not resume practice of patent, trademark, or other non-patent law before the Office until reinstated by order of the OED Director or the USPTO Director.

(b) Petition for reinstatement. An excluded or suspended practitioner shall be eligible to apply for reinstatement only upon expiration of the period of suspension or exclusion and the practitioner's full compliance with §11.58. An excluded practitioner shall be eligible to apply for reinstatement no earlier than at least five years from the effective date of the exclusion. A resigned practitioner shall be eligible to petition for reinstatement and must show compliance with §11.58 no earlier than at least five years from the date the practitioner's resignation is accepted and an order is entered excluding the practitioner on consent.

(c) Review of reinstatement petition. An excluded, suspended or resigned practitioner shall file a petition for reinstatement accompanied by the fee required by §1.21(a)(10) of this subchapter. The petition for reinstatement shall be filed with the OED Director. An excluded or suspended practitioner who has violated any provision of §11.58 shall not be eligible for reinstatement until a continuous period of the time in compliance with §11.58 that is equal to the period of suspension or exclusion has elapsed. A resigned practitioner shall not be eligible for reinstatement until compliance with §11.58 is shown. If the excluded, suspended or resigned practitioner is not eligible for reinstatement, or if the OED Director determines that the petition is insufficient or defective on its face, the OED Director may dismiss the petition. Otherwise the OED Director shall consider the petition for reinstatement. The excluded, suspended or resigned practitioner seeking reinstatement shall have the burden of proof by clear and convincing evidence. Such proof shall be included in or accompany the petition, and shall establish:

(1) That the excluded, suspended or resigned practitioner has the good moral character and reputation, competency, and learning in law required under §11.7 for admission;

(2) That the resumption of practice before the Office will not be detrimental to the administration of justice or subversive to the public interest; and

(3) That the suspended practitioner has complied with the provisions of §11.58 for the full period of suspension, that the excluded practitioner has complied with the provisions of §11.58 for at least five continuous years, or that the resigned practitioner has complied with §11.58 upon acceptance of the resignation.

(d) Petitions for reinstatement—Action by the OED Director granting reinstatement. **(1)** If the excluded, suspended or resigned practitioner is found to have complied with paragraphs (c)(1) through (c)(3) of this section, the OED Director shall enter an order of reinstatement, which shall be conditioned on payment of the costs of the disciplinary proceeding to the extent set forth in paragraphs (d)(2) and (3) of this section.

(2) Payment of costs of disciplinary proceedings. Prior to reinstatement to practice, the excluded or suspended practitioner shall pay the costs of the disciplinary proceeding. The costs imposed pursuant to this section include all of the following:

(i) The actual expense incurred by the OED Director or the Office for the original and copies of any reporter's transcripts of the disciplinary proceeding, and any fee paid for the services of the reporter;

(ii) All expenses paid by the OED Director or the Office which would qualify as taxable costs recoverable in civil proceedings; and

(iii) The charges determined by the OED Director to be "reasonable costs" of investigation, hearing, and review. These amounts shall serve to defray the costs, other than fees for services of attorneys and experts, of the Office of Enrollment and Discipline in the preparation or hearing of the disciplinary proceeding, and costs incurred in the administrative processing of the disciplinary proceeding.

(3) An excluded or suspended practitioner may be granted relief, in whole or in part, only from an order assessing costs under this section or may be granted an extension of time to pay these costs, in the discretion of the OED Director, upon grounds of hardship, special circumstances, or other good cause.

(e) Petitions for reinstatement—Action by the OED Director denying reinstatement. If the excluded, suspended or resigned practitioner is found unfit to resume the practice of patent law before the Office, the OED Director shall first provide the excluded, suspended or resigned practitioner with an opportunity to show cause in writing why the petition should not be denied. Failure to comply with §11.12(c) shall constitute unfitness. If unpersuaded by the showing, the OED Director shall deny the petition. The OED Director may require the excluded, suspended or resigned practitioner, in meeting the requirements of §11.7, to take and pass an examination under §11.7(b), ethics courses, and/or the Multistate Professional Responsibility Examination. The OED Director shall provide findings, together with the record. The findings shall include on the first page, immediately beneath the caption of the case, a separate section entitled "Prior Proceedings" which shall state the docket number of the original disciplinary proceeding in which the exclusion or suspension was ordered.

(f) Resubmission of petitions for reinstatement. If a petition for reinstatement is denied, no further petition for reinstatement may be filed until the expiration of at least one year following the denial unless the order of denial provides otherwise.

(g) Reinstatement proceedings open to public. Proceedings on any petition for reinstatement shall be open to the public. Before reinstating any excluded or suspended practitioner, the OED Director shall publish a notice of the excluded or suspended practitioner's petition for reinstatement and shall permit the public a reasonable opportunity to comment or submit evidence with respect to the petition for reinstatement.

History of 37 C.F.R. §11.60: 73 FR 47689, Sept. 15, 2008.

§§11.61 TO 11.99. RESERVED

SUBPART D. USPTO RULES OF PROFESSIONAL CONDUCT

§11.100. RESERVED

CLIENT-PRACTITIONER RELATIONSHIP

§11.101. COMPETENCE

A practitioner shall provide competent representation to a client. Competent representation requires the legal, scientific, and technical knowledge, skill, thoroughness and preparation reasonably necessary for the representation.

History of 37 C.F.R. §11.101: 78 FR 20202, Apr. 3, 2013.

§11.102. SCOPE OF REPRESENTATION & ALLOCATION OF AUTHORITY BETWEEN CLIENT & PRACTITIONER

(a) Subject to paragraphs (c) and (d) of this section, a practitioner shall abide by a client's decisions concerning the objectives of representation and, as required by §11.104, shall consult with the client as to the means by which they are to be pursued. A practitioner may take such action on behalf of the client as is impliedly authorized to carry out the representation. A practitioner shall abide by a client's decision whether to settle a matter.

(b) [Reserved]

(c) A practitioner may limit the scope of the representation if the limitation is reasonable under the circumstances and the client gives informed consent.

(d) A practitioner shall not counsel a client to engage, or assist a client, in conduct that the practitioner knows is criminal or fraudulent, but a practitioner may discuss the legal consequences of any proposed course of conduct with a client and may counsel or assist a client to make a good-faith effort to determine the validity, scope, meaning or application of the law.

History of 37 C.F.R. §11.102: 78 FR 20202, Apr. 3, 2013.

§11.103. DILIGENCE

A practitioner shall act with reasonable diligence and promptness in representing a client.

History of 37 C.F.R. §11.103: 78 FR 20202, Apr. 3, 2013.

§11.104. COMMUNICATION

(a) A practitioner shall:

(1) Promptly inform the client of any decision or circumstance with respect to which the client's informed consent is required by the USPTO Rules of Professional Conduct;

(2) Reasonably consult with the client about the means by which the client's objectives are to be accomplished;

(3) Keep the client reasonably informed about the status of the matter;

(4) Promptly comply with reasonable requests for information from the client; and

(5) Consult with the client about any relevant limitation on the practitioner's conduct when the practitioner knows that the client expects assistance not permitted by the USPTO Rules of Professional Conduct or other law.

(b) A practitioner shall explain a matter to the extent reasonably necessary to permit the client to make informed decisions regarding the representation.

History of 37 C.F.R. §11.104: 78 FR 20202, Apr. 3, 2013.

§11.105. FEES

(a) A practitioner shall not make an agreement for, charge, or collect an unreasonable fee or an unreasonable amount for expenses. The factors to be considered in determining the reasonableness of a fee include the following:

(1) The time and labor required, the novelty and difficulty of the questions involved, and the skill requisite to perform the legal service properly;

(2) The likelihood, if apparent to the client, that the acceptance of the particular employment will preclude other employment by the practitioner;

(3) The fee customarily charged in the locality for similar legal services;

(4) The amount involved and the results obtained;

(5) The time limitations imposed by the client or by the circumstances;

(6) The nature and length of the professional relationship with the client;

(7) The experience, reputation, and ability of the practitioner or practitioners performing the services; and

(8) Whether the fee is fixed or contingent.

(b) The scope of the representation and the basis or rate of the fee and expenses for which the client will be responsible shall be communicated to the client, preferably in writing, before or within a reasonable time after commencing the representation, except when the practitioner will charge a regularly represented client on the same basis or rate. Any changes in the basis or rate of the fee or expenses shall also be communicated to the client.

(c) A fee may be contingent on the outcome of the matter for which the service is rendered, except in a matter in which a contingent fee is prohibited by law. A contingent fee agreement shall be in a writing signed by the client and shall state the method by which the fee is to be determined, including the percentage or percentages that shall accrue to the practitioner in the event of settlement, trial or appeal; litigation and other expenses to be deducted from the recovery; and whether such expenses are to be deducted before or after the contingent fee is calculated. The agreement must clearly notify the client of any expenses for which the client will be liable whether or not the client is the prevailing party. Upon conclusion of a contingent fee matter, the practitioner shall provide the client with a written statement stating the outcome of the matter and, if there is a recovery, showing the remittance to the client and the method of its determination.

(d) [Reserved]

(e) A division of a fee between practitioners who are not in the same firm may be made only if:

(1) The division is in proportion to the services performed by each practitioner or each practitioner assumes joint responsibility for the representation;

(2) The client agrees to the arrangement, including the share each practitioner will receive, and the agreement is confirmed in writing; and

(3) The total fee is reasonable.

History of 37 C.F.R. §11.105: 78 FR 20202, Apr. 3, 2013.

§11.106. CONFIDENTIALITY OF INFORMATION

(a) A practitioner shall not reveal information relating to the representation of a client unless the client gives informed consent, the disclosure is impliedly authorized in order to carry out the representation, the disclosure is permitted by paragraph (b) of this section, or the disclosure is required by paragraph (c) of this section.

(b) A practitioner may reveal information relating to the representation of a client to the extent the practitioner reasonably believes necessary:

(1) To prevent reasonably certain death or substantial bodily harm;

(2) To prevent the client from engaging in inequitable conduct before the Office or from committing a crime or fraud that is reasonably certain to result in substantial injury to the financial interests or property of another and in furtherance of which the client has used or is using the practitioner's services;

(3) To prevent, mitigate or rectify substantial injury to the financial interests or property of another that is reasonably certain to result or has resulted from the client's commission of a crime, fraud, or inequitable conduct before the Office in furtherance of which the client has used the practitioner's services;

(4) To secure legal advice about the practitioner's compliance with the USPTO Rules of Professional Conduct;

(5) To establish a claim or defense on behalf of the practitioner in a controversy between the practitioner and the client, to establish a defense to a criminal charge or civil claim against the practitioner based upon conduct in which the client was involved, or to respond to allegations in any proceeding concerning the practitioner's representation of the client; or

(6) To comply with other law or a court order.

(c) A practitioner shall disclose to the Office information necessary to comply with applicable duty of disclosure provisions.

History of 37 C.F.R. §11.106: 78 FR 20203, Apr. 3, 2013.

§11.107. CONFLICT OF INTEREST; CURRENT CLIENTS

(a) Except as provided in paragraph (b) of this section, a practitioner shall not represent a client if the representation involves a concurrent conflict of interest. A concurrent conflict of interest exists if:

(1) The representation of one client will be directly adverse to another client; or

(2) There is a significant risk that the representation of one or more clients will be materially limited by the practitioner's responsibilities to another client, a former client or a third person or by a personal interest of the practitioner.

(b) Notwithstanding the existence of a concurrent conflict of interest under paragraph (a) of this section, a practitioner may represent a client if:

(1) The practitioner reasonably believes that the practitioner will be able to provide competent and diligent representation to each affected client;

(2) The representation is not prohibited by law;

(3) The representation does not involve the assertion of a claim by one client against another client represented by the practitioner in the same litigation or other proceeding before a tribunal; and

(4) Each affected client gives informed consent, confirmed in writing.

History of 37 C.F.R. §11.107: 78 FR 20203, Apr. 3, 2013.

§11.108. CONFLICT OF INTEREST; CURRENT CLIENTS; SPECIFIC RULES

(a) A practitioner shall not enter into a business transaction with a client or knowingly acquire an ownership, possessory, security or other pecuniary interest adverse to a client unless:

(1) The transaction and terms on which the practitioner acquires the interest are fair and reasonable to the client and are fully disclosed and transmitted in writing in a manner that can be reasonably understood by the client;

(2) The client is advised in writing of the desirability of seeking and is given a reasonable opportunity to seek the advice of independent legal counsel in the transaction; and

(3) The client gives informed consent, in a writing signed by the client, to the essential terms of the transaction and the practitioner's role in the transaction, including whether the practitioner is representing the client in the transaction.

(b) A practitioner shall not use information relating to representation of a client to the disadvantage of the client unless the client gives informed consent, except as permitted or required by the USPTO Rules of Professional Conduct.

(c) A practitioner shall not solicit any substantial gift from a client, including a testamentary gift, or prepare on behalf of a client an instrument giving the practitioner or a person related to the practitioner any substantial gift unless the practitioner or other recipient of the gift is related to the client. For purposes of this paragraph, related persons include a spouse, child, grandchild, parent, grandparent or other relative or individual with whom the practitioner or the client maintains a close, familial relationship.

(d) Prior to the conclusion of representation of a client, a practitioner shall not make or negotiate an agreement giving the practitioner literary or media rights to a portrayal or account based in substantial part on information relating to the representation.

(e) A practitioner shall not provide financial assistance to a client in connection with pending or contemplated litigation or a proceeding before the Office, except that:

(1) A practitioner may advance court costs and expenses of litigation, the repayment of which may be contingent on the outcome of the matter;

(2) A practitioner representing an indigent client may pay court costs and expenses of litigation or a proceeding before the Office on behalf of the client;

(3) A practitioner may advance costs and expenses in connection with a proceeding before the Office provided the client remains ultimately liable for such costs and expenses; and

(4) A practitioner may also advance any fee required to prevent or remedy an abandonment of a client's application by reason of an act or omission attributable to the practitioner and not to the client, whether or not the client is ultimately liable for such fee.

(f) A practitioner shall not accept compensation for representing a client from one other than the client unless:

(1) The client gives informed consent;

(2) There is no interference with the practitioner's independence of professional judgment or with the client-practitioner relationship; and

(3) Information relating to representation of a client is protected as required by §11.106.

(g) A practitioner who represents two or more clients shall not participate in making an aggregate settlement of the claims of or against the clients, unless each client gives informed consent, in a writing signed by the client. The practitioner's disclosure shall include the existence and nature of all the claims involved and of the participation of each person in the settlement.

(h) A practitioner shall not:

(1) Make an agreement prospectively limiting the practitioner's liability to a client for malpractice unless the client is independently represented in making the agreement; or

(2) Settle a claim or potential claim for such liability with an unrepresented client or former client unless that person is advised in writing of the desirability of seeking and is given a reasonable opportunity to seek the advice of independent legal counsel in connection therewith.

(i) A practitioner shall not acquire a proprietary interest in the cause of action, subject matter of litigation, or a proceeding before the Office which the practitioner is conducting for a client, except that the practitioner may, subject to the other provisions in this section:

(1) Acquire a lien authorized by law to secure the practitioner's fee or expenses;

(2) Contract with a client for a reasonable contingent fee in a civil case; and

(3) In a patent case or a proceeding before the Office, take an interest in the patent or patent application as part or all of his or her fee.

(j) [Reserved]

(k) While practitioners are associated in a firm, a prohibition in paragraphs (a) through (i) of this section that applies to any one of them shall apply to all of them.

History of 37 C.F.R. §11.108: 78 FR 20203, Apr. 3, 2013.

§11.109. DUTIES TO FORMER CLIENTS

(a) A practitioner who has formerly represented a client in a matter shall not thereafter represent another person in the same or a substantially related matter in which that person's interests are materially adverse to the interests of the former client unless the former client gives informed consent, confirmed in writing.

(b) A practitioner shall not knowingly represent a person in the same or a substantially related matter in which a firm with which the practitioner formerly was associated had previously represented a client:

(1) Whose interests are materially adverse to that person; and

(2) About whom the practitioner had acquired information protected by §§11.106 and 11.109(c) that is material to the matter; unless the former client gives informed consent, confirmed in writing.

(c) A practitioner who has formerly represented a client in a matter or whose present or former firm has formerly represented a client in a matter shall not thereafter:

(1) Use information relating to the representation to the disadvantage of the former client except as the USPTO Rules of Professional Conduct would permit or require with respect to a client, or when the information has become generally known; or

(2) Reveal information relating to the representation except as the USPTO Rules of Professional Conduct would permit or require with respect to a client.

History of 37 C.F.R. §11.109: 78 FR 20204, Apr. 3, 2013.

§11.110. IMPUTATION OF CONFLICTS OF INTEREST; GENERAL RULE

(a) While practitioners are associated in a firm, none of them shall knowingly represent a client when any one of them practicing alone would be prohibited from doing so by §§11.107 or 11.109, unless:

(1) The prohibition is based on a personal interest of the disqualified practitioner and does not present a significant risk of materially limiting the representation of the client by the remaining practitioners in the firm; or

(2) The prohibition is based upon §11.109(a) or (b), and arises out of the disqualified practitioner's association with a prior firm, and

(i) The disqualified practitioner is timely screened from any participation in the matter and is apportioned no part of the fee therefrom; and

(ii) Written notice is promptly given to any affected former client to enable the former client to ascertain compliance with the provisions of this section, which shall include a description of the screening procedures employed; a statement of the firm's and of the screened practitioner's compliance with the USPTO Rules of Professional Conduct; a statement that review may be available before a tribunal; and an agreement by the firm to respond promptly to any written inquiries or objections by the former client about the screening procedures.

(b) When a practitioner has terminated an association with a firm, the firm is not prohibited from thereafter representing a person with interests materially adverse to those of a client represented by the formerly associated practitioner and not currently represented by the firm, unless:

(1) The matter is the same or substantially related to that in which the formerly associated practitioner represented the client; and

(2) Any practitioner remaining in the firm has information protected by §§11.106 and 11.109(c) that is material to the matter.

(c) A disqualification prescribed by this section may be waived by the affected client under the conditions stated in §11.107.

(d) The disqualification of practitioners associated in a firm with former or current Federal Government lawyers is governed by §11.111.

History of 37 C.F.R. §11.110: 78 FR 20204, Apr. 3, 2013.

§11.111. FORMER OR CURRENT FEDERAL GOVERNMENT EMPLOYEES

A practitioner who is a former or current Federal Government employee shall not engage in any conduct which is contrary to applicable Federal ethics law, including conflict of interest statutes and regulations of the department, agency or commission formerly or currently employing said practitioner.

History of 37 C.F.R. §11.111: 78 FR 20204, Apr. 3, 2013.

§11.112. FORMER JUDGE, ARBITRATOR, MEDIATOR OR OTHER THIRD-PARTY NEUTRAL

(a) Except as stated in paragraph (d) of this section, a practitioner shall not represent anyone in connection with a matter in which the practitioner participated personally and substantially as a judge or other adjudicative officer or law clerk to such a person or as an arbitrator, mediator or other third-party neutral, unless all parties to the proceeding give informed consent, confirmed in writing.

(b) A practitioner shall not negotiate for employment with any person who is involved as a party or as practitioner for a party in a matter in which the practitioner is participating personally and substantially as a judge or other adjudicative officer or as an arbitrator, mediator or other third-party neutral. A practitioner serving as a law clerk to a judge or other adjudicative officer may negotiate for employment with a party or practitioner involved in a matter in which the clerk is participating personally and substantially, but only after the practitioner has notified the judge, or other adjudicative officer.

(c) If a practitioner is disqualified by paragraph (a) of this section, no practitioner in a firm with which that practitioner is associated may knowingly undertake or continue representation in the matter unless:

(1) The disqualified practitioner is timely screened from any participation in the matter and is apportioned no part of the fee therefrom; and

(2) Written notice is promptly given to the parties and any appropriate tribunal to enable them to ascertain compliance with the provisions of this section.

(d) An arbitrator selected as a partisan of a party in a multimember arbitration panel is not prohibited from subsequently representing that party.

History of 37 C.F.R. §11.112: 78 FR 20204, Apr. 3, 2013.

§11.113. ORGANIZATION AS CLIENT

(a) A practitioner employed or retained by an organization represents the organization acting through its duly authorized constituents.

(b) If a practitioner for an organization knows that an officer, employee or other person associated with the organization is engaged in action, intends to act or refuses to act in a matter related to the representation that is a violation of a legal obligation to the organization, or a violation of law that reasonably might be imputed to the organization, and that is likely to result in substantial injury to the organization, then the practitioner shall proceed as is reasonably necessary in the best interest of the organization. Unless the practitioner reasonably believes that it is not necessary in the best interest of the organization to do so, the practitioner shall refer the matter to higher authority in the organization, including, if warranted by the circumstances, to the highest authority that can act on behalf of the organization as determined by applicable law.

(c) Except as provided in paragraph (d) of this section, if

(1) Despite the practitioner's efforts in accordance with paragraph (b) of this section the highest authority that can act on behalf of the organization insists upon or fails to address in a timely and appropriate manner an action, or a refusal to act, that is clearly a violation of law, and

(2) The practitioner reasonably believes that the violation is reasonably certain to result in substantial injury to the organization, then the practitioner may reveal information relating to the representation whether or not §11.106 permits such disclosure, but only if and to the extent the practitioner reasonably believes necessary to prevent substantial injury to the organization.

(d) Paragraph (c) of this section shall not apply with respect to information relating to a practitioner's representation of an organization to investigate an alleged violation of law, or to defend the organization or an officer, employee or other constituent associated with the organization against a claim arising out of an alleged violation of law.

(e) A practitioner who reasonably believes that he or she has been discharged because of the practitioner's actions taken pursuant to paragraphs (b) or (c) of this section, or who withdraws under circumstances that require or permit the practitioner to take action under either of those paragraphs, shall proceed as the practitioner reasonably believes necessary to assure that the organization's highest authority is informed of the practitioner's discharge or withdrawal.

(f) In dealing with an organization's directors, officers, employees, members, shareholders, or other constituents, a practitioner shall explain the identity of the client when the practitioner knows or reasonably should know that the organization's interests are adverse to those of the constituents with whom the practitioner is dealing.

(g) A practitioner representing an organization may also represent any of its directors, officers, employees, members, shareholders or other constituents, subject to the provisions of §11.107. If the organization's consent to the dual representation is required by §11.107, the consent shall be given by an appropriate official of the organization other than the individual who is to be represented, or by the shareholders.

History of 37 C.F.R. §11.113: 78 FR 20204, Apr. 3, 2013.

§11.114. CLIENT WITH DIMINISHED CAPACITY

(a) When a client's capacity to make adequately considered decisions in connection with a representation is diminished, whether because of minority, mental impairment or for some other reason, the practitioner shall, as far as reasonably possible, maintain a normal client-practitioner relationship with the client.

(b) When the practitioner reasonably believes that the client has diminished capacity, is at risk of substantial physical, financial or other harm unless action is taken and cannot adequately act in the client's own interest, the practitioner may take reasonably necessary protective action, including consulting with individuals or entities that have the ability to take action to protect the client and, in appropriate cases, seeking the appointment of a guardian ad litem, conservator or guardian.

(c) Information relating to the representation of a client with diminished capacity is protected under §11.106. When taking protective action pursuant to paragraph (b) of this section, the practitioner is impliedly authorized under §11.106(a) to reveal information about the client, but only to the extent reasonably necessary to protect the client's interests.

History of 37 C.F.R. §11.114: 78 FR 20205, Apr. 3, 2013.

§11.115. SAFEKEEPING PROPERTY

(a) A practitioner shall hold property of clients or third persons that is in a practitioner's possession in connection with a representation separate from the practitioner's own property. Funds shall be kept in a separate account maintained in the state where the practitioner's office is situated, or elsewhere with the consent of the client or third person. Where the practitioner's office is situated in a foreign country, funds shall be kept in a separate account maintained in that foreign country or elsewhere with the consent of the client or third person. Other property shall be identified as such and appropriately safeguarded. Complete records of such account funds and other property shall be kept by the practitioner and shall be preserved for a period of five years after termination of the representation.

(b) A practitioner may deposit the practitioner's own funds in a client trust account for the sole purpose of paying bank service charges on that account, but only in an amount necessary for that purpose.

(c) A practitioner shall deposit into a client trust account legal fees and expenses that have been paid in advance, to be withdrawn by the practitioner only as fees are earned or expenses incurred.

(d) Upon receiving funds or other property in which a client or third person has an interest, a practitioner shall promptly notify the client or third person. Except as stated in this section or otherwise permitted by law or by agreement with the client, a practitioner shall promptly deliver to the client or third person any funds or other property that the client or third person is entitled to receive and, upon request by the client or third person, shall promptly render a full accounting regarding such property.

(e) When in the course of representation a practitioner is in possession of property in which two or more persons (one of whom may be the practitioner) claim interests, the property shall be kept separate by the practitioner until the dispute is resolved. The practitioner shall promptly distribute all portions of the property as to which the interests are not in dispute.

(f) All separate accounts for clients or third persons kept by a practitioner must also comply with the following provisions:

(1) Required records. The records to be kept include:

(i) Receipt and disbursement journals containing a record of deposits to and withdrawals from client trust accounts, specifically identifying the date, source, and description of each item deposited, as well as the date, payee and purpose of each disbursement;

(ii) Ledger records for all client trust accounts showing, for each separate trust client or beneficiary, the source of all funds deposited, the names of all persons for whom the funds are or were held, the amount of such funds, the descriptions and amounts of charges or withdrawals, and the names of all persons or entities to whom such funds were disbursed;

(iii) Copies of retainer and compensation agreements with clients;

(iv) Copies of accountings to clients or third persons showing the disbursement of funds to them or on their behalf;

(v) Copies of bills for legal fees and expenses rendered to clients;

(vi) Copies of records showing disbursements on behalf of clients;

(vii) The physical or electronic equivalents of all checkbook registers, bank statements, records of deposit, pre-numbered canceled checks, and substitute checks provided by a financial institution;

(viii) Records of all electronic transfers from client trust accounts, including the name of the person authorizing transfer, the date of transfer, the name of the recipient and confirmation from the financial institution of the trust account number from which money was withdrawn and the date and the time the transfer was completed;

(ix) Copies of monthly trial balances and quarterly reconciliations of the client trust accounts maintained by the practitioner; and

(x) Copies of those portions of client files that are reasonably related to client trust account transactions.

(2) Client trust account safeguards. With respect to client trust accounts required by paragraphs (a) through (e) of this section:

(i) Only a practitioner or a person under the direct supervision of the practitioner shall be an authorized signatory or authorize transfers from a client trust account;

(ii) Receipts shall be deposited intact and records of deposit should be sufficiently detailed to identify each item; and

(iii) Withdrawals shall be made only by check payable to a named payee and not to cash, or by authorized electronic transfer.

(3) Availability of records. Records required by paragraph (f)(1) of this section may be maintained by electronic, photographic, or other media provided that they otherwise comply with paragraphs (f)(1) and (f)(2) of this section and that printed copies can be produced. These records shall be readily accessible to the practitioner.

(4) Lawyers. The records kept by a lawyer are deemed to be in compliance with this section if the types of records that are maintained meet the recordkeeping requirements of a state in which the lawyer is licensed and in good standing, the recordkeeping requirements of the state where the lawyer's principal place of business is located, or the recordkeeping requirements of this section.

(5) Patent agents and persons granted limited recognition who are employed in the United States by a law firm. The records kept by a law firm employing one or more registered patent agents or persons granted limited recognition under §11.9 are deemed to be in compliance with this section if the types of records that are maintained meet the recordkeeping requirements of the state where at least one practitioner of the law firm is licensed and in good standing, the recordkeeping requirements of the state where the law firm's principal place of business is located, or the recordkeeping requirements of this section.

History of 37 C.F.R. §11.115: 78 FR 20205, Apr. 3, 2013.

§11.116. DECLINING OR TERMINATING REPRESENTATION

(a) Except as stated in paragraph (c) of this section, a practitioner shall not represent a client, or where representation has commenced, shall withdraw from the representation of a client if:

(1) The representation will result in violation of the USPTO Rules of Professional Conduct or other law;

(2) The practitioner's physical or mental condition materially impairs the practitioner's ability to represent the client; or

(3) The practitioner is discharged.

(b) Except as stated in paragraph (c) of this section, a practitioner may withdraw from representing a client if:

(1) Withdrawal can be accomplished without material adverse effect on the interests of the client;

(2) The client persists in a course of action involving the practitioner's services that the practitioner reasonably believes is criminal or fraudulent;

(3) The client has used the practitioner's services to perpetrate a crime or fraud;

(4) A client insists upon taking action that the practitioner considers repugnant or with which the practitioner has a fundamental disagreement;

(5) The client fails substantially to fulfill an obligation to the practitioner regarding the practitioner's services and has been given reasonable warning that the practitioner will withdraw unless the obligation is fulfilled;

(6) The representation will result in an unreasonable financial burden on the practitioner or has been rendered unreasonably difficult by the client; or

(7) Other good cause for withdrawal exists.

(c) A practitioner must comply with applicable law requiring notice to or permission of a tribunal when terminating a representation. When ordered to do so by a tribunal, a practitioner shall continue representation notwithstanding good cause for terminating the representation.

(d) Upon termination of representation, a practitioner shall take steps to the extent reasonably practicable to protect a client's interests, such as giving reasonable notice to the client, allowing time for employment of other counsel, surrendering papers and property to which the client is entitled and refunding any advance payment of fee or expense that has not been earned or incurred. The practitioner may retain papers relating to the client to the extent permitted by other law.

History of 37 C.F.R. §11.116: 78 FR 20206, Apr. 3, 2013.

§11.117. SALE OF LAW PRACTICE

A practitioner or a law firm may sell or purchase a law practice, or an area of law practice, including good will, if the following conditions are satisfied:

(a) The seller ceases to engage in the private practice of law, or in the area of practice that has been sold, in a geographic area in which the practice has been conducted;

(b)(1) Except as provided in paragraph (b)(2) of this section, the entire practice, or the entire area of practice, is sold to one or more lawyers or law firms;

(2) To the extent the practice or the area of practice involves patent proceedings before the Office, that practice or area of practice may be sold only to one or more registered practitioners or law firms that include at least one registered practitioner;

(c)(1) The seller gives written notice to each of the seller's clients regarding:

(i) The proposed sale;

(ii) The client's right to retain other counsel or to take possession of the file; and

(iii) The fact that the client's consent to the transfer of the client's files will be presumed if the client does not take any action or does not otherwise object within ninety (90) days after receipt of the notice.

(2) If a client cannot be given notice, the representation of that client may be transferred to the purchaser only upon entry of an order so authorizing by a court having jurisdiction. The seller may disclose to the court in camera information relating to the representation only to the extent necessary to obtain an order authorizing the transfer of a file; and

(d) The fees charged clients shall not be increased by reason of the sale.

History of 37 C.F.R. §11.117: 78 FR 20206, Apr. 3, 2013.

§11.118. DUTIES TO PROSPECTIVE CLIENT

(a) A person who discusses with a practitioner the possibility of forming a client-practitioner relationship with respect to a matter is a prospective client.

(b) Even when no client-practitioner relationship ensues, a practitioner who has had discussions with the prospective client shall not use or reveal information learned in the consultation, except as §11.109 would permit with respect to information of a former client.

(c) A practitioner subject to paragraph (b) of this section shall not represent a client with interests materially adverse to those of a prospective client in the same or a substantially related matter if the practitioner received information from the prospective client that could be significantly harmful to that person in the matter, except as provided in paragraph (d) of this section. If a practitioner is disqualified from representation under this paragraph, no practitioner in a firm with which that practitioner is associated may knowingly undertake or continue representation in such a matter, except as provided in paragraph (d) of this section.

(d) When the practitioner has received disqualifying information as defined in paragraph (c) of this section, representation is permissible if:

(1) Both the affected client and the prospective client have given informed consent, confirmed in writing; or

(2) The practitioner who received the information took reasonable measures to avoid exposure to more disqualifying information than was reasonably necessary to determine whether to represent the prospective client; and

(i) The disqualified practitioner is timely screened from any participation in the matter and is apportioned no part of the fee therefrom; and

(ii) Written notice is promptly given to the prospective client.

History of 37 C.F.R. §11.118: 78 FR 20206, Apr. 3, 2013.

§§11.119 TO 11.200. RESERVED

COUNSELOR

§11.201. ADVISOR

In representing a client, a practitioner shall exercise independent professional judgment and render candid advice. In rendering advice, a practitioner may refer not only to law but to other considerations such as moral, economic, social and political factors that may be relevant to the client's situation.

History of 37 C.F.R. §11.201: 78 FR 20207, Apr. 3, 2013.

§11.202. RESERVED

§11.203. EVALUATION FOR USE BY THIRD PERSONS

(a) A practitioner may provide an evaluation of a matter affecting a client for the use of someone other than the client if the practitioner reasonably believes that making the evaluation is compatible with other aspects of the practitioner's relationship with the client.

(b) When the practitioner knows or reasonably should know that the evaluation is likely to affect the client's interests materially and adversely, the practitioner shall not provide the evaluation unless the client gives informed consent.

(c) Except as disclosure is authorized in connection with a report of an evaluation, information relating to the evaluation is otherwise protected by §11.106.

History of 37 C.F.R. §11.203: 78 FR 20207, Apr. 3, 2013.

§11.204. PRACTITIONER SERVING AS THIRD-PARTY NEUTRAL

(a) A practitioner serves as a third-party neutral when the practitioner assists two or more persons who are not clients of the practitioner to reach a resolution of a dispute or other matter that has arisen between them. Service as a third-party neutral may include service as an arbitrator, a mediator or in such other capacity as will enable the practitioner to assist the parties to resolve the matter.

(b) A practitioner serving as a third-party neutral shall inform unrepresented parties that the practitioner is not representing them. When the practitioner knows or reasonably should know that a party does not understand the practitioner's role in the matter, the practitioner shall explain the difference between the practitioner's role as a third-party neutral and a practitioner's role as one who represents a client.

History of 37 C.F.R. §11.204: 78 FR 20207, Apr. 3, 2013.

§§11.205 TO 11.300. RESERVED

ADVOCATE

§11.301. MERITORIOUS CLAIMS & CONTENTIONS

A practitioner shall not bring or defend a proceeding, or assert or controvert an issue therein, unless there is a basis in law and fact for doing so that is not frivolous, which includes a good-faith argument for an extension, modification or reversal of existing law.

History of 37 C.F.R. §11.301: 78 FR 20207, Apr. 3, 2013.

§11.302. EXPEDITING PROCEEDINGS

A practitioner shall make reasonable efforts to expedite proceedings before a tribunal consistent with the interests of the client.

History of 37 C.F.R. §11.302: 78 FR 20207, Apr. 3, 2013.

§11.303. CANDOR TOWARD THE TRIBUNAL

(a) A practitioner shall not knowingly:

(1) Make a false statement of fact or law to a tribunal or fail to correct a false statement of material fact or law previously made to the tribunal by the practitioner;

(2) Fail to disclose to the tribunal legal authority in the controlling jurisdiction known to the practitioner to be directly adverse to the position of the client and not disclosed by opposing counsel in an inter partes proceeding, or fail to disclose such authority in an ex parte proceeding before the Office if such authority is not otherwise disclosed; or

(3) Offer evidence that the practitioner knows to be false. If a practitioner, the practitioner's client, or a witness called by the practitioner, has offered material evidence and the practitioner comes to know of its falsity, the practitioner shall take reasonable remedial measures, including, if necessary, disclosure to the tribunal. A practitioner may refuse to offer evidence that the practitioner reasonably believes is false.

(b) A practitioner who represents a client in a proceeding before a tribunal and who knows that a person intends to engage, is engaging or has engaged in criminal or fraudulent conduct related to the proceeding shall take reasonable remedial measures, including, if necessary, disclosure to the tribunal.

(c) The duties stated in paragraphs (a) and (b) of this section continue to the conclusion of the proceeding, and apply even if compliance requires disclosure of information otherwise protected by §11.106.

(d) In an ex parte proceeding, a practitioner shall inform the tribunal of all material facts known to the practitioner that will enable the tribunal to make an informed decision, whether or not the facts are adverse.

(e) In a proceeding before the Office, a practitioner shall disclose to the Office information necessary to comply with applicable duty of disclosure provisions.

History of 37 C.F.R. §11.303: 78 FR 20207, Apr. 3, 2013.

§11.304. FAIRNESS TO OPPOSING PARTY & COUNSEL

A practitioner shall not:

(a) Unlawfully obstruct another party's access to evidence or unlawfully alter, destroy or conceal a document or other material having potential evidentiary value. A practitioner shall not counsel or assist another person to do any such act;

(b) Falsify evidence, counsel or assist a witness to testify falsely, or offer an inducement to a witness that is prohibited by law;

(c) Knowingly disobey an obligation under the rules of a tribunal except for an open refusal based on an assertion that no valid obligation exists;

(d) Make a frivolous discovery request or fail to make a reasonably diligent effort to comply with a legally proper discovery request by an opposing party;

(e) In a proceeding before a tribunal, allude to any matter that the practitioner does not reasonably believe is relevant or that will not be supported by admissible evidence, assert personal knowledge of facts in issue except when testifying as a witness, or state a personal opinion as to the justness of a cause, the credibility of a witness, the culpability of a civil litigant or the guilt or innocence of an accused; or

(f) Request a person other than a client to refrain from voluntarily giving relevant information to another party unless:

(1) The person is a relative or an employee or other agent of a client; and

(2) The practitioner reasonably believes that the person's interests will not be adversely affected by refraining from giving such information.

History of 37 C.F.R. §11.304: 78 FR 20207, Apr. 3, 2013.

§11.305. IMPARTIALITY & DECORUM OF THE TRIBUNAL

A practitioner shall not:

(a) Seek to influence a judge, hearing officer, administrative law judge, administrative patent judge, administrative trademark judge, juror, prospective juror, employee or officer of the Office, or other official by means prohibited by law;

(b) Communicate ex parte with such a person during the proceeding unless authorized to do so by law, rule or court order; or

(c) [Reserved]

(d) Engage in conduct intended to disrupt any proceeding before a tribunal.

History of 37 C.F.R. §11.305: 78 FR 20208, Apr. 3, 2013.

§11.306. TRIAL PUBLICITY

(a) A practitioner who is participating or has participated in the investigation or litigation of a matter shall not make an extrajudicial statement that the practitioner knows or reasonably should know will be disseminated by means of public communication and will have a substantial likelihood of materially prejudicing an adjudicative proceeding in the matter.

(b) Notwithstanding paragraph (a) of this section, a practitioner may state:

(1) The claim, offense or defense involved and, except when prohibited by law, the identity of the persons involved;

(2) Information contained in a public record;

(3) That an investigation of a matter is in progress;

(4) The scheduling or result of any step in litigation;

(5) A request for assistance in obtaining evidence and information necessary thereto; and

(6) A warning of danger concerning the behavior of a person involved, when there is reason to believe that there exists the likelihood of substantial harm to an individual or to the public interest.

(c) Notwithstanding paragraph (a) of this section, a practitioner may make a statement that a reasonable practitioner would believe is required to protect a client from the substantial undue prejudicial effect of recent publicity not initiated by the practitioner or the practitioner's client. A statement made pursuant to this paragraph shall be limited to such information as is necessary to mitigate the recent adverse publicity.

(d) No practitioner associated in a firm or government agency with a practitioner subject to paragraph (a) of this section shall make a statement prohibited by paragraph (a).

History of 37 C.F.R. §11.306: 78 FR 20208, Apr. 3, 2013.

§11.307. PRACTITIONER AS WITNESS

(a) A practitioner shall not act as advocate at a proceeding before a tribunal in which the practitioner is likely to be a necessary witness unless:

(1) The testimony relates to an uncontested issue;

(2) The testimony relates to the nature and value of legal services rendered in the case; or

(3) Disqualification of the practitioner would work substantial hardship on the client.

(b) A practitioner may act as advocate in a proceeding before a tribunal in which another practitioner in the practitioner's firm is likely to be called as a witness unless precluded from doing so by §§11.107 or 11.109.

History of 37 C.F.R. §11.307: 78 FR 20208, Apr. 3, 2013.

§11.308. RESERVED

§11.309. ADVOCATE IN NONADJUDICATIVE PROCEEDINGS

A practitioner representing a client before a legislative body or administrative agency in a nonadjudicative proceeding shall disclose that the appearance is in a representative capacity and shall conform to the provisions of §§11.303(a) through (c), 11.304(a) through (c), and 11.305.

History of 37 C.F.R. §11.309: 78 FR 20208, Apr. 3, 2013.

§§11.310 TO 11.400. RESERVED

TRANSACTIONS WITH PERSONS OTHER THAN CLIENTS

§11.401. TRUTHFULNESS IN STATEMENTS TO OTHERS

In the course of representing a client, a practitioner shall not knowingly:

(a) Make a false statement of material fact or law to a third person; or

(b) Fail to disclose a material fact to a third person when disclosure is necessary to avoid assisting a criminal or fraudulent act by a client, unless disclosure is prohibited by §11.106.

History of 37 C.F.R. §11.401: 78 FR 20208, Apr. 3, 2013.

§11.402. COMMUNICATION WITH PERSON REPRESENTED BY A PRACTITIONER

(a) In representing a client, a practitioner shall not communicate about the subject of the representation with a person the practitioner knows to be represented by another practitioner in the matter, unless the practitioner has the consent of the other practitioner or is authorized to do so by law, rule, or a court order.

(b) This section does not prohibit communication by a practitioner with government officials who are otherwise represented by counsel and who have the authority to redress the grievances of the practitioner's client, provided that, if the communication relates to a matter for which the government official is represented, then prior to the communication the practitioner must disclose to such government official both the practitioner's identity and the fact that the practitioner represents a party with a claim against the government.

History of 37 C.F.R. §11.402: 78 FR 20208, Apr. 3, 2013.

§11.403. DEALING WITH UNREPRESENTED PERSON

In dealing on behalf of a client with a person who is not represented by a practitioner, a practitioner shall not state or imply that the practitioner is disinterested. When the practitioner knows or reasonably should know that the unrepresented person misunderstands the practitioner's role in the matter, the practitioner shall make reasonable efforts to correct the misunderstanding. The practitioner shall not give legal advice to an unrepresented person, other than the advice to secure counsel, if the practitioner knows or reasonably should know that the interests of such a person are or have a reasonable possibility of being in conflict with the interests of the client.

History of 37 C.F.R. §11.403: 78 FR 20208, Apr. 3, 2013.

§11.404. RESPECT FOR RIGHTS OF THIRD PERSONS

(a) In representing a client, a practitioner shall not use means that have no substantial purpose other than to embarrass, delay, or burden a third person, or use methods of obtaining evidence that violate the legal rights of such a person.

(b) A practitioner who receives a document or electronically stored information relating to the representation of the practitioner's client and knows or reasonably should know that the document or electronically stored information was inadvertently sent shall promptly notify the sender.

History of 37 C.F.R. §11.404: 78 FR 20208, Apr. 3, 2013.

§§11.405 TO 11.500. RESERVED

LAW FIRMS & ASSOCIATIONS

§11.501. RESPONSIBILITIES OF PARTNERS, MANAGERS, & SUPERVISORY PRACTITIONERS

(a) A practitioner who is a partner in a law firm, and a practitioner who individually or together with other practitioners possesses comparable managerial authority in a law firm, shall make reasonable efforts to ensure that the firm has in effect measures giving reasonable assurance that all practitioners in the firm conform to the USPTO Rules of Professional Conduct.

(b) A practitioner having direct supervisory authority over another practitioner shall make reasonable efforts to ensure that the other practitioner conforms to the USPTO Rules of Professional Conduct.

(c) A practitioner shall be responsible for another practitioner's violation of the USPTO Rules of Professional Conduct if:

(1) The practitioner orders or, with knowledge of the specific conduct, ratifies the conduct involved; or

(2) The practitioner is a partner or has comparable managerial authority in the law firm in which the other practitioner practices, or has direct supervisory authority over the other practitioner, and knows of the conduct at a time when its consequences can be avoided or mitigated but fails to take reasonable remedial action.

History of 37 C.F.R. §11.501: 78 FR 20208, Apr. 3, 2013.

§11.502. RESPONSIBILITIES OF A SUBORDINATE PRACTITIONER

(a) A practitioner is bound by the USPTO Rules of Professional Conduct notwithstanding that the practitioner acted at the direction of another person.

(b) A subordinate practitioner does not violate the USPTO Rules of Professional Conduct if that practitioner acts in accordance with a supervisory practitioner's reasonable resolution of an arguable question of professional duty.

History of 37 C.F.R. §11.502: 78 FR 20209, Apr. 3, 2013.

§11.503. RESPONSIBILITIES REGARDING NON-PRACTITIONER ASSISTANCE

With respect to a non-practitioner assistant employed or retained by or associated with a practitioner:

(a) A practitioner who is a partner, and a practitioner who individually or together with other practitioners possesses comparable managerial authority in a law firm shall make reasonable efforts to ensure that the firm has in effect measures giving reasonable assurance that the person's conduct is compatible with the professional obligations of the practitioner;

(b) A practitioner having direct supervisory authority over the non-practitioner assistant shall make reasonable efforts to ensure that the person's conduct is compatible with the professional obligations of the practitioner; and

(c) A practitioner shall be responsible for conduct of such a person that would be a violation of the USPTO Rules of Professional Conduct if engaged in by a practitioner if:

(1) The practitioner orders or, with the knowledge of the specific conduct, ratifies the conduct involved; or

(2) The practitioner is a partner or has comparable managerial authority in the law firm in which the person is employed, or has direct supervisory authority over the person, and knows of the conduct at a time when its consequences can be avoided or mitigated but fails to take reasonable remedial action.

History of 37 C.F.R. §11.503: 78 FR 20209, Apr. 3, 2013.

§11.504. PROFESSIONAL INDEPENDENCE OF A PRACTITIONER

(a) A practitioner or law firm shall not share legal fees with a non-practitioner, except that:

(1) An agreement by a practitioner with the practitioner's firm, partner, or associate may provide for the payment of money, over a reasonable period of time after the practitioner's death, to the practitioner's estate or to one or more specified persons;

(2) A practitioner who purchases the practice of a deceased, disabled, or disappeared practitioner may, pursuant to the provisions of §11.117, pay to the estate or other representative of that practitioner the agreed-upon purchase price;

(3) A practitioner or law firm may include non-practitioner employees in a compensation or retirement plan, even though the plan is based in whole or in part on a profit-sharing arrangement; and

(4) A practitioner may share legal fees, whether awarded by a tribunal or received in settlement of a matter, with a nonprofit organization that employed, retained or recommended employment of the practitioner in the matter and that qualifies under Section 501(c)(3) of the Internal Revenue Code.

(b) A practitioner shall not form a partnership with a non-practitioner if any of the activities of the partnership consist of the practice of law.

(c) A practitioner shall not permit a person who recommends, employs, or pays the practitioner to render legal services for another to direct or regulate the practitioner's professional judgment in rendering such legal services.

(d) A practitioner shall not practice with or in the form of a professional corporation or association authorized to practice law for a profit, if:

(1) A non-practitioner owns any interest therein, except that a fiduciary representative of the estate of a practitioner may hold the stock or interest of the practitioner for a reasonable time during administration;

(2) A non-practitioner is a corporate director or officer thereof or occupies the position of similar responsibility in any form of association other than a corporation; or

(3) A non-practitioner has the right to direct or control the professional judgment of a practitioner.

History of 37 C.F.R. §11.504: 78 FR 20209, Apr. 3, 2013.

§11.505. UNAUTHORIZED PRACTICE OF LAW

A practitioner shall not practice law in a jurisdiction in violation of the regulation of the legal profession in that jurisdiction, or assist another in doing so.

History of 37 C.F.R. §11.505: 78 FR 20209, Apr. 3, 2013.

§11.506. RESTRICTIONS ON RIGHT TO PRACTICE

A practitioner shall not participate in offering or making:

(a) A partnership, shareholders, operating, employment, or other similar type of agreement that restricts the right of a practitioner to practice after termination of the relationship, except an agreement concerning benefits upon retirement; or

(b) An agreement in which a restriction on the practitioner's right to practice is part of the settlement of a client controversy.

History of 37 C.F.R. §11.506: 78 FR 20209, Apr. 3, 2013.

§11.507. RESPONSIBILITIES REGARDING LAW-RELATED SERVICES

A practitioner shall be subject to the USPTO Rules of Professional Conduct with respect to the provision of law-related services if the law-related services are provided:

(a) By the practitioner in circumstances that are not distinct from the practitioner's provision of legal services to clients; or

(b) In other circumstances by an entity controlled by the practitioner individually or with others if the practitioner fails to take reasonable measures to assure that a person obtaining the law-related services knows that the services are not legal services and that the protections of the client-practitioner relationship do not exist.

History of 37 C.F.R. §11.507: 78 FR 20209, Apr. 3, 2013.

§§11.508 TO 11.700. RESERVED

INFORMATION ABOUT LEGAL SERVICES

§11.701. COMMUNICATIONS CONCERNING A PRACTITIONER'S SERVICES

A practitioner shall not make a false or misleading communication about the practitioner or the practitioner's services. A communication is false or misleading if it contains a material misrepresentation of fact or law, or omits a fact necessary to make the statement considered as a whole not materially misleading.

History of 37 C.F.R. §11.701: 78 FR 20209, Apr. 3, 2013.

§11.702. ADVERTISING

(a) Subject to the requirements of §§11.701 and 11.703, a practitioner may advertise services through written, recorded or electronic communication, including public media.

(b) A practitioner shall not give anything of value to a person for recommending the practitioner's services except that a practitioner may:

(1) Pay the reasonable costs of advertisements or communications permitted by this section;

(2) [Reserved]

(3) Pay for a law practice in accordance with §11.117; and

(4) Refer clients to another practitioner or a non-practitioner professional pursuant to an agreement not otherwise prohibited under the USPTO Rules of Professional Conduct that provides for the other person to refer clients or customers to the practitioner, if:

(i) The reciprocal referral agreement is not exclusive, and

(ii) The client is informed of the existence and nature of the agreement.

(c) Any communication made pursuant to this section shall include the name and office address of at least one practitioner or law firm responsible for its content.

History of 37 C.F.R. §11.702: 78 FR 20209, Apr. 3, 2013.

§11.703. DIRECT CONTACT WITH PROSPECTIVE CLIENTS

(a) A practitioner shall not by in-person, live telephone or real-time electronic contact solicit professional employment from a prospective client when a significant motive for the practitioner's doing so is the practitioner's pecuniary gain, unless the person contacted:

(1) Is a practitioner; or

(2) Has a family, close personal, or prior professional relationship with the practitioner.

(b) A practitioner shall not solicit professional employment from a prospective client by written, recorded or electronic communication or by in-person, telephone or real-time electronic contact even when not otherwise prohibited by paragraph (a) of this section, if:

(1) The prospective client has made known to the practitioner a desire not to be solicited by the practitioner; or

(2) The solicitation involves coercion, duress or harassment.

(c) Every written, recorded or electronic communication from a practitioner soliciting professional employment from a prospective client known to be in need of legal services in a particular matter shall include the words "Advertising Material" on the outside envelope, if any, and at the beginning and ending of any recorded or electronic communication, unless the recipient of the communication is a person specified in paragraphs (a)(1) or (a)(2) of this section.

(d) Notwithstanding the prohibitions in paragraph (a) of this section, a practitioner may participate with a prepaid or group legal service plan operated by an organization not owned or directed by the practitioner that uses in-person or telephone contact to solicit memberships or subscriptions for the plan from persons who are not known to need legal services in a particular matter covered by the plan.

History of 37 C.F.R. §11.703: 78 FR 20210, Apr. 3, 2013.

§11.704. COMMUNICATION OF FIELDS OF PRACTICE & SPECIALIZATION

(a) A practitioner may communicate the fact that the practitioner does or does not practice in particular fields of law.

(b) A registered practitioner who is an attorney may use the designation "Patents," "Patent Attorney," "Patent Lawyer," "Registered Patent Attorney," or a substantially similar designation. A registered practitioner who is not an attorney may use the designation "Patents," "Patent Agent," "Registered Patent Agent," or a substantially similar designation. Unless authorized by §11.14(b), a registered patent agent shall not hold himself or herself out as being qualified or authorized to practice before the Office in trademark matters or before a court.

(c) [Reserved]

(d) A practitioner shall not state or imply that a practitioner is certified as a specialist in a particular field of law, unless:

(1) The practitioner has been certified as a specialist by an organization that has been approved by an appropriate state authority or that has been accredited by the American Bar Association; and

(2) The name of the certifying organization is clearly identified in the communication.

(e) An individual granted limited recognition under §11.9 may use the designation "Limited Recognition."

History of 37 C.F.R. §11.704: 78 FR 20210, Apr. 3, 2013.

§11.705. FIRM NAMES & LETTERHEADS

(a) A practitioner shall not use a firm name, letterhead or other professional designation that violates §11.701. A trade name may be used by a practitioner in private practice if it does not imply a connection with a government agency or with a public or charitable legal services organization and is not otherwise in violation of §11.701.

(b) [Reserved]

(c) The name of a practitioner holding a public office shall not be used in the name of a law firm, or in communications on its behalf, during any substantial period in which the practitioner is not actively and regularly practicing with the firm.

History of 37 C.F.R. §11.705: 78 FR 20210, Apr. 3, 2013.

§§11.706 TO 11.800. RESERVED

MAINTAINING THE INTEGRITY OF THE PROFESSION

§11.801. REGISTRATION, RECOGNITION & DISCIPLINARY MATTERS

An applicant for registration or recognition to practice before the Office, or a practitioner in connection with an application for registration or recognition, or a practitioner in connection with a disciplinary or reinstatement matter, shall not:

(a) Knowingly make a false statement of material fact; or

(b) Fail to disclose a fact necessary to correct a misapprehension known by the person to have arisen in the matter, fail to cooperate with the Office of Enrollment and Discipline in an investigation of any matter before it, or knowingly fail to respond to a lawful demand or request for information from an admissions or disciplinary authority, except that the provisions of this section do not require disclosure of information otherwise protected by §11.106.

History of 37 C.F.R. §11.801: 78 FR 20210, Apr. 3, 2013.

§11.802. JUDICIAL & LEGAL OFFICIALS

(a) A practitioner shall not make a statement that the practitioner knows to be false or with reckless disregard as to its truth or falsity concerning the qualifications or integrity of a judge, adjudicatory officer or public legal officer, or of a candidate for election or appointment to judicial or legal office.

(b) A practitioner who is a candidate for judicial office shall comply with the applicable provisions of the Code of Judicial Conduct.

History of 37 C.F.R. §11.802: 78 FR 20210, Apr. 3, 2013.

§11.803. REPORTING PROFESSIONAL MISCONDUCT

(a) A practitioner who knows that another practitioner has committed a violation of the USPTO Rules of Professional Conduct that raises a substantial question as to that practitioner's honesty, trustworthiness or fitness as a practitioner in other respects, shall inform the OED Director and any other appropriate professional authority.

(b) A practitioner who knows that a judge, hearing officer, administrative law judge, administrative patent judge, or administrative trademark judge has committed a violation of applicable rules of judicial conduct that raises a substantial question as to the individual's fitness for office shall inform the appropriate authority.

(c) The provisions of this section do not require disclosure of information otherwise protected by §11.106 or information gained while participating in an approved lawyers assistance program.

History of 37 C.F.R. §11.803: 78 FR 20210, Apr. 3, 2013.

§11.804. MISCONDUCT

It is professional misconduct for a practitioner to:

(a) Violate or attempt to violate the USPTO Rules of Professional Conduct, knowingly assist or induce another to do so, or do so through the acts of another;

(b) Commit a criminal act that reflects adversely on the practitioner's honesty, trustworthiness or fitness as a practitioner in other respects;

(c) Engage in conduct involving dishonesty, fraud, deceit or misrepresentation;

(d) Engage in conduct that is prejudicial to the administration of justice;

(e) State or imply an ability to influence improperly a government agency or official or to achieve results by means that violate the USPTO Rules of Professional Conduct or other law;

(f) Knowingly assist a judge, hearing officer, administrative law judge, administrative patent judge, administrative trademark judge, or judicial officer in conduct that is a violation of applicable rules of judicial conduct or other law;

(g) Knowingly assist an officer or employee of the Office in conduct that is a violation of applicable rules of conduct or other law;

(h) Be publicly disciplined on ethical or professional misconduct grounds by any duly constituted authority of:

(1) A State,

(2) The United States, or

(3) The country in which the practitioner resides; or

(i) Engage in other conduct that adversely reflects on the practitioner's fitness to practice before the Office.

History of 37 C.F.R. §11.804: 78 FR 20211, Apr. 3, 2013.

§§11.805 TO 11.900. RESERVED

§11.901. SAVINGS CLAUSE

(a) A disciplinary proceeding based on conduct engaged in prior to the effective date of these regulations may be instituted subsequent to such effective date, if such conduct would continue to justify disciplinary sanctions under the provisions of this part.

(b) No practitioner shall be subject to a disciplinary proceeding under this part based on conduct engaged in before the effective date hereof if such conduct would not have been subject to disciplinary action before such effective date.

History of 37 C.F.R. §11.901: 78 FR 20211, Apr. 3, 2013.

PARTS 15, 15A. RESERVED

PART 41. PRACTICE BEFORE THE PATENT TRIAL & APPEAL BOARD

SUBPART A. GENERAL PROVISIONS

§41.1. POLICY

(a) Scope. Part 41 governs appeals and interferences before the Patent Trial and Appeal Board. Sections 1.1 to 1.36 and 1.181 to 1.183 of this title also apply to practice before the Board, as do other sections of part 1 of this title that are incorporated by reference into part 41.

(b) Construction. The provisions of Part 41 shall be construed to secure the just, speedy, and inexpensive resolution of every proceeding before the Board.

(c) Decorum. Each party must act with courtesy and decorum in all proceedings before the Board, including interactions with other parties.

History of 37 C.F.R. §41.1: 69 FR 50003, Aug. 12, 2004, as amended at 77 FR 46630, Aug. 6, 2012.

Source of 37 C.F.R. Part 41A: 69 FR 50003, Aug. 12, 2004, unless otherwise noted.

§41.2. DEFINITIONS

Unless otherwise clear from the context, the following definitions apply to proceedings under this part:

Affidavit means affidavit, declaration under §1.68 of this title, or statutory declaration under 28 U.S.C. 1746. A transcript of an ex parte deposition may be used as an affidavit in a contested case.

Board means the Patent Trial and Appeal Board and includes:

(1) For a final Board action:

(i) In an appeal or contested case, a panel of the Board.

(ii) In a proceeding under §41.3, the Chief Administrative Patent Judge or another official acting under an express delegation from the Chief Administrative Patent Judge.

(2) For non-final actions, a Board member or employee acting with the authority of the Board.

Board member means the Under Secretary of Commerce for Intellectual Property and Director of the United States Patent and Trademark Office, the Deputy Under Secretary of Commerce for Intellectual Property and Deputy Director of the United States Patent and Trademark Office, the Commissioner for Patents, the Commissioner for Trademarks, and the administrative patent judges.

Contested case means a Board proceeding other than an appeal under 35 U.S.C. 134 or a petition under §41.3. An appeal in an inter partes reexamination is not a contested case.

Final means, with regard to a Board action, final for the purposes of judicial review. A decision is final only if:

(1) In a panel proceeding. The decision is rendered by a panel, disposes of all issues with regard to the party seeking judicial review, and does not indicate that further action is required; and

(2) In other proceedings. The decision disposes of all issues or the decision states it is final.

Hearing means consideration of the issues of record. Rehearing means reconsideration.

Office means United States Patent and Trademark Office.

Panel means at least three Board members acting in a panel proceeding.

Panel proceeding means a proceeding in which final action is reserved by statute to at least three Board members, but includes a non-final portion of such a proceeding whether administered by a panel or not.

Party, in this part, means any entity participating in a Board proceeding, other than officers and employees of the Office, including:

(1) An appellant;

(2) A participant in a contested case;

(3) A petitioner; and

(4) Counsel for any of the above, where context permits.

History of 37 C.F.R. §41.2: 69 FR 50003, Aug. 12, 2004, as amended at 77 FR 46630, Aug. 6, 2012.

§41.3. PETITIONS

(a) Deciding official. Petitions must be addressed to the Chief Administrative Patent Judge. A panel or an administrative patent judge may certify a question of policy to the Chief Administrative Patent Judge for decision. The Chief Administrative Patent Judge may delegate authority to decide petitions.

(b) Scope. This section covers petitions on matters pending before the Board (§§41.35, 41.64, 41.103, and 41.205); otherwise, see §§1.181 to 1.183 of this title. The following matters are not subject to petition:

(1) Issues committed by statute to a panel, and

(2) In pending contested cases, procedural issues. See §41.121(a)(3) and §41.125(c).

(c) Petition fee. The fee set in §41.20(a) must accompany any petition under this section except no fee is required for a petition under this section seeking supervisory review.

(d) Effect on proceeding. The filing of a petition does not stay the time for any other action in a Board proceeding.

(e) Time for action.

(1) Except as otherwise provided in this part or as the Board may authorize in writing, a party may:

(i) File the petition within 14 days from the date of the action from which the party is requesting relief, and

(ii) File any request for reconsideration of a petition decision within 14 days of the decision on petition or such other time as the Board may set.

(2) A party may not file an opposition or a reply to a petition without Board authorization.

History of 37 C.F.R. §41.3: 69 FR 58260, Sept. 30, 2004.

§41.4. TIMELINESS

(a) Extensions of time. Extensions of time will be granted only on a showing of good cause except as otherwise provided by rule.

(b) Late filings.

(1) A late filing that results in either an application becoming abandoned or a reexamination prosecution becoming terminated under §1.550(d) or 1.957(b) of this title or limited under §1.957(c) of this title may be revived as set forth in §1.137 of this title.

(2) A late filing that does not result in either an application becoming abandoned or a reexamination prosecution becoming terminated under §1.550(d) or 1.957(b) of this title or limited under §1.957(c) of this title will be excused upon a showing of excusable neglect or a Board determination that consideration on the merits would be in the interest of justice.

(c) Scope. This section governs all proceedings before the Board, but does not apply to filings related to Board proceedings before or after the Board has jurisdiction, such as:

(1) Extensions during prosecution (see §1.136 of this title),

(2) Filing of a brief or request for oral hearing (see §§41.37, 41.41, 41.47, 41.67, 41.68, 41.71 and 41.73), or

(3) Seeking judicial review (see §§1.301 to 1.304 of this title).

History of 37 C.F.R. §41.4: 72 FR 18907, May 16, 2007.

§41.5. COUNSEL

While the Board has jurisdiction:

(a) Appearance pro hac vice. The Board may authorize a person other than a registered practitioner to appear as counsel in a specific proceeding.

(b) Disqualification.

(1) The Board may disqualify counsel in a specific proceeding after notice and an opportunity to be heard.

(2) A decision to disqualify is not final for the purposes of judicial review until certified by the Chief Administrative Patent Judge.

(c) Withdrawal. Counsel may not withdraw from a proceeding before the Board unless the Board authorizes such withdrawal. See §11.116 of this subchapter regarding conditions for withdrawal.

(d) Procedure. The Board may institute a proceeding under this section on its own or a party in a contested case may request relief under this section.

(e) Referral to the Director of Enrollment and Discipline. Possible violations of the disciplinary rules in part 11 of this subchapter may be referred to the Office of Enrollment and Discipline for investigation. See §11.22 of this subchapter.

History of 37 C.F.R. §41.5: 73 FR 47704, Sept. 15, 2008; 78 FR 20211, Apr. 3, 2013.

§41.6. PUBLIC AVAILABILITY OF BOARD RECORDS

(a) Publication.

(1) Generally. Any Board action is available for public inspection without a party's permission if rendered in a file open to the public pursuant to §1.11 of this title or in an application that has been published in accordance with §§1.211 to 1.221 of this title. The Office may independently publish any Board action that is available for public inspection.

(2) Determination of special circumstances. Any Board action not publishable under paragraph (a)(1) of this section may be published or made available for public inspection if the Director believes that special circumstances warrant publication and a party does not, within two months after being notified of the intention to make the action public, object in writing on the ground that the action discloses the objecting party's trade secret or other confidential information and states with specificity that such information is not otherwise publicly available. If the action discloses such information, the party shall identify the deletions in the text of the action considered necessary to protect the information. If the affected party considers that the entire action must be withheld from the public to protect such information, the party must explain why. The party will be given time, not less than twenty days, to request reconsideration and seek court review before any contested portion of the action is made public over its objection.

(b) Record of proceeding.

(1) The record of a Board proceeding is available to the public unless a patent application not otherwise available to the public is involved.

(2) Notwithstanding paragraph (b)(1) of this section, after a final Board action in or judgment in a Board proceeding, the record of the Board proceeding will be made available to the public if any involved file is or becomes open to the public under §1.11 of this title or an involved application is or becomes published under §§1.211 to 1.221 of this title.

§41.7. MANAGEMENT OF THE RECORD

(a) The Board may expunge any paper directed to a Board proceeding, or filed while an application or patent is under the jurisdiction of the Board, that is not authorized under this part or in a Board order, or that is filed contrary to a Board order.

(b) A party may not file a paper previously filed in the same Board proceeding, not even as an exhibit or appendix, without Board authorization or as required by rule.

§41.8. MANDATORY NOTICES

(a) In an appeal brief (§§41.37, 41.67, or 41.68) or at the initiation of a contested case (§41.101), and within 20 days of any change during the proceeding, a party must identify:

(1) Its real party-in-interest, and

(2) Each judicial or administrative proceeding that could affect, or be affected by, the Board proceeding.

(b) For contested cases, a party seeking judicial review of a Board proceeding must file a notice with the Board of the judicial review within 20 days of the filing of the complaint or the notice of appeal. The notice to the Board must include a copy of the complaint or notice of appeal. See also §§1.301 to 1.304 of this title.

§41.9. ACTION BY OWNER

(a) Entire interest. An owner of the entire interest in an application or patent involved in a Board proceeding may act in the proceeding to the exclusion of the inventor (see §§3.71 and 3.73 of this title).

(b) Part interest. An owner of a part interest in an application or patent involved in a Board proceeding may petition to act in the proceeding to the exclusion of an inventor or a co-owner. The petition must show the inability or refusal of an inventor or co-owner to prosecute the proceeding or other cause why it is in the interest of justice to permit the owner of a part interest to act in the proceeding. An order granting the petition may set conditions on the actions of the parties during the proceeding.

History of 37 C.F.R. §41.9: 69 FR 50003, Aug. 12, 2004, as amended at 77 FR 48826, Aug. 14, 2012.

§41.10. CORRESPONDENCE ADDRESSES

Except as the Board may otherwise direct,

(a) Appeals. Correspondence in an application or a patent involved in an appeal (subparts B and C of this part) during the period beginning when an appeal docketing notice is issued and ending when a decision has been rendered by the Board, as well as any request for rehearing of a decision by the Board, shall be mailed to: Patent Trial and Appeal Board, United States Patent and Trademark Office, PO Box 1450, Alexandria, Virginia 22313-1450. Notices of appeal, appeal briefs, reply briefs, requests for oral hearing, as well as all other correspondence in an application or a patent involved in an appeal to the Board for which an address is not otherwise specified, should be addressed as set out in §1.1(a)(1)(i) of this title.

(b) Interferences. Mailed correspondence in interference (subpart D of this part) shall be sent to Mail Stop INTERFERENCE, Patent Trial and Appeal Board, United States Patent and Trademark Office, PO Box 1450, Alexandria, Virginia 22313-1450.

(c) Trial Proceedings. Correspondence in trial proceedings (part 42 of this title) are governed by §42.6(b) of this title.

History of 37 C.F.R. §41.10: 77 FR 46630, Sept. 16, 2012.

§41.11. EX PARTE COMMUNICATIONS IN INTER PARTES PROCEEDINGS

An ex parte communication about an inter partes reexamination (subpart C of this part) or about a contested case (subparts D and E of this part) with a Board member, or with a Board employee assigned to the proceeding, is not permitted.

§41.12. CITATION OF AUTHORITY

(a) For any United States Supreme Court decision, citation to the United States Reports is preferred.

(b) For any decision other than a United States Supreme Court decision, citation to the West Reporter System is preferred.

(c) Citations to authority must include pinpoint citations whenever a specific holding or portion of an authority is invoked.

(d) Non-binding authority should be used sparingly. If the authority is not an authority of the Office and is not reproduced in the United States Reports or the West Reporter System, a copy of the authority should be provided.

History of 37 C.F.R. §41.12: 76 FR 72296, Nov. 22, 2011.

A §41.20. FEES

(a) Petition fee. The fee for filing a petition under this part is: $400.00.

(b) Appeal fees. **(1)** For filing a notice of appeal from the examiner to the Patent Trial and Appeal Board:

By a micro entity (§1.29)—$200.00

By a small entity (§1.27(a))—$400.00

By other than a small or micro entity—$800.00

(2)(i) For filing a brief in support of an appeal in an application or ex parte reexamination proceeding: $0.00.

(ii) In addition to the fee for filing a notice of appeal, for filing a brief in support of an appeal in an inter partes reexamination proceeding:

By a micro entity (§1.29)—$500.00

By a small entity (§1.27(a))—$1,000.00

By other than a small or micro entity—$2,000.00

(3) For filing a request for an oral hearing before the Board in an appeal under 35 U.S.C. 134:

By a micro entity (§1.29)—$325.00

By a small entity (§1.27(a))—$650.00

By other than a small or micro entity—$1,300.00

(4) In addition to the fee for filing a notice of appeal, for forwarding an appeal in an application or ex parte reexamination proceeding to the Board:

By a micro entity (§1.29 of this chapter)—$560.00

By a small entity (§1.27(a) of this chapter)—$1,120.00

By other than a small or micro entity—$2,240.00

History of 37 C.F.R. §41.20: 69 FR 52606, Aug. 27, 2004; 69 FR 55506, Sept. 15, 2004; 69 FR 56546, Sept. 21, 2004; 70 FR 3892, Jan. 27, 2005; 72 FR 46903, Sept. 30, 2007; 73 FR 47542, Oct. 2, 2008; 77 FR 54366, Oct. 5, 2012; 78 FR 4290, Mar. 19, 2013; 82 FR 52817, Jan. 16, 2018.

SUBPART B. EX PARTE APPEALS

§41.30. DEFINITIONS

In addition to the definitions in §41.2, the following definitions apply to proceedings under this subpart unless otherwise clear from the context:

Applicant means either the applicant in a national application for a patent or the applicant in an application for reissue of a patent.

Evidence means something (including testimony, documents and tangible objects) that tends to prove or disprove the existence of an alleged fact, except that for the purpose of this subpart Evidence does not include dictionaries, which may be cited before the Board.

Owner means the owner of the patent undergoing ex parte reexamination under §1.510 of this title.

Proceeding means either a national application for a patent, an application for reissue of a patent, an ex parte reexamination proceeding, or a trial before the Patent Trial and Appeal Board. Appeal to the Board in an inter partes reexamination proceeding is controlled by subpart C of this part.

Record means the items listed in the content listing of the Image File Wrapper of the official file of the application or reexamination proceeding on appeal or the official file of the Office if other than the Image File Wrapper, excluding amendments, Evidence, and other documents that were not entered. In the case of an issued patent being reissued or reexamined, the Record further includes the Record of the patent being reissued or reexamined.

History of 37 C.F.R. §41.30: 76 FR 72296, Nov. 22, 2011; 77 FR 46630, Sept. 16, 2012.

Source of 37 C.F.R. Part 41B: 69 FR 50003, Aug. 12, 2004, unless otherwise noted.

§41.31. APPEAL TO BOARD

(a) Who may appeal and how to file an appeal. An appeal is taken to the Board by filing a notice of appeal.

(1) Every applicant, any of whose claims has been twice rejected, may appeal from the decision of the examiner to the Board by filing a notice of appeal accompanied by the fee set forth in §41.20(b)(1) within the time period provided under §1.134 of this title for reply.

(2) Every owner of a patent under ex parte reexamination filed under §1.510 of this title before November 29, 1999, any of whose claims has been twice rejected, may appeal from the decision of the examiner to the Board by filing a notice of appeal accompanied by the fee set forth in §41.20(b)(1) within the time period provided under §1.134 of this title for reply.

(3) Every owner of a patent under ex parte reexamination filed under §1.510 of this title on or after November 29, 1999, any of whose claims has been finally (§1.113 of this title) rejected, may appeal from the decision of the examiner to the Board by filing a notice of appeal accompanied by the fee set forth in §41.20(b)(1) within the time period provided under §1.134 of this title for reply.

(b) The signature requirements of §§1.33 and 11.18(a) of this title do not apply to a notice of appeal filed under this section.

(c) An appeal, when taken, is presumed to be taken from the rejection of all claims under rejection unless cancelled by an amendment filed by the applicant and entered by the Office. Questions relating to matters not affecting the merits of the invention may be required to be settled before an appeal can be considered.

(d) The time periods set forth in paragraphs (a)(1) through (a)(3) of this section are extendable under the provisions of §1.136 of this title for patent applications and §1.550(c) of this title for ex parte reexamination proceedings.

History of 37 C.F.R. §41.31: 76 FR 72296, Nov. 22, 2011.

§41.33. AMENDMENTS & AFFIDAVITS OR OTHER EVIDENCE AFTER APPEAL

(a) Amendments filed after the date of filing an appeal pursuant to §41.31(a)(1) through (a)(3) and prior to the date a brief is filed pursuant to §41.37 may be admitted as provided in §1.116 of this title.

(b) Amendments filed on or after the date of filing a brief pursuant to §41.37 may be admitted:

(1) To cancel claims, where such cancellation does not affect the scope of any other pending claim in the proceeding, or

(2) To rewrite dependent claims into independent form.

(c) All other amendments filed after the date of filing an appeal pursuant to §41.31(a)(1) through (a)(3) will not be admitted except as permitted by §§41.39(b)(1), 41.50(a)(2)(i), and 41.50(b)(1).

(d)(1) An affidavit or other Evidence filed after the date of filing an appeal pursuant to §41.31(a)(1) through (a)(3) and prior to the date of filing a brief pursuant to §41.37 may be admitted if the examiner determines that the affidavit or other Evidence overcomes all rejections under appeal and that a showing of good and sufficient reasons why the affidavit or other Evidence is necessary and was not earlier presented has been made.

(2) All other affidavits or other Evidence filed after the date of filing an appeal pursuant to §41.31(a)(1) through (a)(3) will not be admitted except as permitted by §§41.39(b)(1), 41.50(a)(2)(i), and 41.50(b)(1).

History of 37 C.F.R. §41.33: 76 FR 72296, Nov. 22, 2011.

§41.35. JURISDICTION OVER APPEAL

(a) Beginning of jurisdiction. Jurisdiction over the proceeding passes to the Board upon the filing of a reply brief under §41.41 or the expiration of the time in which to file such a reply brief, whichever is earlier.

(b) End of jurisdiction. The jurisdiction of the Board ends when:

(1) The Director or the Board enters a remand order (see §§41.35(c), 41.35(e), and 41.50(a)(1)),

(2) The Board enters a final decision (see §41.2) and judicial review is sought or the time for seeking judicial review has expired,

(3) An express abandonment which complies with §1.138 of this title is recognized,

(4) A request for continued examination is filed which complies with §1.114 of this title,

(5) Appellant fails to take any required action under §§41.39(b), 41.50(a)(2), 41.50(b), or 41.50(d), and the Board enters an order of dismissal, or

(6) Appellant reopens prosecution pursuant to §41.40(b) or in response to a new ground of rejection entered in a decision of the Board (see §41.50(b)(1)).

(c) Remand ordered by the Director. Prior to the entry of a decision on the appeal by the Board (see §41.50), the Director may sua sponte order the proceeding remanded to the examiner.

(d) Documents filed during Board's jurisdiction. Except for petitions authorized by this part, consideration of any information disclosure statement or petition filed while the Board possesses jurisdiction over the proceeding will be held in abeyance until the Board's jurisdiction ends.

(e) Administrative remands ordered by the Board. If, after receipt and review of the proceeding, the Board determines that the file is not complete or is not in compliance with the requirements of this subpart, the Board may relinquish jurisdiction to the examiner or take other appropriate action to permit completion of the file.

History of 37 C.F.R. §41.35: 76 FR 72297, Nov. 22, 2011.

§41.37. APPEAL BRIEF

(a) Timing. Appellant must file a brief under this section within two months from the date of filing the notice of appeal under §41.31. The appeal brief fee in an application or ex parte reexamination proceeding is $0.00, but if the appeal results in an examiner's answer, the appeal forwarding fee set forth in §41.20(b)(4) must be paid within the time period specified in §41.45 to avoid dismissal of an appeal.

(b) Failure to file a brief. On failure to file the brief within the period specified in paragraph (a) of this section, the appeal will stand dismissed.

(c) Content of appeal brief.

(1) Except as otherwise provided in this paragraph, the brief shall contain the following items under appropriate headings and in the order indicated in paragraphs (c)(1)(i) through (v) of this section, except that a brief filed by an appellant who is not represented by a registered practitioner need only substantially comply with paragraphs (c)(1)(i), (c)(1)(ii), (c)(1)(iv), and (c)(1)(v) of this section:

(i) Real party in interest. A statement identifying by name the real party in interest at the time the appeal brief is filed, except that such statement is not required if the named inventor or inventors are themselves the real party in interest. If an appeal brief does not contain a statement of the real party in interest, the Office may assume that the named inventor or inventors are the real party in interest.

(ii) Related appeals, interferences, and trials. A statement identifying by application, patent, appeal, interference, or trial number all other prior and pending appeals, interferences, trials before the Board, or judicial proceedings (collectively, "related cases") which satisfy all of the following conditions: involve an application or patent owned by the appellant or assignee, are known to appellant, the appellant's legal representative, or assignee, and may be related to, directly affect or be directly affected by or have a bearing on the Board's decision in the pending appeal, except that such statement is not required if there are no such related cases. If an appeal brief does not contain a statement of related cases, the Office may assume that there are no such related cases.

(iii) Summary of claimed subject matter. A concise explanation of the subject matter defined in each of the rejected independent claims, which shall refer to the specification in the Record by page and line number or by paragraph number, and to the drawing, if any, by reference characters. For each rejected independent claim, and for each dependent claim argued separately under the provisions of paragraph (c)(1)(iv) of this section, if the claim contains a means plus function or step plus function recitation as permitted by 35 U.S.C. 112(f), then the concise explanation must identify the structure, material, or acts described in the specification in the Record as corresponding to each claimed function with reference to the specification in the Record by page and line number or by paragraph number, and to the drawing, if any, by reference characters. Reference to the patent application publication does not satisfy the requirements of this paragraph.

(iv) Argument. The arguments of appellant with respect to each ground of rejection, and the basis therefor, with citations of the statutes, regulations, authorities, and parts of the Record relied on. The arguments shall explain why the examiner erred as to each ground of rejection contested by appellant. Except as provided for in §§41.41, 41.47 and 41.52, any arguments or authorities not included in the appeal brief will be refused consideration by the Board for purposes of the present appeal. Each ground of rejection contested by appellant must be argued under a separate heading, and each heading shall reasonably identify the ground of rejection being contested (e.g., by claim number, statutory basis, and applied reference, if any). For each ground of rejection applying to two or more claims, the claims may be argued separately (claims are considered by appellant as separately patentable), as a group (all claims subject to the ground of rejection stand or fall together), or as a subgroup (a subset of the claims subject to the ground of rejection stand or fall together). When multiple claims subject to the same ground of rejection are argued as a group or subgroup by appellant, the Board may select a single claim from the group or subgroup and may decide the appeal as to the ground of rejection with respect to the group or subgroup on the basis of the selected claim alone. Notwithstanding any other provision of this paragraph, the failure of appellant to separately argue claims which appellant has grouped together shall constitute a waiver of any argument that the Board must consider the patentability of any grouped claim separately. Under each heading identifying the ground of rejection being contested, any claim(s) argued separately or as a subgroup shall be argued under a separate subheading that identifies the claim(s) by number. A statement which merely points out what a claim recites will not be considered an argument for separate patentability of the claim.

(v) Claims appendix. An appendix containing a copy of the claims involved in the appeal.

(2) A brief shall not include any new or non-admitted amendment, or any new or non-admitted affidavit or other Evidence. See §1.116 of this title for treatment of amendments, affidavits or other evidence filed after final action but before or on the same date of filing an appeal and §41.33 for treatment of amendments, affidavits or other Evidence filed after the date of filing the appeal. Review of an examiner's refusal to admit an amendment or Evidence is by petition to the Director. See §1.181 of this title.

(d) Notice of non-compliance. If a brief is filed which does not comply with all the requirements of paragraph (c) of this section, appellant will be notified of the reasons for non-compliance and given a time period within which to file an amended brief. If appellant does not, within the set time period, file an amended brief that overcomes all the reasons for non-compliance stated in the notification, the appeal will stand dismissed. Review of a determination of non-compliance is by petition to the Chief Administrative Patent Judge. See §41.3.

(e) Extensions of time. The time periods set forth in this section are extendable under the provisions of §1.136 of this title for patent applications and §1.550(c) of this title for ex parte reexamination proceedings.

History of 37 C.F.R. §41.37: 76 FR 72297, Nov. 22, 2011; 77 FR 46630, Sept. 16, 2012; 78 FR 4291, Mar. 19, 2013; 78 FR 17107, Mar. 20, 2013.

§41.39. EXAMINER'S ANSWER

(a) Content of examiner's answer. The primary examiner may, within such time as may be directed by the Director, furnish a written answer to the appeal brief.

(1) An examiner's answer is deemed to incorporate all of the grounds of rejection set forth in the Office action from which the appeal is taken (as modified by any advisory action and pre-appeal brief conference decision), unless the examiner's answer expressly indicates that a ground of rejection has been withdrawn.

(2) An examiner's answer may include a new ground of rejection. For purposes of the examiner's answer, any rejection that relies upon any Evidence not relied upon in the Office action from which the appeal is taken (as modified by any advisory action) shall be designated by the primary examiner as a new ground of rejection. The examiner must obtain the approval of the Director to furnish an answer that includes a new ground of rejection.

(b) Appellant's response to new ground of rejection. If an examiner's answer contains a rejection designated as a new ground of rejection, appellant must within two months from the date of the examiner's answer exercise one of the following two options to avoid sua sponte dismissal of the appeal as to the claims subject to the new ground of rejection:

(1) Reopen prosecution. Request that prosecution be reopened before the primary examiner by filing a reply under §1.111 of this title with or without amendment or submission of affidavits (§§1.130, 1.131 or 1.132 of this of this[1] title) or other Evidence. Any amendment or submission of affidavits or other Evidence must be relevant to the new ground of rejection. A request that complies with this paragraph will be entered and the application or the patent under ex parte reexamination will be reconsidered by the examiner under the provisions of §1.112 of this title. Any request that prosecution be reopened under this paragraph will be treated as a request to withdraw the appeal.

(2) Maintain appeal. Request that the appeal be maintained by filing a reply brief as set forth in §41.41. Such a reply brief must address as set forth in §41.37(c)(1)(iv) each new ground of rejection and should follow the other requirements of a brief as set forth in §41.37(c). A reply brief may not be accompanied by any amendment, affidavit (§§1.130, 1.131 or 1.132 of this of this[1] title) or other Evidence. If a reply brief filed pursuant to this section is accompanied by any amendment, affidavit or other Evidence, it shall be treated as a request that prosecution be reopened before the primary examiner under paragraph (b)(1) of this section.

(c) Extensions of time. Extensions of time under §1.136(a) of this title for patent applications are not applicable to the time period set forth in this section. See §1.136(b) of this title for extensions of time to reply for patent applications and §1.550(c) of this title for extensions of time to reply for ex parte reexamination proceedings.

1. **Editor's note:** The second "of this" probably should not appear.
History of 37 C.F.R. §41.39: 76 FR 72298, Nov. 22, 2011.

§41.40. TOLLING OF TIME PERIOD TO FILE A REPLY BRIEF

(a) Timing. Any request to seek review of the primary examiner's failure to designate a rejection as a new ground of rejection in an examiner's answer must be by way of a petition to the Director under §1.181 of this title filed within two months from the entry of the examiner's answer and before the filing of any reply brief. Failure of appellant to timely file such a petition will constitute a waiver of any arguments that a rejection must be designated as a new ground of rejection.

(b) Petition granted and prosecution reopened. A decision granting a petition under §1.181 to designate a new ground of rejection in an examiner's answer will provide a two-month time period in which appellant must file a reply under §1.111 of this title to reopen the prosecution before the primary examiner. On failure to timely file a reply under §1.111, the appeal will stand dismissed.

(c) Petition not granted and appeal maintained. A decision refusing to grant a petition under §1.181 of this title to designate a new ground of rejection in an examiner's answer will provide a two-month time period in which appellant may file only a single reply brief under §41.41.

(d) Withdrawal of petition and appeal maintained. If a reply brief under §41.41 is filed within two months from the date of the examiner's answer and on or after the filing of a petition under §1.181 to designate a new ground of rejection in an examiner's answer, but before a decision on the petition, the reply brief will be treated as a request to withdraw the petition and to maintain the appeal.

(e) Extensions of time. Extensions of time under §1.136(a) of this title for patent applications are not applicable to the time period set forth in this section. See §1.136(b) of this title for extensions of time to reply for patent applications and §1.550(c) of this title for extensions of time to reply for ex parte reexamination proceedings.

History of 37 C.F.R. §41.40: 76 FR 72298, Nov. 22, 2011.

§41.41. REPLY BRIEF

(a) Timing. Appellant may file only a single reply brief to an examiner's answer within the later of two months from the date of either the examiner's answer, or a decision refusing to grant a petition under §1.181 of this title to designate a new ground of rejection in an examiner's answer.

(b) Content.

(1) A reply brief shall not include any new or non-admitted amendment, or any new or non-admitted affidavit or other Evidence. See §1.116 of this title for amendments, affidavits or other evidence filed after final action but before or on the same date of filing an appeal and §41.33 for amendments, affidavits or other Evidence filed after the date of filing the appeal.

(2) Any argument raised in the reply brief which was not raised in the appeal brief, or is not responsive to an argument raised in the examiner's answer, including any designated new ground of rejection, will not be considered by the Board for purposes of the present appeal, unless good cause is shown.

(c) Extensions of time. Extensions of time under §1.136(a) of this title for patent applications are not applicable to the time period set forth in this section. See §1.136(b) of this title for extensions of time to reply for patent applications and §1.550(c) of this title for extensions of time to reply for ex parte reexamination proceedings.

History of 37 C.F.R. §41.41: 76 FR 72298, Nov. 22, 2011.

§41.43. REMOVED

§41.45. APPEAL FORWARDING FEE

(a) Timing. Appellant in an application or ex parte reexamination proceeding must pay the fee set forth in §41.20(b)(4) within the later of two months from the date of either the examiner's answer, or a decision refusing to grant a petition under §1.181 of this chapter to designate a new ground of rejection in an examiner's answer.

(b) Failure to pay appeal forwarding fee. On failure to pay the fee set forth in §41.20(b)(4) within the period specified in paragraph (a) of this section, the appeal will stand dismissed.

(c) Extensions of time. Extensions of time under §1.136(a) of this title for patent applications are not applicable to the time period set forth in this section. See §1.136(b) of this title for extensions of time to reply for patent applications and §1.550(c) of this title for extensions of time to reply for ex parte reexamination proceedings.

History of 37 C.F.R. §41.45: 78 FR 4291, Mar. 19, 2013; 78 FR 17107, Mar. 20, 2013.

§41.47. ORAL HEARING

(a) An oral hearing should be requested only in those circumstances in which appellant considers such a hearing necessary or desirable for a proper presentation of the appeal. An appeal decided on the briefs without an oral hearing will receive the same consideration by the Board as appeals decided after an oral hearing.

(b) If appellant desires an oral hearing, appellant must file, as a separate paper captioned "REQUEST FOR ORAL HEARING," a written request for such hearing accompanied by the fee set forth in §41.20(b)(3) within two months from the date of the examiner's answer or on the date of filing of a reply brief, whichever is earlier.

(c) If no request and fee for oral hearing have been timely filed by appellant as required by paragraph (b) of this section, the appeal will be assigned for consideration and decision on the briefs without an oral hearing.

(d) If appellant has complied with all the requirements of paragraph (b) of this section, a date for the oral hearing will be set, and due notice thereof given to appellant. If an oral hearing is held, an oral argument may be presented by, or on behalf of, the primary examiner if considered desirable by either the primary examiner or the Board. A hearing will be held as stated in the notice, and oral argument will ordinarily be limited to twenty minutes for appellant and fifteen minutes for the primary examiner unless otherwise ordered.

(e)(1) Appellant will argue first and may reserve time for rebuttal. At the oral hearing, appellant may only rely on Evidence that has been previously entered and considered by the primary examiner and present argument that has been relied upon in the brief or reply brief except as permitted by paragraph (e)(2) of this section. The primary examiner may only rely on argument and Evidence relied upon in an answer except as permitted by paragraph (e)(2) of this section.

(2) Upon a showing of good cause, appellant and/or the primary examiner may rely on a new argument based upon a recent relevant decision of either the Board or a Federal Court.

(f) Notwithstanding the submission of a request for oral hearing complying with this rule, if the Board decides that a hearing is not necessary, the Board will so notify appellant.

(g) Extensions of time under §1.136(a) of this title for patent applications are not applicable to the time periods set forth in this section. See §1.136(b) of this title for extensions of time to reply for patent applications and §1.550(c) of this title for extensions of time to reply for ex parte reexamination proceedings.

History of 37 C.F.R. §41.47: 76 FR 72298, Nov. 22, 2011.

§41.50. DECISIONS & OTHER ACTIONS BY THE BOARD

(a)(1) Affirmance and reversal. The Board, in its decision, may affirm or reverse the decision of the examiner in whole or in part on the grounds and on the claims specified by the examiner. The affirmance of the rejection of a claim on any of the grounds specified constitutes a general affirmance of the decision of the examiner on that claim, except as to any ground specifically reversed. The Board may also remand an application to the examiner.

(2) If a substitute examiner's answer is written in response to a remand by the Board for further consideration of a rejection pursuant to paragraph (a)(1) of this section, the appellant must within two months from the date of the substitute examiner's answer exercise one of the following two options to avoid sua sponte dismissal of the appeal as to the claims subject to the rejection for which the Board has remanded the proceeding:

(i) Reopen prosecution. Request that prosecution be reopened before the examiner by filing a reply under §1.111 of this title with or without amendment or submission of affidavits (§§1.130, 1.131 or 1.132 of this title) or other Evidence. Any amendment or submission of affidavits or other Evidence must be relevant to the issues set forth in the remand or raised in the substitute examiner's answer. A request that complies with this paragraph (a) will be entered and the application or the patent under ex parte reexamination will be reconsidered by the examiner under the provisions of §1.112 of this title. Any request that prosecution be reopened under this paragraph will be treated as a request to withdraw the appeal.

(ii) Maintain appeal. Request that the appeal be maintained by filing a reply brief as provided in §41.41. If such a reply brief is accompanied by any amendment, affidavit or other Evidence, it shall be treated as a request that prosecution be reopened before the examiner under paragraph (a)(2)(i) of this section.

(b) New ground of rejection. Should the Board have knowledge of any grounds not involved in the appeal for rejecting any pending claim, it may include in its opinion a statement to that effect with its reasons for so holding, and designate such a statement as a new ground of rejection of the claim. A new ground of rejection pursuant to this paragraph shall not be considered final for judicial review. When the Board enters such a non-final decision, the appellant, within two months from the date of the decision, must exercise one of the following two options with respect to the new ground of rejection to avoid termination of the appeal as to the rejected claims:

(1) Reopen prosecution. Submit an appropriate amendment of the claims so rejected or new Evidence relating to the claims so rejected, or both, and have the matter reconsidered by the examiner, in which event the prosecution will be remanded to the examiner. The new ground of rejection is binding upon the examiner unless an amendment or new Evidence not previously of Record is made which, in the opinion of the examiner, overcomes the new ground of rejection designated in the decision. Should the examiner reject the claims, appellant may again appeal to the Board pursuant to this subpart.

(2) Request rehearing. Request that the proceeding be reheard under §41.52 by the Board upon the same Record. The request for rehearing must address any new ground of rejection and state with particularity the points believed to have been misapprehended or overlooked in entering the new ground of rejection and also state all other grounds upon which rehearing is sought.

(c) Review of undesignated new ground of rejection. Any request to seek review of a panel's failure to designate a new ground of rejection in its decision must be raised by filing a request for rehearing as set forth in §41.52. Failure of appellant to timely file such a request for rehearing will constitute a waiver of any arguments that a decision contains an undesignated new ground of rejection.

(d) Request for briefing and information. The Board may order appellant to additionally brief any matter that the Board considers to be of assistance in reaching a reasoned decision on the pending appeal. Appellant will be given a time period within which to respond to such an order. Failure to timely comply with the order may result in the sua sponte dismissal of the appeal.

(e) Remand not final action. Whenever a decision of the Board includes a remand, that decision shall not be considered final for judicial review. When appropriate, upon conclusion of proceedings on remand before the examiner, the Board may enter an order otherwise making its decision final for judicial review.

(f) Extensions of time. Extensions of time under §1.136(a) of this title for patent applications are not applicable to the time periods set forth in this section. See §1.136(b) of this title for extensions of time to reply for patent applications and §1.550(c) of this title for extensions of time to reply for ex parte reexamination proceedings.

History of 37 C.F.R. §41.50: 76 FR 72299, Nov. 22, 2011.

§41.52. REHEARING

(a)(1) Appellant may file a single request for rehearing within two months of the date of the original decision of the Board. No request for rehearing from a decision on rehearing will be permitted, unless the rehearing decision so modified the original decision as to become, in effect, a new decision, and the Board states that a second request for rehearing would be permitted. The request for rehearing must state with particularity the points believed to have been misapprehended or overlooked by the Board. Arguments not raised, and Evidence not previously relied upon, pursuant to §§41.37, 41.41, or 41.47 are not permitted in the request for rehearing except as permitted by paragraphs (a)(2) through (a)(4) of this section. When a request for rehearing is made, the Board shall render a decision on the request for rehearing. The decision on the request for rehearing is deemed to incorporate the earlier opinion reflecting its decision for appeal, except for those portions specifically withdrawn on rehearing, and is final for the purpose of judicial review, except when noted otherwise in the decision on rehearing.

(2) Appellant may present a new argument based upon a recent relevant decision of either the Board or a Federal Court.

(3) New arguments responding to a new ground of rejection designated pursuant to §41.50(b) are permitted.

(4) New arguments that the Board's decision contains an undesignated new ground of rejection are permitted.

(b) Extensions of time under §1.136(a) of this title for patent applications are not applicable to the time period set forth in this section. See §1.136(b) of this title for extensions of time to reply for patent applications and §1.550(c) of this title for extensions of time to reply for ex parte reexamination proceedings.

History of 37 C.F.R. §41.52: 76 FR 72299, Nov. 22, 2011.

§41.54. ACTION FOLLOWING DECISION

After decision by the Board, jurisdiction over an application or patent under ex parte reexamination proceeding passes to the examiner, subject to appellant's right of appeal or other review, for such further action by appellant or by the examiner, as the condition of the application or patent under ex parte reexamination proceeding may require, to carry into effect the decision.

History of 37 C.F.R. §41.54: 76 FR 72299, Nov. 22, 2011.

SUBPART C. INTER PARTES APPEALS

§41.60. DEFINITIONS

In addition to the definitions in §41.2, the following definitions apply to proceedings under this subpart unless otherwise clear from the context:

Appellant means any party, whether the owner or a requester, filing a notice of appeal or cross appeal under §41.61. If more than one party appeals or cross appeals, each appealing or cross appealing party is an appellant with respect to the claims to which his or her appeal or cross appeal is directed.

Filing means filing with a certificate indicating service of the document under §1.903 of this title.

Owner means the owner of the patent undergoing inter partes reexamination under §1.915 of this title.

Proceeding means an inter partes reexamination proceeding. Appeal to the Board in an ex parte reexamination proceeding is controlled by subpart B of this part. An inter partes reexamination proceeding is not a contested case subject to subpart D.

Requester means each party, other than the owner, who requested that the patent undergo inter partes reexamination under §1.915 of this title.

Respondent means any requester responding under §41.68 to the appellant's brief of the owner, or the owner responding under §41.68 to the appellant's brief of any requester. No requester may be a respondent to the appellant brief of any other requester.

Source of 37 C.F.R. Part 41C: 69 FR 50003, Aug. 12, 2004, unless otherwise noted.

§41.61. NOTICE OF APPEAL & CROSS APPEAL TO BOARD

(a)(1) Upon the issuance of a Right of Appeal Notice under §1.953 of this title, the owner may appeal to the Board with respect to the final rejection of any claim of the patent by filing a notice of appeal within the time provided in the Right of Appeal Notice and paying the fee set forth in §41.20(b)(1).

(2) Upon the issuance of a Right of Appeal Notice under §1.953 of this title, the requester may appeal to the Board with respect to any final decision favorable to the patentability, including any final determination not to make a proposed rejection, of any original, proposed amended, or new claim of the patent by filing a notice of appeal within the time provided in the Right of Appeal Notice and paying the fee set forth in §41.20(b)(1).

(b)(1) Within fourteen days of service of a requester's notice of appeal under paragraph (a)(2) of this section and upon payment of the fee set forth in §41.20(b)(1), an owner who has not filed a notice of appeal may file a notice of cross appeal with respect to the final rejection of any claim of the patent.

(2) Within fourteen days of service of an owner's notice of appeal under paragraph (a)(1) of this section and upon payment of the fee set forth in §41.20(b)(1), a requester who has not filed a notice of appeal may file a notice of cross appeal with respect to any final decision favorable to the patentability, including any final determination not to make a proposed rejection, of any original, proposed amended, or new claim of the patent.

(c) The notice of appeal or cross appeal in the proceeding must identify the appealed claim(s) and must be signed by the owner, the requester, or a duly authorized attorney or agent.

(d) An appeal or cross appeal, when taken, must be taken from all the rejections of the claims in a Right of Appeal Notice which the patent owner proposes to contest or from all the determinations favorable to patentability, including any final determination not to make a proposed rejection, in a Right of Appeal Notice which a requester proposes to contest. Questions relating to matters not affecting the merits of the invention may be required to be settled before an appeal is decided.

(e) The time periods for filing a notice of appeal or cross appeal may not be extended.

(f) If a notice of appeal or cross appeal is timely filed but does not comply with any requirement of this section, appellant will be notified of the reasons for non-compliance and given a non-extendable time period within which to file an amended notice of appeal or cross appeal. If the appellant does not then file an amended notice of appeal or cross appeal within the set time period, or files a notice which does not overcome all the reasons for non-compliance stated in the notification of the reasons for non-compliance, that appellant's appeal or cross appeal will stand dismissed.

§41.63. AMENDMENTS & AFFIDAVITS OR OTHER EVIDENCE AFTER APPEAL

(a) Amendments filed after the date of filing an appeal pursuant to §41.61 canceling claims may be admitted where such cancellation does not affect the scope of any other pending claim in the proceeding.

(b) All other amendments filed after the date of filing an appeal pursuant to §41.61 will not be admitted except as permitted by §41.77(b)(1).

(c) Affidavits or other evidence filed after the date of filing an appeal pursuant to §41.61 will not be admitted except as permitted by reopening prosecution under §41.77(b)(1).

§41.64. JURISDICTION OVER APPEAL IN INTER PARTES REEXAMINATION

(a) Jurisdiction over the proceeding passes to the Board upon transmittal of the file, including all briefs and examiner's answers, to the Board.

(b) If, after receipt and review of the proceeding, the Board determines that the file is not complete or is not in compliance with the requirements of this subpart, the Board may relinquish jurisdiction to the examiner or take other appropriate action to permit completion of the file.

(c) Prior to the entry of a decision on the appeal by the Board, the Director may sua sponte order the proceeding remanded to the examiner.

§41.66. TIME FOR FILING BRIEFS

(a) An appellant's brief must be filed no later than two months from the latest filing date of the last-filed notice of appeal or cross appeal or, if any party to the proceeding is entitled to file an appeal or cross appeal but fails to timely do so, no later than two months from the expiration of the time for filing (by the last party entitled to do so) such notice of appeal or cross appeal. The time for filing an appellant's brief or an amended appellant's brief may not be extended.

(b) Once an appellant's brief has been properly filed, any brief must be filed by respondent within one month from the date of service of the appellant's brief. The time for filing a respondent's brief or an amended respondent's brief may not be extended.

(c) The examiner will consider both the appellant's and respondent's briefs and may prepare an examiner's answer under §41.69.

(d) Any appellant may file a rebuttal brief under §41.71 within one month of the date of the examiner's answer. The time for filing a rebuttal brief or an amended rebuttal brief may not be extended.

(e) No further submission will be considered and any such submission will be treated in accordance with §1.939 of this title.

§41.67. APPELLANT'S BRIEF

(a)(1) Appellant(s) may once, within time limits for filing set forth in §41.66, file a brief and serve the brief on all other parties to the proceeding in accordance with §1.903 of this title.

(2) The brief must be signed by the appellant, or the appellant's duly authorized attorney or agent and must be accompanied by the requisite fee set forth in §41.20(b)(2).

(b) An appellant's appeal shall stand dismissed upon failure of that appellant to file an appellant's brief, accompanied by the requisite fee, within the time allowed under §41.66(a).

(c)(1) The appellant's brief shall contain the following items under appropriate headings and in the order indicated in paragraphs (c)(1)(i) through (c)(1)(xi) of this section.

(i) Real party in interest. A statement identifying by name the real party in interest.

(ii) Related appeals, interferences, and trials. A statement identifying by application, patent, appeal, interference, or trial number all other prior and pending appeals, interferences, trials before the Board, or judicial proceedings known to appellant, the appellant's legal representative, or assignee which may be related to, directly affect or be directly affected by or have a bearing on the Board's decision in the pending appeal. Copies of any decisions rendered by a court or the Board in any proceeding identified under this paragraph must be included in an appendix as required by paragraph (c)(1)(xi) of this section.

(iii) Status of claims. A statement of the status of all the claims in the proceeding (*e.g.*, rejected, allowed or confirmed, withdrawn, objected to, canceled). If the appellant is the owner, the appellant must also identify the rejected claims whose rejection is being appealed. If the appellant is a requester, the appellant must identify the claims that the examiner has made a determination favorable to patentability, which determination is being appealed.

(iv) Status of amendments. A statement of the status of any amendment filed subsequent to the close of prosecution.

(v) Summary of claimed subject matter. A concise explanation of the subject matter defined in each of the independent claims involved in the appeal, which shall refer to the specification by column and line number, and to the drawing(s), if any, by reference characters. For each independent claim involved in the appeal and for each dependent claim argued separately under the provisions of paragraph (c)(1)(vii) of this section, every means plus function and step plus function as permitted by 35 U.S.C. 112(f), must be identified and the structure, material, or acts described in the specification as corresponding to each claimed function must be set forth with reference to the specification by page and line number, and to the drawing, if any, by reference characters.

(vi) Issues to be reviewed on appeal. A concise statement of each issue presented for review. No new ground of rejection can be proposed by a third party requester appellant, unless such ground was withdrawn by the examiner during the prosecution of the proceeding, and the third party requester has not yet had an opportunity to propose it as a third party requester proposed ground of rejection.

(vii) Argument. The contentions of appellant with respect to each issue presented for review in paragraph (c)(1)(vi) of this section, and the basis therefor, with citations of the statutes, regulations, authorities, and parts of the record relied on. Any arguments or authorities not included in the brief permitted under this section or §§41.68 and 41.71 will be refused consideration by the Board, unless good cause is shown. Each issue must be treated under a separate heading. If the appellant is the patent owner, for each ground of rejection in the Right of Appeal Notice which appellant contests and which applies to two or more claims, the claims may be argued separately or as a group. When multiple claims subject to the same ground of rejection are argued as a group by appellant, the Board may select a single claim from the group of claims that are argued together to decide the appeal with respect to the group of claims as to the ground of rejection on the basis of the selected claim alone. Notwithstanding any other provision of this paragraph, the failure of appellant to separately argue claims which appellant has grouped together shall constitute a waiver of any argument that the Board must consider the patentability of any grouped claim separately. Any claim argued separately should be placed under a subheading identifying the claim by number. Claims argued as a group should be placed under a subheading identifying the claims by number. A statement which merely points out what a claim recites will not be considered an argument for separate patentability of the claim.

(viii) Claims appendix. An appendix containing a copy of the claims to be reviewed on appeal.

(ix) Evidence appendix. An appendix containing copies of any evidence submitted pursuant to §§1.130, 1.131, or 1.132 of this title or of any other evidence entered by the examiner and relied upon by appellant in the appeal, along with a statement setting forth where in the record that evidence was entered in the record by the examiner. Reference to unentered evidence is not permitted in the brief. See §41.63 for treatment of evidence submitted after appeal. This appendix may also include copies of the evidence relied upon by the examiner in any ground of rejection to be reviewed on appeal.

(x) Related proceedings appendix. An appendix containing copies of decisions rendered by a court or the Board in any proceeding identified pursuant to paragraph (c)(1)(ii) of this section.

(xi) Certificate of service. A certification that a copy of the brief has been served in its entirety on all other parties to the reexamination proceeding. The names and addresses of the parties served must be indicated.

(2) A brief shall not include any new or non-admitted amendment, or any new or non-admitted affidavit or other evidence. See §1.116 of this title for amendments, affidavits or other evidence filed after final action but before or on the same date of filing an appeal and §41.63 for amendments, affidavits or other evidence after the date of filing the appeal.

(d) If a brief is filed which does not comply with all the requirements of paragraph (a) and paragraph (c) of this section, appellant will be notified of the reasons for non-compliance and given a non-extendable time period within which to file an amended brief. If appellant does not file an amended brief within the set time period, or files an amended brief which does not overcome all the reasons for non-compliance stated in the notification, that appellant's appeal will stand dismissed.

History of 37 C.F.R. §41.67: 69 FR 50003, Aug. 12, 2004, as amended at 77 FR 46630, Aug. 6, 2012.

§41.68. RESPONDENT'S BRIEF

(a)(1) Respondent(s) in an appeal may once, within the time limit for filing set forth in §41.66, file a respondent brief and serve the brief on all parties in accordance with §1.903 of this title.

(2) The brief must be signed by the party, or the party's duly authorized attorney or agent, and must be accompanied by the requisite fee set forth in §41.20(b)(2).

(3) The respondent brief shall be limited to issues raised in the appellant brief to which the respondent brief is directed.

(4) A requester's respondent brief may not address any brief of any other requester.

(b)(1) The respondent brief shall contain the following items under appropriate headings and in the order here indicated, and may include an appendix containing only those portions of the record on which reliance has been made.

(i) Real Party in Interest. A statement identifying by name the real party in interest.

(ii) Related Appeals, Interferences, and trials. A statement identifying by application, patent, appeal, interference, or trial number all other prior and pending appeals, interferences or judicial proceedings known to respondent, the respondent's legal representative, or assignee which may be related to, directly affect or be directly affected by or have a bearing on the Board's decision in the pending appeal. Copies of any decisions rendered by a court or the Board in any proceeding identified under this paragraph must be included in an appendix as required by paragraph (b)(1)(ix) of this section.

(iii) Status of claims. A statement accepting or disputing appellant's statement of the status of claims. If appellant's statement of the status of claims is disputed, the errors in appellant's statement must be specified with particularity.

(iv) Status of amendments. A statement accepting or disputing appellant's statement of the status of amendments. If appellant's statement of the status of amendments is disputed, the errors in appellant's statement must be specified with particularity.

(v) Summary of claimed subject matter. A statement accepting or disputing appellant's summary of the subject matter defined in each of the independent claims involved in the appeal. If appellant's summary of the subject matter is disputed, the errors in appellant's summary must be specified.

(vi) Issues to be reviewed on appeal. A statement accepting or disputing appellant's statement of the issues presented for review. If appellant's statement of the issues presented for review is disputed, the errors in appellant's statement must be specified. A counter statement of the issues for review may be made. No new ground of rejection can be proposed by a requester respondent.

(vii) Argument. A statement accepting or disputing the contentions of appellant with each of the issues presented by the appellant for review. If a contention of the appellant is disputed, the errors in appellant's argument must be specified, stating the basis therefor, with citations of the statutes, regulations, authorities, and parts of the record relied on. Each issue must be treated under a separate heading. An argument may be made with each of the issues stated in the counter statement of the issues, with each counter-stated issue being treated under a separate heading.

(viii) Evidence appendix. An appendix containing copies of any evidence submitted pursuant to §§1.130, 1.131, or 1.132 of this title or of any other evidence entered by the examiner and relied upon by respondent in the appeal, along with a statement setting forth where in the record that evidence was entered in the record by the examiner. Reference to unentered evidence is not permitted in the respondent's brief. See §41.63 for treatment of evidence submitted after appeal.

(ix) Related proceedings appendix. An appendix containing copies of decisions rendered by a court or the Board in any proceeding identified pursuant to paragraph (b)(1)(ii) of this section.

(x) Certificate of service. A certification that a copy of the respondent brief has been served in its entirety on all other parties to the reexamination proceeding. The names and addresses of the parties served must be indicated.

(2) A respondent brief shall not include any new or non-admitted amendment, or any new or non-admitted affidavit or other evidence. See §1.116 of this title for amendments, affidavits or other evidence filed after final action but before or on the same date of filing an appeal and §41.63 for amendments, affidavits or other evidence filed after the date of filing the appeal.

(c) If a respondent brief is filed which does not comply with all the requirements of paragraph (a) and paragraph (b) of this section, respondent will be notified of the reasons for non-compliance and given a non-extendable time period within which to file an amended brief. If respondent does not file an amended respondent brief within the set time period, or files an amended respondent brief which does not overcome all the reasons for non-compliance stated in the notification, the respondent brief and any amended respondent brief by that respondent will not be considered.

History of 37 C.F.R. §41.68: 69 FR 50003, Aug. 12, 2004, as amended at 77 FR 46631, Aug. 6, 2012.

§41.69. EXAMINER'S ANSWER

(a) The primary examiner may, within such time as directed by the Director, furnish a written answer to the owner's and/or requester's appellant brief or respondent brief including, as may be necessary, such explanation of the invention claimed and of the references relied upon, the grounds of rejection, and the reasons for patentability, including grounds for not adopting any proposed rejection. A copy of the answer shall be supplied to the owner and all requesters. If the primary examiner determines that the appeal does not comply with the provisions of §§41.61, 41.66, 41.67 and 41.68 or does not relate to an appealable action, the primary examiner shall make such determination of record.

(b) An examiner's answer may not include a new ground of rejection.

(c) An examiner's answer may not include a new determination not to make a proposed rejection of a claim.

(d) Any new ground of rejection, or any new determination not to make a proposed rejection, must be made in an Office action reopening prosecution.

§41.71. REBUTTAL BRIEF

(a) Within one month of the examiner's answer, any appellant may once file a rebuttal brief.

(b)(1) The rebuttal brief of the owner may be directed to the examiner's answer and/or any respondent brief.

(2) The rebuttal brief of the owner shall not include any new or non-admitted amendment, or an affidavit or other evidence. See §1.116 of this title for amendments, affidavits or other evidence filed after final action but before or on the same date of filing an appeal and §41.63 for amendments, affidavits or other evidence filed after the date of filing the appeal.

(c)(1) The rebuttal brief of any requester may be directed to the examiner's answer and/or the respondent brief of the owner.

(2) The rebuttal brief of a requester may not be directed to the respondent brief of any other requester.

(3) No new ground of rejection can be proposed by a requester.

(4) The rebuttal brief of a requester shall not include any new or non-admitted affidavit or other evidence. See §1.116(d) of this title for affidavits or other evidence filed after final action but before or on the same date of filing an appeal and §41.63(c) for affidavits or other evidence filed after the date of filing the appeal.

(d) The rebuttal brief must include a certification that a copy of the rebuttal brief has been served in its entirety on all other parties to the proceeding. The names and addresses of the parties served must be indicated.

(e) If a rebuttal brief is timely filed under paragraph (a) of this section but does not comply with all the requirements of paragraphs (a) through (d) of this section, appellant will be notified of the reasons for non-compliance and provided with a non-extendable period of one month within which to file an amended rebuttal brief. If the appellant does not file an amended rebuttal brief during the one-month period, or files an amended rebuttal brief which does not overcome all the reasons for non-compliance stated in the notification, that appellant's rebuttal brief and any amended rebuttal brief by that appellant will not be considered.

§41.73. ORAL HEARING

(a) An oral hearing should be requested only in those circumstances in which an appellant or a respondent considers such a hearing necessary or desirable for a proper presentation of the appeal. An appeal decided on the briefs without an oral hearing will receive the same consideration by the Board as an appeal decided after an oral hearing.

(b) If an appellant or a respondent desires an oral hearing, he or she must file, as a separate paper captioned "REQUEST FOR ORAL HEARING," a written request for such hearing accompanied by the fee set forth in §41.20(b)(3) within two months after the date of the examiner's answer. The time for requesting an oral hearing may not be extended. The request must include a certification that a copy of the request has been served in its entirety on all other parties to the proceeding. The names and addresses of the parties served must be indicated.

(c) If no request and fee for oral hearing have been timely filed by appellant or respondent as required by paragraph (b) of this section, the appeal will be assigned for consideration and decision on the briefs without an oral hearing.

(d) If appellant or respondent has complied with all the requirements of paragraph (b) of this section, a hearing date will be set, and notice given to the owner and all requesters. If an oral hearing is held, an oral argument may be presented by, or on behalf of, the primary examiner if considered desirable by either the primary examiner or the Board. The notice shall set a non-extendable period within which all requests for oral hearing shall be submitted by any other party to the appeal desiring to participate in the oral hearing. A hearing will be held as stated in the notice, and oral argument will be limited to thirty minutes for each appellant or respondent who has requested an oral hearing, and twenty minutes for the primary examiner unless otherwise ordered. No appellant or respondent will be permitted to participate in an oral hearing unless he or she has requested an oral hearing and submitted the fee set forth in §41.20(b)(3).

(e)(1) At the oral hearing, each appellant and respondent may only rely on evidence that has been previously entered and considered by the primary examiner and present argument that has been relied upon in the briefs except as permitted by paragraph (e)(2) of this section. The primary examiner may only rely on argument and evidence relied upon in an answer except as permitted by paragraph (e)(2) of this section. The Board will determine the order of the arguments presented at the oral hearing.

(2) Upon a showing of good cause, appellant, respondent and/or the primary examiner may rely on a new argument based upon a recent relevant decision of either the Board or a Federal Court.

(f) Notwithstanding the submission of a request for oral hearing complying with this rule, if the Board decides that a hearing is not necessary, the Board will so notify the owner and all requesters.

§41.77. DECISIONS & OTHER ACTIONS BY THE BOARD

(a) The Patent Trial and Appeal Board, in its decision, may affirm or reverse each decision of the examiner on all issues raised on each appealed claim, or remand the reexamination proceeding to the examiner for further consideration. The reversal of the examiner's determination not to make a rejection proposed by the third party requester constitutes a decision adverse to the patentability of the claims which are subject to that proposed rejection which will be set forth in the decision of the Patent Trial and Appeal Board as a new ground of rejection under paragraph (b) of this section. The affirmance of the rejection of a claim on any of the grounds specified constitutes a general affirmance of the decision of the examiner on that claim, except as to any ground specifically reversed.

(b) Should the Board reverse the examiner's determination not to make a rejection proposed by a requester, the Board shall set forth in the opinion in support of its decision a new ground of rejection; or should the Board have knowledge of any grounds not raised in the appeal for rejecting any pending claim, it may include in its opinion a statement to that effect with its reasons for so holding, which statement shall constitute a new ground of rejection of the claim. Any decision which includes a new ground of rejection pursuant to this paragraph shall not be considered final for judicial review. When the Board makes a new ground of rejection, the owner, within one month from the date of the decision, must exercise one of the following two options with respect to the new ground of rejection to avoid termination of the appeal proceeding as to the rejected claim:

(1) Reopen prosecution. The owner may file a response requesting reopening of prosecution before the examiner. Such a response must be either an amendment of the claims so rejected or new evidence relating to the claims so rejected, or both.

(2) Request rehearing. The owner may request that the proceeding be reheard under §41.79 by the Board upon the same record. The request for rehearing must address any new ground of rejection and state with particularity the points believed to have been misapprehended or overlooked in entering the new ground of rejection and also state all other grounds upon which rehearing is sought.

(c) Where the owner has filed a response requesting reopening of prosecution under paragraph (b)(1) of this section, any requester, within one month of the date of service of the owner's response, may once file comments on the response. Such written comments must be limited to the issues raised by the Board's opinion reflecting its decision and the owner's response. Any requester that had not previously filed an appeal or cross appeal and is seeking under this subsection to file comments or a reply to the comments is subject to the appeal and brief fees under §41.20(b)(1) and (2), respectively, which must accompany the comments or reply.

(d) Following any response by the owner under paragraph (b)(1) of this section and any written comments from a requester under paragraph (c) of this section, the proceeding will be remanded to the examiner. The statement of the Board shall be binding upon the examiner unless an amendment or new evidence not previously of record is made which, in the opinion of the examiner, overcomes the new ground of rejection stated in the decision. The examiner will consider any owner response under paragraph (b)(1) of this section and any written comments by a requester under paragraph (c) of this section and issue a determination that the rejection is maintained or has been overcome.

(e) Within one month of the examiner's determination pursuant to paragraph (d) of this section, the owner or any requester may once submit comments in response to the examiner's determination. Within one month of the date of service of comments in response to the examiner's determination, the owner and any requesters may file a reply to the comments. No requester reply may address the comments of any other requester reply. Any requester that had not previously filed an appeal or cross appeal and is seeking under this subsection to file comments or a reply to the comments is subject to the appeal and brief fees under §41.20(b)(1) and (2), respectively, which must accompany the comments or reply.

(f) After submission of any comments and any reply pursuant to paragraph (e) of this section, or after time has expired, the proceeding will be returned to the Board which shall reconsider the matter and issue a new decision. The new decision is deemed to incorporate the earlier decision, except for those portions specifically withdrawn.

(g) The time period set forth in paragraph (b) of this section is subject to the extension of time provisions of §1.956 of this title when the owner is responding under paragraph (b)(1) of this section. The time period set forth in paragraph (b) of this section may not be extended when the owner is responding under paragraph (b)(2) of this section. The time periods set forth in paragraphs (c) and (e) of this section may not be extended.

History of 37 C.F.R. §41.77: 69 FR 50003, Aug. 12, 2004, as amended at 77 FR 46631, Aug. 6, 2012.

§41.79. REHEARING

(a) Parties to the appeal may file a request for rehearing of the decision within one month of the date of:

(1) The original decision of the Board under §41.77(a),

(2) The original §41.77(b) decision under the provisions of §41.77(b)(2),

(3) The expiration of the time for the owner to take action under §41.77(b)(2), or

(4) The new decision of the Board under §41.77(f).

(b)(1) The request for rehearing must state with particularity the points believed to have been misapprehended or overlooked in rendering the Board's opinion reflecting its decision. Arguments not raised in the briefs before the Board and evidence not previously relied upon in the briefs are not permitted in the request for rehearing except as permitted by paragraphs (b)(2) and (b)(3) of this section.

(2) Upon a showing of good cause, appellant and/or respondent may present a new argument based upon a recent relevant decision of either the Board or a Federal Court.

(3) New arguments responding to a new ground of rejection made pursuant to §41.77(b) are permitted.

(c) Within one month of the date of service of any request for rehearing under paragraph (a) of this section, or any further request for rehearing under paragraph (d) of this section, the owner and all requesters may once file comments in opposition to the request for rehearing or the further request for rehearing. The comments in opposition must be limited to the issues raised in the request for rehearing or the further request for rehearing.

(d) If a party to an appeal files a request for rehearing under paragraph (a) of this section, or a further request for rehearing under this section, the Board shall render a decision on the request for rehearing. The decision on the request for rehearing is deemed to incorporate the earlier opinion reflecting its decision for appeal, except for those portions specifically withdrawn on rehearing and is final for the purpose of judicial review, except when noted otherwise in the decision on rehearing. If the Board opinion reflecting its decision on rehearing becomes, in effect, a new decision, and the Board so indicates, then any party to the appeal may, within one month of the new decision, file a further request for rehearing of the new decision under this subsection. Such further request for rehearing must comply with paragraph (b) of this section.

(e) The times for requesting rehearing under paragraph (a) of this section, for requesting further rehearing under paragraph (c) of this section, and for submitting comments under paragraph (b) of this section may not be extended.

§41.81. ACTION FOLLOWING DECISION

The parties to an appeal to the Board may not appeal to the U.S. Court of Appeals for the Federal Circuit under §1.983 of this title until all parties' rights to request rehearing have been exhausted, at which time the decision of the Board is final and appealable by any party to the appeal to the Board.

SUBPART D. CONTESTED CASES

§41.100. DEFINITIONS

In addition to the definitions in §41.2, the following definitions apply to proceedings under this subpart:

Business day means a day other than a Saturday, Sunday, or Federal holiday within the District of Columbia.

Involved means the Board has declared the patent application, patent, or claim so described to be a subject of the contested case.

Source of 37 C.F.R. Part 41D: 69 FR 50003, Aug. 12, 2004, unless otherwise noted.

§41.101. NOTICE OF PROCEEDING

(a) Notice of a contested case will be sent to every party to the proceeding. The entry of the notice initiates the proceeding.

(b) When the Board is unable to provide actual notice of a contested case on a party through the correspondence address of record for the party, the Board may authorize other modes of notice, including:

(1) Sending notice to another address associated with the party, or

(2) Publishing the notice in the Official Gazette of the United States Patent and Trademark Office.

§41.102. COMPLETION OF EXAMINATION

Before a contested case is initiated, except as the Board may otherwise authorize, for each involved application and patent:

(a) Examination or reexamination must be completed, and

(b) There must be at least one claim that:

(1) Is patentable but for a judgment in the contested case, and

(2) Would be involved in the contested case.

§41.103. JURISDICTION OVER INVOLVED FILES

The Board acquires jurisdiction over any involved file when the Board initiates a contested case. Other proceedings for the involved file within the Office are suspended except as the Board may order.

§41.104. CONDUCT OF CONTESTED CASE

(a) The Board may determine a proper course of conduct in a proceeding for any situation not specifically covered by this part and may enter non-final orders to administer the proceeding.

(b) An administrative patent judge may waive or suspend in a proceeding the application of any rule in this subpart, subject to such conditions as the administrative patent judge may impose.

(c) Times set in this subpart are defaults. In the event of a conflict between a time set by rule and a time set by order, the time set by order is controlling. Action due on a day other than a business day may be completed on the next business day unless the Board expressly states otherwise.

§41.106. FILING & SERVICE

(a) General format requirements.

(1) The paper used for filings must be durable and white. A party must choose to file on either A4-sized paper or 8½ inch x 11 inch paper except in the case of exhibits that require a larger size in order to preserve details of the original. A party may not switch between paper sizes in a single proceeding. Only one side of the paper may be used.

(2) In papers, including affidavits, created for the proceeding:

(i) Markings must be in black ink or must otherwise provide an equivalently permanent, dark, high-contrast image on the paper. The quality of printing must be equivalent to the quality produced by a laser printer. Either a proportional or monospaced font may be used, but the proportional font must be 12-point or larger and a monospaced font must not contain more than 4 characters per centimeter (10 characters per inch). Case names must be underlined or italicized.

(ii) Double spacing must be used except in headings, tables of contents, tables of authorities, indices, signature blocks, and certificates of service. Block quotations may be single-spaced and must be indented. Margins must be at least 2.5 centimeters (1 inch) on all sides.

(b) Papers other than exhibits—

(1) Cover sheet.

(i) The cover sheet must include the caption the Board specifies for the proceeding, a header indicating the party and contact information for the party, and a title indicating the sequence and subject of the paper. For example, "JONES MOTION 2, For benefit of an earlier application."

(ii) If the Board specifies a color other than white for the cover sheet, the cover sheet must be that color.

(2) Papers must have two 0.5 cm (¼ inch) holes with centers 1 cm (½ inch) from the top of the page and 7 cm (2¾ inch) apart, centered horizontally on the page.

(3) Incorporation by reference; combined papers. Arguments must not be incorporated by reference from one paper into another paper. Combined motions, oppositions, replies, or other combined papers are not permitted.

(4) Exhibits. Additional requirements for exhibits appear in §41.154(c).

(c) Working copy. Every paper filed must be accompanied by a working copy marked "APJ Copy."

(d) Specific filing forms—

(1) Filing by mail. A paper filed using the Priority Mail Express® service of the United States Postal Service will be deemed to be filed as of "date accepted" on the Priority Mail Express® mailing label; otherwise, mail will be deemed to be filed as of the stamped date of receipt at the Board.

(2) Other modes of filing. The Board may authorize other modes of filing, including electronic filing and hand filing, and may set conditions for the use of such other modes.

(e) Service.

(1) Papers filed with the Board, if not previously served, must be served simultaneously on every opposing party except as the Board expressly directs.

(2) If a party is represented by counsel, service must be on counsel.

(3) Service must be by Priority Mail Express® or by means at least as fast and reliable as Priority Mail Express®. Electronic service is not permitted without Board authorization.

(4) The date of service does not count in computing the time for responding.

(f) Certificate of service.

(1) Papers other than exhibits must include a certificate of service as a separate page at the end of each paper that must be served on an opposing party.

(2) Exhibits must be accompanied by a certificate of service, but a single certificate may accompany any group of exhibits submitted together.

(3) A certificate of service must state:

(i) The date and manner of service,

(ii) The name and address of every person served, and

(iii) For exhibits filed as a group, the name and number of each exhibit served.

(4) A certificate made by a person other than a registered patent practitioner must be in the form of an affidavit.

History of 37 C.F.R. §41.106: 79 FR 63043, Oct. 22, 2014.

§41.108. LEAD COUNSEL

(a) A party may be represented by counsel. The Board may require a party to appoint a lead counsel. If counsel is not of record in a party's involved application or patent, then a power of attorney for that counsel for the party's involved application or patent must be filed with the notice required in paragraph (b) of this section.

(b) Within 14 days of the initiation of each contested case, each party must file a separate notice identifying its counsel, if any, and providing contact information for each counsel identified or, if the party has no counsel, then for the party. Contact information must, at a minimum, include:

(1) A mailing address;

(2) An address for courier delivery when the mailing address is not available for such delivery (for example, when the mailing address is a Post Office box);

(3) A telephone number;

(4) A facsimile number; and

(5) An electronic mail address.

(c) A party must promptly notify the Board of any change in the contact information required in paragraph (b) of this section.

§41.109. ACCESS TO & COPIES OF OFFICE RECORDS

(a) Request for access or copies. Any request from a party for access to or copies of Office records directly related to a contested case must be filed with the Board. The request must precisely identify the records and in the case of copies include the appropriate fee set under §1.19(b) of this title.

(b) Authorization of access and copies. Access and copies will ordinarily only be authorized for the following records:

(1) The application file for an involved patent;

(2) An involved application; and

(3) An application for which a party has been accorded benefit under subpart E of this part.

(c) Missing or incomplete copies. If a party does not receive a complete copy of a record within 21 days of the authorization, the party must promptly notify the Board.

§41.110. FILING CLAIM INFORMATION

(a) Clean copy of claims. Within 14 days of the initiation of the proceeding, each party must file a clean copy of its involved claims and, if a biotechnology material sequence is a limitation, a clean copy of the sequence.

(b) Annotated copy of claims. Within 28 days of the initiation of the proceeding, each party must:

(1) For each involved claim having a limitation that is illustrated in a drawing or biotechnology material sequence, file an annotated copy of the claim indicating in bold face between braces ({ }) where each limitation is shown in the drawing or sequence.

(2) For each involved claim that contains a means-plus-function or step-plus-function limitation in the form permitted under 35 U.S.C. 112(f), file an annotated copy of the claim indicating in bold face between braces ({ }) the specific portions of the specification that describe the structure, material, or acts corresponding to each claimed function.

(c) Any motion to add or amend a claim must include:

(1) A clean copy of the claim,

(2) A claim chart showing where the disclosure of the patent or application provides written description of the subject matter of the claim, and

(3) Where applicable, a copy of the claims annotated according to paragraph (b) of this section.

History of 37 C.F.R. §41.110: 69 FR 50003, Aug. 12, 2004, as amended at 77 FR 46631, Aug. 6, 2012.

§41.120. NOTICE OF BASIS FOR RELIEF

(a) The Board may require a party to provide a notice stating the relief it requests and the basis for its entitlement to relief. The Board may provide for the notice to be maintained in confidence for a limited time.

(b) Effect. If a notice under paragraph (a) of this section is required, a party will be limited to filing substantive motions consistent with the notice. Ambiguities in the notice will be construed against the party. A notice is not evidence except as an admission by a party-opponent.

(c) Correction. A party may move to correct its notice. The motion should be filed promptly after the party becomes aware of the basis for the correction. A correction filed after the time set for filing notices will only be entered if entry would serve the interests of justice.

§41.121. MOTIONS

(a) Types of motions—

(1) Substantive motions. Consistent with the notice of requested relief, if any, and to the extent the Board authorizes, a party may file a motion:

(i) To redefine the scope of the contested case,

(ii) To change benefit accorded for the contested subject matter, or

(iii) For judgment in the contested case.

(2) Responsive motions. The Board may authorize a party to file a motion to amend or add a claim, to change inventorship, or otherwise to cure a defect raised in a notice of requested relief or in a substantive motion.

(3) Miscellaneous motions. Any request for relief other than a substantive or responsive motion must be filed as a miscellaneous motion.

(b) Burden of proof. The party filing the motion has the burden of proof to establish that it is entitled to the requested relief.

(c) Content of motions; oppositions and replies.

(1) Each motion must be filed as a separate paper and must include:

(i) A statement of the precise relief requested,

(ii) A statement of material facts (see paragraph (d) of this section), and

(iii) A full statement of the reasons for the relief requested, including a detailed explanation of the significance of the evidence and the governing law, rules, and precedent.

(2) Compliance with rules. Where a rule in part 1 of this title ordinarily governs the relief sought, the motion must make any showings required under that rule in addition to any showings required in this part.

(3) The Board may order additional showings or explanations as a condition for filing a motion.

(d) Statement of material facts.

(1) Each material fact shall be set forth as a separate numbered sentence with specific citations to the portions of the record that support the fact.

(2) The Board may require that the statement of material facts be submitted as a separate paper.

(e) Claim charts. Claim charts must be used in support of any paper requiring the comparison of a claim to something else, such as another claim, prior art, or a specification. Claim charts must accompany the paper as an appendix. Claim charts are not a substitute for appropriate argument and explanation in the paper.

(f) The Board may order briefing on any issue that could be raised by motion.

§41.122. OPPOSITIONS & REPLIES

(a) Oppositions and replies must comply with the content requirements for motions and must include a statement identifying material facts in dispute. Any material fact not specifically denied shall be considered admitted.

(b) All arguments for the relief requested in a motion must be made in the motion. A reply may only respond to arguments raised in the corresponding opposition.

§41.123. DEFAULT FILING TIMES

(a) A motion, other than a miscellaneous motion, may only be filed according to a schedule the Board sets. The default times for acting are:

(1) An opposition is due 30 days after service of the motion.

(2) A reply is due 30 days after service of the opposition.

(3) A responsive motion is due 30 days after the service of the motion.

(b) Miscellaneous motions.

(1) If no time for filing a specific miscellaneous motion is provided in this part or in a Board order:

(i) The opposing party must be consulted prior to filing the miscellaneous motion, and

(ii) If an opposing party plans to oppose the miscellaneous motion, the movant may not file the motion without Board authorization. Such authorization should ordinarily be obtained through a telephone conference including the Board and every other party to the proceeding. Delay in seeking relief may justify a denial of the motion.

(2) An opposition may not be filed without authorization. The default times for acting are:

(i) An opposition to a miscellaneous motion is due five business days after service of the motion.

(ii) A reply to a miscellaneous motion opposition is due three business days after service of the opposition.

(c) Exhibits. Each exhibit must be filed and served with the first paper in which it is cited except as the Board may otherwise order.

§41.124. ORAL ARGUMENT

(a) Request for oral argument. A party may request an oral argument on an issue raised in a paper within five business days of the filing of the paper. The request must be filed as a separate paper and must specify the issues to be considered.

(b) Copies for panel. If an oral argument is set for a panel, the movant on any issue to be argued must provide three working copies of the motion, the opposition, and the reply. Each party is responsible for providing three working copies of its exhibits relating to the motion.

(c) Length of argument. If a request for oral argument is granted, each party will have a total of 20 minutes to present its arguments, including any time for rebuttal.

(d) Demonstrative exhibits must be served at least five business days before the oral argument and filed no later than the time of the oral argument.

(e) Transcription. The Board encourages the use of a transcription service at oral arguments but, if such a service is to be used, the Board must be notified in advance to ensure adequate facilities are available and a transcript must be filed with the Board promptly after the oral argument.

§41.125. DECISION ON MOTIONS

(a) Order of consideration. The Board may take up motions for decisions in any order, may grant, deny, or dismiss any motion, and may take such other action appropriate to secure the just, speedy, and inexpensive determination of the proceeding. A decision on a motion may include deferral of action on an issue until a later point in the proceeding.

(b) Interlocutory decisions. A decision on motions without a judgment is not final for the purposes of judicial review. A panel decision on an issue will govern further proceedings in the contested case.

(c) Rehearing—

(1) Time for request. A request for rehearing of a decision on a motion must be filed within fourteen days of the decision.

(2) No tolling. The filing of a request for rehearing does not toll times for taking action.

(3) Burden on rehearing. The burden of showing a decision should be modified lies with the party attacking the decision. The request must specifically identify:

(i) All matters the party believes to have been misapprehended or overlooked, and

(ii) The place where the matter was previously addressed in a motion, opposition, or reply.

(4) Opposition; reply. Neither an opposition nor a reply to a request for rehearing may be filed without Board authorization.

(5) Panel rehearing. If a decision is not a panel decision, the party requesting rehearing may request that a panel rehear the decision. A panel rehearing a procedural decision will review the decision for an abuse of discretion.

§41.126. ARBITRATION

(a) Parties to a contested case may resort to binding arbitration to determine any issue in a contested case. The Office is not a party to the arbitration. The Board is not bound and may independently determine questions of patentability, jurisdiction, and Office practice.

(b) The Board will not authorize arbitration unless:

(1) It is to be conducted according to Title 9 of the United States Code.

(2) The parties notify the Board in writing of their intention to arbitrate.

(3) The agreement to arbitrate:

(i) Is in writing,

(ii) Specifies the issues to be arbitrated,

(iii) Names the arbitrator, or provides a date not more than 30 days after the execution of the agreement for the selection of the arbitrator, and

(iv) Provides that the arbitrator's award shall be binding on the parties and that judgment thereon can be entered by the Board.

(4) A copy of the agreement is filed within 20 days after its execution.

(5) The arbitration is completed within the time the Board sets.

(c) The parties are solely responsible for the selection of the arbitrator and the conduct of proceedings before the arbitrator.

(d) Issues not disposed of by the arbitration will be resolved in accordance with the procedures established in this subpart.

(e) The Board will not consider the arbitration award unless it:

(1) Is binding on the parties,

(2) Is in writing,

(3) States in a clear and definite manner each issue arbitrated and the disposition of each issue, and

(4) Is filed within 20 days of the date of the award.

(f) Once the award is filed, the parties to the award may not take actions inconsistent with the award. If the award is dispositive of the contested subject matter for a party, the Board may enter judgment as to that party.

§41.127. JUDGMENT

(a) Effect within Office—

(1) Estoppel. A judgment disposes of all issues that were, or by motion could have properly been, raised and decided. A losing party who could have properly moved for relief on an issue, but did not so move, may not take action in the Office after the judgment that is inconsistent with that party's failure to move, except that a losing party shall not be estopped with respect to any contested subject matter for which that party was awarded a favorable judgment.

(2) Final disposal of claim. Adverse judgment against a claim is a final action of the Office requiring no further action by the Office to dispose of the claim permanently.

(b) Request for adverse judgment. A party may at any time in the proceeding request judgment against itself. Actions construed to be a request for adverse judgment include:

(1) Abandonment of an involved application such that the party no longer has an application or patent involved in the proceeding,

(2) Cancellation or disclaiming of a claim such that the party no longer has a claim involved in the proceeding,

(3) Concession of priority or unpatentability of the contested subject matter, and

(4) Abandonment of the contest.

(c) Recommendation. The judgment may include a recommendation for further action by the examiner or by the Director. If the Board recommends rejection of a claim of an involved application, the examiner must enter and maintain the recommended rejection unless an amendment or showing of facts not previously of record is filed which, in the opinion of the examiner, overcomes the recommended rejection.

(d) Rehearing. A party dissatisfied with the judgment may file a request for rehearing within 30 days of the entry of the judgment. The request must specifically identify all matters the party believes to have been misapprehended or overlooked, and the place where the matter was previously addressed in a motion, opposition, or reply.

History of 37 C.F.R. §41.127: 69 FR 58260, Sept. 30, 2004.

§41.128. SANCTIONS

(a) The Board may impose a sanction against a party for misconduct, including:

(1) Failure to comply with an applicable rule or order in the proceeding;

(2) Advancing a misleading or frivolous request for relief or argument; or

(3) Engaging in dilatory tactics.

(b) Sanctions include entry of:

(1) An order holding certain facts to have been established in the proceeding;

(2) An order expunging, or precluding a party from filing, a paper;

(3) An order precluding a party from presenting or contesting a particular issue;

(4) An order precluding a party from requesting, obtaining, or opposing discovery;

(5) An order excluding evidence;

(6) An order awarding compensatory expenses, including attorney fees;

(7) An order requiring terminal disclaimer of patent term; or

(8) Judgment in the contested case.

§41.150. DISCOVERY

(a) Limited discovery. A party is not entitled to discovery except as authorized in this subpart. The parties may agree to discovery among themselves at any time.

(b) Automatic discovery.

(1) Within 21 days of a request by an opposing party, a party must:

(i) Serve a legible copy of every requested patent, patent application, literature reference, and test standard mentioned in the specification of the party's involved patent or application, or application upon which the party will rely for benefit, and, if the requested material is in a language other than English, a translation, if available, and

(ii) File with the Board a notice (without copies of the requested materials) of service of the requested materials.

(2) Unless previously served, or the Board orders otherwise, any exhibit cited in a motion or in testimony must be served with the citing motion or testimony.

(c) Additional discovery.

(1) A party may request additional discovery. The requesting party must show that such additional discovery is in the interests of justice. The Board may specify conditions for such additional discovery.

(2) When appropriate, a party may obtain production of documents and things during cross examination of an opponent's witness or during testimony authorized under §41.156.

§41.151. ADMISSIBILITY

Evidence that is not taken, sought, or filed in accordance with this subpart shall not be admissible.

§41.152. APPLICABILITY OF THE FEDERAL RULES OF EVIDENCE

(a) Generally. Except as otherwise provided in this subpart, the Federal Rules of Evidence shall apply to contested cases.

(b) Exclusions. Those portions of the Federal Rules of Evidence relating to criminal proceedings, juries, and other matters not relevant to proceedings under this subpart shall not apply.

(c) Modifications in terminology. Unless otherwise clear from context, the following terms of the Federal Rules of Evidence shall be construed as indicated:

Appellate court means United States Court of Appeals for the Federal Circuit or a United States district court when judicial review is under 35 U.S.C. 146.

Civil action, civil proceeding, action, and trial mean contested case.

Courts of the United States, U.S. Magistrate, court, trial court, and trier of fact mean Board.

Hearing means:

(i) In Federal Rule of Evidence 703, the time when the expert testifies.

(ii) In Federal Rule of Evidence 804(a)(5), the time for taking testimony.

Judge means the Board.

Judicial notice means official notice.

Trial or hearing means, in Federal Rule of Evidence 807, the time for taking testimony.

(d) The Board, in determining foreign law, may consider any relevant material or source, including testimony, whether or not submitted by a party or admissible under the Federal Rules of Evidence.

§41.153. RECORDS OF THE OFFICE

Certification is not necessary as a condition to admissibility when the evidence to be submitted is a record of the Office to which all parties have access.

§41.154. FORM OF EVIDENCE

(a) Evidence consists of affidavits, transcripts of depositions, documents, and things. All evidence must be submitted in the form of an exhibit.

(b) Translation required. When a party relies on a document or is required to produce a document in a language other than English, a translation of the document into English and an affidavit attesting to the accuracy of the translation must be filed with the document.

(c) An exhibit must conform with the requirements for papers in §41.106 of this subpart and the requirements of this paragraph.

(1) Each exhibit must have an exhibit label with a unique number in a range assigned by the Board, the names of the parties, and the proceeding number in the following format:

JONES EXHIBIT 2001
Jones v. Smith
Contested Case 104,999

(2) When the exhibit is a paper:

(i) Each page must be uniquely numbered in sequence, and

(ii) The exhibit label must be affixed to the lower right corner of the first page of the exhibit without obscuring information on the first page or, if obscuring is unavoidable, affixed to a duplicate first page.

(d) Exhibit list. Each party must maintain an exhibit list with the exhibit number and a brief description of each exhibit. If the exhibit is not filed, the exhibit list should note that fact. The Board may require the filing of a current exhibit list prior to acting on a motion.

History of 37 C.F.R. §41.154: 69 FR 58260, Sept. 30, 2004.

§41.155. OBJECTION; MOTION TO EXCLUDE; MOTION IN LIMINE

(a) Deposition. Objections to deposition evidence must be made during the deposition. Evidence to cure the objection must be provided during the deposition unless the parties to the deposition stipulate otherwise on the deposition record.

(b) Other than deposition. For evidence other than deposition evidence:

(1) Objection. Any objection must be served within five business days of service of evidence, other than deposition evidence, to which the objection is directed.

(2) Supplemental evidence. The party relying on evidence for which an objection is timely served may respond to the objection by serving supplemental evidence within ten business days of service of the objection.

(c) Motion to exclude. A miscellaneous motion to exclude evidence must be filed to preserve any objection. The motion must identify the objections in the record in order and must explain the objections.

(d) Motion in limine. A party may file a miscellaneous motion in limine for a ruling on the admissibility of evidence.

History of 37 C.F.R. §41.155: 69 FR 58260, Sept. 30, 2004.

§41.156. COMPELLING TESTIMONY & PRODUCTION

(a) Authorization required. A party seeking to compel testimony or production of documents or things must file a miscellaneous motion for authorization. The miscellaneous motion must describe the general relevance of the testimony, document, or thing and must:

(1) In the case of testimony, identify the witness by name or title, and

(2) In the case of a document or thing, the general nature of the document or thing.

(b) Outside the United States. For testimony or production sought outside the United States, the motion must also:

(1) In the case of testimony.

(i) Identify the foreign country and explain why the party believes the witness can be compelled to testify in the foreign country, including a description of the procedures that will be used to compel the testimony in the foreign country and an estimate of the time it is expected to take to obtain the testimony; and

(ii) Demonstrate that the party has made reasonable efforts to secure the agreement of the witness to testify in the United States but has been unsuccessful in obtaining the agreement, even though the party has offered to pay the expenses of the witness to travel to and testify in the United States.

(2) In the case of production of a document or thing.

(i) Identify the foreign country and explain why the party believes production of the document or thing can be compelled in the foreign country, including a description of the procedures that will be used to compel production of the document or thing in the foreign country and an estimate of the time it is expected to take to obtain production of the document or thing; and

(ii) Demonstrate that the party has made reasonable efforts to obtain the agreement of the individual or entity having possession, custody, or control of the document to produce the document or thing in the United States but has been unsuccessful in obtaining that agreement, even though the party has offered to pay the expenses of producing the document or thing in the United States.

§41.157. TAKING TESTIMONY

(a) Form. Direct testimony must be submitted in the form of an affidavit except when the testimony is compelled under 35 U.S.C. 24, in which case it may be in the form of a deposition transcript.

(b) Time and location.

(1) Uncompelled direct testimony may be taken at any time; otherwise, testimony may only be taken during such time period as the Board may authorize.

(2) Other testimony.

(i) Except as the Board otherwise orders, authorized testimony may be taken at any reasonable time and location within the United States before any disinterested official authorized to administer oaths at that location.

(ii) Testimony outside the United States may only be taken as the Board specifically directs.

(c) Notice of deposition.

(1) Prior to the taking of testimony, all parties to the proceeding must agree on the time and place for taking testimony. If the parties cannot agree, the party seeking the testimony must initiate a conference with the Board to set a time and place.

(2) Cross-examination should ordinarily take place after any supplemental evidence relating to the direct testimony has been filed and more than a week before the filing date for any paper in which the cross-examination testimony is expected to be used. A party requesting cross-examination testimony of more than one witness may choose the order in which the witnesses are to be cross-examined.

(3) In the case of direct testimony, at least three business days prior to the conference in paragraph (c)(1) of this section, the party seeking the direct testimony must serve:

(i) A list and copy of each document under the party's control and on which the party intends to rely, and

(ii) A list of, and proffer of reasonable access to, any thing other than a document under the party's control and on which the party intends to rely.

(4) Notice of the deposition must be filed at least two business days before a deposition. The notice limits the scope of the testimony and must list:

(i) The time and place of the deposition,

(ii) The name and address of the witness,

(iii) A list of the exhibits to be relied upon during the deposition, and

(iv) A general description of the scope and nature of the testimony to be elicited.

(5) Motion to quash. Objection to a defect in the notice is waived unless a miscellaneous motion to quash is promptly filed.

(d) Deposition in a foreign language. If an interpreter will be used during the deposition, the party calling the witness must initiate a conference with the Board at least five business days before the deposition.

(e) Manner of taking testimony.

(1) Each witness before giving a deposition shall be duly sworn according to law by the officer before whom the deposition is to be taken. The officer must be authorized to take testimony under 35 U.S.C. 23.

(2) The testimony shall be taken in answer to interrogatories with any questions and answers recorded in their regular order by the officer, or by some other disinterested person in the presence of the officer, unless the presence of the officer is waived on the record by agreement of all parties.

(3) Any exhibits relied upon must be numbered according to the numbering scheme assigned for the contested case and must, if not previously served, be served at the deposition.

(4) All objections made at the time of the deposition to the qualifications of the officer taking the deposition, the manner of taking it, the evidence presented, the conduct of any party, and any other objection to the proceeding shall be noted on the record by the officer. Evidence objected to shall be taken subject to a ruling on the objection.

(5) When the testimony has been transcribed, the witness shall read and sign (in the form of an affidavit) a transcript of the deposition unless:

(i) The parties otherwise agree in writing,

(ii) The parties waive reading and signature by the witness on the record at the deposition, or

(iii) The witness refuses to read or sign the transcript of the deposition.

(6) The officer shall prepare a certified transcript by attaching to the transcript of the deposition a certificate in the form of an affidavit signed and sealed by the officer. Unless the parties waive any of the following requirements, in which case the certificate shall so state, the certificate must state:

(i) The witness was duly sworn by the officer before commencement of testimony by the witness;

(ii) The transcript is a true record of the testimony given by the witness;

(iii) The name of the person who recorded the testimony and, if the officer did not record it, whether the testimony was recorded in the presence of the officer;

(iv) The presence or absence of any opponent;

(v) The place where the deposition was taken and the day and hour when the deposition began and ended;

(vi) The officer has no disqualifying interest, personal or financial, in a party; and

(vii) If a witness refuses to read or sign the transcript, the circumstances under which the witness refused.

(7) The officer must promptly provide a copy of the transcript to all parties. The proponent of the testimony must file the original as an exhibit.

(8) Any objection to the content, form, or manner of taking the deposition, including the qualifications of the officer, is waived unless made on the record during the deposition and preserved in a timely filed miscellaneous motion to exclude.

(f) Costs. Except as the Board may order or the parties may agree in writing, the proponent of the testimony shall bear all costs associated with the testimony, including the reasonable costs associated with making the witness available for the cross-examination.

§41.158. EXPERT TESTIMONY; TESTS & DATA

(a) Expert testimony that does not disclose the underlying facts or data on which the opinion is based is entitled to little or no weight. Testimony on United States patent law will not be admitted.

(b) If a party relies on a technical test or data from such a test, the party must provide an affidavit explaining:

(1) Why the test or data is being used,

(2) How the test was performed and the data was generated,

(3) How the data is used to determine a value,

(4) How the test is regarded in the relevant art, and

(5) Any other information necessary for the Board to evaluate the test and data.

SUBPART E. PATENT INTERFERENCES

§41.200. PROCEDURE; PENDENCY

(a) A patent interference is a contested case subject to the procedures set forth in subpart D of this part.

(b) Any reference to 35 U.S.C. 102 or 135 in this subpart refers to the statute in effect on March 15, 2013, unless otherwise expressly indicated. Any reference to 35 U.S.C. 141 or 146 in this subpart refers to the statute applicable to the involved application or patent.

(c) Patent interferences shall be administered such that pendency before the Board is normally no more than two years.

History of 37 C.F.R. §41.200: 80 FR 17971, May 13, 2015.

Source of 37 C.F.R. Part 41E: 69 FR 50003, Aug. 12, 2004; 75 FR 19559, Apr. 15, 2010, unless otherwise noted.

§41.201. DEFINITIONS

In addition to the definitions in §§41.2 and 41.100, the following definitions apply to proceedings under this subpart:

Accord benefit means Board recognition that a patent application provides a proper constructive reduction to practice under 35 U.S.C. 102(g)(1).

Constructive reduction to practice means a described and enabled anticipation under 35 U.S.C. 102(g)(1), in a patent application of the subject matter of a count. Earliest constructive reduction to practice means the first constructive reduction to practice that has been continuously disclosed through a chain of patent applications including in the involved application or patent. For the chain to be continuous, each subsequent application must comply with the requirements of 35 U.S.C. 119-121, 365, or 386.

Count means the Board's description of the interfering subject matter that sets the scope of admissible proofs on priority. Where there is more than one count, each count must describe a patentably distinct invention.

Involved claim means, for the purposes of 35 U.S.C. 135(a), a claim that has been designated as corresponding to the count.

Senior party means the party entitled to the presumption under §41.207(a)(1) that it is the prior inventor. Any other party is a junior party.

Threshold issue means an issue that, if resolved in favor of the movant, would deprive the opponent of standing in the interference. Threshold issues may include:

(1) No interference-in-fact, and

(2) In the case of an involved application claim first made after the publication of the movant's application or issuance of the movant's patent:

(i) Repose under 35 U.S.C. 135(b) in view of the movant's patent or published application, or

(ii) Unpatentability for lack of written description under 35 U.S.C. 112 of an involved application claim where the applicant suggested, or could have suggested, an interference under §41.202(a).

History of 37 C.F.R. §41.201: 69 FR 50003, Aug. 12, 2004, as amended at 77 FR 46631, Aug. 6, 2012; 80 FR 17971, May 13, 2015.

§41.202. SUGGESTING AN INTERFERENCE

(a) Applicant. An applicant, including a reissue applicant, may suggest an interference with another application or a patent. The suggestion must:

(1) Provide sufficient information to identify the application or patent with which the applicant seeks an interference,

(2) Identify all claims the applicant believes interfere, propose one or more counts, and show how the claims correspond to one or more counts,

(3) For each count, provide a claim chart comparing at least one claim of each party corresponding to the count and show why the claims interfere within the meaning of §41.203(a),

(4) Explain in detail why the applicant will prevail on priority,

(5) If a claim has been added or amended to provoke an interference, provide a claim chart showing the written description for each claim in the applicant's specification, and

(6) For each constructive reduction to practice for which the applicant wishes to be accorded benefit, provide a chart showing where the disclosure provides a constructive reduction to practice within the scope of the interfering subject matter.

(b) Patentee. A patentee cannot suggest an interference under this section but may, to the extent permitted under §1.291 of this title, alert the examiner of an application claiming interfering subject matter to the possibility of an interference.

(c) Examiner. An examiner may require an applicant to add a claim to provoke an interference. Failure to satisfy the requirement within a period (not less than one month) the examiner sets will operate as a concession of priority for the subject matter of the claim. If the interference would be with a patent, the applicant must also comply with paragraphs (a)(2) through (a)(6) of this section. The claim the examiner proposes to have added must, apart from the question of priority under 35 U.S.C. 102(g):

(1) Be patentable to the applicant, and

(2) Be drawn to patentable subject matter claimed by another applicant or patentee.

(d) Requirement to show priority under 35 U.S.C. 102(g).

(1) When an applicant has an earliest constructive reduction to practice that is later than the apparent earliest constructive reduction to practice for a patent or published application claiming interfering subject matter, the applicant must show why it would prevail on priority.

(2) If an applicant fails to show priority under paragraph (d)(1) of this section, an administrative patent judge may nevertheless declare an interference to place the applicant under an order to show cause why judgment should not be entered against the applicant on priority. New evidence in support of priority will not be admitted except on a showing of good cause. The Board may authorize the filing of motions to redefine the interfering subject matter or to change the benefit accorded to the parties.

(e) Sufficiency of showing.

(1) A showing of priority under this section is not sufficient unless it would, if unrebutted, support a determination of priority in favor of the party making the showing.

(2) When testimony or production necessary to show priority is not available without authorization under §41.150(c) or §41.156(a), the showing shall include:

(i) Any necessary interrogatory, request for admission, request for production, or deposition request, and

(ii) A detailed proffer of what the response to the interrogatory or request would be expected to be and an explanation of the relevance of the response to the question of priority.

History of 37 C.F.R. §41.202: 69 FR 50003, Aug. 12, 2004, as amended at 77 FR 42174, July 17, 2012.

§41.203. DECLARATION

(a) Interfering subject matter. An interference exists if the subject matter of a claim of one party would, if prior art, have anticipated or rendered obvious the subject matter of a claim of the opposing party and vice versa.

(b) Notice of declaration. An administrative patent judge declares the patent interference on behalf of the Director. A notice declaring an interference identifies:

(1) The interfering subject matter;

(2) The involved applications, patents, and claims;

(3) The accorded benefit for each count; and

(4) The claims corresponding to each count.

(c) Redeclaration. An administrative patent judge may redeclare a patent interference on behalf of the Director to change the declaration made under paragraph (b) of this section.

(d) A party may suggest the addition of a patent or application to the interference or the declaration of an additional interference. The suggestion should make the showings required under §41.202(a) of this part.

§41.204. NOTICE OF BASIS FOR RELIEF

(a) Priority statement.

(1) A party may not submit evidence of its priority in addition to its accorded benefit unless it files a statement setting forth all bases on which the party intends to establish its entitlement to judgment on priority.

(2) The priority statement must:

(i) State the date and location of the party's earliest corroborated conception,

(ii) State the date and location of the party's earliest corroborated actual reduction to practice,

(iii) State the earliest corroborated date on which the party's diligence began, and

(iv) Provide a copy of the earliest document upon which the party will rely to show conception.

(3) If a junior party fails to file a priority statement overcoming a senior party's accorded benefit, judgment shall be entered against the junior party absent a showing of good cause.

(b) Other substantive motions. The Board may require a party to list the motions it intends to file, including sufficient detail to place the Board and the opponent on notice of the precise relief sought.

(c) Filing and service. The Board will set the times for filing and serving statements required under this section.

§41.205. SETTLEMENT AGREEMENTS

(a) Constructive notice; time for filing. Pursuant to 35 U.S.C. 135(c), an agreement or understanding, including collateral agreements referred to therein, made in connection with or in contemplation of the termination of an interference must be filed prior to the termination of the interference between the parties to the agreement. After a final decision is entered by the Board, an interference is considered terminated when no appeal (35 U.S.C. 141) or other review (35 U.S.C. 146) has been or can be taken or had. If an appeal to the U.S. Court of Appeals for the Federal Circuit (under 35 U.S.C. 141) or a civil action (under 35 U.S.C. 146) has been filed the interference is considered terminated when the appeal or civil action is terminated. A civil action is terminated when the time to appeal the judgment expires. An appeal to the U.S. Court of Appeals for the Federal Circuit, whether from a decision of the Board or a judgment in a civil action, is terminated when the mandate is issued by the Court.

(b) Untimely filing. The Chief Administrative Patent Judge may permit the filing of an agreement under paragraph (a) of this section up to six months after termination upon petition and a showing of good cause for the failure to file prior to termination.

(c) Request to keep separate. Any party to an agreement under paragraph (a) of this section may request that the agreement be kept separate from the interference file. The request must be filed with or promptly after the agreement is filed.

(d) Access to agreement. Any person, other than a representative of a Government agency, may have access to an agreement kept separate under paragraph (c) of this section only upon petition and on a showing of good cause. The agreement will be available to Government agencies on written request.

§41.206. COMMON INTERESTS IN THE INVENTION

An administrative patent judge may decline to declare, or if already declared the Board may issue judgment in, an interference between an application and another application or patent that are commonly owned.

§41.207. PRESUMPTIONS

(a) Priority—

(1) Order of invention. Parties are presumed to have invented interfering subject matter in the order of the dates of their accorded benefit for each count. If two parties are accorded the benefit of the same earliest date of constructive reduction to practice, then neither party is entitled to a presumption of priority with respect to the other such party.

(2) Evidentiary standard. Priority may be proved by a preponderance of the evidence except a party must prove priority by clear and convincing evidence if the date of its earliest constructive reduction to practice is after the issue date of an involved patent or the publication date under 35 U.S.C. 122(b) of an involved application or patent.

(b) Claim correspondence.

(1) For the purposes of determining priority and derivation, all claims of a party corresponding to the count are presumed to stand or fall together. To challenge this presumption, a party must file a timely substantive motion to have a corresponding claim designated as not corresponding to the count. No presumption based on claim correspondence regarding the grouping of claims exists for other grounds of unpatentability.

(2) A claim corresponds to a count if the subject matter of the count, treated as prior art to the claim, would have anticipated or rendered obvious the subject matter of the claim.

(c) Cross-applicability of prior art. When a motion for judgment of unpatentability against an opponent's claim on the basis of prior art is granted, each of the movant's claims corresponding to the same count as the opponent's claim will be presumed to be unpatentable in view of the same prior art unless the movant in its motion rebuts this presumption.

§41.208. CONTENT OF SUBSTANTIVE & RESPONSIVE MOTIONS

The general requirements for motions in contested cases are stated at §41.121(c).

(a) In an interference, substantive motions must:

(1) Raise a threshold issue,

(2) Seek to change the scope of the definition of the interfering subject matter or the correspondence of claims to the count,

(3) Seek to change the benefit accorded for the count, or

(4) Seek judgment on derivation or on priority.

(b) To be sufficient, a motion must provide a showing, supported with appropriate evidence, such that, if unrebutted, it would justify the relief sought. The burden of proof is on the movant.

(c) Showing patentability.

(1) A party moving to add or amend a claim must show the claim is patentable.

(2) A party moving to add or amend a count must show the count is patentable over prior art.

PART 42. TRIAL PRACTICE BEFORE THE PATENT TRIAL & APPEAL BOARD

SUBPART A. TRIAL PRACTICE & PROCEDURE

GENERAL

§42.1. POLICY

(a) Scope. Part 42 governs proceedings before the Patent Trial and Appeal Board. Sections 1.4, 1.7, 1.14, 1.16, 1.22, 1.23, 1.25, 1.26, 1.32, 1.34, and 1.36 of this chapter also apply to proceedings before the Board, as do other sections of part 1 of this chapter that are incorporated by reference into this part.

(b) Construction. This part shall be construed to secure the just, speedy, and inexpensive resolution of every proceeding.

(c) Decorum. Every party must act with courtesy and decorum in all proceedings before the Board, including in interactions with other parties.

(d) Evidentiary standard. The default evidentiary standard is a preponderance of the evidence.

History of 37 C.F.R. §42.1: 77 FR 48670, Sept. 16, 2012.

Source of 37 C.F.R. Part 42: 35 U.S.C. 2(b)(2), 6, 21, 23, 41,135, 311, 312, 316, 321-326 and Public Law 112-29.

§42.2. DEFINITIONS

The following definitions apply to this part:

Affidavit means affidavit or declaration under §1.68 of this chapter. A transcript of an ex parte deposition or a declaration under 28 U.S.C. 1746 may be used as an affidavit.

Board means the Patent Trial and Appeal Board. Board means a panel of the Board, or a member or employee acting with the authority of the Board, including:

(1) For petition decisions and interlocutory decisions, a Board member or employee acting with the authority of the Board.

(2) For final written decisions under 35 U.S.C. 135(d), 318(a), and 328(a), a panel of the Board.

Business day means a day other than a Saturday, Sunday, or Federal holiday within the District of Columbia.

Confidential information means trade secret or other confidential research, development, or commercial information.

Final means final for the purpose of judicial review to the extent available. A decision is final only if it disposes of all necessary issues with regard to the party seeking judicial review, and does not indicate that further action is required.

Hearing means consideration of the trial.

Involved means an application, patent, or claim that is the subject of the proceeding.

Judgment means a final written decision by the Board, or a termination of a proceeding.

Motion means a request for relief other than by petition.

Office means the United States Patent and Trademark Office.

Panel means at least three members of the Board.

Party means at least the petitioner and the patent owner and, in a derivation proceeding, any applicant or assignee of the involved application.

Petition is a request that a trial be instituted.

Petitioner means the party filing a petition requesting that a trial be instituted.

Preliminary Proceeding begins with the filing of a petition for instituting a trial and ends with a written decision as to whether a trial will be instituted.

Proceeding means a trial or preliminary proceeding.

Rehearing means reconsideration.

Trial means a contested case instituted by the Board based upon a petition. A trial begins with a written decision notifying the petitioner and patent owner of the institution of the trial. The term trial specifically includes a derivation proceeding under 35 U.S.C. 135; an inter partes review under Chapter 31 of title 35, United States Code; a post-grant review under Chapter 32 of title 35, United States Code; and a transitional business-method review under section 18 of the Leahy-Smith America Invents Act. Patent interferences are administered under part 41 and not under part 42 of this title, and therefore are not trials.

History of 37 C.F.R. §42.2: 77 FR 48670, Sept. 16, 2012.

§42.3. JURISDICTION

(a) The Board may exercise exclusive jurisdiction within the Office over every involved application and patent during the proceeding, as the Board may order.

(b) A petition to institute a trial must be filed with the Board consistent with any time period required by statute.

History of 37 C.F.R. §42.3: 77 FR 48670, Sept. 16, 2012.

§42.4. NOTICE OF TRIAL

(a) Institution of trial. The Board institutes the trial on behalf of the Director.

(b) Notice of a trial will be sent to every party to the proceeding. The entry of the notice institutes the trial.

(c) The Board may authorize additional modes of notice, including:

(1) Sending notice to another address associated with the party, or

(2) Publishing the notice in the Official Gazette of the United States Patent and Trademark Office or the Federal Register.

History of 37 C.F.R. §42.4: 77 FR 48670, Sept. 16, 2012.

§42.5. CONDUCT OF THE PROCEEDING

(a) The Board may determine a proper course of conduct in a proceeding for any situation not specifically covered by this part and may enter non-final orders to administer the proceeding.

(b) The Board may waive or suspend a requirement of parts 1, 41, and 42 and may place conditions on the waiver or suspension.

(c) Times. **(1)** Setting times. The Board may set times by order. Times set by rule are default and may be modified by order. Any modification of times will take any applicable statutory pendency goal into account.

(2) Extension of time. A request for an extension of time must be supported by a showing of good cause.

(3) Late action. A late action will be excused on a showing of good cause or upon a Board decision that consideration on the merits would be in the interests of justice.

(d) Ex parte communications. Communication regarding a specific proceeding with a Board member defined in 35 U.S.C. 6(a) is not permitted unless both parties have an opportunity to be involved in the communication.

History of 37 C.F.R. §42.5: 77 FR 48670, Sept. 16, 2012.

§42.6. FILING OF DOCUMENTS, INCLUDING EXHIBITS; SERVICE

(a) General format requirements. **(1)** Page size must be 8½ inch x 11 inch except in the case of exhibits that require a larger size in order to preserve details of the original.

(2) In documents, including affidavits, created for the proceeding:

(i) Markings must be in black or must otherwise provide an equivalent dark, high-contrast image;

(ii) 14-point, Times New Roman proportional font, with normal spacing, must be used;

(iii) Double spacing must be used except in claim charts, headings, tables of contents, tables of authorities, indices, signature blocks, and certificates of service. Block quotations may be 1.5 spaced, but must be indented from both the left and the right margins; and

(iv) Margins must be at least 2.5 centimeters (1 inch) on all sides.

(3) Incorporation by reference; combined documents. Arguments must not be incorporated by reference from one document into another document. Combined motions, oppositions, replies, or other combined documents are not permitted.

(4) Signature; identification. Documents must be signed in accordance with §§1.33 and 11.18(a) of this title, and should be identified by the trial number (where known).

(b) Modes of filing. **(1)** Electronic filing. Unless otherwise authorized, submissions are to be made to the Board

See the Office Patent Trial Practice Guide, p. 1336.

electronically via the Internet according to the parameters established by the Board and published on the Web site of the Office.

(2)(i) Filing by means other than electronic filing. A document filed by means other than electronic filing must:

(A) Be accompanied by a motion requesting acceptance of the submission; and

(B) Identify a date of transmission where a party seeks a filing date other than the date of receipt at the Board.

(ii) Mailed correspondence shall be sent to: Mail Stop PATENT BOARD, Patent Trial and Appeal Board, United States Patent and Trademark Office, PO Box 1450, Alexandria, Virginia 22313-1450.

(c) Exhibits. Each exhibit must be filed with the first document in which it is cited except as the Board may otherwise order.

(d) Previously filed paper. A document already in the record of the proceeding must not be filed again, not even as an exhibit or an appendix, without express Board authorization.

(e) Service. **(1)** Electronic or other mode. Service may be made electronically upon agreement of the parties. Otherwise, service may be by Priority Mail Express® or by means at least as fast and reliable as Priority Mail Express®.

(2) Simultaneous with filing. Each document filed with the Board, if not previously served, must be served simultaneously on each opposing party.

(3) Counsel of record. If a party is represented by counsel of record in the proceeding, service must be on counsel.

(4) Certificate of service. **(i)** Each document, other than an exhibit, must include a certificate of service at the end of that document. Any exhibit filed with the document may be included in the certification for the document.

(ii) For an exhibit filed separately, a transmittal letter incorporating the certificate of service must be filed. If more than one exhibit is filed at one time, a single letter should be used for all of the exhibits filed together. The letter must state the name and exhibit number for every exhibit filed with the letter.

(iii) The certificate of service must state:

(A) The date and manner of service; and

(B) The name and address of every person served.

History of 37 C.F.R. §42.6: 77 FR 48670, Sept. 16, 2012; 79 FR 63043, Oct. 22, 2014; 80 FR 28565, May 19, 2015.

§42.7. MANAGEMENT OF THE RECORD

(a) The Board may expunge any paper directed to a proceeding or filed while an application or patent is under the jurisdiction of the Board that is not authorized under this part or in a Board order or that is filed contrary to a Board order.

(b) The Board may vacate or hold in abeyance any non-Board action directed to a proceeding while an application or patent is under the jurisdiction of the Board unless the action was authorized by the Board.

History of 37 C.F.R. §42.7: 77 FR 48671, Sept. 16, 2012.

§42.8. MANDATORY NOTICES

(a) Each notice listed in paragraph (b) of this section must be filed with the Board:

(1) By the petitioner, as part of the petition;

(2) By the patent owner, or applicant in the case of derivation, within 21 days of service of the petition; or

(3) By either party, within 21 days of a change of the information listed in paragraph (b) of this section stated in an earlier paper.

(b) Each of the following notices must be filed:

(1) Real party-in-interest. Identify each real party-in-interest for the party.

(2) Related matters. Identify any other judicial or administrative matter that would affect, or be affected by, a decision in the proceeding.

(3) Lead and back-up counsel. If the party is represented by counsel, then counsel must be identified.

(4) Service information. Identify (if applicable):

(i) An electronic mail address;

(ii) A postal mailing address;

(iii) A hand-delivery address, if different than the postal mailing address;

(iv) A telephone number; and

(v) A facsimile number.

History of 37 C.F.R. §42.8: 77 FR 48671, Sept. 16, 2012.

§42.9. ACTION BY PATENT OWNER

(a) Entire interest. An owner of the entire interest in an involved application or patent may act to the exclusion of the inventor (see §3.71 of this title).

(b) Part interest. An owner of a part interest in the subject patent may move to act to the exclusion of an inventor or a co-owner. The motion must show the inability or refusal of an inventor or co-owner to prosecute the proceeding or other cause why it is in the interests of justice to permit the owner of a part interest to act in the trial. In granting the motion, the Board may set conditions on the actions of the parties.

History of 37 C.F.R. §42.9: 77 FR 48671, Sept. 16, 2012.

§42.10. COUNSEL

(a) If a party is represented by counsel, the party must designate a lead counsel and at least one back-up counsel who can conduct business on behalf of the lead counsel.

(b) A power of attorney must be filed with the designation of counsel, except the patent owner should not file an additional power of attorney if the designated counsel is already counsel of record in the subject patent or application.

(c) The Board may recognize counsel pro hac vice during a proceeding upon a showing of good cause, subject to the condition that lead counsel be a registered practitioner and to any other conditions as the Board may impose. For example, where the lead counsel is a registered practitioner, a motion to appear pro hac vice by counsel who is not a registered practitioner may be granted upon showing that counsel is an experienced litigating attorney and has an established familiarity with the subject matter at issue in the proceeding.

(d) A panel of the Board may disqualify counsel for cause after notice and opportunity for hearing. A decision to disqualify is not final for the purposes of judicial review until certified by the Chief Administrative Patent Judge.

(e) Counsel may not withdraw from a proceeding before the Board unless the Board authorizes such withdrawal.

History of 37 C.F.R. §42.10: 77 FR 48671, Sept. 16, 2012; 80 FR 28565, May 19, 2015.

§42.11. DUTY OF CANDOR; SIGNING PAPERS; REPRESENTATIONS TO THE BOARD; SANCTIONS

(a) Duty of candor. Parties and individuals involved in the proceeding have a duty of candor and good faith to the Office during the course of a proceeding.

(b) Signature. Every petition, response, written motion, and other paper filed in a proceeding must comply with the signature requirements set forth in §11.18(a) of this chapter. The Board may expunge any unsigned submission unless the omission is promptly corrected after being called to the counsel's or party's attention.

(c) Representations to the Board. By presenting to the Board a petition, response, written motion, or other paper—whether by signing, filing, submitting, or later advocating it—an attorney, registered practitioner, or unrepresented party attests to compliance with the certification requirements under §11.18(b)(2) of this chapter.

(d) Sanctions—

(1) In general. If, after notice and a reasonable opportunity to respond, the Board determines that paragraph (c) of this section has been violated, the Board may impose an appropriate sanction on any attorney, registered practitioner, or party that violated the rule or is responsible for the violation.

(2) Motion for sanctions. A motion for sanctions must be made separately from any other motion and must describe the specific conduct that allegedly violates paragraph (c) of this section. The motion must be authorized by the Board under §42.20 prior to filing the motion. At least 21 days prior to seeking authorization to file a motion for sanctions, the moving party must serve the other party with the proposed motion. A motion for sanctions must not be filed or be presented to the Board if the challenged paper, claim, defense, contention, or denial is withdrawn or appropriately corrected within 21 days after service of such motion or within another time the Board sets. If warranted, the Board may award to the prevailing party the reasonable expenses, including attorney's fees, incurred for the motion.

(3) On the Board's initiative. On its own, the Board may order an attorney, registered practitioner, or party to show cause why conduct specifically described in the order has not violated paragraph (c) of this section and why a specific sanction authorized by the Board should not be imposed.

(4) Nature of a sanction. A sanction imposed under this rule must be limited to what suffices to deter repetition of the conduct or comparable conduct by others similarly situated and should be consistent with §42.12.

(5) Requirements for an order. An order imposing a sanction must describe the sanctioned conduct and explain the basis for the sanction.

History of 37 C.F.R. §42.11: 77 FR 48671, Sept. 16, 2012; 81 FR 18765, May 2, 2016.

§42.12. SANCTIONS

(a) The Board may impose a sanction against a party for misconduct, including:

(1) Failure to comply with an applicable rule or order in the proceeding;

(2) Advancing a misleading or frivolous argument or request for relief;

(3) Misrepresentation of a fact;

(4) Engaging in dilatory tactics;

(5) Abuse of discovery;

(6) Abuse of process; or

(7) Any other improper use of the proceeding, including actions that harass or cause unnecessary delay or an unnecessary increase in the cost of the proceeding.

(b) Sanctions include entry of one or more of the following:

(1) An order holding facts to have been established in the proceeding;

(2) An order expunging or precluding a party from filing a paper;

(3) An order precluding a party from presenting or contesting a particular issue;

(4) An order precluding a party from requesting, obtaining, or opposing discovery;

(5) An order excluding evidence;

(6) An order providing for compensatory expenses, including attorney fees;

(7) An order requiring terminal disclaimer of patent term; or

(8) Judgment in the trial or dismissal of the petition.

History of 37 C.F.R. §42.12: 77 FR 48671, Sept. 16, 2012.

§42.13. CITATION OF AUTHORITY

(a) For any United States Supreme Court decision, citation to the United States Reports is preferred.

(b) For any decision other than a United States Supreme Court decision, citation to the West Reporter System is preferred.

See the Office Patent Trial Practice Guide, p. 1336.

(c) Citations to authority must include pinpoint citations whenever a specific holding or portion of an authority is invoked.

(d) Non-binding authority should be used sparingly. If the authority is not an authority of the Office and is not reproduced in the United States Reports or the West Reporter System, a copy of the authority should be provided.

History of 37 C.F.R. §42.13: 77 FR 48672, Sept. 16, 2012.

§42.14. PUBLIC AVAILABILITY

The record of a proceeding, including documents and things, shall be made available to the public, except as otherwise ordered. A party intending a document or thing to be sealed shall file a motion to seal concurrent with the filing of the document or thing to be sealed. The document or thing shall be provisionally sealed on receipt of the motion and remain so pending the outcome of the decision on the motion.

History of 37 C.F.R. §42.14: 77 FR 48672, Sept. 16, 2012.

FEES

A §42.15. FEES

(a) On filing a petition for inter partes review of a patent, payment of the following fees are due:

(1) Inter Partes Review request fee: $15,500.00.

(2) Inter Partes Review Post-Institution fee: $15,000.00.

(3) In addition to the Inter Partes Review request fee, for requesting review of each claim in excess of 20: $300.00.

(4) In addition to the Inter Partes Post-Institution request fee, for requesting review of each claim in excess of 15: $600.00.

(b) On filing a petition for post-grant review or covered business method patent review of a patent, payment of the following fees are due:

(1) Post-Grant or Covered Business Method Patent Review request fee: $16,000.00.

(2) Post-Grant or Covered Business Method Patent Review Post-Institution fee: $22,000.00.

(3) In addition to the Post-Grant or Covered Business Method Patent Review request fee, for requesting review of each claim in excess of 20: $375.00.

(4) In addition to the Post-Grant or Covered Business Method Patent Review Post-Institution fee, for requesting review of each claim in excess of 15: $825.00.

(c) On the filing of a petition for a derivation proceeding, payment of the following fees is due:

(1) Derivation petition fee: $400.00.

(d) Any request requiring payment of a fee under this part, including a written request to make a settlement agreement available: $400.00.

History of 37 C.F.R. §42.15: 77 FR 48672, Sept. 16, 2012; 78 FR 4291, Mar. 19, 2013; 80 FR 28565, May 19, 2015; 82 FR 52817, Jan. 16, 2018.

PETITION & MOTION PRACTICE

§42.20. GENERALLY

(a) Relief. Relief, other than a petition requesting the institution of a trial, must be requested in the form of a motion.

(b) Prior authorization. A motion will not be entered without Board authorization. Authorization may be provided in an order of general applicability or during the proceeding.

(c) Burden of proof. The moving party has the burden of proof to establish that it is entitled to the requested relief.

(d) Briefing. The Board may order briefing on any issue involved in the trial.

History of 37 C.F.R. §42.20: 77 FR 48672, Sept. 16, 2012.

§42.21. NOTICE OF BASIS FOR RELIEF

(a) Notice of request for relief. The Board may require a party to file a notice stating the relief it requests and the basis for its entitlement to relief. A notice must include sufficient detail to place the Board and each opponent on notice of the precise relief requested. A notice is not evidence except as an admission by a party-opponent.

(b) Filing and service. The Board may set the times and conditions for filing and serving notices required under this section. The Board may provide for the notice filed with the Board to be maintained in confidence for a limited time.

(c) Effect. If a notice under paragraph (a) of this section is required:

(1) A failure to state a sufficient basis for relief may result in a denial of the relief requested;

(2) A party will be limited to filing motions consistent with the notice; and

(3) Ambiguities in the notice will be construed against the party.

(d) Correction. A party may move to correct its notice. The motion should be filed promptly after the party becomes aware of the basis for the correction. A correction filed after the time set for filing notices will only be entered if entry would serve the interests of justice.

History of 37 C.F.R. §42.21: 77 FR 48672, Sept. 16, 2012.

§42.22. CONTENT OF PETITIONS & MOTIONS

(a) Each petition or motion must be filed as a separate paper and must include:

(1) A statement of the precise relief requested; and

(2) A full statement of the reasons for the relief requested, including a detailed explanation of the significance of the evidence including material facts, and the governing law, rules, and precedent.

(b) Relief requested. Where a rule in part 1 of this title ordinarily governs the relief sought, the petition or motion must make any showings required under that rule in addition to any showings required in this part.

(c) Statement of material facts. Each petition or motion may include a statement of material fact. Each material fact preferably shall be set forth as a separately numbered sentence with specific citations to the portions of the record that support the fact.

(d) The Board may order additional showings or explanations as a condition for authorizing a motion (see §42.20(b)).

History of 37 C.F.R. §42.22: 77 FR 48672, Sept. 16, 2012.

§42.23. OPPOSITIONS & REPLIES

(a) Oppositions and replies must comply with the content requirements for motions and, if the paper to which the opposition or reply is responding contains a statement of material fact, must include a listing of facts that are admitted, denied, or cannot be admitted or denied. Any material fact not specifically denied may be considered admitted.

(b) All arguments for the relief requested in a motion must be made in the motion. A reply may only respond to arguments raised in the corresponding opposition, patent owner preliminary response, or patent owner response.

History of 37 C.F.R. §42.23: 77 FR 48672, Sept. 16, 2012; 80 FR 28565, May 19, 2015; 81 FR 18765, May 2, 2016.

§42.24. TYPE-VOLUME OR PAGE-LIMITS FOR PETITIONS, MOTIONS, OPPOSITIONS, & REPLIES

(a) Petitions and motions.

(1) The following word counts or page limits for petitions and motions apply and include any statement of material facts to be admitted or denied in support of the petition or motion. The word count or page limit does not include a table of contents, a table of authorities, mandatory notices under §42.8, a certificate of service or word count, or appendix of exhibits or claim listing.

(i) Petition requesting inter partes review: 14,000 words.

(ii) Petition requesting post-grant review: 18,700 words.

(iii) Petition requesting covered business method patent review: 18,700 words.

(iv) Petition requesting derivation proceeding: 14,000 words.

(v) Motions (excluding motions to amend): 15 pages.

(vi) Motions to Amend: 25 pages.

(2) Petitions to institute a trial must comply with the stated word counts but may be accompanied by a motion to waive the word counts. The petitioner must show in the motion how a waiver of the word counts is in the interests of justice and must append a copy of proposed petition exceeding the word count to the motion. If the motion is not granted, the proposed petition exceeding the word count may be expunged or returned. Any other motion to waive word counts or page limits must be granted in advance of filing a motion, opposition, or reply for which the waiver is necessary.

(b) Patent owner responses and oppositions. The word counts or page limits set forth in this paragraph (b) do not include a listing of facts which are admitted, denied, or cannot be admitted or denied.

(1) The word counts for a patent owner preliminary response to petition are the same as the word counts for the petition.

(2) The word counts for a patent owner response to petition are the same as the word counts for the petition.

(3) The page limits for oppositions are the same as those for corresponding motions.

(c) Replies. The following word counts or page limits for replies apply and include any statement of facts in support of the reply. The word counts or page limits do not include a table of contents, a table of authorities, a listing of facts which are admitted, denied, or cannot be admitted or denied, a certificate of service or word count, or appendix of exhibits.

(1) Replies to patent owner responses to petitions: 5,600 words.

(2) Replies to oppositions (excluding replies to oppositions to motions to amend): 5 pages.

(3) Replies to oppositions to motions to amend: 12 pages.

(d) Certification. Any paper whose length is specified by type-volume limits must include a certification stating the number of words in the paper. A party may rely on the word count of the word-processing system used to prepare the paper.

History of 37 C.F.R. §42.24: 77 FR 48673, Sept. 16, 2012; 80 FR 28565, May 19, 2015; 81 FR 18765, May 2, 2016; 81 FR 24703, May 2, 2016.

§42.25. DEFAULT FILING TIMES

(a) A motion may only be filed according to a schedule set by the Board. The default times for acting are:

(1) An opposition is due one month after service of the motion; and

(2) A reply is due one month after service of the opposition.

(b) A party should seek relief promptly after the need for relief is identified. Delay in seeking relief may justify a denial of relief sought.

History of 37 C.F.R. §42.25: 77 FR 48673, Sept. 16, 2012.

TESTIMONY & PRODUCTION

§42.51. DISCOVERY

(a) Mandatory initial disclosures.

(1) With agreement. Parties may agree to mandatory discovery requiring the initial disclosures set forth in the Office Patent Trial Practice Guide.

(i) The parties must submit any agreement reached on initial disclosures by no later than the filing of the patent owner preliminary response or the expiration of the time pe-

See the Office Patent Trial Practice Guide, p. 1336.

riod for filing such a response. The initial disclosures of the parties shall be filed as exhibits.

(ii) Upon the institution of a trial, parties may automatically take discovery of the information identified in the initial disclosures.

(2) Without agreement. Where the parties fail to agree to the mandatory discovery set forth in paragraph (a)(1), a party may seek such discovery by motion.

(b) Limited discovery. A party is not entitled to discovery except as provided in paragraph (a) of this section, or as otherwise authorized in this subpart.

(1) Routine discovery. Except as the Board may otherwise order:

(i) Unless previously served or otherwise by agreement of the parties, any exhibit cited in a paper or in testimony must be served with the citing paper or testimony.

(ii) Cross examination of affidavit testimony prepared for the proceeding is authorized within such time period as the Board may set.

(iii) Unless previously served, a party must serve relevant information that is inconsistent with a position advanced by the party during the proceeding concurrent with the filing of the documents or things that contains the inconsistency. This requirement does not make discoverable anything otherwise protected by legally recognized privileges such as attorney-client or attorney work product. This requirement extends to inventors, corporate officers, and persons involved in the preparation or filing of the documents or things.

(2) Additional discovery. **(i)** The parties may agree to additional discovery between themselves. Where the parties fail to agree, a party may move for additional discovery. The moving party must show that such additional discovery is in the interests of justice, except in post-grant reviews where additional discovery is limited to evidence directly related to factual assertions advanced by either party in the proceeding (see §42.224). The Board may specify conditions for such additional discovery.

(ii) When appropriate, a party may obtain production of documents and things during cross examination of an opponent's witness or during authorized compelled testimony under §42.52.

(c) Production of documents. Except as otherwise ordered by the Board, a party producing documents and things shall either provide copies to the opposing party or make the documents and things available for inspection and copying at a reasonable time and location in the United States.

History of 37 C.F.R. §42.51: 77 FR 48673, Sept. 16, 2012; 80 FR 28565, May 19, 2015.

§42.52. COMPELLING TESTIMONY & PRODUCTION

(a) Authorization required. A party seeking to compel testimony or production of documents or things must file a motion for authorization. The motion must describe the general relevance of the testimony, document, or thing, and must:

(1) In the case of testimony, identify the witness by name or title; and

(2) In the case of a document or thing, the general nature of the document or thing.

(b) Outside the United States. For testimony or production sought outside the United States, the motion must also:

(1) In the case of testimony. **(i)** Identify the foreign country and explain why the party believes the witness can be compelled to testify in the foreign country, including a description of the procedures that will be used to compel the testimony in the foreign country and an estimate of the time it is expected to take to obtain the testimony; and

(ii) Demonstrate that the party has made reasonable efforts to secure the agreement of the witness to testify in the United States but has been unsuccessful in obtaining the agreement, even though the party has offered to pay the travel expenses of the witness to testify in the United States.

(2) In the case of production of a document or thing. **(i)** Identify the foreign country and explain why the party believes production of the document or thing can be compelled in the foreign country, including a description of the procedures that will be used to compel production of the document or thing in the foreign country and an estimate of the time it is expected to take to obtain production of the document or thing; and

(ii) Demonstrate that the party has made reasonable efforts to obtain the agreement of the individual or entity having possession, custody, or control of the document or thing to produce the document or thing in the United States but has been unsuccessful in obtaining that agreement, even though the party has offered to pay the expenses of producing the document or thing in the United States.

History of 37 C.F.R. §42.52: 77 FR 48673, Sept. 16, 2012.

§42.53. TAKING TESTIMONY

(a) Form. Uncompelled direct testimony must be submitted in the form of an affidavit. All other testimony, including testimony compelled under 35 U.S.C. 24, must be in the form of a deposition transcript. Parties may agree to video-recorded testimony, but may not submit such testimony without prior authorization of the Board. In addition, the Board may authorize or require live or video-recorded testimony.

(b) Time and location. **(1)** Uncompelled direct testimony may be taken at any time to support a petition, motion, opposition, or reply; otherwise, testimony may only be taken during a testimony period set by the Board.

(2) Except as the Board otherwise orders, during the testimony period, deposition testimony may be taken at any reasonable time and location within the United States before any disinterested official authorized to administer oaths at that location.

(3) Uncompelled deposition testimony outside the United States may only be taken upon agreement of the parties or as the Board specifically directs.

(c) Duration. **(1)** Unless stipulated by the parties or ordered by the Board, direct examination, cross-examination, and redirect examination for compelled deposition testimony shall be subject to the following time limits: Seven hours for direct examination, four hours for cross-examination, and two hours for redirect examination.

(2) Unless stipulated by the parties or ordered by the Board, cross-examination, redirect examination, and re-cross examination for uncompelled direct testimony shall be subject to the follow[1] time limits: Seven hours for cross-examination, four hours for redirect examination, and two hours for re-cross examination.

(d) Notice of deposition. **(1)** Prior to the taking of deposition testimony, all parties to the proceeding must agree on the time and place for taking testimony. If the parties cannot agree, the party seeking the testimony must initiate a conference with the Board to set a time and place.

(2) Cross-examination should ordinarily take place after any supplemental evidence relating to the direct testimony has been filed and more than a week before the filing date for any paper in which the cross-examination testimony is expected to be used. A party requesting cross-examination testimony of more than one witness may choose the order in which the witnesses are to be cross-examined.

(3) In the case of direct deposition testimony, at least three business days prior to the conference in paragraph (d)(1) of this section, or if there is no conference, at least ten days prior to the deposition, the party seeking the direct testimony must serve:

(i) A list and copy of each document under the party's control and on which the party intends to rely; and

(ii) A list of, and proffer of reasonable access to, anything other than a document under the party's control and on which the party intends to rely.

(4) The party seeking the deposition must file a notice of the deposition at least ten business days before a deposition.

(5) Scope and content—**(i)** For direct deposition testimony, the notice limits the scope of the testimony and must list:

(A) The time and place of the deposition;

(B) The name and address of the witness;

(C) A list of the exhibits to be relied upon during the deposition; and

(D) A general description of the scope and nature of the testimony to be elicited.

(ii) For cross-examination testimony, the scope of the examination is limited to the scope of the direct testimony.

(iii) The notice must list the time and place of the deposition.

(iv) Where an additional party seeks to take direct testimony of a third party witness at the time and place noticed in paragraph (d)(5) of this section, the additional party must provide a counter notice that lists the exhibits to be relied upon in the deposition and a general description of the scope and nature of the testimony to be elicited.

(6) Motion to quash—Objection to a defect in the notice is waived unless the objecting party promptly seeks authorization to file a motion to quash.

(e) Deposition in a foreign language. If an interpreter will be used during the deposition, the party calling the witness must initiate a conference with the Board at least five business days before the deposition.

(f) Manner of taking deposition testimony. **(1)** Before giving deposition testimony, each witness shall be duly sworn according to law by the officer before whom the deposition is to be taken. The officer must be authorized to take testimony under 35 U.S.C. 23.

(2) The testimony shall be taken with any questions and answers recorded in their regular order by the officer, or by some other disinterested person in the presence of the officer, unless the presence of the officer is waived on the record by agreement of all parties.

(3) Any exhibits used during the deposition must be numbered as required by §42.63(c), and must, if not previously served, be served at the deposition. Exhibits objected to shall be accepted pending a decision on the objection.

(4) All objections made at the time of the deposition to the qualifications of the officer taking the deposition, the manner of taking it, the evidence presented, the conduct of any party, and any other objection to the deposition shall be noted on the record by the officer.

(5) When the testimony has been transcribed, the witness shall read and sign (in the form of an affidavit) a transcript of the deposition unless:

(i) The parties otherwise agree in writing;

(ii) The parties waive reading and signature by the witness on the record at the deposition; or

(iii) The witness refuses to read or sign the transcript of the deposition.

(6) The officer shall prepare a certified transcript by attaching a certificate in the form of an affidavit signed and sealed by the officer to the transcript of the deposition. Unless the parties waive any of the following requirements, in which case the certificate shall so state, the certificate must state:

(i) The witness was duly sworn by the officer before commencement of testimony by the witness;

(ii) The transcript is a true record of the testimony given by the witness;

See the Office Patent Trial Practice Guide, p. 1336.

(iii) The name of the person who recorded the testimony, and if the officer did not record it, whether the testimony was recorded in the presence of the officer;

(iv) The presence or absence of any opponent;

(v) The place where the deposition was taken and the day and hour when the deposition began and ended;

(vi) The officer has no disqualifying interest, personal or financial, in a party; and

(vii) If a witness refuses to read or sign the transcript, the circumstances under which the witness refused.

(7) Except where the parties agree otherwise, the proponent of the testimony must arrange for providing a copy of the transcript to all other parties. The testimony must be filed as an exhibit.

(8) Any objection to the content, form, or manner of taking the deposition, including the qualifications of the officer, is waived unless made on the record during the deposition and preserved in a timely filed motion to exclude.

(g) Costs. Except as the Board may order or the parties may agree in writing, the proponent of the direct testimony shall bear all costs associated with the testimony, including the reasonable costs associated with making the witness available for the cross-examination.

1. **Editor's note:** Probably should be "following."

History of 37 C.F.R. §42.53: 77 FR 48674, Sept. 16, 2012; 80 FR 28565, May 19, 2015.

§42.54. PROTECTIVE ORDER

(a) A party may file a motion to seal where the motion to seal contains a proposed protective order, such as the default protective order set forth in the Office Patent Trial Practice Guide. The motion must include a certification that the moving party has in good faith conferred or attempted to confer with other affected parties in an effort to resolve the dispute. The Board may, for good cause, issue an order to protect a party or person from disclosing confidential information, including, but not limited to, one or more of the following:

(1) Forbidding the disclosure or discovery;

(2) Specifying terms, including time and place, for the disclosure or discovery;

(3) Prescribing a discovery method other than the one selected by the party seeking discovery;

(4) Forbidding inquiry into certain matters, or limiting the scope of disclosure or discovery to certain matters;

(5) Designating the persons who may be present while the discovery is conducted;

(6) Requiring that a deposition be sealed and opened only by order of the Board;

(7) Requiring that a trade secret or other confidential research, development, or commercial information not be revealed or be revealed only in a specified way; and

(8) Requiring that the parties simultaneously file specified documents or information in sealed envelopes, to be opened as the Board directs.

(b) [Reserved]

History of 37 C.F.R. §42.54: 77 FR 48675, Sept. 16, 2012.

§42.55. CONFIDENTIAL INFORMATION IN A PETITION

A petitioner filing confidential information with a petition may, concurrent with the filing of the petition, file a motion to seal with a proposed protective order as to the confidential information. The institution of the requested trial will constitute a grant of the motion to seal unless otherwise ordered by the Board.

(a) Default protective order. Where a motion to seal requests entry of the default protective order set forth in the Office Patent Trial Practice Guide, the petitioner must file, but need not serve, the confidential information under seal. The patent owner may only access the filed sealed information prior to the institution of the trial by agreeing to the terms of the default protective order or obtaining relief from the Board.

(b) Protective orders other than default protective order. Where a motion to seal requests entry of a protective order other than the default protective order, the petitioner must file, but need not serve, the confidential information under seal. The patent owner may only access the sealed confidential information prior to the institution of the trial by:

(1) agreeing to the terms of the protective order requested by the petitioner;

(2) agreeing to the terms of a protective order that the parties file jointly; or

(3) obtaining entry of a protective order (e.g., the default protective order).

History of 37 C.F.R. §42.55: 77 FR 48675, Sept. 16, 2012.

§42.56. EXPUNGEMENT OF CONFIDENTIAL INFORMATION

After denial of a petition to institute a trial or after final judgment in a trial, a party may file a motion to expunge confidential information from the record.

History of 37 C.F.R. §42.56: 77 FR 48675, Sept. 16, 2012.

E §42.57. PRIVILEGE FOR PATENT PRACTITIONERS

(a) Privileged communications. A communication between a client and a USPTO patent practitioner or a foreign jurisdiction patent practitioner that is reasonably necessary and incident to the scope of the practitioner's authority shall receive the same protections of privilege under Federal law as if that communication were between a client and an attorney authorized to practice in the United States, including all limitations and exceptions.

(b) Definitions. The term "USPTO patent practitioner" means a person who has fulfilled the requirements to practice patent matters before the United States Patent and Trademark Office under §11.7 of this chapter. "Foreign jurisdiction patent practitioner" means a person who is authorized to provide legal advice on patent matters in a foreign jurisdiction, provided that the jurisdiction establishes professional qualifications and the practitioner satisfies them. For foreign jurisdiction practitioners, this rule applies regardless of whether that jurisdiction provides privilege or an equivalent under its laws.

(c) Scope of coverage. USPTO patent practitioners and foreign jurisdiction patent practitioners shall receive the same treatment as attorneys on all issues affecting privilege or waiver, such as communications with employees or assistants of the practitioner and communications between multiple practitioners.

History of 37 C.F.R. §42.57: 82 FR 51575, Dec. 7, 2017.

§42.61. ADMISSIBILITY

(a) Evidence that is not taken, sought, or filed in accordance with this subpart is not admissible.

(b) Records of the Office. Certification is not necessary as a condition to admissibility when the evidence to be submitted is a record of the Office to which all parties have access.

(c) Specification and drawings. A specification or drawing of a United States patent application or patent is admissible as evidence only to prove what the specification or drawing describes. If there is data in the specification or a drawing upon which a party intends to rely to prove the truth of the data, an affidavit by an individual having first-hand knowledge of how the data was generated must be filed.

History of 37 C.F.R. §42.61: 77 FR 48675, Sept. 16, 2012.

§42.62. APPLICABILITY OF THE FEDERAL RULES OF EVIDENCE

(a) Generally. Except as otherwise provided in this subpart, the Federal Rules of Evidence shall apply to a proceeding.

(b) Exclusions. Those portions of the Federal Rules of Evidence relating to criminal proceedings, juries, and other matters not relevant to proceedings under this subpart shall not apply.

(c) Modifications in terminology. Unless otherwise clear from context, the following terms of the Federal Rules of Evidence shall be construed as indicated:

Appellate court means United States Court of Appeals for the Federal Circuit.

Civil action, civil proceeding, and action mean a proceeding before the Board under part 42.

Courts of the United States, U.S. Magistrate, court, trial court, trier of fact, and judge mean Board.

Hearing means, as defined in Federal Rule of Evidence 804(a)(5), the time for taking testimony.

Judicial notice means official notice.

Trial or hearing in Federal Rule of Evidence 807 means the time for taking testimony.

(d) In determining foreign law, the Board may consider any relevant material or source, including testimony, whether or not submitted by a party or admissible under the Federal Rules of Evidence.

History of 37 C.F.R. §42.62: 77 FR 48675, Sept. 16, 2012.

§42.63. FORM OF EVIDENCE

(a) Exhibits required. Evidence consists of affidavits, transcripts of depositions, documents, and things. All evidence must be filed in the form of an exhibit.

(b) Translation required. When a party relies on a document or is required to produce a document in a language other than English, a translation of the document into English and an affidavit attesting to the accuracy of the translation must be filed with the document.

(c) Exhibit numbering. Each party's exhibits must be uniquely numbered sequentially in a range the Board specifies. For the petitioner, the range is 1001-1999, and for the patent owner, the range is 2001-2999.

(d) Exhibit format. An exhibit must conform with the requirements for papers in §42.6 and the requirements of this paragraph.

(1) Each exhibit must have an exhibit label.

(i) An exhibit filed with the petition must include the petitioner's name followed by a unique exhibit number.

(ii) For exhibits not filed with the petition, the exhibit label must include the party's name followed by a unique exhibit number, the names of the parties, and the trial number.

(2) When the exhibit is a paper:

(i) Each page must be uniquely numbered in sequence; and

(ii) The exhibit label must be affixed to the lower right corner of the first page of the exhibit without obscuring information on the first page or, if obscuring is unavoidable, affixed to a duplicate first page.

(e) Exhibit list. Each party must maintain an exhibit list with the exhibit number and a brief description of each exhibit. If the exhibit is not filed, the exhibit list should note that fact. A current exhibit list must be served whenever evidence is served and the current exhibit list must be filed when filing exhibits.

History of 37 C.F.R. §42.63: 77 FR 48675, Sept. 16, 2012.

§42.64. OBJECTION; MOTION TO EXCLUDE

(a) Deposition evidence. An objection to the admissibility of deposition evidence must be made during the deposition. Evidence to cure the objection must be provided during the deposition, unless the parties to the deposition stipulate otherwise on the deposition record.

(b) Other evidence. For evidence other than deposition evidence:

See the Office Patent Trial Practice Guide, p. 1336.

(1) Objection. Any objection to evidence submitted during a preliminary proceeding must be filed within ten business days of the institution of the trial. Once a trial has been instituted, any objection must be filed within five business days of service of evidence to which the objection is directed. The objection must identify the grounds for the objection with sufficient particularity to allow correction in the form of supplemental evidence.

(2) Supplemental evidence. The party relying on evidence to which an objection is timely served may respond to the objection by serving supplemental evidence within ten business days of service of the objection.

(c) Motion to exclude. A motion to exclude evidence must be filed to preserve any objection. The motion must identify the objections in the record in order and must explain the objections. The motion may be filed without prior authorization from the Board.

History of 37 C.F.R. §42.64: 77 FR 48676, Sept. 16, 2012; 80 FR 28565, May 19, 2015.

§42.65. EXPERT TESTIMONY; TESTS & DATA

(a) Expert testimony that does not disclose the underlying facts or data on which the opinion is based is entitled to little or no weight. Testimony on United States patent law or patent examination practice will not be admitted.

(b) If a party relies on a technical test or data from such a test, the party must provide an affidavit explaining:

(1) Why the test or data is being used;

(2) How the test was performed and the data was generated;

(3) How the data is used to determine a value;

(4) How the test is regarded in the relevant art; and

(5) Any other information necessary for the Board to evaluate the test and data.

History of 37 C.F.R. §42.65: 77 FR 48676, Sept. 16, 2012.

ORAL ARGUMENT, DECISION, & SETTLEMENT

§42.70. ORAL ARGUMENT

(a) Request for oral argument. A party may request oral argument on an issue raised in a paper at a time set by the Board. The request must be filed as a separate paper and must specify the issues to be argued.

(b) Demonstrative exhibits must be served at least seven business days before the oral argument and filed no later than the time of the oral argument.

History of 37 C.F.R. §42.70: 77 FR 48676, Sept. 16, 2012; 81 FR 18765, May 2, 2016.

§42.71. DECISION ON PETITIONS OR MOTIONS

(a) Order of consideration. The Board may take up petitions or motions for decisions in any order, may grant, deny, or dismiss any petition or motion, and may enter any appropriate order.

(b) Interlocutory decisions. A decision on a motion without a judgment is not final for the purposes of judicial review. If a decision is not a panel decision, the party may request that a panel rehear the decision. When rehearing a non-panel decision, a panel will review the decision for an abuse of discretion. A panel decision on an issue will govern the trial.

(c) Petition decisions. A decision by the Board on whether to institute a trial is final and nonappealable. A party may request rehearing on a decision by the Board on whether to institute a trial pursuant to paragraph (d) of this section. When rehearing a decision on petition, a panel will review the decision for an abuse of discretion.

(d) Rehearing. A party dissatisfied with a decision may file a single request for rehearing without prior authorization from the Board. The burden of showing a decision should be modified lies with the party challenging the decision. The request must specifically identify all matters the party believes the Board misapprehended or overlooked, and the place where each matter was previously addressed in a motion, an opposition, or a reply. A request for rehearing does not toll times for taking action. Any request must be filed:

(1) Within 14 days of the entry of a non-final decision or a decision to institute a trial as to at least one ground of unpatentability asserted in the petition; or

(2) Within 30 days of the entry of a final decision or a decision not to institute a trial.

History of 37 C.F.R. §42.71: 77 FR 48676, Sept. 16, 2012; 80 FR 28565, May 19, 2015.

§42.72. TERMINATION OF TRIAL

The Board may terminate a trial without rendering a final written decision, where appropriate, including where the trial is consolidated with another proceeding or pursuant to a joint request under 35 U.S.C. 317(a) or 327(a).

History of 37 C.F.R. §42.72: 77 FR 48676, Sept. 16, 2012.

§42.73. JUDGMENT

(a) A judgment, except in the case of a termination, disposes of all issues that were, or by motion reasonably could have been, raised and decided.

(b) Request for adverse judgment. A party may request judgment against itself at any time during a proceeding. Actions construed to be a request for adverse judgment include:

(1) Disclaimer of the involved application or patent;

(2) Cancellation or disclaimer of a claim such that the party has no remaining claim in the trial;

(3) Concession of unpatentability or derivation of the contested subject matter; and

(4) Abandonment of the contest.

(c) Recommendation. The judgment may include a recommendation for further action by an examiner or by the Director.

(d) Estoppel. **(1)** Petitioner other than in derivation proceeding. A petitioner, or the real party in interest or privy of the petitioner, is estopped in the Office from requesting or maintaining a proceeding with respect to a claim for which it has obtained a final written decision on patentability in an inter partes review, post-grant review, or a covered business method patent review, on any ground that the petitioner raised or reasonably could have raised during the trial, except that estoppel shall not apply to a petitioner, or to the real party in interest or privy of the petitioner who has settled under 35 U.S.C. 317 or 327.

(2) In a derivation, the losing party who could have properly moved for relief on an issue, but did not so move, may not take action in the Office after the judgment that is inconsistent with that party's failure to move, except that a losing party shall not be estopped with respect to any contested subject matter for which that party was awarded a favorable judgment.

(3) Patent applicant or owner. A patent applicant or owner is precluded from taking action inconsistent with the adverse judgment, including obtaining in any patent:

(i) A claim that is not patentably distinct from a finally refused or canceled claim; or

(ii) An amendment of a specification or of a drawing that was denied during the trial proceeding, but this provision does not apply to an application or patent that has a different written description.

History of 37 C.F.R. §42.73: 77 FR 48676, Sept. 16, 2012.

§42.74. SETTLEMENT

(a) Board role. The parties may agree to settle any issue in a proceeding, but the Board is not a party to the settlement and may independently determine any question of jurisdiction, patentability, or Office practice.

(b) Agreements in writing. Any agreement or understanding between the parties made in connection with, or in contemplation of, the termination of a proceeding shall be in writing and a true copy shall be filed with the Board before the termination of the trial.

(c) Request to keep separate. A party to a settlement may request that the settlement be treated as business confidential information and be kept separate from the files of an involved patent or application. The request must be filed with the settlement. If a timely request is filed, the settlement shall only be available:

(1) To a Government agency on written request to the Board; or

(2) To any other person upon written request to the Board to make the settlement agreement available, along with the fee specified in §42.15(d) and on a showing of good cause.

History of 37 C.F.R. §42.74: 77 FR 48677, Sept. 16, 2012.

CERTIFICATE

§42.80. CERTIFICATE

After the Board issues a final written decision in an inter partes review, post-grant review, or covered business method patent review and the time for appeal has expired or any appeal has terminated, the Office will issue and publish a certificate canceling any claim of the patent finally determined to be unpatentable, confirming any claim of the patent determined to be patentable, and incorporating in the patent any new or amended claim determined to be patentable by operation of the certificate.

History of 37 C.F.R. §42.80: 77 FR 48677, Sept. 16, 2012.

SUBPART B. INTER PARTES REVIEW

GENERAL

§42.100. PROCEDURE; PENDENCY

(a) An inter partes review is a trial subject to the procedures set forth in subpart A of this part.

(b) A claim in an unexpired patent that will not expire before a final written decision is issued shall be given its broadest reasonable construction in light of the specification of the patent in which it appears. A party may request a district court-type claim construction approach to be applied if a party certifies that the involved patent will expire within 18 months from the entry of the Notice of Filing Date Accorded to Petition. The request, accompanied by a party's certification, must be made in the form of a motion under §42.20, within 30 days from the filing of the petition.

(c) An inter partes review proceeding shall be administered such that pendency before the Board after institution is normally no more than one year. The time can be extended by up to six months for good cause by the Chief Administrative Patent Judge, or adjusted by the Board in the case of joinder.

History of 37 C.F.R. §42.100: 77 FR 48727, Sept. 16, 2012; 81 FR 18766, May 2, 2016.

§42.101. WHO MAY PETITION FOR INTER PARTES REVIEW

A person who is not the owner of a patent may file with the Office a petition to institute an inter partes review of the patent unless:

(a) Before the date on which the petition for review is filed, the petitioner or real party-in-interest filed a civil action challenging the validity of a claim of the patent;

(b) The petition requesting the proceeding is filed more than one year after the date on which the petitioner, the petitioner's real party-in-interest, or a privy of the petitioner is served with a complaint alleging infringement of the patent; or

(c) The petitioner, the petitioner's real party-in-interest, or a privy of the petitioner is estopped from challenging the claims on the grounds identified in the petition.

History of 37 C.F.R. §42.101: 77 FR 48727, Sept. 16, 2012.

See the Office Patent Trial Practice Guide, p. 1336.

§42.102. TIME FOR FILING

(a) A petition for inter partes review of a patent must be filed after the later of the following dates, where applicable:

(1) If the patent is a patent described in section 3(n)(1) of the Leahy-Smith America Invents Act, the date that is nine months after the date of the grant of the patent;

(2) If the patent is a patent that is not described in section 3(n)(1) of the Leahy-Smith American Invents Act, the date of the grant of the patent; or

(3) If a post-grant review is instituted as set forth in subpart C of this part, the date of the termination of such post-grant review.

(b) The Director may impose a limit on the number of inter partes reviews that may be instituted during each of the first four one-year periods in which the amendment made to chapter 31 of title 35, United States Code, is in effect by providing notice in the Office's Official Gazette or Federal Register. Petitions filed after an established limit has been reached will be deemed untimely.

History of 37 C.F.R. §42.102: 77 FR 48727, Sept. 16, 2012; 78 FR 17874, Mar. 25, 2013.

§42.103. INTER PARTES REVIEW FEE

(a) An inter partes review fee set forth in §42.15(a) must accompany the petition.

(b) No filing date will be accorded to the petition until full payment is received.

History of 37 C.F.R. §42.103: 77 FR 48728, Sept. 16, 2012.

§42.104. CONTENT OF PETITION

In addition to the requirements of §§42.6, 42.8, 42.22, and 42.24, the petition must set forth:

(a) Grounds for standing. The petitioner must certify that the patent for which review is sought is available for inter partes review and that the petitioner is not barred or estopped from requesting an inter partes review challenging the patent claims on the grounds identified in the petition.

(b) Identification of challenge. Provide a statement of the precise relief requested for each claim challenged. The statement must identify the following:

(1) The claim;

(2) The specific statutory grounds under 35 U.S.C. 102 or 103 on which the challenge to the claim is based and the patents or printed publications relied upon for each ground;

(3) How the challenged claim is to be construed. Where the claim to be construed contains a means-plus-function or step-plus-function limitation as permitted under 35 U.S.C. 112(f), the construction of the claim must identify the specific portions of the specification that describe the structure, material, or acts corresponding to each claimed function;

(4) How the construed claim is unpatentable under the statutory grounds identified in paragraph (b)(2) of this section. The petition must specify where each element of the claim is found in the prior art patents or printed publications relied upon; and

(5) The exhibit number of the supporting evidence relied upon to support the challenge and the relevance of the evidence to the challenge raised, including identifying specific portions of the evidence that support the challenge. The Board may exclude or give no weight to the evidence where a party has failed to state its relevance or to identify specific portions of the evidence that support the challenge.

(c) A motion may be filed that seeks to correct a clerical or typographical mistake in the petition. The grant of such a motion does not change the filing date of the petition.

History of 37 C.F.R. §42.104: 77 FR 48728, Sept. 16, 2012.

§42.105. SERVICE OF PETITION

In addition to the requirements of §42.6, the petitioner must serve the petition and exhibits relied upon in the petition as follows:

(a) The petition and supporting evidence must be served on the patent owner at the correspondence address of record for the subject patent. The petitioner may additionally serve the petition and supporting evidence on the patent owner at any other address known to the petitioner as likely to effect service.

(b) Upon agreement of the parties, service may be made electronically. Service may be by Priority Mail Express® or by means at least as fast and reliable as Priority Mail Express®. Personal service is not required.

History of 37 C.F.R. §42.105: 77 FR 48728, Sept. 16, 2012; 79 FR 63043, Oct. 22, 2014.

§42.106. FILING DATE

(a) Complete petition. A petition to institute inter partes review will not be accorded a filing date until the petition satisfies all of the following requirements:

(1) Complies with §42.104;

(2) Effects service of the petition on the correspondence address of record as provided in §42.105(a); and

(3) Is accompanied by the fee to institute required in §42.15(a).

(b) Incomplete petition. Where a party files an incomplete petition, no filing date will be accorded, and the Office will dismiss the petition if the deficiency in the petition is not corrected within one month from the notice of an incomplete petition.

History of 37 C.F.R. §42.106: 77 FR 48728, Sept. 16, 2012.

§42.107. PRELIMINARY RESPONSE TO PETITION

(a) The patent owner may file a preliminary response to the petition. The response is limited to setting forth the reasons why no inter partes review should be instituted under 35 U.S.C. 314 and can include supporting evidence. The preliminary response is subject to the word count under §42.24.

(b) Due date. The preliminary response must be filed no later than three months after the date of a notice indicating that the request to institute an inter partes review has been granted a filing date. A patent owner may expedite the proceeding by filing an election to waive the patent owner preliminary response.

(c) [Reserved]

(d) No amendment. The preliminary response shall not include any amendment.

(e) Disclaim Patent Claims. The patent owner may file a statutory disclaimer under 35 U.S.C. 253(a) in compliance with §1.321(a) of this chapter, disclaiming one or more claims in the patent. No inter partes review will be instituted based on disclaimed claims.

History of 37 C.F.R. §42.107: 77 FR 48728, Sept. 16, 2012; 81 FR 18766, May 2, 2016.

INSTITUTING INTER PARTES REVIEW

§42.108. INSTITUTION OF INTER PARTES REVIEW

(a) When instituting inter partes review, the Board may authorize the review to proceed on all or some of the challenged claims and on all or some of the grounds of unpatentability asserted for each claim.

(b) At any time prior to institution of inter partes review, the Board may deny some or all grounds for unpatentability for some or all of the challenged claims. Denial of a ground is a Board decision not to institute inter partes review on that ground.

(c) Sufficient grounds. Inter partes review shall not be instituted for a ground of unpatentability unless the Board decides that the petition supporting the ground would demonstrate that there is a reasonable likelihood that at least one of the claims challenged in the petition is unpatentable. The Board's decision will take into account a patent owner preliminary response where such a response is filed, including any testimonial evidence, but a genuine issue of material fact created by such testimonial evidence will be viewed in the light most favorable to the petitioner solely for purposes of deciding whether to institute an inter partes review. A petitioner may seek leave to file a reply to the preliminary response in accordance with §§42.23 and 42.24(c). Any such request must make a showing of good cause.

History of 37 C.F.R. §42.108: 77 FR 48728, Sept. 16, 2012; 81 FR 18766, May 2, 2016.

AFTER INSTITUTION OF INTER PARTES REVIEW

§42.120. PATENT OWNER RESPONSE

(a) Scope. A patent owner may file a response to the petition addressing any ground for unpatentability not already denied. A patent owner response is filed as an opposition and is subject to the page limits provided in §42.24.

(b) Due date for response. If no time for filing a patent owner response to a petition is provided in a Board order, the default date for filing a patent owner response is three months from the date the inter partes review was instituted.

History of 37 C.F.R. §42.120: 77 FR 48728, Sept. 16, 2012.

§42.121. AMENDMENT OF THE PATENT

(a) Motion to amend. A patent owner may file one motion to amend a patent, but only after conferring with the Board.

(1) Due date. Unless a due date is provided in a Board order, a motion to amend must be filed no later than the filing of a patent owner response.

(2) Scope. A motion to amend may be denied where:

(i) The amendment does not respond to a ground of unpatentability involved in the trial; or

(ii) The amendment seeks to enlarge the scope of the claims of the patent or introduce new subject matter.

(3) A reasonable number of substitute claims. A motion to amend may cancel a challenged claim or propose a reasonable number of substitute claims. The presumption is that only one substitute claim would be needed to replace each challenged claim, and it may be rebutted by a demonstration of need.

(b) Content. A motion to amend claims must include a claim listing, which claim listing may be contained in an appendix to the motion, show the changes clearly, and set forth:

(1) The support in the original disclosure of the patent for each claim that is added or amended; and

(2) The support in an earlier-filed disclosure for each claim for which benefit of the filing date of the earlier filed disclosure is sought.

(c) Additional motion to amend. In addition to the requirements set forth in paragraphs (a) and (b) of this section, any additional motion to amend may not be filed without Board authorization. An additional motion to amend may be authorized when there is a good cause showing or a joint request of the petitioner and the patent owner to materially advance a settlement. In determining whether to authorize such an additional motion to amend, the Board will consider whether a petitioner has submitted supplemental information after the time period set for filing a motion to amend in paragraph (a)(1) of this section.

History of 37 C.F.R. §42.121: 77 FR 48728, Sept. 16, 2012; 80 FR 28566, May 19, 2015.

§42.122. MULTIPLE PROCEEDINGS & JOINDER

(a) Multiple proceedings. Where another matter involving the patent is before the Office, the Board may during the pendency of the inter partes review enter any appropriate order regarding the additional matter including providing for the stay, transfer, consolidation, or termination of any such matter.

(b) Request for joinder. Joinder may be requested by a patent owner or petitioner. Any request for joinder must be

See the Office Patent Trial Practice Guide, p. 1336.

filed, as a motion under §42.22, no later than one month after the institution date of any inter partes review for which joinder is requested. The time period set forth in §42.101(b) shall not apply when the petition is accompanied by a request for joinder.

History of 37 C.F.R. §42.122: 77 FR 48729, Sept. 16, 2012.

§42.123. FILING OF SUPPLEMENTAL INFORMATION

(a) Motion to submit supplemental information. Once a trial has been instituted, a party may file a motion to submit supplemental information in accordance with the following requirements:

(1) A request for the authorization to file a motion to submit supplemental information is made within one month of the date the trial is instituted.

(2) The supplemental information must be relevant to a claim for which the trial has been instituted.

(b) Late submission of supplemental information. A party seeking to submit supplemental information more than one month after the date the trial is instituted, must request authorization to file a motion to submit the information. The motion to submit supplemental information must show why the supplemental information reasonably could not have been obtained earlier, and that consideration of the supplemental information would be in the interests-of-justice.

(c) Other supplemental information. A party seeking to submit supplemental information not relevant to a claim for which the trial has been instituted must request authorization to file a motion to submit the information. The motion must show why the supplemental information reasonably could not have been obtained earlier, and that consideration of the supplemental information would be in the interests-of-justice.

History of 37 C.F.R. §42.123: 77 FR 48729, Sept. 16, 2012.

SUBPART C. POST-GRANT REVIEW

GENERAL

§42.200. PROCEDURE; PENDENCY

(a) A post-grant review is a trial subject to the procedures set forth in subpart A of this part.

(b) A claim in an unexpired patent that will not expire before a final written decision is issued shall be given its broadest reasonable construction in light of the specification of the patent in which it appears. A party may request a district court-type claim construction approach to be applied if a party certifies that the involved patent will expire within 18 months from the entry of the Notice of Filing Date Accorded to Petition. The request, accompanied by a party's certification, must be made in the form of a motion under §42.20, within 30 days from the filing of the petition.

(c) A post-grant review proceeding shall be administered such that pendency before the Board after institution is normally no more than one year. The time can be extended by up to six months for good cause by the Chief Administrative Patent Judge, or adjusted by the Board in the case of joinder.

(d) Interferences commenced before September 16, 2012, shall proceed under part 41 of this chapter except as the Chief Administrative Patent Judge, acting on behalf of the Director, may otherwise order in the interests-of-justice.

History of 37 C.F.R. §42.200: 77 FR 48729, Sept. 16, 2012; 81 FR 18766, May 2, 2016.

§42.201. WHO MAY PETITION FOR A POST-GRANT REVIEW

A person who is not the owner of a patent may file with the Office a petition to institute a post-grant review of the patent unless:

(a) Before the date on which the petition for review is filed, the petitioner or real party-in-interest filed a civil action challenging the validity of a claim of the patent; or

(b) The petitioner, the petitioner's real party-in-interest, or a privy of the petitioner is estopped from challenging the claims on the grounds identified in the petition.

History of 37 C.F.R. §42.201: 77 FR 48729, Sept. 16, 2012.

§42.202. TIME FOR FILING

(a) A petition for a post-grant review of a patent must be filed no later than the date that is nine months after the date of the grant of a patent or of the issuance of a reissue patent. A petition, however, may not request a post-grant review for a claim in a reissue patent that is identical to or narrower than a claim in the original patent from which the reissue patent was issued unless the petition is filed not later than the date that is nine months after the date of the grant of the original patent.

(b) The Director may impose a limit on the number of post-grant reviews that may be instituted during each of the first four one-year periods in which 35 U.S.C. 321 is in effect by providing notice in the Office's Official Gazette or Federal Register. Petitions filed after an established limit has been reached will be deemed untimely.

History of 37 C.F.R. §42.202: 77 FR 48729, Sept. 16, 2012.

§42.203. POST-GRANT REVIEW FEE

(a) A post-grant review fee set forth in §42.15(b) must accompany the petition.

(b) No filing date will be accorded to the petition until full payment is received.

History of 37 C.F.R. §42.203: 77 FR 48729, Sept. 16, 2012.

§42.204. CONTENT OF PETITION

In addition to the requirements of §§42.6, 42.8, 42.22, and 42.24, the petition must set forth:

(a) Grounds for standing. The petitioner must certify that the patent for which review is sought is available for post-grant review and that the petitioner is not barred or estopped from requesting a post-grant review challenging the patent claims on the grounds identified in the petition.

(b) Identification of challenge. Provide a statement of the precise relief requested for each claim challenged. The statement must identify the following:

(1) The claim;

(2) The specific statutory grounds permitted under 35 U.S.C. 282(b)(2) or (3) on which the challenge to the claim is based;

(3) How the challenged claim is to be construed. Where the claim to be construed contains a means-plus-function or step-plus-function limitation as permitted under 35 U.S.C. 112(f), the construction of the claim must identify the specific portions of the specification that describe the structure, material, or acts corresponding to each claimed function;

(4) How the construed claim is unpatentable under the statutory grounds identified in paragraph (b)(2) of this section. Where the grounds for unpatentability are based on prior art, the petition must specify where each element of the claim is found in the prior art. For all other grounds of unpatentability, the petition must identify the specific part of the claim that fails to comply with the statutory grounds raised and state how the identified subject matter fails to comply with the statute; and

(5) The exhibit number of the supporting evidence relied upon to support the challenge and the relevance of the evidence to the challenge raised, including identifying specific portions of the evidence that support the challenge. The Board may exclude or give no weight to the evidence where a party has failed to state its relevance or to identify specific portions of the evidence that support the challenge.

(c) A motion may be filed that seeks to correct a clerical or typographical mistake in the petition. The grant of such a motion does not change the filing date of the petition.

History of 37 C.F.R. §42.204: 77 FR 48729, Sept. 16, 2012.

§42.205. SERVICE OF PETITION

In addition to the requirements of §42.6, the petitioner must serve the petition and exhibits relied upon in the petition as follows:

(a) The petition and supporting evidence must be served on the patent owner at the correspondence address of record for the subject patent. The petitioner may additionally serve the petition and supporting evidence on the patent owner at any other address known to the petitioner as likely to effect service.

(b) Upon agreement of the parties, service may be made electronically. Service may be by Priority Mail Express® or by means at least as fast and reliable as Priority Mail Express®. Personal service is not required.

History of 37 C.F.R. §42.205: 77 FR 48730, Sept. 16, 2012; 79 FR 63043, Oct. 22, 2014.

§42.206. FILING DATE

(a) Complete petition. A petition to institute a post-grant review will not be accorded a filing date until the petition satisfies all of the following requirements:

(1) Complies with §42.204 or §42.304, as the case may be,

(2) Effects service of the petition on the correspondence address of record as provided in §42.205(a); and

(3) Is accompanied by the filing fee in §42.15(b).

(b) Incomplete petition. Where a party files an incomplete petition, no filing date will be accorded and the Office will dismiss the request if the deficiency in the petition is not corrected within the earlier of either one month from the notice of an incomplete petition, or the expiration of the statutory deadline in which to file a petition for post-grant review.

History of 37 C.F.R. §42.206: 77 FR 48730, Sept. 16, 2012.

§42.207. PRELIMINARY RESPONSE TO PETITION

(a) The patent owner may file a preliminary response to the petition. The response is limited to setting forth the reasons why no post-grant review should be instituted under 35 U.S.C. 324 and can include supporting evidence. The preliminary response is subject to the word count under §42.24.

(b) Due date. The preliminary response must be filed no later than three months after the date of a notice indicating that the request to institute a post-grant review has been granted a filing date. A patent owner may expedite the proceeding by filing an election to waive the patent owner preliminary response.

(c) [Reserved]

(d) No amendment. The preliminary response shall not include any amendment.

(e) Disclaim Patent Claims. The patent owner may file a statutory disclaimer under 35 U.S.C. 253(a) in compliance with §1.321(a), disclaiming one or more claims in the patent. No post-grant review will be instituted based on disclaimed claims.

History of 37 C.F.R. §42.207: 77 FR 48730, Sept. 16, 2012; 81 FR 18766, May 2, 2016.

INSTITUTING POST-GRANT REVIEW

§42.208. INSTITUTION OF POST-GRANT REVIEW

(a) When instituting post-grant review, the Board may authorize the review to proceed on all or some of the challenged claims and on all or some of the grounds of unpatentability asserted for each claim.

(b) At any time prior to institution of post-grant review, the Board may deny some or all grounds for unpatentability for some or all of the challenged claims. Denial of a ground is a Board decision not to institute post-grant review on that ground.

(c) Sufficient grounds. Post-grant review shall not be instituted for a ground of unpatentability unless the Board decides that the petition supporting the ground would, if unrebutted, demonstrate that it is more likely than not that at least one of the claims challenged in the petition is unpatentable.

See the Office Patent Trial Practice Guide, p. 1336.

The Board's decision will take into account a patent owner preliminary response where such a response is filed, including any testimonial evidence, but a genuine issue of material fact created by such testimonial evidence will be viewed in the light most favorable to the petitioner solely for purposes of deciding whether to institute a post-grant review. A petitioner may seek leave to file a reply to the preliminary response in accordance with §§42.23 and 42.24(c). Any such request must make a showing of good cause.

(d) Additional grounds. Sufficient grounds under §42.208(c) may be a showing that the petition raises a novel or unsettled legal question that is important to other patents or patent applications.

History of 37 C.F.R. §42.208: 77 FR 48730, Sept. 16, 2012; 81 FR 18766, May 2, 2016.

AFTER INSTITUTION OF POST-GRANT REVIEW

§42.220. PATENT OWNER RESPONSE

(a) Scope. A patent owner may file a response to the petition addressing any ground for unpatentability not already denied. A patent owner response is filed as an opposition and is subject to the page limits provided in §42.24.

(b) Due date for response. If no date for filing a patent owner response to a petition is provided in a Board order, the default date for filing a patent owner response is three months from the date the post-grant review is instituted.

History of 37 C.F.R. §42.220: 77 FR 48730, Sept. 16, 2012.

§42.221. AMENDMENT OF THE PATENT

(a) Motion to amend. A patent owner may file one motion to amend a patent, but only after conferring with the Board.

(1) Due date. Unless a due date is provided in a Board order, a motion to amend must be filed no later than the filing of a patent owner response.

(2) Scope. A motion to amend may be denied where:

(i) The amendment does not respond to a ground of unpatentability involved in the trial; or

(ii) The amendment seeks to enlarge the scope of the claims of the patent or introduce new subject matter.

(3) A reasonable number of substitute claims. A motion to amend may cancel a challenged claim or propose a reasonable number of substitute claims. The presumption is that only one substitute claim would be needed to replace each challenged claim, and it may be rebutted by a demonstration of need.

(b) Content. A motion to amend claims must include a claim listing, which claim listing may be contained in an appendix to the motion, show the changes clearly, and set forth:

(1) The support in the original disclosure of the patent for each claim that is added or amended; and

(2) The support in an earlier-filed disclosure for each claim for which benefit of the filing date of the earlier filed disclosure is sought.

(c) Additional motion to amend. In addition to the requirements set forth in paragraphs (a) and (b) of this section, any additional motion to amend may not be filed without Board authorization. An additional motion to amend may be authorized when there is a good cause showing or a joint request of the petitioner and the patent owner to materially advance a settlement. In determining whether to authorize such an additional motion to amend, the Board will consider whether a petitioner has submitted supplemental information after the time period set for filing a motion to amend in paragraph (a)(1) of this section.

History of 37 C.F.R. §42.221: 77 FR 48730, Sept. 16, 2012; 80 FR 28566, May 19, 2015.

§42.222. MULTIPLE PROCEEDINGS & JOINDER

(a) Multiple proceedings. Where another matter involving the patent is before the Office, the Board may during the pendency of the post-grant review enter any appropriate order regarding the additional matter including providing for the stay, transfer, consolidation, or termination of any such matter.

(b) Request for joinder. Joinder may be requested by a patent owner or petitioner. Any request for joinder must be filed, as a motion under §42.22, no later than one month after the institution date of any post-grant review for which joinder is requested.

History of 37 C.F.R. §42.222: 77 FR 48731, Sept. 16, 2012.

§42.223. FILING OF SUPPLEMENTAL INFORMATION

(a) Motion to submit supplemental information. Once a trial has been instituted, a party may file a motion to submit supplemental information in accordance with the following requirements:

(1) A request for the authorization to file a motion to submit supplemental information is made within one month of the date the trial is instituted.

(2) The supplemental information must be relevant to a claim for which the trial has been instituted.

(b) Late submission of supplemental information. A party seeking to submit supplemental information more than one month after the date the trial is instituted, must request authorization to file a motion to submit the information. The motion to submit supplemental information must show why the supplemental information reasonably could not have been obtained earlier, and that consideration of the supplemental information would be in the interests-of-justice.

(c) Other supplemental information. A party seeking to submit supplemental information not relevant to a claim for which the trial has been instituted must request authorization to file a motion to submit the information. The motion must show why the supplemental information reasonably could not have been obtained earlier, and that consideration of the supplemental information would be in the interests-of-justice.

History of 37 C.F.R. §42.223: 77 FR 48731, Sept. 16, 2012.

§42.224. DISCOVERY

Notwithstanding the discovery provisions of subpart A:

(a) Requests for additional discovery may be granted upon a showing of good cause as to why the discovery is needed; and

(b) Discovery is limited to evidence directly related to factual assertions advanced by either party in the proceeding.

History of 37 C.F.R. §42.224: 77 FR 48731, Sept. 16, 2012.

SUBPART D. TRANSITIONAL PROGRAM FOR COVERED BUSINESS METHOD PATENTS

§42.300. PROCEDURE; PENDENCY

(a) A covered business method patent review is a trial subject to the procedures set forth in subpart A of this part and is also subject to the post-grant review procedures set forth in subpart C except for §§42.200, 42.201, 42.202, and 42.204.

(b) A claim in an unexpired patent that will not expire before a final written decision is issued shall be given its broadest reasonable construction in light of the specification of the patent in which it appears. A party may a request a district court-type claim construction approach to be applied if a party certifies that the involved patent will expire within 18 months from the entry of the Notice of Filing Date Accorded to Petition. The request, accompanied by a party's certification, must be made in the form of a motion under §42.20, within 30 days from the filing of the petition.

(c) A covered business method patent review proceeding shall be administered such that pendency before the Board after institution is normally no more than one year. The time can be extended by up to six months for good cause by the Chief Administrative Patent Judge, or adjusted by the Board in the case of joinder.

(d) The rules in this subpart are applicable until September 15, 2020, except that the rules shall continue to apply to any petition for a covered business method patent review filed before the date of repeal.

History of 37 C.F.R. §42.300: 77 FR 48731, Sept. 16, 2012; 80 FR 28566, May 19, 2015; 81 FR 18766, May 2, 2016.

§42.301. DEFINITIONS

In addition to the definitions in §42.2, the following definitions apply to proceedings under this subpart D:

(a) Covered business method patent means a patent that claims a method or corresponding apparatus for performing data processing or other operations used in the practice, administration, or management of a financial product or service, except that the term does not include patents for technological inventions.

(b) Technological invention. In determining whether a patent is for a technological invention solely for purposes of the Transitional Program for Covered Business Methods (section 42.301(a)), the following will be considered on a case-by-case basis: whether the claimed subject matter as a whole recites a technological feature that is novel and unobvious over the prior art; and solves a technical problem using a technical solution.

History of 37 C.F.R. §42.301: 77 FR 48753, Aug. 14, 2012.

§42.302. WHO MAY PETITION FOR A COVERED BUSINESS METHOD PATENT REVIEW

(a) A petitioner may not file with the Office a petition to institute a covered business method patent review of the patent unless the petitioner, the petitioner's real party-in-interest, or a privy of the petitioner has been sued for infringement of the patent or has been charged with infringement under that patent. Charged with infringement means a real and substantial controversy regarding infringement of a covered business method patent exists such that the petitioner would have standing to bring a declaratory judgment action in Federal court.

(b) A petitioner may not file a petition to institute a covered business method patent review of the patent where the petitioner, the petitioner's real party-in-interest, or a privy of the petitioner is estopped from challenging the claims on the grounds identified in the petition.

(c) A petitioner may not file a petition to institute a covered business method patent review of the patent where, before the date on which the petition is filed, the petitioner or real party-in-interest filed a civil action challenging the validity of a claim of the patent.

History of 37 C.F.R. §42.302: 77 FR 48731, Sept. 16, 2012; 80 FR 28566, May 19, 2015.

§42.303. TIME FOR FILING

A petition requesting a covered business method patent review may be filed any time except during the period in which a petition for a post-grant review of the patent would satisfy the requirements of 35 U.S.C. 321(c).

History of 37 C.F.R. §42.303: 77 FR 48731, Sept. 16, 2012.

§42.304. CONTENT OF PETITION

In addition to any other notices required by subparts A and C of this part, a petition must request judgment against one or more claims of a patent identified by patent number. In addition to the requirements of §§42.6, 42.8, 42.22, and 42.24 the petition must set forth:

(a) Grounds for standing. The petitioner must demonstrate that the patent for which review is sought is a covered business method patent, and that the petitioner meets the eligibility requirements of §42.302.

(b) Identification of challenge. Provide a statement of the precise relief requested for each claim challenged. The statement must identify the following:

See the Office Patent Trial Practice Guide, p. 1336.

(1) The claim;

(2) The specific statutory grounds permitted under paragraph (2) or (3) of 35 U.S.C. 282(b), except as modified by section 18(a)(1)(C) of the Leahy-Smith America Invents Act (Pub. L. 112-29, 125 Stat. 284 (2011)), on which the challenge to the claim is based;

(3) How the challenged claim is to be construed. Where the claim to be construed contains a means-plus-function or step-plus-function limitation as permitted under 35 U.S.C. 112(f), the construction of the claim must identify the specific portions of the specification that describe the structure, material, or acts corresponding to each claimed function;

(4) How the construed claim is unpatentable under the statutory grounds identified in paragraph (b)(2) of this section. Where the grounds for unpatentability are based on prior art, the petition must specify where each element of the claim is found in the prior art. For all other grounds of unpatentability, the petition must identify the specific part of the claim that fails to comply with the statutory grounds raised and state how the identified subject matter fails to comply with the statute; and

(5) The exhibit number of supporting evidence relied upon to support the challenge and the relevance of the evidence to the challenge raised, including identifying specific portions of the evidence that support the challenge. The Board may exclude or give no weight to the evidence where a party has failed to state its relevance or to identify specific portions of the evidence that support the challenge.

(c) A motion may be filed that seeks to correct a clerical or typographical mistake in the petition. The grant of such a motion does not change the filing date of the petition.

History of 37 C.F.R. §42.304: 77 FR 48731, Sept. 16, 2012.

SUBPART E. DERIVATION

GENERAL

§42.400. PROCEDURE; PENDENCY

(a) A derivation proceeding is a trial subject to the procedures set forth in subpart A of this part.

(b) The Board may for good cause authorize or direct the parties to address patentability issues that arise in the course of the derivation proceeding.

History of 37 C.F.R. §42.400: 77 FR 56090, Mar. 16, 2013.

§42.401. DEFINITIONS

In addition to the definitions in §42.2, the following definitions apply to proceedings under this subpart:

Agreement or understanding under 35 U.S.C. 135(e) means settlement for the purposes of §42.74.

Applicant includes a reissue applicant.

Application includes both an application for an original patent and an application for a reissued patent.

First publication means either a patent or an application publication under 35 U.S.C. 122(b), including a publication of an international application designating the United States as provided by 35 U.S.C. 374.

Petitioner means a patent applicant who petitions for a determination that another party named in an earlier-filed patent application allegedly derived a claimed invention from an inventor named in the petitioner's application and filed the earlier application without authorization.

Respondent means a party other than the petitioner.

Same or substantially the same means patentably indistinct.

History of 37 C.F.R. §42.401: 77 FR 56090, Mar. 16, 2013.

§42.402. WHO MAY FILE A PETITION FOR A DERIVATION PROCEEDING

An applicant for patent may file a petition to institute a derivation proceeding in the Office.

History of 37 C.F.R. §42.402: 77 FR 56090, Mar. 16, 2013.

§42.403. TIME FOR FILING

A petition for a derivation proceeding must be filed within the one-year period beginning on the date of the first publication of a claim to an invention that is the same or substantially the same as the earlier application's claim to the allegedly derived invention.

History of 37 C.F.R. §42.403: 77 FR 56091, Mar. 16, 2013.

§42.404. DERIVATION FEE

(a) A derivation fee set forth in §42.15(c) must accompany the petition.

(b) No filing date will be accorded to the petition until payment is complete.

History of 37 C.F.R. §42.404: 77 FR 56091, Mar. 16, 2013.

§42.405. CONTENT OF PETITION

(a) Grounds for standing. The petition must:

(1) Demonstrate compliance with §§42.402 and 42.403; and

(2) Show that the petitioner has at least one claim that is:

(i) The same or substantially the same as the respondent's claimed invention; and

(ii) The same or substantially the same as the invention disclosed to the respondent.

(b) In addition to the requirements of §§42.8 and 42.22, the petition must:

(1) Provide sufficient information to identify the application or patent for which the petitioner seeks a derivation proceeding;

(2) Demonstrate that a claimed invention was derived from an inventor named in the petitioner's application, and that the inventor from whom the invention was derived did not authorize the filing of the earliest application claiming such invention; and

(3) For each of the respondent's claims to the derived invention,

(i) Show why the claimed invention is the same or substantially the same as the invention disclosed to the respondent, and

(ii) Identify how the claim is to be construed. Where the claim to be construed contains a means-plus-function or step-plus-function limitation as permitted under 35 U.S.C. 112(f), the construction of the claim must identify the specific portions of the specification that describe the structure, material, or acts corresponding to each claimed function.

(c) Sufficiency of showing. A derivation showing is not sufficient unless it is supported by substantial evidence, including at least one affidavit addressing communication of the derived invention and lack of authorization that, if unrebutted, would support a determination of derivation. The showing of communication must be corroborated.

History of 37 C.F.R. §42.405: 77 FR 56091, Mar. 16, 2013.

§42.406. SERVICE OF PETITION

In addition to the requirements of §42.6, the petitioner must serve the petition and exhibits relied upon in the petition as follows:

(a) The petition and supporting evidence must be served on the respondent at the correspondence address of record for the earlier application or subject patent. The petitioner may additionally serve the petition and supporting evidence on the respondent at any other address known to the petitioner as likely to effect service.

(b) Upon agreement of the parties, service may be made electronically. Service may be by Priority Mail Express® or by means at least as fast and reliable as Priority Mail Express®. Personal service is not required.

History of 37 C.F.R. §42.406: 77 FR 56091, Mar. 16, 2013; 79 FR 63043, Oct. 22, 2014.

§42.407. FILING DATE

(a) Complete petition. A petition to institute a derivation proceeding will not be accorded a filing date until the petition satisfies all of the following requirements:

(1) Complies with §§42.404 and 42.405, and

(2) Service of the petition on the correspondence address of record as provided in §42.406.

(b) Incomplete petition. Where the petitioner files an incomplete petition, no filing date will be accorded, and the Office will dismiss the petition if the deficiency in the petition is not corrected within the earlier of either one month from notice of the incomplete petition, or the expiration of the statutory deadline in which to file a petition for derivation.

History of 37 C.F.R. §42.407: 77 FR 56091, Mar. 16, 2013.

INSTITUTING DERIVATION PROCEEDING

§42.408. INSTITUTION OF DERIVATION PROCEEDING

(a) An administrative patent judge institutes, and may as necessary reinstitute, the derivation proceeding on behalf of the Director.

(b) Additional derivation proceeding. The petitioner may suggest the addition of a patent or application to the derivation proceeding. The suggestion should make the showings required under §42.405 and explain why the suggestion could not have been made in the original petition.

History of 37 C.F.R. §42.408: 77 FR 56091, Mar. 16, 2013.

AFTER INSTITUTION OF DERIVATION PROCEEDING

§42.409. SETTLEMENT AGREEMENTS

An agreement or understanding under 35 U.S.C. 135(e) is a settlement for the purposes of §42.74.

History of 37 C.F.R. §42.409: 77 FR 56091, Mar. 16, 2013.

§42.410. ARBITRATION

(a) Parties may resort to binding arbitration to determine any issue. The Office is not a party to the arbitration. The Board is not bound by, and may independently determine, any question of patentability.

(b) The Board will not set a time for, or otherwise modify the proceeding for, an arbitration unless:

(1) It is to be conducted according to Title 9 of the United States Code;

(2) The parties notify the Board in writing of their intention to arbitrate;

(3) The agreement to arbitrate:

(i) Is in writing;

(ii) Specifies the issues to be arbitrated;

(iii) Names the arbitrator, or provides a date not more than 30 days after the execution of the agreement for the selection of the arbitrator;

(iv) Provides that the arbitrator's award shall be binding on the parties and that judgment thereon can be entered by the Board;

(v) Provides that a copy of the agreement is filed within 20 days after its execution; and

(vi) Provides that the arbitration is completed within the time the Board sets.

(c) The parties are solely responsible for the selection of the arbitrator and the conduct of the arbitration.

(d) The Board may determine issues the arbitration does not resolve.

(e) The Board will not consider the arbitration award unless it:

(1) Is binding on the parties;

(2) Is in writing;

(3) States in a clear and definite manner each issue arbitrated and the disposition of each issue; and

(4) Is filed within 20 days of the date of the award.

(f) Once the award is filed, the parties to the award may not take actions inconsistent with the award. If the award is

37 CFR §42.410

See the Office Patent Trial Practice Guide, p. 1336.

dispositive of the contested subject matter for a party, the Board may enter judgment as to that party.

History of 37 C.F.R. §42.410: 77 FR 56091, Mar. 16, 2013.

§42.411. COMMON INTERESTS IN THE INVENTION

The Board may decline to institute, or if already instituted the Board may issue judgment in, a derivation proceeding between an application and a patent or another application that are commonly owned.

History of 37 C.F.R. §42.411: 77 FR 56091, Mar. 16, 2013.

§42.412. PUBLIC AVAILABILITY OF BOARD RECORDS

(a) Publication. **(1)** Generally. Any Board decision is available for public inspection without a party's permission if rendered in a file open to the public pursuant to §1.11 of this chapter or in an application that has been published in accordance with §§1.211 to 1.221 of this chapter. The Office may independently publish any Board decision that is available for public inspection.

(2) Determination of special circumstances. Any Board decision not publishable under paragraph (a)(1) of this section may be published or made available for public inspection if the Director believes that special circumstances warrant publication and a party does not petition within two months after being notified of the intention to make the decision public, objecting in writing on the ground that the decision discloses the objecting party's trade secret or other confidential information and stating with specificity that such information is not otherwise publicly available.

(b) Record of proceeding. **(1)** The record of a Board proceeding is available to the public, unless a patent application not otherwise available to the public is involved.

(2) Notwithstanding paragraph (b)(1) of this section, after a final Board decision in or judgment in a Board proceeding, the record of the Board proceeding will be made available to the public if any involved file is or becomes open to the public under §1.11 of this chapter or an involved application is or becomes published under §§1.211 to 1.221 of this chapter.

History of 37 C.F.R. §42.412: 77 FR 56091, Mar. 16, 2013.

OFFICE PATENT TRIAL PRACTICE GUIDE

Patent and Trademark Office

37 CFR Part 42

[Docket No. PTO-P-2011-0094]

SUMMARY: The Leahy-Smith America Invents Act (AIA) establishes several new trial proceedings to be conducted by the Patent Trial and Appeal Board (Board) including inter partes review, post-grant review, the transitional program for covered business method patents, and derivation proceedings. In separate rulemakings, the United States Patent and Trademark Office (Office or USPTO) is revising the rules of practice to implement these provisions of the AIA that provide for the trial proceedings before the Board. The Office publishes in this notice a practice guide for the trial final rules to advise the public on the general framework of the regulations, including the structure and times for taking action in each of the new proceedings.

DATES: *Effective Date:* This practice guide applies to inter partes review, post-grant review, and covered business method patent review proceedings commencing on or after September 16, 2012, as well as derivation proceedings commencing on or after March 16, 2013.

FOR FURTHER INFORMATION CONTACT: Michael Tierney, Lead Administrative Patent Judge, Board of Patent Appeals and Interferences (will be renamed as Patent Trial and Appeal Board on September 16, 2012), by telephone at (571) 272-9797.

SUPPLEMENTARY INFORMATION:

Executive Summary: The patent trial regulations lay out a framework for conducting the proceedings aimed at streamlining and converging the issues for decision. In doing so, the Office's goal is to conduct proceedings in a timely, fair, and efficient manner. Further, the Office has designed the proceedings to allow each party to determine the preferred manner of putting forward its case, subject to the guidance of judges who determine the needs of a particular case through procedural and substantive rulings throughout the proceedings.

Background: The Leahy-Smith America Invents Act establishes several new trial proceedings to be conducted by the Board including: (1) Inter partes review (IPR); (2) post-grant review (PGR); (3) a transitional program for covered business method patents (CBM); and (4) derivation proceedings. The AIA requires the Office to promulgate rules for the proceedings, with the PGR, IPR, and CBM rules to be in effect one year after AIA enactment and the derivation rules to be in effect 18 months after AIA enactment.

Consistent with the statute, the Office published a number of notices of proposed rulemaking in February of 2012, and requested written comments on the Office's proposed implementation of the new trial proceedings of the AIA. The Office also hosted a series of public educational roadshows, across the country, regarding the proposed rules.

Additionally, the Office published a practice guide based on the proposed trial rules in the Federal Register to provide the public an opportunity to comment. Practice Guide for Proposed Trial Rules, 77 FR 6868 (Feb. 9, 2012) (Request for Comments) (hereafter "Practice Guide for Proposed Trial Rules" or "Office Patent Trial Practice Guide"). This Office Patent Trial Practice Guide is intended to advise the public on the general framework of the rules, including the structure and times for taking action in each of the new proceedings.

In response to the notices of proposed rulemaking and the Practice Guide notice, the Office received 251 submissions of written comments from intellectual property organizations, businesses, law firms, patent practitioners, and others, including a United States senator who was a principal author of section 18 of the AIA. The comments provided support for, opposition to, and diverse recommendations on the proposed rules. The Office appreciates the thoughtful comments, and has considered and analyzed the comments thoroughly. In light of the comments, the Office has made modifications to the proposed rules to provide clarity and to balance the interests of the public, patent owners, patent challengers, and other interested parties, in light of the statutory requirements and considerations, such as the effect of the regulations on the economy, the integrity of the patent system, the efficient administration of the Office, and the ability of the Office to complete the proceedings timely.

For the implementation of sections 3, 6, 7, and 18 of the AIA that are related to administrative trials and judicial review of Board decisions, the Office is publishing the following final rules in separate notices in the Federal Register: (1) Rules of Practice for Trials before the Patent Trial and Appeal Board and Judicial Review of Patent Trial and Appeal Board Decisions (RIN 0651-AC70); (2) Changes to Implement Inter Partes Review Proceedings, Post-Grant Review Proceedings, and Transitional Program for Covered Business Method Patents (RIN 0651-AC71); (3) Transitional Program for Covered Business Method Patents—Definitions of Covered Business Method Patent and Technological Invention (RIN 0651-AC75); and (4) Changes to Implement Derivation Proceedings (RIN 0651-AC74). The Office also provides responses to the public written comments in these final rules in the Response to Comments sections of the notices.

Further, the Office revised the Office Patent Trial Practice Guide based on the final rules. The Office has been working diligently to publish all of the final rules related to the new AIA trial proceedings and the Office Patent Trial Practice Guide in the Federal Register concurrently. Due to certain limitations, however, the Office Patent Trial Practice and the specific final rule for derivation proceedings will be published in the Federal Register after the other final rules. In particular, the specific rules for derivation, i.e., §§42.404 through 42.412, will be published at a later date.

Statutory Requirements: The AIA provides certain minimum requirements for each of the new proceedings. Provided below is a brief overview of these requirements.

Proceedings begin with the filing of a petition to institute a trial. The petition must be filed with the Board consistent with any time period required by statute and be accompanied by the evidence the petitioner seeks to rely upon. See, e.g., 35 U.S.C. 135(a) and 311(c), as amended, and §42.3 (references to §42.x or §1.x refer to title 37 of the Code of Federal Regulations). For IPR, PGR, and CBM, the patent owner is afforded an opportunity to file a preliminary response. 35 U.S.C. 313, as amended, and 35 U.S.C. 323.

The Board acting on behalf of the Director may institute a trial where the petitioner establishes that the standards for instituting the requested trial are met taking into account any preliminary response filed by the patent owner. Conversely, the Board may not authorize a trial where the information presented in the petition, taking into account any patent owner preliminary response, fails to meet the requisite standard for instituting the trial. See e.g., 35 U.S.C. 314, as amended, and 35 U.S.C. 324. Where there are multiple matters in the Office involving the same patent, the Board may determine how the proceedings will proceed, including providing for a stay, transfer, consolidation, or termination of any such matter. See, e.g., 35 U.S.C. 315, as amended, and 35 U.S.C. 325.

The AIA requires that the Board conduct AIA trials and that the Director prescribe regulations concerning the conduct of those trials. 35 U.S.C. 6, 135, and 316, as amended, and 35 U.S.C. 326. For example, for IPR, PGR, and CBM, the AIA mandates the promulgation of rules including motions to seal, procedures for filing supplemental information, standards and procedures for discovery, sanctions for improper use of the proceeding, entry of protective orders, and oral hearings. See, e.g., 35 U.S.C. 316(a), as amended, and 35 U.S.C. 326. Additionally, the AIA mandates the promulgation of rules for IPR, PGR, and CBM concerning the submission of a patent owner response with supporting evidence and allowing the patent owner a motion to amend the patent. Id.

A petitioner and a patent owner may terminate the proceeding with respect to the petitioner by filing a written agreement with the Board, unless the Board has already decided the merits of the proceeding before the request for termination is filed. See, e.g., 35 U.S.C. 317, as amended, and 35 U.S.C. 327. If no petitioner remains in the proceeding, the Board may terminate the review or proceed to a final written decision. For derivation proceedings, the parties may arbitrate issues in the proceeding, but nothing precludes the Office from determining the patentability of the claimed inventions involved in the proceeding. 35 U.S.C. 135, as amended. Where a trial has been instituted and not dismissed, the Board will issue a final written decision with respect to the involved patent and/or applications. 35 U.S.C. 135 and 35 U.S.C. 318, as amended, and 35 U.S.C. 328.

For IPR, PGR, and CBM, the AIA requires that the Office consider the effect of the regulations on the economy, the integrity of the patent system, the efficient administration of the Office, and the ability of the Office to timely complete the proceedings. 35 U.S.C. 316, as amended, and 35 U.S.C. 326. In developing the general trial rules, as well as the specific rules for the individual proceedings, the Office has taken these considerations into account. Further, the specific rules for the individual proceedings take into account the jurisdictional and timing requirements for the particular proceedings.

General Overview of Proceedings: Generally, the proceedings begin with the filing of a petition that identifies all of the claims challenged and the grounds and supporting evidence on a claim-by-claim basis. Within three months of notification of a filing date, the patent owner in an IPR, PGR, or CBM proceeding may file a preliminary response to the petition, including a simple statement that the patent owner elects not to

See the Office Patent Trial Practice Guide, p. 1336.

respond to the petition. The Board acting on behalf of the Director will determine whether to institute a trial within three months of the date the patent owner's preliminary response was due or was filed, whichever is first.

In instituting a trial, the Board will narrow the issues for final decision by authorizing the trial to proceed only on the challenged claims for which the threshold standards for the proceeding have been met. Further, the Board will identify, on a claim-by-claim basis, the grounds on which the trial will proceed. Any claim or issue not included in the authorization for review will not be part of the trial. A party dissatisfied with the Board's determination to institute a trial may request rehearing as to points believed to have been overlooked or misapprehended. See §42.71(d) and (c).

The Board will enter a Scheduling Order (Appendix A) concurrent with the decision to institute a trial. The Scheduling Order will set due dates for the trial taking into account the complexity of the proceeding but ensuring that the trial is completed within one year of institution.

For example, a Scheduling Order for an IPR or PGR might, consistent with §§42.120 and 42.220, provide a three month deadline for patent owner discovery and for filing a patent owner response and motion to amend. Once the patent owner's response and motion to amend have been filed, the Scheduling Order might provide the petitioner with three months for discovery and for filing a petitioner's reply to the response and the petitioner's opposition to the amendment. The Scheduling Order might then provide the patent owner with one month for discovery and for filing a patent owner reply to petitioner's opposition to a patent owner amendment. A representative timeline is provided below:

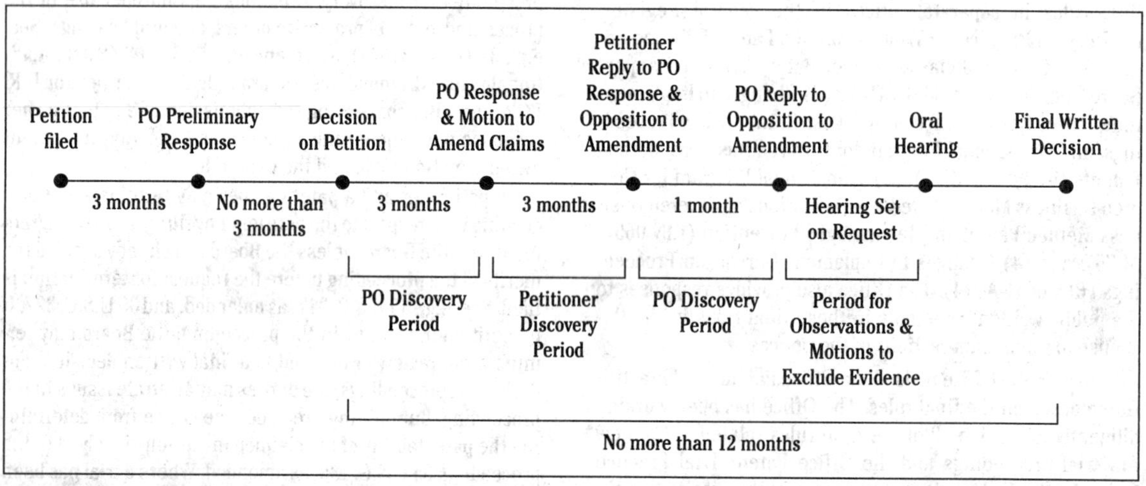

Sequence of discovery. Once instituted, absent special circumstances, discovery will proceed in a sequenced fashion. For example, the patent owner may begin deposing the petitioner's declarants once the proceeding is instituted. After the patent owner has filed a patent owner response and any motion to amend the claims, the petitioner may depose the patent owner's declarants. Similarly, after the petitioner has filed a reply to the patent owner's response and an opposition to an amendment, the patent owner may depose the petitioner's declarants and file a reply in support of its claim amendments. Where the patent owner relies upon new declaration evidence in support of its amendments, the petitioner will be authorized to depose the declarants and submit observations on the deposition. Once the time for taking discovery in the trial has ended, the parties will be authorized to file motions to exclude evidence believed to be inadmissible. Admissibility of evidence is generally governed by the Federal Rules of Evidence.

Sequence of filing responses and motions. An initial conference call will be held about one month from the date of institution to discuss the motions that the parties intend to file and to determine if any adjustment needs to be made to the Scheduling Order. The patent owner may file a patent owner's response and/or a motion to amend the claims by the time set in the Scheduling Order. The petitioner will then file a reply to the patent owner's response and any opposition to the patent owner's amendment. Both parties will then be permitted an opportunity to file motions to exclude an opponent's evidence believed to be inadmissible. After all motions have been filed, the parties will be afforded an opportunity to have an oral argument at the Board.

Summary of the Rules: The following is a general summary of the rules for the proceedings.

I. General Procedures

The rules are to be construed so as to ensure the just, speedy, and inexpensive resolution of a proceeding and, where appropriate, the rules may be modified to accomplish these goals. §42.1(b); §42.5(a) and (b).

A. Jurisdiction and Management of the Record

1. *Jurisdiction:* 35 U.S.C. 6(b), as amended, provides that the Board is to conduct derivation proceedings, inter partes reviews, and post-grant reviews. The Board also conducts the

transitional program for covered business method reviews, which are subject to Board review under 35 U.S.C. 6(b), as amended, 35 U.S.C. 326(c), and Public Law 112-29, section 18. The Board therefore will have exclusive jurisdiction within the Office over every application and patent that is involved in a derivation, IPR, PGR, or CBM proceeding. Ex parte reexamination proceedings and inter partes reexamination proceedings are not "involved" patents (as defined in §42.2) in derivation, IPR, PGR, and CBM proceedings and are thus treated separately except as ordered by the Board.

2. *Prohibition on Ex Parte Communications:* All substantive communications with the Board regarding a proceeding must include all parties to the proceeding, except as otherwise authorized. §42.5(d). The prohibition on ex parte communications does not extend to: (1) Ministerial communications with support staff (for instance, to arrange a conference call); (2) conference calls or hearings in which opposing counsel declines to participate; (3) informing the Board in one proceeding of the existence or status of a related Board proceeding; or (4) reference to a pending case in support of a general proposition (for instance, citing a published opinion from a pending case or referring to a pending case to illustrate a systemic problem).

Arranging a conference call with the Board. The Board encourages the use of conference calls to raise and resolve issues in an expedited manner. The Board envisions that most of the procedural issues arising during a proceeding will be handled during a conference call or shortly thereafter, i.e., in a matter of days. When arranging a conference call, parties should be prepared to discuss with a Trial Section paralegal why the call is needed and what materials may be needed during the call, e.g., a particular exhibit.

Refusal to participate. The Board has the discretion to permit a hearing or conference call to take place even if a party refuses to participate. In such cases, the Board may order as a condition for the call additional safeguards, such as the recording of the communication and the entry of the recording into the record.

B. Counsel

Need for lead and back-up counsel. A party represented by counsel must designate both a lead as well as a back-up counsel who can conduct business on behalf of the lead counsel, as instances may arise where lead counsel may be unavailable. §42.10(a).

Power of attorney. A power of attorney must be filed with the designation of counsel, unless the designated counsel is already counsel of record. §42.10(b).

Pro hac vice. The Board may recognize counsel pro hac vice during a proceeding upon a showing of good cause, and subject to the requirement that lead counsel is a registered practitioner. §42.10(c). The Board may impose other considerations as well. Id. Proceedings before the Office can be technically complex. For example, it is expected that amendments to a patent will be sought. The grant of a motion to appear pro hac vice is a discretionary action taking into account the specifics of the proceedings. Similarly, the revocation of pro hac vice is a discretionary action taking into account various factors, including incompetence, unwillingness to abide by the Office's Rules of Professional Conduct, and incivility.

The Office expects that lead counsel will, and back-up counsel may, participate in all hearings and conference calls with the Board and will sign all papers submitted in the proceeding. In addition, the role of back-up counsel is to conduct business with the Office on behalf of lead counsel when lead counsel is not available. Actions not conducted before the Office (e.g., taking of deposition) may be conducted by lead or back-up counsel.

C. Electronic Filing

Electronic filing is the default manner in which documents are to be filed with the Board. §42.6(b). Electronic filing of legal documents is being implemented across the country in state and federal courts. The use of electronic filing aids in the efficient administration of the proceeding, improves public accessibility, and provides a more effective document management system for the Office and parties. The manner of submission will be established by the Board. The Board will publish electronic submission information on its Web site (www.uspto.gov/PTAB) in August of 2012. Due to system constraints, no single uploaded file may exceed 250 megabytes in size.

Paper filing may be used where appropriate, but must be accompanied by a motion explaining the need for non-electronic filing. §42.6(b). Based upon experience with contested cases, the Board does not expect to receive many requests to file paper submissions. Circumstances where a paper filing may be warranted include those occasions where the Office's electronic filing system is unable to accept filings. Alternatively, if a problem with electronic filing arises during normal business hours, a party may contact the Board and request a one-day extension of time for due dates that are set by rule or orders of the Board. §42.5. In the unlikely event that an administrative patent judge is not available to rule on the extension, the Board may grant an extension the day after the paper is due, which includes situations where electronic filing problems are shown to have occurred.

D. Mandatory Notices

The rules require that parties to a proceeding provide certain mandatory notices, including identification of the real parties-in-interest, related matters, lead and back-up counsel, and service information. §42.8. Where there is a change of information, a party must file a revised notice within 21 days of the change. §42.8(a)(3).

1. *Real Party-in-Interest or Privy:* The core functions of the "real party-in-interest" and "privies" requirement to assist members of the Board in identifying potential conflicts, and to assure proper application of the statutory estoppel provisions. The latter, in turn, seeks to protect patent owners from harassment via successive petitions by the same or re-

See the Office Patent Trial Practice Guide, p. 1336.

lated parties, to prevent parties from having a "second bite at the apple," and to protect the integrity of both the USPTO and Federal Courts by assuring that all issues are promptly raised and vetted. Cf. Fed. R. Civ. P. 17(a) (Advisory Committee Note to 1966 Amendment to Rule 17(a)) ("[T]he modern function of the rule in its negative aspect is simply to protect the defendant against a subsequent action by the party actually entitled to recover, and to insure generally that the judgment will have its proper effect as res judicata."). The USPTO will apply traditional common-law principles with these goals in mind and parties will be well-served to factor in these considerations when determining whom to identify.

Whether a party who is not a named participant in a given proceeding nonetheless constitutes a "real party-in-interest" or "privy" to that proceeding is a highly fact-dependent question. See generally Taylor v. Sturgell, 553 U.S. 880 (2008); 18A Charles Alan Wright, Arthur R. Miller & Edward H. Cooper, Federal Practice & Procedure §§4449, 4451 (2d ed. 2011) (hereinafter "Wright & Miller"). Such questions will be handled by the Office on a case-by-case basis taking into consideration how courts have viewed the terms "real party-in-interest" and "privy." See, e.g., Taylor, 553 U.S. at 893-895 and 893 n.6 (noting that "[t]he list that follows is meant only to provide a framework [for the decision], not to establish a definitive taxonomy"). Courts invoke the terms "real party-in-interest" and "privy" to describe relationships and considerations sufficient to justify applying conventional principles of estoppel and preclusion. Accordingly, courts have avoided rigid definitions or recitation of necessary factors. Similarly, multiple Federal Rules invoke the terms without attempting to define them or what factors trigger their application. See, e.g., Fed. R. Civ. P. 17; Fed. Cir. R. 47.4.

The typical common-law expression of the "real party-in-interest" (the party "who, according to the governing substantive law, is entitled to enforce the right") does not fit directly into the AIA trial context. See 6A Charles Alan Wright, Arthur R. Miller, Mary Kay Kane, & Richard L. Marcus, Federal Practice & Procedure Civil section 1543 (3d ed. 2011) (discussing Fed. R. Civ. P. 17). That notion reflects standing concepts, but no such requirement exists in the IPR or PGR context, although it exists in the CBM context. In an IPR or PGR proceeding, there is no "right" being enforced since any entity (other than the patent owner) may file an IPR or PGR petition. However, the spirit of that formulation as to IPR and PGR proceedings means that, at a general level, the "real party-in-interest" is the party that desires review of the patent. Thus, the "real party-in-interest" may be the petitioner itself, and/or it may be the party or parties at whose behest the petition has been filed. In this regard, the Office's prior application of similar principles in the inter partes reexamination context offers additional guidance. See generally In re Guan et al. Inter Partes Reexamination Proceeding, Control No. 95/001,045, Decision Vacating Filing Date (Aug. 25, 2008). Similar considerations apply to CBM proceedings, although the statute governing those proceedings also requires that the party seeking the proceeding, or its real party-in-interest or privy, have been sued for infringing the subject patent, or been charged with infringement under that patent.

The notion of "privity" is more expansive, encompassing parties that do not necessarily need to be identified in the petition as a "real party-in-interest." The Office intends to evaluate what parties constitute "privies" in a manner consistent with the flexible and equitable considerations established under federal caselaw. Ultimately, that analysis seeks to determine whether the relationship between the purported "privy" and the relevant other party is sufficiently close such that both should be bound by the trial outcome and related estoppels. This approach is consistent with the legislative history of the AIA, which indicates that Congress included "privies" within the parties subject to the statutory estoppel provisions in an effort to capture "the doctrine's practical and equitable nature," in a manner akin to collateral estoppel. In that regard, the legislative history endorsed the expression of "privy" as follows:

The word "privy" has acquired an expanded meaning. The courts, in the interest of justice and to prevent expensive litigation, are striving to give effect to judgments by extending "privies" beyond the classical description. The emphasis is not on the concept of identity of parties, but on the practical situation. Privity is essentially a shorthand statement that collateral estoppel is to be applied in a given case; there is no universally applicable definition of privity. The concept refers to a relationship between the party to be estopped and the unsuccessful party in the prior litigation which is sufficiently close so as to justify application of the doctrine of collateral estoppel.

154 Cong. Rec. S9987 (daily ed. Sept. 27, 2008) (statement of Sen. Kyl) (citing Cal. Physicians' Serv. v. Aoki Diabetes Research Inst., 163 Cal.App.4th 1506 (Cal. App. 2008)); see also 157 Cong. Rec. S1376 (daily ed. Mar. 8, 2011) (incorporating prior 2008 statement). Subsequent legislative history expanded on the prior discussion of "privy" by noting that "privity is an equitable rule that takes into account the 'practical situation,' and should extend to parties to transactions and other activities relating to the property in question." 157 Cong. Rec. S1376 (daily ed. Mar. 8, 2011) (statement of Sen. Kyl).

There are multiple factors relevant to the question of whether a non-party may be recognized as a "real party-in-interest" or "privy." See, e.g., Taylor, 553 U.S. at 893-895 and 893 n.6 (noting that "[t]he list that follows is meant only to provide a framework [for the decision], not to establish a definitive taxonomy"). A common consideration is whether the non-party exercised or could have exercised control over a party's participation in a proceeding. See, e.g., id. at 895; see generally Wright & Miller section 4451. The concept of control generally means that "it should be enough that the nonparty has the actual measure of control or opportunity to control that might reasonably be expected between two formal coparties." Wright & Miller §4451. Courts and commentators agree, however, that there is no "bright-line test" for determining the necessary quantity or degree of participation to qualify as a "real party-in-interest" or "privy" based on the control concept. Gonzalez v. Banco Cent. Corp., 27 F.3d 751, 759 (1st Cir. 1994). See also Wright & Miller section 4451 ("The measure of control by a nonparty that justifies preclusion cannot be defined rigidly."). Accordingly, the rules do not enumerate particular factors regarding a "control" theory of "real party-in-interest" or "privy" under the statute.

Additionally, many of the same considerations that apply in the context of "res judicata" will likely apply in the "real party-in-interest" or "privy" contexts. See Gonzalez, 27 F.3d at 759; see generally Wright & Miller section 4451. Other considerations may also apply in the unique context of statutory estoppel. See generally, e.g., In re Arviv Reexamination Proceeding, Control No. 95/001,526, Decision Dismissing section 1.182 and section 1.183 Petitions, at 6 (Apr. 18, 2011); In re Beierbach Reexamination Proceeding, Control No. 95/000,407, Decision on section 1.182 and section 1.183 Petitions, at 6 (July 28, 2010); In re Schlecht Inter Partes Reexamination Proceeding, Control No. 95/001,206, Decision Dismissing Petition, at 5 (June 22, 2010); In re Guan Inter Partes Reexamination Proceeding, Control No. 95/001,045, Decision Vacating Filing Date, at 8 (Aug. 25, 2008).

The Office has received requests to state whether particular facts will qualify a party as a "real party-in-interest" or "privy." Some fact-combinations will generally justify applying the "real party-in-interest" or "privy" label. For example, a party that funds and directs and controls an IPR or PGR petition or proceeding constitutes a "real party-in-interest," even if that party is not a "privy" of the petitioner. But whether something less than complete funding and control suffices to justify similarly treating the party requires consideration of the pertinent facts. See, e.g., Cal. Physicians, 163 Cal.App.4th at 1523-25 (discussing the role of control in the "privy" analysis, and observing that "preclusion can apply even in the absence of such control"). The Office will handle such questions on a case-by-case basis taking into consideration how courts have viewed the terms. Similarly, while generally a party does not become a "real party-in-interest" or a "privy" of the petitioner merely through association with another party in an unrelated endeavor, slight alterations in the facts, as well as consideration of other facts, might result in a different conclusion. So, for example, if Trade Association X files an IPR petition, Party A does not become a "real party-in-interest" or a "privy" of the Association simply based on its membership in the Association. Similarly, if Party A is part of a Joint Defense Group with Party B in a patent infringement suit, and Party B files a PGR petition, Party A is not a "real party-in-interest" or a "privy" for the purposes of the PGR petition based solely on its participation in that Group. That is not to say that Party A's membership in Trade Association X, or the Joint Defense Group, in those scenarios is irrelevant to the determination; deeper consideration of the facts in the particular case is necessary to determine whether Party A is a "real party-in-interest" or a "privy" of the petitioner. Relevant factors include: Party A's relationship with the petitioner; Party A's relationship to the petition itself, including the nature and/or degree of involvement in the filing; and the nature of the entity filing the petition. In short, because rarely will one fact, standing alone, be determinative of the inquiry, the Office cannot prejudge the impact of a particular fact on whether a party is a "real party-in-interest" or "privy" of the petitioner.

2. *Related Matters:* Parties to a proceeding are to identify any other judicial or administrative matter that would affect, or be affected by, a decision in the proceeding. Judicial matters include actions involving the patent in federal court. Administrative matters include every application and patent claiming, or which may claim, the benefit of the priority of the filing date of the party's involved patent or application as well as any ex parte and inter partes reexaminations for an involved patent.

3. *Identification of Service Information:* Parties are required to identify service information to allow for efficient communication between the Board and the parties. §42.8. Additionally, while the Board is authorized to provide notice by means other than mailing to the correspondence address of record, it is ultimately the responsibility of the applicant or patent owner to maintain a proper correspondence address in the record. Ray v. Lehman, 55 F.3d 606, 610 (Fed. Cir. 1995).

Under §42.6(e), service may be made electronically upon agreement of the parties. For example, the parties could agree that electronic filing with the Board of a document constitutes electronic service.

E. Public Availability and Confidentiality

The rules aim to strike a balance between the public's interest in maintaining a complete and understandable file history and the parties' interest in protecting truly sensitive information.

1. *Public Availability:* The record of a proceeding, including documents and things, shall be made available to the public, except as otherwise ordered. §42.14. Accordingly, a document or thing will be made publicly available, unless a party files a motion to seal that is then granted by the Board.

2. *Confidential information:* The rules identify confidential information in a manner consistent with Federal Rule of Civil Procedure 26(c)(1)(G), which provides for protective orders for trade secret or other confidential research, development, or commercial information. §42.54.

3. *Motion To Seal:* A party intending a document or thing to be sealed may file a motion to seal concurrent with the filing of the document or thing. §42.14. The document or thing will be provisionally sealed on receipt of the motion and remain so pending the outcome of the decision on motion.

4. *Protective Orders:* A party may file a motion to seal where the motion contains a proposed protective order, such as the default protective order in Appendix B. §42.54. Specifically, protective orders may be issued for good cause by the

See the Office Patent Trial Practice Guide, p. 1336.

Board to protect a party from disclosing confidential information. §42.54. Guidelines on proposing a protective order in a motion to seal, including a Standing Protective Order, are provided in Appendix B. The document or thing will be protected on receipt of the motion and remain so, pending the outcome of the decision on motion.

5. *Confidential Information in a Petition:* A petitioner filing confidential information with a petition may, concurrent with the filing of the petition, file a motion to seal with a proposed protective order as to the confidential information. A petitioner filing information under seal with a petition is not required to serve the confidential information. §42.55.

A petitioner may seek entry of the default protective order in Appendix B or may seek entry of an alternative protective order. Where the petitioner seeks entry of the default protective order, the patent owner will be given access to the confidential information prior to institution of the trial by agreeing to the terms of a default order. §42.55(a). The Board anticipates that a patent owner may use the Board's electronic filing system to agree to the default protective order and would, upon confirmation of the agreement by the Board, be given access to the provisionally sealed information.

Where a petitioner files a motion to seal with the petition that seeks entry of a protective order other than the default protective order, a patent owner may only access the sealed confidential information prior to the institution of the trial by:

(1) Agreeing to the terms of the protective order requested by the petitioner;

(2) Agreeing to the terms of a protective order that the parties file jointly; or

(3) Obtaining entry of a protective order (e.g., the default protective order).

For example, the patent owner could arrange a conference call with the Board and opposing party, and provide a suitable basis for entering the default protective order as opposed to the petitioner's proposed protective order. §42.55(b). The Board anticipates that a patent owner may use the Board's electronic filing system to agree to the protective order requested by the petitioner and would, upon confirmation of the agreement by the Board, be given access to the provisionally sealed information. Similarly, the Board anticipates that a patent owner may use the Board's electronic filing system to file a protective order that the parties jointly agree to and would, upon confirmation of the agreement by the Board, be given access to the provisionally sealed information. Alternatively, the patent owner would be given access on entry of a protective order by the Board.

The rule seeks to streamline the process of seeking protective orders prior to the institution of the review while balancing the need to protect confidential information against an opponent's ability to access information used to challenge the opponent's claims.

6. *Expungement of Confidential Information:* Confidential information that is subject to a protective order ordinarily would become public 45 days after denial of a petition to institute a trial or 45 days after final judgment in a trial. There is an expectation that information will be made public where the existence of the information is referred to in a decision to grant or deny a request to institute a review or is identified in a final written decision following a trial. A party seeking to maintain the confidentiality of information, however, may file a motion to expunge the information from the record prior to the information becoming public. §42.56. The rule balances the needs of the parties to submit confidential information with the public interest in maintaining a complete and understandable file history for public notice purposes. The rule encourages parties to redact sensitive information, where possible, rather than seeking to seal entire documents.

7. *Derivation:* A party in a derivation submitting dates of conception to establish inventorship may wish to file the information under seal. Where the dates of conception are filed under seal, a party may request that an opponent not be given access to the conception dates until the opponent's conception dates have been provided to the Board.

F. Discovery

Discovery is a tool to develop a fair record and to aid the Board in assessing the credibility of witnesses. To streamline the proceedings, the rules and Scheduling Order provide a sequenced discovery process upon institution of the trial. Specifically, each party will be provided respective discovery periods, beginning with the patent owner. The sequenced discovery allows parties to conduct meaningful discovery before they are required to submit their respective motions and oppositions during the trial. Thus, discovery before the Board is focused on what the parties reasonably need to respond to the grounds raised by an opponent. In this way, the scope of the trial continually narrows.

1. *Routine Discovery:* Routine discovery includes: (1) Production of any exhibit cited in a paper or testimony; (2) the cross-examination of the other sides[1] declarants; and (3) relevant information that is inconsistent with a position advanced during the proceeding. Routine discovery places the parties on a level playing field and streamlines the proceeding. Board authorization is not required to conduct routine discovery, although the Board will set the times for conducting this discovery in its Scheduling Order.

(a) *Inconsistent Statements:* The following situations exemplify instances where disclosures of inconsistent statements are to be made. Example 1: where a petitioner relies upon an expert affidavit alleging that a method described in a patent cannot be carried out, the petitioner would be required to provide any non-privileged work undertaken by, or on behalf of, the petitioner that is inconsistent with the contentions in the expert's affidavit. Example 2: where a patent owner relies upon surprising and unexpected results to rebut an allegation of obviousness, the patent owner should provide the petitioner with non-privileged evidence that is inconsistent with the contention of unexpected properties.

(b) *Witness Expenses:* The burden and expense of producing a witness for redirect or cross-examination should normally fall on the party presenting the witness. Thus, a party presenting a witness's testimony by affidavit should arrange to make the witness available for cross-examination. This applies to witnesses employed by a party as well as experts and non-party witnesses. If there are associated expenses such as expert witness fees or travel, those should be borne by the party presenting the testimony. Should the witness's testimony be presented by transcript, the same rules apply, and the witness fees and expenses should be borne by the presenting party.

(c) *Document Translation:* All proceedings before the Board will be conducted in English. Translations therefore must be provided for: (1) Those documents produced in discovery under §42.51; and (2) all documents relied on, or otherwise used, during the proceedings. Unless accompanied by an English language translation, such documents in a language other than English will not be considered by the Board.

2. *Additional Discovery:* A request for additional discovery must be in the form of a motion, although the parties may agree to discovery amongst themselves. §42.51(b)(2). The types of discovery available under the Federal Rules of Civil Procedure can be sought by the parties. The standard for granting such requests varies with the proceeding. An "interests of justice" standard applies in IPR and derivations, whereas the more liberal "good cause" standard applies in PGR and CBM. Id. An additional discovery request could be granted under either standard, for example, when a party raises an issue where the evidence on that issue is uniquely in the possession of the party that raised it.

3. *Compelled Testimony:* A party can request authorization to compel testimony under 35 U.S.C. 24. If a motion to compel testimony is granted, testimony may be (1) ex parte, subject to subsequent cross-examination, or (2) inter partes. Therriault v. Garbe, 53 USPQ2d 1179, 1184 (BPAI 1999). Prior to moving for or opposing compelled testimony, the parties should discuss which procedure is appropriate. See Appendix D for guidance on compelled testimony.

4. *Mandatory Initial Disclosures:* Section 42.51(a) provides for mandatory initial disclosures, either by agreement (subparagraph (a)(1)) or, where the parties fail to reach an agreement, by motion, if granted (subparagraph (a)(2)). To proceed under §42.51(a)(1), the parties must submit any agreement reached on initial disclosures no later than the filing of the patent owner's preliminary response, or by the expiration of the time period for filing such a response. See §42.51(a)(1)(i).

Where the parties agree to mandatory initial disclosures under §42.51(a)(1), two options are available as follows:

Option 1

This first option is modeled after Rule 26(a)(1)(A) of the Federal Rules of Civil Procedure, and requires disclosure of the following information: (1) the name and, if known, the address and telephone number of each individual likely to have discoverable information—along with the subjects of that information—that the disclosing party may use to support its claims or defenses, unless the use would be solely for impeachment; and (2) a copy—or a description by category and location—of all documents, electronically stored information, and tangible things that the disclosing party has in its possession, custody, or control and may use to support its claims or defenses, unless the use would be solely for impeachment.

Option 2

This second option is more extensive, and includes the following disclosures listed under both items I and II:

I. If the petition seeks cancellation of one or more claims in whole or part on the basis of the existence of an alleged prior non-published public disclosure, the petitioner will provide a statement: (1) Identifying, to the extent known by the petitioner, the names and information sufficient to contact all persons other than those offering affidavits or declarations who are reasonably likely to know of the alleged prior non-published public disclosure; (2) indicating which of such persons are within the control of petitioner, or who have otherwise consented to appear for a testimony in connection with the proceeding; (3) indicating which, if any, of such persons are represented by petitioner's counsel; (4) identifying all documents and things within petitioner's possession, custody, or control referring to or relating to the alleged prior non-published public disclosure; and (5) identifying all things relating to the alleged prior non-published public disclosure, including a complete description, photographs, the chemical analysis (if the chemical composition is in issue), and computer code (for computer-related subject matter), and their locations, and whether petitioner will produce such things for inspection, analysis, testing, and sampling.

II. If the petition seeks cancellation of one or more claims in whole or in part on the basis of the alleged obviousness of one or more of the claims, the petitioner will provide a statement: (1) Identifying, to the extent known by the petitioner, the names and information sufficient to contact all persons other than those offering affidavits or declarations who are reasonably likely to have information regarding the secondary indicia of non-obviousness; (2) indicating which of such persons are within the control of petitioner, or have otherwise consented to appear for a testimony in connection with the proceeding; (3) indicating which, if any, of such persons are represented by petitioner's counsel; (4) identifying all documents and things within petitioner's possession, custody, or control referring to or relating to such secondary indicia of non-obviousness; and (5) identifying all things relating to the secondary indicia of non-obviousness, including a complete description, photographs, the chemical analysis (if the chemical composition is in issue), and computer code (for computer-related subject matter), and their locations, and whether petitioner will produce such things for inspection, analysis, testing, and sampling.

See the Office Patent Trial Practice Guide, p. 1336.

Under §42.51(a)(1)(ii), upon institution of a trial, the parties may automatically take discovery of the information identified in the initial disclosures. Accordingly, the initial disclosures of a party shall be filed as exhibits as soon as reasonably practicable to permit discovery related to that information. See §42.51(a)(1)(i).

5. *Live Testimony:* Cross-examination may be ordered to take place in the presence of an administrative patent judge, which may occur at the deposition or oral argument. Occasionally, the Board will require live testimony where the Board considers the demeanor of a witness critical to assessing credibility. Examples of where such testimony has been ordered in previous contested cases before the Board include cases where derivation is an issue, where misconduct is alleged to have occurred during the proceeding, or where testimony is given through an interpreter. See Appendix D for guidance on testimony.

6. *Times and Locations for Witness Cross-Examination:* Under §42.53(c)(1), the default time limits for compelled direct examination, cross-examination, and redirect examination are seven hours for direct examination, four hours for cross-examination, and two hours for redirect examination. Similarly, under §42.53(c)(2), the default time limits for cross-examination, redirect examination, and recross-examination for uncompelled direct testimony are seven hours for cross-examination, four hours for redirect examination, and two hours for recross-examination. See Appendix D: Testimony Guidelines, for more information.

The rules do not provide for a specific location for taking testimony other than providing that the testimony may be taken at any reasonable location in the United States. The Board expects that the parties will be able to agree upon a reasonable location but will be available to handle the issue, typically via conference call, where the parties are unable to agree.

7. *E-Discovery:* The cost of e-discovery in patent infringement cases has led a number of courts to adopt special e-discovery rules. Notably, the Federal Circuit Advisory Committee drafted and adopted a Model Order Limiting E-Discovery in Patent Cases that is available on the Federal Circuit's Web site: www.cafc.uscourts.gov. *See also* Federal Rule of Evidence 502. In the interest of promoting economic and procedural efficiency in these proceedings, the Office adopts a default Model Order Regarding E-Discovery (Appendix C) based on the Federal Circuit's Model Order, modified to reflect the differences in statutory requirements. See also Rule 502 of the Federal Rules of Evidence. Except for routine discovery under the provisions of §42.51(b)(1), it is expected that the default Model Order will be entered in a proceeding whenever discovery of Electronically Stored Information (ESI) is sought by the parties, whether under the other discovery provisions of §42.51, or the compelled discovery provisions of §42.52. Should a party desire to obtain production of ESI as part of additional discovery under §42.51, §42.52, or any other provision of the rules, the matter should be raised with the Board in a timely fashion before the discovery is scheduled to take place.

II. Petitions and Motions Practice

A. General Motions Practice Information

1. *Motions practice:* The proceedings begin with the filing of a petition that lays out the petitioner's grounds and supporting evidence for the requested proceeding. Additional relief in a proceeding must be requested in the form of a motion. §42.20(a).

2. *Prior authorization:* Generally, a motion will not be entered without prior Board authorization. §42.20(b). Exceptions include motions where it is impractical for a party to seek prior Board authorization, and motions for which authorization is automatically granted. Motions where it is not practical to seek prior Board authorization include motions to seal and motions filed with a petition, such as motions to waive page limits. Motions where authorization is automatically granted, without a conference with the Board, include requests for rehearing, observations on cross-examination, and motions to exclude evidence. The Board expects that the Scheduling Order will pre-authorize and set times for the filing of observations on cross-examination and motions to exclude evidence based on inadmissibility. See Appendix A, Scheduling Order.

Typically, authorization for a motion is obtained during an initial conference call, which generally occurs within one month of the institution of IPR, PGR, CBM, and derivation proceedings. Additionally, where more immediate relief is required or the request arises after the initial conference call, a party should institute a conference call to obtain such authorization. Typically, the Board will decide procedural issues raised in a conference call during the call itself or shortly thereafter, thereby avoiding the need for additional briefing. The Board has found that this practice simplifies a proceeding by focusing the issues early, reducing costs and efforts associated with motions that are beyond the scope of the proceeding. By taking an active role in the proceeding, the Board can eliminate delay in the proceeding and ensure that attorneys are prepared to resolve the relevant disputed issues.

3. *Page Limits:* Petitions, motions, patent owner preliminary responses, patent owner responses, oppositions, and replies filed in proceedings are subject to page limits in order to streamline the proceedings. §42.24. The rules set a limit of 60 pages for petitions requesting inter partes reviews and derivation proceedings, 80 pages for petitions requesting post-grant review and covered business method patent reviews, and 15 pages for motions. §42.24(a). Patent owner preliminary responses to a petition and patent owner responses to a petition are limited to an equal number of pages as the corresponding petition, and oppositions are limited to an equal number of pages as the corresponding motion. §42.24(b). Re-

plies to patent owner responses to petitions are limited to 15 pages and replies to oppositions are limited to five pages. §42.24(c).

Federal courts routinely use page limits to manage motions practice as "[e]ffective writing is concise writing." Spaziano v. Singletary, 36 F.3d 1028, 1031 n.2 (11th Cir. 1994). Federal courts have found that page limits ease the burden on both the parties and the courts, and patent cases are no exception. Broadwater v. Heidtman Steel Prods., Inc., 182 F.Supp. 2d 705, 710 (S.D. Ill. 2002) ("Counsel are strongly advised, in the future, to not ask this Court for leave to file any memoranda (supporting or opposing dispositive motions) longer than 15 pages. The Court has handled complicated patent cases and employment discrimination cases in which the parties were able to limit their briefs supporting and opposing summary judgment to 10 or 15 pages.").

Although parties are given wide latitude in how they present their cases, the Board's experience is that the presentation of an overwhelming number of issues tends to detract from the argument being presented, and can cause otherwise meritorious issues to be overlooked or misapprehended. Thus, parties should avoid submitting a repository of all the information that a judge could possibly consider, and instead focus on concise, well-organized, easy-to-follow arguments supported by readily identifiable evidence of record. Another factor to keep in mind is that the judges of the Board are familiar with the general legal principles involved in issues which come before the Board. Accordingly, extended discussions of general patent law principles are not necessary.

The Office provides the following practical guidance regarding compliance with the page limits. A party is not required to submit a statement of material fact in its briefing. §42.22. Further, double spacing is not required for claim charts. §42.6(a)(2)(iii).

4. *Testimony Must Disclose Underlying Facts or Data:* The Board expects that most petitions and motions will rely upon affidavits of experts. Affidavits expressing an opinion of an expert must disclose the underlying facts or data upon which the opinion is based. See Fed. R. Evid. 705; and §42.65. Opinions expressed without disclosing the underlying facts or data may be given little or no weight. Rohm & Haas Co. v. Brotech Corp., 127 F.3d 1089, 1092 (Fed. Cir. 1997) (nothing in the Federal Rules of Evidence or Federal Circuit jurisprudence requires the fact finder to credit unsupported assertions of an expert witness).

5. *Tests and Data:* Parties often rely on scientific tests and data to support their positions. Examples include infrared spectroscopy graphs, high-performance liquid-chromatography data, etc. In addition to providing the explanation required in §42.65, a party relying on a test or data should provide any other information the party believes would assist the Board in understanding the significance of the test or the data.

6. *Objective Indicia of Nonobviousness:* The Board expects that most petitions will raise issues of obviousness. In determining whether the subject matter of a claim would have been obvious over the prior art, the Board will review any objective evidence of nonobviousness proffered by the patent owner where appropriate.

B. Petition

Proceedings begin with the filing of a petition. The petition lays out the petitioner's grounds for review and supporting evidence, on a claim-by-claim basis, for instituting the requested proceeding.

1. *Filing date—Minimum Procedural Compliance:* To obtain a filing date, the petition must meet certain minimum standards. See, e.g., §42.106. Generally, the standards required for a petition are those set by statute for the proceeding requested. See, e.g., 35 U.S.C. 312(a). For example, an IPR requires that a complete petition be filed with the required fee, and include a certificate of service for the petition, fee, and evidence relied upon. §42.106. A complete petition for IPR requires that the petitioner certify that the patent is eligible for IPR and that the petitioner is not barred or estopped from requesting the review, and that the petitioner identify the claims being challenged and the specific basis for the challenge. §42.104. Similar petition requirements apply to PGR (§42.204) and derivations (§42.404). CBM proceedings also require a petition demonstrate that the patent for which review is sought is a covered business method patent. §42.304.

2. *Burden of Proof for Statutory Institution Thresholds:* The burden of proof in a proceeding before the Board is a preponderance of the evidence standard. §42.1(d).

3. *Specific Requirements for Petition:* A petitioner must certify that the patent or application is available for review and that the petitioner is not barred or estopped from seeking the proceeding. §§42.104, 42.204, 42.304, and 42.405. Additionally, a petitioner must identify each claim that is challenged and the specific statutory grounds on which each challenge to the claim is based, provide a claim construction for the challenged claims, and state the relevance of the evidence to the issues raised. Id. For IPR, PGR, and CBM proceedings, a petitioner must also identify how the construed claim is unpatentable over the relevant evidence. §§42.104(b), 42.204(b), and 42.304(b).

4. *Covered Business Method/Technological Invention:* A petitioner in a CBM proceeding must demonstrate that the patent for which review is sought is a covered business method patent. §42.304(a). Covered business method patents by definition do not include patents for technological inventions.

The following claim drafting techniques would not typically render a patent a technological invention:

(a) Mere recitation of known technologies, such as computer hardware, communication or computer networks, software, memory, computer-readable storage medium, scanners, display devices or databases, or specialized machines, such as an ATM or point of sale device.

See the Office Patent Trial Practice Guide, p. 1336.

(b) Reciting the use of known prior art technology to accomplish a process or method, even if that process or method is novel and non-obvious.

(c) Combining prior art structures to achieve the normal, expected, or predictable result of that combination.

The following are examples of covered business method patents that are subject to a CBM review proceeding:

(a) A patent that claims a method for hedging risk in the field of commodities trading.

(b) A patent that claims a method for verifying validity of a credit card transaction.

The following are examples of patents that claim a technological invention that would not be subject to a CBM review proceeding:

(a) A patent that claims a novel and non-obvious hedging machine for hedging risk in the field of commodities trading.

(b) A patent that claims a novel and non-obvious credit card reader for verifying the validity of a credit card transaction.

5. *Claim Charts:* While not required, a petitioner may file a claim chart to explain clearly and succinctly what the petitioner believes a claim means in comparison to something else, such as another claim, a reference, or a specification. Where appropriate, claim charts can streamline the process of identifying key features of a claim and comparing those features with specific evidence. Claim charts submitted as part of a petition, motion, patent owner preliminary response, patent owner response, opposition, or reply count towards applicable page limits, but are not required to be double-spaced, e.g., to reduce the number of pages in a petition, claim charts in the petition may be single-spaced. A claim chart from another proceeding that is submitted as an exhibit, however, will not count towards page limits.

6. *Claim Construction:* Regarding the need for a claim construction, where appropriate, it may be sufficient for a party to provide a simple statement that the claim terms are to be given their broadest reasonable interpretation, as understood by one of ordinary skill in the art and consistent with the disclosure. Alternatively, where a party believes that a specific term has meaning other than its plain meaning, the party should provide a statement identifying a proposed construction of the particular term and where the disclosure supports that meaning.

The Office has for decades employed the broadest reasonable interpretation standard to construe claims before the Office, and it will continue to do so in IPR, PGR, and CBM proceedings for construing challenged claims as well as any amended or new claims. §§42.100(b), 42.200(b), and 42.300(b). This approach ensures that the public can clearly understand the outer limits applicants and patentees will attribute to their claims. On the other hand, inconsistent results would become a major issue if the Office adopted a standard of claim construction other than the broadest reasonable interpretation for IPR, PGR, and CBM proceedings. As the AIA contemplates, there may be multiple proceedings involving related patents or patent applications in the Office at a particular time. For example, there may be an IPR of a patent that is also subject to an ex parte reexamination, where the patent is part of a family of co-pending applications all employing the same claim terminology. The Office applies the broadest reasonable interpretation standard in those proceedings, and major difficulties would arise where the Office is handling multiple proceedings with different applicable claim construction standards.

An essential purpose of the broadest reasonable claim interpretation standard in the amendment process is to encourage a patent owner to fashion clear, unambiguous claims. Only through the use of the broadest reasonable claim interpretation standard can the Office ensure that uncertainties of claim scope are removed or clarified. Since patent owners have the opportunity to amend their claims during IPR, PGR, and CBM trials, unlike in district court proceedings, they are able to resolve ambiguities and overbreadth through this interpretive approach, producing clear and defensible patents at the lowest cost point in the system. Patent owners in IPR, PGR, and CBM proceedings will be permitted to file a first motion to amend the patent, after conferring with the Board. §§42.121(a) and 42.221(a). Moreover, although there is no need to permit multiple opportunities to amend to justify the application of the broadest reasonable interpretation standard in an Office proceeding, patent owners in IPR, PGR, and CBM proceedings may file an additional motion to amend when there is a good cause showing, or a joint request of the petitioner and the patent owner to materially advance a settlement. §§42.121(c) and 42.221(c). Thus, the Board will apply the broadest reasonable interpretation standard during IPR, PGR, and CBM proceedings, consistent with the Office's practice in other proceedings.

C. Patent Owner Preliminary Response

For IPR, PGR, and CBM proceedings, a patent owner may file a preliminary response no later than three months after the grant of a filing date. §§42.107(b) and 42.207(b). The preliminary response may present evidence other than new testimonial evidence to demonstrate that no review should be instituted. §§42.107(c) and 42.207(c). New testimonial evidence may be permitted where a party demonstrates that such evidence is in the interests of justice. For example, the Board may permit new testimonial evidence where it addresses issues relating to the petitioner's standing, or where the Board determines that consideration of the identified evidence is necessary in the interests of justice as the evidence demonstrates that the trial may not be instituted.

Potential patent owner preliminary responses include:

(1) The petitioner is statutorily barred from pursuing a review.

(2) The references asserted to establish that the claims are unpatentable are not in fact prior art.

(3) The prior art lacks a material limitation in all of the independent claims.

(4) The prior art teaches or suggests away from a combination that the petitioner is advocating.

(5) The petitioner's claim interpretation for the challenged claims is unreasonable.

(6) If a petition for post-grant review raises 35 U.S.C. 101 grounds, a brief explanation as to how the challenged claims are directed to a patent-eligible invention.

Where a patent owner seeks to expedite the proceeding, the patent owner may file an election to waive the patent owner preliminary response. §§42.107(b) and 42.207(b). No adverse inference will be taken by such an election. Moreover, a patent owner may file a statutory disclaimer of one or more challenged claims to streamline the proceedings. Where no challenged claims remain, the Board would terminate the proceeding. Where one or more challenged claims remain, the Board's decision on institution would be based solely on the remaining claims. See Sony Computer Entm't Am. Inc. v. Dudas, 2006 WL 1472462 (E.D.Va. 2006).

D. Institution of Review

1. *Statutory Threshold Standards:* Generally, the Director may institute a proceeding where a petitioner meets the threshold standards. There is a different statutory threshold standard for institution of each type of proceeding. Each of the statutory threshold standards is summarized below.

(a) *Inter Partes Review:* 35 U.S.C. 314(a), as amended, provides that the Director may not authorize institution of an inter partes review, unless the Director determines that the information presented in the petition filed under 35 U.S.C. 311, as amended, and any response filed under 35 U.S.C. 313, as amended, shows that there is a reasonable likelihood that the petitioner would prevail with respect to at least one of the claims challenged in the petition. The "reasonable likelihood" standard is a somewhat flexible standard that allows the Board room to exercise judgment.

(b) *Post-Grant Review:* 35 U.S.C. 324(a) provides that the Director may not authorize institution of a post-grant review, unless the Director determines that the information presented in the petition filed under 35 U.S.C. 321, if such information is not rebutted, would demonstrate that it is more likely than not that at least one of the claims challenged in the petition is unpatentable. The "more likely than not" standard requires greater than 50% chance of prevailing. In addition, 35 U.S.C. 324(b) provides that the determination required under 35 U.S.C. 324(a) may also be satisfied by a showing that the petition raises a novel or unsettled legal question that is important to other patents or patent applications.

(c) *Covered Business Method Patent Review:* Section 18(a)(1) of the AIA provides that the transitional proceeding for covered business method patents will be regarded as, and will employ the standards and procedures of, a post-grant review under chapter 32 of title 35 United States Code, subject to certain exceptions. Section 18(a)(1)(B) of the AIA specifies that a person may not file a petition for a transitional proceeding with respect to a covered business method patent unless the person or person's real party-in-interest or privy has been sued for infringement of the patent or has been charged with infringement under that patent. A covered business method patent means a patent that claims a method or corresponding apparatus for performing data processing or other operations used in the practice, administration, or management of a financial product or service, except that the term does not include patents for technological inventions.

(d) *Derivation:* 35 U.S.C. 135(a), as amended, provides that an applicant for a patent may file a petition to institute a derivation proceeding. 35 U.S.C. 135(a), as amended, provides that the petition must state with particularity the basis for finding that a named inventor in the earlier application derived the claimed invention from an inventor named in the petitioner's application and, without authorization, filed the earlier application. The petition must be filed within one year of the first publication by the earlier applicant of a claim to the same or substantially the same invention, must be made under oath, and must be supported by substantial evidence. 35 U.S.C. 135(a), as amended, also provides that the Director may institute a derivation proceeding, if the Director determines that the petition demonstrates that the standards for instituting a derivation proceeding are met.

2. *Considerations in Instituting a Review:* The Board institutes the trial on behalf of the Director. §42.4(a). In instituting the trial, the Board will consider whether or not a party has satisfied the relevant statutory institution standard. As part of its consideration, the Board may take into account whether the same or substantially the same prior art or arguments were previously presented to the Office under 35 U.S.C. 325(d).

The Board, in determining whether to institute, may take into account whether the review could be completed timely. For example, the Board may decline to institute a proceeding where the Board determines that it could not complete the proceeding timely. Specifically, the Board could exercise its discretion to decline to institute a petition that seeks review of several hundred claims based upon a thousand references and the patent owner demonstrates that a determination of patentability would require testimony of dozens of non-party controlled witnesses in foreign countries for which the testimony would need to be compelled.

3. *Content of Decision on Whether To Institute:* In instituting a trial, the Board will streamline the issues for final decision by authorizing the trial to proceed only on the challenged claims for which the threshold standards for the proceeding have been met. Further, the Board will identify, on a claim-by-claim basis, the grounds on which the trial will proceed. Any claim or issue not included in the authorization for review is not part of the trial.

Where no trial is instituted, a decision to that effect will be provided. The Board expects that the decision will contain

See the Office Patent Trial Practice Guide, p. 1336.

a short statement as to why the standards were not met, although this may not be necessary in all cases. A party dissatisfied with a decision whether or not to institute may file a request for rehearing before the Board, but the Board's determination on whether to institute a trial is final and nonappealable. 35 U.S.C. 135(a) and 314(d), as amended; 35 U.S.C. 324(e); and §42.71(c).

4. *Scheduling Order:* The Board expects that a Scheduling Order (Appendix A) will be provided concurrent with the decision to institute the proceeding. The Scheduling Order will set due dates for taking action accounting for the complexity of the proceeding but ensuring that the trial is completed within one year of institution. Furthermore, the parties may request changes to the due dates at the initial conference call, and stipulate different dates for Due Dates 1 through 5 (earlier or later, but no later than Due Date 6). See Appendix A.

E. Initial Conference Call (One Month After Instituting Trial)

The Board expects to initiate a conference call within about one month from the date of institution of the trial to discuss the Scheduling Order and any motions that the parties anticipate filing during the trial. Generally, the Board would require a list of proposed motions to be filed no later than two business days prior to the conference call. An accurate motions list is necessary to provide the Board and the opposing parties adequate notice to prepare for the conference call and to plan for the proceeding. The Board's contested cases experience demonstrates that discussing the proposed motions before the motions are authorized to be filed aids the administration of justice by: (1) Helping the Board and counsel adjust the schedule for taking action; (2) permitting the Board to determine whether the listed motions are both necessary and sufficient to resolve the issues raised; and (3) revealing the possibility that there may be a dispositive issue that may aid the settlement of the trial. Submission of a list would not preclude the filing of additional motions not contained in the list. However, the Board may require prior authorization to file an additional motion and the set times are not likely to change as a consequence of the new motion.

F. Patent Owner Response

For IPR, PGR, and CBM, the patent owner will be provided an opportunity to respond to the petition once a trial has been instituted. 35 U.S.C. 316(a)(8), as amended, and 35 U.S.C. 326(a)(8). For a derivation proceeding, the applicant or patent owner alleged to have derived the invention will be provided an opportunity to respond to the petition once the trial has been instituted. 35 U.S.C. 135(b), as amended.

The patent owner response is filed as an opposition to the petition and is subject to the page limits provided in §42.24. §§42.120 and 42.220. The response should identify all the involved claims that are believed to be patentable and state the basis for that belief. Additionally, the response should include any affidavits or additional factual evidence sought to be relied upon and explain the relevance of such evidence. As with the petition, the response may contain a claim chart identifying key features of a claim and comparing those features with specific evidence. Where the patent owner elects not to file a response, the patent owner will arrange for a conference call with the Board to discuss whether or not the patent owner will file a request for adverse judgement. §42.73(b).

G. Motions To Amend

1. *IPR, PGR, and CBM Amendments:* Patent owners in IPR, PGR, and CBM may file motions to amend the claims subject to certain conditions. §§42.121 and 42.221.

First Motion to Amend: Although patent owners may file a first motion to amend and need not obtain prior Board authorization, the patent owner is still required to confer with the Board before filing the motion. §42.121(a) or 42.221(a). During this conference call, it is envisioned that the judge would provide guidance to the patent owner and petitioner regarding the motion including how the filing of the motion will impact the schedule. For example, if a patent holder files a motion to amend the claims, adjustment to the schedule and authorization to conduct additional discovery may be appropriate.

Additional Motion to Amend. Patent owners seeking to file any additional motion to amend claims in the patent under §42.121(c) or 42.221(c) must seek authorization from the Board to file the motion to amend. The filing of the additional motion typically would be authorized if a joint request by the petitioner and patent owner is made to materially advance a settlement. Alternatively, filing of the additional motion may be authorized on a showing of good cause. In determining whether to authorize such an additional motion to amend, the Board will consider, among other factors, whether a petitioner has submitted supplemental information after the time period set for filing a motion to amend in §42.121(a)(1) or 42.221(a)(1). For example, in the event that the petitioner is authorized to submit additional information that was not available to the petitioner before the petition was filed regarding the patentability of an original claim, the entry of the additional evidence will increase the likelihood that an additional motion to amend will be authorized. Other factors, such as the time remaining for the trial, the degree to which the additional evidence impacts the patentability of the claims being sought to be amended, and whether the additional evidence was known to the patent owner before the time period set in §§42.121(a) or 42.221(a) expired, may also be considered in deciding whether the motion should be authorized.

Due Date. A motion to amend must be filed no later than the time period for filing a patent owner response, unless a different due date is provided in a Board order. §42.121(a) or 42.221(a). The Office envisions that most motions to amend will be due three months after a trial is instituted.

Contents of Motion To Amend. Any motion to amend must also comply the[2] content requirements of §§42.121(b) or 42.221(b). Sections 42.121(b) and 42.221(b) require that any motion to amend include a claim listing, show the changes being sought clearly, and describe how the original disclosure of the patent and any relied upon prior application supports each claim that is added or amended. A patent owner may not enlarge the scope of the claims of the patent or add new matter, 35 U.S.C. 316(d)(3) and 326(d)(3), and it is envisioned that the amendment that will be sought by most patent owners is a replacement of a set of broader claims with a set of narrower claims. Where a motion seeks to replace an original patent claim with a new claim, the new claim should be identified as a proposed substitute claim and all changes relative to the original claim clearly discussed. Any motion to amend must also set forth the support in the original disclosure of the patent as well as any application for which benefit of the filing date of the earlier filed disclosure is sought.

Claim Construction. The Board will interpret claims using the broadest reasonable construction, which is consistent with the statute and legislative history of the AIA. See, e.g., 35 U.S.C. 316(a)(2) and (a)(9), as amended, and §42.100(b). In certain circumstances, claim construction under the broadest reasonable interpretation will differ from that of district court. A patent owner, however, will have opportunities to amend its claims during an administrative trial before the Board. See, e.g., §42.121. When filing a motion to amend, a patent owner may demonstrate that the scope of the amended claim is substantially identical to that of the original patent claim, as the original patent claim would have been interpreted by a district court. In such cases, a patent owner may request that the Board determine that the amended claim and original patent claim are substantially identical within the meaning of 35 U.S.C. 252.

2. *Amendments in Derivation Proceedings:* The filing of a motion to amend claims by a petitioner or respondent in a derivation proceeding will be authorized upon a showing of good cause. §42.20. An example of good cause is where the amendment materially advances settlement between the parties or seeks to cancel claims. The Board expects, however, that a request to cancel all of a party's disputed claims will be treated as a request for adverse judgment. §42.73(b).

3. *General Practice Tips on Amendments:* Motions to amend claims are expected to be filed by the due dates set for filing a patent owner response. For authorization to file a motion to amend sought later in the proceeding, a demonstration of good cause will be required. Motions to amend filed late in the proceeding may impair a petitioner's ability to mount a full response in time to meet the statutory deadline for the proceeding. To reduce the number of issues in dispute, however, motions to cancel claims will generally be permitted even late in the proceeding, as will motions to amend to correct simple and obvious typographical errors.

A motion to amend must be accompanied by the proposed amendment. See, e.g., §42.121(b). Claims filed by amendments should be filed as substitute claims. The amendment should clearly state whether each claim is "original," "cancelled," "replaced by proposed substitute," "proposed substitute for original claim X," or "proposed new claim."

Amendments should clearly state where the specification and any drawings support all the limitations in the proposed substitute claims. If the Board is unable to determine how the specification and drawings support the proposed substitute claims, the motion to amend may be denied.

Motions to amend should clearly state the patentably distinct features for proposed substitute claims. This will aid the Board in determining whether the amendment narrows the claims and if the amendment is responsive to the grounds of unpatentability involved in the trial. Moreover, a motion to amend may be denied, without prejudice, if it is determined that patent owner's original claims are patentable.

The number of substitute claims must be "reasonable." There is a general presumption that only one substitute claim would be needed to replace each challenged claim. §§42.121(a) and 42.221(a). This presumption may be rebutted by a demonstration of need. The presumption balances the one-year timeline for final decision against the patent owner's need to appropriately define the invention.

The following is an example of what may be included in a motion to amend. The example sets forth a proposed substitute claim that replaces original patent claims 1-3, a proposed substitute claim that replaces original patent claim 4, and a proposed new claim reciting newly claimed subject matter.

Original patent claims:

Claim 1: A bucket comprising:

A shell; and

an attached handle.

Claim 2: The bucket of claim 1 wherein the shell is made of wood.

Claim 3: The bucket of claim 1 wherein the handle is made of metal.

Claim 4: The bucket of claim 1 wherein the bucket has a volume of 2-5 gallons.

Claim listing in a motion to amend:

Claims 1-4 (cancelled).

Claim 5 (substitute for original claims 1-3): A bucket comprising:

A shell made of wood; and

an attached handle made of metal.

Claim 6 (substitute for original claim 4): The bucket of claim 5 wherein the bucket has a volume of 2-5 gallons.

Claim 7 (new claim): The bucket of claim 5 wherein the metal handle is at least partially made of alloy X.

Discussion of proposed changes:

Proposed claim 5 combines the features originally claimed in claims 1-3 into a single claim. Proposed claim 6 further defines proposed claim 5 by reciting the limitation originally recited in claim 4.

Proposed claim 7 further defines the invention of proposed claim 5 by requiring the metal handle to be at least partially made of alloy X.

See the Office Patent Trial Practice Guide, p. 1336.

Support for claimed subject matter.

Paragraph 14 of the original disclosure of the application which issued as the patent under review describes an embodiment where the shell of the bucket is made of wood and the handle of the bucket is made of metal. Paragraph 15 of the same specification describes a volume of 2-5 gallons as a useful volume for the bucket described in the specification. Paragraph 32 of the same specification describes the use of alloy X in making the metal handle.

Parent application X similarly describes an embodiment where the shell of the bucket is made of wood and the handle is made of metal at paragraph 14. Parent application X does not describe a bucket having a volume of 2-5 gallons or alloy X.

H. Petitioner Opposition to Amendment

A petitioner will be afforded an opportunity to fully respond to a patent owner's motion to amend. The time for filing an opposition generally will be set in a Scheduling Order. No authorization is needed to file an opposition to a motion to amend. Petitioners may respond to new issues arising from proposed substitute claims including evidence responsive to the amendment. 35 U.S.C. 316(a) and 326(a). This includes the submission of new expert declarations that are directed to the proposed substitute claims.

I. Petitioner Reply to Patent Owner Response and Patent Owner Reply to Opposition To Amend

A reply may only respond to arguments raised in the corresponding opposition. §42.23. While replies can help crystalize issues for decision, a reply that raises a new issue or belatedly presents evidence will not be considered and may be returned. The Board will not attempt to sort proper from improper portions of the reply. Examples of indications that a new issue has been raised in a reply include new evidence necessary to make out a prima facie case for the patentability or unpatentability of an original or proposed substitute claim, and new evidence that could have been presented in a prior filing.

J. Other Motions

There are many types of motions that may be filed in a proceeding in addition to motions to amend. Examples of additional motions include motions to exclude evidence, motions to seal, motions for joinder, motions to file supplemental information, motions for judgment based on supplemental information, motions for observations on cross-examination, etc.

Where a party believes it has a basis to request relief on a ground not identified in the rules, the party should contact the Board and arrange for a conference call with the Board and opposing party to discuss the requested relief with the judge handling the proceeding.

When filing the motion, the party must comply with the appropriate requirements. For example, a motion to submit supplemental information must meet the requirements of §42.123 or §42.223: (1) A request for the authorization to file a motion to submit supplemental information is made within one month of the date the trial is instituted; and (2) the supplemental information must be relevant to a claim for which the trial has been instituted. Further, a party seeking to submit supplemental information more than one month after the date the trial is instituted, must request authorization to file a motion to submit the information. Such a motion to submit supplemental information must show why the supplemental information reasonably could not have been obtained earlier, and that consideration of the supplemental information would be in the interests-of-justice. §42.123(b) or §42.223(b).

K. Challenging Admissibility

A party wishing to challenge the admissibility of evidence must object timely to the evidence at the point it is offered and then preserve the objection by filing a motion to exclude the evidence. §42.64(a), (b)(1), and (c). The time for filing a motion to exclude evidence will be set in the Scheduling Order. A motion to exclude evidence must:

(a) Identify where in the record the objection originally was made;

(b) Identify where in the record the evidence sought to be excluded was relied upon by an opponent;

(c) Address objections to exhibits in numerical order; and

(d) Explain each objection.

A motion to exclude must explain why the evidence is not admissible (e.g., relevance or hearsay) but may not be used to challenge the sufficiency of the evidence to prove a particular fact.

L. Observations on Cross-Examination

In the event that cross-examination occurs after a party has filed its last substantive paper on an issue, such cross-examination may result in testimony that should be called to the Board's attention, but the party does not believe a motion to exclude the testimony is warranted. The Board may authorize the filing of observations to identify such testimony and responses to observations, as defined below.

The party taking the cross-examination files the observations. The opposing party may file a response to an observation. The opposing party may not file observations without express prior authorization.

An observation should be a concise statement of the relevance of identified testimony to an identified argument or portion of an exhibit (including another part of the same testimony). Any response should be equally concise. An observation (or response) is not an opportunity to raise new issues, re-argue issues, or pursue objections. Each observation should be in the following form:

In exhibit ____, on page ____, lines ____, the witness testified ____. This testimony is relevant to the ____ on page ____ of ____. The testimony is relevant because ____.

The entire observation should not exceed one short paragraph. The Board may refuse entry of excessively long or argumentative observations (or responses).

M. Oral Argument

Each party to a proceeding will be afforded an opportunity to present their case before at least three members of the Board. The time for requesting an oral argument is normally set in the Scheduling Order but may be modified on a case-by-case basis.

Generally, a petitioner to a hearing will go first followed by the patent owner or respondent after which a rebuttal may be given by the petitioner. The order may be reversed, e.g., where the only dispute is whether the patent owner's proposed substitute claims overcome the grounds for unpatentability set forth in the petition.

Special equipment or needs. A party should advise the Board as soon as possible before an oral argument of any special needs. Examples of such needs include additional space for a wheel chair, an easel for posters, or an overhead projector. Parties should not make assumptions about the equipment the Board may have on hand. Such requests should be directed in the first instance to a Board Trial Division paralegal at 571-272-9797.

Demonstrative exhibits. The Board has found that elaborate demonstrative exhibits are more likely to impede than help an oral argument. The most effective demonstrative exhibits tend to be a handout or binder containing the demonstrative exhibits. The pages of each exhibit should be numbered to facilitate identification of the exhibits during the oral argument, particularly if the argument is recorded.

Live testimony. The Board does not envision that live testimony is necessary at oral argument. However, parties may file a motion for live testimony in appropriate situations.

No new evidence and arguments. A party may rely upon evidence that has been previously submitted in the proceeding and may only present arguments relied upon in the papers previously submitted. No new evidence or arguments may be presented at the oral argument.

N. Settlement

There are strong public policy reasons to favor settlement between the parties to a proceeding. The Board will be available to facilitate settlement discussions, and where appropriate, may require a settlement discussion as part of the proceeding. The Board expects that a proceeding will terminate after the filing of a settlement agreement, unless the Board has already decided the merits of the proceeding. 35 U.S.C. 317(a), as amended, and 35 U.S.C. 327.

O. Final Decision

For IPR, PGR, and CBM, the Board will enter a final written decision not more than one year from the date a trial is instituted, except that the time may be extended up to six months for good cause. The Board expects that a final written decision will address the issues necessary for resolving the proceeding.

In the case of derivation proceedings, although not required by statute, the Board expects to provide a final decision not more than one year from the institution of the proceeding. The Board will provide a final decision as to whether an inventor named in the earlier application derived the claimed invention from an inventor named in the petitioner's application and filed the earlier application claiming such invention without authorization.

P. Rehearing Requests

A party dissatisfied with a decision of the Board may file a request for rehearing. §42.71. The burden of showing that a decision should be modified lies with the party challenging the decision. The request must specifically identify all matters the party believes the Board misapprehended or overlooked, and where each matter was previously addressed in a motion, an opposition, or a reply. Evidence not already of record at the time of the decision will not be admitted absent a showing of good cause. The opposing party should not file a response to a request for rehearing absent a request from the Board. The Board envisions that, absent a need for additional briefing by an opponent, requests for rehearing will be decided approximately one month after receipt of the request.

1. **Editor's note:** Probably should be "other side's."
2. **Editor's note:** Probably should be "comply with the."

APPENDIX A-1: Scheduling Order for Inter Partes Review, Post-Grant Review, and Covered Business Method Patents Review (based on the trial rules)

A. DUE DATES

This order sets due dates for the parties to take action after institution of the proceeding. The parties may stipulate different dates for DUE DATES 1 through 5 (earlier or later, but no later than DUE DATE 6). A notice of the stipulation, specifically identifying the changed due dates, must be promptly filed. The parties may not stipulate an extension of DUE DATES 6-7.

In stipulating different times, the parties should consider the effect of the stipulation on times to object to evidence (§42.64(b)(1)), to supplement evidence (§42.64(b)(2)), to conduct cross-examination, and to draft papers depending on the evidence and cross-examination testimony (see section B, below).

1. DUE DATE 1

The patent owner is not required to file anything in response to the petition. The patent owner may file—

a. A patent owner's response to the petition, and

b. A motion to amend the patent.

Any response or amendment must be filed by DUE DATE 1. If the patent owner elects not to file anything, the patent owner must arrange a conference call with the parties and the Board.

2. DUE DATE 2

Any reply to the patent owner's response, and opposition to the motion to amend, filed by petitioner under §42.23 must be filed by DUE DATE 2.

See the Office Patent Trial Practice Guide, p. 1336.

3. DUE DATE 3

The patent owner must file any reply to the petitioner's opposition to patent owner's motion to amend by DUE DATE 3.

4. DUE DATE 4

a. The petitioner must file any motion for an observation on the cross-examination testimony of a reply witness (see section C, below) by DUE DATE 4. §42.20.

b. Each party must file any motion to exclude evidence (§42.64(c)) and any request for oral argument (§42.70(a)) by DUE DATE 4.

5. DUE DATE 5

a. The patent owner must file any reply to a petitioner observation on cross-examination testimony by DUE DATE 5.

b. Each party must file any opposition to a motion to exclude evidence by DUE DATE 5.

6. DUE DATE 6

Each party must file any reply for a motion to exclude evidence by DUE DATE 6.

B. CROSS-EXAMINATION

Except as the parties might otherwise agree, for each due date—

1. Cross-examination begins after any supplemental evidence is due. §§42.64(b) and 42.53(d)(2).

2. Cross-examination ends no later than a week before the filing date for any paper in which the cross-examination testimony is expected to be used. Id.

C. MOTION FOR OBSERVATION ON CROSS-EXAMINATION

A motion for observation on cross-examination provides the petitioner with a mechanism to draw the Board's attention to relevant cross-examination testimony of a reply witness, since no further substantive paper is permitted after the reply. The observation must be a concise statement of the relevance of the precisely identified testimony to a precisely identified argument or portion of an exhibit. Each observation should not exceed a single, short paragraph. The patent owner may respond to the observation. Any response must be equally concise and specific.

DUE DATE APPENDIX

DUE DATE 1: Patent owner's response to the petition. Patent owner's motion to amend the patent.	3 months.
DUE DATE 2: Petitioner's reply to patent owner response to petition. Petitioner's opposition to motion to amend.	3 months.
DUE DATE 3: Patent owner's reply to petitioner opposition.	1 month.
DUE DATE 4: Petitioner's motion for observation regarding cross-examination of reply witness. Motion to exclude evidence. Request for oral argument.	3 weeks.
DUE DATE 5: Patent owner's response to observation. Opposition to motion to exclude.	2 weeks.
DUE DATE 6: Reply to opposition to motion to exclude.	1 week.
DUE DATE 7: Oral argument.	Set on request.

APPENDIX A-2: Scheduling Order for Derivation Proceedings

A. DUE DATES

This order sets due dates for the parties to take action in this proceeding. The parties may stipulate different dates for DUE DATES 1 through 5 (earlier or later, but not later than DUE DATE 6). A notice of the stipulation, specifically identifying the changed due dates, must be promptly filed. The parties may not stipulate an extension of DUE DATES 6-7.

In stipulating different times, the parties should consider the effect of the stipulation on times to object to evidence (§42.64(b)(1)), to supplement evidence (§42.64(b)(2)), to conduct cross-examination, and to draft papers depending on the evidence and cross-examination testimony (see section B, below).

1. DUE DATE 1

The respondent is not required to file anything in response to the petition. The respondent may file—

a. A response to the petition, and

b. A motion to amend, if authorized.

Any such response or motion to amend must be filed by DUE DATE 1. If the respondent elects not to file anything, the respondent must arrange a conference call with the parties and the Board.

2. DUE DATE 2

The petitioner must file any reply to the respondent's response and opposition to motion to amend by DUE DATE 2.

3. DUE DATE 3

The respondent must file any reply to the petitioner's opposition by DUE DATE 3.

4. DUE DATE 4

a. The petitioner must file any observation on the cross-examination testimony of a reply witness (see section C, below) by DUE DATE 4.

b. Each party must file any motion to exclude evidence (§42.64(c)) and any request for oral argument (§42.70(a)) by DUE DATE 4.

5. DUE DATE 5

a. The respondent must file any response to a petitioner observation on cross-examination testimony by DUE DATE 5.

b. Each party must file any opposition to a motion to exclude evidence by DUE DATE 5.

6. DUE DATE 6

Each party must file any reply for a motion to exclude evidence by DUE DATE 6.

B. CROSS-EXAMINATION

Except as the parties might otherwise agree, for each due date—

1. Cross-examination begins after any supplemental evidence is due. §§42.64(b) and 42.53(d)(2).

2. Cross-examination ends no later than a week before the filing date for any paper in which the cross-examination testimony is expected to be used. Id.

C. MOTION FOR OBSERVATION ON CROSS-EXAMINATION

A motion for observation on cross-examination provides the petitioner with a mechanism to draw the Board's attention to relevant cross-examination testimony of a reply witness, since no further substantive paper is permitted after the reply. The observation must be a concise statement of the relevance of the precisely identified testimony to a precisely identified argument or portion of an exhibit. Each observation should not exceed a single, short paragraph. The patent owner may respond to the observation. Any response must be equally concise and specific.

DUE DATE APPENDIX

DUE DATE 1: Respondent response to the petition. Respondent motion to amend.	3 months.
DUE DATE 2: Petitioner reply to Respondent response to petition. Petitioner opposition to Respondent's motion to amend.	3 months.
DUE DATE 3: Respondent reply to petitioner opposition.	1 month.
DUE DATE 4: Petitioner motion for observation regarding cross-examination of reply witness. Motion to exclude. Request for oral argument.	3 weeks.
DUE DATE 5: Respondent response to observation. Opposition to motion to exclude.	2 weeks.
DUE DATE 6: Reply to opposition to motion to exclude.	1 week.
DUE DATE 7: Oral argument.	Set on request.

See the Office Patent Trial Practice Guide, p. 1336.

APPENDIX B: Protective Order Guidelines (based on the trial rules)

(a) *Purpose.* This document provides guidance on the procedures for filing of motions to seal and the entry of protective orders in proceedings before the Board. The protective order governs the protection of confidential information contained in documents, discovery, or testimony adduced, exchanged, or filed with the Board. The parties are encouraged to agree on the entry of a stipulated protective order. Absent such agreement, the default standing protective order will be automatically entered.

(b) *Timing; lifting or modification of the Protective Order.* The terms of a protective order take effect upon the filing of a Motion to Seal by a party, and remain in place until lifted or modified by the Board either on the motion of a party for good cause shown or sua sponte by the Board.

(c) *Protective Order to Govern Treatment of Confidential Information.* The terms of a protective order govern the treatment of the confidential portions of documents, testimony, and other information designated as confidential, as well as the filing of confidential documents or discussion of confidential information in any papers filed with the Board. The Board shall have the authority to enforce the terms of the Protective Order, to provide remedies for its breach, and to impose sanctions on a party and a party's representatives for any violations of its terms.

(d) *Contents.* The Protective Order shall include the following terms:

(1) *Designation of Confidential Information.* The producing party shall have the obligation to clearly mark as "PROTECTIVE ORDER MATERIAL" any documents or information considered to be confidential under the Protective Order.

(2) *Persons Entitled to Access to Confidential Information.* A party receiving confidential information shall strictly restrict access to that information to the following individuals who first have signed and filed an Acknowledgement as provided herein:

(A) *Parties.* Persons who are owners of a patent involved in the proceeding and other persons who are named parties to the proceeding.

(B) *Party Representatives.* Representatives of record for a party in the proceeding.

(C) *Experts.* Retained experts of a party in the proceeding who further certify in the Acknowledgement that they are not a competitor to any party, or a consultant for, or employed by, such a competitor with respect to the subject matter of the proceeding.

(D) *In-house counsel.* In-house counsel of a party.

(E) *Other Employees of a Party.* Employees, consultants, or other persons performing work for a party, other than in-house counsel and in-house counsel's support staff, who sign the Acknowledgement, shall be extended access to confidential information only upon agreement of the parties or by order of the Board upon a motion brought by the party seeking to disclose confidential information to that person. The party opposing disclosure to that person shall have the burden of proving that such person should be restricted from access to confidential information.

(F) *The Office.* Employees and representatives of the U.S. Patent and Trademark Office who have a need for access to the confidential information shall have such access without the requirement to sign an Acknowledgement. Such employees and representatives shall include the Director, members of the Board and staff, other Office support personnel, court reporters, and other persons acting on behalf of the Office.

(G) *Support Personnel.* Administrative assistants, clerical staff, court reporters, and other support personnel of the foregoing persons who are reasonably necessary to assist those persons in the proceeding. Such support personnel shall not be required to sign an Acknowledgement, but shall be informed of the terms and requirements of the Protective Order by the person they are supporting who receives confidential information.

(3) *Protection of Confidential Information.* Persons receiving confidential information shall take reasonable care to maintain the confidentiality of that information, including:

(A) Maintaining such information in a secure location to which persons not authorized to receive the information shall not have access;

(B) Otherwise using reasonable efforts to maintain the confidentiality of the information, which efforts shall be no less rigorous than those the recipient uses to maintain the confidentiality of information not received from the disclosing party;

(C) Ensuring that support personnel of the recipient who have access to the confidential information understand and abide by the obligation to maintain the confidentiality of information received that is designated as confidential; and

(D) Limiting the copying of confidential information to a reasonable number of copies needed to conduct the proceeding and maintaining a record of the locations of such copies, which similarly must be kept secure.

(4) *Treatment of Confidential Information.* Persons receiving confidential information shall use the following procedures to maintain confidentiality of documents and other information—

(A) *Documents and Information Filed With the Board.*

(i) A party may file documents or information with the Board under seal, together with a non-confidential description of the nature of the confidential information that is under seal and the reasons why the information is confidential and should not be made available to the public. The submission shall be treated as confidential and remain under seal, unless upon motion of a party and after a hearing on the issue, or sua sponte, the Board determines that the documents or information do not qualify for confidential treatment.

(ii) Where confidentiality is alleged as to some but not all of the information submitted to the Board, the submitting party shall file confidential and non-confidential versions of its submission, together with a Motion to Seal the confidential version setting forth the reasons why the information redacted from the non-confidential version is confidential and should not be made publicly available. The non-confidential version of the submission shall clearly indicate the locations of information that has been redacted. The confidential version of the submission shall be filed under seal. The redacted information shall remain under seal, unless upon motion of a party and after a hearing on the issue, or sua sponte, the Board determines that some or all of the redacted information does not qualify for confidential treatment.

(B) *Documents and Information Exchanged Among the Parties.* Information designated as confidential that is disclosed to another party during discovery or other proceedings before the Board shall be clearly marked as "PROTECTIVE ORDER MATERIAL" and shall be produced in a manner that maintains its confidentiality.

(5) *Confidential Testimony.* Any person providing testimony in a proceeding may, on the record during the testimony, preliminarily designate the entirety of the person's testimony and all transcriptions thereof as confidential, pending further review. Within ten days of the receipt of the transcript of the testimony, that person, or that person's representative, shall advise the opposing party of those portions of the testimony to which a claim of confidentiality is to be maintained, and the reasons in support of that claim. Such portions shall be treated as confidential and maintained under seal in any filings to the Board unless, upon motion of a party and after a hearing on the issue, or sua sponte, the Board determines that some or all of the redacted information does not qualify for confidential treatment.

(6) *Other Restrictions Imposed By the Board.* In addition to the foregoing, the Board may, in its discretion, include other terms and conditions in a Protective Order it enters in any proceeding.

(7) *Requirement of Acknowledgement.* Any person receiving confidential information during a proceeding before the Board shall, prior to receipt of any confidential information, first sign an Acknowledgement, under penalty of perjury, stating the following:

(A) The person has read the Protective Order and understands its terms;

(B) The person agrees to be bound by the Protective Order and will abide by its terms;

(C) The person will use the confidential information only in connection with that proceeding and for no other purpose;

(D) The person shall only extend access to the confidential information to support personnel, such as administrative assistants, clerical staff, paralegals, and the like, who are reasonably necessary to assist him or her in the proceeding. The person shall inform such support personnel of the terms and requirements of the Protective Order prior to disclosure of any confidential information to such support personnel and shall be personally responsible for their compliance with the terms of the Protective Order; and

(E) The person agrees to submit to the jurisdiction of the Office for purposes of enforcing the terms of the Protective Order and providing remedies for its breach.

(e) *Filing of Executed Protective Order.* The party filing a Motion to Seal shall include with its supporting papers a copy of a proposed Protective Order, signed by the party or its representative of record, certifying that the party accepts and agrees to the terms of the Protective Order. Prior to the receipt of confidential information, any other party to the proceeding also shall file a copy of the proposed Protective Order, signed by the party or its representative of record, certifying that the party accepts and agrees to the terms of the proposed Protective Order. The proposed Protective Order shall remain in effect until superseded by a Protective Order entered by the Board.

(f) *Duty To Retain Acknowledgements.* Each party to the proceeding shall maintain a signed Acknowledgement from each person acting on its behalf who obtains access to confidential information after signing an Acknowledgement, as set forth herein, and shall produce such Acknowledgements to the Office upon request.

(g) *Motion to Seal.* A party may file an opposition to the motion that may include a request that the terms of the proposed Protective Order be modified including limiting the persons who are entitled to access under the Order. Any such opposition shall state with particularity the grounds for modifying the proposed Protective Order. The party seeking the modification shall have the burden of proving that such modifications are necessary. While the motion is pending, no disclosure of confidential information shall be made to the persons for whom disclosure is opposed, but the filing of the motion shall not preclude disclosure of the confidential information to persons for whom disclosure is not opposed and shall not toll the time for taking any action in the proceeding.

(h) *Other Proceedings.* Counsel for a party who receives confidential information in a proceeding will not be restricted by the Board from representing that party in any other proceeding or matter before the Office. Confidential information received in a proceeding, however, may not be used in any other Office proceeding in which the providing party is not also a party.

(i) *Disposal of Confidential Information.* Within one month after final termination of a proceeding, including any appeals, or within one month after the time for appeal has expired, each party shall assemble all copies of all confidential information it has received, including confidential information provided to its representatives and experts, and shall destroy the confidential information and provide a certification of destruction to the party who produced the confidential information.

DEFAULT PROTECTIVE ORDER

The following Standing Protective Order will be automatically entered into the proceeding upon the filing of a petition for review or institution of a derivation:

Standing Protective Order

This standing protective order governs the treatment and filing of confidential information, including documents and testimony.

1. Confidential information shall be clearly marked "PROTECTIVE ORDER MATERIAL."

2. Access to confidential information is limited to the following individuals who have executed the acknowledgment appended to this order:

(A) *Parties.* Persons who are owners of a patent involved in the proceeding and other persons who are named parties to the proceeding.

(B) *Party Representatives.* Representatives of record for a party in the proceeding.

(C) *Experts.* Retained experts of a party in the proceeding who further certify in the Acknowledgement that they are not a competitor to any party, or a consultant for, or employed by, such a competitor with respect to the subject matter of the proceeding.

(D) *In-house counsel.* In-house counsel of a party.

(E) *Other Employees of a Party.* Employees, consultants or other persons performing work for a party, other than in-house counsel and in-house counsel's support staff, who sign the Acknowledgement shall be extended access to confidential information only upon agreement of the parties or by order of the Board upon a motion brought by the party seeking to disclose confidential information to that person. The party opposing disclosure to that person shall have the burden of proving that such person should be restricted from access to confidential information.

(F) *The Office.* Employees and representatives of the Office who have a need for access to the confidential information shall have such access without the requirement to sign an Acknowledgement. Such employees and representatives shall include the Director, members of the Board and their clerical staff, other support personnel, court reporters, and other persons acting on behalf of the Office.

(G) *Support Personnel.* Administrative assistants, clerical staff, court reporters and other support personnel of the foregoing persons who are reasonably necessary to assist those

See the Office Patent Trial Practice Guide, p. 1336.

persons in the proceeding shall not be required to sign an Acknowledgement, but shall be informed of the terms and requirements of the Protective Order by the person they are supporting who receives confidential information.

3. Persons receiving confidential information shall use reasonable efforts to maintain the confidentiality of the information, including:

(A) Maintaining such information in a secure location to which persons not authorized to receive the information shall not have access;

(B) Otherwise using reasonable efforts to maintain the confidentiality of the information, which efforts shall be no less rigorous than those the recipient uses to maintain the confidentiality of information not received from the disclosing party;

(C) Ensuring that support personnel of the recipient who have access to the confidential information understand and abide by the obligation to maintain the confidentiality of information received that is designated as confidential; and

(D) Limiting the copying of confidential information to a reasonable number of copies needed for conduct of the proceeding and maintaining a record of the locations of such copies.

4. Persons receiving confidential information shall use the following procedures to maintain the confidentiality of the information:

(A) *Documents and Information Filed With the Board.*

(i) A party may file documents or information with the Board under seal, together with a non-confidential description of the nature of the confidential information that is under seal and the reasons why the information is confidential and should not be made available to the public. The submission shall be treated as confidential and remain under seal, unless, upon motion of a party and after a hearing on the issue, or sua sponte, the Board determines that the documents or information do not to qualify for confidential treatment.

(ii) Where confidentiality is alleged as to some but not all of the information submitted to the Board, the submitting party shall file confidential and non-confidential versions of its submission, together with a Motion to Seal the confidential version setting forth the reasons why the information redacted from the non-confidential version is confidential and should not be made available to the public. The non-confidential version of the submission shall clearly indicate the locations of information that has been redacted. The confidential version of the submission shall be filed under seal. The redacted information shall remain under seal unless, upon motion of a party and after a hearing on the issue, or sua sponte, the Board determines that some or all of the redacted information does not qualify for confidential treatment.

(B) *Documents and Information Exchanged Among the Parties.* Information designated as confidential that is disclosed to another party during discovery or other proceedings before the Board shall be clearly marked as "PROTECTIVE ORDER MATERIAL" and shall be produced in a manner that maintains its confidentiality.

(j) *Standard Acknowledgement of Protective Order.* The following form may be used to acknowledge a protective order and gain access to information covered by the protective order:

[CAPTION]

Standard Acknowledgment for Access to Protective Order Material

I _____, affirm that I have read the Protective Order; that I will abide by its terms; that I will use the confidential information only in connection with this proceeding and for no other purpose; that I will only allow access to support staff who are reasonably necessary to assist me in this proceeding; that prior to any disclosure to such support staff I informed or will inform them of the requirements of the Protective Order; that I am personally responsible for the requirements of the terms of the Protective Order and I agree to submit to the jurisdiction of the Office and the United States District Court for the Eastern District of Virginia for purposes of enforcing the terms of the Protective Order and providing remedies for its breach.

[Signature]

APPENDIX C: Model Order Regarding E-Discovery in Trials Before the Patent Trial and Appeal Board

The Board pursuant to §42.5 orders as follows:

1. This Order supplements all other discovery rules and orders. It streamlines Electronically Stored Information (ESI) production to promote "the just, speedy, and inexpensive resolution" of this proceeding in a manner consistent with §42.1.

2. This Order may be modified for good cause. The parties shall jointly submit any proposed modifications within one month after the initiation date of the proceeding or by the date of the initial conference call, whichever is earlier. If the parties cannot resolve their disagreements regarding these modifications, the parties shall submit their competing proposals and a summary of their dispute within the specified time period.

3. Costs will be shifted for disproportionate ESI production requests. Likewise, a party's nonresponsive or dilatory discovery tactics will be cost-shifting considerations. See 35 U.S.C. 316(a)(6), as amended, and 326(a)(6).

4. A party's meaningful compliance with this Order and efforts to promote efficiency and reduce costs will be considered in cost-shifting determinations.

5. Unless otherwise authorized by the Board or agreed to by the parties, any production of ESI pursuant to §§42.51 or 42.52 shall not include metadata. However, fields showing the date and time that the document was sent and received, as well as the complete distribution list, shall generally be included in the production if such fields exist.

6. General ESI production under §§42.51 and 42.52 (with the exception of routine discovery under §42.51(b)(1)) shall not include email or other forms of electronic correspondence (collectively "email"). To obtain additional production of email, absent an agreement between the parties to produce, the parties must propound specific email production requests, which requests require prior Board authorization.

7. Email production requests, where authorized by the Board or permitted by agreement of the parties, shall be propounded for specific issues only, rather than general discovery of a party's products or business.

8. Email production requests, where authorized by the Board or permitted by agreement of the parties, shall be phased to occur after a party's initial production under §42.51(b)(1).

9. Where email production requests are authorized by the Board or permitted by agreement of the parties, such requests shall identify the custodian, search terms, and time frame. The parties shall cooperate to identify proper custodians, proper search terms, and proper time frame.

10. Each requesting party shall limit its email production requests to a total of five custodians per producing party for all such requests. The parties may jointly agree to modify this limit without the Board's leave. The Board shall consider contested requests for up to five additional custodians per producing party, upon showing a need based on the size, complexity, and issues of this specific proceeding.

11. Each party shall limit its email production requests to a total of five search terms per custodian per party. The parties may jointly agree to modify this limit without the Board's leave. The Board shall consider contested requests for up to five additional search terms per custodian, upon showing a need based upon the size, complexity, and issues of this specific proceeding. The search terms shall be narrowly tailored to particular issues. Indiscriminate terms, such as producing company's name or its product name, are inappropriate unless combined with narrowing search criteria that sufficiently reduce the risk of overproduction. A conjunctive combination of multiple words or phrases (e.g., "computer" and "system") narrows the search and shall count as a single search term. A disjunctive combination of multiple words or phrases (e.g., "computer" or "system") broadens the search, and thus each word or phrase shall count as a separate search term unless they are variants of the same word. Use of narrowing search criteria (e.g., "and," "but not," "w/x") is encouraged to limit the production, and shall be considered when determining whether to shift costs for disproportionate discovery.

12. The receiving party shall not use ESI that the producing party asserts is attorney-client privileged or work product protected to challenge the privilege or protection.

13. Pursuant to Federal Rule of Evidence 502(b), the inadvertent production of an attorney-client privileged or work product protected ESI is not a waiver of such protection providing the holder of the privilege or protection took reasonable steps to prevent disclosure and the discloser promptly took reasonable steps to rectify the error.

14. Similar to Federal Rule of Evidence 502(d), the mere production of ESI in the proceeding as part of a mass production shall not itself constitute a waiver of privilege for any purpose before the Office.

APPENDIX D: Testimony Guidelines

Introduction

In trials before the Board, uncompelled direct testimony is almost always presented by affidavit or declaration. §42.53(a). All other testimony (including cross-examination, redirect examination, and compelled direct testimony) occurs by oral examination.

Consistent with the policy expressed in Rule 1 of the Federal Rules of Civil Procedure, and corresponding §42.1(b), unnecessary objections, "speaking" objections, and coaching of witnesses in proceedings before the Board are strictly prohibited. Cross-examination testimony should be a question and answer conversation between the examining lawyer and the witness. The defending lawyer must not act as an intermediary, interpreting questions, deciding which questions the witness should answer, and helping the witness formulate answers while testifying.

The testimony guidelines that follow are based on those set forth in the Federal Rules of Civil Procedure, supplemented by the practices followed in several federal district courts.

Examination and Cross-examination Outside the Presence of the Board

1. The examination and cross-examination of a witness proceed as they would in a trial under the Federal Rules of Evidence, except that Rule 103 (Rulings on Evidence) does not apply. After putting the witness under oath or affirmation, the officer must record the testimony by audio, audiovisual, or stenographic means. Testimony must be recorded by the officer personally, or by a person acting in the presence and under direction of the officer.

2. An objection at the time of the examination—whether to evidence, to a party's conduct, to the officer's qualifications, to the manner of taking the testimony, or any aspect of the testimony—must be noted on the record, but the examination still proceeds; testimony is taken subject to any such objection.

3. An objection must be stated concisely in a non-argumentative and non-suggestive manner. Counsel must not make objections or statements that suggest an answer to a witness. Objections should be limited to a single word or term. Examples of objections that would be properly stated are: "Objection, form"; "Objection, hearsay"; "Objection, relevance"; and "Objection, foundation." Examples of objections that would not be proper are: "Objection, I don't understand the question"; "Objection, vague"; "Objection, take your time answering the question"; and "Objection, look at the docu-

See the Office Patent Trial Practice Guide, p. 1336.

ment before you answer." An objecting party must give a clear and concise explanation of an objection if requested by the party taking the testimony or the objection is waived.

4. Counsel may instruct a witness not to answer only when necessary to preserve a privilege, to enforce a limitation ordered by the Board, or to present a motion to terminate or limit the testimony.

5. Unless otherwise agreed by the parties or ordered by the Board, the testimony is limited in duration to the times set forth in §42.53(c). The Board may allow additional time if needed to examine the witness fairly or if the witness, another person, or any other circumstance impedes or delays the examination.

6. Once the cross-examination of a witness has commenced, and until cross-examination of the witness has concluded, counsel offering the witness on direct examination shall not: (a) Consult or confer with the witness regarding the substance of the witness' testimony already given, or anticipated to be given, except for the purpose of conferring on whether to assert a privilege against testifying or on how to comply with a Board order; or (b) suggest to the witness the manner in which any questions should be answered.

7. An attorney for a witness shall not initiate a private conference with the witness or call for a break in the proceedings while a question is pending, except for the purpose of determining whether a privilege should be asserted.

8. The Board may impose an appropriate sanction—including the reasonable expenses and attorneys' fees incurred by any party—on a person who impedes, delays, or frustrates the fair examination of the witness.

9. At any time during the testimony, the witness or a party may move to terminate or limit the testimony on the ground that it is being conducted in bad faith or in a manner that unreasonably annoys, embarrasses, or oppresses the witness or party. The witness or party must promptly initiate a conference call with the Board to discuss the proposed motion. §42.20(b). If the objecting witness or party so demands, the testimony must be suspended for the time necessary to obtain a ruling from the Board, except as the Board may otherwise order.

PART 90. JUDICIAL REVIEW OF PATENT TRIAL & APPEAL BOARD DECISIONS

§90.1. SCOPE

The provisions herein govern judicial review for Patent Trial and Appeal Board decisions under chapter 13 of title 35, United States Code. Judicial review of decisions arising out of inter partes reexamination proceedings that are requested under 35 U.S.C. 311, and where available, judicial review of decisions arising out of interferences declared pursuant to 35 U.S.C. 135 continue to be governed by the pertinent regulations in effect on July 1, 2012.

History of 37 C.F.R. §90.1: 77 FR 48677, Sept. 16, 2012.

§90.2. NOTICE; SERVICE

(a) For an appeal under 35 U.S.C. 141. **(1)** In all appeals, the notice of appeal required by 35 U.S.C. 142 must be filed with the Director of the United States Patent and Trademark Office as provided in §104.2 of this title. A copy of the notice of appeal must also be filed with the Patent Trial and Appeal Board in the appropriate manner provided in §41.10(a), 41.10(b), or 42.6(b).

(2) In all appeals, the party initiating the appeal must comply with the requirements of the Federal Rules of Appellate Procedure and Rules for the United States Court of Appeals for the Federal Circuit, including:

(i) Serving the requisite number of copies on the Court; and

(ii) Paying the requisite fee for the appeal.

(3) Additional requirements. **(i)** In appeals arising out of an ex parte reexamination proceeding ordered pursuant to §1.525, notice of the appeal must be served as provided in §1.550(f) of this title.

(ii) In appeals arising out of an inter partes review, a post-grant review, a covered business method patent review, or a derivation proceeding, notice of the appeal must provide sufficient information to allow the Director to determine whether to exercise the right to intervene in the appeal pursuant to 35 U.S.C. 143, and it must be served as provided in §42.6(e) of this title.

(b) For a notice of election under 35 U.S.C. 141(d) to proceed under 35 U.S.C. 146. **(1)** Pursuant to 35 U.S.C. 141(d), if an adverse party elects to have all further review proceedings conducted under 35 U.S.C. 146 instead of under 35 U.S.C. 141, that party must file a notice of election with the United States Patent and Trademark Office as provided in §104.2.

(2) A copy of the notice of election must also be filed with the Patent Trial and Appeal Board in the manner provided in §42.6(b).

(3) A copy of the notice of election must also be served where necessary pursuant to §42.6(e).

(c) For a civil action under 35 U.S.C. 146. The party initiating an action under 35 U.S.C. 146 must file a copy of the complaint no later than five business days after filing the complaint in district court with the Patent Trial and Appeal Board in the manner provided in §42.6(b), and the Office of the Solicitor pursuant to §104.2. Failure to comply with this requirement can result in further action within the United States Patent and Trademark Office consistent with the final Board decision.

History of 37 C.F.R. §90.2: 77 FR 48677, Sept. 16, 2012.

§90.3. TIME FOR APPEAL OR CIVIL ACTION

(a) Filing deadline. **(1)** For an appeal under 35 U.S.C. 141. The notice of appeal filed pursuant to 35 U.S.C. 142 must be filed with the Director of the United States Patent and Trademark Office no later than sixty-three (63) days after the date of the final Board decision. Any notice of cross-appeal is controlled by Rule 4(a)(3) of the Federal Rules of Appellate Procedure, and any other requirement imposed by the Rules of the United States Court of Appeals for the Federal Circuit.

(2) For a notice of election under 35 U.S.C. 141(d). The time for filing a notice of election under 35 U.S.C. 141(d) is governed by 35 U.S.C. 141(d).

(3) For a civil action under 35 U.S.C. 145 or 146. **(i)** A civil action must be commenced no later than sixty-three (63) days after the date of the final Board decision.

(ii) The time for commencing a civil action pursuant to a notice of election under 35 U.S.C. 141(d) is governed by 35 U.S.C. 141(d).

(b) Time computation. **(1)** Rehearing. A timely request for rehearing will reset the time for appeal or civil action to no later than sixty-three (63) days after action on the request. Any subsequent request for rehearing from the same party in the same proceeding will not reset the time for seeking judicial review, unless the additional request is permitted by order of the Board.

(2) Holidays. If the last day for filing an appeal or civil action falls on a Federal holiday in the District of Columbia, the time is extended pursuant to 35 U.S.C. 21(b).

(c) Extension of time. **(1)** The Director, or his designee, may extend the time for filing an appeal, or commencing a civil action, upon written request if:

(i) Requested before the expiration of the period for filing an appeal or commencing a civil action, and upon a showing of good cause; or

(ii) Requested after the expiration of the period for filing an appeal of commencing a civil action, and upon a showing that the failure to act was the result of excusable neglect.

(2) The request must be filed as provided in §104.2 of this title.

History of 37 C.F.R. §90.3: 77 FR 48677, Sept. 16, 2012.

SUBCHAPTER B. ADMINISTRATION

PARTS 100, 101. RESERVED

PART 102. DISCLOSURE OF GOVERNMENT INFORMATION

SUBPART A. FREEDOM OF INFORMATION ACT

§102.1. GENERAL

(a) The information in this part is furnished for the guidance of the public and in compliance with the requirements of the Freedom of Information Act (FOIA), as amended (5 U.S.C. 552). This part sets forth the procedures the United States Patent and Trademark Office (USPTO) follows to make publicly available the materials and indices specified in 5 U.S.C. 552(a)(2) and records requested under 5 U.S.C. 552(a)(3). Information routinely provided to the public as part of a regular USPTO activity (for example, press releases issued by the Office of Public Affairs) may be provided to the public without following this part. USPTO's policy is to make discretionary disclosures of records or information exempt from disclosure under FOIA whenever disclosure would not foreseeably harm an interest protected by a FOIA exemption, but this policy does not create any right enforceable in court.

(b) As used in this subpart, FOIA Officer means the USPTO employee designated to administer FOIA for USPTO. To ensure prompt processing of a request, correspondence should be addressed to the FOIA Officer, United States Patent and Trademark Office, P.O. Box 1450, Alexandria, Virginia 22313-1450, or delivered by hand to 10B20, Madison Building East, 600 Dulany Street, Alexandria, Virginia.

History of 37 C.F.R. §102.1: 68 FR 14338, Mar. 25, 2003; 70 FR 10489, Mar. 4, 2005.

Source of 37 C.F.R. Part 102A: 65 FR 52917, Aug. 31, 2000; 66 FR 47390, Sept. 12, 2001, unless otherwise noted.

§102.2. PUBLIC REFERENCE FACILITIES

(a) USPTO maintains a public reference facility that contains the records FOIA requires to be made regularly available for public inspection and copying; furnishes information and otherwise assists the public concerning USPTO operations under FOIA; and receives and processes requests for records under FOIA. The FOIA Officer is responsible for determining which of USPTO's records are required to be made available for public inspection and copying, and for making those records available in USPTO's reference and records inspection facility. The FOIA Officer shall maintain and make available for public inspection and copying a current subject-matter index of USPTO's public inspection facility records. Each index shall be updated regularly, at least quarterly, with respect to newly included records. In accordance with 5 U.S.C. 552(a)(2), USPTO has determined that it is unnecessary and impracticable to publish quarterly, or more frequently, and distribute copies of the index and supplements thereto. The public reference facility is located in the Public Search Room, Madison Building East, First Floor, 600 Dulany Street, Alexandria, Virginia.

(b) The FOIA Officer shall also make public inspection facility records created by USPTO on or after November 1, 1996, available electronically through USPTO's World Wide Web site (http://www.uspto.gov). Information available at the site shall include:

(1) The FOIA Officer's index of the public inspection facility records, which indicates which records are available electronically; and

(2) The general index referred to in paragraph (c)(3) of this section.

(c) USPTO maintains and makes available for public inspection and copying:

(1) A current index providing identifying information for the public as to any matter that is issued, adopted, or promulgated after July 4, 1967, and that is retained as a record and is required to be made available or published. Copies of the index are available upon request after payment of the direct cost of duplication;

(2) Copies of records that have been released and that the FOIA Officer determines, because of their subject matter, have become or are likely to become the subject of subsequent requests for substantially the same records;

(3) A general index of the records described in paragraph (c)(2) of this section;

(4) Final opinions and orders, including concurring and dissenting opinions made in the adjudication of cases;

(5) Those statements of policy and interpretations that have been adopted by USPTO and are not published in the Federal Register; and

(6) Administrative staff manuals and instructions to staff that affect a member of the public.

History of 37 C.F.R. §102.2: 75 FR 36295, June 25, 2010.

§102.3. RECORDS UNDER FOIA

(a) Records under FOIA include all Government records, regardless of format, medium or physical characteristics, and include electronic records and information, audiotapes, videotapes, and photographs.

(b) There is no obligation to create, compile, or obtain from outside USPTO a record to satisfy a FOIA request. With regard to electronic data, the issue of whether records are created or merely extracted from an existing database is not always apparent. When responding to FOIA requests for electronic data where creation of a record or programming becomes an issue, USPTO shall undertake reasonable efforts to search for the information in electronic format.

(c) USPTO officials may, upon request, create and provide new information pursuant to user fee statutes, such as the first paragraph of 15 U.S.C. 1525, or in accordance with authority otherwise provided by law. This is outside the scope of FOIA.

(d) The FOIA Officer shall preserve all correspondence pertaining to the requests received under this subpart, as well as copies of all requested records, until disposition or destruction is authorized by Title 44 of the United States Code or a National Archives and Records Administration's General Records Schedule. The FOIA Officer shall not dispose of records while they are the subject of a pending request, appeal, or lawsuit under FOIA.

§102.4. REQUIREMENTS FOR MAKING REQUESTS

(a) A request for USPTO records that are not customarily made available to the public as part of USPTO's regular informational services must be in writing, and shall be processed under FOIA, regardless of whether FOIA is mentioned in the request. Requests should be sent to the USPTO FOIA Officer, United States Patent and Trademark Office, P.O. Box 1450, Alexandria, Virginia 22313-1450 (records FOIA requires to be made regularly available for public inspection and copying are addressed in §102.2(c)). For the quickest handling, the request letter and envelope should be marked "Freedom of Information Act Request." For requests for records about oneself, §102.24 contains additional requirements. For requests for records about another individual, either a written authorization signed by that individual permitting disclosure of those records to the requester or proof that individual is deceased (for example, a copy of a death certificate or an obituary) facilitates processing the request.

(b) The records requested must be described in enough detail to enable USPTO personnel to locate them with a reasonable amount of effort. Whenever possible, a request should include specific information about each record sought, such as the date, title or name, author, recipient, and subject matter of the record, and the name and location of the office where the record is located. Also, if records about a court case are sought, the title of the case, the court in which the case was filed, and the nature of the case should be included. If known, any file designations or descriptions for the requested records should be included. In general, the more specifically the request describes the records sought, the greater the likelihood that USPTO will locate those records. If the FOIA Officer determines that a request does not reasonably describe records, the FOIA Officer will inform the requester what additional information is needed or why the request is otherwise insufficient. The FOIA Officer also may give the requester an opportunity to discuss the request so that it may be modified to meet the requirements of this section.

History of 37 C.F.R. §102.4: 68 FR 14338, Mar. 25, 2003.

§102.5. RESPONSIBILITY FOR RESPONDING TO REQUESTS

(a) In general. Except as stated in paragraph (b) of this section, the USPTO will process FOIA requests directed to USPTO. In determining records responsive to a request, the FOIA Officer shall include only those records within USPTO's possession and control as of the date the FOIA Officer receives the request.

(b) Consultations and referrals. If the FOIA Officer receives a request for a record in USPTO's possession in which another Federal agency subject to FOIA has the primary interest, the FOIA Officer shall refer the record to that agency for direct response to the requester. The FOIA Officer shall consult with another Federal agency before responding to a requester if the FOIA Officer receives a request for a record in which another Federal agency subject to FOIA has a significant interest, but not the primary interest; or another Federal agency not subject to FOIA has the primary interest or a significant interest. Ordinarily, the agency that originated a record will be presumed to have the primary interest in it.

(c) Notice of referral. Whenever a FOIA Officer refers a document to another Federal agency for direct response to the requester, the FOIA Officer will ordinarily notify the requester in writing of the referral and inform the requester of the name of the agency to which the document was referred.

(d) Timing of responses to consultations and referrals. All consultations and referrals shall be handled according to the date the FOIA request was received by the first Federal agency.

(e) Agreements regarding consultations and referrals. The FOIA Officer may make agreements with other Federal agencies to eliminate the need for consultations or referrals for particular types of records.

§102.6. TIME LIMITS & EXPEDITED PROCESSING

(a) In general. The FOIA Officer ordinarily shall respond to requests according to their order of receipt.

(b) Initial response and appeal. Subject to paragraph (c)(1) of this section, an initial response shall be made within 20 working days (*i.e.*, excluding Saturdays, Sundays, and legal public holidays) of the receipt of a request for a record under this part by the proper FOIA Officer identified in accordance with §102.5(a), and an appeal shall be decided within 20 working days of its receipt by the Office of the General Counsel.

(c) Unusual circumstances.

(1) In unusual circumstances as specified in paragraph (c)(2) of this section, the FOIA Officer may extend the time limits in paragraph (b) of this section by notifying the requester in writing as soon as practicable of the unusual circumstances and of the date by which processing of the request is expected to be completed. Extensions of time for the initial determination and extensions on appeal may not exceed a total of ten working days, unless the requester agrees to a longer extension, or the FOIA Officer provides the requester with an opportunity either to limit the scope of the request so that it may be processed within the applicable time limit, or to arrange an alternative time frame for processing the request or a modified request.

(2) As used in this section, unusual circumstances means, but only to the extent reasonably necessary to properly process the particular request:

(i) The need to search for and collect the requested records from field facilities or other establishments separate from the office processing the request;

(ii) The need to search for, collect, and appropriately examine a voluminous amount of separate and distinct records that are the subject of a single request; or

(iii) The need for consultation, which shall be conducted with all practicable speed, with another Federal agency having a substantial interest in the determination of the request.

(3) Unusual circumstances do not include a delay that results from a predictable workload of requests, unless USPTO demonstrates reasonable progress in reducing its backlog of pending requests. Refusal to reasonably modify the scope of a request or arrange an alternate time frame may affect a requester's ability to obtain judicial review.

(4) If the FOIA Officer reasonably believes that multiple requests submitted by a requester, or by a group of requesters acting in concert, constitute a single request that would otherwise involve unusual circumstances, and the requests involve clearly related matters, the FOIA Officer may aggregate them. Multiple requests involving unrelated matters will not be aggregated.

(d) Multitrack processing.

(1) The FOIA Officer may use two or more processing tracks by distinguishing between simple and more complex requests based on the number of pages involved, or some other measure of the amount of work and/or time needed to process the request, and whether the request qualifies for expedited processing as described in paragraph (e) of this section.

(2) The FOIA Officer may provide requesters in a slower track with an opportunity to limit the scope of their requests in order to qualify for faster processing. The FOIA Officer may contact the requester by telephone or by letter, whichever is most efficient in each case.

(e) Expedited processing.

(1) Requests and appeals shall be taken out of order and given expedited treatment whenever it is determined they involve:

(i) Circumstances in which the lack of expedited treatment could reasonably be expected to pose an imminent threat to the life or physical safety of an individual;

(ii) The loss of substantial due process rights;

(iii) A matter of widespread and exceptional media interest in which there exist questions about the Government's integrity that affect public confidence; or

(iv) An urgency to inform the public about an actual or alleged Federal Government activity, if made by a person primarily engaged in disseminating information.

(2) A request for expedited processing may be made at the time of the initial request for records or at any later time. For a prompt determination, a request for expedited processing should be sent to the FOIA Officer.

(3) A requester who seeks expedited processing must submit a statement, certified to be true and correct to the best of that person's knowledge and belief, explaining in detail the basis for requesting expedited processing. For example, a requester within the category described in paragraph (e)(1)(iv) of this section, if not a full-time member of the news media, must establish that he or she is a person whose main professional activity or occupation is information dissemination, though it need not be his or her sole occupation. A requester within the category described in paragraph (e)(1)(iv) of this section must also establish a particular urgency to inform the public about the Government activity involved in the request, beyond the public's right to know about Government activity generally. The formality of certification may be waived as a matter of administrative discretion.

(4) Within ten calendar days of receipt of a request for expedited processing, the FOIA Officer will decide whether to grant it and shall notify the requester of the decision. If a request for expedited treatment is granted, the request shall be given priority and processed as soon as practicable. If a request for expedited processing is denied, any appeal of that decision shall be acted on expeditiously.

§102.7. RESPONSES TO REQUESTS

(a) Grants of requests. If the FOIA Officer makes a determination to grant a request in whole or in part, the FOIA Officer will notify the requester in writing. The FOIA Officer will inform the requester in the notice of any fee charged under §102.11 and disclose records to the requester promptly upon payment of any applicable fee. Records disclosed in part shall be marked or annotated to show each applicable FOIA exemption and the amount of information deleted, unless doing so would harm an interest protected by an applicable exemption. The location of the information deleted shall also be indicated on the record, if feasible.

(b) Adverse determinations of requests. If the FOIA Officer makes an adverse determination regarding a request, the FOIA Officer will notify the requester of that determination in writing. An adverse determination is a denial of a request in any respect, namely: A determination to withhold any requested record in whole or in part; a determination that a requested record does not exist or cannot be located; a determination that a record is not readily reproducible in the form or format sought by the requester; a determination that what has been requested is not a record subject to FOIA (except that a determination under §102.11(j) that records are to be made available under a fee statute other than FOIA is not an adverse determination); a determination against the requester on any disputed fee matter, including a denial of a request for a fee waiver; or a denial of a request for expedited treatment. Each denial letter shall be signed by the FOIA Officer and shall include:

(1) The name and title or position of the denying official;

(2) A brief statement of the reason(s) for the denial, including applicable FOIA exemption(s);

(3) An estimate of the volume of records or information withheld, in number of pages or some other reasonable form of estimation. This estimate need not be provided if the volume is otherwise indicated through deletions on records disclosed in part, or if providing an estimate would harm an interest protected by an applicable FOIA exemption; and

(4) A statement that the denial may be appealed, and a list of the requirements for filing an appeal under §102.10(b).

§102.9. BUSINESS INFORMATION

(a) In general. Business information obtained by USPTO from a submitter will be disclosed under FOIA only under this section.

(b) Definitions. For the purposes of this section:

(1) Business information means commercial or financial information, obtained by USPTO from a submitter, which may be protected from disclosure under FOIA exemption 4 (5 U.S.C. 552(b)(4)).

(2) Submitter means any person or entity outside the Federal Government from whom USPTO obtains business information, directly or indirectly. The term includes corporations; state, local and tribal governments; and foreign governments.

(c) Designation of business information. A submitter of business information should designate by appropriate markings, either at the time of submission or at a reasonable time thereafter, any portions of its submission that it considers to be protected from disclosure under FOIA exemption 4. These designations will expire ten years after the date of the submission unless the submitter requests, and provides justification for, a longer designation period.

(d) Notice to submitters. The FOIA Officer shall provide a submitter with prompt written notice of a FOIA request or administrative appeal that seeks its business information whenever required under paragraph (e) of this section, except as provided in paragraph (h) of this section, in order to give the submitter an opportunity under paragraph (f) of this section to object to disclosure of any specified portion of that information. Such written notice shall be sent via certified mail, return receipt requested, or similar means. The notice shall either describe the business information requested or include copies of the requested records containing the information. When notification of a large number of submitters is required, notification may be made by posting or publishing the notice in a place reasonably likely to accomplish notification.

(e) When notice is required. Notice shall be given to the submitter whenever:

(1) The information has been designated in good faith by the submitter as protected from disclosure under FOIA exemption 4; or

(2) The FOIA Officer has reason to believe that the information may be protected from disclosure under FOIA exemption 4.

(f) Opportunity to object to disclosure. The FOIA Officer shall allow a submitter seven working days (*i.e.*, excluding Saturdays, Sundays, and legal public holidays) from the date of receipt of the written notice described in paragraph (d) of this section to provide the FOIA Officer with a detailed statement of any objection to disclosure. The statement must specify all grounds for withholding any portion of the information under any exemption of FOIA and, in the case of exemption 4, it must show why the information is a trade secret or commercial or financial information that is privileged or confidential. If a submitter fails to respond to the notice within the time specified, the submitter will be considered to have no objection to disclosure of the information. Information a submitter provides under this paragraph may itself be subject to disclosure under FOIA.

(g) Notice of intent to disclose. The FOIA Officer shall consider a submitter's objections and specific grounds under FOIA for nondisclosure in deciding whether to disclose business information. If the FOIA Officer decides to disclose business information over the objection of a submitter, the FOIA Officer shall give the submitter written notice via certified mail, return receipt requested, or similar means, which shall include:

(1) A statement of reason(s) why the submitter's objections to disclosure were not sustained;

(2) A description of the business information to be disclosed; and

(3) A statement that the FOIA Officer intends to disclose the information seven working days from the date the submitter receives the notice.

(h) Exceptions to notice requirements. The notice requirements of paragraphs (d) and (g) of this section shall not apply if:

(1) The FOIA Officer determines that the information should not be disclosed;

(2) The information has been lawfully published or has been officially made available to the public;

(3) Disclosure of the information is required by statute (other than FOIA) or by a regulation issued in accordance with Executive Order 12600; or

(4) The designation made by the submitter under paragraph (c) of this section appears obviously frivolous, in which case the FOIA Officer shall provide the submitter written notice of any final decision to disclose the information seven working days from the date the submitter receives the notice.

(i) Notice of FOIA lawsuit. Whenever a requester files a lawsuit seeking to compel the disclosure of business information, the FOIA Officer shall promptly notify the submitter.

(j) Corresponding notice to requesters. Whenever a FOIA Officer provides a submitter with notice and an opportunity to object to disclosure under paragraph (d) of this section, the FOIA Officer shall also notify the requester(s). Whenever a submitter files a lawsuit seeking to prevent the disclosure of business information, the FOIA Officer shall notify the requester(s).

§102.10. APPEALS FROM INITIAL DETERMINATIONS OR UNTIMELY DELAYS

(a) If a request for records is initially denied in whole or in part, or has not been timely determined, or if a requester receives an adverse initial determination regarding any other matter under this subpart (as described in §102.7(b)), the requester may file a written appeal, which must be received by the Office of General Counsel within thirty calendar days of the date of the written denial or, if there has been no determination, may be submitted anytime after the due date, including the last extension under §102.6(c), of the determination.

(b) Appeals shall be decided by a Deputy General Counsel. Appeals should be addressed to the General Counsel, United States Patent and Trademark Office, PO Box 1450, Alexandria, Virginia 22313-1450. Both the letter and the appeal envelope should be clearly marked "Freedom of Information Appeal." The appeal must include a copy of the original request and the initial denial, if any, and may include a statement of the reasons why the records requested should be made available and why the initial denial, if any, was in error. No opportunity for personal appearance, oral argument or hearing on appeal is provided.

(c) If an appeal is granted, the person making the appeal shall be immediately notified and copies of the releasable documents shall be made available promptly thereafter upon receipt of appropriate fees determined in accordance with §102.11.

(d) If no determination of an appeal has been sent to the requester within the twenty-working-day period specified in §102.6(b) or the last extension thereof, the requester is deemed to have exhausted his administrative remedies with respect to the request, giving rise to a right of judicial review under 5 U.S.C. 552(a)(6)(C). If the person making a request initiates a civil action against USPTO based on the provision in this paragraph, the administrative appeal process may continue.

(e) A determination on appeal shall be in writing and, when it denies records in whole or in part, the letter to the requester shall include:

(1) A brief explanation of the basis for the denial, including a list of applicable FOIA exemptions and a description of how the exemptions apply;

(2) A statement that the decision is final;

(3) Notification that judicial review of the denial is available in the United States district court for the district in which the requester resides or has its principal place of business, the United States District Court for the Eastern District of Virginia, or the District of Columbia; and

(4) The name and title or position of the official responsible for denying the appeal.

History of 37 C.F.R. §102.10: 68 FR 14338, Mar. 25, 2003.

§102.11. FEES

(a) In general. USPTO shall charge for processing requests under FOIA in accordance with paragraph (c) of this section, except when fees are limited under paragraph (d) of this section or when a waiver or reduction of fees is granted under paragraph (k) of this section. USPTO shall collect all applicable fees before sending copies of requested records to a requester. Requesters must pay fees by check or money order made payable to the Treasury of the United States.

(b) Definitions. For purposes of this section:

(1) Commercial use request means a request from or on behalf of a person who seeks information for a use or purpose that furthers his or her commercial, trade, or profit interests, which can include furthering those interests through litigation. The FOIA Officer shall determine, whenever reasonably possible, the use to which a requester will put the requested records. When it appears that the requester will put the records to a commercial use, either because of the nature of the request itself or because the FOIA Officer has reasonable cause to doubt a requester's stated use, the FOIA Officer shall provide the requester a reasonable opportunity to submit further clarification.

(2) Direct costs means those expenses USPTO incurs in searching for and duplicating (and, in the case of commercial use requests, reviewing) records to respond to a FOIA request. Direct costs include, for example, the labor costs of the employee performing the work (the basic rate of pay for the employee, plus 16 percent of that rate to cover benefits). Not included in direct costs are overhead expenses such as the costs of space and heating or lighting of the facility in which the records are kept.

(3) Duplication means the making of a copy of a record, or of the information contained in it, necessary to respond to a FOIA request. Copies may take the form of paper, microform, audiovisual materials, or electronic records (for example, magnetic tape or disk), among others. The FOIA Officer shall honor a requester's specified preference of form or format of disclosure if the record is readily reproducible with reasonable efforts in the requested form or format.

(4) Educational institution means a preschool, a public or private elementary or secondary school, an institution of undergraduate higher education, an institution of graduate higher education, an institution of professional education, or an institution of vocational education, that operates a program of scholarly research. To be in this category, a requester must show that the request is authorized by and is made under the auspices of a qualifying institution, and that the records are sought to further scholarly research rather than for a commercial use.

(5) Noncommercial scientific institution means an institution that is not operated on a "commercial" basis, as that term is defined in paragraph (b)(1) of this section, and that is operated solely for the purpose of conducting scientific research, the results of which are not intended to promote any particular product or industry. To be in this category, a requester must show that the request is authorized by and is made under the auspices of a qualifying institution and that the records are sought to further scientific research rather than for a commercial use.

(6) Representative of the news media, or news media requester means any person actively gathering news for an entity that is organized and operated to publish or broadcast news to the public. The term "news" means information that is about current events or that would be of current interest to the public. Examples of news media entities include television or radio stations broadcasting to the public at large and publishers of periodicals (but only if they can qualify as disseminators of "news") that make their products available for purchase or subscription by the general public. For "freelance" journalists to be regarded as working for a news organization, they must demonstrate a solid basis for expecting publication through that organization. A publication contract would be the clearest proof, but the FOIA Officer shall also look to the past publication record of a requester in making this determination. To be in this category, a requester must not be seeking the requested records for a commercial use. However, a request for records supporting the news-dissemination function of the requester shall not be considered to be for a commercial use.

(7) Review means the examination of a record located in response to a request in order to determine whether any portion of it is exempt from disclosure. It also includes processing any record for disclosure—for example, doing all that is necessary to redact it and prepare it for disclosure. Review costs are recoverable even if a record ultimately is not disclosed. Review time does not include time spent resolving general legal or policy issues regarding the application of exemptions.

(8) Search means the process of looking for and retrieving records or information responsive to a request. It includes page-by-page or line-by-line identification of information within records and also includes reasonable efforts to locate and retrieve information from records maintained in electronic form or format. The FOIA Officer shall ensure that searches are done in the most efficient and least expensive manner reasonably possible.

(c) Fees. In responding to FOIA requests, the FOIA Officer shall charge the fees summarized in chart form in paragraphs (c)(1) and (c)(2) of this section and explained in paragraphs (c)(3) through (c)(5) of this section, unless a waiver or reduction of fees has been granted under paragraph (k) of this section.

(1) The four categories and chargeable fees are:

CATEGORY	CHARGEABLE FEES
(i) Commercial Use Requesters	Search, Review, and Duplication.
(ii) Educational and Non-Commercial Scientific Institution Requesters	Duplication (excluding the cost of the first 100 pages).
(iii) Representatives of the News Media	Duplication (excluding the cost of the first 100 pages).
(iv) All Other Requesters	Search and Duplication (excluding the cost of the first 2 hours of search and 100 pages).

(2) Uniform fee schedule.

SERVICE	RATE
(i) Manual search	Actual salary rate of employee involved, plus 16 percent of salary rate.
(ii) Computerized search	Actual direct cost, including operator time.
(iii) Duplication of records:	
(A) Paper copy reproduction	$15 per page
(B) Other reproduction (e.g., computer disk or printout, microfilm, microfiche, or microform)	Actual direct cost, including operator time.
(iv) Review of records (includes preparation for release, i.e., excising)	Actual salary rate of employee conducting review, plus 16 percent of salary rate.

(3) Search.

(i) Search fees shall be charged for all requests—other than requests made by educational institutions, noncommercial scientific institutions, or representatives of the news media—subject to the limitations of paragraph (d) of this section. The FOIA Officer will charge for time spent searching even if no responsive records are located or if located records are entirely exempt from disclosure. Search fees shall be the direct costs of conducting the search by the involved employees.

(ii) For computer searches of records, requesters will be charged the direct costs of conducting the search, although certain requesters (as provided in paragraph (d)(1) of this section) will be charged no search fee and certain other requesters (as provided in paragraph (d)(3) of this section) are entitled to the cost equivalent of two hours of manual search time without charge. These direct costs include the costs, attributable to the search, of operating a central processing unit and operator/programmer salary.

(4) Duplication. Duplication fees will be charged to all requesters, subject to the limitations of paragraph (d) of this section. For a paper photocopy of a record (no more than one copy of which need be supplied), the fee shall be $.15 cents per page. For copies produced by computer, such as tapes or printouts, the FOIA Officer shall charge the direct costs, including operator time, of producing the copy. For other forms of duplication, the FOIA Officer will charge the direct costs of that duplication.

(5) Review. Review fees shall be charged to requesters who make a commercial use request. Review fees shall be charged only for the initial record review—the review done when the FOIA Officer determines whether an exemption applies to a particular record at the initial request level. No charge will be made for review at the administrative appeal level for an exemption already applied. However, records withheld under an exemption that is subsequently determined not to apply may be reviewed again to determine whether any other exemption not previously considered applies, and the costs of that review are chargeable. Review fees shall be the direct costs of conducting the review by the involved employees.

(d) Limitations on charging fees.

(1) No search fee will be charged for requests by educational institutions, noncommercial scientific institutions, or representatives of the news media.

(2) No search fee or review fee will be charged for a quarter-hour period unless more than half of that period is required for search or review.

(3) Except for requesters seeking records for a commercial use, the FOIA Officer will provide without charge:

(i) The first 100 pages of duplication (or the cost equivalent); and

(ii) The first two hours of search (or the cost equivalent).

(4) Whenever a total fee calculated under paragraph (c) of this section is $20.00 or less for any request, no fee will be charged.

(5) The provisions of paragraphs (d)(3) and (4) of this section work together. This means that for requesters other than those seeking records for a commercial use, no fee will be charged unless the cost of the search in excess of two hours plus the cost of duplication in excess of 100 pages totals more than $20.00.

(e) Notice of anticipated fees over $20.00. When the FOIA Officer determines or estimates that the fees to be charged under this section will be more than $20.00, the FOIA Officer shall notify the requester of the actual or estimated fees, unless the requester has indicated a willingness to pay fees as high as those anticipated. If only a portion of the fee can be estimated readily, the FOIA Officer shall advise the requester that the estimated fee may be only a portion of the total fee. If the FOIA Officer has notified a requester that actual or estimated fees are more than $20.00, the FOIA Officer shall not consider the request received or process it further until the requester agrees to pay the anticipated total fee. Any such agreement should be in writing. A notice under this paragraph shall offer the requester an opportunity to discuss the matter with USPTO personnel in order to reformulate the request to meet the requester's needs at a lower cost.

(f) Charges for other services. Apart from the other provisions of this section, the FOIA Officer shall ordinarily charge the direct cost of special services. Such special services could include certifying that records are true copies or sending records by other than ordinary mail.

(g) Charging interest. The FOIA Officer shall charge interest on any unpaid bill starting on the 31st calendar day following the date of billing the requester. Interest charges shall be assessed at the rate provided in 31 U.S.C. 3717 and accrue from the date of the billing until payment is received by the FOIA Officer. The FOIA Officer shall follow the provisions of the Debt Collection Improvement Act of 1996 (Pub.L. 104-134), as amended, and its administrative procedures, including the use of consumer reporting agencies, collection agencies, and offset.

(h) Aggregating requests. If a FOIA Officer reasonably believes that a requester or a group of requesters acting together is attempting to divide a request into a series of requests for the purpose of avoiding fees, the FOIA Officer may aggregate those requests and charge accordingly. The FOIA Officer may presume that multiple requests of this type made within a 30-calendar-day period have been made in order to avoid fees. If requests are separated by a longer period, the FOIA Officer shall aggregate them only if a solid basis exists for determining that aggregation is warranted under all the circumstances involved. Multiple requests involving unrelated matters shall not be aggregated.

(i) Advance payments.

(1) For requests other than those described in paragraphs (i)(2) and (3) of this section, the FOIA Officer shall not require the requester to make an advance payment: a payment made before work is begun or continued on a request. Payment owed for work already completed (*i.e.*, a payment before copies are sent to a requester) is not an advance payment.

(2) If the FOIA Officer determines or estimates that a total fee to be charged under this section will be more than $250.00, the requester must pay the entire anticipated fee before beginning to process the request, unless the FOIA Officer receives a satisfactory assurance of full payment from a requester who has a history of prompt payment.

(3) If a requester has previously failed to pay a properly charged FOIA fee to USPTO or another responsible Federal agency within 30 calendar days of the date of billing, the FOIA Officer shall require the requester to pay the full amount due, plus any applicable interest, and to make an advance payment of the full amount of any anticipated fee, before the FOIA Officer begins to process a new request or continues to process a pending request from that requester.

(4) In cases in which the FOIA Officer requires payment under paragraphs (i)(2) or (3) of this section, the request shall not be considered received and further work will not be done on it until the required payment is received.

(5) Upon the completion of processing of a request, when a specific fee is determined to be payable and appropriate notice has been given to the requester, the FOIA Officer shall make records available to the requester only upon receipt of full payment of the fee.

(j) Other statutes specifically providing for fees. The fee schedule of this section does not apply to fees charged under any statute (except for FOIA) that specifically requires USPTO or another responsible Federal agency to set and collect fees for particular types of records. If records responsive to requests are maintained for distribution by agencies operating such statutorily based fee schedule programs, the FOIA Officer shall inform requesters of how to obtain records from those sources.

(k) Requirements for waiver or reduction of fees.

(1) Records responsive to a request will be furnished without charge or at a charge reduced below that established under paragraph (c) of this section if the FOIA Officer determines, based on all available information, that the requester has demonstrated that:

(i) Disclosure of the requested information is in the public interest because it is likely to contribute significantly to public understanding of the operations or activities of the Government; and

(ii) Disclosure of the information is not primarily in the commercial interest of the requester.

(2) To determine whether the first fee waiver requirement is met, the FOIA Officer shall consider the following factors:

(i) The subject of the request: whether the subject of the requested records concerns the operations or activities of the Government. The subject of the requested records must concern identifiable operations or activities of the Federal Government, with a connection that is direct and clear, not remote or attenuated.

(ii) The informative value of the information to be disclosed: whether the disclosure is "likely to contribute" to an understanding of Government operations or activities. The disclosable portions of the requested records must be meaningfully informative about Government operations or activities in order to be "likely to contribute" to an increased public understanding of those operations or activities. The disclosure of information that already is in the public domain, in either a duplicative or a substantially identical form, would not be likely to contribute to such understanding.

(iii) The contribution to an understanding of the subject by the public likely to result from disclosure: whether disclosure of the requested information will contribute to the understanding of a reasonably broad audience of persons interested in the subject, as opposed to the individual understanding of the requester. A requester's expertise in the subject area and ability and intention to effectively convey information to the public shall be considered. It shall be presumed that a representative of the news media satisfies this consideration. It shall be presumed that a requester who merely provides information to media sources does not satisfy this consideration.

(iv) The significance of the contribution to public understanding: whether the disclosure is likely to contribute "significantly" to public understanding of Government operations or activities. The public's understanding of the subject in question prior to the disclosure must be significantly enhanced by the disclosure.

(3) To determine whether the second fee waiver requirement is met, the FOIA Officer shall consider the following factors:

(i) The existence and magnitude of a commercial interest: whether the requester has a commercial interest that would be furthered by the requested disclosure. The FOIA Officer shall consider any commercial interest of the requester (with reference to the definition of "commercial use request" in paragraph (b)(1) of this section), or of any person on whose behalf the requester may be acting, that would be furthered by the requested disclosure. Requesters shall be given an opportunity to provide explanatory information regarding this consideration.

(ii) The primary interest in disclosure: whether any identified commercial interest of the requester is sufficiently large, in comparison with the public interest in disclosure, that disclosure is "primarily in the commercial interest of the requester." A fee waiver or reduction is justified if the public interest standard (paragraph (k)(1)(i) of this section) is satisfied and the public interest is greater than any identified commercial interest in disclosure. The FOIA Officer ordinarily shall presume that if a news media requester has satisfied the public interest standard, the public interest is the primary interest served by disclosure to that requester. Disclosure to data brokers or others who merely compile and market Government information for direct economic return shall not be presumed to primarily serve the public interest.

(4) If only some of the records to be released satisfy the requirements for a fee waiver, a waiver shall be granted for those records.

(5) Requests for the waiver or reduction of fees should address the factors listed in paragraphs (k)(2) and (3) of this section, insofar as they apply to each request.

SUBPART B. PRIVACY ACT

§102.21. PURPOSE & SCOPE

(a) The purpose of this subpart is to establish policies and procedures for implementing the Privacy Act of 1974, as amended (5 U.S.C. 552a) (the Act). The main objectives are to facilitate full exercise of rights conferred on individuals under the Act and to ensure the protection of privacy as to individuals on whom USPTO maintains records in systems of records under the Act. USPTO accepts the responsibility to act promptly and in accordance with the Act upon receipt of any inquiry, request or appeal from a citizen of the United States or an alien lawfully admitted for permanent residence into the United States, regardless of the age of the individual. Further, USPTO accepts the obligations to maintain only such information on individuals as is relevant and necessary to the performance of its lawful functions, to maintain that information with such accuracy, relevancy, timeliness, and completeness as is reasonably necessary to assure fairness in determinations made by USPTO about the individual, to obtain information from the individual to the extent practicable, and to take every reasonable step to protect that information from unwarranted disclosure. USPTO will maintain no record describing how an individual exercises rights guaranteed by the First Amendment unless expressly authorized by statute or by the individual about whom the record is maintained or unless pertinent to and within the scope of an authorized law enforcement activity. An individual's name and address will not be sold or rented by USPTO unless such action is specifically authorized by law; however, this provision shall not be construed to require the withholding of names and addresses otherwise permitted to be made public.

(b) This subpart is administered by the Privacy Officer of USPTO.

(c) Matters outside the scope of this subpart include the following:

(1) Requests for records which do not pertain to the individual making the request, or to the individual about whom the request is made if the requester is the parent or guardian of the individual;

(2) Requests involving information pertaining to an individual which is in a record or file but not within the scope of a system of records notice published in the Federal Register;

(3) Requests to correct a record where a grievance procedure is available to the individual either by regulation or by provision in a collective bargaining agreement with USPTO, and the individual has initiated, or has expressed in writing the intention of initiating, such grievance procedure. An individual selecting the grievance procedure waives the use of the procedures in this subpart to correct or amend a record; and,

(4) Requests for employee-employer services and counseling which were routinely granted prior to enactment of the Act, including, but not limited to, test calculations of retirement benefits, explanations of health and life insurance programs, and explanations of tax withholding options.

(d) Any request for records which pertains to the individual making the request, or to the individual about whom the request is made if the requester is the parent or guardian of the individual, shall be processed under the Act and this subpart and under the Freedom of Information Act and USPTO's implementing regulations at Subpart A of this part, regardless whether the Act or the Freedom of Information Act is mentioned in the request.

Source of 37 C.F.R. Part 102B: 65 FR 52917, Aug. 31, 2000; 66 FR 47390, Sept. 12, 2001, unless otherwise noted.

§102.22. DEFINITIONS

(a) All terms used in this subpart which are defined in 5 U.S.C. 552a shall have the same meaning herein.

(b) As used in this subpart:

(1) Act means the "Privacy Act of 1974, as amended (5 U.S.C. 552a)."

(2) Appeal means a request by an individual to review and reverse an initial denial of a request by that individual for correction or amendment.

(3) USPTO means the United States Patent and Trademark Office.

(4) Inquiry means either a request for general information regarding the Act and this subpart or a request by an individual (or that individual's parent or guardian) that USPTO determine whether it has any record in a system of records which pertains to that individual.

(5) Person means any human being and also shall include but not be limited to, corporations, associations, partnerships, trustees, receivers, personal representatives, and public or private organizations.

(6) Privacy Officer means a USPTO employee designated to administer this subpart.

(7) Request for access means a request by an individual or an individual's parent or guardian to see a record which is in a particular system of records and which pertains to that individual.

(8) Request for correction or amendment means the request by an individual or an individual's parent or guardian that USPTO change (either by correction, amendment, addition or deletion) a particular record in a system of records which pertains to that individual.

§102.23. PROCEDURES FOR MAKING INQUIRIES

(a) Any individual, regardless of age, who is a citizen of the United States or an alien lawfully admitted for permanent residence into the United States may submit an inquiry to USPTO. The inquiry should be made either in person at 10B20, Madison Building East, 600 Dulany Street, Alexandria, Virginia, or by mail addressed to the Privacy Officer, United States Patent and Trademark Office, P.O. Box 1450, Alexandria, Virginia 22313-1450, or to the official identified in the notification procedures paragraph of the systems of records notice published in the Federal Register. If an individual believes USPTO maintains a record pertaining to that individual but does not know which system of records might contain such a record, the USPTO Privacy Officer will provide assistance in person or by mail.

(b) Inquiries submitted by mail should include the words "PRIVACY ACT INQUIRY" in capital letters at the top of the letter and on the face of the envelope. If the inquiry is for general information regarding the Act and this subpart, no particular information is required. USPTO reserves the right to require compliance with the identification procedures appearing at §102.24(d) where circumstances warrant. If the inquiry is a request that USPTO determine whether it has, in a given system of records, a record which pertains to the individual, the following information should be submitted:

(1) Name of individual whose record is sought;

(2) Individual whose record is sought is either a U.S. citizen or an alien lawfully admitted for permanent residence;

(3) Identifying data that will help locate the record (for example, maiden name, occupational license number, period or place of employment, etc.);

(4) Record sought, by description and by record system name, if known;

(5) Action requested (that is, sending information on how to exercise rights under the Act; determining whether requested record exists; gaining access to requested record; or obtaining copy of requested record);

(6) Copy of court guardianship order or minor's birth certificate, as provided in §102.24(f)(3), but only if requester is guardian or parent of individual whose record is sought;

(7) Requester's name (printed), signature, address, and telephone number (optional);

(8) Date; and,

(9) Certification of request by notary or other official, but only if

(i) Request is for notification that requested record exists, for access to requested record or for copy of requested record;

(ii) Record is not available to any person under 5 U.S.C. 552; and

(iii) Requester does not appear before an employee of USPTO for verification of identity.

(c) Any inquiry which is not addressed as specified in paragraph (a) of this section or which is not marked as specified in paragraph (b) of this section will be so addressed and marked by USPTO personnel and forwarded immediately to the Privacy Officer. An inquiry which is not properly addressed by the individual will not be deemed to have been "received" for purposes of measuring the time period for response until actual receipt by the Privacy Officer. In each instance when an inquiry so forwarded is received, the Privacy Officer shall notify the individual that his or her inquiry was improperly addressed and the date the inquiry was received at the proper address.

(d)(1) Each inquiry received shall be acted upon promptly by the Privacy Officer. Every effort will be made to respond within ten working days (*i.e.*, excluding Saturdays, Sundays and legal public holidays) of the date of receipt. If a response cannot be made within ten working days, the Privacy Officer shall send an acknowledgment during that period providing information on the status of the inquiry and asking for such further information as may be necessary to process the inquiry. The first correspondence sent by the Privacy Officer to the requester shall contain USPTO's control number assigned to the request, as well as a note that the requester should use that number in all future contacts in order to facilitate processing. USPTO shall use that control number in all subsequent correspondence.

(2) If the Privacy Officer fails to send an acknowledgment within ten working days, as provided above, the requester may ask the General Counsel to take corrective action. No failure of the Privacy Officer to send an acknowledgment shall confer administrative finality for purposes of judicial review.

(e) An individual shall not be required to state a reason or otherwise justify his or her inquiry.

(f) Special note should be taken of the fact that certain agencies are responsible for publishing notices of systems of records having Government-wide application to other agencies, including USPTO. The agencies known to be publishing these general notices and the types of records covered therein appear in an appendix to this part. The provisions of this section, and particularly paragraph (a) of this section, should be followed in making inquiries with respect to such records. Such records in USPTO are subject to the provisions of this part to the extent indicated in the appendix to this part. The exemptions, if any, determined by an agency publishing a general notice shall be invoked and applied by USPTO after consultation, as necessary, with that other agency.

History of 37 C.F.R. §102.23: 68 FR 14338, Mar. 25, 2003; 70 FR 10489, Mar. 4, 2005.

§102.24. PROCEDURES FOR MAKING REQUESTS FOR RECORDS

(a) Any individual, regardless of age, who is a citizen of the United States or an alien lawfully admitted for permanent residence into the United States may submit a request to the USPTO for access to records. The request should be made either in person at 10B20, Madison Building East, 600 Dulany Street, Alexandria, Virginia, or by mail addressed to the Privacy Officer, United States Patent and Trademark Office, P.O. Box 1450, Alexandria, Virginia 22313-1450.

(b) Requests submitted by mail should include the words "PRIVACY ACT REQUEST" in capital letters at the top of the letter and on the face of the envelope. Any request which is not addressed as specified in paragraph (a) of this section or which is not marked as specified in this paragraph will be so addressed and marked by USPTO personnel and forwarded immediately to the Privacy Officer. A request which is not properly addressed by the individual will not be deemed to have been "received" for purposes of measuring time periods for response until actual receipt by the Privacy Officer. In each instance when a request so forwarded is received, the Privacy Officer shall notify the individual that his or her request was improperly addressed and the date when the request was received at the proper address.

(c) If the request follows an inquiry under §102.23 in connection with which the individual's identity was established by USPTO, the individual need only indicate the record to which access is sought, provide the USPTO control number assigned to the request, and sign and date the request. If the request is not preceded by an inquiry under §102.23, the procedures of this section should be followed.

(d) The requirements for identification of individuals seeking access to records are as follows:

(1) In person. Each individual making a request in person shall be required to present satisfactory proof of identity. The means of proof, in the order of preference and priority, are:

(i) A document bearing the individual's photograph (for example, driver's license, passport or military or civilian identification card);

(ii) A document, preferably issued for participation in a federally sponsored program, bearing the individual's signature (for example, unemployment insurance book, employer's identification card, national credit card, and professional, craft or union membership card); and

(iii) A document bearing neither the photograph nor the signature of the individual, preferably issued for participation in a federally sponsored program (for example, Medicaid card). In the event the individual can provide no suitable documentation of identity, USPTO will require a signed statement asserting the individual's identity and stipulating that the individual understands the penalty provision of 5 U.S.C. 552a(i)(3) recited in §102.32(a). In order to avoid any unwarranted disclosure of an individual's records, USPTO reserves the right to determine the adequacy of proof of identity offered by any individual, particularly when the request involves a sensitive record.

(2) Not in person. If the individual making a request does not appear in person before the Privacy Officer or other employee authorized to determine identity, a certification of a notary public or equivalent officer empowered to administer oaths must accompany the request under the circumstances prescribed in §102.23(b)(9). The certification in or attached to the letter must be substantially in accordance with the following text:

City of ___________

County of ___________:ss

(Name of individual), who affixed (his) (her) signature below in my presence, came before me, a (title), in and for the aforesaid County and State, this _____ day of ______, 20___, and established (his) (her) identity to my satisfaction.

My commission expires ___________.

(Signature)

(3) Parents of minors and legal guardians. An individual acting as the parent of a minor or the legal guardian of the individual to whom a record pertains shall establish his or her personal identity in the same manner prescribed in either paragraph (d)(1) or (d)(2) of this section. In addition, such other individual shall establish his or her identity in the representative capacity of parent or legal guardian. In the case of the parent of a minor, the proof of identity shall be a certified or authenticated copy of the minor's birth certificate. In the case of a legal guardian of an individual who has been de-

clared incompetent due to physical or mental incapacity or age by a court of competent jurisdiction, the proof of identity shall be a certified or authenticated copy of the court's order. For purposes of the Act, a parent or legal guardian may represent only a living individual, not a decedent. A parent or legal guardian may be accompanied during personal access to a record by another individual, provided the provisions of §102.25(f) are satisfied.

(e) When the provisions of this subpart are alleged to impede an individual in exercising his or her right to access, USPTO will consider, from an individual making a request, alternative suggestions regarding proof of identity and access to records.

(f) An individual shall not be required to state a reason or otherwise justify his or her request for access to a record.

History of 37 C.F.R. §102.24: 68 FR 14338, Mar. 25, 2003; 70 FR 10490, Mar. 4, 2005.

§102.25. DISCLOSURE OF REQUESTED RECORDS TO INDIVIDUALS

(a)(1) The Privacy Officer shall act promptly upon each request. Every effort will be made to respond within ten working days (*i.e.*, excluding Saturdays, Sundays, and legal public holidays) of the date of receipt. If a response cannot be made within ten working days due to unusual circumstances, the Privacy Officer shall send an acknowledgment during that period providing information on the status of the request and asking for any further information that may be necessary to process the request. "Unusual circumstances" shall include circumstances in which

(i) A search for and collection of requested records from inactive storage, field facilities or other establishments is required;

(ii) A voluminous amount of data is involved;

(iii) Information on other individuals must be separated or expunged from the particular record; or

(iv) Consultations with other agencies having a substantial interest in the determination of the request are necessary.

(2) If the Privacy Officer fails to send an acknowledgment within ten working days, as provided above in paragraph (a) of this section, the requester may ask the General Counsel to take corrective action. No failure of the Privacy Officer to send an acknowledgment shall confer administrative finality for purposes of judicial review.

(b) Grant of access—

(1) Notification. An individual shall be granted access to a record pertaining to him or her, except where the provisions of paragraph (g)(1) of this section apply. The Privacy Officer will notify the individual of a determination to grant access, and provide the following information:

(i) The methods of access, as set forth in paragraph (b)(2) of this section;

(ii) The place at which the record may be inspected;

(iii) The earliest date on which the record may be inspected and the period of time that the records will remain available for inspection. In no event shall the earliest date be later than thirty calendar days from the date of notification;

(iv) The estimated date by which a copy of the record could be mailed and the estimate of fees pursuant to §102.31. In no event shall the estimated date be later than thirty calendar days from the date of notification;

(v) The fact that the individual, if he or she wishes, may be accompanied by another individual during personal access, subject to the procedures set forth in paragraph (f) of this section; and,

(vi) Any additional requirements needed to grant access to a specific record.

(2) Methods of access. The following methods of access to records by an individual may be available depending on the circumstances of a given situation:

(i) Inspection in person may be had in a location specified by the Privacy Officer during business hours;

(ii) Transfer of records to a Federal facility more convenient to the individual may be arranged, but only if the Privacy Officer determines that a suitable facility is available, that the individual's access can be properly supervised at that facility, and that transmittal of the records to that facility will not unduly interfere with operations of USPTO or involve unreasonable costs, in terms of both money and manpower; and

(iii) Copies may be mailed at the request of the individual, subject to payment of the fees prescribed in §102.31. USPTO, on its own initiative, may elect to provide a copy by mail, in which case no fee will be charged the individual.

(c) Access to medical records is governed by the provisions of §102.26.

(d) USPTO will supply such other information and assistance at the time of access as to make the record intelligible to the individual.

(e) USPTO reserves the right to limit access to copies and abstracts of original records, rather than the original records. This election would be appropriate, for example, when the record is in an automated data media such as tape or diskette, when the record contains information on other individuals, and when deletion of information is permissible under exemptions (for example, 5 U.S.C. 552a(k)(2)). In no event shall original records of USPTO be made available to the individual except under the immediate supervision of the Privacy Officer or the Privacy Officer's designee.

(f) Any individual who requests access to a record pertaining to that individual may be accompanied by another individual of his or her choice. "Accompanied" includes discussion of the record in the presence of the other individual. The individual to whom the record pertains shall authorize the presence of the other individual in writing. The authorization shall include the name of the other individual, a specific description of the record to which access is sought, the USPTO control number assigned to the request, the date, and the signature of the individual to whom the record pertains. The other individual shall sign the authorization in the presence of the Privacy Officer. An individual shall not be required to state a reason or otherwise justify his or her decision to be accompanied by another individual during personal access to a record.

(g) Initial denial of access—

(1) Grounds. Access by an individual to a record which pertains to that individual will be denied only upon a determination by the Privacy Officer that:

(i) The record is exempt under §102.33 or §102.34, or exempt by determination of another agency publishing notice of the system of records, as described in §102.23(f);

(ii) The record is information compiled in reasonable anticipation of a civil action or proceeding;

(iii) The provisions of §102.26 pertaining to medical records temporarily have been invoked; or

(iv) The individual has unreasonably failed to comply with the procedural requirements of this part.

(2) Notification. The Privacy Officer shall give notice of denial of access to records to the individual in writing and shall include the following information:

(i) The Privacy Officer's name and title or position;

(ii) The date of the denial;

(iii) The reasons for the denial, including citation to the appropriate section of the Act and this part;

(iv) The individual's opportunities, if any, for further administrative consideration, including the identity and address of the responsible official. If no further administrative consideration within USPTO is available, the notice shall state that the denial is administratively final; and

(v) If stated to be administratively final within USPTO, the individual's right to judicial review provided under 5 U.S.C. 552a(g)(1), as limited by 5 U.S.C. 552a(g)(5).

(3) Administrative review. When an initial denial of a request is issued by the Privacy Officer, the individual's opportunities for further consideration shall be as follows:

(i) As to denial under paragraph (g)(1)(i) of this section, two opportunities for further consideration are available in the alternative:

(A) If the individual contests the application of the exemption to the records, review procedures in §102.25(g)(3)(ii) shall apply; or

(B) If the individual challenges the exemption itself, the procedure is a petition for the issuance, amendment, or repeal of a rule under 5 U.S.C. 553(e). If the exemption was determined by USPTO, such petition shall be filed with the General Counsel. If the exemption was determined by another agency (as described in §102.23(f)), USPTO will provide the individual with the name and address of the other agency and any relief sought by the individual shall be that provided by the regulations of the other agency. Within USPTO, no such denial is administratively final until such a petition has been filed by the individual and disposed of on the merits by the General Counsel.

(ii) As to denial under paragraphs (g)(1)(ii) of this section, (g)(1)(iv) of this section or (to the limited extent provided in paragraph (g)(3)(i)(A) of this section) paragraph (g)(1)(i) of this section, the individual may file for review with the General Counsel, as indicated in the Privacy Officer's initial denial notification. The procedures appearing in §102.28 shall be followed by both the individual and USPTO to the maximum extent practicable.

(iii) As to denial under paragraph (g)(1)(iii) of this section, no further administrative consideration within USPTO is available because the denial is not administratively final until expiration of the time period indicated in §102.26(a).

(h) If a request is partially granted and partially denied, the Privacy Officer shall follow the appropriate procedures of this section as to the records within the grant and the records within the denial.

§102.26. SPECIAL PROCEDURES: MEDICAL RECORDS

(a) No response to any request for access to medical records by an individual will be issued by the Privacy Officer for a period of seven working days (*i.e.*, excluding Saturdays, Sundays, and legal public holidays) from the date of receipt.

(b) USPTO has published as a routine use, for all systems of records containing medical records, consultations with an individual's physician or psychologist if, in the sole judgment of USPTO, disclosure could have an adverse effect upon the individual. The mandatory waiting period set forth in paragraph (a) of this section will permit exercise of this routine use in appropriate cases. USPTO will pay no cost of any such consultation.

(c) In every case of a request by an individual for access to medical records, the Privacy Officer shall:

(1) Inform the individual of the waiting period prescribed in paragraph (a) of this section;

(2) Obtain the name and address of the individual's physician and/or psychologist, if the individual consents to give them;

(3) Obtain specific, written consent for USPTO to consult the individual's physician and/or psychologist in the event that USPTO believes such consultation is advisable, if the individual consents to give such authorization;

(4) Obtain specific, written consent for USPTO to provide the medical records to the individual's physician or psychologist in the event that USPTO believes access to the record by the individual is best effected under the guidance of the individual's physician or psychologist, if the individual consents to give such authorization; and

(5) Forward the individual's medical record to USPTO's medical expert for review and a determination on whether consultation with or transmittal of the medical records to the individual's physician or psychologist is warranted. If the consultation with or transmittal of such records to the individual's physician or psychologist is determined to be warranted, USPTO's medical expert shall so consult or transmit. Whether or not such a consultation or transmittal occurs, USPTO's medical officer shall provide instruction to the Privacy Officer regarding the conditions of access by the individual to his or her medical records.

(d) If an individual refuses in writing to give the names and consents set forth in paragraphs (c)(2) through (c)(4) of this section and USPTO has determined that disclosure could have an adverse effect upon the individual, USPTO shall give the individual access to said records by means of a copy, provided without cost to the requester, sent registered mail return receipt requested.

§102.27. PROCEDURES FOR MAKING REQUESTS FOR CORRECTION OR AMENDMENT

(a) Any individual, regardless of age, who is a citizen of the United States or an alien lawfully admitted for permanent residence into the United States may submit a request for correction or amendment to USPTO. The request should be made either in person or by mail addressed to the Privacy Officer who processed the individual's request for access to the record, and to whom is delegated authority to make initial determinations on requests for correction or amendment. The office of the Privacy Officer is open to the public between the hours of 9 a.m. and 4 p.m., Monday through Friday (excluding legal public holidays).

(b) Requests submitted by mail should include the words "PRIVACY ACT REQUEST" in capital letters at the top of the letter and on the face of the envelope. Any request which is not addressed as specified in paragraph (a) of this section or which is not marked as specified in this paragraph will be so addressed and marked by USPTO personnel and forwarded immediately to the Privacy Officer. A request which is not properly addressed by the individual will not be deemed to have been "received" for purposes of measuring the time period for response until actual receipt by the Privacy Officer. In each instance when a request so forwarded is received, the Privacy Officer shall notify the individual that his or her request was improperly addressed and the date the request was received at the proper address.

(c) Since the request, in all cases, will follow a request for access under §102.25, the individual's identity will be established by his or her signature on the request and use of the USPTO control number assigned to the request.

(d) A request for correction or amendment should include the following:

(1) Specific identification of the record sought to be corrected or amended (for example, description, title, date, paragraph, sentence, line and words);

(2) The specific wording to be deleted, if any;

(3) The specific wording to be inserted or added, if any, and the exact place at which to be inserted or added; and

(4) A statement of the basis for the requested correction or amendment, with all available supporting documents and materials which substantiate the statement. The statement should identify the criterion of the Act being invoked, that is, whether the information in the record is unnecessary, inaccurate, irrelevant, untimely or incomplete.

§102.28. REVIEW OF REQUESTS FOR CORRECTION OR AMENDMENT

(a)(1)(i) Not later than ten working days (*i.e.*, excluding Saturdays, Sundays and legal public holidays) after receipt of a request to correct or amend a record, the Privacy Officer shall send an acknowledgment providing an estimate of time within which action will be taken on the request and asking for such further information as may be necessary to process the request. The estimate of time may take into account unusual circumstances as described in §102.25(a). No acknowledgment will be sent if the request can be reviewed, processed, and the individual notified of the results of review (either compliance or denial) within the ten working days. Requests filed in person will be acknowledged in writing at the time submitted.

(ii) If the Privacy Officer fails to send the acknowledgment within ten working days, as provided in paragraph (a)(1)(i) of this section, the requester may ask the General Counsel to take corrective action. No failure of the Privacy Officer to send an acknowledgment shall confer administrative finality for purposes of judicial review.

(2) Promptly after acknowledging receipt of a request, or after receiving such further information as might have been requested, or after arriving at a decision within the ten working days, the Privacy Officer shall either:

(i) Make the requested correction or amendment and advise the individual in writing of such action, providing either a copy of the corrected or amended record or a statement as to the means whereby the correction or amendment was effected in cases where a copy cannot be provided (for example, erasure of information from a record maintained only in magnetically recorded computer files); or

(ii) Inform the individual in writing that his or her request is denied and provide the following information:

(A) The Privacy Officer's name and title or position;

(B) The date of the denial;

(C) The reasons for the denial, including citation to the appropriate sections of the Act and this subpart; and

(D) The procedures for appeal of the denial as set forth in §102.29, including the address of the General Counsel.

(3) The term promptly in this section means within thirty working days (*i.e.*, excluding Saturdays, Sundays, and legal public holidays). If the Privacy Officer cannot make the determination within thirty working days, the individual will be advised in writing of the reason therefor and of the estimated date by which the determination will be made.

(b) Whenever an individual's record is corrected or amended pursuant to a request by that individual, the Privacy Officer shall be responsible for notifying all persons and agencies to which the corrected or amended portion of the record had been disclosed prior to its correction or amendment, if an accounting of such disclosure required by the Act was made. The notification shall require a recipient agency maintaining the record to acknowledge receipt of the notification, to correct or amend the record, and to apprise any agency or person to which it had disclosed the record of the substance of the correction or amendment.

(c) The following criteria will be considered by the Privacy Officer in reviewing a request for correction or amendment:

(1) The sufficiency of the evidence submitted by the individual;

(2) The factual accuracy of the information;

(3) The relevance and necessity of the information in terms of purpose for which it was collected;

(4) The timeliness and currency of the information in light of the purpose for which it was collected;

(5) The completeness of the information in terms of the purpose for which it was collected;

(6) The degree of risk that denial of the request could unfairly result in determinations adverse to the individual;

(7) The character of the record sought to be corrected or amended; and

(8) The propriety and feasibility of complying with the specific means of correction or amendment requested by the individual.

(d) USPTO will not undertake to gather evidence for the individual, but does reserve the right to verify the evidence which the individual submits.

(e) Correction or amendment of a record requested by an individual will be denied only upon a determination by the Privacy Officer that:

(1) The individual has failed to establish, by a preponderance of the evidence, the propriety of the correction or amendment in light of the criteria set forth in paragraph (c) of this section;

(2) The record sought to be corrected or amended is part of the official record in a terminated judicial, quasi-judicial, or quasi-legislative proceeding to which the individual was a party or participant;

(3) The information in the record sought to be corrected or amended, or the record sought to be corrected or amended, is the subject of a pending judicial, quasi-judicial, or quasi-legislative proceeding to which the individual is a party or participant;

(4) The correction or amendment would violate a duly enacted statute or promulgated regulation; or

(5) The individual has unreasonably failed to comply with the procedural requirements of this part.

(f) If a request is partially granted and partially denied, the Privacy Officer shall follow the appropriate procedures of this section as to the records within the grant and the records within the denial.

§102.29. APPEAL OF INITIAL ADVERSE DETERMINATION ON CORRECTION OR AMENDMENT

(a) When a request for correction or amendment has been denied initially under §102.28, the individual may submit a written appeal within thirty working days (*i.e.*, excluding Saturdays, Sundays and legal public holidays) after the date of the initial denial. When an appeal is submitted by mail, the postmark is conclusive as to timeliness.

(b) An appeal should be addressed to the General Counsel, United States Patent and Trademark Office, PO Box 1450, Alexandria, Virginia 22313-1450. An appeal should include the words "PRIVACY APPEAL" in capital letters at the top of the letter and on the face of the envelope. An appeal not addressed and marked as provided herein will be so marked by USPTO personnel when it is so identified and will be forwarded immediately to the General Counsel. An appeal which is not properly addressed by the individual will not be deemed to have been "received" for purposes of measuring the time periods in this section until actual receipt by the General Counsel. In each instance when an appeal so forwarded is received, the General Counsel shall notify the individual that his or her appeal was improperly addressed and the date when the appeal was received at the proper address.

(c) The individual's appeal shall include a statement of the reasons why the initial denial is believed to be in error and USPTO's control number assigned to the request. The appeal shall be signed by the individual. The record which the individual requests be corrected or amended and all correspondence between the Privacy Officer and the requester will be furnished by the Privacy Officer who issued the initial denial. Although the foregoing normally will comprise the entire record on appeal, the General Counsel may seek additional information necessary to assure that the final determination is fair and equitable and, in such instances, disclose the additional information to the individual to the greatest extent possible, and provide an opportunity for comment thereon.

(d) No personal appearance or hearing on appeal will be allowed.

(e) The General Counsel shall act upon the appeal and issue a final determination in writing not later than thirty working days (*i.e.*, excluding Saturdays, Sundays and legal public holidays) from the date on which the appeal is received, except that the General Counsel may extend the thirty days upon deciding that a fair and equitable review cannot be made within that period, but only if the individual is advised in writing of the reason for the extension and the estimated date by which a final determination will issue. The estimated date should not be later than the sixtieth working day after receipt of the appeal unless unusual circumstances, as described in §102.25(a), are met.

(f) If the appeal is determined in favor of the individual, the final determination shall include the specific corrections or amendments to be made and a copy thereof shall be transmitted promptly both to the individual and to the Privacy Officer who issued the initial denial. Upon receipt of such final determination, the Privacy Officer promptly shall take the actions set forth in §102.28(a)(2)(i) and (b).

(g) If the appeal is denied, the final determination shall be transmitted promptly to the individual and state the reasons for the denial. The notice of final determination also shall inform the individual of the following:

(1) The right of the individual under the Act to file a concise statement of reasons for disagreeing with the final determination. The statement ordinarily should not exceed one page and USPTO reserves the right to reject a statement of excessive length. Such a statement shall be filed with the General Counsel. It should provide the USPTO control number assigned to the request, indicate the date of the final determination and be signed by the individual. The General Counsel shall acknowledge receipt of such statement and inform the individual of the date on which it was received.

(2) The facts that any such disagreement statement filed by the individual will be noted in the disputed record, that the purposes and uses to which the statement will be put are those applicable to the record in which it is noted, and that a copy of the statement will be provided to persons and agencies to which the record is disclosed subsequent to the date of receipt of such statement;

(3) The fact that USPTO will append to any such disagreement statement filed by the individual, a copy of the final determination or summary thereof which also will be provided to persons and agencies to which the disagreement statement is disclosed; and,

(4) The right of the individual to judicial review of the final determination under 5 U.S.C. 552a(g)(1)(A), as limited by 5 U.S.C. 552a(g)(5).

(h) In making the final determination, the General Counsel shall employ the criteria set forth in §102.28(c) and shall deny an appeal only on the grounds set forth in §102.28(e).

(i) If an appeal is partially granted and partially denied, the General Counsel shall follow the appropriate procedures of this section as to the records within the grant and the records within the denial.

(j) Although a copy of the final determination or a summary thereof will be treated as part of the individual's record for purposes of disclosure in instances where the individual has filed a disagreement statement, it will not be subject to correction or amendment by the individual.

(k) The provisions of paragraphs (g)(1) through (g)(3) of this section satisfy the requirements of 5 U.S.C. 552a(e)(3).

History of 37 C.F.R. §102.29: 68 FR 14339, Mar. 25, 2003.

§102.30. DISCLOSURE OF RECORD TO PERSON OTHER THAN THE INDIVIDUAL TO WHOM IT PERTAINS

(a) USPTO may disclose a record pertaining to an individual to a person other than the individual to whom it pertains only in the following instances:

(1) Upon written request by the individual, including authorization under §102.25(f);

(2) With the prior written consent of the individual;

(3) To a parent or legal guardian under 5 U.S.C. 552a(h);

(4) When required by the Act and not covered explicitly by the provisions of 5 U.S.C. 552a(b); and

(5) When permitted under 5 U.S.C. 552a(b)(1) through (12), which read as follows;[1]

(i) To those officers and employees of the agency which maintains the record who have a need for the record in the performance of their duties;

(ii) Required under 5 U.S.C. 552;

(iii) For a routine use as defined in 5 U.S.C. 552a(a)(7) and described under 5 U.S.C. 552a(e)(4)(D);

(iv) To the Bureau of the Census for purposes of planning or carrying out a census or survey or related activity pursuant to the provisions of Title 13;

(v) To a recipient who has provided the agency with advance adequate written assurance that the record will be used solely as a statistical research or reporting record, and the record is to be transferred in a form that is not individually identifiable;

(vi) To the National Archives and Records Administration as a record which has sufficient historical or other value to warrant its continued preservation by the United States Government, or for evaluation by the Archivist of the United States or the designee of the Archivist to determine whether the record has such value;

(vii) To another agency or to an instrumentality of any governmental jurisdiction within or under the control of the United States for a civil or criminal law enforcement activity if the activity is authorized by law, and if the head of the agency or instrumentality has made a written request to the agency which maintains the record specifying the particular portion desired and the law enforcement activity for which the record is sought;

(viii) To a person pursuant to a showing of compelling circumstances affecting the health or safety of an individual if upon such disclosure notification is transmitted to the last known address of such individual;

(ix) To either House of Congress, or, to the extent of matter within its jurisdiction, any committee or subcommittee thereof, any joint committee of Congress or subcommittee of any such joint committee;

(x) To the Comptroller General, or any of his authorized representatives, in the course of the performance of the duties of the General Accounting Office;

(xi) Pursuant to the order of a court of competent jurisdiction; or

(xii) To a consumer reporting agency in accordance with section 3711(e) of Title 31.

(b) The situations referred to in paragraph (a)(4) of this section include the following:

(1) 5 U.S.C. 552a(c)(4) requires dissemination of a corrected or amended record or notation of a disagreement statement by USPTO in certain circumstances;

(2) 5 U.S.C. 552a(d) requires disclosure of records to the individual to whom they pertain, upon request; and

(3) 5 U.S.C. 552a(g) authorizes civil action by an individual and requires disclosure by USPTO to the court.

(c) The Privacy Officer shall make an accounting of each disclosure by him of any record contained in a system of records in accordance with 5 U.S.C. 552a(c)(1) and (2). Except for a disclosure made under 5 U.S.C. 552a(b)(7), the Privacy Officer shall make such accounting available to any individual, insofar as it pertains to that individual, on request submitted in accordance with §102.24. The Privacy Officer shall make reasonable efforts to notify any individual when any record in a system of records is disclosed to any person under compulsory legal process, promptly upon being informed that such process has become a matter of public record.

1. 5 U.S.C. §552a(b)(4) has no application within USPTO.

§102.31. FEES

The only fees to be charged to or collected from an individual under the provisions of this part are for duplication of records at the request of the individual. The Privacy Officer shall charge fees for duplication of records under the Act in the same way in which they charge duplication fees under §102.11, except as provided in this section.

(a) No fees shall be charged or collected for the following: Search for and retrieval of the records; review of the records; copying at the initiative of USPTO without a request from the individual; transportation of records and personnel; and first-class postage.

(b) It is the policy of USPTO to provide an individual with one copy of each record corrected or amended pursuant to his or her request without charge as evidence of the correction or amendment.

(c) As required by the United States Office of Personnel Management in its published regulations implementing the Act, USPTO will charge no fee for a single copy of a personnel record covered by that agency's Government-wide published notice of systems of records.

§102.32. PENALTIES

(a) The Act provides, in pertinent part:

Any person who knowingly and willfully requests or obtains any record concerning an individual from an agency under false pretenses shall be guilty of a misdemeanor and fined not more than $5,000. (5 U.S.C. 552a(i)(3)).

(b) A person who falsely or fraudulently attempts to obtain records under the Act also may be subject to prosecution under such other criminal statutes as 18 U.S.C. 494, 495 and 1001.

§102.33. GENERAL EXEMPTIONS

(a) Individuals may not have access to records maintained by USPTO but which were provided by another agency which has determined by regulation that such information is subject to general exemption under 5 U.S.C. 552a(j). If such exempt records are within a request for access, USPTO will advise the individual of their existence and of the name and address of the source agency. For any further information concerning the record and the exemption, the individual must contact that source agency.

(b) The general exemption determined to be necessary and proper with respect to systems of records maintained by USPTO, including the parts of each system to be exempted, the provisions of the Act from which they are exempted, and the justification for the exemption, is as follows: Investigative Records—Contract and Grant Frauds and Employee Criminal Misconduct—COMMERCE/DEPT.—12. Pursuant to 5 U.S.C. 552a(j)(2), these records are hereby determined to be exempt from all provisions of the Act, except 5 U.S.C. 552a (b), (c)(1) and (2), (e)(4)(A) through (F), (e)(6), (7), (9), (10), and (11), and (i). These exemptions are necessary to ensure the proper functions of the law enforcement activity, to protect confidential sources of information, to fulfill promises of confidentiality, to prevent interference with law enforcement proceedings, to avoid the disclosure of investigative techniques, to avoid the endangering of law enforcement personnel, to avoid premature disclosure of the knowledge of criminal activity and the evidentiary bases of possible enforcement actions, and to maintain the integrity of the law enforcement process.

§102.34. SPECIFIC EXEMPTIONS

(a)(1) Some systems of records under the Act which are maintained by USPTO contain, from time-to-time, material subject to the exemption appearing at 5 U.S.C. 552a(k)(1), relating to national defense and foreign policy materials. The systems of records published in the Federal Register by USPTO which are within this exemption are: COMMERCE/

PAT-TM-6, COMMERCE/PAT-TM-7, COMMERCE/PAT-TM-8, COMMERCE/PAT-TM-9.

(2) USPTO hereby asserts a claim to exemption of such materials wherever they might appear in such systems of records, or any systems of records, at present or in the future. The materials would be exempt from 5 U.S.C. 552a(c)(3), (d), (e)(1), (e)(4)(G), (H), and (I), and (f) to protect materials required by Executive order to be kept secret in the interest of the national defense and foreign policy.

(b) The specific exemptions determined to be necessary and proper with respect to systems of records maintained by USPTO, including the parts of each system to be exempted, the provisions of the Act from which they are exempted, and the justification for the exemption, are as follows:

(1)(i) Exempt under 5 U.S.C. 552a(k)(2). The systems of records exempt (some only conditionally), the sections of the Act from which exempted, and the reasons therefor are as follows:

(A) Investigative Records—Contract and Grant Frauds and Employee Criminal Misconduct—COMMERCE/DEPT-12, but only on condition that the general exemption claimed in §102.33(b)(3) is held to be invalid;

(B) Investigative Records—Persons Within the Investigative Jurisdiction of USPTO—COMMERCE/DEPT-13;

(C) Litigation, Claims and Administrative Proceeding Records—COMMERCE/DEPT-14;

(D) Attorneys and Agents Registered to Practice Before the Office—COMMERCE/PAT-TM-1;

(E) Complaints, Investigations and Disciplinary Proceedings Relating to Registered Patent Attorneys and Agents—COMMERCE/PAT-TM-2; and

(F) Non-Registered Persons Rendering Assistance to Patent Applicants—COMMERCE/PAT-TM-5.

(ii) The foregoing are exempted from 5 U.S.C. 552a(c)(3), (d), (e)(1), (e)(4)(G), (H), and (I), and (f). The reasons for asserting the exemption are to prevent subjects of investigation from frustrating the investigatory process, to insure the proper functioning and integrity of law enforcement activities, to prevent disclosure of investigative techniques, to maintain the ability to obtain necessary information, to fulfill commitments made to sources to protect their identities and the confidentiality of information and to avoid endangering these sources and law enforcement personnel. Special note is taken of the fact that the proviso clause in this exemption imports due process and procedural protections for the individual. The existence and general character of the information exempted will be made known to the individual to whom it pertains.

(2)(i) Exempt under 5 U.S.C. 552a(k)(5). The systems of records exempt (some only conditionally), the sections of the act from which exempted, and the reasons therefor are as follows:

(A) Investigative Records—Contract and Grant Frauds and Employee Criminal Misconduct—COMMERCE/DEPT-12, but only on condition that the general exemption claimed in §102.33(b)(3) is held to be invalid;

(B) Investigative Records—Persons Within the Investigative Jurisdiction of USPTO—COMMERCE/DEPT-13; and

(C) Litigation, Claims, and Administrative Proceeding Records—COMMERCE/DEPT-14.

(ii) The foregoing are exempted from 5 U.S.C. 552a(c)(3), (d), (e)(1), (e)(4)(G), (H), and (I), and (f). The reasons for asserting the exemption are to maintain the ability to obtain candid and necessary information, to fulfill commitments made to sources to protect the confidentiality of information, to avoid endangering these sources and, ultimately, to facilitate proper selection or continuance of the best applicants or persons for a given position or contract. Special note is made of the limitation on the extent to which this exemption may be asserted. The existence and general character of the information exempted will be made known to the individual to whom it pertains.

(c) At the present time, USPTO claims no exemption under 5 U.S.C. 552a(k)(3), (4), (6) and (7).

APPENDIX TO PART 102—SYSTEMS OF RECORDS NOTICED BY OTHER FEDERAL AGENCIES[1] & APPLICABLE TO USPTO RECORDS & APPLICABILITY OF THIS PART THERETO

CATEGORY OF RECORDS	OTHER FEDERAL AGENCY
Federal Personnel Records	Office of Personnel Management.[2]
Federal Employee Compensation Act Program	Department of Labor.[3]
Equal Employment Opportunity Appeal Complaints	Equal Employment Opportunity Commission.[4]
Formal Complaints/Appeals of Adverse Personnel Actions	Merit Systems Protection Board.[5]

1. Other than systems of records noticed by the Department of Commerce. Where the system of records applies only to USPTO, these regulations apply. Where the system of records applies generally to components of the Department of Commerce, the regulations of that department attach at the point of any denial for access or for correction or amendment.

2. The provisions of this part do not apply to these records covered by notices of systems of records published by the Office of Personnel Management for all agencies. The regulations of OPM alone apply.

3. The provisions of this part apply only initially to these records covered by notices of systems of records published by the U.S. Department of Labor for all agencies. The regulations of that department attach at the point of any denial for access or for correction or amendment.

4. The provisions of this part do not apply to these records covered by notices of systems of records published by the Equal Employment Opportunity Commission for all agencies. The regulations of the Commission alone apply.

5. The provisions of this part do not apply to these records covered by notices of systems of records published by the Merit Systems Protection Board for all agencies. The regulations of the Board alone apply.

PART 104. LEGAL PROCESSES

SUBPART A. GENERAL PROVISIONS

§104.1. DEFINITIONS

Demand means a request, order, or subpoena for testimony or documents for use in a legal proceeding.

Director means the Under Secretary of Commerce for Intellectual Property and Director of the United States Patent and Trademark Office (see §1.9(j)).

Document means any record, paper, and other property held by the Office, including without limitation, official letters, telegrams, memoranda, reports, studies, calendar and diary entries, maps, graphs, pamphlets, notes, charts, tabulations, analyses, statistical or informational accumulations, any kind of summaries of meetings and conversations, film impressions, magnetic tapes, and sound or mechanical reproductions.

Employee means any current or former officer or employee of the Office.

Legal proceeding means any pretrial, trial, and posttrial stages of existing or reasonably anticipated judicial or administrative actions, hearings, investigations, or similar proceedings before courts, commissions, boards or other tribunals, foreign or domestic. This phrase includes all phases of discovery as well as responses to formal or informal requests by attorneys or others involved in legal proceedings.

Office means the United States Patent and Trademark Office, including any operating unit in the United States Patent and Trademark Office, and its predecessors, the Patent Office and the Patent and Trademark Office.

Official business means the authorized business of the Office.

General Counsel means the General Counsel of the Office.

Testimony means a statement in any form, including personal appearances before a court or other legal tribunal, interviews, depositions, telephonic, televised, or videotaped statements or any responses given during discovery or similar proceedings, which response would involve more than the production of documents, including a declaration under 35 U.S.C. 25 or 28 U.S.C. 1746.

United States means the Federal Government, its departments and agencies, individuals acting on behalf of the Federal Government, and parties to the extent they are represented by the United States.

History of 37 C.F.R. §104.1: 68 FR 14339, Mar. 25, 2003.

Source of 37 C.F.R. Part 104A: 66 FR 47390, Sept. 12, 2001, unless otherwise noted.

§104.2. ADDRESS FOR MAIL & SERVICE; TELEPHONE NUMBER

(a) Mail under this part should be addressed to the Office of the General Counsel, United States Patent and Trademark Office, P.O. Box 1450, Alexandria, Virginia 22313-1450.

(b) Service by hand should be made during business hours to the Office of the General Counsel, 10B20, Madison Building East, 600 Dulany Street, Alexandria, Virginia.

(c) The Office of the General Counsel may be reached by telephone at 571-272-7000 during business hours.

History of 37 C.F.R. §104.2: 70 FR 10490, Mar. 4, 2005; 75 FR 36295, June 25, 2010.

§104.3. WAIVER OF RULES

In extraordinary situations, when the interest of justice requires, the General Counsel may waive or suspend the rules of this part, sua sponte or on petition of an interested party to the Director, subject to such requirements as the General Counsel may impose. Any such petition must be accompanied by a petition fee of $130.00.

History of 37 C.F.R. §104.3: 69 FR 56546, Sept. 21, 2004.

§104.4. RELATIONSHIP OF THIS PART TO THE FEDERAL RULES OF CIVIL OR CRIMINAL PROCEDURE

Nothing in this part waives or limits any requirement under the Federal Rules of Civil or Criminal Procedure.

SUBPART B. SERVICE OF PROCESS

§104.11. SCOPE & PURPOSE

(a) This subpart sets forth the procedures to be followed when a summons and complaint is served on the Office or on the Director or an employee in his or her official capacity.

(b) This subpart is intended, and should be construed, to ensure the efficient administration of the Office and not to impede any legal proceeding.

(c) This subpart does not apply to subpoenas, the procedures for which are set out in subpart C.

(d) This subpart does not apply to service of process made on an employee personally on matters not related to official business of the Office or to the official responsibilities of the employee.

Source of 37 C.F.R. Part 104B: 66 FR 47390, Sept. 12, 2001, unless otherwise noted.

§104.12. ACCEPTANCE OF SERVICE OF PROCESS

(a) Any summons and complaint to be served in person or by registered or certified mail or as otherwise authorized by law on the Office, on the Director, or on an employee in his or her official capacity, shall be served as indicated in §104.2.

(b) Any employee of the Office served with a summons and complaint shall immediately notify, and shall deliver the summons and complaint to, the Office of the General Counsel.

(c) Any employee receiving a summons and complaint shall note on the summons and complaint the date, hour, and place of service and whether service was by hand or by mail.

(d) When a legal proceeding is brought to hold an employee personally liable in connection with an action taken in the conduct of official business, rather than liable in an official capacity, the employee by law is to be served personally with process. See Fed. R. Civ. P. 4(e). An employee sued personally for an action taken in the conduct of official business shall immediately notify and deliver a copy of the summons and complaint to the General Counsel.

(e) An employee sued personally in connection with official business may be represented by the Department of Justice at its discretion (28 CFR 50.15 and 50.16).

(f) The Office will only accept service of process for an employee in the employee's official capacity.

SUBPART C. EMPLOYEE TESTIMONY & PRODUCTION OF DOCUMENTS IN LEGAL PROCEEDINGS

§104.21. SCOPE & PURPOSE

(a) This subpart sets forth the policies and procedures of the Office regarding the testimony of employees as witnesses in legal proceedings and the production or disclosure of information contained in Office documents for use in legal proceedings pursuant to a demand.

(b) Exceptions. This subpart does not apply to any legal proceeding in which:

(1) An employee is to testify regarding facts or events that are unrelated to official business; or

(2) A former employee is to testify as an expert in connection with a particular matter in which the former employee did not participate personally while at the Office.

Source of 37 C.F.R. Part 104C: 66 FR 47390, Sept. 12, 2001, unless otherwise noted.

§104.22. DEMAND FOR TESTIMONY OR PRODUCTION OF DOCUMENTS

(a) Whenever a demand for testimony or for the production of documents is made upon an employee, the employee shall immediately notify the Office of the General Counsel at the telephone number or addresses in §104.2 and make arrangements to send the subpoena to the General Counsel promptly.

(b) An employee may not give testimony, produce documents, or answer inquiries from a person not employed by the Office regarding testimony or documents subject to a demand or a potential demand under the provisions of this subpart without the approval of the General Counsel. The General Counsel may authorize the provision of certified copies not otherwise available under Part 1 of this title subject to payment of applicable fees under §1.19.

(c)(1) Demand for testimony or documents. A demand for the testimony of an employee under this subpart shall be addressed to the General Counsel as indicated in §104.2.

(2) Subpoenas. A subpoena for employee testimony or for a document shall be served in accordance with the Federal Rules of Civil or Criminal Procedure or applicable state procedure, and a copy of the subpoena shall be sent to the General Counsel as indicated in §104.2.

(3) Affidavits. Except when the United States is a party, every demand shall be accompanied by an affidavit or declaration under 28 U.S.C. 1746 or 35 U.S.C. 25(b) setting forth the title of the legal proceeding, the forum, the requesting party's interest in the legal proceeding, the reason for the demand, a showing that the desired testimony or document is not reasonably available from any other source, and, if testimony is requested, the intended use of the testimony, a general summary of the desired testimony, and a showing that no document could be provided and used in lieu of testimony.

(d) Failure of the attorney to cooperate in good faith to enable the General Counsel to make an informed determination under this subpart may serve as a basis for a determination not to comply with the demand.

(e) A determination under this subpart to comply or not to comply with a demand is not a waiver or an assertion of any other ground for noncompliance, including privilege, lack of relevance, or technical deficiency.

(f) Noncompliance. If the General Counsel makes a determination not to comply, he or she will seek Department of Justice representation for the employee and will attempt to have the subpoena modified or quashed. If Department of Justice representation cannot be arranged, the employee should appear at the time and place set forth in the subpoena. In such a case, the employee should produce a copy of these rules and state that the General Counsel has advised the employee not to provide the requested testimony nor to produce the requested document. If a legal tribunal rules that the demand in the subpoena must be complied with, the employee shall respectfully decline to comply with the demand, citing *United States ex rel. Touhy v. Ragen*, 340 U.S. 462 (1951).

§104.23. EXPERT OR OPINION TESTIMONY

(a)(1) If the General Counsel authorizes an employee to give testimony in a legal proceeding not involving the United States, the testimony, if otherwise proper, shall be limited to facts within the personal knowledge of the employee. Employees, with or without compensation, shall not provide expert testimony in any legal proceedings regarding Office information, subjects, or activities except on behalf of the United States or a party represented by the United States Department of Justice.

(2) The General Counsel may authorize an employee to appear and give the expert or opinion testimony upon the requester showing, pursuant to §104.3 of this part, that exceptional circumstances warrant such testimony and that the anticipated testimony will not be adverse to the interest of the Office or the United States.

(b)(1) If, while testifying in any legal proceeding, an employee is asked for expert or opinion testimony regarding Office information, subjects, or activities, which testimony has not been approved in advance in writing in accordance with the regulations in this subpart, the witness shall:

(i) Respectfully decline to answer on the grounds that such expert or opinion testimony is forbidden by this subpart;

(ii) Request an opportunity to consult with the General Counsel before giving such testimony; and

(iii) Explain that upon such consultation, approval for such testimony may be provided.

(2) If the tribunal conducting the proceeding then orders the employee to provide expert or opinion testimony regarding Office information, subjects, or activities without the opportunity to consult with the General Counsel, the employee shall respectfully refuse to provide such testimony, citing *United States ex rel. Touhy v. Ragen*, 340 U.S. 462 (1951).

(c) If an employee is unaware of the regulations in this subpart and provides expert or opinion testimony regarding Office information, subjects, or activities in a legal proceeding without the aforementioned consultation, the employee shall, as soon after testifying as possible, inform the General Counsel that such testimony was given and provide a written summary of the expert or opinion testimony provided.

(d) Proceeding where the United States is a party. In a proceeding in which the United States is a party or is representing a party, an employee may not testify as an expert or opinion witness for any party other than the United States.

§104.24. DEMANDS OR REQUESTS IN LEGAL PROCEEDINGS FOR RECORDS PROTECTED BY CONFIDENTIALITY STATUTES

Demands in legal proceedings for the production of records, or for the testimony of employees regarding information protected by the confidentiality provisions of the Patent Act (35 U.S.C. 122), the Privacy Act (5 U.S.C. 552a), the Trade Secrets Act (18 U.S.C. 1905), or any other confidentiality statute, must satisfy the requirements for disclosure set forth in those statutes and associated rules before the records may be provided or testimony given.

SUBPART D. EMPLOYEE INDEMNIFICATION

§104.31. SCOPE

The procedure in this subpart shall be followed if a civil action or proceeding is brought, in any court, against an employee (including the employee's estate) for personal injury, loss of property, or death, resulting from the employee's activities while acting within the scope of the employee's office or employment. When the employee is incapacitated or deceased, actions required of an employee should be performed by the employee's executor, administrator, or comparable legal representative.

Source of 37 C.F.R. Part 104D: 66 FR 47390, Sept. 12, 2001, unless otherwise noted.

§104.32. PROCEDURE FOR REQUESTING INDEMNIFICATION

(a) After being served with process or pleadings in such an action or proceeding, the employee shall within five (5) calendar days of receipt, deliver to the General Counsel all such process and pleadings or an attested true copy thereof, together with a fully detailed report of the circumstances of the incident giving rise to the court action or proceeding.

(b)(1) An employee may request indemnification to satisfy a verdict, judgment, or award entered against that employee only if the employee has timely satisfied the requirements of paragraph (a) of this section.

(2) No request for indemnification will be considered unless the employee has submitted a written request through the employee's supervisory chain to the General Counsel with:

(i) Appropriate documentation, including copies of the verdict, judgment, appeal bond, award, or settlement proposal;

(ii) The employee's explanation of how the employee was acting within the scope of the employee's employment; and

(iii) The employee's statement of whether the employee has insurance or any other source of indemnification.

SUBPART E. TORT CLAIMS

§104.41. PROCEDURE FOR FILING CLAIMS

Administrative claims against the Office filed pursuant to the administrative claims provision of the Federal Tort Claims Act (28 U.S.C. 2672) and the corresponding Department of Justice regulations (28 CFR Part 14) shall be filed with the General Counsel as indicated in §104.2.

Source of 37 C.F.R. Part 104E: 66 FR 47390, Sept. 12, 2001, unless otherwise noted.

§104.42. FINALITY OF SETTLEMENT OR DENIAL OF CLAIMS

Only a decision of the Director or the General Counsel regarding settlement or denial of any claim under this subpart may be considered final for the purpose of judicial review.

SUBCHAPTER C. PROTECTION OF FOREIGN MASK WORKS

PART 150. REQUESTS FOR PRESIDENTIAL PROCLAMATIONS PURSUANT TO 17 U.S.C. 902(a)(2)

§150.1. DEFINITIONS

(a) Director means the Under Secretary of Commerce for Intellectual Property and Director of the United States Patent and Trademark Office (see §1.9(j)).

(b) Foreign government means the duly-constituted executive of a foreign nation, or an international or regional intergovernmental organization which has been empowered by its member states to request issuance of Presidential proclamations on their behalf under this part.

(c) Interim order means an order issued by the Secretary of Commerce under 17 U.S.C. 914.

(d) Mask work means a series of related images, however fixed or encoded—

(1) Having or representing the predetermined, three-dimensional pattern of metallic, insulating, or semiconductor material present or removed from the layers of a semiconductor chip product; and

(2) In which series the relation of the images to one another is that each image has the pattern of the surface of one form of the semiconductor chip product.

(e) Presidential proclamation means an action by the President extending to foreign nationals, domiciliaries and sovereign authorities the privilege of applying for registrations for mask works pursuant to 17 U.S.C. 902.

(f) Request means a request by a foreign government for the issuance of a Presidential proclamation.

(g) Proceeding means a proceeding to issue an interim order extending protection to foreign nationals, domiciliaries and sovereign authorities under 17 U.S.C. Chapter 9.

(h) Secretary means the Secretary of Commerce.

History of 37 C.F.R. §150.1: 68 FR 14339, Mar. 25, 2003.

Source of 37 C.F.R. Part 150: 53 FR 24447, June 29, 1988; 68 FR 14339, Mar. 25, 2003; 70 FR 10490, Mar. 4, 2005, unless otherwise noted.

§150.2. INITIATION OF EVALUATION

(a) The Director independently or as directed by the Secretary, may initiate an evaluation of the propriety of recommending the issuance, revision, suspension or revocation of a section 902 proclamation.

(b) The Director shall initiate an evaluation of the propriety of recommending the issuance of a section 902 proclamation upon receipt of a request from a foreign government.

§150.3. SUBMISSION OF REQUESTS

(a) Requests for the issuance of a section 902 proclamation shall be submitted by foreign governments for review by the Director.

(b) Requests for issuance of a proclamation shall include:

(1) A copy of the foreign law or legal rulings that provide protection for U.S. mask works which provide a basis for the request.

(2) A copy of any regulations or administrative orders implementing the protection.

(3) A copy of any laws, regulations or administrative orders establishing or regulating the registration (if any) of mask works.

(4) Any other relevant laws, regulations or administrative orders.

(5) All copies of laws, legal rulings, regulations or administrative orders submitted must be in unedited, full-text form, and if possible, must be reproduced from the original document.

(6) All material submitted must be in the original language, and if not in English, must be accompanied by a certified English translation.

§150.4. EVALUATION

(a) Upon submission of a request by a foreign government for the issuance of a section 902 proclamation, if an interim order under section 914 has not been issued, the Director may initiate a section 914 proceeding if additional information is required.

(b) If an interim order under section 914 has been issued, the information obtained during the section 914 proceeding will be used in evaluating the request for a section 902 proclamation.

(c) After the Director receives the request of a foreign government for a section 902 proclamation, or after a determination is made by the Director to initiate independently an evaluation pursuant to §150.2(a) of this part, a notice will be published in the Federal Register to request relevant and material comments on the adequacy and effectiveness of the protection afforded U.S. mask works under the system of law described in the notice. Comments should include detailed explanations of any alleged deficiencies in the foreign law or any alleged deficiencies in its implementation. If the alleged deficiencies include problems in administration such as registration, the respondent should include as specifically as possible full detailed explanations, including dates for and the nature of any alleged problems. Comments shall be submitted to the Director within sixty (60) days of publication of the Federal Register notice.

(d) The Director shall notify the Register of Copyrights and the Committees on the Judiciary of the Senate and the House of Representatives of the initiation of an evaluation under these regulations.

(e) If the written comments submitted by any party present relevant and material reasons why a proclamation should not issue, the Director will:

(1) Contact the party raising the issue for verification and any needed additional information;

(2) Contact the requesting foreign government to determine if the issues raised by the party can be resolved; and,

(i) If the issues are resolved, continue with the evaluation; or,

(ii) If the issues cannot be resolved on this basis, hold a public hearing to gather additional information.

(f) The comments, the section 902 request, information obtained from a section 914 proceeding, if any, and information obtained in a hearing held pursuant to paragraph (e)(ii) of this section, if any, will be evaluated by the Director.

(g) The Director will forward the information to the Secretary, together with an evaluation and a draft recommendation.

(h) The Secretary will forward a recommendation regarding the issuance of a section 902 proclamation to the President.

§150.5. DURATION OF PROCLAMATION

(a) The recommendation for the issuance of a proclamation may include terms and conditions regarding the duration of the proclamation.

(b) Requests for the revision, suspension or revocation of a proclamation may be submitted by any interested party. Requests for revision, suspension or revocation of a proclamation will be considered in substantially the same manner as requests for the issuance of a section 902 proclamation.

§150.6. MAILING ADDRESS

Requests and all correspondence pursuant to these guidelines shall be addressed to: Mail Stop Congressional Relations, Director of the United States Patent and Trademark Office, P.O. Box 1450, Alexandria, Virginia 22313-1450.

History of 37 C.F.R. §150.6: 68 FR 14339, Mar. 25, 2003; 70 FR 10490, Mar. 4, 2005.

CHAPTER II. U.S. COPYRIGHT OFFICE, LIBRARY OF CONGRESS

SUBCHAPTER A. COPYRIGHT OFFICE & PROCEDURES

PART 201. GENERAL PROVISIONS

A §201.1. COMMUNICATION WITH THE COPYRIGHT OFFICE

(a) General purpose addresses. Members of the public must use the correct address in order to facilitate timely receipt by the U.S. Copyright Office division or section to which an inquiry should be directed. The address set forth in paragraph (b) may be used for general inquiries made to a particular division or section of the U.S. Copyright Office. Addresses for special, limited purposes are provided below in paragraph (c) of this section. Please note that the Library of Congress no longer accepts direct deliveries from commercial couriers and messengers. For additional address information, including information on courier delivery, mail delays, or disruptions, please visit the "Contact us" section on the Office's website (http://www.copyright.gov). General questions may also be directed to the U.S. Copyright Office website submission form at: http://www.copyright.gov/help/general-form.html.

(b) General purpose address.

(1) Mail and other communications that do not come under the areas listed in paragraph (b)(2) of this section shall be addressed to the Library of Congress, U.S. Copyright Office, 101 Independence Avenue SE., Washington, DC 20559-6000.

(2) Codes to facilitate the routing of mail. To assure that postal mail is routed correctly within the U.S. Copyright Office, applicants should indicate, by the appropriate code, the general subject matter of the correspondence. Such correspondence should be addressed to the Office in the following manner: Library of Congress, U.S. Copyright Office—(Insert appropriate code listed below), 101 Independence Avenue SE., Washington, DC 20559-6000.

Type of Submission	Code
Registration of Literary Works	TX
Registration of Serials	SE
Registration of Visual Arts Works	VA
Registration of Works of the Performing Arts, except Motion Pictures	PA
Registration of Sound Recordings	SR
Registration of Motion pictures	MP
Registration of Renewal claims	RE
Document Recordations	DOC
Registration of Mask Works	MW
Registration of Vessel Designs	VH
Copyright Acquisitions	CAD
Deposit Demands	CAD/AD
Licensing Division	LD
Notice to Libraries and Archives	NLA
Publications Section	PUB

(c) Limited purpose addresses. The following addresses may be used only in the special, limited circumstances given for a particular U.S. Copyright Office service:

(1) Time Sensitive Requests. Notices related to the filing of copyright infringement suits and submitted pursuant to 17 U.S.C. 411(a) and 17 U.S.C. 508; requests pursuant to 17 U.S.C. 411(b)(2) from district courts to the Register of Copyrights, all other correspondence to the Office of the General Counsel and the Office of Policy and International Affairs, and requests for expedited service from the Records Research and Certification Section of the Office of Public Information and Education to meet the needs of pending or prospective litigation, customs matters, or contract or publishing deadlines should be addressed to: U.S. Copyright Office, P.O. Box 70400, Washington, DC 20024-0400. Freedom of Information Act (FOIA) requests and FOIA appeals must also be mailed to: P.O. Box 70400, Washington, DC 20024-0400, but clearly labeled "Freedom of Information Act Request" or "Freedom of Information Act Appeal" as appropriate.

(2) Notices of Termination. Notices of Termination of transfers and licenses under sections 203 and 304 of the Copyright Act should be addressed to: U.S. Copyright Office, Notices of Termination, P.O. Box 71537, Washington, DC 20024-1537.

(3) Reconsiderations of Refusals To Register and Requests for Cancellation. First and second requests for reconsideration of refusal to register a copyright, mask work, or vessel design claim, and requests to cancel registered works should be addressed to: U.S. Copyright Office, RAC Division, P.O. Box 71380, Washington, DC 20024-1380.

(4) Searches and Copies of Records or Deposits. Requests for searches of registrations and recordations in the completed catalogs, indexes, and/or other records of the U.S. Copyright Office as well as requests for copies of records or deposits for use in litigation or other authorized purposes should be addressed to: U.S. Copyright Office, Records Research and Certification Section, P.O. Box 70400, Washington, DC 20559-0400.

(5) Inquiries to Licensing Division. Notices related to statutory licenses under 17 U.S.C. 112, 114, and 115 should be addressed to: U.S. Copyright Office, P.O. Box 70977, Washington, DC 20024-0400. Statements of account related to statutory licenses under 17 U.S.C. 119 and chapter 10 should be addressed to: U.S. Copyright Office, SOA, P.O. Box 70400, Washington, DC 20024-0400. Filings or inquiries related to section 111 licenses should be sent to Library of Congress, U.S. Copyright Office, Attn: 111 Licenses, 101 Independence Avenue SE., Washington, DC 20559.

(6) Copyright Acquisitions. Deposit copies submitted under section 407 of the Copyright Act should be addressed to: Library of Congress, U.S. Copyright Office, Attn: 407 Deposits, 101 Independence Avenue SE., Washington, DC 20559. Serial publishers submitting their required complimentary subscriptions to comply with group registration requirements should address these subscriptions to the Library of Congress, Group Periodicals Registration, 101 Independence Avenue SE., Washington, DC 20540-4161. Newspaper publishers that submit microfilm under §202.4(e) of this chapter should mail their submissions to: Library of Congress, U.S. Copyright Office, Attn: 407 Deposits, 101 Independence Avenue SE, Washington, DC 20559.

(7) Requests to remove PII from registration records. Requests to remove personally identifiable information from registration records pursuant to §§201.2(e) and (f) should be addressed to: U.S. Copyright Office, Associate Register of Copyrights and Director of the Office of Public Information and Education, P.O. Box 70400, Washington, DC 20024-0400. Requests should be clearly labeled "Request to Remove Requested PII," "Request for Reconsideration Following Denial of Request to Remove Requested PII," or "Request to Remove Extraneous PII," as appropriate.

History of 37 C.F.R. §201.1: 24 FR 4955, June 18, 1959; 42 FR 2962, Jan. 14, 1977; 50 FR 30170, July 24, 1985; 60 FR 34168, June 30, 1995; 62 FR 35420, July 1, 1997; 62 FR 35421, July 1, 1997; 62 FR 40457, July 29, 1997; 64 FR 36574, July 7, 1999; 65 FR 39818, June 28, 2000; 66 FR 34372, June 28, 2001; 69 FR 39331, June 30, 2004; 73 FR 37838, July 1, 2008; 74 FR 12556, Mar. 25, 2009; 78 FR 42873, July 18, 2013; 82 FR 9007, Mar. 6, 2017; 82 FR 9355, Mar. 8, 2017; 82 FR 21697, May 10, 2017; 83 FR 4145, Mar. 1, 2018.

Source of 37 C.F.R. Part 201: 24 FR 4955, June 18, 1959; 50 FR 30170, July 24, 1985; 50 FR 52459, Dec. 24, 1985; 56 FR 7812, Feb. 26, 1991; 56 FR 7813, Feb. 26, 1991; 56 FR 27197, June 13, 1991; 56 FR 28959, June 25, 1991; 56 FR 38341, Aug. 13, 1991; 57 FR 3296, Jan. 29, 1992; 57 FR 55465, Nov. 25, 1992; 58 FR 9546, Feb. 22, 1993; 59 FR 12164, Mar. 16, 1994; 59 FR 23981, May 9, 1994; 59 FR 38371, July 28, 1994; 59 FR 67635, Dec. 30, 1994; 60 FR 25998, May 16, 1995; 60 FR 34168, June 30, 1995; 60 FR 50420, Sept. 29, 1995; 60 FR 57937, Nov. 24, 1995; 61 FR 30813, June 18, 1996; 62 FR 18710, Apr. 17, 1997; 62 FR 55739, Oct. 28, 1997; 67 FR 69136, Nov. 15, 2002, unless otherwise noted.

A §201.2. INFORMATION GIVEN BY THE COPYRIGHT OFFICE

(a) In general.

(1) Information relative to the operations of the Copyright Office is supplied without charge. A search of the records, indexes, and deposits will be made for such information as they may contain relative to copyright claims upon application and payment of the statutory fee. The Copyright Office, however, does not undertake the making of comparisons of copyright deposits to determine similarity between works.

(2) The Copyright Office does not furnish the names of copyright attorneys, publishers, agents, or other similar information.

(3) In the administration of the Copyright Act in general, the Copyright Office interprets the Act. The Copyright Office, however, does not give specific legal advice on the rights of persons, whether in connection with particular uses of copyrighted works, cases of alleged foreign or domestic copyright infringement, contracts between authors and publishers, or other matters of a similar nature.

(b) Inspection and copying of records.

(1) Inspection and copying of completed records and indexes relating to a registration or a recorded document, and inspection of copies or identifying material deposited in connection with a completed copyright registration may be undertaken in the Records Research and Certification Section. Since some of these materials are not stored on the immediate premises of the Copyright Office, it is advisable to consult the Records Research and Certification Section to determine the length of time necessary to produce the requested materials.

(2) It is the general policy of the Copyright Office to deny direct public access to in-process files and to any work (or other) areas where they are kept. However, direct public use of computers intended to access the automated equivalent of limited portions of these files is permitted on a specified terminal in the Records Management Section, LM B-14, Monday through Friday, upon payment of applicable fees.

(3) Information contained in Copyright Office in-process files may be obtained by anyone upon payment of applicable fees and request to the Office of Public Information and Education, in accordance with the following procedures:

(i) In general, all requests by the public for information in the in-process and open unfinished business files should be made to the Records Research and Certification Section, which upon receipt of applicable fees will give a report that provides the following for each request:

(A) The date(s) of receipt of:

(1) The application(s) for registration that may have been submitted and is (are) in process;

(2) the document(s) that may have been submitted for recordation and is (are) in process;

(3) the copy or copies (or phonorecords) that may have been submitted;

(B) the title of the work(s); and

(C) the name of the applicant or remitter.

(ii) Such searches of the in-process files will be given priority to the extent permitted by the demands of normal work flow of the affected sections of the Copyright Office.

(4)(i) Access will be afforded as follows to pending applications for registration, the deposit material accompanying them, and pending documents for recordation:

(A) In the case of applications for registration and deposits accompanying them, upon the request of the copyright claimant or his/her authorized representative, and

(B) In the case of documents, upon the request of at least one of the persons who executed the document or by an authorized representative of that person.

(ii) These requests should be made to the Records Research and Certification Section, and the review of the materials will be permitted there. No charge will be made for reviewing these materials; the appropriate search fee identified in §201.3(c) or §201.3(d) will be assessed, and the appropriate copying fee identified in §201.3(c) or §201.3(d) will be assessed if the claimant wants and is entitled to a copy of the material.

(5) In exceptional circumstances, the Register of Copyrights may allow inspection of pending applications and open correspondence files by someone other than the copyright claimant, upon submission of a written request which is deemed by the Register to show good cause for such access and establishes that the person making the request is one properly and directly concerned. The written request should be mailed to the address specified in §201.1(c).

(6) Direct public access will not be permitted to any financial or accounting records, including records maintained on Deposit Accounts.

(7) The Register of Copyrights has issued an administrative manual known as the Compendium of U.S. Copyright Office Practices, Third Edition. The Compendium explains many of the practices and procedures concerning the Office's mandate and statutory duties under title 17 of the United States Code. It is both a technical manual for the Copyright Office's staff, as well as a guidebook for authors, copyright licensees, practitioners, scholars, the courts, and members of the general public. The Third Edition and prior editions of the Compendium may be viewed, downloaded, or printed from the Office's website. They are also available for public inspection and copying in the Records Research and Certification Section.

(c) Correspondence.

(1) Official correspondence, including preliminary applications, between copyright claimants or their agents and the Copyright Office, and directly relating to a completed registration, a recorded document, a rejected application for registration, or a document for which recordation was refused is available for public inspection. Included in the correspondence available for public inspection is that portion of the file directly relating to a completed registration, recorded document, a rejected application for registration, or a document for which recordation was refused which was once open to public inspection as a closed case, even if the case is subsequently reopened. Public inspection is available only for the correspondence contained in the file during the time it was closed because of one of the aforementioned actions. Correspondence relating to the reopening of the file and reconsideration of the case is considered part of an in-process file until final action is taken, and public inspection of that correspondence is governed by §201.2(b). Requests for reproductions of the correspondence shall be made pursuant to paragraph (d) of this section.

(2) Correspondence, application forms, and any accompanying material forming a part of a pending application are considered in-process files and access to them is governed by paragraph (b) of this section.

(3) Correspondence, memoranda, reports, opinions, and similar material relating to internal matters of personnel and procedures, office administration, security matters, and internal consideration of policy and decisional matters including the work product of an attorney, are not open to public inspection.

(4) The Copyright Office will not respond to any abusive or scurrilous correspondence or correspondence where the intent is unknown.

(d) Requests for copies.

(1) Requests for copies of records should include the following:

(i) A clear identification of the type of records desired (for example, additional certificates of registration, copies of correspondence, copies of deposits).

(ii) A specification of whether the copies are to be certified or uncertified.

(iii) A clear identification of the specific records to be copied. Requests should include the following specific information, if possible:

(A) the type of work involved (for example, novel, lyrics, photograph);

(B) the registration number;

(C) the year date or approximate year date of registration;

(D) the complete title of the work;

(E) the author(s) including any pseudonym by which the author may be known; and

(F) the claimant(s); and

(G) if the requested copy is of an assignment, license, contract, or other recorded document, the volume and page number of the recorded document.

(iv) If the copy requested is an additional certificate of registration, include the fee. The Records Research and Certification Section will review requests for copies of other records and quote fees for each.

(v) The telephone number and address of the requestor.

(2) Requests for certified or uncertified reproductions of the copies, phonorecords, or identifying material deposited in connection with a copyright registration of published or unpublished works in the custody of the Copyright Office will be granted only when one of the following three conditions has been met:

(i) The Copyright Office receives written authorization from the copyright claimant of record or his or her designated agent, or from the owner of any of the exclusive rights in the copyright as long as this ownership can be demonstrated by written documentation of the transfer of ownership.

(ii) The Copyright Office receives a written request from an attorney on behalf of either the plaintiff or defendant in connection with litigation, actual or prospective, involving the copyrighted work. The following information must be included in such a request: (A) The names of all the parties involved and the nature of the controversy; (B) the name of the court in which the actual case is pending or, in the case of a prospective proceeding, a full statement of the facts of the controversy in which the copyrighted work is involved; and (C) satisfactory assurance that the requested reproduction will be used only in connection with the specified litigation.

(iii) The Copyright Office receives a court order for reproduction of the deposited copies, phonorecords, or identifying material of a registered work which is the subject of litigation. The order must be issued by a court having jurisdiction of the case in which the reproduction is to be submitted as evidence.

(3) When a request is made for a reproduction of a phonorecord, such as an audiotape or cassette, in which either a sound recording or the underlying musical, dramatic, or literary work is embodied, the Copyright Office will provide proximate reproduction. The Copyright Office reserves the right to substitute a monaural reproduction for a stereo, quadraphonic, or any other type of fixation of the work accepted for deposit.

(e) Requests for removal of requested personally identifiable information from the online public catalog. (1) In general, an author, claimant of record, or the authorized representative of the author or claimant of record may submit a request to remove certain categories of personally identifiable information ("PII") described in paragraph (e)(2) of this section from the Copyright Office's online public catalog by following the procedure set forth in paragraph (e)(3) of this section. Where the requester provides verifiable, non-personally identifiable substitute information to replace the PII being removed, the Office will grant the request unless it determines that the need to maintain the original information in the public record substantially outweighs the safety, privacy, or other stated concern. If the requester does not provide verifiable, non-personally-identifiable substitute information, the Office will grant the request only if the safety, privacy, or other stated concern substantially outweighs the need for the information to remain in the public record. The Office will review requests by joint authors or claimants on a case-by-case basis.

(2) Categories of personally identifiable information that may be removed from the online public catalog include names, home addresses, personal telephone and fax numbers, personal email addresses, and other information that is requested by the Office as part the copyright registration application except that:

(i) Requests for removal of driver's license numbers, social security numbers, banking information, credit card information and other extraneous PII covered by paragraph (f) of this section are governed by the provisions of that paragraph.

(ii) Requests to remove the address of a copyright claimant must be accompanied by a verifiable substitute address. The Office will not remove the address of a copyright claimant unless such a verifiable substitute address is provided.

(iii) Names of authors or claimants may not be removed or replaced with a pseudonym. Requests to substitute the prior name of the author or claimant with the current legal name of the author or claimant must be accompanied by official documentation of the legal name change.

(3) Requests for removal of PII from the online catalog must be in the form of an affidavit, must be accompanied by the non-refundable fee listed in §201.3(c), and must include the following information:

(i) The copyright registration number(s).

(ii) The name of the author and/or claimant of record on whose behalf the request is made.

(iii) Identification of the specific PII that is to be removed.

(iv) If applicable, verifiable non-personally-identifiable substitute information that should replace the PII to be removed.

(v) In the case of requests to replace the names of authors or claimants, the request must be accompanied by a court order granting a legal name change.

(vi) A statement providing the reasons supporting the request. If the requester is not providing verifiable, non-personally-identifiable substitute information to replace the PII to be removed, this statement must explain in detail the specific threat to the individual's personal safety or personal security, or other circumstances, supporting the request.

(vii) The statement, "I declare under penalty of perjury that the foregoing is true and correct."

(viii) If the submission is by an authorized representative of the author or claimant of record, an additional statement, "I am authorized to make this request on behalf of [name of author or claimant of record]."

(ix) The signature of the author, claimant of record, or the authorized representative of the author or claimant of record.

(x) The date on which the request was signed.

(xi) A physical mailing address to which the Office's response may be sent (if no email is provided).

(xii) A telephone number.

(xiii) An email address (if available).

(4) Requests under this paragraph (e) must be mailed to the address listed in §201.1(c).

(5) A properly submitted request will be reviewed by the Associate Register of Copyrights and Director of the Office Public Information and Education or his or her designee(s) to determine whether the request should be granted or denied. The Office will mail its decision to either grant or deny the request to the address indicated in the request.

(6) If the request is granted, the Office will remove the information from the online public catalog. Where substitute information has been provided, the Office will add that information to the online public catalog. In addition, a note indicating that the online record has been modified will be added to the online registration record. A new certificate of registration will be issued that reflects the modified information. The Office will maintain a copy of the original registration record on file in the Copyright Office, and such records shall be open to public inspection and copying pursuant to paragraphs (b), (c), and (d) of this section. The Office will also maintain in its offline records the correspondence related to the request to remove PII.

(7) Requests for reconsideration of denied requests to remove PII from the online public catalog must be made in writing within 30 days from the date of the denial letter. The request for reconsideration, and a non-refundable fee in the amount specified in §201.3(c), must be mailed to the address listed in §201.1(c). The request must specifically address the grounds for denial of the initial request. Only one request for reconsideration will be considered per denial.

(f) Requests for removal of extraneous PII from the public record. Upon written request, the Office will remove driver's license numbers, social security numbers, banking information, credit card information, and other extraneous PII that was erroneously included on a registration application from the public record. There is no fee for this service. To make a request, the author, claimant, or the authorized representative of the author or claimant, must submit the request in writing using the contact information listed in §201.1(c). Such a request must name the author and/or claimant, provide the registration number(s) associated for the record in question, and give a description of the extraneous PII that is to be removed. Once the request is received, the Office will remove the extraneous information from both its online and offline public records. The Office will not include any notation of this action in its records.

History of 37 C.F.R. §201.2: 24 FR 4955, June 18, 1959; 32 FR 9315, June 30, 1967; 42 FR 2962, Jan. 14, 1977; 50 FR 30170, July 24, 1985; 51 FR 30062, Aug. 22, 1986; 62 FR 35421, July 1, 1997; 64 FR 29520, June 1, 1999; 69 FR 39332, June 30, 2004; 69 FR 70377, Dec. 6, 2004; 73 FR 37838, July 1, 2008; 78 FR 42873, July 18, 2013; 82 FR 9007, Mar. 6, 2017; 82 FR 9355, Mar. 8, 2017; 82 FR 21697, May 10, 2017.

A §201.3. FEES FOR REGISTRATION, RECORDATION, & RELATED SERVICES, SPECIAL SERVICES, & SERVICES PERFORMED BY THE LICENSING DIVISION

(a) General. This section prescribes the fees for registration, recordation, and related services, special services, and services performed by the Licensing Division.

(b) Definitions. For purposes of this section, the following definitions apply:

(1) Registration, recordation, and related service fee. This is the fee for a registration or recordation service that the Office is required to perform under 17 U.S.C., or a directly related service. It includes those services described in section 708(a)(1)-(9) and authorized by Pub.L. 105-80.

(2) Special service fee. This is a fee for a special service not specified in title 17, which the Register of Copyrights may fix at any time on the basis of the cost of providing the service, as provided by 17 U.S.C. 708(a).

(3) Licensing Division service fee. This is a fee for a service performed by the Licensing Division.

(c) Registration, recordation, and related service fees. The Copyright Office has established the following fees for these services:

	Registration, Recordation, & Related Services	Fees
(1)	Registration of a standard claim in an original work of authorship: Electronic filing: (i) Single author, same claimant, one work, not for hire (ii) All other filings Paper Filing (Forms PA, SR, TX, VA, SE, SR)	 $35 $55 $85
(2)	Registration of a claim in a group of contributions to periodicals or a group of database updates	$85
(3)	Registration of a claim in a group of published photographs or a claim in a group of unpublished photographs	$55
(4)	Registration for a database that predominantly consists of photographs and updates thereto: (i) Electronic filing (ii) Paper filing	 $55 $65
(5)	Registration of a renewal claim (Form RE): (i) Claim without addendum (ii) Addendum (in addition to the fee for the claim)	 $100 $100
(6)	Registration of a claim in a group of serials (Form SE/Group) (per issue, minimum 2 issues)	$25
(7)	Registration of a claim in a group of newspapers or a group of newsletters	$80
(8)	Registration of a claim in a restored copyright (Form GATT)	$85
(9)	Preregistration of certain unpublished works	$140
(10)	Registration of a correction or amplification to a claim: (i) Supplementary registration: Electronic filing or paper filing (ii) Correction of a design registration: Form DC	 $130 $100
(11)	Registration of a claim in a mask work (Form MW)	$120
(12)	Registration of a claim in a vessel design (Form D/VH)	$400
(13)	Provision of an additional certificate of registration	$40
(14)	Certification of other Copyright Office records, including search reports (per hour)	$200
(15)	Search report prepared from official records other than Licensing Division records (per hour, 2 hour minimum) Estimate of search fee (credited to search fee)	$200 $200
(16)	Retrieval of in-process or completed Copyright Office records or other Copyright Office materials: (i) Retrieval of paper records (per hour, 1 hour minimum) (ii) Retrieval of digital records (per hour, half hour minimum, quarter hour increments)	 $200 $200
(17)	Recordation of a document, including a notice of intention to enforce Single title Additional titles (per group of 1 to 10 titles) Additional titles provided in an electronic title list 1 to 50 additional titles 51 to 500 additional titles 501 to 1,000 additional titles 1,001 to 10,000 additional titles 10,001 or more additional titles Correction of online Public Catalog data due to erroneous electronic title submission (per title)	 $105 $35 $60 $225 $390 $555 $5,550 $7
(18)	Designation of agent under 17 U.S.C. 512(c)(2) to receive notification of claimed infringement, or amendment or resubmission of designation	$6
(19)	Issuance of a receipt for §407 deposit	$30
(20)	Removal of PII from Registration Records (i) Initial request, per registration record (ii) Reconsideration of denied requests, flat fee	 $130 $60

(d) Special service fees. The Copyright Office has established the following fees for special services of the Office:

	Special Services	Fees
(1)	Service charge for deposit account overdraft	$250
(2)	Service charge for dishonored deposit account replenishment check	$100
(3)	Service charge for an uncollectible or non-negotiable payment	$30
(4)	Appeals:	
	(i) First appeal (per claim)	$250
	(ii) Second appeal (per claim)	$500
(5)	Secure test examining fee (per staff member per hour)	$250
(6)	Copying of Copyright Office records by staff:	
	Photocopy (black & white, 8½ x 11) (per page, minimum: $12)	$0.50
	Photocopy (black & white, 11 x 17) (per page, minimum: $12)	$1
	Photocopy (color, 8½ x 11) (per page, minimum: $12)	$2
	Photocopy (color, 11 x 17) (per page, minimum: $12)	$4
	Audiocassette (first 30 minutes)	$75
	Additional 15 minute increments	$20
	Videocassette (first 30 minutes)	$75
	Additional 15 minute increments	$20
	CD or DVD	$30
	Flash drive	$30
	Unsupported formats and other copying of materials by outside providers, at cost of provider	Variable
(7)	Special handling fee for a claim	$800
	Handling fee for each non-special handling claim using the same deposit	$50
(8)	Special handling fee for recordation of a document	$550
(9)	Handling fee for extra deposit copy for certification	$50
(10)	Full-term retention of a published deposit	$540
(11)	Special handling of search report, per hour (for up to 2 hours)	$300
	Additional hours of searching, per hour	$500
(12)	Special handling of retrieval, certification, and copying, per hour	$305
(13)	Notice to libraries and archives	$50
	Each additional title	$20
(14)	Service charge for Federal Express mailing	$45
(15)	Service charge for delivery of documents via facsimile (per page, 7 page maximum)	$1

(e) Licensing Division service fees. The Copyright Office has established the following fees for specific services of the Licensing Division:

	Licensing Division Services	Fees
(1)	Recordation of a notice of intention to make and distribute phonorecords (17 U.S.C. 115)	$75
	Additional titles (per group of 1 to 10 titles) (paper filing)	$20
	Additional titles (per group of 1 to 100 titles) (online filing)	$10
(2)	Statement of account amendment (cable television systems and satellite carriers, 17 U.S.C. 111 and 119; digital audio recording devices or media, 17 U.S.C. 1003)	$150
(3)	Recordation of certain contracts by cable TV systems located outside the 48 contiguous states	$50
(4)	Notice of digital transmission of sound recording (17 U.S.C. 112, 114)	$40
	Amended notice of digital transmission of sound recording	$40

LICENSING DIVISION SERVICES	FEES
(5) Processing of a statement of account based on secondary transmissions of primary transmissions pursuant to 17 U.S.C. 111:	
(i) Form SA1	$15
(ii) Form SA2	$20
(iii) Form SA3	$725
(6) Processing of a statement of account based on secondary transmissions of primary transmissions pursuant to 17 U.S.C. 119 or 122	$725
(7) Search report prepared from Licensing Division records (per hour, 1 hour minimum)	$200

(f) Fees for travel in connection with educational activities. For travel expenses in connection with Copyright Office educational activities when participation by Copyright Office personnel has been requested by another organization or person and that organization or person has agreed to pay such expenses, collection of the fee shall be subject to, and the amount of the fee shall be no greater than, the amount authorized under the Federal Travel Regulations found in Chapters 300 through 304 of Title 41.

History of 37 C.F.R. §201.3: 64 FR 29520, June 1, 1999; 64 FR 36574, July 7, 1999; 65 FR 39819, June 28, 2000; 67 FR 38005, May 31, 2002; 71 FR 31090, June 1, 2006; 71 FR 46402, Aug. 14, 2006; 72 FR 33961, July 1, 2007; 74 FR 12556, Mar. 25, 2009; 74 FR 32807, Aug. 1, 2009; 77 FR 18705, 18707, Mar. 28, 2012; 79 FR 15918, May 1, 2014; 79 FR 24334, Apr. 30, 2014; 79 FR 68623, Nov. 18, 2014; 81 FR 75707, Dec. 1, 2016; 82 FR 9008, Mar. 6, 2017; 82 FR 9356, Mar. 8, 2017; 82 FR 26853, July 12, 2017; 82 FR 27427, July 17, 2017; 82 FR 29413, July 31, 2017; 82 FR 52223, Dec. 18, 2017; 83 FR 2547, Feb. 20, 2018; 83 FR 4146, Mar. 1, 2018.

A §201.4. RECORDATION OF TRANSFERS & OTHER DOCUMENTS PERTAINING TO COPYRIGHT

(a) General. This section prescribes conditions for the recordation of transfers of copyright ownership and other documents pertaining to a copyright under 17 U.S.C. 205. A document is eligible for recordation under this section if it meets the requirements of paragraph (d) of this section, if it is submitted in accordance with the submission procedure described in paragraph (e) of this section, and if it is accompanied by the fee specified in §201.3(c). The date of recordation is the date when all of the elements required for recordation, including a proper document, fee, and any additional required information, are received in the Copyright Office. After recordation the document is returned to the sender with a certificate of recordation. The Office may reject any document submitted for recordation that fails to comply with 17 U.S.C. 205, the requirements of this section, or any relevant instructions or guidance provided by the Office.

(b) Documents not recordable under this section. This section does not govern the filing or recordation of the following documents:

(1) Certain contracts entered into by cable systems located outside of the 48 contiguous States (17 U.S.C. 111(e); see §201.12);

(2) Notices of identity and signal carriage complement, and statements of account of cable systems and satellite carriers and for digital audio recording devices and media (17 U.S.C. 111(d), 119(b), and 1003(c); see §§201.11, 201.17, 201.28);

(3) Notices of intention to obtain a compulsory license to make and distribute phonorecords of nondramatic musical works (17 U.S.C. 115(b); see §201.18);

(4) Notices of termination (17 U.S.C. 203, 304(c) and (d); see §201.10);

(5) Statements regarding the identity of authors of anonymous and pseudonymous works, and statements relating to the death of authors (17 U.S.C. 302);

(6) Documents pertaining to computer shareware and donation of public domain software (Pub. L. 101-650, sec. 805; see §201.26);

(7) Notifications from the clerks of the courts of the United States concerning actions brought under title 17, United States Code (17 U.S.C. 508);

(8) Notices to libraries and archives of normal commercial exploitation or availability at reasonable prices (17 U.S.C. 108(h)(2)(C); see §201.39);

(9) Submission of Visual Arts Registry Statements (17 U.S.C. 113; see §201.25);

(10) Notices and correction notices of intent to enforce restored copyrights (17 U.S.C. 104A(e); see §§201.33, 201.34); and

(11) Designations of agents to receive notifications of claimed infringement (17 U.S.C. 512(c)(2); see §201.38).

(c) Definitions. For purposes of this section:

(1) A transfer of copyright ownership has the meaning set forth in 17 U.S.C. 101.

(2) A document pertaining to a copyright is any document that has a direct or indirect relationship to the existence, scope, duration, or identification of a copyright, or to the ownership, division, allocation, licensing, or exercise of rights under a copyright. That relationship may be past, present, future, or potential.

(3) An actual signature is any legally binding signature, including an electronic signature as defined in 15 U.S.C. 7006.

(4) A sworn certification is a statement made in accordance with 28 U.S.C. 1746 that the copy of the document submitted for recordation is, to the best of the certifier's knowledge, a true copy of the original, signed document. A sworn certification must be signed by one of the parties to the signed document, a successor-in-interest to one of the parties to the signed document, or the authorized representative of such a party or successor. Authorized representatives must state who they represent and successors-in-interest must describe their relationship to the document or the original parties to the document. An authorized representative of a successor-in-interest must describe the successor's relationship to the document or the original parties to the document. A sworn certification may be signed electronically.

(5) An official certification is a certification, by the appropriate governmental official, that the original of the document is on file in a public office and that the copy of the document submitted for recordation is a true copy of the original. An official certification may be signed electronically.

(d) Document requirements—**(1)** Original or certified copy. The remitter must submit either the original document that bears the actual signature(s) of the person(s) who executed it, or a copy of the original, signed document accompanied by a sworn certification or an official certification. Each document submitted for recordation must be certified to either have the actual signature(s) (if it is an original document) or reproduce the actual signature(s) (in the case of a copy of the original document). All documents lacking a handwritten, wet signature (including all documents bearing an electronic signature) are considered to be copies of the original, signed document, and must be accompanied by a sworn certification or an official certification. Where an actual signature on the relevant document is not a handwritten or typewritten name, such as when an individual clicks a button on a Web site or application to indicate agreement to contractual terms, the remitter must submit a description of the nature of the signature and documentation evidencing the existence of the signature (e.g., a database entry or confirmation email showing that a particular user agreed to the terms by clicking "yes" on a particular date). Where such description and evidence are provided, the Office will make them available for public inspection and may presume that the signature requirement for recordation has been satisfied, without prejudice to any party claiming otherwise, including before a court of competent jurisdiction.

(2) Completeness. Each document submitted for recordation must be, and be certified to be, complete by its terms, but need only include referenced schedules, appendices, exhibits, addenda, or other material essential to understanding the copyright-related aspects of the document.

(3) Legibility. Each document submitted for recordation must be, and be certified to be, legible.

(4) Redactions. The Office will accept and make available for public inspection redacted documents certified to be redacted in accordance with this paragraph (d)(4), provided that all of the following conditions are satisfied:

(i) The redactions must be limited to financial terms, trade secret information, Social Security or taxpayer-identification numbers, and financial account numbers. Additional types of information may be redacted on a case-by-case basis if the need for any such redactions is justified to the Office in writing and approved by the Office; such written requests should be included in the remitter's recordation submission to the Office.

(ii) The blank or blocked-out portions of the document must be labeled "redacted" or the equivalent.

(iii) Each portion of the document required by paragraph (d)(2) of this section must be included.

(5) English language requirement. The Office will accept and record non-English language documents and indexing information only if accompanied by an English translation that is either signed by the individual making the translation or, if a publicly available commercial or consumer translation software product or automated service is used, by the individual using such product or service and accompanied by the name of the product or service. All translations will be made available for public inspection and may be redacted in accordance with paragraph (d)(4) of this section.

(e) Paper submission procedure—**(1)** Process. A document may be submitted for recordation by sending it to the appropriate address in §201.1(b) or to such other address as the Office may specify, accompanied by a cover sheet, the proper fee, and, if applicable, any electronic title list. Absent special arrangement with the Office, the Office reserves the right to not process the submission unless all of the items necessary for processing are received together.

(2) Cover sheet required. Submission of a document must include a completed Recordation Document Cover Sheet (Form DCS), available on the Copyright Office Web site. Remitters must follow all instructions provided by the Office in completing Form DCS, including by providing all requested indexing information. Form DCS may be used to provide a sworn certification, if appropriate, and to make any of the other certifications required by this section. Form DCS will not be considered part of the recorded document, but will be used by the Office for examination, indexing, and other administrative purposes. The Office may reject any document submitted for recordation that includes an improperly prepared cover sheet.

(3) Electronic title list. **(i)** In addition to identifying the works to which a document pertains in the paper submission, the remitter may also submit an electronic list setting forth each such work. The electronic list will not be considered part of the recorded document, but will be used by the Office for indexing purposes. Absent special arrangement with the Office, the electronic list must be included in the same package as the paper document to be recorded. The electronic list must be prepared and submitted to the Office in the manner specified by the Copyright Office in instructions made available on its Web site. The Office may reject any document submitted for recordation that includes an improperly prepared electronic title list.

(ii) If a remitter of a recorded document finds that an error or omission in an electronic title list has led to the inaccurate indexing of the document in the public catalog, the remitter may request that the record be corrected by following the instructions provided by the Office on its Web site. Upon receipt of a properly prepared corrective filing and the appropriate fee, the Office will proceed to correct the information in the public catalog, and will make a note in the record indicating that the corrections were made and the date they were made.

(4) Return receipt. If a remitter includes two copies of a properly completed Form DCS indicating that a return receipt is requested, as well as a self-addressed, postage-paid envelope, the remitter will receive a date-stamped return receipt attached to the extra copy acknowledging the Copyright Office's receipt of the enclosed submission. The completed copies of Form DCS and the self-addressed, postage-paid envelope must be included in the same package as the submitted document. A return receipt confirms the Office's receipt of the submission as of the date indicated, but does not establish eligibility for, or the date of, recordation.

(5) Remitter certification. The remitter must certify that he or she has appropriate authority to submit the document for recordation and that all information submitted to the Office by the remitter is true, accurate, and complete to the best of the remitter's knowledge.

(f) Reliance on remitter-provided information. The Copyright Office will rely on the certifications submitted with a document and the information provided by the remitter on Form DCS and, if provided, in an accompanying electronic title list. The Office will not necessarily confirm the accuracy of such certifications or information against the submitted document.

(g) Effect of recordation. The fact that the Office has recorded a document is not a determination by the Office of the document's validity or legal effect. Recordation of a document by the Copyright Office is without prejudice to any party claiming that the legal or formal requirements for recordation have not been met, including before a court of competent jurisdiction.

History of 37 C.F.R. §201.4: 43 FR 35044, Aug. 8, 1978; 53 FR 123, Jan. 5, 1988; 56 FR 59885, Nov. 26, 1991; 64 FR 29521, June 1, 1999; 65 FR 39819, June 28, 2000; 67 FR 69136, Nov. 15, 2002; 70 FR 38022, July 1, 2005; 74 FR 12556, Mar. 25, 2009; 77 FR 71103, Jan. 14, 2013; 79 FR 55635, Sept. 17, 2014; 79 FR 68623, Nov. 18, 2014; 82 FR 9356, Mar. 8, 2017; 82 FR 52219, Dec. 18, 2017.

§201.5. RESERVED

§201.6. PAYMENT & REFUND OF COPYRIGHT OFFICE FEES

(a) In general. All fees sent to the Copyright Office should be in the form of a money order, check or bank draft payable to the U.S. Copyright Office. Coin or currency sent to the Office in letters or packages will be at the remitter's risk. Remittances from foreign countries should be in the form of an International Money Order or Bank Draft payable and immediately negotiable in the United States for the full amount of the fee required. Uncertified checks are accepted subject to collection. Where the statutory fee is submitted in the form of a check, the registration of the copyright claim or other record made by the Office is provisional until payment in money is received. In the event the fee is not paid, the registration or other record shall be expunged.

(b) Deposit accounts. **(1)** Persons or firms having 12 or more transactions a year with the Copyright Office may prepay copyright expenses by establishing a Deposit Account. The Office and the Deposit Account holder will cooperatively determine an appropriate minimum balance for the Deposit Account which, in no case, can be less than $450, and the Office will automatically notify the Deposit Account holder when the account goes below that balance.

(2) The Copyright Office will close a Deposit Account the second time the Deposit Account holder overdraws his or her account within any 12-month period. An account closed for this reason can be re-opened only if the holder elects to fund it through automatic replenishment.

(3) In order to ensure that a Deposit Account's funds are sufficiently maintained, a Deposit Account holder may authorize the Copyright Office to automatically replenish the account from the holder's bank account or credit card. The amount by which a Deposit Account will be replenished will be determined by the deposit account holder. Automatic replenishment will be triggered when the Deposit Account goes below the minimum level of funding established pursuant to paragraph (b)(1) of this section, and Deposit Account holders will be automatically notified that their accounts will be replenished.

(c) Refunds. **(1)** Money remitted to the Copyright Office for basic, supplementary or renewal registration, including mask works and vessel designs, will not be refunded if the claim is rejected because the material deposited does not constitute copyrightable subject matter or because the claim is invalid for any other reason. Payments made by mistake or in excess of the fee will be refunded, but amounts of $50 or less will not be refunded unless specifically requested. Except for services specified in paragraphs (c)(2) and (3) of this section, before making any refund for fees remitted in relation to non-registration copyright services, the Copyright Office shall deduct an administrative processing fee in an amount equivalent to one hour of the requested service, or the minimum charge for the service.

(2) In instances where money has been remitted to pay for recordation of a document, and it is determined that the document cannot be recorded, the basic recordation fee covering one title will be retained as a filing fee. Any additional money over the basic fee for one title will be refunded, but amounts of $50 or less will not be refunded unless specifically requested.

(3) For services where fees are calculated on an hourly basis, such as preparation of a search report, certification of certain Copyright Office records, or location and retrieval of records, in instances where the request is withdrawn before work is begun by the staff member responsible for providing the service, the Copyright Office will retain half of the hourly charge for administrative expenses, and refund the remaining portion of the fee subject to paragraph (c)(1) of this section. In addition, the fee for an estimate of a search fee is non-refundable. This policy applies to requests to the Records Research and Certification Section, and requests to the Licensing Division.

(d) Return of deposit copies. Copies of works deposited in the Copyright Office pursuant to law are either retained in the Copyright Office, transferred for use in the permanent collections or other uses of the Library of Congress, or disposed of according to law. When an application is rejected, the Copyright Office reserves the right to retain the deposited copies.

History of 37 C.F.R. §201.6: 24 FR 4955, June 18, 1959; 46 FR 25442, May 7, 1981; 56 FR 7813, Feb. 26, 1991; 59 FR 38371, July 28, 1994; 74 FR 32809, Aug. 1, 2009; 76 FR 9231, May 1, 2011; 82 FR 9356, Mar. 8, 2017.

A §201.7. CANCELLATION OF COMPLETED REGISTRATIONS

(a) Definition. Cancellation is an action taken by the Copyright Office whereby either the registration is eliminated on the ground that the registration is invalid under the applicable law and regulations, or the registration number is eliminated and a new registration is made under a different class and number.

(b) General policy. The Copyright Office will cancel a completed registration only in those cases where: (1) It is clear that no registration should have been made because the work does not constitute copyrightable subject matter or fails to satisfy the other legal and formal requirements for obtaining copyright; (2) registration may be authorized but the application, deposit material, or fee does not meet the requirements of the law and Copyright Office regulations, and the Office is unable to get the defect corrected; or (3) an existing registration in the wrong class is to be replaced by a new registration in the correct class.

(c) Circumstances under which a registration will be cancelled.

(1) Where the Copyright Office becomes aware after registration that a work is not copyrightable, either because the authorship is insufficiently creative or the work does not contain authorship subject to copyright, the registration will be cancelled. The copyright claimant will be notified by correspondence of the proposed cancellation and the reasons therefor, and be given 30 days, from the date the Copyright Office letter is mailed, to show cause in writing why the cancellation should not be made. If the claimant fails to respond within the 30 day period, or if the Office after considering the response, determines that the registration was made in error and not in accordance with U.S. copyright law, the registration will be cancelled.

(2) When a check received in payment of a registration fee is returned to the Copyright Office marked "insufficient funds" or is otherwise uncollectible the Copyright Office will immediately cancel any registration(s) for which the dishonored check was submitted and will notify the applicant the registration has been cancelled because the check was returned as uncollectible.

(3) Where registration is made in the wrong class, the Copyright Office will cancel the first registration, replace it with a new registration in the correct class, and issue a corrected certificate.

(4) Where registration has been made for a work which appears to be copyrightable but after registration the Copyright Office becomes aware that, on the administrative record before the Office, the statutory requirements have apparently not been satisfied, or that information essential to registration has been omitted entirely from the application or is questionable, or correct deposit material has not been deposited, the Office will correspond with the copyright claimant in an attempt to secure the required information or deposit material or to clarify the information previously given on the application. If the Copyright Office receives no reply to its correspondence within 30 days of the date the letter is mailed, or the response does not resolve the substantive defect, the registration will be cancelled. The correspondence will include the reason for the cancellation. The following are examples of instances where a completed registration will be cancelled unless the substantive defect in the registration can be cured:

(i) Eligibility for registration has not been established.

(ii) A work published before March 1, 1989 was registered more than 5 years after the date of first publication and the deposit copy or phonorecord does not contain a statutory copyright notice.

(iii) The deposit copies or phonorecords of a work published before January 1, 1978 do not contain a copyright notice or the notice is defective.

(iv) A renewal claim was registered after the statutory time limits for registration had apparently expired.

(v) The application and copy(s) or phonorecord(s) do not match each other and the Office cannot locate a copy or phonorecord as described in the application elsewhere in the Copyright Office or the Library of Congress.

(vi) The application for registration does not identify a copyright claimant or it appears from the transfer statement on the application or elsewhere that the "claimant" named in the application does not have the right to claim copyright.

(vii) A claim to copyright is based on material added to a preexisting work and a reading of the application in its totality indicates that there is no copyrightable new material on which to base a claim.

(viii) A work subject to the manufacturing provisions of the Act of 1909 was apparently published in violation of those provisions.

(ix) A work is not anonymous or pseudonymous and statements on the application and/or copy vary so much that the author cannot be identified.

(x) Statements on the application conflict or are so unclear that the claimant cannot be adequately identified.

(xi) The requirements for registering a group of related works under section 408(c) of title 17 of the United States Code have not been met.

(d) Minor substantive errors. Where a registration includes minor substantive errors or omissions which would generally have been rectified before registration, the Copyright Office will attempt to rectify the error through correspondence with the applicant. Except in those cases enumerated in paragraph (c) of this section, if the Office is unable for any reason to obtain the correct information or deposit copy, the registration record will be annotated to state the nature of the informality and show that the Copyright Office attempted to correct the registration.

History of 37 C.F.R. §201.7: 50 FR 40835, Oct. 7, 1985; 60 FR 34168, June 30, 1995; 65 FR 39819, June 28, 2000; 66 FR 34372, June 28, 2001; 82 FR 9356, Mar. 8, 2017; 82 FR 29413, July 31, 2017.

A §201.8. DISRUPTION OF POSTAL OR OTHER TRANSPORTATION OR COMMUNICATION SERVICES

(a) Declaration of disruption. For purposes of 17 U.S.C. 709, when the Register has determined that there is or has been a general disruption or suspension of postal or other transportation or communications services, including a disruption or suspension of a Copyright Office electronic system, that has delayed the receipt by the Copyright Office of applications, fees, deposits, or any other materials, the Register shall publish an announcement of that determination, stating the date on which the disruption or suspension commenced. The announcement may, if appropriate, limit the means of delivery that are subject to relief pursuant to section 709. Following the cessation of the disruption or suspension of services, the Register shall publish an announcement stating the date on which the disruption or suspension has terminated, and may provide specific instructions on how to make a request under paragraph (b)(1) of this section.

(b) Request for earlier filing date due to disruption—(1) When the Register has declared a disruption. When the Register has made a declaration of disruption under paragraph (a) of this section, any person who, in compliance with any instructions provided by the Register, provides satisfactory evidence as described in paragraph (e) of this section that he or she attempted to deliver an application, fee, deposit, or other material to the Copyright Office, but that receipt by the Copyright Office was delayed due to a general disruption or suspension of postal or other transportation or communications services announced under paragraph (a), shall be assigned, as the date of receipt of the application, fee, deposit, or other material, the date on which the Register determines the material would have been received but for the disruption or suspension of services, so long as the application, fee, deposit, or other material was actually received in the Copyright Office within one month after the date the Register identifies pursuant to paragraph (a) of this section that disruption or suspension of services has terminated. Such requests should be mailed to the address specified in §201.1(c)(1), or through any other delivery method the Register specifies in a published announcement under paragraph (a) of this section.

(2) With respect to disruption affecting specific submission. In the absence of a declaration of disruption under paragraph (a) of this section, any person who provides satisfactory evidence as described in paragraph (e) of this section that he or she physically delivered or attempted to physically deliver an application, fee, deposit, or other material to the Copyright Office, but that the Office did not receive that material or that it was lost or misplaced by the Office after its delivery to the Office, shall be assigned, as the date of receipt, the date that the Register determines that the material was received or would have been received. Such requests may be mailed to the address specified in §201.1(c)(1), or through any other delivery method specified by the Copyright Office.

(c) Timing. (1) A request under paragraph (b)(1) of this section shall be made no earlier than the date on which the Register publishes the announcement under paragraph (a) of this section declaring that the disruption or suspension has terminated, and no later than one year after the publication of that announcement.

(2) A request under paragraph (b)(2) of this section shall be made no later than one year after the person physically delivered or attempted to physically deliver the application, fee, deposit, or other material to the Copyright Office.

(d) Return of certificate. In cases where a certificate of registration or a certificate of recordation has already been issued, the original certificate must be returned to the Copyright Office along with the request under paragraph (b) of this section.

(e) Satisfactory evidence. In all cases the Register shall have discretion in determining whether materials submitted with a request under paragraph (b) of this section constitute satisfactory evidence. For purposes of paragraph (b) of this section, satisfactory evidence may include:

(1) A receipt from the United States Postal Service indicating the date on which the United States Postal Service received material for delivery to the Copyright Office by means of first class mail, Priority Mail, or Express Mail;

(2) A receipt from a delivery service such as, or comparable to, United Parcel Service, Federal Express, or Airborne Express, indicating the date on which the delivery service received material for delivery to the Copyright Office; and

(i) The date on which delivery was to be made to the Copyright Office, or

(ii) The period of time (e.g., overnight, or two days) from receipt by the delivery service to the date on which delivery was to be made to the Copyright Office;

(3) A statement under penalty of perjury, pursuant to 28 U.S.C. 1746, from a person with actual knowledge of the facts relating to the attempt to deliver the material to the Copyright Office, setting forth with particularity facts which satisfy the Register that in the absence of the general disruption or suspension of postal or other transportation or communications services, including a disruption or suspension of a Copyright Office electronic system, or but for the misdelivery, misplacement, or loss of materials sent to the Copyright Office, the material would have been received by the Copyright Office by a particular date; or

(4) Other documentary evidence which the Register deems equivalent to the evidence set forth in paragraphs (e)(1) and (2) of this section.

(f) Presumption of receipt. For purposes of paragraph (b) of this section, the Register shall presume that but for the general disruption or suspension of postal or other transportation or communications services, including a disruption or suspension of a Copyright Office electronic system, or but for the misdelivery, misplacement, or loss of materials sent to the Copyright Office:

(1) Materials deposited with the United States Postal Service for delivery by means of first class mail would have been received in the Copyright Office seven days after deposit with the United States Postal Service;

(2) Materials deposited with the United States Postal Service for delivery by means of Priority Mail would have been received in the Copyright Office three days after deposit with the United States Postal Service;

(3) Materials deposited with the United States Postal Service for delivery by means of Express Mail would have been received in the Copyright Office one day after deposit with the United States Postal Service;

(4) Materials deposited with a delivery service such as, or comparable to, United Parcel Service, Federal Express, or Airborne Express, would have been received in the Copyright Office on the date indicated on the receipt from the delivery service;

(5) Materials submitted or attempted to be submitted through a Copyright Office electronic system would have been received in the Copyright Office on the date the attempt was made. If it is unclear when an attempt was made, the Register will determine the effective date of receipt on a case-by-case basis.

History of 37 C.F.R. §201.8: 66 FR 62944, Dec. 4, 2001; 66 FR 63920, Dec. 11, 2001; 73 FR 37838, July 1, 2008; 78 FR 42874, July 18, 2013; 82 FR 9356, Mar. 8, 2017; 82 FR 22887, June 19, 2017.

§201.9. REMOVED & RESERVED

A §201.10. NOTICES OF TERMINATION OF TRANSFERS & LICENSES

This section covers notices of termination of transfers and licenses under 17 U.S.C. 203, 304(c), and 304(d). A termination under section 304(d) is possible only if no termination was made under section 304(c), and federal copyright was originally secured on or between January 1, 1923, and October 26, 1939.

(a) Form. The Copyright Office does not provide printed forms for the use of persons serving notices of termination.

(b) Contents.

(1) A notice of termination covering the extended renewal term under 17 U.S.C. 304(c) and 304(d) must include a clear identification of each of the following:

(i) Whether the termination is made under section 304(c) or under section 304(d);

(ii) The name of each grantee whose rights are being terminated, or the grantee's successor in title, and each address at which service of the notice is being made;

(iii) The title and the name of at least one author of, and the date copyright was originally secured in, each work to which the notice of termination applies; and, if possible and practicable, the original copyright registration number;

(iv) A brief statement reasonably identifying the grant to which the notice of termination applies;

(v) The effective date of termination;

(vi) If termination is made under section 304(d), a statement that termination of renewal term rights under section 304(c) has not been previously exercised; and

(vii) In the case of a termination of a grant executed by a person or persons other than the author, a listing of the surviving person or persons who executed the grant. In the case of a termination of a grant executed by one or more of the authors of the work where the termination is exercised by the successors of a deceased author, a listing of the names and relationships to that deceased author of all of the following, together with specific indication of the person or persons executing the notice who constitute more than one-half of that author's termination interest: That author's surviving widow or widower; and all of that author's surviving children; and, where any of that author's children are dead, all of the surviving children of any such deceased child of that author; however, instead of the information required by this paragraph (vii), the notice may contain both of the following:

(A) A statement of as much of such information as is currently available to the person or persons signing the notice, with a brief explanation of the reasons why full information is or may be lacking; together with

(B) A statement that, to the best knowledge and belief of the person or persons signing the notice, the notice has been signed by all persons whose signature is necessary to terminate the grant under 17 U.S.C. 304 or by their duly authorized agents.

(2) A notice of termination of an exclusive or nonexclusive grant of a transfer or license of copyright or of any right under a copyright, executed by the author on or after January 1, 1978, under 17 U.S.C. 203 must include a clear identification of each of the following:

(i) A statement that the termination is made under section 203;

(ii) The name of each grantee whose rights are being terminated, or the grantee's successor in title, and each address at which service of the notice is being made;

(iii) The date of execution of the grant being terminated and, if the grant covered the right of publication of a work, the date of publication of the work under the grant;

(iv) For each work to which the notice of termination applies, the title of the work and the name of the author or, in the case of a joint work, the authors who executed the grant being terminated; and, if possible and practicable, the original copyright registration number;

(v) A brief statement reasonably identifying the grant to which the notice of termination applies;

(vi) The effective date of termination; and

(vii) In the case of a termination of a grant executed by one or more of the authors of the work where the termination is exercised by the successors of a deceased author, a listing of the names and relationships to that deceased author of all of the following, together with specific indication of the person or persons executing the notice who constitute more than one-half of that author's termination interest: That author's surviving widow or widower; and all of that author's surviving children; and, where any of that author's children are dead, all of the surviving children of any such deceased child of that author; however, instead of the information required by this paragraph (b)(2)(vii), the notice may contain both of the following:

(A) A statement of as much of such information as is currently available to the person or persons signing the notice, with a brief explanation of the reasons why full information is or may be lacking; together with

(B) A statement that, to the best knowledge and belief of the person or persons signing the notice, the notice has been signed by all persons whose signature is necessary to terminate the grant under 17 U.S.C. 203, or by their duly authorized agents.

(3) Clear identification of the information specified by paragraphs (b)(1) and (b)(2) of this section requires a complete and unambiguous statement of facts in the notice itself, without incorporation by reference of information in other documents or records.

(c) Signature.

(1) In the case of a termination of a grant under section 304(c) or section 304(d) executed by a person or persons other than the author, the notice shall be signed by all of the surviving person or persons who executed the grant, or by their duly authorized agents.

(2) In the case of a termination of a grant under section 304(c) or section 304(d) executed by one or more of the authors of the work, the notice as to any one author's share shall be signed by that author or by his or her duly authorized agent. If that author is dead, the notice shall be signed by the number and proportion of the owners of that author's termination interest required under 17 U.S.C. 304(c) or 304(d), whichever applies, or by their duly authorized agents, and shall contain a brief statement of their relationship or relationships to that author.

(3) In the case of a termination of a grant under section 203 executed by one or more of the authors of the work, the notice shall be signed by each author who is terminating the grant or by his or her duly authorized agent. If that author is dead, the notice shall be signed by the number and proportion of the owners of that author's termination interest required under 17 U.S.C. 203, or by their duly authorized agents, and shall contain a brief statement of their relationship or relationships to that author.

(4) Where a signature is by a duly authorized agent, it shall clearly identify the person or persons on whose behalf the agent is acting.

(5) The handwritten signature of each person effecting the termination shall either be accompanied by a statement of the full name and address of that person, typewritten or printed legibly by hand, or shall clearly correspond to such a statement elsewhere in the notice.

(d) Service.

(1) The notice of termination shall be served upon each grantee whose rights are being terminated, or the grantee's successor in title, by personal service, or by first class mail sent to an address which, after a reasonable investigation, is found to be the last known address of the grantee or successor in title.

(2) The service provision of 17 U.S.C. 203, 304(c), or 304(d), whichever applies, will be satisfied if, before the notice of termination is served, a reasonable investigation is made by the person or persons executing the notice as to the current ownership of the rights being terminated, and based on such investigation:

(i) If there is no reason to believe that such rights have been transferred by the grantee to a successor in title, the notice is served on the grantee; or

(ii) If there is reason to believe that such rights have been transferred by the grantee to a particular successor in title, the notice is served on such successor in title.

(3) For purposes of paragraph (d)(2) of this section, a reasonable investigation includes, but is not limited to, a search of the records in the Copyright Office; in the case of a musical composition with respect to which performing rights are licensed by a performing rights society, a reasonable investigation also includes a report from that performing rights society identifying the person or persons claiming current ownership of the rights being terminated.

(4) Compliance with the provisions of paragraphs (d)(2) and (d)(3) of this section will satisfy the service requirements of 17 U.S.C. 203, 304(c), or 304(d), whichever applies. However, as long as the statutory requirements have been met, the failure to comply with the regulatory provisions of paragraph (d)(2) or (d)(3) of this section will not affect the validity of the service.

(e) Harmless errors.

(1) Harmless errors in a notice that do not materially affect the adequacy of the information required to serve the purposes of 17 U.S.C. 203, 304(c), or 304(d), whichever applies, shall not render the notice invalid.

(2) Without prejudice to the general rule provided by paragraph (e)(1) of this section, errors made in giving the date or registration number referred to in paragraph (b)(1)(iii), (b)(2)(iii), or (b)(2)(iv) of this section, or in complying with the provisions of paragraph (b)(1)(vii) or (b)(2)(vii) of this section, or in describing the precise relationships under paragraph (c)(2) or (c)(3) of this section, shall not affect the validity of the notice if the errors were made in good faith and without any intention to deceive, mislead, or conceal relevant information.

(f) Recordation. A copy of a notice of termination shall be recorded in the Copyright Office as required by 17 U.S.C. 203(a)(4)(A), 17 U.S.C. 304(c)(4)(A), or 17 U.S.C. 304(d)(1) if it meets the requirements of paragraph (f)(1) of this section, is submitted in compliance with paragraph (f)(2) of this section, and is accompanied by the fee specified in §201.3(c). The Office may reject any notice submitted for recordation that fails to comply with 17 U.S.C. 203(a), 17 U.S.C. 304(c), 17 U.S.C. 304(d), the requirements of this section, or any relevant instructions or guidance provided by the Office.

(1) Requirements. The following requirements must be met before a copy of a notice of termination may be recorded in the Copyright Office.

(i) What must be submitted—**(A)** Copy of notice of termination. A copy of a notice of termination submitted for recordation must be, and be certified to be, a true, correct, complete, and legible copy of the signed notice of termination as served. Where separate copies of the same notice were served on more than one grantee or successor-in-title, only one copy need be submitted for recordation.

(B) Statement of service. The copy submitted for recordation must be accompanied by a statement setting forth the date on which the notice was served and the manner of service, unless such information is contained in the notice. In instances where service is made by first class mail, the date of service shall be the day the notice of termination was deposited with the United States Postal Service.

(ii) Timeliness. **(A)** The Copyright Office will refuse recordation of a notice of termination as such if, in the judgment of the Copyright Office, such notice of termination is untimely. Conditions under which a notice of termination will be considered untimely include: the effective date of termination does not fall within the five-year period described in section 203(a)(3) or section 304(c)(3), as applicable, of title 17, United States Code; the documents submitted indicate that the notice of termination was served less than two or more than ten years before the effective date of termination; or the date of recordation is after the effective date of termination.

(B) If a notice of termination is untimely, the Office will offer to record the document as a "document pertaining to a copyright" pursuant to §201.4, but the Office will not index the document as a notice of termination.

(C) In any case where an author agreed, prior to January 1, 1978, to a grant of a transfer or license of rights in a work that was not created until on or after January 1, 1978, a notice of termination of a grant under section 203 of title 17 may be recorded if it recites, as the date of execution, the date on which the work was created.

(2) Paper submission procedure—**(i)** Process. A copy of a notice of termination may be submitted for recordation by sending it to the appropriate address in §201.1(c) or to such other address as the Office may specify, accompanied by a cover sheet, the statement of service, and the proper fee.

(ii) Cover sheet required. Submission of a copy of a notice of termination must be accompanied by a completed Recordation Notice of Termination Cover Sheet (Form TCS), available on the Copyright Office Web site. Remitters must follow all instructions provided by the Office in completing Form TCS, including by providing all requested indexing information. Form TCS may be used to provide the statement of service and to make any of the certifications required by this paragraph (f). Form TCS will not be considered part of the recorded notice, but will be used by the Office for examination, indexing, and other administrative purposes. The Office may reject any notice submitted for recordation that includes an improperly prepared cover sheet.

(iii) Return receipt. If a remitter includes two copies of a properly completed Form TCS indicating that a return receipt is requested, as well as a self-addressed, postage-paid envelope, the remitter will receive a date-stamped return receipt attached to the extra copy acknowledging the Copyright Office's receipt of the enclosed submission. The completed copies of Form TCS and the self-addressed, postage-paid envelope must be included in the same package as the submitted notice. A return receipt confirms the Office's receipt of the submission as of the date indicated, but does not establish eligibility for, or the date of, recordation.

(iv) Remitter certification. The remitter must certify that he or she has appropriate authority to submit the notice for recordation and that all information submitted to the Office by the remitter is true, accurate, and complete to the best of the remitter's knowledge.

(3) Date of recordation. The date of recordation is the date when all of the elements required for recordation, including the prescribed fee and, if required, the statement of service, have been received in the Copyright Office. After recordation, the notice, including any accompanying statement, is returned to the sender with a certificate of recordation.

(4) Effect of recordation. The fact that the Office has recorded a notice is not a determination by the Office of the notice's validity or legal effect. Recordation of a notice of termination by the Copyright Office is without prejudice to any party claiming that the legal or formal requirements for effectuating termination (including the requirements pertaining to service and recordation of the notice of termination) have not been met, including before a court of competent jurisdiction.

(5) Reliance on remitter-provided information. The Copyright Office will rely on the certifications submitted with a notice and the information provided by the remitter on Form TCS and, if provided, in an accompanying statement of service. The Office will not necessarily confirm the accuracy of such certifications or information against the submitted notice.

History of 37 C.F.R. §201.10: 42 FR 45920, Sept. 13, 1977; 56 FR 59885, Nov. 26, 1991; 60 FR 34168, June 30, 1995; 64 FR 29521, June 1, 1999; 64 FR 36574, July 7, 1999; 66 FR 34372, June 28, 2001; 67 FR 69136, Nov. 15, 2002; 67 FR 78176, Dec. 23, 2002; 68 FR 16959, Apr. 8, 2003; 71 FR 36486, June 27, 2006; 74 FR 12556, Mar. 25, 2009; 76 FR 32320, June 6, 2011; 78 FR 42874, July 18, 2013; 82 FR 9356, Mar. 8, 2017; 82 FR 52220, Dec. 18, 2017.

§201.11. SATELLITE CARRIER STATEMENTS OF ACCOUNT COVERING STATUTORY LICENSES FOR SECONDARY TRANSMISSIONS

(a) General. This section prescribes rules pertaining to the deposit of Statements of Account and royalty fees in the Copyright Office as required by the satellite carrier license of 17 U.S.C. 119(b)(1), as amended by Public Law 111-175, in order for certain secondary transmissions by satellite carriers for private home viewing to be subject to statutory licensing.

(b) Definitions. **(1)** The terms distributor, network station, private home viewing, satellite carrier, subscribe, subscriber, non-network station, unserved household, primary stream, and multicast stream, have the meanings set forth in 17 U.S.C. 119(d), as amended by Public Law 111-175.

(2) The terms "primary transmission" and "secondary transmission" have the meanings set forth in section 111(f) of title 17 of the United States Code.

(c) Accounting periods and deposit.

(1) Statements of Account shall cover semiannual accounting periods of January 1 through June 30, and July 1 through December 31, and shall be deposited in the Copyright Office, together with the total statutory royalty fee or the confirmed arbitration royalty fee for such accounting periods as prescribed by 17 U.S.C. 119(b)(1)(B), by no later than July 30, if the Statement of Account covers the January 1 through June 30 accounting period, and by no later than the immediately following January 30, if the Statement of Account covers the July 1 through December 31 accounting period.

(2) Upon receiving a Statement of Account and royalty fee, the Copyright Office will make an official record of the actual date when such statement and fee were physically received in the Copyright Office. Thereafter, the Licensing Division of the Copyright Office will examine the statement and fee for obvious errors or omissions appearing on the face of the documents, and will require that any such obvious errors or omissions be corrected before final processing of the documents is completed. If, as the result of communications between the Copyright Office and the satellite carrier, an additional fee is deposited or changes or additions are made in the Statement of Account, the date that additional deposit or information was actually received in the Office will be added to the official record of the case. However, completion by the Copyright Office of the final processing of a Statement of Account and royalty fee deposit shall establish only the fact of such completion and the date or dates of receipt shown in the official record. It shall in no case be considered a determination that the Statement of Account was, in fact, properly prepared and accurate, that the correct amount of the royalty fee had been deposited, that the statutory time limits for filing had been met, or that any other requirements to qualify for a statutory license have been satisfied.

(3) Statements of Account and royalty fees received before the end of the particular accounting period they purport to cover will not be processed by the Copyright Office. Statements of Account and royalty fees received after the filing deadlines of July 30 or January 30, respectively, will be accepted for whatever legal effect they may have, if any.

(4) In the Register's discretion, four years after the close of any calendar year, the Register may close out the royalty payments account for that calendar year, and may treat any funds remaining in such account and any subsequent deposits that would otherwise be attributable to that calendar year as attributable to the succeeding calendar year.

(d) Forms. **(1)** Each Statement of Account shall be furnished on an appropriate form prescribed by the Copyright Office, and shall contain the information required by that form and its accompanying instructions. Computation of the copyright royalty fee shall be in accordance with the procedures set forth in the forms. Copies of Statement of Account forms are available free from the Copyright Office website.

(2) The form prescribed by the Copyright Office is designated "Form SC (Statement of Account for Secondary Transmissions by Satellite Carriers of Distant Television Signals)."

(e) Contents. Each Statement of Account shall contain the following information:

(1) A clear designation of the accounting period covered by the Statement.

(2) The designation "Owner" followed by:

(i) The full legal name of the satellite carrier. If the owner is a partnership, the name of the partnership is to be followed by the name of at least one individual partner;

(ii) Any other name or names under which the owner conducts the business of the satellite carrier; and

(iii) The full mailing address of the owner. Ownership, other names under which the owner conducts the business of the satellite carrier, and the owner's mailing address shall reflect facts existing on the last day of the accounting period covered by the Statement of Account.

(3) The designation "Primary Transmitters," followed by the call signs, broadcast channel numbers, station locations (city and state of license), and a notation whether that primary transmitter is a "non-network station" or "network station" transmitted to any or all of the subscribers of the satellite carrier during any portion of the period covered by the Statement of Account.

(4) The designation "Non-network stations," followed by:

(i) The call sign of each non-network station signal carried for each month of the period covered by the Statement, and

(ii) The total number of subscribers to each non-network station for each month of the period covered by the Statement. This number is the number of subscribers to each non-network station receiving the retransmission on the last day of each month.

(5) The designation "Network Stations," followed by:

(i) The call sign of each network station carried for each month of the period covered by the Statement, and

(ii) The total number of subscribers to each network station for each month of the period covered by the Statement. This number is the number of subscribers to each network station receiving the retransmission on the last day of each month.

(6) The total number of subscribers to each non-network station for the six-month period covered by the Statement multiplied by the statutory royalty rate prescribed in §386.2 of this chapter.

(7) The total number of subscribers to each network station for the six-month period covered by the Statement multiplied by the statutory royalty rate prescribed in §386.2 of this chapter.

(8) The name, address, business title, and telephone number of the individual or individuals to be contacted for information or questions concerning the content of the Statement of Account.

(9) The handwritten signature of:

(i) The owner of the satellite carrier or a duly authorized agent of the owner, if the owner is not a partnership or a corporation; or

(ii) A partner, if the owner is a partnership; or

(iii) An officer of the corporation, if the owner is a corporation. The signature shall be accompanied by:

(A) The printed or typewritten name of the person signing the Statement of Account;

(B) The date of signature;

(C) If the owner of the satellite carrier is a partnership or a corporation, by the title or official position held in the partnership or corporation by the person signing the Statement of Account;

(D) A certification of the capacity of the person signing; and

(E) The following statement:

I, the undersigned Owner or Agent of the Satellite Carrier, or Officer or Partner, if the Satellite Carrier is a Corporation or Partnership, have examined this Statement of Account and hereby declare under penalty of law that all statements of fact contained herein are true, complete, and correct to the best of my knowledge, information, and belief, and are made in good faith.

(f) Royalty fee payment.

(1) All royalty fees shall be paid by a single electronic funds transfer and payment must be received in the designated bank by the filing deadline for the relevant accounting period. The following information shall be provided as part of the EFT and/or as part of the remittance advice as provided for in circulars issued by the Copyright Office:

(i) Remitter's name and address;

(ii) Name of a contact person, telephone number and extension, and email address;

(iii) The actual or anticipated date that the EFT will be transmitted;

(iv) Type of royalty payment (*i.e.* satellite);

(v) Total amount submitted via the EFT;

(vi) Total amount to be paid by year and period;

(vii) Number of Statements of Account that the EFT covers;

(viii) ID numbers assigned by the Licensing Division;

(ix) Legal name of the owner for each Statement of Account.

(2) The remittance advice shall be attached to the Statement(s) of Account. In addition, a copy of the remittance advice shall be emailed or sent by facsimile to the Licensing Division.

(3) The Office may waive the requirement for payment by electronic funds transfer as set forth in paragraph (f)(1) of

this section. To obtain a waiver, the remitter shall submit to the Licensing Division at least 60 days prior to the royalty fee due date a certified statement setting forth the reasons explaining why payment by an electronic funds transfer would be virtually impossible or, alternatively, why it would impose a financial or other hardship on the remitter. The certified statement must be signed by a duly authorized representative of the entity making the payment. A waiver shall cover only a single payment period. Failure to obtain a waiver may result in the remittance being returned to the remitter.

(g) Copies of statements of account. A licensee shall file an original and one copy of the statement of account with the Licensing Division of the Copyright Office.

(h) Corrections, supplemental payments, and refunds.

(1) Upon compliance with the procedures and within the time limits set forth in paragraph (h)(3) of this section, corrections to Statements of Account will be placed on record, supplemental royalty fee payments will be received for deposit, or refunds will be issued, in the following cases:

(i) Where, with respect to the accounting period covered by a Statement of Account, any of the information given in the Statement filed in the Copyright Office is incorrect or incomplete; or

(ii) Where calculation of the royalty fee payable for a particular accounting period was incorrect, and the amount deposited in the Copyright Office for that period was either too high or too low.

(2) Corrections to Statements of Account will not be placed on record, supplemental royalty fee payments will not be received for deposit, and refunds will not be issued, where the information in the Statements of Account, the royalty fee calculations, or the payments were correct as of the date on which the accounting period ended, but changes (for example, addition or deletion of a signal) took place later.

(3) Requests that corrections to a Statement of Account be placed on record, that fee payments be accepted, or requests for the issuance of refunds, shall be made only in the cases mentioned in paragraph (h)(1) of this section. Such requests shall be addressed to the Licensing Division of the Copyright Office, and shall meet the following conditions:

(i) The request must be in writing, must clearly identify its purpose, and, in the case of a request for a refund, must be received in the Copyright Office before the expiration of 30 days from the last day of the applicable Statement of Account filing period, or before the expiration of 30 days from the date of receipt at the Copyright Office of the royalty payment that is the subject of the request, whichever time period is longer. Telephone or similar unsigned requests that meet these conditions may be permitted, where a follow-up written request detailing the same information is received by the Copyright Office within fourteen days after the required thirty-day period.

(ii) The Statement of Account to which the request pertains must be sufficiently identified in the request (by inclusion of the name of the owner of the satellite carrier and the accounting period in question) so that it can be readily located in the records of the Copyright Office.

(iii) The request must contain a clear statement of the facts on which it is based and provide a clear basis on which a refund may be granted, in accordance with the following procedures:

(A) In the case of a request filed under paragraph (h)(1)(i) of this section, where the information given in the Statement of Account is incorrect or incomplete, the request must clearly identify the erroneous or incomplete information and provide the correct or additional information; or

(B) In the case of a request filed under paragraph (h)(1)(ii) of this section, where the royalty fee was miscalculated and the amount deposited in the Copyright Office was either too high or too low, the request must be accompanied by an affidavit under the official seal of any officer authorized to administer oaths within the United States, or a statement in accordance with section 1746 of Title 28 of the United States Code, made and signed in accordance with paragraph (e)(9) of this section. The affidavit or statement shall describe the reasons why the royalty fee was improperly calculated and include a detailed analysis of the proper royalty calculation.

(iv)(A) All requests filed under this paragraph (h) must be accompanied by a filing fee in the amount prescribed in §201.3(e) of this part for each Statement of Account involved. Payment of this fee may be in the form of a personal or company check, or of a certified check, cashier's check or money order, payable to: Register of Copyrights. No request will be processed until the appropriate filing fees are received.

(B) All requests that a supplemental royalty fee payment be received for deposit under this paragraph (h) must be accompanied by a remittance in the full amount of such fee. Payment of the supplemental royalty fee must be in the form of certified check, cashier's check, or money order, payable to: Register of Copyrights; or electronic payment. No such request will be processed until an acceptable remittance in the full amount of the supplemental royalty fee has been received.

(v) All requests submitted under this paragraph (h) must be signed by the satellite carrier owner named in the Statement of Account, or the duly authorized agent of the owner, in accordance with paragraph (e)(9) of this section.

(vi) A request for a refund is not necessary where the Licensing Division, during its examination of a Statement of Account or related document, discovers an error that has resulted in a royalty overpayment. In this case, the Licensing Division will forward the royalty refund to the satellite carrier owner named in the Statement of Account without regard to the time limitations provided for in paragraph (h)(3)(i) of this section.

(4) Following final processing, all requests submitted under this paragraph (h) will be filed with the original Statement of Account in the records of the Copyright Office. Nothing contained in this paragraph shall be considered to relieve satellite carriers from their full obligations under Title 17 of the United States Code, and the filing of a correction or supplemental payment shall have only such effect as may be attributed to it by a court of competent jurisdiction.

(i) Interest.

(1) Interest. Royalty fee payments submitted as a result of late or amended filings will include interest. Interest will begin to accrue beginning on the first day after the close of the period for filing statements of account for all underpayments or late payments of royalties for the satellite carrier statutory license for secondary transmissions for private home viewing and viewing in commercial establishments occurring within that accounting period. The accrual period shall end on the date the electronic payment submitted by a satellite carrier is received by the Copyright Office. In cases where a waiver of the electronic funds transfer requirement is approved by the Copyright Office, and royalties payments are either late or underpaid, the accrual period shall end on the date the payment is postmarked. If the payment is not received by the Copyright Office within five business days of its date, then the accrual period shall end on the date of the actual receipt by the Copyright Office.

(2)(i) The interest rate applicable to a specific accounting period beginning with the 1992/2 period shall be the Current Value of Funds Rate, as established by section 8025.40 of the Treasury Financial Manual and published in the Federal Register, in effect on the first business day after the close of the filing deadline for that accounting period. Satellite carriers wishing to obtain the interest rate for a specific accounting period may do so by consulting the Federal Register for the applicable Current Value of Funds Rate, or by contacting the Licensing Division of the Copyright Office.

(ii) The interest rate applicable to a specific accounting period earlier than the 1992/2 period shall be the rate fixed by the Licensing Division of the Copyright Office pursuant to 37 CFR 201.11(h) in effect on June 30, 1992.

(3) Interest is not required to be paid on any royalty underpayment or late payment from a particular accounting period if the interest charge is less than or equal to five dollars ($5.00).

History of 37 C.F.R. §201.11: 54 FR 27877, July 3, 1989; 55 FR 49998, Dec. 4, 1990; 56 FR 29589, June 28, 1991; 57 FR 61834, Dec. 29, 1992; 59 FR 67635, Dec. 30, 1994; 60 FR 34168, June 30, 1995; 60 FR 57937, Nov. 24, 1995; 63 FR 30635, June 5, 1998; 64 FR 36574, July 7, 1999; 70 FR 30366, May 26, 2005; 70 FR 38022, July 1, 2005; 71 FR 45739, Aug. 10, 2006; 72 FR 33691, July 1, 2007; 73 FR 29072, May 20, 2008; 75 FR 56872, Sept. 17, 2010; 78 FR 42874, July 18, 2013; 82 FR 9357, Mar. 8, 2017.

§201.12. RECORDATION OF CERTAIN CONTRACTS BY CABLE SYSTEMS LOCATED OUTSIDE OF THE FORTY-EIGHT CONTIGUOUS STATES

(a) Written, nonprofit contracts providing for the equitable sharing of costs of videotapes and their transfer, as identified in 17 U.S.C. 111(e)(2), will be filed in the Copyright Office Licensing Division by recordation upon payment of the prescribed fee. The document submitted for recordation shall meet the following requirements:

(1) It shall be an original instrument of contract; or it shall be a legible photocopy or other full-size facsimile reproduction of an original, accompanied by a certification signed by at least one of the parties to the contract, or an authorized representative of that party, that the reproduction is a true copy;

(2) It shall bear the signatures of all persons identified as parties to the contract, or of their authorized agents or representatives;

(3) It shall be complete on its face, and shall include any schedules, appendixes, or other attachments referred to in the instrument as being part of it; and

(4) It shall be clearly identified, in its body or a covering transmittal letter, as being submitted for recordation under 17 U.S.C. 111(e).

(b) The fee for recordation of a document is prescribed in §201.3(e).

(c) The date of recordation is the date when all of the elements required for recordation, including the prescribed fee, have been received in the Copyright Office. A document is filed in the Copyright Office and a filing in the Copyright Office takes place on the date of recordation. After recordation the document is returned to the sender with a certificate of recordation.

History of 37 C.F.R. §201.12: 42 FR 53961, Oct. 4, 1977; 56 FR 59885, Nov. 26, 1991; 64 FR 29521, June 1, 1999; 82 FR 9357, Mar. 8, 2017.

§201.13. NOTICES OF OBJECTION TO CERTAIN NONCOMMERCIAL PERFORMANCES OF NONDRAMATIC LITERARY OR MUSICAL WORKS

(a) Definitions.

(1) A "Notice of Objection" is a notice, as required by 17 U.S.C. 110(4), to be served as a condition of preventing the noncommercial performance of a nondramatic literary or musical work under certain circumstances.

(2) For purposes of this section, the "copyright owner" of a nondramatic literary or musical work is the author of the work (including, in the case of a work made for hire, the employer or other person for whom the work was prepared), or a person or organization that has obtained ownership of the exclusive right, initially owned by the author of performance of the type referred to in 17 U.S.C. 110(4). If the other requirements of this section are met, a Notice of Objection may cover the works of more than one copyright owner.

(b) Form. The Copyright Office does not provide printed forms for the use of persons serving Notices of Objection.

(c) Contents.

(1) A Notice of Objection must clearly state that the copyright owner objects to the performance, and must include all of the following:

(i) Reference to the statutory authority on which the Notice of Objection is based, either by citation of 17 U.S.C. 110(4) or by a more general characterization or description of that statutory provision;

(ii) The date and place of the performance to which an objection is being made; however, if the exact date or place of a particular performance, or both, are not known to the copyright owner, it is sufficient if the Notice describes whatever information the copyright owner has about the date and place of a particular performance, and the source of that information unless the source was considered private or confidential;

(iii) Clear identification, by title and at least one author, of the particular nondramatic literary or musical work or works, to the performance of which the copyright owner thereof is lodging objection; a Notice may cover any number of separately identified copyrighted works owned by the copyright owner or owners serving the objection. Alternatively, a blanket notice, with or without separate identification of certain copyrighted works, and purporting to cover one or more groups of copyrighted works not separately identified by title and author, shall have effect if the conditions specified in paragraph (c)(2) of this section are met; and

(iv) A concise statement of the reasons for the objection.

(2) A blanket notice purporting to cover one or more groups of copyrighted works not separately identified by title and author shall be valid only if all of the following conditions are met:

(i) The Notice shall identify each group of works covered by the blanket notice by a description of any common characteristics distinguishing them from other copyrighted works, such as common author, common copyright owner, common publisher, or common licensing agent;

(ii) The Notice shall identify a particular individual whom the person responsible for the performance can contact for more detailed information about the works covered by the blanket notice and to determine whether a particular work planned for performance is in fact covered by the Notice. Such identification shall include the full name and business and residence addresses of the individual, telephone numbers at which the individual can be reached throughout the period between service of the notice and the performance, and name, addresses, and telephone numbers of another individual to contact during that period in case the first cannot be reached.

(iii) If the copyright owner or owners of all works covered by the blanket notice is not identified in the Notice, the Notice shall include an offer to identify, by name and last known address, the owner or owners of any and all such works, upon request made to the individual referred to in paragraph (c)(2)(ii) of this section.

(3) A Notice of Objection must also include clear and prominent statements explaining that:

(i) A failure to exclude the works identified in the Notice from the performance in question may subject the person responsible for the performance to liability for copyright infringement; and

(ii) The objection is without legal effect if there is no direct or indirect admission charge for the performance, and if the other conditions of 17 U.S.C. 110(4) are met.

(d) Signature and Identification.

(1) A Notice of Objection shall be in writing and signed by each copyright owner, or such owner's duly authorized agent, as required by 17 U.S.C. 110(4)(B)(i).

(2) The signature of each owner or agent shall be an actual handwritten signature of an individual, accompanied by the date of signature and the full name, address, and telephone number of that person, typewritten or printed legibly by hand.

(3) If a Notice of Objection is initially served in the form of an email, fax, or similar communication, as provided by paragraph (e) of this section, the requirement for an individual's handwritten signature shall be considered waived if the further conditions of paragraph (e) are met.

(e) Service.

(1) A Notice of Objection shall be served on the person responsible for the performance at least seven days before the date of the performance, as provided by 17 U.S.C. 110 (4)(B)(ii).

(2) Service of the Notice may be effected by any of the following methods:

(i) Personal service;

(ii) First-class mail;

(iii) Email, fax, or similar form of communication, if: (A) The Notice meets all of the other conditions provided by this section; and (B) before the performance takes place, the person responsible for the performance receives written confirmation of the Notice, bearing the actual handwritten signature of each copyright owner or duly authorized agent.

(3) The date of service is the date the Notice of Objection is received by the person responsible for the performance or any agent or employee of that person.

History of 37 C.F.R. §201.13: 42 FR 64684, Dec. 28, 1977; 82 FR 9357, Mar. 8, 2017.

§201.14. WARNINGS OF COPYRIGHT FOR USE BY CERTAIN LIBRARIES & ARCHIVES

(a) Definitions.

(1) A "Display Warning of Copyright" is a notice under paragraphs (d)(2) and (e)(2) of section 108 of Title 17 of the United States Code. As required by those sections the "Display Warning of Copyright" is to be displayed at the place where orders for copies or phonorecords are accepted by certain libraries and archives.

(2) An "Order Warning of Copyright" is a notice under paragraphs (d)(2) and (e)(2) of section 108 of Title 17 of the United States Code. As required by those sections the "Order Warning of Copyright" is to be included on printed forms supplied by certain libraries and archives and used by their patrons for ordering copies or phonorecords.

(b) Contents. A Display Warning of Copyright and an Order Warning of Copyright shall consist of a verbatim reproduction of the following notice, printed in such size and form and displayed in such manner as to comply with paragraph (c) of this section:

NOTICE WARNING CONCERNING
COPYRIGHT RESTRICTIONS

The copyright law of the United States (Title 17, United States Code) governs the making of photocopies or other reproductions of copyrighted material.

Under certain conditions specified in the law, libraries and archives are authorized to furnish a photocopy or other reproduction. One of these specific conditions is that the photocopy or reproduction is not to be "used for any purpose other than private study, scholarship, or research." If a user makes a request for, or later uses, a photocopy or reproduction for purposes in excess of "fair use," that user may be liable for copyright infringement.

This institution reserves the right to refuse to accept a copying order if, in its judgment, fulfillment of the order would involve violation of copyright law.

(c) Form and Manner of Use.

(1) A Display Warning of Copyright shall be printed on heavy paper or other durable material in type at least 18 points in size, and shall be displayed prominently, in such manner and location as to be clearly visible, legible, and comprehensible to a casual observer within the immediate vicinity of the place where orders are accepted.

(2) An Order Warning of Copyright shall be printed within a box located prominently on the order form itself, either on the front side of the form or immediately adjacent to the space calling for the name or signature of the person using the form. The notice shall be printed in type size no smaller than that used predominantly throughout the form, and in no case shall the type size be smaller than eight points. The notice shall be printed in such manner as to be clearly legible, comprehensible, and readily apparent to a casual reader of the form.

History of 37 C.F.R. §201.14: 42 FR 59265, Nov. 16, 1977; 82 FR 9357, Mar. 8, 2017.

§201.15. ADDED & RESERVED

§201.16. VERIFICATION OF A STATEMENT OF ACCOUNT FOR SECONDARY TRANSMISSIONS MADE BY CABLE SYSTEMS & SATELLITE CARRIERS

(a) General. This section prescribes procedures pertaining to the verification of a Statement of Account filed with the Copyright Office pursuant to sections 111(d)(1) or 119(b)(1) of title 17 of the United States Code.

(b) Definitions. As used in this section:

(1) The term cable system has the meaning set forth in §201.17(b)(2).

(2) Copyright owner means any person or entity that owns the copyright in a work embodied in a secondary transmission made by a statutory licensee that filed a Statement of Account with the Copyright Office for an accounting period beginning on or after January 1, 2010, or a designated agent or representative of such person or entity.

(3) Multiple system operator or MSO means an entity that owns, controls, or operates more than one cable system.

(4) Net aggregate underpayment means the aggregate amount of underpayments found by the auditor less the aggregate amount of any overpayments found by the auditor, as measured against the total amount of royalties reflected on the Statements of Account examined by the auditor.

(5) Participating copyright owner means a copyright owner that filed a notice of intent to audit a Statement of Account pursuant to paragraph (c)(1) or (2) of this section and any other copyright owner that has given notice of its intent to participate in such audit pursuant to paragraph (c)(3) of this section.

(6) The term satellite carrier has the meaning set forth in 17 U.S.C. 119(d)(6).

(7) The term secondary transmission has the meaning set forth in 17 U.S.C. 111(f)(2).

(8) Statement of Account or Statement means a semiannual Statement of Account filed with the Copyright Office under 17 U.S.C. 111(d)(1) or 119(b)(1) or an amended Statement of Account filed with the Office pursuant to §§201.11(h) or 201.17(m).

(9) Statutory licensee or licensee means a cable system or satellite carrier that filed a Statement of Account with the Office under 17 U.S.C. 111(d)(1) or 119(b)(1).

(c) Notice of intent to audit. (1) Any copyright owner that intends to audit a Statement of Account for an accounting period beginning on or after January 1, 2010 must provide written notice to the Register of Copyrights no later than three years after the last day of the year in which the Statement was filed with the Office. The notice must be received in the Office on or after December 1st and no later than December 31st, and a copy of the notice must be provided to the statutory licensee on the same day that it is filed with the Office. Between January 1st and January 31st of the next calendar year the Office will publish a notice in the Federal Register announcing the receipt of the notice of intent to audit. A notice of intent to audit may be filed by an individual copyright owner or a designated agent that represents a group or multiple groups of copyright owners. The notice shall include a statement indicating that it is a "notice of intent to audit" and it shall contain the following information:

(i) It shall identify the licensee that filed the Statement(s) with the Office, and the Statement(s) and accounting period(s) that will be subject to the audit.

(ii) It shall identify the party that filed the notice, including its name, address, telephone number, and email address, and it shall include a statement that the party owns or represents one or more copyright owners that own a work that was embodied in a secondary transmission made by the statutory licensee during one or more of the accounting period(s) specified in the Statement(s) that will be subject to the audit.

(2) Notwithstanding the schedule set forth in paragraph (c)(1) of this section, any copyright owner that intends to audit a Statement of Account pursuant to an expanded audit under paragraph (n) of this section may provide written notice of such to the Register of Copyrights during any month, but no later than three years after the last day of the year in which the Statement was filed with the Office. A copy of the notice must be provided to the licensee on the same day that the notice is filed with the Office. Within thirty days after the notice has been received, the Office will publish a notice in the Federal Register announcing the receipt of the notice of intent to conduct an expanded audit. A notice given pursuant to this paragraph may be provided by an individual copyright owner or a designated agent that represents a group or multiple groups of copyright owners. The notice shall include a statement indicating that it is a "notice of intent to conduct an expanded audit" and it shall contain the information specified in paragraphs (c)(1)(i) and (ii) of this section.

(3) Within thirty days after a notice is published in the Federal Register pursuant to paragraphs (c)(1) or (2) of this section, any other copyright owner that owns a work that was embodied in a secondary transmission made by that statutory licensee during an accounting period covered by the Statement(s) of Account referenced in the Federal Register notice and that wishes to participate in the audit of such Statement(s) must provide written notice of such participation to the Copyright Office as well as to the licensee and party that filed the notice of intent to audit. A notice given pursuant to this paragraph may be provided by an individual copyright owner or a designated agent that represents a group or multiple groups of copyright owners, and shall include the information specified in paragraphs (c)(1)(i) and (ii) of this section.

(4) Notices submitted to the Office under paragraphs (c)(1) through (3) of this section should be addressed to the "U.S. Copyright Office, Office of the General Counsel" and should be sent to the address for time-sensitive requests set forth in §201.1(c)(1).

(5) Once the Office has received a notice of intent to audit a Statement of Account under paragraphs (c)(1) or (2) of this section, a notice of intent to audit that same Statement will not be accepted for publication in the Federal Register.

(6) Once the Office has received a notice of intent to audit two Statements of Account filed by a particular satellite carrier or a particular cable system, a notice of intent to audit that same carrier or that same system under paragraph (c)(1) of this section will not be accepted for publication in the Federal Register until the following calendar year.

(d) Selection of the auditor. **(1)** Within forty-five days after a notice is published in the Federal Register pursuant to paragraph (c)(1) of this section, the participating copyright owners shall provide the statutory licensee with a list of three independent and qualified auditors, along with information reasonably sufficient for the licensee to evaluate the proposed auditors' independence and qualifications, including:

(i) The auditor's curriculum vitae and a list of audits that the auditor has conducted pursuant to 17 U.S.C. 111(d)(6) or 119(b)(2);

(ii) A list and, subject to any confidentiality or other legal restrictions, a brief description of any other work the auditor has performed for any of the participating copyright owners during the prior two calendar years;

(iii) A list identifying the participating copyright owners for whom the auditor's firm has been engaged during the prior two calendar years; and,

(iv) A copy of the engagement letter that would govern the auditor's performance of the audit and that provides for the auditor to be compensated on a non-contingent flat fee or hourly basis that does not take into account the results of the audit.

(2) Within five business days after receiving the list of auditors from the participating copyright owners, the licensee shall select one of the proposed auditors and shall notify the participating copyright owners of its selection. That auditor shall be retained by the participating copyright owners and shall conduct the audit on behalf of all copyright owners who own a work that was embodied in a secondary transmission made by the licensee during the accounting period(s) specified in the Statement(s) of Account identified in the notice of intent to audit.

(3) The auditor shall be independent and qualified as defined in this section. An auditor shall be considered independent and qualified if:

(i) He or she is a certified public accountant and a member in good standing with the American Institute of Certified Public Accountants ("AICPA") and the licensing authority for the jurisdiction(s) where the auditor is licensed to practice;

(ii) He or she is not, for any purpose other than the audit, an officer, employee, or agent of any participating copyright owner;

(iii) He or she is independent as that term is used in the Code of Professional Conduct of the AICPA, including the Principles, Rules, and Interpretations of such Code; and

(iv) He or she is independent as that term is used in the Statements on Auditing Standards promulgated by the Auditing Standards Board of the AICPA and Interpretations thereof issued by the Auditing Standards Division of the AICPA.

(e) Commencement of the audit. **(1)** Within ten days after the selection of the auditor, the auditor shall meet by telephone or in person with designated representatives of the participating copyright owners and the statutory licensee to review the scope of the audit, audit methodology, applicable auditing standard, and schedule for conducting and completing the audit.

(2) Within thirty days after the selection of the auditor, the licensee shall provide the auditor and a representative of the participating copyright owners with a list of all broadcast signals retransmitted pursuant to the statutory license in each community covered by each of the Statements of Account subject to the audit, including the call sign for each broadcast signal and each multicast signal. In the case of an audit involving a cable system or MSO, the list must include the classification of each signal on a community-by-community basis pursuant to §201.17(e)(9)(iv) through (v) and 201.17(h). The list shall be signed by a duly authorized agent of the licensee and the signature shall be accompanied by the following statement "I, the undersigned agent of the statutory licensee, hereby declare under penalty of law that all statements of fact contained herein are true, complete, and correct to the best of my knowledge, information, and belief, and are made in good faith."

(f) Failure to proceed with a noticed audit. If the participating copyright owners fail to provide the statutory licensee with a list of auditors or fail to retain the auditor selected by the licensee pursuant to paragraph (d)(2) of this section, the Statement(s) of Account identified in the notice of intent to audit shall not be subject to audit under this section.

(g) Ex parte communications. Following the initial consultation pursuant to paragraph (e)(1) of this section and until the distribution of the auditor's final report to the participating copyright owners pursuant to paragraph (i)(3) of this section, there shall be no ex parte communications regarding the audit between the auditor and the participating copyright owners or their representatives; provided, however, that the auditor may engage in such ex parte communications where either:

(1) Subject to paragraph (i)(4) of this section, the auditor has a reasonable basis to suspect fraud and that participation by the licensee in communications regarding the suspected fraud would, in the reasonable opinion of the auditor, prejudice the investigation of such suspected fraud; or

(2) The auditor provides the licensee with a reasonable opportunity to participate in communications with the participating copyright owners or their representatives and the licensee declines to do so.

(h) Auditor's authority and access. **(1)** The auditor shall have exclusive authority to verify all of the information reported on the Statement(s) of Account subject to the audit in order to confirm the correctness of the calculations and royalty payments reported therein; provided, however, that the auditor shall not determine whether any cable system properly classified any broadcast signal as required by §201.17(e)(9)(iv) through (v) and 201.17(h) or whether a satellite carrier properly determined that any subscriber or group of subscribers is eligible to receive any broadcast signals under 17 U.S.C. 119(a).

(2) The statutory licensee shall provide the auditor with reasonable access to the licensee's books and records and any other information that the auditor needs in order to conduct the audit. The licensee shall provide the auditor with any information the auditor reasonably requests promptly after receiving such a request.

(3) The audit shall be conducted during regular business hours at a location designated by the licensee with consideration given to minimizing the costs and burdens associated with the audit. If the auditor and the licensee agree, the audit may be conducted in whole or in part by means of electronic communication.

(4) With the exception of its obligations under paragraphs (d) and (e) of this section, a licensee may suspend its participation in an audit for no more than sixty days before the semi-annual due dates for filing Statements of Account by providing advance written notice to the auditor and a representative of the participating copyright owners, provided however, that if the participating copyright owners notify the licensee within ten days of receiving such notice of their good-faith belief that the suspension could prevent the auditor from delivering his or her final report to the participating copyright owners before the statute of limitations may expire on any claims under the Copyright Act related to a Statement of Account covered by that audit, the licensee may not suspend its participation in the audit unless it first executes a tolling agreement to extend the statute of limitations by a period of time equal to the period of the suspension.

(i) Audit report. **(1)** After reviewing the books, records, and any other information received from the statutory licensee, the auditor shall prepare a draft written report setting forth his or her initial conclusions and shall deliver a copy of that draft report to the licensee. The auditor shall then consult with a representative of the licensee regarding the conclusions set forth in the draft report for up to thirty days. If, upon consulting with the licensee, the auditor concludes that there are errors in the facts or conclusions set forth in the draft report, the auditor shall correct those errors.

(2) Within thirty days after the date that the auditor delivered the draft report to the licensee pursuant to paragraph (i)(1) of this section, the auditor shall prepare a final version of the written report setting forth his or her ultimate conclusions and shall deliver a copy of that final version to the licensee. Within fourteen days thereafter, the licensee may provide the auditor with a written rebuttal setting forth its good faith objections to the facts or conclusions set forth in the final version of the report.

(3) Subject to the confidentiality provisions set forth in paragraph (*l*) of this section, the auditor shall attach a copy of any written rebuttal timely received from the licensee to the final version of the report and shall deliver a copy of the complete final report to the participating copyright owners and the licensee. The final report must be delivered by November 1st of the year in which the notice was published in the Federal Register pursuant to paragraph (c)(1) of this section and within five business days after the last day on which the licensee may provide the auditor with a written rebuttal pursuant to paragraph (i)(2) of this section. Upon delivery of the complete and final report, the auditor shall notify the Office that the audit has been completed. The notice to the Office shall specify the date that the auditor delivered the final report to the parties; whether, with respect to each statement examined, the auditor has discovered any underpayment or overpayment; and whether the auditor has received a written rebuttal from the licensee. The notice should be addressed to the "U.S. Copyright Office, Office of the General Counsel" and should be sent to the address for time-sensitive requests specified in §201.1(c)(1).

(4) Prior to the delivery of the final report pursuant to paragraph (i)(3) of this section the auditor shall not provide any draft of his or her report to the participating copyright owners or their representatives; provided, however, that the auditor may deliver a draft report simultaneously to the licensee and the participating copyright owners if the auditor has a reasonable basis to suspect fraud.

(j) Corrections, supplemental payments, and refunds. **(1)** If the auditor concludes in his or her final report that any of the information reported on a Statement of Account is incorrect or incomplete, that the calculation of the royalty fee payable for a particular accounting period was incorrect, or that the amount deposited in the Office for that period was too low, a statutory licensee may cure such incorrect or incomplete information or underpayment by filing an amendment to the Statement and, in case of a deficiency in payment, by depositing supplemental royalty fee payments with the Office using the procedures set forth in §§201.11(h) or 201.17(m); provided, however, that the amendment and/or payments are received within sixty days after the delivery of the final report to the participating copyright owners and the licensee or in the case of an audit of an MSO, within ninety days after the delivery of such report; and further provided that the licensee has reimbursed the participating copyright owners for the licensee's share of the audit costs, if any, determined to be owing pursuant to paragraph (k)(3) of this section. While reimbursement of audit costs shall be paid to a representative of the participating copyright owners, supplemental royalty fee payments made pursuant to this paragraph shall be delivered to the Office and not to the participating copyright owners or their representatives.

(2) Notwithstanding §§201.11(h)(3)(i) and 201.17(m)(4)(i), if the auditor concludes in his or her final report that there was an overpayment on a particular Statement, the licensee may request a refund from the Office using the procedures set forth in §§201.11(h)(3) or 201.17(m)(4), provided that the request is received within sixty days after the delivery of the final report to the participating copyright owners and the licensee or within ninety days after the delivery of the final report in the case of an audit of an MSO.

(k) Costs of the audit. **(1)** No later than the fifteenth day of each month during the course of the audit, the auditor shall provide the participating copyright owners with an itemized statement of the costs incurred by the auditor during the previous month, and shall provide a copy to the licensee that is the subject of the audit.

(2) If the auditor concludes in his or her final report that there was no net aggregate underpayment or a net aggregate underpayment of five percent or less, the participating copyright owners shall pay for the full costs of the auditor. If the auditor concludes in his or her final report that there was a net aggregate underpayment of more than five percent but less than ten percent, the costs of the auditor are to be split evenly between the participating copyright owners and the licensee that is the subject of the audit. If the auditor concludes in his or her final report that there was a net aggregate underpayment of ten percent or more, the licensee will be responsible for the full costs of the auditor.

(3) If a licensee is responsible for any portion of the costs of the auditor, a representative of the participating copyright owners shall provide the licensee with an itemized accounting of the auditor's total costs, the appropriate share of which should be paid by the licensee to such representative no later than sixty days after the delivery of the final report to the participating copyright owners and licensee or within ninety days after the delivery of such report in the case of an audit of an MSO.

(4) Notwithstanding anything to the contrary in paragraph (k) of this section, no portion of the auditor's costs that exceed the amount of the net aggregate underpayment may be recovered from the licensee.

(*l*) Confidentiality. **(1)** For purposes of this section, confidential information shall include any non-public financial or business information pertaining to a Statement of Account that is the subject of an audit under 17 U.S.C. 111(d)(6) or 119(b)(2).

(2) Access to confidential information under this section shall be limited to:

(i) The auditor; and

(ii) Subject to the execution of a reasonable confidentiality agreement, outside counsel for the participating copyright owners and any third party consultants retained by outside counsel, and any employees, agents, consultants, or independent contractors of the auditor who are not employees, officers, or agents of a participating copyright owner for any purpose other than the audit, who are engaged in the audit of a Statement or activities directly related hereto, and who require access to the confidential information for the purpose of performing such duties during the ordinary course of their employment.

(3) The auditor and any person identified in paragraph (*l*)(2)(ii) of this section shall implement procedures to safeguard all confidential information received from any third party in connection with an audit, using a reasonable standard of care, but no less than the same degree of security used to protect confidential financial and business information or similarly sensitive information belonging to the auditor or such person.

(m) Frequency and scope of the audit. **(1)** Except as provided in paragraph (n)(2) of this section with respect to expanded audits, a cable system, MSO, or satellite carrier shall be subject to no more than one audit per calendar year.

(2) Except as provided in paragraph (n)(1) of this section, the audit of a particular cable system or satellite carrier shall include no more than two of the Statements of Account filed by that cable system or satellite carrier that may be timely noticed for audit under paragraph (c)(1) of this section.

(3) Except as provided in paragraph (n)(3)(ii) of this section, an audit of an MSO shall be limited to a sample of no more than ten percent of the MSO's Form 3 cable systems and no more than ten percent of the MSO's Form 2 systems.

(n) Expanded audits. **(1)** If the auditor concludes in his or her final report that there was a net aggregate underpayment of five percent or more on the Statements of Account examined in an initial audit involving a cable system or satellite carrier, a copyright owner may expand the audit to include all previous Statements filed by that cable system or satellite carrier that may be timely noticed for audit under paragraph (c)(2) of this section. The expanded audit shall be conducted using the procedures set forth in paragraphs (d) through (*l*) of this section, with the following exceptions:

(i) The expanded audit may be conducted by the same auditor that performed the initial audit, provided that the participating copyright owners provide the licensee with updated information reasonably sufficient to allow the licensee to determine that there has been no material change in the auditor's independence and qualifications. In the alternative, the expanded audit may be conducted by an auditor selected by the licensee using the procedure set forth in paragraph (d) of this section.

(ii) The auditor shall deliver his or her final report to the participating copyright owners and the licensee within five business days following the last day on which the licensee may provide the auditor with a written rebuttal pursuant to paragraph (i)(2) of this section, but shall not be required to deliver the report by November 1st of the year in which the notice was published in the Federal Register pursuant to paragraph (c) of this section.

(2) An expanded audit of a cable system or a satellite carrier that is conducted pursuant to paragraph (n)(1) of this section may be conducted concurrently with another audit involving that same licensee.

(3) If the auditor concludes in his or her final report that there was a net aggregate underpayment of five percent or more on the Statements of Account examined in an initial audit involving an MSO:

(i) The cable systems included in the initial audit of that MSO shall be subject to an expanded audit in accordance with paragraph (n)(1) of this section; and

(ii) The MSO shall be subject to a new initial audit involving a sample of no more than thirty percent of its Form 3 cable systems and no more than thirty percent of its Form 2 cable systems, provided that the notice of intent to conduct that audit is filed in the same calendar year as the delivery of such final report.

(o) Retention of records. For each Statement of Account or amended Statement that a statutory licensee files with the Office for accounting periods beginning on or after January 1, 2010, the licensee shall maintain all records necessary to confirm the correctness of the calculations and royalty payments reported in each Statement or amended Statement for at least three and one-half years after the last day of the year in which that Statement or amended Statement was filed with the Office and, in the event that such Statement or amended Statement is the subject of an audit conducted pursuant to this section, shall continue to maintain those records until three years after the auditor delivers the final report to the participating copyright owners and the licensee pursuant to paragraph (i)(3) of this section.

History of 37 C.F.R. §201.16: 78 FR 78258, Dec. 26, 2013; 79 FR 68628, Nov. 18, 2014; 82 FR 9357, Mar. 8, 2017.

A §201.17. STATEMENTS OF ACCOUNT COVERING COMPULSORY LICENSES FOR SECONDARY TRANSMISSIONS BY CABLE SYSTEMS

(a) General. This section prescribes rules pertaining to the deposit of Statements of Account and royalty fees in the Copyright Office as required by 17 U.S.C. 111(d)(1) in order for secondary transmissions of cable systems to be subject to compulsory licensing.

(b) Definitions.

(1) Gross receipts for the "basic service of providing secondary transmissions of primary broadcast transmitters" include the full amount of monthly (or other periodic) service fees for any and all services or tiers of services which include one or more secondary transmissions of television or radio broadcast signals, for additional set fees, and for converter fees. In no case shall gross receipts be less than the cost of obtaining the signals of primary broadcast transmitters for subsequent retransmission. All such gross receipts shall be aggregated and the distant signal equivalent (DSE) calculations shall be made against the aggregated amount. Gross receipts for secondary transmission services do not include installation (including connection, relocation, disconnection, or reconnection) fees, separate charges for security, alarm or facsimile services, charges for late payments, or charges for pay cable or other program origination services: Provided That, the origination services are not offered in combination with secondary transmission service for a single fee.

(2) A cable system is a facility, located in any State, Territory, Trust Territory, or Possession, that in whole or in part receives signals transmitted or programs broadcast by one or more television broadcast stations licensed by the Federal Communications Commission, and makes secondary transmissions of such signals or programs by wires, cables, microwave, or other communications channels to subscribing members of the public who pay for such service. A system that meets this definition is considered a "cable system" for copyright purposes, even if the FCC excludes it from being considered a "cable system" because of the number or nature of its subscribers or the nature of its secondary transmissions. The Statements of Account and royalty fees to be deposited under this section shall be recorded and deposited by each individual cable system desiring its secondary transmissions to be subject to compulsory licensing. The owner of each individual cable system on the last day of the accounting period covered by a Statement of Account is responsible for depositing the Statement of Account and remitting the copyright royalty fees. For these purposes, and the purpose of this section, an "individual" cable system is each cable system recognized as a distinct entity under the rules, regulations, and practices of the Federal Communications Commission in effect on the last day of the accounting period covered by a Statement of Account, in the case of the preparation and deposit of a Statement of Account and copyright royalty fee. For these purposes, two or more cable facilities are considered as one individual cable system if the facilities are either:

(i) In contiguous communities under common ownership or control or

(ii) Operating from one headend.

(3) FCC means the Federal Communications Commission.

(4) In the case of cable systems which make secondary transmissions of all available FM radio signals, which signals are not electronically processed by the system as separate and discrete signals, an FM radio signal is "generally receivable" if:

(i) It is usually carried by the system whenever it is received at the system's headend, and

(ii) As a result of monitoring at reasonable times and intervals, it can be expected to be received at the system's headend, with the system's FM antenna, at least three consecutive hours each day at the same time each day, five or more days a week, for four or more weeks during any calendar quarter, with a strength of not less than fifty microvolts per meter measured at the foot of the tower or pole to which the antenna is attached.

(5) The terms primary transmission, secondary transmission, local service area of a primary transmitter, distant signal equivalent, network station, independent station, noncommercial educational station, primary stream, multicast stream, simulcast, primary transmitter, subscriber, and subscribe have the meanings set forth in 17 U.S.C. 111(f), as amended by Public Laws 94-553, 103-369, and 111-175.

(6) A primary transmitter is a "distant" station, for purposes of this section, if the programming of such transmitter is carried by the cable system in whole or in part beyond the local service area of such primary transmitter.

(7) A translator station is, with respect to programs both originally transmitted and retransmitted by it, a primary transmitter for the purposes of this section. A translator station which retransmits the programs of a network station will be considered a network station; a translator station which retransmits the programs of an independent station shall be considered an independent station; and a translator station which retransmits the programs of a noncommercial educational station shall be considered a noncommercial educational station. The determination of whether a translator station should be identified as a "distant" station depends on the local service area of the translator station.

(8) For purposes of this section, the "rules and regulations of the FCC in effect on October 19, 1976," which permitted a cable system, at its election, to omit the retransmission of a particular program and substitute another program in its place, refers to that portion of former 47 CFR 76.61(b)(2), revised June 25, 1981, and §76.63 (referring to §76.61(b)(2)), deleted June 25, 1981, concerning the substitution of a program that is primarily of local interest to the distant community (e.g., a local news or public affairs program).

(9) For purposes of this section, the "rules and regulations of the FCC," which require a cable system to omit the retransmission of a particular program and substitute another program in its place, refers to 47 CFR 76.67.

(10) For purposes of this section, a cable system "lacks the activated channel capacity to retransmit on a full-time basis all signals which it is authorized to carry" only if:

(i) All of its activated television channels are used exclusively for the secondary transmission of television signals; and

(ii) The number of primary television transmitters secondarily transmitted by the cable system exceeds the number of its activated television channels.

(c) Accounting Periods and Deposit.

(1) Statements of Account shall cover semiannual accounting periods of January 1 through June 30, and July 1 through December 31, and shall be deposited in the Copyright

Office, together with the total royalty fee for such accounting periods as prescribed by 17 U.S.C. 111(d)(1)(B) through (F), by no later than the immediately following August 29, if the Statement of Account covers the January 1 through June 30 accounting period, and by no later than the immediately following March 1, if the Statement of Account covers the July 1 through December 31 accounting period.

(2) Upon receiving a Statement of Account and royalty fee, the Copyright Office will make an official record of the actual date when such Statement and fee were received in the Copyright Office. Thereafter, the Office will examine the Statement and fee for obvious errors or omissions appearing on the face of the documents, and will require that any such obvious errors or omissions be corrected before final processing of the documents is completed. If, as the result of communications between the Copyright Office and the cable system, an additional fee is deposited or changes or additions are made in the Statement of Account, the date that additional deposit or information was actually received in the Office will be added to the official record of the case. However, completion by the Copyright Office of the final processing of a Statement of Account and royalty fee deposit shall establish only the fact of such completion and the date or dates of receipt shown in the official record. It shall in no case be considered a determination that the Statement of Account was, in fact, properly prepared and accurate, that the correct amount of the royalty fee had been deposited, that the statutory time limits for filing had been met, or that any other requirements to qualify for a compulsory license have been satisfied.

(3) Statements of Account and royalty fees received before the end of the particular accounting period they purport to cover will not be processed by the Copyright Office. Statements of Account and royalty fees received after the filing deadlines of August 29 or March 1, respectively, will be accepted for whatever legal effect they may have, if any.

(4) In the Register's discretion, four years after the close of any calendar year, the Register may, close out the royalty payments account for that calendar year, and may treat any funds remaining in such account and any subsequent deposits that would otherwise be attributable to that calendar year as attributable to the succeeding calendar year.

(d) Statement of Account forms and submission. Cable systems should submit each Statement of Account using an appropriate form provided by the Copyright Office on its Web site and following the instructions for completion and submission provided on the Office's Web site or the form itself.

(e) Contents. Each Statement of Account shall contain the following information:

(1) A clear designation of the accounting period covered by the Statement.

(2) The designation "Owner," followed by:

(i) The full legal name of the owner of the cable system. The 'owner' of the cable system is the individual or entity that provides the retransmission service and collects payment from the end user either directly or indirectly through a third party. If the owner is a partnership, the name of the partnership is to be followed by the name of at least one individual partner;

(ii) Any other name or names under which the owner conducts the business of the cable system; and

(iii) The full mailing address of the owner.

Ownership, other names under which the owner conducts the business of the cable system, and the owner's mailing address shall reflect facts existing on the last day of the accounting period covered by the Statement of Account.

(3) The designation "System," followed by:

(i) Any business or trade names used to identify the business and operation of the system, unless these names have already been given under the designation "Owner"; and

(ii) The full mailing address of the system, unless such address is the same as the address given under the designation "Owner."

Business or trade names used to identify the business and operation of the system, and the system's mailing address, shall reflect the facts existing on the last day of the accounting period covered by the Statement of Account.

(4) The designation "Area Served," followed by the name of the community or communities served by the system. For this purpose a "community" is the same as a "community unit" as defined in FCC rules and regulations.

(5) The designation "Channels," followed by:

(i) The number of channels including multicast streams on which the cable system made secondary transmissions to its subscribers, and

(ii) The cable system's total activated channel capacity, in each case during the period covered by the Statement.

(iii) A multicast stream is considered a channel for purposes of this section.

(6) The designation "Secondary Transmission Service: Subscribers and Rates," followed by:

(i) A brief description of each subscriber category for which a charge is made by the cable system for the basic service of providing secondary transmissions of primary broadcast transmitters;

(ii) The number of subscribers to the cable system in each such subscriber category; and

(iii) The charge or charges made per subscriber to each such subscriber category for the basic service of providing such secondary transmissions. Standard rate variations within a particular category should be summarized; discounts allowed for advance payment should not be included. For these purposes:

(A) The description, the number of subscribers, and the charge or charges made shall reflect the facts existing on the last day of the period covered by the Statement; and

(B) Each entity (for example, the owner of a private home, the resident of an apartment, the owner of a motel, or the owner of an apartment house) which is charged by the cable system for the basic service of providing secondary transmissions shall be considered one subscriber.

(7) The designation "Gross Receipts", followed by the gross amount paid to the cable system by subscribers for the basic service of providing secondary transmissions of primary broadcast transmissions during the period covered by the Statement of Account.

(i) If the cable system maintains its revenue accounts on an accrual basis, gross receipts for any accounting period includes all such amounts accrued for secondary transmission service furnished during that period, regardless of when accrued:

(A) Less the amount of any bad debts actually written-off during that accounting period;

(B) Plus the amount of any previously written-off bad debts for secondary transmission service which were actually recovered during that accounting period.

(ii) If the cable system maintains its revenue accounts on a cash basis, gross receipts of any accounting period includes all such amounts actually received by the cable system during that accounting period.

(8) The designation "Services Other Than Secondary Transmissions: Rates," followed by a description of each package of service which consists solely of services other than secondary transmission services, for which a separate charge was made or established, and which the cable system furnished or made available to subscribers during the period covered by the Statement of Account, together with the amount of such charge. However, no information need be given concerning services furnished at cost. Specific amounts charged for pay cable programming need not be given if the rates are on a variable, per-program basis. (The fact of such variable charge shall be indicated.)

(9) The designation "Primary Transmitters: Television," followed by an identification of all primary television transmitters whose signals were carried by the cable system during the period covered by the Statement of Account, other than primary transmitters of programs carried by the cable system exclusively pursuant to rules, regulations, or authorizations of the FCC in effect on October 19, 1976, permitting the substitution of signals under certain circumstances, and required to be specially identified by paragraph (e)(11) of this section, together with the information listed below:

(i) The station call sign of the primary transmitter.

(ii) The name of the community to which that primary transmitter is licensed by the FCC (in the case of domestic signals) or with which that primary transmitter is identified (in the case of foreign signals).

(iii) The number of the channel upon which that primary transmitter broadcasts in the community to which that primary transmitter is licensed by the FCC (in the case of domestic signals) or with which that primary transmitter is identified (in the case of foreign signals).

(iv) A designation as to whether that primary transmitter is a "network station," an "independent station," or a "noncommercial educational station."

(v) A designation as to whether that primary transmitter is a "distant" station.

(vi) If that primary transmitter is a "distant" station, a specification of whether the signals of that primary transmitter are carried:

(A) On a part-time basis where full-time carriage is not possible because the cable system lacks the activated channel capacity to retransmit on a full-time basis all signals which it is authorized to carry; or

(B) On any other basis.

If the signals of that primary transmitter are carried on a part-time basis because of lack of activated channel capacity, the Statement shall also include a log showing the dates on which such carriage occurred, and the hours during which such carriage occurred on those dates. Hours of carriage shall be accurate to the nearest quarter-hour, except that, in any case where such part-time carriage extends to the end of the broadcast day of the primary transmitter, an approximate ending hour may be given if it is indicated as an estimate.

(vii) A designation as to whether the channel carried is a multicast stream, and if so, the sub-channel number assigned to that stream by the television broadcast licensee.

(viii) Simulcasts must be reported and labeled on the Statement of Accounts form in an easily identifiable manner (e.g., WETA-simulcast).

(ix) The information indicated by paragraph (e)(9), paragraphs (v) through (viii) of this section, is not required to be given by any cable system that appropriately completed Form SA1-2 for the period covered by the Statement.

(x) Notwithstanding the requirements of this section, where a cable system carried a distant primary transmitter under FCC rules and regulations in effect on October 19, 1976 which permitted carriage of specific network programs on a part-time basis in certain circumstances (former 47 CFR 76.59(d)(2) and (4), 76.61(e)(2) and (4), and 76.63, referring to 76.61(e)(2) and (4), all of which were deleted June 25, 1981), carriage of that primary transmitter on that basis need not be reported, and that carriage is to be excluded in computing the distant signal equivalent of that primary transmitter.

(10) The designation "Primary Transmitters: Radio," followed by an identification of primary radio transmitters whose signals were carried by the cable system during the period covered by the Statement of Account, together with the information listed below:

(i) A designation as to whether each primary transmitter was electronically processed by the system as a separate and discrete signal.

(ii) The station call sign of each:

(A) AM primary transmitter;

(B) FM primary transmitter, the signals of which were electronically processed by the system as separate and discrete signals; and

(C) FM primary transmitter carried on an all-band retransmission basis, the signals of which were generally receivable by the system.

(iii) A designation as to whether the primary transmitter is AM or FM.

(iv) The name of the community to which that primary transmitter is licensed by the FCC (in the case of domestic signals) or with which that primary transmitter is identified (in the case of foreign signals).

(11) A special statement and program log, which shall consist of the information indicated below for all nonnetwork television programming that, during the period covered by the Statement, was carried in whole or in part beyond the local service area of the primary transmitter of such programming under

(i) rules or regulations of the FCC requiring a cable system to omit the further transmission of a particular program and permitting the substitution of another program in place of the omitted transmission; or

(ii) rules, regulations, or authorizations of the FCC in effect on October 19, 1976, permitting a cable system, at its election, to omit the further transmission of a particular program and permitting the substitution of another program in place of the omitted transmission:

(A) The name or title of the substitute program.

(B) Whether the substitute program was transmitted live by its primary transmitter.

(C) The station call sign of the primary transmitter of the substitute program.

(D) The name of the community to which the primary transmitter of the substitute program is licensed by the FCC (in the case of domestic signals) or with which that primary transmitter is identified (in the case of foreign signals).

(E) The date when the secondary transmission of the substitute program occurred, and the hours during which such secondary transmission occurred on that date accurate to the nearest 5 minutes.

(F) A designation as to whether deletion of the omitted program was permitted by the rules, regulations, or authorizations of the FCC in effect on October 19, 1976, or was required by the rules, regulations, or authorizations of the FCC.

(12) A statement of the total royalty fee payable for the period covered by the Statement of Account, together with a royalty fee analysis which gives a clear, complete, and detailed presentation of the determination of such fee. This analysis shall present in appropriate sequence all facts, figures, and mathematical processes used in determining such fee, and shall do so in such manner as required in the appropriate form so as to permit the Copyright Office to verify readily, from the face of the Statement of Account, the accuracy of such determination and fee. The royalty fee analysis is not required to be given by any cable system whose gross receipts from subscribers for the period covered by the Statement of Account, for the basic service of providing secondary transmissions of primary broadcast transmissions, total $137,100 or less.

(13) The name, address, and telephone number of an individual who may be contacted by the Copyright Office for further information about the Statement of Account.

(14) A legally binding signature, including an electronic signature as defined in 15 U.S.C. 7006, of:

(i) The owner of the cable system or a duly authorized agent of the owner, if the owner is not a partnership or a corporation; or

(ii) A partner, if the owner is a partnership; or

(iii) An officer of the corporation, if the owner is a corporation. The signature shall be accompanied by:

(A) The printed name of the person signing the Statement of Account;

(B) The date of signature;

(C) If the owner of the cable system is a partnership or a corporation, by the title or official position held in the partnership or corporation by the person signing the Statement of Account;

(D) A certification of the capacity of the person signing; and

(E) A declaration of the veracity of the statements of fact contained in the Statement of Account and the good faith of the person signing in making such statement of fact.

(f) Computation of Distant Signal Equivalents.

(1) A cable system that elects to delete a particular television program and substitute for that program another television program ("substitute program") under rules, regulations, or authorizations of the FCC in effect on October 19, 1976, which permit a cable system, at its election, to omit the retransmission of a particular program and substitute another program in its place shall compute the distant signal equivalent ("DSE") of each primary transmitter that broadcasts one or more substitute programs by dividing:

(i) The number of the primary transmitter's live, nonnetwork, substitute programs that were carried by the cable system, during the period covered by the Statement of Account, in substitution for programs deleted at the option of the system; by

(ii) The number of days in the year in which the substitution occurred.

(2)(i) Where a cable system carries a primary transmitter on a full-time basis during any portion of an accounting period, the system shall compute a DSE for that primary transmitter as if it was carried full-time during the entire accounting period.

(ii) Where a cable system carries a primary transmitter solely on a substitute or part-time basis, in accordance with paragraph (f)(3) of this section, the system shall compute a DSE for that primary transmitter based on its cumulative carriage on a substitute or part-time basis. If that primary transmitter is carried on a full-time basis as well as on a substitute or part-time basis, the full DSE for that primary transmitter shall be the full DSE type value for that primary transmitter, for the entire accounting period.

(3) In computing the DSE of a primary transmitter in a particular case of carriage on or after July 1, 1981, the cable system may make no prorated adjustments other than those specified in 17 U.S.C. 111(f)(5)(B), and which remain in force under that provision. Two prorated adjustments, as prescribed in that section, are permitted under certain conditions where:

(i) A station is carried on a part-time basis where full-time carriage is not possible because the cable system lacks the activated channel capacity to retransmit on a full-time basis all signals which it is authorized to carry; and

(ii) A station is carried on a "substitute" basis under rules, regulations, or authorizations of the FCC in effect on October 19, 1976 (as defined in 17 U.S.C. 111(f)(5)(B)(ii)), which permitted a cable system, at its election, to omit the retransmission of a particular program and substitute another program in its place.

(4) In computing a DSE, a cable system may round off to the third decimal point. If a DSE is rounded off in any case in a Statement of Account, it must be rounded off throughout the Statement. Where a cable system has chosen to round off, and the fourth decimal point for a particular DSE value would, without rounding off, have been 1, 2, 3, or 4, the third decimal point remains unchanged; if, in such a case, the fourth decimal point would, without rounding off, be 5, 6, 7, 8, or 9, the third decimal point must be rounded off to the next higher number.

(5) For the purposes of computing DSE values, specialty primary television transmitters in the United States and all Canadian and Mexican primary television transmitters shall be assigned a value of one.

(g) Computation of copyright royalty fee: subscriber groups. **(1)** If a cable system provides a secondary transmission of a primary transmitter to some, but not all, communities served by that cable system—

(i) The gross receipts and the distant signal equivalent values for such secondary transmission shall be derived solely on the basis of the subscribers in those communities where the cable system provides such secondary transmission; and

(ii) The total royalty fee for the period paid by such system shall not be less than the minimum fee multiplied by the gross receipts from all subscribers to the system.

(2) A cable system that, on a statement submitted before the date of the enactment of the Satellite Television Extension and Localism Act of 2010, computed its royalty fee consistent with the methodology under paragraph (i)(1) of this section or that amends a statement filed before such date of enactment to compute the royalty fee due using such methodology, shall not be subject to an action for infringement, or eligible for any royalty refund or offset, arising out of the use of such methodology on such statement.

(3) Any royalty fee payments received by the Copyright Office from cable systems for the secondary transmission of primary transmissions that are in addition to the payments calculated and deposited in accordance with this subsection shall be deemed to have been deposited for the particular accounting period for which they are received and shall be distributed as specified under subsection 111(d) of title 17, United States Code. Such payments shall be considered as part of the base rate royalty fund.

(4) The royalty fee rates established by the Satellite Television Extension and Localism Act shall take effect commencing with the first accounting period occurring in 2010.

(h) Computation of the copyright royalty fee: Partially distant stations. A cable system located partly within and partly without the local service area of a primary television transmitter ("partially distant station") computes the royalty fee specified in section 111(d)(1)(B)(ii), (iii), and (iv) of the Copyright Act ("DSE fee") by excluding gross receipts from subscribers located within that station's local service area from total gross receipts. A cable system which carries two or more partially distant stations with local service areas that do not exactly coincide shall compute a separate DSE fee for each group of subscribers who are located outside of the local service areas of exactly the same complement of distant stations. Computation of the DSE fee for each subscriber group is to be based on:

(1) The total distant signal equivalents of that group's complement of distant stations, and

(2) The total gross receipts from that group of subscribers. The copyright royalty fee for that cable system is:

(i) The total of the subscriber group royalty fees thus computed, or

(ii) 1.013 of 1 percent of the system's gross receipts from all subscribers, whichever is larger.

(i) Computation of the copyright royalty fee pursuant to the 1982 cable rate adjustment.

(1) For the purposes of this paragraph, in addition to the definitions of paragraph (b) of this section, the following definitions shall also apply:

(i) "Current base rate" means the applicable royalty rates in effect on December 31, 1982, as reflected in 37 CFR 256.2(a).

(ii) Surcharge means the applicable syndicated exclusivity surcharge established by 37 CFR 308.2(d), in effect on

January 1, 1983. For accounting periods beginning on or after January 1, 1990, "surcharge" refers to the applicable syndicated exclusivity surcharge established by 37 CFR 308.2(d) in effect on January 1, 1990.

(iii) The "3.75% rate" means the rate established by 37 CFR 256.2(c), in effect on March 15, 1983.

(iv) "Top 100 television market" means a television market defined or interpreted as being within either the "top 50 television markets" or "second 50 television markets" in accordance with 47 CFR 76.51, in effect on June 24, 1981.

(v) The "1982 cable rate adjustment" means the rate adjustment adopted by the Copyright Royalty Tribunal on October 20, 1982 (CRT Docket No. 81-2, 47 FR 52146, November 19, 1982).

(2) A cable system filing Form SA3 shall compute its royalty fee in the following manner:

(i) The cable system shall first determine those DSE's to which the 3.75% rate established by 37 CFR 256.2(c) applies.

(ii) If the 3.75% rate does not apply to certain DSE's in the case of a cable system located wholly or in part within a top 100 television market, the current base rate together with the surcharge shall apply. However, the surcharge shall not apply for carriage of a particular signal first carried prior to March 31, 1972. With respect to statements of account covering the filing period beginning January 1, 1990, and subsequent filing periods, the current base rate together with the surcharge shall apply only to those DSE's that represent commercial VHF signals which place a predicted Grade B contour, in whole or in part, over a cable system. The surcharge will not apply if the signal is exempt from the syndicated exclusivity rules in effect on June 24, 1981.

(iii) If the 3.75% rate does not apply to certain DSE's, in the case of a cable system located wholly outside a top 100 television market, the current base rate shall apply.

(iv) Commencing with the semiannual accounting period of January 1, 1998, through June 30, 1998, the 3.75% rate applies to certain DSE's with respect to the communities within the cable system where carriage would not have been permitted under the rules and regulations of the Federal Communications Commission in effect on June 24, 1981, but in all other communities within the cable system, the current base rate and the syndicated exclusivity surcharge, where applicable, shall apply. Such computation shall be made as provided for on Form SA3. The calculations shall be based upon the gross receipts from all subscribers, within the relevant communities, for the basic service of providing secondary transmissions of primary broadcast transmitters, without regard to whether those subscribers actually received the station in question. For partially-distant stations, gross receipts shall be the total gross receipts from subscribers outside the local service area.

(3) It shall be presumed that the 3.75% rate of 37 CFR 308.2(c) applies to DSEs accruing from newly added distant signals, carried for the first time by a cable system after June 24, 1981. The presumption of this section can be rebutted in whole or in part:

(i) By actual carriage of a particular distant signal prior to June 25, 1981, as reported in Statements of Account duly filed with the Copyright Office ("actual carriage"), unless the prior carriage was not permitted by the FCC; or

(ii) By carriage of no more than the number of distant signals which was or would have been allotted to the cable system under the FCC's quota for importation of network and nonspecialty independent stations (47 CFR 76.59(b), 76.61(b) and (c), and 76.63, referring to §76.61(b) and (c), in effect on June 24, 1981).

(4) To qualify as an FCC-permitted signal on the ground of individual waiver of the FCC rules (47 CFR 76.7 in effect on June 24, 1981), the waiver must have actually been granted by the FCC, and the signal must have been first carried by the cable system after April 15, 1976.

(5) Expanded geographic carriage after June 24, 1981, of a signal previously carried within only certain parts of a cable system is governed by the current base rate and the surcharge, if applicable.

(6) In cases of expanded temporal carriage of the same signal, previously carried pursuant to the FCC's former part-time or substitute carriage rules [47 CFR 76.61(b)(2), 76.61(e)(1) and (e)(3), and 76.63, referring to 76.61(e)(1) and (e)(3), in effect on June 24, 1981], the 3.75% rate shall be applied to any additional fraction of a DSE accruing from the expanded temporal carriage of that signal. To identify such additional DSE's, a comparison shall be made of DSE's reported for that signal in any single accounting period prior to the July 1, 1981, to December 31, 1981, period (81-2), as designated by the cable system, with the DSE's for that same signal reported in the current relevant accounting period.

(7) Substitution of like signals pursuant to 37 CFR 256.2(c) is possible at the relevant non-3.75% rate (the surcharge together with the current base rate, or the current base rate alone) only if the substitution does not exceed the number of distant signals which was or would have been allotted to the cable system under the FCC's television market quota for importation of network and nonspecialty independent stations (47 CFR 76.59(b), 76.61(b) and (c), and 76.63, referring to 76.61(b) and (c), in effect on June 24, 1981).

(8) The 3.75% rate does not apply to distant multicast streams retransmitted by cable systems.

(j) Multicasting. **(1)** A royalty payment shall be made for the retransmission of non-network television programming carried on each multicast stream of a distant digital television signal under the following circumstances:

(i) If the distant multicast stream was first retransmitted by a cable system on or after February 27, 2010, or

(ii) If the distant multicast stream is retransmitted by a cable operator on or after July 1, 2010.

(2) In any case in which a distant multicast stream is the subject of a written agreement entered into on or before June 30, 2009, between a cable system or an association representing the cable system and a primary transmitter or an association representing the primary transmitter, a distant signal equivalent value shall not be assigned to a distant multicast stream that is made on or before the date on which such written agreement expires.

(3) No royalties are due for carrying a distant multicast stream that "simulcasts" (i.e., duplicates) a primary stream or another multicast stream of the same station that the cable system is carrying. However, simulcast streams must be reported on the Statement of Accounts.

(4) Multicast streams of digital broadcast programming shall not be subject to the 3.75% fee or the syndicated exclusivity surcharge.

(k) Royalty fee payment.

(1) All royalty fees must be paid by a single electronic funds transfer, and must be received in the designated bank by the filing deadline for the relevant accounting period. The following information must be provided as part of the EFT and/or as part of the remittance advice as provided for in circulars issued by the Copyright Office:

(i) Remitter's name and address;

(ii) Name of a contact person, telephone number and extension, and e-mail address;

(iii) The actual or anticipated date that the EFT will be transmitted;

(iv) Type of royalty payment (*i.e.* cable);

(v) Total amount submitted via the EFT;

(vi) Total amount to be paid by year and period;

(vii) Number of Statements of Account that the EFT covers;

(viii) ID numbers assigned by the Licensing Division;

(ix) Legal name of the owner for each Statement of Account;

(x) Identification of the first community served (city and state).

(2) The remittance advice shall be attached to the Statement(s) of Account. In addition, a copy of the remittance advice shall be emailed or sent by facsimile to the Licensing Division.

(3) The Office may waive the requirement for payment by electronic funds transfer as set forth in paragraph (i)(1) of this section. To obtain a waiver, the remitter shall submit to the Licensing Division at least 60 days prior to the royalty fee due date a certified statement setting forth the reasons explaining why payment by an electronic funds transfer would be virtually impossible or, alternatively, why it would impose a financial or other hardship on the remitter. The certified statement must be signed by a duly authorized representative of the entity making the payment. A waiver shall cover only a single payment period. Failure to obtain a waiver may result in the remittance being returned to the remitter.

(4) Royalty fee payments submitted as a result of late or amended filings shall include interest. Interest shall begin to accrue beginning on the first day after the close of the period for filing statements of account for all late payments and underpayments of royalties for the cable statutory license occurring within that accounting period. The accrual period shall end on the date the electronic payment submitted by a cable operator is received. The accrual period shall end on the date the electronic payment submitted by a satellite carrier is received by the Copyright Office. In cases where a waiver of the electronic funds transfer requirement is approved by the Copyright Office, and royalties payments are either late or underpaid, the accrual period shall end on the date the payment is postmarked. If the payment is not received by the Copyright Office within five business days of its date, then the accrual period shall end on the date of the actual receipt by the Copyright Office. Interest is not required to be paid on any royalty underpayment or late payment from a particular accounting period if the interest charge is less than or equal to five dollars.

(*l*) Corrections, supplemental payments, and refunds.

(1) Royalty fee obligations under 17 U.S.C. 111 prior to the effective date of the Satellite Television Extension and Localism Act of 2010, Public Law 111-175, are determined based on carriage of each distant signal on a system-wide basis. Refunds for an overpayment of royalty fees for an accounting period prior to January 1, 2010, shall be made only when all outstanding royalty fee obligations have been met, including those for carriage of each distant signal on a system-wide basis.

(2) Upon compliance with the procedures and within the time limits set forth in paragraph (m)(4) of this section, corrections to Statements of Account will be placed on record, supplemental royalty fee payments will be received for deposit, or refunds will be issued, in the following cases:

(i) Where, with respect to the accounting period covered by a Statement of Account, any of the information given in the Statement filed in the Copyright Office is incorrect or incomplete; or

(ii) Where, for any reason except that mentioned in paragraph (m)(2)(iii) of this section, calculation of the royalty fee payable for a particular accounting period was incorrect, and the amount deposited in the Copyright Office for that period was either too high or too low.

(3) Corrections to Statements of Account will not be placed on record, supplemental royalty fee payments will not be received for deposit, and refunds will not be issued, where the information in the Statements of Account, the royalty fee calculations, or the payments were correct as of the date on

which the accounting period ended, but changes (for example, addition or deletion of a distant signal) took place later.

(4) Requests that corrections to a Statement of Account be placed on record, that fee payments be accepted, or requests for the issuance of refunds, shall be made only in the cases mentioned in paragraph (m)(2) of this section. Such requests shall be addressed to the Licensing Division of the Copyright Office, and shall meet the following conditions:

(i) The request must be in writing, must clearly identify its purpose, and, in the case of a request for a refund, must be received in the Copyright Office before the expiration of 60 days from the last day of the applicable Statement of Account filing period, or before the expiration of 60 days from the date of receipt at the Copyright Office of the royalty payment that is the subject of the request, whichever time period is longer. Telephone or similar unsigned requests that meet these conditions may be permitted, where a follow-up written request detailing the same information is received by the Copyright Office within fourteen days after the required sixty-day period.

(ii) The Statement of Account to which the request pertains must be sufficiently identified in the request (by inclusion of the name of the owner of the cable system, the community or communities served, and the accounting period in question) so that it can be readily located in the records of the Copyright Office.

(iii) The request must contain a clear statement of the facts on which it is based and provide a clear basis on which a refund may be granted, in accordance with the following procedures:

(A) In the case of a request filed under paragraph (m)(2)(i) of this section, where the information given in the Statement of Account is incorrect or incomplete, the request must clearly identify the erroneous or incomplete information and provide the correct or additional information;

(B) In the case of a request filed under paragraph (m)(2)(ii) of this section, where the royalty fee was miscalculated and the amount deposited in the Copyright Office was either too high or too low, the request must be accompanied by an amended Statement of Account. The amended Statement shall include an explanation of why the royalty fee was improperly calculated and a detailed analysis of the proper royalty calculations.

(iv)(A) All requests filed under this paragraph (m) must be accompanied by a filing fee in the amount prescribed in §201.3(e) of this part for each Statement of Account involved. Payment of this fee may be in the form of a personal or company check, or of a certified check, cashier's check or money order, payable to: Register of Copyrights. No request will be processed until the appropriate filing fees are received; and

(B) All requests that a supplemental royalty fee payment be received for deposit under this paragraph (m) must be accompanied by a remittance in the full amount of such fee. Payment of the supplemental royalty fee must be in the form of a certified check, cashier's check, or money order, payable to: Register of Copyrights; or an electronic payment. No such request will be processed until an acceptable remittance in the full amount of the supplemental royalty fee has been received.

(v) All requests submitted under this paragraph (m) must be signed by the cable system owner named in the Statement of Account, or the duly authorized agent of the owner, in accordance with paragraph (e)(14) of this section.

(vi) A request for a refund is not necessary where the Licensing Division, during its examination of a Statement of Account or related document, discovers an error that has resulted in a royalty overpayment. In this case, the Licensing Division will forward the royalty refund to the cable system owner named in the Statement of Account without regard to the time limitations provided for in paragraph (m)(4)(i) of this section.

(5) Following final processing, all requests submitted under this paragraph (m) will be filed with the original Statement of Account in the records of the Copyright Office. Nothing contained in this paragraph shall be considered to relieve cable systems from their full obligations under Title 17 of the United States Code, and the filing of a correction or supplemental payment shall have only such effect as may be attributed to it by a court of competent jurisdiction.

(m) Satellite carriers not eligible. Satellite carriers and satellite resale carriers are not eligible for the cable compulsory license based upon an interpretation of the whole of section 111 of title 17 of the United States Code.

History of 37 C.F.R. §201.17: 43 FR 27832, June 27, 1978; 45 FR 45274, July 3, 1980; 47 FR 21789, May 20, 1982; 49 FR 13037, Apr. 4, 1984; 49 FR 14952, Apr. 16, 1984; 49 FR 26726, June 29, 1984; 49 FR 33017, Aug. 20, 1984; 50 FR 9273, Mar. 7, 1985; 50 FR 11366, Mar. 21, 1985; 51 FR 30216, Aug. 25, 1986; 51 FR 45112, Dec. 17, 1986; 52 FR 28253, July 29, 1987; 54 FR 14221, Apr. 10, 1989; 55 FR 49999, Dec. 4, 1990; 56 FR 7813, Feb. 26, 1991; 56 FR 29589, June 28, 1991; 57 FR 3296, Jan. 29, 1992; 57 FR 61834, Dec. 29, 1992; 58 FR 40363, July 28, 1993; 58 FR 45263, Aug. 27, 1993; 59 FR 67635, Dec. 30, 1994; 60 FR 34168, June 30, 1995; 60 FR 57937, Nov. 24, 1995; 62 FR 18710, Apr. 17, 1997; 62 FR 23362, Apr. 30, 1997; 63 FR 30635, June 5, 1998; 63 FR 39738, July 24, 1998; 64 FR 36574, July 7, 1999; 65 FR 64623, Oct. 30, 2000; 66 FR 34373, June 28, 2001; 70 FR 30366, May 26, 2005; 70 FR 38022, July 1, 2005; 70 FR 58311, Oct. 6, 2005; 71 FR 45739, Aug. 10, 2006; 72 FR 33691, July 1, 2007; 73 C.F.R. 29073, May 20, 2008; 75 FR 20256, Apr. 20, 2010; 75 FR 56868, Sept. 17, 2010; 78 FR 1759, Feb. 8, 2013; 78 FR 42874, July 18, 2013; 79 FR 68632, Nov. 18, 2014; 82 FR 9357, Mar. 8, 2017; 82 FR 22886, June 19, 2017.

§201.18. Notice of Intention to Obtain a Compulsory License for Making & Distributing Phonorecords of Nondramatic Musical Works

(a) General.

(1) A "Notice of Intention" is a Notice identified in section 115(b) of title 17 of the United States Code, and required by that section to be served on a copyright owner or, in certain cases, to be filed in the Copyright Office, before or within thirty days after making, and before distributing any phonorecords of the work, in order to obtain a compulsory license to make and distribute phonorecords of nondramatic musical works.

(2) A person is entitled to serve or file a Notice of Intention and thereby obtain a compulsory license pursuant to 17 U.S.C. 115 only if the primary purpose in making phonorecords is to distribute them to the public for private use, including by means of a digital phonorecord delivery.

(3) For the purposes of this section, a "digital phonorecord delivery" is each individual delivery of a phonorecord by digital transmission of a sound recording which results in a specifically identifiable reproduction by or for any transmission recipient of a phonorecord of that sound recording, regardless of whether the digital transmission is also a public performance of the sound recording or any nondramatic musical work embodied therein. The reproduction of the phonorecord must be sufficiently permanent or stable to permit it to be perceived, reproduced, or otherwise communicated for a period of more than transitory duration. Such a phonorecord may be permanent or it may be made available to the transmission recipient for a limited period of time or for a specified number of performances. A digital phonorecord delivery includes all phonorecords that are made for the purpose of making the digital phonorecord delivery.

(4) A Notice of Intention shall be served or filed for nondramatic musical works embodied, or intended to be embodied, in phonorecords made under the compulsory license. For purposes of this section and subject to paragraphs (a)(4)(ii) and (iii) of this section, a Notice filed with the Copyright Office which lists multiple works shall be considered a single Notice and fees shall be paid in accordance with the fee schedule set forth in §201.3(e)(1) if filed in the Copyright Office under paragraph (f)(3) of this section. Payment of the applicable fees for a Notice submitted electronically under this paragraph shall be made through a deposit account established under §201.6(b).

(i) Except as provided for in paragraph (a)(7), a Notice of Intention served on a copyright owner or agent of a copyright owner may designate any number of nondramatic musical works provided that the information required under paragraphs (d)(1)(i) through (iv) of this section does not vary and that the copyright owner of each designated work is the same, or in the case of any work having more than one copyright owner, that any one of the copyright owners is the same and is the copyright owner served.

(ii) A Notice of Intention filed in the Copyright Office in paper form may designate any number of nondramatic musical works provided that the information required under paragraphs (d)(1)(i) through (iv) of this section does not vary, and that the copyright owner of each designated work (or, in the case of works having more than one copyright owner, any one of the copyright owners) is the same and the registration records or other public records of the Copyright Office do not identify the copyright owner(s) of such work(s) and include an address for any such owner(s) at which notice can be served. For purposes of this subparagraph, in the case of works having more than one copyright owner, a single Notice must identify an actual person or entity as the common copyright owner; the common copyright owner may not be identified as "unknown." However, a single Notice may include multiple works for which no copyright owners can be identified for any of the listed works.

(iii) A Notice of Intention filed in the Copyright Office through its electronic filing system may designate multiple nondramatic musical works, regardless of whether the copyright owner of each designated work (or, in the case of any work having more than one copyright owner, any one of the copyright owners) is the same, provided that the information required under paragraphs(d)(1)(i) through (iv) of this section does not vary, and that for any designated work, the records of the Copyright Office do not include an address at which notice can be served.

(5) For the purposes of this section, the term copyright owner, in the case of any work having more than one copyright owner, means any one of the co-owners.

(6) For the purposes of this section, service of a Notice of Intention on a copyright owner may be accomplished by means of service of the Notice on either the copyright owner or an agent of the copyright owner with authority to receive the Notice. In the case where the work has more than one copyright owner, the service of the Notice on any one of the co-owners of the nondramatic musical work or upon an authorized agent of one of the co-owners identified in the Notice of Intention shall be sufficient with respect to all co-owners. Notwithstanding paragraph (a)(2) of this section, a single Notice may designate works not owned by the same copyright owner in the case where the Notice is served on a common agent of multiple copyright owners, and where each of the works designated in the Notice is owned by any of the copyright owners who have authorized that agent to receive Notices.

(7) For purposes of this section, a copyright owner or an agent of a copyright owner with authority to receive Notices of Intention may make public a written policy that it will accept Notices of Intention to make and distribute phonorecords pursuant to 17 U.S.C. 115 which include less than all of the information required by this section, in a form different than required by this section, or delivered by means (including electronic transmission) other than those required by this section. Any Notice provided in accordance with such policy shall not be rendered invalid for failing to comply with the specific requirements of this section.

(8) For the purposes of this section, a digital phonorecord delivery shall be treated as a type of phonorecord configuration, and a digital phonorecord delivery shall be treated as a phonorecord manufactured, made, and distributed on the date the phonorecord is digitally transmitted.

(b) Agent. An agent who has been authorized to accept Notices of Intention in accordance with paragraph (a)(6) of this section and who has received a Notice of Intention on behalf of a copyright owner shall provide within two weeks of the receipt of that Notice of Intention the name and address of the copyright owner or its agent upon whom the person or entity intending to obtain the compulsory license shall serve Statements of Account and the monthly royalty in accordance with §210.16(g) of this chapter.

(c) Form. The Copyright Office does not provide printed forms for the use of persons serving or filing Notices of Intention.

(d) Content.

(1) A Notice of Intention shall be clearly and prominently designated, at the head of the notice, as a "Notice of Intention to Obtain a Compulsory License for Making and Distributing Phonorecords," and shall include a clear statement of the following information:

(i) The full legal name of the person or entity intending to obtain the compulsory license, together with all fictitious or assumed names used by such person or entity for the purpose of conducting the business of making and distributing phonorecords;

(ii) The telephone number, the full address, including a specific number and street name or rural route of the place of business, and an e-mail address, if available, of the person or entity intending to obtain the compulsory license, and if a business organization intends to obtain the compulsory license, the name and title of the chief executive officer, managing partner, sole proprietor or other person similarly responsible for the management of such entity. A post office box or similar designation will not be sufficient for this purpose except where it is the only address that can be used in that geographic location.

(iii) The information specified in paragraphs (d)(1)(i) and (ii) of this section for the primary entity expected to be engaged in the business of making and distributing phonorecords under the license or of authorizing such making and distribution (for example: a record company or digital music service), if an entity intending to obtain the compulsory license is a holding company, trust or other entity that is not expected to be actively engaged in the business of making and distributing phonorecords under the license or of authorizing such making and distribution;

(iv) The fiscal year of the person or entity intending to obtain the compulsory license. If that fiscal year is a calendar year, the Notice shall state that this is the case;

(v) For each nondramatic musical work embodied or intended to be embodied in phonorecords made under the compulsory license:

(A) The title of the nondramatic musical work;

(B) The name of the author or authors, if known;

(C) A copyright owner of the work, if known;

(D) The types of all phonorecord configurations already made (if any) and expected to be made under the compulsory license (for example: single disk, long-playing disk, cassette, cartridge, reel-to-reel, a digital phonorecord delivery, or a combination of them);

(E) The expected date of initial distribution of phonorecords already made (if any) or expected to be made under the compulsory license;

(F) The name of the principal recording artist or group actually engaged or expected to be engaged in rendering the performances fixed on phonorecords already made (if any) or expected to be made under the compulsory license;

(G) The catalog number or numbers, and label name or names, used or expected to be used on phonorecords already made (if any) or expected to be made under the compulsory license; and

(H) In the case of phonorecords already made (if any) under the compulsory license, the date or dates of such manufacture.

(vi) In the case where the Notice will be filed with the Copyright Office pursuant to paragraph (f)(3) of this section, the Notice shall include an affirmative statement that with respect to the nondramatic musical work named in the Notice of Intention, the registration records or other public records of the Copyright Office have been searched and found not to identify the name and address of the copyright owner of such work.

(2) A "clear statement" of the information listed in paragraph (d)(1) of this section requires a clearly intelligible, legible, and unambiguous statement in the Notice itself and without incorporation by reference of facts or information contained in other documents or records.

(3) Where information is required to be given by paragraph (d)(1) of this section "if known" or as "expected," such information shall be given in good faith and on the basis of the best knowledge, information, and belief of the person signing the Notice. If so given, later developments affecting the accuracy of such information shall not affect the validity of the Notice.

(e) Signature. The Notice shall be signed by the person or entity intending to obtain the compulsory license or by a duly authorized agent of such person or entity.

(1) If the person or entity intending to obtain the compulsory license is a corporation, the signature shall be that of a duly authorized officer or agent of the corporation.

(2) If the person or entity intending to obtain the compulsory license is a partnership, the signature shall be that of a partner or of a duly authorized agent of the partnership.

(3) If the Notice is signed by a duly authorized agent for the person or entity intending to obtain the compulsory license, the Notice shall include an affirmative statement that the agent is authorized to execute the Notice of Intention on behalf of the person or entity intending to obtain the compulsory license.

(4) If the Notice is served electronically, the person or entity intending to obtain the compulsory license and the copyright owner shall establish a procedure to verify that the Notice is being submitted upon the authority of the person or entity intending to obtain the compulsory license.

(5) If the Notice is filed in the Office electronically, the person or entity intending to obtain the compulsory license or a duly authorized agent of such person or entity shall, rather than signing the Notice, attest that he or she has the appropriate authority of the licensee, including any related entities listed, if applicable, to submit the electronically filed Notice on behalf of the licensee.

(f) Filing and service.

(1) If the registration records or other public records of the Copyright Office identify the copyright owner of the nondramatic musical works named in the Notice of Intention and include an address for such owner, the Notice may be served on such owner by mail sent to, or by reputable courier service at, the last address for such owner shown by the records of the Office. It shall not be necessary to file a copy of the Notice in the Copyright Office in this case.

(2) If the Notice is sent by mail or delivered by reputable courier service to the last address for the copyright owner shown by the records of the Copyright Office and the Notice is returned to the sender because the copyright owner is no longer located at the address or has refused to accept delivery, the original Notice as sent shall be filed in the Copyright Office. Notices of Intention submitted for filing under this paragraph (f)(2) shall be submitted to the Licensing Division of the Copyright Office, shall be accompanied by a brief statement that the Notice was sent to the last address for the copyright owner shown by the records of the Copyright Office but was returned, and may be accompanied by appropriate evidence that it was mailed to, or that delivery by reputable courier service was attempted at, that address. In these cases, the Copyright Office will specially mark its records to consider the date the original Notice was mailed, or the date delivery by courier service was attempted, if shown by the evidence mentioned above, as the date of filing. An acknowledgment of receipt and filing will be provided to the sender.

(3) If, with respect to the nondramatic musical works named in the Notice of Intention, the registration records or other public records of the Copyright Office do not identify the copyright owner of such work and include an address for such owner, the Notice may be filed in the Copyright Office. Notices of Intention submitted for filing shall be accompanied by the fee specified in §201.3(e). A separate fee shall be assessed for each title listed in the Notice. Notices of Intention will be placed in the appropriate public records of the Licensing Division of the Copyright Office. The date of filing will be the date when the Notice and fee are both received in the Copyright Office. An acknowledgment of receipt and filing will be provided to the sender.

(4) Alternatively, if the person or entity intending to obtain the compulsory license knows the name and address of the copyright owner of the nondramatic musical work, or the agent of the copyright owner as described in paragraph (b) of this section, the Notice of Intention may be served on the copyright owner or the agent of the copyright owner by sending the Notice by mail or delivering it by reputable courier service to the address of the copyright owner or agent of the copyright owner. For purposes of section 115(b)(1) of title 17 of the United States Code, the Notice will not be considered properly served if the Notice is not sent to the copyright owner or the agent of the copyright owner as described in paragraph (b) of this section, or if the Notice is sent to an incorrect address.

(5) If a Notice of Intention is sent by certified mail or registered mail, a mailing receipt shall be sufficient to prove that service was timely. If a Notice of Intention is delivered by a reputable courier, documentation from the courier showing the first date of attempted delivery shall also be sufficient to prove that service was timely. In the absence of a receipt from the United States Postal Service showing the date of delivery or documentation showing the first date of attempted delivery by a reputable courier, the compulsory licensee shall bear the burden of proving that the Notice of Intention was served in a timely manner.

(6) If a Notice served upon a copyright owner or an authorized agent of a copyright owner identifies more than 50 works that are embodied or intended to be embodied in phonorecords made under the compulsory license, the copyright owner or the authorized agent may send the person who served the Notice a demand that a list of each of the works so identified be resubmitted in an electronic format, along with a copy of the original Notice. The person who served the Notice must submit such a list, which shall include all of the information required in paragraph (d)(1)(v) of this section, within 30 days after receipt of the demand from the copyright owner or authorized agent. The list shall be submitted on magnetic disk or another medium widely used at the time for electronic storage of data, in the form of a flat file, word processing document or spreadsheet readable with computer software in wide use at such time, with the required information identified and/or delimited so as to be readily discernible. The list may be submitted by means of electronic transmission (such as e-mail) if the demand from the copyright owner or authorized agent states that such submission will be accepted.

(g) Filing date and legal sufficiency of Notices. The Copyright Office will notify a prospective licensee when a Notice was not accompanied by payment of the required fee. Notices shall be deemed filed as of the date the Office receives both the Notice and the fee, if applicable. If the prospective licensee fails to remit the required fee, the Notice will be deemed not to have been filed with the Office. However, the Copyright Office does not review Notices for legal sufficiency or interpret the content of any Notice filed with the Copyright Office under this section. Furthermore, the Copyright Office does not screen Notices for errors or discrepancies and it does not generally correspond with a prospective licensee about the sufficiency of a Notice. If any issue (other than an issue related to fees) arises as to whether a Notice filed in the Copyright Office is sufficient as a matter of law under this section, that issue shall be determined not by the Copyright Office, but shall be subject to a determination of legal sufficiency by a court of competent jurisdiction. Prospective licensees are therefore cautioned to review and scrutinize Notices to assure their legal sufficiency before filing them in the Copyright Office.

(h) Harmless errors. Harmless errors in a Notice that do not materially affect the adequacy of the information required to serve the purposes of section 115(b)(1) of title 17 of the United States Code, shall not render the Notice invalid.

(i) Privacy Act Advisory Statement. The authority for receiving the personally identifying information included within a Notice of Intention to obtain a compulsory license is found in 17 U.S.C. 115 and §201.18. Personally identifying information is any personal information that can be used to identify or trace an individual, such as name, address or telephone numbers. Furnishing the information set forth in §201.18 is voluntary. However, if the information is not furnished, it may affect the sufficiency of Notice of Intention to obtain a compulsory license and may not entitle the prospective licensee to the benefits available under 17 U.S.C. 115. The principal uses of the requested information are the establishment and maintenance of a public record of the Notices of Intention to obtain a compulsory license received in the Licensing Division of the Copyright Office. Other routine uses include public inspection and copying, preparation of public indexes, preparation of public catalogs of copyright records including online catalogs, and preparation of search reports upon request.

History of 37 C.F.R. §201.18: 45 FR 79045, Nov. 28, 1980; 56 FR 59885, Nov. 26, 1991; 63 FR 30635, June 5, 1998; 64 FR 29521, June 1, 1999; 64 FR 36574, July 7, 1999; 64 FR 41288, July 30, 1999; 69 FR 34582, June 22, 2004; 73 FR 66181, Dec. 8, 2008; 77 FR 71103, Jan. 14, 2013; 79 FR 56206, Sept. 18, 2014; 82 FR 9358, Mar. 8, 2017.

§§201.19 TO 201.21. REMOVED & RESERVED

§201.22. ADVANCE NOTICES OF POTENTIAL INFRINGEMENT OF WORKS CONSISTING OF SOUNDS, IMAGES, OR BOTH

(a) Definitions.

(1) An "Advance Notice of Potential Infringement" is a notice which, if served in accordance with section 411(c) of Title 17 of the United States Code, and in accordance with the provisions of this section, enables a copyright owner to institute an action for copyright infringement either before or after the first fixation of a work consisting of sounds, images, or both that is first fixed simultaneously with its transmission, and to enjoy the full remedies of said Title 17 for copyright infringement, provided registration for the work is made within three months after its first transmission.

(2) For purposes of this section, the "copyright owner" of a work consisting of sounds, images, or both, the first fixation of which is made simultaneously with its transmission, is the person or entity that will be considered the author of the work upon its fixation (including, in the case of a work made for hire, the employer or other person or entity for whom the work was prepared), or a person or organization that has obtained ownership of an exclusive right, initially owned by the person or entity that will be considered the author of the work upon its fixation.

(3) A "transmission program" is a body of material that, as an aggregate, has been produced for the sole purpose of transmission to the public in sequence and as a unit.

(b) Form. The Copyright Office does not provide printed forms for the use of persons serving Advance Notices of Potential Infringement.

(c) Contents.

(1) An Advance Notice of Potential Infringement shall be clearly and prominently captioned "ADVANCE NOTICE OF POTENTIAL INFRINGEMENT" and must clearly state that the copyright owner objects to the relevant activities of the person responsible for the potential infringement, and must include all of the following:

(i) Reference to title 17. U.S.C. section 411(c) as the statutory authority on which the Advance Notice of Potential Infringement is based;

(ii) The date, specific time, and expected duration of the intended first transmission of the work or works contained in the specific transmission program;

(iii) The source of the intended first transmission of the work or works;

(iv) Clear identification, by title, of the work or works. A single Advance Notice of Potential Infringement may cover all of the works of the copyright owner embodied in a specific transmission program. If any work is untitled, the Advance Notice of Potential Infringement shall include a detailed description of that work;

(v) The name of at least one person or entity that will be considered the author of the work upon its fixation;

(vi) The identity of the copyright owner, as defined in paragraph (a)(2) of this section. If the copyright owner is not the person or entity that will be considered the author of the work upon its fixation, the Advance Notice of Potential Infringement also shall include a brief, general statement summarizing the means by which the copyright owner obtained ownership of the copyright and the particular rights that are owned; and

(vii) A description of the relevant activities of the person responsible for the potential infringement which would, if carried out, result in an infringement of the copyright.

(2) An Advance Notice of Potential Infringement must also include clear and prominent statements:

(i) Explaining that the relevant activities may, if carried out, subject the person responsible to liability for copyright infringement; and

(ii) Declaring that the copyright owner intends to secure copyright in the work upon its fixation.

(d) Signature and identification.

(1) An Advance Notice of Potential Infringement shall be in writing and signed by the copyright owner, or such owner's duly authorized agent.

(2) The signature of the owner or agent shall be an actual handwritten signature of an individual, accompanied by the date of signature and the full name, address, and telephone number of that person, typewritten or printed legibly by hand.

(3) If an Advance Notice of Potential Infringement is initially served in the form of an email, fax, or similar communication, as provided by paragraph (e)(2)(iii) of this section, the requirement for an individual's handwritten signature shall be considered waived if the further conditions of said paragraph (e) are met.

(e) Service.

(1) An Advance Notice of Potential Infringement shall be served on the person responsible for the potential infringement not less than 48 hours before the first fixation and simultaneous transmission of the work as provided by 17 U.S.C. 411(c)(1).

(2) Service of the Advance Notice may be effected by any of the following methods:

(i) Personal service;

(ii) First-class mail; or

(iii) Email, fax, or similar form of communication, if: (A) The Advance Notice meets all of the other conditions provided by this section; and (B) before the first fixation and simultaneous transmission take place, the person responsible for the potential infringement receives written confirmation of the Advance Notice, bearing the actual handwritten signature of the copyright owner or duly authorized agent.

(3) The date of service is the date the Advance Notice of Potential Infringement is received by the person responsible for the potential infringement or by any agent or employee of that person.

History of 37 C.F.R. §201.22: 46 FR 28849, May 29, 1981; 63 FR 66042, Dec. 1, 1998; 66 FR 34373, June 28, 2001; 82 FR 9358, Mar. 8, 2017.

§201.23. TRANSFER OF UNPUBLISHED COPYRIGHT DEPOSITS TO THE LIBRARY OF CONGRESS

(a) General. This section prescribes rules governing the transfer of unpublished copyright deposits in the custody of the Copyright Office to the Library of Congress. The copyright deposits may consist of copies, phonorecords, or identifying material deposited in connection with registration of claims to copyright under section 408 of Title 17 of the United States Code. These rules establish the conditions under which the Library of Congress is entitled to select deposits of unpublished works for its collections or for permanent transfer to the National Archives of the United States or to a Federal records center in accordance with section 704(b) of Title 17 of the United States Code.

(b) Selection by the Library of Congress. The Library of Congress may select any deposits of unpublished works for the purposes stated in paragraph (a) of this section at the time of registration or at any time thereafter; provided that:

(1) A facsimile reproduction of the entire copyrightable content of the deposit shall be made a part of the Copyright Office records before transfer to the Library of Congress as provided by section 704(c) of Title 17 of the United States Code, unless, within the discretion of the Register of Copyrights, it is considered impractical or too expensive to make the reproduction;

(2) All unpublished copyright deposits retained by the Library of Congress in its collections shall be maintained under the control of the Library of Congress with appropriate safeguards against unauthorized copying or other unauthorized use of the deposits which would be contrary to the rights of the copyright owner in the work under Title 17 of the United States Code; and

(3) At the time selection is made a request for full term retention of the deposit under the control of the Copyright Office has not been granted by the Register of Copyrights, in accordance with section 704(e) of Title 17 of the United States Code.

History of 37 C.F.R. §201.23: 45 FR 41414, June 19, 1980; 82 FR 9358, Mar. 8, 2017.

§201.24. WARNING OF COPYRIGHT FOR SOFTWARE LENDING BY NONPROFIT LIBRARIES

(a) Definition. A Warning of Copyright for Software Rental is a notice under paragraph (b)(2)(A) of section 109 of the Copyright Act, title 17 of the United States Code, as amended by the Computer Software Rental Amendments Act of 1990, Public Law 101-650. As required by that paragraph, the "Warning of Copyright for Software Rental" shall be affixed to the packaging that contains the computer program which is lent by a nonprofit library for nonprofit purposes.

(b) Contents. A Warning of Copyright for Software Rental shall consist of a verbatim reproduction of the following notice, printed in such size and form and affixed in such manner as to comply with paragraph (c) of this section.

Notice: Warning of Copyright Restrictions

The copyright law of the United States (title 17, United States Code) governs the reproduction, distribution, adaptation, public performance, and public display of copyrighted material.

Under certain conditions specified in law, nonprofit libraries are authorized to lend, lease, or rent copies of computer programs to patrons on a nonprofit basis and for nonprofit purposes. Any person who makes an unauthorized copy or adaptation of the computer program, or redistributes the loan copy, or publicly performs or displays the computer program, except as permitted by title 17 of the United States Code, may be liable for copyright infringement.

This institution reserves the right to refuse to fulfill a loan request if, in its judgement, fulfillment of the request would lead to violation of the copyright law.

(c) Form and manner of use. A Warning of Copyright for Software Rental shall be affixed to the packaging that contains the copy of the computer program, which is the subject of a library loan to patrons, by means of a label cemented, gummed, or otherwise durably attached to the copies or to a box, reel, cartridge, cassette, or other container used as a permanent receptacle for the copy of the computer program. The notice shall be printed in such manner as to be clearly legible, comprehensible, and readily apparent to a casual user of the computer program.

History of 37 C.F.R. §201.24: 56 FR 7812, Feb. 26, 1991; 66 FR 34373, June 28, 2001.

§201.25. VISUAL ARTS REGISTRY

(a) General. This section prescribes the procedures relating to the submission of Visual Arts Registry Statements by visual artists and owners of buildings, or their duly authorized representatives, for recordation in the Copyright Office under section 113(d)(3) of Title 17 of the United States Code, as amended by Public Law 101-650, effective June 1, 1991. Statements recorded in the Copyright Office under this regulation will establish a public record of information relevant to an artist's integrity right to prevent destruction or injury to works of visual art incorporated in or made part of a building.

(b) Forms. The Copyright Office does not provide forms for the use of persons recording statements regarding works of visual art that have been incorporated in or made part of a building.

(c) Recordable statements—

(1) General. Any statement designated as a "Visual Arts Registry Statement" and which pertains to a work of visual art that has been incorporated in or made part of a building may be recorded in the Copyright Office provided the statement is accompanied by the fee for recordation of documents specified in section 708(a)(4) of title 17 of the United States Code. Upon their submission, the statements and an accompanying documentation or photographs become the property of the United States Government and will not be returned. Photocopies are acceptable if they are clear and legible. Information contained in the Visual Arts Registry Statement should be as complete as possible since the information may affect the enforceability of valuable rights under the copyright law. Visual Arts Registry Statements which are illegible or fall outside of the scope of section 113(d)(3) of title 17 may be refused recordation by the Copyright Office.

(2) Statements by artists. Statements by artists regarding a work of visual art incorporated or made part of a building should be filed in a document containing the head: "Registry of Visual Art Incorporated in a Building—Artist's Statement." The statement should contain the following information:

(i) Identification of the artist, including name, current address, age, and telephone number, if publicly listed.

(ii) Identification of the work or works, including the title, dimensions, and physical description of the work and the copyright registration number, if known. Additionally, it is recommended that one or more 8 x 10 photographs of the work on good quality photographic paper be included in the submission; the images should be clear and in focus.

(iii) Identification of the building, including its name and address. This identification may additionally include 8 x 10 photographs of the building and the location of the artist's work in the building.

(iv) Identification of the owner of the building, if known.

(3) Statements by the owner of the building. Statements of owners of a building which incorporates a work of visual art should be filed in a document containing the heading: "Registry of Visual Art Incorporated in a Building—Building Owner's Statement." The statement should contain the following information:

(i) Identification of the ownership of the building, the name of a person who represents the owner, and a telephone number, if publicly listed.

(ii) Identification of the building, including the building's name and address. This identification may additionally include 8 x 10 photographs of the building and of the works of visual art which are incorporated in the building.

(iii) Identification of the work or works of visual art incorporated in the building, including the works' title(s), if known, and the dimensions and physical description of the work(s). This identification may include one or more 8 x 10 photographs of the work(s) on high quality photographic paper; the images should be clear and in focus.

(iv) Identification of the artist(s) who have works incorporated in the building, including the current address of each artist, if known.

(v) Photocopy of contracts, if any, between the artist and owners of the building regarding the rights of attribution and integrity.

(vi) Statement as to the measures taken by the owner to notify the artist(s) of the removal or pending removal of the work of visual art, and photocopies of any accompanying documents.

(4) Updating statements. Either the artist or owner of the building or both may record statements updating previously recorded information by submitting an updated statement and paying the recording fee specified in paragraph (d) of this section. Such statements should repeat the information disclosed in the previous filing as regarding the name of the artist(s), the name of the work(s) of visual art, the name and address of the building, and the name of the owner(s) of the building. The remaining portion of the statement should correct or supplement the information disclosed in the previously recorded statement.

(d) Fee. The fee for recording a Visual Arts Registry Statement, a Building Owner's Statement, or an updating statement is the recordation fee for a document, as prescribed in §201.3(c).

(e) Date of recordation. The date of recordation is the date when all of the elements required for recordation, including the prescribed fee have been received in the Copyright Office. After recordation of the statement, the sender will receive a certificate of recordation from the Copyright Office. Any documentation or photographs accompanying any submission will be retained and filed by the Copyright Office. They may also be transferred to the Library of Congress, or destroyed after preparing suitable copies, in accordance with usual procedures.

(f) Effect of recordation. The Copyright Office will record statements in the Visual Arts Registry without examination or verification of the accuracy or completeness of the statement, if the statement is designated as a "Visual Arts Registry Statement" and pertains to a work of visual art incorporated in or made part of a building. Recordation of the statement and payment of the recording fee shall establish only the fact of recordation in the official record. Acceptance for recordation shall not be considered a determination that the statement is accurate, complete, and otherwise in compliance with section 113(d), title 17, U.S. Code. The accuracy and completeness of the statement is the responsibility of the artist or building owner who submits it for recordation. Artists and building owners are encouraged to submit accurate and complete statements. Omission of any information, however, shall not itself invalidate the recordation, unless a court of competent jurisdiction finds the statement is materially deficient and fails to meet the minimum requirements of section 113(d) of title 17, U.S. Code.

History of 37 C.F.R. §201.25: 56 FR 38341, Aug. 13, 1991; 64 FR 29521, June 1, 1999; 65 FR 39819, June 28, 2000; 82 FR 9358, Mar. 8, 2017.

§201.26. RECORDATION OF DOCUMENTS PERTAINING TO COMPUTER SHAREWARE & DONATION OF PUBLIC DOMAIN COMPUTER SOFTWARE

(a) General. This section prescribes the procedures for submission of legal documents pertaining to computer shareware and the deposit of public domain computer software under section 805 of Public Law 101-650, 104 Stat. 5089 (1990). Documents recorded in the Copyright Office under this regulation will be included in the Computer Shareware Registry. Recordation in this Registry will establish a public record of licenses or other legal documents governing the relationship between copyright owners of computer shareware and persons associated with the dissemination or other use of computer shareware. Documents transferring the ownership of some or all rights under the copyright law of computer shareware and security interests in such software should be recorded under 17 U.S.C. 205, as implemented by §201.4.

(b) Definitions.

(1) The term computer shareware is accorded its customary meaning within the software industry. In general, shareware is copyrighted software which is distributed for the purposes of testing and review, subject to the condition that payment to the copyright owner is required after a person who has secured a copy decides to use the software.

(2) A document designated as pertaining to computer shareware means licenses or other legal documents governing the relationship between copyright owners of computer shareware and persons associated with the dissemination or other use of computer shareware.

(3) Public domain computer software means software which has been publicly distributed with an explicit disclaimer of copyright protection by the copyright owner.

(c) Forms. The Copyright Office does not provide forms for the use of persons recording documents designated as pertaining to computer shareware or for the deposit of public domain computer software.

(d) Recordable documents.

(1) Any document clearly designated as a "Document Pertaining to Computer Shareware" and which governs the legal relationship between owners of computer shareware and persons associated with the dissemination or other use of computer shareware may be recorded in the Computer Shareware Registry.

(2) Submitted documents may be a duplicate original, a legible photocopy, or other legible facsimile reproduction of the document, and must be complete on its face.

(3) Submitted documents will not be returned, and the Copyright Office requests that if the document is considered valuable, that only copies of that document be submitted for recordation.

(e) Fee. The fee for recording a document pertaining to computer shareware is the recordation fee for a document, as prescribed in §201.3(c).

(f) Date of recordation. The date of recordation is the date when all of the elements required for recordation, including the prescribed fee have been received in the Copyright Office. After recordation of the statement, the sender will receive a certificate of recordation from the Copyright Office. The submission will be retained and filed by the Copyright Office, and may be destroyed at a later date after preparing suitable copies, in accordance with usual procedures.

(g) Donation of public domain computer software.

(1) Any person may donate a copy of public domain computer software for the benefit of the Machine-Readable Collections Reading Room of the Library of Congress. Decision as to whether any public domain computer software is suitable for accession to the collections rests solely with the Library of Congress. Materials not selected will be disposed of in accordance with usual procedures, including transfer to other libraries, sale, or destruction. Donation of public domain software may be made regardless of whether a document has been recorded pertaining to the software.

(2) In order to donate public domain software, the following conditions must be met:

(i) The copy of the public domain software must contain an explicit disclaimer of copyright protection from the copyright owner.

(ii) The submission should contain documentation regarding the software. If the documentation is in machine-readable form, a print-out of the documentation should be included in the donation.

(iii) If the public domain software is marketed in a box or other packaging, the entire work as distributed, including the packaging, should be deposited.

(iv) If the public domain software is copy protected, two copies of the software must be submitted.

(3) Donations of public domain software with an accompanying letter of explanation must be sent to the following address: Gift Section, Exchange & Gift Division, Library of Congress, Washington, DC 20540-4260.

History of 37 C.F.R. §201.26: 56 FR 50658, Oct. 8, 1991; 58 FR 29107, May 19, 1993; 60 FR 34168, June 30, 1995; 64 FR 29522, June 1, 1999; 65 FR 39819, June 28, 2000; 82 FR 9358, Mar. 8, 2017.

§201.27. INITIAL NOTICE OF DISTRIBUTION OF DIGITAL AUDIO RECORDING DEVICES OR MEDIA

(a) General. This section prescribes rules pertaining to the filing of an Initial Notice of Distribution in the Copyright Office as required by section 1003(b) of the Audio Home Recording Act of 1992, Public Law 102-563, title 17 of the United States Code, to obtain a statutory license to import and distribute, or manufacture and distribute, any digital audio recording device or digital audio recording medium in the United States.

(b) Definitions.

(1) An Initial Notice of Distribution of Digital Audio Recording Devices or Media or Initial Notice is a notice under section 1003(b) of the Audio Home Recording Act of 1992, Public Law 102-563, title 17 of the United States Code, which is required by that section to be filed in the Copyright Office by an importer or manufacturer of a digital audio recording device or digital audio recording medium who has not previously filed notice of the importation or manufacture for distribution of such device or medium in the United States.

(2) The product category of a device or medium is a general class of products made up of functionally equivalent digital audio recording devices or media with substantially the same use in substantially the same environment, including, for example, hand-held portable integrated combination units ("boomboxes"); portable personal recorders; stand-alone home recorders ("tape decks"); home combination systems ("rack systems"); automobile recorders; configurations of tape media (standard cassettes or microcassettes); and configurations of disc media such as 2½", 3" and 5" discs.

(3) The technology of a device or medium is a product type distinguished by different technical processes for digitally recording musical sounds, such as digital audio tape recorders (DAT), digital compact cassette (DCC), or recordable compact discs, including minidiscs (MD).

(4) The terms digital audio recording device, digital audio recording medium, distribute, manufacture, and transfer price, have the meanings of the same terms as they are used in section 1001 of the Copyright Act, title 17 of the United States Code, as amended by Public Law 102-563.

(c) Forms. An Initial Notice form may be obtained from the U.S. Copyright Office free of charge by contacting the address specified in §201.1.

(d) Filing Deadline. Initial Notices shall be filed in the Copyright Office no later than 45 days after the commencement of the first distribution of digital audio recording devices or digital audio recording media in the United States, on or after October 28, 1992. A manufacturer or importer shall file an Initial Notice within 45 days of the first distribution for each new product category and each new technology that the manufacturer or importer has not reported in a previous Initial Notice.

(e) Content of Initial Notices. An Initial Notice of Distribution of Digital Audio Recording Devices or Media shall be identified as such by prominent caption or heading, and shall include the following:

(1) The designation "Importer" or "Manufacturer," or both, whichever is applicable, followed by the full legal name of the importer or manufacturer of the digital audio recording device or medium, or if the party named is a partnership, the name of the partnership followed by the name of at least one individual partner;

(2) Any trade or business name or names, trademarks, or other indicia of origin that the importer or manufacturer uses or intends to use in connection with the importation, manufacture, or distribution of such digital audio recording device or medium in the United States;

(3) The full United States mailing address of the importer or manufacturer, and the full business address, if different;

(4) The product category and technology of the devices or media imported or manufactured;

(5) The first date (day, month, and year) that distribution commenced, or is to commence;

(6) The signature of an appropriate officer, partner, or agent of the importer or manufacturer, as specified by the Initial Notice form; and

(7) Other information relevant to the importation or manufacture for distribution of digital audio recording devices or media as prescribed on the Initial Notice form provided by the Copyright Office.

(f) Amendments.

(1) The Copyright Office will record amendments to Initial Notices submitted to correct an error or omission in the information given in an earlier Initial Notice. An amendment is not appropriate to reflect developments or changes in facts occurring after the date of signature of an Initial Notice.

(2) An amendment shall:

(i) Be clearly and prominently identified as an "Amendment to an Initial Notice of Distribution of Digital Audio Recording Devices or Media";

(ii) Identify the specific Initial Notice intended to be amended so that it may be readily located in the records of the Copyright Office;

(iii) Clearly specify the nature of the amendment to be made; and

(iv) Be signed and dated in accordance with this section.

(3) The recordation of an amendment under this paragraph shall have only such effect as may be attributed to it by a court of competent jurisdiction.

(g) Recordation.

(1) The Copyright Office will record the Initial Notices and amendments submitted in accordance with this section by placing them in the appropriate public files of the Office. The Copyright Office will advise manufacturers and importers of errors or omissions appearing on the face of documents submitted to it, and will require that any such obvious errors or omissions be corrected before the documents will be recorded. However, recordation by the Copyright Office shall establish only the fact and date thereof; such recordation shall in no case be considered a determination that the document was, in fact, properly prepared or that all of the regulatory requirements to satisfy section 1003 of title 17 have been met.

(2) No fee shall be required for the recording of Initial Notices. The fee for filing an Amendment to an Initial Notice of Distribution of Digital Audio Recording Devices or Media is prescribed in §201.3(e).

History of 37 C.F.R. §201.27: 57 FR 55465, Nov. 25, 1992; 64 FR 36575, July 7, 1999; 72 FR 33692, July 1, 2007; 78 FR 42874, July 18, 2013; 82 FR 9358, Mar. 8, 2017.

§201.28. STATEMENTS OF ACCOUNT FOR DIGITAL AUDIO RECORDING DEVICES OR MEDIA

(a) General. This section prescribes rules pertaining to the filing of Statements of Account and royalty fees in the Copyright Office as required by 17 U.S.C. 1003(c) and 1004, in order to import and distribute, or manufacture and distribute, in the United States any digital audio recording device or digital audio recording medium.

(b) Definitions. For purposes of this section, the following definitions apply:

(1) Annual statement of account is the statement required under 17 U.S.C. 1003, to be filed no later than two months after the close of the accounting period covered by the annual statement.

(2) Device and medium have the same meaning as digital audio recording device and digital audio recording medium, respectively, have in 17 U.S.C. 1001.

(3) Digital audio recording product means digital audio recording devices and digital audio recording media.

(4) Generally accepted auditing standards (GAAS), means the auditing standards promulgated by the American Institute of Certified Public Accountants.

(5) Manufacturing or importing party refers to any person or entity that manufactures and distributes, and/or imports and distributes, any digital audio recording device or digital audio recording medium in the United States, and is required under 17 U.S.C. 1003 to file with the Copyright Office quarterly and annual Statements of Account.

(6) Product category of a device or medium is a general class of products made up of functionally equivalent digital audio recording products with substantially the same use in substantially the same environment, including, for example, hand-held portable integrated combination units ("boomboxes"); portable personal recorders; stand-alone home recorders ("tape decks"); home combination systems ("rack systems"); automobile recorders; configurations of tape media (standard cassettes or microcassettes); and configurations of disc media, such as 2½ inch, 3 inch, or 5 inch discs.

(7) Primary auditor is the certified public accountant retained by the manufacturing or importing party to audit the amounts reported in the annual Statement of Account submitted to the Copyright Office. The primary auditor may be the certified public accountant engaged by the manufacturing or importing party to perform the annual audit of the party's financial statement.

(8) Quarterly statement of account is the statement accompanying royalty payments required under 17 U.S.C. 1003, to be filed for each of the first three quarters of the accounting year, and no later than 45 days after the close of the quarterly period covered by the statement.

(9) Technology of a device or medium is a digital audio recording product-type distinguished by different technical processes for digitally recording musical sounds, such as digital audio tape recorders (DAT), digital compact cassettes (DCC), or recordable compact discs, including minidiscs (MD).

(10) Distribute, manufacture, transfer price, and serial copying have the meanings set forth in 17 U.S.C. 1001.

(c) Accounting periods and filing deadlines.

(1) Election of filing basis. Statements of Account may be filed on either a calendar or fiscal year basis at the election of the manufacturing party. The election of a calendar or fiscal year basis must be made when the manufacturing or importing party files its first quarterly Statement of Account by appropriate designation on the Form DART/Q submitted. Thereafter the specific calendar or fiscal-year accounting period must be designated on each quarterly Statement of Account. The filing basis may be changed at any time upon notification in writing to the Register of Copyrights, accompanied by a statement of reasons as to why the change is to be made and a statement that such change will not affect the aggregate royalties due under the earlier basis. The notification of change in filing basis must be made at least two months before the date the next quarterly Statement of Account is due to be filed.

(2) Quarterly filings. Quarterly Statements of Account shall be filed on Form DART/Q and shall cover a three-month period corresponding to the calendar or fiscal year of the filing party. A quarterly statement shall be filed no later than 45 days after the close of the period it covers.

(3) Annual filings. Annual Statements of Account shall be filed on Form DART/A and shall cover both the fourth quarter of an accounting year and the aggregate of the entire year corresponding to the calendar or fiscal accounting year elected. An annual statement shall be filed no later than two months after the close of the period it covers. The appropriate royalty payment, calculated according to the instructions contained in Form DART/A, shall accompany the annual Statement of Account covering royalties due for the filing year: that is, royalties for the fourth quarter and any additional royalties that are due because of adjustments in the aggregate amounts of devices or media distributed.

(4) Early or late filings. Statements of Account and royalty fees received before the end of the particular accounting period covered by the statement will not be processed by the Office. The statement must be filed after the close of the relevant accounting period. Statements of Account and royalty fees received after the 45-day deadline for quarterly statements or the two-month deadline for annual statements will be accepted for whatever legal effect they may have and will be assessed the appropriate interest charge for the late filing.

(d) Forms.

(1) Each quarterly or annual Statement of Account shall be submitted on the appropriate form prescribed by the Copyright Office. Computation of the royalty fee shall be in accordance with the procedures set forth in the forms and this section. Statement of Account forms are available free from the Copyright Office website. Copies of Statement of Account forms transmitted to the Office by fax will not be accepted.

(2) Forms prescribed by the Copyright Office are designated Quarterly Statement of Account for Digital Audio Recording Products (Form DART/Q) and Annual Statement of Account for Digital Audio Recording Products (Form DART/A).

(e) Contents of quarterly Statements of Account.

(1) Quarterly period and filing. Any quarterly Statement of Account shall cover the full quarter of the calendar or fiscal accounting year for the particular quarter for which it is filed. A separate quarterly statement shall be filed for each quarter of the first three quarters of the accounting year during which there is any activity relevant to the payment of royalties under 17 U.S.C. 1004. The annual Statement of Account identified in paragraph (f) of this section incorporates the fourth quarter of the accounting year.

(2) General content. Each quarterly Statement of Account shall be filed on Form DART/Q, the "Quarterly Statement of Account for Digital Audio Recording Products," and shall include a clear statement of the following information:

(i) A designation of the calendar or fiscal year of the annual reporting period;

(ii) A designation of the period, including the beginning and ending day, month, and year of the period covered by the quarter;

(iii) The full legal name of the manufacturing and/or importing party, together with any "doing-business-as" names used by such person or entity for the purpose of conducting the business of manufacturing, importing, or distributing digital audio recording products;

(iv) The full mailing address of the manufacturing or importing party, including a specific number and street name, or rural route and box number, of the place of business of the person or entity. A post office box or similar designation will not be sufficient for this purpose except where it is the only address that can be used in that geographic location;

(v) A designation of the manufacturing or importing party status, *i.e.*, "Manufacturer," "Importer," or "Manufacturer and Importer";

(vi) The designation "Product Categories" together with the product categories of the digital audio recording products manufactured or imported and distributed during the quarter covered by the statement;

(vii) The designation "Technologies" together with the technologies of the digital audio recording products manufactured or imported and distributed under the AHRA during the quarter covered by the statement;

(viii) The designation "Series or Model Number" followed by the model or series numbers of the digital audio recording products manufactured or imported and distributed under the AHRA during the quarter covered by the statement;

(ix) The "fee code" associated with the product;

(x) The "source code" for the product category;

(xi) The "transfer price" of the product;

(xii) The "number of units distributed" for each product;

(xiii) The "minimum fee per unit" for each product;

(xiv) The statutory royalty "rate" for digital audio recording devices or media;

(xv) The "rate fee" for each product;

(xvi) The appropriate "maximum fee per unit" for each product;

(xvii) The "maximum fee" for each product; and

(xviii) A computation of the total royalty payable for the quarter covered by the statement. Filing parties may not round off the figures they list in Space C, the computation section of the form, except for the figure representing the total royalty fee due; in that case, numbers ending in 50 to 99 cents may be rounded up to the next dollar, and numbers ending in one to 49 cents may be rounded down to the next dollar;

(3) Royalty payments and accounting.

(i) The royalty specified in 17 U.S.C. 1004 shall accompany the quarterly and annual Statements of Account. No royalty is payable for redistribution of the same product item unless a credit has been taken for such items. Where royalties are payable for the period covered by the statement, the Statement of Account shall contain the following information for each unique combination of product category, technology, series or model number, fee code, source code, and transfer price:

(A) The total number of digital audio recording media distributed, multiplied by the statutory royalty rate of three percent (3%) of the transfer price;

(B) The total number of digital audio recording devices distributed for which the statutory royalty rate of two percent (2%) of the transfer price is payable, multiplied by such percentage rate of the transfer price;

(C) The total number of digital audio recording devices distributed for which the statutory maximum royalty is limited to eight dollars ($8.00), multiplied by such eight dollar amount;

(D) The total number of digital audio recording devices distributed for which the statutory maximum royalty is limited to twelve dollars ($12.00), multiplied by such twelve dollar amount; and

(E) The total number of digital audio recording devices distributed for which the statutory minimum royalty is limited to one dollar ($1.00), multiplied by such one dollar amount.

(ii) The amount of the royalty payment shall be calculated in accordance with the instructions specified in the quarterly Statement of Account form. Payment shall be made as specified in §201.28(h).

(4) Reduction of royalty fee.

(i) Section 1004(a)(2)(A) of title 17 of the United States Code, provides an instance in which royalty payments may be reduced if the digital audio recording device and such other devices are part of a physically integrated unit, the royalty payment shall be based on the transfer price of the unit, but shall be reduced by any royalty payment made on any digital audio recording device included within the unit that was not first distributed in combination with the unit.

(ii) Notice of this provision together with directions for possible application to a product is contained in the DART/Q Form.

(5) Contact party. Each Statement of Account shall include the name, address, and telephone and fax numbers of an individual whom the Copyright Office can write or call about the Statement of Account.

(6) Credits for returned or exported products. When digital audio recording products first distributed in the United States for ultimate transfer to United States consumers are returned to the manufacturer or importer as unsold or defective merchandise, or are exported, the manufacturing or importing party may take a credit to be deducted from the royalties payable for the period when the products were returned or exported. The credit may be taken only for returns or exports made within two years following the date royalties were paid for the products. This credit must be reflected in the manufacturing or importing party's quarterly or annual Statement of Account. If the manufacturer or importer later redistributes in the United States any products for which a credit has been taken, these products must be listed on the Statement of Account, and a new computation of the royalty fee must be made based on the transfer price of the products at the time of the new distribution.

(7) Oath and signature. Each Statement of Account shall include the handwritten signature of an authorized officer, principal, or agent of the filing party. The signature shall be accompanied by:

(i) The printed or typewritten name of the person signing the quarterly Statement of Account;

(ii) The date the document is signed;

(iii) The following certification:

I, the undersigned, hereby certify that I am an authorized officer, principal, or agent of the "manufacturing or importing party" identified in Space B.

Penalties for fraud and false statements are provided under 18 U.S.C. 1001 et seq.

(f) Contents of annual Statements of Account.

(1) General contents. Each annual Statement of Account shall be filed on form DART/A, "Annual Statement of Account for Digital Audio Recording Products." It must be filed by any importer or manufacturer that distributed in the United States, during a given calendar or fiscal year, any digital audio recording device or digital audio recording medium. The annual statement shall cover the aggregate of the distribution of devices and media for the entire year corresponding to the calendar or fiscal year elected. The annual Statement of Account shall contain the information, oath, and certification prescribed in paragraphs (e)(2)(i) through (e)(7)(iii) of this section, and shall cover the entire accounting year, including the fourth quarter distribution, and shall also provide for the reconciliation of the aggregated accounting of digital audio recording devices and media for the reported accounting year.

(2) Reconciliation. Any royalty payment due under sections 1003 and 1004 of title 17 that was not previously paid with the filing party's first three quarterly Statements of Account, shall be reconciled in the annual statement. Reconciliation in the annual Statement of Account provides for adjustments for reductions, refunds, underpayments, overpayments, credits, and royalty payments paid in Quarters 1, 2, and 3, and shall be computed in accordance with the instructions included in the annual Statement of Account. Errors that require reconciliation shall be corrected immediately upon discovery.

(3) Accountant's opinion. Each annual Statement of Account or any amended annual Statement of Account shall be audited by the primary auditor as defined in paragraph (b)(7) of this section. An amendment may be submitted to the Office either as a result of responses to questions raised by a Licensing Division examiner or on the initiative of the manufacturing or importing party to correct an error in the original Statement of Account.

(i) The audit shall be performed in accordance with generally accepted auditing standards (GAAS). The audit may be performed in conjunction with an annual audit of the manufacturing or importing party's financial statements.

(ii) The CPA shall issue a report, the "primary auditor's report," reflecting his or her opinion as to whether the annual statement presents fairly, in all material respects, the number of digital audio recording devices and media that were imported and distributed, or manufactured and distributed, by the manufacturing or importing party during the relevant year, and the amount of royalty payments applicable to them under 17 U.S.C. chapter 10, in accordance with that law and these regulations.

(iii) The primary auditor's report shall be filed with the Copyright Office together with the annual Statement of Account, within two months after the end of the annual period for which the annual Statement of Account is prepared. The report may be qualified to the extent necessary and appropriate.

(iv) The Copyright Office does not provide a specific form, or require a specific format, for the CPA's review; however, in addition to the above, certain items must be named as audited items. These include the variables necessary to complete Space C of the Statement of Account form. The CPA may place his or her opinion, which will serve as the "primary auditor's report," in the space provided on Form DART/A, or may attach a separate sheet or sheets containing the opinion.

(v) The auditor's report shall be signed by an individual, or in the name of a partnership or a corporation, and shall include city and state of execution, certificate number, jurisdiction of certificate, and date of opinion. The certificate number and jurisdiction are not required if the report is signed in the name of a partnership or a corporation.

(g) Copies of statements of account. A licensee shall file an original and one copy of the statement of account with the Licensing Division of the Copyright Office.

(h) Royalty fee payment.

(1) All royalty fees must be paid by a single electronic funds transfer, and must be received in the designated bank by the filing deadline for the relevant accounting period. The following information must be provided as part of the EFT and/or as part of the remittance advice as provided for in circulars issued by the Copyright Office:

(i) Remitter's name and address;

(ii) Name of a contact person, telephone number and extension, and email address;

(iii) The actual or anticipated date that the EFT will be transmitted;

(iv) Type of royalty payment (*i.e.* DART);

(v) Total amount submitted via the EFT;

(vi) Total amount to be paid by year and period;

(vii) Number of Statements of Account that the EFT covers;

(viii) ID numbers assigned by the Licensing Division;

(ix) Legal name of the owner for each Statement of Account.

(2) The remittance advice shall be attached to the Statement(s) of Account. In addition, a copy of the remittance advice shall be emailed or sent by facsimile to the Licensing Division.

(3) The Office may waive the requirement for payment by electronic funds transfer as set forth in paragraph (1) of this section. To obtain a waiver, the remitter shall submit to the Licensing Division at least 60 days prior to the royalty fee due date a certified statement setting forth the reasons explaining why payment by an electronic funds transfer would be virtually impossible or, alternatively, why it would impose a financial or other hardship on the remitter. The certified statement must be signed by a duly authorized representative of the entity making the payment. A waiver shall cover only a single payment period. Failure to obtain a waiver may result in the remittance being returned to the remitter.

(i) Documentation. All filing parties shall keep and retain in their possession, for at least three years from the date of filing, all records and documents necessary and appropriate to support fully the information set forth in quarterly and annual statements that they file.

(j) Corrections, supplemental payments, and refunds.

(1) General. Upon compliance with the procedures and within the time limits set forth in this paragraph (i), corrections to quarterly and annual Statements of Account will be placed on record, and supplemental royalty fee payments will be received for deposit, or refunds without interest will be issued, in the following cases:

(i) Where, with respect to the accounting period covered by the quarterly or annual Statement of Account, any of the information given in the statement filed in the Copyright Office is incorrect or incomplete; or

(ii) Where, for any reason except that mentioned in paragraph (j)(2) of this section, calculation of the royalty fee payable for a particular accounting period was incorrect, and the amount deposited in the Copyright Office for that period was either too high or too low.

(2) Corrections to quarterly or annual Statements of Account will not be placed on file, supplemental royalty fee payments will not be received for deposit, and refunds will not be issued, where the information in the Statements of Account, the royalty fee calculations, or the payments were correct as of the date on which the accounting period ended, but changes (for example, cases where digital audio recording media were exported) took place later.

(3) Requests that corrections to annual or quarterly Statements of Account be accepted, that fee payments be accepted, or that refunds be issued shall be addressed to the Licensing Division of the Copyright Office, and shall meet the following conditions:

(i) The request shall be made in writing and must clearly identify the manufacturing or importing party making the request, the accounting period in question, and the purpose of the request. A request for a refund must be received in the Copyright Office before the expiration of two months from the last day of the applicable Statement of Account filing period. Telephone or similar unsigned requests that meet these conditions may be permitted, where a follow-up written request detailing the same information is received by the Copyright Office within 14 days after the required 60-day period.

(ii) The request must clearly identify the incorrect or incomplete information formerly filed and must provide the correct or additional information.

(iii) In the case where a royalty fee was miscalculated and the amount deposited with the Copyright Office was too large or too small, the request must be accompanied by an affidavit under the official seal of any officer authorized to administer oaths within the United States, or a statement in accordance with 28 U.S.C. 1746, made and signed in accordance with paragraph (e)(7) of this section. The affidavit or statement shall describe the reasons why the royalty fee was improperly calculated and include a detailed analysis of the proper royalty calculation.

(iv) Following final processing, all requests will be filed with the original Statement of Account in the records of the Copyright Office. Nothing contained in this paragraph shall be considered to relieve manufacturing or importing parties of their full obligations under title 17 of the United States Code, and the filing of a correction or supplemental payment shall have only such effect as may be attributed to it by a court of competent jurisdiction.

(v)(A) The request must be accompanied by a filing fee in the amount prescribed in §201.3(e) for each Statement of Account involved. Payment of this fee may be in the form of a personal or company check, or a certified check, cashier's check, or money order, payable to the Register of Copyrights. No request will be processed until the appropriate filing fees are received.

(B) Requests that a supplemental royalty fee payment be deposited must be accompanied by a remittance in the full amount of such fee. Payment of the supplemental royalty fee must be in the form of a certified check, cashier's check, money order, or electronic payment payable to the Register of Copyrights. No such request will be processed until an acceptable remittance in the full amount of the supplemental royalty fee has been received.

(vi) All requests submitted under paragraph (j) of this section must be signed by the manufacturing or importing party named in the Statement of Account, or the duly authorized agent of that party in accordance with paragraph (e)(7) of this section.

(vii) A request for a refund is not necessary where the Licensing Division, during its examination of a Statement of Account or related document, discovers an error that has resulted in a royalty overpayment. In this case, the Licensing Division will forward the royalty refund to the manufacturing or importing party named in the Statement of Account. The Copyright Office will not pay interest on any royalty refunds.

(k) Examination of Statements of Account by the Copyright Office.

(1) Upon receiving a Statement of Account and royalty fee, the Copyright Office will make an official record of the actual date when such statement and fee were physically received in the Copyright Office. Thereafter, the Licensing Division will examine the statement for obvious errors or omissions appearing on the face of the documents and will require that any such obvious errors or omissions be corrected before final processing of the document is completed. If, as the result of communications between the Copyright Office and the manufacturer or importer, an additional fee is deposited or changes or additions are made in the Statement of Account, the date that additional deposit or information was actually received in the Office will be added to the official record.

(2) Completion by the Copyright Office of the final processing of a Statement of Account and royalty fee deposit shall establish only the fact of such completion and the date or

dates of receipt shown in the official record. It shall not be considered a determination that the Statement of Account was, in fact, properly prepared and accurate, that the correct amount of the royalty was deposited, that the statutory time limits for filing had been met, or that any other requirements of 17 U.S.C. 1001 et seq. were fulfilled.

(*l*) Interest on late payments or underpayments.

(1) Royalty payments submitted as a result of late payments or underpayments shall include interest, which shall begin to accrue on the first day after the close of the period for filing Statements of Account for all late payments or underpayments of royalties for the digital audio recording obligation occurring within that accounting period. The accrual period shall end on the date the electronic payment submitted by the remitter is received. In cases where a waiver of the electronic funds transfer requirement is approved by the Copyright Office, and royalties payments are either late or underpaid, the accrual period shall end on the date the payment is postmarked. If the payment is not received by the Copyright Office within five business days of its date, then the accrual period shall end on the date of the actual receipt by the Copyright Office.

(2) The interest rate applicable to a specific accounting period shall be the Current Value of Funds rate in accordance with the Treasury Financial Manual, at 1 TFM 6-8025.40, in effect on the first business day after the close of the filing deadline for the relevant accounting period. The interest rate for a particular accounting period may be obtained by consulting the Federal Register for the applicable Current Value of Funds Rate, or by contacting the Licensing Division of the Copyright Office.

(3) Interest is not required to be paid on any royalty underpayment or late payment from a particular accounting period if the interest charge is five dollars ($5.00) or less.

(m) Confidentiality of Statements of Account. Public access to the Copyright Office files of Statements of Account for digital audio recording products shall not be provided. Access will only be granted to interested copyright parties in accordance with regulations prescribed by the Register of Copyrights pursuant to 17 U.S.C. 1003(c).

History of 37 C.F.R. §201.28: 58 FR 9546, Feb. 22, 1993; 59 FR 4589, Feb. 1, 1994; 64 FR 36575, July 7, 1999; 65 FR 48914, Aug. 10, 2000; 70 FR 30367, May 26, 2005; 70 FR 38022, July 1, 2005; 71 FR 45740, Aug. 10, 2006; 72 FR 33692, July 1, 2007; 73 FR 29073, May 20, 2008; 82 FR 9358, Mar. 8, 2017.

§201.29. ACCESS TO, & CONFIDENTIALITY OF, STATEMENTS OF ACCOUNT, VERIFICATION AUDITOR'S REPORTS, & OTHER VERIFICATION INFORMATION FILED IN THE COPYRIGHT OFFICE FOR DIGITAL AUDIO RECORDING DEVICES OR MEDIA

(a) General. This section prescribes rules covering access to DART Statements of Account, including the Primary Auditor's Reports, filed under 17 U.S.C. 1003(c) and access to a Verifying Auditor's Report or other information that may be filed in the Office in a DART verification procedure as set out in §201.30. It also prescribes rules to ensure confidential disclosure of these materials to appropriate parties.

(b) Definitions.

(1) Access includes inspection of and supervised making of notes on information contained in Statements of Account including Primary Auditor's Reports, Verification Auditor's Reports, and any other verification information.

(2) Audit and Verification Information means the reports of the Primary Auditor and Verifying Auditor filed with the Copyright Office under §§201.28 and 201.30, and all information relating to a manufacturing or importing party.

(3) DART Access Form means the form provided by the Copyright Office that must be completed and signed by any appropriate party seeking access to DART confidential material.

(4) DART confidential material means the Quarterly and Annual Statements of Account, including the Primary Auditor's Report that is part of the Annual Statements of Account, and the Verifying Auditor's Report and any other verification information filed with the Copyright Office. It also includes photocopies of notes made by requestors who have had access to these materials that are retained by the Copyright Office.

(5) Interested copyright party means a party as defined in 17 U.S.C. 1001(7).

(6) A Representative is someone, such as a lawyer or accountant, who is not an employee or officer of an interested copyright party or a manufacturing or importing party but is authorized to act on that party's behalf.

(7) Statements of Account means Quarterly and Annual Statements of Account as required under 17 U.S.C. 1003(c) and defined in §201.28.

(c) Confidentiality. The Copyright Office will keep all DART confidential materials in locked files and disclose them only in accordance with this section. Any person or entity provided with access to DART confidential material by the Copyright Office shall receive such information in confidence and shall use and disclose it only as authorized in 17 U.S.C. 1001 et seq.

(d) Persons allowed access to DART confidential material. Access to DART Statements of Account filed under 17 U.S.C. 1003(c) and to Verification Auditor's Reports or other verification information is limited to:

(1) An interested copyright party as defined in §201.29(b)(5) or an authorized representative of an interested copyright party, who has been qualified for access pursuant to paragraph (f)(2) of this section;

(2) The Verifying Auditor authorized to conduct verification procedures under §201.30;

(3) The manufacturing or importing party who filed that Statement of Account or that party's authorized representative(s); and

(4) Staff of the Copyright Office or the Library of Congress who require access in the performance of their duties under title 17 U.S.C. 1001 et seq.;

(e) Requests for access. An interested copyright party, manufacturing party, importing party, representative, or Verifying Auditor seeking access to any DART confidential material must complete and sign a "DART Access Form." The requestor must submit a copy of the completed DART Access Form to the Licensing Specialist, Licensing Division. The form must be received in the Licensing Division at least five working days before the date an appointment is requested. The form may be faxed to the Licensing Division to expedite scheduling, but a copy of the form with the original signature must be filed with the Office.

(1) A representative of an interested copyright party, a manufacturing party or an importing party shall submit an affidavit of his or her authority (e.g., in the form of a letter of authorization from the interested copyright party or the manufacturing or importing party).

(2) An auditor selected to conduct a verification procedure under §201.30 shall submit an affidavit of his or her selection to conduct the verification procedure.

(3) DART Access Forms may be requested from, and upon completion returned to the address specified in §201.1.

(f) Criteria for access to DART confidential material.

(1) A Verifying Auditor will be allowed access to any particular Statement of Account and Primary Auditor's Report required to perform his or her verification function;

(2) Interested copyright parties as defined in paragraph (b)(5) of this section will be allowed access to any DART confidential material as defined in paragraph (b)(4) of this section for verification purposes, except that no interested copyright party owned or controlled by a manufacturing or importing party subject to royalty payment obligations under the Audio Home Recording Act, or who owns or controls such a manufacturing or importing party, may have access to DART confidential material relating to any other manufacturing or importing party. In such cases, a representative of the interested copyright party as defined in paragraph (b)(6) of this section may have access for that party, provided that these representatives do not disclose the confidential information contained in the Statement of Account or Primary Auditor's Report to his or her client.

(3) Access to a Verifying Auditor's Report and any other verification material filed in the Office shall be limited to the interested copyright party(s) requesting the verification procedure and to the manufacturing or importing party whose Statement of Account was the subject of the verification procedure.

(g) Denial of access. Any party who does not meet the criteria described in §201.29(f) shall be denied access.

(h) Content of DART Access Form. The DART Access Form shall include the following information:

(1) Identification of the Statement of Account and Primary Auditor's Report, the Verification Auditor's Report and other verification materials, or notes prepared by requestors who earlier accessed the same items, to be accessed, by both the name of the manufacturing party or importing party and the quarter(s) and year(s) to be accessed.

(2) The name of the interested copyright party, manufacturing party, importing party, or verification auditor on whose behalf the request is made, plus this party's complete address, including a street address (not a post office box number), a telephone number, and a fax number, if any.

(3) If the request for access is by or for an interested copyright party, a statement indicating whether the copyright party is owned or controlled by a manufacturing or importing party subject to a royalty payment obligation, or whether the interested copyright party owns or controls a manufacturing or importing party subject to royalty payments.

(4) The name, address, and telephone number of the person making the request for access and his/her relationship to the party on whose behalf the request is made.

(5) The specific purpose for the request for access, for example, access is requested in order to verify a Statement of Account; in order to review the results of a verification audit; for the resolution of a dispute arising from such an audit; or in order for a manufacturing or importing party to review its own Statement of Account, Primary Auditor's Report, Verification Auditor's Report, or related information.

(6) A statement that the information obtained from access to Statements of Account, Primary Auditor's Report, Verification Auditor's Report, and any other verification audit filings will be used only for a purpose permitted under the Audio Home Recording Act and the DART regulations.

(7) The actual signature of the party or the representative of the party requesting access certifying that the information will be held in confidence and used only for the purpose specified by the Audio Home Recording Act and these regulations.

History of 37 C.F.R. §201.29: 60 FR 25998, May 16, 1995; 63 FR 30635, June 5, 1998; 64 FR 36575, July 7, 1999; 73 FR 37839, July 1, 2008; 78 FR 42874, July 18, 2013; 82 FR 9358, Mar. 8, 2017.

§201.30. VERIFICATION OF STATEMENTS OF ACCOUNT

(a) General. This section prescribes rules pertaining to the verification of information contained in the Statements of Account by interested copyright parties pursuant to section 1003(c) of title 17 of the United States Code.

(b) Definitions.

(1) Annual Statement of Account, generally accepted auditing standards (GAAS), and primary auditor have the same meaning as the definition in §201.28 of this part.

(2) Filer is a manufacturer or importer of digital devices or media who is required by 17 U.S.C. 1003 to file with the

Copyright Office Quarterly and Annual Statements of Account and a primary auditor's report on the Annual Statement of Account.

(3) Interested copyright party has the same meaning as the definition in §201.29 of this part.

(4) Verifying auditor is the person retained by interested copyright parties to perform a verification procedure. He or she is independent and qualified as defined in paragraphs (j)(2) and (j)(3) of this section.

(5) Verification procedure is the process followed by the verifying auditor to verify the information reported on an Annual Statement of Account.

(c) Purpose of Verification. The purpose of verification is to determine whether there was any failure of the primary auditor to conduct the primary audit properly or to obtain a reliable result, or whether there was any error in the Annual Statement of Account.

(d) Timing of Verification Procedure.

(1) Requesting a verification procedure. No sooner than three months nor later than three years after the filing deadline of the Annual Statement of Account to be verified, any interested copyright party shall notify the Register of Copyrights of its interest in instituting a verification procedure. Such notification of interest shall also be served at the same time on the filer and the primary auditor identified in the Annual Statement of Account. Such notification shall include the year of the Annual Statement of Account to be verified, the name of the filer, information on how other interested copyright parties may contact the party interested in the verification including name, address, telephone number, facsimile number and electronic mail address, if any, and a statement establishing the party filing the notification as an interested copyright party. The notification of interest may apply to more than one Annual Statement of Account and more than one filer.

(2) Coordination and selection of verifying auditor. The Copyright Office will publish in the Federal Register notice of having received a notification of interest to institute a verification procedure. Interested copyright parties have one month from the date of publication of the Federal Register notice to notify the party interested in instituting the verification procedure of their intent to join with it and to participate in the selection of the verifying auditor. Any dispute about the selection of the verifying auditor shall be resolved by the parties themselves.

(3) Notification of the filer and primary auditor. As soon as the verifying auditor has been selected, and in no case later than two months after the publication in the Federal Register of the notice described in paragraph (d)(2) of this section, the joint interested copyright parties shall notify the Register of Copyrights, the filer, and the primary auditor identified in the Annual Statement of Account to be verified, that they intend or do not intend to initiate a verification procedure.

(4) Commencement of the verification procedure. The verification procedure shall begin no sooner than one month after notice of intent to initiate a verification procedure was given to the filer and the primary auditor by the joint interested copyright parties. The joint interested copyright parties shall grant the filer or the primary auditor a postponement of the beginning of the verification procedure of up to one additional month if either one requests it. Verification procedures shall be conducted at reasonable times during normal business hours.

(5) Anti-duplication rules. A filer shall be subject to no more than one verification procedure per calendar year. An Annual Statement of Account shall be subject to a verification procedure only once.

(e) Scope of verification. The verifying auditor shall limit his or her examination to verifying the information required in the Annual Statement of Account. To the extent possible, the verifying auditor shall inspect the information contained in the primary auditor's report and the primary auditor's working papers. If the verifying auditor believes that access to the records, files, or other materials in the control of the filer is required according to GAAS, he or she may, after consultation with the primary auditor, require the production of these documents as well. The verifying auditor and the primary auditor shall act in good faith using reasonable professional judgment, with the intention of reaching a reasonable accommodation as to the necessity and scope of examination of any additional documents, but the decision to require the production of additional documents is solely that of the verifying auditor.

(f) Verification Report. Upon concluding the verification procedure, the verifying auditor shall render a report enumerating in reasonable detail the procedures performed by the verifying auditor and his or her findings. Such findings shall state whether there was any failure of the primary auditor to conduct properly the primary audit or obtain a reliable result, and whether there was any error in the Annual Statement of Account, itemized by amount and by the filer's elected fiscal year. If there was such failure or error, the report shall specify all evidence from which the verifying auditor reached such conclusions. Such evidence shall be listed and identified in an appendix to the report in sufficient detail to enable a third party to reasonably understand or interpret the evidence on which the verifying auditor based his or her conclusion. If there was no such failure or error, the report shall so state.

(g) Distribution of Report. Copies of the verifying auditor's report shall be subject to the confidentiality provisions of §201.29 and shall be distributed as follows:

(1) One copy, excluding the appendix, if applicable, shall be filed with the Register of Copyrights.

(2) One copy, with the appendix, if applicable, shall be submitted to each of the interested copyright parties who retained the services of the verifying auditor and who are authorized to receive such information according to §201.29.

(3) One copy, with the appendix, if applicable, shall be submitted to the filer of the Annual Statement of Account.

(4) One copy, with the appendix, if applicable, shall be submitted to the primary auditor.

(h) Retention of Report. The Register of Copyrights will retain his or her copy of the verifying auditor's report for three years following the date the copy of the verifying auditor's report is filed.

(i) Costs of Verification. The joint interested copyright parties who requested the verification procedure shall pay the fees of the verifying auditor and the primary auditor for their work performed in connection with the verification procedure, except, if the verification procedure results in a judicial determination or the filer's agreement that royalty payments were understated on the Annual Statement of Account, then,

(1) if the amount is less than five percent (5%) of the amount stated on the Annual Statement of Account, that amount shall first be used to pay the fees of the verifying auditor and the primary auditor, and any remaining amount plus any applicable interest on the total amount shall be deposited, allocated by the filer's elected fiscal year, with the Register of Copyrights, or

(2) if the amount is equal to or greater than five percent (5%) of the amount stated on the Annual Statement of Account, the filer shall pay the fees of the verifying auditor and the primary auditor, and, in addition, shall deposit the amount found to be due plus any applicable interest on the total amount, allocated by the filer's elected fiscal year, with the Register of Copyrights.

(j) Independence and qualifications of verifying auditor.

(1) The verifying auditor shall be qualified and independent as defined in this section. If the filer has reason to believe that the verifying auditor is not qualified or independent, it shall raise the matter with the joint interested copyright parties before the commencement of the verification procedure, and if the matter is not resolved, it may raise the issue with the American Institute of Certified Public Accountants' Professional Ethics Division and/or the verifying auditor's State Board of Accountancy while the verification procedure is being performed.

(2) A verifying auditor shall be considered qualified if he or she is a certified public accountant or works under the supervision of a certified public accounting firm.

(3) A verifying auditor shall be considered independent if:

(i) he or she is independent as that term is used in the Code of Professional Conduct of the American Institute of Certified Public Accountants, including the Principles, Rules and Interpretations of such Code applicable generally to attest engagements (collectively, the "AICPA Code"); and

(ii) he or she is independent as that term is used in the Statements on Auditing Standards promulgated by the Auditing Standards Board of the AICPA and Interpretations thereof issued by the Auditing Standards Division of the AICPA.

History of 37 C.F.R. §201.30: 61 FR 30813, June 18, 1996.

§201.31. REMOVED & RESERVED

§201.32. RESERVED

History of 37 C.F.R. §201.32: 64 FR 29522, June 1, 1999.

§201.33. PROCEDURES FOR FILING NOTICES OF INTENT TO ENFORCE A RESTORED COPYRIGHT UNDER THE URUGUAY ROUND AGREEMENTS ACT

(a) General. This section prescribes the procedures for submission of Notices of Intent to Enforce a Restored Copyright under the Uruguay Round Agreements Act, as required in 17 U.S.C. 104A(a). On or before May 1, 1996, and every four months thereafter, the Copyright Office will publish in the Federal Register a list of works for which Notices of Intent to Enforce have been filed. It will maintain a list of these works. The Office will also make a more complete version of the information contained in the Notice of Intent to Enforce available on its website.

(b) Definitions.

(1) NAFTA work means a work restored to copyright on January 1, 1995, as a result of compliance with procedures contained in the North American Free Trade Agreement Implementation Act of December 8, 1993, Public Law No. 103-182.

(2) Reliance party means any person who—

(i) With respect to a particular work, engages in acts, before the source country of that work becomes an eligible country under the URAA, which would have violated 17 U.S.C. 106 if the restored work had been subject to copyright protection and who, after the source country becomes an eligible country, continues to engage in such acts;

(ii) Before the source country of a particular work becomes an eligible country, makes or acquires one or more copies or phonorecords of that work; or

(iii) As the result of the sale or other disposition of a derivative work, covered under 17 U.S.C. 104A(d)(3), or of significant assets of a person, described in 17 U.S.C. 104A(d)(3)(A) or (B), is a successor, assignee or licensee of that person.

(3) Restored work means an original work of authorship that—

(i) Is protected under 17 U.S.C. 104A(a);

(ii) Is not in the public domain in its source country through expiration of term of protection;

(iii) Is in the public domain in the United States due to—

(A) Noncompliance with formalities imposed at any time by U.S. copyright law, including failure of renewal, lack of proper notice, or failure to comply with any manufacturing requirements;

(B) Lack of subject matter protection in the case of sound recordings fixed before February 15, 1972; or

(C) Lack of national eligibility; and

(iv) Has at least one author or rightholder who was, at the time the work was created, a national or domiciliary of an eligible country, and if published, was first published in an eligible country and not published in the United States during the 30-day period following publication in such eligible country.

(4) Source country of a restored work is—

(i) A nation other than the United States; and

(ii) In the case of an unpublished work—

(A) The eligible country in which the author or rightholder is a national or domiciliary, or, if a restored work has more than one author or rightholder, the majority of foreign authors or rightholders are nationals or domiciliaries of eligible countries; or

(B) If the majority of authors or rightholders are not foreign, the nation other than the United States which has the most significant contacts with the work; and

(iii) In the case of a published work—

(A) The eligible country in which the work is first published; or

(B) If the restored work is published on the same day in two or more eligible countries, the eligible country which has the most significant contacts with the work.

(c) Forms. The Copyright Office does not provide forms for Notices of Intent to Enforce filed with the Copyright Office. It requests that filers of such notices follow the format set out in Appendix A of this section and give all of the information listed in paragraph (d) of this section. Notices of Intent to Enforce must be in English, and should be typed or printed by hand legibly in dark, preferably black, ink, on 8½ by 11 inch white paper of good quality, with at least a one inch (or three cm) margin.

(d) Requirements for Notice of Intent to Enforce a Copyright Restored under the Uruguay Round Agreements Act.

(1) Notices of Intent to Enforce should be mailed to the address specified in §201.1.

(2) The document should be clearly designated as "Notice of Intent to Enforce a Copyright Restored under the Uruguay Round Agreements Act."

(3) Notices of Intent to Enforce must include:

(i) Required information:

(A) The title of the work, or if untitled, a brief description of the work;

(B) An English translation of the title if title is in a foreign language;

(C) Alternative titles if any;

(D) Name of the copyright owner of the restored work, or of an owner of an exclusive right therein;

(E) The address and telephone number where the owner of copyright or the exclusive right therein can be reached; and

(F) The following certification signed and dated by the owner of copyright, or the owner of an exclusive right therein, or the owner's authorized agent:

I hereby certify that for each of the work(s) listed above, I am the copyright owner, or the owner of an exclusive right, or the owner's authorized agent, the agency relationship having been constituted in a writing signed by the owner before the filing of this notice, and that the information given herein is true and correct to the best of my knowledge.

Signature:

___

Name (printed or typed):

___

As agent for (if applicable):

___

Date:

___

(ii) Optional but essential information:

(A) Type of work (painting, sculpture, music, motion picture, sound recording, book, etc.);

(B) Name of author(s);

(C) Source country;

(D) Approximate year of publication;

(E) Additional identifying information (e.g. for movies: director, leading actors, screenwriter, animator; for photographs or books: subject matter; for books: editor, publisher, contributors);

(F) Rights owned by the party on whose behalf the Notice of Intent to Enforce is filed (e.g., the right to reproduce/distribute/publicly display/publicly perform the work, or to prepare a derivative work based on the work, etc.); and

(G) Email address at which owner, exclusive rights holder, or agent thereof can be reached.

(4) Notices of Intent to Enforce may cover multiple works provided that each work is identified by title, all the works are by the same author, all the works are owned by the identified copyright owner or owner of an exclusive right, and the rights owned by the party on whose behalf the Notice of Intent is filed are the same. In the case of Notices of Intent to Enforce covering multiple works, the notice must separately designate for each work covered the title of the work, or if untitled, a brief description of the work; an English translation of the title if the title is in a foreign language; alternative titles, if any; the type of work; the source country; the approximate year of publication; and additional identifying information.

(5) Notices of Intent to Enforce works restored on January 1, 1996, may be submitted to the Copyright Office on or after January 1, 1996, through December 31, 1997.

(e) Fee.

(1) Amount. The filing fee for recording Notices of Intent to Enforce is prescribed in §201.3(c).

(2) Method of payment.

(i) Checks, money orders, or bank drafts. The Copyright Office will accept checks, money orders, or bank drafts made payable to the U.S. Copyright Office. Remittances must be redeemable without service or exchange fees through a United States institution, must be payable in United States dollars, and must be imprinted with American Banking Association routing numbers. International money orders, and postal money orders that are negotiable only at a post office are not acceptable. CURRENCY WILL NOT BE ACCEPTED.

(ii) Copyright Office Deposit Account. The Copyright Office maintains a system of Deposit Accounts for the convenience of those who frequently use its services. The system allows an individual or firm to establish a Deposit Account in the Copyright Office and to make advance deposits into that account. Deposit Account holders can charge copyright fees against the balance in their accounts instead of sending separate remittances with each request for service. For information on Deposit Accounts, see Circular 5 on the Copyright Office's website, or request a copy at the address specified in §201.1(b).

(iii) Credit cards. For URAA filings the Copyright Office will accept most major credit cards. Debit cards cannot be accepted for payment. With the NIE, a filer using a credit card must submit a separate cover letter stating the name of the credit card, the credit card number, the expiration date of the credit card, the total amount, and a signature authorizing the Office to charge the fees to the account. To protect the security of the credit card number, the filer must not write the credit card number on the Notice of Intent to Enforce.

(f) Public access. Notices of Intent to Enforce filed with the Copyright Office are available for public inspection and copying in the Records Research and Certification Section. Some of the information contained in these records is available on the Office's website, including the title of the work or a brief description if the work is untitled and the name of the copyright owner or owner of an exclusive right.

(g) NAFTA work. The copyright owner of a work restored under NAFTA by the filing of a NAFTA Statement of Intent to Restore with the Copyright Office prior to January 1, 1995, is not required to file a Notice of Intent to Enforce under this regulation.

History of 37 C.F.R. §201.33: 60 FR 50420, Sept. 29, 1995; 63 FR 30635, June 5, 1998; 64 FR 12902, Mar. 16, 1999; 71 FR 31092, June 1, 2006; 73 FR 37839, July 1, 2008; 78 FR 42874, July 18, 2013; 82 FR 9358, Mar. 8, 2017.

APPENDIX A TO §201.33—NOTICE OF INTENT TO ENFORCE A COPYRIGHT RESTORED UNDER THE URUGUAY ROUND AGREEMENTS ACT (URAA)

1. Title:

____

(If this work does not have a title, state "No title.") OR

Brief description of work (for untitled works only):

____

2. English translation of title (if applicable):

____

3. Alternative title(s) (if any):

____

4. Type of work:

____

(e.g. painting, sculpture, music, motion picture, sound recording, book)

5. Name of author(s):

____

6. Source country:

____

7. Approximate year of publication:

____

8. Additional identifying information:

____

(e.g. for movies: director, leading actors, screenwriter, animator; for photographs: subject matter; for books: editor, publisher, contributors, subject matter).

9. Name of copyright owner:

____

(Statements may be filed in the name of the owner of the restored copyright or the owner of an exclusive right therein.)

10. If you are not the owner of all rights, specify the rights you own:

____

(e.g. the right to reproduce/distribute publicly display/publicly perform the work, or to prepare a derivative work based on the work)

11. Address at which copyright owner may be contacted:

____

____

____

(Give the complete address, including the country and an "attention" line, or "in care of" name, if necessary.)

12. Telephone number of owner:

____

13. Fax number of owner:

____

14. Certification and Signature:

I hereby certify that, for each of the work(s) listed above, I am the copyright owner, or the owner of an exclusive right, or the owner's authorized agent, the agency relationship having been constituted in a writing signed by the owner before the filing of this notice, and that the information given herein is true and correct to the best of my knowledge.

Signature:

Name (printed or typed):

As agent for (if applicable):

Date:

Note: Notices of Intent to Enforce must be in English, except for the original title, and either typed or printed by hand legibly in dark, preferably black, ink. They should be on 8½" by 11" white paper of good quality, with at least a 1-inch (or 3 cm) margin.

§201.34. PROCEDURES FOR FILING CORRECTION NOTICES OF INTENT TO ENFORCE A COPYRIGHT RESTORED UNDER THE URUGUAY ROUND AGREEMENTS ACT

(a) General. This section prescribes the procedures for submission of corrections of Notices of Intent to Enforce a Copyright (NIEs) Restored under the Uruguay Round Agreements Act of December 8, 1994, as required by 17 U.S.C. 104A(e), as amended by Pub.L. 103-465, 108 Stat. 4809, 4976 (1994).

(b) Definitions. For purposes of this section, the following definitions apply.

(1) Major error. A major error in filing a Notice of Intent to Enforce a Copyright Restored under the Uruguay Round Agreements Act is an error in the name of the copyright owner or rightholder, or in the title of the work (as opposed to its translation, if any) where such error fails to adequately identify the restored work or its owner through a reasonable search of the Copyright Office NIE records. Omission of, or incorrect information regarding, a written agency relationship also constitutes a major error.

(2) Minor error. A minor error in filing a Notice of Intent to Enforce a Copyright Restored under the Uruguay Round Agreements Act is any error that is not a major error.

(3) Restored work. For the definition of works restored under the URAA, see 37 CFR 201.33.

(c) Forms. The Copyright Office does not provide forms for Correction Notices of Intent to Enforce filed with the Copyright Office. It requests that filers of such Correction NIEs follow the format set out in Appendix A of this section and give all information listed in paragraph (d) of this section. Correction NIEs must be in English, and should be typed or legibly printed by hand in dark, preferably black ink, on 8½" by 11" white paper of good quality with at least a 1" (or three cm) margin.

(d) Requirements for Correction Notice of Intent to Enforce a Copyright Restored under the Uruguay Round Agreements Act.

(1) A correction for a Notice of Intent to Enforce should be clearly designated as a "Correction Notice of Intent to Enforce" or "Correction NIE."

(2) Correction Notices of Intent to Enforce should be addressed to Attn: URAA/GATT, NIE and Registrations and mailed to the address specified in §201.1.

(3) A Correction NIE shall contain the following information:

(i) The volume and document number of the previous NIE which is to be corrected;

(ii) The title of the work as it appears on the previous NIE, including alternative titles, if they appear;

(iii) The English translation of the title, if any, as it appears on the previous NIE;

(iv) A statement of the erroneous information as it appears on the previous NIE;

(v) A statement of the correct information as it should have appeared and an optional explanation of its correction; or

(vi) A statement of the information to be added. This includes optional information such as:

(A) Type of work;

(B) Rights owned by the party on whose behalf the Correction Notice is filed;

(C) Name of author;

(D) Source country;

(E) Year of publication;

(F) Alternative titles;

(G) An optional explanation of the added information.

(vii) The name and address:

(A) To which correspondence concerning the document should be sent; and

(B) To which the acknowledgment of the recordation of the Correction NIE should be mailed; and

(viii) A certification. The certification shall consist of:

(A) A statement that, for each of the works named above, the person signing the Correction NIE is the copyright owner, or the owner of an exclusive right, or the owner's authorized agent, and that the information is correct to the best of that person's knowledge;

(B) The typed or printed name of the person whose signature appears;

(C) The signature and date of signature; and

(D) The telephone and fax number at which the owner, rightholder, or agent thereof can be reached.

(4) A Correction NIE may cover multiple works in multiple NIE documents for one fee provided that: each work is identified by title; all the works are by the same author; all the works are owned by the same copyright owner or owner of an exclusive right. In the case of Correction NIEs, the notice must separately designate each title to be corrected, noting the incorrect information as it appeared on the previously filed NIE, as well as the corrected information. A single notice covering multiple titles need bear only a single certification.

(5) Copies, phonorecords or supporting documents cannot be made part of the record of a Correction NIE and should not be submitted with the document.

(6) Time for Submitting Correction NIEs.

(i) Major errors. The Copyright Office will accept a Correction NIE for a major error concerning a restored work during the 24-month period beginning on the date of restoration of the work, as provided for original NIEs in section 104A(d)(2)(A) of title 17.

(ii) Minor errors. The Office will accept a Correction NIE for a minor error or omission concerning a restored work at any time after the original NIE has been filed, as provided in section 104A(e)(1)(A)(iii) of title 17.

(e) Fee—

(1) Amount. The filing fee for recording Correction NIEs is prescribed in §201.3(c).

(2) Method of payment. See 37 CFR 201.33(e)(1), (2).

(f) Public access. Correction Notices of Intent to Enforce filed with the Copyright Office are available for public inspection and copying in the Records Research and Certification Section.

History of 37 C.F.R. §201.34: 62 FR 55739, Oct. 28, 1997; 71 FR 31092, June 1, 2006; 73 FR 37839, July 1, 2008; 78 FR 42874, July 18, 2013; 82 FR 9359, Mar. 8, 2017.

APPENDIX A TO §201.34—CORRECTION NOTICE OF INTENT TO ENFORCE

Correction of Notice of Intent To Enforce

1. Name of Copyright Owner (or owner of exclusive right) (If this correction notice is to cover multiple works, the author and the rights owner must be the same for all works covered by the notice.)

____

2. Title(s) (or brief description)

(a) Work No. 1— __________
Volume and Document Number: __________
English Translation: __________

(b) Work No. 2 (if applicable)— __________
Volume and Document Number: __________
English Translation: __________

(c) Work No. 3 (if applicable)— __________
Volume and Document Number: __________
English Translation: __________

(d) Work No. 4 (if applicable)— __________
Volume and Document Number: __________
English Translation: __________

3. Statement of incorrect information on earlier NIE:

____

4. Statement of correct (or previously omitted) information:

____

Give the following only if incorrect or omitted on earlier NIE:

(a) Type of work __________

(b) Rights owned __________

(c) Name of author (of entire work) __________

(d) Source Country __________

(e) Year of Publication (Approximate if precise year is unknown) __________

(f) Alternative titles __________

5. Explanation of error:

____

6. Certification and Signature: I hereby certify that for each of the work(s) listed above, I am the copyright owner, or the owner of an exclusive right, or the owner's authorized agent, the agency relationship having been constituted in a writing signed by the owner before the filing of this notice, and that the information given herein is true and correct to the best of my knowledge.

____

Name and Address (typed or printed):

____

Telephone/Fax:

____

As agent for:

____

Date and Signature:

____

§§201.35 TO 201.37. RESERVED

History of 37 C.F.R. §§201.35-201.37: 69 FR 11527, Mar. 11, 2004.

A §201.38. DESIGNATION OF AGENT TO RECEIVE NOTIFICATION OF CLAIMED INFRINGEMENT

(a) General. This section prescribes the rules pursuant to which service providers may designate agents to receive notifications of claimed infringement pursuant to section 512 of title 17 of the United States Code. Any service provider seeking to comply with section 512(c)(2) of the statute must:

(1) Designate an agent by making available through its service, including on its website in a location accessible to the public, and by providing to the Copyright Office, the service provider and designated agent information required by paragraph (b) of this section;

(2) Maintain the currency and accuracy of the information required by paragraph (b) both on its website and with the Office by timely updating such information when it has changed; and

(3) Comply with the electronic registration requirements in paragraph (c) to designate an agent with the Office.

(b) Information required to designate an agent. To designate an agent, a service provider must make available through its service, including on its website in a location accessible to the public, and provide to the Copyright Office in accordance with paragraph (c) of this section, the following information:

(1)(i) The full legal name and physical street address of the service provider. Related or affiliated service providers that are separate legal entities (e.g., corporate parents and subsidiaries) are considered separate service providers, and each must have its own separate designation.

(ii) A post office box may not be substituted for the street address for the service provider, except in exceptional circumstances (e.g., where there is a demonstrable threat to an individual's personal safety or security, such that it may be dangerous to publicly publish a street address where such individual can be located) and, upon written request by the service provider, the Register of Copyrights determines that the circumstances warrant a waiver of this requirement. To obtain a waiver, the service provider must send a signed letter, addressed to the "U.S. Copyright Office, Office of the General Counsel" and sent to the address for time-sensitive requests set forth in section 201.1(c)(1), containing the following information: The name of the service provider; the post office box address that the service provider wishes to use; a detailed statement providing the reasons supporting the request, with explanation of the specific threat(s) to an individual's personal safety or security; and an email address for any responsive correspondence from the Office. There is no fee associated with making this request. If the request is approved, the service provider may display the post office box address on its website and will receive instructions from the Office as to how to complete the Office's electronic registration process.

(2) All alternate names that the public would be likely to use to search for the service provider's designated agent in the Copyright Office's online directory of designated agents, including all names under which the service provider is doing business, website names and addresses (i.e., URLs), software application names, and other commonly used names. Separate legal entities are not considered alternate names.

(3) The name of the agent designated to receive notifications of claimed infringement and, if applicable, the name of the agent's organization. The designated agent may be an individual (e.g., "Jane Doe"), a specific position or title held by an individual (e.g., "Copyright Manager"), a specific department within the service provider's organization or within a third-party entity (e.g., "Copyright Compliance Department"), or a third-party entity generally (e.g., "ACME Takedown Service"). Only a single agent may be designated for each service provider.

(4) The physical mail address (street address or post office box), telephone number, and email address of the agent designated to receive notifications of claimed infringement.

(c) Electronic registration with the Copyright Office. Service providers designating an agent with the Copyright Office must do so electronically by establishing an account with and then utilizing the applicable online registration system made available through the Copyright Office's website. Designations, amendments, and resubmissions submitted to the Office in paper or any other form will not be accepted. All electronic registrations must adhere to the following requirements:

(1) Registration information. All required fields in the online registration system must be completed in order for the designation to be registered with the Copyright Office. In addition to the information required by paragraph (b) of this section, the person designating the agent with the Office must provide the following for administrative purposes, and which will not be displayed in the Office's public directory and need not be displayed by the service provider on its website:

(i) The first name, last name, telephone number, and email address of a representative of the service provider who will serve as the primary point of contact for communications with the Office.

(ii) A telephone number and email address for the service provider for communications with the Office.

(2) Attestation. For each designation and any subsequent amendment or resubmission of such designation, the person designating the agent, or amending or resubmitting such designation, must attest that:

(i) The information provided to the Office is true, accurate, and complete to the best of his or her knowledge; and

(ii) He or she has been given authority to make the designation, amendment, or resubmission on behalf of the service provider.

(3) Amendment. All service providers must ensure the currency and accuracy of the information contained in designations submitted to the Office by timely updating information when it has changed. A service provider may amend a designation previously registered with the Office at any time to correct or update information.

(4) Periodic renewal. A service provider's designation will expire and become invalid three years after it is registered with the Office, unless the service provider renews such designation by either amending it to correct or update information or resubmitting it without amendment. Either amending or resubmitting a designation, as appropriate, begins a new three-year period before such designation must be renewed.

(d) Fees. The Copyright Office's general fee schedule, located at section 201.3 of title 37 of the Code of Federal Regulations, sets forth the applicable fee for a service provider to designate an agent with the Copyright Office to receive notifications of claimed infringement and to amend or resubmit such a designation.

(e) Transitional provisions. **(1)** As of December 1, 2016, any designation of an agent pursuant to 17 U.S.C. 512(c)(2) must be made electronically through the Copyright Office's online registration system.

(2) A service provider that has designated an agent with the Office under the previous version of this section, which was effective between November 3, 1998 and November 30, 2016, and desires to remain in compliance with section 512(c)(2) of title 17, United States Code, must submit a new designation electronically using the online registration system by December 31, 2017. Any designation not made through the online registration system will expire and become invalid after December 31, 2017.

(3) During the period beginning with the effective date of this section, December 1, 2016, through December 31, 2017 (the "transition period"), the Copyright Office will maintain two directories of designated agents: the directory consisting of paper designations made pursuant to the prior interim regulations (the "old directory"), and the directory consisting of designations made electronically through the online registration system (the "new directory"). During the transition period, a compliant designation in either the old directory or the new directory will satisfy the service provider's obligation under section 512(c)(2) of title 17, United States Code to designate an agent with the Copyright Office.

History of 37 C.F.R. §201.38: 63 FR 59234, Nov. 3, 1998; 67 FR 38005, May 31, 2002; 72 FR 5932, Feb. 8, 2007; 73 FR 37839, July 1, 2008; 78 FR 42874, July 18, 2013; 81 FR 75707, Dec. 1, 2016; 82 FR 9359, Mar. 8, 2017; 82 FR 21697, May 10, 2017.

§201.39. NOTICE TO LIBRARIES & ARCHIVES OF NORMAL COMMERCIAL EXPLOITATION OR AVAILABILITY AT REASONABLE PRICE

(a) General. This section prescribes rules under which copyright owners or their agents may provide notice to qualified libraries and archives (including a nonprofit educational institution that functions as such) that a published work in its last 20 years of copyright protection is subject to normal commercial exploitation, or that a copy or phonorecord of the work can be obtained at a reasonable price, for purposes of section 108(h)(2) of title 17 of the United States Code.

(b) Format. The Copyright Office provides a required format for a Notice to Libraries and Archives of Normal Commercial Exploitation or Availability at Reasonable Price, and for continuation sheets for group notices. The required format is set out in Appendix A to this section, and is available from the Copyright Office website (http://lcweb.loc.gov/copyright). The Copyright Office does not provide printed forms. The Notice shall be in English (except for an original title, which may be in another language), typed or printed legibly in dark ink, and shall be provided on 8½ x 11 inch white paper with a one-inch margin.

(c) Required Content. A "Notice to Libraries and Archives of Normal Commercial Exploitation or Availability at Reasonable Price" shall be identified as such by prominent caption or heading, and shall include the following:

(1) The acronym NLA in capital, and preferably bold, letters in the top right-hand corner of the page;

(2) A check-box just below the acronym NLA indicating whether continuation sheets for additional works are attached;

(3) The title of the work, or if untitled, a brief description of the work;

(4) The author(s) of the work;

(5) The type of work (e.g., music, motion picture, book, photograph, illustration, map, article in a periodical, painting, sculpture, sound recording, etc.);

(6) The edition, if any (e.g., first edition, second edition, teacher's edition) or version, if any (e.g., orchestral arrangement, translation, French version). If there is no information relating to the edition or version of the work, the notice should so state;

(7) The year of first publication;

(8) The year the work first secured federal copyright through publication with notice or registration as an unpublished work;

(9) The copyright renewal registration number (except this information is not required for foreign works in which copyright is restored pursuant to 17 U.S.C. 104A);

(10) The name of the copyright owner (or the owner of exclusive rights);

(11) If the copyright owner is not the owner of all rights, a specification of the rights owned (e.g., the right to reproduce/distribute/publicly display/publicly perform the work or to prepare a derivative work);

(12) The name, address, telephone number, fax number (if any) and e-mail address (if any) of the person or entity that the Copyright Office should contact concerning the Notice;

(13) The full legal name, address, telephone number, fax number (if any) and e-mail address (if any) of the person or entity that Libraries and Archives may contact concerning the work's normal commercial exploitation or availability at reasonable price; and

(14) A declaration made under penalty of perjury that the work identified is subject to normal commercial exploitation, or that a copy or phonorecord of the work is available at a reasonable price.

(d) Additional content. A Notice to Libraries and Archives of Normal Commercial Exploitation or Availability at Reasonable Price may include the following:

(1) The original copyright registration number of the work; and

(2) Additional information concerning the work's normal commercial exploitation or availability at a reasonable price.

(e) Signature. The Notice to Libraries and Archives of Normal Commercial Exploitation or Availability at Reasonable Price shall include the signature of the copyright owner or its agent. The signature shall be accompanied by the printed or typewritten name and title of the person signing the Notice, and by the date of signature.

(f) Multiple works. A Notice to Libraries and Archives may be filed for more than one work. The first work shall be identified using the format required for all Notices to Libraries and Archives. Each additional work in the group must be identified on a separate continuation sheet. The required format for the continuation sheet is set out in Appendix B to this section, and is available from the Copyright Office website (http://lcweb.loc.gov/copyright). A group filing is permitted provided that:

(1) All the works are by the same author;

(2) All the works are owned by the same copyright owner or owner of the exclusive rights therein. If the claimant is not owner of all rights, the claimant must own the same rights with respect to all works in the group;

(3) All the works first secured federal copyright in the same year, through either publication with notice or registration as unpublished works;

(4) All the works were first published in the same year;

(5) The person or entity that the Copyright Office should contact concerning the Notice is the same for all the works; and

(6) The person or entity that Libraries and Archives may contact concerning the work's normal commercial exploitation or availability at reasonable price is the same for all the works.

(g) Filing—

(1) Method of filing. The Notice to Libraries and Archives of Normal Commercial Exploitation or Availability at Reasonable Price should be addressed to NLA, at the address specified in §201.1.

(2) Amount. The filing fee for recording Notice to Libraries and Archives is prescribed in §201.3(d).

(3) Method of Payment—

(i) Checks, money orders, or bank drafts. The Copyright Office will accept checks, money orders, or bank drafts made payable to the U.S. Copyright Office. Remittances must be redeemable without service or exchange fees through a United States institution, must be payable in United States dollars, and must be imprinted with American Banking Association routing numbers. Postal money orders that are negotiable only at a post office and international money orders are not acceptable. CURRENCY IS NOT ACCEPTED.

(ii) Copyright Office Deposit Account. The Copyright Office maintains a system of Deposit Accounts for the convenience of those who frequently use its services. The system allows an individual or firm to establish a Deposit Account in the Copyright Office and to make advance deposits into that account. Deposit Account holders can charge copyright fees against the balance in their accounts instead of sending separate remittances with each request for service. For information on Deposit Accounts, see Circular 5 on the Copyright Office's website, or request a copy at the address specified in §201.1(b).

History of 37 C.F.R. §201.39: 63 FR 71787, Dec. 30, 1998; 66 FR 34373, June 28, 2001; 71 FR 31092, June 1, 2006; 73 FR 37839, July 1, 2008; 78 FR 42874, July 18, 2013; 82 FR 9359, Mar. 8, 2017.

APPENDIX A TO §201.39—REQUIRED FORMAT OF NOTICE TO LIBRARIES & ARCHIVES OF NORMAL COMMERCIAL EXPLOITATION OR AVAILABILITY AT REASONABLE PRICE

NLA

[ ] Check box if continuation sheets for additional works are attached.

Notice to Libraries and Archives of Normal Commercial Exploitation or Availability at Reasonable Price

1. Title of the work (or, if untitled, a brief description of the work): ________.

2. Author(s) of the work: ________.

3. Type of work (e.g. music, motion picture, book, photograph, illustration, map, article in a periodical, painting, sculpture, sound recording, etc.): ________.

4. Edition, if any (e.g., first edition, second edition, teacher's edition) or version, if any (e.g., orchestral arrangement, English translation of French text). If there is no information available relating to the edition or version of the work, the Notice should state, "No information available": ________.

5. Year of first publication: _____.

6. Year the work first secured federal copyright through publication with notice or registration as an unpublished work: _____.

7. Copyright renewal registration number (not required for foreign works restored under 17 U.S.C. 104A): _____.

8. Full legal name of the copyright owner (or the owner of exclusive rights): _____.

9. The person or entity identified in space #8 owns:

[ ] all rights.

[ ] the following rights (e.g., the right to reproduce/distribute/publicly display/publicly perform the work or to prepare a derivative work): _____.

10. Person or entity that the Copyright Office should contact concerning the Notice:

[ ] Name:

____

[ ] Address:

____

[ ] Telephone:

____

[ ] Fax number (if any):

[ ] E-mail address (if any):

11. Person or entity that libraries and archives may contact concerning the work's normal commercial exploitation or availability at a reasonable price:
[ ] Name:

[ ] Address:

[ ] Telephone:

[ ] Fax number (if any):

[ ] E-mail address (if any):

Additional Content (OPTIONAL):
12. Original copyright registration number: __________
13. Additional information concerning the work's normal commercial exploitation or availability at a reasonable price: __________

Declaration:
I declare under penalty of perjury under the laws of the United States:
[ ] that each work identified in this notice is subject to normal commercial exploitation.
[ ] that a copy or phonorecord of each work identified in this notice is available at a reasonable price.
Signature:

Date:

[ ] Typed or printed name:

[ ] Title:

APPENDIX B TO §201.39—REQUIRED FORMAT FOR CONTINUATION SHEET

NLA CON
Page __ of __ Pages.
Continuation Sheet for NLA Notice to Libraries and Archives of Normal Commercial Exploitation or Availability at Reasonable Price
1. Title of the work (or, if untitled, a brief description of the work): __________.
2. Type of work (e.g. music, motion picture, book, photograph, illustration, map, article in a periodical, painting, sculpture, sound recording, etc.): __________.
3. Edition, if any (e.g., first edition, second edition, teacher's edition) or version, if any (e.g., orchestral arrangement, English translation of French text). If there is no information available relating to the edition or version of the work, the Notice should state, "No information available": __________.
4. Copyright renewal registration number (not required for foreign works restored under 17 U.S.C. 104A): __________.
Additional Content (OPTIONAL):
5. Original copyright registration number: __________.
6. Additional information concerning the work's normal commercial exploitation or availability at a reasonable price: __________.

§201.40. EXEMPTIONS TO PROHIBITION AGAINST CIRCUMVENTION

(a) General. This section prescribes the classes of copyrighted works for which the Librarian of Congress has determined, pursuant to 17 U.S.C. 1201(a)(1)(C) and (D), that noninfringing uses by persons who are users of such works are, or are likely to be, adversely affected. The prohibition against circumvention of technological measures that control access to copyrighted works set forth in 17 U.S.C. 1201(a)(1)(A) shall not apply to such users of the prescribed classes of copyrighted works.

(b) Classes of copyrighted works. Pursuant to the authority set forth in 17 U.S.C. 1201(a)(1)(C) and (D), and upon the recommendation of the Register of Copyrights, the Librarian has determined that the prohibition against circumvention of technological measures that effectively control access to copyrighted works set forth in 17 U.S.C. 1201(a)(1)(A) shall not apply to persons who engage in noninfringing uses of the following classes of copyrighted works:

(1) Motion pictures (including television shows and videos), as defined in 17 U.S.C. 101, where circumvention is undertaken solely in order to make use of short portions of the motion pictures for the purpose of criticism or comment in the following instances:

(i) For use in documentary filmmaking,

(A) Where the circumvention is undertaken using screen-capture technology that appears to be offered to the public as enabling the reproduction of motion pictures after content has been lawfully acquired and decrypted, or

(B) Where the motion picture is lawfully made and acquired on a DVD protected by the Content Scramble System, on a Blu-ray disc protected by the Advanced Access Control System, or via a digital transmission protected by a technological measure, and where the person engaging in circumvention reasonably believes that screen-capture software or other non-circumventing alternatives are unable to produce the required level of high-quality content;

(ii) For use in noncommercial videos (including videos produced for a paid commission if the commissioning entity's use is noncommercial),

(A) Where the circumvention is undertaken using screen-capture technology that appears to be offered to the public as enabling the reproduction of motion pictures after content has been lawfully acquired and decrypted, or

(B) Where the motion picture is lawfully made and acquired on a DVD protected by the Content Scramble System, on a Blu-ray disc protected by the Advanced Access Control System, or via a digital transmission protected by a technological measure, and where the person engaging in circumvention reasonably believes that screen-capture software or other non-circumventing alternatives are unable to produce the required level of high-quality content;

(iii) For use in nonfiction multimedia e-books offering film analysis,

(A) Where the circumvention is undertaken using screen-capture technology that appears to be offered to the public as enabling the reproduction of motion pictures after content has been lawfully acquired and decrypted, or

(B) Where the motion picture is lawfully made and acquired on a DVD protected by the Content Scramble System, on a Blu-ray disc protected by the Advanced Access Control System, or via a digital transmission protected by a technological measure, and where the person engaging in circumvention reasonably believes that screen-capture software or other non-circumventing alternatives are unable to produce the required level of high-quality content;

(iv) By college and university faculty and students, for educational purposes,

(A) Where the circumvention is undertaken using screen-capture technology that appears to be offered to the public as enabling the reproduction of motion pictures after content has been lawfully acquired and decrypted, or

(B) In film studies or other courses requiring close analysis of film and media excerpts where the motion picture is lawfully made and acquired on a DVD protected by the Content Scramble System, on a Blu-ray disc protected by the Advanced Access Control System, or via a digital transmission protected by a technological measure, and where the person engaging in circumvention reasonably believes that screen-capture software or other non-circumventing alternatives are unable to produce the required level of high-quality content;

(v) By faculty of massive open online courses (MOOCs) offered by accredited nonprofit educational institutions to officially enrolled students through online platforms (which platforms themselves may be operated for profit), for educational purposes, where the MOOC provider through the online platform limits transmissions to the extent technologically feasible to such officially enrolled students, institutes copyright policies and provides copyright informational materials to faculty, students and relevant staff members, and applies technological measures that reasonably prevent unauthorized further dissemination of a work in accessible form to others or retention of the work for longer than the course session by recipients of a transmission through the platform, as contemplated by 17 U.S.C. 110(2),

(A) Where the circumvention is undertaken using screen-capture technology that appears to be offered to the public as enabling the reproduction of motion pictures after content has been lawfully acquired and decrypted, or

(B) In film studies or other courses requiring close analysis of film and media excerpts where the motion picture is lawfully made and acquired on a DVD protected by the Content Scramble System, on a Blu-ray disc protected by the Advanced Access Control System, or via a digital transmission protected by a technological measure, and where the person engaging in circumvention reasonably believes that screen-capture software or other non-circumventing alternatives are unable to produce the required level of high-quality content;

(vi) By kindergarten through twelfth-grade educators, including of accredited general educational development (GED) programs, for educational purposes,

(A) Where the circumvention is undertaken using screen-capture technology that appears to be offered to the public as enabling the reproduction of motion pictures after content has been lawfully acquired and decrypted, or

(B) In film studies or other courses requiring close analysis of film and media excerpts where the motion picture is lawfully made and acquired on a DVD protected by the Content Scramble System, or via a digital transmission protected by a technological measure, and where the person engaging in circumvention reasonably believes that screen-capture software or other non-circumventing alternatives are unable to produce the required level of high-quality content;

(vii) By kindergarten through twelfth-grade students, including those in accredited general educational development (GED) programs, for educational purposes, where the circumvention is undertaken using screen-capture technology that appears to be offered to the public as enabling the reproduction of motion pictures after content has been lawfully acquired and decrypted; and

(viii) By educators and participants in nonprofit digital and media literacy programs offered by libraries, museums and other nonprofit entities with an educational mission, in the course of face-to-face instructional activities for educational purposes, where the circumvention is undertaken using screen-capture technology that appears to be offered to the public as enabling the reproduction of motion pictures after content has been lawfully acquired and decrypted.

(2) Literary works, distributed electronically, that are protected by technological measures that either prevent the enabling of read-aloud functionality or interfere with screen readers or other applications or assistive technologies,

(i) When a copy of such a work is lawfully obtained by a blind or other person with a disability, as such a person is defined in 17 U.S.C. 121; provided, however, that the rights owner is remunerated, as appropriate, for the price of the mainstream copy of the work as made available to the general public through customary channels, or

(ii) When such work is a nondramatic literary work, lawfully obtained and used by an authorized entity pursuant to 17 U.S.C. 121.

(3)(i) Computer programs that enable the following types of wireless devices to connect to a wireless telecommunications network, when circumvention is undertaken solely in order to connect to a wireless telecommunications network and such connection is authorized by the operator of such network, and the device is a used device:

(A) Wireless telephone handsets (i.e., cellphones);

(B) All-purpose tablet computers;

(C) Portable mobile connectivity devices, such as mobile hotspots, removable wireless broadband modems, and similar devices; and

(D) Wearable wireless devices designed to be worn on the body, such as smartwatches or fitness devices.

(ii) A device is considered "used" for purposes of this exemption when it has previously been lawfully acquired and activated on the wireless telecommunications network of a wireless carrier.

(4) Computer programs that enable smartphones and portable all-purpose mobile computing devices to execute lawfully obtained software applications, where circumvention is accomplished for the sole purpose of enabling interoperability of such applications with computer programs on the smartphone or device, or to permit removal of software from the smartphone or device. For purposes of this exemption, a "portable all-purpose mobile computing device" is a device that is primarily designed to run a wide variety of programs rather than for consumption of a particular type of media content, is equipped with an operating system primarily designed for mobile use, and is intended to be carried or worn by an individual.

(5) Computer programs that enable smart televisions to execute lawfully obtained software applications, where circumvention is accomplished for the sole purpose of enabling interoperability of such applications with computer programs on the smart television.

(6) Computer programs that are contained in and control the functioning of a motorized land vehicle such as a personal automobile, commercial motor vehicle or mechanized agricultural vehicle, except for computer programs primarily designed for the control of telematics or entertainment systems for such vehicle, when circumvention is a necessary step undertaken by the authorized owner of the vehicle to allow the diagnosis, repair or lawful modification of a vehicle function; and where such circumvention does not constitute a violation of applicable law, including without limitation regulations promulgated by the Department of Transportation or the Environmental Protection Agency; and provided, however, that such circumvention is initiated no earlier than 12 months after the effective date of this regulation.

(7)(i) Computer programs, where the circumvention is undertaken on a lawfully acquired device or machine on which the computer program operates solely for the purpose of good-faith security research and does not violate any applicable law, including without limitation the Computer Fraud and Abuse Act of 1986, as amended and codified in title 18, United States Code; and provided, however, that, except as to voting machines, such circumvention is initiated no earlier than 12 months after the effective date of this regulation, and the device or machine is one of the following:

(A) A device or machine primarily designed for use by individual consumers (including voting machines);

(B) A motorized land vehicle; or

(C) A medical device designed for whole or partial implantation in patients or a corresponding personal monitoring system, that is not and will not be used by patients or for patient care.

(ii) For purposes of this exemption, "good-faith security research" means accessing a computer program solely for purposes of good-faith testing, investigation and/or correction of a security flaw or vulnerability, where such activity is carried out in a controlled environment designed to avoid any harm to individuals or the public, and where the information derived from the activity is used primarily to promote the security or safety of the class of devices or machines on which the computer program operates, or those who use such devices or machines, and is not used or maintained in a manner that facilitates copyright infringement.

(8)(i) Video games in the form of computer programs embodied in physical or downloaded formats that have been lawfully acquired as complete games, when the copyright owner or its authorized representative has ceased to provide access to an external computer server necessary to facilitate an authentication process to enable local gameplay, solely for the purpose of:

(A) Permitting access to the video game to allow copying and modification of the computer program to restore access to the game for personal gameplay on a personal computer or video game console; or

(B) Permitting access to the video game to allow copying and modification of the computer program to restore access to the game on a personal computer or video game console when necessary to allow preservation of the game in a playable form by an eligible library, archives or museum, where such activities are carried out without any purpose of direct or indirect commercial advantage and the video game is not distributed or made available outside of the physical premises of the eligible library, archives or museum.

(ii) Computer programs used to operate video game consoles solely to the extent necessary for an eligible library, archives or museum to engage in the preservation activities described in paragraph (i)(B).

(iii) For purposes of the exemptions in paragraphs (i) and (ii), the following definitions shall apply:

(A) "Complete games" means video games that can be played by users without accessing or reproducing copyrightable content stored or previously stored on an external computer server.

(B) "Ceased to provide access" means that the copyright owner or its authorized representative has either issued an affirmative statement indicating that external server support for the video game has ended and such support is in fact no longer available or, alternatively, server support has been discontinued for a period of at least six months; provided, however, that server support has not since been restored.

(C) "Local gameplay" means gameplay conducted on a personal computer or video game console, or locally connected personal computers or consoles, and not through an online service or facility.

(D) A library, archives or museum is considered "eligible" when the collections of the library, archives or museum are open to the public and/or are routinely made available to researchers who are not affiliated with the library, archives or museum.

(9) Computer programs that operate 3D printers that employ microchip-reliant technological measures to limit the use of feedstock, when circumvention is accomplished solely for the purpose of using alternative feedstock and not for the purpose of accessing design software, design files or proprietary data; provided, however, that the exemption shall not extend to any computer program on a 3D printer that produces goods or materials for use in commerce the physical production of which is subject to legal or regulatory oversight or a related certification process, or where the circumvention is otherwise unlawful.

(10) Literary works consisting of compilations of data generated by medical devices that are wholly or partially implanted in the body or by their corresponding personal monitoring systems, where such circumvention is undertaken by a patient for the sole purpose of lawfully accessing the data generated by his or her own device or monitoring system and does not constitute a violation of applicable law, including without limitation the Health Insurance Portability and Accountability Act of 1996, the Computer Fraud and Abuse Act of 1986 or regulations of the Food and Drug Administration, and is accomplished through the passive monitoring of wireless transmissions that are already being produced by such device or monitoring system.

(c) Persons who may initiate circumvention. To the extent authorized under paragraph (b) of this section, the circumvention of a technological measure that restricts wireless telephone handsets or other wireless devices from connecting to a wireless telecommunications network may be initiated by the owner of any such handset or other device, by another person at the direction of the owner, or by a provider of a commercial mobile radio service or a commercial mobile data service at the direction of such owner or other person, solely in order to enable such owner or a family member of such owner to connect to a wireless telecommunications network, when such connection is authorized by the operator of such network.

History of 37 C.F.R. §201.40: 65 FR 64574, Oct. 27, 2000; 68 FR 62018, Oct. 31, 2003; 71 FR 63247, Oct. 30, 2006; 71 FR 68480, Nov. 27, 2006; 74 FR 55139, Oct. 28, 2009; 75 FR 43839, July 27, 2010; 75 FR 47465, Aug. 6, 2010; 77 FR 65278, Oct. 28, 2012; 79 FR 50553, Aug. 25, 2014; 80 FR 65961, Oct. 28, 2015.

PART 202. PREREGISTRATION & REGISTRATION OF CLAIMS TO COPYRIGHT

§202.1. MATERIAL NOT SUBJECT TO COPYRIGHT

The following are examples of works not subject to copyright and applications for registration of such works cannot be entertained:

(a) Words and short phrases such as names, titles, and slogans; familiar symbols or designs; mere variations of typographic ornamentation, lettering or coloring; mere listing of ingredients or contents;

(b) Ideas, plans, methods, systems, or devices, as distinguished from the particular manner in which they are expressed or described in a writing;

(c) Blank forms, such as time cards, graph paper, account books, diaries, bank checks, scorecards, address books, report forms, order forms and the like, which are designed for recording information and do not in themselves convey information;

(d) Works consisting entirely of information that is common property containing no original authorship, such as, for example: Standard calendars, height and weight charts, tape measures and rulers, schedules of sporting events, and lists or tables taken from public documents or other common sources.

(e) Typeface as typeface.

History of 37 C.F.R. §202.1: 24 FR 4956, June 18, 1959; 38 FR 3045, Feb. 1, 1973; 57 FR 6202, Feb. 21, 1992.

Source of 37 C.F.R. Part 202: 24 FR 4956, June 18, 1959; 50 FR 30172, July 24, 1985; 51 FR 6403, Feb. 24, 1986; 56 FR 7813, Feb. 26, 1991; 56 FR 7815, Feb. 26, 1991; 59 FR 23981, May 9, 1994; 60 FR 34168, June 30, 1995; 60 FR 50422, Sept. 29, 1995; 66 FR 37149, July 17, 2001; 70 FR 61906, Oct. 27, 2005, unless otherwise noted.

A §202.2. COPYRIGHT NOTICE

(a) General.

(1) With respect to a work published before January 1, 1978, copyright was secured, or the right to secure it was lost, except for works seeking ad interim copyright, at the date of publication, *i.e.*, the date on which copies are first placed on sale, sold, or publicly distributed, depending upon the adequacy of the notice of copyright on the work at that time. The adequacy of the copyright notice for such a work is determined by the copyright statute as it existed on the date of first publication.

(2) If before January 1, 1978, publication occurred by distribution of copies or in some other manner, without the statutory notice or with an inadequate notice, as determined by the copyright statute as it existed on the date of first publication, the right to secure copyright was lost. In such cases, copyright cannot be secured by adding the notice to copies distributed at a later date.

(3) Works first published abroad before January 1, 1978, other than works for which ad interim copyright has been obtained, must have borne an adequate copyright notice. The adequacy of the copyright notice for such works is determined by the copyright statute as it existed on the date of first publication abroad.

(b) Defects in notice. Where the copyright notice on a work published before January 1, 1978, does not meet the requirements of Title 17 of the United States Code as it existed on December 31, 1977, the Copyright Office will reject an application for copyright registration. Common defects in the notice include, among others the following:

(1) The notice lacks one or more of the necessary elements (*i.e.*, the word "Copyright," the abbreviation "Copr.," or the symbol ©, or, in the case of a sound recording, the symbol (P) (the letter P in a circle); the name of the copyright proprietor, or, in the case of a sound recording, the name, a recognizable abbreviation of the name, or a generally known alternative designation, of the copyright owner; and, when required, the year date of publication);

(2) The elements of the notice are so dispersed that a necessary element is not identified as a part of the notice; in the case of a sound recording, however, if the producer is named on the label or container, and if no other name appears in conjunction with the notice, the producer's name will be considered a part of the notice;

(3) The notice is not in one of the positions prescribed by law;

(4) The notice is in a foreign language;

(5) The name in the notice is that of someone who had no authority to secure copyright in that person's name;

(6)(i) The year date in the copyright notice is later than the date of the year in which copyright was actually secured, including the following cases:

(A) Where the year date in the notice is later than the date of actual publication;

(B) Where copyright was first secured by registration of a work in unpublished form, and copies of the same work as later published without change in substance bear a copyright notice containing a year date later than the year of unpublished registration; or

(C) Where a book or periodical published abroad, for which ad interim copyright has been obtained, is later published in the United States without change in substance and contains a year date in the copyright notice later than the year of first publication abroad.

(ii) Provided, however, that in each of the three types of cases described in paragraphs (b)(6)(i)(A) through (C) of this section, if the copyright was actually secured not more than one year earlier than the year date in the notice, registration may be considered as a doubtful case;

(7) A notice is permanently covered so that it cannot be seen without tearing the work apart;

(8) A notice is illegible or so small that it cannot be read without the aid of a magnifying glass: Provided, however, That where the work itself requires magnification for its ordinary use (e.g., a microfilm, microcard or motion picture) a notice which will be readable when so magnified, will not constitute a reason for rejection of the claim;

(9) A notice is on a detachable tag and will eventually be detached and discarded when the work is put in use;

(10) A notice is on the wrapper or container which is not a part of the work and which will eventually be removed and discarded when the work is put to use; the notice may be on a container which is designed and can be expected to remain with the work; and

(11) The notice is restricted or limited exclusively to an uncopyrightable element, either by virtue of its position on the work, by the use of asterisks, or by other means.

(c) Methods of affixation and positions of the copyright notice on various types of works—**(1)** General. **(i)** This paragraph specifies examples of methods of affixation and positions of the copyright notice on various types of works that will satisfy the notice requirement of section 401(c) of title 17 of the United States Code, as amended by Public Law 94-553. A notice considered "acceptable" under this regulation shall be considered to satisfy the requirement of that section that it be "affixed to the copies in such manner and location as to give reasonable notice of the claim of copyright." As provided by that section, the examples specified in this regulation shall not be considered exhaustive of methods of affixation and positions giving reasonable notice of the claim of copyright.

(ii) The provisions of this paragraph are applicable to copies publicly distributed on or after December 1, 1981. This paragraph does not establish any rules concerning the form of the notice or the legal sufficiency of particular notices, except with respect to methods of affixation and positions of notice. The adequacy or legal sufficiency of a copyright notice is determined by the law in effect at the time of first publication of the work.

(2) Definitions. For the purposes of this paragraph:

(i) In the case of a work consisting preponderantly of leaves on which the work is printed or otherwise reproduced on both sides, a "page" is one side of a leaf; where the preponderance of the leaves are printed on one side only, the terms "page" and "leaf" mean the same.

(ii) A work is published in book form if the copies embodying it consist of multiple leaves bound, fastened, or assembled in a predetermined order, as, for example, a volume, booklet, pamphlet, or multipage folder. For the purpose of this paragraph, a work need not consist of textual matter in order to be considered published in "book form."

(iii) A title page is a page, or two consecutive pages facing each other, appearing at or near the front of the copies of a work published in book form, on which the complete title of the work is prominently stated and on which the names of the author or authors, the name of the publisher, the place of publication, or some combination of them, are given.

(iv) The meaning of the terms front, back, first, last, and following, when used in connection with works published in book form, will vary in relation to the physical form of the copies, depending upon the particular language in which the work is written.

(v) In the case of a work published in book form with a hard or soft cover, the front page and back page of the copies are the outsides of the front and back covers; where there is no cover, the "front page," and "back page" are the pages visible at the front and back of the copies before they are opened.

(vi) A masthead is a body of information appearing in approximately the same location in most issues of a newspaper, magazine, journal, review, or other periodical or serial, typically containing the title of the periodical or serial, information about the staff, periodicity of issues, operation, and subscription and editorial policies, of the publication.

(vii) A single-leaf work is a work published in copies consisting of a single leaf, including copies on which the work is printed or otherwise reproduced on either one side or on both sides of the leaf, and also folders which, without cutting or tearing the copies, can be opened out to form a single leaf. For the purpose of this paragraph, a work need not consist of textual matter in order to be considered a "single-leaf work."

(viii) A machine-readable copy is a copy from which the work cannot ordinarily be visually perceived except with the aid of a machine or device, such as magnetic tapes or disks, punched cards, or the like. Works published in a form requiring the use of a machine or device for purposes of optical enlargement (such as film, filmstrips, slide films, and works published in any variety of microform) and works published in visually perceptible form but used in connection with optical scanning devices, are not within this category.

(3) Manner of affixation and position generally. (i) In all cases dealt with in this paragraph, the acceptability of a notice depends upon its being permanently legible to an ordinary user of the work under normal conditions of use, and affixed to the copies in such manner and position that, when affixed, it is not concealed from view upon reasonable examination.

(ii) Where, in a particular case, a notice does not appear in one of the precise locations prescribed in this paragraph but a person looking in one of those locations would be reasonably certain to find a notice in another somewhat different location, that notice will be acceptable under this paragraph.

(4) Works published in book form. In the case of works published in book form, a notice reproduced on the copies in any of the following positions is acceptable:

(i) The title page, if any;

(ii) The page immediately following the title page, if any;

(iii) Either side of the front cover, if any; or, if there is no front cover, either side of the front leaf of the copies;

(iv) Either side of the back cover, if any; or, if there is no back cover, either side of the back leaf of the copies;

(v) The first page of the main body of the work;

(vi) The last page of the main body of the work;

(vii) Any page between the front page and the first page of the main body of the work, if:

(A) There are no more than ten pages between the front page and the first page of the main body of the work; and

(B) The notice is reproduced prominently and is set apart from other matter on the page where it appears;

(viii) Any page between the last page of the main body of the work and back page, if:

(A) There are no more than ten pages between the last page of the main body of the work and the back page; and

(B) The notice is reproduced prominently and is set apart from the other matter on the page where it appears.

(ix) In the case of a work published as an issue of a periodical or serial, in addition to any of the locations listed in paragraphs (c)(4)(i) through (viii) of this section, a notice is acceptable if it is located:

(A) As a part of, or adjacent to, the masthead;

(B) On the page containing the masthead if the notice is reproduced prominently and is set apart from the other matter appearing on the page; or

(C) Adjacent to a prominent heading, appearing at or near the front of the issue, containing the title of the periodical or serial and any combination of the volume and issue number and date of the issue.

(x) In the case of a musical work, in addition to any of the locations listed in paragraphs (c)(4)(i) through (ix) of this section, a notice is acceptable if it is located on the first page of music.

(5) Single-leaf works. In the case of single-leaf works, a notice reproduced on the copies anywhere on the front or back of the leaf is acceptable.

(6) Contributions to collective works. For a separate contribution to a collective work to be considered to "bear its own notice of copyright," as provided by 17 U.S.C. 404, a notice reproduced on the copies in any of the following positions is acceptable:

(i) Where the separate contribution is reproduced on a single page, a notice is acceptable if it appears:

(A) Under the title of the contribution on that page;

(B) Adjacent to the contribution; or

(C) On the same page if, through format, wording, or both, the application of the notice to the particular contribution is made clear;

(ii) Where the separate contribution is reproduced on more than one page of the collective work, a notice is acceptable if it appears:

(A) Under a title appearing at or near the beginning of the contribution;

(B) On the first page of the main body of the contribution;

(C) Immediately following the end of the contribution; or

(D) On any of the pages where the contribution appears, if:

(1) The contribution is reproduced on no more than twenty pages of the collective work;

(2) The notice is reproduced prominently and is set apart from other matter on the page where it appears; and

(3) Through format, wording, or both, the application of the notice to the particular contribution is made clear;

(iii) Where the separate contribution is a musical work, in addition to any of the locations listed in paragraphs (c)(6)(i) and (ii) of this section, a notice is acceptable if it is located on the first page of music of the contribution;

(iv) As an alternative to placing the notice on one of the pages where a separate contribution itself appears, the contribution is considered to "bear its own notice" if the notice appears clearly in juxtaposition with a separate listing of the contribution by title, or if the contribution is untitled, by a description reasonably identifying the contribution:

(A) On the page bearing the copyright notice for the collective work as a whole, if any; or

(B) In a clearly identified and readily-accessible table of contents or listing of acknowledgements appearing near the front or back of the collective work as a whole.

(7) Works reproduced in machine-readable copies. For works reproduced in machine-readable copies, each of the following constitutes an example of acceptable methods of affixation and position of notice:

(i) A notice embodied in the copies in machine-readable form in such a manner that on visually perceptible printouts it appears either with or near the title, or at the end of the work;

(ii) A notice that is displayed at the user's terminal at sign on;

(iii) A notice that is continuously on terminal display; or

(iv) A legible notice reproduced durably, so as to withstand normal use, on a gummed or other label securely affixed to the copies or to a box, reel, cartridge, cassette, or other container used as a permanent receptacle for the copies.

(8) Motion pictures and other audiovisual works. (i) The following constitute examples of acceptable methods of affixation and positions of the copyright notice on motion pictures and other audiovisual works: A notice that is embodied in the copies by a photomechanical or electronic process, in such a position that it ordinarily would appear whenever the work is performed in its entirety, and that is located:

(A) With or near the title;

(B) With the cast, credits, and similar information;

(C) At or immediately following the beginning of the work; or

(D) At or immediately preceding the end of the work.

(ii) In the case of an untitled motion picture or other audiovisual work whose duration is sixty seconds or less, in addition to any of the locations listed in paragraph (c)(8)(i) of this section, a notice that is embodied in the copies by a photomechanical or electronic process, in such a position that it ordinarily would appear to the projectionist or broadcaster when preparing the work for performance, is acceptable if it is located on the leader of the film or tape immediately preceding the beginning of the work.

(iii) In the case of a motion picture or other audiovisual work that is distributed to the public for private use, the notice may be affixed, in addition to the locations specified in paragraph (c)(8)(i) of this section, on the housing or container, if it is a permanent receptacle for the work.

(9) Pictorial, graphic, and sculptural works. The following constitute examples of acceptable methods of affixation and positions of the copyright notice on various forms of pictorial, graphic, and sculptural works:

(i) Where a work is reproduced in two-dimensional copies, a notice affixed directly or by means of a label cemented, sewn, or otherwise attached durably, so as to withstand normal use, of the front or back of the copies, or to any backing, mounting, matting, framing, or other material to which the copies are durably attached, so as to withstand normal use, or in which they are permanently housed, is acceptable.

(ii) Where a work is reproduced in three-dimensional copies, a notice affixed directly or by means of a label cemented, sewn, or otherwise attached durably, so as to withstand normal use, to any visible portion of the work, or to any base, mounting, framing, or other material on which the copies are durably attached, so as to withstand normal use, or in which they are permanently housed, is acceptable.

(iii) Where, because of the size or physical characteristics of the material in which the work is reproduced in copies, it is impossible or extremely impracticable to affix a notice to the copies directly or by means of a durable label, a notice is acceptable if it appears on a tag that is of durable material, so as to withstand normal use, and that is attached to the copy with sufficient durability that it will remain with the copy while it is passing through its normal channels of commerce.

(iv) Where a work is reproduced in copies consisting of sheet-like or strip material bearing multiple or continuous reproductions of the work, the notice may be applied:

(A) To the reproduction itself;

(B) To the margin, selvage, or reverse side of the material at frequent and regular intervals; or

(C) If the material contains neither a selvage nor a reverse side, to tags or labels, attached to the copies and to any spools, reels, or containers housing them in such a way that a notice is visible while the copies are passing through their normal channels of commerce.

(v) If the work is permanently housed in a container, such as a game or puzzle box, a notice reproduced on the permanent container is acceptable.

History of 37 C.F.R. §202.2: 24 FR 4956, June 18, 1959; 24 FR 6163, July 31, 1959; 37 FR 3055, Feb. 11, 1972; 46 FR 33249, June 29, 1981; 46 FR 34329, July 1, 1981; 60 FR 34168, June 30, 1995; 66 FR 34373, June 28, 2001; 77 FR 18707, Mar. 28, 2012; 77 FR 20988, Apr. 9, 2012; 80 FR 19206, Apr. 10, 2015; 82 FR 9359, Mar. 8, 2017; 82 FR 42736, Oct. 12, 2017.

A §202.3. REGISTRATION OF COPYRIGHT

(a) General.

(1) This section prescribes conditions for the registration of copyright, and the application to be made for registration under sections 408 and 409 of Title 17 of the United States Code.

(2) For the purposes of this section, the terms audiovisual work, compilation, copy, derivative work, device, fixation, literary work, motion picture, phonorecord, pictorial, graphic and sculptural works, process, sound recording, and their variant forms, have the meanings set forth in section 101 of Title 17. The term author includes an employer or other person for whom a work is "made for hire" under section 101 of Title 17.

(3) For the purposes of this section, a copyright claimant is either:

(i) The author of a work;

(ii) A person or organization that has obtained ownership of all rights under the copyright initially belonging to the author.[1]

(b) Administrative Classification and Application Forms—

(1) Classes of Works. For the purpose of registration, the Register of Copyrights has prescribed the classes of works in which copyright may be claimed. These classes, and examples of works which they include, are as follows:

(i) Class TX: Nondramatic Literary Works. This class includes all published and unpublished nondramatic literary works. Examples: Fiction; nonfiction; poetry; textbooks; reference works; directories; catalogs; advertising copy; and compilations of information.

(ii) Class PA: Works of the Performing Arts. This class includes all published and unpublished works prepared for the purpose of being performed directly before an audience or indirectly by means of a device or process. Examples: Musical works, including any accompanying words; dramatic works, including any accompanying music; pantomimes and choreographic works; and motion pictures and other audiovisual works.

(iii) Class VA: Works of the Visual Arts. This class includes all published and unpublished pictorial, graphic, and sculptural works. Examples: Two dimensional and three dimensional works of the fine, graphic, and applied arts; photographs; prints and art reproductions; maps, globes, and charts; technical drawings, diagrams, and models; and pictorial or graphic labels and advertisements.

(iv) Class SR: Sound Recordings. This class includes all published and unpublished sound recordings fixed on and after February 15, 1972. Claims to copyright in literary, dramatic, and musical works embodied in phonorecords may also be registered in this class under paragraph (b)(4) of this section if: (A) Registration is sought on the same application for both a recorded literary, dramatic, or musical work and a sound recording; (B) the recorded literary, dramatic, or musical work and the sound recording are embodied in the same phonorecord; and (C) the same claimant is seeking registration of both the recorded literary, dramatic, or musical work and the sound recording.

(v) Class SE: Serials. A serial is a work issued or intended to be issued in successive parts bearing numerical or chronological designations and intended to be continued indefinitely. This class includes periodicals (including newspapers); annuals; and the journals, proceedings, transactions, etc. of societies.

(2) Submission of application for registration. For purposes of registration, an applicant may submit an application for registration of individual works and certain groups of works electronically through the Copyright Office's website, or by using the printed forms prescribed by the Register of Copyrights.

(i) Electronic applications.

(A) An applicant may submit an application electronically. For non-group registrations, an applicant may submit a standard electronic application, or an applicant may submit a "single" application.

(B) A "single" application can be made only for a single work by a single author that is owned by the person who created it, and is not a work made for hire. The claimant and the author must be the same. A third party may remit a "single" application on behalf of the author/claimant, provided that party lists itself as the correspondent. The following categories of work may not be registered using the "single" application: collective works, unpublished collections, units of publication, group registration options, databases, websites, works by more than one author, and works with more than one owner. The designation of a work as eligible for a "single" registration does not include work characterized as a "single work" under paragraph (b)(4) of this section.

(C) An online submission requires a payment of the application fee through an electronic fund transfer, credit or debit card, or through a Copyright Office deposit account.

(D) Deposit materials in support of an online application may be submitted electronically in a digital format (if eligible) along with the application and payment, or an applicant may send physical copies or phonorecords as necessary to satisfy the best edition requirements, by mail to the Copyright Office, using the required shipping slip generated during the online registration process.

(ii)(A) Alternatively, an applicant may submit an application on one of the printed forms prescribed by the Register of Copyrights. Each printed form corresponds to a class set forth in paragraph (b)(1) of this section and is so designated ("Form TX"; "Short Form TX", "Form PA"; "Short Form PA", "Form VA"; "Short Form VA", "Form SR"; "Form SE"; "Short Form SE", and "Form SE/Group").

(B) Short form applications may only be used if certain conditions are met. Short Form TX, Short Form PA, and Short Form VA may be used only to register a single work in a case when a living author who is the only author of his or her work is the sole owner of the copyright in the work, the work is not a compilation or derivative work containing a substantial amount of previously published or registered material, and the work is not a work made for hire. Short Form SE may be used only if the claim is in a collective work, the work is essentially an all-new collective work or issue, the author is a citizen or domiciliary of the United States, the work is a work for hire, the author(s) and claimant(s) are the same person(s) or organization(s), and the work was first published in the United States.

(C) Printed form applications should be submitted in the class most appropriate to the nature of the authorship in which copyright is claimed. In the case of contributions to collective works, applications should be submitted in the class representing the copyrightable authorship in the contribution. In the case of derivative works, applications should be submitted in the class most appropriately representing the copyrightable authorship involved in recasting, transforming, adapting, or otherwise modifying the preexisting work. In cases where a work contains elements of authorship in which copyright is claimed which fall into two or more classes, the application should be submitted in the class most appropriate to the predominant type of authorship in the work as a whole. However, in any case where registration is sought for a work consisting of or including a sound recording in which copyright is claimed, the application shall be submitted on Form SR.

(D) Copies of the printed forms are available on the Copyright Office's website (www.copyright.gov) and upon request to the Copyright Public Information Office, Library of Congress. Printed form applications may be completed and submitted by completing a printed version or using a PDF version of the applicable Copyright Office application form and mailing it together with the other required elements, *i.e.*, physically tangible deposit copies and/or materials, and the required filing fee, all elements being placed in the same package and sent by mail or hand-delivered to the Copyright Office.

(3) Continuation sheets. A continuation sheet (Form CON) is appropriate only in the case when a printed form application is used and where additional space is needed by the applicant to provide all relevant information concerning a claim to copyright. An application may include more than one continuation sheet.

(4) Registration as a Single Work.

(i) For the purpose of registration on a single application and upon payment of a single registration fee, the following shall be considered a single work:

(A) In the case of published works: all copyrightable elements that are otherwise recognizable as self-contained works, that are included in a single unit of publication, and in which the copyright claimant is the same; and

(B) In the case of unpublished works: all copyrightable elements that are otherwise recognizable as self-contained works, and are combined in a single unpublished "collection." For these purposes, a combination of such elements shall be considered a "collection" if:

(1) The elements are assembled in an orderly form;

(2) the combined elements bear a single title identifying the collection as a whole;

(3) the copyright claimant in all of the elements, and in the collection as a whole, is the same; and

(4) all of the elements are by the same author, or, if they are by different authors, at least one of the authors has contributed copyrightable authorship to each element.

Registration of an unpublished "collection" extends to each copyrightable element in the collection and to the authorship, if any, involved in selecting and assembling the collection.

(ii) In the case of an application for registration made under paragraphs (b)(4) through (10) of this section or under §202.4, the "year of creation," "year of completion," or "year in which creation of this work was completed" means the latest year in which the creation of any copyrightable element was completed.

(5) Group registration of related works: Automated databases.

(i) Pursuant to the authority granted by section 408(c)(1) of Title 17 of the United States Code, the Register of Copyrights has determined that, on the basis of a single application, deposit, and filing fee, a single registration may be made for automated databases and their updates or other derivative versions that are original works of authorship, if, where a database (or updates or other revisions thereof), if unpublished, is (or are) fixed, or if published is (or are) published only in the form of machine-readable copies, all of the following conditions are met:

(A) All of the updates or other revisions are owned by the same copyright claimant;

(B) All of the updates or other revisions have the same general title;

(C) All of the updates or other revisions are similar in their general content, including their subject;

(D) All of the updates or other revisions are similar in their organization;

(E) Each of the updates or other revisions as a whole, if published before March 1, 1989, bears a statutory copyright notice as first published and the name of the owner of copyright in each work (or an abbreviation by which the name can be recognized, or a generally known alternative designation of the owner) was the same in each notice;

(F) Each of the updates or other revisions if published was first published, or if unpublished was first created, within a three-month period in a single calendar year; and

(G) The deposit accompanying the application complies with §202.20(c)(2)(vii)(D).

(ii) A single registration may be made on one application for both a database published on a single date, or if unpublished, created on a single date, and also for its copyrightable revisions, including updates covering a three-month period in a single calendar year. An application for group registration of automated databases under section 408(c)(1) of Title 17 and this subsection shall consist of:

(A) A form that best reflects the subject matter of the material in the database as set forth in paragraph (b)(2) of this section, completed in accordance with the basic instructions on the form and the Special Instructions for Group Registration of an Automated Database and its Updates or Revisions, except that in the case of an application for group registration of an automated database consisting predominantly of photographs, after consultation and with the permission and under the direction of the Visual Arts Division, the application may be submitted electronically.

(B) The appropriate filing fee, as required in §201.3(c); and

(C) The deposit required by §202.20(c)(2)(vii)(D).

(6) Group registration of related serials.

(i) Pursuant to the authority granted by section 408(c)(1) of title 17 of the United States Code, the Register of Copyrights has determined that, on the basis of a single application, deposit, and filing fee, a single registration may be made for a group of serials published at intervals of a week or longer if all the following conditions are met:

(A) The Library of Congress receives two complimentary copies promptly after publication of each issue of the serial.

(B) The single application covers no more than the issues published in a given three month period.

(C) The claim to copyright for which registration is sought is in the collective work.

(D) The collective work authorship is essentially new material that is being published for the first time.

(E) The collective work is a work made for hire.

(F) The author(s) and claimant(s) of the collective work is the same person(s) or organization(s).

(G) Each issue must have been created no more than one year prior to publication and all issues included in the group registration must have been published in the same calendar year.

(ii) To be eligible for group registration of serials, publishers must submit a letter affirming that two complimentary subscriptions to the particular serial have been entered for the Library of Congress. The letter should be mailed to the address specified in §201.1 of this chapter.

(iii) The complimentary subscription copies must be mailed to the address specified in §201.1 of this chapter.

(iv) The Register of Copyrights may revoke the privilege of group registration of serials for any publisher who fails to submit the required complimentary subscription copies promptly after publication of each issue. Notice of revocation of the group registration of serials privilege shall be given in writing and shall be sent to the individual person or organization applying for group registration of serials, at the last address shown in the records of the Copyright Office. A notice of revocation may be given at any time if the requirements of the regulation are not satisfied, but it shall state a specific date of revocation that is at least 30 days later than the date the notice is mailed.

(v) To apply for registration of a group of serial issues under 17 U.S.C. 408(c)(1) and this section, an applicant may file electronically, or submit a completed Form SE/Group.

(A) For applicants filing electronically:

(1) Furnish the requested information for group of serial issues.

(2) Submit the appropriate filing fee, as required in §201.3(c) of this chapter, for each issue covered by the group registration.

(3) Submit either a digital format which complies with §202.20(b)(2)(iii) or a deposit consisting of one complete copy of the best edition of each issue included in the group registration.

(B) For applicants filing a completed Form SE/Group, the following must be sent together in the same package:

(1) A completed Form SE/Group, providing the requested information.

(2) The appropriate filing fee, as required in §201.3(c) of this chapter, for each issue covered by the group registration.

(3) A deposit consisting of one complete copy of the best edition of each issue included in the group registration.

(7) Reserved.

(8) Reserved.

(9) Group registration of daily newsletters. Pursuant to the authority granted by 17 U.S.C. 408(c)(1), the Register of Copyrights has determined that, on the basis of a single application, deposit, and filing fee, a single registration may be made for a group of two or more issues of a daily newsletter if the following conditions are met:

(i) As used in this regulation, daily newsletter means a serial published and distributed by mail or electronic media (online or telefacsimile), or in any medium including but not limited to, paper, cassette tape, diskette or CD-ROM. Publication must occur on at least two days each week and the newsletter must contain news or information of interest chiefly to a special group (for example, trade and professional associations, corporate in-house groups, schools, colleges, or churches).

(ii) The works must be essentially all new collective works or all new issues that have not been published before.

(iii) Each issue must be a work made for hire.

(iv) The author(s) and claimant(s) must be the same person(s) or organization(s) for all of the issues.

(v) All the items in the group must bear issue dates within a single calendar month under the same continuing title.

(vi) Deposit.

(A) The deposit for newsletters registered under this section is one complete copy of each issue included in the group.

(B) In addition, if requested in writing by the Copyright Acquisitions Division before an application for registration is submitted, the claimant must give the Library of Congress whichever of the following the Library prefers: either as many as two complimentary subscriptions of the newsletter in the edition most suitable to the Library's needs, or a single positive, 35 mm silver halide microfilm meeting the Library's best edition criteria that includes all issues published as final editions in the designated calendar month. Subscription copies must be delivered to the separate address specified by the Copyright Acquisitions Division in its request. Subscription copies or a microfilm are not required unless expressly requested by the Copyright Acquisitions Division.

(C) The copyright owner of any newsletter that cannot meet the criteria set out in this section may continue to register on Form SE or Short Form SE.

(vii) Registration is sought within three months after the publication date of the last issue included in the group.

(viii) A Form G/DN shall be submitted for daily newsletters bearing issue dates within a single month, together with one copy of each issue, and a filing fee. The application shall designate the first and last day that issues in the group were published.

(10) Reserved.

(11) One registration per work. As a general rule only one copyright registration can be made for the same version of a particular work. However:

(i) Where a work has been registered as unpublished, another registration may be made for the first published edition of the work, even if it does not represent a new version;

(ii) Where someone other than the author is identified as copyright claimant in a registration, another registration for the same version may be made by the author in his or her own name as copyright claimant;[2]

(iii) Where an applicant for registration alleges that an earlier registration for the same version is unauthorized and legally invalid, a registration may be made by that applicant.

(c) Application for Registration.

(1) An application for copyright registration may be submitted by any author or other copyright claimant of a work, or the owner of any exclusive right in a work, or the duly authorized agent of any such author, other claimant, or owner.

(2) An application for copyright registration shall be submitted by using one of the methods set forth in paragraph (b) of this section. All completed application forms shall be accompanied by the appropriate filing fee, as required in §201.3(c) of this chapter, and the deposit copies and materials required under 17 U.S.C. 408 and §202.20 or §202.4, as applicable. All applications submitted for registration shall supply the information required by the particular application and shall include a certification. The certification shall consist of:

(i) A designation that the party signing the print application, or submitting the application electronically, falls within an accepted status from among the following: author, claimant, an owner of exclusive rights, or a duly authorized agent of the author, claimant, owner of exclusive rights;

(ii) For print applications, the handwritten signature of the party described in paragraph (c)(2)(i) of this section accompanied by the typed or printed name of that party; or, if an electronically submitted application, a name provided within the certification screen of the electronic application which represents a party described in paragraph (c)(2)(i) of this section;

(iii) A declaration that information provided within the application is correct to the best of that party's knowledge; and,

(iv) For print applications, the date of completion of the application form, with the date (month, day, year) printed, typed, or handwritten; or, if an electronically submitted application, the date of electronic receipt of the application by the

Copyright Office, which date shall be provided automatically by the Copyright Office.

(3) An application for registration of a published work will not be accepted if the date of certification is earlier than the date of publication given in the application.

1. This category includes a person or organization that has obtained, from the author or from an entity that has obtained ownership of all rights under the copyright initially belonging to the author, the contractual right to claim legal title to the copyright in an application for copyright registration.

2. An author includes an employer or other person for whom a work is "made for hire" under 17 U.S.C. §101. This paragraph does not permit an employee or other person working "for hire" under that section to make a later registration in his or her own name. In the case of authors of a joint work, this paragraph does permit a later registration by one author in his or her own name as copyright claimant, where an earlier registration identifies only another author as claimant.

History of 37 C.F.R. §202.3: 43 FR 966, Jan. 5, 1978; 54 FR 13181, Mar. 31, 1989; 54 FR 21059, May 16, 1989; 55 FR 50557, Dec. 7, 1990; 56 FR 7813, Feb. 26, 1991; 56 FR 7815, Feb. 26, 1991; 56 FR 27197, June 13, 1991; 56 FR 59885, Nov. 26, 1991; 56 FR 65190, Dec. 16, 1991; 56 FR 65191, Dec. 16, 1991; 57 FR 39616, Sept. 1, 1992; 58 FR 17778, Apr. 6, 1993; 60 FR 15875, Mar. 28, 1995; 60 FR 34168, June 30, 1995; 62 FR 35421, July 1, 1997; 62 FR 63657, Dec. 2, 1997; 62 FR 66822, Dec. 22, 1997; 64 FR 29522, June 1, 1999; 64 FR 29523, June 1, 1999; 64 FR 36575, July 7, 1999; 65 FR 39819, June 28, 2000; 66 FR 34373, June 28, 2001; 66 FR 37149, July 17, 2001; 67 FR 10329, Mar. 7, 2002; 70 FR 15590, Mar. 28, 2005; 72 FR 36888, July 6, 2007; 72 FR 40746, July 25, 2007; 73 FR 37839, July 1, 2008; 76 FR 4075, Jan. 24, 2011; 77 FR 18707, Mar. 28, 2012; 77 FR 66921, Nov. 8, 2012; 78 FR 38845, June 28, 2013; 78 FR 42875, July 18, 2013; 82 FR 9359, Mar. 8, 2017; 82 FR 27427, July 17, 2017; 82 FR 29413, July 31, 2017; 83 FR 2547, Feb. 20, 2018; 83 FR 4146, Mar. 1, 2018.

E §202.4. GROUP REGISTRATION

(a) General. This section prescribes conditions for issuing a registration for a group of related works under section 408(c) of title 17 of the United States Code.

(b) Definitions. (1) For purposes of this section, unless otherwise specified, the terms used have the meanings set forth in §§202.3, 202.13, and 202.20.

(2) For purposes of this section, the term Library means the Library of Congress.

(3) For purposes of this section, a periodical is a collective work that is issued or intended to be issued on an established schedule in successive issues that are intended to be continued indefinitely. In most cases, each issue will bear the same title, as well as numerical or chronological designations.

(c) [Reserved]

(d) [Reserved]

(e) Group registration of newspapers. Pursuant to the authority granted by 17 U.S.C. 408(c)(1), the Register of Copyrights has determined that a group of newspaper issues may be registered with one application, the required deposit, and the filing fee required by §201.3(c) of this chapter, if the following conditions are met:

(1) Issues must be newspapers. All the issues in the group must be newspapers. For purposes of this section, a newspaper is a periodical (as defined in paragraph (b)(3) of this section) that is mainly designed to be a primary source of written information on current events, either local, national, or international in scope. A newspaper contains a broad range of news on all subjects and activities and is not limited to any specific subject matter. Newspapers are intended either for the general public or for a particular ethnic, cultural, or national group.

(2) Requirements for newspaper issues. Each issue in the group must be an all-new collective work that has not been previously published (except where earlier editions of the same newspaper are included in the deposit together with the final edition), each issue must be fixed and distributed as a discrete, self-contained collective work, and the claim in each issue must be limited to the collective work.

(3) Author and claimant. Each issue in the group must be a work made for hire, and the author and claimant for each issue must be the same person or organization.

(4) Time period covered. All the issues in the group must be published under the same continuing title, and they must be published within the same calendar month and bear issue dates within that month. The applicant must identify the earliest and latest date that the issues were published.

(5) Application. The applicant must complete and submit the online application designated for a group of newspaper issues. The application may be submitted by any of the parties listed in §202.3(c)(1).

(6) Deposit. (i) The applicant must submit one complete copy of the final edition of each issue published in the calendar month designated in the application. Each submission may also include earlier editions of the same newspaper issue, provided that they were published on the same date as the final edition. Each submission may also include local editions of the newspaper issue that were published within the same metropolitan area, but may not include national or regional editions that were distributed outside that metropolitan area.

(ii)(A) The issues must be submitted in a digital form, and each issue must be contained in a separate electronic file. The applicant must use the file-naming convention and submit digital files in accordance with instructions specified on the Copyright Office's website. The files must be submitted in Portable Document Format (PDF), they must be assembled in an orderly form, and they must be uploaded to the electronic registration system as individual electronic files (i.e., not .zip files). The files must be viewable and searchable, contain embedded fonts, and be free from any access restrictions (such as those implemented through Digital Rights Management (DRM)). The file size for each uploaded file must not exceed 500 megabytes, but files may be compressed to comply with this requirement.

(B) Until December 31, 2019, the applicant may also submit the complete issues on positive 35mm silver halide microfilm at the same time as the application, in addition to providing electronic copies of the newspaper issues pursuant to paragraph (e)(6)(ii)(A) of this section. The issues should be arranged on the microfilm in chronological order, and should be sent to: Library of Congress, U.S. Copyright Office, Attn: 407 Deposits, 101 Independence Avenue SE, Washington, DC 20559. Should the applicant submit microfilm copies in addition to electronic files under paragraph (e)(6)(ii)(A) of this section, the effective date of registration for a group registration under paragraph (e) of this section will be the date on which the Office received an acceptable application, the electronic files submitted under paragraph (e)(6)(ii)(A), and the proper filing fee. If the electronic files submitted under paragraph (e)(6)(ii)(A) are deficient and the applicant also submits microfilm copies, the Register shall have discretion in determining whether the microfilm copies may be used to cure deficiencies in the electronic files (e.g., an electronic file is missing some pages from one newspaper issue, but the microfilm contains a complete version of each issue in the group). In cases where the Register determines that microfilm copies can be used to cure deficiencies in the electronic files submitted under paragraph (e)(6)(ii)(A), the effective date of registration for a group registration under paragraph (e) of this section will be the date on which the Office received an acceptable application, the electronic files submitted under paragraph (e)(6)(ii)(A), and the proper filing fee.

(7) The application, the filing fee, and files specified in paragraph (e)(6)(ii)(A) of this section must be received by the Copyright Office within three months after the date of publication for the earliest issue in the group.

(f) [Reserved]

(g) Group registration of contributions to periodicals. Pursuant to the authority granted by 17 U.S.C. 408(c)(2), the Register of Copyrights has determined that a group of contributions to periodicals may be registered in Class TX or Class VA with one application, one filing fee, and the required deposit, if the following conditions are met:

(1) All the contributions in the group must be created by the same individual.

(2) The copyright claimant must be the same person or organization for all the contributions.

(3) The contributions must not be works made for hire.

(4) Each work must be first published as a contribution to a periodical, and all the contributions must be first published within a twelve-month period (e.g., January 1, 2015 through December 31, 2015; February 1, 2015 through January 31, 2016).

(5) If any of the contributions were first published before March 1, 1989, those works must bear a separate copyright notice, the notice must contain the copyright owner's name (or an abbreviation by which the name can be recognized, or a generally known alternative designation for the owner), and the name that appears in each notice must be the same.

(6) The applicant must complete and submit the online application designated for a group of contributions to periodicals. The application must identify each contribution that is included in the group, including the date of publication for each contribution and the periodical in which it was first published. The application may be submitted by any of the parties listed in §202.3(c)(1). The application should be filed in Class TX if a majority of the contributions predominantly consist of text, and the application should be filed in Class VA if a majority of the contributions predominantly consist of photographs, illustrations, artwork, or other works of the visual arts.

(7) The appropriate filing fee, as required by §201.3(c) of this chapter, must be included with the application or charged to an active deposit account.

(8) The applicant must submit one copy of each contribution that is included in the group, either by submitting the entire issue of the periodical where the contribution was first published, the entire section of the newspaper where it was first published, or the specific page(s) from the periodical where the contribution was first published. The contributions must be contained in separate electronic files that comply with §202.20(b)(2)(iii). The files must be submitted in a PDF, JPG, or other electronic format approved by the Office, and they must be uploaded to the electronic registration system, preferably in a .zip file containing all the files. The file size for each uploaded file must not exceed 500 megabytes; the files may be compressed to comply with this requirement.

(9) In an exceptional case, the Copyright Office may waive the online filing requirement set forth in paragraph (g)(6) of this section or may grant special relief from the deposit requirement under §202.20(d), subject to such conditions as the Associate Register of Copyrights and Director of the Office of Registration Policy and Practice may impose on the applicant.

(h) Group registration of unpublished photographs. Pursuant to the authority granted by 17 U.S.C. 408(c)(1), the Register of Copyrights has determined that a group of unpublished photographs may be registered in Class VA with one application, the required deposit, and the filing fee required by §201.3(c) of this chapter, if the following conditions are met:

(1) All the works in the group must be photographs.

(2) The group must include no more than 750 photographs, and the application must specify the total number of photographs that are included in the group.

(3) All the photographs must be created by the same author.

(4) The copyright claimant for all the photographs must be the same person or organization.

(5) The photographs may be registered as works made for hire if all the photographs are identified in the application as such.

(6) All the photographs must be unpublished.

(7) The applicant must provide a title for the group as a whole

(8) The applicant must complete and submit the online application designated for a group of unpublished photographs. (The Office will not register a group of unpublished photographs as an unpublished collection under §202.3(b)(4)(i)(B).) The application may be submitted by any of the parties listed in §202.3(c)(1).

(9) The applicant must submit one copy of each photograph in one of the following formats: JPEG, GIF, or TIFF. The file name for a particular photograph may consist of letters, numbers, and spaces, but the file name should not contain any other form of punctuation. The photographs may be uploaded to the electronic registration system together with the required numbered list, preferably in a .zip file containing all the photographs. The file size for each uploaded file must not exceed 500 megabytes; the photographs may be compressed to comply with this requirement. Alternatively, the photographs and the required numbered list may be saved on a physical storage device, such as a flash drive, CD-R, or DVD-R, and delivered to the Copyright Office together with the required shipping slip generated by the electronic registration system.

(10) The applicant must submit a sequentially numbered list containing a title and file name for each photograph in the group (matching the corresponding file names for each photograph specified in paragraph (h)(9) of this section). The title and file name for a particular photograph may be the same. The numbered list must be contained in an electronic file in Excel format (.xls), Portable Document Format (PDF), or other electronic format approved by the Office, and the file name for the list must contain the title of the group and the case number assigned to the application by the electronic registration system (e.g., "Title Of Group Case Number 16283927239.xls").

(11) In an exceptional case, the Copyright Office may waive the online filing requirement set forth in paragraph (h)(8) of this section or may grant special relief from the deposit requirement under §202.20(d), subject to such conditions as the Associate Register of Copyrights and Director of the Office of Registration Policy and Practice may impose on the applicant.

(i) Group registration of published photographs. Pursuant to the authority granted by 17 U.S.C. 408(c)(1), the Register of Copyrights has determined that a group of published photographs may be registered in Class VA with one application, the required deposit, and the filing fee required by §201.3(c) of this chapter, if the following conditions are met:

(1) All the works in the group must be photographs.

(2) The group must include no more than 750 photographs, and the application must specify the total number of photographs that are included in the group.

(3) All the photographs must be created by the same author.

(4) The copyright claimant for all the photographs must be the same person or organization.

(5) The photographs may be registered as works made for hire if all the photographs are identified in the application as such.

(6) All the photographs must be published within the same calendar year, and the applicant must specify the earliest and latest date that the photographs were published during the year.

(7) The applicant must provide a title for the group as a whole.

(8) The applicant must complete and submit the online application designated for a group of published photographs. The application may be submitted by any of the parties listed in §202.3(c)(1).

(9) The applicant must submit one copy of each photograph in one of the following formats: JPEG, GIF, or TIFF. The file name for a particular photograph may consist of letters, numbers, and spaces, but the file name should not contain any other form of punctuation. The photographs may be uploaded to the electronic registration system together with the required numbered list, preferably in a .zip file containing all the photographs. The file size for each uploaded file must not exceed 500 megabytes; the photographs may be compressed to comply with this requirement. Alternatively, the photographs and the required numbered list may be saved on a physical storage device, such as a flash drive, CD-R, or DVD-R, and delivered to the Copyright Office together with the required shipping slip generated by the electronic registration system.

(10) The applicant must submit a sequentially numbered list containing the title, file name, and month and year of publication for each photograph in the group (matching the corresponding file names for each photograph specified in paragraph (i)(9) of this section). The title and file name for a particular photograph may be the same. The numbered list must be contained in an electronic file in Excel format (.xls), Portable Document Format (PDF), or other electronic format approved by the Office, and the file name for the list must contain the title of the group and the case number assigned to the application by the electronic registration system (e.g., "Title Of Group Case Number 16283927239.xls").

(11) In an exceptional case, the Copyright Office may waive the online filing requirement set forth in paragraph (i)(8) of this section or may grant special relief from the deposit requirement under §202.20(d), subject to such conditions as the Associate Register of Copyrights and Director of the Office of Registration Policy and Practice may impose on the applicant.

(j) [Reserved]

(k) Secure test items. Pursuant to the authority granted by 17 U.S.C. 408(c)(1), the Register of Copyrights has determined that a group of test items may be registered in Class TX with one application, one filing fee, and identifying material, if the conditions set forth in §202.13(c) and (d) have been met.

(*l*) Refusal to register. The Copyright Office may refuse registration if the applicant fails to satisfy the requirements for registering a group of related works under this section or §202.3(b)(5) through (7), or (9).

(m) Cancellation. If the Copyright Office issues a registration for a group of related works and subsequently determines that the requirements for that group option have not been met, and if the claimant fails to cure the deficiency after being notified by the Office, the registration may be cancelled in accordance with §201.7 of this chapter.

(n) The scope of a group registration. When the Office issues a group registration under paragraph (e) of this section, the registration covers each issue in the group and each issue is registered as a separate collective work. When the Office issues a group registration under paragraph (g), (h), (i), or (k) of this section, the registration covers each work in the group and each work is registered as a separate work. For purposes of registration, the group as a whole is not considered a compilation, a collective work, or a derivative work under section 101, 103(b), or 504(c)(1) of title 17 of the United States Code.

History of 37 C.F.R. §202.4: 82 FR 29413, July 31, 2017; 82 FR 52228, Nov. 13, 2017; 83 FR 2547, Feb. 20, 2018; 83 FR 4146, Mar. 1, 2018.

(A) §202.5. RECONSIDERATION PROCEDURE FOR REFUSALS TO REGISTER

(a) General. This section prescribes rules pertaining to procedures for administrative review of the Copyright Office's refusal to register a claim to copyright, a mask work, or a vessel design upon a finding by the Office that the application for registration does not satisfy the legal requirements of title 17 of the United States Code. If an applicant's initial claim is refused, the applicant is entitled to request that the initial refusal to register be reconsidered.

(b) First reconsideration. Upon receiving a written notification from the Registration Program explaining the reasons for a refusal to register, an applicant may request that the Registration Program reconsider its initial decision to refuse registration, subject to the following requirements:

(1) An applicant must request in writing that the Registration Program reconsider its decision. A request for reconsideration must include the reasons the applicant believes registration was improperly refused, including any legal arguments in support of those reasons and any supplementary information. The Registration Program will base its decision on the applicant's written submissions.

(2) The fee set forth in §201.3(d) of this chapter must accompany the first request for reconsideration.

(3) The first request for reconsideration and the applicable fee must be postmarked or dispatched by a commercial carrier, courier, or messenger no later than three months from the date that appears in the written notice from the Registration Program of its decision to refuse registration. When the ending date for the three-month time period falls on a weekend or a Federal holiday, the ending day of the three-month period shall be extended to the next Federal work day.

(4) If the Registration Program decides to register an applicant's work in response to the first request for reconsideration, it will notify the applicant in writing of the decision and the work will be registered. However, if the Registration Program again refuses to register the work, it will send the applicant a written notification stating the reasons for refusal within four months of the date on which the first request for reconsideration is received by the Registration Program. When the ending date for the four-month time period falls on a weekend or a Federal holiday, the ending day of the four-month period shall be extended to the next Federal work day. Failure by the Registration Program to send the written notification within the four-month period shall not result in registration of the applicant's work.

(c) Second reconsideration. Upon receiving written notification of the Registration Program's decision to refuse registration in response to the first request for reconsideration, an applicant may request that the Review Board reconsider the Registration Program's refusal to register, subject to the following requirements:

(1) An applicant must request in writing that the Review Board reconsider the Registration Program's decision to refuse registration. The second request for reconsideration must include the reasons the applicant believes registration was improperly refused, including any legal arguments in support of those reasons and any supplementary information, and must address the reasons stated by the Registration Program for refusing registration upon first reconsideration. The Board will base its decision on the applicant's written submissions.

(2) The fee set forth in §201.3(d) of this chapter must accompany the second request for reconsideration.

(3) The second request for reconsideration and the applicable fee must be postmarked or dispatched by a commercial carrier, courier, or messenger no later than three months from the date that appears in the Registration Program's written notice of its decision to refuse registration after the first request for reconsideration. When the ending date for the three-month time period falls on a weekend or a Federal holiday, the ending day of the three-month period shall be extended to the next Federal work day.

(4) If the Review Board decides to register an applicant's work in response to a second request for reconsideration, it will notify the applicant in writing of the decision and the work will be registered. If the Review Board upholds the refusal to register the work, it will send the applicant a written notification stating the reasons for refusal.

(d) Submission of reconsiderations.

(1) All submissions for reconsideration should be mailed to the address specified in §201.1(c) of this chapter.

(2) The first page of the written request must contain the Copyright Office control number and clearly indicate either "FIRST RECONSIDERATION" or "SECOND RECONSIDERATION," as appropriate, on the subject line.

(e) Suspension or waiver of time requirements. For any particular request for reconsideration, the provisions relating to the time requirements for submitting a request under this section may be suspended or waived, in whole or in part, by the Register of Copyrights upon a showing of good cause. Such suspension or waiver shall apply only to the request at issue and shall not be relevant with respect to any other request for reconsideration from that applicant or any other applicant.

(f) Composition of the Review Board. The Review Board shall consist of three members; the first two members are the Register of Copyrights and the General Counsel or their respective designees. The third member will be designated by the Register.

(g) Final agency action. A decision by the Review Board in response to a second request for reconsideration constitutes final agency action.

History of 37 C.F.R. §202.5: 69 FR 77636, Dec. 28, 2004; 70 FR 7177, Feb. 11, 2005; 73 FR 37839, July 1, 2008; 76 FR 27898, May 13, 2011; 78 FR 42875, July 18, 2013; 81 FR 62373, Sept. 9, 2016; 82 FR 9359, Mar. 8, 2017; 82 FR 21697, May 10, 2017.

E §202.6. SUPPLEMENTARY REGISTRATION

(a) General. This section prescribes conditions relating to the filing of an application for supplementary registration under section 408(d) of title 17 of the United States Code to correct an error in a copyright registration or to amplify the information given in a registration. No correction or amplification of the information in a basic registration will be made except pursuant to the provisions of this section. As an exception, where it is discovered that a basic registration contains an error caused by the Copyright Office's own action, the Office will take appropriate measures to rectify its mistake.

(b) Definitions. (1) A basic registration means any of the following:

(i) A copyright registration made under sections 408, 409, and 410 of title 17 of the United States Code;

(ii) A renewal registration made under section 304 of title 17 of the United States Code; or

(iii) A copyright registration or a renewal registration made under title 17 of the United States Code as it existed before January 1, 1978.

(2) A supplementary registration means a registration issued under section 408(d) of title 17 of the United States Code and the provisions of this section.

(c) Persons entitled to file an application for supplementary registration. Supplementary registration can be made only if a basic copyright registration for the same work has already been completed. After a basic registration has been completed, any author or other copyright claimant of the work, or the owner of any exclusive right in the work, or the duly authorized agent of any such author, other claimant, or owner, who wishes to correct or amplify the information given in the basic registration for the work may file an application for supplementary registration.

(d) Basis for issuing a supplementary registration. (1) Supplementary registration may be made either to correct or to amplify the information in a basic registration.

(2) A correction is appropriate if information in the basic registration was incorrect at the time that basic registration was made.

(3) An amplification is appropriate:

(i) To supplement or clarify the information that was required by the application for the basic registration and should have been provided, such as the identity of a co-author or co-claimant, but was omitted at the time the basic registration was made; or

(ii) To reflect changes in facts, other than those relating to transfer, license, or ownership of rights in the work, that occurred since the basic registration was made.

(4) Supplementary registration is not appropriate:

(i) To reflect a change in ownership that occurred on or after the effective date of the basic registration or to reflect the division, allocation, licensing, or transfer of rights in a work;

(ii) To correct errors in statements or notices on the copies or phonorecords of a work, or to reflect changes in the content of a work; or

(iii) To correct or amplify the information set forth in a basic registration that has been cancelled under §201.7 of this chapter.

(5) If an error or omission in a basic renewal registration is extremely minor, and does not involve the identity of the renewal claimant or the legal basis of the claim, supplementary registration may be made at any time. In an exceptional case, however, supplementary registration may be made to correct the name of the renewal claimant and the legal basis of the claim if clear, convincing, and objective documentation is submitted to the Copyright Office which proves that an inadvertent error was made in failing to designate the correct living statutory renewal claimant in the basic renewal registration.

(6) In general, the Copyright Office will not issue a supplementary registration for a basic registration made under title 17 of the United States Code as it existed before January 1, 1978. In an exceptional case, the Copyright Office may issue a supplementary registration for such a registra-

tion, if the correction or amplification is supported by clear, convincing, and objective documentation.

(e) Application for supplementary registration. **(1)** To seek a supplementary registration for a work registered in Class TX, PA, VA, SR, or SE., an unpublished collection, or a unit of publication registered under §202.3, or a group of related works registered under §202.3(b)(6) through (10) or §202.4, an applicant must complete and submit the online application designated for supplementary registration.

(2) To seek a supplementary registration for a database that consists predominantly of photographs registered under §202.3(b)(5), an applicant must complete and submit the online application designated for supplementary registration after consultation with and under the direction of the Visual Arts Division.

(3) To seek a supplementary registration for a restored work registered under §202.12, a database that does not consist predominantly of photographs registered under §202.3(b)(5), or a renewal registration, an applicant must complete and submit a paper application using Form CA.

(4) Before submitting the application, the applicant must sign a certification stating that the applicant reviewed a copy of the certificate of registration for the basic registration that will be corrected or amplified by the supplementary registration. To obtain a copy of the certificate, the applicant may submit a written request to the Records Research and Certification Section using the procedure set forth in Chapter 2400 of the Compendium of U.S. Copyright Office Practices, Third Edition.

(5) The appropriate filing fee, as required by §201.3(c) of this chapter, must be included with the application or charged to an active deposit account. At the Office's discretion, the applicant may be required to pay an additional fee to make a copy of the certificate of registration for the basic registration that will be corrected or amplified by the supplementary registration.

(6) Copies, phonorecords, or supporting documents cannot be made part of the record for a supplementary registration and should not be submitted with the application.

(7) In an exceptional case, the Copyright Office may waive the requirements set forth in paragraph (e)(1) of this section, subject to such conditions as the Associate Register and Director of the Office of Registration Policy and Practice may impose on the applicant.

(f) Effect of supplementary registration. **(1)** When the Copyright Office completes a supplementary registration, it will issue a certificate of supplementary registration bearing a new registration number in the appropriate class. The Office will cross-reference the records for the basic registration and the supplementary registration by placing a note in each record that identifies the registration number and effective date of registration for the related registration.

(2) As provided in section 408(d) of title 17 of the United States Code, the information contained in a supplementary registration augments but does not supersede that contained in the basic registration. The basic registration will not be expunged or cancelled.

History of 37 C.F.R. §202.6: 82 FR 27427, July 17, 2017; 82 FR 42738, Oct. 12, 2017.

§§202.7 TO 202.9. RESERVED

§202.10. PICTORIAL, GRAPHIC, & SCULPTURAL WORKS

(a) In order to be acceptable as a pictorial, graphic, or sculptural work, the work must embody some creative authorship in its delineation or form. The registrability of such a work is not affected by the intention of the author as to the use of the work or the number of copies reproduced. The availability of protection or grant of protection under the law for a utility or design patent will not affect the registrability of a claim in an original work of pictorial, graphic, or sculptural authorship.

(b) A claim to copyright cannot be registered in a print or label consisting solely of trademark subject matter and lacking copyrightable matter. While the Copyright Office will not investigate whether the matter has been or can be registered at the Patent and Trademark Office, it will register a properly filed copyright claim in a print or label that contains the requisite qualifications for copyright even though there is a trademark on it. However, registration of a claim to copyright does not give the claimant rights available by trademark registrations at the Patent and Trademark Office.

History of 37 C.F.R. §202.10: 46 FR 33249, June 29, 1981; 60 FR 15606, Mar. 24, 1995; 61 FR 5445, Feb. 12, 1996.

§202.11. ARCHITECTURAL WORKS

(a) General. This section prescribes rules pertaining to the registration of architectural works, as provided for in the amendment of title 17 of the United States Code by the Architectural Works Copyright Protection Act, title VII of the Judicial Improvements Act of 1990, Public Law 101-650.

(b) Definitions.

(1) For the purposes of this section, the term architectural work has the same meaning as set forth in section 101 of title 17, as amended.

(2) The term building means humanly habitable structures that are intended to be both permanent and stationary, such as houses and office buildings, and other permanent and stationary structures designed for human occupancy, including but not limited to churches, museums, gazebos, and garden pavilions.

(c) Registration—

(1) Original design. In general, an original design of a building embodied in any tangible medium of expression, including a building, architectural plans, or drawings, may be registered as an architectural work.

(2) Registration limited to single architectural work. For published and unpublished architectural works, a single application may cover only a single architectural work. A group of architectural works may not be registered on a single application form. For works such as tract housing, a single work is one house model, with all accompanying floor plan options, elevations, and styles that are applicable to that particular model.

(3) Application form. Registration should be sought on Form VA. Line one of the form should give the title of the building. The date of construction of the building, if any, should also be designated. If the building has not yet been constructed, the notation "not yet constructed" should be given following the title.

(4) Separate registration for plans. Where dual copyright claims exist in technical drawings and the architectural work depicted in the drawings, any claims with respect to the technical drawings and architectural work must be registered separately.

(5) Publication. Publication of an architectural work occurs when underlying plans or drawings of the building or other copies of the building design are distributed or made available to the general public by sale or other transfer of ownership, or by rental, lease, or lending. Construction of a building does not itself constitute publication for purposes of registration, unless multiple copies are constructed.

(d) Works excluded. The following structures, features, or works cannot be registered:

(1) Structures other than buildings. Structures other than buildings, such as bridges, cloverleafs, dams, walkways, tents, recreational vehicles, mobile homes, and boats.

(2) Standard features. Standard configurations of spaces, and individual standard features, such as windows, doors, and other staple building components.

(3) Pre-December 1, 1990 building designs.

(i) Published building designs. The designs of buildings where the plans or drawings of the building were published before December 1, 1990, or the buildings were constructed or otherwise published before December 1, 1990.

(ii) Unpublished building designs. The designs of buildings that were unconstructed and embodied in unpublished plans or drawings on December 1, 1990, and remained unconstructed on December 31, 2002.

History of 37 C.F.R. §202.11: 57 FR 45310, Oct. 1, 1992; 68 FR 38630, June 30, 2003.

§202.12. RESTORED COPYRIGHTS

(a) General. This section prescribes rules pertaining to the registration of foreign copyright claims which have been restored to copyright protection under section 104A of 17 U.S.C., as amended by the Uruguay Round Agreements Act, Public Law 103-465.

(b) Definitions.

(1) For the purposes of this section, restored work and source country, have the definition given in 17 U.S.C. 104(A)(g)(6) and (8) and §201.33(b) of this chapter.

(2) Descriptive statement for a work embodied solely in machine-readable format is a separate written statement giving the title of the work, nature of the work (for example: computer program, database, videogame, etc.), plus a brief description of the contents or subject matter of the work.

(c) Registration—**(1)** Application. Applications for registration for single works restored to copyright protection under the URAA should be made on Form GATT. Copies of this form may be obtained from the Office's website or by contacting the Public Information Office at (202) 707-3000. Applicants should submit the completed application with the appropriate filing fee and deposit copies and materials required by paragraph (c)(3) of this section in the same package by mail.

(2) Fee.

(i) Amount. The filing fee for registering a copyright claim in a restored work is prescribed in §201.3(c).

(ii) Method of payment.

(A) Checks, money orders, or bank drafts. The Copyright Office will accept checks, money orders, or bank drafts made payable to the U.S. Copyright Office. Remittances must be redeemable without service or exchange fees through a United States institution, must be payable in United States dollars, and must be imprinted with American Banking Association routing numbers. In addition, international money orders, and postal money orders that are negotiable only at a post office are not acceptable. CURRENCY WILL NOT BE ACCEPTED.

(B) Copyright Office Deposit Account. The Copyright Office maintains a system of Deposit Accounts for the convenience of those who frequently use its services. The system allows an individual or firm to establish a Deposit Account in the Copyright Office and to make advance deposits into that account. Deposit Account holders can charge copyright fees against the balance in their accounts instead of sending separate remittances with each request for service. For information on Deposit Accounts, visit the Copyright Office website or write to the address specified in §201.1 of this chapter and request a copy of Circular 5.

(C) Credit cards. For GATT registrations the Copyright Office will accept most major credit cards. Debit cards cannot be accepted for payment. With the registration application, an applicant using a credit card must submit a separate cover letter stating the name of the credit card, the credit card number, the expiration date of the credit card, the total amount authorized and a signature authorizing the Office to charge the fees to the account. To protect the security of the credit card number, the applicant must not write the credit card number on the registration application.

(3) Deposit—

(i) General. The deposit for a work registered as a restored work under 17 U.S.C. 104A, except for those works listed in paragraphs (c)(3)(ii) through (iv) of this section, should consist of one copy or phonorecord which best represents the copyrightable content of the restored work. In descending order of preference, the deposit should be:

(A) The work as first published;

(B) A reprint or re-release of the work as first published;

(C) A photocopy or identical reproduction of the work as first published; or

(D) A revised version which includes a substantial amount of the copyrightable content of the restored work with an indication in writing of the percentage of the restored work appearing in the revision.

(ii) Previously registered works. No deposit is needed for works previously registered in the Copyright Office.

(iii) Works embodied solely in machine-readable format. For works embodied only in machine-readable formats, the deposit requirements are as follows:

(A) One machine-readable copy and a descriptive statement of the work; or

(B) Representative excerpts of the work, such as printouts; or, if the claim extends to audiovisual elements in the work, a videotape of what appears on the screen.

(iv) Pictorial, graphic and sculptural works. With the exception of 3-dimensional works of art, the general deposit preferences specified under paragraph (c)(3)(i) of this section shall govern. For 3-dimensional works of art, the preferred deposit is one or more photographs of the work, preferably in color.

(v) Special relief. An applicant who is unable to submit any of the preferred deposits may submit an alternative deposit under a grant of special relief under §202.20(d). In such a case, the applicant should indicate in writing why the deposit preferences cannot be met, and submit alternative identifying materials clearly showing some portion of the copyrightable contents of the restored work which is the subject of registration.

(vi) Motion pictures. If the deposit is a film print (16 or 35 mm), the applicant should contact the Performing Arts Division of the Registration Program for delivery instructions. The telephone number is: (202) 707-6040; the fax number is: (202) 707-1236.

(5) [Reserved]

(d) Works excluded. Works which are not copyrightable subject matter under title 17 of the U.S. Code, other than sound recordings fixed before February 15, 1972, shall not be registered as restored works.

History of 37 C.F.R. §202.12: 60 FR 50422, Sept. 29, 1995; 64 FR 12902, Mar. 16, 1999; 64 FR 29522, June 1, 1999; 72 FR 36888, July 6, 2001; 71 FR 31092, June 1, 2006; 73 FR 37839, July 1, 2008; 76 FR 27898, May 13, 2011; 78 FR 42875, July 18, 2013; 82 FR 9359, Mar. 8, 2017.

E §202.13. SECURE TESTS

(a) General. This section prescribes rules pertaining to the registration of secure tests or a group of test items prepared for use in a secure test.

(b) Definitions. For purposes of this section—

(1) A secure test is a nonmarketed test administered under supervision at specified centers on scheduled dates, all copies of which are accounted for and either destroyed or returned to restricted locked storage following each administration.

(2) A test is nonmarketed if copies of the test are not sold, but instead are distributed and used in such a manner that the test sponsor or publisher retains ownership and control of the copies.

(3) A test is administered under supervision if test proctors or the equivalent supervise the administration of the test.

(4) A specified center is a place where test takers are physically assembled at the same time.

(5) A test item is comprised of a question (or "stem"), the correct answer to that question, any incorrect answer choices (or "distractors"), and any associated material, such as a narrative passage or diagram, and each item shall be considered one work. A single narrative, diagram, or other prefatory material, followed by multiple sets of related questions and correct or incorrect answers shall together be considered one item.

(c) Deposit requirements. Pursuant to the authority granted by 17 U.S.C. 408(c)(1), the Register of Copyrights has determined that a secure test or a group of test items prepared for use in a secure test may be registered with identifying material, and the filing and examination fees required by §201.3(c) and (d), if the following conditions are met:

(1) The applicant must complete and submit a standard application. The application may be submitted by any of the parties listed in §202.3(c)(1).

(2) In the case of a secure test, the applicant must submit a redacted copy of the entire test. In the case of a group of test items prepared for use in a secure test, the applicant must submit a redacted copy of each test item. In all cases the redacted copy must contain a sufficient amount of visible content to reasonably identify the work(s). In addition, the applicant must complete and submit the secure test questionnaire that is posted on the Copyright Office's Web site. The questionnaire and the redacted copy must be contained in separate electronic files, and each file must be uploaded to the electronic registration system in Portable Document Format (PDF). The Copyright Office will review these materials to determine if the work(s) qualify for an in-person examination. If they appear to be eligible, the Copyright Office will contact the applicant to schedule an appointment to examine an unredacted copy of the work(s) under secure conditions.

(3) On the appointed date, the applicant must bring the following materials to the Copyright Office:

(i) A copy of the completed application.

(ii) The appropriate examination fee, as required by §201.3(d) of this chapter.

(iii) A copy of the redacted version of the work(s) that was uploaded to the electronic registration system.

(iv) A signed declaration confirming that the redacted copy specified in paragraph (c)(3)(iii) of this section is identical to the redacted copy that was uploaded to the electronic registration system.

(v) In the case of a secure test, the applicant must bring an unredacted copy of the entire test. In the case of a group of test items prepared for use in a secure test, the applicant must bring an unredacted copy of all the test items.

(4) The Copyright Office will examine the copies specified in paragraphs (c)(3)(iii) and (v) of this section in the applicant's presence. When the examination is complete, the Office will stamp the date of the appointment on the copies and will return them to the applicant. The Office will retain the signed declaration and the redacted copy that was uploaded to the electronic registration system.

(d) Group registration requirements. The Copyright Office may register a group of test items if the following conditions have been met:

(1) All the test items must be prepared for use in a secure test, and the name of the secure test must be identified in the title of the group.

(2) The group may contain an unlimited amount of works, but the applicant must identify the individual works included within the group by numbering each test item in the deposit.

(3) The applicant must provide a title for the group as a whole, and must append the term "GRSTQ" to the beginning of the title.

(4) The group must contain only unpublished works, or works published within the same three-calendar-month period and the application must identify the earliest date that the works were published.

(5) All the works in the group must have the same author or authors, and the copyright claimant for each work must be the same. Claims in the selection, coordination, or arrangement of the group as a whole will not be permitted on the application. Each item in the group must be separately copyrightable or must be excluded from the group.

History of 37 C.F.R. §202.13: 82 FR 26854, July 12, 2017; 82 FR 52228, Nov. 13, 2017.

§§202.14 TO 202.15. RESERVED

History of 37 C.F.R. §§202.13-202.15: 60 FR 50422, Sept. 29, 1995.

§202.16. PREREGISTRATION OF COPYRIGHTS

(a) General. This section prescribes rules pertaining to the preregistration of copyright claims in works eligible for preregistration under 17 U.S.C. 408(f).

(b) Definitions. For the purposes of this section

(1) A work is in a class of works that the Register of Copyrights has determined has had a history of infringement prior to authorized commercial release if it falls within one of the following classes of works:

(i) Motion pictures;

(ii) Sound recordings;

(iii) Musical compositions;

(iv) Literary works being prepared for publication in book form;

(v) Computer programs (including videogames); or

(vi) Advertising or marketing photographs.

(2) A work is being prepared for commercial distribution if:

(i) The claimant, in a statement certified by the authorized preregistering party, has a reasonable expectation that the work will be commercially distributed to the public; and

(ii) Preparation of the work has commenced and at least some portion of the work has been fixed in a tangible medium of expression, as follows:

(A) For a motion picture, filming of the motion picture must have commenced;

(B) For a sound recording, recording of the sounds must have commenced;

(C) For a musical composition, at least some of the musical composition must have been fixed either in the form of musical notation or in a copy or phonorecord embodying a performance of some or all of the work;

(D) For a literary work being prepared for publication in book form, the actual writing of the text of the work must have commenced;

(E) For a computer program, at least some of the computer code (either source code or object code) must have been fixed; and

(F) For an advertising or marketing photograph, the photograph (or, in the case of a group of photographs intended for simultaneous publication, at least one of the photographs) must have been taken.

(3) A work eligible for preregistration is a work that is:

(i) Unpublished;

(ii) Being prepared for commercial distribution; and

(iii) In a class of works that the Register of Copyrights has determined has had a history of infringement prior to authorized commercial release.

(c) Preregistration.

(1) General. A work eligible for preregistration may be preregistered by submitting an application and fee to the Copyright Office pursuant to the requirements set forth in this section.

(2) Works excluded. Works that are not copyrightable subject matter under title 17 of the U.S. Code may not be preregistered in the Copyright Office.

(3) Application. An application for preregistration must be submitted electronically on the Copyright Office website at: http://www.copyright.gov.

(4) Preregistration as a single work. For the purpose of preregistration on a single application and upon payment of a single preregistration fee, all copyrightable elements that are otherwise recognizable as self-contained works, that are to be included and first published in a single unit of publication, and in which the copyright claimant is the same, shall be considered a single work eligible for preregistration.

(5) Fee.

(i) Amount. The filing fee for preregistration is prescribed in §201.3(c).

(ii) Method of payment.

(A) Copyright Office deposit account. The Copyright Office maintains a system of Deposit Accounts for the convenience of those who frequently use its services and for those who file applications electronically. The system allows an individual or firm to establish a Deposit Account in the Copyright Office and to make advance deposits in that account. Deposit Account holders can charge preregistration fees against the balance in their accounts instead of using credit cards for each request of service. For information on Deposit Accounts, please download a copy of Circular 5, "How to Open and Maintain a Deposit Account in the Copyright Office," or write the Register of Copyrights, Copyright Office, Library of Congress, Washington, D.C. 20559.

(B) Credit cards, debit cards and electronic funds transfer. The online preregistration filing system will provide options for payment by means of credit or debit cards and by means of electronic funds transfers. Applicants will be redirected to the Department of Treasury's Pay.gov website to make payments with credit or debit cards, or directly from their bank accounts by means of ACH debit transactions.

(C) No refunds. The preregistration filing fee is not refundable.

(6) Description. No deposit of the work being preregistered should be submitted with an application for preregistration. The preregistration applicant should submit a detailed description, of not more than 2,000 characters (approximately 330 words), of the work as part of the application. The description should be based on information available at the time of the application sufficient to reasonably identify the work. Generally, the Copyright Office will not review descriptions for adequacy, but in an action for infringement of a preregistered work, the court may evaluate the adequacy of the description to determine whether the preregistration actually describes the work that is alleged to be infringed, taking into account the information available to the applicant at the time of preregistration and taking into account the legitimate interest of the applicant in protecting confidential information.

(i) For motion pictures, the identifying description should include the following information to the extent known at the time of filing: The subject matter, a summary or outline, the director, the primary actors, the principal location of filming, and any other information that would assist in identifying the particular work being preregistered.

(ii) For sound recordings, the identifying description should include the following information to the extent known at the time of filing: the subject matter of the work or works recorded, the performer or performing group, the genre of the work recorded (e.g., classical, pop, musical comedy, soft rock, heavy metal, gospel, rap, hip-hop, blues, jazz), the titles of the musical compositions being recorded, the principal recording location, the composer(s) of the recorded musical compositions embodied on the sound recording, and any other information that would assist in identifying the particular work being preregistered.

(iii) For musical compositions, the identifying description should include the following information to the extent known at the time of filing: The subject matter of the lyrics, if any; the genre of the work (e.g., classical, pop, musical comedy, soft rock, heavy metal, gospel, rap, hip-hop, blues, jazz); the performer, principal recording location, record label, motion picture, or other information relating to any sound recordings or motion pictures that are being prepared for commercial distribution and will include the musical composition; and any other detail or characteristic that may assist in identifying the particular musical composition.

(iv) For literary works in book form, the identifying description should include to the extent known at the time of filing: The genre of the book (e.g., biography, novel, history, etc.), and should include a brief summary of the work including, the subject matter (e.g., a biography of President Bush, a history of the war in Iraq, a fantasy novel); a description (where applicable) of the plot, primary characters, events, or other key elements of the content of the work; and any other salient characteristics of the book (e.g., whether it is a later edition or revision of a previous work, as well as any other detail which may assist in identifying the literary work in book form).

(v) For computer programs (including videogames), the identifying description should include to the extent known at the time of filing: The nature, purpose and function of the computer program, including the programming language in which it is written and any particular organization or structure in which the program has been created; the form in which it is expected to be published (e.g., as an online-only product; whether there have been previous versions and identification of such previous versions); the identities of persons involved in the creation of the computer program; and, if the work is a videogame, also the subject matter of the videogame and the overall object, goal, or purpose of the game, its characters, if any, and the general setting and surrounding found in the game.

(vi) For advertising or marketing photographs, the description should include the subject matter depicted in the photograph or photographs, including information such as the particular product, event, public figure, or other item or occurrence which the photograph is intended to advertise or market. To the extent possible and applicable, the description for photographs should give additional details which will assist in identifying the particular photographs, such as the party for whom such advertising photographs are taken; the approximate time periods during which the photographs are taken; the approximate number of photos which may be included in the grouping; any events associated with the photographs; and the location and physical setting or surrounding depicted in the photographs. The description may also explain the general presentation (e.g., the lighting, background scenery, positioning of elements of the subject matter as it is seen in the photographs), and should provide any locations and events, if applicable, associated with the photographs.

(7) Review of preregistration information. The Copyright Office will conduct a limited review of applications for preregistration, in order to ascertain whether the application describes a work that is in a class of works that the Register of Copyrights has determined has had a history of infringement prior to authorized commercial release. However, a work will not be preregistered unless an applicant has provided all of the information requested on the application and has certified that all of the information provided on the application is correct to the best of the applicant's knowledge.

(8) Certification. The person submitting an application for preregistration must certify on the application that he or she is the author, copyright claimant, or owner of exclusive rights, or the authorized agent of the author, copyright claimant, or owner of exclusive rights, of the work submitted for this preregistration; that the information given in this application is correct to the best of his or her knowledge; that the work is being prepared for commercial distribution; and that he or she has a reasonable expectation that the work will be commercially distributed to the public.

(9) Effective date of preregistration. The effective date of a preregistration is the day on which an application and fee for preregistration of a work, which the Copyright Office later notifies the claimant has been preregistered or which a court of competent jurisdiction has concluded was acceptable for preregistration, have been received in the Copyright Office.

(10) Notification of preregistration. Upon completion of the preregistration, the Copyright Office will email an official notification of the preregistration to the person who submitted the application.

(11) Certification of preregistation.[1] A certified copy of the official notification may be obtained in physical form from the Records Research and Certification Section of the Office of Public Information and Education at the address specified in §201.1 of this chapter.

(12) Public record of preregistration. The preregistration record also will be made available to the public on the Copyright Office website at: http://www.copyright.gov.

(13) Effect of preregistration. Preregistration of a work offers certain advantages to a copyright owner pursuant to 17 U.S.C. 408(f), 411 and 412. However, preregistration of a work does not constitute prima facie evidence of the validity of the copyright or of the facts stated in the application for preregistration or in the preregistration record. The fact that a work has been preregistered does not create any presumption that the Copyright Office will register the work upon submission of an application for registration.

(14) Petition for recognition of a new class of works. At any time an interested party may petition the Register of Copyrights for a determination as to whether a particular class of works has had a history of copyright infringement prior to authorized release that would justify inclusion of that class of works among the classes of works eligible for preregistration.

1. **Editor's note:** Probably should be "preregistration."

History of 37 C.F.R. §202.16: 70 FR 61906, Oct. 27, 2005; 71 FR 31092, June 1, 2006; 73 FR 37839, July 1, 2008; 78 FR 42875, July 18, 2013; 82 FR 9360, Mar. 8, 2017.

§202.17. RENEWALS

(a) General.

(1) This section concerns renewal for copyrights originally secured from January 1, 1964, through December 31, 1977, either by publication with the required copyright notice or by registration as an unpublished work. Renewal registration for these works is optional. As provided in Pub. L. No. 102-307, 106 Stat. 264, enacted June 26, 1992, renewal registration made during the last year of the original 28-year term of copyright differs in legal effect from renewal registration made during the 67-year extended renewal term. In the latter instance, the copyright is renewed automatically at the expiration of the original 28-year term. In the former instance, renewal by registration during the last year of the original 28-year term vested the renewal copyright in the statutory claimant living on the date of registration.

(2) Works for which copyright was secured before 1964 are governed by the provisions of 17 U.S.C. 304(a) in effect prior to the 1992 date of enactment of Pub. L. No. 102-307. The copyrights in such works could have been renewed by registration only within the last calendar year of the original 28-year term of copyright protection. If renewal registration was not made during that period of time, copyright protection was lost when the original term of copyright expired and cannot be regained.

(3) Works restored to copyright by the Uruguay Round Agreements Act are governed in their copyright term of protection by Pub. L. No. 103-465, 108 Stat. 4809, 4976 (December 8, 1994). Under 17 U.S.C. 104A(a)(1)(A) and (B), as amended, any work in which copyright is restored subsists for the remainder of the term of copyright that the work would have been otherwise granted in the United States. Such term includes the remainder of any applicable renewal term.

(4) Automatic restoration of copyright in certain foreign works that were in the public domain in the United States may have occurred under the Uruguay Round Agreements Act and may be protected by copyright or neighboring rights in their "source country," as defined at 17 U.S.C. 104A(h)(8).

(b) Definitions. **(1)** For purposes of this section, the terms assignee and successor, as they pertain to 17 U.S.C. 304(a)(3)(A)(ii), refer to a party which has acquired the renewal copyright in a work by assignment or by other means of legal succession from the statutory claimant (as that claimant is defined in 17 U.S.C. 304(a)(1)(B) and (C)) in whom the renewal copyright vested but in whose name no renewal registration was previously made.

(2) For purposes of this section, a work has been copyrighted when it has been published with a proper copyright notice or, in the case of an unpublished work, when it has been registered for copyright.

(3) For purposes of this section, the term posthumous work means a work that was unpublished on the date of the death of the author and with respect to which no copyright assignment or other contract for exploitation of the work occurred during the author's lifetime.

(4) For purposes of this section, the term statutory claimant means:

(i) A party who was entitled to claim copyright for the renewal term at the time renewal registration was made either as a proprietary claimant, 17 U.S.C. 304(a)(2)(A)(i), or as a personal claimant, 17 U.S.C. 304(a)(2)(B)(i), if registration was made during the original term of copyright; or

(ii) If the original copyright term expired, a party who was entitled to claim copyright for the renewal term as of the last day of the original term of copyright as either a proprietary or a personal claimant, 17 U.S.C. 304(a)(2)(A)(ii) and (a)(2)(B)(ii).

(5) For purposes of this section, the term to vest means to give a fixed, non-contingent right of present or future enjoyment of the renewal copyright in a work. If renewal registration was made during the 28th year of the original term of copyright, the renewal copyright vested in the party or parties entitled to claim such copyright at the time of registration as provided by 17 U.S.C. 304(a)(1)(B) and (C). Although the vested right may have been determined by registration during the 28th year of the original term, the exercise of such right did not commence until the beginning of the renewal term, as provided in 17 U.S.C. 304(a)(2). If renewal registration was not made during the 28th year, the renewal copyright automatically vested upon the beginning of the renewal term in the party or parties entitled to claim such copyright on the last day of the original term as provided by 17 U.S.C. 304(a)(2)(A)(ii) and (B)(ii).

(c) Time limits: original term and renewal term registration. **(1)** Under 17 U.S.C. 304(a), prior to its amendment of June 26, 1992, a registration for the original term of copyright must have been made during the 28 years of that original term, and a renewal registration must also have been made during the 28th year of that term. Pub. L. No. 102-307, 106 Stat. 264 (June 26, 1992) amended section 304(a) for works originally copyrighted from January 1, 1964, through December 31, 1977, and provided for optional original-term registration and optional renewal registration. 17 U.S.C. 304(a)(2), (a)(3) and 409(11). For such works, claims to renewal copyright could have been registered during the last year of the original term but such registration was not required in order to enjoy statutory protection during the renewal term. 17 U.S.C. 304(a)(3)(B).

(2) A renewal registration can be made at any time during the renewal term. 17 U.S.C. 304(a)(3)(A)(ii). If no original-term registration was made, renewal registration remains possible; but the Register may request information, under 17 U.S.C. 409(10), regarding the original term of copyright. Such information must demonstrate that the work complies with all requirements of the 1909 Act with respect to the existence, ownership, or duration of the copyright for the original term of the work. The Form RE/Addendum is used to provide this information.

(3) Renewal registration is currently available for works copyrighted from January 1, 1964, through December 31, 1977. Under the provisions of 17 U.S.C. 304(a)(3)(A)(ii), renewal registration may be made any time during the 67-year renewal term for such works according to the procedure indicated in paragraph (h) of this section. Such renewal registration is optional and is not a condition of the subsistence of the copyright for the 67-year renewal term. 17 U.S.C. 304(a)(3)(B). In the case of such works for which no registration was made during the original term of copyright, renewal registration may be made by submission of a Form RE/Addendum. The Addendum, an adjunct to the renewal form, concerns the facts of first publication for a work and assures the Copyright Office that the work as it existed in its original term of copyright was in compliance with the 1909 copyright law, 17 U.S.C. 1, et. seq. (1909 Act, in effect through December 31, 1977), whose provisions govern such works.

(d) Benefits of 28th-year renewal registration. Prior to January 1, 2006, renewal registration was available during the 28th year of the original term of copyright for works copyrighted from January 1, 1964, through December 31, 1977. As provided in Pub. L. No. 102-307, 106 Stat. 264, registration made during the 28th year of the original term of copyright provided the following benefits to the registrant:

(1) The certificate of registration constituted prima facie evidence as to the validity of the copyright during its renewal term and of the facts stated in the certificate. 17 U.S.C. 304(a)(4)(B).

(2) A derivative work prepared under the authority of a grant of a transfer or license of copyright in a work made before the expiration of the original term of copyright could not continue to be used under the terms of the grant during the renewal term without the authority of the owner of the renewal copyright. 17 U.S.C. 304(a)(4)(A).

(3) The renewal copyright vested upon the beginning of the renewal term in the party entitled to claim the renewal of copyright at the time the application was made as provided under 17 U.S.C. 304(a)(2)(A)(i) and (B)(i).

(e) Statutory parties entitled to claim copyright for the renewal term under section 304(a). **(1)** Renewal claims must be registered in the name of the party or parties entitled to claim copyright for the renewal term as provided in paragraphs (e)(2) through (4) of this section and as specified in 17 U.S.C. 304(a). If a work was a new version of a previously published or registered work, renewal registration may be claimed only in the new matter.

(2) If the renewal claim was submitted during the last, i.e., the 28th, year of the original term of copyright, the claim had to be registered in the name(s) of the statutory claimant(s) entitled to claim the renewal copyright on the date on which the claim was submitted to the Copyright Office. If the renewal claim is submitted during the 67-year extended renewal term, the renewal claim can be registered only in the name(s) of the statutory claimant(s) entitled to claim the renewal on the last day (December 31) of the original term of copyright. These eligible renewal claimants are listed below:

(i) The person who, on the applicable day, was the copyright proprietor is the appropriate renewal claimant in any posthumous work or any periodical, encyclopedia, or other composite work upon which the copyright was originally secured by the proprietor;

(ii) The person who, on the applicable day, was the copyright proprietor is the appropriate claimant in any work copyrighted by a corporate body (otherwise than as assignees or licensees of the individual author), or by an employer for whom such work was made for hire;

(iii) For any other copyrighted work, including a contribution by an individual author to a periodical or to a cyclopedic or other composite work, the appropriate claimants, in descending order of eligibility, are the person who, on the applicable day, was:

(A) The author(s) of the work, if still living;

(B) The widow(er) and/or child(ren) of the author, if the author was deceased on the applicable day;

(C) The author's executor(s), if still acting in that capacity on the applicable day, provided the author had a will and neither the author, nor any widow(er) or child of the author is still living; or

(D) The author's next of kin, in the absence of a will and if neither the author nor any widow, widower or child of the author is living.

(3) The provisions of paragraphs (e)(1) and (2) of this section are subject to the following qualification: Notwithstanding the definition of "posthumous work" in paragraph (b)(3) of this section, a renewal claim may be registered in the name of the proprietor of a work, as well as in the name of the appropriate claimant under paragraph (e)(2)(iii) of this section, in any case in which a contract for exploitation of the work but no copyright assignment in the work has occurred during the author's lifetime. However, registration by the Copyright Office in this case should not be interpreted as evidencing the validity of either claim.

(4) The provisions of paragraphs (e)(2)(iii)(C) and (D) of this section are subject to the following qualifications:

(i) In any case where:

(A) The author has left a will which names no executor;

(B) The author has left a will which names an executor who cannot or will not serve in that capacity; or

(C) The author has left a will which names an executor who has been discharged upon settlement of the estate, removed before the estate has been completely administered, or is deceased at the time of the renewal registration submission, the renewal claim may be registered either in the name of an administrator cum testamento annexo (administrator c.t.a.) or an administrator de bonis non cum testamento annexo (administrator d.b.n.c.t.a.) so appointed by a court of competent jurisdiction.

(ii) In any case described in paragraph (e) of this section, except in the case where the author has left a will without naming an executor and a court-appointed administrator c.t.a. or administrator d.b.n.c.t.a. is in existence at the time of renewal registration, the renewal claim also may be registered in the name of the author's next of kin. However, registration by the Copyright Office of conflicting renewal claims in such a case should not be interpreted as evidencing the validity of either claim.

(f) Successors/assignees entitled to file an application for the renewal term under Section 304(a). The provisions of paragraph (e) of this section are subject to the following qualifications:

(1) Where no renewal registration has been made in the name of a person or entity identified in paragraphs (e)(2)(i), (ii) and (iii) of this section, a renewal application may be filed at any time during the renewal term by any successor or assignee of such person or entity.

(2) In such cases described in paragraph (f)(1) of this section, the renewal application must identify the party in whom the renewal copyright vested; must indicate the basis upon which copyright for the renewal term vested in that party; must identify the party who is the successor or assignee of the statutory claimant under 17 U.S.C. 304(a)(3); and, must give the manner by which such successor/assignee secured the renewal copyright.

(3) When such a claim has been filed by a successor or assignee in the name of the statutory claimant as described in paragraph (e)(2)(i), (ii) and (iii) of this section, generally no subsequent claims may be filed by other successors or assignees whose rights are derived from the same statutory claimant. If a public record of renewal ownership is sought by other successors or assignees of the same statutory claimant, the document of transfer of the renewal copyright, either the renewal in its entirety or in part, may be recorded in the Copyright Office.

(4) Where a successor or assignee claims the renewal right from the same statutory claimant as does another successor or assignee, the Copyright Office may inquire concerning the situation and, if appropriate, may allow adverse renewal claims from the successors/assignees to be placed on the public record. In such cases, correspondence between the parties filing competing renewal claims and the Copyright Office will be, as always, maintained within Office records and subject to public inspection according to regulations found at 37 CFR 201.2.

(g) Application for renewal registration for a work registered in its original 28-year term.

(1) Each application for renewal registration shall be submitted on Form RE. All forms are available free of charge via the Internet by accessing the Copyright Office website at: http://www.copyright.gov. Copies of Form RE are also available free upon request. Requests should be mailed to the address specified in §201.1(b) of this chapter.

(2)(i) An application for renewal registration may be submitted by any eligible statutory renewal claimant as specified in paragraph (e) of this section or by the duly authorized agent of such claimant, or by the successor or assignee of such claimant as provided under paragraph (f) of this section or by the duly authorized agent of such successor or assignee.

(ii) An application for renewal registration shall be accompanied by the required fee as set forth in 37 CFR 201.3. The application shall contain the information required by the form and its accompanying instructions, and shall include a certification. The certification shall consist of:

(A) A designation of whether the applicant is the renewal claimant, or a successor or assignee, or the duly authorized agent of such claimant or of such successor or assignee (whose identity shall also be given);

(B) The handwritten signature of such claimant, successor or assignee, or agent, accompanied by the typewritten or printed name of that person;

(C) A declaration that the statements made in the application are correct to the best of that person's knowledge; and

(D) The date of certification.

(3) Once a renewal registration has been made, the Copyright Office will not accept another application for renewal registration on behalf of the same renewal claimant.

(h) Renewal with addendum registration for an unregistered work. **(1)** General. For published works copyrighted from January 1, 1964, through December 31, 1977, where no registration was made during the original term of copyright and where renewal registration is sought during the 67-year renewal term, the Form RE/Addendum must be used to provide information concerning the original term of copyright. The Form RE/Addendum requires a separate fee and the deposit of one copy or phonorecord of the work as first published (or identifying material in lieu of a copy or phonorecord). The effective date of registration for a renewal claim submitted on a Form RE/Addendum is the date the Copyright Office receives an acceptable completed application, the required fees, and an acceptable deposit for the work.

(2) Time Limits. A renewal claim accompanied by an Addendum to Form RE may be filed at any time during the 67-year renewal term.

(3) Content. The Form RE/Addendum must contain the following information:

(i) The title of the work;

(ii) The name of the author(s);

(iii) The date of first publication of the work;

(iv) The nation of first publication of the work;

(v) The citizenship of the author(s) on the date of first publication of the work;

(vi) The domicile of the author(s) on the date of first publication of the work;

(vii) An averment that, at the time of first publication, and thereafter until March 1, 1989 (effective date of the Berne Implementation Act of 1988), all the copies or phonorecords of the work, including reprints of the work, published, i.e., publicly distributed in the United States or elsewhere, under the authority of the author or other copyright proprietor, bore the copyright notice required by the Copyright Act of 1909 and that United States copyright subsists in the work;

(viii) For works of United States origin which were subject to the manufacturing provisions of section 16 of the Copyright Act of 1909 as it existed at the time the work was published, the Form RE/Addendum must also contain information about the country of manufacture and the manufacturing processes; and

(ix) The handwritten signature of the renewal claimant or successor or assignee, or the duly authorized agent of the claimant or of the successor or assignee. The signature shall be accompanied by the printed or typewritten name of the person signing the Addendum and by the date of the signature; and shall be immediately preceded by a declaration that the statements made in the application are correct to the best of that person's knowledge.

(4) Fees. Form RE and Form RE/Addendum must be accompanied by the required fee for each form as required in 37 CFR 201.3.

(5) Deposit requirement. One copy or phonorecord or identifying material of the work as first published in accordance with the deposit requirements set out in 37 CFR 202.20 and 202.21 is required.

(6) Waiver of the deposit requirement. Where the renewal applicant asserts that it is either impossible or otherwise an undue hardship to satisfy the deposit requirements of 37 CFR 202.20 and 202.21, the Copyright Office, at its discretion, may, upon receipt of an acceptable explanation of the inability to submit such copy or identifying material, permit the deposit of the following in descending order of preference. In every case, however, proof of the copyright notice showing the content and location of the notice as it appeared on copies or phonorecords of the work as first published must be included.

(i) A reproduction of the entire work as first published (e.g., photocopy, videotape, audiotape, CD-ROM, DVD are examples of physical media which may hold reproductions of a work as first published). If the work is a contribution to a periodical, a reproduction of only the contribution (including the relevant copyright notice) will suffice.

(ii) A reprint of the work (e.g., a later edition, a later release of a phonorecord, or the like). The reprint must show the copyright notice as it appeared in the same location within the first published copy of the work as well as the exact content of the copyright notice appearing in the first published edition. If the copyrightable content of the reprint differs from that of the first published edition, an explanation of the differences between the two editions is required.

(iii) Identifying material including a reproduction of the greatest feasible portion of the copyrightable content of a work including a photocopy or photograph of the title page, title screen, record label or the like, as first published, and a photocopy or photograph showing the copyright notice content and location as first published. The Copyright Office may request deposit of additional material if the initial submission is inadequate for examination purposes.

History of 37 C.F.R. §202.17: 43 FR 964, Jan. 5, 1978; 46 FR 58671, Dec. 3, 1981; 56 FR 59885, Nov. 26, 1991; 57 FR 60483, Dec. 21, 1992; 64 FR 29522, June 1, 1999; 64 FR 36575, July 7, 1999; 65 FR 39819, June 28, 2000; 66 FR 24267, May 14, 2001; 66 FR 34373, June 28, 2001; 72 FR 61803, Nov. 1, 2007; 73 FR 37839, July 1, 2008; 78 FR 42875, July 18, 2013; 82 FR 9360, Mar. 8, 2017.

E §202.18. ACCESS TO ELECTRONIC WORKS

(a) Access to electronic works received under §202.4(e) will be available only to authorized users at Library of Congress premises in accordance with the policies listed below. Library staff may access such content off-site as part of their assigned duties via a secure connection.

(b) Access to each individual electronic work received under §202.4(e) will be limited, at any one time, to two Library of Congress authorized users via a secure server over a secure network that serves Library of Congress premises.

(c) The Library of Congress will not make electronic works received under §202.4(e) available to the public over the internet without rightsholders' permissions.

(d) "Authorized user" means Library of Congress staff, contractors, and registered researchers, and Members, staff and officers of the U.S. House of Representatives and the U.S. Senate for the purposes of this section.

(e) "Library of Congress premises" means all Library of Congress premises in Washington, DC, and the Library of Congress Packard Campus for Audio-Visual Conservation in Culpeper, VA.

History of 37 C.F.R. §202.18: 83 FR 4147, Mar. 1, 2018.

A §202.19. DEPOSIT OF PUBLISHED COPIES OR PHONORECORDS FOR THE LIBRARY OF CONGRESS

(a) General. This section prescribes rules pertaining to the deposit of copies and phonorecords of published works for the Library of Congress under section 407 of title 17 of the United States Code. The provisions of this section are not applicable to the deposit of copies and phonorecords for purposes of copyright registration under section 408 of title 17, except as expressly adopted in §202.20.

(b) Definitions. For the purposes of this section:

(1)(i) The "best edition" of a work is the edition, published in the United States at any time before the date of deposit, that the Library of Congress determines to be most suitable for its purposes. The "best edition" requirement is described in detail at Appendix B to this part.

(ii) Criteria for selection of the "best edition" from among two or more published editions of the same version of the same work are set forth in the statement entitled "Best Edition of Published Copyrighted Works for the Collections of the Library of Congress" (hereafter referred to as the "Best Edition Statement") in effect at the time of deposit.

(iii) Where no specific criteria for the selection of the "best edition" are established in the Best Edition Statement, that edition which, in the judgment of the Library of Congress, represents the highest quality for its purposes shall be considered the "best edition." In such cases:

(A) When the Copyright Office is aware that two or more editions of a work have been published it will consult with other appropriate officials of the Library of Congress to obtain instructions as to the "best edition" and (except in cases for which special relief is granted) will require deposit of that edition; and

(B) When a potential depositor is uncertain which of two or more published editions comprises the "best edition," inquiry should be made to the Copyright Acquisitions Division.

(iv) Where differences between two or more "editions" of a work represent variations in copyrightable content, each edition is considered a separate version, and hence a different work, for the purpose of this section, and criteria of "best edition" based on such differences do not apply.

(2) A complete copy includes all elements comprising the unit of publication of the best edition of the work, including elements that, if considered separately, would not be copyrightable subject matter or would otherwise be exempt from the mandatory deposit requirement under paragraph (c) of this section.

(i) In the case of sound recordings, a "complete" phonorecord includes the phonorecord, together with any printed or other visually perceptible material published with such phonorecord (such as textual or pictorial matter appearing on record sleeves or album covers, or embodied in leaflets or booklets included in a sleeve, album, or other container).

(ii) In the case of a musical composition published in copies only, or in both copies and phonorecords:

(A) If the only publication of copies in the United States took place by the rental, lease, or lending of a full score and parts, a full score is a "complete" copy; and

(B) If the only publication of copies in the United States took place by the rental, lease, or lending of a conductor's score and parts, a conductor's score is a "complete" copy.

(iii) In the case of a motion picture, a copy is "complete" if the reproduction of all of the visual and aural elements comprising the copyrightable subject matter in the work is clean, undamaged, undeteriorated, and free of splices, and if the copy itself and its physical housing are free of any defects that would interfere with the performance of the work or that would cause mechanical, visual, or audible defects or distortions.

(iv) In the case of an electronic work published in the United States and available only online, a copy is "complete" if it includes all elements constituting the work in its published form, i.e., the complete work as published, including metadata and formatting codes otherwise exempt from mandatory deposit.

(3) The terms architectural works, copies, collective work, device, fixed, literary work, machine, motion picture, phonorecord, publication, sound recording, useful article, and their variant forms, have the meanings given to them in 17 U.S.C. 101.

(4) For purposes of paragraph (c)(5) of this section, an electronic serial is an electronic work published in the United States and available only online, issued or intended to be issued on an established schedule in successive parts bearing numerical or chronological designations, without subsequent alterations, and intended to be continued indefinitely. This class includes periodicals, newspapers, annuals, and the journals, proceedings, transactions, and other publications of societies.

(5) The term literary monograph means a literary work published in one volume or a finite number of volumes. This category does not include serials, nor does it include legal publications that are published in one volume or a finite number of volumes that contain legislative enactments, judicial decisions, or other edicts of government.

(c) Exemptions from deposit requirements. The following categories of material are exempt from the deposit requirements of section 407(a) of title 17:

(1) Diagrams and models illustrating scientific or technical works or formulating scientific or technical information in linear or three-dimensional form, such as an architectural or engineering blueprint, plan, or design, a mechanical drawing, or an anatomical model.

(2) Greeting cards, picture postcards, and stationery.

(3) Lectures, sermons, speeches, and addresses when published individually and not as a collection of the works of one or more authors.

(4) Literary, dramatic, and musical works published only as embodied in phonorecords. This category does not exempt the owner of copyright, or of the exclusive right of publication, in a sound recording resulting from the fixation of such works in a phonorecord from the applicable deposit requirements for the sound recording.

(5) Electronic works published in the United States and available only online. This exemption includes electronic serials available only online only until such time as a demand is issued by the Copyright Office under the regulations set forth in §202.24. This exemption does not apply to works that are published in both online, electronic formats and in physical formats, which remain subject to the appropriate mandatory deposit requirements.

(6) Three-dimensional sculptural works, and any works published only as reproduced in or on jewelry, dolls, toys, games, plaques, floor coverings, wallpaper and similar commercial wall coverings, textiles and other fabrics, packaging material, or any useful article. Globes, relief models, and similar cartographic representations of area are not within this category and are subject to the applicable deposit requirements.

(7) Prints, labels, and other advertising matter, including catalogs, published in connection with the rental lease, lending, licensing, or sale of articles of merchandise, works of authorship, or services.

(8) Tests, and answer material for tests when published separately from other literary works.

(9) Works first published as individual contributions to collective works. This category does not exempt the owner of copyright, or of the exclusive right of publication, in the collective work as a whole, from the applicable deposit requirements for the collective work.

(10) Works first published outside the United States and later published in the United States without change in copyrightable content, if:

(i) Registration for the work was made under 17 U.S.C. 408 before the work was published in the United States; or

(ii) Registration for the work was made under 17 U.S.C. 408 after the work was published in the United States but before a demand for deposit is made under 17 U.S.C. 407(d).

(11) Works published only as embodied in a soundtrack that is an integral part of a motion picture. This category does not exempt the owner of copyright, or of the exclusive right of publication, in the motion picture, from the applicable deposit requirements for the motion picture.

(12) Motion pictures that consist of television transmission programs and that have been published, if at all, only by reason of a license or other grant to a nonprofit institution of the right to make a fixation of such programs directly from a transmission to the public, with or without the right to make further uses of such fixations.

(d) Nature of required deposit.

(1) Subject to the provisions of paragraph (d)(2) of this section, the deposit required to satisfy the provisions of section 407(a) of title 17 shall consist of:

(i) In the case of published works other than sound recordings, two complete copies of the best edition; and

(ii) In the case of published sound recordings, two complete phonorecords of the best edition.

(2) In the case of certain published works not exempt from deposit requirements under paragraph (c) of this section, the following special provisions shall apply:

(i) In the case of published three-dimensional cartographic representations of area, such as globes and relief models, the deposit of one complete copy of the best edition of the work will suffice in lieu of the two copies required by paragraph (d)(1) of this section.

(ii) In the case of published motion pictures, the deposit of one complete copy of the best edition of the work will suffice in lieu of the two copies required by paragraph (d)(1) of this section. Any deposit of a published motion picture must be accompanied by a separate description of its contents, such as a continuity, pressbook, or synopsis. The Library of Congress may, at its sole discretion, enter into an agreement permitting the return of copies of published motion pictures to the depositor under certain conditions and establishing certain rights and obligations of the Library with respect to such copies. In the event of termination of such an agreement by the Library it shall not be subject to reinstatement, nor shall the depositor or any successor in interest of the depositor be entitled to any similar or subsequent agreement with the Library, unless at the sole discretion of the Library it would be in the best interests of the Library to reinstate the agreement or enter into a new agreement.

(iii) In the case of any published work deposited in the form of a hologram, the deposit shall be accompanied by:

(A) Two sets of precise instructions for displaying the image fixed in the hologram; and

(B) Two sets of identifying material in compliance with §202.21 and clearly showing the displayed image.

(iv) In any case where an individual author is the owner of copyright in a published pictorial or graphic work and:

(A) Less than five copies of the work have been published; or

(B) The work has been published and sold or offered for sale in a limited edition consisting of no more than three hundred numbered copies, the deposit of one complete copy of the best edition of the work or, alternatively, the deposit of photographs or other identifying material in compliance with §202.21, will suffice in lieu of the two copies required by paragraph (d)(1) of this section.

(v) In the case of a musical composition published solely in copies, or in both copies and phonorecords, the deposit of one complete copy of the best edition will suffice in lieu of the two copies required by paragraph (d)(1) of this section.

(vi) In the case of published multimedia kits that include literary works, audiovisual works, sound recordings, or any combination of such works, the deposit of one complete copy of the best edition will suffice in lieu of the two copies required by paragraph (d)(1) of this section.

(vii) In the case of published computer programs and published computerized information works, such as statistical compendia, serials, and reference works that are not copy-protected, the deposit of one complete copy of the best edition as specified in the current Library of Congress Best Edition Statement will suffice in lieu of the two copies required by paragraph (d)(1) of this section. If the works are copy-protected, two copies of the best edition are required.

(viii) In the case of published architectural works, the deposit shall consist of the most finished form of presentation drawings in the following descending order of preference:

(A) Original format, or best quality form of reproduction, including offset or silk screen printing;

(B) Xerographic or photographic copies on good quality paper;

(C) Positive photostat or photodirect positive;

(D) Blue line copies (diazo or ozalid process). If photographs are submitted, they should be 8 x 10 inches and should clearly show several exterior and interior views. The deposit should disclose the name(s) of the architect(s) and draftsperson(s) and the building site.

(ix) In the case of published newspapers, a deposit submitted pursuant to and in compliance with the group registration option under §202.4(e) shall be deemed to satisfy the mandatory deposit obligation under this section.

(e) Special relief.

(1) In the case of any published work not exempt from deposit under paragraph (c) of this section, the Register of Copyrights may, after consultation with other appropriate officials of the Library of Congress and upon such conditions as the Register may determine after such consultation:

(i) Grant an exemption from the deposit requirements of section 407(a) of title 17 on an individual basis for single works or series or groups of works; or

(ii) Permit the deposit of one copy or phonorecord, or alternative identifying material, in lieu of the two copies or phonorecords required by paragraph (d)(1) of this section; or

(iii) Permit the deposit of incomplete copies or phonorecords, or copies or phonorecords other than those normally comprising the best edition; or

(iv) Permit the deposit of identifying material which does not comply with §202.21.

(2) Any decision as to whether to grant such special relief, and the conditions under which special relief is to be granted, shall be made by the Register of Copyrights after consultation with other appropriate officials of the Library of Congress, and shall be based upon the acquisition policies of the Library of Congress then in force.

(3) Requests for special relief under this paragraph shall be made in writing to the Associate Register of Copyrights and Director of the Office of Registration Policy and Practice, shall be signed by or on behalf of the owner of copyright or of the exclusive right of publication in the work, and shall set forth specific reasons why the request should be granted.

(4) The Register of Copyrights may, after consultation with other appropriate officials of the Library of Congress, terminate any ongoing or continuous grant of special relief. Notice of termination shall be given in writing and shall be sent to the individual person or organization to whom the grant of special relief had been given, at the last address shown in the records of the Copyright Office. A notice of termination may be given at any time, but it shall state a specific date of termination that is at least 30 days later than the date the notice is mailed. Termination shall not affect the validity of any deposit made earlier under the grant of special relief.

(f) Submission and receipt of copies and phonorecords.

(1) All copies and phonorecords deposited in the Copyright Office will be considered to be deposited only in compliance with section 407 of title 17 unless they are accompanied by an application for registration of a claim to copyright in the work represented by the deposit, and either a registration fee or a deposit account number. Copies or phonorecords deposited without such an accompanying application and either a fee or a deposit account notation will not be connected with or held for receipt of separate applications, and will not satisfy the deposit provisions of section 408 of title 17 or §202.20.

(2) All copies and phonorecords deposited in the Copyright Office under section 407 of title 17, unless accompanied by written instructions to the contrary, will be considered to be deposited by the person or persons named in the copyright notice on the work.

(3) Upon request by the depositor made at the time of the deposit, the Copyright Office will issue a certificate of receipt for the deposit of copies or phonorecords of a work under this section. Certificates of receipt will be issued in response to requests made after the date of deposit only if the requesting party is identified in the records of the Copyright Office as having made the deposit. In either case, requests for a certificate of receipt must be in writing and accompanied by the appropriate fee, as required in §201.3(c). A certificate of receipt will include identification of the depositor, the work deposited, and the nature and format of the copy or phonorecord deposited, together with the date of receipt.

History of 37 C.F.R. §202.19: 43 FR 41979, Sept. 19, 1978; 51 FR 6403, Feb. 24, 1986; 54 FR 42299, Oct. 16, 1989; 56 FR 47403, Sept. 19, 1991; 56 FR 59885, Nov. 19, 1991; 57 FR 45310, Oct. 1, 1992; 60 FR 34168, June 30, 1995; 64 FR 29522, June 1, 1999; 64 FR 62978, Nov. 18, 1999; 66 FR 34373, June 28, 2001; 73 FR 37839, July 1, 2008; 75 FR 3869, Feb. 24, 2010; 76 FR 27898, May 13, 2011; 82 FR 9360, Mar. 8, 2017; 83 FR 2372, Feb. 16, 2018; 83 FR 4147, Mar. 1, 2018.

A §202.20. DEPOSIT OF COPIES & PHONORECORDS FOR COPYRIGHT REGISTRATION

(a) General. This section prescribes rules pertaining to the deposit of copies and phonorecords of published and unpublished works for the purpose of copyright registration under section 408 of title 17 of the United States Code. The provisions of this section are not applicable to the deposit of copies and phonorecords for the Library of Congress under section 407 of title 17, except as expressly adopted in §202.19.

(b) Definitions. For the purposes of this section:

(1) The best edition of a work has the meaning set forth in §202.19(b)(1). For purposes of this section, if a work is first published in both hard copy, i.e., in a physically tangible format, and also in an electronic format, the current Library of Congress Best Edition Statement requirements pertaining to the hard copy format apply.

(2) A complete copy or phonorecord means the following:

(i) Unpublished works. Subject to the requirements of paragraph (b)(2)(vii) of this section, a "complete" copy or phonorecord of an unpublished work is a copy or phonorecord representing the entire copyrightable content of the work for which registration is sought;

(ii) Published works. Subject to the requirements of paragraphs (b)(2)(iv) through (vii) of this section, a "complete" copy or phonorecord of a published work includes all elements comprising the applicable unit of publication of the work, including elements that, if considered separately, would not be copyrightable subject matter. However, even where certain physically separable elements included in the applicable unit of publication are missing from the deposit, a copy or phonorecord will be considered "complete" for purposes of registration where:

(A) The copy or phonorecord deposited contains all parts of the work for which copyright registration is sought; and

(B) The removal of the missing elements did not physically damage the copy or phonorecord or garble its contents; and

(C) The work is exempt from the mandatory deposit requirements under section 407 of title 17 of the United States Code and §202.19(c) of these regulations, or the copy deposited consists entirely of a container, wrapper, or holder, such as an envelope, sleeve, jacket, slipcase, box, bag, folder, binder, or other receptacle acceptable for deposit under paragraph (c)(2) of this section;

(iii) Works submitted for registration in digital formats. A "complete" electronically filed work is one which is embodied in a digital file which contains:

(A) If the work is unpublished, all authorship elements for which registration is sought; and

(B) If the work is published solely in an electronic format, all elements constituting the work in its published form, i.e., the complete work as published, including metadata and authorship for which registration is not sought. Publication in an electronic only format requires submission of the digital file(s) in exact first-publication form and content.

(C) For works submitted electronically, any of the following file formats are acceptable for registration: PDF, TXT, WPD, DOC, TIF, SVG, JPG, XML, HTML, WAV, and MPEG family of formats, including MP3. This list of file formats is non-exhaustive and it may change, or be added to periodically. Changes will be noted in the list of acceptable formats on the Copyright Office website.

(D) Contact with the registration applicant may be necessary if the Copyright Office cannot access, view, or examine the content of any particular digital file that has been submitted for the registration of a work. For purposes of 17 U.S.C. 410(d), a deposit has not been received in the Copyright Office until a copy that can be reviewed by the Office is received.

(iv) Contributions to collective works. In the case of a published contribution to a collective work, a "complete" copy is one complete copy of the best edition of the entire collective work, the complete section containing the contribution if published in a newspaper, the contribution cut from the paper in which it appeared, or a photocopy of the contribution itself as it was published in the collective work;

(v) Sound recordings. In the case of published sound recordings, a "complete" phonorecord has the meaning set forth in §202.19(b)(2)(i);

(vi) Musical scores. In the case of a musical composition published in copies only, or in both copies and phonorecords:

(A) If the only publication of copies took place by the rental, lease, or lending of a full score and parts, a full score is a "complete" copy; and

(B) If the only publication of copies took place by the rental, lease, or lending of a conductor's score and parts, a conductor's score is a "complete" copy.

(vii) Motion pictures. In the case of a published or unpublished motion picture, a copy is "complete" if the reproduction of all of the visual and aural elements comprising the copyrightable subject matter in the work is clean, undamaged, undeteriorated, and free of splices, and if the copy itself and its physical housing are free of any defects that would interfere with the performance of the work or that would cause mechanical, visual, or audible defects or distortions.

(3) The terms secure test and literary monograph have the meanings set forth in §§202.13(b) and 202.19(b)(5).

(4) Title 17 means title 17 of the United States Code.

(5) For the purposes of determining the applicable deposit requirements under this section only, the following shall be considered unpublished motion pictures: motion pictures that consist of television transmission programs and that have been published, if at all, only by reason of a license or other grant to a nonprofit institution of the right to make a fixation of such programs directly from a transmission to the public, with or without the right to make further uses of such fixations.

(c) Nature of required deposit.

(1) Subject to the provisions of paragraph (c)(2) of this section, the deposit required to accompany an application for registration of claim to copyright under section 408 of title 17 shall consist of:

(i) In the case of unpublished works, one complete copy or phonorecord.

(ii) In the case of works first published in the United States before January 1, 1978, two complete copies or phonorecords of the work as first published.

(iii) In the case of works first published in the United States on or after January 1, 1978, two complete copies or phonorecords of the best edition.

(iv) In the case of works first published outside of the United States, one complete copy or phonorecord of the work either as first published or of the best edition. For purposes of this section, any works simultaneously first published within and outside of the United States shall be considered to be first published in the United States.

(2) In the case of certain works, the special provisions set forth in this clause shall apply. In any case where this clause specifies that one copy or phonorecord may be submitted, that copy or phonorecord shall represent the best edition, or the work as first published, as set forth in paragraph (c)(1) of this section.

(i) General. In the following cases the deposit of one complete copy or phonorecord will suffice in lieu of two copies or phonorecords:

(A) Published three-dimensional cartographic representations of area, such as globes and relief models.

(B) Published diagrams illustrating scientific or technical works or formulating scientific or technical information in linear or other two-dimensional form, such as an architectural or engineering blueprint, or a mechanical drawing.

(C) Published greeting cards, picture postcards, and stationery.

(D) Lectures, sermons, speeches, and addresses published individually and not as a collection of the works of one or more authors.

(E) Musical compositions published solely in copies or in both copies and phonorecords, provided that one complete copy (rather than a phonorecord) is deposited.

(F) Published multimedia kits or any part thereof.

(G) Works exempted from the requirement of depositing identifying material under paragraph (c)(2)(xi)(B) of this section.

(H) Literary, dramatic, and musical works published only as embodied in phonorecords, although this category does not exempt the owner of copyright in a sound recording.

(I) Choreographic works, pantomimes, literary, dramatic, and musical works published only as embodied in motion pictures.

(J) Published works in the form of two-dimensional games, decals, fabric patches or emblems, calendars, instructions for needle work, needle work and craft kits.

(K) Works reproduced on three-dimensional containers such as boxes, cases, and cartons.

(L) Published literary monographs.

(ii) Motion pictures. In the case of published or unpublished motion pictures, the deposit of one complete copy will suffice. The deposit of a copy or copies for any published or unpublished motion picture must be accompanied by a separate description of its contents, such as a continuity, pressbook, or synopsis. In any case where the deposit copy or copies required for registration of a motion picture cannot be viewed for examining purposes on equipment in the Registration Program of the Copyright Office, the description accompanying the deposit must comply with §202.21(h). The Library of Congress may, at its sole discretion, enter into an agreement permitting the return of copies of published motion pictures to the depositor under certain conditions and establishing certain rights and obligations of the Library of Congress with respect to such copies. In the event of termination of such an agreement by the Library, it shall not be subject to reinstatement, nor shall the depositor or any successor in interest of the depositor be entitled to any similar or subsequent agreement with the Library, unless at the sole discretion of the Library it would be in the best interests of the Library to reinstate the agreement or enter into a new agreement. In the case of unpublished motion pictures (including television transmission programs that have been fixed and transmitted to the public, but have not been published), the deposit of identifying material in compliance with §202.21 may be made and will suffice in lieu of an actual copy. In the case of colorized versions of motion pictures made from pre-existing black and white motion pictures, in addition to the deposit of one complete copy of the colorized motion picture and the separate description of its contents as specified above, the deposit shall consist of one complete print of the black and white version of the motion picture from which the colorized version was prepared. If special relief from this requirement is requested and granted, the claimant shall make a good faith effort to deposit the best available, near-archival quality black and white print, as a condition of any grant of special relief.

(iii) Holograms. In the case of any work deposited in the form of a three-dimensional hologram, the copy or copies shall be accompanied by:

(A) Precise instructions for displaying the image fixed in the hologram; and

(B) Photographs or other identifying material complying with §202.21 and clearly showing the displayed image.

The number of sets of instructions and identifying material shall be the same as the number of copies required. In the case of a work in the form of a two-dimensional hologram, the image of which is visible without the use of a machine or device, one actual copy of the work shall be deposited.

(iv) Certain pictorial and graphic works. In the case of any unpublished pictorial or graphic work, deposit of identifying material in compliance with §202.21 may be made and will suffice in lieu of deposit of an actual copy. In the case of a published pictorial or graphic work, deposit of one complete copy, or of identifying material in compliance with §202.21, may be made and will suffice in lieu of deposit of two actual copies where an individual author is the owner of copyright, and either:

(A) Less than five copies of the work have been published; or

(B) The work has been published and sold or offered for sale in a limited edition consisting of no more than 300 numbered copies.

(v) Commercial prints and labels. In the case of prints, labels, and other advertising matter, including catalogs, published in connection with the rental, lease, lending, licensing, or sale of articles of merchandise, works of authorship, or services, the deposit of one complete copy will suffice in lieu of two copies. Where the print or label is published in a larger work, such as a newspaper or other periodical, one copy of the entire page or pages upon which it appears may be submitted in lieu of the entire larger work. In the case of prints or labels physically inseparable from a three-dimensional object, identifying material complying with §202.21 must be submitted rather than an actual copy or copies except under the conditions of paragraph (c)(2)(xi)(B)(4) of this section.

(vi) Tests. In the case of tests, and answer material for tests, published separately from other literary works, the deposit of one complete copy will suffice in lieu of two copies. In the case of any secure test the applicant may submit identifying material in lieu of one complete copy if the conditions set forth in §202.13(c) have been met.

(vii) Computer programs and databases embodied in machine-readable copies other than CD-ROM format. In cases where a computer program, database, compilation, statistical compendium, or the like, if unpublished is fixed, or if published is published only in the form of machine-readable copies (such as magnetic tape or disks, punched cards, semiconductor chip products, or the like) other than a CD-ROM format, from which the work cannot ordinarily be perceived except with the aid of a machine or device, the deposit shall consist of:

(A) For published or unpublished computer programs, one copy of identifying portions of the program, reproduced in a form visually perceptible without the aid of a machine or device, either on paper or in microform. For these purposes "identifying portions" shall mean one of the following:

(1) The first and last 25 pages or equivalent units of the source code if reproduced on paper, or at least the first and last 25 pages or equivalent units of the source code if reproduced in microform, together with the page or equivalent unit containing the copyright notice, if any. If the program is 50 pages or less, the required deposit will be the entire source code. In the case of revised versions of computer programs, if the revisions occur throughout the entire program, the deposit of the page containing the copyright notice and the first and last 25 pages of source code will suffice; if the revisions do not occur in the first and last 25 pages, the deposit should consist of the page containing the copyright notice and any 50 pages of source code representative of the revised material; or

(2) Where the program contains trade secret material, the page or equivalent unit containing the copyright notice, if any, plus one of the following: the first and last 25 pages or equivalent units of source code with portions of the source code containing trade secrets blocked-out, provided that the blocked-out portions are proportionately less than the material remaining, and the deposit reveals an appreciable amount of original computer code; or the first and last 10 pages or equivalent units of source code alone with no blocked-out portions; or the first and last 25 pages of object code, together with any 10 or more consecutive pages of source code with no blocked-out portions; or for programs consisting of, or less than, 50 pages or equivalent units, the entire source code with the trade secret portions blocked-out, provided that the blocked-out portions are proportionately less than the material remaining, and the remaining portion reveals an appreciable amount of original computer code. If the copyright claim is in a revision not contained in the first and last 25 pages, the deposit shall consist of either 20 pages of source code representative of the revised material with no blocked-out portions, or any 50 pages of source code representative of the revised material with portions of the source code containing trade secrets blocked-out, provided that the blocked-out portions are proportionately less than the material remaining and the deposit reveals an appreciable amount of original computer code. Whatever method is used to block out trade secret material, at least an appreciable amount of original computer code must remain visible.

(B) Where registration of a program containing trade secrets is made on the basis of an object code deposit the Copyright Office will make registration under its rule of doubt and warn that no determination has been made concerning the existence of copyrightable authorship.

(C) Where the application to claim copyright in a computer program includes a specific claim in related computer screen displays, the deposit, in addition to the identifying portions specified in paragraph (c)(2)(vii)(A) of this section, shall consist of:

(1) Visual reproductions of the copyrightable expression in the form of printouts, photographs, or drawings no smaller than 3x3 inches and no larger than 9x12 inches; or

(2) If the authorship in the work is predominantly audiovisual, a one-half inch VHS format videotape reproducing the copyrightable expression, except that printouts, photographs, or drawings no smaller than 3x3 inches and no larger than 9x12 inches must be deposited in lieu of videotape where the computer screen material simply constitutes a demonstration of the functioning of the computer program.

(D) For published and unpublished automated databases, compilations, statistical compendia, and the like, so fixed or published, one copy of identifying portions of the work, reproduced in a form visually perceptible without the aid of a machine or device, either on paper or in microform. For these purposes:

(1) Identifying portions shall generally mean either the first and last 25 pages or equivalent units of the work if reproduced on paper or in microform.

(2) Datafile and file shall mean a group of data records pertaining to a common subject matter regardless of their size or the number of data items in them.

(3) In the case of individual registration of a revised version of the works identified in paragraph (c)(2)(vii)(D) of this section, the identifying portions deposited shall contain 50 representative pages or data records which have been added or modified.

(4) If the work is an automated database comprising multiple separate or distinct data files, "identifying portions" shall instead consist of 50 complete data records from each data file or the entire data file, whichever is less, and the descriptive statement required by paragraph (c)(2)(vii)(D)(5) of this section.

(5) In the case of group registration for revised or updated versions of a database, the claimant shall deposit identifying portions that contain 50 representative pages or equivalent units, or representative data records which have been marked to disclose (or do in fact disclose solely) the new material added on one representative publication date if published, or on one representative creation date, if unpublished, or in the case of applications for automated databases that predominantly consist of photographs, the claimant shall deposit identifying portions that comply with (D)(8) of this section; the claimant shall also deposit a brief typed or printed descriptive statement containing the notice of copyright information

required under paragraphs (c)(2)(vii)(D)(6) or (7) of this section, if the work bears a notice, and;

(i) The title of the database;

(ii) A subtitle, date of creation or publication, or other information, to distinguish any separate or distinct data files for cataloging purposes;

(iii) The name and address of the copyright claimant;

(iv) For each separate file, its name and content, including its subject, the origin(s) of the data, and the approximate number of data records it contains; and

(v) In the case of revised or updated versions of an automated database, information as to the nature and frequency of changes in the database and some identification of the location within the database or the separate data files of the revisions.

(6) For a copyright notice embodied in machine-readable form, the statement shall describe exactly the visually perceptible content of the notice which appears in or with the database, and the manner and frequency with which it is displayed (e.g., at user's terminal only at sign-on, or continuously on terminal display, or on printouts, etc.).

(7) If a visually perceptible copyright notice is placed on any copies of the work (or on magnetic tape reels or containers therefor), a sample of such notice must also accompany the statement.

(8) In the case of an application for registration of a database that consists predominantly of photographs (including a group registration for revised or updated versions of such a database), "identifying portions" shall instead consist of all individual photographs included in the claim. Photographs must be submitted in digital form in one of the following formats: JPEG, GIF, or TIFF. In addition, the applicant must submit a sequentially numbered list containing the title and file name—and if the photographs have been published, the month and year of publication—for each photograph in the group. The title and file name for a particular photograph may be the same and may consist of letters, numbers, and spaces, but the file name should not contain any other form of punctuation. The numbered list must be contained in an electronic file in Excel format (.xls), Portable Document Format (PDF), or other electronic format approved by the Office. The file name for the list must contain the title of the database, and the case number assigned to the application by the electronic registration system, if any (e.g., "Title Of Database Case Number 162883927239.xls"). The photographs and the numbered list may be uploaded to the electronic registration system with the permission and under the direction of the Visual Arts Division, preferably in a .zip file containing these materials. The file size for each uploaded file must not exceed 500 megabytes; the photographs may be compressed to comply with this requirement. Alternatively, the photographs and the numbered list may be saved on a physical storage device, such as a flash drive, CD-R, or DVD-R, and delivered to the Copyright Office together with the required shipping slip generated by the electronic registration system or with a paper application submitted on Form VA.

(viii) Machine-readable copies of works other than computer programs, databases, and works fixed in a CD-ROM format. Where a literary, musical, pictorial, graphic, or audiovisual work, or a sound recording, except for works fixed in a CD-ROM format and literary works which are computer programs, databases, compilations, statistical compendia or the like, if unpublished has been fixed or, if published, has been published only in machine-readable form, the deposit must consist of identifying material. The type of identifying material submitted should generally be appropriate to the type of work embodied in machine-readable form, but in all cases should be that which best represents the copyrightable content of the work. In all cases the identifying material must include the title of the work. A synopsis may also be requested in addition to the other deposit materials as appropriate in the discretion of the Copyright Office. In the case of any published work subject to this section, the identifying material must include a representation of the copyright notice, if one exists. Identifying material requirements for certain types of works are specified below. In the case of the types of works listed below, the requirements specified shall apply except that, in any case where the specific requirements are not appropriate for a given work the form of the identifying material required will be determined by the Copyright Office in consultation with the applicant, but the Copyright Office will make the final determination of the acceptability of the identifying material.

(A) For pictorial or graphic works, the deposit shall consist of identifying material in compliance with §202.21.

(B) For audiovisual works, the deposit shall consist of either a videotape of the work depicting representative portions of the copyrightable content, or a series of photographs or drawings, depicting representative portions of the work, plus in all cases a separate synopsis of the work.

(C) For musical compositions, the deposit shall consist of a transcription of the entire work such as a score, or a reproduction of the entire work on a phonorecord.

(D) For sound recordings, the deposit shall consist of a reproduction of the entire work on a phonorecord.

(E) For literary works, the deposit shall consist of a transcription of representative portions of the work including the first and last 25 pages or equivalent units, and five or more pages indicative of the remainder.

(ix) Copies containing both visually-perceptible and machine-readable material other than a CD-ROM format. Where a published literary work is embodied in copies containing both visually-perceptible and machine-readable material, except in the case of a CD-ROM format, the deposit shall consist of the visually-perceptible material and identifying portions of the machine-readable material.

(x) Works reproduced in or on sheetlike materials. In the case of any unpublished work that is fixed, or any published work that is published, only in the form of a two-dimensional reproduction on sheetlike materials such as textiles and other fabrics, wallpaper and similar commercial wall coverings, carpeting, floor tile, and similar commercial floor coverings, and wrapping paper and similar packaging material, the deposit shall consist of one copy in the form of an actual swatch or piece of such material sufficient to show all elements of the work in which copyright is claimed and the copyright notice appearing on the work, if any. If the work consists of a repeated pictorial or graphic design, the complete design and at least part of one repetition must be shown. If the sheetlike material in or on which a published work has been reproduced has been embodied in or attached to a three-dimensional object, such as furniture, or any other three-dimensional manufactured article, and the work has been published only in that form, the deposit must consist of identifying material complying with §202.21 instead of a copy. If the sheetlike material in or on which a published work has been reproduced has been embodied in or attached to a two-dimensional object such as wearing apparel, bed linen, or a similar item, and the work has been published only in that form, the deposit must consist of identifying material complying with §202.21 instead of a copy unless the copy can be folded for storage in a form that does not exceed four inches in thickness.

(xi) Works reproduced in or on three-dimensional objects.

(A) In the following cases the deposit must consist of identifying material complying with §201.21 of this chapter instead of a copy or copies:

(1) Any three-dimensional sculptural work, including any illustration or formulation of artistic expression or information in three-dimensional form. Examples of such works include statues, carvings, ceramics, moldings, constructions, models, and maquettes; and

(2) Any two-dimensional or three-dimensional work that, if unpublished, has been fixed, or, if published, has been published only in or on jewelry, dolls, toys, games, except as provided in paragraph (c)(2)(xi)(B)(3) of this section, or any three-dimensional useful article.

(B) In the following cases the requirements of paragraph (c)(2)(xi)(A) of this section for the deposit of identifying material shall not apply:

(1) Three-dimensional cartographic representations of area, such as globes and relief models;

(2) Works that have been fixed or published in or on a useful article that comprises one of the elements of the unit of publication of an educational or instructional kit which also includes a literary or audiovisual work, a sound recording, or any combination of such works;

(3) Published games consisting of multiple parts that are packaged and published in a box or similar container with flat sides and with dimensions of no more than 12x24x6 inches;

(4) Works reproduced on three-dimensional containers or holders such as boxes, cases, and cartons, where the container or holder can be readily opened out, unfolded, slit at the corners, or in some other way made adaptable for flat storage, and the copy, when flattened, does not exceed 96 inches in any dimension; or

(5) Any three-dimensional sculptural work that, if unpublished, has been fixed, or, if published, has been published only in the form of jewelry cast in base metal which does not exceed four inches in any dimension.

(xii) Soundtracks. For separate registration of an unpublished work that is fixed, or a published work that is published, only as embodied in a soundtrack that is an integral part of a motion picture, the deposit of identifying material in compliance with §202.21 will suffice in lieu of an actual copy of the motion picture.

(xiii) Oversize deposits. In any case where the deposit otherwise required by this section exceeds 96 inches in any dimension, identifying material complying with §202.21 must be submitted instead of an actual copy or copies.

(xiv) Pictorial advertising material. In the case of published pictorial advertising material, except for advertising material published in connection with motion pictures, the deposit of either one copy as published or prepublication material consisting of camera-ready copy is acceptable.

(xv) Contributions to collective works. In the case of published contributions to collective works, the deposit of either one complete copy of the best edition of the entire collective work, the complete section containing the contribution if published in a newspaper, the entire page containing the contribution, the contribution cut from the paper in which it appeared, or a photocopy of the contribution itself as it was published in the collective work, will suffice in lieu of two complete copies of the entire collective work.

(xvi) Phonorecords. In any case where the phonorecord or phonorecords submitted for registration of a claim to copyright is inaudible on audio playback devices in the Registration Program of the Copyright Office, the Office will seek an appropriate deposit in accordance with paragraph (d) of this section.

(xvii) Group registration of serials. For group registration of related serials, as specified in §202.3(b)(6), for applicants filing electronically, the deposit must consist of one complete copy of the best edition of each issue included in the group registration, or a digital format of a complete copy which complies with §202.20(b)(2)(iii). For applicants filing a completed Form SE/Group, the deposit must consist of one complete copy of the best edition of each issue included in the group registration. In addition, for all filings for group registration of serial issues, two complimentary subscriptions to any serial for which group registration is sought must be entered and maintained in the name of the Library of Congress, and the copies must be submitted regularly and promptly after publication.

(xviii) Architectural works.

(A) For designs of unconstructed buildings, the deposit must consist of one complete copy of an architectural drawing or blueprint in visually perceptible form showing the overall form of the building and any interior arrangements of spaces and/or design elements in which copyright is claimed.[6] For archival purposes, the Copyright Office prefers that the drawing submissions consist of the following in descending order of preference:

(1) Original format, or best quality form of reproduction, including offset or silk screen printing;

(2) Xerographic or photographic copies on good quality paper;

(3) Positive photostat or photodirect positive;

(4) Blue line copies (diazo or ozalid process).

(B) For designs of constructed buildings, the deposit must consist of one complete copy of an architectural drawing or blueprint in visually perceptible form showing the overall form of the building and any interior arrangement of spaces and/or design elements in which copyright is claimed. In addition, the deposit must also include identifying material in the form of photographs complying with §202.21, which clearly discloses the architectural works being registered.[7] For archival purposes, the Copyright Office prefers that the drawing submissions constitute the most finished form of presentation drawings and consist of the following in descending order of preference:

(1) Original format, or best quality form of reproduction, including offset or silk screen printing;

(2) Xerographic or photographic copies on good quality paper;

(3) Positive photostat or photodirect positive;

(4) Blue line copies (diazo or ozalid process).

(xix) Works fixed in a CD-ROM format.

(A) Where a work is fixed in a CD-ROM format, the deposit must consist of one complete copy of the entire CD-ROM package, including a complete copy of any accompanying operating software and instructional manual, and a printed version of the work embodied in the CD-ROM, if the work is fixed in print as well as a CD-ROM. A complete copy of a published CD-ROM package includes all of the elements comprising the applicable unit of publication, including elements that if considered separately would not be copyrightable subject matter or could be the subject of a separate registration.

(B) In any case where the work fixed in a CD-ROM package cannot be viewed on equipment available in the Registration Program of the Copyright Office, the Office will seek an appropriate deposit in accordance with paragraph (d) of this section, in addition to the deposit of the CD-ROM package.

(d) Special relief.

(1) In any case the Register of Copyrights may, after consultation with other appropriate officials of the Library of Congress and upon such conditions as the Register may determine after such consultation:

(i) Permit the deposit of one copy or phonorecord, or alternative identifying material, in lieu of the one or two copies or phonorecords otherwise required by paragraph (c)(1) of this section; or

(ii) Permit the deposit of incomplete copies or phonorecords, or copies or phonorecords other than those normally comprising the best edition; or

(iii) Permit the deposit of an actual copy or copies, in lieu of the identifying material otherwise required by this section or §202.4; or

(iv) Permit the deposit of identifying material which does not comply with §202.4 or §202.21.

(2) Any decision as to whether to grant such special relief, and the conditions under which special relief is to be granted, shall be made by the Register of Copyrights after consultation with other appropriate officials of the Library of Congress, and shall be based upon the acquisition policies of the Library of Congress then in force and the archival and examining requirements of the Copyright Office.

(3) Requests for special relief under this paragraph may be combined with requests for special relief under §202.19(e). Whether so combined or made solely under this paragraph, such requests shall be made in writing to the Associate Register of Copyrights and Director of the Office of Registration Policy and Practice, shall be signed by or on behalf of the person signing the application for registration, and shall set forth specific reasons why the request should be granted.

(4) The Register of Copyrights may, after consultation with other appropriate officials of the Library of Congress, terminate any ongoing or continuous grant of special relief. Notice of termination shall be given in writing and shall be sent to the individual person or organization to whom the grant of special relief had been given, at the last address shown in the records of the Copyright Office. A notice of termination may be given at any time, but it shall state a specific date of termination that is at least 30 days later than the date the notice is mailed. Termination shall not affect the validity of any deposit or registration made earlier under the grant of special relief.

(e) Use of copies and phonorecords deposited for the Library of Congress. Copies and phonorecords deposited for the Library of Congress under 17 U.S.C. 407 and §202.19 may be used to satisfy the deposit provisions of this section if they are accompanied by an application for registration of a claim to copyright in the work represented by the deposit, and either a registration fee or a deposit account number.

6. The Copyright Office prefers that the deposit disclose the name(s) of the architect(s) and draftsperson(s) and the building site, if known.

7. With respect to the accompanying photographs, the Copyright Office prefers 8 x 10 inches, good quality photographs, which clearly show several exterior and interior views. The Copyright Office prefers that the deposit disclose the name(s) of the architect(s) and draftsperson(s) and the building site.

History of 37 C.F.R. §202.20: 43 FR 41979, Sept. 19, 1978; 51 FR 6405, Feb. 24, 1986; 53 FR 29890, Aug. 9, 1988; 54 FR 13176, Mar. 31, 1989; 54 FR 13181, Mar. 31, 1989; 54 FR 21059, May 16, 1989; 55 FR 50557, Dec. 7, 1990; 56 FR 47403, Sept. 19, 1991; 56 FR 55632, Oct. 29, 1991; 56 FR 60065, Nov. 27, 1991; 56 FR 65191, Dec. 16, 1991; 57 FR 45310, Oct. 1, 1992; 60 FR 34168, June 30, 1995; 62 FR 35421, July 1, 1997; 64 FR 36575, July 7, 1999; 66 FR 37150, July 17, 2001; 72 FR 36889, July 6, 2007; 72 FR 40746, July 25, 2007; 73 FR 37839, July 1, 2008; 76 FR 4076, Jan. 24, 2011; 76 FR 27898, May 13, 2011; 77 FR 40270, Aug. 8, 2012; 77 FR 66921, Nov. 8, 2012; 82 FR 9361, Mar. 8, 2017; 82 FR 26854, July 12, 2017; 82 FR 29414, July 31, 2017; 83 FR 2372, Feb. 16, 2018; 83 FR 2548, Feb. 20, 2018.

§202.21. DEPOSIT OF IDENTIFYING MATERIAL INSTEAD OF COPIES

(a) General. Subject to the specific provisions of paragraphs (f) and (g) of this section, and §§202.19(e)(1)(iv) and 202.20(d)(1)(iv), in any case where the deposit of identifying material is permitted or required under §202.19 or §202.20 for published or unpublished works, the material shall consist of photographic prints, transparencies, photostats, drawings, or similar two-dimensional reproductions or renderings of the work, in a form visually perceivable without the aid of a machine or device. In the case of pictorial or graphic works, such material should reproduce the actual colors employed in the work. In all other cases, such material may be in black and white or may consist of a reproduction of the actual colors.

(b) Completeness; number of sets. As many pieces of identifying material as are necessary to show the entire copyrightable content in the ordinary case, but in no case less than an adequate representation of such content, of the work for which deposit is being made, or for which registration is being sought shall be submitted. Except in cases falling under the provisions of §202.19(d)(2)(iii) or §202.20(c)(2)(iii) with respect to holograms, only one set of such complete identifying material is required.

(c) Size. Photographic transparencies must be at least 35mm in size and, if such transparencies are 3x3 inches or less, must be fixed in cardboard, plastic, or similar mounts to facilitate identification, handling, and storage. The Copyright Office prefers that transparencies larger than 3x3 inches be mounted in a way that facilitates their handling and preservation, and reserves the right to require such mounting in particular cases. All types of identifying material other than photographic transparencies must be not less than 3x3 inches and not more than 9x12 inches, but preferably 8x10 inches. Except in the case of transparencies, the image of the work must be either lifesize or larger, or if less than lifesize must be large enough to show clearly the entire copyrightable content of the work.

(d) Title and dimensions. At least one piece of identifying material must, on its front, back, or mount, indicate the title of the work; and the indication of an exact measurement of one or more dimensions of the work is preferred.

(e) Copyright notice. In the case of works published with notice of copyright, the notice and its position on the work must be clearly shown on at least one piece of identifying material. Where necessary because of the size or position of the notice, a separate drawing or similar reproduction shall be submitted. Such reproduction shall be no smaller than 3x3 inches and no larger than 9x12 inches, and shall show the exact appearance and content of the notice, and its specific position on the work.

(f) For separate registration of an unpublished work that is fixed, or a published work that is published, only as embodied in a soundtrack that is an integral part of a motion picture, identifying material deposited in lieu of an actual copy of the motion picture shall consist of:

(1) A transcription of the entire work, or a reproduction of the entire work on a phonorecord; and

(2) Photographs or other reproductions from the motion picture showing the title of the motion picture, the soundtrack credits, and the copyright notice for the soundtrack, if any.

The provisions of paragraphs (b), (c), (d), and (e) of this section do not apply to identifying material deposited under this paragraph (f).

(g)(1) In the case of unpublished motion pictures (including transmission programs that have been fixed and transmitted to the public, but have not been published), identifying material deposited in lieu of an actual copy shall consist of either:

(i) An audio cassette or other phonorecord reproducing the entire soundtrack or other sound portion of the motion picture, and a description of the motion picture; or

(ii) A set consisting of one frame enlargement or similar visual reproduction from each 10-minute segment of the motion picture, and a description of the motion picture.

(2) In either case the "description" may be a continuity, a pressbook, or a synopsis but in all cases it must include:

(i) The title or continuing title of the work, and the episode title, if any;

(ii) The nature and general content of the program;

(iii) The date when the work was first fixed and whether or not fixation was simultaneous with first transmission;

(iv) The date of first transmission, if any;

(v) The running time; and

(vi) The credits appearing on the work, if any.

(3) The provisions of paragraphs (b), (c), (d), and (e) of this section do not apply to identifying material submitted under this paragraph (g).

(h) In the case where the deposit copy or copies of a motion picture cannot be viewed for examining purposes on equipment in the Registration Program of the Copyright Office, the "description" required by §202.20(c)(2)(ii) may be a continuity, a press-book, a synopsis, or a final shooting script but in all cases must be sufficient to indicate the copyrightable material in the work and include

(1) The continuing title of the work and the episode title, if any;

(2) The nature and general content of the program and of its dialogue or narration, if any;

(3) The running time; and

(4) All credits appearing on the work including the copyright notice, if any.

The provisions of paragraphs (b), (c), and (d) of this section do not apply to identifying material submitted under this paragraph (h).

History of 37 C.F.R. §202.21: 43 FR 41983, Sept. 19, 1978; 51 FR 6409, Feb. 24, 1986; 73 FR 37839, July 1, 2008; 76 FR 27898, May 13, 2011; 82 FR 9362, Mar. 8, 2017.

§202.22. ACQUISITION & DEPOSIT OF UNPUBLISHED AUDIO & AUDIOVISUAL TRANSMISSION PROGRAMS

(a) General. This section prescribes rules pertaining to the acquisition of phonorecords and copies of unpublished audio and audiovisual transmission programs by the Library of Congress under section 407(e) of title 17 of the United States Code, as amended. It also prescribes rules pertaining to the use of such phonorecords and copies in the registration of claims to copyright, under section 408(b).

(b) Definitions. For purposes of this section:

(1) The terms copies, fixed, phonorecords, publication, and transmission program and their variant forms, have the meanings given to them in section 101 of title 17. The term network station has the meaning given it in section 111(f) of title 17. For the purpose of this section, the term transmission includes transmission via the Internet, cable, broadcasting, and satellite systems, and via any other existing or future devices or processes for the communication of a performance or display whereby images or sounds are received beyond the place from which they are sent.

(2) "Title 17" means Title 17 of the United States Code, as amended.

(c) Recording of transmission programs.

(1) Library of Congress employees, including Library of Congress contractors, acting under the general authority of the Librarian of Congress, may make a fixation of an unpublished audio or audiovisual transmission program directly from a transmission to the public in the United States, in accordance with subsections 407(e)(1) and (4) of title 17 of the United States Code. The choice of programs selected for fixation shall be based on the Library of Congress's acquisition policies in effect at the time of fixation. Specific notice of an intent to record a transmission program will ordinarily not be given. In general, the Library of Congress will seek to record a substantial portion of the television programming transmitted by noncommercial educational broadcast stations as defined in section 397 of title 47 of the United States Code, and will record selected programming transmitted by commercial television broadcast stations, both network and independent. The Library will also record a selected portion of the radio programming transmitted by commercial and noncommercial broadcast stations. Additionally, the Library will record a selected portion of unpublished Internet, cable and satellite programming transmitted to the public in the United States.

(2) Upon written request addressed to the Chief, Motion Picture, Broadcasting and Recorded Sound Division by a broadcast station or other owner of the right of transmission, the Library of Congress will inform the requestor whether a particular transmission program has been recorded by the Library.

(3) The Library of Congress will not knowingly record any unfixed or published transmission program under the recording authority of section 407(e) of Title 17 of the United States Code.

(4) The Library of Congress is entitled under this paragraph (c) to presume that a radio program transmitted to the public in the United States has been fixed but not published at the time of transmission, and that a television program transmitted to the public in the United States by a noncommercial educational broadcast station as defined in section 397 of title 47 of the United States Code has been fixed but not published.

(5) The presumption established by paragraph (c)(4) of this section may be overcome by written declaration and submission of appropriate documentary evidence to the Chief, Motion Picture, Broadcasting and Recorded Sound Division, either before or after recording of the particular transmission program by the Library of Congress. Such written submission shall contain:

(i) The identification, by title and time of broadcast, of the transmission program in question;

(ii) A brief statement declaring either that the program was not fixed or that it was published at the time of transmission;

(iii) If it is declared that the program was published at the time of transmission, a brief statement of the facts of publication, including the date and place thereof, the method of publication, the name of the owner of the right of first publication, and whether the work was published in the United States; and

(iv) The actual handwritten signature of an officer or other duly authorized agent of the organization which transmitted the program in question.

(6) A declaration that the program was unfixed at the time of transmission shall be accepted by the Library of Congress, unless the Library can cite evidence to the contrary, and the copy or phonorecord will either be

(i) Erased; or

(ii) Retained, if requested by the owner of copyright or of any exclusive right, to satisfy the deposit provision of section 408 of Title 17 of the United States Code.

(7) If it is declared that the program was published at the time of transmission, the Library of Congress is entitled under this section to retain the copy or phonorecord to satisfy the deposit requirement of section 407(a) of title 17 of the United States Code.

(8) The Library of Congress shall maintain a list of the radio, cable, Internet and satellite transmission programs that the Library has recorded on the Motion Picture, Broadcasting and Recorded Sound Division website at http://www.loc.gov/rr/record/ for audio transmission programs, or http://www.loc.gov/rr/mopic/ for audiovisual transmission programs, and, in making fixations of such unpublished transmission programs, shall identify a program that the Library has recorded by including that transmission program on the list no later than fourteen days after such fixation has occurred. The Library of Congress in making fixations of unpublished television transmission programs transmitted by commercial broadcast stations shall not do so without notifying the transmitting organization or its agent that such activity is taking place. In the case of television network stations, the notification will be sent to the particular network. In the case of any other commercial television broadcasting station, the notification will be sent to the particular broadcast station that has transmitted, or will transmit, the program. Such notice shall, if possible, be given by the Library of Congress prior to the time of broadcast. In every case, the Library of Congress shall transmit such notice no later than fourteen days after such fixation has occurred. Such notice shall contain:

(i) The identification, by title and time of broadcast, of the transmission program in question;

(ii) A brief statement asserting the Library of Congress' belief that the transmission program has been, or will be by the date of transmission, fixed and is unpublished, together with language converting the notice to a demand for deposit under section 407 (a) and (b) of title 17 of the United States Code, if the transmission program has been published in the United States.

(9) The notice required by paragraph (c)(8) of this section shall not cover more than one transmission program except that the notice may cover up to thirteen episodes of one title if such episodes are generally scheduled to be broadcast at the same time period on a regular basis, or may cover all the episodes comprising the title if they are scheduled to be broadcast within a period of not more than two months.

(d) Demands for deposit of a transmission program.

(1) The Register of Copyrights may make a written demand upon the owner of the right of transmission in the United States to deposit a copy or phonorecord of a specific transmission program for the benefit of the Library of Congress under the authority of section 407(e)(2) of Title 17 of the United States Code.

(2) The Register of Copyrights is entitled to presume, unless clear evidence to the contrary is proffered, that the transmitting organization is the owner of the United States transmission right.

(3) Notices of demand shall be in writing and shall contain:

(i) The identification, by title and time of broadcast, of the work in question;

(ii) An explanation of the optional forms of compliance, including transfer of ownership of a copy or phonorecord to the Library, lending a copy or phonorecord to the Library for reproduction, or selling a copy or phonorecord to the Library at a price not to exceed the cost of reproducing and supplying the copy or phonorecord;

(iii) A ninety-day deadline by which time either compliance or a request for an extension of a request to adjust the scope of the demand or the method for fulfilling it shall have been received by the Register of Copyrights;

(iv) A brief description of the controls which are placed on the use of the copies or phonorecords;

(v) A statement concerning the Register's perception of the publication status of the program, together with language converting this demand to a demand for a deposit, under 17 U.S.C. 407, if the recipient takes the position that the work is published; and

(vi) A statement that a "compliance copy, or in the case of an audio transmission program, a compliance phonorecord," must be made and retained if the notice is received prior to transmission.

(4) With respect to paragraph (d)(3)(ii) of this section, the sale of a copy or phonorecord in compliance with a demand of this nature shall be at a price not to exceed the cost to the Library of reproducing and supplying the copy or phonorecord. The notice of demand should therefore inform the recipient of that cost and set that cost, plus reasonable shipping charges, as the maximum price for such a sale.

(5) Copies and phonorecords transferred, lent, or sold under paragraph (d) of this section shall be of sound physical condition as described in Appendix A to this section.

(6) Special Relief. In the case of any demand made under paragraph (d) of this section the Register of Copyrights may, after consultation with other appropriate officials of the Library of Congress and upon such conditions as the Register may determine after such consultation,

(i) Extend the time period provided in subparagraph (d)(3)(iii);

(ii) Make adjustments in the scope of the demand; or

(iii) Make adjustments in the method of fulfilling the demand. Any decision as to whether to allow such extension or adjustments shall be made by the Register of Copyrights after consultation with other appropriate officials of the Library of Congress and shall be made as reasonably warranted by the circumstances. Requests for special relief under paragraph (d) of this section shall be made in writing to the Copyright

Acquisitions Division, shall be signed by or on behalf of the owner of the right of transmission in the United States and shall set forth the specific reasons why the request should be granted.

(e) Disposition and use of copies and phonorecords.

(1) All copies and phonorecords acquired under this section shall be maintained by the Motion Picture, Broadcasting and Recorded Sound Division of the Library of Congress. The Library may make one archival copy or phonorecord of a program which it has fixed under the provisions of section 407(e)(1) of Title 17 of the United States Code and paragraph (c) of this section.

(2) All copies and phonorecords acquired or made under this section, except copies and phonorecords of transmission programs consisting of a regularly scheduled newscast or on-the-spot coverage of news events, shall be subject to the following restrictions concerning copying and access: in the case of television or other audiovisual transmission programs, copying and access are governed by Library of Congress Regulation 818-17, Policies Governing the Use and Availability of Motion Pictures and Other Audiovisual Works in the Collections of the Library of Congress, or its successors; in the case of audio transmission programs, copying and access are governed by Library of Congress Regulation 818-18.1, Recorded Sound Listening and Duplication Services, or its successors. Transmission programs consisting of regularly scheduled newscasts or on-the-spot coverage of news events are subject to the provisions of the "American Television and Radio Archives Act," 2 U.S.C. 170, and such regulations as the Librarian of Congress shall prescribe.

(f) Registration of claims to copyright.

(1) Copies and phonorecords fixed by the Library of Congress under the provisions of paragraph (c) of this section may be used as the deposit for copyright registration provided that:

(i) The application and fee, in a form acceptable for registration, is received by the Copyright Office no later than ninety days after transmission of the program, and

(ii) Correspondence received by the Copyright Office in the envelope containing the application and fee states that a fixation of the instant work was made by the Library of Congress and requests that the copy or phonorecord so fixed be used to satisfy the registration deposit provisions.

(2) Copies and phonorecords transferred, lent, or sold to the Library of Congress under the provisions of paragraph (d) of this section may be used as the deposit for copyright registration purposes only when the application and fee, in a form acceptable for registration, accompany, in the same container, the copy or phonorecord lent, transferred, or sold, and there is an explanation that the copy or phonorecord is intended to satisfy both the demand issued under section 407(e)(2) of Title 17 of the United States Code and the registration deposit provisions.

(g) Agreements modifying the terms of this section.

(1) The Library of Congress may, at its sole discretion, enter into an agreement whereby the provision of copies or phonorecords of unpublished audio or audiovisual transmission programs on terms different from those contained in this section is authorized.

(2) Any such agreement may be terminated without notice by the Library of Congress.

History of 37 C.F.R. §202.22: 48 FR 37208, Aug. 17, 1983; 56 FR 7815, Feb. 26, 1991; 60 FR 34168, June 30, 1995; 64 FR 36575, July 7, 1999; 65 FR 48914, Aug. 10, 2000; 66 FR 34373, June 28, 2001; 69 FR 62411, Oct. 26, 2004; 82 FR 9362, Mar. 8, 2017.

§202.23. FULL TERM RETENTION OF COPYRIGHT DEPOSITS

(a) General.

(1) This section prescribes conditions under which a request for full term retention, under the control of the Copyright Office, of copyright deposits (copies, phonorecords, or identifying material) of published works may be made and granted or denied pursuant to section 704(e) of Title 17 of the United States Code. Only copies, phonorecords, or identifying material deposited in connection with registration of a claim to copyright under Title 17 of the United States Code are within the provisions of this section. Only the depositor or the copyright owner of record of the work identified by the copyright deposit, or a duly authorized agent of the depositor or copyright owner, may request full term retention. A fee for this service is fixed by this section pursuant to section 708(a) of Title 17 of the United States Code.

(2) For purposes of this section, under the control of the Copyright Office shall mean within the confines of Copyright Office buildings and under the control of Copyright Office employees, including retention in a Federal records center, but does not include transfer to the Library of Congress collections.

(3) For purposes of this section, full term retention means retention for a period of 75 years from the date of publication of the work identified by the particular copyright deposit which is retained.

(4) For purposes of this section, copyright deposit or its plural means the copy, phonorecord, or identifying material submitted to the Copyright Office in connection with a published work that is subsequently registered and made part of the records of the Office.

(b) Form and content of request for full term retention—

(1) Forms. The Copyright Office does not provide printed forms for the use of persons requesting full term retention of copyright deposits.

(2) Requests for full term retention must be made in writing addressed to the Director of the Office of Public Records and Repositories at the address specified in §201.1(b)(1) of this chapter, and shall be signed by or on behalf of the depositor or copyright owner of record, and clearly indicate that full term retention is desired.

(3) The request for full term retention must adequately identify the particular copyright deposit to be retained, preferably by including the title used in the registration application, the name of the depositor or copyright owner of record, the publication date, and, if registration was completed earlier, the registration number.

(c) Conditions under which requests will be granted or denied—

(1) General. A request that meets the requirements of paragraph (b) of this section will generally be granted if the copyright deposit for which full term retention is requested has been continuously in the custody of the Copyright Office and the Library of Congress has not, by the date of the request, selected the copyright deposit for its collections.

(2) Time of request. The request for full term retention of a particular copyright deposit may be made at the time of deposit or at any time thereafter; however, the request will be granted only if at least one copy, phonorecord, or set of identifying material is in the custody of the Copyright Office at the time of the request. Where the request is made concurrent with the initial deposit of the work for registration, the requestor must submit one copy or phonorecord more than the number specified in §202.20 for the particular work.

(3) One deposit retained. The Copyright Office will retain no more than one copy, phonorecord, or set of identifying material for a given registered work.

(4) Denial of request for full term retention. The Copyright Office reserves the right to deny the request for full term retention where:

(i) The excessive size, fragility, or weight of the deposit would, in the sole discretion of the Register of Copyrights, constitute an unreasonable storage burden. The request may nevertheless be granted if, within 60 calendar days of the original denial of the request, the requestor pays the reasonable administrative costs, as fixed in the particular case by the Register of Copyrights, of preparing acceptable identifying materials for retention in lieu of the actual copyright deposit;

(ii) The Library of Congress has selected for its collections the single copyright deposit, or both, if two copies or phonorecords were deposited; or

(iii) Retention would result in a health or safety hazard, in the sole judgment of the Register of Copyrights. The request may nevertheless be granted if, within 60 calendar days of the original denial of the request, the requestor pays the reasonable administrative costs, as fixed in the particular case by the Register of Copyrights of preparing acceptable identifying materials for retention in lieu of the actual copyright deposit.

(d) Form of copyright deposit. If full term retention is granted, the Copyright Office will retain under its control the particular copyright deposit used to make registration for the work. Any deposit made on or after September 19, 1978, shall satisfy the requirements of §§202.20 and 202.21.

(e) Fee for full term retention.

(1) Pursuant to section 708(a) of title 17 of the United States Code, the Register of Copyrights has fixed the fee for full term retention, as prescribed in §201.3(d) of this chapter, for each copyright deposit granted full term retention.

(2) A check or money order in the amount prescribed in §201.3(d) of this chapter payable to the U.S. Copyright Office, must be received in the Copyright Office within 60 calendar days from the date of mailing of the Copyright Office's notification to the requestor that full term retention has been granted for a particular copyright deposit.

(3) The Copyright Office will issue a receipt acknowledging payment of the fee and identifying the copyright deposit for which full term retention has been granted.

(f) Selection by Library of Congress—

(1) General. All published copyright deposits are available for selection by the Library of Congress until the Copyright Office has formally granted a request for full term retention. Unless the requestor has deposited the additional copy or phonorecord specified by paragraph (c)(2) of this section, the Copyright Office will not process a request for full term retention submitted concurrent with a copyright registration application and deposit, until the Library of Congress has had a reasonable amount of time to make its selection determination.

(2) A request for full term retention made at the time of deposit of a published work does not affect the right of the Library to select one or both of the copyright deposits.

(3) If one copyright deposit is selected, the second deposit, if any, will be used for full term retention.

(4) If both copyright deposits are selected, or, in the case where the single deposit made is selected, full term retention will be granted only if the additional copy or phonorecord specified by paragraph (c)(2) was deposited.

(g) Termination of full term storage. Full term storage will cease 75 years after the date of publication of the work identified by the copyright deposit retained, and the copyright deposit will be disposed of in accordance with section 704, paragraphs (b) through (d), of title 17 of the United States Code.

History of 37 C.F.R. §202.23: 48 FR 32777, July 19, 1983; 52 FR 28822, Aug. 4, 1987; 60 FR 34168, June 30, 1995; 63 FR 29139, May 28, 1998; 64 FR 29522, June 1, 1999; 64 FR 36575, July 7, 1999; 65 FR 39819, June 28, 2000; 73 FR 37839, July 1, 2008; 82 FR 9362, Mar. 8, 2017.

§202.24. DEPOSIT OF PUBLISHED ELECTRONIC WORKS AVAILABLE ONLY ONLINE

(a) Pursuant to authority under 17 U.S.C. 407(d), the Register of Copyrights may make written demand to deposit one complete copy or a phonorecord of an electronic work published in the United States and available only online upon the owner of copyright or of the exclusive right of publication in the work, under the following conditions:

(1) Demands may be made only for works in those categories identified in §202.19(c)(5) as being subject to demand.

(2) Demands may be made only for works published on or after February 24, 2010.

(3) The owner of copyright or of the exclusive right of publication must deposit the demanded work within three months of the date the demand notice is received.

(4) Copies or phonorecords deposited in response to a demand must be able to be accessed and reviewed by the Copyright Office, Library of Congress, and the Library's authorized users on an ongoing basis.

(b) Technical standards. Technical standards for the transmission of copies of online-only works to the Copyright Office in response to a demand will be available on the Copyright Office website (www.copyright.gov).

(c) Definitions. **(1)** "Best edition" has the meaning set forth in §202.19(b)(1).

(2) "Complete copy" has the meaning set forth in §202.19(b)(2).

(3) "Electronic works" are works fixed and published solely in an electronic format.

(d) Special relief. **(1)** In the case of any demand made under paragraph (a) of this section, the Register of Copyrights may, after consultation with other appropriate officials of the Library of Congress and upon such conditions as the Register may determine after such consultation,

(i) Extend the time period provided in 17 U.S.C. 407(d);

(ii) Permit the deposit of incomplete copies or phonorecords; or

(iii) Permit the deposit of copies or phonorecords other than those normally comprising the best edition.

(2) Any decision as to whether to grant such special relief, and the conditions under which special relief is to be granted, shall be made by the Register of Copyrights after consultation with other appropriate officials of the Library of Congress, and shall be based upon the acquisition policies of the Library of Congress then in force.

(3) Requests for special relief under this section shall be made in writing to the Copyright Acquisitions Division, shall be signed by or on behalf of the owner of copyright or of the exclusive right of publication in the work, and shall set forth specific reasons why the request should be granted.

History of 37 C.F.R. §202.24: 75 FR 3869, Feb. 24, 2010; 82 FR 9362, Mar. 8, 2017.

APPENDIX A TO PART 202—TECHNICAL GUIDELINES REGARDING SOUND PHYSICAL CONDITION

To be considered a copy "of sound physical condition" within the meaning of 37 CFR 202.22(d)(5), a copy shall conform to all the technical guidelines set out in this Appendix.

A. Physical Condition. All portions of the copy that reproduce the transmission program must be:

1. Clean: Free from dirt, marks, spots, fungus, or other smudges, blotches, blemishes, or distortions;

2. Undamaged: Free from burns, blisters, tears, cuts, scratches, breaks, erasure, or other physical damage. The copies must also be free from:

(i) Any damage that interferes with performance from the tape or other reproduction, including physical damage resulting from earlier mechanical difficulties such as cassette jamming, breaks, tangles, or tape overflow; and

(ii) Any erasures, damage causing visual or audible defects or distortions or any material remaining from incomplete erasure of previously recorded works.

3. Unspliced: Free from splices in any part of the copy reproducing the transmission program, regardless of whether the splice involves the addition or deletion of material or is intended to repair a break or cut.

4. Undeteriorated: Free from any visual or aural deterioration resulting from aging or exposure to climatic, atmospheric, or other chemical or physical conditions, including heat, cold, humidity, electromagnetic fields, or radiation. The copy shall also be free from excessive brittleness or stretching, from any visible flaking of oxide from the tape base or other medium, and from other visible signs of physical deterioration or excessive wear.

B. Physical Appurtenances of Deposit Copy.

1. Physical Housing of Video Tape Copy. (a) In the case of video tape reproduced for reel-to-reel performance, the deposit copy shall consist of reels of uniform size and length. The length of the reels will depend on both the size of the tape and its running time (the last reel may be shorter). (b) In the case of video tape reproduced for cassette, cartridge, or similar performance, the tape drive mechanism shall be fully operable and free from any mechanical defects.

2. "Leader" or Equivalent. The copy, whether housed in reels, cassettes, or cartridges, shall have a leader segment both preceding the beginning and following the end of the recording.

C. Visual and Aural Quality of Copy:

1. Visual Quality. The copy should be equivalent to an evaluated first generation copy from an edited master tape and must reproduce a flawless and consistent electronic signal that meets industry standards for television screening.

2. Aural Quality. The sound channels or other portions must reproduce a flawless and consistent electronic signal without any audible defects.

History of 37 C.F.R. Part 202, App. A: 48 FR 37209, Aug. 17, 1983; 60 FR 34168, June 30, 1995.

APPENDIX B TO PART 202—"BEST EDITION" OF PUBLISHED COPYRIGHTED WORKS FOR THE COLLECTIONS OF THE LIBRARY OF CONGRESS

a. The copyright law (title 17, United States Code) requires that copies or phonorecords deposited in the Copyright Office be of the "best edition" of the work. The law states that "The 'best edition' of a work is the edition, published in the United States at any time before the date of deposit, that the Library of Congress determines to be most suitable for its purposes." (For works first published only in a country other than the United States, the law requires the deposit of the best edition as first published.)

b. When two or more editions of the same version of a work have been published, the one of the highest quality is generally considered to be the best edition. In judging quality, the Library of Congress will adhere to the criteria set forth below in all but exceptional circumstances.

c. Where differences between editions represent variations in copyrightable content, each edition is a separate version and "best edition" standards based on such differences do not apply. Each such version is a separate work for the purpose of the copyright law.

d. The criteria to be applied in determining the best edition of each of several types of material are listed below in descending order of importance. In deciding between two editions, a criterion-by-criterion comparison should be made. The edition which first fails to satisfy a criterion is to be considered of inferior quality and will not be an acceptable deposit. Example: If a comparison is made between two hardbound editions of a book, one a trade edition printed on acid-free paper, and the other a specially bound edition printed on average paper, the former will be the best edition because the type of paper is a more important criterion than the binding.

e. Under regulations of the Copyright Office, potential depositors may request authorization to deposit copies or phonorecords of other than the best edition of a specific work (e.g., a microform rather than a printed edition of a serial), by requesting "special relief" from the deposit requirements. All requests for special relief should be in writing and should state the reason(s) why the applicant cannot send the required deposit and what the applicant wishes to submit instead of the required deposit.

I. Printed Textual Matter

A. Paper, Binding, and Packaging:

1. Archival-quality rather than less-permanent paper.

2. Hard cover rather than soft cover.

3. Library binding rather than commercial binding.

4. Trade edition rather than book club edition.

5. Sewn rather than glue-only binding.

6. Sewn or glued rather than stapled or spiral-bound.

7. Stapled rather than spiral-bound or plastic-bound.

8. Bound rather than looseleaf, except when future looseleaf insertions are to be issued. In the case of looseleaf materials, this includes the submission of all binders and indexes when they are part of the unit as published and offered for sale or distribution. Additionally, the regular and timely receipt of all appropriate looseleaf updates, supplements, and releases including supplemental binders issued to handle these expanded versions, is part of the requirement to properly maintain these publications.

9. Slip-cased rather than nonslip-cased.

10. With protective folders rather than without (for broadsides).

11. Rolled rather than folded (for broadsides).

12. With protective coatings rather than without (except broadsides, which should not be coated).

B. Rarity:

1. Special limited edition having the greatest number of special features.

2. Other limited edition rather than trade edition.

3. Special binding rather than trade binding.

C. Illustrations:

1. Illustrated rather than unillustrated.

2. Illustrations in color rather than black and white.

D. Special Features:

1. With thumb notches or index tabs rather than without.

2. With aids to use such as overlays and magnifiers rather than without.

E. Size:

1. Larger rather than smaller sizes. (Except that large-type editions for the partially-sighted are not required in place of editions employing type of more conventional size.)

II. Photographs

A. Size and finish, in descending order of preference:

1. The most widely distributed edition.

2. 8 x 10-inch glossy print.

3. Other size or finish.

B. Unmounted rather than mounted.

C. Archival-quality rather than less-permanent paper stock or printing process.

III. Motion Pictures

Film medium is considered a better quality than any other medium. The formats under "film" and "video formats" are listed in descending order of preference:

A. Film

1. Preprint material, by special arrangement

2. 70 mm positive print, if original production negative is greater than 35 mm

3. 35 mm positive prints

4. 16 mm positive prints

B. Video Formats

1. Betacam SP

2. Digital Beta (Digibeta)

3. DVD

4. VHS Cassette

IV. Other Graphic Matter

A. Paper and Printing:

1. Archival quality rather than less-permanent paper.

2. Color rather than black and white.

B. Size and Content:

1. Larger rather than smaller size.

2. In the case of cartographic works, editions with the greatest amount of information rather than those with less detail.

C. Rarity:

1. The most widely distributed edition rather than one of limited distribution.

2. In the case of a work published only in a limited, numbered edition, one copy outside the numbered series but otherwise identical.

3. A photographic reproduction of the original, by special arrangement only.

D. Text and Other Materials:

1. Works with annotations, accompanying tabular or textual matter, or other interpretative aids rather than those without them.

E. Binding and Packaging:

1. Bound rather than unbound.

2. If editions have different binding, apply the criteria in I.A.2-I.A.7, above.

3. Rolled rather than folded.

4. With protective coatings rather than without.

V. Phonorecords

A. Compact digital disc rather than a vinyl disc.

B. Vinyl disc rather than tape.

C. With special enclosures rather than without.

D. Open-reel rather than cartridge.

E. Cartridge rather than cassette.

F. Quadraphonic rather than stereophonic.

G. True stereophonic rather than monaural.

H. Monaural rather than electronically rechanneled stereo.

VI. Musical Compositions

A. Fullness of Score:

1. Vocal music:

a. With orchestral accompaniment:

i. Full score and parts, if any, rather than conductor's score and parts, if any. (In cases of compositions published only by rental, lease, or lending, this requirement is reduced to full score only.)

ii. Conductor's score and parts, if any, rather than condensed score and parts, if any. (In cases of compositions published only by rental, lease, or lending, this requirement is reduced to conductor's score only.)

b. Unaccompanied: Open score (each part on separate staff) rather than closed score (all parts condensed to two staves).

2. Instrumental music:

a. Full score and parts, if any, rather than conductor's score and parts, if any. (In cases of compositions published only by rental, lease, or lending, this requirement is reduced to full score only.)

b. Conductor's score and parts, if any, rather than condensed score and parts, if any. (In cases of compositions published only by rental, lease, or lending, this requirement is reduced to conductor's score only.)

B. Printing and Paper:

1. Archival-quality rather than less-permanent paper.

C. Binding and Packaging:

1. Special limited editions rather than trade editions.

2. Bound rather than unbound.

3. If editions have different binding, apply the criteria in I.A.2-I.A.12, above.

4. With protective folders rather than without.

VII. Microforms

A. Related Materials:

1. With indexes, study guides, or other printed matter rather than without.

B. Permanence and Appearance:

1. Silver halide rather than any other emulsion.

2. Positive rather than negative.

3. Color rather than black and white.

C. Format (newspapers and newspaper-formatted serials):

1. Reel microfilm rather than any other microform.

D. Format (all other materials):

1. Microfiche rather than reel microfilm.

2. Reel microfilm rather than microform cassettes.

3. Microfilm cassettes rather than micro-opaque prints.

E. Size:

1. 35 mm rather than 16 mm.

VIII. Machine-Readable Copies

A. Computer Programs

1. With documents and other accompanying material rather than without.

2. Not copy-protected rather than copy-protected (if copy-protected then with a backup copy of the disk(s)).

3. Format:

a. PC-DOS or MS-DOS (or other IBM compatible formats, such as XENIX):

(i) 5¼" Diskette(s).

(ii) 3½" Diskette(s).

(iii) Optical media, such as CD-ROM—best edition should adhere to prevailing NISO standards.

b. Apple Macintosh:

(i) 3½" Diskette(s).

(ii) Optical media, such as CD-ROM—best edition should adhere to prevailing NISO standards.

B. Computerized Information Works, Including Statistical Compendia, Serials, or Reference Works:

1. With documentation and other accompanying material rather than without.

2. With best edition of accompanying program rather than without.

3. Not copy-protected rather than copy-protected (if copy-protected then with a backup copy of the disk(s)).

4. Format:

a. PC-DOS or MS-DOS (or other IBM compatible formats, such as XENIX):

(i) Optical media, such as CD-ROM—best edition should adhere to prevailing NISO standards.

(ii) 5¼" Diskette(s).

(iii) 3½" Diskette(s).

b. Apple Macintosh:

(i) Optical media, such as CD-ROM—best edition should adhere to prevailing NISO standards.

(ii) 3½" Diskette(s).

IX. Electronic Works Published in the United States and Available Only Online

For all deposits, UTF-8 encoding is preferred to ASCII encoding and other non UTF-8 encodings for non-Latin character sets in all categories below.

A. Electronic Serials

1. Content Format

a. Level 1: Serials-specific structured/markup format:

(i) Content compliant with the NLM Journal Archiving (XML) Document Type Definition (DTD), with presentation stylesheet(s), rather than without.

(ii) Other widely used serials or journal XML DTDs/schemas, with presentation stylesheet(s), rather than without.

(iii) Proprietary XML format for serials or journals (with documentation), with DTD/schema and presentation stylesheet(s), rather than without.

b. Level 2: Page-oriented rendition:

(i) PDF/A (Portable Document Format/Archival; compliant with ISO 19005).

(ii) PDF (Portable Document Format, with searchable text, rather than without).

c. Level 3: Other formats:

(i) XHTML/HTML, as made available online, with presentation stylesheets(s), rather than without.

(ii) XML (widely used, publicly documented XML-based word-processing formats, e.g., ODF/OpenDocument Format, Office OpenXML), with presentation stylesheets(s), if appropriate, rather than without.

(iii) Plain text.

(iv) Other formats (e.g., proprietary word processing or page layout formats).

2. Metadata Elements:

If it has already been gathered and is available, descriptive data (metadata) as described below should accompany the deposited material.

a. Title level metadata: serial or journal title, ISSN, publisher, frequency, place of publication.

b. Article level metadata, as relevant/applicable: volume(s), number(s), issue dates(s), article title(s), article author(s), article identifier (DOI, etc.).

c. With other descriptive metadata (e.g., subject heading(s), descriptor(s), abstract(s)), rather than without.

3. Technological measures that control access to or use of the work should be removed.

X. Works Existing in More Than One Medium

Editions are listed below in descending order of preference.

A. Newspapers, dissertations and theses, newspaper-formatted serials:

1. Microform.

2. Printed matter.

B. All other materials:

1. Printed matter.

2. Microform.

3. Phonorecord.

History of 37 C.F.R. Part 202, App. B: 54 FR 42299, Oct. 16, 1989; 62 FR 51603, Oct. 2, 1997; 69 FR 8821, Feb. 26, 2004; 75 FR 3869, Feb. 24, 2010; 82 FR 9362, Mar. 8, 2017.

PART 203. FREEDOM OF INFORMATION ACT: POLICIES & PROCEDURES

ORGANIZATION

§203.1. GENERAL

This information is furnished for the guidance of the public and in compliance with the requirements of the Freedom of Information Act ("FOIA"), 5 U.S.C. 552. The rules contained in this part should be read in conjunction with the text of FOIA and the Uniform Freedom of Information Fee Schedule and Guidelines published by the Office of Management and Budget ("OMB Guidelines"). Requests made by individuals for records pertaining to themselves under the Privacy Act of 1974, 5 U.S.C. 552a, are processed under part 204 of this chapter. Requests for services for which the Copyright Act of 1976, title 17 of the United States Code, requires a fee are not processed under this part, but will be processed under the applicable regulations governing that service (including §201.2 of this chapter). If the Copyright Office receives a request for services for which the Copyright Act requires a fee to be charged, the Office will notify the requester of the procedure established to obtain such services, and the applicable fees under §201.3 of this chapter. Section 706(b) of the Copyright Act and the regulations issued under section 706(b) are not subject to FOIA.

History of 37 C.F.R. §203.1: 66 FR 34373, June 28, 2001; 82 FR 9506, Mar. 9, 2017.

Source of 37 C.F.R. Part 203: 43 FR 774, Jan. 4, 1978; 59 FR 23981, May 9, 1994; 60 FR 34168, June 30, 1995; 62 FR 55742, Oct. 28, 1997; 63 FR 1927, Jan. 13, 1998, unless otherwise noted.

§203.2. AUTHORITY & FUNCTIONS

The administration of the copyright law was entrusted to the Library of Congress by an act of Congress in 1870, and the Copyright Office has been a separate department of the Library since 1897. The statutory functions of the Copyright Office are contained in and carried out in accordance with the Copyright Act.

History of 37 C.F.R. §203.2: 62 FR 35421, July 1, 1997; 82 FR 9362, Mar. 8, 2017.

§203.3. ORGANIZATION

(a) The Office of the Register of Copyrights has overall responsibility for the Copyright Office and its statutory mandate, specifically: For legal interpretation of the copyright law; administering the provisions of title 17 of the U.S.C.; promulgating copyright regulations; advising Congress and other government officials on domestic and international copyright policy and other intellectual property issues; determining personnel and other resource requirements for the Office; organizing strategic and annual program planning; and preparing budget estimates for inclusion in the budget of the Library of Congress and U.S. Government.

(b) The Office of the Chief of Operations is headed by the Chief of Operations ("COO"), who advises the Register on core business functions and coordinates and directs the day-to-day operations of the Copyright Office. The Office of the COO supervises human capital, the administration of certain statutory licenses, mandatory deposits and acquisitions, and strategic planning functions. This Office interacts with every other senior management office that reports to the Register and frequently coordinates and assesses institutional projects. The COO chairs the Copyright Office's operations committee. The following divisions fall under the oversight of the COO:

(1) The Receipt Analysis and Control Division is responsible for sorting, analyzing, and scanning incoming mail; creating initial records; labeling materials; and searching, assembling, and dispatching electronic and hardcopy materials and deposits to the appropriate service areas. The Division is responsible for operating the Copyright Office's central print room, mail functions, and temporary storage. The Division also processes all incoming fees and maintains accounts, related records, and reports involving fees received.

(2) The Licensing Division administers certain statutory licenses set forth in the Copyright Act. The Division collects royalty payments and examines statements of account for the cable statutory license (17 U.S.C. 111), the satellite statutory license for retransmission of distant television broadcast stations (17 U.S.C. 119), and the statutory license for digital audio recording technology (17 U.S.C. chapter 10). The Division also accepts and records documents associated with the use of the mechanical statutory license (17 U.S.C. 115).

(3) The Copyright Acquisitions Division administers the mandatory deposit requirements of the Copyright Act, acting as an intermediary between copyright owners of certain published works and the acquisitions staff in the Library of Congress. 17 U.S.C. 407. This Office creates and updates records for the copies received by the Copyright Office; demands particular works or particular formats of works as necessary; and administers deposit agreements between the Library and copyright owners.

(c) The Office of the General Counsel is headed by the General Counsel and Associate Register of Copyrights, who is an expert copyright attorney and one of four legal advisors to the Register. This Office assists the Register in carrying out critical work of the Copyright Office regarding the legal interpretation of the copyright law. The General Counsel liaises with the Department of Justice, other federal departments, and the legal community on a wide range of copyright matters including litigation and the administration of title 17 of the U.S.C. The General Counsel also has primary responsibility for the formulation and promulgation of regulations and the adoption of legal positions governing policy matters and the practices of the Copyright Office.

(d) The Office of Policy and International Affairs is headed by the Associate Register of Copyrights and Director of Policy and International Affairs, who is an expert copyright attorney and one of four legal advisors to the Register. This Office assists the Register with critical policy functions of the

Copyright Office, including domestic and international policy analyses, legislative support, and trade negotiations. Policy and International Affairs represents the Copyright Office at meetings of government officials concerned with the international aspects of intellectual property protection, and provides regular support to Congress and its committees on statutory amendments and construction.

(e) The Office of Registration Policy and Practice is headed by the Associate Register of Copyrights and Director of Registration Policy and Practice, who is an expert copyright attorney and one of four legal advisors to the Register. This Office administers the U.S. copyright registration system and advises the Register of Copyrights on questions of registration policy and related regulations and interpretations of copyright law. This Office has three divisions: Literary, Performing Arts, and Visual Arts. It also has a number of specialized sections, for example, in the area of motion pictures. This Office executes major sections of the Compendium of Copyright Office Practices, particularly with respect to the examination of claims and related principles of law.

(f) The Office of Public Information and Education is headed by the Associate Register for Public Information and Education, who is an expert copyright attorney and one of four legal advisors to the Register. This Office informs and helps carry out the work of the Register and the Copyright Office in providing authoritative information about the copyright law to the public and establishing educational programs. The Office publishes the copyright law and other provisions of title 17 of the U.S.C.; maintains a robust and accurate public website; creates and distributes a variety of circulars, information sheets, and newsletters, including NewsNet; responds to public inquiries regarding provisions of the law, explaining registration policies, procedures, and other copyright-related topics upon request; plans and executes a variety of educational activities; and engages in outreach with various copyright community stakeholders.

(g) The Office of Public Records and Repositories is headed by the Director, who is an expert in public administration and one of the Register's top business advisors. This Office is responsible for carrying out major provisions of title 17 of the U.S.C., including establishing records policies; ensuring the storage and security of copyright deposits, both analog and digital; recording licenses and transfers of copyright ownership; preserving, maintaining, and servicing copyright related records; researching and providing certified and non-certified reproductions of copyright deposits; and maintaining the official records of the Copyright Office. Additionally, the Office engages regularly in discussions with leaders in the private and public sectors regarding issues of metadata, interoperability, data management, and open government.

(h) The Office of the Chief Information Officer is headed by the Chief Information Officer ("CIO"), who is the Register's top advisor on the development and implementation of technology policy and infrastructure. The Office of the CIO provides strategic leadership and direction for necessary planning, design, development, and implementation of the Copyright Office's automated initiatives. The Office of the CIO is a liaison to the central technology office of the Library of Congress, which administers the Copyright Office's networks and communications. The CIO also supervises the Copyright Technology Office. The Copyright Technology Office maintains certain Copyright Office enterprise-wide IT systems for registration, recordation, public records management and access, and related public services, as well as certain internal and external help-desk functions.

(i) The Chief Financial Officer ("CFO") is a senior staff position that serves under the Register and oversees all fiscal, financial, budgetary, and procurement-related activities for the Copyright Office.

(j) The Office has no field organization.

(k) The Office is located in The James Madison Memorial Building of the Library of Congress, 1st and Independence Avenue, SE., Washington, DC 20559-6000. The Public Information Office is located in Room LM-401. Its hours are 8:30 a.m. to 5 p.m., Monday through Friday except legal holidays. The phone number of the Public Information Office is (202) 707-3000. Informational material regarding the copyright law, the registration process, fees, and related information about the Copyright Office and its functions may be obtained free of charge from the Public Information Office upon request.

(*l*) All Copyright Office forms may be obtained free of charge from the Public Information Office or by calling the Copyright Office Hotline anytime day or night at (202) 707-9100.

History of 37 C.F.R. §203.3: 43 FR 774, Jan. 4, 1978; 47 FR 36820, Aug. 24, 1982; 60 FR 34168, June 30, 1995; 62 FR 55742, Oct. 28, 1997; 63 FR 1927, Jan. 13, 1998; 64 FR 36575, July 7, 1999; 65 FR 39819, June 28, 2000; 66 FR 34373, June 28, 2001; 73 FR 37839, July 1, 2008; 76 FR 27898, May 13, 2011; 82 FR 9362, Mar. 8, 2017; 82 FR 9507, Mar. 9, 2017.

PROCEDURES

§203.4. PROACTIVE DISCLOSURE OF OFFICE RECORDS

Records that are required by FOIA to be made available for public inspection in electronic format may be accessed through the Office's Web site at www.copyright.gov. The Office is responsible for determining which of its records must be made publicly available, for identifying additional records of interest to the public that are appropriate for public disclosure, and for posting and indexing such records. The Office must ensure that its Web site of posted records and indices is reviewed and updated on an ongoing basis. The Office has a FOIA Public Liaison who can assist individuals in locating records particular to the Office. The Office's FOIA Public Liaison contact information may be found at www.copyright.gov /foia.

History of 37 C.F.R. §203.4: 43 FR 774, Jan. 4, 1978; 47 FR 36820, Aug. 24, 1982; 62 FR 55742, Oct. 28, 1997; 63 FR 1927, Jan. 13, 1998; 64 FR 36575, July 7,

1999; 65 FR 39819, June 28, 2000; 65 FR 39820, June 28, 2000; 66 FR 34373, June 28, 2001; 73 FR 37839, July 1, 2008; 82 FR 9363, Mar. 8, 2017; 82 FR 9507, Mar. 9, 2017.

§203.5. REQUIREMENTS FOR MAKING REQUESTS

(a) General information. To be proper, a request must be made in accordance with the rules established under this part.

(1) To make a request for records, a requester should write directly by email to copfoia@loc.gov, by postal mail to the FOIA Requester Service Center, Copyright Office, PIE, P.O. Box 70400, Washington, DC 20024, or submit the request in person between the hours of 8:30 a.m. and 5 p.m. on any working day except legal holidays at Room LM-401, The James Madison Memorial Building, 101 Independence Avenue SE., Washington, DC. If a request is made by mail, both the request and the envelope containing it should include "Freedom of Information Act Request". A request will receive the quickest possible response if it is clearly marked and addressed to the FOIA Requester Service Center. Guidelines for submitting a request can be found at www.copyright.gov/foia.

(2) A requester who is making a request for records about himself or herself must comply with part 204 of this chapter.

(3) Where a request for records pertains to a third party, a requester may receive greater access by submitting either a notarized authorization signed by that individual or a declaration made in compliance with the requirements set forth in 28 U.S.C. 1746 by that individual authorizing disclosure of the records to the requestor, or by submitting proof that the individual is deceased (e.g., a copy of a death certificate or obituary). As an exercise of administrative discretion, the Office can require a requester to supply additional information if necessary in order to verify that a particular individual has consented to disclosure.

(b) Description of records sought. The request must reasonably describe the records sought. A request reasonably describes records if it enables the Office to identify the records requested in such a way that is not unreasonably burdensome or disruptive to Office operations. To the extent possible, requesters should include specific information that may help the agency identify the requested records, such as the date, title or name, author, recipient, subject matter of the record, registration, recordation, or reference number. Before submitting their requests, requesters may contact the FOIA Public Liaison to discuss the records they seek and to receive assistance in describing the records. If after receiving a request the Office determines that it does not reasonably describe the records sought, the Office will inform the requester what additional information is needed or why the request is insufficient. The requester may discuss with the FOIA Public Liaison how to reformulate or modify a request. If a request does not reasonably describe the records sought, the agency's response to the request may be delayed.

(c) Formats. Requests may specify the preferred form or format (including electronic formats) for the records identified. The Office will accommodate the request if the record is readily reproducible in that form or format.

(d) Contact information. Requesters must provide contact information, such as a phone number, email address, and/or mailing address, to assist the Office in communicating with a requester and providing released records.

History of 37 C.F.R. §203.5: 82 FR 9507, Mar. 9, 2017.

§203.6. RESPONSIBILITY FOR RESPONDING TO REQUESTS

(a) In general. The Office is responsible for responding to a request. In determining which records are responsive to a request, the Office ordinarily will include only records in its possession as of the date that it begins its search. If any other date is used, the Office will inform the requester of that date.

(b) Authority to grant or deny requests. The Register of Copyrights, and the Associate Register of Copyrights and Director of Public Information and Education are authorized to grant or to deny any requests for records.

(c) Consultation, referral, and coordination. When reviewing records located by the Office in response to a request, the Office will determine whether another agency of the Federal Government is better able to determine whether the record is exempt from disclosure under FOIA. As to any such record, the Office will proceed in one of the following ways:

(1) Consultation. When records originated with the Office, but contain within them information of interest to another agency or Federal Government office, the Office may consult with the other entity prior to making a release determination.

(2) Referral. **(i)** When the Office believes that a different agency is best able to determine whether to disclose the record, the Office will refer the responsibility for responding to the request regarding that record to that agency. Ordinarily, the Office that originated the record is presumed to be the best agency to make the disclosure determination. If, however, the Office and the originating agency jointly agree that the Office is in the best position to respond, then the record may be handled as a consultation.

(ii) Whenever the Office refers any responsibility for responding to a request to another agency, it will document the referral, maintain a copy of the record that it refers, and notify the requester of the referral. The notification will include the name(s) of the agency to which the record was referred and that agency's FOIA contact information.

(3) Coordination. When the Office believes that a different agency is best able to determine whether to disclose the record, but disclosure of the identity of the different agency could harm an interest protected by an applicable exemption, the Office will coordinate with the originating agency to seek its views of disclosability of the record. The release determination for the record that is the subject of the coordination will then be conveyed to the requester by the Office.

(d) Timing of responses to consultations and referrals. All consultations and referrals received by the Office will be handled according to the date that the first agency received the perfected FOIA request.

(e) Agreements regarding consultations and referrals. The Office may establish agreements with other agencies to eliminate the need for consultations or referrals with respect to particular types of records.

History of 37 C.F.R. §203.6: 43 FR 774, Jan. 4, 1978; 47 FR 36820, Aug. 24, 1982; 53 FR 8456, Mar. 15, 1988; 56 FR 59885, Nov. 26, 1991; 62 FR 55742, Oct. 28, 1997; 63 FR 1927, Jan. 13, 1998; 63 FR 29139, May 28, 1998; 64 FR 29522, June 1, 1999; 66 FR 34373, June 28, 2001; 79 FR 15919, May 1, 2014; 82 FR 9364, Mar. 8, 2017; 82 FR 9507, Mar. 9, 2017.

§203.7. TIMING OF RESPONSES TO REQUESTS

(a) In general. The Office will respond to all properly addressed emailed and mailed requests and all personally delivered written requests for records within 20 working days of receipt. The Office ordinarily will respond to requests according to their order of receipt. In instances involving a misdirected request rerouted to the Office, the response time will commence on the date that the request is received by the Office, but in any event not later than 10 working days after the request is first received by the Library of Congress.

(b) Multitrack processing. The Office will designate a specific track for requests that are granted expedited processing, in accordance with the standards set forth in paragraph (e) of this section. The Office may also designate additional processing tracks that distinguish between simple and more complex requests based on the estimated amount of work or time needed to process the request. Among the factors the Office may consider are the number of records requested, the number of pages involved in processing the request, and the need for consultations or referrals. The Office will advise a requester of the track into which their request falls and, when appropriate, will offer the requester an opportunity to narrow or modify their request so that it can be placed in a different processing track.

(c) Unusual circumstances. **(1)(i)** Whenever the Office cannot meet the statutory time limit for processing a request because of "unusual circumstances," as defined in paragraph (c)(2) of this section, the Office will notify the requester in writing of the unusual circumstances and the estimated date of determination. Where an extension of time greater than 10 days is required, the Office will give the requester the opportunity to:

(A) Limit the scope of the request so that it may be processed within 20 working days; or

(B) Arrange with the Office an alternative time frame for processing the request or a modified request.

(ii) The Office will make available the FOIA Public Liaison to assist the requester in modifying the request.

(2) As used in this paragraph (c), "unusual circumstances" means, only to the extent reasonably necessary to the proper processing of the particular request:

(i) The need to search for and collect the requested records from establishments that are physically separate from the Office;

(ii) The need to search for, collect, and examine a voluminous amount of separate and distinct records which are demanded in a single request; or,

(iii) The need for consultation, which shall be conducted with all practicable speed, with another agency having a substantial interest in the determination of the request or among two or more components of the Copyright Office which have a substantial subject matter interest therein.

(d) Aggregating requests. To satisfy unusual circumstances under the FOIA, the Office may aggregate requests in cases where it reasonably appears that multiple requests, submitted either by a requester or by a group of requesters acting in concert, constitute a single request that would otherwise involve unusual circumstances. The Office will not aggregate multiple requests that involve unrelated matters.

(e) Expedited processing. **(1)** The Office will process requests and appeals on an expedited basis whenever it is determined that the request or appeal involves:

(i) Circumstances in which the lack of expedited processing could reasonably be expected to pose an imminent threat to the life or physical safety of an individual; or,

(ii) An urgency to inform the public about an actual or alleged Federal Government activity, if the request or appeal is made by a person who is primarily engaged in disseminating information.

(2) A request for expedited processing may be made at any time. Requests for expedited processing of initial requests should be made to the FOIA Requester Service Center. Requests for expedited processing of an administrative appeal should be submitted to the Office of the Register of Copyrights.

(3) A requester who seeks expedited processing must submit a statement, certified to be true and correct, setting forth the basis for the claim that a "compelling need" exists for the requested information.

(4) The Office will notify the requester within 10 calendar days of the receipt of a request for expedited processing of its decision whether to grant or deny expedited processing. If expedited processing is granted, the request will be given priority and processed as soon as is practicable. If a request for expedited processing is denied, the requester may submit an appeal to the Office of the Register of Copyrights. The Office will act expeditiously on any appeal of a denial of expedited processing.

History of 37 C.F.R. §203.7: 82 FR 9508, Mar. 9, 2017.

§203.8. RESPONSES TO REQUESTS

(a) In general. The Office, to the extent practicable, will communicate with requesters having access to the Internet electronically, such as email or web portal.

(b) Acknowledgement of requests. The Office will acknowledge a request in writing and assign it an individualized tracking number if it will take longer than 10 working days to process. The Office will include in the acknowledgement a brief description of the records sought.

(c) Estimated dates of completion and interim responses. Upon request, the Office will provide an estimated date by which the Office expects to provide a response to the requester. If a request involves a voluminous amount of material, or searches in multiple locations, the agency may provide interim responses, releasing the records on a rolling basis.

(d) Grants of requests. Once the Office determines it will grant a request in full or in part, it will notify the requester in writing. The Office will also inform the requester of any fees charged under §203.11 and will disclose the requested records to the requester promptly upon payment of any applicable fees. The Office will inform the requester of the availability of the FOIA Public Liaison to offer assistance.

(e) Adverse determinations. If the Office makes an adverse determination denying a request in any respect, it will notify the requester of that determination in writing. Adverse determinations, or denials of requests, include decisions that: The requested record is exempt, in whole or in part; the requested record does not exist, cannot be located, or has been destroyed; or the requested record is not readily reproducible in the form or format sought by the requester. Adverse determinations also include denials involving fees or fee waiver matters or denials of requests for expedited processing.

(f) Content of denial. The denial shall be signed by the Associate Register of Copyrights and Director of Public Information and Education or a designee and shall include:

(1) The name and title or position of the person responsible for the denial;

(2) A brief statement of the reasons for the denial, including any FOIA exemption applied by the agency in denying the request;

(3) When applicable, an estimate of the volume of any records or information withheld, such as the number of pages or some other reasonable form of estimation, although such an estimate is not required if the volume is otherwise indicated by deletions marked on records that are disclosed in part or if providing an estimate would harm an interest protected by an applicable exemption;

(4) A statement that the denial may be appealed under §203.9, and a description of the appeal requirements; and,

(5) A statement notifying the requester of the assistance available from the Office's FOIA Public Liaison and the dispute resolution services offered by the Office of Government Information Services.

(g) Markings on released documents. Records disclosed in part shall be marked clearly to show the amount of information deleted and the exemption under which the deletion was made unless doing so would harm an interest protected by an applicable exemption. The location of the information deleted must also be indicated on the record, if technically feasible.

History of 37 C.F.R. §203.8: 82 FR 9508, Mar. 9, 2017.

§203.9. ADMINISTRATIVE APPEALS

(a) Requirements for making an appeal. A requester may appeal any adverse determination to the Register of Copyrights. Examples of adverse determinations are provided in §203.8(e). Requesters can submit appeals by mail to the Register of Copyrights, Copyright Office, P.O. Box 70400, Washington, DC 20024. The requester must make the appeal in writing and to be considered timely it must be postmarked within 90 calendar days after the date of the Office's response. The appeal should clearly identify the agency determination that is being appealed, include the assigned docket number, and include a statement explaining the basis for the appeal. To facilitate handling, the requester should include on both the appeal letter and envelope "Freedom of Information Act Appeal."

(b) Adjudication of appeals. **(1)** The Register of Copyrights or a designee will adjudicate all appeals under this section.

(2) An appeal ordinarily will not be adjudicated if the request becomes a matter of FOIA litigation.

(c) Decisions on appeals. The Office shall provide its decision on an appeal in writing. A decision that upholds the Office's determination in whole or in part will contain a statement that identifies the reasons for the affirmance, including any FOIA exemptions applied. The decision will provide the requester with notification of the statutory right to file a lawsuit and will inform the requester of the mediation services offered by the Office of Government Information Services (OGIS) of the National Archives and Records Administration as a non-exclusive alternative to litigation. If the Office's decision is remanded or modified on appeal, the Agency will notify the requester of that determination in writing. The Office will then further process the request in accordance with the appeal determination and will respond directly to the requester.

(d) Engaging in dispute resolution. Mediation is a voluntary process. If the Office agrees to participate in the mediation services provided by OGIS, it will actively engage as a partner to the process in an attempt to resolve the dispute.

(e) When an appeal is required. Before seeking review by a court of an agency's adverse determination, a requester must first submit a timely administrative appeal.

History of 37 C.F.R. §203.9: 82 FR 9509, Mar. 9, 2017.

§203.10. PRESERVATION OF RECORDS

The Office must preserve all correspondence pertaining to the requests that it receives under this part, as well as copies of all requested records, until disposition or destruction is authorized pursuant to title 44 of the United States Code or the General Records Schedule 14 of the National Archives and Records Administration. The Office shall not dispose of or destroy records while they are the subject of a pending request, appeal, or lawsuit under FOIA.

History of 37 C.F.R. §203.10: 82 FR 9509, Mar. 9, 2017.

CHARGES FOR RESPONDING TO FOIA REQUESTS

§203.11. FEES

(a) In general. **(1)** The fee schedule of this section does not apply with respect to the charging of fees for those records for which the Copyright Act requires a fee to be charged. The fees required to be charged are contained in §201.3 of this chapter, or have been established by the Register of Copyrights or Library of Congress pursuant to the requirements of that section. The Copyright Office will charge for processing requests under FOIA in accordance with the provisions of this section and with the OMB Guidelines. For purposes of assessing fees for processing requests, FOIA establishes three categories of requesters:

(i) Commercial use requesters;

(ii) Non-commercial scientific or educational institutions or news media requesters; and

(iii) All other requesters.

(2) Different fees are assessed depending on the category. Requesters may seek a fee waiver, which the Office will consider in accordance with paragraph (k) of this section. To resolve any fee issues that arise under this section, an agency may contact a requester for additional information. The Office shall ensure that searches, review, and duplication are conducted in the most efficient and the least expensive manner. The Office will ordinarily collect all applicable fees before sending copies of records to a requester. Requesters must pay fees by check or money order made payable to the United States Copyright Office.

(b) Definitions. For the purpose of this section:

(1) Commercial use request is a request that asks for information for a use or purpose that furthers a commercial, trade, or profit interest, which can include furthering those interests through litigation. The Office's decision to place a requester in the commercial use category will be made on a case-by-case basis based on the requester's intended use of the information. The Office will notify requesters of their placement in this category.

(2) Direct costs are those expenses that the Office incurs in searching for, duplicating, and/or reviewing records in order to respond to a FOIA request. Direct costs do not include overhead expenses such as the costs of space, and of heating or lighting a facility.

(3) Duplication is reproducing a copy of a record, or of the information contained in it, necessary to respond to a FOIA request. Copies can take the form of paper, audiovisual materials, or electronic records, among others.

(4) Educational institution is any school that operates a program of scholarly research. A requester in this fee category must show that the request is made in connection with his or her role at the educational institution. The Office may seek verification from the requester that the request is in furtherance of scholarly research and the Office will advise requesters of their placement in this category.

(5) Noncommercial scientific institution is an institution that is not operated on a commercial basis and is operated solely for the purpose of conducting scientific research the results of which are not intended to promote any particular product or industry. A requester in this category must show that the request is authorized by and is made under the auspices of a qualifying institution that the records are sought to further scientific research and are not for a commercial use. The Office will advise requesters of their placement in this category.

(6) Representative of the news media is any person or entity that gathers information of potential interest to a segment of the public, uses its editorial skills to turn the raw materials into a distinct work, and distributes that work to an audience. The term "news" means information that is about current events or that would be of current interest to the public. A request for records supporting the news-dissemination function of the requester will not be considered to be for a commercial use. "Freelance" journalists who demonstrate a solid basis for expecting publication through a news media entity will be considered as a representative of the news media. A publishing contract would provide the clearest evidence that publication is expected; however, the Office can also consider a requester's past publication record in making this determination. The Office will advise requesters of their placement in this category.

(7) Review is the examination of a record located in response to a request in order to determine whether any portion of it is exempt from disclosure. Review includes taking all necessary steps to prepare a record for disclosure, including the process of redacting the record and marking the appropriate exemptions and time spent obtaining and considering any formal objection to disclosure made by a confidential commercial information submitter under §203.9. Review does not include time spent resolving general legal or policy issues regarding the application of exemptions. Review costs are properly charged even if a record ultimately is not disclosed.

(8) Search is the process of looking for and retrieving records or information responsive to a request. Search includes page-by-page or line-by-line identification of information within records and the reasonable efforts expended to locate and retrieve information from electronic records.

(c) Charging fees. In responding to FOIA requests, the Office will charge the following fees unless a waiver or reduction of fees has been granted under paragraph (k) of this section.

(1) Search. **(i)** Requests made by educational institutions, noncommercial scientific institutions, or representatives of the news media are not subject to search fees. The Office will charge search fees for all other requesters, subject to the restrictions of paragraph (d) of this section. Fees may be assessed for time spent searching even if the search fails to locate any responsive records or where the records located are subsequently determined to be entirely exempt from disclosure.

(ii) For each quarter hour spent by administrative staff in searching for a requested record, $7.50; for each quarter hour spent by professional staff in searching for a requested record, $17.50, with a half hour minimum in both cases.

(iii) For computer searches of records, which may be undertaken through the use of existing programming, the actual direct costs of conducting the search including the cost of operating a central processing unit for that portion of operating time that is directly attributable to searching for records responsive to a request, as well as the direct costs of operator/programmer salary apportionable to search (at no less than $65 per hour or fraction thereof).

(iv) For requests that require the retrieval of records stored by an agency at a Federal records center operated by the National Archives and Records Administration (NARA), agencies will charge additional costs in accordance with the Transactional Billing Rate Schedule established by NARA.

(2) Duplication. The Office will charge duplication fees to all requesters, subject to the restrictions of paragraph (d) of this section. The Office will honor a requester's preference for receiving a record in a particular form or format when the Office can readily reproduce it in the form or format requested. For copies of the public records, deposits, or indexes of the Office, the Office will charge fees according to §201.3 of this chapter. For copies of all other Copyright Office records not otherwise provided for in this section, a minimum fee of $15.00 for up to 15 pages and $.50 per page over 15.

(3) Review. The Office will charge review fees to requesters who make commercial use requests. Review fees will be assessed in connection with the initial review of the record to determine whether an exemption applies to a particular record or portion of a record. No charge will be made for review at the administrative appeal stage of exemptions applied at the initial review stage. If a particular exemption is deemed to no longer apply on appeal, any costs associated with the Office's re-review of the records may be assessed as review fees. Review fees will be charged at the same rates as described in paragraph (c)(1)(ii) of this section.

(4) Other direct costs. Other costs incurred by the Copyright Office in fulfilling a request will be chargeable at the actual cost to the Office.

(d) Restrictions on charging fees. **(1)(i)** If the Copyright Office fails to comply with FOIA's time limits in which to respond to a request, it may not charge search fees or, in the instances of requests from educational institutions, noncommercial scientific institutions, or representatives of the news media, may not charge duplication fees, except as described in this paragraph (d).

(ii) If the Office has determined that unusual circumstances, as defined by FOIA, apply and the agency provides timely written notice to the requester, a failure to comply with the time limit shall be excused for an additional 10 days.

(iii) If the Office has determined that unusual circumstances, as defined by FOIA, apply and more than 5,000 pages are necessary to respond to the request, the Office may charge fees if the Office has provided timely written notice of the unusual circumstances to the requester in accordance with FOIA and the Office has discussed with the requester (or made not less than three good-faith attempts to do so) how the requester could effectively limit the scope of the request in accordance with 5 U.S.C. 552(a)(6)(B)(ii).

(iv) If a court has determined that exceptional circumstances exist, as defined by the FOIA, a failure to comply with the time limits shall be excused for the length of time provided by the court order.

(2) No search or review fees will be charged for a quarter-hour period unless more than half of that period is required for search or review.

(3) Except for requesters seeking records for a commercial use, the Office will provide without charge:

(i) The first 100 pages of duplication (or the cost equivalent for other media); and

(ii) The first two hours of search.

(4) No fee will be charged when the total fee, after deducting the first 100 pages (or its cost equivalent) and the first two hours of search, is equal to or less than $25.00.

(5) No fees will be charged for ordinary packaging and mailing costs.

(e) Notice of anticipated fees in excess of $25.00. **(1)** When the Office determines or estimates that the fees to be assessed will exceed $25.00, the Office shall notify the requester of the actual or estimated amount of the fees, including a breakdown of the fees for search, review or duplication, unless the requester has indicated a willingness to pay fees as high as those anticipated. If only a portion of the fee can be estimated readily, the Office will advise the requester accordingly. If the request is a noncommercial use requester, the notice shall include the services provided without charge indicated in paragraph (d)(3) of this section, and shall advise the requester whether those entitlements have been provided.

(2) When a requester has been provided notice of anticipated fees in excess of $25.00, the request shall not be considered received and further work will not be completed until the requester commits in writing to pay the actual or estimated total fee, to designate which fees the requester is willing to pay, or, for noncommercial requests, to indicate that the requester seeks only the services that can be provided in paragraph (d)(3) of this section without charge. The Office is not required to accept payment in installments.

(3) When the requester has committed to pay some designated amount of fees, but the Office estimates that the total fee will exceed that amount, the Office shall toll processing of the request when it notifies the requester of the estimated fees in excess of the requester's commitment. The Office shall inquire whether the requester wishes to revise the amount of fees the requester is willing to pay or modify the request. Once the requester responds, the time to respond will resume from where it was at the date of the notification.

(4) The Office shall make available the FOIA Public Liaison to assist the requester in reformulating a request to meet the requester's needs at a lower cost.

(f) Charges for other services. Although not required to provide special services, if the Office chooses to do so as a matter of administrative discretion, the direct costs of providing the service shall be charged.

(g) Charging interest. The Office may charge interest on any unpaid bill starting on the 31st day following the date of billing the requester. Interest charges will be assessed at the rate provided in 31 U.S.C. 3717 and will accrue from the billing date until payment is received by the Office.

(h) Aggregating requests. When the Office reasonably believes that a requester or group of requesters acting in concert is attempting to divide a single request into a series of requests for the purpose of avoiding fees, the Office may aggregate those requests and charge accordingly. The Office may presume that multiple requests of this type made within a 30-day period have been made in order to avoid fees. For requests separated by a longer period, agencies will aggregate them only where there is a reasonable basis for determining that aggregation is warranted in view of all the circumstances involved. Multiple requests involving unrelated matters cannot be aggregated.

(i) Advance payments. (1) For requests other than those described in paragraph (i)(2) or (3) of this section, the Copyright Office cannot require the requester to make an advance payment before work is commenced or continued on a request. Payment owed for work already completed is not an advance payment.

(2) When the Office determines or estimates that a total fee to be charged under this section will exceed $250.00, it may require that the requester make an advance payment up to the amount of the entire anticipated fee before beginning to process the request. The Office may elect to process the request prior to collecting fees when it receives a satisfactory assurance of full payment from a requester with a history of prompt payment.

(3) Where a requester has previously failed to pay a properly charged FOIA fee to any agency within 30 calendar days of the billing date, the Office may require that the requester pay the full amount due, plus any applicable interest on that prior request, and the Office may require that the requester make an advance payment of the full amount of any anticipated fee before the Office begins to process a new request or continues to process a pending request or any pending appeal. Where the Office has a reasonable basis to believe that a requester has misrepresented the requester's identity in order to avoid paying outstanding fees, it may require that the requester provide proof of identity.

(4) In cases in which the Office requires advance payment, the request will not be considered received and further work will not be completed until the required payment is received. If the requester does not pay the advance payment within 30 calendar days after the date of the Office's fee determination, the request will be closed.

(j) Other statutes specifically providing for fees. The provisions of this section do not apply with respect to the charging of fees for which the copyright law requires a fee to be charged. Requesters asking for copies of records about themselves shall be processed under the Privacy Act fee schedule found in §204.6 of this chapter. Fees for services by the Office in the administration of the copyright law are contained in §201.3 of this chapter. In instances where records responsive to a request are subject to the statutorily-based fee schedule, the Office will inform the requester of the service and appropriate fee.

(k) Requirements for waiver or reduction of fees. (1) Records responsive to a request shall be furnished without charged[1] or at a reduced rate where the Office determines, based on all available information, that the requester has demonstrated that:

(i) Disclosure of the requested information is in the public interested[2] because it is likely to contribute significantly to the public understanding of the operations or activities of the government; and

(ii) Disclosure of the information is not primarily in the commercial interest of the requester.

(2) In deciding whether the requester has demonstrated the requirement of paragraph (k)(1)(i) of this section, the Office shall consider all four of the following factors:

(i) The subject of the request must concern identifiable operations or activities of the Federal Government, with a connection that is direct and clear, not remote or attenuated.

(ii) Disclosure of the requested records must be meaningfully informative about government operations or activities in order to be "likely to contribute" to an increased public understanding of those operations or activities. The disclosure of information that already is in the public domain, in either the same or a substantially identical form, would not contribute to such understanding where nothing new would be added to the public's understanding.

(iii) The disclosure must contribute to the understanding of a reasonably broad audience of persons interested in the subject, as opposed to the individual understanding of the requester. A requester's expertise in the subject area as well as the requester's ability and intention to effectively convey information to the public shall be considered. It shall be presumed that a representative of the news media will satisfy this consideration.

(iv) The public's understanding of the subject in question must be enhanced by the disclosure to a significant extent. However, the Office shall not make value judgments about whether the information at issue is "important" enough to be made public.

(3) In deciding whether the requester has demonstrated the requirement of paragraph (k)(1)(ii) of this section, the Office shall consider the following two factors:

(i) The Office shall identify any commercial interest of the requester that would be furthered by the requested disclosure. Requesters shall be given an opportunity to provide explanatory information regarding this consideration.

(ii) A waiver or reduction of fees is justified where the public interest is greater than any identified commercial interest in disclosure. The Office ordinarily shall presume that where a news media requester has satisfied the public interest standard, the public interest will be the interest primarily served by disclosure to that requester. Disclosure to data brokers or others who merely compile and market government information for direct economic return shall not be presumed to primarily serve the public interest.

(4) Where only some of the records to be released satisfy the requirements for a waiver of fees, a waiver shall be granted for those records.

(5) Requests for a waiver or reduction of fees should be made when the request is first submitted to the Office and should address the criteria referenced above. A requester may submit a fee waiver request at a later time so long as the underlying record request is pending or on administrative appeal. When a requester who has committed to pay fees subsequently asks for a waiver of those fees and that waiver is denied, the requester shall be required to pay any costs incurred up to the date the fee waiver request was received.

1. **Editor's note:** Probably should be "charge."
2. **Editor's note:** Probably should be "interest."

History of 37 C.F.R. §203.11: 82 FR 9509, Mar. 9, 2017.

PART 204. PRIVACY ACT: POLICIES & PROCEDURES

§204.1. PURPOSES & SCOPE

The purposes of these regulations are:

(a) The establishment of procedures by which an individual can determine if the Copyright Office maintains a system of records in which there is a record pertaining to the individual; and

(b) The establishment of procedures by which an individual may gain access to a record or information maintained on that individual and have such record or information disclosed for the purpose of review, copying, correction, or amendment.

Source of 37 C.F.R. Part 204: 43 FR 776, Jan. 4, 1978; 59 FR 23981, May 9, 1994; 60 FR 34169, June 30, 1995; 65 FR 39820, June 28, 2000, unless otherwise noted.

§204.2. DEFINITIONS

For purposes of this part:

(a) The term "individual" means a citizen of the United States or an alien lawfully admitted for permanent residence;

(b) The term "maintain" includes maintain, collect, use, or disseminate;

(c) The term "record" means any item, collection, or grouping of information about an individual that is maintained by an agency, including, but not limited to, his education, financial transactions, medical history, and criminal or employment history, and that contains his or her name, or the identifying number, symbol, or other identifying particular assigned to the individual, such as a finger or voice print or a photograph;

(d) The term "system of records" means a group of any records under the control of any agency from which information is retrieved by the name of the individual; and

(e) The term "routine use" means, with respect to the disclosure of a record, the use of such record for a purpose which is compatible with the purpose for which it was collected.

§204.3. GENERAL POLICY

The Copyright Office serves primarily as an office of public record. Section 705 of Title 17, United States Code, requires the Copyright Office to open for public inspection all records of copyright deposits, registrations, recordations, and other actions taken under Title 17. Therefore, a routine use of all Copyright Office systems of records created under section 705 of Title 17 is disclosure to the public. All Copyright Office systems of records created under section 705 of Title 17 are also available for public copying as required by section 706(a), with the exception of copyright deposits, whose reproduction is governed by section 706(b) and the regulations issued under that section. In addition to the records mandated by section 705 of Title 17, the Copyright Office maintains other systems of records which are necessary for the Office effectively to carry out its mission. These systems of records are routinely consulted and otherwise used by Copyright Office employees in the performance of their duties. The Copyright Office will not sell, rent, or otherwise make publicly available any mailing list prepared by the Office.

History of 37 C.F.R. §204.3: 43 FR 776, Jan. 4, 1978; 47 FR 36821, Aug. 24, 1982.

§204.4. PROCEDURE FOR NOTIFICATION OF THE EXISTENCE OF RECORDS PERTAINING TO INDIVIDUALS

(a) The Copyright Office will publish in the Federal Register, upon the establishment or revision of the system of records, notices of all Copyright Office systems of records subject to the Privacy Act, as provided by 5 U.S.C., section 552a(e)(4). Individuals desiring to know if a Copyright Office system of records contains a record pertaining to them should submit a written request to that effect either by mail to the Supervisory Copyright Information Specialist, U.S. Copyright Office, P.O. Box 70400, Washington, DC 20024-0400, or in person between the hours of 8:30 a.m. and 5 p.m. on any working day except legal holidays at Room LM-401, The James Madison Memorial Building, 1st and Independence Avenue, SE, Washington, D.C.

(b) The written request should identify clearly the system of records which is the subject of inquiry, by reference, whenever possible, to the system number and title as given in the notices of systems of records in the Federal Register. Both the written request and the envelope carrying it should be plainly marked "Privacy Act Request." Failure to so mark the request may delay the Office's response.

(c) The Office will acknowledge all properly marked requests made by individuals wishing to gain access to view or copy their records or any information pertaining to the individual, within a reasonable time. The Office will acknowledge in writing an individual's request to amend a record pertaining to him or her within ten business days.

(d) Since all Copyright Office records created under section 705 of Title 17 are open to public inspection, no identity verification is necessary for individuals who wish to know whether a system of records created under section 705 pertains to them.

History of 37 C.F.R. §204.4: 43 FR 776, Jan. 4, 1978; 47 FR 36821, Aug. 24, 1982; 50 FR 32697, Aug. 14, 1985; 60 FR 34169, June 30, 1995; 64 FR 36575, July 7, 1999; 65 FR 39820, June 28, 2000; 73 FR 37839, July 1, 2008; 82 FR 9364, Mar. 8, 2017.

§204.5. PROCEDURES FOR REQUESTING ACCESS TO RECORDS

(a) Individuals desiring to obtain access to Copyright Office information pertaining to them in a system of records other than those created under section 705 of Title 17 should make a written request, signed by themselves or their duly authorized agent, to that effect either by mail to the Supervisory Copyright Information Specialist, U.S. Copyright Office, P.O. Box 70400, Washington, DC 20024-0400, or in person between the hours of 8:30 a.m. and 5 p.m. on any working day except legal holidays at Room LM-401, The James Madison Memorial Building, 1st and Independence Avenue SE., Washington, D.C.

(b) The written request should identify clearly the system of records which is the subject of inquiry, by reference, whenever possible, to the system number and title as given in the notices of systems of records in the Federal Register. Both the written request and the envelope carrying it should be plainly marked "Privacy Act Request." Failure to so mark the request may delay the Office's response.

(c) The Office will acknowledge all properly marked requests within 20 working days of receipt; and will notify the requester within 30 working days of receipt when and where access to the record will be granted. If the individual requested a copy of the record, the copy will accompany such notification.

History of 37 C.F.R. §204.5: 43 FR 776, Jan. 4, 1978; 47 FR 36821, Aug. 24, 1982; 60 FR 34169, June 30, 1995; 64 FR 36575, July 7, 1999; 65 FR 39820, June 28, 2000; 73 FR 37839, July 1, 2008; 82 FR 9364, Mar. 8, 2017.

§204.6. FEES

(a) The Copyright Office will provide, free of charge, one copy to an individual of any record pertaining to that individual contained in a Copyright Office system of records, except where the request is for a copy of a record for which a specific fee is required and identified in §201.3 of this chapter, in which case that fee shall be charged. For additional copies of records not covered by section 708 the fee will be a minimum of $15.00 for up to 15 pages and $.50 per page over 15. The Office will require prepayment of fees estimated to exceed $25.00 and will remit any excess paid or bill an additional amount according to the differences between the final fee charged and the amount prepaid. When prepayment is required, a request is not deemed "received" until prepayment has been made.

(b) The Copyright Office may waive the fee requirement whenever it determines that such waiver would be in the public interest.

History of 37 C.F.R. §204.6: 43 FR 776, Jan. 4, 1978; 47 FR 36821, Aug. 24, 1982; 56 FR 59886, Nov. 26, 1991; 63 FR 29139, May 28, 1998; 64 FR 29522, June 1, 1999.

§204.7. REQUEST FOR CORRECTION OR AMENDMENT OF RECORDS

(a) Any individual may request the correction or amendment of a record pertaining to her or him. Requests for the removal of personally identifiable information requested by the Copyright Office as part of an application for copyright registration are governed by §201.2(e) of this chapter. Requests for the removal of extraneous personally identifiable information, such as driver's license numbers, social security numbers, banking information, and credit card information from registration records are governed by §201.2(f) of this chapter. With respect to the correction or amendment of all other information contained in a copyright registration, the set of procedures and related fees are governed by 17 U.S.C. 408(d) and §201.5 of this chapter. With respect to requests to amend any other record that an individual believes is incomplete, inaccurate, irrelevant or untimely, the request shall be in writing and delivered either by mail addressed to the U.S. Copyright Office, Supervisory Copyright Information Specialist, Copyright Information Section, Attn: Privacy Act Request, P.O. Box 70400, Washington, DC 20024-0400, or in person Monday through Friday between the hours of 8:30 a.m. and 5 p.m., eastern time, except legal holidays, at Room LM-401, Library of Congress, U.S. Copyright Office, 101 Independence Avenue SE., Washington, DC 20559-6000. The request shall explain why the individual believes the record to be incomplete, inaccurate, irrelevant, or untimely.

(b) With respect to requests for the correction or amendment of records that are governed by this section, the Office will respond within 10 working days indicating to the requester that the requested correction or amendment has been made or that it has been refused. If the requested correction or amendment is refused, the Office's response will indicate the reason for the refusal and the procedure available to the individual to appeal the refusal.

History of 37 C.F.R. §204.7: 43 FR 776, Jan. 4, 1978; 47 FR 36821, Aug. 24, 1982; 60 FR 34169, June 30, 1995; 64 FR 36575, July 7, 1999; 65 FR 39820, June 28, 2000; 73 FR 37839, July 1, 2008; 82 FR 9009, Mar. 6, 2017; 82 FR 12180, Mar. 1, 2017.

§204.8. APPEAL OF REFUSAL TO CORRECT OR AMEND AN INDIVIDUAL'S RECORD

(a) An individual who disagrees with a refusal of the Copyright Office to amend his or her record may request a review of the denial. The individual should submit a written appeal to the General Counsel of the United States Copyright Office at the address specified in §201.1(c)(1) of this chapter. Appeals, and the envelopes containing them, should be plainly marked "Privacy Act Appeal." Failure to so mark the appeal may delay the General Counsel's response. An appeal should contain a copy of the request for amendment or correction and a copy of the record alleged to be untimely, inaccurate, incomplete, or irrelevant.

(b) The General Counsel will issue a written decision granting or denying the appeal within 30 working days after receipt of the appeal unless, after showing good cause, the General Counsel extends the 30-day period. If the appeal is granted, the requested amendment or correction will be made promptly. If the appeal is denied, in whole or in part, the General Counsel's decision will set forth reasons for the denial. Additionally, the decision will advise the requester that he or she has the right to file with the Copyright Office a concise statement of his or her reasons for disagreeing with the refusal to amend the record and that such statement will be attached to the requester's record and included in any future disclosure of such record. If the requester is dissatisfied with the agency's final determination, the individual may bring a civil action against the Office in the appropriate United States district court.

History of 37 C.F.R. §204.8: 64 FR 36575, July 7, 1999; 65 FR 39820, June 28, 2000; 65 FR 48914, Aug. 10, 2000; 66 FR 34373, June 28, 2001; 73 FR 37840, July 1, 2008; 82 FR 9364, Mar. 8, 2017.

§204.9. JUDICIAL REVIEW

Within two years of the receipt of a final adverse administrative determination, an individual may seek judicial review of that determination as provided in 5 U.S.C. 552a(g)(1).

PART 205. LEGAL PROCESSES

SUBPART A. GENERAL PROVISIONS

§205.1. DEFINITIONS

For the purpose of this part:

Demand means an order, subpoena or any other request for documents or testimony for use in a legal proceeding.

Document means any record or paper held by the Copyright Office, including, without limitation, official letters, deposits, recordations, registrations, publications, or other material submitted in connection with a claim for registration of a copyrighted work.

Employee means any current or former officer or employee of the Copyright Office, as well as any individual subject to the jurisdiction, supervision, or control of the Copyright Office.

General Counsel, unless otherwise specified, means the General Counsel and Associate Register of Copyrights or his or her designee.

Legal proceeding means any pretrial, trial, and post-trial stages of existing or reasonably anticipated judicial or administrative actions, hearings, investigations, or similar proceedings before courts, commissions, boards or other tribunals, foreign or domestic. This phrase includes all phases of discovery as well as responses to formal or informal requests by attorneys or others involved in legal proceedings. This phrase also includes state court proceedings (including grand jury proceedings) and any other state or local legislative and administrative proceedings.

Office means the Copyright Office, including any division, section, or operating unit within the Copyright Office.

Official business means the authorized business of the Copyright Office.

Testimony means a statement in any form, including a personal appearance before a court or other legal tribunal, an interview, a deposition, an affidavit or declaration under penalty of perjury pursuant to 28 U.S.C. 1746, a telephonic, televised, or videotaped statement or any response given during discovery or similar proceeding, which response would involve more than the production of documents, including a declaration under 35 U.S.C. 25 or a declaration under penalty of perjury pursuant to 28 U.S.C. 1746.

United States means the Federal Government, its departments and agencies, individuals acting on behalf of the Federal Government, and parties to the extent they are represented by the United States.

History of 37 C.F.R. §205.1: 82 FR 9364, Mar. 8, 2017.

Source of 37 C.F.R. Part 205A: 59 FR 23981, May 9, 1994; 69 FR 39334, June 30, 2004, unless otherwise noted.

§205.2. ADDRESS FOR MAIL & SERVICE; TELEPHONE NUMBER

(a) Mail under this part should be addressed to the General Counsel at the address specified in §201.1(c)(1) of this chapter.

(b) Service by hand shall be made upon an authorized person from 8:30 a.m. to 5 p.m., Monday through Friday in the Copyright Information Section, U.S. Copyright Office, Library of Congress, James Madison Memorial Building, Room LM-401, 101 Independence Avenue SE., Washington, DC. Persons authorized to accept service of process are the General Counsel of the Copyright Office and his or her designees.

(c) The Office of the General Counsel may be reached by telephone during normal business hours specified in paragraph (b) of this section at 202-707-8380.

History of 37 C.F.R. §205.2: 73 FR 37840, July 1, 2008; 82 FR 9365, Mar. 8, 2017.

§205.3. WAIVER OF RULES

In extraordinary situations, when the interest of justice requires, the General Counsel may waive or suspend the rules of this part, sua sponte or on petition of an interested party, subject to such requirements as the General Counsel may impose on the parties. However, the inclusion of certain legal processes within the scope of these rules, e.g., state legal proceedings, does not represent a waiver of any claim of immunity, privilege, or other defense by the Office in a legal proceeding, including but not limited to, sovereign immunity, preemption, or lack of relevance. This rule does not create any right or benefit, substantive or procedural, enforceable at law by a party against the Copyright Office, the Library of Congress, or the United States.

§205.4. RELATIONSHIP OF THIS PART TO THE FEDERAL RULES OF CIVIL & CRIMINAL PROCEDURE

Nothing in this part waives any requirement under the Federal Rules of Civil or Criminal Procedure.

§205.5. SCOPE OF THIS PART RELATED TO COPYRIGHT OFFICE DUTIES UNDER TITLE 17 OF THE U.S. CODE

This part relates only to legal proceedings, process, requests and demands relating to the Copyright Office's performance of its duties pursuant to title 17 of the United States Code. Legal proceedings, process, requests and demands relating to other matters (e.g., personal injuries, employment matters, etc.) are the responsibility of the General Counsel of the Library of Congress and are governed by 36 CFR part 703.

§§205.6 TO 205.10. ADDED & RESERVED

SUBPART B. SERVICE OF PROCESS

§205.11. SCOPE & PURPOSE

(a) This subpart provides the procedures governing service of process on the Copyright Office and its employees in their official capacity. These regulations provide the identity of Copyright Office officials who are authorized to accept service of process. The purpose of this subpart is to provide a centralized location for receipt of service of process to the Office. Such centralization will provide timely notification of legal process and expedite the Office's response. Litigants also must comply with all requirements pertaining to service of process that are established by statute, court rule and rule of procedure including the applicable provisions of the Federal Rules of Civil Procedure governing service upon the United States.

(b) This subpart does not apply to service of process made on an employee personally for matters not related to official business of the Office. Process served upon a Copyright Office employee in his or her individual capacity must be served in compliance with the applicable requirements for service of process established by statute, court rule, or rule of procedure.

History of 37 C.F.R. §205.11: 82 FR 9365, Mar. 8, 2017.

Source of 37 C.F.R. Part 205B: 59 FR 23981, May 9, 1994; 69 FR 39334, June 30, 2004, unless otherwise noted.

§205.12. PROCESS SERVED ON THE REGISTER OF COPYRIGHTS OR AN EMPLOYEE IN HIS OR HER OFFICIAL CAPACITY

(a) Summonses, complaints and all other process directed to the Copyright Office, the Register of Copyrights or any other Copyright Office employee in his or her official capacity should be served on the General Counsel of the Copyright Office or his or her designee as indicated in §205.2 of this part. To effect proper service, the requirements of Rule 4(i) of the Federal Rules of Civil Procedure must also be satisfied by effecting service on both the United States Attorney for the district in which the action is brought and the Attorney General, Attn: Director of Intellectual Property Staff, Commercial Litigation Branch, Civil Division, Department of Justice, Washington, DC 20530.

(b) If, notwithstanding paragraph (a) of this section, any employee of the Office is served with a summons or complaint in connection with the conduct of official business, that employee shall immediately notify and deliver the summons or complaint to the Office of the General Counsel of the Copyright Office.

(c) Any employee receiving a summons or complaint shall note on the summons or complaint the date, hour, and place of service and mode of service.

(d) The Office will accept service of process for an employee only when the legal proceeding is brought in connection with the conduct of official business carried out in the employee's official capacity.

(e) When a legal proceeding is brought to hold an employee personally liable in connection with an action taken in the conduct of official business, rather than liable in an official capacity, the employee is to be served in accordance with any applicable statute, court rule, or rule of procedure. Service of process in this case is inadequate when made only on the General Counsel. An employee sued personally for an action taken in the conduct of official business shall immediately notify and deliver a copy of the summons or complaint to the General Counsel of the Copyright Office.

§205.13. COMPLAINTS SERVED ON THE REGISTER OF COPYRIGHTS PURSUANT TO 17 U.S.C. 411(a)

When an action has been instituted pursuant to 17 U.S.C. 411(a) for infringement of the copyright of a work for which registration has been refused, notice of the institution of the action and a copy of the complaint must be served on the Register of Copyrights by sending such documents by registered or certified mail to the General Counsel of the Copyright Office at the address specified in §201.1(c)(1) of this chapter, or delivery by hand addressed to the General Counsel of the Copyright Office and delivered to the Copyright Information Section, U.S. Copyright Office, Library of Congress, James Madison Memorial Building, Room LM-401, 101 Independence Avenue SE., Washington, DC. The notice must be in the form of a letter that is clearly identified as a 411(a) notice. Both the letter and the envelope should state: "Section 411(a) Notice to the Register of Copyrights." In compliance with Fed. R. Civ. P. §4(i), a notice of the institution of the action and a copy of the complaint must also be served on both the United States Attorney for the district in which the action is brought and the United States Department of Justice, directed to the Attorney General, Attn: Director of Intellectual Property Staff, Civil Division, Department of Justice, Washington, DC 20530.

History of 37 C.F.R. §205.13: 73 FR 37840, July 1, 2008; 82 FR 9365, Mar. 8, 2017.

§§205.14 TO 205.20. ADDED & RESERVED

SUBPART C. TESTIMONY BY EMPLOYEES & PRODUCTION OF DOCUMENTS IN LEGAL PROCEEDINGS IN WHICH THE OFFICE IS NOT A PARTY

§205.21. SCOPE & PURPOSE

(a) This subpart prescribes policies and procedures of the Copyright Office governing testimony, in legal proceedings in which the Office is not a party, by Office employees in their official capacities and the production of Office documents for use in legal proceedings pursuant to a demand, request, subpoena or order.

(b) The purpose of this subpart is:

(1) To conserve the time of Office employees for conducting official business;

(2) To minimize the possibility of involving the Office in the matters of private parties or other issues which are not related to the mission of the Office;

(3) To prevent the public from confusing personal opinions of Office employees with Office policy;

(4) To avoid spending the time and money of the United States for private purposes;

(5) To preserve the integrity of the administrative process, minimize disruption of the decision-making process, and prevent interference with the Office's administrative functions.

(c) An employee of the Office may not voluntarily appear as a witness or voluntarily testify in a legal proceeding relating to his or her official capacity without proper authorization under this subpart.

(d) This subpart does not apply to any legal proceeding in which:

(1) An employee is to testify regarding facts or events that are unrelated to official business; or

(2) A former employee is asked to testify as an expert on a matter in which that employee did not personally participate while at the Office so long as the former employee testifies concerning his or her personal opinion and does not purport to speak for or on behalf of the Copyright Office.

Source of 37 C.F.R. Part 205C: 59 FR 23981, May 9, 1994; 69 FR 39334, June 30, 2004, unless otherwise noted.

§205.22. PRODUCTION OF DOCUMENTS & TESTIMONY

(a) Generally, all documents and material submitted to the Copyright Office as part of an application to register a claim to copyright are available for public inspection and copying. It is possible, therefore, to obtain those materials without use of a legal process. Anyone seeking such documents must contact the Records Research and Certification Section of the Office. 37 CFR 201.2(b)(1). Certified copies of public documents and public records are self-authenticating. FED. R. EVID. 902 and 1005; see also, FED. R. CIV. P. 44(a)(1). In certain specified circumstances, information contained in the in-process files may be obtained by complying with the procedures of 37 CFR 201.2(b)(3). Correspondence between a copyright claimant or his or her agent and the Copyright Office in a completed registration, recordation, or refusal to register is also available for public inspection. Section 201.2(d) of this chapter prescribes the method for requesting copies of copyright registration records. An attorney engaged in actual or prospective litigation who submits a court order or a completed Litigation Statement may obtain a copy of the deposit if his or her request is found to comply with the requirements set out in 37 CFR 201.2(d)(2). The fees associated with various document requests, searches, copies, and expedited handling are listed in 37 CFR 201.3. Other publications containing Copyright Office procedures and practices are available to the public without charge from the Copyright Office or its website: http://www.copyright.gov. The Office website also allows online searching of copyright registration information and information pertaining to documents recorded with the Copyright Office beginning January 1, 1978. Pre-1978 copyright registration information and document recordation information is available to the public in the Copyright Office during regular business hours. If the information sought to be obtained from the Office is not available through these Office services, demands and subpoenas for testimony or documents may be served as follows:

(1) Demands for testimony or documents. All demands, requests, subpoenas or orders for production of documents or testimony in a legal proceeding directed to the Copyright Office, the Register of Copyrights or any other Copyright Office employee in his or her official capacity must be in writing and should be served on the General Counsel of the Copyright Office as indicated in §205.2 of this part and in accordance with the Federal Rules of Civil or Criminal Procedure.

(2) Affidavits. Except when the Copyright Office is a party to the legal proceeding, every demand, request or subpoena shall be accompanied by an affidavit or declaration under penalty of perjury pursuant to 28 U.S.C. 1746. Such affidavit or declaration shall contain a written statement setting forth the title of the legal proceeding; the forum; the requesting party's interest in the legal proceeding; the reasons for the demand, request, or subpoena; a showing that the desired testimony or document is not reasonably available from any published or other written source, (e.g., 37 CFR, Chapter II; Compendium of U.S. Copyright Office Practices, Third Edition; other written practices of the Office; circulars; the Copyright Office website) and is not available by other established procedure, e.g. 37 CFR 201.2, 201.3. If testimony is requested in the affidavit or declaration, it shall include the intended use of the testimony, a detailed summary of the testimony desired, and a showing that no document could be provided and used in lieu of the requested testimony. The purpose of these requirements is to permit the General Counsel of the Copyright Office to make an informed decision as to whether testimony or production of a document should be authorized. The decision by the General Counsel will be based on consideration of the purposes set forth in §205.21(b) of this part, on the evaluation of the requesting party's need for the testimony and any other factor warranted by the circumstances. Typically, when the information requested is available through other existing Office procedures or materials, the General Counsel will not authorize production of documents or testimony.

(b) No Copyright Office employee shall give testimony concerning the official business of the Office or produce any document in a legal proceeding other than those made available by the Records Research and Certification Section under existing regulations without the prior authorization of the General Counsel. Without prior approval from the General Counsel of the Copyright Office, no Office employee shall answer inquiries from a person not employed by the Library of Congress or the Department of Justice regarding testimony or documents in connection with a demand, subpoena or order. All inquiries involving demands, subpoenas, or orders shall be directed to the General Counsel of the Copyright Office.

(c) Any Office employee who receives a demand, request, subpoena or order for testimony or the production of documents in a legal proceeding shall immediately notify the General Counsel of the Copyright Office at the phone number indicated in §205.2 of this part and shall immediately forward the demand to the General Counsel.

(d) The General Counsel may consult or negotiate with an attorney for a party or the party, if not represented by an attorney, to refine or limit a demand, request or subpoena to address interests or concerns of the Office. Failure of the attorney or party to cooperate in good faith under this part may serve as the basis for the General Counsel to deny authorization for the testimony or production of documents sought in the demand.

(e) A determination under this part regarding authorization to respond to a demand is not an assertion or waiver of privilege, lack of relevance, technical deficiency or any other ground for noncompliance. The Copyright Office reserves the right to oppose any demand on any appropriate legal ground independent of any determination under this part, including but not limited to, sovereign immunity, preemption, privilege, lack of relevance, or technical deficiency.

(f) Office procedures when an employee receives a demand or subpoena. **(1)** If the General Counsel has not acted by the return date, the employee must appear at the time and place set forth in the subpoena (unless otherwise advised by the General Counsel) and inform the court (or other legal authority) that the demand has been referred for the prompt consideration of the General Counsel and shall request the court (or other legal authority) to stay the demand pending receipt of the requested instructions.

(2) If the General Counsel makes a determination not to authorize testimony or the production of documents, but the subpoena is not withdrawn or modified and Department of Justice representation cannot be arranged, the employee should appear at the time and place set forth in the subpoena unless advised otherwise by the General Counsel. If legal counsel cannot appear on behalf of the employee, the employee should produce a copy of these rules and state that the General Counsel has advised the employee not to provide the requested testimony or to produce the requested document. If a court (or other legal authority) rules that the demand in the subpoena must be complied with, the employee shall respectfully decline to comply with the demand, citing *United States ex rel. Touhy v. Ragen*, 340 U.S. 462 (1951).

History of 37 C.F.R. §205.22: 73 FR 37840, July 1, 2008; 82 FR 9365, Mar. 8, 2017.

§205.23. SCOPE OF TESTIMONY

(a)(1) If a Copyright Office employee is authorized to give testimony in a legal proceeding, the testimony, if otherwise proper, shall be limited to facts within the personal knowledge of the Office employee. An Office employee is prohibited from giving expert testimony, or opinion, answering hypothetical or speculative questions, or giving testimony with respect to subject matter which is privileged. If an Office employee is authorized to testify in connection with his or her involvement or assistance in a proceeding or matter before the Office, that employee is further prohibited from giving testimony in response to an inquiry about the bases, reasons, mental processes, analyses, or conclusions of that employee in the performance of his or her official functions.

(2) The General Counsel may authorize an employee to appear and give expert testimony or opinion testimony upon the showing, pursuant to §205.3 of this part, that exceptional circumstances warrant such testimony and that the anticipated testimony will not be adverse to the interest of the Copyright Office or the United States.

(b) If an Office employee is authorized to testify, the employee will generally be prohibited from providing testimony in response to questions which seek, for example:

(1) To elicit information about the employee's:

(i) Qualifications to examine or otherwise consider a particular copyright application.

(ii) Usual practice or whether the employee followed a procedure set out in any Office manual of practice in a particular case.

(iii) Consultation with another Office employee.

(iv) Familiarity with:

(A) Preexisting works that are similar.

(B) Registered works, works sought to be registered, a copyright application, registration, denial of registration, or request for reconsideration.

(C) Copyright law or other law.

(D) The actions of another Office employee.

(v) Reliance on particular facts or arguments.

(2) To inquire into the manner in and extent to which the employee considered or studied material in performing the function.

(3) To inquire into the bases, reasons, mental processes, analyses, or conclusions of that Office employee in performing the function.

(c) In exceptional circumstances, the General Counsel may waive the limitations set forth in paragraph (b) of this section pursuant to §205.3.

History of 37 C.F.R. §205.23: 82 FR 9365, Mar. 8, 2017.

PART 210. COMPULSORY LICENSE FOR MAKING & DISTRIBUTING PHYSICAL & DIGITAL PHONORECORDS OF NONDRAMATIC MUSICAL WORKS

SUBPART A. RESERVED

§§210.1 TO 210.10. RESERVED

SUBPART B. ROYALTIES & STATEMENTS OF ACCOUNT UNDER COMPULSORY LICENSE

§210.11. GENERAL

This subpart prescribes rules for the payment of royalties and the preparation and service of statements of account under the compulsory license for the making and distribution of phonorecords of nondramatic musical works, including by means of a digital phonorecord delivery, pursuant to 17 U.S.C. 115 and the rates and terms in part 385 of this title.

History of 37 C.F.R. §210.11: 79 FR 56207, Sept. 18, 2014.

§210.12. DEFINITIONS

As used in this subpart:

(a) A Monthly Statement of Account or Monthly Statement is a statement accompanying monthly royalty payments identified in 17 U.S.C. 115(c)(5), and required by that section to be filed under the compulsory license to make and distribute phonorecords of nondramatic musical works, including by means of a digital phonorecord delivery.

(b) An Annual Statement of Account or Annual Statement is a statement identified in 17 U.S.C. 115(c)(5), and required by that section to be filed under the compulsory license to make and distribute phonorecords of nondramatic musical works, including by means of a digital phonorecord delivery. Such term, when used in this rule, includes an Amended Annual Statement of Account filed pursuant to §210.17(d)(2)(iii).

(c) A digital phonorecord delivery is each individual delivery of a phonorecord by digital transmission of a sound recording which results in a specifically identifiable reproduction by or for any transmission recipient of a phonorecord of that sound recording, regardless of whether the digital transmission is also a public performance of the sound recording or any nondramatic musical work embodied therein. The reproduction of the phonorecord must be sufficiently permanent or stable to permit it to be perceived, reproduced, or otherwise communicated for a period of more than transitory duration. Such a phonorecord may be permanent or it may be made available to the transmission recipient for a limited period of time or for a specified number of performances. A digital phonorecord delivery includes all phonorecords that are made for the purpose of making the digital phonorecord delivery. A digital phonorecord delivery does not include any transmission that did not result in a specifically identifiable reproduction of the entire product being transmitted, and for which the distributor did not charge, or fully refunded, any monies that would otherwise be due for the relevant transmission.

(d) Ringtone shall have the meaning given in §385.2 of this title.

(e) The term copyright owner, in the case of any work having more than one copyright owner, means any one of the co-owners.

(f) A compulsory licensee is a person or entity exercising the compulsory license to make and distribute phonorecords of nondramatic musical works as provided under 17 U.S.C. 115, including by means of a digital phonorecord delivery.

(g) A phonorecord is considered distributed if the compulsory licensee has voluntarily and permanently parted with possession of the phonorecord, which shall occur as follows:

(1) In the case of physical phonorecords relinquished from possession for purposes other than sale, at the time at which the compulsory licensee actually first parts with possession;

(2) In the case of physical phonorecords relinquished from possession for purposes of sale without a privilege of returning unsold phonorecords for credit or exchange, at the time at which the compulsory licensee actually first parts with possession;

(3) In the case of physical phonorecords relinquished from possession for purposes of sale accompanied by a privilege of returning unsold phonorecords for credit or exchange:

(i) At the time when revenue from a sale of the phonorecord is "recognized" by the compulsory licensee; or

(ii) Nine months from the month in which the compulsory licensee actually first parted with possession, whichever occurs first. For these purposes, a compulsory licensee shall be considered to "recognize" revenue from the sale of a phonorecord when sales revenue would be recognized in accordance with GAAP.

(4) In the case of a digital phonorecord delivery, on the date that the phonorecord is digitally transmitted.

(h) A phonorecord reserve comprises the number of phonorecords made under a particular compulsory license, if any, that have been relinquished from possession for purposes of sale in a given month accompanied by a privilege of return, as described in paragraph (g)(3) of this section, and that have not been considered distributed during the month in which the compulsory licensee actually first parted with their possession. The initial number of phonorecords comprising a phonorecord reserve shall be determined in accordance with GAAP.

(i) A negative reserve balance comprises the aggregate number of phonorecords made under a particular compulsory license, if any, that have been relinquished from possession for purposes of sale accompanied by a privilege of return, as described in paragraph (g)(3) of this section, and that have been returned to the compulsory licensee, but because all available phonorecord reserves have been eliminated, have not been used to reduce a phonorecord reserve.

(j) GAAP means U.S. Generally Accepted Accounting Principles, except that if the U.S. Securities and Exchange Commission permits or requires entities with securities that are publicly traded in the U.S. to employ International Financial Reporting Standards, as issued by the International Accounting Standards Board, or as accepted by the Securities and Exchange Commission if different from that issued by the International Accounting Standards Board, in lieu of Generally Accepted Accounting Principles, then an entity may employ International Financial Reporting Standards as "GAAP" for purposes of this subpart.

History of 37 C.F.R. §210.12: 79 FR 56207, Sept. 18, 2014.

§210.13. ACCOUNTING REQUIREMENTS WHERE SALES REVENUE IS "RECOGNIZED"

Where under §210.12(g)(3)(i), revenue from the sale of phonorecords is "recognized" during any month after the month in which the compulsory licensee actually first parted with their possession, said compulsory licensee shall reduce particular phonorecord reserves by the number of phonorecords for which revenue is being "recognized," as follows:

(a) If the number of phonorecords for which revenue is being "recognized" is smaller than the number of phonorecords comprising the earliest eligible phonorecord reserve, this phonorecord reserve shall be reduced by the number of phonorecords for which revenue is being "recognized." Subject to the time limitations of §210.12(g)(3)(ii), the number of phonorecords remaining in this reserve shall be available for use in subsequent months.

(b) If the number of phonorecords for which revenue is being "recognized" is greater than the number of phonorecords comprising the earliest eligible phonorecord reserve but less than the total number of phonorecords comprising all eligible phonorecord reserves, the compulsory licensee shall first eliminate those phonorecord reserves, beginning with the earliest eligible phonorecord reserve and continuing to the next succeeding phonorecord reserves, that are completely offset by phonorecords for which revenue is being "recognized." Said compulsory licensee shall then reduce the next succeeding phonorecord reserve by the number of phonorecords for which revenue is being "recognized" that have not been used to eliminate a phonorecord reserve. Subject to the time limitations of §210.12(g)(3)(ii), the number of phonorecords remaining in this reserve shall be available for use in subsequent months.

(c) If the number of phonorecords for which revenue is being "recognized" equals the number of phonorecords comprising all eligible phonorecord reserves, the person or entity exercising the compulsory license shall eliminate all of the phonorecord reserves.

(d) Digital phonorecord deliveries shall not be considered as accompanied by a privilege of return as described in §210.12(g)(3), and the compulsory licensee shall not take digital phonorecord deliveries into account in establishing phonorecord reserves.

History of 37 C.F.R. §210.13: 79 FR 56207, Sept. 18, 2014.

§210.14. ACCOUNTING REQUIREMENTS FOR OFFSETTING PHONORECORD RESERVES WITH RETURNED PHONORECORDS

(a) In the case of a phonorecord that has been relinquished from possession for purposes of sale accompanied by a privilege of return, as described in §210.12(g)(3), where the phonorecord is returned to the compulsory licensee for credit or exchange before said compulsory licensee is considered to have "voluntarily and permanently parted with possession" of the phonorecord as described in §210.12(g), the compulsory licensee may use such phonorecord to reduce a "phonorecord reserve," as defined in §210.12(h).

(b) In such cases, the compulsory licensee shall reduce particular phonorecord reserves by the number of phonorecords that are returned during the month covered by the Monthly Statement of Account in the following manner:

(1) If the number of phonorecords that are returned during the month covered by the Monthly Statement is smaller than the number comprising the earliest eligible phonorecord reserve, the compulsory licensee shall reduce this phonorecord reserve by the total number of returned phonorecords. Subject to the time limitations in §210.12(g)(3)(ii), the number of phonorecords remaining in this reserve shall be available for use in subsequent months.

(2) If the number of phonorecords that are returned during the month covered by the Monthly Statement is greater than the number of phonorecords comprising the earliest eligible phonorecord reserve but less than the total number of phonorecords comprising all eligible phonorecord reserves, the compulsory licensee shall first eliminate those phonorecord reserves, beginning with the earliest eligible phonorecord reserve, and continuing to the next succeeding phonorecord reserves, that are completely offset by returned phonorecords. Said compulsory licensee shall then reduce the next succeeding phonorecord reserve by the number of returned phonorecords that have not been used to eliminate a phonorecord reserve. Subject to the time limitations in §210.12(g)(3)(ii), the number of phonorecords remaining in this reserve shall be available for use in subsequent months.

(3) If the number of phonorecords that are returned during the month covered by the Monthly Statement is equal to or is greater than the total number of phonorecords comprising all eligible phonorecord reserves, the compulsory licensee shall eliminate all eligible phonorecord reserves. Where said number is greater than the total number of phonorecords comprising all eligible phonorecord reserves, said compulsory licensee shall establish a "negative reserve balance," as defined in §210.12(i).

(c) Except where a negative reserve balance exists, a separate and distinct phonorecord reserve shall be established for each month during which the compulsory licensee relinquishes phonorecords from possession for purposes of sale accompanied by a privilege of return, as described in §210.12(g)(3). In accordance with §210.12(g)(3)(ii), any phonorecord remaining in a particular phonorecord reserve nine months from the month in which the particular reserve was established shall be considered "distributed"; at that point, the particular monthly phonorecord reserve shall lapse and royalties for the phonorecords remaining in it shall be paid as provided in §210.16(d)(2).

(d) Where a negative reserve balance exists, the aggregate total of phonorecords comprising it shall be accumulated into a single balance rather than being separated into distinct monthly balances. Following the establishment of a negative reserve balance, any phonorecords relinquished from possession by the compulsory licensee for purposes of sale or otherwise, shall be credited against such negative balance, and the negative reserve balance shall be reduced accordingly. Digital phonorecord deliveries may be credited against such negative reserve balance, but only if such digital phonorecord deliveries have the same royalty rate as physical phonorecords under part 385 of this title. The nine-month limit provided in §210.12(g)(3)(ii) shall have no effect upon a negative reserve balance; where a negative reserve balance exists, relinquishment from possession of a phonorecord by the compulsory licensee at any time shall be used to reduce such balance, and such phonorecord shall not be considered "distributed" within the meaning of §210.12(g).

(e) In no case shall a phonorecord reserve be established while a negative reserve balance is in existence; conversely, in no case shall a negative reserve balance be established before all available phonorecord reserves have been eliminated.

History of 37 C.F.R. §210.14: 79 FR 56208, Sept. 18, 2014.

§210.15. SITUATIONS IN WHICH A COMPULSORY LICENSEE IS BARRED FROM MAINTAINING RESERVES

Notwithstanding any other provisions of this section, in any case where, within three years before the phonorecord was relinquished from possession, the compulsory licensee has had final judgment entered against it for failure to pay royalties for the reproduction of copyrighted music on phonorecords, or within such period has been definitively found in any proceeding involving bankruptcy, insolvency, receivership, assignment for the benefit of creditors, or similar action, to have failed to pay such royalties, that compulsory licensee shall be considered to have "permanently parted with possession" of a phonorecord made under the license at the time at which that compulsory licensee actually first parts with possession. For these purposes the compulsory licensee shall include:

(a) In the case of any corporation, the corporation or any director, officer, or beneficial owner of twenty-five percent (25%) or more of the outstanding securities of the corporation;

(b) In all other cases, any entity or individual owning a beneficial interest of twenty-five percent (25%) or more in the entity exercising the compulsory license.

History of 37 C.F.R. §210.15: 79 FR 56208, Sept. 18, 2014; 82 FR 9365, Mar. 8, 2017.

§210.16. MONTHLY STATEMENTS OF ACCOUNT

(a) Forms. The Copyright Office does not provide printed forms for the use of persons serving Monthly Statements of Account.

(b) General content. A Monthly Statement of Account shall be clearly and prominently identified as a "Monthly Statement of Account Under Compulsory License for Making and Distributing Phonorecords," and shall include a clear statement of the following information:

(1) The period (month and year) covered by the Monthly Statement.

(2) The full legal name of the compulsory licensee, together with all fictitious or assumed names used by such person or entity for the purpose of conducting the business of making and distributing phonorecords.

(3) The full address, including a specific number and street name or rural route, of the place of business of the compulsory licensee. A post office box or similar designation will not be sufficient for this purpose, except where it is the only address that can be used in that geographic location.

(4) For each nondramatic musical work that is owned by the same copyright owner being served with the Monthly Statement and that is embodied in phonorecords covered by the compulsory license, a detailed statement of all of the information called for in paragraph (c) of this section.

(5) The total royalty payable to the relevant copyright owner for the month covered by the Monthly Statement, computed in accordance with the requirements of this section and the formula specified in paragraph (d) of this section, including detailed information regarding how the royalty was computed.

(6) The amount of late fees, if applicable, included in the payment associated with the Monthly Statement.

(7) In any case where the compulsory licensee falls within the provisions of §210.15, a clear description of the action or proceeding involved, including the date of the final judgment or definitive finding described in that section.

(8) Detailed instructions on how to request records of any promotional uses of the copyright owner's works that are required to be maintained or provided under §385.14 or §385.24 of this title, or other applicable provision, including, where applicable, records required to be maintained or provided by any third parties that were authorized by the compulsory licensee to engage in promotional uses during any part of the month. If this information is provided, Monthly Statements need not reflect phonorecords subject to the promotional royalty rate provided in §385.14 or §385.24 of this title, or any similar promotional royalty rate of zero that may be provided in part 385 of this title.

(c) Specific content of monthly statements—(1) Accounting of phonorecords subject to a cents rate royalty structure. The information called for by paragraph (b)(4) of this section shall, with respect to each nondramatic musical work as to which the compulsory licensee has made and distributed phonorecords subject to part 385, subpart A of this title or any other provisions requiring computation of applicable royalties on a cents-per-unit basis, include a separate listing of each of the following items of information:

(i) The number of phonorecords made during the month covered by the Monthly Statement.

(ii) The number of phonorecords that, during the month covered by the Monthly Statement and regardless of when made, were either:

(A) Relinquished from possession for purposes other than sale;

(B) Relinquished from possession for purposes of sale without any privilege of returning unsold phonorecords for credit or exchange;

(C) Relinquished from possession for purposes of sale accompanied by a privilege of returning unsold phonorecords for credit or exchange;

(D) Returned to the compulsory licensee for credit or exchange; or

(E) Placed in a phonorecord reserve (except that if a negative reserve balance exists give either the number of phonorecords added to the negative reserve balance, or the number of phonorecords relinquished from possession that have been used to reduce the negative reserve balance).

(iii) The number of phonorecords, regardless of when made, that were relinquished from possession during a month earlier than the month covered by the Monthly Statement but that, during the month covered by the Monthly Statement either have had revenue from their sale "recognized" under §210.12(g)(3)(i), or were comprised in a phonorecord reserve that lapsed after nine months under §210.12(g)(3)(ii).

(iv) The per unit statutory royalty rate applicable to the relevant configuration; and

(v) The total royalty payable for the month covered by the Monthly Statement (i.e., the result in paragraph (d)(2)(v) of this section) for the item described by the set of information called for, and broken down as required, by paragraph (c)(1) of this section.

(vi) The phonorecord identification information required by paragraph (c)(3) of this section.

(2) Accounting of phonorecords subject to a percentage rate royalty structure. The information called for by paragraph (b)(4) of this section shall, with respect to each nondramatic musical work as to which the compulsory licensee has made and distributed phonorecords subject to part 385, subparts B or C of this title, or any other provisions requiring computation of applicable royalties on a percentage-rate basis, include a detailed and step-by-step accounting of the calculation of royalties under §385.12, §385.22, or other provisions of part 385 of this title as applicable, sufficient to allow the copyright owner to assess the manner in which the licensee determined the royalty owed and the accuracy of the royalty calculations, including but not limited to the following information:

(i) The number of plays, constructive plays, or other payable units, of the relevant sound recording for the month covered by the Monthly Statement for the relevant offering.

(ii) The total royalty payable for the month for the item described by the set of information called for, and broken down as required, by paragraph (c)(3) of this section (i.e., the per-work royalty allocation for the relevant sound recording and offering).

(iii) The phonorecord identification information required by paragraph (c)(3) of this section.

(3) Identification of phonorecords in monthly statements. The information required by this paragraph shall include, and if necessary shall be broken down to identify separately, the following:

(i) The title of the nondramatic musical work subject to compulsory license.

(ii) A reference number or code identifying the relevant Notice of Intention, if the compulsory licensee chose to include such a number or code on its relevant Notice of Intention for the compulsory license.

(iii) The International Standard Recording Code (ISRC) associated with the relevant sound recording, if known, and at least one of the following, as applicable and available for tracking sales and/or usage:

(A) The catalog number or numbers and label name or names, associated with the phonorecords;

(B) The Universal Product Code (UPC) or similar code used on or associated with the phonorecords; or

(C) The sound recording identification number assigned by the compulsory licensee or a third-party distributor to the relevant sound recording.

(iv) The names of the principal recording artist or group engaged in rendering the performances fixed on the phonorecords.

(v) The playing time of the relevant sound recording, except that playing time is not required in the case of ringtones or licensed activity to which no overtime adjustment is applicable.

(vi) If the compulsory licensee chooses to allocate its payment between co-owners of the copyright in the nondramatic musical work, as described in paragraph (g)(1) of this section, and thus pays the copyright owner (or agent) receiving the statement less than one hundred percent of the applicable royalty, the percentage share paid.

(vii) The names of the writer or writers of the nondramatic musical work, or the International Standard Name Identifiers (ISNIs) or other unique identifier of the writer or writers, if known.

(viii) The International Standard Musical Work Code (ISWC) or other unique identifier for the nondramatic musical work, if known.

(ix) Identification of the relevant phonorecord configuration (for example: compact disc, permanent digital download, ringtone) or offering (for example: limited download, music bundle) for which the royalty was calculated, including, if applicable and except for physical phonorecords, the name of the third-party distributor of the configuration or offering.

(d) Royalty payment and accounting—**(1)** In general. The total royalty called for by paragraph (b)(5) of this section shall be computed so as to include every phonorecord "distributed" during the month covered by the Monthly Statement.

(2) Phonorecords subject to a cents rate royalty structure. For phonorecords subject to part 385, subpart A of this title, or any other applicable royalties computed on a cents-per-unit basis, the amount of the royalty payment shall be calculated as follows:

(i) Step 1: Compute the number of phonorecords shipped for sale with a privilege of return. This is the total of phonorecords that, during the month covered by the Monthly Statement, were relinquished from possession by the compulsory licensee, accompanied by the privilege of returning unsold phonorecords to the compulsory licensee for credit or exchange. This total does not include:

(A) Any phonorecords relinquished from possession by the compulsory licensee for purposes of sale without the privilege of return; and

(B) Any phonorecords relinquished from possession for purposes other than sale.

(ii) Step 2: Subtract the number of phonorecords reserved. This involves deducting, from the subtotal arrived at in Step 1, the number of phonorecords that have been placed in the phonorecord reserve for the month covered by the Monthly Statement. The number of phonorecords reserved is determined by multiplying the subtotal from Step 1 by the percentage reserve level established under GAAP. This step should be skipped by a compulsory licensee barred from maintaining reserves under §210.15.

(iii) Step 3: Add the total of all phonorecords that were shipped during the month and were not counted in Step 1. This total is the sum of two figures:

(A) The number of phonorecords that, during the month covered by the Monthly Statement, were relinquished from possession by the compulsory licensee for purposes of sale, without the privilege of returning unsold phonorecords to the compulsory licensee for credit or exchange; and

(B) The number of phonorecords relinquished from possession by the compulsory licensee, during the month covered by the Monthly Statement, for purposes other than sale.

(iv) Step 4: Make any necessary adjustments for sales revenue "recognized," lapsed reserves, or reduction of negative reserve balance during the month. If necessary, this step involves adding to or subtracting from the subtotal arrived at in Step 3 on the basis of three possible types of adjustments:

(A) Sales revenue "recognized." If, in the month covered by the Monthly Statement, the compulsory licensee "recognized" revenue from the sale of phonorecords that had been relinquished from possession in an earlier month, the number of such phonorecords is added to the Step 3 subtotal.

(B) Lapsed reserves. If, in the month covered by the Monthly Statement, there are any phonorecords remaining in the phonorecord reserve for the ninth previous month (that is, any phonorecord reserves from the ninth previous month that have not been offset under FOFI, the first-out-first-in accounting convention, by actual returns during the intervening months), the reserve lapses and the number of phonorecords in it is added to the Step 3 subtotal.

(C) Reduction of negative reserve balance. If, in the month covered by the Monthly Statement, the aggregate reserve balance for all previous months is a negative amount, the number of phonorecords relinquished from possession by the compulsory licensee during that month and used to reduce the negative reserve balance is subtracted from the Step 3 subtotal.

(v) Step 5: Multiply by the statutory royalty rate. The total monthly royalty payment is obtained by multiplying the subtotal from Step 3, as adjusted if necessary by Step 4, by the statutory royalty rate set forth in §385.3 or other provisions of part 385 of this title as applicable.

(3) Phonorecords subject to a percentage rate royalty structure. For phonorecords subject to part 385, subparts B or C of this title, or any other applicable royalties computed on a percentage-rate basis, the amount of the royalty payment shall be calculated as provided in §385.12, §385.22, or other provisions of part 385 of this title as applicable. The calculations shall be made in good faith and on the basis of the best knowledge, information, and belief of the licensee at the time payment is due, and subject to the additional accounting and certification requirements of 17 U.S.C. 115(c)(5) and this section. The following additional provisions shall also apply:

(i) A licensee may, in cases where the final public performance royalty has not yet been determined, compute the public performance royalty component based on the interim public performance royalty rate, if established; or alternatively, on a reasonable estimation of the expected royalties to be paid in accordance with GAAP. Royalty payments based on anticipated payments or interim public performance royalty rates must be reconciled on the Annual Statement of Account, or by complying with §210.17(d)(2)(iii) governing Amended Annual Statements of Account.

(ii) When calculating the per-work royalty allocation for each work, as described in §385.12(b)(4), §385.22(b)(3), or any similar provisions of part 385 of this title as applicable, an actual or constructive per-play allocation is to be calculated to at least the hundredth of a cent (i.e., to at least four decimal places).

(e) Clear statements. The information required by paragraphs (b) and (c) of this section requires intelligible, legible, and unambiguous statements in the Monthly Statements of Account without incorporation of facts or information contained in other documents or records.

(f) Certification. (1) Each Monthly Statement of Account shall be accompanied by:

(i) The printed or typewritten name of the person who is signing and certifying the Monthly Statement of Account.

(ii) A signature, which in the case of a compulsory licensee that is a corporation or partnership, shall be the signature of a duly authorized officer of the corporation or of a partner.

(iii) The date of signature and certification.

(iv) If the compulsory licensee is a corporation or partnership, the title or official position held in the partnership or corporation by the person who is signing and certifying the Monthly Statement of Account.

(v) One of the following statements:

(A) I certify that (1) I am duly authorized to sign this Monthly Statement of Account on behalf of the compulsory licensee; (2) I have examined this Monthly Statement of Account; and (3) all statements of fact contained herein are true, complete, and correct to the best of my knowledge, information, and belief, and are made in good faith; or

(B) I certify that (1) I am duly authorized to sign this Monthly Statement of Account on behalf of the compulsory licensee, (2) I have prepared or supervised the preparation of the data used by the compulsory licensee and/or its agent to generate this Monthly Statement of Account, (3) such data is true, complete, and correct to the best of my knowledge, information, and belief, and was prepared in good faith, and (4) this Monthly Statement of Account was prepared by the compulsory licensee and/or its agent using processes and internal controls that were subject to an examination, during the past year, by a licensed Certified Public Accountant in accordance with the attestation standards established by the American Institute of Certified Public Accountants, the opinion of whom was that the processes and internal controls were suitably designed to generate monthly statements that accurately reflect, in all material respects, the compulsory licensee's usage of musical works, the statutory royalties applicable thereto, and any other data that is necessary for the proper calculation of the statutory royalties in accordance with 17 U.S.C. 115 and applicable regulations.

(2) If the Monthly Statement of Account is served by mail or by reputable courier service, certification of the Monthly Statement of Account by the compulsory licensee shall be made by handwritten signature. If the Monthly Statement of Account is served electronically, certification of the Monthly Statement of Account by the compulsory licensee shall be made by electronic signature as defined in section 7006(5) of title 15 of the United States Code.

(g) Service. (1) The service of a Monthly Statement of Account on a copyright owner under this subpart may be accomplished by means of service on either the copyright owner or an agent of the copyright owner with authority to receive Statements of Account on behalf of the copyright owner. In the case where the work has more than one copyright owner, the service of a Statement of Account on at least one co-owner or upon an agent of at least one of the co-owners shall be sufficient with respect to all co-owners. The compulsory licensee may choose to allocate its payment between co-owners. In such a case the compulsory licensee shall provide each co-owner (or its agent) a Monthly Statement reflecting the percentage share paid to that co-owner. Each Monthly Statement of Account shall be served on the copyright owner or the agent to whom or which it is directed by mail, by reputable courier service, or by electronic delivery as set forth in paragraph (g)(2) of this section on or before the 20th day of the immediately succeeding month. The royalty payment for a month also shall be served on or before the 20th day of the immediately succeeding month. The Monthly Statement and payment may be sent together or separately, but if sent separately, the payment must include information reasonably sufficient to allow the payee to match the Monthly Statement to the payment. However, in the case where the compulsory licensee has served its Notice of Intention upon an agent of the copyright owner pursuant to §201.18 of this chapter, the compulsory licensee is not required to serve Monthly Statements of Account or make any royalty payments until the compulsory licensee receives from the agent with authority to receive the Notice of Intention notice of the name and address of the copyright owner or its agent upon whom the compulsory licensee shall serve Monthly Statements of Account and the monthly royalty fees. Upon receipt of this information, the compulsory licensee shall serve Monthly Statements of Account and all royalty fees covering the intervening period upon the person or entity identified by the agent with authority to receive the Notice of Intention by or before the 20th day of the month following receipt of the notification. It shall not be necessary to file a copy of the Monthly Statement in the Copyright Office.

(2) A copyright owner or authorized agent may send a licensee a demand that Monthly Statements of Account be submitted in a readily accessible electronic format consistent with prevailing industry practices applicable to comparable electronic delivery of comparable financial information.

(3) When a compulsory licensee receives a request to deliver or make available Monthly Statements of Account in electronic form, or a request to revert back to service by mail or reputable courier service, the compulsory licensee shall make such a change effective with the first accounting period ending at least 30 days after the compulsory licensee's receipt of the request and any information (such as a postal or email address, as the case may be) that is necessary for the compulsory licensee to make the change.

(4)(i) In any case where a Monthly Statement of Account is sent by mail or reputable courier service and the Monthly Statement of Account is returned to the sender because the copyright owner or agent is no longer located at that address or has refused to accept delivery, or the Monthly Statement of Account is sent by electronic mail and is undeliverable, or in any case where an address for the copyright owner is not known, the Monthly Statement of Account, together with any evidence of mailing or attempted delivery by courier service or electronic mail, may be filed in the Licensing Division of the Copyright Office. Any Monthly Statement of Account submitted for filing in the Copyright Office shall be accompanied by a brief statement of the reason why it was not served on the copyright owner. A written acknowledgment of receipt and filing will be provided to the sender.

(ii) The Copyright Office will not accept any royalty fees submitted with Monthly Statements of Account under this section.

(iii) Neither the filing of a Monthly Statement of Account in the Copyright Office, nor the failure to file such Monthly Statement, shall have effect other than that which may be attributed to it by a court of competent jurisdiction.

(iv) No filing fee will be required in the case of Monthly Statements of Account submitted to the Copyright Office under this section. Upon request and payment of the fee specified in §201.3(e) of this chapter, a Certificate of Filing will be provided to the sender.

(5) Subject to paragraph (g)(6) of this section, a separate Monthly Statement of Account shall be served for each month during which there is any activity relevant to the payment of royalties under 17 U.S.C. 115. The Annual Statement of Account described in §210.17 of this subpart does not replace any Monthly Statement of Account.

(6) Royalties under 17 U.S.C. 115 shall not be considered payable, and no Monthly Statement of Account shall be required, until the compulsory licensee's cumulative unpaid royalties for the copyright owner equal at least one cent. Moreover, in any case in which the cumulative unpaid royalties under 17 U.S.C. 115 that would otherwise be payable by the compulsory licensee to the copyright owner are less than $5, and the copyright owner has not notified the compulsory licensee in writing that it wishes to receive Monthly Statements of Account reflecting payments of less than $5, the compulsory licensee may choose to defer the payment date for such royalties and provide no Monthly Statements of Account until the earlier of the time for rendering the Monthly Statement of Account for the month in which the compulsory licensee's cumulative unpaid royalties under section 17 U.S.C. 115 for the copyright owner exceed $5 or the time for rendering the Annual Statement of Account, at which time the compulsory licensee may provide one statement and payment covering the entire period for which royalty payments were deferred.

(7) If the compulsory licensee is required, under applicable tax law and regulations, to make backup withholding from its payments required hereunder, the compulsory licensee shall indicate the amount of such withholding on the Monthly Statement or on or with the payment.

(8) If a Monthly Statement of Account is sent by certified mail or registered mail, a mailing receipt shall be sufficient to prove that service was timely. If a Monthly Statement of Account is sent by a reputable courier, documentation from the courier showing the first date of attempted delivery shall be sufficient to prove that service was timely. If a Monthly Statement of Account or a link thereto is sent by electronic mail, a return receipt shall be sufficient to prove that service was timely. In the absence of the foregoing, the compulsory licensee shall bear the burden of proving that the Monthly Statement of Account was served in a timely manner.

History of 37 C.F.R. §210.16: 79 FR 56209, Sept. 18, 2014; 79 FR 60978, Oct. 9, 2014.

§210.17. ANNUAL STATEMENTS OF ACCOUNT

(a) Forms. The Copyright Office does not provide printed forms for the use of persons serving Annual Statements of Account.

(b) Annual period. Any Annual Statement of Account shall cover the full fiscal year of the compulsory licensee.

(c) General content. An Annual Statement of Account shall be clearly and prominently identified as an "Annual Statement of Account Under Compulsory License for Making and Distributing Phonorecords," and shall include a clear statement of the following information:

(1) The fiscal year covered by the Annual Statement of Account.

(2) The full legal name of the compulsory licensee, together with all fictitious or assumed names used by such person or entity for the purpose of conducting the business of making and distributing phonorecords.

(3) If the compulsory licensee is a business organization, the name and title of the chief executive officer, managing partner, sole proprietor or other person similarly responsible for the management of such entity.

(4) The full address, including a specific number and street name or rural route, or the place of business of the compulsory licensee (a post office box or similar designation will not be sufficient for this purpose except where it is the only address that can be used in that geographic location).

(5) For each nondramatic musical work that is owned by the same copyright owner being served with the Annual Statement and that is embodied in phonorecords covered by the compulsory license, a detailed statement of all of the information called for in paragraph (d) of this section.

(6) The total royalty payable for the fiscal year covered by the Annual Statement computed in accordance with the requirements of §210.16, and, in the case of offerings for which royalties are calculated pursuant to part 385, subparts B or C of this title, or any other provision requiring computation of applicable royalties on a percentage-rate basis, calculations showing in detail how the royalty was computed (for these purposes, the applicable royalty as specified in part 385, subpart A of this title shall be payable for every phonorecord "distributed" during the fiscal year covered by the Annual Statement).

(7) The total sum paid under Monthly Statements of Account by the compulsory licensee to the copyright owner being served with the Annual Statement during the fiscal year covered by the Annual Statement.

(8) In any case where the compulsory license falls within the provisions of §210.15, a clear description of the action or proceeding involved, including the date of the final judgment or definitive finding described in that section.

(9) Any late fees, if applicable, included in any payment associated with the Annual Statement.

(d) Specific content of annual statements—**(1)** Accounting of phonorecords subject to a cents rate royalty structure. The information called for by paragraph (c)(5) of this section shall, with respect to each nondramatic musical work as to which the compulsory licensee has made and distributed phonorecords subject to part 385, subpart A of this title, or any other provision requiring computation of applicable royalties on a cents-per-unit basis, include a separate listing of each of the following items of information:

(i) The number of phonorecords made through the end of the fiscal year covered by the Annual Statement, including any made during earlier years.

(ii) The number of phonorecords which have never been relinquished from possession of the compulsory licensee through the end of the fiscal year covered by the Annual Statement.

(iii) The number of phonorecords involuntarily relinquished from possession (as through fire or theft) of the compulsory licensee during the fiscal year covered by the Annual Statement and any earlier years, together with a description of the facts of such involuntary relinquishment.

(iv) The number of phonorecords "distributed" by the compulsory licensee during all years before the fiscal year covered by the Annual Statement.

(v) The number of phonorecords relinquished from possession of the compulsory licensee for purposes of sale during the fiscal year covered by the Annual Statement accompanied by a privilege of returning unsold records for credit or exchange, but not "distributed" by the end of that year.

(vi) The number of phonorecords "distributed" by the compulsory licensee during the fiscal year covered by the Annual Statement.

(vii) The per unit statutory royalty rate applicable to the relevant configuration.

(viii) The total royalty payable for the fiscal year covered by the Annual Statement for the item described by the set of information called for, and broken down as required, by this paragraph (d)(1).

(ix) The phonorecord identification information required by paragraph (d)(3) of this section.

(2) Accounting of phonorecords subject to a percentage rate royalty structure. **(i)** The information called for by paragraph (c)(5) of this section shall identify each offering for which royalties are to be calculated separately and, with respect to each nondramatic musical work as to which the compulsory licensee has made and distributed phonorecords subject to part 385, subparts B or C of this title, or any other provision requiring computation of applicable royalties on a percentage-rate basis, include the number of plays, constructive plays, or other payable units during the fiscal year covered by the Annual Statement, together with, and which if necessary shall be broken down to identify separately, the following:

(A) The total royalty payable for the fiscal year for the item described by the set of information called for, and broken down as required, by paragraph (d)(3) of this section (i.e., the per-work royalty allocation for the relevant sound recording and offering).

(B) The phonorecord identification information required by paragraph (d)(3) of this section.

(ii) If the information given under paragraph (d)(2)(i) of this section does not reconcile, the Annual Statement shall also include a clear and detailed explanation of the difference.

(iii) In any case where a licensee serves an Annual Statement of Account based on anticipated payments or interim public performance royalty rates prior to the final determination of final public performance royalties for all musical works used by the service in the relevant fiscal year, the licensee shall serve an Amended Annual Statement of Account within six months from the date such public performance royalties have been established. The Amended Annual Statement of Account shall recalculate the royalty fees reported on the relevant Annual Statement of Account to adjust for any change to the public performance rate used to calculate the royalties reported. Service shall be made in accordance with paragraph (g) of this section. Certification of the Amended Annual Statement shall be made in accordance with paragraph (f) of this section, except that the CPA examination under paragraph (f)(2) of this section may be limited to the licensee's recalculation of royalty fees in accordance with this paragraph.

(3) Identification of phonorecords in annual statements. The information required by this paragraph shall include, and if necessary shall be broken down to identify separately, the following:

(i) The title of the nondramatic musical work subject to compulsory license.

(ii) A reference number or code identifying the relevant Notice of Intention, if the compulsory licensee chose to include such a number or code on its relevant Notice of Intention for the compulsory license.

(iii) The International Standard Recording Code (ISRC) associated with the relevant sound recording, if known; and at least one of the following, as applicable and available for tracking sales and/or usage:

(A) The catalog number or numbers and label name or names, used on or associated with the phonorecords;

(B) The Universal Product Code (UPC) or similar code used on or associated with the phonorecords; or

(C) The sound recording identification number assigned by the compulsory licensee or a third-party distributor to the relevant sound recording;

(iv) The names of the principal recording artist or group engaged in rendering the performances fixed on the phonorecords.

(v) The playing time of the relevant sound recording, except that playing time is not required in the case of ringtones or licensed activity to which no overtime adjustment is applicable.

(vi) If the compulsory licensee chooses to allocate its payments between co-owners of the copyright in the nondramatic musical work as described in paragraph (g)(1) of §210.16, and thus pays the copyright owner (or agent) receiving the statement less than one hundred percent of the applicable royalty, the percentage share paid.

(vii) The names for the writer or writers of the nondramatic musical work, or the International Standard Name Identifiers (ISNIs) or other unique identifier of the writer or writers, if known.

(viii) The International Standard Work Code (ISWC) or other unique identifier for the nondramatic musical work, if known.

(ix) Identification of the relevant phonorecord configuration (for example: compact disc, permanent digital download, ringtone) or offering (for example: limited download, music bundle) for which the royalty was calculated, including, if applicable and except for physical phonorecords, the name of the third-party distributor of the configuration or offering.

(e) Clear statement. The information required by paragraph (c) of this section requires intelligible, legible, and unambiguous statements in the Annual Statement of Account without incorporation by reference of facts or information contained in other documents or records.

(f) Certification. **(1)** Each Annual Statement of Account shall be accompanied by:

(i) The printed or typewritten name of the person who is signing the Annual Statement of Account on behalf of the compulsory licensee.

(ii) A signature, which in the case of a compulsory licensee that is a corporation or partnership, shall be the signature of a duly authorized officer of the corporation or of a partner.

(iii) The date of signature.

(iv) If the compulsory licensee is a corporation or partnership, the title or official position held in the partnership or corporation by the person signing the Annual Statement of Account.

(v) The following statement: I am duly authorized to sign this Annual Statement of Account on behalf of the compulsory licensee.

(2) Each Annual Statement of Account shall also be certified by a licensed Certified Public Accountant. Such certification shall comply with the following requirements:

(i) Except as provided in paragraph (f)(2)(ii) of this section, the accountant shall certify that it has conducted an examination of the Annual Statement of Account prepared by the compulsory licensee in accordance with the attestation standards established by the American Institute of Certified Public Accountants, and has rendered an opinion based on such examination that the Annual Statement conforms with the standards in paragraph (f)(2)(iv) of this section.

(ii) If such accountant determines in its professional judgment that the volume of data attributable to a particular compulsory licensee renders it impracticable to certify the Annual Statement of Account as required by paragraph (f)(2)(i) of this section, the accountant may instead certify the following:

(A) That the accountant has conducted an examination in accordance with the attestation standards established by the American Institute of Certified Public Accountants of the following assertions by the compulsory licensee's management:

(1) That the processes used by or on behalf of the compulsory licensee, including calculation of statutory royalties, generated Annual Statements that conform with the standards in paragraph (f)(2)(iv) of this section; and

(2) That the internal controls relevant to the processes used by or on behalf of the compulsory licensee to generate Annual Statements were suitably designed and operated effectively during the period covered by the Annual Statements.

(B) That such examination included examining, either on a test basis or otherwise as the accountant considered necessary under the circumstances and in its professional judgment, evidence supporting the management assertions in paragraph (f)(2)(ii)(A) of this section, including data relevant to the calculation of statutory royalties, and performing such other procedures as the accountant considered necessary in the circumstances.

(C) That the accountant has rendered an opinion based on such examination that the processes used to generate the Annual Statement were designed and operated effectively to generate Annual Statements that conform with the standards in paragraph (f)(2)(iv) of this section, and that the internal controls relevant to the processes used to generate Annual Statements were suitably designed and operated effectively during the period covered by the Annual Statements.

(iii) In the event a third party or third parties acting on behalf of the compulsory licensee provided services related to the Annual Statement, the accountant making a certification under either paragraph (f)(2)(i) or paragraph (f)(2)(ii) of this section may, as the accountant considers necessary under the circumstances and in its professional judgment, rely on a report and opinion rendered by a licensed Certified Public Accountant in accordance with the attestation standards established by the American Institute of Certified Public Accountants that the processes and/or internal controls of the third party or third parties relevant to the generation of the compulsory licensee's Annual Statements were suitably designed and operated effectively during the period covered by the Annual Statements, if such reliance is disclosed in the certification.

(iv) An Annual Statement of Account conforms with the standards of this paragraph if it presents fairly, in all material respects, the compulsory licensee's usage of the copyright owner's musical works under compulsory license during the period covered by the Annual Statement, the statutory royalties applicable thereto, and such other data as are relevant to the calculation of statutory royalties in accordance with 17 U.S.C. 115 and applicable regulations.

(v) Each certificate shall be signed by an individual, or in the name of a partnership or a professional corporation with two or more shareholders. The certificate number and jurisdiction are not required if the certificate is signed in the name of a partnership or a professional corporation with two or more shareholders.

(3) If the Annual Statement of Account is served by mail or by reputable courier service, the Annual Statement of Account shall be signed by handwritten signature. If the Annual Statement of Account is served electronically, the Annual Statement of Account shall be signed by electronic signature as defined in section 7006(5) of title 15 of the United States Code.

(4) If the Annual Statement of Account is served electronically, the compulsory licensee may serve an electronic facsimile of the original certification of the Annual Statement of Account signed by the licensed Certified Public Accountant. The compulsory licensee shall retain the original certification of the Annual Statement of Account signed by the licensed Certified Public Accountant for the period identified in §210.18, which shall be made available to the copyright owner upon demand.

(g) Service. **(1)** The service of an Annual Statement of Account on a copyright owner under this subpart may be accomplished by means of service on either the copyright owner or an agent of the copyright owner with authority to receive Statements of Account on behalf of the copyright owner. In the case where the work has more than one copyright owner, the service of the Statement of Account on one co-owner or upon an agent of one of the co-owners shall be sufficient with respect to all co-owners. Each Annual Statement of Account shall be served on the copyright owner or the agent to whom or which it is directed by mail, by reputable courier service, or by electronic delivery as set forth in paragraph (g)(2) of this section on or before the 20th day of the sixth month following the end of the fiscal year covered by the Annual Statement. It shall not be necessary to file a copy of the Annual Statement in the Copyright Office. An Annual Statement of Account shall be served for each fiscal year during which at least one Monthly Statement of Account was required to have been served under §210.16(g).

(2) If an Annual Statement of Account is being sent electronically, it may be sent or made available to a copyright owner or its agent in a readily accessible electronic format consistent with prevailing industry practices applicable to comparable electronic delivery of comparable financial information.

(3) If the copyright owner or agent has made a request pursuant to §210.16(g)(3) to receive statements in electronic or paper form, such request shall also apply to Annual Statements to be rendered on or after the date that the request is effective with respect to Monthly Statements.

(4) In any case where the amount required to be stated in the Annual Statement of Account under paragraph (c)(6) of this section (i.e., the total royalty payable) is greater than the amount stated in that Annual Statement under paragraph (c)(7) of this section (i.e., the total sum paid), the difference between such amounts shall also be served on or before the 20th day of the sixth month following the end of the fiscal year covered by the Annual Statement. The Annual Statement and payment may be sent together or separately, but if sent separately, the payment must include information reasonably sufficient to allow the payee to match the Annual Statement and the payment. The delivery of such sum does not require the copyright owner to accept such sum, or to forego any right, relief, or remedy which may be available under law. In any case where the amount required to be stated in the Annual Statement of Account under paragraph (c)(6) of this section is less than the amount stated in that Annual Statement under paragraph (c)(7) of this section, the difference between such amounts shall be available to the compulsory licensee as a credit.

(5)(i) In any case where an Annual Statement of Account is sent by mail or by reputable courier service and is returned to the sender because the copyright owner or agent is no longer located at that address or has refused to accept delivery, or the Annual Statement of Account is sent by electronic mail and is undeliverable, or in any case where an address for the copyright owner is not known, the Annual Statement of Account, together with any evidence of mailing or attempted delivery by courier service or electronic mail, may be filed in the Licensing Division of the Copyright Office. Any Annual Statement of Account submitted for filing shall be accompanied by a brief statement of the reason why it was not served on the copyright owner. A written acknowledgment of receipt and filing will be provided to the sender.

(ii) The Copyright Office will not accept any royalty fees submitted with Annual Statements of Account under paragraph (g)(5)(i) of this section.

(iii) Neither the filing of an Annual Statement of Account in the Copyright Office, nor the failure to file such Annual Statement, shall have any effect other than that which may be attributed to it by a court of competent jurisdiction.

(iv) No filing fee will be required in the case of Annual Statements of Account submitted to the Copyright Office under paragraph (g)(5)(i) of this section. Upon request and payment of the fee specified in §201.3(e) of this chapter, a Certificate of Filing will be provided to the sender.

(6) If an Annual Statement of Account is sent by certified mail or registered mail, a mailing receipt shall be sufficient to prove that service was timely. If an Annual Statement of Account is sent by a reputable courier, documentation from the courier showing the first date of attempted delivery shall be sufficient to prove that service was timely. If an Annual Statement of Account or a link thereto is sent by electronic mail, a return receipt shall be sufficient to prove that service was timely. In the absence of the foregoing, the compulsory licensee shall bear the burden of proving that the Annual Statement of Account was served in a timely manner.

(h) Annual Statements for periods before the effective date of this regulation. If a copyright owner did not receive an Annual Statement of Account from a compulsory licensee for any fiscal year ending after March 1, 2009 and before November 17, 2014, the copyright owner may, at any time before May 17, 2015, make a request in writing to that compulsory licensee requesting an Annual Statement of Account for the relevant fiscal year conforming to the requirements of this section. If such a request is made, the compulsory licensee shall provide the Annual Statement of Account within six months after receiving the request. If such a circumstance and request applies to more than one of the compulsory licensee's fiscal years, such years may be combined on a single statement.

History of 37 C.F.R. §210.17: 79 FR 56212, Sept. 18, 2014; 79 FR 60978, Oct. 9, 2014; 82 FR 9365, Mar. 8, 2017.

§210.18. DOCUMENTATION

All compulsory licensees shall, for a period of at least five years from the date of service of an Annual Statement of Account or Amended Annual Statement of Account, keep and retain in their possession all records and documents necessary and appropriate to support fully the information set forth in such Annual Statement or Amended Annual Statement and in Monthly Statements served during the fiscal year covered by such Annual Statement or Amended Annual Statement.

History of 37 C.F.R. §210.18: 79 FR 56215, Sept. 18, 2014.

§210.19. HARMLESS ERRORS

Errors in a Monthly or Annual Statement of Account that do not materially prejudice the rights of the copyright owner shall be deemed harmless, and shall not render that statement of account invalid or provide a basis for the exercise of the remedies set forth in 17 U.S.C. 115(c)(6).

History of 37 C.F.R. §210.19: 79 FR 56215, Sept. 18, 2014.

PART 211. MASK WORK PROTECTION

§211.1. GENERAL PROVISIONS

(a) Mail and other communications with the Copyright Office concerning the Semiconductor Chip Protection Act of 1984, Pub.L. 98-620, chapter 9 of Title 17 U.S.C., should be sent to the address specified in §201.1(b) of this chapter.

(b) Section 201.2 of this chapter relating to the information given by the Copyright Office, and Parts 203 and 204 of this chapter pertaining to the Freedom of Information Act and Privacy Act, shall apply, where appropriate, to the administration by the Copyright Office of the Semiconductor Chip Protection Act of 1984, Pub.L. 98-620.

(c) For purposes of this part, the terms "semiconductor chip product," "mask work," "fixed," "commercially exploited," and "owner," shall have the meanings set forth in section 901 of Title 17 U.S.C.

History of 37 C.F.R. §211.1: 82 FR 9365, Mar. 8, 2017.

Source of 37 C.F.R. Part 211: 50 FR 271, Jan. 3, 1985; 50 FR 26719, June 28, 1985; 56 FR 7817, Feb. 26, 1991; 59 FR 23981, May 9, 1994, unless otherwise noted.

§211.2. RECORDATION OF DOCUMENTS PERTAINING TO MASK WORKS

The conditions prescribed in section 201.4 of this chapter for recordation of transfers of copyright ownership and other documents pertaining to copyright are applicable to the recordation of documents pertaining to mask works under section 903 of title 17 U.S.C.

History of 37 C.F.R. §211.2: 66 FR 34373, June 28, 2001.

§211.3. MASK WORK FEES

(a) Section 201.3 of this chapter prescribes the fees or charges established by the Register of Copyrights for services relating to mask works.

(b) Section 201.6 of this chapter on the payment and refund of Copyright Office fees shall apply to mask work fees.

History of 37 C.F.R. §211.3: 56 FR 59886, Nov. 26, 1991; 59 FR 38372, July 28, 1994; 63 FR 29139, May 28, 1998; 64 FR 29522, June 1, 1999.

§211.4. REGISTRATION OF CLAIMS OF PROTECTION IN MASK WORKS

(a) General. This section prescribes conditions for the registration of claims of protection in mask works pursuant to section 908 of title 17 U.S.C.

(b) Application for registration.

(1) For purposes of registration of mask work claims, the Register of Copyrights has designated "Form MW" to be used for all applications. Copies of the form are available free from the Copyright Office website or upon request to the Copyright Information Section, U.S. Copyright Office, Library of Congress, Washington, DC 20559-6000.

(2) An application for registration of a mask work claim may be submitted by the owner of the mask work, or the duly authorized agent of any such owner.

(i) The owner of a mask work includes a party that has obtained the transfer of all of the exclusive rights in the work, but does not include the transferee of less than all of the exclusive rights, or the licensee of all or less than all of these rights.

(ii) For purposes of eligibility to claim mask work protection pursuant to section 902(a)(1)(A) of 17 U.S.C., the owner of the mask work must be either the initial owner or a person who has obtained by transfer the totality of rights in the mask work under the Act.

(3) An application for registration shall be submitted on Form MW prescribed by the Register under paragraph (b)(1) of this section, and shall be accompanied by the registration fee and deposit required under 17 U.S.C. 908 and §§211.3 and 211.5 of these regulations. The application shall contain the information required by the form and its accompanying instructions, and shall include a certification. The certification shall consist of:

(i) A declaration that the applicant is authorized to submit the application and that the statements made are correct to the best of that person's knowledge; and

(ii) The handwritten signature of the applicant, accompanied by the typed or printed name of that person.

(c) One registration per mask work.

(1) Subject to the exception specified in paragraph (c)(2) of this section, only one registration can generally be made for the same version of a mask work fixed in an intermediate or final form of any semiconductor chip product. However, where an applicant for registration alleges that an earlier registration for the same version of the work is unauthorized and legally invalid and submits for recordation a signed affidavit, a registration may be made in the applicant's name.

(2) Notwithstanding the general rule permitting only one registration per work, owners of mask works in final forms of semiconductor chip products that are produced by adding metal-connection layers to unpersonalized gate arrays may separately register the entire unpersonalized gate array and the custom metallization layers. Applicants seeking to register separately entire unpersonalized gate arrays or custom metallization layers should make the nature of their claim clear at Space 8 of application Form MW. For these purposes, an "unpersonalized gate array" is an intermediate form chip product that includes a plurality of circuit elements that are adaptable to be personalized into a plurality of different final form chip products, in which some of the circuit elements are, or will be, connected as gates.

(d) Registration as a single work. Subject to the exception specified in paragraph (c)(2) of this section, for purposes of registration on a single application and upon payment of a single fee, the following shall be considered a single work:

(1) In the case of a mask work that has not been commercially exploited: All original mask work elements fixed in a particular form of a semiconductor chip product at the time an application for registration is filed and in which the owner or owners of the mask work is or are the same; and

(2) In the case of a mask work that has been commercially exploited: All original mask work elements fixed in a semiconductor chip product at the time that product was first commercially exploited and in which the owner or owners of the mask work is or are the same.

(e) Registration in most complete form. Owners seeking registration of a mask work contribution must submit the entire original mask work contribution in its most complete form as fixed in a semiconductor chip product. The most complete form means the stage of the manufacturing process which is closest to completion. In cases where the owner is unable to register on the basis of the most complete form because he or she lacks control over the most complete form, an averment of this fact must be made at Space 2 of Form MW. Where such an averment is made, the owner may register on the basis of the most complete form in his or her possession. For applicants seeking to register an unpersonalized gate array or custom metallization layers under paragraph (c)(2) of this section, the most complete form is the entire chip on which the unpersonalized gate array or custom metallization layers reside(s), and registration covers those elements of the chip in which work protection is asserted.

(f) Corrections and amplifications of prior registration. Except for errors or omissions made by the Copyright Office, no corrections or amplifications can be made to the information contained in the record of a completed registration after the effective date of the registration. A document purporting to correct or amplify the information in a completed registration may be recorded in the Copyright Office for whatever effect a court of competent jurisdiction may later give to it, if the document is signed by the owner of the mask work, as identified in the registration record, or by a duly authorized agent of the owner.

History of 37 C.F.R. §211.4: 56 FR 7818, Feb. 26, 1991; 64 FR 36575, July 7, 1999; 66 FR 34373, June 28, 2001; 73 FR 37840, July 1, 2008; 82 FR 9365, Mar. 8, 2017.

§211.5. DEPOSIT OF IDENTIFYING MATERIAL

(a) General. This section prescribes rules pertaining to the deposit of identifying material for registration of a claim of protection in a mask work under section 908 of Title 17 U.S.C.

(b) Nature of required deposit. Subject to the provisions of paragraph (c) of this section, the deposit of identifying material to accompany an application for registration of a mask work claim under §211.4 shall consist of:

(1) In the case of a commercially exploited mask work, four reproductions of the mask work fixed in the form of the semiconductor chip product in which it was first commercially exploited. Defective chips may be deposited under this section provided that the mask work contribution would be revealed in reverse dissection of the chips. The four reproductions shall be accompanied by a visually perceptible representation of each layer of the mask work consisting of:

(i) Sets of plastic color overlay sheets;

(ii) Drawings or plots in composite form on a single sheet or on separate sheets; or

(iii) A photograph of each layer of the work fixed in a semiconductor chip product.

(2) The visually perceptible representation of a mask work deposited under this section shall be reproduced on material which can be readily stored in an 8½ x 11 inch format, and shall be reproduced at a magnification sufficient to reveal the basic circuitry design of the mask work and which shall in all cases be at least 20 times magnification.

(3) In the case of a mask work that has not been commercially exploited, one of the following:

(i) Where the mask work contribution in which registration is sought represents twenty percent or more of the area of the intended final form, a visually perceptible representation of the work in accordance with paragraph (b)(1)(i) or (ii) of this section. In addition to the deposit of visually perceptible representations of the work, an applicant may, at his or her option, deposit four reproductions in the most complete form of the mask work as fixed in a semiconductor product.

(ii) Where the mask work contribution in which registration is sought represents less than twenty percent of the area of the intended final form, a visually perceptible representation of the work which reveals the totality of the mask work contribution to a person trained in the state of the art. The visually perceptible representations may consist of any combination of plastic color overlay sheets, drawing or plots in composite form, or a photograph or photographs of the entire mask set. If the visually perceptible representation fails to identify all of the elements of the mask work contribution, they may be accompanied by additional explanatory material. The visually perceptible representation of a mask work deposited under this section shall be reproduced on material which can be readily stored in an 8½ x 11 inch format and shall be of sufficient magnification and completeness to reveal all elements of the mask work contribution. In addition to the deposit of visually perceptible representations of the work, an applicant may, at his or her option, deposit four reproductions in the most complete form of the mask work as fixed in a semiconductor chip product.

(c) Trade secret protection. Where specific layers of a mask work fixed in a semiconductor chip product contain information in which trade secret protection is asserted, certain material may be withheld as follows:

(1) Mask works commercially exploited. For commercially exploited mask works no more than two layers of each five or more layers in the work. In lieu of the visually perceptible representations required under paragraphs (b)(1) and

(2) of this section, identifying portions of the withheld material must be submitted. For these purposes, "identifying portions" shall mean:

(i) A printout of the mask work design data pertaining to each withheld layer, reproduced in microform; or

(ii) Visually perceptible representations in accordance with paragraphs (b)(1)(i), (ii), or (iii) and (b)(2) of this section with those portions containing sensitive information maintained under a claim of trade secrecy blocked out, provided that the portions remaining are greater than those which are blocked out.

(2) Mask work not commercially exploited. **(i)** For mask works not commercially exploited falling under paragraph (b)(3)(i) of this section, any layer may be withheld. In lieu of the visually perceptible representations required under paragraph (b)(3) of this section, "identifying portions" shall mean:

(A) A printout of the mask work design data pertaining to each withheld layer, reproduced in microform, in which sensitive information maintained under a claim of trade secrecy has been blocked out or stripped; or

(B) Visually perceptible representations in accordance with paragraph (b)(3)(i) of this section with those portions containing sensitive information maintained under a claim of trade secrecy blocked out, provided that the portions remaining are greater than those which are blocked out.

(ii) The identifying portions shall be accompanied by a single photograph of the top or other visible layers of the mask work fixed in a semiconductor chip product in which the sensitive information maintained under a claim of trade secrecy has been blocked out, provided that the blocked out portions do not exceed the remaining portions.

(d) Special relief. The Register of Copyrights may decide to grant special relief from the deposit requirements of this section, and shall determine the conditions under which special relief is to be granted. Requests for special relief under this paragraph shall be made in writing to the Associate Register of Copyrights and Director of Registration Policy and Practice, P.O. Box 70400, Washington, DC 20024-0400, shall be signed by the person signing the application for registration, shall set forth specific reasons why the request should be granted and shall propose an alternative form of deposit.

(e) Retention and disposition of deposits.

(1) Any identifying material deposited under this section, including material deposited in connection with claims that have been refused registration, are the property of the United States Government.

(2) Where a claim of protection in a mask work is registered in the Copyright Office, the identifying material deposited in connection with the claim shall be retained under the control of the Copyright Office, including retention in Government storage facilities, during the period of protection. After that period, it is within the joint discretion of the Register of Copyrights and the Librarian of Congress to order its destruction or other disposition.

History of 37 C.F.R. §211.5: 60 FR 34169, June 30, 1995; 64 FR 36575, July 7, 1999; 73 FR 37840, July 1, 2008; 76 FR 27898, May 13, 2011; 82 FR 9365, Mar. 8, 2017.

§211.6. METHODS OF AFFIXATION & PLACEMENT OF MASK WORK NOTICE

(a) General.

(1) This section specifies methods of affixation and placement of the mask work notice that will satisfy the notice requirement in section 909 of title 17 U.S.C. A notice deemed "acceptable" under this regulation shall be considered to satisfy the requirement of that section that it be affixed "in such manner and location as to give reasonable notice" of protection. As provided in that section, the examples specified in this regulation shall not be considered exhaustive of the methods of affixation and positions giving reasonable notice of the claim of protection in a mask work.

(2) The acceptability of a mask work notice under these regulations shall depend upon its being legible under normal conditions of use, and affixed in such manner and position that, when affixed, it may be viewed upon reasonable examination.

(b) Elements of mask work notice. The elements of a mask work notice shall consist of:

(1) The words "mask work," the symbol 'M' or the symbol (M) (the letter M in a circle); and

(2) The name of the owner or owners of the mask work or an abbreviation by which the name is recognized or is generally known.

(c) Methods of affixation and placement of the notice. In the case of a mask work fixed in a semiconductor chip product, the following locations are acceptable:

(1) A gummed or other label securely affixed or imprinted upon the package or other container used as a permanent receptacle for the product; or

(2) A notice imprinted or otherwise affixed in or on the top or other visible layer of the product.

History of 37 C.F.R. §211.6: 60 FR 34169, June 30, 1995.

§211.7. RECONSIDERATION PROCEDURE FOR REFUSALS TO REGISTER

The requirements prescribed in §202.5 of this chapter for reconsideration of refusals to register copyright claims are applicable to requests to reconsider refusals to register mask works under 17 U.S.C. chapter 9, unless otherwise required by this part.

History of 37 C.F.R. §211.7: 69 FR 77637, Dec. 28, 2004.

PART 212. PROTECTION OF VESSEL DESIGNS

§212.1. SCOPE

The provisions of this part apply to the protection and registration of original designs of vessels under chapter 13 of title 17, United States Code. Design protection and registration under this part are separate from copyright protection and registration. Copyright registration is governed by the provisions of part 202 of this subchapter.

History of 37 C.F.R. §212.1: 82 FR 9366, Mar. 8, 2017.

Source of 37 C.F.R. Part 212: 59 FR 23981, May 9, 1994; 64 FR 36578, July 7, 1999, unless otherwise noted.

§212.2. FEES

Services related to registration of original designs of vessels are subject to fees prescribed in §§201.3(c) and (d).

History of 37 C.F.R. §212.2: 67 FR 38005, May 31, 2002; 71 FR 31092, June 1, 2006; 82 FR 9366, Mar. 8, 2017.

§212.3. REGISTRATION OF CLAIMS FOR PROTECTION OF ELIGIBLE DESIGNS

(a) Limitations. Protection is not available for, and an application for registration will not be accepted for:

(1) An otherwise eligible design made public prior to October 28, 1998;

(2) An otherwise eligible design made public on a date more than two years prior to the filing of an application for registration under this section;

(3) A design ineligible for any of the reasons set forth in 17 U.S.C. 1302.

(b) Required elements of application. An application is considered filed with the Copyright Office on the date on which the following three items have been received by the Copyright Office:

(1) Completed Form D-VH;

(2) Deposit material identifying the design or designs for which registration is sought; and

(3) The appropriate fee.

(c) Application by owner of design. An application for registration under this section may be made only by the owner or owners of the design, or by the duly authorized agent or representative of the owner or owners of the design.

(d) Application form. Registration must be made on Form D-VH. Forms are available from the Copyright Office and may be reprinted from the Copyright Office's website (http://www.loc.gov/copyright/forms/formdvh.pdf).

(e) Deposit material—

(1) In General. Identification of the design to be registered may be made in the form of drawings or photographs. No more than two drawings or photographs of the design may appear on a single sheet. Applicants may submit up to three 8½" x 11" sheets containing drawings or photographs as part of the basic application fee. An additional fee shall be assessed for each page beyond the first three pages. No combinations of drawings and photographs may be submitted on a single sheet. The drawings or photographs that accompany the application must reveal those aspects of the design for which protection is claimed. The registration extends only to those aspects of the design which are adequately shown in the drawings or photographs.

(2) Views. The drawings or photographs submitted should contain a sufficient number of views to make an adequate disclosure of the appearance of the design, *i.e.* front, rear, right and left sides, top and bottom. While not required, it is suggested that perspective views be submitted to show clearly the appearance and shape of the three dimensional designs.

(3) Drawings.

(i) Drawings must be in black ink on white 8½" x 11" unruled paper. A drawing of a design should include appropriate surface shading which shows clearly the character and contour of all surfaces of any 3-dimensional aspects of the design. Surface shading is also necessary to distinguish between any open and solid areas of the design. Solid black surface shading is not permitted except when used to represent the black color as well as color contrast.

(ii) The use of broken lines in drawings depicting the design is understood to be for illustrative purposes only and forms no part of the claimed design. Structure that is not part of the design, but that is considered necessary to show the environment in which the design is used, may be represented in the drawing by broken lines. This includes any portion of the vessel in which the design is embodied or applied that is not considered part of the design. When the claimed design is only surface ornamentation to the vessel, the vessel in which it is embodied must be shown in broken lines.

(iii) When broken lines are used, they should not intrude upon or cross the depiction of the design and should not be of heavier weight than the lines used in depicting the design. Where a broken line showing of environmental structure must necessarily cross or intrude upon the representation of the design and obscure a clear understanding of the design, such an illustration should be included as a separate figure, in addition to other figures which fully disclose the subject matter of the design.

(4) Photographs. High quality black and white or color photographs will be accepted provided that they are mounted on plain white 8½" x 11" unlined paper and do not exceed two photographs per sheet. Photographs must be developed on double weight photographic paper and must be of sufficient quality so that all the details of the design are plainly visible and are capable of reproduction on the registration certificate, if issued.

(f) Multiple claims—

(1) In general. Claims for more than one design may be filed in one of two ways. If multiple designs are contained on a single make and model of a vessel (and therefore, the information in Space 1 of Form D-VH—the make and model of the vessel that embodies the design—is the same for each of the designs), a single application form may be used for all designs, provided that the information in spaces 3 through 9 is the same for each of the designs. If multiple designs are contained on more than one make and model of a vessel, or the information in spaces 3 through 9 is not the same for each of the multiple designs, then separate applications must be used for each design.

(2) Single application. Where a single application for multiple designs is appropriate, a separate Form D-VH/CON must be used for each design beyond the first appearing on Form D-VH. Each Form D-VH/CON must be accompanied by deposit material identifying the design that is the subject of the Form D-VH/CON, and the deposit material must be attached to the Form D-VH/CON. The Form D-VH and all the Form D-VH/CONs for the single application must be submitted together.

(3) Multiple applications. Where multiple applications for more than one design are required, a Form D-VH must be completed for each design. Deposit material identifying the design must accompany each application. Multiple applications may be filed separately.

(4) Fees. The basic application fee prescribed in §201.3(c) of this chapter applies to each design submitted, regardless of whether a single application or multiple applications are used.

(g) Written declaration. In lieu of the oath required by 17 U.S.C. 1312(a), the application shall contain a written declaration, as permitted by 17 U.S.C. 1312(b), signed by the applicant, or the applicant's duly authorized agent or representative. If the design has been made public with the design notice prescribed in 17 U.S.C. 1306, the written declaration shall also describe the exact form and position of the design notice. The written declaration shall read as follows:

The undersigned, as the applicant or the applicant's duly appointed agent or representative, being hereby warned that willful false statements are punishable by fine or imprisonment, or both, under 18 U.S.C. 1001, and that such willful false statements may jeopardize the validity of this application or any resulting registration, hereby declares to the best of his/her knowledge and belief:

(1) That the design has been fixed in a useful article;

(2) That the design is original and was created by the designer(s), or employer if applicable, named in the application;

(3) That those aspects of the design for which registration is sought are not protected by a design patent;

(4) That the design has not previously been registered on behalf of the applicant or the applicant's predecessor in title; and

(5) That the applicant is the person entitled to protection and to registration under chapter 13 of title 17, United States Code.

(h) Priority claims. An applicant seeking the benefit of 17 U.S.C. 1311 because the applicant has, within the previous six months, filed an application for protection of the same design in a foreign country, must provide:

(1) Identification of the filing date of the foreign application;

(2) Identification of the foreign country in which the application was filed;

(3) The serial number or any other identifying number of the foreign application;

(4) A certified copy of the foreign application;

(5) A translation of the foreign application and a statement, signed by the translator, that the translation is accurate, if the foreign application is in a language other than English; and

(6) If requested by the Copyright Office, proof that the foreign country in which the prior application was filed extends to designs of owners who are citizens of the United States, or to applications filed under chapter 13 of title 17, United States Code, similar protection to that provided under chapter 13 of title 17, United States Code.

(i) Effective date of registration. The effective date of registration is the date of publication of the registration by the Copyright Office.

(j) Publication of registration. Publication of registrations of vessel designs shall be made on the Copyright Office website (http://www.loc.gov/copyright/vessels).

History of 37 C.F.R. §212.3: 72 FR 33692, July 1, 2007; 82 FR 9366, Mar. 8, 2017.

§212.4. AFFIXATION & PLACEMENT OF DESIGN NOTICE

(a) General.

(1) This section specifies the methods of affixation and placement of the design notice required by 17 U.S.C. 1306. Sections 1306 and 1307 govern the circumstances under which a design notice must be used and the effect of omission of a design notice. A notice deemed acceptable under this part shall be considered to satisfy the requirements of section 1306 that it be so located and applied as to give reasonable notice of design protection while the useful article embodying the design is passing through its normal channels of commerce. As provided in that section, the examples specified in this part shall not be considered exhaustive of the methods of affixation and locations giving reasonable notice of the claim of protection in the design.

(2) The acceptability of a design notice under these regulations shall depend upon its being legible under normal conditions of use, and affixed in such a manner and position that, when affixed, it may be viewed upon reasonable examination. There is no requirement that a design notice be permanently embossed or engraved into a vessel hull or deck, but it should be affixed in such a manner that, under normal conditions of use, it is not likely to become unattached or illegible.

(b) Elements of a design notice. If the design has been registered, the registration number may be included in the design notice in place of the year of the date on which protection for the design commenced and the name of the owner, an abbreviation by which the name can be recognized, or a generally accepted alternative designation of the owner. The elements of a design notice shall consist of:

(1) The words "Protected Design," the abbreviation "Prot'd Des.," or the letter "D" within a circle, or the symbol *D*;

(2) The year of the date on which protection for the design commenced; and

(3) The name of the owner, an abbreviation by which the name can be recognized, or a generally accepted alternative designation of the owner.

(c) Distinctive identification. Any distinctive identification of an owner may be used for purposes of paragraph (b)(3) of this section if it has been recorded by the Register of Copyrights pursuant to §212.5 before the design marked with such identification is registered.

(d) Acceptable locations of notice. The following are acceptable means of affixing and placement of a design notice:

(1) In close proximity to the identification number required by 33 CFR 181.23;

(2) In close proximity to the driver's console such that it is in plain view from the console;

(3) If the vessel is twenty feet in length or less and is governed by 33 CFR 183.21, in close proximity to the capacity marking; and

(4) In close proximity to the make and/or model designation of the vessel.

History of 37 C.F.R. §212.4: 82 FR 9366, Mar. 8, 2017.

§212.5. RECORDATION OF DISTINCTIVE IDENTIFICATION OF VESSEL DESIGNER

(a) General. Any owner of a vessel design may record a distinctive identification with the Register of Copyrights for purposes of using such distinctive identification in a design protection notice required by 17 U.S.C. 1306. A distinctive identification of an owner may not be used in a design notice before it has first been recorded with the Register.

(b) Forms. The Copyright Office does not provide forms for the use of persons recording distinctive identifications of ownership of a vessel design. However, persons recording distinctive identifications are encouraged to use the suggested format available on the Copyright Office website (http://www.loc.gov/copyright/vessels).

(c) Recording distinctive identifications. Any distinctive identification of an owner of a vessel design may be recorded with the Register of Copyrights provided that a document containing the following is submitted:

(1) The name and address of the owner;

(2) A statement of the owner that he/she is entitled to use the distinctive identification;

(3) A statement or depiction of the identification; and

(4) The recordation fee in the amount prescribed in §201.3 (c) of this chapter.

(d) The document should be mailed to the address specified in §201.1(b)(2) of this chapter.

History of 37 C.F.R. §212.5: 67 FR 38005, May 31, 2002; 72 FR 33692, July 1, 2007; 82 FR 9366, Mar. 8, 2017.

§212.6. RECORDATION OF TRANSFERS & OTHER DOCUMENTS

The conditions prescribed in §201.4 of this chapter for recordation of transfers of copyright ownership and other documents pertaining to copyright are applicable to the recordation of documents pertaining to the protection of vessel designs under 17 U.S.C. chapter 13.

History of 37 C.F.R. §212.6: 82 FR 9366, Mar. 8, 2017.

§212.7. RECONSIDERATION PROCEDURE FOR REFUSALS TO REGISTER

The requirements prescribed in §202.5 of this chapter for reconsideration of refusals to register copyright claims are applicable to requests to reconsider refusals to register vessel designs under 17 U.S.C. chapter 13, unless otherwise required by this part.

History of 37 C.F.R. §212.7: 69 FR 77637, Dec. 28, 2004; 82 FR 9366, Mar. 8, 2017.

§212.8. CORRECTION OF ERRORS IN CERTIFICATES OF REGISTRATION

(a) General.

(1) This section prescribes conditions relating to the correction of clerical or typographical errors in a certificate of registration of a vessel design, under section 1319 of title 17 of the United States Code, as amended by Public Law 105-304.

(2) For the purposes of this section, a basic registration means registration of a vessel design made under sections 1310 through 1314 of title 17 of the United States Code, as amended by Public Law 105-304.

(3) No correction of the information in a basic registration will be made except pursuant to the provisions of this §212.8. As an exception, where it is discovered that the record of a vessel design registration contains a clerical or typographical error made by the Copyright Office, the Office will take appropriate measures to rectify its error. Correction will be made only of clerical or typographical errors; errors of a different nature cannot be corrected and there is no procedure to amplify the registration record with additional information.

(b) Application for correction of error in certificate. At any time after registration of a vessel design, the Copyright Office will correct a clerical or typographical error in the registration upon the application of the owner of the registered design or the owner's authorized agent.

(c) Form and content of application to correct registration.

(1) An application to correct a registration shall be made on a form prescribed by the Copyright Office, shall be accompanied by the appropriate filing fee identified in §201.3(c) and shall contain the following information:

(i) The make and model of the vessel that embodies the registered design;

(ii) The registration number of the basic registration;

(iii) The year when the basic registration was completed;

(iv) The name or names of the designer or designers of the vessel design, and the owner or owners of the vessel design, as they appear in the basic registration;

(v) The space number and heading or description of the part of the basic registration where the error occurred;

(vi) A transcription of the erroneous information as it appears in the basic registration;

(vii) A statement of the correct information as it should have appeared;

(viii) If desired, an explanation of the error or its correction;

(ix) The name and address:

(A) To which the correspondence concerning the application should be sent; and

(B) To which the certificate of correction should be mailed; and

(x) The certification shall consist of:

(A) The handwritten signature of the owner of the registered design or of the duly authorized agent of such owner (who shall also be identified);

(B) The typed or printed name of the person whose signature appears, and the date of signature; and

(C) A statement that the person signing the application is the owner of the registered design or of the duly authorized agent of such owner, and that the statements made in the application are correct to the best of that person's knowledge.

(2) The form prescribed by the Copyright Office for the foregoing purposes is designated "Application to Correct a Design Registration (Form DC)." Copies of the form are available free upon request to the Public Information Office, Library of Congress, Copyright Office, 101 Independence Avenue SE., Washington, DC 20559-6000 or on the Copyright Office website at http://www.copyright.gov/forms/formdc.pdf.

(3) Copies, phonorecords or supporting documents cannot be made part of the record of a corrected certificate of registration and should not be submitted with the application.

(d) Fee. The filing fee for an application to correct a certificate of registration of a vessel design is prescribed in §201.3(c).

History of 37 C.F.R. §212.8: 71 FR 46402, Aug. 14, 2006; 82 FR 9366, Mar. 8, 2017.

PARTS 253 TO 256, 258, 260 TO 263, 270. [REMOVED & RESERVED]

CHAPTER III. COPYRIGHT ROYALTY BOARD, LIBRARY OF CONGRESS

SUBCHAPTER A. GENERAL PROVISIONS

PART 301. ORGANIZATION

§301.1. COPYRIGHT ROYALTY BOARD

The Copyright Royalty Board is the institutional entity in the Library of Congress that will house the Copyright Royalty Judges, appointed pursuant to 17 U.S.C. 801(a), and their staff.

Source of 37 C.F.R. Part 301: 70 FR 30905, May 31, 2005, unless otherwise noted.

A §301.2. OFFICIAL ADDRESSES

All claims, pleadings, and general correspondence intended for the Copyright Royalty Board and not submitted by electronic means through the electronic filing system ("eCRB") must be addressed as follows:

(a) If sent by mail (including overnight delivery using United States Postal Service Express Mail), the envelope should be addressed to: Copyright Royalty Board, P.O. Box 70977, Southwest Station, Washington, DC 20024-0977.

(b) If hand-delivered by a private party, the envelope must be brought to the Copyright Office Public Information Office, Room LM-401 in the James Madison Memorial Building, and be addressed as follows: Copyright Royalty Board, Library of Congress, James Madison Memorial Building, 101 Independence Avenue SE., Washington, DC 20559-6000.

(c) If hand-delivered by a commercial courier (excluding Federal Express, United Parcel Service and similar courier services), the envelope must be delivered to the Congressional Courier Acceptance Site (CCAS) located at Second and D Street NE., Washington, DC, addressed as follows: Copyright Royalty Board, Library of Congress, James Madison Memorial Building, 101 Independence Avenue SE., Washington, DC 20559-6000.

(d) Subject to paragraph (f) of this section, if sent by electronic mail, to crb@loc.gov.

(e) Correspondence and filings for the Copyright Royalty Board may not be delivered by means of:

(1) Overnight delivery services such as Federal Express, United Parcel Service, etc.; or

(2) Fax.

(f) General correspondence for the Copyright Royalty Board may be sent by electronic mail. Claimants or Parties must not send any claims, pleadings, or other filings to the Copyright Royalty Board by electronic mail without specific, advance authorization of the Copyright Royalty Judges.

History of 37 C.F.R. §301.2: 71 FR 53326, Sept. 11, 2006; 82 FR 18570, Apr. 20, 2017.

§301.3. RESERVED

History of 37 C.F.R. §301.3: 71 FR 53326, Sept. 11, 2006.

PART 302. PUBLIC ACCESS TO RECORDS

§302.1. PUBLIC RECORDS & ACCESS

(a) Inspection. Records of proceedings before the Board will be available for public inspection at the Copyright Royalty Board offices.

(b) Requests. Requests for access to records must be directed to the Copyright Royalty Board. No requests for information or access to records shall be directed to or accepted by a Copyright Royalty Judge. Access to records is only available by appointment.

Source of 37 C.F.R. Part 302: 70 FR 30905, May 31, 2005; 71 FR 53326, Sept. 11, 2006, unless otherwise noted.

§302.2. FEES

For services rendered in connection with document location, reproduction, etc., fees shall apply in accordance with §201.3 of this title.

SUBCHAPTER B. COPYRIGHT ROYALTY JUDGES RULES & PROCEDURES

PART 350. GENERAL ADMINISTRATIVE PROVISIONS

§350.1. SCOPE

This subchapter governs procedures generally applicable to proceedings before the Copyright Royalty Judges in making determinations and adjustments pursuant to the Copyright Act, 17 U.S.C. 801(b).

History of 37 C.F.R. §350.1: 71 FR 53327, Sept. 11, 2006.

Source of 37 C.F.R. Part 350: 70 FR 30905, May 31, 2005; 71 FR 53326, Sept. 11, 2006, unless otherwise noted.

§350.2. REPRESENTATION

Individual parties in proceedings before the Judges may represent themselves or be represented by an attorney. All other parties must be represented by an attorney. Cf. Rule 49(c)(11) of the Rules of the District of Columbia Court of Appeals. The appearance of an attorney on behalf of any party constitutes a representation that the attorney is a member of the bar, in one or more states, in good standing.

History of 37 C.F.R. §350.2: 71 FR 53327, Sept. 11, 2006.

§350.3. DOCUMENTS: FORMAT & LENGTH

(a) Format—**(1)** Caption and description. Parties filing pleadings and documents in a proceeding before the Copyright Royalty Judges must include on the first page of each filing a caption that identifies the proceeding by proceeding type and docket number, and a heading under the caption describing the nature of the document. In addition, to the extent technologically feasible using software available to the general public, Parties must include a footer on each page after the page bearing the caption that includes the name and posture of the filing party, e.g., [Party's] Motion, [Party's] Response in Opposition, etc.

(2) Page layout. Parties must submit documents that are typed (double spaced) using a serif typeface (e.g., Times New Roman) no smaller than 12 points for text or 10 points for footnotes and formatted for 8½ by 11 inch pages with no less than 1 inch margins. Parties must assure that, to the extent technologically feasible using software available to the general public, any exhibit or attachment to documents reflects the docket number of the proceeding in which it is filed and that all pages are numbered appropriately. Any party submitting a document to the Copyright Royalty Board in paper format must submit it unfolded and produced on opaque 8½ by 11 inch white paper using clear black text, and color to the extent the document uses color to convey information or enhance readability.

(3) Binding or securing. Parties submitting any paper document to the Copyright Royalty Board must bind or secure the document in a manner that will prevent pages from becoming separated from the document. For example, acceptable forms of binding or securing include: Ring binders; spiral binding; comb binding; and for documents of fifty pages or fewer, a binder clip or single staple in the top left corner of the document. Rubber bands and paper clips are not acceptable means of securing a document.

(b) Additional format requirements for electronic documents—**(1)** In general. Parties filing documents electronically through eCRB must follow the requirements of paragraphs (a)(1) and (2) of this section and the additional requirements in paragraphs (b)(2) through (10) of this section.

(2) Pleadings; file type. Parties must file all pleadings, such as motions, responses, replies, briefs, notices, declarations of counsel, and memoranda, in Portable Document Format (PDF).

(3) Proposed orders; file type. Parties filing a proposed order as required by §350.4 must prepare the proposed order as a separate Word document and submit it together with the main pleading.

(4) Exhibits and attachments; file types. Parties must convert electronically (not scan) to PDF format all exhibits or attachments that are in electronic form, with the exception of proposed orders and any exhibits or attachments in electronic form that cannot be converted into a usable PDF file (such as audio and video files, files that contain text or images that would not be sufficiently legible after conversion, or spreadsheets that contain too many columns to be displayed legibly on an 8½" x 11" page). Participants must provide electronic copies in their native electronic format of any exhibits or attachments that cannot be converted into a usable PDF file. In addition, participants may provide copies of other electronic files in their native format, in addition to PDF versions of those files, if doing so is likely to assist the Judges in perceiving the content of those files.

(5) No scanned pleadings. Parties must convert every filed document directly to PDF format (using "print to pdf" or "save to pdf"), rather than submitting a scanned PDF image. The Copyright Royalty Board will NOT accept scanned documents, except in the case of specific exhibits or attachments that are available to the filing party only in paper form.

(6) Scanned exhibits. Parties must scan exhibits or other documents that are only available in paper form at no less than 300 dpi. All exhibits must be searchable. Parties must scan in color any exhibit that uses color to convey information or enhance readability.

(7) Bookmarks. Parties must include in all electronic documents appropriate electronic bookmarks to designate the tabs and/or tables of contents that would appear in a paper version of the same document.

(8) Page rotation. Parties must ensure that all pages in electronic documents are right side up, regardless of whether they are formatted for portrait or landscape printing.

(9) Signature. The signature line of an electronic pleading must contain "/s/" followed by the signer's typed name. The name on the signature line must match the name of the user logged into eCRB to file the document.

(10) File size. The eCRB system will not accept PDF or Word files that exceed 128 MB, or files in any other format that exceed 500 MB. Parties may divide excessively large files into multiple parts if necessary to conform to this limitation.

(c) Length of submissions. Whether filing in paper or electronically, parties must adhere to the following space limitations or such other space limitations as the Copyright Royalty Judges may direct by order. Any party seeking an enlargement of the applicable page limit must make the request by a motion to the Copyright Royalty Judges filed no fewer than three days prior to the applicable filing deadline. Any order granting an enlargement of the page limit for a motion or response shall be deemed to grant the same enlargement of the page limit for a response or reply, respectively.

(1) Motions. Motions must not exceed 20 pages and must not exceed 5000 words (exclusive of cover pages, tables of contents, tables of authorities, signature blocks, exhibits, and proof of delivery).

(2) Responses. Responses in support of or opposition to motions must not exceed 20 pages and must not exceed 5000 words (exclusive of cover pages, tables of contents, tables of authorities, signature blocks, exhibits, and proof of delivery).

(3) Replies. Replies in support of motions must not exceed 10 pages and must not exceed 2500 words (exclusive of cover pages, tables of contents, tables of authorities, signature blocks, exhibits, and proof of delivery).

History of 37 C.F.R. §350.3: 71 FR 53327, Sept. 11, 2006; 82 FR 18570, Apr. 20, 2017.

E §350.4. CONTENT OF MOTION & RESPONSIVE PLEADINGS

A motion, responsive pleading, or reply must, at a minimum, state concisely the specific relief the party seeks from the Copyright Royalty Judges, and the legal, factual, and evidentiary basis for granting that relief (or denying the relief sought by the moving party). A motion, or a responsive pleading that seeks alternative relief, must be accompanied by a proposed order.

History of 37 C.F.R. §350.4: 82 FR 18571, Apr. 20, 2017.

E §350.5. ELECTRONIC FILING SYSTEM (eCRB)

(a) Documents to be filed by electronic means—**(1)** Transition period. For the period commencing with the initial deployment of the Copyright Royalty Board's electronic filing and case management system (eCRB) and ending January 1, 2018, all parties having the technological capability must file all documents with the Copyright Royalty Board through eCRB in addition to filing paper documents in conformity with applicable Copyright Royalty Board rules. The Copyright Royalty Board must announce the date of the initial deployment of eCRB on the Copyright Royalty Board Web site (www.loc.gov/crb), as well as the conclusion of the dual-system transition period.

(2) Subsequent to transition period. Except as otherwise provided in this chapter, all attorneys must file documents with the Copyright Royalty Board through eCRB. Pro se parties may file documents with the Copyright Royalty Board through eCRB, subject to §350.4(c)(2).

(b) Official record. The electronic version of a document filed through and stored in eCRB will be the official record of the Copyright Royalty Board.

(c) Obtaining an electronic filing password—**(1)** Attorneys. An attorney must obtain an eCRB password from the Copyright Royalty Board in order to file documents or to receive copies of orders and determinations of the Copyright Royalty Judges. The Copyright Royalty Board will issue an eCRB password after the attorney applicant completes the application form available on the CRB Web site.

(2) Pro se parties. A party not represented by an attorney (a pro se party) may obtain an eCRB password from the Copyright Royalty Board with permission from the Copyright Royalty Judges, in their discretion. To obtain permission, the pro se party must submit an application on the form available on the CRB Web site, describing the party's access to the Internet and confirming the party's ability and capacity to file documents and receive electronically the filings of other parties on a regular basis. If the Copyright Royalty Judges grant permission, the pro se party must complete the eCRB training provided by the Copyright Royalty Board to all electronic filers before receiving an eCRB password. Once the Copyright Royalty Board has issued an eCRB password to a pro se party, that party must make all subsequent filings by electronic means through eCRB.

(3) Claimants. Any person desiring to file a claim with the Copyright Royalty Board for copyright royalties may obtain an eCRB password for the limited purpose of filing claims by completing the application form available on the CRB Web site.

(d) Use of an eCRB password. An eCRB password may be used only by the person to whom it is assigned, or, in the case of an attorney, by that attorney or an authorized employee or agent of that attorney's law office or organization. The person to whom an eCRB password is assigned is responsible for any document filed using that password.

(e) Signature. The use of an eCRB password to login and submit documents creates an electronic record. The password operates and serves as the signature of the person to whom the password is assigned for all purposes under this chapter III.

(f) Originals of sworn documents. The electronic filing of a document that contains a sworn declaration, verification, certificate, statement, oath, or affidavit certifies that the original signed document is in the possession of the attorney or pro se party responsible for the filing and that it is available for review upon request by a party or by the Copyright Royalty Judges. The filer must file through eCRB a scanned copy of the signature page of the sworn document together with the document itself.

(g) Consent to delivery by electronic means. An attorney or pro se party who obtains an eCRB password consents to electronic delivery of all documents, subsequent to the petition to participate, that are filed by electronic means through eCRB. Counsel and pro se parties are responsible for monitoring their email accounts and, upon receipt of notice of an electronic filing, for retrieving the noticed filing. Parties and their counsel bear the responsibility to keep the contact information in their eCRB profiles current.

(h) Accuracy of docket entry. A person filing a document by electronic means is responsible for ensuring the accuracy of the official docket entry generated by the eCRB system, including proper identification of the proceeding, the filing party, and the description of the document. The Copyright Royalty Board will maintain on its Web site (www.loc.gov/crb) appropriate guidance regarding naming protocols for eCRB filers.

(i) Documents subject to a protective order. A person filing a document by electronic means must ensure, at the time of filing, that any documents subject to a protective order are identified to the eCRB system as "restricted" documents. This requirement is in addition to any requirements detailed in the applicable protective order. Failure to identify documents as "restricted" to the eCRB system may result in inadvertent publication of sensitive, protected material.

(j) Exceptions to requirement of electronic filing—**(1)** Certain exhibits or attachments. Parties may file in paper form any exhibits or attachments that are not in a format that readily permits electronic filing, such as oversized documents; or are illegible when scanned into electronic format. Parties filing paper documents or things pursuant to this paragraph must deliver legible or usable copies of the documents or things in accordance with §350.6(a)(2) and must file electronically a notice of filing that includes a certificate of delivery.

(2) Pro se parties. A pro se party may file documents in paper form and must deliver and accept delivery of documents in paper form, unless the pro se party has obtained an eCRB password.

(k) Privacy requirements. **(1)** Unless otherwise instructed by the Copyright Royalty Judges, parties must exclude or redact from all electronically filed documents, whether designated "restricted" or not:

(i) Social Security numbers. If an individual's Social Security number must be included in a filed document for evidentiary reasons, the filer must use only the last four digits of that number.

(ii) Names of minor children. If a minor child must be mentioned in a document for evidentiary reasons, the filer must use only the initials of that child.

(iii) Dates of birth. If an individual's date of birth must be included in a pleading for evidentiary reasons, the filer must use only the year of birth.

(iv) Financial account numbers. If a financial account number must be included in a pleading for evidentiary reasons, the filer must use only the last four digits of the account identifier.

(2) Protection of personally identifiable information. If any information identified in paragraph (k)(1) of this section must be included in a filed document, the filing party must treat it as confidential information subject to the applicable protective order. In addition, parties may treat as confidential, and subject to the applicable protective order, other personal information that is not material to the proceeding.

(*l*) Incorrectly filed documents. **(1)** The Copyright Royalty Board may direct an eCRB filer to re-file a document that has been incorrectly filed, or to correct an erroneous or inaccurate docket entry.

(2) After the transition period, if an attorney or a pro se party who has been issued an eCRB password inadvertently presents a document for filing in paper form, the Copyright Royalty Board may direct the attorney or pro se party to file the document electronically. The document will be deemed filed on the date it was first presented for filing if, no later than the next business day after being so directed by the Copyright Royalty Board, the attorney or pro se participant files the document electronically. If the party fails to make the electronic filing on the next business day, the document will be deemed filed on the date of the electronic filing.

(m) Technical difficulties. **(1)** A filer encountering technical problems with an eCRB filing must immediately notify the Copyright Royalty Board of the problem either by email or by telephone, followed promptly by written confirmation.

(2) If a filer is unable due to technical problems to make a filing with eCRB by an applicable deadline, and makes the notification required by paragraph (m)(1) of this section, the filer shall use electronic mail to make the filing with the CRB and deliver the filing to the other parties to the proceeding. The filing shall be considered to have been made at the time it was filed by electronic mail. The Judges may direct the filer to refile the document through eCRB when the technical problem has been resolved, but the document shall retain its original filing date.

(3) The inability to complete an electronic filing because of technical problems arising in the eCRB system may constitute "good cause" (as used in §350.6(b)(4)) for an order enlarging time or excusable neglect for the failure to act within the specified time, provided the filer complies with paragraph (m)(1) of this section. This section does not provide authority to extend statutory time limits.

History of 37 C.F.R. §350.5: 82 FR 18571, Apr. 20, 2017; 82 FR 27018, June 13, 2017.

A §350.6. FILING & DELIVERY

(a) Filing of pleadings—**(1)** Electronic filing through eCRB. Except as described in §350.5(*l*)(2), any document filed by electronic means through eCRB in accordance with §350.5 constitutes filing for all purposes under this chapter, effective as of the date and time the document is received and timestamped by eCRB.

(2) All other filings. For all filings not submitted by electronic means through eCRB, the submitting party must deliver an original, five paper copies, and one electronic copy in Portable Document Format (PDF) on an optical data storage medium such as a CD or DVD, a flash memory device, or an external hard disk drive to the Copyright Royalty Board in accordance with the provisions described in §301.2 of this chapter. In no case will the Copyright Royalty Board accept any document by facsimile transmission or electronic mail, except with prior express authorization of the Copyright Royalty Judges.

(b) Exhibits. Filers must include all exhibits with the pleadings they support. In the case of exhibits not submitted by electronic means through eCRB, whose bulk or whose cost of reproduction would unnecessarily encumber the record or burden the party, the Copyright Royalty Judges will consider a motion, made in advance of the filing, to reduce the number of required copies. See §350.5(j).

(c) English language translations. Filers must accompany each submission that is in a language other than English with an English-language translation, duly verified under oath to be a true translation. Any other party to the proceeding may, in response, submit its own English-language translation, similarly verified, so long as the responding party's translation proves a substantive, relevant difference in the document.

(d) Affidavits. The testimony of each witness must be accompanied by an affidavit or a declaration made pursuant to 28 U.S.C. 1746 supporting the testimony. See §350.5(f).

(e) Subscription—**(1)** Parties represented by counsel. Subject to §350.5(e), all documents filed electronically by counsel must be signed by at least one attorney of record and must list the attorney's full name, mailing address, email address (if any), telephone number, and a state bar identification number. See §350.5(e). Submissions signed by an attorney for a party need not be verified or accompanied by an affidavit. The signature of an attorney constitutes certification that the contents of the document are true and correct, to the best of the signer's knowledge, information, and belief, formed after an inquiry reasonable under the circumstances and:

(i) The document is not being presented for any improper purpose, such as to harass or to cause unnecessary delay or needless increase in the cost of litigation;

(ii) The claims, defenses, and other legal contentions therein are warranted by existing law or by a nonfrivolous argument for the extension, modification, or reversal of existing law or the establishment of new law;

(iii) The allegations and other factual contentions have evidentiary support or, if specifically so identified, are likely to have evidentiary support after a reasonable opportunity for further investigation or discovery; and

(iv) The denials of factual contentions are warranted by the evidence or, if specifically so identified, are reasonably based on a lack of information or belief.

(2) Parties representing themselves. The original of all paper documents filed by a party not represented by counsel must be signed by that party and list that party's full name, mailing address, email address (if any), and telephone number. The party's signature will constitute the party's certification that, to the best of his or her knowledge and belief, there is good ground to support the document, and that it has not been interposed for purposes of delay.

(f) Responses and replies. Responses in support of or opposition to motions must be filed within ten days of the filing of the motion. Replies to responses must be filed within five days of the filing of the response.

(g) Participant list. The Copyright Royalty Judges will compile and distribute to those parties who have filed a valid petition to participate the official participant list for each proceeding, including each participant's mailing address, email address, and whether the participant is using the eCRB system for filing and receipt of documents in the proceeding. For all paper filings, a party must deliver a copy of the document to counsel for all other parties identified in the participant list, or, if the party is unrepresented by counsel, to the party itself. Parties must notify the Copyright Royalty Judges and all parties of any change in the name or address at which they will accept delivery and must update their eCRB profiles accordingly.

(h) Delivery method and proof of delivery—**(1)** Electronic filings through eCRB. Electronic filing of any document through eCRB operates to effect delivery of the document to counsel or pro se participants who have obtained eCRB passwords, and the automatic notice of filing sent by eCRB to the filer constitutes proof of delivery. Counsel or parties who have not yet obtained eCRB passwords must deliver and receive delivery as provided in paragraph (h)(2). Parties making electronic filings are responsible for assuring delivery of all filed documents to parties that do not use the eCRB system.

(2) Other filings. During the course of a proceeding, each party must deliver all documents that they have filed other than through eCRB to the other parties or their counsel by means no slower than overnight express mail sent on the same day they file the documents, or by such other means as the parties may agree in writing among themselves. Parties must include a proof of delivery with any document delivered in accordance with this paragraph.

History of 37 C.F.R. §350.6: 71 FR 53327, Sept. 11, 2006; 71 FR 59010, Oct. 6, 2006; 82 FR 18571, 18572, Apr. 20, 2017.

Ⓐ §350.7. TIME

(a) Computation. To compute the due date for filing and delivering any document or performing any other act directed by an order of the Copyright Royalty Judges or the rules of the Copyright Royalty Board:

(1) Exclude the day of the act, event, or default that begins the period.

(2) Exclude intermediate Saturdays, Sundays, and federal holidays when the period is less than 11 days, unless computation of the due date is stated in calendar days.

(3) Include the last day of the period, unless it is a Saturday, Sunday, federal holiday, or a day on which the weather or other conditions render the Copyright Royalty Board's office inaccessible.

(4) As used in this rule, "federal holiday" means the date designated for the observance of New Year's Day, Inauguration Day, Birthday of Martin Luther King, Jr., George Washington's Birthday, Memorial Day, Independence Day, Labor Day, Columbus Day, Veterans Day, Thanksgiving Day, Christmas Day, and any other day declared a federal holiday by the President or the Congress.

(5) Except as otherwise described in this Chapter or in an order by the Copyright Royalty Judges, the Copyright Royalty Board will consider documents to be timely filed only if:

(i) They are filed electronically through eCRB and time-stamped by 11:59:59 p.m. Eastern time on the due date;

(ii) They are sent by U.S. mail, are addressed in accordance with §301.2(a) of this chapter, have sufficient postage, and bear a USPS postmark on or before the due date;

(iii) They are hand-delivered by private party to the Copyright Office Public Information Office in accordance with §301.2(b) of this chapter and received by 5:00 p.m. Eastern time on the due date; or

(iv) They are hand-delivered by commercial courier to the Congressional Courier Acceptance Site in accordance with §301.2(c) of this chapter and received by 4:00 p.m. Eastern time on the due date.

(6) Any document sent by mail and dated only with a business postal meter will be considered filed on the date it is actually received by the Library of Congress.

(b) Extensions. A party seeking an extension must do so by written motion. Prior to filing such a motion, a party must attempt to obtain consent from the other parties to the proceeding. An extension motion must state:

(1) The date on which the action or submission is due;

(2) The length of the extension sought;

(3) The date on which the action or submission would be due if the extension were allowed;

(4) The reason or reasons why there is good cause for the delay;

(5) The justification for the amount of additional time being sought; and

(6) The attempts that have been made to obtain consent from the other parties to the proceeding and the position of the other parties on the motion.

History of 37 C.F.R. §350.7: 71 FR 53327, Sept. 11, 2006; 82 FR 18571, 18573, Apr. 20, 2017.

Ⓐ §350.8. CONSTRUCTION & WAIVER

The regulations of the Copyright Royalty Judges are intended to provide efficient and just administrative proceedings and will be construed to advance these purposes. For purposes of an individual proceeding, the provisions of this subchapter may be suspended or waived, in whole or in part, upon a showing of good cause, to the extent allowable by law.

History of 37 C.F.R. §350.8: 71 FR 53327, Sept. 11, 2006; 82 FR 18571, Apr. 20, 2017.

PART 351. PROCEEDINGS

Ⓐ §351.1. INITIATION OF PROCEEDINGS

(a) Notice of commencement; solicitation of petitions to participate. All proceedings before the Copyright Royalty Judges to make determinations and adjustments of reasonable terms and rates of royalty payments, and to authorize the distribution of royalty fees, shall be initiated by publication in the Federal Register of a notice of the initiation of proceedings calling for the filing of petitions to participate in the proceeding.

(b) Petitions to participate.

(1) Royalty rate proceedings.

(i) Single petition. Each petition to participate filed in a royalty rate proceeding must include:

(A) The petitioner's full name, address, telephone number, facsimile number (if any), and e-mail address (if any); and

(B) A description of the petitioner's significant interest in the subject matter of the proceeding.

(ii) Joint petition. Petitioners with similar interests may, in lieu of filing individual petitions, file a single petition. Each joint petition must include:

(A) The full name, address, telephone number, facsimile number (if any), and e-mail address (if any) of the person filing the petition;

(B) A list identifying all participants to the joint petition;

(C) A description of the participants' significant interest in the subject matter of the proceeding; and

(D) If the joint petition is filed by counsel or a representative of one or more of the participants that are named in the joint petition, a statement from such counsel or representative certifying that, as of the date of submission of the joint petition, such counsel or representative has the authority and consent of the participants to represent them in the royalty rate proceeding.

(2) Distribution proceedings.

(i) Single petition. Each petition to participate filed in a royalty distribution proceeding must include:

(A) The petitioner's full name, address, telephone number, facsimile number (if any), and e-mail address (if any);

(B) In a cable or satellite royalty distribution proceeding, identification of whether the petition covers a Phase I proceeding (the initial part of a distribution proceeding where royalties are divided among the categories or groups of copyright owners), a Phase II proceeding (where the money allotted to each category is subdivided among the various copyright owners within that category), or both; and

(C) A description of the petitioner's significant interest in the subject matter of the proceeding.

(ii) Joint petition. Petitioners with similar interests may, in lieu of filing individual petitions, file a single petition. Each joint petition must include:

(A) The full name, address, telephone number, facsimile number (if any), and e-mail address (if any) of the person filing the petition;

(B) A list identifying all participants to the joint petition;

(C) In a cable or satellite royalty distribution proceeding, identification of whether the petition covers a Phase I proceeding (the initial part of a distribution proceeding where royalties are divided among the categories or groups of copyright owners), a Phase II proceeding (where the money allotted to each category is subdivided among the various copyright owners within that category), or both;

(D) A description of the participants' significant interest in the subject matter of the proceeding; and

(E) If the joint petition is filed by counsel or a representative of one or more of the participants that are named in the joint petition, a statement from such counsel or representative certifying that, as of the date of submission of the joint petition, such counsel or representative has the authority and consent of the participants to represent them in the royalty distribution proceeding.

(3) Filing deadline. A petition to participate shall be filed by no later than 30 days after the publication of the notice of commencement of a proceeding, subject to the qualified exception set forth in paragraph (d) of this section.

(4) Filing fee. A petition to participate must be accompanied with a filing fee of $150 or the petition will be rejected. For petitions filed electronically through eCRB, payment must be made to the Copyright Royalty Board through the payment portal designated on eCRB. For petitions filed by other means, payment must be made to the Copyright Royalty Board by check or by money order. If a check is subsequently dishonored, the petition will be rejected. If the petitioner believes that the contested amount of that petitioner's claim will be $1,000 or less, the petitioner must so state in the petition to participate and should not include payment of the $150 filing fee. If it becomes apparent during the course of the proceedings that the contested amount of the claim is more than $1,000, the Copyright Royalty Judges will require payment of the filing fee at that time.

(c) Acceptance and rejection of petitions to participate. A petition to participate will be deemed to have been allowed by the Copyright Royalty Judges unless the Copyright Royalty Judges determine the petitioner lacks a significant interest in the proceeding or the petition is otherwise invalid.

(d) Late petitions to participate. The Copyright Royalty Judges may, for substantial good cause shown, and if there is no prejudice to the participants that have already filed petitions, accept late petitions to participate at any time up to the date that is 90 days before the date on which participants in the proceeding are to file their written direct statements. However, petitioners whose petitions are filed more than 30 days after publication of notice of commencement of a proceeding are not eligible to object to a settlement reached during the voluntary negotiation period.

History of 37 C.F.R. §351.1: 71 FR 53327, Sept. 11, 2006; 81 FR 8650, Feb. 22, 2016; 82 FR 18574, Apr. 20, 2017.

Source of 37 C.F.R. Part 351: 70 FR 30905, May 31, 2005; 70 FR 30906, May 31, 2005; 71 FR 53326, Sept. 11, 2006, unless otherwise noted.

§351.2. VOLUNTARY NEGOTIATION PERIOD; SETTLEMENT

(a) Commencement; duration. After the date for filing petitions to participate in a proceeding, the Copyright Royalty Judges will announce the beginning of a voluntary negotiation period and will make a list of the participants available to the participants in the particular proceeding. The voluntary negotiation period shall last three months, after which the parties shall notify the Copyright Royalty Judges in writing as to whether a settlement has been reached.

(b) Settlement.

(1) Distribution proceedings. Pursuant to 17 U.S.C. 801(b)(7)(A), to the extent that a settlement has been

reached in a distribution proceeding, that agreement will provide the basis for the distribution.

(2) Royalty rate proceedings. If, in a proceeding to determine statutory terms and rates, the participating parties report that a settlement has been reached by some or all of the parties, the Copyright Royalty Judges, pursuant to 17 U.S.C. 801(b)(7)(A), will publish the settlement in the Federal Register for notice and comment from those bound by the terms, rates, or other determination set by the agreement. If an objection to the adoption of an agreement is filed, the Copyright Royalty Judges may decline to adopt the agreement as a basis for statutory terms and rates for participants that are not parties to the agreement if the Copyright Royalty Judges conclude that the agreement does not provide a reasonable basis for setting statutory terms or rates.

History of 37 C.F.R. §351.2: 71 FR 53328, Sept. 11, 2006.

§351.3. CONTROVERSY & FURTHER PROCEEDINGS

(a) Declaration of controversy. If a settlement has not been reached within the voluntary negotiation period, the Copyright Royalty Judges will issue an order declaring that further proceedings are necessary. The procedures set forth at §§351.5, et seq., for formal hearings will apply, unless the abbreviated procedures set forth in paragraphs (b) and (c) of this section are invoked by the Copyright Royalty Judges.

(b) Small claims in distribution proceedings.

(1) General. If, in a distribution proceeding, the contested amount of a claim is $10,000 or less, the Copyright Royalty Judges shall decide the controversy on the basis of the filing of the written direct statement by each participant (or participant group filing a joint petition), the response by any opposing participant, and one optional reply by a participant who has filed a written direct statement.

(2) Bad faith inflation of claim. If the Copyright Royalty Judges determine that a participant asserts in bad faith an amount in controversy in excess of $10,000 for the purpose of avoiding a determination under the procedure set forth in paragraph (b)(1) of this section, the Copyright Royalty Judges shall impose a fine on that participant in an amount not to exceed the difference between the actual amount distributed and the amount asserted by the participant.

(c) Paper proceedings—

(1) Standard. The procedure under this paragraph (c) will be applied in cases in which there is no genuine issue of material fact, there is no need for evidentiary hearings, and all participants in the proceeding agree in writing to the procedure. In the absence of an agreement in writing among all participants, this procedure may be applied by the Copyright Royalty Judges either on the motion of a party or by the Copyright Royalty Judges sua sponte.

(2) Procedure. Paper proceedings will be decided on the basis of the filing of the written direct statement by the participant (or participant group filing a joint petition), the response by any opposing participant, and one optional reply by a participant who has filed a written direct statement.

History of 37 C.F.R. §351.3: 71 FR 53328, Sept. 11, 2006.

§351.4. WRITTEN DIRECT STATEMENTS

(a) Required filing; deadline. All parties who have filed a petition to participate in the hearing must file a written direct statement. The deadline for the filing of the written direct statement will be specified by the Copyright Royalty Judges, not earlier than 4 months, nor later than 5 months, after the end of the voluntary negotiation period set forth in §351.2.

(b) Required content.

(1) Testimony. The written direct statement shall include all testimony, including each witness's background and qualifications, along with all the exhibits.

(2) Designated past records and testimony. Each participating party may designate a portion of past records, including records of the Copyright Royalty Tribunal or Copyright Arbitration Royalty Panels, that it wants included in its direct statement. If a party intends to rely on any part of the testimony of a witness in a prior proceeding, the complete testimony of that witness (*i.e.*, direct, cross and redirect examination) must be designated. The party submitting such past records and/or testimony shall include a copy with the written direct statement.

(3) Claim. In the case of a royalty distribution proceeding, each party must state in the written direct statement its percentage or dollar claim to the fund. In the case of a rate (or rates) proceeding, each party must state its requested rate. No party will be precluded from revising its claim or its requested rate at any time during the proceeding up to, and including, the filing of the proposed findings of fact and conclusions of law.

(c) Amended written direct statements. A participant in a proceeding may amend a written direct statement based on new information received during the discovery process, within 15 days after the end of the discovery period. An amended written direct statement must explain how it differs from the written direct statement it will amend and must demonstrate that the amendment is based on new information received during the discovery process. The participant amending its written direct statement may file either the amended portions of the written direct statement or submit complete new copies at its option.

History of 37 C.F.R. §351.4: 71 FR 53328, Sept. 11, 2006; 71 FR 59010, Oct. 6, 2006.

§351.5. DISCOVERY IN ROYALTY RATE PROCEEDINGS

(a) Schedule. Following the submission to the Copyright Royalty Judges of written direct and rebuttal statements by the participants in a royalty rate proceeding, and after conferring with the participants, the Copyright Royalty Judges will issue a discovery schedule.

(b) Document production, depositions and interrogatories—

(1) Document production. A participant in a royalty rate proceeding may request of an opposing participant nonprivileged documents that are directly related to the written direct statement or written rebuttal statement of that participant. Broad, nonspecific discovery requests are not acceptable. All documents offered in response to a discovery request must be furnished in as organized and useable form as possible. Any objection to a request for production shall be resolved by a motion or request to compel production. The motion must include a statement that the parties had conferred and were unable to resolve the matter.

(2) Depositions and interrogatories. In a proceeding to determine royalty rates, the participants entitled to receive royalties shall collectively be permitted to take no more than 10 depositions and secure responses to no more than 25 interrogatories. Similarly, the participants obligated to pay royalties shall collectively be permitted to take no more than 10 depositions and secure responses to no more than 25 interrogatories. Parties may obtain such discovery regarding any matter, not privileged, that is relevant to the claim or defense of any party. Relevant information need not be admissible at hearing if the discovery by means of depositions and interrogatories appears reasonably calculated to lead to the discovery of admissible evidence.

(c) Motions to request other relevant information and materials.

(1) In any royalty rate proceeding scheduled to commence prior to January 1, 2011, a participant may, by means of written or oral motion on the record, request of an opposing participant or witness other relevant information and materials. The Copyright Royalty Judges will allow such request only if they determine that, absent the discovery sought, their ability to achieve a just resolution of the proceeding would be substantially impaired.

(2) In determining whether such discovery motions will be granted, the Copyright Royalty Judges may consider—

(i) Whether the burden or expense of producing the requested information or materials outweighs the likely benefit, taking into account the needs and resources of the participants, the importance of the issues at stake, and the probative value of the requested information or materials in resolving such issues;

(ii) Whether the requested information or materials would be unreasonably cumulative or duplicative, or are obtainable from another source that is more convenient, less burdensome, or less expensive; and

(iii) Whether the participant seeking the discovery had an ample opportunity by discovery in the proceeding or by other means to obtain the information sought.

History of 37 C.F.R. §351.5: 71 FR 53328, Sept. 11, 2006.

§351.6. DISCOVERY IN DISTRIBUTION PROCEEDINGS

In distribution proceedings, the Copyright Royalty Judges shall designate a 45-day period beginning with the filing of written direct statements within which parties may request of an opposing party nonprivileged underlying documents related to the written exhibits and testimony. However, all parties shall be given a reasonable opportunity to conduct discovery on amended statements.

History of 37 C.F.R. §351.6: 71 FR 53328, Sept. 11, 2006.

§351.7. SETTLEMENT CONFERENCE

A post-discovery settlement conference will be held among the participants, within 21 days after the close of discovery, outside of the presence of the Copyright Royalty Judges. Immediately after this conference the participants shall file with the Copyright Royalty Judges a written Joint Settlement Conference Report indicating the extent to which the participants have reached a settlement.

History of 37 C.F.R. §351.7: 71 FR 53329, Sept. 11, 2006.

§351.8. PRE-HEARING CONFERENCE

In the absence of a complete settlement in a proceeding not subject to the abbreviated procedures set forth in §§351.3(b) and (c), a hearing will be scheduled expeditiously so as to allow the Copyright Royalty Judges to conduct hearings and issue its final determination in the proceeding within the time allowed by the Copyright Act. Prior to the hearing, the Copyright Royalty Judges may conduct a prehearing conference to assist in setting the order of presentation of evidence and the appearance of witnesses at the hearing and to provide for the submission of pre-hearing written legal arguments.

History of 37 C.F.R. §351.8: 71 FR 53329, Sept. 11, 2006.

§351.9. CONDUCT OF HEARINGS

(a) By panels. Subject to paragraph (b) of this section, hearings will be conducted by Copyright Royalty Judges sitting en banc.

(b) Role of Chief Judge. The Chief Copyright Royalty Judge, or an individual Copyright Royalty Judge designated by the Chief Judge, may preside over such collateral and administrative proceedings, and over such proceedings under section 803(b)(1) through (5) of the Copyright Act, as the Chief Judge considers appropriate. The Chief Judge, or an individual Copyright Royalty Judge designated by the Chief Judge, shall have the responsibility for:

(1) Administering oaths and affirmations to all witnesses;

(2) Announcing the Copyright Royalty Judges' ruling on objections and motions and all rulings with respect to introducing or excluding documentary or other evidence. In all cases, with the exception of a hearing pursuant to 17 U.S.C. 803(a)(2), it takes a majority vote to grant a motion or sustain an objection. A tie vote will result in the denial of a motion or the overruling of the objection;

(c) Opening statements. In each distribution or rate proceeding, each party may present its opening statement summarizing its written direct statement.

(d) Notice of witnesses and prior exchange of exhibits. Each party must provide all other parties notice of the witnesses who are to be called to testify at least one week in advance of such testimony, unless modified by applicable trial order. Parties must exchange exhibits at least one day in advance of being offered into evidence at a hearing, unless modified by applicable trial order.

(e) Subpoenas. The parties may move the Copyright Royalty Judges to issue a subpoena. The object of the subpoena shall be served with the motion and may appear in response to the motion.

(f) Witnesses sequestered. Subject to applicable trial order, witnesses, other than party representatives, may not be permitted to listen to any testimony and may not be allowed to review a transcript of any prior testimony.

History of 37 C.F.R. §351.9: 71 FR 53329, Sept. 11, 2006.

§351.10. EVIDENCE

(a) Admissibility. All evidence that is relevant and not unduly repetitious or privileged, shall be admissible. Hearsay may be admitted to the extent deemed appropriate by the Copyright Royalty Judges. Written testimony and exhibits must be authenticated or identified in order to be admissible as evidence. The requirement of authentication or identification as a condition precedent to admissibility is satisfied by evidence sufficient to support a finding that the matter in question is what its proponent claims. Extrinsic evidence of authenticity as a condition precedent to admissibility is not required with respect to materials that can be self-authenticated under Rule 902 of the Federal Rules of Evidence such as certain public records. No evidence, including exhibits, may be submitted without a sponsoring witness, except for good cause shown.

(b) Examination of witnesses. All witnesses shall be required to take an oath or affirmation before testifying. Parties are entitled to conduct direct examination (consisting of the testimony of the witness in the written statements and an oral summary of that testimony); cross-examination (limited to matters raised on direct examination); and redirect examination (limited to matters raised on cross-examination). The Copyright Royalty Judges may limit the number of witnesses or limit questioning to avoid cumulative testimony.

(c) Exhibits—

(1) Submission. Writings, recordings and photographs shall be presented as exhibits and marked by the presenting party. "Writings" and "recordings" consist of letters, words, or numbers, or their equivalent, set down by handwriting, typewriting, printing, photostating, photographing, magnetic impulse, mechanical or electronic recording, or other form of data compilation. "Photographs" include still photographs, video tapes, and motion pictures.

(2) Separation of irrelevant portions. Relevant and material matter embraced in an exhibit containing other matter not material or relevant or not intended as evidence must be plainly designated as the matter offered in evidence, and the immaterial or irrelevant parts shall be marked clearly so as to show they are not intended as evidence.

(3) Summary exhibits. The contents of voluminous writings, recordings, or photographs which cannot conveniently be examined in the hearing may be presented in the form of a chart, summary, or calculation. The originals, or duplicates, shall be made available for examination or copying, or both, by other parties at a reasonable time and place. The Copyright Royalty Judges may order that they be produced in the hearing.

(d) Copies. Anyone presenting exhibits as evidence must present copies to all other participants in the proceedings, or their attorneys, and afford them an opportunity to examine the exhibits in their entirety and offer into evidence any other portion that may be considered material and relevant.

(e) Introduction of studies and analyses. If studies or analyses are offered in evidence, they shall state clearly the study plan, the principles and methods underlying the study, all relevant assumptions, all variables considered in the analysis, the techniques of data collection, the techniques of estimation and testing, and the results of the study's actual estimates and tests presented in a format commonly accepted within the relevant field of expertise implicated by the study. The facts and judgments upon which conclusions are based shall be stated clearly, together with any alternative courses of action considered. Summarized descriptions of input data, tabulations of input data and the input data themselves shall be retained.

(f) Objections. Parties are entitled to raise objections to evidence on any proper ground during the course of the hearing and to raise an objection that an opposing party has not furnished unprivileged underlying documents.

(g) New exhibits for use in cross-examination. Exhibits that have not been identified and exchanged in advance may be shown to a witness on cross-examination. However, copies of such exhibits must be distributed to the Copyright Royalty Judges and to the other participants before being shown to the witness at the time of cross-examination, unless the Copyright Royalty Judges direct otherwise. Such exhibits can be used solely to impeach the witness's direct testimony.

History of 37 C.F.R. §351.10: 71 FR 53329, Sept. 11, 2006; 71 FR 59010, Oct. 6, 2006.

§351.11. REBUTTAL PROCEEDINGS

Written rebuttal statements shall be filed at a time designated by the Copyright Royalty Judges upon conclusion of the hearing of the direct case, in the same form and manner as the written direct statement, except that the claim or the requested rate shall not have to be included if it has not changed from the written direct statement. Further proceedings at the rebuttal stage shall follow the schedule ordered by the Copyright Royalty Judges.

History of 37 C.F.R. §351.11: 71 FR 53329, Sept. 11, 2006.

§351.12. CLOSING THE RECORD

To close the record of a proceeding, the presiding Judge shall make an announcement that the taking of evidence has concluded.

History of 37 C.F.R. §351.12: 71 FR 53330, Sept. 11, 2006.

§351.13. TRANSCRIPT & RECORD

(a) An official reporter for the recording and transcribing of hearings shall be designated by the Copyright Royalty Judges. Anyone wishing to inspect the transcript of a hearing may do so at the offices of the Copyright Royalty Board.

(b) The transcript of testimony and written statements, except those portions to which an objection has been sustained, and all exhibits, documents and other items admitted in the course of a proceeding shall constitute the official written record. The written record, along with the Copyright Royalty Judges' final determination, shall be available at the Copyright Royalty Board's offices for public inspection and copying.

History of 37 C.F.R. §351.13: 71 FR 53330, Sept. 11, 2006.

§351.14. PROPOSED FINDINGS OF FACT & CONCLUSIONS OF LAW

(a) Any party to the proceeding may file proposed findings of fact and conclusions, briefs or memoranda of law, or may be directed by the Copyright Royalty Judges to do so. Such filings, and any replies to them, shall take place after the record has been closed.

(b) Failure to file when directed to do so shall be considered a waiver of the right to participate further in the proceeding unless good cause for the failure is shown. A party waives any objection to a provision in the determination unless the provision conflicts with a proposed finding of fact or conclusion of law filed by the party.

(c) Proposed findings of fact shall be numbered by paragraph and include all basic evidentiary facts developed on the record used to support proposed conclusions, and shall contain appropriate citations to the record for each evidentiary fact. Proposed conclusions shall be stated and numbered by paragraph separately. Failure to comply with this paragraph (c) may result in the offending paragraph being stricken.

History of 37 C.F.R. §351.14: 71 FR 53330, Sept. 11, 2006.

§351.15. REMAND

In the event of a remand from the United States Court of Appeals for the District of Columbia Circuit of a final determination of the Copyright Royalty Judges, the parties to the proceeding shall within 45 days from the issuance of the mandate from the Court of Appeals file with the Judges written proposals for the conduct and schedule of the resolution of the remand.

History of 37 C.F.R. §351.15: 74 FR 38533, Aug. 4, 2009.

PART 352. DETERMINATIONS

§352.1. HOW MADE

Except for decisions authorized by law to be made by a single Copyright Royalty Judge, determinations in a proceeding will be made by a majority of the Copyright Royalty Judges. The opinion or opinions of the majority and any dissenting opinion will be included in the determination. Each determination will be transmitted to the Register of Copyrights to enable review for consistency with the Copyright Act on the day it is issued.

History of 37 C.F.R. §352.1: 71 FR 53330, Sept. 11, 2006.

Source of 37 C.F.R. Part 352: 70 FR 30905, May 31, 2005; 70 FR 30910, May 31, 2005; 71 FR 53326, Sept. 11, 2006, unless otherwise noted.

§352.2. TIMING

The Copyright Royalty Judges will issue their determination within 11 months of the date of the post-discovery settlement conference or 15 days before the expiration of the existing rates or terms in a proceeding to determine successors to rates or terms that will expire on a specific date, whichever date first occurs. The date the determination is "issued" refers to the date of the order.

History of 37 C.F.R. §352.2: 71 FR 53330, Sept. 11, 2006.

§352.3. FINAL DETERMINATIONS

Unless a motion for a rehearing is timely filed within 15 days, the determination by the Copyright Royalty Judges pursuant to 17 U.S.C. 803(c) in a proceeding is final when it is issued.

History of 37 C.F.R. §352.3: 71 FR 53330, Sept. 11, 2006.

PART 353. REHEARING

§353.1. WHEN GRANTED

A motion for rehearing may be filed by any participant in the relevant proceeding. The Copyright Royalty Judges may grant rehearing upon a showing that any aspect of the determination may be erroneous.

History of 37 C.F.R. §353.1: 71 FR 53330, Sept. 11, 2006.

Source of 37 C.F.R. Part 353: 70 FR 30905, May 31, 2005; 70 FR 30910, May 31, 2005; 71 FR 53326, Sept. 11, 2006, unless otherwise noted.

§353.2. FORM & CONTENT OF REHEARING MOTIONS

A motion for rehearing shall not exceed 10 pages in length and must set forth, in the beginning of its text, a brief summary statement of the aspects of the determination believed by the moving participant to be without evidentiary support in the record or contrary to legal requirements.

§353.3. PROCEDURE ON REHEARING

Upon receipt of a motion for rehearing, the Copyright Royalty Judges will issue an appropriate order. No participant shall file a response to a rehearing motion, unless such response is allowed by order of the Copyright Royalty Judges.

History of 37 C.F.R. §353.3: 71 FR 53330, Sept. 11, 2006.

§353.4. FILING DEADLINE

A motion for rehearing must be filed within 15 days after the date on which the Copyright Royalty Judges issue an initial determination.

History of 37 C.F.R. §353.4: 71 FR 53330, Sept. 11, 2006.

§353.5. PARTICIPATION NOT REQUIRED

In any case in which a response to a rehearing motion is allowed, or rehearing is granted, an opposing party shall not be required to participate in the rehearing. The Copyright Royalty Judges will not draw any negative inference from a lack of participation in a rehearing. Nonparticipation in rehearing proceedings may limit the scope of their participation in judicial review proceedings as set forth in 17 U.S.C. 803(d)(1).

History of 37 C.F.R. §353.5: 71 FR 53330, Sept. 11, 2006.

PART 354. SUBMISSIONS TO THE REGISTER OF COPYRIGHTS

§354.1. MATERIAL QUESTIONS OF COPYRIGHT LAW

(a) Discretionary referrals. The Copyright Royalty Judges may seek guidance from the Register of Copyrights with respect to a material question of substantive law, concerning an interpretation or construction of those provisions of the Copyright Act, that arises in the course of their proceedings.

(b) How presented. A question of substantive law may be referred to the Register of Copyrights at the request of one or more of the Copyright Royalty Judges. A question of substantive law may also be referred to the Register of Copyrights as a request submitted by motion of a participant, provided that one or more of the Copyright Royalty Judges agrees with the participant's request.

(1) Referral by Judges. One or more of the Copyright Royalty Judges may refer what he or she believes to be a material question of substantive law to the Register of Copyrights at any time during a proceeding by issuing a written referral that is made part of the record of that proceeding. The referral will state the issue(s) to be referred and the schedule for the filing of briefs by the parties of the issue(s). After the briefs and other relevant materials are received, they will be transmitted to the Register of Copyrights.

(2) Motion by participant. Any participant may submit a motion to the Copyright Royalty Judges (but not to the Register of Copyrights) requesting their referral to the Register of Copyrights a question that the participant believes would be suitable for referral under paragraph (a) of this section.

(i) Content. The motion should be captioned "Motion of [Participant(s)] Requesting Referral of Material Question of Substantive Law." The motion should set forth, at the outset, the precise legal question for which the moving party is seeking interlocutory referral to the Register of Copyrights. The motion should then proceed to explain, with brevity, why the issue meets the criteria for potential referral under paragraph (a) of this section and why the interests of fair and efficient adjudication would be best served by obtaining interlocutory guidance from the Register of Copyrights. The motion should not include argument on the merits of the issue, but may include a suggested schedule of briefing that would make reasonable provision for comments and legal arguments, in such a way as to avoid delay and duplication.

(ii) Time of motion. A motion for referral of a material question of substantive law to the Register of Copyrights should be filed as soon as possible in the relevant proceeding, but no later than any deadline set by the Copyright Royalty Judges.

(iii) Action on motion—

(A) Referral granted. Upon consideration of a Motion Requesting Referral of Material Question of Substantive Law, if one or more of the Copyright Royalty Judges agrees with the request, the Chief Judge shall issue an appropriate referral. The referral will state the issue(s) to be referred and the schedule for the filing of briefs by the parties of the issue(s). After the briefs and other relevant materials are received, they will be transmitted to the Register of Copyrights.

(B) Referral denied. If none of the Copyright Royalty Judges agrees with the request, the Board will issue an order denying the request which will provide the basis for the decision. A copy of any order denying a Motion Requesting Referral of Material Question of Substantive Law will be transmitted to the Register of Copyrights.

(c) No effect on proceedings. The issuance of a request to the Register of Copyrights for an interpretive ruling under this part does not delay or otherwise affect the schedule of the participants' obligations in the relevant ongoing proceeding, unless that schedule or those obligations are expressly changed by order of the Copyright Royalty Judges.

(d) Binding effect; time limit. The Copyright Royalty Judges will not issue a final determination in a proceeding where the discretionary referral of a question to the Register of Copyrights under this part is pending, unless the Register has not delivered the decision to the Copyright Royalty Judges within 14 days after the Register receives all of the briefs of the participants. If the decision of the Register of Copyrights is timely delivered to the Copyright Royalty Judges, the decision will be included in the record of the proceeding. The legal interpretation embodied in the timely delivered response of the Register of Copyrights in resolving material questions of substantive law is binding upon the Copyright Royalty Judges and will be applied by them in their final determination in the relevant proceeding.

History of 37 C.F.R. §354.1: 71 FR 53330, Sept. 11, 2006.

Source of 37 C.F.R. Part 354: 70 FR 30905, May 31, 2005; 70 FR 30910, May 31, 2005; 71 FR 53326, Sept. 11, 2006, unless otherwise noted.

§354.2. NOVEL QUESTIONS

(a) Mandatory referrals. If the material question of substantive law described in §354.1(a) is a novel question of law, referral to the Register of Copyrights by the Copyright Royalty Judges is mandatory. A "novel question of law" is a question of law that has not been determined in the prior decisions, determinations, or rulings under the Copyright Act of the Copyright Royalty Judges, the Librarian of Congress, the Register of Copyrights, the Copyright Arbitration Royalty Panels (to the extent they are consistent with the current decisions, determinations, or rulings of the Register of Copyrights or the Librarian of Congress), or the former Copyright Royalty Tribunal.

(b) Procedures. The procedures set forth for the discretionary referral of material questions of copyright law to the Register of Copyrights by the Copyright Royalty Judges, set forth in §354.1, shall also govern the mandatory referral of novel questions, except that the Register of Copyrights' decision will be timely if it is delivered to the Copyright Royalty Judges within 30 days after the Register of Copyrights has received all of the briefs or comments of the participants. The Copyright Royalty Judges will not issue a final determination in a proceeding where the referral of a novel question to the Register of Copyrights under this part is pending, unless this 30-day period has expired. The legal interpretation embodied in the timely delivered response of the Register of Copyrights in resolving material questions of substantive law is binding upon the Copyright Royalty Judges and will be applied by them in their final determination in the relevant proceeding.

History of 37 C.F.R. §354.2: 71 FR 53331, Sept. 11, 2006.

§354.3. REGISTER OF COPYRIGHTS' AUTHORITY TO REDESIGNATE REFERRALS

If, during the 14-day period of a discretionary referral of a material question of law under §354.1, the Register of Copyrights determines that the question is a "novel" one within the meaning of §354.2(a), the Register may notify the Copyright Royalty Judges of that determination. The Copyright Royalty Judges will be bound by such a determination by the Register of Copyrights and will regard the Register's decision as timely delivered if it is received within the 30-day period applicable to novel question referrals.

History of 37 C.F.R. §354.3: 71 FR 53331, Sept. 11, 2006.

§§354.4, 354.5. RESERVED

History of 37 C.F.R. §§354.4, 354.5: 71 FR 53331, Sept. 11, 2006.

SUBCHAPTER C. SUBMISSION OF ROYALTY CLAIMS

Ⓐ PART 360. FILING OF CLAIMS TO ROYALTY FEES COLLECTED UNDER COMPULSORY LICENSE

SUBPART A. CABLE & SATELLITE CLAIMS

Ⓐ §360.1. GENERAL

This subpart prescribes procedures under 17 U.S.C. 111(d)(4)(A) and 17 U.S.C. 119(b)(4) whereby parties claiming entitlement to cable compulsory license royalty fees or satellite compulsory license royalty fees must file claims with the Copyright Royalty Board.

History of 37 C.F.R. §360.1: 82 FR 27018, June 13, 2017.

Ⓐ §360.2. DEFINITIONS

For purposes of this subpart, the following definitions will apply:

Cable compulsory license royalty fees means royalty fees deposited with the Copyright Office pursuant to 17 U.S.C. 111.

Performing rights society has the meaning set forth in 17 U.S.C. 101.

Satellite compulsory license royalty fees means royalty fees deposited with the Copyright Office pursuant to 17 U.S.C. 119.

History of 37 C.F.R. §360.2: 82 FR 27018, June 13, 2017.

Ⓐ §360.3. TIME OF FILING

(a) During the month of July each year, any party claiming to be entitled to cable compulsory license royalty fees or satellite compulsory license royalty fees for secondary transmissions during the preceding calendar year must file a claim or claims with the Copyright Royalty Board. No party will receive royalty fees for secondary transmissions during the specified period unless the party has filed a timely claim to the fees. Claimants may file claims jointly or as a single claim. Claimants must file separate claims for cable compulsory license royalty fees and satellite compulsory license royalty fees. The Copyright Royalty Board will reject any claim that purports to be for both cable and satellite royalty fees.

(b) Claims filed with the Copyright Royalty Board will be considered timely filed only if they are filed online through eCRB or by mail or hand delivery in accordance with §301.2 during the month of July, as determined in accordance with §350.7.

(c) Notwithstanding paragraphs (a) and (b) of this section, in any year in which July 31 falls on a Saturday, Sunday, holiday, or other nonbusiness day within the District of Columbia or the Federal Government, the due date for claims to cable or satellite compulsory license royalty fees will be the first business day in August.

(d) In the event the Copyright Royalty Board does not receive a claim that was properly addressed and mailed, the filer may prove proper filing of the claim if it was sent by certified mail return receipt requested, and the filer produces a receipt bearing a July date stamp of the United States Postal Service. The Copyright Royalty Board will accept no other offer of proof in lieu of the return receipt.

(e) For claims filed electronically through eCRB, the Copyright Royalty Board will accept the confirmation email generated by eCRB as proof of filing. The Copyright Royalty Board will accept no other offer of proof regarding claims filed electronically through eCRB.

History of 37 C.F.R. §360.3: 82 FR 27018, June 13, 2017.

Ⓐ §360.4. FORM & CONTENT OF CLAIMS

(a) Forms. **(1)** Each filer must use the form prescribed by the Copyright Royalty Board to claim cable compulsory license royalty fees or satellite compulsory license royalty fees and must provide all information required by that form and its accompanying instructions.

(2) Copies of claim forms are available:

(i) On the Copyright Royalty Board Web site at http://www.crb.gov/claims/ during the month of July for claims filed with the Copyright Royalty Board by mail or by hand delivery;

(ii) On the Copyright Royalty Board Web site at http://www.crb.gov/cable/ (for cable claims) or http://www.crb.gov/satellite/ (for satellite claims) during the month of July for claims filed online through eCRB; and

(iii) Upon request to the Copyright Royalty Board by mail at the address set forth in §301.2(a), by email at the address set forth in §301.2(d), or by telephone at (202) 707-7658.

(b) Content—**(1)** Single claim. A claim filed on behalf of a single copyright owner of a work or works secondarily transmitted by a cable system or satellite carrier must include the following information:

(i) The full legal name, address, and email address of the copyright owner entitled to claim the royalty fees.

(ii) A statement of the nature of the copyright owner's work(s) that has (have) been secondarily transmitted by a cable system or satellite carrier establishing a basis for the claim.

(iii) The name, telephone number, full mailing address, and email address of the person or entity filing the single claim. The information contained in a filer's eCRB profile shall fulfill this requirement for claims submitted through eCRB.

(iv) The name, telephone number, and email address of the person whom the Copyright Royalty Board can contact regarding the claim.

(v) An original signature of the copyright owner or of a duly authorized representative of the copyright owner, except for claims filed online through eCRB.

(vi) A declaration of authority to file the claim and a certification of the veracity of the information contained in the claim and the good faith of the person signing in providing the information. Penalties for fraud and false statements are provided under 18 U.S.C. 1001 et seq.

(2) Joint claim. A claim filed on behalf of more than one copyright owner whose works have been secondarily transmitted by a cable system or satellite carrier must include the following information:

(i) With the exception of joint claims filed by a performing rights society on behalf of its members, a list including the full legal name, address, and email address of each copyright owner whose claim(s) are included in the joint claim. Claims filed online through eCRB must include an Excel spreadsheet containing the information if the number of joint claimants is in excess of ten. For claims filed by mail or hand delivery, the list containing the name of each claimant to the joint claim may be provided in a single Excel spreadsheet on CD, DVD, or other electronic storage medium.

(ii) A general statement of the nature of the copyright owners' works that have been secondarily transmitted by a cable system or satellite carrier establishing a basis for the joint claim.

(iii) The name, telephone number, full mailing address, and email address of the person or entity filing the joint claim. The information contained in a filer's eCRB profile shall fulfill this requirement for claims submitted through eCRB.

(iv) The name, telephone number, and email address of a person whom the Copyright Royalty Board can contact regarding the claim.

(v) Original signatures of the copyright owners identified on the joint claim or of a duly authorized representative or representatives of the copyright owners, except for claims filed online through eCRB.

(vi) A declaration of authority to file the claim and a certification of the veracity of the information contained in the claim and the good faith of the person signing in providing the information. Penalties for fraud and false statements are provided under 18 U.S.C. 1001 et seq.

(c) Changes. In the event the legal name and/or address of the copyright owner entitled to royalties or the person or entity filing the claim changes after the filing of the claim, the filer or the copyright owner shall notify the Copyright Royalty Board of the change. Any other proposed changes or amendments must be submitted in accordance with 37 CFR 360.30. If the good faith efforts of the Copyright Royalty Board to contact the copyright owner or filer are frustrated because of outdated or otherwise inaccurate contact information, the claim may be subject to dismissal. A person or entity that filed a claim online through eCRB must notify the Copyright Royalty Board of any change of name or address by updating the eCRB profile for that person or entity through eCRB as required by 37 CFR 350.5(g).

History of 37 C.F.R. §360.4: 82 FR 27018, June 13, 2017.

Ⓐ §360.5. COPIES OF CLAIMS

Following the instructions outlined in 37 CFR 301.2, a claimant must file an original and one copy of the claim to cable or satellite compulsory license royalty fees at the address(es) listed for each claim submitted to the Copyright Royalty Board by hand delivery or by U.S. mail.

History of 37 C.F.R. §360.5: 82 FR 27018, June 13, 2017.

SUBPART B. DIGITAL AUDIO RECORDING DEVICES & MEDIA (DART) ROYALTY CLAIMS

Ⓐ §360.20. GENERAL

This subpart prescribes procedures whereby an interested copyright party, as defined in 17 U.S.C. 1001(7), claiming to be entitled to royalty payments made for the importation and distribution in the United States, or the manufacture and distribution in the United States, of digital audio recording devices and media (DART) pursuant to 17 U.S.C. 1006, shall file claims with the Copyright Royalty Board.

History of 37 C.F.R. §360.20: 82 FR 27018, June 13, 2017.

A §360.21. TIME OF FILING

(a) General. During January and February of each year, every interested copyright party claiming to be entitled to DART royalty payments made for quarterly periods ending during the previous calendar year must file a claim with the Copyright Royalty Board. Claimants may file claims jointly or as a single claim.

(b) Consequences of an untimely filing. No royalty payments for the previous calendar year will be distributed to any interested copyright party who has not filed a claim to those royalty payments during January or February of the following calendar year.

(c) Authorization. Any organization or association acting as a common agent for collection and distribution of DART royalty fees must obtain from its members or affiliates separate, specific, and written authorization, signed by members, affiliates, or their representatives, apart from their standard affiliation agreements, for purposes of royalties claim filing and fee distribution relating to the DART Musical Works Fund or Sound Recordings Fund. The written authorization, however, will not be required for claimants to the Musical Works Fund when either:

(1) The agreement between the organization or association and its members or affiliates specifically authorizes the entity to represent its members or affiliates as a common agent before the Copyright Royalty Board in royalty claims filing and fee distribution proceedings; or

(2) The agreement between the organization or association and its members or affiliates, as specified in a court order issued by a court with authority to interpret the terms of the contract, authorizes the entity to represent its members or affiliates as a common agent before the Copyright Royalty Board in royalty claims filing and fee distribution proceedings.

History of 37 C.F.R. §360.21: 82 FR 27018, June 13, 2017.

A §360.22. FORM & CONTENT OF CLAIMS

(a) Forms. **(1)** Each claim to DART royalty payments must be furnished on a form prescribed by the Copyright Royalty Board and must contain the information required by that form and its accompanying instructions.

(2) Copies of DART claim forms are available:

(i) On the Copyright Royalty Board's Web site at http://www.crb.gov/claims for claims filed with the Copyright Royalty Board by mail or by hand delivery;

(ii) On the Copyright Royalty Board's Web site at http://www.crb.gov/dart/ during the months of January and February for claims filed online through eCRB; and

(iii) Upon request to the Copyright Royalty Board, by mail at the address set forth in §301.2(a), by email at the address set forth in §301.2(d), or by telephone at (202) 707-7658.

(b) Content. Claims filed by interested copyright parties for DART royalty payments must include the following information:

(1) The full legal name and address of the person or entity claiming royalty payments.

(2) The name, telephone number, full mailing address, and email address of the person or entity filing the claim. The information contained in a filer's eCRB profile will fulfill this requirement for claims submitted through eCRB.

(3) The name, telephone number, and email address of a person whom the Copyright Royalty Board can contact regarding the claim.

(4) A statement as to how the claimant fits within the definition of interested copyright party.

(5) A statement as to whether the claim is being made against the Sound Recordings Fund or the Musical Works Fund, as set forth in 17 U.S.C. 1006(b), and as to which Subfund the claim is made. The Subfunds for the Sound Recordings Fund are the Copyright Owners Subfund and the Featured Recording Artists Subfund, The Subfunds for the Musical Works Fund are the Music Publishers Subfund and the Writers Subfund, as described in 17 U.S.C. 1006(b)(1) through (2).

(6) Identification, establishing a basis for the claim, of at least one musical work or sound recording embodied in a digital musical recording or an analog musical recording lawfully made under title 17 of the United States Code that has been distributed (as that term is defined in 17 U.S.C. 1001(6)), and that, during the period to which the royalty payments claimed pertain, has been:

(i) Distributed (as that term is defined in 17 U.S.C. 1001(6)) in the form of digital musical recordings or analog musical recordings; or

(ii) Disseminated to the public in transmissions.

(7) A declaration of the authority to file the claim and of the veracity of the information contained in the claim and the good faith of the person signing in providing the information. Penalties for fraud and false statements are provided under 18 U.S.C. 1001 et seq.

(c) Signature. Claims must bear the original signature of the claimant or of a duly authorized representative of the claimant, except for claims filed online through eCRB.

(d) Changes. In the event that the legal name and/or address of the claimant changes after the filing of the claim, the claimant must notify the Copyright Royalty Board of the change. Any other proposed changes or amendments must be submitted in accordance with 37 CFR 360.30. If the good faith efforts of the Copyright Royalty Board to contact the claimant are frustrated because of failure to notify the Copyright Royalty Board of a name and/or address change, the claim may be subject to dismissal. A person or entity that filed a claim online through eCRB must notify the Copyright Royalty Board of any change of name or address by updating that person or entity's eCRB profile as required by §350.5(g).

(e) List of claimants. If the claim is a joint claim, it must include the name of each claimant participating in the joint claim. Filers submitting joint claims online through eCRB on behalf of ten or fewer claimants, must list the name of each claimant included in the joint claim directly on the filed joint claim. Filers submitting joint claims on behalf of more than ten claimants must include an Excel spreadsheet listing the name of each claimant included in the joint claim. For joint claims filed by mail or hand delivery, the filer may submit the list containing the name of each claimant included in the joint claim in a single Excel spreadsheet on CD, DVD, or other electronic storage medium.

(f) Subfunds. If an interested copyright party intends to file claims against more than one Subfund, each Subfund claim must be filed separately with the Copyright Royalty Board. The Copyright Royalty Board will reject any claim that purports to claim funds from more than one Subfund.

History of 37 C.F.R. §360.22: 82 FR 27018, June 13, 2017; 82 FR 55323, Nov. 21, 2017.

Ⓐ §360.23. COPIES OF CLAIMS

Following the instructions outlined in 37 CFR 301.2, a claimant must file an original and one copy of the claim to DART royalty fees at the address(es) listed for each claim submitted to the Copyright Royalty Board by hand delivery or by U.S. mail.

History of 37 C.F.R. §360.23: 82 FR 27018, June 13, 2017.

Ⓐ §360.24. CONTENT OF NOTICES REGARDING INDEPENDENT ADMINISTRATORS

(a) The independent administrator jointly appointed by the interested copyright parties, as defined in 17 U.S.C. 1001(7)(A), and the American Federation of Musicians (or any successor entity) for the purpose of managing and ultimately distributing royalty payments to nonfeatured musicians as defined in 17 U.S.C. 1006(b)(1), must file a notice informing the Copyright Royalty Board of his/her appointment.

(b) The independent administrator jointly appointed by the interested copyright parties, as defined in 17 U.S.C. 1001(7)(A) and the American Federation of Television and Radio Artists (or any successor entity) for the purpose of managing and ultimately distributing royalty payments to nonfeatured vocalists as defined in 17 U.S.C. 1006(b)(1), must file a notice informing the Copyright Royalty Board of his/her appointment.

(c) A notice filed under paragraph (a) or (b) of this section must include the full name, telephone number, mailing address, and email address of the place of business of the independent administrator.

(d) The independent administrator must file the notices identified in paragraphs (a) and (b) of this section through eCRB no later than March 31 of each year, commencing with March 31, 2018.

History of 37 C.F.R. §360.24: 82 FR 27018, June 13, 2017.

SUBPART C. RULES OF GENERAL APPLICATION

Ⓐ §360.30. AMENDMENT OF CLAIMS

Any claimant may amend a filed claim as of right by filing a Notice of Amendment during the statutory period for filing annual claims. After the expiration of the time for filing claims, a claimant may amend a filed claim as of right to correct the general description of the nature of the claimant's work(s), to fix typographical or other nonsubstantive errors in other portions of the claim, or to strike a claimant or interested copyright party that was erroneously included in a joint claim. No filer may amend a filed claim to add additional claimants or interested copyright parties after the expiration of the time for filing claims.

History of 37 C.F.R. §360.30: 82 FR 27018, June 13, 2017.

Ⓐ §360.31. WITHDRAWAL OF CLAIMS

Any claimant may withdraw its claim for any royalty year as of right by filing a Notice of Withdrawal of Claim(s). If a single claimant filed a Petition to Participate in a proceeding, withdrawal of the claim shall serve to dismiss the Petition to Participate. If the claimant withdrawing a claim was included on the Petition to Participate of another entity, withdrawal of the claim shall not affect the Petition to Participate as to other claims listed thereon.

History of 37 C.F.R. §360.31: 82 FR 27018, June 13, 2017.

Ⓐ §360.32. REINSTATEMENT OF PREVIOUSLY WITHDRAWN CLAIMS

Once a claimant has withdrawn a claim, that claim may be reinstated only by order of the Copyright Royalty Judges, on motion showing good cause and lack of prejudice to other claimants to the applicable year's royalty funds.

History of 37 C.F.R. §360.32: 82 FR 27018, June 13, 2017.

SUBCHAPTER D. NOTICE & RECORDKEEPING REQUIREMENTS FOR STATUTORY LICENSES

PART 370. NOTICE & RECORDKEEPING REQUIREMENTS FOR STATUTORY LICENSES

§370.1. GENERAL DEFINITIONS

For purposes of this part, the following definitions apply:

(a) A Notice of Use of Sound Recordings Under Statutory License is a written notice to sound recording copyright owners of the use of their works under section 112(e) or 114(d)(2) of title 17, United States Code, or both, and is required under this part to be filed by a Service in the Copyright Office.

(b) A Service is an entity engaged in either the digital transmission of sound recordings pursuant to section 114(d)(2) of title 17 of the United States Code or making ephemeral phonorecords of sound recordings pursuant to section 112(e) of title 17 of the United States Code or both. The definition of a Service includes an entity that transmits an AM/FM broadcast signal over a digital communications network such as the Internet, regardless of whether the transmission is made by the broadcaster that originates the AM/FM signal or by a third party, provided that such transmission meets the applicable requirements of the statutory license set forth in 17 U.S.C. 114(d)(2). A Service may be further characterized as either a preexisting subscription service, preexisting satellite digital audio radio service, nonsubscription transmission service, new subscription service, business establishment service or a combination of those.

(c) A Preexisting Subscription Service is defined in 17 U.S.C. 114(j)(11).

(d) A New Subscription Service is defined in 17 U.S.C. 114(j)(8).

(e) A Nonsubscription Transmission Service is a service that makes noninteractive nonsubscription digital audio transmissions that are not exempt under section 114(d)(1) of title 17 of the United States Code and are made as part of a service that provides audio programming consisting, in whole or in part, of performances of sound recordings, including transmissions of broadcast transmissions, if the primary purpose of the service is to provide to the public such audio or other entertainment programming, and the primary purpose of the service is not to sell, advertise, or promote particular products or services other than sound recordings, live concerts, or other music-related events.

(f) A Preexisting Satellite Digital Audio Radio Service is defined in 17 U.S.C. 114(j)(10).

(g) A Business Establishment Service is a service that makes ephemeral phonorecords of sound recordings pursuant to section 112(e) of title 17 of the United States Code and is exempt under section 114(d)(1)(C)(iv) of title 17 of the United States Code.

(h) A Collective is a collection and distribution organization that is designated under one or both of the statutory licenses by determination of the Copyright Royalty Judges.

(i) A Report of Use is a report required to be provided by a Service that is transmitting sound recordings pursuant to the statutory license set forth in section 114(d)(2) of title 17 of the United States Code or making ephemeral phonorecords of sound recordings pursuant to the statutory license set forth in section 112(e) of title 17 of the United States Code, or both.

History of 37 C.F.R. §370.1: 74 FR 52423, Nov. 12, 2009; 79 FR 25010, May 2, 2014.

§370.2. NOTICE OF USE OF SOUND RECORDINGS UNDER STATUTORY LICENSE

(a) General. This section prescribes rules under which copyright owners shall receive notice of use of their sound recordings when used under either section 112(e) or 114(d)(2) of title 17, United States Code, or both.

(b) Forms and content. A Notice of Use of Sound Recordings Under Statutory License shall be prepared on a form that may be obtained from the Copyright Office Web site or from the Licensing Division, and shall include the following information:

(1) The full legal name of the Service that is either commencing digital transmissions of sound recordings or making ephemeral phonorecords of sound recordings under statutory license or doing both.

(2) The full address, including a specific number and street name or rural route, of the place of business of the Service. A post office box or similar designation will not be sufficient except where it is the only address that can be used in that geographic location.

(3) The telephone number and facsimile number of the Service.

(4) Information on how to gain access to the online Web site or homepage of the Service, or where information may be posted under this section concerning the use of sound recordings under statutory license.

(5) Identification of each license under which the Service intends to operate, including identification of each of the following categories under which the Service will be making digital transmissions of sound recordings: Preexisting subscription service, preexisting satellite digital audio radio service, nonsubscription transmission service, new subscription service or business establishment service.

(6) The date or expected date of the initial digital transmission of a sound recording to be made under the section 114 statutory license and/or the date or the expected date of the initial use of the section 112(e) license for the purpose of making ephemeral phonorecords of the sound recordings.

(7) Identification of any amendments required by paragraph (e) of this section.

(c) Signature. The Notice shall include the signature of the appropriate officer or representative of the Service that is either transmitting the sound recordings or making ephemeral phonorecords of sound recordings under statutory license or doing both. The signature shall be accompanied by the printed or typewritten name and the title of the person signing the Notice and by the date of the signature.

(d) Filing notices; fees. The original and three copies shall be filed with the Licensing Division of the Copyright Office and shall be accompanied by the filing fee set forth in §201.3(e) of this title. Notices shall be placed in the public records of the Licensing Division. The Notice and filing fee shall be sent to the Licensing Division at either the address listed on the form obtained from the Copyright Office or to: Library of Congress, Copyright Office, Licensing Division, 101 Independence Avenue, SE., Washington, DC 20557-6400. A Service that, on or after July 1, 2004, shall make digital transmissions and/or ephemeral phonorecords of sound recordings under statutory license shall file a Notice of Use of

Sound Recordings under Statutory License with the Licensing Division of the Copyright Office prior to the making of the first ephemeral phonorecord of the sound recording and prior to the first digital transmission of the sound recording.

(e) Amendment. A Service shall file a new Notice of Use of Sound Recordings under Statutory License within 45 days after any of the information contained in the Notice on file has changed, and shall indicate in the space provided by the Copyright Office that the Notice is an amended filing. The Licensing Division shall retain copies of all prior Notices filed by the Service.

History of 37 C.F.R. §370.2: 74 FR 52423, Nov. 12, 2009; 79 FR 25010, May 2, 2014.

§370.3. REPORTS OF USE OF SOUND RECORDINGS UNDER STATUTORY LICENSE FOR PREEXISTING SUBSCRIPTION SERVICES

(a) General. This section prescribes the rules for the maintenance and delivery of reports of use for sound recordings under section 112(e) or section 114(d)(2) of title 17 of the United States Code, or both, by preexisting subscription services.

(b) Delivery. Reports of Use shall be delivered to Collectives that are identified in the records of the Licensing Division of the Copyright Office as having been designated by determination of the Copyright Royalty Judges. Reports of Use shall be delivered on or before the forty-fifth day after the close of each month.

(c) Posting. In the event that no Collective is designated under the statutory license, or if all designated Collectives have terminated collection and distribution operations, a preexisting subscription service transmitting sound recordings under statutory license shall post and make available online its Reports of Use. Preexisting subscription services shall post their Reports of Use online on or before the forty-fifth day after the close of each month, and continue to make them available thereafter to all sound recording copyright owners for a period of 90 days. Preexisting subscription services may require use of passwords for access to posted Reports of Use, but must make passwords available in a timely manner and free of charge or other restrictions. Preexisting subscription services may predicate provision of a password upon:

(1) Information relating to identity, location and status as a sound recording copyright owner; and

(2) A "click-wrap" agreement not to use information in the Report of Use for purposes other than royalty collection, royalty distribution, and determining compliance with statutory license requirements, without the express consent of the preexisting subscription service providing the Report of Use.

(d) Content. A "Report of Use of Sound Recordings under Statutory License" shall be identified as such by prominent caption or heading, and shall include a preexisting subscription service's "Intended Playlists" for each channel and each day of the reported month. The "Intended Playlists" shall include a consecutive listing of every recording scheduled to be transmitted, and shall contain the following information in the following order:

(1) The name of the preexisting subscription service or entity;

(2) The channel;

(3) The sound recording title;

(4) The featured recording artist, group, or orchestra;

(5) The retail album title (or, in the case of compilation albums created for commercial purposes, the name of the retail album identified by the preexisting subscription service for purchase of the sound recording);

(6) The marketing label of the commercially available album or other product on which the sound recording is found;

(7) The catalog number;

(8) The International Standard Recording Code (ISRC) embedded in the sound recording, where available and feasible;

(9) Where available, the copyright owner information provided in the copyright notice on the retail album or other product (e.g., following the symbol (P), that is the letter P in a circle) or, in the case of compilation albums created for commercial purposes, in the copyright notice for the individual sound recording;

(10) The date of transmission; and

(11) The time of transmission.

(e) Signature. Reports of Use shall include a signed statement by the appropriate officer or representative of the preexisting subscription service attesting, under penalty of perjury, that the information contained in the Report is believed to be accurate and is maintained by the preexisting subscription service in its ordinary course of business. The signature shall be accompanied by the printed or typewritten name and title of the person signing the Report, and by the date of signature.

(f) Format. Reports of Use should be provided on a standard machine-readable medium, such as diskette, optical disc, or magneto-optical disc, and should conform as closely as possible to the following specifications:

(1) ASCII delimited format, using pipe characters as delimiter, with no headers or footers;

(2) Carats should surround strings;

(3) No carats should surround dates and numbers;

(4) Dates should be indicated by: YYYY/MM/DD;

(5) Times should be based on a 24-hour clock: HH:MM:SS;

(6) A carriage return should be at the end of each line; and

(7) All data for one record should be on a single line.

(g) Confidentiality. Copyright owners, their agents and Collectives shall not disseminate information in the Reports of Use to any persons not entitled to it, nor utilize the information for purposes other than royalty collection and distribution, and determining compliance with statutory license requirements, without express consent of the preexisting subscription service providing the Report of Use.

(h) Documentation. All compulsory licensees shall, for a period of at least three years from the date of service or posting of the Report of Use, keep and retain a copy of the Report of Use.

(i) In any case in which a preexisting subscription service has not provided a report of use required under this section for use of sound recordings under section 112(e) or section 114 of title 17 of the United States Code, or both, prior to January 1, 2010, reports of use for the corresponding calendar year filed by other preexisting subscription services shall serve as the reports of use for the non-reporting service, solely for purposes of distribution of any corresponding royalties by the Collective.

History of 37 C.F.R. §370.3: 74 FR 52424, Nov. 12, 2009; 76 FR 45696, Aug. 1, 2011; 79 FR 25010, May 2, 2014.

§370.4. REPORTS OF USE OF SOUND RECORDINGS UNDER STATUTORY LICENSE FOR NONSUBSCRIPTION TRANSMISSION SERVICES, PREEXISTING SATELLITE DIGITAL AUDIO RADIO SERVICES, NEW SUBSCRIPTION SERVICES & BUSINESS ESTABLISHMENT SERVICES

(a) General. This section prescribes rules for the maintenance and delivery of Reports of Use of sound recordings under section 112(e) or section 114 of title 17 of the United States Code, or both, by nonsubscription transmission services, preexisting satellite digital audio radio services, new subscription services, and business establishment services.

(b) Definitions. For purposes of this section, the following definitions apply:

Aggregate Tuning Hours means the total hours of programming that a nonsubscription transmission service, preexisting satellite digital audio radio service, new subscription service or business establishment service has transmitted during the reporting period identified in paragraph (d)(3) of this section to all listeners within the United States over the relevant channels or stations, and from any archived programs, that provide audio programming consisting, in whole or in part, of eligible nonsubscription service, preexisting satellite digital audio radio service, new subscription service or business establishment service transmissions, less the actual running time of any sound recordings for which the service has obtained direct licenses apart from 17 U.S.C. 114(d)(2) or which do not require a license under United States copyright law. For example, if a nonsubscription transmission service transmitted one hour of programming to 10 simultaneous listeners, the nonsubscription transmission service's Aggregate Tuning Hours would equal 10. If 3 minutes of that hour consisted of transmission of a directly licensed recording, the nonsubscription transmission service's Aggregate Tuning Hours would equal 9 hours and 30 minutes. If one listener listened to the transmission of a nonsubscription transmission service for 10 hours (and none of the recordings transmitted during that time was directly licensed), the nonsubscription transmission service's Aggregate Tuning Hours would equal 10.

AM/FM Webcast means a transmission made by an entity that transmits an AM/FM broadcast signal over a digital communications network such as the Internet, regardless of whether the transmission is made by the broadcaster that originates the AM/FM signal or by a third party, provided that such transmission meets the applicable requirements of the statutory license set forth in 17 U.S.C. 114(d)(2).

Broadcaster means an entity that:

(i) Has a substantial business owning and operating one or more terrestrial AM or FM radio stations that are licensed as such by the Federal Communications Commission;

(ii) Has obtained a compulsory license under 17 U.S.C. 112(e) and 114 and the implementing regulations therefor to make Eligible Transmissions and related ephemeral recordings;

(iii) Complies with all applicable provisions of Sections 112(e) and 114 and applicable regulations; and

(iv) Is not a noncommercial webcaster as defined in 17 U.S.C. 114(f)(5)(E)(i).

Eligible Minimum Fee Webcaster means a nonsubscription transmission service whose payments for eligible transmissions do not exceed the annual minimum fee established for licensees relying upon the statutory licenses set forth in 17 U.S.C. 112(e) and 114; and:

(i) Is a licensee that owns and operates a terrestrial AM or FM radio station that is licensed by the Federal Communications Commission; or

(ii) Is directly operated by, or affiliated with and officially sanctioned by, a domestically accredited primary or secondary school, college, university, or other post-secondary degree-granting institution; and

(A) The digital audio transmission operations of which are, during the course of the year, staffed substantially by students enrolled in such institution;

(B) Is exempt from taxation under section 501 of the Internal Revenue Code, has applied for such exemption, or is operated by a State or possession or any governmental entity or subordinate thereof, or by the United States or District of Columbia, for exclusively public purposes; and

(C) Is not a "public broadcasting entity" (as defined in 17 U.S.C. 118(f)) qualified to receive funding from the Corporation for Public Broadcasting pursuant to the criteria set forth in 47 U.S.C. 396.

Performance means each instance in which any portion of a sound recording is publicly performed to a Listener by means of a digital audio transmission or retransmission (e.g., the delivery of any portion of a single track from a compact disc to one Listener) but excluding the following:

(i) A performance of a sound recording that does not require a license (e.g., the sound recording is not copyrighted);

(ii) A performance of a sound recording for which the service has previously obtained a license from the Copyright Owner of such sound recording; and

(iii) An incidental performance that both:

(A) Makes no more than incidental use of sound recordings including, but not limited to, brief musical transitions in and out of commercials or program segments, brief performances during news, talk and sports programming, brief background performances during disk jockey announcements, brief performances during commercials of sixty seconds or less in duration, or brief performances during sporting or other public events; and

(B) Other than ambient music that is background at a public event, does not contain an entire sound recording and does not feature a particular sound recording of more than thirty seconds (as in the case of a sound recording used as a theme song).

Play frequency means the number of times a sound recording is publicly performed by a Service during the relevant period, without respect to the number of listeners receiving the sound recording. If a particular sound recording is transmitted to listeners on a particular channel or program only once during the reporting period, then the play frequency is one. If the sound recording is transmitted 10 times during the reporting period, then the play frequency is 10.

(c) *Delivery*. Reports of Use shall be delivered to Collectives that are identified in the records of the Licensing Division of the Copyright Office as having been designated by determination of the Copyright Royalty Judges. Reports of Use shall be delivered on or before the forty-fifth day after the close of each reporting period identified in paragraph (d)(3) of this section.

(d) *Report of Use*. (1) *Separate reports not required*. A nonsubscription transmission service, preexisting satellite digital audio radio service or a new subscription service that transmits sound recordings pursuant to the statutory license set forth in section 114(d)(2) of title 17 of the United States Code and makes ephemeral phonorecords of sound recordings pursuant to the statutory license set forth in section 112(e) of title 17 of the United States Code need not maintain a separate Report of Use for each statutory license during the relevant reporting periods.

(2) *Content*. For a nonsubscription transmission service, preexisting satellite digital audio radio service, new subscription service or business establishment service that transmits sound recordings pursuant to the statutory license set forth in section 114(d)(2) of title 17 of the United States Code, or the statutory license set forth in section 112(e) of title 17 of the United States Code, or both, each Report of Use shall contain the following information, in the following order, for each sound recording transmitted during the reporting periods identified in paragraph (d)(3) of this section:

(i) The name of the nonsubscription transmission service, preexisting satellite digital audio radio service, new subscription service or business establishment service making the transmissions, including the name of the entity filing the Report of Use, if different;

(ii) The category transmission code for the category of transmission operated by the nonsubscription transmission service, preexisting satellite digital audio radio service, new subscription service or business establishment service:

(A) For eligible nonsubscription transmissions other than broadcast simulcasts and transmissions of non-music programming;

(B) For eligible nonsubscription transmissions of broadcast simulcast programming not reasonably classified as news, talk, sports or business programming;

(C) For eligible nonsubscription transmissions of non-music programming reasonably classified as news, talk, sports or business programming;

(D) to (G) [Reserved]

(H) For transmissions other than broadcast simulcasts and transmissions of non-music programming made by an eligible new subscription service;

(I) For transmissions of broadcast simulcast programming not reasonably classified as news, talk, sports or business programming made by an eligible new subscription service;

(J) For transmissions of non-music programming reasonably classified as news, talk, sports or business programming made by an eligible new subscription service; and

(K) For eligible transmissions by a business establishment service making ephemeral recordings;

(iii) The featured artist;

(iv) The sound recording title;

(v) The International Standard Recording Code (ISRC) or, alternatively to the ISRC, the:

(A) Album title; and

(B) Marketing label;

(vi) For a nonsubscription transmission service except those qualifying as eligible minimum fee webcasters: The actual total performances of the sound recording during the reporting period.

(vii) For a preexisting satellite digital audio radio service, a new subscription service, a business establishment service or a nonsubscription service qualifying as an eligible minimum fee webcaster: The actual total performances of the sound recording during the reporting period or, alternatively, the

(A) Aggregate Tuning Hours;

(B) Channel or program name; and

(C) Play frequency.

(3) Reporting period. A Report of Use shall be prepared:

(i) For each calendar month of the year by all services other than a nonsubscription service qualifying as an eligible minimum fee webcaster; or

(ii) For a two-week period (two periods of 7 consecutive days) for each calendar quarter of the year by a nonsubscription service qualifying as an eligible minimum fee webcaster and the two-week period need not consist of consecutive weeks, but both weeks must be completely within the calendar quarter.

(4) Signature. Reports of Use shall include a signed statement by the appropriate officer or representative of the service attesting, under penalty of perjury, that the information contained in the Report is believed to be accurate and is maintained by the service in its ordinary course of business. The signature shall be accompanied by the printed or typewritten name and the title of the person signing the Report, and by the date of the signature.

(5) Confidentiality. Copyright owners, their agents and Collectives shall not disseminate information in the Reports of Use to any persons not entitled to it, nor utilize the information for purposes other than royalty collection and distribution, without consent of the service providing the Report of Use.

(6) Documentation. A Service shall, for a period of at least three years from the date of service or posting of a Report of Use, keep and retain a copy of the Report of Use.

(e) Format and delivery. (1) Electronic format only. Reports of use must be maintained and delivered in electronic format only, as prescribed in paragraphs (e)(2) through (8) of this section. A hard copy report of use is not permissible.

(2) ASCII text file delivery; facilitation by provision of spreadsheet templates. All report of use data files must be delivered in ASCII format. However, to facilitate such delivery, SoundExchange shall post and maintain on its Internet Web site a template for creating a report of use using Microsoft's Excel spreadsheet and Corel's Quattro Pro spreadsheet and instruction on how to convert such spreadsheets to ASCII text files that conform to the format specifications set forth below. Further, technical support and cost associated with the use of spreadsheets is the responsibility of the service submitting the report of use.

(3) Delivery mechanism. The data contained in a report of use may be delivered by File Transfer Protocol (FTP), e-mail, or CD-ROM according to the following specifications:

(i) A service delivering a report of use via FTP must obtain a username, password and delivery instructions from SoundExchange. SoundExchange shall maintain on a publicly available portion of its Web site instructions for applying for a username, password and delivery instructions. SoundExchange shall have 15 days from date of request to respond with a username, password and delivery instructions.

(ii) A service delivering a report of use via e-mail shall append the report as an attachment to the e-mail. The main body of the e-mail shall identify:

(A) The full name and address of the service;

(B) The contact person's name, telephone number and e-mail address;

(C) The start and end date of the reporting period;

(D) The number of rows in the data file. If the report of use is a file using headers, counting of the rows should begin with row 15. If the report of use is a file without headers, counting of the rows should begin with row 1; and

(E) The name of the file attached.

(iii) A service delivering a report of use via CD-ROM must compress the reporting data to fit onto a single CD-ROM per reporting period. Each CD-ROM shall be submitted with a cover letter identifying:

(A) The full name and address of the service;

(B) The contact person's name, telephone number and e-mail address;

(C) The start and end date of the reporting period;

(D) The number of rows in the data file. If the report of use is a file using headers, counting of the rows should begin with row 15. If the report of use is a file without headers, counting of the rows should begin with row 1; and

(E) The name of the file attached.

(4) Delivery address. Reports of use shall be delivered to SoundExchange at the following address: SoundExchange, Inc., 1121 14th Street, NW., Suite 700, Washington, DC 20005; (Phone) (202) 640-5858; (Facsimile) (202) 640-5859; (E-mail) *reports@soundexchange.com*. SoundExchange shall forward electronic copies of these reports of use to all other collectives defined in this section.

(5) File naming. Each data file contained in a report of use must be given a name by the service followed by the start and end date of the reporting period. The start and end date must be separated by a dash and in the format of year, month, and day (YYYYMMDD). Each file name must end with the file type extension of ".txt". (*Example*: AcmeMusicCo20050101-20050331.txt.

(6) File type and compression. (i) All data files must be in ASCII format.

(ii) A report of use must be compressed in one of the following zipped formats:

(A) .zip—generated using utilities such as WinZip and/or UNIX zip command;

(B) .Z—generated using UNIX compress command; or

(C) .gz—generated using UNIX gzip command.

(iii) Zipped files shall be named in the same fashion as described in paragraph (e)(5) of this section, except that such zipped files shall use the applicable file extension compression name described in this paragraph (e)(6).

(7) Files with headers. (i) If a service elects to submit files with headers, the following elements, in order, must occupy the first 14 rows of a report of use:

(A) Name of service;

(B) Name of contact person;

(C) Street address of the service;

(D) City, state and zip code of the service;

(E) Telephone number of the contact person;

(F) E-mail address of the contact person;

(G) Start of the reporting period (YYYYMMDD);

(H) End of the reporting period (YYYYMMDD);

(I) Report generation date (YYYYMMDD);

(J) Number of rows in data file, beginning with 15th row;

(K) Text indicator character;

(L) Field delimiter character;

(M) Blank line; and

(N) Report headers (Featured Artist, Sound Recording Title, etc.).

(ii) Each of the rows described in paragraphs (e)(7)(i)(A) through (F) of this section must not exceed 255 alphanumeric characters. Each of the rows described in paragraphs (e)(7)(i)(G) through (I) of this section should not exceed eight alphanumeric characters.

(iii) Data text fields, as required by paragraph (d) of this section, begin on row 15 of a report of use with headers. A carriage return must be at the end of each row thereafter. Abbreviations within data fields are not permitted.

(iv) The text indicator character must be unique and must never be found in the report's data content.

(v) The field delimiter character must be unique and must never be found in the report's data content. Delimiters must be used even when certain elements are not being reported; in such case, the service must denote the blank data field with a delimiter in the order in which it would have appeared.

(8) Files without headers. If a service elects to submit files without headers, the following format requirements must be met:

(i) ASCII delimited format, using pipe (|) characters as delimiters, with no headers or footers;

(ii) Carats (^) should surround strings;

(iii) No carats (^) should surround dates and numbers;

(iv) A carriage return must be at the end of each line;

(v) All data for one record must be on a single line; and

(vi) Abbreviations within data fields are not permitted.

(f) In any case in which a nonsubscription transmission service, preexisting satellite digital audio radio service, new subscription service, or business establishment service has not provided a report of use required under this section for use of sound recordings under section 112(e) or section 114 of title 17 of the United States Code, or both, prior to January 1, 2010, reports of use for the corresponding calendar year filed by other services of the same type shall serve as the reports of use for the non-reporting service, solely for purposes of distribution of any corresponding royalties by the Collective.

History of 37 C.F.R. §370.4: 74 FR 52425, Nov. 12, 2009; 76 FR 45696, Aug. 1, 2011; 81 FR 31510, May 19, 2016; 81 FR 40190, June 21, 2016; 81 FR 89868, Dec. 13, 2016.

§370.5. DESIGNATED COLLECTION & DISTRIBUTION ORGANIZATIONS FOR REPORTS OF USE OF SOUND RECORDINGS UNDER STATUTORY LICENSE

(a) General. This section prescribes rules under which reports of use shall be collected and distributed under section 114(f) of title 17 of the United States Code, and under which reports of such use shall be kept and made available.

(b) Notice of Designation as Collective under Statutory License. A Collective shall file with the Licensing Division of the Copyright Office and post and make available online a "Notice of Designation as Collective under Statutory License," which shall be identified as such by prominent caption or heading, and shall contain the following information:

(1) The Collective name, address, telephone number and facsimile number;

(2) A statement that the Collective has been designated for collection and distribution of performance royalties under statutory license for digital transmission of sound recordings; and

(3) Information on how to gain access to the online Web site or home page of the Collective, where information may be posted under this part concerning the use of sound recordings under statutory license. The address of the Licensing Division is: Library of Congress, Copyright Office, Licensing Division, 101 Independence Avenue, SE., Washington, DC 20557-6400.

(c) Annual Report. The Collective will post and make available online, for the duration of one year, an Annual Report on how the Collective operates, how royalties are collected and distributed, and what the Collective spent that fiscal year on administrative expenses.

(d) Inspection of Reports of Use by copyright owners. The Collective shall make copies of the Reports of Use for the preceding three years available for inspection by any sound recording copyright owner, without charge, during normal office hours upon reasonable notice. The Collective shall predicate inspection of Reports of Use upon information relating to identity, location and status as a sound recording copyright owner, and the copyright owner's written agreement not to utilize the information for purposes other than royalty collection and distribution, and determining compliance with statutory license requirements, without express consent of the Service providing the Report of Use. The Collective shall render its best efforts to locate copyright owners in order to make available reports of use, and such efforts shall include searches in Copyright Office public records and published directories of sound recording copyright owners.

(e) Confidentiality. Copyright owners, their agents, and Collectives shall not disseminate information in the Reports of Use to any persons not entitled to it, nor utilize the information for purposes other than royalty collection and distribution, and determining compliance with statutory license requirements, without express consent of the Service providing the Report of Use.

(f) Termination and dissolution. If a Collective terminates its collection and distribution operations prior to the close of its term of designation, the Collective shall notify the Licensing Division of the Copyright Office, the Copyright Royalty Board and all Services transmitting sound recordings under statutory license, by certified or registered mail. The dissolving Collective shall provide each such Service with information identifying the copyright owners it has served.

History of 37 C.F.R. §370.5: 74 FR 52427, Nov. 12, 2009; 79 FR 25010, May 2, 2014.

SUBCHAPTER E. RATES & TERMS FOR STATUTORY LICENSES

PART 380. RATES & TERMS FOR TRANSMISSIONS BY ELIGIBLE NONSUBSCRIPTION SERVICES & NEW SUBSCRIPTION SERVICES & FOR THE MAKING OF EPHEMERAL REPRODUCTIONS TO FACILITATE THOSE TRANSMISSIONS

SUBPART A. REGULATIONS OF GENERAL APPLICATION

§380.1. SCOPE & COMPLIANCE

(a) Scope. Subparts A and B of this part codify rates and terms of royalty payments for the public performance of sound recordings in certain digital transmissions by certain Licensees in accordance with the applicable provisions of 17 U.S.C. 114 and for the making of Ephemeral Recordings by those Licensees in accordance with the provisions of 17 U.S.C. 112(e), during the period January 1, 2016, through December 31, 2020.

(b) Limited application of terms and definitions. The terms and definitions in Subpart A apply only to Subpart B, except as expressly adopted and applied in subpart C or subpart D of this part.

(c) Legal compliance. Licensees relying upon the statutory licenses set forth in 17 U.S.C. 112(e) and 114 must comply with the requirements of this part 380 and any other applicable regulations.

(d) Voluntary agreements. Notwithstanding the royalty rates and terms established in any subparts of this part 380, the rates and terms of any license agreements entered into by Copyright Owners and Licensees may apply in lieu of these rates and terms.

History of 37 C.F.R. §380.1: 81 FR 26406, May 2, 2016.

§380.2. MAKING PAYMENT OF ROYALTY FEES

(a) Payment to the Collective. A Licensee must make the royalty payments due under subpart B to SoundExchange, Inc., which is the Collective designated by the Copyright Royalty Board to collect and distribute royalties under this part 380.

(b) Monthly payments. A Licensee must make royalty payments on a monthly basis. Payments are due on or before the 45th day after the end of the month in which the Licensee made Eligible Transmissions.

(c) Minimum payments. A Licensee must make any minimum annual payments due under Subpart B by January 31 of the applicable license year. A Licensee that as of January 31 of any year has not made any eligible nonsubscription transmissions, noninteractive digital audio transmissions as part of a new subscription service, or Ephemeral Recordings pursuant to the licenses in 17 U.S.C. 114 and/or 17 U.S.C. 112(e), but that begins making such transmissions after that date must make any payment due by the 45th day after the end of the month in which the Licensee commences making such transmissions.

(d) Late fees. A Licensee must pay a late fee for each payment and each Statement of Account that the Collective receives after the due date. The late fee is 1.5% (or the highest lawful rate, whichever is lower) of the late payment amount per month. The late fee for a late Statement of Account is 1.5% of the payment amount associated with the Statement of Account. Late fees accrue from the due date until the date that the Collective receives the late payment or late Statement of Account.

(1) Waiver of late fees. The Collective may waive or lower late fees for immaterial or inadvertent failures of a Licensee to make a timely payment or submit a timely Statement of Account.

(2) Notice regarding noncompliant Statements of Account. If it is reasonably evident to the Collective that a timely-provided Statement of Account is materially noncompliant, the Collective must notify the Licensee within 90 days of discovery of the noncompliance.

History of 37 C.F.R. §380.2: 81 FR 26406, May 2, 2016.

§380.3. DELIVERING STATEMENTS OF ACCOUNT

(a) Statements of Account. Any payment due under this Part 380 must be accompanied by a corresponding Statement of Account that must contain the following information:

(1) Such information as is necessary to calculate the accompanying royalty payment;

(2) The name, address, business title, telephone number, facsimile number (if any), electronic mail address (if any) and other contact information of the person to be contacted for information or questions concerning the content of the Statement of Account;

(3) The signature of:

(i) The Licensee or a duly authorized agent of Licensee;

(ii) A partner or delegate if the Licensee is a partnership; or

(iii) An officer of the corporation if the Licensee is a corporation.

(4) The printed or typewritten name of the person signing the Statement of Account;

(5) If the Licensee is a partnership or corporation, the title or official position held in the partnership or corporation by the person signing the Statement of Account;

(6) A certification of the capacity of the person signing;

(7) The date of signature; and

(8) An attestation to the following effect:

I, the undersigned owner/officer/partner/agent of the Licensee have examined this Statement of Account and hereby state that it is true, accurate, and complete to my knowledge after reasonable due diligence and that it fairly presents, in all material respects, the liabilities of the Licensee pursuant to 17 U.S.C. 112(e) and 114 and applicable regulations adopted under those sections.

(b) Certification. Licensee's Chief Financial Officer or, if Licensee does not have a Chief Financial Officer, a person authorized to sign Statements of Account for the Licensee must submit a signed certification on an annual basis attesting that Licensee's royalty statements for the prior year represent a true and accurate determination of the royalties due and that any method of allocation employed by Licensee was applied in good faith and in accordance with U.S. GAAP.

History of 37 C.F.R. §380.3: 81 FR 26406, May 2, 2016.

§380.4. DISTRIBUTING ROYALTY FEES

(a) Distribution of royalties. (1) The Collective must promptly distribute royalties received from Licensees to Copyright Owners and Performers that are entitled thereto, or to their designated agents. The Collective shall only be responsible for making distributions to those who provide the Collective with information as is necessary to identify and pay the correct recipient. The Collective must distribute royalties on a basis that values all performances by a Licensee equally based upon the information provided under the Reports of Use requirements for Licensees pursuant to §370.4 of this chapter and this subpart.

(2) The Collective must use its best efforts to identify and locate copyright owners and featured artists in order to distribute royalties payable to them under §112(e) or 114(d)(2) of title 17, United States Code, or both. Such efforts must include, but not be limited to, searches in Copyright Office public records and published directories of sound recording copyright owners.

(b) Unclaimed funds. If the Collective is unable to identify or locate a Copyright Owner or Performer who is entitled to receive a royalty distribution under this part 380, the Collective must retain the required payment in a segregated trust account for a period of three years from the date of the first distribution of royalties from the relevant payment by a Licensee. No claim to distribution shall be valid after the expiration of the three-year period. After expiration of this period, the Collective must handle unclaimed funds in accordance with applicable federal, state, or common law.

(c) Retention of records. Licensees and the Collective shall keep books and records relating to payments and distributions of royalties for a period of not less than the prior three calendar years.

(d) Designation of the Collective. (1) The Judges designate SoundExchange, Inc., as the Collective to receive Statements of Account and royalty payments from Licensees and to distribute royalty payments to each Copyright Owner and Performer (or their respective designated agents) entitled to receive royalties under 17 U.S.C. 112(e) or 114(g).

(2) If SoundExchange, Inc. should dissolve or cease to be governed by a board consisting of equal numbers of representatives of Copyright Owners and Performers, then it shall be replaced for the applicable royalty term by a successor Collective according to the following procedure:

(i) The nine Copyright Owner representatives and the nine Performer representatives on the SoundExchange board as of the last day preceding SoundExchange's cessation or dissolution shall vote by a majority to recommend that the Copyright Royalty Judges designate a successor and must file a petition with the Copyright Royalty Judges requesting that the Judges designate the named successor and setting forth the reasons therefor.

(ii) Within 30 days of receiving the petition, the Copyright Royalty Judges must issue an order designating the recommended Collective, unless the Judges find good cause not to make and publish the designation in the Federal Register.

History of 37 C.F.R. §380.4: 81 FR 26407, May 2, 2016.

§380.5. HANDLING CONFIDENTIAL INFORMATION

(a) Definition. For purposes of this part 380, "Confidential Information" means the Statements of Account and any information contained therein, including the amount of royalty payments and the number of Performances, and any information pertaining to the Statements of Account reasonably designated as confidential by the party submitting the statement. Confidential Information does not include documents or information that at the time of delivery to the Collective is public knowledge. The party seeking information from the Collective based on a claim that the information sought is a matter of public knowledge shall have the burden of proving to the Collective that the requested information is in the public domain.

(b) Use of Confidential Information. The Collective may not use any Confidential Information for any purpose other than royalty collection and distribution and activities related directly thereto.

(c) Disclosure of Confidential Information. The Collective shall limit access to Confidential Information to:

(1) Those employees, agents, consultants, and independent contractors of the Collective, subject to an appropriate written confidentiality agreement, who are engaged in the collection and distribution of royalty payments hereunder and activities related directly thereto who require access to the Confidential Information for the purpose of performing their duties during the ordinary course of their work;

(2) A Qualified Auditor or outside counsel who is authorized to act on behalf of:

(i) The Collective with respect to verification of a Licensee's statement of account pursuant to this part 380; or

(ii) A Copyright Owner or Performer with respect to the verification of royalty distributions pursuant to this part 380;

(3) Copyright Owners and Performers, including their designated agents, whose works a Licensee used under the statutory licenses set forth in 17 U.S.C. 112(e) and 114 by the Licensee whose Confidential Information is being supplied, subject to an appropriate written confidentiality agreement, and including those employees, agents, consultants, and independent contractors of such Copyright Owners and Performers and their designated agents, subject to an appropriate written confidentiality agreement, who require access to the Confidential Information to perform their duties during the ordinary course of their work;

(4) Attorneys and other authorized agents of parties to proceedings under 17 U.S.C. 8, 112, 114, acting under an appropriate protective order.

(d) Safeguarding Confidential Information. The Collective and any person authorized to receive Confidential Information from the Collective must implement procedures to safeguard against unauthorized access to or dissemination of Confidential Information using a reasonable standard of care, but no less than the same degree of security that the recipient uses to protect its own Confidential Information or similarly sensitive information.

History of 37 C.F.R. §380.5: 81 FR 26407, May 2, 2016.

§380.6. AUDITING PAYMENTS & DISTRIBUTIONS

(a) General. This section prescribes procedures by which any entity entitled to receive payment or distribution of royalties may verify payments or distributions by auditing the payor or distributor. The Collective may audit a Licensee's payments of royalties to the Collective, and a Copyright Owner or Performer may audit the Collective's distributions of royalties to the owner or performer. Nothing in this section shall preclude a verifying entity and the payor or distributor from agreeing to verification methods in addition to or different from those set forth in this section.

(b) Frequency of auditing. The verifying entity may conduct an audit of each licensee only once a year for any or all of the prior three calendar years. A verifying entity may not audit records for any calendar year more than once.

(c) Notice of intent to audit. The verifying entity must file with the Copyright Royalty Judges a notice of intent to audit the payor or distributor, which notice the Judges must publish in the Federal Register within 30 days of the filing of the notice. Simultaneously with the filing of the notice, the verifying entity must deliver a copy to the payor or distributor.

(d) The audit. The audit must be conducted during regular business hours by a Qualified Auditor who is not retained on a contingency fee basis and is identified in the notice. The auditor shall determine the accuracy of royalty payments or distributions, including whether an underpayment or overpayment of royalties was made. An audit of books and records, including underlying paperwork, performed in the ordinary course of business according to generally accepted auditing standards by a Qualified Auditor, shall serve as an acceptable verification procedure for all parties with respect to the information that is within the scope of the audit.

(e) Access to third-party records for audit purposes. The payor or distributor must use commercially reasonable efforts to obtain or to provide access to any relevant books and records maintained by third parties for the purpose of the audit.

(f) Duty of auditor to consult. The auditor must produce a written report to the verifying entity. Before rendering the report, unless the auditor has a reasonable basis to suspect fraud on the part of the payor or distributor, the disclosure of which would, in the reasonable opinion of the auditor, prejudice any investigation of the suspected fraud, the auditor must review tentative written findings of the audit with the appropriate agent or employee of the payor or distributor in order to remedy any factual errors and clarify any issues relating to the audit; Provided that an appropriate agent or employee of the payor or distributor reasonably cooperates with the auditor to remedy promptly any factual error[s] or clarify any issues raised by the audit. The auditor must include in the written report information concerning the cooperation or the lack thereof of the employee or agent.

(g) Audit results; underpayment or overpayment of royalties. If the auditor determines the payor or distributor underpaid royalties, the payor or distributor shall remit the amount of any underpayment determined by the auditor to the verifying entity, together with interest at the rate specified in §380.2(d). In the absence of mutually-agreed payment terms, which may, but need not, include installment payments, the payor or distributor shall remit promptly to the verifying entity the entire amount of the underpayment determined by the auditor. If the auditor determines the payor or distributor overpaid royalties, however, the verifying entity shall not be required to remit the amount of any overpayment to the payor or distributor, and the payor or distributor shall not seek by any means to recoup, offset, or take a credit for the overpayment, unless the payor or distributor and the verifying entity have agreed otherwise.

(h) Paying the costs of the audit. The verifying entity must pay the cost of the verification procedure, unless the auditor determines that there was an underpayment of 10% or more, in which case the payor or distributor must bear the reasonable costs of the verification procedure, in addition to paying or distributing the amount of any underpayment.

(i) Retention of audit report. The verifying party must retain the report of the audit for a period of not less than three years from the date of issuance.

History of 37 C.F.R. §380.6: 81 FR 26407, May 2, 2016.

§380.7. DEFINITIONS

Aggregate Tuning Hours (ATH) means the total hours of programming that the Licensee has transmitted during the relevant period to all listeners within the United States from all channels and stations that provide audio programming consisting, in whole or in part, of eligible nonsubscription transmissions or noninteractive digital audio transmissions as part of a new subscription service, less the actual running time of any sound recordings for which the Licensee has obtained direct licenses apart from 17 U.S.C. 114(d)(2) or which do not require a license under United States copyright law. By way of example, if a service transmitted one hour of programming containing Performances to 10 listeners, the service's ATH would equal 10 hours. If three minutes of that hour consisted of transmission of a directly-licensed recording, the service's ATH would equal nine hours and 30 minutes (three minutes times 10 listeners creates a deduction of 30 minutes). As an additional example, if one listener listened to a service for 10 hours (and none of the recordings transmitted during that time was directly licensed), the service's ATH would equal 10 hours.

Collective means the collection and distribution organization that is designated by the Copyright Royalty Judges, and which, for the current rate period, is SoundExchange, Inc.

Commercial Webcaster means a Licensee, other than a Noncommercial Webcaster or Public Broadcaster, that makes Ephemeral Recordings and eligible digital audio transmissions of sound recordings pursuant to the statutory licenses under 17 U.S.C. 112(e) and 114(d)(2).

Copyright owners means sound recording copyright owners who are entitled to royalty payments made under Part 380 pursuant to the statutory licenses under 17 U.S.C. 112(e) and 114.

Digital audio transmission has the same meaning as in 17 U.S.C. 114(j).

Eligible nonsubscription transmission has the same meaning as in 17 U.S.C. 114(j).

Eligible Transmission means a subscription or nonsubscription transmission made by a Licensee that is subject to licensing under 17 U.S.C. 114(d)(2) and the payment of royalties under this part.

Ephemeral recording has the same meaning as in 17 U.S.C. 112.

Licensee means a Commercial Webcaster, a Noncommercial Webcaster, or any entity operating a noninteractive Internet streaming service that has obtained a license under Section 112 or 114 to transmit eligible sound recordings.

New subscription service has the same meaning as in 17 U.S.C. 114(j).

Noncommercial webcaster has the same meaning as in 17 U.S.C. 114(f)(5)(E).

Nonsubscription has the same meaning as in 17 U.S.C. 114(j).

Performance means each instance in which any portion of a sound recording is publicly performed to a listener by means of a digital audio transmission (e.g., the delivery of any portion of a single track from a compact disc to one listener), but excludes the following:

(1) A performance of a sound recording that does not require a license (e.g., a sound recording that is not copyrighted);

(2) A performance of a sound recording for which the service has previously obtained a license from the Copyright Owner of such sound recording; and

(3) An incidental performance that both:

(i) Makes no more than incidental use of sound recordings including, but not limited to, brief musical transitions in and out of commercials or program segments, brief performances during news, talk and sports programming, brief background performances during disk jockey announcements, brief performances during commercials of sixty seconds or less in duration, or brief performances during sporting or other public events; and

(ii) Does not contain an entire sound recording, other than ambient music that is background at a public event, and does not feature a particular sound recording of more than thirty seconds (as in the case of a sound recording used as a theme song).

Performers means the independent administrators identified in 17 U.S.C. 114(g)(2)(B) and (C) and the parties identified in 17 U.S.C. 114(g)(2)(D).

Public broadcaster means a Covered Entity under subpart D of this part.

Qualified auditor means an independent Certified Public Accountant licensed in the jurisdiction where it seeks to conduct a verification.

Transmission has the same meaning as in 17 U.S.C. 114(j).

History of 37 C.F.R. §380.7: 81 FR 26408, May 2, 2016.

SUBPART B. COMMERCIAL WEBCASTERS & NONCOMMERCIAL WEBCASTERS

A §380.10. ROYALTY FEES FOR THE PUBLIC PERFORMANCE OF SOUND RECORDINGS & THE MAKING OF EPHEMERAL RECORDINGS

(a) Royalty fees. For the year 2018, Licensees must pay royalty fees for all Eligible Transmissions of sound recordings at the following rates:

(1) Commercial Webcasters: $0.0023 per performance for subscription services and $0.0018 per performance for nonsubscription services.

(2) Noncommercial webcasters. $500 per year for each channel or station and $0.0018 per performance for all digital audio transmissions in excess of 159,140 ATH in a month on a channel or station.

(b) Minimum fee. Licensees must pay the Collective a minimum fee of $500 each year for each channel or station. The Collective must apply the fee to the Licensee's account as credit towards any additional royalty fees that Licensees may incur in the same year. The fee is payable for each individual channel and each individual station maintained or operated by the Licensee and making Eligible Transmissions during each calendar year or part of a calendar year during which it is a Licensee. The maximum aggregate minimum fee in any calendar year that a Commercial Webcaster must pay is $50,000. The minimum fee is nonrefundable.

(c) Annual royalty fee adjustment. The Copyright Royalty Judges shall adjust the royalty fees each year to reflect any changes occurring in the cost of living as determined by the most recent Consumer Price Index (for all consumers and for all items) (CPI-U) published by the Secretary of Labor before December 1 of the preceding year. The adjusted rate shall be rounded to the nearest fourth decimal place. To account more accurately for cumulative changes in the CPI-U over the rate period, the calculation of the rate for each year shall be cumulative based on a calculation of the percentage increase in the CPI-U from the CPI-U published in November, 2015 (237.838), according to the formula $(1 + (Cy - 237.838)/237.838) \times R_{2016}$, where Cy is the CPI-U published by the Secretary of Labor before December 1 of the preceding year, and R_{2016} is the royalty rate for 2016 (i.e., $0.0022 per subscription performance or $0.0017 per nonsubscription performance). By way of example, if the CPI-U published in November 2016 is 242.083, the adjusted rate for nonsubscription services in 2017 will be computed as (1 + (242.083 – 237.838)/237.838) × $0.0017 and will equal $0.00173 ($0.0017 when rounded to the nearest fourth decimal place). If the CPI-U published in November 2017 is 249.345, the rate for nonsubscription services for 2018 will be computed as (1 + (249.345 – 237.838)/237.838) × $0.0017 and will equal $0.00179 ($0.0018 when rounded to the nearest fourth decimal place). The Judges shall publish notice of the adjusted fees in the Federal Register at least 25 days before January 1. The adjusted fees shall be effective on January 1.

(d) Ephemeral recordings royalty fees. The fee for all Ephemeral Recordings is part of the total fee payable under this section and constitutes 5% of it. All ephemeral recordings that a Licensee makes which are necessary and commercially reasonable for making noninteractive digital transmissions are included in the 5%.

History of 37 C.F.R. §380.10: 81 FR 26409, May 2, 2016; 81 FR 87456, Jan. 1, 2017; 82 FR 55946, Jan. 1, 2018.

SUBPART C. NONCOMMERCIAL EDUCATIONAL WEBCASTERS

§380.20. GENERAL

(a) Scope. This subpart establishes rates and terms, including requirements for royalty payments, recordkeeping and reports of use, for the public performance of sound recordings in certain digital transmissions made by Noncommercial Educational Webcasters as set forth herein in accordance with the provisions of 17 U.S.C. 114, and the making of Ephemeral Recordings by Noncommercial Educational Webcasters as set forth herein in accordance with the provisions of 17 U.S.C. 112(e), during the period January 1, 2016, through December 31, 2020.

(b) Legal compliance. Noncommercial Educational Webcasters relying upon the statutory licenses set forth in 17 U.S.C. 112(e) and 114 shall comply with the requirements of those sections, the rates and terms of this subpart, and any other applicable regulations not inconsistent with the rates and terms set forth herein.

(c) Relationship to voluntary agreements. Notwithstanding the royalty rates and terms established in this subpart, the rates and terms of any license agreements entered into by Copyright Owners and digital audio services shall apply in lieu of the rates and terms of this subpart to transmissions within the scope of such agreements.

History of 37 C.F.R. §380.20: 76 FR 13054, Mar. 9, 2011; 79 FR 23135, Apr. 25, 2014; 80 FR 58205, Jan. 1, 2016.

§380.21. DEFINITIONS

For purposes of this subpart, the following definitions shall apply:

ATH or Aggregate Tuning Hours means the total hours of programming that a Noncommercial Educational Webcaster has transmitted during the relevant period to all listeners within the United States over all channels and stations that provide audio programming consisting, in whole or in part, of Eligible Transmissions, including from any archived programs, less the actual running time of any sound recordings for which the Noncommercial Educational Webcaster has obtained direct licenses apart from 17 U.S.C. 114(d)(2) or which do not require a license under United States copyright law. By way of example, if a Noncommercial Educational Webcaster transmitted one hour of programming to 10 simultaneous listeners, the Noncommercial Educational Webcaster's Aggregate Tuning Hours would equal 10. If three minutes of that hour consisted of transmission of a directly licensed recording, the Noncommercial Educational Webcaster's Aggregate Tuning Hours would equal 9 hours and 30 minutes. As an additional example, if one listener listened to a Noncommercial Educational Webcaster for 10 hours (and none of the recordings transmitted during that time was directly licensed), the Noncommercial Educational Webcaster's Aggregate Tuning Hours would equal 10.

Collective is the collection and distribution organization specified in §380.2.

Copyright Owners are sound recording copyright owners who are entitled to royalty payments made under this subpart pursuant to the statutory licenses under 17 U.S.C. 112(e) and 114(f).

Eligible Transmission means an eligible nonsubscription transmission made by a Noncommercial Educational Webcaster over the Internet.

Ephemeral Recording is a phonorecord created for the purpose of facilitating an Eligible Transmission of a public performance of a sound recording under a statutory license in accordance with 17 U.S.C. 114(f), and subject to the limitations specified in 17 U.S.C. 112(e).

Noncommercial Educational Webcaster means a Noncommercial Webcaster (as defined in 17 U.S.C. 114(f)(5)(E)(i)) that

(1) Has obtained a compulsory license under 17 U.S.C. 112(e) and 114 and the implementing regulations therefor to make Eligible Transmissions and related ephemeral recordings;

(2) Complies with all applicable provisions of Sections 112(e) and 114 and applicable regulations;

(3) Is directly operated by, or is affiliated with and officially sanctioned by, and the digital audio transmission operations of which are staffed substantially by students enrolled at, a domestically accredited primary or secondary school, college, university or other post-secondary degree-granting educational institution;

(4) Is not a "public broadcasting entity" (as defined in 17 U.S.C. 118(f)) qualified to receive funding from the Corporation for Public Broadcasting pursuant to the criteria set forth in 47 U.S.C. 396; and

(5) Takes affirmative steps not to make total transmissions in excess of 159,140 Aggregate Tuning Hours on any individual channel or station in any month, if in any previous calendar year it has made total transmissions in excess of 159,140 Aggregate Tuning Hours on any individual channel or station in any month.

Performance is each instance in which any portion of a sound recording is publicly performed to a listener by means of a digital audio transmission (e.g., the delivery of any portion of a single track from a compact disc to one listener) but excluding the following:

(1) A performance of a sound recording that does not require a license (e.g., a sound recording that is not copyrighted);

(2) A performance of a sound recording for which the Noncommercial Educational Webcaster has previously obtained a license from the Copyright Owner of such sound recording; and

(3) An incidental performance that both:

(i) Makes no more than incidental use of sound recordings, including, but not limited to, brief musical transitions in and out of commercials or program segments, brief performances during news, talk and sports programming, brief background performances during disk jockey announcements, brief performances during commercials of sixty seconds or less in duration, or brief performances during sporting or other public events; and

(ii) Other than ambient music that is background at a public event, does not contain an entire sound recording and does not feature a particular sound recording of more than thirty seconds (as in the case of a sound recording used as a theme song).

Performers means the independent administrators identified in 17 U.S.C. 114(g)(2)(B) and (C) and the parties identified in 17 U.S.C. 114(g)(2)(D).

Qualified Auditor is a Certified Public Accountant.

History of 37 C.F.R. §380.21: 76 FR 13054, Mar. 9, 2011; 79 FR 23135, Apr. 25, 2014; 80 FR 58205, Jan. 1, 2016.

§380.22. ROYALTY FEES FOR THE PUBLIC PERFORMANCE OF SOUND RECORDINGS & FOR EPHEMERAL RECORDINGS

(a) Minimum fee for eligible Noncommercial Educational Webcasters. Each Noncommercial Educational Webcaster that did not exceed 159,140 total ATH for any individual channel or station for more than one calendar month in the immediately preceding calendar year and does not expect to make total transmissions in excess of 159,140 Aggregate Tuning Hours on any individual channel or station in any calendar month during the applicable calendar year shall pay an annual, nonrefundable minimum fee of $500 (the "Minimum Fee") for each of its individual channels, including each of its individual side channels, and each of its individual stations, through which (in each case) it makes Eligible Transmissions, for each calendar year it makes Eligible Transmissions subject to this subpart. For clarity, each individual stream (e.g., HD radio side channels, different stations owned by a single licensee) will be treated separately and be subject to a separate minimum. The Minimum Fee shall constitute the annual per channel or per station royalty for all Eligible Transmissions totaling not more than 159,140

Aggregate Tuning Hours in a month on any individual channel or station, and for Ephemeral Recordings to enable such Eligible Transmissions. In addition, a Noncommercial Educational Webcaster electing the reporting waiver described in §380.23(g)(1), shall pay a $100 annual fee (the "Proxy Fee") to the Collective.

(b) Consequences of unexpectedly exceeding ATH cap. In the case of a Noncommercial Educational Webcaster eligible to pay royalties under paragraph (a) that unexpectedly makes total transmissions in excess of 159,140 Aggregate Tuning Hours on any individual channel or station in any calendar month during the applicable calendar year:

(1) The Noncommercial Educational Webcaster shall, for such month and the remainder of the calendar year in which such month occurs, pay royalties in accordance, and otherwise comply, with the provisions of Part 380 Subparts A and B applicable to Noncommercial Webcasters;

(2) The Minimum Fee paid by the Noncommercial Educational Webcaster for such calendar year will be credited to the amounts payable under the provisions of Part 380 Subparts A and B applicable to Noncommercial Webcasters; and

(3) The Noncommercial Educational Webcaster shall, within 45 days after the end of each month, notify the Collective if it has made total transmissions in excess of 159,140 Aggregate Tuning Hours on a channel or station during that month; pay the Collective any amounts due under the provisions of Part 380 Subparts A and B applicable to Noncommercial Webcasters; and provide the Collective a statement of account pursuant to part 380, subpart A.

(c) Royalties for other Noncommercial Educational Webcasters. A Noncommercial Educational Webcaster that is not eligible to pay royalties under paragraph (a) of this section shall pay royalties in accordance, and that otherwise comply, with the provisions of subparts A and B of this part applicable to Noncommercial Webcasters.

(d) Estimation of performances. In the case of a Noncommercial Educational Webcaster that is required to pay royalties under paragraph (b) or (c) on a per-performance basis, that is unable to calculate actual total performances, and that is not required to report actual total performances under §380.23(g)(3), the Noncommercial Educational Webcaster may pay its applicable royalties on an ATH basis, provided that the Noncommercial Educational Webcaster shall pay such royalties at the applicable per-performance rates based on the assumption that the number of sound recordings performed is 12 per hour. The Collective may distribute royalties paid on the basis of ATH hereunder in accordance with its generally applicable methodology for distributing royalties paid on such basis. In addition, and for the avoidance of doubt, a Noncommercial Educational Webcaster offering more than one channel or station shall pay per-performance royalties on a per-channel or -station basis.

(e) Ephemeral royalty. The royalty payable under 17 U.S.C. 112(e) for any ephemeral reproductions made by a Noncommercial Educational Webcaster is deemed to be included within the royalty payments set forth in paragraphs (a) through (c) of this section and to equal 5% of the total royalties payable under such paragraphs.

History of 37 C.F.R. §380.22: 76 FR 13055, Mar. 9, 2011; 79 FR 23135, Apr. 25, 2014; 80 FR 58205, Jan. 1, 2016; 81 FR 26409, May 2, 2016.

§380.23. TERMS FOR MAKING PAYMENT OF ROYALTY FEES & STATEMENTS OF ACCOUNT

(a) Payment to the Collective. A Noncommercial Educational Webcaster shall make the royalty payments due under §380.22 to the Collective.

(b) Designation of the Collective. **(1)** The Copyright Royalty Judges designate SoundExchange, Inc., as the Collective to receive statements of account and royalty payments from Noncommercial Educational Webcasters due under §380.22 and to distribute royalty payments to each Copyright Owner and Performer, or their designated agents, entitled to receive royalties under 17 U.S.C. 112(e) or 114(g).

(2) If SoundExchange, Inc., should dissolve or cease to be governed by a board consisting of equal numbers of representatives of Copyright Owners and Performers, then it shall be replaced by a successor Collective upon the fulfillment of the requirements set forth in paragraph (b)(2)(i) of this section.

(i) By a majority vote of the nine Copyright Owner representatives and the nine Performer representatives on the SoundExchange board as of the last day preceding the condition precedent in this paragraph (b)(2), such representatives shall file a petition with the Copyright Royalty Board designating a successor to collect and distribute royalty payments to Copyright Owners and Performers entitled to receive royalties under 17 U.S.C. 112(e) or 114(g) that have themselves authorized such Collective.

(ii) The Copyright Royalty Judges shall publish in the Federal Register within 30 days of receipt of a petition filed under paragraph (b)(2)(i) of this section an order designating the Collective named in such petition.

(c) Minimum fee. Noncommercial Educational Webcasters shall submit the Minimum Fee, and Proxy Fee if applicable, accompanied by a statement of account, by January 31st of each calendar year, except that payment of the Minimum Fee, and Proxy Fee if applicable, by a Noncommercial Educational Webcaster that was not making Eligible Transmissions or Ephemeral Recordings pursuant to the licenses in 17 U.S.C. 114 and/or 17 U.S.C. 112(e) as of said date but begins doing so thereafter shall be due by the 45th day after the end of the month in which the Noncommercial Educational Webcaster commences doing so. At the same time the Noncommercial Educational Webcaster must identify all its stations making Eligible Transmissions and identify which of the reporting options set forth in paragraph (g) of this section it elects for the relevant year (provided that it must be eligible for the option it elects).

(d) [Reserved]

(e) Late fees. A Noncommercial Educational Webcaster shall pay a late fee for each instance in which any payment, any statement of account or any report of use is not received by the Collective in compliance with the applicable regulations by the due date. The amount of the late fee shall be 1.5% of the late payment, or 1.5% of the payment associated with a late statement of account or report of use, per month, compounded monthly for the balance due, or the highest lawful rate, whichever is lower. The late fee shall accrue from the due date of the payment, statement of account or report of use until a fully compliant payment, statement of account or report of use (as applicable) is received by the Collective, provided that, in the case of a timely provided but noncompliant statement of account or report of use, the Collective has notified the Noncommercial Educational Webcaster within 90 days regarding any noncompliance that is reasonably evident to the Collective.

(f) Statements of account. Any payment due under §380.22(a) shall be accompanied by a corresponding statement of account on a form provided by the Collective. A statement of account shall contain the following information:

(1) The name of the Noncommercial Educational Webcaster, exactly as it appears on the notice of use, and if the statement of account covers a single station only, the call letters or name of the station;

(2) [Removed & reserved]

(3) The name, address, business title, telephone number, facsimile number (if any), electronic mail address (if any) and other contact information of the person to be contacted for information or questions concerning the content of the statement of account;

(4) The signature of a duly authorized representative of the applicable educational institution;

(5) The printed or typewritten name of the person signing the statement of account;

(6) The date of signature;

(7) The title or official position held by the person signing the statement of account;

(8) A certification of the capacity of the person signing; and

(9) A statement to the following effect:

I, the undersigned duly authorized representative of the applicable educational institution, have examined this statement of account; hereby state that it is true, accurate, and complete to my knowledge after reasonable due diligence; and further certify that the licensee entity named herein qualifies as a Noncommercial Educational Webcaster for the relevant year, and did not exceed 159,140 total ATH in any month of the prior year for which the Noncommercial Educational Webcaster did not submit a statement of account and pay any required additional royalties.

(g) Reporting by Noncommercial Educational Webcasters in general—

(1) Reporting waiver. In light of the unique business and operational circumstances with respect to Noncommercial Educational Webcasters, and for the purposes of this subpart only, a Noncommercial Educational Webcaster that did not exceed 80,000 total ATH for any individual channel or station for more than one calendar month in the immediately preceding calendar year and that does not expect to exceed 80,000 total ATH for any individual channel or station for any calendar month during the applicable calendar year may elect to pay to the Collective a nonrefundable, annual Proxy Fee of $100 in lieu of providing reports of use for the calendar year pursuant to the regulations §370.4 of this chapter. In addition, a Noncommercial Educational Webcaster that unexpectedly exceeded 80,000 total ATH on one or more channels or stations for more than one month during the immediately preceding calendar year may elect to pay the Proxy Fee and receive the reporting waiver described in paragraph (g)(1) of this section during a calendar year, if it implements measures reasonably calculated to ensure that it will not make Eligible Transmissions exceeding 80,000 total ATH during any month of that calendar year. The Proxy Fee is intended to defray the Collective's costs associated with this reporting waiver, including development of proxy usage data. The Proxy Fee shall be paid by the date specified in paragraph (c) of this section for paying the Minimum Fee for the applicable calendar year and shall be accompanied by a certification on a form provided by the Collective, signed by a duly authorized representative of the applicable educational institution, stating that the Noncommercial Educational Webcaster is eligible for the Proxy Fee option because of its past and expected future usage and, if applicable, has implemented measures to ensure that it will not make excess Eligible Transmissions in the future.

(2) Sample-basis reports. A Noncommercial Educational Webcaster that did not exceed 159,140 total ATH for any individual channel or station for more than one calendar month in the immediately preceding calendar year and that does not expect to exceed 159,140 total ATH for any individual channel or station for any calendar month during the applicable calendar year may elect to provide reports of use on a sample basis (two weeks per calendar quarter) in accordance with the regulations at §370.4 of this chapter, except that, notwithstanding §370.4(d)(2)(vi), such an electing Noncommercial Educational Webcaster shall not be required to include ATH or actual total performances and may in lieu thereof provide channel or station name and play frequency. Notwithstanding the foregoing, a Noncommercial Educational Webcaster that is able to report ATH or actual total performances is encouraged to do so. These reports of use shall be submitted to the Collective no later than January 31st of the year immediately following the year to which they pertain.

(3) Census-basis reports. If any of the following three conditions is satisfied, a Noncommercial Educational Webcaster must report pursuant to paragraph (g)(3) of this section:

(i) The Noncommercial Educational Webcaster exceeded 159,140 total ATH for any individual channel or station for more than one calendar month in the immediately preceding calendar year;

(ii) The Noncommercial Educational Webcaster expects to exceed 159,140 total ATH for any individual channel or station for any calendar month in the applicable calendar year; or

(iii) The Noncommercial Educational Webcaster otherwise does not elect to be subject to paragraph (g)(1) or (2) of this section.

A Noncommercial Educational Webcaster required to report pursuant to paragraph (g)(3) of this section shall provide reports of use to the Collective quarterly on a census reporting basis in accordance with §370.4 of this chapter, except that, notwithstanding §370.4(d)(2), such a Noncommercial Educational Webcaster shall not be required to include ATH or actual total performances, and may in lieu thereof provide channel or station name and play frequency, during the first calendar year it reports in accordance with paragraph (g)(3) of this section. For the avoidance of doubt, after a Noncommercial Educational Webcaster has been required to report in accordance with paragraph (g)(3) of this section for a full calendar year, it must thereafter include ATH or actual total performances in its reports of use. All reports of use under paragraph (g)(3) of this section shall be submitted to the Collective no later than the 45th day after the end of each calendar quarter.

(h) Distribution of royalties.

(1) The Collective shall promptly distribute royalties received from Noncommercial Educational Webcasters to Copyright Owners and Performers, or their designated agents, that are entitled to such royalties. The Collective shall only be responsible for making distributions to those Copyright Owners, Performers, or their designated agents who provide the Collective with such information as is necessary to identify and pay the correct recipient. The Collective shall distribute royalties on a basis that values all performances by a Noncommercial Educational Webcaster equally based upon the information provided under the report of use requirements for Noncommercial Educational Webcasters contained in §370.4 of this chapter and this subpart, except that in the case of Noncommercial Educational Webcasters that elect to pay a Proxy Fee in lieu of providing reports of use pursuant to paragraph (g)(1) of this section, the Collective shall distribute the aggregate royalties paid by electing Noncommercial Educational Webcasters based on proxy usage data in accordance with a methodology adopted by the Collective's Board of Directors.

(2) If the Collective is unable to locate a Copyright Owner or Performer entitled to a distribution of royalties under paragraph (h)(1) of this section within 3 years from the date of payment by a Noncommercial Educational Webcaster, such distribution may first be applied to the costs directly attributable to the administration of that distribution. The foregoing shall apply notwithstanding the common law or statutes of any State.

(i) Server logs. Noncommercial Educational Webcasters shall retain for a period of no less than three full calendar years server logs sufficient to substantiate all information relevant to eligibility, rate calculation and reporting under this subpart. To the extent that a third-party Web hosting or service provider maintains equipment or software for a Noncommercial Educational Webcaster and/or such third party creates, maintains, or can reasonably create such server logs, the Noncommercial Educational Webcaster shall direct that such server logs be created and maintained by said third party for a period of no less than three full calendar years and/or that such server logs be provided to, and maintained by, the Noncommercial Educational Webcaster.

(ii) [Reserved]

History of 37 C.F.R. §380.23: 76 FR 13055, Mar. 9, 2011; 79 FR 23136, Apr. 25, 2014; 80 FR 58206, Jan. 1, 2016; 81 FR 26409, May 2, 2016.

§380.24. CONFIDENTIAL INFORMATION

(a) Definition. For purposes of this subpart, "Confidential Information" shall include the statements of account and any information contained therein, including the amount of Usage Fees paid, and any information pertaining to the statements of account reasonably designated as confidential by the Noncommercial Educational Webcaster submitting the statement.

(b) Exclusion. Confidential Information shall not include documents or information that at the time of delivery to the Collective are public knowledge. The party claiming the benefit of this provision shall have the burden of proving that the disclosed information was public knowledge.

(c) Use of Confidential Information. In no event shall the Collective use any Confidential Information for any purpose other than royalty collection and distribution and activities related directly thereto.

(d) Disclosure of Confidential Information. Access to Confidential Information shall be limited to:

(1) Those employees, agents, attorneys, consultants and independent contractors of the Collective, subject to an appropriate confidentiality agreement, who are engaged in the collection and distribution of royalty payments hereunder and activities related thereto, for the purpose of performing such duties during the ordinary course of their work and who require access to Confidential Information;

(2) An independent Qualified Auditor, subject to an appropriate confidentiality agreement, who is authorized to act on behalf of the Collective with respect to verification of a Noncommercial Educational Webcaster's statement of account pursuant to §380.25 or on behalf of a Copyright Owner or Performer with respect to the verification of royalty distributions pursuant to §380.26;

(3) Copyright Owners and Performers, including their designated agents, whose works have been used under the statutory licenses set forth in 17 U.S.C. 112(e) and 114(f) by the Noncommercial Educational Webcaster whose Confidential Information is being supplied, subject to an appropriate confidentiality agreement, and including those employees, agents, attorneys, consultants and independent contractors of such Copyright Owners and Performers and their designated agents, subject to an appropriate confidentiality agreement, for the purpose of performing their duties during the ordinary course of their work and who require access to the Confidential Information; and

(4) In connection with future proceedings under 17 U.S.C. 112(e) and 114(f) before the Copyright Royalty Judges, and under an appropriate protective order, attorneys, consultants and other authorized agents of the parties to the proceedings or the courts.

(e) Safeguarding of Confidential Information. The Collective and any person identified in paragraph (d) of this section shall implement procedures to safeguard against unauthorized access to or dissemination of any Confidential Information using a reasonable standard of care, but no less than the same degree of security used to protect Confidential Information or similarly sensitive information belonging to the Collective or person.

History of 37 C.F.R. §380.24: 76 FR 13057, Mar. 9, 2011; 79 FR 23138, Apr. 25, 2014.

§380.25. VERIFICATION OF ROYALTY PAYMENTS

(a) General. This section prescribes procedures by which the Collective may verify the royalty payments made by a Noncommercial Educational Webcaster.

(b) Frequency of verification. The Collective may conduct a single audit of a Noncommercial Educational Webcaster, upon reasonable notice and during reasonable business hours, during any given calendar year, for any or all of the prior 3 calendar years, but no calendar year shall be subject to audit more than once.

(c) Notice of intent to audit. The Collective must file with the Copyright Royalty Board a notice of intent to audit a particular Noncommercial Educational Webcaster, which shall, within 30 days of the filing of the notice, publish in the Federal Register a notice announcing such filing. The notification of intent to audit shall be served at the same time on the Noncommercial Educational Webcaster to be audited. Any such audit shall be conducted by an independent Qualified Auditor identified in the notice and shall be binding on all parties.

(d) Acquisition and retention of report. The Noncommercial Educational Webcaster shall use commercially reasonable efforts to obtain or to provide access to any relevant books and records maintained by third parties for the purpose of the audit. The Collective shall retain the report of the verification for a period of not less than 3 years.

(e) Acceptable verification procedure. An audit, including underlying paperwork, which was performed in the ordinary course of business according to generally accepted auditing standards by an independent Qualified Auditor, shall serve as an acceptable verification procedure for all parties with respect to the information that is within the scope of the audit.

(f) Consultation. Before rendering a written report to the Collective, except where the auditor has a reasonable basis to suspect fraud and disclosure would, in the reasonable opinion of the auditor, prejudice the investigation of such suspected fraud, the auditor shall review the tentative written findings of the audit with the appropriate agent or employee of the Noncommercial Educational Webcaster being audited in order to remedy any factual errors and clarify any issues relating to the audit; Provided that an appropriate agent or employee of the Noncommercial Educational Webcaster reasonably cooperates with the auditor to remedy promptly any factual errors or clarify any issues raised by the audit.

(g) Costs of the verification procedure. The Collective shall pay the cost of the verification procedure, unless it is finally determined that there was an underpayment of 10% or more, in which case the Noncommercial Educational Webcaster shall, in addition to paying the amount of any underpayment, bear the reasonable costs of the verification procedure.

History of 37 C.F.R. §380.25: 76 FR 13058, Mar. 9, 2011; 79 FR 23138, Apr. 25, 2014.

§380.26. VERIFICATION OF ROYALTY DISTRIBUTIONS

(a) General. This section prescribes procedures by which any Copyright Owner or Performer may verify the royalty distributions made by the Collective; provided, however, that nothing contained in this section shall apply to situations where a Copyright Owner or Performer and the Collective have agreed as to proper verification methods.

(b) Frequency of verification. A Copyright Owner or Performer may conduct a single audit of the Collective upon reasonable notice and during reasonable business hours, during any given calendar year, for any or all of the prior 3 calendar years, but no calendar year shall be subject to audit more than once.

(c) Notice of intent to audit. A Copyright Owner or Performer must file with the Copyright Royalty Board a notice of intent to audit the Collective, which shall, within 30 days of the filing of the notice, publish in the Federal Register a notice announcing such filing. The notification of intent to audit shall be served at the same time on the Collective. Any audit shall be conducted by an independent Qualified Auditor identified in the notice, and shall be binding on all Copyright Owners and Performers.

(d) Acquisition and retention of report. The Collective shall use commercially reasonable efforts to obtain or to provide access to any relevant books and records maintained by third parties for the purpose of the audit. The Copyright Owner or Performer requesting the verification procedure shall retain the report of the verification for a period of not less than 3 years.

(e) Acceptable verification procedure. An audit, including underlying paperwork, which was performed in the ordinary course of business according to generally accepted auditing standards by an independent Qualified Auditor, shall serve as an acceptable verification procedure for all parties with respect to the information that is within the scope of the audit.

(f) Consultation. Before rendering a written report to a Copyright Owner or Performer, except where the auditor has a reasonable basis to suspect fraud and disclosure would, in the reasonable opinion of the auditor, prejudice the investigation of such suspected fraud, the auditor shall review the tentative written findings of the audit with the appropriate agent or employee of the Collective in order to remedy any factual errors and clarify any issues relating to the audit; Provided that the appropriate agent or employee of the Collective reasonably cooperates with the auditor to remedy promptly any factual errors or clarify any issues raised by the audit.

(g) Costs of the verification procedure. The Copyright Owner or Performer requesting the verification procedure shall pay the cost of the procedure, unless it is finally determined that there was an underpayment of 10% or more, in which case the Collective shall, in addition to paying the amount of any underpayment, bear the reasonable costs of the verification procedure.

History of 37 C.F.R. §380.26: 76 FR 13058, Mar. 9, 2011; 79 FR 23138, Apr. 25, 2014.

§380.27. UNCLAIMED FUNDS

If the Collective is unable to identify or locate a Copyright Owner or Performer who is entitled to receive a royalty distribution under this subpart, the Collective shall retain the required payment in a segregated trust account for a period of 3 years from the date of distribution. No claim to such distribution shall be valid after the expiration of the 3-year period. After expiration of this period, the Collective may apply the unclaimed funds to offset any costs deductible under 17 U.S.C. 114(g)(3). The foregoing shall apply notwithstanding the common law or statutes of any State.

History of 37 C.F.R. §380.27: 76 FR 13058, Mar. 9, 2011; 79 FR 23139, Apr. 25, 2014.

SUBPART D. PUBLIC BROADCASTERS

§380.30. GENERAL

(a) Scope. This subpart establishes rates and terms of royalty payments for the public performance of sound recordings in certain digital transmissions, through Authorized Web sites, by means of Web site Performances, by certain Covered Entities as set forth in this subpart in accordance with the provisions of 17 U.S.C. 114, and the making of Ephemeral Recordings by Covered Entities in accordance with the provisions of 17 U.S.C. 112(e) solely as necessary to encode Sound Recordings in different formats and at different bit rates as necessary to facilitate Web site Performances, during the period January 1, 2016, through December 31, 2020. The provisions of this subpart shall apply to the Covered Entities in lieu of other rates and terms applicable under 17 U.S.C. 112(e) and 114.

(b) Legal compliance. Licensees relying upon the statutory licenses set forth in 17 U.S.C. 112(e) and 114 shall comply with the requirements of those sections, the rates and terms of this subpart, and any other applicable regulations.

(c) Relationship to voluntary agreements. Notwithstanding the royalty rates and terms established in this subpart, the rates and terms of any license agreements entered into by Copyright Owners and Licensees shall apply in lieu of the rates and terms of this subpart to transmission within the scope of such agreements.

History of 37 C.F.R. §380.30: 80 FR 59590, Jan. 1, 2016.

§380.31. DEFINITIONS

For purposes of this subpart, the following definitions shall apply:

Aggregate Tuning Hours (ATH) means the total hours of programming that Covered Entities have transmitted during the relevant period to all listeners within the United States from all Covered Entities that provide audio programming consisting, in whole or in part, of Web site Performances, less the actual running time of any sound recordings for which the Covered Entity has obtained direct licenses apart from this Agreement. By way of example, if a Covered Entity transmitted one hour of programming to ten (10) simultaneous listeners, the Covered Entity's Aggregate Tuning Hours would equal ten (10). If three (3) minutes of that hour consisted of transmission of a directly licensed recording, the Covered Entity's Aggregate Tuning Hours would equal nine (9) hours and thirty (30) minutes. As an additional example, if one listener listened to a Covered Entity for ten (10) hours (and none of the recordings transmitted during that time was directly licensed), the Covered Entity's Aggregate Tuning Hours would equal 10.

Authorized Web site is any Web site operated by or on behalf of any Covered Entity that is accessed by Web site Users through a Uniform Resource Locator ("URL") owned by such Covered Entity and through which Web site Performances are made by such Covered Entity.

CPB is the Corporation for Public Broadcasting.

Collective is the collection and distribution organization that is designated by the Copyright Royalty Judges.

Copyright Owners are Sound Recording copyright owners who are entitled to royalty payments made under this subpart pursuant to the statutory licenses under 17 U.S.C. 112(e) and 114(f).

Covered Entities are NPR, American Public Media, Public Radio International, and Public Radio Exchange, and up to 530 Originating Public Radio Stations as named by CPB. CPB shall notify SoundExchange annually of the eligible Originating Public Radio Stations to be considered Covered Entities hereunder (subject to the numerical limitations set forth herein). The number of Originating Public Radio Stations treated hereunder as Covered Entities shall not exceed 530 for a given year without SoundExchange's express written approval, except that CPB shall have the option to increase the number of Originating Public Radio Stations that may be considered Covered Entities as provided in section 380.32(c).

Ephemeral Phonorecords are Phonorecords of all or any portion of any Sound Recordings; provided that:

(1) Such Phonorecords are limited solely to those necessary to encode Sound Recordings in different formats and at different bit rates as necessary to facilitate Web site Performances covered by this subpart;

(2) Such Phonorecords are made in strict conformity with the provisions set forth in 17 U.S.C. 112(e)(1)(A)-(D); and

(3) The Covered Entities comply with 17 U.S.C. 112(a) and (e) and all of the terms and conditions of this Agreement.

Music ATH is ATH of Web site Performances of Sound Recordings of musical works.

NPR is National Public Radio, Inc.

Originating Public Radio Station is a noncommercial terrestrial radio broadcast station that—

(1) Is licensed as such by the Federal Communications Commission;

(2) Originates programming and is not solely a repeater station;

(3) Is a member or affiliate of NPR, American Public Media, Public Radio International, or Public Radio Exchange, a member of the National Federation of Community Broadcasters, or another public radio station that is qualified to receive funding from CPB pursuant to its criteria;

(4) Qualifies as a "noncommercial webcaster" under 17 U.S.C. 114(f)(5)(E)(i); and

(5) Either—

(i) Offers Web site Performances only as part of the mission that entitles it to be exempt from taxation under section 501 of the Internal Revenue Code of 1986 (26 U.S.C. 501); or

(ii) In the case of a governmental entity (including a Native American Tribal governmental entity), is operated exclusively for public purposes.

Performers means the independent administrators identified in 17 U.S.C. 114(g)(2)(B) and (C) and the individuals and entities identified in 17 U.S.C. 114(g)(2)(D).

Person is a natural person, a corporation, a limited liability company, a partnership, a trust, a joint venture, any governmental authority or any other entity or organization.

Phonorecords have the meaning set forth in 17 U.S.C. 101.

Qualified Auditor is a Certified Public Accountant, or a person, who by virtue of education or experience, is appropriately qualified to perform an audit to verify royalty payments related to performances of sound recordings.

Side Channel is any Internet-only program available on an Authorized Web site or an archived program on such Authorized Web site that, in either case, conforms to all applicable requirements under 17 U.S.C. 114.

Sound Recording has the meaning set forth in 17 U.S.C. 101.

Term is the period January 1, 2016, through December 31, 2020.

Web site is a site located on the World Wide Web that can be located by a Web site User through a principal URL.

Web site Performances are all public performances by means of digital audio transmissions of Sound Recordings, including the transmission of any portion of any Sound Recording, made through an Authorized Web site in accordance with all requirements of 17 U.S.C. 114, from servers used by a Covered Entity (provided that the Covered Entity controls the content of all materials transmitted by the server), or by a contractor authorized pursuant to Section 380.32(f), that consist of either the retransmission of a Covered Entity's over-the-air terrestrial radio programming or the digital transmission of nonsubscription Side Channels that are programmed and controlled by the Covered Entity. This term does not include digital audio transmissions made by any other means.

Web site Users are all those who access or receive Web site Performances or who access any Authorized Web site.

History of 37 C.F.R. §380.31: 80 FR 59590, Jan. 1, 2016.

§380.32. ROYALTY FEES FOR THE PUBLIC PERFORMANCE OF SOUND RECORDINGS & FOR EPHEMERAL RECORDINGS

(a) Royalty rates. The total license fee for all Web site Performances by Covered Entities during the Term, up to a total Music ATH of 285,132,065 per calendar year, and Ephemeral Phonorecords made by Covered Entities solely to facilitate such Web site Performances, during the Term shall be $2,800,000 (the "License Fee"), unless additional payments are required as described in paragraph (c) of this section.

(b) Calculation of License Fee. It is understood that the License Fee includes:

(1) An annual minimum fee of $500 for each Covered Entity for each year during the Term;

(2) Additional usage fees for certain Covered Entities; and

(3) A discount that reflects the administrative convenience to the Collective of receiving annual lump sum payments that cover a large number of separate entities, as well as the protection from bad debt that arises from being paid in advance.

(c) Increase in Covered Entities. If the total number of Originating Public Radio Stations that wish to make Web site Performances in any calendar year exceeds the number of such Originating Public Radio Stations considered Covered Entities in the relevant year, and the excess Originating Public Radio Stations do not wish to pay royalties for such Web site Performances apart from this subpart, CPB may elect by written notice to the Collective to increase the number of Originating Public Radio Stations considered Covered Entities in the relevant year effective as of the date of the notice. To the extent of any such elections, CPB shall make an additional payment to the Collective for each calendar year or part thereof it elects to have an additional Originating Public Radio Station considered a Covered Entity, in the amount of $500 per Originating Public Radio Station per year. Such payment shall accompany the notice electing to have an additional Originating Public Radio Station considered a Covered Entity.

(d) Ephemeral recordings. The royalty payable under 17 U.S.C. 112(e) for the making of all Ephemeral Recordings used by Covered Entities solely to facilitate Web site Performances for which royalties are paid pursuant to this subpart shall be included within, and constitute 5% of, the total royalties payable under 17 U.S.C. 112(e) and 114.

(e) Effect of non-performance by any Covered Entity. In the event that any Covered Entity violates any of the material provisions of 17 U.S.C. 112(e) or 114 or this subpart that it is required to perform, the remedies of the Collective shall be specific to that Covered Entity only, and shall include, without limitation, termination of that Covered Entity's right to be treated as a Covered Entity hereunder upon written notice to CPB. The Collective and Copyright Owners also shall have whatever rights may be available to them against that Covered Entity under applicable law. The Collective's remedies for such a breach or failure by an individual Covered Entity shall not include termination of the rights of other Covered Entities to be treated as Covered Entities hereunder, except that if CPB fails to pay the License Fee or otherwise fails to perform any of the material provisions of this subpart, or such a breach or failure by a Covered Entity results from CPB's inducement, and CPB does not cure such breach or failure within 30 days after receiving notice thereof from the Collective, then the Collective may terminate the right of all Covered Entities to be treated as Covered Entities hereunder upon written notice to CPB. In such a case, a prorated portion of the License Fee for the remainder of the Term (to the extent paid by CPB) shall, after deduction of any damages payable to the Collective by virtue of the breach or failure, be credited to statutory royalty obligations of Covered Entities to the Collective for the Term as specified by CPB.

(f) Use of contractors. The right to rely on this subpart is limited to Covered Entities, except that a Covered Entity may employ the services of a third Person to provide the technical services and equipment necessary to deliver Web site Performances on behalf of such Covered Entity, but only through an Authorized Web site. Any agreement between a Covered Entity and any third Person for such services shall:

(1) Obligate such third Person to provide all such services in accordance with all applicable provisions of the statutory licenses and this subpart;

(2) Specify that such third Person shall have no right to make Web site Performances or any other performances or Phonorecords on its own behalf or on behalf of any Person or entity other than a Covered Entity through the Covered Entity's Authorized Web site by virtue of its services for the Covered Entity, including in the case of Phonorecords, pre-encoding or otherwise establishing a library of Sound Recordings that it offers to a Covered Entity or others for purposes of making performances, but instead must obtain all necessary licenses from the Collective, the copyright owner or another duly authorized Person, as the case may be;

(3) Specify that such third Person shall have no right to grant any sublicenses under the statutory licenses; and

(4) Provide that the Collective is an intended third-party beneficiary of all such obligations with the right to enforce a breach thereof against such third Person.

History of 37 C.F.R. §380.32: 80 FR 59591, Jan. 1, 2016.

§380.33. TERMS FOR MAKING PAYMENT OF ROYALTY FEES & STATEMENTS OF ACCOUNT

(a) Payment to the Collective. CPB shall pay the License Fee to the Collective in five equal installments of $560,000 each, which shall be due December 31, 2015, and annually thereafter through December 31, 2019.

(b) Designation of the Collective. (1) The Copyright Royalty Judges designate SoundExchange, Inc., as the Collective to receive statements of account and royalty payments for Covered Entities under this subpart and to distribute royalty payments to each Copyright Owner and Performer, or their designated agents, entitled to receive royalties under 17 U.S.C. 112(e) or 114(g).

(2) If SoundExchange, Inc. should dissolve or cease to be governed by a board consisting of equal numbers of representatives of Copyright Owners and Performers, then it shall be replaced by a successor Collective upon the fulfillment of the requirements set forth in paragraph (b)(2)(i) of this section.

(i) By a majority vote of the nine Copyright Owner representatives and the nine Performer representatives on the SoundExchange board as of the last day preceding the condition precedent in this paragraph (b)(2), such representatives shall file a petition with the Copyright Royalty Judges designating a successor to collect and distribute royalty payments to Copyright Owners and Performers entitled to receive royalties under 17 U.S.C. 112(e) or 114(g) that have themselves authorized the Collective.

(ii) The Copyright Royalty Judges shall publish in the Federal Register within 30 days of receipt of a petition filed under paragraph (b)(2)(i) of this section an order designating the Collective named in such petition.

(c) Reporting. CPB and Covered Entities shall submit reports of use and other information concerning Web site Performances as agreed upon with the Collective.

(d) Late payments and statements of account. A Licensee shall pay a late fee of 1.5% per month, or the highest lawful rate, whichever is lower, for any payment and/or statement of account received by the Collective after the due date. Late fees shall accrue from the due date until payment and the related statement of account are received by the Collective.

(e) Distribution of royalties.

(1) The Collective shall promptly distribute royalties received from CPB to Copyright Owners and Performers, or their designated agents, that are entitled to such royalties. The Collective shall only be responsible for making distributions to those Copyright Owners, Performers, or their designated agents who provide the Collective with such information as is necessary to identify the correct recipient. The Collective shall distribute royalties on a basis that values all Web site Performances by Covered Entities equally based upon the reporting information provided by CPB/NPR.

(2) If the Collective is unable to locate a Copyright Owner or Performer entitled to a distribution of royalties under paragraph (e)(1) of the section within 3 years from the date of payment by a Licensee, such royalties shall be handled in accordance with §380.37.

(f) Retention of records. Books and records of CPB and Covered Entities and of the Collective relating to payments of and distributions of royalties shall be kept for a period of not less than the prior 3 calendar years.

History of 37 C.F.R. §380.33: 80 FR 59591, Jan. 1, 2016; 81 FR 26409, May 2, 2016.

§380.34. CONFIDENTIAL INFORMATION

(a) Definition. For purposes of this subpart, "Confidential Information" shall include the statements of account and any information contained therein, including the amount of royalty payments, and any information pertaining to the statements of account reasonably designated as confidential by the Licensee submitting the statement.

(b) Exclusion. Confidential Information shall not include documents or information that at the time of delivery to the Collective are public knowledge, or documents or information that become publicly known through no fault of the Collective or are known by the Collective when disclosed by CPB/NPR. The party claiming the benefit of this provision shall have the burden of proving that the disclosed information was public knowledge.

(c) Use of Confidential Information. In no event shall the Collective use any Confidential Information for any purpose other than royalty collection and distribution and activities related directly thereto and enforcement of the terms of the statutory licenses.

(d) Disclosure of Confidential Information. Access to Confidential Information shall be limited to:

(1) Those employees, agents, attorneys, consultants and independent contractors of the Collective, subject to an appropriate confidentiality agreement, who are engaged in the collection and distribution of royalty payments hereunder and activities related thereto, for the purpose of performing such duties during the ordinary course of their work and who require access to the Confidential Information;

(2) An independent and Qualified Auditor, subject to an appropriate confidentiality agreement, who is authorized to act on behalf of the Collective with respect to verification of a Licensee's statement of account pursuant to §380.35 or on behalf of a Copyright Owner or Performer with respect to the verification of royalty distributions pursuant to §380.36;

(3) Copyright Owners and Performers, including their designated agents, whose works have been used under the statutory licenses set forth in 17 U.S.C. 112(e) and 114 by the Licensee whose Confidential Information is being supplied, subject to an appropriate confidentiality agreement, and including those employees, agents, attorneys, consultants and independent contractors of such Copyright Owners and Performers and their designated agents, subject to an appropriate confidentiality agreement, for the purpose of performing their duties during the ordinary course of their work and who require access to the Confidential Information; and

(4) In connection with future proceedings under 17 U.S.C. 112(e) and 114 before the Copyright Royalty Judges, and under an appropriate protective order, attorneys, consultants and other authorized agents of the parties to the proceedings or the courts, subject to the provisions of any relevant agreements restricting the activities of CPB, Covered Entities or the Collective in such proceedings.

(e) Safeguarding of Confidential Information. The Collective and any person identified in paragraph (d) of this section shall implement procedures to safeguard against unauthorized access to or dissemination of any Confidential Information using a reasonable standard of care, but no less than the same degree of security used to protect Confidential Information or similarly sensitive information belonging to the Collective or person.

History of 37 C.F.R. §380.34: 80 FR 59592, Jan. 1, 2016.

§380.35. VERIFICATION OF ROYALTY PAYMENTS

(a) General. This section prescribes procedures by which the Collective may verify the royalty payments made by CPB.

(b) Frequency of verification. The Collective may conduct a single audit of any Covered Entities, upon reasonable notice and during reasonable business hours, during any given calendar year, for any or all of the prior 3 calendar years, but no calendar year shall be subject to audit more than once.

(c) Notice of intent to audit. The Collective must file with the Copyright Royalty Judges a notice of intent to audit CPB and Covered Entities, which shall, within 30 days of the filing of the notice, publish in the Federal Register a notice announcing such filing. The notification of intent to audit shall be served at the same time on CPB. Any such audit shall be conducted by an independent and Qualified Auditor identified in the notice, and shall be binding on all parties.

(d) Acquisition and retention of report. CPB and Covered Entities shall use commercially reasonable efforts to obtain or to provide access to any relevant books and records maintained by third parties for the purpose of the audit. The Collective shall retain the report of the verification for a period of not less than 3 years.

(e) Consultation. Before rendering a written report to the Collective, except where the auditor has a reasonable basis to suspect fraud and disclosure would, in the reasonable opinion of the auditor, prejudice the investigation of such suspected fraud, the auditor shall review the tentative written findings of the audit with the appropriate agent or employee of CPB in order to remedy any factual errors and clarify any issues relating to the audit; Provided that an appropriate agent or employee of CPB reasonably cooperates with the auditor to remedy promptly any factual errors or clarify any issues raised by the audit.

(f) Costs of the verification procedure. The Collective shall pay the cost of the verification procedure, unless it is finally determined that there was an underpayment of 10% or more, in which case CPB shall, in addition to paying the amount of any underpayment, bear the reasonable costs of the verification procedure.

History of 37 C.F.R. §380.35: 80 FR 59592, Jan. 1, 2016.

§380.36. VERIFICATION OF ROYALTY DISTRIBUTIONS

(a) General. This section prescribes procedures by which any Copyright Owner or Performer may verify the royalty distributions made by the Collective; provided, however, that nothing contained in this section shall apply to situations where a Copyright Owner or Performer and the Collective have agreed as to proper verification methods.

(b) Frequency of verification. A Copyright Owner or Performer may conduct a single audit of the Collective upon reasonable notice and during reasonable business hours, during any given calendar year, for any or all of the prior 3 calendar years, but no calendar year shall be subject to audit more than once.

(c) Notice of intent to audit. A Copyright Owner or Performer must file with the Copyright Royalty Judges a notice of intent to audit the Collective, which shall, within 30 days of the filing of the notice, publish in the Federal Register a notice announcing such filing. The notification of intent to audit shall be served at the same time on the Collective. Any audit shall be conducted by an independent and Qualified Auditor identified in the notice, and shall be binding on all Copyright Owners and Performers.

(d) Acquisition and retention of report. The Collective shall use commercially reasonable efforts to obtain or to provide access to any relevant books and records maintained by third parties for the purpose of the audit. The Copyright Owner or Performer requesting the verification procedure shall retain the report of the verification for a period of not less than 3 years.

(e) Consultation. Before rendering a written report to a Copyright Owner or Performer, except where the auditor has a reasonable basis to suspect fraud and disclosure would, in the reasonable opinion of the auditor, prejudice the investigation of such suspected fraud, the auditor shall review the tentative written findings of the audit with the appropriate agent or employee of the Collective in order to remedy any factual errors and clarify any issues relating to the audit; Provided that the appropriate agent or employee of the Collective reasonably cooperates with the auditor to remedy promptly any factual errors or clarify any issues raised by the audit.

(f) Costs of the verification procedure. The Copyright Owner or Performer requesting the verification procedure shall pay the cost of the procedure, unless it is finally determined that there was an underpayment of 10% or more, in which case the Collective shall, in addition to paying the amount of any underpayment, bear the reasonable costs of the verification procedure.

History of 37 C.F.R. §380.36: 80 FR 59593, Jan. 1, 2016.

§380.37. UNCLAIMED FUNDS

If the Collective is unable to identify or locate a Copyright Owner or Performer who is entitled to receive a royalty distribution under this subpart, the Collective shall retain the required payment in a segregated trust account for a period of 3 years from the date of distribution. No claim to such distribution shall be valid after the expiration of the 3-year period. After expiration of this period, the Collective may apply the unclaimed funds to offset any costs deductible under 17 U.S.C. 114(g)(3). The foregoing shall apply notwithstanding the common law or statutes of any State.

History of 37 C.F.R. §380.37: 80 FR 59593, Jan. 1, 2016.

PART 381. USE OF CERTAIN COPYRIGHTED WORKS IN CONNECTION WITH NONCOMMERCIAL EDUCATIONAL BROADCASTING

A §381.1. GENERAL

This part establishes terms and rates of royalty payments for certain activities using published nondramatic musical works and published pictorial, graphic and sculptural works during a period beginning on January 1, 2018, and ending on December 31, 2022. Upon compliance with 17 U.S.C. 118, and the terms and rates of this part, a public broadcasting entity may engage in the activities with respect to such works set forth in 17 U.S.C. 118(c).

History of 37 C.F.R. §381.1: 72 FR 67647, Jan. 1, 2008; 77 FR 71105, Jan. 1, 2013; 83 FR 2740, Jan. 19, 2018.

§381.2. DEFINITION OF PUBLIC BROADCASTING ENTITY

As used in this part, the term public broadcasting entity means a noncommercial educational broadcast station as defined in section 397 of title 47 and any nonprofit institution or organization engaged in the activities described in 17 U.S.C. 118(c).

History of 37 C.F.R. §381.2: 72 FR 67647, Jan. 1, 2008.

§381.3. RESERVED

A §381.4. PERFORMANCE OF MUSICAL COMPOSITIONS BY PBS, NPR & OTHER PUBLIC BROADCASTING ENTITIES ENGAGED IN THE ACTIVITIES SET FORTH IN 17 U.S.C. 118(c)

(a) Determination of royalty rate. The following rates and terms shall apply to the performance by PBS, NPR and other public broadcasting entities engaged in activities set forth in 17 U.S.C. 118(c) of copyrighted published nondramatic musical compositions, except for public broadcasting entities covered by §§381.5 and 381.6, and except for compositions which are the subject of voluntary license agreements: The royalty shall be $1.

(1) For performance of such work in a feature presentation of PBS:

2013-2017 .... $232.18

(2) For performance of such a work as background or theme music in a PBS program:

2013-2017 .... $58.51

(3) For performance of such a work in a feature presentation of a station of PBS:

2013-2017 .... $19.84

(4) For performance of such a work as background or theme music in a program of a station of PBS:

2013-2017 .... $4.18

(5) For the performance of such a work in a feature presentation of NPR:

2013-2017 .... $23.53

(6) For the performance of such a work as background or theme music in an NPR program:

2013-2017 .... $5.70

(7) For the performance of such a work in a feature presentation of a station of NPR:

2013-2017 .... $1.66

(8) For the performance of such a work as background or theme music in a program of a station of NPR:

2013-2017 .... $.59

(9) For purposes of this schedule the rate for the performance of theme music in an entire series shall be double the single program theme rate.

(10) In the event the work is first performed in a program of a station of PBS or NPR, and such program is subsequently distributed by PBS or NPR, an additional royalty payment shall be made equal to the difference between the rate specified in this section for a program of a station of PBS or NPR, respectively, and the rate specified in this section for a PBS or NPR program, respectively.

(b) Payment of royalty rate. The required royalty rate shall be paid to each known copyright owner not later than July 31 of each calendar year for uses during the first six months of that calendar year, and not later than January 31 for uses during the last six months of the preceding calendar year.

(c) Records of use. PBS and NPR shall, upon the request of a copyright owner of a published musical work who believes a musical composition of such owner has been performed under the terms of this schedule, permit such copyright owner a reasonable opportunity to examine their standard cue sheets listing the nondramatic performances of musical compositions on PBS and NPR programs. Any local PBS and NPR station that shall be required by the provisions of any voluntary license agreement with ASCAP, BMI or SESAC covering the license period January 1, 2018, to December 31, 2022, to provide a music use report shall, upon request of a copyright owner who believes a musical composition of such owner has been performed under the terms of this schedule, permit such copyright owner to examine the report.

History of 37 C.F.R. §381.4: 72 FR 67647, Jan. 1, 2008; 77 FR 71105, Jan. 1, 2013; 83 FR 2740, Jan. 19, 2018.

A §381.5. PERFORMANCE OF MUSICAL COMPOSITIONS BY PUBLIC BROADCASTING ENTITIES LICENSED TO COLLEGES & UNIVERSITIES

(a) Scope. This section applies to the performance of copyrighted published nondramatic musical compositions by noncommercial radio stations which are licensed to accredited colleges, accredited universities, or other accredited nonprofit educational institutions and which are not affiliated with National Public Radio. For purposes of this section, accreditation of institutions providing post-secondary education shall be determined by a regional or national accrediting agency recognized by the Council for Higher Education Accreditation or the United States Department of Education; and accreditation of institutions providing elementary or secondary education shall be as recognized by the applicable state licensing authority.

(b) Voluntary license agreements. Notwithstanding the schedule of rates and terms established in this section, the rates and terms of any license agreements entered into by copyright owners and colleges, universities, and other nonprofit educational institutions concerning the performance of copyrighted musical compositions, including performances by noncommercial radio stations, shall apply in lieu of the rates and terms of this section.

(c) Royalty rate. A public broadcasting entity within the scope of this section may perform published nondramatic musical compositions subject to the following schedule of royalty rates:

(1) For all such compositions in the repertory of ASCAP, the royalty rates shall be as follows:

(i) Music fees.

Number of Full-Time Students		2018	2019	2020	2021	2022
Level 1	<1,000	$352	$359	$366	$373	$380
Level 2	1,000-4,999	407	415	423	431	440
Level 3	5,000-9,999	557	568	579	591	603
Level 4	10,000-19,999	722	736	751	766	781
Level 5	20,000+	908	926	945	964	983

(ii) Level 1 rates as set forth in paragraph (c)(1)(i) of this section, shall also apply to College Radio Stations with an authorized effective radiated power (ERP), as that term is defined in 47 CFR 73.310(a), of 100 Watts or less, as specified on its current FCC license, regardless of the size of the student population.

(2) For all such compositions in the repertory of BMI, the royalty rates shall be as follows:

(i) Music fees.

Number of Full-Time Students		2018	2019	2020	2021	2022
Level 1	<1,000	$352	$359	$366	$373	$380
Level 2	1,000-4,999	407	415	423	431	440
Level 3	5,000-9,999	557	568	579	591	603
Level 4	10,000-19,999	722	736	751	766	781
Level 5	20,000+	908	926	945	964	983

(ii) Level 1 rates, as set forth in paragraph (c)(2)(i) of this section, shall also apply to College Radio Stations with an authorized effective radiated power (ERP), as that term is defined in 47 CFR 73.310(a), of 100 Watts or less, as specified on its current FCC license, regardless of the size of the student population.

(3) For all such compositions in the repertory of SESAC, the royalty rates shall be as follows:

(i) 2018: The 2017 rate, subject to an annual cost of living adjustment in accordance with paragraph (c)(3)(vi) of this section.

(ii) 2019: The 2018 rate, subject to an annual cost of living adjustment in accordance with paragraph (c)(3)(vi) of this section.

(iii) 2020: The 2019 rate, subject to an annual cost of living adjustment in accordance with paragraph (c)(3)(vi) of this section.

(iv) 2021: The 2020 rate, subject to an annual cost of living adjustment in accordance with paragraph (c)(3)(vi) of this section.

(v) 2022: The 2021 rate, subject to an annual cost of living adjustment in accordance with paragraph (c)(3)(vi) of this section.

(vi) Such cost of living adjustment to be made in accordance with the greater of:

(A) The change, if any, in the Consumer Price Index (all consumers, all items) published by the U.S. Department of Labor, Bureau of Labor Statistics during the twelve (12) month period from the most recent Index, published before December 1 of the year immediately prior to the applicable year; or

(B) One and one-half percent (1.5%).

(4) For the performance of any other such compositions: $1.

(d) Payment of royalty rate. The public broadcasting entity shall pay the required royalty rate to ASCAP, BMI and SESAC not later than January 31 of each year. Each annual payment to ASCAP, BMI and SESAC shall be accompanied by a signed declaration stating the number of full-time students enrolled in the educational entity operating the station and/or the effective radiated power (ERP) as specified in its current FCC license. An exact copy of such declaration shall be furnished to each of ASCAP, BMI and SESAC.

(e) Records of use. A public broadcasting entity subject to this section shall furnish to ASCAP, BMI and SESAC, upon request, a music-use report during one week of each calendar year. ASCAP, BMI and SESAC shall not in any one calendar year request more than 10 stations to furnish such reports.

History of 37 C.F.R. §381.5: 72 FR 67648, Jan. 1, 2008; 73 FR 72726, Jan. 1, 2009; 74 FR 62705, Jan. 1, 2010; 75 FR 74623, Jan. 1, 2011; 76 FR 74703, Dec. 1, 2011; 77 FR 71105, Jan. 1, 2013; 78 FR 71501, Dec. 30, 2013; 79 FR 71319, Dec. 2, 2014; 80 FR 73118, Dec. 24, 2015; 81 FR 84478, Jan. 1, 2017; 83 FR 2740, Jan. 19, 2018.

A §381.6. PERFORMANCE OF MUSICAL COMPOSITIONS BY OTHER PUBLIC BROADCASTING ENTITIES

(a) Scope. This section applies to the performance of copyrighted published nondramatic musical compositions by radio stations not licensed to colleges, universities, or other nonprofit educational institutions and not affiliated with NPR. In the event that a station owned by a public broadcasting entity broadcasts programming by means of an in-band, on-channel ("IBOC") digital radio signal and such programming is different than the station's analog broadcast programming, then any such programming shall be deemed to be provided by a separate station requiring a separate royalty payment.

(b) Definitions. As used in paragraphs (d) and (e) of this section, the following terms and their variant forms mean the following:

(1) Feature Music shall mean any performance of a musical work, whether live or recorded, that is the principal focus of audience attention. Feature Music does not include bridge, background, or underscore music, themes or signatures, interstitial music between programs such as in public service announcements or program sponsorship identifications, brief musical transitions in and out of program segments (not to exceed 60 seconds in duration), incidental performances of music during broadcasts of public, religious, or sports events, or brief performances during news, talk, religious, and sports programming of no more than 30 seconds in duration.

(2) Population Count. The combination of:

(i) The number of persons estimated to reside within a station's Predicted 60 dBu Contour, based on the most recent available census data; and

(ii) The nonduplicative number of persons estimated to reside in the Predicted 60 dBu Contour of any Translator or Booster Station that extends a public broadcasting entity's signal beyond the contours of a station's Predicted 60 dBu Contour.

(iii) In determining Population Count, a station or a Translator or Booster Station may use and report the total population data, from a research company generally recognized in the broadcasting industry, for the radio market within which the station's community license is located.

(3) Predicted 60 dBu Contour shall be calculated as set forth in 47 CFR 73.313.

(4) Talk Format Station shall mean a noncommercial radio station:

(i) Whose program content primarily consists of talk shows, news programs, sports, community affairs or religious sermons (or other non-music-oriented programming);

(ii) That performs Feature Music in less than 20% of its programming annually; and

(iii) That performs music-oriented programming for no more than four (4) programming hours during the hours from 6 a.m. to 10 p.m. each weekday, with no two (2) hours of such programming occurring consecutively, with the exception of up to five (5) weekdays during the year.

(5) Weekday shall mean the 24-hour period starting at 12 a.m. through 11:59 p.m. on Mondays, Tuesdays, Wednesdays, Thursdays and Fridays occurring between January 1 of a given year up to and including Thanksgiving day of that year.

(6) Translator Station and Booster Station shall have the same meanings as set forth in 47 CFR 74.1201.

(c) Voluntary license agreements. Notwithstanding the schedule of rates and terms established in this section, the rates and terms of any license agreements entered into by copyright owners and noncommercial radio stations within the scope of this section concerning the performance of copyrighted musical compositions, including performances by noncommercial radio stations, shall apply in lieu of the rates and terms of this section.

(d) Royalty rate. A public broadcasting entity within the scope of this section may perform published nondramatic musical compositions subject to the following schedule of royalty rates:

(1) For all such compositions in the repertory of ASCAP, the royalty rates shall be as follows:

(i) Music Fees (Stations with 20% or more programming containing Feature Music):

POPULATION COUNT		2018	2019	2020	2021	2022
Level 1	0-249,999	$697	$711	$725	$739	$754
Level 2	250,000-499,999	1,243	1,268	1,294	1,319	1,346
Level 3	500,000-999,999	1,864	1,901	1,939	1,978	2,017
Level 4	1,000,000-1,499,999	2,486	2,535	2,586	2,638	2,691
Level 5	1,500,000-1,999,999	3,107	3,169	3,232	3,297	3,363
Level 6	2,000,000-2,499,999	3,728	3,803	3,879	3,956	4,035
Level 7	2,500,000-2,999,999	4,349	4,436	4,525	4,615	4,708
Level 8	3,000,000 and above	6,214	6,338	6,465	6,594	6,726

(ii) Talk Format Station Fees (Stations with <20% Feature Music programming):

POPULATION COUNT		2018	2019	2020	2021	2022
Level 1	0-249,999	$697	$711	$725	$739	$754
Level 2	250,000-499,999	697	711	725	739	754
Level 3	500,000-999,999	697	711	725	739	754
Level 4	1,000,000-1,499,999	870	887	905	923	942
Level 5	1,500,000-1,999,999	1,087	1,109	1,131	1,154	1,177
Level 6	2,000,000-2,499,999	1,305	1,331	1,357	1,384	1,412

POPULATION COUNT		2018	2019	2020	2021	2022
Level 7	2,500,000-2,999,999	1,522	1,552	1,583	1,615	1,647
Level 8	3,000,000 and above	2,175	2,218	2,262	2,308	2,354

(2) For all such compositions in the repertory of BMI, the royalty rates shall be as follows:

(i) Music Fees (Stations with 20% or more programming containing Feature Music):

POPULATION COUNT		2018	2019	2020	2021	2022
Level 1	0-249,999	$697	$711	$725	$739	$754
Level 2	250,000-499,999	1,243	1,268	1,294	1,319	1,346
Level 3	500,000-999,999	1,864	1,901	1,939	1,978	2,017
Level 4	1,000,000-1,499,999	2,486	2,535	2,586	2,638	2,691
Level 5	1,500,000-1,999,999	3,017	3,169	3,232	3,297	3,363
Level 6	2,000,000-2,499,999	3,728	3,803	3,879	3,956	4,035
Level 7	2,500,000-2,999,999	4,349	4,436	4,525	4,615	4,708
Level 8	3,000,000 and above	6,214	6,338	6,465	6,594	6,726

(ii) Talk Format Station Fees (Stations with <20% Feature Music programming):

POPULATION COUNT		2018	2019	2020	2021	2022
Level 1	0-249,999	$697	$711	$725	$739	$754
Level 2	250,000-499,999	697	711	725	739	754
Level 3	500,000-999,999	697	711	725	739	754
Level 4	1,000,000-1,499,999	870	887	905	923	942
Level 5	1,500,000-1,999,999	1,087	1,109	1,131	1,154	1,177
Level 6	2,000,000-2,499,999	1,305	1,331	1,357	1,384	1,412
Level 7	2,500,000-2,999,999	1,522	1,552	1,583	1,615	1,647
Level 8	3,000,000 and above	2,175	2,218	2,262	2,308	2,354

(3) For all such compositions in the repertory of SESAC, the royalty rates shall be as follows:

(i) Music fees for stations with >=20% Feature Music programming:

POPULATION COUNT		2018	2019	2020	2021	2022
Level 1	0-249,999	$152	$155	$158	$161	$164
Level 2	250,000-499,999	253	258	263	268	274
Level 3	500,000-999,999	380	388	396	403	411
Level 4	1,000,000-1,499,999	507	517	527	538	548
Level 5	1,500,000-1,999,999	634	647	660	673	686
Level 6	2,000,000-2,499,999	760	775	790	806	822
Level 7	2,500,000-2,999,999	887	905	923	941	960
Level 8	3,000,000 and above	1,268	1,293	1,318	1,344	1,371

(ii) Talk fees for stations with <20% Feature Music programming:

POPULATION COUNT		2018	2019	2020	2021	2022
Level 1	0-249,999	$152	$155	$158	$161	$164
Level 2	250,000-499,999	152	155	158	161	164
Level 3	500,000-999,999	152	155	158	161	164
Level 4	1,000,000-1,499,999	177	181	185	188	192
Level 5	1,500,000-1,999,999	222	227	231	236	240
Level 6	2,000,000-2,499,999	266	271	277	282	288
Level 7	2,500,000-2,999,999	311	317	323	330	336
Level 8	3,000,000 and above	444	452	461	470	480

(4) For the performance of any other such compositions, in 2018 through 2022, $1.

(e) Payment of royalty rate. The public broadcasting entity shall pay the required royalty rate to ASCAP, BMI and SESAC not later than January 31 of each year. Each annual payment shall be accompanied by a signed declaration stating the Population Count of the public broadcasting entity and the source for such Population Count. An exact copy of such declaration shall be furnished to each of ASCAP, BMI and SESAC. Upon prior written notice thereof from ASCAP, BMI and SESAC, a public broadcasting entity shall make its books and records relating to its Population Count available for inspection. In the event that a public broadcasting entity wishes to be deemed a Talk Format Station, then such entity shall provide a signed declaration stating that Feature Music is performed in less than 20% of its annual programming and that it complies with the caps set forth in paragraph (b)(4) of this section. An exact copy of such declaration shall be furnished to each of ASCAP, BMI and SESAC. Upon prior written notice thereof from ASCAP, BMI or SESAC, a public broadcasting entity shall make its program schedule or other documentation supporting its eligibility as a Talk Format Station available for inspection.

(f) Records of use. A public broadcasting entity subject to this section shall furnish to ASCAP, BMI and SESAC, upon request, a music-use report during one week of each calendar year. ASCAP, BMI and SESAC each shall not in any one calendar year request more than 10 stations to furnish such reports.

History of 37 C.F.R. §381.6: 72 FR 67648, Jan. 1, 2008; 77 FR 71106, Jan. 1, 2013; 83 FR 2741, Jan. 19, 2018.

A §381.7. RECORDING RIGHTS, RATES & TERMS

(a) Scope. This section establishes rates and terms for the recording of nondramatic performances and displays of musical works, other than compositions subject to voluntary license agreements, on and for the radio and television programs of public broadcasting entities, whether or not in synchronization or timed relationship with the visual or aural content, and for the making, reproduction, and distribution of copies and phonorecords of public broadcasting programs containing such nondramatic performances and displays of musical works solely for the purpose of transmission by public broadcasting entities. The rates and terms established in this schedule include the making of the reproductions described in 17 U.S.C. 118(c)(3).

(b) Royalty rate. **(1)(i)** For uses described in paragraph (a) of this section of a musical work in a PBS-distributed program, the royalty fees shall be calculated by multiplying the following per-composition rates by the number of different compositions in that PBS-distributed program:

	2018-2022
(A) Feature	$118.70
(B) Concert feature (per minute)	35.65
(C) Background	59.99
(D) Theme:	
(1) Single program or first series program	59.99
(2) Other series program	24.36

(ii) For such uses other than in a PBS-distributed television program, the royalty fee shall be calculated by multiplying the following per-composition rates by the number of different compositions in that program:

	2018-2022
(A) Feature	$9.81
(B) Concert feature (per minute)	2.58
(C) Background	4.26
(D) Theme:	
(1) Single program or first series program	4.26
(2) Other series program	1.69

(iii) In the event the work is first recorded other than in a PBS-distributed program, and such program is subsequently distributed by PBS, an additional royalty payment shall be made equal to the difference between the rate specified in this section for other than a PBS-distributed program and the rate specified in this section for a PBS-distributed program.

(2) For uses licensed herein of a musical work in a NPR program, the royalty fees shall be calculated by multiplying the following per-composition rates by the number of different compositions in any NPR program distributed by NPR. For purposes of this schedule "National Public Radio" programs include all programs produced in whole or in part by NPR, or by any NPR station or organization under contract with NPR.

	2018-2022
(i) Feature	$12.85
(ii) Concert feature (per minute)	18.86
(iii) Background	6.44
(iv) Theme:	
(A) Single program or first series program	6.44
(B) Other series program	2.57

(3) For purposes of this schedule, a "Concert Feature" shall be deemed to be the nondramatic presentation in a program of all or part of a symphony, concerto, or other serious work originally written for concert performance, or the nondramatic presentation in a program of portions of a serious work originally written for opera performance.

(4) For such uses other than in an NPR-produced radio program:

	2018-2022
(i) Feature	$.81
(ii) Feature (concert) (per half hour)	1.69
(iii) Background	.41

(5) The schedule of fees covers use for a period of three years following the first use. Succeeding use periods will require the following additional payment: Additional one-year period—25 percent of the initial three-year fee; second three-year period—50 percent of the initial three-year fee; each three-year fee thereafter—25 percent of the initial three-year fee; provided that a 100 percent additional payment prior to the expiration of the first three-year period will cover use during all subsequent use periods without limitation. Such succeeding uses which are subsequent to December 31, 2017, shall be subject to the royalty rates established in this schedule.

(c) Payment of royalty rates. The required royalty rates shall be paid to each known copyright owner not later than July 31 of each calendar year for uses during the first six months of that calendar year, and not later than January 31 for uses during the last six months of the preceding calendar year.

(d) Records of use—(1) Maintenance of cue sheets. PBS and its stations, NPR, or other public broadcasting entities shall maintain and make available for examination pursuant to paragraph (e) of this section copies of their standard cue sheets or summaries of same listing the recording of the musical works of such copyright owners.

(2) Content of cue sheets or summaries. Such cue sheets or summaries shall include:

(i) The title, composer and author to the extent such information is reasonably obtainable.

(ii) The type of use and manner of performance thereof in each case.

(iii) For Concert Feature music, the actual recorded time period on the program, plus all distribution and broadcast information available to the public broadcasting entity.

(e) Filing of use reports with the Copyright Royalty Judges. Deposit of cue sheets or summaries. PBS and its stations, NPR, or other television public broadcasting entity shall deposit with the Copyright Royalty Judges one electronic copy in Portable Document Format (PDF) on compact disk (an optical data storage medium such as a CD-ROM, CD-R or CD-RW) or floppy diskette of their standard music cue sheets or summaries of same listing the recording pursuant to this schedule of the musical works of copyright owners. Such cue sheets or summaries shall be deposited not later than July 31 of each calendar year for recordings during the first six months of the calendar year and not later than January 31 of each calendar year for recordings during the second six months of the preceding calendar year. PBS and NPR shall maintain at their offices copies of all standard music cue sheets from which such music use reports are prepared. Such music cue sheets shall be furnished to the Copyright Royalty Judges upon their request and also shall be available during regular business hours at the offices of PBS or NPR for examination by a copyright owner who believes a musical composition of such owner has been recorded pursuant to this schedule.

History of 37 C.F.R. §381.7: 72 FR 67649, Jan. 1, 2008; 77 FR 71108, Jan. 1, 2013; 83 FR 2742, Jan. 19, 2018.

§381.8. TERMS & RATES OF ROYALTY PAYMENTS FOR THE USE OF PUBLISHED PICTORIAL, GRAPHIC, & SCULPTURAL WORKS

(a) Scope. This section establishes rates and terms for the use of published pictorial, graphic, and sculptural works by public broadcasting entities for the activities described in 17 U.S.C. 118. The rates and terms established in this schedule include the making of the reproductions described in 17 U.S.C. 118(c).

(b) Royalty rate. (1) The following schedule of rates shall apply to the use of works within the scope of this section:

(i) For such uses in a PBS-distributed program:

	2013-2017
(A) For featured display of a work	$70.75
(B) For background and montage display	34.50
(C) For use of a work program identification or for thematic use	139.46
(D) For the display of an art reproduction copyrighted separately from the work of fine art from which the work was reproduced irrespective of whether the reproduced work of fine art is copyrighted so as to be subject also to payment of a display fee under the terms of the schedule	45.82

(ii) For such uses in other than PBS-distributed programs:

	2013-2017
(A) For featured display of a work	$45.82
(B) For background and montage display	23.48
(C) For use of a work program identification or for thematic use	93.65
(D) For the display of an art reproduction copyrighted separately from the work of fine art from which the work was reproduced irrespective of whether the reproduced work of fine art is copyrighted so as to be subject also to payment of a display fee under the terms of the schedule	23.49

(2) For the purposes of the schedule in paragraph (b)(1) of this section the rate for the thematic use of a work in an entire series shall be double the single program theme rate. In the event the work is first used other than in a PBS-distributed program, and such program is subsequently distributed by PBS, an additional royalty payment shall be made equal to the difference between the rate specified in this sec-

tion for other than a PBS-distributed program and the rate specified in this section for a PBS-distributed program.

(3) "Featured display" for purposes of this schedule means a full-screen or substantially full-screen display appearing on the screen for more than three seconds. Any display less than full-screen or substantially full-screen, or full-screen for three seconds or less, is deemed to be a "background or montage display."

(4) "Thematic use" is the utilization of the works of one or more artists where the works constitute the central theme of the program or convey a story line.

(5) "Display of an art reproduction copyrighted separately from the work of fine art from which the work was reproduced" means a transparency or other reproduction of an underlying work of fine art.

(c) Payment of royalty rate. PBS or other public broadcasting entity shall pay the required royalty fees to each copyright owner not later than July 31 of each calendar year for uses during the first six months of that calendar year, and not later than January 31 for uses during the last six months of the preceding calendar year.

(d) Records of use. (1) PBS and its stations or other public broadcasting entity shall maintain and furnish either to copyright owners, or to the offices of generally recognized organizations representing the copyright owners of pictorial, graphic and sculptural works, copies of their standard lists containing the pictorial, graphic, and sculptural works displayed on their programs. Such notice shall include the name of the copyright owner, if known, the specific source from which the work was taken, a description of the work used, the title of the program on which the work was used, and the date of the original broadcast of the program.

(2) Such listings shall be furnished not later than July 31 of each calendar year for displays during the first six months of the calendar year, and not later than January 31 of each calendar year for displays during the second six months of the preceding calendar year.

(e) Filing of use reports with the Copyright Royalty Judges. (1) PBS and its stations or other public broadcasting entity shall deposit with the Copyright Royalty Judges one electronic copy in Portable Document Format (PDF) on compact disk (an optical data storage medium such as a CD-ROM, CD-R or CD-RW) or floppy diskette of their standard lists containing the pictorial, graphic, and sculptural works displayed on their programs. Such notice shall include the name of the copyright owner, if known, the specific source from which the work was taken, a description of the work used, the title of the program on which the work was used, and the date of the original broadcast of the program.

(2) Such listings shall be furnished not later than July 31 of each calendar year for displays during the first six months of the calendar year, and not later than January 31 of each calendar year for displays during the second six months of the preceding calendar year.

(f) Terms of use. (1) The rates of this schedule are for unlimited use for a period of three years from the date of the first use of the work under this schedule. Succeeding use periods will require the following additional payment: Additional one-year period—25 percent of the initial three-year fee; second three-year period—50 percent of the initial three-year fee; each three-year period thereafter—25 percent of the initial three-year fee; provided that a 100 percent additional payment prior to the expiration of the first three-year period will cover use during all subsequent use periods without limitation. Such succeeding uses which are subsequent to December 31, 2017, shall be subject to the rates established in this schedule.

(2) Pursuant to the provisions of 17 U.S.C. 118(e), nothing in this schedule shall be construed to permit, beyond the limits of fair use as provided in 17 U.S.C. 107, the production of a transmission program drawn to any substantial extent from a published compilation of pictorial, graphic, or sculptural works.

History of 37 C.F.R. §381.8: 72 FR 67651, Jan. 1, 2008; 77 FR 71108, Jan. 1, 2013.

§381.9. Unknown Copyright Owners

If PBS and its stations, NPR and its stations, or other public broadcasting entity is not aware of the identity of, or unable to locate, a copyright owner who is entitled to receive a royalty payment under this part, they shall retain the required fee in a segregated trust account for a period of three years from the date of the required payment. No claim to such royalty fees shall be valid after the expiration of the three-year period. Public broadcasting entities may establish a joint trust fund for the purposes of this section. Public broadcasting entities shall make available to the Copyright Royalty Judges, upon request, information concerning fees deposited in trust funds.

History of 37 C.F.R. §381.9: 72 FR 67652, Jan. 1, 2008.

A §381.10. Cost of Living Adjustment

(a) On or before December 1, 2018, the Copyright Royalty Judges shall publish in the Federal Register a notice of the change in the cost of living as determined by the Consumer Price Index (all consumers, all items) during the period from the most recent Index published prior to December 1, 2017, to the most recent Index published prior to December 1, 2018. On or before each December 1 thereafter the Copyright Royalty Judges shall publish a notice of the change in the cost of living during the period from the most recent index published prior to the previous notice, to the most recent Index published prior to December 1, of that year.

(b) On the same date of the notices published pursuant to paragraph (a) of this section, the Copyright Royalty Judges shall publish in the Federal Register a revised schedule of the rates for §381.5(c)(3), the rate to be charged for compositions in the repertory of SESAC, which shall adjust the royalty amounts established in a dollar amount according to the greater of:

(1) The change in the cost of living determined as provided in paragraph (a) of this section; or

(2) One-and-a-half percent (1.5%).

(3) Such royalty rates shall be fixed at the nearest dollar.

(c) The adjusted schedule for the rates for §381.5(c)(3) shall become effective thirty (30) days after publication in the Federal Register.

History of 37 C.F.R. §381.10: 72 FR 67652, Jan. 1, 2008; 77 FR 71109, Jan. 1, 2013; 83 FR 2743, Jan. 19, 2018.

§381.11. NOTICE OF RESTRICTIONS ON USE OF REPRODUCTIONS OF TRANSMISSION PROGRAMS

Any public broadcasting entity which, pursuant to 17 U.S.C. 118, supplies a reproduction of a transmission program to governmental bodies or nonprofit institutions shall include with each copy of the reproduction a warning notice stating in substance that the reproductions may be used for a period of not more than seven days from the specified date of transmission, that the reproductions must be destroyed by the user before or at the end of such period, and that a failure to fully comply with these terms shall subject the body or institution to the remedies for infringement of copyright.

History of 37 C.F.R. §381.11: 72 FR 67652, Jan. 1, 2008.

PART 382. RATES & TERMS FOR DIGITAL TRANSMISSIONS OF SOUND RECORDINGS & THE REPRODUCTION OF EPHEMERAL RECORDINGS BY PREEXISTING SUBSCRIPTION SERVICES & PREEXISTING SATELLITE DIGITAL AUDIO RADIO SERVICES

SUBPART A. PREEXISTING SUBSCRIPTION SERVICES

§382.1. GENERAL

(a) This subpart establishes rates and terms of royalty payments for the public performance of sound recordings by nonexempt preexisting subscription services in accordance with the provisions of 17 U.S.C. 114, and the making of Ephemeral Recordings in connection with the public performance of sound recordings by nonexempt preexisting subscription services in accordance with the provisions of 17 U.S.C. 112(e).

(b) Upon compliance with 17 U.S.C. 114 and the terms and rates of this subpart, nonexempt preexisting subscription services may engage in the activities set forth in 17 U.S.C. 114(d)(2).

(c) Upon compliance with 17 U.S.C. 112(e) and the terms and rates of this subpart, nonexempt preexisting subscription services may engage in the activities set forth in 17 U.S.C. 112(e) without limit to the number of Ephemeral Recordings made.

History of 37 C.F.R. §382.1: 72 FR 71796, Jan. 1, 2008; 78 FR 23096, Apr. 17, 2013.

§382.2. DEFINITIONS

For purposes of this subpart, the following definitions shall apply:

Collective is the collection and distribution organization that is designated by the Copyright Royalty Judges. For the 2013-2017 license term, the Collective is SoundExchange, Inc.

Copyright Owners are sound recording copyright owners who are entitled to royalty payments made under this subpart pursuant to the statutory licenses under 17 U.S.C. 112(e) and 114.

Ephemeral Recording is a phonorecord created for the purpose of facilitating a transmission of a public performance of a sound recording under a statutory license in accordance with 17 U.S.C. 114 and subject to the limitations specified in 17 U.S.C. 112(e).

GAAP shall mean generally accepted accounting principles in effect from time to time in the United States.

Gross Revenues.

(1) Gross Revenues shall mean all monies derived from the operation of the programming service of the Licensee and shall be comprised of the following:

(i) Monies received by Licensee from Licensee's carriers and directly from residential U.S. subscribers for Licensee's programming service;

(ii) Licensee's advertising revenues (as billed), or other monies received from sponsors, if any, less advertising agency commissions not to exceed 15% of those fees incurred to a recognized advertising agency not owned or controlled by Licensee;

(iii) Monies received for the provision of time on the programming service to any third party;

(iv) Monies received from the sale of time to providers of paid programming such as infomercials;

(v) Where merchandise, service, or anything of value is received by Licensee in lieu of cash consideration for the use of Licensee's programming service, the fair market value thereof or Licensee's prevailing published rate, whichever is less;

(vi) Monies or other consideration received by Licensee from Licensee's carriers, but not including monies received by Licensee's carriers from others and not accounted for by Licensee's carriers to Licensee, for the provision of hardware by anyone and used in connection with the programming service;

(vii) Monies or other consideration received for any references to or inclusion of any product or service on the programming service; and

(viii) Bad debts recovered regarding paragraphs (1)(i) through (vii) of this definition.

(2) Gross Revenues shall include such payments as set forth in paragraphs (1)(i) through (viii) of this definition to which Licensee is entitled but which are paid to a parent, subsidiary, division, or affiliate of Licensee, in lieu of payment to Licensee but not including payments to Licensee's carriers for the programming service. Licensee shall be allowed a deduction from "Gross Revenues" as defined in paragraph (1) of this definition for affiliate revenue returned during the reporting period and for bad debts actually written off during reporting period.

Licensee means any preexisting subscription service as defined in 17 U.S.C. 114(j)(11).

Performers means the independent administrators identified in 17 U.S.C. 114(g)(2)(B) and (C), and the parties identified in 17 U.S.C. 114(g)(2)(D).

Qualified Auditor is a Certified Public Accountant.

History of 37 C.F.R. §382.2: 78 FR 23096, Apr. 17, 2013.

§382.3. ROYALTY FEES FOR THE DIGITAL PERFORMANCE OF SOUND RECORDINGS & THE MAKING OF EPHEMERAL RECORDINGS BY PREEXISTING SUBSCRIPTION SERVICES

(a) Commencing January 1, 2013, and continuing through December 31, 2017, the monthly royalty fee to be paid by a Licensee for the public performance of sound recordings pursuant to 17 U.S.C. 114 and the making of any number of Ephemeral Recordings to facilitate such performances pursuant to 17 U.S.C. 112(e) shall be a percentage of monthly Gross Revenues resulting from residential services in the United States as follows: for 2013, 8%; and for 2014 through 2017, 8.5%.

(b) Each Licensee making digital performances of sound recordings pursuant to 17 U.S.C. 114 and Ephemeral Recordings pursuant to 17 U.S.C. 112(e) shall make an advance payment to the Collective of $100,000 per year, payable no later than January 20th of each year. The annual advance payment shall be nonrefundable, but it may be counted as an advance of the section 112 royalties due and payable for a given year or any month therein under paragraph (a) of this section; Provided, however, that any unused portion of an annual advance payment for a given year shall not carry over into a subsequent year.

(c) The royalty payable under 17 U.S.C. 112(e) for the making of phonorecords used by the Licensee solely to facilitate transmissions for which it pays royalties as and when provided in this subpart shall be included within, and constitute 5% of, the total royalties payable under 17 U.S.C. 112(e) and 114.

(d) A Licensee shall pay a late fee of 1.5% per month, or the highest lawful rate, whichever is lower, for each payment or statement of account, or either of them, received by the Collective after the due date. Late fees shall accrue from the due date until payment and the statement of account are received.

History of 37 C.F.R. §382.3: 72 FR 71796, Jan. 1, 2008; 78 FR 23096, Apr. 17, 2013.

§382.4. TERMS FOR MAKING PAYMENT OF ROYALTY FEES & STATEMENTS OF ACCOUNT

(a) Payment to the Collective. A Licensee shall make the royalty payments due under §382.3 to the Collective.

(b) Timing of payment. A Licensee shall make any payments due under §382.3 on a monthly basis on or before the 45th day after the end of each month for that month.

(c) Statements of Account. Licensees shall submit monthly statements of account on a form provided by the Collective. A statement of account shall contain the following information:

(1) Such information as is necessary to calculate the accompanying royalty payments;

(2) The name, address, business title, telephone number, facsimile (if any), electronic mail address and other contact information of the person to be contacted for information or questions concerning the content of the statement of account;

(3) The signature of a duly authorized officer or representative of the Licensee;

(4) The printed or typewritten name of the person signing the statement of account;

(5) The date of signature;

(6) The title or official position held in relation to the Licensee by the person signing the statement of account;

(7) A certification of the capacity of the person signing; and

(8) A statement to the following effect:

I, the undersigned officer or representative of the Licensee, have examined this statement of account and hereby state that it is true, accurate, and complete to my knowledge after reasonable due diligence.

(d) Distribution of royalties.

(1) The Collective shall promptly distribute royalties received from Licensees to Copyright Owners and Performers, or their designated agents, that are entitled to such royalties. The Collective shall be responsible only for making distributions to those Copyright Owners, Performers, or their designated agents who provide the Collective with such information as is necessary to identify the correct recipient. The Collective shall distribute royalties on a basis that values all performances by a Licensee equally based upon the information provided under the reports of use requirements for Licensees contained in §370.3 of this chapter.

(2) If the Collective is unable to locate a Copyright Owner or Performer entitled to a distribution of royalties under paragraph (d)(1) of this section within 3 years from the date of payment by a Licensee, such royalties shall be handled in accordance with §382.8.

(e) Retention of records. Both Licensees and the Collective shall maintain books and records relating to the payment of the license fees in accordance with generally accepted accounting principles for a period of three years after the end of the period for which the payment is made. These records shall include, but are not limited to, the statements of account, records documenting an interested party's share of the royalty fees, and the records pertaining to the administration of the collection process and the further distribution of the royalty fees to those interested parties entitled to receive such fees.

History of 37 C.F.R. §382.4: 72 FR 71797, Jan. 1, 2008; 76 FR 45696, Aug. 1, 2011; 78 FR 23097, Apr. 17, 2013.

§382.5. CONFIDENTIAL INFORMATION

(a) For purposes of this subpart, confidential information shall include statements of account and any information pertaining to the statements of account designated as confidential by the nonexempt preexisting subscription service filing the statement. Confidential information shall also include any information so designated in a confidentiality agreement duly executed between a nonexempt preexisting subscription service and an interested party, or between one or more interested parties; Provided that all such information shall be made available, for the verification proceedings provided for in §§382.6 and 382.7.

(b) Access to the confidential information pertaining to the royalty payments shall be subject to an appropriate confidentiality agreement and limited to:

(1) Those employees, agents, consultants and independent contractors of the Collective who are engaged in the collection and distribution of royalty payments hereunder and activities directly related hereto, who are not also employees or officers of a sound recording Copyright Owner or Performer, and who, for the purpose of performing such duties during the ordinary course of employment, require access to the records; and

(2) An independent and Qualified Auditor who is not an employee or officer of a sound recording Copyright Owner or Performer, but is authorized to act on behalf of the interested Copyright Owners with respect to the verification of the royalty payments; and

(3) Copyright Owners and Performers whose works have been used under the statutory licenses set forth in 17 U.S.C. 112(e) and 114 by the Licensee whose Confidential Information is being supplied, or agents thereof provided that the only confidential information that may be shared pursuant to this paragraph (b)(3) are the monthly statements of account that accompany royalty payments.

(c) The Collective or any person identified in paragraph (b) of this section shall implement procedures to safeguard all confidential financial and business information, including, but not limited to royalty payments, submitted as part of the statements of account, using a reasonable standard of care, but no less than the same degree of security used to protect confidential financial and business information or similarly sensitive information belonging to the Collective or such person.

History of 37 C.F.R. §382.5: 72 FR 71797, Jan. 1, 2008; 78 FR 23097, Apr. 17, 2013.

§382.6. VERIFICATION OF STATEMENTS OF ACCOUNT

(a) General. This section prescribes general rules pertaining to the verification of the statements of account by interested parties according to terms promulgated by the Copyright Royalty Board.

(b) Frequency of verification. Interested parties may conduct a single audit of a nonexempt preexisting subscription service during any given calendar year.

(c) Notice of intent to audit. Interested parties must submit a notice of intent to audit a particular service to the Copyright Royalty Board, which shall publish in the Federal Register a notice announcing the receipt of the notice of intent to audit within 30 days of the filing of the interested party's notice. Such notification of intent to audit shall also be delivered at the same time to the party to be audited.

(d) Retention of records. The party requesting the verification procedure shall retain the report of the verification for a period of three years from the date of completion of the verification process.

(e) Acceptable verification procedure. An audit, including underlying paperwork, which was performed in the ordinary course of business according to generally accepted auditing standards by an independent and Qualified Auditor, shall serve as an acceptable verification procedure for all parties.

(f) Costs of the verification procedure. The interested party or parties requesting the verification procedure shall pay all costs of the verification procedure, unless an independent and Qualified Auditor concludes that during the period audited, the Licensee underpaid royalties by an amount of five (5) percent or more; in which case, the service that made the underpayment shall bear the costs of the verification procedure.

(g) Interested parties. For purposes of this section, interested parties are those Copyright Owners who are entitled to receive royalty fees pursuant to 17 U.S.C. 114(g), their designated agents, or the Collective.

History of 37 C.F.R. §382.6: 72 FR 71797, Jan. 1, 2008; 78 FR 23097, Apr. 17, 2013.

§382.7. VERIFICATION OF ROYALTY PAYMENTS

(a) General. This section prescribes general rules pertaining to the verification of the payment of royalty fees to those parties entitled to receive such fees, according to terms promulgated by the Copyright Royalty Board.

(b) Frequency of verification. Interested parties may conduct a single audit of the Collective during any given calendar year.

(c) Notice of intent to audit. Interested parties must submit a notice of intent to audit the entity making the royalty payment to the Copyright Royalty Board, which shall publish in the Federal Register a notice announcing the receipt of the notice of intent to audit within 30 days of the filing of the interested party's notice. Such notification of intent shall also be delivered at the same time to the party to be audited.

(d) Retention of records. The interested party requesting the verification procedure shall retain the report of the verification for a period of three years after completion of the verification process.

(e) Acceptable verification procedure. An audit, including underlying paperwork, which was performed in the ordinary course of business according to generally accepted auditing standards by an independent and Qualified Auditor, shall serve as an acceptable verification procedure for all interested parties.

(f) Costs of the verification procedure. The interested party or parties requesting the verification procedure shall pay for all costs associated with the verification procedure, unless an independent and Qualified Auditor concludes that, during the period audited, the Licensee underpaid royalties in the amount of five (5) percent or more, in which case, the entity that made the underpayment shall bear the costs of the verification procedure.

(g) Interested parties. For purposes of this section, interested parties are those who are entitled to receive royalty payments pursuant to 17 U.S.C. 114(g)(2), or their designated agents.

History of 37 C.F.R. §382.7: 72 FR 71798, Jan. 1, 2008; 78 FR 23098, Apr. 17, 2013.

§382.8. UNCLAIMED FUNDS

If the Collective is unable to identify or locate a Copyright Owner or Performer who is entitled to receive a royalty distribution under this subpart, the Collective shall retain the required payment in a segregated trust account for a period of 3 years from the date of the last distribution from the royalty fund at issue. No claim to such distribution shall be valid after the expiration of the 3-year period. After expiration of the three-year claim period, the Collective may apply the unclaimed funds to offset any costs deductible under 17 U.S.C. 114(g)(3). The foregoing shall apply notwithstanding the common law or statutes of any State.

History of 37 C.F.R. §382.8: 72 FR 71798, Jan. 1, 2008; 78 FR 23098, Apr. 17, 2013.

SUBPART B. PREEXISTING SATELLITE DIGITAL AUDIO RADIO SERVICES

§382.10. GENERAL

(a) Scope. This subpart establishes rates and terms of royalty payments for the public performance of sound recordings in certain digital transmissions by Licensees in accordance with the provisions of 17 U.S.C. 114, and the making of Ephemeral Recordings by Licensees in accordance with the provisions of 17 U.S.C. 112(e), during the period from January 1, 2013, through December 31, 2017.

(b) Legal compliance. Licensees relying upon the statutory licenses set forth in 17 U.S.C. 112(e) and 114 shall comply with the requirements of those sections, the rates and terms of this subpart, and any other applicable regulations.

(c) Relationship to voluntary agreements. Notwithstanding the royalty rates and terms established in this subpart, the rates and terms of any voluntary license agreements entered into by Copyright Owners and Licensees shall apply in lieu of the rates and terms of this subpart to transmission within the scope of such agreements.

History of 37 C.F.R. §382.10: 73 FR 4102, Jan. 24, 2008; 78 FR 23098, Apr. 17, 2013.

§382.11. DEFINITIONS

For purposes of this subpart, the following definitions shall apply:

Collective is the collection and distribution organization that is designated by the Copyright Royalty Judges. For the 2013-2017 license term, the Collective is SoundExchange, Inc.

Copyright Owners are sound recording copyright owners who are entitled to royalty payments made under this subpart pursuant to the statutory licenses under 17 U.S.C. 112(e) and 114.

Directly-Licensed Recording is a sound recording for which the Licensee has previously obtained a license of all relevant rights from the Copyright Owner of such sound recording.

Ephemeral Recording is a phonorecord created for the purpose of facilitating a transmission of a public performance of a sound recording under a statutory license in accordance with 17 U.S.C. 114 and subject to the limitations specified in 17 U.S.C. 112(e).

GAAP shall mean generally accepted accounting principles in effect from time to time in the United States.

Gross Revenues.

(1) Gross Revenues shall mean revenue recognized by the Licensee in accordance with GAAP from the operation of an SDARS, and shall be comprised of the following:

(i) Subscription revenue recognized by Licensee directly from U.S. subscribers for Licensee's SDARS; and

(ii) Licensee's advertising revenues, or other monies received from sponsors, if any, attributable to advertising on channels other than those that use only incidental performances of sound recordings, less advertising agency and sales commissions.

(2) Gross Revenues shall include such payments as set forth in paragraphs (1)(i) and (ii) of the definition of "Gross Revenues" to which Licensee is entitled but which are paid to a parent, wholly-owned subsidiary or division of Licensee.

(3) Gross Revenues shall exclude:

(i) Monies or other consideration attributable to the sale and/or license of equipment and/or other technology, including but not limited to bandwidth, sales of devices that receive the Licensee's SDARS and any taxes, shipping and handling fees therefor;

(ii) Royalties paid to Licensee for intellectual property rights;

(iii) Monies or other consideration received by Licensee from the sale of phonorecords and digital phonorecord deliveries;

(iv) Sales and use taxes, shipping and handling, credit card, invoice, and fulfillment service fees;

(v) Bad debt expense, and

(vi) Revenues recognized by Licensee for the provision of

(A) Current and future data services offered for a separate charge (e.g., weather, traffic, destination information, messaging, sports scores, stock ticker information, extended program associated data, video and photographic images, and such other telematics and/or data services as may exist from time to time);

(B) Channels, programming, products and/or other services offered for a separate charge where such channels use only incidental performances of sound recordings;

(C) Channels, programming, products and/or other services provided outside of the United States; and

(D) Channels, programming, products and/or other services for which the performance of sound recordings and/or the making of Ephemeral Recordings is exempt from any license requirement or is separately licensed, including by a statutory license and, for the avoidance of doubt, webcasting, audio services bundled with television programming, interactive services, and transmissions to business establishments.

Licensee is a person that has obtained a statutory license under 17 U.S.C. 114, and the implementing regulations, to make transmissions over a preexisting satellite digital audio radio service, and has obtained a statutory license under 17 U.S.C. 112(e), and the implementing regulations, to make Ephemeral Recordings for use in facilitating such transmissions.

Performers means the independent administrators identified in 17 U.S.C. 114(g)(2)(B) and (C), and the parties identified in 17 U.S.C. 114(g)(2)(D).

Pre-1972 Recording is a sound recording fixed before February 15, 1972.

Qualified Auditor is a Certified Public Accountant.

SDARS means the preexisting satellite digital audio radio services as defined in 17 U.S.C. 114(j)(10).

Term means the period commencing January 1, 2013, and continuing through December 31, 2017.

History of 37 C.F.R. §382.11: 73 FR 4102, Jan. 24, 2008; 78 FR 23098, Apr. 17, 2013.

§382.12. ROYALTY FEES FOR THE PUBLIC PERFORMANCE OF SOUND RECORDINGS & THE MAKING OF EPHEMERAL RECORDINGS

(a) In general. The monthly royalty fee to be paid by a Licensee for the public performance of sound recordings pursuant to 17 U.S.C. 114(d)(2) and the making of any number of Ephemeral Recordings to facilitate such performances pursuant to 17 U.S.C. 112(e) shall be a percentage of monthly Gross Revenues as follows: for 2013, 9.0%; for 2014, 9.5%; for 2015, 10.0%; for 2016, 10.5%; and for 2017, 11.0%, except that the royalty fee so determined may be reduced by the Direct License Share or the Pre-1972 Recording Share as described in paragraphs (d) and (e), respectively, of this section.

(b) Ephemeral recordings. The royalty payable under 17 U.S.C. 112(e) for the making of phonorecords used by the Licensee solely to facilitate transmissions for which it pays royalties as and when provided in this subpart shall be included within, and constitute 5% of, the total royalties payable under 17 U.S.C. 112(e) and 114.

(c) Ephemeral recordings minimum fee. Each Licensee making Ephemeral Recordings pursuant to 17 U.S.C. 112(e) shall make an advance payment to the Collective of $100,000 per year, payable no later than January 20th of each year. The annual advance payment shall be nonrefundable, but it shall be considered as an advance of the Ephemeral Recordings royalties due and payable for a given year or any month therein under paragraphs (a) and (b) of this section; Provided, however, that any unused annual advance payment for a given year shall not carry over into a subsequent year.

(d) Direct license share. The percentage of monthly Gross Revenues royalty fee specified in paragraph (a) of this section may be reduced by a percentage as set forth in this paragraph (referred to herein as the "Direct License Share").

(1) Subject to paragraph (d)(3) of this section, for each month, the Direct License Share is the result of dividing the Internet Performances of Directly-Licensed Recordings on the Reference Channels by the total number of Internet Performances of all sound recordings on the Reference Channels.

(2) For purposes of paragraph (d)(1) of this section:

(i) A "Performance" is each instance in which any portion of a sound recording is publicly performed to a listener within the United States by means of a digital audio transmission or retransmission (e.g., the delivery of any portion of a single track from a compact disc to one listener) but excluding an incidental performance that both:

(A) Makes no more than incidental use of sound recordings including, but not limited to, brief musical transitions in and out of commercials or program segments, brief performances during news, talk and sports programming, brief background performances during disk jockey announcements, brief performances during commercials of sixty seconds or less in duration, or brief performances during sporting or other public events; and

(B) Other than ambient music that is background at a public event, does not contain an entire sound recording and does not feature a particular sound recording of more than thirty seconds (as in the case of a sound recording used as a theme song).

(ii) The "Reference Channels" are Internet webcast channels offered by the Licensee that directly correspond to channels offered on the Licensee's SDARS that are capable of being received on all models of Sirius radio, all models of XM radio, or either or both, and on which the programming consists primarily of music.

(3) A Direct License Share adjustment as described in paragraph (d) of this section is available to a Licensee only if—

(i) The Reference Channels constitute a large majority of the music channels offered on the Licensee's SDARS and are generally representative of the music channels offered on the Licensee's SDARS; and

(ii) The Licensee timely provides the relevant information required by §382.13(h).

(4) No performance shall be credited as an Internet Performance of a Directly-Licensed Sound Recording under this section if that performance is separately credited as an Internet Performance of a Pre-1972 sound recording under paragraph (e)(1) of this section.

(e) Pre-1972 Recording Share. The percentage of monthly Gross Revenues royalty fee specified in paragraph (a) of this section may be reduced by a percentage as set forth in this paragraph (referred to herein as the "Pre-1972 Recording Share").

(1) Subject to paragraph (e)(3) of this section, for each month, the Pre-1972 Recording Share is the result of dividing the Internet Performances of Pre-1972 Sound Recordings on the Reference Channels by the total number of Internet Performances of all sound recordings on the Reference Channels.

(2) For purposes of paragraph (e)(1) of this section:

(i) A "Performance" is each instance in which any portion of a sound recording is publicly performed to a listener within the United States by means of a digital audio transmission or retransmission (e.g., the delivery of any portion of a single track from a compact disc to one listener) but excluding an incidental performance that both:

(A) Makes no more than incidental use of sound recordings including, but not limited to, brief musical transitions in and out of commercials or program segments, brief performances during news, talk and sports programming, brief background performances during disk jockey announcements, brief performances during commercials of sixty seconds or less in duration, or brief performances during sporting or other public events; and

(B) Other than ambient music that is background at a public event, does not contain an entire sound recording and does not feature a particular sound recording of more than thirty seconds (as in the case of a sound recording used as a theme song).

(ii) The "Reference Channels" are Internet webcast channels offered by the Licensee that directly correspond to channels offered on the Licensee's SDARS that are capable of being received on all models of Sirius radio, all models of XM radio or both, and on which the programming consists primarily of music.

(3) A Pre-1972 Recording Share adjustment as described in paragraph (e) of this section is available to a Licensee only if—

(i) The Reference Channels constitute a large majority of the music channels offered on the Licensee's SDARS and are generally representative of the music channels offered on the Licensee's SDARS; and

(ii) The Licensee timely provides the relevant information required by §382.13(h).

History of 37 C.F.R. §382.12: 73 FR 4102, Jan. 24, 2008; 75 FR 5513, Mar. 5, 2010; 78 FR 23098, Apr. 17, 2013.

§382.13. TERMS FOR MAKING PAYMENT OF ROYALTY FEES & STATEMENTS OF ACCOUNT

(a) Payment to the Collective. A Licensee shall make the royalty payments due under §382.12 to the Collective.

(b) Designation of the Collective.

(1) Until such time as a new designation is made, SoundExchange, Inc., is designated as the Collective to receive statements of account and royalty payments from Licensees due under §382.12 and to distribute such royalty payments to each Copyright Owner and Performer, or their designated agents, entitled to receive royalties under 17 U.S.C. 112(e) or 114.

(2) If SoundExchange, Inc. should dissolve or cease to be governed by a board consisting of equal numbers of representatives of Copyright Owners and Performers, then it shall be replaced by a successor Collective upon the fulfillment of the requirements set forth in paragraph (b)(2)(i) of this section.

(i) By a majority vote of the nine Copyright Owner representatives and the nine Performer representatives on the SoundExchange board as of the last day preceding the condition precedent in paragraph (b)(2) of this section, such representatives shall file a petition with the Copyright Royalty Judges designating a successor to collect and distribute royalty payments to Copyright Owners and Performers entitled to receive royalties under 17 U.S.C. 112(e) or 114 that have themselves authorized the Collective.

(ii) The Copyright Royalty Judges shall publish in the Federal Register within 30 days of receipt of a petition filed under paragraph (b)(2)(i) of this section an order designating the Collective named in such petition.

(c) Monthly payments. A Licensee shall make any payments due under §382.12 on a monthly basis on or before the 45th day after the end of each month for that month. All payments shall be rounded to the nearest cent.

(d) Late payments and statements of account. A Licensee shall pay a late fee of 1.5% per month, or the highest lawful rate, whichever is lower, each for any payment or statement of account, or either of them received by the Collective after the due date. Late fees shall accrue from the due date until payment and the statement of account are received by the Collective.

(e) Statements of account. Any payment due under §382.12 shall be accompanied by a corresponding statement of account. A statement of account shall contain the following information:

(1) Such information as is necessary to calculate the accompanying royalty payments;

(2) The name, address, business title, telephone number, facsimile number (if any), electronic mail address and other contact information of the person to be contacted for information or questions concerning the content of the statement of account;

(3) The signature of a duly authorized officer or representative of the Licensee;

(4) The printed or typewritten name of the person signing the statement of account;

(5) The date of signature;

(6) The title or official position held in relation to the Licensee by the person signing the statement of account;

(7) A certification of the capacity of the person signing; and

(8) A statement to the following effect:

I, the undersigned officer or representative of the Licensee, have examined this statement of account and hereby state that it is true, accurate, and complete to my knowledge after reasonable due diligence.

(f) Distribution of royalties. **(1)** The Collective shall promptly distribute royalties received from Licensees to Copyright Owners and Performers, or their designated agents, that are entitled to such royalties. The Collective shall only be responsible for making distributions to those Copyright Owners, Performers, or their designated agents who provide the Collective with such information as is necessary to identify the correct recipient. The Collective shall distribute royalties on a basis that values all performances by a Licensee equally based upon the information provided under the reports of use requirements for Licensees contained in §370.4 of this chapter.

(2) If the Collective is unable to locate a Copyright Owner or Performer entitled to a distribution of royalties under paragraph (f)(1) of this section within 3 years from the date of payment by a Licensee, such royalties shall be handled in accordance with §382.17.

(g) Retention of records. Books and records of a Licensee and of the Collective relating to payments of and distributions of royalties shall be kept for a period of not less than the prior 3 calendar years.

(h) Notification of exclusions.

(1) As a condition to a Licensee's taking a Direct License Share adjustment as described in §382.12(d), by no later than the due date for the relevant payment under paragraph (c) of this section, the Licensee must provide the Collective a list of each Copyright Owner from which the Licensee claims to have a direct license of rights to Directly-Licensed Recordings that is in effect for the month for which the payment is made, and of each sound recording as to which the Licensee takes such an adjustment (identified by featured artist name, sound recording title, and International Standard Recording Code (ISRC) number or, alternatively to the ISRC, album title and copyright owner name). Notwithstanding §382.14, the Collective may disclose such information as reasonably necessary for it to confirm whether a claimed direct license exists and claimed sound recordings are properly excludable.

(2) As a condition to a Licensee's taking a Pre-1972 Recording Share adjustment as described in §382.12(e), by no later than the due date for the relevant payment under paragraph (c) of this section, the Licensee must provide the Collective a list of each Pre-1972 Recording as to which the Licensee takes such an adjustment (identified by featured artist name, sound recording title, and International Standard Recording Code (ISRC) number or, alternatively to the ISRC, album title and copyright owner name).

History of 37 C.F.R. §382.13: 73 FR 4103, Jan. 24, 2008; 76 FR 45696, Aug. 1, 2011; 78 FR 23099, Apr. 17, 2013.

§382.14. CONFIDENTIAL INFORMATION

(a) Definition. For purposes of this subpart, "Confidential Information" shall include the statements of account and any information contained therein, including the amount of royalty payments, and any information pertaining to the statements of account reasonably designated as confidential by the Licensee submitting the statement.

(b) Exclusion. Confidential Information shall not include documents or information that at the time of delivery to the Collective are public knowledge. The party claiming the benefit of this provision shall have the burden of proving that the disclosed information was public knowledge.

(c) Use of Confidential Information. In no event shall the Collective use any Confidential Information for any purpose other than royalty collection and distribution and activities related directly thereto.

(d) Disclosure of Confidential Information. Access to Confidential Information shall be limited, subject to an appropriate confidentiality agreement, to:

(1) Those employees, agents, attorneys, consultants and independent contractors of the Collective who are engaged in the collection and distribution of royalty payments hereunder and activities related thereto, for the purpose of performing such duties during the ordinary course of their work and who require access to the Confidential Information;

(2) An independent and Qualified Auditor who is authorized to act on behalf of the Collective with respect to verification of a Licensee's statement of account pursuant to §382.15 or on behalf of a Copyright Owner or Performer with respect to the verification of royalty distributions pursuant to §382.16;

(3) Copyright Owners and Performers, including their designated agents, whose works have been used under the statutory licenses set forth in 17 U.S.C. 112(e) and 114 by the Licensee whose Confidential Information is being supplied and including those employees, agents, attorneys, consultants and independent contractors of such Copyright Owners and Performers and their designated agents for the purpose of performing their duties during the ordinary course of their work and who require access to the Confidential Information; and

(4) In connection with future proceedings under 17 U.S.C. 112(e) and 114 before the Copyright Royalty Judges, and under an appropriate protective order, attorneys, consultants and other authorized agents of the parties to the proceedings or the courts.

(e) Safeguarding of Confidential Information. The Collective and any person identified in paragraph (d) of this section shall implement procedures to safeguard against unauthorized access to or dissemination of any Confidential Information using a reasonable standard of care, but no less than the same degree of security used to protect Confidential Information or similarly sensitive information belonging to the Collective or person.

History of 37 C.F.R. §382.14: 73 FR 4103, Jan. 24, 2008; 78 FR 23099, Apr. 17, 2013.

§382.15. VERIFICATION OF ROYALTY PAYMENTS

(a) General. This section prescribes procedures by which the Collective may verify the royalty payments made by a Licensee.

(b) Frequency of verification. The Collective may conduct a single audit of a Licensee, upon reasonable notice and during reasonable business hours, during any given calendar year, for any or all of the prior 3 calendar years, but no calendar year shall be subject to audit more than once.

(c) Notice of intent to audit. The Collective must file with the Copyright Royalty Judges a notice of intent to audit a particular Licensee, which shall, within 30 days of the filing of the notice, publish in the Federal Register a notice announcing such filing. The notification of intent to audit shall be served at the same time on the Licensee to be audited. Any such audit shall be conducted by an independent and Qualified Auditor identified in the notice, and shall be binding on all parties.

(d) Acquisition and retention of report. The Licensee shall use commercially reasonable efforts to obtain or to provide access to any relevant books and records maintained by third parties for the purpose of the audit. The Collective shall retain the report of the verification for a period of not less than 3 years.

(e) Acceptable verification procedure. An audit, including underlying paperwork, which was performed in the ordinary course of business according to generally accepted auditing standards by an independent and Qualified Auditor, shall serve as an acceptable verification procedure for all parties with respect to the information that is within the scope of the audit.

(f) Consultation. Before rendering a written report to the Collective, except where the auditor has a reasonable basis to suspect fraud and disclosure would, in the reasonable opinion of the auditor, prejudice the investigation of such suspected fraud, the auditor shall review the tentative written findings of the audit with the appropriate agent or employee of the Licensee being audited in order to remedy any factual errors and clarify any issues relating to the audit; Provided that an appropriate agent or employee of the Licensee reasonably cooperates with the auditor to remedy promptly any factual errors or clarify any issues raised by the audit.

(g) Costs of the verification procedure. The Collective shall pay all costs associated with the verification procedure, unless it determines that the Licensee underpaid royalties in an amount of 10% or more, in which case the Licensee shall, in addition to paying the amount of any underpayment, bear the reasonable costs of the verification procedure.

History of 37 C.F.R. §382.15: 73 FR 4104, Jan. 24, 2008; 78 FR 23099, Apr. 17, 2013.

§382.16. VERIFICATION OF ROYALTY DISTRIBUTIONS

(a) General. This section prescribes procedures by which any Copyright Owner or Performer may verify the royalty distributions made by the Collective; Provided, however, that nothing contained in this section shall apply to situations where a Copyright Owner or Performer and the Collective have agreed as to proper verification methods.

(b) Frequency of verification. A Copyright Owner or Performer may conduct a single audit of the Collective upon reasonable notice and during reasonable business hours, during any given calendar year, for any or all of the prior 3 calendar years, but no calendar year shall be subject to audit more than once.

(c) Notice of intent to audit. A Copyright Owner and Performer must file with the Copyright Royalty Judges a notice of intent to audit the Collective, which shall, within 30 days of the filing of the notice, publish in the Federal Register a notice announcing such filing. The notification of intent to audit shall be served at the same time on the Collective. Any audit shall be conducted by an independent and Qualified Auditor identified in the notice, and shall be binding on all Copyright Owners and Performers.

(d) Acquisition and retention of report. The Collective shall use commercially reasonable efforts to obtain or to provide access to any relevant books and records maintained by third parties for the purpose of the audit. The Copyright Owner or Performer requesting the verification procedure shall retain the report of the verification for a period of not less than 3 years.

(e) Acceptable verification procedure. An audit, including underlying paperwork, which was performed in the ordinary course of business according to generally accepted auditing standards by an independent and Qualified Auditor, shall serve as an acceptable verification procedure for all parties with respect to the information that is within the scope of the audit.

(f) Consultation. Before rendering a written report to a Copyright Owner or Performer, except where the auditor has a reasonable basis to suspect fraud and disclosure would, in the reasonable opinion of the auditor, prejudice the investigation of such suspected fraud, the auditor shall review the tentative written findings of the audit with the appropriate agent or employee of the Collective in order to remedy any factual errors and clarify any issues relating to the audit; Provided that the appropriate agent or employee of the Collective reasonably cooperates with the auditor to remedy promptly any factual errors or clarify any issues raised by the audit.

(g) Costs of the verification procedure. The Copyright Owner or Performer requesting the verification procedure shall pay all costs associated with the procedure, unless it is finally determined that the Licensee underpaid royalties in an amount of 10% or more, in which case the Collective shall, in addition to paying the amount of any underpayment, bear the reasonable costs of the verification procedure.

History of 37 C.F.R. §382.16: 73 FR 4104, Jan. 24, 2008; 78 FR 23100, Apr. 17, 2013.

§382.17. UNCLAIMED FUNDS

If the Collective is unable to identify or locate a Copyright Owner or Performer who is entitled to receive a royalty distribution under this subpart, the Collective shall retain the required payment in a segregated trust account for a period of 3 years from the date of distribution. No claim to such distribution shall be valid after the expiration of the 3-year period. After expiration of this period, the Collective may apply the unclaimed funds to offset any costs deductible under 17 U.S.C. 114(g)(3). The foregoing shall apply notwithstanding the common law or statutes of any State.

History of 37 C.F.R. §382.17: 73 FR 4104, Jan. 24, 2008.

PART 383. RATES & TERMS FOR SUBSCRIPTION TRANSMISSIONS & THE REPRODUCTION OF EPHEMERAL RECORDINGS BY CERTAIN NEW SUBSCRIPTION SERVICES

§383.1. GENERAL

(a) Scope. This part 383 establishes rates and terms of royalty payments for the public performance of sound recordings in certain digital transmissions by Licensees in accordance with the provisions of 17 U.S.C. 114, and the making of certain ephemeral recordings by Licensees in accordance with the provisions of 17 U.S.C. 112(e), during the period commencing January 1, 2016, and continuing through December 31, 2020.

(b) Legal compliance. Licensees relying upon the statutory licenses set forth in 17 U.S.C. 112(e) and 114 shall comply with the requirements of those sections and the rates and terms of this part.

(c) Relationship to voluntary agreements. Notwithstanding the royalty rates and terms established in this part, the rates and terms of any voluntary license agreements entered into by Copyright Owners and Licensees shall apply in lieu of the rates and terms of this part to transmissions with the scope of such agreements.

History of 37 C.F.R. §383.1: 72 FR 72254, Jan. 22, 2008; 75 FR 14075, Jan. 1, 2011; 80 FR 36928, Jan. 1, 2016.

§383.2. DEFINITIONS

For purposes of this part, the following definitions shall apply:

(a) Bundled Contracts means contracts between the Licensee and a Provider in which the Service is not the only content licensed by the Licensee to the Provider.

(b) Copyright Owner is a sound recording copyright owner who is entitled to receive royalty payments made under this part pursuant to statutory licenses under 17 U.S.C. 112(e) and 114.

(c) License Period means the period commencing January 1, 2016, and continuing through December 31, 2020.

(d) Licensee is a person that has obtained statutory licenses under 17 U.S.C. 112(e) and 114, and the implementing regulations, to make digital audio transmissions as part of a Service (as defined in paragraph (f) of this section), and ephemeral recordings for use in facilitating such transmissions.

(e) Provider means a "multichannel video programming distributor" as that term is defined in 47 CFR 76.1000(e); notwithstanding such definition, for purposes of this part, a Provider shall include only a distributor of programming to televisions, such as a cable or satellite television provider.

(f) A Service is a non-interactive (consistent with the definition of "interactive service" in 17 U.S.C. 114(j)(7)) audio-only subscription service (including accompanying information and graphics related to the audio) that is transmitted to residential subscribers of a television service through a Provider which is marketed as and is in fact primarily a video service where

(1) Subscribers do not pay a separate fee for audio channels.

(2) The audio channels are delivered by digital audio transmissions through a technology that is incapable of tracking the individual sound recordings received by any particular consumer.

(3) However, paragraph (f)(2) of this section shall not apply to the Licensee's current contracts with Providers that are in effect as of the effective date of this part if such Providers become capable in the future of tracking the individual sound recordings received by any particular consumer, provided that the audio channels continued to be delivered to Subscribers by digital audio transmissions and the Licensee remains incapable of tracking the individual sound recordings received by any particular consumer.

(g) Subscriber means every residential subscriber to the underlying service of the Provider who receives Licensee's Service in the United States for all or any part of a month; provided, however, that for any Licensee that is not able to track the number of subscribers on a per-day basis, "Subscribers" shall be calculated based on the average of the number of subscribers on the last day of the preceding month and the last day of the applicable month, unless the Service is paid by the Provider based on end-of-month numbers, in which event "Subscribers" shall be counted based on end-of-month data.

(h) Stand-Alone Contracts means contracts between the Licensee and a Provider in which the only content licensed to the Provider is the Service.

History of 37 C.F.R. §383.2: 72 FR 72254, Jan. 22, 2008; 75 FR 14075, Jan. 1, 2011; 80 FR 36928, Jan. 1, 2016.

§383.3. ROYALTY FEES FOR PUBLIC PERFORMANCES OF SOUND RECORDINGS & THE MAKING OF EPHEMERAL RECORDINGS

(a) Royalty rates. Royalty rates for the public performance of sound recordings by eligible digital transmissions made over a Service pursuant to 17 U.S.C. 114, and for ephemeral recordings of sound recordings made pursuant to 17 U.S.C. 112(e) to facilitate such transmissions during the License Period, are as follows. Each Licensee will pay, with respect to content covered by the statutory licenses that is provided via the Service of each such Licensee:

(1) For Stand-Alone Contracts, the following monthly payment per Subscriber to the Service of such Licensee:

(i) 2016: $0.0179;

(ii) 2017: $0.0185;

(iii) 2018: $0.0190;

(iv) 2019: $0.0196;

(v) 2020: $0.0202;

(2) For Bundled Contracts, the following monthly payment per Subscriber to the Service of such Licensee:

(i) 2016: $0.0299;

(ii) 2017: $0.0308;

(iii) 2018: $0.0317;

(iv) 2019: $0.0326;

(v) 2020: $0.0336;

(b) Minimum fee. Each Licensee will pay an annual, non-refundable minimum fee of one hundred thousand dollars ($100,000), payable on January 31 of each calendar year in which the Service is provided pursuant to the section 112(e) and 114 statutory licenses. Such fee shall be recoupable and credited against royalties due in the calendar year in which it is paid.

(c) Ephemeral recordings. The royalty payable under 17 U.S.C. 112(e) for the making of phonorecords used by the Licensee solely to facilitate transmissions during the License Period for which it pays royalties as and when provided in this part shall be included within, and constitute 5% of, such royalty payments.

History of 37 C.F.R. §383.3: 72 FR 72255, Jan. 22, 2008; 75 FR 14075, Jan. 1, 2011; 80 FR 36928, Jan. 1, 2016.

§383.4. TERMS FOR MAKING PAYMENT OF ROYALTY FEES

(a) Terms in general. Subject to the provisions of this section, terms governing timing and due dates of royalty payments to the Collective, late fees, statements of account, audit and verification of royalty payments and distributions, cost of audit and verification, record retention requirements, treatment of Licensees' confidential information, distribution of royalties by the Collective, unclaimed funds, designation of the Collective, and any definitions for applicable terms not defined herein and not otherwise inapplicable shall be those adopted by the Copyright Royalty Judges for subscription transmissions and the reproduction of ephemeral recordings by preexisting satellite digital audio radio services in 37 CFR part 382, subpart B of this chapter, for the license period 2013-2017. For purposes of this section, the term "Collective" refers to the collection and distribution organization that is designated by the Copyright Royalty Judges. For the License Period through 2020, the sole Collective is SoundExchange, Inc.

(b) Reporting of performances. Without prejudice to any applicable notice and recordkeeping provisions, statements of account shall not require reports of performances.

(c) Applicable regulations. To the extent not inconsistent with this part, all applicable regulations, including part 370 of this chapter, shall apply to activities subject to this part.

History of 37 C.F.R. §383.4: 72 FR 72256, Jan. 22, 2008; 75 FR 14075, Jan. 1, 2011; 80 FR 36928, Jan. 1, 2016.

PART 384. RATES & TERMS FOR THE MAKING OF EPHEMERAL RECORDINGS BY BUSINESS ESTABLISHMENT SERVICES

§384.1. GENERAL

(a) Scope. This part 384 establishes rates and terms of royalty payments for the making of Ephemeral Recordings by a Business Establishment Service, as defined in §384.2, in accordance with the provisions of 17 U.S.C. 112(e), during the period January 1, 2014, through December 31, 2018 (the "License Period").

(b) Legal compliance. Licensees relying upon the statutory license set forth in 17 U.S.C. 112(e) shall comply with the requirements of that section, the rates and terms of this part and any other applicable regulations.

(c) Relationship to voluntary agreements. Notwithstanding the royalty rates and terms established in this part, the rates and terms of any license agreements entered into by Copyright Owners and Licensees shall apply in lieu of the rates and terms of this part to the making of Ephemeral Recordings within the scope of such agreements.

History of 37 C.F.R. §384.1: 73 FR 16200, Jan. 1, 2009; 78 FR 66277, Jan. 1, 2014.

§384.2. DEFINITIONS

For purposes of this part, the following definitions shall apply:

Business Establishment Service means a service making transmissions of sound recordings under the limitation on exclusive rights specified by 17 U.S.C. 114(d)(1)(C)(iv).

Collective is the collection and distribution organization that is designated by the Copyright Royalty Judges. For the License Period, the Collective is SoundExchange, Inc.

Copyright Owners are sound recording copyright owners who are entitled to royalty payments made under this part pursuant to the statutory license under 17 U.S.C. 112(e).

Ephemeral Recording is a phonorecord created for the purpose of facilitating a transmission of a public performance of a sound recording under the limitations on exclusive rights specified by 17 U.S.C. 114(d)(1)(C)(iv), and subject to the limitations specified in 17 U.S.C. 112(e).

Licensee is a Business Establishment Service that has obtained a compulsory license under 17 U.S.C. 112(e) and the implementing regulations therefor to make Ephemeral Recordings.

Performers means the independent administrators identified in 17 U.S.C. 114(g)(2)(B) and (C) and the parties identified in 17 U.S.C. 114(g)(2)(D).

Qualified Auditor is a certified public accountant.

History of 37 C.F.R. §384.2: 73 FR 16200, Jan. 1, 2009; 78 FR 66277, Jan. 1, 2014.

§384.3. ROYALTY FEES FOR EPHEMERAL RECORDINGS

(a) Basic royalty rate. For the making of any number of Ephemeral Recordings in the operation of a Business Establishment Service, a Licensee shall pay 12.5% of such Licensee's "Gross Proceeds" derived from the use in such service of musical programs that are attributable to copyrighted recordings. "Gross Proceeds" as used in this section means all fees and payments, including those made in kind, received from any source before, during or after the License Period that are derived from the use of copyrighted sound recordings during the License Period pursuant to 17 U.S.C. 112(e) for the sole purpose of facilitating a transmission to the public of a performance of a sound recording under the limitation on exclusive rights specified in 17 U.S.C. 114(d)(1)(C)(iv). The attribution of Gross Proceeds to copyrighted recordings may be made on the basis of:

(1) For classical programs, the proportion that the playing time of copyrighted classical recordings bears to the total playing time of all classical recordings in the program, and

(2) For all other programs, the proportion that the number of copyrighted recordings bears to the total number of all recordings in the program.

(b) Minimum fee. Each Licensee shall pay a minimum fee of $10,000 for each calendar year of the License Period in which it makes Ephemeral Recordings for use to facilitate transmissions under the limitation on exclusive rights specified by 17 U.S.C. 114(d)(1)(C)(iv), whether or not it does so for all or any part of the year. These minimum fees shall be nonrefundable, but shall be fully creditable to royalty payments due under paragraph (a) of this section for the same calendar year (but not any subsequent calendar year).

(c) Other royalty rates and terms. This part 384 does not apply to persons or entities other than Licensees, or to Licensees to the extent that they make other types of ephemeral recordings beyond those set forth in paragraph (a) of this section. For ephemeral recordings other than those governed by paragraph (a) of this section, persons making such ephemeral recordings must pay royalties, to the extent (if at all) applicable, under 17 U.S.C. 112(e) or as prescribed by other law, regulation or agreement.

History of 37 C.F.R. §384.3: 73 FR 16200, Jan. 1, 2009; 78 FR 66277, Jan. 1, 2014.

§384.4. TERMS FOR MAKING PAYMENT OF ROYALTY FEES & STATEMENTS OF ACCOUNT

(a) Payment to the Collective. A Licensee shall make the royalty payments due under §384.3 to the Collective.

(b) Designation of the Collective. **(1)** Until such time as a new designation is made, SoundExchange, Inc., is designated as the Collective to receive statements of account and royalty payments from Licensees due under §384.3 and to distribute such royalty payments to each Copyright Owner, or their designated agents, entitled to receive royalties under 17 U.S.C. 112(e).

(2) If SoundExchange, Inc. should dissolve or cease to be governed by a board consisting of equal numbers of representatives of Copyright Owners and Performers, then it shall be replaced by a successor Collective upon the fulfillment of the requirements set forth in paragraph (b)(2)(i) of this section.

(i) By a majority vote of the nine Copyright Owner representatives and the nine Performer representatives on the SoundExchange board as of the last day preceding the condition precedent in this paragraph (b)(2), such representatives shall file a petition with the Copyright Royalty Judges designating a successor to collect and distribute royalty payments to Copyright Owners entitled to receive royalties under 17 U.S.C. 112(e) that have themselves authorized the Collective.

(ii) The Copyright Royalty Judges shall publish in the Federal Register within 30 days of receipt of a petition filed under paragraph (b)(2)(i) of this section an order designating the Collective named in such petition.

(c) Monthly payments. A Licensee shall make any payments due under §384.3(a) on a monthly basis on or before the 45th day after the end of each month for that month. All monthly payments shall be rounded to the nearest cent.

(d) Minimum payments. A Licensee shall make any minimum payment due under §384.3(b) by January 31 of the applicable calendar year, except that payment by a Licensee that has not previously made Ephemeral Recordings pursuant to the license under 17 U.S.C. 112(e) shall be due by the 45th day after the end of the month in which the Licensee commences to do so.

(e) Late payments. A Licensee shall pay a late fee of 1.0% per month, or the highest lawful rate, whichever is lower, if either or both a required payment or statement of account for a required payment is received by the Collective after the due date. Late fees shall accrue from the due date until both the payment and statement of account are received by the Collective.

(f) Statements of account. For any part of the License Period during which a Licensee operates a Business Establishment Service, at the time when a minimum payment is due under paragraph (d) of this section, and by 45 days after the end of each month during the period, the Licensee shall deliver to the Collective a statement of account containing the information set forth set forth[1] in this paragraph (f) on a form prepared, and made available to Licensees, by the Collective. In the case of a minimum payment, or if a payment is owed for such month, the statement of account shall accompany the payment. A statement of account shall contain only the following information:

(1) Such information as is necessary to calculate the accompanying royalty payment, or if no payment is owed for the month, to calculate any portion of the minimum fee recouped during the month;

(2) The name, address, business title, telephone number, facsimile number (if any), electronic mail address and other contact information of the person to be contacted for information or questions concerning the content of the statement of account;

(3) The signature of:

(i) The owner of the Licensee or a duly authorized agent of the owner, if the Licensee is not a partnership or corporation;

(ii) A partner or delegee, if the Licensee is a partnership; or

(iii) An officer of the corporation, if the Licensee is a corporation;

(4) The printed or typewritten name of the person signing the statement of account;

(5) The date of signature;

(6) If the Licensee is a partnership or corporation, the title or official position held in the partnership or corporation by the person signing the statement of account;

(7) A certification of the capacity of the person signing; and

(8) A statement to the following effect:

I, the undersigned owner or agent of the Licensee, or officer or partner, have examined this statement of account and hereby state that it is true, accurate and complete to my knowledge after reasonable due diligence.

(g) Distribution of royalties.

(1) The Collective shall promptly distribute royalties received from Licensees directly to Copyright Owners, or their designated agents, that are entitled to such royalties. The Collective shall only be responsible for making distributions to those Copyright Owners or their designated agents who provide the Collective with such information as is necessary to identify the correct recipient. The Collective shall distribute royalties on a basis that values all Ephemeral Recordings by a Licensee equally based upon the information provided under the reports of use requirements for Licensees contained in §370.4 of this chapter.

(2) If the Collective is unable to locate a Copyright Owner entitled to a distribution of royalties under paragraph (g)(1) of this section within 3 years from the date of payment by a Licensee, such royalties shall be handled in accordance with §384.8.

(h) Retention of records. Books and records of a Licensee and of the Collective relating to payments of and distributions of royalties shall be kept for a period of not less than the prior 3 calendar years.

1. **Editor's note:** "Set forth" probably should appear only once.

History of 37 C.F.R. §384.4: 73 FR 16200, Jan. 1, 2009; 78 FR 66278, Jan. 1, 2014.

§384.5. CONFIDENTIAL INFORMATION

(a) Definition. For purposes of this section, "Confidential Information" shall include the statements of account and any information contained therein, including the amount of royalty payments, and any information pertaining to the statements of account reasonably designated as confidential by the Licensee submitting the statement.

(b) Exclusion. Confidential Information shall not include documents or information that at the time of delivery to the Collective are public knowledge. The party claiming the benefit of this provision shall have the burden of proving that the disclosed information was public knowledge.

(c) Use of Confidential Information. In no event shall the Collective or any other person or entity authorized to have access to Confidential Information pursuant to paragraph (d) of this section use any Confidential Information for any purpose other than royalty collection and distribution and activities related directly thereto.

(d) Disclosure of Confidential Information. Access to Confidential Information shall be limited to:

(1) Those employees, agents, attorneys, consultants and independent contractors of the Collective, subject to an appropriate confidentiality agreement, who are engaged in the collection and distribution of royalty payments hereunder and activities related thereto, who are not also employees or officers of a Copyright Owner or Performer, and who, for the purpose of performing such duties during the ordinary course of their work require access to Confidential Information;

(2) Board members of the Collective, and members of the Collective committees whose primary functions are directly related to royalty collection and distribution, subject to an appropriate confidentiality agreement and for the sole purpose of performing their duties as board or committee members of the Collective, as applicable, provided that the sole Confidential Information that may be shared pursuant to this paragraph (d)(2) is Confidential Information contained in monthly statements of accounts provided pursuant to §384.4(f) that accompany royalty payments;

(3) An independent and Qualified Auditor, subject to an appropriate confidentiality agreement, who is authorized to act on behalf of the Collective with respect to verification of a Licensee's statement of account pursuant to §384.6 or on behalf of a Copyright Owner with respect to the verification of royalty distributions pursuant to §384.7;

(4) Copyright Owners, including their designated agents, whose works have been used under the statutory license set forth in 17 U.S.C. 112(e) by the Licensee whose Confidential Information is being supplied, subject to an appropriate confidentiality agreement, provided that the sole Confidential Information that may be shared pursuant to paragraph (d)(4) of this section are monthly statements of account provided pursuant to §384.4(f) that accompany royalty payments;

(5) In connection with future proceedings under 17 U.S.C. 112(e) before the Copyright Royalty Judges, and under an appropriate protective order, attorneys, consultants and other authorized agents of the parties to the proceedings or the courts; and

(6) In connection with bona fide royalty disputes or claims that are the subject of the procedures under §384.6 or §384.7, and under an appropriate confidentiality agreement or protective order, the specific parties to such disputes or claims, their attorneys, consultants or other authorized agents, and/or arbitration panels or the courts to which disputes or claims may be submitted.

(e) Safeguarding of Confidential Information. The Collective and any person or entity identified in paragraph (d) of this section shall implement procedures to safeguard against unauthorized access to or dissemination of any Confidential Information using a reasonable standard of care, but no less than the same degree of security used to protect Confidential Information or similarly sensitive information belonging to the Collective, person, or entity.

History of 37 C.F.R. §384.5: 73 FR 16201, Jan. 1, 2009; 78 FR 66278, Jan. 1, 2014.

§384.6. VERIFICATION OF ROYALTY PAYMENTS

(a) General. This section prescribes procedures by which the Collective may verify the royalty payments made by a Licensee.

(b) Frequency of verification. The Collective may conduct a single audit of a Licensee, upon reasonable notice and during reasonable business hours, during any given calendar year, for any or all of the prior 3 calendar years, but no calendar year shall be subject to audit more than once.

(c) Notice of intent to audit. The Collective must file with the Copyright Royalty Judges a notice of intent to audit a particular Licensee, which shall, within 30 days of the filing of the notice, publish in the Federal Register a notice announcing such filing. The notification of intent to audit shall be served at the same time on the Licensee to be audited. Any such audit shall be conducted by an independent and Qualified Auditor identified in the notice, and shall be binding on all parties.

(d) Acquisition and retention of report. The Licensee shall use commercially reasonable efforts to obtain or to provide access to any relevant books and records maintained by third parties for the purpose of the audit. The Collective shall retain the report of the verification for a period of not less than 3 years.

(e) Acceptable verification procedure. An audit, including underlying paperwork, which was performed in the ordinary course of business according to generally accepted auditing standards by an independent and Qualified Auditor, shall serve as an acceptable verification procedure for all parties with respect to the information that is within the scope of the audit.

(f) Consultation. Before rendering a written report to the Collective, except where the auditor has a reasonable basis to suspect fraud and disclosure would, in the reasonable opinion of the auditor, prejudice the investigation of such suspected fraud, the auditor shall review the tentative written findings of the audit with the appropriate agent or employee of the Licensee being audited in order to remedy any factual errors and clarify any issues relating to the audit; Provided that the appropriate agent or employee of the Licensee reasonably cooperates with the auditor to remedy promptly any factual errors or clarify any issues raised by the audit.

(g) Costs of the verification procedure. The Collective shall pay the cost of the verification procedure, unless it is finally determined that there was an underpayment of 10% or more, in which case the Licensee shall, in addition to paying the amount of any underpayment, bear the reasonable costs of the verification procedure.

History of 37 C.F.R. §384.6: 73 FR 16202, Jan. 1, 2009; 78 FR 66278, Jan. 1, 2014.

§384.7. VERIFICATION OF ROYALTY DISTRIBUTIONS

(a) General. This section prescribes procedures by which any Copyright Owner may verify the royalty distributions made by the Collective; provided, however, that nothing contained in this section shall apply to situations where a Copyright Owner and the Collective have agreed as to proper verification methods.

(b) Frequency of verification. A Copyright Owner may conduct a single audit of the Collective upon reasonable notice and during reasonable business hours, during any given calendar year, for any or all of the prior 3 calendar years, but no calendar year shall be subject to audit more than once.

(c) Notice of intent to audit. A Copyright Owner must file with the Copyright Royalty Judges a notice of intent to audit the Collective, which shall, within 30 days of the filing of the notice, publish in the Federal Register a notice announcing such filing. The notification of intent to audit shall be served at the same time on the Collective. Any such audit shall be conducted by an independent and Qualified Auditor identified in the notice, and shall be binding on all Copyright Owners.

(d) Acquisition and retention of record. The Collective shall use commercially reasonable efforts to obtain or to provide access to any relevant books and records maintained by third parties for the purpose of the audit. The Copyright Owner requesting the verification procedure shall retain the report of the verification for a period of not less than 3 years.

(e) Acceptable verification procedure. An audit, including underlying paperwork, which was performed in the ordinary course of business according to generally accepted auditing standards by an independent and Qualified Auditor, shall serve as an acceptable verification procedure for all parties with respect to the information that is within the scope of the audit.

(f) Consultation. Before rendering a written report to a Copyright Owner, except where the auditor has a reasonable basis to suspect fraud and disclosure would, in the reasonable opinion of the auditor, prejudice the investigation of such suspected fraud, the auditor shall review the tentative written findings of the audit with the appropriate agent or employee of the Collective in order to remedy any factual errors and clarify any issues relating to the audit; Provided that the appropriate agent or employee of the Collective reasonably cooperates with the auditor to remedy promptly any factual errors or clarify any issues raised by the audit.

(g) Costs of the verification procedure. The Copyright Owner requesting the verification procedure shall pay the cost of the procedure, unless it is finally determined that there was an underpayment of 10% or more, in which case the Collective shall, in addition to paying the amount of any underpayment, bear the reasonable costs of the verification procedure.

History of 37 C.F.R. §384.7: 73 FR 16202, Jan. 1, 2009; 78 FR 66278, Jan. 1, 2014.

§384.8. UNCLAIMED FUNDS

If the Collective is unable to identify or locate a Copyright Owner who is entitled to receive a royalty distribution under this part, the Collective shall retain the required payment in a segregated trust account for a period of 3 years from the date of distribution. No claim to such distribution shall be valid after the expiration of the 3-year period. After expiration of this period, the Collective may apply the unclaimed funds to offset any costs deductible under 17 U.S.C. 114(g)(3). The foregoing shall apply notwithstanding the common law or statutes of any State.

History of 37 C.F.R. §384.8: 73 FR 16202, Jan. 1, 2009; 78 FR 66278, Jan. 1, 2014.

PART 385. RATES & TERMS FOR USE OF MUSICAL WORKS UNDER COMPULSORY LICENSE FOR MAKING & DISTRIBUTING OF PHYSICAL & DIGITAL PHONORECORDS

SUBPART A. PHYSICAL PHONORECORD DELIVERIES, PERMANENT DIGITAL DOWNLOADS & RINGTONES

§385.1. GENERAL

(a) Scope. This subpart establishes rates and terms of royalty payments for making and distributing phonorecords, including by means of digital phonorecord deliveries, in accordance with the provisions of 17 U.S.C. 115.

(b) Legal compliance. Licensees relying upon the compulsory license set forth in 17 U.S.C. 115 shall comply with the requirements of that section, the rates and terms of this subpart, and any other applicable regulations.

(c) Relationship to voluntary agreements. Notwithstanding the royalty rates and terms established in this subpart, the rates and terms of any license agreements entered into by Copyright Owners and Licensees shall apply in lieu of the rates and terms of this subpart to use of musical works within the scope of such agreements.

History of 37 C.F.R. §385.1: 74 FR 4529, Mar. 1, 2009.

§385.2. DEFINITIONS

For purposes of this subpart, the following definitions apply:

Copyright Owners are nondramatic musical work copyright owners who are entitled to royalty payments made under this subpart pursuant to the compulsory license under 17 U.S.C. 115.

Digital phonorecord delivery means a digital phonorecord delivery as defined in 17 U.S.C. 115(d).

Licensee is a person or entity that has obtained a compulsory license under 17 U.S.C. 115, and the implementing regulations, to make and distribute phonorecords of a nondramatic musical work, including by means of a digital phonorecord delivery.

Permanent digital download means a digital phonorecord delivery that is distributed in the form of a download that may be retained and played on a permanent basis.

Ringtone means a phonorecord of a partial musical work distributed as a digital phonorecord delivery in a format to be made resident on a telecommunications device for use to announce the reception of an incoming telephone call or other communication or message or to alert the receiver to the fact that there is a communication or message.

History of 37 C.F.R. §385.2: 74 FR 4529, Mar. 1, 2009.

§385.3. ROYALTY RATES FOR MAKING & DISTRIBUTING PHONORECORDS

(a) Physical phonorecord deliveries and permanent digital downloads. For every physical phonorecord and permanent digital download made and distributed, the royalty rate payable for each work embodied in such phonorecord shall be either 9.1 cents or 1.75 cents per minute of playing time or fraction thereof, whichever amount is larger.

(b) Ringtones. For every ringtone made and distributed, the royalty rate payable for each work embodied therein shall be 24 cents.

History of 37 C.F.R. §385.3: 74 FR 4529, Mar. 1, 2009.

§385.4. LATE PAYMENTS

A Licensee shall pay a late fee of 1.5% per month, or the highest lawful rate, whichever is lower, for any payment received by the Copyright Owner after the due date set forth in §210.16(g)(1) of this title. Late fees shall accrue from the due date until payment is received by the Copyright Owner.

History of 37 C.F.R. §385.4: 74 FR 4529, Mar. 1, 2009; 78 FR 67942, Jan. 1, 2014; 82 FR 15299, Mar. 28, 2017.

SUBPART B. INTERACTIVE STREAMING & LIMITED DOWNLOADS

§385.10. GENERAL

(a) Scope. This subpart establishes rates and terms of royalty payments for interactive streams and limited downloads of musical works by subscription and nonsubscription digital music services in accordance with the provisions of 17 U.S.C. 115.

(b) Legal compliance. A licensee that, pursuant to 17 U.S.C. 115, makes or authorizes interactive streams or limited downloads of musical works through subscription or nonsubscription digital music services shall comply with the requirements of that section, the rates and terms of this subpart, and any other applicable regulations, with respect to such musical works and uses licensed pursuant to 17 U.S.C. 115.

(c) Interpretation. This subpart is intended only to set rates and terms for situations in which the exclusive rights of a copyright owner are implicated and a compulsory license pursuant to 17 U.S.C. 115 is obtained. Neither this subpart nor the act of obtaining a license under 17 U.S.C. 115 is intended to express or imply any conclusion as to the circumstances in which any of the exclusive rights of a copyright owner are implicated or a license, including a compulsory license pursuant to 17 U.S.C. 115, must be obtained.

History of 37 C.F.R. §385.10: 74 FR 4529, Mar. 1, 2009; 78 FR 67942, Jan. 1, 2014.

§385.11. DEFINITIONS

For purposes of this subpart, the following definitions shall apply:

Affiliate means an entity controlling, controlled by, or under common control with another entity, except that an affiliate of a record company shall not include a copyright owner of musical works to the extent it is engaging in business as to musical works.

Applicable consideration means anything of value given for the identified rights to undertake the licensed activity, including, without limitation, ownership equity, monetary advances, barter or any other monetary and/or nonmonetary consideration, whether such consideration is conveyed via a single agreement, multiple agreements and/or agreements that do not themselves authorize the licensed activity but nevertheless provide consideration for the identified rights to undertake the licensed activity, and including any such value given to an affiliate of a record company for such rights to undertake the licensed activity. For the avoidance of doubt, value given to a copyright owner of musical works that is controlling, controlled by, or under common control with a record company for rights to undertake the licensed activity shall not be considered value given to the record company. Notwithstanding the foregoing, applicable consideration shall not include in-kind promotional consideration given to a record company (or affiliate thereof) that is used to promote the sale or paid use of sound recordings embodying musical works or the paid use of music services through which sound recordings embodying musical works are available where such in-kind promotional consideration is given in connection with a use that qualifies for licensing under 17 U.S.C. 115.

GAAP means U.S. Generally Accepted Accounting Principles, except that if the U.S. Securities and Exchange Commission permits or requires entities with securities that are publicly traded in the U.S. to employ International Financial Reporting Standards, as issued by the International Accounting Standards Board, or as accepted by the Securities and Exchange Commission if different from that issued by the International Accounting Standards Board, in lieu of Generally Accepted Accounting Principles, then an entity may employ International Financial Reporting Standards as "GAAP" for purposes of this subpart.

Interactive stream means a stream of a sound recording of a musical work, where the performance of the sound recording by means of the stream is not exempt under 17 U.S.C. 114(d)(1) and does not in itself or as a result of a program in which it is included qualify for statutory licensing under 17 U.S.C. 114(d)(2).

Licensee means a person that has obtained a compulsory license under 17 U.S.C. 115 and its implementing regulations.

Licensed activity means interactive streams or limited downloads of musical works, as applicable.

Limited download means a digital transmission of a sound recording of a musical work to an end user, other than a stream, that results in a specifically identifiable reproduction of that sound recording that is only accessible for listening for—

(1) An amount of time not to exceed 1 month from the time of the transmission (unless the service provider, in lieu of retransmitting the same sound recording as another limited download, separately and upon specific request of the end user made through a live network connection, reauthorizes use for another time period not to exceed 1 month), or in the case of a subscription transmission, a period of time following the end of the applicable subscription no longer than a subscription renewal period or 3 months, whichever is shorter; or

(2) A specified number of times not to exceed 12 (unless the service provider, in lieu of retransmitting the same sound recording as another limited download, separately and upon specific request of the end user made through a live network connection, reauthorizes use of another series of 12 or fewer plays), or in the case of a subscription transmission, 12 times after the end of the applicable subscription.

(3) A limited download is a general digital phonorecord delivery under 17 U.S.C. 115(c)(3)(C) and (D).

Offering means a service provider's offering of licensed activity that is subject to a particular rate set forth in §385.13(a) (e.g., a particular subscription plan available through the service provider).

Promotional royalty rate means the statutory royalty rate of zero in the case of certain promotional interactive streams and certain promotional limited downloads, as provided in §385.14.

Record company means a person or entity that

(1) Is a copyright owner of a sound recording of a musical work;

(2) In the case of a sound recording of a musical work fixed before February 15, 1972, has rights to the sound recording, under the common law or statutes of any State, that are equivalent to the rights of a copyright owner of a sound recording of a musical work under title 17, United States Code;

(3) Is an exclusive licensee of the rights to reproduce and distribute a sound recording of a musical work; or

(4) Performs the functions of marketing and authorizing the distribution of a sound recording of a musical work under its own label, under the authority of the copyright owner of the sound recording.

Relevant page means a page (including a Web page, screen or display) from which licensed activity offered by a service provider is directly available to end users, but only where the offering of licensed activity and content that directly relates to the offering of licensed activity (e.g., an image of the artist or artwork closely associated with such offering, artist or album information, reviews of such offering, credits and music player controls) comprises 75% or more of the space on that page, excluding any space occupied by advertising. A licensed activity is directly available to end users from a page if sound recordings of musical works can be accessed by end users for licensed activity from such page (in most cases this will be the page where the limited download or interactive stream takes place).

Service provider means that entity (which may or may not be the licensee) that, with respect to the licensed activity,

(1) Contracts with or has a direct relationship with end users in a case where a contract or relationship exists, or otherwise controls the content made available to end users;

(2) Is able to report fully on service revenue from the provision of the licensed activity to the public, and to the extent applicable, verify service revenue through an audit; and

(3) Is able to report fully on usage of musical works by the service, or procure such reporting, and to the extent applicable, verify usage through an audit.

Service revenue. **(1)** Subject to paragraphs (2) through (5) of the definition of "Service revenue," and subject to GAAP, service revenue shall mean the following:

(i) All revenue recognized by the service provider from end users from the provision of licensed activity;

(ii) All revenue recognized by the service provider by way of sponsorship and commissions as a result of the inclusion of third-party "in-stream" or "in-download" advertising as part of licensed activity (i.e., advertising placed immediately at the start, end or during the actual delivery, by way of interactive streaming or limited downloads, as applicable, of a musical work); and

(iii) All revenue recognized by the service provider, including by way of sponsorship and commissions, as a result of the placement of third-party advertising on a relevant page of the service or on any page that directly follows such relevant page leading up to and including the limited download or interactive streaming, as applicable, of a musical work; provided that, in the case where more than one service is actually available to end users from a relevant page, any advertising revenue shall be allocated between such services on the basis of the relative amounts of the page they occupy.

(2) In each of the cases identified in paragraph (1) of the definition of "Service revenue," such revenue shall, for the avoidance of doubt,

(i) Include any such revenue recognized by the service provider, or if not recognized by the service provider, by any associate, affiliate, agent or representative of such service provider in lieu of its being recognized by the service provider;

(ii) Include the value of any barter or other nonmonetary consideration;

(iii) Not be reduced by credit card commissions or similar payment process charges; and

(iv) Except as expressly set forth in this subpart, not be subject to any other deduction or set-off other than refunds to end users for licensed activity that they were unable to use due to technical faults in the licensed activity or other bona fide refunds or credits issued to end users in the ordinary course of business.

(3) In each of the cases identified in paragraph (1) of the definition of "Service revenue," such revenue shall, for the avoidance of doubt, exclude revenue derived solely in connection with services and activities other than licensed activity, provided that advertising or sponsorship revenue shall be treated as provided in paragraphs (2) and (4) of the definition of "Service revenue." By way of example, the following kinds of revenue shall be excluded:

(i) Revenue derived from non-music voice, content and text services;

(ii) Revenue derived from other non-music products and services (including search services, sponsored searches and click-through commissions); and

(iii) Revenue derived from music or music-related products and services that are not or do not include licensed activity.

(4) For purposes of paragraph (1) of the definition of "Service revenue," advertising or sponsorship revenue shall be reduced by the actual cost of obtaining such revenue, not to exceed 15%.

(5) Where the licensed activity is provided to end users as part of the same transaction with one or more other products or services that are not a music service engaged in licensed activity, then the revenue deemed to be recognized from end users for the service for the purpose of the definition in paragraph (1) of the definition of "Service revenue" shall be the revenue recognized from end users for the bundle less the standalone published price for end users for each of the other component(s) of the bundle; provided that, if there is no such standalone published price for a component of the bundle, then the average standalone published price for end users for the most closely comparable product or service in the U.S. shall be used or, if more than one such comparable exists, the average of such standalone prices for such comparables shall be used.

Stream means the digital transmission of a sound recording of a musical work to an end user—

(1) To allow the end user to listen to the sound recording, while maintaining a live network connection to the transmitting service, substantially at the time of transmission, except to the extent that the sound recording remains accessible for future listening from a streaming cache reproduction;

(2) Using technology that is designed such that the sound recording does not remain accessible for future listening, except to the extent that the sound recording remains accessible for future listening from a streaming cache reproduction; and

(3) That is also subject to licensing as a public performance of the musical work.

Streaming cache reproduction means a reproduction of a sound recording of a musical work made on a computer or other receiving device by a service solely for the purpose of permitting an end user who has previously received a stream of such sound recording to play such sound recording again from local storage on such computer or other device rather than by means of a transmission; provided that the user is only able to do so while maintaining a live network connection to the service, and such reproduction is encrypted or otherwise protected consistent with prevailing industry standards to prevent it from being played in any other manner or on any device other than the computer or other device on which it was originally made.

Subscription service means a digital music service for which end users are required to pay a fee to access the service for defined subscription periods of 3 years or less (in contrast to, for example, a service where the basic charge to users is a payment per download or per play), whether such payment is made for access to the service on a standalone basis or as part of a bundle with one or more other products or services, and including any use of such a service on a trial basis without charge as described in §385.14(b).

History of 37 C.F.R. §385.11: 74 FR 4529, Mar. 1, 2009; 74 FR 6834, Mar. 1, 2009; 78 FR 67942, Jan. 1, 2014.

§385.12. CALCULATION OF ROYALTY PAYMENTS IN GENERAL

(a) Applicable royalty. Licensees that make or authorize licensed activity pursuant to 17 U.S.C. 115 shall pay royalties therefor that are calculated as provided in this section, subject to the minimum royalties and subscriber-based royalty floors for specific types of services provided in §385.13, except as provided for certain promotional uses in §385.14.

(b) Rate calculation methodology. Royalty payments for licensed activity shall be calculated as provided in paragraph (b) of this section. If a service includes different offerings, royalties must be separately calculated with respect to each such offering taking into consideration service revenue and expenses associated with such offering. Uses subject to the promotional royalty rate shall be excluded from the calculation of royalties due, as further described in this section and the following §385.13.

(1) Step 1: Calculate the All-In Royalty for the Offering. For each accounting period, the all-in royalty for each offering of the service provider is the greater of

(i) The applicable percentage of service revenue associated with the relevant offering as set forth in paragraph (c) of this section (excluding any service revenue derived solely from licensed activity uses subject to the promotional royalty rate), and

(ii) The minimum specified in §385.13 of the offering involved.

(2) Step 2: Subtract Applicable Performance Royalties. From the amount determined in step 1 in paragraph (b)(1) of this section, for each offering of the service provider, subtract the total amount of royalties for public performance of musical works that has been or will be expensed pursuant to public performance licenses in connection with uses of musical works through such offering during the accounting period that constitute licensed activity (other than licensed activity subject to the promotional royalty rate). Although this amount may be the total of the service's payments for that offering for the accounting period, it will be less than the total of such public performance payments if the service is also engaging in public performance of musical works that does not constitute licensed activity. In the case where the service is also engaging in the public performance of musical works that does not constitute licensed activity, the amount to be subtracted for public performance payments shall be the amount of such payments allocable to licensed activity uses (other than promotional royalty rate uses) through the relevant offering, as determined in relation to all uses of musical works for which the public performance payments are made for the accounting period. Such allocation shall be made on the basis of plays of musical works or, where per-play information is unavailable due to bona fide technical limitations as described in step 4 in paragraph (b)(4) of this section, using the same alternative methodology as provided in step 4.

(3) Step 3: Determine the Payable Royalty Pool. The payable royalty pool is the amount payable for the reproduction and distribution of all musical works used by the service provider by virtue of its licensed activity for a particular offering during the accounting period. This amount is the greater of

(i) The result determined in step 2 in paragraph (b)(2) of this section, and

(ii) The subscriber-based royalty floor resulting from the calculations described in §385.13.

(4) Step 4: Calculate the Per-Work Royalty Allocation for Each Relevant Work. This is the amount payable for the reproduction and distribution of each musical work used by the service provider by virtue of its licensed activity through a particular offering during the accounting period. To determine this amount, the result determined in step 3 in paragraph (b)(3) of this section must be allocated to each musical work used through the offering. The allocation shall be accomplished by dividing the payable royalty pool determined in step 3 for such offering by the total number of plays of all musical works through such offering during the accounting period (other than promotional royalty rate plays) to yield a per-play allocation, and multiplying that result by the number of plays of each musical work (other than promotional royalty rate plays) through the offering during the accounting period. For purposes of determining the per-work royalty allocation in all calculations under this step 4 only (i.e., after the payable royalty pool has been determined), for sound recordings of musical works with a playing time of over 5 minutes, each play shall be counted as provided in paragraph (d) of this section. Notwithstanding the foregoing, if the service provider is not capable of tracking play information due to bona fide limitations of the available technology for services of that nature or of devices useable with the service provider, the per-work royalty allocation may instead be accomplished in a manner consistent with the methodology used by the service provider for making royalty payment allocations for the use of individual sound recordings.

(c) Percentage of service revenue. The percentage of service revenue applicable under paragraph (b) of this section is 10.5%.

(d) Overtime adjustment. For purposes of the calculations in step 4 in paragraph (b)(4) of this section only, for sound recordings of musical works with a playing time of over 5 minutes, adjust the number of plays as follows:

(1) 5:01 to 6:00 minutes—Each play = 1.2 plays

(2) 6:01 to 7:00 minutes—Each play = 1.4 plays

(3) 7:01 to 8:00 minutes—Each play = 1.6 plays

(4) 8:01 to 9:00 minutes—Each play = 1.8 plays

(5) 9:01 to 10:00 minutes—Each play = 2.0 plays

(6) For playing times of greater than 10 minutes, continue to add .2 for each additional minute or fraction thereof.

History of 37 C.F.R. §385.12: 74 FR 4531, Mar. 1, 2009; 78 FR 67943, Jan. 1, 2014; 78 FR 76987, Jan. 1, 2014.

§385.13. MINIMUM ROYALTY RATES & SUBSCRIBER-BASED ROYALTY FLOORS FOR SPECIFIC TYPES OF SERVICES

(a) In general. The following minimum royalty rates and subscriber-based royalty floors shall apply to the following types of licensed activity:

(1) Standalone non-portable subscription—streaming only. Except as provided in paragraph (a)(4) of this section, in the case of a subscription service through which an end user can listen to sound recordings only in the form of interactive streams and only from a non-portable device to which such streams are originally transmitted while the device has a live network connection, the minimum for use in step 1 of §385.12(b)(1)(ii) is the lesser of subminimum II as described in paragraph (c) of this section for the accounting period and the aggregate amount of 50 cents per subscriber per month. The subscriber-based royalty floor for use in step 3 of §385.12(b)(3)(ii) is the aggregate amount of 15 cents per subscriber per month.

(2) Standalone non-portable subscription—mixed. Except as provided in paragraph (a)(4) of this section, in the case of a subscription service through which an end user can listen to sound recordings either in the form of interactive streams or limited downloads but only from a non-portable device to which such streams or downloads are originally transmitted, the minimum for use in step 1 of §385.12(b)(1)(ii) is the lesser of the subminimum I as described in paragraph (b) of this section for the accounting period and the aggregate amount of 50 cents per subscriber per month. The subscriber-based royalty floor for use in step 3 of §385.12(b)(3)(ii) is the aggregate amount of 30 cents per subscriber per month.

(3) Standalone portable subscription service. Except as provided in paragraph (a)(4) of this section, in the case of a subscription service through which an end user can listen to sound recordings in the form of interactive streams or limited downloads from a portable device, the minimum for use in step 1 of §385.12(b)(1)(ii) is the lesser of subminimum I as described in paragraph (b) of this section for the accounting period and the aggregate amount of 80 cents per subscriber per month. The subscriber-based royalty floor for use in step 3 of §385.12(b)(3)(ii) is the aggregate amount of 50 cents per subscriber per month.

(4) Bundled subscription services. In the case of a subscription service providing licensed activity that is made available to end users with one or more other products or services (including products or services subject to other subparts) as part of a single transaction without pricing for the subscription service providing licensed activity separate from the product(s) or service(s) with which it is made available (e.g., a case in which a user can buy a portable device and one-year access to a subscription service providing licensed activity for a single price), the minimum for use in step 1 of §385.12(b)(1)(ii) is subminimum I as described in paragraph (b) of this section for the accounting period. The subscriber-based royalty floor for use in step 3 of §385.12(b)(3)(ii) is the aggregate amount of 25 cents per month for each end user who has made at least one play of a licensed work during such month (each such end user to be considered an "active subscriber").

(5) Free nonsubscription/ad-supported services. In the case of a service offering licensed activity free of any charge to the end user, the minimum for use in step 1 of §385.12(b)(1)(ii) is subminimum II described in paragraph (c) of this section for the accounting period. There is no subscriber-based royalty floor for use in step 3 of §385.12(b)(3)(ii).

(b) Computation of subminimum I. For purposes of paragraphs (a)(2), (3), and (4) of this section, subminimum I for an accounting period means the aggregate of the following with respect to all sound recordings of musical works used in the relevant offering of the service provider during the accounting period—

(1) In cases in which the record company is the licensee under 17 U.S.C. 115 and the record company has granted the rights to make interactive streams or limited downloads of a sound recording through the third-party service together with the right to reproduce and distribute the musical work embodied therein, 17.36% of the total amount expensed by the service provider or any of its affiliates in accordance with GAAP for such rights for the accounting period, which amount shall equal the applicable consideration for such rights at the time such applicable consideration is properly recognized as an expense under GAAP.

(2) In cases in which the record company is not the licensee under 17 U.S.C. 115 and the record company has granted the rights to make interactive streams or limited downloads of a sound recording through the third-party service without the right to reproduce and distribute the musical work embodied therein, 21% of the total amount expensed by the service provider or any of its affiliates in accordance with GAAP for such rights for the accounting period, which amount shall equal the applicable consideration for such rights at the time such applicable consideration is properly recognized as an expense under GAAP.

(c) Computation of subminimum II. For purposes of paragraphs (a)(1) and (5) of this section, subminimum II for an accounting period means the aggregate of the following with respect to all sound recordings of musical works used in the relevant offering of the service provider during the accounting period—

(1) In cases in which the record company is the licensee under 17 U.S.C. 115 and the record company has granted the rights to make interactive streams and limited downloads of a sound recording through the third-party service together with the right to reproduce and distribute the musical work embodied therein, 18% of the total amount expensed by the service provider or any of its affiliates in accordance with GAAP for such rights for the accounting period, which amount shall equal the applicable consideration for such rights at the time such applicable consideration is properly recognized as an expense under GAAP.

(2) In cases in which the record company is not the licensee under 17 U.S.C. 115 and the record company has granted the rights to make interactive streams or limited downloads of a sound recording through the third-party service without the right to reproduce and distribute the musical work embodied therein, 22% of the total amount expensed by the service provider or any of its affiliates in accordance with GAAP for such rights for the accounting period, which amount shall equal the applicable consideration for such rights at the time such applicable consideration is properly recognized as an expense under GAAP.

(d) Payments made by third parties. If a record company providing sound recording rights to the service provider for a licensed activity—

(1) Recognizes revenue (in accordance with GAAP, and including for the avoidance of doubt all applicable consideration with respect to such rights for the accounting period, regardless of the form or timing of payment) from a person or entity other than the service provider providing the licensed activity and its affiliates, and

(2) Such revenue is received, in the context of the transactions involved, as applicable consideration for such rights,

(3) Then such revenue shall be added to the amounts expensed by the service provider solely for purposes of paragraphs(b)(1), (b)(2), (c)(1), or (c)(2) of this section, as applicable, if not already included in such expensed amounts. Where the service provider is the licensee, if the service provider provides the record company all information necessary for the record company to determine whether additional royalties are payable by the service provider hereunder as a result of revenue recognized from a person or entity other than the service provider as described in the immediately preceding sentence, then the record company shall provide such further information as necessary for the service provider to calculate the additional royalties and indemnify the service provider for such additional royalties. The sole obligation of the record company shall be to pay the licensee such additional royalties if actually payable as royalties hereunder; provided, however, that this shall not affect any otherwise existing right or remedy of the copyright owner nor diminish the licensee's obligations to the copyright owner.

(e) Computation of subscriber-based royalty rates. For purposes of paragraph (a) of this section, to determine the minimum or subscriber-based royalty floor, as applicable to any particular offering, the total number of subscriber-months for the accounting period, shall be calculated, taking into account all end users who were subscribers for complete calendar months, prorating in the case of end users who were subscribers for only part of a calendar month, and deducting on a prorated basis for end users covered by a free trial period subject to the promotional royalty rate as described in §385.14(b)(2), except that in the case of a bundled subscription service, subscriber-months shall instead be determined with respect to active subscribers as defined in paragraph (a)(4) of this section. The product of the total number of subscriber-months for the accounting period and the specified number of cents per subscriber (or active subscriber, as the case may be) shall be used as the subscriber-based component of the minimum or subscriber-based royalty floor, as applicable, for the accounting period.

History of 37 C.F.R. §385.13: 74 FR 4532, Mar. 1, 2009; 78 FR 67943, Jan. 1, 2014.

§385.14. PROMOTIONAL ROYALTY RATE

(a) General provisions. (1) This section establishes a royalty rate of zero in the case of certain promotional interactive streaming activities, and of certain promotional limited downloads offered in the context of a free trial period for a digital music subscription service under a license pursuant to 17 U.S.C. 115. Subject to the requirements of 17 U.S.C. 115 and the additional provisions of paragraphs (b) through (e) of this section, the promotional royalty rate shall apply to a musical work when a record company transmits or authorizes the transmission of interactive streams or limited downloads of a sound recording that embodies such musical work, only if—

(i) The primary purpose of the record company in making or authorizing the interactive streams or limited downloads is to promote the sale or other paid use of sound recordings by the relevant artists, including such sound recording, through established retail channels or the paid use of one or more established retail music services through which the sound recording is available, and not to promote any other good or service;

(ii) Either—

(A) The sound recording (or a different version of the sound recording embodying the same musical work) is being lawfully distributed and offered to consumers through the established retail channels or services described in paragraph (a)(1)(i) of this section; or

(B) In the case of a sound recording of a musical work being prepared for commercial release but not yet released, the record company has a good faith intention of lawfully distributing and offering to consumers the sound recording (or a different version of the sound recording embodying the same musical work) through the established retail channels or services described in paragraph (a)(1)(i) of this section within 90 days after the commencement of the first promotional use authorized under this section (and in fact does so, unless it can demonstrate that notwithstanding its bona fide intention, it unexpectedly did not meet the scheduled release date);

(iii) In connection with authorizing the promotional interactive streams or limited downloads, the record company has obtained from the service provider it authorizes a written representation that—

(A) In the case of a promotional use other than interactive streaming subject to paragraph (d) of this section, the service provider agrees to maintain for a period of no less than 5 years from the conclusion of the promotional activity complete and accurate records of the relevant authorization and dates on which the promotion was conducted, and identifying each sound recording of a musical work made available through the promotion, the licensed activity involved, and the number of plays of such recording;

(B) The service provider is in all material respects operating with appropriate license authority with respect to the musical works it is using for promotional and other purposes; and

(C) The representation is signed by a person authorized to make the representation on behalf of the service provider;

(iv) Upon receipt by the record company of written notice from the copyright owner of a musical work or agent of the copyright owner stating in good faith that a particular service is in a material manner operating without appropriate license authority from such copyright owner, the record company shall within 5 business days withdraw by written notice its authorization of such uses of such copyright owner's musical works under the promotional royalty rate by that service;

(v) The interactive streams or limited downloads are offered free of any charge to the end user and, except in the case of interactive streaming subject to paragraph (d) of this section in the case of a free trial period for a digital music subscription service, no more than 5 sound recordings at a time are streamed in response to any individual request of an end user;

(vi) The interactive streams and limited downloads are offered in a manner such that the user is at the same time (e.g., on the same Web page) presented with a purchase opportunity for the relevant sound recording or an opportunity to subscribe to a paid service offering the sound recording, or a link to such a purchase or subscription opportunity, except—

(A) In the case of interactive streaming of a sound recording being prepared for commercial release but not yet released, certain mobile applications or other circumstances in which the foregoing is impracticable in view of the current state of the relevant technology; and

(B) In the case of a free trial period for a digital music subscription service, if end users are periodically offered an opportunity to subscribe to the service during such free trial period; and

(vii) The interactive streams and limited downloads are not provided in a manner that is likely to cause mistake, to confuse or to deceive, reasonable end users as to the endorsement or association of the author of the musical work with any product, service or activity other than the sale or paid use of sound recordings or paid use of a music service through which sound recordings are available. Without limiting the foregoing, upon receipt of written notice from the copyright owner of a musical work or agent of the copyright owner stating in good faith that a particular use of such work under this section violates the limitation set forth in this paragraph (a)(1)(vii), the record company shall promptly cease such use of that work, and within 5 business days withdraw by written notice its authorization of such use by all relevant third parties it has authorized under this section.

(2) To rely upon the promotional royalty rate, a record company making or authorizing interactive streams or limited downloads shall keep complete and accurate contemporaneous written records of such uses, including the sound recordings and musical works involved, the artists, the release dates of the sound recordings, a brief statement of the promotional activities authorized, the identity of the service or services where each promotion is authorized (including the Internet address if applicable), the beginning and end date of each period of promotional activity authorized, and the representation required by paragraph (a)(1)(iii) of this section; provided that, in the case of trial subscription uses, such records shall instead consist of the contractual terms that bear upon promotional uses by the particular digital music subscription services it authorizes; and further provided that, if the record company itself is conducting the promotion, it shall also maintain any additional records described in paragraph (a)(1)(iii)(A) of this section. The records required by this paragraph (a)(2) shall be maintained for no less time than the record company maintains records of usage of royalty-bearing uses involving the same type of licensed activity in the ordinary course of business, but in no event for less than 5 years from the conclusion of the promotional activity to which they pertain. If the copyright owner of a musical work or its agent requests a copy of the information to be maintained under this paragraph (a)(2) with respect to a specific promotion or relating to a particular sound recording of a musical work, the record company shall provide complete and accurate documentation within 10 business days, except for any information required under paragraph (a)(1)(iii)(A) of this section, which shall be provided within 20 business days, and provided that if the copyright owner or agent requests information concerning a large volume of promotions or sound recordings, the record company shall have a reasonable time, in view of the amount of information requested, to respond to any request of such copyright owner or agent. If the record company does not provide required information within the required time, and upon receipt of written notice citing such failure does not provide such information within a further 10 business days, the uses will be considered not to be subject to the promotional royalty rate and the record company (but not any third-party service it has authorized) shall be liable for any payment due for such uses; provided, however, that all rights and remedies of the copyright owner with respect to unauthorized uses shall be preserved.

(3) If the copyright owner of a musical work or its agent requests a copy of the information to be maintained under paragraph (a)(1)(iii)(A) of this section by a service authorized by a record company with respect to a specific promotion, the service provider shall provide complete and accurate documentation within 20 business days, provided that if the copyright owner or agent requests information concerning a large volume of promotions or sound recordings, the service provider shall have a reasonable time, in view of the amount of information requested, to respond to any request of such copyright owner or agent. If the service provider does not provide required information within the required time, and upon receipt of written notice citing such failure does not provide such information within a further 10 business days, the uses will be considered not to be subject to the promotional royalty rate and the service provider (but not the record company) will be liable for any payment due for such uses; provided, however, that all rights and remedies of the copyright owner with respect to unauthorized uses shall be preserved.

(4) The promotional royalty rate is exclusively for audio-only interactive streaming and limited downloads of musical works subject to licensing under 17 U.S.C. 115. The promotional royalty rate does not apply to any other use under 17 U.S.C. 115; nor does it apply to public performances, audiovisual works, lyrics or other uses outside the scope of 17 U.S.C. 115. Without limitation, uses subject to licensing under 17 U.S.C. 115 that do not qualify for the promotional royalty rate (including without limitation interactive streaming or limited downloads of a musical work beyond the time limitations applicable to the promotional royalty rate) require payment of applicable royalties. This section is based on an understanding of industry practices and market conditions at the time of its development, among other things. The terms of this section shall be subject to de novo review and consideration (or elimination altogether) in future proceedings before the Copyright Royalty Judges. Nothing in this section shall be interpreted or construed in such a manner as to nullify or diminish any limitation, requirement or obligation of 17 U.S.C. 115 or other protection for musical works afforded by the Copyright Act, 17 U.S.C. 101 et seq.

(b) Interactive streaming and limited downloads of full-length musical works through third-party services. In addition to those of paragraph (a) of this section, the provisions of this paragraph (b) apply to interactive streaming, and limited downloads (in the context of a free trial period for a digital music subscription service), authorized by record companies under the promotional royalty rate through third-party services (including Web sites) that is not subject to paragraphs (c) or (d) of this section. Such interactive streams and limited downloads may be made or authorized by a record company under the promotional royalty rate only if—

(1) No applicable consideration for making or authorizing the relevant interactive streams or limited downloads is received by the record company, any of its affiliates, or any other person or entity acting on behalf of or in lieu of the record company, except for in-kind promotional consideration given to a record company (or affiliate thereof) that is used to promote the sale or paid use of sound recordings or the paid use of music services through which sound recordings are available;

(2) In the case of interactive streaming and limited downloads offered in the context of a free trial period for a digital music subscription service, the free trial period does not exceed 30 consecutive days per subscriber per two-year period; and

(3) In contexts other than a free trial period for a digital music subscription service, interactive streaming subject to paragraph (b) of this section of a particular sound recording is authorized by the record company on no more than 60 days total for all services (i.e., interactive streaming under paragraph (b) of this section of a particular sound recording may be authorized on no more than a total of 60 days, which need not be consecutive, and on any one such day, interactive streams may be offered on one or more services); provided, however, that an additional 60 days shall be available each time the sound recording is re-released by the record company in a remastered form or as a part of a compilation with a different set of sound recordings than the original release or any prior compilation including such sound recording.

(4) In the event that a record company authorizes promotional uses in excess of the time limitations of paragraph (b) of this section, the record company, and not the third-party service it has authorized, shall be liable for any payment due for such uses; provided, however, that all rights and remedies of the copyright owner with respect to unauthorized uses shall be preserved. In the event that a third-party service exceeds the scope of any authorization by a record company, the service provider, and not the record company, shall be liable for any payment due for such uses; provided, however, that all rights and remedies of the copyright owner with respect to unauthorized uses shall be preserved.

(c) Interactive streaming of full-length musical works through record company and artist services. In addition to those of paragraph (a) of this section, the provisions of this paragraph (c) apply to interactive streaming conducted or authorized by record companies under the promotional royalty rate through a service (e.g., a Web site) directly owned or operated by the record company, or directly owned or operated by a recording artist under the authorization of the record company, and that is not subject to paragraph (d) of this section. For the avoidance of doubt and without limitation, an artist page or site on a third-party service (e.g., a social networking service) shall not be considered a service operated by the record company or artist. Such interactive streams may be made or authorized by a record company under the promotional royalty rate only if—

(1) The interactive streaming subject to this paragraph (c) of a particular sound recording is offered or authorized by the record company on no more than 90 days total for all services (i.e., interactive streaming under this paragraph (c) of a particular sound recording may be authorized on no more than a total of 90 days, which need not be consecutive, and on any such day, interactive streams may be offered on one or more services operated by the record company or artist, subject to the provisions of paragraph (b)(2) of this section); provided, however, that an additional 90 days shall be available each time the sound recording is re-released by the record company in a remastered form or as part of a compilation with a different set of sound recordings than prior compilations that include that sound recording;

(2) In the case of interactive streaming through a service devoted to one featured artist, the interactive streams subject to this paragraph (c) of this section of a particular sound recording are made or authorized by the record company on no more than one official artist site per artist and are recordings of that artist; and

(3) In the case of interactive streaming through a service that is not limited to a single featured artist, all interactive streaming on such service (whether eligible for the promotional royalty rate or not) is limited to sound recordings of a single record company and its affiliates and the service would not reasonably be considered to be a meaningful substitute for a paid music service.

(d) Interactive streaming of clips. In addition to those in paragraph (a) of this section, the provisions of this paragraph (d) apply to interactive streaming conducted or authorized by record companies under the promotional royalty rate of segments of sound recordings of musical works with a playing time that does not exceed 90 seconds. Such interactive streams may be made or authorized by a record company under the promotional royalty rate without any of the temporal limitations set forth in paragraphs (b) and (c) of this section (but subject to the other conditions of paragraphs (b) and (c) of this section, as applicable). For clarity, this paragraph (d) is strictly limited to the uses described herein and shall not be construed as permitting the creation or use of an excerpt of a musical work in violation of 17 U.S.C. 106(2) or 115(a)(2) or any other right of a musical work owner.

History of 37 C.F.R. §385.14: 74 FR 4533, Mar. 1, 2009; 74 FR 6834, Mar. 1, 2009; 78 FR 67944, Jan. 1, 2014.

§385.15. REMOVED & RESERVED

§385.16. REPRODUCTION & DISTRIBUTION RIGHTS COVERED

A compulsory license under 17 U.S.C. 115 extends to all reproduction and distribution rights that may be necessary for the provision of the licensed activity, solely for the purpose of providing such licensed activity (and no other purpose).

History of 37 C.F.R. §385.16: 74 FR 4536, Mar. 1, 2009.

§385.17. EFFECT OF RATES

In any future proceedings under 17 U.S.C. 115(c)(3)(C) and (D), the royalty rates payable for a compulsory license shall be established de novo.

History of 37 C.F.R. §385.17: 74 FR 4536, Mar. 1, 2009.

SUBPART C. LIMITED OFFERINGS, MIXED SERVICE BUNDLES, MUSIC BUNDLES, PAID LOCKER SERVICES & PURCHASED CONTENT LOCKER SERVICES

§385.20. GENERAL

(a) Scope. This subpart establishes rates and terms of royalty payments for certain reproductions or distributions of musical works through limited offerings, mixed service bundles, music bundles, paid locker services and purchased content locker services provided in accordance with the provisions of 17 U.S.C. 115. For the avoidance of doubt, to the extent that product configurations for which rates are specified in subpart A of this part are included within licensed subpart C activity, as defined in §385.21, the rates specified in subpart A of this part shall not apply, except that in the case of a music bundle the compulsory licensee may elect to pay royalties for the music bundle pursuant to subpart C of this part or for the components of the bundle pursuant to subpart A of this part.

(b) Legal compliance. A licensee that, pursuant to 17 U.S.C. 115, makes or authorizes reproduction or distribution of musical works in limited offerings, mixed service bundles, music bundles, paid locker services or purchased content locker services shall comply with the requirements of that section, the rates and terms of this subpart, and any other applicable regulations, with respect to such musical works and uses licensed pursuant to 17 U.S.C. 115.

(c) Interpretation. This subpart is intended only to set rates and terms for situations in which the exclusive rights of a copyright owner are implicated and a compulsory license pursuant to 17 U.S.C. 115 is obtained. Neither this subpart nor the act of obtaining a license under 17 U.S.C. 115 is intended to express or imply any conclusion as to the circumstances in which any of the exclusive rights of a copyright owner are implicated or a license, including a compulsory license pursuant to 17 U.S.C. 115, must be obtained.

History of 37 C.F.R. §385.20: 78 FR 67945, Jan. 1, 2014.

§385.21. DEFINITIONS

For purposes of this subpart, the following definitions shall apply:

Affiliate shall have the meaning given in §385.11.

Applicable consideration shall have the meaning given in §385.11, except that for purposes of this subpart C, references in the definition of "Applicable consideration" in §385.11 to licensed activity shall mean licensed subpart C activity, as defined in this section.

Free trial royalty rate means the statutory royalty rate of zero in the case of certain free trial periods, as provided in §385.24.

GAAP shall have the meaning given in §385.11.

Interactive stream shall have the meaning given in §385.11.

Licensee shall have the meaning given in §385.11.

Licensed subpart C activity means, referring to subpart C of this part—

(1) In the case of a limited offering, the applicable interactive streams or limited downloads;

(2) In the case of a locker service, the applicable interactive streams, permanent digital downloads, restricted downloads or ringtones;

(3) In the case of a music bundle, the applicable reproduction or distribution of a physical phonorecord, permanent digital download or ringtone; and

(4) In the case of a mixed service bundle, the applicable—

(i) Permanent digital downloads;

(ii) Ringtones;

(iii) To the extent a limited offering is included in a mixed service bundle, interactive streams or limited downloads; or

(iv) To the extent a locker service is included in a mixed service bundle, interactive streams, permanent digital downloads, restricted downloads or ringtones.

Limited download shall have the meaning given in §385.11.

Limited offering means a subscription service providing interactive streams or limited downloads where—

(1) An end user is not provided the opportunity to listen to a particular sound recording chosen by the end user at a time chosen by the end user (i.e., the service does not provide interactive streams of individual recordings that are on-demand, and any limited downloads are rendered only as part of programs rather than as individual recordings that are on-demand); or

(2) The particular sound recordings available to the end user over a period of time are substantially limited relative to services in the marketplace providing access to a comprehensive catalog of recordings (e.g., a service limited to a particular genre, or permitting interactive streaming only from a monthly playlist consisting of a limited set of recordings).

Locker service means a service providing access to sound recordings of musical works in the form of interactive streams, permanent digital downloads, restricted downloads or ringtones, where the service has reasonably determined that phonorecords of the applicable sound recordings have been purchased by the end user or are otherwise in the possession of the end user prior to the end user's first request to access such sound recordings by means of the service. The term locker service does not extend to any part of a service otherwise meeting this definition as to which a license is not obtained for the applicable reproductions and distributions of musical works.

Mixed service bundle means an offering of one or more of permanent digital downloads, ringtones, locker services or limited offerings, together with one or more of non-music services (e.g., Internet access service, mobile phone service) or non-music products (e.g., a device such as a phone) of more than token value, that is provided to users as part of one transaction without pricing for the music services or music products separate from the whole offering.

Music bundle means an offering of two or more of physical phonorecords, permanent digital downloads or ringtones provided to users as part of one transaction (e.g., download plus ringtone, CD plus downloads). A music bundle must contain at least two different product configurations and cannot be combined with any other offering containing licensed activity under subpart B of this part or subpart C of this part.

(1) In the case of music bundles containing one or more physical phonorecords, the physical phonorecord component of the music bundle must be sold under a single catalog number, and the musical works embodied in the digital phonorecord delivery configurations in the music bundle must be the same as, or a subset of, the musical works embodied in the physical phonorecords; provided that when the music bundle contains a set of digital phonorecord deliveries sold by the same record company under substantially the same title as the physical phonorecord (e.g., a corresponding digital album), up to 5 sound recordings of musical works that are included in the stand-alone version of such set of digital phonorecord deliveries but are not included on the physical phonorecord may be included among the digital phonorecord deliveries in the music bundle. In addition, the seller must permanently part with possession of the physical phonorecord or phonorecords sold as part of the music bundle.

(2) In the case of music bundles composed solely of digital phonorecord deliveries, the number of digital phonorecord deliveries in either configuration cannot exceed 20, and the musical works embodied in each configuration in the music bundle must be the same as, or a subset of, the musical works embodied in the configuration containing the most musical works.

Paid locker service means a locker service that is a subscription service.

Permanent digital download shall have the meaning given in §385.2.

Purchased content locker service means a locker service made available to end-user purchasers of permanent digital downloads, ringtones or physical phonorecords at no incremental charge above the otherwise applicable purchase price of the permanent digital downloads, ringtones or physical phonorecords, with respect to the sound recordings embodied in permanent digital downloads or ringtones or physical phonorecords purchased from a qualifying seller as described in paragraph (1) of this definition of "Purchased content locker service," whereby the locker service enables the purchaser to engage in one or both of the qualifying activities indentified[1] in paragraph (2) of this definition of "Purchased content locker service." In addition, in the case of a locker service made available to end-user purchasers of physical phonorecords, the seller must permanently part with possession of the physical phonorecords.

(1) A qualifying seller for purposes of this definition of "purchased content locker service" is the same entity operating such locker service, one of its affiliates or predecessors, or—

(i) In the case of permanent digital downloads or ringtones, a seller having another legitimate connection to the locker service provider set forth in one or more written agreements (including that the locker service and permanent digital downloads or ringtones are offered through the same third party); or

(ii) In the case of physical phonorecords, a seller having an agreement with—

(A) The locker service provider whereby such parties establish an integrated offer that creates a consumer experience commensurate with having the same service both sell the physical phonorecord and offer the locker service; or

(B) A service provider that also has an agreement with the entity offering the locker service, where pursuant to those agreements the service provider has established an integrated offer that creates a consumer experience commensurate with having the same service both sell the physical phonorecord and offer the locker service.

(2) Qualifying activity for purposes of this definition of "purchased content locker service" is enabling the purchaser to—

(i) Receive one or more additional phonorecords of such purchased sound recordings of musical works in the form of permanent digital downloads or ringtones at the time of purchase, or

(ii) Subsequently access such purchased sound recordings of musical works in the form of interactive streams, additional permanent digital downloads, restricted downloads or ringtones.

Record company shall have the meaning given in §385.11.

Restricted download means a digital phonorecord delivery distributed in the form of a download that may not be retained and played on a permanent basis. The term restricted download includes a limited download.

Ringtone shall have the meaning given in §385.2.

Service provider shall have the meaning given in §385.11, except that for purposes of this subpart references in the definition of "Service provider" in §385.11 to licensed activity and service revenue shall mean licensed subpart C activity, as defined in this section, and subpart C service revenue, as defined in this section, respectively.

Subpart C offering means, referring to subpart C of this part, a service provider's offering of licensed subpart C activity, as defined in this section, that is subject to a particular rate set forth in §385.23(a) (e.g., a particular subscription plan available through the service provider).

Subpart C relevant page means, referring to subpart C of this part, a page (including a Web page, screen or display) from which licensed subpart C activity, as defined in this section, offered by a service provider is directly available to end users, but only where the offering of licensed subpart C activity, as defined in this section, and content that directly relates to the offering of licensed subpart C activity, as defined in this section, (e.g., an image of the artist or artwork closely associated with such offering, artist or album information, reviews of such offering, credits and music player controls) comprises 75% or more of the space on that page, excluding any space occupied by advertising. A licensed subpart C activity, as defined in this section, is directly available to end users from a page if sound recordings of musical works can be accessed by end users for licensed subpart C activity, as defined in this section, from such page (in most cases this will be the page where the transmission takes place).

Subpart C service revenue.

(1) Subject to paragraphs (2) through (6) of the definition of "Subpart C service revenue," as defined in this section, and subject to GAAP, subpart C service revenue shall mean, referring to subpart C of this part, the following:

(i) All revenue recognized by the service provider from end users from the provision of licensed subpart C activity, as defined in this section;

(ii) All revenue recognized by the service provider by way of sponsorship and commissions as a result of the inclusion of third-party "in-stream" or "in-download" advertising as part of licensed subpart C activity, as defined in this section, (i.e., advertising placed immediately at the start, end or during the actual delivery, by way of transmissions of a musical work that constitute licensed subpart C activity, as defined in this section); and

(iii) All revenue recognized by the service provider, including by way of sponsorship and commissions, as a result of the placement of third-party advertising on a subpart C relevant page, as defined in this section, of the service or on any page that directly follows such subpart C relevant page, as defined in this section, leading up to and including the transmission of a musical work that constitutes licensed subpart C activity, as defined in this section; provided that, in the case where more than one service is actually available to end users from a subpart C relevant page, as defined in this section, any advertising revenue shall be allocated between such services on the basis of the relative amounts of the page they occupy.

(2) In each of the cases identified in paragraph (1) of the definition of "Subpart C service revenue," of this section such revenue shall, for the avoidance of doubt,

(i) Include any such revenue recognized by the service provider, or if not recognized by the service provider, by any associate, affiliate, agent or representative of such service provider in lieu of its being recognized by the service provider;

(ii) Include the value of any barter or other nonmonetary consideration;

(iii) Not be reduced by credit card commissions or similar payment process charges; and

(iv) Except as expressly set forth in this subpart, not be subject to any other deduction or set-off other than refunds to end users for licensed subpart C activity, as defined in this section, that they were unable to use due to technical faults in the licensed subpart C activity, as defined in this section, or other bona fide refunds or credits issued to end users in the ordinary course of business.

(3) In each of the cases identified in paragraph (1) of the definition of "Subpart C service revenue" of this section, such revenue shall, for the avoidance of doubt, exclude revenue derived solely in connection with services and activities other than licensed subpart C activity, as defined in this section, provided that advertising or sponsorship revenue shall be treated as provided in paragraphs (2) and (4) of the definition of "Subpart C service revenue" of this section. By way of example, the following kinds of revenue shall be excluded:

(i) Revenue derived from non-music voice, content and text services;

(ii) Revenue derived from other non-music products and services (including search services, sponsored searches and click-through commissions);

(iii) Revenue generated from the sale of actual locker service storage space to the extent that such storage space is sold at a separate retail price;

(iv) In the case of a locker service, revenue derived from the sale of permanent digital downloads or ringtones; and

(v) Revenue derived from other music or music-related products and services that are not or do not include licensed subpart C activity, as defined in this section.

(4) For purposes of paragraph (1) of the definition of "Subpart C service revenue" of this section, advertising or sponsorship revenue shall be reduced by the actual cost of obtaining such revenue, not to exceed 15%.

(5) In the case of a mixed service bundle, the revenue deemed to be recognized from end users for the service for the purpose of the definition in paragraph (1) of the definition of "Subpart C service revenue" of this section shall be the greater of—

(i) The revenue recognized from end users for the mixed service bundle less the standalone published price for end users for each of the non-music product or non-music service components of the bundle; provided that, if there is no such standalone published price for a non-music component of the bundle, then the average standalone published price for end users for the most closely comparable non-music product or non-music service in the U.S. shall be used or, if more than one such comparable exists, the average of such standalone prices for such comparables shall be used; and

(ii) Either—

(A) In the case of a mixed service bundle that either has 750,000 subscribers or other registered users, or is reasonably expected to have 750,000 subscribers or other registered users within 1 year after commencement of the mixed service bundle, 40% of the standalone published price of the licensed music component of the bundle (i.e., the permanent digital downloads, ringtones, locker service or limited offering); provided that, if there is no such standalone published price for the licensed music component of the bundle, then the average standalone published price for end users for the most closely comparable licensed music component in the U.S. shall be used or, if more than one such comparable exists, the average of such standalone prices for such comparables shall be used; and further provided that in any case in which royalties were paid based on this paragraph due to a reasonable expectation of reaching 750,000 subscribers or other registered users within 1 year after commencement of the mixed service bundle and that does not actually happen, applicable payments shall, in the accounting period next following the end of such 1-year period, retroactively be adjusted as if paragraph (5)(ii)(B) of the definition of "Subpart C service revenue" of this section applied; or

(B) Otherwise, 50% of the standalone published price of the licensed music component of the bundle (i.e., the permanent digital downloads, ringtones, locker service or limited offering); provided that, if there is no such standalone published price for the licensed music component of the bundle, then the average standalone published price for end users for the most closely comparable licensed music component in the U.S. shall be used or, if more than one such comparable exists, the average of such standalone prices for such comparables shall be used.

(6) In the case of a music bundle containing a physical phonorecord, where the music bundle is distributed by a record company for resale and the record company is the compulsory licensee—

(i) Service revenue shall be 150% of the record company's wholesale revenue from the music bundle; and

(ii) The times at which distribution and revenue recognition are deemed to occur shall be in accordance with §201.19 of this title.

Subscription service means a digital music service for which end users are required to pay a fee to access the service for defined subscription periods of 3 years or less (in contrast to, for example, a service where the basic charge to users is a payment per download or per play), whether such payment is made for access to the service on a standalone basis or as part of a bundle with one or more other products or services, and including any use of such a service on a trial basis without charge as described in §385.24.

1. **Editor's note:** Probably should be "identified."

History of 37 C.F.R. §385.21: 78 FR 67945, Jan. 1, 2014.

§385.22. CALCULATION OF ROYALTY PAYMENTS IN GENERAL

(a) Applicable royalty. Licensees that make or authorize licensed subpart C activity, as defined in §385.21, pursuant to 17 U.S.C. 115 shall pay royalties therefor that are calculated as provided in this section, subject to the royalty rates and subscriber-based royalty floors for specific types of services provided in §385.23, except as provided for certain free trial periods in §385.24.

(b) Rate calculation methodology. Royalty payments for licensed subpart C activity, as defined in §385.21, shall be calculated as provided in this paragraph (b). If a service provides different subpart C offerings, as defined in §385.21, royalties must be separately calculated with respect to each such subpart C offering, as defined in §385.21, taking into consideration service revenue and expenses associated with such offering. Uses subject to the free trial royalty rate shall be excluded from the calculation of royalties due, as further described in this section and §385.23.

(1) Step 1: Calculate the All-In Royalty for the Subpart C Offering, as Defined in §385.21. For each accounting period, the all-in royalty for each subpart C offering, as defined in §385.21, of the service provider is the greater of:

(i) The applicable percentage of subpart C service revenue, as defined in §385.21, associated with the relevant offering as set forth in §385.23(a) (excluding any subpart C service revenue, as defined in §385.21, derived solely from licensed subpart C activity, as defined in §385.21, uses subject to the free trial royalty rate); and

(ii) The minimum specified in §385.23(a) for the subpart C offering, as defined in §385.21, involved.

(2) Step 2: Subtract applicable performance royalties to determine the payable royalty pool, which is the amount payable for the reproduction and distribution of all musical works used by the service provider by virtue of its licensed subpart C activity, as defined in §385.21, for a particular subpart C offering, as defined in §385.21, during the accounting period. From the amount determined in step 1 in paragraph (b)(1) of this section, for each subpart C offering, as defined in §385.21, of the service provider, subtract the total amount of royalties for public performance of musical works that has been or will be expensed pursuant to public performance licenses in connection with uses of musical works through such subpart C offering, as defined in §385.21, during the accounting period that constitute licensed subpart C activity, as defined in §385.21, (other than licensed subpart C activity, as defined in §385.21, subject to the free trial royalty rate), or in connection with previewing of such subpart C offering, as defined in §385.21, during the accounting period. Although this amount may be the total of the payments with respect to the service for that subpart C offering, as defined in §385.21, for the accounting period, it will be less than the total of such public performance payments if the service is also engaging in public performance of musical works that does not constitute licensed subpart C activity, as defined in §385.21, or previewing of such licensed subpart C activity, as defined in §385.21. In the case where the service is also engaging in the public performance of musical works that does not constitute licensed subpart C activity, as defined in §385.21, the amount to be subtracted for public performance payments shall be the amount of such payments allocable to licensed subpart C activity, as defined in §385.21, uses (other than free trial royalty rate uses), and previewing of such uses, in connection with the relevant subpart C offering, as defined in §385.21, as determined in relation to all uses of musical works for which the public performance payments are made for the accounting period. Such allocation shall be made on the basis of plays of musical works or, where per-play information is unavailable due to bona fide technical limitations as described in step 3 in paragraph (b)(3) of this section, using the same alternative methodology as provided in step 3 in paragraph (b)(3) of this section.

(3) Step 3: Calculate the Per-Work Royalty Allocation for Each Relevant Work. This is the amount payable for the reproduction and distribution of each musical work used by the service provider by virtue of its licensed subpart C activity, as defined in §385.21, through a particular subpart C offering, as defined in §385.21, during the accounting period. To determine this amount, the result determined in step 2 in paragraph (b)(2) of this section must be allocated to each musical work used through the subpart C offering, as defined in §385.21. The allocation shall be accomplished as follows:

(i) In the case of limited offerings (but not limited offerings that are part of mixed service bundles), by dividing the payable royalty pool determined in step 2 in paragraph (b)(2) of this section for such offering by the total number of plays of all musical works through such offering during the accounting period (other than free trial royalty rate plays) to yield a per-play allocation, and multiplying that result by the number of plays of each musical work (other than free trial royalty rate plays) through the offering during the accounting period. For purposes of determining the per-work royalty allocation in all calculations under this step 3 only (i.e., after the payable royalty pool has been determined), for sound recordings of musical works with a playing time of over 5 minutes, each play shall be counted as provided in paragraph (c) of this section. Notwithstanding the foregoing, if the service provider is not capable of tracking play information due to bona fide limitations of the available technology for services of that nature or of devices usable with the service, the per-work royalty allocation may instead be accomplished in a manner consistent with the methodology used by the service provider for making royalty payment allocations for the use of individual sound recordings.

(ii) In the case of mixed service bundles and locker services, by—

(A) Determining a constructive number of plays of all licensed musical works that is the sum of the total number of interactive streams of all licensed musical works made through such offering during the accounting period (other than free trial royalty rate interactive streams), plus the total number of plays of restricted downloads of all licensed musical works made through such offering during the accounting period as to which the service provider tracks plays (other than free trial royalty rate restricted downloads), plus 5 times the total number of downloads of all licensed musical works made through such offering during the accounting period as to which the service provider does not track plays (other than free trial royalty rate downloads);

(B) Determining a constructive per-play allocation that is the payable royalty pool determined in step 2 of paragraph (b)(2) of this section for such offering divided by the constructive number of plays of all licensed musical works determined in paragraph (b)(3)(ii)(A) of this section;

(C) For each licensed musical work, determining a constructive number of plays of that musical work that is the sum of the total number of interactive streams of such licensed musical work made through such offering during the accounting period (other than free trial royalty rate interactive streams), plus the total number of plays of restricted downloads of such licensed musical work made through such offering during the accounting period as to which the service provider tracks plays (other than free trial royalty rate restricted downloads), plus 5 times the total number of downloads of such licensed musical work made through such offering during the accounting period as to which the service provider does not track plays (other than free trial royalty rate downloads); and

(D) For each licensed musical work, determining the per-work royalty allocation by multiplying the constructive per-play allocation determined in paragraph (b)(3)(ii)(B) of this section by the constructive number of plays of that musical work determined in paragraph (b)(3)(ii)(C) of this section.

(E) Notwithstanding the foregoing, if a service provider offers both a paid locker service and a purchased content locker service, and with respect to the purchased content locker service there is no subpart C service revenue, as defined in §385.21, and the applicable subminimum is zero dollars, then the service provider shall be permitted to include within the calculation of constructive plays under paragraphs (b)(3)(ii)(A) and (C) of this section for the paid locker service, the licensed subpart C activity, as defined in §385.21, made through the purchased content locker service (i.e., the total number of interactive streams of all licensed musical works made through the purchased content locker service during the accounting period (other than free trial royalty rate interactive streams), plus the total number of plays of restricted downloads of all licensed musical works made through the purchased content locker service during the accounting period as to which the service provider tracks plays (other than free trial royalty rate restricted downloads), plus 5 times the total number of downloads of all licensed musical works made through the purchased content locker service during the accounting period as to which the service provider does not track plays (other than free trial royalty rate downloads)); provided that the relevant licensed subpart C activity, as defined in §385.21, made through the purchased content locker service is similarly included within the play calculation for the paid locker service for the corresponding sound recording rights.

(iii) In the case of music bundles, by—

(A) Allocating the payable royalty pool determined in step 2 of paragraph (b)(2) of this section to separate pools for each type of product configuration included in the music bundle (e.g., CD, permanent digital download, ringtone) in accordance with the ratios that the standalone published prices of the products that are included in the music bundle bear to each other; provided that, if there is no such standalone published price for such a product, then the average standalone published price for end users for the most closely comparable product in the U.S. shall be used or, if more than one such comparable exists, the average of such standalone prices for such comparables shall be used; and

(B) Allocating the product configuration pools determined in paragraph (b)(3)(iii)(A) of this section to individual musical works by dividing each such pool by the total number of sound recordings of musical works included in products of that configuration in the music bundle.

(c) Overtime adjustment. For purposes of the calculations in step 3 of paragraph (b)(3)(i) of this section only, for sound recordings of musical works with a playing time of over 5 minutes, adjust the number of plays as follows:

(1) 5:01 to 6:00 minutes—Each play = 1.2 plays

(2) 6:01 to 7:00 minutes—Each play = 1.4 plays

(3) 7:01 to 8:00 minutes—Each play = 1.6 plays

(4) 8:01 to 9:00 minutes—Each play = 1.8 plays

(5) 9:01 to 10:00 minutes—Each play = 2.0 plays

(6) For playing times of greater than 10 minutes, continue to add .2 plays for each additional minute or fraction thereof.

History of 37 C.F.R. §385.22: 78 FR 67947, Jan. 1, 2014.

§385.23. ROYALTY RATES & SUBSCRIBER-BASED ROYALTY FLOORS FOR SPECIFIC TYPES OF SERVICES

(a) In general. The following royalty rates and subscriber-based royalty floors shall apply to the following types of licensed subpart C activity, as defined in §385.21:

(1) Mixed service bundle. In the case of a mixed service bundle, the percentage of subpart C service revenue, as defined in §385.21, applicable in step 1 of §385.22(b)(1)(i) is 11.35%. The minimum for use in step 1 of §385.22(b)(1)(ii) is the appropriate subminimum as described in paragraph (b) of this section for the accounting period, where the all-in percentage applicable to §385.23(b)(1) is 17.36%, and the sound recording-only percentage applicable to §385.23(b)(2) is 21%.

(2) Music bundle. In the case of a music bundle, the percentage of subpart C service revenue, as defined in §385.21, applicable in step 1 of §385.22(b)(1)(i) is 11.35%. The minimum for use in step 1 of §385.22(b)(1)(ii) is the appropriate subminimum as described in paragraph (b) of this section for the accounting period, where the all-in percentage applicable to §385.23(b)(1) and (3) is 17.36%, and the sound recording-only percentage applicable to §385.23(b)(2) is 21%.

(3) Limited offering. In the case of a limited offering, the percentage of subpart C service revenue, as defined in §385.21, applicable in step 1 of §385.22(b)(1)(i) is 10.5%. The minimum for use in step 1 of §385.22(b)(1)(ii) is the greater of—

(i) The appropriate subminimum as described in paragraph (b) of this section for the accounting period, where the all-in percentage applicable to §385.23(b)(1) is 17.36%, and the sound recording-only percentage applicable to §385.23(b)(2) is 21%; and

(ii) The aggregate amount of 18 cents per subscriber per month.

(4) Paid locker service. In the case of a paid locker service, the percentage of subpart C service revenue, as defined in §385.21, applicable in step 1 of §385.22(b)(1)(i) is 12%. The minimum for use in step 1 of §385.22(b)(1)(ii) is the greater of—

(i) The appropriate subminimum as described in paragraph (b) of this section for the accounting period, where the all-in percentage applicable to §385.23(b)(1) is 17.11%, and the sound recording-only percentage applicable to §385.23(b)(2) is 20.65%; and

(ii) The aggregate amount of 17 cents per subscriber per month.

(5) Purchased content locker service. In the case of a purchased content locker service, the percentage of subpart C service revenue, as defined in §385.21, applicable in step 1 of §385.22(b)(1)(i) is 12%. For the avoidance of doubt, paragraph (1)(i) of the definition of "Subpart C service revenue," as defined in §385.21, shall not apply. The minimum for use in step 1 in §385.22(b)(1)(ii) is the appropriate subminimum as described in paragraph (b) of this section for the accounting period, where the all-in percentage applicable to §385.23(b)(1) is 18%, and the sound recording-only percentage applicable to §385.23(b)(2) is 22%, except that for purposes of paragraph (b) of this section the applicable consideration expensed by the service for the relevant rights shall consist only of applicable consideration expensed by the service, if any, that is incremental to the applicable consideration expensed for the rights to make the relevant permanent digital downloads and ringtones.

(b) Computation of subminima. For purposes of paragraph (a) of this section, the subminimum for an accounting period is the aggregate of the following with respect to all sound recordings of musical works used in the relevant subpart C offering, as defined in §385.21, of the service provider during the accounting period—

(1) Except as provided in paragraph (b)(3) of this section, in cases in which the record company is the licensee under 17 U.S.C. 115 and the record company has granted the rights to engage in licensed subpart C activity, as defined in §385.21, with respect to a sound recording through the third-party service together with the right to reproduce and distribute the musical work embodied therein, the appropriate all-in percentage from paragraph (a) of this section of the total amount expensed by the service provider or any of its affiliates in accordance with GAAP for such rights for the accounting period, which amount shall equal the applicable consideration for such rights at the time such applicable consideration is properly recognized as an expense under GAAP.

(2) In cases in which the record company is not the licensee under 17 U.S.C. 115 and the record company has granted the rights to engage in licensed subpart C activity, as defined in §385.21, with respect to a sound recording through the third-party service without the right to reproduce and distribute the musical work embodied therein, the appropriate sound recording-only percentage from paragraph (a) of this section of the total amount expensed by the service provider or any of its affiliates in accordance with GAAP for such rights for the accounting period, which amount shall equal the applicable consideration for such rights at the time such applicable consideration is properly recognized as an expense under GAAP.

(3) In the case of a music bundle containing a physical phonorecord, where the music bundle is distributed by a record company for resale and the record company is the compulsory licensee, the appropriate all-in percentage from paragraph (a) of this section of the record company's total wholesale revenue from the music bundle in accordance with GAAP for the accounting period, which amount shall equal the applicable consideration for such music bundle at the time such applicable consideration is properly recognized as revenue under GAAP, subject to the provisions of §201.19 of this title concerning the times at which distribution and revenue recognition are deemed to occur.

(4) If a record company providing sound recording rights to the service provider for a licensed subpart C activity, as defined in §385.21—

(i) Recognizes revenue (in accordance with GAAP, and including for the avoidance of doubt all applicable consideration with respect to such rights for the accounting period, regardless of the form or timing of payment) from a person or entity other than the service provider providing the licensed subpart C activity, as defined in §385.21, and its affiliates, and

(ii) Such revenue is received, in the context of the transactions involved, as applicable consideration for such rights,

(iii) Then such revenue shall be added to the amounts expensed by the service provider solely for purposes of paragraph (b)(1) or (2) of this section, as applicable, if not already included in such expensed amounts. Where the service provider is the licensee, if the service provider provides the record company all information necessary for the record company to determine whether additional royalties are payable by the service provider hereunder as a result of revenue recognized from a person or entity other than the service provider as described in the immediately preceding sentence, then the record company shall provide such further information as necessary for the service provider to calculate the additional royalties and indemnify the service provider for such additional royalties. The sole obligation of the record company shall be to pay the licensee such additional royalties if actually payable as royalties hereunder; provided, however, that this shall not affect any otherwise existing right or remedy of the copyright owner nor diminish the licensee's obligations to the copyright owner.

(c) Computation of subscriber-based royalty rates. For purposes of paragraphs (a)(3) and (4) of this section, to determine the subscriber-based minimum applicable to any particular subpart C offering, as defined in §385.21, the total number of subscriber-months for the accounting period shall be calculated, taking into account all end users who were subscribers for complete calendar months, prorating in the case of end users who were subscribers for only part of a calendar month, and deducting on a prorated basis for end users covered by a free trial period subject to the free trial royalty rate as described in §385.24. The product of the total number of subscriber-months for the accounting period and the specified number of cents per subscriber shall be used as the subscriber-based component of the minimum for the accounting period.

History of 37 C.F.R. §385.23: 78 FR 67949, Jan. 1, 2014.

§385.24. FREE TRIAL PERIODS

(a) General provisions. This section establishes a royalty rate of zero in the case of certain free trial periods for mixed service bundles, paid locker services and limited offerings under a license pursuant to 17 U.S.C. 115. Subject to the requirements of 17 U.S.C. 115 and the additional provisions of paragraphs (b) through (e) of this section, the free trial royalty rate shall apply to a musical work when a record company transmits or authorizes the transmission, as part of a mixed service bundle, paid locker service or limited offering, of a sound recording that embodies such musical work, only if—

(1) The primary purpose of the record company in providing or authorizing the free trial period is to promote the applicable subpart C offering, as defined in §385.21;

(2) No applicable consideration for making or authorizing the transmissions is received by the record company, or any other person or entity acting on behalf of or in lieu of the record company, except for in-kind promotional consideration used to promote the sale or paid use of sound recordings or audiovisual works embodying musical works or the paid use of music services through which sound recordings or audiovisual works embodying musical works are available;

(3) The free trial period does not exceed 30 consecutive days per subscriber per two-year period;

(4) In connection with authorizing the transmissions, the record company has obtained from the service provider it authorizes a written representation that—

(i) The service provider agrees to maintain for a period of no less than 5 years from the end of each relevant accounting period complete and accurate records of the relevant authorization, and identifying each sound recording of a musical work made available through the free trial period, the licensed subpart C activity, as defined in §385.21, involved, and the number of plays or downloads, as applicable, of such recording;

(ii) The service is in all material respects operating with appropriate license authority with respect to the musical works it is using; and

(iii) The representation is signed by a person authorized to make the representation on behalf of the service provider;

(5) Upon receipt by the record company of written notice from the copyright owner of a musical work or agent of the copyright owner stating in good faith that a particular service is in a material manner operating without appropriate license authority from such copyright owner, the record company shall within 5 business days withdraw by written notice its authorization of such uses of such copyright owner's musical works under the free trial royalty rate by that service;

(6) The free trial period is offered free of any charge to the end user; and

(7) End users are periodically offered an opportunity to subscribe to the service during such free trial period.

(b) Recordkeeping by record companies. To rely upon the free trial royalty rate for a free trial period, a record company making or authorizing the free trial period shall keep complete and accurate contemporaneous written records of the contractual terms that bear upon the free trial period; and further provided that, if the record company itself is conducting the free trial period, it shall also maintain any additional records described in paragraph (a)(4)(i) of this section. The records required by this paragraph (b) shall be maintained for no less time than the record company maintains records of usage of royalty-bearing uses involving the same type of licensed subpart C activity, as defined in §385.21, in the ordinary course of business, but in no event for less than 5 years from the conclusion of the licensed subpart C activity, as defined in §385.21, to which they pertain. If the copyright owner of a musical work or its agent requests a copy of the information to be maintained under this paragraph (b) with respect to a specific free trial period, the record company shall provide complete and accurate documentation within 10 business days, except for any information required under paragraph (a)(4)(i) of this section, which shall be provided within 20 business days, and provided that if the copyright owner or agent requests information concerning a large volume of free trial periods or sound recordings, the record company shall have a reasonable time, in view of the amount of information requested, to respond to any request of such copyright owner or agent. If the record company does not provide required information within the required time, and upon receipt of written notice citing such failure does not provide such information within a further 10 business days, the uses will be considered not to be subject to the free trial royalty rate and the record company (but not any third-party service it has authorized) shall be liable for any payment due for such uses; provided, however, that all rights and remedies of the copyright owner with respect to unauthorized uses shall be preserved.

(c) Recordkeeping by services. If the copyright owner of a musical work or its agent requests a copy of the information to be maintained under paragraph (a)(4)(i) of this section by a service authorized by a record company with respect to a specific promotion, the service provider shall provide complete and accurate documentation within 20 business days, provided that if the copyright owner or agent requests information concerning a large volume of free trial periods or sound recordings, the service provider shall have a reasonable time, in view of the amount of information requested, to respond to any request of such copyright owner or agent. If the service provider does not provide required information within the required time, and upon receipt of written notice citing such failure does not provide such information within a further 10 business days, the uses will be considered not to be subject to the free trial royalty rate and the service provider (but not the record company) will be liable for any payment due for such uses; provided, however, that all rights and remedies of the copyright owner with respect to unauthorized uses shall be preserved.

(d) Interpretation. The free trial royalty rate is exclusively for audio-only licensed subpart C activity, as defined in §385.21, involving musical works subject to licensing under 17 U.S.C. 115. The free trial royalty rate does not apply to any other use under 17 U.S.C. 115; nor does it apply to public performances, audiovisual works, lyrics or other uses outside the scope of 17 U.S.C. 115. Without limitation, uses subject to licensing under 17 U.S.C. 115 that do not qualify for the free trial royalty rate (including without limitation licensed subpart C activity, as defined in §385.21, beyond the time limitations applicable to the free trial royalty rate) require payment of applicable royalties. This section is based on an understanding of industry practices and market conditions at the time of its development, among other things. The terms of this section shall be subject to de novo review and consideration (or elimination altogether) in future proceedings before the Copyright Royalty Judges. Nothing in this section shall be interpreted or construed in such a manner as to nullify or diminish any limitation, requirement or obligation of 17 U.S.C. 115 or other protection for musical works afforded by the Copyright Act, 17 U.S.C. 101, et seq.

History of 37 C.F.R. §385.24: 78 FR 67950, Jan. 1, 2014.

§385.25. REPRODUCTION & DISTRIBUTION RIGHTS COVERED

A compulsory license under 17 U.S.C. 115 extends to all reproduction and distribution rights that may be necessary for the provision of the licensed subpart C activity, as defined in §385.21, solely for the purpose of providing such licensed subpart C activity, as defined in §385.21 (and no other purpose).

History of 37 C.F.R. §385.25: 78 FR 67951, Jan. 1, 2014.

§385.26. EFFECT OF RATES

In any future proceedings under 17 U.S.C. 115(c)(3)(C) and (D), the royalty rates payable for a compulsory license shall be established de novo.

History of 37 C.F.R. §385.26: 78 FR 67951, Jan. 1, 2014.

PART 386. ADJUSTMENT OF ROYALTY FEES FOR SECONDARY TRANSMISSIONS BY SATELLITE CARRIERS

§386.1. GENERAL

This part 386 adjusts the rates of royalties payable under the statutory license for the secondary transmission of broadcast stations under 17 U.S.C. 119.

History of 37 C.F.R. §386.1: 75 FR 53198, Aug. 31, 2010.

A §386.2. ROYALTY FEE FOR SECONDARY TRANSMISSION BY SATELLITE CARRIERS

(a) General. **(1)** For purposes of this section, Per subscriber per month shall mean for each subscriber subscribing to the station in question (or to a package including such station) on the last day of a given month.

(2) In the case of a station engaged in digital multicasting, the rates set forth in paragraph (b) of this section shall apply to each digital stream that a satellite carrier or distributor retransmits pursuant to 17 U.S.C. 119, provided however that no additional royalty shall be paid for the carriage of any material related to the programming on such stream.

(b) Rates—**(1)** Private home viewing. The rates applicable to Satellite Carriers' carriage of each broadcast signal for private home viewing shall be as follows:

(i) 2010: 25 cents per subscriber per month (for each month of 2010);

(ii) 2011: 25 cents per subscriber per month;

(iii) 2012: 26 cents per subscriber per month;

(iv) 2013: 27 cents per subscriber per month;

(v) 2014: 27 cents per subscriber per month.

(vi) 2015: 27 cents per subscriber per month (for each month of 2015).[1]

(vii) 2016: 27 cents per subscriber per month (for each month of 2016).[3]

(viii) 2017: 27 cents per subscriber per month.

(ix) 2018: 28 cents per subscriber per month.

(2) Viewing in commercial establishments. The rates applicable to Satellite Carriers' carriage of each broadcast signal for viewing in commercial establishments shall be as follows:

(i) 2010: 50 cents per subscriber per month (for each month of 2010);

(ii) 2011: 51 cents per subscriber per month;

(iii) 2012: 53 cents per subscriber per month;

(iv) 2013: 54 cents per subscriber per month;

(v) 2014: 55 cents per subscriber per month.

(vi) 2015: 56 cents per subscriber per month (for each month of 2015).[2]

(vii) 2016: 56 cents per subscriber per month (for each month of 2016).[4]

(viii) 2017: 57 cents per subscriber per month.

(ix) 2018: 58 cents per subscriber per month.

1. This is the 2014 rate adjusted for the amount of inflation as measured by the change in the Consumer Price Index for All Urban Consumers All Items from October 2013 to October 2014.

2. This is the 2014 rate adjusted for the amount of inflation as measured by the change in the Consumer Price Index for All Urban Consumers All Items from October 2013 to October 2014.

3. This is the 2015 rate adjusted for the amount of inflation as measured by the change in the Consumer Price Index for All Urban Consumers All Items from October 2014 to October 2015.

4. This is the 2015 rate adjusted for the amount of inflation as measured by the change in the Consumer Price Index for All Urban Consumers All Items from October 2014 to October 2015.

History of 37 C.F.R. §386.2: 75 FR 53198, Aug. 31, 2010; 75 FR 75624, Dec. 6, 2010; 76 FR 74704, Dec. 1, 2011; 77 FR 70374, Jan. 1, 2013; 78 FR 71502, Jan. 1, 2014; 80 FR 22418, Apr. 22, 2015; 80 FR 73119, Jan. 1, 2016; 81 FR 84479, Jan. 1, 2017; 82 FR 55947, Jan. 1, 2018.

PART 387. ADJUSTMENT OF ROYALTY FEE FOR CABLE COMPULSORY LICENSE

§387.1. GENERAL

This part establishes adjusted terms and rates for royalty payments in accordance with the provisions of 17 U.S.C. 111 and 801(b)(2)(A), (B), (C), and (D). Upon compliance with 17 U.S.C. 111 and the terms and rates of this part, a cable system shall be subject to a statutory license authorizing secondary transmissions of broadcast signals to the extent provided in 17 U.S.C. 111.

History of 37 C.F.R. §387.1: 81 FR 62813, Sept. 13, 2016.

§387.2. ROYALTY FEE FOR COMPULSORY LICENSE FOR SECONDARY TRANSMISSION BY CABLE SYSTEMS

(a) Royalty fee rates. Commencing with the first semiannual accounting period of 2015 and for each semiannual accounting period thereafter, the royalty fee rates for secondary transmission by cable systems not subject to paragraph (b) of this section are those established by 17 U.S.C. 111(d)(1)(B)(i)-(iv), as amended.

(b) Rates for certain classes of cable systems. Commencing with the first semiannual accounting period of 2015 and for each semiannual accounting period thereafter, the alternate tiered royalty fee rates for cable systems with certain levels of gross receipts as described in 17 U.S.C. 111(d)(1)(E) and (F), are those described therein.

(c) 3.75 percent rate. Commencing with the first semiannual accounting period of 2015, and for each semiannual accounting period thereafter, and notwithstanding paragraphs (a) and (d) of this section, for each distant signal equivalent or fraction thereof not represented by the carriage of:

(1) Any signal that was permitted (or, in the case of cable systems commencing operations after June 24, 1981, that would have been permitted) under the rules and regulations of the Federal Communications Commission in effect on June 24, 1981 (former 47 CFR 76.1 through 76.617 (1980)); or

(2) A signal of the same type (that is, independent, network, or non-commercial educational) substituted for such permitted signal; or

(3) A signal that was carried pursuant to an individual waiver of (former 47 CFR 76.1 through 76.617 (1980)); in lieu of the royalty rates specified in paragraphs (a) and (d) of this section, the royalty rate shall be 3.75 percent of the gross receipts of the cable system for each distant signal equivalent. Any fraction of a distant signal equivalent shall be computed at its fractional value.

(d) Syndicated exclusivity surcharge. Commencing with the first semiannual accounting period of 2015 and for each semiannual accounting period thereafter, in the case of a cable system located outside the 35-mile specified zone of a commercial VHF station that places a predicted Grade B contour, in whole or in part, over the cable system, and that is not significantly viewed or otherwise exempt from the FCC's syndicated exclusivity rules in effect on June 24, 1981 (former 47 CFR 76.151 through 76.617 (1980)), for each distant signal equivalent or fraction thereof represented by the carriage of such commercial VHF station, the royalty rate shall be, in addition to the amount specified in paragraph (a) of this section:

(1) For cable systems located wholly or in part within a top 50 television market:

(i) 0.599 percent of such gross receipts for the first distant signal equivalent;

(ii) 0.377 percent of such gross receipts for each of the second, third, and fourth distant signal equivalents; and

(iii) 0.178 percent of such gross receipts for the fifth distant signal equivalent and each additional distant signal equivalent thereafter;

(2) For cable systems located wholly or in part within a second 50 television market:

(i) 0.300 percent of such gross receipts for the first distant signal equivalent;

(ii) 0.189 percent of such gross receipts for each of the second, third, and fourth distant signal equivalents; and

(iii) 0.089 percent of such gross receipts for the fifth distant signal equivalent and each additional distant signal equivalent thereafter;

(3) For purposes of this section "first 50 major television markets" and "second 50 major television markets" shall be defined as those terms are defined or interpreted in accordance with the Federal Communications Commission rule "Major television markets" in effect on June 24, 1981 (47 CFR 76.51 (1980)).

(e) Computation of rates. Computation of royalty fees shall be governed by 17 U.S.C. 111(d) and 111(f) and 37 CFR 201.17.

History of 37 C.F.R. §387.2: 81 FR 62813, Sept. 13, 2016.

Part 388. Adjustment of Royalty Rate for Coin-Operated Phonorecord Players

§388.1. General

This part 388 establishes the compulsory license fees for coin-operated phonorecord players beginning on January 1, 1982, in accordance with the provisions of 17 U.S.C. 116.

History of 37 C.F.R. §388.1: 81 FR 83141, Nov. 21, 2016.

§388.2. Definition of Coin-Operated Phonorecord Player

As used in this part, the term coin-operated phonorecord player is a machine or device that:

(a) Is employed solely for the performance of nondramatic musical works by means of phonorecords upon being activated by insertion of coins, currency, tokens, or other monetary units or their equivalent;

(b) Is located in an establishment making no direct or indirect charge for admission;

(c) Is accompanied by a list of the titles of all the musical works available for performance on it, which list is affixed to the phonorecord player or posted in the establishment in a prominent position where it can be readily examined by the public; and

(d) Affords a choice of works available for performance and permits the choice to be made by the patrons of the establishment in which it is located.

History of 37 C.F.R. §388.2: 81 FR 83142, Nov. 21, 2016.

§388.3. Compulsory License Fees for Coin-Operated Phonorecord Players

(a) Commencing January 1, 1982, the annual compulsory license fee for a coin-operated phonorecord player shall be $25.

(b) Commencing January 1, 1984, the annual compulsory license fee for a coin-operated phonorecord player shall be $50.

(c) Commencing January 1, 1987, the annual compulsory license fee for a coin-operated phonorecord player shall be $63.

(d) If performances are made available on a particular coin-operated phonorecord player for the first time after July 1 of any year, the compulsory license fee for the remainder of that year shall be one half of the annual rate of paragraph (a), (b), or (c) of this section, whichever is applicable.

(e) Commencing January 1, 1990, the annual compulsory license fee for a coin-operated phonorecord player is suspended through December 31, 1999, or until such earlier or later time as the March 1990 license agreement between AMOA and ASCAP/BMI/SESAC is terminated.

History of 37 C.F.R. §388.3: 81 FR 83142, Nov. 21, 2016.

Chapter IV. National Institute of Standards & Technology, Department of Commerce

Part 400. Reserved

Part 401. Rights to Inventions Made by Nonprofit Organizations & Small Business Firms Under Government Grants, Contracts, & Cooperative Agreements

§401.1. Scope

(a) Traditionally there have been no conditions imposed by the government on research performers while using private facilities which would preclude them from accepting research funding from other sources to expand, to aid in completing or to conduct separate investigations closely related to research activities sponsored by the government. Notwithstanding the right of research organizations to accept supplemental funding from other sources for the purpose of expediting or more comprehensively accomplishing the research objectives of the government sponsored project, it is clear that the ownership provisions of these regulations would remain applicable in any invention "conceived or first actually reduced to practice in performance" of the project. Separate accounting for the two funds used to support the project in this case is not a determining factor.

(1) To the extent that a non-government sponsor established a project which, although closely related, falls outside the planned and committed activities of a government-funded project and does not diminish or distract from the performance of such activities, inventions made in performance of the non-government sponsored project would not be subject to the conditions of these regulations. An example of such related but separate projects would be a government sponsored project having research objectives to expand scientific understanding in a field and a closely related industry sponsored project having as its objectives the application of such new knowledge to develop usable new technology. The time relationship in conducting the two projects and the use of new fundamental knowledge from one in the performance of the other are not important determinants since most inventions rest on a knowledge base built up by numerous independent research efforts extending over many years. Should such an invention be claimed by the performing organization to be the product of non-government sponsored research and be challenged by the sponsoring agency as being reportable to the government as a "subject invention," the challenge is appealable as described in §401.11(d).

(2) An invention which is made outside of the research activities of a government-funded project is not viewed as a "subject invention" since it cannot be shown to have been "conceived or first actually reduced to practice" in performance of the project. An obvious example of this is a situation where an instrument purchased with government funds is later used, without interference with or cost to the government-funded project, in making an invention all expenses of which involve only non-government funds.

(b) This part implements 35 U.S.C. 202 through 204 and is applicable to all Federal agencies. It applies to all funding agreements with small business firms and nonprofit organizations executed after the effective date of this part, except for a funding agreement made primarily for educational purposes. Certain sections also provide guidance for the administration of funding agreements which predate the effective date of this part. In accordance with 35 U.S.C. 212, no scholarship, fellowship, training grant, or other funding agreement made by a Federal agency primarily to an awardee for educational purposes will contain any provision giving the Federal agency any rights to inventions made by the awardee.

(c) The "march-in" and appeals procedures in §§401.6 and 401.11 shall apply to any march-in or appeal proceeding under a funding agreement subject to Chapter 18 of Title 35, U.S.C., initiated after the effective date of this part even if the funding agreement was executed prior to that date.

(d) At the request of the contractor, a funding agreement for the operation of a government-owned facility which is in effect on the effective date of this part shall be promptly amended to include the provisions required by §401.3(a) unless the agency determines that one of the exceptions at 35 U.S.C. 202(a)(i) through (iv) §401.3(a)(8) through (iv) of this part) is applicable and will be applied. If the exception at §401.3(a)(iv) is determined to be applicable, the funding agreement will be promptly amended to include the provisions required by §401.3(c).

(e) This regulation supersedes OMB Circular A-124 and shall take precedence over any regulations dealing with ownership of inventions made by small businesses and nonprofit organizations which are inconsistent with it. This regulation will be followed by all agencies pending amendment of agency regulations to conform to this part and amended Chapter 18 of Title 35. Only deviations requested by a contractor and not inconsistent with Chapter 18 of Title 35, United States Code, may be made without approval of the Secretary. Modifications or tailoring of clauses as authorized by §401.5 or §401.3, when alternative provisions are used under §401.3(a)(1) through (4), are not considered deviations requiring the Secretary's approval. Three copies of proposed and final agency regulations supplementing this part shall be submitted to the Secretary at the office set out in §401.16 for approval for consistency with this part before they are submitted to the Office of Management and Budget (OMB) for review under Executive Order 12291 or, if no submission is required to be made to OMB, before their submission to the Federal Register for publication.

(f) In the event an agency has outstanding prime funding agreements that do not contain patent flow-down provisions consistent with this part or earlier Office of Federal Procurement Policy regulations (OMB Circular A-124 or OMB Bulletin 81-22), the agency shall take appropriate action to ensure that small business firms or nonprofit organizations that are subcontractors under any such agreements and that received their subcontracts after July 1, 1981, receive rights in their subject inventions that are consistent with Chapter 18 and this part.

(g) This part is not intended to apply to arrangements under which nonprofit organizations, small business firms, or others are allowed to use government-owned research facilities and normal technical assistance provided to users of those facilities, whether on a reimbursable or nonreimbursable basis. This part is also not intended to apply to arrangements under which sponsors reimburse the government or facility contractor for the contractor employee's time in performing work for the sponsor. Such arrangements are not considered "funding agreements" as defined at 35 U.S.C. 201(b) and §401.2(a) of this part.

Source of 37 C.F.R. Part 401: 52 FR 8554, Mar. 18, 1987; 55 FR 38983, Sept. 24, 1990, unless otherwise noted.

§401.2. DEFINITIONS

As used in this part—

(a) The term "funding agreement" means any contract, grant, or cooperative agreement entered into between any Federal agency, other than the Tennessee Valley Authority, and any contractor for the performance of experimental, developmental, or research work funded in whole or in part by the Federal government. This term also includes any assignment, substitution of parties, or subcontract of any type entered into for the performance of experimental, developmental, or research work under a funding agreement as defined in the first sentence of this paragraph.

(b) The term "contractor" means any person, small business firm or nonprofit organization which is a party to a funding agreement.

(c) The term "invention" means any invention or discovery which is or may be patentable or otherwise protectable under Title 35 of the United States Code, or any novel variety of plant which is or may be protectable under the Plant Variety Protection Act (7 U.S.C. 2321 et seq.).

(d) The term "subject invention" means any invention of a contractor conceived or first actually reduced to practice in the performance of work under a funding agreement; provided that in the case of a variety of plant, the date of determination (as defined in section 41(d) of the Plant Variety Protection Act, 7 U.S.C. 2401(d)) must also occur during the period of contract performance.

(e) The term "practical application" means to manufacture in the case of a composition of product, to practice in the case of a process or method, or to operate in the case of a machine or system; and, in each case, under such conditions as to establish that the invention is being utilized and that its benefits are, to the extent permitted by law or government regulations, available to the public on reasonable terms.

(f) The term "made" when used in relation to any invention means the conception or first actual reduction to practice of such invention.

(g) The term "small business firm" means a small business concern as defined at section 2 of Pub.L. 85-536 (15 U.S.C. 632) and implementing regulations of the Administrator of the Small Business Administration. For the purpose of this part, the size standards for small business concerns involved in government procurement and subcontracting at 13 CFR 121.5 will be used.

(h) The term "nonprofit organization" means universities and other institutions of higher education or an organization of the type described in section 501(c)(3) of the Internal Revenue Code of 1954 (26 U.S.C. 501(c)) and exempt from taxation under section 501(a) of the Internal Revenue Code (26 U.S.C. 501(a)) or any nonprofit scientific or educational organization qualified under a state nonprofit organization statute.

(i) The term "Chapter 18" means Chapter 18 of Title 35 of the United States Code.

(j) The term Secretary means the Director of the National Institute of Standards and Technology.

(k) The term "electronically filed" means any submission of information transmitted by an electronic or optical-electronic system.

(*l*) The term "electronic or optical-electronic system" means a software-based system approved by the agency for the transmission of information.

(m) The term "patent application" or "application for patent" includes a provisional or nonprovisional U.S. national application for patent as defined in 37 CFR 1.9 (a)(2) and (a)(3), respectively, or an application for patent in a foreign country or in an international patent office.

(n) "The term initial patent application" means a nonprovisional U.S. national application for patent as defined in 37 CFR 1.9(a)(3).

History of 37 C.F.R. §401.2: 60 FR 41812, Aug. 14, 1995; 78 FR 4766, Jan. 23, 2013.

§401.3. USE OF THE STANDARD CLAUSES AT §401.14

(a) Each funding agreement awarded to a small business firm or nonprofit organization (except those subject to 35 U.S.C. 212) shall contain the clause found in §401.14(a) with such modifications and tailoring as authorized or required elsewhere in this part. However, a funding agreement may contain alternative provisions—

(1) When the contractor is not located in the United States or does not have a place of business located in the United States or is subject to the control of a foreign government; or

(2) In exceptional circumstances when it is determined by the agency that restriction or elimination of the right to retain title to any subject invention will better promote the policy and objectives of Chapter 18 of Title 35 of the United States Code; or

(3) When it is determined by a government authority which is authorized by statute or executive order to conduct foreign intelligence or counterintelligence activities that the restriction or elimination of the right to retain title to any subject invention is necessary to protect the security to such activities; or

(4) When the funding agreement includes the operation of the government-owned, contractor-operated facility of the Department of Energy primarily dedicated to that Department's naval nuclear propulsion or weapons related programs and all funding agreement limitations under this subparagraph on the contractor's right to elect title to a subject invention are limited to inventions occurring under the above two programs.

(5) If any part of the contract may require the contractor to perform work on behalf of the Government at a Government laboratory under a Cooperative Research and Development Agreement (CRADA) pursuant to the statutory authority of 15 U.S.C. 3710a, the contracting officer may include alternate paragraph (b) in the basic patent rights clause in §401.14. Because the use of the alternate is based on a determination of exceptional circumstances under §401.3(a)(2), the contracting officer shall ensure that the appeal procedures of §401.4 are satisfied whenever the alternate is used.

(b) When an agency exercises the exceptions at §401.3(a)(2) or (3), it shall use the standard clause at §401.14(a) with only such modifications as are necessary to address the exceptional circumstances or concerns which led to the use of the exception. For example, if the justification relates to a particular field of use or market, the clause might be modified along lines similar to those described in §401.14(b). In any event, the clause should provide the contractor with an opportunity to receive greater rights in accordance with the procedures at §401.15. When an agency justifies and exercises the exception at §401.3(a)(2) and uses an alternative provision in the funding agreement on the basis of national security, the provision shall provide the contractor with the right to elect ownership to any invention made under such funding agreement as provided by the Standard Patent Rights Clause found at §401.14(a) if the invention is not classified by the agency within six months of the date it is reported to the agency, or within the same time period the Department of Energy does not, as authorized by regulation, law or Executive Order or implementing regulations thereto, prohibit unauthorized dissemination of the invention. Contracts in support of DOE's naval nuclear propulsion program are exempted from this paragraph.

(c) When the Department of Energy exercises the exception at §401.3(a)(4), it shall use the clause prescribed at §401.14(b) or substitute thereto with such modification and tailoring as authorized or required elsewhere in this part.

(d) When a funding agreement involves a series of separate task orders, an agency may apply the exceptions at §401.3(a)(2) or (3) to individual task orders, and it may structure the contract so that modified patent rights provisions will apply to the task order even though the clauses at either §401.14(a) or (b) are applicable to the remainder of the work. Agencies are authorized to negotiate such modified provisions with respect to task orders added to a funding agreement after its initial award.

(e) Before utilizing any of the exceptions in §401.3(a) of this section, the agency shall prepare a written determination, including a statement of facts supporting the determination, that the conditions identified in the exception exist. A separate statement of facts shall be prepared for each exceptional circumstances determination, except that in appropriate cases a single determination may apply to both a funding agreement and any subcontracts issued under it or to any funding agreement to which such an exception is applicable. In cases when §401.3(a)(2) is used, the determination shall also include an analysis justifying the determination. This analysis should address with specificity how the alternate provisions will better achieve the objectives set forth in 35 U.S.C. 200. A copy of each determination, statement of facts, and, if applicable, analysis shall be promptly provided to the contractor or prospective contractor along with a notification to the contractor or prospective contractor of its rights to appeal the determination of the exception under 35 U.S.C. 202(b)(4) and §401.4 of this part.

(f) Except for determinations under §401.3(a)(3), the agency shall also provide copies of each determination, statement of fact, and analysis to the Secretary. These shall be sent within 30 days after the award of the funding agreement to which they pertain. Copies shall also be sent to the Chief Counsel for Advocacy of the Small Business Administration if the funding agreement is with a small business firm. If the Secretary of Commerce believes that any individual determination or pattern of determinations is contrary to the policies and objectives of this chapter or otherwise not in conformance with this chapter, the Secretary shall so advise the head of the agency concerned and the Administrator of the Office of Federal Procurement Policy and recommend corrective actions.

(g) To assist the Comptroller General of the United States to accomplish his or her responsibilities under 35 U.S.C. 202, each Federal agency that enters into any funding agreements with nonprofit organizations or small business firms shall accumulate and, at the request of the Comptroller General, provide the Comptroller General or his or her duly authorized representative the total number of prime agreements entered into with small business firms or nonprofit organizations that contain the patent rights clause in this part or under OMB Circular A-124 for each fiscal year beginning with October 1, 1982.

(h) To qualify for the standard clause, a prospective contractor may be required by an agency to certify that it is either a small business firm or a nonprofit organization. If the agency has reason to question the status of the prospective contractor as a small business firm, it may file a protest in accordance with 13 CFR 121.9. If it questions nonprofit status, it may require the prospective contractor to furnish evidence to establish its status as a nonprofit organization.

History of 37 C.F.R. §401.3: 69 FR 17301, Apr. 2, 2004.

§401.4. CONTRACTOR APPEALS OF EXCEPTIONS

(a) In accordance with 35 U.S.C. 202(b)(4) a contractor has the right to an administrative review of a determination to use one of the exceptions at §401.3(a)(1) through (4) if the contractor believes that a determination is either contrary to the policies and objectives of this chapter or constitutes an abuse of discretion by the agency. Paragraph (b) of this section specifies the procedures to be followed by contractors and agencies in such cases. The assertion of such a claim by the contractor shall not be used as a basis for withholding or delaying the award of a funding agreement or for suspending performance under an award. Pending final resolution of the claim the contract may be issued with the patent rights provision proposed by the agency; however, should the final decision be in favor of the contractor, the funding agreement will be amended accordingly and the amendment made retroactive to the effective date of the funding agreement.

(b)(1) A contractor may appeal a determination by providing written notice to the agency within 30 working days from the time it receives a copy of the agency's determination, or within such longer time as an agency may specify in its regulations. The contractor's notice should specifically identify the basis for the appeal.

(2) The appeal shall be decided by the head of the agency or by his/her designee who is at a level above the person who made the determination. If the notice raises a genuine dispute over the material facts, the head of the agency or the designee shall undertake, or refer the matter for, fact-finding.

(3) Fact-finding shall be conducted in accordance with procedures established by the agency. Such procedures shall be as informal as practicable and be consistent with principles of fundamental fairness. The procedures should afford the contractor the opportunity to appear with counsel, submit documentary evidence, present witnesses and confront such persons as the agency may rely upon. A transcribed record shall be made and shall be available at cost to the contractor upon request. The requirement for a transcribed record may be waived by mutual agreement of the contractor and the agency.

(4) The official conducting the fact-finding shall prepare or adopt written findings of fact and transmit them to the head of the agency or designee promptly after the conclusion of the fact-finding proceeding along with a recommended decision. A copy of the findings of fact and recommended decision shall be sent to the contractor by registered or certified mail.

(5) Fact-finding should be completed within 45 working days from the date the agency receives the contractor's written notice.

(6) When fact-finding has been conducted, the head of the agency or designee shall base his or her decision on the facts found, together with any argument submitted by the contractor, agency officials or any other information in the administrative record. In cases referred for fact-finding, the agency head or the designee may reject only those facts that have been found to be clearly erroneous, but must explicitly state the rejection and indicate the basis for the contrary finding. The agency head or the designee may hear oral arguments after fact-finding provided that the contractor or contractor's attorney or representative is present and given an opportunity to make arguments and rebuttal. The decision of the agency head or the designee shall be in writing and, if it is unfavorable to the contractor shall include an explanation of the basis of the decision. The decision of the agency or designee shall be made within 30 working days after fact-finding or, if there was no fact-finding, within 45 working days from the date the agency received the contractor's written notice. A contractor adversely affected by a determination under this section may, at any time within sixty days after the determination is issued, file a petition in the United States Claims Court, which shall have jurisdiction to determine the appeal on the record and to affirm, reverse, remand, or modify as appropriate, the determination of the Federal agency.

§401.5. MODIFICATION & TAILORING OF CLAUSES

(a) Agencies should complete the blank in paragraph (g)(2) of the clauses at §401.14 in accordance with their own or applicable government-wide regulations such as the Federal Acquisition Regulation. In grants and cooperative agreements (and in contracts, if not inconsistent with the Federal Acquisition Regulation) agencies wishing to apply the same clause to all subcontractors as is applied to the contractor may delete paragraph (g)(2) of the clause and delete the words "to be performed by a small business firm or domestic nonprofit organization" from paragraph (g)(1). Also, if the funding agreement is a grant or cooperative agreement, paragraph (g)(3) may be deleted. When either paragraph (g)(2) or paragraphs (g) (2) and (3) are deleted, the remaining paragraph or paragraphs should be renumbered appropriately.

(b) Agencies should complete paragraph (*l*), "Communications," at the end of the clauses at §401.14 by designating a central point of contact for communications on matters relating to the clause. Additional instructions on communications may also be included in paragraph (*l*).

(c) Agencies may replace the italicized words and phrases in the clauses at §401.14 with those appropriate to the particular funding agreement. For example, "contracts" could be replaced by "grant," "contractor" by "grantee," and "contracting officer" by "grants officer." Depending on its use, "Federal agency" can be replaced either by the identification of the agency or by the specification of the particular office or official within the agency.

(d) When the agency head or duly authorized designee determines at the time of contracting with a small business firm or nonprofit organization that it would be in the national interest to acquire the right to sublicense foreign governments or international organizations pursuant to any existing treaty or international agreement, a sentence may be added at the end of paragraph (b) of the clause at §401.14 as follows:

This license will include the right of the government to sublicense foreign governments, their nationals, and international organizations, pursuant to the following treaties or international agreements:

______________________________.

The blank above should be completed with the names of applicable existing treaties or international agreements, agreements of cooperation, memoranda of understanding, or similar arrangements, including military agreements relating to weapons development and production. The above language is not intended to apply to treaties or other agreements that are in effect on the date of the award but which are not listed. Alternatively, agencies may use substantially similar language relating the government's rights to specific treaties or other agreements identified elsewhere in the funding agreement. The language may also be modified to make clear that the rights granted to the foreign government, and its nationals or an international organization may be for additional rights beyond a license or sublicense if so required by the applicable treaty or international agreement. For example, in some exclusive licenses or even the assignment of title in the foreign country involved might be required. Agencies may also modify the language above to provide for the direct licensing by the contractor of the foreign government or international organization.

(e) If the funding agreement involves performance over an extended period of time, such as the typical funding agreement for the operation of a government-owned facility, the following language may also be added:

The agency reserves the right to unilaterally amend this funding agreement to identify specific treaties or international agreements entered into or to be entered into by the government after the effective date of this funding agreement and effectuate those license or other rights which are necessary for the government to meet its obligations to foreign governments, their nationals and international organizations under such treaties or international agreements with respect to subject inventions made after the date of the amendment.

(f) Agencies may add additional subparagraphs to paragraph (f) of the clauses at §401.14 to require the contractor to do one or more of the following:

(1) Provide a report prior to the close-out of a funding agreement listing all subject inventions or stating that there were none.

(2) Provide, upon request, the filing date, patent application number and title; a copy of the patent application; and patent number and issue date for any subject invention in any country in which the contractor has applied for a patent.

(3) Provide periodic (but no more frequently than annual) listings of all subject inventions which were disclosed to the agency during the period covered by the report.

(g) If the contract is with a nonprofit organization and is for the operation of a government-owned, contractor-operated facility, the following will be substituted for paragraph (k)(3) of the clause at §401.14(a):

(3) After payment of patenting costs, licensing costs, payments to inventors, and other expenses incidental to the administration of subject inventions, the balance of any royalties or income earned and retained by the contractor during any fiscal year on subject inventions under this or any successor contract containing the same requirement, up to any amount equal to five percent of the budget of the facility for that fiscal year, shall be used by the contractor for scientific research, development, and education consistent with the research and development mission and objectives of the facility, including activities that increase the licensing potential of other inventions of the facility. If the balance exceeds five percent, 75 percent of the excess above five percent shall be paid by the contractor to the Treasury of the United States and the remaining 25 percent shall be used by the contractor only for the same purposes as described above. To the extent it provides the most effective technology transfer, the licensing of subject inventions shall be administered by contractor employees on location at the facility.

(h) If the contract is for the operation of a government-owned facility, agencies may add the following at the end of paragraph (f) of the clause at §401.14(a):

(5) The contractor shall establish and maintain active and effective procedures to ensure that subject inventions are promptly identified and timely disclosed and shall submit a description of the procedures to the contracting officer so that the contracting officer may evaluate and determine their effectiveness.

History of 37 C.F.R. §401.5: 60 FR 41812, Aug. 14, 1995.

§401.6. EXERCISE OF MARCH-IN RIGHTS

(a) The following procedures shall govern the exercise of the march-in rights of the agencies set forth in 35 U.S.C. 203 and paragraph (j) of the clause at §401.14.

(b) Whenever an agency receives information that it believes might warrant the exercise of march-in rights, before initiating any march-in proceeding, it shall notify the contractor in writing of the information and request informal written or oral comments from the contractor as well as information relevant to the matter. In the absence of any comments from the contractor within 30 days, the agency may, at its discretion, proceed with the procedures below. If a comment is received within 30 days, or later if the agency has not initiated the procedures below, then the agency shall, within 60 days after it receives the comment, either initiate the procedures below or notify the contractor, in writing, that it will not pursue march-in rights on the basis of the available information.

(c) A march-in proceeding shall be initiated by the issuance of a written notice by the agency to the contractor and its assignee or exclusive licensee, as applicable and if known to the agency, stating that the agency is considering the exercise of march-in rights. The notice shall state the reasons for the proposed march-in in terms sufficient to put the contractor on notice of the facts upon which the action would be based and shall specify the field or fields of use in which the agency is considering requiring licensing. The notice shall advise the contractor (assignee or exclusive licensee) of its rights, as set forth in this section and in any supplemental agency regulations. The determination to exercise march-in rights shall be made by the head of the agency or his or her designee.

(d) Within 30 days after the receipt of the written notice of march-in, the contractor (assignee or exclusive licensee) may submit in person, in writing, or through a representative, information or argument in opposition to the proposed march-in, including any additional specific information which raises a genuine dispute over the material facts upon which the march-in is based. If the information presented raises a genuine dispute over the material facts, the head of the agency or designee shall undertake or refer the matter to another official for fact-finding.

(e) Fact-finding shall be conducted in accordance with the procedures established by the agency. Such procedures shall be as informal as practicable and be consistent with principles of fundamental fairness. The procedures should afford the contractor the opportunity to appear with counsel, submit documentary evidence, present witnesses and confront such persons as the agency may present. A transcribed record shall be made and shall be available at cost to the contractor upon request. The requirement for a transcribed record may be waived by mutual agreement of the contractor and the agency. Any portion of the march-in proceeding, including a fact-finding hearing that involves testimony or evidence relating to the utilization or efforts at obtaining utilization that are being made by the contractor, its assignee, or licensees shall be closed to the public, including potential licensees. In accordance with 35 U.S.C. 202(c)(5), agencies shall not disclose any such information obtained during a march-in proceeding to persons outside the government except when such release is authorized by the contractor (assignee or licensee).

(f) The official conducting the fact-finding shall prepare or adopt written findings of fact and transmit them to the head of the agency or designee promptly after the conclusion of the fact-finding proceeding along with a recommended determination. A copy of the findings of fact shall be sent to the contractor (assignee or exclusive licensee) by registered or certified mail. The contractor (assignee or exclusive licensee) and agency representatives will be given 30 days to submit written arguments to the head of the agency or designee; and, upon request by the contractor oral arguments will be held before the agency head or designee that will make the final determination.

(g) In cases in which fact-finding has been conducted, the head of the agency or designee shall base his or her determination on the facts found, together with any other information and written or oral arguments submitted by the contractor (assignee or exclusive licensee) and agency representatives, and any other information in the administrative record. The consistency of the exercise of march-in rights with the policy and objectives of 35 U.S.C. 200 shall also be considered. In cases referred for fact-finding, the head of the agency or designee may reject only those facts that have been found to be clearly erroneous, but must explicitly state the rejection and indicate the basis for the contrary finding. Written notice of the determination whether march-in rights will be exercised shall be made by the head of the agency or designee and sent to the contractor (assignee of exclusive licensee) by certified or registered mail within 90 days after the completion of fact-finding or 90 days after oral arguments, whichever is later, or the proceedings will be deemed to have been terminated and thereafter no march-in based on the facts and reasons upon which the proceeding was initiated may be exercised.

(h) An agency may, at any time, terminate a march-in proceeding if it is satisfied that it does not wish to exercise march-in rights.

(i) The procedures of this Part shall also apply to the exercise of march-in rights against inventors receiving title to subject inventions under 35 U.S.C. 202(d) and, for that purpose, the term "contractor" as used in this section shall be deemed to include the inventor.

(j) An agency determination unfavorable to the contractor (assignee or exclusive licensee) shall be held in abeyance pending the exhaustion of appeals or petitions filed under 35 U.S.C. 203(2).

(k) For purposes of this section the term "exclusive licensee" includes a partially exclusive licensee.

(l) Agencies are authorized to issue supplemental procedures not inconsistent with this part for the conduct of march-in proceedings.

§401.7. SMALL BUSINESS PREFERENCE

(a) Paragraph (k)(4) of the clauses at §401.14 Implements the small business preference requirement of 35 U.S.C. 202(c)(7)(D). Contractors are expected to use efforts that are reasonable under the circumstances to attract small business licensees. They are also expected to give small business firms that meet the standard outlined in the clause a preference over other applicants for licenses. What constitutes reasonable efforts to attract small business licensees will vary with the circumstances and the nature, duration, and expense of efforts needed to bring the invention to the market. Paragraph (k)(4) is not intended, for example, to prevent nonprofit organizations from providing larger firms with a right of first refusal or other options in inventions that relate to research being supported under long-term or other arrangements with larger companies. Under such circumstances it would not be reasonable to seek and to give a preference to small business licensees.

(b) Small business firms that believe a nonprofit organization is not meeting its obligations under the clause may report their concerns to the Secretary. To the extent deemed appropriate, the Secretary will undertake informal investigation of the concern, and, if appropriate, enter into discussions or negotiations with the nonprofit organization to the end of improving its efforts in meeting its obligations under the clause. However, in no event will the Secretary intervene in ongoing negotiations or contractor decisions concerning the licensing of a specific subject invention. All the above investigations, discussions, and negotiations of the Secretary will be in coordination with other interested agencies, including the Small Business Administration; and in the case of a contract for the operation of a government-owned, contractor operated research or production facility, the Secretary will coordinate with the agency responsible for the facility prior to any discussions or negotiations with the contractor.

§401.8. REPORTING ON UTILIZATION OF SUBJECT INVENTIONS

(a) Paragraph (h) of the clauses at §401.14 and its counterpart in the clause at Attachment A to OMB Circular A-124 provides that agencies have the right to receive periodic reports from the contractor on utilization of inventions. Agencies exercising this right should accept such information, to the extent feasible, in the format that the contractor normally prepares it for its own internal purposes. The prescription of forms should be avoided. However, any forms or standard questionnaires that are adopted by an agency for this purpose must comply with the requirements of the Paperwork Reduction Act. Copies shall be sent to the Secretary.

(b) In accordance with 35 U.S.C. 202(c)(5) and the terms of the clauses at §401.14, agencies shall not disclose such information to persons outside the government. Contractors will continue to provide confidential markings to help prevent inadvertent release outside the agency.

§401.9. RETENTION OF RIGHTS BY CONTRACTOR EMPLOYEE INVENTOR

Agencies which allow an employee/inventor of the contractor to retain rights to a subject invention made under a funding agreement with a small business firm or nonprofit organization contractor, as authorized by 35 U.S.C. 202(d), will impose upon the inventor at least those conditions that would apply to a small business firm contractor under paragraphs (d)(1) and (3); (f)(4); (h); (i); and (j) of the clause at §401.14(a).

§401.10. GOVERNMENT ASSIGNMENT TO CONTRACTOR OF RIGHTS IN INVENTION OF GOVERNMENT EMPLOYEE

In any case when a Federal employee is a co-inventor of any invention made under a funding agreement with a small business firm or nonprofit organization and the Federal agency employing such co-inventor transfers or reassigns the right it has acquired in the subject invention from its employee to the contractor as authorized by 35 U.S.C. 202(e), the assignment will be made subject to the same conditions as apply to the contractor under the patent rights clause of its funding agreement. Agencies may add additional conditions as long as they are consistent with 35 U.S.C. 201-206.

§401.11. APPEALS

(a) As used in this section, the term "standard clause" means the clause at §401.14 of this part and the clauses previously prescribed by either OMB Circular A-124 or OMB Bulletin 81-22.

(b) The agency official initially authorized to take any of the following actions shall provide the contractor with a written statement of the basis for his or her action at the time the action is taken, including any relevant facts that were relied upon in taking the action.

(1) A refusal to grant an extension under paragraph (c)(4) of the standard clauses.

(2) A request for a conveyance of title under paragraph (d) of the standard clauses.

(3) A refusal to grant a waiver under paragraph (i) of the standard clauses.

(4) A refusal to approve an assignment under paragraph (k)(1) of the standard clauses.

(5) A refusal to grant an extension of the exclusive license period under paragraph (k)(2) of the clauses prescribed by either OMB Circular A-124 or OMB Bulletin 81-22.

(c) Each agency shall establish and publish procedures under which any of the agency actions listed in paragraph (b) of this section may be appealed to the head of the agency or designee. Review at this level shall consider both the factual and legal basis for the actions and its consistency with the policy and objectives of 35 U.S.C. 200-206.

(d) Appeals procedures established under paragraph (c) of this section shall include administrative due process procedures and standards for fact-finding at least comparable to those set forth in §401.6 (e) through (g) whenever there is a dispute as to the factual basis for an agency request for a conveyance of title under paragraph (d) of the standard clause, including any dispute as to whether or not an invention is a subject invention.

(e) To the extent that any of the actions described in paragraph (b) of this section are subject to appeal under the Contract Dispute Act, the procedures under the Act will satisfy the requirements of paragraphs (c) and (d) of this section.

§401.12. LICENSING OF BACKGROUND PATENT RIGHTS TO THIRD PARTIES

(a) A funding agreement with a small business firm or a domestic nonprofit organization will not contain a provision allowing a Federal agency to require the licensing to third parties of inventions owned by the contractor that are not subject inventions unless such provision has been approved by the agency head and a written justification has been signed by the agency head. Any such provision will clearly state whether the licensing may be required in connection with the practice of a subject invention, a specifically identified work object, or both. The agency head may not delegate the authority to approve such provisions or to sign the justification required for such provisions.

(b) A Federal agency will not require the licensing of third parties under any such provision unless the agency head determines that the use of the invention by others is necessary for the practice of a subject invention or for the use of a work object of the funding agreement and that such action is necessary to achieve practical application of the subject invention or work object. Any such determination will be on the record after an opportunity for an agency hearing. The contractor shall be given prompt notification of the determination by certified or registered mail. Any action commenced for judicial review of such determination shall be brought within sixty days after notification of such determination.

§401.13. ADMINISTRATION OF PATENT RIGHTS CLAUSES

(a) In the event a subject invention is made under funding agreements of more than one agency, at the request of the contractor or on their own initiative the agencies shall designate one agency as responsible for administration of the rights of the government in the invention.

(b) Agencies shall promptly grant, unless there is a significant reason not to, a request by a nonprofit organization under paragraph (k)(2) of the clauses prescribed by either OMB Circular A-124 or OMB Bulletin 81-22 inasmuch as 35 U.S.C. 202(c)(7) has since been amended to eliminate the limitation on the duration of exclusive licenses. Similarly, unless there is a significant reason not to, agencies shall promptly approve an assignment by a nonprofit organization to an organization which has as one of its primary functions the management of inventions when a request for approval has been necessitated under paragraph (k)(1) of the clauses prescribed by either OMB Circular A-124 or OMB Bulletin 81-22 because the patent management organization is engaged in or holds a substantial interest in other organizations engaged in the manufacture or sale of products or the use of processes that might utilize the invention or be in competition with embodiments of the invention. As amended, 35 U.S.C. 202(c)(7) no longer contains this limitation. The policy of this subsection should also be followed in connection with similar approvals that may be required under Institutional Patent Agreements, other patent rights clauses, or waivers that predate Chapter 18 of Title 35, United States Code.

(c) The President's Patent Policy Memorandum of February 18, 1983, states that agencies should protect the confidentiality of invention disclosure, patent applications, and utilization reports required in performance or in consequence of awards to the extent permitted by 35 U.S.C. 205 or other applicable laws. The following requirements should be followed for funding agreements covered by and predating this Part 401.

(1) To the extent authorized by 35 U.S.C. 205, agencies shall not disclose to third parties pursuant to requests under the Freedom of Information Act (FOIA) any information disclosing a subject invention for a reasonable time in order for a patent application to be filed. With respect to subject inventions of contractors that are small business firms or nonprofit organizations, a reasonable time shall be the time during which an initial patent application may be filed under paragraph (c) of the standard clause found at §401.14(a) or such other clause may be used in the funding agreement. However, an agency may disclose such subject inventions under the FOIA, at its discretion, after a contractor has elected not to retain title or after the time in which the contractor is required to make an election if the contractor has not made an election within that time. Similarly, an agency may honor a FOIA request at its discretion if it finds that the same information has previously been published by the inventor, contractor, or otherwise. If the agency plans to file itself when the contractor has not elected title, it may, of course, continue to avail itself of the authority of 35 U.S.C. 205.

(2) In accordance with 35 U.S.C. 205, agencies shall not disclose or release for a period of 18 months from the filing date of the patent application to third parties pursuant to requests under the Freedom of Information Act, or otherwise, copies of any document which the agency obtained under this clause which is part of an application for patent with the U.S. Patent and Trademark Office or any foreign patent office filed by the contractor (or its assignees, licensees, or employees) on a subject invention to which the contractor has elected to retain title. This prohibition does not extend to disclosure to other government agencies or contractors of government agencies under an obligation to maintain such information in confidence.

(3) A number of agencies have policies to encourage public dissemination of the results of work supported by the agency through publication in government or other publications of technical reports of contractors or others. In recognition of the fact that such publication, if it included descriptions of a subject invention could create bars to obtaining patent protection, it is the policy of the executive branch that agencies will not include in such publication programs copies of disclosures of inventions submitted by small business firms or nonprofit organizations, pursuant to paragraph (c) of the standard clause found at §401.14(a), except that under the same circumstances under which agencies are authorized to release such information pursuant to FOIA requests under paragraph (c)(1) of this section, agencies may publish such disclosures.

(4) Nothing in this paragraph is intended to preclude agencies from including in the publication activities described in the first sentence of paragraph (c)(3), the publication of materials describing a subject invention to the extent such materials were provided as part of a technical report or other submission of the contractor which were submitted independently of the requirements of the patent rights provisions of the contract. However, if a small business firm or nonprofit organization notifies the agency that a particular report or other submission contains a disclosure of a subject invention to which it has elected title or may elect title, the agency shall use reasonable efforts to restrict its publication of the material for six months from date of its receipt of the report or submission or, if earlier, until the contractor has filed an initial patent application. Agencies, of course, retain the discretion to delay publication for additional periods of time.

(5) Nothing in this paragraph is intended to limit the authority of agencies provided in 35 U.S.C. 205 in circumstances not specifically described in this paragraph.

History of 37 C.F.R. §401.13: 60 FR 41812, Aug. 14, 1995.

§401.14. STANDARD PATENT RIGHTS CLAUSES

(a) The following is the standard patent rights clause to be used as specified in §401.3(a).

Patent Rights (Small Business Firms and Nonprofit Organizations)

(a) Definitions

(1) "Invention" means any invention or discovery which is or may be patentable or otherwise protectable under Title 35 of the United States Code, or any novel variety of plant which is or may be protected under the Plant Variety Protection Act (7 U.S.C. 2321 et seq.).

(2) "Subject invention" means any invention of the contractor conceived or first actually reduced to practice in the performance of work under this contract, provided that in the case of a variety of plant, the date of determination (as defined in section 41(d) of the Plant Variety Protection Act, 7 U.S.C. 2401(d)) must also occur during the period of contract performance.

(3) "Practical Application" means to manufacture in the case of a composition or product, to practice in the case of a process or method, or to operate in the case of a machine or system; and, in each case, under such conditions as to establish that the invention is being utilized and that its benefits are, to the extent permitted by law or government regulations, available to the public on reasonable terms.

(4) "Made" when used in relation to any invention means the conception or first actual reduction to practice of such invention.

(5) "Small Business Firm" means a small business concern as defined at section 2 of Pub.L. 85-536 (15 U.S.C. 632) and implementing regulations of the Administrator of the Small Business Administration. For the purpose of this clause, the size standards for small business concerns involved in government procurement and subcontracting at 13 CFR 121.3-8 and 13 CFR 121.3-12, respectively, will be used.

(6) "Nonprofit Organization" means a university or other institution of higher education or an organization of the type described in section 501(c)(3) of the Internal Revenue Code of 1954 (26 U.S.C. 501(c)) and exempt from taxation under section 501(a) of the Internal Revenue Code (25 U.S.C. 501(a)) or any nonprofit scientific or educational organization qualified under a state nonprofit organization statute.

(b) Allocation of Principal Rights

The Contractor may retain the entire right, title, and interest throughout the world to each subject invention subject to the provisions of this clause and 35 U.S.C. 203. With respect to any subject invention in which the Contractor retains title, the Federal government shall have a nonexclusive, nontransferable, irrevocable, paid-up license to practice or have practiced for or on behalf of the United States the subject invention throughout the world.

(c) Invention disclosure, Election of Title and Filing of Patent Application by Contractor.

(1) The contractor will disclose each subject invention to the Federal Agency within two months after the inventor discloses it in writing to contractor personnel responsible for patent matters. The disclosure to the agency shall be in the form of a written report and shall identify the contract under which the invention was made and the inventor(s). It shall be sufficiently complete in technical detail to convey a clear understanding to the extent known at the time of the disclosure, of the nature, purpose, operation, and the physical, chemical, biological or electrical characteristics of the invention. The disclosure shall also identify any publication, on sale or public use of the invention and whether a manuscript describing the invention has been submitted for publication and, if so, whether it has been accepted for publication at the time of disclosure. In addition, after disclosure to the agency, the Contractor will promptly notify the agency of the acceptance of any manuscript describing the invention for publication or of any on sale or public use planned by the contractor.

(2) The Contractor will elect in writing whether or not to retain title to any such invention by notifying the Federal agency within two years of disclosure to the Federal agency. However, in any case where publication, on sale or public use has initiated the one year statutory period wherein valid patent protection can still be obtained in the United States, the period for election of title may be shortened by the agency to a date that is no more than 60 days prior to the end of the statutory period.

(3) The contractor will file its initial patent application on a subject invention to which it elects to retain title within one year after election of title or, if earlier, prior to the end of any statutory period wherein valid patent protection can be obtained in the United States after a publication, on sale, or public use. The contractor will file patent applications in additional countries or international patent offices within either ten months of the corresponding initial patent application or six months from the date permission is granted by the Commissioner of Patents and Trademarks to file foreign patent applications where such filing has been prohibited by a Secrecy Order.

(4) Requests for extension of the time for disclosure, election, and filing under subparagraphs (1), (2), and (3) may, at the discretion of the agency, be granted.

(d) Conditions When the Government May Obtain Title

The contractor will convey to the Federal agency, upon written request, title to any subject invention—

(1) If the contractor fails to disclose or elect title to the subject invention within the times specified in (c), above, or elects not to retain title; provided that the agency may only request title within 60 days after learning of the failure of the contractor to disclose or elect within the specified times.

(2) In those countries in which the contractor fails to file patent applications within the times specified in (c) above; provided, however, that if the contractor has filed a patent application in a country after the times specified in (c) above, but prior to its receipt of the written request of the Federal agency, the contractor shall continue to retain title in that country.

(3) In any country in which the contractor decides not to continue the prosecution of any application for, to pay the maintenance fees on, or defend in reexamination or opposition proceeding on, a patent on a subject invention.

(e) Minimum Rights to Contractor and Protection of the Contractor Right to File

(1) The contractor will retain a nonexclusive royalty-free license throughout the world in each subject invention to which the Government obtains title, except if the contractor fails to disclose the invention within the times specified in (c), above. The contractor's license extends to its domestic subsidiary and affiliates, if any, within the corporate structure of which the contractor is a party and includes the right to grant sublicenses of the same scope to the extent the contractor was legally obligated to do so at the time the contract was awarded. The license is transferable only with the approval of the Federal agency except when transferred to the successor of that party of the contractor's business to which the invention pertains.

(2) The contractor's domestic license may be revoked or modified by the funding Federal agency to the extent necessary to achieve expeditious practical application of the subject invention pursuant to an application for an exclusive license submitted in accordance with applicable provisions at 37 CFR Part 404 and agency licensing regulations (if any). This license will not be revoked in that field of use or the geographical areas in which the contractor has achieved practical application and continues to make the benefits of the invention reasonably accessible to the public. The license in any foreign country may be revoked or modified at the discretion of the funding Federal agency to the extent the contractor, its licensees, or the domestic subsidiaries or affiliates have failed to achieve practical application in that foreign country.

(3) Before revocation or modification of the license, the funding Federal agency will furnish the contractor a written notice of its intention to revoke or modify the license, and the contractor will be allowed thirty days (or such other time as may be authorized by the funding Federal agency for good cause shown by the contractor) after the notice to show cause why the license should not be revoked or modified. The contractor has the right to appeal, in accordance with applicable regulations in 37 CFR Part 404 and agency regulations (if any) concerning the licensing of Government-owned inventions, any decision concerning the revocation or modification of the license.

(f) Contractor Action to Protect the Government's Interest

(1) The contractor agrees to execute or to have executed and promptly deliver to the Federal agency all instruments necessary to (i) establish or confirm the rights the Government has throughout the world in those subject inventions to which the contractor elects to retain title, and (ii) convey title to the Federal agency when requested under paragraph (d) above and to enable the government to obtain patent protection throughout the world in that subject invention.

(2) The contractor agrees to require, by written agreement, its employees, other than clerical and nontechnical employees, to disclose promptly in writing to personnel identified as responsible for the administration of patent matters and in a format suggested by the contractor each subject invention made under contract in order that the contractor can comply with the disclosure provisions of paragraph (c), above, and to execute all papers necessary to file patent applications on subject inventions and to establish the government's rights in the subject inventions. This disclosure format should require, as a minimum, the information required by (c)(1), above. The contractor shall instruct such employees through employee agreements or other suitable educational programs on the importance of reporting inventions in sufficient time to permit the filing of patent applications prior to U.S. or foreign statutory bars.

(3) The contractor will notify the Federal agency of any decisions not to continue the prosecution of a patent application, pay maintenance fees, or defend in a reexamination or opposition proceeding on a patent, in any country, not less than thirty days before the expiration of the response period required by the relevant patent office.

(4) The contractor agrees to include, within the specification of any United States patent applications and any patent issuing thereon covering a subject invention, the following statement, "This invention was made with government support under (identify the contract) awarded by (identify the Federal agency). The government has certain rights in the invention."

(g) Subcontracts

(1) The contractor will include this clause, suitably modified to identify the parties, in all subcontracts, regardless of tier, for experimental, developmental or research work to be performed by a small business firm or domestic nonprofit organization. The subcontractor will retain all rights provided for the contractor in this clause, and the contractor will not, as part of the consideration for awarding the subcontract, obtain rights in the subcontractor's subject inventions.

(2) The contractor will include in all other subcontracts, regardless of tier, for experimental developmental or research work the patent rights clause required by (cite section of agency implementing regulations or FAR).

(3) In the case of subcontracts, at any tier, when the prime award with the Federal agency was a contract (but not a grant or cooperative agreement), the agency, subcontractor, and the contractor agree that the mutual obligations of the parties created by this clause constitute a contract between the subcontractor and the Federal agency with respect to the matters covered by the clause; provided, however, that nothing in this paragraph is intended to confer any jurisdiction under the Contract Disputes Act in connection with proceedings under paragraph (j) of this clause.

(h) Reporting on Utilization of Subject Inventions

The Contractor agrees to submit on request periodic reports no more frequently than annually on the utilization of a subject invention or on efforts at obtaining such utilization that are being made by the contractor or its licensees or assignees. Such reports shall include information regarding the status of development, date of first commercial sale or use, gross royalties received by the contractor, and such other data and information as the agency may reasonably specify. The contractor also agrees to provide additional reports as may be requested by the agency in connection with any march-in proceeding undertaken by the agency in accordance with paragraph (j) of this clause. As required by 35 U.S.C. 202(c)(5), the agency agrees it will not disclose such information to persons outside the government without permission of the contractor.

(i) Preference for United States Industry

Notwithstanding any other provision of this clause, the contractor agrees that neither it nor any assignee will grant to any person the exclusive right to use or sell any subject inventions in the United States unless such person agrees that any products embodying the subject invention or produced through the use of the subject invention will be manufactured substantially in the United States. However, in individual cases, the requirement for such an agreement may be waived by the Federal agency upon a showing by the contractor or its assignee that reasonable but unsuccessful efforts have been made to grant licenses on similar terms to potential licensees that would be likely to manufacture substantially in the United States or that under the circumstances domestic manufacture is not commercially feasible.

(j) March-in Rights

The contractor agrees that with respect to any subject invention in which it has acquired title, the Federal agency has the right in accordance with the procedures in 37 CFR 401.6 and any supplemental regulations of the agency to require the contractor, an assignee or exclusive licensee of a subject invention to grant a nonexclusive, partially exclusive, or exclusive license in any field of use to a responsible applicant or applicants, upon terms that are reasonable under the circumstances, and if the contractor, assignee, or exclusive licensee refuses such a request the Federal agency has the right to grant such a license itself if the Federal agency determines that:

(1) Such action is necessary because the contractor or assignee has not taken, or is not expected to take within a reasonable time, effective steps to achieve practical application of the subject invention in such field of use.

(2) Such action is necessary to alleviate health or safety needs which are not reasonably satisfied by the contractor, assignee or their licensees;

(3) Such action is necessary to meet requirements for public use specified by Federal regulations and such requirements are not reasonably satisfied by the contractor, assignee or licensees; or

(4) Such action is necessary because the agreement required by paragraph (i) of this clause has not been obtained or waived or because a licensee of the exclusive right to use or sell any subject invention in the United States is in breach of such agreement.

(k) Special Provisions for Contracts with Nonprofit Organizations

If the contractor is a nonprofit organization, it agrees that:

(1) Rights to a subject invention in the United States may not be assigned without the approval of the Federal agency, except where such assignment is made to an organization which has as one of its primary functions the management of inventions, provided that such assignee will be subject to the same provisions as the contractor;

(2) The contractor will share royalties collected on a subject invention with the inventor, including Federal employee co-inventors (when the agency deems it appropriate) when the subject invention is assigned in accordance with 35 U.S.C. 202(e) and 37 CFR 401.10;

(3) The balance of any royalties or income earned by the contractor with respect to subject inventions, after payment of expenses (including payments to inventors) incidental to the administration of subject inventions, will be utilized for the support of scientific research or education; and

(4) It will make efforts that are reasonable under the circumstances to attract licensees of subject invention that are small business firms and that it will give a preference to a small business firm when licensing a subject invention if the contractor determines that the small business firm has a plan or proposal for marketing the invention which, if executed, is equally as likely to bring the invention to practical application as any plans or proposals from applicants that are not small business firms; provided, that the contractor is also satisfied that the small business firm has the capability and resources to carry out its plan or proposal. The decision whether to give a preference in any specific case will be at the discretion of the contractor. However, the contractor agrees that the Secretary may review the contractor's licensing program and decisions regarding small business applicants, and the contractor will negotiate changes to its licensing policies, procedures, or practices with the Secretary when the Secretary's review discloses that the contractor could take reasonable steps to implement more effectively the requirements of this paragraph (k)(4).

(*l*) Communication

(Complete According to Instructions at 401.5(b))

(b) When the Department of Energy (DOE) determines to use alternative provisions under §401.3(a)(4), the standard clause at §401.14(a), of this section, shall be used with the following modifications unless a substitute clause is drafted by DOE:

(1) The title of the clause shall be changed to read as follows: Patent Rights to Nonprofit DOE Facility Operators

(2) Add an "(A)" after "(1)" in paragraph (c)(1) and add subparagraphs (B) and (C) to paragraph (c)(1) as follows:

(B) If the subject invention occurred under activities funded by the naval nuclear propulsion or weapons related programs of DOE, then the provisions of this subparagraph (c)(1)(B) will apply in lieu of paragraphs (c)(2) and (3). In such cases the contractor agrees to assign the government the entire right, title, and interest thereto throughout the world in and to the subject invention except to the extent that rights are retained by the contractor through a greater rights determination or under paragraph (e), below. The contractor, or an employee-inventor, with authorization of the contractor, may submit a request for greater rights at the time the invention is disclosed or within a reasonable time thereafter. DOE will process such a request in accordance with procedures at 37 CFR 401.15. Each determination of greater rights will be subject to paragraphs (h)-(k) of this clause and such additional conditions, if any, deemed to be appropriate by the Department of Energy.

(C) At the time an invention is disclosed in accordance with (c)(1)(A) above, or within 90 days thereafter, the contractor will submit a written statement as to whether or not the invention occurred under a naval nuclear propulsion or weapons-related program of the Department of Energy. If this statement is not filed within this time, subparagraph (c)(1)(B) will apply in lieu of paragraphs (c)(2) and (3). The contractor statement will be deemed conclusive unless, within 60 days thereafter, the Contracting Officer disagrees in writing, in which case the determination of the Contracting Officer will be deemed conclusive unless the contractor files a claim under the Contract Disputes Act within 60 days after the Contracting Officer's determination. Pending resolution of the matter, the invention will be subject to subparagraph (c)(1)(B).

(3) Paragraph (k)(3) of the clause will be modified as prescribed at §401.5(g).

(c) As prescribed in §401.3, replace (b) of the basic clause with the following paragraphs (1) and (2):

(b) Allocation of principal rights. **(1)** The Contractor may retain the entire right, title, and interest throughout the world to each subject invention subject to the provisions of this clause, including (2) below, and 35 U.S.C. 203. With respect to any subject invention in which the Contractor retains title, the Federal Government shall have a nonexclusive, nontransferable, irrevocable, paid-up license to practice or have practiced for or on behalf of the United States the subject invention throughout the world.

(2) If the Contractor performs services at a Government owned and operated laboratory or at a Government owned and contractor operated laboratory directed by the Government to fulfill the Government's obligations under a Cooperative Research and Development Agreement (CRADA) authorized by 15 U.S.C. 3710a, the Government may require the Contractor to negotiate an agreement with the CRADA collaborating party or parties regarding the allocation of rights to any subject invention the Contractor makes, solely or jointly, under the CRADA. The agreement shall be negotiated prior to the Contractor undertaking the CRADA work or, with the permission of the Government, upon the identification of a subject invention. In the absence of such an agreement, the Contractor agrees to grant the collaborating party or parties an option for a license in its inventions of the same scope and terms set forth in the CRADA for inventions made by the Government.

History of 37 C.F.R. §401.14: 69 FR 17301, Apr. 2, 2004.

§401.15. DEFERRED DETERMINATIONS

(a) This section applies to requests for greater rights in subject inventions made by contractors when deferred determination provisions were included in the funding agreement because one of the exceptions at §401.3(a) was applied, except that the Department of Energy is authorized to process deferred determinations either in accordance with its waiver regulations or this section. A contractor requesting greater rights should include with its request information on its plans and intentions to bring the invention to practical application. Within 90 days after receiving a request and supporting information, or sooner if a statutory bar to patenting is imminent, the agency should seek to make a determination. In any event, if a bar to patenting is imminent, unless the agency plans to file on its own, it shall authorize the contractor to file a patent application pending a determination by the agency. Such a filing shall normally be at the contractor's own risk and expense. However, if the agency subsequently refuses to allow the contractor to retain title and elects to proceed with the patent application under government ownership, it shall reimburse the contractor for the cost of preparing and filing the patent application.

(b) If the circumstances of concerns which originally led the agency to invoke an exception under §401.3(a) are not applicable to the actual subject invention or are no longer valid because of subsequent events, the agency should allow the contractor to retain title to the invention on the same conditions as would have applied if the standard clause at §401.14(a) had been used originally, unless it has been licensed.

(c) If paragraph (b) is not applicable the agency shall make its determination based on an assessment whether its own plans regarding the invention will better promote the policies and objectives of 35 U.S.C. 200 than will contractor ownership of the invention. Moreover, if the agency is concerned only about specific uses or applications of the invention, it shall consider leaving title in the contractor with additional conditions imposed upon the contractor's use of the invention for such applications or with expanded government license rights in such applications.

(d) A determination not to allow the contractor to retain title to a subject invention or to restrict or condition its title with conditions differing from those in the clause at §401.14(a), unless made by the head of the agency, shall be appealable by the contractor to an agency official at a level above the person who made the determination. This appeal shall be subject to the procedures applicable to appeals under §401.11 of this part.

§401.16. ELECTRONIC FILING

Unless otherwise requested or directed by the agency,

(a) The written report required in (c)(1) of the standard clause in §401.14(a) may be electronically filed;

(b) The written election required in (c)(2) of the standard clause in §401.14(a) may be electronically filed; and

(c) The close-out report in (f)(1) and the information identified in (f)(2) and (f)(3) of §401.5 may be electronically filed.

History of 37 C.F.R. §401.16: 60 FR 41812, Aug. 14, 1995.

§401.17. SUBMISSIONS & INQUIRIES

All submissions or inquiries should be directed to the Chief Counsel for NIST, National Institute of Standards and Technology, 100 Bureau Drive, Mail Stop 1052, Gaithersburg, Maryland 20899-1052; telephone: (301) 975-2803; email: nistcounsel@nist.gov.

History of 37 C.F.R. §401.17: 60 FR 41812, Aug. 14, 1995; 78 FR 4766, Jan. 23, 2013.

PARTS 402, 403. RESERVED

PART 404. LICENSING OF GOVERNMENT OWNED INVENTIONS

§404.1. SCOPE OF PART

This part prescribes the terms, conditions, and procedures upon which a federally owned invention, other than an invention in the custody of the Tennessee Valley Authority, may be licensed. This part does not affect licenses which:

(a) Were in effect prior to April 7, 2006;

(b) May exist at the time of the Government's acquisition of title to the invention, including those resulting from the allocation of rights to inventions made under Government research and development contracts;

(c) Are the result of an authorized exchange of rights in the settlement of patent disputes, including interferences; or

(d) Are otherwise authorized by law or treaty, including 35 U.S.C. 202(e), 35 U.S.C. 207(a)(3) and 15 U.S.C. 3710a, which also may authorize the assignment of inventions. Although licenses on inventions made under a cooperative research and development agreement (CRADA) are not subject to this regulation, agencies are encouraged to apply the same policies and use similar terms when appropriate. Similarly, this should be done for licenses granted under inventions where the agency has acquired rights pursuant to 35 U.S.C. 207(a)(3).

History of 37 C.F.R. §404.1: 71 FR 11512, Mar. 8, 2006.

Source of 37 C.F.R. Part 404: 50 FR 6802, Feb. 15, 1985; 50 FR 9802, Mar. 12, 1985; 55 FR 38983, Sept. 24, 1990; 66 FR 34546, June 29, 2001; 71 FR 11512, Mar. 8, 2006, unless otherwise noted.

§404.2. POLICY & OBJECTIVE

It is the policy and objective of this subpart to use the patent system to promote the utilization of inventions arising from federally supported research or development.

§404.3. DEFINITIONS

(a) Government owned invention means an invention, whether or not covered by a patent or patent application, or discovery which is or may be patentable or otherwise protectable under Title 35, the Plant Variety Protection Act (7 U.S.C. 2321 et seq.) or foreign patent law, owned in whole or in part by the United States Government.

(b) "Federal agency" means an executive department, military department, Government corporation, or independent establishment, except the Tennessee Valley Authority, which has custody of a federally owned invention.

(c) "Small business firm" means a small business concern as defined in section 2 of Pub.L. 85-536 (15 U.S.C. 632) and implementing regulations of the Administrator of the Small Business Administration.

(d) "Practical application" means to manufacture in the case of a composition or product, to practice in the case of a process or method, or to operate in the case of a machine or system; and, in each case, under such conditions as to establish that the invention is being utilized and that its benefits are to the extent permitted by law or Government regulations available to the public on reasonable terms.

(e) "United States" means the United States of America, its territories and possessions, the District of Columbia, and the Commonwealth of Puerto Rico.

History of 37 C.F.R. §404.3: 71 FR 11512, Mar. 8, 2006.

§404.4. AUTHORITY TO GRANT LICENSES

Federally owned inventions shall be made available for licensing as deemed appropriate in the public interest and each agency shall notify the public of these available inventions. The agencies having custody of these inventions may grant nonexclusive, co-exclusive, partially exclusive, or exclusive licenses thereto under this part. Licenses may be royalty-free or for royalties or other consideration. They may be for all or less than all fields of use or in specified geographic areas and may include a release for past infringement. Any license shall not confer on any person immunity from the antitrust laws or from a charge of patent misuse, and the exercise of such rights pursuant to this part shall not be immunized from the operation of state or federal law by reason of the source of the grant.

History of 37 C.F.R. §404.4: 71 FR 11512, Mar. 8, 2006.

§404.5. RESTRICTIONS & CONDITIONS ON ALL LICENSES GRANTED UNDER THIS PART

(a)(1) A license may be granted only if the applicant has supplied the Federal agency with a satisfactory plan for development or marketing of the invention, or both, and with information about the applicant's capability to fulfill the plan. The plan for a non-exclusive research license may be limited to describing the research phase of development.

(2) A license granting rights to use or sell under a Government owned invention in the United States shall normally be granted only to a licensee who agrees that any products embodying the invention or produced through the use of the invention will be manufactured substantially in the United

States. However, this condition may be waived or modified if reasonable but unsuccessful efforts have been made to grant licenses to potential licensees that would be likely to manufacture substantially in the United States or if domestic manufacture is not commercially feasible.

(b) Licenses shall contain such terms and conditions as the Federal agency determines are appropriate for the protection of the interests of the Federal Government and the public and are not in conflict with law or this part. The following terms and conditions apply to any license:

(1) The duration of the license shall be for a period specified in the license agreement, unless sooner terminated in accordance with this part.

(2) Any patent license may grant the licensee the right of enforcement of the licensed patent without joining the Federal agency as a party as determined appropriate in the public interest.

(3) The license may extend to subsidiaries of the licensee or other parties if provided for in the license but shall be nonassignable without approval of the Federal agency, except to the successor of that part of the licensee's business to which the invention pertains.

(4) The license may provide the licensee the right to grant sublicenses under the license, subject to the approval of the Federal agency. Each sublicense shall make reference to the license, including the rights retained by the Government, and a copy of such sublicense with any modifications thereto, shall be promptly furnished to the Federal agency.

(5) The license shall require the licensee to carry out the plan for development or marketing of the invention, or both, to bring the invention to practical application within a reasonable time as specified in the license, and continue to make the benefits of the invention reasonably accessible to the public.

(6) The license shall require the licensee to report periodically on the utilization or efforts at obtaining utilization that are being made by the licensee, with particular reference to the plan submitted but only to the extent necessary to enable the agency to determine compliance with the terms of the license.

(7) Where an agreement is obtained pursuant to §404.5(a)(2) that any products embodying the invention or produced through the use of the invention will be manufactured substantially in the United States, the license shall recite such an agreement.

(8) The license shall provide for the right of the Federal agency to terminate the license, in whole or in part, if the agency determines that:

(i) The licensee is not executing its commitment to achieve practical application of the invention, including commitments contained in any plan submitted in support of its request for a license and the licensee cannot otherwise demonstrate to the satisfaction of the Federal agency that it has taken, or can be expected to take within a reasonable time, effective steps to achieve practical application of the invention;

(ii) Termination is necessary to meet requirements for public use specified by Federal regulations issued after the date of the license and such requirements are not reasonably satisfied by the licensee;

(iii) The licensee has willfully made a false statement of or willfully omitted a material fact in the license application or in any report required by the license agreement;

(iv) The licensee commits a substantial breach of a covenant or provision contained in the license agreement, including the requirement in §404.5(a)(2); or

(v) The licensee has been found by a court of competent jurisdiction to have violated the Federal antitrust laws in connection with its performance under the license agreement.

(9) The license may be modified or terminated, consistent with this part, upon mutual agreement of the Federal agency and the licensee.

(10) The license may be modified or terminated, consistent with this part, upon mutual agreement of the Federal agency and the licensee.

(11) Nothing relating to the grant of a license, nor the grant itself, shall be construed to confer upon any person any immunity from or defenses under the antitrust laws or from a charge of patent misuse, and the acquisition and use of rights pursuant to this part shall not be immunized from the operation of state or Federal law by reason of the source of the grant.

History of 37 C.F.R. §404.5: 71 FR 11512, Mar. 8, 2006.

§404.6. NONEXCLUSIVE LICENSES

Nonexclusive licenses may be granted under Government owned inventions without a public notice of a prospective license.

History of 37 C.F.R. §404.6: 71 FR 11513, Mar. 8, 2006.

§404.7. EXCLUSIVE, CO-EXCLUSIVE & PARTIALLY EXCLUSIVE LICENSES

(a)(1) Exclusive, co-exclusive or partially exclusive domestic licenses may be granted on Government owned inventions, only if;

(i) Notice of a prospective license, identifying the invention and the prospective licensee, has been published in the Federal Register, providing opportunity for filing written objections within at least a 15-day period;

(ii) After expiration of the period in §404.7(a)(1)(i) and consideration of any written objections received during the period, the Federal agency has determined that;

(A) The public will be served by the granting of the license, in view of the applicant's intentions, plans and ability to bring the invention to the point of practical application or otherwise promote the invention's utilization by the public.

(B) Exclusive, co-exclusive or partially exclusive licensing is a reasonable and necessary incentive to call forth the investment capital and expenditures needed to bring the invention to practical application or otherwise promote the invention's utilization by the public; and

(C) The proposed scope of exclusivity is not greater than reasonably necessary to provide the incentive for bringing the invention to practical application, as proposed by the applicant, or otherwise to promote the invention's utilization by the public;

(iii) The Federal agency has not determined that the grant of such a license will tend substantially to lessen competition or create or maintain a violation of the Federal antitrust laws; and

(iv) The Federal agency has given first preference to any small business firms submitting plans that are determined by the agency to be within the capability of the firms and as having equal or greater likelihood as those from other applicants to bring the invention to practical application within a reasonable time.

(2) In addition to the provisions of §404.5, the following terms and conditions apply to domestic exclusive, co-exclusive and partially exclusive licenses:

(i) The license shall be subject to the irrevocable, royalty-free right of the Government of the United States to practice or have practiced the invention on behalf of the United States and on behalf of any foreign government or international organization pursuant to any existing or future treaty or agreement with the United States.

(ii) The license shall reserve to the Federal agency the right to require the licensee to grant sublicenses to responsible applicants, on reasonable terms, when necessary to fulfill health or safety needs.

(iii) The license shall be subject to any licenses in force at the time of the grant of the exclusive, co-exclusive or partially exclusive license.

(b)(1) Exclusive, co-exclusive or partially exclusive foreign licenses may be granted on a Government owned invention provided that;

(i) Notice of the prospective license, identifying the invention and prospective licensee, has been published in the Federal Register, providing opportunity for filing written objections within at least a 15-day period and following consideration of such objections received during the period;

(ii) The agency has considered whether the interests of the Federal Government or United States industry in foreign commerce will be enhanced; and

(iii) The Federal agency has not determined that the grant of such a license will tend substantially to lessen competition or create or maintain a violation of the Federal antitrust laws.

(2) In addition to the provisions of §404.5, the following terms and conditions apply to foreign exclusive, co-exclusive and partially exclusive licenses:

(i) The license shall be subject to the irrevocable, royalty-free right of the Government of the United States to practice and have practiced the invention on behalf of the United States and on behalf of any foreign government or international organization pursuant to any existing or future treaty or agreement with the United States.

(ii) The license shall be subject to any licenses in force at the time of the grant of the exclusive, co-exclusive or partially exclusive license.

(iii) The license may grant the licensee the right to take any suitable and necessary actions to protect the licensed property, on behalf of the Federal Government.

(c) Federal agencies shall maintain a record of determinations to grant exclusive, co-exclusive or partially exclusive licenses.

History of 37 C.F.R. §404.7: 66 FR 34546, June 29, 2001; 71 FR 11513, Mar. 8, 2006.

§404.8. APPLICATION FOR A LICENSE

An application for a license should be addressed to the Federal agency having custody of the invention and shall normally include:

(a) Identification of the invention for which the license is desired including the patent application serial number or patent number, title, and date, if known;

(b) Identification of the type of license for which the application is submitted;

(c) Name and address of the person, company, or organization applying for the license and the citizenship or place of incorporation of the applicant;

(d) Name, address, and telephone number of the representative of the applicant to whom correspondence should be sent;

(e) Nature and type of applicant's business, identifying products or services which the applicant has successfully commercialized, and approximate number of applicant's employees;

(f) Source of information concerning the availability of a license on the invention;

(g) A statement indicating whether the applicant is a small business firm as defined in §404.3(c)

(h) A detailed description of applicant's plan for development or marketing of the invention, or both, which should include:

(1) A statement of the time, nature and amount of anticipated investment of capital and other resources which applicant believes will be required to bring the invention to practical application;

(2) A statement as to applicant's capability and intention to fulfill the plan, including information regarding manufacturing, marketing, financial, and technical resources;

(3) A statement of the fields of use for which applicant intends to practice the invention; and

(4) A statement of the geographic areas in which applicant intends to manufacture any products embodying the invention and geographic areas where applicant intends to use or sell the invention, or both;

(i) Identification of licenses previously granted to applicant under federally owned inventions;

(j) A statement containing applicant's best knowledge of the extent to which the invention is being practiced by private industry or Government, or both, or is otherwise available commercially; and

(k) Any other information which applicant believes will support a determination to grant the license to applicant.

§404.9. RESERVED

History of 37 C.F.R. §404.9: 71 FR 11514, Mar. 8, 2006.

§404.10. MODIFICATION & TERMINATION OF LICENSES

Before modifying or terminating a license, other than by mutual agreement, the Federal agency shall furnish the licensee and any sublicensee of record a written notice of intention to modify or terminate the license, and the licensee shall be allowed 30 days after such notice to remedy any breach of the license or show cause why the license shall not be modified or terminated.

History of 37 C.F.R. §404.10: 71 FR 11514, Mar. 8, 2006.

§404.11. APPEALS

(a) In accordance with procedures prescribed by the Federal agency, the following parties may appeal to the agency head or designee any decision or determination concerning the grant, denial, modification, or termination of a license:

(1) A person whose application for a license has been denied;

(2) A licensee whose license has been modified or terminated, in whole or in part; or

(3) A person who timely filed a written objection in response to the notice required by §404.7(a)(1)(i) or §404.7(b)(1)(i) and who can demonstrate to the satisfaction of the Federal agency that such person may be damaged by the agency action.

(b) An appeal by a licensee under paragraph (a)(2) of this section may include a hearing, upon the request of the licensee, to address a dispute over any relevant fact. The parties may agree to Alternate Dispute Resolution in lieu of an appeal.

History of 37 C.F.R. §404.11: 71 FR 11514, Mar. 8, 2006.

§404.12. PROTECTION & ADMINISTRATION OF INVENTIONS

A Federal agency may take any suitable and necessary steps to protect and administer rights to Government owned inventions, either directly or through contract.

History of 37 C.F.R. §404.12: 71 FR 11514, Mar. 8, 2006.

§404.13. TRANSFER OF CUSTODY

A Federal agency having custody of a federally owned invention may transfer custody and administration, in whole or in part, to another Federal agency, of the right, title, or interest in such invention.

§404.14. CONFIDENTIALITY OF INFORMATION

Title 35, United States Code, section 209, requires that any plan submitted pursuant to §404.8(h) and any report required by §404.5(b)(6) shall be treated as commercial or financial information obtained from a person and privileged and confidential and not subject to disclosure under section 552 of Title 5 of the United States Code.

History of 37 C.F.R. §404.14: 71 FR 11514, Mar. 8, 2006.

PART 501. UNIFORM PATENT POLICY FOR RIGHTS IN INVENTIONS MADE BY GOVERNMENT EMPLOYEES

§501.1. PURPOSE

The purpose of this part is to provide for the administration of a uniform patent policy for the Government with respect to the rights in inventions made by Government employees and to prescribe rules and regulations for implementing and effectuating such policy.

History of 37 C.F.R. §501.1: 61 FR 40999, Aug. 7, 1996.

Source of 37 C.F.R. Part 501: 53 FR 39735, Oct. 11, 1988; 55 FR 38983, Sept. 24, 1990; 61 FR 40999, Aug. 7, 1996, unless otherwise noted.

§501.2. SCOPE

This part applies to any invention made by a Government employee and to any action taken with respect thereto.

§501.3. DEFINITIONS

(a) The term Secretary, as used in this part, means the Director of the National Institute of Standards and Technology.

(b) The term Government agency, as used in this part, means any Executive department or independent establishment of the Executive branch of the Government (including any independent regulatory commission or board, any corporation wholly owned by the United States, and the Smithsonian Institution), but does not include the Department of Energy for inventions made under the provisions of 42 U.S.C. 2182, the Tennessee Valley Authority, or the Postal Service.

(c) The term Government employee, as used in this part, means any officer or employee, civilian or military, of any Government agency, including any special Government employee as defined in 18 U.S.C. 202 or an individual working for a Federal agency pursuant to the Intergovernmental Personnel Act (IPA), 5 U.S.C. 1304 and 3371-3376, or a part-time consultant or part-time employee as defined in 29 U.S.C. 2101(a)(8) except as may otherwise be provided by agency regulation approved by the Secretary.

(d) The term invention, as used in this part, means any art or process, machine, manufacture, design, or composition of matter, or any new and useful improvement thereof, or any variety of plant, which is or may be patentable under the patent laws of the United States.

(e) The term made as used in this part in relation to any invention, means the conception or first actual reduction to practice of such invention as stated in *In re King*, 3 USPQ2d (BNA) 1747 (Comm'r Pat. 1987).

History of 37 C.F.R. §501.3: 55 FR 38983, Sept. 24, 1990; 61 FR 40999, Aug. 7, 1996; 78 FR 4766, Jan. 23, 2013.

§501.4. DETERMINATION OF INVENTIONS & RIGHTS

Each Government agency has the approval of the Secretary to determine whether the results of research, development, or other activity in the agency constitute an invention within the purview of Executive Order 10096, as amended by Executive Order 10930 and Executive Order 10695, and to determine the rights in and to the invention in accordance with the provisions of §§501.6 and 501.7.

History of 37 C.F.R. §501.4: 61 FR 40999, Aug. 7, 1996.

§501.5. AGENCY LIAISON OFFICER

Each Government agency shall designate a liaison officer to represent the agency before the Secretary; Provided, however, that the Departments of the Army, the Navy, and the Air Force may each designate a liaison officer.

§501.6. CRITERIA FOR THE DETERMINATION OF RIGHTS IN & TO INVENTIONS

(a) The following rules shall be applied in determining the respective rights of the Government and of the inventor in and to any invention that is subject to the provisions of this part:

(1) The Government shall obtain, except as herein otherwise provided, the entire right, title and interest in and to any invention made by any Government employee:

(i) During working hours, or

(ii) With a contribution by the Government of facilities, equipment, materials, funds or information, or of time or services of other Government employees on official duty, or

(iii) Which bears a direct relation to or is made in consequence of the official duties of the inventor.

(2) In any case where the contribution of the Government, as measured by any one or more of the criteria set forth in paragraph (a)(1) of this section, to the invention is insufficient equitably to justify a requirement of assignment to the Government of the entire right, title and interest in and to such invention, or in any case where the Government has insufficient interest in an invention to obtain the entire right, title and interest therein (although the Government could obtain same under paragraph (a)(1) of this section), the Government agency concerned shall leave title to such invention in the employee, subject however, to the reservation to the Government of a nonexclusive, irrevocable, royalty-free license in the invention with power to grant licenses for all governmental purposes. The terms of such reservation will appear, where practicable, in any patent, domestic or foreign, which may issue on such invention. Reference is made to section 15 of the Federal Technology Transfer Act of 1986 (15 U.S.C. 3710d) which requires a Government agency to allow the inventor to retain title to any covered invention when the agency does not intend to file a patent application or otherwise promote commercialization.

(3) In applying the provisions of paragraphs (a)(1) and (2) of this section to the facts and circumstances relating to the making of a particular invention, it shall be presumed that an invention made by an employee who is employed or assigned:

(i) To invent or improve or perfect any art or process, machine, design, manufacture, or composition of matter;

(ii) To conduct or perform research, development work, or both,

(iii) To supervise, direct, coordinate, or review Government financed or conducted research, development work, or both, or

(iv) To act in a liaison capacity among governmental or non-governmental agencies or individuals engaged in such research or development work, falls within the provisions of paragraph (a)(1) of this section, and it shall be presumed that any invention made by any other employee falls within the provisions of paragraph (a)(2) of this section. Either presumption may be rebutted by a showing of the facts and circumstances in the case and shall not preclude a determination that these facts and circumstances justify leaving the entire right, title and interest in and to the invention in the Government employee, subject to law.

(4) In any case wherein the Government neither:

(i) Obtains the entire right, title and interest in and to an invention pursuant to the provisions of paragraph (a)(1) of this section nor

(ii) Reserves a nonexclusive, irrevocable, royalty-free license in the invention, with power to grant licenses for all governmental purposes, pursuant to the provisions of paragraph (a)(2) of this section, the Government shall leave the entire right, title and interest in and to the invention in the Government employee, subject to law.

History of 37 C.F.R. §501.6: 61 FR 40999, Aug. 7, 1996.

§501.7. AGENCY DETERMINATION

(a) If the agency determines that the Government is entitled to obtain title pursuant to §501.6(a)(1) and the employee does not appeal, no further review is required.

(b) In the event that a Government agency determines, pursuant to paragraph (a)(2) or (a)(4) of §501.6, that title to an invention will be left with the employee, the agency shall notify the employee of this determination. In cases pursuant to §501.6(a)(2) where the Government's insufficient interest in the invention is evidenced by its decision not to file a patent application, the agency may impose on the employee any one or all of the following conditions or any other conditions that may be necessary in a particular case:

(1) That a patent application be filed in the United States and/or abroad, if the Government has determined that it has or may need to practice the invention;

(2) That the invention not be assigned to any foreign-owned or controlled corporation without the written permission of the agency; and

(3) That any assignment or license of rights to use or sell the invention in the United States shall contain a requirement that any products embodying the invention or produced through the use of the invention be substantially manufactured in the United States. The agency shall notify the employee of any conditions imposed.

(c) In the case of a determination under either paragraph (a) or (b) of this section, the agency shall promptly provide the employee with:

(1) A signed and dated statement of its determination and reasons therefor; and

(2) A copy of 37 CFR part 501.

History of 37 C.F.R. §501.7: 61 FR 40999, Aug. 7, 1996.

§501.8. APPEALS BY EMPLOYEES

(a) Any Government employee who is aggrieved by a Government agency determination pursuant to §§501.6(a)(1) or (a)(2), may obtain a review of any agency determination by filing, within 30 days (or such longer period as the Secretary may, for good cause shown in writing, fix in any case) after receiving notice of such determination, two copies of an appeal with the Secretary. The Secretary then shall forward one copy of the appeal to the liaison officer of the Government agency.

(b) On receipt of a copy of an appeal filed pursuant to paragraph (a) of this section, the agency liaison officer shall, subject to considerations of national security, or public health, safety or welfare, promptly furnish both the Secretary and the inventor with a copy of a report containing the following information about the invention involved in the appeal:

(1) A copy of the agency's statement specified in §501.7(c);

(2) A description of the invention in sufficient detail to identify the invention and show its relationship to the employee's duties and work assignments;

(3) The name of the employee and employment status, including a detailed statement of official duties and responsibilities at the time the invention was made; and

(4) A detailed statement of the points of dispute or controversy, together with copies of any statements or written arguments filed with the agency, and of any other relevant evidence that the agency considered in making its determination of Government interest.

(c) Within 25 days (or such longer period as the Secretary may, for good cause shown, fix in any case) after the transmission of a copy of the agency report to the employee, the employee may file a reply with the Secretary and file one copy with the agency liaison officer.

(d) After the time for the inventor's reply to the Government agency's report has expired and if the inventor has so requested in his or her appeal, a date will be set for hearing of oral arguments before the Secretary, by the employee (or by an attorney whom he or she designates by written power of attorney filed before, or at the hearing) and a representative of the Government agency involved. Unless it shall be otherwise ordered before the hearing begins, oral arguments will be limited to thirty minutes for each side. The employee need not retain an attorney or request an oral hearing to secure full consideration of the facts and his or her arguments. The employee may expedite such consideration by notifying the Secretary when he or she does not intend to file a reply to the agency report.

(e) After a hearing on the appeal, if a hearing was requested, or after expiration of the period for the inventor's reply to the agency report if no hearing is set, the Secretary shall issue a decision on the matter within 120 days, which decision shall be final after a thirty day period for requesting reconsideration expires or on the date that a decision on a petition for reconsideration is finally disposed of. Any request for reconsideration or modification of the decision must be filed within 30 days from the date of the original decision (or within such an extension thereof as may be set by the Secretary before the original period expires). The decision of the Secretary shall be made after consideration of the statements of fact in the employee's appeal, the agency's report, and the employee's reply, but the Secretary at his or her discretion and with due respect to the rights and convenience of the inventor and the Government agency, may call for further statements on specific questions of fact or may request additional evidence in the form of affidavits or depositions on specific facts in dispute.

History of 37 C.F.R. §501.8: 61 FR 41000, Aug. 7, 1996.

§501.9. PATENT PROTECTION

(a) A Government agency, upon determining that an invention coming within the scope of §§501.6(a)(1) or (a)(2) has been made, shall promptly determine whether patent protection will be sought in the United States by or on behalf of the agency for such invention. A controversy over the respective rights of the Government and of the employee shall not unnecessarily delay the filing of a patent application by the agency to avoid the loss of patent rights. In cases coming within the scope of §501.6(a)(2), the filing of a patent application shall be contingent upon the consent of the employee.

(b) Where there is an appealed dispute as to whether §§501.6 (a)(1) or (a)(2) applies in determining the respective rights of the Government and of an employee in and to any invention, the agency may determine whether patent protection will be sought in the United States pending the Secretary's decision on the dispute. If the agency decides that an application for patent should be filed, the agency will take such rights as are specified in §501.6(a)(2), but this shall be without prejudice to acquiring the rights specified in paragraph (a)(1) of that section should the Secretary so decide.

(c) Where an agency has determined to leave title to an invention with an employee under §501.6(a)(2), the agency will, upon the filing of an application for patent, take the rights specified in that paragraph without prejudice to the subsequent acquisition by the Government of the rights specified in paragraph (a)(1) of that section should the Secretary so decide.

(d) Where an agency has filed a patent application in the United States, the agency will, within 8 months from the filing date of the U.S. application, determine if any foreign patent applications should also be filed. If the agency chooses not to file an application in any foreign country, the employee may request rights in that country subject to the conditions stated in §501.7(b) that may be imposed by the agency. Alternatively, the agency may permit the employee to retain foreign rights by including in any assignment to the Government of an unclassified U.S. patent application on the invention an option for the Government to acquire title in any foreign country within 8 months from the filing date of the U.S. application.

History of 37 C.F.R. §501.9: 61 FR 41000, Aug. 7, 1996.

§501.10. DISSEMINATION OF THIS PART & OF IMPLEMENTING REGULATIONS

Each Government agency shall disseminate to its employees the provisions of this part, and any appropriate implementing agency regulations and delegations. Copies of any such regulations shall be sent to the Secretary. If the Secretary identifies an inconsistency between this part and the agency regulations or delegations, the agency, upon being informed by the Secretary of the inconsistency, shall take prompt action to correct it.

§501.11. SUBMISSIONS & INQUIRIES

All submissions or inquiries should be directed to the Chief Counsel for NIST, National Institute of Standards and Technology, 100 Bureau Drive, Mail Stop 1052, Gaithersburg, MD 20899-1052; telephone: (301) 975-2803; email: nistcounsel@nist.gov.

History of 37 C.F.R. §501.11: 61 FR 41000, Aug. 7, 1996; 78 FR 4766, Jan. 23, 2013.

INDEX

INDEX

Notes

Notes

Notes

Notes